THE ZONDERVAN
EXPANDED
CONCORDANCE

THE ZONDERVAN
EXPANDED
CONCORDANCE

ZONDERVAN PUBLISHING HOUSE
GRAND RAPIDS, MICHIGAN

ACKNOWLEDGMENTS

Appreciation is expressed to the following publishers for permission to reprint selections from their translations of the New Testament or the complete Bible:

DIVISION OF CHRISTIAN EDUCATION, NATIONAL COUNCIL OF THE CHURCHES OF CHRIST IN THE UNITED STATES OF AMERICA. *The Revised Standard Version of the Bible.* Copyright © 1952 by The Division of Christian Education, National Council of Churches of Christ in the United States of America.

THE MACMILLAN COMPANY. *The New Testament in Modern English.* Copyright © 1958, 1959, 1960 by J. B. Phillips.

OXFORD UNIVERSITY PRESS. *The New Scofield Reference Bible.* Copyright © 1967 by Oxford University Press, Inc.

OXFORD UNIVERSITY PRESS and CAMBRIDGE UNIVERSITY PRESS. *The New English Bible: New Testament.* Copyright © 1961 by The Delegates of the Oxford University Press and The Syndics of the Cambridge University Press.

ZONDERVAN PUBLISHING HOUSE. *The Amplified New Testament.* Copyright © 1954 and 1958 by the Lockman Foundation. *The Amplified Bible.* Old Testament, copyright © 1962, 1964 and 1965 by Zondervan Publishing House.

ZONDERVAN PUBLISHING HOUSE. *The Holy Bible, The Berkeley Version in Modern English* by Gerrit Verkuyl. Copyright © 1959 by Zondervan Publishing House.

FOREWORD

One of the blessings of our day is the great interest in modern speech translations of the Bible. There is probably a greater wealth of modern translations today than at any time in Christian history. The availability of these translations, however, has created some confusion in the mind of the Bible student, especially in an effort to remember just which translation gives a particularly helpful rendition of some specific passage. The *Zondervan Expanded Concordance* will, therefore, render a great and much needed service to the Bible student. Its need is so obvious that I have long wished for such a concordance. It goes without saying then that I am delighted that Zondervan has issued such a work. The work is clearly arranged, which in itself is a significant achievement.

I commend Zondervan for the vision of bringing out this work, and I commend the Concordance to all serious students of God's Word.

Dr. Charles W. Conn
General Overseer, Church of God

PREFACE

THE ZONDERVAN EXPANDED CONCORDANCE is an important new tool for all who would know their Bibles better. This *Expanded* concordance includes key words from six recent Bible translations and the King James Version (including the new words from the New Scofield Bible). Among the translations (and their abbreviations) included are:

> The King James Version of the Bible
> The Amplified Bible (A)
> The Berkeley Version in Modern English (B)
> American Standard Version (E)
> The New English Bible (N)
> Phillips (P)
> Revised Standard Version of the Bible (R)
> New Scofield Bible (S)

The type selected for this new concordance was chosen with the reader in mind. Key words stand out in clear-cut, boldfaced type for easy location. The word headings are centered in columns so that words and passages are easily found. By a careful use of italics for emphasis, only the key word is emphasized, with generous space provided between entries to make it easy for the reader to find the particular reference for which he is searching. Each entry is clearly identified as to its location in the Scriptures.

The paper on which this Concordance is printed is chosen for its opacity and its glare-free quality.

Another outstanding feature of this new Concordance is the separating of modifying adjectives and adverbs with key words, according to the alphabetizing of the modifying word. This makes it doubly easy to pick out a particular reference. For example:

> *All*
> According to *all*
> After *all*
> At *all*
> Before *all*
> For *all*
> From *all*
> etc.

Here is a reference tool which is easy to use and is exhaustive.

THE PUBLISHERS

ABBREVIATIONS OF THE NAMES OF THE BOOKS OF THE BIBLE

Ge	=Genesis.	Isa	=Isaiah.	Ro	=Romans.
Ex	=Exodus.	Jer	=Jeremiah.	1Co	=I. Corinthians.
Le	=Leviticus.	La	=Lamentations.	2Co	=II. Corinthians.
Nu	=Numbers.	Eze	=Ezekiel.	Ga	=Galatians.
De	=Deuteronomy.	Da	=Daniel.	Eph	=Ephesians.
Jos	=Joshua.	Ho	=Hosea.	Ph'p	=Phillipians.
J'g	=Judges.	Joe	=Joel.	Col	=Colossians.
Ru	=Ruth.	Am	=Amos.	1Th	=I. Thessalonians.
1Sa	=I. Samuel.	Ob	=Obadiah.	2Th	=II. Thessalonians.
2Sa	=II. Samuel.	Jon	=Jonah.	1Ti	=I. Timothy.
1Ki	=I. Kings.	Mic	=Micah.	2Ti	=II. Timothy.
2Ki	=II. Kings.	Na	=Nahum.	Tit	=Titus.
1Ch	=I. Chronicles.	Hab	=Habakkuk.	Ph'm	=Philemon.
2Ch	=II. Chronicles.	Zep	=Zephaniah.	Heb	=Hebrews.
Ezr	=Ezra.	Hag	=Haggai.	Jas	=James.
Ne	=Nehemiah.	Zec	=Zechariah.	1Pe	=I. Peter.
Es	=Esther.	Mal	=Malachi.	2Pe	=II. Peter.
Job	=Job.	M't	=Matthew.	1Jo	=I. John.
Ps	=Psalms.	M'k	=Mark.	2Jo	=II. John.
Pr	=Proverbs.	Lu	=Luke.	3Jo	=III. John.
Ec	=Ecclesiastes.	Joh	=John.	Jude	=Jude.
Ca	=Canticles.	Ac	=Acts.	Re	=Revelation.

THE ZONDERVAN
EXPANDED
CONCORDANCE

AARON

Is not *A.* the Levite thy brother   *Ex 4:14*
they met Moses and *A.* who stood in way   *Ex 5:20*
A. took Elisheba to wife   *Ex 6:23*
A. thy brother shall be thy prophet   *Ex 7:1*
A. laid pot of manna before testimony   *Ex 16:34*
A. and Hur stayed up his hands   *Ex 17:12*
come up, thou and *A.* with thee   *Ex 19:24*
A. and Hur are with you   *Ex 24:14*
A. shall bear their names   *Ex 28:12; 28:29, 30*
holy garment of *A.*   *Ex 29:29*
A. shall burn incense every morning   *Ex 30:7*
when *A.* lighteth the lamps at even   *Ex 30:8*
A. shall make atonement once a year   *Ex 30:10*
they made the calf which *A.* had made   *Ex 32:35*
Moses and *A.* and sons washed thereat   *Ex 40:31*
he sprinkled blood on *A.* and sons   *Le 8:30*
A. lifted up right hand, blessed them   *Le 9:22*
And *A.* held his peace   *Le 10:3*
Thus shall *A.* come into the holy place   *Le 16:3*
A. shall cast lots upon the two goats   *Le 16:8*
A. shall lay hands on head of the goat   *Le 16:21*
A. shall number them by their armies   *Nu 1:3*
A. shall offer Levites before the Lord   *Nu 8:11*
what is *A.* that ye murmur against him   *Nu 16:11*
come thou, they, and *A.* to-morrow   *Nu 16:16*
Moses and *A.* came before tabernacle   *Nu 16:43*
thou and *A.* speak to the rock   *Nu 20:8*
A. died in the top of the mount   *Nu 20:28; 33:38*
A. was 120 years old when he died in Hor   *Nu 33:29*
the Lord was very angry with *A.*   *De 9:20*
sent Moses and *A.*   *Jos 24:5; 1Sa 12:8; Mic 6:4*
the Lord that advanced Moses and *A.*   *1Sa 12:6*
sons of Amram, *A.* and Moses   *1Ch 6:3; 23:13*
leddest Thy people by Moses and *A.*   *Ps 77:20*
Moses and *A.* among His priests   *Ps 99:6*
they envied *A.* the saint of the Lord   *Ps 106:16*
O house of *A.* trust in the Lord   *Ps 115:10*
the Lord bless the house of *A.*   *Ps 115:12*
let house of *A.* say, his mercy endureth   *Ps 118:3*
bless the Lord, O house of *A.*   *Ps 135:19*
his wife was of the daughters of *A.*   *Lu 1:5*
saying to *A.* make us gods to go   *Ac 7:40*
he that is called of God, as was *A.*   *Heb 5:4*
not be called after the order of *A.*   *Heb 7:11*

AARONITES

Jehoida was the leader of the *A.*   *1Ch 12:27*
the son of Kemuel; of the *A.*   *1Ch 27:17*

AARON'S

Eleazar *A.* son took him one of the   *Ex 6:25*
A. rod swallowed up their rods   *Ex 7:12*
Eleazar and Ithamar; *A.* sons   *Ex 28:1*

that they make *A.* garments   *Ex 28:3*
they shall be upon *A.* heart   *Ex 28:30*
it shall be upon *A.* forehead   *Ex 28:38*
for *A.* sons make coats   *Ex 28:40*
the ram of *A.* consecration   *Ex 29:26*
it shall be *A.* and his sons   *Ex 29:28; Le 24:9*
the priests, *A.* sons   *Le 1:5; 1:8, 11*
A. sons   *Le 2:2; 2:3, 10; 3:2, 5, 8; 9:12*
breast shall be *A.* and his sons'   *Le 7:31*
the anointing oil upon *A.* head   *Le 8:12*
Moses brought *A.* sons   *Le 8:13; 8:24*
upon the tip of *A.* right ear   *Le 8:23*
he put all upon *A.* hands   *Le 8:27*
thou shalt write *A.* name upon rod   *Nu 17:3*
Bring *A.* rod again before the   *Nu 17:10*
upon the beard, even *A.* beard   *Ps 133:2*
pot that had the manna, and *A.* rod   *Heb 9:4*

ABADDON

A. has no covering (A)(E)(R)   *Job 26:6*
A. and death say (A)(E)(R)   *Job 28:22*
name in the Hebrew tongue is *A.*   *Re 9:11*

ABAGTHA

Bigtha, and *A.*, Zethar and Carcas   *Es 1:10*

ABANA

Are not *A.* and Pharpar rivers of   *2Ki 5:12*

ABANDONED

A. their idols (B)(R)   *2Sa 5:21*
A. my soul (B)   *Ac 2:27*
A. to unbridled sensuality (A)(E)(R)   *Eph 4:19*
A. to vice (N)   *Eph 4:19*
A. proper dwelling place (A)(B)(N)(P)(R)   *Jude 6*

ABANDONS

who *A.* me (B)   *Eze 14:7*

ABARIM

Get thee up into this mount *A.*   *Nu 27:12*
pitched in the mountains of *A.*   *Nu 33:47*
departed from the mountains of *A.*   *Nu 33:48*
get thee up into this mountain *A.*   *De 32:49*

ABASE

every one that is proud, and *A.* him   *Job 40:11*
as the lion will not *a.* himself   *Isa 31:4*
nor daunted at their noise (A)(B)(R)   *Isa 31:4*
exalt low, and *a.* him that is high   *Eze 21:26*
the high is to be brought low (A)   *Eze 21:26*
that walk in pride, is able to *a.*   *Da 4:37*

ABASED

a. themselves to Sheol (B)   *Isa 57:9*
despised and *a.* (A)(B)(R)   *Mal 2:9*
shall exalt himself shall be *a.*   *M't 23:12; Lu 14:11; 18:14*
whoever exalts himself shall be humbled (A)(B)   *M't 23:12*
be humbled (A)(B)(E)(N)(P)(R)   *Lu 14:11; 18:14*
I know how to be *a.*, how to abound   *Ph'p 4:12*
how to live simply, relish plenty (B)   *Ph'p 4:12*
what it is to be brought low (N)   *Ph'p 4:12*

how live when things are difficult (P)   *Ph'p 4:12*

ABASING

have I committed offence in *a.* myself   *2Co 11:7*
wrong, debasing, cheapening myself (A)   *2Co 11:7*
erred in humbling myself (B)   *2Co 11:7*
offence in lowering myself (N)   *2Co 11:7*

ABATE

waters continued to *a.* (R)   *Ge 8:5*

ABATED

after 150 days were waters *a.*   *Ge 8:3; 8:11*
waters receded (A)   *Ge 8:3*
steadily the waters moved back (B)   *Ge 8:3*
the waters decreased (E)   *Ge 8:3*
it shall be *a.* from thy estimation   *Le 27:18*
it shall be deducted (A)   *Le 27:18*
deduct from the evaluation (B)   *Le 27:18*
an abatement from thy estimation (E)   *Le 27:18*
deduction from your evaluation (R)   *Le 27:18*
nor was Moses' natural force *a.*   *De 34:7*
then their anger was *a.* toward him   *J'g 8:3*
anger of the king *a.* (R)   *Es 7:10*

ABATEMENT

a. from thy estimation (E)   *Le 27:18*

ABBA

He said, *A.*, Father, all things are   *M'k 14:36*
spirit of adoption, whereby we cry *A.*   *Ro 8:15*
into your hearts, crying, *A.*, Father   *Ga 4:6*

ABDA

Adoniram the son of *A.*   *1Ki 4:6*
A. the son of Shammua   *Ne 11:17*

ABDEEL

Shelemiah the son of *A.*   *Jer 36:26*

ABDI

the son of Kishi, the son of *A.*   *1Ch 6:44*
Kish the son of *A.*, and Azariah   *2Ch 29:12*
Jehiel, and *A.*, and Jeremoth   *Ezr 10:26*

ABDIEL

Ahi the son of *A.*   *1Ch 5:15*

ABDOMEN

thy *a.* to swell (S)   *Nu 5:21; 5:22, 27*
thrust through the *a.* (S)   *Nu 25:8*
passes into the *a.* (A)   *M't 15:17*

ABDON

Mishal with her suburbs, *A.* with   *Jos 21:30*
after him *A.* the son of Hillel   *J'g 12:13; 12:15*
Moshal and her suburbs, and *A.* with   *1Ch 6:74*
Eliel and *A.*, and Zichri and Hanan   *1Ch 8:23*
his firstborn son *A.*, and Zur   *1Ch 8:30; 9:36*
and *A.* the son of Micah   *2Ch 34:20*

ABED-NEGO

he gave to Azariah the name *A.*   *Da 1:7*

set *A.* over affairs of   *Da 2:49;*
province   *Da 3:12-14, 16, 19-20, 22, 26,*
       28-30

ABEL

bare his brother *A.* And *A.*   *Ge 4:2*
was keeper
A. also brought. Lord had   *Ge 4:4*
respect to *A.*
Cain talked with *A.*, rose   *Ge 4:8*
against *A.*
Lord said unto Cain, Where   *Ge 4:9*
is *A.*
appointed me another seed   *Ge 4:25*
instead of *A.*
even unto the great stone   *1Sa 6:18*
of *A.*
all the tribes unto *A.*,   *2Sa 20:14*
besieged in *A.*
shall surely ask counsel at   *2Sa 20:18*
A.
from blood of righteous *A.*   *M't 23:35;*
       Lu 11:51
By faith *A.* offered unto   *Heb 11:4*
God a more
better things than that of   *Heb 12:24*
A.

ABEL-BETH-MAACHAH

smote Ijon, Dan, and *A.*   *1Ki 15:20;*
       2Ki 15:29

ABEL-MAIM

smote Ijon, Dan, and *A.*   *2Ch 16:4*

ABEL-MEHOLAH

and to the border of *A.* unto   *J'g 7:22*
from Beth-shean to *A.*, even   *1Ki 4:12*
unto
Elisha the son of Shaphat   *1Ki 19:16*
of *A.*

ABEL-MIZRAIM

name of it was called *A.*   *Ge 50:11*

ABEL-SHITTIM

from Beth-jesimoth even   *Nu 33:49*
unto *A.*

ABEZ

And Rabbith, and Kishion,   *Jos 19:20*
and *A.*

ABHOR

and my soul shall not *a.*   *Le 26:11*
you
will not despise or reject or   *Le 26:11*
separate itself from you (A)
My soul will not reject you   *Le 26:11*
(B)
if your soul *a.* my   *Le 26:15*
judgments
my soul shall *a.* you   *Le 26:30*
my soul shall *a.* you   *Le 26:30*
(B)
nor will I *a.* them, to   *Le 26:44*
destroy them
I will not spurn them (A)(R)   *Le 26:44*
thou shalt utterly *a.* it, a   *De 7:26*
cursed
Utterly detest and loathe it   *De 7:26*
(B)
not *a.* Edomite, not *a.* an   *De 23:7*
Egyptian
detest an Edomite (B)   *De 23:7*
he hath made his people *a.*   *1Sa 27:12*
him
brought himself in bad   *1Sa 27:12*
repute (B)
mine own clothes shall *a.* me   *Job 9:31*
my familiar friends *a.* me   *Job 19:19*
(A)(E)
They *a.* me, they flee from   *Job 30:10*
me
they despise Me (B)   *Job 30:10*
I *a.* myself, and repent in   *Job 42:6*
dust and
I retract and repent (B)   *Job 42:6*
I despise myself and repent   *Job 42:6*
(R)

the Lord will *a.* the bloody   *Ps 5:6*
man
I hate, *a.* lying, but love   *Ps 119:163*
thy law
I hate, I despise falsehood   *Ps 119:163*
(B)
nations shall *a.* him   *Pr 24:24*
do not *a.* us for thy name's   *Jer 14:21*
sake
do not reject the throne (B)   *Jer 14:21*
do not spurn us, for thy   *Jer 14:21*
name's (R)
they *a.* him that speaketh   *Am 5:10*
uprightly
I *a.* the excellency of Jacob   *Am 6:8*
I detest the pride of Jacob   *Am 6:8*
(B)
hear, ye that *a.* judgment,   *Mic 3:9*
pervert
spurn justice, twist everything   *Mic 3:9*
(B)
a. that which is evil, cleave   *Ro 12:9*
to good
hate what is evil (A)(R)   *Ro 12:9*
loathing evil, clinging to good   *Ro 12:9*
(N)
a genuine break with evil (P)   *Ro 12:9*

ABHORRED

have made our savour to be   *Ex 5:21*
a.
made us a rotten stench to be   *Ex 5:21*
detested (A)
spoiling prospects with   *Ex 5:21*
Pharoah (B)
made us offensive in sight of   *Ex 5:21*
(R)
committed, and therefore I   *Le 20:23*
a. them
I am wearied and grieved by   *Le 20:23*
them (A)
their soul *a.* my statutes   *Le 26:43*
they despised and rejected   *Le 26:43*
(A)
when Lord saw it, he *a.*   *De 32:19*
them
He spurned and rejected   *De 32:19*
them (A)
when Lord saw he spurned   *De 32:19*
them (B)(R)
men *a.* the offering of the   *1Sa 2:17*
Lord
they despised the offering   *1Sa 2:17*
(A)
people came to scorn   *1Sa 2:17*
sacrifices (B)
men despised offering of   *1Sa 2:17*
Jehovah (E)
treated offering with   *1Sa 2:17*
contempt (R)
shall hear, thou art *a.* of   *2Sa 16:21*
thy father
made yourself detestable   *2Sa 16:21*
to your (B)
made yourself odious to   *2Sa 16:21*
father (R)
Hadad *a.* Israel, and   *1Ki 11:25*
reigned over
he loathed Israel (B)   *1Ki 11:25*
all my inward friends *a.* me   *Job 19:19*
all my intimate friends   *Job 19:19*
avoid me (B)
nor *a.* affliction of the   *Ps 22:24*
afflicted
he was wroth, and greatly *a.*   *Ps 78:59*
Israel
Abhorring and loathing her   *Ps 78:59*
ways (A)
He utterly rejected Israel   *Ps 78:59*
(R)
Thou hast cast off and *a.*   *Ps 89:38*
You have cast off and   *Ps 89:38*
rejected (A)(R)
he *a.* his own inheritance   *Ps 106:40*
He regarded heritage with   *Ps 106:40*
disgust (B)
who is *a.* of Lord shall fall   *Pr 22:14*
therein
he who is cursed of Lord   *Pr 22:14*
falls (B)
he whom Lord is angry with   *Pr 22:14*
falls (R)
the Lord hath *a.* his   *La 2:7*
sanctuary
He has repudiated his holy   *La 2:7*
place (B)
He has disowned his sanctuary   *La 2:7*
(R)

thou hast made thy beauty   *Eze 16:25*
to be *a.*
made your beauty an   *Eze 16:25*
abomination (A)(E)
prostituting your beauty   *Eze 16:25*
(B)(R)
their soul also *a.* me   *Zec 11:8*
they also loathed me   *Zec 11:8*
(A)(B)(E)
they also detested me (R)   *Zec 11:8*

ABHORRENCE

an *a.* to the Lord (B)   *De 7:25; 27:15*
a. to all flesh (S)   *Isa 66:24*

ABHORRENT

are *a.* to the Lord (B)   *De 23:18*

ABHORREST

the land that thou *a.* shall be   *Isa 7:16*
you feel a sickening dread   *Isa 7:16*
(B)
before kings you are in dread   *Isa 7:16*
(R)
thou that *a.* idols, dost thou   *Ro 2:22*
commit
You that abominate false   *Ro 2:22*
(B)
You that abominate false   *Ro 2:22*
gods (N)
You loathe idolatry (P)   *Ro 2:22*

ABHORRETH

So that his life *a.* bread   *Job 33:20*
his desire makes him loathe   *Job 33:20*
food (A)(R)
blesseth covetous whom the   *Ps 10:3*
Lord *a.*
deviseth mischief on bed, he   *Ps 36:4*
a. not evil
he does not reject or despise   *Ps 36:4*
evil (A)
he does not loathe evil (B)   *Ps 36:4*
he does not spurn evil (R)   *Ps 36:4*
their soul *a.* all manner of   *Ps 107:18*
meat
to him whom the nation *a.*   *Isa 49:7*
him who man rejects,   *Isa 49:7*
despises (A)

ABHORRING

A. and loathing her ways   *Ps 78:59*
(A)
they shall be an *a.* unto all   *Isa 66:24*
flesh

ABI

his mother's name also was   *2Ki 18:2*
A.

ABIA

A. his son, Asa his son   *1Ch 3:10*
Roboam begat *A.*; and *A.*   *M't 1:7*
begat
Zacharias, of the course of *A.*   *Lu 1:5*
the *A.* week of series (B)   *Lu 1:5*

ABIAH

the name of the second, *A.*   *1Sa 8:2*
A. Hezron's wife bare him   *1Ch 2:24*
Ashur
the firstborn Vashni, and *A.*   *1Ch 6:28*
Jerimoth, and *A.*, and   *1Ch 7:8*
Anathoth

ABI-ALBON

A. the Arbathite   *2Sa 23:31*

ABIASAPH

Assir, Elkanah, and *A.*   *Ex 6:24*

ABIATHAR

A. escaped and fled to   *1Sa 22:20;*
David   *1Sa 22:21-22; 23:6*
David said to *A.*, Bring   *1Sa 23:9;*
the ephod   *30:7*
Ahimelech the son of *A.*   *2Sa 8:17;*
       1Ch 24:6
A. went up until all the   *2Sa 15:24*
people

Jonathan the son of *A.* 2Sa 15:27; 1Ki 1:42

Zadok and *A.* were priests 2Sa 15:29; 15:35; 17:15; 19:11; 20:25; 1Ki 4:4; 1Ch 15:11

A. the priest 1Ki 1:7; 1Ki 1:19, 25; 2:22, 26

Solomon thrust out *A.* from 1Ki 2:27 being

did the king put in room of 1Ki 2:35 *A.*

Abimelech the son 1Ch 18:16; 24:6 of *A.*

the son of Benaiah, and 1Ch 27:34 *A.*

in the days of *A.* the high M'k 2:26 priest

ABIATHAR'S

Zadok's son, and Jonathan 2Sa 15:36 *A.* son

ABIB

ye came out in the month *A.* Ex 13:4; 34:18

time appointed of the Ex 23:15; month *A.* 34:18

Observe the month *A.,* keep De 16:1 passover

ABIDA

Epher, Henoch, and *A.* 1Ch 1:33

ABIDAH

Hanoch, and *A.* Ge 25:4

ABIDAN

A. the son of Gideoni Nu 1:11; 7:65

of the sons of Benjamin shall Nu 2:22 be *A.*

On the ninth day *A.* the son Nu 7:60 of

of the children of Benjamin Nu 10:24 was *A.*

ABIDE

we will *a.* in the street all Ge 19:2 night

spend the night in the square Ge 19:2 (A)

a. you here with the ass, I Ge 22:5 and lad

stay here with the ass (A) Ge 22:5

let the damsel *a.* with us a Ge 24:55 few days

it is better I give her to Ge 29:19 thee, *a.* with

stay and live with me (A) Ge 29:19

let thy servant *a.* instead of Ge 44:33 the lad

remain instead of the youth Ge 44:33 (A)

a. every man in his place Ex 16:29

a. at the door of the Le 8:35 tabernacle

wages of him hired shall not Le 19:13 *a.* with

a. to the death of the high Nu 35:25 priest

a. here fast by my maidens Ru 2:8

appear before Lord, and *a.* 1Sa 1:22 for ever

ark of God shall not *a.* with 1Sa 5:7 us

a. with me, fear not, for he 1Sa 22:23

whom they had made *a.* at 1Sa 30:21 brook Besor

his will I be, with him will 2Sa 16:18 I *a.*

a. with (B) 1Ki 6:13; Ps 37:27

they rebel, nor *a.* in paths Job 24:13 of light

a. in the covert to lie in Job 38:40 wait

will unicorn be willing to *a.* Job 39:9 by crib

who shall *a.* in thy tabernacle Ps 15:1

I will *a.* in thy tabernacle for Ps 61:4 ever

he shall *a.* before God for Ps 61:7 ever

shall *a.* under shadow of Ps 91:1 Almighty

remain stable and fixed under Ps 91:1 (A)

lodges in shadow of the Ps 91:1 Almighty (B)

her feet *a.* not in her house Pr 7:11

he that hath it shall *a.* Pr 19:23 satisfied

that shall *a.* with him of his Ec 8:15 labour

nations not able to *a.* his Jer 10:10 indignation

if ye *a.* in land I will build Jer 42:10 you

no man shall *a.* there Jer 49:18; Jer 49:33; 50:40

thou shalt *a.* for me many Ho 3:3 days

children of Israel shall *a.* Ho 3:4 many days

dwell, sit deprived many days Ho 3:4 (A)(R)

continue many days without a Ho 3:4 king (B)

the sword shall *a.* on his Ho 11:6 cities

the day is terrible, who can Joe 2:11 *a.* it

shall *a.* for now shall he be Mic 5:4 great

who can *a.* fierceness of his Na 1:6 anger

who may *a.* the day of his Mal 3:2 coming

Who can endure day of Mal 3:2 coming (A)(B)(R)

there *a.* M't 10:11; M'k 6:10; Lu 9:4

abide (E) M't 26:38; M'k 13:34; Lu 24:49; Joh 4:49; Ac 18:20

for to-day I must *a.* at thy Lu 19:5 house

a. with us, it is toward Lu 24:29 evening

believe on me, not *a.* in Joh 12:46 darkness

no believer remain in Joh 12:46 darkness (B)(N)(P)(R)

another Comforter may *a.* Joh 14:16 for ever

He may remain with you Joh 14:16 for ever (A)

Comforter stay with you for Joh 14:16 ever (B)

He may be with you for Joh 14:16 ever (E)(N)(R)

to stand with you, be with Joh 14:16 you always (P)

a. in me, and I in you Joh 15:4

except it *a.* in the vine Joh 15:4

Dwell with me, I will dwell Joh 15:4 in you (A)(E)

Remain in me, I in you Joh 15:4; (B) Joh 15:6-7, 10

go on growing in me, I Joh 15:4 will grow in you (P)

If a man *a.* not in me, he is Joh 15:6 cast

If ye *a.* in me, my words *a.* Joh 15:7 in you

a. in my love, *a.* in his love Joh 15:10

it pleased Silas to *a.* there Ac 15:34 still

come into my house and *a.* Ac 16:15 there

bonds and afflictions *a.* me Ac 20:23

except *a.* in ship, cannot be Ac 27:31 saved

if any man's work *a.* he 1Co 3:14 shall receive

survives this test 1Co 3:14 (A)(B)(P)(R)

If a man's building stands 1Co 3:14 (E)

good for them to *a.* even as I 1Co 7:8

let every man *a.* in same 1Co 7:20 calling

she is happier if she so *a.* 1Co 7:40

to *a.* in flesh is more Ph'p 1:24 needful

I know I shall *a.* with you Ph'p 1:25 all

I besought thee to *a.* at 1Ti 1:3 Ephesus

let that *a.* in you which ye 1Jo 2:24 heard

ye shall *a.* in him 1Jo 2:27

little children, *a.* in him 1Jo 2:28

ABIDES

God *a.* in us (A)(E)(R) 1Jo 4:12

ABIDETH

all that *a.* not the fire ye Nu 31:23 shall

Ziba said, he *a.* at Jerusalem 2Sa 16:3

man being in honour *a.* not Ps 49:12

God hear, even he that *a.* of Ps 55:19 old

thou hast established earth, Ps 119:90 it *a.*

be as mount Zion, which *a.* Ps 125:1 ever

heareth reproof, *a.* among Pr 15:31 wise

cometh, but the earth *a.* for Ec 1:4 ever

earth remains for ever Ec 1:4 (A)(B)(R)

he that *a.* in city shall die by Jer 21:9 sword

the wrath of God *a.* on him Joh 3:36

servant *a.* not, but Son *a.* Joh 8:35 for ever

except corn of wheat die, it Joh 12:24 *a.* alone

we have heard that Christ Joh 12:34 *a.* for ever

he *a.* with you (E) Joh 14:17

a. in me bringeth forth much Joh 15:5 fruit

now *a.* faith, hope, charity 1Co 13:13

if we believe not, he *a.* 2Ti 2:13 faithful

Melchizedec *a.* a priest Heb 7:3 continually

by word of God which *a.* 1Pe 1:23 for ever

saith he *a.* in him ought to 1Jo 2:6 walk

that loveth his brother *a.* in 1Jo 2:10 light

strong, and the word of God 1Jo 2:14 *a.* in you

he that doeth will of God 1Jo 2:17 *a.* for ever

anointing *a.* in you and 1Jo 2:27 teacheth you

whosoever *a.* in him sinneth 1Jo 3:6 not

loveth not his brother *a.* in 1Jo 3:14 death

hereby we know he *a.* in us 1Jo 3:24

whoso *a.* not in doctrine of 2Jo 9 Christ, he that *a.* hath Father and Son

ABIDING

Balaam saw Israel *a.* in his Nu 24:2 tents

a. with her in chamber J'g 16:9; 16:12

from *a.* in inheritance of 1Sa 26:19 Lord

shepherds *a.* in the field Lu 2:8

have not his word *a.* in you Joh 5:38

Father *a.* in me (E) Joh 14:10

were in city *a.* certain days Ac 16:12

no murderer hath eternal life 1Jo 3:15 *a.* in

ABIEL

Kish, the son of *A.* 1Sa 9:1; 14:51

Hurai of brooks of Gaash, 1Ch 11:32 *A.*

ABIEZER

the children of *A.* Jos 17:2

A. was gathered after him J'g 6:34

is not better than vintage of J'g 8:2 *A.*

A. the Anethothite 2Sa 23:27; 1Ch 11:28

Hammoleketh bare Ishod, *A.* 1Ch 7:18

captain for ninth month 1Ch 27:12 was *A.*

ABI-EZRITE

pertained unto Joash the *A.* J'g 6:11

ABI-EZRITES

it is yet in Ophrah of the *A.* J'g 6:24

his father, in Ophrah of the J'g 8:32 *A.*

ABIGAIL

Nabal: name of his wife *A.*   *1Sa 25:3;*
    1Sa 27:3; 30:5; 2Sa 2:2; 3:3
one of the young men told *1Sa 25:14;*
A.   *25:18, 23, 32, 36, 39-40, 42*
in to *A.* the daughter of   *2Sa 17:25*
Nahash
sisters were Zeruiah and *A.* *1Ch 2:16*
A. bare Amasa; and the   *1Ch 2:17*
father
the second Daniel, of *A.* the *1Ch 3:1*

ABIHAIL

Zuriel the son of *A.*   *Nu 3:35*
name of wife of Abishur   *1Ch 2:29*
was *A.*
These are children of *A.* the *1Ch 5:14*
son
A. daughter of Eliab   *2Ch 11:18;*
      Es 2:15; 9:29

ABIHU

she bare him Nadab and *A.* *Ex 6:23;*
  Le 10:1; Nu 26:60; 1Ch 6:3; 24:1
Aaron, Nadab, and *A.*   *Ex 24:1;*
    Ex 24:9; 28:1
Nadab the firstborn, and *A.* *Nu 3:2;*
        26:60
Nadab and *A.* died before the *Nu 3:4;*
Lord   *Nu 26:61; 1Ch 24:2*

ABIHUD

Addar, and Gera, and *A.*   *1Ch 8:3*

ABIJAH

A. the son of Jeroboam was *1Ki 14:1*
sick
seventh to Hakkoz, eighth *1Ch 24:10*
to *A.*
which bare him *A.*, and   *2Ch 11:20*
Attai
Rehoboam made *A.* chief *2Ch 11:22*
ruler
A. his son reigned in his *2Ch 12:16;*
stead   *2Ch 13:1-4, 15, 17, 19-22*
So *A.* slept with his fathers *2Ch 14:1*
And his mother's name was *2Ch 29:1*
A.
Meshullam, *A.*, Mijamin   *Ne 10:7*
Iddo, Ginnetho, *A.*   *Ne 12:4*
Of *A.*, Zichri   *Ne 12:17*

ABIJAM

A. his son reigned in his *1Ki 14:31;*
stead   *1Ki 15:1, 7-8*

ABILENE

Lysanias the tetrarch of *A.*   *Lu 3:1*

ABILITY

filled them with *a.* (R)   *Ex 35:35*
put *a.* and intelligence (R)   *Ex 36:1;*
        36:2
according to his *a.* that   *Le 27:8*
vowed
mighty man of *a.* (A)(R)   *1Ch 26:6;*
     1Ch 26:30-32
They gave after their *a.*   *Ez 2:69*
We after our *a.* have redeemed *Ne 5:8*
such as had *a.* in them   *Da 1:4*
according to his several *a.* *M't 25:15*
have *a.* to escape (B)   *Lu 21:36*
granted *a.* to become sons *Joh 1:12*
(B)
every man according to his *Ac 11:29*
a.
a. to heal (P)   *1Co 12:9*
according to the *a.* (A)   *2Co 8:3*
as of the *a.* which God   *1Pe 4:11*
giveth

ABIMAEL

Obal, *A.*, and Sheba   *Ge 10:28;*
      1Ch 11:22

ABIMELECH

A. king of Gerar   *Ge 20:2;*
20:3-4, 8-10, 14-15, 17-18; 21:22, 25-27,
        29, 32

A. king of Philistines   *Ge 26:1;*
    Ge 26:8-11, 16, 26
A. the son of Gideon   *J'g 8:31;*
9:1, 3-4, 6, 16, 18-25, 27-29, 31, 34-35,
38-42, 44-45, 47-50, 52, 55-56; 10:1;
        2Sa 11:21
A. the son of Abiathar   *1Ch 18:16*
changed his behavior   *Ps 34 title*
before *A.* (S)

ABIMELECH'S

A. servants had violently *Ge 21:25*
taken
a piece of millstone upon *A.* *J'g 9:53*
head

ABINADAB

brought it into the house of *1Sa 7:1*
A.
Jesse called *A.* and made *1Sa 16:8*
him pass
next unto him *A.*   *1Sa 17:13*
Philistines slew Jonathan *1Sa 31:2;*
and *A.*   *1Ch 10:2*
brought it out of house of *A.* *2Sa 6:3;*
     2Sa 6:4; 1Ch 13:7
son of *A.* in all region of *1Ki 4:11*
Dor
begat his firstborn Eliab, *1Ch 2:13*
and *A.*
Saul begat *A.*   *1Ch 8:33; 9:39*

ABINOAM

Barak son of *A.* *J'g 4:6; 4:12; 5:1, 12*

ABIRAM

Dathan and *A.*   *Nu 16:1;*
16:12, 24-25, 27; 26:9; De 11:6; Ps 106:17
laid the foundation thereof *1Ki 16:34*
in *A.*

ABISHAG

found *A.* the Shunamite *1Ki 1:3; 1:15*
give me *A.* to wife   *1Ki 2:17; 2:21-22*

ABISHAI

A. the son of Zeruiah   *1Sa 26:6;*
26:7-9; 2Sa 2:18, 24; 3:30; 16:9; 19:21;
20:10; 21:17; 23:18; 1Ch 2:16; 11:20;
        18:12
delivered into the hand of *2Sa 10:10*
A.
then fled they also before *2Sa 10:14*
A.
David said to *A.*, and to *2Sa 16:11;*
all his   *20:6*
third part under the hand of *2Sa 18:2*
A.
he delivered unto the hand *1Ch 19:11*
of *A.*
likewise fled before *A.* his *1Ch 19:15*
brother

ABISHALOM

Maachah, daughter of *A.*   *1Ki 15:2;*
        15:10

ABISHUA

begat Phinehas, Phinehas *1Ch 6:4;*
begat *A.*   *6:50*
A. begat Bukki   *1Ch 6:5*
A., and Naaman, and Ahoah *1Ch 8:4*
The son of *A.*, the son of *Ezr 7:5*
Phinehas

ABISHUR

sons of Shammar; Nadab *1Ch 2:28*
and *A.*
name of wife of *A.* was   *1Ch 2:29*
Abihail

ABITAL

Shephatiah son of *A.*   *2Sa 3:4;*
        1Ch 3:3

ABITUB

Hushim begat *A.*   *1Ch 8:11*

ABIUD

Zorobabel begat *A.*; and *A.* *M't 1:13*
begat

ABJECT

I am become *a.* (A)(B)   *La 1:11*

ABJECTS

a. gathered together against *Ps 35:15*
me
smiters, slanderers and   *Ps 35:15*
revilers (A)
Slanderers (B)   *Ps 35:15*
cripples (R)   *Ps 35:15*

ABLE

who are *a.* men (S)   *Ge 47:6*
provide out of people *a.* men *Ex 18:21*
two pigeons, as he is *a.* to *Le 14:22;*
get   *14:31*
all *a.* to go to war   *Nu 1:3;*
1:20, 22, 24, 26, 28, 30, 32, 34, 36, 38,
    40, 42, 45; 26:2
we are well *a.* to overcome *Nu 13:30*
it
every man give as he is *a.* *De 16:17*
no man been *a.* to stand *Jos 23:9*
before you
who is *a.* to stand before *1Sa 6:20*
holy God
who is *a.* to judge so great *1Ki 3:9*
people
who is *a.* to build him an *2Ch 2:6*
house
none is *a.* to withstand thee *2Ch 20:6*
Lord is *a.* to give thee much *2Ch 25:9*
more
who is *a.* to stand before *Job 41:10*
me
who is *a.* to stand before envy *Pr 27:4*
offering be as he is *a.* to *Eze 46:11*
give
God whom we serve is *a.* to *Da 3:17*
deliver
is God *a.* to deliver thee *Da 6:20*
from lions
God is *a.* of these stones   *M't 3:9;*
        Lu 3:8
believe that I am *a.*   *M't 9:28*
to do this
fear him who is *a.* to   *M't 10:28*
destroy soul in hell
he that is *a.* to receive it, *M't 19:12*
let him
are ye *a.* to drink of the *M't 20:22*
cup I shall drink
no man *a.* to answer him a *M't 22:46*
word
spake he, as they were *a.* to *M'k 4:33*
hear it
no man *a.* to pluck them out *Joh 10:29*
of my
yoke fathers nor we were *a.* *Ac 15:10*
to bear
word of his grace *a.* to build *Ac 20:32*
you
which among you *a.* go down *Ac 25:5*
with me
he promised, he was *a.* to *Ro 4:21*
perform
God is *a.* to graff them in *Ro 11:23*
again
for God is *a.* to make him *Ro 14:4*
stand
ye are *a.* also to admonish *Ro 15:14*
one another
ye not *a.* nor yet now are ye *1Co 3:2*
a.
not suffer to be tempted *1Co 10:13*
above that are *a.*
hath made us *a.* ministers of *2Co 3:6*
new testament
God is *a.* to make all grace *2Co 9:8*
abound
to him that is *a.* to do   *Eph 3:20*
abundantly
he is *a.* to subdue all   *Ph'p 3:21*
things to himself
he is *a.* to keep that I   *2Ti 1:12*
committed
never *a.* to come to   *2Ti 3:7*
knowledge of truth
scriptures *a.* to make wise to *2Ti 3:15*
salvation
is *a.* to succour them that *Heb 2:18*
are tempted

to him that was *a.* to save   *Heb 5:7*
from death
he is *a.* to save to the   *Heb 7:25*
uttermost that
accounting God was *a.* to   *Heb 11:19*
raise him up
word which is *a.* to save   *Jas 1:21*
your souls
is *a.* also to bridle the whole   *Jas 3:2*
body
one lawgiver *a.* to save and   *Jas 4:12*
destroy
to him that is *a.* to keep   *Jude 24*
from falling
no man *a.* to open the book   *Re 5:3*
nor look
who is *a.* to make war with   *Re 13:4*
beast
no man *a.* to enter into the   *Re 15:8*
temple

BE ABLE

himself *be a.* to redeem it   *Le 25:26*
not any man *be a.* to stand   *De 7:24;*
before thee   *11:25; Jos 1:5*
if Lord be with me I shall *Jos 14:12*
be a. to drive
if he *be a.* to fight with me   *1Sa 17:9*
and kill me
we should *be a.* to offer   *1Ch 29:14*
willingly
your God should be *a.* to   *2Ch 32:14*
deliver
if thou *be a.* to profit   *Isa 47:12*
nor shall righteous *be a.* to   *Eze 33:12*
live
whether he *be a.* with   *Lu 14:31*
10,000 to meet
be a. to separate us from   *Ro 8:39*
love of God
that ye may *be a.* to bear   *1Co 10:13*
it
may *be a.* to comprehend   *Eph 3:18*
with all
may *be a.* to stand against   *Eph 6:11*
the devil
wherewith ye shall *be a.* to   *Eph 6:16*
quench
shall *be a.* to teach others   *2Ti 2:2*
also
may *be a.* with sound doctrine   *Tit 1:9*
may *be a.* after my decease   *2Pe 1:15*
to have
wrath is come, who shall *be*   *Re 6:17*
a. to

NOT BE ABLE

not be a. to deliver   *2Ki 18:29;*
   Isa 36:14
cast down, shall *not be a.* to   *Ps 36:12*
rise
shall *not be a.* to find it   *Ec 8:17*
shalt *not be a.* to put it off   *Isa 47:11*
they shall *not be a.* to   *Jer 11:11*
escape
he shall *not be a.* to hide   *Jer 49:10*
himself
gold shall *not be a.* to   *Eze 7:19*
deliver them
to enter in, and shall *not be*   *Lu 13:24*
a.
wisdom adversaries *not be a.*   *Lu 21:15*
to gainsay

NOT ABLE

if he be *not a.* to bring a lamb   *Le 5:7*
we be *not a.* to go up   *Nu 13:31*
because Lord was *not a.*   *Nu 14:16;*
   De 9:28
ships *not a.* to go to   *2Ch 20:37*
Tarshish
we are *not a.* to stand   *Ezr 10:13*
without
we were *not a.* to build the   *Ne 4:10*
wall
wounded that were *not a.* to   *Ps 18:38*
rise
device they are *not a.* to   *Ps 21:11*
perform
I am *not a.* to look up   *Ps 40:12*
land is *not a.* to bear his   *Am 7:10*
words
if ye *not a.* to do that   *Lu 12:26*
thing
laid foundation, *not a.* to   *Lu 14:29*
finish

were *not a.* to draw it for   *Joh 21:6*
the fishes
were *not a.* to resist the   *Ac 6:10*
wisdom

ABLUTIONS

various *a.,* physical   *Heb 9:10*
regulations (B)(R)

ABNER

captain of his host was *A.*   *1Sa 14:50;*
   1Sa 17:55; 26:5; 2Sa 2:8
A. son of Ner   *1Sa 14:51;*
26:5; 2Sa 2:8, 12; 3:23, 25; 1Ki 2:5,
   32; 1Ch 26:28
A. whose son is this   *1Sa 17:55*
youth
A. took him, and brought   *1Sa 17:57*
him to Saul
A. and people lay round   *1Sa 26:7*
about him
David cried, Answerest   *1Sa 26:14;*
thou not *A.*   *26:15*
A. said, Let the young men   *2Sa 2:14;*
play   *2Sa 2:17, 19-26, 29-30*
A. made himself strong for   *2Sa 3:6*
house of Saul
A. turned against Ishbosheth   *2Sa 3:7;*
3:8-12, 16-17, 19-28, 30-33, 37
Saul's son heard that *A.* was   *2Sa 4:2*
dead
buried it in the sepulchre of   *2Sa 4:12*
A.
Jaasiel the son of *A.*   *2Sa 27:21*

ABNER'S

of Benjamin, and of *A.* men   *2Sa 2:31*

ABODE

Jacob *a.* with him a month   *Ge 29:14*
his bow *a.* in strength, and   *Ge 49:24*
the arms
thy holy *a.* (R)   *Ex 15:13*
glory of the Lord *a.* on Sinai   *Ex 24:16*
because the cloud *a.* thereon   *Ex 40:35*
his *a.* outside the camp   *Le 13:46*
(A)(B)
where cloud *a.* Israel pitched   *Nu 9:17*
   9:18-22
people journeyed, and *a.* in   *Nu 11:35*
Hazeroth
people *a.* in Kadesh   *Nu 20:1;*
   De 1:46; J'g 11:17
princes of Moab *a.* with   *Nu 22:8*
Balaam
Israel *a.* in Shittim, began   *Nu 25:1*
to commit
we *a.* in valley over against   *De 3:29*
Beth-peor
I *a.* in the mount forty days   *De 9:9*
they *a.* in their places in the   *Jos 5:8*
camp
Gilead *a.* beyond Jordan, *a.*   *J'g 5:17*
in breaches
the Levite *a.* with him three   *J'g 19:4*
days
a. in the rock Rimmon four   *J'g 20:47*
months
woman *a.* and gave her son   *1Sa 1:23*
suck
while the ark *a.* in   *1Sa 7:2*
Kirjath-jearim
Saul and Jonathan *a.* in   *1Sa 13:16;*
Gibeah   *22:6*
David *a.* in wood   *1Sa 23:14;*
   1Sa 23:18, 25; 26:3
David *a.* two days in Ziklag   *2Sa 1:1*
Uriah *a.* in Jerusalem that   *2Sa 11:12*
day
servant vowed while I *a.* at   *2Sa 15:8*
Geshur
carried him to loft where   *1Ki 17:19*
he *a.*
I know thy *a.*   *2Ki 19:27; Isa 37:28*
a fitting *a.* (A)   *2Ch 6:2*
the *a.* of the righteous (R)   *Pr 3:33*
holy and glorious *a.* (B)(R)   *Isa 63:15*
Jeremiah *a.* in court of the   *Jer 38:28*
prison
while they *a.* in Galilee,   *M't 17:22*
Jesus said
Mary *a.* with her about three   *Lu 1:56*
months
nor *a.* in any house, but in   *Lu 8:27*
the tombs

I saw the Spirit, it *a.* upon   *Joh 1:32*
him
they came and *a.* with him   *Joh 1:39*
that day
when he said these words he   *Joh 7:9*
a. in Galilee
he was a murderer, *a.* not in   *Joh 8:44*
truth
come and make our *a.* with   *Joh 14:23*
him
an upper room where *a.*   *Ac 1:13*
Peter, James
long time they *a.* speaking   *Ac 14:3*
boldly
Paul *a.* with them and   *Ac 18:3*
wrought
we came and *a.* with brethren   *Ac 21:7*
one day
entered house of Philip and   *Ac 21:8*
a. with him
a. two whole years (E)   *Ac 28:30*
I went and *a.* with Peter   *Ga 1:18*
fifteen days
a fixed *a.* of God (A)   *Eph 2:22*

ABODE THERE

according to days ye *a. there*   *De 1:46*
came to mountain, *a. there*   *Jos 2:22*
three days
people *a. there* till even   *J'g 21:2*
before God
came to Jerusalem *a. there*   *Ezr 8:32*
three days
Jesus *a. there* two days   *Joh 4:40*
Silas and Timotheus *a. there*   *Ac 17:14*
still

THERE ABODE

there a. we in tents three   *Ezr 8:15*
days
where John first baptized,   *Joh 10:40*
there a.
Herod went to Caesarea,   *Ac 12:19*
and *there a.*
there a. long time with the   *Ac 14:28*
disciples

ABODEST

a. thou among the sheepfolds   *J'g 5:15*

ABOLISH

the idols he shall utterly (B)   *Isa 2:18*
every one shall vanish (B)   *Isa 2:18*
idols shall utterly pass away   *Isa 2:18*
(E)(R)

ABOLISHED

my righteousness shall not be   *Isa 51:6*
My victory shall never be   *Isa 51:6*
annulled (B)
My deliverance shall never be   *Isa 51:6*
ended (R)
and your works may be *a.*   *Eze 6:6*
Handiworks wiped away,   *Eze 6:6*
blotted out (A)
your evil doings ended (B)   *Eze 6:6*
your works wiped out (R)   *Eze 6:6*
look to end of that which is   *2Co 3:13*
a.
gaze upon finish of the   *2Co 3:13*
vanishing (A)
finishing of something faded   *2Co 3:13*
(B)
that which is passing away   *2Co 3:13*
(E)
end of the fading splendor   *2Co 3:13*
(R)
a. the hostile dividing wall   *Eph 2:14*
(A)
having *a.* in his flesh the   *Eph 2:15*
enmity
ended the feud, demolished   *Eph 2:15*
the law (B)
broken down enmity,   *Eph 2:15*
annulled law (N)
removed hostility of the law   *Eph 2:15*
(P)
Jesus Christ, who hath *a.*   *2Ti 1:10*
death
annulled death, made it of   *2Ti 1:10*
no effect (A)
rendered death ineffectual (B)   *2Ti 1:10*
broken the power of death   *2Ti 1:10*
(N)

ABOMINABLE

shall touch any *a.* unclean thing · *Le 7:21*
shall not make yourselves *a.* · *Le 11:43; 20:25*
Do not defile yourselves (B) · *Le 11:43*
not any one of these *a.* customs · *Le 18:30*
it is *a.*; it shall not be accepted · *Le 19:7*
it is loathsome (A) · *Le 19:7*
shalt not eat any *a.* thing · *De 14:3*
your *a.* practices (A) · *De 18:9; 2Ki 16:3*
an *a.* idol (A) · *2Ki 11:7; 23:13*
king's word was *a.* to Joab · *1Ch 21:6*
was detestable to Joab (A) · *1Ch 21:6*
put away the *a.* idols out of · *2Ch 15:8*
remove the detestable things (B) · *2Ch 15:8*
much more *a.* and filthy is man · *Job 15:16*
they have done *a.* works · *Ps 14:1*
and have done *a.* iniquity · *Ps 53:1*
thy grave like an *a.* branch · *Isa 14:19*
a. things is in their vessels · *Isa 65:4*
detestable and *a.* things · *Jer 16:18*
do not this *a.* thing that I hate · *Jer 44:4*
neither came *a.* flesh into · *Eze 4:14*
saw *a.* beasts and all idols · *Eze 8:10*
loathsome, *a.* impurities (B) · *Eze 11:18*
thy sins committed more *a.* than they · *Eze 16:52*
the scant measure that is *a.* · *Mic 6:10*
I will cast *a.* filth upon thee · *Na 3:6*
in works deny him, being *a.* · *Tit 1:16*
detestable and loathsome (A) · *Tit 1:16*
detestable and disobedient (B)(R) · *Tit 1:16*
vile and rebellious (P) · *Tit 1:16*
banquetings, and *a.* idolatries · *1Pe 4:3*
indulging in unbridled lusts (B) · *1Pe 4:3*
walked in lasciviousness (E) · *1Pe 4:3*
lived in license and debauchery (N) · *1Pe 4:3*
living in lawless idolatry (R) · *1Pe 4:3*
follow their *a.* lusts (N) · *2Pe 3:10*
fearful, unbelieving, and *a.* · *Re 21:8*
defiled with abominations (A) · *Re 21:8*
the depraved (B) · *Re 21:8*
the vile (N) · *Re 21:8*
the corrupt (P) · *Re 21:8*
the polluted (R) · *Re 21:8*

ABOMINABLY

did very *a.* in following idols · *1Ki 21:26*

ABOMINATE

You that *a.* false gods (N) · *Ro 2:22*

ABOMINATION

is an *a.* to the Egyptians · *Ge 43:32*
offence to Egyptians (B) · *Ge 43:32; 46:34*
we shall sacrifice *a.* of Egyptians · *Ex 8:26*
something offensive to Egyptians (B) · *Ex 8:26*
it shall be an *a.* · *Le 7:18; 11:41-42*
disgusting, repulsive, loathsome (B) · *Le 7:18*
they shall be *a.* to you · *Le 11:10; 12:20, 23*
offensive, repulsive, loathsome (B) · *Le 11:10*
as with womankind it is *a.* · *Le 18:22; 20:13*
it is detestable; perverse (B) · *Le 18:22; 20:13*
it is *a.* to the Lord · *De 7:25; 17:1*
it is an abhorrence (B) · *De 7:25; 22:5*
nor shall bring an *a.* into thy house · *De 7:26*
every *a.* they have done to their gods · *De 12:31*
that such *a.* is wrought among you · *De 13:14; 17:4*
all that do these things are *a.* · *De 18:12; 22:5*
both are an *a.* to the Lord · *De 23:18*

both are abhorrent to the Lord (B) · *De 23:18*
for that is an *a.* before the Lord · *De 24:4*
all that do unrighteously are *a.* · *De 25:16*
cursed be man that maketh *a.* to Lord · *De 27:15*
makes an abhorrence to the Lord (B) · *De 27:15*
a. and wantonness (R) · *J'g 20:6*
Israel was had in *a.* with Philistines · *1Sa 13:4*
became odious to Philistines (B)(R) · *1Sa 13:4*
Milcom the *a.* of Ammonites · *1Ki 11:5; 11:7*
high place for Chemosh *a.* of Moab · *1Ki 11:7*
abominable idol of Moab (A) · *1Ki 11:7; 11:5*
Ashtaroth the *a.* of Zidonians · *2Ki 23:13*
the abominable goddess of Sidonians (A) · *2Ki 23:13*
thou hast made me an *a.* to them · *Ps 88:8*
an object of loathing (B) · *Ps 88:8*
a thing of horror to them (R) · *Ps 88:8*
the froward is an *a.* to the Lord · *Pr 3:32*
seven things are an *a.* to him · *Pr 6:16*
speak truth, wickedness is *a.* to my lips · *Pr 8:7*
is detestable and loathsome to my (A) · *Pr 8:7*
a false balance is an *a.* to the Lord · *Pr 11:1*
extremely offensive, shamefully sinful (A) · *Pr 11:1; 11:20 12:22*
they of a froward heart are *a.* to Lord · *Pr 11:20*
lying lips are an *a.* to the Lord · *Pr 12:22*
it is *a.* to fools to depart from evil · *Pr 13:19*
hateful, exceedingly offensive (A) · *Pr 13:19; 16:5*
sacrifice of wicked is an *a.* · *Pr 15:8; 21:27*
way of wicked is an *a.* to the Lord · *Pr 15:9*
thoughts of wicked are *a.* to the Lord · *Pr 15:26*
shamefully vile, exceedingly offensive (A) · *Pr 15:26*
every one proud in heart is an *a.* · *Pr 16:5*
is an *a.* for kings to commit wickedness · *Pr 16:12*
they both are an *a.* to the Lord · *Pr 17:15*
both of them are alike *a.* to the Lord · *Pr 20:10*
exceedingly offensive, abhorrent (A) · *Pr 20:10*
divers weights are an *a.* to the Lord · *Pr 20:23*
the scorner is an *a.* to men · *Pr 24:9*
even his prayer shall be *a.* · *Pr 28:9*
an unjust man is *a.* to the just · *Pr 29:27*
the upright in the way is *a.* to wicked · *Pr 29:27*
incense is *a.* to me, the new moons · *Isa 1:13*
an *a.* is he that chooseth you · *Isa 41:24*
an offence is he who chooses you (B) · *Isa 41:24*
shall I make residue an *a.* · *Isa 44:19*
eating swine's flesh, and *a.*, and mouse · *Isa 66:17*
swine's flesh, vermin, and mice (B) · *Isa 66:17*
ye made my heritage an *a.* · *Jer 2:7*
ashamed when they committed *a.* · *Jer 6:15; 8:12*
make them an *a.* (B) · *Jer 25:9*
that they should do these *a.* to cause · *Jer 32:35*
made beauty an *a.* (A)(E) · *Eze 16:25*
they were haughty and committed *a.* · *Eze 16:50*
lift up eyes to idols, committed *a.* · *Eze 18:12*
committed *a.* with neighbor's wife · *Eze 22:11*
ye work *a.*, and defile every · *Eze 33:26*

place the *a.* that maketh desolate · *Da 11:31*
the *a.* that maketh desolate set up · *Da 12:11*
an *a.* is committed in Israel · *Mal 2:11*
see *a.* of desolation · *M't 24:15; M'k 13:14*
appalling sacrilege spoken by (A) · *M't 24:15*
desolating sacrilege spoken (R) · *M't 24:15*
esteemed among men is *a.* with God · *Lu 16:15*
detestable and abhorrent (A) · *Lu 16:15*
disgusting in sight of God (B) · *Lu 16:15*
no wise enter that worketh *a.* · *Re 21:27*
practicing lewdness and falsehood (B) · *Re 21:27*

ABOMINATIONS

not learn to do after *a.* of nations · *De 18:9*
abominable practices (A) · *De 18:9*
obnoxious ways of the nations (B) · *De 18:9*
with *a.* provoked him to anger · *De 32:16*
did according to all *a.* of nations · *1Ki 14:24*
through fire according to *a.* · *2Ki 16:3; 2Ch 28:3*
abominable idolatrous practices (A) · *2Ki 16:3*
did evil after *a.* of heathen · *2Ki 21:2; 2Ch 33:2*
idolatrous practices of nations (A) · *2Ki 21:2*
a. did Josiah put away · *2Ki 23:24; 2Ch 34:33*
acts of Jehoiakim and his *a.* he did · *2Ch 36:8*
his detestable practices (B) · *2Ch 36:8; 36:14*
people transgressed after all *a.* of heathen · *2Ch 36:14*
there are seven *a.* in his heart · *Pr 26:25*
Lord could not bear for the *a.* · *Jer 44:22*
alas for all evil *a.* of Israel · *Eze 6:11*
see *a.*, shalt see greater *a.* · *Eze 8:6; 8:13, 15*
behold wicked *a.* that they do here · *Eze 8:9*
is it a light thing to commit *a.* here · *Eze 8:17*
that sigh and cry for all *a.* done · *Eze 9:4*
offences that are practiced (B) · *Eze 9:4*
take away all *a.* from thence · *Eze 11:18*
detestable, offensive impurities (B) · *Eze 11:18*
turn away faces from all your *a.* · *Eze 14:6*
cause Jerusalem to know their *a.* · *Eze 16:2*
when righteous do according to *a.* · *Eze 18:24*
cause them to know *a.* of fathers · *Eze 20:4*
cast away every man *a.* of his eyes · *Eze 20:7*
detestable things you love (B) · *Eze 20:7*
did not cast away *a.* of their eyes · *Eze 20:8*
detestable things they loved (B) · *Eze 20:8*
shalt show her all her *a.* · *Eze 22:2*
loathe yourselves for all your *a.* · *Eze 36:31*
let it suffice you for all your *a.* · *Eze 44:6*
have broken my covenant for all *a.* · *Eze 44:7*
for the overspreading of *a.* · *Da 9:27*
on wing of horrors shall desolator come (B) · *Da 9:27*
take his *a.* from between teeth · *Zec 9:7*
golden cup in hand full of *a.* · *Re 17:4*
full of accursed offences (A) · *Re 17:4*
full of offences, impurities (B) · *Re 17:4*

full of obscenities and foulness (N)   Re 17:4

full of filthiness, foul impurity (P)   Re 17:4

mother of harlots and *a.* of earth   Re 17:5

of the atrocities of the earth (B)   Re 17:5

of every obscenity on earth (N)   Re 17:5

THEIR ABOMINATIONS

teach not to do after all *their a.*   De 20:18

abominable practices (A)   De 20:18

have seen *their a.* and their idols   De 29:17

seen their detestable things (B)(R)   De 29:17

people doing according to *their a.*   Ezr 9:1

their wicked practices (B)   Ezr 9:1; 9:11

with *their a.* which filled the land   Ezr 9:11

their soul delighteth in *their a.*   Isa 66:3

set *their a.* in the house   Jer 7:30; 32:34

for the evils committed in *their a.*   Eze 6:9

they made images of *their a.*   Eze 7:20

made detestable, loathsome images (B)   Eze 7:20

whose heart walketh after *their a.*   Eze 11:21

they may declare all *their a.*   Eze 12:16

yet hast thou done after *their a.*   Eze 16:47

commit whoredom after *their a.*   Eze 20:30

after loathsome detestable things (A)   Eze 20:30

declare to them *their a.*   Eze 23:36

land desolate because of *their a.*   Eze 33:29

have defiled my holy name by *their a.*   Eze 43:8

shall bear their shame and *their a.*   Eze 44:13

their a. were according as they loved   Ho 9:10

became detestable and loathsome like that which they loved (A)   Ho 9:10

THESE ABOMINATIONS

shall not commit any of *these a.*   Le 18:26

commit any of these offences (B)   Le 18:26

all *these a.* have the men done   Le 18:27

whosoever shall commit any *these a.*   Le 18:29

because of *these a.* Lord hath driven out   De 18:12

Manasseh hath done *these a.*   2Ki 21:11

done these detestable things (B)   2Ki 21:11

join affinity with people of *these a.*   Ezr 9:14

we are delivered to do all *these a.*   Jer 7:10

hath done all *these a.* shall die   Eze 18:13

all these evils; he shall die (B)   Eze 18:13

THINE ABOMINATIONS

if thou wilt put away *thine a.*   Jer 4:1

I have seen *thine a.* on the hills   Jer 13:27

detestable acts, adulteries, lewdness (A)   Jer 13:27

seen your detestable behavior (B)   Jer 13:27

the like, because of *thine a.*   Eze 5:9

I will recompense all *thine a.*   Eze 7:3; 7:4, 8-9

in all thine *a.* thou hast not remembered   Eze 16:22

with all the idols of *thine a.*   Eze 16:36

commit this lewdness above all *thine a.*   Eze 16:43

multiplied *thine a.* more than they   Eze 16:51

hast borne *thine a.*   Eze 16:58

THY ABOMINATIONS

hast defiled my sanctuary with *thy a.*   Eze 5:11

with detestable, loathsome impurities (B)   Eze 5:11

ABOUND

a. in prosperity (R)   De 28:11

faithful man shall *a.* with blessings   Pr 28:20

because iniquity shall *a.*   M't 24:12

love of many

multiplied lewdness and iniquity (A)   M't 24:12

due to excessive lawlessness (B)   M't 24:12

iniquity shall be multiplied (E)(R)   M't 24:12

as lawlessness spreads, men's love (N)(P)   M't 24:12

law entered that offence might *a.*   Ro 5:20

to expand, increase the trespass (A)   Ro 5:20

to make trespass more serious (B)   Ro 5:20

to multiply law-breaking (N)   Ro 5:20

to point the vast extent of sin (P)   Ro 5:20

to increase the trespass (R)   Ro 5:20

shall we continue in sin, that grace may *a.*   Ro 6:1

that grace may multiply, overflow (A)   Ro 6:1

that grace become more plentiful (B)   Ro 6:1

that there may be all the more grace (N)   Ro 6:1

see how far we can exploit grace (P)   Ro 6:1

that ye may *a.* in hope   Ro 15:13

as sufferings *a.* consolation abounds   2Co 1:5

sufferings fall to our lot abundantly (A)   2Co 1:5

experience richly the sufferings (B)   2Co 1:5

as Christ's cup of sufferings overflow (N)   2Co 1:5

share abundantly in Christ's suffering (R)   2Co 1:5

as you *a.* in every thing, see that ye *a.*   2Co 8:7

you are ahead in every thing (B)   2Co 8:7

you are so rich in every thing (N)   2Co 8:7

you excell in every thing (R)   2Co 8:7

God is able to make all grace *a.*   2Co 9:8

grace come to you in abundance (A)   2Co 9:8

pour out on you richly every grace (B)   2Co 9:8

provide richly every good gift (N)   2Co 9:8

God can give you every thing (P)   2Co 9:8

provide every blessing in abundance (R)   2Co 9:8

pray that your love may *a.* more   Ph'p 1:9

love grows richer and richer (B)(N)   Ph'p 1:9

I know how to *a.*, both to *a.* and suffer   Ph'p 4:12

I know how to enjoy plenty (A)   Ph'p 4:12

I know how to relish plenty (B)   Ph'p 4:12

desire fruit may *a.* to your account   Ph'p 4:17

I have all and *a.* I am full   Ph'p 4:18

Lord make you to *a.* in love one   1Th 3:12

increase, excell, overflow with love (A)   1Th 3:12

abundant and overrunning love (B)   1Th 3:12

love mount and overflow (N)   1Th 3:12

increasing and overflowing love (P)   1Th 3:12

so ye would *a.* more and more   1Th 4:1

if these things be in you and *a.*   2Pe 1:8

possess these qualities increasingly (B)   2Pe 1:8

if you possess and foster them (N)   2Pe 1:8

qualities existing and growing (P)   2Pe 1:8

ABOUNDED

hath more *a.* through my lie unto   Ro 3:7

grace hath *a.* unto many   Ro 5:15

much more profusely did grace overflow (A)   Ro 5:15

more richly did the grace overflow (B)   Ro 5:15

vastly exceeded by grace (N)   Ro 5:15

free giving of grace overflowed (P)   Ro 5:15

where sin *a.* grace did much more   Ro 5:20

sin *a.* grace superabounded (A)   Ro 5:20

grace overflows the more (B)   Ro 5:20

a. unto riches of their liberality   2Co 8:2

Wherein he hath *a.* toward us in   Eph 1:8

He lavish upon us in every (A)(N)(B)   Eph 1:8

poured out upon us wisdom (B)   Eph 1:8

ABOUNDETH

furious man *a.* in transgression   Pr 29:22

consolation also *a.* by Christ   2Co 1:5

charity toward each other *a.*   2Th 1:3

mutual love increasing (B)(R)   2Th 1:3

love grows ever greater (N)   2Th 1:3

love reached such proportions (P)   2Th 1:3

ABOUNDING

a. in loving-kindness (A)(E)(R)   Ps 86:15

a. in mercy (B)   Ps 103:8

no fountains *a.* with water   Pr 8:24

fountains laden with water (A)   Pr 8:24

springs abundantly flowing (B)   Pr 8:24

always *a.* in work of Lord   1Co 15:58

a. therein with thanksgiving   Col 2:7

overflowing with thanksgiving (A)(B)(N)(P)   Col 2:7

ABOUT

a. three months after was told Judah   Ge 38:24

God shewed Pharaoh what he is *a.* to do   Ge 41:25

turned *a.* from them and wept   Ge 42:24

thy servant's trade hath been *a.* cattle   Ge 46:34

a. midnight will I go out into Egypt   Ex 11:4

a. six hundred thousand on foot that   Ex 12:37

God led people *a.* through the way   Ex 13:18

set bounds *a.* the mount, sanctify it   Ex 19:23

there fell that day *a.* 3,000 men   Ex 32:28

all *a.* which he had sworn falsely   Le 6:5

from *a.* the tabernacle of Korah   Nu 16:24

led him *a.* and instructed him   De 32:12

sun hasted not to go down *a.* a day   Jos 10:13

it was *a.* an ephah of barley   Ru 2:17

let ark of God be carried *a.* to Gath   1Sa 5:8

women kept from us *a.* three days   1Sa 21:5

kingdom is turned *a.* and become   1Ki 2:15

a. going down of sun   *1Ki 22:36;*
    2Ch 18:34
a. this season according to   *2Ki 4:16*
the time
house which I am *a.* to build   *2Ch 2:9*
when he is *a.* to fill his   *Job 20:23*
belly
bind them *a.* thy neck   *Pr 3:3; 6:21*
that goeth *a.* as a tale-bearer *Pr 20:19*
like a heap of wheat set *a.*   *Ca 7:2*
with lilies
that compass yourselves *a.*   *Isa 50:11*
with sparks
why gaddest *a.* so much to   *Jer 2:36*
change
how long wilt thou go *a.*   *Jer 31:22*
a. in rioting (B)   *Eze 22:5*
their own doings have beset   *Ho 7:2*
them *a.*
he went out *a.* the third   *M't 20:3*
hour
set an hedge *a.* it   *M'k 12:1*
I must be *a.* my Father's   *Lu 2:49*
business
Jesus began to be *a.* thirty   *Lu 3:23*
years
let loins be girded *a.* and   *Lu 12:35*
lights
arose a question *a.* purifying *Joh 3:25*
why go ye *a.* to kill me   *Joh 7:19*
number of men was *a.* 5,000   *Ac 4:4*
when he was *a.* 100 years old *Ro 4:19*
going *a.* to establish own   *Ro 10:3*
righteousness
have we not power to lead *a.* *1Co 9:5*
a sister
always bearing *a.* in body   *2Co 4:10*
the dying
having loins girt *a.* with   *Eph 6:14*
truth
wandering *a.* from house to   *1Ti 5:13*
house
when he was *a.* to make   *Heb 8:5*
tabernacle
and *a.* the elders and the four *Re 7:11*
beasts
silence in heaven *a.* space of   *Re 8:1*
half hour
I was *a.* to write, I heard a   *Re 10:4*
voice
prophesy *a.* many peoples   *Re 10:11*
(S)

ABOVE

the waters *a.* the firmament   *Ge 1:7*
fowl may fly *a.* the earth in   *Ge 1:20*
open
serpent cursed *a.* cattle, *a.*   *Ge 3:14*
beast
a cubit finish it *a.*   *Ge 6:16*
ark was lifted up *a.* the earth *Ge 7:17*
commune with you from *a.*   *Ex 25:22*
mercy seat
a. the curious girdle of the   *Ex 28:27*
ephod
have legs *a.* the feet to leap *Le 11:21*
heart not be lifted up *a.*   *De 17:20*
brethren
shalt be *a.* only, not beneath *De 28:13*
multiply thee *a.* thy fathers   *De 30:5*
waters that came down from *Jos 3:13;*
a.   *3:16*
blessed shall she be *a.* women *J'g 5:24*
He sent from *a.*   *2Sa 22:17; Ps 18:16*
cherubim covered ark *a.*   *1Ki 8:7;*
    2Ch 5:8
a. throne of kings *2Ki 25:28; Jer 52:32*
Judah prevailed *a.* his   *1Ch 5:2*
brethren
Levites numbered from 20 *1Ch 23:27*
years and *a.*
priest, which stood *a.* the   *2Ch 24:20*
people
he had advanced him *a.* the   *Es 5:11*
princes
let not God regard it from *a.*   *Job 3:4*
price of wisdom is *a.* rubies *Job 28:18*
what portion of God from *a.* *Job 31:2*
I should have denied God *Job 31:28*
a.
thy judgments are *a.* out of   *Ps 10:5*
sight
Thou liftest me *a.* enemies   *Ps 18:48;*
    27:6
oil of gladness *a.* thy fellows *Ps 45:7;*
    Heb 1:9
he commanded the clouds   *Ps 78:23*
from *a.*

I love thy comandments *a.*   *Ps 119:27*
gold
stretched out earth *a.* waters *Ps 136:6*
his glory is *a.* earth and   *Ps 148:13*
heaven
when he established clouds *a.*   *Pr 8:28*
way of life is *a.* to the wise *Pr 15:24*
for her price is far *a.* rubies *Pr 31:10*
man hath no preeminence *a.* *Ec 3:19*
beast
mountains exalted *a.* the hills *Isa 2:2*
a. it stood the seraphims, each *Isa 6:2*
had
ask in depth or in the height *Isa 7:11*
a.
widows increased *a.* sand of *Jer 15:8*
the seas
as appearance of man *a.*   *Eze 1:26*
upon it
glory of God was over   *Eze 10:19;*
them *a.*   *11:22*
nor exalt itself any more *a.* *Eze 29:15*
nations
Daniel was preferred *a.* the   *Da 6:3*
presidents
king magnify himself *a.*   *Da 11:36*
every god
a. the waters (S)   *Da 12:6; 12:7*
I destroyed his fruit from *a.*   *Am 2:9*
multiplied thy merchants *a.* *Na 3:16*
the stars
disciple is not *a.* his master *M't 10:24;*
    Lu 6:40
I am from *a.*, ye are of this *Joh 8:23*
world
except it were given him   *Joh 19:11*
from *a.*
the man was *a.* forty years   *Ac 4:22*
old
I saw light *a.* brightness of *Ac 26:13*
the sun
that is to bring Christ down *Ro 10:6*
from *a.*
one man esteemeth one day *Ro 14:5*
a. another
not to think of men *a.* what   *1Co 4:6*
is written
to be temped *a.* that ye   *1Co 10:13*
are able
was seen of *a.* 500 brethren *1Co 15:6*
at once
in stripes *a.* measure   *2Co 11:23*
a. fourteen years ago,   *2Co 12:2*
whether in body
but Jerusalem which is *a.* is   *Ga 4:26*
free
given him a name *a.* every   *Ph'p 2:9*
name
seek those things which are *a.* *Col 3:1*
set affections on things *a.* not *Col 3:2*
on
now not as servant, but *a.*   *Ph'm 16*
servant
a. when he said, sacrifice   *Heb 10:8*
and
every good and perfect gift   *Jas 1:17*
from *a.*
this wisdom descendeth not   *Jas 3:15*
from *a.*

ABOVEBOARD

absolutely *a.* (P)   *2Co 8:21*

ABOVE ALL

serpent cursed *a. all* cattle   *Ge 3:14*
Moses was meek *a. all* men   *Nu 12:3*
shalt be blessed *a. all* people *De 7:14*
chose you *a. all* people   *De 10:15;*
    De 14:2; 26:19; 28:1
done evil *a. all* before him   *1Ki 14:9;*
    16:30
provoked *a. all* that fathers *1Ki 14:22*
had done
done wickedly *a. all*   *2Ki 21:11*
Amorites did
Thou art exalted as head *a.* *1Ch 29:11*
all
loved Maachah *a. all* his   *2Ch 11:21*
wives
Ezra was *a. all* the people   *Ne 8:5*
king loved Esther *a. all*   *Es 2:17*
women
Lord art high *a. all* the earth *Ps 97:9*
He is high *a. all* people   *Ps 99:2;*
    113:4
magnified thy word *a. all* thy *Ps 138:2*
name

a. all that were before me   *Ec 2:7*
heart is deceitful *a. all* things *Jer 17:9*
commit this lewdness *a. all* *Eze 16:43*
height was exalted *a. all* the *Eze 31:5*
trees
he shall magnify himself *a.* *Da 11:37*
all
Herod added yet this *a. all*   *Lu 3:20*
sinners *a. all* the Galileans   *Lu 13:2;*
    13:4
He that cometh from heaven *Joh 3:31*
is *a. all*
far *a. all* principality and   *Eph 1:21*
power
a. all that we ask or think   *Eph 3:20*
one God *a. all* and through   *Eph 4:6*
all
a. all taking shield of faith   *Eph 6:16*
to quench
a. all things put on charity   *Col 3:14*
exalteth himself *a. all* called   *2Th 2:4*
God
a. all things swear not   *Jas 5:12*
a. all things that thou mayest *1Pe 4:8*
prosper
I wish *a. all* things that thou   *3Jo 2*
mayest

ABRAHAM

name shall be A.   *Ge 17:5;*
    1Ch 1:27; Ne 9:7
God said to A.   *Ge 17:9;*
    Ge 17:15; 18:13; 21:12; 22:15
A. fell upon his face, and   *Ge 17:17*
laughed
A. said unto God   *Ge 17:18; 18:23*
God went up from A.   *Ge 17:22;*
    18:33
A. took Ishmael and   *Ge 17:23*
circumcised
A. was 99 years old when   *Ge 17:24;*
circumcised   *17:26*
A. hastened into the tent   *Ge 18:6*
unto
A. ran unto the herd, and   *Ge 18:7*
fetched
shall I hide from A. that   *Ge 18:17*
thing
A. stood yet before the Lord *Ge 18:22*
God remembered A. and   *Ge 19:29*
sent Lot
A. said of Sarah, She is my *Ge 20:2*
sister
A. prayed and God healed   *Ge 20:17*
Philistines
A. called his son   *Ge 21:2;*
Isaac, circumcised, made   *21:5-14*
feast for Isaac
A. makes covenant with   *Ge 21:22;*
Philistines   *21:24*
God did tempt A.   *Ge 22:1*
Sarah died and A. came to   *Ge 23:2*
mourn for
A. buried Sarah his wife   *Ge 23:19;*
    Ge 23:5-20; 49:31
Lord had blessed A. in all   *Ge 24:1;*
things   *24:2-48*
A. took a wife. Gave all to   *Ge 25:1;*
Isaac   *25:5*
A. gave up the ghost *Ge 25:8; 25:10-12*
A. obeyed my voice   *Ge 26:5*
give thee the blessing of A.   *Ge 28:4*
I am the Lord God of A.   *Ge 28:13;*
31:42, 53; 32:9; Ex 3:6, 15-16; 4:5;
    1Ki 18:36; 1Ch 29:18; M't 22:32;
    Ac 3:13; 7:32
land he sware to A.   *Ge 50:24;*
15:18-21; 17:8; 26:3; 28:4; 35:12;
    Ex 33:1; De 34:4
remembered his covenant   *Ex 2:24;*
with A.   *Le 26:42; 2Ki 13:23;*
    1Ch 16:16; Ps 105:9
Remember A.   *Ex 32:13;*
    De 9:27; Ps 105:9
Lord sware to A.   *De 1:8;*
6:10; 9:5; 29:13; 30:20; Lu 1:73; Ac 7:17
I took your father A. from   *Jos 24:3*
Abram; the same is A.   *1Ch 1:27*
The sons of A.; Isaac and   *1Ch 1:28;*
Ishmael   *1:34*
the people of the God of A.   *Ps 47:9*
saith the Lord, who   *Isa 29:22*
redeemed A.
though A. be ignorant of us *Isa 51:2*
A. was one, and he   *Eze 33:24*
inherited
truth to Jacob, and mercy to *Mic 7:20*
A.

the son of David, the son of *A.* — *M't 1:1*

the generations from *A.* to David — *M't 1:17*

We have *A.* to our father — *M't 3:9*

God able to raise children to *A.* — *M't 3:9; Lu 3:8*

sit down with *A.* in kingdom of heaven — *M't 8:11*

which was the son of *A.* — *Lu 3:34*

this woman, being a daughter of *A.* — *Lu 13:16*

when ye see *A.* in the kingdom of God — *Lu 13:28*

and seeth *A.* afar off — *Lu 16:23*

A. saith, They have Moses and prophets — *Lu 16:29*

forasmuch as he also is a son of *A.* — *Lu 19:9*

this did not *A.* — *Joh 8:40*

A. is dead, and the prophets — *Joh 8:52*

and hast thou seen *A.* — *Joh 8:57*

Before *A.* was, I am — *Joh 8:58*

children of the stock of *A.* — *Ac 13:26*

if *A.* were justified by works — *Ro 4:2*

A. believed God, it was counted to him — *Ro 4:3; 4:9; Ga 3:6; Jas 2:23*

who are of faith are children of *A.* — *Ga 3:7*

preached before gospel unto *A.* — *Ga 3:8*

they of faith are blessed with *A.* — *Ga 3:9*

blessing of *A.* might come on Gentiles — *Ga 3:14*

God gave it to *A.* by promise — *Ga 3:18; Heb 6:13*

A. had two sons, the one by — *Ga 4:22*

A. returning from slaughter of kings — *Heb 7:1*

To whom *A.* gave a tenth of spoils — *Heb 7:2; 7:4*

they came out of loins of *A.* — *Heb 7:5*

Levi paid tithes in *A.* — *Heb 7:9*

By faith *A.* — *Heb 11:8; Heb 11:9, 11, 17; Jas 2:23*

Sarah obeyed *A.*, calling him lord — *1Pe 3:6*

ABRAHAM with *FATHER*

I will perform oath to *A.* thy father — *Ge 26:3*

I am the God of *A.* thy father — *Ge 26:24; 28:13*

O God of my father *A.* God of Isaac — *Ge 32:9*

I took your father *A.* from other side — *Jos 24:3*

look to *A.* your father, to Sarah — *Isa 51:2*

we have *A.* to our father — *M't 3:9; Lu 3:8*

oath which he sware to our father *A.* — *Lu 1:73*

he said, father *A.* have mercy on me — *Lu 16:24*

nay, father *A.* but if one went from dead — *Lu 16:30*

they said to him, *A.* is our father — *Joh 8:39*

art Thou greater than our father *A.* — *Joh 8:53*

your father *A.* rejoiced to see my day — *Joh 8:56*

God of glory appeared to our father *A.* — *Ac 7:2*

what say that *A.* our father hath found — *Ro 4:1*

Walk in steps of faith of our father *A.* — *Ro 4:12*

faith of *A.* who is father of us all — *Ro 4:16*

was not *A.* our father justified by works — *Jas 2:21*

ABRAHAM with *SEED*

gavest it to *seed* of *A.* thy friend — *2Ch 20:7*

O ye *seed* of *A.* his servant — *Ps 105:6*

thou Israel, the *seed* of *A.* my friend — *Isa 41:9*

rulers over the *seed* of *A.* — *Jer 33:26*

as he spake to *A.* and his *seed* — *Lu 1:55*

promise not to *A.* or his *seed* through law — *Ro 4:13*

neither because they are *seed* of *A.* — *Ro 9:7*

I also am *seed* of *A.* — *Ro 11:1; 2Co 11:22*

to *A.* and his *seed* were promises — *Ga 3:16*

he took on him the *seed* of *A.* — *Heb 2:16*

ABRAHAM'S

every male among men of *A.* house — *Ge 17:23*

because of Sarah *A.* wife — *Ge 20:18*

thing was grievous in *A.* sight — *Ge 21:11*

Nahor, *A.* brother — *Ge 22:23; 24:15*

I am *A.* servant — *Ge 24:34; 24:52, 59*

these are days of years of *A.* life — *Ge 25:7*

A. son — *Ge 25:12; 25:19; 28:9*

my servant *A.* sake — *Ge 26:24*

sons of Keturah, *A.* concubine — *1Ch 1:32*

carried by angels into *A.* bosom — *Lu 16:22*

A. seed — *Joh 8:33; 8:37; Ga 3:29*

if ye were *A.* children, ye would do — *Joh 8:39*

ABRAM

lived seventy years, begat *A.* — *Ge 11:26; 11:27*

A. and Nahor took them wives — *Ge 11:29*

Terah took *A.* his son, and Lot — *Ge 11:31*

Lord had said to *A.*, Get thee out of — *Ge 12:1*

A. departed, as the Lord had said — *Ge 12:4*

A. was seventy five years old when he — *Ge 12:4*

A. passed through the land unto — *Ge 12:6; 12:9*

Lord appeared unto *A.* — *Ge 12:7; Ge 15:1-18; 17:1-5*

A. went down into Egypt — *Ge 12:10; Ge 12:14, 16, 18*

A. went up out of Egypt, he — *Ge 13:1*

A. was very rich in cattle and — *Ge 13:2*

A. called on the name of the Lord — *Ge 13:4*

A. dwelled in the land of Canaan — *Ge 13:12*

Lord said unto *A.*, after that — *Ge 13:14*

A. removed his tent and dwelt in — *Ge 13:18*

A. rescues Lot and captives — *Ge 14:13; 14:14-23*

word of Lord came unto *A.* — *Ge 15:1*

saying a deep sleep fell upon *A.* — *Ge 15:12; 15:2-18*

Sarai gives Hagar to *A.* — *Ge 16:2; 16:3-16*

A. was 85 years old when Ishmael born — *Ge 16:16*

when *A.* was 90 years old Lord appeared — *Ge 17:1*

thy name any more be called *A.* — *Ge 17:5; 1Ch 1:27; Ne 9:7*

ABRAM'S

name of *A.* wife was Sarai — *Ge 11:29; 11:31; 12:17*

strife between herdmen of *A.* cattle — *Ge 13:7*

took Lot *A.* brother's son — *Ge 14:12*

Now *A.* wife bare no children — *Ge 16:1*

Sarai *A.* wife took Hagar her maid — *Ge 16:3*

ABROAD

of the Canaanites spread *a.* — *Ge 10:18*

lest we be scattered *a.* upon earth — *Ge 11:4*

Lord scattered them *a.* upon face of earth — *Ge 11:8*

he brought him forth *a.* — *Ge 15:5; 19:17*

carry forth aught of flesh *a.* — *Ex 12:46*

if it spread *a.* — *Le 13:7; 13:12, 22, 27*

whether she be born at home *A.* — *Le 18:9*

then shall he go *a.* out of camp — *De 23:10*

when thou wilt ease thyself — *De 23:13*

eagle spreadeth *a.* her wings — *De 32:11*

took daughters from *a.* for sons — *J'g 12:9*

borrow vessels *a.* from neighbors — *2Ki 4:3*

as soon as commandment came *a.* — *2Ch 31:5*

this deed of queen come *a.* — *Es 1:17*

he wandereth *a.* for bread — *Job 15:23*

when he goeth *a.* he telleth it — *Ps 41:6*

let thy fountains be dispersed *a.* — *Pr 5:16*

that spreadeth *a.* earth by myself — *Isa 44:24*

began to blaze *a.* the matter — *M'k 1:45*

nor kept secret, but it should come *a.* — *M'k 4:22*

these sayings were come *a.* — *Lu 1:65*

made known *a.* saying of this child — *Lu 2:17*

when this was noised *a.* the multitude — *Ac 2:6*

we went *a.*, and set forth — *Ac 21:2*

love of God shed *a.* in our hearts — *Ro 5:5*

faith to God-ward is spread *a.* — *1Th 1:8*

12 tribes which are scattered *a.* — *Jas 1:1*

ABROGATED

a. the law (B) — *Ro 3:31*

ABSALOM

A. the son of Maacah — *2Sa 3:3; 1Ch 3:2*

A. the son of David — *2Sa 13:1; 18:33; 19:4*

A. spake to Amnon neither good or bad — *2Sa 13:22*

A. had sheepshearers in Baal-hazor — *2Sa 13:23*

A. hath slain all the king's sons — *2Sa 13:30*

David longed to go forth unto *A.* — *2Sa 13:39*

king's heart was toward *A.* — *2Sa 14:1*

Joab arose and brought *A.* to Jerusalem — *2Sa 14:23*

none praised as *A.* for his beauty — *2Sa 14:25*

the king kissed *A.* — *2Sa 14:33'*

A. stole hearts of men of Israel — *2Sa 15:1-37; 16:8-23; 17:1-28; 18:5-33*

A. went in unto his father's concubines — *2Sa 16:22*

Ahithophel's counsel pleased *A.* well — *2Sa 17:4*

Lord might bring evil upon *A.* — *2Sa 17:14*

A. passed over Jordan — *2Sa 17:24; 17:26*

deal gently for my sake with *A.* — *2Sa 18:5*

I saw *A.* hanged in an oak — *2Sa 18:10*

thrust three darts in heart of *A.* — *2Sa 18:14*

Is the young man *A.* safe — *2Sa 18:29; 18:32*

king weepeth, mourneth for *A.* — *2Sa 19:1*

if *A.* had lived, and we had all died — *2Sa 19:6*

do us more harm than did *A.* — *2Sa 20:6*

I fled because of *A.* thy brother — *1Ki 2:7*

turned after Adonijah, not after *A.* — *1Ki 2:28*

Maachah daughter of *A.* — *2Ch 11:20; 11:21*

ABSALOM'S

I love Tamar, *A.* sister — *2Sa 13:4*

desolate in her brother *A.* — *2Sa 13:20*

A. servants set the field on fire — *2Sa 14:30*

A. servants came to the woman 2Sa 17:20
it is called unto this day 2Sa 18:18
A. place

ABSENCE

in the *a.* of the multitude Lu 22:6
now much more in my *a.* Ph'p 2:12

ABSENT

when we are *a.* one from another Ge 31:49
For I verily as *a.* in body 1Co 5:3
we are *a.* from the Lord 2Co 5:6
rather to be *a.* from the 2Co 5:8; 5:9
being *a.* am bold toward you 2Co 10:1; 10:11; 13:2, 10; Ph'p 1:27; Col 2:5

ABSOLUTELY

a. aboveboard (P) 2Co 8:21

ABSOLVE

wishing to *a.* himself (B) Lu 10:29

ABSOLVED

every believer is *a.* Ac 13:39
(A)(B)(P)

ABSTAIN

a. from pollutions of idols Ac 15:20
a. from meats offered to idols Ac 15:29
that ye should *a.* from fornication 1Th 4:3
a. from all appearance of evil 1Th 5:22
commanding to *a.* from meats 1Ti 4:3
a. from fleshly lusts, which war 1Pe 2:11

ABSTINENCE

after long *a.* Paul stood forth in Ac 27:21

ABSURD

senseless and *a.* (A) Ac 25:27
a., utterly nonsense 1Co 1:23
(A)(B)(N)(P)(R)

ABSURDITY

a. and folly (A)(B)(N)(R) 1Co 1:18

ABUNDANCE

an *a.* of good things (B) De 28:11
servedst not God for the *a.* of all De 28:47
a. of the everlasting hills De 33:15
(A)(B)(E)(R)
shall suck of *a.* of the seas De 33:19
out of the *a.* of my complaint 1Sa 1:16
spoil of the city in great *a.* 2Sa 12:30
came no more such *a.* of spices 1Ki 10:10
sycamore trees for *a.* 1Ki 10:27; 2Ch 1:15; 9:27
there is a sound of *a.* of rain 1Ki 18:41
all this *a.* (S) 1Ch 29:16
a. of waters cover Job 22:11; 38:34
a. of mercy (A)(E)(R) Ps 5:7
the *a.* of the wicked (E)(R) Ps 37:16
a. of their riches (A)(B)(R) Ps 49:6
to an overflowing *a.* (B) Ps 66:12
my heart observed *a.* (B) Ec 1:16
an *a.* of rubies (S) Pr 20:15
for *a.* of milk that they shall give Isa 7:22
great *a.* of thine enchantments Isa 47:9
a. of the sea shall be converted to thee Isa 60:5
with the *a.* of her glory Isa 66:11
I will reveal to them *a.* of peace Jer 33:6

a. of idleness was in her Eze 16:49
by reason of *a.* of his horses Eze 26:10
gold, silver, apparel in great *a.* Zec 14:14
out of *a.* of heart M't 12:34; Lu 6:45
he shall have more *a.* M't 13:12; 25:29
cast in of their *a.* M'k 12:44; Lu 21:4
from his *a.* all have (B) Joh 1:16
they which receive *a.* of grace Ro 5:17
a. of joy, of supply 2Co 8:2; 8:14, 20
grace come to you in *a.* 2Co 9:8
(A)(R)
exalted through *a.* of revelations 2Co 12:7
the *a.* of her delicacies Re 18:3

IN ABUNDANCE

David prepared iron, brass, cedar trees, workmen in *a.* 1Ch 22:3; 22:4, 14-15; 29:2, 21
Solomon prepared timber, vessels, spices, gold in *a.* 2Ch 1:15; 2:9; 4:18; 9:1, 9, 27
Rehoboam gave them victual in *a.* 2Ch 11:23
fell to Asa out of Israel in *a.* 2Ch 15:9
Jehoshaphat had riches and honour in *a.* 2Ch 17:5; 18:1-2; 20:25
Ahab killed sheep in *a.* 2Ch 18:2
Joash gathered money in *a.* 2Ch 24:11
Hezekiah had burnt offerings, tithes, weapons in *a.* 2Ch 29:35; 31:5; 32:5, 29
vineyards and fruit trees in *a.* Ne 9:25
royal wine in *a.* Es 1:7
delight in *a.* of peace Ps 37:11; 72:7
trusted in *a.* of riches Ps 52:7; Ec 5:12
land brought forth frogs in *a.* Ps 105:30
life consisteth not in *a.* of possessions Lu 12:15

ABUNDANT

seven *a.* years (B) Ge 41:34; 41:47
Lord God *a.* in goodness and truth Ex 34:6
a. in mercy (A) Ps 86:5
a. in love (E)(R) Ps 86:5
a. in loving kindness (E) Ps 103:8
a. redemption (B) Ps 130:7
many waters *a.* in treasures Jer 51:13
your *a.* wealth (B)(R) Eze 27:33
army with *a.* supplies (R) Da 11:13
harvest is *a.* (B) M't 9:27
a. blessing of the gospel Ro 15:29
(A)(B)
we bestow more *a.* honour 1Co 12:23; 12:24
have more *a.* comeliness 1Co 12:23
more *a.* grace 2Co 4:15; 1Ti 1:14
is *a.* also by many thanksgivings 2Co 9:12
in labours more *a.;* in stripes frequent 2Co 11:23
may be more *a.* in Jesus Christ Ph'p 1:26
a. and overflowing love (B) 1Th 3:12
according to his *a.* mercy 1Pe 1:3

ABUNDANTLY

Let waters bring forth *a.* Ge 1:20; 1:21
they may breed *a.* in the earth Ge 8:17; 9:7
children of Israel increased *a.* Ex 1:7
river shall bring forth frogs *a.* Ex 8:3
the water came out *a.* Nu 20:11
prosper you *a.* (B) De 30:9
brought oil, oxen, and sheep *a.* 1Ch 12:40
David prepared *a.* before his death 1Ch 22:5
Thou hast shed blood *a.* 1Ch 22:8
all things brought they in *a.* 2Ch 31:5
whose hand God bringeth *a.* Job 12:5
clouds drop and distil upon man *a.* Job 36:28
They shall be *a.* satisfied with fatness Ps 36:8
Thou waterest the ridges *a.* Ps 65:10
I will *a.* bless her provision Ps 132:15

a. utter memory of thy goodness Ps 145:7
springs *a.* flowing (B) Pr 8:24
O friends drink *a.*, O beloved Ca 5:1
every one shall howl, weeping *a.* Isa 15:3
it shall blossom *a.* and rejoice Isa 35:2
to our God, for he will *a.* pardon Isa 55:7
that they might have life more *a.* Joh 10:10
I laboured more *a.* than they all 1Co 15:10
sufferings fall to our lot *a.* 2Co 1:5
(A)(R)
conversation, and more *a.* to you 2Co 1:12
know the love I have more *a.* to you 2Co 2:4
enlarged according to our rule *a.* 2Co 10:15
the more *a.* I love you, the less 2Co 12:15
him that is able to do exceeding *a.* Eph 3:20
endeavoured more *a.* to see your face 1Th 2:17
which he shed on us *a.* through Jesus Tit 3:6
God willing more *a.* to shew heirs Heb 6:17
so an entrance be ministered to you *a.* 2Pe 1:11

ABUSE

heap no *a.* upon judges (B) Ex 22:28
thrust me through, and *a.* me 1Sa 31:4
these uncircumcised come and *a.* me 1Ch 10:4
strife and *a.* will cease Pr 22:10
(A)(B)(R)
they *a.* me (B)(R) Jer 38:19
hurled *a.* at him (N)(P) M't 27:39; M'k 15:29, 32
they covered him with *a.* Lu 23:39
(P)
insult, *a.,* molest (A)(B) Ac 14:5
I *a.* not my power in the gospel 1Co 9:18
foul mouthed *a.* (A) Col 3:8
who *a.* themselves (A) 1Ti 1:10
quarrels, dissension, *a.* (A) 1Ti 6:4
bearing *a.* for him (R) Heb 13:13
a. with *a.* 1Pe 3:9
censured and suffer *a.* (A) 1Pe 4:14

ABUSED

knew her and *a.* her all night J'g 19:25
they *a.* him (B)(N) Joh 9:28
abuses of those *a.* (B) Ro 15:3

ABUSERS

a. of themselves with mankind 1Co 6:9
a. of themselves (E) 1Ti 1:10

ABUSES

a. of those abused (B) Ro 15:3

ABUSING

that use this world, as not *a.* it 1Co 7:31

ABUSIVE

an *a.* man (B) 1Co 5:11
violent and *a.* work (A) Eph 6:9
a. condemnation against (A) Jude 9

ABUSIVELY

spake *a.*, jeered him (A) M't 27:39

ABYSS

The *a.* says, It is not in me Job 28:14
(B)
the *a.* surrounded me (A) Jon 2:5
key to the *a.* Re 9:1
(A)(B)(E)(N)(P)(R)
opened the *a.* (A)(N)(R) Re 9:2

angel of the *a.*   *Re 9:11*
(A)(B)(E)(N)
come out of the *a.*   *Re 11:7*
(A)(B)(E)(N)(P)(R)
come up out of the *a.*   *Re 17:8*
(A)(E)(P)
key of the *a.* (A)(B)(E)(P)   *Re 20:1*
hurled into the *a.* (A)(B)(E)(N) *Re 20:3*

ACACIA

and *a.* wood (S)   *Ex 25:5;*
25:10, 13, 23, 28; 26:15, 26, 32, 37; 27:1,
6; 30:1, 5; 35:7, 24; 36:20, 31, 36; 37:1,
4, 10, 15, 25, 28; 38:1, 6; De 10:3
I will plant the *a.* (S)   *Isa 41:19*

ACCAD

Babel, Erech, and *A.*   *Ge 10:10*

ACCENT

your *a.* shows   *M't 26:13*
(A)(B)(N)(P)(R)

ACCEPT

peradventure he will *a.* of   *Ge 32:20*
me
the owner shall *a.* thereof   *Ex 22:11*
they *a.* the punishment *Le 26:41; 26:43*
bless and *a.* the work of his   *De 33:11*
hands
let him *a.* an offering   *1Sa 26:19*
Araunah said, The Lord   *2Sa 24:23*
God *a.* thee
will ye *a.* his person   *Job 13:8*
reprove you if ye secretly *a.* *Job 13:10*
persons
let me not *a.* any man's   *Job 32:21*
person
Job will pray for you, for   *Job 42:8*
him will I *a.*
a freewill offerings of my   *Ps 119:108*
mouth
not good to *a.* person of the *Pr 18:5*
wicked
Lord doth not *a.* them   *Jer 14:10;*
Jer 14:12; Mal 1:10
there will I *a.* them   *Eze 20:40;*
Eze 20:41; 43:27
will he be pleased or *a.* thy *Mal 1:8*
person
we *a.* it always, and in all   *Ac 24:3*
places

ACCEPTABLE

it shall not be *a.* for you   *Le 22:20*
let Ashur be *a.* to his   *De 33:24*
brethren
let meditation of my heart   *Ps 19:14*
be *a.*
my prayer is to thee in an   *Ps 69:13*
a. time
to do justice, judgment is   *Pr 21:3*
more *a.*
the preacher sought out *a.*   *Ec 12:10*
words
in an *a.* time have I heard   *Isa 49:8*
thee
wilt thou call this an *a.* day *Isa 58:5*
to Lord
to proclaim *a.* year of Lord *Isa 61:2;*
Lu 4:19
your burnt offerings are not *Jer 6:20*
a.
let my counsel be *a.* to thee *Da 4:27*
bodies living sacrifice, holy, *Ro 12:1*
a. to God
that good and *a.* will of God *Ro 12:2*
is *a.* to God and approved *Ro 14:18*
of men
offering up of Gentiles be *a.* *Ro 15:16*
proving what is *a.* unto the *Eph 5:10*
Lord
a sacrifice *a.* well-pleasing to *Ph'p 4:18*
God
this is *a.* in the sight of God *1Ti 2:3;*
5:4
sacrifices *a.* to God by Jesus *1Pe 2:5*
Christ
if take patiently, this is *a.* to *1Pe 2:20*
God

ACCEPTABLY

serve God *a.* with   *Heb 12:28*
reverence

ACCEPTANCE

come up with *a.* on mine   *Isa 60:7*
altar

ACCEPTATION

a saying worthy of all *a.* *1Ti 1:15; 4:9*

ACCEPTED

if doest well, shalt thou not   *Ge 4:7*
be *a.*
I have *a.* thee concerning   *Ge 19:21*
this
that they may be *a.* before *Ex 28:38*
Lord
offering shall be *a.* for him   *Le 1:4;*
22:27
it shall not be *a.*   *Le 7:18;*
Le 19:7; 22:23, 25
should it have been *a.* in   *Le 10:19*
sight of Lord
an offering shall be perfect *Le 22:21*
to be *a.*
shall wave the sheaf to be *a.* *Le 23:11*
he was *a.* in sight of all   *1Sa 18:5*
people
David said, see I have *a.*   *1Sa 25:35*
thy person
he *a.* it not (S)   *Es 4:4*
a. of multitude of his   *Es 10:3*
the Lord also *a.* Job   *Job 42:9*
sacrifice shall be *a.* on mine *Isa 56:7*
altar
let my supplication be *a.*   *Jer 37:20;*
42:2
no prophet is *a.* in own   *Lu 4:24*
country
he that worketh   *Ac 10:35*
righteousness is *a.*
heard in a time *a.*; now is *a.* *2Co 6:2*
time
another gospel which ye   *2Co 11:4*
have not *a.*
a. us as sons (N)   *Eph 1:5*
he hath made us *a.* in the   *Eph 1:6*
beloved

ACCEPTEST

neither *a.* thou person of   *Lu 20:21*
any man

ACCEPTETH

to him that *a.* not persons *Job 34:19*
of princes
eat with joy, for God *a.* thy *Ec 9:7*
works
they sacrifice, but Lord *a.*   *Ho 8:13*
them not
God *a.* no man's person   *Ga 2:6*

ACCEPTING

tortured, not *a.* deliverance *Heb 11:35*

ACCESS

by whom also we have *a.* by *Ro 5:2*
faith
through him we both have   *Eph 2:18*
a. to Father
in whom we have boldness *Eph 3:12*
and *a.* by

ACCESSARIES

the *a.* or instruments   *Nu 3:36*
(A)(B)(R)

ACCHO

nor did Asher drive out   *J'g 1:31*
inhabitants of *A.*

ACCIDENTALLY

accidentally (B)   *Nu 35:15;*
De 14:42; Jos 20:3, 9

ACCOMPANIED

certain brethren from Joppa *Ac 10:23*
a. him
these six brethren *a.* me   *Ac 11:12*
Sopater of Berea *a.* Paul into *Ac 20:4*
Asia
they *a.* him to the ship   *Ac 20:38*

ACCOMPANY

things that *a.* salvation   *Heb 6:9*

ACCOMPANYING

a. the ark of God   *2Sa 6:4*

ACCOMPLISH

offereth a sacrifice to *a.* his *Le 22:21*
vow
shalt *a.* my desire in giving *1Ki 5:9*
food
till he shall *a.* as an hireling *Job 14:6*
they *a.* a diligent search   *Ps 64:6*
it shall *a.* that which I   *Isa 55:11*
please
ye will surely *a.* your vows *Jer 44:25*
thus will I *a.* my fury upon *Eze 6:12*
them
now will I *a.* mine anger   *Eze 7:8*
upon
thus will I *a.* my wrath   *Eze 13:15*
upon wall
I will pour out fury to *a.*   *Eze 20:8;*
anger   *20:21*
that he would *a.* seventy years *Da 9:2*
which he should *a.* at   *Lu 9:31*
Jerusalem

ACCOMPLISHED

the word by Jeremiah   *2Ch 36:22*
might be *a.*
days of purification were *a.*   *Es 2:12;*
Lu 2:22
it shall be *a.* before his   *Job 15:32*
time
desire *a.* is sweet to the soul *Pr 13:19*
cry unto her, that her   *Isa 40:2*
warfare is *a.*
when seventy years are *a.*   *Jer 25:12;*
29:10
days of your dispersions are *Jer 25:34*
a.
my words shall be *a.* before *Jer 39:16*
thee
the Lord hath *a.* his fury   *La 4:11*
punishment of thine iniquity *La 4:22*
is *a.*
when *a.* them, lie on right   *Eze 4:6*
side
thus shall mine anger be *a.* *Eze 5:13*
prosper, till indignation be   *Da 11:36*
a.
a. to scatter power of holy *Da 12:7*
people
days of his ministration were *Lu 1:23*
a.
days were *a.* she should be   *Lu 2:6*
delivered
eight days were *a.* for   *Lu 2:21*
circumcising
how am I straitened till it   *Lu 12:50*
be *a.*
concerning the Son of man *Lu 18:31*
shall be *a.*
that is written must yet be *Lu 22:37*
a. in me
knowing that all things   *Joh 19:28*
were now *a.*
when we had *a.* those days *Ac 21:5*
same afflictions are *a.* in   *1Pe 5:9*
brethren

ACCOMPLISHING

a. the service of God   *Heb 9:6*

ACCOMPLISHMENT

a. of the days of purification *Ac 21:26*

ACCORD

groweth of its own *a.* not   *Le 25:5*
reap
what grows of itself   *Le 25:5*
(A)(E)(R)
the volunteer growth (B)   *Le 25:5*
to fight with Israel with one *Jos 9:2*
a.
all continued with one *a.*   *Ac 1:14;*
Ac 2:1, 46; 4:24; 5:12; 15:25
ran upon Stephen with one *a.* *Ac 7:57*
people with one *a.* gave heed *Ac 8:6*
gate opened of his own *a.*   *Ac 12:10*

they came with one *a.* to him — Ac 12:20

Jews with one *a.* made insurrection — Ac 18:12

they rushed with one *a.* into theatre — Ac 19:29

what *a.* has Christ with Belial (R) — 2Co 6:15

being more forward of his own *a.* — 2Co 8:17

being of one *a.* of one mind — Ph'p 2:2

ACCORDING

a. to all that God commanded him — Ge 6:22

a. unto all that the Lord commanded — Ge 7:5

a. to the time of life, and Sarah shall — Ge 18:14

done altogether *a.* to the cry of it — Ge 18:21

a. to the kindness that I have done — Ge 21:23

have done *a.* as thou biddest me — Ge 27:19

began to come *a.* as Joseph said — Ge 41:54

land of Egypt *a.* to their armies — Ex 6:26

Lord will give *a.* as he has promised — Ex 12:25

be great, *a.* as thou hast spoken — Nu 14:17

his inheritance *a.* as God promised — De 10:9

a. as the Lord hath blessed thee — De 16:10

a. as he walked before thee in truth — 1Ki 3:6

a. to the custom (S) — 2Ki 11:14

a. to the ordinance (S) — 2Ch 4:20

that they might give *a.* to the divisions — 2Ch 35:12

a. to their families (S) — Ne 4:13

cause every man to find *a.* — Job 34:11;

to his ways — Jer 17:10; 21:14; 32:19

did *a.* as the Lord commanded — Job 42:9

judge me, *a.* to my righteousness — Ps 7:8

will praise Lord *a.* to his righteousness — Ps 7:17

a. to thy mercy remember thou me — Ps 25:7; 51:1; 106:45; 109:26; 119:124

give them *a.* to their deeds, and *a.* to — Ps 28:4

mercy be upon us *a.* as we hope in — Ps 33:22

Judge me, *a.* to thy righteousness — Ps 35:24

a. to thy name, so is thy praise — Ps 48:10

reward every man *a.* to his work — Ps 62:12; Pr 24:12, 29; M't 16:27; Ro 2:6; Re 2:23

a. to the greatness of thy power — Ps 79:11

a. to thy fear, so is thy wrath — Ps 90:11

nor rewarded us *a.* to our iniquities — Ps 103:10

a. to thy word — Ps 119:25; 119:28, 41, 58, 65, 76, 107, 116, 154, 169, 170

quicken me *a.* to thy kindness — Ps 119:159; Isa 63:7

before thee: deliver me *a.* to thy word — Ps 119:170

praise him *a.* to his excellent greatness — Ps 150:2

if they speak not *a.* to this word — Isa 8:20

they joy *a.* to the joy in harvest — Isa 9:3

a. to all Lord has bestowed on them — Isa 63:7

recompense her *a.* to her work — Jer 50:29

shall rule, and do *a.* to his will — Da 11:3

a. to love of Lord to Israel — Ho 3:1

Lord will punish Jacob *a.* to his ways — Ho 12:2

A. to days of coming out of Egypt — Mic 7:15

a. to your faith be it unto you — M't 9:29

nor did *a.* to his will, shall be beaten — Lu 12:47

judge not *a.* to appearance, but judge — Joh 7:24

to every man *a.* as he had need — Ac 4:35

made of seed of David *a.* to flesh — Ro 1:3

who are called *a.* to his purpose — Ro 8:28

gifts differing *a.* to grace given to us — Ro 12:6

be like-minded *a.* to Jesus Christ — Ro 15:5

Christ died *a.* to scriptures — 1Co 15:3; 15:4

every man *a.* as he purposeth — 2Co 9:7

whose end shall be *a.* to their works — 2Co 11:15

gave himself *a.* to will of God — Ga 1:4

Abrahams's seed, heirs *a.* to promise — Ga 3:29

a. as he hath chosen us in him before — Eph 1:4

a. to the good pleasure of his will — Eph 1:5

a. to the riches of his grace — Eph 1:7

predestinated *a.* to the purpose of him — Eph 1:11

a. to the power that worketh in us — Eph 3:20

a. to the working whereby he is able — Ph'p 3:21

God supply our need *a.* to his riches — Ph'p 4:19

called not *a.* to our works, but *a.* to — 2Ti 1:9

a. to mercy he saved us by washing — Tit 3:5

not *a.* to covenant made with fathers — Heb 8:9

a. to mercy hath begotten us again — 1Pe 1:3

live *a.* to God in the Spirit — 1Pe 4:6

A. as his divine power hath given us — 2Pe 1:3

we *a.* to promise look for new heaven — 2Pe 3:13

dead judged *a.* to their works — Re 20:12; 20:13

I come to give *a.* as his work shall be — Re 22:12

ACCORDING TO THAT

my voice *a. to that* I command thee — Ge 27:8

do to me *a. to that* which proceeded — J'g 11:36

slew not *a. to that* which is written — 2Ki 14:6

a. to that which was written — 2Ch 35:26

Tatnai did *a. to that* Darius had sent — Ezr 6:13

a. to that which was spoken — Ro 4:18

a. to that he hath done, good or bad — 2Co 5:10

a. to that man hath, not *a. to that* he — 2Co 8:12

ACCORDINGLY

a. he will repay fury to his enemies — Isa 59:18

ACCOUNT

of every one that passeth the *a.* — 2Ki 12:4

Money assessed on all bound by vows (A) — 2Ki 12:4

levied according to valuation (B) — 2Ki 12:4

Money of persons each rated (E) — 2Ki 12:4

Money each man is assessed (R) — 2Ki 12:4

neither was the number put in the *a.* — 1Ch 27:24

Number not recorded (A) — 1Ch 27:24

total was not entered into figures (B) — 1Ch 27:24

number not entered in chronicle (R) — 1Ch 27:24

according to number of their *a.* — 2Ch 26:11

to the number as recorded (A) — 2Ch 26:11

according to number of their levy (B) — 2Ch 26:11

according to number of reckoning (E) — 2Ch 26:11

the number of the muster made by (R) — 2Ch 26:11

he giveth not *a.* of his matters — Job 33:13

son of man that thou makest *a.* — Ps 144:3

son of man, that thou considerest (B) — Ps 144:3

son of man, that thou dost think (R) — Ps 144:3

counting one by one to find out the *a.* — Ec 7:27

God will call you to *a.* (B) — Ec 11:9

give *a.* thereof in day of judgment — M't 12:36

be answerable in day of judgment (B) — M't 12:36

to answer at day of judgment (P) — M't 12:36

which would take *a.* of his servants — M't 18:23

give an *a.* of thy stewardship — Lu 16:2

the former *a.* (A) — Ac 1:1

whereby we may give *a.* of this — Ac 19:40

take no *a.* or reckon (A)(B) — Ro 4:8

every one give *a.* of himself to God — Ro 14:12

on *a.* of bodily ailment (A)(N)(P)(R) — Ga 4:17

desire fruit may abound to your *a.* — Ph'p 4:17

if he oweth thee, put that on my *a.* — Ph'm 18

they watch that they must give *a.* — Heb 13:17

who shall give *a.* to him that — 1Pe 4:5

a. that the longsuffering of Lord — 2Pe 3:15

ACCOUNTED

Which also were *a.* as giants — De 2:11

known as Rephaim (A)(R) — De 2:11

regarded as Rephaim (B) — De 2:11

also *a.* as a land of giants — De 2:20

known as a land of Rephaim (A)(R) — De 2:20

regarded as the land of Rephaim (B) — De 2:20

silver was nothing *a.* of — 1Ki 10:21; 2Ch 9:20

be *a.* to Lord for a generation — Ps 22:30

tell of Lord to next generation (A)(R) — Ps 22:30

told of Lord to next generation (B) — Ps 22:30

wherein is he to be *a.* of — Isa 2:22

what sense can he be counted as having intrinsic worth (A) — Isa 2:22

for what should he be valued (B) — Isa 2:22

for what account is he (R) — Isa 2:22

which are *a.* to rule Gentiles — M'k 10:42

recognized as governing (A) — M'k 10:42

supposed to rule Gentiles (B)(R) — M'k 10:42

recognized rulers lord it over (N) — M'k 10:42

so-called rulers of the heathen (P) — M'k 10:42

be *a.* worthy to obtain that world — Lu 20:35

considered worthy to gain that (A)(B)(P) — Lu 20:35

judged worthy of a place in (N) — Lu 20:35

be *a.* worthy to escape all these things — Lu 21:36

have ability to escape (B) — Lu 21:36

may prevail to escape (E) — Lu 21:36

strength to pass safely through (N) — Lu 21:36

strong enough to come safely through (R) — Lu 21:36

strength to escape (R) — Lu 21:36

which of them should be *a.* the greatest — Lu 22:24

considered and reputed greatest (A)(B) — Lu 22:24

rank the highest (P) — Lu 22:24

regarded the greatest (R)   *Lu 22:24*
faith *a.* to Abraham (B)   *Ro 4:9;*
                          4:10
are *a.* as sheep for slaughter   *Ro 8:36*
regarded and counted as   *Ro 8:36*
sheep (A)(R)
been treated like sheep for   *Ro 8:36*
(N)
was *a.* to him for   *Ga 3:6*
righteousness
accredited to him for   *Ga 3:6*
righteousness (B)
reckoned to him for   *Ga 3:6*
righteousness (E)(R)
counted to him for   *Ga 3:6*
righteousness (N)(P)

ACCOUNTETH

a. anything unclean (E)   *Ro 14:14*

ACCOUNTING

require an *a.* (A)(B)(R)   *2Ki 12:15*
a. that God was able to   *Heb 11:19*
raise him up
a. the reproach of Christ   *Heb 11:26*
(E)

ACCOUNTS

that the princes might give *a.*   *Da 6:2*
came and settled *a.*   *M't 25:19*
(A)(B)(N)(P)(R)
whom God *a.* righteous (P)   *Ro 4:6*

ACCREDITED

righteousness might be *a.* (B)   *Ro 4:11*
was *a.* to him (B)   *Ro 4:22; 4:23*
granted and *a.* (A)(B)   *Ro 4:24*
a. to him for righteousness (B)   *Ga 3:6*

ACCURATE

an *a.* weight is his delight   *Pr 11:1*
(B)

ACCURATELY

explained more *a.*   *Ac 18:26*
(A)(B)(E)(P)(R)

ACCURSED

he that is hanged is *a.* of   *De 21:23*
God
city shall be *a.,* it and all   *Jos 6:17*
in any wise keep from the *a.*   *Jos 6:18*
thing
trespass in the *a.* thing;   *Jos 7:1;*
Achan took *a.* thing   *Jos 7:11-13, 15;*
              22:20; 1Ch 2:7
secretly violated the devoted   *Jos 7:1;*
portion (B)(E)(R)   *7:11-13, 15; 22:20*
who transgressed in the thing   *1Ch 2:7*
a.
consecrated, devoted things   *1Ch 2:7*
(B)(E)(R)
sinner an hundred years old   *Isa 65:20*
shall be *a.*
I could wish myself *a.* from   *Ro 9:3*
Christ
no man by the Spirit calleth   *1Co 12:3*
Jesus *a.*
any other gospel, let him be   *Ga 1:8;*
a.   *1:9*
full of *a.* offenses (A)   *Re 17:4*

ACCUSATION

wrote to him an *a.* against   *Ezr 4:6*
Judah
bring *a.* against me (B)   *Ne 6:13*
has an *a.* against (B)   *Mic 6:2*
set over his head this *a.*   *M't 27:37;*
                     M'k 15:26
that they might find an *a.*   *Lu 6:7*
against
if I have taken any thing by   *Lu 19:8*
false *a.*
what *a.* bring ye against   *Joh 18:29*
this man
the *a.* laid against him (S)   *Ac 25:16*
they brought no *a.* as I   *Ac 25:18*
supposed
against an elder receive not   *1Ti 5:19*
an *a.*

bring not a railing *a.* against   *2Pe 2:11*
them
Michael durst not bring a   *Jude 9*
railing *a.*

ACCUSATIONS

many grave *a.* (A)   *Ac 25:7*
state the *a.* (A)   *Ac 25:27*
the *a.* laid against him (S)   *Ac 25:27*

ACCUSE

to *a.* him (R)   *De 19:16*
king *a.* his servant (B)   *1Sa 22:15*
conscience does not *a.* (B)   *Job 27:6*
a. not a servant to his   *Pr 30:10*
master
that they might *a.* him   *M't 12:10;*
   M'k 3:2; Lu 11:54; 23:2, 14; Joh 8:6
nor *a.* any falsely   *Lu 3:14*
that I will *a.* you to the   *Joh 5:45*
Father
let them *a.* one another (E)   *Ac 19:38*
Tertullus began to *a.* him   *Ac 24:2;*
                     24:8, 13
let them go down and *a.* this   *Ac 25:5*
man
if there be none whereof   *Ac 25:11*
these *a.* me
not that I had ought to *a.*   *Ac 28:19*
my nation
falsely *a.* your good   *1Pe 3:16*
conversation
a. your Christian conduct   *1Pe 3:16*
(B)(N)

ACCUSED

a. his brother falsely   *Le 19:18*
(A)(B)(R)
a. him severely (B)   *J'g 8:1*
Chaldeans came near and *a.*   *Da 3:8*
Jews
brought them which had *a.*   *Da 6:24*
Daniel
When He was *a.* He   *M't 27:12*
answered nothing
a. Him of many things   *M'k 15:3;*
                     Lu 23:10
was *a.* that he had wasted his   *Lu 16:1*
goods
the certainty wherefore he   *Ac 22:30;*
was *a.*   *Ac 23:28, 29; 25:16; 26:2, 7*
not *a.* of riot, or unruly   *Tit 1:6*
accuser, who *a.* them before   *Re 12:10*
God

ACCUSER

agree with your *a.*   *M't 5:25;*
(A)(R)   *Lu 12:58*
your *a.* the devil (B)   *1Pe 5:8*
the *a.* of the brethren is cast   *Re 12:10*
out

ACCUSERS

woman, where are those   *Joh 8:10*
thine *a.*
gave commandment to his   *Ac 23:30;*
a.   *Ac 23:35; 24:8; 25:16, 18*
trucebreakers, false *a.*   *2Ti 3:3*
not false *a.,* not given to much   *Tit 2:3*
wine

ACCUSETH

there is one that *a.* you,   *Joh 5:45*
even Moses

ACCUSING

a. you wrongfully (A)   *Lu 3:14*
their thoughts *a.* or excusing   *Ro 2:15*
one

ACCUSTOMED

a. to push with horns (S)   *Ex 21:29*
was I ever *a.* to do so (S)   *Nu 22:30*
David was *a.* to (S)   *1Sa 30:31*
were *a.* to speak in old   *2Sa 20:18*
time (S)
ye that are *a.* to do evil   *Jer 13:23*
a. to releasing one (S)   *M't 27:15*
went as he was *a.* (S)   *Lu 22:39*
where prayer was *a.* to be   *Ac 16:13*
made (S)

ACELDAMA

A., that is to say, The field   *Ac 1:19*
of

ACHAIA

when Gallio was deputy of   *Ac 18:12*
A.
Apollos was disposed to   *Ac 18:27*
pass into *A.*
it pleased them of *A.* to   *Ro 15:26*
make contribution
the first-fruits of *A.*   *Ro 16:5;*
                     1Co 16:15
saints which are in all *A.*   *2Co 1:1*
that *A.* was ready a year ago   *2Co 9:2*
no man stop me in regions   *2Co 11:10*
of *A.*
ye were ensamples to all in   *1Th 1:7*
A.
from you word sounded not   *1Th 1:8*
only in *A.*

ACHAICUS

I am glad of the coming of   *1Co 16:17*
A.

ACHAN

A. the son of Carmi   *Jos 7:1*
A. of tribe of Judah was   *Jos 7:18;*
taken   *7:19*
A. answered Joshua, and said   *Jos 7:20*
all Israel with him, took *A.*   *Jos 7:24*
and stoned
did not *A.* the son of Zerah   *Jos 22:20*
commit

ACHAR

A. the troubler of Israel who   *1Ch 2:7*
transgressed

ACHAZ

Joatham begat *A.,* and *A.*   *M't 1:9*
begat

ACHBOR

Baal-hanan son of *A.*   *Ge 36:38;*
                Ge 36:39; 1Ch 1:49
A. son of Michaiah   *2Ki 22:12; 22:14*
Elnathan son of *A.*   *Jer 26:22; 36:12*

ACHIEVE

possibly *a.* resurrection (B)   *Ph'p 3:11*

ACHIEVING

a. something among you (N)   *Ro 1:13*

ACHIM

Sadoc begat *A.;* and *A.*   *M't 1:14*
begat Eliud

ACHISH

David fled and went to *A.*   *1Sa 21:10;*
                     21:11, 14
David was sore afraid of *A.*   *1Sa 21:12*
David dwelt with *A.*   *1Sa 27:3;*
               27:2, 5-6, 9-10, 12
A. said to David, Know   *1Sa 28:1;*
thou   *28:2; 29:2-9*
servants of Shimei ran away   *1Ki 2:39;*
to *A.*   *2:40*

ACHMETHA

there was found at *A.*   *Ezr 6:2*

ACHOR

them into the valley of *A.*   *Jos 7:24;*
                     7:26; 15:7
the valley of *A.* a place for   *Isa 65:10*
the valley of *A.* for a door   *Ho 2:15*
of hope

ACHSA

the daughter of Caleb was   *1Ch 2:49*
A.

ACHSAH

will I give *A.* my daughter   *Jos 15:16;*
                          J'g 1:1<
he gave him *A.*   *Jos 15:17; J'g 1:13*

ACHSHAPH

to the king of *A.*   *Jos 11:1; 12:20*
Hali, and Beten, and *A.*   *Jos 19:25*

ACHZIB

Keilah, and *A.*   *Jos 15:44;*
              Jos 19:29; J'g 1:31
the houses of *A.* shall be a   *Mic 1:14*
lie

ACKNOWLEDGE

shall *a.* son of the hated   *De 21:17*
woman
neither did he *a.* his brethren   *De 33:9*
a. you to be right (B)(R)   *Job 27:5*
a. that your own right hand   *Job 40:14*
(A)(R)
I *a.* my transgressions   *Ps 51:3*
in all thy ways *a.* him, he shall   *Pr 3:6*
direct
ye that are near, *a.* my   *Isa 33:13*
might
all that see them, shall *a.*   *Isa 61:9*
them
Thou art our Father, though   *Isa 63:16*
Israel *a.* us not
Only *a.* thine iniquity   *Jer 3:13*
We *a.,* O Lord, our   *Jer 14:20*
wickedness
so will I *a.* them that are   *Jer 24:5*
carried away
strange god whom he shall   *Da 11:39*
a.
I will go till they *a.* their   *Ho 5:15*
offence
you *a.* me (B)(N)(P)(R)   *M't 10:32*
a. Jesus to be Christ   *Joh 9:22*
(A)(N)
see fit to *a.*   *Ro 1:28*
(A)(B)(N)(P)(R)
let him *a.* the things that I   *1Co 14:37*
write
a. ye them that are such   *1Co 16:18*
what ye *a.* and I trust shall   *2Co 1:13*
a.

ACKNOWLEDGED

And Judah *a.* them   *Ge 38:26*
I *a.* my sin unto Thee   *Ps 32:5*
ye have *a.* us in part   *2Co 1:14*
God *a.* his gifts (B)   *Heb 11:4*

ACKNOWLEDGETH

he that *a.* Son hath the   *1Jo 2:23*
Father

ACKNOWLEDGING

a. that God is true (P)   *Joh 3:33*
repentance to *a.* of the truth   *2Ti 2:25*
a. of the truth which is   *Tit 1:1*
godliness
by the *a.* of every good thing   *Ph'm 6*

ACKNOWLEDGMENT

to *a.* of the mystery of God   *Col 2:2*

ACQUAINT

a. now thyself with him   *Job 22:21*

ACQUAINTANCE

priests take it, every man of   *2Ki 12:5*
his *a.*
receive no more money of   *2Ki 12:7*
your *a.*
mine *a.* are estranged from   *Job 19:13*
me
all that had been of his *a.*   *Job 42:11*
I was reproach and fear of   *Ps 31:11*
mine *a.*
mine equal, and mine *a.*   *Ps 55:13*
hast put away mine *a.* far   *Ps 88:8*
from me
lover put from me, my *a.*   *Ps 88:18*
into darkness
they sought him among   *Lu 2:44*
their *a.*

all his *a.* stood far off   *Lu 23:49*
should forbid none of his *a.*   *Ac 24:23*
to come

ACQUAINTED

art *a.* with all my ways   *Ps 139:3*
man of sorrows, and *a.* with   *Isa 53:3*
grief

ACQUAINTING

a. mine heart with wisdom   *Ec 2:3*

ACQUIRE

a. the property (B)   *Ge 34:10*

ACQUIT

may *a.* the innocent (B)   *De 25:1*
a. yourselves like men (S)   *1Sa 4:9*
thou wilt not *a.* me from   *Job 10:14*
will not at all *a.* the wicked   *Na 1:3*
who *a.* the guilty (B)(R)   *Isa 5:23*
your words will *a.* you (P)   *M't 12:3*
a. himself of reproach (A)   *Lu 10:29*

ACQUITS

who *a.* the guilty (N)   *Ro 4:5*

ACQUITTAL

a., right standing (A)(N)(R)   *Ro 5:18*
God who pronounces the *a.*   *Ro 8:33*
(N)

ACQUITTED

by your words be *a.* (B)   *M't 12:37*
went home *a.* of sins (N)   *Lu 18:14*
every believer is *a.* of   *Ac 13:39*
everything (N)
freely *a.* before God (P)   *Ro 5:18*

AQUITTER

God is the *A.* (B)   *Ro 8:33*

ACQUITTING

a. the innocent (R)   *De 25:1*
a. the righteous (B)   *1Ki 8:32*

ACRE

as it were an half *a.* of   *1Sa 14:14*
land

ACRES

ten *a.* of vineyard shall yield   *Isa 5:10*

ACT

committed such wicked *a.*   *Jos 19:23*
(B)
this disgraceful *a.* (B)   *2Sa 13:12*
to pass His *a.,* His   *Isa 28:21*
strange *a.*
a. of violence is in their   *Isa 59:6*
hands
taken in adultery, in the very   *Joh 8:4*
a.

ACTED

way your servants *a.* (B)   *2Sa 19:19*
a. insincerely (A)(R)   *Ga 2:13*
a. immorally (R)   *Jude 7*

ACTION

powerful in speech and *a.*   *Lu 24:19*
(N)
let them take legal *a.* (P)   *Ac 19:38*
merciful in *a.* (P)   *Col 3:12*
stripped for *a.* (N)   *1Pe 1:13*

ACTIONS

by him *a.* are weighed   *1Sa 2:3*
his *a.* were good (B)   *Ne 6:9*
wisdom stands or falls by *a.*   *M't 11:19*
(B)
due reward for his *a.*   *Lu 23:41*
(A)(R)

ACTIVITY

if thou knowest any men of   *Ge 47:6*
a.

ACTIVITIES

his *a.* exposed (E)   *Joh 3:20*
our *a.* in the world (P)   *2Co 1:12*
a. of lower nature (P)   *Ga 5:19*
all their impious *a.* (E)(P)   *Jude 15*

ACTS

His *a.* which He did in   *De 11:3;*
Egypt   *11:7*
righteous *a.* of the Lord   *J'g 5:11;*
                      1Sa 12:7
who had done many *a.*   *2Sa 23:20;*
                    1Ch 11:22
a. of Solomon   *1Ki 11:41;*
           1Ki 10:6; 2Ch 9:5, 29
in the book of the *a.* of   *1Ki 11:41*
Solomon
rest of the *a.* of Jeroboam   *1Ki 14:19*
rest of the *a.* of Rehoboam   *1Ki 14:29;*
                    1Ch 12:15
rest of the *a.* of Abijam   *1Ki 15:7,*
                    1Ch 13:22
rest of the *a.* of Asa   *1Ki 15:23;*
                    2Ch 16:11
rest of the *a.* of Nadab   *1Ki 15:31*
rest of the *a.* of Baasha   *1Ki 16:5*
rest of the *a.* of Elah   *1Ki 16:14*
rest of the *a.* of Zimri   *1Ki 16:20*
rest of the *a.* of Omri   *1Ki 16:27*
rest of the *a.* of Ahab   *1Ki 22:39*
rest of *a.* of Jehoshaphat   *1Ki 22:45;*
                    2Ch 20:34
rest of the *a.* of Ahaziah   *2Ki 1:18*
rest of the *a.* of Joram   *2Ki 8:23*
rest of the *a.* of Jehu   *2Ki 10:34*
rest of the *a.* of Joash   *2Ki 12:19;*
                      13:12
rest of the *a.* of Jehoahaz   *2Ki 13:8*
rest of the *a.* of Jehoash   *2Ki 14:15*
rest of the *a.* of Amaziah   *2Ki 14:18;*
                    2Ch 25:26
rest of the *a.* of Jeroboam   *2Ki 14:28*
rest of the *a.* of Azariah   *2Ki 15:6;*
                    2Ch 26:22
rest of the *a.* of Zachariah   *2Ki 15:11*
rest of the *a.* of Shallum   *2Ki 15:15*
rest of the *a.* of Menahem   *2Ki 15:21*
rest of the *a.* of Pekahiah   *2Ki 15:26*
rest of the *a.* of Pekah   *2Ki 15:31*
rest of the *a.* of Jotham   *2Ki 15:36;*
                     2Ch 27:7
rest of the *a.* of Ahaz   *2Ki 16:19*
rest of the *a.* of Hezekiah   *2Ki 20:20;*
                     2Ch 32:32
rest of the *a.* of Manasseh   *2Ki 21:17;*
                     2Ch 33:18
rest of the *a.* of Amon   *2Ki 21:25*
rest of the *a.* of Josiah   *2Ki 23:19;*
                     2Ch 35:26
rest of the *a.* of Jehoiakim   *2Ki 24:5;*
                      2Ch 36:8
proclaim his *a.* (B)   *1Ch 16:8*
the *a.* of David the king,   *1Ch 29:29*
first
all the *a.* of his power   *Es 10:2*
His *a.* unto the children of   *Ps 103:7*
Israel
Who can utter the mighty *a.*   *Ps 106:2*
of
shall declare thy mighty *a.*   *Ps 145:4;*
                     145:12
the might of thy terrible *a.*   *Ps 145:6*
Praise him for his mighty *a.*   *Ps 150:2*
she has committed wicked *a.*   *Jer 11:15*
(B)
signs, miracles, *a.* of power   *2Co 12:12*

ADADAH

and Dimonah, and *A.*   *Jos 15:22*

ADAH

name of one was *A.*   *Ge 4:19;*
                    4:20, 23
A. daughter of Elon   *Ge 36:2;*
              36:4, 10, 12, 16

ADAIAH

Jedidah, daughter of *A.*   *2Ki 22:1*
son of Zerah, son of *A.*   *1Ch 6:41*

ADAIAH *(continued)*

A., and Beraiah, and Shimrath	*1Ch 8:21*
A., the son of Jeroham	*1Ch 9:12; Ne 11:5, 12*
Maaseiah the son of *A.*	*2Ch 23:1*
Malluch, and *A.*	*Ezr 10:29; 10:39*

ADALIA

Poratha, and *A.*	*Es 9:8*

ADAM

brought them unto *A.* to see what	*Ge 2:19*
A. gave names to all cattle	*Ge 2:20*
a deep sleep fall upon *A.*	*Ge 2:21*
A. said, This is now bone of my bones	*Ge 2:23*
A. and his wife hid themselves	*Ge 3:8; Ge 3:9, 17*
A. called his wife's name Eve	*Ge 3:20; 3:21*
A. knew Eve his wife	*Ge 4:25; 1Ch 1:1*
book of generations of *A.*	*Ge 5:1; 5:2-5*
when he separated the sons of *A.*	*De 32:8*
very far from the city of *A.*	*Jos 3:16*
I covered my transgressions as *A.*	*Job 31:33*
which was the son of *A.* the son of God	*Lu 3:38*
death reigned from *A.* to Moses	*Ro 5:14*
as in *A.* all die, even so in Christ	*1Co 15:22*
The first man *A.* was made a living soul	*1Co 15:45*
last *A.* was made quickening Spirit	*1Co 15:45*
A. was first formed, *A.* not deceived	*1Ti 2:13*
Enoch also, the seventh from *A.*	*Jude 14*

ADAMAH

and *A.*, and Ramah, and Hazor	*Jos 19:36*

ADAMANT

As an *a.* harder than flint	*Eze 3:9*
made their hearts as an *a.* stone	*Zec 7:12*

ADAMI

from Allon Zaanannim, and *A.*	*Jos 19:33*

ADAM'S

similitude of *A.* transgression	*Ro 5:14*

ADAR

went up to *A.* and fetched a	*Jos 15:3*
on the third day of the month *A.*	*Ezr 6:15; Es 3:7, 13; 8:12; 9:1, 15, 17, 21*

ADBEEL

Kedar, *A.*, and Mibsam	*Ge 25:13; 1Ch 1:29*

ADD

Lord shall *a.* to me another son	*Ge 30:24*
shall *a.* a fifth part thereto	*Le 5:16; 6:5; 27:13, 15, 19, 27, 31; Nu 5:7*
a. forty-two cities of refuge	*Nu 35:6*
ye shall not *a.* to the word	*De 4:2; 12:32*
shalt *a.* three cities more of refuge	*De 19:9*
a. drunkenness to thirst	*De 29:19*
Lord God *a.* to the people	*2Sa 24:3*
will *a.* to your yoke	*1Ki 12:11; 2Ch 10:14*
a. to thy days 15 years	*2Ki 20:6; Isa 38:5*
thou mayest *a.* thereto	*1Ch 22:14*

ye intend to *a.* more to our sins	*2Ch 28:13*
a. iniquity to their iniquity	*Ps 69:27*
long life, peace shall they *a.* to thee	*Pr 3:2*
a. not to his words, lest he reprove	*Pr 30:6*
a. year to year, let them kill sacrifices	*Isa 29:1*
that they may *a.* sin to sin	*Isa 30:1*
a. one cubit to his stature	*M't 6:27; Lu 12:25*
supposing to *a.* affliction to my bonds	*Ph'p 1:16*
a. lustre to the doctrine (N)	*Tit 2:10*
besides this *a.* to your faith virtue	*2Pe 1:5*
if any man *a.* to these God shall *a.*	*Re 22:18*

ADDAN

Tel-harsa, Cherub, *A.*	*Ezr 2:59*

ADDAR

sons of Bela were *A.* and Gera	*1Ch 8:3*

ADDED

with great voice, and he *a.* no more	*De 5:22*
we have *a.* unto all our sins	*1Sa 12:19*
there were *a.* besides unto them	*Jer 36:32*
Lord hath *a.* grief to my sorrow	*Jer 45:3*
excellent majesty was *a.* to me	*Da 4:36*
all these things shall be *a.*	*M't 6:33; Lu 12:31*
Herod *a.* yet this above all	*Lu 3:20*
He *a.* and spake a parable	*Lu 19:11*
same day there were *a.* 3000 souls	*Ac 2:41*
Lord *a.* to church daily such as	*Ac 2:47*
believers were the more *a.* to the Lord	*Ac 5:14*
much people was *a.* to the Lord	*Ac 11:24*
in conference *a.* nothing to me	*Ga 2:6*
law was *a.* because of transgressions	*Ga 3:19*

ADDER

an *a.* in the path	*Ge 49:17*
deaf *a.* that stoppeth her ear	*Ps 58:4*
tread upon lion and *a.*	*Ps 91:13*
a serpent, and stingeth like an *a.*	*Pr 23:32*
the *a.* (A)(B)(E)(R)	*Isa 14:29; Jer 8:17*
come forth an *a.* (S)	*Isa 14:29*

ADDERS

I will send serpents and *a.* (S)	*Jer 8:17*

ADDERS'

a. poison is under their lips	*Ps 140:3*
hand on the *a.* den (S)	*Isa 11:8*
they hatch *a.* eggs (S)	*Isa 59:5*

ADDETH

he *a.* rebellion unto his sin	*Job 34:37*
he *a.* no sorrow with it	*Pr 10:22*
a. learning to his lips	*Pr 16:23*
no man disannulleth, or *a.*	*Ga 3:15*

ADDI

which was the son of *A.*	*Lu 3:28*

ADDICTED

have *a.* themselves to ministry	*1Co 16:15*

ADDITION

at the side of every *a.*	*1Ki 7:30*
in *a.* to the daughter of (S)	*1Ki 11:1*

ADDITIONS

certain *a.* made of thin work	*1Ki 7:29*
and *a.* round about	*1Ki 7:36*

ADDON

Tel-haresha, Cherub, *A.*	*Ne 7:61*

ADDRESS

made a public *a.* (B)	*Ac 12:21*
Paul's *a.* became longer and longer (P)	*Ac 20:9*
a. him as father (B)	*1Ti 5:1*

ADER

and Arad, and *A.*	*1Ch 8:15*

ADHERE

bones *a.* to my skin (S)	*Ps 102:5*
Not *a.* one to another (S)	*Da 2:43*
a. to the true doctrine (P)	*Tit 1:9*

ADHERED

hand *a.* to sword (S)	*2Sa 23:10*
men *a.* to him (B)	*Ac 5:36*
a. to and relied on (A)	*Eph 1:13*

ADHERING

a. to traditions of elders (A)	*M'k 7:3*

ADIEL

and Asaiah, and *A.*	*1Ch 4:36*
Maasiai the son of *A.*	*1Ch 9:12*
Azmaveth the son of *A.*	*1Ch 27:25*

ADIN

children of *A.*, four hundred	*Ezr 2:15*
Of the son also of *A.*	*Ezr 8:6*
children of *A.*, six hundred	*Ne 7:20*
Adonijah, Bigvai,	*Ne 10:16*

ADINA

A. the son of Chiza	*1Ch 11:42*

ADINO

the same was *A.* the Eznite	*2Sa 23:8*

ADITHAIM

Sharaim, and *A.*	*Jos 15:36*

ADJOURNED

a. the case (B)(N)(P)	*Ac 24:22*

ADJUDGE

let us *a.* the matter (B)	*Isa 1:18*

ADJURATION

voice of *a.* (E)(R)	*Le 5:1*

ADJURE

many times shall I *a.* thee	*1Ki 22:16; 2Ch 18:15*
many times must I charge you (A)	*1Ki 22:16*
I *a.* thee by the living God	*M't 26:63*
I call upon you to swear by (A)	*M't 26:63*
I charge you on oath (B)	*M't 26:63*
I command you by (P)	*M't 26:63*
I *a.* thee by God, torment me not	*M'k 5:7*
I solemnly implore you (A)	*M'k 5:7; Ac 19:13*
for God's sake don't torture me (P)	*M'k 5:7*
we *a.* thee by Jesus whom Paul	*Ac 19:13*

ADJURED

Joshua *a.* them at that time	*Jos 6:26*
Joshua laid this oath upon them (A)(R)	*Jos 6:26*

for Saul had *a.* the people   *1Sa 14:24*
Saul caused men to take   *1Sa 14:24*
an oath (A)(B)(R)

ADLAI

was Shaphat the son of A.   *1Ch 27:29*

ADMAH

Sodom, Gomorrha, A.   *Ge 10:19; 14:2, 8*
A. and Zeboim, which the   *De 29:23*
Lord
how shall I make thee as A.   *Ho 11:8*

ADMATHA

Shethar, A., Tarshish, Meros   *Es 1:14*

ADMINISTER

a. justice (B)   *Ex 18:13; 18:16, 22*
a. retribution (B)   *Le 26:25*
a. proper justice (B)   *De 16:18*
a. justice (A)(E)   *Pr 31:9*

ADMINISTERED

a. justice, equity (R)   *2Sa 8:15*
a. by us to the glory of God   *2Co 8:19*
abundance which is *a.* by us   *2Co 8:20*
administration of this large   *2Co 8:20*
contribution (A)
our handling of this liberal   *2Co 8:20*
collection (B)(N)
gift ministered by us (E)   *2Co 8:20*
liberal gift we are   *2Co 8:20*
ministering (R)

ADMINISTERING

a. the priest's office (B)   *Lu 1:8*

ADMINISTRATING

administrating (B)   *1Co 12:28*

ADMINISTRATION

the *a.* of the law (P)   *2Co 3:7*
the *a.* of the Spirit (P)   *2Co 3:8*
the *a.* of contribution (A)   *2Co 8:20*
For the *a.* of this service   *2Co 9:12*
ministering of this fund (A)   *2Co 9:12*
service this fund renders   *2Co 9:12*
(B)(E)(N)
the *a.* of divine grace (B)   *Eph 3:2*

ADMINISTRATIONS

are differences of *a.*, but the   *1Co 12:5*
same
varieties of service and   *1Co 12:5*
ministration (A)
Distinctive ministries (B)   *1Co 12:5*
diversities of ministrations   *1Co 12:5*
(E)
varieties of service (N)(R)   *1Co 12:5*

ADMINISTRATOR

as *a.* of all things (B)   *Heb 8:2*
a. of the new agreement (P)   *Heb 9:15*

ADMINISTRATORS

administrators (A)(R)   *1Co 12:28*
under guardians and *a.* (A)   *Ga 4:2*

ADMIRABLE

excellent and *a.* (N)   *Ph'p 4:8*

ADMIRATION

having men's persons in *a.*   *Jude 16*
pay people flattering   *Jude 16*
compliments (A)(B)(R)
court favor to gain their ends   *Jude 16*
(N)
her, I wondered with great *a.*   *Re 17:6*

ADMIRED

a. their looks (B)   *Ge 6:2*
to be *a.* in all them that   *2Th 1:10*
believe

ADMONISH

discipline, *a.* (A)   *Ge 4:36*
I *a.* you this day (B)   *De 32:46*
my emotions *a.* me (B)   *Ps 16:7*
I *a.* you (A)(R)   *Ps 81:8*
able also to *a.* one another   *Ro 15:14*
over you in the Lord, and *a.*   *1Th 5:12*
you
a. the careless (N)(R)   *1Th 5:14*
but *a.* him as a brother   *2Th 3:15*

ADMONISHED

and *a.* thee (S)   *1Ki 2:42*
who will no more be *a.*   *Ec 4:1*
by these, my son, be *a.*   *Ec 12:12*
know certainly that I have   *Jer 42:19*
a. you
already past, Paul *a.* them   *Ac 27:9*
as Moses was *a.* of God   *Heb 8:5*

ADMONISHING

a. one another in psalms and   *Col 3:16*

ADMONITION

they are written for our *a.*   *1Co 10:11*
the nurture and *a.* of the   *Eph 6:4*
Lord
after first and second *a.*   *Tit 3:10*
reject

ADNA

A. and Chelal   *Ezr 10:30*
Of Hiram, A.   *Ne 12:15*

ADNAH

fell to him of Manasseh, A.   *1Ch 12:20*
A. the chief, and with him   *2Ch 17:14*

ADO

Why make ye this *a.* and   *M'k 5:39*
weep

ADONI-BEZEK

they found A. in Bezek   *J'g 1:5*
A. fled, A. said, threescore   *J'g 1:6;*
ten   *1:7*

ADONIJAH

A. son of Haggith   *2Sa 3:4; 1Ki 1:5; 2:13; 1Ch 3:2*
they following A. helped him   *1Ki 1:7; 1:8, 9, 11, 13, 18, 24-25, 41-43, 49-51*
speak unto him for A.   *1Ki 2:19; 1Ki 2:21-24, 28*
Jehonathan, and A.   *2Ch 17:8*
A., Bigvai, Adin   *Ne 10:16*

ADONIKAM

children of A. six hundred   *Ezr 2:13; Ne 7:18*
of the last sons of A.   *Ezr 8:13*

ADONIRAM

A. son of Abda was over levy   *1Ki 4:6; 5:14*

ADONI-ZEDEK

A. king of Jerusalem   *Jos 10:1; 10:3*

ADOPTION

have received the Spirit of *a.*   *Ro 8:15*
spirit of sonship (B)   *Ro 8:15*
Spirit that makes us sons   *Ro 8:15*
(N)(R)
waiting for the *a.* to wit, the   *Ro 8:23*
the right of sonship (B)   *Ro 8:23*
wait for God to make us   *Ro 8:23*
sons (N)
realize our full sonship (P)   *Ro 8:23*
to whom pertaineth the *a.*   *Ro 9:4*
Theirs is the sonship (B)   *Ro 9:4*
they were made sons (N)   *Ro 9:4*
to them belong the sonship   *Ro 9:4*
(R)

we might receive the *a.* of   *Ga 4:5*
sons
might attain status of sons   *Ga 4:5*
(N)
unto the *a.* of children by   *Eph 1:5*
Jesus
predestined us for sonship   *Eph 1:5*
(B)
accepted us as sons (N)   *Eph 1:5*
destined us to be his sons   *Eph 1:5*
(R)

ADORAIM

A., and Lachish, and   *2Ch 11:9*
Azekah

ADORAM

A. was over the tribute   *2Sa 20:24; 1Ki 12:18*

ADORN

that women *a.* themselves in   *1Ti 2:9*
modest
dress themselves modestly   *1Ti 2:9*
(B)(N)(P)
may *a.* the doctrine of God   *Tit 2:10*
do credit to the teaching (A)   *Tit 2:10*
beautify the teaching of God   *Tit 2:10*
(B)
add lustre to the doctrine   *Tit 2:10*
(N)
be living testimonial to (P)   *Tit 2:10*

ADORNED

she *a.* her head (B)(R)   *2Ki 9:30*
he *a.* the house (A)(S)   *2Ch 3:6*
shalt again be *a.* with thy   *Jer 31:4*
temple was *a.* with goodly   *Lu 21:5*
stones
decorated with handsome   *Lu 21:5*
stones (A)
a. themselves, being in   *1Pe 3:5*
subjection
were to beautify themselves   *1Pe 3:5*
(A)
were to beautify themselves   *1Pe 3:5*
as a bride *a.* for her husband   *Re 21:2*
beautified for her husband   *Re 21:2*
(B)
dressed in beauty for her (P)   *Re 21:2*
a. with all manner of   *Re 21:19*
(E)(N)(R)

ADORNETH

a bride *a.* herself with   *Isa 61:10*
jewels

ADORNING

a. let it not be outward *a.*   *1Pe 3:3*
beauty not dependant on   *1Pe 3:3*
elaborate coiffure, jewelry,
fine clothes (P)

ADRAMMELECH

burnt children in fire to A.   *2Ki 17:31*
A. and Sharezer his sons   *2Ki 19:37; Isa 37:38*

ADRAMYTTIUM

entering into a ship of A.   *Ac 27:2*

ADRIA

driven up and down in A.   *Ac 27:27*

ADRIEL

she was given unto A.   *1Sa 18:19*
whom she brought up for A.   *2Sa 21:8*

ADULLAM

the king of A.   *Jos 12:15*
Jarmuth, and A.   *Jos 15:35; 2Ch 11:7; Ne 11:30*
escaped to cave A.   *1Sa 22:1; 2Sa 23:13*
rock to David, into the   *1Ch 11:15*
cave of A.
he shall come unto A. the   *Mic 1:15*
glory

ADULLAMITE

turned in to a certain *A.*   *Ge 38:1;*
          38:12, 20

ADULT

we are spiritually *a.* (P)   *Ph'p 3:15*

ADULTERER

a. and adulteress shall be   *Le 20:10*
put to
eye of the *a.* waiteth for   *Job 24:15*
the seed of the *a.* and the   *Isa 57:3*
whore

ADULTERERS

hast been partaker with *a.*   *Ps 50:18*
they be all *a.*   *Jer 9:2; Ho 7:4*
the land is full of *a.*   *Jer 23:10*
the sorcerers, and against the   *Mal 3:5*
a.
extortioners, unjust, *a.*   *Lu 18:11*
nor idolaters, nor *a.*   *1Co 6:9*
whoremongers and *a.* God   *Heb 13:4*
will judge
Ye *a.* and adulteresses know   *Jas 4:4*
ye not

ADULTERESS

adulterer and *a.* shall surely   *Le 20:10*
the *a.* will hunt for souls   *Pr 6:26*
beloved of her friend, yet an   *Ho 3:1*
a.
she shall be called an *a.*   *Ro 7:3*

ADULTERESSES

after the manner of *a.,*   *Eze 23:45*
they are *a.*
Ye adulterers and *a.* know ye   *Jas 4:4*
not

ADULTERIES

I have seen thine *a.*   *Jer 13:27*
her that was old in *a.*   *Eze 23:43*
out of her sight, and her *a.*   *Ho 2:2*
murders, *a.,* fornications   *M't 15:19;*
          M'k 7:21

ADULTEROUS

such is the way of an *a.*   *Pr 30:20*
woman
their *a.* hearts (B)(S)   *Eze 6:9*
An evil and *a.* generation   *M't 12:39*
seeketh
A wicked and *a.* generation   *M't 16:4*
in this *a.* and sinful   *M'k 8:38*
generation

ADULTEROUSLY

a. courting (B)   *Le 17:7*
turned *a.* after other gods   *1Ch 5:25*
(B)

ADULTERY

shalt not commit *a.*   *Ex 20:14;*
De 5:18; M't 5:27; 19:18; Lu 18:20;
          Ro 13:9; Jas 2:11
committeth *a.* shall be put to   *Le 20:10*
death
commits *a.* lacketh   *Pr 6:32*
understanding
Israel committed *a.*   *Jer 3:8;*
3:9; 5:7; 7:9; 23:14; 29:32; Eze 23:37;
          Ho 4:13
as a wife that committeth   *Eze 16:32*
a.
commit *a.* with her (B)   *Eze 23:43*
by lying and committing *a.*   *Ho 4:2*
they
not punish them when they   *Ho 4:14*
commit *a.*
hath committed *a.* in his   *M't 5:28*
heart
whosoever marry her   *M't 5:32; 19:9;*
that is divorced committeth   *M'k 10:11,*
a.   *12; Lu 16:18*
a woman taken in *a.*   *Joh 8:3; 8:4*
should not commit *a.* dost   *Ro 2:22*
thou
A., fornication, uncleanness   *Ga 5:19*
having eyes full of *a.*   *2Pe 2:14*
them that commit *a.* with her   *Re 2:22*
poisoned earth with *a.* (A)   *Re 19:2*

ADUMMIM

going up to *A.*   *Jos 15:7; 18:17*

ADVANCE

you will *a.* (B)(R)   *Eze 38:9*
entered for us in *a.* (B)   *Heb 6:20*

ADVANCED

well *a.* in years (A)   *Ge 18:11;*
24:1; Jos 23:1, 2; 1Ki 1:1; Lu 1:7, 18
well *a.* in years (B)   *Ge 18:11;*
          1Ki 1:1; Lu 1:18
a. in age (R)   *Ge 18:11;*
24:1; 13:1; 23:1, 2; 1Ki 1:1; Lu 1:7, 18
Lord that *a.* Moses and   *1Sa 12:6*
Aaron (A)
appointed Moses and Aaron   *1Sa 12:6*
(B)(E)(R)
a. him and set his seat above   *Es 3:1*
princes
promoted Haman   *Es 3:1*
(A)(B)(E)(R)
he had *a.* him above the   *Es 5:11*
princes
king had promoted him   *Es 5:11*
(A)(B)(E)(R)
whereunto the king *a.* him   *Es 10:2*
the king raised Mordecai (B)   *Es 10:2*

ADVANTAGE

what *a.* will it be to thee   *Job 35:3*
a. of man over the beast   *Ec 3:19*
(B)(R)
What *a.* then hath the Jew   *Ro 3:1*
Lest Satan should get an *a.*   *2Co 2:11*
of us
took *a.* of a brother   *2Co 7:2*
(A)(E)(N)(R)
take *a.* of a brother (B)   *1Th 4:6*
bring no *a.* (N)(R)   *Heb 13:17*
in admiration because of *a.*   *Jude 16*

ADVANTAGED

For what is a man *a.* if he   *Lu 9:25*
gain world
what does it profit (A)(R)   *Lu 9:25*
what will it benefit (B)   *Lu 9:25*
what will a man gain (N)   *Lu 9:25*
what is use of gaining whole   *Lu 9:25*
world (P)

ADVANTAGETH

what *a.* it me, if the dead   *1Co 15:32*
rise not
what do I gain if the dead   *1Co 15:32*
(A)(R)
what good is my fighting if   *1Co 15:32*
(B)
what doth it profit me if   *1Co 15:32*
(E)
what have I gained by it if   *1Co 15:32*
(N)
what is the good of an   *1Co 15:32*
ordeal (P)

ADVENTURE

would not *a.* to set the sole   *De 28:56*
of her
venture to set the sole of   *De 28:56*
her (A)(B)(R)
not *a.* himself into the   *Ac 19:31*
theatre
venturing into the theatre   *Ac 19:31*
(A)
risked himself in the theatre   *Ac 19:31*
(B)(P)
venture in the theatre   *Ac 19:31*
(N)(R)

ADVENTURED

my father *a.* his life for you   *J'g 9:17*
father jeopardized his life   *J'g 9:17*
(A)
father risked his life for you   *J'g 9:17*
(B)(R)

ADVENTURESS

the *a.* (B)(R)   *Pr 2:16; 5:20; 7:5*
tongue of an *a.* (B)   *Pr 6:24; 23:27*

ADVERSARIES

an adversary unto thine *a.*   *Ex 23:22*
a. should behave themselves   *De 32:27*
strangely
He will render vengeance to   *De 32:43*
His *a.*
art thou for us, or for our *a.*   *Jos 5:13*
the *a.* of the Lord shall be   *1Sa 2:10*
broken
ye should this day be *a.* to   *2Sa 19:22*
me
when *a.* of Judah and   *Ezr 4:1*
Benjamin heard
our *a.* said, They shall not   *Ne 4:11*
know
render evil for good, they   *Ps 38:20*
are my *a.*
mine *a.* are all before me   *Ps 69:19*
be confounded that are *a.* to   *Ps 71:13*
my soul
turned my hand against their   *Ps 81:14*
a.
hast set up right hand of his   *Ps 89:42*
a.
for my love they are my *a.*   *Ps 109:4*
let this be the reward of my   *Ps 109:20*
a.
let my *a.* be clothed with   *Ps 109:29*
shame
I will ease me of my *a.*   *Isa 1:24*
Lord shall set up the *a.* of   *Isa 9:11*
Rezin
the *a.* of Judah shall be cut   *Isa 11:13*
off
he will repay fury to his *a.*   *Isa 59:18*
our *a.* have trodden down   *Isa 63:18*
sanctuary
make thy name known to   *Isa 64:2*
thine *a.*
all thine *a.* shall go into   *Jer 30:16*
captivity
that he may avenge him of   *Jer 46:10*
his *a.*
their *a.* said, We offend not   *Jer 50:7*
her *a.* are the chief, her   *La 1:5*
enemies
the *a.* saw her, did mock at   *La 1:7*
her
that his *a.* should be round   *La 1:17*
about
He hath set up horn of thine   *La 2:17*
a.
Noph shall have *a.* (A)(E)   *Ez 30:16*
hand be lifted up upon thy *a.*   *Mic 5:9*
Lord take vengeance on his *a.*   *Na 1:2*
all his *a.* were ashamed   *Lu 13:17*
all your *a.* not be able to   *Lu 21:15*
gainsay
there are many *a.*   *1Co 16:9*
nothing terrified by your *a.*   *Ph'p 1:28*
indignation which shall   *Heb 10:27*
devour the *a.*

ADVERSARY

I will be an *a.* to thine   *Ex 23:22*
adversaries
opponent to your opponents   *Ex 23:22*
(B)
enemy to your enemies   *Ex 23:22*
(E)(R)
angel stood for an *a.*   *Nu 22:22*
against Balaam
her *a.* provoked her sore   *1Sa 1:6*
her rival provoked her   *1Sa 1:6*
(A)(B)(R)
lest in battle he be an *a.* to   *1Sa 29:4*
us
there is neither *a.* nor evil   *1Ki 5:4*
occurrent
stirred up an *a.* to   *1Ki 11:14;*
Solomon   *11:23, 25*
the *a.* is this wicked Haman   *Es 7:6*
An oppressor, and enemy is   *Es 7:6*
this (B)
Haman is a foe and an enemy   *Es 7:6*
(R)
that my *a.* had written in a   *Job 31:35*
book
how long shall the *a.*   *Ps 74:10*
reproach
who is my *a.*? Let him come   *Isa 50:8*
near
the *a.* hath spread out his   *La 1:10*
hand
stood with right hand as an *a.*   *La 2:4*
that the *a.* should have   *La 4:12*
entered gates

an *a.* shall be round about the land	*Am 3:11*
agree with *a.* quickly, *a.* deliver thee	*M't 5:25*
agree with your accuser (A)(R)	*M't 5:25*
Come to terms with opponent (B)(P)	*M't 5:25*
when thou goest with thine *a.*	*Lu 12:58*
as you go with your accuser (A)(R)	*Lu 12:58*
go with your opponent (B)(N)(P)	*Lu 12:58*
widow, saying, Avenge me of mine *a.*	*Lu 18:3*
Do justice to my opponent (B)(N)	*Lu 18:3*
give no occasion to *a.* to speak	*1Ti 5:14*
not give opponents occasion (A)(B)(N)	*1Ti 5:14*
give the enemy no occasion (P)(R)	*1Ti 5:14*
your *a.* the devil as a roaring lion	*1Pe 5:8*
enemy of yours, the devil (A)(N)(P)	*1Pe 5:8*
your accuser, the devil (B)	*1Pe 5:8*

ADVERSE

heard this *a.* message (B)	*Ex 33:4*

ADVERSITIES

saved you out of all your *a.*	*1Sa 10:19*
saved from all calamities (A)(B)(E)(R)	*1Sa 10:19*
hast known my soul in *a.*	*Ps 31:7*
taken note of my life in distresses (A)	*Ps 31:7*
known afflictions of my soul (B)	*Ps 31:7*
consider my *a.* (E)	*Ps 31:7*

ADVERSITY

redeemed my soul out of all *a.*	*2Sa 4:9*
redeemed from all *a.* (B)(E)(R)	*1Ki 1:29*
God did vex them with all *a.*	*2Ch 15:6*
let not *a.* (B)	*Ne 9:32; Ps 25:19; Jer 14:32*
opens their ears by *a.* (A)(R)	*Job 36:15*
I shall never be in *a.*	*Ps 10:6*
But in mine *a.* they rejoiced	*Ps 35:15*
in my stumbling, limping (A)(B)(R)	*Ps 35:15*
give him rest from the days of *a.*	*Ps 94:13*
security in days of distress (B)	*Ps 94:13*
respite from days of trouble (R)	*Ps 94:13*
a brother is born for *a.*	*Pr 17:17*
If thou faint in the day of *a.*	*Pr 24:10*
in the day of *a.* consider	*Ec 7:14*
Lord give you the bread of *a.*	*Isa 30:20*
remember them which suffer *a.*	*Heb 13:3*
those who are ill-treated (A)(E)(R)	*Heb 13:3*
the maltreated as suffering (B)(N)	*Heb 13:3*
those who suffer (P)	*Heb 13:3*

ADVERTISE

I will *a.* what this people shall	*Nu 24:14*
I will tell you what this (A)	*Nu 24:14*
let me inform you what this (B)	*Nu 24:14*
I will let you know what this (R)	*Nu 24:14*
I thought to *a.* thee	*Ru 4:4*
I thought to let you hear of it (A)	*Ru 4:4*
let you know about it (B)	*Ru 4:4*
disclose it unto thee (E)	*Ru 4:4*
tell you of it (R)	*Ru 4:4*
a. your goodness before men (P)	*Lu 16:15*

ADVICE

take *a.* and speak your minds	*J'g 19:30*
take counsel, and speak your minds (A)	*J'g 19:30*
give here your *a.* and counsel	*J'g 20:7*
blessed be thy *a.* and	*1Sa 25:33*
blessed be thou	
a. into foolishness (A)(B)	*2Sa 15:31*
that our *a.* should not be first	*2Sa 19:43*
let me give *a.* (B)	*1Ki 1:12; 12:8; 2Ki 18:20; 2Ch 22:5*
What *a.* give ye, that we may	*2Ch 10:9*
answered them as *a.* of young men	*2Ch 10:14*
give heed to my *a.* (B)	*2Ch 25:16*
King Amaziah took *a.* and sent to	*2Ch 25:17*
king of Judah took counsel (A)	*2Ch 25:17*
the *a.* of the wicked (B)	*Ps 1:1*
with good *a.* make war	*Pr 20:18*
I give my own *a.* (A)(B)(P)(R)	*1Co 7:25*
herein I give my *a.*	*2Co 8:10*
my *a.* to you to buy (P)	*Re 3:18*

ADVISE

I will *a.* (S)	*Nu 24:14*
a. and see what answer I shall give	*2Sa 24:13*
consider and decide (B)(R)	*2Sa 24:13*
let me *a.* you (A)	*1Ki 1:12*
How do ye *a.* that I may answer	*1Ki 12:6*
a. thyself what word I shall	*1Ch 21:12*
I *a.* you to buy of me (B)(N)	*Re 3:18*

ADVISED

with the well *a.* is wisdom	*Pr 13:10*
the more part *a.* to depart	*Ac 27:12*

ADVISEMENT

the Philistines upon *a.* sent him	*1Ch 12:19*
Philistines after consultation (B)	*1Ch 12:19*
Philistines took counsel and sent (R)	*1Ch 12:19*

ADVISERS

conferring with *a.* (N)(P)	*Ac 25:12*

ADVOCATE

by my *a.* (B)	*1Sa 24:15*
your *a.* (N)	*Joh 14:16; 14:26; 15:26; 16:7*
an *a.* named Tertullis (A)(N)	*Ac 24:1*
we have an *a.* with the Father, Jesus	*1Jo 2:1*
We have a counsel for defense (B)	*1Jo 2:1*
One to plead our cause (N)	*1Jo 2:1*

AENEAS

a certain man named *A.*	*Ac 9:33; 9:34*

AENON

baptizing in *A.* near Salim	*Joh 3:23*

AFAR OFF

Abraham saw the place *a. off*	*Ge 22:4*
his brethren saw Joseph *a. off*	*Ge 37:18*
stood *a. off*	*Ex 2:4; 20:18, 21; 1Sa 26:13; 2Ki 2:7; Lu 17:12; 23:49; Re 18:17*
worship ye *a. off*	*Ex 24:1*
pitched it without the camp *a. off*	*Ex 33:7*
be in a journey *a. off*	*Nu 9:10*
when the man of God saw her *a. off*	*2Ki 4:25*
was heard *a. off*	*Ezr 3:13; Ne 12:43*
lifted up eyes *a. off*	*Job 2:12*
behold it *a. off*	*Job 36:25; 39:29; M't 27:55*
he smelleth the battle *a. off*	*Job 39:25*
standest *a. off*	*Ps 10:1; 38:11; Isa 59:14*

them that are *a. off*	*Ps 65:5; Isa 66:19; Jer 31:10*
knoweth proud-thought *a. off*	*Ps 138:6; 139:2*
her own feet carry her *a. off*	*Isa 23:7*
not a God *a. off*	*Jer 23:23*
I will save thee from *a. off*	*Jer 30:10; 46:27*
remember the Lord *a. off*	*Jer 51:50*
rebuke strong nations *a. off*	*Mic 4:3*
followed *a. off*	*M't 26:58; M'k 14:54; Lu 22:54*
saw Jesus *a. off*	*M'k 5:6*
seeing the fig tree *a. off*	*M'k 11:13*
looking on *a. off*	*M'k 15:40*
seeth Abraham *a. off*	*Lu 16:23*
all that are *a. off*	*Ac 2:39; Eph 2:17*
having seen them *a. off*	*Heb 11:13*
is blind, and cannot see *a. off*	*2Pe 1:9*
standing *a. off*	*Re 18:10; 18:15*

AFFAIRS

pertaining to God, and *a.* of the king	*1Ch 26:32*
his *a.* from first to last (B)	*2Ch 35:27*
he will guide *a.* with discretion	*Ps 112:5*
conducts *a.* with justice (A)(R)	*Ps 112:5*
set Shadrach over *a.* of the province	*Da 2:49*
Jews whom thou hast set over *a.* of	*Da 3:12*
also may know of my *a.*	*Eph 6:21; 6:22*
I may hear of your *a.*	*Ph'p 1:27*
entangleth himself with *a.* of life	*2Ti 2:4*

AFFECT

zealously *a.* you, that ye might *a.*	*Ga 4:17*
zealously trying to dazzle you-paying court to you, making much of you (A)	*Ga 4:17*
you may be infatuated with them (B)	*Ga 4:17*
zealously seek you in no good way (E)	*Ga 4:17*
envious of you, but not with honest envy (N)	*Ga 4:17*

AFFECTED

made their minds evil (A)	*Ac 14:2*
be zealously *a.* always in a good	*Ga 4:18*

AFFECTETH

Mine eye *a.* mine heart	*La 3:51*

AFFECTION

I have set my *a.* to house of God	*1Ch 29:3*
my deep interest in God's temple (B)	*1Ch 29:3*
my devotion to house of God (N)	*1Ch 29:3*
my *a.* is stirred (A)	*Jer 31:20*
without natural *a.*	*Ro 1:31; 2Ti 3:3*
heartless and loveless (A)(R)	*Ro 1:31*
your yearning *a.* (A)	*2Co 7:7*
his inward *a.* is more abundant	*2Co 7:15*
his heart goes out to you (A)(R)	*2Co 7:15*
his feelings go out to you (B)	*2Co 7:15*
his heart warms all the more (N)	*2Co 7:15*
deep *a.* of Christ (N)	*Ph'p 1:8*
depth of *a.* (A)(B)(N)(R)	*Ph'p 2:1*
set your *a.* on things above, not on	*Col 3:2*
set your minds, keep them (A)(E)(N)	*Col 3:2*
apply your minds to things above (B)	*Col 3:2*
thoughts dwell on higher realm (N)	*Col 3:2*
give your heart to heavenly things (P)	*Col 3:2*
mortify therefore inordinate *a.*	*Col 3:5*
sensual appetites (A)	*Col 3:5*
passion (B)(E)(P)(R)	*Col 3:5*
lust (N)	*Col 3:5*

AFFECTIONATELY

being *a.* desirous of you,   1Th 2:8
willing

AFFECTIONED

Be kindly *a.* one to another   Ro 12:10

AFFECTIONS

a. centered upon (B)   Ge 34:8
God gave them up to vile *a.*   Ro 1:26
to shameful passions (B)(N)   Ro 1:26
to vile passions (E)   Ro 1:26
to disgraceful passions (P)   Ro 1:26
to dishonorable passions (R)   Ro 1:26
your own *a.* (A)(E)(R)   2Co 6:12
have crucified flesh with *a.*   Ga 5:24
and lusts
passions, appetites, and   Ga 5:24
desires (A)
with passions and desires   Ga 5:24
(B)(N)(R)
with passions and lusts (E)   Ga 5:24

AFFINITY

Solomon made *a.* with   1Ki 3:1
Pharaoh (A)
marriage alliance   1Ki 3:1;
(A)(B)(R)
joined *a.* with Ahab   2Ch 18:1
was allied by marriage (A)   2Ch 18:1
join in *a.* with the people   Ez 9:14
intermarrying with the people   Ez 9:14
(A)(B)(R)

AFFIRM

and as some *a.* that we say   Ro 3:8
they say, nor whereof they *a.*   1Ti 1:7
I will that thou *a.* constantly   Tit 3:8

AFFIRMED

about an hour after another   Lu 22:59
a.
she constantly *a.* that it was   Ac 12:15
even
a. the truth (N)   Ac 23:11
whom Paul *a.* to be alive   Ac 25:19

AFFIRMS

a. the warnings to them   Job 33:16
(B)
he who *a.* this (B)   Re 22:20

AFFLICT

shall *a.* them four hundred   Ge 15:13
years
be afflicted and oppressed   Ge 15:13
(A)
they shall oppress them   Ge 15:13
(B)(R)
if thou *a.* my daughters, or   Ge 31:50
take
if you will ill treat (B)(R)   Ge 31:50
set over them taskmasters to   Ex 1:11
a. them
make life hard for them (B)   Ex 1:11
a. country with frogs (B)   Ex 8:2
shall not *a.* any widow   Ex 22:22;
  22:23
cause distress to (B) Ex 22:22; 22:23
a. souls   Le 16:29; 16:31; 23:27, 32;
Nu 29:7; 30:13; Ps 143:12; Isa 58:5
humble yourselves (B)   Le 16:29;
Ezr 8:21
ships from Chittim shall *a.*   Nu 24:24
Ashur
every binding oath to *a.* the   Nu 30:13
soul
that we bind him to *a.* him   J'g 16:5
bind him to subdue him (A)   J'g 16:5;
  16:6
thou mightest be bound to *a.*   J'g 16:6
thee
render helpless   J'g 16:6; 16:19 (B)
she began to *a.* him   J'g 16:19
torment him (A)(R)   J'g 16:19
nor children of wickedness a.   2Sa 7:10
them
I will for this *a.* the seed of   1Ki 11:39
David
turn when thou dost *a.*   2Ch 6:26;
  1Ki 8:35
we might *a.* ourselves before   Ezr 8:21
God

might humble ourselves (A)   Ezr 8:21
touching the Almighty, He   Job 37:23
will not *a.*
He does no violence (A)   Job 37:23
how thou didst *a.* the people   Ps 44:2
God shall hear and *a.* them   Ps 55:19
God shall humble them   Ps 55:19
(A)(B)(R)
pursue and *a.*   Ps 83:10;
(A)(B)(E)(R)   La 3:66
nor the son of wickedness *a.*   Ps 89:22
him
they *a.* thine heritage   Ps 94:5
destroy all them that *a.* my   Ps 143:12
soul
afterward did more grievously   Isa 9:1
a. her
put into hand of them that   Isa 51:23
a. thee
a day for a man to *a.* his   Isa. 58:5
soul
to humble himself (A)(R)   Isa 58:5
wilt Thou *a.* us very sore   Isa 64:12
as I watched to destroy and   Jer 31:28
to *a.*
the Lord doth not *a.* willingly   La 3:33
they *a.* the just   Am 5:12
they shall *a.* you from   Am 6:14
Hemath
have afflicted, I will *a.* thee   Na 1:12
no more
I will undo all that *a.* thee   Zep 3:19
a. oppress, torment (A)   Ac 12:1
those that *a.* you (A)(R)   2Th 1:6

AFFLICTED

the Lord *a.* Pharaoh (R)   Ge 12:17
more they *a.* them the more   Ex 1:12
they grew
more they were oppressed   Ex 1:12
(A)(R)
more they held them down   Ex 1:12
(B)
soul that shall not be *a.* that   Le 23:29
day
does not humble himself (B)   Le 23:29
wherefore hast thou *a.* thy   Nu 11:11
servant
dealt ill with thy servant   Nu 11:11
(A)(R)
Egyptians *a.* us and laid on   De 26:6
us
treated us harshly (B)(R)   De 26:6
dealt ill with us (E)   De 26:6
a. and oppressed them (R)   J'g 2:18
the Almighty hath *a.* me   Ru 1:21
the Lord *a.* me   Ru 1:21
Lord terrified and *a.* them   1Sa 5:6;
(R)   5:8; Job 2:7
Lord *a.* the men (A)   1Sa 5:9
the *a.* people thou wilt save   2Sa 22:28
a. in all wherein my father   1Ki 2:26
was *a.*
Lord rejected Israel, and *a.*   2Ki 17:20
them
to him that is *a.* pity should   Job 6:14
be
about to faint and despair   Job 6:14
(A)
He hath loosed my cords,   Job 30:11
and *a.* me
He has humbled me   Job 30:11
(B)(R)
He heareth the cry of the *a.*   Job 34:28
the cry of the *a.* (R)   Ps 9:6
pursue the *a.* (B)(R)   Ps 10:2
forget not the *a.* (B)(R)   Ps 10:12
longing of the *a.* (B)   Ps 10:17
planning of the *a.* (B)   Ps 14:6
for thou wilt save the *a.*   Ps 18:27
people
nor abhorred affliction of the   Ps 22:24
a.
I am desolate and *a.*   Ps 25:16
a. hear and be glad (R)   Ps 34:2
do justice to the *a.* and needy   Ps 82:3
thou hast *a.* me with all thy   Ps 88:7
waves
keeping me down with thy   Ps 88:7
waves (B)
overwhelm me with thy waves   Ps 88:7
(R)
I am *a.* and ready to die   Ps 88:15
according to days thou hast   Ps 90:15
a. us
fools because of iniquities   Ps 107:17
are *a.*
illness because of wicked   Ps 107:17
ways (B)

I was greatly *a.*   Ps 116:10
before I was *a.* I went   Ps 119:67
astray
good for me that I have   Ps 119:71
been *a.*
thou in faithfulness hast *a.*   Ps 119:75
me
I am *a.* very much,   Ps 119:107
quicken me
Many a time have they *a.*   Ps 129:1
me
Lord will maintain cause of   Ps 140:12
the *a.*
all the days of the *a.* are evil   Pr 15:15
days of poor are   Pr 15:15
unfortunate (B)
neither oppress the *a.* in the   Pr 22:22
gate
lying tongue hateth those   Pr 26:28
that are *a.*
those that it has wounded   Pr 26:28
(A)(E)
those it crushes (B)   Pr 26:28
hates its victims (R)   Pr 26:28
lest they pervert judgment of   Pr 31:5
the *a.*
when at first he lightly *a.* land   Isa 9:1
of
Lord will have mercy on   Isa 49:13
His *a.*
hear now, thou *a.* and   Isa 51:21
drunken
did esteem him smitten of   Isa 53:4
God and *a.*
he was oppressed, he was *a.*   Isa 53:7
yet
he was maltreated (B)   Isa 53:7
O thou *a.* tossed with   Isa 54:11
tempest
wherefore have we *a.* our   Isa 58:3
souls
if thou satisfy the *a.* soul,   Isa 58:10
thy light
sons of them that *a.* thee   Isa 60:14
shall come
in all their affliction he was   Isa 63:9
a.
her virgins are *a.*   La 1:4
the Lord hath *a.* her   La 1:5; 1:12
I will gather her that I have   Mic 4:6
a.
Though I have *a.* I will afflict   Na 1:12
no more
I will leave in thee an *a.*   Zep 3:12
people
a. and hurt (A)(B)(E)(R)   Zec 10:2
shall deliver you up to be *a.*   M't 24:9
a. with the unclean spirits   Ac 5:16
(R)
whether we be *a.* it is for   2Co 1:6
your
if we are troubled, it is for   2Co 1:6
(A)(B)(P)
if distress is our lot, it is   2Co 1:6
(N)
a. in every way (R)   2Co 4:8;
  2Co 7:5; 2Th 1:7
if she have relieved the *a.*   1Ti 5:10
helped relieve distressed   1Ti 5:10
(A)(B)(N)(P)
being destitute, *a.* and   Heb 11:37
tormented
utterly desitute, oppressed   Heb 11:37
(A)(B)(N)
be *a.* and mourn, and weep   Jas 4:9
be deeply penitent (A)   Jas 4:9
Feel for your misery (B)   Jas 4:9
be sorrowful (N)   Jas 4:9
Be wretched (R)   Jas 4:9
Is any among you *a.* let him   Jas 5:13
pray
suffering trouble, pray   Jas 5:13
(B)(N)(P)
any among you suffering   Jas 5:13
(E)(R)

AFFLICTEST

their sin, when Thou *a.* them   1Ki 8:35

AFFLICTING

pursuing and *a.* them   Ps 35:6
(A)(B)(E)(R)

AFFLICTION

the Lord hath heard thy *a.*   Ge 16:11
noticed your harsh treatment   Ge 16:11
(B)

the Lord hath looked upon *Ge 29:32*
my *a.*
noticed my trouble (B) *Ge 29:32*
God hath seen mine *a.* and *Ge 31:42*
labour
saw my misery (B) *Ge 31:42*
to be fruitful in the land of *Ge 41:52*
a.
I have seen *a.* of my people *Ex 3:7;*
    Ac 7:34
observed the misery of (B) *Ex 3:7*
I will bring you out of *a.* of *Ex 3:17*
Egypt
He hath looked on their *a.* *Ex 4:31*
bread of *a.*
   1Ki 22:27; 2Ch 18:26
Lord heard and looked on *De 26:7*
our *a.*
every sickness and *a.* *De 28:61*
(A)(R)
if thou wilt indeed look on *1Sa 1:11*
our *a.*
may be Lord will look on *2Sa 16:12*
my *a.*
look on the iniquity done *2Sa 16:12*
me (A)
look on my misery (B) *2Sa 16:12*
the Lord saw the *a.* of Israel *2Ki 14:26*
affliction (E)
  Ps 9:13; 2Co 1:4, 8; 2Th 1:6
own *a.* and sorrow (A)(R) *2Ch 6:29*
bread and water of *a.* *2Ch 18:26*
cry to thee in our *a.* thou *2Ch 20:9*
wilt hear
Manasseh was in *a.* and *2Ch 33:12*
sought Lord
remnant are in great *a.* and *Ne 1:3*
reproach
are in great trouble and *Ne 1:3*
reproach (A)
didst see the *a.* of our fathers *Ne 9:9*
though *a.* cometh not forth of *Job 5:6*
dust
calamity does not spring (B) *Job 5:6*
I am full of confusion, see *Job 10:15*
mine *a.*
seeing my misery (B) *Job 10:15*
days of *a.* have taken hold *Job 30:16*
upon me
the days of *a.* prevented me *Job 30:27*
if they be holden in cords *Job 36:8*
of *a.*
he delivereth the poor in *Job 36:15*
his *a.*
this hast thou chosen rather *Job 36:21*
than *a.*
were tested by suffering (B) *Job 36:21*
look upon my *a.* and pain, *Ps 25:18*
forgive
considered my *a.* (A)(R) *Ps 31:7*
forgettest our *a.* and *Ps 44:24*
oppression
thou laidst *a.* upon our loins *Ps 66:11*
heavy burden upon our loins *Ps 66:11*
(A)(B)(E)
mine eye mourneth by reason *Ps 88:9*
of *a.*
because of sorrow (B)(R) *Ps 88:9*
He regarded their *a.* when *Ps 106:44*
he heard
being bound in *a.* and iron *Ps 107:10*
in irons and misery (B) *Ps 107:10*
they are brought low *Ps 107:39*
through *a.*
bowed down through *Ps 107:39*
oppression (A)(B)(E)(R)
setteth he the poor on high *Ps 107:41*
from *a.*
this is my comfort in my *a.* *Ps 119:50*
I should have perished in *Ps 119:92*
mine *a.*
consider mine *a.* and *Ps 119:153*
deliver me
it is a sore *a.* (A)(R) *Ec 6:2*
though Lord give you water *Isa 30:20*
of *a.*
I have chosen thee in *Isa 48:10*
furnace of *a.*
in all the *a.* he was afflicted *Isa 63:9*
published *a.* from mount *Jer 4:15*
Ephraim
intreat thee well in time of *Jer 15:11*
a.
my refuge in the day of *a.* *Jer 16:19*
why criest thou for thine *a.* *Jer 30:15*
Moab's calamity is near, *a.* *Jer 48:16*
hasteth
Judah gone into captivity *La 1:3*
because of *a.*

Jerusalem remembered in days *La 1:7*
of *a.*
had no comforter, behold mine *La 1:9*
a.
I am the man that hath seen *La 3:1*
a.
remembering my *a.* and my *La 3:19*
misery
my *a.* and anguish (B) *La 3:19*
in *a.* they will seek me early *Ho 5:15*
when trouble comes, they will *Ho 5:15*
(B)
not grieved for the *a.* of *Am 6:6*
Joseph
shouldest not looked on their *a.* *Ob 13*
I cried by reason of my *a.* *Jon 2:2*
I cried in my distress (A) *Jon 2:2*
I cried out in anguish (B) *Jon 2:2*
a. shall not rise up the second *Na 1:9*
time
I saw the tents of Cushan in *Hab 3:7*
a.
they helped forward the *a.* *Zec 1:15*
went out and came in *Zec 8:10*
because of *a.*
he shall pass through sea *Zec 10:11*
with *a.*
when *a.* and trouble comes *M't 13:21*
(A)
after the great *a.* (B) *M't 24:29*
when *a.* ariseth for word's *M'k 4:17*
sake
trouble or persecution *M'k 4:17*
(A)(B)(N)(P)
tribulation, persecution *M'k 4:17*
ariseth (E)(R)
healed of her *a.* (B) *M'k 5:29; 5:34*
in those days shall be *a.* *M'k 13:19*
such as
misery of those days (B) *M'k 13:19*
shall be tribulation (E)(R) *M'k 13:19*
distress such as never been *M'k 13:19*
(N)
utter misery in those days *M'k 13:19*
(P)
remember her *a.* (B) *Joh 16:21*
came a dearth and great *a.* *Ac 7:11*
a. and anxiety to (B) *Ro 2:9*
comfort in *a.* (E)(R) *2Co 1:4;*
    1:8
out of such *a.* I wrote to you *2Co 2:4*
great sorrow and deep *2Co 2:4*
distress (A)
in deep distress (B)(P) *2Co 2:4*
out of distress and anxiety *2Co 2:4*
(N)
a. and anxiety (R) *2Co 2:4*
our light *a.* which is but for *2Co 4:17*
a moment
light, momentary trouble *2Co 4:17*
(B)
troubles are slight, *2Co 4:17*
short-lived (N)
these little troubles (P) *2Co. 4:17*
in all our *a.* (E) *2Co 7:4;*
   1Th 3:4; 2Th 1:6
how that in a great trial of *a.* *2Co 8:2*
supposing to add *a.* to my *Ph'p 1:16*
bonds.
ye communicate with me in *Ph'p 4:14*
my *a.*
having received word with *1Th 1:6*
much *a.*
message in much persecution *1Th 1:6*
(A)
message with grave suffering *1Th 1:6*
(N)
message meant bitter *1Th 1:6*
persecution (P)
suffer *a.* (A)(R) *1Th 3:4*
comforted over you in all our *1Th 3:7*
a.
repay with *a.* (A)(R) *2Th 1:6*
choosing to suffer *a.* with *Heb 11:25*
people of
rather to share oppression *Heb 11:25*
(A)
sharing maltreatment (B) *Heb 11:25*
sharing ill-treatment (E) *Heb 11:25*
preferring to suffer *Heb 11:25*
hardship (P)
sharing burden of God's *Heb 11:25*
people (P)
to visit fatherless in their *a.* *Jas 1:27*
widows in their trouble (B) *Jas 1:27*
widows in their distress *Jas 1:27*
(N)(P)
for an example of suffering *Jas 5:10*
a. and

suffering ill-treatment (A)(B) *Jas 5:10*
example of suffering *Jas 5:10*
(E)(P)(R)
patience under ill treatment *Jas 5:10*
(N)
ten days have *a.* (A) *Re 2:10; 2:22*

AFFLICTIONS

known *a.* of my soul (B) *Ps 31:7*
many are *a.* of the righteous *Ps 34:19*
remember David and all his *Ps 132:1*
a.
delivered him out of all his *a.* *Ac 7:10*
enter the kingdom by *a.* (B) *Ac 14:22*
that bonds and *a.* abide me *Ac 20:23*
we exult in *a.* (B) *Ro 5:3*
approving in much patience, *2Co 6:4*
in *a.*
fill up of the *a.* of Christ *Col 1:24*
no man be moved by these *a.* *1Th 3:3*
crushing distresses and *a.* *2Th 1:4*
(A)(E)(R)
be partakers of *a.* of the *2Ti 1:8*
gospel
a. which came to me at *2Ti 3:11*
Antioch
watch in all things, endure *a.* *2Ti 4:5*
ye endured a great fight of *Heb 10:32*
a.
made a gazing stock by *a.* *Heb 10:33*
the same *a.* accomplished in *1Pe 5:9*
brethren

AFFORDING

garners full *a.* all manner of *Ps 144:13*
store

AFFRIGHT

to *a.* them, and trouble *2Ch 32:18*
them
to frighten, demoralize *2Ch 32:18*
them (B)
frighten and terrorize them *2Ch 32:18*
(R)

AFFRIGHTED

shalt not be *a.* at them *De 7:21*
Do not dread them *De 7:21*
(A)(B)(R)
they that went before were *Job 18:20*
a.
seized with terror (A) *Job 18:20*
filled with horror (B)(R) *Job 18:20*
he mocketh at fear, and is *Job 39:22*
not *a.*
not dismayed or terrified *Job 39:22*
(A)(B)(R)
my heart panted, fearfulness *Isa 21:4*
a. me
horror terrifies me (A) *Isa 21:4*
horror appals me (B)(R) *Isa 21:4*
as a man *a.* (E) *Jer 14:9*
reeds are burnt, men of war *Jer 51:32*
are *a.*
men of war frightened (A) *Jer 51:32*
men of war panicky (B) *Jer 51:32*
soldiers are in panic (R) *Jer 51:32*
they were *a.* *M'k 16:5; Lu 24:37*
utterly amazed, struck with *M'k 16:5*
terror (A)
struck with terror (B) *M'k 16:5*
they were amazed (E)(R) *M'k 16:5*
they were dumbfounded (N) *M'k 16:5*
they were simply astonished *M'k 16:5*
(P)
be not *a.* ye seek Jesus *M'k 16:6*
crucified
Do not be amazed or *M'k 16:6*
terrified (A)(R)
Be not terrified (B) *M'k 16:6*
Fear nothing (E) *M'k 16:6*
no need to be astonished *M'k 16:6*
(P)
the remnant were *a.* and *Re 11:13*
gave glory
filled with dread and terror *Re 11:13*
(A)
survivors grew awe-stricken *Re 11:13*
(B)
rest in terror did homage *Re 11:13*
(N)
rest were terrified (P)(R) *Re 11:13*

AFOOT

many ran *a.* out of all cities   *M'k 6:33*
on foot (A)(B)(E)(P)(R)   *M'k 6:33;*
  Ac 20:13
Paul minding himself to go   *Ac 20:13*
a.

AFORE

a. Isaiah was gone out into   *2Ki 20:4*
the court
before Isaiah had left   *2Ki 20:4*
(B)(E)(R)
withereth *a.* it groweth up   *Ps 129:6*
a. harvest when the bud is   *Isa 18:5*
perfect
before the harvest   *Isa 18:5*
(A)(B)(E)(N)(P)(R)
a. he that was escaped   *Eze 33:22*
which he had promised *a.*   *Ro 1:2*
by prophets
which he had *a.* prepared   *Ro 9:23*
unto glory
mystery, as I wrote *a.* in few   *Eph 3:3*
words

AFOREHAND

she is come *a.* to anoint my   *M'k 14:8*
body
came beforehand   *M'k 14:8*
(A)(B)(E)(N)(P)(R)

AFORETIME

a. they laid the meat offerings   *Ne 13:5*
and *a.* I was as a tabret   *Job 17:6*
My people went down *a.* into   *Isa 52:4*
Egypt
went down first into Egypt   *Isa 52:4*
(A)(E)(R)
went down long ago into   *Isa 52:4*
Egypt (B)
their children also shall be   *Jer 30:20*
as *a.*
he prayed before God, as he   *Da 6:10*
did *a.*
brought him that *a.* was   *Joh 9:13*
blind
whatsoever things were   *Ro 15:4*
written *a.*

AFRAID

saw bundles of money, they   *Ge 42:35*
were *a.*
they were *a.* to come nigh   *Ex 34:30*
him
none shall make you *a.*   *Le 26:6;*
  Job 11:19
were not *a.* to speak against   *Nu 12:8*
Moses
do to all people of whom   *De 7:19*
thou art *a.*
whosoever is fearful, and *a.*   *J'g 7:3*
Philistines were *a.* for they   *1Sa 4:7*
said
Saul was yet more *a.* of   *1Sa 18:29*
David
how wast thou not *a.* to   *2Sa 1:14*
destroy
the people have made me *a.*   *2Sa 14:15*
I will come on him, and make   *2Sa 17:2*
him *a.*
ungodly men made me *a.*   *2Sa 22:5;*
  Ps 18:4
they all made us *a.*   *Ne 6:9*
I am *a.* of all my sorrows   *Job 9:28*
none shall make thee *a.*   *Job 11:19*
shall not his excellency   *Job 13:11*
make you *a.*
let not thy dread make me   *Job 13:21*
a.
trouble and anguish shall   *Job 15:24;*
make him *a.*   *Job 18:11; 33:7*
I am *a.*   *Job 21:6;*
23:15; Ps 56:3; 119:120; Jer 38:19;
  Ga 4:11
a. to show opinion (R)   *Job 32:6*
canst make him *a.* as a   *Job 39:20*
grasshopper
the mighty are *a.*   *Job 41:25*
the waters saw thee, and   *Ps 77:16*
were *a.*
make them *a.* with thy storm   *Ps 83:15*
be not *a.* (B)   *Isa 7:4*
none shall make them *a.*   *Isa 17:2;*
  Eze 34:28; Mic 4:4; Zep 3:13
sinners in Zion are *a.*   *Isa 33:14*

the ends of the earth were *a.*   *Isa 41:5*
of whom hast thou been *a.*   *Isa 57:11*
none shall make him *a.*   *Jer 30:10*
they were not *a.* nor rent   *Jer 36:24*
garments
the men, of whom thou art   *Jer 39:17*
a.
none made them *a.*   *Eze 39:26; Na 2:11*
I saw a dream, which made   *Da 4:5*
me *a.*
then the mariners were *a.*   *Jon 1:5;*
  1:10
made *a.*, because of men's   *Hab 2:17*
blood
they were *a.*   *M'k 5:15;*
  M'k 9:32; 10:32; 16:8; Lu 8:35
they were all *a.* of Saul   *Ac 9:26*
they with me saw light, and   *Ac 22:9*
were *a.*
not *a.* of the king's   *Heb 11:23*
commandment
are not *a.* with any   *1Pe 3:6*
amazement
not *a.* to speak evil of   *2Pe 2:10*
dignities

BE AFRAID

neither *be a.*   *De 1:29;*
  De 31:6; Isa 8:12; 44:8
we *be a.* here in Judah   *1Sa 23:3*
be a. out of close places   *2Sa 22:46;*
  Ps 18:45
was he hired that I should   *Ne 6:13*
be a.
nor shalt thou *be a.* of   *Job 5:21*
destruction
be a. of the sword, for   *Job 19:29*
wrath bringeth
my strength, of whom shall I   *Ps 27:1*
be a.
maketh mention, shall *be a.*   *Isa 19:17*
that thou shouldest *be a.* of   *Isa 51:12*
man
if do that which is evil, *be a.*   *Ro 13:4*

BE NOT AFRAID

be not a. of them   *De 20:1;*
  Jos 11:6; Ne 4:14; Jer 10:5; Lu 12:4
Saul said *be not a.* what   *1Sa 28:13*
sawest thou
go down, *be not a.* of him   *2Ki 1:15*
be not a. when one is made   *Ps 49:16*
rich
Be not a. of sudden fear   *Pr 3:25*
lift up thy voice, *be not a.*   *Isa 40:9*
am
Be not a. of their faces, for I   *Jer 1:8*
son of man, *be not a.* of   *Eze 2:6*
them
It is I, *be not a.*   *M't 14:27;*
  M'k 6:50; Joh 6:20
Jesus touched them, Arise *be*   *M't 17:7*
not a.
be not a. go tell my   *M't 28:10*
brethren that
saith to ruler, *Be not a.* only   *M'k 5:36*
believe
be not a. but speak, hold not   *Ac 18:9*
peace
be not a. of their terror, nor   *1Pe 3:14*
be

NOT BE AFRAID

you shall *not be a.* of face of   *De 1:17*
man
thou shalt *not be a.* of them   *De 7:18;*
  18:22
I will *not be a.* of ten   *Ps 3:6*
thousands
I will *not be a.* what man   *Ps 56:11*
can do
shalt *not be a.* for the terror   *Ps 91:5*
by night
he shall *not be a.* of evil   *Ps 112:7*
tidings
heart is established, he shall   *Ps 112:8*
not be a.
when liest down, shalt *not be*   *Pr 3:24*
a.
I will trust and *not be a.*   *Isa 12:2*
he will *not be a.* of their   *Isa 31:4*
voice
trumpet blown, and people   *Am 3:6*
not be a.
wilt thou *not be a.* of the   *Ro 13:3*
power

SORE AFRAID

told these things, men were   *Ge 20:8*
sore a.
Egyptians marched, they   *Ex 14:10*
were *sore a.*
Moab was *sore a.* of the   *Nu 22:3*
people
we were *sore a.* of our lives   *Jos 9:24*
fled from Goliath, and were   *1Sa 17:24*
sore a.
Saul fell on earth, was *sore*   *1Sa 28:20*
a.
his armourbearer was *sore*   *1Sa 31:4;*
a.   *1Ch 10:4*
nothing but sorrow, was *sore*   *Ne 2:2*
a.
wist not what to say, were   *M'k 9:6*
sore a.
shone upon them, were *sore a.*   *Lu 2:9*

WAS AFRAID

I heard thy voice, I *was a.*   *Ge 3:10*
saying, I laughed not, for   *Ge 18:15*
she *was a.*
Jacob *was a.* and distressed   *Ge 32:7*
Moses hid his face, *was a.* to   *Ex 3:6*
look on
I *was a.* of the anger and   *De 9:19*
displeasure
at midnight the man *was a.*   *Ru 3:8*
Saul *was a.* of David   *1Sa 18:12; 18:15*
Ahimelech *was a.* at meeting   *1Sa 21:1*
David
Saul saw Philistines, he *was*   *1Sa 28:5*
a.
David *was a.* of Lord   *2Sa 6:9;*
  1Ch 13:12
David could not go, he *was*   *1Ch 21:30*
a.
that which I *was a.* of is   *Job 3:25*
come
I *was a.* and durst not shew   *Job 32:6*
opinion
when Urijah heard it, he   *Jer 26:21*
was a.
when he came, I *was a.* and   *Da 8:17*
fell
I heard thy speech, and *was a.*   *Hab 3:2*
he feared me, and *was a.* of   *Mal 2:5*
my name
Joseph *was a.* to go thither   *M't 2:22*
saw the wind boisterous,   *M't 14:30*
was a.
I *was a.* and hid my talent   *M't 25:25*
in earth
when Pilate heard, he *was a.*   *Joh 19:8*
when Cornelius looked, he   *Ac 10:4*
was a.

AFRESH

crucify Son of God *a.* and   *Heb 6:6*

AFTER

man in our image, *a.* our   *Ge 1:26*
likeness
a. name of   *Ge 4:17;*
  48:6; Jos 19:47; Lu 1:59
his own likeness, *a.* his image   *Ge 5:3*
a. he had begotten Seth   *Ge 5:4*
a. he begat   *Ge 5:7;*
5:10, 13, 16, 19, 22, 26, 30; 11:11, 13,
  15, 17, 19, 21, 23, 25
a. seven days   *Ge 7:10; 31:23; Ex 7:25*
with seed *a.* you   *Ge 9:9;*
  Ge 17:7-10, 19; 35:12; 48:4
Noah lived *a.* the flood three   *Ge 9:28*
hundred
sons born *a.* the flood   *Ge 10:1*
a. tongue, *a.* families   *Ge 10:5;*
10:20, 31; Nu 1:2, 22, 24, 26, 28, 30,
32, 34, 36, 38, 40, 42; 2:34; 4:2, 29, 34,
44, 46; 26:12, 15, 20, 23, 26, 28, 38,
  37, 38, 41, 42, 44, 48, 57
divided in the earth *a.* the   *Ge 10:32*
flood
a. his return from slaughter   *Ge 14:17*
of
A. these things   *Ge 15:1;*
22:1, 20; 39:7; 40:1; 48:1; De 12:8;
Jos 24:29; 1Ki 17:17; 2Ch 32:1; Ezr 7:1;
Es 2:1; 3:1; Lu 5:27; 10:1; Joh 3:22;
6:1; 7:1; 21:1; Ac 19:21; Re 7:1; 18:1;
  19:1
be with Sarah *a.* the manner   *Ge 18:11*
a. I am waxed old shall I   *Ge 18:12*

to do *a.* this manner   Ge 18:25
come in unto us *a.* the   Ge 19:31
manner of all
a. the death of   Ge 25:11;
Le 16:1;   Nu 35:28; Jos 1:1; J'g 1:1;
2Sa 1:1; 2Ki 1:1; 2Ch 22:4; 24:17; 25:25
thou dost ask *a.* my name   Ge 32:29
A. this manner   Ge 39:19;
Nu 15:13;   28:24;   1Ki 7:37; Ezr 5:4;
Isa 5:17;   10:24,   26; Jer 13:9; 1Pe 3:5
came up *a.* them   Ge 41:3;
41:6, 19, 23; Ex 10:14; 14:4, 9, 10, 23,
                                28
a. the pattern of the   Ex 25:9
tabernacle
a. the shekel   Ex 30:13;
30:24;   38:24,   26;   Le 5:15;   27:3;
Nu 3:47;   7:19,   25, 31, 37, 43, 49, 55,
        61, 67, 73, 79, 85, 86; 18:16
a. their gods   Ex 34:15;
34:16;   De 12:30;   13:2;   1Ki 11:2; 2Ch
                              25:15,20
made *a.* the fashion   Ex 37:19
A. the doings of land of   Le 18:3
Egypt
go a whoring *a.*   Le 20:5;
                20:6; J'g 8:27, 33
the morrow *a.* the sabbath   Le 23:15;
                             23:16
years *a.* the jubilee   Le 25:15; 27:18
a. their generations   Nu 1:24; 1:26, 28
he must do *a.* the law   Nu 6:21
a. own heart   Nu 15:39;
              1Sa 13:14; Ac 13:22
a. other gods   De 6:14;
8:19;   11:28;   28:14;   31:16;   J'g 2:17;
Jer 7:6, 9; 11:10; 13:10, 16:11; 25:6
soul lusteth *a.*   De 12:15;
             12:20, 21; 14:26
walk *a.* the Lord   De 13:4;
2Ki 23:6; 2Ch 34:31; Ho 11:10
a. the abominations   De 18:9;
2Ki 21:2; 2Ch 28:3; Eze 20:30
pursued *a.*   Jos 2:7;
8:16,   17;   24:6;   J'g 1:6;   7:23;   8:12;
20:45; 1Sa 23:25; 2Sa 2:19, 24, 28; 20:10
a. the ark   Jos 6:9; 6:13
pursue *a.*   Jos 8:16;
10:19;   20:5; 1Sa 26:18; 30:8; 2Sa. 17:1;
                        20:6, 7, 13
and cut themselves *a.* their   1Ki 18:28
manner
and not *a.* the doings of   2Ch 17:4
Israel
a. him repaired   Ne 3:16;
         Ne 3:17-18, 20-27, 29-31
thou inquirest *a.* mine   Job 10:6
iniquity
a. my skin worms destroy   Job 19:26
cried *a.* them, as *a.* thief   Job 30:5
lest I deal with you *a.* your   Job 42:8
folly
will not seek *a.* God   Ps 10:4
they seek *a.* my life   Ps 38:12;
Ps 40:14; 54:3; 70:2; 86:14
As hart panteth *a.* water   Ps 42:1;
brooks   Ps 63:8; 143:6
not dealt with us *a.* our   Ps 103:10
sins; nor
priest *a.* order of   Ps 110:4;
Melchizedek   Heb 5:6, 10; 6:20; 7:11,
                    15, 17, 21
The proud, which are not   Ps 119:85
a. thy law
if thou criest *a.* knowledge   Pr 2:3
followeth *a.*   Pr 21:21; 28:19; Isa 1:23
not judge *a.* sight of His eyes   Isa 11:3
a. the imagination   Jer 3:17;
                  Jer 9:14; 16:12
a. many days;   M't 13:6;
       Ec 11:1; Isa 24:22; Eze 38:8
come *a.* me   M't 16:24;
M'k 1:17; 8:34; Lu 9:23; 14:27
a. I am risen   M't 26:32;
M'k 14:28; Joh 21:14
out of graves *a.* his   M't 27:53
resurrection
a. three days I will rise   M'k 8:31
again
a. that he is killed, he shall   M'k 9:31
rise
a. the sop Satan entered   Joh 13:27
into him
a. the manner of men   Ro 6:19
a. the flesh   Ro 8:1;
8:4-5,   12-13;   1Co 1:26;   2Co 5:16;
          10:3; 11:18; Ga 4:23, 29
a. the Spirit   Ro 8:5; Ga 4:29
Follow *a.* charity, and desire   1Co 14:1

made sorry *a.* a godly   2Co 7:9;
manner   7:11
follow *a.* righteousness,   1Ti 6:11
godliness
For if *a.* they have escaped   2Pe 2:20
world wondered *a.* the beast   Re 13:3

AFTER HIS KIND

fruit tree yielding fruit *a. his*   Ge 1:11
kind
herb yielding seed *a. his kind*   Ge 1:12
seed was in itself, *a. his kind*   Ge 1:12
every winged fowl *a. his kind*   Ge 1:21;
                          7:14
the living creature *a. his kind*   Ge 1:24
beast of the earth *a. his kind*   Ge 1:24;
                          7:14
creepeth *a. his kind*   Ge 1:25;
                  Ge 6:20; 8:19
fowls *a.* their kind   Ge 6:20
kite *a. his kind*   Le 11:14
raven *a. his kind*   Le 11:15; De 14:14
hawk *a. his kind*   Le 11:16; De 14:15
heron *a. his kind*   Le 11:19; De 14:18
bald locust *a. his kind*   Le 11:22
tortoise *a. his kind*   Le 11:29
vulture *a. his kind*   De 14:13

AFTER THAT

and also *a. that*, when sons of   Ge 6:4
God
a. that Lot was separated   Ge 13:14
from
a. that he will let you go   Ex 3:20
a. that I will go out   Ex 11:8
a. that he shall come into   Le 14:8
camp
a. that the Nazarite may   Nu 6:20
drink
a. that shall the Levites go   Nu 8:15;
                          8:22
a. that let her be received in   Nu 12:14
not take her *a. that* she is   De 24:4
defiled
be avenged, and *a. that* I will   J'g 15:7
cease
a. that God was intreated   2Sa 21:14
for land
a. that I have spoken, mock   Job 21:3
on
a. that they go to the dead   Ec 9:3
a. that I was turned, I   Jer 31:19
repented
a. that have no more they   Lu 12:4
can do
a. that thou shalt cut it down   Lu 13:9
a. that which is lost, until he   Lu 15:4
find it
a. that he through the Holy   Ac 1:2
Ghost
receive power, *a. that* the Holy   Ac 1:8
a. that they shall come forth   Ac 7:7
a. that he shewed wonders in   Ac 7:36
the
a. that he was seen of above   1Co 15:6
500
a. that he must be loosed a   Re 20:3
little

AFTER THIS

a. this Abraham buried   Ge 23:19
Sarah
a. this David inquired of   2Sa 2:1
Lord
A. this Job opened his mouth   Job 3:1
A. this lived Job an   Job 42:16
hundred and
A. this there was a feast of   Joh 5:1
a. this, Jesus knowing that   Joh 19:38
all
a. this I will return, and   Ac 15:16
build again
A. this I looked, and, behold,   Re 4:1
A. this, I beheld a great   Re 7:9
multitude

AFTERNOON

tarried until *a.* and did eat   J'g 19:8

AFTERWARD

a. were the families of   Ge 10:18
Canaanites
a. shall they come out with   Ge 15:14
great
a. I shall see his face   Ge 32:20

a. came out his brother, that   Ge 38:30
had
a. Moses and Aaron went in   Ex 5:1
a. all the children of Israel   Ex 34:32
came
a. he shall kill burnt   Le 14:19;
offering   14:36
a. he shall come into camp   Le 16:26;
               Le 16:28; Nu 19:7; 31:24
a. eat of the holy things   Le 22:7
a. shall cause the woman to   Nu 5:26
drink
a. shall be gathered unto thy   Nu 31:2
a. ye shall return, and be   Nu 32:22
guiltless
a. the hands of all the people   De 17:7
thou shalt not glean it *a.*   De 24:21
a. he read all the words of   Jos 8:34
the law
a. shall hands be strengthened   J'g 7:11
a. that David's heart smote   1Sa 24:5
a. receive me to glory   Ps 73:24
a. thou shalt be called, The   Isa 1:26
city of
a. did more grievously afflict   Isa 9:1
them
a. I will bring again the   Jer 49:6
captivity of
A. he brought me to   Eze 41:1;
                         43:1; 47:1
A. he brought me (S)   Eze 46:19
a. I rose and did the king's   Da 8:27
business
A. shall children of Israel   Ho 3:5
return
come to pass *a.*, that I will   Joe 2:28
pour
He was *a.* an hungered   M't 4:2;
                            Lu 4:2
a. repented, repented not   M't 21:29;
a.   21:32
A. came also the other   M't 25:11
virgins
a., when affliction or   M'k 4:17
persecution
A. he appeared unto the   M'k 16:14
eleven
but *a.* he said within himself   Lu 18:4
A. Jesus findeth him in the   Joh 5:14
temple
a. they desired a king; and   Ac 13:21
God gave
a. they that are Christ's at   1Co 15:23
his coming
a. that which is spiritual.   1Co 15:46
would he not *a.* have spoken   Heb 4:8
of
a. it yieldeth peaceable   Heb 12:11
fruit
a. when he would have   Heb 12:17
inherited a
a. destroyed them that   Jude 5
believed

AFTERWARDS

a. she bare a daughter   Ge 30:21
a. he will let you go   Ex 11:1
a. the hand of all the people   De 13:9
a. they eat that be bidden   1Sa 9:13
a. we will speak   Job 18:2
a. his mouth be filled with   Pr 20:17
gravel
a. build thine house   Pr 24:27
rebuketh a man *a.* shall find   Pr 28:23
favour
a wise man keepeth it in till   Pr 29:11
a.
A. the Spirit took me up   Eze 11:24
but thou shalt follow me *a.*   Joh 13:36
A. I came into the regions of   Ga 1:21
Syria
which should *a.* be revealed   Ga 3:23

AGABUS

one of them named *A.*   Ac 11:28;
                          21:10

AGAG

His king shall be higher than   Nu 24:7
A.
took, spared, brought *A.*   1Sa 15:8;
                     1Sa 15:9, 20, 32
A. came and said, Surely   1Sa 15:32
bitterness
Samuel hewed *A.* in pieces   1Sa 15:33

AGAGITE

son of Hammedatha the *A.*   *Es* 3:1;
           Es 8:5; 9:24
away the mischief of Haman *Es* 8:3
the *A.*

AGAIN

she *a.* bare his brother Abel *Ge* 4:2
Adam knew his wife *a.*   *Ge* 4:25
a. he sent forth the dove *Ge* 8:10;
                  8:12
I will not *a.* curse the ground *Ge* 8:21
they shall come hither *a.* *Ge* 15:16;
               28:15
ran *a.* unto the well to draw *Ge* 24:20
water
Then *a.* Abraham took a wife *Ge* 25:1
Isaac digged *a.* the wells of *Ge* 26:18
water
she conceived *a.*   *Ge* 29:33;
 Ge 29:34, 35; 30:7, 19; 38:4, 5
God appeared unto Jacob *a.* *Ge* 35:9
he knew her *a.* no more   *Ge* 38:26
I will see *a.* thy face no *Ex* 10:29;
more   14:13
Moses put the vail upon his *Ex* 34:35
face *a.*
may be redeemed *a.*   *Le* 25:48;
             25:51, 52
Israel wept *a.*   *Nu* 11:4
not till Miriam was brought *Nu* 12:15
in *a.*
Israel did evil *a.*   *J'g* 3:12;
   J'g 4:1; 8:33; 10:6; 13:1
a. the anger of the Lord was *2Sa* 24:1
kindled
king's hand was restored him *1Ki* 13:6
a.
child's soul come into him *1Ki* 17:21;
a.   17:22
a. take root downward   *2Ki* 19:30;
             Isa 37:31
For *a.* the Edomites had   *2Ch* 28:17
come
should we *a.* break   *Ezr* 9:14
commandments
if a man die shall he live *a.* *Job* 14:14
bring me up *a.* from the   *Ps* 71:20
depths
Turn us *a.*, O God   *Ps* 80:3; 80:7, 19
Wilt thou not revive us *a.* *Ps* 85:6
seven times, and riseth up *a.* *Pr* 24:16
return *a.* to me   *Jer* 3:1; 25:5
I will bring them *a.*   *Jer* 12:15;
*15:19; 16:15; 23:3; 24:6; 27:16; 28:4;
29:14; 30:3, 18; 31:16, 17, 23; 32:37;
33:12; 50:19; Eze 16:53; 29:14; Joe 3:1;*
              Am 9:14
A. when a righteous man   *Eze* 3:20
doth sin
A. the word of the Lord   *Eze* 11:14
came unto
A. when a wicked man   *Eze* 18:27
turneth
A. the word of Lord came   *Eze* 21:8;
*12:26; 14:12; 18:1; 21:18; 23:1; 25:1;
27:1; 28:1, 20; 30:1; 33:1; 37:15;*
          Hag 2:20; *Zech* 8:1
It is written *a.*, thou shalt not *M't* 4:7
A., the kingdom of heaven *M't* 13:44;
           M't 13:45, 47
be raised *a.* the third day *M't* 26:21;
17:9, 23; 27:63; M'k 8:31; 10:34;
          Lu 18:33; 24:7
her spirit came *a.*, and she *Lu* 8:55
arose
the seventy returned *a.* with *Lu* 10:17
joy
Except a man be born *a.* *Joh* 3:3; 3:7
I will come *a.* and receive *Joh* 14:3
you
will build *a.* the tabernacle *Ac* 15:16
of David
raised *a.* for our justification *Ro* 4:25
able to graff them in *a.*   *Ro* 11:23
come together *a.* that Satan *1Co* 7:5
tempt
rose *a.* the third day   *1Co* 15:4
according
if I build *a.* the things which *Ga* 2:18
I once
how turn *a.* to the weak and *Ga* 4:9
ye desire *a.* to be in bondage *Ga* 4:9
I travail in birth *a.* until *Ga* 4:19
Christ be
not entangled *a.* with the yoke *Ga* 5:1
of
a., I will be to him a Father *Heb* 1:5

a., when he bringeth in the *Heb* 1:6
first
a., I will put my trust in *Heb* 2:13
him
a., Behold I and the   *Heb* 2:13
children God
ye have need that one teach *Heb* 5:12
you *a.*
not laying *a.* the foundation *Heb* 6:1
of
to renew them *a.* unto   *Heb* 6:6
repentance
begotten us *a.* unto a living *1Pe* 1:3
Being born *a.* not of   *1Pe* 1:23
they are *a.* entangled therein *2Pe* 2:20
dog is turned to his own   *2Pe* 2:22
vomit *a.*
prophesy *a.* before many *Re* 10:11
peoples
a. they said Alleluia   *Re* 19:3
rest of the dead lived not *a.* *Re* 20:5
until

AGAINST

Cain rose up *a.* Abel his   *Ge* 4:8
brother
his hand will be *a.* every *Ge* 16:12
man
his anger was kindled *a.* *Ge* 30:2
Rachel
that he prevailed not *a.* him *Ge* 32:25
Do not sin *a.* the child   *Ge* 42:22
anger of Lord kindled *a.*   *Ex* 4:14;
*Nu 11:33; 25:3; 32:13; Jos 7:1; 23:16;
J'g 2:14, 20; 3:8; 10:7; 2Sa 6:7; 12:5;
24:1; 2Ki 13:3; 23:26; 2Ch 13:10;*
             Isa 5:25
people murmured *a.* Moses *Ex* 15:24;
*16:2, 7, 8; 17:3; Nu 14:2, 27, 29, 36;
      16:11, 41; 17:5; Jos 9:18*
my wrath may wax hot *a.* *Ex* 32:10;
32:11; De 11:17; 2Ki 22:17; 2Ch 36:16;
             Job 42:7
Whosoever hath sinned *a.* *Ex* 32:33
me
sin through ignorance *a.* any *Le* 4:2;
of the commandments *4:13, 14, 22, 27*
nor bear any grudge *a.* the *Le* 19:18
people
I will set my face *a.*   *Le* 20:3;
     Le 20:5, 6; 26:17
anger of the Lord was   *Nu* 12:9
kindled *a.* them
rebel not *a.* the Lord   *Nu* 14:9
ye rebelled *a.* my   *Nu* 27:14;
commandment   *De* 1:26; 9:23-24;
             1Sa 12:15
we have sinned *a.* the Lord *De* 1:41;
           Da 9:8, 11
over to fight *a.* the children *J'g* 12:1
of Ammon
the hand of the Lord was *a.* *1Sa* 5:9
Satan stood up *a.* Israel to *1Ch* 21:1
provoke
Meshullam over *a.* his   *Ne* 3:30
chamber
counsel *a.* the Lord, and *a.* *Ps* 2:2;
             Ac 4:26
many are they that rise up *a.* *Ps* 3:1
me
a. whom there is no rising *Pr* 30:31
up
nation shall not lift up sword *a.* *Isa* 2:4
And I will set my face *a.* *Eze* 14:8
that man
shall draw their swords *a.* *Eze* 30:11
Egypt
was gallery *a.* gallery in *Eze* 42:3
three
speak great words *a.* most *Da* 7:25
high
stand up *a.* the Prince of *Da* 8:25
princes
nations come *a.* Jerusalem *Zec* 12:9;
            14:2, 16
dash thy foot *a.* a stone   *M't* 4:6
gave them power *a.* unclean *M't* 10:1
spirits
rise up *a.* parents   *M't* 10:21;
    M't 10:35; *Lu* 12:53
kingdom, house divided *a.* *M't* 12:25;
itself cannot stand   *M'k* 3:24-26;
           Lu 11:17-18
blasphemy *a.* the Holy   *M't* 12:31;
Ghost   *12:32; M'k 3:29; Lu 12:10*
ye be witnesses *a.* yourselves *M't* 23:31
(S)

wrath from heaven *a.* all   *Ro* 1:18
ungodliness
who *a.* hope believed in hope *Ro* 4:18
If God be for us, who can be *Ro* 8:31
a. us
puffed up for one *a.* another *1Co* 4:6
flesh lusteth *a.* Spirit; Spirit *Ga* 5:17
a. flesh
be able to stand *a.* wiles of *Eph* 6:11
devil
wrestle not *a.* flesh and *Eph* 6:12
blood, but *a.*
fleshly lusts which war *a.* the *1Pe* 2:11
soul
rust of them shall be a   *Jas* 5:3
witness *a.* you
I have somewhat *a.* thee   *Re* 2:4;
           Re 2:14, 20
opened mouth in blasphemy *Re* 13:6
a. God
war *a.* him that sat on the *Re* 19:19
horse and *a.*

AGAR

gendereth to bondage, which *Ga* 4:24
is *A.*
For this *A.* is mount Sinai in *Ga* 4:25
Arabia

AGATE

the third row a ligure, an *a.* *Ex* 28:19;
             39:12
fine linen, and coral, and *a.* *Eze* 27:16

AGATES

I will make thy windows *a.* *Isa* 54:12

AGE

shalt be buried in good old *Ge* 15:15
a.
well stricken in *a.*   *Ge* 18:11;
 21:2, 7; 24:1; 25:8; 37:3; 44:20
whole *a.* of Jacob was 147 *Ge* 47:28
years
eyes of Israel were dim   *Ge* 48:10
with *a.*
from the *a.* of 50 years cease *Nu* 8:25
Joshua stricken in *a.* *Jos* 23:1; 23:2
Gideon died in good old *a.* *J'g* 8:32
nourisher of thine old *a.* *Ru* 4:15
shall die in flower of their *a.* *1Sa* 2:33
Ahijah's eyes set by reason *1Ki* 14:4
of his *a.*
in the time of his old *a.* he *1Ki* 15:23
was
from the *a.* of thirty years *1Ch* 23:3
from the *a.* of twenty years *1Ch* 23:24
died in good old *a.*   *1Ch* 29:28
him that stooped for *a.* *2Ch* 36:17
come to thy grave in full *a.* *Job* 5:26
I pray thee, of the former *a.* *Job* 8:8
in whom old *a.* was perished *Job* 30:2
mine *a.* is as nothing before *Ps* 39:5
thee
Cast me not off in time of *Ps* 71:9
old *a.*
still bring forth fruit in old *Ps* 92:14
a.
Mine *a.* is departed, and is *Isa* 38:12
removed
even to your old *a.* I am he *Isa* 46:4
which are of your *a.* (S) *Da* 1:10
his staff in hand for very *a.* *Zec* 8:4
this *a.* (S)   *M't* 12:32;
*Lu 16:8; 20:34; 1Co 1:20; 2:6, 8; 3:18;
2Co 4:4; Ga 1:4; Eph 1:21; 1Ti 6:17;*
             Tit 2:12
the *a.* to come (S)   *M't* 12:32
    M'k 10:30; Lu 20:35; Eph 1:21
the care of this *a.* (S)   *M't* 13:22;
            M'k 4:19
the end of the *a.* (S)   *M't* 13:39;
    13:40, 49; 24:3; 28:20
she was of the *a.* of twelve *M'k* 5:42
years
conceived a son in her old *a.* *Lu* 1:36
was of great *a.* and lived *Lu* 2:36
with an
Jesus about thirty years of *a.* *Lu* 3:23
about twelve years of *a.* and *Lu* 8:42
she lay
we know not: he is of *a.* *Joh* 9:21;
            9:23
since the *a.* began   *Joh* 9:32;
(S)   *Ac* 3:21; 15:18

she pass the flower of her *a.*   *1Co 7:36*
to them that are of full *a.*   *Heb 5:14*
when she was past *a.*   *Heb 11:11*
because she

AGED

Barzillai was a very *a.* man   *2Sa 19:32*
taketh away understanding   *Job 12:20*
of the *a.*
the grayheaded and very *a.*   *Job 15:10*
men
the *a.* arose, and stood up   *Job 29:8*
neither do the *a.* understand   *Job 32:9*
judgment
the *a.* with him that is full of   *Jer 6:11*
days
That the *a.* men be sober,   *Tit 2:2*
grave
The *a.* women likewise, that   *Tit 2:3*
they
being such an one as Paul the   *Ph'm 9*
a.

AGEE

Shammah the son of *A.*   *2Sa 23:11*

AGENT

he is God's *a.* (B)(N)   *Ro 13:4*

AGENTS

a. in guise (N)   *Lu 20:20*
a. of wrath (B)   *Ro 9:22*
they are God's *a.* (B)   *Ro 13:6*
his *a., a.* of good (N)   *2Co 11:15*

AGES

since the *a.* began (S)   *Lu 1:70*
before the *a.* began (S)   *1Co 2:7*
on whom the ends of the *a.*   *1Co 10:11*
are come (S)
That in the *a.* to come he   *Eph 2:7*
might
which in other *a.* was not   *Eph 3:5*
made known
in past generations   *Eph 3:5*
(A)(B)(E)(N)(P)(R)
from the beginning of the *a.*   *Eph 3:9*
(S)
throughout all *a.,* world   *Eph 3:21*
without end
throughout all generations   *Eph 3:21*
(A)(B)(E)(N)(R)
for ever and ever (P)   *Eph 3:21*
since the foundation of the   *Heb 9:26*
a. (S)

AGHAST

gaze stupified and *a.* (A)   *Isa 13:8*

AGITATED

terribly *a.* (P)   *Lu 1:12*
the city was *a.* (B)   *Ac 19:29*

AGITATION

Jesus exclaimed in deep *a.*   *Joh 13:21*
(N)

AGITATOR

an *a.* to all the Jews (A)   *Ac 24:5*

AGLOW

keep spiritually *a.* (B)(R)   *Ro 12:11*

AGO

asses that were lost three   *1Sa 9:20*
days *a.*
Hast thou not heard long   *2Ki 19:25;*
a.   *Isa 37:26*
was builded these many   *Ezr 5:11*
years *a.*
unto him that fashioned it   *Isa 22:11*
long *a.*
repented long *a.* in   *M't 11:21;*
sackcloth   *Lu 10:13*
How long *a.* is it since this   *M'k 9:21*
came
Cornelius said, Four days *a.*   *Ac 10:30*
I was
how that a good while *a.*   *Ac 15:7*
God made

also to be forward a year   *2Co 8:10;*
a.   *9:2*
in Christ above fourteen   *2Co 12:2*
years *a.*

AGONE

because three days *a.* I fell   *1Sa 30:13*
sick
fell sick three days ago   *1Sa 30:13*
(B)(E)(R)

AGONIES

pains and *a.* seize them (B)   *Isa 13:8*
a. are turned (B)   *Da 10:16*
my *a.* of mind (P)   *1Ti 6:10*
suffering spiritual *a.* (P)   *2Pe 2:8*

AGONIZED

then *a.* David (B)   *2Sa 10:6*

AGONIZING

a. longings never (P)   *Ro 8:26*

AGONY

this *a.* is come upon us (B)   *Ge 42:21*
saw the *a.* of his soul (B)   *Ge 42:21*
a. will seize them (R)   *Isa 13:8*
Pelusium shall be in *a.* (R)   *Eze 30:4*
paralyzed and in *a.* (B)   *M't 8:6*
a. in this fire (N)(P)   *Lu 16:24*
being in an *a.* he prayed   *Lu 22:44*
more
remember her *a.* (P)   *Joh 16:21*
gnawed their tongues in *a.*   *Re 16:10*
(N)(P)

AGREE

A. with thine adversary   *M't 5:25*
quickly
a. with your accuser (A)(R)   *M't 5:25;*
  Lu 12:58
That if two of you shall *a.*   *M't 18:19*
on earth
didst not thou *a.* with me   *M't 20:13*
for a penny
neither so did their witness   *M'k 14:59*
a.
this *a.* all the words of the   *Ac 15:15*
prophets
I *a.* with the law   *Ro 7:16*
only too ready to *a.* (P)   *Ga 2:10*
blood; and these three *a.* in   *1Jo 5:8*
one
fulfill his will, and to *a.* to   *Re 17:17*
give

AGREEABLE

an *a.* person (S)   *1Sa 16:18*
a. mutually in mind, attitude   *1Co 1:10*
(B)

AGREED

a. on a signal (B)   *J'g 20:38*
walk together, except they be   *Am 3:3*
a.
when he had *a.* with them   *M't 20:2*
he sent
their witness *a.* not together   *M'k 14:56*
for the Jews had *a.* already   *Joh 9:22*
if any
How is it ye have *a.* together   *Ac 5:9*
to tempt
to him they *a.* and when they   *Ac 5:40*
had
a. to send contribution (N)   *Ac 11:29*
they *a.* that Paul (N)   *Ac 15:2*
The Jews have *a.* to desire   *Ac 23:20*
thee to
they *a.* not among   *Ac 28:25*
themselves

AGREEMENT

make an *a.* by a present   *2Ki 18:31;*
  Isa 36:16
with hell are we at *a.*   *Isa 28:15; 28:18*
to king of the north to make   *Da 11:6*
an *a.*
flood of the new *a.* (P)   *M't 26:28*
walking in *a.* with (B)   *Lu 1:6*
in full *a.* (A)   *1Co 1:10*

administrators of the new *a.*   *2Co 3:6*
(P)
what *a.* hath temple of God   *2Co 6:16*
with idols
a guarantee of a better *a.*   *Heb 7:22*
(A)(P)
transgressors of the first *a.*   *Heb 9:15*
(B)(P)
a. God made with you (P)   *Heb 9:18*
the ark of his *a.* (P)   *Re 11:19*

AGREETH

thy speech *a.* thereto   *M'k 14:70*
out of new, *a.* not with the   *Lu 5:36*
old

AGRIPPA

king *A.* and Bernice came   *Ac 25:13;*
  25:22-24
specially before thee, O king   *Ac 25:26*
A., that
Then *A.* said unto Paul, Thou   *Ac 26:1*
art
I think myself happy, king   *Ac 26:2;*
A.   *Ac 26:7, 19*
King *A.,* believest thou the   *Ac 26:27*
prophets
Then said *A.* unto   *Ac 26:28;*
  26:32

AGROUND

they ran the ship *a.*   *Ac 27:41*

AGUE

I will appoint terror, the   *Le 26:16*
burning *a.*
the burning fever   *Le 26:16*
(B)(E)(R)

AGUR

the words of *A.* the son of   *Pr 30:1*
Jakeh

AH

not say, *A.,* so would we   *Ps 35:25*
have it
A. sinful nation, a people   *Isa 1:4*
laden
A., I will ease me of mine   *Isa 1:24*
adversaries
A., Lord God   *Jer 1:6;*
4:10; 14:13; 32:17; Eze 4:14; 9:8; 11:13;
  20:49
A. my brother! or, *A.* sister!   *Jer 22:18*
saying, *A.* Lord! or *A.* glory!   *Jer 22:18*
will lament thee, saying, *A.*   *Jer 34:5*
Lord!
a! it is made bright   *Eze 21:15*
A., thou that destroyest the   *M'k 15:29*
temple

AHA

said *A., a.,* our eye hath seen it   *Ps 35:21*
that say unto me, *A., a.*   *Ps 40:15*
reward of shame that say, *A.,*   *Ps 70:3*
a.
said *A.,* I am warm, I have   *Isa 44:16*
seen
Because thou saidst, *A.,*   *Eze 25:3*
against my
A., she is broken that was the   *Eze 26:2*
gates
enemy hath said against you,   *Eze 36:2*
A., the

AHAB

A. his son reigned in his stead   *1Ki 16:28;*
  16:29
A. the son of Omri did   *1Ki 16:30;*
evil   *16:33*
Elijah said unto *A.,* As the   *1Ki 17:1*
Lord
Go, shew thyself to *A.*   *1Ki 18:1; 18:2*
A. called Obadiah, *A.* said   *1Ki 18:3;*
  18:5
A. went one way by himself,   *1Ki 18:6*
and
deliver me into hand of *A.*   *1Ki 18:9;*
  1Ki 18:12, 16
A. saw Elijah, *A.* said, Art   *1Ki 18:17*
thou he

AHAB

A. sent unto all the   *1Ki 18:20*
children of
Elijah said unto A., Get   *1Ki 18:41;*
thee up, eat   *1Ki 18:42, 44-46*
A. told Jezebel all that   *1Ki 19:1*
Elijah had
sent messengers to A.   *1Ki 20:2;*
    1Ki 20:13-14, 34
A. spake to Naboth   *1Ki 21:2;*
  21:3-4, 15-16, 18, 20-21, 24-25, 27, 29
Who will persuade A.   *1Ki 22:20;*
    2Ch 18:19
A. slept with his fathers   *1Ki 22:40;*
    1Ki 22:39, 41, 49
Ahaziah the son of A.   *1Ki 22:51*
began to reign
Moab rebelled after death of *2Ki 1:1;*
A.   *6:5*
Jehoram son of A. began to *2Ki 6:1;*
reign   *8:16, 18, 25, 27, 28, 29; 9:29;*
    2Ch 22:5-8
smite the house of A.   *2Ki 9:7;*
 9:8-9, 25; 10:1, 10-11, 17-18, 30; 21:13;
    2Ch 22:8
made a grove as did A.   *2Ki 21:3;*
  2Ch 21:6, 13; 22:3, 4; Mic 6:16
joined affinity with A.   *2Ch 18:1;*
    18:2-3
of A. the son of Kolaiah *Jer 29:21;*
    29:22

AHAB'S

she wrote letters in A. name *1Ki 21:8*
them that brought up A.   *2Ki 10:1*
children

AHARAH

the second, and A. the third *1Ch 8:1*

AHARHEL

families of A. the son of   *1Ch 4:8*
Harum

AHASAI

the son of Azareel, the son *Ne 11:13*
of A.

AHASBAI

Eliphalet the son of A.   *2Sa 23:34*

AHASUERUS

reign of A.   *Ezr 4:6;*
   Es 1:1-2, 9-10, 15-16
king A. commanded Vashti *Es 1:17;*
    Es 1:19; 2:1
Esther was taken in to A. *Es 2:16;*
    2:12
sougt to lay hand on king A. *Es 2:21;*
    6:2
After these things did king A. *Es 3:1;*
    Es 3:6-8, 12
Then king A. answered *Es 7:5; 8:1, 7*
all provinces of king A.   *Es 8:12;*
    Es 9:2, 20, 30
king A. laid a tribute upon *Es 10:1*
Mordecai the Jew was next *Es 10:3*
unto A.
first year of Darius the son of *Da 9:1*
A.

AHASUERUS'

he wrote in king A. name   *Es 8:10*

AHAVA

river of A.   *Ezr 8:21; 8:15, 31*

AHAZ

A. his son reigned in his *2Ki 15:38;*
stead   *16:1-2; 18:1; 2Ch 27:9; 28:1*
they besieged A., but could *2Ki 16:5*
not
A. sent messengers to   *2Ki 16:7;*
    16:8; 2Ch 28:16
A. went to Damascus to *2Ki 16:10*
meet
A. sent from Damascus   *2Ki 16:11;*
    16:15-17
rest of the acts of A. which *2Ki 16:19*
he did
A. slept with his fathers   *2Ki 16:20;*
    2Ch 28:27

In the twelfth year of A.   *2Ki 17:1*
sun gone down on dial of *2Ki 20:11;*
A.   *Isa 38:8*
top of the upper chamber *2Ki 23:12*
of A.
A. his son, Hezekiah his son *1Ch 3:13*
Melech, Tarea, and A. *1Ch 8:35; 9:41*
A. begat Jehoadah, Jarah *1Ch 8:36;*
    9:42
brought Judah low because *2Ch 28:19;*
of A.   *28:21*
against the Lord: this is *2Ch 28:22*
that king A.
A. gathered together the *2Ch 28:24;*
vessels   *29:19*
in the days of Uzziah,   *Isa 1:1;*
Jotham, A. *Isa 7:1; Ho 1:1; Mic 1:1*
Go forth to meet A., thou and *Isa 7:3*
the Lord spake again unto A. *Isa 7:10*
year that king A. died was *Isa 14:28*
this burden

AHAZIAH

A. reigned in his stead   *1Ki 22:40;*
    1Ki 22:49, 51
A. fell down through a lattice *2Ki 1:2*
rest of the acts of A. which *2Ki 1:18*
he did
A. his son reigned in his   *2Ki 8:24;*
stead   *8:25-26*
A. the son of Jehoram king *2Ki 8:25;*
of Judah *8:26, 29; 9:16, 21, 23, 27, 29;*
    2Ch 22:1-2
Jehu met with brethren of *2Ki 10:13*
A.
mother of A., son of A.   *2Ki 11:1;*
 11:2; 12:18; 13:1; 14:13; 1Ch 3:11;
    2Ch 22:8-11
join with A. king of Israel *2Ch 20:35;*
    20:37
destruction of A. was of God *2Ch 22:7;*
    22:8-11

AHBAN

she bare him A. and Molid *1Ch 2:29*

AHEAD

went a. (S) *Lu 18:39; 19:4, 28; Ac 20:13*

AHER

the sons of A.   *1Ch 7:12*

AHI

A. the son of Abdiel *1Ch 5:15; 7:34*

AHIAH

And A., the son of Ahitub *1Sa 14:3*
Saul said unto A., bring   *1Sa 14:18*
hither the ark
Elihoreph and A. were scribes *1Ki 4:3*
Naaman, and A., and Gera *1Ch 8:7*

AHIAM

A. the son of Sharar the   *2Sa 23:33*
Hararite
A. the son of Sacar the   *1Ch 11:35*
Hararite

AHIAN

sons of Shemidah were A., *1Ch 7:19*

AHIEZER

A. the son of Ammishaddai *Nu 1:12*
of the children of Dan shall *Nu 2:25*
be A.
On the tenth day A. the son *Nu 7:66;*
of   *7:71*
over his host was A. the son *Nu 10:25*
of
The chief was A. then Joash *1Ch 12:3*

AHIHUD

A. the son of Shelomi   *Nu 34:27*
and begat Uzza, and A.   *1Ch 8:7*

AHIJAH

prophet A. found him in *1Ki 11:29;*
the way *11:30; 12:15; 14:2, 4-6, 18;*
  15:29; 2Ch 9:29; 10:15

Baasha the son of A.   *1Ki 15:27;*
began to reign *15:33; 21:22; 2Ki 9:9*
Ozem, and A. *1Ch 2:25; 11:36; 26:20*
And A., Hanan, Anan   *Ne 10:26*

AHIKAM

Hilkiah the priest, and A. *2Ki 22:12;*
   2Ki 22:14; 2Ch 34:20
he made Gedaliah the son *2Ki 25:22;*
of A. *Jer 39:14; 40:5-7, 9, 11, 14, 16;*
   41:1-2, 6, 10, 16, 18; 43:6
the hand of A. the son of *Jer 26:24*
Shaphan

AHILUD

Jehoshaphat the son of A.   *2Sa 8:16;*
  2Sa 20:24; 1Ki 4:3; 1Ch 18:15
Baana the son of A.   *1Ki 4:12*

AHIMAAZ

Ahinoam, the daughter of *1Sa 14:50*
A.
A. Zadok's son   *2Sa 15:27;*
 15:36; 17:17, 20; 18:19, 22; 1Ch 6:8, 53
A. ran by the way of the *2Sa 18:23;*
plain   *18:27*
A. called, and said unto the *2Sa 18:28*
king
A. answered, When Joab *2Sa 18:29*
sent the
A. was in Naphtali; he also *1Ki 4:15*
took

AHIMAN

A. was of children of Anak *Nu 13:22;*
    Jos 15:14
Judah slew A. and Talmai *J'g 1:10*
porters were Talmon, and *1Ch 9:17*
A., and

AHIMELECH

A. the priest *1Sa 21:1; 21:2, 8; 22:9*
Then the king sent to call *1Sa 22:11;*
A.   *1Sa 22:14, 16*
one of the sons of A.   *1Sa 22:20;*
    23:6; 26:6
Ahitub and A. *2Sa 8:17; 1Ch 24:31*
A. of the sons of Ithamar *1Ch 24:3;*
    24:6
David is come to the   *Ps 52 title*
house of A.

AHIMELECH'S

to Abiathar the priest A., son *1Sa 30:7*

AHIMOTH

sons of Elkanah; Amasai   *1Ch 6:25*
and A.

AHINADAB

A. the son of Iddo   *1Ki 4:14*

AHINOAM

name of Saul's wife was A. *1Sa 14:50*
David also took A. of   *1Sa 25:43;*
Jezreel *27:3; 30:5; 2Sa 2:2; 3:2; 1Ch 3:1*

AHIO

Uzzah and A. *2Sa 6:3; 6:4; 1Ch 13:7*
A., Shashak, and Jeremoth *1Ch 8:14*
Gedor, A., and Zacher *1Ch 8:31; 9:37*

AHIRA

A. son of Enan   *Nu 1:15;*
   Nu 2:29; 7:78, 83; 10:27

AHIRAM

A., the family of Ahiramites *Nu 26:38*

AHIRAMITES

of Ahiram, the family of the *Nu 26:38*
A.

AHISAMACH

Aholiab, son of A.   *Ex 31:6;*
   Ex 35:34; 38:23

AHISHAHAR

Zethan, and Tharshish, and *1Ch 7:10*
A.

AHISHAR

A. was over the household   *1Ki 4:6*

AHITHOPHEL

Absalom sent for A. the   *2Sa 15:12*
Gilonite
A. is among the   *2Sa 15:31;*
conspirators with   *16:15*
turn counsel of A. into   *2Sa 15:31;*
foolishness   *15:34*
said Absalom to A., give   *2Sa 16:20*
counsel
A. said unto Absalom, Go   *2Sa 16:21*
in unto
counsel of A. was as if a   *2Sa 16:23*
man inquired
A. said unto Absalom, Let   *2Sa 17:1*
me now
The counsel that A. hath   *2Sa 17:7*
given is
is better than the counsel of *2Sa 17:14*
A.
Thus and thus did A.   *2Sa 17:15;*
counsel   *17:21, 23*
Eliam the son of A. the   *2Sa 23:34*
Gilonite
A. was the king's counsellor *1Ch 27:33;*
   27:34

AHITUB

Ahiah, the son of A.,   *1Sa 14:3*
Ichabod's
Ahimelech the son of A.   *1Sa 22:9;*
   22:11-12, 20
Zadok the son of A.   *2Sa 8:17;*
   1Ch 6:8; 18:16
Amariah begat A.   *1Ch 6:7; 6:11, 52*
A. begat Zadok   *1Ch 6:12; Ezr 7:2*
A., the ruler of the house of *1Ch 9:11*
God
son of A. was ruler of house *Ne 11:11*
of God

AHLAB

nor of A., nor of Achzib   *J'g 1:31*

AHLAI

the children of Sheshan; A.   *1Ch 2:31*
the Hittite, Zabad the son   *1Ch 11:41*
of A.

AHOAH

Abishua, and Naaman, and   *1Ch 8:4*
A.

AHOHITE

Eleazar son of Dodo the A.   *2Sa 23:9;*
   1Ch 11:12
Zalmon the A.   *2Sa 23:28*
Ilai the A.   *1Ch 11:29*
the second month was   *1Ch 27:4*
Dodai an A.

AHOLAH

names of them were A.;   *Eze 23:4*
Samaria is A.
A. played the harlot   *Eze 23:5;*
   Eze 23:36, 44

AHOLIAB

have given him A.   *Ex 31:6;*
   Ex 35:34; 36:1-2; 38:23

AHOLIBAH

A. her sister: Jerusalem is *Eze 23:4;*
A.   *23:11*
A. the lewd woman   *Eze 23:44;*
   Eze 23:22, 36

AHOLIBAMAH

A., daughter of Anah   *Ge 36:2;*
   Ge 36:5, 14, 18, 25
duke A,. duke Elah   *Ge 36:41;*
   1Ch 1:52

AHUMAI

Jahath begat A. and Lahad   *1Ch 4:2*

AHUZAM

Naarah bare him A.   *1Ch 4:6*

AHUZZATH

A. one of his friends   *Ge 26:26*

AI

sent men from Jericho to A.   *Jos 7:2;*
   7:2-5
arise, go up to A.   *Jos 8:1;*
8:2-3, 9-12, 14, 16-18, 20-21, 23-26,
   28-29
had done to Jericho and A.   *Jos 9:3;*
   10:1-2
king of A., which is beside   *Jos 12:9*
Beth-el
men of Beth-el and A.   *Ezr 2:28;*
   Ne 7:32
Howl, O Heshbon, for A. is   *Jer 49:3*
spoiled

AIAH

daughter of A.   *2Sa 3:7; 21:8, 10-11*
sons of Zibeon; A. and   *1Ch 1:40*
Anah

AIATH

He is come to A., he is   *Isa 10:28*
passed to

AID

came to a. (S)   *2Sa 8:5; 18:3; 21:17*

AIDED

which a. him in the killing   *J'g 9:24*

AIJA

Geba dwelt at Michmash,   *Ne 11:31*
and A.

AIJALON

A. with her suburbs   *Jos 21:24;*
   1Ch 6:69
would dwell in mount Heres   *J'g 1:35*
in A.
buried in A. in country of   *J'g 12:12*
Zebulun
that day from Michmash to *1Sa 14:31*
A.
the fathers of the   *1Ch 8:13*
inhabitants of A.
and Zorah, and A., and   *2Ch 11:10*
Hebron

AIJELETH

chief musician upon A.   *Ps 22 title*
Shahar

AILED

What a. thee, O thou sea   *Ps 114:5*
that

AILETH

What a. thee   *J'g 18:23; 18:24*
What a. the people that they *1Sa 11:5*
king said, What a. thee   *2Sa 14:5;*
   2Ki 6:28
What a. thee now, that thou *Isa 22:1*
art

AILMENT

healed of her a. (A)   *M'k 5:29*
of what a. he suffered (B)   *Joh 5:3*
on account of bodily a.   *Ga 4:13*
(N)(R)

AILMENTS

all who suffered a. (B)   *M't 14:34*
healed of a. (N)   *Lu 5:15*
your frequent a. (N)(R)   *1Ti 5:23*

AIM

a. hard at choicest graces *1Co 12:31*
(B)(N)

AIN

to Riblah, on the east side *Nu 34:11,*
of A.
A. and Rimmon *Jos 15:32; 19:7; 21:16*
their villages were Etam and *1Ch 4:32*
A.

AIR

the fowl of the a.   *Ge 1:26;*
Ge 1:29-30; 2:19-20; 9:2; Ps 8:8
the fowl of the a.   *Ge 1:26;*
7:3; De 28:26; 1Sa 17:44, 46; 1Ki 14:11;
16:4; 21:24; Job 12:7; 28:21; M't 6:26;
M'k 4:4, 32, Lu 8:5; 13:19; Ac 10:12;
   11:6
winged fowl that flieth in the *De 4:17*
a.
the birds of the a.   *2Sa 21:10;*
   M't 8:20; 13:32; Lu 9:58
no a. can come between   *Job 41:16*
them
The way of an eagle in the   *Pr 30:19*
a.
bird of the a. shall carry the *Ec 10:20*
voice
comfort with hot a. (B)   *Zec 10:2*
threw dust in the a.   *Ac 22:23*
not as one beateth the a.   *1Co 9:26*
sun and the a. were darkened *Re 9:2*
poured out his vial into the *Re 16:17*
a.

AJAH

children of Zibeon; both A. *Ge 36:24*
and

AJALON

thou, moon, in the valley of *Jos 10:12*
A.
Shaalabbin, and A. and   *Jos 19:42*
Jethlah
had taken Beth-shemesh   *2Ch 28:18*
and A.

AKAN

Bilhan, and Zaavan, and A.   *Ge 36:27*

AKKUB

Pelaiah, and A. and   *1Ch 3:24*
Johanan
Shallum, and A. and Talmon *1Ch 9:17*
of Talmon, the children of   *Ezr 2:42*
A.
of Hagabah, the children of *Ezr 2:45*
A.
the children of A.   *Ne 7:45*
Sherebiah, Jamin, A.   *Ne 8:7*
the porters, A., Talmon   *Ne 11:19;*
   12:25

AKRABBIM

from the south to the ascent *Nu 34:4*
of A.
from the going up to A.   *J'g 1:36*

ALABASTER

having an a. box of   *M't 26:7;*
ointment   *M'k 14:3; Lu 7:37*
a. of pure nard   *M'k 14:3*
(A)(B)(E)(N)(R)

ALAMETH

and Abiah, and Anathoth,   *1Ch 7:8*
and A.

ALAMMELECH

A., and Amad, and Mishael *Jos 19:26*

ALAMOTH

with psalteries on A.   *1Ch 15:20*
A song upon A.   *Ps 46 title*

ALARM

blow an a.   *Nu 10:5; 10:6-7, 9*
with sounding trumpets to *2Ch 13:12*
cry a.

sound of a trumpet, the *a.*   *Jer 4:19*
of war
I will cause an *a.* of war to   *Jer 49:2*
be
sound an *a.* in my holy   *Joe 2:1*
mountain
A day of the trumpet and *a.*   *Zep 1:16*
seized with *a.* (A)   *Lu 8:25*

ALARMED

were vexed and *a.* (A)   *Ex 1:12*
be not *a.* or terrified (B)   *De 20:3*
they became *a.* (B)   *Da 3:24*
thoughts *a.* him (B)   *Da 5:6; 7:28*
a. him (R)   *Da 5:6;*
5:7; 7:15, 28; M't 24:6; M'k 13:7
don't be *a.* (N)(P)   *M't 24:6; M'k 13:7*
deeply *a.* and distressed   *M'k 14:33*
(B)

ALAS

Aaron said to Moses, *A.,*   *Nu 12:11*
my lord
A., who shall live when God   *Nu 24:23*
doeth
A., my Lord   *Jos 7:7; J'g 6:22*
A., my daughter! thou hast   *J'g 11:35*
brought
mourned over him, saying,   *1Ki 13:20*
A.
the king of Israel said, *A.!*   *2Ki 3:10*
A., master   *2Ki 6:5; 6:15*
A! for the day is great   *Jer 30:7; Joe 1:15*
A. for all the evil   *Eze 6:11*
abominations
A. for the day (S)   *Eze 30:2*
say in all the highways, *A! a!*   *Am 5:16*
A., A., that great city   *Re 18:10;*
18:16, 19

ALBEIT

Lord saith it; *a.* I have not   *Eze 13:7*
spoken
a. I do not say to thee how   *Ph'm 19*
thou

ALCOHOLIC

mixing *a.* drinks (A)   *Isa 5:22*

ALEMETH

A. with her suburbs   *1Ch 6:60*
Jehoadah begat *A.* and   *1Ch 8:36*
Azmaveth
Jarah begat *A.* and   *1Ch 9:42*
Azmaveth

ALERT

be on the *a.* (N)   *1Pe 5:8*

ALEXANDER

the father of *A.* and Rufus   *M'k 15:21*
John and *A.,* and as many as   *Ac 4:6*
were
drew *A.* out of multitude   *Ac 19:33*
of whom is Hymeneus and   *1Ti 1:20*
A.
A. the coppersmith did me   *2Ti 4:14*
much harm

ALEXANDRIA

Apollos, born at *A.,* an   *Ac 18:24*
eloquent
a ship of *A.* sailing into Italy   *Ac 27:6*
we departed in a ship of *A.*   *Ac 28:11*

ALEXANDRIANS

A., and of them of Cilicia   *Ac 6:9*

ALGUM

and *a.* trees out of Lebanon   *2Ch 2:8*
a. trees and precious stones   *2Ch 9:10*
king made of the *a.* trees   *2Ch 9:11*
terraces

ALIAH

duke Timnah, duke *A.*   *1Ch 1:51*

ALIAN

of Shobal; *A.* and Manahath   *1Ch 1:40*

ALIEN

an *a.* in a strange land (S)   *Ex 2:22*
an *a.* live among you (B)   *Ex 12:48;*
Le 17:8; 10; 19:33; 25:45; Nu 15:14
I have been an *a.* in a   *Ex 18:3*
strange
not maltreat an *a.* (B)   *Ex 22:21*
and the *a.* (A)   *Ex 23:12; Isa 62:8*
the *a.* (B)(R)   *Ex 23:12; De 1:16;*
Job 19:15; Jer 7:6; 22:3; Eze 47:23
the *a.* rabble (B)(R)   *Nu 11:4*
thou mayest sell it unto *a.*   *De 14:21*
justice due an *a.* (A)(B)   *De 27:19*
I am an *a.* in their sight   *Job 19:15*
an *a.* unto my mother's   *Ps 69:8*
children
people of an *a.* speech (R)   *Ps 114:1*
hostile *a.* tribes (A)   *Ps 144:7*
house of an *a.* (S)   *Pr 5:10*
the *a.* woman (R)   *Pr 7:5*
an *a.* woman (R)(S)   *Pr 23:27; 27:13*
an *a.* god (B)   *Isa 17:10*
an *a.* work (B)   *Isa 28:21*
the *a.* shall be your   *Isa 61:5*
ploughmen
an *a.* vine (R)   *Jer 2:21*
a. children (A)(B)   *Ho 5:7*
an *a.* in a foreign land   *Ac 7:6*
(B)(R)
a. teachings (A)   *Heb 13:9*

ALIENATE

a. me as your enemy (A)   *Job 13:24*
a. a close friend (B)(R)   *Pr 17:9*
nor *a.* the first fruits of the   *Eze 48:14*
land

ALIENATED

her mind was *a.* from them   *Eze 23:17*
then my mind was *a.* from   *Eze 23:18*
her
whom thy mind is *a.*   *Eze 23:22; 23:28*
being *a.* from the life of   *Eph 4:18*
God
were sometime *a.* and   *Col 1:21*
enemies

ALIENATION

know my *a.* (E)   *Nu 14:34*

ALIENS

hand of *a.* (E)(R)(S)   *Ps 144:7*
noise of *a.* (S)   *Isa 25:5*
our houses are turned to *a.*   *La 5:2*
a. in a land belonging to (R)   *Ac 7:6*
living as *a.* in Egypt (N)   *Ac 13:7*
being *a.* from the   *Eph 2:12*
commonwealth
exiles, migrants, *a.*   *Eph 2:19*
(A)(N)(P)
turned to flight armies of   *Heb 11:34*
the *a.*
as *a.* in a foreign land   *1Pe 2:11*
(N)(R)

ALIEN'S

the *a.* children (B)   *Ps 144:7*

ALIGHTED

they *a.* from (S)   *Ge 24:64;*
Jos 15:18; J'g 1:14; 4:15; 1Sa 25:23;
2Ki 5:21

ALIKE

the clean shall eat of them   *De 12:22;*
a.   *15:22*
they shall part *a.*   *1Sa 30:24*
They shall lie down *a.* in   *Job 21:26*
the dust
He fashioneth their hearts *a.*   *Ps 33:15*
darkness and light are both   *Ps 139:12*
a.
both of them are *a.*   *Pr 20:10*
abomination
a contentious woman are *a.*   *Pr 27:15*
All things come *a.* to all   *Ec 9:2*
whether they both shall be *a.*   *Ec 11:6*
good
another esteemeth every day *a.*   *Ro 14:5*

ALIVE

to keep them *a.*   *Ge 6:19; 6:20; 7:3*
Noah only remained *a.,* and   *Ge 7:23*
but they will save thee *a.*   *Ge 12:12*
to save much people *a.*   *Ge 50:20*
but saved the men children   *Ex 1:17;*
a.   *1:18*
every daughter ye shall save   *Ex 1:22*
a.
be certainly found in his   *Ex 22:4*
hand *a.*
sons of Aaron which were   *Le 10:16*
left *a.*
to take two birds *a.* and clean   *Le 14:4*
be presented *a.* before the   *Le 16:10*
Lord
upon them that are left *a.*   *Le 26:36*
they went down *a.* into the   *Nu 16:33*
pit
go down *a.* into the pit (S)   *Nu 16:30;*
Ps 55:15
smote Og until there were   *Nu 21:35*
none left *a.*
I had slain thee, and saved   *Nu 22:33*
her *a.*
Have ye saved all the   *Nu 31:15*
women *a.*
are *a.* every one of you this   *De 4:4*
day
who are all of us *a.* here this   *De 5:3*
day
that he might preserve us *a.*   *De 6:24*
at this
shall save *a.* nothing that   *De 20:16*
breatheth
I kill, and make *a.*   *De 32:39; 1Sa 2:6*
that ye will save *a.* my father   *Jos 2:13*
Joshua saved Rahab the   *Jos 6:25*
harlot *a.*
the king of Ai they took *a.*   *Jos 8:23*
Lord hath kept me *a.* as he   *Jos 14:10*
said
if ye had saved them *a.* I   *J'g 8:19*
would not
gave them wives which they   *J'g 21:14*
saved *a.*
took Agag the king of   *1Sa 15:8*
Amalek *a.*
David left neither man nor   *2Sa 27:9*
woman *a.*
to save the horses and mules   *1Ki 18:5*
a.
whether come for peace or   *1Ki 20:18*
war take *a.*
for Naboth is not *a.* but   *1Ki 21:15*
dead
Am I God to kill and make   *2Ki 5:7*
a.
if they save us *a.* we shall live   *2Ki 7:4*
when they come out catch   *2Ki 7:12*
them *a.*
take them *a.* and they took   *2Ki 10:14*
them *a.*
and other ten thousand left   *2Ch 25:12*
a.
thou hast kept me *a.* that I   *Ps 30:3*
swallowed us up *a.* (S)   *Ps 124:3*
let us swallow them up *a.* as   *Pr 1:12*
the
the fatherless I will preserve   *Jer 49:11*
a.
will ye save souls *a.* that   *Eze 13:18*
come
to save souls *a.* that should   *Eze 13:19*
not live
doeth what is right, shall   *Eze 18:27*
save his soul *a.*
whom he would he kept *a.*   *Da 5:19*
when they heard that he   *M'k 16:11*
was *a.*
my son was dead and is *a.*   *Lu 15:24;*
15:32
had seen angels who said he   *Lu 24:23*
was *a.*
make me *a.*   *Joh 5:2;*
(A)(B)(N)(P)(R)   *Joh 6:63; Ro 4:17*
shewed himself *a.* after his   *Ac 1:3*
passion
had called the widow,   *Ac 9:41*
presented her *a.*
they brought the young man   *Ac 20:12*
a.
Jesus, whom Paul affirmed   *Ac 25:19*
to be *a.*
but *a.* to God through Christ   *Ro 6:11*
as those that are *a.* from the   *Ro 6:13*
dead

for I was *a*. without the law   *Ro 7:9*
once
so in Christ shall all be   *1Co 15:22*
made *a*.
that sown is not made *a*.   *1Co 15:36*
except (S)
you hath he made. (S)   *Eph 2:1;*
    Eph 2:5; Col 2:13; 1Pe 3:18
he made *a*. (A)(E)(R)   *Col 2:1; 2:25*
that we which are *a*. and   *1Th 4:15;*
remain   *4:17*
maketh all things *a*. (S)   *1Ti 6:13*
made *a*. in spirit   *1Pe 3:18*
(A)(B)(E)(R)
behold I am *a*. for evermore   *Re 1:18*
first and last which was dead,   *Re 2:8*
is *a*.
were both cast *a*. into lake   *Re 19:20*
of fire

YET ALIVE

is your father *yet a*.   *Ge 43:7;*
    Ge 43:27, 28
Joseph is *yet a*. *Ge 45:26; 45:28; 46:30*
let me go see whether they be   *Ex 4:18*
yet a.
while I am *yet a*. with you   *De 31:27*
this day
while the child was *yet a*.   *2Sa 12:18;*
    12:21-22
while *yet a*. in the midst of   *2Sa 18:14*
the oak
is he *yet a*.? he is my   *1Ki 20:32*
brother
more than living which are *yet* *Ec 4:2*
a.
although they were *yet a*.   *Eze 7:13*
deceiver said, while he was   *M't 27:63*
yet a.

ALL

the cattle, and over *a*. the   *Ge 1:26*
earth
upon the face of *a*. the earth *Ge 1:29;*
    11:8-9
finished, and *a*. the host of   *Ge 2:1*
them
seventh day from *a*. His work   *Ge 2:2;*
    2:3
cursed above *a*. cattle   *Ge 3:14*
a. the days of thy life   *Ge 3:14; 3:17*
she was the mother of *a*.   *Ge 3:20;*
living   *5:4*
a. the days   *Ge 5:5;*
  5:8, 11, 14, 17, 20, 23, 27, 31
end of *a*. flesh is come   *Ge 6:13;*
    Ge 6:17; 7:21-22
a. their substance that they   *Ge 12:5*
had
and his wife, and *a*. that he   *Ge 13:1*
had
a. nations of the earth   *Ge 18:18; 26:4*
Shall not judge of *a*. earth   *Ge 18:25*
do right
after the manner of *a*. the   *Ge 19:31*
earth
with thee in *a*. that thou   *Ge 21:22*
doest
a. the nations of the earth   *Ge 22:18*
be blessed
of *a*. that went in at the   *Ge 23:10*
gate
before *a*. that went in at the *Ge 23:18*
gate
had blessed Abraham in *a*.   *Ge 24:1*
things
that ruled over *a*. that he had *Ge 24:2*
a. the goods of his master   *Ge 24:10*
were in his
and drew for *a*. his camels   *Ge 24:20*
to him he hath given *a*. that   *Ge 24:36*
he hath
Jacob loved Joseph more   *Ge 37:3*
than *a*. his
Lord made *a*. he did to   *Ge 39:3*
prosper
and *a*. the souls that came out *Ex 1:5*
of
and smite Egypt with *a*. my   *Ex 3:20*
wonders
a. the men are dead which   *Ex 4:19*
sought
throughout *a*. the land of   *Ex 8:16*
Egypt
throughout *a*. the land of   *Ex 8:21*
Egypt
none like it in *a*. the land of *Ex 9:24*
Egypt

they said. We be *a*. dead   *Ex 12:33*
men
seen with thee in *a*. thy   *Ex 13:7*
quarters
made heaven, earth, sea, and   *Ex 20:11*
a. in
Moses wrote *a*. the words of   *Ex 24:4*
the law
make *a*. my goodness pass   *Ex 33:19*
before thee
shall pour out *a*. the blood   *Le 4:34*
thereof
Lord appeared unto *a*. the   *Le 9:23*
people
it is *a*. turned white: he is   *Le 13:13*
clean
assembled *a*. congregation   *Nu 1:18;*
1:20, 22, 24, 26, 28, 30, 32, 34, 36, 38, 40
Number *a*. the firstborn   *Nu 3:40;*
    Nu 3:41-43, 45
A. the days of separation   *Nu 6:4;*
    Nu 6:5-6, 8
and *a*. that were numbered   *Nu 14:29*
of you
we die, we perish, we *a*.   *Nu 17:12*
perish
according to *a*. that   *Nu 30:2*
proceedeth out
keep *a*. the commandments   *De 11:8;*
  De 11:22; 13:18; 19:9; 26:18; 27:1
But *a*. the princes said unto   *Jos 9:19*
a. the
the trumpet throughout *a*.   *1Sa 13:3*
the land
And *a*. the people brought   *1Sa 14:34*
every man
And according to *a*. this   *2Sa 7:17*
vision, so
but who slew *a*. these   *2Ki 10:9*
in the purifying of *a*. holy   *1Ch 23:28*
things
So *a*. Israel went to their   *2Ch 10:16*
tents
and *a*. Israel with him   *2Ch 12:1*
and *a*. the store cities of   *2Ch 16:4*
Naphtali
over *a*. the kingdoms of the   *2Ch 20:6*
heathen
a. gone aside, *a*. become   *Ps 14:3*
filthy
Lord delivereth out of them   *Ps 34:19*
a.
out thine anger to *a*.   *Ps 85:5*
generations
thee, to keep thee in *a*. thy   *Ps 91:11*
ways
his judgments are in *a*. the   *Ps 105:7*
earth
I have seen an end of *a*.   *Ps 119:96*
perfection
thy word above *a*. thy name   *Ps 138:2*
the earth, ye dragons, and *a*. *Ps 148:7*
deeps
her breasts satisfy thee at *a*. *Pr 5:19*
times
a. of the dust, *a*. turn to dust *Ec 3:20*
again
and *a*. the daughters of   *Ec 12:4*
musick shall
a. the sighing thereof have I   *Isa 21:2*
made
They were *a*. ashamed of a   *Isa 30:5*
people
by the hand of *a*. the sons   *Isa 51:18*
that she
shall *a*. bow down to the   *Isa 65:12*
slaughter
And *a*. nations shall serve   *Jer 27:7*
him, and
king of Babylon and *a*. his   *Jer 39:1*
army
heart because of *a*. the   *La 3:51*
daughters
they are *a*. estranged from   *Eze 14:5*
me
and madest *a*. their loins to   *Eze 29:7*
be at a
Seir, and *a*. Idumea, even   *Eze 35:15*
a. of it
and, behold, *a*. the earth   *Zec 1:11*
sitteth still
a. Judea, *a*. region about   *M't 3:5*
pass from law, till *a*. be   *M't 5:18*
fulfilled
His sisters, are they not *a*.   *M't 13:56*
with us
she cast in *a*. she had   *M'k 12:44;*
    Lu 21:4
except ye repent, ye shall *a*.   *Lu 13:3*
perish

of his fulness have *a*. we   *Joh 1:16*
He told me *a*. that ever I   *Joh 4:29*
did
ye are clean but not *a*.   *Joh 13:10*
great grace was upon them *a*.   *Ac 4:33*
a. things are yours   *1Co 3:22*
that they *a*. might be   *2Th 2:12*
damned
Are they not *a*. ministering   *Heb 1:14*
spirits
chastisement, *a*. are   *Heb 12:8*
partakers
that *a*. should come to   *2Pe 3:9*
repentance
ye to be in *a*. holy   *2Pe 3:11*
conversation
cleanseth us from *a*. sin   *1Jo 1:7; 1:9*
A. unrighteousness is sin   *1Jo 5:17*
I wish above *a*. things that thou *3Jo 3*

ACCORDING TO ALL

did *according to a*.   *Ge 6:22;*
commanded   *Ge 7:5; Ex 31:11; 36:1;*
  39:32, 42; 40:16; Nu 2:34; 8:20; 9:5;
    29:40; De 1:3, 41
took land *according to a*.   *Jos 11:23*
Lord said
rest *according to a*. He   *1Ki 8:56*
promised
reign *according to a*. soul   *1Ki 11:37*
desireth
according to a. father done   *1Ki 22:53;*
  2Ki 23:32, 37; 24:9, 19; 2Ch 26:4; 27:2
done *according to a*. in my   *2Ki 10:30*
heart
according to a. David did   *2Ki 18:3;*
    1Ch 29:2
according to a. words,   *1Ch 17:15*
according to a.
think on me, *according to a*.   *Ne 5:19*
I have done
deal *according to a*. his   *Jer 21:2*
works
according to a. Lord shall   *Jer 42:20*
say
according to a. Babylon   *Jer 50:29*
hath done, do
according to a. he hath   *Eze 24:24*
done, shall
according to a. thy   *Da 9:16*
righteousness

AFTER ALL

not do *after a*. their   *De 20:18*
abominations
not kept the word to do   *2Ch 34:21*
after a.
after a. that is come on us   *Ezr 9:13*
for deeds
after a. thy wickedness   *Eze 16:23*
after a. these things do   *M't 6:32*
Gentiles
for he longed *after a*.   *Ph'p 2:26*

AT ALL

nor delivered thy people *at a*. *Ex 5:23*
if thou afflict, and they cry   *Ex 22:23*
at a. to
but if he will *at a*. redeem it *Le 27:13*
have I now any power *at a*.   *Nu 22:38*
to say
if thou do *at a*. forget the   *De 8:19*
Lord
if thy father *at a*. miss me,   *1Sa 20:6*
then
if ye shall *at a*. turn from   *1Ki 9:6*
following
they shall not save them *at*   *Jer 11:12*
a.
cometh in mind shall not *at*   *Eze 20:32*
a.
none *at a*. would exalt him   *Ho 11:7*
weep ye not *at a*., roll in   *Mic 1:10*
dust
Lord not *at a*. acquit the   *Na 1:3*
wicked
couldst have no power *at a*.   *Joh 19:11*
his will was not *at a*. to   *1Co 16:12*
come
in him is no darkness *at a*.   *1Jo 1:5*
Babylon be found no more   *Re 18:21*
at a.
sound be heard no more *at*   *Re 19:22*
a. in thee

BEFORE ALL

before *a.* that went in at   *Ge 23:18*
gates of city
before *a.* people I will be   *Le 10:3*
glorified
Jerusalem I have chosen   *2Ch 33:7*
before a.
shall be to me an honour   *Jer 33:9*
before a.
he denied *before a.* saying   *M't 26:70*
I said to Peter *before a.*   *Ga 2:14*
them that sin rebuke *before*   *1Ti 5:20*
a. that

FOR ALL

have taken Levites *for a.*   *Nu 8:18*
firstborn
for a. that do so are   *De 22:5;*
abomination   *25:16*
hide my face in that day *for*   *De 31:18*
a. evils
as *for a.* his enemies he   *Ps 10:5*
puffeth at
for a. this they sinned still   *Ps 78:32*
what render to Lord *for a.*   *Ps 116:12*
his benefits
the profit of the earth is *for a.*   *Ec 5:9*
for a. these God will bring to   *Ec 11:9*
judgment
hath received double *for a.*   *Isa 40:2*
her sins
alas *for a.* the evil   *Eze 6:11*
abominations
shall loathe yourselves *for*   *Eze 20:43*
a. evils
in it was meat *for a.*   *Da 4:21*
for a. the evils Herod had   *Lu 3:19*
done
God of the living *for a.* live   *Lu 20:38*
unto
for a. have sinned and come   *Ro 3:23*
short
if one died *for a.* then were   *2Co 5:14*
all dead
for a. seek their own, not   *Ph'p 2:21*
the things
who gave himself a ransom   *1Ti 2:6*
for a.
for a. shall know me, from   *Heb 8:11*
least to
offering the body of Christ   *Heb 10:10*
once *for a.*

FROM ALL

angel who redeemed me   *Ge 48:16*
from a. evil
that ye may be clean *from a.*   *Le 16:30*
sins
delivered me *from a.* my fears   *Ps 34:4*
from a. lands whither he   *Jer 16:15*
had driven
it was diverse *from a.* beasts   *Da 7:7*
before it
God rested seventh day *from*   *Heb 4:4*
a. works

IN ALL

in a. that Sarah hath said,   *Ge 21:12*
hearken
God is with thee *in a.* thou   *Ge 21:22*
doest
that ye may prosper *in a.*   *De 29:9*
that ye do
have obeyed my voice *in a.*   *Jos 22:2*
that
mighty men, thirty seven *in*   *2Sa 23:39*
a.
thou mayest prosper *in a.*   *1Ki 2:3*
thou doest
afflicted *in a.* my father was   *1Ki 2:23*
afflicted
sons of Zerah, five of them *in*   *1Ch 2:6*
a.
Thou art just *in a.* brought   *Ne 9:33*
upon us
God is not *in a.* his thoughts   *Ps 10:4*
in a. thy ways acknowledge   *Pr 3:6*
him
nothing *in a.* dominion   *Isa 39:2*
shewed not
in a. their afflictions he was   *Isa 63:9*
afflicted
have done evil *in a.* they   *Jer 38:9*
have done
in a. your doings your sins   *Eze 21:24*
appear

in a. my labours shall find no   *Ho 12:8*
iniquity
we were *in a.* 276 souls   *Ac 27:37*
in a. these more than   *Ro 8:37*
conquerors
to be admired *in a.* them   *2Th 1:10*
that believe
marriage is honorable *in a.*   *Heb 13:4*
as also *in a.* his epistles   *2Pe 3:16*

ALL IN ALL

the same God worketh *all in*   *1Co 12:6*
a.
put *a.* under, that God be   *1Co 15:28*
all in a.
the fulness of him that   *Eph 1:23*
filleth *all in a.*
but Christ is *all in a.*   *Col 3:11*

OF ALL

took them wives *of a.* they   *Ge 6:2*
chose
he gave him tithes of *a.*   *Ge 14:20;*
   Heb 7:2
of a. give me, I will give   *Ge 28:22*
tenth
nothing die *of a.* is Israel's   *Ex 9:4*
not a word *of a.* Moses   *Jos 8:35*
commanded
of a. I said to woman,   *J'g 13:13*
beware
shall hands *of a.* be strong   *2Sa 16:21*
Jehu said, to which *of a.* us   *2Ki 9:5*
let nothing fail *of a.* hast   *Es 6:10*
spoken
so are paths *of a.* that forget   *Job 8:13*
God
wanteth nothing *of a.* he   *Ec 6:2*
desireth
if be ashamed *of a.* they   *Eze 43:11*
have done
you only have I known *of a.*   *Am 3:2*
families
same shall be servant *of a.*   *M'k 9:35;*
   10:44
of a. given me, lose nothing   *Joh 6:39*
peace by Jesus Christ, Lord   *Ac 10:36*
of a.
he is convinced of *a.,*   *1Co 14:24*
judged *of a.*
the heir, though he be lord *of*   *Ga 4:1*
a.
God who is Father *of a.,*   *Eph 4:6*
above all
to God the Judge *of a.*   *Heb 12:23*
offend in one point is guilty   *Jas 2:10*
of a.

OVER ALL

that thou mayest reign *over*   *2Sa 3:21*
a.
thou reignest *over a.*   *1Ch 29:12*
His kingdom ruleth *over a.*   *Ps 103:19*
make him ruler *over a.*   *M't 24:47;*
   Lu 12:44
as thou hast given him   *Joh 17:2*
power *over a.*
who is *over a.,* God blessed   *Ro 9:5*
for ever
same Lord *over a.* is rich to   *Ro 10:12*
a.

TO ALL

Lord is good *to a.*   *Ps 145:9*
one event happeneth *to a.*   *Ec 2:14;*
   Ec 9:2, 3. 11
so is Pharaoh *to a.* that trust   *Isa 36:6*
in him
speakest to us, or even *to a.*   *Lu 12:41*
promise is *to a.* that are afar   *Ac 2:39*
off
manifest *to a.* in Jerusalem   *Ac 4:16*
render *to a.* their dues   *Ro 13:7*
that thy profiting may appear   *1Ti 4:15*
to a.

UNTO ALL

what I say to you, I say   *M'k 13:37*
unto a.
Lord is rich *unto a.* that   *Ro 10:12*
call on him
I made myself a servant   *1Co 9:19*
unto a.

UPON ALL

blessing of Lord *upon a.* he   *Ge 39:5*
had
for *upon a.* glory shall be a   *Isa 4:5*
defence
set heart *upon a.* that I   *Eze 40:4*
shall shew
unto *a., upon a.* them that   *Ro 3:22*
believe
that he might have mercy   *Ro 11:32*
upon a.
to execute judgment *upon a.*   *Jude 15*
hour of temptation come   *Re 3:10*
upon a.

WITH ALL

with *a.* that appertain to   *Nu 16:30*
them
love Lord *with a.* thy heart,   *De 6:5;*
with a. thy soul   *De 11:13; M't 22:37*
with a. the children of   *2Ch 25:7*
Ephraim
with a. getting, get   *Pr 4:7*
understanding
feared God *with a.* house   *Ac 10:2;*
   16:34
with a. in every place call on   *1Co 1:2*
Jesus
shall abide, continue *with a.*   *Ph'p 1:25*
I joy and rejoice *with you*   *Ph'p 2:17*

ALL THAT HE HAD

Pharaoh sent him and *a.*   *Ge 12:20*
that he had
Abram went out and *a. that*   *Ge 13:1*
he had
Abraham gave *a. that he had*   *Ge 25:5*
to Isaac
Jacob fled with *a. that he*   *Ge 31:21*
had
a. that he had in Joseph's   *Ge 39:4;*
hand   *39:5-6*
be sold and *a. that he had*   *M't 18:25*

ALL THAT SHE HAD

she spent *a. that she had,*   *M'k 5:26*
nothing
cast in *a. that she had*   *M'k 12:44;*
   Lu 21:4

ALL THE WHILE

a. the while David was in   *1Sa 22:4*
the hold
nothing missing *a. the while*   *1Sa 25:7*
in Carmel
his manner *a. the while* he   *1Sa 27:11*
dwelleth
a. the while my breath is in   *Job 27:3*
me

ALL THESE

he took to him *a. these* and   *Ge 15:10*
divided
a. these things are against   *Ge 42:36*
me
a. these are twelve tribes of   *Ge 49:28*
Israel
God spake *a. these* words   *Ex 20:1*
who knoweth not that in *a.*   *Job 12:9*
these
for *a. these* nations are   *Jer 9:26*
uncircumcised
shall not *a. these* take up a   *Hab 2:6*
parable
a. these be added to you   *M't 6:33;*
   Lu 12:31
a. these are beginning of   *M't 24:8*
sorrows
a. these evil things come   *M'k 7:23*
from within
are not *a. these* which speak   *Ac 2:7*
a. these worketh that   *1Co 12:11*
self-same Spirit
put off *a. these,* anger, wrath,   *Col 3:8*
filthy
a. these died in faith, not   *Heb 11:13*
having

ALL THIS

as God hath shewed thee *a.*   *Ge 41:39*
this

the Lord hath not done *a.*   *De 32:27*
this
why then is *a. this* befallen   *J'g 6:13*
us?
thy servant knew nothing of   *1Sa 22:15*
a. this
is not the hand of Joab in   *2Sa 14:19*
a. this
a. this the Lord made me   *1Ch 28:19*
understand
after *a. this* the Lord smote   *2Ch 21:18*
him
a. this continued till the   *2Ch 29:28*
burnt offering
a. this was a burnt offering   *Ezr 8:35*
to Lord
because of *a. this* we make   *Ne 9:38*
covenant
yet *a. this* availeth me   *Es 5:13*
nothing
in *a. this* Job sinned not   *Job 1:22;*
  2:10
mine eye hath seen *a. this*   *Job 13:1*
a. this is come upon us   *Ps 44:17*
for *a. this* they sinned still   *Ps 78:32*
a. this have I proved by   *Ec 7:23*
wisdom
a. this have I seen, and   *Ec 8:9*
applied
a. this I considered in my   *Ec 9:1*
heart
for *a. this* His anger is not   *Isa 5:25;*
turned away   *Isa 9:12, 17, 21; 10:4*
thou hast heard, see *a. this*   *Isa 48:6*
a. this came upon   *Da 4:28*
Nebuchadnezzar
hast not humbled, though   *Da 5:22*
knew *a. this*
came and asked the truth of   *Da 7:16*
a. this
do not return, nor seek for *a.*   *Ho 7:10*
this
for transgression of Jacob is   *Mic 1:5*
a. this
a. this was done that the   *M't 1:22;*
prophets might be fulfilled   *21:4; 26:56*
besides *a. this* there is a gulf   *Lu 16:26*
fixed
besides *a. this* today is the   *Lu 24:21*
third day

ALL YE

a. ye assemble and hear   *Isa 48:14*
a. ye that kindle a fire   *Isa 50:11*
a. ye that love her   *Isa 66:10*
hear the word, *a. ye* in   *Jer 29:20*
captivity
is it nothing to you, *a. ye*   *La 1:12*
that pass by
come to me, *a. ye* that   *M't 11:28*
labour
one your master: *a. ye* are   *M't 23:8*
brethren
a. ye shall be offended   *M't 26:31;*
  M'k 14:27
a. ye that dwell at Jerusalem   *Ac 2:14*

ALLEGIANCE

kept their *a.* (A)(R)   *1Ch 12:29*

ALLEGING

a. Christ must needs have   *Ac 17:3*
suffered
setting forth and proving (A)   *Ac 17:3*
he established that Christ (B)   *Ac 17:3*
applied to show that the   *Ac 17:3*
Messiah (N)
to prove the necessity for the   *Ac 17:3*
(P)
proving it was necessary for   *Ac 17:3*
Christ (R)

ALLEGORIES

an inventor of *a.* (B)   *Eze 20:49*

ALLEGORY

speak an *a.* (R)   *Eze 17:2*
propound an *a.* (B)(R)   *Eze 24:3*
which things are an *a.* for   *Ga 4:24*
these are

ALLELUIA

people in heaven saying *A.*   *Re 19:1;*
  19:3-4, 6

ALLEYS

streets and *a.* of the city   *Lu 14:21*
(B)(N)

ALLIANCE

marriage *a.* with (A)(B)(R)(S)   *1Ki 3:1;*
  2Ch 18:1
made an *a.* with (B)   *2Ch 20:35;*
  Da 11:6
they make an *a.* (B)   *Ps 83:5*
time an *a.* was made   *Da 11:23*
(A)(B)

ALLIED

was *a.* with Ahab (A)   *2Ch 18:1*
the priest was *a.* with Tobiah   *Ne 13:4*
related by marriage to Tobiah   *Ne 13:4*
(A)
being connected with Tobiah   *Ne 13:4*
(B)(R)
be *a.* with (A)(R)   *Ps 94:20*
Syria *a.* with Ephraim (A)(B)   *Isa 7:2*
number of men *a.* themselves   *Ac 5:36*
(A)

ALLIES

the *a.* of Abraham   *Ge 14:13*
(A)(B)(R)
all your *a.* pushed (B)(R)   *Ob 7*

ALLOCATIONS

a. Moses made (B)   *Jos 13:32*

ALLON

from *A.* to Zaanannim   *Jos 19:33*
the son of *A.*   *1Ch 4:37*

ALLON-BACHUTH

the name of it was called *A.*   *Ge 35:8*

ALLOTMENT

with me in my *a.* (S)   *J'g 1:3*

ALLOTTED

a. to them (B)   *Jos 14:1*
a. to him (A)   *1Co 7:17; 2Co 12:13*
God has *a.* to (B)   *2Co 10:13*

ALLOW

did not *a.* (A)   *Ge 31:7;*
  2Sa 21:10; M'k 1:34
not *a.* (A)   *Ex 12:23;*
22:18; Le 2:13; Nu 21:23; Jos 10:19;
J'g 1:34; 15:1; Job 9:18; 1Ki 15:17;
Ps 55:22; 89:33; 121:3; Pr 10:3; Ec 5:6;
Eze 44:20; M't 23:13; M'k 7:12;
  Ac 13:35; Re 11:9
not *a.* (B)   *Ex 12:23;*
Ps 16:10; 55:22; 121:3; Ec 5:6;
M'k 11:16; Ac 13:35; 1Ti 2:12; Re 11:9
not *a.* (R)   *Ex 12:23;*
  Nu 21:23; J'g 1:34; 15:1; M'k 11:16
allow (B)   *Ex 22:18;*
Job 21:3; M't 19:14; M'k 10:14;
M'k 7:12; 10:14; Lu 9:59; 18:16; 22:51
allow (S)   *Le 2:13;*
19:17; 22:16; J'g 1:34; 15:1; 1Ki 15:17;
Ps 89:33; M'k 11:16; Lu 8:32; Ac 2:27;
  13:35
allow (A)   *J'g 16:26;*
Job 21:3; M't 19:14; M'k 10:14;
  Lu 18:16; Ac 21:39; 1Ti 2:12
a. neither birds (R)   *2Sa 21:10*
allow (B)   *Ps 66:9; 107:38; Ac 28:4*
allow (P)   *M't 23:13; Lu 8:32*
not *a.* (P)   *M'k 1:34*
allow (N)   *M'k 5:19; Ac 16:7*
  Lu 4:41; 8:51; Ac 16:7; 19:30
not *a.* (N)   *M'k 11:16; 1Co 10:13*
did not *a.* (S)   *Lu 4:41*
ye *a.* the deeds of your   *Lu 11:48*
father
give your full approval and   *Lu 11:48*
consent (A)
consenting to your father's   *Lu 11:48*
works (B)
consent unto father's works   *Lu 11:48*
(E)(R)

approve of the deeds of   *Lu 11:48*
(N)(P)
Spirit *a.* them   *Ac 16:7*
which they themselves also   *Ac 24:15*
a.
these hold and look for (A)   *Ac 24:15*
they hold as their own (B)   *Ac 24:15*
these also themselves look   *Ac 24:15*
for (E)
my accusers also accept   *Ac 24:15*
(N)(R)
they themselves hold (P)   *Ac 24:15*
wind did not *a.* (R)   *Ac 27:7*
for that which I do, I *a.* not   *Ro 7:15*
not *a.* (P)   *1Co 10:13;*
  1Ti 2:12; Re 11:9

ALLOWANCE

his *a.* was a continual *a.*   *2Ki 25:30*
be content with your *a.* (A)   *Lu 3:14*

ALLOWANCES

making *a.* for (P)   *Eph 4:2*

ALLOWED

allowed (S)   *Ge 20:6;*
31:7; 2Sa 21:10; M't 24:43; Lu 8:51;
  Ac 14:16; 16:7; Heb 7:23
allowed (A)   *De 8:3;*
1Ch 16:21; Ps 105:14; M't 24:43;
  M'k 10:4
not *a.* thee (A)   *De 18:14*
not *a.* (R)   *De 18:14;*
  J'g 3:28; 1Ch 16:21; Ps 105:14
a. not our feet (A)   *Ps 66:9*
he *a.* no man (B)   *Ps 105:14;*
  M't 24:43; Lu 8:51; Ac 28:16
allowed (P)   *M't 19:8;*
  24:43; M'k 5:37; Ac 14:16
allowed (R)   *M't 19:8;*
  M'k 5:37; 10:4; Ac 14:16; 28:16
not *a.* him to live (R)   *Ac 28:4*
But as we were *a.* of God to   *1Th 2:4*
be
approved by God   *1Th 2:4*
(A)(E)(N)(R)
divinely approved (B)   *1Th 2:4*
being entrusted by God (P)   *1Th 2:4*

ALLOWEST

a. that woman Jezebel (S)   *Re 2:20*

ALLOWETH

a. not to live (S)   *Ac 28:4*
in the thing which he *a.*   *Ro 14:22*
judge what he approves   *Ro 14:22*
(A)(E)(R)
make decision with clear   *Ro 14:22*
conscience (N)

ALLURE

I will *a.* her and bring into   *Ho 2:14*
wilderness
they *a.* through the lusts of the   *2Pe 2:18*
flesh
lure with lustful desires (A)   *2Pe 2:18*
entice to immoral passions   *2Pe 2:18*
(B)(E)(R)
make sensual lusts a bait   *2Pe 2:18*
(N)

ALLURING

flirtatious, *a.* eyes (A)   *Isa 3:16*

ALLUSIONS

rotted with lust's *a.* (P)   *Eph 4:22*

ALMIGHTY

I am the *A.* God   *Ge 17:1;*
  Ge 28:3; 35:11; 43:14; 48:3
by the *A.* who shall bless   *Ge 49:25*
thee
appeared by the name of *A.*   *Ex 6:3*
God
which saw a vision of the *A.*   *Nu 24:4;*
  24:16
the *A.* hath dealt bitterly   *Ru 1:20;*
with me   *1:21*
despise not chastening of the   *Job 5:17*
A.
the arrows of the *A.* are   *Job 6:4*
within me

he forsaketh the fear of the *Job 6:14*
A.
doth the A. pervert justice *Job 8:3*
make thy supplication to the *Job 8:5*
A.
find out the A. to perfection *Job 11:7*
Surely I would speak to the *Job 13:3*
A.
he strengthened himself *Job 15:25*
against the A.
What is the A. that we *Job 21:15*
should serve
he shall drink the wrath of *Job 21:20*
the A.
is it pleasure to the A. thou *Job 22:3*
art right.
what can the A. do for *Job 22:17*
them
if thou return to the A. *Job 22:23*
thou shalt be
A. shall be thy defence, *Job 22:25*
thou
then shalt have delight in *Job 22:26*
the A.
the A. troubleth me *Job 23:16*
seeing times are not hid *Job 24:1*
from the A.
the A. who hath vexed my *Job 27:2*
soul
will he delight himself in *Job 27:10*
the A.
with the A. I will not *Job 27:11*
conceal
which they shall receive of *Job 27:13*
the A.
when the A. was yet with me *Job 29:5*
what inheritance of the A. *Job 31:2*
from on
my desire is, that the A. *Job 31:35*
answer me
inspiration of A. giveth *Job 32:8*
understanding
breath of the A. hath given *Job 33:4*
me life
far be it from A. to commit *Job 34:10*
iniquity
neither will the A. pervert *Job 34:12*
judgment
surely the A. will not *Job 35:13*
regard vanity
touching A. we cannot find *Job 37:23*
him out
he that contendeth with A. *Job 40:2*
instruct
when the A. scattered kings *Ps 68:14*
in it
shall abide under shadow of *Ps 91:1*
the A.
shall come as destruction *Isa 13:6*
from the A.
I heard as the voice of A. *Eze 1:24;*
10:5
as destruction from A. shall *Joe 1:15*
it come
shall be my sons, saith Lord *2Co 6:18*
A.
sustains universe with a. *Heb 1:3*
work (B)
which is, was, and is to come *Re 1:8*
the A.
the Lord God A. which was, *Re 4:8;*
is *11:17*
Lord A. just and true are *Re 15:3;*
ways *16:7*
battle of that great day of *Re 16:14*
God A.
treadeth winepress of wrath *Re 19:15*
of A. God
God A. and Lamb are *Re 21:22*
temple of it

ALMODAD

Joktan begat A. *Ge 10:26; 1Ch 1:20*

ALMON

A. with her suburbs *Jos 21:18*

ALMOND

and of the a. (S) *Ge 30:37*
the a. tree shall flourish *Ec 12:5*
I see a rod of an a. tree *Jer 1:11*

ALMON-DIBLATHAIM

encamped in A. *Nu 33:46*
they removed from A. *Nu 33:47*

ALMONDS

Myrrh, nuts, and a. *Ge 43:11*
Three bowls made like unto *Ex 25:33;*
a. *Ex 25:34; 37:19, 20*
blossoms, and yielded a. *Nu 17:8*

ALMOST

they be a. ready to stone me *Ex 17:4*
as for me, my feet were a. *Ps 73:2*
gone (S)
my soul had a. dwelt in *Ps 94:17*
silence
they had a. consumed me *Ps 119:87*
upon earth
I was a. in all evil in the *Pr 5:14*
midst
came a. the whole city *Ac 13:44*
together
only at Ephesus, but a. *Ac 19:26*
through all Asia
when the seven days were a. *Ac 21:27*
ended
a. thou persuadest me to be *Ac 26:28*
a Christian
were both and a. altogether *Ac 26:29*
as I am
a. all things by the law are *Heb 9:22*
purged

ALMS

do not your a. before men *M't 6:1*
not do good deeds publicly *M't 6:1*
(A)(P)
not perform good works *M't 6:1*
publicly (B)
do not your righteousness *M't 6:1*
before (E)
make a show of your religion *M't 6:1*
(N)
practicing your piety before *M't 6:1*
men (R)
when thou doest a. do not *M't 6:2*
sound a
that thine a. may be in secret, *M't 6:4*
and
give a. of such things as you *Lu 11:41*
have
give donations to the poor *Lu 11:41*
(A)
better bestow in kindness *Lu 11:41*
(B)
what is in the cup be given *Lu 11:41*
(N)
by doing good to others (P) *Lu 11:41*
Sell that ye have, and give a. *Lu 12:33*
give donations to the poor *Lu 12:33*
(A)
practice benevolence (B) *Lu 12:33*
give in charity (N) *Lu 12:33*
Sell possessions; give money *Lu 12:33*
away (P)
they laid, to ask a. of them *Ac 3:2*
that
to beg charitable gifts (A) *Ac 3:2*
to ask for charity (B) *Ac 3:2*
to beg from people (N)(P) *Ac 3:2*
who seeing Peter and John *Ac 3:3*
asked an a.
knew that it was he which *Ac 3:10*
sat for a.
Cornelius gave much a. to the *Ac 10:2*
people
practiced liberal benevolence *Ac 10:2*
(B)
gave generously to help (N) *Ac 10:2*
made many charitable gifts *Ac 10:2*
(P)
a. are come up for memorial *Ac 10:4;*
10:31
came to bring a. to my *Ac 24:17*
nation and
bring contributions of *Ac 24:17*
charity (A)
bring charitable gifts *Ac 24:17*
(N)(P)

ALMSDEEDS

full of good works and a. *Ac 9:36*

ALMUG

great plenty of a. trees *1Ki 10:11;*
10:12

ALOES

as the trees of lign a. which *Nu 24:6*
garments smell of Myrrh, and *Ps 45:8*
a.
I have perfumed my bed with *Pr 7:17*
a.
and a. with all the chief *Ca 4:14*
spices
brought a mixture of myrrh *Joh 19:39*
and a.

ALONE

not good the man should be *Ge 2:18*
a.
not able to perform it *Ex 18:18*
thyself a.
Moses a. shall come near the *Ex 24:2*
Lord
leper dwell a. without the *Le 13:46*
camp
not able to bear people a. *Nu 11:14;*
De 1:9, 12
that thou bear it not thyself *Nu 11:17*
a.
people dwell a. not be *Nu 23:9*
reckoned
so the Lord a. did lead them *De 32:12*
Israel then shall dwell in *De 33:28*
safety a.
Achan perished not a. in his *Jos 22:20*
iniquity
die a. because of wickedness *Jos 22:20*
(B)
behold, a man running a. *2Sa 18:24;*
18:26
if he be a. there is tidings *2Sa 18:25*
in his mouth
they two were a. in the *1Ki 11:29*
field
art God a. *2Ki 19:15;*
Isa 37:16; Ps 86:10
Solomon, whom a. God hath *1Ch 29:1*
chosen
scorn to lay hands on *Es 3:6*
Mordecai a.
I am escaped a. to tell *Job 1:15;*
Job 1:16, 17, 19
God a. spreadeth out the *Job 9:8*
heavens
to whom a. the earth was *Job 15:19*
given
have I eaten my morsel *Job 31:17*
myself a.
thou whose name a. is *Ps 83:18*
Jehovah
I watch as a sparrow a. on *Ps 102:7*
the housetop
to him who a. doeth great *Ps 136:4*
wonders
for his name a. is excellent *Ps 148:13*
there is one a. and not a *Ec 4:8*
second
woe to him that is a. when *Ec 4:10*
he falleth
Lord a. be exalted in that *Isa 2:11;*
day *2:17*
none be a. in his appointed *Isa 14:31*
times
I called him a. and blessed *Isa 51:2*
him
I have trodden the winepress *Isa 63:3*
a.
how sits she all a. (B) *La 1:1*
he sitteth a. and keepeth *La 3:28*
silence
I Daniel a. saw the vision *Da 10:7*
a wild ass a. by himself *Ho 8:9*
who live a. in the forest (B) *Mic 7:14*
man not live by bread a. *M't 4:4;*
Lu 4:4
evening came, He was a. *M't 14:23;*
Lu 9:18
tell his fault between thee *M't 18:15*
and him a.
when they were a. he *M'k 4:34*
expounded
ship in midst of sea, he a. *M'k 6:47*
on land
who can forgive sins but God *Lu 5:21*
a.?
not lawful to eat, but priests *Lu 6:4*
a.
as Jesus was a. praying *Lu 9:18*
when voice was past, Jesus *Lu 9:36*
was found a.
that my sister left me to *Lu 10:40*
serve a.

he departed into a mountain *Joh 6:15* *a.*
his disciples were gone away *Joh 6:22* *a.* to
am not *a.* but I and the *Joh 8:16; 16:32* Father
neither pray for these *a.* *Joh 17:20* but for them
ye see and hear that not *a.* *Ac 19:26* at Ephesus
it was written for his sake *a.* *Ro 4:23*
shall have rejoicing in himself *Ga 6:4* *a.*
went high priest *a.* once *Heb 9:7* every year
faith if hath not works is *Jas 2:17* dead, being *a.*

LEFT ALONE

Jacob was *left a.* and there *Ge 32:24* wrestled
brother is dead, he is *left a.* *Ge 42:38; 44:20*
I was *left a.* *Isa 49:21; Da 10:8; Ro 11:3*
Jesus was *left a.* and the *Joh 8:9* woman
Father hath not *left* me *a.* *Joh 8:29* for I do

LET HER ALONE

let her a. for her soul is *2Ki 4:27* vexed in her
let her a. why trouble her? *M'k 14:6*
let her a.; against day of my *Joh 12:7* burying

LET HIM ALONE

let him a. and let him curse *2Sa 16:11*
Ephraim is joined to idols, *Ho 4:17* *let him a.*
if we *let him a.* all men *Joh 11:48* will believe

LET ME ALONE

let me a. that my wrath may *Ex 32:10* wax hot
let me a. that I may destroy *De 9:14* them
let me a. two months, that I *J'g 11:37* may go
let me a. that I may take *Job 10:20* comfort
let me a. that I may speak *Job 13:13*

LET THEM ALONE

let them a. they be blind *M't 15:14* leaders of
let them a. for if this *Ac 5:38* counsel be of

LET US ALONE

let us a. that we may serve *Ex 14:12* Egyptians
let us a. Jesus of Nazareth *M'k 1:24; Lu 4:34*

ALONG

walked *a.* by the river's side *Ex 2:5*
the fire ran *a.* upon the *Ex 9:23* ground
will go *a.* by the king's *Nu 21:22* highway
chased them *a.* the way *Jos 10:10*
passed *a.* *Jos 15:3; Jos 15:6, 10-11; 16:2; 18:18-19*
robbed all that came *a.* that *J'g 9:25* way
went *a.* the highway, lowing *1Sa 6:12*
Saul fell straightway *a.* on *1Sa 28:20* the earth
went with her *a.* weeping *2Sa 3:16*
Shimei went *a.* on the hill's *2Sa 16:13* side
a. by altar and temple *2Ki 11:11; 2Ch 23:10*
weeping all *a.* as he went *Jer 41:6*

ALONGSIDE

a. the oblation of holy *Eze 45:6; 48:18* portion (S)

ALOOF

my friends stand *a.* from my *Ps 38:11* sore

ALOTH

Hushai was in Asher and in *1Ki 4:16* *A.*

ALOUD

And he wept *a.* *Ge 45:2*
wept *a.* (A) (R) *1Sa 11:4*
Cry *a.*: for he is a god *1Ki 18:27*
they cried *a.* and cut *1Ki 18:28*
many shouted *a.* for joy *Ezr 3:12*
I cry *a.*, but there is no *Job 19:7*
will I pray, and cry *a.* *Ps 51:14*
my tongue shall sing *a.* of *Ps 55:17*
I will sing *a.* of thy mercy *Ps 59:16*
Sing *a.* unto God our strength *Ps 81:1*
her saints shall shout *a.* for *Ps 132:16* joy
let them sing *a.* upon beds *Ps 149:5*
they shall cry *a.* from the *Isa 24:14* sea
break forth into singing, cry *Isa 54:1* *a.*
Cry *a.*, spare not, lift up thy *Isa 58:1*
an herald cried *a.*, To you *Da 3:4*
He cried *a.*, and said thus, *Da 4:14* Hew
The king cried *a.* to bring in *Da 5:7*
cry *a.* at Beth-aven *Ho 5:8*
cry out *a.*? is there no king *Mic 4:9*
multitude crying *a.* began to *M'k 15:8*

ALPHA

I am *A.* and Omega *Re 1:8; Re 1:11; 21:6; 22:13*

ALPHAEUS

James the son of *A.* *M't 10:3; M'k 3:18; Lu 6:15; Ac 1:13*
Levi the son of *A.* sitting at *M'k 2:14* the

ALREADY

for Joseph was in Egypt *a.* *Ex 1:5*
offended against the Lord *2Ch 28:13* *a.*
are brought into bondage *a.* *Ne 5:5*
it hath been *a.* of old time *Ec 1:10*
even that which hath been *a.* *Ec 2:12* done
which is to be hath *a.* been *Ec 3:15; 6:10*
I have cursed them *a.* because *Mal 2:2*
committed adultery *a.* with *M't 5:28* her
Elias is come *a.* and they *M't 17:12* knew him
marvelled if he were *a.* *M'k 15:44* dead
what will I, if it be *a.* *Lu 12:49* kindled
believeth not is condemned *Joh 3:18* *a.*
they are white *a.* to harvest *Joh 4:35*
for the Jews had agreed *a.* *Joh 9:22*
lain in the grave four days *Joh 11:17* *a.*
saw that he was dead *a.* *Joh 19:33*
were three men *a.* come *Ac 11:11* unto me
because the fast was now *a.* *Ac 27:9* past
have judged *a.* as though I *1Co 5:3* were
many which have sinned *a.* *2Co 12:21*
Not as though I had *a.* *Ph'p 3:12;* attained *3:16*
mystery of iniquity doth *a.* *2Th 2:7* work
For some are *a.* turned aside *1Ti 5:15* after
that the resurrection is past *2Ti 2:18* *a.*
even now *a.* is it in the world *1Jo 4:3*
that which ye have *a.* hold *Re 2:25* fast

ALSO

He made the stars *a.* *Ge 1:16*
life *a.* in the midst of the *Ge 2:9* garden

a. unto her husband with her *Ge 3:6*
Unto Adam *a.* and to his *Ge 3:21* wife did
take *a.* of the tree of life, *Ge 3:22* and live
he *a.* brought of the firstlings *Ge 4:4* of
for that he *a.* is flesh *Ge 6:3*
giants in earth in those days, *Ge 6:4* and *a.*
I *a.* withheld thee from *Ge 20:6* sinning
I will give thy camels drink *Ge 24:14* *a.*
I will draw water for thy *Ge 24:19* camels *a.*
and I will *a.* draw for thy *Ge 24:44* camels
and I will give thy camels *Ge 24:46* drink *a.*
and she made the camels *Ge 24:46* drink *a.*
and *a.* the ground whereon *Ex 8:21* they are
this people shall *a.* go to *Ex 18:23* their place
a. in the iniquities of their *Le 26:39* fathers
seek ye the priesthood *a.* *Nu 16:10*
God do so and more *a.* *1Sa 14:44; 2Sa 3:35; 19:13*
if we sit still here, we die *a.* *2Ki 7:4*
he *a.* is to be feared above *1Ch 16:25* all gods
gifts, yea, for the rebellious *Ps 68:18* *a.*
the world *a.* is stablished, that *Ps 93:1* it
but will ye weary my God *a.* *Isa 7:13*
I have sent *a.* unto you all *Jer 35:15* my servants
death: *a.* what the king said *Jer 38:25* unto thee
a. I gave them my *Eze 20:12* sabbaths, to be
to seek the Lord I will go *a.* *Zec 8:21*
there will heart be *a.* *M't 6:21; Lu 12:34*
surely thou art *a.* one of *M't 26:73* them
that I preach there *a.* *M'k 1:38*
Son of man is Lord *a.* of *M'k 2:28;* sabbath *Lu 6:5*
Jesus *a.* being baptized *Lu 3:21*
thus saying, reproachest us *Lu 11:45* *a.*
for they *a.* went unto the *Joh 4:45* feast
what he doeth, these *a.* *Joh 5:19* doeth the Son
where I am, there shall *a.* *Joh 12:26* my servant
that where I am, there ye *Joh 14:3* may be *a.*
and Judas *a.* which betrayed *Joh 18:2* him
he proceeded to take Peter *a.* *Ac 12:3*
Jews and *a.* of the Greeks *Ac 14:1* believed
to the Jews, and *a.* to the *Ac 20:21* Greeks
are ye *a.* the called of Jesus *Ro 1:6* Christ
preach to you that are at *Ro 1:15* Rome *a.*
By whom *a.* we have access by *Ro 5:2* faith
shall he not with him *a.* *Ro 8:32* freely give
and they *a.* if they abide not *Ro 11:23* still
mercy they *a.* may obtain *Ro 11:31* mercy
succourer of many, myself *a.* *Ro 16:2*
who *a.* were in Christ before *Ro 16:7* me
or saith not the law the same *1Co 9:8* *a.*
and last of all, he was seen *1Co 15:8* of me *a.*
that I *a.* myself shall come *Ph'p 2:24* shortly
knowing that ye *a.* have a *Col 4:1* Master
I am persuaded that in thee *a.* *2Ti 1:5*
we *a.* were sometimes *Tit 3:3* foolish
let ours *a.* learn to maintain *Tit 3:14* good

now *a.* a prisoner of Jesus   *Ph'm 9*
Christ
commit adultery, said *a.* Do   *Jas 2:11*
not kill
faith without works is dead   *Jas 2:26*
a.
that loveth God, love brother   *1Jo 4:21*
a.
they *a.* which pierced him   *Re 1:7*
I *a.* will keep thee from hour   *Re 3:10*
of
even as I *a.* overcame, and   *Re 3:21*
am set
where *a.* our Lord was   *Re 11:8*
crucified

ALTAR

Noah builded an *a.* unto the   *Ge 8:20*
Lord
Abraham builded an *a.*   *Ge 12:7;*
    Ge 12:8; 13:4, 18; 22:9; Jas 2:21
Isaac builded an *a.* there   *Ge 26:25*
Jacob erected there an *a.*   *Ge 33:20;*
    Ge 35:1, 3, 7
Moses built an *a.*   *Ex 17:15; 24:4-6*
An *a.* of earth make   *Ex 20:24;*
    20:25-26
shalt take him from mine *a.*   *Ex 21:14*
to die
thou shalt make a brazen *a.*   *Ex 27:1;*
    27:5-7
put blood on horns of the   *Ex 29:12;*
a. 29:13, 16, 18; Le 4:7, 18, 25, 30, 34;
    8:15; 9:9; 16:18
cleanse, make atonement for   *Ex 29:36;*
a.   *29:37*
thou shalt make a golden *a.*   *Ex 30:1;*
    40:5, 26
a. of incense   *Ex 30:27;*
31:8; 35:15; 37:25; 39:38; 1Ch 6:49;
28:18; 2Ch 4:19; 26:16, 19; Lu 1:11
the *a.* of burnt offering   *Ex 30:28;*
31:9; 35:16; 38:1-7; 40:6; 10:29;
Le 4:10, 19; 1Ch 16:40; 22:1; 2Ch 29:18,
    27; 35:16
Aaron built an idol *a.*   *Ex 32:5*
the brasen *a.*   *Ex 38:30;*
    39:39; 2Ch 1:5, 6; 4:1; Eze 9:2
set up golden and brazen *a.*   *Ex 40:5;*
    40:6-7, 10, 26, 29-33
anoint the *a.* of burnt   *Ex 40:10;*
offering   *Le 8:11*
put blood round about upon *a.* Le 1:5;
1:11; 3:2; 4:18; 7:2; 8:11, 19, 24, 30;
9:18; 17:6; Nu 18:17; 2Ch 29:22, 24
put fire upon *a.*   *Le 1:7;*
1:8-9, 12, 17; 2:2, 9, 12; 3:5, 11, 16;
4:10, 19, 35; 5:12; 6:9-13, 15; 7:5, 31;
8:16, 21, 28; 9:10; .13:14, 17, 24;
    Ex 29:20-21; Nu 5:26; 16:46
eat it without leaven beside   *Le 10:12*
the *a.*
on golden *a.* they shall   *Nu 4:11*
spread a cloth
this is the dedication of the   *Nu 7:84;*
a.   *7:10-11*
plates for covering of *a.*   *Nu 16:38;*
    16:39
they shall not come nigh the   *Nu 18:3*
a.
offer burnt offerings upon   *De 12:27;*
the *a.*   *33:10*
not plant trees near the *a.*   *De 16:21*
built an *a.* of stones   *De 27:5;*
    De 27:6; Jos 8:31
Joshua built an *a.*   *Jos 8:30*
Israel built an *a.* near   *Jos 22:10;*
Jordan *22:11, 16, 19, 23, 26, 28, 29, 34*
Gideon built an *a.*   *J'g 6:24*
the *a.* of Baal was cast down   *J'g 6:28;*
    6:30-32
flame went up from the *a.*   *J'g 13:20*
Israel built an *a.* there   *J'g 21:4*
I shall not cut off from mine   *1Sa 2:33*
a.
Samuel built an *a.*   *1Sa 7:17*
Saul built an *a.*   *1Sa 14:35*
David built an *a.*   *1Sa 14:18;*
1Sa 24:21, 25; 1Ch 21:18, 22, 26, 29
caught hold of horns of *a.*   *1Ki 1:50;*
    1Ki 1:51, 53; 2:28, 29
Solomon offered upon that *a.*   *1Ki 3:4;*
    12:32-33
a. and table of gold   *1Ki 7:48; 9:25*
Solomon stood before the *a.*   *1Ki 8:22;*
1Ki 8:31, 54; 2Ch 5:12; 6:12. 22
Solomon built brazen *a.*   *1Ki 9:25;*
    1Ki 8:64; 2Ch 7:7

Jeroboam stood by the *a.*   *1Ki 13:1*
he cried against the *a.* O   *1Ki 13:2;*
a. a.   *13:4, 32; 2Ki 23:15-17*
the *a.* was rent   *1Ki 13:3; 13:4, 5*
Ahab reared up the *a.* of   *1Ki 16:32*
Baal
they leaped upon the *a.*   *1Ki 18:26*
Elijah repaired the *a.* of   *1Ki 18:30;*
the Lord   *18:32*
water ran round about the *a.*   *1Ki 18:35*
Ahaz and Urijah built a   *2Ki 16:10;*
pagan *a.*   *2Ki 16:11-15*
Hezekiah restored worship   *2Ki 18:22;*
at true *a.*   *2Ch 32:12; Isa 36:7*
kept the dedication of the   *2Ch 7:9*
renewed the *a.* of the Lord   *2Ch 15:8;*
    2Ch 8:12; 29:19, 21, 22
Manasseh repaired the *a.*   *2Ch 33:16*
of the Lord
Israel built the *a.* of the Lord *Ezr 3:2;*
    Ezr 3:3; 7:17; Ne 10:34
so will I compass Thine *a.* O   *Ps 26:6*
Lord
Then will I go unto *a.* of God   *Ps 43:4*
offer bullocks upon Thine *a.*   *Ps 51:19*
unto the horns of the *a.*   *Ps 118:27*
with the tongs from off the *a.*   *Isa 6:6*
an *a.* to Lord in midst of   *Isa 19:19*
Egypt
maketh all the stones of the   *Isa 27:9*
a.
sacrifices be accepted upon   *Isa 56:7;*
mine *a.*   *60:7*
The Lord hath cast off His *a.*   *La 2:7*
between porch and *a.* 25   *Eze 8:16*
men
the millennial *a.*   *Eze 40:46;*
40:47; 41:22; 43:13, 15-16, 18, 22, 26,
    27; 45:19; 47:1
howl, ye ministers of the *a.*   *Joe 1:13;*
    2:17
clothes laid to pledge by every   *Am 2:8*
a.
the horns of the *a.* be cut off   *Am 3:14*
the Lord standing upon the *a.*   *Am 9:1*
as the corners of the *a.*   *Zec 9:15*
be like bowls before the *a.*   *Zec 14:20*
ye offer polluted bread upon   *Mal 1:7*
mine *a.*
do ye kindle fire on mine *a.*   *Mal 1:10*
covering the *a.* of the Lord   *Mal 2:13*
with tears
bring thy gift to the *a.*   *M't 5:23;*
    M't 5:24; 23:19
whoso shall swear by the   *M't 23:18;*
a.   *23:20*
slew between temple and *a.*   *M't 23:35;*
    Lu 11:51
an *a.* to the unknown God   *Ac 17:23*
wait at *a.* partakers with *a.*   *1Co 9:13;*
    10:18
no man gave attendance at   *Heb 7:13*
the *a.*
We have an *a.* whereof   *Heb 13:10*
they have no
offered Isaac his son upon   *Jas 2:21*
the *a.*
I saw under the *a.* the souls of   *Re 6:9*
them
angel stood at the *a.* offering   *Re 8:3;*
    8:5
voice from four horns of   *Re 9:13*
golden *a.*
the temple of God, and the *a.*   *Re 11:1*
another angel came out   *Re 14:18*
from the *a.*
I heard another out of the *a.*   *Re 16:7*
say

ALTARS

But ye shall destroy their *a.*   *Ex 34:13;*
    De 7:5; 12:3; J'g 2:2
the candlestick and the *a.*   *Nu 3:31*
Build me here seven *a.*   *Nu 23:1;*
    23:4, 14, 29
Israel has thrown down   *1Ki 19:10;*
thine *a.*   *19:14*
his *a.* and his images brake   *2Ki 11:18*
they
whose *a.* Hezekiah hath   *2Ki 18:22*
taken away
Manasseh reared up the *a.*   *2Ki 21:3;*
of Baal   *21:4*
Manasseh built *a.* for all   *2Ki 21:5;*
host of heaven   *23:12, 20; 2Ch 33:3-5*
Asa took away *a.* of strange   *2Ch 14:3*
gods
Israel brake the *a.* of Baal   *2Ch 23:17*
Ahaz made *a.* to false gods   *2Ch 28:24*

Hezekiah took away *a.* of   *2Ch 30:14;*
Baal   *32:12*
Israel brake *a.* of false gods   *2Ch 31:1*
Manasseh took away *a.* of   *2Ch 33:15*
false gods
Josiah destroyed *a.* of   *2Ch 34:4;*
Baalim   *34:7*
Burned bones of priests   *2Ch 34:5*
upon the *a.*
even thine *a.* O Lord of hosts   *Ps 84:3*
he shall not look to the *a.*   *Isa 17:8*
burneth incense on *a.* of   *Isa 65:3*
brick
set up *a.* to that shameful   *Jer 11:13*
thing
upon the horns of your *a.*   *Jer 17:1*
their children remember their   *Jer 17:2*
a.
your *a.* shall be desolate   *Eze 6:4;*
    6:5-6, 13
Ephraim hath made many *a.*   *Ho 8:11;*
    10:1-2
thorn and thistle come on   *Ho 10:8*
their *a.*
their *a.* are as heaps   *Ho 12:11*
I will also visit the *a.* of   *Am 3:14*
Beth-el
they have digged down thine   *Ro 11:3*
a.

AL-TASCHITH

In titles of Ps 57, 58, 59, 75

ALTER

He shall not *a.* it nor change   *Le 27:10*
it
whosoever shall *a.* his word   *Eze 6:11;*
    6:12
covenant will I not break,   *Ps 89:34*
nor *a.*

ALTERED

it be not *a.*, that Vashti come   *Es 1:19*
not
fashion of his countenance   *Lu 9:29*
was *a.*

ALTERETH

according to law which *a.* not   *Da 6:8*

ALTHOUGH

a. that was near; for God   *Ex 13:17*
said
a. there was a plague in the   *Jos 22:17*
a. my house be not so with   *2Sa 23:5*
God
A. I have sent unto thee   *1Ki 20:5*
saying
held my tongue, *a.* the enemy   *Es 7:4*
integrity, *a.* thou movedst me   *Job 2:3*
A. affliction cometh not forth   *Job 5:6*
A. thou sayest thou shalt   *Job 35:14*
a. I was an husband unto   *Jer 31:32*
them
is sold, *a.* they were yet alive   *Eze 7:13*
A. I have cast them far off   *Eze 11:16*
A. the fig tree shall not   *Hab 3:17*
blossom
A. all shall be offended, yet   *M'k 14:29*
not I
a. the works were finished   *Heb 4:3*
from

ALTOGETHER

whether they have done *a.*   *Ge 18:21*
according
thrust you out hence *a.*   *Ex 11:1*
mount Sinai was on fire *a.*   *Ex 19:18*
make thyself *a.* a prince   *Nu 16:13*
over us
which is *a.* just shall thou   *De 16:20*
follow
judgments of Lord are   *Ps 19:9*
righteous *a.*
every man at his best is *a.*   *Ps 39:5*
vanity
that I was *a.* such an one as   *Ps 50:21*
thyself
Thou knowest thoughts *a.*   *Ps 139:4*
he is *a.* lovely   *Ca 5:16*
thou wast *a.* born in sins   *Joh 9:34*
both almost and *a.* such as I   *Ac 26:29*
am

Yet not *a*. with the   *1Co 5:10*
fornicators of this
Or saith he it *a*. for our   *1Co 9:10*
sake

ALUSH

Israel encamped in *A*.   *Nu 33:13*
removed from *A*.   *Nu 33:14*

ALVAH

duke Timnah, duke *A*.   *Ge 36:40*

ALVAN

children of Shobal; *A*.   *Ge 36:23*

ALWAY

table of shewbread before   *Ex 25:30*
me *a*.
So it was *a*.: the cloud   *Nu 9:16*
covered it
keep his commandments *a*.   *De 11:1*
be oppressed and crushed *a*.   *De 28:33*
have a light *a*. before me   *1Ki 11:36*
I would not live *a*.   *Job 7:16*
inclined to perform   *Ps 119:112*
statutes *a*.
Happy is man that feareth *a*.   *Pr 28:14*
I am with you *a*., even unto   *M't 28:20*
the end
your time is *a*. ready   *Joh 7:6*
prayed to God *a*.   *Ac 10:2*
bow down their back *a*.   *Ro 11:10*
we which live are *a*.   *2Co 4:11*
delivered
As sorrowful, yet *a*.   *2Co 6:10*
rejoicing
Rejoice in the Lord *a*.   *Ph'p 4:4*
Let your speech be *a*. with   *Col 4:6*
grace
to fill up their sins *a*.   *1Th 2:16*
bound to give thanks *a*. to   *2Th 2:13*
God
The Cretians are *a*. liars   *Tit 1:12*
They do *a*. err in their   *Heb 3:10*
hearts

ALWAYS

My spirit not *a*. strive with   *Ge 6:3*
man
to cause the lamp to burn *a*.   *Ex 27:20*
it shall be *a*. upon his   *Exr 28:38*
forehead
keep all my commandments   *De 5:29*
a.
eyes of the Lord *a*. upon it   *De 11:12*
to fear the Lord thy God *a*.   *De 14:23*
Be ye mindful *a*. of his   *1Ch 16:15*
covenant
never prophesied good, but   *2Ch 18:7*
a. evil
will he *a*. call upon God   *Job 27:10*
Great men are not *a*. wise   *Job 32:9*
neither do
have set the Lord *a*. before   *Ps 16:8*
me
He will not *a*. chide; neither   *Ps 103:9*
will
be thou ravished *a*. with her   *Pr 5:19*
love
rejoicing *a*. before him   *Pr 8:30*
Let thy garments be *a*. white   *Ec 9:8*
their angels do *a*. behold   *M't 18:10*
face of
have poor *a*. with   *M't 26:11;*
    M'k 14:7; Joh 12:8
a. night and day, he was in the   *M'k 5:5*
tombs
men ought *a*. to pray and not to   *Lu 18:1*
faint
pray *a*. that he may be   *Lu 21:36*
worthy to
I do *a*. those things that   *Joh 8:29*
please him
I knew that thou hearest   *Joh 11:42*
me *a*.
I foresaw the Lord *a*. before   *Ac 2:25*
me
ye do *a*. resist the Holy   *Ac 7:51*
Ghost
a. a conscience void of   *Ac 24:16*
offence
mention of you *a*. in my   *Ro 1:9*
prayers

thank God *a*. on your behalf   *1Co 1:4*
a. abounding in the work   *1Co 15:58*
of Lord
a. causeth us to triumph in   *2Co 2:14*
Christ
A. bearing about in body   *2Co 4:10*
the dying
we are *a*. confident, knowing   *2Co 5:6*
that
ye *a*. having all sufficiency in   *2Co 9:8*
all
affected *a*. in a good thing   *Ga 4:18*
Giving thanks *a*. for all   *Eph 5:20*
things
Praying *a*. with all   *Eph 6:18*
supplication
A. in every prayer of mine   *Ph'p 1:4*
for you
praying *a*. for you   *Col 1:3*
a. labouring fervently for you   *Col 4:12*
We give thanks to God *a*. for   *1Th 1:2*
you
have good remembrance of us   *1Th 3:6*
a.
bound to thank God *a*. for   *2Th 1:3*
you
mention thee *a*. in my prayers   *Ph'm 4*
went *a*. into the first   *Heb 9:6*
tabernacle
be ready *a*. to give an   *1Pe 3:15*
answer
a. in remembrance of these   *2Pe 1:12;*
things   *1:15*

AM

surety bear a child, which *a*.   *Ge 18:13*
old
speak unto the Lord, which   *Ge 18:27*
a. but dust
I only *a*. escaped   *Job 1:15;*
    Job 1:16, 17, 19
I the Lord *a*. thy Saviour   *Isa 49:26;*
    60:16
I the Lord their God *a*.   *Eze 34:30*
with them
he is tempted I *a*. tempted of   *Jas 1:13*
God

I AM used of Christ

I am meek and lowly in   *M't 11:29*
heart
I am the Son of God   *M't 27:43;*
    Joh 10:36
I am the bread of life   *Joh 6:35;*
    6:41, 48
I am the living bread   *Joh 6:51*
I am the light of the world   *Joh 8:12;*
    12:46
I am he   *Joh 8:28; 13:19; 18:5-6, 8*
I am the door of the sheep   *Joh 10:7;*
    10:9
I am the good shepherd   *Joh 10:11;*
    10:14
I am the resurrection and   *Joh 11:25*
the life
I am the way, the truth, and   *Joh 14:6*
the life
I am the true vine   *Joh 15:1; 15:5*
I am a King   *Joh 19:21*
I am Jesus   *Ac 9:5; 22:8*
I am Alpha and Omega   *Re 1:8;*
    Re 1:11; 21:6, 13
I am the first and the last   *Re 1:17*
I am he that liveth, and was   *Re 1:18*
dead; *I am* alive forevermore
I am he that searcheth   *Re 2:23*
hearts
I am the root and offspring   *Re 22:16*
of David

I AM used of God

I am thy shield   *Ge 15:1*
I am the Lord   *Ge 15:7;*
*Ex 6:2, 8, 29; 7:5, 17; 10:2; 12:12; 14:4,
18; 15:26; 29:46 31:13; Le 11:45; 18:5,
6, 21; 19:12, 14, 16, 30, 32; 20:8;
21:12; 22:2, 3, 8, 30-33; 26:2, 45;
Nu 3:13, 41, 45; 1Ki 20:13, 28;
Isa 42:8; 43:11, 15; 44:24; 45:5-6, 18;
Jer 9:24; 24:7; Eze 6:7, 14, 10, 13; 7:4,
9, 27; 11:10, 12; 12:15, 16, 20, 25;
13:9, 14, 21, 23; 14:8; 15:7; 16:62;
20:26, 38, 42, 44; 22:16; 23:49; 24:24,
27; 25:5, 7, 11; 26:6; 28:22-24; 29:6, 9,*

*21; 30:8, 19, 25-26; 32:15; 33:29; 34:27;
35:4, 9, 12, 15; 36:11, 23, 38; 37:6, 13;
38:23; 39:6-7, 28; Mal 3:6*
I am Almighty God   *Ge 17:1*
I am the God of Abraham   *Ge 26:24*
I am the Lord God of   *Ge 28:13;*
Abraham   *M't 22:32; M'k 12:26;*
I am the God of Beth-el   *Ge 31:13*
I am God Almighty   *Ge 35:11*
I am God   *Ge 46:3; Isa 45:22; 46:9*
I am the God of thy father   *Ex 3:6*
I am that *I am*   *Ex 3:14; 6:14*
I am the Lord your God   *Ex 6:7;
16:12; Le 11:44; 18:2, 4, 30; 19:2-3, 10,
25, 31, 34; 20:7, 24; 23:22, 43; 24:22;
25:17, 38, 55; 26:1, 13; Nu 10:10;
15:41; De 5:6; 29:6; J'g 6:10; Eze 20:5,
7, 19; Joe 2:27; 3:17*
I am the Lord thy God   *Ex 20:2;
20:5; Ps 81:10; Isa 43:3; 48:17; 51:15;
Ho 12:9; 13:4*
I am holy   *Le 11:44*
neighbour as thyself; *I am*   *Le 19:18*
the Lord
any marks upon you: *I am*   *Le 19:28*
the Lord
I am he   *De 32:39;
Isa 41:4; 43:10, 13, 25; 48:12*
am not *I* grieved with those   *Ps 139:21*
that rise
I am the first, *I am* the last   *Isa 44:5;*
    48:12
I am the God of Israel   *Isa 45:3*
Behold, *I am* against thee   *Jer 50:31*
I am broken with their   *Eze 6:9*
whorish heart
I am the God of thy fathers   *Ac 7:32*

I AM used of natural man

I am waxed old   *Ge 18:12;
18:13; 27:2; Jos 23:2; 1Sa 12:2; Ps 71:18*
I am a stranger and a   *Ge 23:4*
sojourner
I am faint   *Ge 25:30*
I am at the point to die   *Ge 25:32;*
    Ps 88:15
I am weary of my life   *Ge 27:46;*
    Ps 6:6; 69:3
I am not able   *Nu 11:14; De 1:9*
I am thirsty   *J'g 4:19*
I am a poor man   *1Sa 18:23*
I am sore distressed   *1Sa 28:15;*
    2Sa 1:26
I am weak   *2Sa 3:39; Ps 6:2*
I am in a great straight   *1Ch 21:13*
I am ashamed and blush to   *Ezr 9:6*
lift up
I am full of tossings to and   *Job 7:4*
fro
I am a burden to myself   *Job 7:20*
I am afraid of all my   *Job 9:28;*
sorrows   *23:15*
I am full of confusion   *Job 10:15*
I am troubled   *Job 23:15;*
    Ps 38:6; Ps 77:4; 102:2
I am vile   *Job 40:4*
I am desolate and afflicted   *Ps 25:16*
I am bowed down greatly   *Ps 38:6*
I am feeble and sore broken   *Ps 38:8*
I am not able to look up   *Ps 40:12*
I am poor and needy   *Ps 40:17;
Ps 70:5; 86:1; 109:22*
I am full of heaviness   *Ps 69:20*
I am withered like grass   *Ps 102:11*
I am a man of unclean lips   *Isa 6:5*
I am holier than thou   *Isa 65:5*

I AM used of spiritual man

I am helped   *Ps 28:7*
I am like a green olive tree   *Ps 52:8*
I am a debtor   *Ro 1:14*
I am ready to preach the   *Ro 1:15*
gospel
I am not ashamed of the   *Ro 1:16*
gospel
I am crucified with Christ   *Ga 2:20*
I am an ambassador   *Eph 6:20*

AM *I*

am I my brother's keeper   *Ge 4:9*
am I in God's stead   *Ge 30:2*
am I God, to kill and make   *2Ki 5:7*
alive
am I come without the   *2Ki 18:25;*
Lord   *Isa 36:10*

am I a God at hand	Jer 23:23
am I not an apostle? *am I*	1Co 9:1
not free	

AMAD

and A., and Misheal — Jos 19:26

AMAL

Imna, and Shelesh, and A. — 1Ch 7:35

AMALEK

Timna bare to Eliphaz	Ge 36:12
Esau's son A.	
then came A. and fought with	Ex 17:8
Israel	
utterly put out remembrance	Ex 17:14
of A.	
sworn he will have war with	Ex 17:16
A.	
when he looked on A. he	Nu 24:20
said, A. was first of the nations	
remember what A. did	De 25:17;
	1Sa 15:2
shalt blot out remembrance	De 25:19
of A.	
out of Ephraim was a root	J'g 5:14
against A.	
Smite A. and utterly destroy	1Sa 15:3
didst not execute his wrath	1Sa 28:18
on A.	
Gebal, Ammon, A. are	Ps 83:7
confederate	

AMALEKITE

man of Egypt, servant to an	1Sa 30:13
A.	
I am an A.	2Sa 1:8; 1:13

AMALEKITES

smote all the country of the	Ge 14:7
A.	
A. dwell in the land of the	Nu 13:29
south	
the A. and the Canaanites	Nu 14:25;
	14:43
the A. came down and	Nu 14:45
smote Israel	
A. and children of east	J'g 6:3;
	J'g 6:33; 7:12
The Sidonians also, and the	J'g 10:12;
A.	12:15
smote the A.	1Sa 14:48;
	1Sa 15:6-8, 15, 18, 20, 32
the Gezrites, and the A.	1Sa 27:8
The A. invaded the south	1Sa 30:1;
	30:18
from the slaughter of the A.	2Sa 1:1;
	1Ch 4:43

AMAM

A., and Shema, and — Jos 15:26
Moladah

AMANA

look from the top of A. — Ca 4:8

AMARIAH

Meraioth begat A., and A.	1Ch 6:7
begat	
Azariah begat A., and A.	1Ch 6:11
begat	
Meraioth his son, A. his son	1Ch 6:52
Jeriah the first, A. the	1Ch 23:19
second	
A. the second, Jahaziel the	1Ch 24:23
A. the chief priest was over	2Ch 19:11
Shemaiah, A., and	2Ch 31:15
Shecaniah	
the son of A., the son of	Ezr 7:3
Shallum, A., and Joseph	Ezr 10:42
Pashur, A., Malchijah	Neh 10:3
son of A., the son of	Ne 11:4
A., Malluch, Hattush	Ne 12:2
A., Jehohanan	Ne 12:13
the son of A.	Zep 1:1

AMASA

Absalom made A. captain	2Sa 17:25
say ye to A., Art thou not	2Sa 19:13
Then said the king to A.	2Sa 20:4;
	20:5, 8, 9

A. wallowed in his blood	2Sa 20:12
A. the son of Jether	1Ki 2:5;
	1Ki 2:32; 1Ch 2:17
A. the son of Hadlai, stood	2Ch 28:12
up against	

AMASAI

oi Elkanah, A., and	1Ch 6:25
Ahimoth	
the son of Mahath, son of	1Ch 6:35
A.	
Then the Spirit came upon	1Ch 12:18
A.	
Nethaneel, and A., and	1Ch 15:24
Zechariah	
Levites arose, Mahath, son	2Ch 29:12
of A.	

AMASHAI

and A. the son of Azareel — Ne 11:13

AMASIAH

next to him was A. — 2Ch 17:16

AMAZED

dukes of Edom shall be a.	Ex 15:15
the men of Benjamin were	J'g 20:41
a.	
men were overcome with	J'g 20:41
fear (B)	
men were dismayed (E)(R)	J'g 20:41
they were a., they answered	Job 32:15
no more	
Dismayed they stand (B)	Job 32:15
They were discomfited (R)	Job 32:15
they were a. (A)(B)(E)	Ps 48:5
be not a. at the matter (R)	Ec 5:8
they shall be a. one at	Isa 13:8
another	
gaze stupified and aghast	Isa 13:8
(A)(R)	
gaze in amazement at	Isa 13:8
another (B)(E)	
was a. (B)	Isa 59:16; Rev. 17:6
was a. and appalled (B)(R)	Isa 63:5
I will make many people a.	Eze 32:10
at thee	
make many people	Eze 32:10
astonished (B)	
make many people appalled	Eze 32:10
(R)	
a., the man exclaimed (B)	M't 8:27
the multitude was a. (A)	M't 15:31;
	Ac 8:13
disciples were exceedingly a.	M't 19:25
were utterly puzzled (A)	M't 19:25
were utterly dumbfounded	M't 19:25
(B)	
were astonished exceedingly	M't 19:25
(E)(R)	
were all a. and glorified	M'k 2:12;
God	Lu 5:26
they were astounded (N)	M'k 2:12
all were a. (N)(P)	M'k 5:20
He began to be sore a. and	M'k 14:33
very heavy	
struck with terror (A)	M'k 14:33
deeply alarmed and	M'k 14:33
distressed (B)	
horror and dismay came	M'k 14:33
over (N)	
became horror-stricken (P)	M'k 14:33
distressed and troubled (R)	M'k 14:33
were utterly a. (A) (E) (S)	M'k 16:5
(R)	
they were a. (P)	Lu 2:18; 4:22
a. at what was said (P)	Lu 2:33
they were a. (S)	Lu 2:47;
	Lu 5:9; 8:56; 24:22
all a. and spake among	Lu 4:36
themselves	
were all a. at the mighty	Lu 9:43
power of God	
the Jews were a. (P)	Joh 7:15
they were a.	Ac 2:6
(B)(E)(N)(P)(R)	
they were a. (B)(N)(P)(R)	Ac 2:7
(E)(R)	
he a. the people of Samaria	Ac 8:9
he a. them with sorceries (E)	Ac 8:11
was a. (S)	Ac 8:13
all that heard Saul were a.	Ac 9:21
I am a. that you are so soon	Ga 1:6
(B)(P)	
why are you a. (B)(P)	Re 17:7

AMAZEMENT

looked in a. (R)	Ge 43:33
became an a. (A)	De 28:37
gaze in a. (B)(E)	Isa 13:8
make them an a. (A)	Jer 25:9
the governor's a.	M't 27:14
astonished with a. (A)(R)	M'k 5:42
beside themselves with a. (A)	Ac 2:7
were filled with a. at what	Ac 3:10
happened	
filled with awe and a. (B)	Ac 3:10
to the utter a. of (A)	Ac 8:9
are not afraid with any a.	1Pe 3:6

AMAZIAH

A. reigned in his stead	2Ki 12:21;
	1Ki 14:1; 2Ch 24:27; 25:1; 26:1
A. sent messengers to	2Ki 14:8;
Jehoash	14:9, 11, 13, 15, 17-18, 21, 23
as his father A. had done	2Ki 15:3;
	2Ch 26:4
A. his son	1Ch 3:12; 2Ch 24:27
Joshah the son of A.	1Ch 4:34; 6:45
A. gathered all Judah	2Ch 25:5;
	25:9-27
A. the priest of Beth-el	Am 7:10;
	7:12, 14

AMBASSADOR

a faithful a. is health	Pr 13:17
an a. sent to the heathen	Jer 49:14;
	Ob 1
for which I am an a. in	Eph 6:20
bonds	

AMBASSADORS

made as if they had been a.	Jos 9:4
the business of the a. of	2Ch 32:31
Babylon	
he sent a. to him	2Ch 35:21
that sendeth a. by the sea in	Isa 18:2
vessels	
princes of Zoan, his a. came	Isa 30:4
to Hanes	
a. of peace wept bitterly	Isa 33:7
he rebelled in sending a. to	Eze 17:15
Egypt	
now then we are a. for	2Co 5:20
Christ	

AMBASSAGE

he sendeth an a.	Lu 14:32
he sends an envoy (A)(N)	Lu 14:32
he will send a delegation	Lu 14:32
(B)	
he sends messengers (P)	Lu 14:32
he sends an embassy (R)	Lu 14:32

AMBER

as the color of a. — Eze 1:4; 1:27; 8:2

AMBITION

governed by selfish a. (N) — Ro 2:8

AMBITIONS

a. to be teachers (B) — 2Ti 1:7

AMBITIOUS

a. to be teachers (B) — 1Ti 1:7

AMBUSH

lay thee an a. for the city	Jos 8:2;
	8:9, 12, 14
ambush (B)	Jos 8:4;
	8:13; J'g 9:25, 34, 43; 20:29, 33, 36, 37,
	38; 1Sa 15:5; 22:8; Pr 7:12; Jer 9:8;
	Ac 23:16; 25:3
ye shall lie in a. (E)	Jos 8:4
shall rise up from the a.	Jos 8:7; 8:19
saw that the a. had taken the	Jos 8:21
city	

AMBUSHERS

trusted the a. (S) — J'g 20:36; 20:37

AMBUSHES

delivered from the a. by the	Ezr 8:31
way (R)	
set up watchmen, prepare	Jer 51:12
the a.	

AMBUSHMENT

Jeroboam caused an *a.*   *2Ch 13:13*

AMBUSHMENTS

the Lord set *a.* against   *2Ch 20:22*
Ammon

AMEN

the women shall say, A., *a.*   *Nu 5:22*
the people shall say, A.   *De 27:15;*
                 27:16-26
answered the king, and said,   *1Ki 1:36*
A.
all the people said, A.   *1Ch 16:36;*
           Ne 5:13; 8:6
everlasting to everlasting. A.   *Ps 41:13*
and A.
filled with his glory; A.   *Ps 72:19*
and A.
for evermore. A. and A.   *Ps 89:52*
A., Praise ye the Lord   *Ps 106:48*
the prophet Jeremiah said, A.   *Jer 28:6*
and the glory, for ever. A.   *M't 6:13*
unto the end of the world. *M't 28:20*
A.
the word with signs   *M'k 16:20*
following. A.
praising and blessing God.   *Lu 24:53*
A.
book that should be   *Joh 21:25*
written. A.
Creator, who is blessed for   *Ro 1:25;*
ever. A.   *9:5; 11:36; 16:27; Ga 1:5;*
Eph 3:21; 6:24; Ph'p 4:20; 1Ti 1:17;
6:16; 2Ti 4:18; Heb 13:21; 1Pe 4:11;
5:11, 14; 2Pe 3:18; Jude 25; Re 1:6; 7:12
God of peace be with you *Ro 15:33*
all. A.
Jesus Christ be with you. A.   *Ro 16:20;*
16:24; Ga 6:18; Ph'p 4:23; 1Th 5:28;
      2Th 3:18; Ph'm 23; Re 22:21
unlearned say A. at thy   *1Co 14:16*
giving of thanks
yea, and in him A. unto the   *2Co 1:20*
glory of
Holy Ghost be with you all. *2Co 13:14*
A.
Grace be with you all. A.   *Col 4:18;*
1Ti 6:21; 2Ti 4:22; Tit 3:15; Heb 13:25
keep yourselves from idols.   *1Jo 5:21*
A.
of thy elect sister greet thee.   *2Jo 13*
A.
wail because of him. Even so,   *Re 1:7*
A.
I am alive for evermore,   *Re 1:18*
A.
These things saith the A.   *Re 3:14*
the four beasts said, A.   *Re 5:14*
multitude saying, A.   *Re 7:12*
Sat on the throne, saying, A.   *Re 19:4*
A. Even so come Lord   *Re 22:20*
Jesus

AMEND

to repair and to *a.* the   *2Ch 34:10*
house
A. your ways, and your   *Jer 7:3;*
doings   *Jer 7:5; 26:13; 35:15*
the hour when he began to   *Joh 4:52*
a.

AMENDS

he shall make *a.* for the harm   *Le 5:16*

AMERCE

shall *a.* him in an hundred   *De 22:19*
shekels

AMETHYST

agate, and an *a.*   *Ex 28:19; 39:12*
a jacinth; the twelfth, an *a.*   *Re 21:20*

AMI

the children of A.   *Ezr 2:57*

AMIABLE

How *a.* are Thy tabernacles   *Ps 84:1*

AMINADAB

Aram begat A., and A. begat *M't 1:4*
Naasson
Which was the son of A.   *Lu 3:33*

AMISS

we have sinned, we have   *2Ch 6:37*
done *a.*
we have done wrong (A)   *2Ch 6:37*
we have done perversely   *2Ch 6:37*
(B)(E)(R)
speak anything *a.* against   *Da 3:29*
God
this man hath done nothing *Lu 23:41*
a.
receive not, because ye ask *a.*   *Jas 4:3*

AMITTAI

Jonah, the son of A.   *2Ki 14:25;*
            Jon 1:1

AMMAH

were come to the hill of A.   *2Sa 2:24*

AMMI

say ye unto your brethren, A.   *Ho 2:1*

AMMIEL

of Dan, A. the son of   *Nu 13:12*
Gemalli
house of Machir, the son of   *2Sa 9:4*
A.
Machir the son of A. of   *2Sa 17:27*
Lo-debar
Bath-shua the daughter of A.   *1Ch 3:5*
A. the sixth   *1Ch 26:5*

AMMIHUD

Elishama the son of A.   *Nu 1:10;*
     Nu 2:18; 7:48, 53; 10:22
Simeon, Shemuel the son of *Nu 34:20*
A.
Pedahel the son of A.   *Nu 34:28*
went to Talmai, the son of   *2Sa 13:37*
A.
Laadan his son, A. his son   *1Ch 7:26*
Uthai the son of A., the son *1Ch 9:4*
of

AMMINADAB

Elisheba, daughter of A.   *Ex 6:23*
Nahshon the son of A.   *Nu 1:7;*
2:3; 7:12; 7:17; 10:14; Ru 4:19-20;
            1Ch 2:10
A. his son, Korah his son   *1Ch 6:22*
A. the chief, and his brethren *1Ch 15:10;*
            15:11

AMMI-NADIB

made me like the chariots of   *Ca 6:12*
A.

AMMISHADDAI

Ahiezer, son of A.   *Nu 1:12;*
      Nu 2:25; 7:66, 71; 10:25

AMMIZABAD

in his course was A. his son *1Ch 27:6*

AMMON

the children of A.   *Ge 19:38;*
De 2:19, 37; 3:11; Jos 12:2; 13:10;
J'g 3:13; 2Ch 20:10, 22-23; 27:5
the children of A. was strong   *Nu 21:24*
the border of the children of   *De 3:16;*
A.   *Jos 12:2; 13:10*
the land of the children of   *Jos 13:25;*
A. `   *2Sa 10:2; 1Ch 19:2*
the gods of the children of   *J'g 10:6;*
A.   *1Ki 11:33*
into the hands of the children *J'g 10:7*
of A.
the children of A. fought   *J'g 10:17;*
against Israel   *10:18; 11:4-36; 12:1-3;*
1Sa 14:47; 2Sa 8:12; 10:1-19; 1Ch 19:1-
            19; 20:1
the king of the children of   *1Sa 12:12;*
A.   *2Sa 10:1; 1Ch 19:1*
princes of children of A.   *2Sa 10:2;*
            1Ch 19:3
slain Uriah with sword of   *2Sa 12:9*
children of A.
cities of A. *2Sa 12:26; 12:31; 1Ch 20:3*

abomination of A.   *1Ki 11:7;*
           2Ki 23:13
bands of the children of A. *1Ki 24:2*
A. sent a thousand talents   *1Ch 19:6*
Syrians help the children of *1Ch 19:19*
A.
Married wives of Ashdod, of *Ne 13:23*
A.
Gebal, and A., and Amalek   *Ps 83:7*
children of A. shall obey   *Isa 11:14*
them
of A. and Moab   *Jer 9:26; 25:21*
the captivity of the children   *Jer 49:6*
of A.
the chief of the children of   *Da 11:41*
A.
transgressions of the children *Am 1:13*
of A.
revilings of the children of A.   *Zep 2:8*
of A. as Gomorrah, even the   *Zep 2:9*

AMMONITE

An A. or Moabite shall not   *De 23:3*
enter the congregation of Lord   *Ne 13:1*
the A. came up and   *1Sa 11:1*
encamped
Nahash the A. answered   *1Sa 11:2*
them
Zelek the A.   *2Sa 23:37; 1Ch 11:39*
Tobiah the servant, the A.   *Ne 2:10;*
           Ne 2:19; 4:3

AMMONITES

the A. call them   *De 2:20*
Zamzummims
slew the A. until the heat of   *1Sa 11:11*
the day
women of the Moabites, A.   *1Ki 11:1*
Milcom the abomination of   *1Ki 11:5*
the A.
with them other beside the A.   *2Ch 20:1*
A. gave gifts to Uzziah   *2Ch 26:8*
fought also with the king of   *2Ch 27:5*
the A.
the Perizzites, the Jebusites,   *Ezr 9:1*
the A.
the Arabians, and the A.   *Ne 4:7*
to the king of the A.   *Jer 27:3;*
        Jer 40:11, 14
departed to go over to A.   *Jer 41:10;*
        41:15; 49:1-2
come to Rabbath of the A.   *Eze 21:20;*
     Eze 21:28; 25:2, 3, 5, 10

AMMONITESS

Naamah an A.   *1Ki 14:21;*
     1Ki 14:31; 2Ch 12:13
Zabad the son of Shimeath, *2Ch 24:26*
an A.

AMNON

his firstborn was A.   *2Sa 3:2; 1Ch 3:1*
A. the son of David loved *2Sa 13:1;*
her   *13:2-10, 15, 20, 22, 26-29, 32-33, 39*
sons of Shimon were A.,   *1Ch 4:20*
Rinnah

AMNON'S

Go now to thy brother A.   *2Sa 13:7;*
house   *13:8*
when A. heart is merry   *2Sa 13:28*
with wine

AMOK

Sallu, A., Hilkiah   *Ne 12:7*
of Sallai, Kallai; of A., Eber *Ne 12:20*

AMON

carry him back to A.   *1Ki 22:26;*
           2Ch 18:25
A. his son reigned in his   *2Ki 21:18;*
stead   *2Ki 21:19; 2Ch 33:20-21*
servants of A. conspired   *2Ki 21:23;*
against him   *2Ki 21:24; 2Ch 33:25*
rest of the acts of A.   *2Ki 21:25*
A. his son, Josiah his   *1Ch 3:14*
A. sacrificed to all carved   *2Ch 33:22*
images
A. transgressed more and   *2Ch 33:23*
more
the children of A.   *Ne 7:59*
in days of Josiah the son of   *Jer 1:2;*
A.   *25:3*

the son of A., king of Judah   Zep 1:1
Manasses begat A.; A. begat   M't 1:10
Josias

AMONG

child a. you be circumcised   Ge 17:10
   17:12
my signs which I have done   Ex 10:2
a. them
the poor a. you (S)   Ex 22:25
heard that thou, Lord, art   Nu 14:14
a. them
Is Saul also a. the prophets   1Sa 10:11;
   10:12
he hath hid himself a. the   1Sa 10:22
stuff
there is none like him a. all   1Sa 10:24
the people
a. the sons of the priests   Ezr 10:18
were found
a. many nations there was   Ne 13:26
no king
If an interpreter, one a. a   Job 33:23
thousand
their life is a. the unclean   Job 36:14
there is an evil common a.   Ec 6:1
men
one a. a thousand, but a   Ec 7:28
woman a.
the chiefest a. ten thousand   Ca 5:10
a. my people are found   Jer 5:26
wicked men
people a. whom they (S)   Eze 29:13
there is none upright a. men   Mic 7:2
manner of disease a. the   M't 4:23;
people   9:35
A. them that are born of   M't 11:11
women
blessed art thou a. women   Lu 1:28
send you forth as lambs a.   Lu 10:3
wolves
what are they a. so many?   Joh 6:9
there be no divisions a. you   1Co 1:10;
   11:18
many weak and sickly a.   1Co 11:30
you
is any a. you afflicted? let   Jas 5:13
him pray
Is any sick a. you? let him   Jas 5:14
call
God shall dwell a. them   Re 7:15
were redeemed from a. men   Re 14:4

AMONGST

a. the trees of the garden   Ge 3:8
possession of a burying place   Ge 23:9
a. the

AMORITE

the Jebusite, and the A.   Ge 10:16;
   1Ch 1:14
dwelt in the plain of Mamre   Ge 14:13
the A.
I took out of the hand of   Ge 48:22
the A.
drive out the Canaanite, the   Ex 33:2;
A.   Ex 34:11; Nu 32:39; Jos 9:1; 11:3
given into thine hand Sihon   De 2:24
the A.
thy father was an A.   Eze 16:3; 16:45
destroyed I the A. before   Am 2:9;
them   2:10

AMORITES

the A. that dwell in   Ge 14:7
Hazezon-tamar
iniquity of the A. not yet   Ge 15:16
full
the A. and Canaanites   Ge 15:21;
Ex 3:8, 17; 13:5; De 7:1; 20:17;
Jos 3:10; 12:8; J'g 3:5; 2Ch 8:7; Eze 9:1;
   Ne 9:8
I bring thee in unto the A.   Ge 23:23
the A. dwell in the   Nu 13:29
mountains
cometh out of the coasts of   Nu 21:13
the A.
Sihon king of the A.   Nu 21:21;
21:26, 29, 34; 32:33; De 1:4; 4:46;
Jos 12:2; 13:10, 21; J'g 11:19; 1Ki 4:19;
   Ps 135:11; 136:19
drove out the A.   Nu 21:32; 22:2
the mount of the A.   De 1:7;
   De 1:19-20, 44
the A. which dwell at Heshbon   De 3:2

the two kings of the A.   De 3:8;
   4:47; 31:4; Jos 2:10; 9:10; 24:12
all the kings of the A.   Jos 5:1; 10:5-6
the gods of the A.   Jos 24:15; J'g 6:10
the A. forced the children of   J'g 1:34
Dan
peace between Israel and the   1Sa 7:14
A.
the remnant of the A.   2Sa 21:2;
   1Ki 9:20
wickedly above all that the   2Ki 21:11
A. did

AMOS

the words of A.   Am 1:1
the Lord said unto me, A.   Am 7:8
A. hath conspired against   Am 7:10
thus A. saith, Jeroboam shall   Am 7:11
Amaziah said unto A.   Am 7:12
answered A., and said to   Am 7:14
Amaziah
and he said, A., what seest   Am 8:2
which was the son of A.   Lu 3:25

AMOUNT

a certain a. (S)   Ex 16:47;
   1Ki 10:25 2Ch 9:24
reckon the a. of (S)   2Ki 22:4

AMOUNTING

a. to six hundred talents   2Ch 3:8

AMOURS

came into her bed a. (B)   Eze 23:17

AMOZ

Isaiah the prophet, son of   1Ki 19:2;
A.   19:20; 20:1; 2Ch 26:22; 32:20, 32;
   Isa 1:1; 2:1; 13:1; 20:2; 37:2, 21; 38:1

AMPHIPOLIS

when they were passed   Ac 17:1
through A.

AMPLE

gave a. proof that (N)   Ac 1:3

AMPLIAS

Greet A. my beloved in the   Ro 16:8
Lord

AMRAM

the sons of Kohath; A. and   Ex 6:18;
Izhar   Nu 26:58; 1Ch 6:2, 18; 23:12
A. took him Jochebed   Ex 6:20;
   Nu 26:59; 1Ch 6:3; 23:13; 24:30
the years of the life of A.   Ex 6:20
were
of Kohath by their families;   Nu 3:19
A.
A., and Eshban, and Ithran   1Ch 1:41
sons of Bani, A. and Uel   Ezr 10:34

AMRAMITES

Kohath was the family of A.   Nu 3:27
of the A., and Izharites   1Ch 26:23

AMRAM'S

name of A. wife was   Nu 26:59
Jochebed

AMRAPHEL

in the day of A.   Ge 14:1; 14:9

AMULETS

and the a. (S)   Isa 3:20
a. upon all wrists (S)   Eze 13:18;
   13:20

AMZI

The son of A., son of Bani   1Ch 6:46
son of A., son of Zechariah   Ne 11:12

ANAB

from A., and from all the   Jos 11:21
And A., and Eshtemoh   Jos 15:50

ANAH

Aholibamah, the daughter of   Ge 36:2;
A.   Ge 36:14, 18, 25
Shobal, and Zibeon, and A.   Ge 36:20;
   36:24, 29; 1Ch 1:38, 40, 41
this was that A. that found   Ge 36:24
the mules

ANAHARATH

Shihon, and A.   Jos 19:19

ANAIAH

Shema, and A.   Ne 8:4
Pelatiah, Hanan, A.   Ne 10:22

ANAK

giants, sons of A.   Nu 13:33;
   Nu 13:22, 28; Jos 15:14
stand before the children of   De 9:2
city of Arba the father of   Jos 15:13;
A.   21:11
drove three sons of A.   Jos 15:14;
   J'g 1:20

ANAKIMS

seen the sons of the A. there   De 1:28
many, and tall, as the A.   De 2:10; 9:2
were accounted giants, as the   De 2:11;
A.   2:21
cut off the A. from the   Jos 11:21;
mountains   11:22
was great man among the   Jos 14:15;
A.   14:12

ANALYZING

correctly a. message (B)   2Ti 2:15

ANAMIM

A. and Lehabim   Ge 10:13; 1Ch 1:11

ANAMMELECH

and A. the gods of   2Ki 17:31
Sepharvaim

ANAN

And Ahijah, Hanan, A.   Ne 10:26

ANANI

Johanan, and Dalaiah, and   1Ch 3:24
A.

ANANIAH

son of Maaseiah, son of A.   Ne 3:23
at Anathoth, Nob, A.   Ne 11:32

ANANIAS

a certain man named A.   Ac 5:1;
   5:3, 5
a disciple at Damascus   Ac 9:10;
named A.   Ac 9:12, 13, 17; 22:12
the high priest A.   Ac 23:2; 24:1

ANARCHY

lawlessness, moral a. (N)   Ro 6:19

ANATH

Shamgar the son of A.   J'g 3:31; 5:6

ANATHEMA

let him be A. Maran-atha   1Co 16:22

ANATHOTH

A. with her suburbs   Jos 21:18;
   1Ch 6:60
Get thee to A. unto thine   1Ki 2:26
own fields
Abiah, A., and Alameth   1Ch 7:8
A. an hundred and twenty   Ezr 2:23;
   Ne 7:27
be heard unto Laish, O   Isa 10:30
poor A.
A. in the land of Benjamin   Jer 1:1

ANATHOTH (continued)

will bring evil upon the   *Jer 11:23;*
men of *A.*   *11:21*
thou not reproved Jeremiah   *Jer 29:27*
of *A.*
Buy my field that is in *A.*   *Jer 32:7;*
   32:8-9

ANCESTOR

our human *a.* (B)(N)(P)   *Ro 4:1*

ANCESTORS

remember covenant of their   *Le 26:45*
a.

ANCESTRY

the *a.* of Jesus Christ (A)(P)   *M't 1:1*

ANCHOR

hope we have as an *a.* of   *Heb 6:19*
the soul

ANCHORS

they cast four *a.* out   *Ac 27:29; 27:30*
they had taken up the *a.*   *Ac 27:40*

ANCIENT

chief things of the *a.*   *De 33:15*
mountains
that *a.* river, the river Kishon   *J'g 5:21*
Hast thou not heard of a.   *2Ki 19:25*
times
these are *a.* things   *1Ch 4:22*
fathers were *a.* men   *Ezr 3:12; Eze 9:6*
With the *a.* is wisdom   *Job 12:12*
the years of *a.* times   *Ps 77:5*
remove not the *a.* landmark   *Pr 22:28*
the prudent, and the *a.*   *Isa 3:2*
behave himself proudly against   *Isa 3:5*
a.
the *a.* and honourable, he is   *Isa 9:15*
head
son of *a.* kings   *Isa 19:11*
whose antiquity is of *a.* days   *Isa 23:7*
Hast thou not heard of *a.*   *Isa 37:26*
things
since I appointed the *a.*   *Isa 44:7*
people
hath declared this from *a.*   *Isa 45:21*
time
a. times the things that are   *Isa 46:10*
not
upon *a.* hast laid   *Isa 47:6*
a. days, in the generations of   *Isa 51:9*
old
it is an *a.* nation   *Jer 5:15*
in their ways from the *a.*   *Jer 18:15*
paths
they began at the *a.* men   *Eze 9:6*
the *a.* high places are ours in   *Eze 36:2*
A. of days did sit   *Da 7:9; 7:13, 22*
refused to follow *a.* customs   *M'k 7:5*
(P)

ANCIENTS

As saith the proverb of the   *1Sa 24:13*
a.
I understand more than   *Ps 119:100*
the *a.*
enter into judgment with the   *Isa 3:14*
a.
Lord shall reign before his   *Isa 24:23*
a.
take of the *a.* of the   *Jer 19:1*
people, *a.* of
priest, and counsel from the   *Eze 7:26*
a.
seventy men of the *a.* of the   *Eze 8:11*
people
the *a.* of the house of Israel   *Eze 8:12*
do
a. of Gebal and the wise   *Eze 27:9*
men

ANCLE

feet and *a.* bone received   *Ac 3:7*
strength

ANCLES

the waters were to the *a.*   *Eze 47:3*

ANDREW

Simon called Peter and *A.*   *M't 4:18;*
his brother   *10:2; M'k 1:16, 29;*
   Lu 6:14; Joh 1:40, 44; 6:8
A., and Philip, and   *M'k 3:18*
Bartholomew
John and *a.* asked him   *M'k 13:3*
privately
Philip cometh and telleth *a.*   *Joh 12:22*
A., Philip, and Thomas   *Ac 1:13*

ANDRONICUS

Salute *A.* and Junia, my   *Ro 16:7*
kinsmen

ANEM

A. with her suburbs   *1Ch 6:73*

ANER

Eshcol, the brother of *A.*   *Ge 14:13;*
   14:24
A. with her suburbs   *1Ch 6:70*

ANETHOTHITE

Abiezer the *A.*   *2Sa 23:27*

ANETOTHITE

Abiezer the *A.*   *1Ch 27:12*

ANGEL

he shall send his *a.* before   *Ge 24:7;*
thee   *24:40*
The *A.* that redeemed me   *Ge 48:16*
from
I send an *a.* before thee   *Ex 23:20;*
   23:23; 32:34; 33:2; Nu 20:16
The *a.* did wondrously   *J'g 13:19*
when *a.* stretched forth his   *2Sa 24:16;*
hand   *24:17; 1Ch 21:12, 15-16, 18, 20,*
   27, 30
an *a.* spake unto me by the   *1Ki 13:18*
an *a.* touched him, and said   *1Ki 19:5*
the Lord sent an *a.* which   *2Ch 32:21*
cut off
an *a.,* a mediator (R)   *Job 33:23*
neither say thou before the *a.*   *Ec 5:6*
it was
the *a.* of his presence saved   *Isa 63:9*
them
who has sent his *a.* and   *Da 3:28*
delivered
My God has sent his *a.* and   *Da 6:22*
hath
he had power over the *a.*   *Ho 12:4*
a. that talked with me   *Zec 1:9*
1:11-14, 19; 2:3; 3:3, 5-6; 4:1, 4-5; 5:5,
   10; 6:4-5
the *a.* answered and said   *M't 28:5*
unto them
the *a.* Gabriel was sent from   *Lu 1:26*
God
the *a.* departed from her   *Lu 1:38*
the *a.* said unto them, Fear   *Lu 2:10*
not
a. a multitude of heavenly   *Lu 2:13*
host
which was so named of the *a.*   *Lu 2:21*
a. went down at a certain   *Joh 5:4*
season
others said, An *a.* spake   *Joh 12:29*
unto him
as it had been the face of an   *Ac 6:15*
a.
the hand of the *a.* which   *Ac 7:35*
appeared
with the *a.* which spake to   *Ac 7:38*
him
warned from God by an   *Ac 10:22*
holy *a.*
said they, It is his *a.*   *Ac 12:15*
neither *a.* nor spirit   *Ac 23:8*
transformed into an *a.* of   *2Co 11:14*
light
we, or an *a.* from heaven,   *Ga 1:8*
preach
received me as an *a.* of God   *Ga 4:14*
he sent and signified it by his   *Re 1:1*
a.
the *a.* of the church of   *Re 2:1;*
   2:8, 12, 18; 3:1, 7, 14
I saw a strong *a.* proclaiming   *Re 5:2*
another *a.* ascending from the   *Re 7:2*
east
a. came and stood at the altar   *Re 8:3;*
   8:5

The first *a.,* second *a.,* third   *Re 8:7;*
a., fourth *a.,* fifth *a.,* sixth *a.,*
seventh *a.* sounded   *8:8, 10, 12; 9:1,*
   13, 14; 10:7; 11:15
an *a.* flying through the midst   *Re 8:13*
of
which is the *a.* of the   *Re 9:11*
bottomless pit
I saw another mighty *a.*   *Re 10:1;*
come   *10:5, 8-9*
the *a.* stood, saying, Rise,   *Re 11:1*
measure
I saw another *a.* fly   *Re 14:6;*
   14:8-9, 15, 17-19
first *a.,* second., third *a.,*   *Re 16:3;*
fourth *a.,* fifth *a.,* sixth *a.,*
seventh *a.* poured out   *16:4, 8, 10, 12, 17*
I heard the *a.* of the waters   *Re 16:5*
say
the *a.* said unto me   *Re:17:7*
I saw another *a.* come down   *Re 18:1;*
   20:1
a mighty *a.* took up a stone   *Re 18:21*
I saw an *a.* standing in the   *Re 19:17*
sun
measure of a man, that is,   *Re 21:17*
of the *a.*
his *a.* to shew unto his   *Re 22:6*
servants
fell down before the feet of   *Re 22:8*
the *a.*
have sent mine *a.* to testify   *Re 22:16*
unto

ANGEL *OF GOD*

the *a.* *of God* called Hagar   *Ge 21:17*
the *a.* *of God* speaks in a   *Ge 31:11*
dream
the *a.* *of God* which went   *Ex 14:19*
before
the *a.* *of God* stood in the   *Nu 22:22*
way
the *a.* *of God* said unto him   *J'g 6:20*
the *a.* *of God* came again   *J'g 13:9*
unto the
good in my sight, as an *a.*   *1Sa 29:9;*
of God   *2Sa 14:7, 20; 19:27*
an *a.* *of God* coming to him   *Ac 10:3;*
   11:13
stood by me this night an *a.*   *Ac 27:23*
of God

ANGEL *OF THE LORD*

the *a.* *of the Lord* found her   *Ge 16:7;*
   16:9-11
the *a.* *of the Lord* called   *Ge 22:11;*
   22:15
the *a.* *of the Lord* appeared   *Ex 3:2;*
J'g 6:12; 13:3; M't 1:20; 2:13, 19;
   Lu 1:11; 22:43
the *a.* *of the Lord* stood   *Nu 22:22;*
   Nu 22:32; 1Ch 21:15
ass saw the *a.* *of the Lord*   *Nu 22:23;*
   22:25, 27
Balaam saw the *a.* *of the*   *Nu 22:31*
Lord standing
the *a.* *of the Lord* said   *Nu 22:32;*
22:35; J'g 5:23; 13:13, 16, 18; 2Ki 1:3,
   15
an *a.* *of the Lord* came   *J'g 2:1;*
   6:11; Lu 2:9; Ac 12:7
the *a.* *of the Lord* spake   *J'g 2:4;*
the *a.* *of the Lord* put forth   *J'g 6:21*
the end
the *a.* *of the Lord* departed   *J'g 6:21*
I have seen the *a.* *of the Lord*   *J'g 6:22*
Manoah said unto the *a.* of   *J'g 13:15;*
the Lord   *13:17*
the *a.* *of the Lord* ascended   *J'g 13:20*
the *a.* *of the Lord* was by   *2Sa 24:16*
the threshing
the *a.* *of the Lord* came   *1Ki 19:7*
again
the *a.* *of the Lord* went   *1Ki 19:35;*
out   *Isa 37:36*
the *a.* *of the Lord*   *1Ch 21:12*
destroying
saw the *a.* *of the Lord*   *1Ch 21:16*
stand
the *a.* *of the Lord*   *1Ch 21:18;*
commanded   *21:27*
the sword of the *a.* *of the*   *1Ch 21:30*
Lord
the *a.* *of the Lord* encampeth   *Ps 34:7*
round
let the *a.* *of the Lord* chase   *Ps 35:5*
them

let the *a. of the Lord* persecute Ps 35:6
them
the *a. of the Lord*, and Satan Zec 3:1
as the *a. of the Lord* before Zec 12:8
them
did as the *a. of the Lord* M't 1:24
had bidden
the *a. of the Lord* descended M't 28:2
the *a. of the Lord* by night Ac 5:19
opened
an *a. of the Lord* in a flame Ac 7:30
the *a. of the Lord* spake unto Ac 8:26
Philip
the *a. of the Lord* came Ac 12:7
the *a. of the Lord* smote Ac 12:23
him

ANGELIC

a. rulers (A)(N)(P)   Eph 3:10

ANGELS

there came two *a.* to Sodom Ge 19:1;
                              19:15
which of the holy *a.* (A) Job 5:1
made lower than *a.* Ps 8:5; Heb 2:7, 9
thousand, even thousands of Ps 68:17
a.
by sending evil *a.* among Ps 78:49
them
a. came and ministered M't 4:11;
                          M'k 1:13
the reapers are the *a.* M't 13:39
the *a.* shall come forth, and M't 13:49
sever
in heaven their *a.* do M't 18:10
always behold
no not the *a.* of heaven M't 24:36;
                          M'k 13:32
and all the holy *a.* with him M't 25:31
hell prepared for the devil M't 25:41
and his *a.*
more than twelve legions of M't 26:53
a.
glory of Father with the M'k 8:38
holy *a.*
are as the *a.* which are in M'k 12:25
heaven
as the *a.* were gone away into Lu 2:15
heaven
in his Father's, and of the Lu 9:26
holy *a.*
carried by the *a.* into Lu 16:22
Abraham's bosom
they are equal unto the *a.* Lu 20:36
had also seen a vision of the Lu 24:23
seeth two *a.* sitting in white Joh 20:12
received law by the Ac 7:53
disposition of *a.*
nor life, not *a.*, nor Ro 8:38
principalities
to the world, and to *a.*, and 1Co 4:9
to men
know ye not, we shall judge 1Co 6:3
a.
on her head because of the 1Co 11:10
a.
the tongues of men and of 1Co 13:1
a.
law ordained by *a.* in the Ga 3:19
hand of
humility and worshipping of Col 2:18
a.
seen of *a.*, preached to the 1Ti 3:16
Gentiles
Jesus Christ, and the elect *a.* 1Ti 5:21
made so much better than Heb 1:4
the *a.*
unto which of the *a.* said he Heb 1:5;
                               1:13
of *a.* he saith, who maketh *a.* Heb 1:7
spirits
if the word spoken by *a.* was Heb 2:2
stedfast
unto the *a.* hath he not put Heb 2:5
took not on him the nature Heb 2:16
of *a.*
an innumerable company Heb 12:22
of *a.*
some have entertained *a.* Heb 13:2
unawares
things *a.* desire to look into 1Pe 1:12
a. and authorities and 1Pe 3:22
powers being
if God spared not *a.* that 2Pe 2:4
sinned
Whereas *a.* which are greater 2Pe 2:11
a. which kept not their first Jude 6
estate

the *a.* of the seven churches Re 1:20
my Father, and before his *a.* Re 3:5
I heard the voice of many *a.* Re 5:11
round
I saw four *a.* standing on four Re 7:1
corners
with a loud voice to the four Re 7:2
a.
all *a.* stood round about the Re 7:11
throne
I saw seven *a.* which stood Re 8:2
before God
a. which had the seven Re 8:6
trumpets
the trumpet of the three *a.* Re 8:13
which are
Loose the four *a.* which are Re 9:14
bound
and the four *a.* were loosed Re 9:15
Michael and his *a.* fought Re 12:7
against
the dragon fought and his *a.* Re 12:7
his *a.* were cast out with him Re 12:9
in the presence of the holy Re 14:10
a.
seven *a.* having the seven last Re 15:1
plagues
seven *a.* came out of the Re 15:6
temple
gave unto the seven *a.* seven Re 15:7
golden
of the seven *a.* were fulfilled Re 15:8
saying to the seven *a.*, Go Re 16:1
your ways
one of the seven *a.* which Re 17:1
had the
unto me one of the seven *a.* Re 21:9
which
at the gates twelve *a.* Re 21:12

ANGELS *OF GOD*

the *a. of God* ascending Ge 28:12;
                          Joh 1:51
Jacob went on his way, and Ge 32:1
a. of God
but as *a. of God* in heaven M't 22:30;
                              M'k 12:25
the Son confess before *a. of* Lu 12:8
God in
shall be denied before *a. of* Lu 12:9
God in
joy in presence of the *a.* of Lu 15:10
God
let all the *a. of God* worship Heb 1:6
him

HIS ANGELS

his a. he charged with folly Job 4:18
give *his a.* charge over thee Ps 91:11;
                               M't 4:6; Lu 4:10
ye *his a.* which excell Ps 103:20
in strength
who maketh *his a.* spirits Ps 104:4;
                             Heb 1:7
praise ye him all *his a.* Ps 148:2
Son of man shall send forth M't 13:41
his a.
come in glory of Father M't 16:27
with *his a.*
send *his a.* with great M't 24:31;
sound   M'k 13:27
fire prepared for devil and M't 25:41
his a.
from heaven with *his* mighty 2Th 1:7
a.
will confess before Father and Re 3:5
his a.
Michael, *his a.*, dragon, *his* Re 12:7
a.
great dragon cast out, and *his* Re 12:9
a.

ANGEL'S

before God out of the *a.* Re 8:4
hand
the little book out of the Re 10:10
a. hand

ANGELS'

Man did eat *a.* food Ps 78:25

ANGER

till thy brother's *a.* is turned Ge 27:45
away

let not thine *a.* burn against Ge 44:18
me
cursed be their *a.* for it was Ge 49:7
fierce
anger (E)   Ge 49:7;
2Ch 29:10; Job 36:13; 37:8; Pr 14:29;
          15:1; Isa 14:6; Jer 21:5; 32:37; 44:8
anger (R)   Ge 49:7
2Sa 11:20; 2Ch 29:10; Es 2:1; 7:10;
Job 36:13; Ps 37:8; Pr 14:39; 30:33;
Isa 14:6; 44:8; Ga 5:20; Eph 4:26; 6:4;
Col 3:8; 1Ti 2:8; Heb 11:27; Jas 1:19,
                                        20
anger (A)   Ex 32:12;
Ps 85:3; 88:16; 90:7, 11; Jer 18:20;
                               Hab 3:8
saw dancing, Moses' *a.*   Ex 32:19
waxed hot
let not *a.* of my lord wax hot Ex 32:22
Lord's *a.* flared up (B)   Num 11:32
I was afraid of the *a.* and De 9:19
displeasure
Lord turn away fierceness of De 13:17
his *a.*
a. and indignation (B)   De 29:23
what meaneth heat of this De 29:24
great *a.*
Lord turned from fierceness Jos 7:26
of his *a.*
Then their *a.* was abated J'g 8:3
toward him
anger (A)   2Sa 11:20;
2Ch 28:13; 29:10; Job 36:13; Ps 37:8;
14:29; Pr 21:14; 27:4; Isa 14:6; Jer 44:8;
Ro 9:22; Ga 5:20; Eph 6:4; 1Ti 2:8;
                          Jas 1:20; Re 12:12
anger (B)   1Ki 23:26;
1Ch 27:24; 2Ch 19:10; 24:18; 28:13;
29:10; Es 2:1; 3:5; 7:10; Ps 37:8;
Pr 14:29; 19:12; 21:14; 30:33; Jer 21:5;
32:37; Lu 21:23; Ro 2:5; Eph 4:31; 6:4;
Col 3:8; 1Ti 2:8; Heb 11:27; Jas 1:20;
                                Re 12:12
anger (B)   2Ch 12:7;
                                Ho 13:11; Heb 4:3
till *a.* of God be turned (B) Ezr 10:14
Ahasuerus, his *a.* burned Es 1:12
within him
the *a.* of the king abated (R) Es 7:10
if God will withdraw his *a.* Job 9:13
the proud
increase thine *a.* toward Job 10:17
(B)
send his fierce *a.* (R) Job 20:23;
                          Pr 24:18
anger (R)   Job 40:11;
                Ps 38:1; 79:6; 102:10
as a fiery oven in time of Ps 21:9
thine *a.*
for his *a.* endureth but a Ps 30:5
moment
cease from *a.* and forsake Ps 37:8
wrath
no soundness in flesh because Ps 38:3
of thine *a.*
let thy wrathful *a.* take hold Ps 69:24
on them
why doth thine *a.* smoke Ps 74:1
against sheep
a. also came up against Ps 78:21
Israel
the *a.* of God abideth (E) Ps 78:31
many a time turned he his *a.* Ps 78:38
away
He cast on them fierceness Ps 78:49
of his *a.*
made a way to his *a.* he Ps 78:50
spared not
turned from the fierceness of Ps 85:3
thine *a.*
cause thine *a.* towards us to Ps 85:3
cease
wilt thou draw out thine *a.* Ps 85:5
to all
for we are consumed by thine Ps 90:7
a.
who knoweth the power of Ps 90:11
thine *a.*
nor will he keep his *a.* for Ps 103:9;
ever   Jer 3:5
grievous words stir up *a.* Pr 15:1
discretion of a man deferreth Pr 19:11
his *a.*
a gift in secret pacifieth *a.* Pr 21:14
the rod of his *a.* shall fail Pr 22:8
wrath is cruel, *a.* is Pr 27:4
outrageous
a. resteth in the bosom of Ec 7:9
fools

for all this his *a.* is not   *Isa 5:25;*
turned away   *9:12, 17, 21; 10:4*
fear not for the *a.* of Resin   *Isa 7:4*
O Assyrian, the rod of mine   *Isa 10:5*
a.
and mine *a.* in their   *Isa 10:25*
destruction
though thou wast angry,   *Isa 12:1*
thine *a.* is
day of Lord cometh with   *Isa 13:9;*
wrath and fierce *a.*   *13:13; Lam 1:12;*
   Jer 25:38; 49:37
name of Lord cometh   *Isa 30:27*
burning with *a.*
Lord shall shew indignation   *Isa 30:30*
of his *a.*
he poured on him fury of   *Isa 42:25*
his *a.*
for my name's sake I defer   *Isa 48:9*
mine *a.*
Lord will come to render   *Isa 66:15*
his *a.* with
surely his *a.* shall turn from   *Jer 2:35*
me
I will not cause mine *a.* to   *Jer 3:12*
fall on you
I will not keep mine *a.* for   *Jer 3:12*
ever
cities were broken down by   *Jer 4:26*
his *a.*
Mine *a.* shall be poured on   *Jer 7:20*
this place
deal with them in time of   *Jer 18:23*
thine *a.*
city has been a provocation   *Jer 32:31*
of mine *a.*
great is *a.* the Lord hath   *Jer 36:7*
pronounced
as mine *a.* hath been poured   *Jer 42:18*
on Jerusalem
wherefore mine *a.* was   *Jer 44:6*
poured forth
remembered not in the day of   *La 2:1*
a.
Lord despised in indignation   *La 2:6*
of his *a.*
slain them in the day of   *La 2:21;*
thine *a.*   *2:22*
Thou hast covered with *a.*   *La 3:43*
and
he hath poured out his fierce   *La 4:11*
a.
thus shall mine *a.* be   *Eze 5:13*
accomplished
I will send mine *a.* upon thee   *Eze 7:3*
accomplish mine *a.* on thee   *Eze 7:8;*
   20:8, 21
shall do in Edom according   *Eze 25:14*
to mine *a.*
I will do according to thine   *Eze 35:11*
a.
moved with *a.* (A)(E)(S)   *Da 8:7*
let thine *a.* be turned away   *Da 9:16*
moved with *a.* (A)(E)   *Da 11:11*
not execute fierceness of mine   *Ho 11:9*
a.
Mine *a.* is turned away from   *Ho 14:4*
him
his *a.* did tear perpetually   *Am 1:11*
if God will turn from his   *Jon 3:9*
fierce *a.*
he retained not his *a.* for   *Mic 7:18*
ever
who can abide fierceness of   *Na 1:6*
his *a.*
was thine *a.* against the   *Hab 3:8*
rivers
pour upon them all my fierce   *Zep 3:8*
a.
when he had looked on them   *M'k 3:5*
with *a.*
against the day of *a.* (B)   *Ro 2:5*
let all *a.* be put away   *Eph 4:31;*
   Col 3:8
without *a.* (A)(B)(R)   *1Ti 2:8*

ANGER *KINDLED*

a. of Jacob was *kindled*   *Ge 30:2*
against Rachel
the *a.* of Lord was *kindled*   *Ex 4:14;*
Nu 11:1, 10; 12:9; 22:22; 25:3; 32:10,
13; De 6:15; 7:4; 29:27; Jos 7:1;
2Sa 6:7; 2Ki 13:3; 1Ch 13:10; 2Ch 25:15;
   Isa 5:25
Balaam's *a.* was *kindled,* he   *Nu 22:27*
smote
Balak's *a.* was *kindled*   *Nu 24:10*
against Balaam
lest *a.* of the Lord be *kindled*   *De 6:15*

so will *a.* of the Lord be   *De 7:4*
kindled
mine *a.* shall be *kindled*   *De 31:17;*
   Jos 23:16
a fire is *kindled* in mine *a.*   *De 32:22;*
   Jer 15:14
Zebul's *a.* was *kindled* against   *J'g 9:30*
Gaal
Samson's *a. kindled* and he   *J'g 14:19*
Saul's *a.* was *kindled*   *1Sa 11:6; 20:30*
Eliab's *a.* was *kindled*   *1Sa 17:28*
against David
David's *a.* was *kindled*   *2Sa 12:5*
wrath wherewith his *a.* was   *2Ki 23:26*
kindled
their *a.* was *kindled* against   *2Ch 25:10*
Judah
Ye have *kindled* a fire in   *Jer 17:4*
mine *a.*
mine *a.* is *kindled* against   *Ho 8:5*
them
Mine *a. kindled*   *Zec 10:3*
against shepherds

ANGER *OF THE LORD*

fierce *a.* of the Lord   *Nu 25:4*
to augment *a.* of the Lord   *Nu 32:14*
on Israel
a. of the Lord shall smoke   *De 29:20*
against
a. of the Lord against   *J'g 2:14*
   2:20; 3:8; 10:7
through *a.* of the Lord it   *2Ki 24:20;*
became   *Jer 52:3*
fierce *a.* of the Lord turned   *Jer 4:8*
away
because of fierce *a.* of the   *Jer 12:13;*
Lord   *25:37*
a. of the Lord not return   *Jer 23:20;*
   30:24
deliver soul from fierce *a.* of   *Jer 51:45*
the Lord
a. of the Lord hath divided   *La 4:16*
them
before fierce *a.* of the Lord   *Zep 2:2*
come on
be hid in day of *a.* of the   *Zep 2:3*
Lord

IN ANGER

for *in a.* they slew a man   *Ge 49:6*
went out from Pharaoh in   *Ex 11:8*
which the Lord overthrew *in*   *De 29:23*
a.
Lord rooted them out of   *De 29:28*
land *in a.*
Jonathan rose from the   *1Sa 20:34*
table *in a.*
they returned home *in a.*   *2Ch 25:10*
which overturneth them *in a.*   *Job 9:5*
he teareth himself *in a.*   *Job 18:4*
God distributeth sorrows *in*   *Job 21:17*
a.
He hath visited *in a.*   *Job 35:15*
rebuke me not *in a.*   *Ps 6:1; Jer 10:24*
arise, *in a.* lift up thyself   *Ps 7:6*
put not thy servant away *in a.*   *Ps 27:9*
in a. cast down the people, O   *Ps 56:7*
God
hath he *in a.* shut up mercies   *Ps 77:9*
I have called my mighty ones   *Isa 13:3*
in a.
he that ruled the nations *in*   *Isa 14:6*
a.
I will tread them *in a.*   *Isa 63:3;*
   63:6; Re 19:15
I will fight against you *in a.*   *Jer 21:5*
I have driven them *in a.*   *Jer 32:37*
whom I have slain *in a.* and   *Jer 33:5*
in fury
Lord covered Zion with cloud   *La 2:1*
in a.
He hath cut off *in a.* all the   *La 2:3*
horn
Persecute and destroy them *in*   *La 3:66*
a.
when I execute judgments *in*   *Eze 5:15*
thee *in a.*
shall be overflowing shower   *Eze 13:13*
in a.
I will gather you *in a.* and   *Eze 22:20*
fury
I have consumed them *in a.*   *Eze 43:8*
neither *in a.* nor in battle   *Da 11:20*
I gave thee a king *in a.*   *Ho 13:11*
I will execute vengeance *in*   *Mic 5:15*
a.

thou didst thresh the   *Hab 3:12*
heathen *in a.*

PROVOKE TO ANGER

to *provoke* him *to a.*   *De 4:25;*
   9:18; 31:29
I will *provoke* them *to a.*   *De 32:21*
with
images, to *provoke* me *to a.*   *1Ki 14:9;*
14:15; 16:2, 7, 26; 2Ki 17:11, 17; 22:17;
23:19; 2Ch 33:6; 34:25; Jer 7:18-19;
11:17; 25:7; 32:29, 32; 44:3; Eze 8:17;
   16:26
provoke me not *to a.*   *Jer 25:6*
provoke not your children *to*   *Col 3:21*
a.

PROVOKED TO ANGER

provoked him *to a.*   *De 32:16;*
   Ps 78:58; 106:29; Ho 12:14
They *provoked* me *to a.*   *De 32:21;*
   1Ki 21:22; 2Ki 21:15; Jer 32:30
provoked the Lord *to a.*   *J'g 2:12;*
   1Ki 22:53; 2Ch 28:25
they have *provoked* thee *to a.*   *Ne 4:5*
Why have they *provoked* me   *Jer 8:19*
to a.

PROVOKETH TO ANGER

whoso *provoketh* him *to a.*   *Pr 20:2*
sinneth
A people that *provoketh* me   *Isa 65:3*
to a.

SLOW TO ANGER

art a God ready to pardon,   *Ne 9:17*
slow to a.
slow to a. plenteous in   *Ps 103:9;*
mercy   *145:8*
he that is *slow to a.*   *Pr 15:18*
appeaseth wrath
he that is *slow to a.* is better   *Pr 16:32*
than
slow to a. and of great   *Joe 2:13;*
kindness   *Jon 4:2*
Lord is *slow to a.* and great   *Na 1:3*
in power

ANGERED

a. the Lord (B)   *J'g 2:12;*
   1Ki 22:53; 2Ki 21:15
a. him also at waters of   *Ps 106:32*
strife
your fathers *a.* me (B)   *Zec 8:14*

ANGERING

a. me with sins (B)   *1Ki 16:2;*
   6:26, 33; 2Ki 23:19

ANGLE

they that cast *a.* into brooks   *Isa 19:8*
fishermen shall lament   *Isa 19:8*
(A)(B)(R)
fishers shall lament (E)   *Isa 19:8*
they take up all of them   *Hab 1:15*
with
take up with the hook   *Hab 1:15*
(A)(B)(R)

ANGRY

Cain was *a.* (S)   *Ge 4:5*
let not the Lord be *a.*   *Ge 18:30; 18:32*
Jacob was *a.* (S)   *Ge 31:36*
they were very *a.* (B)(R)(S)   *Ge 34:7*
Pharaoh was *a.* (S)   *Ge 40:2; 41:10*
grieved, nor *a.* with   *Ge 45:5*
yourselves
Moses was *a.* (S)   *Ex 16:20;*
   Nu 16:15; 31:14
was *a.* with Eleazar and   *Le 10:16*
Ithamar
Lord wilt thou be *a.* (S)   *Nu 16:22*
the Lord was *a.* (S)   *De 1:34;*
   3:26; 9:19
was *a.* with me for your   *De 1:37;*
sakes   *4:21*
Lord was *a.*   *De 9:8;*
   9:20; 1Ki 11:9; 2Ki 17:18
he will be *a.* with the   *Jos 22:18*
congregation (S)
lest *a.* fellows run upon thee   *J'g 18:25*

ANGRY (continued)

Saul was very *a*. (S)   *1Sa 18:8; 20:7*
the princes were very *a*. (S)   *1Sa 29:4*
Abner was very *a*. (S)   *2Sa 3:8*
the king is *a*. (S)   *2Sa 11:20*
the king was very *a*. (S)   *2Sa 13:21*
then be ye *a*. for this   *2Sa 19:42*
matter
he was very *a*. (S)   *2Sa 22:8*
and thou be *a*. with them   *1Ki 8:46*
Naaman was very *a*. (S)   *2Ki 5:11*
the man of God was very   *2Ki 13:19*
a. (S)
be *a*. with them, and deliver   *2Ch 6:36*
them
Asa was very *a*. (S)   *2Ch 16:10*
Uzziah was *a*. (S)   *2Ch 26:19*
God of your fathers was *a*.   *2Ch 28:9*
(S)
wouldst not thou be *a*. with   *Ezr 9:14*
us
Sanballat was *a*. (A)(R)(S)   *Ne 4:1*
they were very *a*.   *Ne 4:7*
very *a*. when I heard their cry   *Ne 5:6*
they were very *a*. (S)   *Es 2:21*
Kiss the Son, lest he be *a*.   *Ps 2:12*
God is *a*. with the wicked   *Ps 7:11*
every day
because he was *a*. (S)   *Ps 18:7*
thou hast been *a*.   *Ps 60:1*
(A)(B)(P)(R)
in thy sight when once thou   *Ps 76:7*
art *a*.
the Lord was very *a*. (S)   *Ps 78:21;*
   78:59, 62; 89:38
wilt thou be *a*. for ever   *Ps 79:5;*
   80:4; 85:5
the wicked sees it and is *a*.   *Ps 112:11*
(R)
that is soon *a*. dealeth   *Pr 14:17*
foolishly
a contentious and an *a*.   *Pr 21:19*
woman
whom the Lord is *a*. with   *Pr 22:14*
falls (R)
make no friendship with an   *Pr 22:24*
a. man
so doth an *a*. countenance a   *Pr 25:23*
An *a*. man stirreth up strife   *Pr 29:22*
should God be *a*. at thy voice   *Ec 5:6*
Be not hasty in spirit to be *a*.   *Ec 7:9*
my mother's children were *a*.   *Ca 1:6*
though thou was *a*. with me   *Isa 12:1*
the Lord shall be *a*. (S)   *Isa 28:21*
I was *a*. with my people (S)   *Isa 47:6*
I would not be *a*. at thee (S)   *Isa 54:9*
neither will I always be *a*.   *Isa 57:16*
(S)
for iniquity I was *a*. (S)   *Isa 57:17*
thou art *a*. (S)   *Isa 64:5*
Be not exceedingly *a*. (S)   *Isa 64:9*
the princes were *a*. (S)   *Jer 37:15*
thou art very *a*. (S)   *La 5:22*
be quiet and be no more *a*.   *Eze 16:42*
king was *a*. and very furious   *Da 2:12*
he was very *a*.   *Joh 4:1; 4:4, 9*
the Lord was very *a*.   *Zec 1:2*
(A)(B)(R)
Herod was exceedingly *a*.   *M't 2:16*
(S)
whosoever is *a*. with his   *M't 5:22*
brother
his lord was *a*. (S)   *M't 18:34*
the king was very *a*. (S)   *M't 22:7*
the master of the house   *Lu 14:21*
being *a*.
he was *a*. and would not   *Lu 15:28*
go in
are ye *a*. with me, because   *Joh 7:23*
I have
a. with the people   *Ac 12:20*
(N)(P)(R)
Be ye *a*. and sin not: let not   *Eph 4:26*
the sun
not soon *a*., not given to wine   *Tit 1:7*
not be quick-tempered (A)(R)   *Tit 1:7*
not hot-tempered (B)(P)   *Tit 1:7*
not overbearing, short-tempered   *Tit 1:7*
(N)
slow to get *a*.   *Jas 2:19*
nations were *a*., thy wrath is   *Re 11:18*
come
the heathen raged   *Re 11:18*
(A)(B)(N)(R)
the nations were wroth (E)   *Re 11:18*
the nations full of fury (P)   *Re 11:18*
the dragon was *a*. (S)   *Re 12:17*

ANGUISH

guilty, in that we saw the *a*.   *Ge 42:21*
of his
saw agony of his soul (B)   *Ge 42:21*
saw distress of his soul   *Ge 42:21*
(E)(R)
they hearkened not to Moses   *Ex 6:9*
for *a*.
downed by cruel slavery (B)   *Ex 6:9*
broken spirit and cruel   *Ex 6:9*
bondage (R)
a. take hold (B)   *Ex 15:14*
tremble, and be in *a*. because   *De 2:25*
of thee
tremble and shake (B)   *De 2:25*
when *a*. is yours (B)   *De 5:30*
slay me, for *a*. is come upon   *2Sa 1:9*
me
weakness has seized me (B)   *2Sa 1:9*
in my *a*. I cried (A)   *2Sa 22:7*
I will speak in *a*. of my   *Job 7:11*
spirit
trouble and *a*. shall make   *Job 15:24*
him afraid
trouble and worry threaten   *Job 15:24*
(B)
I am in *a*. (B)   *Ps 31:9;*
   107:26; 116:3; Da 12:1
my heart is in *a*. (R)   *Ps 55:4*
trouble and *a*. (R)   *Ps 116:3*
trouble and *a*. have taken   *Ps 119:143*
hold of me
when distress and *a*. come   *Pr 1:27*
upon you
distress and despair come (B)   *Pr 1:27*
look to earth, behold dimness   *Isa 8:22*
of *a*.
my loins filled with *a*.   *Isa 21:3*
(A)(B)(E)(R)
be in *a*. over the (R)   *Isa 23:5*
into the land of trouble and   *Isa 30:6*
a.
a day of *a*. (B)   *Isa 37:3*
a. of spirit (R)   *Isa 65:14*
my *a*., my *a*. (E)(N)(R)   *Jer 4:19*
a. as of her that bringeth   *Jer 4:31*
forth child
woman in labor, a cry as of   *Jer 4:31*
one (B)
a. hath taken hold of us   *Jer 6:24;*
   49:24; 50:43
compassed with *a*. (A)   *La 3:5*
a. upon Ethiopia (B)(E)(R)   *Eze 30:4*
Pelusium shall have great *a*.   *Eze 30:16*
(A)
Sin shall have great *a*. (E)   *Eze 30:16*
people are in *a*.   *Joe 2:6*
(A)(B)(E)(R)
I cried in *a*. (B)   *Jon 2:2*
a. in all loins (A)(B)(E)(R)   *Na 2:10*
intolerable *a*. (A)   *M't 24:10;*
in *a*. and dismay (N)   *M't 26:37*
   M'k 13:18
you are in *a*.   *Lu 16:25*
(A)(B)(E)(R)
he was in *a*. of soul (P)   *Joh 13:21*
she remembereth no more   *Joh 16:21*
her *a*. for
no longer remembers her   *Joh 16:21*
pain (A)
remembers her affliction   *Joh 16:21*
(B)
remembers her agony (P)   *Joh 16:21*
tribulation and *a*. upon every   *Ro 2:9*
soul
affliction and anxiety (B)   *Ro 2:9*
grinding misery for every soul   *Ro 2:9*
(N)
bitter pain and fearful undoing   *Ro 2:9*
(P)
tribulation and distress (R)   *Ro 2:9*
out of much *a*. of heart   *2Co 2:4*
wrote to you
out of great sorrow and   *2Co 2:4*
distress (A)
out of great distress and   *2Co 2:4*
anxiety (N)
deep distress, most unhappy   *2Co 2:4*
heart (P)
much affliction and anxiety   *2Co 2:4*
(R)
in *a*. of her delivery (A)(N)   *Re 12:2*
gnawed tongues in *a*. (R)   *Re 16:10*
their *a*. and ulcers (A)   *Re 16:11*

ANIAM

Shechem, and Likhi, and A.   *1Ch 7:19*

ANIM

Anab and Eshtemoh, and A.   *Jos 15:50*

ANIMAL

slaughter an *a*. (S)   *Ge 43:16*
their *a*. cravings (A)   *Eze 7:19*
an *a*. mind be given (B)(R)   *Da 4:16*

ANIMALISTIC

is earthly, *a*. (B)   *Jas 3:15*

ANIMOSITY

from *a*. strikes (B)   *Nu 35:21*
cherished bitter *a*. (A)   *Ac 12:20*

ANKLETS

beauty of their *a*.   *Isa 3:18;*
(A)(B)(E)(R)(S)   *3:20*

ANISE

tithe of mint, and *a*., and   *M't 23:23*
cummin
mint, dill, and cummin   *M't 23:23*
(A)(B)(N)(R)

ANNA

there was one A., a   *Lu 2:36*
prophetess

ANNAS

A. and Caiaphas being the   *Lu 3:2*
high
led him away to A. first   *Joh 18:13*
A. had sent him bound   *Joh 18:24*
unto
A. the high priest, and   *Ac 4:6*
Caiaphas

ANNIHILATE

completely *a*. the nations (B)   *De 7:1*
to *a*. them (B)   *2Ch 20:23*
to *a*. Jews (R)   *Es 3:13; 8:11*

ANNIHILATED

to be *a*. (R)   *Es 7:4*

ANNIHILATION

a. is determined (B)   *Isa 10:22*

ANNOUNCE

a. in hearing of people (B)   *J'g 7:3*
a. it in the streets (A)   *2Sa 1:20*
set up prophets to *a*. (A)   *Ne 6:7*
go *a*. these words (B)   *Jer 3:12*
a. in Decapolis (B)   *M'k 5:20*
a. good news (N)   *Lu 4:18*
to *a*. the kingdom (B)(N)   *Lu 9:2*

ANNOUNCED

prophets *a*. these times (B)   *Ac 3:24*
forgiveness of sins *a*. (B)   *Ac 13:38*

ANNOUNCING

a. the good news (B)   *M't 4:23*
a. the gospel (B)(N)   *M't 9:35*
a. the good news (A)   *Ac 10:36*

ANNOYANCE

in his *a*. at Jesus (P)   *Lu 13:14*

ANNOYED

Paul sorely *a*. (A)(B)   *Ac 16:18*

ANNUL

make void, *a*. the vow   *Nu 30:8*
(A)(E)(R)
a., set aside, render void   *Job 40:8*
(A)(E)(S)
who will *a*. it   *Isa 14:27*
(A)(B)(E)(R)(S)
cannot *a*. the covenant   *Ga 3:17*
(A)(B)(R)(S)

ANNULLED

covenant with death a.   Isa 28:18
(A)(B)(E)(R)(S)
victory never be a. (B)   Isa 51:6
a. the law (N)   Eph 2:15
a. death (A)   2Ti 1:10

ANNULLETH

no man a. (S)   Ga 3:15

ANNULLING

an a. of the commandment   Heb 7:18
(S)

ANNULS

no one a. or adds to it (R)   Ga 3:15

ANOINT

shalt a. and consecrate   Ex 28:41;
    29:7; 30:30; 40:15; Le 16:32
shalt a. the altar and   Ex 29:36;
sanctify it   40:10
shalt a. the tabernacle   Ex 30:26; 40:9
shalt a. the laver and his   Ex 40:11
foot
shalt not a. self with oil   De 28:40;
    2Sa 14:2
trees went to a. a king over   J'g 9:8;
them   9:15
wash thyself and a. thee   Ru 3:3
shalt a. him captain over   1Sa 9:16
Israel
Lord sent me to a. thee king   1Sa 15:1
over Israel
shalt a. him whom I name   1Sa 16:3
unto thee
Lord said, Arise, a. him,   1Sa 16:12
this is he
let Zadok a. him king over   1Ki 1:34
Israel
a. Hazael king over Syria   1Ki 19:15
a. Jehu king, a. Elisha   1Ki 19:16
prophet
arise ye princes, and a. the   Isa 21:5
shield
seal up the vision, a. the   Da 9:24
most holy
neither did I a. myself at all,   Da 10:3
till
a. themselves with chief   Am 6:6
ointments
shalt tread olives, but not a.   Mic 6:15
thee
when thou fastest a. thine   M't 6:17
head
perfume your head (A)   M't 6:17
wash your face (P)   M't 6:17
had brought spices they   M't 16:1
might a. him
My head with oil thou didst   Lu 7:46
not a.
a. thine eyes with eyesalve   Re 3:18
salve to put on your eyes   Re 3:18
(A)(B)(P)
ointment for your eyes (N)   Re 3:18

ANOINTED

wafers, unleavened a. with   Ex 29:2;
oil   Le 2:4; 7:12; Nu 6:15
Aaron's sons after him, to   Ex 29:29
be a.
if the priest that is a. do sin   Le 4:3;
    4:5, 16; 6:22; Nu 3:3
offering of Aaron, when he is   Le 6:20
a.
in the day that he a. them   Le 7:36
a. the tabernacle, altar   Le 8:10;
    8:11; Nu 7:1, 10, 84, 88
poured oil on Aaron's head, a.   Le 8:12
him
names of Aaron's sons which   Nu 3:3
were a.
high priest which was a. in   Nu 35:25
those
Lord a. thee captain over his   1Sa 10:1
Lord a. Saul king over   1Sa 15:17
Israel
David a. king   1Sa 16:13;
2Sa 2:4, 7; 5:3, 17; 12:7; 2Ki 9:3, 6, 12;
    1Ch 11:3; 14:8
house of Judah have a. me   2Sa 2:7
king
I am weak though a. king   2Sa 3:39

David rose from the earth,   2Sa 12:20
and a.
David the a. of God   2Sa 23:1
Lord hath a. me to preach   Isa 61:1;
    Lu 4:18
thou art the a. cherub that   Eze 28:14
covereth
these are the two a. ones   Zec 4:14
which stand
she kissed his feet and a.   Lu 7:38;
them   7:46
he a. the eyes of the blind   Joh 9:6
man with clay   9:11
it was that Mary which a.   Joh 11:2;
the Lord   12:3
holy child Jesus, whom thou   Ac 4:27
hast a.
How God a. Jesus of   Ac 10:38
Nazareth with
he which hath a. us is God   2Co 1:21

ANOINTED WITH OIL

wafers a. with oil   Ex 29:2; Le 2:4
death of high priest a. with   Nu 35:25
oil
as though he had not been   2Sa 1:21
a. with oil
God a. with oil of gladness   Ps 45:7;
    Heb 1:9
with holy oil have I a. him   Ps 89:20
I shall be a. with fresh oil   Ps 92:10

HIS ANOINTED

give strength, exalt horn of   1Sa 2:10
his a.
witness before the Lord and   1Sa 12:3
his a.
Lord and his a. is witness   1Sa 12:5
this day
sheweth mercy to his a.   2Sa 22:51;
    Ps 18:50
against Lord and against his a.   Ps 2:2
the Lord saveth his a.   Ps 20:6
he is the saving strength of   Ps 28:8
his a.
saith Lord to his a., to Cyrus   Isa 45:1

LORD'S ANOINTED

surely the Lord's a. is before   1Sa 16:6
him
do this to my master, the   1Sa 24:6
Lord's a.
against my lord, for he is   1Sa 24:10
the Lord's a.
stretch forth his hand   1Sa 26:9
against the Lord's a.
ye have not kept the Lord's   1Sa 26:16
a.
not afraid to destroy the   2Sa 1:14
Lord's a.
death because he cursed the   2Sa 19:21
Lord's a.

MINE ANOINTED

he shall walk before mine a.   1Sa 2:35
for ever
touch not mine a.   1Ch 16:22;
    Ps 105:15
have ordained a lamp for   Ps 132:17
mine a.

THINE ANOINTED

the face of thine a.   2Ch 6:42;
    Ps 132:10
God, look on the face of   Ps 84:9
thine a.
thou hast been wroth with   Ps 89:38
thine a.
reproached the footsteps of   Ps 89:51
thine a.
even for salvation with thine a.   Hab 3:13

ANOINTEDST

I am God of Bethel, where   Ge 31:13
thou a.

ANOINTEST

thou a. my head with oil   Ps 23:5

ANOINTING

their a. be an everlasting   Ex 40:15
priesthood

is the portion of the a. of   Le 7:35
Aaron
given by reason of the a.   Nu 18:8
be destroyed because of the   Isa 10:27
a.
the a. which ye have received   1Jo 2:27
same a. teachest you all   1Jo 2:27
things

ANOINTING OIL

spices of a. oil, and for   Ex 25:6;
sweet incense   31:11; 35:8, 15, 28; 39:38
take the a. oil   Ex 29:7;
    29:21; 40:9; Le 8:2, 10, 30; Nu 4:16
it shall be an holy a. oil Ex 30:25; 30:31
he made the holy a. oil   Ex 37:29
he poured the a. oil on   Le 8:12;
Aaron's head   10:7; 21:10; Ps 133:2
to office of Eleazar pertaineth   Nu 4:16
a. oil
a. him with oil in name of   Jas 5:14
the Lord

ANON

and a. with joy receiveth it   M't 13:20
a. they tell him of her   M'k 1:30

ANOTHER

appointed me a. seed instead   Ge 4:25
of Abel
and sware to one a.   Ge 26:31
Lord shall add to me a. son   Ge 30:24
man asked, Have ye a.   Ge 43:7
brother
because he had a. spirit   Nu 14:24
a. generation that knew not   J'g 2:10
Lord
then shall I be weak as a.   J'g 16:7
man
shalt be turned into a. man   1Sa 10:6
God gave him a. heart   1Sa 10:9
answered one a. as they   1Sa 18:7
played
encamped opposite one a.   1Ki 20:29
(S)
repaired a. portion (S)   Ne 3:20
let king give her royal estate   Es 1:19
to a.
whom mine eyes shall   Job 19:27
behold and not a.
let a. take his office Ps 109:8; Ac 1:20
discover not a secret to a.   Pr 25:9
let a. praise thee, not own   Pr 27:2
mouth
my glory will I not give a.   Isa 42:8;
    48:11
turned in fear to one a. (S)   Jer 36:16
a. Jesus, a. spirit, a. gospel   2Co 11:4
rejoicing in himself and not in   Ga 6:4
a.
exhort one a.   Heb 3:13; 10:25
he would have spoken of a.   Heb 4:8
day
a. angel   Re 7:2;
    8:3; 10:1; 14:6, 8, 15, 17-18; 18:1

AGAINST ANOTHER

if one man sin against a. the   1Sa 2:25
judge
dash them one against a.   Jer 13:14
puffed up one against a.   1Co 4:6
grudge not one against a.   Jas 5:9

ONE FOR ANOTHER

when ye come to eat, tarry   1Co 11:33
one for a.
members have same care   1Co 12:25
one for a.
pray one for a. to be healed   Jas 5:16

ANOTHER'S

not understand one a. speech   Ge 11:7
if one man's ox hurt a.   Ex 21:35
ye also ought to wash one   Joh 13:14
a. feet
by every man a. wealth   1Co 10:24
Bear ye one a. burdens, and   Ga 6:2
so fulfil

ANSWER

shall my righteousness a. for   Ge 30:33
me

God shall give Pharaoh an   Ge 41:16
a. of peace
if the city make an a. of   De 20:11
peace
people shall a. and say,   De 27:15
Amen
see what a. I shall return to   2Sa 24:13
him
my servant, and he gave me   Job 19:16
no a.
because they had found no   Job 32:3
a.
demand of thee, and a. thou   Job 38:3
me
I am vile; what shall I a.   Job 40:4
thee
once have I spoken, but I   Job 40:5
will not a.
have mercy upon me, a. me   Ps 27:7;
108:6
wilt thou a. us, O God   Ps 65:5
call upon thee: for thou wilt   Ps 86:7
a. me
call upon me, and I will a.   Ps 91:15
him
the day when I call a. me   Ps 102:2
speedily
in thy faithfulness a. me   Ps 143:1
a. me quickly (B)(R)   Ps 143:7
call upon me, but I will not   Pr 1:28
a.
A soft a. turneth away wrath   Pr 15:1
hath joy by the a. of his   Pr 15:23
mouth
the righteous studieth to a.   Pr 15:28
a. of the tongue is from the   Pr 16:1
Lord
kiss his lips that giveth a   Pr 24:26
right a.
A. not a fool according to his   Pr 26:4
folly
A. a fool according to his   Pr 26:5
folly
called him, but he gave me no a.   Ca 5:6
then call, and the Lord shall   Isa 58:9
a.
before they call, I will a.   Isa 65:24
when I called none did a.   Isa 66:4
Call unto me, and I will a.   Jer 33:3
thee
I the Lord will a. him   Eze 14:4; 14:7
careful to a. thee in this matter   Da 3:16
for there is no a. of God   Mic 3:7
a beam out of the timber shall   Hab 2:1
a.
then he shall a., those with   Zec 13:6
no man was able to a. him   M't 22:46
a word
Then shall the righteous a.   M't 25:37
Then shall the wicked a.   M't 25:44
Then shall he a. them   M't 25:45;
25:40
ask you one question, and   M'k 11:29;
a. me   11:30; Lu 20:3
wist they what to a. him   M'k 14:40
shall a. and say, Trouble me   Lu 11:7
not
how and what thing ye shall   Lu 12:11
a.
could not a. him again to   Lu 14:6
these
they marvelled at his a. and   Lu 20:26
held
meditate before what ye   Lu 21:14
shall a.
ye will not a. me, nor let me   Lu 22:68
go
gave an a. to them that sent   Joh 1:22
us
Jesus gave him no a.   Joh 19:9
a. for myself   Ac 24:10; 25:16; 26:2
what saith the a. of God   Ro 11:4
unto him
a. to them that do examine   1Co 9:3
me
somewhat to a. them which   2Co 5:12
glory
how ye ought to a. every man   Col 4:6
first a. no man stood with   2Ti 4:16
me
a. to every man that asketh   1Pe 3:15
you
a. of a good conscience   1Pe 3:21

ANSWERABLE

a. to the hangings of the   Ex 38:18
court
be a. in the day of   M't 12:36
judgment (B)(P)

ANSWERED

Abraham a. and said, I have   Ge 18:27
taken
children of Heth a. Abraham   Ge 23:5;
23:10, 14
Laban and Bethuel a., The   Ge 24:50
thing
Isaac a. Esau and said   Ge 27:37;
27:39
unto God, who a. me in the   Ge 35:3
day of
God a. him by a voice   Ex 19:19
the Lord a.   1Sa 10:22;
23:4; 2Sa 21:1; 2Ki 7:19; 1Ch 21:28
Job 38:1; 40:1, 6
the Lord a. him not   1Sa 28:6
14:37; 2Sa 22:42; Ps 18:41
which he a. not (S)   1Ki 10:3; 2Ch 9:2
Satan a. the Lord   Job 1:7; 1:9; 2:2, 4
Job a. the Lord   Job 40:3; 42:1
I a. thee in the secret place of   Ps 81:7
upon the Lord, and he a.   Ps 99:6
them
Lord a. me, and set me in a   Ps 118:5
large
what hath the Lord a.   Jer 23:35; 23:37
And the Lord a. and said   Joe 2:19
(S)
the Lord a. me, and said,   Hab 2:2
Write the
they a. the angel of the Lord   Zec 1:11
Then the angel of the Lord a.   Zec 1:12
the Lord a. the angel   Zec 1:13
I a. and spake to the angel   Zec 4:4;
4:5-6, 11-13; 5:2; 6:4-5
Jesus a. Satan and said, It is   M't 4:4
written
Jesus a. and said   M't 11:4;
11:25; 15:28; 16:17; 17:11, 17; 20:22;
21:21, 24; 22:1; 24:4; M'k 10:5, 29, 51;
11:14, 29; 12:29, 35; 14:48; Lu 4:4, 8;
10:41; 22:51; Joh 1:48, 50; 2:19; 3:3, 5,
10; 4:10, 13; 5:17; 6:26, 29, 43, 70; 7:16,
21; 8:14, 19, 34, 49, 54; 9:3; 10:25, 32-34;
11:9; 12:23, 30; 13:7-8, 26, 36, 38; 14:23;
16:31; 18:8, 20, 23, 34, 36-37; 19:11
he a. and said   M't 12:39;
12:48; 13:11, 37; 15:3, 13, 24, 26; 16:2;
19:4; 21:29-30; 25:12; 26:23; M'k 6:37;
7:6; 10:3, 20; 14:20; Lu 8:21; 17:37;
19:40; 20:3; 23:3
Peter a.   M't 14:28; 15:15; 16:16; 17:4;
19:27;   26:33;   M'k 9:5;   Lu 7:43;
Joh 6:68; Ac 4:19; 5:8; 8:24; 10:46
He a. him never a word   M't 27:14;
Lu 23:9
the angel a. and said unto   M't 28:5
the women
John a.   M'k 9:38;
Lu 3:16; 9:49; Joh 1:26; 3:27
the angel a. and said unto   Lu 1:35
her
Philip a. him, Two hundred   Joh 6:7
James a. saying, Men and   Ac 15:13
brethren
the evil spirit a. and said,   Ac 19:15
Jesus I know
Then Paul a., What mean ye   Ac 21:13
to break
one of the elders a. saying   Re 7:13
unto

ANSWEREDST

Thou a. them, O Lord   Ps 99:8
the day when I cried thou a.   Ps 138:3
me

ANSWEREST

A. thou not, Abner   1Sa 26:14
emboldeneth thee that thou   Job 16:3
a.
said unto him, A. thou   M't 26:62;
nothing   M'k 14:60; 15:4
A. thou the high priest so   Joh 18:22

ANSWERETH

a. me no more, neither by   1Sa 28:15
prophets
the God that a. by fire, let   1Ki 18:24
him
calleth upon God, and he a.   Job 12:4
him
He that a. a matter before   Pr 18:13
he heareth
the rich a. roughly   Pr 18:23

As in water face a. to face,   Pr 27:19
God a. him in the joy of his   Ec 5:20
but money a. to all things   Ec 10:19
Peter a. and saith unto him,   M'k 8:29
Thou
But Jesus a. again, and   M'k 10:24
saith unto
He a. him, and saith, O   M'k 9:19
faithless
He a. and saith unto them   Lu 3:11
a. to Jerusalem which now is   Ga 4:25

ANSWERING

Jesus a. said   M't 3:15;
M'k 11:22, 33; 12:17, 24; 13:2, 5; 15:2;
Lu 4:12; 5:22, 31; 6:3; 7:22, 40; 9:41;
10:27, 30; 13:2; 14:3; 17:17; 20:34
the angel a. said unto him   Lu 1:19
Simon a. said unto him,   Lu 5:5;
Master   9:20
They a. said, John the Baptist   Lu 9:19
he a. said to his father   Lu 15:29
certain of the scribes a. said   Lu 20:39
the other a. rebuked him   Lu 23:40
Cleopas a. said unto him   Lu 24:18
well in a. things; not a. again   Tit 2:9

ANSWERS

a. there remaineth falsehood   Job 21:34
of his a. for wicked men   Job 34:36
astonished at his understanding   Lu 2:47
and a.

ANT

Go to the a. thou sluggard   Pr 6:6

ANTAGONISTIC

a. to each other (A)   Ga 5:17

ANTAGONIZED

how serious they had a. (B)   1Ch 19:6

ANTELOPE

of the a. and deer (B)   De 12:15;
12:22
skip like an a. (B)   Ps 29:6
the a. in a net (S)   Isa 51:20

ANTICHRIST

ye have heard that a. shall come   1Jo 2:18
He is a. that denieth the   1Jo 2:22
Father and
this is that spirit of a.   1Jo 4:3
whereof ye
This a deceiver and an a.   2Jo 7

ANTICHRISTS

even now there are many a.   1Jo 2:18

ANTICIPATE

mine eyes a. the night   Ps 119:148
watches (S)
a. the hope of (B)   Ga 5:5

ANTICIPATED

I a. the dawning of day (S)   Ps 119:147
a. what he was (P)   M't 17:25

ANTICIPATES

My eyes a. night watches   Ps 119:148
(A)(E)

ANTIOCH

Nicolas a proselyte of A.   Ac 6:5
travelled as far as A.   Ac 11:19;
11:20, 22, 26-27
in the church that was at A.   Ac 13:1
they came to A. in Pisidia   Ac 13:14
certain Jews from A.   Ac 14:19;
14:21, 26
men of their own company   Ac 15:22;
to A.   15:23
were dismissed, they came to   Ac 15:30
A.
Barnabas continued in A.   Ac 15:35
teaching
the church, he went down to   Ac 18:22
A.
when Peter was come to A.   Ga 2:11
which came unto me at A.   2Ti 3:11

ANTIPAS

A. was my faithful martyr　　Re 2:13

ANTIPATRIS

brought him by night to A.　　Ac 23:31

ANTIQUITY

whose a. is of ancient days　　Isa 23:7

ANTOTHIJAH

Hananiah, and Elam, and A.　1Ch 8:24

ANTOTHITE

the Tekoite, Abi-ezer the A.　1Ch 11:28
Berachah, and Jehu the A.　　1Ch 12:3

ANTS

The a. are a people not
strong　　　　　　　　　　Pr 30:25

ANUB

Coz begat A. and Zobebah　　1Ch 4:8

ANVIL

hammer him that smote the a.　Isa 41:7

ANXIETY

dwelt in a. (S)　　　　　　　J'g 18:7
a day of a. (B)　　　　　　　Ps 86:7
trouble and a. (A)　　　　　Jer 49:23
eat with a. (S)　　　Eze 12:18; 12:19
searching with great a. (N)　Lu 2:48
live in a state of a. (P)　　Lu 12:29
great distress and a. (N)　　Ro 2:9

ANXIOUS

he became a. (S)　　　　　　1Sa 9:6
I am a. because of (B)　　　Ps 38:18
not be a. in drouth (S)　　　Jer 17:8
spirit in me was a. (R)　　　Da 7:15
be not a. (S)　　　　　　　M't 6:25;
　　　　　　　　6:31; 10:19; Lu 12:22
being a. (S)　　　　　　　　M't 6:27
are you a. (S)　　M't 6:28; Lu 12:26
be not a. about (S)　　　　M't 6:34
the morrow will be a. (S)　　M't 6:34
a. and bustling (B)(S)　　　Lu 10:41
be not a. (S)　　　　　　　Lu 12:11
by being a. (S)　　　　　　Lu 12:25
neither be a. (A)(B)(R)　　　Lu 12:29
love not a. to impress (P)　　1Co 13:4
be not a. (S)　　　　　　　Ph'p 4:6

ANXIOUSLY

waited a. for (S)　　　　　　Mic 1:12

ANY

was more subtle than a. beast　Ge 3:1
of
a mark upon Cain, lest a.　　Ge 4:15
finding
five times as much as a. of　Ge 43:34
theirs
when there falleth out a. war,　Ex 1:10
they join
ought changed to a. (S)　　　Ex 5:11;
12:46; 29:34; Le 11:25; 27:31; 1Sa 30:22;
　　　　　　　　　　　　　Ac 4:32
there remained not a. green　Ex 10:15
thing
against a. of the children of　Ex 11:7
Israel
prepared for themselves a.　Ex 12:39
victual
a. graven image, a. thing　　Ex 20:4;
　　　　　　　　　　　20:10, 17
If thou lend money to a. of　Ex 22:25
my people
if a soul sin against a.　　　Le 4:2;
commandments　　　4:13, 22, 27; 5:17
may be used in a. other use　Le 7:24
vessel it be, wherein a. work　Le 11:32
is done
if a. say, I have sinned　　Job 33:27
who will show us a. good　　Ps 4:6
a lion turneth not away from　Pr 30:30
a.

there is no God, I know not　Isa 44:8
a.
is the vine tree more than a.　Eze 15:2
tree
cause thy nations to fall a.　Eze 36:15
more
and into a. city of the　　　M't 10:5
Samaritans enter
forgive, if ye have ought　M'k 11:25
against a.
that had a. sick with divers　Lu 4:40
diseases
if a. man thirst, let him　　Joh 7:37
come to me
if he found a. of this way　　Ac 9:2
if a. lack wisdom, let him ask　Jas 1:5
God
not willing that a. should　　2Pe 3:9
perish
if we ask a. thing　1Jo 5:14; Joh 14:14
if a. man hear my voice, and　Re 3:20
open
If a. man add, take away　Re 22:18;
from　　　　　　　　　　　22:19

ANYTHING

ought changed to a. (S)　　Ge 39:6;
47:18; Ex 5:8; 22:11; Le 19:6; 25:14;
Nu 15:24, 30; 30:6; De 4:2; 15:2; 26:14;
Ru 1:17; 1Sa 12:4-5; 25:7; 2Sa 3:35;
14:10, 19; M't 5:23; 21:3; M'k 7:12;
8:23; 11:25; Ac 24:19; 28:19; Ph'm 18
If thou hast a. to say　　　Job 33:32
a. to eat (S)　　　　　　　Lu 24:41

ANYWHERE

who comes a. near (S)　　　Nu 17:13
from there a. (S)　　　　　1Ki 2:36
walketh abroad a. (S)　　　1Ki 2:42

APACE

he came a., and drew near　2Sa 18:25
Kings of armies did flee a.　Ps 68:12
their mighty ones are fled a.　Jer 46:5

APART

set a. the sabbath (A)　　　Ge 2:3
sat her down a. from (S)　　Ge 21:16
I will set a. this day (S)　　Ex 8:22
set a. the cattle of Israel (S)　Ex 9:4
set a. the first-born (A)(R)　Ex 13:2
set a. all that open the　　Ex 13:12
matrix
set yourselves a. (B)　　　Le 11:44
she shall be put a. seven days　Le 15:19
not approach, as long as she is　Le 18:19
a.
set a. the tabernacle (B)　　Nu 7:1
Lord set a. (S)　　　　　　De 10:8;
　　　　　　　　　19:2, 7; 29:21
males you shall set a. (A)　　De 15:19
set a. cities (A)(B)(E)(R)　　De 19:2;
　　　　　　　　　　　　　19:7
set him a. from all (B)(R)　De 29:21
Aaron was set a. (R)　　　1Ch 23:13
priests set a. themselves (A)　2Ch 31:18
set a. for Levites　　　　　Ne 12:47
(A)(B)(E)(R)
Lord hath set a. him that is　Ps 4:3
godly
a. from any fault of mine (S)　Ps 59:4
I set you a. (A)　　　　　　Jer 1:5
they humbled her that was　Eze 22:10
set a.
set them a. (A)　　　Eze 28:22; 28:25
set a. and consecrate (A)　Eze 37:28
set a. for the task (S)　　　Eze 39:14
every family a.　　　Zec 12:12; 12:13-14
into a desert place a.　　　M't 14:13;
　　　　　　　　　　　　　M'k 6:31
into a mountain a. to pray　M't 14:23
into a high mountain a.　　M't 17:1;
　　　　　　　　　　　　　M'k 9:2
the disciples to Jesus a.　　M't 17:19;
　　　　　　　　　　　　　20:17
Father set a.　　　　　　　Joh 10:36
(A)(N)(P)(R)
set a. Barnabas and Paul　　Ac 13:2
(B)(N)(P)(R)
all God's set a. ones (A)　　Ac 20:32
a. from the law (S)　　　　Ro 3:21;
　　　　　　　　　　3:28; 7:8-9
a. from works (S)　　　　　Ro 4:6
you were set a. (A)　　　　1Co 6:11
husband, wife set a. (A)　　1Co 7:14
set a. for pure living (A)　　1Th 4:3

vessel set a. and useful　　2Ti 2:21
(A)(B)
Wherefore lay a. all filthiness　Jas 1:21
set Christ a. as holy (A)　　1Pe 3:15
those who are set a. (A)(B)　Jude 1

APELLES

Salute A. approved in　　　Ro 16:10
Christ

APES

ivory, a., and peacocks　　1Ki 10:22;
　　　　　　　　　　　　　2Ch 9:21

APHARSACHITES

his companions the A.　Ezr 5:6; 6:6

APHARSATHCHITES

the A., the Tarpelites　　　Ezr 4:9

APHARSITES

Tarpelites, the A., the　　　Ezr 4:9
Archevites

APHEK

The king of A., one　　　　Jos 12:18
unto A. to the borders of the　Jos 13:4
Ummah also, and A., and　　Jos 19:30
Rehob
the Philistines pitched in A.　1Sa 4:1
together all their armies to　1Sa 29:1
A.
up to A. to fight against　1Ki 20:26;
Israel　　　　　　　　　　　20:30
shalt smite the Syrians in　2Ki 13:17
A.

APHEKAH

Janum, Beth-tappuah, and　Jos 15:53
A.

APHIAH

son of A. a Benjamite　　　1Sa 9:1

APHIK

nor of A. nor of Rehob　　　J'g 1:31

APHRAH

house of A. roll thyself in　Mic 1:10
dust

APHSES

Hezir, the eighteenth to A.　1Ch 24:15

APIECE

take five shekels a. by the　Nu 3:47
poll
ten shekels a. after the shekel　Nu 7:86
their princes gave him a rod　Nu 17:6
a.
eighteen cubits high a.　　　1Ki 7:15
Every one had four faces　Eze 10:21
a.
and the doors had two　　Eze 41:24
leaves a.
money, neither have two coats　Lu 9:3
a.
containing two or three firkins　Joh 2:6
a.

APOLLONIA

through Amphipolis and A.　Ac 17:1

APOLLOS

a certain Jew named A.　　Ac 18:24
while A. was at Corinth　　Ac 19:1
and I of A.; and I of　　　1Co 1:12
Cephas
another, I am of A.; are ye not　1Co 3:4
Who then is Paul, and who is　1Co 3:5
A.
A. watered: but God gave the　1Co 3:6
Whether Paul, or A. or　　1Co 3:22
Cephas
and to A. for your sakes　　1Co 4:6
touching our brother A.　　1Co 16:12
Bring Zenas the lawyer and　Tit 3:13
A.

APOLLYON

Greek tongue hath this name *Re 9:11*
A.

APOSTASIES

their sinful *a*. (B) *Eze 37:23*

APOSTASY

a. is to come first (B) *2Th 2:3*

APOSTATES

a. and sinners (B) *Isa 1:28; 46:8*

APOSTLE

position of an *a*. (A) *Ac 1:25*
called to be an *a*., separated *Ro 1:1*
unto
as I am the *a*. of the *Ro 11:13*
Gentiles
called to be an *a*. of Jesus *1Co 1:1*
Christ
Am I not an *a*? am I not *1Co 9:1*
free
If I be not an *a*. unto others *1Co 9:2*
not meet to be called an *a*. *1Co 15:9*
Paul, an *a*. of Jesus Christ by *2Co 1:1*
the signs of an *a*. were *2Co 12:12*
wrought
Paul, an *A*. (not of men, *Ga 1:1*
neither by
Paul, an *a*. of Jesus Christ *Eph 1:1*
Paul, an *a*. of Jesus Christ by *Col 1:1*
Paul, an *a*. of Jesus Christ by *1Ti 1:1*
am ordained a preacher, and *1Ti 2:7*
an *a*.
Paul, an *a*. of Jesus Christ *2Ti 1:1*
appointed a preacher, and an *a*. *2Ti 1:11*
an *a*. of Jesus Christ, *Tit 1:1*
according to
consider the *A*. and High *Heb 3:1*
Priest
Peter, an *a*. of Jesus Christ *1Pe 1:1*
a servant and an *a*. of Jesus *2Pe 1:1*

APOSTLES

names of the twelve *a*. are *M't 10:2*
these
the *a*. gathered themselves *M'k 6:30*
together
whom also he named *a*. *Lu 6:13*
the *a*. when they were *Lu 9:10*
returned
I will send them prophets *Lu 11:49*
and *a*.
the *a*. said unto the Lord *Lu 17:5*
the twelve *a*. with him *Lu 22:14*
told these things unto the *a*. *Lu 24:10*
commandments unto the *a*. *Ac 1:2*
whom
numbered with the eleven *a*. *Ac 1:26*
Peter, and to the rest of the *Ac 2:37*
a.
and signs were done by the *a*. *Ac 2:43*
the *a*. witness of the *Ac 4:33*
resurrection
by the *a*. was surnamed *Ac 4:36*
Barnabas
hands of the *a*. were many *Ac 5:12*
signs
laid their hands on the *a*. *Ac 5:18*
Peter and the other *a*. answered *Ac 5:29*
to put the *a*. forth a little space *Ac 5:34*
called the *a*. and beaten them *Ac 5:40*
Whom they set before the *a*. *Ac 6:6*
Judaea and Samaria, except *Ac 8:1*
the *a*.
the *a*. which were at *Ac 8:14*
Jerusalem
him and brought him to the *Ac 9:27*
a.
a. and brethren that were in *Ac 11:1*
Judaea
with the Jews, and part with *Ac 14:4*
the *a*.
when the *a*. Barnabas and *Ac 14:14*
Paul
unto the *a*. and elders about *Ac 15:2*
this
of the *a*. and elders, and they *Ac 15:4*
the *a*. and elders came together *Ac 15:6*
Then pleased it the *a*. and *Ac 15:22*
elders
The *a*. and elders and *Ac 15:23*
brethren

the brethren unto the *a*. *Ac 15:33*
were ordained of the *a*. and *Ac 16:4*
elders
who are of note among the *a*. *Ro 16:7*
God hath set forth us the *a*. *1Co 4:9*
last
as well as other *a*. and as the *1Co 9:5*
first *a*. secondarily prophets *1Co 12:28*
Are all *a*.? are all *1Co 12:29*
prophets
of James; then of all the *a*. *1Co 15:7*
I am the least of the *a*. that *1Co 15:9*
a whit behind the very *2Co 11:5*
chiefest *a*.
are false *a*. deceitful workers *2Co 11:13*
themselves into the *a*. of *2Co 11:13*
Christ
the very chiefest *a*. though *2Co 12:11*
I be
to them which were *a*. before *Ga 1:17*
me
other of the *a*. saw I none *Ga 1:19*
foundation of the *a*. and *Eph 2:20*
prophets
revealed unto his holy *a*. *Eph 3:5*
gave some, *a*.; and some, *Eph 4:11*
prophets
burdensome, as the *a*. of *1Th 2:6*
Christ
the *a*. of the Lord and *2Pe 3:2*
Saviour
before of the *a*. of our Lord *Jude 17*
Jesus
them which say they are *a*. *Re 2:2*
ye holy *a*. and prophets *Re 18:20*
names of the twelve *a*. of the *Re 21:14*
Lamb

APOSTLES'

in the *a*. doctrine and *Ac 2:42*
fellowship
laid them down at the *a*. *Ac 4:35*
feet
the money, and laid it at the *Ac 4:37*
a. feet
part, and laid it at the *a*. feet *Ac 5:2*
through laying on of the *a*. *Ac 8:18*
hands

APOSTLESHIP

take part of this ministry and *Ac 1:25*
a.
position of an apostle (A) *Ac 1:25*
position of this apostolate *Ac 1:25*
(B)
apostle's ministry which *Ac 1:25*
Judas (P)
by whom we have received *Ro 1:5*
grace and *a*.
privileges of a commission *Ro 1:5*
(N)(P)
seal of mine *a*. are ye in the *1Co 9:2*
Lord
the seal of my apostolate (N) *1Co 9:2*
samples of my work in the *1Co 9:2*
Lord (P)
wrought effectually in Peter to *Ga 2:8*
the *a*.
for the mission of the *Ga 2:8*
circumcision (A)
actuated Peter to the *Ga 2:8*
apostolate (B)
the mission to the circumcised *Ga 2:8*
(R)

APOSTOLATE

position in the *a*. (B) *Ac 1:25*
seal of my *a*. (N) *1Co 9:2*
actuate to the *a*. (B) *Ga 2:8*

APOTHECARIES

Hananiah the son of one of *Ne 3:8*
the *a*.

APOTHECARIES'

spices prepared by the *a*. *2Ch 16:14*
art

APOTHECARY

compound after the art of *Ex 30:25*
the *a*.
confection after the art of *Ex 30:35*
the *a*.

according to the work of the *Ex 37:29*
a.
the ointment of the *a*. *Ec 10:1*

APPAIM

the sons of Nadab; Seled, *1Ch 2:30*
and *A*.
the sons of *A*.; Ishi. And *1Ch 2:31*
the sons

APPALLED

sat down *a*. (A)(R)(S) *Ezr 9:3*
men are *a*. (B) *Job 17:8; 18:20*
fearfulness *a*. me (S) *Isa 21:4;*
Eze 32:10
be *a*. (S) *Jer 2:12;*
18:16; 19:8; 49:17; 50:13; Eze 26:16;
27:35; 28:19

APPALLING

the *a*. sacrilege (A) *M't 24:15*
an *a*. thing (S) *Jer 5:30*

APPAREL

and a suit of *a*., and thy *J'g 17:10*
victuals
the camels, and the *a*. *1Sa 27:9*
ornaments of gold upon your *2Sa 1:24*
a.
himself, and changed his *a*. *2Sa 12:20*
put on now mourning *a*. *2Sa 14:2*
his ministers, and their *a*. *1Ki 10:5*
his ministers, and their *a*.; his *2Ch 9:4*
cupbearers also, and their *a*. *2Ch 9:4*
they set the priests in their *Ezr 3:10*
a.
that Esther put on her royal *a*. *Es 5:1*
Let the royal *a*. be brought *Es 6:8*
let this *a*. and horse be *Es 6:9*
delivered
take the *a*. and the horse *Es 6:10*
Then took Haman the *a*. *Es 6:11*
in royal *a*. of blue and white *Es 8:15*
The changeable suits of *a*. *Isa 3:22*
own bread, and wear our own *Isa 4:1*
a.
your glorious *a*. (B) *Isa 52:1; 63:1*
this that is glorious in his *a*. *Isa 63:1*
Wherefore art thou red in *Isa 63:2*
thine *a*.
in chests of rich *a*., bound *Eze 27:24*
with
as are clothed with strange *a*. *Zep 1:8*
gold, and silver, and *a*. *Zec 14:14*
cast lots upon my *a*. (A) *M't 27:35*
wear fine *a*. (A)(P) *Lu 7:25*
men stood by them in white *Ac 1:10*
a.
Herod, arrayed in royal *a*. *Ac 12:21*
no man's silver, or gold, or *Ac 20:33*
a.
adorn themselves in modest *a*. *1Ti 2:9*
gold ring, in goodly *a*. *Jas 2:2*
in vile *a*. *Jas 2:2*
of gold or of putting on of *a*. *1Pe 3:3*

APPARELLED

daughters that were virgins *2Sa 13:18*
a.
they which are gorgeously *a*. *Lu 7:25*

APPARENT

fasting be *a*. and seen (A) *M't 6:16*

APPARENTLY

speak mouth to mouth, even *Nu 12:8*
a.

APPEAL

a. for mercy (A) *Job 9:15*
I *a*. unto Caesar *Ac 25:11*
constrained to *a*. unto *Ac 28:19*
Caesar
we humbly make our *a*. (N) *1Co 4:13*
I *a*. to your reason (A)(B) *1Co 10:15*
a. to him as a father (N)(P) *1Ti 5:1*

APPEALED

a. to the king (S) *2Ki 8:5*
because you *a*. to me (N) *M't 8:32*

Hast thou a. unto Caesar | Ac 25:12
when Paul had a. to be | Ac 25:21
reserved
himself hath a. to Augustus | Ac 25:25
if he had not a. unto Caesar | Ac 26:32

APPEAR

let the dry land a.: and it was | Ge 1:9
so
made the white a. which | Ge 30:37
was in
none shall a. before me | Ex 23:15
empty
all thy males shall a. before | Ex 23:17
none shall a. before me | Ex 34:20
empty
menchildren a. before the | Ex 34:23
Lord
to a. before the Lord thy | Ex 34:24
God
to day the Lord will a. unto | Le 9:4
you
glory of the Lord shall a. unto | Le 9:6
you
if it a. still in the garment | Le 13:57
I will a. in the cloud upon | Le 16:2
males a. before the Lord thy | De 16:16
God
they shall not a. empty | De 16:16
Israel is come to a. before | De 31:11
the Lord
a. before the assembly for | Jos 20:6
trial (B)
angel of the Lord did no | J'g 13:21
more a
that he may a. before the | 1Sa 1:22
Lord
Did I plainly a. unto the | 1Sa 2:27
house of
night did God a. unto | 2Ch 1:7
Solomon
shall I come and a. before | Ps 42:2
God
behold the face of God | Ps 42:2
(A)(R)
let thy work a. to thy | Ps 90:16
servants
let work be revealed (A)(B) | Ps 90:16
let work be manifest (R) | Ps 90:16
he shall a. in his glory | Ps 102:16
The flowers a. on the earth | Ca 2:12
goats, that a. from mount | Ca 4:1
Gilead
of goats that a. from Gilead | Ca 6:5
whether the tender grape a. | Ca 7:12
When ye come to a. before | Isa 1:12
me
but he shall a. to your joy | Isa 65:5
that thy shame may a. | Jer 13:26
so that your sins do a. | Eze 21:24
they may a. unto men to fast | M't 6:16
fasting may be apparent and | M't 6:16
seen (A)
make looks unsightly | M't 6:16
(B)(N)
disfigure faces to be seen | M't 6:16
(E)(P)(R)
even so ye outwardly a. | M't 23:28
righteous
outwardly seem just, upright | M't 23:28
(A)(B)
look like honest men (N) | M't 23:28
look fine on the outside (P) | M't 23:28
then shall a. sign of Son of | M't 24:30
man in
Son of man shown in the | M't 24:30
sky (B)
ye are as graves which a. | Lu 11:44
not
like graves which are not | Lu 11:44
marked (A)
like unseen tombs (B)(R) | Lu 11:44
like unmarked graves | Lu 11:44
(N)(P)
thought kingdom of God | Lu 19:11
should a.
brought to light, shown forth | Lu 19:11
(A)
might dawn at any moment | Lu 19:11
(N)
of things in which I will a. | Ac 26:16
to thee
but sin, that it might a. sin, | Ro 7:13
working
sin be shown up as sin | Ro 7:13
(B)(E)(R)
sin become more sinful (N) | Ro 7:13
show the sinful nature of sin | Ro 7:13
(P)

we must all a. before | 2Co 5:10
judgment seat of Christ
must all be shown as we are | 2Co 5:10
(B)
be manifest before the | 2Co 5:10
judgment (E)
lives laid open before the | 2Co 5:10
tribunal (N)
stand without pretense | 2Co 5:10
before Christ (P)
a. as discredited (S) | 2Co 13:7
when Christ who is our life | Col 3:4
shall a.
shall make his appearance | Col 3:4
(B)
shall be manifested (E)(N) | Col 3:4
will show himself openly (P) | Co 3:4
that thy profiting may a. to | 1Ti 4:15
all
progress may be evdient to | 1Ti 4:15
many (A)
advance may be evident to | 1Ti 4:15
everyone (B)
progress may be manifest to | 1Ti 4:15
all (E)(R)
progress may be plain to all | 1Ti 4:15
(N)(P)
now to a. in the presence of | Heb 9:24
God for
shall he a. second time | Heb 9:28
without sin
show himself the second | Heb 9:28
time (B)
were not made of things | Heb 11:3
which do a.
not made of visible things | Heb 11:3
(A)(B)
visible came from the | Heb 11:3
invisible (N)
from principles which are | Heb 11:3
invisible (P)
where shall ungodly and | 1Pe 4:18
sinner a.
what will become of godless | 1Pe 4:18
(A)
what chance have impious | 1Pe 4:18
(B)(N)
what will be fate of wicked | 1Pe 4:18
(P)
when chief Shepherd shall a. | 1Pe 5:4
when the chief Shepherd is | 1Pe 5:4
revealed (A)(P)
with the appearing of the | 1Pe 5:4
Chief Shepherd (B)
Chief Shepherd be manifested | 1Pe 5:4
(E)(R)
when he shall a. | 1Jo 2:28; 3:2
when he is made visible (A) | 1Jo 2:28
doth not yet a. what we shall | 1Jo 3:2
be
it is not yet disclosed what we | 1Jo 3:2
(A)(N)
has not yet been shown (B) | 1Jo 3:2
not yet manifest what we | 1Jo 3:2
shall be (E)
don't know what we shall | 1Jo 3:2
become (P)
shame of thy nakedness do | Re 3:18
not a.
shame of nudity being seen | Re 3:18
(A)(B)(R)
shame of nakedness not be | Re 3:18
manifest (E)
hide shame of thy nakedness | Re 3:18
(N)(P)

APPEAR used of God

today the Lord will a. to you | Le 9:4; 9:6
I will a. in the cloud on | Le 16:2
mercy seat
Did I plainly a. to thy father | 1Sa 2:27
that night God did a. to | 2Ch 1:7
Solomon
build up Zion, he shall a. in | Ps 102:16
glory
He shall a. to your joy | Isa 66:5
those things in which I will | Ac 26:16
a.

APPEARANCE

on tabernacle as the a. of | Nu 9:15; 9:16
fire
of a fierce a. (B) | De 28:50
the a. of an angel (B) | J'g 13:6
man looketh on outward a. | 1Sa 16:7

a handsome a. (B)(R) | 1Sa 16:12
of what a. is he (B)(R) | 1Sa 28:14
my sad a. (B) | Ne 2:3
discern the a. | Job 4:16
(A)(B)(E)(R)
you change his a. (A) | Job 14:20
rebuke of thy a. (B) | Ps 80:16
a. like Lebanon (A)(R) | Ca 5:15
his whole a. (A)(B)(R) | Isa 52:14
this was their a. | Eze 1:5;
1:13-14, 16, 26-28; 8:2; 10:1, 9; 40:3; 41:31
like the a. of the chambers | Eze 42:11
according to the a. of the | Eze 43:3
vision
our a. and the a. of youths | Da 1:13
better in a. than (R) | Da 1:15
the a. of the fourth is like | Da 3:25
(B)(R)
as the a. of a man | Da 8:15
his face as the a. of the | Da 10:6
lightning
like the a. of a man, and he | Da 10:18
a. of them is as the a. of | Joe 2:4
horses
the a. like lightning | M't 28:3
(A)(B)(E)(P)(R)
his a. altered (S) | Lu 9:29
Judge not according to the a. | Joh 7:24
glory in a. and not in heart | 2Co 5:12
on things after the outward | 2Co 10:7
a.
Abstain from all a. of evil | 1Th 5:22
its a. is ruined (B) | Jas 1:11

APPEARANCES

And as for their a. they | Eze 10:10
four had
Chebar, their a. and | Eze 10:22
themselves

APPEARED

And the Lord a. unto Abram | Ge 12:7
And when, the Lord a. to | Ge 17:1
Abram
And the Lord a. unto him | Ge 18:1
And the Lord a. unto him | Ge 26:2
a. unto him the same night | Ge 26:24
God, that a. unto thee when | Ge 35:1
thou
because there God a. unto | Ge 35:7
him
And God a. unto Jacob again | Ge 35:9
God Almighty a. unto me at | Ge 48:3
Luz
And the angel of the Lord a. | Ex 3:2
The Lord God of your | Ex 3:16
fathers a.
The Lord hath not a. unto thee | Ex 4:1
God of Jacob, hath a. unto thee | Ex 4:5
And I a. unto Abraham | Ex 6:3
strength when the morning | Ex 14:27
a.
glory of the Lord a. in the | Ex 16:10
cloud
and the glory of the Lord a. | Le 9:23
the glory of the Lord a. in the | Nu 14:10
Lord a. unto all the | Nu 16:19
congregation
and the glory of the Lord a. | Nu 16:42
the glory of the Lord a. unto | Nu 20:6
them
And the Lord a. in the | De 31:15
tabernacle
the angel of the Lord a. unto | J'g 6:12
him
a. unto the woman, and said | J'g 13:3
unto
the man hath a. unto me | J'g 13:10
the Lord a. again in Shiloh | 1Sa 3:21
And the channels of the sea | 2Sa 22:16
a.
In Gibeon the Lord a. to | 1Ki 3:5
Solomon
the Lord a. to Solomon the | 1Ki 9:2
second
as he had a. unto him at | 1Ki 9:2
Gibeon
Lord God of Israel, which | 1Ki 11:9
had a.
behold, there a. a chariot of | 2Ki 2:11
fire
where the Lord a. unto David | 2Ch 3:1
the Lord a. to Solomon by | 2Ch 7:12
night

of the morning till the stars *a.*   *Ne 4:21*
The Lord hath *a.* of old   *Jer 31:3*
there *a.* over them as it were *a.*   *Eze 10:1*
And there *a.* in the cherubims   *Eze 10:8*
and she *a.* in her height   *Eze 19:11*
countenances *a.* fairer and fatter   *Da 1:15*
a. unto me, after that which *a.*   *Da 8:1*
behold, the angel of the Lord *a.*   *M't 1:20*
what time the star *a.*   *M't 2:7*
a. a preacher in the wilderness (N)   *M't 3:11*
then *a.* the tares also   *M't 13:26*
a. unto them Moses and Elias   *M't 17:3*
into the holy city, and *a.* unto   *M't 27:53*
a. unto them Elias with Moses   *M'k 9:4*
he *a.* first to Mary Magdalene   *M'k 16:9*
a. in another form unto two of   *M'k 16:12*
Afterward he *a.* unto the eleven   *M'k 16:14*
there *a.* unto him an angel   *Lu 1:11*
of some, that Elias had *a.*   *Lu 9:8*
Who *a.* in glory, and spake of his   *Lu 9:31*
And there *a.* an angel unto him   *M'k 22:43*
and hath *a.* to Simon   *M'k 24:34*
there *a.* unto them cloven tongues   *Ac 2:3*
God of glory *a.* unto our father   *Ac 7:2*
there *a.* to him in the wilderness   *Ac 7:30*
angel which *a.* to him in the bush   *Ac 7:35*
Jesus, that *a.* unto thee in the way   *Ac 9:17*
a vision *a.* to Paul in the night   *Ac 16:9*
I *a.* unto thee for this purpose   *Ac 26:16*
nor stars in many days *a.*   *Ac 27:20*
salvation hath *a.* to all men   *Tit 2:11*
of God our Saviour toward man *a.*   *Tit 3:4*
hath he *a.* to put away sin by   *Heb 9:26*
Christ *a.* to do away with (N)(R)   *1Jo 3:5*
a. to break up works of (B)(N)(R)   *1Jo 3:8*
a. a great wonder in heaven   *Re 12:1*
a. another wonder in heaven   *Re 12:3*

APPEARETH

when raw flesh *a.* in him   *Le 13:14*
a. in the skin of the flesh   *Le 13:43*
into thy hands, as *a.* this day   *De 2:30*
every one of them in Zion *a.*   *Ps 84:7*
The hay *a.* and the tender grass   *Pr 27:25*
evil *a.* out of the north   *Jer 6:1*
who shall stand when he *a.*   *Mal 3:2*
angel of the Lord *a.* to Joseph in   *M't 2:13*
a. in a dream to Joseph in Egypt   *M't 2:19*
a vapour, that *a.* for a little time   *Jas 4:14*

APPEARING

the *a.* of our Lord Jesus Christ   *1Ti 6:14*
the *a.* of our Saviour Jesus Christ   *2Ti 1:10*
at his *a.* and his kingdom   *2Ti 4:1*
by his coming and his kingdom (A)   *2Ti 4:1*
at his coming appearance (N)(R)   *2Ti 4:1*
to all them that love his *a.*   *2Ti 4:8*
looking for glorious *a.* of God   *Tit 2:13*
glory at the *a.* of Jesus Christ   *1Pe 1:7*
when Christ is revealed (A)(B)(N)   *1Pe 1:7*
at revelation of Jesus (E)(R)   *1Pe 1:7*
when Jesus reveals himself (P)   *1Pe 1:7*

APPEASE

will *a.* him with the present   *Ge 32:20*
I will *a.* myself (A)   *Isa 1:24*

APPEASED

wrath of king Ahasuerus was *a.*   *Es 2:1*
the townclerk had *a.* the people   *Ac 19:35*

APPEASETH

he that is slow to anger *a.* strife   *Pr 15:18*

APPERTAIN

with all that *a.* unto them   *Nu 16:30*
with all their possessions (B)   *Nu 16:30*
with all that belongs to them (R)   *Nu 16:30*
for to thee doth it *a.*   *Jer 10:7*
for toward thee it is fitting (B)   *Jer 10:7*
for this is to thy due (R)   *Jer 10:7*

APPERTAINED

all the men that *a.* to Korah   *Nu 16:32; 16:33*
all their households, goods (B)(R)   *Nu 16:32*
palace which *a.* to the house   *Ne 2:8*

APPERTAINETH

give it to him to whom it *a.*   *Le 6:5*
giving it to whom it belongs (B)(R)   *Le 6:5*
It *a.* not unto thee, Uzziah   *2Ch 26:18*
It is not for you, Uzziah (B)(R)   *2Ch 26:18*

APPETITE

or fill the *a.* of the young lions   *Job 38:39*
satisfy his own *a.* (R)   *Pr 6:30; Pr 13:25; Job 6:7*
if thou be a man given to *a.*   *Pr 23:2*
the *a.* is not filled   *Ec 6:7*
he is faint, and his soul hath *a.*   *Isa 29:8*
whose god is their *a.* (N)(P)(S)   *Ph'p 3:19*

APPETITES

satisfying bodily *a.* (N)   *Ro 13:14*
serve own *a.* (A)(B)(N)(R)   *Ro 16:18*

APPETIZING

I ate no *a.* food (B)   *Da 10:3*

APPHIA

to our beloved *A.* and Archippus   *Ph'm 2*

APPII

to meet us as far as *A.* forum   *Ac 28:15*

APPLE

he kept him as the *a.* of his eye   *De 32:10*
Keep me as the *a.* of the eye   *Ps 17:8*
my law as the *a.* of thine eye   *Pr 7:2*
as the *a.* tree among the trees   *Ca 2:3*
I raised thee up under the *a.* tree   *Ca 8:5*
not the *a.* of thine eye cease   *La 2:18*
palm tree also, and the *a.* tree   *Joe 1:12*
toucheth the *a.* of his eye   *Zec 2:8*

APPLES

May *a.* (B)   *Ge 30:14; 30:15-16*
A word fitly spoken is like *a.*   *Pr 25:11*
flagons, comfort me with *a.*   *Ca 2:5*
the smell of thy nose like *a.*   *Ca 7:8*

APPLIED

I *a.* mine heart to know, and   *Ec 7:25*
and *a.* my heart unto every work   *Ec 8:9*
I *a.* mine heart to know wisdom   *Ec 8:16*

APPLY

may *a.* our hearts unto wisdom   *Ps 90:12*
a. thine heart to understanding   *Pr 2:2*
a. thine heart unto my   *Pr 22:17*
A. thine heart unto instruction   *Pr 23:12*
A. your mind to things above (B)   *Col 3:2*

APPOINT

a. me my wages   *Ge 30:28*
State your salary (A)   *Ge 30:28*
name me my wages (B)(R)   *Ge 30:28*
let Pharaoh *a.* officers over the land   *Ge 41:34*
I will *a.* over you terror, consumption   *Le 26:16*
I will visit you with (B)   *Le 26:16*
a. every one to service   *Nu 4:19*
assign each individual his service (B)   *Nu 4:19*
a. form among you (S)   *Jos 18:4*
to *a.* me ruler over the people   *2Sa 6:21*
chose me in preference (B)(E)(R)   *2Sa 6:21*
I will *a.* a place for my people   *2Sa 7:10*
establish a place for Israel (B)   *2Sa 7:10*
I will *a.* a place (A)(E)(R)   *1Ch 17:9*
wouldst *a.* me a set time   *Job 14:13*
set a definite time (A)(B)   *Job 14:13*
Salvation will God *a.* for walls   *Isa 26:1*
sets up salvation as walls (A)(B)(R)   *Isa 26:1*
to *a.* them that mourn in Zion   *Isa 61:3*
grant consolation and joy to (A)   *Isa 61:3*
to settle mourners in Zion (B)   *Isa 61:3*
grant to those who mourn (R)   *Isa 61:3*
I will *a.* over them four kinds   *Jer 15:3*
who will *a.* me the time   *Jer 49:19; 50:44*
will the kingdoms *a.* a captain   *Jer 51:27*
a. thee two ways   *Eze 21:19; 21:20*
mark out two ways (A)(R)   *Eze 21:19*
trace two ways (B)   *Eze 21:19*
they shall *a.* themselves one head   *Ho 1:11*
choose one head (B)   *Ho 1:11*
a. him his portion with hypocrites   *M't 24:51*
put him with pretenders (A)   *M't 24:51*
put him with the hypocrites (B)(R)   *M't 24:51*
find his place among the (N)   *M't 24:51*
send him off to share the penalty (P)   *M't 24:51*
a. him his portion with unbelievers   *Lu 12:46*
assign his lot with unfaithful (A)   *Lu 12:46*
make him share the fate of (B)(P)   *Lu 12:46*
find his place with the (N)   *Lu 12:46*
put him with the unfaithful (R)   *Lu 12:46*
I *a.* you a kingdom, as my Father   *Lu 22:29*
I confer on you and decree (A)   *Lu 22:29*
so I assign to you (B)   *Lu 22:29*
I vest in you the kingship (N)   *Lu 22:29*
I give you the right (P)   *Lu 22:29*
seven men we may *a.* over this business   *Ac 6:3*
may assign to look after this (A)   *Ac 6:3*
we will put in charge of (P)   *Ac 6:3*
a. elder in every city (A)(B)(E)(P)(R)   *Tit 1:5*

APPOINTED

hath a. me another seed	Ge 4:25
thou hast a. for my servant	Ge 24:14
thou hast designated for (B)	Ge 24:14
Keep the passover in a.	Nu 9:2;
seasons	9:3, 7
these were cities a. for refuge	Jos 20:9
there was an a. sign between	J'g 20:38
Israel	
agreed upon a signal (B)	J'g 20:38
a. Moses and Aaron	1Sa 12:1
(A)(B)(E)(R)	
Jeroboam a. a feast	1Ki 12:32
(A)(R)	
a. to burn incense (B)	2Ki 23:5
the seer had a. (B)	1Ch 9:22
as the king a. (S)	2Ch 10:12
he a. his own priests	2Ch 11:15
(A)(E)(R)(S)	
a. you priests (S)	2Ch 13:9
Esther had a. them (B)	Es 9:3
wearisome nights are a. me	Job 7:3
nights of trouble apportioned	Job 7:3
me (B)(R)	
hast a. his bounds that he	Job 14:5
the heritage a. unto him by	Job 20:29
God	
to the house a. for all living	Job 30:23
who a. God his way (A)	Job 36:23
given us like sheep a. for	Ps 44:11
meat	
intended for mutton (A)	Ps 44:11
surrendered us as	Ps 44:11
slaughter-sheep (B)	
made us like sheep for	Ps 44:11
slaughter (R)	
a. a law in Israel, which he	Ps 78:5
preserve those that are a. to	Ps 79:11
die	
to loose those a. to death	Ps 102:20
who are destined to die (B)	Ps 102:20
who are doomed to die (R)	Ps 102:20
He a. the moon for seasons	Ps 104:19
will come home at the day a.	Pr 7:20
when he a. the foundations of	Pr 8:29
all such as are a. to	Pr 31:8
destruction	
new moons and your a.	Isa 1:14
feasts	
shall be alone in his a.	Isa 14:31
times	
wheat and the a. barley	Isa 28:25
since I a. the ancient people	Isa 44:7
established people of	Isa 44:7
antiquity (A)(E)	
directed the ancient people	Isa 44:7
(B)	
a. you a prophet (A)(E)(R)	Jer 1:5
reserveth unto us the a.	Jer 5:24
weeks	
the stork knoweth her a.	Jer 8:7
times	
if I have not a. the	Jer 33:25
ordinances	
he hath passed the time a.	Jer 46:17
there hath he a. it	Jer 47:7
have a. thee each day for a	Eze 4:6
year	
have a. my land into their	Eze 36:5
the a. feasts (B)(E)(R)	Eze 36:38;
	46:9, 11
he shall burn it in the a.	Eze 43:21
place	
all a. feasts (A)(B)(E)(R)	Eze 45:17
And the king a. them a daily	Da 1:5
who hath a. your meat and	Da 1:10
a. to destroy (A)(B)(E)(R)	Da 2:24
at the time a. the end shall	Da 8:19
be	
but the time a. was long	Da 10:1
the end shall be at the time	Da 11:27
a.	
At the time a. he shall	Da 11:29
return	
it is yet for a time a.	Da 11:35
the a. feast (R)	Ho 12:9
the rod, and who hath a. it	Mic 6:9
the vision is yet for an a.	Hab 2:3
time	
disciples did as Jesus had a.	M't 26:19
them	
as the Lord a. me	M't 27:10
as the Lord directed	M't 27:10
(A)(B)(N)(R)	
he a. the twelve to	M'k 3:14
(A)(E)(N)(P)(R)(S)	
exact no more than which is	Lu 3:13
a. you	

the Lord a. other seventy	Lu 10:1
Lord commissioned seventy	Lu 10:1
others (B)(P)	
to you a kingdom, as my	Lu 22:29
Father a. me	
assigned to me a kingdom	Lu 22:29
(B)	
kingship my Father vested in	Lu 22:29
me (N)	
Father given to me my	Lu 22:28
kingdom (P)	
I have a. you	Joh 15:16
(A)(B)(E)(N)(P)(R)	
they a. two, Joseph and	Ac 1:23
Matthias	
proposed (nominated) two	Ac 1:23
men (A)	
they put up two names (B)	Ac 1:23
they put forward two	Ac 1:23
(E)(N)(P)(R)	
Christ who has been a.	Ac 3:20
(E)(N)(R)	
a. by God a judge (P)	Ac 10:42
a. for eternal life (N)	Ac 13:48
a. them elders	Ac 14:23
(E)(N)(P)(R)	
they a. Paul (E)(R)	Ac 15:2
He hath a. a day he will	Ac 17:31
judge world	
He has fixed a day	Ac 17:31
(A)(B)(N)(P)(R)	
destined and a. a man	Ac 17:31
(A)(P)(R)	
a. and foreknown (A)(P)	Ro 11:2
resist what God has a.	Ro 13:2
(A)(R)	
God set us apostles last, a. to	1Co 4:9
death	
sentenced to death (A)(R)	1Co 4:9
as men doomed to death (E)	1Co 4:9
condemned to death in the	1Co 4:9
arena (N)	
like men who are to die in	1Co 4:9
the arena (P)	
you know that we are a.	1Th 3:3
thereto	
God hath not a. us to wrath	1Th 5:9
not destined for	1Th 5:9
indignation (B)(N)	
did not choose us to	1Th 5:9
condemn us (P)	
destined us for wrath (R)	1Th 5:9
I was a. a preacher	1Ti 2:7;
(A)(B)(E)(N)(P)(R)	Heb 5:1; 8:3
Whereunto I am a. a	2Ti 1:11
preacher	
as I had a. thee	Tit 1:5
he hath a. heir of all things	Heb 1:2
faithful to him that a. him	Heb 3:2
as it is a. unto men once to	Heb 9:27
die	
whereunto also they were a.	1Pe 2:8

APPOINTED TIME

at the time a. will I return	Ge 18:14
eat unleavened bread in time	Ex 23:15
a.	
Jonathan went into field at	1Sa 20:35
time a.	
tarried longer than the set	2Sa 20:5
time a.	
according to their a. time	Es 9:27
is there not an a. time to men	Job 7:1
all the days of my a. time	Job 14:14
blow up the trumpet in the	Ps 81:3
time a.	
he hath passed the a. time	Jer 46:17
for at the time a. the end	Da 8:19
shall be	
the time a. was long	Da 10:1
for yet the end shall be at	Da 11:27
the time a.	
At the time a. shall return	Da 11:29
time of end, it is yet for	Da 11:35
time a.	
vision is yet for an a. time	Hab 2:3
under tutors, until time a.	Ga 4:2

APPOINTED TIMES

none shall be alone in his a.	Isa 14:31
stork in heaven knoweth her	Jer 8:7
a times	
God determined before times	Ac 17:26
a.	

APPOINTETH

he a. the number of stars	Ps 147:4
(S)	
he a. over it whomsoever he	Da 5:21
will	

APPOINTMENT

At the a. of Aaron and his	Nu 4:27
sons	
by the a. of Absalom this	2Sa 13:32
hath	
according to the a. of the	Ezr 6:9
priests	
for they had made an a.	Job 2:11
together	
by their a. they stand (R)	Ps 119:91
by God's a. (B)	Ro 13:1
resisting God's a. (B)	Ro 13:2
by divine a. (B)	Col 1:25

APPORTION

a. the contributions	2Ch 31:14
(A)(B)(R)	

APPORTIONED

God has a. a measure	2Co 10:13
(A)(R)	

APPORTIONS

a. each person (A)(R)	1Co 12:11

APPRAISE

priest a. it (A)	Le 27:14

APPRECIATION

without a. of the body (B)	1Co 11:29

APPREHEND

desirous to a. me	2Co 11:32
to arrest me	2Co 11:32
(A)(B)(N)(P)	
in order to take me (E)	2Co 11:32
to seize me (R)	2Co 11:32
a. and grasp with (A)(E)	Eph 3:18

APPREHENDED

when he had a. him	Ac 12:4
for which also I am a. of	Ph'p 3:12
Christ	
I count not myself to have	Ph'p 3:13
a.	
to have captured and made	Ph'p 3:13
my own (A)	
to have laid hold (B)(E)	Ph'p 3:13
got hold of it yet (N)	Ph'p 3:13
to have fully grasped it even	Ph'p 3:13
now (P)	
made it my own (R)	Ph'p 3:13

APPROACH

None of you shall a. to any	Le 18:6
thou shalt not a. to his wife	Le 18:14
thou shalt not a. unto a	Le 18:19
woman	
if a woman a. unto any beast	Le 20:16
let him not a. to offer the	Le 21:17
bread	
hath a. blemish, he shall not	Le 21:18
a.	
they a. unto the most holy	Nu 4:19
things	
that the priest shall a. and	De 20:2
speak	
Israel, ye a. this day unto	De 20:3
battle	
thy days a. that thou must die	De 31:14
people that are with me will	Jos 8:5
a.	
make his sword to a. unto	Job 40:19
him	
thou choosest and causest to a.	Ps 65:4
and he shall a. unto me	Jer 30:21
engaged his heart to a. unto	Jer 30:21
me	
the priests that a. unto the	Eze 42:13
Lord	
shall a. to those things	Eze 42:14
which are	

the Levites, which *a.* unto   *Eze 43:19*
me
a. this Christ (P)   *Ac 8:29*
in the light which no man   *1Ti 6:16*
can *a.*

APPROACHABLE

peace-loving, gentle, *a.* (P)   *Jas 3:17*

APPROACHED

Wherefore *a.* ye so nigh   *2Sa 11:20*
unto the
and the king *a.* to the altar   *2Ki 16:12*

APPROACHETH

where no thief *a.* neither   *Lu 12:33*
moth

APPROACHING

they take delight in *a.* to   *Isa 58:2*
God
the more, as ye see the day   *Heb 10:25*
a.

APPROPRIATE

stir up to *a.* (A)   *Ro 11:4*
received *a.* a penalty (A)(P)   *Heb 2:2*

APPROVE

Lord did not *a.* of Cain (B)   *Ge 4:5*
their posterity *a.* their   *Ps 49:13*
sayings
whosoever ye shall *a.*   *1Co 16:3*
by, letters
may *a.* things that are   *Ph'p 1:10*
excellent

APPROVED

the Lord *a.* of Abel (B)   *Ge 4:4*
a man *a.* of God among you   *Ac 2:22*
acceptable to God, and *a.* of   *Ro 14:18*
men
Salute Apelles *a.* in Christ   *Ro 16:10*
which, *a.* may be made   *1Co 11:19*
manifest
ye have *a.* yourselves to be   *2Co 7:11*
clear
he that commendeth   *2Co 10:18*
himself is *a.*
not that we should appear *a.*   *2Co 13:7*
a. by God   *1Th 2:4*
(A)(B)(E)(N)(R)
Study to shew thyself *a.* unto   *2Ti 2:15*
God

APPROVEDNESS

stedfastness, *a.,* hope (E)   *Ro 5:4*

APPROVEST

a. the things that are more   *Ro 2:18*

APPROVETH

in his cause, the Lord *a.* not   *La 3:36*

APPROVING

a. ourselves as the ministers   *2Co 6:4*

APRONS

together, and made themselves *a.*   *Ge 3:7*
handkerchiefs or *a.* and the   *Ac 19:12*

APT

all that were strong and *a.*   *2Ki 24:16*
for war
that were *a.* to the war and   *1Ch 7:40*
given to hospitality, *a.* to   *1Ti 3:2*
teach
unto all men, *a.* to teach,   *2Ti 2:24*
patient

AQUEDUCT

stood at the *a.* (B)   *2Ki 18:17;*
     2Ki 20:20; Isa 7:3

AQUILA

a certain Jew named *A.* born   *Ac 18:2*
in
with him Priscilla and *A.*   *Ac 18:18*
when *A.* and Priscilla had   *Ac 18:26*
heard
Greet Priscilla and *A.* my   *Ro 16:3*
helpers
A. and Priscilla salute you   *1Co 16:19*
much
Salute Prisca and *A.*   *2Ti 4:19*

AR

goeth down to the dwelling   *Nu 21:15*
of *A.*
it hath consumed *A.* of   *Nu 21:28*
Moab.
I have given *A.* unto the   *De 2:9*
children
Thou art to pass over   *De 2:18*
through *A.*
the Moabites which dwell in   *De 2:29*
A.
in the night *A.* of Moab is   *Isa 15:1*
laid

ARA

Jephunneh, and Pispah, and   *1Ch 7:38*
A.

ARAH

A. and Dumah, and Eshean   *Jos 15:52*

ARABAH

the *A.* (S)   *De 1:1;*
1:7; 2:8; 3:17; 4:49; 11:30; Jos 3:16;
8:14; 11:2, 16; 12:1, 3, 8; 1Sa 23:24;
2Sa 2:29; 4:7; 2Ki 14:25; 25:4; Jer 17:26;
     39:4; 52:7; Zec 14:10
living in the *A.*   *De 11:30*
(B)(E)(R)(S)
over against *A.* northward   *Jos 18:18*
and went down unto *A.*   *Jos 18:18*
go down into the *A.* (S)   *Eze 47:8*
the brook of the *A.* (B)(S)   *Am 6:14*

ARABIA

of all the kings of *A.* and   *1Ki 10:15*
all the kings of *A.* and   *2Ch 9:14*
governors
In the forest in *A.* shall ye   *Isa 21:13*
lodge
And all the kings of *A.* and   *Jer 25:24*
A. and all the princes of   *Eze 27:21*
Kedar
I went into *A.* and returned   *Ga 1:17*
this Agar is mount Sinai in   *Ga 4:25*
A.

ARABIAN

and Geshem the *A.* heard it   *Ne 2:19*
Geshem the *A.* and the rest of   *Ne 6:1*
neither shall the *A.* pitch   *Isa 13:20*
tent
thou sat for them, as the *A.*   *Jer 3:2*
in the

ARABIANS

and the *A.* brought him   *2Ch 17:11*
flocks
of the Philistines, and of   *2Ch 21:16*
the *A.*
band of men that came with   *2Ch 22:1*
the *A.*
the *A.* that dwelt in   *2Ch 26:7*
Gur-baal
and the *A.* and the Ammonites   *Ne 4:7*
Cretes and *A.* we do hear   *Ac 2:11*
them

ARAD

And when king *A.* the   *Nu 21:1*
Canaanite
A. the Canaanite, which   *Nu 33:40*
dwelt in
Hormah, one; the king of   *Jos 12:14*
A. one
which lieth in the south of *A.*   *J'g 1:16*
And Zebadiah, and *A.* and   *1Ch 8:15*
Ader

ARAH

the sons of Ulla; *A.* and   *1Ch 7:39*
Haniel
A. seven hundred seventy and   *Ezr 2:5*
five
in law of Shechaniah son of   *Ne 6:18*
A.
the children of *A.* six   *Ne 7:10*
hundred

ARAM

and Arphaxad, and Lud,   *Ge 10:22*
and *A.*
the children of *A.:* Uz, and   *Ge 10:23*
Hul
and Kemuel the father of *A.*   *Ge 22:21*
of Moab that brought me   *Nu 23:7*
from *A.*
Arphaxad, and Lud, and *A.*   *1Ch 1:17*
and Uz
he took Geshur, and *A.* with   *1Ch 2:23*
the
Rohgah, Jehubbah, and *A.*   *1Ch 7:34*
the field of *A.* (S)   *Ho 12:12*
Esrom begat *A.*   *M't 1:3*
A. begat Aminadab   *M't 1:4*
which was the son of *A.*   *Lu 3:33*

ARAMAIC

speak in *A.* (A)(B)(P)(S)   *2Ki 18:26;*
     Isa 36:11
the *A.* tongue (S)   *Ezr 4:7*
to the king in *A.* (S)   *Da 2:4*

ARAMITESS

his concubine the *A.* bare   *1Ch 7:14*
Machir

ARAM-NAHARAIM

when he strove with *A.*   *Ps 60 title*

ARAM-ZOBAH

and with *A.*   *Ps 60 title*

ARAN

of Dishan are these; Uz and   *Ge 36:28*
A.
The sons of Dishan; Uz   *1Ch 1:42*
and *A.*

ARARAT

upon the mountains of *A.*   *Ge 8:4*
the land of *A.* (S)   *2Ki 19:37; Isa 37:38*
against her the kingdoms of   *Jer 51:27*
A.

ARAUNAH

threshing place of *A.* the   *2Sa 24:16;*
Jehusite   *2Sa 24:18, 20-24*

ARBA

which *A.* was a great man   *Jos 14:15*
among
even the city of *A.* the   *Jos 15:13*
father of
they gave them the city of   *Jos 21:11*
A.

ARBAH

the city of *A.* which is   *Ge 35:27*
Hebron.

ARBATHITE

Abi-albon the *A.* Azmaveth   *2Sa 23:31*
brooks of Gaash, Abiel the   *1Ch 11:32*
A.

ARBITE

the Carmelite, Paarai the *A.*   *2Sa 23:35*

ARBITRATE

a. between me and my (B)   *Isa 5:3*
judge or *a.* (N)   *Lu 12:14*

ARBITRATOR

judge or *a.* (P)   *Lu 12:14*

ARCHANGEL

with the voice of the *a.*   *1Th 4:16*
Michael the *a.* when   *Jude 9*
contending

ARCHELAUS

heard that *A.* did reign in   *M't 2:22*
Judaea

ARCHER

he grew, and became an *a.*   *Ge 21:20*
let the *a.* bend his bow   *Jer 51:3*

ARCHERS

a. have sorely grieved him   *Ge 49:23*
are delivered from the noise   *J'g 5:11*
of *a.*
the *a.* hit him; and he   *1Sa 31:3*
sore wounded of the *a.*   *1Sa 31:3*
mighty men of valour, *a.*   *1Ch 8:40*
the *a.* hit him   *1Ch 10:3*
he was wounded of the *a.*   *1Ch 10:3*
the *a.* shot at king Josiah   *2Ch 35:23*
His *a.* compass me round   *Job 16:13*
about
the residue of the number   *Isa 21:17*
of *a.*
they are bound by the *a.*   *Isa 22:3*
Call together the *a.* against   *Jer 50:29*

ARCHES

the *a.* (colonades)   *Eze 40:16; 40:21-22,*
     24-26, 29-31, 33-34, 36
pool with five *a.* (P)   *Joh 5:2*

ARCHEVITES

the Apharsites, the *A.,* the   *Ezr 4:9*

ARCHI

along unto the borders of *A.*   *Jos 16:2*

ARCHIPPUS

say to *A.,* Take heed to the   *Col 4:17*
A. our fellowsoldier   *Ph'm 2*

ARCHITE

Hushai the *A.* came to   *2Sa 15:32*
meet him
Hushai the *A.* David's   *2Sa 16:16*
friend
Call now Hushai the *A.* also   *2Sa 17:5*
counsel of Hushai the *A.* is   *2Sa 17:14*
better
Hushai the *A.* was the   *1Ch 27:33*
king's

ARCHITECT

a skilled *a.* (B)   *1Co 3:10*

ARCHIVES

search in the *a.*   *Ezr 6:1*
(S)

ARCTURUS

maketh *A.,* Orion, and   *Job 9:9*
Pleiades
thou guide *A.* with his sons   *Job 38:32*

ARD

Muppim, and Huppim,   *Ge 46:21*
and *A.*
sons of Bela were *A.* and   *Nu 26:40*
Naaman
of *A.* the family of the   *Nu 26:40*
Ardites

ARDENT

exciting his *a.* anger (B)   *1Ki 14:22*

ARDITES

of Ard, the family of the *A.*   *Nu 26:40*

ARDON

Jesher, and Shobab, and *A.*   *1Ch 2:18*

ARDOUR

keep in *a.* of spirit (N)   *Ro 12:11*

ARE

for the fifty righteous that *a.*   *Ge 18:24*
therein
a. we not counted of him   *Ge 31:15*
strangers
all these things *a.* against us   *Ge 42:36*
as ye *a.* so shall the stranger   *Nu 15:15*
be
there they *a.* to this day   *1Ki 8:8*
may go and say to thee,   *Job 38:35*
here we *a.*
a. at their wit's end   *Ps 107:27*
a. ye not much better than   *M't 6:26*
they
a. as the angels of God in   *M't 22:30*
heaven
a. not his sisters here with us   *M'k 6:3*
I am not as other men *a.*   *Lu 18:11*
tempted like as we *a.* yet   *Heb 4:15*
without sin
write the things which *a.*   *Re 1:19*
for thy pleasure they *a.* and   *Re 4:11*
created heaven and all things   *Re 10:6*
therein *a.*

ARELI

Ezbon, Eri, and   *Ge 46:16*
Arodi, and *A.*
of *A.* the family of the   *Nu 26:17*
Arelites

ARELITES

of Areli, the family of the   *Nu 26:17*
A.

AREOPAGITE

which was Dionysius, the *A.*   *Ac 17:34*

AREOPAGUS

took him, and brought him   *Ac 17:19*
unto *A.*

ARETAS

under *A.* the king kept the   *2Co 11:32*
city

ARGOB

all the region of *A.* the   *De 3:4*
kingdom
the region of *A.* with all   *De 3:13*
Bashan
Manasseh took all the   *De 3:14*
country of *A.*
him also pertained the region   *1Ki 4:13*
of *A.*
with *A.* and Arieh, and   *2Ki 15:25*

ARGUE

a. my case with God (B)(R)   *Job 13:3*
who will *a.* (S)   *Job 13:19*
a. with unprofitable talk (R)   *Job 15:3*
a. your cause (A)(B)(R)   *Ps 25:9*
let us *a.* together (A)   *Isa 43:26*
a. with thee about justice   *Jer 12:1*
(B)
talk and *a.* with (P)   *Ac 9:29*
a. about uprightness (A)   *Ac 24:25*

ARGUED

a. among themselves (B)   *M't 16:7;*
     M't 21:15; M'k 11:31; Lu 20:5, 14
a. among themselves   *M't 21:25*
(N)(P)(R)
a. in his mind (B)   *M'k 2:6*
a. with one another (B)   *M'k 9:34*
a. with themselves (A)   *Lu 20:14*
a. from the scriptures   *Ac 17:2*
(N)(P)(R)
reasoned and *a.* with   *Ac 17:17*
(A)(N)(R)
a. about justice (R)   *Ac 24:25*
a. about the body of Moses   *Jude 9*
(A)(B)

ARGUING

a. with Moses (B)   *Nu 20:3*
what doth your *a.* reprove   *Job 6:25*
a. with pointless talk (B)   *Job 15:3*
speaking boldly *a.* (A)(R)   *Ac 19:8*
a. and disputing (A)   *Ac 28:29*
a. about on the way (N)(P)   *M'k 9:34*
without *a.* (P)   *Ph'p 2:14*

ARGUMENT

why all the *a.* (P)   *M't 16:8*
an *a.* arose (N)(R)   *Lu 9:46*
using *a.* and persuasion   *Ac 19:8*
(N)(P)

ARGUMENTATIONS

became factuous in *a.* (P)   *Ro 1:21*

ARGUMENTATIVE

still *a.* (P)   *Tit 2:10*

ARGUMENTS

fill may mouth with *a.*   *Job 23:4*
plausible, attractive *a.* (P)   *Ro 16:18*
a. of the wise are futile (N)   *1Co 3:20*
refute *a.* theories (A)   *2Co 10:5*
a., jealousy (P)   *2Co 12:20*
groundless *a.* (A)(P)(N)   *Eph 5:6*
steer clear of stupid *a.* (P)   *Tit 3:9*

ARIDAI

Parmashta, and Arisai, and *A.*   *Es 9:9*

ARIDATHA

Poratha, and Adalia, and *A.*   *Es 9:8*

ARIEH

with Argob and *A.* and   *2Ki 15:25*
with him

ARIEL

the two sons of *A.* (S)   *2Sa 23:20*
Then sent I for Eliezer, for   *Ezr 8:16*
A.
Woe to *A.* to *A.,* the city   *Isa 29:1*
where
Yet I will distress *A.* and there   *Isa 29:2*
it shall be unto me as *A.*   *Isa 29:2*
the nations that fight against   *Isa 29:7*
A.

ARIGHT

that ordereth his   *Ps 50:23*
conversation *a.*
that set not their heart *a.*   *Ps 78:8*
of the wise useth knowledge   *Pr 15:2*
a.
the cup, when it moveth   *Pr 23:31*
itself *a.*
his God teaches him *a.* (R)   *Isa 28:26*
heard, but they spake not *a.*   *Jer 8:6*

ARIMATHAEA

there came a rich man of   *M't 27:57*
A.
Joseph of *A.* an honourable   *M'k 15:43*
A. a city of the Jews   *Lu 23:51*
Joseph of *A.* being a   *Joh 19:38*
disciple of

ARIOCH

A. king of Ellasar,   *Ge 14:1*
Chedorlaomer
and *A.* king of Ellasar; four   *Ge 14:9*
kings
A. the captain of the king's   *Da 2:14*
guard
He answered and said to *A.*   *Da 2:15*
A. made the thing known to   *Da 2:15*
Daniel
Therefore Daniel went in   *Da 2:24*
unto *A.*
Then *A.* brought in Daniel   *Da 2:25*
before

ARISAI

Parmashta, and *A.* and Aridai   *Es 9:9*

ARISE

A. walk through the land	Ge 13:17
A. take thy wife, and thy two	Ge 19:15
A. lift up the lad, and hold him in	Ge 21:18
A. go up to Beth-el, and dwell	Ge 35:1
And let us a. and go up to Beth-el	Ge 35:3
And there shall a. after them	Ge 41:30
with me, and we will a. and go	Ge 43:8
Take also your brother, and a.	Ge 43:13
A. get thee down quickly from	De 9:12
A. take thy journey before	De 10:11
If there a. among you a prophet	De 13:1
there a. a matter too hard for thee	De 17:8
then shalt thou a. and get thee	De 17:8
therefore a. go over this Jordan	Jos 1:2
and a. go up to Ai: see, I have	Jos 8:1
a. Barak, and lead thy captivity	J'g 5:12
and a. go seek the asses	1Sa 9:3
A. anoint him: for this is he	1Sa 16:12
A. go down to Keilah	1Sa 23:4
Let the young men now a.	2Sa 2:14
A. go up to meet the messengers	2Ki 1:3
A. and go thou and thine	2Ki 8:1
A. up from among his brethren	2Ki 9:2
A. therefore, and be doing	1Ch 22:16
a. therefore, and build ye the	1Ch 22:19
Now therefore a. O Lord God	2Ch 6:41
A.; for this matter belongeth unto	Ezr 10:4
we his servants will a. and build	Ne 2:20
a. too much contempt and wrath	Es 1:18
and deliverance a. to the Jews	Es 4:14
When shall I a. and the night	Job 7:4
upon whom doth not his light a.	Job 25:3
A. O Lord; save me, O my God	Ps 3:7
A. O Lord, in thine anger	Ps 7:6
A. O Lord; let not man prevail	Ps 9:19
A. O Lord; O God, lift up thine	Ps 10:12
now will I a. saith the Lord	Ps 12:5
A. O Lord, disappoint him	Ps 17:13
why sleepest thou, O Lord? a.	Ps 44:23
A. for our help, and redeem us	Ps 44:26
Let God a. let his enemies be	Ps 68:1
A. O God, a. plead thine own cause	Ps 74:22
who should a. and declare them to	Ps 78:6
A., O Lord, into thy rest	Ps 132:8
shall the dead a. and praise thee	Ps 88:10
when the waves thereof a. thou	Ps 89:9
Thou shalt a. and have mercy	Ps 102:13
they a. let them be ashamed	Ps 109:28
A., O Lord, into thy rest	Ps 132:8
when wilt thou a. out of thy sleep	Pr 6:9
children a. up, and call her	Pr 31:28
A. my love, my fair one, and	Ca 2:13
a. ye princes, and anoint the	Isa 21:5
a. pass over to Chittim	Isa 23:12
with my dead body shall they a.	Isa 26:19
but will a. against the house of	Isa 31:2
Kings shall see and a.	Isa 49:7
a. and sit down, O Jerusalem	Isa 52:2
A. shine; for thy light is come	Isa 60:1
but the Lord shall a. upon thee	Isa 60:2
gird up thy loins, and a.	Jer 1:17
they will say, A. and save us	Jer 2:27

let them a. if they can save thee	Jer 2:28
a. and let us go up at noon	Jer 6:4
A. and let us go by night	Jer 6:5
Shall they fall, and not a.	Jer 8:4
and a. go to Euphrates, and hide	Jer 13:4
A. go to Euphrates, and take	Jer 13:6
A. and go down to the potter's	Jer 18:2
A. ye, and let us go up to Zion	Jer 31:6
A. and let us go again to our own	Jer 46:16
A. ye, go up to Kedar	Jer 49:28
A. get you up unto the wealthy	Jer 49:31
A. cry out in the night	La 2:19
A. go forth into the plain	Eze 3:22
And after thee shall a.	Da 2:39
A. devour much flesh	Da 7:5
which shall a. out of the earth	Da 7:17
ten kings that shall a.	Da 7:24
a tumult a. among thy people	Ho 10:14
by whom shall Jacob a.	Am 7:2; 7:5
A. ye, and let us rise up against	Ob 1
A. go to Nineveh, that great city	Jon 1:2
a. call upon thy God	Jon 1:6
A. go unto Nineveh	Jon 3:2
when the sun did a.	Jon 4:8
A. ye, and depart, for this is not	Mic 2:10
A. and thresh, O daughter of	Mic 4:13
A. contend thou before the	Mic 6:1
enemy: when I fall, I shall a.	Mic 7:8
A. it shall teach! Behold it is	Hab 2:19
shall the Sun of righteousness a.	Mal 4:2
A. and take the young child	M't 2:13
A. and take the young child	M't 2:20
or to say, A. and walk	M't 9:5
A. take up thy bed, and go	M't 9:6
said, A. and be not afraid	M't 17:7
For there shall a. false Christs	M't 24:24
or to say, A. and take up thy bed	M'k 2:9
unto thee, A. and take up thy bed	M'k 2:11
Damsel, I say unto thee, a.	M'k 5:41
A. Peter; slay and eat	Ac 11:7
raised him up, saying, A. up	Ac 12:7
of your own selves, shall men a.	Ac 20:30
me, A. and go unto Damascus	Ac 22:10
a. and be baptized, and wash away	Ac 22:16
a. from the dead, and Christ shall	Eph 5:14
the day star a. in your hearts	2Pe 1:19

ARISETH

a. a little cloud out of the sea	1Ki 18:44
sun a. they gather themselves	Ps 104:22
Unto the upright there a. light	Ps 112:4
The sun also a. and the sun	Ec 1:5
when he a. to shake terribly	Isa 2:19; 2:21
when the sun a. they flee away	Nah 3:17
tribulation or persecution a.	M't 13:21
affliction or persecution a. for	M'k 4:17
for out of Galilee a. no prophet	Joh 7:52
there a. another priest	Heb 7:15

ARISING

the king a. from the banquet	Es 7:7

ARISTARCHUS

having caught Gaius and A.	Ac 19:29
Thessalonians, A. and Secundus	Ac 20:4
A. a Macedonian of Thessalonica	Ac 27:2
my fellowprisoner saluteth you	Col 4:10
Marcus, A., Demas	Ph'm 24

ARISTOBULUS'

them which are of A. household.	Ro 16:10

ARK

Make thee an a. of gopher wood	Ge 6:14; 6:15-16, 18-19; 7:1, 7, 9, 13, 15, 17-18, 23; 8:1, 4, 6, 9-10, 13, 16, 19; 9:10, 18
an a. of bulrushes	Ex 2:3; 2:5
make an a. of shittim wood	Ex 25:10; Ex 25:14-16, 21; 26:33; 37:1, 5; 40:3
the a. of the testimony	Ex 25:22; 26:34; 30:6; 31:7; 39:35; 40:3, 5, 21; Nu 4:5
the a. of the covenant	Nu 10:33; 14:44; De 10:8; 31:25-26; Jos 3:3, 6, 8; 4:7-8; 6:6; 1Sa 4:4-5; 2Sa 15:24; 1Ki 3:15; 5:19; 8:1, 6; 1Ch 15:25, 29; 16:6; 17:1; 22:19; 28:18; 2Ch 5:2; Jer 3:16; Heb 9:4; Re 11:19
the a. of the Lord	Jos 3:13; 4:5, 11; 6:6; 7:6; J'g 20:27; 1Sa 4:6; 5:3; 6:2, 8, 11, 15, 18-19, 21; 7:1; 2Sa 6:9-11, 13, 15-17; 1Ki 8:4; 1Ch 15:3, 12-14; 2Ch 8:11
the a. of God	1Sa 3:3; 4:13, 17-19, 21-22; 5:1, 8, 10-11; 14:18; 2Sa 6:2-7, 12; 7:2; 15:24-25, 29; 1Ch 13:5, 6-7, 14; 15:1-2; 16:1; 2Ch 1:4
the a. of the God of Israel	1Sa 5:7; 6:3
the a. of the Lord God	1Ki 2:26
the a. of our God	1Ch 13:3
the holy a.	2Ch 35:3
delivered his a. (B)	Ps 78:61
the a. of his strength	Ps 132:8
Noe entered into the a.	M't 24:38; Lu 17:27
Noah prepared an a. to the saving of	Heb 11:7
while the a. was preparing	1Pe 3:20

ARKITE

Hivite, the A., and the Sinite	Ge 10:17
the A. and the Sinite	1Ch 1:15

ARM

by the greatness of thine a.	Ex 15:16
A. some of yourselves unto the	Nu 31:3
teareth the a. with the crown	De 33:20
I will cut off thine a., the a. of	1Sa 2:31
the bracelet that was on his a.	2Sa 1:10
With him is an a. of flesh	2Ch 32:8
the a. that hath no strength	Job 26:2
a. fall from my shoulder blade	Job 31:22
mine a. be broken from the bone	Job 31:22
by reason of the a. of the mighty	Job 35:9
and the high a. shall be broken	Job 38:15
Hast thou an a. like God	Job 40:9
Break thou the a. of the wicked	Ps 10:15
neither did their own a. save them	Ps 44:3
but thy right hand, and thine a.	Ps 44:3
with thine a. redeemed thy people	Ps 77:15
thine enemies with thy strong a.	Ps 89:10
Thou hast a mighty a.	Ps 89:13
mine a. also shall strengthen him	Ps 89:21
a. hath gotten him the victory	Ps 98:1
as a seal upon thine a.	Ca 8:6
every man the flesh of his own a.	Isa 9:20
and reapeth the ears with his a.	Isa 17:5
shew the lighting down of his a.	Isa 30:30
be thou their a. every morning	Isa 33:2
and his a. shall rule for him	Isa 40:10
shall gather the lambs with his a.	Isa 40:11
his a. shall be on the Chaldeans	Isa 48:14

on mine *a.* shall they trust — *Isa 51:5*
put on strength, O *A.* of the — *Isa 51:9*
Lord
Lord hath made bare his — *Isa 52:10*
holy *a.*
to whom is the *a.* of the — *Isa 53:1*
Lord
his *a.* brought salvation — *Isa 59:16*
unto him
and by the *a.* of his strength — *Isa 62:8*
own *a.* brought salvation — *Isa 63:5*
unto me
Moses with his glorious *a.*, — *Isa 63:12*
dividing
and maketh flesh his *a.* — *Jer 17:5*
and with a strong *a.* — *Jer 21:5*
and with a stretched out *a.* — *Jer 32:21*
his *a.* is broken, saith the — *Jer 48:25*
Lord
and thine *a.* shall be — *Eze 4:7*
uncovered
I have broken the *a.* of — *Eze 30:21*
Pharaoh
and they that were his *a.* — *Eze 31:17*
not retain the power of the — *Da 11:6*
a.
neither shall he stand, nor his — *Da 11:6*
a.
the sword shall be upon his — *Zec 11:17*
a.
his *a.* shall be clean dried — *Zec 11:17*
up
hath shewed strength with his — *Lu 1:51*
a.
to whom hath the *a.* of the — *Joh 12:38*
Lord
with an high *a.* brought he — *Ac 13:17*
them
a. yourselves likewise with the — *1Pe 4:1*

ARM STRETCHED OUT

you with a *stretched out a.* — *Ex 6:6;*
De 26:8; Ps 136:12; Jer 32:21; Eze 20:33-34
by a *stretched out a.* — *De 4:34;*
De 5:15; 9:29
and the *stretched out a.* — *De 7:19*
his *stretched out a.* — *De 11:2*
of thy *stretched out a.* — *1Ki 8:42;*
2Ch 6:32
power, *stretched out a.* — *2Ki 17:36;*
Jer 32:17

ARMAGEDDON

in the Hebrew tongue *A.* — *Re 16:16*

ARMED

when, he *a.* his trained — *Ge 14:14*
servants
went up *a.* (S) — *Ex 13:18*
twelve thousand *a.* for war — *Nu 31:5*
we ourselves will go ready — *Nu 32:17*
a.
if ye will go *a.* before the Lord — *Nu 32:20*
go all of you *a.* over Jordan — *Nu 32:21*
every man *a.* for war — *Nu 32:27*
every man *a.* to battle — *Nu 32:29*
they will not pass over with — *Nu 32:30*
you *a.*
will pass over *a.* before the — *Nu 32:32*
Lord
pass over *a.* before your — *De 3:18*
brethren
the *a.* forces (B) — *De 10:24*
pass before your brethren *a.* — *Jos 1:14*
Manasseh, passed over *a.* — *Jos 4:12*
before
that is *a.* pass on before the — *Jos 6:7*
ark
the *a.* men went before the priest — *Jos 6:9*
the *a.* men went before them; — *Jos 6:13*
but
the *a.* men that were in the — *J'g 7:11*
host
he was *a.* with a coat of — *1Sa 17:5*
mail
Saul *a.* David with his — *1Sa 17:38*
armour
also he *a.* him with a coat of — *1Sa 17:38*
mail
a. with iron (S) — *2Sa 23:7*
They were *a.* with bows — *1Ch 12:2*
that were ready *a.* to the — *1Ch 12:23*
war
ready *a.* to the war — *1Ch 12:24*
a. men with bow and shield — *2Ch 17:17*
the *a.* men left the captives — *2Ch 28:14*

he goeth on to meet the *a.* — *Job 39:21*
men
The children of Ephraim, — *Ps 78:9*
being *a.*
and thy want as an *a.* man — *Pr 6:11*
and thy want as an *a.* man — *Pr 24:34*
a. soldiers of Moab shall cry — *Isa 15:4*
out
strong man *a.* keepeth his — *Lu 11:21*
palace
a. with power from (N) — *Lu 24:49*
a. with faith (N)(P) — *1Ti 1:19*

ARMENIA

they escaped into the land — *2Ki 19:37;*
of *A.* — *Isa 37:38*

ARMHOLES

rotten rags under thine *a.* — *Jer 38:12*
sew pillows to all *a.* — *Eze 13:18*

ARMIES

from, Egypt according to — *Ex 6:26;*
their *a. 7:4; 12:17, 51; Nu 1:3; 2:3,*
9-10, 16, 18, 24-25; 10:14, 18, 22, 28;
33:1
make captains of the *a.* to — *De 20:9*
lead
together their *a.* to battle — *1Sa 17:1;*
17:8, 10, 23, 26, 36, 45; 23:3; 28:1;
29:1
the captains of the *a.* they — *2Ki 25:23*
captains of the *a.* arose — *2Ki 25:26*
the valiant men of the *a.* — *1Ch 11:26*
of his *a.* against the cities — *2Ch 16:4*
Is there any number of his — *Job 25:3*
a.
goest not forth with our *a.* — *Ps 44:9*
didst not go out with our *a.* — *Ps 60:10*
Kings of *a.* did flee apace — *Ps 68:12*
As it were the company of — *Ca 6:13*
two *a.*
his fury upon all their *a.:* he — *Isa 34:2*
he sent forth his *a.* and — *M't 22:7*
destroyed
Jerusalem compassed with *a.* — *Lu 21:20*
turned to flight the *a.* of — *Heb 11:34*
the aliens
And the *a.* which were in — *Re 19:14*
heaven
and their *a.* gathered — *Re 19:19*
together

ARMLETS

the *a.* (E)(R) — *Ex 35:22; Nu 31:50*
the *a.* (S) — *Isa 3:20*

ARMONI

unto Saul, *A.* and — *2Sa 21:8*
Mephibosheth

ARMOR

girdeth on his *a.* (S) — *1Ki 20:11*
joints of his *a.* (S) — *1Ki 22:34;*
2Ch 18:33
and raiment, and *a.* (S) — *2Ch 9:24*

ARMOUR

the young man that bare his — *1Sa 14:1*
a.
that bare his *a.,* Come, and — *1Sa 14:6*
let us
Saul armed David with his — *1Sa 17:38*
a.
girded his sword upon his *a.* — *1Sa 17:39*
he put his *a.* in his tent — *1Sa 17:54*
his head, and stripped off his — *1Sa 31:9*
a.
his *a.* in the house of — *1Sa 31:10*
Ashtaroth
take thee his *a.* But Asahel — *2Sa 2:21*
would
young men that bare Joab's — *2Sa 18:15*
a.
garments, and *a.* and spices — *1Ki 10:25*
they washed his *a.;* — *1Ki 22:38*
according
all that were able to put on — *2Ki 3:21*
horses, a fenced city also, — *2Ki 10:2*
and *a.*

of his *a.* and all that was — *2Ki 20:13*
found
they took his head, and his — *1Ch 10:9*
a.
his *a.* in the house of their — *1Ch 10:10*
gods
the *a.* of the house of the forest — *Isa 22:8*
the house of his *a.* and all — *Isa 39:2*
that
clothed with all sorts of *a.* — *Eze 38:4*
even
him all his *a.* wherein he — *Lu 11:22*
trusted
let us put on the *a.* of light — *Ro 13:12*
by the *a.* of righteousness — *2Co 6:7*
on the
Put on the whole *a.* of God — *Eph 6:11*
that
take unto you the whole *a.* of — *Eph 6:13*
God

ARMOURBEARER

the young man his *a.* — *J'g 9:54*
his *a.* said unto him — *1Sa 14:7;*
1Sa 14:12-14, 17
he became his *a.* — *1Sa 16:21*
Then said Saul unto his *a.* — *1Sa 31:4*
his *a.* would not; for he was — *1Sa 31:4*
a. saw that Saul was dead — *1Sa 31:5*
Saul died, and his *a.* and — *1Sa 31:6*
a. to Joab the son of — *2Sa 23:37*
Zeruiah
Then said Saul to his *a.* — *1Ch 10:4*
his *a.* would not — *1Ch 10:4*
his *a.* saw that Saul was — *1Ch 10:5*
dead
a. of Joab the son of — *1Ch 11:39*
Zeruiah

ARMOURY

going up to the *a.* at the — *Ne 3:19*
turning
builded for an *a.* whereon — *Ca 4:4*
there
The Lord hath opened his *a.* — *Jer 50:25*

ARMPITS

under thine *a.* (S) — *Jer 38:12*

ARMS

the *a.* of his hands were — *Ge 49:24*
made
underneath are the — *De 33:27*
everlasting *a.*
the cords that were upon his — *J'g 15:14*
a.
he brake them from off his — *J'g 16:12*
a. like
bow of steel is broken by — *2Sa 22:35*
mine *a.*
stood beside the *a.* (S) — *1Ki 10:19*
smote Jehoram between his — *2Ki 9:24*
a.
the *a.* of the fatherless have — *Job 22:9*
been
bow of steel is broken by — *Ps 18:34*
mine *a.*
For the *a.* of the wicked — *Ps 37:17*
shall be
strength, and strengtheneth — *Pr 31:17*
her *a.*
it with the strength of his *a.* — *Isa 44:12*
bring thy sons in their *a.* — *Isa 49:22*
mine *a.* shall judge the — *Isa 51:5*
people
carried in the *a.* (E)(R) — *Isa 60:4*
I will tear them from your — *Eze 13:20*
a.
of Egypt, and will break his — *Eze 30:21*
a.
I will strengthen the *a.* of — *Eze 30:24*
the king
but I will break Pharaoh's — *Eze 30:24*
I will strengthen the *a.* of — *Eze 30:25*
the king
the *a.* of Pharaoh shall fall — *Eze 30:25*
down
his breast and his *a.* of silver — *Da 2:32*
his *a.* and his feet like in — *Da 10:6*
colour
and the *a.* of the south shall — *Da 11:15*
not
with the *a.* of a flood shall — *Da 11:22*
they be

And *a*. shall stand on his   *Da 11:31*
part
bound and strengthened their   *Ho 7:15*
a.
taking them by their *a*.; but   *Ho 11:3*
they
when he had taken him in   *M'k 9:36*
his *a*.
he took them up in his *a*.   *M'k 10:16*
put his
took he him up in his *a*.   *Lu 2:28*

ARMY

the chief captain of his *a*.   *Ge 26:26*
making a formidable *a*. (B)   *Ge 50:9*
and his horsemen, and his *a*.   *Ex 14:9*
what he did unto the *a*. of   *De 11:4*
Egypt
Sisera, the captain of Jabin's *a*   *J'g 4:7*
should give bread unto thine *a*.   *J'g 8:6*
Increase thine *a*. and come   *J'g 9:29*
out
they slew of the *a*. in the field   *1Sa 4:2*
a man of Benjamin out of   *1Sa 4:12*
the *a*.
I am he that came out of   *1Sa 4:16*
the *a*.
I fled to day out of the *a*.   *1Sa 4:16*
battle in array, *a*. against   *1Sa 17:21*
a.
and ran into the *a*. and   *1Sa 17:22*
came and
David hasted and ran   *1Sa 17:48*
toward the *a*.
and the *a*. which followed   *1Ki 20:19*
them
number thee an *a*.   *1Ki 20:25*
like the *a*. that thou hast   *1Ki 20:25*
lost
the *a*. of the Chaldees   *2Ki 25:5*
pursued
all his *a*. were scattered   *2Ki 25:5*
from him
And all the *a*. of the   *2Ki 25:10*
Chaldees
units of the *a*. for war   *1Ch 7:4*
(A)(R)
Joab led forth the power of   *1Ch 20:1*
the *a*.
the general of the king's *a*.   *1Ch 27:34*
in array with an *a*. of   *2Ch 13:3*
valiant
Asa had an *a*. of men that   *2Ch 14:8*
bare
they went out before the *a*.   *2Ch 20:21*
a. of the Syrians came with   *2Ch 24:24*
a.
let not the *a*. of Israel go   *2Ch 25:7*
with
I have given to the *a*. of   *2Ch 25:9*
Israel
the *a*. that was come to   *2Ch 25:10*
him out
But the soldiers of the *a*.   *2Ch 25:13*
which
the men of the *a*. (E)(R)   *2Ch 25:13*
under their hand was an *a*.   *2Ch 26:13*
had sent captains of the *a*.   *Ne 2:9*
the *a*. of Samaria, and said,   *Ne 4:2*
What
dwelt as a king in the *a*.   *Job 29:25*
terrible as an *a*. with   *Ca 6:4, 10*
banners
king Hezekiah with a great *a*.   *Isa 36:2*
horse, the *a*. and the power   *Isa 43:17*
Babylon's *a*. besieged   *Jer 32:2*
Jerusalem
king of Babylon, and all his   *Jer 34:1*
a.
the king of Babylon's *a*.   *Jer 34:7*
fought
hand of the king of   *Jer 34:21*
Babylon's *a*.
for fear of the *a*. of the   *Jer 35:11*
Chaldeans
for fear of the *a*. of the   *Jer 35:11*
Syrians
Pharaoh's *a*. was come forth   *Jer 37:5*
out
Pharaoh's *a*. which is come   *Jer 37:7*
ye had smitten the whole *a*.   *Jer 37:10*
when the *a*. of the   *Jer 37:11*
Chaldeans was
for fear of Pharaoh's *a*.   *Jer 37:11*
the king of Babylon's *a*.   *Jer 38:3*
all his *a*. against Jerusalem   *Jer 39:1*
Chaldeans' *a*. pursued after   *Jer 39:5*
them
against the *a*. of Pharaoh-necho   *Jer 46:2*

they shall march with an *a*.   *Jer 46:22*
he and all his *a*. against   *Jer 52:4*
Jerusalem
a. of the Chaldeans pursued   *Jer 52:8*
after
all his *a*. was scattered from   *Jer 52:8*
him
all the *a*. of the Chaldeans   *Jer 52:14*
Pharaoh with his mighty *a*.   *Eze 17:17*
Lud and Phut were in thine   *Eze 27:10*
a.
The men of Arvad with   *Eze 27:11*
thine *a*.
caused his *a*. to serve a   *Eze 29:18*
great service
yet had he no wages, nor   *Eze 29:18*
his *a*.
and it shall be the wages   *Eze 29:19*
for his *a*.
Pharaoh and all his *a*. slain   *Eze 32:31*
an exceeding great *a*.   *Eze 37:10*
all thine *a*. horses and   *Eze 38:4*
horsemen
a great company, and a   *Eze 38:15*
mighty *a*.
mighty men that were in his   *Da 3:20*
a.
according to his will in the *a*.   *Da 4:35*
of
which shall come with an *a*.   *Da 11:7*
after certain years with a   *Da 11:13*
great *a*.
of the south with a great *a*.   *Da 11:25*
with a very great and   *Da 11:25*
and his *a*. shall overflow   *Da 11:26*
shall utter his voice before   *Joe 2:11*
his *a*.
far off from you the northern   *Joe 2:20*
a.
my great *a*. which I sent   *Joe 2:25*
among
mine house because of the *a*.   *Zec 9:8*
then came I with an *a*. and   *Ac 23:27*
number of the *a*. of the   *Re 9:16*
horsemen
sat on the horse, and against   *Re 19:19*
his *a*.

ARNAN

the sons of *A*. the sons of   *1Ch 3:21*
Obadiah

ARNON

and pitched on the other   *Nu 21:13*
side of *A*.
for *A*. is the border of   *Nu 21:13*
Moab
Red sea, and in the brooks   *Nu 21:14*
of *A*.
possessed his land from *A*.   *Nu 21:24*
unto
land out of his hand, even   *Nu 21:26*
unto *A*.
the lords of the high places   *Nu 21:28*
of *A*.
Moab, which is in the   *Nu 22:36*
border of *A*.
and pass over the river *A*.   *De 2:24*
is by the brink of the river of   *De 2:36*
A.
river of *A*. unto mount   *De 3:8*
Hermon
Aroer, which is by the river   *De 3:12*
from Gilead even unto the   *De 3:16*
river *A*.
is by the bank of the river *A*.   *De 4:48*
rising of the sun, from the   *Jos 12:1*
river *A*.
is upon the bank of the river   *Jos 12:2*
A.
is upon the bank of the river   *Jos 13:9*
A.
the river *A*. and the city   *Jos 13:16*
that is
from *A*. even unto Jabbok,   *J'g 11:13*
and
and pitched on the other   *J'g 11:18*
side of *A*.
for *A*. was the border of   *J'g 11:18*
Moab
from *A*. even unto Jabbok,   *J'g 11:22*
and
that be along by the coasts   *J'g 11:26*
of *A*.
by the river *A*. even Gilead   *2Ki 10:33*
and

of Moab shall be at the fords   *Isa 16:2*
of *A*.
tell ye it in *A*. that Moab is   *Jer 48:20*
spoiled

AROD

A. the family of the   *Nu 26:17*
Arodites

ARODI

Ezbon, Eri, and *A*. and   *Ge 46:16*
Areli

ARODITES

Of Arod, the family of the   *Nu 26:17*
A.

AROER

built Dibon, and Ataroth,   *Nu 32:34*
and *A*.
From *A*. which is by the   *De 2:36*
brink of
we possessed at that time,   *De 3:12*
from *A*.
From *A*. which is by the   *De 4:48*
bank of
in Heshbon, and ruled from   *Jos 12:2*
A.
From *A*. that is upon the   *Jos 13:9*
bank
And their coast was from   *Jos 13:16*
A. that
unto *A*. that is before   *Jos 13:25*
Rabbah
towns, and in *A*. and her   *J'g 11:26*
towns
And he smote them from *A*.   *J'g 11:33*
even
And to them which were in   *1Sa 30:28*
A.
over Jordan, and pitched in   *2Sa 24:5*
A.
from *A*. which is by the   *2Ki 10:33*
river
the son of Joel, who dwelt in   *1Ch 5:8*
A.
The cities of *A*. are forsaken   *Isa 17:2*
O inhabitant of *A*. stand by   *Jer 48:19*
the

AROERITE

Jehiel the sons of Hothan   *1Ch 11:44*
the *A*.

AROMA

the *a*. of Christ (R)   *2Co 12:15*

AROMATICS

had brought *a*. (B)(N)   *M'k 16:1*

AROSE

he perceived not when she   *Ge 19:33;*
a.   *19:35*
my sheaf *a*. and stood   *Ge 37:7*
upright
there *a*. new king who knew   *Ex 1:8;*
   Ac 7:18
a. a generation knew not the   *J'g 2:10*
Lord
till I Deborah *a*., till I *a*. in   *J'g 5:7*
all the people *a*. as one man   *J'g 20:8*
they *a*. early   *1Sa 9:26; Isa 37:36*
when he *a*. against me, I   *1Sa 17:35*
slew him
neither after him *a*. there   *2Ki 23:25*
any like
till the wrath of the Lord   *2Ch 36:16*
a.
young men hid, aged men *a*.   *Job 29:8*
when God *a*. in judgment to   *Ps 76:9*
save
sun hasteth to go down where   *Ec 1:5*
he *a*.
the king *a*. early and went to   *Da 6:19*
the den
he *a*., took the young child   *M't 2:14;*
   2:21
she *a*. and ministered   *M't 8:15; Lu 4:39*
a. rebuked winds   *M't 8:26;*
   M'k 4:39; Lu 8:24
   M't 9:9;
a. and followed him   *M't 9:19; M'k 2:14*

took her by hand and maid   *M't 9:25* *a.*
many bodies of saints   *M't 27:52* which slept *a.*
Jesus lifted him up, and he   *M'k 9:27* *a.*
when the flood *a.* the stream   *Lu 6:48* beat
he *a.* and came to his father   *Lu 15:20*
the persecution which *a.*   *Ac 11:19*
there *a.* no small stir about   *Ac 19:23*
when he so said there *a.* a   *Ac 23:7* dissension
there *a.* smoke out of the pit   *Re 9:2*

AROSE *AND WENT*

Samuel *a.* and went to Eli   *1Sa 3:6*
Jonathan *a.* and went to   *1Sa 23:16* David
David *a. and went* to the   *1Sa 25:1* wilderness
Elisha *a. and went* after   *1Ki 19:21* Elijah
so Jonah *a., and went* to   *Jon 3:3* Nineveh
then Peter *a. and went* with   *Ac 9:39* them

AROUSE

a. them to jealousy   *Ro 11:11;* (A)(B)(R)   *11:14*
do not *a.* children's anger   *Eph 6:4* (B)
a. others to love (N)   *Heb 11:24*

AROUSED

a. David to number Israel   *1Ch 21:1* (B)
a. his temper (B)   *Ps 106:29; 106:33*
a. the emotions (B)   *Ac 17:8*

ARPAD

the gods of Hamath, and of   *2Ki 18:34* *A.*
of Hamath, and the king of   *2Ki 19:13* *A.*
not Hamath as *A.?* is not   *Isa 10:9* Samaria
Hamath is confounded, and   *Jer 49:23* *A.*

ARPHAD

are the gods of Hamath and   *Isa 36:19* *A.*
of Hamath, and the king of   *Isa 37:13* *A.*

ARPHAXAD

Elam, Asshur, and *A.*   *Ge 10:22;* *10:24; 11:10-13; 1Ch 1:17-18, 24*
which was the son of *A.*   *Lu 3:36*

ARRANGE

a. wood on the fire (B)   *Le 1:7;* *Le 1:12; 6:12; 24:8*

ARRANGED

a. to have Paul (B)(N)   *Ac 15:2*

ARRANGEMENT

under this *a.* (N)(P)   *Heb 9:6*

ARRANGING

a. upon it the bread (B)   *Ex 40:23*

ARRAY

put themselves in *a.*   *J'g 20:20; 20:22,* *30, 33; 1Sa 4:2*
battle in *a.*   *1Sa 17:2;* *17:8, 21; 2Sa 10:8; 1Ch 19:9, 17;* *2Ch 13:3*
set themselves in *a.* against   *Job 6:4* me
he shall *a.* himself with   *Jer 43:12*
yourselves in *a.* against   *Jer 50:14*
gold, or pearls, or costly *a.*   *1Ti 2:9*

ARRAYED

Pharaoh *a.* Joseph in fine   *Ge 41:42* linen

dressed him in fine linen   *Ge 41:42* (B)
took captives, with spoil *a.*   *2Ch 28:15* them
clothed them and gave   *2Ch 28:15* them (B)(E)(R)
was not *a.* like one of these   *M't 6:29;* *Lu 12:27*
dressed like one of these (B)   *M't 6:29*
attired like one of these (N)   *M't 6:29*
Herod and his men of war   *Lu 23:11* *a.* Christ
dressing him up in bright   *Lu 23:11* (A)(P)(R)
put a bright robe upon him   *Lu 23:11* (B)
dressed in a gorgeous robe   *Lu 23:11* (N)
Herod *a.* in royal apparel   *Ac 12:21* sat
what are these *a.* in white   *Re 7:13* robes
clothed in long white robes   *Re 7:13* (A)(R)
robed in long white robes   *Re 7:13* (B)
robed in white (N)   *Re 7:13*
dressed in white robes (P)   *Re 7:13*
woman was *a.* in purple,   *Re 17:4* scarlet color
robed in purple and scarlet   *Re 17:4* (A)(B)
clothed in purple and scarlet   *Re 17:4* (P)
to her was granted to be *a.*   *Re 19:8* in fine
to dress in fine linen   *Re 19:8* (A)(B)(N)
dressed in linen (P)   *Re 19:8*
clothed in fine linen (R)   *Re 19:8*

ARREST

a. Jesus by (A)(B)(N)(P)(R)   *M't 26:4*
a. Jesus (A)(B)(N)   *M'k 14:1*
to *a.* us (A)(B)(N)(R)   *2Co 11:32*

ARRESTED

then we *a.* him (N)   *Ac 24:6*

ARRIVE

finally *a.* at resurrection   *Ph'p 3:11* (N)

ARRIVED

a. at the country of   *Lu 8:26* Gadarenes
the next day we *a.* at Samos   *Ac 20:15*

ARROGANCE

your *a.* and careless ease   *2Ki 19:28;* (A)(E)   *Isa 37:29*
your *a.* has come up   *Ps 37:29* (B)(E)(R)
nothing prompted by empty   *Ph'p 2:3* *a.* (A)

ARROGANCY

let not *a.* come out of your   *1Sa 2:3* mouth
let not arrogance come from   *1Sa 2:3* (A)(R)
no more taunts from mouth   *1Sa 2:3* (B)
pride, and *a.* and the evil way   *Pr 8:13*
the *a.* of the proud to cease   *Isa 13:11*
his *a.* and his pride   *Jer 48:29*

ARROGANT

envious at the *a.* (B)(E)   *Ps 73:3*
a. men have risen (B)   *Ps 86:14*
conceited and *a.* (B)(R)   *Ps 101:5*
the *a.* (B)   *Ps 119:21;* *Ps 119:51, 69, 78, 122; 123:4*
a. men have hidden (R)   *Ps 140:5*
   Mal 3:15; 4:1
the *a.* men (B)   *Jer 43:2*
we call the *a.* happy (B)(R)   *Mal 3:15*
a. and all evildoers (R)   *Mal 4:1*
conceited and *a.* (A)(R)   *1Co 4:18*
proud and *a.* (A)(R)   *1Co 5:2*
love is not *a.* or rude (R)   *1Co 13:4*
God opposes the *a.* (B)(N)   *1Pe 5:5*
utter *a.* nonsense (B)   *2Pe 2:18*

ARROGANTLY

deal not *a.* (A)(E)   *Ps 75:4*
so you may not be *a.* (B)   *1Co 4:6*

ARROW

he shot an *a.* beyond him   *1Sa 20:36*
was come to the place of   *1Sa 20:37* the *a.*
is not the *a.* beyond thee   *1Sa 20:37*
the *a.* went out at his heart   *2Ki 9:24*
The *a.* of the Lord's   *2Ki 13:17* deliverance
and the *a.* of deliverance   *2Ki 13:17*
nor shoot an *a.* there   *2Ki 19:32*
a. goes through his back   *Job 20:25* (B)
a. cannot make him flee   *Job 41:28*
they make ready their *a.*   *Ps 11:2*
God shall shoot at them with   *Ps 64:7* an *a.*
for the *a.* that flieth by day   *Ps 91:5*
a sword, and a sharp *a.*   *Pr 25:18*
nor shoot an *a.* there   *Isa 37:33*
made me a polished *a.*   *Isa 49:2* (A)(B)(R)
Their tongue is as an *a.*   *Jer 9:8*
set me as a mark for the *a.*   *La 3:12*
his *a.* shall go forth   *Zec 9:14*

ARROWS

pierce them through with his   *Nu 24:8* *a.*
I will spend mine *a.* upon   *De 32:23* them
make mine *a.* drunk with   *De 32:42* blood
I will shoot three *a.* on the   *1Sa 20:20* side
Go, find out the *a.*   *1Sa 20:21*
the *a.* are on this side of   *1Sa 20:21* thee
the *a.* are beyond thee   *1Sa 20:22*
find out now the *a.* which I   *1Sa 20:36* shoot
Jonathan's lad gathered up   *1Sa 20:38* the *a.*
he sent out *a.* and scattered   *2Sa 22:15* them
Take bow and *a.*   *2Ki 13:15*
And he took unto him bow   *2Ki 13:15* and *a.*
he said, Take the *a.*   *2Ki 13:18*
in hurling stones and shooting   *1Ch 12:2* *a.*
to shoot *a.* and great stones   *2Ch 26:15*
For the *a.* of the Almighty   *Job 6:4* are
he ordaineth his *a.* against   *Ps 7:13*
Yea, he sent out his *a.*   *Ps 18:14*
ready thine *a.* upon thy   *Ps 21:12* strings
For thine *a.* stick fast in me   *Ps 38:2*
Thine *a.* are sharp in the   *Ps 45:5* heart
whose teeth are spears and *a.*   *Ps 57:4*
bendeth his bow to shoot his   *Ps 58:7* *a.*
bend their bows to shoot their   *Ps 64:3* *a.*
brake he the *a.* of the bow   *Ps 76:3*
thine *a.* also went abroad   *Ps 77:17*
Sharp *a.* of the mighty   *Ps 120:4*
As *a.* are in the hand of a   *Ps 127:4* mighty
shoot out thine *a.* and   *Ps 144:6* destroy
casteth firebrands, *a.* and   *Pr 26:18* death
Whose *a.* are sharp   *Isa 5:28*
With *a.* and with bows shall   *Isa 7:24* men
their *a.* shall be as of a   *Jer 50:9* mighty
shoot at her, spare no *a.*   *Jer 50:14*
Make bright the *a.*   *Jer 51:11*
hath caused the *a.* of his   *La 3:13* quiver
send upon them the evil *a.*   *Eze 5:16*
he made his *a.* bright, he   *Eze 21:21*
and will cause thine *a.* to   *Eze 39:3* fall
the bows and the *a.* and the   *Eze 34:9*
at the light of thine *a.* they   *Hab 3:11* went
with his *a.* (A)   *Hab 3:14*
flaming *a.* of the evil one   *Eph 6:16* (N)

ART

and said unto him, Where *a.*   Ge 3:9
thou
dust thou *a.* and dust thou   Ge 3:19
Whose daughter *a.* thou   Ge 24:23;
   24:47
a. thou my very son Esau   Ge 27:24
a bloody husband thou *a.*   Ex 4:26
a. thou for us, or our   Josh 5:13
adversaries
I am as thou *a.*   1Ki 22:4; 2Ki 3:7
a. thou also become weak   Isa 14:10
as we
a. thou he that should come   Lu 7:19
Thou *a.* the Son of God   Joh 1:49
tell me, *a.* thou a Roman   Ac 22:27
thou *a.* inexcusable   Ro 2:1
a. thou bound to a wife   1Co 7:27
Thou *a.* my Son, this day   Heb 1:5;
have I begotten thee   Heb 15:5;
   Ac 13:33; Ps 2:7
Thou *a.* a priest for ever   Heb 5:6;
after order of   Heb 7:17, 21;
Melchisedec   Ps 110:4
nor faint when thou *a.*   Heb 12:5
rebuked of him
thou *a.* neither cold nor hot   Re 3:15;
   3:16
Thou *a.* worthy   Re 4:11; 5:9
which *a.* and *a.* to come   Re 11:17;
   16:5
Thou *a.* righteous, O God   Re 16:5

ARTAXERXES

in the day of *A.* wrote   Ezr 4:7
Bishlam
unto *A.* king of Persia; and   Ezr 4:7
to *A.* the king in this sort   Ezr 4:8
they sent unto him, even   Ezr 4:11
unto *A.*
and Darius, and *A.* king of   Ezr 6:14
Persia
in the reign of *A.* king of   Ezr 7:1
Persia
in the seventh year of *A.* the   Ezr 7:7
king
that the king *A.* gave unto   Ezr 7:11
Ezra
A. king of kings, unto Ezra   Ezr 7:12
the
And I, even I *A.* the king   Ezr 7:21
in the reign of *A.* the king   Ezr 8:1
in the twentieth year of *A.* the   Ne 2:1
king
the two and thirtieth year of   Ne 5:14
A.
in the two and thirtieth year   Ne 13:6
of *A.*

ARTAXERES'

copy of king *A.* letter was   Ezr 4:23
read

ARTEMAS

When I shall send *A.* unto   Tit 3:12
thee

ARTFULLY

tales *a.* spun (N)   2Pe 1:16

ARTICLES

a. of silver (B)   Ge 24:53
borrowed gold *a.* (B)   Ex 3:22
money or *a.* to keep (B)   Ex 22:7
articles (B)   Ex 39:40;
Nu 18:3; 2Sa 8:10; 1Ki 7:45, 47-48, 51;
8:4; 2Ki 12:13; 25:16; 1Ch 18:10;
2Ch 4:18; 5:5; 24:7; 15:18; Ezr 1:6;
   Da 11:8; Re 18:12
all wrought *a.* (A)(R)   Nu 31:51
gold *a.* for atonement (A)   1Sa 6:8
a. of silver (B)   2Sa 8:10;
   1Ki 10:25; 1Ch 18:10; 2Ch 9:24;
   Re 18:12
all these *a.* (A)   2Ki 25:16;
   2Ch 9:24; Re 18:12
found precious *a.* (B)   2Ch 20:25;
   32:27
all kinds of precious *a.* (B)   2Ch 32:27

ARTIFICER

an instructer of every *a.*   Ge 4:22
and the cunning *a.* and the   Isa 3:3

ARTIFICERS

by the hands of *a.*   1Ch 29:5
Even to the *a.* and builders   2Ch 34:11

ARTILLERY

Jonathan gave his *a.* unto   1Sa 20:40
his lad

ARTISAN

the skilled *a.* (B)   Re 18:22

ARTS

his magic *a.* (A)(B)(R)   Ac 8:11; 8:9
them also which used   Ac 19:19
curious *a.*
their magic *a.* (B)   Re 9:21

ARUBOTH

The son of Hesed, in *A.*   1Ki 4:10

ARUMAH

And Abimelech dwelt at *A.*   J'g 9:41

ARVAD

The inhabitants of Zidon   Eze 27:8
and *A.*
The men of *A.* with thine   Eze 27:11
army

ARVADITE

And the *A.* and the   Ge 10:18
Zemarite
And the *A.* and the   1Ch 1:16
Zemarite

ARZA

himself drunk in the house   1Ki 16:9
of *A.*

ASA

A. his son reigned in his stead   1Ki 15:8
15:9, 11, 13, 16-18, 20, 22-25, 28, 32-33;
2Chr 14: 1-13; 15:2-19; 16:1-13
In the twenty and sixth year   1Ki 16:8
of *A.*
twenty and seventh year of   1Ki 16:10;
A.   16:15
In the thirty and first year   1Ki 16:23
of *A.*
in the thirty and eighth   1Ki 16:29
year of *A.*
the son of *A.* began to   1Ki 22:41
reign
he walked in all the ways   1Ki 22:43
of *A.* his
in the days of his father *A.*   1Ki 22:46
Abia his son, *A.* his son   1Ch 3:10
and Berechiah, the son of *A.*   1Ch 9:16
which *A.* his father had   1Ch 17:2
taken.
walked in the way of *A.*   1Ch 20:32
his father
the ways of *A.* king of   1Ch 21:12
Judah
which *A.* the king had made   Jer 41:9
for
and Abia begat *A.*   M't 1:7
and *A.* begat Josaphat   M't 1:8

ASAHEL

there, Joab, Abishai, and *A.*   2Sa 2:18;
   2:19-23, 30, 32
for the blood of *A.* his   2Sa 3:27
brother
slain their brother *A.* at   2Sa 3:30
Gibeon
A. the brother of Joab was   2Sa 23:24
one
Abishai, and Joab, and *A.*   1Ch 2:16
three
were, *A.* the brother of   1Ch 11:26
Joab
for the fourth month, was   1Ch 27:7
A. the
and Zebadiah, and *A.* and   2Ch 17:8
and Nahath, and *A.* and   2Ch 31:13
Jerimoth
Only Jonathan the son of   Ezr 10:15
A. and

ASAHIAH

and *A.* a servant of the   2Ki 22:12
king's
and *A.* went unto Huldah   2Ki 22:14
the

ASAIAH

and *A.* and Adiel, and   1Ch 4:36
Jesimiel
Haggiah his son, *A.* his son   1Ch 6:30
A. the first born, and his   1Ch 9:5
sons.
sons of Merari; *A.* the chief   1Ch 15:6
Uriel, *A.* and Joel,   1Ch 15:11
Shemaiah
the scribe, and *A.* a servant   2Ch 34:20
of

ASAPH

Joah son of *A.*   2Ki 18:18; Isa 36:32
A. son of Berechiah   1Ch 6:39;
   1Ch 9:15; 15:7
David delivered this psalm   1Ch 16:7;
to *A.*   16:37
sons of *A.*   1Ch 25:1;
25:2, 6, 9; 26:1; 2Ch 5:12; 20:14; 29:13;
35:15; Ezr 2:41; 3:10; Ne 7:44; 11:17,
   22; 12:35
words of David, and of *A.*   2Ch 29:30;
   35:15
A. the keeper of the king's   Ne 2:8
forest
days of David and of *A.* of   Ne 12:46
old
were written by *A.*   Ps 50, 73-83

ASAPH'S

the scribe, and Joah, *A.* son   Isa 36:3

ASAREEL

Ziph, and Ziphah, Tiria, and   1Ch 4:16
A.

ASARELAH

Joseph, and Nethaniah, and   1Ch 25:2
A.

ASA'S

nevertheless *A.* heart was   1Ki 15:14
perfect

ASCEND

people *a.* up every man   Jos 6:5
straight
each one moving straight   Jos 6:5
ahead (B)
go up straight before him   Jos 6:5
(E)(R)
who shall *a.* into hill of the   Ps 24:3
Lord
go up to mountain of Lord   Ps 24:3
(A)(B)
he causeth vapours to *a.*   Ps 135:7;
   Jer 10:13; 51:16
causes vapors to arise   Ps 135:7
(A)(B)(R)
if I *a.* into heaven thou art   Ps 139:8
there
Lucifer said, I will *a.* into   Isa 14:13;
heaven   14:14
I will scale the heavens (B)   Isa 14:13
thou shalt *a.* and come like   Eze 38:9
a storm
you will advance, coming   Eze 38:9
like (B)(R)
if ye shall see the Son of   Joh 6:62
man *a.* up
I *a.* to my Father, and your   Joh 20:17
Father
beast shall *a.* out of bottomless   Re 17:8
pit
come up out of the abyss   Re 17:8
(A)(E)(P)

ASCENDED

smoke *a.*   Ex 19:18; Jos 8:20-21
angel of the Lord *a.* in   J'g 13:20
flame
angel went up to heaven   J'g 13:20
(R)

Thou hast *a.* on high | *Ps 68:18; Eph 4:8*
who hath *a.* up to heaven, or | *Pr 30:4*
descended
no man hath *a.* to heaven, | *Joh 3:13*
but he
has gone up to heaven | *Joh 3:13*
(A)(B)
ever went up into heaven | *Joh 3:13*
(N)
ever been up to heaven (P) | *Joh 3:13*
I am not yet *a.* to my | *Joh 20:17*
Father
David is not yet *a.* into the | *Ac 2:34*
heavens
when he *a.* on high, he led | *Eph 4:8;*
captivity | *4:9-10; Ps 68:18*
smoke of the incense *a.* before | *Re 8:4*
God
incense rose in presence of | *Re 8:4*
God (A)(B)(R)
incense went up before God | *Re 8:4*
(E)(N)(P)
they *a.* up to heaven in a | *Re 11:12*
cloud

ASCENDETH

that *a.* out of the bottomless | *Re 11:7*
pit
comes up out of abyss | *Re 11:7*
(A)(B)(E)(N)(P)(R)
smoke of their torment *a.* | *Re 14:11*
for ever
smoke of torment goes up | *Re 14:11*
(E)(N)(R)

ASCENDING

angels of God *a.* and | *Ge 28:12*
descending
I saw gods *a.* out of the | *1Sa 28:13*
earth
god-like form rising from | *1Sa 28:13*
earth (B)(E)(R)
He went before *a.* up to | *Lu 19:28*
Jerusalem
going up to Jerusalem | *Lu 19:28*
(A)(B)(E)(R)
angels of God *a.* and | *Joh 1:51*
descending on
another angel *a.* from the east | *Re 7:2*
coming from the east (A) | *Re 7:2*
angel rising out of the east (N) | *Re 7:2*

ASCENT

to the *a.* of Akrabbim | *Nu 34:4*
the *a.* of (S) | *Jos 15:3; 15:7; 18:17;*
J'g 1:36; 2Ki 9:27; Ne 3:19; 31-32; 12:37;
Isa 15:5; Jer 48:5; Eze 40:31, 34, 37
up by the *a.* of mount Olivet | *2Sa 15:30*
and his *a.* by which he went | *1Ki 10:5*
up
and his *a.* by which he went | *2Ch 9:4*
up

ASCRIBE

a. ye greatness unto our God | *De 32:3*
a. righteousness to my | *Job 36:3*
Maker
A. ye strength unto God | *Ps 68:34*

ASCRIBED

They have *a.* unto David | *1Sa 18:8*
to me they have *a.* but | *1Sa 18:8*
thousands

ASENATH

and he gave him to wife *A.* | *Ge 41:45*
the
A. the daughter of | *Ge 41:50*
Poti-pherah
Manasseh and Ephraim, | *Ge 46:20*
which *A.*

ASER

of the tribe of *A.* | *Lu 2:36*
Of the tribe of *A.* were sealed | *Re 7:6*

ASH

he planteth an *a.* and the | *Isa 44:14*
rain

ASH-COLORED

an *a.* horse (B) | *Re 6:8*

ASHAMED

naked, man and wife were | *Ge 2:25*
not *a.*
they felt no shame (B) | *Ge 2:25*
they tarried till they were *a.* | *J'g 3:25*
they were embarrassed (B) | *J'g 3:25*
were utterly at a loss (R) | *J'g 3:25*
men were greatly *a.* | *2Sa 10:5;*
| *1Ch 19:5*
greatly humiliated (B) | *2Sa 10:5;*
| *1Ch 19:5*
they urged him till he was *a.* | *2Ki 2:17*
urged him until he relented | *2Ki 2:17*
(B)
priests and Levites were *a.* | *2Ch 30:15*
I was *a.* to require of the | *Ezr 8:22*
king a band
they came thither, and were | *Job 6:20*
a.
were bitterly disappointed | *Job 6:20*
(A)(B)(R)
were lightened, and faces not | *Ps 34:5*
a.
faces shall never blush (A) | *Ps 34:5*
faces never be confounded | *Ps 34:5*
(E)
a. and terrified (B) | *Ps 83:17*
she that maketh *a.* is as | *Pr 12:4*
rottenness
who acts disgracefully (B) | *Pr 12:4*
will be *a.* (A)(B)(E)(R) | *Isa 1:29*
shall be *a.* of Ethiopia | *Isa 20:5*
dismayed and confounded | *Isa 20:5*
(A)(B)(E)(R)
sun shall be *a.* when the | *Isa 24:23*
Lord reigns
a. of people that could not | *Isa 30:5*
profit
all come to shame (B)(R) | *Isa 30:5*
Lebanon is *a.* and hewn | *Isa 33:9*
down
Lebanon is confounded | *Isa 33:9*
(A)(E)(R)
as the thief is *a.* when found | *Jer 2:26*
thief brought to shame (A) | *Jer 2:26*
we are utterly *a.* (B)(R) | *Jer 9:19;*
| *Jer 50:12*
they are *a.* of their might | *Eze 32:30*
put to shame | *Eze 32:30*
(A)(B)(E)(R)
the nations be *a.* (A)(R) | *Mic 7:16*
all his adversaries were *a.* | *Lu 13:17*
opponents put to shame | *Lu 13:17*
(A)(E)(P)(R)
covered with confusion (N) | *Lu 13:17*
hope maketh not *a.* because | *Ro 5:5*
hope never disappoints, | *Ro 5:5*
deludes, or shames (A)(B)
hope putteth not to shame (E) | *Ro 5:5*
hope *is no* mockery (N) | *Ro 5:5*
hope will never disappoint | *Ro 5:5*
(P)(R)
what fruit in things ye are | *Ro 6:21*
now *a.*
if I have boasted, I am not | *2Co 7:14*
a.
disappointed, put to shame | *2 Co 7:14*
(A)(E)
told him of my pride in you | *2Co 7:14*
(N)(P)(R)
I am not *a.* (S) | *2Co 11:29*
God make me *a.* (P) | *2Co 12:21*
suffer, nevertheless I am not | *2Ti 1:12*
a.
Onesiphorus was not *a.* of my | *2Ti 1:16*
chain
He is not *a.* to call them | *Heb 2:11*
brethren
God is not *a.* to be called | *Heb 11:16*
their God

BE ASHAMED

let her take it, lest we *be a.* | *Ge 38:23*
do not want to be ridiculed | *Ge 38:23*
(B)
lest we be laughed at (R) | *Ge 38:23*
let none that wait on thee *be* | *Ps 25:3*
not be put to shame | *Ps 25:3*
(A)(E)(R)
let me never *be a.* | *Ps 31:1*
put to shame (A)(B)(E)(R) | *Ps 31:1;*
| *31:17; 69:6*
they shall *be a.* | *Isa 1:29;*
23:4; 26:11; 42:17; 44:11; 45:24; 65:13;
66:5; Jer 2:36; 12:13; 17:13; 20:11;
50:12; Eze 43:11; Ho 4:19; 10:6

whore's forehead, refused to | *Jer 3:3*
be a.
My people shall never *be a.* | *Joe 2:26;*
| *2:27*
be a. of me and my words | *M'k 8:38;*
| *Lu 9:26*
believeth on him not *be a.* | *Ro 9:33;*
| *10:11*
in nothing I shall not *be a.* | *Ph'p 1:20*
may *be a.* that falsely accuse | *1Pe 3:16*

NOT BE ASHAMED

should she *not be a.* seven | *Nu 12:14*
days
let me *not be a.* | *Ps 25:2;*
| *Ps 31:17; 119:116*
they shall *not be a.* in evil | *Ps 37:19*
time
speak of thy testimonies, | *Ps 119:46*
not be a.
they shall *not be a.,* but | *Ps 127:5*
shall speak
Jacob *not be a.* | *Isa 29:22;*
| *Isa 45:17; 49:23; 54:4*
believeth on him shall *not* | *Ro 9:33;*
be a. | *10:11*
workman that needeth *not be* | *2Ti 2:15*
a.
suffer as a Christian, let him | *1Pe 3:16*
not be a.
not be a. before him at his | *1Jo 2:28*
coming

ASHAN

Libnah, and Ether, and *A.* | *Jos 15:42*
Ain, Remmon, and Ether, | *Jos 19:7*
and *A*
Rimmon, and Tochen, and | *1Ch 4:32*
A. five
And *A.* with her suburbs | *1Ch 6:59*

ASHBEA

of the house of *A.* | *1Ch 4:21*

ASHBEL

Becher, and *A.,* Gera, and | *Ge 46:21*
Naaman
of *A.* the family of the | *Nu 26:38*
Ashbelites
Bela his firstborn, *A.* the | *1Ch 8:1*
second

ASHBELITES

of Ashbel, the family of the | *Nu 26:38*
A.

ASHCHENAZ

sons of Gomer; *A.* and | *1Ch 1:6*
Riphath
kingdoms of Ararat, Minni, | *Jer 51:27*
and *A.*

ASHDOD

only in Gaza, in Gath, and | *Jos 11:22*
in *A.*
lay near *A.* with their | *Jos 15:46*
villages
A. with her towns and her | *Jos 15:47*
villages
brought it from Eben-ezer | *1Sa 5:1*
unto *A.*
of *A.* rose early on the morrow | *1Sa 5:3*
the threshold of Dagon in *A.* | *1Sa 5:5*
was heavy upon them of *A.* | *1Sa 5:6*
and
even *A.* and the coasts thereof | *1Sa 5:6*
when the men of *A.* saw that | *1Sa 5:7*
for *A.* one, for Gaza one | *1Sa 6:17*
of *A.* and built cities about | *2Ch 26:6*
A.
Jews that had married wives | *Ne 13:23*
of *A.*
spake half in the speech of | *Ne 13:24*
A.
year that Tartan came unto *A.* | *Isa 20:1*
and fought against *A.* and | *Isa 20:1*
took it
and Ekron, and the remnant | *Jer 25:20*
of *A.*
cut off the inhabitant from *A.* | *Am 1:8*
Publish in the palaces at *A.* | *Am 3:9*
shall drive out *A.* at the | *Zep 2:4*
noonday
And a bastard shall dwell in | *Zec 9:6*
A.

ASHDODITES

and the A. heard that the   Ne 4:7
walls

ASHDOTHITES

A. the Eshkalonites, the   Jos 13:3
Gittites

ASHDOTH-PISGAH

salt sea, under A. eastward   De 3:17
from the south, under A.   Jos 12:3
And Beth-peor, and A. and   Jos 13:20

ASHER

and she called his name A.   Ge 30:13
Leah's handmaid; Gad, and   Ge 35:26
A.
sons of A.; Jimnah, and   Ge 46:17
Ishuah
Out of A. his bread shall be   Ge 49:20
fat
Dan, and Naphtali, Gad, and   Ex 1:4
A.
Of A.; Pagiel the son of   Nu 1:13
Ocran
children of A. by their   Nu 1:40
generations
of the tribe of A. were forty   Nu 1:41
by him shall be the tribe of   Nu 2:27
A.
captain of the children of A.   Nu 2:27
prince the children of A.   Nu 7:72
offered
tribe of the children of A.   Nu 10:26
of A. Sethur the son of   Nu 13:13
Michael
children of A. after their   Nu 26:44
families
of the daughter of A. was   Nu 26:46
Sarah
are the families of the sons   Nu 26:47
of A.
of A. Ahihud the son of   Nu 34:27
Shelomi
Reuben, Gad, and A. and   De 27:13
Zebulun
of A. he said, Let A. be   De 33:24
blessed
coast of Manasseh was from   Jos 17:7
A. to
met together in A. on the   Jos 17:10
north
Manasseh had in Issachar   Jos 17:11
and in A.
tribe of the children of A.   Jos 19:24
according
of the tribe of the children   Jos 19:31
of A.
reacheth to A. on the west   Jos 19:34
side
out of the tribe of A. and   Jos 21:6
out of
of A. Mishal with her   Jos 21:30
suburbs
did A. drive out the   J'g 1:31
inhabitants of
A. continued on the sea shore   J'g 5:17
and he sent messengers unto A.   J'g 6:35
of A. and out of all   J'g 7:23
Manasseh
son of Hushai was in A. and   1Ki 4:16
Benjamin, Naphtali, Gad, and   1Ch 2:2
A.
out of the tribe of A. and   1Ch 6:62
of A.; Mashal with her   1Ch 6:74
suburbs
sons of A.; Imnah, and   1Ch 7:30
Isuah
All these were the children   1Ch 7:40
of A.
of A. such as went forth to   1Ch 12:36
battle
divers of A. and Manasseh   2Ch 30:11
the west side, a portion for   Eze 48:2
A.
border of A. from the east   Eze 48:3
side
gate of A. one gate of   Eze 48:34
Naphtali

ASHERAH

do not plant an A.   De 16:21
(A)(B)(E)(R)
wood of the A. (A)   J'g 6:25

made an A.   1Ki 15:13;
(A)(B)(E)(R)   16:33
prophets of A.   1Ki 18:19
(A)(B)(E)(R)
remained the A. (A)(E)(R)   2Ki 13:6;
   17:16; 21:3; 23:4-5, 15
cut down the A. (A)(E)(R)   2Ki 18:4

ASHERAHS

chopped down the A.   2Ch 14:3
(B)(E)(R)
destroyed the A. (R)   2Ch 19:3; 33:3

ASHERIM

cut down their A.   Ex 34:13
(A)(E)(R)
made their A.   1Ki 14:15
(A)(B)(E)(R)
high places, pillars of A.   1Ki 14:23
(A)(B)(E)(R)
cut down the A.   2Ki 23:14
(A)(E)(R)
pillars, obelisks, A. (A)   2Ch 14:3
took away the A.   2Ch 17:6;
(A)(E)(R)   2Ch 31:1; 34:3, 7
the A. (A)(E)(R)   Isa 17:8;
   Isa 27:9; Mic 5:14
the A., sin-images (A)(E)   Isa 27:9
their A. (B)(E)(R)   Jer 17:2
root out your A. (A)(R)   Mic 5:14

ASHERITES

A. dwelt among the   J'g 1:32
Canaanites

ASHEROTH

served Balaam and A. (E)(R)   J'g 3:7

ASHES

which am but dust and a.   Ge 18:27
you handfuls of a. of the   Ex 9:8
furnace
And they took a. of the   Ex 9:10
furnace
pans to receive his a.   Ex 27:3
by the place of the a.   Le 1:16
where the a. are poured out   Le 4:12
take up the a.   Le 6:10
carry forth the a.   Le 6:11
And they shall take away the   Nu 4:13
a.
the a. of the heifer   Nu 19:9
he that gathereth the a. of   Nu 19:10
they shall take of the a. of   Nu 19:17
the
Tamar put a. on her head   2Sa 13:19
the a. that are upon it   1Ki 13:3
the a. poured out from the   1Ki 13:5
altar
disguised himself with a.   1Ki 20:38
upon
took the a. away from his   1Ki 20:41
face
the a. of them unto Beth-el   2Ki 23:4
put on sackcloth with a.   Es 4:1
many lay in sackcloth and a.   Es 4:3
he sat down among the a.   Job 2:8
remembrances are like unto   Job 13:12
a.
I am become like dust and   Job 30:19
a.
repent in dust and a.   Job 42:6
For I have eaten a. like   Ps 102:9
bread
he scattereth the hoarfrost   Ps 147:16
like a.
He feedeth on a.   Isa 44:20
spread sackcloth and a.   Isa 58:5
under him
to give unto them beauty for   Isa 61:3
a.
wallow thyself in a.   Jer 6:26
and wallow yourselves in the   Jer 25:34
a.
and of the a. and all the   Jer 31:40
fields
he hath covered me with a.   La 3:16
wallow themselves in the a.   Eze 27:30
I will bring thee to a.   Eze 28:18
with fasting, and sackcloth,   Da 9:3
and a.
and sat in a.   Jon 3:6
for they shall be a.   Mal 4:3

long ago in sackcloth and   M't 11:21
a.
sitting in sackcloth and a.   Lu 10:13
the a. of an heifer   Heb 9:13
sprinkling the
Sodom and Gomorrha into a.   2Pe 2:6

ASHIMA

and the men of Hamath   2Ki 17:30
made A.

ASHKELON

and he went down to A. and   J'g 14:19
slew
A. and Azzah, and Ekron   Jer 25:20
A. is cut off with the   Jer 47:5
remnant
A. and against the sea shore   Jer 47:7
that holdeth the sceptre from   Am 1:8
A.
Gaza shall be forsaken, and   Zep 2:4
A.
houses of A. shall they lie   Zep 2:7
down
A. shall see it, and fear   Zec 9:5
and A. shall not be inhabited   Zec 9:5

ASHKENAZ

sons of Gomer; A. and   Ge 10:3
Riphath

ASHNAH

Eshtaol, and Zoreah, and   Jos 15:33
A.
Jiphtah, and A. and Nezib   Jos 15:43

ASHPENAZ

the king spake unto A. the   Da 1:3
master

ASHRIEL

of Manasseh; A. whom she   1Ch 7:14
bare

ASHTAROTH

king of Bashan, which was   Jos 9:10
at A.
that dwelt at A. and at Edrei   Jos 12:4
Og in Bashan, which   Jos 13:12
reigned in A.
half Gilead, and A. and   Jos 13:31
Edrei
the Lord, and served Baal and   J'g 2:13
A.
served Baals and A. (A)(B)   J'g 3:17
served Baalim, and A. and   J'g 10:6
the
put away the strange gods   1Sa 7:3
and A.
Israel did put away Baalim and   1Sa 7:4
A.
and have served Baalim and   1Sa 12:10
A.
put his armour in the house   1Sa 31:10
of A.
and A. with her suburbs   1Ch 6:71

ASHTERATHITE

Uzzia and A., Shama and   1Ch 11:44
Jehiel

ASHTEROTH

and smote the Rephaims in   Ge 14:5
A.
images of the A. (B)   Isa 17:8
the goddess A. (A)   Jer 17:2

ASHTORETH

Solomon went after A. the   1Ki 11:5
A. the goddess of the   1Ki 11:33
Sidonians
for A. the abomination of   2Ki 23:13

ASHUR

Hezron's wife bare him A.   1Ch 2:24
A. the father of Tekoa had   1Ch 4:5
two

ASHURITES

over the A. and over Jezreel	2Sa 2:9
the A. have made thy benches	Eze 27:6

ASHVATH

and A. These are the children	1Ch 7:33

ASHY

a. pale horse (A)	Re 6:8

ASIA

Pontus, and A.	Ac 2:9; 6:9
to preach the word in A.	Ac 16:6
all they which dwelt in A.	Ac 19:10
stayed in A. for a season	Ac 19:22
but almost throughout all A.	Ac 19:26
all A. and the world worshippeth	Ac 19:27
certain of the chief of A.	Ac 19:31
accompanied him into A.	Ac 20:4
of A. Tychicus and Trophimus	Ac 20:4
would not spend the time in A.	Ac 20:16
that I came into A.	Ac 20:18
the Jews which were of A.	Ac 21:27
certain Jews from A.	Ac 24:18
by the coasts of A.	Ac 27:2
The churches of A. salute you	1Co 16:19
which came to us in A.	2Co 1:8
all they which are in A.	2Ti 1:15
A. and Bithynia	1Pe 1:1
seven churches which are in A.	Re 1:4
seven churches which are in A.	Re 1:11

ASIDE

turn a. and see this sight	Ex 3:3; 3:4
have turned a. quickly out	Ex 32:8;
of way	De 9:12, 16; 11:16; 31:29
turned a. there (S)	J'g 18:15
shalt set a. that which is full	2Ki 4:4
all gone a.	Ps 14:3;
	40:4; 78:57; 125:5
called disciples a. (S)	M't 20:17;
	M'k 6:31
laying a. commandment of God	M'k 7:8
turned a. unto vain jangling	1Ti 1:6
some are already turned a.	1Ti 5:15
let us lay a. every weight	Heb 12:1
laying a. all malice	1Pe 2:1
things we a. for (N)	1Jo 5:15

ASIEL

of Seraiah, the son of A.	1Ch 4:35

ASK

thou dost a. after my name	Ge 32:29
A. me never so much dowry	Ge 34:12
who shall a. counsel for him	Nu 27:21
a. now of the days that are past	De 4:32
a. from the one side of heaven	De 4:32
enquire, and make search, and a.	De 13:14
a. thy father, and he will shew	De 32:7
your children a. their fathers	Jos 4:6
When your children shall a.	Jos 4:21
she moved him to a. of her	Jos 15:18
she moved him to a. of her	J'g 1:14
A. counsel, we pray thee, of God	J'g 18:5
our sins this evil, to a. us a king	1Sa 12:19
A. thy young men, and they will	1Sa 25:8
Wherefore then dost thou a. of me	1Sa 28:16
thee, the thing that I shall a. thee	2Sa 14:18
shall surely a. counsel at Abel	2Sa 20:18
I a. one petition of thee	1Ki 2:16
the king said unto her, A. on, my	1Ki 2:20
why dost thou a. Abishag	1Ki 2:22
a. for him the kingdom also	1Ki 2:22
A. what I shall give thee	1Ki 3:5

cometh to a. a thing of thee for	1Ki 14:5
A. what I shall do for thee	2Ki 2:9
A. what I shall give thee	2Ch 1:7
to a. help of the Lord	2Ch 20:4
a. now the beasts, and they shall	Job 12:7
A. of me, and I shall give thee	Ps 2:8
A. thee a sign of the Lord	Isa 7:11
a. it either in the depth, or in the	Isa 7:11
Ahaz said, I will not a.	Isa 7:12
A. me of things to come	Isa 45:11
A. of me the ordinances of justice	Isa 58:2
and a. for the old paths	Jer 6:16
who shall go aside to a. how thou	Jer 15:5
A. ye now among the heathen	Jer 18:13
prophet, or a priest, shall a. thee	Jer 23:33
A. ye now, and see	Jer 30:6
I will a. thee a thing	Jer 38:14
a. him that fleeth	Jer 48:19
They shall a. the way to Zion	Jer 50:5
the young children a. bread	La 4:4
whosoever shall a. a petition of	Da 6:7
every man that shall a. a petition	Da 6:12
My people a. counsel at their	Ho 4:12
A. now the priests concerning	Hag 2:11
A. ye of the Lord rain	Zec 10:1
have need of, before ye a. him	M't 6:8
A. and it shall be given you	M't 7:7
if his son a. bread, will he give	M't 7:9
Or if he a. a fish, will he give him	M't 7:10
good things to them that a. him	M't 7:11
give her whatsoever she would a.	M't 14:7
any thing that they shall a.	M't 18:19
said, Ye know not what ye a.	M't 20:22
whatsoever ye shall a. in prayer	M't 21:22
I also will a. you one thing	M't 21:24
a. him any more questions	M't 22:46
that they should a. Barabbas	M't 27:20
A. of me whatsoever thou wilt	M'k 6:22
Whatsoever thou shalt a. of me	M'k 6:23
unto her mother, What shall I a.	M'k 6:24
saying, and were afraid to a. him	M'k 9:32
Ye know not what ye a.	M'k 10:38
I will also a. of you one question	M'k 11:29
And no man after that durst a.	M'k 12:34
I will a. you one thing; Is it	Lu 6:9
away thy goods a. them not	Lu 6:30
they feared to a. him of that	Lu 9:45
A. and it shall be given you	Lu 11:9
If a son shall a. bread of any	Lu 11:11
if he a. a fish will he for a fish	Lu 11:11
Or if he shall a. an egg, will	Lu 11:12
Holy Spirit to them that a. him	Lu 11:13
of him they will a. the more	Lu 12:48
if any man a. you	Lu 19:31
I will also a. you one thing	Lu 20:3
they durst not a. him any	Lu 20:40
And if I also a. you	Lu 22:68
from Jerusalem to a. him, Who	Joh 1:19
he is of age; a. him: he shall	Joh 9:21
his parents, He is of age; a. him	Joh 9:23
whatsoever thou wilt a. of God	Joh 11:22
that he should a. who it should	Joh 13:24
whatsoever ye shall a. in my	Joh 14:13
If ye shall a. any thing in my	Joh 14:14
abide in you, ye shall a.	Joh 15:7

whatsoever ye shall a. of the	Joh 15:16
they were desirous to a. him	Joh 16:19
ye shall a. me nothing	Joh 16:23
Whatsoever ye shall a. the	Joh 16:23
a. and ye shall receive, that your	Joh 16:24
At that day ye shall a. in my name	Joh 16:26
that any man should a. thee	Joh 16:30
Why askest thou me? a. them	Joh 18:21
none of the disciples durst a.	Joh 21:12
to a. alms of them that entered	Ac 3:2
I a. therefore for what intent	Ac 10:29
let them a. their husbands	1Co 14:35
above all that we a. or think	Eph 3:20
you lack wisdom, let him a. of	Jas 1:5
But let him a. in faith	Jas 1:6
ye have not, because ye a. not	Jas 4:2
Ye a. and receive not, because	Jas 4:3
ye a. amiss, that ye may	Jas 4:3
whatsoever we a. we receive	1Jo 3:22
if we a. any thing according to his	1Jo 5:14
we a. we know that we have the	1Jo 5:15
not unto death, he shall a. and	1Jo 5:16

ASKED

and I a. her, and said	Ge 24:47
the men of the place a. him	Ge 26:7
And Jacob a. him	Ge 32:29
and the man a. him	Ge 37:15
Then he a. the men of that place	Ge 38:21
And he a. Pharaoh's officers	Ge 40:7
The man a. us straitly	Ge 43:7
And he a. them of their welfare	Ge 43:27
My lord a. his servants	Ge 44:19
they a. of neighbors (S)	Ex 3:22;
	Ex 11:2; 12:35
they a. each other of their welfare	Ex 18:7
a. not counsel at the mouth of the	Jos 9:14
gave him the city which he a.	Jos 19:50
that the children of Israel a.	J'g 1:1
a. water, and she gave him milk	J'g 5:25
And when they enquired and a.	J'g 6:29
I a. him not whence he was	J'g 13:6
and a. counsel of God	J'g 20:18
and a. counsel of the Lord	J'g 20:23
thy petition that thou hast a.	1Sa 1:17
I have a. him of the Lord	1Sa 1:20
my petition which I a. of him	1Sa 1:27
the people that a. of him a king	1Sa 8:10
the king a. for (A)(E)(R)	1Sa 12:13
And Saul a. counsel of God	1Sa 14:37
and he a. and said	1Sa 19:22
David earnestly a. leave	1Sa 20:6
a. leave of me to go to Beth-lehem	1Sa 20:28
Solomon had a. this thing	1Ki 3:10
Because thou hast a. this thing	1Ki 3:11
hast not a. for thyself long life	1Ki 3:11
neither hast a. riches for thyself	1Ki 3:11
hast a. the life of thine enemies	1Ki 3:11
hast a. for thyself understanding	1Ki 3:11
thee that which thou hast not a.	1Ki 3:13
whatsoever she a.	1Ki 10:13
Thou hast a. a hard thing	2Ki 2:10
when the king a. the woman	2Ki 8:6
thou hast not a. riches	2Ch 1:11
neither yet hast a. long life	2Ch 1:11
hast a. wisdom and knowledge	2Ch 1:11
all her desire, whatsoever she a.	2Ch 9:12
Then a. we those elders	Ezr 5:9
We a. their names also	Ezr 5:10

and I *a.* them concerning the   *Ne 1:2*
Jews
Have ye not *a.* them that   *Job 21:29*
go by
He *a.* life of thee   *Ps 21:4*
The people *a.* and he   *Ps 105:40*
brought
have not *a.* at my mouth   *Isa 30:2*
when I *a.* of them, could   *Isa 41:28*
answer
I am sought of them that *a.*   *Isa 65:1*
not
they *a.* Baruch   *Jer 36:17*
the king *a.* him secretly in   *Jer 37:17*
his
the princes unto Jeremiah,   *Jer 38:27*
and *a.*
a. such things at any   *Da 2:10*
magician
and *a.* him the truth of all   *Da 7:16*
this
they *a.* him, saying   *M't 12:10*
he *a.* his disciples, saying,   *M't 16:13*
Whom
his disciples *a.* him, saying   *M't 17:10*
a. him for something   *M't 20:20*
(A)(E)(R)
is no resurrection, and *a.*   *M't 22:23*
him
them, which was a lawyer,   *M't 22:35*
a. him
gathered together, Jesus *a.*   *M't 22:41*
them
and the governor *a.* him,   *M't 27:11*
saying
about him with the twelve *a.*   *M'k 4:10*
of
And he *a.* him, What is thy   *M'k 5:9*
name
unto the king, and *a.* saying   *M'k 6:25*
Pharisees and scribes *a.* him   *M'k 7:5*
his disciples *a.* him   *M'k 7:17*
concerning the
he *a.* them, How many loaves   *M'k 8:5*
he *a.* him if he saw ought   *M'k 8:23*
by the way he *a.* his   *M'k 8:27*
disciples
And they *a.* him saying,   *M'k 9:11*
Why say
And he *a.* the scribes, What   *M'k 9:16*
And he *a.* his father, How   *M'k 9:21*
long is it
his disciples *a.* him privately,   *M'k 9:28*
Why
being in the house he *a.*   *M'k 9:33*
them
Pharisees came to him, and   *M'k 10:2*
a. him
disciples *a.* him again of   *M'k 10:10*
the same
and *a.* him, Good Master,   *M'k 10:17*
what
no resurrection; and they *a.*   *M'k 12:18*
him
a. him, Which is the first   *M'k 12:28*
John and Andrew *a.* him   *M'k 13:3*
privately
the midst, and *a.* Jesus,   *M'k 14:60*
saying
Again the high priest *a.* him   *M'k 14:61*
And Pilate *a.* him, Art thou   *M'k 15:2*
the
And Pilate *a.* him again,   *M'k 15:4*
saying
he *a.* him whether he had   *M'k 15:44*
been
a. body of Jesus   *M'k 15:45*
(A)(B)(E)(N)(P)(R)(S)
he *a.* for a writing table, and   *Lu 1:63*
wrote
And the people *a.* him, saying   *Lu 3:10*
a. him to thrust out the ship   *Lu 3:10*
(S)
And his disciples *a.* him,   *Lu 8:9*
saying
And Jesus *a.* him, saying,   *Lu 8:30*
What is
and he *a.* them, saying,   *Lu 9:18*
Whom say
and *a.* what these things   *Lu 15:26*
meant
a certain ruler *a.* him, saying   *Lu 18:18*
pass by, he *a.* what it meant   *Lu 18:36*
he was come near, he *a.* him   *Lu 18:40*
they *a.* him, saying, Master,   *Lu 20:21*
we
any resurrection; and they *a.*   *Lu 20:27*
him

And they *a.* him, saying,   *Lu 21:7*
Master
Satan *a.* excessively   *Lu 22:31*
(A)(B)(E)(R)
and *a.* him, saying,   *Lu 22:64*
Prophesy, who
And Pilate *a.* him, saying,   *Lu 23:3*
Art
he *a.* whether the man were a   *Lu 23:6*
And they *a.* him, What then   *Joh 1:21*
they *a.* him, and said   *Joh 1:25*
thou wouldest have *a.* of him   *Joh 4:10*
Then *a.* they him, What man   *Joh 5:12*
is
his disciples *a.* him   *Joh 9:2*
the Pharisees also *a.* him   *Joh 9:15*
a. them, saying, Is this your   *Joh 9:19*
son
have ye *a.* nothing in my   *Joh 16:24*
name
Then *a.* he them again,   *Joh 18:7*
Whom
The high priest then *a.*   *Joh 18:19*
Jesus of
they *a.* of him, saying, Lord,   *Ac 1:6*
wilt
to go into the temple an   *Ac 3:3*
alms
a. a murderer (E)(R)   *Ac 3:14*
they *a.*, By what power, or by   *Ac 4:7*
and the high priest *a.* them   *Ac 5:27*
and *a.* whether Simon   *Ac 10:18*
they *a.* him to tarry (S)   *Ac 10:48*
a. for peace (A)(E)(R)   *Ac 12:20*
a. for a king   *Ac 13:21*
(A)(B)(E)(N)(R)
aside privately, and *a.* him   *Ac 23:19*
he *a.* of what province he   *Ac 23:34*
was
a. me to bring this man (S)   *Ac 25:18*
I *a.* him whether he would   *Ac 25:20*
go
unto them that *a.* not after   *Ro 10:20*
me
a. for Titus (N)(P)   *2Co 8:6*

ASKEST

Why *a.* thou thus after my   *J'g 13:18*
name
being a Jew, *a.* drink of   *Joh 4:9*
me
Why *a.* thou me? ask them   *Joh 18:21*
which

ASKETH

my brother meeteth thee,   *Ge 32:17*
and *a.*
when thy son *a.* thee   *Ex 13:14*
thy son *a.* thee in time to come   *De 6:20*
hands earnestly, the prince   *Mic 7:3*
a.
and the judge *a.* for a reward   *Mic 7:3*
Give to him that *a.* thee   *M't 5:42*
every one that *a.* receiveth   *M't 7:8*
Give to every man that *a.* of   *Lu 6:30*
thee
every one that *a.* receiveth   *Lu 11:10*
none of you *a.* me   *Joh 16:5*
every man that *a.* you a   *1Pe 3:15*
reason

ASKING

in *a.* you a king   *1Sa 12:17*
for *a.* counsel of one that   *1Ch 10:13*
had a.
tempted God in their heart   *Ps 78:18*
by *a.*
them, and *a.* them questions   *Lu 2:46*
So when they continued *a.*   *Joh 8:7*
him
a. no question for   *1Co 10:25*
conscience sake
eat, *a.* no question for   *1Co 10:27*
conscience

ASKELON

and *A.* with the coast thereof   *J'g 1:18*
for Gaza one, for *A.* one,   *1Sa 6:17*
for Gath
publish it not in the streets   *2Sa 1:20*
of *A.*

ASKING

and *a.* peace   *Lu 14:32*
(A)(E)(N)(P)(R)

ASLEEP

he was fast *a.* and weary   *J'g 4:21*
in deep sleep (B)(E)   *J'g 4:21*
lips of those that are *a.* to   *Ca 7:9*
speak
of those sleeping (B)   *Ca 7:9*
but Jonah lay, and was fast *a.*   *Jon 1:5*
arose storm, he was *a.*   *M't 8:24;*
   M'k 4:38
He was sleeping (A)(B)(N)(P)   *M't 8:24*
He findeth disciples *a.*   *M't 26:40;*
   M'k 14:40
found them sleeping   *M't 26:40*
(A)(E)(R)
when Stephen said this, he   *Ac 7:60*
fell *a.*
with that he died (N)   *Ac 7:60*
fell in sleep of death (P)   *Ac 7:60*
fell *a.* (S)   *Ac 13:36*
part remain, but some are   *1Co 15:6*
fallen *a.*
some have died (N)(P)   *1Co 15:6*
they which are fallen *a.* in   *1Co 15:18*
Christ
those who have died   *1Co 15:18*
(A)(N)(P)
ignorant concerning them   *1Th 4:13*
that are *a.*
we alive not prevent them *a.*   *1Th 4:15*
since fathers fell *a.* all things   *2Pe 3:4*

ASNAH

The children of *A.* the   *Ezr 2:50*
children

ASNAPPER

great and noble *A.* brought   *Ezr 4:10*
over

ASP

shall play on the hole of the   *Isa 11:8*
a.

ASPATHA

and Dalphon, and *A.*   *Es 9:7*

ASPECT

his *a.* like Lebanon (E)   *Ca 5:15*
the *a.* of the fourth is like (E)   *Da 3:25*

ASPHALT

a. for mortar (B)   *Ge 11:3*

ASPS

and the cruel venom of *a.*   *De 32:33*
venon of serpents   *De 32:33*
(B)(E)(R)
the gall of *a.* within him   *Job 20:14*
He shall suck the poison of   *Job 20:16*
a.
poison of *a.* is under their   *Ro 3:13*
lips

ASRIEL

of *A.* the family of the   *Nu 26:31*
Asrielites
and for the children of *A.*   *Jos 17:2*

ASRIELITES

of Asriel, the family of the   *Nu 26:31*
A.

ASS

a wild *a.* among men   *Ge 16:12*
(A)(B)(E)(R)
saddled his *a.* and took two   *Ge 22:3*
saddled his donkey (B)   *Ge 22:3; 22:5*
Issachar is a strong *a.*   *Ge 49:14*
crouching
Issachar is a big-boned   *Ge 49:14*
donkey (B)
every firstling of an *a.* shalt   *Ex 13:13*
a donkey (B)   *Ex 13:13;*
   23:4, 12; De 22:10; Jos 15:18; J'g 15:16;
   1Ki 13:28
meet thine enemy's *a.* going   *Ex 23:4*
astray
that thine ox and *a.* may   *Ex 23:12*
rest

I have not taken one *a.*   *Nu 16:15*
from them
saddled his *a.* and went   *Nu 22:21;*
with   *22:22*
the *a.* saw angel standing   *Nu 22:23;*
  22:25, 27
Lord opened the mouth of   *Nu 22:28*
the *a.*
the *a.* said to Balaam   *Nu 22:30;*
  2Pe 2:16
not plow ox and *a.* together   *De 22:10*
lighted off her *a.*   *Jos 15:18;*
  J'g 1:14; 1Sa 25:23
sons that rode on thirty *a.*   *J'g 10:4;*
colts   *12:14*
slew with the jawbone of   *J'g 15:16*
an *a.*
whose *a.* have I taken   *1Sa 12:3*
the lion had not torn the *a.*   *1Ki 13:28*
they drive away the *a.* of   *Job 24:3*
fatherless
a donkey (A)(B)   *Job 24:3;*
Pr 26:3; Isa 1:3; 32:20; Jer 2:24; 22:19;
Zec 9:9; 14:15
hath sent out the wild *a.* free   *Job 39:5*
loosed the bands of the wild   *Job 39:5*
a.
a bridle for the *a.*   *Pr 26:3*
and the *a.* his masters crib   *Isa 1:3*
the feet of the ox and the *a.*   *Isa 32:20*
A wild *a.* used to the   *Jer 2:24*
wilderness
buried with the burial of an   *Jer 22:19*
a.
a wild *a.* alone by himself   *Ho 8:9*
lowly, and riding upon an *a.*   *Zec 9:9*
and upon a colt the foal of   *Zec 9:9*
an *a.*
mule, of the camel, and of   *Zec 14:15*
the *a.*
ye shall find an *a.* tied   *M't 21:2*
meek, and sitting upon an *a.*   *M't 21:5*
and a colt the foal of an *a.*   *M't 21:5*
And brought the *a.* and the   *M't 21:7*
colt
loose his ox or his *a.* from   *Lu 13:15*
the stall
Which of you shall have an   *Lu 14:5*
a. or
when he had found a young   *Joh 12:14*
a.
a. speaking with man's voice   *2Pe 2:16*

WILD ASS

doth the *wild a.* bray when he   *Job 6:5*
hath grass
a wild donkey (A)(B)   *Job 6:5; Jer 2:24*
sent out the *wild a.* free   *Job 39:5*
the swift donkey (A)(B)   *Job 39:5*
a *wild a.* used to the   *Jer 2:24*
wilderness
a wild donkey (B)   *Jer 2:24*
a *wild a.* alone by himself   *Ho 8:9*

ASSAIL

a. him with questions (N)   *Lu 11:53*

ASSASSINATED

his own offspring *a.* him   *2Ch 32:21*
(A)(B)

ASSAULT

the people, that would *a.*   *Es 8:11*
them
that armed against them (B)   *Es 8:11*
that might attack them (R)   *Es 8:11*
when there was an *a.* made   *Ac 14:5*
insult, abuse, and molest (A)   *Ac 14:5*
abuse and stone (B)   *Ac 14:5*
treat them shamefully (E)   *Ac 14:5*
maltreat them (N)   *Ac 14:5*
insult and stone them (P)   *Ac 14:5*
molest and stone them (R)   *Ac 14:5*

ASSAULTED

a. the house of Jason, and   *Ac 17:5*
sought
attack the house of Jason   *Ac 17:5*
(A)(B)(P)(R)
mobbed Jason's house (N)   *Ac 17:5*

ASSAY

If we *a.* to commune with   *Job 4:2*
thee

ASSAYED

hath God *a.* to go and take   *De 4:34*
him
venture to go take a nation   *De 4:34*
(B)
attempted to go and take (R)   *De 4:34*
and he *a.* to go; for he had   *1Sa 17:39*
not
tried walking for he had   *1Sa 17:39*
never (B)
he tried in vain to go (R)   *1Sa 17:39*
a. to join himself to the   *Ac 9:26*
disciples
he tried to associate himself   *Ac 9:26*
(A)(B)(N)(P)
he attempted to join (R)   *Ac 9:26*
they *a.* to go into Bithynia   *Ac 16:7*
tried to go to Bithynia   *Ac 16:7*
(A)(B)(N)(P)
attempted to go to Bithynia   *Ac 16:7*
(R)

ASSAYING

Egyptians *a.* to do were   *Heb 11:29*
tried to do the same thing   *Heb 11:29*
(A)(B)(P)
attempted the crossing   *Heb 11:29*
(N)(R)

ASSEMBLE

shall *a.* themselves to thee   *Nu 10:3*
A. me the men of Judah   *2Sa 20:4*
went to *a.* the men of Judah   *2Sa 20:5*
shall *a.* the outcasts of   *Isa 11:12*
Israel
A. yourselves and come   *Isa 45:20*
All ye, *a.* yourselves, and   *Isa 48:14*
hear
and say, *A.* yourselves, and let   *Jer 4:5*
us
do we sit still? *a.* yourselves   *Jer 8:14*
a. all the beasts of the field   *Jer 12:9*
and I will *a.* them into the   *Jer 21:4*
midst
and *a.* you out of the   *Eze 11:17*
countries
A. yourselves, and come   *Eze 39:17*
a. a multitude of great   *Da 11:10*
forces
they *a.* themselves for corn   *Ho 7:14*
Gather the people, *a.* the   *Joe 2:16*
elders
A. yourselves, and come, all   *Joe 3:11*
ye
A. yourselves upon the   *Am 3:9*
mountain
surely *a.* O Jacob, all of   *Mic 2:12*
thee
will I *a.* her that halteth   *Mic 4:6*
that I may *a.* the kingdoms   *Zep 3:8*

ASSEMBLED

a. at the door of the   *Ex 38:8*
tabernacle
they *a.* all the congregation   *Nu 1:18*
congregation, *a.* together at   *Jos 18:1*
of Israel *a.* themselves   *J'g 10:17*
together
a. at the door of the   *1Sa 2:22*
tabernacle
all the people, *a.*   *1Sa 14:20*
themselves
Solomon *a.* the elders of   *1Ki 8:1*
Israel
a. themselves unto king   *1Ki 8:2*
Solomon
that were *a.* unto him   *1Ki 8:5*
he *a.* all the house of Judah   *1Ki 12:21*
David *a.* the children of   *1Ch 15:4*
Aaron
David *a.* all the princes of   *1Ch 28:1*
Israel
Solomon *a.* the elders of   *2Ch 5:2*
Israel
all the men of Israel *a.*   *2Ch 5:3*
themselves
were *a.* unto him before the   *2Ch 5:6*
ark
they *a.* themselves in the   *2Ch 20:26*
valley
a. at Jerusalem much   *2Ch 30:13*
people
Then were *a.* unto me every   *Ezr 9:4*
one
there *a.* unto him, a very   *Ezr 10:1*
great

the children of Israel were *a.*   *Ne 9:1*
that were at Shushan, *a.*   *Es 9:18*
together
kings were *a.*, they passed by   *Ps 48:4*
and let the people be *a.*   *Isa 43:9*
and *a.* themselves by troops   *Jer 5:7*
company that are *a.* unto   *Eze 38:7*
thee
presidents and princes *a.*   *Da 6:6*
together
these men *a.* and found   *Da 6:11*
Daniel
Then these men *a.* unto the   *Da 6:15*
king
a. together the chief priests   *M't 26:3*
scribes and the elders were   *M't 26:57*
a.
they were *a.* with the   *M't 28:12*
elders
were *a.* all the chief priests   *M'k 14:53*
where the disciples were *a.*   *Joh 20:19*
And being *a.* together with   *Ac 1:4*
them
when they were *a.* together   *Ac 4:31*
a. themselves with the   *Ac 11:26*
church
being *a.* with one accord   *Ac 15:25*

ASSEMBLIES

and the *a.* of violent men   *Ps 86:14*
fastened by the masters of *a.*   *Ec 12:11*
calling of *a.*, I cannot away   *Isa 1:13*
with
her *a.* a cloud of smoke by   *Isa 4:5*
day
my statutes in all mine *a.*   *Eze 44:24*
not smell in your solemn *a.*   *Am 5:21*

ASSEMBLING

glasses of the women *a.*   *Ex 38:8*
the *a.* of ourselves together   *Heb 10:25*

ASSEMBLY

into their secret; unto their *a.*   *Ge 49:6*
a. of the congregation of   *Ex 12:6*
Israel
an holy *a.* (A)(R)   *Ex 12:16; Le 23:21*
kill this whole *a.* with hunger   *Ex 16:3*
be hid from the eyes of the *a.*   *Le 4:13*
the *a.* was gathered together   *Le 8:4*
a solemn *a.* (A)   *Le 23:21*
it is a solemn *a.*   *Le 26:36*
thou shalt gather the whole *a.*   *Nu 8:9*
the calling of the *a.* and for   *Nu 10:2*
the
a. shall assemble themselves   *Nu 10:3*
to
on their faces before all the   *Nu 14:5*
a.
princes of the *a.* famous   *Nu 16:2*
went from the presence of   *Nu 20:6*
the *a.*
gather thou the *a.* together   *Nu 20:8*
the holy *a.* (A)   *Nu 28:18;*
  Nu 28:25-26; 29:1, 7, 12
ye shall have a solemn *a.*   *Nu 29:35*
stood trial before the *a.* (B)   *Nu 35:12*
the *a.* shall decide (B)   *Nu 35:24*
the Lord spake unto all your   *De 5:22*
a.
fire in the day of the *a.*   *De 9:10*
of the fire, in the day of the *a.*   *De 10:4*
a solemn *a.* to the Lord thy   *De 16:8*
God
Horeb in the day of the *a.*   *De 18:16*
appear before the *a.* for trial   *Jos 20:6*
(B)
themselves in the *a.* of the   *J'g 20:2*
people
from Jabesh-gilead to the *a.*   *J'g 21:8*
this *a.* shall know that the   *1Sa 17:47*
Lord
Proclaim a solemn *a.* for   *2Ki 10:20*
Baal
they made a solemn *a.*   *2Ch 7:9*
the whole *a.* took counsel   *2Ch 30:23*
And I set a great *a.* against   *Ne 5:7*
them
the eighth day was a solemn   *Ne 8:18*
a.
a. of the wicked have   *Ps 22:16*
enclosed me
in the midst of thine *a.* (E)   *Ps 74:4*
to be feared in the *a.* of the   *Ps 89:7*
saints
and praise him in the *a.* of   *Ps 107:32*
in the *a.* of the upright   *Ps 111:1*

midst of the congregation and *Pr 5:14*
a.
the *a.* of young men together *Jer 6:11*
an *a.* of treacherous men *Jer 9:2*
I sat not in the *a.* of the *Jer 15:17*
mockers
spake to all the *a.* of the *Jer 26:17*
people
Babylon an *a.* of great *Jer 50:9*
nations
he hath called an *a.* against *La 1:15*
me
destroyed his places of the *a.* *La 2:6*
not be in the *a.* of my *Eze 13:9*
people
and with an *a.* of people *Eze 23:24*
bring up an *a.* (B) *Eze 23:46*
the great *a.* day (B) *Ho 9:5*
call a solemn *a.*, gather the *Joe 1:14*
elders
sanctify a fast, call a solemn *a.* *Joe 2:15*
are sorrowful for the solemn *Zep 3:18*
a.
for the *a.* was confused *Ac 19:32*
determined in a lawful *a.* *Ac 19:39*
thus spoken, he dismissed the *Ac 19:41*
a.
a. and church of the *Heb 12:23*
firstborn
there come unto your *a.* a *Jas 2:2*
man

ASSENT

good to the king with one *2Ch 18:12*
a.

ASSENTED

And the Jews also *a.* saying *Ac 24:9*

ASS'S

his *a.* colt unto the choice *Ge 49:11*
vine
donkey's foal (B) *Ge 49:11*
an *a.* head was sold for *2Ki 6:25*
fourscore
man be born like a wild *a.* *Job 11:12*
colt
King cometh, sitting on an *Joh 12:15*
a. colt
sitting on a donkey's colt (A) *Joh 12:15*

ASSES

he *a.* and menservants *Ge 12:16*
donkeys, she-donkeys (B) *Ge 12:16;*
30:43; 36:24; 47:17; J'g 5:10; 1Sa 8:16;
9:3, 20; 2Sa 16:2; 1Ch 27:30; 2Ch 28:15;
Job 42:12; Isa 21:7; Eze 23:20
maidservants, and camels, *Ge 24:35*
and *a.*
menservants, and camels, *Ge 30:43*
and *a.*
I have oxen, and *a.* flocks *Ge 32:5*
twenty she *a.* and ten foals *Ge 32:15*
their oxen, and their *a.* *Ge 34:28*
as he fed the *a.* of Zibeon *Ge 36:24*
they laded their *a.* with the *Ge 42:26*
corn
take us for bondmen, and *Ge 43:18*
our *a.*
he gave their *a.* provender *Ge 43:24*
sent away, they and their *a.* *Ge 44:3*
ten *a.* laden with the good *Ge 45:23*
things
she *a.* laden with corn and *Ge 45:23*
bread
herds, and for the *a.* *Ge 47:17*
upon the horses, upon the *a.* *Nu 31:28*
of the beeves, and of the *a.* *Nu 31:30*
of the *a.* and of the flocks *Nu 31:34*
threescore and one thousand
a.
And the *a.* were thirty *Nu 3:39*
thousand
thousand *a.* and five *Nu 31:45*
hundred
his oxen, and his *a.* *Jos 7:24*
took old sacks upon their *a.* *Jos 9:4*
speak, ye that ride on white *J'g 5:10*
a.
goodliest young men, and *1Sa 8:16*
your *a.*
a. of Kish, Saul's father were *1Sa 9:3*
lost
and of *a.* two thousand *1Ch 5:21*
brought bread on *a.* *1Ch 12:40*
and over the *a.* was *1Ch 27:30*
Jehdeiah

all the feeble of them upon *2Ch 28:15*
a.
six thousand seven *Ezr 2:67*
hundred
seven hundred and twenty *a.* *Ne 7:69*
bringing in sheaves, and *Ne 13:15*
lading *a.*
five hundred she *a.* *Job 1:3*
and the *a.* feeding beside *Job 1:14*
them
a thousand she *a.* *Job 42:12*

WILD ASSES

as *wild a.* in the desert go *Job 24:5*
forth
wild donkeys (B) *Job 24:5;*
Ps 104:11; Isa 32:14; Da 5:21
forts shall be a joy of *wild* *Isa 32:14*
a.
wild a. snuffed up the wind *Jer 14:6*
Nebuchadnezzar's dwelling *Da 5:21*
with *wild a.*

YOUNG ASSES

carry their riches on *young a.* *Isa 30:6*
young a. that ear the ground *Isa 30:24*

ASSESSED

money *a.* each man (A)(R) *2Ki 12:4*
what was the *a.* on Israel *2Ch 24:9*
(B)

ASSHUR

Out of that land went forth *Ge 10:11*
A.
Elam, and *A.* and Arphaxad, *Ge 10:22*
and
A. shall carry thee away *Nu 24:22*
captive
afflict *A.* and shall afflict *Nu 24:24*
Eber
The sons of Shem; Elam, *1Ch 1:17*
and *A.*
the merchants of Sheba, *A.* *Eze 27:23*
and
A. is there and all her *Eze 32:22*
company
A. shall not save us; we will *Hos 14:3*
not

ASSHURIM

the sons of Dedan were *A.* *Ge 25:3*
and

ASSIGN

a. each his service (B) *Nu 4:19*
a. the articles (A)(B)(R) *Nu 4:32*
a. for the manslayer (S) *Nu 35:6;*
Jos 20:2
a. to him his way (B) *Job 36:23*
a. his lot with unfaithful (A) *Lu 22:29*

ASSIGNED

priests had a portion *a.* *Ge 47:22*
them
they *a.* Bezer in the wilderness *Jos 20:8*
that he *a.* Uriah unto a *2Sa 11:16*
place
a. to the king's gate (A) *1Ch 9:18*
a. to Joseph (E) *Ps 81:5*
a. to me a kingdom (B) *Lu 22:29*
life Lord as him (R) *1Co 7:17*
a. the gift of grace (N) *Eph 1:10*
the task *a.* to me (N) *Col 1:25*

ASSIR

A. and Elkanah, and *Ex 6:24*
Abiasaph
Jeconiah; *A.* Salathiel his *1Ch 3:17*
son
Korah his son, *A.* his son *1Ch 6:22*
Ebiasaph his son, and *A.* his *1Ch 6:23*
son
The son of Tahath, the son *1Ch 6:37*
of *A.*

ASSIST

and that ye *a.* her in *Ro 16:2*
whatsoever

ASSISTANT

chief *a.* about David (S) *2Sa 20:26*
John as their *a.* (N)(P) *Ac 13:5*
been an *a.* to many (B) *Ro 16:2*

ASSISTANTS

a. of God (B) *2Co 6:4*

ASSIZE

day to hold *a.* (N) *1Pe 2:12*

ASSOCIATE

not *a.* with him (A)(B)(R) *Pr 20:19*
do not *a.* with one (B) *Pr 22:24*
do not *a.* with those (B) *Pr 24:21*
A. yourselves, O ye people *Isa 8:9*
man is my *a.* (A)(B) *Zec 13:7*
made effort to *a.* with them *Ac 9:26*
(B)
a. with the lowly (R) *Ro 12:16*
not *a.* with (A)(R) *1Co 5:11; 5:9*
Titus may *a.* (B)(N)(R) *2Co 8:23*
do not *a.* with (A)(P) *2Th 3:14*

ASSOCIATED

a. with pagans (B) *Ps 106:35*
tribes of Israel *a.* (B) *Eze 37:19*
a. with him (A)(B) *Ac 17:4*
a. with him (B) *Ac 17:34*

ASSOCIATES

to be my *a.* (B) *Ps 101:6*
a. with harlots (A)(B) *Pr 29:3*
all his *a.* shall be (B) *Isa 44:11*
not been their *a.* (B) *M't 23:30*

ASSOCIATION

a. between light and *2Co 6:14*
darkness (B)

ASSOCIATIONS

bad *a.* corrupt (B) *1Co 15:33*

ASSOS

sailed unto *A.* there *Ac 20:13*
intending to
he met with us at *A.* *Ac 20:14*

ASSUAGE

would *a.* your pain (R) *Job 16:5*

ASSUR

days of Esar-haddon king of *Ezr 4:2*
A.
A. also is joined with them: *Ps 83:8*
they

ASSURANCE

shalt have none *a.* of thy *De 28:66*
life
quietness and *a.* for ever *Isa 32:17*
he hath given *a.* unto all *Ac 17:31*
men
it was with *a.* (A)(B) *2Co 1:15*
of the full *a.* of understanding *Col 2:2*
and in much *a.*; as ye know *1Th 1:5*
the full *a.* of hope unto the *He 6:11*
end
in full *a.* of faith, having *He 10:22*
our
faith is the *a.* *He 11:1*
(A)(B)(E)(R)

ASSURE

to *a.* you continuance (B) *Ge 45:7*
a. him of your love (A)(N) *2Co 2:8*
I *a.* every person (B) *Ga 5:3*
and shall *a.* our hearts *1Jo 3:19*
before him

ASSURED

a. it shall be mine (B) *Ge 15:8*
and it shall be *a.* to him *Le 27:19*
a. peace in this place *Jer 14:13*
and hast been *a.* of *2Ti 3:14*

ASSUREDLY

know thou *a.* that thou shalt go	1Sa 28:1
A. Solomon thy son shall reign	1Ki 1:13
saying, *A.* Solomon thy son	1Ki 1:17; 1:30
a. with my whole heart	Jer 32:41
wilt *a.* go forth unto the king	Jer 38:17
of the cup have *a.* drunken	Jer 49:12
house of Israel know *a.*	Ac 2:36
a. gathering that the Lord had	Ac 16:10

ASSWAGE

my lips should *a.* your grief	Job 16:5

ASSWAGED

and the waters *a.*	Ge 8:1
my grief is not *a.*	Job 16:6

ASSYRIA

Hiddekel goeth toward east of *A.*	Ge 2:14
Ishmael's sons dwelt as thou goest to *A.*	Ge 25:18
Pul king of *A.*	2Ki 15:19; 1Ch 5:26
came Tiglath-pileser king of *A.*	2Ki 15:29; 16:7-18; 1Ch 5:6, 26; 2Ch 28:20
came Shalmaneser king of *A.*	2Ki 17:3; 17:4-6, 23-27; 8:7-11
Sennacherib king of *A.*	2Ki 18:13;
come	18:17-33; 19:4-36; 20:6; 2Ch 32:1-22; 33:11; Isa 36:1-18; 37:4-37; 38:6
turned the heart of the king of *A.*	Ezr 6:22
since the time of the kings of *A.*	Ne 9:32
from Judah; even the king of *A.*	Isa 7:17; 7:18, 20; 8:4, 7; 10:12
to recover remnant from *A.*	Isa 11:11; 11:16
an highway for his people left from *A.*	Isa 11:16; Isa 19:23; 35:8
Israel be third with Egypt and *A.*	Isa 19:24
A. the work of my hands	Isa 19:25
Sargon king of *A.* sent him	Isa 20:1; 20:5-6
ready to perish in the land of *A.*	Isa 27:13
what hast thou to do in the way of *A.*	Jer 2:18
Egypt as thou wast ashamed of *A.*	Jer 2:36
king of *A.* hath devoured him	Jer 50:17; 50:18
that were the chosen men of *A.*	Eze 23:7
they go to *A.*	Ho 7:11; 8:9; 9:3; 10:6
tremble as a dove in land of *A.*	Ho 11:11
A. shall not save us (S)	Ho 14:3
they shall waste the land of *A.*	Mic 5:6
they shall come to thee from *A.*	Mic 7:12
shepherds slumber, O king of *A.*	Na 3:18
he shall destroy *A.* and Nineveh	Zep 2:13
gather them out of *A.*	Zec 10:10
the pride of *A.* shall be brought down	Zec 10:11

ASSYRIAN

O *A.* the rod of mine anger	Isa 10:5
in Zion, be not afraid of the *A.*	Isa 10:24
I will break the *A.* in my land	Isa 14:25
and the *A.* shall come into Egypt	Isa 19:23
till the *A.* founded it for them that	Isa 23:13
shall the *A.* be beaten down	Isa 30:31
shall the *A.* fall with the sword	Isa 31:8
A. oppressed them without cause	Isa 52:4
the *A.* was a cedar in Lebanon with	Eze 31:3
then went Ephraim to the *A.*	Ho 5:13
but the *A.* shall be his king, the *A.* shall come into our land	Ho 11:5; Mic 5:5

thus shall he deliver us from the *A.*	Mic 5:6

ASSYRIANS

and smote in the camp of the *A.*	2Ki 19:35
shall serve with the *A.*	Isa 19:23
and smote in the camp of the *A.*	Isa 37:36
and to the *A.*, to be satisfied with	La 5:6
the whore also with the *A.*	Eze 16:28
her lovers, on the *A.* her neighbours	Eze 23:5
into the hand of the *A.* upon	Eze 23:9
upon the *A.* her neighbours	Eze 23:12
and Koa, and all the *A.* with them	Eze 23:23
I do make a covenant with the *A.*	Ho 12:1

ASTAROTH

king of Bashan, which dwelt at *A.*	De 1:4

ASTONIED

of my beard, and sat down *a.*	Ezr 9:3
sat down appalled (A)(R)	Ezr 9:3
sat down confounded (B)(E)	Ezr 9:3; 9:4
sat *a.* until the evening sacrifice	Ezr 9:4
sat astounded (A)	Ezr 9:4
sat appalled (R)	Ezr 9:4; Job 17:8; 18:20
upright men shall be *a.* at	Job 17:8
men shall be astonished	Job 17:8; 18:20; Isa 52:14; Dan 3:24; 4:19; 5:9
men are appalled (B)	Job 17:8; 18:20
that come after him shall be *a.*	Job 18:20
As many were *a.* at thee	Isa 52:14
astonished at him (B)	Isa 52:14
were astonished at him (R)	Isa 52:14; Da 3:24
shouldest thou be as a man *a.*	Jer 14:9
like a man stunned and confused (A)	Isa 14:9
like a man surprised (B)	Isa 14:9
as a man affrighted (E)	Jer 14:9
a. one with another, and look at one another	Eze 4:17; Eze 4:17
dismayed (A)(B)(E)	
Nebuchadnezzar the king was *a.*	Da 3:24
became alarmed (B)	Da 3:24
Daniel, was *a.* for one hour	Da 4:19
was stunned and stood aghast (B)	Da 4:19
was stricken dumb for a while (E)	Da 4:19
was dismayed (R)	Da 4:19
in him, and his lords were *a.*	Da 5:9
rulers were at their wits end (B)	Da 5:9
rulers were perplexed (E)(R)	Da 5:9

ASTONISHED

and your enemies, shall be *a.*	Le 26:32
passeth by it shall be *a.*	1Ki 9:8
men be *a.* (A)	Job 17:8; 18:20; Isa 52:14; Dan 3:24; 4:19; 5:9
Mark me, and be *a.* and lay your	Job 21:5
and are *a.* at his reproof	Job 26:11
be not *a.*, at the matter (B)	Ec 5:8
that we may be *a.* (B)	Isa 41:23
many be *a.* at him (B)(R)	Isa 52:14
Be *a.* O ye heavens, at this	Jer 2:12
and the priests shall be *a.*	Jer 4:9
that passeth thereby shall be *a.*	Jer 18:16
that passeth thereby shall be *a.*	Jer 19:8
that goeth by it shall be *a.*	Jer 49:17
that goeth by Babylon shall be *a.*	Jer 50:13
remained there *a.* among them	Eze 3:15
every monent, and be *a.* at thee	Eze 26:16
inhabitants of the isles shall be *a.*	Eze 27:35
the people shall be *a.* at thee	Eze 28:19

make many *a.* (B)	Eze 32:10
and I was *a.* at the vision	Da 8:27
be *a.*, be dismayed (A)(B)	Hab 1:5
the people were *a.* at his doctrine	M't 7:28
men were *a.* (N)	M't 8:27
insomuch that they were *a.*	M't 13:54
the multitude was *a.* (P)	M't 15:31
were *a.* exeeedingly (E)(R)(S)	M't 19:25
they were *a.* at his doctrine	M't 22:33
they were *a.* at his doctrine	M'k 1:22
they were *a.* (N)	M'k 2:12
they were all *a.* (B)	M'k 5:20
a. with a great astonishment	M'k 5:42
were *a.* with amazement (A)(R)	M'k 5:42
many hearing him were *a.*	M'k 6:2
lack of faith *a.* him (P)	M'k 6:6
were *a.* exceedingly (A)	M'k 6:51
were beyond measure *a.*	M'k 7:37
disciples were *a.* at his words	M'k 10:24
they were *a.* out of measure	M'k 10:26
the people was *a.* at his doctrine	M'k 11:18
were simply *a.* (P)	M'k 16:5
no need to be *a.* (P)	M'k 16:6
they were *a.* (A)	Lu 1:65
they were *a.* (N)	Lu 2:18; 8:25; 11:14
were *a.* at his understanding	Lu 2:47
they were *a.* at his doctrine	Lu 4:32
For he was *a.* and all that	Lu 5:9
her parents were *a.*	Lu 8:56
noticed and was *a.* (A)(R)	Lu 11:38
made us *a.* which were early	Lu 24:22
you ought not to be *a.* (P)	Joh 3:7
they were *a.* (A)(N)	Joh 7:15
they were *a.* and bewildered (A)	Ac 2:6
And he trembling and *a.* said	Ac 9:6
were *a.* as many as came with	Ac 10:45
saw him, they were *a.*	Ac 12:16
a. at the doctrine of the Lord	Ac 13:12
I am *a.* to find you so soon (R)	Ga 2:6
will be *a.* (A)(P)(R)	Re 17:8

ASTONISHING

speak *a.* things (A)(R)	Da 11:36
this is *a.* (A)	Joh 9:30

ASTONISHMENT

and *a.* of heart	De 28:28
with confusion (B)(R)	De 28:28
shalt become an *a.* and a proverb	De 28:37
become an amazement (A)	De 28:37
become an object of horror (B)(R)	De 28:37
this house shall be an *a.* to every one	2Ch 7:21
hath delivered them to *a.* and hissing	2Ch 29:8
made us to drink wine of *a.*	Ps 60:3
made us reel and be dazed (A)(B)(R)	Ps 60:3
wine of staggering (E)	Ps 60:3
I am black, *a.* hath taken hold of me	Jer 8:21
dismay has taken hold (A)(E)(R)	Jer 8:21
confusion has overwhelmed (B)	Jer 8:21
make them an *a.* and a hissing	Jer 25:9; 25:18
make them an amazement (A)	Jer 25:9
make them an abomination (B)	Jer 25:9
make them a horror (R)	Jer 25:9
whole land be desolation and *a.*	Jer 25:11
make them a ruin and a waste (B)(R)	Jer 25:11
deliver them to be a curse and an *a.*	Jer 29:18
an execration, terror (B)	Jer 29:18
a curse, and a terror (R)	Jer 29:18
shall be an excration and an *a.*	Jer 42:18; 44:12
a desolation, curse, reproach (B)	Jer 42:18
your land an *a.* and a curse	Jer 44:22
an astonishing waste (A)(B)(R)	Jer 44:22

Babylon shall be heaps and an *a.*   *Jer 51:37*
an astonishing desolation (A)   *Jer 51:37; 51:41*
a horror, and a hissing (B)(R)   *Jer 51:37*
drink water with *a.*   *Eze 4:16; 12:19*
drink water in dismay (A)(B)(E)(R)   *Eze 4:16*
it shall be an *a.* to the nations   *Eze 5:15*
an horror to the nations (B)(R)   *Eze 5:15*
cup of *a.* and desolation (B)   *Eze 23:33*
cup of horror and terror   *Eze 23:33*
cup of horror and desolation (R)   *Eze 23:33*
I will smite every horse with *a.*   *Zec 12:4*
horse with terror and panic (A)(R)   *Zec 12:4*
horse with bewilderment (B)   *Zec 12:4*
horse with terror (E)   *Zec 12:4*
were filled with *a.* (P)   *M't 8:27*
the governor's *a.* (N)   *M't 27:14*
astonished with great *a.*   *M'k 5:42*
utterly astonished with amazement (A)   *M'k 5:42*
astonished beyond all expression (B)   *M'k 5:42*
overcome with amazement (R)   *M'k 5:42*
to the *a.* of them all (N)   *Lu 1:65*

ASTOUNDED

they sat *a.* (B)   *Ezr 9:4*
be *a.* at this (S)   *Job 17:8; Job 18:20; Isa 52:14; Da 3:24*
prophets *a.* and dazed (A)(B)(R)   *Jer 4:9*
priests shall be *a.* (S)   *Jer 4:9*
wonder and *a.* (R)   *Hab 1:5*
were utterly *a.* (R)   *M'k 6:5*
a. and marvelled (A)   *Lu 2:18; Ac 7:31*
they were *a.* (B)   *Ac 2:6*

ASTOUNDING

a. them by magic (P)   *Ac 8:11*

ASTRAY

enemy's ox or his ass going *a.*   *Ex 23:4*
not see thy brother's ox go *a.*   *De 22:1*
they go *a.* as soon as they be born   *Ps 58:3*
Before I was afflicted I went *a.*   *Ps 119:67*
I have gone *a.* like a lost sheep   *Ps 119:176*
of his folly he shall go *a.*   *Pr 5:23*
go not *a.* in her paths   *Pr 7:25*
causeth the righteous to go *a.*   *Pr 28:10*
led *a.* (A)(B)(E)(R)   *Isa 19:13; Pr 12:26; M'k 13:22*
knowledge led you *a.* (A)(R)   *Isa 47:10*
All we like sheep have gone *a.*   *Isa 53:6*
gone *a.* at cost of lives (B)(R)   *Jer 42:20*
have caused them to go *a.*   *Jer 50:6*
Israel may go no more *a.* from me   *Eze 14:11*
when Israel went *a.*   *Eze 44:10*
the children of Israel went *a.*   *Eze 44:15*
which went not *a.*   *Eze 48:11*
when the children of Israel went *a.*   *Eze 48:11*
as the Levites went *a.*   *Eze 48:11*
and one of them be gone *a.*   *M't 18:12*
and seeketh that which is gone *a.*   *M't 18:12*
ninety and nine which went not *a.*   *M't 18:13*
ye were as sheep going *a.*   *1Pe 2:25*
and are gone *a.* following the way   *2Pe 2:15*

ASTROLOGER

things at any magician, or *a.*   *Da 2:10*

ASTROLOGERS

now the *a.* the stargazers   *Isa 47:13*
a. that were in all his realm   *Da 1:20*
the magicians, and the *a.*   *Da 2:2*
cannot the wise men, the *a.*   *Da 2:27*
came in the magicians, the *a.*   *Da 4:7*
cried aloud to bring in the *a.*   *Da 5:7*
master of the magicians, *a.*   *Da 5:11*
the *a.* have been brought in   *Da 5:15*
a tricked him (N)   *M't 2:16*

ASTUTELY

for acting so *a.* (N)   *Le 16:8*

ASUNDER

shall not divide it *a.*   *Le 1:17*
his neck, but shall not divide it *a.*   *Le 5:8*
the ground clave *a.* that was   *Nu 16:31*
and parted them both *a.*   *2Ki 2:11*
but he hath broken me *a.*   *Job 16:12*
about, he cleaveth my reins *a.*   *Job 16:13*
Let us break their bands *a.* and   *Ps 2:3*
he hath cut *a.* the cords of   *Ps 129:4*
hammer of the whole earth cut *a.*   *Jer 50:23*
No shall be rent *a.*   *Eze 30:16*
and drove *a.* the nations   *Hab 3:6*
and cut it *a.* that I might break   *Zec 11:10*
Then I cut *a.* mine other staff   *Zec 11:14*
together, let not man put *a.*   *M't 19:6*
shall cut him *a.* and appoint him   *M't 24:51*
had been plucked *a.* by him   *M'k 5:4*
'et not man put *a.*   *M'k 10:9*
he burst *a.* in the midst   *Ac 1:18*
they departed *a.* one from   *Ac 15:39*
even to the dividing *a.* of soul and   *Heb 4:12*
they were sawn *a.*, were tempted   *Heb 11:37*

ASUPPIM

to his sons the house of *A.*   *1Ch 26:15*
and toward *A* two and two   *1Ch 26:17*

ASYNCRITUS

Salute *A.*, Phlegon, Hermas   *Ro 16:14*

AT

placed cherubims *a.* east of Eden   *Ge 3:24*
sin lieth *a.* the door   *Ge 4:7*
judge the people *a.* all seasons   *Ex 18:22; 18:26*
a. the door of the tabernacle   *Ex 29:42; 33:9-10; Le 4:18; Nu 6:18; 1Sa 2:22*
a. commandment of Lord   *Nu 3:39; 9:18, 23*
a. mouth of two or three witnesses   *De 17:6; 19:15*
ask counsel *a.* mouth of Lord   *Jos 9:14*
receive good *a.* the hand of God   *Job 2:10*
kingdom of heaven is *a.* hand   *M't 3:2; 4:17*
astonished *a.* his doctrine   *M't 7:28; 22:33; M'k 1:15; 10:24; 11:18; Lu 4:32*
astonished *a.* his understanding   *Lu 2:47*
God who *a.* sundry times and   *Heb 1:1*
glory *a.* the appearing of Jesus   *1Pe 1:7; 1:13*
found no more *a.* all   *Re 18:21; 18:14, 22-23*
the time is *a.* hand   *Re 22:10*

ATAD

came to the threshingfloor of *A.*   *Ge 50:10*
saw the mourning in the floor of *A.*   *Ge 50:11*

ATARAH

another wife, whose name was *A.*   *1Ch 2:26*

ATAROTH

A. and Dibon, and Jazer   *Nu 32:3*
of Gad built Dibon, and *A.*   *Nu 37:34*
unto the borders of Archi to *A.*   *Jos 16:2*
went down from Janohah to *A.*   *Jos 16:7*
A. the house of Joab, and half   *1Ch 2:54*

ATAROTH-ADAR

the border descended to *A.*   *Jos 18:13*

ATAROTH-ADDAR

on the east side was *A.* unto   *Jos 16:5*

ATE

and *a.* the sacrifices of the dead   *Ps 106:28*
I *a.* no pleasant bread, neither   *Da 10:3*
of the angel's hand, and *a.* it up   *Re 10:10*

ATER

The children of *A.* of Hezekiah   *Ezr 2:16*
the children of *A.*, the children of   *Ezr 2:42*
The children of *A.* of Hezekiah   *Ne 7:21*
of Shallum, the children of *A.*   *Ne 7:45*
A. Hizkijah, Azzur   *Ne 10:17*

ATHACH

and to them which were in *A.*   *1Sa 30:30*

ATHAIAH

of Judah; *A.* the son of Uzziah   *Ne 11:4*

ATHALIAH

and his mother's name was *A.*   *2Ki 8:26*
And when *A.* the mother of   *2Ki 11:1*
from *A.* so that he was not slain   *2Ki 11:2*
And *A.* did reign over the land   *2Ki 11:3*
when *A.* heard the noise of the   *2Ki 11:13*
and *A.* rent her clothes, and cried   *2Ki 11:14*
and they slew *A.* with the sword   *2Ki 11:20*
and Shehariah, and *A.*   *1Ch 8:26*
was *A.* the daughter of Omri   *2Ch 22:2*
when *A.* the mother of Ahaziah   *2Ch 22:10*
hid him from *A.* so that she slew   *2Ch 22:11*
house of God in six years: and *A.*   *2Ch 22:12*
Now when *A.* heard the noise   *2Ch 23:12*
A. rent her clothes, and said   *2Ch 23:13*
they had slain *A.* with the sword   *2Ch 23:21*
sons of *A.* that wicked woman   *2Ch 24:7*
of Elam; Jeshaiah the son of *A.*   *Ezr 8:7*

ATHENIANS

(For all the *A.* and strangers   *Ac 17:21*

ATHENS

brought him unto *A.*   *Ac 17:15*
while Paul waited for them at *A.*   *Ac 17:16*
Ye men of *A.* I perceive   *Ac 17:22*
Paul departed from *A.*   *Ac 18:1*
it good to be left at *A.* alone   *1Th 3:1*

ATHIRST

he was sore *a.* and called on   *J'g 15:18*

thou art *a.*, go unto the vessels *Ru 2:9*
saw we thee an hungered, *M't 25:44*
or *a.*
I will give to him that is *a.* *Re 21:6*
let him that is *a.* come *Re 22:17*

ATHLAI

Hananiah, Zabbai, and *A.* *Ezr 10:28*

ATHLETIC

brave and *a.* man (A) *1Sa 14:52*

ATONE

to *a.* for guilt (B)(R) *Eze 45:15*

ATONEMENT

wherewith the *a.* was made *Ex 29:33*
a bullock for a sin offering *Ex 29:36*
for *a.*
when thou hast made an *a.* *Ex 29:36*
for it
shalt make an *a.* for the *Ex 29:37*
altar
shall make an *a.* upon the *Ex 30:10*
horns
once in the year shall he *Ex 30:10*
make *a.*
to make *a.* for your souls *Ex 30:15*
take the *a.* money of the *Ex 30:16*
children
to make an *a.* for your souls *Ex 30:16*
I shall make an *a.* for your *Ex 32:30*
sin
to make *a.* for him *Le 1:4*
priest shall make an *a.* for *Le 4:20*
them
and the priests shall make an *a.* *Le 4:26*
priest shall make an *a.* for *Le 4:31*
him
shall make an *a.* for his sin *Le 4:35*
shall make an *a.* for him *Le 5:6, 10, 13*
the priest shall make an *a.* *Le 5:16*
an *a.* for him concerning his *Le 5:18*
an *a.* for him before the Lord *Le 6:7*
the priest that maketh *a.* *Le 7:7*
to make *a.* for *Le 8:15;*
(A)(B)(E)(R) *Eze 45:15, 17*
to make an *a.* for you *Le 8:34*
and make an *a.* for thyself *Le 9:7*
and make an *a.* for them *Le 9:7*
make *a.* for them before the *Le 10:17*
Lord
and make an *a.* for her *Le 12:7*
priest shall make an *a.* for *Le 12:8*
her
and the priest shall make an *Le 14:18*
a.
and make an *a.* for him *Le 14:19*
and the priest shall make an *Le 14:20*
a.
to make an *a.* for him *Le 14:21;*
14:29
and the priest shall make an *Le 14:31*
a.
and make an *a.* for the *Le 14:53*
house
priest shall make an *a.* for *Le 15:15;*
15:30
and make an *a.* for himself *Le 16:6*
to make an *a.* with him *Le 16:10*
and shall make an *a.* for *Le 16:11*
himself
shall make an *a.* for the holy *Le 16:16*
place
to make an *a.* in the holy *Le 16:17*
place
and have made an *a.* for *Le 16:17*
himself
and make an *a.* for it *Le 16:18*
completed the *a.* (A)(B)(E)(R) *Le 16:20*
and make an *a.* for himself *Le 16:24*
blood was brought in to make *Le 16:27*
a.
the priest make an *a.* for *Le 16:30*
you
And the priest, shall make *Le 16:32*
the *a.*
make an *a.* for the holy *Le 16:33*
sanctuary
shall make an *a.* for the *Le 16:33*
tabernacle
and he shall make an *a.* for *Le 16:33*
the
an *a.* for the children of Israel *Le 16:34*
to make an *a.* for your souls *Le 17:11*
the blood that maketh an *a.* *Le 17:11*
for

the priest shall make an *a.* *Le 19:22*
for
there shall be a day of *a.* *Le 23:27*
it is a day of *a.* *Le 23:28*
to make an *a.* for you *Le 23:28*
the day of *a.* shall you make *Le 25:9*
the ram of the *a.* *Nu 5:8*
an *a.* shall be made for him *Nu 5:8*
and make an *a.* for him *Nu 6:11*
to make an *a.* for the Levites *Nu 8:12*
and to make an *a.* for the *Nu 8:19*
children
and Aaron made an *a.* *Nu 8:21*
And the priest shall make an *Nu 15:25*
a.
shall make an *a.* for the *Nu 15:28*
soul
to make an *a.* for him *Nu 15:28*
and make an *a.* for them *Nu 16:46*
and made an *a.* for the people *Nu 16:47*
an *a.* for the children of *Nu 25:13*
Israel
sin offering, to make an *a.* *Nu 28:22*
for you
the goats; to make an *a.* for *Nu 28:30*
you
offering to make an *a.* for *Nu 29:5*
you
the sin offering of *a.* *Nu 29:11*
to make an *a.* for our souls *Nu 31:50*
wherewith shall I make the *2Sa 21:3*
a.
and to make an *a.* for Israel *1Ch 6:49*
to make an *a.* for all Israel *2Ch 29:24*
to make an *a.* for Israel *Ne 10:33*
we have now received the *a.* *Ro 5:11*
for *a.* of transgressions (B) *Heb 9:15*
make *a.* for sins *Heb 12:17*
(A)(B)(P)
made personal *a.* for our *1Jo 2:21*
sins (P)

ATONEMENTS

the sin offering of *a.* *Ex 30:10*

ATONING

a. sacrifice for our sins (B) *1Jo 2:2;*
4:10

ATROTH

And *A.*, Shophan, and Jaazer *Nu 32:35*

ATTACHED

will grow *a.* to me (B) *Ge 29:34*
a. himself to one (N) *Lu 15:15*
a. to the word of life (B) *Ph'p 2:16*

ATTACK

go up and *a.* Ai (A)(R) *Jos 7:3*
attack (B) *J'g 1:8; 20:39; 2Ch 28:17*
a. the Philistines (R) *1Sa 23:2*
do not *a.* anyone (B) *1Ki 22:31*
made an *a.* on Paul *Ac 18:12*
(A)(P)(R)

ATTACKED

a. and subdued (A) *Ge 14:5; 14:15*
they bitterly *a.* (A) *Ge 14:29*
attacked (R) *J'g 8:11;*
2Sa 21:17; 2Ki 3:24; Jon 4:7
a. him (A) *2Ki 15:25*
a. them brutally (N) *M't 22:6*

ATTAI

to wife, and she bare him *1Ch 2:35*
A.
And *A.* begat Nathan, and *1Ch 2:36*
Nathan
A. the sixth, Eliel the *1Ch 12:11*
seventh
which bare him Abijah, *2Ch 11:20*
and *A.*

ATTAIN

it is high, I cannot *a.* unto it *Ps 139:6*
I cannot reach it (A)(B) *Ps 139:6*
a man of understanding shall *Pr 1:5*
as his hand shall *a.* unto *Eze 46:7*
will it be ere they *a.* to *Ho 8:5*
innocence

will a pure heart be *Ho 8:5*
impossible (B)
until they are pure (R) *Ho 8:5*
all means might *a.* to *Ac 27:12*
Phenice
to reach Phenice (A) *Ac 27:12*
I might *a.* unto the *Ph'p 3:11*
resurrection
possibly achieve resurrection *Ph'p 3:11*
(B)
finally arrive at resurrection *Ph'p 3:11*
(N)

ATTAINED

not *a.* unto the days of the *Ge 47:9*
years
he *a.* not unto the first three *2Sa 23:19*
he *a.* not to the first *2Sa 23:23*
howbeit he *a.* not to the *1Ch 11:21*
first three
but *a.* not to the first three *1Ch 11:25*
have *a.* to righteousness *Ro 9:30*
not *a.* to the law of *Ro 9:31*
righteousness
did not succeed fulfilling law *Ro 9:31*
(A)(R)
failed to come up to it (B) *Ro 9:31*
did not arrive at that law *Ro 9:31*
(E)
failed to reach the goal (P) *Ro 9:31*
might *a.* the status of sons *Ga 4:5*
(N)
Not as though I had *Ph'p 3:12*
already *a.*
not already reached *Ph'p 3:12*
perfection (B)(N)
not already made perfect *Ph'p 3:12*
(E)(R)
whereto we have already *a.* *Ph'p 3:16*
where we have arrived (B) *Ph'p 3:16*
level we have already *Ph'p 3:16*
reached (N)
whereunto thou hast *a.* *1Ti 4:6*
which you have closely *1Ti 4:6*
followed (A)(R)
you have been conforming *1Ti 4:6*
your life (B)
thou hast followed until now *1Ti 4:6*
(E)(N)

ATTALIA

they went down into *A.* *Ac 14:25*

ATTEMPT

a. to plot against you (A)(R) *Na 1:9*

ATTEMPTED

he *a.* to go (S) *1Sa 17:39; Ac 16:7*
a. to join (R) *Ac 9:26*
a. to go (R) *Ac 16:7*
a. the crossing (N)(R) *Heb 11:29*

ATTEMPTING

a. to do so (S) *Heb 11:29*

ATTEND

a. to the office (A)(B)(R) *Nu 3:10*
he had appointed to *a.* upon *Es 4:5*
her
a. unto my cry, give ear unto *Ps 17:1*
my
A. unto me, and hear me *Ps 55:2*
a. unto my prayer *Ps 61:1*
a. to the voice of my *Ps 86:6*
supplications
A. unto my cry; for I am *Ps 142:6*
brought
and *a.* to know understanding *Pr 4:1*
My son, *a.* to my words *Pr 4:20*
My son, *a.* unto my wisdom *Pr 5:1*
and *a.* to the words of my *Pr 7:24*
mouth
that ye may *a.* upon the *1Co 7:35*
Lord

ATTENDANCE

and the *a.* of his ministers *1Ki 10:5*
and the *a.* of his ministers *2Ch 9:4*
Till I come, give *a.* to *1Ti 4:13*
reading
no man gave *a.* at the altar *Heb 7:13*

ATTENDANT

Joshua his *a.* (A)   *Ex 24:13*
gave it back to the *a.*   *Lu 4:20*
(A)(E)(N)(P)(R)
John as an *a.* (A)(B)(E)   *Ac 13:5*

ATTENDANTS

had many *a.* (A)   *2Ch 9:1*
a. of the word (B)   *Lu 1:2*
his personal *a.* (A)(B)   *Ac 10:7*

ATTENDED

Yea, I *a.* unto you, and,   *Job 32:12*
behold
hath *a.* to the voice of my   *Ps 66:19*
prayer
she *a.* unto the things which   *Ac 16:14*
were

ATTENDING

a. continually upon this very   *Ro 13:6*
thing

ATTENT

thine ears be *a.* unto the   *2Ch 6:40*
prayer
mine ears *a.* unto the prayer   *2Ch 7:15*

ATTENTION

pay strict *a.* to (B)   *Ex 23:13*
to the *a.* of (S)   *Es 1:17*
fools pay *a.* (R)   *Pr 8:5*
give full *a.* to (P)   *1Ti 4:15*
careful *a.* to (B)(P)   *Heb 2:1*

ATTENTIVE

ears be *a.* to my prayer (S)   *2Ch 6:40;*
    7:15
let now thine ear be *a.*   *Ne 1:6*
now thine ear be *a.* to the   *Ne 1:11*
prayer
were *a.* unto the book of the   *Ne 8:3*
law
let thine ears be *a.* to the   *Ps 130:2*
voice
were very *a.* to hear him   *Lu 19:48*

ATTENTIVELY

Hear *a.* the noise of his   *Job 37:2*
voice

ATTEST

a. that God is true (P)   *Joh 3:33*
we *a.* that the Father set the   *Joh 4:14*
Son (N)
to *a.* the good news (A)   *Ac 20:24*

ATTESTED

and *a.* character and repute   *Ac 6:3*
(A)

ATTIRE

the *a.* of an harlot   *Pr 7:10*
dressed as an harlot (A)(R)   *Pr 7:10*
can a bride forget her *a.*   *Jer 2:32*
a bride her marriage girdle   *Jer 2:32*
(A)
in dyed *a.* upon their heads   *Eze 23:15*
flowing turbans on heads   *Eze 23:15*
(A)(B)(E)(R)

ATTIRED

the linen mitre shall he be *a.*   *Le 16:4*
wear the linen turban (B)(R)   *Le 16:4*
a. her head (E)   *2Ki 9:30*
a. like one of these (N)   *M't 6:29*

ATTITUDE

a. not as it used to be (B)   *Ge 31:2*
test my soul and *a.* (B)   *Ps 26:2*
carnal *a.* is opposed to God   *Ro 8:7*
(P)
renewed in mental *a.* (B)   *Eph 4:23*

ATTRACTIVE

beautiful and *a.* (A)   *Ge 29:1*
an *a.* mantle (A)   *Jos 7:21*

ATTRIBUTES

God *a.* righteousness (B)   *Ro 4:6*

AUDIBLY

wept *a.* (B)   *1Sa 11:4*

AUDIENCE

in *a.* of children of Heth   *Ge 23:13;*
    23:10, 16
said in the presence of the   *Ge 23:13*
people (A)
in hearing of people   *Ge 23:13;*
(B)(R)   *23:16*
took book of covenant, read   *Ex 24:7*
in *a.*
let thine handmaid speak in   *1Sa 25:24*
thy *a.*
in the *a.* of our God   *1Ch 28:8*
in the hearing of God   *1Ch 28:8*
(A)(B)(R)
read book of Moses in *a.* of   *Ne 13:1*
people
ended sayings in the *a.* of   *Lu 7:1*
people
in the hearing of people   *Lu 7:1*
(A)(R)
to the listening people (B)   *Lu 7:1*
in the ears of the people (E)   *Lu 7:1*
addressing the people (N)   *Lu 7:1*
finished his talks to people (P)   *Lu 7:1*
in *a.* of people he said to   *Lu 20:45*
disciples
all the people listening (A)   *Lu 20:45*
in hearing of people   *Lu 20:45*
(B)(E)(N)(R)
while everybody was   *Lu 20:45*
listening (P)
ye that fear God, give *a.*   *Ac 13:16*
reverence and fear God,   *Ac 13:16*
listen (A)(N)
all the multitude gave *a.* to   *Ac 15:12*
Barnabas
listened attentively (A)(N)(P)   *Ac 15:12*
(R)
kept quiet and heard (B)   *Ac 15:12*
they hearkened (E)   *Ac 15:12*
they gave *a.* to this word   *Ac 22:22*
the people listened   *Ac 22:22*
(A)(B)(P)(R)
gave him a hearing (N)   *Ac 22:22*

AUGMENT

to *a.* yet the fierce anger of   *Nu 32:14*
the

AUGUSTUS

a decree from Caesar *A.*   *Lu 2:1*
reserved unto the hearing of   *Ac 25:21*
A.
himself hath appealed to *A.*   *Ac 25:25*

AUGUSTUS'

a centurion of *A.* band   *Ac 27:1*

AUL

bore his ear through with an   *Ex 21:6*
a.
Then thou shalt take an *a.*   *De 15:17*

AUNT

she is thine *a.*   *Le 18:14*

AUSTERE

because thou art an *a.* man   *Lu 19:21*
a stern man (A)   *Lu 19:21*
a harsh man (B)   *Lu 19:21*
a hard man (N)(P)   *Lu 19:21*
a severe man (R)   *Lu 19:21*

AUTHOR

God is not the *a.* of   *1Co 14:33*
confusion, but
became the *a.* of eternal   *Heb 5:9*
salvation
the *a.* and finisher of our   *Heb 12:2*
faith

AUTHORITIES

rulers and *a.* (B)(E)(R)   *Lu 12:11*
before the *a.* (B)(P)   *Ac 16:20*

the governing *a.*   *Ro 13:1;*
(A)(B)(N)(P)(R)   *Eph 3:10; Col 1:16;*
    Tit 3:1
civil *a.* in God's service   *Ro 13:6*
(N)(P)
angelic rulers and *a.*   *Eph 3:10*
(A)(B)(N)
rulers and *a.* (A)(B)(N)   *Col 1:16*
authority over all *a.* (P)   *Col 2:10*
princes and *a.* (B)   *Col 2:15*
subject to ruling *a.*   *Tit 3:1*
(B)(E)(N)(R)
a. and powers being made   *1Pe 3:22*
subject

AUTHORITY

have complete *a.* over (A)   *Ge 1:26*
Mordecai the Jew, with all   *Es 9:29*
a.
When the righteous are in *a.*   *Pr 29:2*
the
commit *a.* to (A)(B)(R)   *Isa 22:21*
taught them as one having *a.*   *M't 7:29*
For I am a man under *a.*   *M't 8:9*
a. to forgive   *M't 9:6*
(A)(B)(E)(P)(R)(S)
that are great exercise *a.*   *M't 20:25*
upon
what *a.* doest thou these   *M't 21:23*
things
and who gave thee this *a.*   *M't 21:23*
by what *a.* I do these   *M't 21:24;*
things   *21:27*
all *a.* is given to me   *M't 28:18*
(A)(B)(E)(N)(R)(S)
as one that had *a.*   *M'k 1:22*
for with *a.* commandeth he   *M'k 1:27*
a. to forgive sins (S)   *M'k 2:10*
a. to heal (S)   *M'k 3:15; 6:7*
their great ones exercise *a.*   *M'k 10:42*
upon
what *a.* doest thou these   *M'k 11:28*
things
and who gave thee this *a.*   *M'k 11:28*
by what *a.* I do these   *M'k 11:29;*
things   *11:33*
gave *a.* to his servants   *M'k 13:34*
Continued under their *a.* (N)   *Lu 2:51*
a. I will give thee (S)   *Lu 4:6*
his word was with *a.*   *Lu 4:32*
(A)(B)(E)(N)(R)
with *a.* and power he   *Lu 4:36*
commandeth
am a man set under *a.*   *Lu 7:8*
gave them power and *a.* over   *Lu 9:1*
all
a. to tread on serpents   *Lu 10:19*
(B)(E)(R)
have thou *a.* over ten cities   *Lu 19:17*
what *a.* doest thou these   *Lu 20:2*
things
who is he that gave thee this   *Lu 20:2*
a.
by what *a.* I do these things   *Lu 20:8*
power and *a.* of the   *Lu 20:20*
governor
that exercise *a.* upon them   *Lu 22:25*
are
he gave *a.* to become sons (A)   *Joh 1:12*
a. to judge (P)   *Joh 5:27*
a. to lay down life (B)   *Joh 10:18*
a. over all flesh to give   *Joh 17:2*
(A)(B)(E)(P)
under his personal *a.*   *Ac 1:7*
(B)(E)(P)
eunuch of great *a.* under   *Ac 8:27*
Candace
he hath *a.* from the chief   *Ac 9:14*
priests
having received *a.* from the   *Ac 26:10*
chief
went to Damascus with *a.*   *Ac 26:12*
from *a.* of Satan to God   *Ac 26:18*
(B)
law exercises *a.* over (P)   *Ro 7:1*
no *a.* but of God   *Ro 13:1*
(A)(B)(N)(R)
a., authorities   *Ro 13:2;*
(A)(B)(N)(P)(R)
a token of *a.*   *1Co 11:10*
(A)(B)(E)(N)(P)(R)(S)
all rule and all *a.* and power   *1Co 15:24*
somewhat more of our *a.*   *2Co 10:8*
under *a.* of basic principles   *Ga 4:3*
(P)
all government, *a.*, power   *Eph 1:21*
(A)(B)(E)(P)(R)
head of all rule and *a.*   *Col 2:10*
(A)(B)(N)(R)

AUTHORITY (continued)

a. over all authorities (P) — *Col 2:10*
and for all that are in *a.* — *1Ti 2:2*
nor to usurp *a.* over the man, but — *1Ti 2:12*
have *a.* over men (A)(P)(R) — *1Ti 2:12*
will not recognize *a.* (P) — *Tit 1:10*
exhort, and rebuke with all *a.* — *Tit 2:15*
obey every man made *a.* (P) — *1Pe 2:13*
despise *a.* (B)(N)(P)(R) — *2Pe 2:10*
a. over the Gentiles (B)(E)(N)(P) — *Re 2:26*
a. was granted him (B)(E) — *Re 6:8*
power, and his seat, and great *a.* — *Re 13:2*
to exercise *a.* of the beast (A)(E)(N)(P)(R) — *Re 13:12*
receive royal *a.* (B)(E)(N)(P) — *Re 17:12*
exercise royal *a.* (N)(P) — *Re 17:13*
a. to act as judges (A)(B) — *Re 20:4*

AVA

and from Cuthah, and from A. — *2Ki 17:24*

AVAIL

it shall *a.* nothing (B) — *Isa 16:12*

AVAILETH

all this *a.* me nothing — *Es 5:13*
neither circumcision *a.* any thing — *Ga 5:6*
neither circumcision *a.* any thing — *Ga 6:15*
prayer of a righteous man *a.* much — *Jas 5:16*

AVARICIOUS

the *a.* grasping (B) — *1Co 5:10; 6:10*

AVEN

young men of A. and of Pi-beseth — *Eze 30:17*
high places also of A. the sin of — *Ho 10:8*
inhabitant from the plain of A. — *Am 1:5*

AVENGE

Thou shalt not *a.* nor bear any — *Le 19:18*
a sword, that shall *a.* the quarrel — *Le 26:25*
A. the children of Israel of — *Nu 31:2*
and *a.* the Lord of Midian — *Nu 31:3*
will *a.* the blood of his servants — *De 32:43*
and the Lord *a.* me of thee — *1Sa 24:12*
I may *a.* the blood of my servants — *2Ki 9:7*
to *a.* themselves on their enemies — *Es 8:13*
and *a.* me of mine enemies — *Isa 1:24*
a. me of my persecutors (S) — *Jer 15:15*
he may *a.* him of his adversaries — *Jer 46:10*
and I will *a.* the blood of Jezreel — *Ho 1:4*
I will *a.* their blood (S) — *Joe 3:21*
saying, A. me of mine adversary — *Lu 18:3*
I will *a.* her, lest by her continual — *Lu 18:5*
not God *a.* his own elect — *Lu 18:7*
he will *a.* them speedily — *Lu 18:8*
Dearly beloved, *a.* not yourselves — *Ro 12:19*
dost thou not judge and *a.* our — *Re 6:10*

AVENGED

If Cain shall be *a.* sevenfold — *Ge 4:24*
the people had *a.* themselves — *Jos 10:13*
yet will I be *a.* of you — *J'g 15:7*
that I may be at once *a.* of — *J'g 16:28*
that I may be *a.* on mine enemies — *1Sa 14:24*
to be *a.* of the king's enemies — *1Sa 18:25*
or that my Lord hath *a.* himself — *1Sa 25:31*
the Lord hath *a.* my lord — *2Sa 4:8*

hath *a.* him of his enemies — *2Sa 18:19*
Lord hath *a.* thee this day of all — *2Sa 18:31*
shall not my soul be *a.* on such — *Jer 5:9; 5:29*
shall not my soul be *a.* on such — *Jer 9:9*
I have not *a.* (S) — *Joe 3:21*
a. him that was oppressed — *Ac 7:24*
God hath *a.* you on her — *Re 18:20*
hath *a.* the blood of his servants — *Re 19:2*

AVENGER

for refuge from the *a.*; that — *Nu 35:12*
the *a.* of blood (S) — *Nu 35:19; 35:21, 24-25, 27*
Lest the *a.* of the blood pursue the — *De 19:6*
into the hand of the *a.* of blood — *De 19:12*
your refuge from the *a.* of blood — *Jos 20:3*
if the *a.* of blood pursue after him — *Jos 20:5*
by the hand of the *a.* of blood — *Jos 20:9*
still the enemy and the *a.* — *Ps 8:2*
enemy and the revengeful (B) — *Ps 8:2*
by reason of the enemy and *a.* — *Ps 44:16*
enemy and the revengeful (A) — *Ps 44:16*
a. evil-doings (A) — *Ps 99:8*
the *a.* of wrath (E)(S) — *Ro 13:4*
the Lord is the *a.* of all such — *1Th 4:6*
punisher in such cases (B) — *1Th 4:6*
punishes all such offences (N) — *1Th 4:6*
God will punish all who do (P) — *1Th 4:6*

AVENGERS

the *a.* of blood (S) — *2Sa 14:11*

AVENGETH

It is God that *a.* me — *2Sa 22:48*
It is God that *a.* me — *Ps 18:47*
the Lord *a.* (S) — *Na 1:2*

AVENGING

Praise ye the Lord for the *a.* — *J'g 5:2*
from *a.* thyself with thine own — *1Sa 25:26*
taking law in hands (B) — *1Sa 25:26; 25:33*
from taking vengeance (R) — *1Sa 25:26*
from *a.* myself with mine own — *1Sa 25:33*

AVERSE

by securely as men *a.* from war — *Mic 2:8*
with no thought of war (R) — *Mic 2:8*

AVERTED

plague was *a.* (S) — *2Sa 24:21; 2Sa 24:25; 1Ch 21:22*

AVIM

And A., and Parah, and Ophrah — *Jos 18:23*

AVIMS

And the A. which dwelt in — *De 2:23*

AVITES

and the Ekronites; also the A. — *Jos 13:3*
the A. made Nibhaz and Tartak — *2Ki 17:31*

AVITH

and the name of his city was A. — *Ge 36:35*
and the name of his city was A. — *1Ch 1:46*

AVOID

my intimate friends *a.* me (B)(R) — *Job 19:19*

A. it, pass not by it, turn from it — *Pr 4:15*
which ye have learned; and *a.* — *Ro 16:17*
Nevertheless, to *a.* fornication — *1Co 7:2*
a. irreverent legends - profane — *1Ti 4:7*
and impure and godless fictions, grandmother's tales - silly myths (A) — *1Ti 4:7*
and unlearned questions *a.* — *2Ti 2:23*
But *a.* foolish questions, and — *Tit 3:9*

AVOIDED

And David *a.* out of his presence — *1Sa 18:11*

AVOIDING

A. this, that no man should — *2Co 8:20*
a. profane and vain babblings — *1Ti 6:20*

AVOUCHED

Thou hast *a.* the Lord this day to — *De 26:17*
the Lord hath *a.* thee this day — *De 26:18*

AVOWED

you have *a.* this day (S) — *De 26:17; 26:18*

AWAIT

laying *a.* was known of Saul — *Ac 9:24*
afflictions *a.* me (S) — *Ac 20:23*

AWAITS

a. precious produce (B) — *Jas 5:7*

AWAKE

A., *a.*, Deborah; *a.*, *a.*, utter a — *J'g 5:12*
surely now he would *a.* for thee — *Job 8:6*
they shall not *a.* nor be raised — *Job 14:12*
and *a.* for me to the judgment — *Ps 7:6*
I shall be satisfied, when I *a.* with — *Ps 17:15*
Stir up thyself, and *a.* to my — *Ps 35:23*
A., why sleepest thou, O Lord — *Ps 44:23*
A., up, my glory — *Ps 57:8*
a. psaltery and harp — *Ps 57:8*
I myself will *a.* early — *Ps 57:8*
a. to help me, and behold — *Ps 59:4*
a. to visit all the heathen — *Ps 59:5*
A. psaltery and harp — *Ps 108:2*
I myself will *a.* early — *Ps 108:2*
when I *a.* I am still with thee — *Ps 139:18*
when shall I *a.*? I will seek it yet — *Pr 23:35*
nor *a.* my love, till he please — *Ca 2:7*
not up, nor *a.* my love, till he — *Ca 3:5*
A., O north wind; and come — *Ca 4:16*
ye stir not up, nor *a.* my love — *Ca 8:4*
A. and sing, ye that dwell in dust — *Isa 26:19*
A., *a.*, put on strength, O arm — *Isa 51:9*
the Lord; *a.* as in the ancient — *Isa 51:9*
A., *a.*, stand up, O Jerusalem — *Isa 51:17*
A., *a.*; put on thy strength — *Isa 52:1*
in the dust of the earth shall *a.* — *Da 12:2*
A. ye drunkards, and weep — *Joe 1:5*
and *a.* that shall vex thee — *Hab 2:7*
him that saith to the wood, A. — *Hab 2:19*
A., O sword, against my shepherd — *Zec 13:7*
they *a.* him, and say unto him — *M'k 4:38*
when they were *a.* they saw — *Lu 9:32*
that I may *a.* him out of sleep — *Joh 11:11*
is high time to *a.* out of sleep — *Ro 13:11*
A. to righteousness, and sin not — *1Co 15:34*
A. thou that sleepest, and arise — *Eph 5:14*

AWAKED

And Jacob *a.* out of his sleep — *Ge 28:16*

And he *a.* out of his sleep *J'g 16:14*
saw it, nor knew it, neither *1Sa 26:12*
a.
he sleepeth, and must be *a.* *1Ki 18:27*
The child is not *a.* *2Ki 4:31*
I *a.;* for the Lord sustained me *Ps 3:5*
the Lord *a.* as one out of *Ps 78:65*
sleep
Upon this I *a.* and beheld *Jer 31:26*

AWAKENED

I *a.* thee under the apple tree *Ca 8:5*
(S)

AWAKENETH

he *a.* morning by morning *Isa 50:4*
(S)

AWAKEST

when thou *a.* thou shalt *Ps 73:20*
despise
when thou *a.* it shall talk with *Pr 6:22*

AWAKETH

As a dream when one *a.* *Ps 73:20*
but he *a.* and his soul is *Isa 29:8*
empty
but he *a.* and, behold, he is *Isa 29:8*
faint

AWAKING

a. out of his sleep, and *Ac 16:27*

AWARE

was not *a.* of it (B) *Ex 34:29*
was not *a.* of it (A) *Le 5:17*
thine heart is *a.* of (S) *1Ki 2:44*
Or ever I was *a.* my soul *Ca 6:12*
made
thou wast not *a.;* thou art *Jer 50:24*
found
in an hour that he is not *a.* *M't 24:50*
of
over them are not *a.* of *Lu 11:44*
them
and at an hour when he is *Lu 12:46*
not *a.*
they were *a.* of it (S) *Ac 14:6*

AWAY

they sent him *a.* and his *Ge 12:20*
wife
Abraham drove the fowls *a.* *Ge 15:11*
Take the child *a.* and nurse it *Ex 2:9*
put *a.* leaven *Ex 12:15*
shall send him *a.* by the *Le 16:21*
hand of a fit man
put evil *a.* *De 17:7;*
17:12; 19:19; 21:21; 22:21-24; J'g 20:13;
1Sa 1:16
put *a.* guilt of innocent *De 19:13;*
blood *21:9*
put *a.* gods *Jos 24:14;*
J'g 10:16; 1Sa 7:3
put *a.* those with familiar *1Sa 28:3*
spirits
for he had sent him *a.* and *2Sa 3:22*
he is gone
put *a.* the image of Baal *2Ki 3:2*
carried Israel *a.* captive *2Ki 17:6;*
17:11, 23, 28, 33; 18:11; 24:14; 1Ch 5:6,
26; 9:1; 2Ch 6:36; M't 1:11, 17
put *a.* abominable idols *2Ch 15:8*
put *a.* iniquity *Job 22:23*
Put *a.* the froward mouth *Pr 4:24*
put *a.* abominations *Jer 4:1*
captivity *a.* from his land *Am 7:17*
(S)
whosoever shall put *a.* his *M't 5:31;*
wife *5:32; 19:3, 7-9; M'k 10:2, 4, 11-12;*
Lu 16:18; 1Co 7:11-12
put *a.* from among you that *1Co 5:13*
evil
old things are passed *a.* *2Co 5:17*
putting *a.* lying, evil *Eph 4:25*
speaking
come a falling *a.* first *2Th 2:3*
if they shall fall *a.* *Heb 6:6; 10:35*
carried me *a.* in the Spirit *Re 17:3;*
21:10
first earth were passed *a.* *Re 21:1*
former things are passed *a.* *Re 21:4*
God take *a.* part out of *Re 22:19*
book

AWE

work of God inspires *a.* (B) *Ex 34:10*
Stand in *a.* and sin not *Ps 4:4*
of the world stand in *a.* *Ps 33:8*
heart standeth in *a.* of thy *Ps 119:161*
word
hearts filled with *a.* (B) *Isa 60:5*
filled with *a.* and amazement *Ac 3:10*
(B)
reverence, *a.* and mixed *Eph 6:5*
motives (B)

AWE-INSPIRING

awe-inspiring (S) *Ex 34:10;*
De 10:21; 2Sa 7:23; Ne 1:5; 4:14; 9:32;
Job 37:22; Ps 45:5; 47:2; 66:3; 68:35;
99:3; 145:6
a. terror (B)(S) *De 26:8*
angel very *a.* (B) *J'g 13:6*
a. deeds (B) *Ps 45:4;*
65:5; 66:3; 68:35; 99:3; 106:22; 145:6
a. God (B) *Ps 47:2*
a. is his name (B) *Ps 111:9*

AWE-STRICKEN

survivors were *a.* *Re 11:13*
(B)

AWE-STRUCK

neighbors were *a.* (N) *Lu 1:65*

AWESOME

How *a.* is this place (S) *Ge 28:17;*
De 10:17
mighty God and *a.* (S) *De 7:21;*
Ps 65:5; 66:5; 106:22
great *a.* power (A) *De 26:8*
a. and fearfully glorious (A) *Ps 66:3*
he is *a.* (B) *Ps 66:5*
a. reverence inspiring (A) *Ps 99:3*
great and *a.* God (S) *Da 9:4;*
De 10:17; J'g 13:6

AWOKE

And Noah *a.* from his wine *Ge 9:24*
and fat kine. So Pharaoh *a.* *Ge 41:4*
and Pharaoh *a.* and, behold, *Ge 41:7*
it
as at the beginning, So I *a.* *Ge 41:21*
And he *a.* out of his sleep *J'g 16:20*
And Solomon *a.;* and, *1Ki 3:15*
behold, it
a. him, saying, Lord, save us *M't 8:25*
they came to him, and *a.* him *Lu 8:24*

AXE

with the *a.* to cut down the *De 19:5*
tree
by forcing an *a.* against *De 20:19*
them
Abimelech took an *a.* in his *J'g 9:48*
hand
to sharpen every man, his *1Sa 13:20*
a.
neither hammer nor *a.* nor any *1Ki 6:7*
the *a.* head fell into the water *2Ki 6:5*
Shall the *a.* boast itself *Isa 10:15*
of the workman, with the *a.* *Isa 10:3*
Thou art my battle *a.* and *Jer 51:20*
now also the *a.* is laid unto *M't 3:10*
now also the *a.* is laid unto *Lu 3:9*

AXES

for the forks, and for the *a.* *1Sa 13:21*
and under *a.* of iron *2Sa 12:31*
with harrows of iron, and *1Ch 20:3*
with *a.*
he had lifted up *a.* upon the *Ps 74:5*
thick
with *a.* and hammers *Ps 74:6*
and come against her with *Jer 46:22*
a.
with his *a.* he shall break *Eze 26:9*
down

AXLES

and *a.* of brass (S) *1Ki 7:30*
the *a.* of the wheels (S) *1Ki 7:32;*
7:33

AXLETREES

and the *a.* of the wheels *1Ki 7:32*
their *a.* and their naves *1Ki 7:33*

AZAL

mountains shall reach unto *Zec 14:5*
A.

AZALIAH

king sent Shaphan the son of *2Ki 22:3*
A.
the son of *A.* and Maaseiah *2Ch 34:8*

AZANIAH

both Jeshua the son of *A.* *Ne 10:9*

AZARAEL

his brethren, Shemaiah, and *Ne 12:36*
A.

AZAREEL

and *A.* and Joezer, and *1Ch 12:6*
The eleventh to *A.* he, his *1Ch 25:18*
sons
Of Dan, *A.* the son of *1Ch 27:22*
Jeroham
A. and Shelemiah, *Ezr 10:41*
Shemariah
and Amashai the son of *A.* *Ne 11:13*
the son

AZARIAH

A. the son of Zadok the *1Ki 4:2*
priest
And *A.* the son of Nathan *1Ki 4:5*
all the people of Judah *2Ki 14:21*
took *A*
began *A.* son of Amaziah *2Ki 15:1*
king of
And the rest of the acts of *2Ki 15:6*
A. and
So *A.* slept with his fathers *2Ki 15:7*
In the thirty and eighth year *2Ki 15:8*
of *A.*
In the nine and thirtieth *2Ki 15:17*
year of *A.*
In the fiftieth year of *A.* *2Ki 15:23*
king of
In the two and fiftieth year *2Ki 15:27*
of *A.*
And the sons of Ethan; *A.* *1Ch 2:8*
begat Jehu, and Jehu begat *1Ch 2:38*
A.
And *A.* begat Helez, and *1Ch 2:39*
Helez
Amaziah his son, *A.* his son *1Ch 3:12*
And Ahimaaz begat *A.* *1Ch 6:9*
And *A.* begat Johanan *1Ch 6:9*
and Johanan begat *A.* (he it *1Ch 6:10*
is
And *A.* begat Amariah, and *1Ch 6:11*
and Hilkiah begat *A.* *1Ch 6:13*
and *A.* begat Seraiah, and *1Ch 6:14*
the son of Joel, the son of *1Ch 6:36*
A.
And *A.* the son of Hilkiah, *1Ch 9:11*
the son
the Spirit of God came *2Ch 15:1*
upon *A.*
the sons of Jehoshaphat, *A.* *2Ch 21:2*
Zechariah, and *A.* and *2Ch 21:2*
Michael
And *A.* the son of Jehoram *2Ch 22:6*
king
A. the son of Jeroham, and *2Ch 23:1*
A. the son of Obed, and *2Ch 23:1*
Maaseiah
A. the priest went in after *2Ch 26:17*
him
And *A.* the chief priest, *2Ch 26:20*
and all
A. the son of Johanan, *2Ch 28:12*
Berechiah
Amasai, and Joel the son *2Ch 29:12*
of *A.*
and *A.* the son of Jehalelel *2Ch 29:12*
And *A.* the chief priest of *2Ch 31:10*
and *A.* the ruler of the *2Ch 31:13*
house of
the son of Seraiah, the son of *Ezr 7:1*
A.
The son of Amariah, the son *Ezr 7:3*
of *A.*

AZARIAH (cont.)

After him repaired *A.* the son of · Ne 3:23

from the house of *A.* unto · Ne 3:24
Nehemiah, *A.,* Raamiah · Ne 7:7
Kelita, *A.,* Jozabad, Hanan · Ne 8:7
Seraiah, *A.,* Jeremiah · Ne 10:2
And *A.,* Ezra, and Meshullam · Ne 12:33
spake *A.* the son of Hoshaiah · Jer 43:2
Daniel, Hananiah, Mishael, and *A.* · Da 1:6
and to *A.* of Abed-nego · Da 1:7
Daniel, Hananiah, Mishael, and *A.* · Da 1:11
and *A.*: therefore stood they · Da 1:19
Mishael, and *A.* his companions · Da 2:17

AZAZ

And Bela the son of *A.,* the son of · 1Ch 5:8

AZAZEL

the other *A.* (A)(B)(E)(R) · Le 16:8; 16:10, 26

AZAZIAH

A. with harps on the Sheminith · 1Ch 15:21
Ephraim, Hoshea the son of *A.* · 1Ch 27:20
And Jehiel, and *A.* and Nahath · 2Ch 31:13

AZBUK

Nehemiah the son of *A.* the ruler · Ne 3:16

AZEKAH

and smote them to *A.* and unto · Jos 10:10
from heaven upon them unto *A.* · Jos 10:11
and Adullam, Socoh, and *A.* · Jos 15:35
pitched between Shochoh and *A.* · 1Sa 17:1
Adoraim, and Lachish, and *A.* · 2Ch 11:9
and the fields thereof, at *A.* · Ne 11:30
against Lachish, and against *A.* · Jer 34:7

AZEL

Eleasah his son, *A.* his son · 1Ch 8:37
A. had six sons, whose names are · 1Ch 8:38
All these were the sons of *A.* · 1Ch 8:38
Eleasah his son, *A.* his son · 1Ch 9:43
A. had six sons, whose names are · 1Ch 9:44
these were the sons of *A.* · 1Ch 9:44

AZEM

Baalah, and Iim, and *A.* · Jos 15:29
Hazar-shual, and Balah, and *A.* · Jos 19:3

AZGAD

The children of *A.* a thousand · Ezr 2:12
And of the sons of *A.*; Johanan · Ezr 8:12
The children of *A.* two thousand · Ne 7:17
Bunni, *A.* Bebai · Ne 10:15

AZIEL

And Zechariah, and *A.* and · 1Ch 15:20

AZIZA

and Jeremoth, and Zabad, and *A.* · Ezr 10:27

AZMAVETH

Abi-albon the Arbathite, *A.* the · 2Sa 23:31
Jehoadah begat Alemeth, and *A.* · 1Ch 8:36

and Jarah begat Alemeth, and *A.* · 1Ch 9:42
A. the Baharumite, Eliahba · 1Ch 11:33
Jeziel, and Pelet, the sons of · 1Ch 12:3
over the king's treasures was *A.* · 1Ch 27:25
The children of *A.* forty and two · Ezr 2:24
out of the fields of Geba and *A.* · Ne 12:29

AZMON

Hazar-addar, and pass on to *A.* · Nu 34:4
shall fetch a compass from *A.* · Nu 34:5
From thence it passed toward *A.* · Jos 15:4

AZNOTH-TABOR

the coast turneth westward to *A.* · Jos 19:34

AZOR

and Eliakim begat *A.* · M't 1:13
And *A.* begat Sadoc · M't 1:14

AZOTUS

But Philip was found at *A.* · Ac 8:40

AZRIEL

and Ishi, and Eliel, and *A.* · 1Ch 5:24
Naphtali, Jerimoth the son of *A.* · 1Ch 27:19
and Seraiah the son of *A.* and · Jer 36:26

AZRIKAM

Elioenai, and Hezekiah, and *A.* · 1Ch 3:23
whose names are these, *A.* · 1Ch 8:38
son of *A.* the son of Hashabiah · 1Ch 9:14
sons, whose names are these, · 1Ch 9:44
A. the governor of the house · 2Ch 28:7
the son of Hashub, the son of · Ne 11:15

AZUBAH

And his mother's name was *A.* · 1Ki 22:42
son of Hezron begat children of *A.* · 1Ch 2:18
And when *A.* was dead, Caleb · 1Ch 2:19
And his mother's name was *A.* · 2Ch 20:31

AZUR

that Hananiah the son of *A.* the · Jer 28:1
I saw Jaazaniah the son of *A.* · Eze 11:1

AZZAH

dwelt in Hazerim, even unto *A.* · De 2:23
from Tiphsah even to *A.* over all · 1Ki 4:24
and Ashkelon, and *A.* and · Jer 25:20

AZZAN

Paltiel the son of *A.* · Nu 34:26

AZZUR

Ater, Hizkijah, *A.* · Ne 10:17

B

BAAL

up into the high places of *B.* · Nu 22:41
Lord, and served *B.* and Ashtaroth · J'g 2:13

and throw down the altar of *B.* · J'g 6:25
the altar of *B.* was cast down · J'g 6:28
hath cast down the altar of *B.* · J'g 6:30
Will ye plead for *B.*? will ye save · J'g 6:31
Let *B.* plead against him · J'g 6:32
and served *B.* and worshipped · 1Ki 16:31
he reared up an altar for *B.* · 1Ki 16:32
in the house of *B.* · 1Ki 16:32
the prophets of *B.* four hundred · 1Ki 18:19
but if *B.* then follow him · 1Ki 18:21
Elijah said unto the prophets of *B.* · 1Ki 18:25
and called on the name of *B.* · 1Ki 18:26
saying, O *B.* hear us · 1Ki 18:26
them, Take the prophets of *B.* · 1Ki 18:40
which have not bowed unto *B.* · 1Ki 19:18
For he served *B.* and worshipped · 1Ki 22:53
he put away the image of *B.* · 2Ki 3:2
Ahab served *B.* · 2Ki 10:18; 10:19-23, 25-28
the land went into the house of *B.* · 2Ki 11:18
and slew Mattan the priest of *B.* · 2Ki 11:18
the host of heaven, and served *B.* · 2Ki 17:16
and he reared up altars for *B.* · 2Ki 21:3
the vessels that were made for *B.* · 2Ki 23:4
also that burned incense unto *B.* · 2Ki 23:5
about the same cities, unto *B.* · 1Ch 4:33
Reaia his son, *B.* his son · 1Ch 5:5
and Kish, and *B.* and Nadab · 1Ch 8:30
Kish, and *B.* and Ner, and Nadab · 1Ch 9:36
the people went to the house of *B.* · 2Ch 23:17
and slew Mattan the priest of *B.* · 2Ch 23:17
the prophets prophesied by *B.* · Jer 2:8
falsely, and burn incense unto *B.* · Jer 7:9
altars to burn incense unto *B.* · Jer 11:13
anger in offering incense unto *B.* · Jer 11:17
taught my people to swear by *B.* · Jer 12:16
built also the high places of *B.* · Jer 19:5
fire for burnt offerings unto *B.* · Jer 19:5
they prophesied in *B.* and caused · Jer 23:13
have forgotten my name for *B.* · Jer 23:27
they have offered incense unto *B.* · Jer 32:29
they build the high places of *B.* · Jer 32:35
gold, which they prepared for *B.* · Ho 2:8
when he offended in *B.,* he died · Ho 13:1
I will cut off the remnant of *B.* · Zep 1:4
bowed the knee to the image of *B.* · Ro 11:4

BAALAH

and the border was drawn to *B.* · Jos 15:9
the border compassed from *B.* · Jos 15:10
and passed along to mount *B.* · Jos 15:11
B., and Iim, and Azem · Jos 15:29
went up, and all Israel, to *B.* · 1Ch 13:6

BAALATH

Eltekeh, and Gibbethon, and *B.* · Jos 19:44
B. and Tadmor in the wilderness · 1Ki 9:18
B. and all the store cities · 2Ch 8:6

BAALATH-BEER

round about these cities to B.   *Jos 19:8*

BAAL-BERITH

and made B. their god   *J'g 8:33*
of silver out of the house of B.   *J'g 9:4*

BAALE

people that were with him from B.   *2Sa 6:2*

BAAL-GAD

even unto B. in the valley of   *Jos 11:17*
the west, from B. in the valley   *Jos 12:7*
from B. under mount Hermon   *Jos 13:5*

BAAL-HAMON

Solomon had a vineyard at B.   *Ca 8:11*

BAAL-HANAN

B. the son of Achbor reigned   *Ge 36:38*
And B. the son of Achbor died   *Ge 36:39*
when Shaul was dead, B the son   *1Ch 1:49*
when B. was dead, Hadad reigned   *1Ch 1:50*
the low plains was B. the Gederite   *1Ch 27:28*

BAAL-HAZOR

Absalom had sheepshearers in B.   *2Sa 13:23*

BAAL-HERMON

from mount B. unto the entering   *J'g 3:3*
from Bashan unto B. and Senir   *1Ch 5:23*

BAALI

and shalt call me no more B.   *Hos 2:16*

BAALIM

sight of the Lord, and served B.   *J'g 2:11*
and served B. and the groves   *J'g 3:7*
went a whoring after B. and made   *J'g 8:33*
and served B. and Ashtaroth   *J'g 10:6*
our God, and also served B.   *J'g 10:10*
children of Israel did put away B.   *1Sa 7:4*
have served B. and Ashtaroth   *1Sa 12:10*
and thou hast followed B.   *1Ki 18:18*
David, and sought not unto B.   *2Ch 17:3*
Lord did they bestow upon B.   *2Ch 24:7*
made also molten images for B.   *2Ch 28:2*
and he reared up altars for B.   *2Ch 33:3*
they brake down the altars of B.   *2Ch 34:4*
polluted, I have not gone after B.   *Jer 2:23*
after B. which their fathers   *Jer 9:14*
I will visit upon her the days of B.   *Ho 2:13*
I will take away the names of B.   *Ho 2:17*
sacrificed unto B. and burned   *Ho 11:2*

BAALIS

B. the king of the Ammonites   *Jer 40:14*

BAAL-MEON

Nebo, and B. (their names being   *Nu 32:38*
even unto Nebo and B.   *1Ch 5:8*
Beth-jeshimoth, B. and   *Eze 25:9*

BAAL-PEOR

Israel joined himself unto B.   *Nu 25:3*
his men that were joined unto B.   *Nu 25:5*
what the Lord did because of B.   *De 4:3*
for all the men that followed B.   *De 4:3*
joined themselves also unto B.   *Ps 106:28*
they went to B. and separated   *Ho 9:10*

BAAL-PERAZIM

David came to B. and David   *2Sa 5:20*
called the name of that place B.   *2Sa 5:20*
So they came up to B.; and David   *1Ch 14:11*
called the name of that place B.   *1Ch 14:11*

BAALS

served B. and Ashtaroth (A)(B)   *J'g 3:7*
turned to the B. (B)   *Jg 8:33*
followed after B. (B)   *Jer 2:23*

BAAL'S

but B. prophets are four hundred   *1Ki 18:22*

BAAL-SHALISHA

there came a man from B.   *2Ki 4:42*

BAAL-TAMAR

put themselves in array at B.   *J'g 20:33*

BAAL-ZEBU

Go, enquire of B. the god of Ekron   *2Ki 1:2*
that ye go to enquire of B. the god   *2Ki 1:3*
that thou sendest to enquire of B.   *2Ki 1:6*
sent messengers to enquire of B.   *2Ki 1:16*

BAAL-ZEPHON

and the sea, over against B.   *Ex 14:2*
beside Pi-hahiroth, before B.   *Ex 14:9*
Pi-hahiroth, which is before B.   *Nu 33:7*

BAANA

B. the son of Ahilud: to him   *1Ki 4:12*
repaired Zadok the son of B.   *Ne 3:4*

BAANAH

the name of the one was B.   *2Sa 4:2*
Rechab and B. went, and   *2Sa 4:5*
Rechab and B. his brother   *2Sa 4:6*
David answered Rechab and B.   *2Sa 4:9*
Heleb the son of B. a Netophathite   *2Sa 23:29*
B. the son of Hushai was in Asher   *1Ki 4:16*
Netophathite, Heled the son of B.   *1Ch 11:30*
Mizpar, Bigvai, Rehum, B.   *Ezr 2:2*
Mispereth, Bigvai, Nehum, B.   *Ne 7:7*
Malluch, Harim, B.   *Ne 10:27*

BAARA

Hushim and B. were his wives   *1Ch 8:8*

BAASEIAH

the son of B. the son of Malchiah   *1Ch 6:40*

BAASHA

reign of B.   *1Ki 15:16; 15:17, 19, 21-22, 27-28, 32-33; 16:1, 3, 4-8, 11-13; 21:22; 2Ch 16:1-6*
like the house of B.   *2Ki 9:9*
king had made for fear of B.   *Jer 41:9*

BABBLER

and a b. is no better   *Ec 10:11*
the slanderer is no better (A)   *Ec 10:11*
charmer's skill does not benefit (B)   *Ec 10:11*
no advantage in the charmer (E)(R)   *Ec 10:11*
What will this b. say   *Ac 17:18*
amateur talker trying to say (A)   *Ac 17:18*
charlatan be trying to say (N)   *Ac 17:18*
cock-sparrow trying to say (P)   *Ac 17:18*

BABBLING

who hath b.? who hath wounds   *Pr 23:29*
who has complaining (A)(E)(R)   *Pr 23:29*
who has complaints (B)   *Pr 23:29*

BABBLINGS

avoiding profane and vain b.   *1Ti 6:20*
irreverent babble, godless chatter (A)   *1Ti 6:20*
irreligious empty discussions (B)   *1Ti 6:20*
empty and worldly chatter (E)   *1Ti 6:20*
godless mixture of contradictory notions (P)   *1Ti 6:20*
godless chatter and contradictions (R)   *1Ti 6:20*
shun profane and vain b. (A)   *2Ti 2:16*
all empty talk (A)   *2Ti 2:16*
those unholy, empty discussions (B)   *2Ti 2:16*
empty and worldly chatter (N)   *2Ti 2:16*
avoid godless chatter (R)   *2Ti 2:16*
steer clear of unchristian b. (P)   *2Ti 2:16*

BABE

behold, the b. wept   *Ex 2:6*
the b. leaped in her womb   *Lu 1:41*
baby leaped in her womb (A)(N)   *Lu 1:41; 1:44*
the child leaped (P)   *Lu 1:41*
the b. leaped in my womb for joy   *Lu 1:44*
the b. wrapt in swaddling clothes   *Lu 2:12*
baby wrapped (A)(B)(N)(P)   *Lu 2:12*
Mary, and Joseph, and the b. lying   *Lu 2:16*
from a b. thou hast (E)   *2Tim 3:15*
of righteousness; for he is a b.   *Heb 5:13*
he a mere infant (A)(B)(N)   *Heb 5:13*
he simply has not grown up (P)   *Heb 5:13*
he is a child (R)   *Heb 5:13*

BABEL

beginning of his kingdom was B.   *Ge 10:10*
is the name of it called B.   *Ge 11:9*

BABES

of the mouth of b. and sucklings   *Ps 8:2*
out of mouths of children (B)   *Ps 8:2*
rest of their substance to their b.   *Ps 17:14*
remainder to their young ones (B)   *Ps 17:14*
and b. shall rule over them   *Isa 3:4*
hast revealed them unto b. (A)   *M't 11:25*
revealed them to babies (A)   *M't 11:25*
revealing them to the simple (N)   *M't 11:25*
showing them to mere children (P)   *M't 11:25*
Out of the mouth of b.   *M't 21:16*
hast revealed them unto b.   *Lu 10:21*
teacher of b. which hast the form   *Ro 2:20*
teacher of the childish (A)   *Ro 2:20*
teacher of the immature   *Ro 2:20*

(B)(N)
those who have no spiritual | Ro 2:20
wisdom (P)
teacher of children (R) | Ro 2:20
as unto b. in Christ | 1Co 3:1
as to mere infants in Christ | 1Co 3:1
(A)(N)
babies in the Christian life | 1Co 3:1
(P)
continue to be b. in evil | 1Co 14:20
(A)(R)
As newborn b. desire the | 1Pe 2:2
sincere
like newborn babies (A)(P) | 1Pe 2:2
Like the newborn infants (N) | 1Pe 2:2

BABY

b. leaped in the womb (A)(N) | Lu 1:41;
| 1:44
b. wrapped (A)(B)(N)(P) | Lu 2:12

BABYLON

of Assyria brought men | 2Ki 17:24
from B.
men of B. made | 2Ki 17:30
Succoth-benoth
king of B. sent messengers | 2Ki 20:12;
| 2Ki 20:14, 17-18
king of B. came up against | 2Ki 24:1;
Jehoiakim | 24:7, 10-12, 15-17, 20
king of B. came against | 2Ki 25:1;
Judah 25:6-13, 20-24, 27-28; | 1Ch 9:1;
2Ch 32:31; 33:11; 36:6-7, 10, 18, 20
Judah went up from B. to | Ezr 1:11
Jerusalem 2:1; 5:12-17; 6:1-5; 7:6-9, 16;
| 8:1; Ne 13:6
king of B. | Es 2:6;
Jer 20:4-6; 21:2-7, 10; 22:25; 24:1; 25:1,
9, 11-12; 27:6-22; 28:2-14; 29:1-28;
32:3-5, 29, 36; 34:1-3; 35:11; 36:29;
37:1, 17, 19; 38:23; 39:1-11; 40:1-11;
41:2, 18; 42:11; 43:3, 10; 44:30; 46:2,
13, 26; 49:28-30; Eze 12:13; 17:12-20;
19:9; 21:19-21; 24:2; 26:7; 29:18-19;
30:10, 24-25; 32-11; Da 1:1; Mic 4:10;
| M't 1:11-17; Ac 7:43
make mention of Rahab and | Ps 87:4
B.
the rivers of B. there we sat | Ps 137:1
down
O daughter of B. who art to | Ps 137:8
be
The burden of B. which | Isa 13:1
Isaiah
And B. the glory of | Isa 13:19
kingdoms
this proverb against the king | Isa 14:4
of B.
and cut off from B. the | Isa 14:22
name
and said, B. is fallen, is | Isa 21:9
fallen
king of B. sent letters and a | Isa 39:1
far country unto me, even | Isa 39:3
from B.
this day, shall be carried to | Isa 39:6
B.
in the palace of the king of | Isa 39:7
B.
For your sake I have sent | Isa 43:14
to B.
O virgin daughter of B. sit | Isa 47:1
on the
he will do his pleasure on | Isa 48:14
B.
Go ye forth of B. flee ye | Isa 48:20
the Lord spake against B. | Jer 50:1
B. is taken, destroyed | Jer 50:2;
50:8-9, 13-14, 16-18, 23-24, 28-29, 34-35,
42-43, 46; 51:1-9, 11-12, 24, 28-29, 35,
| 42-43, 45-46
rebelled against B. | Jer 52:3;
| 52:4, 9-12, 15, 26-27, 31-32, 34
destroy all wise men of B. | Da 2:12;
| 2:14, 24
ruler over whole province of | Da 2:48;
B. | 2:49
image in the province of B. | Da 3:1;
| 3:12, 30
bring in all the wise men of | Da 4:6;
B. | 5:7
palace of the kingdom of B. | Da 4:29;
| 4:30
first year of Belshazzar king of | Da 7:1
B.
and thou shall go even to B. | Mic 4:10
with the daughter of B. | Zec 2:7
which are come from B. | Zec 6:10

they were carried away to B. | M't 1:11
after they were brought to B. | M't 1:12
the carrying away into B. | M't 1:17
carrying away into B. unto | M't 1:17
Christ
carry you away beyond B. | Ac 7:43
The church that is at B. | 1Pe 5:13
B. is fallen, is fallen | Re 14:8
great B. came in | Re 16:19
remembrance
B. the great, the mother of | Re 17:5
B. the great is fallen | Re 18:2
that great city B. that | Re 18:10
mighty city
great city B. be thrown | Re 18:21
down

BABYLONIANS

the B. the Susanchites, the | Ezr 4:9
manner of the B. of | Eze 23:15
Chaldea
the B. came to her into the | Eze 23:17
The B. and all the | Eze 23:23
Chaldeans

BABYLONISH

spoils a goodly B. garment | Jos 7:21

BABYLON'S

the king of B. army besieged | Jer 32:2
When the king of B. army | Jer 34:7
fought
the hand of the king of B. | Jer 34:21
of B. army, which shall take | Jer 38:3
it
go forth unto the king of B. | Jer 38:17
princes
to the king of B. princes, | Jer 38:18
then shall
forth to the king of B. | Jer 38:22
princes
and all the king of B. | Jer 39:13
princes

BACA

passing through the valley of | Ps 84:6
B.

BACHRITES

of Becher, the family of the | Nu 26:35
B.

BACK

money put b. (R) | Ge 42:28
Zipporah, after he had sent | Ex 18:2
her b.
ass going astray, thou shalt | Ex 23:4
bring it b.
over the b. of the tabernacle | Ex 26:12
(S)
if it displease thee, I will | Nu 22:34
get me b.
the Lord hath kept thee b. | Nu 24:11
from honour
Joshua drew not his hand b. | Jos 8:26
till he
he himself turned b. (S) | J'g 3:19
the Moabitish damsel that | Ru 2:6
came b.
return, and take b. thy | 2Sa 15:20
brethren
why speak ye not of | 2Sa 19:10
bringing king b.
when Judah looked b. | 2Ch 13:14
behold
but the soldiers that | 2Ch 25:13
Amaziah sent b.
give b. his wealth | Job 20:10
(A)(B)(E)(K)
shall he give it b. (A)(R) | Job 20:18
arrow goes through his b. | Job 20:25
(B)
he holdeth b. the face of his | Job 26:9
throne
make them turn their b. | Ps 21:12
plowed upon my b.: they | Ps 129:3
made
rod for b. of him that is | Pr 10:13
cast all my sins behind thy | Isa 38:17
b.
gave my b. to the smiters | Isa 50:6
have turned their b. upon me | Jer 2:27
shew me the b., and not | Jer 18:17

turn me b. and I shall be | Jer 31:18
restored (S)
have turned unto me the b. | Jer 32:33
turned about and came b. | Jer 41:14
(S)
they look not b. | Jer 46:5
hath Moab turned b. with | Jer 48:39
which had upon the b. of it | Da 7:6
Israel slideth b. as backsliding | Ho 4:16
heifer
stand, shall they cry, none | Na 2:8
shall look b.
nor let him that is in field | M't 24:18
return b.
angel rolled b. the stone from | M't 28:21
the door
went into ship, and returned b. | Lu 8:37
again
put his hand to plough, and | Lu 9:62
looking b.
let him likewise not return | Lu 17:31
b.
bow down their b. alway | Ro 11:10
if any man draw b., my | Heb 10:38
soul
not of them who draw b. | Heb 10:39
to
you kept b. by fraud | Jas 5:4
on the b. sealed with (S) | Re 5:1

BACKBITERS

B., haters of God, despiteful | Ro 1:30
Slanderers (A)(R) | Ro 1:30
gossips, slanderers (B) | Ro 1:30
scandal-mongers (N) | Ro 1:30
stabbers-in-the-back (P) | Ro 1:30

BACKBITETH

He that b. not with his | Ps 15:3
tongue
not slander with tongue | Ps 15:3
(A)(B)(E)(R)

BACKBITING

angry countenance a b. | Pr 25:23
tongue
a concealed tongue (B) | Pr 25:23

BACKBONE

it shall he take off hard by b. | Le 3:9

BACKS

all thine enemies turn their | Ex 23:27
b.
when Israel turneth their b. | Jos 7:8
their b. before their enemies | Jos 7:12
Therefore they turned their | J'g 20:42
b.
of the Lord, and turned their | 2Ch 29:6
b.
cast thy law behind their b. | Ne 9:26
with their b. toward the | Eze 8:16
temple
and their b. and their hands | Eze 10:12

BACKSIDE

flock to the b. of the desert, | Ex 3:1
and
over the b. of the tabernacle | Ex 26:12
book written within and on b. | Re 5:1

BACKSLIDER

The b. in heart shall be | Pr 14:14
filled

BACKSLIDING

he went on b. (S) | Isa 57:17
that which b. Israel hath done | Jer 3:6
b. Israel committed adultery | Jer 3:8
The b. Israel hath justified | Jer 3:11
herself
Return, thou b. Israel, saith | Jer 3:12
the
Turn, O b. children, saith | Jer 3:14
the
Return, ye b. children, and I | Jer 3:22
will
slidden back by a perpetual | Jer 8:5
b.
perpetual turning away (A) | Jer 8:5
perpetual b. (B)(R) | Jer 8:5
O thou b. daughter | Jer 31:22

thy flowing valley, O *b.* daughter — Jer 49:4

Israel slideth back as *b.* heifer — Ho 4:16

like a stubborn heifer (A)(B)(E)(R) — Ho 4:16

my people are bent to *b.* from me — Ho 11:7

I will heal their *b.* — Ho 14:4

heal their faithlessness (A)(R) — Ho 14:4

BACKSLIDINGS

and thy *b.* shall reprove thee — Jer 2:19
and I will heal your *b.* — Jer 3:22
their *b.* are increased — Jer 5:6
our *b.* are many — Jer 14:7

BACKWARD

both their shoulders, and went *b.* — Ge 9:23
their faces were *b.* and they — Ge 9:23
so that his rider shall fall *b.* — Ge 49:17
he fell from off the seat *b.* — 1Sa 4:18
shadow return *b.* ten degrees — 2Ki 20:10
brought the shadow ten degrees *b.* — 2Ki 20:11
and *b.* but I cannot perceive — Job 23:8
them be driven *b.* and put to shame — Ps 40:14
be turned *b.* and put to confusion — Ps 70:2
unto anger, they are gone away *b.* — Isa 1:4
that they might go, and fall *b.* — Isa 28:13
sun dial of Ahaz, ten degrees *b.* — Isa 38:8
that turneth wise men *b.* — Isa 44:25
neither turned *b.* (S) — Isa 50:5
Judgment is turned away *b.* — Isa 59:14
went *b.* and not forward — Jer 7:24
saith the Lord, thou art gone *b.* — Jer 15:6
she sigheth, and turneth *b.* — La 1:8
they went *b.* and fell to — Joh 18:6

BAD

cannot speak unto thee *b.* or good — Ge 24:50
not to Jacob either good or *b.* — Ge 31:24; 31:29
nor change it, a good for a *b.* — Le 27:10
or a *b.* for a good: and if he — Le 27:10
value it, whether it be good or *b.* — Le 27:12
estimate it, whether it be good or *b.* — Le 27:14
not search whether it be good or *b.* — Le 27:33
whether it be good or *b.*; and what — Nu 13:19
good or *b.* of mine own mind — Nu 24:13
brought himself in *b.* repute (B) — 1Sa 27:12
brother Amnon neither good nor *b.* — 2Sa 13:22
the king to discern good and *b.* — 2Sa 14:17
discern between good and *b.* — 1Ki 3:9
the water is *b.* (S) — 2Ki 2:19
the rebellious and the *b.* city — Ezr 4:12
seemed *b.* to me (B) — Ec 2:17
very *b.* figs (A)(B)(E)(R)(S) — Jer 24:2
not be eaten, they were so *b.* — Jer 24:2
b. figs (S) — Jer 24:3; 24:8
they are so *b.* (S) — Jer 29:17
b. fruit — M't 7:7; M't 7:17, 18
both tree and fruit *b.* (B)(N)(R) — M't 12:33
into vessels, but cast the *b.* away — M't 13:48
has *b.* fits (N) — M't 17:15
as they found, both *b.* and good — M't 22:10
done, whether it be good or *b.* — 2Co 5:10
no *b.* language (N) — Eph 4:29

BADE

did as Joseph *b.*; and the man — Ge 43:17

up till the morning, as Moses *b.* — Ex 16:24
congregation *b.* stone them with — Nu 14:10
unto them as the Lord *b.* him — Jos 11:9
all that her mother in law *b.* her — Ru 3:6
and some *b.* me kill thee — 1Sa 24:10
b. them teach the children of Judah — 2Sa 1:18
thy servant Joab, he *b.* me — 2Sa 14:19
the king *b.* saying, Come again — 2Ch 10:12
Then Esther *b.* them return — Es 4:15
they how that he *b.* them not — M't 16:12
And he that *b.* thee and him come — Lu 14:9
when he that *b.* thee cometh, he — Lu 14:10
said he also to him that *b.* him — Lu 14:12
made a great supper, and *b.* many — Lu 14:16
the spirit *b.* me go with them — Ac 11:12
b. them farewell, saying, I must — Ac 18:21
b. that he should be examined — Ac 22:24

BADEST

done according as thou *b.* me — Ge 27:19

BADGE

on forehead a *b.* (B) — De 6:8

BADGER

the rock *b.* (S) — Le 11:5; De 14:7

BADGERS

the *b.* are a feeble fold (S) — Pr 30:26

BADGERS'

b. skins, and shittim wood — Ex 25:5
a covering above of *b.* skins — Ex 26:14
dyed red, and *b.* skins, and — Ex 35:7; 35:23
a covering of *b.* skins above that — Ex 36:19
the covering of *b.* skins — Ex 39:34
the covering of *b.* skins — Nu 4:6; Nu 4:8, 10-12, 14, 25
shod thee with *b.* skin — Eze 16:10

BADLY

b. treated (S) — Ex 5:22; De 26:6

BADNESS

in all the land of Egypt for *b.* — Ge 41:19

BAFFLING

prayers go *b.* like heathen (N) — M't 6:7

BAG

not have in thy *b.* divers weights — De 25:13
bread in our *b.* (B) — 1Sa 9:7
the shepherd *b.* (B)(E)(R) — 1Sa 17:4
in a shepherd's *b.* which he had — 1Sa 17:40
David put his hand in his *b.* — 1Sa 17:49
transgression is sealed up in *b.* — Job 14:17
sealed up in a sack (B) — Job 14:17
taken a *b.* of money with thee — Pr 7:20
weights of the *b.* are his work — Pr 16:11
They lavish gold out of the *b.* — Isa 46:6
with the *b.* of deceitful weights — Mic 6:11
to put it into a *b.* with holes — Hag 1:6
b. or wallet (A)(B)(R) — M't 10:10; M'k 6:8; Lu 9:3
bag (S) — M't 10:10; M'k 6:8; Lu 9:3; 10:4; 22:35-36

provisions *b.* (A)(P)(R) — Lu 10:4; 22:35-36
and *b.* (B)(R) — Lu 22:35; 22:36
he was a thief, and had the *b.* — Joh 12:6
thought, because Judas had the *b.* — Joh 13:29
had the money box (A)(R) — Joh 13:29

BAGGAGE

their *b.* (A)(S) — Jos 7:11; 1Sa 25:13; 30:24; Eze 12:3-4, 7
hid among the *b.* (B) — 1Sa 10:22; 30:24
the *b.* (E) — 1Sa 10:22; 25:13; 30:24
the *b.* (R) — 1Sa 10:22; 25:13; 30:24; Eze 12:3-4, 7
his *b.* (S) — 1Sa 17:22; Isa 10:28

BAGS

fruits in your *b.* (R) — Ge 43:11
food *b.* and utensils (A) — 2Sa 21:5
two talents of silver in two *b.* — 2Ki 5:23
they put up in *b.* and told — 2Ki 12:10
make it into ingots (B) — 2Ki 12:10
provide yourselves *b.* which wax — Lu 12:33
provide with purses and handbags (A) — Lu 12:33
make purses for yourselves (B)(E)(N)(P)(R) — Lu 12:33

BAHARUMITE

Azmaveth the *B.*, Eliahba — 1Ch 11:33

BAHURIM

along weeping behind her to *B.* — 2Sa 3:16
And when king David came to *B.* — 2Sa 16:5
and came to a man's house in *B.* — 2Sa 17:18
a Benjamite, which was of *B.* — 2Sa 19:16
a Benjamite of *B.* which cursed — 1Ki 2:8

BAIL

required *b.* from Jason (B) — Ac 17:9

BAIT

no *b.* in it (B) — Am 3:5

BAJITH

is gone up to *B.* and to Dibon — Isa 15:2

BAKBAKKAR

B., Heresh, and Galal, and — 1Ch 9:15

BAKBUK

The children of *B.* the children — Ezr 2:51; Ne 7:53

BAKBUKIAH

B. the second among his — Ne 11:17
B. and Unni, their breathren — Ne 12:9
Mattaniah, and *B.* Obadiah — Ne 12:25

BAKE

did *b.* unleavened bread, and they — Ge 19:3
b. that which ye will *b.* — Ex 16:23
and *b.* twelve cakes thereof — Le 24:5
ten women shall *b.* your bread in — Le 26:26
did *b.* unleavened bread thereof — 1Sa 28:24
in his sight, and did *b.* the cakes — 2Sa 13:8
thou shalt *b.* it with dung that — Eze 4:12
they shall *b.* the meat offering — Eze 46:20

BAKED

And they *b.* unleavened cakes — Ex 12:39

b. it in pans, and made cakes *Nu 11:8*
for that which is *b.* in the *1Ch 23:29*
pan
I have *b.* bread upon the *Isa 44:19*
coals

BAKEMEATS

of *b.* for Pharaoh *Ge 40:17*
baker's delicacies (B) *Ge 40:17*

BAKEN

a meat offering *b.* in the oven *Le 2:4*
be a meat offering *b.* in a pan *Le 2:5*
offering *b.* in the frying pan *Le 2:7*
It shall not be *b.* with leaven *Le 6:17*
when it is *b.* thou shalt *Le 6:21*
the *b.* pieces of the meat *Le 6:21*
offering
all the meat offering that is *b.* *Le 7:9*
they shall be *b.* with leaven *Le 23:17*
there was a cake *b.* on the *1Ki 19:6*
coals

BAKER

and his *b.* had offended their *Ge 40:1*
lord
and the *b.* of the king of *Ge 40:5*
Egypt
When the chief *b.* saw that *Ge 40:16*
of the chief *b.* among his *Ge 40:20*
servants
But he hanged the chief *b.* *Ge 40:22*
both me and the chief *b.* *Ge 41:10*
as an oven heated by the *b.* *Ho 7:4*
their *b.* sleepeth all the night *Ho 7:6*

BAKERS

against the chief of the *b.* *Ge 40:2*
and to be cooks, and to be *1Sa 8:13*
b.
perfumers, cooks, *b.* *1Sa 8:13*
(A)(B)(E)(R)

BAKER'S

b. delicacies (B) *Ge 40:17*
piece of bread out of the *b.* *Jer 37:21*
street

BAKING

of the *b.* pan (E) *Le 2:5; 6:21; 7:9*
a *b.* pan (B) *Le 11:35*
bread of a new *b.* (N) *1Co 5:6*

BALAAM

B. the son of Beor *Nu 22:5; 22:7-8*
God came to *B.* *Nu 22:9;*
      22:10, 12, 20; 23:4, 16
B. rose up in morning *Nu 22:13;*
      Nu 22:14, 16, 18, 21
B. smote the ass *Nu 22:23; 22:29-30*
the ass said to *B.* *Nu 22:28 22:29-30*
Lord opened the eyes of *B.* *Nu 22:31*
B. said to angel of the *Nu 22:34;*
Lord   *22:35*
B. went with princes of *Nu 22:35;*
Balak   *22:36-41; 23:1-5, 11, 25-30;*
      24:10, 12
B. saw that it pleased the *Nu 24:1;*
Lord   *24:2-3*
B. rose up returned to his *Nu 24:25*
place
B. the son of Beor they slew *Nu 31:8*
with
through the counsel of *B.* *Nu 31:16*
they hired against thee *B.* *De 23:4;*
   23:5; Jos 13:22; 24:9-10; Ne 13:2;
      Mic 6:5
following the way of *B.* *2Pe 2:15*
the error of *B.* for reward *Jude 11*
the doctrine of *B.,* who *Re 2:14*
taught Balac

BALAAM'S

and crushed *B.* foot against *Nu 22:25*
and *B.* anger was kindled *Nu 22:27*
the Lord put a word in *B.* *Nu 23:5*
mouth

BALAC

taught *B.* to cast a *Re 2:14*
stumblingblock

BALADAN

the son of *B.* king of *2Ki 20:12*
Babylon
Merodach-baladan, the son of *Isa 39:1*
B.

BALAH

Hazar-shual, and *B.* and *Jos 19:3*
Azem

BALAK

B. the son of Zippor *Nu 22:2;*
  22:4, 7, 10, 13-16; Jos 24:9; Mic 6:5
if *B.* would give me a house *Nu 22:18*
full
Balaam went with princes *Nu 22:35;*
of *B.*   *22:36*
B. heard that Balaam had *Nu 22:37;*
come *22:38-41; 23:1-3, 5, 7, 11, 13, 15-*
      18, 25-30; 24:10-13, 25
art thou better than *B.* *J'g 11:25*

BALAK'S

And *B.* anger was kindled *Nu 24:10*
against

BALANCE

Let me be weighed in an *Job 31:6*
even *b.*
to be laid in the *b.* they are *Ps 62:9*
false *b.* is abomination to the *Pr 11:1*
just weight and *b.* are the *Pr 16:11*
Lord's
and a false *b.* is not good *Pr 20:23*
and the hills in a *b.* *Isa 40:12*
count as the small dust of *Isa 40:15*
the *b.*
weigh silver in the *b.* and *Isa 46:6*
hire a.
thrown off *b.* (P) *2Th 2:2*

BALANCES

Just *b.,* just weights, a just *Le 19:36*
my calamity laid in the *b.* *Job 6:2*
together
weighed him the money in *Jer 32:10*
the *b.*
then take the *b.* to weigh *Eze 5:1*
Ye shall have just *b.* *Eze 45:10*
Thou art weighed in the *b.* *Da 5:27*
b. of deceit are in his *Ho 12:7*
hand
falsifying the *b.* by deceit *Am 8:5*
pure with the wicked *b.* *Mic 6:11*
had a pair of *b.* in his hand *Re 6:5*

BALANCINGS

thou know the *b.* of the *Job 37:16*
clouds

BALD

the *b.* locust after his kind *Le 11:22*
he is *b.*; yet is he clean *Le 13:40*
he is forehead *b.* *Le 13:41; 13:42-43*
b. head; go up, thou *b.* head *2Ki 2:23*
make themselves *b.* for them *Jer 16:6*
every head shall be *b.* and *Jer 48:37*
every
themselves utterly *b.* for *Eze 27:31*
thee
every head was made *b.* and *Eze 29:18*
Make thee *b.* and poll thee *Mic 1:16*
for thy

BALDNESS

They shall not make *b.* upon *Le 21:5*
their
nor make any *b.* between *De 14:1*
your
instead of well set hair *b.* *Isa 3:24*
on all their heads shall be *b.* *Isa 15:2*
to mourning, and to *b.* *Isa 22:12*
B. is come upon Gaza *Jer 47:5*
b. upon all their heads *Eze 7:18*
b. upon every head; and I will *Am 8:10*
enlarge thy *b.* as the eagle *Mic 1:16*

BALL

and toss thee like a *b.* into *Isa 22:18*
a

BALLADS

those who sing *b.* *Nu 21:27*
(A)(B)(R)

BALM

spicery and *b.* and myrrh, *Ge 37:25*
going
a little *b.* and a little honey *Ge 43:11*
Is there no *b.* in Gilead *Jer 8:22*
Go up into Gilead, and take *Jer 46:11*
b.
take *b.* for her pain, if so be *Jer 51:8*
she
and honey, and oil, and *b.* *Eze 27:17*

BALMS

with *b.* and perfumes (B)(S) *Es 2:12*

BALSAM

the *b.* trees (B)(R) *2Sa 5:23; 5:24*

BAMAH

thereof is called *B.* unto *Eze 20:29*
this day

BAMOTH

from Nahaliel to *B.* *Nu 21:19*
And from *B.* in the valley, *Nu 21:20*
that is

BAMOTH-BAAL

Dibon, and *B.* and *Jos 13:17*

BAN

b. your name as infamous *Lu 6:22*
(N)

BAND

a *b.* round about the hole, *Ex 39:23*
that it
meet a *b.* of prophets *1Sa 10:5*
(E)(R)
him a *b.* of men, whose *1Sa 10:26*
hearts
lead you to this *b.* *1Sa 30:15*
(A)(B)(R)
captain over a *b.,* when *1Ki 11:24*
David
they spied a *b.* of men; and *2Ki 13:21*
they
made them captains of the *1Ch 12:18*
b.
David against the *b.* of the *1Ch 12:21*
the *b.* of men that came *2Ch 22:1*
with the
the king a. *b.* of soldiers and *Ezr 8:22*
unicorn with his *b.* in the *Job 39:10*
furrow
a *b.* of twelve cubits (S) *Jer 52:21*
even with a *b.* of iron and *Da 4:15*
brass
in the earth, even with a *b.* *Da 4:23*
of iron
gathered unto him the *M't 27:27*
whole *b.*
they call together the whole *M'k 15:16*
b.
having received a *b.* of men *Joh 18:3*
Then the *b.* and the captain *Joh 18:12*
of the *b.* called the Italian *b.* *Ac 10:1*
chief captain of the *b.* that *Ac 21:31*
Julius, a centurion of *Ac 27:1*
Augustus' *b.*

BANDAGE

put a *b.* to bind (S) *Eze 30:21*

BANDED

b. with silver (S) *Ex 27:17; 38:17, 28*
of the Jews *b.* together *Ac 23:12*
b. together and grows (N) *Eph 2:21;*
      4:16

BANDIT

poverty come as a *b.* (B) *Pr 6:11;*
      24:34

BANDS

herds, and the camels, into *Ge 32:7*
two *b.*
and now I am become two *Ge 32:10*
b.
their *b.* (B) *Ex 27:10;*
36:38; 38:10-12, 17, 19, 28
their *b.* (S) *Ex 27:10;*
27:11; 36:38; 38:10-12, 17, 19
have broken the *b.* of your *Le 26:13*
yoke
his *b.* loosed from off his *J'g 15:14*
hands
two men that were captains *2Sa 4:2*
of *b.*
So the *b.* of Syria came no *2Ki 6:23*
more
And the *b.* of the Moabites *2Ki 13:20*
invaded
Pharaoh-nechoh put him in *2Ki 23:33*
b. at
against him *b.* of the *2Ki 24:2*
Chaldees
were *b.* of soldiers for war *1Ch 7:4*
of the *b.* that were ready *1Ch 12:23*
armed
went out to war by *b.* *2Ch 26:11*
Chaldeans made out three *b.* *Job 1:17*
Pleiades, or loose the *b.* of *Job 38:31*
Orion
hath loosed the *b.* of the *Job 39:5*
wild ass
b. make traffic of him (E) *Job 41:6*
break their *b.* asunder, and *Ps 2:3*
cast
the cords or *b.* of death (A) *Ps 18:4*
there are no *b.* in their death *Ps 73:4*
and break their *b.* in sunder *Ps 107:14*
The *b.* of the wicked have *Ps 119:61*
robbed
go they forth all of them by *Pr 30:27*
b.
and nets, and her hands as *b.* *Ec 7:26*
lest your *b.* be made strong *Isa 28:22*
loose thyself from the *b.* of *Isa 52:2*
loose the *b.* of wickedness, to *Isa 58:6*
thy yoke, and burst thy *b.* *Jer 2:20*
they shall put *b.* upon thee *Eze 3:25*
I will lay *b.* upon thee, and *Eze 4:8*
to help him, and all his *b.* *Eze 12:14*
with all his *b.* shall fall *Eze 17:21*
have broken the *b.* of their *Eze 34:27*
yoke
Gomer, and all his *b.* *Eze 38:6;*
38:9, 22
of Israel, thou, and all thy *b.* *Eze 39:4*
of a man, with *b.* of love *Ho 11:4*
Beauty, the other I called *B.* *Zec 11:7*
asunder, mine other staff, *Zec 11:14*
even *B.*
he brake the *b.* and was *Lu 8:29*
driven
and every one's *b.* were loosed *Ac 16:26*
he loosed him from his *Ac 22:30*
b.
loosed the rudder *b.* and *Ac 27:40*
hoised
the body by joints and *b.* *Col 2:19*

BANEFUL

any *b.* motive (B) *Ps 139:24*

BANI

Nathan of Zobah, *B.* the *2Sa 23:36*
Gadite
The son of *B.* the son of *1Ch 6:46*
Shamer
the son of *B.* of the children *1Ch 9:4*
of
The children of *B.* six *Ezr 2:10*
hundred
sons of *B.;* Meshullam *Ezr 10:29;*
10:34, 38
Rehum the son of *B.* Next *Ne 3:17*
Jeshua, and *B.* and Sherebiah *Ne 8:7;*
9:4-5
Levites, Jeshua, and *B.* *Ne 9:4*
Hodijah, *B.,* Beninu *Ne 10:13;*
10:14
Uzzi the son of *B.* the son *Ne 11:22*
of

BANISHED

fetch home again his *b.* *2Sa 14:13;*
14:14

BANISHMENT

it be unto death, or to *b.* *Ezr 7:26*
false burdens and causes of *b.* *La 2:14*

BANK

I stood upon the *b.* of the *Ge 41:17*
river
is by the *b.* of the river Arnon *De 4:48*
upon the *b.* of the river Arnon *Jos 12:2*
is upon the *b.* of the river *Jos 13:9;*
Arnon *13:16*
cast up a *b.* against the city *2Sa 20:15*
and stood by the *b.* of *2Ki 2:13*
Jordan
shield, nor cast a *b.* against it *2Ki 19:32*
shields, nor cast a *b.* against *Isa 37:33*
it
at the *b.* of the river were *Eze 47:7*
very
by the river upon the *b.* *Eze 47:12*
thereof
this side of the *b.* of the *Da 12:5*
river
money into the *b.* that at my *Lu 19:23*

BANKS

overfloweth all his *b.* all the *Jos 3:15*
time
flowed over all his *b.,* as they *Jos 4:18*
did
it had overflown all his *b.* *1Ch 12:15*
channels, and go over all his *Isa 8:7*
b.
man's voice between the *b.* of *Da 8:16*
Ulai

BANNER

with the *b.* of father's house *Nu 2:2*
(S)
given a *b.* to them that fear *Ps 60:4*
and his *b.* over me was love *Ca 2:4*
Lift ye up a *b.* upon the high *Isa 13:2*
lift up a *b.* (B) *Isa 62:10*
set up a *b.* (R) *Jer 50:2*

BANNERED

terrible as a *b.* host (A) *Ca 6:4*

BANNERS

set up our *b.* the Lord fulfil *Ps 20:5*
all
the set *b.* for signs (S) *Ps 74:4*
terrible as an army with *b.* *Ca 6:4*
terrible as a bannered host (A) *Ca 6:4*
and terrible as an army with *b.* *Ca 6:10*

BANQUET

made a *b.* (B) *Ge 26:30*
29:22; 40:20; Es 1:9; 2:18; Ec 10:19
gave a *b.* (R) *Es 1:3; 1:5, 9; 2:18*
Haman come this day unto *Es 5:4;*
the *b.* 5:5-6, 8, 12, 14
hasted to bring Haman unto *Es 6:14*
the *b.*
the king and Haman came to *Es 7:1;*
b. 7:2, 7-8
Shall the companions make *Job 41:6*
a *b.*
his lord, came into the *b.* house *Da 5:10*
the *b.* of them that stretched *Am 6:7*
made a wedding *b.* (A)(B) *M't 22:2*
to the *b.* (B) *M't 22:8*
went into the *b.* (B) *M't 25:10*
made a *b.* (A)(B)(N)(R) *M'k 6:21*
made a great *b.* (A)(B) *Lu 5:29*
made a *b.* (R) *Lu 14:12; 14:16-17, 24*
give a *b.* (A) *Lu 14:13*
shall taste my *b.* (N) *Lu 14:24*
the wedding *b.* (B) *Re 19:7; 19:9*
into the *b.* (B) *Re 19:9; 19:17*

BANQUETING

b. in his house (B) *1Sa 25:36*
He brought me to the *b.* house *Ca 2:4*

BANQUETINGS

b. and abominable idolatries *1Pe 4:3*

BAPTISM

and Sadducees come to his *b.* *M't 3:7*
the *b.* that I am baptized *M't 20:22*

with
be baptized with the *b.* that *M't 20:23*
I am
The *b.* of John, whence was *M't 21:25*
it
preach the *b.* of repentance *M'k 1:4*
the *b.* that I am baptized *M'k 10:38*
with
with the *b.* that I am *M'k 10:39*
baptized
The *b.* of John, was it from *M'k 11:30*
heaven
preaching the *b.* of repentance *Lu 3:3*
being baptized with the *b.* of *Lu 7:29*
John
I have a *b.* to be baptized with *Lu 12:50*
The *b.* of John, was it from *Lu 20:4*
heaven
Beginning from the *b.* of *Ac 1:22*
John
after the *b.* which John *Ac 10:37*
preached
the *b.* of repentance to all *Ac 13:24*
the people
Lord, knowing only the *b.* *Ac 18:25*
of John
And they said, Unto John's *Ac 19:3*
b.
with the *b.* of repentance, *Ac 19:4*
saying
buried with him by *b.* into *Ro 6:4*
death
One Lord, one faith, one *b.* *Eph 4:5*
Buried with him in *b.* *Col 2:12*
wherein
even *b.* doth also now save *1Pe 3:21*
us

BAPTISMS

Of the doctrine of *b.* and of *Heb 6:2*
laying

BAPTIST

In those days came John the *M't 3:1*
B.
risen a greater than John *M't 11:11*
the *B.*
from the days of John the *M't 11:12*
B. until
This is John the *B.;* he is *M't 14:2*
risen
Some say that thou art *M't 16:14*
John the *B.*
he spake unto them of John *M't 17:13*
the *B.*
That John the *B.* was risen *M'k 6:14*
she said, The head of John *M'k 6:24*
the *B.*
a charger the head of John *M'k 6:25*
the *B.*
they answered, John the *B.* *M'k 8:28*
John *B.* hath sent us unto *Lu 7:20*
thee
greater prophet than John the *Lu 7:28*
B.
John the *B.* came neither *Lu 7:33*
eating
answering said, John the *B.* *Lu 9:19*

BAPTIST'S

Give me here John *B.* head *M't 14:8*

BAPTIZE

I indeed *b.* you with water *M't 3:11*
he shall *b.* you with the *M't 3:11*
Holy Ghost
John did *b.* in the wilderness *M'k 1:4*
he shall *b.* you with the Holy *M'k 1:8*
Ghost
I indeed *b.* you with water *Lu 3:16*
he shall *b.* you with the Holy *Lu 3:16*
Ghost
saying, I *b.* with water: but *Joh 1:26*
he that sent me to *b.* with *Joh 1:33*
water
Christ sent me not to *b.* but *1Co 1:17*
to

BAPTIZED

And were *b.* of him in Jordan *M't 3:6*
Jordan unto John, to be *b.* *M't 3:13*
of him
I have need to be *b.* of *M't 3:14*
thee, and
Jesus, when he was *b.* went *M't 3:16*
up

BAPTIZED (continued)

I shall drink of, and to be *b.* — M't 20:22
the baptism that I am *b.* with — M't 20:22
and be *b.* with the baptism that I am *b.* with — M't 20:23
all *b.* of him in the river of Jordan — M'k 1:5
I indeed have *b.* you with water — M'k 1:8
and was *b.* of John in Jordan — M'k 1:9
and be *b.* with the baptism that I am *b.* with — M'k 10:38
and with the baptism that I am *b.* — M'k 10:39
withal shall ye be *b.* — M'k 10:39
believeth and is *b.* shall be saved — M'k 16:16
came forth to be *b.* of him — Lu 3:7
Then came also publicans to be *b.* — Lu 3:12
when all the people were *b.* it came — Lu 3:21
that Jesus also being *b.* — Lu 3:21
being *b.* with the baptism of John — Lu 7:29
themselves, being not *b.* of him — Lu 7:30
I have a baptism to be *b.* with — Lu 12:50
there he tarried with them, and *b.* — Joh 3:22
and they came, and were *b.* — Joh 3:23
Jesus made and *b.* more disciples — Joh 4:1
(Though Jesus himself *b.* not — Joh 4:2
place where John at first *b.* — Joh 10:40
John truly *b.* with water — Ac 1:5
ye shall be *b.* with the Holy Ghost — Ac 1:5
Repent, and be *b.* every one of you — Ac 2:38
gladly received his word were *b.* — Ac 2:41
were *b.* both men and women — Ac 8:12
he was *b.* he continued with Philip — Ac 8:13
only they were *b.* in the name — Ac 8:16
what doth hinder me to be *b.* — Ac 8:36
and the eunuch; and he *b.* him — Ac 8:38
forthwith, and arose, and was *b.* — Ac 9:18
water, that these should not be *b.* — Ac 9:47
commanded them to be *b.* in — Ac 10:48
John indeed *b.* with water — Ac 11:16
ye shall be *b.* with the Holy Ghost — Ac 11:16
when she was *b.* and her household — Ac 16:15
was *b.* he and all his, straightway — Ac 16:33
hearing believed, and were *b.* — Ac 18:8
Unto what then were ye *b.* — Ac 19:3
John verily *b.* with the baptism of — Ac 19:4
heard this, they were *b.* in the name — Ac 19:5
and be *b.* and wash away thy sins — Ac 22:16
of us as were *b.* into Jesus Christ — Ro 6:3
were *b.* into his death — Ro 6:3
or were ye *b.* in the name of Paul — 1Co 1:13
I thank God that I *b.* none of you — 1Co 1:14
say that I had *b.* in mine own name — 1Co 1:15
I *b.* also the household of Stephanas — 1Co 1:16
I know not whether I *b.* any other — 1Co 1:16
were all *b.* unto Moses in the cloud — 1Co 10:2
For by one Spirit are we all *b.* into — 1Co 12:13
they do which are *b.* for the dead — 1Co 15:29
why are they then *b.* for the dead — 1Co 15:29
as have been *b.* into Christ have put — Ga 3:27

BAPTIZEST

said unto him, Why *b.* thou then — Joh 1:25

BAPTIZETH

is he which *b.* with the Holy Ghost — Joh 1:33
behold, the same *b.* and all men — Joh 3:26

BAPTIZING

b. them in the name of the Father — M't 28:19
Jordan, where John was *b.* — Joh 1:28
therefore am I come *b.* with water — Joh 1:31
John also was *b.* in Ænon — Joh 3:23

BAR

And the middle *b.* in the midst of — Ex 26:28
he made the middle *b.* to shoot — Ex 36:33
skins, and shall put it upon a *b.* — Nu 4:10
skins, and shall put them on a *b.* — Nu 4:12
away with them, *b.*, and all — J'g 16:3
them shut the doors, and *b.* them — Ne 7:3
handles of the *b.* (B) — Ca 5:5
break also the *b.* of Damascus — Am 1:5

BARABBAS

a notable prisoner called B. — M't 27:16; 27:17, 20-21, 26; M'k 15:7, 11, 15; Lu 23:18; Joh 18:40

BARACHEL

Elihu the son of B. — Job 32:2; 32:6

BARACHIAS

Zacharias son of B. whom ye slew — M't 23:35

BARAK

called B. the son of Abinoam — J'g 4:6; 4:8-10, 12, 14-16, 22; 5:1, 12, 15
to tell of Gideon and of B. — Heb 11:32

BARBARIAN

unto him that speaketh a *b.* — 1Co 14:11
that speaketh shall be a *b.* unto me — 1Co 14:11
seem a foreigner (A)(B)(P)(R) — 1Co 14:11
will be gibberish (N) — 1Co 14:11
B., Scythian, bond nor free — Col 3:11
foreigner (P) — Col 3:11

BARBARIANS

when the *b.* saw the venomous — Ac 28:4
When natives saw (A)(B)(P)(R) — Ac 28:4
islanders, seeing snake (N) — Ac 28:4
to the Greeks, and to the B. — Ro 1:14

BARBAROUS

the *b.* people shewed us no little — Ac 28:2
the natives showed (A)(B)(P)(R) — Ac 28:2
the islanders (N) — Ac 28:2

BARBED

thou fill his skin with *b.* irons — Job 41:7

BARBER'S

sharp knife, take thee a *b.* rasor — Eze 5:1

BARBS

be as *b.* in your eyes (B) — Nu 33:55

BARE

she conceived and *b.* — Ge 4:1; 4:2, 17, 20, 22, 25; 6:4; 16:1, 15:16;
19:37-38; 20:17; 21:2-3; 22:24; 24:24, 36, 47; 25:2
b. the ark — Ge 7:17; De 31:9, 25; Jos 3:15; 4:10; 8:33; 2Sa 6:13; 1Ch 15:15, 26-27
I *b.* the loss of it — Ge 31:39
I *b.* you on eagles' wings — Ex 19:4; De 1:31
his head *b.* — Le 13:45
they *b.* it between two — Nu 13:23
the people that *b.* the present — J'g 3:18
the young man that *b.* his armour — 1Sa 14:1; 14:61; 17:41; 2Sa 18:15
laid *b.* (S) — 2Sa 22:16; Ps 18:15
ten thousand *b.* burdens — 1Ki 5:15; 1Ki 9:23; Ne 4:17
camels that *b.* spices — 1Ki 10:2; 2Ch 9:1
b. shields — 1Ch 12:24; 2Ch 14:8
b. rule — 2Ch 8:10; Ne 5:15; Eze 19:11
an army that *b.* targets — 2Ch 14:8
strippeth *b.* (S) — Ps 29:5
strip you, make you *b.* — Isa 32:11; 47:2
Lord made *b.* his holy arm — Isa 52:10
b. the sin of many — Isa 53:12
He *b.* them, and carried them — Isa 63:9
I have made Esau *b.* — Jer 49:10
foundations laid *b.* (B)(R) — Eze 13:14
leave thee naked and *b.* — Eze 23:29
He hath made clean *b.* — Joe 1:7
lay *b.* her foundations (A)(B) — Mic 1:6
laying *b.* (S) — Hab 3:13
our infirmities, and *b.* our sicknesses — M't 8:17
b. false witness — M't 14:56; 14:57
all *b.* witness, and wondered — Lu 4:22
b. fruit — Lu 8:8; 1Co 15:37; Re 22:2
b. witness of him — Joh 1:15; Joh 5:33; Ac 15:8
b. record — Joh 1:32; Joh 1:34; 12:17; 19:35; Re 1:2
b. and exposed (B)(R) — Heb 4:13
b. our sins in his own body on tree — 1Pe 2:24

BAREFOOT

head covered, and he went *b.* — 2Sa 15:30
lead counsellors away *b.* (B) — Job 12:7; 12:19
he did so, walking naked and *b.* — Isa 20:2
Isaiah hath walked naked and *b.* — Isa 20:3
young and old, naked and *b.* — Isa 20:4

BAREST

because thou *b.* the ark of the — 1Ki 2:26
thou never *b.* rule over them — Isa 63:19
to whom thou *b.* witness, behold — Joh 3:26

BARGAINED

the *b.* with him (S) — M't 26:15

BARHUMITE

Azmaveth the B. — 2Sa 23:31

BARIAH

Hattush, and Igeal, and B. and — 1Ch 3:22

BAR-JESUS

a Jew, whose name was B. — Ac 13:6

BAR-JONA

Blessed art thou, Simon B. — M't 16:17

BARK

all dumb dogs, they cannot *b.* — Isa 56:10

BARKED

and *b.* my fig tree: he hath — Joe 1:7

BARKOS

The children of B. the *Ezr 2:53*
children
The children of B. *Ne 7:55*

BARLEY

the flax and the b. was smitten *Ex 9:31*
an homer of b. seed shall be *Le 27:16*
valued
tenth part of an ephah of b. *Nu 5:15*
meal
A land of wheat, and b. and *De 8:8*
vines
and, lo, a cake of b. bread *J'g 7:13*
tumbled
in the beginning of b. harvest *Ru 1:22*
and it was about an ephah of *Ru 2:17*
b.
to glean unto the end of b. *Ru 2:23*
harvest
he winnoweth b. tonight in *Ru 3:2*
he measured six measures of *Ru 3:15*
b.
six measures of b. gave he *Ru 3:17*
me
he hath b. there; go and set *2Sa 14:30*
it on
wheat, and b. and flour *2Sa 17:28*
beginning of b. harvest *2Sa 21:9*
B. also and straw for the *1Ki 4:28*
horses
twenty loaves of b. and full *2Ki 4:42*
ears
two measures of b. for a *2Ki 7:1*
shekel
two measures of b. for a *2Ki 7:16*
shekel
saying, Two measures of b. *2Ki 7:18*
for a
parcel of ground full of b. *1Ch 11:13*
twenty thousand measures of *2Ch 2:10*
b.
and the b., the oil, and the *2Ch 2:15*
wine
of wheat, and ten thousand *2Ch 27:5*
of b.
cockle instead of b. The *Job 31:40*
words
and the appointed b. and *Isa 28:25*
the rie
of wheat, and of b. and of *Jer 41:8*
oil
unto thee wheat, and b. and *Eze 4:9*
beans
thou shalt eat is as b. cakes *Eze 4:12*
for handfuls of b. and for *Eze 13:19*
pieces
part of an ephah of an *Eze 45:13*
homer of b.
and for an homer of b. *Ho 3:2*
for the wheat and for the b. *Joe 1:11*
which hath five b. loaves and *Joh 6:9*
two
the fragments of the five b. *Joh 6:13*
loaves
three measures of b. for *Re 6:6*
a penny

BARN

seed, and gather it into thy *Job 39:12*
b.
Is the seed yet in the b. *Hag 2:19*
gather wheat into the b. (A) *M't 3:12*
but gather the wheat into *M't 13:30*
my b.
neither have storehouse nor b. *Lu 12:24*

BARNABAS

by the apostles was surnamed *Ac 4:36*
B.
But B. took him and brought *Ac 9:27*
him
Then departed B. to Tarsus *Ac 11:25*
it to the elders by the hands *Ac 11:30*
of B.
And B. and Saul returned *Ac 12:25*
from
as B. and Simeon that was *Ac 13:1*
called
Separate me B. and Saul for *Ac 13:2*
the
called for B. and Saul, and *Ac 13:7*
desired
proselytes followed Paul and *Ac 13:43*
B.

Then Paul and B. waxed *Ac 13:46*
bold
persecution against Paul and *Ac 13:50*
B.
And they called B. Jupiter *Ac 14:12*
when the apostles, B. and *Ac 14:14*
Paul
he departed with B. to *Ac 14:20*
Derbe
When therefore Paul and B. *Ac 15:2*
had
and gave audience to B. and *Ac 15:12*
Paul
to Antioch with Paul and B. *Ac 15:22*
with our beloved B. and *Ac 15:25*
Paul
also and B. continued in *Ac 15:35*
Antioch
some days after, Paul said *Ac 15:36*
unto B.
B. determined to take with *Ac 15:37*
them
and so B took Mark, and *Ac 15:39*
sailed
Or I only and B. have not we *1Co 9:6*
up again to Jerusalem with B. *Ga 2:1*
gave to me and B. the right *Ga 2:9*
hands
that B. also was carried away *Ga 2:13*
and Marcus, sister's son to B. *Col 4:10*

BARNFLOOR

the b. or out of the *2Ki 6:27*
winepress

BARNS

shall thy b. be filled with *Pr 3:10*
plenty
b. are broken down *Joe 1:17*
do they reap, nor gather into *M't 6:26*
b.
I will pull down my b. and *Lu 12:18*
build

BARRACKS

into the b. (S) *Ac 21:34;*
 21:37; 22:24; 23:10, 16, 32

BARREL

a handful of meal in a b. *1Ki 17:12*
and a
The b. of meal shall not *1Ki 17:14*
waste
the b. of meal wasted not *1Ki 17:16*

BARRELS

20,000 b. of oil (B) *1Ki 5:11*
Fill four b. with water, and *1Ki 18:33*
pour
gathered the good into h. (P) *M't 13:48*
a hundred b. of oil (B) *Lu 16:6*

BARREN

Sarai was b.; she had no *Ge 11:30*
child
for his wife, because she *Ge 25:21*
was b.
but Rachel was b. *Ge 29:31*
nothing cast their young, nor *Ex 23:26*
be b.
shall not be male or female *De 7:14*
b.
his wife was b. and bare not *J'g 13:2*
Behold now, thou art b. *J'g 13:3*
so that the b. hath born seven *1Sa 2:5*
is naught, and the ground b. *2Ki 2:19*
any more death or b. land *2Ki 2:21*
let that night be b. (B)(E)(R) *Job 3:7*
He evil entreateth the b. *Job 24:21*
and the b. land his dwellings *Job 39:6*
maketh the b. woman to keep *Ps 113:9*
The grave; and the b. womb *Pr 30:16*
and none is b. among them *Ca 4:2*
there is not one b. among *Ca 6:6*
them
Sing, O b. thou that didst *Isa 54:1*
not
him into a land b. and *Joe 2:20*
desolate
it proves b. (N) *M't 13:22; M'k 4:19*
because that Elisabeth was b. *Lu 1:7*
month with her, who was *Lu 1:36*
called b.

Blessed are the b. and the *Lu 23:29*
wombs
not proved a b. gift (P) *1Co 15:2*
Rejoice, thou b. that bearest *Ga 4:27*
not
b. deeds of darkness (N) *Eph 5:11*
faith is b. (N)(R) *Jas 2:20*
neither be b. nor unfruitful in *2Pe 1:8*
the
useless or b. (N) *2Pe 1:8*

BARRENNESS

A fruitful land into b. for *Ps 107:34*

BARRIER

breaking down the b. (P) *Eph 2:14*

BARS

shalt make b. of shittim *Ex 26:26;*
wood *26:27, 29; 35:11; 36:31-34; 39:33;*
 40:18; Nu 3:36; 4:31
cities with walls, gates, and b. *De 3:5;*
1Sam 23:7; 1Ki 4:13; 2Ch 8:5; 14:7;
 Ne 3:3, 6, 13-15
shall go down to the b. of *Job 17:16*
the pit
place, and set b. and doors *Job 38:10*
his bones are like b. of iron *Job 40:18*
and cut the b. of iron in *Ps 107:16*
sunder
strengthened the b. of thy *Ps 147:13*
gates
are like the b. of a castle *Pr 18:19*
and cut in sunder the b. of *Isa 45:2*
iron
which have neither gates nor *Jer 49:31*
b.
dwellingplaces; her b. are *Jer 51:30*
broken
hath destroyed and broken her *La 2:9*
b.
broken the b. (S) *Eze 34:27*
having neither b. nor gates *Eze 38:11*
the earth with her b. was *Jon 2:6*
about me
the fire shall devour thy b. *Na 3:13*

BARSABAS

B. who was surnamed Justus *Ac 1:23*
namely, Judas surnamed B *Ac 15:22*

BARTER

b. your wares (R) *Eze 27:9*

BARTHOLOMEW

Philip, and B.; Thomas *M't 10:3*
Philip, and B. and Matthew *M'k 3:18*
Philip and B. *Lu 6:14*
Philip, and Thomas, B. *Ac 1:13*

BARTIMAEUS

blind B. the son of *M'k 10:46*
Timaeus, sat

BARUCH

After him B. the son of *Ne 3:20*
Zabbai
Daniel, Ginnethon, B. *Ne 10:6*
Maaseiah the son of B. the *Ne 11:5*
son of
evidence of the purchase *Jer 32:12;*
unto B. *32:13, 16; 36:4-5, 8, 10, 13-19,*
 26-27, 32; 43:3, 6; 45:1-2

BARZILLAI

B. the Gileadite *2Sa 17:27;*
 19:31-34, 39
brought up for Adriel son of *2Sa 21:8*
B.
shew kindness unto the sons of *1Ki 2:7*
B.
the children of B. *Ezr 2:61; Ne 7:63*

BASE

the b. of the mountain (B) *Ex 19:17*
b. fellows are gone (A)(E)(R) *De 13:13*
certain b. fellows (E)(R)(S) *J'g 19:22*
deliver to us the b. fellows *J'g 20:13*
(S)

BASE

a *b.* woman (R)	*1Sa 1:16; 20:13*
wicked men, *b.* fellows (A)(E)(R)	*1Sa 30:22*
will be *b.* in mine own sight	*2Sa 6:22*
humbled in my own eyes (B)	*2Sa 6:22*
b. fellow (A)(E)	*2Sa 20:1*
b. for the lavers	*1Ki 7:27; 7:29-35*
b. fellows (A)(E)(R)	*1Ki 21:10; 21:13*
gathered *b.* fellows (S)	*2Ch 13:7*
worthless men, *b.* fellows (A)(E)	*2Ch 21:13*
yea, children of *b.* men	*Job 30:8*
worthless and nameless men (A)	*Job 30:8*
worthless and infamous men (B)	*Job 30:8*
senseless, disreputable brood (R)	*Job 30:8*
the *b.* against the honourable	*Isa 3:5*
lowborn against the honorable (A)	*Isa 3:5*
dishonorable over honorable (B)	*Isa 3:5*
sons of *b.* men (E)	*Jer 30:8*
That the kingdom might be *b.*	*Eze 17:14*
exist under treaty obligations (B)	*Eze 17:14*
that his covenant might stand (R)	*Eze 17:14*
they shall be there a *b.* kingdom	*Eze 29:14*
be there a lowly kingdom (A)(R)	*Eze 29:14*
abide an insignificant kingdom (B)	*Eze 29:14*
and set there upon her own *b.*	*Zec 5:11*
and *b.* before all the people	*Mal 2:9*
despised and abased (A)(B)(R)	*Mal 2:9*
not *b.* born (N)	*Joh 8:41*
a *b.* and condemned mind (A)(R)	*Ro 1:28*
And *b.* things of the world	*1Co 1:28*
lowborn and insignificant (A)	*1Co 1:28*
lowborn and contemptible (B)(N)	*1Co 1:28*
low and despised (R)	*1Co 1:28*
who in presence am *b.* among	*2Co 10:1*
lowly enough among you (A)(E)	*2Co 10:1*
so meek when face to face (B)	*2Co 10:1*
so feeble when face to face (N)	*2Co 10:1*
humble enough in our presence (P)	*2Co 10:1*
humble when face to face (R)	*2Co 10:1*
slander, *b.* suspicions (N)(R)	*1Ti 6:5*
for *b.* gain (R)	*Tit 1:11*

BASER

lewd fellows of the *b.* sort	*Ac 17:5*
loungers, ruffians, and rascals (A)	*Ac 17:5*
loungers of the market place (B)	*Ac 17:5*
fellows of the rabble (E)(R)	*Ac 17:5*
low fellows from the dregs of the (N)	*Ac 17:5*
unprincipled loungers (P)	*Ac 17:5*

BASES

scorching the *b.* of the hills (B)	*De 32:22*
b. for the lavers	*1Ki 7:27; 7:28, 37-39, 43*
Ahaz cut off the borders of the *b.*	*1Ki 16:17*
and the *b.* and the brasen sea	*1Ki 25:13*
the *b.* which Solomon had made	*1Ki 25:16*
He made also *b.*	*2Ch 4:14*
they set the altar upon his *b.*	*Ezr 3:3*
concerning the *b.* and concerning	*Jer 27:19*
and the *b.* and the brasen sea	*Jer 52:17*
bulls that were under the *b.*	*Jer 52:20*

BASELESS

not hear a *b.* cry (B)	*Job 35:13*

BASELESSLY

unless you believed *b.* (B)	*1Co 15:2*

BASENESS

with inner *b.* comes outer shame (A)	*Ps 18:3*

BASEST

shall be the *b.* of the kingdoms	*Eze 29:15*
setteth up over it the *b.* of men	*Da 4:17*

BASHAN

and went up by the way of *B.*	*Nu 21:33; 32:33; De 1:4; 3:1-4, 10-13; 4:47; 29:7; Jos 9:10; 12:4; 13:12, 30-31; 1Ki 4:19; Ne 9:22; Ps 135:11*
Golan in *B.*	*De 4:43; Jos 20:8; 21:27; 1Ch 6:71*
rams of the breed of *B.*	*De 32:14*
lion's whelp: he shall leap from *B.*	*De 33:22*
land of *B.*	*Jos 13:11; 13:30; 17:1, 5; 1Ch 5:11-12*
half of tribe of Manasseh in *B.*	*Jos 21:6; Jos 22:7; 1Ch 6:62*
region of Argob, which is in *B.*	*1Ki 4:13*
river Arnon, even Gilead and *B.*	*2Ki 10:33*
bulls of *B.* have beset me round	*Ps 22:19*
the hill of God is as the hill of *B.*	*Ps 68:15*
I will bring again from *B.*, I will	*Ps 68:22*
Amorites, and Og king of *B.*	*Ps 135:11*
Og the king of *B.* for his mercy	*Ps 136:20*
up, and upon all the oaks of *B.*	*Isa 2:13*
Sharon is like a wilderness; and *B.*	*Isa 33:9*
cry; and lift up thy voice in *B.*	*Jer 22:20*
feed on Carmel and *B.* and his	*Jer 50:19*
of *B.* have they made thine oars	*Eze 27:6*
bullocks, all of them fatlings of *B.*	*Eze 39:18*
Hear this word, ye kine of *B.* that	*Am 4:1*
let them feed in *B.* and Gilead	*Mic 7:14*
B. languisheth, and Carmel	*Na 1:4*
howl, O ye oaks of *B.*, for the	*Zec 11:2*

BASHAN-HAVOTH-JAIR

own name, *B.*, unto this day	*De 3:14*

BASHEMATH

and *B.* the daughter of Elon	*Ge 26:34*
B. Ishmael's daughter, sister of	*Ge 36:3*
Esau Eliphaz; and *B.* bare Ruvel	*Ge 36:4*
the son of *B.* the wife of Esau	*Ge 36:10*
were the sons of *B.* Esau's wife	*Ge 36:13*
are the sons of *B.* Esau's wife	*Ge 36:17*

BASIN

made a wash *b.* (B)	*Ex 30:18; Ex 38:8; 40:7, 11*
the *b.* and its base (B)	*Le 8:11*
cover with a *b.* (N)(P)	*Lu 8:16*

BASINS

and the *b.* (S)	*2Ki 25:15*
pots and *b.* (P)	*M'k 7:4*

BASIS

the *b.* of true knowledge (P)	*Ro 2:20*

BASKET

And in the uppermost *b.*	*Ge 40:17*
birds did eat them out of the *b.*	*Ge 40:17*
thou shalt put them into one *b.*	*Ex 29:3*
and bring them in the *b.*	*Ex 29:3*
wafer out of the *b.* of unleavened	*Ex 29:23*
and the bread that is in the *b.*	*Ex 29:32*
and a *b.* of unleavened bread	*Le 8:2*
out of the *b.* of unleavened bread	*Le 8:26*
that is in the *b.* of consecrations	*Le 8:31*
And a *b.* of unleavened bread	*Nu 6:15*
with the *b.* of unleavened bread	*Nu 6:17*
one unleavened cake out of the *b.*	*Nu 6:19*
shalt put it in a *b.* and shalt	*De 26:2*
the priest shall take the *b.*	*De 26:4*
Blessed shall be thy *b.* and thy	*De 28:5*
Cursed shall be thy *b.* and	*De 28:17*
the flesh he put in a *b.* and	*J'g 6:19*
delivered from the *b.* (S)	*Ps 81:6*
One *b.* had very good figs	*Jer 24:2*
other *b.* had very naughty figs	*Jer 24:2*
behold a *b.* of summer fruit	*Am 8:1*
And I said, A. *b.* of summer fruit	*Am 8:2*
let him down by the wall in a	*Ac 9:25*
in a *b.* was I let down by the wall	*2Co 11:33*

BASKETS

I had three white *b.* on my head	*Ge 40:16*
The three *b.* are three days	*Ge 40:18*
put their heads in *b.* and sent	*2Ki 10:7*
as a grapegatherer into the *b.*	*Jer 6:9*
two *b.* of figs were set before (B)	*Jer 24:1*
gathered the good into *b.*	*M't 13:48*
that remained twelve *b.* full	*M't 14:20*
meat that was left seven *b.* full	*M't 15:37*
and how many *b.* ye took up	*M't 16:9; M't 16:10*
twelve *b.* full of the fragments	*M'k 6:43*
meat that was left seven *b.*	*M'k 8:8; 8:19-20*
remained to them twelve *b.*	*Lu 9:17*
and filled twelve *b.* with the	*Joh 6:13*

BASMATH

took *B.* the daughter of Solomon	*1Ki 4:15*

BASON

in the blood that is in the *b.*	*Ex 12:22; b.*
gave gold by weight for every *b.*	*1Ch 28:17*
that he poureth water into a *b.*	*Joh 13:5*

BASONS

half of the blood, and put it in *b.*	*Ex 24:6; 27:3; 38:3; Nu 4:14; 2Sa 17:28; 1Ki 7:40, 45, 50; 2Ki 12:13*
golden *b.*	*1Ch 28:17; 2Ch 4:8, 22; Ezr 1:10; 8:27; Ne 7:70*
the *b.* and the firepans	*Jer 52:19*

BASTARD

A *b.* shall not enter into the	*De 23:2*
turn into *b.* shoots (B)	*Jer 2:21*
and a *b.* shall dwell in Ashdod	*Zec 9:6*

BASTARDS

then are ye *b.* and not sons	*Heb 12:8*

BAT

kind, and the lapwing, and *Le 11:19*
the *b.*
the lapwing, and the *b.* *De 14:18*

BATALLION

b. of conscript laborers (B) *1Ki 5:13;*
 5:14

BATCH

the whole *b.* (B) *1Co 5:6*

BATH

of vineyard shall yield one *Isa 5:10;*
b. *Eze 43:10-11, 14*

BATH-RABBIM

Heshbon, by the gate of *B.*: *Ca 7:4*
thy

BATH-SHEBA

one said, Is not this *B.* the *2Sa 11:3*
David comforted *B.* his *2Sa 12:24*
wife
Nathan spake unto *B.* the *1Ki 1:11;*
 1:15-16, 28, 31; 2:13, 18-19; Ps 51 title

BATH-SHUA

Solomon, four, of *B.* the *1Ch 3:5*
daughter

BATHE

b. himself in water *Le 15:5;*
 15:6-8, 10-11, 13, 18, 21-22, 27

BATHED

my steps *b.* in cream (B) *Job 29:6*
my sword shall be *b.* in *Isa 34:5*
heaven

BATHING

b. of regeneration (B) *Tit 3:5*

BATHS

it contained two thousand *b.* *1Ki 7:26*
one laver contained forty *b.* *1Ki 7:38*
twenty thousand *b.* of wine *2Ch 2:10*
received and held three *2Ch 4:5*
thousand *b.*
and to a hundred *b.* of *Ezr 7:22*
wine
and to an hundred *b.* of oil *Ezr 7:22*
an homer of ten *b.* *Eze 45:14*
for ten *b.* are an homer *Eze 45:14*

BATS

to the moles and to the *b.* *Isa 2:20*

BATTERED

b. the wall, to throw it *2Sa 20:15*
down
gates *b.* to ruins (B)(R) *Isa 24:14*

BATTERING

set *b.* rams against it *Eze 4:2*
appoint *b.* rams against the *Eze 21:22*
gates
b. rams shall pound (B)(R) *Eze 26:9*

BATTLE

joined *b.* *Ge 14:8; 1Sa 4:2; 1Ki 20:29*
will pass over before Lord *Nu 32:27*
to *b.*
rise up, contend with Sihon *De 2:24*
in *b.*
O Israel, you approach this *De 20:3*
day to *b.*
let him return, lest he die in *De 20:5;*
b. *6:7*
of Gibeon, all other they *Jos 11:19*
took in *b.*
shall I yet again go out to *J'g 20:28*
b.
they turned, but the *b.* *J'g 20:42*
overtook them

followed after Philistines in *1Sa 14:22*
b.
as the host shouted for the *1Sa 17:20*
b.
for thou art come down to *1Sa 17:28*
see the *b.*
for the *b.* is the Lord's *1Sa 17:47;*
 2Ch 20:15
he shall descend into *b.* and *1Sa 26:10*
perish
thou shalt go out with me to *1Sa 28:1*
b.
lest in *b.* he be an adversary *1Sa 29:4*
to us
when kings go forth to *b.* *2Sa 11:1;*
 1Ch 20:1
set Uriah in the forefront *2Sa 11:15*
of the hottest *b.*
Absalom is dead in *b.* *2Sa 19:10*
if people go out to *b.* *1Ki 8:44*
thy servant went out into *1Ki 20:39*
midst of *b.*
wilt thou go with me to *b.* *1Ki 22:4;*
 2Ki 3:7
for they cried to God in the *1Ch 5:20*
b.
Gadites, men of war fit for *1Ch 12:8*
the *b.*
David set *b.* in array *1Ch 19:17;*
against the Syrians *2Ch 13:3; 14:10*
if thou wilt go, be strong *2Ch 25:8*
for *b.*
shall prevail, as a king *Job 15:24*
ready to *b.*
and he smelleth the *b.* afar *Job 39:25*
off
remember the *b.* do no more *Job 41:8*
hast girded me with strength *Ps 18:39*
to *b.*
King of glory, Lord mighty in *Ps 24:8*
b.
he hath delivered my soul *Ps 55:18*
from *b.*
he brake the shield, the *Ps 76:3*
sword, and *b.*
and hast not made him to *Ps 80:43*
stand in *b.*
no discharge in this *b.* (A)(B) *Ec 8:8*
race not to swift, nor *b.* to *Ec 9:11*
strong
every *b.* of the warrior is with *Isa 9:5*
noise
the Lord mustereth the host *Isa 13:4*
of the *b.*
the press of the *b.* (B)(R) *Isa 21:15*
thy slain men are not dead in *Isa 22:2*
b.
set briars and thorns against *Isa 27:4*
me in *b.*
strength to them that turn *b.* *Isa 28:6*
to gate
hath poured on him *Isa 42:25*
strength of *b.*
the shout of *b.* (B) *Jer 4:19*
turned as the horse rusheth *Jer 8:6*
into *b.*
let young men be slain in *b.* *Jer 18:21*
order buckler and shield, *Jer 46:3*
draw near to *b.*
come against her, and rise up *Jer 49:14*
to *b.*
a sound of *b.* is in land, and *Jer 50:22*
destruction
put in array, like a man to *Jer 50:42*
b. against thee
have blown, but none goeth *Eze 7:14*
to *b.*
to stand in the *b.* in the day *Eze 13:5*
of the Lord
I will not save them by bow *Ho 1:7*
nor by *b.*
I will break bow and *b.* out *Ho 2:18*
of earth
b. in Gibeah did not overtake *Ho 10:9*
them
as a strong people set in *b.* *Joe 2:5*
let us rise up against Edom *Ob 1*
in *b.*
made them as his goodly *Zec 10:3*
horse in *b.*
which tread down their *Zec 10:5*
enemies in the *b.*
gather all nations against *Zec 14:2*
Jerusalem to *b.*
who shall prepare himself to *1Co 14:8*
b.
shapes of locusts like horses *Re 9:7*
prepared to *b.*

sound of chariots many horses *Re 9:9*
running to *b.*
gather to *b.* of great day *Re 16:14;*
 20:8
massed together for *b.* (P) *Re 19:19*

DAY OF BATTLE

so it came to pass in *day of* *1Sa 13:22*
b. that
I reserved against *day of b.* *Job 38:23*
and war
Ephraim turned back in *day* *Ps 78:9*
of b.
thou hast covered my head in *Ps 140:7*
day of b.
the horse is prepared against *Pr 21:31*
day of b.
Shalman spoiled Beth-arbel *Ho 10:14*
in *day of b.*
devour with shouting in *day* *Am 1:14*
of b.
as when he fought in *day of* *Zec 14:3*
b.

BATTLEMENT

thou shalt make a *b.* for thy *De 22:8*
roof

BATTLEMENTS

take away her *b.* *Jer 5:10*

BATTLES

go out before us, and fight *1Sa 8:20*
our *b.*
fight the Lord's *b.* For Saul *1Sa 18:17*
my lord fighteth the *b.* of *1Sa 25:28*
the Lord
spoils won in *b.* did they *1Ch 26:27*
dedicate
and to fight our *b.* And the *2Ch 32:8*
people
and in *b.* of shaking will he *Isa 30:32*
fight
not fight wordy *b.* (P) *2Ti 2:14*

BATTLING

b. with a head-wind (N) *M't 14:24*

BAVAI

B. the son of Henadad, the *Ne 3:18*
ruler

BAY

the *b.* that looketh southward *Jos 15:2*
the *b.* of the sea at the *Jos 15:5*
uttermost
the north *b.* of the salt sea *Jos 18:19*
himself like a green *b.* tree *Ps 37:35*
fourth chariot grisled and *b.* *Zec 6:3*
horses
And the *b.* went forth, and *Zec 6:7*
noticed a *b.* (A)(N)(R) *Ac 27:39*

BAZAAR

standing in the *b.* (B) *M't 20:3;*
 Lu 7:32

BAZLITH

the children of *B.*, the *Ne 7:54*
children

BAZLUTH

the children of *B.*, the *Ezr 2:52*
children

BDELLIUM

there is *b.* and the onyx *Ge 2:12*
stone
colour thereof as the colour *Nu 11:7*
of *b.*

BE

not good that man *b.* alone *Ge 2:18*
to *b.* unfaithful (S) *2Ch 21:11*
if I *b.* wicked; if I *b.* *Job 10:15*
righteous
if there *b.* any wicked way *Ps 139:24*
in me

b. converted (S)   *Isa 6:10*
if thou *b.* the Son of God   *M't 4:3;*
           M't 4:6; 27:40
calleth those things which *b.*   *Ro 4:17*
not as
if God *b.* for us, who can *b.*   *Ro 8:31*
against
let him *b.* unjust, *b.* filthy   *Re 22:11*
still

BE *NOT*

b. not   *2Ch 30:7;*
Ps 22:19; 35:22; 38:21; 71:12; Isa 28:22;
Zec 1:4; Ro 12:16; 1Co 14:20; 2Co 6:14;
      Eph 5:7, 17; Tit 3:14; 1Pe 3:3

I *WILL* BE

I will *b.* their God   *Ge 17:8;*
Ex 29:45; Jer 24:7; 32:38; 2Co 6:16;
              Heb 8:10
I will *b.* with thee   *Ge 26:3;*
   31:3; Ex 3:12; J'g 6:16; 1Ki 11:38
I will *b.* your God   *Jer 7:23; 30:22*
I will *b.* as the dew to Israel   *Ho 14:5*
I will *b.* a wall of fire, I   *Zec 2:5*
will *b.* the
I will *be* a Father to you   *2Co 6:18;*
              Heb 1:5
I will *b.* his God   *Re 21:7*

IF IT BE

if it *b.*   *Ge 23:8;*
25:22; Ex 1:16; 2Ki 10:15; Zec 8:6;
  M't 14:28; Ac 5:39; 18:15; Ga 3:4

LET THERE BE

let there *b.*   *Ge 1:3;*
   Ge 13:8; 26:28; Ex 5:9; Ezr 5:17

NOT BE

not *b.*   *Ge 21:12;*
24:5; 38:9; 44:30; Le 26:13; Nu 12:12;
16:40; Jos 7:12; Ru 3:18; 2Ch 30:7;
Ps 22:19; Isa 28:22; Zec 8:11; Lu 13:33;
14:26; Joh 1:25; Ro 12:16; 1Co 9:2;
14:20; 2Co 6:14; Ga 1:10; Eph 5:7, 17;
   Tit 3:14; Ph'm 14; Heb 8:4; 1Pe 3:3

BEACON

left as a *b.* upon the top of a   *Isa 30:17*

BEADS

strings of *b.* (B)   *Ca 1:10*

BEALIAH

Eluzai, and Jerimoth, and *B.*   *1Ch 12:5*

BEALOTH

Ziph, and Telem, and *B.*   *Jos 15:24*

BEAM

went away with the pin of   *J'g 16:14*
the *b.*
of his spear was like a   *1Sa 17:7*
weaver's *b.*
whose spear was like a   *2Sa 21:9*
weaver's *b.*
the thick *b.* were before them   *1Ki 7:6*
take thence every man a *b.*   *2Ki 6:2*
as one was felling a *b.* the   *2Ki 6:5*
axe head
was a spear like a weaver's *1Ch 11:23*
b.
spear staff was like a weaver's *1Ch 20:5*
b.
b. out of the timber shall   *Hab 2:11*
answer
considerest not the *b.* that is   *M't 7:3*
behold, a *b.* is in thine own   *M't 7:4*
eye
cast out the *b.* out of thine   *M't 7:5*
own eye
perceivest not the *b.* that is   *Lu 6:41*
beholdest not the *b.* that is in   *Lu 6:42*
cast out first the *b.* out of   *Lu 6:42*
thine

BEAMS

that the *b.* should not be   *1Ki 6:6*
fastened

covered the house with *b.* and   *1Ki 6:9*
stone, and a row of cedar *b.*   *1Ki 6:36*
with cedar *b.* upon the pillars   *1Ki 7:2*
with cedar above upon the *b.*   *1Ki 7:3*
a row of cedar *b.* both for   *1Ki 7:12*
the *b.*, the posts, and the   *2Ch 3:7*
walls
give me timber to make *b.* for   *Ne 2:8*
Who layeth the *b.* of his   *Ne 3:3*
they laid the *b.* thereof, and   *Ne 3:6*
set up
Who layeth the *b.* of his   *Ps 104:3*
chambers
The *b.* of our house are   *Ca 1:17*
cedar
healing in its *b.* (B)   *Mal 4:2*

BEANS

flour, and parched corn,   *2Sa 17:28*
and *b.*
barley, and *b.*, and lentiles   *Eze 4:9*

BEAR

punishment greater than I   *Ge 4:13*
can *b.*
land was not able to *b.* them   *Ge 13:6;*
                36:7
let me *b.* the blame for ever   *Ge 43:9;*
               44:32
Issachar bowed his shoulder *Ge 49:15*
to *b.*
they shall *b.* the burden   *Ex 18:22*
with thee
to *b.* the ark   *Ex 25:27;*
   27:7; 30:4; 37:5; De 10:8; Jos 3:3, 8,
       13-14; 4:16; 2Sa 15:24
Aaron shall *b.* their names   *Ex 28:12*
before Lord
with which to *b.* it (S)   *Ex 30:4*
shalt not *b.* any grudge   *Le 19:18*
against
not able to *b.* this people   *Nu 11:14;*
               De 1:9
how long shall I *b.*   *Nu 14:27*
congregation
children *b.* your whoredoms *Nu 14:33;*
             Eze 23:35
b. alone the weight (R)   *De 1:12*
God bare as a man *b.* his   *De 1:31*
son
let me run and *b.* king   *2Sa 18:19*
tidings
which thou puttest on me, I *2Ki 18:14*
will *b.*
b. with (R)   *Job 21:3;*
36:2; M't 17:17; M'k 9:19; Lu 9:41;
     2Co 11:19-20; Heb 13:22
b. me that I may speak (S)   *Job 21:3*
B. with (B)   *Job 36:2;*
         Ps 88:15; Pr 19:19
B. with me a little (S)   *Job 36:2*
I *b.* up the pillars of the   *Ps 75:3*
earth
how I do *b.* in my bosom   *Ps 89:50*
reproach
they shall *b.* thee up   *Ps 91:12;*
           M't 4:6; Lu 4:11
if thou scornest, thou alone   *Pr 9:12*
shalt *b.* it
but a wounded spirit who   *Pr 18:14*
can *b.*
and for four which it cannot *Pr 30:21*
b.
I cannot *b.* (S)   *Isa 1:13*
your feasts, I am weary to *b.*   *Isa 1:14*
them
I have made and I will *b.*   *Isa 46:4*
you
him upon shoulder, they   *Isa 46:7*
carry him
be ye clean that *b.* the   *Isa 52:11*
vessels of Lord
O barren, thou that didst not *Isa 54:1*
b.
truly this is a grief, and I   *Jer 10:19*
must *b.* it
b. no burden on the   *Jer 17:21;*
sabbath-day   *17:27*
because I did *b.* the reproach *Jer 31:19*
of my youth
so that the Lord could no   *Jer 44:22*
longer *b.*
it is good to *b.* yoke in his   *La 3:27*
youth
in their sight shalt thou *b.*   *Eze 12:6*
on shoulders
prince shall *b.* upon his   *Eze 12:12*
shoulder

shall *b.* punishment of their   *Eze 14:10*
iniquity
b. thou thine own shame   *Eze 16:52*
for thy sins
b. their shame with them   *Eze 32:30;*
            36:7; 44:13
nor *b.* the shame of the   *Eze 34:29;*
heathen   *36:15*
the land is not able to *b.* his   *Am 7:10*
words
ye shall *b.* the reproach of   *Mic 6:16*
my people
I will *b.* indignation of the   *Mic 7:9*
Lord
if one *b.* holy flesh in the   *Hag 2:12*
skirt of his
whither do these *b.* the   *Zec 5:10*
ephah
shall *b.* glory, and rule on   *Zec 6:13*
his throne
whose shoes I am not worthy *M't 3:11*
to *b.*
how long shall I *b.* with you *M't 17:17;*
(S)   *Lu 9:41*
hard to *b.* (A)(R)   *M't 23:4*
they found Simon, they   *M't 27:32;*
compelled him to *M'k 15:21; Lu 23:26*
b. his cross
b. with (A)   *M'k 9:19;*
   Lu 9:41; 2Co 11:19; Heb 13:22
whosoever doth not *b.* his   *Lu 14:27*
cross
avenge elect, tho he *b.* long   *Lu 18:7*
with them
many things, ye cannot *b.*   *Joh 16:12*
them now
is a chosen vessel to *b.* my   *Ac 9:15*
name
yoke fathers nor we were   *Ac 15:10*
able to *b.*
reason would I should *b.*   *Ac 18:14*
with you
b. the family likeness (P)   *Ro 8:29*
we ought to *b.* infirmities of *Ro 15:1*
the weak
hitherto ye were not able to *1Co 3:2*
b. it
b. all things (S)   *1Co 13:7*
way to escape, that may be *1Co 10:13*
able to *b.* it
we shall also *b.* image of   *1Co 15:49*
heavenly
would to God ye could *b.*   *2Co 11:1*
with me
not accepted, ye might well *2Co 11:4*
b. with him
b. with (N)(S)   *2Co 11:19; Heb 13:22*
b. one another's burdens   *Ga 6:2*
for every man shall *b.* his own *Ga 6:5*
burden
I *b.* in my body marks of the   *Ga 6:17*
Lord
b. with one another (A)   *Eph 4:2*
can the fig tree *b.*   *Jas 3:12*
olive-berries
thou canst not *b.* them that   *Re 2:2*
are evil

BEAR birth to

and shall Sarah that is 90   *Ge 17:17*
years old *b.*
shall I of a surety *b.* a   *Ge 18:13*
child, which am old
but if she a maid child,   *Le 12:5*
then unclean
and toward her children she *De 28:57*
shall *b.*
but thou shalt conceive and   *J'g 13:3*
b. a son
it was not my son that I did *1Ki 3:21*
b.
sheep, whereof every one *b.*   *Ca 4:2;*
twins   *6:6*
a virgin shall conceive and *b.* *Isa 7:14*
a son, and
sing, O barren, thou that   *Isa 54:1*
didst not *b.*
that they may *b.* sons and   *Jer 29:6*
daughters
thy wife Elisabeth shall *b.* a *Lu 1:13*
son
younger women marry, *b.*   *1Ti 5:14*
children

BEAR *INIQUITY*

Aaron may *b. iniquity* of   *Ex 28:38*
holy things

Aaron and his son *b.* not   *Ex 28:43* *iniquity*
he shall *b.* his *iniquity*   *Le 5:1;*
    5:17; 7:18; 17:16; 19:8; 20:17
hath given to you to *b.*   *Le 10:17*
iniquity of the congregation
goat shall *b.* upon him all   *Le 16:22*
their *iniquities*
they shall *b.* their *iniquity*   *Le 20:19;*
    Nu 18:23; Eze 44:10, 12
or suffer them to *b. iniquity Le 22:16*
of their trespass
this woman shall *b.* her   *Nu 5:31*
iniquity
b. your *iniquity* even forty   *Nu 14:34*
years
Aaron and his sons *b.*   *Nu 18:1*
iniquity of the sanctuary
after he heard he shall *b.*   *Nu 30:15*
her *iniquity*
my righteous servant shall *b.*   *Isa 53:11*
their *iniquity*
number of days, thou shalt   *Eze 4:4;*
b. their *iniquity*   *4:5*
why doth not son *b.*   *Eze 18:19*
iniquity of the father
the son shall not *b.* the   *Eze 18:20*
iniquity of the father

BEAR *JUDGMENT*

Aaron shall *b. judgment* of   *Ex 28:30*
children
that troubleth you shall *b.* his   *Ga 5:10*
judgment

BEAR *RULE*

every man *b. rule* his house   *Es 1:22*
hand of the diligent shall *b.*   *Pr 12:24*
rule
priests *b. rule* by their means *Jer 5:31*
had strong rods for them   *Eze 19:11*
that *b. rule*
kingdom of brass shall *b. rule Da 2:39*

BEAR *SIN*

they shall *b.* their *sin,* they   *Le 20:20*
shall die
lest they *b. sin* for it, and die, *Le 22:9*
therefore
whosoever curseth his God,   *Le 24:15*
shall *b.* his *sin*
shall be cut off, that man   *Nu 9:13*
shall *b.* his *sin*
not come nigh, lest they *b.*   *Nu 18:22*
sin and die
ye shall *b.* no *sin* when ye *Nu 18:32*
heaved the best of it
and ye shall *b.* the *sin* of   *Eze 23:49*
your idols
so Christ was once offered   *Heb 9:28*
to *b. sin*

BEAR *WITNESS*

thou shalt not *b.* false   *Ex 20:16;*
witness   *De 5:20; M't 19:18; Ro 13:9*
set two men sons of Belial *1Ki 21:10*
to *b. witness*
do not *b.* false *witness*   *M'k 10:19;*
         Lu 18:20
truly ye *b. witness* that ye   *Lu 11:48*
allow deeds
the same came for a witness, *Joh 1:7*
to *b. witness*
he was sent to *b. witness* of *Joh 1:8*
that light
ye yourselves *b.* me *witness Joh 1:28*
that I said
if *b. witness* of myself, my   *Joh 5:31*
witness not true
works that I do, *b. witness Joh 5:36;*
of me   *10:25*
I am one that *b. witness* of   *Joh 8:18*
myself
ye shall also *b. witness*   *Joh 15:27*
because ye have been
if I have spoken evil, *b.*   *Joh 18:23*
witness of the evil
cause came I, that I should *Joh 18:37*
b.witness
also the high priest doth *b.*   *Ac 22:5*
me *witness*
so must thou *b. witness* also *Ac 23:11*
at Rome
have seen it, and *b. witness,* *1Jo 1:2*
and shew
are three that *b. witness* in   *1Jo 5:8*
earth

BEAR an animal

slew both the lion and the   *1Sa 17:34*
b.
out of the paw of the *b.*   *1Sa 17:37*
as a *b.* robbed of her whelps *2Sa 17:8*
Let a *b.* robbed of her   *Pr 17:12*
whelps
roaring lion, and a ranging   *Pr 28:15*
b.
the cow and the *b.* shall feed *Isa 11:7*
beast, a second like to a *b.*   *Da 7:5*
from a lion, and a *b.* met   *Am 5:19*
him
his feet as the feet of a *b.*   *Re 13:2*

BEARABLE

judgment more *b.* (N)   *M't 10:15;*
    M't 11:22, 24; Lu 10:12, 14
judgment more *b.* (P) *M't 11:22; 11:24*
it will be more *b.* (P)   *M't 11:22;*
         Lu 10:14

BEARD

plague upon the head or the   *Le 13:29*
b.
a leprosy upon the head or *b.* *Le 13:30*
head and his *b.* and his   *Le 14:9*
eyebrows
thou mar the corners of thy *Le 19:27*
b.
shave off the corner of their   *Le 21:5*
b.
him by his *b.* and smote   *1Sa 17:35*
him
his spittle fall down upon   *1Sa 21:13*
his *b.*
his feet, nor trimmed his *b.* *2Sa 19:24*
And Joab took Amasa by   *2Sa 20:9*
the *b.*
of my *b.* and sat down   *Ezr 9:3*
astonied
that ran down upon the *b.*   *Ps 133:2*
even Aaron's *b.:* that went   *Ps 133:2*
down
and it shall also consume the *Isa 7:20*
b.
be baldness, and every *b.* cut *Isa 15:2*
off
shall be bald and every *b.*   *Jer 48:37*
clipped
upon thine head and upon thy *Eze 5:1*
b.

BEARDS

shaved off the one half of   *2Sa 10:4*
their *b.*
at Jericho until your *b.* be   *2Sa 10:5*
grown
Jericho until your *b.* be   *1Ch 19:5*
grown
b. shaven, and their clothes *Jer 41:5*
rent

BEARERS

of them to be *b.* of burdens *2Ch 2:18*
they were over the *b.* of   *2Ch 34:13*
burdens
of the *b.* of burdens is   *Ne 4:10*
decayed

BEAREST

thou art barren and *b.* not   *J'g 13:3*
the favour that thou *b.* unto *Ps 106:4*
Thou *b.* record of thyself   *Joh 8:13*
thou *b.* not the root, but the *Ro 11:18*
root
Rejoice, thou barren that *b.*   *Ga 4:27*
not

BEARETH

whosoever *b.* ought of the   *Le 11:25*
he that *b.* the carcase of   *Le 11:28*
them
he also that *b.* the carcase   *Le 11:40*
of it
and he that *b.* any of those *Le 15:10*
things
a nursing father *b.* the   *Nu 11:12*
sucking
the firstborn which she *b.*   *De 25:6*
shall
a root that *b.* gall and   *De 29:18*
wormwood

is not sown, nor *b.* nor any *De 29:23*
grass
b. them on her wings   *De 32:11*
rising up in me by *b. witness Job 16:8*
entreateth the barren that   *Job 24:21*
b. not
A man that *b.* false witness *Pr 25:18*
but when the wicked *b.* rule *Pr 29:2*
every one *b.* twins, and there *Ca 6:6*
is
tree that *b.* her fruit, the fig *Joe 2:22*
tree
also *b.* fruit, and bringeth   *M't 13:23*
forth
another that *b.* witness of   *Joh 5:32*
me
that sent me *b.* witness of me *Joh 8:18*
branch in me that *b.* not   *Joh 15:2*
fruit
branch that *b.* fruit, he   *Joh 15:2*
purgeth it
The Spirit itself *b.* witness   *Ro 8:16*
with
for he *b.* not the sword in   *Ro 13:4*
vain
B. all things, believeth all   *1Co 13:7*
things
that which *b.* thorns and   *Heb 6:8*
briers
it is the Spirit that *b.* witness *1Jo 5:6*

BEARING

given you every herb *b.* seed   *Ge 1:29*
Lord hath restrained me from *Ge 16:2*
b.
prevented me from *b.* (B)(R) *Ge 16:2*
his name Judah; and left *b.* *Ge 29:35*
Leah saw that she had left *b.* *Ge 30:9*
b. spicery and balm and   *Ge 37:25*
myrrh
set forward, *b.* the   *Nu 10:17*
tabernacle
set forward, *b.* the sanctuary *Nu 10:21*
b. poisonous bitter fruit (R) *De 29:18*
the priests the Levites *b.* it *Jos 3:3*
priests *b.* the ark of the   *Jos 3:14*
covenant
seven priests *b.* the seven   *Jos 6:8*
trumpets
seven priests *b.* seven   *Jos 6:13*
trumpets
one *b.* a shield went before *1Sa 17:7*
him
b. the ark of the covenant *2Sa 15:24*
of God
b. precious seed, shall   *Ps 126:6*
doubtless
weary *b.* them (S)   *Isa 1:14*
a man *b.* a pitcher of water *M'k 14:13*
meet you, *b.* a pitcher of   *Lu 22:10*
water
b. his cross went forth   *Joh 19:17*
conscience also *b.* witness,   *Ro 2:15*
and
conscience also *b.* me witness *Ro 9:1*
Always *b.* about in the body *2Co 4:10*
the
b. children for (S)   *Ga 4:24*
b. with one another (A)   *Eph 4:2*
God also *b.* them witness   *Heb 2:4*
both
without the camp, *b.* his   *Heb 13:13*
reproach

BEARS

forth two she *b.* out of the *2Ki 2:24*
wood
b. burdens and carries us   *Ps 68:19*
(A)(B)(E)
daily *b.* us up (R)   *Ps 68:19*
We roar all like *b.* and   *Isa 59:11*
mourn

BEAST

let the earth bring forth the *Ge 1:24*
b.
God made *b.* of the earth   *Ge 1:25*
after his kind
the serpent was more subtil   *Ge 3:1*
than any *b.*
some evil *b.* hath devoured *Ge 37:20;*
him   *37:33*
every firstling that cometh of *Ex 13:12*
a *b.*
put his *b.* in another man's *Ex 22:5*
field
deliver to his neighbour any *Ex 22:10*
b. to keep

whoso lieth with *b.* shall be   Ex 22:19;
put to death   Le 18:23; 20:15-16;
       De 27:21
b. of the field multiply   Ex 23:29
against thee
b. that may be eaten, and *b.*   Le 11:47
that may
if it be a *b.* whereof men bring   Le 27:9
the likeness of any *b.* on the   De 4:17
earth
smote them, as well the men   J'g 20:48
as *b.*
nor any *b.* save the *b.* I rode   Ne 2:12
on
so ignorant, I was as a *b.*   Ps 73:22
before thee
he giveth to the *b.* his food,   Ps 147:9
and to ravens
righteous man regards life of   Pr 12:10
his *b.*
man hath no pre-eminence   Ec 3:19
above *b.*
b. of the field shall honour   Isa 43:20
me
as a *b.* that goeth into the   Isa 63:14
valley
dead or torn, whether fowl   Eze 44:31
or *b.*
let a *b.* heart be given to him   Da 4:16
I beheld even till the *b.* was   Da 7:11
slain
I would know the truth of   Da 7:19
the fourth *b.*
set him on his own *b.*   Lu 10:34
Paul shook off the *b.* into the   Ac 28:5
fire
if so much as a *b.* touch   Heb 12:20
mountain
first *b.* like a lion, second *b.,*   Re 4:7
third *b.*
I heard the second *b.* say,   Re 6:3
Come and see
b. that ascendeth out of the   Re 11:7
bottomless pit
and I saw a *b.* rise up out of   Re 13:1
the sea
I beheld a *b.* coming out of   Re 13:11
the earth
them that had got the victory   Re 15:2
over the *b.*
unclean spirits came out of   Re 16:13
mouth of *b.*
the *b.* that was, and is not   Re 17:8
I saw the *b.* and the kings   Re 19:19
of the earth
where the *b.* and false   Re 20:10
prophet are

EVERY BEAST

to *every b.* I have given green   Ge 1:30
herb
out of the ground God   Ge 2:19
formed *every b.*
Adam gave names to *every b.*   Ge 2:20
of the field
thou art cursed above *every*   Ge 3:14
b. of the field
of *every* clean *b.* take to thee   Ge 7:2
by sevens
they and *every b.* after his   Ge 7:14
kind
every b. after their kinds   Ge 8:19
went out of ark
of *every* clean *b.* and clean   Ge 8:20
fowl he offered
dread of you shall be on *every*   Ge 9:2
b.
blood will I require at hand of   Ge 9:5
every b.
with *every b.* I establish my   Ge 9:10
covenant
shall not *every b.* of theirs   Ge 34:23
be ours
every b. which divideth the   Le 11:26;
hoof, nor cheweth the cud   De 14:6
for *every b.* of the forest is   Ps 50:10
mine
they give drink to *every b.*   Ps 104:11
of the field
my flock became meat to   Eze 34:8
every b.
speak to *every b.* of the   Eze 39:17
field

BEAST with *MAN*

I will destroy both *man* and *b.*   Ge 6:7
dust, it became lice in *man* and   Ex 8:17
b.

boil blains upon *man* and *b.*   Ex 9:9
hail come down on *man* and   Ex 9:19
b.
no dog move tongue against   Ex 11:7
man or *b.*
will smite all first born in   Ex 12:12;
Egypt, both of *man*   13:15; Ps 135:8
and *b.*
first born of *man* and *b.* is   Ex 13:2;
mine   Nu 8:17
whether *man* or *b.* it shall   Ex 19:13
not live
no devoted thing of *man* or   Le 27:28
b.
hallowed to me first born of   Nu 3:13
man and *b.*
prey taken, both of *man* and   Nu 31:26
b.
Lord, thou preservest *man*   Ps 36:6
and *b.*
fury on *man* and *b.*   Jer 7:20;
21:6; 36:29; Eze 14:13, 17, 19, 21;
      25:13; 29:8; Zep 1:3
I have made *man* and *b.*   Jer 27:5
sow Judah with seed of *man*   Jer 31:27
and *b.*
ye say, It is desolate   Jer 32:43;
without *man* or *b.*   33:10, 12; 36:29;
      51:62
they shall depart, both *man*   Jer 50:3
and *b.*
multiply upon you *man* and   Eze 36:11
b.
let not *man* nor *b.* taste   Jon 3:7
any thing

UNCLEAN BEAST

if a soul touch any *unclean b.*   Le 5:2;
      7:21
unclean b. of which they do   Le 27:11
not offer

WILD BEAST

there passed by *wild b.* of   2Ki 14:9;
Lebanon, and trod   2Ch 25:18
down thistle
forgetteth *wild b.* may   Job 39:15
break them
wild b. of the field doth   Ps 80:13
devour it
the *wild b.* shall tear them   Ho 13:8

BEASTS

that which was torn of *b.*   Ge 31:39;
    Ex 22:31; Le 7:24; 17:15; 22:8
Esau took all his *b.* and his   Ge 36:6
substance
lade your *b.* and go to   Ge 45:17
Canaan
all the first born of *b.* shall   Ex 11:5
die
these *b.* ye shall eat   Le 11:2;
      De 14:4
chew cud among *b.* shall ye   Le 11:3;
eat   De 14:6
for *b.* shall the increase   Le 25:7
thereof be meat
I will rid evil *b.* out of the   Le 26:6
land
give the congregation and *b.*   Nu 20:8
drink
of all *b.* give a portion to   Nu 31:30
the Levites
I will send teeth of *b.* on   De 32:24
them
Solomon spake of *b.* and of   1Ki 4:33
fowl
find grass, that we lose not   1Ki 18:5
all the *b.*
drink both your cattle and *b.*   2Ki 3:17
help him goods, and with *b.*   Ezr 1:4
ask *b.* and they shall teach   Job 12:7
thee
wherefore are we counted as   Job 18:3
b.
then the *b.* go into dens, and   Job 37:8
man is like the *b.* that   Ps 49:12;
perish   49:20
rebuke the wild *b.* (A)(B)(E)   Ps 68:30
(R)
wherein all the *b.* of the   Ps 104:20
forest creep
in sea, are both small and   Ps 104:25
great *b.*

b. and all cattle, praise the   Ps 148:10
Lord
wisdom hath killed her *b.*   Pr 9:2
a lion, which is strongest   Pr 30:30
among *b.*
might see that themselves are   Ec 3:18
b.
show that they are *b.* (R)   Ec 3:18
that which befalleth men,   Ec 3:19
befalleth *b.*
the burden of the *b.* of the   Isa 30:6
south
nor *b.* thereof for a   Isa 40:16
burnt-offering
their idols were on the *b.*   Isa 46:1
and cattle
upon swift *b.* to my holy   Isa 66:20
mountain
the *b.* are fled   Jer 9:10
send famine and evil *b.*   Eze 5:17;
      14:15
fill *b.* of whole earth with   Eze 32:4
thee
destroy all the *b.* thereof   Eze 32:13;
      34:25, 28
let the *b.* get away from   Da 4:14
under it
let his portion be with the *b.*   Da 4:15
these four great *b.* are four   Da 7:17
kings
so that no *b.* might stand   Da 8:4
before him
how do the *b.* groan   Joe 1:18
nor regard peace-offerings of   Am 5:22
fat *b.*
spoil of *b.* made them   Hab 2:17
afraid
become a place for *b.* to lie   Zep 2:15
down
so shall be the plague of all   Zec 14:15
b.
have ye offered to me slain *b.*   Ac 7:42
provide them *b.* that ye may   Ac 23:24
set Paul
changed into image made like   Ro 1:23
b.
if I have fought with *b.* at   1Co 15:32
Ephesus
for every king of *b.* is tamed   Jas 3:7
these as natural brute *b.*   2Pe 2:12
speak evil
what they know naturally as   Jude 10
brute *b.*
four *b.* full of eyes before and   Re 4:6
behind
four *b.* had each six wings   Re 4:8
about him
when those *b.* give glory and   Re 4:9
honour
in midst of throne and four *b.*   Re 5:6
stood a Lamb
four *b.* said, Amen, and the   Re 5:14
24 elders fell
one of four *b.* saying, Come   Re 6:1;
      15:7
angels stood about throne   Re 7:11
and four *b.*
new song before throne and   Re 14:3
four *b.*
24 elders and four *b.* fell   Re 19:4
down

BEASTS *OF THE EARTH*

carcase be meat to all *b.* of   De 28:26
earth
carcases of Philistines to *b.*   1Sa 17:46
of earth
nor shalt be afraid of the *b.*   Job 5:22
of earth
who teacheth us more than   Job 35:11
b. of earth
flesh of thy saints to the *b.* of   Ps 79:2
earth
they shall be left to *b.* of   Isa 18:6
earth
carcases of the people meat   Jer 7:33;
for *b. of the earth*   16:4; 19:7; 34:20
appoint over them *b. of earth*   Jer 15:3
to devour
all manner of *b. of earth*   Ac 10:12;
      11:6
kill with hunger and with *b.* of   Re 6:8
earth

BEASTS *OF THE FIELD*

what poor leave, *b.* of field   Ex 23:11
may eat

lest *b. of the field* increase De 7:22
upon thee
I will give thy flesh to *b. of* 1Sa 17:44
field
birds by day, *b. of the field* 2Sa 21:10
by night
b. of the field shall be at Job 5:23
peace with thee
mountains, where all *b. of* Job 40:20
the field play
hast put *b. of the field* under Ps 8:7
his feet
all ye *b. of the field* come to Isa 56:9
devour
assemble all *b. of the field* to Jer 12:9
devour
b. of field given him Jer 27:6;
            Jer 28:14; Da 2:38
given thee for meat to *b. of* Eze 29:5;
the field 34:5; 39:4
under his branches *b. of the* Eze 31:6
field
all *b. of field* be on his Eze 31:13
branches
b. of the field shake at my Eze 38:20
presence
b. of the field had shadow Da 4:12
under it
dwelling shall be with *b. of* Da 4:25;
field 4:32
make covenant with *b. of* Ho 2:18
field
shall the land mourn with *b.* Ho 4:3
of field
b. of field cry also to thee Joe 1:20
be not afraid, ye *b. of field* Joe 2:22

WILD BEASTS

I will also send *wild b.* Le 26:22
among you
gave carcases to *wild b.* 1Sa 17:46
the *wild b.* of the field are Ps 50:11
mine
wild b. of desert shall lie Isa 13:21
there
the *wild b.* of the islands Isa 13:22
shall cry
wild b. of desert shall also Isa 34:14;
meet with *wild b.* of the Jer 50:39
island
Christ was there with the M'k 1:13
wild b.
sheet, wherein were all *wild* Ac 10:12;
b. 11:6

BEASTS'

let a *b.* heart be given unto Da 4:16
him

BEAT

shalt *b.* some of it very Ex 30:36
small
did *b.* the gold into thin Ex 39:3
plates
it in mills, or *b.* it in a Nu 11:8
mortar
and *b.* him above these with De 25:3
he *b.* down the tower of J'g 8:17
Penuel
and *b.* down the city, and J'g 9:45
sowed
b. at the door, and spake to J'g 19:22
the
and *b.* out that she had Ru 2:17
gleaned
b. them (B) 1Sa 7:11;
    1Sa 14:31; Ps 14:31; 78:66; Jer 20:2
Then did I *b.* them as small 2Sa 22:43
as
they *b.* down the cities, and 2Ki 3:25
Three times did Joash *b.* 2Ki 13:25
him
b. it to dust (A)(B)(E)(R) 2Ki 23:6
did the king *b.* down, and 2Ki 23:12
brake
b. certain of them (A) Ne 13:25;
             Jer 20:2
beat (R) Ne 13:25;
    Ca 5:7; Jer 20:2; Lu 18:13; 23:48
I *b.* them small as the dust Ps 18:42
b. down his foes before his Ps 89:23
face
Thou shalt *b.* him with the Pr 23:14
rod
b. their swords into Isa 2:4
plowshares
ye *b.* my people to pieces, Isa 3:15

and
Lord shall *b.* off from the Isa 27:12
channel
and *b.* them small, and shalt Isa 41:15
make
princes *b.* him (A)(B)(R) Jer 37:15
B. your plowshares into Joe 3:10
swords
the sun *b.* upon the head of Jon 4:8
Jonah
b. their swords into Mic 4:3
plowshares
shalt *b.* in pieces many Mic 4:13
people
winds blew, and *b.* upon that M't 7:25
fell
b. upon that house; and it M't 7:27
took his servants, and *b.* M't 21:35
one
b. him on the head (N) M't 27:30
and the waves *b.* into the M'k 4:37
ship
they caught him, and *b.* him M'k 12:3
stream *b.* vehemently upon Lu 6:48
against which the stream did Lu 6:49
b.
they *b.* him (E)(R) Lu 10:30
shall begin to *b.* the Lu 12:45
menservants
the husbandmen *b.* him, and Lu 20:10
servant: and they *b.* him Lu 20:11
also
and commanded to *b.* them Ac 16:22
b. him before the judgment Ac 18:17
seat
and *b.* in every synagogue Ac 22:19
b. the breast over her (B) Re 18:9

BEATEN

had set over them, were *b.* Ex 5:14
and, behold, thy servants are Ex 5:16
b.
beaten (B) Ex 9:31; 22:2; De 1:42;
  J'g 20:36; 1Sa 4:2; 13:4; 1Ch 18:10;
        2Ch 20:22; 25:19
of *b.* work shalt thou make Ex 25:18
them
of *b.* work shall the Ex 25:31
candlestick
one *b.* work of pure gold Ex 25:36
pure oil olive *b.* for the light Ex 27:20
fourth part of an hin of *b.* Ex 29:40
oil
of gold, *b.* out of one piece Ex 37:7
b. work made he the Ex 37:17
candlestick
it was one *b.* work of pure Ex 37:22
gold
even corn *b.* out of full ears Le 2:14
of the *b.* corn thereof, and Le 2:14
part
full of sweet incense *b.* small Le 16:12
pure oil olive *b.* for the light Le 24:2
the candlestick was of *b.* gold Nu 8:4
the flowers thereof, was *b.* Nu 8:4
work
fourth part of an hin of *b.* Nu 28:5
oil
the wicked man be worthy to De 25:2
be *b.*
made as if they were *b.* Jos 8:15
and Abner was *b.*, and the 2Sa 2:17
men
two hundred targets of *b.* 1Ki 10:16
gold
three hundred shields of *b.* 1Ki 10:17
gold
measures of *b.* wheat 2Ch 2:10
two hundred targets of *b.* 2Ch 9:15
gold
hundred shekels of *b.* gold 2Ch 9:15
three hundred shields made 2Ch 9:16
he of *b.*
b. the graven images into 2Ch 34:7
powder
they have *b.* me, and I felt it Pr 23:35
not
b. in the house of friends Isa 13:16
(B)
chalkstones that are *b.* in Isa 27:9
sunder
the fitches are *b.* out with a Isa 28:27
staff
shall the Assyrian be *b.* Isa 30:31
down
silver *b.* into plates (S) Jer 10:9

and their mighty ones are *b.* Jer 46:5
down
images thereof shall be *b.* to Mic 1:7
pieces
in the synagogues ye shall be M'k 13:9
b.
shall be *b.* with many stripes Lu 12:47
shall be *b.* with few stripes Lu 12:48
called the apostles, and *b.* Ac 5:40
them
have *b.* us openly Ac 16:37
uncondemned
Thrice was I. *b.* with rods, 2Co 11:25
once

BEATEST

When thou *b.* thine olive De 24:20
tree
if thou *b.* him with the rod Pr 23:13

BEATETH

not as one that *b.* the air 1Co 9:26

BEATING

Egyptian *b.* a Hebrew (A)(B) Ex 2:11
him that is *b.* him De 25:11
(A)(B)(R)
went on *b.* down one 1Sa 14:16
another
b. them to dust (A)(E)(R) 2Ch 15:16
b. upon their breasts Na 2:7
(A)(B)(R)(E)(R)(S)
others; *b.* some, and killing M'k 12:5
some
b. breasts (A)(B) Lu 23:4
the soldiers, they left *b.* of Ac 21:32
Paul
box as one *b.* the air 1Co 9:26
(A)(B)(R)

BEATS

my heart *b.* fast (B) Ps 38:10

BEAUTIES

in the *b.* of holiness from Ps 110:3

BEAUTIFICATION

ointments for *b.* (S) Es 2:9
their *b.* accomplished (S) Es 2:12

BEAUTIFIED

b. her head (A) 2Ki 9:30
b. for her husband (B) Re 21:2

BEAUTIFUL

beautiful (A) Ge 12:14;
  16:7; 1Ki 1:4; Es 2:2, 3; Ca 1:15;
          Eze 31:7; Ac 7:20
beautiful (B) Ge 12:14;
  26:7; 2Sa 13:1; 1Ki 1:4; Es 2:2, 3;
  Job 42:15; Pr 11:22; Ca 1:15; Eze 31:7;
              Ac 7:20
beautiful (R) Ge 12:14;
  1Sa 13:1; 1Ki 1:4; Es 2:2, 3; Pr 11:22;
           Ca 1:15; Ac 7:20
Rachel was *b.* and well Ge 29:17
beautiful (S) Ge 49:21;
      Ex 2:2; Jos 7:21; Jer 3:19
among the captives a *b.* De 21:11
woman
a *b.* robe (B) Jos 7:21
withal of a *b.* countenance 1Sa 16:12
and of a *b.* countenance 1Sa 25:3
was very *b.* to look upon 2Sa 11:2
the maid was fair and *b.* Es 2:7
B. for situation, the joy of the Ps 48:2
b. woman who neglects (B) Pr 11:22
made every thing *b.* in his Ec 3:11
time
are *b.* (A) Ca 1:15;
           Ac 7:30
Thou are *b.* O my love Ca 6:4
How *b.* are thy feet with shoes Ca 7:1
shall the branch of the Lord Isa 4:2
be *b.*
put on thy *b.* garments, O Isa 52:1
How *b.* upon the mountains Isa 52:7
are
Our holy and our *b.* house Isa 64:11
your *b.* crown (A)(R) Jer 13:18
was given thee, thy *b.* flock Jer 13:20

strong staff broken, and the *Jer 48:17*
b. rod
a *b.* crown upon thine *Eze 16:12*
head
thou wast exceeding *b.* and *Eze 16:13*
thou
b. crowns upon their heads *Eze 23:42*
which indeed appear *b.* *M't 23:27*
outward
the temple which is called *B.* *Ac 3:2*
sat for alms at the *B.* gate *Ac 3:10*
How *b.* are the feet of them *Ro 10:15*
that
a *b.* child (S) *Heb 11:23*

BEAUTIFULLY

b. wrought, woven (S) *Ex 28:8;*
28:27-28; 29:5; 35:32, 35; 39:5, 20-21;
Le 8:7

BEAUTIFY

to *b.* the house of the Lord *Ezr 7:27*
he will *b.* the meek with *Ps 149:4*
salvation
to *b.* the place of my *Isa 60:13*
sanctuary
b. the teaching of God (B) *Tit 2:10*
were to *b.* themselves (A) *1Pe 3:5*

BEAUTIFYING

b. ointments (S) *Es 2:3*
b. of women (S) *Es 2:12*

BEAUTY

thy brother, for glory and for *Ex 28:2*
b.
for them, for glory and for *Ex 28:40*
b.
its *b.* faded away (A) *Jos 1:11*
The *b.* of Israel is slain *2Sa 1:19*
upon thy
praised as Absalom for his *2Sa 14:25*
b.
the Lord in the *b.* of *1Ch 16:29*
holiness
house with precious stones *2Ch 3:6*
for *b.*
should praise the *b.* of *2Ch 20:21*
holiness
the people and the princes her *Es 1:11*
b.
array thyself with glory and *Job 40:10*
b.
to behold the *b.* of the Lord *Ps 27:4*
the Lord in the *b.* of holiness *Ps 29:2*
makest his *b.* to consume *Ps 39:11*
away
the king greatly desire thy *b.* *Ps 45:11*
and their *b.* shall consume in *Ps 49:14*
the
out of Zion, the perfection of *Ps 50:2*
b.
let the *b.* of the Lord our *Ps 90:17*
God
and *b.* are in his sanctuary *Ps 96:6*
the Lord in the *b.* of holiness *Ps 96:9*
finds great *b.* (B) *Ps 119:162*
Lust not after her *b.* in thine *Pr 6:25*
b. of old men is the gray *Pr 20:29*
head
Favour is deceitful, and *b.* is *Pr 31:30*
vain
burning instead of *b.* *Isa 3:24*
the *b.* of the Chaldees' *Isa 13:19*
excellency
glorious *b.* is a fading flower *Isa 28:1*
glorious *b.* which is on the *Isa 28:4*
head
of glory, and for a diadem of *Isa 28:5*
b.
eyes shall see the king in his *Isa 33:17*
b.
all the *b.* is as (S) *Isa 40:6*
according to the *b.* of a *Isa 44:13*
man
no *b.* that we should desire *Isa 53:2*
him
to give unto the *b.* for ashes *Isa 61:3*
your crown of *b.* (B) *Jer 13:18*
her *b.* is departed: her princes *La 1:6*
the *b.* of Israel, and *La 2:1*
remembered
the perfection of *b.* The joy *La 2:15*
As for the *b.* of his ornament *Eze 7:20*
among the heathen for thy *Eze 16:14*
b.

---

thou didst trust in thine *Eze 16:15*
own *b.*
hast made thy *b.* to be *Eze 16:25*
abhorred
thou hast said, I am of *Eze 27:3*
perfect *b.*
thy builders have perfected *Eze 27:4*
thy *b.*
they have made thy *b.* *Eze 27:11*
perfect
against the *b.* of thy wisdom *Eze 28:7*
full of wisdom, and perfect *Eze 28:12*
in *b.*
was lifted up because of thy *Eze 28:17*
b.
God was like unto him in *Eze 31:8*
his *b.*
Whom dost thou pass in *b.* *Eze 32:19*
his *b.* shall be as the olive *Ho 14:6*
tree
goodness, how great is his *b.* *Zec 9:17*
the one I called *B.*, and the *Zec 11:7*
other
I took my staff, even *B.* *Zec 11:10*
and cut
only for *b.* (R) *Ro 9:21*
b. not dependent on coiffure, *1Pe 3:3*
jewelry, fine clothes (P)
secret of the *b.* of (P) *1Pe 3:5*
dressed in *b.* for her (P) *Re 21:2*

BEBAI

The children of *B.* six *Ezr 2:11*
hundred
And of the sons of *B.* *Ezr 8:11*
the sons also of *B.*; *Ezr 10:28*
Jehohanan
The children of *B.* six *Ne 7:16*
hundred
Bunni, Azgad, *B.* *Ne 10:15*

BECAME

man *b.* a living soul *Ge 2:7*
the same *b.* mighty men which *Ge 6:4*
she *b.* a pillar of salt *Ge 19:26*
in the wilderness, and *b.* an *Ge 21:20*
archer
became (S) *Ge 26:13;*
Ex 1:7, 20; 16:21; 19:19; 2Sa 16:14;
2Ki 4:34; 2Ch 13:21; 17:12; Ne 9:21;
Ps 32:3; Jer 50:43; Lu 1:80; 2:40; 13:19;
Heb 11:34
a servant under tribute *Ge 49:15*
Pharoah's daughter, he *b.* her *Ex 2:10*
son
it *b.* a serpent, it *b.* a rod *Ex 4:3;*
4:4; 7:10
magician's rods *b.* serpents *Ex 7:10*
it *b.* lice, *b.* boil *Ex 8:17;*
8:24
Miriam *b.* leprous, white as *Nu 12:10*
snow
it *b.* the inheritance *Jos 14:14; 24:32*
they *b.* tributaries *J'g 1:30; 1:33, 35*
Nabal *b.* as stone *1Sa 25:37*
it *b.* a sin *1Ki 12:30; 13:34*
b. David's servants *1Ch 18:2; 18:6, 13*
the Edomites *b.* David's *1Ch 18:13*
servants
people of the land *b.* Jews *Es 8:17*
it *b.* a proverb *Ps 69:11; 1Sa 10:12*
keepers did shake and *b.* as *M't 28:4*
dead
His raiment *b.* shining *M'k 9:3*
exceeding
b. vain in their imaginations *Ro 1:21*
unto the Jews I *b.* a Jew *1Co 9:20*
b. obedient unto death, even *Ph'p 2:8*
b. the author of eternal *Heb 5:9*
salvation
sun *b.* black, moon *b.* as *Re 6:12;*
blood *8:8, 11; 16:3-4*
it *b.* as blood of a dead man *Re 16:3*

BECAMEST

and thou, Lord, *b.* their *1Ch 17:22*
God
and thou *b.* mine *Eze 16:8*

BECAUSE

b. that in it he had rested *Ge 2:3*
b. thou hast done this *Ge 3:14;*
Ge 3:17; 22:16
b. she was the mother of all *Ge 3:20*
living

---

b. there they sware both of *Ge 21:31*
them
b. thou hast obeyed *Ge 22:18; 26:5*
b. thou hast despised my *Le 26:43*
judgments
b. of all your sins which ye *De 9:18*
sinned
b. the Lord had said he *De 9:25*
would
B. the Lord was not able to *De 9:28*
bring
b. he hated them, he hath *De 9:28*
brought
b. they hired against thee *De 23:4*
Balaam
b. our God is not among us *De 31:17*
ye sanctified me not in the *De 32:51*
b. thou hast rejected word *1Sa 15:23*
of Lord
thy words: *b.* I feared the *1Sa 15:24*
people
b. they forsook the Lord *1Ki 9:9;*
11:9, 33-34; 2Ki 18:12; 22:17;
2Ch 7:22; 24:16, 20, 24; 28:6; 34:25
b. he humbled himself *1Ki 23:29*
him, *b.* he was the son in law *Ne 6:18*
of
B. Haman the son of *Es 9:24*
Hammedatha
b. our days upon earth are a *Job 8:9*
shadow
taken hold upon me *b.* of *Ps 119:53*
the wicked
B. they hated knowledge (S) *Pr 1:29*
b. thou hast put thy trust in *Jer 39:18*
me
B. thou hast had a perpetual *Eze 35:5*
b. thou hast spoiled many *Hab 2:8*
nations
b. of men's blood, and for *Hab 2:8*
the violence
b. of the crowd (S) *Lu 8:19; 19:3*
b. I go to my Father *Joh 14:12;*
Joh 14:28; 16:10, 16-17
b. your sins are forgiven *1Jo 2:12*
b. ye have known him *1Jo 2:13*
b. we love the brethren *1Jo 3:14*
b. we keep his *1Jo 3:22*
commandments

BECHER

Belah, and *B.*, and Ashbel, *Ge 46:21*
Gera
of *B.* the family of the *Nu 26:35*
Bachrites
Bela, and *B.*, and Jediael, *1Ch 7:6*
three
the sons of *B.*; Zemira, and *1Ch 7:8*
Joash
All these are the sons of *B.* *1Ch 7:8*

BECHORATH

Zeror, the son of *B.* the son *1Sa 9:1*
of

BECKONED

he *b.* unto them, and *Lu 1:22*
remained
they *b.* unto their partners *Lu 5:7*
Peter therefore *b.* to him, *Joh 13:24*
that
Alexander *b.* with the hand, *Ac 19:33*
and
b. with the hand unto the *Ac 21:40*
people
after that the governor had *Ac 24:10*
b.

BECKONING

b. unto them with the hand *Ac 12:17*
and *b.* with his hand, said *Ac 13:16*

BECOME

man is *b.* as one of us *Ge 3:22*
I have *b.* old *Ge 18:12*
Abraham shall surely *b.* *Ge 18:18;*
great *48:19*
the cry has *b.* great (S) *Ge 19:13*
husband *b.* attached to me *Ge 29:34*
(S)
He is *b.* my salvation *Ex 15:2;*
Ps 118:14, 21; Isa 12:2
brother *b.* poor (S) *Le 25:25;*
25:35, 39
become (S) *Le 25:47;*

Nu 11:23;   De 32:15;   Job 6:17;
Ps 102:26;   Isa 17:4;   Eze 16:7;
    M't 13:15;   2Ti 3:13;   Heb 1:11
thou art b. the people of the   De 27:9
Lord
have not b. old (S)   De 29:5
Israel had b. strong (S)   Jos 17:13
had b. odious (S)   2Sa 10:6; Ex 16:24
young b. strong (S)   Job 39:4
have him b. his son at the   Pr 29:21
length
b. fools (S)   Jer 50:36
converted, and b. as little   M't 18:3
children
b. the head of the corner   M't 21:42;
    M'k 12:10; Lu 20:17; Ac 4:11
power to b. the sons of God   Joh 1:12
b. obtuse (S)   Ac 28:27
behold, all things are b. new   2Co 5:17
kingdoms of this world are   Re 11:15
b. the

BECOMETH

holiness b. thine house, O   Ps 93:5
Lord
b. poor that dealeth with slack   Pr 10:4
hand
Excellent speech b. not a fool   Pr 17:7
it b. us to fulfill all   M't 3:15
righteousness
word b. unfruitful M't 13:22; M'k 4:19
b. saints, b. the gospel, b.   Eph 5:3;
holiness   Ph'p 1:27; 1Ti 2:10; Tit 2:3

BECOMING

b. confident by my bonds   Ph'p 1:14
(S)

BED

and sat upon the b.   Ge 48:2;
    1Sa 28:23
went to father's b.   Ge 49:4; 1Ch 5:1
die not, but keepeth his b.   Ex 21:18
b. he lieth on is unclean   Le 15:4;
    15:21, 23-24, 26
an image laid in the b.   1Sa 19:13;
    19:15-16
lay on a b.   2Sa 4:5;
4:7, 11; 11:13; 13:5; 1Ki 17:19, 21;
    2Ch 16:14
not come down from b.   2Ki 1:4;
    1:6, 16
My b. shall comfort me   Job 7:13
made my b. in darkness   Job 17:13
in slumberings upon the b.   Job 33:15
also with pain upon the b.   Job 33:19
commune with own heart upon   Ps 4:4
your b.
He deviseth mischief upon his   Ps 36:4
b.
make all his b. in sickness   Ps 41:3
if I make my b. in hell   Ps 139:8
decked my b. with coverings   Pr 7:16;
    7:17
why should he take away thy   Pr 22:27
b.
So doth the slothful upon his   Pr 26:14
b.
our b. is green   Ca 1:16
by night on my b. I sought   Ca 3:1
him
his b. which is Solomon's   Ca 3:7
the b. is shorter than man   Isa 28:20
can stretch
came to her in the b. of   Eze 23:17
love
visions of thy head upon thy   Da 2:28;
b.   Da 2:29; 4:5, 10, 13; 7:1
take up thy b.   M't 9:6;
    M'k 2:9, 11-12; Joh 5:8-12; Ac 9:34
candle put under a b.   M'k 4:21;
    Lu 8:16
my children are with me in b.   Lu 11:7
two men in one b.   Lu 17:34
Aeneas, which had kept his   Ac 9:33
b.
b. undefiled: but   Heb 13:4
whoremongers
I will cast her into a b.   Re 2:22

BEDAD

and Hadad the son of B.   Ge 36:35
who
Hadad the son of B. which   1Ch 1:46
smote

BEDAN

the Lord sent Jerubbaal,   1Sa 12:11
and B.
sons of Ulam; B. These   1Ch 7:17
were

BEDCHAMBER

into thy b. and upon thy bed   Ex 8:3
he lay on his bed in his b.   2Sa 4:7
that thou speakest in thy b.   2Ki 6:12
in the b. from Athalia   2Ki 11:2
put him and his nurse in   2Ch 22:11
a b.
curse not the rich in thy b.   Ec 10:20

BEDECKED

b. with gold (A)(R)   Re 17:4
b. with gold (S)   Re 17:4; 18:16
b. with gold (A)(P)(R)   Re 18:16

BEDEIAH

Benaiah, B., Chelluh   Ezr 10:35

BEDEZENED

b. with gold (N)   Re 18:16; 17:4

BEDS

b. and basons, and earthen   2Sa 17:28
the b. were of gold and silver   Es 1:6
let them sing aloud upon   Ps 149:5
their b.
to the b. of spices, to feed in   Ca 6:2
they shall rest in their b. each   Isa 57:2
they howled upon their b.   Ho 7:14
That lie upon b. of ivory   Am 6:4
and work evil upon their b.   Mic 2:1
and began to carry about in   M'k 6:55
b.
and laid them on b. and   Ac 5:15
couches

BED'S

bowed himself upon the b.   Ge 47:31
head

BEDSTEAD

his b. was a b. of iron   De 3:11

BEE

and for the b. that is in the   Isa 7:18
land

BEELIADA

Elishama, and B. and   1Ch 14:7
Eliphalet

BEELZEBUB

called the master of the   M't 10:25
house B.
but by B. the prince of the   M't 12:24
devils
And if I by B. cast out   M't 12:27
devils
said, He hath B. and by the   M'k 3:22
prince
He casteth out devils   Lu 11:15
through B.
I cast out devils through B.   Lu 11:18
And if I by B. cast out   Lu 11:19
devils

BEEN

their trade hath b. to feed   Ge 46:32
cattle
Hazor had b. the head (S)   Jos 11:10
b. speaking (S)   1Sa 1:16
Saul was as though he had   1Sa 10:27
b. deaf
very pleasant hast thou b. to   2Sa 1:26
me
if that had b. too little, I   2Sa 12:8
would have
have slept, then had I b. at   Job 3:13
rest
hast b. my help, leave me not   Ps 27:9;
    63:7
unless Lord had b. my help,   Ps 94:17
my soul

I have b. still, and refrained   Isa 42:14
then had thy peace b. as a   Isa 48:18
river
left alone; these, where had   Isa 49:21
they b.
she hath b. ashamed and   Jer 15:9
confounded
Hebrew, which hath b. sold   Jer 34:14
unto thee
hath not b. emptied from   Jer 48:11
vessel to
hast not b. as an harlot, in   Eze 16:31
if we had b. in days of our   M't 23:30
fathers
but we trusted that it had b.   Lu 24:21
he
took knowledge they had b.   Ac 4:13
with Jesus
had b. as Sodom, and like   Ro 9:29
Gomorrah
ye had heard that he had b.   Ph'p 2:26
sick
widow, having b. the wife of   1Ti 5:9
one man
it had b. better not to have   2Pe 2:21
known
if they had b. of us, no   1Jo 2:19
doubt they

HATH BEEN

God of my fathers hath b.   Ge 31:5
with me
the Lord thy God hath b. with   De 2:7
thee
see wherein this sin hath b.   1Sa 14:38
Israel hath b. without true   2Ch 15:3
God
that which hath b. is now,   Ec 3:15
and that which is to be hath
already b.
precept hath b. upon   Isa 28:10
this hath b. thy manner   Jer 22:21
from youth
hath this b. in your days of   Joe 1:2
fathers
for he hath b. dead four   Joh 11:39
days
or who hath b. his counsellor   Ro 11:34

HAVE BEEN

not servants to Hebrews as   1Sa 4:9
have b.
have b. with thee whither   1Ch 17:8
walkedst
since days of fathers have   Ezr 9:7
we b.
I should have b. as if I   Job 10:19
had not been
thy tender mercies have b.   Ps 25:6
ever of old
have b. young, and now old,   Ps 37:25
yet not seen
my tears have b. my meat day   Ps 42:3
and night
have b. as Sodom, have b. as   Isa 1:9
Gomorrah
so have we b. in thy sight,   Isa 26:17
O Lord
have b. with child, have b.   Isa 26:18
in pain
all those things have b. saith   Isa 66:2
the Lord
have I b. a wilderness to   Jer 2:31
Israel
the prophets that have b.   Jer 28:8
before me
though I have b. a rebuker of   Ho 5:2
them all
but have b. partial in the law   Mal 2:9
they have b. with me three   M'k 8:2
days
which have b. since the world   Lu 1:70
began
have I b. so long time with   Joh 14:9
you
ye have b. with me from   Joh 15:27
the begin
after what manner I have b.   Ac 20:18
with you
a night and a day I have   2Co 11:25
b. in deep
righteousness should have b.   Ga 3:21
by law

NOT BEEN

to rain hail such as not b. in   Ex 9:18
Egypt

yet hast *not b.* as my   *1Ki 14:8*
servant David
as an hidden untimely birth   *Job 3:16*
I had *not b.*
I should have been as tho'   *Job 10:19*
I had *not b.*
if it had *not b.* Lord on our   *Ps 124:1;*
side   *124:2*
better than both is he that   *Ec 4:3*
hath *not b.*
they shall be as though they had   *Ob 16*
not b.
good for that man he had   *M't 26:24*
not b. born
if therefore ye have *not b.*   *Lu 16:11;*
faithful   *16:12*

BEER

from thence they went to *B.*   *Nu 21:16*
ran away, and fled, and went   *J'g 9:21*
to *B.*

BEERA

Shilshah, and Ithran, and *B.*   *1Ch 7:37*

BEERAH

B. his son, when   *1Ch 5:6*
Tilgath-pilneser

BEER-ELIM

and the howling thereof unto   *Isa 15:8*
B.

BEERI

the daughter of *B.* the   *Ge 26:34*
Hittite
Hosea, the son of *B.* in the   *Ho 1:1*
days

BEER-LAHAI-ROI

Wherefore the well was   *Ge 16:14*
called *B.*

BEEROTH

took their journey from *B.* of   *De 10:6*
and *B.*, and Kirjath-jearim   *Jos 9:17*
Gibeon, and Ramah, and *B.*   *Jos 18:25*
B. also was reckoned to   *2Sa 4:2*
Benjamin
Kirjath-arim, Chephirah, and   *Ezr 2:25*
B.
Kirjath-jearim, Chephirah,   *Ne 7:29*
and *B.*

BEEROTHITE

the sons of Rimmon a *B.* of   *2Sa 4:2*
the
Rimmon the *B.*, Rechab and   *2Sa 4:5*
brother, the sons of Rimmon   *2Sa 4:9*
the *B.*
Nahari the *B.*,   *2Sa 23:37*
armourbearer

BEEROTHITES

the *B.* fled to Gittaim, and were   *2Sa 4:3*

BEER-SHEBA

wandered in the wilderness   *Ge 21:14*
of *B.*
Wherefore he called that   *Ge 21:31*
place *B.*
Thus they made a covenant   *Ge 21:32*
at *B.*
Abraham planted a grove in   *Ge 21:33*
B.
up and went together to *B.*   *Ge 22:19*
Abraham dwelt at *B.*   *Ge 22:19*
he went up from thence to   *Ge 26:23*
B.
therefore the name of the   *Ge 26:33*
city is *B.*

BEES

you, as *b.* do, and destroyed   *De 1:44*
you
of *b.* and honey in the   *J'g 14:8*
carcase
They compassed me about   *Ps 118:12*
like *b.*

BEESH-TERAH

and *B.* with her suburbs;   *Jos 21:27*
two

BEETLE

the *b.* after his kind, and the   *Le 11:22*

BEEVES

blemish, of the *b.* of the   *Le 22:19*
sheep
a freewill offering in *b.* or   *Le 22:21*
sheep
of persons, and of the *b.*   *Nu 31:28*
of the persons, of the *b.*   *Nu 31:30*
threescore and twelve   *Nu 31:33*
thousand *b.*
And the *b.* were thirty and six   *Nu 31:38*
And thirty and six thousand   *Nu 31:44*
b.

BEFALL

peradventure mischief *b.* him   *Ge 42:4*
if mischief *b.* him by the   *Ge 42:38*
way
mischief *b.* him, ye shall   *Ge 44:29*
bring
tell you that which shall *b.*   *Ge 49:1*
you
evils and troubles shall *b.*   *De 31:17*
them
will *b.* you in the latter days   *De 31:29*
There shall be no evil *b.* thee   *Ps 91:10*
what shall *b.* thy people   *Da 10:14*
the things that shall *b.* me   *Ac 20:22*

BEFALLEN

and such things have *b.* me   *Le 10:19*
travel that hath *b.* us   *Nu 20:14*
many evils and troubles are *b.*   *De 31:21*
why then is all this *b.* us   *J'g 6:13*
Something hath *b.* him, he   *1Sa 20:26*
is not
everything that had *b.* him   *Es 6:13*
b. to the possessed of the   *M't 8:33*
devils

BEFALLETH

b. the sons of men *b.* beasts   *Ec 3:19*
even one thing *b.* them   *Ec 3:19*

BEFELL

told him all that *b.* unto   *Ge 42:29*
them
told him all things that *b.*   *Jos 2:23*
them
evil that *b.* thee from thy   *2Sa 19:7*
youth
b. to him that was possessed   *M'k 5:16*
and temptations, which *b.*   *Ac 20:19*
me by

BEFITTING

praise is *b.* to the upright (S)   *Ps 33:1*

BEFORE

b. it was in the earth, *b.* it   *Ge 2:5*
grew
earth was also corrupt *b.*   *Ge 6:11;*
God   *6:13*
mighty hunter *b.* the Lord   *Ge 10:9*
sinners *b.* the Lord   *Ge 13:13*
exceedingly
walk *b.* me and be thou   *Ge 17:1*
perfect
Abraham stood yet *b.* the   *Ge 18:22*
Lord
to pass, *b.* he had done   *Ge 24:15*
speaking
delivered *b.* midwives come in   *Ex 1:19*
(S)
I send my angel *b.* thee to   *Ex 23:20;*
keep   *23:23*
b. it was chewed (S)   *Nu 11:33*
how long *b.* they believe (S)   *Nu 14:11*
praying *b.* the Lord   *1Sa 1:12; 1:15, 19*
b. the lamp of God went out   *1Sa 3:3*
(S)
b. you bid people return (S)   *2Sa 2:26*
but dead men *b.* my lord   *2Sa 19:28*
the king

he bowed himself *b.* the king   *1Ki 1:23*
with his
b. the messenger came (S)   *2Ki 6:32*
made it *b.* king Ahaz came   *2Ki 16:11*
(S)
why lodge *b.* the wall (S)   *Ne 13:21*
nor trembled *b.* him (S)   *Es 5:9*
to present himself *b.* the Lord   *Job 2:1*
as one *b.* whom men spit   *Job 17:6*
(S)
Hell is naked *b.* him, and   *Job 26:6*
set the Lord always *b.* me   *Ps 16:8;*
  Ac 2:25
pay my vows *b.* them that   *Ps 22:25*
fear
mine adversaries are all *b.*   *Ps 69:19*
thee
my prayer come *b.* thee (S)   *Ps 88:13*
his throne as the sun *b.* me   *Ps 89:36*
set no wicked thing *b.* mine   *Ps 101:3*
eyes
withereth *b.* it groweth up   *Ps 129:6*
(S)
and destruction are *b.* the   *Pr 15:11*
Lord
B. I was aware (S)   *Ca 6:12*
For *b.* the harvest (S)   *Isa 18:5*
all nations *b.* him are as   *Isa 40:17*
nothing
grow up *b.* him as a tender   *Isa 53:2*
plant
B. I formed thee in the belly   *Jer 1:5*
shall be as *b.* (S)   *Jer 30:20*
how long *b.* be quiet (S)   *Jer 47:6*
b. he that was escaped came   *Eze 33:22*
(S)
which was *b.* the building   *Eze 42:1*
toward
and said unto him that   *Da 10:16*
stood *b.* me
B. the decree bring forth   *Zep 2:2*
forth, *b.* the day pass as the   *Zep 2:2*
chaff
b. the fierce anger of the   *Zep 2:2*
Lord
b. the day of the Lord's anger   *Zep 2:2*
b. they came together, she   *M't 1:18*
was
let your light shine *b.* men   *M't 5:16; 6:1*
ye have need *b.* ye ask him   *M't 6:8*
and went *b.* them (S)   *M'k 6:33*
after me is preferred *b.* me   *Joh 1:15; 1:27, 30*
come down *b.* child dies (S)   *Joh 4:49*
promised *b.* by prophets (S)   *Ro 1:2*
world may become guilty *b.*   *Ro 3:18*
God
he had prepared *b.* (S)   *Ro 9:23*
God ordained *b.* the world   *1Co 2:7; Eph 1:4*
I wrote *b.* in few words (S)   *Eph 3:3*
spirits which are *b.* his throne   *Re 1:4*
b. the Father and *b.* his angels   *Re 3:5*
small and great stand *b.*   *Re 20:12*
God

BEFOREHAND

hated not *b.* (S)   *Jos 20:5*
take no thought *b.* what ye   *M'k 13:11*
shall
told everything *b.*   *M'k 13:23*
(A)(E)(R)
loved *b.* (A)(B)   *Ro 8:29*
b. he had in mind (B)   *Ro 11:2*
and make up *b.* your bounty   *2Co 9:5*
tell you *b.* (S)   *2Co 13:2*
Some men's sins are open *b.*   *1Ti 5:24*
works of some are manifest   *1Ti 5:25*
b.
testified *b.* the sufferings of   *1Pe 1:11*
Christ

BEFORETIME

The Horims also dwelt in   *De 2:12*
Seir *b.*
for Hazor *b.* was the head of   *Jos 11:10*
and hated him not *b.*   *Jos 20:5*
B. in Israel, when a man   *1Sa 9:9*
a Prophet was *b.* called a Seer   *1Sa 9:9*
when all that knew him *b.*   *1Sa 10:11*
afflict them any more, or *b.*   *2Sa 7:10*
dwelt in their tents, as *b.*   *2Ki 13:5*
Now I had not been *b.* sad   *Ne 2:1*
and *b.* that we may say, He   *Isa 41:26*
is
called Simon, which *b.* in the   *Ac 8:9*
same

BEFOULED

b. with your feet (B)　　　　Eze 34:19

BEG

be continually vagabonds,　　Ps 109:10
and b.
therefore shall he b. in the　　Pr 20:4
harvest
cannot dig; to b. I am　　Lu 16:3
ashamed
to b. from people (N)(P)　　Ac 3:2
we b. you, be reconciled (S)　2Co 5:20
b. that nothing more be　　Heb 12:19
(A)

BEGAN

then b. men to call upon the　Ge 4:26
Lord
b. Moses to declare this law　De 1:5
Spirit of Lord b. to move　　J'g 13:25
him
Lord b. to cut Israel short　2Ki 10:32;
　　　　　　　　　　　　　15:37
when they b. to sing and　　2Ch 20:22
praise
b. to seek after the God of　2Ch 34:1
David
Jesus b. to preach　　M't 4:17; 11:7
Jesus b. to teach　　M'k 4:1;
　　　　M'k 6:2, 34; 8:31; Ac 1:1
since the world b.　　Joh 9:32;
　　Ac 3:21; Ro 16:25; 2Ti 1:9; Tit 1:2

BEGAT

b. a son　　Ge 4:18;
　　5:3-32; 11:10-27; Ru 4:18-22;
　1Ch 1:10-13; 2:10-46; 4:2-14; 6:4-14;
　　8:1-11, 32-37; 9:38-43; M't 1:2-16
not mindful of the Rock　　De 32:18
that b. thee
of his own will b. he us　　Jas 1:18
with word
every one that loveth him that　1Jo 5:1
b.

BEGET

twelve princes shall he b.　　Ge 17:20
thou shalt b.　　De 4:25;
　28:41; 2Ki 20:18; Isa 39:7; Eze 47:22
If a man b. an hundred　　Ec 6:3
children
Take ye wives and b. sons　Jer 29:6
If he b. a son that is a　　Eze 18:10;
robber　　　　　　　　　　18:14

BEGETTEST

issue, which thou b. after　Ge 48:6
them
unto his father, What b.　　Isa 45:10
thou

BEGETTETH

He that b. a fool doeth it to　Pr 17:21
his
and he that b. a wise child　Pr 23:24
shall
he b. a son, and there is　　Ec 5:14
nothing

BEGGAR

up the b. from the dunghill　1Sa 2:8
was a certain b. named　　Lu 16:20
Lazarus
that the b. died, and was　　Lu 16:22
carried

BEGGARLY

to the weak and b. elements　Ga 4:9
b. rudiments of world (B)(E)　Ga 4:9
b. spirits of the elements (N)　Ga 4:9
b. elementary spirits (R)　　Ga 4:9

BEGGED

because you b. me　　M't 18:32
(A)(B)(P)
b. a favor (N)(P)　　M't 20:20
Pilate, and b. the body of　M't 27:58
Jesus

Pilate, and b. the body of　Lu 23:52
Jesus
Is not this he that sat and b.　Joh 9:8
you b. us a favor (N)(P)　　Ac 3:14
b. him for letters (P)　　Ac 9:2
b. for peace (P)　　Ac 12:20
b. for a king (P)　　Ac 13:21
she b. us (B)　　Ac 16:15
I b. titus (N)　　2Co 12:18
b. to hear no more (N)　　Heb 12:19

BEGGING

forsaken, nor his and b.　　Ps 37:25
bread
sat by the highway side b.　M'k 10:46
man sat by the wayside b.　Lu 18:35

BEGIN

this they b. to do; and now　Ge 11:6
nothing
b. to possess the land　　De 2:24;
　　　　　　　　　　　　2:25, 31
b. to number the seven weeks　De 16:9
This day will I b. to magnify　Jos 3:7
thee
when I b. I will make a full　1Sa 3:12
end
Did I then b. to enquire of　1Sa 22:15
God
to b. thanksgiving in prayer　Ne 11:17
I b. to bring evil on the city　Jer 25:29
and b. at my sanctuary　　Eze 9:6
b. not to say within yourselves　Lu 3:8
b. to stand without and　　Lu 13:25;
knock　　　　　　　　　　13:26
behold it b. to mock him　　Lu 14:29
these things b. to come to　Lu 21:28
pass
Do we b. to commend　　2Co 3:1
ourselves
judgment must b. at house　1Pe 4:17
of God
shall b. to sound, the mystery　Re 10:7
of God

BEGINNEST

from such time thou b. to　De 16:9
put

BEGINNING

In the b.　　Ge 1:1;
　　Pr 8:22-23; Joh 1:1-2; Ph'p 4:15;
　　　　　　　　　　　　Heb 1:10
the b. of my strength　　Ge 49:3;
　　　　　　　　　　　　De 21:17
the b. of months　　Ex 12:2
end of Job more　than　　Job 42:12
the b.
fear of Lord is b. of　　Ps 111:10;
wisdom　　　　　　　　　Pr 9:10
b. of strife is as one letteth　Pr 17:14
out water
better is the end than the b.　Ec 7:8
from the b.　　Isa 18:2;
　De 11:12; 32:42; Ps 119:160; Pr 8:23;
　Ec 3:11; Isa 40:21; 41:26; 46:10; 48:16;
　Jer 17:12; M't 19:8; M'k 10:6; 13:19;
　Lu 1:2; Joh 6:64; 8:25, 44; 15:27;
　Ac 11:4; 15:18; 26:5; Eph 3:9;
　2Th 2:13; 2Pe 3:4; 1Jo 1:1; 2:7, 13-14,
　　　　　　　24; 3:8, 11; 2Jo 5-6
at the b.　　Da 9:21;
　9:23; M't 19:4; Joh 2:10; 16:4; Ac 11:15
The b. of the word of the　Ho 1:2
Lord
these are the b. of sorrows　M't 24:8
since the b. of the world　　M't 24:21;
　　　　　　　　　　　　Isa 64:4
The b. of the gospel of Jesus　M'k 1:1
Christ
This b. of miracles did Jesus　Joh 2:11
B. from the baptism of John　Ac 1:22
who is the b., the firstborn　Col 1:18;
　　　　　　　　　　　　Re 3:14
if we hold the b. of our　　Heb 3:14
confidence
having neither b. of days, nor　Heb 7:3
end of
from the b. of the world　Heb 9:26
(P)
is worse with them than the　2Pe 2:20
b.
the b. and the ending　　Re 1:8;
　　　　　　　　21:6; 22:13

BEGINNINGS

and in the b. of your　　Nu 10:10
months
And in the b. of your　　Nu 28:11
months
better unto you than at　　Eze 36:11
your b.
these are the b. of sorrows　M'k 13:8
the elementary b. (B)　　Heb 5:12

BEGONE

B. Satan (S)　　M't 4:10

BEGOTTEN

days of Adam after he had b.　Ge 5:4
Seth
b. of thy father, she is thy　Le 18:11
sister
I b. them, that thou　　Nu 11:12
shouldest
The children that are b. of　De 23:8
them
and ten sons of his body b.　J'g 8:30
who hath b. the drops of　Job 38:28
dew
my son; this day have I b. thee　Ps 2:7
Who hath b. me these,　　Isa 49:21
seeing I
for they have b. strange　Ho 5:7
children
as of the only b. of the　Joh 1:14
Father
the only b. Son, which is　Joh 1:18
who only b. Son, that　　Joh 3:16
whosoever
name of the only b. Son of　Joh 3:18
God
my Son, this day have I b.　Ac 13:33
thee
I have b. you through the　1Co 4:15
gospel
whom I have b. in my bonds　Ph'm 10
my Son, this day have I b.　Heb 1:5
thee
my Son, to day have I b.　Heb 5:5
thee
offered up his only b. son　Heb 11:17
b. us again unto a lively hope　1Pe 1:3
God sent his only b. Son　1Jo 4:9
loveth him also that is b. of　1Jo 5:1
him
but he that is b. of God　1Jo 5:18
keepeth
first b. of the dead, and the　Re 1:5
prince

BEGUILE

lest any man should b. you　Col 2:4
with
Let no man b. you of your　Col 2:18
reward

BEGUILED

The serpent b. me, and I did　Ge 3:13
eat
wherefore then hast thou b.　Ge 29:25
me?
they have b. you in the　Nu 25:18
matter of
Wherefore have ye b. us,　Jos 9:22
saying
as the serpent b. Eve　　2Co 11:3
through his

BEGUILING

b. unstable souls: an heart　2Pe 2:14
they
teaching and b. (R)　　Re 2:20

BEGUN

from the Lord: the plague is　Nu 16:46
b.
plague was b. among the　Nu 16:47
people
I have b. to give Sihon　De 2:31
his
thou hast b. to shew thy servant　De 3:24
before whom thou hast b. to　Es 6:13
fall
undertook to do as they had　Es 9:23
b.
when he had b. to reckon,　M't 18:24
one was

that as he had *b.* so he would also   *2Co 8:6*

who have *b.* before, not only to do   *2Co 8:10*

having *b.* in the Spirit, are ye now   *Ga 3:3*

that he which hath *b.* a good   *Ph'p 1:6*

when they have *b.* to wax wanton   *1Ti 5:11*

BEHALF

on the *b.* of the children of Israel   *Ex 27:21*

messengers to David on his *b.*   *2Sa 3:12*

to shew himself strong in the *b.*   *2Ch 16:9*

I have yet to speak on God's *b.*   *Job 36:2*

on *b.* of (S)   *Isa 8:19*

but a prince for his own *b.* shall   *Da 11:18*

I am glad therefore on your *b.*   *Ro 16:19*

thank my God always on your *b.*   *1Co 1:4*

may be given by many on our *b.*   *2Co 1:11*

you occasion to glory on our *b.*   *2Co 5:12*

and of our boasting on your *b.*   *2Co 8:24*

you should be in vain in this *b.*   *2Co 9:3*

it is given in the *b.* of Christ   *Ph'p 1:29*

let him glorify God on this *b.*   *1Pe 4:16*

BEHAVE

lest their adversaries should *b.*   *De 32:27*

b. worse than fathers (B)(R)   *J'g 19:2*

and let us *b.* ourselves valiantly   *1Ch 19:13*

I will *b.* myself wisely in a perfect   *Ps 101:2*

the child shall *b.* himself proudly   *Isa 3:5*

Doth not *b.* itself unseemly   *1Co 13:5*

to *b.* thyself in the house of God   *1Ti 3:15*

BEHAVED

have *b.* wickedly (B)   *Ex 32:7*

BEHAVED

sent him, and *b.* himself wisely   *1Sa 18:5*

David *b.* himself wisely in all his   *1Sa 18:14*

saw that he *b.* himself very wisely   *1Sa 18:15*

David *b.* himself more wisely than   *1Sa 18:30*

I *b.* myself as though he had been   *Ps 35:14*

I have *b.* and quieted myself   *Ps 131:2*

as they have *b.* themselves ill   *Mic 3:4*

b. ourselves (S)   *1Co 1:12*

unblameably we *b.* ourselves   *1Th 2:10*

for we *b.* not ourselves disorderly   *2Th 3:7*

BEHAVETH

think that he *b.* himself uncomely   *1Co 7:36*

BEHAVIOUR

he changed his *b.* before them   *1Sa 21:13*

when he changed his *b.* before   *Ps 34 title*

choice *b.* (B)   *1Co 7:35*

vigilant, sober, of good *b.*   *1Ti 3:2*

that they be in *b.* as becometh   *Tit 2:3*

by his good *b.* (B)   *Jas 3:13*

holy in all *b.* (N)   *1Pe 1:15*

having *b.* seemly (E)(N)(S)   *1Pe 2:12*

b. of wives (E)(N)(P)(R)(S)   *1Pe 3:1*

chaste, respectful *b.* (B)(E)(N)(P)(R)   *1Pe 3:2*

revile your right *b.* (A)(P)(R)   *1Pe 3:16*

immoral *b.* of the lawless (B)   *2Pe 2:7*

holy *b.* (A)(B)   *2Pe 3:11*

BEHEADED

the heifer that is *b.* in the valley   *De 21:6*

and slew him, and *b.* him   *2Sa 4:7*

he sent, and *b.* John in the prison   *M't 14:10*

It is John, whom I *b.*   *M'k 6:16*

he went and *b.* him in the prison   *M'k 6:27*

Herod said, John have I *b.*   *Lu 9:9*

the souls of them that were *b.*   *Re 20:4*

BEHELD

the Egyptians *b.* the woman   *Ge 12:14*

when he *b.* the serpent of brass   *Nu 21:9*

He hath not *b.* iniquity in Jacob   *Nu 23:21*

the Lord *b.* and he repented him   *1Ch 21:15*

I *b.* but there was no man   *Ps 142:4; Isa 41:28*

And *b.* among the simple ones   *Pr 7:7*

Then I *b.* all the work of God   *Ec 8:17*

I *b.* the earth and it was without form and void   *Jer 4:23; 4:24-26*

I *b.*   *Da 7:4; 7:6, 9, 11, 21; Re 5:6, 11; 6:5, 12; 7:9; 8:13; 11:12; 13:11*

I *b.* Satan as lightning fall from heaven   *Lu 10:18*

b. the city and wept over it   *Lu 19:41*

we *b.* his glory, the glory as   *Joh 1:14*

while they *b.* he was taken to heaven   *Ac 1:9*

passed by, and *b.* your devotions   *Ac 17:23*

BEHEMOTH

Behold now *b.*, which I made   *Job 40:15*

BEHIND

heard in tent door *b.* him   *Ge 18:10*

look not *b.*, wife looked *b.*   *Ge 19:17; 19:26*

b. him a ram caught in the thicket   *Ge 22:13*

left *b.* (S)   *Ex 10:24*

not a hoof be left *b.*   *Ex 10:26*

lay ambush *b.* city   *Jos 8:2; 8:4, 14, 20*

looked *b.* him   *1Sa 24:8; 2Sa 1:7; 2:20*

hast cast me *b.* thy back   *1Ki 14:9; Ne 9:26; Ps 50:17; Eze 23:35*

close *b.* (S)   *Ps 63:8*

hast cast all my sins *b.* thy back   *Isa 38:17*

I heard *b.* me a voice   *Eze 3:12; Re 1:10*

came *b.* him and touched the hem   *M't 9:20; M'k 5:27; Lu 8:44*

Get *b.* me Satan   *M't 16:23; M'k 8:33; Lu 4:8*

Jesus tarried *b.* in Jerusalem   *Lu 2:43*

So that ye come *b.* in no gift   *1Co 1:7*

not a whit *b.* the chiefest   *2Co 11:5; 12:11*

forgetting those things which are *b.*   *Ph'p 3:13*

fill up what is *b.* of afflictions of   *Col 1:24*

beasts full of eyes before and *b.*   *Re 4:6*

BEHOLD

B. I have given you, *b.* very good   *Ge 1:29*

B. the man is become as one of us   *Ge 3:22*

he said, *B.* the fire and the wood   *Ge 22:7*

and *b.* behind him a ram caught in   *Ge 22:13*

B. Milcah, she hath also born   *Ge 22:20*

B., I stand here by the well   *Ge 24:13*

that, *b.*, Rebekah came out, who was   *Ge 24:15*

and. *b.*, he stood by the camels at   *Ge 24:30*

B., I stand by the well of water; and   *Ge 24:43*

b., Rebekah came forth with her   *Ge 24:45*

and, *b.*, Joseph was not in the pit   *Ge 37:29*

B., I have brought you this day   *Ge 47:23*

B., the people of the children of   *Ex 1:9*

the child: and, *b.*, the babe wept   *Ex 2:6*

b. the bush burned with fire   *Ex 3:2*

B., the hand of the Lord is upon thy   *Ex 9:3*

and, *b.*, they had done it as the Lord   *Ex 39:43*

b. if the plague   *Le 13:5; 13:6, 8, 10, 13, 17, 20-21, 25-26, 30-32, 34, 36, 39, 53-56; 14:3, 37, 39, 44, 48; Nu 16:47*

and, *b.*, if the rising of the sore be   *Le 13:43*

similitude of the Lord shall he *b.*   *Nu 12:8*

B., I have given thee the charge   *Nu 18:8*

B., there is a people come out from   *Nu 22:5*

b., they cover the face of the earth   *Nu 22:5*

b., thou hast altogether blessed   *Nu 24:10*

and, *b.*, it is a stiffnecked people   *De 9:13*

B. the heaven of heavens cannot   *De 10:14*

B., here I am: witness against me   *1Sa 12:3*

b., he set him up a place   *1Sa 15:12*

B., to obey is better than sacrifice   *1Sa 15:22*

B., David is at Naioth in Ramah   *1Sa 19:19*

and said, *B.*, I saw Absalom hanged   *2Sa 18:10*

B. a child shall be born to house of   *1Ki 13:2*

B. I was shapen in iniquity   *Ps 51:5; 51:6*

B. a virgin shall conceive   *Isa 7:14; M't 1:23*

B., I will deliver them into the hand   *Jer 29:21*

B., he shall come up like a lion   *Jer 49:19*

B., a people shall come from   *Jer 50:41*

and *b.* a shaking, and the bones   *Eze 37:7*

For, *b.*, in those days, and in that   *Joe 3:1*

For, *b.*, the Lord commandeth, and   *Am 6:11*

b. I send my messenger   *Mal 3:1; 4:5; M't 11:10*

b. my hands and my feet   *Lu 24:39*

b. I send the promise of my Father   *Lu 24:49*

b. the Lamb of God   *Joh 1:29; 1:36*

b. what manner of love the Father   *1Jo 3:1*

b. I stand at the door and knock   *Re 3:20*

b. I come as a thief   *Re 16:15; 22:7, 12*

BEHOLDEST

thou *b.* mischief and spite, to   *Ps 10:14*

why *b.* thou the mote that is in thy   *M't 7:3*

And why *b.* thou the mote that is   *Lu 6:41*

when thou thyself *b.* not the beam   *Lu 6:42*

BEHOLDETH

b. not the the way of the vineyards   *Job 24:18*

He *b.* all high things: he is   *Job 41:34*

heaven; he *b.* all the sons of men   *Ps 33:13*

For he *b.* himself, and goeth his   *Jas 1:24*

BEHOLDING

Turn away mine eyes from *b.*   *Ps 119:37*

every place, *b.* the evil and   *Pr 15:3*
the *b.* of them with their eyes *Ec 5:11*
women were there *b.* afar off *M't 27:55*
Jesus *b.* him loved him, and *M'k 10:21*
said
the people stood *b.* And the *Lu 23:35*
b. the things which were *Lu 23:48*
done
stood afar off *b.* these things *Lu 23:49*
b. the man which was healed *Ac 4:14*
b. the miracles and signs *Ac 8:13*
which
who stedfastly *b.* him and *Ac 14:9*
Paul, earnestly *b.* the council *Ac 23:1*
b. as in a glass the glory of *2Co 3:18*
joying and *b.* your order, and *Col 2:5*
like unto a man *b.* his *Jas 1:23*
natural

BEHOVED

thus it *b.* Christ to suffer *Lu 24:46*
in all things it *b.* him to be *Heb 2:17*
made

BEING

man became a living *b.* *Ge 2:7*
(A)(R)
I have pleasure, my lord *b.* *Ge 18:12*
old
the Lord *b.* merciful unto *Ge 19:16*
him
died, *b.* one hundred ten *Ge 50:26;*
years *Jos 24:29*
heart and entire *b.* (A) *De 10:12;*
               De 26:16; 30:2, 10
the vessels *b.* diverse one from *Es 1:7*
man *b.* in honor abideth not *Ps 49:12*
my inner *b.* (A) *Ps 71:23*
my whole *b.* (A) *Jer 32:41; Lam 3:24*
which *b.* brought forth into *Eze 47:8*
the sea
in danger of *b.* broken (S) *Jon 1:4*
Joseph her husband *b.* a just *M't 1:19*
man
no human *b.* endure *M't 24:22*
(A)(P)(R)
woman, *b.* a daughter of *Lu 13:16*
Abraham
b. seen of them forty days *Ac 1:3*
b. full of the Holy Ghost *Ac 7:55*
b. sent by the Holy Ghost *Ac 13:4*
But Paul, *b.* grieved, turned *Ac 16:18*
and said
after *b.* long without food *Ac 27:21*
(S)
no human *b.* justify himself *Ro 3:20*
(P)
B. justified freely by his *Ro 3:24;*
grace *5:1, 9*
bring to whole *b.* new (P) *Ro 8:11*
the complete *b.* of God (N) *Col 1:19;*
                  2:9
B. made so much better than *Heb 1:4*
b. born again, not of *1Pe 1:23*
corruptible seed
b. the firstfruits unto God *Re 14:4*
and to

BEKAH

A. *b.* for every man, that is *Ex 38:26*

BEL

B. boweth down. Nebo *Isa 46:1*
stoopeth
Babylon is taken. *B.* is *Jer 50:2*
confounded
I will punish *B.* in Babylon *Jer 51:44*

BELA

and the king of *B.* which is *Ge 14:2*
Zoar
the king of *B.* (the same is *Ge 14:8*
Zoar
And *B.* the son of Beor *Ge 36:32*
reigned in
And *B.* died, and Jobab the *Ge 36:33*
son of
of *B.* the family of the *Nu 26:38*
Belaites
sons of *B.* were Ard and *Nu 26:40*
Naaman
B. the son of Beor: and the *1Ch 1:43*
name
And when *B.* was dead, *1Ch 1:44*
Jobab the

And *B.* the son of Azaz, the *1Ch 5:8*
son of
sons of Benjamin; *B.* and *1Ch 7:6*
Becher
the sons of *B.*; Ezbon, and *1Ch 7:7*
Uzzi
Benjamin begat *B.* his *1Ch 8:1*
firstborn
sons of *B.* were, Addar, and *1Ch 8:3*
Gera

BELAH

sons of Benjamin were *B.* *Ge 46:21*

BELAITES

the family of the *B.* *Nu 26:38*

BELCH

they *b.* out with their mouth *Ps 59:7*

BELIAL

the children of *B.* are gone *De 13:13*
out
base fellows are gone *De 13:13*
(A)(E)(R)
wicked men have arisen (B) *De 13:13*
certain sons of *B.*, beset the *J'g 19:22*
house
certain worthless fellows *J'g 19:22*
(A)
certain perverted men (B) *J'g 19:22*
certain base fellows (E)(R) *J'g 19:22*
the children of *B.*, which are *J'g 20:13*
in
perverted fellows (B) *J'g 20:13*
the base fellows (E)(R) *J'g 20:13*
handmaid for a daughter of *1Sa 1:16*
B.
a wicked woman (A)(E) *1Sa 1:16*
your maid a *1Sa 1:16*
good-for-nothing (B)
a base woman (R) *1Sa 1:16*
the sons of Eli were sons of *1Sa 2:12*
B.
base men (A)(E) *1Sa 2:12*
worthless men (R)(S) *1Sa 2:12;*
         10:27; 25:17, 25
for he is such a son of *B.* *1Sa 25:17;*
                 25:25
such a wicked man (A) *1Sa 25:17*
men of *B.*, of those that *1Sa 30:22*
went
wicked men and base *1Sa 30:22*
fellows (A)(E)(R)
worthless characters (B) *1Sa 30:22*
come out, thou man of *B.* *2Sa 16:7*
base fellow (A)(E) *2Sa 16:7*
you worthless scoundrel (B) *2Sa 16:7*
worthless fellow (R) *2Sa 16:7*
there a man of *B.*, whose *2Sa 20:1*
name was
base and contemptible fellow *2Sa 20:1*
(A)
worthless fellow (B)(R) *2Sa 20:1*
base fellow (E) *2Sa 20:1*
the sons of *B.* shall be all of *2Sa 23:6*
wicked, godless, worthless *2Sa 23:6*
lives (A)
the worthless (B) *2Sa 23:6*
the ungodly (E) *2Sa 23:6*
the godless (R) *2Sa 23:6*
set two men, sons of *B.* *1Ki 21:10;*
before *21:13*
base fellows (A)(E)(R) *1Ki 21:10*
unprincipled men (B) *1Ki 21:10*
him vain men, the children *2Ch 13:7*
of *B.*
worthless men, base fellows *2Ch 13:7*
(A)(E)
good-for-nothing, *2Ch 13:7*
ne'er-do-wells (B)
worthless scoundrels (R) *2Ch 13:7*
what concord hath Christ *2Co 6:15*
with *B.*

BELIED

They have *b.* the Lord, and *Jer 5:12*
said
acted deceptively against *Jer 5:12*
Lord (B)
they have denied Jehovah *Jer 5:12*
(E)
spoken falsely of the Lord *Jer 5:12*
(R)

BELIEF

of the Spirit and *b.* of the *2Th 2:13*
truth

BELIEVE

they will not *b.* me, nor *Ex 4:1*
hearken
That they may *b.* that the *Ex 4:5*
Lord
if they will not *b.* thee, neither *Ex 4:8*
that they will *b.* the voice of *Ex 4:8*
if they will not *b.* also these *Ex 4:9*
two
with thee, and *b.* thee for *Ex 19:9*
ever
how long will it be ere they *Nu 14:11*
b. me
ye did not *b.* the Lord your *De 1:32*
God
that did not *b.* in the Lord *2Ki 17:14*
their
B. in the Lord your God, *2Ch 20:20*
so shall
b. his prophets, so shall ye *2Ch 20:20*
prosper
on this manner, *2Ch 32:15*
neither yet *b.* him
I not *b.* that he had *Job 9:16*
hearkened
Wilt thou *b.* him, that he *Job 39:12*
will
When he speaketh fair, *b.* *Pr 26:25*
him not
If ye will not *b.* surely ye *Isa 7:9*
shall not
that ye may know and *b.* *Isa 43:10*
me, and
b. them not, though they *Jer 12:6*
speak
ye will not *b.* though it be *Hab 1:5*
told
B. ye that I am able to do *M't 9:28*
this
little ones which *b.* in me, it *M't 18:6*
were
Why did ye not then *b.* him *M't 21:25*
afterwards, that ye might *b.* *M't 21:32*
him
here is Christ, or there, *b.* *M't 24:23*
it not
in the secret chambers; *b.* it *M't 24:26*
not
and we will *b.* him *M't 27:42*
repent ye, and *b.* the gospel *M'k 1:15*
Be not afraid, only *b.* *M'k 5:36*
If thou canst *b.* all things *M'k 9:23*
are
Lord, I *b.*; help thou mine *M'k 9:24*
little ones that *b.* in me *M'k 9:42*
but shall *b.* that those *M'k 11:23*
things which
b. that ye receive them, and *M'k 11:24*
ye
say, Why then did ye not *b.* *M'k 11:31*
him
or, lo, he is there; *b.* him *M'k 13:21*
not
that we may see and *b.* *M'k 15:32*
And they
signs shall follow them that *M'k 16:17*
b.
lest they should *b.* and be *Lu 8:12*
saved
which for a while *b.* and in *Lu 8:13*
time
b. only, and she shall be *Lu 8:50*
made
ye will not *b.* *Lu 22:67*
fools, and slow of heart to *Lu 24:25*
all men through him might *b.* *Joh 1:7*
even to them that *b.* on his *Joh 1:12*
name
and ye *b.* not *Joh 3:12*
how shall ye *b.* if I tell you *Joh 3:12*
of
Woman, *b.* me, the hour *Joh 4:21*
cometh
Now we *b.* not because of *Joh 4:42*
thy
signs and wonders, ye will *Joh 4:48*
not *b.*
whom he hath sent, him ye *Joh 5:38*
b. not
How can ye *b.* which receive *Joh 5:44*
But if ye *b.* not his writings *Joh 5:47*
how shall ye *b.* my words *Joh 5:47*

ye *b*. on him whom he hath sent	Joh 6:29	upon him, because he *b*. in his	Da 6:23
that we may see, and *b*. thee	Joh 6:30	So the people of Nineveh *b*. God	Jon 3:5
ye also have seen me, and *b*. not	Joh 6:36	and as thou hast *b*. so be it	M't 8:13
there are some of you that *b*. not	Joh 6:64	and ye *b*. him not: but the	M't 21:32
And we *b*. and are sure that thou	Joh 6:69	publicans and the harlots *b*. him	M't 21:32
neither did his brethren *b*. in him	Joh 7:5	and had been seen of her, *b*. not	M'k 16:11
which they that *b*. on him should	Joh 7:39	unto the residue: neither *b*. they	M'k 16:13
if ye *b*. not that I am he, ye shall	Joh 8:24	because they *b*. not them which	M'k 16:14
I tell you the truth, ye *b*. me not	Joh 8:45	things which are most surely *b*.	Lu 1:1
the truth, why do ye not *b*. me	Joh 8:46	blessed is she that *b*.: for there	Lu 1:45
the Jews did not *b*. concerning	Joh 9:18	say, Why then *b*. ye him not	Lu 20:5
Dost thou *b*. on the Son of God	Joh 9:35	idle tales, and they *b*. them not	Lu 24:11
he, Lord, that I might *b*. on him	Joh 9:36	while they yet *b*. not for joy	Lu 24:41
Lord, I *b*. And he worshipped	Joh 9:38	his disciples *b*. on him	Joh 2:11
But ye *b*. not, because ye are not	Joh 10:26	and they *b*. the scripture, and the	Joh 2:22
the works of my Father, *b*. me not	Joh 10:37	many *b*. in his name, when they	Joh 2:23
though ye *b*. not me	Joh 10:38	already, because he hath not	Joh 3:18
b. the works; that ye may know	Joh 10:38	of the Samaritans of that city *b*. on	Joh 4:39
and *b*. that the Father	Joh 10:38	many more *b*. because of his own	Joh 4:41
to the intent ye may *b*.; nevertheless	Joh 11:15	the man *b*. the word that Jesus had	Joh 4:50
I *b*. that thou art the Christ, the	Joh 11:27	himself. and his whole house	Joh 4:53
thou wouldest *b*. thou shouldest	Joh 11:40	had ye *b*. Moses	Joh 5:46
by I said it, that they may *b*. that	Joh 11:42	ye would have *b*. me	Joh 5:46
thus alone, all men will *b*. on him	Joh 11:48	who they were that *b*. not, and who	Joh 6:64
b. in the light, that ye may be	Joh 12:36	And many of the people *b*. on him	Joh 7:31
Therefore they could not *b*.	Joh 12:39	or of the Pharisees *b*. on him	Joh 7:48
man hear my words, and *b*. not	Joh 12:47	spake these words, many *b*. on	Joh 8:30
come to pass, ye may *b*. that I am he	Joh 13:19	to those Jews which *b*. on	Joh 8:31
ye *b*. in God, *b*. also in me	Joh 14:1	ye *b*. not: the works that I do	Joh 10:25
B. me that I am in the Father	Joh 14:11	And many *b*. on him there	Joh 10:42
else *b*. me for the very works' sake	Joh 14:11	things which Jesus did, *b*. on him	Joh 11:45
it is come to pass, ye might *b*.	Joh 14:29	of the Jews went away, and *b*. on	Joh 12:11
because they *b*. not on me	Joh 16:9	before them, yet they *b*. not on him	Joh 12:37
by this we *b*. that thou camest	Joh 16:30	Lord, who hath *b*. our report	Joh 12:38
answered them, Do ye now *b*.	Joh 16:31	chief rulers also many *b*. on him	Joh 12:42
for them also which shall *b*. on me	Joh 17:20	have *b*. that I came out from God	Joh 16:27
that the world may *b*. that thou	Joh 17:21	and they have *b*. that thou didst	Joh 17:8
he saith true, that ye might *b*.	Joh 19:35	the sepulchre, and he saw, and *b*.	Joh 20:8
my hand into his side, I will not *b*.	Joh 20:25	thou hast *b*.: blessed are they	Joh 20:29
might *b*. that Jesus is the Christ	Joh 20:31	have not seen, and yet have *b*.	Joh 20:29
I *b*. that Jesus Christ is the Son of	Ac 8:37	And all that *b*. were together	Ac 2:44
by him all that *b*. are justified	Ac 13:39	of them which heard the word *b*.	Ac 4:4
which ye shall in no wise *b*.	Ac 13:41	of them that *b*. were of one heart	Ac 4:32
hear the word of the gospel, and *b*.	Ac 15:7	But when they *b*. Philip preaching	Ac 8:12
But we *b*. that through the grace	Ac 15:11	Then Simon himself *b*. also	Ac 8:13
B. on the Lord Jesus Christ	Ac 16:31	and *b*. not that he was a disciple	Ac 9:26
that they should *b*. on him which	Ac 19:4	Joppa; and many *b*. in the Lord	Ac 9:42
of Jews there are which *b*.	Ac 21:20	they of the circumcision which *b*.	Ac 10:45
touching the Gentiles which *b*.	Ac 21:25	who *b*. on the Lord Jesus Christ	Ac 11:17
for I *b*. God, that it shall be even	Ac 27:25	a great number *b*. and turned	Ac 11:21
For what if some did not *b*.	Ro 3:3	when he saw what was done, *b*.	Ac 13:12
unto all and upon all them that *b*.	Ro 3:22	as were ordained to eternal life *b*.	Ac 13:48
be the father of all them that *b*.	Ro 4:11	Jews and also of the Greeks *b*.	Ac 14:1
if we *b*. on him that raised up	Ro 4:24	them to the Lord, on whom they *b*.	Ac 14:23
we *b*. that we shall also live with	Ro 6:8	of the Pharisees which *b*. saying	Ac 15:5
shalt *b*. in thine heart that God	Ro 10:9	which was a Jewess, and *b*.	Ac 16:1
not believed? and how shall they *b*.	Ro 10:14		
them that do not *b*. in Judæa	Ro 15:31		
preaching to save them that *b*.	1Co 1:21		
If any of them that *b*. not bid you	1Co 10:27		
and I partly *b*. it	1Co 11:18		
not to them that *b*.	1Co 14:22		
but to them that *b*. not	1Co 14:22		
serveth not for them that *b*. not	1Co 14:22		
but for them which *b*.	1Co 14:22		
minds of them which *b*. not	2Co 4:4		
spoken; we also *b*. and therefore	2Co 4:13		
might be given to them that *b*.	Ga 3:22		
to us-ward who *b*. according to	Eph 1:19		
not only to *b*. on him, but also to	Ph'p 1:29		
were ensamples to all that *b*.	1Th 1:7		
ourselves among you that *b*.	1Th 2:10		
worketh also in you that *b*.	1Th 2:13		
if we *b*. that Jesus died and rose	1Th 4:14		
be admired in all them that *b*.	2Th 1:10		
delusion, that they should *b*. a lie	2Th 2:11		
should hereafter *b*. on him to life	1Ti 1:16		
them which *b*. and know the truth	1Ti 4:3		
all men, specially of those that *b*.	1Ti 4:10		
If we *b*. not, yet he abideth	2Ti 2:13		
of them that *b*. to the saving	Heb 10:39		
must *b*. that he is, and that he is	Heb 11:6		
the devils also *b*. and tremble	Jas 2:19		
Who by him do *b*. in God, that	1Pe 1:21		
Unto you therefore which *b*. he is	1Pe 2:7		
That we should *b*. on the name of	1Jo 3:23		
Beloved, *b*. not every spirit, but	1Jo 4:1		
unto you that *b*. on the name of	1Jo 5:13		
ye may *b*. on the name of the Son	1Jo 5:13		

BELIEVED

And he *b*. in the Lord; and he	Ge 15:66		
Jacob's heart fainted, for he *b*.	Ge 45:26		
And the people *b*.: and when they	Ex 4:31		
and *b*. the Lord, and his servant	Ex 14:31		
Because ye *b*. me not, to sanctify	Nu 20:12		
and ye *b*. him not, nor hearkened	De 9:23		
And Achish *b*. David, saying, He	1Sa 27:12		
Howbeit I *b*. not the words, until	1Ki 10:7		
Howbeit I *b*. not their words, until	2Ch 9:6		
I laughed on them, they *b*. it not	Job 29:24		
unless I had *b*. to see the goodness	Ps 27:13		
Because they *b*. not in God	Ps 78:22		
b. not for his wondrous works	Ps 78:32		
Then *b*. they his words; they sang	Ps 106:12		
pleasant land they *b*. not his word	Ps 106:24		
I *b*. therefore have I spoken: I	Ps 116:10		
for I have *b*. thy commandments	Ps 119:66		
Who hath *b*. our report? and to	Isa 53:1		
the son of Ahikam, *b*. them not	Jer 40:14		
of the world, would not have *b*. that	La 4:12		

And some of them *b.* and   *Ac 17:4*
the Jews which *b.* not, moved *Ac 17:5*
Therefore many of them *b.*; *Ac 17:12*
also
certain men clave unto him, *Ac 17:34*
and *b.*
b. on the Lord with all his *Ac 18:8*
house
of the Corinthians hearing *b.* *Ac 18:8*
helped them much which *Ac 18:27*
had *b.*
received the Holy Ghost since *Ac 19:2*
ye *b.*
divers were hardened, and *b.* *Ac 19:9*
not
And many that *b.* came, and *Ac 19:18*
every synagogue them that *Ac 22:19*
b. on
the centurion *b.* the master *Ac 27:11*
And some *b.* the things *Ac 28:24*
which
were spoken, and some *b.* not *Ac 28:24*
Abraham *b.* God, and it was *Ro 4:3*
before him whom he *b.* even *Ro 4:17*
God
who against hope *b.* in hope *Ro 4:18*
on him in whom they have *Ro 10:14*
not *b.*
saith, Lord, who hath *b.* *Ro 10:16*
our report
ye in times past have not *b.* *Ro 11:30*
God
so have these also now not *b.* *Ro 11:31*
b.
salvation nearer than when *Ro 13:11*
we *b.*
ministers by whom ye *b.* even *1Co 3:5*
as
unless ye have *b.* in vain *1Co 15:2*
or they, so we preach, and *1Co 15:11*
so ye *b.*
I *b.* and therefore have I *2Co 4:13*
spoken
even we have *b.* in Jesus *Ga 2:16*
Christ
as Abraham *b.* God, and it *Ga 3:6*
was
in whom also after that ye *Eph 1:13*
b.
our testimony among you *2Th 1:10*
was *b.*
who *b.* not the truth, but *2Th 2:12*
had
b. on in the world, received *1Ti 3:16*
up into
I know whom I have *b.* and *2Ti 1:12*
am
that they which have *b.* in *Tit 3:8*
God
his rest, but to them that *b.* *Heb 3:18*
not
which have *b.* do enter into *Heb 4:3*
rest
he *b.* God to be *Heb 11:11*
trustworthy (P)
perished not with them *Heb 11:31*
that *b.*
Abraham *b.* God, and it was *Jas 2:23*
we have known and *b.* the *1Jo 4:16*
love
destroyed them that *b.* not *Jude 5*

BELIEVERS

And *b.* were the more added *Ac 5:14*
be thou an example of the *b.* *1Ti 4:12*
in

BELIEVEST

because thou *b.* not my words *Lu 1:20*
thee under the fig tree, *b.* *Joh 1:50*
thou
in me shall never die. *B.* *Joh 11:26*
thou
B. thou not that I am in *Joh 14:10*
If thou *b.* with all thine heart *Ac 8:37*
King Agrippa, *b.* thou the *Ac 26:27*
prophets
I know that thou *b.* *Ac 26:27*
Thou *b.* that there is one *Jas 2:19*
God

BELIEVETH

He *b.* not that he shall *Job 15:22*
return
neither *b.* he that it is the *Job 39:24*
sound
The simple *b.* every word *Pr 14:15*

he that *b.* shall not make *Isa 28:16*
haste
are possible to him that *b.* *M'k 9:23*
He that *b.* and is baptized *M'k 16:16*
shall
he that *b.* not shall be *M'k 16:16*
damned
whosoever *b.* in him *Joh 3:15;*
should *3:16*
He that *b.* on him is not *Joh 3:18*
but he that *b.* not is *Joh 3:18*
condemned
He that *b.* on the Son hath *Joh 3:36*
that *b.* not the Son shall not *Joh 3:36*
see
and *b.* on him that sent me *Joh 5:24*
he that *b.* on me shall never *Joh 6:35*
thirst
and *b.* on him, may have *Joh 6:40*
He that *b.* on me hath *Joh 6:47*
everlasting
He that *b.* on me, as the *Joh 7:38*
scripture
he that *b.* in me, though he *Joh 11:25*
were
and *b.* in me shall never die *Joh 11:26*
He that *b.* on me, *b.* not on *Joh 12:44*
me, but
that whosoever *b.* on me *Joh 12:46*
should not
He that *b.* on me, the *Joh 14:12*
works that I
whosoever *b.* in him shall *Ac 10:43*
receive
unto salvation to every one *Ro 1:16*
that *b.*
justifier of him which *b.* in *Ro 3:26*
but *b.* on him that justifieth *Ro 4:5*
whosoever *b.* on him shall *Ro 9:33*
not be
righteousness to every one *Ro 10:4*
that *b.*
For with the heart man *b.* *Ro 10:10*
unto
Whosoever *b.* on him shall *Ro 10:11*
not be
For one *b.* that he may eat *Ro 14:2*
all
hath a wife, that *b.* not, and *1Co 7:12*
she
hath an husband that *b.* not *1Co 7:13*
b. all things, hopeth all *1Co 13:7*
things
there come in one that *b.* *1Cor 14:24*
not, or
hath he that *b.* with an *2Co 6:15*
infidel
If any man or woman that *1Ti 5:16*
b.
and he that *b.* on him shall *1Pe 2:6*
not be
Whosoever *b.* that Jesus is the *1Jo 5:1*
he that *b.* that Jesus is the Son *1Jo 5:5*
He that *b.* on the Son of *1Jo 5:10*
God
he that *b.* not God hath *1Jo 5:10*
made
because he *b.* not the record *1Jo 5:10*

BELIEVING

ye shall ask in prayer, *b.* ye *M't 21:22*
shall
and be not faithless, but *b.* *Joh 20:27*
and that *b.* ye might have *Joh 20:31*
life
rejoiced, *b.* in God with all *Ac 16:34*
his
b. all things which are *Ac 24:14*
written
you with all joy and peace *Ro 15:13*
in *b.*
And they that have *b.* masters *1Ti 6:2*
yet *b.* ye rejoice with joy *1Pe 1:8*

BELL

b. and a pomegranate *Ex 28:34*
a golden *b.* *Ex 28:34*
A *b.* and a pomegranate, a *b* *Ex 39:26*

BELLIES

always liars, evil beasts, slow *Tit 1:12*
b.

BELLOW

as the heifer at grass, and *Jer 50:11*
b. as

BELLOWS

The *b.* are burned, the lead is *Jer 6:29*

BELLS

and *b.* of gold between them *Ex 28:33*
b. of pure gold, and put the *Ex 39:25*
b.
there be upon the *b.* of the *Zec 14:20*
horses

BELLY

upon thy *b.* shalt thou go *Ge 3:14*
goeth upon the *b.* and *Le 11:42*
whatsoever
thy thigh to rot, and thy *b.* *Nu 5:21*
to
to make thy *b.* to swell, and *Nu 5:22*
thy
her *b.* shall swell, and her *Nu 5:27*
thigh
and the woman through her *Nu 25:8*
b
thrust it into his *b.* *J'g 3:21*
not draw the dagger out of *J'g 3:22*
his *b.*
over against the *b.* which *1Ki 7:20*
was by
ghost when I came out of *Job 3:11*
the *b.*
when my mother bore me *Job 3:11*
(A)(E)
came forth from the womb *Job 3:11*
(B)(R)
fill his *b.* with the east wind *Job 15:2*
their *b.* prepareth deceit *Job 15:35*
God shall cast them out of *Job 20:15*
his *b.*
ejects them from his *Job 20:15*
stomach (B)
shall not feel quietness in *Job 20:20*
his *b.*
quietness within him *Job 20:20*
(A)(E)
no rest within him (B) *Job 20:20*
he is about to fill his *b.* *Job 20:23*
about to gorge himself (B) *Job 20:23*
my *b.* is as wine which hath *Job 32:19*
no vent
my breast is as wine (A) *Job 32:19*
whose *b.* thou fillest with thy *Ps 17:14*
hid treasure
whose stomach thou dost fill *Ps 17:14*
(B)
Thou art my God from my *Ps 22:10*
mother's *b.*
from my mother's womb *Ps 22:10*
(A)(E)
from my birth (B)(R) *Ps 22:10*
our *b.* cleaveth to the earth *Ps 44:25*
body cleaves to the ground *Ps 44:25*
(A)(B)(E)(R)
the *b.* of the wicked shall *Pr 13:25*
want
the stomach of the wicked *Pr 13:25*
(A)(B)
go into innermost parts of *Pr 18:8;*
the *b.* *26:22*
innermost parts of the body *Pr 18:8*
(A)(B)(E)(R)
man's *b.* shall be satisfied *Pr 18:20*
with fruit
A man's moral self shall (A) *Pr 18:20*
a man's stomach is filled (B) *Pr 18:20*
searching all inward parts of *Pr 20:27*
the *b.*
searching innermost parts *Pr 20:27*
(A)(B)(E)(R)
so do stripes the inward *Pr 20:30*
parts of *b.*
reach innermost parts *Pr 20:30*
(A)(B)(E)(R)
his *b.* is as bright ivory *Ca 5:14*
overlaid with
his body as bright ivory *Ca 5:14*
(A)(B)(E)(R)
thy *b.* is like an heap of wheat *Ca 7:2*
set
body like a round goblet *Ca 7:2*
(A)(E)
navel like a rounded bowl *Ca 7:2*
(B)(R)
which are born by me from *Isa 46:3*
the *b.*
borne me from your birth *Isa 46:3*
(A)(B)(E)(R)
before I formed thee in the *b.* *Jer 1:5*
I knew

formed thee in the womb | Jer 1:5
(A)(B)(R)
hath filled his *b.* with my | Jer 51:34
delicates
filled his stomach (B) | Jer 51:34
filled his maw with (E) | Jer 51:34
son of man, cause thy *b.* to | Eze 3:3
eat
fill your stomach with | Eze 3:3
(A)(B)(R)
fill thy bowels with (E) | Eze 3:3
his *b.* and his thighs of brass | Da 2:32
in *b.* of fish three days | Jon 1:17;
| M't 12:40
out of the *b.* of hell cried I | Jon 2:2
innermost part of Sheol (B) | Jon 2:2
when I heard my *b.* | Hab 3:16
trembled
my whole inner self | Hab 3:16
trembled (A)
my body trembles | Hab 3:16
(B)(E)(R)
b. of the great fish (S) | M't 12:40
enters mouth goes into *b.* | M't 15:17;
| M'k 7:19
passes into the abdomen | M't 15:17
(A)
passes into the stomach | M't 15:17
(B)(N)(P)(R)
fain have filled his *b.* with | Lu 15:16
husks
get his stomach filled (B) | Lu 15:16
longing to stuff himself (P) | Lu 15:16
out of *b.* flow rivers of living | Joh 7:38
water
from his innermost being | Joh 7:38
(A)(B)
from within him shall flow | Joh 7:38
(E)(N)
from his innermost heart | Joh 7:38
(P)
out of his heart shall flow | Joh 7:38
(R)
serve not Lord but their own | Ro 16:18
b.
serve own appetites | Ro 16:18
(A)(B)(N)(R)
are utterly self-centered (P) | Ro 16:18
meats for *b.* and *b.* for | 1Co 6:13
meats
meats for stomach | 1Co 6:13
(A)(B)(P)(R)
whose god is their *b.* | Ph'p 3:19
god is their stomach | Ph'p 3:19
(A)(B)
god is their appetite | Ph'p 3:19
(N)(P)
it shall make thy *b.* bitter | Re 10:9;
| 10:10
embitter your stomach | Re 10:9
(A)(B)(N)(R)

BELONG

Do not interpretations *b.* to | Ge 40:8
God
the possession of the land | Le 27:24
did *b.*
and over all things that *b.* to | Nu 1:50
it
The secret things *b.* unto the | De 29:29
Lord
things which are revealed *b.* | De 29:29
unto
shields of the earth *b.* unto | Ps 47:9
God
the Lord *b.* the issues from | Ps 68:20
death
preparations of heart *b.* to | Pr 16:1
man (S)
These things also *b.* to the | Pr 24:23
wise
To the Lord our God *b.* | Da 9:9
mercies
because ye *b.* to Christ, | M'k 9:41
verily I
things which *b.* unto thy | Lu 19:42
peace
careth for the things that *b.* | 1Co 7:32
to

BELONGED

b. to the children of Ephraim | Jos 17:8
the herdmen that *b.* to Saul | 1Sa 21:7
mighty men which *b.* to | 1Ki 1:8
David
which *b.* to the Philistines | 1Ki 15:27
which *b.* to the Philistines | 1Ki 16:15

and Hamath, which *b.* to | 2Ki 14:28
Judah
these *b.* to the sons of | 1Ch 2:23
Machir
Kirjath-jearim, which *b.* to | 1Ch 13:6
Judah
the burial which *b.* to the | 2Ch 26:23
kings
house which *b.* to king | Es 1:9
Ahasuerus
things as *b.* to her, and seven | Es 2:9
he *b.* unto Herod's | Lu 23:7
jurisdiction.

BELONGEST

unto him, To whom *b.* thou | 1Sa 30:13

BELONGETH

This is it that *b.* unto the | Nu 8:24
Levites
To me *b.* vengeance, and | De 32:35
by Gibeah, which *b.* to | J'g 19:14
Benjamin
into Gibeah that *b.* to | J'g 20:4
Benjamin
at Shochoh, which *b.* to | 1Sa 17:1
Judah
the coast which *b.* to | 1Sa 30:14
Judah, and
Zarephath, which *b.* to Zidon | 1Ki 17:9
Beer-sheba, which *b.* to | 1Ki 19:3
Judah
Beth-shemesh, which *b.* to | 2Ki 14:11
Judah
Beth-shemesh, which *b.* to | 2Ch 25:21
Judah
for this matter *b.* unto thee | Ezr 10:4
Salvation *b.* unto the Lord: thy | Ps 3:8
heard this; that power *b.* | Ps 62:11
unto God
unto thee, O Lord, *b.* mercy: | Ps 62:12
for thou
O Lord God, to whom | Ps 94:1
vengeance *b.*
O God, to whom | Ps 94:1
vengeance *b.* shew
O Lord, righteousness *b.* unto | Da 9:7
thee
O Lord, to us *b.* confusion of | Da 9:8
face
But strong meat *b.* to them | Heb 5:14
that
Vengeance *b.* unto me, I | Heb 10:30
will

BELONGING

service of the sanctuary *b.* | Nu 7:9
unto
on the side *b.* to Israel (S) | Jos 22:11
a part of the field *b.* unto | Ru 2:3
Boaz
of the Philistines *b.* to the | 1Sa 6:18
five lords
with strife *b.* not to him, is | Pr 26:17
like
desert place *b.* to the city | Lu 9:10
called

BELONGINGS

their *b.* (B) | Jos 7:11
prepare *b.* (A)(B) | Eze 12:3;
| Eze 12:4, 7; Lu 17:31
rob his *b.* (B) | M't 12:29
your *b.* (B) | Lu 6:30;
| Lu 11:21; 16:1; 19:8
his *b.* (N) | Lu 17:21
give all my *b.* (B) | Ac 13:3

BELOVED

wives, one *b.* and another | De 21:15
hated
The *b.* of the Lord shall | De 33:12
dwell in
were *b.* and lovely | 2Sa 1:23
(A)(B)(R)
was *b.* of his God, and God | Ne 13:26
made
That thy *b.* may be delivered | Ps 60:5;
| 108:6
so he giveth his *b.* sleep | Ps 127:2
only *b.* in the sight of his | Pr 4:3
mother
My *b.* | Ca 1:14;
| 1:16; 2:3, 8-10, 16-17; 4:16; 5:1-2,
4-6, 8-10, 16; 6:1-3; 7:9, 11, 13; 8:5, 14

to my wellbeloved a song of | Isa 5:1
my *b.*
man greatly *b.* | Da 9:23;
| 10:11, 19
This is my *b.* Son | M't 3:17;
M't 17:5; M'k 1:11; 9:7; Lu 3:22; 9:35;
| 2Pe 1:17
I will send them my *b.* son | Lu 20:13
beloved (used of Christians) | Ac 15:25;
Ro 1:7; 9:25; 11:28; 12:19; 16:8-9, 12;
1Co 4:14, 17; 10:14; 15:58; 2Co 7:1;
12:19; Eph 6:21; Ph'p 2:12; 4:1;
Col 3:12 4:7, 9, 14; 1Th 1:4;
2Th 2:13; 1Ti 6:2; 2Ti 1:2; Ph'm 1-2,
16; Heb 6:9; Jas 1:16, 19; 2:5; 1Pe 2:11;
4:12; 2Pe 3:1, 8, 14-15, 17; 1Jo 3:2,
21; 4:1, 7, 11; 3Jo 2, 5, 11; Jude 3,
| 17, 20
hath been accepted in the *b.* | Eph 1:6
b. children (E)(R) | Eph 5:1
b. servant (A)(E)(P)(R) | Col 1:7
his *b.* son (P)(R) | Col 1:13
of the saints and the *b.* city | Re 20:9

BELOVED'S

my *b.* and my beloved is mine | Ca 6:3
I am my *b.* and his desire is | Ca 7:10

BELSHAZZAR

B. the king made a great feast | Da 5:1
to
B. whiles he tasted the wine | Da 5:2
was king *B.* greatly troubled | Da 5:9
B. hast not humbled thine | Da 5:22
heart
B. and they clothed Daniel | Da 5:29
B. the king of the Chaldeans | Da 5:30
slain
B. king of Babylon Daniel had | Da 7:1
B. a vision appeared unto me | Da 8:1

BELT

and his *b.* (S) | 1Sa 18:4; 1Ki 2:5
just below the *b.* (B) | 2Sa 10:4
and a *b.* (S) | 2Sa 18:11;
2Sa 20:8; 1Ki 2:5; 2Ki 2:8; Jer 13:1
with a leather *b.* (S) | 2Ki 1:8;
| M't 3:4; M'k 1:6
I bought a *b.* (S) | Jer 13:2
take the *b.* and go (S) | Jer 13:4; 13:6
I took the *b.* and went (S) | Jer 13:7;
| 13:11
even as this *b.* (S) | Jer 13:10; Ac 21:11
the *b.* of truth | Eph 6:14
(A)(B)(N)(P)
buckle on the *b.* of truth | Eph 6:19
(N)(P)

BELTESHAZZAR

gave unto Daniel the name of | Da 1:7
B.
to Daniel, whose name was | Da 2:26
B.
in before me whose name was | Da 4:8
B.
O *B.* master of the magicians | De 4:9
B. declare the interpretation | Da 4:18
whose name was *B.* was | Da 4:19
astonied
and said, *B.* let not the | Da 4:19
dream
B. answered and said, My | Da 4:19
lord
Daniel, whom the king | Da 5:12
named *B.*
Daniel, whose name was | Da 10:1
called *B.*

BELTS

with *b.* upon their loins (S) | Eze 23:15

BEMOAN

to *b.* him (E) | Job 2:11
who shall *b.* for (E) | Isa 51:19
who shall *b.* thee? or who | Jer 15:5
shall go
neither go to lament nor *b.* | Jer 16:5
him
ye not for the dead, neither *b.* | Jer 22:10
him
All ye that are about him, *b.* | Jer 48:17
him
is laid waste: who will *b.* her | Na 3:7

BEMOANED

b. him 70 days (A)(B)   Ge 50:3
and they b. him, and   Job 42:11
comforted

BEMOANING

heard Ephraim b. himself   Jer 31:18
thus

BEMOANS

his soul b. himself (B)   Job 14:22

BEN

second degree, Zechariah,   1Ch 15:18
B. and

BENAIAH

And B. the son of Jehoiada   2Sa 8:18;
was   2Sa 20:23; 23:20
These things did B. the   2Sa 23:22
son of
B. the Pirathonite, Hiddai of   2Sa 23:30
priest, and B. the son of   1Ki 1:8;
Jehoiada   1:10, 26, 32, 36, 38, 44; 2:25,
           29-30, 34-35, 46
B. the son of Jehoiada was   1Ki 4:4
over
and Adiel, and Jesimiel, and   1Ch 4:36
B.
B. the son of Jehoiada, the   1Ch 11:22
son of
These things did B. the   1Ch 11:24
son of
of Benjamin, B. the   1Ch 11:31
Pirathonite
Eliab, and B. and Maaseiah   1Ch 15:18
and Eliab, and Maaseiah,   1Ch 15:20
and B.
Zechariah, and B. and   1Ch 15:24
Eliezer
and Eliab, and B. and   1Ch 16:5
Obed-edom
B. also and Jahaziel the   1Ch 16:6
priests
And B. the son of Jehoiada   1Ch 18:17
was
for the third month was B.   1Ch 27:5
the son
This is that B. who was   1Ch 27:6
mighty
month was B. the Pirathonite   1Ch 27:14
was Jehoiada the son of B.   1Ch 27:34
of Zechariah, the son of B.   2Ch 20:14
Mahath, and B. were   2Ch 31:13
overseers
Eleazar, and Malchijah, and   Ezr 10:25
B.
Chelal, B., Maaseiah,   Ezr 10:30
Mattaniah
B., Bedeiah, Chelluh   Ezr 10:35
Zebina, Jadau, and Joel, B.   Ezr 10:43
and Pelatiah the son of B.   Eze 11:1
that Pelatiah the son of B.   Eze 11:13
died

BEN-AMMI

bare a son, and called his   Ge 19:38
name B.

BENCH

sitting on the b. (P)   M't 27:19
in full view of the b. (N)   Ac 18:17

BENCHES

made thy b. of ivory,   Eze 27:6
brought out

BEND

the wicked b. their bow, they   Ps 11:2
b. their bows to shoot their   Ps 64:3
they b. their tongues like their   Jer 9:3
Lydians, that handle and b.   Jer 46:9
all ye that b. the bow   Jer 50:14
Babylon: all ye that b. the   Jer 50:29
bow
bendeth let the archer b. his   Jer 51:3
bow
vine did b. her roots toward   Eze 17:7
him

BENDETH

he b. his bow to shoot his   Ps 58:7
arrows
Against him that b. let the   Jer 51:3
archer

BENDING

b. their bodies (B)   Ge 43:28
thee shall come b. unto thee   Isa 60:14

BENEATH

and she was buried b. Beth-el   Ge 35:8
or that is in the earth b. or   Ex 20:4;
that   26:24; 27:5; 28:33; 32:19; 36:29;
            38:4
that is in the waters b. the   De 4:18
earth
upon the earth b.: there is   De 4:39
none
or that is in the earth b.   De 5:8
above only, thou shalt not   De 28:13
be b.
and for the deep that   De 33:13
coucheth b.
in heaven above, and in   Jos 2:11
earth b.
the host of Midian was b. him   J'g 7:8
which is by Zartanah b.   1Ki 4:12
Jezreel
and b. the lions and oxen   1Ki 7:29
were
in heaven above, or on earth   1Ki 8:23
b.
sackcloth b. upon his flesh (S)   2Ki 6:30
His roots shall be dried up   Job 18:16
b. and
that he may depart from hell   Pr 15:24
b.
Hell from b. is moved for   Isa 14:9
thee to
and look upon the earth b.   Isa 51:6
of the earth searched out b.   Jer 31:37
from above, and his roots   Am 2:9
from b.
And as Peter was b. in the   M'k 14:66
palace
Ye are from b.; I am from   Joh 8:23
above
and signs in the earth b.;   Ac 2:19
blood

BENE-BERAK

Jehud, and B. and   Jos 19:45
Gath-rimmon

BENEFACTORS

authority upon them are   Lu 22:25
called b.

BENEFICIAL

b. to spiritual progress (A)   Eph 4:29

BENEFICIENT

b. and gracious contribution   2Co 8:6
(A)

BENEFIT

cannot b. (B)   1Sa 12:2
according to the b. done   2Ch 32:25
unto
wherewith I said I would b.   Jer 18:10
them
what will it b. (B)   Lu 9:25
what b. did you get (A)(B)   Ro 6:1
that ye might have a second   2Co 1:15
b.
double favor and token of   2Co 1:15
grace (A)
enjoy a double blessing (B)   2Co 1:15
give you a double treat (P)   2Co 1:15
might have a double   2Co 1:15
pleasure (R)
and beloved, partakers of the   1Ti 6:2
b.
that thy b. should not be as it   Ph'm 14
your benevolence might not   Ph'm 14
seem (A)
your kind action may not   Ph'm 14
(B)
your goodness should not   Ph'm 14
(E)(R)

your kindness may be a matter   Ph'm 14
(N)
have a favor to give me (P)   Ph'm 14

BENEFITS

who daily loadeth us with b.   Ps 68:19
bears burdens and carries us   Ps 68:19
(A)(B)
beareth our burden (E)   Ps 68:19
daily bears us up (R)   Ps 68:19
and forget not all his b.   Ps 103:2
Lord for all his b. toward   Ps 116:12
me
for all his founties (B)(R)   Ps 116:12

BENE-JAAKAN

from Moseroth, and pitched   Nu 33:31
in B.
removed from B. and   Nu 33:32
encamped

BENEVOLENCE

practice b. (B)   Lu 12:33
practiced liberal b. (B)   Ac 10:2
render unto the wife due b.   1Co 7:3
your b. might (A)   Ph'm 14

BENEVOLENCES

b. and contributions (B)   Heb 13:16

BENEVOLENT

b. service I have (B)   Ne 13:14

BEN-HADAD

and king Asa sent them to B.   1Ki 15:18
so B. hearkened   1Ki 15:20
unto king Asa
B. the king of Syria   1Ki 20:1;
20:2, 5, 9-10, 12, 16-17, 20, 26, 30, 32-34
after this, that B. king of   2Ki 6:24
Syria
and B. the king of Syria was   2Ki 8:7
sick
and said, Thy son B. king of   2Ki 8:9
Syria
the hand of B. the son   2Ki 13:3
of Hazael
and B. his son reigned in   2Ki 13:24
his stead
of the hand of B. the son   2Ki 13:25
of Hazael
and sent to B. king of Syria,   2Ch 16:2
that
And B. hearkened unto king   2Ch 16:4
Asa
shall consume the palaces of   Jer 49:27
B.
shall devour the palaces of B.   Am 1:4

BEN-HAIL

sent to his princes, even to   2Ch 17:7
B.

BEN-HANAN

Amnon, and Rinnah, B., and   1Ch 4:20

BENINU

Hodijah, Bani, B.   Ne 10:13

BENJAMIN

but his father called him B.   Ge 35:18
the sons of Rachel, Joseph   Ge 35:24;
and B.   46:19
Joseph is not, and ye will   Ge 42:36
take B. also
he may send away your   Ge 43:14
brother and B.
when Joseph saw B. with them   Ge 43:16
sons of B.   Ge 46:21;
Nu 26:38, 41; 1Ch 7:6; 8:1, 40; 9:7;
           Ne 11:7
B. shall ravin as a wolf   Ge 49:27
the prince of B. was Abidan   Nu 1:11
these stand to bless Joseph,   De 27:12
B.
of B. Moses said, beloved of   De 33:12
Lord
after thee, B. among thy   J'g 5:14
people
were by Gibeah, which   J'g 19:14
belongs to B.

men of Israel went to battle *J'g 20:20*
against *B.*
the Lord smote *B.* before *J'g 20:35*
Israel
all that fell that day of *B.* *J'g 20:46*
were 25,000 men
not any of us give his *J'g 21:1;*
daughter to *B.* *21:18*
seeing the women are *J'g 21:16*
destroyed out of *B.*
ran a man of *B.* out of the *1Sa 4:12*
army
a man of *B.* whose name was *1Sa 9:1*
Kish
by Rachel's sepulchre, in the *1Sa 10:2*
border of *B.*
in Gibeah of *B.* *1Sa 13:2; 14:16; 15:16*
there arose by number twelve *2Sa 2:15*
of *B.*
Abner also spake in the *2Sa 3:19*
ears of *B.*
were a thousand men of *B.* *2Sa 19:17*
with him
the bones of Saul buried *2Sa 21:14*
they in *B.*
Shimei son of Elah officer in *1Ki 4:18*
B.
sons of Bilhan, Jeush and *B.* *1Ch 7:10*
Levi and *B.* counted he not *1Ch 21:6*
among them
over *B.* was Jaasiel son of *1Ch 27:21*
Abner
of *B.* Eliada a mighty man *2Ch 17:17*
caused all in Jerusalem and *2Ch 34:32*
B. to stand
after him repaired *B.* and *Ne 3:23*
Hashub
there is little *B.* with their *Ps 68:27*
ruler
before *B.* and Manasseh, stir *Ps 80:2*
up
when Jeremiah was in gate *Jer 37:13*
of *B.*
king then sitting in the gate *Jer 38:7*
of *B.*
B. have a portion *Eze 48:23*
cry aloud at Beth-aven O *B.* *Ho 5:8*
B. shall possess Gilead *Ob 19*

BENJAMIN with *JUDAH*

Ammon passed to fight *Judah* *J'g 10:9*
and *B.*
speak to house of *Judah* and *1Ki 12:23;*
B. *2Ch 11:3*
came of *B.* and *Judah* to *1Ch 12:16*
David
Rehoboam having *Judah* *2Ch 11:12*
and *B.*
hear ye me all *Judah* and *B.* *2Ch 15:2*
put away idols out of *Judah* *2Ch 15:8*
and *B.*
made captains thro' *Judah* *2Ch 25:5*
and *B.*
threw down altars of *Judah* *2Ch 31:1*
and *B.*
money gathered of *Judah* *2Ch 34:9*
and *B.*
rose up chief fathers of *Judah* *Ezr 1:5*
and *B.*
adversaries of *Judah* and *B.* *Ezr 4:1*
heard
at Jerusalem dwelt of *Judah* *Ne 11:4*
and *B.*
after them went *Judah*, *B.* *Ne 12:34*
between border of *Judah* *Eze 48:22*
and *B.*

LAND OF *BENJAMIN*

take wife go into the *land* *J'g 21:21*
of *B.*
send a man out of the *land* *1Sa 9:16*
of *B.*
put away idols out of the *2Ch 15:8*
land of B.
come from *land of B.* *Jer 17:26*
bringing
shall take witnesses in *land* *Jer 32:44*
of *B.*
in the *land of B.* shall flocks *Jer 33:13*
pass again
Jeremiah went to go into *Jer 37:12*
the *land of B.*

TRIBE OF BENJAMIN

of *tribe of B.* numbered *Nu 1:37*
35,400

captain of *tribe of B.* *Nu 2:22;*
Abidan *10:24*
of *tribe of B.* to spy the *Nu 13:9*
land, Palti
of the *tribe of B.* to divide, *Nu 34:21*
Eliad
the lot of the *tribe of B.* *Jos 18:11*
came up
the cities of the *tribe of B.* *Jos 18:21*
were Jericho
cities to the Levites out of *Jos 21:4;*
the tribe of Judah and *1Ch 6:60, 65*
the *tribe of B.*
Israel sent men thro' *tribe* *J'g 20:12*
of *B.*
am least of families of *tribe* *1Sa 9:21*
of *B.*
tribes come near, *tribe of* *1Sa 10:20*
B. was taken
Saul a man of the *tribe of* *Ac 13:21*
I am the *tribe of B.* *Ro 11:1;*
sealed 12,000 *Ph'p 3:5*

BENJAMIN'S

but *B.* mess was five times *Ge 43:34*
so
the cup was found in *B.* *Ge 44:12*
sack
he fell upon his brother *B.* *Ge 45:14*
neck
inhabited in her place, from *Zec 14:10*
B.

BENJAMITE

Ehud the son of Gera, a *B.* a *J'g 3:15*
man
the son of Aphiah, a *B.* a *1Sa 9:1*
mighty
Am not I a *B.* of the *1Sa 9:21*
smallest of
much more now may this *2Sa 16:11*
B. do it
Shimei the son of Gera, a *B.* *2Sa 19:16*
Sheba, the son of Bichri, a *2Sa 20:1*
B.
the son of Gera, a *B.* of *1Ki 2:8*
Bahurim
Shimei, the son of Kish, a *B.* *Es 2:5*
the words of Cush the *B.* *Ps 7 title*

BENJAMITES

but the men of the place *J'g 19:16*
were *B.*
Israel destroyed of the *B.* *J'g 20:35*
that
Israel gave place to the *B.* *J'g 20:36*
pillars of smoke, the *B.* *J'g 20:40*
looked
thus they inclosed the *B.* *J'g 20:43*
round
passed through the land of *1Sa 9:4*
the *B.*
Hear now, ye *B.*; will the *1Sa 22:7*
son of
Abiezer the Anetothite, of *1Ch 27:12*
the *B.*

BENO

Mushi: the sons of *1Ch 24:26*
Jaaziah; *B.*
B. and Shoham, and *1Ch 24:27*
Zaccur, and

BEN-ONI

she called his name *B.*: but *Ge 35:18*
his

BENT

he hath *b.* his bow, and made *Ps 7:12*
it
and have *b.* their bow, to *Ps 37:14*
cast
b. over and heard my cry (B) *Ps 40:1*
all their bows *b.* their horses *Isa 5:28*
drawn sword, and from the *Isa 21:15*
b. bow
He hath *b.* his bow like an *La 2:4*
enemy
He hath *b.* his bow, and set *La 3:12*
me as

my people are *b.* to *Ho 11:7*
backsliding
When I have *b.* Judah for *Zec 9:13*
me
b. on perverted sensuality (B) *Jude 9*

BENUMBED

I am *b.* (B) *Ps 38:8*

BEN-ZOHETH

sons of Ishi were, Zoheth, *1Ch 4:20*
and *B.*

BEON

and Shebam, and Nebo, and *Nu 32:3*
B.

BEOR

And Bela the son of *B.* *Ge 36:32*
reigned in
Balaam the son of *B.* *Nu 22:5*
to Pethor
Balaam the son of *B.* hath *Nu 24:3*
said
the son of *B.* hath said, *Nu 24:15*
and
Balaam also the son of *B.* *Nu 31:8*
they
against thee Balaam the son *De 23:4*
of *B.*
Balaam also the son of *B.* *Jos 13:22*
called Balaam the son of *B.* *Jos 24:9*
to
Bela the son of *B.*: and the *1Ch 1:43*
name
Balaam the son of *B.* *Mic 6:5*
answered

BERA

these made war with *B.* king *Ge 14:2*
of

BERACHAH

Azmaveth; and *B.* and Jehu *1Ch 12:3*
themselves in the valley of *2Ch 20:26*
B.

BERACHIAH

even Asaph the son of *B.* *1Ch 6:39*
the son

BERAIAH

Adaiah, and *B.* and *1Ch 8:21*
Shimrath

BEREA

Paul and Silas by night unto *Ac 17:10*
B.
was preached of Paul at *B.*, *Ac 17:13*
they
him into Asia Sopater of *B.* *Ac 20:4*

BEREAVE

I labour and *b.* my soul of *Ec 4:8*
good
I will *b.* them of children, I *Jer 15:7*
will
beasts, and they shall *b.* thee *Eze 5:17*
no more henceforth *b.* them *Eze 36:12*
of
neither *b.* thy nations any *Eze 36:14*
yet will I *b.* them, that there *Ho 9:12*
shall

BEREAVED

Me have ye *b.* of my children *Ge 42:36*
I be *b.* of my children, I am *b.* *Ge 43:14*
wives be *b.* of their children *Jer 18:21*
up men, and hast *b.* thy *Eze 36:13*
nations
as a bear that is *b.* of her *Ho 13:8*
whelps

BEREAVEMENT

to my personal *b.* *Ps 55:12*
(A)(B)(E)

BEREAVETH

abroad the sword b. at home | La 1:20

BERECHIAH

and Ohel, and B. and | 1Ch 3:20
Hasadiah
B. the son of Asa, the son | 1Ch 9:16
of
his brethren, Asaph the son | 1Ch 15:17
of B.
B. and Elkanah were | 1Ch 15:23
doorkeepers
B. the son of Meshillemoth | 2Ch 28:12
Meshullam the son of B. the | Ne 3:4
son
son of B. over against his | Ne 3:30
chamber
of Meshullam the son of B. | Ne 6:18
the son of B. the son of Iddo | Zec 1:1;
| 1:7

BERED

it is between Kadesh and B. | Ge 16:14
Shuthelah, and B. his son | 1Ch 7:20

BEREFT

was b. of her sons (S) | Ru 1:5
b. of truth (A)(E)(N) | 1Ti 6:5

BERI

Shual, and B. and Imrah | 1Ch 7:36

BERIAH

and B. and Serah their sister | Ge 46:17
Jesuites: of B. the family of | Nu 26:44
Of the sons of B.: of Heber | Nu 26:45
he called his name B. | 1Ch 7:23
because it
and B. and Serah their sister | 1Ch 7:30
sons of B.; Heber, and | 1Ch 7:31
Malchiel
B. also, and Shema, who | 1Ch 8:13
were
Ispah, and Joha, the sons of | 1Ch 8:16
B.
Jahath, Zina, and Jeush, | 1Ch 23:10
and B.
Jeush and B. had not many | 1Ch 23:11
sons

BERIITES

of Beriah, the family of the | Nu 26:44
B.

BERITES

to Beth-maachah, and all | 2Sa 20:14
the B.

BERITH

hold of the house of the god | J'g 9:46
B.

BERNICE

and B. came unto Cæsarea | Ac 25:13
to
come, and B. with great | Ac 25:23
pomp
B. and they that sat with | Ac 26:30
them

BERODACH-BALADAN

At that time B. the son of | 2Ki 20:12

BEROTHAH

Hamath, B., Sibraim | Eze 47:16

BEROTHAI

and from B. cities of | 2Sa 8:8
Hadadezer

BEROTHITE

Naharai the B. the | 1Ch 11:39
armourbearer

BERRIES

two or three b. in the top of | Isa 17:6
tree, my brethren, bear | Jas 3:12
olive b.

BERYL

the fourth row a b. and an | Ex 28:20
onyx
a b., an onyx, and a jasper: | Ex 39:13
they
are as gold rings set with the | Ca 5:14
b.
was like unto the colour of a | Eze 1:16
b.
was as the colour of a b. stone | Eze 10:9
topaz, and the diamond, the | Eze 28:13
b.
His body also was like the b. | Da 10:6
seventh, chrysolyte; the | Re 21:20
eighth, b.

BESAI

of Paseah, the children of B. | Ezr 2:49
of B. the children of Meunim | Ne 7:52

BESEECH

I b. thee (used in prayer | Ex 33:18;
to God) Nu 12:13; 14:17, 19; 2Sa 24:10;
2Ki 19:19; 20:3; 1Ch 21:8; 2Ch 6:40;
Ne 1:5, 8, 11; Job 10:9; 42:4; Ps 80:14;
116:4; 118:25; 119:108; Isa 38:3; 64:9;
Da 9:16; Am 7:2, 5; Jon 1:14; 4:3
I b. thee (used of man to man) Nu 2:11;
1Sa 23:11; 2Sa 13:24; 16:4; Jer 38:20;
Da 1:12
I b. thee (used in prayer to | Lu 8:28;
Christ) | 9:38
I b. thee (used in addressing Ac 21:39;
man) | 26:3
I. b. thee (S) | Ac 24:4; 27:34
I b. thee (used in exhortations Ro 12:1;
to Christians) | 15:30; 16:17;
1Co 1:10; 4:16; 16:15; 2Co 2:8; 6:1;
10:1-2; Ga 4:12; Eph 4:1; Ph'p 4:2;
1Th 4:1, 10; 5:12; 2Th 2:1; Ph'm 9-10;
Heb 13:19, 22; 1Pe 2:11; 2Jo 5

BESEECHING

unto him a centurion, b. him | M't 8:5
there came a leper to him, | M'k 1:40
b. him
b. him that he would come | Lu 7:3
b. him (S) | Ac 16:9;
| 19:31; 2Co 8:4

BESET

Belial, b. the house round | J'g 19:22
about
and b. the house round about | J'g 20:5
of Bashan have b. me round | Ps 22:12
hast b. me behind and before | Ps 139:5
own doings have b. them | Ho 7:2
about
the sin which doth so easily | Heb 12:1
b. us

BESIDE

b. the first famine that was | Ge 26:1
b. the bottom of the altar | Ex 29:12
Le 1:16; 6:10; 10:12; Jos 22:19; 2Ki 12:9
b. the sabbaths, b. gifts, | Le 23:38
b. vows
b. the continual burnt | Nu 28:10
offering; 28:15, 23-24, 31; 29:6, 11;
| 34:38-39
God; there is none else b. | De 4:35
him; 2Sa 7:22; 1Ch 17:20; Isa 43:11;
44:6, 8; 45:5-6, 21; 47:8-10; Ho 13:4
b. the covenant he made in | De 29:1
Horeb
leadeth me b. the still waters | Ps 23:2
Blessed are ye that sow b. | Isa 32:20
all waters
beside (S) | Eze 1:20;
| 1:21; 3:13; 48:13
He is b. himself | M'k 3:21
| Ac 26:24; 2Co 5:13
b. all this, between us and | Lu 16:26
you
b. those things that are | 2Co 11:28
without
And b. all this, giving all | 2Pe 1:5
diligence

BESIDES

Lot, Hast thou here any b. | Ge 19:12
b. Jacob's sons' wives, all | Ge 46:26

B. the cakes, he shall offer | Le 7:13
for
not here a prophet of the | 1Ki 22:7
Lord b.
here a prophet of the Lord | 2Ch 18:6
b.
and there were added b. | Jer 36:32
unto
b. I know not whether I | 1Co 1:16
And b. they learn to be idle | 1Ti 5:13
(S)
unto me even thine own self | Ph'm 19
b.

BESIEGE

thee, then thou shalt b. it | De 20:12
When thou shalt b. a city a | De 20:19
long
And he shall b. thee in all thy | De 28:52
b. thee in all thy gates | De 28:52
to b. David and his men | 1Sa 23:8
if their enemy b. them in the | 1Ki 8:37
city, and his servants did b. | 2Ki 24:11
if their enemies b. them in | 2Ch 6:28
Go up, O Elam: b. O Media | Isa 21:2
the Chaldeans, which b. you | Jer 21:4
to the Chaldeans that b. you | Jer 21:9

BESIEGED

of Ammon, and b. Rabbah | 2Sa 11:1
And they came and b. | 2Sa 20:15
with him, and they b. | 1Ki 16:17
Tirzah
and he went up and b. | 1Ki 20:1
Samaria
and went up, and b. Samaria | 2Ki 6:24
and, behold, they b. it, until | 2Ki 6:25
they b. Ahaz, but could not | 2Ki 16:5
Samaria, and b. it three | 2Ki 17:5
years
came up against Samaria, | 2Ki 18:9
and b.
up all the rivers of b. | 2Ki 19:24
places
and the city was b. | 2Ki 24:10
And the city was b. unto the | 2Ki 25:2
and came and b. Rabbah | 1Ch 20:1
of cucumbers, as a b. city | Ec 9:14
all the rivers of the b. | Isa 1:8
places
the king of Babylon's army b. | Isa 37:25
the Chaldeans that b. | Jer 32:2
Jerusalem | Jer 37:5
against Jerusalem, and they b. | Jer 39:1
it
city was b. unto the eleventh | Jer 52:5
it shall be b. and thou shalt | Eze 4:3
he that remaineth and is b. | Eze 6:12
shall
unto Jerusalem, and it b. | Da 1:1

BESIEGERS

that b. come (A)(B)(R) | Jer 4:16

BESMEAR

b. me with lies (R) | Ps 119:69

BESODEIAH

and Meshullam the son of B. | Ne 3:6

BESOM

it with the b. of destruction | Isa 14:23

BESOR

and came to the brook B. | 1Sa 30:9
could not go over the brook | 1Sa 30:10
B.
also to abide at the brook | 1Sa 30:21
B.

BESOUGHT

when he b. us, we would not | Ge 42:21
Moses b. the Lord | Ex 32:11;
| De 3:23
David b. God for the child | 2Sa 12:16
the man of God b. the Lord | 1Ki 13:6
cantain b. Elijah | 2Ki 1:13
Jehoahaz b. Lord, Lord | 2Ki 13:4
hearkened

BESOUGHT

Manasseh *b.* the Lord his God *2Ch 33:12*
Ezra *b.* our God for this *Ez 8:23*
Esther *b.* him with tears to put away *Es 8:3*
Hezekiah *b.* the Lord *Jer 26:19*
devils *b.* him, *M't 8:31; M'k 5:12; Lu 8:31-32*
disciples *b.* him, Send her away *M't 15:23*
leper *b.* Jesus *Lu 5:12*
b. him to eat (S) *Joh 4:31; Ac 8:31; 2Co 8:6*
Gentiles *b.* that these words be *Ac 13:42*
she *b.* us saying, If ye have judged me *Ac 16:15*
b. him not to go to Jerusalem *Ac 21:12*
I *b.* the Lord thrice *2Co 12:8*

BESOUGHTEST

because you *b.* me (S) *M't 18:32*

BEST

take *b.* fruits of the land *Ge 43:11; 47:6*
in the *b.* of the land dwell *Ge 47:11*
of the *b.* of his own field *Ex 22:5*
the *b.* spices (A) *Ex 30:23*
all the *b.* of the oil, wine *Nu 18:12; 18:29-32*
let them marry to whom think *b.* *Nu 36:6*
dwell where it likes him *b.* *De 23:16*
king *b.* of your oliveyards *1Sa 8:14*
spared *b.* of sheep *1Sa 15:9; 15:15*
the *b.* that were doomed (B)(R) *1Sa 15:21*
What seemeth you *b.* I will do *2Sa 8:14*
man at *b.* state is altogether vanity *Ps 39:5*
the *b.* (S) *Eze 27:22*
the *b.* seats (A)(R) *M't 23:26*
Bring forth the *b.* robe, and put *Lu 15:22*
but covet earnestly the *b.* gifts *1Co 12:31*

BESTEAD

shall pass through it, hardly *b.* *Isa 8:21*

BESTIR

then thou shalt *b.* thyself: for *2Sa 5:24*

BESTOW

he may *b.* upon you a blessing *Ex 32:29*
And thou shalt *b.* that money for *De 14:26*
of the Lord they *b.* upon *2Ch 24:7*
thou shalt have occasion to *b.* *Ezr 7:20*
b. it out of the king's treasure *Ezr 7:20*
I have no more room where to *b.* *Lu 12:17*
there will I *b.* all my fruits and my *Lu 12:18*
upon these we *b.* more abundant *1Co 12:23*
And though I *b.* all my goods *1Co 13:3*

BESTOWED

horsemen, whom he *b.* in the *1Ki 10:26*
their hand, and *b.* them in the *2Ki 5:24*
the money to be *b.* on workmen *2Ki 12:15*
b. upon him such royal majesty *1Ch 29:25*
whom he *b.* in the chariot cities *2Ch 9:25*
b. upon Mordecai (S) *Es 6:3*
to all that the Lord hath *b.* on us *Isa 63:7*
he hath *b.* on them according *Isa 63:7*
whereon ye *b.* no labour: other *Joh 4:38*
Mary, who *b.* much labour on us *Ro 16:6*
his grace which was *b.* upon me *1Co 15:10*
that for the gift *b.* upon us by *2Co 1:11*
grace of God *b.* on the churches *2Co 8:1*
lest I have *b.* upon you labour in *Ga 4:11*
of love the Father hath *b.* on us *1Jo 3:1*

BETAH

And from *B.* and from Berothai *2Sa 8:8*

BETEN

and Hali, and *B.* and Achshaph *Jos 19:25*

BETHABARA

These things were done in *B.* *Joh 1:28*

BETH-ANATH

Harem, and *B.* and *Jos 19:38*
nor the inhabitants of *B.*; but he *J'g 1:33*
Beth-shemesh, and of *B.* became *J'g 1:33*

BETH-ANOTH

Maarath, and *B.* and Eltekon *Jos 15:59*

BETHANY

and went out of the city into *B.* *M't 21:17*
Now when Jesus was in *B.* in *M't 26:6*
unto Bethphage and *B.* at the *M'k 11:1*
he went out unto *B.* with the *M'k 11:11*
when they were come from *B.* he *M'k 11:12*
And being in *B.* in the house *M'k 14:3*
come nigh to Bethphage and *B.* *Lu 19:29*
he led them out as far as to *B.* *Lu 24:50*
named Lazarus, of *B.* the town *Joh 11:1*
Now *B.* was nigh unto Jerusalem *Joh 11:18*
before the passover came to *B.* *Joh 12:1*

BETH-ARABAH

passed along by the north of *B.* *Jos 15:6*
In the wilderness, *B.*, Middin *Jos 15:61*
B. and Zemaraim, and Beth-el *Jos 18:22*

BETH-ARAM

And in the valley, *B.* and *Jos 13:27*

BETH-ARBEL

Shalman spoiled *B.* in the day *Ho 10:14*

BETH-AVEN

to Ai, which is beside *B.* on the *Jos 7:2*
were at the wilderness of *B.* *Jos 18:12*
in Michmash, eastward from *B.* *1Sa 13:5*
and the battle passed over unto *B.* *1Sa 14:23*
neither go ye up to *B.* nor swear *Ho 4:15*
cry aloud at *B.* after thee, O *Ho 5:8*
because of the calves of *B.* *Ho 10:5*

BETH-AZMAVETH

The men of *B.* forty and two *Ne 7:28*

BETH-BAAL-MEON

Dibon, and Bamoth-baal, and *B.* *Jos 13:17*

BETH-BARAH

before them the waters unto *B.* *J'g 7:24*
and took the waters unto *B.* *J'g 7:24*

BETH-BIREI

Hazar-susim, and at *B.* and at *1Ch 4:31*

BETH-CAR

them, until they came under *B.* *1Sa 7:11*

BETH-DAGON

And Gederoth, *B.* and Naamah *Jos 15:41*
toward the sunrising to *B.* *Jos 19:27*

BETH-DIBLATHAIM

and upon Nebo, and upon *B.* *Jer 48:22*

BETH-EL

a mountain on the east of *B.* *Ge 12:8*
from the south even to *B.* *Ge 13:3*
called name of that place *B.* *Ge 28:19*
I am the God of *B.* *Ge 31:13; Ho 12:4*
Arise and go up to *B.* *Ge 35:1; 35:3, 6, 8, 15-16*
ambush between *B.* and Ai *Jos 8:9; 8:12-17*
king of Ai and *B.* *Jos 12:9; 12:16*
mount *B.* *Jos 16:1; J'g 4:5; 1Sa 13:2*
Luz which is *B.* *Jos 18:13; 16:2*
from year to year in circuit to *B.* *1Sa 7:16*
golden calf in *B.* *1Ki 12:29; 12:32-33; 2Ki 10:29*
idol altar in *B.* *1Ki 13:4; 13:1, 10-11, 32; 2Ki 23:4, 15-19; Am 3:14*
Lord hath sent me to *B.* *2Ki 2:2; 2:3, 23*
B. and the towns thereof *1Ch 7:28*
men of *B.* *Ezr 2:28; Ne 7:32*
house of Israel ashamed of *B.* *Jer 48:13*
Come to *B.* and transgress *Am 3:14*
But seek not *B.* *Am 5:5; 5:6*
prophesy not again any more at *B.* *Am 7:13*

BETH-ELITE

did Hiel the *B.* build Jericho *1Ki 16:34*

BETH-EMEK

toward the north side of *B.* *Jos 19:27*

BETHER

hart upon the mountains of *B.* *Ca 2:17*

BETHESDA

is called in the Hebrew tongue *B.* *Joh 5:2*

BETH-EZEL

not forth in the mourning of *B.* *Mic 1:11*

BETH-GADER

Hareph the father of *B.* *1Ch 2:51*

BETH-GAMUL

upon *B.* and upon Beth-meon *Jer 48:23*

BETH-HACCEREM

Rechab, the ruler of part of *B.* *Ne 3:14*
and set up a sign of fire in *B.* *Jer 6:1*

BETH-HARAN

Beth-nimrah, and *B.* fenced *Nu 32:36*

BETH-HOGLA

went up to *B.* and passed *Jos 15:6*

BETH-HOGLAH

along to the side of *B.* northward *Jos 18:19*
Jericho, and *B.* and the valley of *Jos 18:21*

BETH-HORON

the way that goeth up to *B.* *Jos 10:10*
and were in the going down to *B.* *Jos 10:11*
the coast of *B.* the nether, and *Jos 16:3*
Ataroth-addar, unto *B.* the upper *Jos 16:5*

on the south side of the   *Jos 18:13*
nether *B.*
hill that lieth before *B.*   *Jos 18:14*
southward
B. with her suburbs; four   *Jos 21:22*
cities
company turned the way to   *1Sa 13:18*
B.
built Gezer, and *B.* the nether   *1Ki 9:17*
B. with her suburbs   *1Ch 6:68*
Sherah, who built *B.* the   *1Ch 7:24*
nether
Also he built *B.* the upper, and *2Ch 8:5*
B. the nether, fenced cities   *2Ch 8:5*
from Samaria even unto *B.*   *2Ch 25:13*

BETHINK

b. themselves in the   *1Ki 8:47;*
                                   2Ch 6:37

BETH-JESHIMOTH

sea on the east, the way to B   *Jos 12:3*
Ashdoth-pisgah, and *B.*   *Jos 13:20*
of the country, *B.* Baal-meon   *Eze 25:9*

BETH-JESIMOTH

from *B.* even unto   *Nu 33:49*
Abel-shittim

BETH-LEBAOTH

And *B.* and Sharuhen   *Jos 19:6*

BETH-LEHEM

way to Ephrath which is *B.*   *Ge 35:19;*
                                   Ge 48:7
Ibzan of *B.* judged Israel   *J'g 12:8;*
                                   J'g 12:10
two came to *B.*   *Ru 1:19;*
                                   Ru 1:22; 2:4; 4:11
Samuel came to *B.* the elders   *1Sa 16:4*
trembled
to feed his father's sheep in   *1Sa 17:15*
B.
David asked leave to go to *B.*   *1Sa 20:6;*
                                   20:28
Philistines were in *B.*   *1Sa 23:14;*
                                   1Ch 11:16
drew water of well of *B.*   *1Sa 23:16;*
                                   1Ch 11:18
Salma the father of *B.*   *1Ch 2:51;*
                                   1Ch 2:54; 4:4
Rehoboam built *B.* and Etam   *2Ch 11:6*
children of *B.*   *Ezr 2:21;*
                                   Ne 7:26
thou *B.* Ephratah, though thou   *Mic 5:2*
be
Jesus was born in *B.*   *M't 2:1;*
M't 2:5-6, 8, 16; Lu 2:4, 15; Joh 7:42

BETH-LEHEMITE

I will send thee to Jesse the *B.* *1Sa 16:1*
I have seen a son of Jesse the   *1Sa 16:18*
B.
the son of thy servant Jesse   *1Sa 17:58*
the *B.*
the son of Jaare-oregim, a *B.*   *2Sa 21:19*

BETH-LEHEM-JUDAH

there was a young man out of   *J'g 17:7*
B.
from *B.* to sojourn where he   *J'g 17:8*
could
I am a Levite of *B.* and I   *J'g 17:9*
to him a concubine out of B   *J'g 19:1*
unto her father's house to *B.*   *J'g 19:2*
We are passing from *B.*   *J'g 19:18*
toward
and I went to *B.* but I   *J'g 19:18*
a certain man of *B.* went to   *Ru 1:1*
and Chilion, Ephrathites of *B.*   *Ru 1:2*
son of that Ephrathite of *B.*   *1Sa 17:12*

BETH-MAACHAH

unto Abel, and to *B.*, and all   *2Sa 20:14*
and besieged him in Abel of   *2Sa 20:15*
B.

BETH-MARCABOTH

Ziklag, and *B.* and   *Jos 19:5*
Hazar-susah
at *B.* and Hazar-susim, and at   *1Ch 4:31*

BETH-MEON

upon Beth-gamul, and upon   *Jer 48:23*
B.

BETH-NIMRAH

B. and Beth-haran, fenced   *Nu 32:36*
cities
in the valley, Beth-aram, and   *Jos 13:27*
B.

BETH-PALET

and Heshmon, and *B.*   *Jos 15:27*

BETH-PAZZEZ

and En-haddah, and *B.*   *Jos 19:21*

BETH-PEOR

in the valley over against *B.*   *De 3:29*
against *B.* in the land of Sihon *De 4:46*
the land of Moab, over against   *De 34:6*
B.
And *B.* and Ashdoth-pisgah   *Jos 13:20*

BETHPHAGE

were come to *B.* unto the   *M't 21:1*
mount
Jerusalem, unto *B.* and   *M'k 11:1*
Bethany
was come nigh to *B.* and   *Lu 19:29*
Bethany

BETH-PHELET

and at Moladah, and at *B.*   *Ne 11:26*

BETH-RAPHA

And Eshton begat *B.* and   *1Ch 4:12*

BETH-REHOB

was in the valley that lieth by   *J'g 18:28*
B.
sent and hired the Syrians of   *2Sa 10:6*
B.

BETHSAIDA

woe unto thee, *B.*! for if the   *M't 11:21*
go to the other side before   *M'k 6:45*
unto *B.*
And he cometh to *B.*; and   *M'k 8:22*
they
belonging to the city called *B.* *Lu 9:10*
woe unto thee, *B.*! for if the   *Lu 10:13*
mighty
Now Philip was of *B.* the city   *Joh 1:44*
of
therefore to Philip, which   *Joh 12:21*
was of *B.*

BETH-SHAN

his body to the wall of *B.*   *1Sa 31:10*
of his sons from the wall of   *1Sa 31:12*
B.
stolen them from the street   *2Sa 21:12*
of *B.*

BETH-SHEAN

B. and her towns, and Ibleam   *Jos 17:11*
both they who are of *B.* and   *Jos 17:16*
her
drive out the inhabitants of *B.* *J'g 1:27*
and all *B.* which is by   *1Ki 4:12*
Zartanah
Jezreel, from *B.* to   *1Ki 4:12*
Abel-meholah
children of Manasseh, *B.* and   *1Ch 7:29*
her

BETH-SHEMESH

and went down to *B.* and   *Jos 15:10*
passed
to Tabor, Shahazimah, and   *Jos 19:22;*
B.   *Jos 19:38*
Juttah with her suburbs, and   *Jos 21:16*
B.
drive out the inhabitants of *B.* *J'g 1:33*
the inhabitants of *B.* and of   *J'g 1:33*
by way of own coast to *B.*   *1Sa 6:9;*
                                   1Sa 6:12, 13, 15, 19, 20

Makaz, and in Shaalbim, and   *1Ki 4:9*
B.
looked one another in the   *2Ki 14:11*
face at *B.*
the son of Ahaziah, at *B.* and   *2Ki 14:13*
Ashan with her suburbs, and   *1Ch 6:59*
B.
Amaziah king of Judah, at   *2Ch 25:21;*
B.   *25:23*
Judah, and had taken *B.* and   *2Ch 28:18*
break also the images of *B.*   *Jer 43:13*
that is

BETH-SHEMITE

the field of Joshua, a *B.* and   *1Sa 6:14*
day in the field of Joshua, the   *1Sa 6:18*
B.

BETH-SHITTAH

and the host fled to *B.* in   *J'g 7:22*

BETH-TAPPUAH

And Janum, and *B.* and   *Jos 15:53*
Aphekah

BETHUEL

Pildash, Jidlaph, and *B.*   *Ge 22:22;*
                                   22:23
who was born to *B.* son of   *Ge 24:15*
Milcah
I am the daughter of *B.*   *Ge 24:24;*
                                   Ge 24:47
Then Laban and *B.* answered   *Ge 24:50*
daughter of *B.* the Syrian of   *Ge 25:20*
unto Laban, son of *B.* the   *Ge 28:2*
Syrian
And at *B.* and at Hormah   *1Ch 4:30*

BETHUL

And Eltolad, and *B.* and   *Jos 19:4*
Hormah

BETH-ZUR

Halhul, *B.* and Gedor   *Jos 15:58*
and Maon was the father of   *1Ch 2:45*
B.
and *B.* and Shoco, and   *2Ch 11:7*
Adullam
the ruler of the half part of *B.* *Ne 3:16*

BETIMES

and they rose up *b.* in the   *Ge 26:31*
rising up early in the morning   *Ge 26:31*
(A)(B)(R)
rising up *b.* and sending   *2Ch 36:15*
sent to them persistently   *2Ch 36:15*
(A)(R)
rising early and sending them   *2Ch 36:15*
(B)(E)
thou wouldest seek unto God *b.*   *Job 8:5*
seek diligently (A)(B)(E)   *Job 8:5*
rising *b.* for a prey: the   *Job 24:5*
seeking diligently for prey (A)   *Job 24:5*
loveth him chasteneth him *b.*   *Pr 13:24*
punishes him early (A)   *Pr 13:24*

BETONIM

unto Ramath-mizpeh, and *B.*   *Jos 13:26*

BETRAY

if ye come to *b.* me to   *1Ch 12:17*
enemies
talebearers *b.* confidence (B)   *Pr 11:13*
b. not him that wandereth (S)   *Isa 16:3*
many shall *b.* one another   *M't 24:10*
Judas sought opportunity to   *M't 26:16;*
b. M't 26:21, 23, 46; M'k 14:11, 18;
                                   Lu 22:4, 6
brother shall *b.* brother   *M'k 13:12*
Jesus knew who should *b.*   *Joh 6:64;*
                                   Joh 6:71; 12:4; 13:2, 11, 21

BETRAYED

Judas, who also *b.* him   *M't 10:4*
M't 26:25, 48; 27:3; M'k 3:19
Son of man shall be *b.*   *M't 17:22*
M't 20:18; 26:2, 24, 45; M'k 14:21, 41,
                                   44; Lu 22:22; Joh 18:2, 5
sinned in that I have *b.*   *M't 27:4*
innocent

ye shall be *b.* both by parents *Lu 21:16*
same night in which he was *1Co 11:23*
b. took

BETRAYERS

ye have been now the *b.* and *Acts 7:52*

BETRAYEST

b. thou the Son of man with a *Lu 22:48*

BETRAYETH

which *b.* (S) *Pr 27:16; M't 26:73*
lo, he that *b.* me is at hand *M'k 14:42*
the hand of him that *b.* me is *Lu 22:21*
with
Lord, which is he that *b.* thee *Joh 21:20*

BETRAYS

right hand *b.* them (B) *Pr 27:16*
accent *b.* you (A)(R) *M't 26:73*

BETROTH

Thou shalt *b.* a wife, and *De 28:30*
another
And I will *b.* thee unto me *Ho 2:19;*
2:20

BETROTHED

who hath *b.* her to himself *Ex 21:8*
And if he have *b.* her unto his *Ex 21:9*
maid that is not *b.* and lie *Ex 22:16*
with
that is a bondmaid, *b.* to an *Le 19:20*
that hath *b.* a wife, and hath *De 20:7*
not
that is a virgin be *b.* *De 22:23;*
De 22:25, 27-28
I *b.* to me (S) *2Sa 3:14*

BETTER

b. I give her to thee than to *Ge 29:19*
another
b. for us to have served the *Ex 14:12*
Egyptians
were it not *b.* for us to return *Nu 14:3*
to Egypt
gleanings of Ephraim *b.* than *J'g 8:2*
vintage
nor art thou any thing *b.* than *J'g 11:25*
Balak
b. looking (B) *J'g 15:2*
am not I *b.* to thee than ten *1Sa 1:8*
sons
how much *b.* (S) *1Sa 14:30*
nothing *b.* than to go to *1Sa 27:1*
the Philistines
God make the name of king *1Ki 1:47*
Solomon *b.*
who tell upon two men *b.* than *1Ki 2:32*
he, and slew
Elijah said, I am not *b.* *1Ki 19:4*
my fathers
I will give thee for it a *b.* *1Ki 21:2*
vineyard than it
rivers of Damascus *b.* than *2Ki 5:12*
Jordan
hast slain brethren *b.* than *2Ch 21:13*
thyself
iniquities got the *b.* of me (B) *Ps 65:3*
shall please Lord *b.* than an ox *Ps 69:31*
wisdom *b.* than folly (A)(B) *Ec 2:15*
nothing *b.* for a man than *Ec 2:24*
to eat
nothing *b.* than to rejoice in his *Ec 3:22*
works
b. is he than both they, which *Ec 4:3*
have not been
two are *b.* than one *Ec 4:9*
that the former days were *b.* *Ec 7:10*
than these
serpent will bite, a babbler is *Ec 10:11*
no *b.*
give a name *b.* than of sons *Isa 56:5*
they that be slain with sword *La 4:9*
are *b.*
I will settle you, and do *b.* to *Eze 36:11*
you
b. looking (A) *Da 1:15*
b. condition (B) *Da 1:15*
b. appearance (R) *Da 1:15*
in all matters he found them *Da 1:20*
ten times *b.*

then was it *b.* with me than now *Ho 2:7*
be they *b.* than these kingdoms *Am 6:2*
art thou *b.* than populous No *Na 3:8*
are ye not much *b.* than they *M't 6:26;*
Lu 12:24
fare *b.* in judgment (B) *M't 10:15*
how much is a man *b.* than *M't 12:12*
a sheep
it were *b.* that a millstone *M't 18:6;*
were hanged *M'k 9:42; Lu 17:2*
and no *b.* (S) *M'k 5:26*
are we *b.* than they? no, in no *Ro 3:9*
wise
giveth her not in marriage, *1Co 7:38*
doth *b.*
for neither if we eat are we the *1Co 8:8*
b.
b. for me to die, than make *1Co 9:15*
my glorying void
come together not for *b.* but *1Co 11:17*
for worse
let each esteem other *b.* than *Ph'p 2:3*
himself
being made so much *b.* than *Heb 1:4*
the angels
we are persuaded *b.* things of *Heb 6:9*
you
the less is blessed of the *b.* *Heb 7:7*
perfect, but bringing in of *b.* *Heb 7:19*
hope did
Jesus was made a surety of a *Heb 7:22*
b. testament
he is Mediator of a *b.* *Heb 8:6*
covenant, established on *b.* promises
but heavenly things with *b.* *Heb 9:23*
sacrifices
in heaven a *b.* and enduring *Heb 10:34*
substance
they desire a *b.* country, an *Heb 11:16*
heavenly
that they might obtain a *b.* *Heb 11:35*
resurrection
God having provided some *Heb 11:40*
b. thing for us
that speaketh *b.* things than *Heb 12:24*
that of Abel
b. for them not to have known *2Pe 2:21*
way

BETTER IS

b. is little with the fear of the *Pr 15:16*
Lord
b. is a dinner of herbs where *Pr 15:17*
love is
b. is little with righteousness *Pr 16:8*
than
how much *b. is* it to get *Pr 16:16*
wisdom than gold
b. is a dry morsel and quietness *Pr 17:1*
b. is the poor that walks in *Pr 19:1;*
integrity *28:6*
for *b. is* a neighbour that is *Pr 27:10*
near, than
b. is an handful with quietness *Ec 4:6*
than
b. is a poor wise child that a *Ec 4:13*
foolish king
b. is sight of the eyes than *Ec 6:9*
wandering
b. is the end of a thing than the *Ec 7:8*
beginning
how much *b. is* thy love than *Ca 4:10*
wine

IS BETTER, IS IT BETTER

whether *is b.* for you that all *J'g 9:2*
reign
is it b. to be a priest to one, *J'g 18:19*
than to a tribe
daughter *is b.* to thee than *Ru 4:15*
seven
behold, to obey *is b.* than *1Sa 15:22*
sacrifice
given to a neighbor that *is* *1Sa 15:28*
b. than thou
counsel of Hushai the *2Sa 17:14*
Archite *is b.*
estate to another that *is b.* *Es 1:19*
than she
a little a righteous man hath *is* *Ps 37:16*
b.
thy loving-kindness *is b.* than *Ps 63:3*
life
a day in thy courts *is b.* than *Ps 84:10*
law of thy mouth *is b.* to me *Ps 119:72*
for the merchandise of wisdom *Pr 3:14*
is b.

wisdom *is b.* than rubies, and *Pr 8:11*
all things
my fruit *is b.* than gold *Pr 8:19*
is b. than he that honoureth *Pr 12:9*
himself
slow to anger *is b.* than the *Pr 16:32*
mighty
and a poor man *is b.* than a *Pr 19:22*
liar
open rebuke *is b.* than secret *Pr 27:5*
love
an untimely birth *is b.* than he *Ec 6:3*
a good name *is b.* than precious *Ec 7:1*
ointment
sorrow *is b.* than laughter, for *Ec 7:3*
the heart *is* made *b.*
the patient in spirit *is b.* than *Ec 7:8*
the proud in spirit
a living dog *is b.* than a dead *Ec 9:4*
lion
then said I, Wisdom *is b.* than *Ec 9:16*
strength
wisdom *is b.* than weapons of *Ec 9:18*
war
for thy love *is b.* than wine *Ca 1:2*
for he saith, The old *is b.* *Lu 5:39*
to be with Christ, which *Ph'p 1:23*
is far b.

IT IS BETTER, BETTER IT IS

it is b. I give her to thee than *Ge 29:19*
another
b. it is thou succour us out of *2Sa 18:3*
city
it is b. to trust in Lord *Ps 118:8*
b. it is to be of an humble *Pr 16:19*
spirit
it is b. to dwell in a corner of *Pr 21:9;*
house *25:24*
it is b. to dwell in wilderness *Pr 21:19*
b. it is that it be said to thee, *Pr 25:7*
Come
b. it is that thou shouldest not *Ec 5:5*
vow
it is b. to go to the house of *Ec 7:2*
mourning
it is b. to hear the rebuke of the *Ec 7:5*
wise
it is b. for me to die than to *Jon 4:3;*
live *4:8*
it is b. for thee to enter into *M't 18:8;*
life *M'k 9:43, 45, 47*
for *it is b.* to marry than to *1Co 7:9*
burn
it is b. ye suffer for well doing *1Pe 3:17*

BETTERED

nothing *b.,* but rather grew *M'k 5:26*
worse

BETWEEN

put enmity *b.* thee and the *Ge 3:15*
woman
covenant *b.* me and you *Ge 9:12;*
Ge 9:13-17; 17:2, 7, 10
strife *b.* me and thee *Ge 13:7; 13:8*
lamp *b.* those pieces of *Ge 15:17*
sacrifice
Lord judge *b.* me and thee *Ge 16:5;*
1Sa 24:12, 15
witness *b.* me and thee *Ge 31:44;*
Ge 31:48, 49
lawgiver *b.* his feet until *Ge 49:10*
Shiloh come
division *b.* my people and *Ex 8:23;*
Egyptians *11:7*
the Lord shall sever *b.* the cattle *Ex 9:4*
of
memorial *b.* thine eye *Ex 13:9;*
Ex 13:16; De 6:8; 11:18
sabbath a sign *b.* me and you *Ex 31:13;*
Ex 31:17; Eze 20:12, 20
difference *b.* clean and *Le 10:10;*
unclean *Le 11:47; 20:25*
judge righteously *b.* brethren *De 1:16*
and buried him *b.* Zorah and *J'g 16:31*
Eshtaol
how long halt ye *b.* two *1Ki 18:21*
opinions
put his face *b.* his knees *1Ki 18:42*
dwellest *b.* cherubims *2Ki 19:15;*
2Sa 6:2; 1Ch 13:6; Ps 80:1; 99:1;
Isa 37:16
b. the ranks (S) *2Ch 23:14*
between (S) *Job 9:33;*
Job 36:32; Ca 1:13; Isa 5:3; Jer 39:4;
Ph'p 1:23

three ribs b. the teeth of it	Da 7:5
a notable horn b. his eyes	Da 8:5
brotherhood b. Judah and Israel	Zec 11:14
fault b. thee and him alone	M't 18:15
slew b. altar and temple	M't 23:35; Lu 11:51
great gulf b. us and you	Lu 16:26
contention was so sharp b. them	Ac 15:39
dishonor own bodies b. themselves	Ro 1:24
no difference b. Jews and Gentiles	Ro 10:12
able to judge b. his brethren	1Co 6:5
There is a difference b. a wife	1Co 7:34
middle wall of partition b. us	Eph 2:14
one God, and one mediator b. God	1Ti 2:5

BETWIXT

token of covenant b. me and you	Ge 17:11
may judge b. us both	Ge 31:37; 31:50-53
is there any daysman b. us	Job 9:33
I am in a strait b. two, having a	Ph'p 1:23

BEULAH

call thy land B.	Isa 62:4

BEWAIL

whole house of Israel b.	Le 10:6
shall bemoan the flame (B)	Le 10:6
b. her father and her mother	De 21:13
and b. her virginity	J'g 11:37
all Israel b. him (B)	1Ki 14:13
I will b. her weeping	Isa 16:9
weep with weeping of Jazer (A)(B)(E)(R)	Isa 16:9
I shall b. many which have sinned	2Co 12:21
sorrow over many (A)	2Co 12:21
saddened over many (B)	2Co 12:21
mourn for many of them (E)(R)	2Co 12:21
have tears to shed over many (N)	2Co 12:21
grieve over many who have (P)	2Co 12:21
shall b. her when they see smoke of	Re 18:9
weep and beat their breasts (A)(B)	Re 18:9
weep and wail over her (E)(N)(R)	Re 18:9
wail and lament over her (P)	Re 18:9

BEWAILED

companions, and b. her virginity	J'g 11:38
And all wept and b. her	Lu 8:52
which also b. and lamented	Lu 23:27

BEWAILETH

daughter of Zion, that b. herself	Jer 4:31

BEWARE

b. that thou bring not my son thither	Ge 24:6
b. of him, and obey his voice	Ex 23:21
b. lest thou forget the Lord	De 6:12; 8:11
b. that there be not a thought in	De 15:9
b., drink no wine	J'g 13:4; J'g 13:13
b. that none touch the young man	2Sa 18:12
b. lest he take away with his stroke	Job 36:18
smite a scorner, and the simple will b.	Pr 19:2
b. of false prophets	M't 7:15; M't 10:17
b. of leaven of Pharisees	M't 16:6; M't 16:11-12; M'k 8:15; Lu 12:1
b. of scribes	M'k 12:38; Lu 20:46
b. of covetousnes	Lu 12:15
b. therefore, lest that come upon	Ac 13:40
b. of dogs, b. of evil workers,	Ph'p 3:2
b. of	

b. lest any man spoil you through	Col 2:8
do thou b. (S)	2Ti 4:15
b. lest ye also, being led away with	2Pe 3:17

BEWILDERED

were stunned and b. (A)	M't 8:27
brightened and b. (P)	Lu 8:25; Lu 24:41
b. and dazzled them (A)	Ac 8:11

BEWILDERMENT

horses with b. (B)	Zec 12:4
looked in b. (N)	Joh 13:22

BEWITCHED

b. the people of Samaria	Ac 8:9
to the utter amazement (A)	Ac 8:9
astonishing the Samaritan nation (B)	Ac 8:9
amazed the people of Samaria (E)(R)	Ac 8:9
swept the Samaritans off their feet (N)	Ac 8:9
mystifying the people of Samaria (P)	Ac 8:9
had b. them with sorceries	Ac 8:11
bewildered and dazzled them (A)	Ac 8:11
kept them excited with magic arts (B)	Ac 8:11
amazed them with his sorceries (E)	Ac 8:11
carried away by his magic (N)	Ac 8:11
astounding them by magical practices (P)	Ac 8:11
amazed them with his magic (R)	Ac 8:11
foolish Galatians, who hath b. you	Ga 3:1
casting a spell over you (P)	Ga 3:1

BEWRAY

the outcasts; b. not him that	Isa 16:3
betray not the fugitive (A)(B)(E)(R)	Isa 16:3

BEWRAYETH

his right hand, which b. itself	Pr 27:16
his right hand betrays him (B)	Pr 27:16
his right hand encountereth oil (E)	Pr 27:16
grasp oil in his right hand (R)	Pr 27:16
heareth cursing, and b. if not	Pr 29:24
thy speech b. thee	M't 26:73
your accent betrays you (A)(R)	M't 26:73
your accent shows you up (B)	M't 26:73
thy speech maketh thee known (E)	M't 26:73
your accent gives you away (N)	M't 26:73
it's obvious from your accent (P)	M't 26:73

BEYOND

spread his tent b. the tower of Edar	Ge 35:21
may give light b. (S)	Ex 25:37
I cannot go b. the word of Lord	Nu 22:18; Nu 24:13
b. Jordan (S)	Nu 32:19
b. Jordan	De 3:20; 3:25; Jos 13:8; J'g 5:17; Isa 9:1; M't 4:15, 25; 19:1; M'k 3:8; Joh 1:28; 3:26; 10:40
Neither is it b. the sea	De 30:13; 2Ch 20:2; Jer 25:22
the arrows are b. thee	1Sa 20:22; 1Sa 20:36-37
b. the river	2Sa 10:16; 1Ki 14:15; 1Ch 19:16; Ezr 4:17, 20; 6:6, 8; 7:21, 25; Ne 2:7, 9; Isa 7:20
b. the ranks	2Ki 11:15
vessel b. weight (S)	2Ki 25:16; 1Ch 22:2, 14
b. the rivers of Ethiopia	Isa 18:1; Zep 3:10
b. measures	M'k 6:51; M'k 7:37; 2Co 8:3; 10:14; Ga 1:13
carry you away b. Babylon	Ac 7:43

the gospel in the regions b. you	2Co 10:16
no man go b. and defraud his brother	1Th 4:6

BEZAI

The children of B. three	Ezr 2:17
children of B. three hundred	Ne 7:23
Hodijah, Hashum, B.	Ne 10:18

BEZALEEL

I have called by name B. the son	Ex 31:2
the Lord hath called by name B.	Ex 35:30
Then wrought B. and Aholiab	Ex 36:1
Moses called B. and Aholiab	Ex 36:2
B. made the ark of shittim wood	Ex 37:1
B. the son of Uri, the son of Hur	Ex 38:22
Hur begat Uri, and Uri begat B.	1Ch 2:20
Moreover the brasen altar, that B.	2Ch 1:5
Mattaniah, B. and Binnui	Ezr 10:30

BEZEK

they slew of them in B. ten	J'g 1:4
And they found Adoni-bezek in B.	J'g 1:5
And when he numbered them in B.	1Sa 11:8

BEZER

Namely, B. in the wilderness	De 4:43
assigned B. in the wilderness	Jos 20:8
Reuben, B. with her suburbs	Jos 21:36
B. in the wilderness with her	1Ch 6:78
B. and Hod, and Shamma	1Ch 7:37

BICHRI

the son of B. a Benjamite	2Sa 20:1; 2Sa 20:2, 6-7, 10, 13, 21-22

BID

and b. them that they make them	Nu 15:38
until the day I b. you shout	Jos 6:10
B. the servant pass on before us	1Sa 9:27
long shall it be then, ere thou b.	2Sa 2:26
riding for me, except I b. thee	2Ki 4:24
if the prophet had b. thee do	2Ki 5:13
will do all that thou shalt b. us	2Ki 10:5
the preaching that I b. thee	Jon 3:2
prepared a sacrifice, he hath b.	Zep 1:7
b. me come unto thee on the	M't 14:28
ye shall find, b. to the marriage	M't 22:9
therefore whatsoever they b. you	M't 23:3
let me first go b. them farewell	Lu 9:61
b. her therefore that she help me	Lu 10:40
lest they also b. thee again	Lu 14:12
any of them that believe not b.	1Co 10:27
house, neither b. him God speed	2Jo 10

BIDDEN

afterwards they eat that be b. which	1Sa 9:13
among them that were b.	1Sa 9:22
for the Lord hath b. him	2Sa 16:11
hath b. his guests (S)	Zep 1:7
angel of the Lord had b. him	M't 1:24
to call them that were b.	M't 22:3
Tell them which are b.	M't 22:4
Behold, I which were b. were not worthy	M't 22:8
the Pharisee which had b. him	Lu 7:39
a parable to those which were b.	Lu 14:7
When thou art b. of any man	Lu 14:8
when thou art b. go and sit down	Lu 14:10
to say to them that were b.	Lu 14:17
none of those men which were b.	Lu 14:24

BIDDETH

For he that b. him God speed   2Jo 11

BIDDING

and goeth at thy b. and is   1Sa 22:14

BIDKAR

said Jehu to B. his captain   2Ki 9:25

BIER

king David himself followed the b.   2Sa 3:31
And he came and touched the b.   Lu 7:14

BIG

knowledge may make man look b. (P)   1Co 8:1

BIGOTED

b. and wicked men (P)   2Th 3:2

BIGTHA

Harbona, B. and Abagtha   Es 1:10

BIGTHAN

king's chamberlains, B. and   Es 2:21

BIGTHANA

Mordecai had told of B. and   Es 6:2

BIGVAI

Mizpar, B., Rehum, Baanah   Ezr 2:2
The children of B. two thousand   Ezr 2:14
Of the sons also of B.; Uthai   Ezr 8:14
Bilshan, Mispereth, B., Nehum   Ne 7:7
The children of B. two thousand   Ne 7:19
Adonijah, B., Adin   Ne 10:16

BILDAD

B. the Shuhite   Job 2:11; 8:1; 18:1; 25:1; 42:9

BILEAM

suburbs, and B. with her suburbs   1Ch 6:70

BILGAH

The fifteenth to B. the   1Ch 24:14
Miamin, Maadiah, B.   Ne 12:5
Of B. Shammua; of Shemaiah   Ne 12:18

BILGAI

Maaziah, B., Shemaiah: these   Ne 10:8

BILHAH

B. his handmaid to be her   Ge 29:29
Behold my maid B., go in unto   Ge 30:3; Ge 30:4-5, 7; 35:25
went and lay with B. his father's   Ge 35:22
the lad was with the sons of B.   Ge 37:2
These are the sons of B. which   Ge 46:25
And at B. and at Ezem, and at   1Ch 4:29
and Shallum, the sons of B.   1Ch 7:13

BILHAN

B. and Zaavan, and Akan   Ge 36:27
Ezer; B. and Zavan, and Jakan   1Ch 1:42
The sons also of Jediael; B.   1Ch 7:10
and the sons of B.; Jeush   1Ch 7:10

BILL

write her a b. of divorcement   De 24:1
and write her a b. of divorcement   De 24:3

Where is the b. of your mother's   Isa 50:1
and given her a b. of divorce   Jer 3:8
to write a b. of divorcement   M'k 10:4
said unto him, Take thy b.   Lu 16:6; Lu 16:7

BILLOWS

all thy waves and thy b. are   Ps 42:7
all thy b. and thy waves passed   Jon 2:3

BILSHAN

Reelaiah, Mordecai, B., Mizpar   Ezr 2:2
Nahamani, Mordecai, B.   Ne 7:7

BIMHAL

Pasach, and B. and Ashvath   1Ch 7:33

BIND

they shall b. the breastplate   Ex 28:28
And they did b. the breastplate   Ex 39:21
swear an oath to b. his soul   Nu 30:2
Lord, and b. herself by a bond   Nu 30:3
thou shalt b. them for a sign   De 6:8
and b. them for a sign upon   De 11:18
b. up the money in thine hand   De 14:25
thou shalt b. this line of scarlet   Jos 2:18
To b. Samson are we come   J'g 15:10; up   J'g 15:12-13; 16:5, 7, 11
and b. it as a crown to me   Job 31:36
Canst thou b. the sweet   Job 38:31
Canst thou b. the unicorn with   Job 39:10
and b. their faces in secret   Job 40:13
or wilt thou b. him for thy   Job 41:5
To b. his princes at his pleasure   Ps 105:22
b. the sacrifice with cords, even   Ps 118:27
To b. their kings with chains   Ps 149:8
b. them about thy neck; write   Pr 3:3
B. them continually upon thine   Pr 6:21
B. them upon thy fingers, write   Pr 7:3
B. up the testimony, seal the law   Isa 8:16
and b. them on thee, as a bride   Isa 49:18
to b. up the brokenhearted   Isa 61:1
thou shalt b. a stone to it, and   Jer 51:63
and shall b. thee with them   Eze 3:25
and b. them in thy skirts   Eze 5:3
b. the tire of thine head upon   Eze 24:17
to put a roller to b. it, to make   Eze 30:21
b. up that which was broken   Eze 34:16
were in his army to b. Shadrach   Da 3:20
smitten, and he will b. us up   Ho 6:1
when they shall b. themselves   Ho 10:10
b. the chariot to the swift beast   Mic 1:13
except he first b. the strong man   M't 12:29
b. them in bundles to burn them   M't 13:30
whatsoever thou shalt b. on earth   M't 16:19
shall b. on earth shall be bound in   M't 18:18
B. him hand and foot, and take   M't 22:13
For they b. heavy burdens and   M't 23:4
he will first b. the strong man   M'k 3:27
no man could b. him, no, not with   M'k 5:3
to b. all that call on thy name   Ac 9:14
thyself, and b. on thy sandals   Ac 12:8
the Jews at Jerusalem b. the man   Ac 21:11

BINDETH

for he maketh sore, and b. up   Job 5:18
He b. up the waters in his thick   Job 26:8
b. the floods from overflowing   Job 28:11
it b. me about as the collar of my   Job 30:18
they cry not when he b. them   Job 36:13
nor he that b. sheaves his bosom   Ps 129:7

in heart, and b. up their wounds   Ps 147:3
As he that b. a stone in a sling   Pr 26:8
that the Lord b. up the breach   Isa 30:26

BINDING

For, behold, we were b. sheaves   Ge 37:7
B. his foal unto the vine, and his   Ge 49:11
it shall have a b. of woven work   Ex 28:32
every b. oath to afflict the soul   Nu 30:13
b. them over (P)   Ac 17:9
b. and delivering into prisons   Ac 22:4
law in b. over a person (R)   Ro 7:1

BINEA

Moza begat B.: Rapha was his   1Ch 8:37
Moza begat B.; and Rephaiah   1Ch 9:43

BINNUI

Noadiah the son of B., Levites   Ezr 8:33
Mattaniah, Bezaleel, and B.   Ezr 10:30
And Bani, and B., Shimei   Ezr 10:38
After him repaired B. the son of   Ne 3:24
The children of B. six hundred   Ne 7:15
the son of Azaniah, B. of the sons   Ne 10:9
Moreover the Levites: Jeshua, B.   Ne 12:8

BIRD

his kind, every b. of every sort   Ge 7:14
As for the living b. he shall take   Le 14:6; 14:7, 51-53
thou play with him as with a   Job 41:5
Flee as a b. to your mountain   Ps 11:1
b. out of the snare of the fowlers   Ps 124:7
spread in the sight of any b.   Pr 1:17
a b. from the hand of the fowler.   Pr 6:5
as a b. hasteth to the snare, and   Pr 7:23
As the b. by wandering, as the   Pr 26:2
As a b. that wandereth from   Pr 27:8
b. of the air shall carry the voice   Ec 10:20
the voice of the b. and all the   Ec 12:4
wandering b. cast out of the nest   Isa 16:2
a ravenous b. from the east   Isa 46:11
heritage is unto me as a speckled b.   Jer 12:9
enemies chased me sore, like a b.   La 3:52
their glory shall fly away like a b.   Ho 9:11
shall tremble as a b. out of Egypt   Ho 11:11
Can a b. fall in a snare upon   Am 3:5
of every unclean and hateful b.   Re 18:2

BIRDS

another: but the b. divided he not   Ge 15:10
and the b. did eat them out of   Ge 40:17
b. shall eat thy flesh from off thee   Ge 40:19
cleansed two b. alive and clean   Le 14:4; Le 14:5, 49-50
Of all clean b. ye shall eat   De 14:11
neither the b. of the air to rest   2Sa 21:10
greater wisdom than b. (B)   Job 35:11
Where the b. make their nests   Ps 104:17
and as the b. that are caught in   Ec 9:12
time of the singing of b. is come   Ca 2:12
As b. flying, so will the Lord of   Isa 31:5
the b. of the heavens were fled   Jer 4:25
As a cage is full of b. so are their   Jer 5:27
beasts are consumed, and the b.   Jer 12:4
as a speckled bird, the b. round   Jer 12:9

BIRDS

give thee unto the ravenous *b.*   *Eze 39:4*
and the *b.* of the air have nests *M't 8:20*
so that the *b.* of the air come *M't 13:32*
holes, and *b.* of air have nests *Lu 9:58*
like to corruptible man, and to *Ro 1:23*
b.
of fishes, and another of *b.* *1Co 15:39*
every kind of beasts, and of *b.* *Jas 3:7*

BIRD'S

b. nest chance to be before *De 22:6*
thee

BIRDS'

and his nails like *b.* claws *Da 4:33*

BIRSHA

and with *B.* king of Gomorrah *Ge 14:2*

BIRTH

the land of *b.* (A)(R)˙   *Ge 11:28;*
   Jer 46:16
the order of their *b.* (A)(B) *Ex 6:16*
other stone, according to their *Ex 28:10*
b.
in the land of your *b.* (A)(B) *Ru 2:11*
hath given *b.* (S) *Ru 4:15*
for the children are come to *2Ki 19:3*
the *b.*
untimely *b.* I had not been *Job 3:16*
from my *b.* (B)(R) *Ps 22:10*
like the untimely *b.* of a woman *Ps 58:8*
an untimely *b.* is better than he *Ec 6:3*
of death than the day of one's *Ec 7:1*
b.
the children are come to the *b.* *Isa 37:3*
borne from my *b.* *Isa 46:3*
(A)(B)(E)(R)
I bring to the *b.* and not cause *Isa 66:9*
man give *b.* to a child (A) *Jer 30:6*
Thy *b.* and thy nativity is of *Eze 16:3*
spiritual origin and *b.* *Eze 16:3*
(A)(B)(R)
in the land of *b.* (A) *Eze 21:30*
from the *b.* and from the *Ho 9:11*
womb
the *b.* of Jesus Christ was on *M't 1:18*
this
and many shall rejoice at his *b.* *Lu 1:14*
man which was blind from his *Joh 9:1*
b.
I travail in *b.* again until *Ga 4:19*
Christ
power of the new *b.* (P) *Ga 6:15*
cleansing of the new *b.* (A)(P) *Tit 3:5*
cried, travailing in *b.* and *Re 12:2*
pained

BIRTHDAY

which was Pharaoh's *b.* *Ge 40:20*
when Herod's *b.* was kept, the *M't 14:6*
Herod on his *b.* made a *M'k 6:21*
supper

BIRTH-PANGS

suffer *b.* (B) *Ge 3:16*
Rachel felt *b.* (B) *Ge 35:16*
b. came upon her (B) *1Sa 4:19*
beginning of *b.* (A)(P) *M't 24:8;*
   M'k 13:8
b. of a new age (N) *M't 24:8;*
   M'k 13:8
b. of a woman (B)(R) *1Th 5:3*

BIRTHRIGHT

said, Sell me this day thy *b.* *Ge 25:31*
what profit shall this *b.* do to *Ge 25:32*
me
and he sold his *b.* unto Jacob *Ge 25:33*
way; thus Esau despised his *b.* *Ge 25:34*
he took away my *b.*; and, *Ge 27:36*
behold
the firstborn according to his *Ge 43:33*
b.
his *b.* was given unto the sons *1Ch 5:1*
is not to be reckoned after the *1Ch 5:1*
b.
ruler; but the *b.* was *1Ch 5:2*
Joseph's:)
for one morsel of meat sold *Heb 12:16*
his *b.*

BIRTHSTOOLS

upon *b.* (A)(B)(E)(R) *Ex 1:16*

BIRZAVITH

Malchiel, who is the father of *1Ch 7:31*
B.

BISHLAM

days of Artaxerxes, wrote B. *Ezr 4:7*

BISHOP

If a man desire the office of a *1Ti 3:1*
b.
A *b.* then must be blameless *1Ti 3:2*
For a *b.* must be blameless, as *Tit 1:7*
Shepherd and *B.* of your *1Pe 2:25*
souls

BISHOPRICK

therein: and his *b.* let another *Ac 1:20*
his position or overseership *Ac 1:20*
(A)
take his charge (B)(N) *Ac 1:20*
his office let another take *Ac 1:20*
(E)(P)(R)

BISHOPS

made *b.* and guardians *Ac 20:28*
(A)(E)
Philippi, with the *b.* and *Ph'p 1:1*
deacons

BIT

people, and they *b,* the people *Nu 21:6*
be held in with *b.* and bridle *Ps 32:9*
on the wall, and a serpent *b.* *Am 5:19*
him

BITE

a *b.* of bread (B) *Ge 18:5; J'g 19:5*
an hedge, a serpent shall *b.* him *Ec 10:8*
will *b.* without enchantment *Ec 10:11*
be charmed, and they shall *b.* *Jer 8:17*
you
the serpent, and he shall *b.* *Am 9:3*
them
that *b.* with their teeth, and cry *Mic 3:5*
up suddenly that shall *b.* thee *Hab 2:7*
if ye *b.* and devour one *Ga 5:15*
another

BITETH

the path, that *b.* the horse *Ge 49:17*
heels
it *b.* like a serpent, and *Pr 23:32*
stingeth

BITHIAH

the sons of *B.* the daughter of *1Ch 4:18*

BITHRON

went through all *B.* and they *2Sa 2:29*

BITHYNIA

Mysia, they assayed to go into *Ac 16:7*
B.
Galatia, Cappadocia, Asia, and *1Pe 1:1*
B.

BITS

we put *b.* in the horses' mouths *Jas 3:3*

BITTEN

every one that is *b.* when he *Nu 21:8*
if a serpent had *b.* any man, *Nu 21:9*
when

BITTER

made life *b.* (R) *Ge 26:35*
b.
with a great and exceeding *b.* *Ge 27:34*
cry
made their lives *b.* with hard *Ex 1:14*
with *b.* herbs they shall eat it *Ex 12:8*

waters of Marah, for they *Ex 15:23*
were *b.*
b. water that causeth the *Nu 5:18;*
curse *Nu 5:19, 23-24, 27*
unleavened bread and *b.* herbs *Nu 9:11*
heat, and with *b.* destruction *De 32:24;*
   32:32
it is exceedingly *b.* (A)(R) *Ru 1:13*
complaint and *b.* *1Sa 1:16*
provocation (A)(E)
people *b.* in soul (R) *1Sa 30:6*
soul in *b.* distress (R)(S) *2Ki 4:27*
of Israel, that it was very *b.* *2Ki 14:26*
cried with a loud and a *b.* cry *Es 4:1*
and life unto the *b.* in soul *Job 3:20*
thou writest *b.* things against *Job 13:26*
me
Even to day is my complaint *Job 23:2*
b.
make my soul *b.* (R) *Job 27:2*
to shoot their arrows, even *b.* *Ps 64:3*
my heart was *b.* (B) *Ps 73:21*
her end is *b.* as wormwood, *Pr 5:4*
sharp
to the hungry soul every *b.* *Pr 27:7*
thing
more *b.* than death the woman *Ec 7:26*
put *b.* for sweet, and sweet for *Isa 5:20*
b.
strong drink shall be *b.* to *Isa 24:9*
them
it is an evil thing and *b.* that *Jer 2:19*
thou
is thy wickedness, because it is *Jer 4:18*
b.
an only son, most *b.* *Jer 6:26*
lamentation
in Ramah, lamentation, and *Jer 31:15*
b.
bitterness of heart and *b.* *Eze 27:31*
wailing
and the end thereof as a *b.* *Am 8:10*
day
Chaldeans, that *b.* and hasty *Hab 1:6*
wives, and be not *b.* against *Col 3:19*
them
same place sweet water and *b.* *Jas 3:11*
if ye have *b.* envying and strife *Jas 3:14*
shall have *b.* sorrow (P) *Re 1:7*
waters, because they were *Re 8:11*
made *b.*
it shall make thy belly *b,* but it *Re 10:9*
I had eaten it, my belly was *b.* *Re 10:10*

BITTERLY

b. attacked (A) *Ge 49:23*
curse ye *b.* the inhabitants *J'g 5:23*
thereof
wept *b.* (S) *J'g 21:2;*
1Sa 1:10; Ezr 10:1; Isa 38:3; Jer 13:17;
   22:10; La 1:2
Almighty hath dealt very *b.* *Ru 1:20*
with
I will weep *b.* labor not to *Isa 22:4*
comfort
of peace shall weep *b.* *Isa 33:7*
and shall cry *b.* and shall cast *Eze 27:30*
up
provoked him to anger most *Ho 12:14*
b.
the mighty man shall cry there *Zep 1:14*
b.
And he went out, and wept *b.* *M't 26:75*
Peter went out, and wept *b.* *Lu 22:62*

BITTERN

make it a possession for the *Isa 14:23*
b.
cormorant and the *b.* shall *Isa 34:11*
cormorant and the *b.* shall *Zep 2:14*
lodge

BITTERNESS

she was in *b.* of soul, and *1Sa 1:10*
prayed
said, Surely the *b.* of death is *1Sa 15:32*
past
that it will be *b.* in the latter *2Sa 2:26*
end
I will complain in the *b.* of my *Job 7:11*
breath, but filleth me with *b.* *Job 9:18*
I will speak in the *b.* of my *Job 10:1*
soul
another dieth in the *b.* of his *Job 21:25*
soul
The heart knoweth his own *b.* *Pr 14:10*
father, and *b.* to her that bare *Pr 17:25*

my years in the *b.* of my soul   *Isa 38:15*
Behold, for peace I had great   *Isa 38:17*
b.
are afflicted, and she is in *b.*   *La 1:4*
compassed with *b.* (A)(B)   *La 3:5*
He hath filled me with *b.*   *La 3:15*
my affliction and *b.* (R)   *La 3:19*
took me away, and I went in   *Eze 3:14*
b.
and with *b.* sigh before their   *Eze 21:6*
eyes
they shall weep for thee with   *Eze 27:31*
b.
and shall be in *b.* for him   *Zec 12:10*
as one that is in *b.*   *Zec 12:10*
thou art in the gall of *b.* and in   *Ac 8:23*
mouth is full of cursing and *b.*   *Ro 3:14*
let all *b.* and wrath, and anger   *Eph 4:31*
lest any root of *b.* springing   *Heb 12:15*
up

BITUMEN

b. for mortar (R)   *Ge 11:3*
slime or *b.* pits (A)(B)   *Ge 14:10*

BIZJOTHJAH

and Beer-sheba, and *B.*   *Jos 15:28*

BIZTHA

he commanded Mehuman, *B.*   *Es 1:10*

BLACK

the *b.* eagle (B)   *Le 11:13*
that there is no *b.* hair in it   *Le 13:31;*
  13:37
heaven was *b.* with clouds   *IKi 18:45*
of red, and blue, and white, and   *Es 1:6*
b.
My skin is *b.* upon me, and   *Job 30:30*
my
in the evening in the *b.* and   *Pr 7:9*
I am *b.* but comely, O ye   *Ca 1:5; 1:6*
his locks are bushy, and *b.* as a   *Ca 5:11*
and the heavens above be *b.*   *Jer 4:28*
I am *b.*; astonishment hath   *Jer 8:21*
taken
they are *b.* unto the ground   *Jer 14:2*
Our skin was *b.* like an oven   *La 5:10*
in the second chariot *b.* horses   *Zec 6:2;*
  6:6
not make one hair white or *b.*   *M't 5:36*
b. dungeons of Tartarus (B)   *2Pe 2:4*
And I beheld, and lo a *b.* horse   *Re 6:5*
sun became *b.* as sackcloth of   *Re 6:12*

BLACKER

Their visage is *b.* than a coal   *La 4:8*

BLACKISH

Which are *b.* by reason of the   *Job 6:16*
ice

BLACKMAIL

no bullying, no *b.* (N)   *Lu 3:14*

BLACKNESS

let the *b.* of the day terrify it   *Job 3:5*
put out in *b.* of darkness (E)   *Pr 20:20*
I clothe the heavens with *b.*   *Isa 50:3*
pained: all faces shall gather *b.*   *Joe 2:6*
the faces of them all gather *b.*   *Na 2:10*
nor unto *b.* and darkness   *Heb 12:18*
to whom is reserved the *b.* of   *Jude 13*

BLACKSMITH

no *b.* to be found (B)   *2Ki 13:19*

BLADE

the haft also went in after the   *J'g 3:22*
b.
arm fall from my shoulder *b.*   *Job 31:22*
But when the *b.* was sprung   *M't 13:26*
up
first the *b*, then the ear, after   *M'k 4:28*

BLAINS

be a boil breaking forth with *b.*   *Ex 9:9*
break out in open sores (B)(R)   *Ex 9:9*
a boil breaking forth with *b.*   *Ex 9:10*

BLAME

then let me bear the *b.* for ever   *Ge 43:9*
then I shall bear the *b.* to my   *Ge 44:32*
why does God *b.* men (N)(P)   *Ro 9:19*
that no man should *b.* us in   *2Co 8:20*
this
be holy and without *b.*   *Eph 1:4*

BLAMED

that the ministry be not *b.*   *2Co 6:3*
the face, because he was to be   *Ga 2:11*
b.

BLAMELESS

righteous and *b.* (A)(R)   *Ge 6:9*
b. among fellowmen (B)   *Ge 6:9*
walk before me and be *b.* (R)   *Ge 17:1*
stay a *b.* people (B)(R)   *Ge 20:4*
my servant; and ye shall be *b.*   *Ge 44:10*
be *b.* before the Lord   *De 18:13*
(A)(B)(R)
We will be *b.* of this thine oath   *Jos 2:17*
Now shall I be more *b.* than   *J'g 15:3*
b. before him (A)   *J'g 22:24;*
  Ps 19:13
hast been *b.* (R)   *J'g 22:24; 22:26;*
Job 12:4; Ps 18:23, 25; 19:13; Pr 11:20;
  29:10, 27
he guides the *b.* (A)   *2Sa 22:33*
heart to *b.* (A)   *IKi 8:61*
heart not *b.* (A)   *IKi 15:3*
Asa's heart was *b.* (A)   *1Ki 15:14*
You are *b.* (B)   *2Ki 10:9*
with a *b.* heart (A)   *1Ch 12:38;*
  1Ch 29:9; 2Ch 19:9; 25:2
to Solomon a *b.* heart (A)   *1Ch 29:19*
whose heart was *b.* (A)(R)   *2Ch 16:9*
b. and upright (B)   *Job 1:1;*
  Job 1:8; 2:3
never cast away a *b.* man   *Job 8:20*
(A)(R)
though I am *b.*   *Job 9:20; 9:21*
destroys the *b.* with the   *Job 9:22*
wicked (B)
make your ways *b.* (R)   *Job 22:3*
b. in the way (B)   *Ps 13:6;*
  29:10
mark the *b.* man (A)(R)   *Ps 37:37*
shoot at the *b.* (A)(R)   *Ps 64:4*
b. way, *b.* heart (A)(R)   *Ps 101:2*
heart be *b.* (R)   *Ps 119:80*
b. shall remain (A)   *Pr 2:21*
righteousness of the *b.*   *Pr 11:5*
(A)(B)(R)
b. in your ways (A)(R)   *Eze 28:15*
I was found *b.* (R)   *Da 6:22*
profane the sabbath, and are   *M't 12:5*
b.
and ordinances of the Lord *b.*   *Lu 1:6*
that ye may be *b.* in the day of   *1Co 1:8*
live sincere and *b.*   *Ph'p 1:10*
(A)(B)(N)(P)(R)
that ye may be *b.* and   *Ph'p 2:15*
harmless
which is in the law, *b.*   *Ph'p 3:6*
present you *b.* (B)   *Col 1:22*
upright, *b.* (A)(N)(R)   *1Th 2:10*
holy and *b.* (P)   *1Th 3:13*
be preserved *b.* unto the   *1Th 5:23*
coming
maintained *b.* (B)(R)   *1Th 5:23*
a bishop then must be *b.* the   *1Ti 3:2*
office of a deacon, being found   *1Ti 3:10*
b.
in charge, that they may be *b.*   *1Ti 5:7*
if any be *b.* the husband of one   *Tit 1:6;*
  1:7
in peace, without spot, and *b.*   *2Pe 3:14*
spotless and *b.* (B)(P)   *2Pe 3:14*

BLAMELESSLY

he who walks *b.* (R)   *Ps 15:2*

BLAMING

people *b.* each other (B)   *2Sa 19:9*

BLASPHEME

the enemies of the Lord to *b.*   *2Sa 12:14*
Thou didst *b.* God and the   *1Ki 21:10*
king
Naboth did *b.* God and the   *1Ki 21:13*
king
shall the enemy *b.* thy name   *Ps 74:10*
for

wherewith soever they shall *b.*   *M'k 3:28*
he that shall *b.* against the   *M'k 3:29*
Holy
and compelled them to *b.*   *Ac 26:11*
that they may learn not to *b.*   *1Ti 1:20*
Do not they *b.* that worthy   *Jas 2:7*
name
to *b.* his name, and his   *Re 13:6*
tabernacle

BLASPHEMED

Israelitish woman's son *b.* the   *Le 24:11*
of the king of Assyria have *b.*   *2Ki 19:6*
me
hast thou reproached and *b.*   *2Ki 19:22*
defied and *b.* (E)   *2Ki 19:22; 19:23*
the foolish people have *b.* thy   *Ps 74:18*
of the king of Assyria have *b.*   *Isa 37:6*
me
hast thou reproached and *b.*   *Isa 37:23*
name continually every day is   *Isa 52:5*
b.
upon the mountains, and *b.* me   *Isa 65:7*
in this your fathers have *b.*   *Eze 20:27*
me
they opposed themselves, and *b.*   *Ac 18:6*
the name of God is *b.* among   *Ro 2:24*
God and his doctrine be not *b.*   *1Ti 6:1*
that the word of God be not   *Tit 2:5*
b.
heat, and *b.* the name of God   *Re 16:9*
b. the God of heaven because   *Re 16:11*
of
men *b.* God because of the   *Re 16:21*
plague

BLASPHEMER

is a *b.* against the Lord (B)   *Nu 15:30*
Who was before a *b.* and a   *1Ti 1:13*

BLASPHEMERS

churches, nor yet *b.* of your   *Ac 19:37*
covetous, boasters, proud, *b.*   *2Ti 3:2*

BLASPHEMEST

Thou *b.*; because I said, I am   *Joh 10:36*

BLASPHEMETH

he that *b.* the name of the   *Le 24:16*
Lord
the same *b.* Jehovah (E)   *Nu 15:30*
of him that reproacheth and *b.*   *Ps 44:16*
within themselves, This man *b.*   *M't 9:3*
unto him that *b.* against the   *Lu 12:10*
Holy

BLASPHEMIES

I have heard all thy *b.* which   *Eze 35:12*
thou
thefts, false witness, *b.*   *M't 15:19*
Why doth this man thus speak   *M'k 2:7*
b.
b. wherewith soever they shall   *M'k 3:28*
Who is this which speaketh *b.*   *Lu 5:21*
mouth speaking great things   *Re 13:5*
and *b.*

BLASPHEMING

sons *b.* (R)   *1Sa 3:13*
by Paul, contradicting and *b.*   *Ac 13:45*

BLASPHEMOUS

we have heard him speak *b.*   *Ac 6:11*
words
ceaseth not to speak *b.* words   *Ac 6:13*

BLASPHEMOUSLY

things *b.* spake they against   *Lu 22:65*
him

BLASPHEMY

of trouble, and of rebuke,   *2Ki 19:3*
and *b.*
trouble, and of rebuke, and of   *Isa 37:3*
b.
All manner of sin and *b.*   *M't 12:31*
shall be
the *b.* against the Holy Ghost   *M't 12:31*
clothes, saying, He hath   *M't 26:65*
spoken *b.*
behold, now ye have heard   *M't 26:65*
his *b.*

an evil eye, b., pride,   M'k 7:22
foolishness
Ye have heard the b.: what   M'k 14:64
think
for b.; and because that thou Joh 10:33
anger, wrath, malice, b., filthy Col 3:8
I know the b. of them which say Re 2:9
and upon his heads the name   Re 13:1
of b.
And he opened his mouth in b. Re 13:6
full of names of b. having   Re 17:3
seven

BLAST

And with the b. of thy nostrils Ex 15:8
lengthy b. of ram's horn (B)   Ex 19:13
when they make a long b. with Jos 6:5
at the b. of the breath of his   2Sa 22:16
I will send a b. upon him   2Ki 19:7
put a spirit in him   2Ki 19:7
(A)(B)(E)(R)
By the b. of God they perish   Job 4:9
b. of his anger (A)(B)(E)(R)   Job 4:9
b. of his mouth (A)   Job 15:30
at the b. of the breath of thy Ps 18:15
when the b. of the terrible ones Isa 25:4
I will send a b. upon him, and Isa 37:7
b. of a trumpet (A)(N)(P)   Heb 12:19
announce by trumpet (P)   Re 10:7

BLASTED

seven thin ears and b. with the Ge 41:6
seven ears, withered, thin,   Ge 41:23
and b.
seven empty ears b. with the Ge 41:27
east
as corn b. before it be grown 2Ki 19:26
scorched before it comes up   2Ki 19:26
(B)
blighted before it is grown   2Ki 19:26
(R)
and as corn b. before it be   Isa 37:27
grown

BLASTING

sword, and with b. and with   De 28:22
with blight and mildew (B)   De 28:22
famine, if there be pestilence, 1Ki 8:37
b.
blight and mildew (A)(B)(R) 1Ki 8:37
there be b. or mildew, locusts 2Ch 6:28
I have smitten you with b. and Am 4:9
with blight and mildew   Am 4:9
(A)(B)(R)
I smote you with b. and with Hag 2:17
blight and mildew   Hag 2:17
(A)(B)(R)

BLASTUS

and having made B. the   Ac 12:20
king's

BLAZE

my wrath shall b. hot (A)   Ex 32:11
my anger b. hot (A)(B)   Ex 32:22
like a b. of flames (B)   Da 7:9
chariots b. with fire of steel (A) Na 2:8
and to b. abroad the matter M'k 1:45

BLAZING

a b. furnace (A)(B)(R)   Ps 2:19
the b. flame (S)   Eze 20:47

BLEACH

any bleacher could b.   M'k 9:3
(B)(N)(P)

BLEACHER

any b. could bleach   M'k 9:3
(B)(N)(P)

BLEATING

What meaneth then this b. of 1Sa 15:14

BLEATINGS

to hear the b. of the flocks   J'g 5:16

BLEEDING

fresh and b. stripes (A)(E)(R) Isa 1:6

BLEMISH

lamb without b.   Ex 12:5;
Le 14:10; 23:12, 18; Nu 6:14; 29:2, 8,
  13, 20, 23, 29, 32, 36; Eze 46:4, 13
rams without b.   Ex 29:1;
Eze 5:15, 18; Eze 43:23, 25; 45:23; 46:6
offer a male without b.   Le 1:3;
  Le 1:10; 4:23; 22:19-21; De 15:21
offer it without b.   Le 3:1;
    Le 3:6; Nu 28:19, 31
young bullock without b.   Le 4:3;
  De 17:1; Eze 43:23; 45:18
a female without b.   Le 4:28; 4:32
burnt offering without b.   Le 9:2; 9:3
man that hath a b.   Le 21:18;
    Le 21:20-21, 23
man cause a b. to neighbour Le 24:19;
    24:20
red heifer without b.   Nu 19:2
without b., defect (B)(R)   Nu 19:2
without b. (B)   Nu 28:9, 11; 29:17; Heb 9:14
without b. (R)   Nu 28:3;
Nu 28:9, 11; 29:17; Job 11:15; Heb 9:14;
    1Pe 1:19
that is their b. (A)(B)(R)   De 32:5
Absalom was without b.   2Sa 14:25
there is no b. in you (B)   Ca 4:7
offer kid without b.   Eze 43:22
children in whom was no b. Da 1:4
church should be holy   Eph 5:27
without b.
present you without b. (E)   Col 1:22
offered himself without b.   Heb 9:14
(E)(N)(R)
as of a lamb without b.,   1Pe 1:19
without spot
without mark or b. (N)   1Pe 1:19
without b. (A)(E)   Re 14:5

BLEMISHES

corruption in them, and b. be Le 22:25
Spots they are and b.,   2Pe 2:13
sporting
blots and b. (A)(B)(R)   2Pe 2:13

BLENDED

b. together (R)   Ex 30:35

BLESS God being agent

Lord said, I will b. thee   Ge 12:2;
    Ge 26:3, 24
I will b. them that bless thee Ge 12:3
will b. her, and give a son of Ge 17:16
her
in blessing I will b. thee   Ge 22:17;
    Heb 6:14
God almighty b. and multiply Ge 28:3
not let thee go, except thou b. Ge 32:26
me
b. the lads, let my name be   Ge 48:16
named
by the Almighty who shall b. Ge 49:25
thee
I will come to thee, I will b. Ex 20:24
thee
he shall b. thy bread and thy Ex 23:25
water
the Lord b. thee and keep thee Nu 6:24
put my name on Israel, I will Nu 6:27
b. them
saw it pleased Lord to b. Israel Nu 24:1
b. you as he hath promised De 1:11
you
will b. thee, b. fruit of womb De 7:13
Lord may b. thee   De 14:29;
    De 23:20; 24:19
shall be no poor, for Lord shall De 15:4
b. thee
for this thing Lord b. thee   De 15:10
God shall b. thee in all   De 15:18;
    30:16
because Lord shall b. thee in De 16:15
all
look down and b. thy people De 26:15
Israel
he shall b. thee in the land he De 28:8
giveth
and to b. all the work of thine De 28:12
hand
b. Lord, his substance, and De 33:11
accept
the Lord b. thee   Ru 2:4;
    Jer 31:23
let it please thee to b. house 1Sa 7:29;
of thy servant   1Ch 17:27

that he might b. him (S)   1Sa 13:10
that thou wouldest b. me   1Ch 4:10
indeed
Thou, Lord, wilt b. the   Ps 5:12
righteous
save thy people, b. thine   Ps 28:9
inheritance
Lord will b. his people with Ps 29:11
peace
even our God shall b. us   Ps 67:6;
    67:7
Lord will b. us, b. the house Ps 115:12
of Israel, the house of Aaron
he will b. them that fear the Ps 115:13
Lord
the Lord shall b. thee out of Ps 128:5
Zion
I will abundantly b. her   Ps 132:15
provision.
the Lord b. thee out of Zion Ps 134:3
whom the Lord of hosts shall Isa 19:25
b.
from this day will I b. you   Hag 2:19
sent him to b. you in turning Ac 3:26
you

BLESS God being the object

art full, then thou shalt b.   De 8:10
Lord
b. ye the Lord   J'g 5:9; Ps 103:21; 134:1
David said, Now b. Lord   1Ch 29:20
your God
b. Lord for ever and ever   Ne 9:5
b. Lord who hath given counsel Ps 16:7
in the congregations will I b. Ps 26:12
Lord
I will b. the Lord at all times Ps 34:1
thus will I b. thee while I live Ps 63:4
b. our God, make his praise Ps 66:8
heard
b. ye God in congregations, Ps 68:26
sing to Lord, b. his name   Ps 96:2
be thankful to him, b. his   Ps 100:4;
name   103:1
b. the Lord, O my soul   Ps 103:1;
   Ps 12:22; 104:1, 35
b. Lord, ye his angels   Ps 103:20
b Lord all his works in all   Ps 103:22
places
we will b. Lord from this   Ps 115:18
time
lift up your hands, and b.   Ps 134:2
b. Lord, O house of Israel   Ps 135:19
ye that fear the Lord, b. the Ps 135:20
Lord
I will b. thy name for ever and Ps 145:1
ever
every day will I b. thee   Ps 145:2
O Lord, thy saints shall b.   Ps 145:10
thee
let all flesh b. his holy name Ps 145:21
for ever
therewith b. God, even the   Jas 3:9
Father

BLESS man agent and object

soul may b. thee before I die Ge 27:4
b. me, even me also, O my   Ge 27:34
father
bring them to me, I will b.   Ge 48:9
them
in thee shall Israel b. saying, Ge 48:20
take flocks and begone, b. me Ex 12:32
also
on this wise ye shall b. Israel Nu 6:23
I have received commandment Nu 23:20
to b.
neither curse them nor b.   Nu 23:25
them
the Lord separated Levi to b. De 10:8;
    21:5
sleep in own raiment, and b. De 24:13
thee
these stand on mount   De 27:12
Gerizim, to b.
heareth words of curse, he b. De 29:19
himself
as Moses commanded they   Jos 8:33
should b.
because he doth b. the sacrifice 1Sa 9:13
b. his household 2Sa 6:20; 1Ch 16:43
Toi sent Joram his son to   2Sa 8:10
David
ye may b. inheritance of Lord 2Sa 21:3
servants came to b. king David 1Ki 1:47
to b. in his name for ever   1Ch 23:13

they *b.* with mouths, but curse   *Ps 62:4*
let them curse, but *b.* thou   *Ps 109:28*
we *b.* you in name of the Lord   *Ps 129:8*
a generation that curseth   *Pr 30:11*
father, doth not *b,* their mother
shall *b.* himself in God of   *Isa 65:16*
truth
nations shall *b.* themselves in   *Jer 4:2*
him
b. them that curse you   *M't 5:44;*
  Lu 6:28
b. those persecute you, *b.* and   *Ro 12:14*
curse not
being reviled we *b.* being   *1Co 4:12*
persecuted
else when thou shalt *b.* with   *1Co 14:16*
spirit

BLESSED man agent and object

Melchisedek *b.* Abram, and   *Ge 14:19*
said, *B.,* be
they *b.* Rebekah, and said   *Ge 24:60*
unto her
so Isaac *b.* Jacob, and said   *Ge 27:23;*
  27:27
and *b.* be he that blesseth thee   *Ge 27:29*
I have *b.* him, yea, and he   *Ge 27:33*
shall be *b.*
blessing wherewith his father   *Ge 27:41*
b. him
Isaac called Jacob, *b.* him   *Ge 28:1*
b. him he gave him charge   *Ge 28:6;*
  Heb 11:20
for the daughters will call me   *Ge 30:13*
b.
kissed sons and daughters,   *Ge 31:55*
and *b.*
Jacob *b.* Pharaoh   *Ge 47:7;*
  47:10
Jacob *b.* Manasseh and   *Ge 48:20;*
Ephraim   *Heb 11:21*
Jacob *b.* his sons, every one   *Ge 49:28*
he *b.*
and Moses *b.* them   *Ex 39:43; De 33:1*
Aaron lift up hands and *b.*   *Le 9:22*
them
Moses and Aaron *b.* the people   *Le 9:23*
he whom thou blessest is *b.*   *Nu 22:6*
thou hast *b.* them altogether   *Nu 23:11;*
  24:10
b. be he that enlargeth Gad   *De 33:20*
let Asher be *b.* with children   *De 33:24*
Joshua *b.* Caleb, gave Hebron   *Jos 14:13*
Joshua *b.* and sent them away   *Jos 22:6;*
  22:7
therefore Balaam *b.* you still   *Jos 24:10*
b. above women shall Jael be   *J'g 5:24*
b. be he that took knowledge   *Ru 2:19*
Eli *b.* Elkanah and wife   *1Sa 2:20*
b. be thy advice, and *b.* be   *1Sa 25:33*
thou
b. be thou, my son David   *1Sa 26:25*
David *b.* people   *2Sa 6:18; 1Ch 16:2*
howbeit he would not go, but   *2Sa 13:25*
b. him
the king kissed Barzillai, and   *2Sa 19:39*
b. him
and king Solomon shall be *b.*   *1Ki 2:45*
Solomon *b.* all congregation   *1Ki 8:14;*
  8:55
congregation *b.* Solomon   *1Ki 8:66;*
  2Ch 6:3
priests and Levites *b.* people   *2Ch 30:27*
people *b.* all that willingly   *Ne 11:2*
offered
blessed (B)   *Job 5:17;*
Ps 127:5;   137:8-9;   144:15;   146:5;
Pr 3:13;   28:14;   Joh 13:17;   Jas 5:11;
  1Pe 3:14; 4:14
when the ear heard me, it *b.*   *Job 29:11*
me
if his loins have not *b.* me   *Job 31:20*
while he lived he *b.* his soul   *Ps 49:18*
men be *b.* in him, call him *b.*   *Ps 72:17*
b. be he that cometh in name   *Ps 118:26*
of Lord, we *b.* you out of
house of Lord
children arise, and call her *b.*   *Pr 31:28*
b. art thou when thy king   *Ec 10:17*
daughters saw her, and *b.* her   *Ca 6:9*
burneth incense, as if *b.* an   *Isa 66:3*
idol
let not day mother bare me be   *Jer 20:14*
b.
and all nations shall call you   *Mal 3:12*
b.

b. be the kingdom of our   *M'k 11:10*
father
all generations shall call me *b.*   *Lu 1:48*
Simeon *b.* them, and said to   *Lu 2:34*
Mary
more *b.* to give than to   *Ac 20:35*
receive
looking for that *b.* hope   *Tit 2:13*
Melchisedek met Abraham *b.*   *Heb 7:1*
him
without contradiction less *b.*   *Heb 7:7*
of better
b. who are stedfast   *Jas 5:11*
(A)(B)(E)(P)
you will be *b.* (R)   *1Pe 3:14; 4:14*

BLESSED God the agent

God *b.* them, saying, Be   *Ge 1:22;*
fruitful   *Ge 1:28;   5:2*
God *b.* seventh day   *Ge 2:3; Ex 20:11*
God *b.* Noah and sons, and said   *Ge 9:1*
in thee all families be *b.* 18:18;   *Ge 12:3;*
18:18;   22:18;   26:4;   28:14;   Ac 3:25;
  Ga 3:8
I have *b.* Ishmael   *Ge 17:20*
he said, Come in thou *b.* of   *Ge 24:31*
Lord
after death of Abraham God   *Ge 25:11;*
b. Isaac   *26:12*
thou art now the *b.* of the   *Ge 26:29*
Lord
smell of a field which Lord *b.*   *Ge 27:27*
that Lord *b.* me for thy sake   *Ge 30:27*
Lord hath *b.* thee since my   *Ge 30:30*
coming
he *b.* Jacob there   *Ge 32:29;*
  Ge:35:9; 48:3
Lord *b.* the Egyptian's house   *Ge 39:5*
shalt not curse, people are *b.*   *Nu 22:12*
hath *b.* and I cannot reverse   *Nu 23:20*
it
God hath *b.* thee   *De 2:7;*
  De 12:7; 15:14; 16:10
thou shalt be *b.* above all   *De 7:14*
people
if place be too far, when Lord   *De 14:24*
b.
b. shalt thou be in city, *b,* in   *De 28:3*
field
b. shalt be fruit of thy body   *De 28:4*
of Joseph be land, *B.* of Lord   *De 33:13*
forasmuch as Lord hath *b.* me   *Jos 17:14*
Samson grew, and Lord *b.*   *J'g 13:24*
him
b. be thou of Lord   *J'g 17:2; Ru 3:10;*
  1Sa 15:13
b. be he of Lord who hath not   *Ru 2:20*
b. be thou of the Lord, my   *Ru 3:10*
daughter
b. be ye of Lord   *1Sa 23:21; 2Sa 2:5*
Lord *b.* Obed-edom, and all   *2Sa 6:11;*
his household   *1Ch 13:14; 26:5*
house of thy servant be *b.* for   *2Sa 7:29*
ever
blessest, and it shall be *b.*   *1Ch 17:27*
the Lord hath *b.* his people   *2Ch 31:10*
thou hast *b.* the work of his   *Job 1:10*
hands
the Lord *b.* the latter end of   *Job 42:12*
Job
for thou hast made him most   *Ps 21:6*
b.
b. is nation whose God is   *Ps 33:12*
Lord
for such as be *b.* of him shall   *Ps 37:22*
inherit
merciful and lendeth, his seed   *Ps 37:26*
is *b.*
Lord keep him, and he shall be   *Ps 41:2*
b.
therefore God hath *b.* thee for   *Ps 45:2*
ever
b. is people that know joyful   *Ps 89:15*
sound
generation of the upright shall   *Ps 112:2*
be *b.*
you are *b.* of Lord who made   *Ps 115:15*
heaven
b. are the undefiled in the way   *Ps 119:1*
b. is every one that feareth the   *Ps 128:1*
Lord
shall man be *b.* that feareth   *Ps 128:4*
Lord
he hath *b.* thy children within   *Ps 147:13*
thee
let thy fountain be *b.* and   *Pr 5:18*
rejoice

the memory of the just is *b.*   *Pr 10:7*
just man's children are *b.* after   *Pr 20:7*
him
but the end thereof shall not   *Pr 20:21*
be *b.*
he that hath a bountiful eye   *Pr 22:9*
shall be
saying, *B.* be Egypt my people *Isa 19:25*
for I called him alone and *b.*   *Isa 51:2*
him
they are seed Lord hath *b.*   *Isa 61:9;*
  65:23
B. are the poor in spirit; for   *M't 5:3*
their's
B. are they that mourn: for   *M't 5:4*
they
B. are the meek, for they shall   *M't 5:5*
B. are they which do hunger   *M't 5:6*
and
B. are the merciful: for they   *M't 5:7*
B. are the pure in heart: for   *M't 5:8*
they
B. are the peacemakers, for   *M't 5:9*
they
B. are they which are   *M't 5:10*
persecuted
B. are ye, when men shall   *M't 5:11*
revile
b. is he, whosoever shall not   *M't 11:6*
be
b. are your eyes, for they see *M't 13:16*
He *b.* the bread   *M't 14:19;*
M't 26:26;   M'k 6:41;   14:22;   Lu 9:16;
  24:30
Jesus said, *B.* art thou, Simon *M't 16:17*
Bar-jona
b. is that servant   *M't 24:46; Lu 12:43*
come, *b.* of my Father,   *M't 25:34*
inherit kingdom
took them up in arms, and   *M'k 10:16*
b. them
thou art Christ, the Son of   *M'k 14:61*
the *b.*
b. art thou among women   *Lu 1:28;*
  1:48
b. is she that believed   *Lu 1:45*
b. is womb that bare thee,   *Lu 11:27*
and paps
b. are those servants   *Lu 12:37; 12:38*
thou shalt be *b.* they cannot   *Lu 14:14*
recompense
b. be King that cometh in   *Lu 19:38*
name of Lord
b. are the barren that never   *Lu 23:29*
bare
he *b.* them   *Lu 24:50*
they are *b.* with faithful   *Ga 3:9*
Abraham
who hath *b.* us with spiritual   *Eph 1:3*
blessings
this man shall be *b.* in his deed *Jas 1:25*
b. are the dead that die in   *Re 14:13*
Lord

BLESSED God the object

he said, *B.* be the Lord   *Ge 9:26;*
24:27;   Ex 18:10;   Ru 4:14;   1Sa 25:32;
2Sa 18:28; 1Ki 1:48; 5:7; 8:15, 56; 10:9;
1Ch 16:36; 2Ch 2:12; 6:4; 9:8; Ezr 7:27;
Ps 28:6;   31:21;   41:13;   68:19;   72:18;
89:52;   106:48;   124:6;   135:21;   144:1;
  Zec 11:5; Lu 1:68
b. be most high God who   *Ge 14:20*
delivered
the children of Israel *b.* God   *Jos 22:33*
b. be my rock   *2Sa 22:47; Ps 18:46*
David *b.* Lord, *B.* thou, O   *1Ch 29:10*
Lord
all congregation *b.* the Lord   *1Ch 29:20*
God
for there they *b.* the Lord   *2Ch 20:26*
they saw the heaps, they *b.*   *2Ch 31:8*
Lord
Ezra *b.* the Lord, the great God   *Ne 8:6*
b. be thy glorious name   *Ne 9:5;*
  Ps 72:19
b. be name of Lord *Job 1:21; Ps 113:2*
b. be God   *Ps 66:20; Ps 68:35; 2Co 1:3*
b. art thou, teach me thy   *Ps 119:12*
statues
saying, *B.* the glory of Lord   *Eze 3:12*
Daniel *b.* God of heaven   *Da 2:19;*
  4:20
Nebuchadnezzar *b.* the most   *Da 4:34*
High
took him in his arms and *b.*   *Lu 2:28*
God
b. is King of Israel that   *Joh 12:13*
cometh

than Creator, who is *b.* for ever   *Ro 1:25*
Christ, over all, God *b.* for ever   *Ro 9:5*
is *b.* for evermore, knoweth   *2Co 11:31*
b. be Father of our   *Eph 1:3; 1Pe 1:3*
Lord
glorious gospel of *b.* God   *1Ti 1:11*
who is the *b.* and only   *1Ti 6:15*
Potentate

BLESSED *ARE THEY*

b. are they that put trust in him   *Ps 2:12*
b. are they that dwell in thy   *Ps 84:4*
house
b. are they that keep judgment   *Ps 106:3*
b. are they that keep his   *Ps 119:2*
testimonies
for *b. are they* that keep my   *Pr 8:32*
ways
b. are they that wait for him   *Isa 30:18*
b. are they that mourn,   *M't 5:4*
shall be
b. are they who hunger   *M't 5:6*
b. are they who are persecuted   *Lu 5:10*
rather *b. are they* that hear   *Lu 11:28*
word
b. are they that have not seen   *Joh 20:29*
b. are they iniquities are   *Ro 4:7*
forgiven
b. are they called to marriage   *Re 19:9*
supper
b. are they that do his   *Re 22:14*
commandments

BLESSED *ARE YE*

b. are ye that sow beside   *Isa 32:20*
all waters
b. are ye when men shall   *M't 5:11*
revile you
b. are ye that hunger now,   *Lu 6:21*
b. are ye that weep now   *Lu 6:22*
b. are ye when men shall hate   *Lu 6:22*
you

BLESSED *IS HE*

b. is he that blesseth thee   *Nu 24:9*
b. is he transgression is   *Ps 32:1*
forgiven
b. is he that considereth the   *Ps 41:1*
poor
b. is he that waiteth, cometh   *Da 12:12*
to
b. is he whosoever shall not   *M't 11:6;*
be offended in me   *Lu 7:23*
b. is he that cometh in name   *M't 21:9;*
of Lord   *M't 23:39; M'k 11:9;*
  Lu 13:35
b. is he that eat bread in   *Lu 14:15*
kingdom
b. is he that readeth, and hear   *Re 1:3*
b. is he that watcheth, and   *Re 16:15*
keepeth
b. is he hath part in first   *Re 20:6*
resurrection
b. is he that keepeth sayings of   *Re 22:7*
prophecy

BLESSED *IS THE MAN*

b. is the man walketh not in   *Ps 1:1*
counsel
b. is the man to whom Lord   *Ps 32:2;*
imputeth not iniquity   *Ro 4:8*
b. is man that trusteth   *Ps 34:8;*
  Ps 84:12; Jer 17:7
b is the man that maketh Lord   *Ps 40:4*
his trust
b. is the man whom thou   *Ps 65:4*
choosest
b. is the man whose strength   *Ps 84:5*
is in thee
b. is the man whom thou   *Ps 94:12*
chastenest
b. is the man that feareth   *Ps 112:1*
Lord
b. is the man, that heareth me   *Pr 8:34*
b. is the man that doth this   *Isa 56:2*
b. is the man endureth   *Jas 1:12*
temptation

BLESSEDNESS

even as David describeth the *b.*   *Ro 4:6*
cometh this *b.* on the   *Ro 4:9*
circumcision only
crown of eternal *b.* (A)   *1Co 9:25*
where is then the *b.* ye spake   *Ga 4:15*
of

BLESSEST

I wot that he whom thou *b.* is   *Nu 22:6*
blessed
thou *b.* O Lord, and it shall   *1Ch 17:27*
be blessed
thou *b.* the springing thereof   *Ps 65:10*

BLESSETH

and blessed be he that *b.* thee   *Ge 27:29*
Blessed is he that *b.* thee, and   *Nu 24:9*
the Lord thy God *b.* thee, as he   *De 15:6*
b. the covetous, whom the Lord   *Ps 10:3*
He *b.* them also, so that they   *Ps 107:38*
are
but he *b.* the habitation of the   *Pr 3:33*
just
that *b.* his friend with a loud   *Pr 27:14*
voice
That he who *b.* himself in the   *Isa 65:16*
earth

BLESSING

great; and thou shalt be a *b.*   *Ge 12:2*
That in *b.* I will bless thee   *Ge 22:17*
and in
a curse upon me, and not a   *Ge 27:12;*
b.   *Ge 27:30, 35-36, 38, 41*
and give thee the *b.* of   *Ge 28:4*
Abraham
Take, I pray thee, my *b.* that   *Ge 33:11*
is
the *b.* of the Lord was upon all   *Ge 39:5*
every one according to his *b.*   *Ge 49:28*
he
he may bestow upon you a *b.*   *Ex 32:29*
I will command my *b.* upon   *Le 25:21*
you
you this day a *b.* and a curse   *De 11:26;*
Lord   *16:17*
according to the *b.* of the   *De 12:15;*
Lord   *16:17*
thy God turned the curse into   *De 23:5*
a *b.*
The Lord shall command the *b.*   *De 28:8*
the *b.* and the curse, which I   *De 30:1*
have
life and death, *b.* and cursing   *De 30:19*
this is *b.* Moses   *De 33:1;*
  De 33:7, 16, 23
b. is your (B)   *De 33:29*
Who answereth, Give me a *b.*   *Jos 15:19*
Give me a *b.:* for thou hast   *J'g 1:15*
given
now this *b.* with thine   *1Sa 25:27*
handmaid
and with thy *b.* let the house   *2Sa 7:29*
of
thee, take a *b.* of thy servant   *2Ki 5:15*
is exalted above all *b.* and   *Ne 9:5*
praise
God turned the curse into a *b.*   *Ne 13:2*
b. of him that was ready to   *Job 29:13*
perish
thy *b.* is upon thy people   *Ps 3:8*
shall receive the *b.* from the   *Ps 24:5*
Lord
as he delighted not in *b.* so   *Ps 109:17*
let it
The *b.* of the Lord be upon   *Ps 129:8*
you
there the Lord commanded   *Ps 133:3*
the *b.*
The *b.* of the Lord, it maketh   *Pr 10:22*
rich
By the *b.* of the upright the   *Pr 11:11*
city is
but *b.* shall be upon the head   *Pr 11:26*
of
a good *b.* shall come upon   *Pr 24:25*
them
even a *b.* in the midst of the   *Isa 19:24*
land
and my *b.* upon thine offspring   *Isa 44:3*
Destroy it not; for a *b.* is in it   *Isa 65:8*
places round about my hill a   *Eze 34:26*
b.
there shall be showers of *b.*   *Eze 34:26*
that he may cause the *b.* to   *Eze 44:30*
rest
repent, and leave a *b.* behind   *Joe 2:14*
him
I save you, and ye shall be a *b.*   *Zec 8:13*
pour you out a *b.* that there   *Mal 3:10*
shall
in the temple, praising and *b.*   *Lu 24:53*
God

the fulness of the *b.* of the   *Ro 15:29*
gospel
we return a *b.* (P)   *1Co 4:13*
The cup of *b.* which we bless   *1Co 10:16*
a double *b.* (B)   *2Co 1:15*
the *b.* of Abraham might come   *Ga 3:14*
is dressed, receiveth *b.* from   *Heb 6:7*
God
Saying, Surely *b.* I will bless   *Heb 6:14*
thee
would have inherited the *b.*   *Heb 12:17*
mouth proceedeth *b.* and   *Jas 3:10*
cursing
contrariwise *b.*   *1Pe 3:9*
inherit *b.*   *1Pe 3:9*
and honour, and glory, and *b.*   *Re 5:12*
B., and honour, and glory   *Re 5:13*
B., and glory, and wisdom   *Re 7:12*

BLESSINGS

bless thee with *b.* of heaven   *Ge 49:25;*
above   *49:26*
all these *b.* shall come on thee   *De 28:2*
the *b.* and cursings, according   *Jos 8:34*
b. I will give Israel (B)   *1Sa 2:32*
preventest with the *b.* of   *Ps 21:3*
goodness
B. are upon the head of the just   *Pr 10:6*
faithful man shall abound   *Pr 28:20*
with *b.*
I will curse your *b.;* yea, I have   *Mal 2:2*
with all spiritual *b.* in heavenly   *Eph 1:3*

BLEW

b. with the trumpets   *Jos 6:8;*
Jos 6:9, 13, 16, 20; J'g 3:27; 6:34; 7:19-
  20, 22
b. the trumpet throughout all   *1Sa 13:3*
So Joab *b.* a trumpet, and all   *2Sa 2:28*
And Joab *b.* the trumpet, and   *2Sa 18:16*
and he *b.* a trumpet, and said   *2Sa 20:1*
And he *b.* a trumpet, and   *2Sa 20:22*
they
And they *b.* the trumpet; and   *1Ki 1:39*
of the stairs, and *b.* with   *2Ki 9:13*
trumpets
rejoiced, and *b.* with   *2Ki 11:14*
trumpets
b. trumpets (A)(B)   *2Ch 7:6; 13:14*
winds *b.* and beat upon that   *M't 7:25*
b. and beat upon that house   *M't 7:27*
by reason of a great wind that   *Joh 6:18*
b.
south wind *b.* softly,   *Ac 27:13*
supposing
one day the south wind *b.* and   *Ac 28:13*
b. his trumpet (A)(B)(N)(P)(R)   *Re 8:7;*
  Re 8:9-10, 12; 9:1, 13; 11:15

BLIGHT

with *b.* and mildew (B)(S)   *De 28:22*
b. and mildew (A)(B)(R)   *1Ki 8:37*
I will send *b.* (S)   *2Ki 19:7*
if there be *b.* (S)   *2Ch 6:28*
with *b.* and mildew   *Am 4:9;*
(A)(B)(R)(S)   *Hag 2:17*
fall into *b.* and decay (P)   *Jas 1:11*
b. fell on the sun (B)   *Re 8:12*

BLIGHTED

blighted (S)   *Ge 41:6; 41:23, 27*
b. before it is grown (R)(S)   *2Ki 19:26*
b. before it is grown (S)   *Isa 37:27*

BLIGHTING

pestilence, *b.,* mildew (S)   *1Ki 8:37*

BLIND

or deaf, or the seeing, or the *b.*   *Ex 4:11*
a stumblingblock before the   *Le 9:14*
b.
a *b.* man, or a lame, or he that   *Le 21:18*
B., or broken, or maimed, or   *Le 22:22*
it be lame, or *b.* or have any   *De 15:21*
ill
a gift doth *b.* the eyes of the   *De 16:19*
wise
he that maketh the *b.* to   *De 27:18*
wander
b. gropeth in darkness, and   *De 28:29*
thou
bribe *b.* mine eyes   *1Sa 12:3*
therewith
take away *b.* and the lame   *2Sa 5:6;*
  5:8

I was eyes to the *b.* and feet *Job 29:15*
was I
Lord openeth the eyes of the *Ps 146:8*
b.
the *b.* shall see out of *Isa 29:18*
obscurity
eyes of the *b.* shall be opened *Isa 35:5*
open the *b.* eyes, to bring *Isa 42:7,*
out the *42:16, 18-19*
forth the *b.* people that have *Isa 43:8*
eyes
His watchmen are *b.*: they *Isa 56:10*
are all
for the wall like the *b.* and we *Isa 59:10*
and with them the *b.* and the *Jer 31:8*
lame
wandered as *b.* men in the *La 4:14*
streets
walk like *b.* men, because they *Zep 1:17*
the *b.* for sacrifice, is it not evil *Mal 1:8*
two *b.* men followed him, *M't 9:27*
crying
the house, the *b.* men came to *M't 9:28*
him
The *b.* receive their sight, and *M't 11:5*
one possessed with a devil, *b.* *M't 12:22*
b. leaders of the *b.* *M't 15:14;*
23:16-17. 24, 26
the lame, *b.*, maimed *M't 15:30;*
Lu 14:13, 21; Joh 5:3
the *b.* see *M't 15:31; Lu 7:21-22*
two *b.* men sitting by way *M't 20:30*
side
b. and lame came to him in *M't 21:14*
temple
they bring a *b.* man to him *M'k 8:22;*
8:23
b. Bartimaeus *M'k 10:46;*
10:49, 51
recovering sight to *b.* *Lu 4:18;*
Isa 61:1-3
Can the *b.* lead the *b.* *Lu 6:39*
a certain *b.* man sat by way *Lu 18:35*
side
which was *b.* from birth *Joh 9:1;*
Joh 9:2, 6, 8, 13, 17-20, 24-25, 32, 39-41
can devil open eyes of the *b.* *Joh 10:21*
opened the eyes of the *b.* *Joh 11:37*
have
shall be *b.* not seeing the sun *Ac 13:11*
thou thyself art a guide of the *Ro 2:19*
b.
he that lacketh these things is *2Pe 1:9*
b.
and poor, and *b.* and naked *Re 3:17*

BLINDED

He hath *b.* their eyes, and *Joh 12:40*
obtained it, and the rest were *Ro 11:7*
b.
But their minds were *b.*: for *2Co 3:14*
until
of this world hath *b.* the minds *2Co 4:4*
b. in world of allusion (P) *Eph 4:17*
that darkness hath *b.* his eyes *1Jo 2:11*

BLINDETH

b. the wise, and perverteth the *Ex 23:8*

BLINDFOLDED

And when they had *b.* him, *Lu 22:64*
they

BLINDNESS

at the door of the house with *Ge 19:11*
b.
smite thee with madness, and *De 28:28*
b.
this people, I pray thee, with *2Ki 6:18*
b.
And he smote them with *b.* *2Ki 6:18*
every horse of the people with *Zec 12:4*
b.
b. in part is happened to *Ro 11:25*
Israel
because of the *b.* of their *Eph 4:18*
heart

BLOCK

worship a *b.* of wood (A)(B) *Isa 44:19*
take up the stumbling *b.* out *Isa 57:14*

BLOCKED

snares of death *b.* me (B) *2Sa 22:6;*
18:18
b. me when distressed (B) *2Sa 22:19*

BLOOD

of thy brother's *b.* crieth unto *Ge 4:10*
me
thy brother's *b.* from thy hand *Ge 4:11*
thereof, which is the *b.* thereof *Ge 9:4*
surely your *b.* of your lives will *Ge 9:5*
sheddeth man's *b.*, his *b.* be *Ge 9:6*
shed
Shed no *b.* but cast him into *Ge 37:22*
goats, and dipped the coat in *Ge 37:31*
the *b.*
and his clothes in the *b.* of *Ge 49:11*
grapes
become *b.* upon the dry land *Ex 4:9*
a *b.* bridegroom to me *Ex 4:26*
(B)(E)(R)
rivers turned to *b.* *Ex 7:17; 7:19-21*
b. as token on posts *Ex 12:7;*
Ex 12:13, 22-23
not offer the *b.* of my sacrifice *Ex 23:18*
took half of *b.* and put it *Ex 24:6;*
24:8
pour *b.* *Ex 29:12;*
Le 4:7, 18, 25, 30, 34; 8:15; 9:9; 17:13;
Jer 18:21
b. of the sin offering *Ex 30:10*
b. of my sacrifice *Ex 34:25; 2Ki 16:15*
dip finger in *b.* *Le 4:6; 4:17; 9:9*
b. of the peace offerings *Le 7:33*
put *b.* on the altar *Le 8:24; 8:30*
b. of purifying *Le 12:4; 12:5*
issue of *b.* *Le 12:7;*
Le 15:25; M't 9:20; M'k 5:25; Le 8:43-44
dip living bird in *b.* *Le 14:6; 14:51*
b. of tresspass offerings *Le 14:14;*
Le 14:17, 25
b. imputed unto man *Le 17:4;*
Le 20:9, 11-13, 16, 27; Jos 2:19;
Eze 33:4-6, 8, 25
life of flesh is in the *b.* *Le 17:11;*
Le 17:14; De 12:23
the *b.* that maketh atonement *Le 17:11*
the fountain of her *b.* *Le 20:18;*
M'k 5:29
the revenger of *b.* *Nu 35:19;*
Nu 35:21, 24-25, 27; De 19:6, 12;
Jos 20:5, 9; 2Sa 14:11
the *b.* shall be forgiven *De 21:8*
drink the pure *b.* of the grape *De 32:14*
Amasa wallowed in *b.* in *2Sa 20:12*
highway
the *b.* of war *1Ki 2:5*
dogs licked the *b.* *1Ki 21:19; 22:38*
Moabites saw waters red as *2Ki 3:22;*
b. *3:23*
the *b.* of the burnt-offering *2Ki 16:15*
Her young ones suck up *b.* *Job 39:30*
What profit is there in my *b.* *Ps 30:9*
or drink the *b.* of goats *Ps 50:13*
wash his feet in *b.* of wicked *Ps 58:10;*
68:23
precious shall their *b.* be in *Ps 72:14*
his sight
had turned their rivers into *b.* *Ps 78:44*
revenging of the *b.* of thy *Ps 79:10*
servants
and condemn the innocent *b.* *Ps 94:21*
turned their waters into *b.* *Ps 105:29*
even the *b.* of their sons *Ps 106:38*
the land was polluted with *b.* *Ps 106:38*
let us lay wait for *b.* let us look *Pr 1:11*
they lay wait for their own *b.* *Pr 1:18*
to lie in wait for *b.*: but the *Pr 12:6*
mouth
violence to the *b.* of any *Pr 28:17*
person
of the nose bringeth forth *b.* *Pr 30:33*
delight not in the *b.* of *Isa 1:11*
bullocks
hear: your hands are full of *b.* *Isa 1:15*
have purged the *b.* of Jerusalem *Isa 4:4*
noise, and garments rolled in *b.* *Isa 9:5*
of Dimon shall be full of *b.* *Isa 15:9*
the earth also shall disclose *Isa 26:21*
her *b.*
his ears from hearing of *b.* *Isa 33:15*
shall be melted with their *b.* *Isa 34:3*
sword of Lord is filled with *b.* *Isa 34:6;*
34:7
be drunken with their own *b.* *Isa 49:26*
your hands are defiled with *b.* *Isa 59:3*
as if he offered swine's *b.*: he *Isa 66:3*
that
skirts is found the *b.* of the *Jer 2:34*
souls
this place with the *b.* of *Jer 19:4*
innocents
and made drunk with their *b.* *Jer 46:10*

keepeth back his sword from *Jer 48:10*
b.
and my *b.* upon the *Jer 51:35*
inhabitants of
that have shed the *b.* of the just *La 4:13*
polluted themselves with *b.* so *La 4:14*
but his *b.* will I require at *Eze 3:18;*
thine *3:20*
pestilence and *b.* shall pass *Eze 5:17*
city of *b.* guiltiness (R) *Eze 7:23*
the land is full of *b.* and the *Eze 9:9*
city
and pour out my fury upon it *Eze 14:19*
in *b.*
polluted in thine own *b.* I said *Eze 16:6*
Eze 16:9, 22, 36, 38
that is a robber, a shedder of *Eze 18:10*
b.
surely die; his *b.* shall be *Eze 18:13*
upon him
Thy mother is like a vine in *Eze 19:10*
thy *b.*
thy *b.* shall be in the midst of *Eze 21:32*
the
and *b.* is in their hands, and *Eze 23:37*
with
the manner of women that *Eze 23:45*
shed *b.*
are adulteresses, and *b.* is in *Eze 23:45*
their
For her *b.* is in the midst of *Eze 24:7*
her
I have set her *b.* upon the top *Eze 24:8*
of a
her pestilence, and *b.* into *Eze 28:23*
I will also water with thy *b.* *Eze 32:6*
his *b.* shall be upon him *Eze 33:5;*
Eze 33:6, 8, 25
him with pestilence and with *Eze 38:22*
b.
eat flesh, and drink *b.* *Eze 39:17;*
Eze 39:18-19
thou shalt take of the *b.* *Eze 43:20*
thereof
my bread, the fat and the *b.* *Eze 44:7*
offer unto me the fat and the *Eze 44:15*
b.
the priest shall take of the *b.* *Eze 45:19*
of the
I will avenge the *b.* of Jezreel *Ho 1:4*
upon
they break out, and *b.* toucheth *Ho 4:2*
b.
iniquity, and is polluted with *b.* *Ho 6:8*
therefore shall he leave his *b.* *Ho 12:14*
upon
b. and fire, and pillars of *Joe 2:30*
smoke.
darkness, and the moon into *Joe 2:31*
b.
they have shed innocent *b.* in *Joe 3:19*
their
For I will cleanse their *b.* that *Joe 3:21*
I
and lay not upon us innocent *Jon 1:14*
b.
They build up Zion with *b.* *Mic 3:10*
they all lie in wait for *b.*; they *Mic 7:2*
because of men's *b.* and for *Hab 2:8*
him that buildeth a town with *Hab 2:12*
b.
them afraid, because of men's *Hab 2:17*
b.
and their *b.* shall be poured *Zep 1:17*
out as
I will take away his *b.* out of *Zec 9:7*
his
by the *b.* of thy covenant I *Zec 9:11*
have
for flesh and *b.* hath not *M't 16:17*
revealed
with them in the *b.* of the *M't 23:30*
prophets
the righteous *b.* shed upon *M't 23:35*
from the *b.* of righteous Abel *M't 23:35*
unto the *b.* of Zacharias son *M't 23:35*
of
for this is my *b.* of the new *M't 26:28;*
testament *Lu 22:20*
because it is the price of *b.* *M't 27:6*
was called, The field of *b.* *M't 27:8*
unto this
I am innocent of the *b.* of *M't 27:24*
this just
His *b.* be on us, and on our *M't 27:25*
children
This is my *b.* of the new *M'k 14:24*
testament

the *b.* of all the prophets, *Lu 11:50*
which
From the *b.* of Abel *Lu 11:51*
unto the *b.* of Zacharias *Lu 11:51*
whose *b.* Pilate had mingled *Lu 13:1*
with
great drops of *b.* falling down *Lu 22:44*
to
Which were born, not of *b.* *Joh 1:13*
nor of
Son of man, and drink his *b.* *Joh 6:53*
he
eateth my flesh, and drinketh *Joh 6:54*
my *b.*
is meat indeed, and my *b.* is *Joh 6:55*
drink
eateth my flesh, and drinketh *Joh 6:56*
my *b.*
forthwith came there out *b.* *Joh 19:34*
that is to say, The field of *b.* *Ac 1:19*
b. and fire, an vapour of *Ac 2:19*
smoke
into darkness, and the moon *Ac 2:20*
into *b.*
intend to bring this man's *b.* *Ac 5:28*
upon
from things strangled, and *Ac 15:20*
from *b.*
offered to idols, and from *b.* *Ac 15:29*
hath made of one *b.* all *Ac 17:26*
nations of
Your *b.* be upon your own *Ac 18:6*
heads; I
that I am pure from the *b.* of *Ac 20:26*
all
hath purchased with his own *Ac 20:28*
b.
from *b.* and from strangled *Ac 21:25*
the *b.* of thy martyr Stephen *Ac 22:20*
was
Their feet are swift to shed *b.* *Ro 3:15*
through faith in his *b.* to *Ro 3:25*
declare
then, being now justified by his *Ro 5:9*
b.
the communion of the *b.* of *1Co 10:16*
Christ
the new testament in my *b.* *1Co 11:25*
of the body and *b.* of the *1Co 11:27*
Lord
that flesh and *b.* cannot *1Co 15:50*
inherit the
I conferred not with flesh and *Ga 1:16*
b.
have redemption through his *b.* *Eph 1:7*
are made nigh by the *b.* of *Eph 2:13*
Christ
wrestle not against flesh and *Eph 6:12*
b.
redemption through his *b.* even *Col 1:14*
made peace through the *b.* of *Col 1:20*
his
partakers of flesh and *b.* he *Heb 2:14*
also
once every year, not without *b.* *Heb 9:7*
neither by the *b.* of goats and *Heb 9:12*
calves, but by his own *b.* he *Heb 9:12*
For if the *b.* of bulls and of *Heb 9:13*
goats
How much more shall the *b.* *Heb 9:14*
testament was dedicated *Heb 9:18*
without *b.*
he took the *b.* of calves and *Heb 9:19*
Saying, This is the *b.* of the *Heb 9:20*
sprinkled with *b.* both the *Heb 9:21*
are by the law purged with *b.* *Heb 9:22*
without shedding of *b.* is no *Heb 9:22*
the holy place every year with *Heb 9:25*
b. of
that the *b.* of bulls and of *Heb 10:4*
goats
to enter into the holiest by *Heb 10:19*
the *b.* of
and hath counted the *b.* of *Heb 10:29*
passover, and the sprinkling *Heb 11:28*
of *b.*
not yet resisted unto *b.* *Heb 12:4*
striving
to the *b.* of sprinkling, that *Heb 12:24*
those beasts, whose *b.* is *Heb 13:11*
brought
sanctify the people with his *Heb 13:12*
own *b.*
through the *b.* of the *Heb 13:20*
everlasting
sprinkling of the *b.* of Jesus *1Pe 1:2*
Christ
with the precious *b.* of Christ, *1Pe 1:19*
as of
the *b.* of Jesus Christ his Son *1Jo 1:7*

water and *b.* even Jesus Christ *1Jo 5:6*
by water only, but by water and *1Jo 5:6*
b.
spirit, and the water, and the *b.* *1Jo 5:8*
us from our sins in his own *b.* *Re 1:5*
redeemed us to God by thy *b.* *Re 5:9*
out of
thou not judge and avenge our *Re 6:10*
b.
of hair, and the moon became *Re 6:12*
as *b.*
them white in the *b.* of the *Re 7:14*
Lamb
hail and fire mingled with *b.* and *Re 8:7*
third part of the sea became *b.* *Re 8:8*
over waters to turn them to *b.* *Re 11:6*
by the *b.* of the Lamb, and by *Re 12:11*
the city, and *b.* came out of *Re 14:20*
it became as the *b.* of a dead *Re 16:3*
man
of waters; and they became *b.* *Re 16:4*
shed the *b.* of saints and *Re 16:6*
prophets
thou hast given them *b.* to *Re 16:6*
drink
drunken with the *b.* of the *Re 17:6*
saints
and with the *b.* of the martyrs *Re 17:6*
of
And in her was found the *b.* *Re 18:24*
of
avenged the *b.* of his servants *Re 19:2*
at
clothed with a vesture dipped *Re 19:13*
in *b.*

BLOOD *BE UPON*

that curseth parents, his *b.* be *Le 20:9*
upon him
incest, his *b.* be *upon* him *Le 20:11*
sodomy, his *b.* be *upon* him *Le 20:13*
bestiality, his *b.* be *upon* him *Le 20:16*
wizard, their *b.* be *upon* them *Le 20:27*
innocent *b.* shed be *upon* thee *De 19:10*
abominations, his *b.* be *upon* *Eze 18:13*
him
warning, his *b.* shall *be upon* *Eze 33:5*
him

BLOOD *OF BULLOCK*

take *b.* of bullock *Ex 29:12;*
Le 4:5; 16:14, 18
pour *b.* of bullock at bottom of *Le 4:7*
altar
do with that as he did with *b.* *Le 16:15*
of bullock
I delight not in *b.* of bullocks *Isa 1:11*

BLOOD *OF CHRIST*

is it not communion of *b.* of *1Co 10:16*
Christ
far off, made nigh by *b.* of *Eph 2:13*
Christ
much more shall *b.* of Christ *Heb 9:14*
purge
with precious *b.* of Christ as a *1Pe 1:19*
lamb
b. of Christ cleanseth from all *1Jo 1:7*
sin

BLOOD *OF THE COVENANT*

Moses said, Behold *b.* of the *Ex 24:8*
covenant
as for thee also by the *b.* of *Zec 9:11*
covenant
counted *b.* of covenant an *Heb 10:29*
unholy thing
through *b.* of the everlasting *Heb 13:20*
covenant

BLOOD *with EAT*

statute that ye *eat* neither fat *Le 3:17*
nor *b.*
eat no manner of *b.* *Le 7:26;*
Le 7:27; 17:14; De 12:16, 23; 15:23
eateth b. shall be cut off *Le 7:27; 17:10*
people did *eat* them with the *1Sa 14:32*
b.
ye *eat* with *b.* and lift up *Eze 33:25*
your eyes

BLOOD *SPRINKLED*

b. Moses *sprinkled* on altar *Ex 24:6;*
Le 8:19, 24
Moses took *b.* and *sprinkled* *Ex 24:8*
on people

when there is *sprinkled b.* on *Le 6:27*
garment
Moses took *b.* and *sprinkled* on *Le 8:30*
Aaron
sons presented him *b.* he *Le 9:12;*
sprinkled *9:18*
Athaliah's *b.* *sprinkled* *2Ki 9:33*
on wall
Ahaz *sprinkled* the *b.* of *2Ki 16:13*
peace-offering
sprinkled b. of bullocks *2Ch 29:22;*
30:16
priests *sprinkled b.* from *2Ch 35:11*
hands
b. shall be *sprinkled* on my *Isa 63:3*
garment
he *sprinkled* with *b.* the *Heb 9:21*
tabernacle

FOR BLOOD

pollute land, *for b.* it defileth *Nu 35:33*
land
died *for b.* of Asahel his *2Sa 3:27*
brother
for the *b.* of sons of *2Ch 24:25*
Jehoiada
when he maketh inquisition *for Ps 9:12*
b.
come let us lay wait *for b.* *Pr 1:11;*
1:18
words of wicked to lie in wait *Pr 12:6*
for b.
they all lie in wait *for b.* they *Mic 7:2*
hunt

HIS BLOOD

if slay brother and conceal *his Ge 37:26*
b.
therefore behold *his b.* is *Ge 42:22*
required
his b. shall be upon his head *Jos 2:19*
shall I not require *his b.* of *2Sa 4:11*
your hand
Lord return *his b.* on his head *1Ki 2:32*
but *his b.* will require *Eze 3:18;*
at thy hand *Eze 33:4, 6, 8*
shall he leave *his b.* on him *Ho 12:14*
his b. be on us and our *M't 27:25*
children
church he hath purchased *Ac 20:28*
with *his b.*
propitiation through faith in *Ro 3:25*
his b.
being now justified by *his b.* *Ro 5:9*
have redemption thro *his b.* *Eph 1:7;*
Col 1:14
but by *his* own *b.* he entered *Heb 9:12*
in once
he might sanctify people *Heb 13:12*
with *his b.*
washed us from our sins in *his Re 1:5*
b.

INNOCENT BLOOD

innocent b. be not shed in *De 19:10*
land
put away guilt of *innocent b.* *De 19:13;*
21:9
lay not *innocent b.* to people *De 21:8*
wilt thou sin against *innocent 1Sa 19:5*
b.
take away *innocent b.* Joab *1Ki 2:31*
shed
Manasseh shed *innocent b.* *2Ki 21:16;*
24:4
gather and condemn *innocent Ps 94:21*
b.
shed *innocent b.* even blood *Ps 106:38*
of sons
Lord hateth hands shed *Pr 6:17*
innocent b.
make haste to shed *innocent b.* *Isa 59:7*
oppress not, shed not *innocent Jer 7:6;*
b. *22:3*
eyes and heart are to shed *Jer 22:17*
innocent b.
bring *innocent b.* on *Jer 26:15*
yourselves
they have shed *innocent b.* *Joe 3:19*
we beseech, lay not on us *Jon 1:14*
innocent b.
sinned I have betrayed *M't 27:4*
innocent b.

SHED BLOOD

man's *b.* by man his *b.* shed *Ge 9:6*
Reuben said to them, Shed no *Ge 37:22*
b.

there shall no *b.* be *shed* for   *Ex 22:2* him
risen upon him, *b.* be *shed* for *Ex 22:3* him
he hath *shed b.* that man shall *Le 17:4* be
cleansed of *b. shed* but by *b. Nu 35:33*
our hands have not *shed* this *b. De 21:7*
withholden from coming to *1Sa 25:26* *shed b.*
he slew and *shed b.* of   *1Ki 2:5* war
hast *shed b.* much *b.*   *1Ch 22:8;* 28:3
b. shed like water round   *Ps 79:3* Jerusalem
by revenging *b.* of thy servants *Ps 79:10* *shed*
make haste to *shed b.*   *Pr 1:16; Ro 3:15*
prophets have *shed b.* of just *La 4:13*
judge women that *shed b.*   *Eze 16:38;* 23:45
guilty in thy *b.* thou hast *shed Eze 22:4*
princes in the power to *shed Eze 22:6* *b.*
manner of women that *shed Eze 23:45* *b.*
shed b. and shall ye possess *Eze 33:25* land
hast *shed b.* of children of   *Eze 35:5* Israel
poured fury on them for *b. Eze 36:18* *shed*
on you come all righteous *b. M't 23:35* *shed*
this is my *b. shed M'k 14:24; Lu 22:20*
b. of all prophets which was *Lu 11:59* *shed*
when *b.* of Stephen was *shed Ac 22:20*
for they have *shed* the *b.* of the *Re 16:6* saints

SPRINKLE BLOOD

take ram's *b.* and *sprinkle* it   *Ex 29:16* on altar
sprinkle b. on altar round   *Ex 29:20;* about   *Le 1:5, 11; 3:2, 8, 13; 7:2; 17:6;* *Nu 18:17*
priest *sprinkle b.* seven times   *Le 4:6;* *Le 17; 16:14, 19*
sprinkle b. of sin-offering on   *Le 5:9* side of altar
it shall be priest's that *sprinkle Le 7:14* the *b.*
sprinkle of *b.* before   *Nu 19:4* tabernacle
sprinkle on it *b.* of   *2Ki 16:15* burnt-offering
when make an altar to   *Eze 43:18* *sprinkle b.*

WITH BLOOD

Aaron make atonement *with*   *Ex 30:10* *b.*
cleanse house *with b.* of bird *Le 14:52*
ye shall not eat any thing *with Le 19:26* *b.*
hoary head bring down *with b. 1Ki 2:9*
the land was polluted *with b. Ps 106:38*
sword filled *with b.* made fat *Isa 34:6* *with b.*
and their land shall be soaked *Isa 34:7* *with b.*
they shall be drunken *with Isa 49:26* their own *b.*
for your hands are defiled *with Isa 59:3* *b.*
filled place *with b.* of innocents *Jer 19:4*
it shall be made drunk *with Jer 46:10* their *b.*
have polluted themselves *with La 4:14* *b.*
I will plead against him *with Eze 38:22* *b.*
Gilead is a city polluted *with b. Ho 6:8*
build up Zion *with b.* and   *Mic 3:10* Jerusalem
woe to him that buildeth town *Hab 2:12* *with b.*
immediately I conferred not   *Ga 1:16* *with b.*
all things by law purged   *Heb 9:22* *with b.*
followed hail and fire, mingled *Re 8:7* *with b.*

saw woman drunken *with b.* of *Re 17:6* saints

BLOODGUILTINESS

Deliver me from *b.* O God   *Ps 51:14*

BLOODSHED

looking for justice, see *b.*   *Isa 5:7* (B)(R)

BLOODTHIRSTY

The *b.* hate the upright: but   *Pr 29:10*

BLOODY

Surely a *b.* husband art thou to *Ex 4:25*
A *b.* husband thou art because *Ex 4:26* of
come out, thou *b.* man, and   *2Sa 16:7* thou
because thou art a *b.* man   *2Sa 16:8*
for Saul, and for his *b.* house *2Sa 21:1*
Lord will abhor the *b.* and   *Ps 5:6*
with sinners, nor my life with *Ps 26:9* *b.*
b. and deceitful men shall not *Ps 55:23*
iniquity, and save me from *b. Ps 59:2*
depart from me therefore, ye *Ps 139:19* *b.*
the land is full of *b.* crimes *Eze 7:23*
wilt thou judge the *b.* city   *Eze 22:2*
Woe to the *b.* city, to the pot *Eze 24:6*
Woe to the *b.* city! I will even *Eze 24:9*
Woe to the *b.* city! it is full   *Nah 3:1*
lay sick of a fever and of a *b. Ac 28:8* flux

BLOOM

vines blossom and *b.* (B)(R)   *Ca 2:13*
b. of her youth (A)(B)   *1Co 7:36*

BLOOMED

and *b.* blossoms, and yielded   *Nu 17:8*

BLOSSOM

whom I shall choose, shall *b. Nu 17:5*
vines *b.* and bloom (B)(R)   *Ca 2:13;* *Ca 2:15; 7:12*
and their *b.* shall go up as dust *Isa 5:24*
Israel shall *b.* and bud, and fill *Isa 27:6*
shall rejoice, and *b.* as the rose *Isa 35:1*
It shall *b.* abundantly, and   *Isa 35:2* rejoice
Although the fig tree shall not *Hab 3:17* *b.*

BLOSSOMED

rod hath *b.* pride hath budded *Eze 7:10*

BLOSSOMS

it budded, and her *b.* shot   *Ge 40:10* forth
and bloomed *b.* and yielded   *Nu 17:8*
cast off *b.* (A)(B)(R)   *Job 15:33*

BLOT

b. me, I pray thee, out of thy *Ex 32:32* book
him will I *b.* out of my book *Ex 32:33*
and he shall *b.* them out with *Nu 5:23*
and *b.* out their name from   *De 9:14* under
b. out the remembrance of   *De 25:19* Amalek
the Lord shall *b.* out his name *De 29:20*
he would *b.* out the name of *2Ki 14:27* Israel
if any *b.* hath cleaved to mine *Job 31:7*
mercies *b.* out of my   *Ps 51:1* transgressions
sins, and *b.* out all mine   *Ps 51:9* iniquities
wicked man getteth himself a *b. Pr 9:7*
neither *b.* out their sin from   *Jer 18:23* thy
an ugly *b.* on your company   *2Pe 2:13* (N)
a *b.* on your love feasts (N)   *Jude 12*
I will not *b.* out his name out of *Re 3:5*

BLOTTED

let not their sin be *b.* out from *Ne 4:5*
the sin of his mother be *b. Ps 109:14* out
b. out, as a thick cloud, thy   *Isa 44:22*
Handiworks *b.* out (A)   *Eze 6:6*
your sins may be *b.* out, when *Ac 3:19*

BLOTTETH

he that *b.* out thy   *Isa 43:25* transgressions

BLOTTING

B. out the handwriting of   *Col 2:14*

BLOTS

b. and blemishes (A)(B)(R)   *2Pe 2:13*

BLOW

Thou didst *b.* with thy wind   *Ex 15:10*
when they shall *b.* with them   *Nu 10:3;* *Nu 10:4-10*
the trumpets to *b.* in his hand *Nu 31:6*
I will *b.* them away (B)   *De 32:26*
priests shall *b.* with the   *Jos 6:4* trumpets
When I *b.* with the trumpet, I   *J'g 7:18*
with me, then *b.* ye the   *J'g 7:18* trumpets
trumpets in their right hands to *J'g 7:20* *b.*
and *b.* ye with the trumpet   *1Ki 1:34*
did *b.* with the trumpets   *1Ch 15:24* before
I am consumed by the *b.* of   *Ps 39:10* thine
He caused an east wind to *b. Ps 78:26*
B. up the trumpet in the new *Ps 81:3*
he causeth his wind to *b.* and *Ps 147:18*
b. upon my garden, that the   *Ca 4:16*
he shall also *b.* upon them   *Isa 40:24*
B. ye the trumpet in the land   *Jer 4:5*
b. the trumpet in Tekoa, and set *Jer 6:1*
breach, with a very grievous *Jer 14:17* *b.*
b. the trumpet among the   *Jer 51:27* nations
I will *b.* against thee in the   *Eze 21:31* fire
to *b.* the fire upon it, to melt *Eze 22:20* it
I will gather you, and *b.*   *Eze 22:21* upon
upon the land, he *b.* the   *Eze 33:3* trumpet
b. not the trumpet, and the   *Eze 33:6*
B. ye the cornet in Gibeah, and *Ho 5:8*
B. ye the trumpet in Zion   *Joe 2:1*
B. the trumpet in Zion,   *Joe 2:15* sanctify
brought it home, I did *b.* upon *Hag 1:9* it
Lord God shall *b.* the trumpet *Zec 9:14*
when ye see the south wind *b. Lu 12:55*
wind should not *b.* on the earth *Re 7:1*

BLOWETH

when he *b.* a trumpet, hear ye *Isa 18:3*
the spirit of the Lord *b.* upon *Isa 40:7* it
the smith that *b.* the coals in *Isa 54:16*
the wind *b.* where it listeth   *Joh 3:8*

BLOWING

a memorial of *b.* of trumpets *Le 23:24*
a day of *b.* the trumpets unto *Nu 29:1* you
on and *b.* with trumpets   *Jos 6:9;* 6:13

BLOWN

a fire not *b.* shall consume *Job 20:26* him
the great trumpet shall be *b. Isa 27:13*
They have *b.* the trumpet, even *Eze 7:14*
Shall a trumpet be *b.* in the   *Am 3:6* city

BLUE

And *b.* and purple, and   *Ex 25:4;*
scarlet   *Ex 26:1, 31; 28:5-6, 8, 15, 28;* 35:6; 25; 36:8, 35; 39:1-3, 5, 8, 29

make loops of *b.*   *Ex 26:4; 36:11*
door of tabernacle of *b.,*   *Ex 26:36;*
and purple   *27:16; 36:37*
robe of the ephod all of *b.*   *Ex 28:31;*
    39:21-22
make pomegranates of *b.*   *Ex 28:33;*
    39:24
put it on a lace of *b.*   *Ex 28:37;*
    39:31
veil of *b.* and purple   *Ex 36:35;*
    2Ch 3:14
the court was needlework of   *Ex 38:18*
b.
ribband of *b.*   *Nu 15:38*
man of cunning work in *b.*   *2Ch 2:7;*
    2:14
white, green, and *b.* hangings   *Es 1:6*
b. and white, and black,   *Es 7:6*
marble
the king in royal apparel of   *Es 8:15*
b.
b. and purple is their clothing   *Jer 10:9*
were clothed with *b.* captains   *Eze 23:6*
b. and purple from the isles   *Eze 27:7*
in *b.* clothes, and broidered   *Eze 27:24*
work
b. and yellow (P)   *Re 9:17*

BLUENESS

b. of a wound cleanseth   *Pr 20:30*
away

BLUNDERING

know my folly and *b.*   *Ps 69:5*
(A)(B)(R)

BLUNT

If the iron be *b.* and he do   *Ec 10:10*
not

BLUSH

I am ashamed and *b.* to lift   *Ezr 9:6*
faces shall never *b.* (A)   *Ps 34:5*
ashamed, neither could they   *Jer 6:15*
b.
neither could they *b.:*   *Jer 8:12*
therefore

BOANERGES

he surnamed them *B.* which   *M'k 3:17*
is

BOAR

b. out of the wood doth   *Ps 80:13*
waste it

BOARD

cubits shall be the length of   *Ex 26:16;*
a *b.*   *Ex 26:17, 19, 21, 25; 36:21-22,*
    24, 26, 30
room and *b.* (B)   *J'g 17:10*
he put us on *b.* (S)   *Ac 27:6*
placed on *b.* (S)   *Ac 28:10*

BOARDS

make *b.* for the tabernacle   *Ex 26:15;*
Ex 26:17-20, 22-23, 25-29; 27:8; 35:11;
36:20, 22-25, 27-28, 30-34; 38:7; 39:33;
    40:18; Nu 3:36; 4:31
the house with beams and *b.*   *1Ki 6:9*
of
walls of the house within   *1Ki 6:15*
with *b.*
and the walls with *b.* of   *1Ki 6:16*
cedar
we will inclose her with *b.* of   *Ca 8:9*
thy ship *b.* of fir trees of   *Eze 27:5*
Senir
And the rest, some on *b.*   *Ac 27:44*

BOAST

Israel *b.* about (A)   *J'g 7:2*
that girdeth on his harness   *1Ki 20:11*
b.
thine heart lifteth thee up   *2Ch 25:19*
to *b.*
My soul shall make her *b.* in   *Ps 34:2*
In God we *b.* all the day long   *Ps 44:8*
trust in their wealth, and *b.*   *Ps 49:6*
workers of iniquity *b.*   *Ps 94:4*
themselves
images, that *b.* themselves of   *Ps 97:7*

B. not thyself of to morrow;   *Pr 27:1*
for
Shall the ax *b.* itself against   *Isa 10:15*
him
their glory shall ye *b.*   *Isa 61:6*
yourselves
they *b.* of wisdom (N)   *Ro 1:22*
law and makest thy *b.* of God   *Ro 2:17*
Thou that makest thy *b.* of the   *Ro 2:23*
B. not against the branches   *Ro 11:18*
if thou *b.* thou bearest not   *Ro 11:18*
no mortal man should *b.*   *1Co 1:29*
(A)(P)(R)
make my *b.* an empty *b.*   *1Co 9:15*
(N)(P)
for which I *b.* of you to   *2Co 9:2*
them of
an empty *b.* (A)(B)(N)   *2Co 9:3*
though I should *b.*   *2Co 10:8*
somewhat
we will not *b.* of things   *2Co 10:13*
without
not to *b.* in another man's   *2Co 10:16*
line
me, that I may *b.* myself a   *2Co 11:16*
little
b. of worldly things   *2Co 11:18*
(A)(B)(R)
of works, lest any man   *Eph 2:9*
should *b.*

BOASTED

with your mouth ye have *b.*   *Eze 35:13*
have scoffed and *b.* (R)   *Zep 2:10*
I have *b.* anything to him of   *2Co 7:14*

BOASTERS

despiteful, proud, *b.* inventors   *Ro 1:30*
covetous, *b.,* proud,   *2Ti 3:2*
blasphemers

BOASTEST

Why *b.* thou thyself in   *Ps 52:1*
mischief

BOASTETH

wicked *b.* of his heart's desire   *Ps 10:3*
he is gone his way, then he   *Pr 20:14*
b.
Whoso *b.* himself of a false   *Pr 25:14*
gift
little member, and *b.* great   *Jas 3:5*

BOASTFUL

Israel became *b.* (B)   *J'g 7:2*
said to the *b.* (A)(B)(R)   *Ps 75:4*
love is not *b.* (A)(N)(R)   *1Co 13:4*

BOASTING

the arrogant *b.* of (B)   *Isa 10:12*
the *b.* of the violent (B)   *Isa 13:11*
Theudas, *b.* himself to be   *Ac 5:36*
Where is *b.* then? It is   *Ro 3:27*
excluded
even so our *b.* which I made   *2Co 7:14*
love, and of our *b.* on your   *2Co 8:24*
behalf
lest our *b.* of you should be   *2Co 9:3*
in this same confident *b.*   *2Co 9:4*
Not *b.* of things without   *2Co 10:15*
our
no man shall stop me of   *2Co 11:10*
this *b.*
in this confidence of *b.*   *2Co 11:17*

BOASTINGS

now ye rejoice in your *b.:* all   *Jas 4:16*

BOASTLESS

that all humanity be *b.* (B)   *1Co 1:29*

BOASTS

utter monstrous *b.* (B)   *Da 11:36*
made *b.* against territory (R)   *Zep 2:8*
loud *b.* of folly (A)(R)   *2Pe 2:18*

BOAT

And there went over a ferry   *2Sa 19:18*
b.
boat (S)   *M't 4:21;*

M't 4:22; 8:23-24; 9:1; 13:2; 14:13, 22,
24, 29, 32; 15:39; M'k 1:19-20; 3:9;
4:1, 36-38; 5:2, 18, 21; 6:32, 45, 47, 51,
54; 8:10, 13-14; Lu 5:3, 7; 8:22, 37;
    Joh 6:17, 19, 21; 21:3, 6, 8
that there was none other *b.*   *Joh 6:22*
there
with his disciples into the *b.*   *Joh 6:22*
much work to come by the   *Ac 27:16*
b.
when they had let down the   *Ac 27:30*
b.
cut off the ropes of the *b.*   *Ac 27:32*

BOATS

boats (S)   *M'k 4:36;*
    Lu 5:2-3, 7, 11; Joh 6:24
Howbeit there came other *b.*   *Joh 6:23*

BOAZ

Elimelech; and his name was   *Ru 2:1;*
B.   *Ru 2:3-5, 8, 11, 14-15, 19, 23; 3:2,*
    7; 4:1, 5, 8-9, 13, 21
and called the name thereof   *1Ki 7:21*
B.
begat Salma, and Salma   *1Ch 2:11*
begat *B.*
B. begat Obed, and Obed   *1Ch 2:12*
begat
the name of that on the left   *2Ch 3:17*
B.

BOCHERU

these, Azrikam, *B.* and   *1Ch 8:38*
Ishmael
B. and Ishmael, and   *1Ch 9:44*
Sheariah

BOCHIM

came up from Gilgal to *B.* and   *J'g 2:1*
called the name of the place   *J'g 2:5*
B.

BODIES

bending their *b.* (B)   *Ge 43:28*
lord, but our *b.* and our   *Ge 47:18*
lands
body of Saul and the *b.* of   *1Sa 31:12*
his
All were dead *b.* (A)(S)   *2Ki 19:35;*
    Isa 37:36
away the body of Saul, and   *1Ch 10:12*
the *b.*
they have dominion over our   *Ne 9:37*
b.
ashes, your *b.* to *b.* of clay   *Job 13:12*
another, and two covered   *Eze 1:11*
their *b.*
covered on that side, their *b.*   *Eze 1:23*
upon whose *b.* the fire had   *Da 3:27*
no
and yielded their *b.* that they   *Da 3:28*
and many *b.* of the saints   *M't 27:52*
which
the *b.* should not remain   *Joh 19:31*
upon
to dishonour their own *b.*   *Ro 1:24*
between
shall also quicken your   *Ro 8:11*
mortal *b.*
that ye present your *b.* a   *Ro 12:1*
living
that your *b.* are the   *1Co 6:15*
members of
also celestial *b.* and *b.*   *1Co 15:40*
terrestrial
to love their wives as their   *Eph 5:28*
own *b.*
and our *b.* washed with   *Heb 10:22*
pure
For the *b.* of those beasts,   *Heb 13:11*
whose
defiling *b.* of filthy fantasies   *Jude 8*
(P)

DEAD BODIES

they were *dead b.* fallen   *2Ch 20:24*
they found *dead b.* precious   *2Ch 20:25*
jewels
dead b. of servants given to   *Ps 79:2*
be meat
he shall fill the places with   *Ps 110:6*
the *dead b.*
whole valley of *dead b.* be   *Jer 31:40*
holy

it is to fill them with *dead b.*   *Jer 33:5*
of men
dead b. shall be for meat to   *Jer 34:20*
fowls
pit wherein Ishmael cast *dead*   *Jer 41:9*
b.
shall be many *dead b.* in   *Am 8:3*
every place
their *dead b.* shall lie in   *Re 11:8*
street of city
nations see their *dead b.*   *Re 11:9*
three days
not suffer their *dead b.* be put   *Re 11:9*
in graves

BODILY

sustain in *b.* pain (A)   *Ps 18:14*
Holy Ghost descended in a *b.*   *Lu 3:22*
satisfying *b.* appetites (N)   *Ro 13:14*
on account of *b.* ailment   *Ga 4:13*
(A)(N)(P)(R)
but his *b.* presence is weak   *2Co 10:10*
all the fulness of the Godhead   *Col 2:9*
b.
For *b.* exercise profiteth little   *1Ti 4:8*
b. pollution (N)   *1Pe 3:21*

BODY

from your own *b.* (A)(B)   *Ge 15:4*
as it were *b.* of heaven   *Ex 24:10*
he shall come at no dead *b.*   *Nu 6:6*
we are defiled by the dead *b.*   *Nu 9:7*
Whosoever toucheth a dead   *Nu 19:13;*
b.   *19:16*
in the fruit of thy *b.*   *De 30:9*
took the *b.* of Saul   *1Sa 31:12;*
  1Ch 10:12
proceed from own *b.*   *2Sa 7:12*
(B)(R)(S)
come from own *b.* (B)   *2Sa 16:11*
my mother's *b.* (S)   *Job 3:11;*
  Ps 22:10; Ro 16:18; 1Co 6:13
the *b.* shall grieve (A)   *Job 14:22*
children's sake of mine own   *Job 19:17*
b.
worms destroy this *b.*, yet   *Job 19:26*
in flesh
drawn, and cometh out of   *Job 20:25*
the *b.*
b. cleaves to the ground   *Ps 44:25*
(A)(B)(E)(R)
when thy flesh and thy *b.* are   *Pr 5:11*
innermost parts of the *b.*   *Pr 18:8*
(A)(B)(E)(R)
his *b.* as bright ivory   *Ca 5:14*
(A)(B)(E)(R)
consume both soul and *b.*   *Isa 10:18*
offspring of your *b.* (B)(S)   *Isa 48:19*
your *b.* (S)   *Isa 49:1;*
  Job 20:16
thou hast laid thy *b.* as the   *Isa 51:23*
ground
they were more ruddy in *b.*   *La 4:7*
than
their whole *b.* was full of   *Eze 10:12*
eyes
in my spirit in the midst of   *Da 7:15*
my *b.*
my *b.* trembles (B)(E)(R)   *Hab 3:16*
unclean by a dead *b.* touch   *Hag 2:13*
any
thy whole *b.* cast into hell   *M't 5:29;*
  5:30
light of the *b.* is the eye   *M't 6:22;*
  M't 6:23, 25; Lu 11:34, 36
destroy *b.* and soul in hell   *M't 10:28;*
  Lu 12:4
took the *b.* of John the   *M't 14:12*
Baptist
poured ointment on my *b.*   *M't 26:26;*
  M'k 14:8
Take eat; this is my *b.*   *M't 26:26;*
  Lu 22:19
begged the *b.* of Jesus   *M't 27:58;*
M't 27:59; M'k 15:43; 45;   Lu 23:52;
  Joh 19:38, 40
she felt in her *b.* that she   *M'k 5:29*
was
took up John's *b.*   *M'k 6:29*
(A)(B)(N)(P)(R)
cloth cast about his naked   *M'k 15:43*
b.
b. more than raiment   *Lu 12:23;*
  Lu 12:22
Wheresoever the *b.* is thither   *Lu 17:37*
will
found not *b.* of the Lord   *Lu 24:3;*
  Joh 20:12

Peter turning to the *b.* said,   *Ac 9:40*
Tabitha
the *b.* of sin might be   *Ro 6:6*
destroyed
reign in your mortal *b.* that   *Ro 6:12*
ye
dead to the law by the *b.* of   *Ro 7:4*
Christ
shall deliver me from the *b.*   *Ro 7:24*
of this
the *b.* is dead because of sin;   *Ro 8:10*
but
do mortify the deeds of the   *Ro 8:13*
b., ye
to wit, the redemption of our   *Ro 8:23*
b.
we have many members in   *Ro 12:4*
one *b.*
being many, are one *b.* in   *Ro 12:5*
Christ
For I verily, as absent in *b.*   *1Co 5:3*
but
b. experience powers of sin   *1Co 5:5*
(P)
Now the *b.* is not for   *1Co 6:13;*
fornication   *1Co 6:16, 18-20*
wife hath not power of her   *1Co 7:4*
own *b.*
she may be holy both in *b.*   *1Co 7:34*
and in
But I keep under my *b.* and   *1Co 9:27*
bring
is it not the communion of   *1Co 10:16*
the *b.*
many are one bread, and   *1Co 10:17*
one *b.*
Take, eat: this is my *b.*   *1Co 11:24*
which is
shall be guilty of the *b.*   *1Co 11:27*
and blood
not discerning the Lord's   *1Co 11:29*
b.
blind to presence of Lord's   *1Co 11:29*
b. (P)
For as the *b.* is one, and   *1Co 12:12;*
hath many members   *1Co 12:14-20,*
  22-25, 27
all baptized into one *b.*   *1Co 12:13*
though I give my *b.* to be   *1Co 13:3*
burned
with what *b.* do they come   *1Co 15:35;*
  1Co 15:37
God giveth it a *b.* every   *1Co 15:38*
seed
sown natural *b.*, raised   *1Co 15:44*
spiritual *b.*
bearing about in the *b.* the   *2Co 4:10*
dying
might be made manifest in   *2Co 4:10*
our *b.*
whilst we are at home in the   *2Co 5:6*
b. we
rather to be absent from the   *2Co 5:8*
b.
the *b.* I cannot tell   *2Co 12:2*
or whether out of the *b.*   *2Co 12:2*
in the *b.* or out of the *b.* I   *2Co 12:3*
cannot
I bear in my *b.* the marks of   *Ga 6:17*
Which is his *b.* the fulness of   *Eph 1:23*
him
unto God in one *b.* by the   *Eph 2:16*
cross
fellow heirs, and of the same   *Eph 3:6*
b.
There is one *b.* and one   *Eph 4:4*
Spirit
ministry, for the edifying of   *Eph 4:12*
the *b.*
building up *b.* of Christ   *Eph 4:12*
(A)(B)(E)(N)(P)(R)
From whom the whole *b.*   *Eph 4:16*
fitly
maketh increase of the *b.*   *Eph 4:16*
unto
and he is the saviour of the   *Eph 5:23*
b.
For we are members of his   *Eph 5:30*
b. of
Christ shall be magnified in   *Ph'p 1:20*
my *b.*
mutilators of your *b.* (P)   *Ph'p 3:2*
Who shall change our vile   *Ph'p 3:21*
b. that
And he is the head of the *b.*   *Col 1:18*
In the *b.* of his flesh through   *Col 1:22*
putting off the *b.* of the sins   *Col 2:11*
of the
of things to come; but the *b.*   *Col 2:17*
is of

from which all the *b.* by   *Col 2:19*
joints and
humility, and neglecting of   *Col 2:23*
the *b.*
which also ye are called in   *Col 3:15*
one *b.*
possess his own *b.*   *1Th 4:4*
(A)(N)(P)
and *b.* be preserved   *1Th 5:23*
blameless
but in a *b.* hast thou   *Heb 10:5*
prepared me
through the offering of the   *Heb 10:10*
b. of
as being yourselves also in   *Heb 13:3*
the *b.*
things which are needful to   *Jas 2:16*
the *b.*
as the *b.* without the spirit is   *Jas 2:26*
dead
able also to bridle the whole   *Jas 3:2*
b.
and to turn about their whole   *Jas 3:3*
b.
that it defileth the whole *b.*   *Jas 3:6*
pay honor to a woman's *b.*   *1Pe 3:7*
(N)(R)
washing of a dirty *b.*   *1Pe 3:21*
(P)(R)
corrupt the *b.* (A)(B)(N)   *Jude 8*
he disputed about the *b.* of   *Jude 9*
Moses

DEAD BODY

nor go in to any *dead b.*   *Le 21:11;*
  Nu 6:6
certain men defiled by a *dead*   *Nu 9:6*
b.
any be unclean by a *dead b.*   *Nu 9:10;*
  Hag 2:13
toucheth *dead b.* be unclean   *Nu 19:11;*
  19:16
how he restored *dead b.* to   *2Ki 8:5*
life
with my *dead b.* shall they   *Isa 26:19*
arise
and cast his *dead b.* into   *Jer 26:23*
the graves
his *dead b.* shall be cast out   *Jer 36:30*
in the day

FRUIT OF BODY

blessed shall be the *fruit of*   *De 28:4*
thy b.
plenteous in *fruit of thy b.*   *De 28:11;*
  De 30:9
cursed shall be *fruit of thy*   *De 28:18*
b.
thou shalt eat the *fruit of*   *De 28:53*
thy b.
fruit of thy b. will I set on   *Ps 132:11*
throne
give *fruit of my b.* for sin of   *Mic 6:7*
my soul

HIS BODY

his *b.* not remain all night   *De 21:23*
on tree
Gideon had 70 sons of *his b.*   *J'g 8:30*
fastened *his b.* to wall of   *1Sa 31:10*
Bethshan
his *b.* wet with dew of   *Da 4:33;*
heaven   *Da 5:21*
till beast was slain, and *his*   *Da 7:11*
b. destroyed
his *b.* also was like the beryl   *Da 10:6*
women beheld now *his b.*   *Lu 23:55*
laid
when they found not *his b.*   *Lu 24:23*
they came
he spake of the temple of   *Joh 2:21*
his b.
from *his b.* were brought to   *Ac 19:12*
sick
he considered not *his b.* now   *Ro 4:19*
dead
fornication sinneth against   *1Co 6:18*
his b.
husband hath not power of   *1Co 7:4*
his b.
may receive things done in   *2Co 5:10*
his b.
which is *his b.* fulness of   *Eph 1:23*
him
be fashioned like to *his*   *Ph'p 3:21*
glorious *b.*
bare our sins in *his b.* on   *1Pe 2:24*
tree

IN BODY

more ruddy *in b.* than rubies   *La 4:7*
let not sin reign *in* your   *Ro 6:12*
mortal *b.*
I verily as absent *in b.* have   *1Co 5:3*
judged
glorify God *in* your *b.* and   *1Co 6:20*
spirit
that she may be holy *in b.*   *1Co 7:34*
and in spirit
God hath set members   *1Co 12:18*
every one *in* the *b.*
that there should be no   *1Co 12:25*
schism *in* the *b.*
bearing *in b.* dying of Lord   *2Co 4:10*
that life of Jesus might be
manifest *in b.*
knowing that whilst we are at   *2Co 5:6*
home *in b.*
whether *in b.* or whether out   *2Co 12:2*
of the body
I bear *in b.* marks of the   *Ga 6:17*
Lord
Christ shall be magnified *in*   *Ph'p 1:20*
my *b.*
reconciled *in b.* of flesh thro'   *Col 1:22*
death
as being yourselves also *in*   *Heb 13:3*
the *b.*

ONE BODY

we have many members in   *Ro 12:4*
one *b.*
we are *one b.* in Christ   *Ro 12:5;*
     1Co 10:17
he that is joined to an harlot, *1Co 6:16*
is *one b.*
as *b.* is *one,* and hath   *1Co 12:12*
many members
we are baptized into *one b.*   *1Co 12:13*
whether Jews
now are they many   *1Co 12:20*
members, yet but *one b.*
he might reconcile both to   *Eph 2:16*
God in *one b.*
there is *one b.* and one Spirit   *Eph 4:4*
to which ye are also called   *Col 3:15*
in *one b.*

BODY'S

in my flesh for his *b.* sake,   *Col 1:24*
which

BOHAN

border went up to the stone   *Jos 15:6*
of *B.*
and descended to the stone   *Jos 18:17*
of *B.*

BOIL

a *b.* breaking forth with   *Ex 9:9;*
blains   *9:10-11*
boil (A)(E)(R)   *Ex 16:23;*
Ex 23:19;   *29:31;*   *34:26;*   *De:14:21*
boil (S)   *Ex 16:23;*
23:19; 29:31; 34:26; De 14:21; 2Ki 4:38;
     Eze 24:5; Zec 14:21
boil (B)   *Ex 23:19;*
     Ex 29:31; 34:26; De 14:21
B. the flesh at the door of the *Le 8:31*
in the skin thereof, was a *b.* *Le 13:18;*
     Le 13:19-23
smite thee with *b.* (S)   *De 28:27;*
     28:35
b. stew, pottage (B)(E)(R) *2Ki 4:38*
And they took and laid it on *2Ki 20:7*
the *b.*
He maketh the deep to *b.* *Job 41:31*
like a
lay it for a plaister upon   *Isa 38:21*
the *b.*
the fire causeth the waters to *b. Isa 64:2*
make it *b.* well, and let them *Eze 24:5*
and *b.* well (E)   *Eze 24:5*
the priests shall *b.* the   *Eze 46:20*
trespass
b. their sacrifices   *Zec 14:21*
(A)(B)(E)(R)

BOILED

b. pottage, offerings (S)   *Ge 25:29;*
     2Ch 35:13
boiled (A)(E)(R)(S)   *Ex 12:9;*
Le 6:28; Nu 6:19; 1Sa 2:15; La 4:10

boiled (B)   *Nu 6:19;*
     1Sa 2:15; La 4:10
b. their flesh with the   *1Ki 19:21*
instruments
So we *b.* my son, and did   *2Ki 6:29*
eat him
b. in pots (B)(E)(R)   *2Ch 35:13*
My bowels *b.* and rested   *Job 30:27*
not

BOILING

Jacob *b.* pottage (B)(E)(R)   *Ge 25:29*
while flesh was *b.*   *1Sa 2:13*
(A)(B)(E)(R)(S)
b. pot (B)(E)(R)(S)   *Job 41:20;*
     Jer 1:13
and it was made with *b.*   *Eze 46:23*
places

BOILS

before Moses because of the *Ex 9:11*
b.
with *b.* of Egypt   *De 28:27*
(A)(B)(E)(R)
smote Job with sore *b.* from *Job 2:7*
my inside *b.* (B)   *Job 30:27*

BOISTEROUS

when he saw the wind *b.* he *M't 14:30*
was
felt a strong wind (A)   *M't 14:30*
saw the strength of the gale *M't 14:30*
(N)
saw the fury of the wind   *M't 14:30*
(P)

BOLD

but the righteous are *b.* as a *Pr 28:1*
lion
Paul and Barnabas waxed *b.* *Ac 13:46*
Esaias is very *b.* and saith, *Ro 10:20*
I was
we speak very *b.* (R)   *2Co 3:12*
being absent am *b.* toward *2Co 10:1;*
you   *2Co 10:2; 11:21*
much more *b.* to speak the *Ph'p 1:14*
word
we were *b.* in our God to   *1Th 2:2*
speak
I might be much *b.* in Christ *Ph'm 8*
b. and wilful (R)   *2Pe 2:10*

BOLDLY

came upon the city *b.* and   *Ge 34:25*
slew
and went in *b.* unto Pilate   *M'k 15:43*
But, lo, he speaketh *b.* and *Joh 7:26*
they
he had preached *b.* at   *Ac 9:27*
Damascus
spake *b.* in the name of the *Ac 9:29*
Lord
speaking *b.* in the Lord, which *Ac 14:3*
to speak *b.* in the synagogue *Ac 18:26*
spake *b.* for the space of three *Ac 19:8*
spoke *b.* arguing, pleading (A) *Ac 19:8*
I have written the more *b.*   *Ro 15:15*
unto
speak out *b.* (N)   *2Co 3:12*
may open my mouth *b.* to   *Eph 6:19*
make
may speak *b.* as I ought to   *Eph 6:20*
speak
b. confessed your loyalty (P) *1Ti 6:12*
Let us therefore come *b.*   *Heb 4:16*
unto
So that we may *b.* say, The *Heb 13:6*
Lord

BOLDNESS

the *b.* of his face shall be   *Ec 8:1*
changed
they saw the *b.* of Peter and *Ac 4:13*
John
all *b.* they may speak thy   *Ac 4:29*
word
they saw the *b.* of Peter and *Ac 4:13*
with *b.*
with *b.* openly (A)(E)   *Ac 28:31*
Great is my *b.* of speech   *2Co 7:4*
toward
In whom we have *b.* and   *Eph 3:12*
access

but that with all *b.* as   *Ph'p 1:20*
always
great *b.* in the faith which is *1Ti 3:13*
b. to enter into the holiest *Heb 10:19*
by the
have *b.* in the day of   *1Jo 4:17*
judgment

BOLLED

in the ear, and the flax was   *Ex 9:31*
b.

BOLSTER

pillow of goats' hair for his *1Sa 19:13;*
b.   *19:16*
stuck in the ground at his   *1Sa 26:7;*
b.   *1Sa 26:11-12, 16*

BOLT

woman out from me, and   *2Sa 13:17*
b. the
handles of the *b.* (A)(E)(R)   *Ca 5:5*

BOLTED

out and *b.* the door after   *2Sa 13:18*
her

BOLTS

fiery *b.* went forth (E)   *Hab 3:5*

BOND

bind soul with a *b.*   *Nu 30:2;*
     Nu 30:3-4, 10-12
b. servants (S)   *De 20:11*
and free (S)   *2Ki 9:8*
He looseth the *b.* of kings *Job 12:18*
put to *b.* service (B)   *Isa 31:8*
I will bring you into the *b.* *Eze 20:37*
of the
be loosed from this *b.* on   *Lu 13:16*
bitterness, and in the *b.* of   *Ac 8:23*
whether we be *b.* or free   *1Co 12:13*
there is neither *b.* nor free,   *Ga 3:28*
there
of the Spirit in the *b.* of   *Eph 4:3*
peace
Lord, whether he be *b.* or   *Eph 6:8*
free
Barbarian, Scythian, *b.* nor *Col 3:11*
free
which is the *b.* of perfectness *Col 3:14*
rich and poor, free and *b.* to *Re 13:16*
flesh of all men, both free   *Re 19:18*
and *b.*

BONDAGE

their lives bitter with hard *b.* *Ex 1:14*
sighed by reason of the *b.*   *Ex 2:23*
up unto God by reason of the *Ex 2:23*
b.
whom the Egyptians keep in *b. Ex 6:5*
and I will rid you out of their *Ex 6:6*
b.
anguish of spirit, and for cruel *Ex 6:9*
b.
for cruel *b.* (R)   *Ex 6:9*
out of house of *b.*   *Ex 13:3,*
Ex 13:3, 14; 20:2; De 5:6; 6:12; 8:14;
     13:5, 10; Jos 24:17; J'g 6:8
out of the house of *b.* (S)   *De 7:8;*
     Jer 34:13
give us a little reviving in our *Ezr 9:8*
b.
hath not forsaken us in our *b. Ezr 9:9*
we bring into *b.* our sons and *Ne 5:5*
our
our daughters are brought   *Ne 5:5*
unto *b.*
because the *b.* was heavy   *Ne 5:18*
upon
a captain to return to their *b. Ne 9:17*
the hard *b.* wherein thou   *Isa 14:3*
wast
and were never in *b.* to any *Joh 8:33*
man
they should bring them into *b. Ac 7:6*
to whom they shall be in *b.* *Ac 7:7*
will
received the spirit of *b.* again *Ro 8:15*
to
brought under *b.* (B)   *Ro 8:20*
shall be delivered from the *b. Ro 8:21*

a sister is not under b. in   *1Co 7:15*
such
if a man bring you into b.   *2Co 11:20*
that they might bring us into   *Ga 2:4*
b.
were in b. under the elements   *Ga 4:3*
of
ye desire again to be in b.   *Ga 4:9*
which gendereth to b. which   *Ga 4:24*
is
and is in b. with her children   *Ga 4:25*
again with the yoke of   *Ga 5:1*
all their lifetime subject to   *Heb 2:15*
b.
of the same is he brought in   *2Pe 2:19*
b.

BONDED

b. and knit together (N)   *Eph 4:16*

BONDMAID

is a b. betrothed to an   *Le 19:20*
husband
two sons, the one by a b. the   *Ga 4:22*

BONDMAIDS

Both thy bondmen, and thy   *Le 25:44*
b.
them shall ye buy bondmen   *Le 25:44*
and b.

BONDMAN

Instead of the lad a b. to   *Ge 44:33*
my lord
remember that thou wast a   *De 15:15;*
b. in   *16:12*
thou wast a b. in Egypt, and   *De 24:18*
a b. in the land of Egypt   *De 24:22*
every b. and every free man,   *Re 6:15*
hid

BONDMEN

and take us for b. and our   *Ge 43:18*
asses
and we also will be my lord's   *Ge 44:9*
b.
Egypt: they shall not be sold   *Le 25:42*
as b.
Both thy b. and thy   *Le 25:44*
bondmaids.
they shall be your b. for ever   *Le 25:46*
that ye should not be their   *Le 26:13*
b.
We were Pharaoh's b. in   *De 6:21*
Egypt
you out of the house of b.   *De 7:8*
be sold unto your enemies   *De 28:68*
for b.
none of you be freed from   *Jos 9:23*
being b.
Israel did Solomon make no   *1Ki 9:22*
b.
unto him my two sons to be   *2Ki 4:1*
b.
of Judah and Jerusalem for   *2Ch 28:10*
b.
For we were b.; yet our God   *Ezr 9:9*
hath
But if we had been sold for b.   *Es 7:4*
of Egypt, out of the house   *Jer 34:13*
of b.

BONDS

or of her b. wherewith she   *Nu 30:5;*
   Nu 30:7, 12, 14
and her b. wherewith she   *Nu 30:7*
bound
or all her b. which are upon   *Nu 30:14*
her
put him in b. (S)   *2Ki 23:33*
find the b. of Pleiades (B)   *Job 38:31*
handmaid, hast loosed my   *Ps 116:16*
b.
broken the yoke and burst the   *Jer 5:5*
b.
Make thee b. and yokes, and   *Jer 27:2*
put
burst thy b. and strangers   *Jer 30:8*
shall
and will burst thy b. in   *Na 1:13*
sunder
broke the b. (S)   *Lu 8:29*
saying that b. and afflictions   *Ac 20:23*
charge worthy of death or   *Ac 23:29*
of b.

a certain man left in b. by   *Ac 25:14*
Felix
such as I am, except these   *Ac 26:29*
b.
nothing worthy of death or   *Ac 26:31*
of b.
which I am an ambassador   *Eph 6:20*
in b.
as both in my b. and in the   *Ph'p 1:7;*
   Ph'p 1:13-14, 16
for which I am also in b.   *Col 4:3*
Remember my b. Grace b.   *Col 4:18*
with
as an evil doer, even unto b.   *2Ti 2:9*
whom I have begotten in my   *Ph'm 10*
b.
have ministered unto me in   *Ph'm 13*
the b.
had compassion of me in   *Heb 10:34*
my b.
moreover of b. and   *Heb 11:36*
imprisonment
Remember them that are in   *Heb 13:3*
b.

BONDSERVANT

compel him to serve as a b.   *Le 25:39*

BONDSERVICE

Solomon levy a tribute of b.   *1Ki 9:21*

BONDWOMAN

Cast out this b. and her   *Ge 21:10;*
son   *Ge 21:12-13; Ga 4:23, 30-31*

BONDWOMEN

for bondmen and b. and no   *De 28:68*
man
for bondmen and b. unto   *2Ch 28:10*
you
bondmen and b. I had held my   *Es 7:4*

BONE

This is now b. of my bones   *Ge 2:23*
thou art my b. and my flesh   *Ge 29:14*
neither shall ye break a b.   *Ex 12:46*
thereof
nor break any b. of it   *Nu 9:12*
a dead body, or a b. of a   *Nu 19:16*
man
him that touched a b. or   *Nu 19:18*
one slain
that I am your b. and your   *J'g 9:2*
flesh
Behold, we are thy b. and thy   *2Sa 5:1*
flesh
Art thou not of my b. and   *2Sa 19:13*
of my
Behold, we are thy b. and   *1Ch 11:1*
thy flesh
touch his b. and his flesh,   *Job 2:5*
and he
My b. cleaveth to my skin   *Job 19:20*
and to
mine arm be broken from   *Job 31:22*
the b.
all mine enemies upon the   *Ps 3:7*
cheek b.
a soft tongue breaketh the b.   *Pr 25:15*
bones came together, b. to   *Eze 37:7*
his b.
when any seeth a man's b.   *Eze 39:15*
then
A b. of him shall not be   *Joh 19:36*
broken

BONES

bone of my b. and flesh of   *Ge 2:23*
my
shall carry up my b. from   *Ge 50:25*
hence
took the b. of Joseph with   *Ex 13:19*
him
ye shall carry up my b.   *Ex 13:19*
away hence
break their b. and pierce   *Nu 24:8*
them
b. of Joseph, which the   *Jos 24:32*
children
divided her, together with   *J'g 19:29*
her b.
took their b. and buried   *1Sa 31:13*
them
ye are my b. and my flesh   *2Sa 19:12*
went and took the b. of   *2Sa 21:12;*

Saul   *21:13-14*
men's b. shall be burnt upon   *1Ki 13:2*
thee
buried; lay my b. beside his   *1Ki 13:31*
b.
and touched the b. of   *2Ki 13:21*
Elisha
their places with b. of men   *2Ki 23:14;*
   2Ki 23:16, 18, 20
buried their b. under the   *1Ch 10:12*
oak in
b. of the priests upon their   *2Ch 34:5*
altars
which made all my b. to   *Job 4:14*
shake
fenced me with b. and   *Job 10:11*
sinews
His b. are full of the sin of   *Job 20:11*
his
his b. are moistened with   *Job 21:24*
marrow
My b. are pierced in me in   *Job 30:17*
and my b. are burned with   *Job 30:30*
heat
of his b. with strong pain   *Job 33:19*
b. that were not seen stick   *Job 33:21*
out
b. are as strong as pieces of   *Job 40:18*
his b. are like bars of iron   *Job 40:18*
heal me; for my b. are vexed   *Ps 6:2*
all my b. are out of joint   *Ps 22:14*
all my b. they look and   *Ps 22:17*
stare
and my b. are consumed   *Ps 31:10*
b. waxed old through my   *Ps 32:3*
roaring
He keepeth all his b.: not   *Ps 34:20*
one of
All my b. shall say, Lord,   *Ps 35:10*
who is
neither is there any rest in my   *Ps 38:3*
b.
with a sword in my b.   *Ps 42:10*
the b. which thou hast broken   *Ps 51:8*
God hath scattered the b. of   *Ps 53:5*
him
my b. are burned as an   *Ps 102:3*
hearth
my b. cleave to my skin   *Ps 102:5*
water, and like oil into his   *Ps 109:18*
b.
Our b. are scattered at the   *Ps 141:7*
grave's
thy navel, and marrow to thy   *Pr 3:8*
is as rottenness in his b.   *Pr 12:4*
but envy the rottenness of   *Pr 14:30*
the b.
a good report maketh the b.   *Pr 15:30*
fat
to the soul and health to the   *Pr 16:24*
b.
a broken spirit drieth the b.   *Pr 17:22*
how the b. do grow in the   *Ec 11:5*
womb
lion, so will he break all my   *Isa 38:13*
b.
drought and make fat thy b.   *Isa 58:11*
and your b. shall flourish   *Isa 66:14*
like an
the b. of the kings of Judah   *Jer 8:1*
as a burning fire shut up in   *Jer 20:9*
my b.
all my b. shake; I am like a   *Jer 23:9*
king of Babylon hath   *Jer 50:17*
broken his b.
he sent fire into my b. and it   *La 1:13*
made old; he hath broken my   *La 3:4*
b.
their skin cleaveth to their b.   *La 4:8*
scatter your b. round about   *Eze 6:5*
your
fill it with the choice b.   *Eze 24:4*
burn b. under it   *Eze 24:5*
seethe b. of it   *Eze 24:5*
it well, and let the b. be   *Eze 24:10*
burned
iniquities shall be upon   *Eze 32:27*
their b.
the valley which was full of   *Eze 37:1*
b.
Son of man, can these b. live   *Eze 37:3*
O ye dry b. hear the word   *Eze 37:4*
b. came together bone to his   *Eze 37:7*
bone
these b. are the whole   *Eze 37:11*
house of
and brake all their b. in   *Da 6:24*
pieces or

— — —

burned the *b.* of the king of   *Am 2:1*
Edom
to bring out the *b.* out of   *Am 6:10*
the house
their flesh from off their *b.*   *Mic 3:2*
they break their *b.* and chop   *Mic 3:3*
them
rottenness entered into my   *Hab 3:16*
b. and
gnaw not the *b.* till the   *Zep 3:3*
morrow
full of dead men's *b.* and   *M't 23:27*
of all
hath not flesh and *b.* as ye   *Lu 24:39*
see
feet and ancle *b.* received   *Ac 3:7*
body, of his flesh, and of   *Eph 5:30*
his *b.*
commandment concerning   *Heb 11:22*
his *b.*

BONNETS

and *b.* shalt thou make for   *Ex 28:40*
them
caps for glory and honor   *Ex 28:40*
(A)
turbans for honor and   *Ex 28:40*
beauty (B)
head-tires shall thou make   *Ex 28:40*
(E)
caps you shall make (R)   *Ex 28:40*
put the *b.* on them: and the   *Ex 29:9*
bind caps on them (A)(R)   *Ex 29:9*
bind the turbans on them (B)   *Ex 29:9*
bind head-tires on them (E)   *Ex 29:9*
goodly *b.* of fine linen   *Ex 39:28*
linen
caps of fine linen (A)(R)   *Ex 39:28*
lovely caps of fine linen (B)   *Ex 39:28*
goodly head-tires of linen   *Ex 39:28*
(E)
put *b.* upon them; as the   *Le 8:13*
Lord
The *b.* and the ornaments of   *Isa 3:20*
The headbands (A)(B)   *Isa 3:20*
the head-tires (E)   *Isa 3:20*
the head-dresses (R)   *Isa 3:20*
They shall have linen *b.*   *Eze 44:18*
upon
linen turbans on their heads   *Eze 44:18*
(A)(B)(R)
linen tires on their heads   *Eze 44:18*
(E)

BOOK

b. of the generations of Adam   *Ge 5:1*
for a memorial in a *b.*   *Ex 17:14*
b. of the covenant   *Ex 24:7;*
  2Ki 23:2-3, 21, 24; 2Ch 34:30
blot me out of thy *b.*   *Ex 32:32;*
  Ps 69:28
whosoever hath sinned will I   *Ex 32:33*
blot out of my *b.*
curses in a *b.* *Nu 5:23; De 29:20-21, 27*
b. of the wars of the Lord   *Nu 21:14*
copy of law in *b.*   *De 17:18*
this *b.*   *De 28:58;*
De 29:20, 27; 30:10; 2Ki 22:13; 23:3;
2Ch 34:21; Jer 25:13; 51:63; Joh 20:30;
  Re 22:7, 9-10, 18-19
b. of law   *De 28:61;*
De 29:21; 31:26; Jos 1:8; 8:34; 23:6;
2Ki 14:6; 22:8, 10-13; 2Ch 34:15;
  Ne 8:1, 3
b. of Jasher   *Jos 10:13; 2Sa 1:18*
Joshua wrote in *b.* of law   *Jos 24:26;*
of God   *Ne 8:8, 18*
Samuel wrote in a *b.*   *1Sa 10:25;*
  1Ch 29:29
b. of the acts of Solomon   *1Ki 11:41*
b. of the chronicles of the   *1Ki 14:19;*
kings of Israel *1Ki 15:31; 16:5, 14, 20,*
27; 22:39; 2Ki 1:18; 10:34; 13:8, 12;
14:15, 28; 15:11, 15, 21, 26, 31
b. of the chronicles of the   *1Ki 14:29;*
kings of Judah *1Ki 15:7, 23; 22:45;*
2Ki 8:23; 12:19; 14:18; 15:6, 36; 16:19;
  20:20; 21:17, 25; 23:28; 24:5
b. of the kings of Israel   *1Ch 9:1;*
and Judah *2Ch 16:11; 27:7; 35:27;*
  36:8
b. of Nathan the prophet   *1Ch 29:29;*
  2Ch 9:29
b. of Gad the seer   *1Ch 29:29*
b. of the prophecy of Ahijah   *2Ch 9:29*
b. of the visions of Iddo the   *2Ch 9:29*
seer

b. of Shemaiah the prophet   *2Ch 12:15*
b. of the law of the   *2Ch 17:9;*
Lord   *34:14; Ne 9:3*
b. of Jehu   *2Ch 20:34*
b. of the kings of Israel   *2Ch 20:34;*
  33:18
b. of the kings   *2Ch 24:27*
b. of Moses   *2Ch 25:4; 35:12;*
  Ezr 6:18; Ne 13:1; M'k 12:26
b. of the kings of Judah   *2Ch 25:26;*
and Israel   *2Ch 28:26; 32:32*
b. of the records of thy   *Ezr 4:15*
fathers
b. of the chronicles   *Ne 12:23; Es 2:23*
b. of the records of the   *Es 6:1*
chronicles
b. of the chronicles of the   *Es 10:2*
kings of Media and Persia
oh that they were printed in   *Job 19:23*
a *b.*
mine adversary had written   *Job 31:35*
a *b.*
in the volume of the *b.* it is   *Ps 40:7;*
  Heb 10:7
thy bottle: are they not in thy   *Ps 56:8*
b.
Let them be blotted out of   *Ps 69:28*
the *b.* of
in thy *b.* all my members   *Ps 139:16*
were
the words of a *b.* that is   *Isa 29:11*
sealed
And the *b.* is delivered to   *Isa 29:12*
him that
the deaf hear the words of   *Isa 29:18*
the *b.*
and note it in a *b.* that it   *Isa 30:8*
may be
Seek ye out of the *b.* of the   *Isa 34:16*
Lord
I have spoken unto thee in a   *Jer 30:2*
b.
subscribed the *b.* of the   *Jer 32:12*
purchase
Take a roll of a *b.* and   *Jer 36:2;*
write   *36:4*
reading in the *b.* the words   *Jer 36:8*
of the
Then read Baruch in the *b.*   *Jer 36:10*
out of the *b.* all the words   *Jer 36:11*
of the
Baruch read the *b.* in the   *Jer 36:13*
ears of
I wrote them with ink in the *b. Jer 36:18*
all the words of the *b.*   *Jer 36:32*
which
he had written these words in   *Jer 45:1*
a *b.*
Jeremiah wrote in a *b.* all the   *Jer 51:60*
evil
lo. a roll of a *b.* was therein   *Eze 2:9*
writing or *b.* of truth   *Da 10:21*
(A)(B)(R)
shall be found written in the   *Da 12:1*
b.
shut up the words, and seal   *Da 12:4*
the *b.*
The *b.* of the vision of Nahum   *Na 1:1*
and a *b.* of remembrance   *Mal 3:16*
was
The *b.* of the generation of   *M't 1:1*
Jesus
As it is written in the *b.* of   *Lu 3:4;*
  2Ch 32:32
delivered unto him the *b.* of   *Lu 4:17*
when he had opened the *b.*   *Lu 4:17*
he closed the *b.* and gave it   *Lu 4:20*
again
David himself saith in *b.* of   *Lu 20:42*
Psalms
in my first *b.* (P)(R)   *Ac 1:1*
it is written in the *b.* of   *Ac 1:20*
Psalms
written in the *b.* of the   *Ac 7:42*
prophets
b. of life   *Ph'p 4:3;*
Re 3:5; 13:8; 17:8; 20:12, 15; 21:27;
  22:19
sprinkled *b.* and all the   *Heb 9:19*
people
What thou seest, write in a *b. Re 1:11*
a *b.* written within and   *Re 5:1;*
without   *Re 5:2-5, 7-9; 10:2, 8-10*
and another *b.* was opened   *Re 20:12*
take away words of the *b.*   *Re 22:19*
of this

BOOKS

making many *b.* there is no   *Ec 12:12*
end
judgment was set. and the *b.*   *Da 7:10*
I Daniel understood by *b.* the   *Da 9:2*
could not contain the *b.*   *Joh 21:25*
that
brought their *b.* together and   *Ac 19:19*
bring with thee, and the *b.*   *2Ti 4:13*
but
the *b.* were opened: and   *Re 20:12*
another
which were written in the *b.*   *Re 20:12*

BOOM

b. of sounding waves (A)   *Re 19:9*

BOOTH

and as a *b.* that the keeper   *Job 27:18*
as or like a *b.* (S)   *Isa 1:8; 24:20*
and there made him a *b.* and   *Jon 4:5*
sat

BOOTHS

made *b.* for his cattle: *Ge 33:17*
therefore
Ye shall dwell in *b.* seven   *Le 23:42*
days
are Israelites born shall   *Le 23:42*
dwell in *b.*
children of Israel do dwell in   *Le 23:43*
b.
children of Israel should   *Ne 8:14*
dwell in *b.*
branches of thick trees, to   *Ne 8:15*
make *b.*
made themselves *b.* every one   *Ne 8:16*
again out of the captivity   *Ne 8:17*
made *b.*
make us *b.* (S)   *M't 17:4;*
  M'k 9:5; Lu 9:33

BOOTIES

thou shalt be for *b.* unto   *Hab 2:7*
them

BOOTY

booty (A)   *Nu 31:9; 31:53;*
  De 2:35; 2Ch 14:13
booty (B)   *Nu 31:9; 31:11-12,*
53; De 2:35; 20:14; J'g 4:30; 1Sa 30:19;
2Sa 8:12; 23:10; 2Ch 14:14; 28:8;
Ps 68:12; Isa 9:3; 10:6; Eze 25:7; 38:12
the *b.* being the rest of the   *Nu 31:32*
prey
booty (E)(R)   *Nu 31:53; 2Ch 14:13*
their camels shall be a *b.*   *Jer 49:32*
spoil, *b.*, property (B)   *Da 11:24*
with much *b.* (A)   *Da 11:28*
dens with plenty of *b.* (B)   *Na 2:12*
shall be her *b.* (S)   *Hab 2:7*
their goods shall become a   *Zep 1:13*
b.

BOOZ

And Salmon begat *B.* of   *M't 1:5*
Rachab
which was the son of *B.*   *Lu 3:32*
which

BORDER

b. of Canaanites   *Ge 10:19*
b. of Zebulun   *Ge 49:13; Jos 19:10*
locusts in thy *b.* (E)   *Ex 10:4*
into thy *b.* (S)   *Ex 10:4; 34:11;*
  De 11:24; 16:4; 19:8; Jos 1:4
b. of Sinai   *Ex 19:12*
b. of furniture   *Ex 25:25;*
  Ex 25:27; 37:12, 14
b. of garments   *Ex 28:26;*
  Ex 39:19; M'k 6:56; Lu 8:44
by the *b.* of Edom (S)   *Nu 20:23;*
  Jos 15:21
on the *b.* (S)   *Nu 33:37*
the outmost *b.* (S)   *Nu 34:3*
b. of Canaan (S)   *Nu 34:3; 34:4-12*
the *b.* of thy brethren (S)   *De 11:24;*
your *b.* (E)   *De 11:24;*
Jos 1:4; 18:5; J'g 11:20; 1Sa 6:9
the *b.* of Moab (S)   *De 12:18*
enlarge your *b.* (E)(R)   *De 19:8*
the *b.* of Og (S)   *Jos 12:4*
their *b.* (S)   *Jos 13:16;*

Jos 13:25, 30; 18:5, 11; 19:22, 29, 33, 34, 41; J'g 1:18
b. of Judah — *Jos 15:1; 15:2-47*
the south b. — *Jos 15:1; 15:4; 18:9*
the b. of the sea (S) — *Jos 15:4;*
Jos 15:12; Eze 25:15; Zep 2:5, 6, 7;
M't 4:13; Lu 6:17
the b. of Judah (S) — *Jos 15:12;*
1Sa 30:14
the b. of Japhleti (S) — *Jos 16:3*
b. of Ephraim — *Jos 16:6*
the b. of Manasseh (S) — *Jos 17:7;*
16:9
b. of Manasseh — *Jos 17:8*
b. of Benjamin — *Jos 18:12; 18:13-20*
the b. of Dan (S) — *Jos 19:4*
the b. of the Amorites (S) — *J'g 1:36*
his b. (S) — *J'g 11:20; 1Sa 6:9*
the b. of Israel (E)(S) — *1Sa 7:13;*
1Sa 27:1; 2Ki 14:25
enlarge my b. (S) — *1Ch 4:10*
b. of Israel — *Eze 11:10;*
Eze 11:11; 45:7; 47:13-20; 48:1-28;
Joe 3:6; Zep 2:8; Zec 9:2; Mal 1:4
b. of Ethiopia — *Eze 29:10*
b. of the altar — *Eze 43:13;*
43:17, 20
the b. of Hauran (R) — *Eze 47:16*
the b. of Hethlon — *Eze 48:1*
the b. of Hamath — *Eze 48:1*
the b. of wickedness — *Mal 1:4*
the b. of Tyre (S) — *M't 15:21;*
M'k 7:31
the b. of Magdala (S) — *M't 15:39*
the b. of Caesarea (S) — *M't 16:13*
the b. of Judea (S) — *M't 19:1;*
M'k 10:1; Ac 26:20
the b. of Decapolis (A) — *M'k 7:31*
the upper b. (A) — *Ac 19:1*

BORDERS

the b. of the Gentiles (S) — *Ge 10:5*
trees in all b. were made — *Ge 23:17*
sure
in the b. of Egypt (S) — *Ex 10:14;*
10:19
till they come to b. of — *Ex 16:35*
Canaan
I will cast out nations, — *Ex 34:24*
enlarge thy B.
in b. of their garments — *Nu 15:38;*
M't 23:5
until we have passed thy b. — *Nu 20:17*
within thy b. (S) — *Nu 32:33*
with the b. (S) — *Nu 34:2; 34:12;*
Jos 18:20; 1Sa 5:6; 7:14; 2Ki 15:16;
1Ch 6:54, 66; M't 2:16; 15:22; M'k 5:17
the b. of Geshuri (S) — *De 3:14*
divide the b. (S) — *De 19:3*
all the b. Jos (S) — *De 28:40; 9:1*
the b. of it shall be (S) — *Jos 17:18*
the b. of the Amorites (S) — *J'g 11:22*
the b. of Arnon (S) — *J'g 11:26*
their b. (S) — *J'g 18:2;*
2Ch 11:13; Ps 105:31, 33; Eze 33:2;
M't 8:34; M'k 5:17; Ac 13:50
the b. of Israel — *J'g 19:29; 1Sa 11:3, 7;*
(S) — *2Sa 21:5; 1Ki 1:3; 2Ki 10:32;*
1Ch 21:12
b. between ledges — *1Ki 7:28*
7:29-36
b. of the bases — *2Ki 16:17; 19:23*
thou hast set the b. of the — *Ps 74:17*
earth
He maketh peace in thy b. — *Ps 147:14*
b. of gold with studs of silver — *Ca 1:11*
I will make thy b. of — *Isa 54:12*
pleasant stones
for all thy sins, even in all — *Jer 15:13*
b.
the b. of the earth (S) — *Jer 25:30;*
Jer 31:8; 50:41
this shall be holy in all the — *Eze 45:1*
b.
the b. of Palestine (S) — *Joe 3:4*
when he treadeth within our — *Mic 5:6*
b.
in b. of Zabulon and — *M't 4:13*
Nephthalim

BORE

master shall b. his ear — *Ex 21:6*
through
b. his jaw through with a — *Job 41:2*
thorn
he b. their manners (S) — *Ac 13:18*
doesn't b. me to repeat (P) — *Ph'p 3:1*

BORED

and b. a hole in the lid of it — *2Ki 12:9*

BORN

sons b. — *Ge 4:18; 4:26; 10:1, 25;*
Ru 4:17; 1Sa 4:20; 2Sa 3:2; 1Ch 2:3;
26:6
daughters b. unto men — *Ge 6:1*
children b. — *Ge 10:21;*
Ge 22:20; Jer 16:3
b. in house — *Ge 14:14;*
Ge 15:3; 17:12-13, 17, 23, 27
b. unto him — *Ge 21:3;*
Ge 21:5, 7, 9; 36:5; 1Ch 2:9; 3:1, 4-5;
Job 1:2
b. of thee (S) — *Ge 25:25*
b. him — *Ge 29:34;*
Ge 30:20; 46:27; Ex 21:4; Ru 4:15
b. in the land — *Ex 12:19;*
Ex 12:48; Le 24:16; Nu 9:14; 15:30
b. a man child — *Le 12:2; Jer 20:15*
b. a male — *Le 12:7*
b. at home or abroad — *Le 18:9*
not b. in the yoke (S) — *De 21:3*
b. unto Israel — *J'g 18:29*
sons and daughters b. — *2Sa 5:13*
be b. to (A) — *2Sa 7:12; 16:11*
b. to the giant — *2Sa 21:20;*
2Sa 21:22; 1Ch 20:8
the day perish wherein I was — *Job 3:3*
b.
man is b. in trouble as sparks — *Job 5:7*
man be b. like a wild ass's — *Job 11:12*
colt
man that is b. of a woman — *Job 14:1;*
Job 15:14; 25:4; M't 11:11; Lu 7:28
people that shall be b. — *Ps 22:31*
sinful state I was b. (B) — *Ps 51:5*
go astray as soon as they be b. — *Ps 58:3*
this man was b. there — *Ps 87:4;*
Ps 87:5, 6
a brother is b. for adversity — *Pr 17:17*
a time to be b. — *Ec 3:2*
unto us a child is b., a son is — *Isa 9:6*
given
shall a nation be b. at once — *Isa 66:8*
of whom was b. Jesus — *M't 1:16;*
M't 2:1-2, 4; Lu 1:35, 2:11
so b. from their mother's — *M't 19:12*
womb
that man if he had not — *M't 26:24;*
been b. — *M'k 14:21*
which were b., not of blood, — *Joh 1:13*
nor of
Except a man be b. again — *Joh 3:3;*
Joh 3:5, 7
which is b. of the flesh is — *Joh 3:6*
flesh
which is b. of the Spirit is — *Joh 3:6;*
spirit — *3:8*
We be not b. of fornication — *Joh 8:41*
b. blind — *Joh 9:2; 9:19-20, 32*
b. in sins — *Joh 9:34*
joy that a man is b. into — *Joh 16:21*
world
to this end was I b. — *Joh 18:37*
own tongue, wherein we were — *Ac 2:8*
b.
In which time Moses was b. — *Ac 7:20*
Aquila, b. in Pontus, lately — *Ac 18:2*
come
named Apollos, b. at — *Ac 18:24*
Alexandria
which am a Jew, b. in Tarsus — *Ac 22:3*
Paul said, But I was free b. — *Ac 22:28*
(For the children being not — *Ro 9:11*
yet b.
also, as one b. out of due — *1Co 15:8*
time
bondwoman was b. after the — *Ga 4:23*
flesh
he that was b. after the flesh — *Ga 4:29*
him that was b. after the — *Ga 4:29*
Spirit
By faith Moses, when he — *Heb 11:23*
was b.
b. again not of corruptible — *1Pe 1:23*
seed
doeth righteousness is b. of — *1Jo 2:29*
him
Whosoever is b. of God doth — *1Jo 3:9*
not
sin, because he is b. of God — *1Jo 3:9*
every one that loveth is b. of — *1Jo 4:7*
God
Jesus is the Christ is b. of — *1Jo 5:1*
God
For whatsoever is b. of God — *1Jo 5:4*

whosoever is b. of God — *1Jo 5:18*
sinneth not
her child as soon as it was b. — *Re 12:4*

BORNE

the ark may be b. with them — *Ex 25:14*
the table may be b. with — *Ex 25:28*
them
and on which it was b. up — *J'g 16:29*
I have b. chastisement, I — *Job 34:31*
will not
then I could have b. it: — *Ps 55:12*
neither
I have b. reproach; shame — *J'g 69:7*
hath
are b. by me from the belly — *Isa 46:3*
Surely he hath b. our griefs — *Isa 53:4*
ye shall be b. upon her sides — *Isa 66:12*
have b. witness of thy charity — *3Jo 6*
And hast b. and hast patience — *Re 2:3*

BORROW

woman shall b. of her — *Ex 3:22*
neighbour
b. gold articles (B) — *Ex 3:22*
every man b. of his neighbour — *Ex 11:2*
b. ought of his neighbour — *Ex 22:14*
nations, but thou shalt not b. — *De 15:6*
nations, and thou shalt not — *De 28:12*
b.
b. thee vessels abroad of all — *2Ki 4:3*
thy
from him that would b. of — *M't 5:42*
thee

BORROWED

they b. of the Egyptians — *Ex 12:35*
jewels
Alas, master! for it was b. — *2Ki 6:5*
We have b. money for the — *Ne 5:4*
king's

BORROWER

the b. is servant to the lender — *Pr 22:7*
so with the b.; as with the — *Isa 24:2*
taker

BORROWETH

The wicked b. and payeth — *Ps 37:21*
not

BOSCATH

the daughter of Adaiah of B. — *2Ki 22:1*

BOSOM

I have given my maid into — *Ge 16:5*
thy b.
Put now thine hand into thy — *Ex 4:6;*
b. — *4:7*
Carry them in thy b. as a — *Nu 11:12*
nursing
or the wife of thy b. or thy — *De 13:6*
friend
toward the wife of his b. — *De 28:54*
evil toward the husband of — *De 28:56*
her b.
laid it in her b. and became — *Ru 4:16*
nurse
lay in his b. and was unto — *2Sa 12:3*
him
thy master's wives into thy — *2Sa 12:8*
b.
let her lie in thy b. that my — *1Ki 1:2*
lord
and laid it in her b. and laid — *1Ki 3:20*
her
he took him out of her b. — *1Ki 17:19*
by hiding mine iniquity in — *Job 31:33*
my b.
prayer returned into mine — *Ps 35:13*
own b.
hand? pluck it out of thy b. — *Ps 74:11*
sevenfold into their b. their — *Ps 79:12*
I do bear in my b. the — *Ps 89:50*
reproach of
he that bindeth sheaves his — *Ps 129:7*
b.
and embrace his b. of a — *Pr 5:20*
stranger
Can a man take fire in his b. — *Pr 6:27*
man taketh a gift out of the — *Pr 17:23*
b. to
man hideth in his hand in — *Pr 19:24*
his b.

a reward in the b. strong wrath | Pr 21:14
slothful hideth his hand in his b. | Pr 26:15
anger resteth in the b. of fools | Ec 7:9
and carry them in his b. | Isa 40:11 and shall
even recompense into their b. | Isa 65:6
into the b. of their children after | Jer 32:18
poured out into their mother's b. | La 2:12
handle b. girlish breasts (A) | Eze 23:3
b. pressed, nipples stroked (B) | Eze 23:3
breasts pressed, b. handled (E) | Eze 23:3
handled breasts, girlish b. (B)(S) | Eze 23:21
handled b., pressed breasts (R) | Eze 23:21
from her that lieth in thy b. | Mic 7:5
shall men give into your b. | Lu 6:38
by the angels into Abraham's b. | Lu 16:22
afar off, and Lazarus in his b. | Lu 16:23
which is in the b. of the Father | Joh 1:18
leaning on Jesus b. one of his | Joh 13:23

BOSOMS

b. pressed, breasts handled (A)(R) | Eze 23:3

BOSOR

Balaam the son of B. who loved | 2Pe 2:15

BOSSES

upon the thick b. of his bucklers | Job 15:26

BOTCH

smite thee with the b. of Egypt | De 28:27
with boils of Egypt (A)(B)(E)(R) | De 28:27
with a sore b. that cannot be | De 28:35

BOTH

they were b. naked, the man | Ge 2:25
the eyes of them b. were opened | Ge 3:7
b. man, and beast | Ge 6:7; Ge 7:21, 23; 8:17
b. daughters of Lot with child | Ge 19:36
b. in vessels of wood, and in vessels | Ex 7:19
all, in the field, b. man and beast | Ex 9:25
firstborn of Egypt, b. man and beast | Ex 12:12
b. be put to death | Le 20:11; Le 20:12; De 22:22
five lords, b. of fenced cities, and of | 1Sa 6:18
distributed them. b. Zadok of the sons | 1Ch 24:3
darkness and light are b. alike to | Ps 139:12
they b. are abomination | Pr 17:15; 20:10
b. he that helpeth shall fall, and he | Isa 31:3
counsel of peace between them b. | Zec 6:13
destroy b. soul and body in hell | M't 10:28
b. fall into ditch | M't 15:14; Lu 6:39
Jesus began b. to do and teach | Ac 1:1
b. Jews and Gentiles under sin | Ro 3:9
Lord b. of dead and living | Ro 14:9
who hath made b. one | Eph 2:14; 2:16
he hath b. Father and Son | 2Jo 9
b. small and great | Re 13:16; Re 19:5, 18
b. cast alive into lake of fire | Re 19:20

BOTTLE

took bread, and b. of water | Ge 21:14; Ge 21:15, 19

took a skin of water (B)(R) | Ge 21:14
she opened a b. of milk | J'g 4:19
opened a skin of milk (A)(R) | J'g 4:19
b. of wine | 1Sa 1:24; 1Sa 10:3; 16:20; 2Sa 16:1
skin of wine (A)(B)(R) | 1Sa 1:24; 1Sa 10:3; 16:20; 2Sa 16:1
the b. of water (A) | 1Sa 26:11
a b. of honey (A) | 1Ki 14:3
oil in a b. (A) | 1Ki 17:12
put my tears into thy b. | Ps 56:8
like a b. in the smoke | Ps 119:83
like a wineskin in smoke (B)(E)(R) | Ps 119:83
every b. shall be filled with wine | Jer 13:12
every jar shall be filled with (B)(R) | Jer 13:12
get a potter's earthen b. | Jer 19:1; 19:10
a potter's earthen jar (B) | Jer 19:1
a potter's earthen flask (R) | Jer 19:1
puttest b. to him and makest drunken | Hab 2:15
put your wineskin (B) | Hab 2:15
giveth his neighbor drink (E)(R) | Hab 2:15

BOTTLES

Gibeonites took wine b. and rent | Jos 9:4; 9:13
took old wineskins (A)(B)(E)(R) | Jos 9:4; 9:13
Abigail took two b. of wine | 1Sa 25:18
two skins of wine (A)(B)(R) | 1Sa 25:18
belly ready to burst like new b. | Job 32:19
like new wineskins (A)(B)(E)(R) | Job 32:19
who can stay the b. of heaven | Job 38:37
pitchers of heaven (B) | Job 38:37
waterskins of the heavens (R) | Job 38:37
empty his vessels, and break b. | Jer 48:12
dash their jars in pieces (B)(R) | Jer 48:12
make him sick with b. of wine | Ho 7:5
sick with the heat of wine (A)(E)(R) | Ho 7:5
sick with the fever of wine (B) | Ho 7:5
put new wine into old b., | M't 9:17; else b. break | M'k 2:22; Lu 5:37-38
old wineskins | M't 9:17; (A)(B)(E)(N)(P)(R) | M'k 2:22; Lu 5:37

BOTTOM

they sank into b. as a stone | Ex 15:5
blood beside b. of altar | Ex 29:12; Le 4:7, 18, 25, 30, 34; 5:9; 8:15; 9:9
and covereth the b. of the sea | Job 36:30
b. thereof of gold, the covering | Ca 3:10
even the b. shall be a cubit | Eze 43:13
And from the b. upon the ground | Eze 43:14
and the b. therefore shall be a cubit | Eze 43:17
or ever they came at the b. of the | Dan 6:24
in the b. of the sea, thence will I | Am 9:3
myrtle trees that were in the b. | Zec 1:8
from the top to the b.; and | M't 27:51
in twain from the top to the b. | M'k 15:38

BOTTOMLESS

was given the key of the b. pit | Re 9:1
And he opened the b. pit | Re 9:2
the angel of the b. pit, whose | Re 9:11
that ascendeth out of the b. pit | Re 11:7
and shall ascend out of the b. pit | Re 17:8
having the key of the b. pit | Re 20:1
and a cast him into the b. pit, and shut | Re 20:3

BOTTOMS

I went down to the b. of the | Jon 2:6

BOUGH

Joseph is a fruitful b. | Ge 49:22
even a fruitful b. by a well | Ge 49:22
and cut down a b. from the trees | J'g 9:48
cut down every man his b. | J'g 9:49
the Lord of hosts, shall lop the b. | Isa 10:33
the top of the uppermost b. four | Isa 17:6
strong cities be as a forsaken b. | Isa 17:9

BOUGHS

the b. of goodly trees, branches | Le 23:40
and the b. of thick trees | Le 23:40
thou shalt not go over the b. | De 24:20
the thick b. of a great oak | 2Sa 18:9
will bud, and bring forth b. like | Job 14:9
and the b. thereof were like | Ps 80:10
She sent out her b. unto the sea | Ps 80:11
I will take hold of the b. thereof | Ca 7:8
When the b. thereof are | Isa 27:11
it shall bring forth b. and bear | Eze 17:23
his top was among the thick b. | Eze 31:3; Eze 31:5-6, 8, 10, 12, 14
birds of heaven dwelt in the b. | Da 4:12

BOUGHT

b. with money of stranger | Ge 17:12; Ge 17:13, 23, 27
he b. parcel of a field | Ge 33:19; Ge 49:30; 50:13
b. him of the hands of the | Ge 39:1
for the corn which they b. | Ge 47:14; Ge 47:20-23
man's servant that is b. for | Ex 12:44
hand of him that b. it | Le 25:28, 50-51
field which he hath b. which is | Le 27:22
unto him of whom it was b. even | Le 27:24
he thy father that hath b. | De 32:6 thee
which Jacob b. of the sons of | Jos 24:32
that I have b. all that was | Ru 4:9
which he had b. and nourished up | 2Sa 12:3
So David b. the threshing floor and | 2Sa 24:24
And he b. the hill Samaria | 1Ki 16:24
of this wall, neither b. we any | Ne 5:16
Thou hast b. me no sweet cane | Isa 43:24
thou hast b. (S) | Jer 13:4
And I b. the field of Hanameel mv | Jer 32:9
And fields shall be b. in this land | Jer 32:43
So I b. her to me for fifteen pieces | Ho 3:2
and sold all that he had, and b. it | M't 13:46
sold and b. in the temple | M't 21:12
b. with them the potter's field, to | M't 27:7
cast out them that sold and b. in | M'k 11:15
he b. fine linen, and took him | M'k 15:46
had b. sweet spices, that they | M'k 16:1
I have b. a piece of ground, and I | Lu 14:18
I have b. five yoke of oxen, and I go | Lu 14:19
they did eat, they drank, they b. | Lu 17:28
that sold therein, and them that b. | Lu 19:45
Abraham b. for a sum of money of | Ac 7:16
For ye are b. with a price | 1Co 6:20

Ye are *b*. with a price; be 1Co 7:23
not ye
denying the Lord that *b*. them 2Pe 2:1

BOUND

and *b*. Isaac his son, and laid Ge 22:9
and *b*. upon his hand a Ge 38:28
scarlet
where the king's prisoners Ge 39:20
were *b*.
the place where Joseph was Ge 40:3;
b. 40:5
Egypt, which were *b*. in the Ge 40:5
prison
let one of your brethren be Ge 42:19
b. in
Simeon, and *b*. him before Ge 42:24
their
seeing that his life is *b*. up Ge 44:30
in the
the utmost *b*. of the Ge 49:26
everlasting
their kneadingtroughs being Ex 12:34
b.
b. it unto him therewith Le 8:7
vessel, which hath no Nu 19:15
covering *b*.
her bond wherein she hath Nu 30:4;
b. her soul 30:5-11
she *b*. scarlet line in window Jos 2:21
wine bottles, old, and rent, and Jos 9:4
b.
they *b*. Samson J'g 15:13;
J'g 16:6, 8, 10, 13, 21
new ropes, and *b*. him J'g 16:12
therewith
b. with fetters 2Ki 25:7;
2Ch 33:11; 33:6; Job 36:8
b. with chains Ps 68:6;
Jer 39:7; 40:1; Na 3:10; M'k 5:4;
Lu 8:29; Ac 21:33; 28:20
being *b*. in affliction and Ps 107:10
iron
a city *b*. together (B)(R) Ps 122:3
Foolishness is *b*. in the heart Pr 22:15
of a
who hath *b*. the water in a Pr 30:4
have not been closed, neither Isa 1:6
b.
they are *b*. by the archers Isa 22:3
all that are found in thee are Isa 22:3
b.
of the prison to them that Isa 61:1
are *b*.
the *b*. of the sea by a Jer 5:22
perpetual
thy cause, that thou mayest Jer 30:13
be *b*.
yoke of my transgressions is La 1:14
b. by
apparel, *b*. with cords, and Eze 27:24
made
it shall not be *b*. up to be Eze 30:21
healed
neither have ye *b*. up that Eze 34:4
which
Then these men were *b*. in Da 3:21
their
fell down *b*. into the midst of Da 3:23
Did not we cast three men *b*. Da 3:24
into
The wind hath *b*. her up in Ho 4:19
her
them that remove the *b*. Ho 5:10
I have *b*. and strengthened Ho 7:15
their
The iniquity of Ephraim is Ho 13:12
b. up
and all her great men were *b*. Na 3:10
laid hold on John, and *b*. M't 14:3
him
on earth shall be *b*. in M't 16:19
heaven
on earth shall be *b*. in M't 18:18
heaven
he is *b*. (S) M't 23:18
when they had *b*. him, they M't 27:2
led him
had been often *b*. with fetters M'k 5:4
laid hold upon John, and *b*. M'k 6:17
him in
and *b*. Jesus, and carried M'k 15:1
him
Barabbas, which lay *b*. with M'k 15:7
them
he was kept *b*. with chains Lu 8:29
and in
And went to him, and *b*. up Lu 10:34
his

whom Satan hath *b*. lo, Lu 13:16
these
b. hand and foot with Joh 11:44
his face was *b*. about with Joh 11:44
the Jews took Jesus and *b*. Joh 18:12
him
Now Annas had sent him *b*. Joh 18:24
unto
b. in linen clothes Lu 19:4
(A)(E)(R)
he might bring them *b*. unto Ac 9:2;
9:21
b. with two chains: and the Ac 12:6
b. over Jason (N) Ac 17:9
I go *b*. in the spirit unto Ac 20:22
b. his own hands and Ac 21:11
feet, and
I am ready not to be *b*. Ac 21:13
only, but
commanded him to be *b*. Ac 21:33
with
b. unto Jerusalem, for to be Ac 22:5
as they *b*. him with thongs, Ac 22:25
Paul
a Roman, and because he Ac 22:29
had *b*.
and *b*. themselves under a Ac 23:12
curse
b. ourselves under a great Ac 23:14
curse
have *b*. themselves with an Ac 23:21
oath
the Jews a pleasure, left Ac 24:27
Paul *b*.
hope of Israel I am *b*. with Ac 28:20
this
which hath an husband is *b*. Ro 7:2
by
Art thou *b*. unto a wife? 1Co 7:27
seek not
The wife is *b*. by the law as 1Co 7:39
long as
We are *b*. to thank God 2Th 1:3
always
we are *b*. to give thanks 2Th 2:13
always
but the word of God is not *b*. 2Ti 2:9
them that are in bonds, as Heb 13:3
b.
Loose the four angels which Re 9:14
are *b*.
Satan, and *b*. him a thousand Re 20:2

BOUNDARIES

your *b*. (B) De 19:8; 1Sa 7:13
compassed waters with *b*. Job 26:10
(S)
removed the *b*. of the Isa 10:13
people (S)

BOUNDARY

in the utmost *b*. (S) Nu 22:36;
De 3:17
remove the *b*. (S) Ho 5:10

BOUNDING

the *b*. chariots (S) Na 3:2

BOUNDLESS

b. riches of Christ (A) Eph 3:8

BOUNDS

thou shalt set *b*. unto the Ex 19:12
people
Set *b*. about the mount, and Ex 19:23
set thy *b*. from the Red sea Ex 23:31
even
he set the *b*. of the people De 32:8
hast appointed his *b*. that he Job 14:5
waters with *b*. until the day Job 26:10
removed the *b*. of the Isa 10:13
people
and the *b*. of their Ac 17:26
habitation

BOUNTIES

for all his *b*. (B)(R) Ps 116:12

BOUNTIFUL

hath a *b*. eye shall be blessed Pr 22:9
nor the churl said to be *b*. Isa 32:5

BOUNTIFULLY

he hath dealt *b*. with me Ps 13:6
the Lord hath dealt *b*. with Ps 116:7
thee
Deal *b*. with thy servant, Ps 119:17
that I
thou shalt deal *b*. with me Ps 142:7
which soweth *b*. shall reap 2Co 9:6
also *b*.

BOUNTIFULNESS

thing to all *b*. which causeth 2Co 9:11

BOUNTY

Solomon gave her of his 1Ki 10:13
royal *b*.
the *b*. of the king (S) Es 1:7; 2:18
your *b*. to Jerusalem (E) 1Co 16:3
your *b*. whereof ye had notice 2Co 9:5
might be ready, as a matter 2Co 9:5
of *b*.

BOW

I do set my *b*. in the cloud, Ge 9:13
and it
the *b*. shall be seen in the Ge 9:14
cloud
And the *b*. shall be in the Ge 9:16
cloud
thy weapons, thy quiver and Ge 27:3
thy *b*.
cried before him, B. the Ge 41:43
knee
with my sword and with my Ge 48:22
b.
his *b*. abode in strength, and Ge 49:24
Thou shalt not *b*. down thyself De 5:9
with thy sword, nor with thy De 24:12
b.
b. down for a mite 1Sa 2:36
(B)(E)(S)
and to his *b*. and to his 1Sa 18:4
girdle
of Judah the use of the *b*. 2Sa 1:18
the *b*. of Jonathan turned 2Sa 1:22
not back
a *b*. of steel is broken by 2Sa 22:35
mine
certain man drew a *b*. at a 1Ki 22:34
venture
with thy sword and with thy 2Ki 6:22
b.
drew a *b*. with his full 2Ki 9:24
strength
said unto him, Take *b*. and 2Ki 13:15
arrows
he took unto him *b*. and 2Ki 13:15
arrows
Put thine hand upon the *b*. 2Ki 13:16
other gods, nor *b*. 2Ki 17:35
yourselves to
Lord, *b*. down thine ear 2Ki 19:16
to shoot with *b*. and skilful 1Ch 5:18
arrows out of a *b*. even of 1Ch 12:2
Saul's
armed men with *b*. and 2Ch 17:17
shield
certain man drew a *b*. at a 2Ch 18:33
venture
the *b*. of steel shall strike Job 20:24
him
my *b*. was renewed in my Job 29:20
hand
b. themselves, they bring Job 39:3
bent his *b*. and made it ready Ps 7:12
bend their *b*. they make ready Ps 11:2
a *b*. of steel is broken by Ps 18:34
mine
all that go down to dust *b*. Ps 22:29
I have bent their *b*. to cast Ps 37:14
down
I will not trust in my *b*. Ps 44:6
neither
he breaketh the *b*. and cutteth Ps 46:9
bendeth his *b*. to shoot his Ps 58:7
arrows
dwell in wilderness *b*. before Ps 72:9
the arrows of the *b*. the shield Ps 76:3
turned aside like a deceitful Ps 78:57
b.
B. down thine ear, O Lord, Ps 86:1
hear
b. heavens, O Lord, come Ps 144:5
b. ear to my understanding Pr 5:1
evil *b*. before the good Pr 14:19
strong men shall *b*. themselves Ec 12:3

sword, and from the bent *b.*   *Isa 21:15*
and as driven stubble to his   *Isa 41:2*
b.
unto me every knee shall *b.*   *Isa 45:23*
every
Pul, and Lud, that draw the   *Isa 66:19*
b.
shall lay hold on *b.* and spear   *Jer 6:23*
bend their tongues like their *b.*   *Jer 9:3*
that handle and bend the *b.*   *Jer 46:9*
I will break the *b.* of Elam   *Jer 49:35*
all ye that bend the *b.* shoot at *Jer 50:14*
all ye that bend the *b.* camp   *Jer 50:29*
shall hold the *b.* and the   *Jer 50:42*
lance
hold the *b.* and spear   *Jer 50:42*
(B)(E)(R)
bend his *b.* and against him   *Jer 51:3*
hath bent his *b.* like an enemy *La 2:4*
He hath bent his *b.* and set   *La 3:12*
me as
As the appearance of the *b.*   *Eze 1:28*
that is
smite thy *b.* out of thy left   *Eze 39:3*
hand
I will break the *b.* of Israel   *Ho 1:5*
not save them by *b.* nor by   *Ho 1:7*
sword
and I will break the *b.* and   *Ho 2:18*
they are like a deceitful *b.*   *Ho 7:16*
he stand that handleth the *b.*   *Am 2:15*
b. myself before high God   *Mic 6:6*
perpetual hills did *b.*   *Hab 3:6*
Thy *b.* was made quite naked *Hab 3:9*
and the battle *b.* shall be cut   *Zec 9:10*
off
filled the *b.* with Ephraim   *Zec 9:13*
out of him the battle *b.* out   *Zec 10:4*
of
the *b.* stuck (S)   *Ac 27:41*
every knee shall *b.* to me   *Ro 14:11*
I *b.* my knees unto the   *Eph 3:14*
Father
of Jesus every knee should   *Ph'p 2:10*
b.
he that sat on him had a *b.*   *Re 6:2*

BOW *DOWN*

nations *b. down*, mother's   *Ge 27:29*
sons *b. down*
shall I, thy mother, brethren   *Ge 37:10*
b. down
father's children *b. down*   *Ge 49:8*
before me
these servants *b. down* to me   *Ex 11:8*
not *b. down* thyself to them   *Ex 20:5;*
  De 5:9
thou shalt not *b. down* to   *Ex 23:24*
their gods
neither set up image to *b.*   *Le 26:1*
down
in following other gods to *b.*   *J'g 2:19*
down
when *b. down* in house of   *2Ki 5:18*
Rimmon
b. down thine ear, hear   *2Ki 19:16;*
  Ps 86:1
let others *b. down* upon her *Job 31:10*
forth
b. down ear to me   *Ps 31:2; Pr 22:17*
let us worship and *b. down*   *Ps 95:6*
without me they *b. down*   *Isa 10:4*
under prisoners
they stoop, *b. down* together *Isa 46:2*
kings and queens shall *b.*   *Isa 49:23*
down to thee
said, *b. down* that we   *Isa 51:23*
may go over
is it to *b. down* his head as *Isa 58:5*
a bulrush
they that despised thee shall *Isa 60:14*
b. down
shall all *b. down* to   *Isa 65:12*
slaughter
eyes darkened, *b. down* back *Ro 11:10*
alway

BOW *KNEE*

they cried before him, *b.* the *Ge 41:43*
knee
to me every *knee* shall *b.*   *Isa 45:23;*
  Ro 14:11
I *b. knee* to Father of our   *Eph 3:14*
Lord

at name of Jesus every *knee* *Ph'p 2:10*
shall *b.*

BOWED

b. himself with face toward   *Ge 19:1*
b. himself to the people   *Ge 23:7*
the man *b.* down his head   *Ge 24:26*
b. down my head, and   *Ge 24:48*
worshipped
children, and they *b.*   *Ge 33:6*
themselves
came near, and *b.* themselves *Ge 33:7*
and Rachel, and they *b.*   *Ge 33:7*
themselves
b. down (A)(B)(R)   *Ge 37:7; 37:9*
b. themselves to him to the   *Ge 43:26*
Israel *b.* himself upon the   *Ge 47:31*
bed's
b. himself with his face to   *Ge 48:12*
and *b.* his shoulder to bear   *Ge 49:15*
b. the head and worshipped   *Ex 12:27*
b. in homage (A)(B)   *Ex 18:7*
gods, and *b.* yourselves to   *Jos 23:16*
them
and *b.* themselves unto them   *J'g 2:12*
and *b.* themselves unto them   *J'g 2:17*
he *b.* he fell, he lay down   *J'g 5:27*
at her feet he *b.* he fell   *J'g 5:27*
where he *b.* there he fell   *J'g 5:27*
and *b.* herself to the ground   *Ru 2:10*
she *b.* herself and travailed   *1Sa 4:19*
and *b.* himself three times   *1Sa 20:41*
and *b.* herself to the ground *1Sa 25:23*
b. herself on her face to the *1Sa 25:41*
earth
b. to the ground (B)   *2Sa 1:2*
he *b.* the heart of all the   *2Sa 19:14*
men
He *b.* the heavens also, and   *2Sa 22:10*
Bath-sheba *b.* and did   *1Ki 1:16*
obeisance
Bath-sheba *b.* with her face *1Ki 1:31*
to
king *b.* himself upon the   *1Ki 1:47*
bed.
which have not *b.* unto   *1Ki 19:18*
Baal
and *b.* themselves to ground   *2Ki 2:15*
and *b.* herself to the ground   *2Ki 4:37*
b. himself to David with   *1Ch 21:21*
his face
the house, they *b.* themselves *2Ch 7:3*
b. down to the king (B)   *2Ch 24:17*
present with him *b.*   *2Ch 29:29*
themselves
b. their heads, and worshipped *Ne 8:6*
b. and reverenced Haman   *Es 3:2*
Mordecai *b.* not, nor did him *Es 3:2*
Haman saw that Mordecai *b.*   *Es 3:5*
not
He *b.* the heavens also, and   *Ps 18:9*
raiseth them that are *b.*   *Ps 146:8*
down
and they *b.* the knee before *M't 27:29*
him
was *b.* together and could in *Lu 13:11*
no
have not *b.* the knee to   *Ro 11:4*

BOWED *DOWN*

Abraham *b. down* before   *Ge 23:12*
people
Joseph's brethren *b. down*   *Ge 42:6;*
  Ge 43:28
people did eat, and *b. down* *Nu 25:2*
to gods
rest of people *b. down* on   *J'g 7:6*
knees
set them up to be gods, *b.*   *2Ch 25:14*
down
b. down heavily as one that *Ps 35:14*
mourneth
b. down greatly, mourning all *Ps 38:6*
day
our soul is *b. down* to dust, *Ps 44:25*
our belly
my soul is *b. down*, have   *Ps 57:6*
digged a pit
raiseth up all *b. down*   *Ps 145:14;*
  146:8
haughtiness of man shall be *b.* *Isa 2:11*
down
and the loftiness of man shall *Isa 2:17*
be *b. down*
I was *b. down* at the hearing *Isa 21:3*
of it
were afraid and *b. down* their *Lu 24:5*
faces

BOWED *HEAD*

man *b. head* and worshipped   *Ge 24:26*
b. their *heads* and made   *Ge 43:28*
obeisance
b. their *heads* and   *Ex 4:31;*
worshipped   *Ex 12:27; Ne 8:6*
Moses *b.* his *head* to earth   *Ex 34:8*
Balaam *b.* his *head* and fell *Nu 22:31*
flat
b. down their *heads* and   *1Ch 29:20*
worshipped
Jehoshaphat *b.* his *head* to   *2Ch 20:18*
ground
they sang praises and *b.*   *2Ch 29:30*
their *heads*
Jesus *b. head* and gave up   *Joh 19:30*
ghost

BOWED *HIMSELF*

Abraham, Lot, Jacob, Joseph *Ge 18:2;*
b. himself   *Ge 19:1; 23:7, 12; 33:3;*
  47:31; 48:12
Samson *b. himself* with all   *J'g 16:30*
his might
David stooped and *b. himself* *1Sa 24:8*
Saul *b. himself* to Samuel   *1Sa 28:14*
Mephibosheth *b. himself* to   *2Sa 9:8*
David
Joab, Absalom *b. himself*   *2Sa 14:22;*
  14:33
Cushi, Araunah *b. himself*   *2Sa 18:21;*
  24:20
Nathan, Adonijah, Solomon   *1Ki 1:23;*
b. himself   *1Ki 1:53; 2:19*
the king *b. himself* on his bed *1Ki 1:47*

BOWELS

out of own *b.* shall be thine *Ge 15:4*
heir
from your own body (A)(B)   *Ge 15:4*
your own son shall be heir   *Ge 15:4*
(R)
two manner of people from   *Ge 25:23*
thy *b.*
his *b.* did yearn upon his   *Ge 43:30*
brother
heart yearned for brother   *Ge 43:30*
(A)(E)(R)
was deeply moved (B)   *Ge 43:30*
this water shall go into thy *b.* *Nu 5:22*
go into thy stomach   *Nu 5:22*
thy seed which proceed out *2Sa 7:12*
of thy *b.*
who shall be born of you   *2Sa 7:12*
(A)
proceed from your own body *2Sa 7:12*
(B)(R)
my son which came of my   *2Sa 16:11*
b.
who was born of me (A)   *2Sa 16:11*
came from my own body   *2Sa 16:11*
(B)
my own son (R)   *2Sa 16:11*
Joab shed forth Amasa's *b.* *2Sa 20:10*
on ground
his intestines poured out   *2Sa 20:10*
(B)
her *b.* yearned upon her son *1Ki 3:26*
motherly compassion went out *1Ki 3:26*
(B)
her heart yearned over son *1Ki 3:26*
(A)(E)(R)
great sickness of thy *b.*   *2Ch 21:15*
intestinal disease (A)   *2Ch 21:15*
your vitals fall out (B)   *2Ch 21:15*
smote him in his *b.*, his   *2Ch 21:18*
b. fell out
an incurable intestinal   *2Ch 21:18*
disease (A)
with incurable disease (B)   *2Ch 21:18*
they that came of his own   *2Ch 32:21*
b. slew him
his own offspring   *2Ch 32:21*
assassinated (A)(B)
his own sons struck him   *2Ch 32:21*
down (R)
his meat in his *b.* turned   *Job 20:14*
turns in his own stomach   *Job 20:14*
(A)(B)(R)
my *b.* boiled and rested not *Job 30:27*
my heart is troubled   *Job 30:27*
(A)(E)(R)
my inside boils (B)   *Job 30:27*
it is melted in the midst of *Ps 22:14*
my *b.*
melted within me   *Ps 22:14*
(A)(B)(E)(R)

art he that took me out of   *Ps 71:6*
mother's *b.*
my mother's womb (A)(R)   *Ps 71:6*
from the maternal womb (B)   *Ps 71:6*
let it come into *b.* like   *Ps 109:18*
water
seeped into inward life (A)   *Ps 109:18*
sink into flesh like water   *Ps 109:18*
(B)
into his inward parts (E)   *Ps 109:18*
soak into body like water   *Ps 109:18*
(R)
my *b.* were moved for him   *Ca 5:4*
heart was moved for him   *Ca 5:4*
(A)(E)
heart grew desirous of him   *Ca 5:4*
(B)
heart was thrilled within (R)   *Ca 5:4*
my *b.* shall sound like a   *Isa 16:11*
harp
heart sounds like a harp   *Isa 16:11*
(A)(E)
feelings moved like a lyre (R)   *Isa 16:11*
(B)
soul moans like a lyre (R)   *Isa 16:11*
offspring of thy *b.* like the   *Isa 48:19*
gravel
offspring of your body (B)   *Isa 48:19*
from *b.* of my mother he made *Isa 49:1*
called me from womb   *Isa 49:1*
(A)(E)(R)
from body of my mother (B)   *Isa 49:1*
where is sounding of *b.* and *Isa 63:15*
mercies
your yearning pity   *Isa 63:15*
(A)(B)(E)(R)
my *b.* my *b.*, I am pained at *Jer 4:19*
heart
my anguish, my anguish   *Jer 4:19*
(A)(E)(R)
my feelings, my feelings (B)   *Jer 4:19*
my *b.* are troubled for him   *Jer 31:20*
my affection is stirred (A)   *Jer 31:20*
my emotions stir (B)   *Jer 31:20*
heart yearneth for him   *Jer 31:20*
(E)(R)
my *b.* are troubled   *La 1:20; 2:11*
my vital parts are in tumult (A) *La 1:20*
I am in distress (B)(E)(R)   *La 1:20*
fill thy *b.* with this roll I give *Eze 3:3*
thee
fill your stomach with it   *Eze 3:3*
(A)(B)(R)
till *b.* with (E)   *Eze 3:3*
not satisfy souls, nor fill *b.*   *Eze 7:19*
fill their stomachs   *Eze 7:19*
(A)(B)(R)
Judas burst, all his *b.* gushed *Ac 1:18*
out
his intestines poured out   *Ac 1:18*
(A)(B)
his entrails poured out (N)   *Ac 1:18*
his intestines burst (P)   *Ac 1:18*
ye are straitened in your   *2Co 6:12*
own *b.*
your own affections (A)(E)(R) *2Co 6:12*
open wide your own hearts   *2Co 6:12*
(B)
constraint in yourselves (N)   *2Co 6:12*
any stiffness between us (P)   *2Co 6:12*
long after you in *b.* of Christ *Ph'p 1:8*
tender mercies of Jesus   *Ph'p 1:8*
Christ (A)(R)
deep-felt affection of Jesus   *Ph'p 1:8*
Christ (B)
deep yearning of Jesus Christ *Ph'p 1:8*
(N)
deepest Christian love and   *Ph'p 1:8*
affection (P)
if there be any *b.* of mercies *Ph'p 2:1*
put on *b.* of mercies,   *Col 3:12*
kindness
tenderhearted pity and mercy *Col 3:12*
(A)
tenderness of heart (B)   *Col 3:12*
heart of compassion   *Col 3:12*
(E)(N)(R)
merciful in action (P)   *Col 3:12*
b. of the saints are refreshed *Ph'm 7*
by thee
hearts of the saints   *Ph'm 7*
(A)(B)(E)(R)
been much refreshed (N)   *Ph'm 7*
cheers the hearts of fellow   *Ph'm 7*
(P)
receive him that is my own   *Ph'm 12*
b.
my very heart   *Ph'm 12*
(A)(B)(E)(R)

part of myself (N)(P)   *Ph'm 12*
refresh my *b.* in the Lord   *Ph'm 20*
refresh my heart (A)(E)(R)   *Ph'm 20*
buoy up my deepest feelings   *Ph'm 20*
(B)
relieve my anxiety (N)   *Ph'm 20*
do my old heart good (P)   *Ph'm 20*
shutteth up his *b.* of   *1Jo 3:17*
compassion
his heart of compassion (A)   *1Jo 3:17*
deep sympathies (B)   *1Jo 3:17*
shutteth up his compassion   *1Jo 3:17*
(E)
shuts up his heart (N)(R)   *1Jo 3:17*
shuts his eyes and his heart   *1Jo 3:17*
(P)

BOWETH

every one that *b.* down upon *J'g 7:5*
And the mean man *b.* down   *Isa 2:9*
Bel *b.* down, Nebo stoopeth   *Isa 46:1*

BOWING

worshipped the Lord *b.*   *Ge 24:52*
have set their eyes *b.* down   *Ps 17:11*
as a *b.* wall shall ye be, and *Ps 62:3*
as a
b. their knees worshipped   *M'k 15:19*
him

BOWL

bowl   *Nu 7:13;*
19, 25, 31, 37, 43, 49, 55, 61, 67, 73
bowl (A)   *Nu 7:14;*
20, 26, 32, 38, 44, 50, 56, 62, 68, 74, 80
one silver *b.* of seventy   *Nu 7:79*
shekels
and thirty shekels, each *b.*   *Nu 7:85*
seventy
of the fleece, a *b.* full of   *J'g 6:38*
water
in a lordly *b.* (B)(R)   *J'g 5:25*
or the golden *b.* be broken   *Ec 12:6*
with a *b.* upon the top of it, *Zec 4:2*
and his
upon the right side of the *b.* *Zec 4:3*
a *b.* of vinegar (R)   *Joh 19:29*
poured out his *b.*   *Re 16:2-4;*
(A)(B)(E)(N)(P)(R)(S)   8, 10, 12, 17

BOWLS

covers thereof, and *b.*   *Ex 25:29;*
thereof   *Ex 25:31, 33-34*
bowls (A)   *Ex 25:29*
   Ex 37:16; Nu 4:7; 7:84, 86
bowls (B)   *Ex 25:29;*
   Ex 37:16; 2 Ki 25:14; 2 Ch 24:14
his spoons, and his *b.* and   *Ex 37:16;*
his   *Ex 37:17, 19-20*
the spoons, and the *b.* and   *Nu 4:7*
twelve silver *b.* twelve spoons *Nu 7:84*
the two *b.* of the chapiters   *1Ki 7:41*
that
the two *b.* of the chapiters   *1Ki 7:41*
which
cover the two *b.* of the   *1Ki 7:42*
chapiters
And the *b.* and the snuffers   *1Ki 7:50*
house of the Lord *b.* of   *2Ki 12:13*
silver
firepans, and the *b.* and   *2Ki 25:15*
such
for the fleshhooks, and the   *1Ch 28:17*
b.
the two *b.* (S)   *2Ch 4:12; 4:13*
from *b.* and pitchers (B)   *Isa 22:24*
the snuffers, and the *b.* and *Jer 52:18*
the firepans, and the *b.* and *Jer 52:19*
That drink wine in *b.* and   *Am 6:6*
anoint
they shall be filled like *b.*   *Zec 9:15*
and as
shall be like *b.* before the   *Zec 14:20*
altar
golden *b.* full of   *Re 5:8;*
(A)(B)(E)(N)(P)(R)(S)   *Re 15:7;*
   16:1; 17:1; 21:9

BOWMEN

of the horsemen and *b.*   *Jer 4:29*

BOWS

b. of the mighty men are   *1Sa 2:4*
broken

They were armed with *b.*   *1Ch 12:2*
bare shields and drew *b.*   *2Ch 14:8*
helmets, and habergeons,   *2Ch 26:14*
and *b.*
swords, their spears, and   *Ne 4:13*
their *b.*
spears, the shields, and the *b.* *Ne 4:16*
and their *b.* shall be broken   *Ps 37:15*
and bend their *b.* to shoot   *Ps 64:3*
their
being armed, and carrying *b.* *Ps 78:9*
all their *b.* bent, their horses *Isa 5:28*
With arrows and with *b.*   *Isa 7:24*
shall
Their *b.* also shall dash the   *Isa 13:18*
young
every one of their *b.* is   *Jer 51:56*
broken
bucklers, the *b.* and the   *Eze 39:9*
arrows

BOWSHOT

way off, as it were a *b.*   *Ge 21:16*

BOWSTRING

seven fresh *b.* (B)(R)   *J'g 16:1;*
   16:8-9
loose my *b.* (A)(B)   *Job 30:11*

BOX

a *b.* (A)(B)(R)   *1Sa 6:8; 6:11, 15*
in a *b.* (S)   *1Sa 6:8; 6:11, 15*
take this *b.* of oil in thine   *2Ki 9:1*
hands
Then take the *b.* of oil, and   *2Ki 9:3*
pour
pine, and the *b.* tree   *Isa 41:19*
together
and the *b.* together, to   *Isa 60:13*
beautify
having an alabaster *b.* of   *M't 26:7*
very
having an alabaster *b.* of   *M'k 14:3*
she brake the *b.* and poured   *M'k 14:3*
it
brought an alabaster *b.* of   *Lu 7:37*

BOXER

I am like a *b.* (N)   *1Co 9:26*

BOXES

perfume *b.*   *Isa 3:20*
(A)(B)(E)(R)(S)

BOY

death of the *b.* (B)   *Ge 21:16*
the *b.* is not here (A)   *Ge 27:30*
the *b.* girded (R)   *1Sa 2:18*
called the *b.* (A)(R)   *1Sa 3:8*
the *b.* was sick (B)   *2Sa 12:15;*
   12:19
behind a little *b.* (B)   *1Ki 2:11*
given a *b.* for an harlot, and *Joe 3:3*
the *b.* was cured   *M't 17:18*
(A)(B)(E)(N)(P)(R)
a little *b.* (A)   *M'k 9:21*
whatever the little *b.* be (A)   *Lu 1:66;*
   1:80

BOYS

And the *b.* grew: and Esau   *Ge 25:27*
was
b. and girls playing in the   *Zec 8:5*
streets

BOZEZ

the name of the one was B.   *1Sa 14:4*

BOZKATH

Lachish, and B. and Eglon   *Jos 15:39*

BOZRAH

the son of Zerah of B.   *Ge 36:33*
reigned
Jobab the son of Zerah of   *1Ch 1:44*
B.
the Lord hath a sacrifice in B. *Isa 34:6*
with dyed garments from B.   *Isa 63:1*

And upon Kerioth, and upon B.	Jer 48:24
that B. shall become a desolation	Jer 49:13
and spread his wings over B.	Jer 49:22
shall devour the palaces of B.	Am 1:12
them together as the sheep of B.	Mic 2:12

BRACELET

the b. that was on his arm	2Sa 1:10

BRACELETS

two b. for her hands of ten	Ge 24:22
b. upon his sister's hands	Ge 24:30
and the b. upon her hands	Ge 24:47
Thy signet, and thy b. and thy	Ge 38:18
the signet, and b. and staff	Ge 38:25
brought b. and earrings, and	Ex 35:22
jewels of gold, chains, and b.	Nu 31:50
The chains, and the ·b. and	Isa 3:19
I put b. upon thy hands	Eze 16:11
b. upon their hands, and	Eze 23:42

BRACING

b. up your minds (A)(B)(R)	1Pe 1:13

BRAG

b. of empty distinctions (N)	2Co 11:18

BRAIDED

of gold b. work (S)	Ex 28:14; Ex 28:22, 24-25; 39:15, 17-18; 2Ki 25:17
b. hair (S)	1Ti 2:9

BRAIDING

b. the hair (S)	1Pe 3:3

BRAKE

b. every tree of the field	Ex 9:25
people b. off the golden earrings	Ex 32:3
and b. them beneath the mount	Ex 32:19
and b. them before your eyes	De 9:17
the trumpets, and b. the pitchers	J'g 7:19; 7:20
head, and all to b. his skull	J'g 9:53
And he b. the withs, as a thread	J'g 16:9
he b. them from off his arms	J'g 16:12
and his neck b. and he died	1Sa 4:18
three mighty men b. through	2Sa 23:16
and b. in pieces the rocks before	1Ki 19:11
they b. down the image of Baal	2Ki 10:27
and b. down the house of Baal	2Ki 10:27
house of Baal, and b. it down	2Ki 11:18
his images b. they in pieces	2Ki 11:18
b. down the wall of Jerusalem	2Ki 14:13
and b. the images, and cut down	2Ki 18:4
b. in pieces the brasen serpent	2Ki 18:4
And he b. down the houses of	2Ki 23:7 2Ki 23:8, 12, 14-15
b. down the walls of Jerusalem	2Ki 25:10
b. faith with God (B)	1Ch 5:25
And the three b. through the host	1Ch 11:18
and b. down the images, and cut	2Ch 14:3
and b. into it, and carried away	2Ch 21:17
the house of Baal, and b. it down	2Ch 23:17
b. down the wall of Jerusalem	2Ch 25:23
and b. down the wall of Gath	2Ch 26:6
and b. the images in pieces	2Ch 31:1

they b. down the altars of Baalim	2Ch 34:4
b. down the wall of Jerusalem	2Ch 36:19
I b. the jaws of the wicked	Job 29:17
when it b. forth, as if it had	Job 38:8
b. up for it my decreed place	Job 38:10
b. he the arrows of the bow	Ps 76:3
he b. the whole staff of bread	Ps 105:16
and b. the trees of their coasts	Ps 105:33
inventions: and the plague b. in	Ps 106:29
and b. their bands in sunder	Ps 107:14
off Jeremiah's neck, and b. it	Jer 28:10
my covenant they b. although	Jer 31:32
b. down the walls of Jerusalem	Jer 39:8
b. down all the walls of Jerusalem	Jer 52:14
the Chaldeans b. and carried	Jer 52:17
whose covenant he b. even with	Eze 17:16
and his sleep b. from him	Da 2:1
and clay, and b. them to pieces	Da 2:34
that it b. in pieces the iron	Da 2:45
and b. all their bones in pieces	Da 6:24
it devoured and b. in pieces	Da 7:7
which devoured, b. in pieces	Da 7:19
the ram, and b. his two horns	Da 8:7
he blessed, and b. and gave	M't 14:19
and gave thanks, and b. them	M't 15:36
bread, and blessed it, and b.	M't 26:26
and b. the loaves and gave them	M'k 6:41
and gave thanks, and b. and	M'k 8:6
When I b. the five loaves among	M'k 8:19
and she b. the box, and poured	M'k 14:3
took bread, and blessed, and b.	M'k 14:22
on fishes: and their net b.	Lu 5:6
he b. the bands, and was	Lu 8:29
he blessed them, and b. and	Lu 9:16
and gave thanks, and b. it	Lu 22:19
and blessed it, and b. and gave	Lu 24:30
and b. the legs of the first, and of	Joh 19:32
already, they b. not his legs	Joh 19:33
he b. it, and said, Take, eat	1Co 11:24

BRAKEST

the first tables, which thou b.	Ex 34:1
the first tables which thou b.	De 10:2
thou b. the heads of the dragons	Ps 74:13
Thou b. the heads of leviathan	Ps 74:14
they leaned upon thee, thou b.	Eze 29:7

BRAMBLE

said all the trees unto the b.	J'g 9:14
the b. said unto the trees, If	J'g 9:15
let fire come out of the b.	J'g 9:15
of a b. bush gather they grapes	Lu 6:44

BRAMBLES

lily among b. (R)	Ca 2:2
nettles and b. in the fortresses	Isa 34:13

BRANCH

in one b.; and three bowls made	Ex 25:33
his shaft, his b. his bowls	Ex 37:17; 37:19
cut down from thence a b. with	Nu 13:23
b. shooteth forth in his garden	Job 8:16
his shoots go forth (A)(B)(E)(R)	Job 8:16

tender b. thereof will not cease	Job 14:7
the tender shoots of it (A)(B)(R)	Job 14:7
and his b. shall not be green	Job 15:32
above shall his b. be cut off	Job 18:16
dew lay all night upon my b.	Job 29:19
the b. that thou madest strong	Ps 80:15
the son whom thou hast raised (B)	Ps 80:15
the stock which thy right hand (R)	Ps 80:15
righteous shall flourish as a b.	Pr 11:28
flourish like a green bough (A)	Pr 11:28
flourish like a fresh leaf (B)	Pr 11:28
flourish like a green leaf (E)(R)	Pr 11:28
day shall the b. of the Lord	Isa 4:2
head and tail, b. and rush	Isa 9:14
B. shall grow out of his roots	Isa 11:1
like an abominable b. and as the	Isa 14:19
bough, and an uppermost b.	Isa 17:9
the head or tail, b. or rush, may	Isa 19:15
the b. of the terrible one shall	Isa 25:5
the b. of my planting, the work of	Isa 60:21
raise unto David a righteous B.	Jer 23:5
at that time, will I cause the B. to	Jer 33:15
and, lo, they put the b. to their	Eze 8:17
a b. which is among the trees of	Eze 15:2
and took the highest b. of	Eze 17:3
top of the cedar tree (A)(E)(R)	Eze 17:3
the crest of a cedar (B)	Eze 17:3
the highest b. of the high cedar	Eze 17:22
out of a b. of her roots shall	Da 11:7
bring forth my servant the B.	Zec 3:8
the man whose name is The B.	Zec 6:12
leave them neither root nor	Mal 4:1
When his b. is yet tender	M't 24:32
young shoots become soft (A)(N)	M't 24:32
When her b. is yet tender	M'k 13:28
Every b. in me that beareth not	Joh 15:2
and every b. that beareth fruit	Joh 15:2
As the b. cannot bear fruit of	Joh 15:4
he is cast forth as a b. and is	Joh 15:6
as a root-sprout (B)	Joh 15:6

BRANCHES

in the vine were three b.	Ge 40:10; Ge 40:12
a well; whose b. run over	Ge 49:22
his b., his bowls Ex 25:31; 25:32, 33, 35	
and their b. shall be of the same	Ex 25:36
six b. going out of sides	Ex 37:18; Ex 37:19, 21-22
b. of palm trees and the boughs	Le 23:40
and fetch olive b. and pine b.	Ne 8:15
the flame shall dry up his b. and	Job 15:30
as flame consumes a dry tree (A)	Job 15:30
flame shall shrivel his roots (B)	Job 15:30
unto the sea, and her b. unto	Ps 80:11
which sing among the b.	Ps 104:12
find festal procession b. (R)	Ps 118:27
her b. are stretched out, they	Isa 16:8
in the outmost fruitful b. thereof	Isa 17:6
in the uppermost bough (A)(E)	Isa 17:6
on the topmost bough (B)	Isa 17:6
on the highest bough (R)	Isa 17:6
take away and cut down the b.	Isa 18:5

lie down, and consume the *Isa 27:10*
b.
eat the twigs of it (B) *Isa 27:10*
it, and the *b.* of it are *Jer 11:16*
broken
b. turned toward him *Eze 17:6;*
Eze 17:7, 8, 23
fruitful and full of *b.* by *Eze 19:10;*
reason *Eze 19:11, 14*
a cedar in Lebanon with fair *Eze 31:3*
b. *Eze 31:5-9, 12-13*
ye shall shoot forth your *b.* *Eze 36:8*
cut off his *b.*, shake off his *Da 4:14*
leaves
and upon whose *b.* the fowls *Da 4:21*
of
consume his *b.* and devour *Ho 11:6*
them
His *b.* shall spread, and his *Ho 14:6*
his suckers and shoots shall *Ho 14:6*
(A)
his shoots shall spread out *Ho 14:6*
(B)
the *b.* thereof are made white *Joe 1:7*
out, and marred their vine *b.* *Na 2:2*
these two olive *b.* which *Zec 4:12*
through
come and lodge in the *b.* *M't 13:32*
thereof
others cut down *b.* from the *M't 21:8*
trees
shooteth out great *b.*; so *M'k 4:32*
that
others cut down *b.* off the *M'k 11:8*
trees
fowls of the air lodged in *Lu 13:19*
the *b.*
Took *b.* of palm trees, and *Joh 12:13*
went
I am the vine, ye are the *b.* *Joh 15:5*
if the root be holy so are *Ro 11:16*
the *b.*
if some of the *b.* be broken *Ro 11:17*
off
Boast not against the *b.* But *Ro 11:18*
if
The *b.* were broken off, that *Ro 11:19*
I
if God spared not the *Ro 11:21*
natural *b.*
these, which be the natural *Ro 11:24*
b. be

BRAND

is not this a *b.* plucked out of *Zec 3:2*

BRANDED

b. in conscience (E)(N) *1Ti 4:2*

BRANDING

b. instead of beauty (S) *Isa 3:24*

BRANDISH

I shall *b.* my sword before *Eze 32:10*
them

BRANDS

when he had set the *b.* on *J'g 15:5*
fire, he

BRASEN

make four *b.* rings in the *Ex 27:4*
four
burnt offering with his *b.* *Ex 35:16*
grate
he made for the altar a *b.* *Ex 38:4*
grate
their *b.* sockets twenty; the *Ex 38:10*
and the *b.* altar, and the *b.* *Ex 38:30*
grate
b. altar, and his grate of *Ex 39:39*
brass
sodden in a *b.* pot, it shall be *Le 6:28*
both
the priest took the *b.* *Nu 16:39*
censers
great cities walls and *b.* bars *1Ki 4:13*
every base had four *b.* *1Ki 7:30*
wheels
b. altar that was before the *1Ki 8:64*
Lord
made in their stead *b.* *1Ki 14:27*
shields
he brought also the *b.* altar *2Ki 16:14*

the *b.* altar shall be for me *2Ki 16:15*
to
down the sea from off the *2Ki 16:17*
b. oxen
brake in pieces the *b.* *2Ki 18:4*
serpent that
the *b.* sea that was in the *2Ki 25:13*
house of
wherewith Solomon made *1Ch 18:8*
the *b.*
Moreover the *b.* altar, that *2Ch 1:5*
Bezaleel
the *b.* altar before the Lord, *2Ch 1:6*
which
Solomon had made a *b.* *2Ch 6:13*
scaffold
b. altar which Solomon had *2Ch 7:7*
made
an iron pillar, and *b.* walls *Jer 1:18*
unto this people a fenced *Jer 15:20*
b. wall
the *b.* sea that was in the *Jer 52:17*
house of
twelve *b.* bulls that were *Jer 52:20*
under the
and stood beside the *b.* altar *Eze 9:2*
of cups, and pots, *b.* vessels *M'k 7:4*

BRASS

of every artificer in *b.* and *Ge 4:22*
iron
of them; gold and silver, and *Ex 25:3*
b.
thou shalt make fifty taches *Ex 26:11*
of *b.*
cast five sockets of *b.* for *Ex 26:37*
them
and thou shalt overlay it *Ex 27:2;*
with *b.* 27:6
thereof thou shalt make of *b.* *Ex 27:3*
for it a grate of network of *Ex 27:4*
b.
their twenty sockets shall be *Ex 27:10*
of *b.*
and their twenty sockets of *Ex 27:11*
b.
of silver and their sockets of *Ex 27:17*
b.
twined linen, and their *Ex 27:18*
sockets of *b.*
the pins of the court, shall *Ex 27:19*
be of *b.*
Thou shalt also make a *Ex 30:18*
laver of *b.*
and his foot also of *b.* *Ex 30:18*
in gold, and in silver, and in *Ex 31:4*
b.
the Lord; gold and silver, and *Ex 35:5*
b.
an offering of silver and *b.* *Ex 35:24*
in gold and in silver, and in *Ex 35:32*
b.
he made fifty taches of *b.* to *Ex 36:18*
couple
but their five sockets were of *Ex 36:38*
b.
he overlaid it with *b.* *Ex 38:2;*
38:6
the vessels thereof made *Ex 38:3;*
he of *b.* *Ex 38:5, 8, 11, 17, 19-20, 29*
brasen altar, and his grate *Ex 39:39*
of *b.*
as iron, and your earth as *b.* *Le 26:19*
Moses made a serpent of *b.* *Nu 21:9*
the gold, and the silver, the *Nu 31:22*
b.
of whose hills thou mayest dig *De 8:9*
b.
that is over thy head shall *b.* *De 28:23*
Thy shoes shall be iron and *Nu 33:25*
vessels of *b.* and iron, are *Jos 6:19*
the vessels of *b.* and of iron, *Jos 6:24*
they
with gold, and with *b.* and *Jos 22:8*
with
bound him with fetters of *J'g 16:21*
b.; and
an helmet of *b.* upon his *1Sa 17:5;*
head *1Sa 17:6, 38*
David took exceeding much *b.* *2Sa 8:8*
vessels of gold and vessels of *2Sa 8:10*
b.
bow of *b.* (E) *2Sa 20:24*
three hundred shekels of *b.* *2Sa 21:16*
in
a man of Tyre, a worker in *1Ki 7:14*
b.
cunning to work all works *1Ki 7:14;*

in *b.* *1Ki 7:15, 16, 27, 30, 38, 45, 47*
bound him with fetters of *b.* *2Ki 25:7*
pillars of *b.* that were in *2Ki 25:13*
the house
all the vessels of *b.* *2Ki 25:14*
wherewith
b. of all these vessels was *2Ki 25:16*
without
and the chapiter upon it *2Ki 25:17*
was *b.*
to sound with cymbals of *1Ch 15:19*
b.
brought David very much *b.* *1Ch 18:8*
the pillars, and the vessels *1Ch 18:8*
of *b.*
vessels of gold and silver *1Ch 18:10*
and *b.*
b. in abundance without *1Ch 22:3*
weight;
and of *b.* and iron without *1Ch 22:14*
weight
the gold, the silver, and the *1Ch 22:16*
b.
the *b.* for things of *b.* the *1Ch 29:2*
iron for
of *b.* eighteen thousand *1Ch 29:7*
talents
in silver, and in *b.* and in *2Ch 2:7*
iron
in gold, and in silver, and in *2Ch 2:14*
b.
made an altar of *b.* twenty *2Ch 4:1*
cubits
overlaid the doors of them *2Ch 4:9*
with *b.*
house of the Lord, of bright *2Ch 4:16*
b.
the weight of the *b.* could *2Ch 4:18*
not be
king Rehoboam made *2Ch 12:10*
shields of *b.*
also such as wrought iron *2Ch 24:12*
and *b.*
fine bright *b.* (B)(E) *Ezr 8:27*
of stones? or is my flesh of *Job 6:12*
b.
b. is molten out of the stone *Job 28:2*
bones are as strong pieces *Job 40:18*
of *b.*
as straw, and *b.* as rotten *Job 41:27*
wood
bow of *b.* (E)(R) *Ps 18:34*
he hath broken the gates of *Ps 107:16*
b.
break in pieces the gates of *Isa 45:2*
b.
is an iron sinew, and thy *Isa 48:4*
brow *b.*
For *b.* I will bring gold, and *Isa 60:17*
for
bring silver, and for wood *Isa 60:17*
b.
they are *b.* and iron; they are *Jer 6:28*
all
Also the pillars of *b.* that *Jer 52:17*
were in
and carried all the *b.* of *Jer 52:17*
them to
of *b.* wherewith they *Jer 52:18*
ministered
the *b.* of all these vessels *Jer 52:20*
was
a chapiter of *b.* was upon *Jer 52:22*
it; and
like the colour of burnished *Eze 1:7*
b.
all they are *b.* and tin, and *Eze 22:18*
iron
they gather silver, and *b.* *Eze 22:20*
and iron
that the *b.* of it may be *Eze 24:11*
hot, and
persons of men and vessels *Eze 27:13*
of *b.*
was like the appearance of *Eze 40:3*
b.
his belly and his thighs of *b.* *Da 2:32*
the clay, the *b.* the silver *Da 2:35*
another third kingdom of *b.* *Da 2:39*
the iron, the *b.* the clay, the *Da 2:45*
with a band of iron and *b.* *Da 4:15, 23*
gods of gold, and of silver, of *Da 5:4*
b.
the gods of silver, and gold, of *Da 5:23*
b.
were of iron, and his nails of *Da 7:19*
b.
feet like in colour to polished *Da 10:6*
b.
I will make thy hoofs *b.* *Mic 4:13*

mountains were mountains of *Zec 6:1*
b.
nor silver, nor b. in your *M't 10:9*
purses
I am become as sounding b. *1Co 13:1*
and his feet like unto fine b. *Re 1:15*
and his feet are like fine b. *Re 2:18*
idols of gold, and silver, and *Re 9:20*
b.
and of b. and iron, and *Re 18:12*
marble

BRAVE

b. men (A) *J'g18:2*
a b. hero (B) *J'g 21:10*
a b. man (B) *2Sa 13:28*
a b. man (A) *2Sa 17:10*
b. warriors (B) *1Ch 5:24;*
           1Ch 7:7, 9, 40
mighty and b. warriors (A) *1Ch 12:25*
b. men (B) *2Ch 17:4; 17:16, 17*

BRAVERY

a woman of b. (A) *Ru 3:11*
b. of their tinkling ornaments *Isa 3:18*
finery of their anklets *Isa 3:18*
(A)(B)(R)
beauty of their anklets (E) *Isa 3:18*

BRAVEST

sent the b. of men (A)(R) *J'g 21:10*
his b. men (A) *Na 2:5*

BRAWLER

patient, not a b. not covetous *1Ti 3:3*
not combative but gentle (A) *1Ti 3:3*
not a fist-fighter, but genial *1Ti 3:3*
(B)
neither intemperate nor *1Ti 3:3*
violent (P)
not violent, but gentle (R) *1Ti 3:3*
not a b. (N) *1Ti 3:3*

BRAWLERS

evil of no man, to be no b., *Tit 3:2*
but

BRAWLING

with a b. woman in a wide *Pr 25:24;*
house *21:9*
disagreeing, quarrelsome, *Pr 25:24*
scolding (A)
a contentious woman *Pr 25:24*
(B)(E)(R)

BRAY

Doth the wild ass b. when he *Job 6:5*
hath
shouldst b. a fool in a *Pr 27:22*
mortar
pound a fool in a mortar *Pr 27:22*
(A)
crush the fool (B)(R) *Pr 27:22*

BRAYED

Among the bushes they b. *Job 30:7*
they howl (B) *Job 30:7*

BRAZENFACED

a b. harlot (B)(R) *Eze 16:30*

BREACH

this b. be upon thee; *Ge 38:29*
therefore
every b. of trust (R) *Ex 22:9*
commits a b. of faith (R) *Le 6:2*
B. for b., eye for eye, tooth for *Le 24:20*
fracture for fracture *Le 24:20*
(A)(B)(R)
ye shall know my b. of *Nu 14:34*
promise
know my displeasure, the *Nu 14:34*
revoking of my promise and my
estrangement (A)
realize what it means to *Nu 14:34*
have me against you (B)
shall know my alienation *Nu 14:34*
(E)
shall know my discipline *Nu 14:34*
(R)

made a b. in the tribes of *J'g 21:15*
Israel
made a gap among the *J'g 21:15*
tribes (B)
before me, as the b. of *2Sa 5:20*
waters
like the bursting forth of *2Sa 5:20*
waters (A)
like a breakthrough of *2Sa 5:20*
water (B)
like a bursting flood (R) *2Sa 5:20*
Lord made b. upon Uzzah *2Sa 6:8;*
           1Ch 13:11
broken forth against Uzzah *2Sa 6:8*
(A)(E)(R)
outbreak against Uzzah (B) *2Sa 6:8*
where any b. shall be found *2Ki 12:5*
wherever there is any *2Ki 12:5*
damage (B)
any need of repairs is *2Ki 12:5*
discovered (R)
our God made a b. upon *1Ch 15:13*
us
broke forth upon us *1Ch 15:13*
outbreak against us (B) *1Ch 15:13*
there was no b. left therein *Ne 6:1*
He breaketh me with b. *Job 16:14*
upon b.
chosen stood before him in *Ps 106:23*
the b.
therein is a b. in the spirit *Pr 15:4*
breaks down the spirit *Pr 15:4*
(A)(B)
breaking of the spirit (E) *Pr 15:4*
breaks the spirit (R) *Pr 15:4*
let us make a b. therein for us *Isa 7:6*
as a b. ready to fall *Isa 30:13*
broken section of the wall *Isa 30:13*
(A)(B)
break in a high wall (R) *Isa 30:13*
bindeth up the b. of his *Isa 30:26*
people
binds up hurt of people *Isa 30:26*
(A)(E)(R)
heals the severe wounds of *Isa 30:26*
(B)
repairer of b., restorer of *Isa 58:12*
paths
people broken with a great *Jer 14:17*
b.
smitten with a great wound *Jer 14:17*
(A)(R)
thy b. is great like the sea *La 2:13*
ruin is measureless as sea *La 2:13*
(A)
the sea is your ruin (B)(R) *La 2:13*
into the city wherein is *Eze 26:10*
made a b.

BREACHES

seashore, and abode in his b. *J'g 5:17*
abode by his creeks (A)(E) *J'g 5:17*
by its bays he remained (B) *J'g 5:17*
settling down by his landings *J'g 5:17*
(R)
repaired the b. of the city *1Ki 11:27*
of David
closed the breaks in (B) *1Ki 11:27*
repair b. of house *2Ki 12:5;*
       2Ki 12:6-8, 12; 22:5
damage of the house (B) *2Ki 12:5;*
       2Ki 12:8-12; 22:5
whatever needed repair (R) *2Ki 12:5*
the b. began to be stopped *Ne 4:7*
the broken places (B) *Ne 4:7*
heal the b. thereof; for it *Ps 60:2*
shaketh
b. of the city of David, that *Isa 22:9*
they
And ye shall go out at the b. *Am 4:3*
smite the great house with b. *Am 6:11*
great house into ruins (A) *Am 6:11*
smitten into fragments (R) *Am 6:11*
close up the b. thereof *Am 9:11*
repair the breaks (B) *Am 9:11*

BREAD

Salem brought forth b. and *Ge 14:18*
wine
I will fetch a morsel of b. *Ge 18:5*
and took b. and a bottle of *Ge 21:14*
water
Jacob gave Esau b. and *Ge 25:34*
pottage
gave the savoury meat and *Ge 27:17*
the b.
all the land of Egypt there *Ge 41:54*
was b.

the people cried to Pharoah *Ge 41:55*
for b.
laden with corn and b. and *Ge 45:23*
meat
with b. according to their *Ge 47:12*
unto Joseph, and said, Give *Ge 47:15*
us b.
Joseph gave them b. in *Ge 47:17*
exchange
fed them with b. for all *Ge 47:17*
their cattle
buy us and our land for b. *Ge 47:19*
and we
Out of Asher his b. shall be *Ge 49:20*
fat
I will rain b. from heaven for *Ex 16:4*
you
and in the morning b. to the *Ex 16:8*
full
morning ye shall be filled *Ex 16:12*
with b.
they gathered twice as much *Ex 16:22*
b.
on the sixth day the b. of *Ex 16:29*
two days
the b. wherewith I have fed *Ex 16:32*
shall bless thy b. and thy *Ex 23:25*
water
the b. that is in thy basket *Ex 29:32*
the b. remain until morning *Ex 29:34*
he set the b. in order upon *Ex 40:23*
it
a cake of oiled b., and one *Le 8:26*
wafer
of the b. shall ye burn with *Le 8:32*
fire
the b. of their God *Le 21:6;*
         Le 21:8, 17, 21
the b. of your God of any *Le 22:25*
of these
feast of unleavened b. unto *Le 23:6*
ye must eat unleavened b. *Le 23:6*
offer with the b. seven *Le 23:18*
lambs
b. of first fruits for a wave *Le 23:20*
may be on the b. for a *Le 24:7*
memorial
continual b. shall be thereon *Nu 4:7*
they are b. for us: their *Nu 14:9*
defence
our soul loatheth this light b. *Nu 21:5*
my b. for my sacrifices made *Nu 28:2*
by
shall unleavened b. be eaten *Nu 28:17*
man doth not live by b. only *De 8:3*
I neither did eat b. nor drink *De 9:9*
I did neither eat b. nor drink *De 9:18*
shalt eat no leavened b. with *De 16:3*
it
shalt thou eat unleavened b. *De 16:3*
even the b. of affliction; for *De 16:3*
thou
there shall be no leavened b. *De 16:4*
the feast of unleavened b. *De 16:16*
and in
they met you not with b. and *De 23:4*
with
Ye have not eaten b. neither *De 29:6*
have
all the b. of their provision *Jos 9:5*
was
This our b. we took hot for *Jos 9:12*
our
and, lo, a cake of barley b. *J'g 7:13*
should give b. unto thine army *J'g 8:6*
we should give b. unto thy men *J'g 8:15*
thine heart with a morsel of *J'g 19:5*
b.
there is b. and wine also for *J'g 19:19*
me
visited his people in giving *Ru 1:6*
them b.
hired out themselves for b. *1Sa 2:5*
the b. is spent in our vessels *1Sa 9:7*
an ass laden with b. and a *1Sa 16:20*
bottle of
but there is hallowed b. *1Sa 21:4;*
              21:5
in that thou hast given him *1Sa 22:13*
b.
Shall I then take my b. and *1Sa 25:11*
my
let me set a morsel of b. *1Sa 28:22*
before
to David, and gave him b. *1Sa 30:11*
on the sword, or that lacketh *2Sa 3:29*
if I taste b., or ought else *2Sa 3:35*
till the

to every one a cake of *b.*   2Sa 6:19
thy master's son eat *b.*   2Sa 9:10
always
ravens brought *b.* and flesh   1Ki 17:6
me, I pray thee, a morsel   1Ki 17:11
of *b.*
fed them on *b.* and water   1Ki 18:4;
   1Ki 18:13; 22:27
a land of *b.* and vineyards   2Ki 18:32
b. on asses, and camels   1Ch 12:40
in the feast of unleavened *b.*   2Ch 8:13
feed him with *b.* of   2Ch 18:26
affliction and
the feast of unleavened *b.*   2Ch 30:13
in the
feast of unleavened *b.*   2Ch 30:21
seven days
feast of unleavened *b.*   2Ch 35:17
seven days
feast of unleavened *b.* seven   Ezr 6:22
days
brethren have not eaten the   Ne 5:14
b. of
had taken of them *b.* and   Ne 5:15
wine
the *b.* of the governor,   Ne 5:18
because
And gavest them *b.* from   Ne 9:15
heaven
not the children of Israel   Ne 13:2
with *b.*
wandereth abroad for *b.*   Job 15:23
saying
thou hast withholden *b.* from   Job 22:7
shall not be satisfied with *b.*   Job 27:14
for the earth, out of it   Job 28:5
cometh *b.*
his life abhorreth *b.* and his   Job 33:20
soul
forsaken, nor his seed   Ps 37:25
begging *b.*
eat up my people as they eat   Ps 53:4
b.
he give *b.* also? can he   Ps 78:20
provide
feedest them with the *b.* of   Ps 80:5
tears
I have eaten ashes like *b.*   Ps 102:9
and *b.* which strengtheneth   Ps 104:15
man's
and satisfied them with the   Ps 105:40
b. of
and beg: let them seek their   Ps 109:10
b. also
I will satisfy her poor with   Ps 132:15
b.
are sweet, and *b.* eaten in   Pr 9:17
secret is
honoureth himself, and   Pr 12:9
lacketh *b.*
his land shall be satisfied   Pr 12:11
with *b.*
and thou shalt be satisfied   Pr 20:13
with *b.*
B. of deceit is sweet to a   Pr 20:17
man
for he giveth of his *b.* to the   Pr 22:9
poor
his land shall have plenty of   Pr 28:19
b.
and eateth not the *b.* of   Pr 31:27
idleness
neither yet *b.* to the wise, nor   Ec 9:11
Cast thy *b.* upon the waters: Ec 11:1
for
the whole stay of *b.* and the   Isa 3:1
whole
house is neither *b.* nor   Isa 3:7
clothing
they prevented with their *b.*   Isa 21:14
him
the *b.* of adversity, and the   Isa 30:20
water
and *b.* of the increase of the   Isa 30:23
earth
of rocks: *b.* shall be given   Isa 33:16
him
wine, a land of *b.* and   Isa 36:17
vineyards
he kindleth it and baketh   Isa 44:15
b.; yea
I have baked *b.* upon the coals   Isa 44:19
pit, nor that his *b.* should   Isa 51:14
fail
money for that which is not   Isa 55:2
b.
seed to the sower, and *b.* to   Isa 55:10
to deal thy *b.* to the hungry   Isa 58:7
nor have hunger of *b.*; and   Jer 42:14
there

there was no *b.* for the   Jer 52:6
people of
did continually eat *b.* before   Jer 52:33
him
All her people sigh, they seek   La 1:11
b.
where is *b.* and wine (B)(R)   La 2:12
the young children ask *b.* and   La 4:4
no
Assyrians, to be satisfied with   La 5:6
b.
We gat our *b.* with the peril of   La 5:9
make thee *b.* thereof,   Eze 4:9
according
will break the staff of the   Eze 14:13
b.
fulness of *b.* and abundance   Eze 16:49
of
given his *b.* to the hungry   Eze 18:7
hath given his *b.* to the   Eze 18:16
hungry
your lips, nor eat the *b.* of   Eze 18:22
men
when ye offer my *b.* the fat   Eze 44:7
give me my *b.* and my water   Ho 2:5
unto them as the *b.* of   Ho 9:4
mourners
their *b.* for their soul shall not   Ho 9:4
and want of *b.* in all your   Am 4:6
places
not a famine of *b.* nor a   Am 8:11
thirst for
and with his skirt do touch   Hag 2:12
b.
Ye offer polluted *b.* upon   Mal 1:7
mine
that these stones be made *b.*   M't 4:3
Man shall not live by *b.* alone   M't 4:4
Give us this day our daily *b.*   M't 6:11
whom if his son ask *b.* will he   M't 7:9
not meet to take the   M't 15:26
children's *b.*
should we have so much *b.*   M't 15:33
in
they had forgotten to take *b.*   M't 16:5
because ye have brought no   M't 16:8
b.
not to you concerning *b.*   M't 16:11
that
not beware of the leaven of   M't 16:12
b. but
the feast of unleavened *b.*   M't 26:17
Jesus took *b.* and blessed it   M't 26:26
two hundred pennyworth of   M'k 6:37
b.
but eat *b.* with unwashen   M'k 7:5
hands
not meet to take the   M'k 7:27
children's *b.*
satisfy these men with *b.* here   M'k 8:4
in
disciples had forgotten to   M'k 8:14
take *b.*
saying, It is because we   M'k 8:16
have no *b.*
reason ye, because ye have   M'k 8:17
no *b.*?
the first day of unleavened   M'k 14:12
b.
Jesus took *b.* and blessed   M'k 14:22
this stone that it be made *b.*   Lu 4:3
man shall not live by *b.* alone,   Lu 4:4
but
neither eating *b.* nor drinking   Lu 7:33
scrip, neither *b.* neither money   Lu 9:3
Give us day by day our daily   Lu 11:3
b.
If a son shall ask *b.* of any   Lu 11:11
of you
servants of my father's have   Lu 15:17
b.
Now the feast of unleavened   Lu 22:1
b. drew
he took *b.* and gave thanks   Lu 22:19
he took *b.* and blessed it   Lu 24:30
known of them in breaking   Lu 24:35
of *b.*
Two hundred pennyworth of   Joh 6:7
b.
my Father giveth you the   Joh 6:32
true *b.*
For the *b.* of God is he   Joh 6:33
which
Lord, evermore give us this   Joh 6:34
b.
I am the *b.* of life: he that   Joh 6:35
cometh
I am the *b.* which came   Joh 6:41
down from
I am that *b.* of life   Joh 6:48

This is the *b.* which cometh   Joh 6:50
down
I am the living *b.* which   Joh 6:51
came
if any man eat of this *b.* he   Joh 6:51
shall
the *b.* that I will give is my   Joh 6:51
flesh
This is that *b.* which came   Joh 6:58
down
he that eateth of this *b.* shall   Joh 6:58
live
He that eateth *b.* with me   Joh 13:18
hath
there, and fish laid thereon,   Joh 21:9
and *b.*
Jesus then cometh, and   Joh 21:13
taketh *b.*
in breaking of *b.* and in   Ac 2:42
prayers
breaking *b.* from house to   Ac 2:46
house
were the days of unleavened   Ac 12:3
b.
came together to break *b.*   Ac 20:7
Paul
had broken *b.* and eaten   Ac 20:11
he took *b.* and gave thanks   Ac 27:35
to God
b. of a new baking (N)   1Co 5:6
new unleavened *b.* (P)   1Co 5:6
The *b.* which we break, is   1Co 10:16
it not
we being many are one *b.*   1Co 10:17
are all partakers of that   1Co 10:17
one *b.*
which he was betrayed   1Co 11:23
took *b.*
so let him eat of that *b.*   1Co 11:28
and drink
minister *b.* for your food   2Co 9:10

BREAD *CORN*

b. corn is bruised, because   Isa 28:28
he will

BREAD with *EAT*

in sweat of face shalt thou   Ge 3:19
eat b.
if Lord will give me *b.* to   Ge 28:20
eat
Jacob called his brethren to   Ge 31:54
eat b.
Joseph's brethren sat down   Ge 37:25
to *eat b.*
knew not he had, save *b.* he   Ge 39:6
did *eat*
they heard that they should   Ge 43:25
eat b. there
Egyptians might not *eat b.*   Ge 43:32
with Hebrews
call him that he may *eat b.*   Ex 12:20
and when we did *eat b.* to   Ex 16:3
the full
this is *b.* the Lord hath   Ex 16:15
given to *eat*
came to *eat b.* with Moses'   Ex 18:12
father-in-law
he did not *eat b.* forty days   Ex 34:28;
   De 9:9. 18
there *eat* it, with *b.* in the   Le 8:31
basket
he shall *eat* the *b.* of his   Le 21:22
God
ye shall neither *eat b.* nor   Le 23:14
parched corn
ye shall *eat* your *b.* to full   Le 26:5
and dwell
when ye *eat* the *b.* of the   Nu 15:19
land
thou shalt *eat b.* without   De 8:9
scarceness
tho' thou detain me, I will   J'g 13:16
not *eat b.*
at meal-time come thou, and   Ru 2:14
eat b.
thou shalt *eat b.* at my   2Sa 9:7;
table   9:10
neither did he *eat b.* with   2Sa 12:17
them
set *b.* and he did *eat*   2Sa 12:20
b. summer fruit for young   2Sa 16:2
men to *eat*
nor *eat b.* nor drink water   1Ki 13:8;
   13:16
charged me by Lord, *eat* no   1Ki 13:9
b.

come home with me and   *1Ki 13:15*
eat b.
neither *eat b.* nor drink   *1Ki 13:16;*
     1Ki 13:17-18, 22-23
arise, *eat b.* let thy heart be   *1Ki 21:7*
merry
Shunamite constrained Elisha   *2Ki 4:8*
to *eat b.*
set *b.* and water, they may   *2Ki 6:22*
eat and drink
but they did *eat* of the   *2Ki 23:9*
unleavened *b.*
did *eat b.* continually   *2Ki 25:29;*
before him   *Jer 52:33*
and did *eat b.* with Job in his   *Job 42:11*
house
eat up people, as they *eat b.*   *Ps 14:4;*
     53:4
did *eat* of my *b.* hath lifted   *Ps 41:9*
up his heel
heart smitten, so I forget to *eat*   *Ps 102:4*
my b.
vain to sit up late, to *eat b.*   *Ps 127:2*
of sorrows
for they *eat* the *b.* of   *Pr 4:17*
wickedness
eat of my *b.* and drink of the   *Pr 9:5*
wine
eat not *b.* of him that hath   *Pr 23:6*
evil eye
if thy enemy hunger, give   *Pr 25:21*
him *b.* to eat
go thy way, *eat* thy *b.* with joy   *Ec 9:7*
will *eat* our *b.* and wear our   *Isa 4:1*
apparel
they shall *eat* up thy harvest   *Jer 5:17*
and thy *b.*
there they did *eat b.* together   *Jer 41:1*
in Mizpah
thus shall they *eat* their   *Eze 4:13*
defiled *b.*
they shall *eat b.* by weight   *Eze 4:16*
and with care
eat b. with quaking   *Eze 12:18;*
     12:19
cover not lips, *eat* not *b.*   *Eze 24:17;*
of men   *24:22*
prince sit in it to *eat b.*   *Eze 44:3*
before Lord
flee into Judah, there *eat b.*   *Am 7:12*
and prophesy
they that *eat* thy *b.* have laid a   *Ob 7*
wound
wash not hands when they   *M't 15:2*
eat b.
they could not so much as   *M'k 3:20*
eat b.
buy *b.* for they have nothing   *M'k 6:36*
to *eat*
saw disciples *eat b.* with   *M'k 7:2;*
defiled hands   *7:5*
to Pharisee's house to *eat b.*   *Lu 14:1*
on sabbath
blessed is he that shall *eat*   *Lu 14:15*
b. in kingdom
shall we buy *b.* that these   *Joh 6:5*
may *eat*
nigh to the place where they   *Joh 6:23*
did *eat b.*
he gave them *b.* from heaven   *Joh 6:31*
to *eat*
if any man *eat* of this *b.* he   *Joh 6:51*
shall live
as often as ye *eat* this *b.*   *1Co 11:26*
and drink
whosoever shall *eat* this *b.*   *1Co 11:27*
and drink this cup
did we *eat* any man's *b.* for   *2Th 3:8*
nought
that with quietness they   *2Th 3:12*
work and eat *b.*

LEAVENED BREAD

eateth *leavened b.* that soul   *Ex 12:15*
be cut off
there shall no *leavened b.* be   *Ex 13:3*
eaten
there shall no *leavened b.* be   *Ex 13:7;*
seen   *De 16:3-4*
not offer blood with *leavened*   *Ex 23:18*
b.
he shall offer for his offering   *Le 7:13*
leavened b.

LOAF, LOAVES OF BREAD

loaf of *b.* with ram of   *Ex 29:23*
consecration

loaves of *b.* to people that   *J'g 8:5*
follow me
another carrying three *loaves*   *1Sa 10:3*
of *b.*
they salute, and give thee   *1Sa 10:4*
two *loaves of b.*
give me five *loaves of b.* in   *1Sa 21:3*
my hand
upon asses two hundred   *2Sa 16:1*
loaves of b.
dealt to every one of Israel   *1Ch 16:3*
loaf of b.

NO BREAD

there was *no b.* in all the   *Ge 47:13*
land
there is *no b.* and our soul   *Nu 21:5*
loatheth
no common *b.* under my   *1Sa 21:4*
hand
there was *no b.* there, but   *1Sa 21:6*
shew-bread
Saul had eaten *no b.* all the   *1Sa 28:20*
day
Egyptian had eaten *no b.*   *1Sa 30:12*
three days
eat *no b.* nor drink water   *1Ki 13:9;*
     17:22
turned away face, and would   *1Ki 21:4*
eat *no b.*
why spirit so sad, that thou   *1Ki 21:5*
eatest *no b.*
was *no b.* for the people   *2Ki 25:3;*
     Jer 52:6
when he came thither, he did   *Ezr 10:6*
eat *no b.*
for there is *no* more *b.* in the   *Jer 38:9*
city
I ate *no* pleasant *b.* nor came   *Da 10:3*
flesh
reasoned, it is because we   *M't 16:7;*
have taken *no b.*   *M'k 8:16-17*
take no scrip, *no b.* no   *M'k 6:8*
money in purse

PIECE, PIECES OF BREAD

I pray that I may eat a   *1Sa 2:36*
piece of b.
by means of a whorish   *Pr 6:26*
woman a man is brought to a
piece of b.
for a *piece of b.* that man   *Pr 28:21*
will transgress
to give Jeremiah daily a   *Jer 37:21*
piece of b.
will ye pollute me for   *Eze 13:19*
pieces of b.

STAFF OF BREAD

when I have broken *staff of*   *Le 26:26*
your *b.*
moreover, he brake whole   *Ps 105:16*
staff of b.
I will break *staff of b.*   *Eze 14:16;*
     Eze 5:16; 14:13

UNLEAVENED BREAD

did bake *unleavened b.* they   *Ge 19:3*
did eat
eat *unleavened*   *Ex 12:8;*
b.   *Nu 9:11*
seven days eat *unleavened*   *Ex 12:15;*
b. Ex 13:6, 7; 23:15; 34:18; Le 23:6;
     Nu 28:17; De 16:3
fourteenth day of month eat   *Ex 12:18*
unleavened b.
in all habitations eat   *Ex 12:20*
unleavened b.
feast of *unleavened b.*   *Ex 23:15;*
     23:18
unleavened b. and cakes   *Ex 29:2;*
     Ex 29:23; 34:18
with *unleavened b.* shall it be   *Le 6:16;*
     Le 8:2, 26
wafers of *unleavened b.*   *Nu 6:15*
anointed with oil
six days eat *unleavened b.*   *De 16:8*
witch of Endor did bake   *1Sa 18:24*
unleavened b.
did eat *unleavened b.* among   *2Ki 23:9*
brethren
on passover of *unleavened*   *Eze 45:21*
b. be eaten
first day of *unleavened b.*   *M'k 14:12*
when they killed
the days of *unleavened b.*   *Lu 22:7;*
     Ac 12:3

after days of *unleavened b.*   *Ac 20:6*
we sailed
but with *unleavened b.* of   *1Co 5:8*
sincerity

BREADTH

the *b.* of it fifty cubits   *Ge 6:15*
length and *b.* of land   *Ge 13:17;*
     Isa 8:8
cubit and half the *b.*   *Ex 25:10;*
thereof   *Ex 37:1, 6*
cubit the *b.* thereof   *Ex 25:23;*
     30:2; 37:10, 25
border a hand *b.* round   *Ex 25:25*
b. of one curtain   *Ex 26:2;*
     Ex 26:8; 36:9
the *b.* of the court   *Ex 27:12;*
     Ex 27:13, 18
a span the *b.* thereof   *Ex 28:16;*
     39:9
b. of the board one cubit   *Ex 30:21*
five cubits the *b.* thereof   *Ex 38:1*
so much as a foot *b.*   *De 2:5*
four cubits the *b.* of bed   *De 3:11*
sling stones an hair *b.*   *J'g 20:16*
twenty cubits the *b.* thereof   *1Ki 6:2;*
    1Ki 6:20; 2Ch 3:4, 8; 4:1
the *b.* fifty cubits   *1Ki 7:2; 1Ki 7:6*
four cubits the *b.* thereof   *1Ki 7:27*
threescore cubits the *b.*   *2Ch 3:3;*
     Ezr 6:3
the *b.* of the waters is   *Job 37:10*
Hast thou perceived *b.* of   *Job 38:18*
earth
by the cubit and an hand *b.*   *Eze 40:5*
b. of the gate   *Eze 40:11;*
    Eze 40:13, 19-21, 48
the *b.* of the porch   *Eze 40:49*
b. of the   *Eze 41:1;*
tabernacle *Eze 41:2-7, 11, 14; 42:2, 4;*
     43:13-14
b. of the holy oblation   *Eze 45:1;*
     45:2-5
the *b.* of the city   *Eze 48:8; 48:9-15*
threescore cubits, and the *b.*   *Da 3:1*
through the *b.* of the land, to   *Hab 1:6*
to see what is the *b.* thereof   *Zec 2:2*
twenty cubits, and the *b.*   *Zec 5:2*
thereof
what is the *b.* and length   *Eph 3:18*
they went up on the *b.* of the   *Re 20:9*
the length is as large as the   *Re 21:16*
b.
and the *b.* and the height of   *Re 21:16*
it are

BREAK

they came near to *b.* the door   *Ge 19:9*
shalt *b.* his yoke from off   *Ge 27:40*
thy neck
nor shall ye *b.* a bone   *Ex 12:46;*
     Nu 9:12
then thou shalt *b.* his neck   *Ex 13:13;*
     34:20
let them *b.* loose (E)(R)   *Ex 32:25*
ye shall *b.* their images   *Ex 34:13*
b. down altars (B)(E)   *Ex 34:13*
earthen vessel unclean ye   *Le 11:33*
shall *b.*
I will *b.* the pride of your   *Le 26:19*
power
Israel shall *b.* their bones   *Nu 24:8*
if a man vow, be shall not *b.*   *Nu 30:2*
his word
ye shall *b.* their pillars   *De 12:3*
b. my covenant (B)   *Jos 23:16*
dawn began to *b.* (A)(R)   *J'g 19:25*
b. away every man from   *1Sa 25:10*
his master
b. thy league with Baasha   *1Ki 15:19;*
     2Ch 16:3
should we again *b.* thy   *Ezr 9:14*
commandments
wilt thou *b.* a leaf driven to   *Job 13:25*
and fro
forgetteth that wild beast   *Job 39:15*
may *b.* them
let us *b.* their bands asunder   *Ps 2:3*
thou shalt *b.* them with a rod   *Ps 2:9*
of iron
b. thou the arm of the   *Ps 10:15*
wicked
he shall *b.* them down   *Ps 28:5*
(A)(E)(R)
b. their teeth, O God, in   *Ps 58:6*
their mouth
b. open the fountain (B)(S)   *Ps 74:15*

if they *b.* my statutes and   *Ps 89:31*
keep not
be an oil which shall not *b.*   *Ps 141:5*
my head
until day *b.* and shadows flee   *Ca 2:17;*
  4:6
I will *b.* the Assyrian in my   *Isa 14:25*
land
b. in the wall (A)(B)(R)   *Isa 7:4*
b. the clods   *Isa 28:22, 24*
b. it as the breaking of a   *Isa 30:14*
potter's vessel
as a lion so will he *b.* all   *Isa 38:13*
my bones
bruised reed will he not *b.*   *Isa 42:3;*
  M't 12:20
is not this the fast, that ye *b.*   *Isa 58:6*
every yoke
shall iron *b.* northern iron   *Jer 15:12*
and steel
b. the bottle, so will I *b.*   *Jer 19:10;*
this people   *19:11*
I will *b.* yoke of king of   *Jer 28:4;*
Babylon   *30:8*
he shall *b.* the images of   *Jer 43:13*
Beth-shemesh
send wanderers and *b.*   *Jer 48:12*
Moab's bottles
I will *b.* the bow of Elam   *Jer 49:35*
I will *b.* the staff of bread   *Eze 4:16;*
  Eze 5:16; 14:13
shall *b.* it (S)   *Eze 13:11; 13:13*
judge thee as women that   *Eze 16:38*
b. wedlock
thou shalt *b.* the sherds   *Eze 23:34*
thereof
when they took hold of thee   *Eze 29:7*
thou didst *b.*
when I shall *b.* the yokes of   *Eze 30:18*
Egypt
and I will *b.* Pharaoh's   *Eze 30:22;*
arms   *30:24*
I will *b.* the bow of Israel in   *Ho 1:5*
Jezreel
I will *b.* the bow, the sword   *Ho 2:18*
and battle
Judah shall plow, Jacob   *Ho 10:11*
shall *b.* his clods
they shall march and not *b.*   *Joe 2:7*
their ranks
I will *b.* the bar of Damascus   *Am 1:5*
who flay their skin, and *b.*   *Mic 3:3*
their bones
now will I *b.* his yoke from   *Na 1:13*
off thee
that I might *b.* the   *Zec 11:14*
brotherhood
b. one of these least   *M't 5:19*
commandments
else bottles *b.* and the wine   *M't 9:17*
runneth
b. my sabbath (B)(N)(P)   *M't 12:5*
b. with grief (N)   *M't 26:38*
the disciples came together to   *Ac 20:7*
b. bread
what mean ye to weep and   *Ac 21:13*
b. my heart
a genuine *b.* with evil (P)   *Ro 12:9*
b. down the work of God   *Ro 14:20*
(B)
the bread which we *b.* is it   *1Co 10:16*
not
b. the power of him (N)   *Heb 2:14*
b. up works of the devil (B)   *1Jo 3:8*
b. the law   *Re 2:27*
(A)(B)(N)(P)(R)

BREAK OF DAY

came to Hebron at *b. of day*   *2Sa 2:32*
long while, even to *b. of day*   *Ac 20:11*

BREAK COVENANT

but that ye *b.* my *covenant*   *Le 26:15;*
  26:44
this people will *b.* my   *De 31:16;*
covenant I made   *De 31:20*
I said, I will never *b.* my   *J'g 2:1*
covenant with you
my *covenant* will I not *b.*   *Ps 89:34*
nor alter the thing
remember, *b.* not thy   *Jer 14:21*
covenant with us
if ye can *b.* my *covenant* of   *Jer 33:20*
the day and night
shall he *b. covenant* and be   *Eze 17:15*
delivered
that I might *b.* my *covenant*   *Zec 11:10*
I made

BREAK DOWN

quite *b. down* their images   *Ex 23:24;*
  De 7:5
and he shall *b. down* house   *Le 14:45*
when I come I will *b. down*   *J'g 8:9*
tower
if a fox go up, he shall *b.*   *Ne 4:3*
down stone wall
now they *b. down* the carved   *Ps 74:6*
work
time to *b. down* and a time   *Ec 3:3*
to build
I will *b. down* wall of the   *Isa 5:5*
vineyard
I have watched over them   *Jer 31:28*
to *b. down*
that which I have built will I   *Jer 45:4*
b. down
b. down wall ye have   *Eze 13:14*
daubed
they shall *b. down* thy high   *Eze 16:39*
places
they shall *b. down* the   *Eze 26:4*
towers of Tyrus
and they shall *b. down* thy   *Eze 26:12*
walls
he shall *b. down* their altars   *Ho 10:2*

BREAK FORTH

lest Lord *b. forth* upon   *Ex 19:22;*
them   *19:24*
they *b. forth* into singing   *Isa 14:7;*
  Isa 41:23; 49:13; 54:1
b. forth into joy, sing   *Isa 52:9*
thou shalt *b. forth* on right   *Isa 54:3*
hand
hills *b. forth* before you into   *Isa 55:12*
singing
thy light *b. forth* as the   *Isa 58:8*
morning
out of the north an evil shall   *Jer 1:14*
b. forth
b. forth thou that travailest   *Ga 4:27*
not

BREAK IN PIECES

b. in pieces pillars of brass   *2Ki 25:13*
ye *b.* me *in pieces* with   *Job 19:2*
words
shall *b. in pieces* mighty   *Job 34:24*
men
he shall *b. in pieces* the   *Ps 72:4*
oppressor
they *b. in pieces* thy people   *Ps 94:5*
I will *b. in pieces* gates of   *Isa 45:2*
brass
with thee will I *b. in pieces*   *Jer 51:20*
nations
b. in pieces horse and rider   *Jer 51:21*
b. in pieces man, woman,   *Jer 51:22*
old and young
b. in pieces and bruise   *Da 2:40;*
kingdoms   *2:44*
fourth beast *b. in pieces*   *Da 7:23*
whole earth

BREAK OFF

thou shalt *b.* his yoke *off*   *Ge 27:40*
thy neck
b. off the golden ear rings   *Ex 32:2;*
  32:24
b. off thy sins by   *Da 4:27*
righteousness

BREAK OUT

if fire *b. out*   *Ex 22:6*
if plague *b. out*   *Le 14:43;*
  13:12
b. out the great teeth of the   *Ps 58:6*
young lion
in the wilderness shall waters   *Isa 35:6*
b. out
they *b. out*, and blood   *Ho 4:2*
toucheth blood
lest he *b. out* like fire in the   *Am 5:6*
house of Joseph

BREAK THROUGH

lest they *b. through* to Lord   *Ex 19:21*
to gaze
let not priests and people *b.*   *Ex 19:24*
through
to *b. through* to the king of   *2Ki 3:26*
Edom
thieves *b. through*   *M't 6:19; 6:20*

BREAK UP

b. up fallow ground   *Jer 4:3; Ho 10:12*

BREAKAGE

b. of your idols (B)(E)(R)   *Le 26:30*

BREAKDOWN

guard against *b.* of faith (N)   *Jer 16:1*

BREAKER

The *b.* is come up before   *Mic 2:13*
them
but if thou be a *b.* of the law   *Ro 2:25*

BREAKERS

the *b.* of death (B)   *2Sa 22:5*

BREAKEST

Thou *b.* the ships of Tarshish   *Ps 48:7*

BREAKETH

he said, Let me go, for the   *Ge 32:26*
day *b.*
he *b.* me with a tempest, and   *Job 9:17*
Behold, he *b.* down, and it   *Job 12:14*
He *b.* me with breach upon   *Job 16:14*
The flood *b.* out from the   *Job 28:4*
The voice of the Lord *b.* the   *Ps 29:5*
he *b.* the bow, and cutteth the   *Ps 46:9*
My soul *b.* for the longing   *Ps 119:20*
that it
and a soft tongue *b.* the   *Pr 25:15*
bone
whoso *b.* an hedge, a serpent   *Ec 10:8*
is crushed *b.* out into a viper   *Isa 59:5*
as one *b.* a potter's vessel   *Jer 19:11*
like a hammer that *b.* the   *Jer 23:29*
rock in
ask bread, and no man *b.* it   *La 4:4*
unto
forasmuch as iron *b.* in   *Da 2:40*
pieces

BREAKFAST

come have *b.*   *Joh 21:12*
(A)(B)(N)(P)(R)
when they had *b.* (P)(R)   *Joh 21:15*

BREAKFASTED

when they had *b.* (B)   *Joh 21:15*

BREAKING

a man with him until the *b.*   *Ge 32:24*
of
a boil *b.* forth with blains   *Ex 9:9*
upon
If a thief be found *b.* up, and   *Ex 22:2*
be
like the *b.* forth of waters   *1Ch 14:11*
me as a wide *b.* in of   *Job 30:14*
waters
that there be no *b.* in, nor   *Ps 144:14*
going
b. down the walls, and of   *Isa 22:5*
crying
whose *b.* cometh suddenly at   *Isa 30:13*
as the *b.* of the potters'   *Isa 30:14*
vessel
despised the oath in *b.* the   *Eze 16:59*
by *b.* the covenant, when,   *Eze 17:18*
lo, he
with the *b.* of thy loins; and   *Eze 21:6*
b. heart (S)   *Eze 21:6*
the *b.* up of the power (S)   *Da 12:7*
in the place of the *b.* forth   *Ho 13:13*
heart nearly *b.* (P)   *M't 26:28;*
  M'k 14:34
known of them in *b.* of   *Lu 24:35*
bread
in *b.* of bread, and in prayers   *Ac 2:42*
and *b.* bread from house to   *Ac 2:46*
house
b. the law dishonourest thou   *Re 2:23*

BREAKINGS

by reason of *b.* they purify   *Job 41:25*

BREAKS

b. the spirit (A)(B)(E)(R)   *1Ch 15:4*
repair the *b.* (B)   *Am 9:11*

BREAST

thou shalt take the *b.* of the   *Ex 29:26*
sanctify the *b.* of the wave   *Ex 29:27*
the fat with the *b.* it shall he   *Le 7:30*
that the *b.* may be waved   *Le 7:30*
but the *b.* shall be Aaron's   *Le 7:31*
and his
the wave *b.* and the heave   *Le 7:34*
Moses took the *b.* and waved   *Le 8:29*
it
the wave *b.* and heave   *Le 10:14*
shoulder
heave shoulder and the wave   *Le 10:15*
b.
priest, with the wave *b.* and   *Nu 6:20*
heave
as the wave *b.* and as the   *Nu 18:18*
right
pluck the fatherless from the   *Job 24:9*
b.
my *b.* is as wine (A)   *Job 32:19*
shalt suck the *b.* of kings   *Isa 60:16*
the sea monsters draw out the   *La 4:3*
b.
his *b.* and his arms of silver,   *Da 2:32*
his
but smote upon his *b.* saying   *Lu 18:13*
He then lying on Jesus' *b.*   *Joh 13:25*
saith
which also leaned on his *b.*   *Joh 21:20*
at
girdle of gold about *b.*   *Re 1:13*
(A)(B)(E)(N)(P)(R)
beat of the *b.* (B)   *Re 18:9*

BREASTPLATE

be set in the ephod, and in   *Ex 25:7*
the *b.*
they shall make; a *b.*   *Ex 28:4;*
    Ex 28:15, 22-24, 26, 28-30
the ephod, and the *b.* and   *Ex 29:5*
gird
set for the ephod, and for   *Ex 35:9*
the *b.*
he made the *b.* of cunning   *Ex 39:8;*
work   *Ex 39:9, 15-17, 19, 21*
he put the *b.* upon him   *Le 8:8*
also he put in the *b.* the Urim   *Le 8:8*
put on righteousness as a *b.*   *Isa 59:17*
having on the *b.* of   *Eph 6:14*
righteousness
putting on the *b.* of faith and   *1Th 5:8*
love

BREASTPLATES

b., as it were *b.* of iron;   *Re 9:9*
b. of fire, and of jacinth, and   *Re 9:17*

BREASTS

blessings of the *b.* and of   *Ge 49:25*
they put the fat upon the *b.*   *Le 9:20*
the *b.* and the right shoulder   *Le 9:21*
b. themselves (S)   *Ne 4:17*
or why the *b.* that I should   *Job 3:12*
suck
His *b.* are full of milk, and   *Job 21:24*
his
when I was upon my mother's   *Ps 22:9*
b.
let her *b.* satisfy thee at all   *Pr 5:19*
times
shall lie all night betwixt my   *Ca 1:13*
b.
Thy two *b.* are like two young   *Ca 4:5*
roes
thy two *b.* are like two young   *Ca 7:3*
roes
and thy *b.* to clusters of   *Ca 7:7*
grapes
thy *b.* shall be as clusters of   *Ca 7:8*
that sucked the *b.* of my   *Ca 8:1*
mother
little sister, and she hath no *b.*   *Ca 8:8*
and my *b.* like towers: then   *Ca 8:10*
was
the milk, and drawn from the   *Isa 28:9*
b.
beat your *b.* (A)(B)(E)(R)   *Isa 32:12*
satisfied with the *b.* of her   *Isa 66:11*
thy *b.* are fashioned, and   *Eze 16:7*
thine
there were their *b.* pressed   *Eze 23:3*
b. handled (A)(E)(R)(S)   *Eze 23:3*
bruised the *b.* of her   *Eze 23:8*
virginity
handled your girlish *b.*   *Eze 23:21*
(A)(B)(E)(R)(S)

and pluck off thine own *b.*   *Eze 23:34*
adulteries from between her *b.*   *Ho 2:2*
miscarrying womb and dry *b.*   *Ho 9:14*
and those that suck the *b.*   *Joe 2:16*
of doves, tabering upon their   *Na 2:7*
b. that gave suck   *Lu 11:27;*
(A)(B)(E)(N)(R)(S)   *23:29*
smote their *b.* and returned   *Lu 23:48*
beat their *b.* (A)(B)   *Re 1:7*
about the *b.* a girdle (S)   *Re 1:13*
their *b.* girded with golden   *Re 15:6*
girdles

BREATH

into his nostrils the *b.* of life   *Ge 2:7*
wherein is the *b.* of life, from   *Ge 6:17*
flesh, wherein is the *b.* of life   *Ge 7:15*
in whose nostrils was the *b.*   *Ge 7:22*
of life
at the blast of the *b.* of his   *2Sa 22:16*
nostrils
that there was no *b.* left in   *1Ki 17:17*
him
and by the *b.* of his nostrils   *Job 4:9*
are
blast of his anger   *Job 4:9*
(A)(E)(R)
blast of his nostrils (B)   *Job 4:9*
my life is a *b.* (S)   *Job 7:7*
my days an a *b.* (A)(R)   *Job 7:16*
will not suffer me to take   *Job 9:18*
my *b.*
and the *b.* of all mankind   *Job 12:10*
spirit of every mortal (B)   *Job 12:10*
by the *b.* of his mouth,   *Job 15:30*
shall he go
blast of his mouth (A)   *Job 15:30*
swept away by the wind   *Job 15:30*
(B)
My *b.* is corrupt, my days   *Job 17:1*
are
My spirit is broken (A)(R)   *Job 17:1*
My life is ruined (B)   *Job 17:1*
My spirit is consumed (E)   *Job 17:1*
My *b.* is strange to my wife   *Job 19:17*
I am repulsive to my wife   *Job 19:17*
(A)(R)
by his *b.* the heavens are   *Job 26:13*
(A)(B)
while my *b.* is in me, and   *Job 27:3*
and the *b.* of the Almighty   *Job 33:4*
hath
Spirit of God made me   *Job 33:4*
(A)(B)(E)(R)
unto himself his spirit and   *Job 34:14*
his *b.*
By the *b.* of God frost is   *Job 37:10*
given
His *b.* kindleth coals, and a   *Job 41:21*
flame
the blast of the *b.* of thy   *Ps 18:15*
nostrils
the host of them by the *b.*   *Ps 33:6*
of his
man is *b.* (A)(B)(R)   *Ps 39:4;*
    39:11
they are *b.* (R)   *Ps 62:9;*
  Ps 78:33; 144:5; Isa 51:13
thou takest away their *b.*   *Ps 104:29*
they
neither is their any *b.* in   *Ps 135:17*
His *b.* goeth forth, he   *Ps 146:4*
returneth
every thing that hath *b.*   *Ps 150:6*
praise
fragrance of thy *b.* (S)   *Ca 7:8*
yea they have all one *b.*; so   *Ec 3:19*
that
from man, whose *b.* is in his   *Isa 2:22*
and with the *b.* of his lips   *Isa 11:4*
shall
And his *b.* as an   *Isa 30:28*
overflowing
the *b.* of the Lord, like a   *Isa 30:33*
stream
your *b.* as fire, shall devour   *Isa 33:11*
the *b.* of the Lord (S)   *Isa 40:7*
he that giveth *b.* unto the   *Isa 42:5*
people
a *b.* shall take them (E)   *Isa 57:13*
falsehood, and there is no   *Jer 10:14;*
b. in   *51:17*
b. of our nostrils, the   *La 4:20*
anointed
I will cause *b.* to enter into   *Eze 37:5*
you

and put *b.* in you, and ye   *Eze 37:6*
shall
but there was no *b.* in them   *Eze 37:8*
the four winds, O *b.* and   *Eze 37:9*
breathe
the *b.* came into them, and   *Eze 37:10*
they
God in whose hand thy *b.* is   *Da 5:23*
me, neither is there *b.* left   *Da 10:17*
in me
there is no *b.* at all in the   *Hab 2:19*
midst
he giveth to all life, and   *Ac 17:25*
the *b.* of life (A)   *Heb 4:12*

BREATHE

there was not any left to *b.*   *Jos 11:11*
them, neither left they any   *Jos 11:14*
to *b.*
me, and such as *b.* out of   *Ps 27:12*
cruelty
and *b.* upon these slain, that   *Eze 37:9*

BREATHED

and *b.* into his nostrils the   *Ge 2:7*
breath
he *b.* his last (A)(B)(R)   *Ge 49:33*
utterly destroyed all that *b.*   *Jos 10:40*
as
left not to Jeroboam any   *1Ki 15:29*
that *b.*
said this, he *b.* on them,   *Joh 20:22*
and said

BREATHETH

shalt save alive nothing that   *De 20:16*
b.

BREATHING

hide not thine ear at my *b.* at   *La 3:56*
Saul, yet *b.* out threatenings   *Ac 9:1*
b. out threats and murder   *Ac 9:1*
(B)(R)

BRED

morning, and it *b.* worms   *Ex 16:20*

BREECHES

thou shalt make them linen   *Ex 28:42*
b. to
linen trunks (B)   *Ex 28:42;*
    Ex 39:28; Le 6:10; 16:4
they shall have linen *b.* on   *Eze 44:18*
loins
their *b.* (E)   *Da 3:27*

BREED

that they may *b.* abundantly   *Ge 8:17*
in
rams of the *b.* of Bashan   *De 32:14*
they *b.* strifes (S)   *2Ti 2:23*

BREEDER

a sheep *b.* (S)   *2Ki 3:4*

BREEDING

the *b.* of nettles, and salt pits   *Zep 2:9*
possessed by nettles (A)(R)   *Zep 2:9*
possession of nettles (B)(E)   *Zep 2:9*

BREEDS

knowledge *b.* conceit (N)   *1Co 8:1*

BRETHREN

we are *b.*   *Ge 13:8*
we are kinsmen (B)(R)   *Ge 13:8*
pray you, *b.* do not so   *Ge 19:7*
wickedly
to the house of my master's   *Ge 24:27*
died in the presence of all   *Ge 25:18*
his *b.*
be lord over thy *b.* and let   *Ge 27:29*
thy
all his *b.* have I given to   *Ge 27:37*
him for
unto them, My *b.* whence be   *Ge 29:4*
ye
he took his *b.* with him,   *Ge 31:23;*
and   *Ge 31:25, 32, 37, 46, 54*

unto her father and unto   Ge 34:11;
her b.   34:25
Joseph's ten b. went down to   Ge 42:3;
buy corn   Ge 42:6, 13, 32; 45:16; 49:5
Joseph's b. saw their father   Ge 50:15
was dead
give us possession among the   Nu 27:4
b.
among father's relatives   Nu 27:4;
(B)   27:7
b. dwell together and one die   De 25:5
Rahab brought out her father   Jos 6:23
and b.
he gave them an inheritance   Jos 17:4
among the b.
Abimelech went to his   J'g 9:1
mother's b.
his mother's b. spake of him   J'g 9:3
to men of Shechem
they answered, b. of   2Ki 10:13
Ahaziah
we are relatives of Ahaziah   2Ki 10:13
(B)
kinsmen of Ahaziah (R)   2Ki 10:13
there came to David of   1Ch 12:2
Saul's b.
fellow tribesmen of Saul (B)   1Ch 12:2
Saul's kinsmen (R)   1Ch 12:2
sons of Shemaiah, whose b.   1Ch 26:7
were strong
of Judah, Elihu, one of b.   1Ch 27:18
of David
he had b. the sons of   2Ch 21:2
Jehoshaphat
when Jehu found the b. of   2Ch 22:8
Ahaziah
pleasant b. to dwell together   Ps 133:1
in unity
he that soweth discord   Pr 6:19
among b.
shall have part of inheritance   Pr 17:2
among b.
all b. of the poor do hate   Pr 19:7
him
Jesus saw two b.   M't 4:18;
  4:21
every one that hath   M't 19:29
forsaken houses, b.
moved with indignation   M't 20:24
against two b.
there were with us seven b.   M't 22:25;
  M'k 12:20
one is your Master, Christ,   M't 23:8
all ye are b.
left house or b.   M'k 10:29; Lu 18:29
receive an hundred-fold,   M'k 10:30
houses, b.
if any come, and hate not   Lu 14:26
children b.
for I have five b. that he   Lu 16:28
may testify to them
ye shall be betrayed by   Lu 21:16
parents and b.
this saying went abroad   Joh 21:23
among the b.
b. I wot that through   Ac 3:17
ignorance ye did it
wherefore b. look out among   Ac 6:3
you seven men
certain b. from Joppa   Ac 10:23
accompanied him
moreover these six b.   Ac 11:12
accompanied me
they determined to send   Ac 11:29
relief to the b.
shew these things to James   Ac 12:17
and the b.
made minds evil-affected   Ac 14:2
against the b.
certain men from Judea   Ac 15:1
taught the b.
and they caused great joy to   Ac 15:3
all the b.
Barsabas and Silas chief   Ac 15:22
among the b.
apostles and elders and b.   Ac 15:23
send greeting
Timotheus was well reported   Ac 16:2
of by the b.
when they had seen the b.   Ac 16:40
they comforted
they drew Jason and certain   Ac 17:6
b. to the rulers
the b. immediately sent away   Ac 17:10;
Paul   17:14
Paul then took his leave of   Ac 18:18
the b.
the b. wrote exhorting to   Ac 18:27
receive Apollos

now b. I commend you to   Ac 20:32
God and his grace
we came to Ptolemais and   Ac 21:7
saluted the b.
come to Jerusalem, b.   Ac 21:17
received us gladly
from whom also I received   Ac 22:5
letters to the b.
I wist not b. that he was the   Ac 23:5
high-priest
where we found b. and were   Ac 28:14
desired to tarry
now I would not have you   Ro 1:13;
ignorant, b.   Ro 11:25;
  1Co 10:1; 12:1; 1Th 4:13
know ye not, b. the law hath   Ro 7:1
dominion
b. we are debtors, not to the   Ro 8:12
flesh, to live
he might be firstborn   Ro 8:29
among many b.
b. my prayer to God for Israel   Ro 10:1
is
I beseech you b. by mercies   Ro 12:1;
of God   Ro 15:30; 16:17; 1Co 1:10
  16:15; Ga 4:12; Heb 13:22
for ye see your calling, b.   1Co 1:26
b. when I came to you, came   1Co 2:1
not with
could not speak to you as to   1Co 3:1
spiritual
these things, b. I have in a   1Co 4:6
figure transferred
this I say b. the time is short   1Co 7:29;
  15:50
when sin against b. ye sin   1Co 8:12
against Christ
as the b. of the Lord and   1Co 9:5
Cephas
I praise you, b. that ye   1Co 11:2
remember me
how is it, b. when ye come   1Co 14:26
together
after he was seen of above   1Co 15:6
500 b. at once
my beloved, b. be stedfast   1Co 15:58;
  Jas 2:5
for I look for him with the   1Co 16:11
b.
I desired him to come to   1Co 16:12
you with the b.
all the b. greet you   1Co 16:20;
  Ph'p 4:21
yet have I sent b. lest   2Co 9:3
boasting
I thought it necessary to   2Co 9:5
exhort the b.
b. which came from   2Co 11:9
Macedonia supplied
I have been in perils   2Co 11:26
among false b.
finally b. farewell, be perfect   2Co 13:11
all b. that are with me to   Ga 1:2
churches
because of false b. unawares   Ga 2:4
brought in
peace be to b. and love with   Eph 6:23
faith
many of the b. waxing   Ph'p 1:14
confident
to saints and faithful b. in   Col 1:2
Christ
we beseech you b.   1Th 4:1;
  1Th 5:12; 2Th 2:1
indeed ye do it towards all   1Th 4:10
b.
b. pray for us   1Th 5:25; 2Th 3:1
greet all the b. with an holy   1Th 5:26
kiss
that this epistle be read to   1Th 5:27
all holy b.
put b. in remembrance of   1Ti 4:6
these things
intreat him as a father,   1Ti 5:1
younger men as b.
not despise them because they   1Ti 6:2
are b.
he is not ashamed to call   Heb 2:11
them b.
holy b., partakers, consider   Heb 3:1
the Apostle
unto unfeigned love of the b.   1Pe 1:22
be of one mind, love as b. be   1Pe 3:8
pitiful
from death to life, because   1Jo 3:14
we love b.
we ought to lay down our   1Jo 3:16
lives for the b.
rejoiced greatly when b. testified   3Jo 3
of truth

whatsoever thou doest to b. and   3Jo 5
strangers
neither doth he himself receive   3Jo 10
the b.

HIS BRETHREN

Ham told *his* two b. without   Ge 9:22
a servant of servants shall be   Ge 9:25
to *his* b.
dwell in presence of *his* b.   Ge 16:12;
  25:18
his b. have: given to him for   Ge 27:37
servants
Joseph was feeding the flock   Ge 37:2
with *his* b.
Joseph dreamed a dream and   Ge 37:5
told it *his* b.
his b. envied him, father   Ge 37:11
observed saying
Reuben returned to *his* b.   Ge 37:30
and said, child
for he said, lest he die also   Ge 38:11
as *his* b. did
and let the lad go up with   Ge 44:33
his b.
Joseph nourished his father   Ge 47:12
and *his* b.
was separate from *his* b.   Ge 49:26;
  De 33:16
Joseph died, *his* b. and that   Ex 1:6
generation
Moses went out to *his* b. and   Ex 2:11
looked on
he that is high-priest among   Le 21:10
his b.
one of *his* b. may redeem   Le 25:48
him
brought to *his* b. Midianitish   Nu 25:6
woman
shall ye give inheritance to   Nu 27:9
his b.
Levi hath no part with *his* b.   De 10:9
heart be not lifted up above   De 17:20
his b.
he shall minister as all *his* b.   De 18:7
do
if a man be found stealing   De 24:7
any of *his* b.
nor did he acknowledge *his*   De 33:9
b. nor knew
let Asher be acceptable to   De 33:24
his b.
Abimelech slew *his* b., 70   J'g 9:5
persons
Gaal came with *his* b. to   J'g 9:26
Shechem
he did to his father in slaying   J'g 9:56
his 70 b.
Jephthah fled from *his* b. and   J'g 11:3
to Tob
name of dead be not cut off   Ru 4:10
from *his* b.
anointed him in midst of   1Sa 16:13
his b.
when *his* b. and father's   1Sa 22:1
house heard it
make him rise up from   2Ki 9:2
among *his* b.
Jabez more honourable than   1Ch 4:9
his b.
for Judah prevailed above *his*   1Ch 5:2
b.
Ephraim mourned, *his* b.   1Ch 7:22
came to comfort
with *his* b. and sons were   1Ch 25:9
twelve
Jehoram slew all *his* b. with   2Ch 21:4
sword
Mordecai was accepted of *his*   Es 10:3
b.
though he be fruitful among   Ho 13:15
his b.
remnant of *his* b. shall return   Mic 5:3
to Israel
his b. stood without   M't 12:46;
  M'k 3:31; Lu 8:19
for neither did *his* b. believe   Joh 7:5
in him
Joseph was made known to   Ac 7:13
his b.
it came into Moses' heart to   Ac 7:23
visit *his* b.
supposed *his* b. would have   Ac 7:25
understood
not one able to judge   1Co 6:5
between *his* b.
behoved him to be made   Heb 2:17
like to *his* b.

MEN AND BRETHREN

men and b. this scripture   *Ac 1:16*
must be
men and b. let me freely   *Ac 2:29*
speak
men and b. what shall we do   *Ac 2:37*
men, b and fathers, hearken   *Ac 7:2*
men and b. if ye have any   *Ac 13:15*
word
men and b. children of   *Ac 13:26*
Abraham
be it known to you, *men*   *Ac 13:38*
and b.
men and b. G. made choice   *Ac 15:7*
among us
men and b. hearken unto me   *Ac 15:13*
men b. and fathers, hear   *Ac 22:1*
my defence
men and b. I have lived in   *Ac 23:1*
all good
men and b. I am a Pharisee,   *Ac 23:6*
the son of
men and b. I have   *Ac 28:17*
committed nothing

MY BRETHREN

Jacob said to them, *my b.*   *Ge 29:4*
whence be ye
set here before *my b.* and   *Ge 31:37*
thy brethren
I seek *my b.* tell me where   *Ge 37:16*
they feed
my b. and father's house   *Ge 46:31;*
are come   *47:1*
let me go and return to *my b.*   *Ex 4:18*
will save alive my father and   *Jos 2:13*
my b.
my b. made the heart of the   *Jos 14:8*
people melt
Gideon said, they were *my b.*   *J'g 8:19*
my b. I pray you, do not so   *J'g 19:23*
wickedly
let me get away and see *my*   *1Sa 20:29*
b.
David said, ye shall not do   *1Sa 30:23*
so, *my b.*
ye are *my b.* my bones, my   *2Sa 19:12*
flesh
David said, hear *my b.* and   *1Ch 28:2*
people
Hanani, one of *my b.* came   *Ne 1:2*
and men
I nor *my b.* nor guard put off   *Ne 4:23*
our clothes
I and *my b.* might exact of   *Ne 5:10*
them money
I and *my b.* have not eaten   *Ne 5:14*
bread of
my b. have dealt deceitfully   *Job 6:15*
he hath put *my b.* far from   *Job 19:13*
me
declare thy name to *my b.*   *Ps 22:22;*
    Heb 2:12
I am become a stranger to   *Ps 69:8*
my b.
for *my b.* and companions'   *Ps 122:8*
sake
who are *my b.*   *M't 12:48;*
    M'k 3:33
behold my mother and *my*   *M't 12:49;*
b.   *M'k 3:34*
ye have done it to least of   *M't 25:40*
these *my b.*
go tell *my b.* they go into   *M't 28:10*
Galilee
my b. are these which hear   *Lu 8:21*
word of
go to *my b.* and say, I   *Joh 20:17*
ascend
myself accursed from Christ   *Ro 9:3*
for *my b.*
take *my b.* the prophets who   *Jas 5:10*
have
but above all things, *my b.*   *Jas 5:12*
swear not

OUR BRETHREN

before *our b* discern what is   *Ge 31:32*
thine
when *our b.* died before the   *Nu 20:3*
Lord
our b. have discouraged our   *De 1:28*
hearts
why have *our b.* stolen thee   *2Sa 19:41*
away
send abroad to *our b.* every   *1Ch 13:2*
where

yet now our flesh is as the   *Ne 5:5*
flesh of *our b.*
after our ability have   *Ne 5:8*
redeemed *our b.*
let us go again visit *our b.*   *Ac 15:36*
in every city
our b. be inquired of, are   *2Co 8:23*
messengers
the accuser of *our b.* is cast   *Re 12:10*
down

THEIR BRETHREN

but shall minister with *their*   *Nu 8:26*
b.
Levites no inherit. among   *De 18:2*
their b.
will raise a prophet from   *De 18:18*
among *their b.*
not hearken to the voice of   *J'g 20:13*
their b.
when *their b.* come to us to   *J'g 21:22*
complain
people return from following   *2Sa 2:26*
their b.
did eat unleavened bread   *2Ki 23:9*
among *their b.*
dwelt with *their b.*   *1Ch 8:32;*
    9:38
all *their b.* were at their   *1Ch 12:32*
commandment
for *their b.* had prepared   *1Ch 12:39*
for them
brought them to *their b.* to   *2Ch 28:15*
Jericho
was a great cry against *their*   *Ne 5:1*
b.
office was to distribute to   *Ne 13:13*
their b.
gave them inheritance among   *Job 42:15*
their b.
for he slew them not among   *Jer 41:8*
their b.
till *their b.* be killed as they   *Re 6:11*
were

THY BRETHREN

be lord over *thy b.* let   *Ge 27:29*
mother's sons
set it before *thy b.* that may   *Ge 31:37*
judge
I and *thy b.* come to bow   *Ge 37:10*
ourselves to thee
do not *thy b.* feed flock in   *Ge 37:13*
Shechem
whether it be well with *thy*   *Ge 37:14*
b. and flocks
I have given one portion   *Ge 48:22*
above *thy b.*
thou art he whom *thy b.*   *Ge 49:8*
shall praise
for poor man of *thy b.* be   *De 15:7*
within gates
from among *thy b.* set king   *De 17:15*
over
raise up a prophet of *thy b.*   *De 18:15*
like me
not oppress poor of *thy b.*   *De 24:14*
or stranger
thou shalt bring *thy b.* home   *Jos 2:18*
no woman among daughters   *J'g 14:3*
of *thy b.*
for *thy b.* run to camp to   *1Sa 17:17*
thy b.
look how *thy b.* fare, and   *1Sa 17:18*
take pledge
return, take back *thy b.*   *2Sa 15:20*
with thee
slain *thy b.* better than   *2Ch 21:13*
thyself
thy b. dealt treacherously with   *Jer 12:6*
thee
thy b. even *thy b.* men of   *Eze 11:15*
kindred
behold, thy mother and *thy*   *M't 12:47;*
b. stand without   *M'k 3:32; Lu 8:20*
call not *thy b.* lest they bid   *Lu 14:12*
again
when art converted,   *Lu 22:32*
strengthen *thy b.*
see do it not, I am of *thy*   *Re 19:10;*
b.   *22:9*

YOUR BRETHREN

let one of *your b.* be bound   *Ge 42:19*
in prison

leave one of *your b.* here   *Ge 42:33*
with me
carry *your b.* from before   *Le 10:4*
sanctuary
let *your b.* bewail the burning   *Le 10:6*
the Lord
over *your b.* ye shall not   *Le 25:46*
rule with rigour
I have taken *your b.* the   *Nu 18:6*
Levites
shall *your b.* go to war and   *Nu 32:6*
ye sit here
hear causes between *your b.*   *De 1:16*
pass over armed before your   *De 3:18;*
b.   *Jos 1:14*
hath given rest to *your b.*   *De 3:20;*
    Jos 1:15
not left *your b.* these many   *Jos 22:3*
days
Lord hath given rest to *your*   *Jos 22:4*
b.
divide spoil of enemies with   *Jos 22:8*
your b.
not fight against *your b.*   *1Ki 12:24;*
    2Ch 11:4
what cause come to you of   *2Ch 19:10*
your b. so wrath come upon
you and *your b.*
deliver captives ye have   *2Ch 28:11*
taken of *your b.*
be not ye like *your b.* which   *2Ch 30:7*
trespassed
if ye turn, *your b.* shall find   *2Ch 30:9*
compassion
and fight for *your b.* your   *Ne 4:14*
sons
will you even sell *your b.*   *Ne 5:8*
your b. that hated you, that   *Isa 66:5*
cast you out
they shall bring *your b.* for   *Isa 66:20*
an offering
cast out as I cast out *your b.*   *Jer 7:15*
say to *your b.* Ammi, to   *Ho 2:1*
sisters, Ruhamah
if ye salute *your b.* only,   *M't 5:47*
what do you more
prophet shall Lord raise of   *Ac 3:22;*
your b.   *7:37*
ye do wrong and defraud and   *1Co 6:8*
that *your b.*
same afflictions accomplished   *1Pe 5:9*
in *your b.*

BRETHREN'S

lest his *b.* heart faint as well   *De 20:8*
as

BRIBE

who hate a *b.* (R)   *Ex 18:21*
bribe (S)   *Ex 23:8;*
    De 16:19; Pr 17:8, 23
not take a *b.* (A)(R)   *De 10:17*
b. to murder (B)   *De 19:6*
who take a *b.*   *De 27:25*
(A)(B)(E)(R)
hand have I received any *b.*   *1Sa 12:3*
have I accepted a present   *1Sa 12:3*
(B)
taken a ransom (E)   *1Sa 12:3*
pay a *b.* on my account   *Job 6:22*
(A)(B)(R)
who will not take a *b.*   *Ps 15:5*
(A)(B)(R)
they take a *b.* and they turn   *Am 5:12*
judge ask for a *b.*   *Mic 7:3*
(A)(B)(R)

BRIBED

nor can be *b.* (B)   *De 10:17*
the *b.* men (P)   *Ac 6:11*

BRIBERY

consume the tabernacles of   *Job 15:34*
b.

BRIBES

aside after lucre, and took *b.*   *1Sa 8:3*
they accepted presents (B)   *1Sa 8:3*
turn aside after gain (R)   *1Sa 8:3*
nor making *b.* (S)   *2Ch 19:7*
and their right hand is full   *Ps 26:10*
of *b.*
loves *b.* (A)(B)(E)(R)(S)   *Isa 1:23*
his hands from holding of *b.*   *Isa 33:15*

BRICK

Go to, let us make *b*. and burn   Ge 11:3
they had *b*. for stone, and slime   Ge 11:3
in morter, and in *b*. and in all   Ex 1:14
give the people straw to make *b*.   Ex 5:7
fulfilled your task in making *b*.   Ex 5:14
and they say to us, Make *b*.   Ex 5:16
burneth incense upon altars of *b*.   Isa 65:3
the pavement of *b*. (A)(E)   Jer 43:9
take a *b*. (R)   Eze 4:1

BRICKKILN

made them pass through the *b*.   2Sa 12:31
the clay in the *b*. which is at   Jer 43:9
in the pavement of brick (A)(R)   Jer 43:9
in mortar under the pavement (B)   Jer 43:9
mortar in the brickwork (E)   Jer 43:9
morter, make strong the *b*.   Na 3:14

BRICKS

the tale of the *b*. which they did   Ex 5:8
yet shall ye deliver the tale of *b*.   Ex 5:18
from your *b*. of your daily task   Ex 5:19
The *b*. are fallen down, but we will   Isa 9:10

BRIDE

my *b*. (A)(B)(E)   Ca 4:8; Ca 4:9-12; 5:1
bind them on thee, as a *b*. doeth   Isa 49:18
a *b*. adorneth herself with jewels   Isa 61:10
bridegroom rejoiceth over the *b*.   Isa 62:5
maid forget her ornaments, or a *b*.   Jer 2:32
bridegroom, and the voice of the *b*.   Jer 7:34
and the voice of the *b*.   Jer 16:9
the voice of the *b*. the sound of   Jer 25:10
the voice of the *b*. the voice of   Jer 33:11
and the *b*. out of her closet   Joe 2:16
that hath the *b*. is the bridegroom   Joh 3:29
as a pure *b*. (R)   2Co 11:2
of the *b*. shall be heard no more   Re 18:23
prepared as a *b*. adorned for her   Re 21:2
shew thee the *b*. the Lamb's wife   Re 21:9
the Spirit and the *b*. say, Come   Re 22:17

BRIDECHAMBER

Can the children of the *b*. mourn   M't 9:15
wedding guests (A)(B)(P)(R)   M't 9:15
bridegroom's friends (N)   M't 9:15
Can the children of the *b*. fast   M'k 2:19
make the children of the *b*. fast   Lu 5:34

BRIDEGROOM

a *b*. coming out of his chamber   Ps 19:5
as a *b*. decketh himself with   Isa 61:10
the *b*. rejoiceth over the bride, so   Isa 62:5
the voice of the *b*. and the voice   Jer 7:34
of gladness, the voice of the *b*.   Jer 16:9; 25:10; 33:11
let the *b*. go forth of his chamber   Joe 2:16
as long as the *b*. is with them   M't 9:15

and went forth to meet the *b*.   M't 25:1
While the *b*. tarried, they all   M't 25:5
Behold, the *b*. cometh; go ye out   M't 25:6
they went to buy, the *b*. came   M't 25:10
while the *b*. is with them   M'k 2:19
when the *b*. shall be taken away   M'k 2:20
fast, while the *b*. is with them   Lu 5:34
governor of the feast called the *b*.   Joh 2:9
that hath the bride is the *b*.   Joh 3:29
but the friend of the *b*.   Joh 3:29
and the voice of the *b*. and of the   Re 18:23

BRIDEGROOM'S

greatly because of the *b*. voice   Joh 3:29

BRIDESMAIDS

ten *b*. (P)   M't 25:1; 25:7, 11

BRIDLE

my *b*. in thy lips, and I will turn   2Ki 19:28
they have also let loose the *b*.   Job 30:11
come to him with his double *b*.   Job 41:13
must be held in with bit and *b*.   Ps 32:9
I will keep my mouth with a *b*.   Ps 39:1
a *b*. for the ass, and a rod for the   Pr 26:3
be a *b*. in the jaws of the people   Isa 30:28
in thy nose, and my *b*. in thy lips   Isa 37:29
able also to *b*. the whole body   Jas 3:2

BRIDLES

even unto the horse *b*. by   Re 14:20

BRIDLETH

b. not his tongue, but deceiveth   Jas 1:26

BRIEFLY

b. comprehended in this saying   Ro 13:9
I have written *b*. exhorting   1Pe 5:12

BRIER

a *b*. to prick (R)   Pr 28:24
instead of the *b*. shall come up   Isa 55:13
shall be no more a pricking *b*.   Eze 28:24
a *b*. to prick (A)   Eze 28:24
The best of them is as a *b*.   Mic 7:4

BRIERS

of the wilderness and with *b*.   J'g 8:7
thorns of the wilderness, and *b*.   J'g 8:16
thorns and painful *b*. (B)   Pr 28:24
but there shall come up *b*. and   Isa 5:6
it shall even be for *b*. and thorns   Isa 7:23
all the land shall become *b*.   Isa 7:24
come thither the fear of *b*.   Isa 7:25
it shall devour the *b*. and thorns   Isa 9:18
and devour his thorns and *b*.   Isa 10:17
who would set the *b*. and thorns   Isa 27:4
shall come up thorns and *b*.   Isa 32:13
b. and thorns be with thee   Eze 2:6
which beareth thorns and *b*.   Heb 6:8

BRIGANDINE

that lifteth himself up in his *b*.   Jer 51:3
coat of mail (A)(B)(E)(R)   Jer 51:3

BRIGANDINES

the spears, and put on the *b*.   Jer 46:4
put on coats of mail (A)(B)(E)(R)   Jer 46:4

BRIGANDS

ransom me from *b*. (B)(R)   Job 6:23

BRIGHT

a rising, a scab, a *b*. spot   Le 13:2; Le 13:4, 19, 23-26, 28, 38-39; 14:56
his eyes became *b*. (R)   1Sa 14:27
became *b*. (S)   1Sa 14:29
of the Lord, were of *b*. brass   1Ki 7:45
for the house of the Lord of *b*.   2Ch 4:16
he scattereth his *b*. cloud   Job 37:11
now men see not the *b*. light   Job 37:21
his belly is as *b*. ivory overlaid   Ca 5:14
Make *b*. the arrows; gather   Jer 51:11
and the fire was *b*. and out of   Eze 1:13
ah! it is made *b*. it is wrapped   Eze 21:15
he made his arrows *b*. he   Eze 21:21
b. iron, cassia, and calamus   Eze 27:19
All the *b*. lights of heaven will I   Eze 32:8
both the *b*. sword and the   Na 3:3
so the Lord shall make *b*. clouds   Zec 10:1
behold, a *b*. cloud overshadowed   M't 17:5
as when the *b*. shining of a candle   Lu 11:36
stood before me in *b*. clothing   Ac 10:30
made *b*. (S)   Re 18:1
and the *b*. and morning star   Re 22:16

BRIGHTENED

his eyes *b*. (A)(B)(S)   1Sa 14:27

BRIGHTNESS

Through the *b*. before him were   2Sa 22:13
shined, or the moon walking in his   Job 31:26
At the *b*. that was before him   Ps 18:12
for *b*. but we walk in darkness   Isa 59:9
and kings to the *b*. of thy rising   Isa 60:3
neither for *b*. shall the moon give   Isa 60:19
righteousness thereof go forth as *b*.   Isa 62:1
and a *b*. was about it and out of   Eze 1:4
of fire, and it had *b*. round about   Eze 1:27
the appearance of the *b*. round   Eze 1:28
as the appearance of *b*. as the   Eze 8:2
the court was full of the *b*. of the   Eze 10:4
wisdom, they shall defile thy *b*.   Eze 28:7
thy wisdom by reason of thy *b*.   Eze 28:17
This great image, whose *b*. was   Da 2:31
mine honour and *b*. returned   Da 4:36
shall shine as the *b*. of the   Da 12:3
even very dark, and no *b*. in it   Am 5:20
And his *b*. was as the light   Hab 3:4
light from heaven, above the *b*. of   Ac 26:13
with the *b*. of his coming: 2Th 2:8
Who being the *b*. of his glory   Heb 1:3

BRILLIANCE

my *b*. of speech (P)   1Co 2:1

BRIM

were dipped in the *b*. of the   Jos 3:15
ten cubits from the one *b*. to the   1Ki 7:23
under the *b*. of it round about   1Ki 7:24

and the *b.* thereof was   *1Ki 7:26*
wrought
like the *b.* of a cup   *1Ki 7:26*
from *b.* to *b.* round in   *2Ch 4:2*
compass
and the *b.* of it like the work   *2Ch 4:5*
And they filled them up to   *Joh 2:7*
the *b.*

BRIMSTONE

Sodom and upon Gomorrah   *Ge 19:24*
b.
rained sulphur **(B)**   *Ge 19:24*
the whole land is *b.* and salt   *De 29:23*
b. shall be scattered on his   *Job 18:15*
habitation
sulphur shall be scattered   *Job 18:15*
(A)(B)
rain snare, fire, and *b.*   *Ps 11:6;*
  Eze 38:22
rain burning sulphur **(B)**   *Ps 11:6*
breath of Lord like a stream   *Isa 30:33*
of *b.*
the dust thereof turned to *b.*   *Isa 34:9*
out of mouths issued fire and   *Re 9:17*
b.
sapphire blue and sulphur   *Re 9:17*
(A)(R)
sulphur-yellow **(B)(N)**   *Re 9:17*
blue and yellow **(P)**   *Re 9:17*
third part of men killed by   *Re 9:18*
the *b.*
by smoke and sulphur   *Re 9:18*
(A)(B)(N)(P)(R)
shall be tormented with fire   *Re 14:10*
and *b.*
cast into lake of fire,   *Re 19:20*
burning with *b.*
that burns with sulphur   *Re 19:20*
(B)(P)
burns with sulphurous flames   *Re 19:20*
(N)
the lake of fire and *b.*,   *Re 20:10*
where the
lake of fire and sulphur   *Re 20:10*
(B)(N)(P)
lake which burneth with fire   *Re 21:8*
and *b.*
burns with fire and sulphur   *Re 21:8*
(B)(P)
burns with sulphurous flames   *Re 21:8*
(N)

BRING

I do *b.* a flood of waters on   *Ge 6:17*
earth
two of every sort *b.* into the   *Ge 6:19*
ark
when I *b.* a cloud over earth,   *Ge 9:14*
the bow
Abraham did *b.* them on   *Ge 18:16*
their way
b. on Abraham what he   *Ge 18:19*
hath spoken
and *b.* it to me that I may   *Ge 27:4;*
eat   *27:25*
b. your youngest brother to   *Ge 42:20;*
me   *42:34*
if I *b.* him not to thee   *Ge 42:37;*
  Ge 43:9; 44:32
b. these men home, stay and   *Ge 43:16*
make ready
take waggons and *b.* your   *Ge 45:19*
father
b. them, I pray, to me, and I   *Ge 48:9*
will bless
to morrow I will *b.* the   *Ex 10:4*
locusts
yet will I *b.* one plague more   *Ex 11:1*
on
when the Lord shall *b.* thee   *Ex 13:5;*
  13:11
that thou mayest *b.* the   *Ex 18:19*
causes to God
his master shall *b.* him to the   *Ex 21:6*
judges
if it be torn in pieces, *b.* it   *Ex 22:13*
for witness
thou shalt surely *b.* it back to   *Ex 23:4*
him again
first of first-fruits of land   *Ex 23:19;*
shalt *b.*   *34:26*
send an Angel to *b.* thee   *Ex 23:20*
into the place
whoso is of a willing heart,   *Ex 35:5*
let him *b.*
the people *b.* much more than   *Ex 36:5*
enough

if he be not able to *b.* a lamb   *Le 5:7;*
  12:8
and he shall *b.* them to the   *Le 5:8;*
priest   *5:12*
b. fire and incense within the   *Le 16:12*
veil
that Israel may *b.* their   *Le 17:5*
sacrifices
and thou shalt *b.* the Levites   *Nu 8:9;*
  8:10
it Lord delight in us   *Nu 14:8*
he will *b.* us
because Lord not able to *b.*   *Nu 14:16;*
  De 9:28
Caleb, him will I *b.* into the   *Nu 14:24*
land
b. before Lord every man   *Nu 16:17*
his censer
shall *b.* unto the Lord   *Nu 18:13*
ye shall not *b.* congregation   *Nu 20:12*
into land
give land, and *b.* us not over   *Nu 32:5*
Jordan
cause too hard for you *b.* to   *De 1:17*
me
when Lord shall *b.* thee into   *De 7:1*
the land
thou shalt *b.* her home to   *De 21:12*
thy house
shalt *b.* it unto thine own   *De 22:2*
house
b. to us, that we may hear   *De 30:12;*
and do   *30:13*
hear, Lord, and *b.* Judah to   *De 33:7*
his people
child be weaned, then I will   *1Sa 1:22*
b. him
said, what shall we *b.* the   *1Sa 9:7*
man
b. the portion I gave thee, of   *1Sa 9:23*
which
b. men we may put them to   *1Sa 11:12*
death
why shouldest *b.* me to thy   *1Sa 20:8*
father
my hand with thee, to *b.*   *2Sa 3:12*
Israel to
except thou *b.* Michal when   *2Sa 3:13*
thou comest
whosoever saith aught *b.*   *2Sa 14:10*
him to me
why are ye last to *b.* the   *2Sa 19:11*
king back
the king said, *b.* me a sword   *1Ki 3:24*
the wicked, to *b.* his way on   *1Ki 8:32*
his head
b. him back with thee to   *1Ki 13:18*
thine house
b. me a morsel of bread in   *1Ki 17:11*
thine hand
then he said, go ye *b.* him   *1Ki 20:33*
b. me a new cruse, and put   *2Ki 2:20*
salt
I will *b.* you to man whom   *2Ki 6:19*
ye seek
b. an offering and come   *1Ch 16:29*
before him
b. the number of them to   *1Ch 21:2*
me, that I may
since the people began to   *2Ch 31:10*
b. offerings
did not our God *b.* this evil   *Ne 13:18*
on us
did I say *b.* unto me, or give   *Job 6:22*
reward
wilt thou *b.* me into the dust   *Job 10:9*
again
who can *b.* a clean thing out   *Job 14:4*
of an unclean
it shall *b.* him to the king   *Job 18:14*
of terrors
for I know thou wilt *b.* me   *Job 30:23*
to death
to *b.* back his soul from the   *Ne 33:30*
pit
let them *b.* me to thy holy hill   *Ps 43:3*
who will *b.* me into strong   *Ps 60:9;*
city   *108:10*
the mountains shall *b.* peace   *Ps 72:3*
to the people
he shall *b.* on them their   *Ps 94:23*
own iniquity
scornful men *b.* a city into a   *Pr 29:8*
snare
who shall *b.* him to see what   *Ec 3:22*
shall be
know that God will *b.* thee   *Ec 11:9*
into judgment
God shall *b.* every work into   *Ec 12:14*
judgment

would *b.* thee into mother's   *Ca 8:2*
house
Lord shall *b.* on thee and my   *Isa 7:17*
people
the people shall *b.* them to   *Isa 14:2*
their place
I will *b.* more upon Dimon,   *Isa 15:9*
lions on him
shall *b.* to the ground,   *Isa 25:12*
even to the
tell ye and *b.* them near, let   *Isa 45:21*
them take
I *b.* near my righteousness   *Isa 46:13*
even them will I *b.* to my   *Isa 56:7*
holy mountain
that thou *b.* the poor to thy   *Isa 58:7*
house
for brass I will *b.* gold, for   *Isa 60:17*
iron *b.* silver
I will *b.* their fears upon   *Isa 66:4*
them
I will take you and *b.* you to   *Jer 3:14*
Zion
not in anger, lest thou *b.* me   *Jer 10:24*
to nothing
b. on them all words of this   *Jer 11:8*
covenant
b. upon them day of evil   *Jer 17:18*
I will *b.* them from the north   *Jer 31:8*
country
I will *b.* on them all good   *Jer 32:42*
promised
I will *b.* it health and cure   *Jer 33:6*
them that shall *b.* sacrifice   *Jer 33:11*
of praise
I will *b.* a fear upon thee   *Jer 49:5*
I, even I, will *b.* a sword   *Eze 6:3*
upon you
I will *b.* you out of the   *Eze 11:9*
midst thereof
that I would not *b.* them   *Eze 20:15*
into the land
b. on necks of them that   *Eze 21:29*
are slain
b. them against thee on   *Eze 23:22*
every side
b. them to their   *Eze 34:13;*
land   *Eze 36:24; 37:21*
that I would *b.* thee against   *Eze 38:17*
them
I will allure and *b.* her to   *Ho 2:14*
wilderness
yet will I *b.* an heir to thee   *Mic 1:15*
I will *b.* them, and they shall   *Zec 8:8*
dwell
B. all the tithes into the   *Mal 3:10*
storehouse
be thou there till I *b.* thee   *M't 2:13*
word
therefore if thou *b.* thy gift   *M't 5:23*
to the altar
b. him hither to me   *M't 17:17;*
  M'k 9:19
an ass and a colt, loose   *Mt 21:2;*
them and *b.* them to me   *M'k 11:2;*
  Lu 19:30
they *b.* to him one that was   *M'k 7:32*
deaf
I *b.* you good tidings of great   *Lu 2:10*
joy
choked with cares *b.* no fruit   *Lu 8:14*
to perfection
when they *b.* you unto the   *Lu 12:11*
synagogues
other sheep, them also I   *Joh 10:16*
must *b.*
b. all things to your   *Joh 14:26*
remembrance
Pilate said, what accusation   *Joh 18:29*
b. you
b. of fish which ye have   *Joh 21:10*
now caught
ye intend to *b.* this man's   *Ac 5:28*
blood on us
that they should *b.* them into   *Ac 7:6*
bondage
he might *b.* them bound to   *Ac 9:2*
Jerusalem
I went to Damascus to *b.*   *Ac 22:5*
them bound
commanded to *b.* Paul into   *Ac 23:10*
the castle
b. this young man to the   *Ac 23:17*
chief captain
will *b.* to nothing the   *1Co 1:19*
understanding
b. to nought things that are   *1Co 1:28*
b. you into remembrance of   *1Co 4:17*
my ways

keep under body, *b.* it into 1Co 9:27
subjection
that ye may *b.* me on my 1Co 16:6
journey whither I go
suffer, if man *b.* you into 2Co 11:20
bondage
our schoolmaster to *b.* us to Ga 3:24
Christ
that sleep will God *b.* with 1Th 4:14
him
take Mark and *b.* him with 2Ti 4:11
thee
suffered that he might *b.* us 1Pe 3:18
to God
if any come and *b.* not this 2Jo 10
doctrine
if thou *b.* forward on their 3Jo 6
journey
and kings do *b.* their glory Re 21:24
to it
they shall *b.* the glory of Re 21:26
nations into it

BRING *AGAIN*

must I *b.* thy son *again* to Ge 24:5
the land
beware that thou *b.* not my Ge 24:6
son *again*
will *b. again* into this land Ge 28:15;
Ge 48:21
well with brethren *b.* word Ge 37:14
again
deliver and *b.* him to thee Ge 42:37
again
surely *b.* it back to him *again* Ex 23:4
b. Aaron's rod *again* before Nu 17:10
testimony
lodge this night and *b.* you Nu 22:8
word *again*
b. word *again* what way we De 1:22
must go
in any case *b.* them *again* to De 22:1
thy brother
the Lord shall *b.* thee into De 28:68
Egypt *again*
if ye *b.* me home *again* to J'g 11:9
fight
husband arose and went to *b.* J'g 19:3
her *again*
can I *b.* him *again*, I shall 2Sa 12:23
go to him
b. the young man Absalom 2Sa 14:21
again
if Lord shall *b.* me *again* to 2Sa 15:8
Jerusalem
he will *b.* me *again* and 2Sa 15:25
shew me it
forgive and *b.* them *again* 1Ki 8:34;
2Ch 6:25
to *b.* kingdom *again* 1Ki 12:21;
2Ch 11:1
let us *b. again* the ark of 1Ch 13:3
our God
advise what word I shall *b.* 1Ch 21:12
again to him
he sent prophets to *b.* them 2Ch 24:19
again
mightest *b.* them *again* to thy Ne 9:29
law
I will *b. again* from Bashan Ps 68:22
I will *b. again* my people from
depths of sea
not so much as *b.* it to Pr 19:24
mouth *again*
grieveth him to *b.* it *again* to Pr 26:15
his mouth
I will *b. again* shadow of Isa 38:8
degrees
b. it *again* to mind, O ye Isa 46:8
transgressors
saith lord, to *b.* Jacob *again* Isa 49:5
to him
when the Lord shall *b. again* Isa 52:8
Zion
will return and *b.* them Jer 12:15;
again 50:19
if thou return, then will I *b.* Jer 15:19
thee *again*
b. them *again* to their land Jer 16:15;
Jer 24:6; 32:37
b. them *again* into their folds Jer 23:3
in two years will I *b. again* Jer 28:3
the vessels
I will *b. again* to this place Jer 28:4;
Jeconiah 28:6
b. again captivity of my Jer 30:3;
people Jer 31:23; Eze 39:25; Am 9:14
will I *b. again* captivity of Jer 48:47
Moab

b. again captivity of Ammon Jer 49:6
I *b. again* their captivity Eze 16:53
I will *b. again* the captivity Eze 29:14
of Egypt
I will *b. again* that which Eze 34:16
was driven
at that time I will *b.* you Zec 3:20
again
I will *b.* them *again* to place Zec 10:6
them
I will *b.* them *again* out of Zec 10:10
land of Egypt
b. me word *again* that I may M't 2:8
worship

BRING *DOWN*

b. down my grey hairs Ge 42:38;
Ge 44:29, 31
would say, *b.* your brother Ge 43:7;
down 44:21
ye shall haste and *b. down* Ge 45:13
my father
he shall *b.* them *down* before De 9:3
thy face
b. them *down* to the water J'g 7:4
canst *b.* me *down*, I will *b.* 1Sa 30:15
thee *down*
eyes on haughty to *b.* them 2Sa 22:28
down
Solomon *b.* him *down* to 1Ki 1:33
Gibon
his hoary head *b. down* with 1Ki 2:9
blood
save afflicted, *b. down* high Ps 18:27
looks
b. them *down* to pit of Ps 55:23
destruction
shalt *b. down* noise of Isa 25:5
strangers
he shall *b. down* their pride Isa 25:11
high fort of walls shall he *b.* Isa 25:12
down
I will *b. down* their strength Isa 63:6
to the earth
b. thee *down* from thence Jer 49:16;
Ob 4
b. them *down* like lambs to Jer 51:40
slaughter
I shall *b.* thee *down* with Eze 26:20
them
they shall *b.* thee *down* to Eze 28:8
pit
b. them *down* as fowls of Ho 7:12
heaven
b. them *down* to valley of Joe 3:2
Jehoshaphat
he shall *b. down* thy strength Am 3:11
climb to heaven, thence will Am 9:2
b. them *down*
saith in heart, who shall *b.* me Ob 3
down
he *b.* him *down* to you Ac 23:15
to-morrow
Jews desire thou wouldest *b.* Ac 23:20
down Paul
that is, to *b.* Christ *down* Ro 10:6
from above

BRING *FORTH*

let earth *b. forth* Ge 1:11;
1:20, 24
in sorrow thou shalt *b. forth* Ge 3:16
children
thorns and thistles shall it *b.* Ge 3:18
forth
b. forth every living thing Ge 8:17
with thee
b. forth abundantly in the Ge 9:7
earth
b. her *forth*, and let her be Ge 38:24
burnt
thou mayest *b. forth* my Ex 3:10
people
who am I, that I should *b.* Ex 3:11
forth Israel
that I may *b. forth* my armies Ex 7:4
and people
river shall *b. forth* frogs Ex 8:3
abundantly
magicians did so to *b. forth* Ex 8:18
lice
b. forth him that hath Le 24:14;
cursed 24:23
it shall *b. forth* fruit for Le 25:21
three years
eat and *b. forth* old, Le 26:10
because of new

shalt *b. forth* water out of Nu 20:8
rock
shalt *b. forth* all tithe of De 14:28
increase
then shalt thou *b. forth* that De 17:5
man
b. forth tokens of damsel's De 22:15
virginity
b. forth the men that are Jos 2:3
come to thee
till I come and *b. forth* my J'g 6:18
present
b. forth the man that came J'g 19:22
to thy house
b. forth vestments for 2Ki 10:22
worshippers
no strength to *b. forth* 2Ki 19:3;
Isa 37:3
b. forth all vessels made for 2Ki 23:4
Baal
those did Cyrus *b. forth* by Ezr 1:8
Mithredath
it will bud and *b. forth* Job 14:9
boughs
conceive mischief, *b. forth* Job 15:35
vanity
canst *b. forth* Mazzaroth in Job 38:32
season
knowest when wild goats *b.* Job 39:1;
forth 39:2-3
the mountains *b.* him *forth* Job 40:20
food
shall *b. forth* righteousness as Ps 37:6
light
they shall still *b. forth* fruit Ps 92:14
in old age
he may *b. forth* food out of Ps 104:14
earth
that our sheep may *b. forth* Ps 144:13
thousands
knowest not what a day may Pr 27:1
b. forth
looked it should *b. forth* Isa 5:2;
grapes 5:4
I travail not, nor *b. forth* Isa 23:4
children
conceive chaff, and *b. forth* Isa 33:11
stubble
b. forth your strong reasons, Isa 41:21
saith King
let them *b. forth* what shall Isa 41:22
happen
he shall *b. forth* judgment to Isa 42:1
the Gentiles
he shall *b. forth* judgment Isa 42:3
unto truth
b. forth blind people that Isa 43:8
have eyes
let them *b. forth* their Isa 43:9
witnesses, that
let them *b. forth* salvation Isa 45:8
watereth earth, and maketh Isa 55:10
it *b. forth*
conceive mischief, *b. forth* Isa 59:4
iniquity
I will *b. forth* a seed out of Isa 65:9
Jacob
not labour in vain, nor *b.* Isa 65:23
forth for trouble
shall earth be made to *b.* Isa 66:8
forth in one day
bring to birth, and not cause Isa 66:9
to *b. forth*
they grow, yea, they *b. forth* Jer 12:2
fruit
b. forth out of mouth what Jer 51:44
swallowed
thou shalt *b. forth* thy stuff Eze 12:4
by day
it shall *b. forth* boughs and Eze 17:23
bear fruit
to *b.* them *forth* of the land Eze 20:6
of Egypt
I will *b.* them *forth* out of Eze 20:38
the country
will I *b. forth* a fire in the Eze 28:18
midst of
I will *b.* thee *forth*, army Eze 38:4
and horsemen
b. forth new fruit according Eze 47:12
to months
Ephraim shall *b. forth* his Ho 9:13
children
tho' they *b. forth*, yet will I Ho 9:16
slay beloved
be in pain and labour to *b.* Mic 4:10
forth
he will *b.* me *forth* to the Mic 7:9
light
before the decree *b. forth* Zep 2:2

will *b. forth* my servant the   *Zec 3:8*
BRANCH
b. forth head-stone with   *Zec 4:7*
shoutings
b. forth a curse, it shall enter   *Zec 5:4*
house
a virgin shall *b. forth* a son   *M't 1:23;*
  1:21
b. forth fruit meet for   *M't 3:8;*
repentance   *Lu 3:8*
good tree cannot *b. forth*   *M't 7:18;*
evil fruit   *Lu 6:43*
b. forth fruit, some 30 fold,   *M'k 4:20*
some
b. forth a son, call name   *Lu 1:31*
JESUS
heard word, keep it, and *b.*   *Lu 8:15*
forth fruit
b. forth the best robe and   *Lu 15:22*
put it on him
that it may *b. forth* more   *Joh 15:2*
fruit
I ordained you, should *b.*   *Joh 15:16*
forth fruit
I *b.* him *forth* to you that ye   *Joh 19:4*
may know
after Easter *b.* him *forth* to   *Ac 12:4*
people
we should *b. forth* fruit unto   *Ro 7:4*
God
motions of sin *b. forth* fruit   *Ro 7:5*
unto death

BRING IN

I will *b.* you *in* unto land I   *Ex 6:8*
swear
b. in and plant them in the   *Ex 15:17*
mountain
on the sixth day prepare that   *Ex 16:5*
they *b. in*
mine Angel go before and *b.*   *Ex 23:23*
thee *in*
your little ones, them will I   *Nu 14:31*
b. in
they made proclamation to   *2Ch 24:9*
b. in
ye shall not *b. in* the   *2Ch 28:13*
captives hither
b. in no burden on the   *Jer 17:24*
sabbath-day
b. me *in* before king, I will   *Da 2:24*
shew
the king cried to *b. in* the   *Da 5:7*
astrologers
to *b. in* everlasting   *Da 9:24*
righteousness
ye have sown much and *b. in*   *Hag 1:6*
little
sought means to *b.* him *in*   *Lu 5:18*
and lay
b. in hither poor, maimed,   *Lu 14:21*
and halt
privily *b. in* damnable   *2Pe 2:1*
heresies

BRING OUT

b. them *out* to us that we   *Ge 19:5;*
may   *19:8. 12*
make mention, and *b.* me   *Ge 40:14*
out of this house
God will visit and *b.* you   *Ge 50:24*
out of land
I will *b.* you *out* from under   *Ex 6:6*
burden
gave charge to *b.* children of   *Ex 6:13;*
Israel *out* of Egypt   *Ex 26:27;*
  Ex 7:5; 12:51; Jer 31:32
for mischief did *b.* them *out*   *Ex 32:12*
to slay
lay hold and *b. out* to the   *De 21:19*
elders
b. out the damsel   *De 22:21*
shall *b. out* pledge abroad to   *De 24:11*
thee
b. out thence Rahab and all   *Jos 6:22*
she
b. out those five kings out   *Jos 10:22*
of the cave
b. out thy son that he may   *J'g 6:30*
die
I will *b. out*, and humble ye   *J'g 19:24*
them
b. thou me *out* of my distresses   *Ps 25:17*
b. my soul *out* of prison,   *Ps 142:7*
that I may
O Lord, *b.* my soul *out* of   *Ps 143:11*
trouble

to *b. out* prisoners from   *Isa 42:7*
prison
shall *b. out* bones of kings of   *Jer 8:1*
Judah
b. out wives and children to   *Jer 38:23*
Chaldeans
I will *b.* you forth *out* of   *Eze 11:7*
midst of it
I will *b.* you *out* from the   *Eze 20:34;*
people   *34:13*
accept you, when I *b. out*   *Eze 20:41*
from people
b. it *out* piece by piece, let   *Eze 24:6*
no lot fall
that burneth him to *b. out*   *Am 6:10*
the bones
sought to *b.* them *out* to   *Ac 17:5*
people

BRING TO PASS

dream, God will shortly *b.* it   *Ge 41:32*
to pass
b. to pass as at this day, to   *Ge 50:20*
save people
trust in him, he shall *b.* it *to*   *Ps 37:5*
pass
b. to pass his act, his   *Isa 28:21*
strange act
I have spoken, I will also *b.*   *Isa 46:11*
it *to pass*

BRING UP

I will also surely *b.* thee *up*   *Ge 46:4*
again
to *b.* them *up* out of that land   *Ex 3:8*
I will *b.* you *up* out of   *Ex 3:17*
affliction
thou sayest to me, *b. up* this   *Ex 33:12*
people
men that *b. up* evil report   *Nu 14:37*
on land
b. up Aaron and son to   *Nu 20:25*
mount Hor
b. up an evil name on her   *De 22:14*
did not Lord *b.* us *up* from   *J'g 6:13*
Egypt
b. him *up* in bed, I may   *1Sa 19:15*
slay
whom shall I *b. up*, B. *up*   *1Sa 28:11*
Samuel
his men did David *b. up*   *2Sa 2:3*
every man
b. up ark of God   *2Sa 6:2;*
1Ki 8:1, 4; 1Ch 13:6; 15:3, 12, 14, 25;
  2Ch 5:2, 5
since I did *b. up* Israel to   *1Ch 17:5*
this day
did Sheshbazzar *b. up* with   *Ezr 1:11*
them
shall *b. up* tithes to house of   *Ne 10:38*
God
nor bring forth children nor   *Isa 23:4*
b. up virgins
then will I *b.* them *up* and   *Jer 27:22*
restore
shall *b. up* a company   *Eze 16:40*
against thee
I will *b. up* a company   *Eze 23:46*
upon them
when I shall *b. up* the deep   *Eze 26:19*
upon thee
will *b.* thee *up* out of midst   *Eze 29:4*
of rivers
a company shall *b.* thee *up*   *Eze 32:3*
in my net
I will *b. up* flesh on you,   *Eze 37:6*
and cover you
though *b. up* children, I will   *Ho 9:12*
bereave
I will *b. up* sackcloth upon   *Am 8:10*
all loins
to *b. up* Christ again from   *Ro 10:7*
the dead
b. them *up* in the nurture of   *Eph 6:4*
the Lord

BRINGERS

b. up of children sent to   *2Ki 10:5*
Jehu

BRINGEST

and *b.* me into judgment   *Job 14:3*
with thee
O Jerus, that *b.* good tidings   *Isa 40:9*
thou *b.* strange things to our   *Ac 17:20*
ears

b. you out from under burden   *Ex 6:7*
the Lord that *b.* you out of   *Le 11:45*
Egypt
b. it not to door of tabernacle   *Le 17:4;*
  17:9
the Lord *b.* thee into a good   *De 8:7*
land
he *b.* down to grave, and *b.*   *1Sa 2:6*
up
Lord maketh poor, *b.* low,   *1Sa 2:7*
lifteth up
b. down the people under   *2Sa 22:48*
me
that *b.* me forth from mine   *2Sa 22:49*
enemies
into whose hand God *b.*   *Job 12:6*
abundantly
he *b.* out to light the   *Job 12:22*
shadow of death
wrath *b.* punishments of the   *Job 19:29*
sword
thing that is hid *b.* he forth   *Job 28:11*
to light
that *b. forth* his fruit in his   *Ps 1:3*
season
when Lord *b.* back captivity   *Ps 14:7;*
  53:6
b. counsel of heathen to   *Ps 33:10*
nought
the man who *b.* wicked   *Ps 37:7*
devices to pass
b. out them that are bound   *Ps 68:6*
with chains
and *b.* them out of their   *Ps 107:28*
distresses
so he *b.* them to their   *Ps 107:30*
desired haven
b. wind out of treasuries   *Ps 135:7;*
  Jer 10:13; 51:16
mouth of just *b. forth*   *Pr 10:31*
wisdom
moving his lips he *b.* evil to   *Pr 16:30*
pass
a man's gift *b.* him before   *Pr 18:6*
great men
son that causeth shame, *b.*   *Pr 19:26*
reproach
a wise king *b.* the wheel   *Pr 20:26*
over them
much more when he *b.* it   *Pr 21:27*
with a wicked
but a child left, *b.* his   *Pr 29:15*
mother to shame
delicately *b. up* his servant   *Pr 29:21*
from a child
fear of man *b.* a snare, but   *Pr 29:25*
whoso trusts
b. forth butter, *b.* blood, *b.*   *Pr 30:33*
forth strife
like ships, she *b.* her food   *Pr 31:14*
from afar
to water the wood that *b.*   *Ec 2:6*
forth trees
Lord *b.* on them waters of the   *Isa 8:7*
river
b. down them that dwell on   *Isa 26:5*
high, *b.* to
that *b.* the princes to   *Isa 40:23*
nothing, he makes
that *b. out* their host by   *Isa 40:26*
number
which *b. forth* the chariot   *Isa 43:17*
and horse
the smith that *b. forth* an   *Isa 54:16*
instrument
for as the earth *b. forth* her   *Isa 61:11*
bud
anguish of her that *b. forth*   *Jer 4:31*
first child
which *b.* iniquity to   *Eze 29:16*
remembrance
Israel *b. forth* fruit to   *Ho 10:1*
himself
drought on which ground *b.*   *Hag 1:11*
forth
tree *b.* not forth good fruit   *M't 3:10;*
is hewn down   *M't 7:19; Lu 3:9*
every good tree *b. forth*   *M't 7:17*
good fruit
good man out of heart *b.*   *M't 12:35;*
forth good things, evil man   *Lu 6:45*
b. forth evil things
b. forth an hundred fold,   *M't 13:23*
some sixty
b. out of treasure things   *M't 13:52*
new and old

BRINGETH

Jesus *b.* them up into an high mountain   *M't 17:1*
the earth *b.* forth fruit of herself   *M'k 4:28*
a good tree *b.* not forth corrupt fruit   *Lu 6:43*
if it die, it *b.* forth much fruit   *Joh 12:24; 15:5*
gospel *b.* forth fruit, as in you   *Col 1:6*
the grace of God that *b.* salvation   *Tit 2:11*
b. in first-begotten into the world   *Heb 1:6*
the earth *b.* forth herbs meet for them   *Heb 6:7*
lust *b.* forth sin, and sin *b.* forth death   *Jas 1:15*

BRINGING

much observed for *b.* them out   *Ex 12:42*
so the people were restrained from *b.*   *Ex 36:6*
offering *b.* iniquity to remembrance   *Nu 5:15*
by *b.* up a slander upon the land   *Nu 14:36*
speak not of *b.* king back   *2Sa 19:10; 19:43*
navy *b.* gold and silver   *1Ki 10:22; 2Ch 9:21*
I am *b.* such evil on Jerusalem   *2Ki 21:12*
some on the sabbath *b.* in sheaves   *Ne 13:15*
rejoicing, *b.* his sheaves with him   *Ps 126:6*
b. burnt offerings, *b.* sacrifices of praise   *Jer 17:26*
I made myself known in *b.* them out   *Eze 20:9*
his word by *b.* upon us great evil   *Da 9:12*
to a nation *b.* forth the fruit thereof   *M't 21:43*
b. one sick of the palsy borne of four   *M'k 2:3*
b. spices which they prepared   *Lu 24:1*
a multitude *b.* sick folks   *Ac 5:16*
b. me into captivity to the law of sin   *Ro 7:23*
and *b.* into captivity every thought   *2Co 10:5*
b. many sons unto glory to make   *Heb 2:10*
but the *b.* in of a better hope did   *Heb 7:19*
b. in flood on world of ungodly   *2Pe 2:5*

BRINK

stood by other kine on *b.* of river   *Ge 41:3*
laid the ark in flags by river's *b.*   *Ex 2:3*
stand by the river's *b.* when he comes   *Ex 7:15*
from Aroer by the *b.* of the river   *De 2:36*
when ye are come to the *b.* of Jordan   *Jos 3:8*
caused me return to the *b.* of river   *Eze 47:6*

BROAD

make censers, *b.* plates for covering   *Nu 16:38*
make *b.* plates for the covering of the altar   *Nu 16:39*
fortified Jerusalem to *b.* wall   *Ne 3:8; 12:38*
removed out of strait into *b.* place   *Job 36:16*
thy commandment is exceeding *b.*   *Ps 119:96*
in the *b.* ways I will seek him   *Ca 3:2*
Lord will be a place of *b.* rivers   *Isa 33:21*
know and seek in *b.* places thereof   *Jer 5:1*
b. walls of Babylon shall be broken   *Jer 51:58*
chariots shall justle in *b.* ways   *Na 2:4*
b. is way that leadeth to destruction   *M't 7:13*
they make *b.* their phylacteries   *M't 23:5*

BROADCAST

b. in all the camp (B)   *Ex 36:6*
b. at appointed times (B)   *Le 23:4*
b. the news (B)   *1Sa 31:9*
the more they *b.* it (B)(P)   *M'k 7:36*

BROADER

measure thereof is *b.* than the sea   *Job 11:9*

BROIDED

not with *b.* hair, or gold   *1Ti 2:9*

BROIDERED

make a *b.* coat, a mitre, a girdle   *Ex 28:4*
a coat of checker work (E)(R)   *Ex 28:4*
I clothed thee also with *b.* work   *Eze 16:10*
embroidered cloth (A)(B)(R)   *Eze 16:10; 16:13, 18; 26:16; 27:16, 24*
thy raiment was of silk and *b.* work   *Eze 16:13*
took thy *b.* garments and covered them   *Eze 16:18*
princes shall put off their *b.* garments   *Eze 26:16*
lined with *b.* work from Egypt   *Eze 27:7*
occupied in thy fairs with *b.* work   *Eze 27:16*
merchants in blue clothes and *b.* work   *Eze 27:24*

BROILED

they gave him a piece of a *b.* fish   *Lu 24:42*

BROKE

God *b.* forth (S)   *1Ch 15:13*
acted wickedly and *b.* faith (A)   *Ezr 10:10*

BROKEN

he hath *b.* my covenant   *Ge 17:14; Ps 55:20; Isa 24:5; 33:8; Jer:11:10*
for *b.* spirit (R)   *Ex 6:9*
vessel wherein sodden, shall *b.*   *Le 6:28*
the vessel that he touched shall be *b.*   *Le 15:12*
that hath his stones *b.* let him not offer   *Le 21:20*
b. or maimed, ye shall not offer   *Le 22:22; 22:24*
I have *b.* the bands of your yoke   *Le 26:13*
when I have *b.* the staff of your bread   *Le 26:26*
because he hath *b.* his commandment   *Nu 15:31*
then were the horse-hoofs *b.* by prancings   *J'g 5:22*
brake withs, as a thread of tow is *b.*   *J'g 16:9*
bowls of the mighty men are *b.*   *1Sa 2:4*
had *b.* forth upon Uzziah (S)   *2Sa 6:8; 1Ch 13:11*
that a bow of steel is *b.*   *2Sa 22:35; Ps 18:34*
ships were *b.* at Ezion-geber   *1Ki 22:48*
God hath *b.* in upon mine enemies   *1Ch 14:11*
Lord hath *b.* thy works, ships *b.*   *2Ch 20:37*
also he built up all the wall that was *b.*   *2Ch 32:5*
the *b.* places (B)   *Ne 4:7*
the teeth of the young lions *b.*   *Job 4:10*
my skin is *b.* and become loathsome   *Job 7:5*
was at ease, but he hath *b.* me asunder   *Job 16:12*
my spirit is *b.* (A)(R)   *Job 17:1*
b. me down (A)(B)(E)   *Job 19:10*
the arms of the fatherless have been *b.*   *Job 22:9*
my heart is *b.* (A)   *Job 23:16*
and wickedness shall be *b.* as a tree   *Job 24:20*
and let mine arm by *b.* from the bone   *Job 31:22*

and the high arm shall be *b.*   *Job 38:15*
hast *b.* the teeth of the ungodly   *Ps 3:7*
b. without remedy (B)(R)   *Ps 29:1*
I am forgotten, I am like a *b.* vessel   *Ps 31:12*
Lord is nigh them of *b.* heart   *Ps 34:18; 51:17*
keepeth his bones, not one is *b.*   *Ps 34:20*
their bows shall be *b.*   *Ps 37:15; 37:17*
am feeble and sore *b.* I have roared   *Ps 38:8*
thou hast *b.* us in place of dragons   *Ps 44:19*
that the bones thou hast *b.* may rejoice   *Ps 51:8*
sacrifices of God are *b.* spirit, contrite   *Ps 51:17*
made earth to tremble, thou hast *b.* it   *Ps 60:2*
reproach hath *b.* my heart   *Ps 69:20*
he hath *b.* gates of brass and bars   *Ps 107:16*
that he might even slay the *b.* in heart   *Ps 109:16*
b. thy law (R)   *Ps 119:126*
the snare is *b.* and we are escaped   *Ps 124:7*
He healeth *b.* in heart, bindeth up   *Ps 147:3*
suddenly be *b.* without remedy   *Pr 6:15*
by sorrow of heart the spirit is *b.*   *Pr 15:13*
but a *b.* spirit drieth the bones   *Pr 17:22*
a *b.* spirit (A)(B)(E)(R)   *Pr 18:14*
is like *b.* tooth and foot out of joint   *Pr 25:19*
a threefold cord is not quickly *b.*   *Ec 4:12*
golden bowl be *b.* or pitcher be *b.*   *Ec 12:6*
the latchet of their shoes be *b.*   *Isa 5:27*
within sixty-five years Ephraim be *b.*   *Isa 7:8*
many among them shall fall and be *b.*   *Isa 8:15*
thou hast *b.* the yoke of his burden   *Isa 9:4*
Lord hath *b.* the staff of the wicked   *Isa 14:5*
the rod of him that smote thee is *b.*   *Isa 14:29*
they shall be *b.* in purposes thereof   *Isa 19:10*
graven images he hath *b.* to ground   *Isa 21:9*
they might fall backward and be *b.*   *Isa 28:13*
he hath *b.* covenant, regardeth no man   *Isa 33:8*
nor shall any of the cords thereof be *b.*   *Isa 33:20*
trustest in the staff of this *b.* reed   *Isa 36:6*
b. or wounded spirit (A)   *Isa 66:2*
hewed *b.* cisterns that hold no water   *Jer 2:13*
children have *b.* crown of thy head   *Jer 2:16*
of old I have *b.* thy yoke, burst bands   *Jer 2:20*
these have *b.* thy yoke, burst thy bonds   *Jer 5:5*
all my cords are *b.* my children gone   *Jer 10:20*
kindled a fire, branches of it are *b.*   *Jer 11:16*
virgin daughter of my people is *b.*   *Jer 14:17*
is this man Coniah a despised *b.* idol   *Jer 22:28*
mine heart is *b.* because of the prophets   *Jer 23:9*
I have *b.* yoke of the king of Babylon   *Jer 28:2*
thou hast *b.* the yokes of wood   *Jer 28:13*
may my covenant be *b.* with David   *Jer 33:21*
how is the strong staff *b.*   *Jer 48:17*
the arm of Moab is *b.* saith the Lord   *Jer 48:25*
I have *b.* Moab like a vessel   *Jer 48:38*
Nebuchadnezzar hath *b.* Israel's bones   *Jer 50:17*

hammer of whole earth cut   Jer 50:23
asunder and b.
Babylon, every one of their   Jer 51:56
bows is b.
broad walls of Babylon shall   Jer 51:58
be b.
he hath destroyed and b. her   La 2:9
bars
hath b. my bones   La 3:4; 3:16
altars, and images shall be b.   Eze 6:4;
                               6:6
because I am b. with their   Eze 6:9
whorish heart
my covenant that he hath b.   Eze 17:19
her strong rods were b. and   Eze 19:12
withered
she is b. that was gates of   Eze 26:2
people
the east-wind hath b. thee   Eze 27:26
in the seas
time when thou shalt be b.   Eze 27:34
by seas
have b. arm of Pharaoh   Eze 30:21
king of Egypt
break strong and that which   Eze 30:22
was b.
his boughs are b. by all   Eze 31:12
rivers of land
be b. in the midst of the   Eze 32:28
uncircumcised
nor have ye bound up that   Eze 34:4
which was b.
I will bind up that which   Eze 34:16
was b.
when I have b. the bands   Eze 34:27
of their yoke
and they have b. my   Eze 44:7
covenant
kingdom partly strong, partly   Da 2:42
b.
when he was strong, the great   Da 8:8
horn was b.
that being b. whereas four   Da 8:22
stood up for it
but he shall be b. without   Da 8:25
hand
his kingdom shall be b. and   Da 11:4
be divided
arms of a flood be   Da 11:22
overflown and b.
be b. and swept away   Da 11:22
(A)(R)
Ephraim is oppressed and b.   Ho 5:11
so that the ship was like to   Jon 1:4
be b.
it was b. in that day, and   Zec 11:11
so poor
shepherd shall not heal that   Zec 11:16
which is b.
took up of the b. meat   M't 15:37;
                           M'k 8:8
fall on this stone, shall be   M't 21:44;
b.
those b. down with (A)(N)   Lu 20:18
not have suffered house to   Lu 4:18
be b.   Lu 12:39
he had not only b. sabbath   Joh 5:18
that the law of Moses should   Joh 7:23
not be b.
the scripture cannot be b.   Joh 10:35
that their legs might be b.   Joh 19:31
scripture fulfilled, a bone   Joh 19:36
shall not be b.
for all so many, yet was   Joh 21:11
not the net b.
had b. bread and talked a   Ac 20:11
long while
gave thanks, when he had b.   Ac 27:35
it he began
the hinder part was b. with   Ac 27:41
the waves
this is my body which is b.   1Co 11:24
for you
b. the power of death (N)   1Ti 1:10
stretched and b. on wheel   Heb 11:10
(B)
as vessels of potter shall be b.   Re 2:27

BROKEN DOWN

ranges b. down for they are   Le 11:35
unclean
repaired altar that   1Ki 18:30
was b. down
keep watch, that it be not b.   2Ki 11:6
down
high places Hezekiah had b.   2Ch 33:3
down

Josiah had b. down the   2Ch 34:7
altars and groves
wall of Jerusalem is b. down   Ne 1:3
I viewed walls which were b.   Ne 2:13
down
why hast thou b. down her   Ps 80:12
hedges
thou hast b. down all his   Ps 89:40
hedges
stone wall thereof was b.   Pr 24:31
down
no rule over spirit, like a   Pr 25:28
city b. down
have b. down principal plants   Isa 16:8
houses b. down to fortify   Isa 22:10
wall
city of confusion is b. down   Isa 24:10
earth is utterly b. down, it   Isa 24:19
is dissolved
cities were b. down   Jer 4:26
and her foundations shall be   Eze 30:4
b. down
barns are b. down, corn   Joe 1:17
withered
Christ hath b. down middle   Eph 2:14
wall

BROKEN FORTH

how hast thou b. forth   Ge 38:29
Lord hath b. forth on mine   2Sa 5:20
enemies

BROKEN IN

God hath b. in on mine   1Ch 14:11
enemies

BROKEN OFF

days are past, my purposes   Job 17:11
b. off
boughs withered, shall be b. off   Isa 27:11
if some of branches be b.   Ro 11:17
off
because of unbelief were b.   Ro 11:20;
off   11:19

BROKEN OUT

plague of leprosy b. out of   Le 13:20;
the boil   13:25

BROKEN IN, TO PIECES

adversaries of Lord be b. to   1Sa 2:10
pieces
cast from rock, were b. in   2Ch 25:12
pieces
hast b. Rahab in pieces as one   Ps 89:10
slain
people, ye shall be b. in pieces   Isa 8:9
break as potter's vessel b. in   Isa 30:14
pieces
Merodach b. in pieces, images   Jer 50:2
b. in pieces
brass, silver, gold, b. to   Da 2:35
pieces
calf of Samaria shall be b. in   Ho 8:6
pieces
bound, and fetters b. in   M'k 5:4
pieces

BROKEN UP

fountains of great deep b. up   Ge 7:11
Jerusalem b. up   2Ki 25:4;
                      Jer 39:2; 52:7
by his knowledge depths b.   Pr 3:20
up
when army of Chaldeans b.   Jer 37:11
up
they have b. up and passed   Mic 2:13
the gate
not suffered house be b. up   M't 24:43
when b. roof up they let   M'k 2:4
down
when the congregation was   Ac 13:43
b. up

BROKENFOOTED

Or a man that is b.   Le 21:19

BROKENHANDED

that is brokenfooted, or b.   Le 21:19

BROKENHEARTED

Lord sent me to bind up b.   Isa 61:1
heal b., to preach deliverance   Lu 4:18

BRONZE

bronze (S)   Ge 4:22; Ex 25:3; 26:11, 37;
27:2, 3, 4, 6, 10, 11, 17, 18, 19; 30:18;
31:4; 35:5, 24, 32; 36:18, 38; 38:2, 3,
5, 6, 8, 11, 17, 19, 20, 29; 39:39;
Le 26:19; Nu 21:9; 31:22; De 8:9;
28:23; 33:25; Jos 6:19, 24; 22:8;
J'g 16:21; 1Sa 17:5, 38; 2Sa 8:8, 10;
21:16; 1Ki 7:14, 27, 30, 38, 45, 47; 7:15,
16; 2Ki 25:7, 13, 14, 16, 17; 1Ch 15:19;
18:8, 10; 22:3, 14, 16; 29:2, 7, 14; 4:1,
9, 18; 12:10; 24:12; Job 6:12; 28:2;
40:18; 41:27; Ps 107:16; Isa 45:2; 48:4;
60:17; Jer 6:28; 52:17, 18, 20, 22;
Eze 1:7; 22:18, 20; 24:11; 27:13; 40:3;
Da 2:32, 35; 39, 45; 4:15, 23; 5:4, 23;
7:19; 10:6; Mic 4:13; Zec 6:1; M't 10:9;
1Co 13:1; Re 1:15; 2:18; 9:20; 18:12
bronze (S) (adjective)   Ex 27:4;
Ex 35:16; 38:4, 10, 30; 39:39; Le 6:28;
Nu 16:39; 1Ki 4:13; 7:30; 8:64; 14:27;
2Ki 16:14, 15, 17; 18:4; 25:13; Ch 18:8;
2Ch 1:5, 6; 6:13; 7:7; Jer 1:18; 15:20;
            52:17, 20; Eze 9:2; M'k 7:4
b. chains (B)   J'g 16:21
b. leggings, sin armor   1Sa 17:6
(B)(S)
b. javelin (A)(B)(E)(R)(S)   1Sa 17:6
a b. arrow (B)   2Sa 20:24
a b. bow (R)   2Sa 20:24
a bow of b. (A)(B)(E)(R)   2Sa 22:35
a bow of b. (S)   2Sa 22:35;
         Job 20:24; Ps 18:34; Jer 15:12
melted b. (S)   1Ki 4:16
polished b. (S)   2Ch 4:16
burnished, fine b. (A)(R)(S)   Ezr 8:27
a b. (A)(B)   Ps 18:34
feet like burnished b.   Da 10:6
(A)(E)(R)

BROOD

children of sin, disloyal b.   Isa 57:4
(B)
senseless, disreputable b. (R)   Jer 30:8
you viper b.   M't 3:7
(A)(B)(N)(P)(R)
as a hen gathers b. under   Lu 13:34
wings
hen gathers her young (A)   Lu 13:34

BROOK

took and sent them over b.   Ge 32:23
take willows of the b. and   Le 23:40
rejoice
came to b. Eshcol and cut a   Nu 13:23
branch
b. Eshcol because of cluster   Nu 13:24
of grapes
get over b. Zered   De 2:13;
                               2:14
I cast the dust thereof into   De 9:21
the b.
chose five smooth stones   1Sa 17:40
out of b.
David and 600 men came to   1Sa 30:9
b. Besor
king passed over b. Kidron   2Sa 15:23
they be gone over the b. of   2Sa 17:20
water
on the day thou passest over   1Ki 2:37
the b.
idol burnt by b. Kidron   1Ki 15:13;
                           2Ch 15:16
hide thyself by b. Cherith   1Ki 17:3;
                              17:5
ravens brought bread, he   1Ki 17:6
drank of b.
Elijah brought them to the   1Ki 18:40
b. Kishon
he burnt grove at b. Kidron   2Ki 23:6
cast dust into b. Kidron   2Ki 23:12;
                           2Ch 30:14
shall find them at end of b.   2Ch 20:16
Levites carried it to the b.   2Ch 29:16
Kidron
much people gathered and   2Ch 32:4
stopped the b.
went up by b. and viewed   Ne 2:15
wall
my brethren dealt deceitfully   Job 6:15
as a b.

willows of the *b*. compass　*Job 40:22*
him about
break open the fountain and　*Ps 74:15*
b. (B)
do to them as to Jabin at *b*.　*Ps 83:9*
Kison
shall drink of the *b*. in the　*Ps 110:7*
way
wellspring of wisdom as　*Pr 18:4*
flowing *b*.
shall carry away to *b*. of　*Isa 15:7*
willows
fields to *b*. Kidron be holy　*Jer 31:40*
to Lord
the *b*. of the Arabah (B)　*Am 6:14*
went with disciples over *b*.　*Joh 18:1*
Cedron

BROOKS

he did in Red sea and *b*. of　*Nu 21:14*
Arnon
at the stream of *b*. that　*Nu 21:15*
goeth to Ar
to land of *b*. of water and　*De 8:7*
fountains
of *b*. of Gaash　*2Sa 23:30; 1Ch 11:32*
Ahab said, go unto all *b*. of　*1Ki 18:5*
water
as stream of *b*. they pass　*Job 6:15*
away
shall not see *b*. of honey　*Job 20:17*
and butter
lay up gold as stones of the　*Job 22:24*
b.
as hart panteth after water *b*.　*Ps 42:1*
cleave springs and *b*. (R)　*Ps 74:15*
b. of defence be emptied and　*Isa 19:6*
dried
paper-reeds by the mouth of　*Isa 19:7*
the *b*. and every thing sown
by *b*. shall wither
they that cast angle into *b*.　*Isa 19:8*
shall lament

BROOM

under the *b*. bush (B)(R)　*1Ki 19:4*
roots of the *b*.　*Job 30:4*
(A)(B)(E)(R)
the *b*. tree (A)(B)(R)　*Ps 120:4*
sweep it with a *b*. (S)　*Isa 14:23*

BROTH

Gideon put *b*. in a pot,　*J'g 6:19*
brought it
angel said, pour out *b*. and　*J'g 6:20*
he did so
b. of abominable things in　*Isa 65:4*
their vessels

BROTHEL

b., vaulted place　*Eze 16:24; 16:31, 39*
(A)(B)(E)(R)

BROTHER

at hand of every man's *b*. will　*Ge 9:5*
I
Rebekah had *b*. name Laban　*Ge 24:29*
gave her *b*. and mother　*Ge 24:53*
precious things
Jacob told Rachel he was　*Ge 29:12*
father's *b*.
every man his *b*. (A)(B)(R)　*Ex 32:27*
husband's *b*. shall go in to　*De 25:5*
her
blood laid on Abimelech their　*J'g 9:24*
b.
Israel repented for Benjamin　*J'g 21:6*
their *b*.
b. to dragons, companion　*Job 30:29*
to owls
and a *b*. is born for　*Pr 17:17*
adversity
slothful is *b*. to him that is a　*Pr 18:9*
waster
b. offended is harder won　*Pr 18:9*
than city
a friend that sticketh closer　*Pr 18:24*
than a *b*.
better neighbour near than *b*.　*Pr 27:10*
far off
he hath neither child nor *b*.　*Ec 4:8*
trust not in *b*. for *b*. will　*Jer 9:4*
supplant
for *b*. they may defile　*Eze 44:25*
themselves

Was not Esau Jacob's *b*.　*Mal 1:2*
b. shall deliver up *M't 10:21; M'k 13:12*
b.
if a man's *b*. die　*M'k 12:19; Lu 20:28*
Mary, whose *b*. Lazarus was　*Joh 11:2*
sick
B. Saul, receive thy sight　*Ac 9:17;*
　　　　　　　　　　　　22:13
killed James the *b*. of John　*Ac 12:2*
with sword
seest, *b*. how many　*Ac 21:20*
thousands believe
Quartus a *b*. saluteth you　*Ro 16:23*
if any man called *b*. be　*1Co 5:11*
fornicator
b. goeth to law with *b*.　*1Co 6:6*
before unbelievers
if any *b*. hath a wife that　*1Co 7:12*
believeth not
b. or sister not under　*1Co 7:15*
bondage in such
thro' thy knowledge a weak　*1Co 8:11*
b. perish
and we have sent with him　*2Co 8:18*
the *b*.
that ye withdraw from every　*2Th 3:6*
b.
count not an enemy, but　*2Th 3:15*
admonish as a *b*.
bowels of saints refreshed by　*Ph'm 7*
thee, *b*.
but above a servant, a *b*.　*Ph'm 16*
beloved to me

HIS BROTHER

and after that came *his b*.　*Ge 25:26*
out
lest that he should give seed　*Ge 38:9*
to *his b*.
his b. is dead, he is left　*Ge 42:38;*
alone　　　　　　　　　　　　*44:20*
slay every man *his b*.　*Ex 32:27*
for father or *his b*. may be　*Le 21:2*
defiled
not make himself unclean for　*Nu 6:7*
his b.
not exact of neighbour or *his*　*De 15:2*
b.
as he thought to do to *his b*.　*De 19:19*
first-born succeed in name of　*De 25:6*
his b.
his eye shall be evil toward　*De 28:54*
his b.
Jotham fled for fear of　*J'g 9:21*
Abimelech *his b*.
smote him for blood of　*2Sa 3:27*
Asahel *his b*.
but Solomon *his b*. he called　*1Ki 1:10*
not
you exact usury every one of　*Ne 5:7*
his b.
none can by any means　*Ps 49:7*
redeem *his b*.
when a man shall take hold of　*Isa 3:6*
his b.
people be as fuel, no man　*Isa 9:19*
shall spare *his b*.
shall fight every one against　*Isa 19:2*
his b.
one said to *his b*. be of good　*Isa 41:6*
courage
teach no more every man　*Jer 31:34;*
his b.　　　　　　　　　　*Heb 8:11*
that none serve himself of a　*Jer 34:9*
Jew *his b*.
let ye go every man *his b*.　*Jer 34:14*
an Hebrew
in proclaiming liberty every　*Jer 34:17*
one to *his b*.
because he spoiled *his b*. by　*Eze 18:18*
violence
speak every one to *his b*.　*Eze 33:30*
saying, come
Jacob took *his b*. by heel in　*Ho 12:3*
womb
he did pursue *his b*. with　*Am 1:11*
sword
they hunt every man *his b*.　*Mic 7:2*
with a net
every one by the sword of　*Hag 2:22*
his b.
shew mercy every man to *his b*.　*Zec 7:9*
none imagine evil against *his*　*Zec 7:10*
b. in heart
why deal treacherously　*Mal 2:10*
against *his b*.
whoso is angry, sayeth Raca to　*M't 5:22*
his b.
forgive not every one *his b*.　*M't 18:35*

raise seed to *his b*.　*M't 22:24;*
　　　　　　　　　M'k 12:19; Lu 20:28
having no issue, left his　*M't 22:25*
wife to *his b*.
he findeth *his b*. Simon, and　*Joh 1:41*
saith
no man defraud *his b*. in　*1Th 4:6*
any matter
speak evil of *his b*. and judge　*Jas 4:11*
his b.
in the light, and hateth *his b*.　*1Jo 2:9;*
　　　　　　　　　　　　　2:11
he that loveth *his b*. abideth　*1Jo 2:10*
in the light
neither he that loveth not　*1Jo 3:10;*
his b.　　　　　　　　　　*3:14*
and slew *his b*.　*1Jo 3:12*
whoso hateth *his b*. is a　*1Jo 3:15;*
murderer　　　　　　　　*4:20*
he who loveth God love his　*1Jo 4:21*
b. also
if any see *his b*. sin a sin　*1Jo 5:16*
not to death

MY BROTHER

herself said, he is *my b*.　*Ge 20:5;*
　　　　　　　　　　　　1Ki 20:32
Esau said, then will I slay　*Ge 27:41*
my b. Jacob
Lahan said, because thou art　*Ge 29:15*
my b.
battle against Benjamin *my*　*J'g 20:23;*
b.
distressed for thee, *my b*.　*2Sa 1:26*
Jonathan
my b. do not force me, do　*2Sa 13:12*
not this
mourned, saying, alas *my b*.　*1Ki 13:30*
behaved as though had been　*Ps 35:14*
my b.
that thou wert as *my b*. that　*Ca 8:1*
sucked
not lament, saying, ah *my b*.　*Jer 22:18*
same is *my b*. and sister　*M't 12:50;*
　　　　　　　　　　　　M'k 3:35
how oft shall *my b*. sin　*M't 18:21*
against me
speak to *my b*. that he　*Lu 12:13*
divide inheritance
had been here, *my b*. had　*Joh 11:21*
not died
if meat make *my b*. to　*1Co 8:13*
offend, eat
because I found not Titus　*2Co 2:13*
my b.

OUR BROTHER

what profit is it if we slay　*Ge 37:26*
our b.
for he is *our b*. and our　*Ge 37:27;*
flesh　　　　　　　　　　*J'g 9:3*
we are guilty concerning *our*　*Ge 42:21*
b.
if thou send *our b*. with us,　*Ge 43:4*
we will go
we have sent with them *our*　*2Co 8:22*
b.
and Timothy *our b*. to　*Ph'm 1*
Philemon

THY BROTHER

Lord said, where is Abel *thy*　*Ge 4:9*
b.
live by thy sword, and serve　*Ge 27:40*
thy b.
is not Aaron the Levite *thy b*.　*Ex 4:14*
take to thee Aaron *thy b*. and　*Ex 28:1*
his sons
not hate *thy b*. in thine　*Le 19:17*
heart
that *thy b*. may live with　*Le 25:36*
thee
Aaron *thy b*. was gathered　*Nu 27:13;*
　　　　　　　　　　　　De 32:50
if *thy b*. entice thee secretly　*De 13:6*
open thy hand wide to *thy*　*De 15:11*
b.
if *thy b*. an Hebrew be sold　*De 15:12*
to thee
in any case bring them again　*De 22:1*
to *thy b*.
in like manner with lost　*De 22:3*
things of *thy b*.
not abhor an Edomite, for he　*De 23:7*
is *thy b*.
shalt not lend upon usury to　*De 23:19*
thy b.

hold up my face to Joab *thy*   2Sa 2:22
b.
hold thy peace, my sister,   2Sa 13:20
he is *thy b.*
and they said, *thy b.*   1Ki 20:33
Benhadad
taken pledge from *thy b.* for   Job 22:6
nought
sittest and speakest against   Ps 50:20
thy b.
for violence against *thy b.*   Ob 10
Jacob
should not have looked on day   Ob 12
of *thy b.*
remember *thy b.* hath ought   M't 5:23
against
be reconciled to *thy b.* then   M't 5:24
offer gift
wilt thou say to *thy b.*   M't 7:4;
  Lu 6:42
if *thy b.* trespass   M't 18:15; Lu 17:3
Jesus saith, *thy b.* shall rise   Joh 11:23
again
why judge *thy b.*   Ro 14:10

YOUR BROTHER

bring *your b.* so will I   Ge 42:34
deliver
see my face, except *your b.*   Ge 43:3
be with you
take *your b.* and go again   Ge 43:13
unto man
I am Joseph *your b.* whom   Ge 45:4
ye sold
Abimelech king, he is *your b.*   J'g 9:18
John, who also am *your b.*   Re 1:9

BROTHERHOOD

break *b.* between Judah and   Zec 11:14
Israel
love *b.* fear God, honour   1Pe 2:17
king

BROTHERLY

they remembered not the *b.*   Am 1:9
covenant
be kindly affectioned, with   Ro 12:10
b. love
touching *b.* love, ye need not   1Th 4:9
that I
let *b.* love continue   Heb 13:1
to godliness *b.* kindness, to   2Pe 1:7
kindness

BROTHERS

b. and relatives (B)   J'g 16:31

BROTHER'S

Am I my *b.* keeper   Ge 4:9
voice of thy *b.* blood crieth   Ge 4:10
receive thy *b.* blood   Ge 4:11
his *b.* name was Jubal   Ge 4:21
his *b.* name was Joktan   Ge 10:25;
  1Ch 1:19
Lot his *b.* son   Ge 12:5
they took Lot, Abram's *b.*   Ge 14:12
son
take my master's *b.* daughter   Ge 24:48
thy *b.* anger   Ge 27:44; 27:45
unto thy *b.* wife   Ge 38:8;
Ge 38:9; Le 20:21; De 25:7-9; M'k 6:18
nakedness of thy *b.* wife   Le 18:16
b. ox, ass   De 22:1; 22:3-4
turned about, become my *b.*   1Ki 2:15
drinking in eldest *b.* house   Job 1:13;
  1:18
neither go into thy *b.* house   Pr 27:10
mote in thy *b.* eye   M't 7:3; 7:5;
  Lu 6:41-42
occasion to fall in his *b.*   Ro 14:13
way
were evil, and his *b.*   1Jo 3:12
righteous

BROTHERS'

unto their father's *b.* sons   Nu 36:11

BROUGHT

b. on me and my kingdom   Ge 20:9
great sin
because the Lord thy God *b.*   Ge 27:20
it to me

that torn of beasts I *b.* not   Ge 31:39
to thee
they *b.* him the present in   Ge 43:26
their hand
beast in field not *b.* home   Ex 9:19
shall die
Lord *b.* east wind, east wind   Ex 10:13
b. locusts
the hard causes they *b.* to   Ex 18:26
Moses
how I bare you and *b.* you   Ge 19:4
to myself
man that *b.* us out of Egypt   Ge 32:1;
  32:23
thou hast *b.* so great a sin   Ge 32:21
on them
they that had purple and   Ge 35:23
scarlet *b.* them
shall be *b.* to Aaron the   Le 13:2;
priest   13:9
till ye have *b.* an offering to   Le 23:14
God
they *b.* the blasphemer to   Le 24:11
Moses
shall be *b.* to door of   Nu 6:13
tabernacle
because *b.* not offering in his   Nu 9:13
season
wherefore hath Lord *b.* us to   Nu 14:3
this land
and he hath *b.* thee near to   Nu 16:10
him
Moses *b.* their cause before   Nu 27:5
the Lord
we have *b.* an oblation for   Nu 31:50
Lord
till we have *b.* them to their   Nu 32:17
place
Lord thy God *b.* thee out   De 5:15
thence
I have *b.* the first-fruits of   De 26:10
the land
I have *b.* away the hallowed   De 26:13
thing:
in the morning ye shall be *b.*   Jos 7:14
they took and *b.* them to   Jos 7:23
Joshua
they *b.* them to the valley of   Jos 7:24
Achor
Lord *b.* sea upon them,   Jos 24:7
covered them
I have *b.* you unto land I   J'g 2:1
sware
Philistines *b.* money in their   J'g 16:18
hand
who *b.* thee hither? What   J'g 18:3
makest thou
she *b.* Samuel to house of   1Sa 1:24
Lord
they slew bullock, and *b.*   1Sa 1:25
child to Eli
they despised him, *b.* him   1Sa 10:27
no presents
wherefore then have ye *b.*   1Sa 21:14
him to me
David received what Abigail   1Sa 25:35
b. him
found and *b.* an Egyptian   1Sa 30:11
crown and bracelet, *b.* to my   2Sa 1:10
lord
thou hast *b.* me hitherto   2Sa 7:18;
  1Ch 17:16
Lord *b.* on them evil   1Ki 9:9;
  2Ch 7:22
they *b.* each his present   1Ki 10:25;
  2Ch 9:24
hast thou also *b.* evil upon   1Ki 17:20
the widow
the king died, and was *b.*   1Ki 22:37
to Samaria
Hoshea *b.* no presents to   2Ki 17:4
king of Assyria
carry thither priest *b.* from   2Ki 17:27
thence
he *b.* shadow ten degrees   2Ki 20:11
backward
craftsmen king *b.* captive to   2Ki 24:16
Babylon
with jeopardy of lives they   1Ch 11:19
b. it
Lord *b.* fear of him on all   1Ch 14:17
nations
children of Israel were *b.*   2Ch 13:18
under
all Judah *b.* to Jehoshaphat   2Ch 17:5
presents
b. Ahaziah to Jehu, and   2Ch 22:9
when had slain

king of Syria *b.* Israel to   2Ch 28:5
Damascus
b. captives to Jericho to   2Ch 28:15
their brethren
many *b.* gifts to Lord to   2Ch 32:23
Jerusalem
they *b.* us a man of   Ezr 8:18
understanding
God had *b.* counsel to nought   Ne 4:15
people *b.* them and made   Ne 8:16
booths
thou art just in all that is *b.*   Ne 9:33
upon us
Judah *b.* tithe of corn and   Ne 13:12
new wine
b. the book (S)   Es 6:1
let royal apparel be *b.* king   Es 6:8
number of slain in Shushan *b.*   Es 9:11
to king
now a thing was secretly *b.*   Job 4:12
to me
yet shall he be *b.* to grave   Job 21:32
let them be *b.* to confusion   Ps 35:4
with gladness shall they be *b.*   Ps 45:15
are *b.* to shame that seek my   Ps 71:24
hurt
a man is *b.* to a piece of   Pr 6:26
bread
he *b.* me to the   Ca 2:4
banqueting house
Kir of Moab is *b.* to silence   Isa 15:1
b. land of Chaldæans to   Isa 23:13
ruin
for the terrible one is *b.* to   Isa 29:20
nought
thou hast not *b.* small cattle   Isa 43:23
to me
I have called him, I have *b.*   Isa 48:15
him
he is *b.* as a lamb to slaughter   Isa 53:7
therefore his arm *b.*   Isa 59:16;
salvation   63:5
and that their kings may be   Isa 60:11
b.
that *b.* it shall drink it in   Isa 62:9
courts
as an ox that is *b.* to   Jer 11:19
slaughter
have *b.* on them a spoiler at   Jer 15:8
noonday
as I have *b.* all this evil on   Jer 32:42
this people
Lord hath *b.* it and done as   Jer 40:3
he said
be comforted concerning   Eze 14:22
evil I *b.*
the high be *b.* low (A)   Eze 21:26
nor left her whoredoms *b.*   Eze 23:8
from Egypt
shalt not be *b.* together nor   Eze 29:5
gathered
I might shew them, art thou   Eze 40:4
b. hither
he *b.* me through waters to   Eze 47:3;
ankles   47:4
instruments of music *b.*   Da 6:18
before him
b. him near before the   Da 7:13
ancient of days
Lord watched on the evil,   Da 9:14
and *b.* it on us
she be given up, and they   Da 11:6
that *b.* her
when ye *b.* it home I did   Hag 1:9
blow on it
ye *b.* what was torn, lame,   Mal 1:13
sick
shall be *b.* before kings   M't 10:18;
for my sake for a   M'k 13:9; Lu 21:12
test against them
kingdom is *b.* to desolation   M't 12:25;
  Lu 11:17
she *b.* John Baptist's head   M't 14:11
to her mother
I *b.* him to disciples, could   M't 17:16
not cure him
one was *b.* that owed him   M't 18:24
10,000 talents
were *b.* to him little   M't 19:13;
children   M'k 10:13
a candle *b.* to be put under   M'k 4:21
a bushel
the king commanded his   M'k 6:27
head to be *b.*
the disciples rebuked those   M'k 10:13
that *b.* them
b. him to Jerusalem to   Lu 2:22
present him
a woman *b.* an alabaster box   Lu 7:37
of ointment

b. him to an inn and took　　　*Lu* 10:34
care of him
they said, why have ye not　　　*Joh* 7:45
b. him
sent to the prison to have　　　*Ac* 5:21
them *b.*
Barnabas *b.* him to apostles　　　*Ac* 9:27
and being *b.* on their way by　　*Ac* 15:3
the church
who *b.* her masters gain by　　　*Ac* 16:16
soothsaying
b. them to the magistrates　　　*Ac* 16:20
from his body were *b.* to　　　*Ac* 19:12
sick, aprons
b. books, and burned them　　　*Ac* 19:19
before all
Demetrius *b.* no small gain　　　*Ac* 19:24
to craftsmen
b. these men, no robbers of　　　*Ac* 19:37
churches
they *b.* the young man alive　　　*Ac* 20:12
they all *b.* us on our way,　　　*Ac* 21:5
with wives
next day commanded Paul to　　*Ac* 25:6
be *b.*
fear not, Paul, thou must be　　　*Ac* 27:24
b. before Cæsar
b. under bondage (B)　　　　*Ro* 8:20
to be *b.* on my way thither　　　*Ro* 15:24
by you
I will not be *b.* under power　　*1Co* 6:12
of any
of you to be *b.* on my way　　　*2Co* 1:16
to Judaea
what it is to be *b.* low (N)　　　*Ph'p* 4:12
hath *b.* life and immortality　　　*2Ti* 1:10
to light
for the grace that is to be *b.*　　*1Pe* 1:13
to you
of the same is he *b.* in　　　　*2Pe* 2:19
bondage

BROUGHT *AGAIN*

Abram *b.* again his brother　　　*Ge* 14:16
Lot
the money that was *b.* again　　*Ge* 43:12
in sacks
Moses and Aaron *b.* again to　　*Ex* 10:8
Pharaoh
Lord *b.* again waters of sea　　　*Ex* 15:19
on them
b. us word again and said, it　　*De* 1:25
is a good land
b. word again as it was in　　　*Jos* 14:7
my heart
the Lord hath *b.* me home　　　*Ru* 1:21
again empty
Philistines *b.* again ark of　　　*1Sa* 6:21
Lord
b. again Abner from well of　　　*2Sa* 3:26
Sirah
b. the king word again　　　　*2Ki* 22:9;
　　　　　　　　　1Ki 20:9; *2Ch* 34:28
b. Manasseh again to　　　　*2Ch* 33:13
Jerusalem
b. again vessels of the house　　*Ne* 13:9
vessels shall shortly be *b.*　　　*Jer* 27:16
again
have not *b.* again what was　　　*Eze* 34:4
driven
when I have *b.* them again　　　*Eze* 39:27
from people
b. again 30 pieces of silver　　　*M't* 27:3
God of peace *b.* again　　　　*Heb* 13:20
from dead

BROUGHT *BACK*

Abram *b.* back all goods and　　*Ge* 14:16
Lot
b. back word to　　　　　　*Nu* 13:26
congregation
the prophet whom he had　　　*1Ki* 13:23
b. back
Jehoshaphat *b.* them back to　　*2Ch* 19:4
Lord
hast *b.* back captivity of　　　*Ps* 85:1
Jacob
come into land *b.* back from　　*Eze* 38:8
sword

BROUGHT *DOWN*

Joseph was *b.* down into　　　*Ge* 39:1
Egypt
he *b.* down people to the　　　*J'g* 7:5
waters
Philistines *b.* down Samson　　*J'g* 16:21
to Gaza

when he had *b.* him down　　　*1Sa* 30:16
they
b. Adonijah down from altar　　*1Ki* 1:53
b. child down out of　　　　*1Ki* 17:23
chamber
b. down to brook Kishon　　　*1Ki* 18:40
slew them
they are *b.* down and fallen　　*Ps* 20:8
he *b.* down their heart with　　*Ps* 107:12
labour
mean man shall be *b.* down　　*Isa* 5:15
pomp is *b.* down to the　　　*Isa* 14:11
grave
thou shalt be *b.* down to　　　*Isa* 14:15
hell
be *b.* down and speak out of　*Isa* 29:4
ground
for your sake I have *b.*　　　*Isa* 43:14
down nobles
he hath *b.* them down to　　　*La* 2:2
ground
Lord have *b.* down high　　　*Eze* 17:24
tree
be *b.* down with trees of　　　*Eze* 31:18
Eden
pride of Assyria be *b.* down　　*Zec* 10:11
Capernaum be *b.* down to　　　*M't* 11:23
hell
brethren *b.* him down to　　　*Ac* 9:30
Cesarea

BROUGHT *FORTH*

the earth *b.* forth grass and　　*Ge* 1:12
herbs
waters *b.* forth after their　　　*Ge* 1:21
kind
king of Salem *b.* forth　　　*Ge* 14:18
bread, wine
Lord *b.* forth Abram abroad,　*Ge* 15:5
and said
angels *b.* Lot forth without　　*Ge* 19:16
city
servant *b.* forth jewels of　　　*Ge* 24:53
silver and
when *b.* forth sent to her　　　*Ge* 38:25
father-in-law
plenteous years earth *b.*　　　*Ge* 41:47
forth handfuls
when thou hast *b.* forth　　　*Ex* 3:12
people
ye have *b.* us forth into　　　*Ex* 16:3
wilderness
know I am Lord who *b.*　　　*Ex* 29:46;
them forth out of Egypt　　　*Le* 25:38;
　　　　　　　　　　　26:13, 45
Aaron's rod *b.* forth buds　　*Nu* 17:8
sent angel, *b.* us forth out　　*Nu* 20:16
of Egypt
God *b.* him forth out of　　　*Nu* 24:8
Egypt
lest forget Lord who *b.* forth　*De* 6:12;
　　　　　　　　　　　8:14
who *b.* forth water out of　　*De* 8:15
rock of flint
people thou *b.* forth have　　　*De* 9:12
corrupted
Lord *b.* us forth with a　　　*De* 26:8
mighty hand
covenant made when *b.*　　　*De* 29:25
them forth
precious fruits *b.* forth by　　*De* 33:14
the sun
b. forth five kings out of　　　*Jos* 10:23
cave
she *b.* forth butter in lordly　*J'g* 5:25
dish
b. you forth out of house of　*J'g* 6:8
bondage
sent Moses, who *b.* forth　　*1Sa* 12:8
your fathers
b. forth into large place　　　*2Sa* 22:20;
　　　　　　　　　　　Ps 18:19
forsook lord who *b.* forth　　*1Ki* 9:9;
fathers out of land of Egypt　*2Ch* 7:22
b. forth vestments for　　　*2Ki* 10:22
worshippers
b. forth king's son, and put　*2Ki* 11:12
crown on
hast *b.* me forth out of　　　*Job* 10:18
womb
wicked be *b.* forth to day　　*Job* 21:30
of wrath
conceived mischief, *b.* forth　*Ps* 7:14
falsehood
before mountains *b.* forth, art　*Ps* 90:2
God
land *b.* forth frogs in　　　*Ps* 105:30
abundance

b. forth people with joy and　*Ps* 105:43
gladness
when no depths, I was *b.*　　*Pr* 8:24
forth
before the hills was I *b.* forth　*Pr* 8:25
mother *b.* thee forth, she *b.*　*Ca* 8:5
forth
looked for grapes, *b.* forth　　*Isa* 5:2
wild grapes
b. forth wind　　　　　　*Isa* 26:18
guide her among sons, she　　*Isa* 51:18
b. forth
before she travailed, she *b.*　*Isa* 66:7
forth
soon as Zion travailed, she *b.*　*Isa* 66:8
forth children
saying to stone, thou hast *b.*　*Jer* 2:27
me forth
I commanded in today I *b.*　*Jer* 11:4;
them forth　　　　　　　34:13
b. forth Jeremiah out of　　　*Jer* 20:3
stocks
b. forth people Israel with　　*Jer* 32:21
signs
Lord *b.* forth weapons of　　*Jer* 50:25
his indignation
Lord hath *b.* forth our　　　*Jer* 51:10
righteousness
b. forth stuff by day in their　*Eze* 12:7
sight
remnant *b.* forth both sons　　*Eze* 14:22
and daughters
heathen in whose sight I *b.*　*Eze* 20:22
them forth
till time she which travaileth　*Mic* 5:3
b. forth
the olive tree hath not *b.*　　*Hag* 2:19
forth
till she had *b.* forth her　　　*M't* 1:25
first-born son
fell in ground, *b.* forth fruit　*M't* 13:8;
　　　　　　　　　　　M'k 4:8
Elisabeth's time came, she *b.*　*Lu* 1:57
forth son
she *b.* forth her first-born son　*Lu* 2:7
ground of rich man *b.* forth　*Lu* 12:16
plentifully
Pilate heard that, he *b.*　　　*Joh* 19:13
forth Jesus
opened prison doors *b.* them　*Ac* 5:19
forth
when Herod would have *b.*　*Ac* 12:6
him forth
I commanded the man to be　*Ac* 25:17
b. forth
he prayed and earth *b.* forth　*Jas* 5:18
fruit
b. forth man child, who was　*Re* 12:5
to rule
dragon persecuted woman　　*Re* 12:13
which *b.* forth

BROUGHT *IN*

hath *b.* in an Hebrew to　　　*Ge* 39:14
mock us
Joseph *b.* in Jacob his father　*Ge* 47:7
blood was not *b.* in holy　　　*Le* 10:18
place
bullock and goat, whose　　　*Le* 16:27
blood was *b.* in
journeyed not till Miriam　　　*Nu* 12:15
was *b.* in
for my righteousness Lord *b.*　*De* 9:4
me in
when Lord hath *b.* thee in　　*De* 11:29
to land
Joab *b.* in a great spoil with　*2Sa* 3:22
him
they *b.* in ark of Lord　　　*2Sa* 6:17;
　　　　　　　　　　　1Ki 8:6
no burden *b.* in on　　　　*Ne* 13:19
sabbath day
by his power he *b.* in south　*Ps* 78:26
wind
then was Daniel *b.* in before　*Da* 5:13
king
John's head was *b.* in in　　*M't* 14:11
charger
b. in with Jesus into　　　　*Ac* 7:45
possession
false brethren *b.* in to spy　　*Ga* 2:4

BROUGHT *INTO*

not *b.* us *into* land that　　　*Nu* 16:14
floweth
when Lord hath *b.* thee *into*　*De* 6:10;
　　　　　　　　　　　31:20
b. ark *into* Dagon's house　　*1Sa* 5:2

b. them *into* parlour, made   1Sa 9:22
them sit
b. thy servant *into* covenant   1Sa 20:8
with thee
sin money not *b. into* house   2Ki 12:16
of Lord
hast *b.* me *into* dust of death   Ps 22:15
king hath *b.* me *into* his   Ca 1:4
chambers
I *b.* you *into* a plentiful   Jer 2:7
country
b. me *into* darkness, but not   La 3:2
light
rowers have *b.* thee *into*   Eze 27:26
waters
have *b. into* my sanctuary   Eze 44:7
strangers
led him and *b.* him *into*   Ac 9:8
Damascus
b. Greeks *into* temple,   Ac 21:28
polluted it
for we *b.* nothing *into* this   1Ti 6:7
world
whose blood is *b. into*   Heb 13:11
sanctuary

BROUGHT *LOW*

daughter, thou hast *b.* me   J'g 11:35
very *low*
b. Judah *low*, because of   2Ch 28:19
Ahaz
they are *b. low*, he   Job 14:21
perceiveth it not
wicked are gone and *b. low*   Job 24:24
let mercies prevent us, we are   Ps 79:8
b. low
were *b. low* for their   Ps 106:43
iniquity
they are *b. low*, through   Ps 107:39
oppression
I was *b. low*, and he helped   Ps 116:6
me
attend to my cry, for I am   Ps 142:6
b. very *low*
all daughters of music shall be   Ec 12:4
b. low
upon every one lifted up   Isa 2:12
shall be *b. low*
branch of terrible ones shall   Isa 25:5
be *b. low*
every mountain and hill *b.*   Lu 3:5;
low   Isa 40:4

BROUGHT *OUT*

that *b.* thee *out* of Ur of   Ge 15:7
Chaldees
they *b.* him hastily *out* of   Ge 41:14
dungeon
he *b.* Simeon *out* unto them   Ge 43:23
by strength of hand Lord *b.*   Ex 13:3;
you *out* from this   Ex 13:9,
place   14, 16; De 6:21
I am Lord God, which *b.*   Ex 20:2;
thee *out* Le 19:36; Nu 15:41; De 5:6;
  Ps 81:10
when I *b.* them *out* of   Le 23:43;
remember that Lord *b.* thee   De 5:15
out
b. them *out* to slay them in   De 9:28
wilderness
young men *b. out* Rahab and   Jos 6:23
all she hath
plagued Egypt, afterward I *b.*   Jos 24:5
you *out*
servant *b.* her *out*, bolted   2Sa 13:18
door
b. out grove from house of   2Ki 23:6
Lord
b. out people that were in   1Ch 20:3
it
then they *b. out* the king's   2Ch 23:11
son
priests *b. out* all   2Ch 29:16
uncleanness they found
he *b.* streams also *out* of   Ps 78:16
rock
thou hast *b.* a vine *out* of   Ps 80:8
Egypt
he *b.* them *out* of darkness,   Ps 107:14
and brake
b. out Israel from among   Ps 136:11
them
in the day I *b.* them *out* of   Jer 7:22
Egypt
king my father *b. out* of   Da 5:13
Jewry
by a prophet Lord *b.* Israel   Ho 12:13
out

this Moses, which *b.* us *out*   Ac 7:40
of Egypt
declared how Lord *b.* him   Ac 12:17
out of prison
with an high arm *b.* them   Ac 13:17
out of Egypt
b. out, said, what must I do   Ac 16:30
to be saved
besought them, and *b.* them   Ac 16:39
out

BROUGHT *TO PASS*

now have I *b.* it *to pass*   2Ki 19:25;
  Isa 37:26
it cometh, and shall be *b. to*   Eze 21:7
pass
then shall be *b. to pass* the   1Co 15:54
saying

BROUGHT *UP*

wherefore hast thou *b.* us   Ex 17:3;
up   Nu 21:5
Moses, the man that *b.* us   Ex 32:1;
up   32:23
thy gods which *b.* thee *up*   Ex 32:4;
  1Ki 12:28
thou and people which thou   Ex 33:1
hast *b. up*
they *b. up* an evil report of   Nu 13:32
land
small thing thou hast *b.* us   Nu 16:13
up
why have ye *b. up*   Nu 20:4
congregation of Lord
Lord is with thee, which *b.*   De 20:1
thee *up*
he *b. up* an evil name on a   De 22:19
virgin
he it is that *b.* us *up* and   Jos 24:17
fathers
bones of Joseph *b. up*   Jos 28:32
buried in Shechem
I *b.* you *up* from Egypt   J'g 6:8;
  1Sa 10:18
b. Samson *up* and buried   J'g 15:13;
  16:31
lords *b. up* to her seven green   J'g 16:8
withs
all fleshhook *b. up* priest   1Sa 2:14
took
since the day I *b.* them *up*   1Sa 8:8;
  2Sa 7:6; 1Ch 17:5
Lord *b.* your fathers *up* out   1Sa 12:6
of Egypt
David went and *b. up* ark   2Sa 6:12;
2Sa 6:15; 1Ki 8:4; 1Ch 15:28; 2Ch 1:4
them that *b. up* Ahab's   2Ki 10:1
children
Israel sinned against Lord   2Ki 17:7
who *b.* them *up*
Lord who *b.* you *up*, him   2Ki 17:36
fear
b. up Zedekiah to king of   2Ki 25:6;
Babylon   Jer 39:5
Solomon *b. up* daughter of   2Ch 8:11
Pharaoh
counsel with young men *b.*   2Ch 10:8
up with him
these vessels *b. up* from   Ezr 1:11
Babylon
Esar-haddon king of Assur *b.*   Ezr 4:2
us *up*
this is God that *b.* thee *up*   Ne 9:18
out of Egypt
Mordecai *b. up* Esther   Es 2:7
like as when she was *b. up*   Es 2:20
with him
from youth he was *b. up*   Job 31:18
with me
hast *b. up* my soul from grave   Ps 30:3
b. me *up* out of a horrible   Ps 40:2
pit
I was by him, as one *b. up*   Pr 8:30
with him
have nourished and *b. up*   Isa 1:2
children
who hath *b. up* these   Isa 49:21
where is he that *b.* them   Isa 63:11;
up   Jer 2:6
I protested in day I *b.* them   Jer 11:7
up
Lord *b. up* Israel out of   Jer 16:14;
Egypt   23:7
Lord *b. up* Israel from   Jer 16:15;
north   23:8
those I *b. up* my enemy   La 2:22
consumed

that were *b. up* in scarlet   La 4:5
embrace
she *b. up* one of her whelps   Eze 19:3
when *b.* you *up* out of your   Eze 37:13
graves
I *b.* you *up*   Am 2:10;
  Am 3:1; 9:7; Mic 6:4
hast *b. up* my life from   Jon 2:6
corruption
she shall be *b. up*, and her   Na 2:7
maids
Nazareth, where been *b. up*   Lu 4:16
been *b. up* with Herod the   Ac 13:1
tetrarch
b. up in this city at feet of   Ac 22:3
Gamaliel
widow, if she have *b. up*   1Ti 5:10
children

BROUGHTEST

people thou *b.* out have   Ex 32:7
corrupted
b. up this people in thy   Nu 14:13
might
lest land whence thou *b.* us   De 9:28
out say
inheritance thou *b.* out   De 9:29;
  1Ki 8:51
wast he that *b.* in Israel   2Sa 5:2;
  1Ch 11:2
thou *b.* our fathers out of   1Ki 8:53
Egypt
b. him forth out of Ur of   Ne 9:7
Chaldees
thou *b.* forth water for them   Ne 9:15
out of rock
b. them into the land hadst   Ne 9:23
promised
b. us into the net, thou   Ps 66:11
laidst
but thou *b.* us out into a   Ps 66:12
wealthy place

BROW

sweat of your *b.* (B)   Ge 3:19
neck is an iron sinew, thy *b.*   Isa 48:4
brass
they led him to the *b.* of the   Lu 4:29
hill

BROWN

all *b.* cattle among the   Ge 30:32;
sheep   35:40
every one that is not *b.* be   Ge 30:33
accounted stolen

BRUISE

it shall *b.* thy head   Ge 3:15
cart nor *b.* it with his   Isa 28:28
horsemen
Yet it pleased the Lord to   Isa 53:10
b. him
Thy *b.* is incurable, and thy   Jer 30:12
shall it break in pieces and *b.*   Da 2:40
no healing of thy *b.*; thy   Na 3:19
wound
b. Satan under your feet   Re 16:20
shortly

BRUISED

unto the Lord that which is   Le 22:24
b.
the staff of this *b.* reed,   2Ki 18:21
even
Bread corn is *b.*, because he   Isa 28:28
A *b.* reed shall he not break,   Isa 42:3
and
he was *b.* for our iniquities   Isa 53:5
they *b.* the teats of their   Eze 23:3
virginity
b. the breasts of her virginity   Eze 23:8
A *b.* reed shall he not   M't 12:20
break and
to set at liberty them that are   Lu 4:18
b.
those *b.*, crushed (A)   Lu 4:18

BRUISES

and *b.* and putrifying sores   Isa 1:6
b. welts and raw wounds   Isa 1:6
(B)(R)

BRUISING

in *b*. thy teats by the   *Eze 23:21*
Egyptians
b. him hardly departeth from   *Lu 9:39*

BRUIT

the noise of the *b*. is come,   *Jer 10:22*
and
the sound of a rumor   *Jer 10:22*
(A)(R)
great commotion is coming   *Jer 10:22*
(B)
the voice of tidings (E)   *Jer 10:22*
all that hear the *b*. of thee,   *Na 3:19*
shall clap
all who hear the news   *Na 3:19*
(A)(R)
all who hear this report   *Na 3:19*
(B)(E)

BRUTAL

the *b*. men (S)   *Eze 21:31*
in *b*. rage he butted (B)   *Da 8:7*

BRUTALLY

attacked them *b*. (N)   *M't 22:6*

BRUTE

as natural *b*. beasts, made to   *2Pe 2:12*
be
know naturally, as *b*. beasts   *Jude 10*

BRUTISH

the fool and the *b*. person   *Ps 49:10*
perish
the fool and the stupid   *Ps 49:10*
(A)(R)
a *b*. man knoweth not: *Ps 92:6*
neither a fool
rude and uncultivated state (A) *Ps 92:6*
An unthinking person (B)   *Ps 92:6*
the dull man cannot know   *Ps 92:6*
(R)
he that hateth reproof is *b*.   *Pr 12:1*
is like a brute beast, stupid   *Pr 12:1*
and indiscriminating (A)
he who hates reproof is like a *Pr 12:1*
cow (R)
he who hates reproof is   *Pr 12:1*
stupid (R)
Surely I am more *b*. than any *Pr 30:2*
man
I am too stupid to be a man   *Pr 30:2*
(B)(R)
counsellors of Pharaoh is   *Isa 19:11*
become *b*.
counsel has become witless   *Isa 19:11*
(A)
advice is folly (B)   *Isa 19:11*
give stupid counsel (R)   *Isa 19:11*
they are altogether *b*. and   *Jer 10:8*
foolish
altogether irrational and   *Jer 10:8*
stupid (A)
both stupid and foolish   *Jer 10:8;*
(B)(R)   *Jer 10:14*
every man is *b*. in his   *Jer 10:14*
knowledge
the pastors are become *b*.   *Jer 10:21*
and
deliver thee into hands of   *Eze 21:31*
b. men
hand of brutal men (B)(R)   *Eze 21:31*

BUBBLES

water that *b*. up (B)   *Joh 4:14*

BUCKET

the nations are as a drop of   *Isa 40:15*
a *b*.
put in a cupboard or *b*. (P)   *Lu 11:33*

BUCKETFULS

draw out fifty *b*. (A)   *Hag 2:16*

BUCKETS

pour the water out of his *b*.   *Nu 24:7*

BUCKLER

a *b*. to all that trust in   *2Sa 22:31;*
him   *Ps 18:30*

a shield (B)   *2Sa 22:31;*
   1Ch 5:18; Ps 18:2; 35:2; 91:4; Pr 2:7
a shield (E)   *2Sa 22:31; Ps 18:2; Pr 2:7*
a shield (R)   *2Sa 22:31;*
   1Ch 5:18; Ps. 18:2
gold for each *b*. (B)(E)(S)   *1Ki 10:16*
men able to bear *b*. and   *1Ch 5:18;*
sword   *12:8*
gold for each *b*. (E)   *2Ch 9:16*
Lord is my God, my *b*., my   *Ps 18:2*
high tower
is a shield (A)   *Ps 18:2; Pr 2:7*
Take hold of shield and *b*.   *Ps 35:2*
truth shall be thy shield and *Ps 91:4*
a *b*. to them that walk   *Pr 2:7*
uprightly
Order ye the *b*. and shield   *Jer 46:3*
set against thee *b*. and   *Eze 23:24*
shield
and lift up the *b*. against   *Eze 26:8*
thee

BUCKLERS

200 *b*. of gold (B)(E)   *1Ki 10:16*
200 shields or *b*.   *2Ch 9:15*
(A)(B)(E)(R)
200 *b*. (S)   *2Ch 9:15;*
   2Ch 14:8; 1Ki 10:16
that bare *b*. (A)(E)(R)   *2Ch 14:8*
spears, and *b*. and shields,   *2Ch 23:9*
that
upon the thick bosses of his   *Job 15:26*
b.
a thickly ornamented shield   *Job 15:26*
(A)
whereon hanged a thousand *b*. *Ca 4:4*
a thousand shields (B)   *Ca 4:4*
company with *b*. and   *Eze 38:4*
shields
the shields and the *b*. the   *Eze 39:9*
bows

BUD

flax was in *b*. (S)   *Ex 9:31*
the scent of water it will *b*.   *Job 14:9*
to cause the *b*. of the   *Job 38:27*
tender herb
I make the horn of David   *Ps 132:17*
to *b*.
the pomegranates *b*. forth: *Ca 7:12*
there
when the *b*. is perfect, and the *Isa 18:5*
b. becomes a ripening grape *Isa 18:5*
(B)
Israel shall blossom and *b*.   *Isa 27:6*
maketh it bring forth and *b*.   *Isa 55:10*
that
the earth bringeth forth her *b*. *Isa 61:11*
to multiply as the *b*. of the   *Eze 16:7*
field
of the house of Israel to *b*.   *Eze 29:21*
forth
the *b*. shall yield no meal: *Ho 8:7*
if so

BUDDED

it was as though it *b*. and her *Ge 40:10*
rod of Aaron was *b*.   *Nu 17:8*
and the pomegranates *b*.   *Ca 6:11*
hath blossomed, pride hath   *Eze 7:10*
b.
Aaron's rod that *b*. and the *Heb 9:4*
tables

BUDS

was budded, and brought   *Nu 17:8*
forth *b*.

BUFFALO

the *b*. (B)   *Nu 23:22; Nu 24:8*

BUFFET

to cover his face, and to *b*.   *M'k 14:65*
him
messenger of Satan to *b*. me *2Co 12:7*
lest

BUFFETED

they spit in his face and *b*.   *M't 26:67*
him
and are *b*. and have no   *1Co 4:11*
certain
when ye be *b*. for your   *1Pe 2:20*
faults

BUILD

go to, let us *b*. us a city and   *Ge 11:4*
tower
and they left off to *b*. the city *Ge 11:8*
will *b*. sheep folds for cattle *Nu 32:16*
b. cities for your little ones   *Nu 32:24*
shalt *b*. bulwarks against   *De 20:20*
city
to *b*. in Jerusalem   *1Ki 9:19; 2Ch 8:6*
Solomon did *b*.   *1Ki 11:7; 9:24*
in Ahab's days Hiel did *b*.   *1Ki 16:34*
Jericho
b. the sanctuary of Lord   *1Ch 22:19*
God
give Solomon an heart to   *1Ch 29:19*
b. palace
let us *b*. cities and make   *2Ch 14:7*
walls
let us *b*. with you, we seek   *Ezr 4:2*
your God
and *b*. the house that was   *Ezr 5:11*
builded
let us *b*. the wall   *Ne 2:17; 2:18, 20*
b. if a fox go up he shall   *Ne 4:3*
break down
so that we are not able to *b*.   *Ne 4:10*
the wall
house, they labor in vain   *Ps 127:1*
that *b*. it
time to break down, time to *b*. *Ec 3:3*
up
if she be a wall, we will *b*.   *Ca 8:9*
upon her
the bricks are fallen, but we   *Isa 9:10*
will *b*.
have raised him up, he shall *Isa 45:13*
b. my city
shall *b*. the old waste   *Isa 58:12;*
places   *61:4*
sons of strangers shall *b*. up *Isa 60:10*
walls
they shall not *b*. and   *Isa 65:22*
another inhabit
set these over nations to *b*.   *Jer 1:10*
and plant
lay siege, *b*. a fort against it *Eze 4:2;*
   21:22
restore and *b*. Jerusalem to *Da 9:25*
Messiah
I will *b*. it as in the days of *Am 9:11*
old
b. the waste cities and   *Am 9:14*
inhabit them
they *b*. up Zion with blood *Mic 3:10*
he shall *b*. the temple of   *Zec 6:12;*
Lord   *6:13*
that are far off shall *b*. in   *Zec 6:15*
temple of Lord
Tyrus did *b*. herself a strong *Zec 9:3*
hold
shall *b*. but I will throw   *Mal 1:4*
down
b. tombs of prophets   *M't 23:29;*
   Lu 11:47-48
pull down barns and *b*.   *Lu 12:18*
greater
which of you intending to *b*. *Lu 14:28*
a tower
began to *b*. and not able to *Lu 14:30*
finish
word of his grace, able to   *Ac 20:32*
b. you up
b. up the common life (N)   *Ro 14:9;*
   15:2
b. up spiritually (A)   *Ro 15:2*
b. up characters (P)   *Ro 15:2*
lest I *b*. on another man's   *Ro 15:20*
foundation
if any *b*. on this foundation, *1Co 3:12*
gold, silver
in ways that *b*. up (A)(N)   *1Co 14:12*
b. up the church (N)   *1Co 14:26*
to *b*. you up (E)(N)(P)(R)   *2Co 10:8*
in order to *b*. you up   *2Co 12:19*
(A)(N)
if I *b*. again things which I   *Ga 2:18*
destroyed
b. up one the other   *1Th 5:11*
(B)(E)(R)

BUILD referred to God

will *b*. him a sure house   *1Sa 2:35;*
   2Sa 7:27; 1Ki 11:38
the Lord will *b*. thee an   *1Ch 17:10*
house
hast told that thou wilt *b*.   *1Ch 17:25*
him an house

he shall destroy, not *b.*   *Ps 28:5*
them up
do good to Sion, *b.* walls of *Ps 51:18*
Jerusalem
for God will *b.* the cities of *Ps 69:35*
Judah
b. up thy throne to all   *Ps 89:4*
generations
when Lord shall *b.* up Zion *Ps 102:16*
except Lord *b.* house, they *Ps 127:1*
labour in vain
Lord doth *b.* up Jerusalem *Ps 147:2*
I speak concerning a nation *Jer 18:9*
to *b.* it
I will *b.* and not pull them *Jer 24:6;*
down   *31:28*
again I will *b.* thee, O virgin *Jer 31:4*
of Israel
I will *b.* Judah and Israel as *Jer 33:7*
at the first
if ye abide in this land I *Jer 42:10*
will *b.* you
I the Lord *b.* the ruined *Eze 36:36*
places
I will *b.* it as in the days of *Am 9:11*
old
on this rock will I *b.* my *M't 16:18*
church
able to *b.* it in three days *M't 26:61;*
                   M'k 14:58
I will *b.* again tabernacle of *Ac 15:16*
David

BUILD *ALTARS*

shalt not *b.* an *altar* of hewn *Ex 20:25*
stone
Balaam said, *b.* me seven *Nu 23:1;*
altars   *23:29*
shalt *b.* an *altar* to the Lord *De 27:5;*
                   27:6
God forbid, we rebel and *b.* *Jos 22:29*
an *altar*

BUILD *HOUSE*

man that will not *b.* brother's *De 25:9*
house
b. an *house*, not dwell in it *De 28:30;*
                 Zep 1:13
which two did *b. house* of *Ru 4:11*
Israel
thou *b.* me an *house* to dwell *2Sa 7:5*
in
why *b.* ye not me a *house* of *2Sa 7:7*
cedar
thy seed *b.* an *house* for my *2Sa 7:13;*
name *1Ki 5:5; 8:19; 1Ch 17:12; 22:10*
b. thee an *house* in *1Ki 2:36*
Jerusalem
David could not *b.* an *house* *1Ki 5:3*
for wars
purpose to *b.* an *house* to *1Ki 5:5;*
Lord   *2Ch 2:1*
I chose no city to *b.* an *1Ki 8:16;*
house   *2Ch 6:5*
was in heart of David to *b.* *1Ki 8:17;*
an *house* for God of Israel *1Ch 28:2;*
                 2Ch 6:7
shall *b.* me an *house* *1Ch 17:12;*
                 2Ch 6:9
not *b.* an *house* because *1Ch 22:8*
shed blood
my son, *b.* the *house* of Lord *1Ch 22:11*
Solomon shall *b.* my *house* *1Ch 28:6*
I *b.* an *house* to Lord my *2Ch 2:4*
God
house I *b.* is great, for great *2Ch 2:5*
is God
b. him an *house? b.* an *house* *2Ch 2:6*
charged me to *b.* him a *2Ch 36:23;*
house   *Ezr 1:2*
go to Jerusalem *b. house* of *Eze 1:3*
Lord
who commanded you to *b.* *Eze 5:3*
this *house*
let the governor of Jews *b.* *Eze 6:7*
this *house*
labour in vain that *b.* the *Ps 127:1*
house
prepare, afterwards *b.* thy *Pr 24:27*
house
shall *b. houses* and inhabit *Isa 65:21*
them
where is the *house* that ye *b.* *Isa 66:1*
unto me?
will *b.* wide *house* and large *Jer 22:14*
chambers
b. houses and dwell in them, *Jer 29:5*
and plant

neither shall ye *b. house* nor *Jer 35:7*
sow seed
say, it is not near, let us *b.* *Eze 11:3*
houses
shall dwell safely, and shall *Eze 28:26*
b. houses
go to mountain, bring wood, *Hag 1:8*
b. house
to *b.* it an *house* in land of *Zec 5:11*
Shinar
what *house* will ye *b.* me *Ac 7:49*

BUILDED

Cain *b.* a city, and called it *Ge 4:17*
Enoch
Noah *b.* an altar to the Lord *Ge 8:20*
Asher *b.* Nineveh, Rehoboth *Ge 10:11*
came to see tower children of *Ge 11:5*
men *b.*
Abram *b.* an altar to Lord *Ge 12:7;*
                  13:18
Isaac *b.* an altar *Ge 26:25*
Moses *b.* an altar under the *Ex 24:4*
hill
in that ye have *b.* an altar *Jos 22:16*
much less this house I have *1Ki 8:27*
b.
the stones wherewith *1Ki 15:22*
Baasha had *b.*
Solomon had *b.* for *2Ki 23:13*
Ashtoreth
house to be *b.* must be *1Ch 22:5*
magnifical
when adversaries heard they *Ezr 4:1*
b.
be it known, if this city be *Ezr 4:13;*
b.   *4:16*
give commandment this city *Ezr 4:21*
be not *b.*
went to house of great God *Ezr 5:8*
which is *b.*
build house that was *b.* *Ezr 5:11*
many years ago
let house of God be *b.* in *Ezr 5:15;*
place   *6:3*
elders of the Jews *b.* and *Ezr 6:14*
they prospered
every one had sword girded, *Ne 4:18*
and *b.*
hath taken away house he *Job 20:19*
b. not
Jerusalem is *b.* a city that is *Ps 122:3*
compact
Wisdom hath *b.* her house *Pr 9:1*
through wisdom is an house *Pr 24:3*
b.
I *b.* me houses, I planted *Ec 2:4*
vineyards
neck like tower of David *Ca 4:4*
city shall be *b.* on her own *Jer 30:18*
heap
hath *b.* against me, and *La 3:5*
compassed me
the wastes shall be *b.* *Eze 36:10;*
                 36:33
they sold, they planted, they *Lu 17:28*
in whom ye are *b.* together *Eph 2:22*
for
who *b.* house hath more *Heb 3:3*
honour
every house is *b.* by some *Heb 3:4*
man

BUILDEDST

give goodly cities thou *b.* not *De 6:10*

BUILDER

whose *b.* and maker is God *Heb 11:10*

BUILDERS

Solomon's *b.* and Hiram's *b.* *1Ki 5:18*
to the carpenters and *b.* *2Ki 12:11*
that
Unto carpenters, and *b.* and *2Ki 22:6*
to the artificers and *b.* gave *2Ch 34:11*
they it
when the *b.* laid the *Ezr 3:10*
foundation
thee to anger before the *b.* *Ne 4:5*
For the *b.* every one had his *Ne 4:18*
the stone which the *b.* *Ps 118:22*
refused

thy *b.* have perfected thy *Eze 27:4*
beauty
The stone which the *b.* *M't 21:42*
rejected
The stone which the *b.* *M'k 12:10*
rejected
The stone which the *b.* *Lu 20:17*
rejected
which was set at nought of *Ac 4:11*
you *b.*
the stone which the *b.* *1Pe 2:7*
disallowed

BUILDEST

When thou *b.* a new house *De 22:8*
which cause thou *b.* the wall *Ne 6:6*
In that thou *b.* thine *Eze 16:31*
eminent
temple and *b.* it in three *M't 27:40*
days
temple, and *b.* it in three *M'k 15:29*
days

BUILDETH

and *b.* this city Jericho: he *Jos 6:26*
shall
he *b.* his house as a moth *Job 27:18*
Every wise woman *b.* her *Pr 14:1*
house
Woe unto him that *b.* his *Jer 22:13*
house
and *b.* temples; and Judah *Ho 8:14*
that *b.* his stories in the *Am 9:6*
heaven
Woe to him that *b.* a town *Hab 2:12*
with
foundation, and another *b.* *1Co 3:10*

BUILDING

in *b.* you an altar beside the *Jos 22:19*
made an end of *b.* his own *1Ki 3:1*
when it was in *b.* *1Ki 6:7;*
                1Ki 6:12, 38
Solomon was *b.* his own *1Ki 7:1*
house
Solomon had finished the *b.* *1Ki 9:1*
of
that he left off *b.* of Ramah *1Ki 15:21*
and had made ready for the *1Ch 28:2*
b.
for the *b.* of the house of *2Ch 3:3*
God
that he left off *b.* of Ramah *2Ch 16:5*
wherewith Baasha was *b.* *2Ch 16:6*
Judah, and troubled them in *2Ch 4:4*
b.
b. the rebellious and the bad *Ezr 4:12*
of the men that make this *b.* *Ezr 5:4*
even until now hath it been *Ezr 5:16*
in *b.*
for the *b.* of this house of *Ezr 6:8*
God
By much slothfulness the *b.* *Ec 10:18*
and *b.* forts, to cut off *Eze 17:17*
many
the breadth of the *b.*, one *Eze 40:5*
reed
Now the *b.* that was *Eze 41:12;*
before the   *Eze 41:13, 15*
before the *b.* toward the *Eze 42:1*
north
and than the middlemost of *Eze 42:5*
the *b.*
therefore the *b.* was *Eze 42:6*
straitened
place, and over against the *Eze 42:10*
b.
there was a row of *b.* *Eze 46:23*
round about
was this temple in *b.* and *Joh 2:20*
wilt
for mutual *b.* up (A)(R) *Ro 14:19*
husbandry, ye are God's *b.* *1Co 3:9*
the *b.* of the community *1Co 10:23*
(N)
b. up faith (P) *1Co 14:3*
we have a *b.* of God, an *2Co 5:1*
house
for *b.* you up (A)(E)(N) *2Co 13:10*
(P)(R)
in whom all the *b.* fitly *Eph 2:21*
framed
b. up itself in love *Eph 4:16*
(A)(E)(N)(R)
that is to say, not of this *b.* *Heb 9:11*

b. up yourselves on your most *Jude 20*
the *b.* of the wall of it was *Re 21:18*
of

BUILDINGS

to shew him the *b.* of the *M't 24:1*
temple
stones and what *b.* are here *M'k 13:1*
him, Seest thou these great *b. M'k 13:2*

BUILT

shall be an heap, not *b. De 13:16*
again
cities that Ahab *b.* are *1Ki 22:39*
written
b. houses for himself (S) *1Ch 15:1*
rest on every side, so they *b. 2Ch 14:7*
they have *b.* thee a *2Ch 20:8*
sanctuary therein
Uzziah *b.* towers in *2Ch 26:9;*
Jerusalem *26:10*
Jotham *b.* in forests castles *2Ch 27:4*
and towers
b. desolate places for *Job 3:14*
themselves
breaketh down, it cannot be *Job 12:14*
b. again
if return to Almighty, shalt *Job 22:23*
be *b.* up
b. his sanctuary like high *Ps 78:69*
palaces
said, mercy shall be *b.* up *Ps 89:2*
for ever
b. tower in midst of his *Isa 5:2*
vineyard
saith to cities of Judah, ye *Isa 44:26*
shall be *b.*
saying to Jerusalem, thou *Isa 44:28*
shalt be *b.*
shall be *b.* in midst of my *Jer 12:16*
people
thou shalt be *b.* O virgin of *Jer 31:4*
Israel
as provocation from day *Jer 32:31*
they *b.* it
which I have *b.* will I break *Jer 45:4*
down
hast *b.* to thee an eminent *Eze 16:24*
place
b. high place at every head *Eze 16:25*
of way
thou shalt be *b.* no more, *Eze 26:14*
saith Lord
is not this great Babylon I *Da 4:30*
have *b.*
street shall be *b.* again and *Da 9:25*
the wall
hands be strong, that temple *Zec 8:9*
be *b.*
dig a winepress, *b.* a *M't 21:33;*
tower *M'k 12:1*
centurion hath *b.* us a *Lu 7:5*
synagogue
if work abide which he *b. 1Co 3:14*
thereon
b. on foundation of the *Eph 2:20*
apostles
rooted and *b.* in him, *Col 2:7*
established
but he that *b.* all things is *Heb 3:4*
God

BUILT *ALTAR*

Abram *b.* an *altar* unto the *Ge 13:18;*
Lord *22:9*
Jacob *b.* there an *altar Ge 35:7*
Moses *b.* an *altar Ex 17:15*
Aaron *b.* an *altar* before calf *Ex 32:5*
Joshua *b.* an *altar* unto the *Jos 8:30*
Lord
Manasseh *b.* there an *altar Jos 22:10;*
22:11, 23
Gideon *b.* an *altar* there *J'g 6:24;*
6:28
Israel *b.* there an *altar J'g 21:4*
Samuel *b.* an *altar* unto the *1Sa 7:17*
Lord
Saul *b.* an *altar* unto the *1Sa 14:35*
Lord
David *b.* there an *altar 2Sa 24:25*
unto the Lord
Solomon *b.* an *altar* unto the *1Ki 9:25*
Lord
Elijah *b.* an *altar* unto the *1Ki 18:32*
Lord
Urijah the priest *b.* an *altar 2Ki 16:11*

BUILT *ALTARS*

Balak *b.* seven *Nu 23:14*
altars
Manasseh *b. altars,* and *2Ki 21:4;*
offered *21:5; 2Ch 33:5, 15*

BUILT *CITIES*

b. for Pharaoh treasure *Ex 1:11*
cities
given you *cities* ye *b.* not *Jos 24:13*
the *cities* which Asa *b. 1Ki 15:23;*
2Ch 14:6
Solomon and Rehoboam *b. 2Ch 8:2;*
cities 11:5
Jehoshaphat, Uzziah and *2Ch 17:12*
Jotham *b. cities 2Ch 26:6; 27:4*

BUILT *CITY*

let the *city* of Sihon be *b. Nu 21:27*
Joshua *b.* the *city* and dwelt *Jos 19:50*
there
Danites *b.* a *city J'g 18:28*
David *b.* a *city* round about *1Ch 11:8*
Millo
a *city* shall be *b.* to the *Jer 31:38*
Lord
to brow of hill whereon *city Lu 4:29*
was *b.*

BUILT *HIGH PLACES*

Judah *b. high places* for *1Ki 14:23*
images
Israel *b. high places* in the *2Ki 17:9*
cities
Manasseh *b. high places 2Ki 21:3;*
2Ch 33:3
b. high places of Tophet *Jer 7:31*

BUILT *HOUSE*

what man hath *b.* a new *De 20:5*
house
no *house b.* to name of the *1Ki 3:2*
Lord
have *b.* an *house* to name *1Ki 8:20;*
of the Lord *1Ki 8:44;*
48; 2Ch 6:18, 34, 38
b. a sure *house,* as I built *1Ki 11:38*
for David
why have ye not *b.* me an *1Ch 17:6*
house
time that Lord's *house* should *Hag 1:2*
be *b.*
my *house* be *b.* in it *Zec 1:16*
wise man *b.* his *house* on a *M't 7:24;*
rock *Lu 6:48*
foolish man *b.* his *house* on *M't 7:26;*
sand *Lu 6:49*
Solomon *b.* him an *house Ac 7:47*
ye also are *b.* up a spiritual *1Pe 2:5*
house

BUILT *HOUSES*

when thou hast *b.* goodly *De 8:12*
houses
ye have *b. houses* of hewn *Am 5:11*
stone

BUILT *WALL*

Solomon *b.* the *walls* of *1Ki 6:15*
house
on *walls* of Ophel he *b. 2Ch 27:3*
much
Hezekiah *b.* up *wall* that *2Ch 32:5*
was broken
Manasseh *b. wall* without *2Ch 33:14*
city of David
so *b.* we the *wall Ne 4:6*
one *b.* up *wall,* another *Eze 13:10*
daubed it
street shall be *b.* again and *Da 9:25*
wall
in day that thy *walls* are to *Mic 7:11*
be *b.*

BUKKI

of Dan, *B.* the son of Jogli *Nu 34:22*
Abishua begat *B.* and *B. 1Ch 6:5*
begat
B. his son, Uzzi his son, *1Ch 6:51*
Zerahiah
the son of Uzzi, the son of *B. Ezr 7:4*

BUKKIAH

B. Mattaniah, Uzziel, *1Ch 25:4*
Shebuel
The sixth to *B.* he, his sons *1Ch 25:13*

BUL

in the month *B.* which is the *1Ki 6:38*

BULGING

flasks and *b.* bottles (A) *Isa 22:24*

BULL

Their *b.* gendereth, and *Job 21:10*
faileth
as a wild *b.* in a net: they *Isa 51:20*
are

BULLOCK

Take one young *b.* and two *Ex 29:1*
rams *Ex 29:3, 10-12, 14, 36*
kill *b.* before Lord *Le 1:5;*
Le 4:4, 15; 16:11; Ex 29:11
young *b.* without blemish *Le 4:3;*
Le 4:14; 16:3; Nu 7:15, 21, 27, 33, 39,
45, 51, 57, 63, 69, 75, 81; 2Ch 13:9;
Eze 45:18; 46:6
take blood of *b. Le 4:7;*
Le 16:14, 15, 18
b. for a sin offering *Le 4:8;*
Le 8:2, 14; 16:3, 6, 11, 27; Eze 43:19,
21
the whole *b.* shall he carry *Le 4:12;*
4:21
burn him as he burned the *Le 4:21*
first *b.*
hands upon the head of the *b. Le 8:14*
b. and ram for peace offering *Le 9:4;*
9:18-19
Aaron shall bring the *b.* and *Le 16:11*
kill
Either a *b.* or a *Le 22:23;*
lamb *Le 22:27; 23:18*
with a *b.* a meat offering *Nu 15:9;*
Nu 15:11; 28:12, 14, 20, 28; 29:2-3, 8-9,
14, 36-37
b. for a burnt offering *Nu 15:24*
offered on every altar a *b. Nu 23:2*
offered upon every altar a *b. Nu 23:4*
offered *b.* and ram on *Nu 23:14;*
Nu 23:30
mingled with oil, for one *b. Nu 28:12*
half an hin of wine unto a *Nu 28:14*
b. and
tenth deals shall ye offer for *Nu 28:20*
a *b.*
three tenth deals unto one *Nu 28:28*
b. two
one young *b.,* one ram, and *Nu 29:2*
seven
three tenth deals for a *b.,* and *Nu 29:3*
two
for a sweet savour; one *Nu 29:8*
young *b.*
three tenth deals to a *b.* and *Nu 29:9*
two
deals unto every *b.* of the *Nu 29:14*
thirteen
one *b.,* one ram, seven lambs *Nu 29:36*
of
for the *b.,* for the ram, and *Nu 29:37*
the firstling of thy *b.* nor *De 15:19*
shear
any *b.* or sheep, wherein is *De 17:1*
like the firstling of his *b. De 33:17*
and his
Take thy father's young *b. J'g 6:25*
even the second *b.* of seven *J'g 6:25*
years
and take the second *b.* and *J'g 6:26*
offer
the second *b.* was offered *J'g 6:28*
upon the
And they slew a *b.* and *1Sa 1:25*
brought
and let them choose one *b. 1Ki 18:23*
for
and I will dress the other *b. 1Ki 18:23*
Choose you one *b.* for *1Ki 18:25*
yourselves
they took the *b.* which was *1Ki 18:26*
given
and cut the *b.* in pieces; *1Ki 18:33*
and laid
consecrate himself with a *2Ch 13:9*
young *b.*

I will take no b. out of thy house   *Ps 50:9*
or b. that hath horns and hoofs   *Ps 69:31*
lion shall eat straw like the b.   *Isa 65:25*
a b. unaccustomed to the yoke   *Jer 31:18*
a young b. for a sin offering   *Eze 43:19*
take the b. also of the sin offering   *Eze 43:21*
as they did cleanse it with the b.   *Eze 43:22*
offer a young b. without blemish   *Eze 43:23*
they shall also prepare a young b.   *Eze 43:25*
take a young b. without blemish   *Eze 45:18*
for all the people of the land a b.   *Eze 45:22*
an ephah for a b. and an ephah   *Eze 45:24*
a young b. without blemish   *Eze 46:6*
an ephah for a b. and an ephah   *Eze 46:7*
shall be an ephah to a b.   *Eze 46:11*

BULLOCKS

were twelve b. the rams twelve   *Nu 7:87*
were twenty and four b. the rams   *Nu 7:88*
upon the heads of the b.   *Nu 8:12*
prepare me here seven b.   *Nu 23:29*
unto the Lord; two young b.   *Nu 28:11*
two young b. and one ram   *Nu 28:19*
unto the Lord; two young b.   *Nu 28:27*
thirteen young b. two rams   *Nu 29:13*
every bullock of the thirteen b.   *Nu 29:14*
ye shall offer twelve young b.   *Nu 29:17*
their drink offerings for the b.   *Nu 29:18*
the third day eleven b. two rams   *Nu 29:20*
for the b. for the rams, and for   *Nu 29:21*
on the fourth day ten b. two rams   *Nu 29:23*
drink offerings for the b. for   *Nu 29:24*
And on the fifth day nine b., two   *Nu 29:26*
offerings for the b. for the rams   *Nu 29:27*
on the sixth day eight b. two   *Nu 29:29*
b. for the rams, and for the lambs   *Nu 29:30*
And on the seventh day seven b.   *Nu 29:32*
and their drink offerings for the b.   *Nu 29:33*
him up with her, with three b.   *1Sa 1:24*
them therefore give us two b.   *1Ki 18:23*
they offered seven b. and seven   *1Ch 15:26*
a thousand b. a thousand rams   *1Ch 29:21*
they brought seven b. and seven   *2Ch 29:21*
they killed the b. and the priests   *2Ch 29:22*
threescore and ten b. an hundred   *2Ch 29:32*
thousand b. and seven thousand   *2Ch 30:24*
to the congregation a thousand b.   *2Ch 30:24*
three thousand b.; these were   *2Ch 35:7*
both young b. and rams, and   *Ezr 6:9*
an hundred b. two hundred rams   *Ezr 6:17*
buy speedily with this money b.   *Ezr 7:17*
twelve b. for all Israel, ninety   *Ezr 8:35*
take unto you now seven b.   *Job 42:8*
then shall they offer b. upon thine   *Ps 51:19*
I will offer b. with goats   *Ps 66:15*
I delight not in the blood of b.   *Isa 1:11*
and the b. with the bulls   *Isa 34:7*

in the midst of her like fatted b.   *Jer 46:21*
Slay all her b.; let them go down   *Jer 50:27*
of lambs, and of goats, of b. all of   *Eze 39:18*
seven b. and seven rams without   *Eze 45:23*
they sacrifice b. in Gilgal; yea   *Ho 12:11*

BULLOCK'S

his hand upon the b. head   *Le 4:4*
shall take of the b. blood   *Le 4:5*
anointed, shall bring of the b.   *Le 4:16*

BULLS

forty kine, and ten b., twenty   *Ge 32:15*
Many b. have compassed me   *Ps 22:12*
strong b. of Bashan have beset me   *Ps 22:12*
Will I eat the flesh of b., or drink   *Ps 50:13*
the multitude of the b. with   *Ps 68:30*
the bullocks with the b.; and their   *Isa 34:7*
heifer at grass, and bellow as b.   *Jer 50:11*
and twelve brasen b. that were   *Jer 52:20*
if the blood of b. and of goats   *Heb 9:13*
not possible that the blood of b.   *Heb 10:4*

BULLY

Don't b. people (P)   *Lu 3:14*

BULLYING

no b., no blackmail (N)   *Lu 3:14*

BULRUSH

bow down his head as a b.   *Isa 58:5*
bow down his head like a rush (B)(E)(R)   *Isa 58:5*

BULRUSHES

took for him an ark of b.   *Ex 2:3*
got for him a reed basket (B)   *Ex 2:3*
in vessels of b. upon the waters   *Isa 18:2*
vessels of papyrus (A)(B)(E)(R)   *Isa 18:2*

BULWARK

founded a b. (R)   *Ps 8:2*

BULWARKS

shalt build b. against the city   *De 20:20*
build siege works (B)(R)   *De 20:20*
be on the towers and upon the b.   *2Ch 26:15*
Mark ye well her b.   *Ps 48:13*
built great b. against it   *Ec 9:14*
building great siege-works (R)   *Ec 9:14*
will God appoint for walls and b.   *Isa 26:1*

BUNAH

Ram the firstborn, and B.   *1Ch 2:25*

BUNCH

ye shall take a b. of hyssop   *Ex 12:22*

BUNCHES

an hundred b. of raisins   *2Sa 16:1*
cakes of figs, and b. of raisins   *1Ch 12:40*
upon the b. of camels, to a   *Isa 30:6*
on the humps of their camels (A)(B)(R)(S)   *Isa 30:6*

BUNDLE

every man's b. of money was in   *Ge 42:35*
bound in the b. of life with   *1Sa 25:29*

A b. of myrrh is my well-beloved   *Ca 1:13*
gathered a b. of sticks, and laid   *Ac 28:3*

BUNDLES

their father saw the b. of money   *Ge 42:35*
bind them in b. to burn them   *M't 13:30*

BUNNI

Shebaniah, B. Sherebiah, Bani   *Ne 9:4*
B. Azgad, Bebai   *Ne 10:15*
son of Hashabiah, the son of B.   *Ne 11:15*

BURDEN

they shall bear the b. with thee   *Ex 18:22*
lying under his b. and wouldest   *Ex 23:5*
the b. of the sons of Kohath in the   *Nu 4:15*
one to his service and to his b.   *Nu 4:19*
And this is the charge of their b.   *Nu 4:31*
of the charge of their b.   *Nu 4:32*
service of the b. in the tabernacle   *Nu 4:47*
according to his b.: thus were they   *Nu 4:49*
the b. of all this people upon me   *Nu 11:11*
they shall bear the b. of the people   *Nu 11:17*
and your b., and your strife   *De 1:12*
then thou shalt be a b. unto me   *2Sa 15:33*
should thy servant be yet a b.   *2Sa 19:35*
my father did b. (S)   *1Ki 12:11*
servant two mules' b. of earth   *2Ki 5:17*
forty camels' b. and came and   *2Ki 8:9*
the Lord laid this b. upon him   *2Ki 9:25*
not be a b. upon your shoulders   *2Ch 35:3*
there should no b. be brought in   *Ne 13:19*
so that I am a b. to myself   *Job 7:20*
as an heavy b. they are too heavy   *Ps 38:4*
Cast thy b. upon the Lord, and he   *Ps 55:22*
heavy b. upon loins (A)(B)(E)   *Ps 66:11*
removed his shoulder from the b.   *Ps 81:6*
and the grasshopper shall be a b.   *Ec 12:5*
they were an oppressive b. (A)(B)(R)   *Isa 1:14*
broken the yoke of his b. and   *Isa 9:4*
his b. shall be taken away from off   *Isa 10:27*
The b. of Babylon, which Isaiah   *Isa 13:1*
and his b. depart from off their   *Isa 14:25*
that king Ahaz died was this b.   *Isa 14:28*
The b. of Moab. Because in   *Isa 15:1*
The b. of Damascus. Behold   *Isa 17:1*
The b. of Egypt. Behold, the Lord   *Isa 19:1*
The b. of the desert of the sea   *Isa 21:1*
The b. of Dumah. He calleth to   *Isa 21:11*
The b. upon Arabia. In the forest   *Isa 21:13*
The b. of the valley of vision   *Isa 22:1*
fall; and the b. that was upon it   *Isa 22:25*
The b. of Tyre. Howl, ye ships   *Isa 23:1*
The b. of the beasts of the south   *Isa 30:6*
the b. thereof is heavy: his lips   *Isa 30:27*
they are a b. to the weary beast   *Isa 46:1*
they could not deliver the b. but   *Isa 46:2*

The *b.* of the word of the Lord *Zec 9:1* in

The *b.* of the word of the   *Zec 12:1* Lord

all that *b.* themselves with it *Zec 12:3*

The *b.* of the word of the   *Mal 1:1* Lord to

yoke is easy, and my *b.* is   *M't 11:30* light

which have borne the *b.*   *M't 20:12* and heat

upon you no greater *b.* than   *Ac 15:28* these

the ship was to unlade her *b.*   *Ac 21:3*

may not *b.* your (S)   *2Co 2:5*

I did not *b.* you: *2Co 12:16* nevertheless

every man shall bear his own   *Ga 6:5* *b.*

sharing *b.* of God's people   *Heb 11:25* (P)

will put upon you none   *Re 2:24* other *b.*

BURDENED

our oxen well *b.* (B)   *Ps 144:14*

b. me (S)   *Isa 43:24*

do groan, being *b.*: not for   *2Co 5:4* that

other men be eased, and ye   *2Co 8:13* *b.*

BURDENS

crouching down between two   *Ge 49:14* *b.*

to afflict them with their *b.*   *Ex 1:11*

looked on their *b.*: and he   *Ex 2:11* spied

their works? get you into your   *Ex 5:4* *b.*

ye make them rest from their   *Ex 5:5* *b.*

from under the *b.* of the   *Ex 6:6* Egyptians

bringeth you out from under   *Ex 6:7* the *b.*

Gershonites, to serve, and for   *Nu 4:24* *b.*

the Gershonites, in all their   *Nu 4:27* *b.*

unto them in charge all their   *Nu 4:27* *b.*

and ten thousand that bare   *1Ki 5:15* *b.*

ten thousand men to bear *b.*   *2Ch 2:2*

to be bearers of *b.* and   *2Ch 2:18* fourscore

the greatness of the *b.* laid   *2Ch 24:27* upon

over the bearers of *b.* and   *2Ch 34:13* were

The strength of the bearers   *Ne 4:10* of *b.*

and they that bare *b.* with   *Ne 4:17* those

all manner of *b.* which they   *Ne 13:15* bears

b. and carries us   *Ps 68:19* (A)(B)(E)

to undo the heavy *b.* and to   *Isa 58:6*

false *b.* and causes of   *La 2:14* banishment

ye take from him *b.* of   *Am 5:11* wheat

For they bind heavy *b.* and   *M't 23:4*

with *b.* grievous to be borne   *Lu 11:46*

ye yourselves touch not the   *Lu 11:46* *b.*

Bear ye one another's *b.* and   *Ga 6:2*

BURDENSOME

lest we be *b.* (S)   *1Sa 13:25*

will I make Jerusalem a *b.*   *Zec 12:3* stone

kept myself from being *b.*   *2Co 11:9* unto

I myself was not *b.* to you   *2Co 12:13*

I will not be *b.* to you: for   *2Co 12:14* I seek

we might have been *b.* as the   *1Th 2:6*

orders are not *b.*   *1Jo 5:3* (A)(N)(P)(R)(S)

BURGLARY

catch them in *b.* (B)   *Jer 2:34*

BURIAL

in the field of the *b.* which   *2Ch 26:23*

good, and also that ye have no   *Ec 6:3* *b.*

not be joined with them in   *Isa 14:20* *b.*

with the *b.* of an ass, drawn   *Jer 22:19*

b. place (R)(S)   *Jer 26:23*

for *b.* in Israel   *Eze 39:1* (A)(B)(E)(R)

my body, she did it for my   *M't 26:12* *b.*

for the *b.* (S)   *M'k 14:8; Joh 12:7*

men carried Stephen to his *b.*   *Ac 8:2*

refuse them *b.* (N)(P)   *Re 11:9*

BURIED

thou shalt be *b.* in a good   *Ge 15:15* old age

Abraham *b.* Sarah his wife   *Ge 23:19* in the

his sons Isaac and Ishmael *b.*   *Ge 25:9* him

there was Abraham *b.* and   *Ge 25:10* Sarah

nurse died, and she was *b.*   *Ge 35:8*

Rachel died, and was *b.* in   *Ge 35:19*

his sons Esau and Jacob *b.*   *Ge 35:29* him

and I *b.* her there in the way   *Ge 48:7* of

There they *b.* Abraham and   *Ge 49:31* Sarah

there they *b.* Isaac and   *Ge 49:31* Rebekah

and there I *b.* Leah   *Ge 49:31*

and *b.* him in the cave of   *Ge 50:13* the field

after he had *b.* his father   *Ge 50:14*

because there they *b.* the   *Nu 11:34* people

Miriam died there, and was   *Nu 20:1* *b.*

For the Egyptians *b.* all their *Nu 33:4*

Aaron died, and there he was   *De 10:6* *b.*

And he *b.* him in a valley in   *De 34:6*

And they *b.* him in the   *Jos 24:30* border of

b. they in Shechem, in a   *Jos 24:32* parcel

and they *b.* him in a hill   *Jos 24:33* that

And they *b.* him in the border   *J'g 2:9* of

died in a good old age, and was   *J'g 8:32* *b.*

and died, and was *b.* in   *J'g 10:2* Shamir

Jair died, and was *b.* in   *J'g 10:5* Camon

the Gileadite, and was *b.* in   *J'g 12:7* one of

Ibzan, and was *b.* at   *J'g 12:10* Beth-lehem

died, and was *b.* in Aijalon   *J'g 12:12*

died, and was *b.* in Pirathon   *J'g 12:15*

b. him between Zorah and   *J'g 16:31* Eshtaol

and there will I be *b.*: the   *Ru 1:17* Lord

and *b.* him in his house at   *1Sa 25:1* Ramah

and *b.* him in Ramah, even   *1Sa 28:3* in

b. them under a tree at   *1Sa 31:13* Jabesh

Jabesh-gilead were they that   *2Sa 2:4* *b.*

even unto Saul, and have *b.*   *2Sa 2:5* him

and *b.* him in the sepulchre   *2Sa 2:32* of his

And they *b.* Abner in   *2Sa 3:32* Hebron

head of Ish-bosheth, and *b.*   *2Sa 4:12* it

and was *b.* in the sepulchre   *2Sa 17:23* of his

be *b.* by the grave of my   *2Sa 19:37* father

and Jonathan his son *b.*   *2Sa 21:14* they

slept with his fathers, and   *1Ki 2:10* was *b.*

and he was *b.* in his own   *1Ki 2:34* house

slept with his fathers, and   *1Ki 11:43* was *b.*

after he had *b.* him, that he   *1Ki 13:31* spake

wherein the man of God is   *1Ki 13:31* *b.*

And they *b.* him; and all   *1Ki 14:18* Israel

slept with his fathers, and   *1Ki 14:31* was *b.*

they *b.* him in the city of   *1Ki 15:8* David

slept with his fathers, and   *1Ki 15:24* was *b.*

with his fathers, and was *b.* in *1Ki 16:6;*
                                  16:28

and they *b.* the king in   *1Ki 22:37* Samaria

slept with his fathers, and   *1Ki 22:50* was *b.*

slept with his fathers, and   *2Ki 8:24* was *b.*

and *b.* him in his sepulchre   *2Ki 9:28* with

fathers: and they *b.* him in   *2Ki 10:35*

and they *b.* him with his   *2Ki 12:21* fathers

and they *b.* him in Samaria   *2Ki 13:9*

and Joash was *b.* in   *2Ki 13:13* Samaria with

And Elisha died, and they   *2Ki 13:20* *b.* him

slept with his fathers, and   *2Ki 14:16* was *b.*

and he was *b.* at Jerusalem   *2Ki 14:20* with

and they *b.* him with his   *2Ki 15:7* fathers

slept with his fathers, and   *2Ki 15:38* was *b.*

slept with his fathers, and   *2Ki 16:20* was *b.*

slept with his fathers, and   *2Ki 21:18* was *b.*

And he was *b.* in his   *2Ki 21:26* sepulchre

and *b.* him in his own   *2Ki 23:30* sepulchre

and *b.* their bones under   *1Ch 10:12* the oak

and he was *b.* in the city of   *2Ch 9:31* David

slept with his fathers, and   *2Ch 12:16* was *b.*

they *b.* him in the city of   *2Ch 14:1* David

b. him in his own   *2Ch 16:14* sepulchres

slept with his fathers, and   *2Ch 21:1* was *b.*

Howbeit they *b.* him in the   *2Ch 21:20* city of

they had slain him, they *b.*   *2Ch 22:9* him

they *b.* him in the city of   *2Ch 24:16* David

and they *b.* him in the city   *2Ch 24:25* of David

they *b.* him not in the   *2Ch 24:25* sepulchres

and *b.* him with his fathers   *2Ch 25:28* in the

b. him with his fathers in   *2Ch 26:23* the field

they *b.* him in the city of   *2Ch 27:9* David

and they *b.* him in the city,   *2Ch 28:27* even

and they *b.* him in the   *2Ch 32:33* chiefest of

and they *b.* him in his own   *2Ch 33:20* house

and was *b.* in one of the   *2Ch 35:24* sepulchres

remain of him shall be *b.*   *Job 27:15* in death

And so I saw the wicked *b.*   *Ec 8:10* who

shall not be gathered, nor be   *Jer 8:2* *b.*

lamented; neither shall they   *Jer 16:4* be *b.*

they shall not be *b.* neither   *Jer 16:6* shall

thou shalt die, and shalt be *b.* *Jer 20:6*

He shall be *b.* with the   *Jer 22:19* burial of an

lamented, neither gathered,   *Jer 25:33* nor *b.*

till the buriers have *b*. it in   *Eze 39:15*
and *b*. it, and went and   *M't 14:12*
told Jesus
rich man also died, and was   *Lu 16:22*
b.
those dead and *b*. (P)   *Joh 5:28*
he is both dead and *b*. and   *Ac 2:29*
his
and carried him out, and *b*.   *Ac 5:6*
him
the feet of them which have *b*.   *Ac 5:9*
thy
carrying her forth, *b*. her by   *Ac 5:10*
her
we are *b*. with him by baptism   *Ro 6:4*
And that he was *b*. and that   *1Co 15:4*
he
B. with him in baptism,   *Col 2:12*
wherein

BURIERS

till the *b*. have buried it in   *Eze 39:15*

BURN

let us make brick and *b*.   *Ge 11:3*
them
anger *b*.   *Ge 44:18*
b. with fire   *Ex 12:10; 29:14,*
34; Le 8:32; De 13:16; Jos 11:6, 13;
J'g 9:52; Jer 34:22; 37:8, 10; 38:18;
43:13; Eze 5:2; 39:9-10; Na 2:13
my wrath shall *b*.   *Ex 22:24;*
(A)(B)(R)(S)   *Ex 32:10*
lamp to *b*. always   *Ex 27:20; Le 24:2*
b. upon the altar   *Ex 29:13;*
29:18, 25; Le 1:9, 13, 17; 2:9; 3:5,
11, 16; 4:10, 12, 19, 31, 35; 5:12; 6:12,
15; 7:5; 16:25; Nu 5:26; 2Ki 16:15;
Ne 10:34
b. incense   *Ex 30:1; 30:7-8;*
1Sa 2:28; 1Ki 13:1-2; 2Ki 18:4; 23:5;
1Ch 23:13; 2Ch 2:4; 13:11; 26:16, 18-19;
28:25; 29:11; 32:12; Jer 7:9; 11:13;
44:3, 5, 17-18, 25; Ho 4:13; Hab 1:16;
Lu 1:9
b. offering made by fire   *Ex 30:20*
anger *b*. (S)   *Ex 32:10; 32:11, 22*
b. the memorial   *Le 2:2; 2:16*
ye shall *b*. no leaven   *Le 2:11*
b. without the camp   *Le 4:21; 16:27*
b. the fat   *Le 6:12;*
7:31; 17:6; Nu 18:17; 1Sa 2:16
b. that garment   *Le 13:52; 13:55, 57*
one shall *b*. the heifer   *Nu 19:5*
mountain did *b*. with fire   *De 5:23*
b. graven images   *De 7:5; 7:25; 12:3*
b. their sacred trees (B)   *De 12:3*
b. their Asherim (A)(E)(R)   *De 12:3*
b. unto the lowest hell   *De 32:32*
will *b*. thine house upon thee   *J'g 12:1*
lest we *b*. thee and thy   *J'g 14:15*
father's house
shall thy jealousy *b*. like fire   *Ps 79:5*
wrath *b*. like fire   *Ps 89:46;*
Jer 15:14; 17:4
and they shall both *b*.   *Isa 1:31*
together
and it shall *b*. and devour   *Isa 10:17*
his
I would *b*. them together   *Isa 27:4*
Lebanon is not sufficient to   *Isa 40:16*
b.
shall it be for a man to *b*.:   *Isa 44:15*
for he
the fire shall *b*. them; they   *Isa 47:14*
shall
and *b*. that none can quench   *Jer 4:4*
it
and it shall *b*. and shall not   *Jer 7:20*
be
b. their sons and their   *Jer 7:31*
daughters
to *b*. their sons with fire for   *Jer 19:5*
and he shall *b*. it with fire   *Jer 21:10*
and *b*. that none can quench   *Jer 21:12*
it
and *b*. it with the houses,   *Jer 32:29*
upon
b. cereal offerings, oblations   *Jer 33:18*
(A)(B)(E)(R)
and he shall *b*. it with fire   *Jer 34:2*
so shall they *b*. odours for   *Jer 34:5*
thee
that he would not *b*. the roll   *Jer 36:25*
Thou shalt *b*. with fire a third   *Eze 5:2*
and *b*. them in the fire; for   *Eze 5:4*
And they shall *b*. thine   *Eze 16:41*
houses

and *b*. up their houses with   *Eze 23:47*
fire
b. also the bones under it   *Eze 24:5*
may be hot, and may *b*.   *Eze 24:11*
to *b*. you up (B)   *Eze 28:18*
set on fire and *b*. the   *Eze 39:9*
weapons
and he shall *b*. it in the   *Eze 43:21*
appointed
b. with rage (B)   *Da 11:30*
and I will *b*. her chariots in   *Na 2:13*
and *b*. incense unto their   *Hab 1:16*
drag
that shall *b*. as an oven; and   *Mal 4:1*
all
and the day that cometh shall   *Mal 4:1*
b.
but he will *b*. up the chaff   *M't 3:12*
with
bind them in bundles to   *M't 13:30*
b.
his lot was to *b*. incense when   *Lu 1:9*
but the chaff he will *b*. with   *Lu 3:17*
fire
Did not our heart *b*. within   *Lu 24:32*
us
it is better to marry than to   *1Co 7:9*
b.
who is offended, and I *b*.   *2Co 11:29*
not
and *b*. her with fire   *Re 17:16*

BURNED

the bush *b*. with fire, and the   *Ex 3:2*
anger *b*. (S)   *Ex 32:19*
him as he *b*. the first bullock   *Le 4:21*
and Moses *b*. it upon the   *Le 8:16*
altar
the mountain *b*. with fire   *De 4:11*
unto
and the mount *b*. with fire   *De 9:15*
and *b*. them with fire, after   *Jos 7:25*
israel *b*. none of them, save   *Jos 11:13*
Hazor
Ziklag, and *b*. it with fire   *1Sa 30:1*
behold, it was *b*. with fire   *1Sa 30:3*
Caleb; and we *b*. Ziklag   *1Sa 30:14*
with fire
and David and his men *b*.   *2Sa 5:21*
them
they shall be utterly *b*. with   *2Sa 23:7*
fire
the house of Baal, and *b*.   *2Ki 10:26*
them
b. incense still in the high   *2Ki 15:35*
places
have *b*. incense unto other   *2Ki 22:17*
gods
he *b*. them without   *2Ki 23:4*
Jerusalem
also that *b*. incense unto   *2Ki 23:5*
Baal
and *b*. it at the brook   *2Ki 23:6*
Kidron
where the priest had *b*.   *2Ki 23:8*
incense
and *b*. the chariots of the   *2Ki 23:11*
sun
to powder, and *b*. the grove   *2Ki 23:15*
and *b*. them upon the altar   *2Ki 23:16*
and *b*. men's bones upon   *2Ki 23:20*
them
and they were *b*. with fire   *1Ch 14:12*
them, *b*. incense unto them   *2Ch 25:14*
have not *b*. incense nor   *2Ch 29:7*
offered
have *b*. incense unto other   *2Ch 34:25*
gods
gates thereof are *b*. with fire   *Ne 1:3*
and the gates thereof are *b*.   *Ne 2:17*
with
heaps of rubbish which are *b*.   *Ne 4:2*
wroth, and his anger *b*. in   *Es 1:12*
him
and hath *b*. up the sheep   *Job 1:16*
and my bones are *b*. with   *Job 30:30*
heat
while I was musing the fire *b*.   *Ps 39:3*
have *b*. up all the synagogues   *Ps 74:8*
It is *b*. with fire, it is cut   *Ps 80:16*
down
and my bones are *b*. as an   *Ps 102:3*
hearth
the flame *b*. up the wicked   *Ps 106:18*
and his clothes not be *b*.   *Pr 6:27*
hot coals, and his feet not be   *Pr 6:28*
b.
your cities are *b*. with fire: *Isa 1:7*
your

inhabitants of the earth are   *Isa 24:6*
b.
as thorns cut up shall they   *Isa 33:12*
be *b*.
and it *b*. him, yet he laid it   *Isa 42:25*
not
thou shalt not be *b*.; neither   *Isa 43:2*
you shall not be *b*. (B)   *Isa 43:2*
I have *b*. part of it in the   *Isa 44:19*
fire
is *b*. up with fire: and all   *Isa 64:11*
our
b. incense upon the mountains   *Isa 65:7*
have *b*. incense unto other   *Jer 1:16*
gods
cities are *b*. without   *Jer 2:15*
inhabitant
The bellows are *b*. the lead is   *Jer 6:29*
they are *b*. up, so that none   *Jer 9:10*
can
the land perisheth and is *b*.   *Jer 9:12*
up
they have *b*. incense to   *Jer 18:15*
vanity
b. incense in it unto other   *Jer 19:4*
gods
they have *b*. incense unto all   *Jer 19:13*
after that the king had *b*.   *Jer 36:27*
the roll
the king of Judah hath *b*.   *Jer 36:28*
Thou hast *b*. this roll,   *Jer 36:29*
saying
Jehoiakim king of Judah   *Jer 36:32*
had *b*.
this city shall not be *b*. with   *Jer 38:17*
fire
cause this city to be *b*. with   *Jer 38:23*
fire
the Chaldeans *b*. the king's   *Jer 39:8*
house
wives had *b*. incense unto   *Jer 44:15*
other
b. incense to the queen of   *Jer 44:19*
heaven
that ye *b*. in the cities of   *Jer 44:21*
Judah
Because ye have *b*. incense   *Jer 44:23*
her daughters shall be *b*. with   *Jer 49:2*
fire
they have *b*. her   *Jer 51:30*
dwellingplaces
the reeds they have *b*. with   *Jer 51:32*
fire
high gates shall be *b*. with   *Jer 51:58*
fire
And *b*. the house of the   *Jer 52:13*
Lord
of the great men, *b*. he with   *Jer 52:13*
fire
he *b*. against Jacob like a   *La 2:3*
flaming
of it, and the midst of it is   *Eze 15:4*
b.
fire hath devoured it, and it is   *Eze 15:5*
b.
the south to the north shall   *Eze 20:47*
be *b*.
it well, and let the bones be   *Eze 24:10*
b.
all impurities *b*. up (B)   *Eze 24:11*
wherein she *b*. incense to   *Ho 2:13*
them
and *b*. incense to graven   *Ho 11:2*
images
the flame hath *b*. all the   *Joe 1:19*
trees of
b. the bones of the king of   *Am 2:1*
Edom
the hires thereof shall be *b*.   *Mic 1:7*
with
the earth is *b*. at his presence   *Na 1:5*
the tares are gathered and   *M't 13:40*
b. in
murderers, and *b*. up their   *M't 22:7*
city
into the fire, and they are *b*.   *Joh 15:6*
and *b*. them before all men   *Ac 19:19*
b. in their lust one toward   *Ro 1:27*
If any man's work shall be *b*.   *1Co 3:15*
b. he
I give my body to be *b*. and   *1Co 13:3*
have
cursing, whose end is to be   *Heb 6:8*
b.
and that *b*. with fire, nor   *Heb 12:18*
unto
high priest for sin, are *b*.   *Heb 13:11*
without
works that are therein shall   *2Pe 3:10*
be *b*.

as if they *b.* in a furnace;   *Re 1:15*
and his
she shall be utterly *b.* with   *Re 18:8*
fire

BURNETH

that *b.* have a white bright   *Le 13:24*
spot
And he that *b.* them shall   *Le 16:28*
wash
And he that *b.* her shall   *Nu 19:8*
wash his
he *b.* the chariot in the fire   *Ps 46:9*
As the fire *b.* a wood, and   *Ps 83:14*
as the
A fire goeth before him, and   *Ps 97:3*
b. up
For wickedness *b.* as a fire: *Isa 9:18*
it shall
He *b.* part thereof in the   *Isa 44:16*
fire
thereof as a lamp that *b.*   *Isa 62:1*
As when the melting fire *b.*   *Isa 64:2*
b. incense upon altars of   *Isa 65:3*
brick
nose, a fire that *b.* all the   *Isa 65:5*
day
he that *b.* incense, as if he   *Isa 66:3*
and him that *b.* incense to   *Jer 48:35*
his gods
in the morning it *b.* as a   *Ho 7:6*
flaming
behind them a flame *b.*: the   *Joe 2:3*
land
that *b.* him, to bring out the   *Am 6:10*
bones
in the lake which *b.* with fire   *Re 21:8*

BURNING

a *b.* lamp that passed   *Ge 15:17*
between
B. for *b.*, wound for wound   *Ex 21:25*
because of the *b.* upon the   *Le 6:9*
altar
the fire of the altar shall be *b.*   *Le 6:9*
in
the fire upon the altar shall   *Le 6:12*
be *b.*
The fire shall ever be *b.* upon   *Le 6:13*
b. which the Lord hath   *Le 10:6*
kindled
it is a *b.* boil; and the priest   *Le 13:23*
skin thereof there is a hot *b.*   *Le 13:24*
a leprosy broken out of the   *Le 13:25*
b.
a rising of the *b.* and the   *Le 13:28*
priest
it is an inflammation of the   *Le 13:28*
b.
shall take a censer full of *b.*   *Le 16:12*
coals
consumption, and the *b.*   *Le 26:16*
ague
the *b.* fever (B)   *Le 26:16*
take up the censers out of   *Nu 16:37*
the *b.*
cast it into the midst of the   *Nu 19:6*
b. of
and with an extreme *b.* and   *De 28:22*
with
brimstone, and salt, and *b.*   *De 29:23*
that
devoured with *b.* heat, and   *De 32:24*
with
they made a very great *b.*   *2Ch 16:14*
for him
his people made no *b.* for   *2Ch 21:19*
him
like the *b.* of his fathers   *2Ch 21:19*
Out of his mouth go *b.*   *Job 41:19*
lamps
feeled with *b.* (E)(R)   *Ps 38:7*
Let *b.* coals fall upon them: *Ps 140:10*
let
in his lips there is as a *b.*   *Pr 16:27*
fire
As coals are to *b.* coals, and   *Pr 26:21*
B. lips and a wicked heart   *Pr 26:23*
are
and *b.* instead of beauty   *Isa 3:24*
and by the spirit of *b.*   *Isa 4:4*
but this shall be with *b.* and   *Isa 9:5*
fuel
kindle a *b.* like the *b.* of a   *Isa 10:16*
b. with his anger, and the   *Isa 30:27*
burden

land thereof shall become *b.*   *Isa 34:9*
pitch
was in mine heart as a *b.* fire   *Jer 20:9*
fire on the hearth *b.* before   *Jer 36:22*
him
b. incense unto other gods in   *Jer 44:8*
like *b.* coals of fire, and like   *Eze 1:13*
into the midst of a *b.* fiery   *Da 3:6*
furnace
should be cast into the midst   *Da 3:11*
of a *b.*
same hour into the midst of   *Da 3:15*
a *b.*
able to deliver us from the *b.*   *Da 3:17*
fiery
cast them into the *b.* fiery   *Da 3:20*
furnace
the midst of the *b.* fiery   *Da 3:21;*
furnace   *Da 3:23*
to the mouth of the *b.* fiery   *Da 3:26*
furnace
flame, and his wheels as *b.* fire   *Da 7:9*
and given to the *b.* flame   *Da 7:11*
firebrand plucked out of the   *Am 4:11*
b.
b. coals went forth at his   *Hab 3:5*
feet
girded about, and your lights   *Lu 12:35*
b.
He was a *b.* and a shining   *Joh 5:35*
light
with *b.* spirit (B)   *Ac 18:25*
b. with the spirit (A)(P)   *Ro 12:11*
b. missle of the enemy (P)   *Eph 6:16*
b. wrath (A)   *Heb 10:27*
b. indignation (B)   *Heb 10:27*
no sooner risen with a *b.*   *Jas 1:11*
heat
lamps of fire *b.* before the   *Re 4:5*
throne
a great mountain *b.* with fire   *Re 8:8*
was
b. as it were a lamp, and it   *Re 8:10*
fell
they shall see the smoke of   *Re 18:9*
her *b.*
saw the smoke of her *b.*   *Re 18:18*
saying
a lake of fire *b.* with   *Re 19:20*
brimstone

BURNINGS

people shall be as the *b.* of   *Isa 33:12*
lime
us shall dwell with   *Isa 33:14*
everlasting *b.*
and with the *b.* of thy fathers   *Jer 34:5*

BURNISHED

b. bronze (S)   *Ezr 8:27*
like the colour of *b.* brass   *Eze 1:7*
feet like *b.* bronze   *Da 10:6*
(A)(E)(R)

BURNS

b. both ends (B)   *Eze 15:4*

BURNT

said, bring her forth, let her   *Ge 38:24*
be *b.*
but they shall not be *b.* on   *Le 2:12*
altar
meat offering be wholly *b.*   *Le 6:22;*
  Le 6:23; 8:21
Moses sought the goat, and   *Le 10:16*
it was *b.*
they that were *b.* had   *Nu 16:39*
offered
be *b.* with hunger, and   *De 32:24*
devoured
before *b.* fat, priest's servant   *1Sa 2:15*
came
David and his men *b.* their   *2Sa 5:21*
images
mens' bones shall be *b.* upon   *1Ki 13:2*
the
Asa *b.* her idol by brook   *1Ki 15:13;*
  2Ch 15:16
he *b.* grove at brook Kidron   *2Ki 23:6*
she *b.* high place, stamped   *2Ki 23:15*
it small
took bones out of   *2Ki 23:16*
sepulchres *b.* them
b. house of Lord   *2Ki 25:9;*
  2Ch 36:19; Jer 52:13
my bones are *b.* with heat   *Job 30:30*

skin black, bones are *b.* as   *Ps 102:3*
an hearth
take fire, and his clothes not   *Pr 6:27*
be *b.*
can one go on coals and feet   *Pr 6:28*
not be *b.*
his cities are *b.*   *Jer 2:15*
in the roll which Jehoiakim   *Jer 36:28*
hath *b.*
and I will make thee a *b.*   *Jer 51:25*
mountain
and all faces shall be *b.*   *Eze 20:47*
therein
kindle the fire, and let the   *Eze 24:10*
bones be *b.*
flame hath *b.* all trees of   *Joe 1:19*
field
he *b.* bones of king of Edom   *Am 2:1*
the earth is *b.* at his presence   *Na 1:5*
if work be *b.* shall suffer   *1Co 3:15*
loss
those beasts are *b.* without   *Heb 13:11*
camp

BURNT with *FIRE*

flesh be *b.* with *fire*   *Le 7:17; Le 19:6*
be *b.* with *fire*, both he and   *Le 20:14*
they
the whore, she shall be *b.*   *Le 21:9*
with *fire*
the mountain *b.* with *fire*   *De 4:11*
sons and daughters they *b.*   *De 12:31*
in *fire*
b. Jericho with *fire* and all   *Jos 16:24*
therein
accursed thing shall be *b.*   *Jos 7:15*
with *fire*
Joshua *b.* their chariots with   *Jos 11:9*
fire
he took Hazor and *b.* it   *Jos 11:11*
with *fire*
they *b.* her and her father   *J'g 15:6*
with *fire*
cords became as flax *b.* with   *J'g 15:14*
fire
came to Laish and *b.* it with   *J'g 18:27*
fire
Amalekites *b.* Ziklag with   *1Sa 30:1*
fire
they shall be utterly *b.* with   *2Sa 23:7*
fire
Pharaoh had *b.* Gezer with   *1Ki 9:16*
fire
Zimri *b.* the king's house   *1Ki 16:18*
with *fire*
fire from heaven *b.* up   *2Ki 1:14*
captains
Sepharvites *b.* children with   *2Ki 17:31*
fire
b. the chariots of the sun   *2Ki 23:11*
with *fire*
every great man's house *b.*   *2Ki 25:9*
with *fire*
their gods were *b.* with *fire*   *1Ch 14:12*
Ahaz *b.* his children in *fire*   *2Ch 28:3*
gates thereof are *b.* with *fire*   *Ne 1:3;*
  2:17
it is *b.* with *fire*, it is cut   *Ps 80:16*
down
your cities are *b.* with *fire*   *Isa 1:7*
when walkest thro' *fire* not   *Isa 43:2*
be *b.*
holy and beautiful house *b.*   *Isa 64:11*
with *fire*
this city shall not be *b.* with   *Jer 38:17*
fire
cause this city to be *b.* with   *Jer 38:23*
fire
her daughters shall be *b.* with   *Jer 49:2*
fire
the reeds they have *b.* with   *Jer 51:32*
fire
Babylon's high gates shall be   *Jer 51:58*
b. with *fire*
hires thereof be *b.* with the   *Mic 1:7*
fire
she shall be utterly *b.* with   *Re 18:8*
fire

BURNT *INCENSE*

b. sweet *incense* as   *Ex 40:27*
commanded
Solomon *b.* *incense* in high   *1Ki 3:3*
places
Solomon *b.* *incense* on altar   *1Ki 9:25*
before Lord
Jeroboam offered on altar   *1Ki 12:33*
and *b.* *incense*

people *b. incense*   *1Ki 22:43;*
     2Ki 12:3; 14:4; 15:4, 35
Ahaz *b. incense* in high   *2Ki 16:4;*
places   *2Ch 28:3, 4*
put out lamps, have not *b. 2Ch 29:7*
incense
which have *b. incense* on the *Isa 65:7*
mountains
my people have *b. incense*   *Jer 18:15*
to vanity
men knew their wives had   *Jer 44:15*
b. incense
days wherein she *b. incense* *Ho 2:13*
to them
sacrificed and *b. incense* to *Ho 11:2*
graven images

BURNT *OFFERING*

where is lamb for *b. offering*   *Ge 22:7*
God will provide lamb for *b. Ge 22:8*
offering
offered him for *b. offering*   *Ge 22:13*
instead of
Jethro took a *b. offering* for *Ex 18:12*
God
ram is a *b. offering* unto the *Ex 29:18*
Lord
put hand on head of *b.*   *Le 1:4*
offering
slay sin offering in place of *b. Le 4:29;*
offering   *Le 6:25; 7:2; 14:13*
this is law of *b. offering*   *Le 6:9;*
     7:37
priest have skin of *b. offering Le 7:8*
a ram for a *b. offering*   *Le 9:2;*
     Le 16:3, 5; 23:18
calf and lamb for *b. offering Le 9:5;*
     Le 12:6; 23:12
lamb of first year for *b. Nu 17:15;*
offering Nu 7:21, 27, 33, 39, 51, 57, 63,
     69, 75, 81; Eze 45:15
stand by *b. offering*   *Nu 23:3;*
     23:15
this is *b. offering* of every *Nu 28:10*
sabbath
b. offering of sweet savour *Nu 28:13*
unto Lord
this is the *b. offering* of *Nu 28:14*
every month
beside meat offering and   *Nu 29:6*
daily *b. offering*
build an altar not for *b.*   *Jos 22:26*
offering
not received *b. offering* at *J'g 13:23*
our hands
Samuel was offering up *b. 1Sa 7:10*
offering
forced myself and offered *b. 1Sa 13:12*
offering
offered him for *b. offering 2Ki 3:27*
on wall
fire came down consumed *b. 2Ch 7:1*
offering
b. offering should be made *2Ch 29:24*
for all Israel
b. offerings hast thou not   *Ps 40:6*
required
for thou delightest not in *b. Ps 51:16*
offering
pleased with *b. offering* and *Ps 51:19*
whole *b. offering*
nor beasts thereof for *b.*   *Isa 40:16*
offering
I the Lord hate robbery for *Isa 61:8*
b. offering
shall slay *b. offering* and   *Eze 44:11*
sacrifice
prince prepare *b. offering*   *Eze 45:17*
for Israel
priest prepare prince's *b. Eze 46:2*
offering
daily prepare *b. offering* to *Eze 46:13*
Lord

CONTINUAL BURNT
OFFERING

a *continual b. offering*   *Ex 29:42;*
Nu 28:3, 6, 10, 15, 24, 31; 29:11, 16,
   19, 22; Ezr 3:5; Ne:10:33; Eze 46:15

OFFER BURNT *OFFERING*

Isaac and *offer* him for *b. Ge 22:2*
offering
go to altar and *offer b.*   *Le 9:7*
offering

in beginnings of months   *Nu 28:11*
offer b. offering
offer these besides the *b. Nu 28:23*
offering
I will *offer* it up for *b. J'g 11:31*
offering
if *offer* a *b. offering* offer to *J'g 13:16*
Lord
offered kine for *b. offering 1Sa 6:14*
Samuel *offered* lamb for *b. 1Sa 7:9*
offering
henceforth *offer* neither *b. 2Ki 5:17*
offering
Hezekiah commanded to *2Ch 29:27*
offer b. offering
offer up for yourselves *b. Job 42:8*
offering
b. offering prince shall *offer Eze 46:4*

BURNT *OFFERINGS*

Noah offered *b. offerings* on *Ge 8:20*
altar
give us sacrifices and *b. Ex 10:25*
offerings
sacrifice thereon thy *b. Ex 20:24*
offerings
blow trumpets over your *b. Nu 10:10*
offerings
thither bring *b. offerings De 12:6;*
     De 12:11, 14, 24
do service of Lord with *b. Jos 22:27*
offerings
hath Lord delight in *b.*   *1Sa 15:22*
offerings
Solomon offered *b. offerings 1Ki 3:15*
middle of court offered *b. 1Ki 8:64*
offerings
offered *b. offerings* to Lord *1Ch 29:21*
I build an house for *b.*   *2Ch 2:4*
offerings
brazen altar not able to   *2Ch 7:7*
receive *b. offerings*
not offered *b. offerings* in *2Ch 29:7*
holy place
priests could not slay all *b. 2Ch 29:34*
offerings
Levites were ashamed,   *2Ch 30:15*
brought *b. offerings*
sons of Aaron busied in *b. 2Ch 35:14*
offerings
offered daily *b. offerings* by *Ezr 3:4*
number
that they have need of for *b. Ezr 6:9*
offerings
offered *b. offerings* according *Job 1:5*
to number
will not reprove thee for *b. Ps 50:8*
offerings
go into thy house with *b. Ps 66:13*
offerings
am full of *b. offerings* of   *Isa 1:11*
rams
nor brought me small cattle *Isa 43:23*
of thy *b. offerings*
b. offerings be accepted on *Isa 56:7*
mine altar
your *b. offerings* are not   *Jer 6:20*
acceptable
put *b. offerings* to your   *Jer 7:21*
sacrifices
spake not to fathers   *Jer 7:22*
concerning *b. offerings*
come from south bringing *b. Jer 17:26*
offerings
burn sons for *b. offerings* to *Jer 19:5*
Baal
be prince's part to give *b. Eze 45:17*
offerings
knowledge of God more than *Ho 6:6*
b. offerings
shall I come before him with *Mic 6:6*
b. offerings
love neighbour is more   *M'k 12:33*
than *b. offerings*
in *b. offerings* for sin had *Heb 10:6*
no pleasure

OFFER BURNT OFFERINGS

come down to *offer b. offerings 1Sa 10:8*
nor *offer b. offerings*   *2Sa 24:24;*
     1Ch 21:24
thousand *b. offerings* did   *1Ki 3:4*
Solomon *offer*
three times year Solomon   *1Ki 9:25*
offer b. offerings
Jeshua builded altar to *offer Ezr 3:2*
b. offerings

Levites not want man to   *Jer 33:18*
offer b. offerings
in day make it to *offer b. Eze 43:18*
offerings
though ye *offer* me *b.*   *Am 5:22*
offerings I will not

BURNT *SACRIFICE*

offer no strange incense, nor *Ex 30:9*
b. sacrifice
priest burn all to be *b.*   *Le 1:9;*
sacrifice   *3:5*
stood by his *b. sacrifice* and *Nu 23:6*
princes
shall put whole *b. sacrifice De 33:10*
on altar
here be oxen for *b. sacrifice 2Sa 24:22*
fire fell and consumed *b.*   *1Ki 18:38*
sacrifice
on great altar burn king's   *2Ki 16:15*
b. sacrifice
remember offerings, accept *b. Ps 20:3*
sacrifice

BURNT *SACRIFICES*

to offer all *b. sacrifices* in *1Ch 23:31*
sabbaths
burn morning and evening *2Ch 13:11*
b. sacrifices
offer to thee *b. sacrifices* of *Ps 66:15*
fatlings

BURNT *UP*

foxes *b. up* the shocks and *J'g 15:5*
corn
fire came down, and *b. up 2Ki 1:14*
captains
fire of God hath *b. up* sheep *Job 1:16*
they have *b. up* all synagogues *Ps 74:8*
fire kindled, flame *b. up*   *Ps 106:18*
wicked
our holy and beautiful   *Isa 64:11*
house is *b. up*
b. up that none can pass   *Jer 9:10;*
     Jer 9:12
king sent and *b. up* their city *M't 22:7*
earth and works therein be *2Pe 3:10*
b. up
trees *b. up* and all grass *b. up Re 8:7*

BURST

it is ready to *b.* like new   *Job 32:19*
bottles
and thy presses shall *b.* out *Pr 3:10*
thy yoke and *b.* thy bands   *Jer 2:20*
broken the yoke, and *b.* the *Jer 5:5*
bonds
and will *b.* thy bonds, and *Jer 30:8*
and will *b.* thy bonds in   *Na 1:13*
sunder
doth *b.* the bottles, and the *M'k 2:22*
wine
new wine will *b.* the bottles *Lu 5:37*
he *b.* asunder in the midst *Ac 1:18*

BURSTING

shall not be found in the *b. Isa 30:14*
of it
b. with futile conceit (P)   *Col 2:18*

BURY

I may *b.* my dead out of my *Ge 23:4*
sight
of our sepulchres *b.* thy dead *Ge 23:6;*
     Ge 23:11, 15
mind that I should *b.* my   *Ge 23:8;*
dead   *23:13*
b. me not, I pray thee, in   *Ge 47:29*
Egypt
and *b.* me in their burying- *Ge 47:30*
place
b. me with my fathers in the *Ge 49:29*
Canaan there shalt thou *b. Ge 50:5;*
me   *Ge 50:5-7, 14*
shalt in any wise *b.* him   *De 21:23*
that day
and fall upon him, and *b. 1Ki 2:31*
him
host was gone up to *b.* the *1Ki 11:15*
slain
the city, to mourn and to *1Ki 13:29*
b. him
When I am dead, then *b. 1Ki 13:31*
me in

shall mourn for him, and *b.*   *1Ki 14:13*
him
and there shall be none to *b.*   *2Ki 9:10*
her
and *b.* her: for she is the   *2Ki 9:34*
king's
they went to *b.* her: but they   *2Ki 9:35*
and there was none to *b.*   *Ps 79:3*
them
for they shall *b.* in Tophet   *Jer 7:32*
they shall have none to *b.*   *Jer 14:16*
them
they shall *b.* them in Tophet   *Jer 19:11*
till there be no place to *b.*   *Jer 19:11*
and there shall they *b.* Gog   *Eze 39:11*
all the people of the land   *Eze 39:13*
shall *b.*
to *b.* with the passengers   *Eze 39:14*
those
them up, Memphis shall *b.*   *Ho 9:6*
them
me first to go and *b.* my   *M't 8:21*
father
and let the dead *b.* their   *M't 8:22*
dead
potter's field, to *b.* strangers   *M't 27:7*
in
me first to go and *b.* my   *Lu 9:59*
father
Let the dead *b.* their dead   *Lu 9:60*
the manner of the Jews is   *Joh 19:40*
to *b.*

BURYING

as they were *b.* a man, that   *2Ki 13:21*
house of Israel be *b.* of them   *Eze 39:12*
to anoint my body to the *b.*   *M'k 14:8*
against the day of my *b.*   *Joh 12:7*
hath she

BURYINGPLACE

give me a possession of a *b.*   *Ge 23:4*
possession of a *b.* amongst   *Ge 23:9*
you
possession of a *b.* by the   *Ge 23:20*
sons
bury me in their *b.* And he   *Ge 47:30*
said
Hittite for a possession of a   *Ge 49:30*
b.
for a possession of a *b.* of   *Ge 50:13*
Ephron
in the *b.* of Manoah his   *J'g 16:31*
father

BUSH

fire out of the midst of a *b.*   *Ex 3:2*
behold, the *b.* burned with fire   *Ex 3:2*
and the *b.* was not consumed   *Ex 3:2*
sight, why the *b.* is not burnt   *Ex 3:3*
him out of the midst of the *b.*   *Ex 3:4*
will of him that dwelt in the   *De 33:16*
b.
how in the *b.* God spake   *M'k 12:26*
unto him
of a bramble *b.* gather they   *Lu 6:44*
grapes
even Moses shewed at the *b.*   *Lu 20:37*
Lord in a flame of fire in a   *Ac 7:30*
b.
which appeared to him in the   *Ac 7:35*
b.

BUSHEL

an honest *b.* (B)   *Le 19:36*
fifth of a *b.* (B)   *Le 23:13;*
    Le 23:17; 24:5
a candle, and put it under a   *M't 5:15*
b.
brought to be put under a *b.*   *M'k 4:21*
neither under a *b.* but on a   *Lu 11:33*
put it under a *b.* (A)(E)(R)   *Lu 11:33*

BUSHELS

ten *b.* (B)   *Le 27:16;*
    Isa 5:10; Eze 45:11, 13, 14
two *b.* of roasted grain (B)   *1Sa 25:18*
195 *b.* of fine flour, 390 *b.* of   *1Ki 4:22*
meal (B)
two *b.* of seed (B)   *1Ki 18:32*
125 *b.* of wheat (B)   *Ezr 7:22*
fifteen *b.* (B)   *Ho 3:2*
a heap of twenty *b.* (B)   *Hag 2:16*
a thousand *b.* of wheat   *Lu 16:7*
(N)(P)

BUSHES

Who cut up mallows by the   *Job 30:4*
b.
Among the *b.* they brayed;   *Job 30:7*
under
all thorns, and upon all *b.*   *Isa 7:19*

BUSHY

his locks are *b.* and black as   *Ca 5:11*

BUSIED

priests the sons of Aaron   *2Ch 35:14*
were *b.*

BUSINESS

stay and do *b.* (B)   *Ge 32:21*
went into the house to do   *Ge 39:11*
his *b.*
do *b.* in the land (A)(S)   *Ge 42:34*
shall he be charged with any   *De 24:5*
b.
yours, if ye utter not this our   *Jos 2:14*
b.
if thou utter this our *b.*, then   *Jos 2:20*
we
and had no *b.* with any man   *J'g 18:7*
they had no *b.* with any   *J'g 18:28*
man
when the *b.* was in hand   *1Sa 20:19*
hath commanded me a *b.*   *1Sa 21:2*
man know any thing of the   *1Sa 21:2*
b.
the king's *b.* required haste   *1Sa 21:8*
his sons were for the   *1Ch 26:29*
outward *b.*
westward in all the *b.* of   *1Ch 26:30*
the Lord
the Levites wait upon their   *2Ch 13:10*
b.
much *b.* in the cities of   *2Ch 17:13*
Judah
in the *b.* of the   *2Ch 32:31*
ambassadors of
outward *b.* of the house of   *Ne 11:16*
God
over the *b.* of the house of   *Ne 11:22*
God
Levites, every one in his *b.*   *Ne 13:30*
that have the charge of the *b.*   *Es 3:9*
ships, that do *b.* in great   *Ps 107:23*
waters
conducts *b.* with fairness (B)   *Ps 112:5*
thou a man diligent in his *b.*   *Pr 22:29*
a miserable *b.* (A)(R)   *Ec 1:13*
the *b.* which God (R)   *Ec 3:10*
through the multitude of *b.*   *Ec 5:3*
the *b.* that is done upon the   *Ec 8:16*
earth
rose up, and did the king's *b.*   *Da 8:27*
did *b.* with them   *M't 25:16*
(B)(N)(P)
must be about my father's *b.*   *Lu 2:49*
b. they had transacted (B)   *Lu 19:15*
we may appoint over this *b.*   *Ac 6:3*
b. and industry (N)   *Ac 19:25*
Not slothful in *b.*; fervent in   *Ro 12:11*
in whatsoever *b.* she hath   *Ro 16:2*
need of
I made it my *b.* (N)   *Ga 2:10*
to do your own *b.* and to   *1Th 4:11*
work
make these matters your *b.*   *1Ti 4:16*
(N)
whose *b.* is upon the sea   *Re 18:17*
(P)

BUSTLING

anxious and *b.* about (B)   *Lu 10:41*

BUSY

servant was *b.* here and   *1Ki 20:40*
there

BUSYBODIES

working not at all, but are   *2Th 3:11*
b.
but tattlers also and *b.*   *1Ti 5:13*
speaking

BUSYBODY

or as a *b.* in other men's   *1Pe 4:15*
matters

BUT

b. a step between me and   *1Sa 20:3*
death
if they kill us, we shall *b.* die   *2Ki 7:4*
mouths *b.* speak not; eyes *b.*   *Ps 115:5*
see not
ears *b.* hear not; noses *b.*   *Ps 115:6*
smell not
hands *b.* handle not; feet *b.*   *Ps 115:7*
walk not
b. of that day and hour   *M't 24:36*
knoweth
b. as days of Noe were, so   *M't 24:37*
shall
said, if I may touch *b.* his   *M'k 5:28*
clothes
B. if: *b.* only (S)   *Ro 2:17;*
    Lu 4:26-27
know not speech, *b.* the   *1Co 4:19*
power
b. ye are washed   *1Co 6:11*
b. same Spirit; *b.* same   *1Co 6:12;*
Lord   *12:5*
b. it is the same God which   *1Co 12:6*
worketh all
he hath not grieved me *b.* in   *2Co 2:5*
part
light affliction, which is *b.*   *2Co 4:17*
for moment
b. by the revelation of Jesus   *Ga 1:12*
Christ

BUTCHER

b. the sin offering (B)   *Le 4:20*

BUTCHERING

see to the *b.* (B)   *Ge 43:16*

BUTLER

the *b.* of the king of Egypt   *Ge 40:1;*
    Ge 40:5, 9, 13, 20, 21, 23
spake the chief *b.* unto   *Ge 41:9*
Pharaoh

BUTLERS

against the chief of the *b.*   *Ge 40:2*

BUTLERSHIP

the chief butler unto his *b.*   *Ge 40:21*

BUTT

with the *b.* of the spear (S)   *2Sa 2:23*

BUTTED

in brutal rage he *b.* (B)   *Da 8:7*

BUTTER

he took *b.* and milk, and the   *Ge 18:8*
calf
B. of kine, and milk of   *De 32:14*
sheep
brought forth *b.* in a lordly   *J'g 5:25*
dish
honey, and *b.* and sheep   *2Sa 17:29*
floods, the brooks of honey   *Job 20:17*
and *b.*
When I washed my steps   *Job 29:6*
with *b.*
his mouth were smoother   *Ps 55:21*
than *b.*
of milk bringeth forth *b.* and   *Pr 30:33*
B. and honey shall he eat,   *Isa 7:15*
that he
they shall give, he shall eat *b.*   *Isa 7:22*

BUTTOCKS

in the middle, even to their   *2Sa 10:4*
b.
just below the belt (B)   *2Sa 10:4*
cut off garments in the   *2Sa 10:4*
middle (E)(R)
in the midst hard by their *b.*   *1Ch 19:4*
with their *b.* uncovered, to   *Isa 20:4*

BUY

Egypt to Joseph for to *b.*   *Ge 41:57*
corn
b. for us from thence: that   *Ge 42:2*
we

went down to *b*. corn in   *Ge 42:3;*
Egypt   *Ge 42:5, 7, 10; 43:20, 22*
Go again, *b*. us a little food   *Ge 43:2*
we will go down and *b*. thee *Ge 43:4*
food
Go again, and *b*. us a little *Ge 44:25*
food
b. us and our land for bread *Ge 47:19*
If thou *b*. an Hebrew servant *Ex 21:2*
But if the priest *b*. any soul *Le 22:11*
with
thou shalt *b*. of thy   *Le 25:15*
neighbour
of them shall ye *b*. bondmen *Le 25:44*
of them shall ye *b*. and of *Le 25:45*
their
shall *b*. meat of them for   *De 2:6*
money
ye shall also *b*. water of them *De 2:6*
for
bondwomen, and no man   *De 28:68*
shall *b*.
B. it before the inhabitants   *Ru 4:4*
b. it also of Ruth the   *Ru 4:5*
Moabitess
said unto Boaz, *B*. it for thee *Ru 4:8*
To *b*. the threshingfloor of *2Sa 24:21*
thee to
will surely *b*. it of thee at a *2Sa 24:24*
price
to *b*. timber and hewed   *2Ki 12:12*
stone
and to *b*. timber and hewn *2Ki 22:6*
stone
I will verily *b*. it for the   *1Ch 21:24*
full price
to *b*. hewn stone, and   *2Ch 34:11*
timber for
b. speedily with this money *Ezr 7:17*
that we might *b*. corn, because *Ne 5:3*
not *b*. it of them on the   *Ne 10:31*
sabbath
B. the truth, and sell it not *Pr 23:23*
come ye, *b*. and eat   *Isa 55:1*
yea, come, *b*. wine and milk *Isa 55:1*
B. thee my field that is in   *Jer 32:7*
of redemption is thine to *b*. *Jer 32:7*
it
B. my field, I pray thee, that *Jer 32:8*
is in
is thine; *b*. it for thyself   *Jer 32:8*
B. thee the field for money *Jer 32:25*
Men shall *b*. fields for   *Jer 32:44*
money
That we may *b*. the poor for *Am 8:6*
silver
villages, and *b*. themselves *M't 14:15*
victuals
that sell, and *b*. for   *M't 25:9*
yourselves
while they went to *b*., the *M't 25:10*
villages, and *b*. themselves *M'k 6:36*
bread
b. two hundred pennyworth *M'k 6:37*
of bread
go and *b*. meat for all this *Lu 9:13*
people
let him sell his garment, and *Lu 22:36*
b. one
away unto the city to *b*. meat *Joh 4:8*
Whence shall we *b*. bread, *Joh 6:5*
that
B. those things that we   *Joh 13:29*
have need
they that *b*. as though they *1Co 7:30*
and *b*. and sell, and get   *Jas 4:13*
gain
I counsel thee to *b*. of me   *Re 3:18*
gold
that no man might *b*. or sell *Re 13:17*

BUYER

it is naught, saith the *b*.: but *Pr 20:14*
as with the *b*. so with the *Isa 24:2*
seller
let not the *b*. rejoice, nor the *Eze 7:12*
seller

BUYEST

b. ought of thy neighbour's *Le 25:14*
hand
What day thou *b*. the field of *Ru 4:5*

BUYETH

She considereth a field, and *Pr 31:16*
b. it

all that he hath, and *b*. that *M't 13:44*
field
for no man *b*. their   *Re 18:11*
merchandise

BUYING

made by *b*. and selling (A) *Lu 19:15*

BUZ

his firstborn, and *B*. his   *Ge 22:21*
brother
the son of Jahdo, the son of *1Ch 5:14*
B.
Dedan, and Tema, and *B*.   *Jer 25:23*

BUZI

Ezekiel the priest, the son of *Eze 1:3*
B.

BUZITE

of Barachel the *B*. of the   *Job 32:2*
kindred
Elihu the son of Barachel *Job 32:6*
the *B*.

BUZZARD

the *b*. (S)   *De 14:13*

BUZZARDS

every species of *b*. (B)   *Le 11:14*
the *b*. (A)(B)(R)   *De 14:13*

BY

b. the oaks (S)   *Ge 13:18;*
          Ge 14:13; 18:1
b. what means (S)   *1Ki 22:22;*
          2Ch 18:20
those who pass *b*. (S)   *Pr 9:15*

BY-AND-BY

b. and *b*. is offended   *M't 13:21*
give me *b*. and *b*. in a   *M'k 6:25*
charger
say to him *b*. and *b*. sit down *Lu 17:7*
to
come to pass, but end is not *Lu 21:9*
b. and *b*.

BYWAYS

travellers walked through *b*. *J'g 5:6*

BYWORD

a *b*. among all nations   *De 28:37*
whither
and a *b*. among all people *1Ki 9:7*
and a *b*. among all nations *2Ch 7:20*
made me also a *b*. of the *Job 17:6*
people
made me a *b*.   *Job 17:6*
(A)(B)(E)(R)
their song, yea, I am their *b*. *Job 30:9*
us a *b*. among the heathen *Ps 44:14*
I became a *b*. (A)(B)(R) *Ps 69:11*
sign and a *b*. (A)(B)(R)   *Eze 14:8*
became a *b*. (S)   *Eze 23:10*

C

CAB

fourth part of a *c*. of dove's *2Ki 6:25*
dung

CABBON

C. and Lahmam, and   *Jos 15:40*
Kithlish

CABINS

into the *c*. and Jeremiah *Jer 37:16*

CABUL

goeth out to *C*. on the left *Jos 19:27*
hand
he called them the land of *C*. *1Ki 9:13*

CAESAR

to give tribute unto *C*. or *M't 22:17*
not
unto *C*. the things which *M't 22:21*
are
to give tribute to *C*. or not *M'k 12:14*
C. the things that are   *M'k 12:17*
Caesar's
a decree from *C*. Augustus *Lu 2:1*
the reign of Tiberius *C*.   *Lu 3:1*
Pontius
to give tribute unto *C*. or no *Lu 20:22*
C. the things which be Cæsar's *Lu 20:25*
forbidding to give tribute to *Lu 23:2*
C.
himself a king speaketh   *Joh 19:12*
against *C*.
answered, We have no king *Joh 19:15*
but *C*.
pass in the days of Claudius *Ac 11:28*
C.
contrary to the decrees of *C*. *Ac 17:7*
not yet against *C*. have I   *Ac 25:8*
offended
unto them. I appeal unto *C*. *Ac 25:11;*
           25:12
be kept till I might send   *Ac 25:21*
him to *C*.
if he had not appealed unto *Ac 26:32*
C.
thou must be brought before *Ac 27:24*
C.
constrained to appeal unto *Ac 28:19*
C.

CAESAREA

into the coasts of *C*.   *M't 16:13*
Philippi
into the towns of *C*. Philippi *M'k 8:27*
all the cities, till he came to *Ac 8:40*
C.
they brought him down to *C*. *Ac 9:30*
certain man in *C*. called   *Ac 10:1*
Cornelius
morrow after they entered *Ac 10:24*
into *C*.
I was, sent from *C*. unto me *Ac 11:11*
went down from Judæa to *C*. *Ac 12:19*
he had landed at *C*. and   *Ac 18:22*
gone up
came unto *C*.: and we entered *Ac 21:8*
of the disciples of *C*. and *Ac 21:16*
brought
soldiers to go to *C*.   *Ac 23:23*
they came to *C*. and   *Ac 23:33*
delivered
ascended from *C*. to   *Ac 25:1*
Jerusalem
that Paul should be kept at *C*. *Ac 25:4*
ten days he went down unto *Ac 25:6*
C.
Bernice came unto *C*. to salute *Ac 25:13*

CAESAR'S

They say unto him, *C*. Then *M't 22:21*
C. the things which are *M't 22:21*
C.
And they said unto him, *C*. *M'k 12:16*
to Caesar the things that *M'k 12:17*
are *C*.
They answered and said, *C*. *Lu 20:24*
unto Caesar the things   *Lu 20:25*
which be *C*.
thou art not *C*. friend: *Jo 19:12*
whosoever
I stand at *C*. judgment seat *Ac 25:10*
they that are of *C*.   *Ph'p 4:22*
household

CAGE

As a *c*. is full of birds, so *Jer 5:27*
are their
put them in a *c*. (S)   *Eze 19:9*
a *c*. of every unclean and *Re 18:2*
hateful

CAIAPHAS

high priest, who was called *M't 26:3*
C.
led him away to *C*. the   *M't 26:57*
high priest
Annas and *C*. being the high *Lu 3:2*
And one of them, named *C*. *Joh 11:49*
he was father in law to *C*. *Joh 18:13*
C. was he, which gave   *Joh 18:14*
counsel to

CAIAPHAS

Annas had sent him bound *Joh 18:24*
unto C.
Then led they Jesus from C. *Joh 18:28*
unto
Annas the high priest, and C. *Ac 4:6*

CAIN

she conceived, and bare C. *Ge 4:1;*
  Ge 4:2-3, 5-6, 8-9, 13, 15-17, 24-25
C., Gibeah, and Timnah; ten *Jos 15:57*
cities
a more excellent sacrifice *Heb 11:4*
than C.
Not as C. who was of that *1Jo 3:12*
wicked
gone in the way of C. and *Jude 11*
ran

CAINAN

lived ninety years, and begat *Ge 5:9;*
C. *5:10-14*
Which was the son of C. *Lu 3:36;*
  3:37

CAKE

one c. of oiled bread, and *Ex 29:23*
one
he took one unleavened c. *Le 8:26*
and a c. of oiled bread *Le 8:26*
two tenth deals shall be in *Le 24:5*
one c.
unleavened c. out of the *Nu 6:19*
basket
Ye shall offer up a c. of the *Nu 15:20*
first
a c. of barley bread tumbled *J'g 7:13*
into
gave him a piece of a c. of *1Sa 30:12*
figs
to every one a c. of bread, *2Sa 6:19*
and a
a c. of raisins (S) *2Sa 6:19; 1Ch 16:3*
I have not a c. but an *1Ki 17:12*
handful of
make me thereof a little c. *1Ki 17:13*
first
there was a c. baken on the *1Ki 19:6*
coals
take a c. of figs (A)(B)(E)(R) *2Ki 20:7;*
  Isa 38:21
Ephraim is a c. not turned *Ho 7:8*

CAKES

it, and make c. upon the *Ge 18:6*
hearth
baked unleavened c. of the *Ex 12:39*
dough
bread, and c. unleavened *Ex 29:2*
unleavened c. of fine flour *Le 2:4*
unleavened c. mingled with oil *Le 7:12*
Besides the c. he shall offer *Le 7:13*
for
bake twelve c. thereof: two *Le 24:5*
tenth
c. of fine flour mingled with *Nu 6:15*
oil
baked it in pans, and make *Nu 11:8*
c. of it
unleavened c. and parched *Jos 5:11*
corn
unleavened c. of flour *J'g 6:19; 6:20-21*
two hundred c. of figs, and *1Sa 25:18*
laid
make me a couple of c. in *2Sa 13:6;*
my sight *13:8*
Tamar took the c. which *2Sa 13:10*
she had
ten loaves and c. *1Ki 14:3*
(A)(B)(E)(R)(S)
meal, c. of figs, and *1Ch 12:40*
bunches of
for the unleavened c. and *1Ch 23:29*
c. of raisins (S) *Ca 2:5; Ho 3:1*
make c. to the queen of *Jer 7:18*
heaven
we make her c. to worship *Jer 44:19*
her
And thou shalt eat it as *Eze 4:12*
barley c.
love raisin c. (A)(B)(E)(R) *Ho 3:1*

CALAH

and the city Rehoboth, and *Ge 10:11*
C.
Resen between Nineveh and *Ge 10:12*
C.

CALAMITIES

I will heap up c. (B) *De 32:23*
saved from c. *1Sa 10:19*
(A)(B)(E)(R)
refuge, until these c. be *Ps 57:1*
overpast
prayer also shall be in their *Ps 141:5*
c.
he that is glad at c. shall not *Pr 17:5*
be
in her c. (S) *La 1:3*

CALAMITY

the day of their c. is at *De 32:35*
hand, and
calamity (B) *Jos 7:25;*
J'g 11:35; Job 5:6; Isa 65:23; Jer 2:27,
28; 11:12
prevented me in the day of *2Sa 22:19*
my c.
c. does not spring from *Job 5:6*
ground (B)
and my c. laid in the balances *Job 6:2*
Cannot my taste discern c. *Job 6:30*
(R)
mocks at c. of the innocent *Job 9:23*
(R)
c. ready at his side *Job 18:12*
(A)(E)(R)
c. comes upon them *Job 21:17*
(A)(B)(E)(R)
eyes see their c. (B) *Job 21:20*
in the day of their c. *Job 21:30*
(B)(E)(R)
they set forward my c., they *Job 30:13*
have
in his c. will he (A)(B)(E) *Job 30:24*
c. befalls the righteous *Job 31:3*
(A)(B)(E)(R)
c. from God a terror *Job 31:23*
(A)(B)(E)(R)
happy at c. of him (B) *Job 31:29*
prevented me in the day of *Ps 18:18*
my c.
I also will laugh at your c., I *Pr 1:26*
will
shall his c. come suddenly *Pr 6:15*
certain c. comes (A)(R) *Pr 11:15*
foolish son is the c. of his *Pr 19:13*
father
reap c. and futility *Pr 22:8*
(A)(E)(R)
wicked falls into c. *Pr 24:16*
(A)(E)(R)
For their c. shall rise *Pr 24:22*
suddenly
brother's house in the day of *Pr 27:10*
thy c.
bring forth c. (E)(R) *Isa 65:23*
the face, in the day of their *Jer 18:17*
c.
I will regret the c. (B) *Jer 42:10*
the day of their c. was come *Jer 46:21*
upon
The c. of Moab is near to *Jer 48:16*
come
will bring the c. of Esau *Jer 49:8*
upon him
bring their c. from all sides *Jer 49:32*
thereof
a day of c. (A) *Jer 51:2*
c. upon c. (A) *Eze 7:26*
the sword in the time of *Eze 35:5*
their c.
in the day of their c.; yea, *Ob 13*
thou
grieved at c. (B) *Jon 4:2*
broken down with c. (A) *Lu 4:18*
c. is upon them (N) *1Th 5:3*

CALAMUS

of sweet c. two hundred and *Ex 30:23*
fifty
and saffron; c. and cinnamon *Ca 4:14*
cassia, and c. were in thy *Eze 27:19*
market

CALCOL

and Heman, and C. and Dara *1Ch 2:6*

CALCULATE

c. the number (A)(B)(P) *Re 13:18*

CALCULATIONS

tear down c. (B) *2Co 10:5*

CALDRON

the pan, or kettle, or c., or *1Sa 2:14*
pot
as out of a seething pot or *Job 41:20*
c.
city is the c. and we be the *Eze 11:3*
flesh
this city is the c.: but I will *Eze 11:7*
bring
This city shall not be your *Eze 11:11*
c.
the pot, and as flesh within *Mic 3:3*
the c.

CALDRONS

sod they in pots, and in c. *2Ch 35:13*
and in
the c. also, and the shovels *Jer 52:18*
the c. and the candlesticks *Jer 52:19*

CALEB

Judah, C. the son of *Nu 13:6*
Jephunneh
C. stilled the people before *Nu 13:30*
Moses
Joshua the son of Nun, and *Nu 14:6;*
C. *Nu 14:24, 30, 38*
not left a man of them, *Nu 26:65;*
save C. *Nu 32:12; De 1:36*
Judah, C. the son of *Nu 34:19*
Jephunneh
c. the son of Jephunneh the *Jos 14:6*
blessed him, and gave unto *Jos 14:13;*
C. *14:14*
unto C. the son of Jephunneh *Jos 15:13*
he
C. drove thence the three sons *Jos 15:14*
of
And C. said, He that smiteth *Jos 15:16*
Kenaz, the brother of C. took *Jos 15:17*
C. said unto her, What *Jos 15:18*
wouldest
villages thereof, gave they to *Jos 21:12*
C.
And C. said, He that smiteth *J'g 1:12*
C. said unto her, What wilt *J'g 1:14*
thou
And C. gave her the upper *J'g 1:15*
springs
they gave Hebron unto C. as *J'g 1:20*
and he was of the house of C. *1Sa 25:3*
Judah, and upon the south of *1Sa 30:14*
C.
And C. the son of Hezron *1Ch 2:18*
begat
Azubah was dead, C. took *1Ch 2:19*
unto
Now the sons of C. the brother *1Ch 2:42*
of
and the daughter of C. was *1Ch 2:49*
Achsa
These were the sons of C. the *1Ch 2:50*
son
sons of C. the son of *1Ch 4:15*
Jephunneh
villages thereof, they gave to *1Ch 6:56*
C.

CALEB-EPHRATAH

after that Hezron was dead *1Ch 2:24*
in C.

CALEB'S

son of Kenaz, C. younger *J'g 1:13*
brother
son of Kenaz, C. younger *J'g 3:9*
brother
Ephah, C. concubine, bare *1Ch 2:46*
Haran
Maachah, C. concubine, bare *1Ch 2:48*

CALF

fetchted a c. tender and good *Ge 18:7;*
18:8
after he had made it a molten *Ex 32:4;*
c. *Ex 32:8; 19-20, 24, 35*
a young c. for a sin offering *Le 9:2;*
9:3, 8
and had made you a molten c. *De 9:16;*
9:21
woman had a fat c. in the *1Sa 28:24*
house
They had made them a molten *Ne 9:18*
c.

cow calveth, and casteth not *Job 21:10*
her *c.*
maketh them also to skip like *Ps 29:6*
a *c.*
They made a *c.* in Horeb, and *Ps 106:19*
and the *c.* and the young lion *Isa 11:6*
wilderness: there shall be *c.* *Isa 27:10*
feed
when they cut the *c.* in twain *Jer 34:18*
passed between the parts of *Jer 34:19*
the *c.*
Thy *c.* O Samaria, hath cast *Ho 8:5*
thee
the *c.* of Samaria shall be *Ho 8:6*
broken
bring hither the fatted *c.* and *Lu 15:23*
kill
thy father hath killed the *Lu 15:27*
fatted *c.*
hast killed for him the fatted *Lu 15:30*
c.
they made a *c.* in those days *Ac 7:41*
the second beast like a *c.* and *Re 4:7*

CALF'S

feet was like the sole of a *c.* *Eze 1:7*
foot

CALKERS

thereof were in thee thy *c.* *Eze 27:9*
mariners, and thy pilots, thy *Eze 27:27*
c.

CALL

to see what he would *c.* them *Ge 2:19*
c. a nurse of Hebrew women *Ex 2:7*
c. him that he may eat bread *Ex 2:20*
Moses sent to *c.* Dathan and *Nu 16:12*
if men *c.* thee, rise up and go *Nu 22:20*
as God is in all things we *c.* on *De 4:7*
I *c.* heaven and earth to *De 4:26;*
witness this day *De 30:19; 31:28*
c. for Samson he may make *J'g 16:25*
sport
they sent to *c.* peaceably unto *J'g 21:13*
them
here am I, thou didst *c.* me *1Sa 3:6;*
3:8
c. Jesse to sacrifice, I will *1Sa 16:3*
shew thee
then king sent to *c.* *1Sa 22:11*
Ahimelech
said Absalom, *c.* now Hushai *2Sa 17:5*
c. Bathsheba, Zadok, Nathan *1Ki 1:28;*
1:32
hearken to them in all they *1Ki 8:52*
c. for
to *c.* my sin to remembrance *1Ki 17:18*
c. ye on name of your gods *1Ki 18:24;*
18:25
Elisha said, *c.* this *2Ki 4:12*
Shunammite
c. unto me all the prophets of *2Ki 10:19*
Baal
c. now if be any that will answer *Job 5:1*
then *c.* thou, and I will *Job 13:22;*
answer *14:15*
hear when I *c.* O God *Ps 4:1*
Lord will hear when I *c.* unto *Ps 4:3*
him
eat up my people, *c.* not upon *Ps 14:4*
Lord
save, Lord, hear us when we *Ps 20:9*
c.
they *c.* their lands after own *Ps 49:11*
names
c. to remembrance my song in *Ps 77:6*
night
plenteous in mercy to all that *Ps 86:5*
c. on
Samuel among them that on *Ps 99:6*
his name
when I *c.* answer me speedily *Ps 102:2*
therefore will I *c.* upon him as *Ps 116:2*
long
Lord is nigh all them that *c.* *Ps 145:18*
on him
to you, O men, I *c.* *Pr 8:4*
c. passengers who go right their *Pr 9:15*
ways
her children arise, and *c.* her *Pr 31:28*
blessed
woe to them that *c.* evil good *Isa 5:20*
in that day did Lord *c.* to *Isa 22:12*
weeping
I the Lord which *c.* thee by *Isa 45:3*
thy name

they *c.* themselves of the holy *Isa 48:2*
city
when I *c.* they stand up *Isa 48:13*
together
c. ye upon him while he is near *Isa 55:6*
wilt thou *c.* this a fast to the *Isa 58:5*
Lord
c. sabbath a delight, holy of *Isa 58:13*
the Lord
c. his servants by another *Isa 65:15*
name
that before they *c.* I will *Isa 65:24*
answer
consider and *c.* for mourning *Jer 9:17*
women
c. unto me, and I will answer *Jer 33:3*
thee
city men *c.* perfection of beauty *La 2:15*
Lord said, *c.* his name Jezreel *Ho 1:4*
God said, *c.* her name *Ho 1:6*
Lo-ruhamah
c. name Lo-ammi, ye are not my *Ho 1:9*
people
they *c.* to Egypt, they go to *Ho 7:11*
Assyria
sanctify fast *c.* solemn *Joe 1:14;*
assembly *2:15*
sleeper, arise, *c.* upon thy God *Jon 1:6*
c. every man his neighbour *Zec 3:10*
we *c.* proud happy, they that *Mal 3:15*
work
not come to *c.* righteous, but *M't 9:13;*
sinners to repentance *M'k 2:17; Lu 5:32*
shall they *c.* them of his *M't 10:25*
household
c. labourers and give them *M't 20:8*
their hire
servants to *c.* them that were *M't 22:3*
bidden
how doth David in spirit *c.* *M't 22:43*
him Lord
c. no man your father upon *M't 23:9*
I *c.* upon you to swear by (A) *M't 26:63*
why *c.* me Lord and do not *Lu 6:46*
things I say
when thou makest a feast *c.* *Lu 14:13*
poor
c. thy husband, and come *Joh 4:16*
hither
ye *c.* me Master and Lord and *Joh 13:13*
say
to bind all that *c.* on thy name *Ac 9:14*
c. over them which had evil *Ac 19:13*
spirits
that after way they *c.* heresy *Ac 24:14*
Lord rich to all that *c.* on him *Ro 10:12*
c. God for a record upon my *2Co 1:23*
soul
when I *c.* to remembrance *2Ti 1:5*
the faith
follow peace with them that *c.* *2Ti 2:22*
on Lord
not ashamed to *c.* them *Heb 2:11*
brethren
but *c.* to remembrance *Heb 10:32*
former days
let him *c.* elders of church *Jas 5:14*
if ye *c.* on Father who judgeth *1Pe 1:17*

CALL ON,
UPON NAME OF LORD

began men to *c.* *upon name* *Ge 4:26*
of Lord
will *c.* on name of Lord *1Ki 18:24;*
Ps 116:17
come out and *c.* on name of *2Ki 5:11*
Lord
c. upon his name *1Ch 16:8; Ps 105:1;*
Isa 12:4
whosoever *c.* on name of Lord *Joe 2:32;*
shall be delivered *Ac 2:21; Ro 10:13*
may all *c. upon* name of Lord *Zep 3:9*
in every place *c.* on name of *1Co 1:2*
Lord

CALL *UPON ME*

c. upon me in day of trouble *Ps 50:15*
c. upon me, and I will *Ps 91:15*
answer
c. upon me, and I will not *Pr 1:28*
answer
c. upon me, and I will *Jer 29:12*
hearken

not c. her name Sarai, but *Ge 17:15*
Sarah
didst *not c.* us to go with thee *J'g 12:1*
c. me *not* Naomi, call me *Ru 1:20*
Mara
they *c. not* upon the Lord *Ps 14:4*
he will *not c.* back his words *Isa 31:2*
upon families that *c. not* upon *Jer 10:25*
c. not thy friends, nor *Lu 14:12*
brethren
henceforth I *c.* you *not* *Joh 15:15*
servants
that *c. not* thou common *Ac 10:15;*
Ac 11:9
shewed me *not* to *c.* any man *Ac 10:28*
common

SHALL, SHALT CALL

thou *shalt c.* his name Isaac *Ge 17:19*
elders of his city *shall c.* him *De 25:8*
shalt c. to mind among *De 30:1*
nations
shall c. people to mountain *De 33:19*
shalt c. and I will answer *Job 14:15*
thee
shall c. to heavens from above *Ps 50:4*
all nations *shall c.* him *Ps 72:17*
blessed
shall c. name Emmanuel *Isa 7:14;*
M't 1:23
shall c. nobles to the *Isa 34:12*
kingdom
from rising of sun *shall c.* *Isa 41:25*
on my name
shall c. himself by name of *Isa 44:5*
Jacob
shall c. and shall declare it *Isa 44:7*
shalt c. nation thou knowest *Isa 55:5*
not
shalt thou *c.* and Lord shall *Isa 58:9*
answer
shall c. thee city of the Lord *Isa 60:14*
shalt c. walls salvation, and *Isa 60:18*
gates praise
shall c. you ministers of our *Isa 61:6*
God
shall c. them holy people *Isa 62:12*
shall c. Jerusalem throne of *Jer 3:17*
Lord
shalt c. me, my father *Jer 3:19*
reprobate silver *shall* men *c.* *Jer 6:30*
them
shalt c. to them, they will not *Jer 7:27*
answer
thou *shalt c.* me no more *Ho 2:16*
Baali
the remnant whom Lord *Joe 2:32*
shall c.
shall c. husbandman to *Am 5:16*
mourning
shall c. on my name and I *Zec 13:9*
will hear
shall c. them border of *Mal 1:4*
wickedness
all nations *shall c.* you *Mal 3:12*
blessed
shalt c. his name Jesus *M't 1:21*
much more *shall c.* them of *M't 10:25*
household
thou *shalt c.* his name John *Lu 1:13*
all generations *shall c.* me *Lu 1:48*
blessed
as many as Lord our God *Ac 2:39*
shall c.
how *shall* they *c.* on him in *Ro 10:14*
whom

WILL CALL

will *c.* damsel and inquire at *Ge 24:57*
her
the daughters will *c.* me *Ge 30:13*
blessed
will *c.* unto Lord, and he *1Sa 12:17*
shall send
will *c.* on Lord *2Sa 22:4; Ps 18:3*
will hypocrite always *c.* on *Job 27:10*
God
I *will c.* upon God *Ps 55:16; 86:7*
quicken us, we *will c.* on thy *Ps 80:18*
name
therefore *will* I *c.* on him as *Ps 116:2*
long
I *will c.* my servant Eliakim *Isa 22:20*
I *will c.* all families of the *Jer 1:15*
north

I *will* c. for a sword — *Jer 25:29; Eze 38:21*

will c. to remembrance iniquity — *Eze 21:23*

will c. for corn, and will increase it — *Eze 36:29*

convenient season I *will* c. for thee — *Ac 24:25*

will c. them my people which were — *Ro 9:25*

CALLED

therefore is name of it c. Babel — *Ge 11:9*

angel of God c. to Hagar — *Ge 21:17*

angel c. to Abraham out of heaven — *Ge 22:11*

name not be c. any more Jacob — *Ge 35:10*

c. him Ben-oni, father c. for Benjamin — *Ge 35:18*

she c. to the men of her house — *Ge 39:14*

king of Egypt c. for midwives — *Ex 1:18*

Pharaoh c. for Moses — *Ex 8:8; Ex 9:27; 10:16, 24; 12:31*

Moses c. Oshea, Jehoshua — *Nu 13:16*

Moses c. all Israel and said — *De 5:1; 29:2*

not exact it, it is c. Lord's release — *De 15:2*

thou art c. by name of Lord — *De 28:10*

have ye c. us to take what we have — *J'g 14:15*

cast away jaw-bone, and c. place — *J'g 15:17*

Samson was sore athirst, c. on Lord — *J'g 15:18*

Samson c. to the Lord and said — *J'g 16:28*

now c. a prophet, was c. a seer — *1Sa 9:9*

whose name is c. by name of Lord — *2Sa 6:2*

I take city, it be c. after my name — *2Sa 12:28*

watchman c. to porter, and said — *2Sa 18:26*

king c. Gibeonites, and said to them — *2Sa 21:2*

Adonijah c. all his brethren — *1Ki 1:9; 19:25*

Ahab c. Obadiah, who was governor — *1Ki 18:3*

c. on name of Baal from morning — *1Ki 18:26*

she c. to her husband and said — *2Ki 4:22*

they came and c. to porter of city — *2Ki 7:10*

Jabez c. on God of Israel — *1Ch 4:10*

bring ark of God, whose name is c. on it — *1Ch 13:6*

where the name is c., on (S) — *1Ch 13:6*

David c. on Lord, he answered him — *1Ch 21:26*

came no more, except c. by name — *Es 2:14*

who is not c. I have not been — *Es 4:11*

they have not c. upon God — *Ps 53:4*

kingdoms have not c. on thy name — *Ps 79:6*

shepherds is c. forth against him — *Isa 31:4*

but thou hast not c. on me, O Jacob — *Isa 43:22*

ye that are c. by name of Israel — *Isa 48:1*

hearken O Jacob, and Israel my c. — *Isa 48:12*

might be c. trees of righteousness — *Isa 61:3*

it shall no more be c. Tophet — *Jer 7:32*

wilt bring day that thou hast c. — *La 1:21*

hast c. as a solemn day my terrors — *La 2:22*

the name thereof is c. Bamah — *Eze 20:29*

let Daniel be c. and he will shew — *Da 5:12*

was born Jesus, who is c. Christ — *M't 1:16*

the first Simon, who is c. Peter — *M't 10:2*

said, is not his mother c. Mary — *M't 13:55*

Jesus c. a little child unto him — *M't 18:2*

many be c. but few chosen — *M't 20:16; 22:14*

Jesus stood still, and c. them — *M't 20:32*

be not c. Rabbi, one is your Master — *M't 23:8*

one of twelve c. Judas Iscariot — *M't 26:14*

shall I release Jesus, c. Christ — *M't 27:17*

Jesus commanded him to be c. — *M'k 10:49*

Peter c. to mind word Jesus said — *M'k 14:72*

none of kindred is c. by name — *Lu 1:61*

made signs how he would have him c. — *Lu 1:62*

no more worthy to be c. thy son — *Lu 15:19*

commanded the servants to be c. — *Lu 19:15*

when come to place c. Calvary — *Lu 23:33*

before Philip c. thee I saw thee — *Joh 1:48*

Messiah cometh, who is c. Christ — *Joh 4:25*

man c. Jesus made clay anointed eyes — *Joh 9:11*

go into street c. Straight, one c. Saul — *Ac 9:11*

disciples c. Christians first at Antioch — *Ac 11:26*

c. for Barnabas and Saul, desired to hear — *Ac 13:7*

Saul, c. Paul, filled with Holy Ghost — *Ac 13:9*

all Gentiles on whom my name is c. — *Ac 15:17*

be c. in question for uproar — *Ac 19:40*

I am c. in question by you — *Ac 23:6; 24:21*

Paul c. and prayed me to bring — *Ac 23:18*

Paul c. to be an apostle — *Ro 1:1; 1Co 1:1*

among whom are ye c. of Jesus — *Ro 1:6*

to them c. to be saints — *Ro 1:7; 1Co 1:2*

art c. a Jew, and restest in law — *Ro 2:17*

who are c. according to his purpose — *Ro 8:28*

by whom ye were c. to fellowship — *1Co 1:9*

to them c. both Jews and Greeks — *1Co 1:24*

not many mighty, not many noble c. — *1Co 1:26*

if any man c. brother be fornicator — *1Co 5:11*

is any c. being circumcised? is any c. — *1Co 7:18*

art c. being servant care not — *1Co 7:21*

every man wherein he is c. abide — *1Co 7:24*

soon removed from him that c. — *Ga 1:6*

ye have been c. to liberty — *Ga 5:13*

who are c. uncircumcision by that c. — *Eph 2:11*

walk worthy of vocation wherewith c. — *Eph 4:1*

as ye are c. in one hope of calling — *Eph 4:4*

to which ye are c. in one body — *Col 3:15*

Jesus, c. Justus, saluteth you — *Col 4:11*

exalteth above all that is c. God — *2Th 2:4*

eternal life, whereto thou art c. — *1Ti 6:12*

avoiding oppositions of science, falsely c. — *1Ti 6:20*

exhort daily while it is c. to-day — *Heb 3:13*

tabernacle which is c. the sanctuary — *Heb 9:2*

they that are c. might receive promise — *Heb 9:15*

God is not ashamed to be c. their God — *Heb 11:16*

Moses refused to be c. son of Pharaoh's — *Heb 11:24*

blaspheme name by which ye are c. — *Jas 2:7*

him who hath c. you out of darkness — *1Pe 2:9*

hereunto c. because Christ suffered — *1Pe 2:21*

knowing that ye are thereunto c. — *1Pe 3:9*

hath c. us to glory and virtue — *2Pe 1:3*

that we should be c. sons of God — *1Jo 3:1*

sanctified, preserved in Christ, and c. — *Jude 1*

name of star is c. wormwood — *Re 8:11*

city spiritually c. Sodom and Egypt — *Re 11:8*

old serpent c. the Devil, and Satan — *Re 12:9*

that are with him, are c. and chosen — *Re 17:14*

blessed that are c. to marriage supper — *Re 19:9*

GOD, LORD CALLED

God c. light day, darkness c. night — *Ge 1:5*

God c. the firmament, heaven — *Ge 1:8*

God c. dry land earth, waters c. he seas — *Ge 1:10*

God blessed them, and c. name Adam — *Ge 5:2*

God c. to him out of midst of bush — *Ex 3:4*

Lord c. to him out of the mountain — *Ex 19:3*

Lord c. Moses up to top of mount — *Ex 19:20*

Lord c. to Moses out of cloud — *Ex 24:16*

see, Lord hath c. my name Bezaleel — *Ex 35:30*

Lord c. Aaron and Miriam — *Nu 12:5*

Lord c. Samuel — *1Sa 3:4; 3:6, 8, 10*

Lord hath c. these three kings — *2Ki 3:10*

Lord hath c. for famine on land — *2Ki 8:1*

Lord c. earth from rising of sun — *Ps 50:1*

Lord raised, and c. him — *Isa 41:2*

Lord have c. thee in righteousness — *Isa 42:6*

Lord hath c. me from the womb — *Isa 49:1*

Lord hath c. thee as woman forsaken — *Isa 54:6*

Lord c. thy name a green olive tree — *Jer 11:16*

Lord hath not c. thy name Pashur — *Jer 20:3*

Lord God c. to contend by fire — *Am 7:4*

gathering that the Lord had c. us — *Ac 16:10*

God hath c. us to peace — *1Co 7:15*

as Lord c. every one, let him walk — *1Co 7:17*

it pleased God, who c. me by grace — *Ga 1:15*

God c. you to his kingdom and glory — *1Th 2:12*

for God hath not c. us to uncleanness — *1Th 4:7*

God c. you by our gospel — *2Th 2:14*

God hath c. us with a holy calling — *2Ti 1:9*

he that is c. of God, as was Aaron — *Heb 5:4*

c. of God an high priest after Melchisedek — *Heb 5:10*

God of all grace, who hath c. us — *1Pe 5:10*

HE CALLED

he c. that place Beer-sheba — *Ge 21:31*

he c. names as his father called — *Ge 26:18*

he c. his name Israel — *Ge 35:10*

on that day he c. him Jerubbaal — *J'g 6:32*

he saw me and c. to me — *2Sa 1:7*

he c. servant that ministered to him — *2Sa 13:17*

his brother he c. not — *1Ki 1:10; 1:19, 26*

he c. them land of Cabul to this day — *1Ki 9:13*

he c. to Gehazi, so he c. her — *2Ki 4:36*

brazen serpent, he c. it Nehushtan — *2Ki 18:4*

he c. for a famine on the land — *Ps 105:16*

c. he Johanan and all captains   Jer 42:8
he *c.* an assembly against me   La 1:15
he *c.* to man clothed with linen   Eze 9:3
he *c.* the twelve   M't 10:1
he *c.* them and they left   M'k 1:20
Jesus saw her, he *c.* her to him   Lu 13:12
if he *c.* them gods, to whom word   Joh 10:35
when he had *c.* saints and widows   Ac 9:41
c. he them in, and lodged them   Ac 10:23
then he *c.* for a light, and sprang in   Ac 16:29
whom he *c.* together with the workmen   Ac 19:25
he *c.* unto him two centurions   Ac 23:23
them he also *c.* whom he *c.*   Ro 8:30
he justified
whom he hath *c.* not of Jews only   Ro 9:24
as he which hath *c.* you is holy   1Pe 1:15

CALLED *BY MY NAME*

people *c.* by my name humble   2Ch 7:14
every one that is *c.* by my name   Isa 43:7
to a nation that was not *c.* by my name   Isa 65:1
house *c.* by my name   Jer 7:10; 7:11, 14, 30; 32:34; 34:15
the city which is *c.* by my name   Jer 25:29
remnant of heathen *c.* by my name   Am 9:12

CALLED *BY THY NAME*

house *c.* by thy name 1Ki 8:43; 2Ch 6:33
let us be *c.* by thy name to take reproach   Isa 4:1
I have *c.* thee by thy name   Isa 43:1; 45:4
they were not *c.* by thy name Isa 63:19
we are *c.* by thy name leave us Jer 14:9 not
I am *c.* by thy name O Lord Jer 15:16 God
the city which is *c.* by thy name Da 9:18
thy city and people are *c.* by Da 9:19 thy name

CALLED *HIS NAME*

Jacob, he *c.* his name Israel   Ge 35:10
he *c.* his name Benoni, but   Ge 35:18
father Benjamin
his mother *c.* his name Jabez   1Ch 4:9
she *c.* his name Peresh   1Ch 7:16
he *c.* his name Beriah   1Ch 7:23
first born son, *c.* his name   M't 1:25
Jesus
his name is *c.* the Word of   Re 19:13 God

CALLED *THE NAME*

c. the name of place Beth-el Ge 28:19; 35:15
Israel *c.* the name thereof   Ex 16:31 Manna
he *c.* the name of place   Ex 17:7 Massah
c. the name of altar   Ex 17:15 Jehovah-nissi
Samson *c.* the name   J'g 15:19 En-hakkore
c. the name of place   2Sa 5:20 Baal-perazim
c. the name Jachin 1Ki 7:21; 2Ch 3:17
and he *c.* the name of the   Job 42:14 first Jemima

I CALLED, I HAVE CALLED

I c. thee to curse mine   Nu 24:10 enemies
when *I c.* you, ye delivered   J'g 12:2 me not
I c. not, lie down again   1Sa 3:5
I have c. thee, thou mayest 1Sa 28:15 make known
in my distress *I c.*   2Sa 22:7; Ps 18:6; 118:5
I c. priests, took an oath of Ne 5:12 them

if *I* had *c.* and he had   Job 9:16 answered me
I c. servant, he gave no   Job 19:16 answer
I have c. on thee, for thou   Ps 17:6 wilt hear
not be ashamed, for *I have*   Ps 31:17 *c.* upon thee
Lord, *I have c.* daily upon   Ps 88:9 thee
then *c. I* upon the name of   Ps 116:4 the Lord
because *I have c.* and ye   Pr 1:24 refused
I c. him, but he gave me no   Ca 5:6 answer
I have c. mighty ones for   Isa 13:3 mine anger
I c. thee from chief   Isa 41:9 men thereof
I c. thee by thy name Isa 43:1; 45:4
I have c. him, I have   Isa 48:15 brought him
when *I c.* was there none to Isa 50:2 answer
for *I c.* him alone, and   Isa 51:2 blessed him
when *I c.* ye did not   Isa 65:12; answer   Jer 7:13
because when *I c.* none did Isa 66:4 answer
because *I have c.* to them   Jer 35:17
I c. for my lovers, but they   La 1:19 deceived me
I c. on thy name out of low   La 3:55 dungeon
drewest near in day *I c.* upon La 3:57 thee
I c. my Son out of Egypt   Ho 11:1; M't 2:15
I c. for a drought upon land Hag 1:11
one *I c.* Beauty, the other *I* Zec 11:7 *c.* Bands
servants, *I have c.* you   Joh 15:15 friends
for work whereto *I have c.*   Ac 13:2 them
this cause have *I c.* you to Ac 28:20 see

SENT AND CALLED

she *sent and c.* Jacob   Ge 27:42
Jacob *sent and c.* Rachel and Ge 31:4 Leah
then Pharaoh *sent and c.*   Ge 41:14 Joseph
Balak *sent and c.* Balaam to Jos 24:9 curse
she *sent and c.* Barak of   J'g 4:6 Kadesh
sent and c. lords of   J'g 16:18 Philistines
sent and c. his name   2Sa 12:25 Jedidiah
the king *sent and c.* Shimei 1Ki 2:36; 12:42
sent and c. Jeroboam   1Ki 12:3; 2Ch 10:3
Haman *sent and c.* for friends Es 5:10
sent to Ephesus, *and c.*   Ac 20:17 elders

SHALL BE CALLED

shall be c. woman, because   Ge 2:23 taken out of
thy name *shall be c.*   Ge 17:5 Abraham, for a father
hearken to Sarah's voice,   Ge 21:12; for in Isaac *shall* seed *be c.* Ro 9:7; Heb 11:18
shall be c. no more Jacob,   Ge 32:28 but Israel
issue *shall be c.* after their   Ge 48:6 brethren
his name *shall be c.* in   De 25:10 Israel
wise in heart *shall be c.*   Pr 16:21 prudent
evil, *shall be c.* mischievous Pr 24:8 person
remaineth in Jerusalem *shall* Isa 4:3 *be c.* holy
his name *shall be c.*   Isa 9:6 Wonderful
one *shall be c.* city of   Isa 19:18 destruction
vile person *shall* no more be Isa 32:5 *c.* liberal

a way, and *shall be c.* way of Isa 35:8 holiness
God of whole earth *shall* he Isa 54:5 *be c.*
shall be c. house of prayer   Isa 56:7; M't 21:13
it *shall* no more *be c.*   Jer 7:32; Tophet   19:6
he *shall be c.* Lord our   Jer 23:6; Righteousness   33:16
Jerusalem *shall be c.* city of Zec 8:3 truth
be fulfilled, *shall be c.* a   M't 2:23 Nazarene
peacemakers *shall be c.*   M't 5:9 children of God
he *shall be c.* least in   M't 5:19 kingdom of
he *shall be c.* Son of Highest Lu 1:32
holy thing *shall be c.* Son of Lu 1:35 God
said, Not so; but he *shall be* Lu 1:60 *c.* John
every male *shall be c.* holy to Lu 2:23 Lord
if married, *shall be c.* an   Ro 7:3 adulteress
they *shall be c.* the children Ro 9:26 of God

SHALT BE CALLED

shalt be c. city of   Isa 1:26 righteousness
shalt be c. no more tender   Isa 47:1 and delicate
shalt no more *be c.* lady of Isa 47:5 kingdoms
shalt be c. repairer of the   Isa 58:12 breach
shalt be c. by a new name   Isa 62:2
shalt be c. Hephzi-bah, land Isa 62:4 Beulah
shalt be c. sought for, city Isa 62:12 not forsaken
shalt be c. Prophet of Highest Lu 1:76
shalt be c. Cephas, which is, Joh 1:42 a stone

THEY CALLED

they c. Lot, where are the men Ge 19:5
they c. the people to the   Nu 25:2 sacrifices
they c. for Samson out of   J'g 16:25 the prison
they c. these days Purim,   Es 9:26 after Pur
they c. upon Lord, he   Ps 99:6 answered
they have c. a multitude after Jer 12:6 thee
they c. thee an outcast,   Jer 30:17 saying
they c. to them, so they   Ho 11:2 went from
though *they c.* them to the   Ho 11:7 most High
if *they have c.* master   M't 10:25 Beelzebub
they c. him Zacharias, after Lu 1:59 his father
they c. parents of him that Joh 9:18 received
then again *they c.* man that Joh 9:24 was blind
they c. them, and commanded Ac 4:18 not to
when *they* had *c.* apostles,   Ac 5:40 and beaten
they c. Barnabas, Jupiter;   Ac 14:12 Paul, Mercurius

WAS CALLED

which *was c.* the land of   De 3:13 giants
place *was c.* valley of   2Ch 20:26 Berachah
was c. after their name   Ezr 2:61; Ne 7:63
was c. a transgressor from   Isa 48:8 womb
whose name *was c.*   Da 10:1 Belteshazzar
high priest, who *was c.*   M't 26:3 Caiaphas
was c. field of blood, to this M't 27:8 day
sixth month with her who   Lu 1:36 *was c.* barren

name *was* c. Jesus, named   *Lu 2:21*
of angel
Jesus *was* c. and disciples to *Joh 2:2*
marriage
in church Simeon, that *was* c. *Ac 13:1*
Niger
when he *was* c. forth,   *Ac 24:2*
Tertullus
knew that island *was* c.   *Ac 28:1*
Melita
abide in calling wherein he *1Co 7:20*
was c.
Abraham when he *was* c.   *Heb 11:8*
obeyed
he *was* c. the friend of God *Jas 2:23*
that sat on him *was* c.   *Re 19:11*
Faithful

CALLEDST

that thou c. us not, when thou *J'g 8:1*
for thou c. me. And he said, *1Sa 3:5*
I
c. in trouble, and I delivered *Ps 81:7*
thee
Thus thou c. to   *Eze 23:21*
remembrance the

CALLEST

Why c. thou me good?   *M't 19:17*
there is
unto him, Why c. thou me *M'k 10:18*
good
Why c. thou me good? none *Lu 18:19*
is

CALLETH

that the stranger c. to thee *1Ki 8:43;*
for   *2Ch 6:33*
c. upon God, and he   *Job 12:4*
answereth
Deep c. unto deep at the *Ps 42:7*
noise
he c. them all by their names *Ps 147:4*
and his mouth c. for strokes *Pr 18:6*
He c. to me out of Seir,   *Isa 21:11*
Watchman
he c. them all by names by *Isa 40:26*
None c. for justice, nor any *Isa 59:4*
there is none that c. upon *Isa 64:7*
thy
there is none among them *Ho 7:7*
that c.
that c. for the waters of the *Am 5:8*
sea
he that c. for the waters of *Am 9:6*
the sea
that, said, This man c. for *M't 27:47*
Elias
and c. unto him whom he *M'k 3:13*
would
of good comfort, rise; he c. *M'k 10:49*
thee
therefore himself c. him *M'k 12:37*
Lord
heard it, said, Behold, he c. *M'k 15:35*
Elias
home, he c. together his *Lu 15:6*
friends
c. her friends and her   *Lu 15:9*
neighbours
c. the Lord the God of   *Lu 20:37*
Abraham
David therefore c. him Lord, *Lu 20:44*
how
and he c. his own sheep by *Joh 10:3*
name
The Master is come, and c. *Joh 11:28*
for thee
c. those things which be not *Ro 4:17*
as
not of works, but of him that *Ro 9:11*
c.
c. Jesus accursed; and that *1Co 12:3*
no
cometh not of him that c. you *Ga 5:8*
Faithful is he that c. you, *1Th 5:24*
who
which c. herself a prophetess, *Re 2:20*
to

CALLING

for the c. of the assembly, *Nu 10:2*
and for
the c. of assemblies, I cannot *Isa 1:13*
c. the generations from the *Isa 41:4*
C. a ravenous bird from the *Isa 46:11*
east,

---

in c. to remembrance the *Eze 23:19*
days of
and c. unto their fellows *M't 11:16*
without, sent unto him, c. *M'k 3:31*
him
Peter c. to remembrance *M'k 11:21*
saith
and c. unto him the   *M'k 15:44*
centurion, he
And John c. unto him two of *Lu 7:19*
his
c. one to another, and saying *Lu 7:32*
stoned Stephen, c. upon God *Ac 7:59*
sins, c. on the name of the *Ac 22:16*
Lord
gifts and c. of God are *Ro 11:29*
without
For ye see your c. brethren, *1Co 1:26*
how
abide in the same c. wherein *1Co 7:20*
he
what is the hope of his c. *Eph 1:18*
and
worthy of c.   *Eph 4:1*
(A)(B)(E)(P)(R)
are called in one hope of *Eph 4:4*
your c.
for the prize of the high c. *Ph'p 3:14*
of
would count you worthy of *2Th 1:11*
this c.
us, and called us with an holy *2Ti 1:9*
c.
partakers of the heavenly c. *Heb 3:1*
Even as Sara obeyed   *1Pe 3:6*
Abraham, c. him lord
give diligence to make your *2Pe 1:10*
c.

CALLOUSNESS

vexed at their c. (B)   *M'k 3:5*

CALM

He maketh the storm a c. *Ps 107:29*
so that
c. undisturbed mind (A) *Pr 14:30*
unto thee, that the sea may *Joh 1:11*
be c.
so shall the sea be c. unto *Joh 1:12*
you
the sea; and there was a *M't 8:26*
great c.
ceased, and there was a *M'k 4:39*
great c.
they ceased, and there was a *Lu 8:24*
c.

CALMED

king's anger c. down (B) *Es 7:10*

CALNEH

and Erech, and Accad, and *Ge 10:10*
C.
Pass ye unto C. and see; and *Am 6:2*

CALNO

Is not C. as Carchemish? is *Isa 10:9*
not

CALVARY

which is called C. there they *Lu 23:33*

CALVE

thou mark when the hinds *Job 39:1*
do c.
the Lord maketh the hinds to *Ps 29:9*
c.

CALVED

the hind also c. in the field *Jer 14:5*

CALVES

bring their c. home from *1Sa 6:7*
them
and shut up their c. at home *1Sa 6:10*
took sheep, and oxen, and *1Sa 14:32*
c.
made two c. of gold, and *1Ki 12:28*
said
unto the c. that he had *1Ki 12:32*
made
golden c. that were in *2Ki 10:29*
Beth-el

---

them molten images, even *2Ki 17:16*
two c.
and for the c. which he had *2Ch 11:15*
made
there are with you golden c. *2Ch 13:8*
which
with the c. of the people, till *Ps 68:30*
shall fear because of the c. *Ho 10:5*
of
the men that sacrifice kiss *Ho 13:2*
the c.
will we render the c. of our *Ho 14:2*
lips
the c. out of the midst of the *Am 6:4*
stall
offerings, with c. of a year *Mic 6:6*
old
and grow up as c. of the stall *Mal 4:2*
by the blood of goats and c. *Heb 9:12*
took the blood of c. and of *Heb 9:19*
goats

CALVETH

their cow c. and casteth not *Job 21:10*
her

CAME

of whom c. Philistine   *Ge 10:14;*
                 1Ch 1:12
two angels c. to Sodom at *Ge 19:1*
even
God c. to Abimelech in a *Ge 20:3*
dream
brother c. with subtilty took *Ge 27:35*
blessing
c. to a certain place (S) *Ge 28:11*
God c. to Laban in dream *Ge 31:24*
c. to thy brother Esau, he *Ge 32:6*
cometh
it c. to pass, when she was *Ge 35:17*
in hard
it c. to pass, as her soul was *Ge 35:18*
in
these are the dukes that c. *Ge 36:30*
of Hori
laid up garment until lord c. *Ge 39:16*
home
c. down (B)   *Ex 18:18; 33:9; De 2:23*
it c. to pass on the eighth day *Le 9:1*
c. to land whither thou *Nu 13:27*
sentest us
red heifer, upon which never *Nu 19:2*
c. yoke
God c. to Balaam at night *Nu 22:9;*
                    22:20
Spirit c. on him   *Nu 24:2;*
     J'g 3:10; 1Sa 10:10
and we c. to Kadesh-barnea *De 1:19*
Lord c. from Sinai, rose from *De 33:2*
Seir
as she c. she moved   *Jos 15:18;*
                 J'g 1:14
kings c. and fought   *J'g 5:19*
cake of bread c. to tent smote it *J'g 7:13*
robbed all that c. along that *J'g 9:25*
way
upon them c. course of Jotham *J'g 9:57*
but c. not within the border *J'g 11:18*
of Moab
man that c. to me the other *J'g 13:10*
day
Manoah arose and c. to the *J'g 13:11*
man
bring forth the man that c. *J'g 19:22*
into thy house
Israel smote Benjamin, all *J'g 20:48*
that c.
it is Moabitish damsel that c. *Ru 2:6*
back
custom was, priest's servant *1Sa 2:13*
c.
they did to Israelites that c. *1Sa 2:14*
thither
there c. a man of God to *1Sa 2:27*
Eli, and said
the word of Samuel c. to all *1Sa 4:1*
Israel
they c. no more into coast *1Sa 7:13*
of Israel
Lord told Samuel before *1Sa 9:15*
Saul c.
saw asses no where, c. to *1Sa 10:14*
Samuel
Samuel c. not, people *1Sa 13:8*
scattered
c. lion and bear, and took *1Sa 17:34*
lamb

Judah *c.* and anointed David   *2Sa 2:4* king
knowest Abner, that *c.* to   *2Sa 3:25* deceive thee
while in way tidings *c.* to   *2Sa 13:30* David
king's sons *c.* and wept, king   *2Sa 13:30* wept
when any *c.* to king for   *2Sa 15:2* judgment
Absalom and Ahithophel *c.*   *2Sa 16:15* to Jerusalem
every one that *c.* by him   *2Sa 20:12* stood still
upon (S)   *2Sa 22:6;*
    2Sa 22:19; Job 20:27; Ps 18:18
while he spake, Jonathan son   *1Ki 1:42* of Abiathar *c.*
c. people to hear wisdom of   *1Ki 4:34* Solomon
there *c.* no more such   *1Ki 10:10* spices as these
c. no such almug-trees   *1Ki 10:12*
returned not by way he *c.*   *1Ki 13:10* to Bethel
c. to a cave and lodged there   *1Ki 19:9*
And, behold, there *c.* a   *1Ki 19:13* voice unto him
king of Israel *c.* heavy to   *1Ki 20:43* Samaria
it fell on day he *c.* thither   *2Ki 4:11*
she *c.* to man of God to hill   *2Ki 4:27*
Naaman *c.* and stood   *2Ki 5:15* before Elisha
bands of Syria *c.* no more   *2Ki 6:23* into Israel
ere messenger *c.* he said to   *2Ki 6:32* elders
Hazael departed from Elisha,   *2Ki 8:14* *c.* to
wherefore *c.* this mad fellow   *2Ki 9:11* to thee
Jehu arose, and *c.* to   *2Ki 10:12* Samaria
he *c.* upon Jehonadab (S)   *2Ki 10:15*
worshippers of Baal *c.*   *2Ki 10:21* house full
one of priests *c.* dwelt in   *2Ki 17:28* Beth-el
by way that he *c.* shall he   *2Ki 19:33* return
at command of Lord *c.* this   *2Ki 24:3* on Judah
these *c.* in days of Hezekiah   *1Ch 4:41*
Judah prevailed, of him *c.*   *1Ch 5:2* chief ruler
Ephraim's brethren *c.* to   *1Ch 7:22* comfort him
these are they that *c.* day by   *1Ch 12:1* day
c. to David to help him a   *1Ch 12:22* great host
that the word of God *c.* to   *1Ch 17:3* Nathan
Levites left all and *c.* to   *2Ch 11:14* Judah
guard *c.* and fetched the   *2Ch 12:11* shields
for fear of Lord *c.* upon   *2Ch 14:14* them
band of men that *c.* with   *2Ch 22:1* Arabians
wrath *c.* on Judah and   *2Ch 24:18* Jerusalem for trespass
Amaziah would not hear,   *2Ch 25:20* for it *c.* of God
divers humbled themselves   *2Ch 30:11* and *c.*
as soon as commandment *c.*   *2Ch 31:5* abroad
c. with Zerubbabel, Mordecai   *Ezr 2:2*
cause to cease till *c.* to Darius   *Ezr 5:5*
seventh month *c.* were in   *Ne 7:73* cities
Vashti be brought in, she *c.*   *Es 1:17* not
then thus *c.* every maiden to   *Es 2:13* the king
Mordecai *c.* even before king's   *Es 4:2* gate
whither king's decree *c.* Jews   *Es 8:17* had joy
not in safety, yet trouble *c.*   *Job 3:26*
blessing of him ready to   *Job 29:13* perish is *c.*
I looked for good, evil *c.*   *Job 30:26* darkness *c.*
cry *c.* before me, even to ears   *Ps 18:6*

when foes *c.* upon me they   *Ps 27:2* stumbled
wrath *c.* upon them, and   *Ps 78:31* slew them
until his word *c.* word   *Ps 105:19* tried them
he spake, and there *c.*   *Ps 105:31* divers sorts of flies
he spake, and locusts *c.* and   *Ps 105:34* caterpillars
go as he *c.* and take nothing   *Ec 5:15;*
    5:16
in year Tartan *c.* to Ashdod   *Isa 20:1*
his ambassadors *c.* to Hanes   *Isa 30:4*
earth were afraid, drew near   *Isa 41:5* and *c.*
nor *c.* it into my mind   *Jer 7:31;*
    Jer 19:5; 32:35
we looked for peace, but no   *Jer 8:15* good *c.*
nor *c.* abominable flesh into   *Eze 4:14* mouth
c. to Lebanon took highest   *Eze 17:3* branch
afore he that was escaped   *Eze 33:22* *c.* opened
bones *c.* together, bone to   *Eze 37:7* his bone
breath *c.* into them, they   *Eze 37:10* lived and stood
glory of God of Israel *c.*   *Eze 43:2* from east
all this *c.* on king   *Da 4:28* Nebuchadnezzar
one like Son of Man *c.* with   *Da 7:13* clouds
till ancient of days *c.*   *Da 7:22* judgment given
to whom the house of Israel   *Am 6:1* *c.*
for word *c.* to king of   *Jon 3:6* Nineveh
God *c.* from Teman, and   *Hab 3:3* Holy One
looked for much, lo it *c.* to   *Hag 1:9* little
when one *c.* to pressfat to   *Hag 2:16* draw out
c. great wrath from Lord of   *Zec 7:12* hosts
all nations *c.* against   *Zec 14:16* Jerusalem
there *c.* wise men from east   *M't 2:1* to Jerusalem
till it *c.* and stood over where   *M't 2:9* child was
those days *c.* John Baptist   *M't 3:1* preaching
rains descended, floods *c.*   *M't 7:25;*
    7:27
passed over and *c.* into own   *M't 9:1* city
woman *c.* touched hem of   *M't 9:20* garment
come into house, blind men   *M't 9:28* *c.*
Son of man *c.* not to be   *M't 20:28* ministered to
c. to first son, go work   *M't 21:28* to-day
he *c.* to second, and said   *M't 21:30* likewise
John *c.* to you in way of   *M't 21:32* righteousness
they went to buy,   *M't 25:10* bridegroom *c.*
was in prison, and ye *c.*   *M't 25:36* to me
he *c.* to Jesus and kissed him   *M't 26:49*
false witnesses *c.* yet found   *M't 26:60* they none
disciples *c.* by night, stole   *M't 28:13* him away
heard what great things he   *M'k 3:8* did *c.*
how long is it since this *c.*   *M'k 9:21* to him
one of the scribes *c.* and   *M'k 12:28* asked him
c. certain poor widow   *M'k 12:42* threw two mites
Elisabeth's full time *c.* to be   *Lu 1:57*
c. cloud and overshadowed   *Lu 9:34* them
there *c.* voice out of cloud   *Lu 9:35*
when he *c.* to himself, he said,   *Lu 15:17* how
he arose and *c.* to his father   *Lu 15:20*
same *c.* to bear witness of   *Joh 1:7* light

c. to own, own received him   *Joh 1:11* not
grace and truth *c.* by Jesus   *Joh 1:17* Christ
c. to Jesus by night   *Joh 3:2;*
    Joh 7:50; 19:39
they *c.* and were baptized   *Joh 3:23*
upon this *c.* disciples, and   *Joh 4:27* marvelled
called gods to whom word   *Joh 10:35* of God *c.*
voice *c.* not because of me,   *Joh 12:30* but for
at even *c.* Jesus, and stood   *Joh 20:19* in midst
preached in all cities, *c.* to   *Ac 8:40* Caesarea
c. for that intent, to bring   *Ac 9:21* bound
many as *c.* with Peter were   *Ac 10:45* astonished
vessel descended, and *c.* to   *Ac 11:5* me
he *c.* and had seen grace of   *Ac 11:23* God
many that believed *c.* and   *Ac 19:18* confessed
brethren that *c.* spake any   *Ac 28:21* harm
judgment *c.* free gift *c.* on all   *Ro 5:18*
when the commandment *c.* sin   *Ro 7:9* revived
of whom, as concerning flesh,   *Ro 9:5* Christ *c.*
by man *c.* death, by man *c.*   *1Co 15:21* also
before that certain *c.* from   *Ga 2:12* James
before faith *c.* we were kept   *Ga 3:23* under law
c. preached peace to you   *Eph 2:17* afar off
gospel *c.* not in word only   *1Th 1:5* but in
that Christ *c.* to save sinners   *1Ti 1:15*
persecutions which *c.* at   *2Ti 3:11* Antioch
there *c.* such a voice to   *2Pe 1:17* him
voice *c.* from heaven we   *2Pe 1:18* heard
prophecy *c.* not in by will of   *2Pe 1:21* man
this is he that *c.* by water   *1Jo 5:6* and blood
brethren *c.* and testified of truth   *3Jo 3*
great Babylon *c.* in   *Re 16:19* remembrance

CAME *AGAIN*

angel *c. again* to the woman   *J'g 13:9*
his spirit *c. again* to him   *J'g 15:19;*
    1Sa 30:12
Benjamin *c. again* at   *J'g 21:14* that time
soul of child *c.* into him   *1Ki 17:22* *again*
angel of Lord *c. again*   *1Ki 19:7* second time
flesh *c. again* like   *2Ki 5:14* flesh of child
lepers *c. again*, entered   *2Ki 7:8* another tent
c. again to Judah   *Ezr 2:1; Ne 7:6*
Mordecai *c. again* to king's   *Es 6:12* gate
c. again touched me one   *Da 10:18* like man
angel *c. again* and waked me   *Zec 4:1*
spirit *c. again*, she arose   *Lu 8:55* straightway
early he *c. again* into temple   *Joh 8:2*

CAME *DOWN*

Lord *c. down* to see city   *Ge 11:5*
when fowls *c. down*   *Ge 15:11* on carcases
we *c. down* at first to buy   *Ge 43:20* food
Lord *c. down* upon mount   *Ex 19:20* Sinai
Moses *c. down* from mount   *Ex 34:29* Sinai
Aaron *c. down* from offering   *Le 9:22*
Lord *c. down* in cloud   *Nu 11:25; 12:5*
then Amalekites *c. down*   *Nu 14:45* and smote

out of Machir *c. down*   *J'g 5:14*
governors
bowed heavens *c. down*   *2Sa 22:10;*
                   Ps 18:9
c. down fire from heaven   *2Ki 1:10;*
              2Ki 1:12, 14
men of Gath *c. down* to take *1Ch 7:21*
cattle
made end of praying, fire *c.* *2Ch 7:1*
down
therefore she *c. down*   *La 1:9*
wonderfully
an holy one *c. down* from   *Da 4:13*
heaven
evil *c. down* from Lord to   *Mic 1:12*
gate
as *c. down* from mountain   *M't 17:9;*
                   M'k 9:9
c. down certain priest that *Lu 10:31*
way
he made haste and *c. down* *Lu 19:6*
he that *c. down* from heaven *Joh 3:13*
c. down from heaven, not to *Joh 6:38*
do own will
bread *c. down* from heaven *Joh 6:41;*
               Joh 6:51, 58
men *c. down* from Judaea   *Ac 15:1*
taught
c. down from Judaea certain *Ac 21:10*
prophet
fire *c. down* from God and   *Re 20:9*
devoured

CAME *FORTH*

Lord did when I *c. forth* out *Ex 13:8*
of Egypt
wept, why *c. forth* out of   *Nu 11:20*
Egypt
Aaron and Miriam, both *c.*   *Nu 12:5*
forth
not with water when *c. forth* *De 23:4*
bread hot on day *c. forth* to *Jos 9:12*
you
out of the eater *c. forth* meat, *J'g 14:14*
and out of the strong *c. forth*
sweetness
Shimei *c. forth* cursed as he   *2Sa 16:5*
came
son *c. forth* of my bowels   *2Sa 16:11*
seeketh my life
c. forth spirit, stood before *1Ki 22:21*
Lord
c. forth children mocked him *2Ki 2:23*
c. forth two she-bears and   *2Ki 2:24*
tare 42 children
fathers *c. forth* out of Egypt *2Ki 21:15;*
                   Jer 7:25
c. forth of his bowels slew *2Ch 32:21*
him
therefore *c.* I *forth* to meet *Pr 7:15*
thee
as *c. forth* naked, shall return *Ec 5:15*
c. I *forth* out of the womb *Jer 20:18*
they *c. forth* of midst of fire   *Da 3:26*
c. forth fingers and wrote on   *Da 5:5*
plaster
fiery stream *c. forth* before   *Da 7:10*
him
out of one of them *c. forth*   *Da 8:9*
little horn
command *c. forth* I am come *Da 9:23*
to shew
out of him *c. forth* corner   *Zec 10:4*
that I may preach, *c.* I *forth* *M'k 1:38*
he that was dead *c. forth*   *Joh 11:44*
bound
I *c. forth* from Father into   *Joh 16:28*
world
Jesus *c. forth* wearing crown *Joh 19:5*
of thorns

CAME *IN*

sons of God *c. in* to daughters *Ge 6:4*
of men
where are men that *c. in* to   *Ge 19:5*
thee
Judah *c. in* unto her, she   *Ge 38:18*
conceived
c. in to lie with me, I cried *Ge 39:14*
loud
if *c. in* by himself, he shall go *Ex 21:3*
none went out, none *c. in* to   *Jos 6:1*
Jericho
out and *c. in* before people *1Sa 18:13;*
                   18:16
she *c. in* to him, he lay with *2Sa 11:4*
her
as she *c. in* at the door   *1Ki 14:6*

no peace to him that *c. in*   *2Ch 15:5;*
                   Zec 8:10
c. in to king no more except *Es 2:14*
they *c. in* and possessed it   *Jer 32:23*
now Jeremiah *c. in* and went *Jer 37:4*
out
return by way of gate he *c.* *Eze 46:9*
in
then *c. in* the magicians   *Da 4:7; 5:8*
but at last Daniel *c. in* before *Da 4:8*
me
my prayer *c. in* to holy   *Jon 2:7*
temple
when king *c. in* to see   *M't 22:11*
guests
angel *c. in* to Mary, and said *Lu 1:28*
woman since I *c. in* kissed   *Lu 7:45*
my feet
wife not knowing what was   *Ac 5:7*
done *c. in*
young men *c. in* and found   *Ac 5:10*
her dead
c. in privily to spy our liberty *Ga 2:4*

CAME *NEAR*

pressed, *c. near* to break door *Ge 19:9*
one *c.* not *near* other all   *Ex 14:20*
night
when *c. near* altar, they   *Ex 40:32*
washed
captains *c. near* to Moses   *Nu 31:48*
chief of Joseph *c. near* before *Nu 36:1*
Moses
c. near to me every one   *De 1:22; 5:23*
c. near put your feet on   *Jos 10:24*
necks
c. near before Eleazar priest *Jos 17:4;*
                   21:1
Elijah *c. near* and said   *1Ki 18:36*
Gehazi *c. near* to thrust her *2Ki 4:27*
away
Zedekiah *c. near* smote   *2Ch 18:23*
Micaiah
from least even to greatest   *Jer 42:1*
c. near
Chaldeans *c. near* accused   *Da 3:8*
Jews
Nebuchadnezzar *c. near* to   *Da 3:26*
the furnace
c. near Damascus, there shined *Ac 9:3*
light

CAME *NIGH*

as he *c. nigh* he saw calf   *Ex 32:19*
all children of Israel *c. nigh* *Ex 34:32*
when any *c. nigh* to do   *2Sa 15:5*
obeisance
Jesus *c. nigh* to sea of   *M't 15:29*
Galilee
when they *c. nigh* to   *M'k 11:1*
Jerusalem
when he *c. nigh* to gate of city *Lu 7:12*

CAME *OUT*

Rebekah *c. out* with her   *Ge 24:15*
pitcher
first *c. out* red, all over like *Ge 25:25*
a hairy
the midwife said, this *c. out* *Ge 38:28*
first
all the souls which *c. out* of *Ge 46:26*
his loins
remember day in which *c.*   *Ex 13:3;*
out   *13:4*
fire *c. out* from Lord   *Le 9:24;*
                   Nu 16:35
Lord spake suddenly, they *c.* *Nu 12:4*
out
Dathan and Abiram *c. out* *Nu 16:27*
and stood
smote rock, water *c. out*   *Nu 20:11*
abundantly
not as Egypt whence ye *c.*   *De 11:10*
out
all that *c. out* were   *Jos 5:4;*
circumcised
till all that *c. out* of Egypt *Jos 5:6*
were consumed
Jael *c. out* to meet him   *J'g 4:22*
I am *c. out* of the army   *1Sa 4:16*
about these three days since I *1Sa 21:5*
c. out
spear *c. out* behind him, he *2Sa 2:23*
fell
Michal *c. out* to meet   *2Sa 6:20*
David

men prevailed against us,   *2Sa 11:23*
and *c. out*
all the people *c. out* by   *2Sa 18:4*
hundreds
they *c. out* of Egypt   *1Ki 8:9; 2Ch 5:10*
young men princes of   *1Ki 20:19*
provinces *c. out*
Israel invade, when they *c.* *2Ch 20:10*
out
naked *c.* I *out* of mother's   *Job 1:21*
womb
give up ghost when *c. out* of *Job 3:11*
belly
which *c. out* of my lips was *Jer 17:16*
right
whirlwind *c. out* of north, a *Eze 1:4*
cloud
c. out as whirlwind to   *Hab 3:14*
scatter
c. out two women, wind in *Zec 5:9*
wings
the whole city *c. out* to meet *M't 8:34*
Jesus
return to house I *c. out*   *M't 12:44;*
                   Lu 11:24
as they *c. out* found Simon *M't 27:32*
of
c. out of graves after   *M't 27:53*
resurrection
unclean spirit cried, he *c.*   *M'k 1:26;*
out   *9:26*
when he *c. out*, he saw much *M'k 6:34*
people
voice *c. out* of cloud, saying, *M'k 9:7*
when he *c. out* he could not *Lu 1:22*
speak
he *c. out* of him, and hurt   *Lu 4:35*
him not
c. out his father, and   *Lu 15:28*
entreated
ye believed I *c. out* from   *Joh 16:27*
God
they have known I *c. out*   *Joh 17:8*
from thee
forthwith *c. out* blood and *Joh 19:34*
water
unclean spirits *c. out* of many *Ac 8:7*
the spirit *c. out* the same   *Ac 16:18*
hour
c. word of God *out* from   *1Co 14:36*
you
all that *c. out* of Egypt by *Heb 3:16*
Moses
these *c. out* of great   *Re 7:14*
tribulation
another angel *c. out* of   *Re 14:15;*
temple   *14:17*
another angel *c. out* from *Re 14:18*
the altar
seven angels *c. out* of the   *Re 15:6*
temple
voice *c. out* of throne, praise *Re 19:5*
God

CAME *OVER*

Israel *c. over* Jordan on dry *Jos 4:22*
land
Levite *c. over* against Jebus *J'g 19:10*
they *c. over* to other side of *M'k 5:1*
sea

CAME *TO PASS*

it *c. to pass* at end of 430   *Ex 12:41*
years, self-same day it *c. to pass*
so it *c. to pass*   *De 2:16;*
1Sa 13:22; 2Ki 15:12; Es 2:8; Ac 27:44
it *c. to pass* when Israel   *Jos 17:13*
grew strong
failed not any thing; all *c.* *Jos 21:45*
to pass
it *c. to pass*   *J'g 15:1;*
              1Ki 11:4, 15;
it *c. to pass*   *J'g 15:1;*
2Ki 3:5; Ne 2:1; 4:1, 7; 6:1; 7:1;
                   Jer 35:11
it *c. to pass* when time was *1Sa 1:20*
come
all those signs *c. to pass* that *1Sa 10:9*
day
it *c. to pass* evil spirit from *1Sa 16:23*
God
it *c. to pass* after this   *2Sa 2:1;*
      8:1; 10:1; 2Ki 6:24; 2Ch 20:1
it *c. to pass* on the morrow *2Ki 8:15;*
       1Ch 10:8; Jer 20:3; Ac 4:5
I did them suddenly, they *c.* *Isa 48:3*
to pass

before it *c. to pass* I shewed   *Isa* 48:5
it thee
even as it *c. to pass* and ye   *1Th* 3:4
know

I CAME

I *c.* this day to the well   *Ge* 24:42
little thou hadst before I *c.*   *Ge* 30:30
were born before I *c.* into   *Ge* 48:5
Egypt
when I *c.* from Padan,   *Ge* 48:7
Rachel died
I *c.* to speak to Pharaoh in   *Ex* 5:23
thy name
I *c.* found her not a maid   *De* 22:14
I *c.* into Gibeah of Benjaman   *J'g* 20:4
I believed not till I *c.*   *1Ki* 10:7;
  2Ch 9:6
I *c.* to the house of Shemaiah *Ne* 6:10
I *c.* to the king and obtained   *Ne* 13:6
leave
I *c.* to Jerusalem and   *Ne* 13:7
understood evil
when I *c.* was there no man   *Isa* 50:2
then I *c.* to them of the   *Eze* 3:15
captivity
when I *c.* to destroy the city *Eze* 43:3
I *c.* not to send peace, but *M't* 10:34
sword
I *c.* not to call righteous   *M'k* 2:17;
  Lu 5:32
I know whence I *c.* whither *Joh* 8:14
I go
I *c.* from God, nor *c.* I of *Joh* 8:42
myself
for this cause I *c.* to this   *Joh* 12:27
hour
I *c.* not to judge world, but *Joh* 12:47
save
this cause *c.* I into world   *Joh* 18:37
c. I. as soon as I was sent *Ac* 10:29
from the first day I *c.* into *Ac* 20:18
Asia
being led by hand, I *c.* to *Ac* 22:11
Damascus
c. I with an army and   *Ac* 23:27
rescued him
I *c.* to bring alms to my nation *Ac* 24:17
when I *c.* I *c.* not with   *1Co* 2:1
excellency
to spare you I *c.* not to   *2Co* 1:23
Corinth
lest when I *c.* I should have *2Co* 2:3
sorrow
I *c.* to Troas to preach   *2Co* 2:12
Christ's gospel
afterwards I *c.* into regions *Ga* 1:21
of Syria

THEN CAME

then *c.* Amalek and fought   *Ex* 17:8
Israel
then *c.* daughters of   *Nu* 27:1
Zelophehad
then *c.* David to Ahimelech *1Sa* 21:1
then *c.* all tribes to David   *2Sa* 5:1
then *c.* to Gilead, numbered *2Sa* 24:6
people
then *c.* Eliakim and   *2Ki* 18:37;
Shebna   *Isa* 36:22
then *c.* Solomon from   *2Ch* 1:13
journey
then *c.* Shemaiah to   *2Ch* 12:5
Rehoboam
then *c.* Sheshbazzar, laid   *Ezr* 5:16
foundation
then Hanani one of my   *Ne* 1:2
brethren *c.*
then I *c.* to governors beyond *Ne* 2:9
the river
when I looked for good,   *Job* 30:26
then evil *c.*
then *c.* Jeremiah from   *Jer* 19:14
Tophet
then *c.* all the princes to   *Jer* 38:27
Jeremiah
then *c.* certain elders of   *Eze* 14:1
Israel
then they *c.* same day into *Eze* 23:39
sanctuary
then *c.* to him disciples of *M't* 9:14
John
then *c.* to Jesus scribes and *M't* 15:1
Pharisees
then *c.* disciples, said to   *M't* 15:12;
him   17:19
then *c.* she, worshipped   *M't* 15:25;
him   *M'k* 7:25

then *c.* Peter to him, and   *M't* 18:21
said, Lord, how oft
then *c.* mother of Zebedee's *M't* 20:20
children
then *c.* and laid hands on   *M't* 26:50
Jesus
then *c.* publicans to be   *Lu* 3:12
baptized
then *c.* the day of unleavened *Lu* 22:7
bread
then *c.* officers to the chief *Joh* 7:45
priests
then there *c.* a voice from *Joh* 12:28
heaven
then *c.* Jesus, doors being *Joh* 20:26
shut, stood

THEY CAME, CAME THEY

they *c.* to Haran and dwelt *Ge* 11:31
there
into the land of Canaan they *Ge* 12:5
c.
they *c.* to place God told   *Ge* 22:9
them
till they *c.* to a land   *Ex* 16:35
inhabited
c. they into wilderness of   *Ex* 19:1
Sinai
when they *c.* he lay on bed, *2Sa* 4:7
slew him
Zadok and Nathan, they *c.* *1Ki* 1:32
they *c.* to me, when I fled *1Ki* 2:7
from Absalom
they *c.* and told it in city *1Ki* 13:25
not leave, so they *c.* to   *2Ki* 2:4
Jericho
they *c.* to Jordan, cut down *2Ki* 6:4
wood
men whence *c.* they   *2Ki* 20:14;
  Isa 39:3
out of Judah they *c.* to seek *2Ch* 20:4
on eighth day *c.* they to   *2Ch* 29:17
porch
some when they *c.* offered *Ezr* 2:68
freely
from that time forth *c.* they *Ne* 13:21
they *c.* thither and were   *Job* 6:20
ashamed
they *c.* upon me as wide   *Job* 30:14
breaking in
they *c.* round about me like *Ps* 88:17
water
they *c.* to pits found no   *Jer* 14:3
water
thus *c.* they even to   *Jer* 43:7
Tahpanhes
a messenger was sent, lo   *Eze* 23:40
they *c.*
they *c.* and stood before the *Da* 2:2
king
ever they *c.* at bottom of den *Da* 6:24
before they *c.* together she *M't* 1:18
was
they *c.* into the land of   *M't* 14:34
Gennesaret
they *c.* and told Lord all   *M't* 18:31;
  Lu 14:21
after a while *c.* they that *M't* 26:73
stood by
they *c.* to him from every *M'k* 1:45
quarter
called whom he would, and *M'k* 3:13
they *c.*
they *c.* with haste, found   *Lu* 2:16
Mary
they *c.* saying, they had seen *Lu* 24:23
vision
they *c.* not for Jesus' sake *Joh* 12:9
only
they *c.* unto a certain water, *Ac* 8:36
eunuch
they *c.* to iron gate which *Ac* 12:10
opened
they *c.* with one accord and *Ac* 12:20
desired peace
they *c.* and stirred up people *Ac* 17:13
they *c.* to chief priests and *Ac* 23:14
elders
when they *c.* to Caesarea, *Ac* 23:33
presented Paul
what are these, and whence *c.* *Re* 7:13
they

WORD OF THE LORD CAME

word of Lord *c.* to Abraham *Ge* 15:1;
  15:4
word of Lord *c.* to Samuel *1Sa* 15:10
c. the word of Lord to Gad *2Sa* 24:11

word of Lord *c.* to Solomon *1Ki* 6:11
word of Lord *c.* to Jehu   *1Ki* 16:1;
against Baasha   16:7
the word of Lord *c.* unto   *1Ki* 17:2;
Elijah   17:8; 18:1; 19:9; 21:17, 28
the word of the Lord *c.*,   *1Ki* 18:31
saying
word of Lord *c.* to Isaiah *2Ki* 20:4;
  Isa 38:4
word of Lord *c.* to Nathan *1Ch* 17:3
word of Lord *c.* to David   *1Ch* 22:8
word of Lord *c.* to   *2Ch* 11:2
Shemaiah   12:7; *1Ki* 12:22
word of Lord *c.* to Jeremiah   *Jer* 1:2;
  1:4; 2:1; 14:1; 29:30; 33:1, 19; *Da* 9:2
word of Lord *c.* to Ezekiel   *Eze* 1:3;
  3:16
word of Lord *c.* to Hosea   *Ho* 1:1
word of the Lord *c.* to Joel *Joe* 1:1
word of the Lord *c.* to Jonah *Jon* 1:1;
  3:1
word of the Lord *c.* to Micah *Mic* 1:1
word of Lord *c.* to   *Zep* 1:1
Zephaniah
word of the Lord *c.* to   *Hag* 1:1;
Haggai   1:3
word of Lord *c.* to Zechariah *Zec* 1:1;
  7:4; 8:1

CAMEL

saw Isaac, she lighted off   *Ge* 24:64
the *c.*
c. because he cheweth the cud *Le* 11:4
the *c.* and the hare, and the *De* 14:7
suckling, ox and sheep, *c.* *1Sa* 15:3
and ass
of the mule, of the *c.*   *Zec* 14:15
easier for a *c.* to go   *M't* 19:24
through the
at a gnat, and swallow a *c.* *M't* 23:24
easier for a *c.* to go   *M'k* 10:25
through the
easier for a *c.* to go through *Lu* 18:25

CAMELS

and she asses, and *c.*   *Ge* 12:16
took ten *c.* of the *c.* of   *Ge* 24:10;
his master   24:11, 14, 19-20, 22, 30-32,
  35, 44, 46, 61, 63
menservants, and *c.* and   *Ge* 30:43
asses
set his sons and his wives   *Ge* 31:17
upon *c.*
herds, and the *c.* into two   *Ge* 32:7
bands
Thirty milch *c.* with their   *Ge* 32:15
colts
came from Gilead with their *Ge* 37:25
c.
upon the asses, upon the *c.* *Ex* 9:3
upon
both they and their *c.* were *J'g* 6:5
and their *c.* were without   *J'g* 7:12
number
the asses, and the *c.* and the *1Sa* 27:9
young men, which rode   *1Sa* 30:17
upon *c.*
with *c.* that bare spices, and *1Ki* 10:2
very
cattle; of their *c.* fifty   *1Ch* 5:21
thousand
bread on asses, and on *c.*   *1Ch* 12:40
and on
Over the *c.* also was Obil *1Ch* 27:30
the
company, and *c.* that bare *2Ch* 9:1
spices
carried away sheep and *c.* *2Ch* 14:15
Their *c.* four hundred thirty *Ezr* 2:67
and
c. four hundred thirty and   *Ne* 7:69
five
c. and young dromedaries   *Es* 8:10
rode upon mules and *c.* went *Es* 8:14
out
three thousand *c.* and five   *Job* 1:3
fell upon the *c.* and have   *Job* 1:17
carried
six thousand *c.* and a   *Job* 42:12
thousand
of asses, and a chariot of *c.* *Isa* 21:7
treasures upon the bunches   *Isa* 30:6
of *c.*
The multitude of *c.* shall   *Isa* 60:6
cover
and all their vessels, and   *Jer* 49:29
their *c.*

And their *c.* shall be a   *Jer 49:32*
booty, and
make Rabbah a stable for *c.*   *Eze 25:5*

CAMEL'S

put them in the *c.* furniture   *Ge 31:34*
his raiment of *c.* hair, and a   *M't 3:4*
clothed with *c.* hair, and with   *M'k 1:6*

CAMELS'

that were on their *c.* necks   *J'g 8:21*
chains that were about their   *J'g 8:26*
c.
of Damascus, forty *c.* burden   *2Ki 8:9*

CAMEST

whence *c.* thou? and whither   *Ge 16:8*
wilt
the land from whence thou *c.*   *Ge 24:5*
eaten of all before thou *c.*   *Ge 27:33*
in it thou *c.* out from Egypt   *Ex 23:15*
Abib thou *c.* out from Egypt   *Ex 34:18*
wherefore *c.* thou not unto   *Nu 22:37*
me
children of Ammon thou *c.*   *De 2:37*
not
for thou *c.* forth out of the   *De 16:3*
land of
season that thou *c.* forth out   *De 16:6*
thou *c.* not within the days   *1Sa 13:11*
Why *c.* thou down hither   *1Sa 17:28*
C. thou not from thy   *2Sa 11:10*
journey
Whereas thou *c.* but yesterday *2Sa 15:20*
by the same way that thou *c.* *1Ki 13:9*
man of God that *c.* from   *1Ki 13:14*
Judah
to go by the way that thou   *1Ki 13:17*
c.
But *c.* back, and hast eaten   *1Ki 13:22*
bread
back by the way by which   *2Ki 19:28*
thou *c.*
Thou *c.* down also upon   *Ne 9:13*
mount
back by the way by which   *Isa 37:29*
thou *c.*
thou *c.* down, the mountains   *Isa 64:3*
before thou *c.* forth out of the *Jer 1:5*
thou *c.* forth with thy rivers   *Eze 32:2*
Friend, how *c.* thou in   *M't 22:12*
hither
him, Rabbi, when *c.* thou   *Joh 6:25*
hither
that thou *c.* forth from God   *Joh 16:30*
in the way as thou *c.* hath   *Ac 9:17*
sent

CAMON

Jair died, and was buried in *J'g 10:5*
C.

CAMP

come upon one *c.* (B)   *Ge 38:8; 32:21*
angel of Lord went before *c.*   *Ex 14:19*
quails came up and covered   *Ex 16:13*
c.
there is a noise of war in   *Ex 32:17*
the *c.*
go thro' *c.* and slay every   *Ex 32:27*
man his
caused it to be proclaimed   *Ex 36:6*
thro' *c.*
what man killeth any goat in   *Le 17:3*
c.
they strove together in the *c.* *Le 24:10*
pitch every one by his own *c.* *Nu 1:52*
on east side shall *c.* of Judah *Nu 2:3*
pitch
when *c.* setteth forward,   *Nu 4:5*
Aaron shall
as *c.* is to set forward, after   *Nu 4:15*
that
consumed in the utmost parts *Nu 11:1*
of *c.*
Eldad and Medad   *Nu 11:26*
prophesied in *c.*
in *c.* (S)   *Nu 13:19; 2Ch 31:2*
he shall not come within *c.*   *De 23:10*
Lord walked in the midst of   *De 23:14*
thy *c.*
make the *c.* of Israel a curse *Jos 6:18*
when I come to the outside   *J'g 7:17*
of *c.*
Spirit of God began to move *J'g 13:25*
him in *c.*

there came none to *c.* from   *J'g 21:8*
Jabesh
young virgins, they brought   *J'g 21:12*
them to *c.*
noise of this great shout in *c.* *1Sa 4:6*
run to the *c.* to thy   *1Sa 17:17*
brethren
plundered their *c.* (S)   *1Sa 17:53*
Israel made Omri king in *c.* *1Ki 16:16*
in such and such place shall   *2Ki 6:8*
be *c.*
they left *c.* as it was, and fled *2Ki 7:7*
for life
when these lepers came to the *2Ki 7:8*
c.
angel of Lord smote in the   *2Ki 19:35;*
c. of Assyrians, 185,000   *Isa 37:36*
band came with Arabians to *2Ch 22:1*
c.
let it fall in the midst of   *Ps 78:28*
their *c.*
they envied Moses also in   *Ps 106:16*
the *c.*
I will *c.* against thee round   *Isa 29:3*
c. against it round about   *Jer 50:29*
lay siege, set *c.* also against it *Eze 4:2*
his *c.* is very great, he is   *Joe 2:11*
strong
c. in the hedges in the cold   *Na 3:17*
day
compassed *c.* of saints about *Re 20:9;*
     20:18, 22, 25, 34

INTO CAMP

after that come *into c.*   *Le 14:8;*
     16:26, 28
again
Moses gat *into c.* he and   *Nu 11:30*
elders
sun is down come *into c.*   *De 23:11*
again
Philistines said, God is come   *1Sa 4:7*
into c.

OUT OF CAMP

Moses brought people *out of*   *Ex 19:17*
c.
carry your brethren *out of c.* *Le 10:4*
priest go forth *out of c.* and   *Le 14:3*
look
man soever killeth goat *out*   *Le 17:3*
of c.
bring him that cursed *out of*   *Le 24:23*
c.
they put ever leper *out of c.* *Nu 5:2*
Miriam be shut *out of c.*   *Nu 12:14*
seven days
ark and Moses departed not   *Nu 14:44*
out of c.
unclean person shall go   *De 23:10*
abroad *out of c.*
spoilers *out of c.* of   *1Sa 13:17*
Philistines
man came *out of c.* from   *2Sa 1:2*
Saul
out of c. of Israel am I   *2Sa 1:3*
escaped

ROUND ABOUT CAMP

quails fell, spread them   *Nu 11:31*
round about c.
stood every man *round about c.* *J'g 7:21*

WITHOUT CAMP

flesh of bullock shalt thou   *Ex 29:14;*
burn *without c.*   *Le 8:17; 9:11; 16:27*
sought Lord, went without *c.* *Ex 33:7*
shall carry forth ashes   *Le 6:11*
without c.
that hath plague dwell   *Le 13:46*
without c.
leper shall be put out *without* *Nu 5:3*
c.
gatherer of sticks stoned   *Nu 15:35*
without c.
bring red heifer *without c.*   *Nu 19:3*
and slay
do ye abide *without c.* seven *Nu 31:19*
days
shalt have place also *without* *De 23:12*
c.
Rahab left her kindred   *Jos 6:23*
without c.
bodies of beasts burnt   *Heb 13:11*
without c.
go forth to him *without c.*   *Heb 13:13*
bearing

CAMPAIGN

starting a whispering *c.* (B) *Nu 14:36*

CAMPED

and there Israel *c.* before the *Ex 19:2*

CAMPHIRE

a cluster of *c.* in the   *Ca 1:14*
vineyards
c. with spikenard   *Ca 4:13*

CAMPS

that were numbered of the *c.* *Nu 2:32*
that they defile not their *c.* in *Nu 5:3*
for the journeying of the *c.*   *Nu 10:2*
then the *c.* that lie on the   *Nu 10:5*
east
then the *c.* that lie on the   *Nu 10:6*
south
the rereward of all the *c.*   *Nu 10:25*
the stink of your *c.* to come   *Am 4:10*
up

CAN

c. we find such a one as this *Ge 41:38*
How *c.* I myself alone bear   *De 1:12*
your
I *c.* no more go out and come *De 31:2*
in
dead, *c.* I bring him back   *2Sa 12:23*
again
c. I discern, *c.* I hear voice *2Sa 19:35*
of singing
not among us any that *c.* skill *1Ki 5:6*
to hew
c. that which is unsavoury be *Job 6:6*
eaten
c. rush grow without mire?   *Job 8:11*
c. flag
c. a man be profitable to   *Job 22:2*
God
c. he judge through dark   *Job 22:13*
cloud
c. any understand spreading *Job 36:29*
of clouds
said, *c.* God furnish a table   *Ps 78:19*
c. give bread also? *c.* provide *Ps 78:20*
flesh
c. be compared? *c.* be likened *Ps 89:6*
to Lord
c. a man take fire in his   *Pr 6:27*
bosom
c. one go on hot coals and   *Pr 6:28*
not be burnt
death *c.* not celebrate thee: *Isa 38:18*
they that
one shall cry, yet *c.* he not   *Isa 46:7*
answer
c. a woman forget her   *Isa 49:15*
sucking child
c. maid forget her ornaments *Jer 2:32*
c. any hide himself in secret *Jer 23:24*
places
c. two walk together except   *Am 3:3*
they be agreed
c. a bird fall in a snare where *Am 3:5*
no gin is
God hath spoken, who *c.* but *Am 3:8*
prophesy
who *c.* be saved   *M't 19:25;*
     M'k 10:26; Lu 18:26
make it as sure as you *c.*   *M't 27:65*
c. children of bridechamber   *M'k 2:19*
fast
this kind *c.* come forth but   *M'k 9:29*
by prayer
c. ye drink of cup that I   *M'k 10:38*
drink of
parable, *c.* blind lead blind   *Lu 6:39*
c. any good come out of   *Joh 1:46*
Nazareth
this is an hard saying, who   *Joh 6:60*
c. hear it
c. a devil open eyes of the   *Joh 10:21*
blind
no more *c.* ye, except ye   *Joh 15:4*
abide in me
c. any man forbid water   *Ac 10:47*
mind not subject to law, nor   *Ro 8:7*
c. be
have not works, *c.* faith save *Jas 2:14*
him
c. fig tree bear olive berries *Jas 3:12*

HOW CAN

how c. I bear your cumbrance   *De 1:12*
how c. I go, if Saul hear, he will   *1Sa 16:2*
how c. I endure to see evil   *Es 8:6*
how c. man be justified with God   *Job 25:4*
how c. this man give us his way   *Joh 6:52*
but *how c.* one be warm alone   *Ec 4:11*
how c. it be quiet seeing Lord   *Jer 47:7*
how c. ye being evil speak good   *M't 12:34*
how c. man be born when old   *Joh 3:4*
said, *How c.* these things be   *Joh 3:9*
how c. this man give us his flesh to eat   *Joh 6:52*
said, Lord, *how c.* we know the way   *Joh 14:5*
how c. I, except some man guide   *Ac 8:31*

CANA

there was a marriage in *C.*   *Joh 2:1*
beginning of miracles did Jesus in *C.*   *Joh 2:11*
Jesus came again into *C.* of Galilee   *Joh 4:46*
Thomas and Nathanael of *C.*   *Joh 21:22*

CANAAN

Ham is the father of *C.*   *Ge 9:18*
Ham father of *C.* saw nakedness   *Ge 9:22*
cursed be *C.*   *Ge 9:25; 9:26, 27*
C. begat Sidon his firstborn   *Ge 10:15; 1Ch 1:13*
not take wife of daughters of *C.*   *Ge 28:1; 21:6*
the inhabitants of *C.* shall melt   *Ex 15:15*
had not known all wars of *C.*   *J'g 3:1*
Lord sold them to Jabin king of *C.*   *J'g 4:2*
God subdued Jabin king of *C.*   *J'g 4:23; 4:24*
then fought kings of *C.*   *J'g 5:19*
they sacrificed to idols of *C.*   *Ps 106:38*
who smote all kingdoms of *C.*   *Ps 135:11*
five cities speak language of *C.*   *Isa 19:18*
O *C.* I will even destroy thee   *Zep 12:5*
woman of *C.* cried to Jesus   *M't 15:22*

LAND OF CANAAN

went forth to go into *land of C.*   *Ge 12:5*
Abraham dwelt ten years in *land of C.*   *Ge 16:3*
I will give thee *land of C.*   *Ge 17:8; Le 25:38; Nu 34:2; De 32:49; 1Ch 16:18; Ps 105:11*
Jacob dwelt in the *land of C.*   *Ge 37:1*
the famine was in the *land of C.*   *Ge 42:5*
whence come ye? from *land of C.*   *Ge 42:7*
are sons of one man in *land of C.*   *Ge 42:13*
go, get ye up into *land of C.*   *Ge 45:17*
sons carried him into *land of C.*   *Ge 50:13*
when ye come into *land of C.*   *Le 14:34*
do not after doings of *land of C.*   *Le 18:3*
Moses sent them to spy *land of C.*   *Nu 13:17*
pass over armed into *land of C.*   *Nu 32:32*
did eat fruit of *land of C.*   *Jos 5:12*
built altar over against *land of C.*   *Jos 22:11*
I led him through all the *land of C.*   *Jos 24:3*
thy nativity is of the *land of C.*   *Eze 16:3*
came dearth over all *land of C.*   *Ac 7:11*
destroyed seven nations in *land of C.*   *Ac 13:19*

CANAANITE

the *C.* was then in the land   *Ge 12:6; 13:7*
certain *C.* whose name was Shuah   *Ge 38:2*
drive out the Hivite, the *C.*   *Ex 23:28; 33:2; 34:11; Jos 9:1; 11:3; 13:3*
king Arad the *C.*   *Nu 21:1; 33:40*
no *C.* in the house of the Lord   *Zec 14:21*
Simon the *C.*   *M't 10:4; M'k 3:18*

CANAANITES

families of the *C.* spread abroad   *Ge 10:18*
border of the *C.* was from Sidon   *Ge 10:19*
the Amorites, the *C.*   *Ge 15:21; 34:30; Ex 3:8, 17; 13:5, 11; 23:23; De 7:1; 20:17; Jos 5:1; 7:9; 12:8; 24:11; J'g 3:3, 5; 2Sa 24:7*
daughters of the *C.*   *Ge 24:3; 24:37*
the *C.* saw the mourning in the   *Ge 50:11*
the *C.* dwelt by the sea   *Nu 13:29; 14:25, 43, 45; Jos 16:10; 17:12, 16; J'g 1:27, 29-30, 32-33*
delivered up the *C.*   *Nu 21:3; J'g 1:4-5*
the land of the *C.*   *De 1:7; 11:30; Jos 13:4; Ne 9:8, 24*
put the *C.* to tribute   *Jos 17:13; J'g 1:28*
go up against the *C.*   *J'g 1:1; 1:3, 9-10, 17*
slain the *C.* that dwelt in the city   *1Ki 9:16*
their abominations, even of the *C.*   *Ezr 9:1*
Israel shall possess that of the *C.*   *Ob 20*

CANAANITESS

of the daughter of Shua the *C.*   *1Ch 2:3*

CANAANITISH

Shaul the son of a *C.* woman   *Ge 46:10*
Shaul the son of a *C.* woman   *Ex 6:15*

CANAL

c. of the upper pool (A)   *2Ki 18:17*

CANCELLATION

a definite *c.* (P)   *Heb 7:18*

CANCELLED

c. decrees of the law (N)   *Col 2:14*
the command is *c.* (A)   *Heb 7:18*

CANCER

eat like a *c.* (A)   *2Ti 2:17*

CANDACE

under *C.* queen of the Ethiopians   *Ac 8:27*

CANDLE

and his *c.* shall be put out   *Job 18:6*
is the *c.* of the wicked put out   *Job 21:17*
When his *c.* shined upon my   *Job 29:3*
For thou wilt light my *c.*   *Ps 18:28*
the *c.* of the Lord, searching   *Pr 20:27*
c. of the wicked shall be put out   *Pr 24:20*
her *c.* goeth not out by night   *Pr 31:18*
and the light of the *c.*   *Jer 25:10*
men light a *c.* and put it under   *M't 5:15*
Is a *c.* brought to be put under   *M'k 4:21*
when he hath lighted a *c.*   *Lu 8:16*
when he hath lighted a *c.*   *Lu 11:33*
the bright shining of a *c.* doth   *Lu 11:36*
doth not light a *c.* and sweep   *Lu 15:8*
And the light of a *c.* shall shine   *Re 18:23*
they need no *c.* neither light   *Re 22:5*

CANDLES

I will search Jerusalem with *c.*   *Zep 1:12*

CANDLESTICK

make a *c.* of pure gold   *Ex 25:31; 25:31-35*
the *c.* over against the table   *Ex 26:35*
the *c.* and his vessels, and   *Ex 30:27*
the pure *c.* with all his furniture   *Ex 31:8*
The *c.* also for the light   *Ex 35:14*
he made *c.* of pure gold   *Ex 37:17; 37:18-20*
The pure *c.* with the lamps   *Ex 39:37*
thou shalt bring in the *c.*   *Ex 40:4*
he put the *c.* in the tent of   *Ex 40:24*
the lamps upon the pure *c.*   *Le 24:4*
c. and the altars, and the vessels   *Nu 3:31*
and cover the *c.* of the light   *Nu 4:9*
give light over against the *c.*   *Nu 8:2*
over against the *c.* as the Lord   *Nu 8:3*
work of the *c.* was of beaten gold   *Nu 8:4*
a table, a stool, and a *c.*   *2Ki 4:10*
by weight for every *c.* and   *1Ch 28:15*
for the *c.* and also for the lamps   *1Ch 28:15*
according to the use of every *c.*   *1Ch 28:15*
and the *c.* of gold with the lamps   *2Ch 13:11*
and wrote over against the *c.*   *Da 5:5*
a *c.* all of gold, with a bowl   *Zec 4:2*
upon the right side of the *c.*   *Zec 4:11*
but on a *c.; and it giveth light*   *M't 5:15*
and not to be set on a *c.*   *M'k 4:21*
but setteth it on a *c.* that they   *Lu 8:16*
but on a *c.* that they which   *Lu 11:33*
wherein was the *c.* and the table   *Heb 9:2*
remove thy *c.* out of his place   *Re 2:5*

CANDLESTICKS

the *c.* of pure gold, five on   *1Ki 7:49*
the weight for the *c.* of gold, and   *1Ch 28:15*
he made ten *c.* of gold according   *2Ch 4:7*
the *c.* with their lamps, that they   *2Ch 4:20*
the *c.* and the spoons, and   *Jer 52:19*
turned, I saw seven golden *c.*   *Re 1:12*
in the midst of the seven *c.*   *Re 1:13*
one hand, and the seven golden *c.*   *Re 1:20*
the midst of the seven golden *c.*   *Re 2:1*
and the two *c.* standing before the   *Re 11:4*

CANE

a *c.* lift him up (B)   *Isa 10:15*
Thou hast bought me no sweet *c.*   *Isa 43:24*
Sheba, and the sweet *c.* from a far   *Jer 6:20*

CANKER

their word will eat as doth a *c.*   *2Ti 2:17*
eat like cancer; spread like gangrene (A)   *2Ti 2:17*
teaching spreads like gangrene (B)(N)   *2Ti 2:17*
will eat as doth gangrene (E)(R)   *2Ti 2:17*
dagnerous as blood poisoning to body; spread like sepsis from a wound (P)   *2Ti 2:17*

CANKERED

Your gold and silver is *c.*   *Jas 5:3*
is completely rusted through (A)(E)   *Jas 5:3*
is covered with rust (B)   *Jas 5:3*
silver and gold is rusted away (N)(R)   *Jas 5:3*
gold and silver are tarnished (P)   *Jas 5:3*

CANKERWORM

hath the *c.* eaten   *Joe 1:4*
the hopping locust has eaten   *Joe 1:4*
(A)(B)(R)
the *c.* and the caterpillar   *Joe 2:25*
it shall eat thee up like the   *Joe 3:15;*
c.   *3:16*
licking locusts, swarming   *Joe 3:15-16*
locusts (A)
young locusts,   *Joe 3:15-16*
grasshoppers (B)(R)

CANNEH

C. and Eden, the merchants   *Eze 27:23*

CANNOT

be poor, and *c.* get so much   *Le 14:21*
c. support himself among   *Le 25:35*
you (S)
fenced up my way that I *c.*   *Job 19:8*
pass
I am shut up, and I *c.* come   *Ps 88:8*
forth
calling assemblies I *c.* away   *Isa 1:13*
with
read this: he saith, I *c.* for   *Isa 29:11*
it is sealed
death *c.* celebrate thee: they   *Isa 38:18*
that go
perpetual decree, that it *c.*   *Jer 5:22*
pass it
c. I do with you as this   *Jer 18:6*
potter
secret king demanded, *c.*   *Da 2:27*
astrologers shew
c. ye discern the signs of the   *M't 16:3*
times
it *c.* be a prophet perish out   *Lu 13:33*
of Jerusalem
which would pass from   *Lu 16:26*
hence to you *c.*
of which we *c.* now speak   *Heb 9:5*
particularly

CANST

thou *c.* not see my face and   *Ex 33:20*
live
itch, whereof thou *c.* not be   *De 28:27*
healed
if thou *c.* answer, set words   *Job 33:5*
in order
How *c.* thou say, I am not   *Jer 2:23*
polluted
if thou wilt, thou *c.* make me   *M't 8:2*
clean
if thou *c.* do any thing, have   *M'k 9:22*
compassion
chief captain said, *c.* thou   *Ac 21:37*
speak Greek

CAPABILITY

a woman of *c.* (A)   *Ru 3:11*

CAPERNAUM

he came and dwelt in *C.*   *M't 4:13*
which is
when Jesus was entered into   *M't 8:5*
C.
And thou, *C.*, which art   *M't 11:23*
exalted
were come to *C.* they that   *M't 17:24*
they went into *C.*; and   *M'k 1:21*
straightway
he entered into *C.* after some   *M'k 2:1*
days
he came to *C.*: and being in   *M'k 9:33*
have heard done in *C.* do   *Lu 4:23*
also here
And came down to *C.* a city   *Lu 4:31*
of the people, he entered into   *Lu 7:1*
C.
And thou, *C.*, which art   *Lu 10:15*
exalted to
After this he went down to   *Joh 2:12*
C.
whose son was sick at *C.*   *Joh 4:46*
and went over the sea   *Joh 6:17*
toward *C.*
came to *C.* seeking for Jesus   *Joh 6:24*
synagogue, as he taught in   *Joh 6:59*
C.

CAPHTHORIM

came the Philistines, and *C.*   *1Ch 1:12*

CAPHTOR

which came forth out of *C.*   *De 2:23*
the remnant of the country   *Jer 47:4*
of *C.*
the Philistines from *C.* and   *Am 9:7*

CAPHTORIM

came Philistim,) and *C.*   *Ge 10:14*

CAPHTORIMS

the *C.* which came forth out   *De 2:23*

CAPITAL

upon the *c.* (S)   *1Ki 7:31;*
  2Ki 25:17; 2Ch 3:15; Je 52:22
in Susa the *c.* (R)   *Ne 1:1; Es 1:2, 5*
Susa the *c.* (A)(R)   *Es 1:2;*
  1:5; 2:3, 5, 8; 3:15; 8:14; 9:6, 11-12
put *c.* in his hands (N)   *M't 25:14*
If I am guilty of any *c.* crime   *Ac 25:11*
(N)

CAPITALS

overlaid their *c.* (S)   *Ex 36:38;*
38:17, 19, 28; 1Ki 7:16-20, 41-42;
  2Ch 4:12-13
smite the *c.* of the door (S)   *Am 9:1*
desolation in the *c.* (S)   *Zep 2:14*

CAPPADOCIA

and *C.*, in Pontus, and Asia   *Ac 2:9*
Galatia, *C.*, Asia, and Bithynia   *1Pe 1:1*

CAPS

c. you shall make (R)   *Ex 28:40*
bind *c.* on them (A)(R)   *Ex 29:9*
lovely *c.* of fine linen   *Ex 39:28*
(A)(B)(R)

CAPTAIN

sold Joseph to *c.* of guard   *Ge 37:36*
c. of guard charged Joseph   *Ge 49:4*
with them
Nahshon, *c.* of children of   *Nu 2:3*
Israel
Nethaneel, *c.* of children of   *Nu 2:5*
Issachar
let us make a *c.* and return   *Nu 14:4;*
  Ne 9:17
but as *c.* of host of the Lord   *Jos 5:14*
c. of the Lord's host said to   *Jos 5:15*
Joshua
c. of Jabin's host was Sisera   *J'g 4:2;*
  1Sa 12:9
they said to Jephthah, come   *J'g 11:6*
and be our *c.*
people made him head and   *J'g 11:11*
c.
anoint him *c.* over my   *1Sa 9:16;*
people   *10:1*
command him to be *c.*   *1Sa 13:14*
over his people
carry ten cheeses to *c.* of   *1Sa 17:18*
thousand
David became a *c.* over them   *1Sa 22:2*
feed, and be a *c.* over Israel   *2Sa 5:2*
he shall be chief and *c.*   *2Sa 5:8;*
  1Ch 11:6
if thou be not *c.* of host in   *2Sa 19:13*
room of Joab
Abishai was therefore their   *2Sa 23:19*
c.
Israel made Omri, *c.* of the   *1Ki 16:16*
host
the king sent a *c.* with his   *2Ki 1:9*
fifty
sent another *c.* with his fifty   *2Ki 1:11;*
  1:13
thou be spoken for to *c.* of   *2Ki 4:13*
host
Naaman, *c.* of host of king of   *2Ki 5:1*
Syria
I have an errand to thee, O *c.*   *2Ki 9:5*
Pekah, *c.* of his, conspired   *2Ki 15:25*
against him
turn away face of one *c.*   *2Ki 18:24;*
  Isa 36:9
tell Hezekiah the *c.* of my   *2Ki 20:5*
people
came Nebuzar-adan, *c.* of   *2Ki 25:8;*
guard   *Jer 52:12*
more honourable, he was *c.*   *1Ch 11:21*

killed Shophach *c.* of host   *1Ch 19:18;*
  2Sa 10:18
third *c.* Benaiah   *1Ch 27:5; 27:7-15*
God is with us for our *c.*   *2Ch 13:12*
Lord doth take away *c.* of fifty   *Isa 3:3*
c. of ward Irijah took   *Jer 37:13*
Jeremiah
c. of guard took Jeremiah,   *Jer 40:2*
and said
c. gave vituals and a reward   *Jer 40:5*
call together, appoint a *c.*   *Jer 51:27*
against her
the *c.* came to him   *Jon 1:6*
(A)(B)(R)
the band and *c.* took Jesus   *Joh 18:12*
the *c.* with officers went and   *Ac 5:26*
brought
to make *c.* of salvation   *Heb 2:10*
perfect

CAPTAINS

chosen *c.* drowned in Red sea   *Ex 15:4*
Moses wroth with *c.* of   *Nu 31:14*
thousands
made wise men *c.* over   *De 1:15*
thousands
make *c.* of army lead people   *De 20:9*
will appoint *c.* over thousands   *1Sa 8:12*
will son of Jesse make you   *1Sa 22:7*
all *c.*
when king gave all *c.* charge   *2Sa 18:5*
sat in the seat chief among   *2Sa 23:8*
the *c.*
knowest what Joab did to *c.*   *1Ki 2:5*
were his princes, and *c.* and   *1Ki 9:22*
rulers
take kings away, put *c.* in   *1Ki 20:24*
their rooms
when *c.* perceived he was   *1Ki 22:33;*
not king of Israel, they   *2Ch 18:32*
turned back
Jehoiada commanded *c.*   *2Ki 11:15*
having for *c.* Pelatiah and   *1Ch 4:42*
three of 30 *c.* went down   *1Ch 11:15*
to David
of Naphtali a thousand *c.*   *1Ch 12:34*
and with them
into the hands of the *c.*   *2Ch 12:10*
(S)
Jehoram smote Edomites   *2Ch 21:9*
and *c.*
Lord brought on them *c.* of   *2Ch 33:11*
host
king had sent *c.* of army with   *Ne 2:9*
thunder of *c.* and shouting   *Job 39:25*
thou hast taught them to be   *Jer 13:21*
c.
with thee will I break *c.*   *Jer 51:23*
and rulers
I will make drunk her *c.*   *Jer 51:57*
and rulers
c. to open mouth in   *Eze 21:22*
slaughter
c. desirable young men   *Eze 23:6;*
  23:12, 23
c. saw men on whose bodies   *Da 3:27*
c. have consulted to establish   *Da 6:7*
a statute
thy *c.* as-great grasshoppers   *Na 3:17*
Herod on birthday made   *M'k 6:21*
supper to *c.*
Judas went and communed   *Lu 22:4*
with *c.*
all the ship *c.* (A)   *Re 18:17*
may eat flesh of *c.* and   *Re 19:18*
mighty

CAPTIVATING

c. as an army (B)   *Ca 6:4; 6:10*

CAPTIVE

heard his brother was taken *c.*   *Ge 14:14*
their wives took they *c.* and   *Ge 34:29*
spoiled
unto firstborn of *c.* in   *Ex 12:29*
dungeon
thou hast taken them *c.*   *De 21:10*
had brought away *c.* little   *2Ki 5:2*
maid
smite those thou hast taken   *2Ki 6:22*
c. with thy
the *c.* Salathiel his son (S)   *1Ch 3:17*
taken *c.* by his own lust (R)   *Pr 11:6*
am desolate, a *c.* removing   *Isa 49:21*
shall the lawful *c.* be   *Isa 49:24*
delivered

c. exile hasteneth, he may   Isa 51:14
be loosed
loose thyself, O c. daughter   Isa 52:2
of Zion
a c. and a prey (A)   Jer 2:14
shall go c. with first that go c.   Am 6:7
taken c. by him at his will   2Ti 2:26

CARRY, CARRIED CAPTIVE

until Ashur shall carry thee   Nu 24:22
away c.
Tiglath-pileser carried them   2Ki 15:29
c.
carried people of Damascus   2Ki 16:9
c. to Kir
whom king of Assyria carried   1Ch 5:6
c.
other 10,000 did Judah   2Ch 25:12
carry c.
Israel carried c. of their   2Ch 28:8
brethren 200,000
they that carried us c.   Ps 137:3
required a song
Lord's flock is carried c.   Jer 13:17
Judah be wholly carried   Jer 13:19
away c.
shall carry them c. to   Jer 20:4
Babylon
acknowledge them that are   Jer 24:5
carried c.
took not when he carried c.   Jer 27:20
Jeconiah
I caused you to be carried c.   Jer 29:14
  52:27
Judah were carried away c.   Jer 40:1;
  52:27
them that were not carried c.   Jer 40:7
Ishmael carried away c. all   Jer 41:10
residue
shall carry Egyptians c.   Jer 43:12
Nebuchadrezzar carried c.   Jer 52:29;
from Jerusalem   52:30
whither they shall be carried   Eze 6:9
c.
shall also carry c. into Egypt   Da 11:8
because they carried c. the   Am 1:6
captivity
in the day that strangers   Ob 11
carried c.

LEAD, LED CAPTIVE

lead captivity c. son of   J'g 5:12
Abinoam
their enemies who led them   1Ki 8:48
c.
compassion before them that   2Ch 30:9
lead c.
thou hast led captivity c.   Ps 68:18;
  Eph 4:8
die in place whither they led   Jer 22:12
c.
Israel be led c. out of their   Am 7:11
land
Huzzab shall be led c.   Na 2:7
be led away c. into all   Lu 21:24
nations
lead c. silly women laden with   2Ti 3:6
sins

CAPTIVES

Israel took all women of   Nu 31:9
Midian c.
they brought the c.   Nu 31:12; 31:19
seest among c. a beautiful   De 21:11
woman
mine arrows drunk with blood   De 32:42
of c.
David's two wives were   1Sa 30:5
taken c.
carried from Jerusalem   2Ki 24:14
10,000 c.
hear and deliver c. again   2Ch 28:11
ye shall not bring in c.   2Ch 28:13
hither
carried with the c. (S)   Es 2:6
take them c. whose c. they   Isa 14:2
were
lead away Ethiopians c.   Isa 20:4
young and old
shall let go my c. not for   Isa 45:13
price nor
c. of mighty shall be taken   Isa 49:25
to proclaim liberty to c.   Isa 61:1;
  Lu 4:18
sons and daughters are   Jer 48:46
taken c.
all that took them c. held   Jer 50:33
them fast

as I was among c. by river   Eze 1:1
Chebar
I will bring again captivity   Eze 16:53
of c.
have found man of c. of   Da 2:25
Judah
gather the c. (S)   Hab 1:9
the c. of this host of Israel   Ob 20
and the c. of Jerusalem (S)

CAPTIVITY

given his daughters into c.   Nu 21:29
shall put raiment of c. from   De 21:13
her
Lord will turn thy c.   De 30:3
till the day of c. of the land   J'g 18:30
carried he into c. to   2Ki 24:15
Babylon
thirty-seventh year of c.   2Ki 25:25;
  Jer 52:31
dwelt in their steads until c.   1Ch 5:22
Jehozadak went into c. when   1Ch 6:15
Lord
if they pray in land of c.   2Ch 6:37
if they return to thee in   2Ch 6:38
land of their c.
sons and wives are in c. for   2Ch 29:9
this
been delivered to c. and spoil   Ezr 9:7
the Jews which were left of   Ne 1:2
the c.
give them for a prey in land   Ne 4:4
of their c.
Mordecai carried away with   Es 2:6
the c.
the Lord turned the c. of Job   Job 42:10
when Lord bringeth back c.   Ps 14:7
  85:1
delivered his strength into c.   Ps 78:61
when Lord turned again c.   Ps 126:1
of Zion
turn again our c. O Lord, as   Ps 126:4
streams in south
my people are gone into c.   Isa 5:13
carry thee away with mighty   Isa 22:17
c.
but themselves are gone into   Isa 46:2
c.
such as are for c. to c.   Jer 15:2; 43:11
I will turn away your c.   Jer 29:14;
saith the Lord   30:3; 32:44; 33:7, 11, 26
hear ye, all ye of c.   Jer 29:20
be taken up a curse by all   Jer 29:22
c.
to all them of c. saying   Jer 29:31
thy seed from land of c.   Jer 30:10;
  46:27
Moab is at ease, nor hath   Jer 48:11
gone into c.
Judah is gone into c. because   La 1:3
her children are gone into c.   La 1:5
not discovered, to turn away   La 2:14
thy c.
no more carry thee away into   La 4:22
c.
was fifth year of Jehoiachin's   Eze 1:2
c.
get to them of c. and speak   Eze 3:11
to them
then I came to them of the   Eze 3:15;
  11:24
I spake to them of c. all   Eze 11:25
things
I brought forth my stuff, as   Eze 12:7
stuff for c.
shall bring again their c.   Eze 16:53
the c. of Sodom, and c. of Samaria
when they went into c. thou   Eze 25:3
saidst, Aha
in twelfth year of c. one   Eze 33:21
escaped
that house of Israel went   Eze 39:23
into c.
in five and twentieth year of   Eze 40:1
our c.
Daniel which is of c. of   Da 6:13
Judah
shall fall by c. and spoil   Da 11:33
many days
when I returned c. of my   Ho 6:11
people
c. of this host, c. of Jerusalem   Ob 20
for they are gone into c.   Mic 1:16
from
She went into c. her children   Na 3:10
dashed
they shall gather c. as the   Hab 1:9
sand

Lord shall turn away their c.   Zep 2:7;
  3:20
take of them of c.   Zec 6:10
bringing me into c. to law of   Ro 7:23
sin
bringing into c. every   2Co 10:5
thought to

BRING, BRINGETH CAPTIVITY

he did bring up with them of   Ezr 1:11
the c.
when God bringeth back c. of   Ps 53:6
his
I will bring again c. of   Jer 30:18
Jacob
when I shall bring again   Jer 31:23
their c.
yet will I bring again their   Jer 48:47
c. of Moab
I will bring again the c. of   Jer 49:6
Ammon
I will bring again c. of   Jer 49:39
Elam
I will bring again c. of   Eze 29:14
Egypt
now will I bring again c. of   Eze 39:25
Jacob
when I bring again c. of   Joe 3:1
Judah
I will bring again c. of my   Am 9:14

CHILDREN OF CAPTIVITY

heard that children of c   Ezr 4:1
builded
rest of children of c. kept   Ezr 6:16
children of c. kept passover on   Ezr 6:19
14th
kill passover for children of   Ezr 6:20
c.
made proclamation to   Ezr 10:7
children of c.
children of c. did so, and   Ezr 10:16
all were
Daniel of children of c. of   Da 5:13
Judah

GO INTO CAPTIVITY

sons and daughters go into   De 28:41
c.
all in thine house shall go in   Jer 20:6
c.
thy lovers shall go in. c.   Jer 22:22
every one of them shall go   Jer 30:16
in. c.
daughter, furnish thyself to   Jer 46:19
go into c.
Chemosh go into c.   Jer 48:7; 49:3
go forth, as they that go into   Eze 12:4
c.
these cities shall go into c.   Eze 30:17
Egypt her daughters shall   Eze 30:18
go into c.
people of Syria shall go into   Am 1:5
c.
their king shall go into c.   Am 1:15
Gilgal shall go into c.   Am 5:5
will I cause you to go into   Am 5:27
c.
Israel shall go into c.   Am 7:17
though they go into c. before   Am 9:4
enemies
half of city shall go into c.   Zec 14:2
he that leadeth into captivity   Re 13:10
shall go into c.

LED CAPTIVITY

he led c. captive, and gave   Eph 4:8
gifts

OUT OF CAPTIVITY

now these went up out of c.   Ezr 2:1;
  Ne 7:6
all come up out of c.   Ezr 3:8; Ne 8:17
children of Israel were come   Ezr 6:21
out of c.
were come out of c. offered   Ezr 8:35
to God

CAPTURED

c. Ijon (B)   1Ki 15:20
c. horses (R)   1Ki 20:21

CAPTURES

c. human lives for God (A)   Pr 11:30

CARAVAN

to be in the c. (A)(B)   Lu 2:44

CARBUNCLE

topaz, and a c.: this shall be   Ex 28:17
was a sardius, a topaz, and   Ex 39:10
a c.
emerald, and the c. and   Eze 28:13
gold

CARBUNCLES

and thy gates of c. and all   Isa 54:12
thy

CARCAS

Abagtha, Zethar, and C.   Es 1:10

CARCASE

a c. of an unclean beast   Le 5:2
c. of unclean beast not touch   Le 11:8;
   11:24-25, 27-28, 35-40; De 14:8
thy c. shall be meat for all   De 28:26
fowls
they should take his c. down   Jos 8:29
from
aside to see c. of the lion   J'g 14:8;
                 14:9
c. of the man of God slain   1Ki 13:22;
by lion   13:24-25, 28-30
the c. of Jezebel shall be as   2Ki 9:37
dung
as a c. trodden under feet   Isa 14:19
For wheresoever the c. is,   M't 24:28
there

CARCASES

the fowls came down upon   Ge 15:11
the c.
shall have their c. in   Le 11:11
abomination
The c. of every beast which   Le 11:26
divideth
cast your c. upon the c. of   Le 26:30
your
Your c. shall fall in   Nu 14:29;
wilderness   14:32-33
the c. of the host of the   1Sa 17:46
Philistines
their c. were torn in the   Isa 5:25
midst of
stink shall come up out of   Isa 34:3
their c.
upon the c. of the men that   Isa 66:24
have
the c. of this people shall be   Jer 7:33
meat
the c. of men shall fall as   Jer 9:22
dung
their c. shall be meat for   Jer 16:4
the fowls
with the c. of their   Jer 16:18
detestable
their c. will I give to be meat   Jer 19:7
dead c. of the children of   Eze 6:5
Israel
nor by the c. of their kings   Eze 43:7
the c. of their kings, far   Eze 43:9
from me
slain, and a great number of c.   Na 3:3
whose c. fell in the   Heb 3:17
wilderness

CARCHEMISH

Is not Calno as C? is not   Isa 10:9
Hamath
was by the river Euphrates in   Jer 46:2
C.

CARE

hath left the c. of the asses   1Sa 10:2
they will not c. for us   2Sa 18:3
been careful for us with all   2Ki 4:13
this c.
thy c. has preserved me (S)   Job 10:12
Lord take c. of the helpless   Ps 116:6
(B)
nation, that dwelleth without   Jer 49:31
c.
eat bread by weight, and   Eze 4:16
with c.
the c. of this world, and the   M't 13:22
to an inn, and took c. of   Lu 10:34
him

Take c. of him; and   Lu 10:35
whatsoever
Lord, dost thou not c. that   Lu 10:40
my
being a servant? c. not for it   1Co 7:21
have you without c. (S)   1Co 7:32
Doth God take c. for oxen   1Co 9:9
the same c. one for another   1Co 12:25
or c. for you in the sight of   2Co 7:12
God
earnest c. into the heart of   2Co 8:16
Titus
daily, the c. of all the   2Co 11:28
churches
will naturally c. for your   Ph'p 2:20
state
your c. of me hath   Ph'p 4:10
flourished
shall he take c. of the church   1Ti 3:5
Casting all your c. upon him   1Pe 5:7

CAREAH

and Johanan the son of C.   2Ki 25:23

CARED

c. for him (E)(R)   De 32:10
failed me; no man c. for my   Ps 142:4
soul
not that he c. for the poor   Joh 12:6
Gallio c. for none of those   Ac 18:17
things

CAREER

previous c. (B)(P)   Ga 1:13

CAREFUL

thou hast been c. for us with   2Ki 4:13
all
not be c. in the year of   Jer 17:8
drought
we are not c. to answer thee   Da 3:16
Martha, thou art c. and   Lu 10:41
troubled
c. of his own future (P)   Lu 16:8
Be c. for nothing; but in   Ph'p 4:6
wherein ye were also c. but   Ph'p 4:10
ye
be c. to maintain good works   Tit 3:8

CAREFULLY

asked us c. (S)   Ge 43:7
Only if thou c. hearken unto   De 15:5
inhabitant of Maroth waited   Mic 1:12
c.
conduct yourselves c. (B)   Eph 5:15
sent him therefore the more   Ph'p 2:28
c.
though he sought it c. with   Heb 12:17
tears

CAREFULNESS

water with trembling and   Eze 12:18
with c.
eat their bread with c. and   Eze 12:19
drink
But I would have you   1Co 7:32
without c.
sort, what c. it wrought in   2Co 7:11
you

CARELESS

how they dwelt c. after the   J'g 18:7
ye c. daughters; give ear unto   Isa 32:9
my
ye be troubled, ye c.   Isa 32:10
women; for
at ease; be troubled, ye c.   Isa 32:11
ones
to make the c. Ethiopians   Eze 30:9
afraid
every c. word give account   M't 12:36
(P)(R)
admonish the c. (N)   1Th 5:14

CARELESSLY

that dwellest c. that sayest in   Isa 47:8
and among them that dwell c.   Eze 39:6
in
is the rejoicing city that   Zep 2:15
dwelt c.
eats and drinks c. (P)   1Co 11:29

CARES

laying c. within me (A)   Ps 13:2
perplexing c. crowd me   Ps 94:19
(B)(R)
the c. of this world, and the   M'k 4:19
are choked with c. and riches   Lu 8:14
and c. of this life, and so   Lu 21:34
that day
provides and c. for it (N)   Eph 5:29

CARESSING

c. his wife (A)(B)(S)   Ge 26:8

CAREST

neither c. thou for any   M't 22:16
man: for
Master, c. thou not that we   M'k 4:38
perish
thou art true, and c. for no   M'k 12:14
man

CARETH

which the Lord thy God c.   De 11:12
for
hireling, and c. not for the   Joh 10:13
sheep
He that is unmarried c. for   1Co 7:32
he that is married c. for the   1Co 7:33
unmarried woman c. for the   1Co 7:34
married c. for the things of   1Co 7:34
upon him, for he c. for you   1Pe 5:7

CARGO

unloaded her c.   Ac 21:3
(A)(B)(N)(P)(R)
not only of the c. (S)   Ac 27:10
buys freight, c.   Re 18:11
(A)(B)(N)(P)(R)

CARING

lest my father leave c. for the   1Sa 9:5
asses

CARMEL

the king of Jokneam of C.   Jos 12:22
one
Maon, C. and Ziph, and   Jos 15:55
Juttah
Misheal; and reacheth to C.   Jos 19:26
Samuel, saying, Saul came   1Sa 15:12
to C.
possessions were in C.   1Sa 25:2;
           1Sa 25:5, 7, 40
to me all Israel unto mount   1Ki 18:19
C.
prophets together unto   1Ki 18:20
mount c.
Elijah went up to the top   1Ki 18:42
of C.
he went from thence to   2Ki 2:25
mount C.
unto the man of God to   2Ki 4:25
mount C.
and into the forest of his   2Ki 19:23
C.
in the mountains, and in C.   2Ch 26:10
Thine head upon thee is like   Ca 7:5
C.
and C. shake off their fruits   Isa 33:9
the excellency of C. and   Isa 35:2
Sharon
border, and the forests of   Isa 37:24
his C.
and as C. by the sea, so   Jer 46:18
shall he
he shall feed on C. and   Jer 50:19
Bashan
shall mourn, and the top of   Am 1:2
C.
hide themselves in the top of   Am 9:3
C.
in the wood, in the midst of   Mic 7:14
C.
Bashan languisheth, and C.   Na 1:4
and

CARMELITE

Abigail the wife of Nabal   1Sa 30:5
the C.
and Abigail Nabal's wife the   2Sa 2:2
C.
Abigail the wife of Nabal the   2Sa 3:3
C.

Hezrai the *C*. Paarai the   *2Sa 23:35*
Arbite
Hezro the *C*. Naarai the   *1Ch 11:37*
son of

CARMELITESS

and Abigail the *C*. Nabal's   *1Sa 27:3*
wife
second Daniel, of Abigail the   *1Ch 3:1*
C.

CARMI

and Phallu, and Hezron, and   *Ge 46:9*
C.
Hanoch, and Pallu, Hezron,   *Ex 6:14*
and *C*.
Hezronites; of *C*. the family   *Nu 26:6*
of
for Achan, the son of *C*. the   *Jos 7:1*
son
by man; and Achan, the son   *Jos 7:18*
of *C*.
And the sons of *C*.; Achar   *1Ch 2:7*
of Judah; Pharez, Hezron,   *1Ch 4:1*
and *C*.
Hanoch, and Pallu, Hezron,   *1Ch 5:3*
and *C*.

CARMITES

of Carmi, the family of the   *Nu 26:6*
C.

CARNAL

but I am *C*. sold under sin   *Ro 7:14*
Because the *c*. mind is enmity   *Ro 8:7*
to minister unto them in *c*.   *Ro 15:27*
things
but as unto *c*. even as unto   *1Co 3:1*
For ye are yet *c*.   *1Co 3:3; 3:4*
if we shall reap your *c*.   *1Co 9:11*
things
weapons of our warfare are   *2Co 10:4*
not *c*.
the law of a *c*. commandment   *Heb 7:16*
and *c*. ordinances, imposed   *Heb 9:10*
on

CARNALLY

thou shalt not lie *c*. with thy   *Le 18:20*
whosoever lieth *c*. with a   *Le 19:20*
And a man lie with her *c*.   *Nu 5:13*
to be *c*. minded is death; but   *Ro 8:6*
to

CAROB

with *c*. pods (A)   *Lu 15:16*

CAROUSINGS

c. and the like (A)(B)(R)   *Ga 5:21*
c. and abominable idolatries   *1Pe 4:3*
(S)

CARPENTER

the *c*. encouraged the   *Isa 41:7*
goldsmith
The *c*. stretched out his rule   *Isa 44:13*
Is not this the *c*. the son of   *M'k 6:3*

CARPENTERS

c. and masons: and they   *2Sa 5:11*
they laid it out to the *c*.   *2Ki 12:11*
Unto *c*. and builders, and   *2Ki 22:6*
with masons and *c*. to build   *1Ch 14:1*
and hired masons and *c*. to   *2Ch 24:12*
repair
unto the masons, and to the   *Ezr 3:7*
c.
with the *c*. and smiths,   *Jer 24:1*
from
and the *c*. and the smiths,   *Jer 29:2*
And the Lord shewed me   *Zec 1:20*
four *c*.

CARPENTER'S

Is not this the *c*. son? is   *M't 13:55*
not his

CARPETED

c. the road (N)(P)   *M't 21:8;*
   M'k 11:8

CARPUS

cloak that I left at Troas   *2Ti 4:13*
with *C*.

CARRIAGE

the cattle and the *c*. before   *J'g 18:21*
them
David left his *c*. in the   *1Sa 17:22*
hand
the hand of the keeper of   *1Sa 17:22*
the *c*.

CARRIAGES

Michmash he hath laid up   *Isa 10:28*
his *c*.
your *c*. were heavy loaden   *Isa 46:1*
we took up our *c*. and   *Ac 21:15*
went up

CARRIED

sons of Israel *c*. Jacob   *Ge 46:5; 50:13*
c. them in their coats out of   *Le 10:5*
camp
they *c*. the stones over with   *Jos 4:8*
them
he *c*. them up to top of an   *J'g 16:3*
hill
let ark of God be *c*. unto   *1Sa 5:8*
Gath
c. out orders (B)   *1Sa 15:11; 15:13*
David *c*. ark aside   *2Sa 6:10;*
   1Ch 13:13
Abiathar *c*. ark of God to   *2Sa 15:29*
Jerusalem
c. him into a loft and laid   *1Ki 17:19*
him
they *c*. Naboth forth and   *1Ki 21:13*
stoned him
c. silver and gold and hid it   *2Ki 7:8*
his servants *c*. him in a   *2Ki 9:28;*
chariot   *23:30*
shall be *c*. to Babylon   *2Ki 20:17;*
   Isa 39:6
c. ashes of the vessels to   *2Ki 23:4*
Beth-el
he *c*. out thence all the   *2Ki 24:13*
treasures
bound Zedekiah and *c*. him   *2Ki 25:7*
to Babylon
c. them captive (S)   *1Ch 8:6*
c. the chest to his place   *2Ch 24:11*
again
c. all the feeble of them   *2Ch 28:15*
upon asses
who took and *c*. Manasseh   *2Ch 33:11*
to Babylon
Shaphan *c*. the book to the   *2Ch 34:16*
king
Necho took and *c*. Jehoahaz   *2Ch 36:4*
to Egypt
counsel of froward is *c*.   *Job 5:13*
headlong
I should have been *c*. from   *Job 10:19*
the womb
tho' the mountains be *c*. into   *Ps 46:2*
the sea
remnant of Israel are *c*. from   *Isa 46:3*
womb
thy daughters shall be *c*. on   *Isa 49:22*
thy shoulders
he hath borne our griefs, *c*.   *Isa 53:4*
our sorrows
daughters *c*. on hips (B)   *Isa 60:4*
bare and *c*. them all the days   *Isa 63:9*
of old
be *c*. into Babylon   *Jer 27:22;*
   Jer 28:3; 52:11, 17
he *c*. twigs into a land of   *Eze 17:4*
traffic
c. me out in Spirit of the   *Eze 37:1*
Lord
which he *c*. into the land of   *Da 1:2*
Shinar
be also *c*. into Assyria for a   *Ho 10:6*
present
make covenant, and oil is *c*.   *Ho 12:1*
into Egypt
ye have *c*. into your temples   *Joe 3:5*
there was a dead man *c*. out   *Lu 7:12*
the beggar was *c*. by the   *Lu 16:22*
angels
parted from them, and *c*.   *Lu 24:51*
into heaven
lame from mother's womb was   *Ac 3:2*
c.

young men *c*. Ananias and   *Ac 5:6*
buried him
our fathers were *c*. over into   *Ac 7:16*
Sychem
devout men *c*. Stephen to his   *Ac 8:2*
burial
c. away by magic (N)   *Ac 8:11*
commanded him to be *c*.   *Ac 21:34*
into the castle
c. about with every wind of   *Eph 4:14*
doctrine
be not *c*. about with divers   *Heb 13:9*
doctrines
clouds that are *c*. with a   *2Pe 2:17*
tempest
clouds without water, *c*.   *Jude 12*
about of winds

CARRIED AWAY

Jacob *c*. *away* all cattle and   *Ge 31:18*
goods
c. *away* my daughters as   *Ge 31:26*
captives
slew not any, but *c*. them   *1Sa 30:2*
away
c. Israel *away* into Assyria   *2Ki 17:6*
heathen Lord *c*. *away*   *2Ki 17:11*
before them
one of priests, whom they   *2Ki 17:28*
c. *away*
c. *away* all Jerusalem and   *2Ki 24:14*
all princes
c. *away* Jehoiachin to   *2Ki 24:15*
Babylon
Judah was *c*. *away* out of   *2Ki 25:21*
their land
c. *away* Reubenites   *1Ch 5:26*
Lord *c*. *away* Judah and   *1Ch 6:15*
Jerusalem
who were *c*. *away* for their   *1Ch 9:1*
transgression
Shishak *c*. *away* shields of   *2Ch 12:9*
gold
Asa *c*. *away* much spoil   *2Ch 14:13;*
   21:17
c. *away* sheep and camels   *2Ch 14:15*
these had been *c*. *away*   *Ezr 2:1;*
   Ne 7:6
transgressions of those *c*. *away*   *Ezr 9:4;*
   10:6
separated from congregation   *Ezr 10:8*
him
fell upon camels, *c*. them   *Job 1:17*
away
I have caused to be *c*. *away*   *Jer 29:4*
captive
iron, gold broken, winds *c*.   *Da 2:35*
them *away*
She was *c*. *away* into   *Na 3:10*
captivity
time they were *c*. *away* to   *M't 1:11*
Babylon
c. Jesus *away* and delivered   *M'k 15:1*
him
Gentiles *c*. *away* to dumb   *1Co 12:2*
idols
Barnabas *c*. *away* with   *Ga 2:13*
dissimulation
cause her to be *c*. *away* of   *Re 12:15*
flood
he *c*. me *away* in the Spirit   *Re 17:3;*
   21:10

CARRIES

c. a rich reward (B)(P)   *Heb 10:35*

CARRIEST

c. them away as with a flood   *Ps 90:5*

CARRIETH

chaff that the storm *c*. away   *Job 21:18*
The east wind *c*. him away   *Job 27:21*
and of the beast that *c*. her   *Re 17:7*

CARRION

the *c*. vulture (S)   *Le 11:18; De 14:17*

CARRY

Ishmaelites going to *c*.   *Ge 37:25*
spicery
go *c*. corn for famine of   *Ge 42:19*
your houses
c. a present, a little balm,   *Ge 43:11*
honey

money *c.* it again in your Ge 43:12
hand
fill sacks with as much as can Ge 44:1
c.
saw waggons sent to *c.* him Ge 45:27;
46:5
shall *c.* up my bones Ge 50:25;
Ex 13:19
presence go not, *c.* us not up Ex 33:15
hence
c. your brethren out of camp Le 10:4
should say, C. them in thy Nu 11:12
bosom
so that thou art not able to De 14:24
c. it
c. twelve stones over with you Jos 4:3
c. these ten cheeses to 1Sa 17:18
captain
Jonathan said, Go, *c.* them 1Sa 20:40
to city
ferry boat to *c.* over king's 2Sa 19:18
house
c. out my judgments (B) 1Ki 6:12
Spirit of Lord shall *c.* thee 1Ki 18:12
father said, C. him to mother 2Ki 4:19
c. Jehu to an inner chamber 2Ki 9:2
saying, C. thither one of the 2Ki 17:27
priests
sent to Philistines to *c.* 1Ch 10:9
tidings
none ought to *c.* ark but 1Ch 15:2
Levites
Levites shall no more *c.* 1Ch 23:26
tabernacle
c. wood up to Jerusalem 2Ch 2:16
bound to *c.* him to Babylon 2Ch 36:6;
Jer 39:7
c. these vessels into temple Ezr 5:15
c. silver and gold freely Ezr 7:15
offered
bird of air shall *c.* the voice Ec 10:20
own feet *c.* her afar off to Isa 23:7
sojourn
will *c.* their riches on young Isa 30:6
asses
he shall *c.* the lambs in his Isa 40:11
bosom
even to hoary hairs will I *c.* Isa 46:4
you
they *c.* him and set him in Isa 46:7
his place
will *c.* them to Babylon Jer 20:5
Gedaliah should *c.* Jer 39:14
Jeremiah home
men *c.* tales to shed blood Eze 22:9
c. his goods (A) M't 12:29
began to *c.* about in beds M'k 6:55
sick
not suffer to *c.* vessel thro' M'k 11:16
temple
c. neither purse, nor scrip Lu 10:4
not lawful to *c.* thy bed Joh 5:10
c. thee whither thou Joh 21:18
wouldest not

CARRY AWAY

king of Assyria *c.* away 2Ki 18:11
Israel
fugitives did Nebuzar-adan 2Ki 25:11
c. away
more than they could *c.* 2Ch 20:25
away
why doth thine heart *c.* Job 15:12
thee *away*
when dieth shall *c.* nothing Ps 49:17
away
nothing left he may *c. away* in Ec 5:15
hand
they shall *c.* the prey *away* Isa 5:29
safe
have laid up, shall they *c.* Isa 15:7
away
the Lord will *c.* thee *away* Isa 22:17
wind shall *c.* them *away* Isa 41:16;
57:13
he will no more *c.* thee *away* La 4:22
art thou come to *c. away* Eze 38:13
silver
I will *c.* you *away* beyond Ac 7:43
Babylon

CARRY BACK

c. back the ark of God into 2Sa 15:25
city
c. Micaiah *back* to Amon 1Ki 22:26;
2Ch 18:25

CARRY FORTH

not *c. forth* aught of Ex 12:46
passover
dealt to *c.* us *forth* out of Ex 14:11
Egypt
whole bullock shall he *c.* Le 4:12;
forth 4:21
c. forth ashes without camp Le 6:11;
Le 14:45; 16:27
c. forth filthiness out of holy 2Ch 29:5
place
nor *c. forth* burden on Jer 17:22
sabbath day
in their sight, *c.* it *forth* in Eze 12:6
twilight

CARRY OUT

thou shalt *c.* me *out* of Ge 47:30
Egypt
c. much seed *out,* gather De 28:38
little
then *c.* him *out* and stone 1Ki 21:10
him
c. me *out* of host 1Ki 22:34;
2Ch 18:33
c. it *out* into brook Kidron 2Ch 29:16
dig through wall, and *c. out* Eze 12:5
feet at door, and shall *c.* thee Ac 5:9
out
certain we can *c.* nothing *out* 1Ti 6:7

CARRYING

one *c.* three kids, and 1Sa 10:3
another
c. bows, turned back in the Ps 78:9
day
c. away of Jerusalem captive Jer 1:3
from David until the *c.* M't 1:17
away
c. her forth, buried her by Ac 5:10
her
c. you captive (B) Col 2:8

CARSHENA

And the next unto him was Es 1:14
C.

CART

make a new *c.* 1Sa 6:7; 6:8, 10-11, 14
set the ark of God upon a 2Sa 6:3
new *c.*
carried the ark of God in a 1Ch 13:7
new *c.*
And Uzza and Ahio drave 1Ch 13:7
the *c.*
and sin as it were with a *c.* Isa 5:18
rope
neither is a *c.* wheel turned Isa 28:27
about
break it with the wheel of Isa 28:28
his *c.*
as a *c.* is pressed that is full Am 2:13

CARVE

c. upon it the inscription (A) Zec 3:9

CARVED

any *c.* image (S) Ex 20:4;
26:1; De 4:16, 23, 25; 5:8; 27:15;
J'g 17:3, 4; 18:14, 17, 20, 30, 31;
2Ki 21:7; Isa 40:20; 44:9, 15, 17; 45:20;
48:5; 51:47; Na 1:14; Hab 2:18
any *c.* images (S) De 7:5;
7:25; 12:3; 2Ki 17:41; 2Ch 33:19; 34:7;
Ps 78:58; 97:7; Isa 10:10; 21:9; 30:22;
42:8, 17; Jer 8:19; 50:38; 51:52;
Ho 11:2; Mic 1:7; 5:13
make a *c.* image (B) De 27:15
fetched the *c.* image, the J'g 18:18
ephod
house within was *c.* with 1Ki 6:18;
6:29, 32, 35
he *c.* cherubims (S) 1Ki 7:36; 2Ch 3:7
he set a *c.* image, the idol 2Ch 33:7
which
sacrificed unto all the *c.* 2Ch 33:22
images
the *c.* images, and the molten 2Ch 34:3
the groves, and the *c.* images 2Ch 34:4
now they break down the *c.* Ps 74:6
work
with *c.* works, with fine linen Pr 7:16

stone, *c.* by art and man's Ac 17:29
(S)

CARVING

and in *c.* of timber, to work Ex 31:5
in all
and in *c.* of wood, to make Ex 35:33
any
c. all kinds of (B)(R) 2Ch 2:14

CARVINGS

c. of cherubims and palm 1Ki 6:32
trees
c. with their borders (S) 1Ki 7:31

CARVETH

c. and habitation for himself Isa 22:16
(S)

CASE

did see that they were in evil Ex 5:19
c.
shall in no *c.* eat of it (S) Le 7:24
this is the *c.* of the slayer, De 19:4
which
thou shalt in any *c.* bring De 22:1
them
In any *c.* thou shalt deliver De 24:13
him
that people, that is in such Ps 144:15
a *c.*
ye shall in no *c.* enter into M't 5:20
If the *c.* of the man be so M't 19:10
with his
a long time in that *c.* he saith Joh 5:6
determine your *c.* (S) Ac 24:22

CASEMENT

I looked through my *c.* Pr 7:6

CASES

is not under bondage in 1Co 7:15
such *c.*

CASIPHIA

Iddo the chief at the place C. Ezr 8:17
the Nethinims, at the place Ezr 8:17
C.

CASLUHIM

and C. (out of whom came Ge 10:14
and C. (of whom came the 1Ch 1:12

CASSIA

And of *c.* five hundred Ex 30:24
shekels
smell of myrrh, and aloes, Ps 45:8
and *c.*
bright iron, *c.* and calamus Eze 27:19

CAST

Hagar *c.* child under a Ge 21:15
shrub
she goats have not *c.* their Ge 31:38
young
slay him, *c.* him into some Ge 37:20
pit
master's wife *c.* eyes upon Ge 39:7
Joseph
every son ye shall *c.* into Ex 1:22
river
c. it, and he *c.* rod on ground Ex 4:3
Zipporah *c.* the foreskin at Ex 4:25
his feet
locusts and *c.* them into Red Ex 10:19
sea
Pharaoh's chariots he *c.* into Ex 15:4
the sea
when he had *c.* the tree into Ex 15:25
the waters
not eat flesh torn of beasts, Ex 22:31
c. it to dogs
nothing *c.* their young, nor be Ex 23:26
c. four rings of gold Ex 25:12;
Ex 37:3, 13; 38:5
Moses *c.* tables out of hand, Ex 32:19
brake
I *c.* into fire, there came out Ex 32:24
calf

priest *c.* cedar wood into　*Nu 19:6*
burning
c. any thing on him without　*Nu 35:22*
laying wait
him not, *c.* it on him that　*Nu 35:23*
he die
Lord *c.* them into another　*De 29:28*
land
c. king of Ai at gate of city　*Jos 8:29*
c. them into cave　*Jos 10:27*
c. every one earrings of his　*J'g 8:25*
prey
woman *c.* piece of millstone　*J'g 9:53;*
　2Sa 11:21
Saul *c.* the javelin　*1Sa 18:11; 20:33*
Shimei *c.* stones at David　*2Sa 16:6;*
　16:13
they *c.* Absalom into great　*2Sa 18:17*
pit in wood
Joab's man *c.* a cloth upon　*2Sa 20:12*
Amasa
metal melted and *c.* (S)　*1Ki 7:33;*
2Ch 4:2; 28:2; 34:3-4; Isa 41:29; 44:10;
　Ho 13:2
in plain of Jordan *c.*　*1Ki 7:46;*
　2Ch 4:17
thou hast *c.* me behind thy　*1Ki 14:9*
back
Elijah *c.* his mantle upon　*1Ki 19:19*
Elisha
lest Lord *c.* him on　*2Ki 2:16*
mountain
went to spring and *c.* salt in　*2Ki 2:21*
there
piece of land *c.* each his　*2Ki 3:25*
stone
then bring meal, and he *c.* it　*2Ki 4:41*
into pot
he *c.* in stick, and the iron　*2Ki 6:6*
swam
c. him in portion of field of　*2Ki 9:25*
Naboth
c. man into the sepulchre　*2Ki 13:21*
of Elisha
neither *c.* them from his　*2Ki 13:23*
presence
have *c.* their gods into fire　*2Ki 19:18;*
　Isa 37:19
nor *c.* a bank against it　*2Ki 19:32;*
　Isa 37:33
c. thy law behind their backs　*Ne 9:26*
they *c.* Pur, that is, the lot　*Es 3:7*
Haman had *c.* Pur, that is　*Es 9:24*
he is *c.* into the net by　*Job 18:8*
God *c.* the fury of wrath　*Job 20:23*
upon him
God shall *c.* upon him and　*Job 27:22*
spare not
he hath *c.* me into the mire　*Job 30:19*
c. abroad the rage of thy　*Job 40:11*
wrath
I was *c.* upon thee from the　*Ps 22:10*
womb
they *c.* iniquity upon me, hate　*Ps 55:3*
me
c. thy burden on the Lord,　*Ps 55:22*
he shall
have *c.* fire into thy sanctuary　*Ps 74:7*
chariot and horse *c.* into a　*Ps 76:6*
sleep
c. off and rejected (A)(R)　*Ps 89:38*
let them be *c.* into the fire　*Ps 140:10*
C. in thy lot among us, let us　*Pr 1:14*
the lot is *c.* into the lap　*Pr 16:33*
C. thy bread upon the waters　*Ec 11:1*
man shall *c.* his idols to bats　*Isa 2:20*
face of covering *c.* over all　*Isa 25:7*
people
hast *c.* all my sins behind　*Isa 38:17*
thy back
are *c.* into the land which　*Jer 22:28*
they know
c. Urijah's body into the　*Jer 26:23*
graves
c. it into the fire that was　*Jer 36:23*
on the
they *c.* Jeremiah into a　*Jer 38:6*
dungeon
Ishmael *c.* them into a pit　*Jer 41:7;*
　41:9
c. into a cistern (A)(B)(R)　*Jer 41:7*
c. a stone upon me　*La 3:53*
shall *c.* their silver into the　*Eze 7:19*
streets
I have *c.* them far off　*Eze 11:16*
among heathen
the vine tree is *c.* into the　*Eze 15:4*
fire
hast *c.* me behind thy back　*Eze 23:35*

I will *c.* thee to the ground　*Eze 28:17*
be *c.* into a fiery furnace　*Da 3:6; 3:20*
we *c.* three men bound into　*Da 3:24*
the fire
he shall be *c.* into den of　*Da 6:7;*
lions　*6:24*
thou hadst *c.* me into the　*Jon 2:3*
deep
I am *c.* out of thy sight　*Jon 2:4*
make her *c.* off strong nation　*Mic 4:7*
wilt *c.* all their sins into the　*Mic 7:19*
sea
I will *c.* abominable filth on　*Na 3:6*
thee
c. it into the ephah; *c.* the　*Zec 5:8*
weight
C. it to potter, *c.* them to　*Zec 11:13*
the potter
nor vine *c.* her fruit before　*Mal 3:11*
time
hewn down and *c.* into fire　*M't 3:10;*
　7:19
and be *c.* into prison　*M't 5:25*
pluck out, *c.* from thee　*M't 5:29;*
　M't 5:30; 18:8-9
to-morrow is *c.* into oven　*M't 6:30;*
　Lu 12:28
nor *c.* pearls before swine,　*M't 7:6*
lest
children's bread and *c.* it　*M't 15:26;*
to the dogs　*M'k 7:27*
c. an hook, take first fish　*M't 17:27*
c. him into prison, till pay　*M't 18:30*
debt
say to mountain, be *c.* into　*M't 21:21*
the sea
c. him into outer darkness　*M't 22:13;*
　25:30
thieves *c.* the same in his　*M't 27:44*
teeth
ofttimes *c.* into the fire　*M'k 9:22*
better he were *c.* into sea　*M't 9:42;*
　Lu 17:2
two eyes to be *c.* into hell　*M'k 9:45;*
　9:47
c. their garments on him　*M'k 11:7;*
　Lu 19:35
at him they *c.* stones　*M'k 12:4*
c. money into treasury　*M'k 12:41;*
　Lu 21:4
poor widow *c.* more than　*M'k 12:43;*
all　*12:44*
c. into fire　*Lu 3:9; M't 3:10*
reviled and *c.* out your name　*Lu 6:22*
(R)
who hath power to *c.* into　*Lu 12:5*
hell
enemies *c.* a trench about　*Lu 19:43*
thee
for murder was *c.* into　*Lu 23:19*
prison
John was not yet *c.* into　*Joh 3:24*
prison
let him first *c.* a stone at her　*Joh 8:7*
Peter did *c.* himself into the　*Joh 21:7*
sea
c. thy garment about thee,　*Ac 12:8*
follow
c. Paul and Silas into prison　*Ac 16:23*
must be *c.* upon a certain　*Ac 27:26*
island
c. themselves into the sea　*Ac 27:43*
tnat I may *c.* a snare upon　*1Co 7:35*
you
devil *c.* some of you into　*Re 2:10*
prison
taught Balak to *c.* a　*Re 2:14*
stumblingblock
will *c.* her into bed, and them　*Re 2:22*
that
elders *c.* their crowns before　*Re 4:10*
throne
hail and fire were *c.* on earth　*Re 8:7*
mountain burning *c.* into sea　*Re 8:8*
dragon saw he was *c.* to　*Re 12:13*
earth
millstone, and *c.* it into the sea　*Re 18:21*
both were *c.* alive into lake　*Re 19:20*
of
the devil *c.* into lake of fire　*Re 20:10*
death and hell were *c.* into　*Re 20:14*
lake
c. into the lake of fire　*Re 20:15*

CAST *AWAY*

I will not *c.* them *away*　*Le 26:44*
c. away jawbone out of　*J'g 15:17*
hand

shield of mighty is *c. away*　*2Sa 1:21*
vessels Syrians *c. away* in　*2Ki 7:15*
haste
vessels Ahaz in his reign *c.*　*2Ch 29:19*
away
c. them *away* for　*Job 8:4*
transgression
God will not *c. away* perfect　*Job 8:20*
man
let us *c. away* their cords　*Ps 2:3*
from us
c. me not *away* from thy　*Ps 51:11*
presence
time to *c. away* stones　*Ec 3:5*
because they have *c. away* law　*Isa 5:24*
c. them *away* as menstruous　*Isa 30:22*
cloth
every man *c. away* idols of　*Isa 31:7*
silver
chosen thee, and not *c.* thee　*Isa 41:9*
away
cut thy hair, and *c.* it *away*　*Jer 7:29*
then will I *c. away* seed　*Jer 33:26*
of Jacob
c. away all your　*Eze 18:31*
transgressions
c. away every man　*Eze 20:7*
abominations
they did not *c. away*　*Eze 20:8*
abominations
my God will *c.* them *away*　*Ho 9:17*
gathered good, *c.* bad *away*　*M't 13:48*
if man lose himself, or be *c.*　*Lu 9:25*
away
hath God *c. away* his people　*Ro 11:1*
God hath not *c. away* his　*Ro 11:2*
people
c. not *away* your　*Heb 10:35*
confidence

CAST *DOWN*

c. down his rod. They *c. down*　*Ex 7:10;*
　7:12
c. down great stones upon　*Jos 10:11*
them
altar of Baal was *c. down*　*J'g 6:28*
Elijah *c.* himself *down* on　*1Ki 18:42*
earth
God hath power to *c. down*　*2Ch 25:8*
c. them *down* from top of　*2Ch 25:12*
rock
were *c. down* in their own　*Ne 6:16*
eyes
his own counsel shall *c.* him　*Job 18:7*
down
when men are *c. down,*　*Job 22:29*
then say
my countenance they *c.* not　*Job 29:24*
down
not one be *c. down* at sight　*Job 41:9*
of him
Lord, disappoint him, *c.*　*Ps 17:13*
down
are *c. down* and not able to　*Ps 36:12*
rise
bent bow to *c. down* poor and　*Ps 37:14*
needy
fall, he shall not be utterly *c.*　*Ps 37:24*
down
why art thou *c. down*　*Ps 42:5;*
　Ps 42:11; 43:5
my soul is *c. down* within me　*Ps 42:6*
in anger *c. down* people, O　*Ps 56:7*
Lord
to *c.* him *down* from　*Ps 62:4*
excellency
c. his throne *down* to ground　*Ps 89:44*
lifted me up, and *c.* me　*Ps 102:10*
down
she hath *c. down* many　*Pr 7:26*
wounded
Lord *c. down* with his hand　*Isa 28:2*
visit, they shall be *c. down*　*Jer 6:15;*
　8:12
c. down to earth beauty of　*La 2:1*
Israel
I will *c. down* slain before　*Eze 6:4*
idols
mother was *c. down* to　*Eze 19:12*
ground
when I *c.* Assyrian *down* to　*Eze 31:16*
hell
wail for Egypt, and *c.* her　*Eze 32:18*
down
beheld till thrones were *c.*　*Da 7:9*
down
he goat *c. down* ram to　*Da 8:7*
ground

c. down some of host, and stars   Da 8:10

sanctuary was *c. down*   Da 8:11

he shall *c. down* many ten thousands   Da 11:12

if Son of God, *c.* self *down*   M't 4:6; Lu 4:9

c. down at Jesus' feet, he healed   M't 15:30

c. down pieces of silver in temple   M't 27:5

they might *c.* Jesus *down* headlong   Lu 4:29

c. down, but not destroyed   2Co 4:9

God comforteth those *c. down*   2Co 7:6

but *c.* the angels *down* to hell   2Pe 2:4

accuser of our brethren is *c. down*   Re 12:10

CAST *FORTH*

I *c. forth* household stuff of Tobias   Ne 13:8

c. forth lightning, scatter them   Ps 144:6

Jehoiakim *c. forth* beyond gates   Jer 22:19

c. thee *forth* upon open field   Eze 32:4

shall *c. forth* roots as Lebanon   Ho 14:5

mariners *c. forth* wares in ship   Jon 1:5

into sea

c. me *forth* into sea, so sea be calm   Jon 1:12

took Jonah and *c.* him *forth* into sea   Jon 1:15

c. forth devil out of daughter   M'k 7:26

c. forth as branch and withered   Joh 15:6

CAST *LOTS*

Aaron *c. lots* on two goats   Le 16:8

Joshua *c. lots* for them in Shiloh   Jos 18:10

c. lots between me and Jonathan   1Sa 14:42

c. lots as well small as great   1Ch 26:13

part my garments and *c.*   Ps 22:18;

lots upon my vesture   M't 27:35; Joh 19:24

he hath *c.* the *lot* for them   Isa 34:17

they have *c. lots* for my people   Joe 3:3

in the day foreigners *c. lots* upon   Ob 11

let us *c. lots* that we may know   Jon 1:7

they *c. lots* for her honourable men   Na 3:10

CAST *OFF*

I will *c. off* this city Jerusalem   2Ki 23:27

if forsake, *c.* thee *off* for ever   1Ch 28:9

Jeroboam and sons *c.* them *off*   2Ch 11:14

shall *c. off* he flower as olive   Job 15:33

why dost thou *c.* me *off*   Ps 43:2

thou hast *c. off*   Ps 44:9; Ps 60:1, 10; 89:38; 108:11

awake, *c.* us not *off* for ever   Ps 44:23

c. me not *off* in the time of old age   Ps 71:9

why hast thou *c.* us *off* for ever   Ps 74:1

will the Lord *c. off* for ever   Ps 77:7

Lord will not *c. off* people   Ps 94:14; La 3:31

c. Hananiah *off* from earth   Jer 28:16

I will *c. off* the seed of Israel   Jer 31:37; 33:24

Lord hath *c. off* his altar   La 2:7

Israel *c. off* thing that is good   Ho 8:3

thy calf, O Samaria, hath *c.* thee *off*   Ho 8:5

because Edom did *c. off* all pity   Am 1:11

be as though I had not *c. off*   Zec 10:6

as they cried and *c. off* clothes   Ac 22:23

let us *c. off* works of darkness   Ro 13:12

because they *c. off* first faith   1Ti 5:12

CAST *OUT*

c. out this bondwoman and son   Ge 21:10

I will *c. out* nations before thee   Ex 34:24

nations are defiled which I *c. out* before you   Le 18:24; Le 20:23; De 7:1

I *c.* two tables *out* of my hands   De 9:17

these two Moses smite, and *c.* them *out*   Jos 13:12

c. out Sheba's head to Joab   2Sa 20:22

this house will I *c. out*   1Ki 9:7; 2Ch 7:20

whom the Lord *c. out*   1Ki 21:26; 2Ki 16:3

captains *c.* them *out* and went   2Ki 10:25

c. them *out* of his sight   2Ki 17:20; 24:20

have *c. out* priests of the Lord   2Ch 13:9

come to *c.* us *out* of thy possession   2Ch 20:11

if ye turn, though they were *c. out*   Ne 1:9

God shall *c.* them *out* of his belly   Job 20:15

bow themselves, they *c. out* sorrows   Job 39:3

c. them *out* in their transgressions   Ps 5:10

I did *c.* them *out* as dirt in streets   Ps 18:42

didst afflict people and *c.* them *out*   Ps 44:2

over Edom will I *c. out* my shoe   Ps 60:8; 108:9

c. out heathen before them   Ps 78:55; 80:8

c. out the scorner, and contention go out   Pr 22:10

but thou art *c. out* of thy grave   Isa 14:19

as wandering bird *c. out* of nest   Isa 16:2

the earth shall *c. out* the dead   Isa 26:19

slain also shall be *c. out* and stink   Isa 34:3

that thou bring poor that are *c. out*   Isa 58:7

that *c.* you *out* for my name's sake   Isa 66:5

c. you *out* of my sight, as I *c. out*   Jer 7:15

because our dwellings have *c.* us *out*   Jer 9:19

c. them *out* of my sight   Jer 15:1; Jer 23:39; 52:3

therefore will I *c.* you *out* of land   Jer 16:13

I will *c.* thee *out*, and thy *out* in the day   Jer 22:26

his dead body shall be *c.*   Jer 36:30

Nebuchadnezzar hath *c.* me *out*   Jer 51:34

thou wast *c. out* in open field   Eze 16:5

will *c.* thee as profane *out* of mount   Eze 28:16

land shall be *c. out* and drowned   Am 8:8

women of my people ye *c. out*   Mic 2:9

Lord hath *c. out* thine enemy   Zep 3:15

to *c. out* the horns of Gentiles   Zec 1:21

Lord will *c.* her *out*, smite her power   Zec 9:4

salt unsavoury be *c. out*   M't 5:13; Lu 14:35

hypocrite, first *c. out* beam   M't 7:5; Lu 6:42

have we not in thy name *c. out* devils   M't 7:22

children of kingdom shall be *c. out*   M't 8:12

and he *c. out* the spirits with his word   M't 8:16

if *c.* us *out*, suffer us to go into swine   M't 8:31

when devil was *c. out* dumb spake   M't 9:33

gave power against spirits to *c. out*   M't 10:1

heal sick, raise dead, *c. out* devils   M't 10:8

c. out devils by Beelzebub   M't 12:24; Lu 11:18

if Satan *c. out* Satan, divided against himself   M't 12:26

if I by Spirit of God *c. out* devils   M't 12:28

into belly, and *c. out* into draught   M't 15:17

why could not we *c.* him *out*   M't 17:19; M'k 9:28

c. out all that sold   M't 21:12; M'k 11:15; Lu 19:45

c. out of vineyard   M't 21:39; M'k 12:8; Lu 20:15

healed and *c. out* devils   M'k 1:34; 6:13

have power to heal and *c. out* devils   M'k 3:15

how can Satan *c. out* Satan   M'k 3:23

out of whom he *c.* seven devils   M'k 16:9

in my name shall they *c. out* devils   M'k 16:17

c. out your name as evil   Lu 6:22

if I with finger of God *c. out* devils   Lu 11:20

I *c. out* devils, and do cures to-day   Lu 13:32

wounded him and *c.* him *out*   Lu 20:12

cometh I will in no wise *c. out*   Joh 6:37

dost thou teach us? they *c.* him *out*   Joh 9:34

now shall prince of world be *c. out*   Joh 12:31

they *c. out* their young children   Ac 7:19

Moses was *c. out* Pharaoh's daughter   Ac 7:21

c. Stephen *out* of city and stoned him   Ac 7:58

third day we *c. out* tackling of ship   Ac 27:19

c. four anchors *out*   Ac 27:29; 27:38

c. out bondwoman and her son   Ga 4:30

great dragon was *c. out*, the devil   Re 12:9

serpent *c. out* of mouth waters   Re 12:15; 12:16

LORD CAST OUT

Lord *c. out* before Israel   2Ki 17:8; 14:24; 16:3; 2Ch 28:3; 33:2

Lord will *c.* her *out* and smite   Zec 9:4

CAST UP

they *c. up* a bank against city   2Sa 20:15

c. ye *up*, prepare way   Isa 57:14; 62:10

troubled sea, whose waters *c. up*   Isa 57:20

walk in paths, in way not *c. up*   Jer 18:15

c. her *up* as heaps, and destroy her   Jer 50:26

c. up dust on heads   La 2:10; Eze 27:30

king of north shall *c. up* mount   Da 11:15

CASTAWAY

to others, I myself should be a *c.*   1Co 9:27

CASTEDST

c. them down into destruction   Ps 73:18

CASTEST

thou *c. off* fear, and restrainest   Job 15:4

instruction, and *c.* my words   Ps 50:17

Lord, why *c.* thou off my soul   Ps 88:14

CASTETH

their cow calveth, and *c.* not her   Job 21:10

he *c.* the wicked down to the   Ps 147:6

He *c. forth* his ice like morsels   Ps 147:17

but he *c.* away the substance   Pr 10:3

Slothfulness *c.* into a deep sleep   Pr 19:15

and c. down the strength of *Pr 21:22*
with c. firebrands, arrows *Pr 26:18*
with gold, and c. silver *Isa 40:19*
chains
As a fountain c. out her *Jer 6:7*
waters
so she c. out her wickedness *Jer 6:7*
He c. out devils through the *M't 9:34*
prince
prince of the devils c. he *M'k 3:22*
out devils
He c. out devils through *Lu 11:15*
Beelzebub
perfect love c. out fear: *1Jo 4:18*
because
and c. them out of the church *3Jo 10*
as a fig tree c. her untimely *Re 6:13*
figs

CASTING

c. them down to the ground *2Sa 8:2*
all of them had one c., one *1Ki 7:37*
c. himself down before the *Ezr 10:1*
house
ye see my c. down, and are *Job 6:21*
afraid
sanctuary, have they defiled *Ps 74:7*
by c.
his crown by c. it to the *Ps 89:39*
ground
melteth and c. (S) *Isa 40:19*
by c. up mounts, and *Eze 17:17*
building
and thy c. down shall be in *Mic 6:14*
c. a net into the sea: for *M't 4:18*
they were
parted his garments, c. lots: *M't 27:35*
that
Andrew his brother c. a net *M'k 1:16*
into
we saw one c. out devils in *M'k 9:38*
thy
he, c. away his garment, *M'k 10:50*
rose, and
parted his garments, c. lots *M'k 15:24*
upon
we saw one c. out devils in *Lu 9:49*
thy
he was c. out a devil, and it *Lu 11:14*
was
the rich men c. their gifts *Lu 21:1*
into the
a certain poor widow c. in *Lu 21:2*
thither
For if the c. away of them *Ro 11:15*
be the
C. down imaginations, and *2Co 10:5*
every
C. all your care upon him; *1Pe 5:7*
for he

CASTLE

c. of the king's house (E) *1Ki 16:18;*
15:25
David took the c. of Zion, *1Ch 11:5*
which
David dwelt in the c.; *1Ch 11:7*
therefore
the c. of Shushan (A) *Ne 1:1*
the gates of the c. (E) *Ne 2:8*
the ruler of the c. (A)(E)(R) *Ne 7:2*
contentions are like the bars *Pr 18:19*
of a c.
guard his own c. (N) *Lu 11:21*
him to be carried into the *Ac 21:34*
Paul was to be led into the *Ac 21:37*
c. he
to be brought into the c. *Ac 22:24*
and bade
and to bring him into the c. *Ac 23:10*
he went and entered into the *Ac 23:16*
c.
and returned to the c. *Ac 23:32*

CASTLES

by their towns, and by their *Ge 25:16*
c.
they dwelt, and all their *Nu 31:10*
goodly c.
c. and strongholds of iron *De 33:25*
(A)
places throughout their c. *1Ch 6:54*
in the villages, and in the *1Ch 27:25*
c.
he built in Judah c. and *2Ch 17:12*
cities

and in the forests he built c. *2Ch 27:4*
and
cry in deserted c. (A)(B) *Isa 13:22*

CASTOR

whose sign was C. and *Ac 28:11*
Pollux

CASTS

c. ice like crumbs (A) *Ps 147:17*

CASUALTIES

with heavy c. (B) *J'g 11:3*

CATARACTS

at the noise of thy c. (B)(R) *Ps 42:7*

CATASTROPHE

c. sweep down upon them *1Th 5:3*
(P)

CATCH

If fire break out, and c. in *Ex 22:6*
and c. you every man his *J'g 21:21*
wife of
from him, and did hastily *1Ki 20:33*
c. it
we shall c. them alive, and *2Ki 7:12*
get
in wait to c. the poor: he *Ps 10:9*
doth c.
let his net that he hath hid c. *Ps 35:8*
Let the extortioner c. all *Ps 109:11*
that he
snares; they set a trap, they c. *Jer 5:26*
it learned to c. the prey *Eze 19:3*
and learned to c. the prey *Eze 19:6*
they c. them in their net *Hab 1:15*
of the Herodians, to c. him *M'k 12:13*
in his
henceforth thou shalt c. men *Lu 5:10*
seeking to c. something out *Lu 11:54*
of his

CATCHETH

which hunteth and c. any *Le 17:13*
beast
cometh the wicked one, and *M't 13:19*
c.
the wolf c. them, and *Joh 10:12*
scattereth

CATERPILLER

if there be c.; if their enemy *1Ki 8:37*
their increase unto the c. and *Ps 78:46*
the gathering of the c. as the *Isa 33:4*
cankerworm hath left hath the *Joe 1:4*
c.
cankerworm, and the c. and *Joe 2:25*

CATERPILLERS

mildew, locusts, or c.; if their *2Ch 6:28*
the locusts came, and c. *Ps 105:34*
fill thee with men, as with c. *Jer 51:14*
horses to come up as the *Jer 51:27*
rough c.

CATTLE

God made c. after their kind *Ge 1:25*
thou art cursed above all c. *Ge 3:14*
all flesh died, both of fowl *Ge 7:21*
and c.
God remembered Noah, and c. *Ge 8:1*
with him
I establish my covenant with *Ge 9:10*
fowls, c.
Abram was very rich in c. *Ge 13:2*
Jacob put them not to *Ge 30:40*
Laban's c.
hath taken away c. of our *Ge 31:9*
father
these c. are my c. all thou *Ge 31:43*
seest
his sons were with c. in the *Ge 34:5*
field
for their trade hath been to *Ge 46:32*
feed c.
then make them rulers over *Ge 47:6*
my c.

Joseph gave bread in *Ge 47:17*
exchange for c.
sever between c. of Israel and *Ex 9:4*
c. of Egypt
made servants and c. flee into *Ex 9:20*
houses
Lord smote all the firstborn *Ex 12:29*
of c.
bring your offering of c. *Le 1:2*
take c. of Levites instead of *Nu 3:41*
all
if I and my c. drink, I will *Nu 20:19*
pay for it
is a land for c., thy servants *Nu 32:4*
have c.
the c. we took for a prey *De 2:35; 3:7*
increase of thy c. (S) *De 7:13*
cattle (A)(B)(R) *De 28:4; 28:51*
only c. take for a prey *Jos 8:2*
only c. Israel took for prey *Jos 8:27;*
11:14
Adonijah slew oxen and c. *1Ki 1:9*
19:25
the c. also concerning the *Job 36:33*
vapour
c. upon a thousand hills is *Ps 50:10*
mine
causeth the grass to grow *Ps 104:14*
for c.
c. heavy with young (R) *Ps 144:14*
beasts and all c. praise the *Ps 148:10*
Lord
had great possessions of c. *Ec 2:7*
and for the treading of lesser *Isa 7:25*
c.
thou hast not brought me *Isa 43:23*
small c.
their idols were upon beasts *Isa 46:1*
and c.
nor can men hear voice of c. *Jer 9:10*
I judge between c. and c *Eze 34:17;*
34:20, 22
called for drought upon land *Hag 1:11*
and c.
for multitude of men and c. *Zec 2:4*
taught me to keep c. from *Zec 13:5*
youth
having servant feeding c. will *Lu 17:7*
say
Jacob, his children drank, *Joh 4:12*
and c.
wheat and c. (S) *Re 18:13*

MUCH CATTLE

Jacob increased and had *Ge 30:43*
much c.
went out of Egypt with *Ex 12:38*
much c.
for I know that ye have *De 3:19*
much c.
return to tents with very *Jos 22:8*
much c.
Uzziah had much c. in *2Ch 26:10*
plains
spare Nineveh, wherein is *Jon 4:11*
much c.

OUR CATTLE

our c. also shall go with us *Ex 10:26*
to kill us and our c. with *Ex 17:3*
thirst
that we and our c. should die *Nu 20:4*
build sheepfolds for our c *Nu 32:16*
all our c. shall be there in *Nu 32:26*
Gilead
give us cities for our c. *Jos 21:2*
dominion over our bodies *Ne 9:37*
and our c.
to bring our sons and our c. *Ne 10:36*

THEIR CATTLE

their c. and substance be *Ge 34:23*
ours
slew Midianites, took spoil of *Nu 31:9*
their c.
suburbs shall be for their c. *Nu 35:3;*
Jos 14:4
Midianites came up with their *J'g 6:5*
c.
David fought, and brought *1Sa 23:5*
their c.
because their c. were *1Ch 5:9*
multiplied
they came down to take *1Ch 7:21*
their c.
gave up their c. also to hail *Ps 78:48*

suffered not *their c.* to decrease   *Ps 107:38*

camels a booty, *their c.* a spoil   *Jer 49:32*

THY CATTLE

knowest how *thy c.* was with me   *Ge 30:29*

I served thee six years for *thy c.*   *Ge 31:41*

hand of the Lord is on *thy c.*   *Ex 9:3*

send therefore now and gather *thy c.*   *Ex 9:19*

servant nor *thy c.* do work   *Ex 20:10; De 5:14*

every firstling among *thy c.* is mine   *Ex 34:19*

let not *thy c.* gender with diverse   *Le 19:19*

sabbath of land be meat for *thy c.*   *Le 25:7*

send grass in fields for *thy c.*   *De 11:15*

blessed shall be fruit of *thy c.*   *De 28:4; 30:9*

eat fruit of *thy c.* and thy land   *De 28:51*

shall *thy c.* feed in large pastures   *Isa 30:23*

YOUR CATTLE

give *your c.* give you for *your c.*   *Ge 47:16*

if not hearken, will destroy *your c.*   *Le 26:22*

your c. abide in cities   *De 3:19; Jos 1:14*

male nor female be barren among *your c.*   *De 7:14*

ye may drink, both ye and *your c.*   *2Ki 3:17*

CAUGHT

ram *c.* in a thicket by his horns   *Ge 22:13*

And she *c.* him by his garment   *Ge 39:12*

put forth his hand, and *c.* it   *Ex 4:4*

which the men of war had *c.*   *Nu 31:32*

pursued after him, and *c.* him   *J'g 1:6*

And *c.* a young man of the men   *J'g 8:14*

went and *c.* three hundred foxes   *J'g 15:4*

whom they *c.*: and they went *J'g 21:23*

he arose against me, I *c.* him   *1Sa 17:35*

And they *c.* every one his fellow   *2Sa 2:16*

and his head *c.* hold of the oak   *2Sa 18:9*

and *c.* hold on the horns of *1Ki 1:50*

he hath *c.* hold on the horns *1Ki 1:51*

and *c.* hold on the horns of *1Ki 2:28*

And Ahijah *c.* the new garment   *1Ki 11:30*

she *c.* him by the feet: but *2Ki 4:27*

sought Ahaziah: and they *c.* him   *2Ch 22:9*

So she *c.* him, and kissed him *Pr 7:13*

birds that are *c.* in the snare *Ec 9:12*

thou art found, and also *c.* *Jer 50:24*

c. him, and said unto him *M't 14:31*

they *c.* him, and cast him out *M't 21:39*

And they *c.* him and beat him *M'k 12:3*

For oftentimes it had *c.* him *Lu 8:29*

and that night they *c.* nothing *Joh 21:3*

the fish which we have now *c.*   *Joh 21:10*

c. him, and brought him to *Ac 6:12*

Spirit of the Lord *c.* away Philip   *Ac 8:39*

they *c.* Paul and Silas, and drew   *Ac 16:19*

c. Gaius and Aristarchus, men   *Ac 19:29*

the Jews *c.* me in the temple *Ac 21:30*

And when the ship was *c.* *Ac 27:15*

one *c.* up to the third heaven   *2Co 12:2*

he was *c.* up into paradise *2Co 12:4*

being crafty, I *c.* you with guile   *2Co 12:16*

shall be *c.* up together with *1Th 4:17*

her child was *c.* up unto God *Re 12:5*

CAUL

the *c.* that is above the liver *Ex 29:13*

and the *c.* above the liver *Ex 29:22*

c. above the liver, with the kidneys   *Le 3:4*

and the *c.* above the liver *Le 3:10*

c. above the liver, with the kidneys   *Le 3:15*

c. above the liver, with the kidneys   *Le 4:9*

and the *c.* that is above the liver   *Le 7:4*

and the *c.* above the liver *Le 8:16*

the *c.* above the liver, and the two   *Le 8:25*

and the *c.* above the liver of *Le 9:10*

and the *c.* above the liver *Le 9:19*

and will rend *c.* of their heart   *Ho 13:8*

CAULS

about their feet, and their *c.* *Isa 3:18*

CAUSE

I will *c.* it to rain upon the earth   *Ge 7:4*

C. every man to go out from me   *Ge 45:1*

and *c.* frogs to come up upon *Ex 8:5*

I will *c.* it to rain a very grievous   *Ex 9:18*

shall *c.* him to be thoroughly healed   *Ex 21:19*

c. a field or vineyard to be eaten   *Ex 22:5*

the *c.* of both parties shall come   *Ex 22:9*

speak in a *c.* to decline after *Ex 23:2*

countenance a poor man in his *c.*   *Ex 23:3*

the judgment of thy poor in his *c.*   *Ex 23:6*

to *c.* the lamp to burn always   *Ex 27:20*

shalt *c.* a bullock to be brought   *Ex 29:10*

he shall *c.* the house to be scraped   *Le 14:41*

to *c.* her to be a whore; lest *Le 19:29*

the light to *c.* the lamps to burn   *Le 24:2*

c. a blemish in his neighbor *Le 24:19*

Then shalt thou *c.* the *Le 25:9*

trumpet the eyes, and *c.* sorrow of heart   *Le 26:16*

he shall *c.* the woman to drink   *Nu 5:24*

and will *c.* him to come near *Nu 16:5*

which *c.* both thou and all thy   *Nu 16:11*

brought their *c.* before the Lord   *Nu 27:5*

shalt *c.* the inheritance *Nu 27:7; 27:8*

shalt thou *c.* the strong wine *Nu 28:7*

any person to *c.* him to die *Nu 35:30*

the *c.* that is too hard for you *De 1:17*

he shall *c.* Israel to inherit it *De 1:38*

he shall *c.* them to inherit the land   *De 3:28*

choose to *c.* his name to dwell   *De 12:11*

nor *c.* the people to return to Egypt   *De 17:16*

thou shalt not *c.* the land to sin   *De 24:4*

the judge shall *c.* him to lie down   *De 25:2*

shall *c.* thine enemies that rise   *De 28:7*

shall *c.* thee to be smitten before   *De 28:25*

thou shalt *c.* them to inherit it   *De 31:7*

the *c.* why Joshua did circumcise   *Jos 5:4*

his *c.* in the ears of the elders   *Jos 20:4*

nor *c.* to swear, by them *Jos 23:7*

shed blood without *c.* (S) *1Sa 15:31*

now done? Is there not a *c.* *1Sa 17:29*

pleaded the *c.* of my reproach   *1Sa 25:39*

for my life to *c.* me to die *1Sa 28:9*

to *c.* David to eat meat while it   *2Sa 3:35*

whither shall I *c.* my shame *2Sa 13:13*

said unto him, There is no *c.*   *2Sa 13:16*

suit or *c.* might come unto me   *2Sa 15:4*

and *c.* Solomon my son to ride   *1Ki 1:33*

c. them to be discharged there *1Ki 5:9*

laid upon him to *c.* him to *1Ki 8:31*

swear   *8:45, 49, 59; 2Ch 6:35, 39*

the *c.* that he lifted up his *1Ki 11:27* hand

the *c.* was from the Lord *1Ki 12:15*

c. him to fall by the sword *2Ki 19:7*

he be a *c.* of trespass to Israel   *1Ch 21:3*

for the *c.* was of God, that *2Ch 10:15*

And what *c.* soever shall come   *2Ch 19:10*

which *c.* was this city destroyed   *Ezr 4:15*

c. these men to cease   *Ezr 4:21; Ezr 5:5; Ne 4:11*

for which *c.* thou buildest the wall   *Ne 6:6*

did outlandish women *c.* to sin   *Ne 13:26*

and to *c.* to perish, all Jews *Es 3:13*

C. Haman to make haste *Es 5:5*

to slay, and to *c.* to perish, all the   *Es 8:11*

unto God would I commit my *c.*   *Job 5:8*

and *c.* me to understand wherein   *Job 6:24*

I have ordered my *c.*; I know   *Job 13:18*

I would order my *c.* before him   *Job 23:4*

They *c.* the naked to lodge *Job 24:7; 24:10*

and the *c.* which I knew not I   *Job 29:16*

If I did despise the *c.* of my   *Job 31:13*

To *c.* it to rain on the earth   *Job 38:26*

and to *c.* the bud of the tender   *Job 38:27*

maintained my right and my *c.* *Ps 9:4*

my judgment, even unto my *c.*   *Ps 35:23*

glad, that favour my righteous *c.*   *Ps 35:27*

c. his face to shine   *Ps 67:1; 80:3, 7, 19*

they hate me without a *c.* *Ps 69:4*

Lord will maintain the *c.* of *Ps 140:12*

C. me to hear thy lovingkindness   *Ps 143:8*

away, unless they *c.* some to fall   *Pr 4:16*

That I may *c.* those that love me   *Pr 8:21*

He that is first in his own *c.* *Pr 18:17*

Debate thy *c.* with thy neighbour   *Pr 25:9*

The righteous considereth the *c.*   *Pr 29:7*

dumb in the *c.* of all such as are   *Pr 31:8*

to *c.* my heart to despair of all   *Ec 2:20*

Suffer not thy mouth to *c.* thy *Ec 5:6*

c. the ointment of the apothecary   *Ec 10:1*

He shall *c.* them that come of   *Isa 27:6*

ye may *c.* the weary to rest *Isa 28:12*

he will *c.* the drink of the thirsty   *Isa 32:6*

Produce your *c.* saith the Lord   *Isa 41:21*

nor *c.* his voice to be heard in the   *Isa 42:2*

thy God that pleadeth the *c.* *Isa 51:22*

and I will *c.* thee to ride upon   *Isa 58:14*

the Lord God will *c.* righteousness   *Isa 61:11*

to the birth, and not *c.* to bring   *Isa 66:9*

and I will not *c.* mine anger to   *Jer 3:12*

judge not the *c.* the *c.* of the *Jer 5:28*

and I will *c.* you to dwell in this   *Jer 7:3*

Then will I *c.* to cease from the   *Jer 7:34*

unto thee have I revealed *Jer 11:20*
my *c.*
of the Gentiles that can *c.* *Jer 14:22*
rain
And I will *c.* them to be *Jer 15:4*
removed
c. the enemy to entreat thee *Jer 15:11*
well
I will this once *c.* them to *Jer 16:21*
know
and I will *c.* thee to serve *Jer 17:4*
thine
and there I will *c.* thee to *Jer 18:2*
hear
and I will *c.* them to fall by *Jer 19:7*
And I will *c.* them to eat the *Jer 19:9*
flesh
unto thee have I opened my *Jer 20:12*
c.
He judged the *c.* of the *Jer 22:16*
poor and
which think to *c.* my peole *Jer 23:27*
to
and *c.* my people to err by *Jer 23:32*
their
and *c.* all the nations, to *Jer 25:15*
whom I
to your dreams which ye *c.* *Jer 29:8*
to be
I will *c.* them to return *Jer 30:3*
to
and I will *c.* him to draw *Jer 30:21*
near
when I went to *c.* him to rest *Jer 31:2*
I will *c.* them to walk by the *Jer 31:9*
c. their sons and their *Jer 32:35*
daughters
I will *c.* their captivity to *Jer 32:44*
return
And I will *c.* the captivity of *Jer 33:7;*
Jer 33:11, 26; 34:22; 42:12; Eze 29:14
c. the Branch of *Jer 33:15*
righteousness
c. them to know the *Eze 20:4*
abominations
I will *c.* you to pass under *Eze 20:37*
the rod
and I will *c.* my fury to *Eze 21:17;*
rest *5:13*
Thus will I *c.* lewdness to *Eze 23:48*
cease out of
That it might *c.* fury to come *Eze 24:8*
up
Behold, I will *c.* breath to *Eze 37:5*
enter into
open your graves, and *c.* *Eze 37:12*
you to come
also he shall *c.* craft to *Da 8:25*
prosper in
and *c.* thy face to shine upon *Da 9:17*
thy
shall *c.* the sacrifice and the *Da 9:27*
oblation
c. to be panic-stricken (A) *Zec 1:21*
saving for the *c.* of *M't 5:32*
fornication
and *c.* them to be put to *M't 10:21*
death
put away his wife for every *M't 19:3*
c.
For this *c.* shall a man leave *M'k 10:7*
his
shall *c.* them to be put to *M'k 13:12*
death
for what *c.* she had touched *Lu 8:47*
him
some of you shall they *c* to *Lu 21:16*
be put
I have found no *c.* of death *Lu 23:22*
in him
For this *c.* the people also *Joh 12:18*
met him
law, They hated me without *Joh 15:25*
a *c.*
what is the *c.* wherefore ye *Ac 10:21*
are
though they found no *c.* of *Ac 13:28*
death
there being no *c.* whereby *Ac 19:40*
we may
when I would have known the *Ac 23:28*
c.
Festus declared Paul's *c.* *Ac 25:14*
there was no *c.* of death in *Ac 28:18*
me
For this *c.* therefore have I *Ac 28:20*
called
For which *c.* also I have *Ac 28:22*
been

mark them which *c.* divisions *Ro 16:17*
For this *c.* have i sent unto *1Co 4:17*
For this *c.* ought the *1Co 11:10*
woman
For which *c.* we faint not; *2Co 4:16*
but
we be sober, it is for your *c.* *2Co 5:13*
not for his *c.* that had done *2Co 7:12*
For this *c.* I Paul, the *Eph 3:1*
prisoner of
For this *c.* shall a man leave *Eph 5:31*
his
For the same *c.* also do ye *Ph'p 2:18*
joy
For this *c.* we also, since *Col 1:9*
c. that it be read also in the *Col 4:16*
For this *c.* when I could no *1Th 3:5*
longer
For the which *c.* I also suffer *2Ti 1:12*
For this *c.* left I thee in Crete *Tit 1:5*
for which *c.* he is not *Heb 2:11*
ashamed to
he might *c.* her to be carried *Re 12:15*
and *c.* that as many as *Re 13:15*
would not

FOR THIS CAUSE

for this c. have I raised up *Ex 9:16*
Pharaoh
for this c. Hezekiah prayed *2Ch 32:20*
for this c. king was angry *Da 2:12*
for this c. man leave father *M't 19:5;*
and mother, cleave to wife *M'k 10:7;*
Eph 5:31
but *for this c.* came I unto *Joh 12:27*
this hour
for this c. came I into the *Joh 18:37*
world
for this c. God gave up to vile *Ro 1:26*
affections
for this c. pay ye tribute also *Ro 13:6*
for this c. I will confess to *Ro 15:9*
thee among
for this c. many weak and *1Co 11:30*
sickly
for this c. I bow my knees *Eph 3:14*
to Father
for this c. thank God *1Th 2:13*
without
for this c. God send strong *2Th 2:11*
delusion
for this c. I obtained mercy *1Ti 1:16*
for this c. he is mediator of *Heb 9:15*
new
for this c. was gospel *1Pe 4:6*
preached

PLEAD CAUSE

the Lord be judge, and *1Sa 24:15;*
plead my *c.* *Ps 35:1; 43:1; 119:154*
arise, O God, *plead* thine *Ps 74:22*
own *c.*
for the Lord will *plead* their *Pr 22:23*
c.
he shall *plead* their *c.* with *Pr 23:11*
thee
open thy mouth, *plead c.* of *Pr 31:9*
poor
there is none to *plead* thy *c.* *Jer 30:13*
Lord shall thoroughly *plead* *Jer 50:34*
their *c.*
I will *plead* thy *c.* and take *Jer 51:36*
vengeance
until he *plead* my *c.* and *Mic 7:9*
execute

WITHOUT CAUSE

wilt thou slay David *without* *1Sa 19:5*
a *c.*
movedst me to destroy him *Job 2:3*
without c.
multiplieth my wounds *Job 9:17*
without c.
delivered him that *without c.* *Ps 7:4*
is my enemy
be ashamed that transgress *Ps 25:3*
without c.
without c. hid for me net, *Ps 35:7*
digged pit *without c.*
hate me *without c.* *Ps 35:19;*
Ps 69:4; Joh 15:25
fought against me *without c.* *Ps 109:3*
proud dealt perversely with *Ps 119:78*
me *without c.*
princes have persecuted me *Ps 119:61*
without c.

lurk for innocent *without c.* *Pr 1:11*
strive not with a man *without* *Pr 3:30*
c.
sorrow, who hath wounds, *Pr 23:29*
without c.
witness against neighbour *Pr 24:28*
without c.
Assyrian oppressed them *Isa 52:4*
without c.
enemies chased me *without c.* *La 3:52*
not done *without c.* all *Eze 14:23*
I have done
whoso is angry with brother *M't 5:22*
without c.

CAUSED

the Lord God had not *c.* it to *Ge 2:5*
rain
And the Lord God *c.* a deep *Ge 2:21*
sleep to
when God *c.* me to wander *Ge 20:13*
from my
God hath *c.* me to be *Ge 41:52*
fruitful
and the Lord *c.* the sea to *Ex 14:21*
go
as he hath *c.* a blemish in a *Le 24:20*
man
I have *c.* thee to see it with *De 34:4*
she *c.* him to shave off the *J'g 16:19*
seven
when Samuel had *c.* all the *1Sa 10:20*
tribes
When he had *c.* the tribe of *1Sa 10:21*
Benjamin
Jonathan *c.* David to swear *1Sa 20:17*
again
and have *c.* thee to rest from *2Sa 7:11*
all
c. Solomon to ride upon *1Ki 1:38;*
king's mule *1:44*
and *c.* a seat to be set for *1Ki 2:19*
the king's
he *c.* him to come up into *1Ki 20:33*
the chariot
they *c.* sons to pass *2Ki 17:17;*
through fire *33:6*
and *c.* the children of Israel *2Ch 8:2*
to dwell
Jeroboam *c.* an *2Ch 13:13*
ambushment to come
c. the inhabitants of *2Ch 21:11*
Jerusalem
And he *c.* all to stand to *2Ch 34:32*
it
God that hath *c.* his name to *Ezr 6:12*
dwell
c. people to understand the *Ne 8:7;*
law *8:8*
and he *c.* the gallows to be *Es 5:14*
made
I *c.* the widow's heart to *Job 29:13*
sing for joy
have *c.* the eyes of the *Job 31:16*
widow to fail
and *c.* the light of his cloud *Job 37:15*
to
c. the dayspring to know *Job 38:12*
his place
Thou hast *c.* men to ride *Ps 66:12*
over our
and *c.* waters to run down *Ps 78:16*
like rivers
He *c.* an east wind to blow *Ps 78:26*
With her much fair speech *Pr 7:21*
she *c.*
and they have *c.* Egypt to *Isa 19:14*
err
I have not *c.* thee to serve *Isa 43:23*
with
he *c.* the waters to flow out *Isa 48:21*
of the rock
Spirit of the Lord *c.* him to *Isa 63:14*
rest
I have *c.* my people Israel *Jer 12:14*
to inherit
so have I *c.* to cleave unto *Jer 13:11*
me
I have *c.* him to fall upon it *Jer 15:8*
they have *c.* them to *Jer 18:15*
stumble in
and *c.* my people Israel to *Jer 23:13*
err
had *c.* my people to hear *Jer 23:22*
my words
I have *c.* to be carried away *Jer 29:4;*
Jer 29:7, 14
him not, and he *c.* you to *Jer 29:31*
trust in a lie

therefore thou hast c. all   Jer 32:23
this evil to
c. the servants and the   Jer 34:11
handmaids
c. every man his servant,   Jer 34:16
and every
little ones have c. a cry to be   Jer 48:4
heard
I have c. wine to fail from   Jer 48:33
shepherds have c. them to go   Jer 50:6
astray
As Babylon hath c. the slain   Jer 51:49
c. the solemn feasts and   La 2:6
sabbaths to
he hath c. thine enemy to   La 2:17
rejoice
He hath c. the arrows of his   La 3:13
quiver
mouth, and he c. me to eat   Eze 3:2
that roll
I have c. thee to multiply as   Eze 16:7
Wherefore I c. them to go   Eze 20:10
forth out of
in that they c. to pass   Eze 20:26
through the fire
and thou hast c. thy days to   Eze 22:4
draw near
c. their sons, whom they   Eze 23:37
bare unto me
have c. my fury to rest   Eze 24:13
upon thee
king of Babylon c. his army   Eze 29:18
to serve
down to the grave I c. a   Eze 31:15
mourning
and I c. Lebanon to mourn   Eze 31:15
for him
c. terror in land of living   Eze 32:23;
       Eze 32:24-26. 32
which c. their terror in the   Eze 32:24
land
And c. me to pass by them   Eze 37:2
round
which c. them to be led   Eze 39:28
into captivity
c. the house of Israel to fall   Eze 44:12
into
and c. me to pass by the   Eze 46:21
four corners
and c. me to return to the   Eze 47:6
brink
being c. to fly swiftly,   Da 9:21
touched me
hath c. them to err, and they   Ho 4:12
have
and their lies c. them to err,   Am 2:4
after the
and I c. it to rain upon one   Am 4:7
city
And he c. it to be proclaimed   Jon 3:7
c. thine iniquity to pass from   Zec 3:4
thee
ye have c. many to stumble   Mal 2:8
at the law
eyes of the blind, have c.   Joh 11:37
that
they c. great joy unto all the   Ac 15:3
if any have c. grief, he hath   2Co 2:5
not

CAUSELESS

that thou hast shed blood c.   1Sa 25:31
by flying, so the curse c. shall   Pr 26:2

CAUSES

that thou mayest bring the c.   Ex 18:19
hard c. they brought unto   Ex 18:26
Moses
Hear the c. between your   De 1:16
brethren
I saw, when for all the c.   Jer 3:8
whereby
for thee false burdens and c.   La 2:14
of
O Lord, thou hast pleaded   La 3:58
the c.
whoever c. little one (R)   M't 18:6
For these c. the Jews caught   Ac 26:21
me

CAUSEST

thou c. me to ride upon it   Job 30:22
man whom thou choosest, and   Ps 65:4
c. to

CAUSETH

bitter water that c. curse   Nu 5:18;
       Nu 5:19, 22, 24, 27
c. them to wander in a   Job 12:24
wilderness
my understanding c. me to   Job 20:3
answer
He c. it to come, whether   Job 37:13
for
He c. the grass to grow for   Ps 104:14
the cattle
c. them to wander in the   Ps 107:40
wilderness,
He c. the vapours to ascend   Ps 135:7
from the
he c. his wind to blow, and   Ps 147:18
in harvest is a son that c.   Pr 10:5
shame
winketh with the eye c.   Pr 10:10
sorrow
wrath is against him that c.   Pr 14:35
shame
have rule over a son that c.   Pr 17:2
shame
The lot c. contentions to   Pr 18:18
cease
a son that c. shame, and   Pr 19:26
bringeth
hear the instruction that c.   Pr 19:27
to err
c. the righteous to go astray   Pr 28:10
in an
the garden c. the things that   Isa 61:11
are
fire burneth, the fire c. the   Isa 64:2
waters to
and he c. the vapours to   Jer 10:13
ascend from
in the heavens; and he c.   Jer 51:16
the vapours
as the sea c. his waves to   Eze 26:3
come up
gird themselves with   Eze 44:18
anything that c.
c. her to commit adultery: M't 5:32
and
c. us to triumph in Christ   2Co 2:14
c. through us thanksgiving   2Co 9:11
to
beast before him, and c. the   Re 13:12
he c. all, both small and   Re 13:16
great

CAUSEWAY

by the c. of the going up,   1Ch 26:16
ward
four at the c. and two at   1Ch 26:18
Parbar

CAUSING

c. the lips of those that are   Ca 7:9
asleep
in the jaws of the people, c   Isa 30:28
them
in c. you to return to this   Jer 29:10
place
of shepherds, c. their flocks   Jer 33:12
to lie

CAUTIONED

c. the king (B)   Jer 36:25

CAVE

he dwelt in a c. he and his   Ge 19:30
two
that he may give me c. of   Ge 23:9;
Machpelah   23:11, 17, 19-20; 25:9;
       49:29-32
buried him in the c. of the   Ge 50:13
field
hid in a c.   Jos 10:16;
       10:17-18, 22-23, 27
escaped to c. of Adullam   1Sa 22:1;
       1Ch 11:15
Saul went in the c.   1Sa 24:3;
       1Sa 24:7-8, 10
in harvest time unto the c.   2Sa 23:13
hid them by fifty in a c.   1Ki 18:4;
       18:13
Elijah came unto a c.   1Ki 19:9
stood in the entering in of   1Ki 19:13
the c.
he fled from Saul in the c.   Ps 57 title

A prayer when he was in   Ps 142 title
the c.
It was a c., a stone lay   Joh 11:38
upon it

CAVES

in the mountains, and c. and   J'g 6:2
living in mountain c. (B)   J'g 6:2
people did hide themselves in   1Sa 13:6
c.
cliffs of the valleys, in c. of   Job 30:6
the
into the c. of the earth, for   Isa 2:19
fear
in c. of the rocks (S)   Isa 2:19
in the forts and in the c.   Eze 33:27
shall die
mountains, and in dens   Heb 11:38
and c.

CAVE'S

laid great stones in the c.   Jos 10:27

CAVILLETH

he that c. contend with (E)   Job 40:2

CEASE

day and night shall not c.   Ge 8:22
as I am gone the thunder   Ex 9:29
shall c.
from age of fifty years shall   Nu 8:25
c.
seventy elders prophesied,   Nu 11:25
did not c.
I will make to c. the   Nu 17:5
murmurings
poor shall never c. out of   De 15:11
land
make remembrance of them   De 32:26
to c.
make children c. from   Jos 22:25
fearing Lord
yet will I be avenged, after I   J'g 15:7
will c.
shall I yet go to battle, or c.   J'g 20:28
c. not to cry to Lord for us   1Sa 7:8
not c. from house of Jacob   2Sa 3:29
(S)
when Baasha heard it, let   2Ch 16:5
his work c.
c. opposing God (R)   2Ch 35:21
made them to c. by force   Ezr 4:23
and power
c. their exacting of interest   Ne 5:10
(S)
why should work c. while I   Ne 6:3
come
there the wicked c. from   Job 3:17
troubling
my days few, c. them, let   Job 10:20
me alone
that tender branch thereof   Job 14:7
will not c.
c. from anger, and forsake   Ps 37:8
wrath
maketh wars to c. to end of   Ps 46:9
earth
thou hast made his glory to   Ps 89:44
c.
c. to hear instruction that   Pr 19:27
causeth
it is honour for man to c.   Pr 20:3
from strife
cast scorner, strife shall c.   Pr 22:10
labour to be rich, c. from thy   Pr 23:4
wisdom
grinders c. because they are   Ec 12:3
few
c. to do evil   Isa 1:16
yet little while indignation   Isa 10:25
shall c.
made their vintage shouting   Isa 16:10
to c.
fortress also shall c. from   Isa 17:3
Ephraim
all sighing thereof have I   Isa 21:2
made to c.
when c. to spoil, shalt be   Isa 33:1
spoiled
let tears run down and not c.   Jer 1:17
leaf green, nor c. yielding   Jer 17:8
fruit
then the seed of Israel shall   Jer 31:36
c.
let not the apple of thine eye   La 2:18
c.

that your idols be broken and *Eze 6:6* c.
I will make pomp of strong *Eze 7:24* to c.
Lord, I will make this *Eze 12:23* proverb c.
thus will I make thy *Eze 23:27* lewdness to c.
make the multitude of *Eze 30:10* Egypt to c.
pomp of her strength shall *Eze 30:18; 33:28*
God, c. by whom shall Jacob *Am 7:5* arise
will not c. to pervert right *Ac 13:10* ways
whether be tongues, they *1Co 13:8* shall c.
I c. not to give thanks for *Eph 1:16* you
not c. to pray for you to be *Col 1:9* filled
having eyes that cannot c. *2Pe 2:14* from sin

CAUSE TO CEASE

cause to c. city be not built *Ezr 4:21*
could not *cause to c.* till *Ezr 5:5* matter
slay them and *cause* the work *Ne 4:11* to c.
cause anger toward us *to c.* *Ps 85:4*
the lot *causeth* contentions *Pr 18:18* to c.
cause the arrogancy of *Isa 13:11* proud *to c.*
cause holy One of Israel *to* *Isa 30:11* c. before us
cause mirth *to c.* from cities *Jer 7:34* of
cause to c. man and beast *Jer 36:29; Ho 2:11*
cause to c. in Moab him *Jer 48:35* that offereth
cause to c. from playing *Eze 16:41* harlot
thus will I *cause* lewdness *Eze 23:48* to c.
I will *cause* the noise of thy *Eze 26:13* songs to c.
cause images *to c.* out of *Eze 30:13* Noph
cause to c. from feeding *Eze 34:10* flock
he shall *cause* the oblation *to* *Da 9:27* c.
cause the reproach offered *Da 11:18* by him *to c.*
cause to c. kingdom of Israel *Ho 1:4*

CEASED

they c. building (S) *Ge 11:8; 1Ki 15:21*
he c. talking (S) *Ge 17:22; Ru 1:18; Jer 38:27; Lu 5:4*
it c. to be with Sarah after *Ge 18:11*
he c. talking (S) *Ge 18:33*
and c. bearing (S) *Ge 29:35; 30:9*
he c. numbering (S) *Ge 41:49*
he c. at the youngest (S) *Ge 44:12*
and the thunders and hail c. *Ex 9:33*
hail and the thunders were c. *Ex 9:34*
he c. communing with (S) *Ex 31:18*
and the manna c. on the *Jos 5:12* morrow
when Israel c. slaying (S) *Jos 8:24; 10:20*
c. not from their own doings *J'g 2:19*
the villages c. they c. in Israel *J'g 5:7*
they that were hungry c.: *1Sa 2:5* so that
he c. prophesying (S) *1Sa 10:13*
he c. offering (S) *1Sa 13:10; 2Ki 10:25; 2Ch 29:29*
he c. speaking (S) *1Sa 18:1; 24:16; 2Sa 13:36; Jer 26:8; 43:1*
in the name of David, and c. *1Sa 25:9*
he c. praying (S) *2Ch 7:1*
Then c. the work of the *Ezr 4:24* house of
So it c. unto the second year *Ezr 4:24*
these three men c. to answer *Job 32:1* Job
they did tear me, and c. not *Ps 35:15*
he c. to be wise (S) *Ps 36:3*
my sore ran in the night, and *Ps 77:2* c.
How hath the oppressor c. *Isa 14:4*

the golden city c. *Isa 14:4*
he c. to burn incense (S) *Jer 44:18*
The elders have c. from the *La 5:14* gate
The joy of our heart is c.; *La 5:15* our
he c. to take heed to Lord *Ho 4:10* (S)
he c. eating (S) *Am 7:2*
and the sea c. from her raging *Joh 1:15*
he c. commanding his *M't 11:1* disciples (S)
come into the siip, the wind *M't 14:32* c.
the wind c. and there was a *M'k 4:39* great
the wind c.: and they were *M'k 6:51* sore
came in hath not c. to kiss *Lu 7:45* my feet
they c. and there was a calm *Lu 8:24*
when he c. one of his *Lu 11:1* disciples
they c. not to teach and *Ac 5:42* preach
And after the uproar was c. *Ac 20:1* Paul
I c. not to warn every one *Ac 20:31* night
not be persuaded, we c. *Ac 21:14* saying
they c. beating Paul (S) *Ac 21:32*
then is the offence of the *Ga 5:11* cross c.
he also hath c. from his *Heb 4:10* own
would they not have c. to *Heb 10:2* be
suffered in the flesh hath c. *1Pe 4:1* from

CEASETH

Help, Lord; for the godly *Ps 12:1* man c.
is precious, and it c. for *Ps 49:8* ever:)
there is no talebearer, the *Pr 26:20* strife c.
the spoiler c. the oppressors *Isa 16:4* are
The mirth of tabrets c. the *Isa 24:8* noise
endeth, the joy of the harp c. *Isa 24:8*
lie waste, the wayfaring man *Isa 33:8* c.
eye trickleth down, and c. not *La 3:49*
who c. from raising after he *Ho 7:4* hath
This man c. not to speak *Ac 6:13*

CEASING

the Lord in c. to pray for *1Sa 12:23* you
prayer was made without c. *Ac 12:5* of
that without c. I make *Ro 1:9* mention of
Remembering without c. your *1Th 1:3*
also thank we God without *1Th 2:13* c.
Pray without c. *1Th 5:17*
without c. I have *2Ti 1:3* remembrance

CEDAR

c. wood, and scarlet, and *Le 14:4;* hyssop *Le 14:6, 49, 51-52*
the priest shall take c. wood *Nu 19:6*
and as c. trees beside the *Nu 24:6* waters
c. trees, and carpenters, and *2Sa 5:11*
I dwell in an house of c. but *2Sa 7:2*
build ye not me an house of *2Sa 7:7* c.
from the c. tree that is in *1Ki 4:33* Lebanon
hew me c. trees out of *1Ki 5:6* Lebanon
concerning timber of c. and *1Ki 5:8*
Hiram gave Solomon c. trees *1Ki 5:10* and fir
house with beams and boards *1Ki 6:9;* of c. *6:10, 15-16, 20, 36; 7:2-3, 7, 12*
furnished Solomon with c. *1Ki 9:11* trees
sent to the c. that was in *2Ki 14:9* Lebanon

and will cut down the tall *2Ki 19:23* c. trees
Also c. trees in abundance: *1Ch 22:4* for the
they of Tyre brought much *1Ch 22:4* c. wood
c. trees made he as the *2Ch 1:15* sycomore
Send me also c. trees, fir *2Ch 2:8* trees, and
in Jerusalem as stones, and *2Ch 9:27* c.
was in Lebanon sent to the *2Ch 25:18* c. that
to bring c. trees from *Ezr 3:7* Lebanon
He moveth his tail like a *Job 40:17* c.
he shall grow like a c. in *Ps 92:12* Lebanon
The beams of our house are *Ca 1:17* c.
we will inclose her with *Ca 8:9* boards of c.
plant in the wilderness the *Isa 41:19* c.
cieled with c. and painted *Jer 22:14* with
thou closest thyself in c.? *Jer 22:15* did not
took the highest branch of *Eze 17:3*
top of the c. (A)(B)(E)(R) *Eze 17:3*
the highest branch of the *Eze 17:22* high c.
be a goodly c.: and under it *Eze 17:23* shall
bound with cords, and *Eze 27:24* made of c.
the Assyrian was a c. in *Eze 31:3* Lebanon
for he shall uncover the c. *Zep 2:14* work
for the c. is fallen; because *Zec 11:2*

CEDARS

and devour the c. of Lebanon *J'g 9:15*
measures of hewed stones, *1Ki 7:11* and c.
c. made he to be as the *1Ki 10:27* sycomore
timber of c. with masons *1Ch 14:1* and
I dwell in an house of c. *1Ch 17:1* but the
ye not built me an house of *1Ch 17:6* c.
send him c. to build him an *2Ch 2:3* house
the Lord breaketh the c.: yea *Ps 29:5*
the Lord breaketh the c. of *Ps 29:5*
thereof were like the goodly *Ps 80:10* c.
c. of Lebanon, which he *Ps 104:16* hath
all hills: fruitful trees, and *Ps 148:9* all c.
as Lebanon, excellent as the *Ca 5:15* c.
upon all the c. of Lebanon, *Isa 2:13* that
but we will change them into *Isa 9:10* c.
the c. of Lebanon, saying, *Isa 14:8* Since
cut down the tall c. thereof *Isa 37:24*
He heweth him down c. and *Isa 44:14* taketh
shall cut down thy choice c. *Jer 22:7*
that makest thy nest in the c. *Jer 22:23*
they have taken c. from *Eze 27:5* Lebanon to
The c. in the garden of God *Eze 31:8* could
like the height of the c. and *Am 2:9* he
that the fire may devour thy *Zec 11:1* c.

CEDRON

over the brook C. where was *Joh 18:1* a

CELEBRATE

even, shall ye c. your *Le 23:32* sabbath

CELEBRATE (continued)

shall *c.* it in the seventh month   *Le 23:41*
praise thee, death can not *c.* thee   *Isa 38:18*

CELESTIAL

There are also *c.* bodies   *1Co 15:40*
but the glory of the *c.* is one   *1Co 15:40*

CELIBACY

on the question of *c.* (N)   *1Co 7:25*

CELIBATES

they are *c.* (B)(P)   *Re 14:4*

CELLAR

in a *c.* or bushel (A)(E)(N)(R)   *Lu 11:33*

CELLARS

for the wine *c.* was Zabdi   *1Ch 27:27*
and over the *c.* of oil was Joash   *1Ch 27:28*

CELLS

Jeremiah entered the *c.* (S)   *Jer 37:16*

CEMETERY

into the *c.* (B)   *Jer 26:23*

CENCHREA

having shorn his head in *C.*   *Ac 18:18*
of the church which is at *C.*   *Ro 16:1*

CENSER

took either of them his *c.* and put   *Le 10:1*
shall take a *c.* full of burning coals   *Le 16:12*
take every man his *c.* and put   *Nu 16:17;*
  Nu 16:18, 46
a *c.* in his hand to burn incense   *2Ch 26:19*
with every man his *c.* in his hand   *Eze 8:11*
Which had the golden *c.* and   *Heb 9:4*
at the altar, having a golden *c.*   *Re 8:3*
took the *c.* and filled it with fire   *Re 8:5*

CENSERS

the *c.*, the fleshhooks, and the   *Nu 4:14*
Take you *c.* Korah   *Nu 16:6;*
  Nu 16:17, 37:39
spoons, and the *c.* of pure gold   *1Ki 7:50*
spoons, and the *c.* of pure gold   *2Ch 4:22*

CENSURE

c. the eater (B)   *Ro 14:3; 14:13*
this *c.* of many (A)(B)   *2Co 2:6*
irrefutable above *c.* (A)   *Tit 2:8*

CENSURED

they *c.* her (A)   *M'k 14:5*
be *c.* and suffer abuse (A)   *1Pe 4:14*

CENTER

in the *c.* of the highway   *2Sa 20:12*
in the *c.* of the ground (S)   *2Sa 23:12*
in the *c.* of Samaria (S)   *2Ki 6:20*
in the *c.* of the court (S)   *2Ch 6:13*
in the *c.* of the city   *Es 4:1; Jer 41:7*
Jesus in the *c.* (S)   *Joh 19:18*

CENTURION

unto him a *c.* beseeching him   *M't 8:5*
The *c.* answered and said, Lord   *M't 8:8*
Jesus said unto the *c.*, Go thy way   *M't 8:13*
c. and they that were with him   *M't 27:54*
c. which stood over against him   *M'k 15:39*

calling unto him the *c.*, he asked   *M'k 15:44*
when he knew it of the *c.* he gave   *M'k 15:45*
the *c.* sent friends to him, saying   *Lu 7:6*
when the *c.* saw what was done   *Lu 23:47*
c. of the band called the Italian   *Ac 10:1*
they said, Cornelius the *c.*, a just   *Ac 10:22*
Paul said unto the *c.* that stood by   *Ac 22:25*
When the *c.* heard that, he went   *Ac 22:26*
commanded a *c.* to keep Paul   *Ac 24:23*
Julius, a *c.* of Augustus' band   *Ac 27:1*
there the *c.* found a ship of   *Ac 27:6*
the *c.* believed the master   *Ac 27:11*
Paul said to the *c.* and to   *Ac 27:31*
the *c.* willing to save Paul, kept   *Ac 27:43*
the *c.* delivered the prisoners to   *Ac 28:16*

CENTURIONS

immediately took soldiers and *c.*   *Ac 21:32*
Paul called one of the *c.* unto him   *Ac 23:17*
he called unto him two *c.* saying   *Ac 23:23*

CENTURION'S

a certain *c.* servant, who was dear   *Lu 7:2*

CEPHAS

thou shalt be called *C.* which is   *Joh 1:42*
and I of Apollos; and I of *C.*   *1Co 1:12*
Whether Paul, or Apollos, or *C.*   *1Co 3:22*
as the brethren of the Lord, and *C.*   *1Co 9:5*
he was seen of *C.* then of   *1Co 15:5*
And when James, *C.* and John   *Ga 2:9*

CEREAL

the *c.* offering (A)(B)(R)   *Ex 29:41; 40:29; Eze 42:13; 44:29; 45:17, 25; 46:5, 7*
the *c.* offering (A)(R)   *Ex 30:9; Nu 4:16; 15:6; 28:8; 29:6; J'g 13:9, 23; Ne 10:33; Isa 57:6; Joe 1:9; 2:14*
the *c.* offering (A)(R)   *Le 2:1; Le 2:3; 6:14; 14:10; 28:26*
the *c.* offering (A)(R)   *Nu 29:39; Jos 22:29*
the *c.* offering (A)   *Nu 29:6*
the *c.* offering (A)(R)   *1Ki 8:64; Ne 13:5; Am 5:22*
the *c.* offering (B)(R)   *Eze 45:17*

CEREMONIES

all the *c.* thereof shall ye keep it   *Nu 9:3*

CERTAIN

And he lighted upon a *c.* place   *Ge 28:11*
shall gather a *c.* rate every day   *Ex 16:4*
Korah rose with *c.* of children of   *Nu 16:2*
c. children of Belial are gone   *De 13:13*
the wicked man be beaten by a *c.* number   *De 25:2*
a *c.* rate every day offering   *2Ch 8:13*
Hanani came, *c.* men of Judah   *Ne 1:2*
I mourned *c.* days, and fasted   *Ne 1:4*
c. portion should be for singers   *Ne 11:23*
smote *c.* of them, plucked off hair   *Ne 13:25*
came *c.* from Shechem, from Shiloh   *Jer 41:5*
carried away *c.* of poor people   *Jer 52:15*
Daniel fainted and was sick *c.* days   *Da 8:27*

king of north come after *c.* years   *Da 11:13*
kingdom likened to *c.* king   *M't 18:23; 22:2*
she and sons desiring *c.* thing of him   *M't 20:20*
came *c.* poor widow   *M'k 12:42; Lu 21:2*
c. and bare false witness against him   *M'k 14:57*
to pass when he was in a *c.* city   *Lu 5:12*
by *c.* thy mother stands to see thee   *Lu 8:20*
as he went into a *c.* village   *Lu 10:38; 17:12*
c. woman lifted up her voice and said   *Lu 11:27*
c. Pharisee besought him to dine with him   *Lu 11:37*
parable to *c.* who trusted in themselves   *Lu 18:9*
who for *c.* sedition and murder   *Lu 23:19*
c. women also made us astonished   *Lu 24:22*
c. of them went to the sepulchre   *Lu 24:24*
angel went down at a *c.* season   *Joh 5:4*
Saul was *c.* days with disciples   *Ac 9:19*
they prayed Peter to tarry *c.* days   *Ac 10:48*
Herod to vex *c.* of the church   *Ac 12:1*
c. went from us troubled us   *Ac 15:24*
c. of your own poets have said   *Ac 17:28*
to make *c.* contribution for saints   *Ro 15:26*
for before that *c.* came from James   *Ga 2:12*
I am *c.* (N)   *Ph'p 1:6*
but one in a *c.* place testified   *Heb 2:6*
spake in *c.* place of 7th day on this wise   *Heb 4:4*
limiteth *c.* day, saying in David   *Heb 4:7*
but *c.* fearful looking for judgment   *Heb 10:27*
there are *c.* men crept in unawares   *Jude 4*

CERTAINLY

I will *c.* return unto thee   *Ge 18:10*
We saw *c.* that the Lord was with   *Ge 26:28*
could we *c.* know that he would   *Ge 43:7*
such a man as I can *c.* divine   *Ge 44:15*
will *c.* requite us all the evil   *Ge 50:15*
he said, *C.* I will be with thee   *Ex 3:12*
If the theft be *c.* found in his   *Ex 22:4*
hath *c.* trespassed against the Lord   *Le 5:19*
the congregation shall *c.* stone him   *Le 24:16*
Because it was *c.* told thy   *Jos 9:24*
if ye can *c.* declare it me   *J'g 14:12*
Thy father *c.* knoweth that I within   *1Sa 20:3*
if I knew *c.* that evil were   *1Sa 20:9*
thy servant hath *c.* heard   *1Sa 23:10*
Lord will *c.* make my lord a sure   *1Sa 25:28*
I will *c.* deliver the Philistines (S)   *2Sa 5:19*
even so will I *c.* do this day   *1Ki 1:30*
him, Thou mayest *c.* recover   *2Ki 8:10*
If thou *c.* return in peace   *2Ch 18:27*
riches *c.* make themselves wings   *Pr 23:5*
Lo, *c.* in vain made he it   *Jer 8:8*
Do we not *c.* know that every   *Jer 13:12*
Lord of hosts; Ye shall *c.* drink   *Jer 25:28*
king of Babylon shall *c.* come   *Jer 36:29*
Dost thou *c.* know that Baalis   *Jer 40:14*
know *c.* that I have admonished you   *Jer 42:19*
Now therefore know *c.* that ye shall   *Jer 42:22*
we will *c.* do whatsoever thing goeth   *Jer 44:17*

CERTAINLY (cont.)

c. this is the day that we looked — La 2:16
one shall c. come, and overflow — Da 11:10
c. come after certain years — Da 11:13
C. this was a righteous man — Lu 23:47

CERTAINTY

Know for a c. that the Lord your — Jos 23:13
come ye again to me with the c. — 1Sa 23:23
the c. of the words of truth; that — Pr 22:21
I know of c. that ye would gain — Da 2:8
know the c. of those things — Lu 1:4
not know the c. for the tumult — Ac 21:34
he would have known the c. — Ac 22:30

CERTIFICATE

my c. of apostleship (B) — 1Co 9:2

CERTIFIED

have we sent and c. the king — Ezr 4:14
and Esther c. the king thereof — Es 2:22

CERTIFIES

c. that God is true (N) — Joh 3:33

CERTIFY

come word from you to c. me — 2Sa 15:28
We c. the king that, if this city — Ezr 4:16
asked their names also, to c. thee — Ezr 5:10
Also we c. you that touching any — Ezr 7:24
But I c. you, brethren, that — Ga 1:11

CHAFED

be c. in their minds, as a bear — 2Sa 17:8
embittered and enraged (A) — 2Sa 17:8
embittered in their minds (B) — 2Sa 17:8
they are enraged (R) — 2Sa 17:8

CHAFF

c. that the storm carrieth away — Job 21:18
c. which the wind driveth away — Ps 1:4
Let them be as c. before the wind — Ps 35:5
and the flame consumeth the c. — Isa 5:24
chased as the c. of the mountains — Isa 17:13
the terrible ones shall be as c. — Isa 29:5
Ye shall conceive c., ye shall — Isa 33:11
and shalt make the hills as c. — Isa 41:15
What is the c. to the wheat — Jer 23:28
like the c. of the summer — Da 2:35
as the c. that is driven with — Ho 13:3
before the day pass as the c. — Zep 2:2
burn up the c. with unquenchable — M't 3:12
the c. he will burn with fire — Lu 3:17

CHAGRINED

they were c. (B) — M't 21:15
c. because then (E) — Ac 4:2

CHAIN

put a gold c. about his neck — Ge 41:42
twined c. (B) — Ex 28:14; Ex 28:22, 25; 39:15
two ends of the two wreathen c. thou — Ex 28:25
bronze c. (B) — J'g 16:21; 2Ki 25:7; 2Ch 36:6
wreaths of c. work, for the — 1Ki 7:17
took Manasseh in c. (E) — 2Ch 33:11
the c. of Pleiades (A)(E) — Job 38:3
compasseth them about as a c. — Ps 73:6

CHAINS

two c. of pure gold at ends — Ex 28:14; 24:14
upon the breastplate c. at the ends — Ex 28:22
thou shalt put the two wreathen c. — Ex 28:24
upon the breastplate c. at the ends — Ex 39:15
c. of gold in the two rings — Ex 39:17
the two wreathen c. they fastened — Ex 39:18
of gold, c. and bracelets, rings — Nu 31:50
c. that were about their camels — J'g 8:26
made a partition by the c. of gold — 1Ki 6:21
and set thereon palm trees and c. — 2Ch 3:5
And he made c. as in the oracle — 2Ch 3:16
and put them on the c. — 2Ch 3:16
those which are bound with c. — Ps 68:6
To bind their kings with c. — Ps 149:8
thy head, and c. about thy neck — Pr 1:9
jewels, thy neck with c. of gold — Ca 1:10
neck with strings of jewels (A)(E)(R) — Ca 1:10
neck with strings of beads (B) — Ca 1:10
The c., and the bracelets, and — Isa 3:19
the pendants (A)(B)(E) — Isa 3:19
with gold, and casteth silver c. — Isa 40:19
in c. they shall come over — Isa 45:14
and bound him with c. to carry — Jer 39:7
being bound in c. among all that — Jer 40:1
I loose thee this day from the c. — Jer 40:4
king of Babylon bound him in c. — Jer 52:11
brought him with c. unto the land — Eze 19:4
put him in ward in c. and — Eze 19:9
her great men were bound in c. — Na 3:10
could bind him, no, not with c. — M'k 5:3
often bound with fetters and c. — M'k 5:4
he was kept bound with c. and in — Lu 8:29
two soldiers, bound with two c. — Ac 12:6
And his c. fell off from his hands — Ac 12:7
him to be bound with two c. — Ac 21:33
delivered them into c. of darkness — 2Pe 2:4
in pits of gloom (A) — 2Pe 2:4
to the black dungeons (B) — 2Pe 2:4
down to pits of darkness (E) — 2Pe 2:4
to the dark pits of hell (N) — 2Pe 2:4
the dark imprisonment of hell (P) — 2Pe 2:4
to pits of nether gloom (R) — 2Pe 2:4
hath reserved in everlasting c. — Jude 6

CHALCEDONY

the third, a c.; the fourth — Re 21:19

CHAINS (continued, col 2)

eyes, with one c. of thy neck — Ca 4:9
with one jewel of necklace (A)(R) — Ca 4:9
with single bead of necklace (B) — Ca 4:9
limbs like jeweled c. (A)(B) — Ca 7:1
he hath made my c. heavy — La 3:7
Make a c.: for the land is full of — Eze 7:23
thy hands, and a c. on thy neck — Eze 16:11
have a c. of gold about his neck — Da 5:7
have a c. of gold about thy neck — Da 5:16
put a c. of gold about his neck — Da 5:29
of Israel I am bound with — Ac 28:20
this c. — Ac 28:20
and was not ashamed of my c. — 2Ti 1:16
pit and a great c. in his hand — Re 20:1

CHALCOL

the Ezrahite, and Heman, and C. — 1Ki 4:31

CHALDAEANS

out of the land of the C. — Ac 7:4

CHALDEA

And C. shall be a spoil: all that — Jer 50:10
the inhabitants of C. all their evil — Jer 51:24
blood upon the inhabitants of C. — Jer 51:35
vision by the Spirit of God into C. — Eze 11:24
in the land of Canaan unto C. — Eze 16:29
manner of the Babylonians of C. — Eze 23:15
messengers unto them into C. — Eze 23:16

CHALDEAN

the C. who destroyed this house — Ezr 5:12
any magician, or astrologer, or C. — Da 2:10

CHALDEANS

The C. made out three bands — Job 1:17
Behold the land of the C., this — Isa 23:13
nobles, and the C. whose cry is in — Isa 43:14
no throne, O daughter of the C. — Isa 47:1; 47:5
and his arm shall be on the C. — Isa 48:14
flee ye from the C. with a voice of — Isa 48:20
and against the C. which besiege — Jer 21:4
out, and falleth to the C. that — Jer 21:9
and into the hand of the C. — Jer 22:25
the land of the C. for their good — Jer 24:5
iniquity, and the land of the C. — Jer 25:12
escape out of the hand of the C. — Jer 32:4; 32:5, 24-25, 28-29, 43
They come to fight with the C. — Jer 33:5
for fear of the army of the C. — Jer 35:11
the C. that besieged Jerusalem — Jer 37:5
the C. shall come again, and fight — Jer 37:8
The C. shall surely depart from us — Jer 37:9
smitten the whole army of the C. — Jer 37:10
the army of the C. was broken up — Jer 37:11
saying, Thou fallest away to the C. — Jer 37:13
is false: I fall not away to the C. — Jer 37:14
goeth forth to the C. shall live — Jer 38:2
be given into the hand of the C. — Jer 38:18
the Jews that are fallen to the C. — Jer 38:19
wives and thy children to the C. — Jer 38:23
And the C. burned the king's house — Jer 39:8
saying, Fear not to serve the C. — Jer 40:9
dwell at Mizpah, to serve the C. — Jer 40:10
and the C. that were found there — Jer 41:3
Because of the C.: for they were — Jer 41:18
deliver us into the hand of the C. — Jer 43:3
and against the land of the C. — Jer 50:1
go forth out of the land of the C. — Jer 50:8
God of hosts in the land of the C. — Jer 50:25

A sword is upon the *C.* *Jer 50:35*
saith the
purposed against the land of *Jer 50:45*
the *C.*
shall fall in the land of the *Jer 51:4*
C.
destruction from the land of *Jer 51:54*
the *C.*
C. were by the city round *Jer 52:7*
about
of the *C.* pursued after the *Jer 52:8*
king
the *C.* that were with the *Jer 52:14*
captain
C. brake, and carried all the *Jer 52:17*
brass
land of the *C.* by the river *Eze 1:3*
Chebar
to Babylon to the land of *Eze 12:13*
the *C.*
images of the *C.* pourtrayed *Eze 23:14*
with
The Babylonians, and all *Eze 23:23*
the *C.*
learning and the tongue of the *Da 1:4*
C.
C. for to shew the king his *Da 2:2*
dreams
Then spake the *C.* to the king *Da 2:4*
king answered and said to the *Da 2:5*
C.
C. answered before the king *Da 2:10*
at that time certain *C.* came *Da 3:8*
near
magicians, the astrologers, the *Da 4:7*
C.
to bring in the astrologers, the *Da 5:7*
C.
astrologers, *C.* and *Da 5:11*
soothsayers
Belshazzar the king of the *C.* *Da 5:30*
slain
king over the realm of the *C.* *Da 9:1*
For, lo, I raise up the *C.* *Hab 1:6*
that

CHALDEANS'

the *C.* army pursued after *Jer 39:5*
them

CHALDEES

of his nativity, in Ur of the *Ge 11:28*
C.
forth with them from Ur of *Ge 11:31*
the *C.*
brought thee out of Ur of the *Ge 15:7*
C.
sent against him bands of *2Ki 24:2*
the *C.*
the *C.* were against the city *2Ki 25:4*
round
of the *C.* pursued after the *2Ki 25:5*
king
And all the army of the *C.* *2Ki 25:10*
that
C. break in pieces, and *2Ki 25:13*
carried
to be the servants of the *C.* *2Ki 25:24*
Jews and the *C.* that were *2Ki 25:25*
with
for they were afraid of the *2Ki 25:26*
C.
upon them the king of the *2Ch 36:17*
C.
him forth out of Ur of the *C.* *Ne 9:7*

CHALDEES'

the beauty of the *C.* *Isa 13:19*
excellency

CHALKSTONES

of the altar as *c.* that are *Isa 27:9*
beaten

CHALLENGE

do not *c.* them (B) *De 2:5*
who will *c.* me (B) *Job 9:19*

CHALLENGETH

which another *c.* to be his *Ex 22:9*

CHAMBER

Joseph entered *c.* and wept *Ge 43:30*
I will go in to my wife into *c.* *J'g 15:1*

liers in wait abiding in *c.* *J'g 16:9*
bring meat into *c.* I may *2Sa 13:10*
eat
Elisha turned into *c.* and lay *2Ki 4:11*
the inner *c.* (B) *2Ch 5:7*
he prepared for Tobiah a *Ne 13:5*
great *c.*
cast forth household stuff out *Ne 13:8*
of *c.*
as bridegroom cometh out of *Ps 19:5*
c.
into *c.* of her that conceived *Ca 3:4*
me
read book in *c.* of Gemariah *Jer 36:10*
laid up roll in *c.* of *Jer 36:20*
Elishama
c. whose prospect toward *Eze 40:45*
south
c. whose prospect toward *Eze 40:46*
north
windows being open in his *c.* *Da 6:10*
let bridegroom go forth of *Joe 2:16*
his *c.*
builds his upper *c.* *Am 9:6*
(A)(B)(E)
enter inner *c.* (E) *M't 6:6; Lu 12:3*

INNER CHAMBER

Benhadad came into *inner* *1Ki 20:30*
c.
go into *inner c.* to hide *1Ki 22:25;*
2Ch 18:24
carry Jehu into *inner c.* and *2Ki 9:2*
take

LITTLE CHAMBER

let us make a *little c.* on *2Ki 4:10*
wall
little c. was one reed long *Eze 40:7*
measured gate from roof of *Eze 40:13*
little c

SIDE CHAMBER

breadth of every *side c.* four *Eze 41:5*
cubits
thickness of wall for *side c.* *Eze 41:9*
without

UPPER CHAMBER

Ahaz fell thro' lattice in *2Ki 1:2*
upper c.
altars in top of *upper c.* *2Ki 23:12*
Josiah beat
washed, laid Dorcas in *upper* *Ac 9:37*
c.
brought Peter, when come *Ac 9:39*
into *upper c.*
many lights in *upper c.* were *Ac 20:8*
gathered

CHAMBERING

not in *c.* and wantonness, *Ro 13:13*
nor in
not in immorality (A) *Ro 13:13*
not in prostitution (B) *Ro 13:13*
vice (N) *Ro 13:13*
playing with sex (P) *Ro 13:13*
licentiousness (R) *Ro 13:13*

CHAMBERLAIN

chamber of Nathan-melech *2Ki 23:11*
the *c.*
the eunuch (B)(R) *2Ki 23:11;*
Es 1:10; 2:15, 21
custody of Hege the king's *c.* *Es 2:3*
of Shaashgaz, the king's *c.* *Es 2:14*
which
Hegai the king's *c.* the keeper *Es 2:15*
of
Blastus the king's *c.* *Es 12:20*
Erastus the *c.* of city *Ro 16:23*
saluteth
the city treasurer *Ro 16:23*
(A)(B)(E)(N)(R)
our town clerk (P) *Ro 16:23*

CHAMBERLAINS

the seven *c.* that served in the *Es 1:10*
king's commandment by his *c.* *Es 1:12*
of the king Ahasuerus by the *Es 1:15*
c.

two of the king's *c.* Bigthan *Es 2:21*
and
maids and her *c.* came and *Es 4:4*
told it
for Hatach, one of the king's *Es 4:5*
c.
two of the king's *c.* the *Es 6:2*
keepers of
came the king's *c.* and hasted *Es 6:14*
Harbonah, one of the *c.* said *Es 7:9*

CHAMBERS

built *c.* round about, against *1Ki 6:5*
of the oracle: and he made *c.* *1Ki 6:5*
he built *c.* against all the *1Ki 6:10*
house
were over the *c.* and *1Ch 9:26*
treasuries
Levites, who remaining in *1Ch 9:33*
the *c.*
in the courts, and in the *c.* *1Ch 23:28*
and of the upper *c.* thereof *1Ch 28:11*
all the *c.* round about, of *1Ch 28:12*
he overlaid the upper *c.* with *2Ch 3:9*
gold
to prepare *c.* in the house *2Ch 31:11*
of the
the *c.* of the house of the *Ezr 8:29*
Lord
to the *c.* of the house of our *Ne 10:37*
God
the *c.* into the treasure *Ne 10:38*
house
the *c.* where are the vessels *Ne 10:39*
of the
the *c.* for the treasures, for *Ne 12:44*
and they cleansed the *c.* *Ne 13:9*
Pleiades, and the *c.* of the *Job 9:9*
south
Who layeth the beams of his *Ps 104:3*
c.
He watereth the hills from *Ps 104:13*
his *c.*
abundance, in the *c.* of *Ps 105:30*
their
going down to the *c.* of death *Pr 7:27*
by knowledge shall the *c.* be *Pr 24:4*
filled
king hath brought me into his *Ca 1:4*
c.
people, enter thou into my *Isa 26:20*
c. and
and his *c.* by wrong *Jer 22:13*
a wide house and large *c.* *Jer 22:14*
into one of the *c.* and give *Jer 35:2*
them
man in the *c.* of his imagery *Eze 8:12*
which entereth into their *Eze 21:14*
privy *c.*
the little *c.* *Eze 40:7;*
40:10, 12, 16-17, 21, 29, 33, 36, 38, 44
the side *c.* *Eze 41:6;*
41:7-11, 26; 42:4-13
the upper *c.* (S) *Eze 42:6*
in the holy *c.* and they shall *Eze 44:19*
put
for a possession for twenty *Eze 45:5*
c.
into the holy *c.* of the *Eze 46:19*
priests
the *c.* of heaven (S) *Am 9:6*
behold, he is in the secret *M't 24:26*
c.

CHAMELEON

ferret, and the *c.* and the *Le 11:30*
lizard

CHAMOIS

and the wild ox, and the *c.* *De 14:5*
the *c.* (B)(E) *De 14:5*

CHAMPAIGN

in the *c.* over against Gilgal *De 11:30*
dwell in the Arabah over *De 11:30*
(A)(E)(R)
dwell in the plain over (B) *De 11:30*

CHAMPION

went out a *c.* out of the *1Sa 17:4*
camp
the *c.* the Philistine of Gath *1Sa 17:23*
when the Philistines saw *1Sa 17:51*
their *c.*

CHANAAN

over all the land of Egypt and C. *Ac 7:11*

seven nations in the land of C. *Ac 13:19*

CHANCE

If a bird's nest c. to be before thee *De 22:6*

it was a c. that happened to us *1Sa 6:9*

I happened by c. upon mount *2Sa 1:6*

time and c. happeneth to them *Ec 9:11*

watched for a c. (B) *M't 26:16; Lu 22:6*

by c. there came down a certain *Lu 10:31*

grain, it may c. of wheat *1Co 15:37*

CHANCELLOR

Rehum the c. and Shimshai *Ezr 4:8*

the Persian commander (A) *Ezr 4:8*

Rehum the governor (B) *Ezr 4:8; 4:17*

Rehum the commander (R) *Ezr 4:8; 4:17*

Then wrote Rehum the c. *Ezr 4:9*

an answer unto Rehum the c. *Ezr 4:17*

CHANCETH

by reason of uncleanness that c. *De 23:10*

CHANGE

be clean, and c. your garments *Ge 35:2*

people c. their purpose (A) *Ex 13:17*

c. their mind (A)(B) *Ex 32:12*

nor c. it, a good for a bad *Le 27:10; 27:33*

c. his mind (B) *Nu 23:19; 1Sa 15:29*

and thirty c. of garments *J'g 14:12; 14:13*

gave c. of garments unto them *J'g 14:19*

c. the face of the matter (S) *2Sa 14:20*

time will I wait, till my c. come *Job 14:14*

They c. the night into day: and *Job 17:12*

as a vesture shalt thou c. them *Ps 102:26*

will not revoke or c. (A)(B)(R) *Ps 110:4*

with them that are given to c. *Pr 24:21*

but we will c. them into cedars *Isa 9:10*

about so much to c. thy way *Jer 2:36*

Can the Ethiopian c. his skin, or *Jer 13:23*

then will I c. from (B) *Jer 18:10*

and think to c. times and laws *Da 7:25*

will I c. their glory into shame *Ho 4:7*

God will c. his mind (A)(R) *Jon 3:9*

Then shall his mind c. and he *Hab 1:11*

clothe thee with c. of raiment *Zec 3:4*

I am the Lord, I c. not; therefore *Mal 3:6*

underwent a c. (A) *M't 17:2*

c. your whole outlook (P) *M't 18:3*

shall c. the customs which Moses *Ac 6:14*

their women did c. the natural *Ro 1:26*

with you now, and to c. my voice *Ga 4:20*

Who shall c. our vile body, that it *Ph'p 3:21*

of necessity a c. also of the law *Heb 7:12*

beyond c. or decay (A)(P) *1Pe 1:4*

CHANGEABLE

The c. suits of apparel, and *Isa 3:22*

CHANGED

and c. my wages ten times; but *Ge 31:7*

thou hast c. my wages ten times *Ge 31:41*

c. his raiment, and came in unto *Ge 41:14*

turn again, and be c. unto white *Le 13:16*

the plague have not c. his colour *Le 13:55*

(their names being c.) and *Nu 32:38*

he c. his behaviour before them *1Sa 21:13*

c. his apparel, and came into the *2Sa 12:20*

and c. his name (S) *2Ki 23:34; 2Ch 36:4*

and c. his name to Zedekiah *2Ki 24:17*

c. his prison garments: and he *2Ki 25:29*

of my disease is my raiment c. *Job 30:18*

when he c. his behaviour *Ps 34 title*

and they shall be c. *Ps 102:26*

Thus they c. their glory into *Ps 106:20*

boldness of his face shall be c. *Ec 8:1*

have transgressed the laws, c. *Isa 24:5*

Hath a nation c. their gods *Jer 2:11*

my people have c. their glory for *Jer 2:11*

in him, and his scent is not c. *Jer 48:11*

And c. his prison garments *Jer 52:33*

how is the most fine gold c. *La 4:1*

And she had c. my judgments *Eze 5:6*

before me, till the time be c. *Da 2:9*

the form of his visage was c. *Da 3:19*

neither were their coats c. nor *Da 3:27*

and have c. the king's word *Da 3:28*

Let his heart be c. from man's *Da 4:16*

the king's countenance was c. *Da 5:6*

his countenance was c. in him *Da 5:9*

nor let thy countenance be c. *Da 5:10*

that it be not c. according to *Da 6:8*

the king establisheth may be c. *Da 6:15*

might not be c. concerning Daniel *Da 6:17*

my countenance c. in me: but I *Da 7:28*

hath c. the portion of my people *Mic 2:4*

they c. their minds, and said that *Ac 28:6*

c. the glory of the uncorruptible *Ro 1:23*

Who c. the truth of God into *Ro 1:25*

all sleep, but we shall all be c. *1Co 15:51*

incorruptible, and we shall be c. *1Co 15:52*

are c. into the same image from *2Co 3:18*

them up, and they shall be c. *Heb 1:12*

priesthood being c. there is made *Heb 7:12*

CHANGERS

doves, and the c. of money sitting *Joh 2:14*

CHANGERS'

poured out the c. money *Joh 2:15*

CHANGES

he gave each man c. of raiment *Ge 45:22*

of silver, and five c. of raiment *Ge 45:22*

c. of new suits (S) *Ge 45:22*

c. of raiment (S) *J'g 14:12; 14:13, 19*

of gold, and ten c. of raiment *2Ki 5:5*

of silver, and two c. of garments. *2Ki 5:22*

two bags, with two c. of garments *2Ki 5:23*

me; c. and war are against me *Job 10:17*

Because they have no c. therefore *Ps 55:19*

CHANGEST

thou c. his countenance *Job 14:20*

CHANGETH

to his own hurt, and c. not *Ps 15:4*

he c. the times and the seasons *Da 2:21*

CHANGING

redeeming and concerning c. *Ru 4:7*

CHANNEL

c. for torrents of rain (A)(E)(R) *Job 38:25*

from the c. of the river unto *Isa 27:12*

CHANNELS

the c. of the sea appeared *2Sa 22:16*

Then the c. of waters were seen *Ps 18:15*

he shall come up over all his c. *Isa 8:7*

CHANT

That c. to the sound of the viol *Am 6:5*

sing idle songs to the sound (A)(E)(R) *Am 6:5*

who croon to the sound (B) *Am 6:5*

CHAOS

confusion, c., worthlessness (A) *Isa 44:9*

CHAPEL

it is the king's c. and it is *Am 7:13*

CHAPTER

the height of the one c. was *1Ki 7:16*

and the height of the other c. *1Ki 7:16*

seven for the one c. *1Ki 7:17*

and seven for the other c. *1Ki 7:17*

and so he did for the other c. *1Ki 7:18*

round about upon the other c. *1Ki 7:20*

the mouth, of it within the c. and *1Ki 7:31*

and the c. upon it was brass *2Ki 25:17*

the height of the c. three cubits *2Ki 25:17*

the pomegranates upon the c. *2Ki 25:17*

the c. that was on the top of each *2Ch 3:15*

And a c. of brass was upon it *Jer 52:22*

and the height of one c. was five *Jer 52:22*

CHAPTERS

he overlaid their c. and their *Ex 36:38*

overlaying c. of silver *Ex 38:17; Ex 38:19, 28*

he made two c. of molten brass *1Ki 7:16; 7:17-20, 41-42*

the c. which were on the top *2Ch 4:12; 4:13*

and pomegranates upon the c. *Jer 52:22*

CHAPLET

a c. of grace upon (A)(E) *Pr 1:9*

a c. of grace (E) *Pr 4:9*

CHAPMEN

c. and merchants brought *2Ch 9:14*

CHAPT

Because the ground is c. for *Jer 14:4*

the ground is cracked (A)(E) *Jer 14:4*

CHARACTER

a wife of good c. (B) *Pr 12:4; 31:10*

develops maturity of c., c. produces hope (A)(B)(P)(R) *Ro 5:4*

growth of another's c. (P) *Ro 14:19*

c. or moral disposition (A) *Heb 13:5*

good and holy c. (P) *2Pe 3:11*

CHARACTERS

worthless c. (B)   1Sa 30:22

CHARASHIM

of C.; for they were   1Ch 4:14

craftsmen

CHARCHEMISH

to fight against C. by   2Ch 35:20
Euphrates

CHARGE

obeyed my voice, and kept   Ge 26:5
my c.
he blessed him, he gave him a   Ge 28:6
c.
gave them a c. unto the   Ex 6:13
children
c. the people, lest they break   Ex 19:21
keep the c. of the Lord, that   Le 8:35
ye
Levites shall keep the c. of   Nu 1:53
they shall keep his c.   Nu 3:7;
3:8, 25, 28, 31-32, 36, 38; 4:27-28,
                         31-32
the priest shall c. her by an   Nu 5:19
oath
the priest shall c. the woman   Nu 5:21
congregation, to keep the c.   Nu 8:26
the Levites touching their c.   Nu 8:26
the children of Israel kept the   Nu 9:19
c.
they kept the c. of the Lord   Nu 9:23
keep thy c. and the c. of   Nu 18:3;
                    Nu 18:4-5, 8
and give him a c. in their   Nu 27:19
sight
and gave him a c. as the   Nu 27:23
Lord
keep the c. of the   Nu 31:30;
tabernacle   Nu 31:47, 49
c. Joshua, and encourage him   De 3:28
keep his c. and his statutes   De 11:1
unto thy people of Israel's c.   De 21:8
that I may give him a c.   De 31:14
gave Joshua the son of Nun   De 31:23
a c.
kept the c. of the   Jos 22:3
commandment
I will give c. concerning thee   2Sa 14:8
the king gave all the   2Sa 18:5
captains c.
keep the c. of the Lord thy   1Ki 2:3
God
every man according to his   1Ki 4:28
c.
had c. over the people (R)   1Ki 9:23
times I must c. you (A)   1Ki 22:16
hand he leaned to have the   2Ki 7:17
c.
in their set c. (S)   1Ch 9:22; 9:26, 31
because the c. was upon   1Ch 9:27
them
And certain of them had the   1Ch 9:28
c.
give thee c. concerning   1Ch 22:12
Israel
the c. of the tabernacle of   1Ch 23:32
for we keep the c. of the   2Ch 13:11
Lord
Levites had the c. of the   2Ch 30:17
killing
the palace, c. over Jerusalem   Ne 7:2
to c. ourselves yearly with   Ne 10:32
kept the c. of the Lord (S)   Ne 12:45
that have the c. of the business   Es 3:9
to c. her that she should go in   Es 4:8
Who hath given him a c.   Job 34:13
over
Lord does not c. iniquity (B)   Ps 32:2
to my c. things that I knew   Ps 35:11
not
shall give his angels c. over   Ps 91:11
thee
I c. you, O ye daughters   Ca 2:7;
                    Ca 3:5; 5:8; 8:4
beloved, that thou dost so c.   Ca 5:9
us
of my wrath will I give him   Isa 10:6
a c.
King of Babylon gave c.   Jer 39:11
concerning
the Lord had given it a c.   Jer 47:7
against
which had the c. of the men   Jer 52:25

them that have c. over the   Eze 9:1
city
keepers of the c. of the   Eze 40:45
house
the keepers of the c. of the   Eze 40:46
altar
kept the c. of mine holy   Eze 44:8;
things   Eze 44:11, 14-16
which have kept my c.   Eze 48:11
which
keep my c. then thou shalt   Zec 3:7
also
give his angels c. concerning   M't 4:6
I c. you on oath (B)(N)   M't 26:63
I c. thee, come out of him   M'k 9:25
shall give his angels c. over   Lu 4:10
thee
a c. of subversion (N)   Lu 23:14
take his c. (B)(N)   Ac 1:20
Lord, lay not this sin to their   Ac 7:60
c.
who had the c. of all her   Ac 8:27
treasure
Who, having received such a   Ac 16:24
to have nothing laid to his c.   Ac 23:29
concerning the c.   Ac 25:16
(A)(B)(N)(P)(R)
shall lay anything to the c. of   Ro 8:33
the gospel of Christ without   1Co 9:18
c.
I c. you by the Lord that   1Th 5:27
this
that thou mightest c. some   1Ti 1:3
that
This c. I commit unto thee,   1Ti 1:18
son
And these things give in c.   1Ti 5:7
that
I c. thee before God, and the   1Ti 5:21
Lord
I give thee c. in the sight of   1Ti 6:13
God
C. them that are rich in this   1Ti 6:17
world
I c. thee therefore before God   2Ti 4:1
it may not be laid to their c.   2Ti 4:16
I c. you to do (A)   Ph'm 8
domineering over those in   1Pe 5:3
your c. (A)

CHARGEABLE

now go, lest we be c. unto   2Sa 13:25
thee
before me were c. unto the   Ne 5:15
people
I was c. to no man: for that   2Co 11:9
not be c. unto any of you   1Th 2:9
that we might not be c. to   2Th 3:8
any

CHARGED

And Abimelech c. all his   Ge 26:11
people
and c. him, and said unto   Ge 28:1
him
the captain of the guard c.   Ge 40:4
Joseph
he c. them, and said unto   Ge 49:29
them
Pharaoh c. all his people,   Ex 1:22
saying
I c. your judges at that time   De 1:16
be c. with any business   De 24:5
Moses c. the people the   De 27:11
same day
Joshua c. them (S)   Jos 6:26
and Joshua c. them that went   Jos 18:8
Moses the servant of the   Jos 22:5
Lord c.
have I not c. the young men   Ru 2:9
Saul c. the people (S)   1Sa 14:24
father c. the people with   1Sa 14:27
the oath
straitly c. the people with   1Sa 14:28
an oath
And c. the messenger,   2Sa 11:19
saying
c. thee and Abishai and   2Sa 18:12
Ittai
he c. Solomon his son, saying   1Ki 2:1
that I have c. thee with   1Ki 2:43
For so was it c. me by the   1Ki 13:9
word
the Lord had c. them, that   2Ki 17:15
they
had made a covenant, and   2Ki 17:35
c. them

and c. him to build an   1Ch 22:6
house
c. Moses with concerning   1Ch 22:13
Israel
c. them, saying. Thus shall   2Ch 19:9
ye do
hath c. me to build him an   2Ch 36:23
house
and he hath c. me to build   Ezr 1:2
him
c. that they should not be   Ne 13:19
opened
Mordecai had c. her that she   Es 2:10
Mordecai had c. her: for   Es 2:20
Esther
sinned not, nor c. God   Job 1:22
foolishly
and his angels he c. with   Job 4:18
folly
And I c. Baruch before   Jer 32:13
them
he hath c. us, to drink no   Jer 35:8
wine
Jesus straitly c. them, saying   M't 9:30
And c. them that they   M't 12:16
should not
Then c. he his disciples that   M't 16:20
they
Jesus c. them, saying, Tell   M't 17:9
he straitly c. him, and   M'k 1:43
forthwith
straitly c. them that they   M'k 3:12
should
he c. them straitly that no   M'k 5:43
man
c. them that they should tell   M'k 7:36
no
but the more he c. them   M'k 7:36
he c. them, saying, Take   M'k 8:15
heed
he c. them that they should   M'k 8:30
tell
c. them they should tell no   M'k 9:9
man
And many c. him that he   M'k 10:48
should
And he c. him to tell no man   Lu 5:14
but he c. them that they   Lu 8:56
should
straitly c. them, and   Lu 9:21
commanded
c. earnestly and warned (B)   Ac 2:40
c. him, See thou tell no man   Ac 23:22
he was c. with   Ac 23:29
(A)(B)(E)(N)(R)
sin not c. to men (A)(B)   Ro 5:13
c. every one of you, as a   1Th 2:11
father
and let not the church be c.   1Ti 5:16

CHARGEDST

thou c. us, saying, Set   Ex 19:23
bounds

CHARGER

And his offering was one   Nu 7:13
silver c.
for his offering one silver c.   Nu 7:19;
         7:25, 31, 37, 43, 49, 55, 61, 67, 73, 79
c. of silver weighing an   Nu 7:85
hundred
here John Baptist's head in   M't 14:8
a c.
was brought in a c. and   M't 14:11
given to
by and by in a c. the head   M'k 6:25
of John
brought his head in a c., and   M'k 6:28
gave

CHARGERS

c. of silver, twelve silver   Nu 7:84
bowls
thirty c. of gold, and a   Ezr 1:9
thousand
c. of silver, nine and twenty   Ezr 1:9

CHARGES

c. her with shameful things   De 22:4
(B)(R)
made shameful c. (A)(R)   De 22:17
more violent than the c.   2Sa 19:43
(A)(B)
the Levites to their c. to   2Ch 8:14
praise

service in their c. according   2Ch 31:16
to
in their c. by their courses   2Ch 31:17
And he set the priests in   2Ch 35:2
their c.
don't bring false c. (P)   Lu 3:14
let them bring c.   Ac 19:38
(A)(B)(N)(R)
c. with them, that they may   Ac 21:24
shave
present to me c. (B)   Ac 25:7
signifying the c.   Ac 25:27
(B)(E)(N)(P)(R)
warfare any time at his own   1Co 9:7
c.
lording it over your c.   1Pe 5:3
(B)(R)

CHARGEST

thou c. me to day with a   2Sa 3:8
fault

CHARGING

a c. bear (A)(R)   .   Pr 28:15
c. the jailor to keep them   Ac 16:23
safely
c. them before the Lord that   2Ti 2:14
they

CHARIOT

made him to ride in the   Ge 41:43
second c.
Joseph made ready his c.   Ge 46:29
ready his c. and took his   Ex 14:6
people
their c. wheels, that they   Ex 14:25
drave
Sisera lighted down off his c.   J'g 4:15
Why is his c. so long in   J'g 5:28
coming
David houghed all the c.   2Sa 8:4
horses
like the work of a c. wheel   1Ki 7:33
c. came up and went out of   1Ki 10:29
Egypt
speed to get him up to his   1Ki 12:18
c.
say unto Ahab, Prepare thy   1Ki 18:44
c.
horse for horse, and c. for   1Ki 20:25
c.
caused him to come up into   1Ki 20:33
the c.
he said unto the driver of   1Ki 22:34
his c.
the king was stayed up in   1Ki 22:35
his c.
wound into the midst of the   1Ki 22:35
c.
the c. in the pool of   1Ki 22:38
Samaria
appeared a c. of fire, and   2Ki 2:11
horses
c. of Israel, and the   2Ki 2:12
horsemen
with his horses and with his   2Ki 5:9
c.
down from the c. to meet   2Ki 5:21;
him   5:26
took therefore two c. horses   2Ki 7:14
Jehu rode in a c. and went   2Ki 9:16
to Jezreel
of Judah went out, each in   2Ki 9:21
his c.
heart, and he sunk down in   2Ki 9:24
his c.
and said, Smite him also in   2Ki 9:27
the c.
carried him in a c. to   2Ki 9:28
Jerusalem,
took him up to him into   2Ki 10:15
the c.
So they made him ride in   2Ki 10:16
his c.
c. of Israel, and the   2Ki 13:14
horsemen
servants carried him in a c.   2Ki 23:30
dead
also houghed all the c.   1Ch 18:4
horses
c. of the cherubims, that   1Ch 28:18
spread
which he placed in the c.   2Ch 1:14
cities
brought forth out of Egypt a   2Ch 1:17
c.
all the c. cities, and the cities   2Ch 8:6

in the c. cities, and with the   2Ch 9:25
king
speed to get him up to his   2Ch 10:18
c.
to his c. man, Turn thine   2Ch 18:33
hand
Israel stayed himself up in   2Ch 18:34
his c.
therefore took him out of   2Ch 35:24
that c.
him in the second c. that   2Ch 35:24
he had
he burneth the c. in the fire   Ps 46:9
the c. and horse are cast into   Ps 76:6
who maketh the clouds his c.   Ps 104:3
King Solomon made himself a   Ca 3:9
c.
a c. with a couple of   Isa 21:7
horsemen
behold, here cometh a c. of   Isa 21:9
men
bringeth forth the c. and   Isa 43:17
horse
thee will I break in pieces   Jer 51:21
the c.
bind the c. to the swift beast   Mic 1:13
In the first c. were red horses   Zec 6:2
and in the second c. black   Zec 6:2
horses
in the third c. white horses   Zec 6:3
in the fourth c. grisled and   Zec 6:3
bay
will cut off the c. from   Zec 9:10
Ephraim
and sitting in his c. read   Ac 8:28
Esaias
Go near, and join thyself to   Ac 8:29
this c.
he commanded the c. to stand   Ac 8:38
still

CHARIOTS

there went up with him both   Ge 50:9
c.
he took six hundred chosen c.   Ex 14:7
c. of Pharaoh   Ex 14:9;
   14:17-18, 23, 26, 28; 15:4, 19
unto their horses, and to   De 11:4
their c.
seest horses, and c. and   De 20:1
a people
with horses and c. very many   Jos 11:4
and burn their c. with fire   Jos 11:6;
   11:9
have c. of iron   Jos 17:16;
   17:18; 4:3, 13
c. and horsemen unto the   Jos 24:6
Red sea
because they had c. of iron   J'g 1:19
Jabin's army, with his c. and   J'g 4:7
his
Sisera gathered together all   J'g 4:13
his c.
discomfited Sisera, and all his   J'g 4:15
c.
Barak pursued after the c.   J'g 4:16
why tarry the wheels of   J'g 5:28
his c.
them for himself, for his c.   1Sa 8:11;
   1Sa 8:12
with Israel, thirty thousand   1Sa 13:5
c.
c. and horsemen followed   2Sa 1:6
hard
took from him a thousand c.   2Sa 8:4
of seven hundred c. of the   2Sa 10:18
Syrians
prepared him c. and horses   2Sa 15:1
prepared him c. and horsemen   1Ki 1:5
stalls of horses for his c.   1Ki 4:26
cities for his c. and cities for   1Ki 9:19
his
his captains, and rulers of   1Ki 9:22
his c.
Solomon gathered together   1Ki 10:26
c.
Zimri, captain of half his c.   1Ki 16:9
with him, and horses, and c.   1Ki 20:1
and c. and slew the Syrians   1Ki 20:21
captains that had rule over   1Ki 22:31
his c.
captains of c. saw   1Ki 22:32;
Jehosaphat   22:33
sent he thither horses, and c.   2Ki 6:14
the city both with horses   2Ki 6:15
and c.
mountain was full of horses   2Ki 6:17
and c.

noise of c. and a noise of   2Ki 7:6
horses
went over to Zair, and all   2Ki 8:21
the c.
there are with you c. and   2Ki 10:2
horses,
but fifty horsemen, and ten   2Ki 13:7
c.
put thy trust on Egypt for   2Ki 18:24
c.
the multitude of my c. I am   2Ki 19:23
come
burned the c. of the sun   2Ki 23:11
with fire
c. and seven thousand   1Ch 18:4
horsemen
hire them c. and horsemen   1Ch 19:6;
out of   1Ch 19:7
thousand men which fought   1Ch 19:18
in c.
gathered c. and horsemen   2Ch 1:14
captains of his c. and   2Ch 8:9
horsemen
thousand stalls for horses and   2Ch 9:25
c.
twelve hundred c. and   2Ch 12:3
threescore
and three hundred c.; and   2Ch 14:9
came
with very many c. and   2Ch 16:8
horsemen
of the c. that were with   2Ch 18:30;
him   2Ch 18:31-32
princes, and all his c. with   2Ch 21:9
him
trust in c. and some in horses   Ps 20:7
c. of God are twenty   Ps 68:17
thousand
company of horses in   Ca 1:9
Pharaoh's c.
my soul made me like the c.   Ca 6:12
of
neither is there any end of   Isa 2:7
their c.
Elam bare the quiver with c.   Isa 22:6
of
choicest valleys shall be full   Isa 22:7
of c.
c. of thy glory shall be the   Isa 22:18
shame
trust in c. because they are   Isa 31:1
and put thy trust on Egypt for   Isa 36:9
c.
By the multitude of my c.   Isa 37:24
am I
with his c. like a whirlwind,   Isa 66:15
to
upon horses, and in c. and   Isa 66:20
his c. shall be as a whirlwind   Jer 4:13
riding in c. and on horses,   Jer 17:25
they
David, riding in c. and on   Jer 22:4
horses
rage, ye c.; and let the   Jer 46:9
mighty
the rushing of his c. and at   Jer 47:3
upon their c. and upon all   Jer 50:37
come against thee with c.   Eze 23:24
with horses, and with c. and   Eze 26:7
of the wheels, and of the c.   Eze 26:10
when
in precious clothes for c.   Eze 27:20
with horses and c. with   Eze 39:20
mighty
with c. and with horsemen   Da 11:40
Like the noise of c. on the   Joe 2:5
tops of
I will destroy thy c.   Mic 5:10
c. shall be with flaming   Na 2:3
torches
The c. shall rage in the streets   Na 2:4
I will burn her c. in the   Na 2:13
smoke
horses, and of the jumping c.   Na 3:2
thine horses and thy c. of   Hab 3:8
I will overthrow the c. and   Hag 2:22
those
came four c. out from   Zec 6:1
between
as the sound of c. of many   Re 9:9
horses
and horses, and c. and   Re 18:13
slaves

CHARITABLE

the c. soul will be (B)   Pr 11:25
made many c. gifts (P)   Ac 10:2
bring c. gifts (N)(P)   Ac 24:17

CHARITABLY

meat, now walkest thou not   *Ro 14:15*
c.

CHARITY

give in c. (N)	*Lu 12:33*
ask c. (A)(B)	*Ac 3:2*
Knowledge puffeth up, but c.	*1Co 8:1*
love, goodwill, benevolence edifies (A)	*1Co 8:1*
love builds up (B)(N)(R)	*1Co 8:1*
love edifieth (E)	*1Co 8:1*
love that can make him grow (P)	*1Co 8:1*
of angels, and have not c.	*1Co 13:1;*
	13:2-3
love	*1Co 13:1*
(A)(B)(E)(N)(P)(R)	*1Co 13:2, 4, 8,*
13; 14:1; 16:14; Col 3:13; 1Th 3:6;	
2Th 1:3; 1Ti 1:5; 2:15; 4:12; 2Ti 2:22;	
3:10; Tit 2:2; 1Pe 4:8; 5:14; Re 2:19	
C. suffereth long, c. envieth	*1Co 13:4*
not c. vaunteth not	
C. never faileth: but whether	*1Co 13:8*
now abideth faith, hope. c.	*1Co 13:13*
these	
the greatest of these is c.	*1Co 13:13*
Follow after c. and desire	*1Co 14:1*
the gift of c.	*1Co 16:3*
(A)(B)(N)(P)(R)	
all your things be done	*1Co 16:14*
with c.	
above all these things put on	*Col 3:14*
c.	
good tidings of your faith	*1Th 3:6*
and c.	
the c. of every one of you all	*2Th 1:3*
commandment is c. out of a	*1Ti 1:5*
in faith and c. and holiness	*1Ti 2:15*
with	
in conversation, in c., in	*1Ti 4:12*
spirit, in	
follow righteousness, faith, c.	*2Ti 2:22*
faith, longsuffering, c.,	*2Ti 3:10*
patience	
temperate, sound in faith, in	*Tit 2:2*
c.	
fervent c. among yourselves	*1Pe 4:8*
for c. shall cover the	*1Pe 4:8*
multitude	
ye one another with a kiss	*1Pe 5:14*
of c.	
and to brotherly kindness c.	*2Pe 1:7*
Christian love (A)(P)	*2Pe 1:7*
affection with love	*2Pe 1:7*
(B)(E)(R)	
brotherly kindness with love	*2Pe 1:7*
(N)	
borne witness of thy c.	*3Jo 6*
your love and friendship (A)	*3Jo 6*
your friendship (B)	*3Jo 6*
love before the church	*3Jo 6*
(E)(P)(R)	
kindness before the	*3Jo 6*
congregation (N)	
spots in your feasts of c.	*Jude 12*
your love-feasts	*Jude 12*
(A)(B)(E)(N)(R)	
your feasts (P)	*Jude 12*
I know thy works, and c. and	*Re 2:19*

CHARLATAN

you utter imposter and c.	*Ac 13:10*
(N)	
this c. trying to say (N)	*Ac 17:18*
c. will make progress (N)	*2Ti 3:13*

CHARMED

which will not be c. and they	*Jer 8:17*

CHARMER

Or a c. or a consulter with	*De 18:11*
the c. no advantage (E)(R)	*Ec 10:11*

CHARMERS

hearken to the voice of c.	*Ps 58:5*
seek to the idols, and to the	*Isa 19:3*
c.	

CHARMING

to the voice of charmers, c.	*Ps 58:5*

CHARMS

mistress of deadly c. (A)(R)	*Na 3:4*

CHARRAN

before he dwelt in C.	*Ac 7:2*
and dwelt in C.: and from thence	*Ac 7:4*

CHASE

And ye shall c. your enemies	*Le 26:7*
And five of you shall c. an hundred	*Le 26:8*
the sound of a shaken leaf shall c.	*Le 26:36*
How should one c. a thousand	*De 32:30*
man of you shall c. a thousand	*Jos 23:10*
and let the angel of the Lord c.	*Ps 35:5*
c. and seize them (B)	*Ps 71:11*

CHASED

came out against you, and c. you	*De 1:44*
for they c. them from before the	*Jos 7:5*
the wilderness wherein they c.	*Jos 8:24*
and c. them along the way that	*Jos 10:10*
and c. them unto great Zidon	*Jos 11:8*
And Abimelech c. him, and he	*J'g 9:40*
c. them, and trode them down	*J'g 20:43*
Horonite: therefore I c. him from	*Ne 13:28*
into darkness, and c. out of	*Job 18:18*
he shall be c. away as a vision of	*Job 20:8*
it shall be as the c. roe, and as a	*Isa 13:14*
and shall be as the chaff of the	*Isa 17:13*
Mine enemies c. me sore, like	*La 3:52*

CHASETH

c. away his mother, is a son that	*Pr 19:26*

CHASING

of Israel returned from c after	*1Sa 17:53*
worthlessness, c. wind (B)	*Ec 1:14;*
	2:19
futility and c. wind (B)	*Ec 4:4; 4:16*

CHASTE

present you as a c. virgin to	*2Co 11:2*
a pure virgin (B)(E)	*2Co 11:2*
like a fresh, unspoiled girl (P)	*2Co 11:2*
a pure bride to her one husband (A)	*2Co 11:2*
discreet, c., keepers at home	*Tit 2:5*
they behold your c. conversation	*1Pe 3:2*
pure and modest way (A)	*1Pe 3:2*
pure and reverent behaviour (P)	*1Pe 3:2*
c. respectful behaviour (B)(E)(N)(R)	*1Pe 3:2*
they are c. (N)(R)	*Re 14:4*

CHASTEN

I will c. him with the rod of men	*2Sa 7:14*
I will correct him with a rod (B)	*2Sa 7:14*
neither c. me in hot displeasure	*Ps 6:1;*
	38:1
discipline me in hot displeasure (B)	*Ps 6:1*
C. thy son while there is hope	*Pr 19:18*
discipline your son (A)(B)(R)	*Pr 19:18*
I will c. them (B)	*Jer 50:31*
to c. thyself before thy God	*Da 10:12*
humble thyself before God (A)(B)(E)	*Da 10:12*
humbled thyself before God (N)	*Da 10:12*
many as I love, I rebuke and c.	*Re 3:19*
I discipline and instruct (A)	*Re 3:19*
I correct and discipline (B)(P)	*Re 3:19*
I reprove and discipline (N)	*Re 3:19*

CHASTENED

when they have c. him, will not	*De 21:18*
they discipline him (B)	*De 21:18*
He is c. with pain upon his bed	*Job 33:19*
When I wept and c. my soul	*Ps 69:10*
humbled myself with fasting (A)(R)	*Ps 69:10*
mourned with fasting (B)	*Ps 69:10*
have I been plagued, and c. every	*Ps 73:14*
c. the nations (R)	*Ps 94:10*
The Lord hath c. me sore: but he	*Ps 118:18*
we are c. of the Lord, that we	*1Co 11:32*
Lord serve to discipline us (B)	*1Co 11:32*
he is disciplining us (N)	*1Co 11:32*
he disciplines us (P)	*1Co 11:32*
as c., and not killed	*2Co 6:9*
disciplined but not done to death (B)	*2Co 6:9*
disciplined by suffering (N)	*2Co 6:9*
punished and yet not killed (R)	*2Co 6:9*
for a few days c. us after their own	*Heb 12:10*
disciplined us (A)(B)(N)(R)	*Heb 12:10*
used to correct us (P)	*Heb 12:10*

CHASTENEST

Blessed is the man whom thou c.	*Ps 94:12*
you discipline and instruct (A)(B)	*Ps 94:12*

CHASTENETH

as a man c. his son, so God c. thee	*De 8:5*
disciplines and instructs his son (A)	*De 8:5*
disciplines his son (B)(R)	*De 8:5*
he that loveth him c. him	*Pr 13:24*
disciplines and punishes (A)	*Pr 13:24*
diligent to discipline him (R)	*Pr 13:24*
For whom the Lord loveth he c.	*Heb 12:6*
corrects and disciplines (A)(B)(N)(R)	*Heb 12:6*
son is he whom the father c. not	*Heb 12:7*
train, correct, and discipline (A)	*Heb 12:7*
does not discipline (B)(R)	*Heb 12:7*
not disciplined by father (N)	*Heb 12:7*
uncorrected by his father (P)	*Heb 12:7*

CHASTENING

despise not c. of the Almighty	*Job 5:17;*
	Pr 3:11; Heb 12:5
do not despise correction of (A)	*Job 5:17*
a prayer when thy c. was upon them	*Isa 26:16*
your punishment was upon them (B)	*Isa 26:16*
If ye endure c. God dealeth with you	*Heb 12:7*
no c. for the present seems to be	*Heb 12:11*
no discipline brings joy (A)(B)(N)(R)	*Heb 12:11*

CHASTISE

I, even I, will c. you seven times	*Le 26:28*
punish you sevenfold (B)	*Le 26:28*
city shall take that man and c. him	*De 22:18*
rebuke and whip him (A)	*De 22:18*
whip him (R)	*De 22:18*
c. you with scorpions	*1Ki 12:11;*
	1Ki 12:14; 2Ch 10:11, 14
flog you with scorpions (B)	*1Ki 12:11;*
	12:14
does he not c. (R)	*Ps 94:10*
I will c. them, as their	*Ho 7:12*
I will punish them (B)	*Ho 7:12*

CHASTISE (cont.)

in my desire that I should *c.*   *Ho 10:10*
I will *c.* him and release   *Lu 23:16;*
  23:22
after a whipping (B)   *Lu 23:16; 23:22*
let him off with flogging   *Lu 23:16;*
(N)   *23:22*
teach him a sharp lesson   *Lu 23:16;*
(P)   *23:22*

CHASTISED

c. you with whips   *1Ki 12:11;*
  2Ch 10:11, 14
flogged you with whips   *1Ki 12:11;*
(B)   *12:14*
Thou hast *c.* me, and I was   *Jer 31:18*
c.
hast disciplined me (B)   *Jer 31:18*

CHASTISEMENT

not seen the *c.* of the Lord   *De 11:2*
your
seen the instruction and   *De 11:2*
discipline (A)
not seen his greatness (B)   *De 11:2*
discipline of the Lord (R)   *De 11:2*
I have borne *c.*, I will not   *Job 34:31*
offend
I have felt discipline (B)   *Job 34:31*
folly is *c.* of fools (B)(R)   *Pr 16:22*
the *c.* of our peace was upon   *Isa 53:5*
him
punishment procured our   *Isa 53:5*
peace (B)
the *c.* of a cruel one. for the   *Jer 30:14*
punishment of a merciless   *Jer 30:14*
one (B)
But if ye be without *c.*,   *Heb 12:8*
whereof all
exempt from correction and   *Heb 12:8*
left without discipline (A)
if you receive no correction   *Heb 12:8*
(B)
if you escape discipline (N)   *Heb 12:8*
had no experience of   *Heb 12:8*
correction (P)
if you are left without   *Heb 12:8*
discipline (R)

CHASTISETH

He that *c.* the heathen, shall   *Ps 94:10*
not
disciplines and instructs   *Ps 94:10*
nations (A)
discipline the nations (B)   *Ps 94:10*
chastens the nations (R)   *Ps 94:10*

CHASTITY

evidence of her *c.* (B)   *De 22:20*

CHATTER

so did I *c.*: I did mourn as   *Isa 38:14*
a crane
like a twittering swallow I   *Isa 38:14*
chirp (B)
like a swallow or crane I   *Isa 38:14*
clamor (R)
this godless *c.* (A)(E)(R)   *1Ti 6:20*
empty and worldly *c.*   *2Ti 2:16*
(N)(R)

CHEAPENING

debasing *c.* myself (A)   *2Co 11:7*
mistake in *c.* myself (E)(R)   *2Co 11:7*

CHEAT

Do not *c.* (B)(P)   *M'k 10:19*
not *c.* of normal sexual (P)   *1Co 7:5*
c. of your joy in Christ (P)   *Col 2:18*

CHEATED

be wronged or *c.* (P)   *1Co 6:8*
c. or take advantage (A)(P)   *2Co 7:2*

CHEATS

thieves, *c.* (B)   *Lu 18:11*
c. or thieves (A)(P)   *1Co 5:10*

CHEBAR

the river *c.*   *Eze 1:1;*
  1:3; 3:15, 23; 10:15, 20, 22; 43:3

CHECK

heard the *c.* of my reproach   *Job 20:3*

CHECKED

the plague be *c.* (R)   *Le 13:5; 13:37*
the plague was *c.* (B)   *Nu 16:48;*
  Ps 106:30
the plague was *c.* (S)   *Ps 106:30*

CHECKER

nets of *c.* work, and wreaths   *1Ki 7:17*
of

CHEDORLAOMER

C. king of Elam   *Ge 14:1;*
  Ge 14:4-5, 9, 17

CHEEK

and smote Micaiah on the   *1Ki 22:24*
c. and
and smote Micaiah upon   *2Ch 18:23*
the *c.*
they have smitten me upon   *Job 16:10*
the *c.*
all mine enemies upon the *c.*   *Ps 3:7*
bone
He giveth his *c.* to him that   *La 3:30*
hath the *c.* teeth of a great   *Joe 1:6*
lion
Israel with a rod upon the *c.*   *Mic 5:1*
smite thee upon thy right *c.*   *M't 5:39*
smiteth thee on the one *c.*   *Lu 6:29*

CHEEKS

the shoulder, and the two *c.*   *De 18:3*
Thy *c.* are comely with rows   *Ca 1:10*
of
His *c.* are as a bed of spices,   *Ca 5:13*
as
and my *c.* to them that   *Isa 50:6*
plucked
and her tears are on her *c.*   *La 1:2*

CHEER

and shall *c.* up his wife   *De 24:5*
which he
eat and be of good *c.* (B)   *1Ki 21:7*
and let thy heart *c.* thee in   *Ec 11:9*
be of good *c.*; thy sins be   *M't 9:2*
forgiven
Be of good *c.*; it is I; be   *M't 14:27*
not afraid
saith unto them, Be of good   *M'k 6:50*
c.
but be of good *c.*; I have   *Joh 16:33*
overcome
Be of good *c.*, Paul: for as   *Ac 23:11*
thou
be of good *c.*   *Ac 27:22 27:25, 36*

CHEERETH

which *c.* God and man, and   *J'g 9:13*
go to

CHEERFUL

let your heart be *c.* (R)   *1Ki 21:7*
A merry heart maketh a *c.*   *Pr 15:13*
a *c.* heart has continual feast   *Pr 15:15*
(E)(R)
a *c.* happy heart   *Pr 17:22*
(A)(B)(E)(R)
drink wine with a *c.* heart (A)   *Ec 9:7*
gladness, and *c.* feasts;   *Zec 8:19*
therefore
shall make the young men *c.*   *Zec 9:17*
for God loveth a *c.* giver   *2Co 9:7*
is anyone feeling *c.*   *Jas 5:13*
(B)(E)(R)

CHEERFULLY

c. approached   *1Sa 15:32*
(A)(B)(E)(R)(S)
the more *c.* answer for   *Ac 24:10*
myself

CHEERFULNESS

he that sheweth mercy, with   *Ro 12:8*
c.

CHEERING

c. one another (P)   *2Th 5:11*

CHEERLESS

make her *c.* (A)   *Re 17:16*

CHEESE

sheep, and *c.* of kine, for   *2Sa 17:29*
David
as milk, and curdled me   *Job 10:10*
like *c.*

CHEESES

carry these ten *c.* unto the   *1Sa 17:18*

CHELAL

Adna, and *C.*, Benaiah,   *Ezr 10:30*
Maaseiah

CHELLUH

Benaiah, Bedeiah, *C.*   *Ezr 10:35*

CHELUB

And *C.* the brother of Shuah   *1Ch 4:11*
the ground was Ezri the   *1Ch 27:26*
son of *C.*

CHELUBAI

Jerahmeel, and Ram, and *C.*   *1Ch 2:9*

CHEMARIMS

name of the *C.* with the   *Zep 1:4*
priests

CHEMOSH

thou art undone, O people   *Nu 21:29*
of *C.*
that which *C.* thy god giveth   *J'g 11:24*
Solomon build an high place   *1Ki 11:7*
for *C.*
C. the god of the Moabites,   *1Ki 11:33*
C. the abomination of the   *2Ki 23:13*
Moabites
C. shall go forth into   *Jer 48:7*
captivity
Moab shall be ashamed of   *Jer 48:13*
C. as
O Moab! the people of *C.*   *Jer 48:46*
perisheth

CHENAANAH

C. made him horns of iron   *1Ki 22:11*
C. went near, and smote   *1Ki 22:24*
Micaiah
Benjamin, and Ehud, and *C.*   *1Ch 7:10*
C. had made him horns of   *2Ch 18:10*
iron
Zedekiah the son of *C.*   *2Ch 18:23*
came near

CHENANI

Bani, and *C.* and cried with   *Ne 9:4*

CHENANIAH

And *C.* chief of the   *1Ch 15:22*
Levites, was
and *C.* the master of the   *1Ch 15:27*
song
C. and his sons were for   *1Ch 26:29*

CHEPHAR-HAAMMONAI

And *C.*, and Ophni, and   *Jos 18:24*
Gaba

CHEPHIRAH

their cities were Gibeon, and   *Jos 9:17*
C.
Mizpeh, and *C.* and Mozah,   *Jos 18:26*
Kirjath-arim, and *C.* and Beeroth   *Ezr 2:25*
of Kirjath-jearim, *C.* and   *Ne 7:29*
Beeroth

CHERAN

and Eshban, and	Ge 36:26
Ithran, and C.	
and Eshban, and Ithran, and	1Ch 1:41
C.	

CHERETHIMS

I will cut off the C. and	Eze 25:16
destroy	
cut off the Cherethites	Eze 25:16
(A)(B)(E)(R)	

CHERETHITES

invasion upon the south of	1Sa 30:14
the C.	
both the C. and the	2Sa 8:18
Pelethites	
all the C. and all the	2Sa 15:18
Pelethites	
and the C. and the Pelethites	2Sa 20:7
was over the C. and over	2Sa 20:23
and the C. and the Pelethites	1Ki 1:38
and the C. and the	1Ki 1:44
Pelethites,	
was over the C. and the	1Ch 18:17
Pelethites	
cut off C. (A)(B)(E)(R)	Eze 25:11
the nation of the C.! the word	Zep 2:5
of	

CHERISH

let her c. him, and let her lie	1Ki 1:2
in	
love does not c. inflated	1Co 13:4
ideas of its own importance (P)	

CHERISHED

was very fair, and c. the king	1Ki 1:4
waited on and nursed him	1Ki 1:4
(A)	
served him (B)	1Ki 1:4
ministered to him (R)	1Ki 1:4
c. place laid waste (B)	Isa 64:11

CHERISHETH

but nourisheth and c. it,	Eph 5:29
even	
carefully protects it (B)	Eph 5:29
provides and cares for it	Eph 5:29
(N)	
to enfold her (P)	Eph 5:29
even as a nurse c. her	1Th 2:7
children	
tenderly fostering (B)	1Th 2:7
caring fondly for (N)	1Th 2:7
taking care of her children	1Th 2:7
(R)	

CHERITH

and hide thyself by the	1Ki 17:3
brook C.	
went and dwelt by the brook	1Ki 17:5
C.	

CHERUB

one c. on the one end; the	Ex 25:19
other c.	37:8
he rode upon a c. and did	1Sa 22:11
fly	
one wing of the c., and five	1Ki 6:24;
	2Ch 3:11-12
the other c. was ten cubits:	1Ki 6:25;
both	1Ki 6:26-27
up from Tel-melah,	Ezr 2:59
Tel-harsa, C.	
from Tel-melah, Tel-haresha,	Ne 7:61
C.	
he rode upon c. and did fly	Ps 18:10
was gone up from the c.	Eze 9:3
under the c. and fill thine	Eze 10:2
hand	
went up from the c. and	Eze 10:4
stood	
one c. stretched forth his	Eze 10:7
hand	
one wheel by one c. and	Eze 10:9
another	
the first face was the face	Eze 10:14
of a c.	
Thou art the anointed c.	Eze 28:14
that	

I will destroy thee, O	Eze 28:16
covering c.	
between a c. and a c.; and	Eze 41:18
every c. had two faces	Eze 41:18

CHERUBIM

c. skilfully embroidered (A)	Ex 26:1
c. were carved (B)(R)	2Ch 3:7

CHERUBIMS

of the garden of Eden C. and	Ge 3:24
thou shalt make two c. of	Ex 25:18;
gold	25:19-22; 26:1, 31; 36:8, 35; 37:7-9
from between the two c.	Nu 7:89
which dwelleth between the c.	1Sa 4:4
that dwelleth between the c.	2Sa 6:2
oracle he made two c. of	1Ki 6:23;
olive	6:25, 27-29, 32, 35
ledges were lions, oxen, and	1Ki 7:29
c.	
graved c. lions, and palm	1Ki 7:36
trees	
even under the wings of the c.	1Ki 8:6
c. spread forth their two	1Ki 8:7
wings	
which dwellest between the	2Ki 19:15
c.	
that dwelleth between the c.	1Ch 13:6
the chariot of the c., that	1Ch 28:18
spread	
gold; and graved c. on the	2Ch 3:7
walls	
he made two c. of image	2Ch 3:10;
work	2Ch 3:11, 13-14; 5:7-8
that dwellest between the c.	Ps 80:1
he sitteth between the c. let	Ps 99:1
that dwellest between the c.	Isa 37:16
head of the c. there	Eze 10:1
appeared	
coals of fire from between	Eze 10:2
the c.	
c. stood on the right side of	Eze 10:3
the wheels, from between the	Eze 10:6
c.	
from between the c. unto the	Eze 10:7
fire	
the fire that was between the	Eze 10:7
c.	
there appeared in the c.	Eze 10:8
form	
behold the four wheels by	Eze 10:9
the c.	
the c. were lifted up. This is	Eze 10:15
when the c. went, the	Eze 10:16
wheels	
them: and when the c. lifted	Eze 10:16
house, and stood over the c.	Eze 10:18
the c. lifted up their wings	Eze 10:19
and I knew that they were	Eze 10:20
the c.	
the c. lift up their wings	Eze 11:22
was made with c. and palm	Eze 41:18
trees	
door were c. and palm trees	Eze 41:20
c. and palm trees, like as	Eze 41:25
were	
c. of glory shadowing the	Heb 9:5

CHERUBIMS'

sound of the c. wings was	Eze 10:5
heard	

CHESALON

of mount Jearim, which is	Jos 15:10
C.	

CHESED

And C., and Hazo, and	Ge 22:22
Pildash	

CHESIL

And Eltolad, and C. and	Jos 15:30
Hormah	

CHEST

Jehoiada the priest took a c.	2Ki 12:9
much money in the c. that	2Ki 12:10
made a c. and set it without	2Ch 24:8
at the	
cast into the c. until they	2Ch 24:10
had	
c. was brought unto the	2Ch 24:11
king's	

CHESTNUT

and of the hazel and c. tree	Ge 30:37
plane trees (B)(E)(R)	Ge 30:37
c. trees were not like his	Eze 31:8
branches	
plane trees (A)(B)(E)(R)	Eze 31:8

CHESTS

in c. of rich apparel, bound	Eze 27:24
with	

CHESULOTH

was toward Jezreel, and C.	Jos 19:18

CHEW

shall ye not eat of them that	Le 11:4
c.	
of them that c. the cud, or of	De 14:7
them	
c. the cud, but divide not the	De 14:7
hoof	

CHEWED

between their teeth, ere it was	Nu 11:33
c.	

CHEWETH

c. the cud, among the beasts	Le 11:3;
	Le 11:4-7, 26; De 14:6, 8

CHEZIB

he was at C. when she bare	Ge 38:5
him	

CHICKENS

as a hen gathereth her c.	M't 23:37
under	

CHIDE

Wherefore the people did c.	Ex 17:2
with	
people contended with Moses	Ex 17:2
(A)	
quarreled with Moses (B)	Ex 17:2
strove with Moses, strive	Ex 17:2
with (E)	
found fault, find fault (R)	Ex 17:2
men of Ephraim did c. with	J'g 8:1
Gideon	
quarreled with him furiously	J'g 8:1
(A)	
they accused him severely (B)	J'g 8:1
upbraided him violently (R)	J'g 8:1
he will not always c. nor	Ps 103:9
keep anger	
show hostility (B)	Ps 103:9

CHIDED

they c. her (B)	M'k 14:5
c. their unbelief (B)	M'k 16:14

CHIDING

called Meribah, because of c.	Ex 17:7
because of the faultfinding of	Ex 17:7
(A)	
because of Israelites	Ex 17:7
quarreling (B)	
striving of Israel (E)	Ex 17:7
faultfinding of Israel (R)	Ex 17:7

CHIDON

unto the threshing floor of C.	1Ch 13:9

CHIEF

chief (S)	Ge 36:15
Ge 36:16-19, 21, 29-30, 40-43; Ex 15:15;	
	1Ch 1:51-54
c. butler told his dream to	Ge 40:9
Joseph	
restored c. butler to	Ge 40:21
butlershop	
hanged c. baker as Joseph	Ge 40:22
interpreted	
Eleazar be c. over c. of	Nu 3:32
Levites	
took c. of tribes, wise men	De 1:15
heads of your tribes	De 1:15
(B)(E)(R)	

people took c. of the things | 1Sa 15:21
which
the best that was doomed | 1Sa 15:21
(B)(R)
Abishai brother of Joab c. | 2Sa 23:18
among
these were the c. of the | 1Ki 9:23
officers
for of Judah came the c. | 1Ch 5:2
ruler
shall be c., Joab went first | 1Ch 11:6
and was c.
shall be generalissimo (B) | 1Ch 11:6
sons of David were c. | 1Ch 18:17
about the king
tho' not firstborn his father | 1Ch 26:10
made him c.
rulers have been c. in this | Ezr 9:2
trespass
foremost in this wicked act | Ezr 9:2
and direct violation of God's
will (A)
were first offenders (B) | Ezr 9:2
these are c. of the province | Ne 11:3
that
heads of the province (A) | Ne 11:3
Asaph was the c. (S) | Ne 11:17
he taketh away heart of the | Job 12:24
people
the leaders of the people | Job 12:24
(A)
I sat c. and dwelt as a king | Job 29:25
behemoth is c. of the ways | Job 40:19
of God
first of the works of God | Job 40:19
(A)(R)
foremost of the ways of | Job 40:19
God (B)
He smote c. of their | Ps 78:51;
strength | 105:36
if I prefer not Jerusalem | Ps 137:6
above c. joy
Wisdom crieth in c. place of | Pr 1:21
concourse
a whisperer separateth c. | Pr 16:28
friends
separates close friends | Pr 16:28
(A)(R)
separates familiar friends | Pr 16:28
(B)
an orchard with all the c. | Ca 4:14
spices
he stirreth up c. ones of | Isa 14:9
earth
hast taught them as c. over | Jer 13:21
thee
ye c. of the flock (S) | Jer 25:34;
| 25:35-36
sing and shout among c. of | Jer 31:7
nations
to be head over you (A) | Jer 31:7
for the leader of the nations | Jer 31:7
(B)
the c. of the children of | Da 11:41
Ammon
the main kernel of Ammon | Da 11:41
(A)
prominent Ammonites shall | Da 11:41
escape (B)
main part of the Ammonites | Da 11:41
(R)
which are named the c. of | Am 6:1
nations
anoint themselves with c. | Am 6:6
ointments
anoint with the finest oils | Am 6:6
(A)(R)
anoint with choicest | Am 6:6
ointments (B)
whosoever will be c. among | M't 20:27
you
desires to be first | M't 20:27
(A)(B)(E)(N)(P)(R)
c. seats in synagogues | M't 23:6;
| M'k 12:39
best seats (A)(R) | M't 23:6
front seats (B) | M't 23:6
seats of honor (P) | M't 23:6
Herod made a supper to his | M'k 6:21
c. estates
casteth out devils through c. | Lu 11:15
of devils
through prince of demons | Lu 11:15
(A)(B)(E)(N)(R)
c. seats in the synagogue (S) | Lu 11:43
went into house of c. | Lu 14:1
Pharisee
how they chose c. rooms | Lu 14:7;
| 20:46

the c. seat (S) | Lu 14:8
he that is c. as he that doth | Lu 22:26
serve
among c. rulers many | Joh 12:42
believed
because Paul was the c. | Ac 14:12
speaker
led the speech (A)(B) | Ac 14:12
he was the spokesman (N) | Ac 14:12
some believed, of c. women | Ac 17:4
not a
the leading women (A)(R) | Ac 17:4
prominent women (B) | Ac 17:4
influential women (N)(P) | Ac 17:4
Jesus Christ c. corner stone | Eph 2:20;
| 1Pe 2:6
came to save sinners of | 1Ti 1:15
whom I am c.
I am foremost (A)(B)(R) | 1Ti 1:15
I stand first (N) | 1Ti 1:15
I was worst of all (P) | 1Ti 1:15
when the c. Shepherd shall | 1Pe 5:4
appear

CHIEF CAPTAIN, CAPTAINS

who smiteth shall be c. and | 2Sa 5:8
captain
Adino the Tachmonite sat c. | 2Sa 23:8
captain
c. captain for first month | 1Ch 27:3
chief of all the commanders | 1Ch 27:3
(A)
commander of all officers | 1Ch 27:3
(B)
c. of Solomon's captains | 2Ch 8:9
tidings came to c. captain of | Ac 21:31
band
commandant (A)(B) | Ac 21:31;
| 21:32; 23:17; 24:7, 22
officer commanding the | Ac 21:31
cohort (N)
colonel of the regiment (P) | Ac 21:31
tribune of the cohort (R) | Ac 21:31
when saw c. captain they | Ac 21:32
left beating
bring this young man to c. | Ac 23:17
captain
c. captain Lysias came upon | Ac 24:7
us, took him
c. captain shall come, I will | Ac 24:22
know
Agrippa entered with c. | Ac 25:23
captains
military commandants (A) | Ac 25:23
the military tribunes (R) | Ac 25:23
rich men and c. captains hid | Re 6:15
the generals (B)(R) | Re 6:15
marshals (N) | Re 6:15
the captains (P) | Re 6:15

CHIEF FATHERS

the c. fathers of | Nu 31:26
congregation
tribal leaders (B) | Nu 31:26
heads of the fathers' houses | Nu 31:26
(E)(R)
c. fathers of Levites | 1Ch 9:34
clan leaders (B) | 1Ch 9:34;
| 1Ch 24:31; 26:32; 2Ch 26:12
heads of fathers' houses | 1Ch 9:34;
(E)(R) | 1Ch 24:31; 26:32; 2Ch 26:12;
| Ezr 1:5; Ne 7:70
the c. fathers of the priests | 1Ch 24:31
c. fathers David made | 1Ch 26:32
rulers
whole number of c. fathers | 2Ch 26:12
rose up c. of the fathers | Ezr 1:5
c. of fathers gave to the | Ne 7:70;
work | 7:71

CHIEF HOUSE

the c. of house of | Nu 3:24
Gershonites
clan leader (B) | Nu 3:24;
| Nu 3:30, 35; 25:14
prince of the fathers' house | Nu 3:24;
(E) | Nu 3:30, 35; 25:14
head of fathers' house (R) | Nu 3:24;
| Nu 3:30, 35; 25:14
the c. of house of the | Nu 3:30
Kohathites
c. of the house of the | Nu 3:35
Merarites
Zimri the c. house among | Nu 25:14
Simeonites
Cozbi, of a c. house in Midian | Nu 25:15
head of clans (B) | Nu 25:15
head of the people (E)(R) | Nu 25:15

of each c. house a prince | Jos 22:14
was sent

CHIEF MAN, MEN

not defile himself, being a c. | Le 21:4
man
As a family man (B) | Le 21:4
husband among his people | Le 21:4
(R)
sons of Uzzi, all c. men | 1Ch 7:3
leaders (B) | 1Ch 7:3; 24:4; Ezr 5:10
heads of the fathers' houses | 1Ch 7:3;
(R) | 24:4
more c. men of Eleazar than | 1Ch 24:4
of Ithamar
the names of the men that | Ezr 5:10
were c.
I gathered together c. men to | Ezr 7:28
go
leading men (B)(R) | Ezr 7:28
I called thee from c. men | Isa 41:9
thereof
the Jews stirred up the c. | Ac 13:50
men
outstanding men (A)(B) | Ac 13:50
leading men (N)(R) | Ac 13:50
leading citizens (P) | Ac 13:50
Judas and Silas, c. men | Ac 15:22
among brethren
possessions of c. man of island | Ac 28:7

CHIEF MUSICIAN

In the titles of | Ps 4:6, 8-9,
| 11-14, 18-22, 31, 36, 39-42, 44-47, 49,
| 51-62, 64-70, 75-77, 80-81, 84-85, 88,
| 109, 139-140

CHIEF PRIEST

took Seraiah the c. priest | 2Ki 25:18
Benaiah a c. priest was third | 1Ch 27:5
anointed Zadok to be c. | 1Ch 29:22
priest
Amariah c. priest is over you | 2Ch 19:11
Azariah the c. priest looked | 2Ch 26:20
on him

CHIEF PRIESTS

I separated twelve of c. of | Ezr 8:24
priests
made c. priests and all Israel | Ezr 10:5
to swear
were c. priests in days of | Ne 12:7
Joshua
suffer many thing of c. | M't 16:21
priests
multitude with staves from | M't 26:47
c. priests
he was accused of c. | M't 27:12;
priests | M'k 15:3
c. priests mocking with | M't 27:41;
scribes | M'k 15:31
c. priests sought to put him | M'k 14:1;
to death | M'k 14:55; M't 26:59;
| Lu 9:22; 22:2
voices of them and c. priests | Lu 23:23
prevailed
c. priests sent officers to take | Joh 7:32
him
c. priests answered, we have | Joh 19:15
no king
hath authority from c. | Ac 9:14;
priests | Ac 26:10
commended c. priests and | Ac 22:30
council to appear

CHIEF PRINCE, PRINCES

were children of Asher, c. of | 1Ch 7:40
princes
heads of the clans (B) | 1Ch 7:40
heads of the fathers' houses | 1Ch 7:40
(E)(R)
Gog c. prince of Meshech | Eze 38:2;
| Eze 38:3; 39:1
Michael one of c. princes | Da 10:13
came

CHIEF SINGER, SINGERS

in days of David were c. of | Ne 12:46
singers
to the c. singer on my | Hab 3:19
instruments

CHIEFEST

make yourselves fat with c. | 1Sa 2:29
offerings

best of the offerings (B)   1Sa 2:29
choicest parts of offerings   1Sa 2:29
(R)
Samuel made them sit in c.   1Sa 9:22
place
Doeg an Edomite, c. of   1Sa 21:7
herd men to Saul
Hezekiah buried in c. of   2Ch 32:33
sepulchres
my beloved is the c. among   Ca 5:10
10,000
who will be c. shall be   M'k 10:44
servant of all
first in rank   M'k 10:44
(A)(B)(E)(N)(P)(R)
not a whit behind c. of   2Co 11:5;
apostles   12:11
extra-super (false) apostles   2Co 11:5
(A)
most eminent apostles (B)   2Co 11:5
superlative apostles (N)(R)   2Co 11:5
extraspecial messengers (P)   2Co 11:5

CHIEFLY

c. because to them were   Ro 3:2
committed, oracles
to begin with, to the Jews (A)   Ro 3:2
Primarily, that they were   Ro 3:2
entrusted (B)
first of all, that they were (E)   Ro 3:2
In the first place, Jews were   Ro 3:2
(N)
to begin with, it was the Jews   Ro 3:2
(P)(R)
c. they that are of Caesar's   Ph'p 4:22
household
especially those of Caesar's   Ph'p 4:22
(A)(B)(E)(R)
particularly those who   Ph'p 4:22
belong (N)(P)
but c. them that walk after   2Pe 2:10
the flesh
particularly those who walk   2Pe 2:10
(A)
especially true of those   2Pe 2:10
(B)(R)
Above all will he punish (N)   2Pe 2:10

CHIEFS

These were c. (S)   Ge 36:15;
Ge 36:19, 21, 29-30, 40, 43; Ex 15:15;
   1Ch 1:51
the c. of Judah (A)(B)(E)   Zec 12:5;
   12:6

CHIEFTAN

he shall be c. (A)(E)   Zec 9:7

CHILD

God appointed another c.   Ge 4:25;
(A)   Ge 15:3; Le 12:21
Shall a c. be born unto him   Ge 17:17
that is an
Shall I of a surety bear a c.   Ge 18:13
Hagar cast c. under shrubs   Ge 21:15
cast the youth (A)(B)   Ge 21:15
let me not see death of the c.   Ge 21:16
death of the lad (A)   Ge 21:16
death of the boy (B)   Ge 21:16
the c. is not, whither shall I   Ge 37:30
go
the boy is not here (A)   Ge 37:30
the lad is not (B)(R)   Ge 37:30; 42:22
do not sin against the c.   Ge 42:22
do not sin against the boy   Ge 42:22
(A)
Do not sin against the lad   Ge 42:22
(B)
shall not afflict any   Ex 22:22
fatherless c.
any orphan (B)(R)   Ex 22:22
Jephthah's daughter was   J'g 11:34
only c.
teach us what to do to the c.   J'g 13:8
they brought the c. to Eli   1Sa 1:25
the lad to Eli (B)   1Sa 1:25; 3:8
Eli perceived Lord called the   1Sa 3:8
c.
called the boy (A)(R)   1Sa 3:8
the c. that is born to thee   2Sa 12:14
shall die
the son born to thee (B)   2Sa 12:14
the Lord struck the c.   2Sa 12:15;
   2Sa 12:16, 19
the boy (B)   2Sa 12:15; 12:19
nurse my c. (S)   1Ki 3:21

divide the living c. in two   1Ki 3:25
what shall become of the c.   1Ki 14:3
the lad (B)   1Ki 14:3
soul of the c. came into   1Ki 17:22
him again
told him, the c. is not   2Ki 4:31
awaked
c. sneezed, c. opened his eyes   2Ki 4:35
withhold not correction from   Pr 23:13
c.
he hath neither c. nor brother   Ec 4:8
with second c. that shall   Ec 4:15
stand up in his stead
the youth (A)(B)(E)(R)   Ec 4:15
c. shall behave proudly   Isa 3:5
for before c. shall know to   Isa 7:16
refuse evil
before c. know to cry, my   Isa 8:4
father
weaned c. put hand on   Isa 11:8
cockatrice den
c. shall die an hundred   Isa 65:20
years old
as of her that bringeth forth   Jer 4:31
first c.
is Ephraim my son?   Jer 31:20
pleasant c.
cut off man, woman, and c.   Jer 44:7
father shall deliver c. to   M't 10:21
death
c. was cured from very   M't 17:18
hour
the boy   M't 17:18
(A)(B)(E)(N)(P)(R)
twofold more the c. of hell   M't 23:15
a son of perdition (B)   M't 23:15
a son of hell (E)   M't 23:15
the c. (B)(N)(P)(R)   M'k 5:39; 5:40
he c. is not dead (S)   M'k 5:39;
   M'k 5:41-42, 49
the c. leaped in her womb   Lu 1:41
(P)
on eighth day came to   Lu 1:59
circumcise c.
what manner of c. shall this   Lu 1:66
be
little boy (A)   Lu 1:66; 1:80
thou c. shall be called   Lu 1:76
Prophet of
little one (A)(B)   Lu 1:76
c. grew, waxed strong in   Lu 1:80;
spirit   2:40
when parents brought in c.   Lu 2:27
Jesus
Master, look on my son, my   Lu 9:38
only c.
Jesus healed c. delivered him   Lu 9:42
to father
sir, come down ere my c. die   Joh 4:49
as soon as she is delivered   Joh 16:21
of c.
of a truth against thy holy   Ac 4:27
c. Jesus
signs be done by name of c.   Ac 4:30
Jesus
Saul said, thou c. of the   Ac 13:10
devil
son of the devil   Ac 13:10
(A)(B)(E)(N)(P)(R)
he is a c. (R)   Heb 5:13
to devour her c. as soon as   Re 12:4
born
c. caught up to God and his   Re 12:5
throne

A CHILD

shall I bear a c. who am old   Ge 18:13
a c. of his old age, a little   Ge 44:20
one
saw he was a goodly c.   Ex 2:2;
   Heb 11:23
a c. girded with a linen   1Sa 2:18
ephod
the lad (B)   1Sa 2:18
the boy (R)   1Sa 2:18
delivered of a c. with her in   1Ki 3:17
house
a c. be born to house of   1Ki 13:2
David, Josiah
his flesh shall be fresher   Job 33:25
than a c.
quieted myself as a c. a   Ps 131:2
weaned c.
even a c. is known by his   Pr 20:11
doings
train up a c. in the way he   Pr 22:6
should go
foolishness is bound in the   Pr 22:15
heart of a c.

a c. left to himself bringeth   Pr 29:15
shame
bringeth up his servant from   Pr 29:21
a c.
better a wise c. than a foolish   Ec 4:13
king
woe to thee, when thy king   Ec 10:16
is a c.
to us a c. is born, a son is   Isa 9:6
given
trees be few, a c. may write   Isa 10:19
them
I cannot speak, for I am a c.   Jer 1:6;
   1:7
a man c. is born to thee   Jer 20:15
a son is born (A)(B)(R)   Jer 20:15
when Israel was a c. then I   Ho 11:1
loved
was a youth (A)   Ho 11:1
how long since this came?   M'k 9:21
of a c.
a little boy (A)   M'k 9:21
from early childhood   M'k 9:21
(B)(N)(R)
took a c. set him in midst   M'k 9:36;
   Lu 9:47
when I was a c. I spake as   1Co 13:11
a c. I understood as a c. I
thought as a c.
heir as long as he is a c.   Ga 4:1
differs not
from a. c. known holy   2Ti 3:15
scriptures
from childhood   2Ti 3:15
(A)(N)(P)(R)
from infancy (B)   2Ti 3:15
from a babe (E)   2Ti 3:15
Sarah delivered of a c.   Heb 11:11
when past age
brought forth a man c. who   Re 12:5
was

LITTLE CHILD

am a little c. I know not how   1Ki 3:7
to
a mere lad (A)(B)   1Ki 3:7
fled into Egypt, being a   1Ki 11:17
little c.
a little boy (B)   1Ki 11:17
came again like flesh of a   2Ki 5:14
little c.
and a little c. shall lead them   Isa 11:6
Jesus called a little c. to   M't 18:2
him
who shall receive one such   M't 18:5
little c.
whosoever shall not receive   M'k 10:15;
the kingdom as a little c.   Lu 18:17
shall not enter

NO CHILD

Sarai was barren, she had   Ge 11:30
no c.
but if priest's daughter have   Le 22:13
no c.
if one brother die, and have   De 25:5
no c.
Michal had no c. to day of   2Sa 6:23
death
Gehazi answered, she hath   2Ki 4:14
no c.
they had no c. because   Lu 1:7
Elisabeth
promised when as yet he had   Ac 7:5
no c.

SUCKING CHILD

as nursing father beareth   Nu 11:12
sucking c.
sucking c. shall play on hole   Isa 11:8
of asp
can a woman forget her   Isa 49:15
sucking c.
tongue of sucking c. cleaveth   La 4:4
to roof

THIS CHILD

take this c. and nurse him for   Ex 2:9
me
which was told concerning   Lu 2:17
this c.
this c. set for fall and rising   Lu 2:34
of many
whoso shall receive this c. my   Lu 9:48
name

WITH CHILD

angel said, Hagar, thou art with c. — Ge 16:11
daughters were *with* c. by father — Ge 19:36
conceived by their fathers (A)(B) — Ge 19:36
Tamar is *with* c. by whoredom — Ge 38:24
by the man whose these are am I *with* c. — Ge 38:25
if men strive and hurt woman with c. — Ex 21:22
a pregnant woman (A)(B) — Ex 21:22
daughter, Phinehas' wife, was *with* c. — 1Sa 4:19
was pregnant (B) — 1Sa 4:19
Bath-sheba said, I am *with* c. — 2Sa 11:5
rip up their women *with* c. — 2Ki 8:12; 15:16
their pregnant women (A)(B) — 2Ki 8:12
bones grow in womb of her *with* c. — Ec 11:5
like woman *with* c. draweth near — Isa 26:17
we have been *with* c. we have been — Isa 26:18
sing, that didst not travail *with* c. — Isa 54:1
see whether man doth travail *with* c. — Jer 30:6
bring forth from north woman *with* c. — Jer 31:8
women *with* c. shall be ripped up — Ho 13:16
their pregnant women (A)(R) — Ho 13:16
they ripped up women *with* c. — Am 1:13
she was found *with* c. of Holy Ghost — M't 1:18
found to be pregnant (A)(R) — M't 1:18
virgin shall be *with* c. and bring forth — M't 1:23
shall become pregnant (A) — M't 1:23
conceive and bear a son (B) — M't 1:23
woe to them *with* c. in those days — M't 24:19; M'k 13:17; Lu 21:23
women who are pregnant (A)(P) — M't 24:19
the childbearing (B) — M't 24:19
Mary, being great *with* c. — Lu 2:5
about to become a mother (A) — Lu 2:5
whose pregnancy was advanced (B) — Lu 2:5
she was pregnant (N) — Lu 2:5
in latter stages of her pregnancy (P) — Lu 2:5
as travail upon a woman *with* c. — 1Th 5:3
she being *with* c. cried, travailing — Re 12:2
she was pregnant (A)(B)(N)(P) — Re 12:2

YOUNG CHILD

brought him, and c. was *young* — 1Sa 1:24
go and search diligently for *young* c. — M't 2:8
take *young* c. and mother, and flee — M't 2:13
took *young* c. and mother by night — M't 2:14

CHILDBEARING

multiply pain in c. (A)(R) — Ge 3:16
alas for the c. (B) — M't 24:19
she shall be saved in c. — 1Ti 2:15

CHILDBIRTH

as a woman in c. (A)(B) — Ps 48:6; Jer 6:24; 22:23; 49:24; 50:43; Mic 4:10
never writhed in c. (B) — Isa 54:1
woman in c. has anguish (B)(P) — Joh 16:21
pain of c. (P) — Ga 4:19

CHILDHOOD

walked before you from my c. — 1Sa 12:2

---

for c. and youth are vanity — Ec 11:10
youth and the dawn of life (A)(B)(E)(R) — Ec 11:10
from early c. (B)(N)(R) — M'k 9:21
from c. (A)(N)(P)(R) — 2Ti 3:15

CHILDISH

teacher of the c. (A) — Ro 2:20
when a man, I put away c. things — 1Co 13:11

CHILDLESS

what wilt thou give me, seeing I go c. — Ge 15:2
shall bear their sin, they shall die c. — Le 20:20
as thy sword hath made women c. so shall thy mother be c. — 1Sa 15:33
saith Lord, write you this man c. — Jer 22:30
the second took her to wife, and died c. — Lu 20:30

CHILDREN

in sorrow shalt thou bring forth c. — Ge 3:16
suffering in pregnancy (A) — Ge 3:16
will suffer birth-pangs (B) — Ge 3:16
may be I may obtain c. by her — Ge 16:2
obtain children by her (A) — Ge 16:2
build up a family through her (B) — Ge 16:2
c. struggled together within her — Ge 25:22
Rachel said, Give me c. or I die — Ge 30:1
denied you c. (A) — Ge 30:2
c. God hath given thy servant — Ge 33:5
children (R) — Ge 48:11; Le 18:21; Isa 59:21
father's c. bow down before thee — Ge 49:8
journeyed 600,000 men, besides c. — Ex 12:37
visiting iniquity of fathers upon c. — Ex 20:5; Ex 34:7; Nu 14:18; De 5:9
wife and c. shall be her master's — Ex 21:4
children (A) — Le 18:21; Job 5:25; Isa 59:21
children (R) — Le 21:15; Le 20:2; Ps 25:13; 37:25-26; Jer 22:28; 49:10
children (R) — Nu 5:28; Ru 4:12; 1Sa 2:20; Ps 37:28; 69:36; 102:28; Mk 12:20; Ro 9:29
we saw the c. of Anak there — Nu 13:28
notwithstanding c. of Korah died not — Nu 26:11
given Ar to c. of Lot — De 2:9; 2:19
who can stand before c. of Anak — De 9:2
c. of Belial are gone from you — De 13:13
ye are the c. of Lord your God — De 14:1
born him c. both beloved and hated — De 21:15
c. begotten of them shall enter into — De 23:8
fathers shall not be put to death for c. nor c. for fathers — De 24:16; 2Ch 25:4
their sons, nor sons for c. — De 24:16
children (B) — De 30:19; Isa 59:21
children (B) — De 31:21; 2Ki 17:20; Job 21:8; Isa 57:4
c. in whom there is no faith — De 32:20
of Asher, let Asher be blessed c. — De 33:24
c. of Reuben and Gad return and built there an altar — Jos 22:9; 10:11
take 10,000 men of c. of Naphtali — J'g 4:6
men of Naphtali (A)(B)(R) — J'g 4:6
each one resembled c. of a king — J'g 8:18
the sons of a king (A)(B)(R) — J'g 8:18
put forth a riddle to c. of people — J'g 14:16
now deliver us the men, the c. of Belial — J'g 20:13
the base fellows (A)(E)(R) — J'g 20:13
the perverted fellows (B) — J'g 20:13

---

she that hath many c. is feeble — 1Sa 2:5
children (A) — 1Sa 2:20; Ps 69:36; 102:28; M'k 12:20; Ro 9:8
c. of Belial said, How shall this man — 1Sa 10:27
worthless fellows (A)(E)(R) — 1Sa 10:27
sons of Belial (B) — 1Sa 10:27
c. of wickedness afflict — 2Sa 7:10; 1Ch 17:9
wicked men shall not afflict (A) — 2Sa 7:10
by the unrighteous (B) — 2Sa 7:10
violent men shall not (R) — 2Sa 7:10
came in two men, c. of Belial — 1Ki 21:13
the base fellows (A)(E)(R) — 1Ki 21:13
two scoundrels, rascals (B) — 1Ki 21:13
two she-bears came and tare 42 c. — 2Ki 2:24
Elisha called one of c. of prophets — 2Ki 9:1
to salute c. of king, c. of queen — 2Ki 10:13
c. of murderers slew not — 2Ki 14:6; 2Ch 25:4
as Lord commanded c. of Jacob — 2Ki 17:31
for c. are come to birth — 2Ki 19:3; Isa 37:3
but Seled died without c. — 1Ch 2:30
and Jether died without c. — 1Ch 2:32
Shimei's brethren had not many c. — 1Ch 4:27
ye c. of Jacob his chosen — 1Ch 16:13; Ps 105:6
gathered to Jeroboam c. of Belial — 2Ch 13:7
worthless men, base fellows (A)(E) — 2Ch 13:7
good-for-nothing ne'er-do-wells (B) — 2Ch 13:7
worthless scoundrels (R) — 2Ch 13:7
Lord is not with all c. of Ephraim — 2Ch 25:7
Amaziah smote of c. of Seir 10,000 — 2Ch 25:11
these are c. of province — Ezr 2:1; Ne 7:6
some had wives by whom had c. — Ezr 10:44
c. multipliedst thou as stars — Ne 9:23
intreated for c. sake of my body — Job 19:17
make supplication for the c. (S) — Job 19:17
were c. of fools, c. of base men — Job 30:8
he is king over all the c. of pride — Job 41:34
sons of pride (A)(B)(E)(R) — Job 41:34
out of the mouths of c. (B) — Ps 8:2
are full of c. and leave rest — Ps 17:14
come ye c. I will teach you — Ps 34:11
I am become an alien to mother's c. — Ps 69:8
he shall save the c. of the needy — Ps 72:4
c. which should be born might know — Ps 78:6
and all of you are c. of the most High — Ps 82:6
they have holpen the c. of Lot — Ps 83:8
c. of thy servants shall continue — Ps 102:28
makes barren be joyful mother of c. — Ps 113:9
lo c. are an heritage of the Lord — Ps 127:3
as arrows in hand, so are c. of youth — Ps 127:4
remember, O Lord, the c. of Edom — Ps 137:7
let old men and c. praise the Lord — Ps 148:12
c. of Zion be joyful in their king — Ps 149:2
hear, ye c., instruction — Pr 4:1; Pr 5:7; 7:24; 8:32
my sons (A)(B)(E)(R) — Pr 4:1
the glory of c. are their fathers — Pr 17:6
c. arise up and call her blessed — Pr 31:28
if a man beget 100 c. and live years — Ec 6:3
my mother's c. were angry with me — Ca 1:6

have brought up *c.* and they *Isa 1:2*
rebelled
sons (A)(B) *Isa 1:2; 1:4*
ah sinful nations, *c.* that are *Isa 1:4*
corrupters
please themselves in *c.* of *Isa 2:6*
strangers
I will give *c.* to be their *Isa 3:4*
princes
as for my people, *c.* are their *Isa 3:12*
oppressors
and *c.* whom Lord given me *Isa 8:18;*
Heb 2:13
have no pity, their eye not *Isa 13:18*
spare *c.*
mighty men of *c.* of Kedar *Isa 21:17*
be
saying, I travail not, nor *Isa 23:4*
bring forth *c.*
woe to rebellious *c.* saith *Isa 30:1*
Lord
lying *c., c.* that will not hear *Isa 30:9*
the law
father to *c.* make known *Isa 38:19*
truth
neither shall I know the loss *Isa 47:8*
of *c.*
come in one day loss of *c.* *Isa 47:9*
c. which thou shalt have, *Isa 49:20*
shall say
sing, O barren, for more are *Isa 54:1;*
c. of desolate than *c.* of married *Ga 4:27*
are ye not *c.* of transgression *Isa 57:4*
c. of sin, disloyal brood *Isa 57:4*
(B)(R)
slaying *c.* in valleys under *Isa 57:5*
clifts
my people, *c.* that will not *Isa 63:8*
lie
soon as Zion travailed, *Isa 66:8*
brought forth *c.*
turn, O backsliding *c.* *Jer 3:14; 3:22*
how shall I put thee among *Jer 3:19*
c.
people is foolish, they are *Jer 4:22*
sottish *c.*
I will pour it out upon the *Jer 6:11*
c. abroad
c. gather wood, fathers kindle *Jer 7:18*
fire
death entered to cut off *c.* *Jer 9:21*
from without
I will fan them, I will *Jer 15:7*
bereave them of *c.*
Rachel weeping for her *c.* *Jer 31:15;*
M't 2:18
shall women eat *c.* of span *La 2:20*
long
men to grind, *c.* fell under *La 5:13*
wood
they are impudent *c.* and *Eze 2:4*
stiff-hearted
c. rebelled against me, they *Eze 20:21*
walked
c. are talking against thee *Eze 33:30*
by walls
to strangers that shall beget *Eze 47:22*
c. among you
c. in whom was no blemish *Da 1:4*
countenances fairer, fatter than *Da 1:15*
all *c.*
these four *c.* God gave *Da 1:17*
knowledge
Michael stand for *c.* of thy *Da 12:1*
people
take unto thee *c.* of *Ho 1:2*
whoredoms
not have mercy on her *c.* for *Ho 2:4*
they be *c.*
battle against *c.* of iniquity *Ho 10:9*
did not
mother dashed in pieces upon *Ho 10:14*
her *c.*
the *c.* shall tremble from the *Ho 11:10*
west
stay in place of breaking *Ho 13:13*
forth of *c.*
gather *c.* and those that suck *Joe 2:16*
the breasts
be glad then ye *c.* of Zion, *Joe 2:23*
and rejoice
ye not as *c.* of Ethiopians to *Am 9:7*
me
make bald, and poll thee for *Mic 1:16*
delicate *c.*
punish the princes and king's *Zep 1:8*
c.
turn heart of fathers to *c.* and *Mal 4:6;*
heart of *c.* to fathers *Lu 1:17*

Herod slew all *c.* in *M't 2:16*
Bethlehem
able of stones to raise up *c.* *M't 3:9;*
Lu 3:8
that ye may be the *c.* of *M't 5:45*
your Father
c. of kingdom shall be cast *M't 8:12*
out
can *c.* of bride chamber *M't 9:15;*
mourn while bridegroom *M'k 2:19;*
with them *Lu 5:34*
wedding guests *M't 9:15*
(A)(B)(P)(R)
sons of the bridechamber *M't 9:15*
(E)
the bridegroom's friends (N) *M't 9:15*
c. rise against parents *M't 10:21;*
M'k 13:12
Wisdom is justified of her *M't 11:19;*
c. *Lu 7:35*
wisdom justified by deeds *M't 11:19*
(A)(R)
wisdom justified by her *M't 11:19*
effects (B)
wisdom is justified by her *M't 11:19*
works (E)
wisdom is proved by results *M't 11:19*
(N)
wisdom stands or falls by *M't 11:19*
her actions (P)
showing to mere *c.* (P) *M't 11:25*
good seed are *c.* of *M't 13:38*
kingdom, but tares are *c.*
of wicked one
sons of the kingdom *M't 13:38*
(E)(P)(R)
c. free
Jesus saith to him, Then are *M't 17:26*
c. free
forsaken wife or *c.* *M't 19:29;*
M'k 10:29
then came the mother of *M't 20:20*
Zebedee's *c.*
priests and scribes saw *c.* *M't 21:15*
crying
c. of them that killed *M't 23:31*
prophets
descendants of those who *M't 23:31*
murdered (A)
sons of the prophets' *M't 23:31*
murderers (B)
sons of those who murdered *M't 23:31*
(E)(N)(P)(R)
Jesus said, Let *c.* first be *M'k 7:27*
filled
receive such *c.* in my name *M'k 9:37;*
9:41
ye shall be *c.* of Highest *Lu 6:35*
sons of the highest *Lu 6:35*
(A)(B)(E)(N)(R)
c. of this world wiser than *c.* *Lu 16:8*
of light
sons of this age, world *Lu 16:8*
(A)(B)(E)(R)
first took wife and died *Lu 20:29*
without *c.*
c. of this world marry, and *Lu 20:34*
are given
people of this world (A)(P) *Lu 20:34*
sons of this world (B)(E) *Lu 20:34*
men and women of this *Lu 20:34*
world (N)
sons of this age (R) *Lu 20:34*
the *c.* of God (S) *Joh 1:12;*
Ph'p 2:15; 1Jo 3:1-2
if ye were Abraham's *c.* *Joh 8:39*
would do
Jesus saith, C. have ye any *Joh 21:5*
meat
c. of prophets and covenant *Ac 3:25*
descendants of the prophets *Ac 3:25*
(A)
heirs of the prophets (B)(N) *Ac 3:25*
sons of the prophets *Ac 3:25*
(E)(P)(R)
teacher of *c.* (R) *Ro 2:20*
if *c.* then heirs, heirs of God *Ro 8:17*
because seed of Abraham are *Ro 9:7*
they all *c.*
c. not yet born, nor done *Ro 9:11*
good or evil
not *c.* in understanding, in *1Co 14:20*
malice *c.*
for *c.* ought not to lay up *2Co 12:14*
for parents, but parenst for *c.*
of faith, same are *c.* of *Ga 3:7*
Abraham
when we were *c.* were in *Ga 4:3*
bondage
bearing *c.* for (S) *Ga 4:24*

Jerusalem, which is in bondage *Ga 4:25*
with *c.*
not *c.* of bondwoman, but of *Ga 4:31*
free
predestinated us to adoption *Eph 1:5*
of *c.*
spirit worketh in *c.* of *Eph 2:2*
disobedience
by nature *c.* of wrath, even *Eph 2:3*
as others
henceforth no more *c.* tossed *Eph 4:14*
to and fro
be ye followers of God as *Eph 5:1*
dear *c.*
wrath on *c.* of disobedience *Eph 5:6;*
Col 3:6
c. obey parents in Lord *Eph 6:1;*
Col 3:20
if any widow have *c.* or *1Ti 5:4*
nephews
if she brought up *c.,* if she *1Ti 5:10*
lodged
that younger women marry, *1Ti 5:14*
bear *c.*
as *c.* partakers of flesh and *Heb 2:14*
blood
exhortation speaketh to you *Heb 12:5*
as to *c.*
as obedient *c.* not fashioning *1Pe 1:14*
eyes full of adultery, cursed *c. 2Pe 2:14*
c. of God manifest, and *c.* *1Jo 3:10*
of devil
elder to elect lady and *c.* *2Jo 1*
c. of thy elect sister greet thee *2Jo 13*
I will kill her *c.* with death *Re 2:23*

CHILDREN *OF BENJAMIN*

of *c.* of *Benjamin* by genealogy *Nu 1:36*
35,400
c. of *Benjamin* did not drive *J'g 1:21*
out Jebusites
c. of *Benjamin* would not *J'g 20:13*
hearken
c. of *Benjamin* gathered *2Sa 2:25*
together
dwelt of *c.* of *Benjamin* *1Ch 9:3;*
Ne 11:4
there came of *c.* of *Benjamin* *1Ch 12:16*
to the hold
c. of *Benjamin* gather yourselves *Jer 6:1*
to flee

CHILDREN *OF GOD*

peacemakers called the *c.* of *M't 5:9*
God
sons of God *M't 5:9*
(A)(B)(E)(N)(P)(R)
are *c.* of *God* being children *Lu 20:36*
of resurrection
should gather together *c.* of *Joh 11:52*
God
beareth witness we are *c.* of *Ro 8:16*
God
delivered into glorious liberty *Ro 8:21*
of *c.* of *God*
children of flesh, these are not *Ro 9:8*
c. of *God*
shall be called *c.* of living *Ro 9:26*
God
sons of living God *Ro 9:26*
(A)(B)(E)(N)(P)(R)
are all *c.* of *God* by faith in *Ga 3:26*
Christ
c. of *God* manifest, and *1Jo 3:10*
children of devil
by this we know that we love *1Jo 5:2*
the *c.* of *God*

CHILDREN *OF ISRAEL*

Joseph took an oath of *c.* of *Ge 50:25*
Israel
c. of *Israel* fruitful and *Ex 1:7*
increased
grieved because of *c.* of *Israel Ex 1:12*
c. of *Israel* sighed *Ex 2:23*
God looked on *c.* of *Israel* *Ex 2:25*
they heard Lord visited *c.* of *Ex 4:31*
Israel
also heard groaning of *c.* of *Ex 6:5*
Israel
bring *c.* of *Israel* out of *Ex 6:13;*
Egypt *Ex 6:26-27; 12:51*
nothing die of all *c.* of *Israel* *Ex 9:4*
c. of *Israel* journeyed *Ex 12:37*
about 600,000
their I will meet with *c.* of *Ex 29:43*
Israel

sign between me and *c. of*   *Ex 31:17*
Israel
whosoever he be, *c. of Israel*   *Le 17:13*
for to me the *c. of Israel* are   *Le 25:55*
servants
glory appeared before *c. of*   *Nu 14:10*
Israel
c. of Israel could not stand   *Jos 7:12*
before
numbered *c. of Israel* 300,000 *1Sa 11:8*
Gibeonites were not of *c. of*   *2Sa 21:2*
Israel
placed them instead of *c. of*   *2Ki 17:24*
Israel
that day had not *c. of Israel*   *Ne 8:17*
done
made known his acts to *c.*   *Ps 103:7*
of Israel
even of *c. of Israel* a   *Ps 148:14*
people near
be gathered one by one, *c.*   *Isa 27:12*
of Israel
when *c. of Israel* went astray *Eze 44:15;*
  48:11
is it not even thus, O ye *c.*   *Am 2:11*
of Israel
this liketh you, *c. of Israel* saith *Am 4:5*
Lord
many of *c. of Israel* shall   *Lu 1:16*
turn to Lord
to visit his brethren the *c. of*   *Ac 7:23*
Israel
this is that Moses which said *Ac 7:37*
to *c. of Israel*
chosen to bear my name   *Ac 9:15*
before *c. of Israel*
word God sent to *c. of Israel*   *Ac 10:36*
preaching
number of *c. of Israel* be as   *Ro 9:27*
sand
c. of Israel could not behold *2Co 3:7*
face
mention of departing of *c.*   *Heb 11:22*
of Israel
cast a stumbling block before *Re 2:14*
c. of Israel
sealed 144,000 of all tribes of   *Re 7:4*
c. of Israel
names of twelve tribes of *c.*   *Re 21:12*
of Israel

CHILDREN *OF JUDAH*

c. of Judah by their   *Nu 1:26*
generations
c. of Judah came to Joshua   *Jos 14:6*
bade teach *c. of Judah*   *2Sa 1:18*
use of bow
c. of Judah prevailed,   *2Ch 13:18*
because relied
10,000 did *c. of Judah* carry *2Ch 25:12*
captive
purpose to keep under *c. of* *2Ch 28:10*
Judah
because of all evil of *c. of*   *Jer 32:32*
Judah
they and *c. of Judah* going   *Jer 50:4*
weeping
Israel and *c. of Judah*   *Jer 50:33*
oppressed together
for violence against *c. of*   *Joe 3:19*
Judah

CHILDREN *OF LIGHT*

children of world wiser than   *Lu 16:8*
c. of light
sons of light (A)(B)(E)(R)   *Lu 16:8*
believe, that ye may be *c.*   *Joh 12:36*
of light
sons of light   *Joh 12:36*
(A)(B)(E)(P)(R)
men of light (N)   *Joh 12:36*
now light in Lord, walk as *c.*   *Eph 5:8*
of light
as Christians you are light   *Eph 5:8*
(N)
are all *c. of light,* children of   *1Th 5:5*
day
sons of light   *1Th 5:5*
(A)(B)(E)(P)(R)

CHILDREN *OF MEN*

to see tower *c. of men* built   *Ge 11:5*
if they be *c. of men,* cursed   *1Sa 26:19*
chastise with stripes of *c. of* *2Sa 7:14*
men
knowest hearts of *c. of men* *1Ki 8:39;*

  2Ch 6:30
his eyelids try *c. of men*   *Ps 11:4*
for faithful fail among *c. of*   *Ps 12:1*
men
looked from heaven upon *c.*   *Ps 14:2;*
of men   *53:2*
c. of men put trust under   *Ps 36:7*
shadow
fairer than *c. of men* grace   *Ps 45:2*
is poured
wonderful works to *c. of*   *Ps 107:8,*
men   *107:15, 21, 31*
earth hath he given to *c. of*   *Ps 115:16*
men
much more hearts of *c. of*   *Pr 15:11*
men
doth not afflict, nor grieve *c.*   *La 3:33*
of men
wherever *c. of men* dwell   *Da 2:38*
hath

CHILDREN *OF PROMISE*

c. of promise are counted   *Ro 9:8*
for seed
we, brethren, as Isaac was,   *Ga 4:28*
are *c. of promise*

CHILDREN'S CHILDREN

be near, thou and thy   *Ge 45:10*
children's c.
iniquity of fathers on *children's Ex 34:7*
c.
when thou shalt beget   *De 4:25*
children and *children's c.*
served images their   *2Ki 17:41*
children and *children's c.*
his righteousness unto   *Ps 103:17*
children's c.
see *children's c.* and peace on *Ps 128:6*
Israel
leaveth inheritance to his   *Pr 13:22*
children's c.
children's c. are crown of old *Pr 17:6*
men, glory of
with you *children's c.* will   *Jer 2:9*
I plead
dwell, and their *children's c. Eze 37:25*
for ever

FATHERLESS CHILDREN

nor let there be any to   *Ps 109:12*
favour *fatherless c.*
leave *fatherless c.* I will   *Jer 49:11*
preserve them

HIS CHILDREN

Abraham will command *his Ge 18:19*
c.
Israel loved Joseph more than *Ge 37:3*
all *his c.*
prolong days, he and *his c.*   *De 17:20*
their spot is not the spot of *De 32:5*
his c.
neither acknowledge, nor   *De 33:9*
knew *his c.*
every man his wife and *his 1Sa 30:22*
c.
little ewe lamb grew up with *2Sa 12:3*
his c.
give him always light, and to *2Ki 8:19*
his c.
burnt *his c.* in fire after   *2Ch 28:3*
heathen
he caused *his c.* to pass   *2Ch 33:6*
thro' the fire
his c. are far from safety   *Job 5:4*
even the eyes of *his c.* shall *Job 17:5*
fail
his c. shall seek to please   *Job 20:10*
the poor
God layeth up his iniquity   *Job 21:19*
for *his c.*
if *his c.* be multiplied, it is *Job 27:14*
for sword
if *his c.* forsake my law, and *Ps 89:30*
walk
like as father pitieth *his c.*   *Ps 103:13*
so Lord
let *his c.* be fatherless, wife   *Ps 109:9*
a widow
let *his c.* be vagabonds, and *Ps 109:10*
beg bread
his c. shall have place of   *Pr 14:26*
refuge
just man, *his c.* blessed after *Pr 20:7*
him

prepare slaughter for *his c.*   *Isa 14:21*
when he seeth *his c.* in   *Isa 29:23*
midst of
Ephraim shall bring forth his *Ho 9:13*
c.
his c. and cattle drank   *Joh 4:12*
thereof
charged you as father *his c.* *1Th 2:11*
his c. in subjection with   *1Ti 3:4*
gravity

LITTLE CHILDREN

little *c.* stood in door of   *Nu 16:27*
tents
their little ones (B)(E)(R)   *Nu 16:27*
came forth *little c.* and   *2Ki 2:23*
mocked
some youths (B)   *2Ki 2:23*
young lads (E)   *2Ki 2:23*
small boys (R)   *2Ki 2:23*
in one day to destroy *little c.* *Es 3:13*
slay utterly maids, *little c.*   *Eze 9:6*
except converted, become as *M't 18:3*
little c.
there brought to him *little c.* *M't 19:13*
suffer *little c.* to come   *M't 19:14;*
  M'k 10:14; Lu 18:16
little c. a little while I am *Joh 13:33*
with
my *little c.* of whom I travail *Ga 4:19*
in birth
little c. I write to you   *1Jo 2:1, 12, 13*
are of God, *little c.* overcome *1Jo 4:4*
world
little c. keep yourselves from *1Jo 5:21*
idols

MEN CHILDREN

midwives saved *men c.* alive   *Ex 1:17;*
  1:18
male babies (B)   *Ex 1:17*
all *men c.* shall appear   *Ex 34:23*
before Lord
your males shall appear   *Ex 34:23*
(B)(E)(R)

MEN, WOMEN, CHILDREN

Bashan we destroyed *men*   *De 3:6*
women, and *c.*
gather *men, women,* and *c.* to *De 31:12*
hear
smote Nob *men, women* and *1Sa 22:19*
c.
great congregation of *men,*   *Ezr 10:1*
women, and *c.*
committed to Gedaliah *men,*   *Jer 40:7*
women, and *c.*
they that had eaten were   *M't 14:21;*
about 5000 *men,* beside   *15:38*
women and *c.*

MY CHILDREN

give me my wives and *my c. Ge 30:26*
for whom
these *c.* are *my c.* these   *Ge 31:43*
cattle my cattle
Jacob said, ye have bereaved *Ge 42:36*
of *my c.*
if I be bereaved of *my c.* I   *Ge 43:14*
am bereaved
firstborn of *my c.* I redeem   *Ex 13:15*
I love my master, wife. and   *Ex 21:5*
my c.
he sent to me for my wives *1Ki 20:7*
and *my c.*
that I were as when *my c.*   *Job 29:5*
were
seeing I have lost *my c.*   *Isa 49:21*
my c. are gone forth of me *Jer 10:20*
my c. are desolate   *La 1:16*
that thou hast slain *my c.*   *Eze 16:21*
bed
trouble not, *my c.* with me in *Lu 11:7*
bed
speak as to *my c.* be   *2Co 6:13*
enlarged
joy to hear that *my c.* walk in   *3Jo 4*
truth

NO CHILDREN

Sarai Abram's wife bare him *Ge 16:1*
no c.
when Rachel saw she bare   *Ge 30:1*
Jacob *no c.*
Nadab and Abihu died, had   *Nu 3:4*
no c.

Peninnah had, but Hannah   *1Sa 1:2*
had *no c.*
if man die having *no c.*   *M't 22:24;*
     M'k 12:19
seven took her, and left *no*   *Lu 20:31*
c.

OUR CHILDREN

all the riches are ours and   *Ge 31:16*
our c.
to kill us, and *our c.* and   *Ex 17:3*
cattle
our wives and *our c.* be a   *Nu 14:3*
prey
belong to us and *our c.* for   *De 29:29*
ever
your *c.* speak to *our.*   *Jos 22:24*
saying
your *c.* make *our c.* cease   *Jos 22:25*
fearing Lord
as flesh of brethren, *our c.* as   *Ne 5:5*
their *c.*
his blood be on us and *our*   *M't 27:25*
c.

STRANGE CHILDREN

deliver me from *strange c.*   *Ps 144:7;*
     144:11
for they have begotten *strange*   *Ho 5:7*
c.

THEIR CHILDREN

what can I do to daughters or   *Ge 31:43*
their *c.*
that they may teach *their c.*   *De 4:10*
that it might be well with   *De 5:29*
their *c.*
that *their c.* learn to fear   *De 31:13*
Lord
their c. them Joshua   *Jos 5:7*
circumcised
of *their* c. did Solomon levy   *1Ki 9:21*
tribute
wilt dash *their c.* and rip   *2Ki 8:12*
women
burnt *their c.* in fire to gods   *2Ki 17:31*
their c. served images as   *2Ki 17:41*
did their fathers
before Lord with wives and   *2Ch 20:13*
their c.
slew not *their c.* but did as   *2Ch 25:4*
written
their c. thou multipliedst as   *Ne 9:23*
stars
their c. spake half in speech   *Ne 13:24*
of Ashdod
send little ones, *their c.*   *Job 21:11*
dance
wilderness yieldeth food for   *Job 24:5*
their c.
we will not hide them from   *Ps 78:4*
their c.
should arise and declare them   *Ps 78:6*
to *their c.*
let thy glory appear to *their*   *Ps 90:16*
c.
their c. sit on thy throne   *Ps 132:12*
for ever
their c. shall be dashed to   *Isa 13:16*
pieces
whilst *their c.* remember their   *Jer 17:2*
altars
therefore deliver up *their c.*   *Jer 18:21*
to famine
their c. also shall be as   *Jer 30:20*
aforetime
iniquity of fathers into   *Jer 32:18*
bosom of *their c.*
for good of them and *their*   *Jer 32:39*
c. after them
fathers not look back to *their*   *Jer 47:3*
c.
hands of women sodden *their*   *La 4:10*
c.
I said to *their c.* in   *Eze 20:18*
wilderness
they had slain *their c.* to   *Eze 23:39*
idols
they and *their c.* shall dwell   *Eze 37:25*
therein
cast them and *their c.* into   *Da 6:24*
den of lions
tho' bring up *their c.* I will   *Ho 9:12*
let *c.* tell *their c.* and *their c.*   *Joe 1:3*
another
their c. have ye taken away   *Mic 2:9*
my glory

yea, *their c.* shall see it and   *Zec 10:7*
be glad
shall live with *their c.* and   *Zec 10:9*
turn again
God fulfilled same to us   *Ac 13:33*
their *c.*
deacons rule *their c.* and   *1Ti 3:12*
houses
young women love husbands   *Tit 2:4*
and *their c.*

THY CHILDREN

firstborn among *thy c.*   *Ex 13:13*
redeem
go well with *thy c.*   *De 4:40; 12:25, 28*
teach them diligently to *thy c.*   *De 6:7*
thou and *thy c.* obey with all   *De 30:2*
heart
land be thine and *thy c.* for   *Jos 14:9*
ever
Samuel said, are here all   *1Sa 16:11*
thy c.
if *thy c.* take heed to their   *1Ki 2:4*
way to walk
so that *thy c.* take heed   *1Ki 8:25;*
     2Ch 6:16
thy wives also and *thy c.* are   *1Ki 20:3*
mine
live thou and *thy c.* of the   *2Ki 4:7*
rest
thy c. of fourth generation   *2Ki 10:30*
sit on throne
Lord will smite *thy* people   *2Ch 21:14*
and *c.*
if *thy c.* have sinned against   *Job 8:4*
him
instead of fathers be *thy c.*   *Ps 45:16*
offend against generation of   *Ps 73:15*
thy c.
thy c. like olive plants round   *Ps 128:3*
table
if *thy c.* will keep my   *Ps 132:12*
covenant
he hath blessed *thy c.*   *Ps 147:13*
within thee
thy c. shall make haste   *Isa 49:17*
I will contend, and I will   *Isa 49:25*
save *thy c.*
all *thy* c. be taught of Lord,   *Isa 54:13*
and great shall be peace of *thy c.*
thy c. have forsaken me   *Jer 5:7*
hope that *thy c.* come again   *Jer 31:17*
bring out *thy c.* to   *Jer 38:23*
Chaldeans
by blood of *thy c.* didst   *Eze 16:36*
give
forgotten law, I will forget   *Ho 4:6*
thy c.
how often gathered *thy c.*   *M't 23:37;*
as hen gathereth her chickens *Lu 13:34*
they shall lay *thy c.* within *Lu 19:44*
thee
I found *thy c.* walking in truth   *2Jo 4*

YOUNG CHILDREN

young c. despised he, they   *Job 19:18*
spake
young c. ask bread, no man   *La 4:4*
breaketh
her *young c.* were dashed in   *Na 3:10*
pieces
brought *young* c. to him to   *M'k 10:13*
touch them
so that they cast out their   *Ac 7:19*
young c.

YOUR CHILDREN

when *your c.* shall say unto   *Ex 12:26*
you
wives, widows, *your c.*   *Ex 22:24*
fatherless
take as inheritance for *your*   *Le 25:46*
c.
wild beasts shall rob you of   *Le 26:22*
your c.
your c. wander in wilderness   *Nu 14:33*
your c. shall go in and   *De 1:39*
possess
not with *your c.* who have   *De 11:2*
not known
my words, ye shall teach   *De 11:19*
your c.
that days of *your c.* be   *De 11:21*
multiplied
generation to come of *your*   *De 29:22*
c. say

shall command *your c.* to   *De 32:46*
observe
when *your c.* ask their fathers   *Jos 4:6;*
     Jos 4:21
then ye shall let *your c.*   *Jos 4:22*
know
if *your c.* turn from following   *1Ki 9:6*
me
for an inherit, to *your c.*   *1Ch 28:8;*
     Ezr 9:12
your c. find compassion   *2Ch 30:9*
before
Lord increase you and *your*   *Ps 115:14*
c.
in vain have I smitten *your c.*   *Jer 2:30*
give good gifts to *your c.*   *M't 7:11;*
     Lu 11:13
by whom do *your c.* cast   *M't 12:27*
them out
but weep for yourselves and   *Lu 23:28*
your c.
the promise is to you and   *Ac 2:39*
your c.
else *your c.* unclean, but   *1Co 7:14*
now holy
provoke not *your c.* to wrath   *Eph 6:4;*
     Col 3:21

CHILDREN'S

father, that is ours, and our   *Ge 31:16*
c.
thy c. children, and thy   *Ge 45:10*
flocks
die of all that is the *c.* of   *Ex 9:4*
Israel
the *c.* children, unto the third   *Ex 34:7*
inheritance, and thy *c.* for   *Jos 14:9*
ever
children, and their *c.*   *2Ki 17:41*
children
I entreated for the *c.* sake   *Job 19:17*
of
righteousness unto *c.*   *Ps 103:17*
children
see thy *c.* children, and   *Ps 128:6*
peace
leaveth an inheritance to his *c.* *Pr 13:22*
C. children are the crown of   *Pr 17:6*
old men
and with your *c.* children will   *Jer 2:9*
and the *c.* teeth are set on   *Jer 31:29*
edge
the *c.* teeth are set on edge   *Eze 18:2*
their *c.* children for ever: *Eze 37:25*
and my
It is not meet to take the *c.*   *M't 15:26*
bread
it is not meet to take the *c.*   *M'k 7:27*
bread
the table eat of the *c.*   *M'k 7:28*
crumbs

CHILD'S

went and called the *c.* mother   *Ex 2:8*
let this *c.* soul come into   *1Ki 17:21*
him again
flesh shall be fresher than a   *Job 33:25*
c.
which sought the young *c.*   *M't 2:20*
life

CHILEAB

And his second, *C.,* of Abigail   *2Sa 3:3*

CHILION

of his two sons Mahlon and   *Ru 1:2*
And Mahlon and *C.* died also   *Ru 1:5*

CHILION'S

Elimelech's, and all that was   *Ru 4:9*
C.

CHILMAD

of Sheba, Asshur, and *C.*   *Eze 27:23*

CHIMHAM

But behold thy servant *C.;*   *2Sa 19:37*
let
the king answered, *C.* shall   *2Sa 19:38*
go
and *C.* went on with him: *2Sa 19:40*
and all
and dwelt in the habitation   *Jer 41:17*
of *C.*

CHIMNEY

and as the smoke out of the c.	Ho 13:3

CHINNERETH

the side of the sea of C. eastward	Nu 34:11
C. even unto the sea of the plain	De 3:17
even unto the edge of the sea of C.	Jos 13:27
and Hammath, Rakkath, and C.	Jos 19:35

CHINNEROTH

and the plains south of C.	Jos 11:2
from the plain to the sea of C.	Jos 12:3

CHIOS

the next day over against C.	Ac 20:15

CHIP

as a c. on waters (B)(R)	Ho 10:7

CHIRP

who c. and mutter (A)(B)(E)(R)	Isa 8:19
like a twittering swallow I c. (B)	Isa 38:14

CHIRPED

opened mouth and c. (A)(B)(E)(R)	Isa 10:14

CHISELS

shapes it with c. (B)	Isa 44:13

CHISLEU

month C. in the twentieth year	Ne 1:1
of the ninth month, even in C.	Zec 7:1

CHISLON

Benjamin, Elidad the son of C.	Nu 34:21

CHISLOTH-TABOR

sunrising unto the border of C.	Jos 19:12

CHITTIM

shall come from the coast of C.	Nu 24:24
from the land of C. it is revealed	Isa 23:1
pass over to C.; there also shalt	Isa 23:12
For pass over the isles of C.	Jer 2:10
brought out of the isles of C.	Eze 27:6
ships of C. shall come against him	Da 11:30

CHIUN

tabernacle of your Moloch and C.	Am 5:26

CHLOE

which are of the house of C.	1Co 1:11

CHODE

was wroth, and c. with Laban	Ge 31:36
Jacob reprimanded Laban (B)	Ge 31:36
upbraided Laban (R)	Ge 31:36
And the people c. with Moses	Nu 20:3
arguing with Moses (B)	Nu 20:3
people strove with Moses (E)	Nu 20:3
people contended with Moses (R)	Nu 20:3

CHOICE

c. of our sepulchres bury thy dead	Ge 23:6
all sorts of c. gifts (R)	Ge 24:10
his ass's colt unto the c. vine	Ge 49:11
your c. vows which ye vow unto	De 12:11
a c. young man, and a goodly	1Sa 9:2
chose of all the c. men of Israel	2Sa 10:9
fenced city, and every c. city	2Ki 3:19
and the c. fir trees thereof	2Ki 19:23
c. and mighty men of valour	1Ch 7:40
all the c. of Israel, and put them	1Ch 19:10
three hundred thousand c. men	2Ch 25:5
one ox and six c. sheep; also	Ne 5:18
knowledge rather than c. gold	Pr 8:10
and my revenue than c. silver	Pr 8:19
tongue of the just is as c. silver	Pr 10:20
is the c. one of her that bare her	Ca 6:9
the c. fir trees thereof: and I will	Isa 37:24
shall cut down thy c. cedars	Jer 22:7
like a c. vessel (A)(B)	Jer 25:34
like c. rams (R)	Jer 25:34
shoulder, fill it with the c. bones	Eze 24:4
Take the c. of the flock, and burn	Eze 24:5
Eden, the c. and best of Lebanon	Eze 31:16
God made c. among us, that	Ac 15:7
God's c. (B)	Ro 9:11; 11:5; 1Th 1:4
agreement with his gracious c. (B)	Ro 11:5
make sinfulness their c. (N)	2Th 2:12

CHOICEST

the c. raiment (S)	Ge 27:15
the c. spices (B)	Ex 30:23
the c. young men (S)	1Sa 8:16
planted it with the c. vine	Isa 5:2
c. valleys shall be full of chariots	Isa 22:7
anoint with c. ointments (B)	Am 6:6
the c. graces (S)	1Co 12:31

CHOKE

deceitfulness of riches, c entering in, c. the word, and it	M't 13:22 M'k 4:19

CHOKED

thorns sprung up, and c. them	M't 13:7
c. it, and it yielded no fruit	M'k 4:7
and were c. in the sea	M'k 5:13
sprang up with it, and c. it	Lu 8:7
and are c. with cares and riches	Lu 8:14
place into the lake, and were c.	Lu 8:33

CHOLER

was moved with c. against him	Da 8:7
moved with anger (A)(E)	Da 8:7
In brutal rage he butted him (B)	Da 8:7
was enraged against him (R)	Da 8:7
the south shall be moved with c.	Da 11:11
moved with anger (A)(E)(R)	Da 11:11
enraged, shall march forth (B)	Da 11:11

CHOOSE

C. us out men, and go out	Ex 17:9
the man whom the Lord doth c.	Nu 16:7
the man's rod, whom I shall c.	Nu 17:5
nor c. you, because ye were more	De 7:7
the Lord your God shall c.	De 12:5; 12:11, 14, 18, 26; 14:23, 25; 15:20; 16:2, 6-7, 15-16; 17:8, 10, 15; 18:6
that place which he shall c. in one	De 23:16
God shall c. to place his name	De 26:2

therefore c. life, that both	De 30:19
in the place which he shall c.	De 31:11
in the place which he should c.	Jos 9:27
c. you this day whom ye will serve	Jos 24:15
did I c. him out of all the tribes	1Sa 2:28
c. you a man for you, and let	1Sa 17:8
and all the men of Israel, c.	2Sa 16:18
Let me now c. out twelve thousand	2Sa 17:1
of Saul, whom the Lord did c.	2Sa 21:6
c. thee one of them, that I may do	2Sa 24:12
which the Lord did c. out of all	1Ki 14:21
and let them c. one bullock for	1Ki 18:23; 1Ki 18:25
c. thee one of them, that I may	1Ch 21:10
Thus saith the Lord, C. thee	1Ch 21:11
the God, who didst c. Abram	Ne 9:7
and c. out my words to reason	Job 9:14
Let us c. to us judgment: let us	Job 34:4
thou refuse, or whether thou c.	Job 34:33
teach in the way that he shall c.	Ps 25:12
He shall c. our inheritance for us	Ps 47:4
did not c. the fear of the Lord	Pr 1:29
oppressor, and c. none of his ways	Pr 3:31
refuse the evil, and c. the good	Isa 7:15; 7:16
and will yet c. Israel, and set them	Isa 14:1
of Israel, and he shall c. thee	Isa 49:7
and c. the things that pleases me	Isa 56:4
c. that wherein I delighted not	Isa 65:12
I also will c. their delusions	Isa 66:4
c. thou a place, c. it at the head	Eze 21:19
c. one head (B)	Ho 1:11
Zion, and shall yet c. Jerusalem	Zec 1:17
and shall c. Jerusalem again	Zec 2:12
c. men from (N)(P)(R)	Ac 15:22
yet what I shall c. I wot not	Ph'p 1:22
not c. to condemn us (P)	1Th 5:9

CHOOSES

what course helmsman c. (N)	Jas 3:4

CHOOSEST

thou c. the tongue of the crafty	Job 15:5
Blessed is the man whom thou c.	Ps 65:4

CHOOSETH

so that my soul c. strangling	Job 7:15
he hath no oblation c. a tree that	Isa 40:20
an abomination is he that c. you	Isa 41:24

CHOOSING

by a man of his c. (N)	Ac 17:31
C. rather to suffer affliction with	Heb 11:25

CHOP

their bones, and c. them in pieces	Mic 3:3

CHOPPED

c. down the Asherahs (B)	2Ch 14:3

CHOR-ASHAN

and to them which were in C.	1Sa 30:30

CHORAZIM

Woe unto thee, C.! woe unto   *M't* 11:21
Woe unto thee, C.! woe unto   *Lu* 10:13

CHOSE

them wives of all which they   *Ge* 6:2 c.
Lot c. him all the plain of   *Ge* 13:11 Jordan
Moses c. able men out of all   *Ex* 18:25 Israel
therefore he c. their seed   *De* 4:37 after them
and he c. their seed after   *De* 10:15 them
Joshua c. out thirty thousand   *Jos* 8:3
They c. new gods; then was   *J'g* 5:8 war in
Saul c. him three thousand   *1Sa* 13:2 men
and c. him five smooth   *1Sa* 17:40 stones out
which c. me before thy   *2Sa* 6:21 father
c. me in preference   *2Sa* 6:21 (B)(E)(R)
behind, he c. of all the   *2Sa* 10:9 choice men
I c. no city out of all the   *1Ki* 8:16 tribes of
but I c. David to be over   *1Ki* 8:16 my people
David my servant's sake   *1Ki* 11:34 whom I c.
c. out of all the choice of   *1Ch* 19:10 Israel
the Lord God of Israel c. me   *1Ch* 28:4 before
I c. no city among all the   *2Ch* 6:5 tribes
neither c. I any man to be a   *2Ch* 6:5 ruler
I c. out their way, and sat   *Job* 29:25 chief
and c. not the tribe of   *Ps* 78:67 Ephraim
But c. the tribe of Judah, the   *Ps* 78:68
He c. David also his servant   *Ps* 78:70
and c. that in which I   *Isa* 66:4 delighted not
In the day when I c. Israel   *Eze* 20:5
of them he c. twelve, whom   *Lu* 6:13 also
they c. out the chief rooms;   *Lu* 14:7 saying
they c. Stephen, a man full of   *Ac* 6:5 faith
c. our fathers, and exalted   *Ac* 13:17
c. elders for them (B)   *Ac* 14:23
And Paul c. Silas, and   *Ac* 15:40 departed
full nature of God c. to live   *Col* 1:19 (P)
c. long ago (P)   *1Pe* 1:2; 1:20

CHOSEN

his c. captains drowned in sea   *Ex* 15:4
whom he hath c. cause to   *Nu* 16:5 come
c. from the congregation (S)   *Nu* 26:9
have c. you Lord to serve   *Jos* 24:22 him
go and cry to gods ye have   *J'g* 10:14 c.
because of the king ye have   *1Sa* 8:18; c.   *1Sa* 12:13
know thou hast c. the son   *1Sa* 20:30 of Jesse
c. great people, cannot be   *1Ki* 3:8
city thou hast c.   *1Ki* 8:44; *2Ch* 6:34, 38
children of Jacob his c.   *1Ch* 16:13 ones
hast thou c. rather than   *Job* 36:21 affliction
people hath c. for   *Ps* 33:12 inheritance
have made a covenant with   *Ps* 89:3 my c.
have exalted one c. out of   *Ps* 89:19 the people
seed of Abraham, Jacob his   *Ps* 105:6 c.
he brought forth his c.   *Ps* 105:43 with gladness
that I may see the good of   *Ps* 106:5 thy c.

had not Moses his c. stood   *Ps* 106:23 before him
rather to be c. than silver   *Pr* 16:16
good name rather be c. than   *Pr* 22:1 riches
give drink to my people,   *Isa* 43:20 my c.
my c. (A)(B)(E)(R)   *Isa* 45:4
leave your name a curse to   *Isa* 65:15 my c.
they have c. their own ways   *Isa* 66:3
death shall be c. rather than   *Jer* 8:3 life
who is c. man I may   *Jer* 49:19; appoint   *Jer* 50:44
many called, but few c.   *M't* 20:16; *M't* 22:14
his c. (B) (N)(P)   *M't* 24:31; *Lu* 18:7; *Ro* 8:33
elect's sake whom he hath   *M'k* 13:20 c.
to mislead God's c. (N)   *M'k* 13:22
Mary hath c. that good part   *Lu* 10:42
shew whether of two hast c.   *Ac* 1:24
for he is a c. vessel to me   *Ac* 9:15
salute Rufus, c. in the Lord   *Ro* 16:13
c. ones (A)(B)(N)(R)   *Col* 3:12; *1Pe* 1:2; 2:6
who was c. of churches   *2Co* 8:19 to travel
please him who hath c. him   *2Ti* 2:4 soldier
c. and foreknown of God   *1Pe* 1:2 (A)(N)
ye are a c. generation, a royal   *1Pe* 2:9
course c. by helmsman (P)   *Jas* 3:4
those who have been c. (B)   *Jude* 1
they are called, c. and   *Re* 17:14 faithful

CHOSEN MEN

seven hundred c. men   *J'g* 20:16 left handed
of Judah 180,000 c. men,   *1Ki* 12:21; *2Ch* 11:1
Abijah with 400,000 c. men,   *2Ch* 13:3
Jeroboam with 800,000 c. men
wrath smote down c. men of   *Ps* 78:31 Israel
send c. men of their   *Ac* 15:22; company   *Ac* 15:25

CHOSEN OF GOD

if he be Christ, c. of God   *Lu* 23:35
but to witnesses c. before of   *Ac* 10:41 God
living stone, c. of God and   *1Pe* 2:4 precious

GOD HATH CHOSEN

God hath c. to put name   *De* 12:21; there   *De* 16:11
them God hath c. to minister   *De* 21:5 unto him
Solomon whom God hath c.   *1Ch* 29:1
God of our fathers hath c.   *Ac* 22:14 thee
God hath c. foolish things,   *1Co* 1:27 God hath c. weak things
things despised God hath c.   *1Co* 1:28 and things
God from beginning hath c.   *2Th* 2:13 you
hath not God c. poor of world   *Jas* 2:5

I HAVE CHOSEN

for David's sake I have c.   *1Ki* 11:13; *2Ki* 21:7; 23:27; *2Ch* 6:6
city which I have c. out of   *1Ki* 11:32 all tribes
bring them to place I have c.   *Ne* 1:9
I have c. way of truth   *Ps* 119:30; *Ps* 119:173
Jacob whom I have c. the   *Isa* 41:8 seed
I have c. thee, and not cast   *Isa* 41:9 thee away
servant whom I have c.   *Isa* 43:10; *M't* 12:18
Israel whom I have c.   *Isa* 44:1; 44:2
I have c. thee in furnace of   *Isa* 48:10 afflicton
is not this the fast that I   *Isa* 58:5; have c.   *Isa* 58:6
I have c. thee, saith the   *Hag* 2:23 Lord

I know whom I have c.   *Joh* 13:18
ye have not c. me, but I   *Joh* 15:16 have c. you
I have c. you out of world   *Joh* 15:19

LORD HATH CHOSEN

Lord hath c. special people   *De* 7:6; *De* 14:2
Lord hath c. him out of all   *De* 18:5 tribes
see him whom Lord hath c.   *1Sa* 10:24
he said, neither hath Lord c.   *1Sa* 16:8 this
Samuel said, The Lord hath   *1Sa* 16:10 not c. these
them Lord hath c. to carry   *1Ch* 15:2 ark
Lord hath c. Judah ruler   *1Ch* 28:4
Lord hath c. Solomon to   *1Ch* 28:5; build house   *1Ch* 28:10
Lord hath c. you to serve   *2Ch* 29:11
he sent Aaron whom he   *Ps* 105:26 had c.
Lord hath c. Zion   *Ps* 132:13
the Lord hath c. Jacob   *Ps* 135:4
two families which Lord   *Jer* 33:24 hath c.
Lord that hath c. Jerusalem   *Zec* 3:2 rebuke
according as he hath c. us in   *Eph* 1:4 him

CHOZEBA

the men of C., and Joash   *1Ch* 4:22

CHRIST

demanded where C. should be   *M't* 2:4 born
art C. the Son of the   *M't* 16:16 living God
one is your Master, even C.   *M't* 23:8; *M't* 23:10
many shall come, saying, I   *M't* 24:5; am C. and shall   *M'k* 13:6; *Lu* 21:8 deceive many
prophesy to us, thou C.   *M't* 26:68 who smote
in my name because belong   *M'k* 9:41 to C.
let C. descend now from   *M'k* 15:32 the cross
not die, before he had seen   *Lu* 2:26 C.
devils, they knew that he was   *Lu* 4:41 C.
save himself, if he be C.   *Lu* 23:35
if thou be C. save thyself   *Lu* 23:39 and us
ought not C. to have   *Lu* 24:26 suffered these
it behoved C. to suffer and   *Lu* 24:46 rise from
Messias cometh, which is   *Joh* 4:25 called C.
when C. cometh no man   *Joh* 7:27 knoweth
when C. cometh, will he do   *Joh* 7:31 more miracles
some said, Shall C. come out   *Joh* 7:41 of Galilee
that C. cometh of the seed   *Joh* 7:42 of David
if any man did confess he   *Joh* 9:22 was C.
have heard that C. abideth   *Joh* 12:34 for ever
would raise up C. to sit on   *Ac* 2:30 throne
God made Jesus both Lord   *Ac* 2:36 and C.
God before shewed C. should   *Ac* 3:18 suffer
Philip went and preached C.   *Ac* 8:5 to them
straightway he preached C.   *Ac* 9:20
alleging C. must needs have   *Ac* 17:3 suffered
that C. should suffer, and   *Ac* 26:23 rise from
in due time C. died for the   *Ro* 5:6 ungodly
while we were sinners C. died   *Ro* 5:8 for us
like C. was raised up from dead   *Ro* 6:4 by
knowing C. being raised, dieth   *Ro* 6:9 no more

become dead to law by body *Ro 7:4* of *C.*

if any have not Spirit of *C.* he *Ro 8:9* is none

if *C.* in you, body dead *Ro 8:10* because of sin

that raised *C.* from dead *Ro 8:11* shall quicken

could wish myself accursed *Ro 9:3* from *C.*

of whom *C.* came, who is over *Ro 9:5* all

C. is end of law for *Ro 10:4* righteousness

that is, to bring up *C.* down *Ro 10:6* from above

that is, to bring *C.* again *Ro 10:7* from dead

to this end *C.* died, and rose *Ro 14:9*

destroy not him with meat *Ro 14:15* for whom *C.*

he that in these things *Ro 14:18* serveth *C.* is

for even *C.* pleased not *Ro 15:3* himself

as *C.* also received us, to *Ro 15:7* glory of God

of things *C.* hath not *Ro 15:18* wrought by me

strived to preach, not where *Ro 15:20* *C.* was named

Epenetus the firstfruits of *Ro 16:5* Achaia to *C.*

but we preach *C.* crucified *1Co 1:23*

C. the power of God, *1Co 1:24* wisdom of God

and ye are *C.* and *C.* is *1Co 3:23* God's

C. our passover sacrificed for *1Co 5:7* us

weak brother perish, for *1Co 8:11* whom *C.* died

under law to *C.* that I might *1Co 9:21* gain

all drank of rock, that rock *1Co 10:4* was *C.*

nor let us tempt *C.* as some *1Co 10:9* also tempted

delivered to you, how *C.* *1Co 15:3* died for sins

if *C.* be preached he rose *1Co 15:12* from dead

if dead rise not, then is not *1Co 15:16* *C.* raised

if *C.* be not raised, your *1Co 15:17* faith is vain

every man in own order, *C.* *1Co 15:23* firstfruits

such trust have we thro' *C.* *2Co 3:4* to God

tho' we have known *C.* after *2Co 5:16* flesh

what concord hath *C.* with *2Co 6:15* Belial

present you as chaste virgin *2Co 11:2* to *C.*

I live, yet not I, but *C.* liveth *Ga 2:20* in

if righteousness come by law *Ga 2:21* *C.* died in vain

C. redeemed us from curse of *Ga 3:13* law

law our schoolmaster, to *Ga 3:24* bring us to *C.*

if ye be *C.* then are *Ga 3:29* Abraham's seed

if son, then an heir of God *Ga 4:7* through *C.*

I travail, till *C.* be formed in *Ga 4:19* you

liberty wherewith *C.* made us *Ga 5:1* free

if be circumcised, *C.* shall *Ga 5:2* profit nothing

C. is become of no effect unto *Ga 5:4* you

at that time ye were without *Eph 2:12* *C.*

C. may dwell in your hearts *Eph 3:17* by faith

grow in him which is head, *Eph 4:15* even *C.*

but ye have not so learned *Eph 4:20* *C.*

as *C.* also loved us, hath *Eph 5:2* given himself

arise from dead, *C.* give thee *Eph 5:14* light

as *C.* is head of the church *Eph 5:23*

as church is subject to *C.* so *Eph 5:24* let wives

love wives, as *C.* also loved *Eph 5:25* church

I speak concerning *C.* and *Eph 5:32* the church

obedient, in singleness of *Eph 6:5* heart as to *C.*

some preach *C.* of envy and *Ph'p 1:15* strife

one preach *C.* of *Ph'p 1:16* contention, not sincerely

C. is preached, and I *Ph'p 1:18* therein do rejoice

so now *C.* shall be *Ph'p 1:20* magnified in my body

I count dung, that I may *Ph'p 3:8* win *C.*

I can do all through *C.* who *Ph'p 4:13* strengtheneth me

after rudiments of world, not *Col 2:8* after *C.*

C. sitteth on right hand of *Col 3:1* God

when *C.* who is our life shall *Col 3:4* appear

bond nor free, but *C.* is all *Col 3:11* and in all

even as *C.* forgave you, so *Col 3:13* also do ye

receive reward, for ye serve *Col 3:24* Lord *C.*

C. as a son over his own *Heb 3:6* house

C. glorified not himself to be *Heb 5:5* high priest

C. being come an high *Heb 9:11* priest of good

C. not entered into holy *Heb 9:24* places made with hands

C. once offered to bear sins *Heb 9:28* of many

because *C.* also suffered for *1Pe 2:21* us

C. once suffered for sins, *1Pe 3:18* just for

C. suffered for us in the flesh *1Pe 4:1*

kingdoms of our Lord and *Re 11:15* *C.*

now is come kingdom of *Re 12:10* God power of *C.*

AGAINST CHRIST

rulers gathered *against* his *C.* *Ac 4:26*

sin against brethren sin *1Co 8:12* *against C.*

was wanton *against C* will *1Ti 5:11* marry

BY CHRIST

our consolation aboundeth *by* *2Co 1:5* *C.*

but if while we seek to be *Ga 2:17* justified *by C.*

be glory in church *by C.* *Eph 3:21* Jesus

FOR CHRIST, CHRIST'S

for C. sent me not to baptize *1Co 1:17*

fools *for C.* sake, wise in *1Co 4:10* Christ

we are ambassadors *for C.* *2Co 5:20*

take pleasure in distresses *2Co 12:10* *for C.* sake

God *for C.* sake hath *Eph 4:32* forgiven you

gain to me, I counted loss *Ph'p 3:7* *for C.*

direct to patient waiting *for* *2Th 3:5* *C.*

JESUS with CHRIST

Jesus, who is called *C.* *M't 1:16* 27:17, 22

grace and truth came by *Joh 1:17* *Jesus C.*

Jesus C. whom thou sent *Joh 17:3*

be baptized in name of *Jesus* *Ac 2:38* *C.*

in name of *Jesus C.* rise up *Ac 3:6* and walk

send *Jesus C.* who was *Ac 3:20* preached to

name of *Jesus C.* doth this *Ac 4:10* man stand

daily ceased not to preach *Ac 5:42* *Jesus C.*

believed Philip preaching *Ac 8:12* things concerning name of *Jesus C.* were baptized

I believe that *Jesus C.* is the *Ac 8:37* Son of God

Eneas, *Jesus C.* maketh thee *Ac 9:34* whole

preaching peace by *Jesus C.* *Ac 10:36* he is Lord

command in name of *Jesus* *Ac 16:18* *C.* come out

that this *Jesus* I preach to *Ac 17:3* you is *C.*

Paul testified that *Jesus* was *C. Ac 18:5*

shewing by scriptures *Jesus* *Ac 18:28* was *C.*

that they should believe on *C. Ac 19:4* *Jesus*

Paul servant of *Jesus C.* *Ro 1:1;* *Ph'p 1:1*

concerning his Son *Jesus C.* *Ro 1:3* our Lord, of seed

among whom are ye called of *Ro 1:6* *Jesus C.*

thank my God through *Jesus* *Ro 1:8* *C.* for all

judge secrets of men by *Jesus Ro 2:16* *C.*

righteousness, by faith of *Ro 3:22* *Jesus C.*

justified through redemption *Ro 3:24* in *Jesus C.*

gift by grace, which is by *Ro 5:15* *Jesus C.*

much more reign in life by *Ro 5:17* *Jesus C.*

many as were baptized into *Ro 6:3* *Jesus C.*

no condemnation to them in *Ro 8:1* *C. Jesus*

Spirit of life in *C. Jesus* *Ro 8:2* made me free

separate from love of God in *Ro 8:39* *C. Jesus*

Priscilla and Aquila, helpers *Ro 16:3* in *C. Jesus*

apostle of *Jesus C.* *1Co 1:1;* *2Co 1:1; Eph 1:1*

all that call on the name of *1Co 1:2* *Jesus C.*

the grace of God given you *1Co 1:4* by *Jesus C.*

of him are ye in *C. Jesus,* *1Co 1:30* who is made

know any thing, save *Jesus* *1Co 2:2* *C.* crucified

in *C. Jesus* have I begotten *1Co 4:15* thro' gospel

knowledge of God in face of *2Co 4:6* *Jesus C.*

reconciled us to himself if by *2Co 5:18* *Jesus C.*

know ye how *Jesus C.* is in *2Co 13:5* you

man justified by faith of *Ga 2:16* *Jesus C.*

blessing on Gentiles thro' *Ga 3:14* *Jesus C.*

female, for ye are all one in *Ga 3:28* *C. Jesus*

received me as an angel, as *Ga 4:14* *C. Jesus*

sit in heavenly places in *C.* *Eph 2:6* *Jesus*

Jesus C. being the chief *Eph 2:20* corner stone

long after you in bowels of *Ph'p 1:8* *Jesus C.*

mind in you, which was in *Ph'p 2:5* *C. Jesus*

Jesus C. is Lord, to glory *Ph'p 2:11* of God

count loss for excellency of *Ph'p 3:8* *C. Jesus*

which I am apprehended of *Ph'p 3:12* *C. Jesus*

according to riches in glory *Ph'p 4:19* by *C. Jesus*

have received *C. Jesus* walk *Col 2:6* in him

C. Jesus came to save sinners *1Ti 1:15*

mediator between God and *1Ti 2:5* men, *C. Jesus*

before *C. Jesus* witnessed *1Ti 6:13* good confession

according to grace given in *C.* *2Ti 1:9* *Jesus*

faith and love, which is in *C.*   *2Ti 1:13*
Jesus
Paul a prisoner of *Jesus C.*   *Ph'm 1;*
     9, 23
Jesus C. same yesterday, for   *Heb 13:8*
ever
blood of *Jesus C.* cleanseth all   *1Jo 1:7*
sin
an advocate, *Jesus C.* the   *1Jo 2:1*
righteous
came by water and blood,   *1Jo 5:6*
Jesus C.
we are in him, even in his   *1Jo 5:20*
Son *Jesus C.*

LORD JESUS CHRIST

us who believed on *Lord*   *Ac 11:17*
Jesus C.
thro' grace of *Lord Jesus C.*   *Ac 15:11*
be saved
believe on *Lord Jesus C.*   *Ac 16:31*
shalt be saved
testifying faith toward *Lord*   *Ac 20:21*
Jesus C.
peace with God, thro' *Lord*   *Ro 5:1*
Jesus C.
we joy in God, thro' *Lord*   *Ro 5:11*
Jesus C.
gift of God eternal life thro'   *Ro 6:23*
Lord Jesus C.
put ye on *Lord Jesus C.* and   *Ro 13:14*
make not provision
grace of *Lord Jesus C.* be   *Ro 16:20;*
with you   *16:24; 2Co 13:14; Ga 6:18;*
     2Th 3:18; Re 22:21
waiting for coming of *Lord*   *1Co 1:7*
Jesus C.
but to us one *Lord Jesus C.*   *1Co 8:6*
by whom
God giveth us victory thro'   *1Co 15:57*
Lord Jesus C.
if any man love not *Lord*   *1Co 16:22*
Jesus C.
grace and peace from God,   *2Co 1:2;*
and from *Lord Jesus C.*   *Ga 1:3;*
     Eph 1:2; Col 1:2
for ye know grace of our   *2Co 8:9*
Lord Jesus C.
glory save in cross of *Lord*   *Ga 6:14*
Jesus C.
blessed be Father of our *Lord*   *Eph 1:3*
Jesus C.
God of our *Lord Jesus C.*   *Eph 1:17*
give spirit of wisdom
patience of hope in our *Lord*   *1Th 1:3*
Jesus C.
ye are our joy in presence   *1Th 2:19*
of *Lord Jesus C.*
establish you at coming of   *1Th 3:13*
Lord Jesus C.
preserved unto coming of   *1Th 5:23*
Lord Jesus C.
beseech by coming of *Lord*   *2Th 2:1*
Jesus C.
our *Lord Jesus C.* hath   *2Th 2:16*
given us consolation
charge before *Lord Jesus C.*   *1Ti 5:21;*
     2 Ti 4:1
Lord Jesus C. be with thy   *2Ti 4:22*
spirit
entrance into kingdom of   *2Pe 1:11*
Lord Jesus C.
grow in grace, knowledge of   *2Pe 3:18*
Lord Jesus C.

IN CHRIST

heard him concerning faith   *Ac 24:24*
in *C.*
I say truth *in C.* I lie not   *Ro 9:1*
so we being many are one   *Ro 12:5*
body *in C.*
who also were *in C.* before   *Ro 16:7*
me
salute Urbane, our helper in   *Ro 16:9*
C.
salute Apelles approved in   *Ro 16:10*
C.
speak even as unto babes in   *1Co 3:1*
C.
we are fools, but ye are   *1Co 4:10*
wise *in C.*
tho' ye have 10,000 instruct,   *1Co 4:15*
in C.
they that are fallen asleep   *1Co 15:18*
in C.
if in this life only we have   *1Co 15:19*
hope *in C.*

even so *in C.* shall all be   *1Co 15:22*
made alive
stablisheth us with you *in C.*   *2Co 1:21*
God who causeth us to   *2Co 2:14*
triumph *in C.*
in sight of God speak we *in*   *2Co 2:17*
C.
untaken away, vail is done   *2Co 3:14*
away *in C.*
if any man be *in C.* he is   *2Co 5:17*
new creature
that God was *in C.*   *2Co 5:19*
reconciling world
pray *in C.* stead, be   *2Co 5:20*
reconciled to God.
knew man *in C.* fourteen   *2Co 12:2*
years ago
we speak before God, *in C.*   *2Co 12:19*
unknown to churches *in C.*   *Ga 1:22*
covenant confirmed before *in*   *Ga 3:17*
C.
as many as have been   *Ga 3:27*
baptized *into C.*
blessed with spiritual   *Eph 1:3*
blessings *in C.*
might gather in one all   *Eph 1:10*
things *in C.*
be to His glory, who first   *Eph 1:12*
trusted *in C.*
which He wrought *in C.*   *Eph 1:20*
when raised
partakers of promise *in C.* by   *Eph 3:6*
gospel
so that my bonds *in C.* are   *Ph'p 1:13*
manifest in
if there be any consolation   *Ph'p 2:1*
in C.
beholding stedfastness of your   *Col 2:5*
faith *in C.*
the dead *in C.* shall rise first   *1Th 4:16*
speak truth *in C.* and lie not   *1Ti 2:7*
accuse good conversation *in*   *1Pe 3:16*
C.

IS CHRIST

if any say, here *is C.*   *M't 24:23;*
     M'k 13:21
C. is son of David   *M'k 12:35;*
     Lu 20:41
born a Saviour which *is C.*   *Lu 2:11*
the Lord
saying, that he himself *is C.*   *Lu 23:2*
a king
others said, this *is the C.*   *Joh 7:41*
Saul increased, proving this *is*   *Ac 9:22*
C.
Jesus whom I preach *is C.*   *Ac 17:3*
is C. that died, rather risen   *Ro 8:34*
again
is C. divided? was Paul   *1Co 1:13*
crucified
the head of every man *is C.*   *1Co 11:3*
members are one body, so   *1Co 12:12*
if dead rise not, then *is C.*   *1Co 15:13;*
not risen   *15:16*
now *is C.* risen from dead   *1Co 15:20*
if any man trust that he *is C.*   *2Co 10:7*
is therefore *C.* the minister   *Ga 2:17*
of sin
as of one, to thy seed, which   *Ga 3:16*
is C.
for to me to live *is C.* but   *Ph'p 1:21*
to die
which *is C.* in you, hope of   *Col 1:27*
glory

OF CHRIST

John heard in prison works   *M't 11:2*
of *C.*
what think you *of C.*?   *M't 22:42*
whose son
if any man have not Spirit *of*   *Ro 8:9*
C.
who shall spearate us from   *Ro 8:35*
love *of C.*
all stand before judgment   *Ro 14:10*
seat *of C.*
cross *of C.* made of none   *1Co 1:17*
effect
but we have the mind *of C.*   *1Co 2:16*
your bodies are members *of*   *1Co 6:15*
C.
is it not communion of   *1Co 10:16*
blood *of C.*
is it not the communion of   *1Co 10:16*
body *of C.*

be followers of me, even as   *1Co 11:1*
I am *of C.*
head *of C.* is God   *1Co 11:3*
now ye are the body *of C.*   *1Co 12:27*
as sufferings *of C.* abound in   *2Co 1:5*
us
forgave I it in the person   *2Co 2:10*
of C.
for we are to God a sweet   *2Co 2:15*
savour *of C.*
ye are epistle *of C.*   *2Co 3:3*
ministered by us
lest light of glorious gospel *of*   *2Co 4:4*
C.
love *of C.* constraineth us   *2Co 5:14*
our brethren, they are glory   *2Co 8:23*
of C.
by meekness and gentleness   *2Co 10:1*
of C.
every thought to obedience   *2Co 10:5*
of C.
as the truth *of C.* is in me,   *2Co 11:10*
power *of C.* rest on me   *2Co 12:9;*
     Re 12:10
seek proof *of C.* speaking in   *2Co 13:3*
me
if pleased men, not be   *Ga 1:10*
servants *of C.*
be justified by faith *of C.*   *Ga 2:16*
lest suffer persecution for   *Ga 6:12*
cross *of C.*
made nigh by the blood *of*   *Eph 2:13*
C.
understand knowledge in   *Eph 3:4*
mystery *of C.*
preach unsearchable riches *of*   *Eph 3:8*
C.
love *of C.* which passeth   *Eph 3:19*
knowledge
according to measure of gift   *Eph 4:7*
of C.
inheritance in the kingdom *of*   *Eph 5:5*
C.
as servants *of C.* doing will   *Eph 6:6*
of God
be without offence till day   *Ph'p 1:10*
of C.
to you it is given in behalf   *Ph'p 1:29*
of C.
that I may rejoice in the   *Ph'p 2:16*
day *of C.*
for the work *of C.* he was   *Ph'p 2:30*
nigh to death
they are enemies of cross   *Ph'p 3:18*
of C.
what is behind of afflictions   *Col 1:24*
of C.
mystery of God, and *of C.*   *Col 2:2*
a shadow of things, but the   *Col 2:17*
body is *of C.*
let word *of C.* dwell in you   *Col 3:16*
richly
open a door, to speak mystery   *Col 4:3*
of C.
every one nameth name *of C.*   *2Ti 2:19*
are made partakers *of C.* if   *Heb 3:14*
we hold
how much more blood *of C.*   *Heb 9:14*
purge
reproach *of C.* greater   *Heb 11:26*
riches than
what time Spirit *of C.* did   *1Pe 1:11*
signify
redeemed with precious   *1Pe 1:19*
blood *of C.*
partakers *of C.* sufferings   *1Pe 4:13*
if ye be reproached for the   *1Pe 4:14*
name *of C.*
shall be priests of God and   *Re 20:6*
of C.

THAT CHRIST

if be not *that C.* nor Elias   *Joh 1:25*
thou art *that C.* the Son of   *Joh 6:69*
God

THE CHRIST

tell no man that he was *the*   *M't 16:20*
C.
tell whether thou be *the C.*   *M't 26:63*
Peter saith, thou art *the C.*   *M'k 8:29*
art thou *the C.*, Son of the   *M'k 14:61*
Blessed
mused, whether he were *the*   *Lu 3:15*
C.
Peter said, thou art *the C.* of   *Lu 9:20*
God

scribes, saying, art thou *the*   *Lu 22:67*
C.
but he confessed, I am not   *Joh 1:20*
the C.
have found Messias, which is   *Joh 1:41*
the C.
I said, I am not *the C.* but   *Joh 3:28*
sent
man told me all, is not this   *Joh 4:29*
the C.
we know that this is indeed   *Joh 4:42;*
the C.   *7:26*
others said, this is *the C.* but   *Joh 7:41*
some said
if thou be *the C.* tell us plainly   *Joh 10:24*
thou art *the C.* the Son of   *Joh 11:27*
God
that ye might believe Jesus   *Joh 20:31*
is *the C.*
he that denieth Jesus is *the*   *1Jo 2:22*
C.
believeth Jesus is *the C.* is   *1Jo 5:1*
born of God

WITH CHRIST

if we be dead *with C.* we shall   *Ro 6:8*
live
if children, then joint-heirs   *Ro 8:17*
with C.
crucified *with C.* I live,   *Ga 2:20*
Christ liveth
hath quickened us together   *Eph 2:5*
with C.
desire to depart and be   *Ph'p 1:23*
with C.
if ye be dead *with C.* from   *Col 2:20*
world
if risen *with C.* seek things   *Col 3:1*
above
your life is hid *with C.* in   *Col 3:3*
God
they reigned *with C.* 1000   *Ro 20:4*
years

CHRISTIAN

thou persuadest me to be a   *Ac 26:28*
C.
C. grace (A)   *1Co 1:7*
bring them up in C. teaching   *Eph 6:4*
(P)
accuse your good C. conduct   *1Pe 3:16*
(B)(N)(P)
if any man suffer as a C. let   *1Pe 4:16*
him

CHRISTIANITY

the rudiments of C. (N)   *Heb 6:1*

CHRISTIANS

disciples were called C. first   *Ac 11:26*
in
give freely to fellow C. in   *Ro 12:13*
want (P)

CHRISTS

For there shall arise false   *M't 24:24*
C.
For false C. and false   *M'k 13:22*
prophets

CHRIST'S

for the Lord Jesus C. sake,   *Ro 15:30*
and
ye are C.; and Christ is   *1Co 3:23*
God's
for C. sake, but ye are wise   *1Co 4:10*
in
is called, being free, is C.   *1Co 7:22*
servant
fruits; afterward they that   *1Co 15:23*
are C.
C. gospel, and a door was   *2Co 2:12*
opened
in C. stead, be ye reconciled   *2Co 5:20*
to
man trust to himself that he   *2Co 10:7*
is C.
in distresses for C. sake: *2Co 12:10*
if ye be C. then are ye   *Ga 3:29*
Abraham's
are C. have crucified the   *Ga 5:24*
flesh
God for C. sake hath   *Eph 4:32*
forgiven

not the things which are   *Ph'p 2:21*
Jesus C.
as ye are partakers of C.   *1Pe 4:13*

CHRONICLE

number not entered into c.   *1Ch 27:24*
(R)

CHRONICLES

c. of the kings of Israel   *1Ki 14:19;*
15:31; 16:4, 14, 20, 27; 22:29; *2Ki 1:18;*
10:34; 13:8, 12; 14:15, 28; 15:11, 15,
                        21, 26, 31
c. of the kings of Judah   *1Ki 14:29;*
15:7, 23, 45; *2Ki 8:23;* 12:19; 14:18;
   15:6, 36; 20:20; 21:17, 25; 23:28; 24:5
c. of King David   *1Ch 27:24*
book of the c. even until   *Ne 12:23*
bock of the c. before the king   *Es 2:23*
records of the c. and they   *Es 6:1*
c. of the kings of Media and   *Es 10:2*

CHRYSOLITE

the seventh, c.; the eighth,   *Re 21:20*
beryl

CHRYSOPRASUS

the tenth, a c.; the eleventh   *Re 21:20*

CHUB

all the mingled people, and C.   *Eze 30:5*

CHUN

from Tibhath, and from C.   *1Ch 18:8*
cities

CHURCH

upon this rock I will build   *M't 16:18*
my c.
tell it unto the c.   *M't 18:17*
but if he neglect to hear the   *M't 18:17*
c.
the Lord added to the c.   *Ac 2:47*
daily
fear came upon all the c. and   *Ac 5:11*
he, that was in the c. in the   *Ac 7:38*
against the c. which was at   *Ac 8:1*
he made havock of the c.   *Ac 8:3*
the c. which was in   *Ac 11:22*
Jerusalem
assembled themselves with   *Ac 11:26*
the c.
his hands to vex certain of   *Ac 12:1*
the c.
without ceasing of the c.   *Ac 12:5*
unto God
Now there were in the c.   *Ac 13:1*
that was
ordained them elders in   *Ac 14:23*
every c.
and had gathered the c.   *Ac 14:27*
together
brought on their way by the   *Ac 15:3*
c.
they were received of the c.   *Ac 15:4*
and elders, with the whole c.   *Ac 15:22*
gone up, and saluted the c.   *Ac 18:22*
and called the elders of the   *Ac 20:17*
c.
overseers, to feed the c. of   *Ac 20:28*
God
is a servant of the c. which   *Ro 16:1*
is at
greet the c. that is in their   *Ro 16:5*
house
mine host and of the whole   *Ro 16:23*
c.
Unto the c. of God which is   *1Co 1:2*
at
I teach everywhere in every   *1Co 4:17*
c.
who are least esteemed in the   *1Co 6:4*
c.
Gentiles; nor to the c. of   *1Co 10:32*
God
when ye come together in   *1Co 11:18*
the c.
or despise ye the c. of God   *1Co 11:22*
God hath set some in the   *1Co 12:28*
c.
that prophesieth edifieth the   *1Co 14:4*
c.

interpret, that the c. may   *1Co 14:5*
receive
excel to the edifying of the   *1Co 14:12*
c.
in the c. I had rather speak   *1Co 14:19*
five
therefore the whole c. be   *1Co 14:23*
come
let him keep silence in the   *1Co 14:28*
c.
for women to speak in the   *1Co 14:35*
c.
I persecuted the c. of God   *1Co 15:9*
with the c. that is in their   *1Co 16:19*
house
unto the c. of God which is   *2Co 1:1*
I persecuted the c. of God   *Ga 1:13*
the head over all things to   *Eph 1:22*
the c.
might be known by the c.   *Eph 3:10*
glory in the c. by Christ   *Eph 3:21*
Jesus
Christ is the head of the c.   *Eph 5:23*
Therefore as the c. is   *Eph 5:24*
subject unto
as Christ also loved the c.   *Eph 5:25*
present it to himself a   *Eph 5:27*
glorious c.
even as the Lord the c.   *Eph 5:29*
concerning Christ and the c.   *Eph 5:32*
Concerning zeal, persecuting   *Ph'p 3:6*
the c.
no c. communicated with   *Ph'p 4:15*
me
the head of the body, the c.   *Col 1:18*
for his body's sake, which is   *Col 1:24*
the c.
and the c. which is in his   *Col 4:15*
house
it be read also in the c. of   *Col 4:16*
unto the c. of the   *1Th 1:1*
Thessalonians
unto the c. of the   *2Th 1:1*
Thessalonians
take care of the c. of God   *1Ti 3:5*
the c. of the living God, the   *1Ti 3:15*
pillar
let not the c. be charged   *1Ti 5:16*
to the c. in thy house   *Ph'm 2*
in the midst of the c. will I   *Heb 2:12*
sing
general assembly and c. of   *Heb 12:23*
call for the elders of the c.   *Jas 5:14*
The c. that is at Babylon,   *1Pe 5:13*
elected
of thy charity before the c.   *3Jo 6*
I wrote unto the c. but   *3Jo 9*
and casteth them out of the c.   *3Jo 10*
the angel of the c. of Ephesus   *Re 2:1*
the angel of the c. in Smyrna   *Re 2:8*
to the angel of the c. in   *Re 2:12*
Pergamos
the angel of the c. in Thyatira   *Re 2:18*
the angel of the c. in Sardis   *Re 3:1*
write
the angel of the c. in   *Re 3:7*
Philadelphia
the angel of the c. of the   *Re 3:14*
Laodiceans

CHURCHES

Then had the c. rest   *Ac 9:31*
throughout
and Cilicia, confirming the c.   *Ac 15:41*
so were the c. established in   *Ac 16:5*
which are neither robbers of   *Ac 19:37*
c.
but also all the c. of the   *Ro 16:4*
Gentiles
The c. of Christ salute you   *Ro 16:16*
And so ordain I in all c.   *1Co 7:17*
custom, neither the c. of   *1Co 11:16*
God
of peace, as in all c. of the   *1Co 14:33*
saints
your women keep silence   *1Co 14:34*
in the c.
I have given order to the c.   *1Co 16:1*
The c. of Asia salute you.   *1Co 16:19*
bestowed on the c. of   *2Co 8:1*
Macedonia
gospel throughout all the c.   *2Co 8:18*
was also chosen of the c. to   *2Co 8:19*
travel
they are the messengers of   *2Co 8:23*
the c.
ye to them, and before the   *2Co 8:24*
c.

CHURCHES (cont.)

I robbed other *c*. taking wages of | 2Co 11:8
me daily, the care of all the *c*. | 2Co 11:28
ye were inferior to other *c*. | 2Co 12:13
unto the *c*. of Galatia | Ga 1:2
unto the *c*. of Judæa which were | Ga 1:22
became followers of the *c*. of God | 1Th 2:14
glory in you in the *c*. of God | 2Th 1:4
John to the seven *c*. which are in | Re 1:4
and send it unto the seven *c*. | Re 1:11
are the angels of the seven *c*. | Re 1:20
which thou sawest are the seven *c*. | Re 1:20
what the Spirit saith unto the *c*. | Re 2:7; 2:11, 17, 29; 3:6 13, 22
all the *c*. shall know that I am he | Re 2:23
unto you these things in the *c*. | Re 22:16

CHURL

nor the *c*. said to be bountiful | Isa 32:5
instruments also of a *c*. are evil | Isa 32:7

CHURLISH

man Nabal was *c*. and evil in his doings | 1Sa 25:3
behaviour was rough and uncouth (B) | 1Sa 25:3

CHURNING

the *c*. of milk bringeth butter | Pr 30:33

CHUSHAN-RISHATHAIM

he sold them into the hand of *C*. | J'g 3:8
of Israel served *C*. eight years. | J'g 3:8
Lord delivered *C*. into his hand | J'g 3:10

CHUZA

the wife of *C*. Herod's steward | Lu 8:3

CEILED

greater house he *c*. with fir tree | 2Ch 3:5
it is *c*. with cedar, and painted | Jer 22:14
door, *c*. with wood round about | Eze 41:16
to dwell in your *c*. houses | Hag 1:4

CEILING

the house, and the walls of the *c*. | 1Ki 6:15

CILICIA

and of them of *C*. and of Asia, | Ac 6:9
in Antioch and Syria and *C*. | Ac 15:23
And he went through Syria and *C*. | Ac 15:41
am a Jew of Tarsus, a city in *C*. | Ac 21:39
born in Tarsus, a city in *C*. | Ac 22:3
he understood that he was of *C*. | Ac 23:34
we had sailed over the sea of *C*. | Ac 27:5
into the regions of Syria and *C*. | Ga 1:21

CINNAMON

and of sweet *c*. half so much | Ex 30:23
my bed with myrrh, aloes, and *c*. | Pr 7:17
calamus and *c*. with all trees of | Ca 4:14
c. and odours, and ointments | Re 18:13

CINNEROTH

and all *C*. with all the land | 1Ki 15:20

CIRCLE

c. them in the rear (B) | 2Sa 6:23
draws a *c*. over the days (B) | Joh 26:10
drew a *c*. upon the (A)(B)(E)(R) | Pr 8:27
sitteth upon the *c*. of the earth | Isa 40:22

CIRCLED

c. around the hill country (B) | De 2:1

CIRCLES

c. about continually (A) | Ec 1:6

CIRCUIT

he went from year to year in *c*. | 1Sa 7:16
made the rounds annually (B) | 1Sa 7:16
make, made a *c*. (S) | 2Sa 5:23; 2Ki 3:9
make a *c*. behind (E) | 2Sa 6:23
make a *c*. seven days (A)(E)(R) | 2Ki 3:9
he walketh in the *c*. of heaven | Job 22:14
vault of the heavens (A)(E)(R) | Job 22:14
on the arch of heaven (B) | Job 22:14
and his *c*. unto the ends of it | Ps 19:6
on its circling the wind returns (A) | Ps 19:6
made a *c*. (A)(E)(R) | Ac 28:13

CIRCUITED

c. for seven days (B) | Heb 11:30

CIRCUITS

agains according to his *c*. | Ec 1:6

CIRCUMCISE

shall *c*. the flesh of your foreskin | Ge 17:11
C. therefore the foreskin of your | De 10:16
And the Lord thy God will *c*. thine | De 30:6
c. again the children of Israel the | Jos 5:2
is the cause why Joshua did *c*. | Jos 5:4
C. yourselves to the Lord, and | Jer 4:4
day they came to *c*. the child; | Lu 1:59
ye on the sabbath day *c*. a man. | Joh 7:22
That it was needful to *c*. them | Ac 15:5
saying that they ought not to *c*. | Ac 21:21

CIRCUMCISED

man child among you shall be *c*. | Ge 17:10
that is eight days old shall be *c*. | Ge 17:12; 17:13-14, 23-27
And Abraham *c*. his son Isaac | Ge 21:4
that every male of you be *c*. | Ge 34:15; 34:17, 22, 24
when thou hast *c*. him, then | Ex 12:44
let all his males be *c*. and | Ex 12:48
flesh of his foreskin shall be *c*. | Le 12:3
c. the children of Israel at the hill | Jos 5:3; 5:5, 7
all them which are *c*. with | Jer 9:25
Isaac, and *c*. him the eighth day | Ac 7:8
be *c*. after the manner of Moses | Ac 15:1
Ye must be *c*. and keep the law | Ac 15:24
and took and *c*. him because | Ac 16:3
believe, though they be not *c*. | Ro 4:11
Is any man called being *c*. | 1Co 7:18
let him not be *c*. | 1Co 7:18
a Greek, was compelled to be *c*. | Ga 2:3
if ye be *c*. Christ shall profit you | Ga 5:2
again to every man that is *c*. | Ga 5:3
they constrain you to be *c*.; only | Ga 6:12

they themselves who are *c*. keep | Ga 6:13
desire to have you *c*. that they may | Ga 6:13
C. the eighth day, of the stock of | Ph'p 3:5
In whom also ye are *c*. with | Col 2:11

CIRCUMCISING

they had done *c*. all the people | Jos 5:8
accomplished for the *c*. of the | Lu 2:21

CIRCUMCISION

husband thou art, because of the *c*. | Ex 4:26
Moses therefore gave unto you *c*. | Joh 7:22
man on the sabbath day receive *c*. | Joh 7:23
he gave him the covenant of *c*. | Ac 7:8
they of the *c*. which believed | Ac 10:45
they that were of the *c*. contended | Ac 11:2
For *c*. verily profiteth, if thou keep | Ro 2:25
thy *c*. is made uncircumcision | Ro 2:25
uncircumcision be counted for *c*. | Ro 2:26
the letter and *c*. dost transgress | Ro 2:27
is that *c*. which is outward in | Ro 2:28
c. is that of the heart, in the spirit | Ro 2:29
what profit is there of *c*. | Ro 3:1
shall justify the *c*. by faith | Ro 3:30
blessedness then upon the *c*. only | Ro 4:9
when he was in *c*. or in | Ro 4:10
And he received and sign of *c*. | Ro 4:11
the father of *c*. to them who are not | Ro 4:12
a minister of the *c*. for the truth | Ro 15:8
C. is nothing, and uncircumcision | 1Co 7:19
gospel of the *c*. was unto Peter | Ga 2:7
Peter to the apostleship of the *c*. | Ga 2:8
heathen, and they unto the *c*. | Ga 2:9
fearing them which were of the *c*. | Ga 2:12
neither *c*. availeth any thing | Ga 5:6
if I yet preach *c*. why do I yet | Ga 5:11
neither *c*. availeth any thing | Ga 6:15
C. in the flesh made by hands | Eph 2:11
For we are the *c*. which worship | Ph'p 3:3
with the *c*. made without hands | Col 2:11
sins of the flesh by the *c*. of Christ | Col 2:11
c. nor uncircumcision, Barbarian | Co 3:11
called Justus, who are of the *c*. | Col 4:11
deceivers, specially they of the *c*. | Tit 1:10

CIRCUMSPECT

that I have said unto you be *c*. | Ex 23:13
Pay strict attention to (B) | Ex 23:13
take ye heed to (E)(R) | Ex 23:13
c., temperate (A) | 1Ti 3:2

CIRCUMSPECTLY

that ye walk *c*. not as fools | Eph 5:15
Look carefully then how you walk (A)(E)(R) | Eph 5:15
conduct yourselves ever so carefully (B) | Eph 5:15
Be most careful how you conduct (N) | Eph 5:15
with a due sense of responsibility (P) | Eph 5:15

CIS

Saul the son of *C*. a man of the | Ac 13:21

CISTERN

spring, c., reservoir   *Le 11:36*
(A)(B)(R)
slew at the c. of (A)   *2Ki 10:14*
every one the waters of his   *2Ki 18:31*
c.
out of his own well (B)   *2Ki 18:31*
Drink waters out of thine own   *Pr 5:15*
c.
or the wheel broken at the c.   *Ec 12:6*
dip water from a c.   *Isa 30:14*
(A)(B)(E)(R)
will make the c. of Judah   *Isa 9:11*
desolate,
cistern   *Jer 38:6;*
(A)(B)(R)   *39:10, 11, 13*
cast into a c. (A)(B)(R)   *Jer 41:7;*
    41:9

CISTERNS

c. hewn out (S)   *Ne 9:25*
hewed them out c., broken c.   *Jer 2:13*
came to the c. (A)(E)(R)   *Jer 14:3*
they came to the c. (S)   *Jer 14:3*

CITADEL

c. of the king's house   *1Ki 15:25*
(A)(B)(R)
c. of the king's palace   *1Ki 16:18*
(B)(R)

CITIES

when God destroyed c. of   *Ge 19:29*
plain
terror of God was upon c.   *Ge 35:5*
round about
Joseph laid up the food in   *Ge 41:48*
the c.
people, he removed them to   *Ge 47:21*
c.
c. of Levites may be   *Le 25:32*
redeemed
what c. that they dwell in   *Nu 13:19*
every one give of his c. to   *Nu 35:8*
Levites
nor camest to c. in mountains *De 2:37*
c. gave I to Reubenites and   *De 3:12*
Gadites
abide in c. which I have   *De 3:19*
given you
into land to give great and   *De 6:10*
goodly c.
shall flee to one of these c.   *De 19:5*
and live
Israel came to c. on third   *Jos 9:17*
day
suffer them not to enter into *Jos 10:19*
their c.
c. that stood still in their   *Jos 11:13*
strength
described by c. in seven parts *Jos 18:9*
in book
Jephthah was buried in one   *J'g 12:7*
of c.
men of Israel set fire on all   *J'g 20:48*
the c. they came to
they repaired c. and dwelt in *J'g 21:23*
them
Israelites forsook the c. and *1Sa 31:7*
fled
for c. of our God   *2Sa 10:12;*
    1Ch 19:13
Hiram came from Tyre to   *1Ki 9:12*
see c.
what c. thou hast given me   *1Ki 9:13*
c. my father took I will   *1Ki 20:34*
restore
Jair had 23 c. in land of   *1Ch 2:22*
Gilead
were their c. to reign of   *1Ch 4:31*
David
so did he in c. of Manasseh *2Ch 34:6*
Israelites were in their c.   *Ezr 3:1;*
    Ne 7:73
nine parts to dwell in other c. *Ne 11:1*
dwelleth in desolate c. and   *Job 15:28*
houses
O enemy, thou hast destroyed *Ps 9:6*
c.
answered, till c. be wasted   *Isa 6:11*
nor fill face of world with c.   *Isa 14:21*
in that day five c. in land of   *Isa 19:18*
Egypt
hath despised c. he regardeth *Isa 33:8*
no man

thy holy c. are a   *Isa 64:10*
made land waste, his c. are   *Jer 2:15*
burnt
according to number of thy   *Jer 2:28;*
c.   *11:13*
c. of south be shut up, none   *Jer 13:19*
open
man be as c. Lord   *Jer 20:16*
overthrew
turn again Israel, to these   *Jer 31:21*
thy c.
kindle fire in c. it shall   *Jer 50:32*
devour
like the c. that are not   *Eze 26:19*
inhabited
these c. shall go into   *Eze 30:17*
captivity
I will send fire upon his c.   *Ho 8:14*
sword shall abide on his c.   *Ho 11:6*
three c. wand. unto one for   *Am 4:8*
water
I will cut off the c. of thy   *Mic 5:11*
land
pluck groves, so will I   *Mic 5:14*
destroy thy c.
c. are destroyed, there is no   *Zep 3:6*
man
c. shall yet spread abroad   *Zec 1:17*
not have gone over c. of   *M't 10:23*
Israel
departed to teach and preach *M't 11:1*
in c.
persecuted them even to   *Ac 26:11*
strange c.
c. of Sodom and Gomor, to   *2Pe 2:6*
ashes
c. about them in like manner *Jude 7*
c. of the nations fell and   *Re 16:19*
Babylon

ALL CITIES

Israel took *all* these c. and   *Nu 21:25;*
dwelt in cities of   *De 2:34; 3:4;*
Amorites   *Jos 10:39*
they burnt *all* their c.   *Nu 31:10;*
    J'g 20:48
all c. of Levites shall be 48 *Nu 35:7*
do to *all* c. afar off from   *De 20:15*
thee
all c. of Kings utterly   *Jos 11:12*
destroy
all c. of children of Aaron *Jos 21:19*
13 c.
all c. of Gershonites were 13 *Jos 21:33*
c.
all c. of children of Merari *Jos 21:40*
by lot 12 c.
all c. of the Levites were 48 *Jos 21:41*
cities
women out of *all* c. of Israel *1Sa 18:6*
did he to *all* c. of Ammon   *2Sa 12:31*
they came to *all* c. of Hivites *2Sa 24:7*
all c. Ahab built are written *1Ki 22:39*
Asa smote *all* c. about   *2Ch 14:14*
Garar
have tithes in *all* c. of tillage *Ne 10:37*
c. thereof were broken   *Jer 4:26*
down
in *all* c. an habitation of   *Jer 33:12*
shepherds
all c. thereof be perpetual   *Jer 49:13*
wastes
that may save thee in *all* c.   *Ho 13:10*
preached in *all* c. till he came *Ac 8:40*
to

DEFENCED CITIES

Sennacherib cometh against   *Isa 36:1*
defenced c.
shouldest lay waste *defenced* *Isa 37:26*
c.
let us go into *defenced* c.   *Jer 4:5; 8:14*
these *defenced* c. remained in *Jer 34:7*
Judah

FENCED CITIES

little ones dwell in *fenced* c. *Nu 32:17*
all c. *fenced* with high walls *De 3:5*
c. *fenced* up to heaven   *De 9:1;*
    Jos 14:12
rest of them entered *fenced* *Jos 10:20*
c.
lest he get *fenced* c. and   *2Sa 20:6*
escape
Shishak took *fenced* c. of   *2Ch 12:4*
Judah
Asa built *fenced* c. in Judah, *2Ch 14:6*

Jehoshaphat placed forces in *2Ch 17:2*
fenced c.
set judges through all *fenced* *2Ch 19:5*
c.
Jehoshaphat gave his sons   *2Ch 21:3*
fenced c.
shall impoverish thy *fenced* c. *Jer 5:17*
king of north take most   *Da 11:15*
fenced c.
Judah hath multiplied *fenced* *Ho 8:14*
c.
day of an alarm against   *Zep 1:16*
fenced c.

YOUR CITIES

your c. are burnt with fire   *Isa 1:7*
dwell in *your* c. ye have   *Jer 40:10*
taken
cleanness of teeth in all *your* *Am 4:6*
c.

CITIES OF JUDAH

I go up to any of c. of Judah *2Sa 2:1*
that burnt incense in c. of   *2Ki 23:5*
Judah
to sons of Aaron gave c. of   *1Ch 6:57*
Judah
to teach in c. of Judah   *2Ch 17:7*
set judges in c. of Judah   *2Ch 19:5*
gather Levites out of all c.   *2Ch 23:2*
of Judah
Israel in c. of Judah brought *2Ch 31:6*
tithes
put captains of war in c. of   *2Ch 33:14*
Judah
in c. of Judah each dwelt   *Ne 11:3*
God will save Zion, and   *Ps 69:35*
build c. of Judah
say to c. of Judah, Behold your *Isa 40:9*
God
saith to c. of Judah, Ye shall *Isa 44:26*
be built
families of north against c.   *Jer 1:15*
of Judah
give out their voice against   *Jer 4:16*
c. of Judah
seest what they do in c. of   *Jer 7:17*
Judah
make c. of Judah desolate   *Jer 9:11;*
    10:22; 34:22
then c. of Judah go and cry to *Jer 11:12*
gods
buy fields, take witness in   *Jer 32:44*
c. of Judah
without man and beast, even *Jer 33:10*
in c. of Judah
in c. of Judah flocks pass   *Jer 33:13*
under hands
fury and anger kindled in c. *Jer 44:6*
of Judah
incense he burnt in c. of   *Jer 44:21*
Judah
they ravished maids in c. of *La 5:11*
Judah
have mercy on c. of Judah   *Zec 1:12*

CITIES OF REFUGE

shall be six c. *for refuge*   *Nu 35:6;*
    35:13, 14
appoint for you c. *of refuge* *Nu 35:11;*
    Jos 20:2
gave sons of Kohath c. of   *1Ch 6:67*
refuge

CITIES with SUBURBS

suburbs of c. may not be   *Le 25:34*
sold
give to Levites *suburbs* for c. *Nu 35:2*
Israel gave Levites c. and   *Jos 21:3*
suburbs
c. of Levites forty-eight with *Jos 21:41*
suburbs

CITIES with VILLAGES

fenced c. and country   *1Sa 6:18*
villages
store-houses in c. and   *1Ch 27:25*
villages
Jesus went about c. and   *M't 9:35;*
villages teaching and preaching *Lu 13:22*
he entered into *villages* or   *M'k 6:56*
c.

CITIES with WASTE

I will make your c. *waste*   *Le 26:31;*
    26:33

repair the *waste c.*	*Isa 61:4*
desolations	
c. be laid *waste* without	*Jer 4:7*
inhabitants	
your *c.* shall be *waste*	*Eze 6:6;*
	19:7; 35:4
waste c. fenced and	*Eze 36:35;*
inhabited	*36:38*
they shall build thy *waste c.*	*Am 9:14*

CITIZEN

himself to a *c.* of that	*Lu 15:15*
country	
in Cilicia, a *c.* of no mean	*Ac 21:39*
city	

CITIZENS

But his *c.* hated him, and	*Lu 19:14*
the leading (P)	*Ac 13:50*
conduct as *c. of* Christ (B)	*Ph'p 1:27*
c. of a new state (A)(E)	*Ph'p 3:20*

CITIZENSHIP

Israel's *c.* (B)	*Eph 2:12*
our *c.* is in heaven (E)	*Ph'p 3:20*
our *c.* is in heaven (S)	*Ph'p 3:20*

CITY

Cain built a *c.* and called it	*Ge 4:17*
Enoch	
let us build us a *c.* and a	*Ge 11:4*
tower	
Lord came down to see *c.*	*Ge 11:5*
and tower	
scattered them, they left off to	*Ge 11:8*
build *c.*	
if I find fifty righteous	*Ge 18:26*
within *c.*	
destroy all *c.* for lack of five	*Ge 18:28*
daughters of *c.* come to	*Ge 24:13*
draw water	
all that went out of gate of	*Ge 34:24*
c.	
came upon *c.* boldly, and	*Ge 34:25*
slew males	
flame gone out from *c.* of	*Nu 21:28*
Sihon	
not one *c.* too strong for us	*De 2:36*
not a *c.* we took not from	*De 3:4*
them	
surely smite inhabitants of	*De 13:15*
that *c.*	
c. next to slain man take	*De 21:3;*
heifer	*31:6*
an heap very far from *c.*	*Jos 3:16*
Adam	
compass *c.* and go round six	*Jos 6:3*
days	
they burnt *c.* with fire	*Jos 6:24;*
De 13:16; Jos 8:8, 19; J'g 1:8; 18:27	
lay an ambush for *c.* behind it	*Jos 8:2*
left *c.* open, and pursued	*Jos 8:17*
after Israel	
smoke of *c.* ascended up to	*Jos 8:20*
heaven	
was not a *c.* made peace,	*Jos 11:19*
save the Hivites	
to Caleb *c.* of Arba, which	*Jos 15:13*
c. is Heb.	
gave Joshua *c.* which he	*Jos 19:50*
asked	
stand at entry of gate of *c.*	*Jos 20:4*
because he feared men of *c.*	*J'g 6:27*
Gideon slew the men of the	*J'g 8:17*
c.	
beat down *c.* sowed it with	*J'g 9:45*
salt	
they of *c.* fled, and shut it to	*J'g 9:51*
them	
flame of *c.* ascended up to	*J'g 20:40*
heaven	
all *c.* was moved about them	*Ru 1:19*
all *c.* of my people know that	*Ru 3:11*
went out of *c.* yearly to	*1Sa 1:3*
worship	
when the man told it, all *c.*	*1Sa 4:13*
cried out	
was a deadly destruction	*1Sa 5:11*
thro' all *c.*	
Samuel said to Israel, go	*1Sa 8:22;*
every man to his *c.* 1Ki 22:36; Ezr 2:1;	
	Ne 7:6
Israel buried him in Ramah,	*1Sa 28:3*
his own *c.*	
two men in *c.* one rich,	*2Sa 12:1*
other poor	

Absalom called, of what *c.*	*2Sa 15:2*
art thou	
may die in own *c.* and be	*2Sa 19:37*
buried	
seekest to destroy *c.* and	*2Sa 20:19*
mother in Israel	
rejoicing, so that *c.* rang	*1Ki 1:45*
again	
for Jerusalem's sake, *c.* I	*1Ki 11:32*
have chosen	
neither is this the *c.* follow	*2Ki 6:19*
me	
people rejoiced, and *c.* was	*2Ki 11:20*
quiet	
c. Jerusalem was besieged	*2Ki 24:10;*
	25:2
destroyed of *c.* for God did	*2Ch 15:6*
vex	
he set judges in the land	*2Ch 19:5*
by *c.*	
so the posts passed from *c.*	*2Ch 30:10*
to *c.*	
to trouble them that they	*2Ch 32:18*
might take *c.*	
Jews are building rebellious	*Ezr 4:12*
c.	
why not sad, when *c.* lieth	*Ne 2:3*
waste	
Judah son of Senuah second	*Ne 11:9*
over *c.*	
in the *c.* (S)	*Ne 13:16*
but *c.* Shushan was perplexed	*Es 3:15*
c. Shushan rejoiced and	*Es 8:15*
was glad	
the *c.* of the great king	*Ps 48:2;*
	M't 5:35
they go round about the *c.*	*Ps 59:6;*
	59:14
they of *c.* flourish like grass	*Ps 72:16*
of earth	
wandered, they found no *c.*	*Ps 107:4*
to dwell in	
Jerusalem is builded as a *c.*	*Ps 122:3*
compact	
except Lord keep *c.*	*Ps 127:1*
watchmen vain	
Wisdom crieth at entry of *c.*	*Pr 8:3*
rich man's wealth strong *c.*	*Pr 10:15;*
	18:11
when well with righteous *c.*	*Pr 11:10*
rejoiceth	
by blessing of upright *c.* is	*Pr 11:11*
exalted	
ruleth spirit, than he that	*Pr 16:32*
taketh *c.*	
like *c.* broken down without	*Pr 25:28*
walls	
scornful men bring a *c.* into a	*Pr 29:8*
snare	
a little *c.* and few men in it	*Ec 9:14*
the poor wise man delivered	*Ec 9:15*
the *c.*	
c. of righteousness, faithful *c.*	*Isa 1:26*
howl, O gate, cry O *c.*	*Isa 14:31*
whole Palestina	
Damascus taken away from	*Isa 17:1*
being a *c.*	
fight *c.* against *c.* kingdom	*Isa 19:2*
against kingdom	
c. of confusion is broken	*Isa 24:10*
down	
made of a *c.* an heap. to be	*Isa 25:2*
no *c.*	
look on Zion, *c.* of our	*Isa 33:20*
solemnities	
they shall call thee *c.* of the	*Isa 60:14*
Lord	
shalt be called a *c.* not	*Isa 62:12*
forsaken	
take you one of a *c.* two of	*Jer 3:14*
a tribe	
whole *c.* flee from noise of	*Jer 4:29*
horsemen	
will I do, even make *c.* as	*Jer 19:12*
Tophet	
bring evil on *c.* called by	*Jer 25:29*
my name	
are come to *c.* and *c.* is	*Jer 32:24*
given	
c. broken up, men of war	*Jer 39:2;*
fled	*52:7*
I will destroy *c.* and	*Jer 46:8*
inhabitants	
how is *c.* of praise not left,	*Jer 49:25*
c. of joy	
c. sit solitary, full of people	*La 1:1*
this *c.* men called perfection	*La 2:15*
of beauty	
portray on it *c.* even	*Eze 4:1*
Jerusalem	

make a chain, for *c.* is full	*Eze 7:23*
of violence	
cause them that have charge	*Eze 9:1*
over *c.*	
go thro' midst of *c.* set mark	*Eze 9:4*
land full of blood, *c.* full of	*Eze 9:9*
perverseness	
scatter coals of fire over the	*Eze 10:2*
c.	
what *c.* is like Tyrus in	*Eze 27:32*
midst of sea	
one came saying, *c.* is	*Eze 33:21*
smitten	
name of *c.* be, Lord is	*Eze 48:35*
there	
the *c.* called by thy name	*Da 9:18;*
	9:19
Gilead a *c.* of them that work	*Ho 6:8*
iniquity	
to ram on one *c.* not on	*Am 4:7*
another	
c. that went out by thousand	*Am 5:3*
shall	
woe to him that stablisheth	*Hab 2:12*
c. by	
woe to filthy, polluted,	*Zep 3:1*
oppressing *c.*	
Jerusalem be called *c.* of truth	*Zec 8:3*
streets of *c.* be full of boys	*Zec 8:5*
and girls	
c. be taken and houses rifled,	*Zec 14:2*
residue not be cut off from *c.*	
c. set on a hill cannot be hid	*M't 5:14*
by Jerusalem, for it is *c.* of	*M't 5:35*
great king	
whole *c.* came out to meet	*M't 8:34*
Jesus	
into whatsoever *c.* ye enter,	*M't 10:11*
inquire	
than for that *c.* M't 10:15; M'k 6:11;	
	Lu 10:12
all *c.* was moved, saying,	*M't 21:10*
who is this	
the king sent and burnt up	*M't 22:7*
their *c.*	
and persecute them from *c.*	*M't 23:34*
to *c.*	
all *c.* gathered together at	*M'k 1:33*
door	
they that fed swine told it	*M'k 5:14;*
in *c.*	*Lu 8:34*
went out to be taxed, every one to	*Lu 2:3*
own *c.*	
much people of *c.* with her	*Lu 7:12*
he beheld the *c.* and wept	*Lu 19:41*
over it	
Joseph was of Arimathea, *c.*	*Lu 23:51*
of Jews	
many of that *c.* believed on	*Joh 4:39*
him	
there was great joy in that *c.*	*Ac 8:8*
together almost whole *c.* to	*Ac 13:44*
hear	
were abiding in that *c.*	*Ac 16:12*
certain days	
set all *c.* in uproar and	*Ac 17:5*
assaulted	
whole *c.* was filled with	*Ac 19:29*
confusion	
all *c.* was moved, and people	*Ac 21:30*
ran	
looked for *c.* that hath	*Heb 11:10*
foundations	
for he hath prepared for	*Heb 11:16*
them a *c.*	
are come to the *c.* of living	*Heb 12:22*
God	
for here we have no	*Heb 13:14*
continuing *c.*	
will go into such *c.* buy and	*Jas 4:13*
sell	
went and compassed beloved	*Re 20:9*
c.	
wall of *c.* had twelve	*Re 21:14*
foundations	
c. was pure gold, like clear	*Re 21:18*
glass	
c. had no need of the sun	*Re 21:23*
nor moon	

BLOODY CITY

wilt thou judge *bloody c.*	*Eze 22:2*
woe to *bloody c.*	*Eze 24:6*

DEFENCED CITY

hast made of a *defenced c.* a	*Isa 25:2*
ruin	

defenced c. shall be desolate Isa 27:10
I have made thee a defenced Jer 1:18
c.

CITY OF DAVID

called it c. of David   2Sa 5:9;
                                 1Ch 11:7
would not remove ark into c.   2Sa 6:10
of David
brought up ark into c. of   2Sa 6:12;
David   6:16
David was buried in c. of   1Ki 2:10
David
Solomon brought her into c.   1Ki 3:1
of David
bring ark out of c. of David   1Ki 8:1;
                                 2Ch 5:2
buried in the c. of David   1Ki 11:43;
14:31; 15:8; 22:50; 2Ki 8:24; 9:28;
12:21; 14:20; 15:7, 38; 16:20; 2Ch 9:31;
    12:16; 14:1; 21:1, 20; 24:16, 25; 27:9
see the breeches of the c. of   Isa 22:9
David
Joseph also went into the c. of Lu 2:4
David
to you is born in c. of David   Lu 2:11
a Saviour

CITY OF GOD

streams make glad c. of God   Ps 46:4
Lord greatly praised in c. of   Ps 48:1
God
the c. of God, God will   Ps 48:8
establish for ever
glorious things spoken of c.   Ps 87:3
of God
come to the c. of the living   Heb 12:22
God
write on him name of c. of   Re 3:12
God

CITY OF THE LORD

cut off wicked from c. of the   Ps 101:8
Lord
shall call thee the c. of the   Isa 60:14
Lord

CITY OF REFUGE

restore him to c. of refuge   Nu 35:25;
if come without c. of   Nu 35:26;
refuge   35:26
should have remained in c.   Nu 35:28
of refuge
for him that is fled to c. of   Nu 35:32
refuge
gave to be c. of refuge   Jos 21:13;
    21:21, 27, 32, 38; 1Ch 6:57

ELDERS with CITY

elders of his c. shall fetch   De 19:12
him
elders of that c. next to slain De 21:6
man
say to elders of c. our son is   De 21:20
stubborn
spread cloth before elders of   De 22:17
c.
then elders of his c. shall call De 25:8
him
declare his cause to elders of   Jos 20:4
c.
Gideon took the elders of the   J'g 8:16
c.
Boaz took ten men of elders   Ru 4:2
of c.
with them elders of every c.   Ezr 10:14

EVERY CITY

smote as well the men of   J'g 20:48
every c.
ye shall smite every fenced c.   2Ki 3:19
in every c. Rehoboam put   2Ch 11:12
shields
in every c. of Judah made   2Ch 28:25
high places
sons of Aaron which were   2Ch 31:19
in every c.
with them elders of every c.   Ezr 10:14
every c. shall be forsaken   Jer 4:29
spoiler shall come upon every   Jer 48:8
c.
every c. divided against   M't 12:25
itself

sent them two and two into   Lu 10:1
every c.
in every c. them that preach   Ac 15:21
him
let us go visit our brethren   Ac 15:36
in every c.
Holy Ghost witnesseth in   Ac 20:23
every c.
thou ordain elders in every c.   Tit 1:5

FENCED CITY

with you fenced c. and   2Ki 10:2
armor
from tower of watchmen to   2Ki 17:9
fenced c.
dispersed children to every   2Ch 11:23
fenced c.

GREAT CITY

Ashur builded Resen, a   Ge 10:12
great c.
feared, because Gibeon was   Jos 10:2
great c.
c. was large and great, but   Ne 7:4
people
why Lord done thus to great   Jer 22:8
c.
go to Nineveh, that great c.   Jon 1:2;
                                     3:2
Nineveh was an exceeding   Jon 3:3
great c.
should I not spare Nineveh,   Jon 4:11
that great c.
dead bodies lie in street of   Re 11:8
great c.
Babylon fallen, great c.   Re 14:8;
                          18:10, 16, 19, 21
great c. divided into three   Re 16:19
parts
woman thou sawest, is that   Re 17:18
great c.
shewed me great c. holy   Re 21:10
Jerusalem

HOLY CITY

cast lots to dwell in the holy   Ne 11:1
c.
all Levites of holy c. were   Ne 11:18
284
they call themselves of the   Isa 48:2
holy c.
put on beautiful garments, O   Isa 52:1
holy c.
seventy weeks determined on   Da 9:24
holy c.
devil taketh him up into holy   M't 4:5
c.
went into holy c. appeared   M't 27:53
to many
holy c. shall tread under foot   Re 11:2
John saw holy c. coming   Re 21:2
down from God
God take his part out of   Re 22:19
holy c.

IN, INTO THE CITY

whatsoever thou hast in the   Ge 19:12
c.
all in the c. take to thyself   De 20:14
blessed shalt thou be in the c. De 28:3
and field
cursed shalt thou be in the   De 28:16
c. and field
so the people went into the   Jos 6:20
c.
destroyed all that was in the   Jos 6:21
c.
entered into the c. and set it   Jos 8:19
on fire
shew us the entrance into the   J'g 1:24
c.
Gideon put ephod in his c. in   J'g 8:27
Ophrah
man came into the c. and   1Sa 4:13
told
carry back ark of God into   2Sa 15:25
the c.
return into the c., your sons   2Sa 15:27
with you
they came and told it in the   1Ki 13:25
c.
dieth of Jeroboam in the c.   1Ki 14:11
dogs eat
when thy feet enter into the   1Ki 14:12
c.

that dieth of Baasha in the   1Ki 16:4
c. dogs eat
came into the c. into inner   1Ki 20:30
chamber
dieth of Ahab, in the c.   1Ki 21:24
dogs eat
if we say, we will enter into   2Ki 7:4
the c.
we shall catch them, and get   2Ki 7:12
into the c.
Hezekiah brought water   2Ki 20:20
into the c.
famine prevailed in the c.   2Ki 25:3;
                                 Jer 52:6
Lord shewed me kindness in   Ps 31:21
strong c.
I have seen violence and strife Ps 55:9
in the c.
in the c. wisdom uttereth   Pr 1:21
words
than ten mighty men in the c.   Ec 7:19
the wicked were forgotten in   Ec 8:10
the c.
in the c. is left desolation   Isa 24:12
if I enter into the c. then   Jer 14:18
sick
there is no more bread in the   Jer 38:9
c.
elders gave up ghost in the c.   La 1:19
in the c. famine shall devour   Eze 7:15
him
they went forth and slew in   Eze 9:7
the c.
I will not enter into the c.   Ho 11:9
run to and fro in the c. on   Joe 2:9
the wall
shall trumpet be blown in the   Am 3:6
c., be evil in a c. and Lord hath
not done it
thy wife shall be an harlot   Am 7:17
in the c.
Jonah began to enter into the   Jon 3:4
c.
came into his own c.   M't 9:1
into any c. of the Samaritans   M't 10:5
enter not
into whatsoever c. ye shall   M't 10:11
enter
go into the c. to such a   M't 26:18
man, and say
behold, some of the watch   M't 28:11
came into the c.
he saith, Go into the c.   M'k 14:13;
                                 Ac 9:6
went to be taxed, every one   Lu 2:3
into his c.
woman in the c. which was a   Lu 7:37
sinner
in a c. a judge, who feared   Lu 18:2
not God
there was a window in that c.   Lu 18:3
when ye are entered into the   Lu 22:10
c.
tarry ye in the c. of   Lu 24:49
Jerusalem
his disciples were gone into   Joh 4:8
the c.
I was in the c. of Joppa,   Ac 11:5
praying
he rose up and came into   Ac 14:20
the c.
had seen Trophimus with   Ac 21:29
him in the c.
neither in synagogues nor in   Ac 24:12
the c.
I have been in perils in the   2Co 11:26
c.
may enter thro' gates into   Re 22:14
the c.

OUT OF THE CITY

when they were gone out of   Ge 44:4
the c.
as soon as I am gone out of   Ex 9:29
the c.
Moses went out of the c.   Ex 9:33
from Pharaoh
shall carry them forth out of   Le 14:45
the c.
other side issued out of the   Jos 8:22
c.
spies saw man come out of   J'g 1:24
the c.
better succour us out of the   2Sa 18:3
c.
then cried a wise woman   2Sa 20:16
out of the c.
carried Naboth out of the   1Ki 21:13
c.

when they come *out of the* c.	2Ki 7:12
Jehu said, let none escape *out of the* c.	2Ki 9:15
brought much spoil *out of* the c.	1Ch 20:2
Josiah cast idols *out of the* c.	2Ch 33:15
men groan from *out of* the	Job 24:12
Zedekiah went *out of the* c.	Jer 39:4; 52:7
these are the goings *out of* the c.	Eze 48:30
now shalt thou go *out of the* c.	Mic 4:10
He left them, and went *out of the* c.	M't 21:17
even was come, went *out of the* c.	M'k 11:19
they thrust him *out of the* c.	Lu 4:29
when ye go *out of the* c. shake off dust	Lu 9:5
then they went *out of the* c.	Joh 4:30
cast Stephen *out of the* c. and stoned him	Ac 7:58
stoned Paul, drew him *out of the* c.	Ac 14:19
on sabbath we went *out of the* c.	Ac 16:13
brought us, till we were *out of the* c.	Ac 21:5

THIS CITY

Lot said, will destroy *this* c.	Ge 19:14
this c. is near to flee unto	Ge 19:20
he said, I will not overthrow *this* c.	Ge 19:21
cursed be he that buildeth *this* c.	Jos 6:26
come, let us turn unto *this* c.	J'g 19:11
there is in *this* c. a man of God	1Sa 9:6
situation of *this* c. is pleasant	2Ki 2:19
this c. not be delivered	2Ki 18:20; Isa 36:15
not come into *this* c.	2Ki 19:32; Isa 37:34
I will cast off *this* c.	2Ki 23:27
will defend *this* c.	2Ki 34:1; 20:6; Isa 37:35; 38:6
pray to thee toward *this* c.	2Ch 6:34
if *this* c. be builded again	Ezr 4:13; 4:16
know that *this* c. is a rebellious city	Ezr 4:15
did not God bring evil upon *this* c.	Ne 13:18
this is the c. to be visited	Jer 6:6
Jerusalem, *this* c. remain for ever	Jer 17:25
I will make *this* c. desolate	Jer 19:8
will I break this people and *this* c.	Jer 19:11
bring upon *this* c. all the evil	Jer 19:15
I will deliver all strength of *this* c.	Jer 20:5
he that abideth in *this* c. die by sword	Jer 21:9
I set my face against *this* c. for evil	Jer 21:10
why hath Lord done thus to *this* c.	Jer 22:8
I will make *this* c. a curse to nations	Jer 26:6
shall bring innocent blood on *this* c.	Jer 26:15
wherefore should *this* c. be laid waste	Jer 27:17
give *this* c. to Chaldeans	Jer 32:3; 32:24-28; 34:2
this c. hath been to me a a provocation	Jer 32:31
for wickedness I hid face from *this* c.	Jer 33:5
cause them to return to *this* c.	Jer 34:22
this c. shall not be burnt with fire	Jer 38:17
cause *this* c. to be burnt with fire	Jer 38:23
will bring my words on *this* c. for evil	Jer 39:16
men give wicked counsel in *this* c.	Eze 11:2

this c. is caldron, we be flesh	Eze 11:3; 11:7
this c. not be caldron, nor ye flesh	Eze 11:11
when persecute in *this* c. flee	M't 10:23
for I have much people in *this* c.	Ac 18:10
brought up in *this* c. at feet of Gamaliel	Ac 22:3

WITHOUT CITY

the men set him *without* c.	Ge 19:16
into an unclean place *without* c.	Le 14:40; 14:41
ye shall measure from *without* c.	Nu 35:5
to stop the fountains *without* c.	2Ch 32:3
wine-press was trodden *without* c.	Re 14:20

CLAD

c. himself with a new garment	1Ki 11:29
and was c. with zeal as a cloke	Isa 59:17

CLAIM

in this c. you are not fair (B)	Job 33:12
many who lay c. to (N)	1Ti 6:21

CLAIMED

some people have c. (B)	1Ti 6:21

CLAIMING

c. to be wise (A)(B)(R)	Ro 1:22

CLAIRVOYANT

a c. spirit (B)(P)	Ac 16:16

CLAMOR

c. of the nations (B)	Ps 65:7; 74:23
c. of enemies (B)(R)	Ps 74:23
like a swallow or crane (R)	Isa 38:14

CLAMOROUS

foolish woman is c.: she is simple	Pr 9:13

CLAMOUR

anger, and c. and evil speaking	Eph 4:31

CLAN

leader of his c. (B)	Nu 1:4
the c. leader (B)	Nu 3:24; 3:30, 35; 25:14
a rod for each c. (B)	Nu 17:2
the c. leaders (B)	1Ch 9:34; 24:31; 26:32; 2Ch 26:12
he shall be the c. head (B)	Zec 9:7
it shall be like a c. (R)	Zec 9:7

CLANS

tribes, c. (B)	Ge 10:5; 10:20
according to families and c. (B)	Nu 1:2; 3:15
according to respective c. (B)	Nu 2:2; 34:14
the c. of Judah (R)	Zec 12:5; 12:6

CLAP

Men shall c. their hands at him	Job 27:23
O c. your hands, all ye people	Ps 47:1
Let the floods c. their hands	Ps 98:8
of the field shall c. their hands	Isa 55:12
pass by c. their hands at thee	La 2:15
shall c. the hands over thee	Na 3:19

CLAPPED

and they c. their hands, and	2Ki 11:12
thou hast c. thine hands, and	Eze 25:6

CLAPPETH

he c. his hands among us	Job 34:37

CLASH

sharp c. of opinion (P)	Ac 15:39

CLASPS

clasps (A)(B)(E)(R)	Ex 26:2; 26:11, 33; 36:13, 18; 39:33
clasps (S)	Ex 26:6; 26:11, 33; 35:11; 36:13, 18; 39:33
two gold c. (B)	Ex 39:16; 39:18

CLASS

in same c. as a destroyer (A)	Pr 28:24

CLAUDA

certain island which is called C.	Ac 27:16

CLAUDIA

and C. and all the brethren	2Ti 4:21

CLAUDIUS

to pass in the days of C. Cæsar	Ac 11:28
C. had commanded all Jews to	Ac 18:2
C. Lysias unto the most excellent	Ac 23:26

CLAVE

and c. the wood for the burnt	Ge 22:3
split the wood (A)(B)	Ge 22:3
cut the wood (R)	Ge 22:3
And his soul c. unto Dinah	Ge 34:3
ground c. asunder that was under	Nu 16:31
the ground split open (A)(B)(R)	Nu 16:31
But God c. an hollow place that	J'g 15:19
split open a hollow place (A)(R)	J'g 15:19
caused a fissure in a hollow place (B)	J'g 15:19
but Ruth c. unto her	Ru 1:14
Ruth clung closely to her (A)(R)	Ru 1:14
and they c. the wood of the cart	1Sa 6:14
split the wood of the cart (A)(B)(R)	1Sa 6:14
men of Judah c. unto their king	1Sa 20:2
men of Judah stayed faithfully with (A)	2Sa 20:2
men of Judah kept following David (B)	2Sa 20:2
followed their king stedfastly (R)	2Sa 20:2
and his hand c. unto the sword	2Sa 23:10
clung to the sword (A)	2Sa 23:10
stuck to this sword (B)	2Sa 23:10
clove to his sword (R)	2Sa 23:10
Solomon c. unto these in love	1Ki 11:2
clung to these in love (A)(R)	1Ki 11:2
held fast to them in love (B)	1Ki 11:2
he c. to the Lord, and departed not	2Ki 18:6
he clung to the Lord (B)	2Ki 18:6
held fast to the Lord (R)	2Ki 18:6
They c. to their brethren	Ne 10:29
joined with their brothers (A)(B)(R)	Ne 10:29
He c. the rocks in the wilderness	Ps 78:15
he c. the rock also, and the	Isa 48:21
men c. unto him, and believed	Ac 17:34
joined him (A)(N)(P)(R)	Ac 17:34
associated with him (B)	Ac 17:34

CLAWS

cleaveth the cleft into two *c.*   De 14:6
feathers, and his nails, like   Da 4:33
birds
fat, and tear their *c.* in   Zec 11:16
pieces

CLAY

king cast them, in the *c.*   1Ki 7:46
ground
in the *c.* ground between   2Ch 4:17
Succoth
them that dwell in houses of   Job 4:19
c.
thou hast made me as the *c.*   Job 10:9
ashes, your bodies to bodies   Job 13:12
of *c.*
and prepare raiment as the   Job 27:16
c.
I also am formed out of the   Job 33:6
c.
It is turned as *c.* to the   Job 38:14
seal; and
out of the miry *c.* and set my   Ps 40:2
feet
be esteemed as the potter's   Isa 29:16
c.
considered equal with *c.* (B)   Isa 29:16
and as the potter treadeth *c.*   Isa 41:25
c. say to him that fashioneth   Isa 45:9
it
thou art our father; we are   Isa 64:8
the *c.*
that he made of *c.* was   Jer 18:4
marred
as the *c.* is in the potter's   Jer 18:6
hand
them in the *c.* in the brick kiln   Jer 43:9
feet part of iron and part of   Da 2:33
c.
were of iron and *c.* and   Da 2:34
brake them
iron, the *c.* the brass, the   Da 2:35
silver
part of potter's *c.* and part of   Da 2:41
iron
sawest the iron mixed with   Da 2:41
miry *c.*
were part of iron, and part   Da 2:42
of *c.*
sawest iron mixed with miry   Da 2:43
c.
even as iron is not mixed   Da 2:43
with *c.*
in pieces the iron, the brass,   Da 2:45
the *c.*
go into *c.* and tread the   Na 3:14
mortar
that ladeth himself with thick   Hab 2:6
c.
and made *c.* of the spittle, and   Joh 9:6
eyes of the blind man with   Joh 9:6
the *c.*
made *c.* with saliva (B)   Joh 9:6
man that is called Jesus made   Joh 9:11
c.
when Jesus made the *c.* and   Joh 9:14
He put *c.* upon mine eyes   Joh 9:15
not the potter power over the   Ro 9:21
c.
as *c.* jars broken (B)   Re 2:27

CLEAN

Of every *c.* beast thou shalt   Ge 7:2;
take   7:8
every *c.* beast, and of every   Ge 8:20
c. fowl
go *c.* and change your   Ge 35:2
garments
a *c.* place where the ashes are   Le 4:12
without the camp unto a *c.*   Le 6:11
place
all that be *c.* shall eat thereof   Le 7:19
and between unclean and *c.*   Le 10:10
shoulder shall ye eat in a *c.*   Le 10:14
place
is plenty of water, shall be *c.*   Le 11:36
which is to be sown, it shall   Le 11:37
be *c.*
between the unclean and the   Le 11:47
c.
for her, and she shall be *c.*   Le 12:8
the priest shall pronounce   Le 13:6;
him *c.*   13:13, 17, 23, 28, 34, 37, 39,
40-41, 58-59; 14:4, 7-9, 11, 20, 48, 53,
57; 15:8, 18, 28

ye may be *c.* from all your   Le 16:30
sins
until the even: then shall he   Le 17:15
be *c.*
between *c.* beasts and   Le 20:25
unclean
and between unclean fowls   Le 20:25
and *c.*
of the holy things, until he be   Le 22:4
c.
the sun is down, he shall be   Le 22:7
c.
thou shalt not make *c.*   Le 23:22
riddance
woman be not defiled, but be   Nu 5:28
c.
and so make themselves *c.*   Nu 8:7
But the man that is *c.* and is   Nu 9:13
not
every one that is *c.* in thy   Nu 18:11
house
every one that is *c.* in thine   Nu 18:13
house
a man that is *c.* shall gather   Nu 19:9
up
up without the camp in a *c.*   Nu 19:9
place
on the seventh day he shall   Nu 19:12
be *c.*
the seventh day he shall not   Nu 19:12
be *c.*
a *c.* person shall take   Nu 19:18
hyssop, and
and the *c.* person shall   Nu 19:19
sprinkle
himself in water, and shall   Nu 19:19
be *c.*
through the fire, and it shall   Nu 31:23
be *c.*
and ye shall be *c.* and   Nu 31:24
afterward
the unclean and the *c.* may   De 12:15
eat
the unclean, and the *c.* shall   De 12:22
eat of
Of all *c.* birds ye shall eat   De 14:11
But of all *c.* fowls ye may   De 14:20
eat
unclean and the *c.* person   De 15:22
shall
not *c.* by reason of   De 23:10
uncleanness
all the people were passed *c.*   Jos 3:17
over
people were *c.* passed over   Jos 4:11
Jordan
people were *c.* passed over   Jos 4:11
he is not *c.;* surely he is   1Sa 20:26
not *c.*
again to thee, and thou shalt   2Ki 5:10
be *c.*
may I not wash in them,   2Ki 5:12
and be *c.*
he saith to thee, Wash, and   2Ki 5:13
be *c.*
of a little child, and he was   2Ki 5:14
c.
for every one that was not   2Ch 30:17
c. to
began to *c.* up Judah (B)   2Ch 34:3
and make my hands never so   Job 9:30
c.
doctrine is pure, and I am *c.*   Job 11:4
Who can bring a *c.* thing   Job 14:4
out of an
What is man, that he   Job 15:14
should be *c.*
the heavens are not *c.* in   Job 15:15
his sight
and he that hath *c.* hands   Job 17:9
shall
or how can he be *c.* that is   Job 25:4
born
I am *c.* without transgression, I   Job 33:9
The fear of the Lord is *c.*   Ps 19:9
He that hath *c.* hands, and a   Ps 24:4
pure
me with hyssop, and I shall   Ps 51:7
be *c.*
Create in me a *c.* heart, O   Ps 51:10
God
even to such as are of a *c.*   Ps 73:1
heart
Is his mercy *c.* gone for ever   Ps 77:8
Where no oxen are, the crib   Pr 14:4
is *c.*
ways of a man are *c.* in his   Pr 16:2
own
can say, I have made my   Pr 20:9
heart *c.*

to the good and to the *c.* and   Ec 9:2
Wash you, make you *c.;* put   Isa 1:16
away
broken down, the earth is *c.*   Isa 24:19
so that there is no place *c.*   Isa 28:8
that ear the ground shall eat   Isa 30:24
c.
be ye *c.* that bear the   Isa 52:11
vessels of
bring an offering in a *c.*   Isa 66:20
vessel
wilt thou not be made *c.*   Jer 13:27
between the unclean and   Eze 22:26
the *c.*
Then will I sprinkle *c.*   Eze 36:25
water
and ye shall be *c.:* from all   Eze 36:25
your
between the unclean and   Eze 44:23
the *c.*
he hath made it *c.* bare, and   Joe 1:7
cast
a *c.* turban (S)   Zec 3:5
his arm shall be *c.* dried   Zec 11:17
up, and
thou wilt, thou canst make   M't 8:2
me *c.*
him, saying, I will; be thou *c.*   M't 8:3
swept *c.* and tidy (N)   M't 12:44
for ye make *c.* the outside   M't 23:25
of the
the outside of them may be   M't 23:26
c.
the body, he wrapped it in   M't 27:59
a *c.*
wilt, thou canst make me *c.*   M'k 1:40
saith unto him, I will; be   M'k 1:41
thou *c.*
thou wilt, thou canst make   Lu 5:12
me *c.*
him, saying, I will: be thou *c.*   Lu 5:13
Now do ye Pharisees make   Lu 11:39
c.
behold, all things are *c.* unto   Lu 11:41
you
but is *c.* every whit   Joh 13:10
and ye are *c.* but not all   Joh 13:10
therefore said he, Ye are   Joh 13:11
not all *c.*
Now ye are *c.* through the   Joh 15:3
word
upon your own heads; I am   Ac 18:6
c.
be *c.* from your sins (P)   Ac 22:16
c. and above reproach (P)   1Ti 6:14
those that were *c.* escaped   2Pe 2:18
from
c. and blameless (P)   2Pe 3:14
arrayed in fine linen, *c.* and   Re 9:8
white
clothed in fine linen, white   Re 19:14
and *c.*

CLEANED

c. and orderly (B)(P)   M't 12:44

CLEANNESS

to the *c.* of my hands hath   2Sa 22:21
he
according to my *c.* in his   2Sa 22:25
eye sight
to the *c.* of my hands hath   Ps 18:20
he
the *c.* of my hands in his   Ps 18:24
eyesight
I also have given you *c.* of   Am 4:6
teeth

CLEANSE

and thou shalt *c.* the altar   Ex 29:36
he shall take to *c.* the house   Le 14:49
two
And he shall *c.* the house   Le 14:52
with the
seven times, and *c.* it, and   Le 16:19
hallow
an atonement for you, to *c.*   Le 16:30
you
children of Israel, and *c.* them   Nu 8:6
shalt thou do unto them, to *c.*   Nu 8:7
and thou shalt *c.* them, and   Nu 8:15
offer
an atonement for them to *c.*   Nu 8:21
them
of the Lord, to *c.* the house   2Ch 29:15
house of the Lord, to *c.* it   2Ch 29:16
the Levites that they should   Ne 13:22
c.

c. thou me from secret faults *Ps 19:12*
mine iniquity, and *c.* me from *Ps 51:2*
my
Wherewithal shall a young *Ps 119:9*
man *c.*
people, not to fan, nor to *c.* *Jer 4:11*
And I will *c.* them from all *Jer 33:8*
their
water to *c.* you *Eze 16:4*
(A)(B)(E)(R)(S)
from all your idols, will I *c.* *Eze 36:25*
you
they have sinned, and will *Eze 37:23*
c. them
of them, that they may *c.* *Eze 39:12*
the land
upon the face of the earth, *Eze 39:14*
to *c.* it
Thus shall they *c.* the land *Eze 39:16*
thus shalt thou *c.* and purge *Eze 43:20*
it
and they shall *c.* the altar *Eze 43:22*
as they did *c.* it with the *Eze 43:22*
bullock
blemish, and *c.* the *Eze 45:18*
sanctuary
For I will *c.* their blood that *Joe 3:21*
I
c. the lepers, raise the dead, *M't 10:8*
cast
c. first that which is within *M't 23:26*
the
let us *c.* ourselves from all *2Co 7:1*
That he might sanctify and *Eph 5:26*
c. it
C. your hands, ye sinners; and *Jas 4:8*
to *c.* us from all *1Jo 1:9*
unrighteousness

CLEANSED

until the even; so it shall be *Le 11:32*
c.
and she shall be *c.* from *Le 12:7*
take for him that is to be *c.* *Le 14:4;*
two   *14:7-8, 14, 17-19, 25, 28-29, 31*
when he that hath an issue *Le 15:13*
is *c.*
if she be *c.* of her issue, *Le 15:28*
then she
the land cannot be *c.* of the *Nu 35:33*
blood
which we are not *c.* until *Jos 22:17*
this day
have *c.* all the house of the *2Ch 29:18*
Lord
not *c.* themselves, yet did *2Ch 30:18*
they eat
though he be not *c.* *2Ch 30:19*
according to
their altars, and *c.* Judah and *2Ch 34:5*
and they *c.* the chambers *Ne 13:9*
Thus *c.* I them from all *Ne 13:30*
strangers
I have, if I be *c.* from my *Job 35:3*
sin
Verily I have *c.* my heart in *Ps 73:13*
vain
Thou art the land that is *Eze 22:24*
not *c.*
In the day that I shall have *Eze 36:33*
c. you
after he is *c.* they shall *Eze 44:26*
reckon
then shall the sanctuary be *c.* *Da 8:14*
their blood that I have not *c.* *Joe 3:21*
immediately his leprosy was *c.* *M't 8:3*
lepers are *c.* and the deaf *M't 11:5*
hear
departed from him and he *M'k 1:42*
was *c.*
and none of them was *c.* *Lu 4:27*
saving
the lepers are *c.* the deaf hear *Lu 7:22*
to pass, as they went, they *Lu 17:14*
were *c.*
Were there not ten *c.*? but *Lu 17:17*
where
What God hath *c.* that call *Ac 10:15;*
not thou   *11:9*
be *c.* from sins (B) *Ac 22:16*

CLEANSETH

the wind passeth, and *c.* *Job 37:21*
them
blueness of a wound *c.* away *Pr 20:30*
evil
blood of Jesus Christ his Son *1Jo 1:7*
c. us

CLEANSING

been seen of the priest for his *Le 13:7*
c.
much in the skin after his *c.* *Le 13:35*
law of the leper in the day *Le 14:2*
of his *c.*
them on the eighth day for *Le 14:23*
his *c.*
get that which pertaineth to *Le 14:32*
his *c.*
to himself seven days for his *Le 15:13*
c.
shave his head in the day of *Nu 6:9*
his *c.*
When thou hast made an *Eze 43:23*
end of *c.*
and offer for thy *c.* those *M'k 1:44*
things
and offer for thy *c.* according *Lu 5:14*
as
c. of the new birth (A) *Tit 3:5*
various rights of *c.* (N) *Heb 9:10*

CLEAR

c. from this my oath *Ge 24:8; 24:41*
or how shall we *c.* ourselves *Ge 44:16*
he that smote him be *c.* (S) *Ex 21:19*
owner of the ox be *c.* (S) *Ex 21:28*
will by no means *c.* the guilty *Ex 34:7*
the earth by *c.* shining after *2Sa 23:4*
rain
speakest, and be *c.* when thou *Ps 51:4*
fair as the moon, *c.* as the *Ca 6:10*
sun
like a *c.* heat upon herbs, *Isa 18:4*
and like
will darken the earth in the *c.* *Am 8:9*
day
the light shall not be *c.* nor *Zec 14:6*
dark
approved yourselves to be *c.* *2Co 7:11*
in
steer *c.* of unchristian *2Ti 2:16*
babblings (P)
steer *c.* of foolish speculations *Tit 3:9*
(N)
keep *c.* of desires of lower *1Pe 2:11*
nature (P)
like a jasper stone, *c.* as *Re 21:11*
crystal
was pure gold, like unto *c.* *Re 21:18*
glass
river of water of life, *c.* as *Re 22:1*
crystal

CLEARED

by his breath skies are *c.* *Job 26:13*
(A)(B)

CLEARER

age shall be *c.* than the *Job 11:17*
noonday

CLEARING

no means *c.* the guilty, *Nu 14:18*
visiting
in you, yea, what *c.* of *2Co 7:11*
yourselves

CLEARLY

my lips shall utter knowledge *Job 33:3*
c.
then shalt thou see *c.* to cast *M't 7:5*
out
restored, and saw every man *M'k 8:25*
c.
then shalt thou see *c.* to pull *Lu 6:42*
out
are *c.* seen, being understood *Ro 1:20*
by
make this *c.* known (B)(R) *Col 4:4*

CLEARNESS

were the body of heaven in *Ex 24:10*
his *c.*

CLEAVE

shall *c.* unto his wife: and *Ge 2:24*
shall *c.* it with the wings *Le 1:17*
thereof
But ye that did *c.* unto the *De 4:4*
Lord

to him shalt thou *c.* and *De 10:20*
swear by
in all his ways, and to *c.* *De 11:22*
unto him
shall serve him, and *c.* unto *De 13:4*
him
shall *c.* nought of the cursed *De 13:17*
thing
make the pestilence *c.* unto *De 28:21*
thee
they shall *c.* unto thee *De 28:60*
and that thou mayest *c.* *De 30:20*
unto him
to *c.* unto him and to serve *Jos 22:5*
him
But *c.* unto the Lord your *Jos 23:8*
God, as
and *c.* unto the remnant of *Jos 23:12*
these
of Naaman shall *c.* unto thee *2Ki 5:27*
and the clods *c.* fast *Job 38:38*
together
c. the fountain and the flood *Ps 74:15*
it shall not *c.* to me *Ps 101:3*
groaning my bones *c.* to my *Ps 102:5*
skin
tongue *c.* to the roof of my *Ps 137:6*
mouth
they shall *c.* to the house of *Isa 14:1*
Jacob
so have I caused to *c.* unto *Jer 13:11*
me the
tongue *c.* to the roof of thy *Eze 3:26*
mouth
they shall not *c.* one to *Da 2:43*
another
shall *c.* to them with *Da 11:34*
flatteries
didst *c.* the earth with rivers *Hab 3:9*
of Olives shall *c.* in the *Zec 14:4*
midst
c. to his wife: and they *M't 19:5*
twain
and mother, and *c.* to his *M'k 10:7*
wife
they would *c.* unto the Lord *Ac 11:23*
c. to that which is good *Ro 12:9*

CLEAVED

Nevertheless he *c.* unto the *2Ki 3:3*
sins
tongue *c.* to the roof of *Job 29:10*
their
if any blot hath *c.* to mine *Job 31:7*
hands

CLEAVETH

and *c.* the cleft into two *De 14:6*
claws
he *c.* my reins asunder, and *Job 16:13*
doth
My bone *c.* to my skin and *Job 19:20*
to my
and my tongue *c.* to my jaws *Ps 22:15*
disease, say they, *c.* fast unto *Ps 41:8*
him
our belly *c.* unto the earth *Ps 44:25*
My soul *c.* unto the dust; *Ps 119:25*
when one cutteth and *c.* *Ps 141:7*
wood
that *c.* wood shall be *Ec 10:9*
endangered
the girdle *c.* to the loins of *Jer 13:11*
a man
The tongue of the sucking *La 4:4*
child *c.*
their skin *c.* to their bones; it *La 4:8*
is
dust of your city, which *c.* *Lu 10:11*
on us

CLEFT

cleaveth the *c.* into two claws *De 14:6*
he *c.* the rock (S) *Isa 48:21*
a *c.* in the rock (S) *Jer 13:4*
the valleys shall be *c.* as wax *Mic 1:4*

CLEFTS

dwell in the *c.* of the valley *Job 30:6*
(S)
in the *c.* of the rock, in the *Ca 2:14*
secret
To go into the *c.* of the *Isa 2:21*
rocks
in *c.* of the rocks (S) *Isa 7:19;*
                                   Jer 16:16

CLEFTS

the *c.* of the rocks (S)   *Isa 57:5*
thou that dwellest in the *c.*   *Jer 49:16*
of the
and the little house with *c.*   *Am 6:11*
that dwellest in the *c.* of the   *Ob 3*
rock

CLEMENCY

hear us of thy *c.* a few   *Ac 24:4*
words.

CLEMENT

in the gospel, with *C.* also   *Ph'p 4:3*

CLEOPAS

one of them, whose name   *Lu 24:18*
was *C.*

CLEOPHAS

Mary the wife of *C.* and   *Joh 19:25*

CLEVER

counsel of the *c.* is carried   *Job 5:13*
(S)
wise, *c.* learning (A)(P)   *M't 11:25*
cleverness of the *c.* (N)(R)   *1Co 1:19*
no hocus-pocus, no *c.* tricks   *2Co 4:2*
(P)
c. devised stories   *2Pe 1:16*
(A)(B)(P)(R)

CLIFF

they come up by the *c.* of   *2Ch 20:16*
Ziz
on the *c.* he dwells (A)(E)   *Job 39:28*

CLIFFS

in the *c.* of the valleys, in   *Job 30:6*
caves

CLIFT

put thee in a *c.* of the rock   *Ex 33:22*

CLIFTS

under the *c.* of the rocks   *Isa 57:5*

CLIMB

and *c.* up upon the rocks   *Jer 4:29*
shall *c.* the wall like men of   *Joe 2:7*
war
they shall *c.* up upon the   *Joe 2:9*
houses
though they *c.* up to heaven   *Am 9:2*

CLIMAX

the *c.* of the ages (A)   *Eph 1:10*

CLIMBED

Jonathan *c.* up upon his   *1Sa 14:13*
hands
c. up into a sycamore tree to   *Lu 19:4*
see

CLIMBETH

c. up some other way, the   *Joh 10:1*
same

CLING

c. nothing of the cursed   *De 13:17*
thing (S)
pestilence *c.* to thee   *De 28:21; 28:60*
c. to the Lord (S)   *Jos 23:8*
leprosy *c.* to thee (S)   *2Ki 5:27*
it shall not *c.* to me (S)   *Ps 101:3*
they shall *c.* to Jacob (S)   *Isa 14:1*
I have caused to *c.* to me   *Jer 13:11*
(S)
tongue *c.* to roof of mouth   *Eze 3:26*
(S)
many shall *c.* to them (S)   *Da 11:34*
would *c.* to the Lord (S)   *Ac 11:23*
c. to that which is good (S)   *Ro 12:9*

CLINGETH

my soul *c.* to the dust (S)   *Ps 119:25*
garment *c.* to man (S)   *Jer 13:11*

tongue *c.* to roof of mouth   *La 4:4*
(S)
skin *c.* to their bones (S)   *La 4:8*
dust *c.* on us (S)   *Lu 10:11*

CLIPPED

shall be bald, and every   *Jer 48:37*
beard *c.*

CLIQUES

there must be *c.* (P)   *1Co 11:19*

CLOAK

four corners of the *c.*   *De 22:12*
(A)(B)(R)
bring the *c.* that is upon thee   *Ru 3:15*
(S)
touched the edge of his *c.*   *M't 9:20*
(N)(P)
touched the edge of his *c.*   *M'k 9:16*
(E)(P)
sell *c.* to buy a sword   *Lu 22:26*
(E)(N)
wrap *c.* around you (N)(P)   *Ac 12:8*
as a *c.* (N)   *Heb 1:12*
clothed in a *c.* (P)   *Re 19:13; 19:16*

CLOAKS

the *c.* (R)(S)   *Isa 3:22*
found in their *c.* (A)   *Da 3:21*

CLODS

with worms and *c.* of dust   *Job 7:5*
The *c.* of the valley shall be   *Job 21:33*
sweet
and the *c.* cleave fast   *Job 38:38*
together
and break the *c.* of his   *Isa 28:24*
ground
and Jacob shall break his *c.*   *Ho 10:11*
seed is rotten under their *c.*   *Joe 1:17*

CLOKE

was clad with zeal as a *c.*   *Isa 59:17*
thy coat, let him have thy *c.*   *M't 5:40*
also
let him have your coat also   *M't 5:40*
(A)(B)(N)
let him have your overcoat   *M't 5:40*
(P)
him that taketh away thy *c.*   *Lu 6:29*
takes away your outer   *Lu 6:29*
garment (A)
who takes thy coat   *Lu 6:29*
(B)(N)(P)
they have no *c.* for their sin   *Joh 15:22*
no excuse for sin   *Joh 15:22*
(A)(B)(E)(N)(P)(R)
nor a *c.* of covetousness; God   *1Th 2:5*
is
some pretext after money (B)   *1Th 2:5*
to conceal greedy motives   *1Th 2:5*
(P)
The *c.* that I left at Troas   *2Ti 4:13*
with
liberty for a *c.* of   *1Pe 2:16*
maliciousness
as a pretext for wickedness   *1Pe 2:16*
(A)
to cover up wickedness (B)   *1Pe 2:16*
a screen for wrongdoing (N)   *1Pe 2:16*
as an excuse for doing   *1Pe 2:16*
wrong (P)
a pretext for evil (R)   *1Pe 2:16*

CLOISTER

Solomon's *c.* (N)   *Joh 10:23;*
    Ac 3:11; 5:12

CLOSE

c. to the backbone (S)   *Le 3:9*
of her husband, and be kept   *Nu 5:13*
c.
abide *c.* by (S)   *Ru 2:8; 2:21, 23*
be afraid out of their *c.*   *2Sa 22:46*
places
c. by the palace (S)   *1Ki 21:1*
he yet kept himself *c.* because   *1Ch 12:1*
of
kept *c.* from the fowls of   *Job 28:21*
the air

shut up together as with a   *Job 41:15*
c. seal
be afraid out of their *c.*   *Ps 18:45*
places
followed *c.* behind (S)   *Ps 63:8*
c. after you there in Egypt   *Jer 42:16*
saw him come *c.* unto the ram   *Da 8:7*
and *c.* up the breaches   *Am 9:11*
thereof
And they kept it *c.* and told   *Lu 9:36*
no
thence, they sailed *c.* by   *Ac 27:13*
Crete

CLOSED

c. up the flesh instead thereof   *Ge 2:21*
the Lord had fast *c.* up all   *Ge 20:18*
and the earth *c.* upon them   *Nu 16:33*
and the fat *c.* upon the blade   *J'g 3:22*
breaches began to be *c.* (S)   *Ne 4:7*
they have not been *c.* neither   *Isa 1:6*
sleep, and hath *c.* your eyes   *Isa 29:10*
the words are *c.* up and   *Da 12:9*
sealed
the depth *c.* me round about   *Jon 2:5*
their eyes they have *c.; lest*   *M't 13:15*
c. the book, and he gave it   *Lu 4:20*
again
their eyes have they *c.; lest*   *Ac 28:27*
they

CLOSELY

Ruth clung *c.* (A)(B)(R)   *Ru 1:14*
evil disease cleaveth *c.* to him   *Ps 41:8*
(S)

CLOSER

that sticketh *c.* than a   *Pr 18:24*
brother

CLOSES

c. his heart (R)   *1Jo 3:17*

CLOSEST

because thou *c.* thyself in   *Jer 22:15*
cedar

CLOSET

and the bride out of her *c.*   *Joe 2:16*
thou prayest, enter into thy *c.*   *M't 6:6*
private room (A)   *M't 6:6*
your inner room (B)   *M't 6:6*
thine inner chamber (E)   *M't 6:6*
into a room by yourself (N)   *M't 6:6*
into your own room (P)(R)   *M't 6:6*

CLOSETS

ye have spoken in the ear in *c.*   *Lu 12:3*
behind closed doors (A)(N)   *Lu 12:3*
within a private room (B)   *Lu 12:3*
in the inner chambers (E)   *Lu 12:3*
within four walls (P)   *Lu 12:3*
in private rooms (R)   *Lu 12:3*

CLOTH

spread over it a *c.* of blue   *Nu 4:6;*
    4:7, 9, 11-12
spread upon them a *c.* of   *Nu 4:8*
scarlet
and spread a purple *c.*   *Nu 4:13*
thereon
spread the *c.* before the   *De 22:17*
elders
bolster, and covered it with   *1Sa 19:13*
a *c.*
wrapped in a *c.* behind the   *1Sa 21:9*
ephod
cast a *c.* upn him, when he   *2Sa 20:12*
saw
he took a thick *c.* and   *2Ki 8:15*
dipped it
weave cotten *c.* (S)   *Isa 19:9*
them away as a menstruous   *Isa 30:22*
c.
of new *c.* unto an old   *M't 9:16*
garment
wrapped it in a clean linen   *M't 27:59*
c.
of new *c.* on an old garment   *M'k 2:21*
linen *c.* cast about his   *M'k 14:51*
naked body

And he left the linen *c.* and | *M'k 14:52*
fled
face wrapped in a *c.* | *Joh 11:44*
(N)(R)
bound with a *c.* (S) | *Joh 11:44*

CLOTHE

his sons, and *c.* them with | *Ex 40:14*
coats
she sent raiment to *c.* | *Es 4:4*
Mordecai
also *c.* her priests with | *Ps 132:16*
salvation
His enemies will I *c.* with | *Ps 132:18*
shame
shall *c.* a man with rags | *Pr 23:21*
And I will *c.* him with thy | *Isa 22:21*
robe
shalt surely *c.* thee with | *Isa 49:18*
them all
I *c.* the heavens with | *Isa 50:3*
blackness
c. themselves with trembling | *Eze 26:16*
ye *c.* you with the wool, ye | *Eze 34:3*
kill them
ye *c.* you, but there is none | *Hag 1:6*
warm
c. thee with change of | *Zec 3:4*
raiment
if God so *c.* grass | *M't 6:30; Lu 12:28*

CLOTHED

make coats of skins, and *c.* | *Ge 3:21*
them
and *c.* him with the robe, and | *Le 8:7*
over Saul, who *c.* you in | *2Sa 1:24*
scarlet
was *c.* with a robe of fine | *1Ch 15:27*
linen
the elders of Israel, who | *1Ch 21:16*
were *c.*
thy priests, be *c.* with | *2Ch 6:41*
salvation
c. in their robes, and they | *2Ch 18:9*
sat
c. all that were naked | *2Ch 28:15*
among them
c. them and gave | *2Ch 28:15*
(B)(E)(R)
the king's gate *c.* with | *Es 4:2*
sackcloth
My flesh is *c.* with worms and | *Job 7:5*
hate thee shall be *c.* with | *Job 8:22*
shame
hast *c.* me with skin and | *Job 10:11*
flesh
on righteousness, and it *c.* | *Job 29:14*
me
thou *c.* his neck with | *Job 39:19*
thunder
let them be *c.* with shame | *Ps 35:26*
The pastures are *c.* with | *Ps 65:13*
flocks
He is *c.* with majesty | *Ps 93:1*
the Lord is *c.* with strength | *Ps 93:1*
art *c.* with honour and | *Ps 104:1*
majesty
As he *c.* himself with | *Ps 109:18*
cursing
mine adversaries be *c.* with | *Ps 109:29*
shame
priests be *c.* with | *Ps 132:9*
righteousness
her household are *c.* with | *Pr 31:21*
scarlet.
he hath *c.* me with the | *Isa 61:10*
garments of
prince shall be *c.* with | *Eze 7:27*
desolation
among them was *c.* with | *Eze 9:2;*
linen | *9:3, 11; 10:2, 6-7*
c. thee also with broidered | *Eze 16:10*
work
c. with blue, captains and | *Eze 23:6*
rulers
and rulers *c.* most | *Eze 23:12*
gorgeously
c. with all sorts of armour | *Eze 38:4*
shall be *c.* with linen | *Eze 44:17*
garments
shall be *c.* with scarlet, and | *Da 5:7*
thou shalt be *c.* with scarlet | *Da 5:16*
and they *c.* Daniel with | *Da 5:29*
scarlet
behold a certain man *c.* in | *Da 10:5*
linen
one said to the man *c.* in | *Da 12:6*
linen

I heard the man *c.* in linen | *Da 12:7*
as are *c.* with strange apparel | *Zep 1:8*
Joshua was *c.* with filthy | *Zec 3:3*
garments
head, and *c.* him with | *Zec 3:5*
garments
or, Wherewithal shall we be | *M't 6:31*
c.
A man *c.* in soft raiment | *M't 11:8*
Naked, and ye *c.* me, I was | *M't 25:36*
sick
thee in? or naked, and *c.* | *M't 25:38*
thee
naked and ye *c.* me not: sick | *M't 25:43*
And John was *c.* with camel's | *M'k 1:6*
hair
and *c.* and in his right mind | *M'k 5:15*
c. him with purple, and | *M'k 15:17*
platted
c. in a long white garment | *M'k 16:5*
see? A man *c.* in soft raiment | *Lu 7:25*
at the feet of Jesus, *c.* and in | *Lu 8:35*
his
was *c.* in purple and fine | *Lu 16:19*
linen
c. with power | *Lu 24:49*
(A)(B)(E)(P)(R)
earnestly desiring to be *c.* | *2Co 5:2*
upon
being *c.* we shall not be | *2Co 5:3*
found
would be unclothed, but *c.* | *2Co 5:4*
upon
be *c.* with humility: for | *1Pe 5:5*
God
c. with a garment down to | *Re 1:13*
the
shall be *c.* in white raiment | *Re 3:5*
raiment, that thou mayest be | *Re 3:18*
c.
sitting, *c.* in white raiment | *Re 4:4*
c. with white robes, and palms | *Re 7:9*
in
c. in white robes (A)(R) | *Re 7:13*
from heaven, *c.* with a cloud | *Re 10:1*
threescore days, *c.* in sackcloth | *Re 11:3*
a woman *c.* with the sun, and | *Re 12:1*
the
c. in pure and white linen | *Re 15:6*
c. in purple (P) | *Re 17:4*
c. in fine linen (R) | *Re 19:8*
c. with a vesture dipped in | *Re 19:13*
blood
c. in fine linen, white and | *Re 19:14*
clean

CLOTHES

clothes | *Ge 24:53;*
27:15, 27; 28:20; 41:14; J'g 3:16; 1Sa 28:8
in the pit, and he rent his *c.* | *Ge 37:29*
And Jacob rent his *c.* and put | *Ge 37:34*
Then they rent their *c.* and | *Ge 44:13*
in wine, and his *c.* in the | *Ge 49:11*
blood
being bound up in their *c.* | *Ex 12:34*
upon
let them wash their *c.* | *Ex 19:10*
people, and they washed | *Ex 19:14*
their *c.*
your heads, neither rend your | *Le 10:6*
c.
wash his *c.* and be unclean | *Le 11:25;*
11:28, 40; 15:5-8, 11, 13, 21-22, 27;
16:26, 28; Nu 19:7-8, 10, 19, 21
wash his *c.* and be clean | *Le 13:6;*
13:34; 14:8-9; 17:15
c. shall be rent, and his head | *Le 13:45*
bare
wash his *c.* and shave off all | *Le 14:8*
his hair
eateth in the house shall | *Le 14:48*
wash his *c.*
shall put on the linen *c.* even | *Le 16:32*
he shall both wash his *c.* | *Le 17:15*
uncover his head, nor rend | *Le 21:10*
his *c.*
let them wash their *c.* and so | *Nu 8:7*
make
purified, and they washed | *Nu 8:21*
their *c.*
that searched the land, rent | *Nu 14:6*
their *c.*
wash your *c.* on the seventh | *Nu 21:24*
day
c. are not waxen old upon | *De 29:5*
you

Joshua rent his *c.* and fell to | *Jos 7:6*
the
that he rent his *c.* and said, | *J'g 11:35*
Alas
with his *c.* rent, and with | *1Sa 4:12*
earth
he stripped off his *c.* also | *1Sa 19:24*
camp from Saul with his *c.* | *2Sa 1:2*
rent
David took hold on his *c.* | *2Sa 1:11*
and rent
Rend your *c.* and gird you | *2Sa 3:31*
with
servants stood by with their | *2Sa 13:31*
c. rent
nor washed his *c.* from the | *2Sa 19:24*
day
they covered him with *c.* but | *1Ki 1:1*
he gat
that he rent his *c.* and put | *1Ki 21:27*
he took hold of his own *c.* | *2Ki 2:12*
that he rent his *c.* and said, | *2Ki 5:7*
Am I
the king of Israel had rent his | *2Ki 5:8*
c.
the woman, that he rent his | *2Ki 6:30*
c.
Athaliah rent her *c.* and | *2Ki 11:14*
cried
to Hezekiah with their *c.* | *2Ki 18:37*
rent
rent his *c.* and covered | *2Ki 19:1*
himself
book of the law, that he | *2Ki 22:11*
rent his *c.*
hast rent thy *c.* and wept | *2Ki 22:19*
before
Then Athaliah rent her *c.* | *2Ch 23:13*
and said
words of the law, that he | *2Ch 34:19*
rent his *c.*
before me, and didst rend | *2Ch 34:27*
thy *c.*
none of us put off our *c.* | *Ne 4:23*
saving
their *c.* waxed not old, and | *Ne 9:21*
their
Mordecai rent his *c.* and put | *Es 4:1*
on
and mine own *c.* shall abhor | *Job 9:31*
me
made clouds its *c.* (B) | *Job 38:9*
bosom, and his *c.* not be | *Pr 6:27*
burned
to Hezekiah with their *c.* | *Isa 36:22*
rent
heard it, that he rent his *c.* | *Isa 37:1*
and their *c.* rent, and having | *Jer 41:5*
cut
shall strip thee also of thy | *Eze 16:39*
c.
c. naked with a robe (B) | *Eze 18:7*
strip thee out of thy *c.* and | *Eze 23:26*
take
in precious *c.* for chariots | *Eze 27:20*
in blue *c.* and broidered | *Eze 27:24*
work
lay themselves down upon *c.* | *Am 2:8*
laid
clothes (B) | *M't 6:28;*
11:8; 17:2; 27:31; M'k 9:3; Lu 23:34;
Joh 19:24; Ac 22:20; Jas 2:2; Re 3:18
dressed in fine *c.* (P) | *M't 11:8;*
Lu 7:25
put on them their *c.* and | *M't 21:7*
they
field return back to take his | *M't 24:18*
c.
Then the high priest rent | *M't 26:65*
his *c.*
cast lots for my *c.* | *M't 27:35*
(B)(N)(P)
if I may but touch his *c.* I | *M'k 5:28*
shall
and said, Who touched my | *M'k 5:30*
c.
Then the high priest rent | *M'k 14:63*
his *c.*
and put his own *c.* on him | *M'k 15:20*
and wrapped him in swaddling | *Lu 2:7*
c.
the babe wrapped in | *Lu 2:12*
swaddling *c.*
for grand *c.* (N) | *Lu 7:25*
and ware no *c.* neither abode | *Lu 8:27*
in
clothes (A) | *Lu 10:30;*
12:23; Re 3:18
and wound it in linen *c.* | *Joh 19:40*
with the

saw the linen *c.* lying   *Joh 20:5; 20:6-7*
the witnesses laid down their   *Ac 7:58*
c.
rent their *c.* and ran in   *Ac 14:14*
among
the magistrates rent off their   *Ac 16:22*
c.
cast off their *c.* and threw   *Ac 22:23*
dust

CLOTHEST

thou *c.* thyself with crimson   *Jer 4:30*

CLOTHING

clothing (B)   *Ex 21:10;*
     Le 11:32; De 8:4; 10:18; J'g 8:26
and stripped the naked of   *Job 22:6*
their *c.*
the naked to lodge without   *Job 24:7;*
c.   *24:10*
seen any perish for want of   *Job 31:19*
c.
were sick, my *c.* was   *Ps 35:13*
sackcloth
within: her *c.* is of wrought   *Ps 45:13*
gold
sackcloth for *c.*   *Ps 69:11*
(A)(B)(E)(R)
lambs are for thy *c.* and the   *Pr 27:26*
goats
her *c.* is silk and purple   *Pr 31:22*
Strength and honour are her *c.*   *Pr 31:25*
Thou hast *c.* be thou our   *Isa 3:6;*
ruler   *3:7*
sufficiently, and for durable   *Isa 23:18*
c.
clothing (B)   *Isa 59:6; 63:3; Lu 24:4*
the garments of vengeance   *Isa 59:17*
for *c.*
blue and purple for their *c.*   *Jer 10:9*
c. white as snow (B)   *Da 7:9*
covers *c.* with cruelty (B)   *Mal 2:16*
clothing (A)   *M't 6:28;*
     17:2; 28:3; Ac 18:6; 1Ti 6:8; Re 4:4
come to you in sheep's *c.* but   *M't 7:15*
wear soft *c.* are in kings'   *M't 11:8*
houses
which love to go in long *c.*   *M'k 12:38*
stood before men in bright *c.*   *Ac 10:30*
to him that weareth the gay *c.*   *Jas 2:3*
loathing the *c.* polluted   *Jude 23*
(B)(N)

CLOTHS

the *c.* of service, and the   *Ex 31:10*
holy
The *c.* of service, to do   *Ex 35:19*
service in
they made *c.* of service, to do   *Ex 39:1*
The *c.* of service to do   *Ex 39:41*
service in

CLOUD

I do set my bow in the *c.*   *Ge 9:13;*
     9:14, 16
them by day in a pillar of a   *Ex 13:21;*
c.   *13:22; 14:24; Nu 14:14*
the *c.* went from before   *Ex 14:19*
their face
it was a *c.* and darkness to   *Ex 14:20*
them
of the Lord appeared in the   *Ex 16:10*
c.
I come unto thee in a thick   *Ex 19:9;*
c.   *19:16*
a *c.* covered the mount   *Ex 24:15;*
     24:16
Moses out of the midst of   *Ex 24:16;*
the *c.*   *24:18*
the Lord descended in the *c.*   *Ex 34:5;*
     Nu 11:25
a *c.* covered the tent   *Ex 40:34;*
     40:35-38
in the *c.* upon the mercy seat   *Le 16:2*
that the *c.* of the incense may   *Le 16:13*
c. covered the tabernacle   *Nu 9:15;*
     9:16-22
that the *c.* was taken up   *Nu 10:11*
the *c.* rested in the   *Nu 10:12*
wilderness of
the *c.* of the Lord was upon   *Nu 10:34*
them
came down in the pillar of   *Nu 12:5*
the *c.*

And the *c.* departed from   *Nu 12:10*
off the
that thy *c.* standeth over   *Nu 14:14*
them
behold, the *c.* covered it   *Nu 16:42*
ye should go, and in a *c.* by   *De 1:33*
day
the *c.* and of the thick   *De 5:22*
darkness
the tabernacle in a pillar of   *De 31:15*
a *c.*
c. filled house of Lord   *1Ki 8:10;*
     2Ch 5:13
stand to minister because of   *1Ki 8:11;*
c.   *2 Ch 5:14*
ariseth a little *c.* out of the   *1Ki 18:44*
sea
the pillar of the *c.* departed   *Ne 9:19*
not
let a *c.* dwell upon it; let the   *Job 3:5*
c. is consumed and vanisheth   *Job 7:9*
away
he judge through the dark   *Job 22:13*
c.
the *c.* is not rent under them   *Job 26:8*
and spreadeth his *c.* upon it   *Job 26:9*
my welfare passeth away   *Job 30:15*
as a *c.*
by the *c.* that cometh   *Job 36:32*
betwixt
he wearieth the thick *c.*   *Job 37:11*
he scattereth his bright *c.*   *Job 37:11*
caused the light of his *c.* to   *Job 37:15*
shine
made the *c.* the garment   *Job 38:9*
thereof
daytime also he led them   *Ps 78:14*
with a *c.*
He spread a *c.* for a   *Ps 105:39*
covering; and
favour is as a *c.* of the latter   *Pr 16:15*
rain
a *c.* and smoke by day, and   *Isa 4:5*
a *c.* of dew in the heat of   *Isa 18:4*
harvest
the Lord rideth upon a swift   *Isa 19:1*
c.
the heat with the shadow of   *Isa 25:5*
a *c.*
I have blotted out, as a   *Isa 44:22*
thick *c.*
as a *c.* thy sins: return unto   *Isa 44:22*
me
Who are these that fly as *c.*   *Isa 60:8*
the daughter of Zion with a *c.*   *La 2:1*
hast covered thyself with a *c.*   *La 3:44*
a great *c.* and a fire infolding   *Eze 1:4*
itself
that is in the *c.* in the day   *Eze 1:28*
of rain
and a thick *c.* of incense   *Eze 8:11*
went up
and the *c.* filled the inner   *Eze 10:3*
court
the house was filled with the   *Eze 10:4*
c.
as for her, a *c.* shall cover   *Eze 30:18*
her
I will cover the sun with a   *Eze 32:7*
c. and
shalt be like a *c.* to cover   *Eze 38:9*
the land
as a *c.* to cover the land; it   *Eze 38:16*
shall
your goodness is as a morning   *Ho 6:4*
c.
they shall be as the morning   *Ho 13:3*
c.
c. overshadowed them   *M't 17:5;*
     M'k 9:7; Lu 9:34
a voice out of *c.*   *M't 17:5;*
     M'k 9:7; Lu 9:35
ye see a *c.* rise out of the   *Lu 12:54*
west
in a *c.* with power and great   *Lu 21:27*
glory
a *c.* received him out of their   *Ac 1:9*
sight
all our fathers were under   *1Co 10:1*
the *c.*
Moses in the *c.* and in the   *1Co 10:2*
sea
with so great a *c.* of   *Heb 12:1*
witnesses
from heaven, clothed with a   *Re 10:1*
c.
ascended up to heaven in a   *Re 11:12*
c.
and behold a white *c.* and   *Re 14:14*
upon the

upon the *c.* one sat like unto   *Re 14:14*
the Son
to him that sat on the *c.,*   *Re 14:15*
Thrust
sat on the *c.* thrust in his   *Re 14:16*
sickle

CLOUDBURST

like a *c.* (B)   *Pr 28:3*

CLOUDS

darkness, *c.* and thick   *De 4:11*
darkness
the *c.* also dropped water   *J'g 5:4*
waters, and thick *c.* of the   *2Sa 22:12*
skies
even a morning without *c.*   *2Sa 23:4*
was black with *c.* and wind   *1Ki 18:45*
and his head reached unto   *Job 20:6*
the *c.*
Thick *c.* are a covering to   *Job 22:14*
him
up the waters in his thick *c.*   *Job 26:8*
c. which are higher than   *Job 35:5*
thou
c. do drop and distil upon   *Job 36:28*
man
the spreadings of the *c.*   *Job 36:29*
With *c.* he covereth the   *Job 36:32*
light
know the balancings of the   *Job 37:16*
c.
bright light which is in the   *Job 37:21*
c.
thou lift up thy voice to the   *Job 38:34*
c.
can number the *c.* in   *Job 38:37*
wisdom
waters and thick *c.* of the   *Ps 18:11*
skies
before him his thick *c.*   *Ps 18:12*
passed
faithfulness reacheth unto the   *Ps 36:5*
c.
and thy truth unto the *c.*   *Ps 57:10*
and his strength is in the *c.*   *Ps 68:34*
The *c.* poured out water: the   *Ps 77:17*
commanded the *c.* from   *Ps 78:23*
above
C. and darkness are round   *Ps 97:2*
about
who maketh the *c.* his   *Ps 104:3*
chariot
thy truth reacheth unto the   *Ps 108:4*
c.
makes *c.* arise (R)   *Ps 135:7*
Who covereth the heaven   *Ps 147:8*
with *c.*
and the *c.* drop down the dew   *Pr 3:20*
When he established the *c.*   *Pr 8:28*
above
is like *c.* and wind without rain *Pr 25:14*
If the *c.* be full of rain, they   *Ec 11:3*
empty
regardeth the *c.* shall not reap   *Ec 11:4*
nor the *c.* return after the   *Ec 12:2*
rain
I will also command the *c.*   *Isa 5:6*
that
ascend above the heights of   *Isa 14:14*
the *c.*
he shall come up as *c.* and   *Jer 4:13*
his
of man came with the *c.* of   *Da 7:13*
heaven
a day of *c.* and of thick   *Joe 2:2*
darkness
and the *c.* are the dust of his   *Na 1:3*
feet
a day of *c.* and thick   *Zep 1:15*
darkness
the Lord shall make bright *c.*   *Zec 10:1*
in the *c.* of heaven with   *M't 24:30*
power
and coming in the *c.* of   *M't 26:64*
heaven
the Son of man coming in   *M'k 13:26*
the *c.*
and coming in the *c.* of   *M'k 14:62*
heaven
up together with them in the   *1Th 4:17*
c.
c. that are carried with a   *2Pe 2:17*
c. they are without water,   *Jude 12*
carried
Behold he cometh with *c.*   *Re 1:7*

CLOUDY

c. pillar descended, and stood *Ex 33:9*
the people saw the c. pillar *Ex 33:10* stand
them in the day by a c. pillar *Ne 9:12*
spake unto them in the c. *Ps 99:7* pillar
day of the Lord is near, a c. *Eze 30:3* day
scattered in the c. and dark *Eze 34:12* day
sky red and c. (B) *M't 16:3*

CLOUTED

old shoes and c. upon their *Jos 9:5* feet

CLOUTS

old cast c. and old rotten *Jer 38:11* rags
Put now these old cast c. *Jer 38:12*

CLOVEN

or of them that divide the c. *De 14:7* hoof
appeared unto them c. tongues *Ac 2:3*
resembling fire, separated *Ac 2:3* (A)(P)
like flames were distributed *Ac 2:3* (B)(R)
parting asunder (E) *Ac 2:3*
like flames, dispersed among *Ac 2:3* (N)

CLOVENFOOTED

the hoof, and is c. *Le 11:3; 11:7, 26*

CLUB

as a scattering c. (B)(R) *Ps 25:18*
c. of war (S) *Pr 25:18*

CLUBS

multitudes with c. *M't 26:47;*
(A)(B)(S) *26:55*

CLUNG

his soul c. to Dinah (S) *Ge 34:3*
Ruth c. closely to her *Ru 1:14* (A)(B)(R)(S)
c. to the sword (A) *2Sa 23:10*
c. to them in love *1Ki 11:2* (A)(R)(S)
he c. to sins of Jeroboam (S) *2Ki 3:3*
he c. to the Lord (B)(S) *2Ki 18:6*
I have c. to thy testimonies *Ps 119:31* (S)

CLUSTER

a branch with one c. of *Nu 13:23* grapes
the c. of grapes which the *Nu 13:24* children
bind the c. of Pleiades (E) *Job 38:31*
My beloved is unto me as a *Ca 1:13* c. of
As the new wine is found in *Isa 65:8* the c.
there is no c. to eat: my soul *Mic 7:1*

CLUSTERS

the c. thereof brought forth *Ge 40:10* ripe
grapes of gall, their c. are *De 32:32* bitter
and an hundred c. of *1Sa 25:18* raisins
cake of figs, and two c. of *1Sa 30:12* raisins
and thy breasts to c. of *Ca 7:7* grapes
breasts shall be as c. of the *Ca 7:8* vine
the c. of the vine of the *Re 14:18* earth

CNIDUS

scarce were come over *Ac 27:7* against C.

COAL

so they shall quench my c. *2Sa 14:7* which
having a live c. in his hand *Isa 6:6*
there shall not be a c. to *Isa 47:14* warm at
Their visage is blacker than a *La 4:8* c.

COALS

take a censer full of burning *Le 16:12* c.
devoured: c. were kindled by *2Sa 22:9* it
before him were c. of fire *2Sa 22:13*
there shall be a cake baken on *1Ki 19:6* the c.
His breath kindleth c. and *Job 41:21*
devoured: c. were kindled by it *Ps 18:8*
passed, hail stones and c. of *Ps 18:12* fire
his voice; hail stones and c. *Ps 18:13* of fire
of the mighty, with c. of *Ps 120:4* juniper
let burning c. fall upon *Ps 140:10* them: let
Can one go upon hot c. and *Pr 6:28*
thou shalt heap c. of fire *Pr 25:22* upon his
As c. are to burning *Pr 26:21*
are to burning c. and wood *Pr 26:21* to
the c. thereof are c. of fire *Ca 8:6*
the tongs both worketh in *Isa 44:12* the c.
baked bread upon the c. *Isa 44:19* thereof
the smith that bloweth the *Isa 54:16* c.
was like burning c. of fire *Eze 1:13*
and fill thine hand with c. of *Eze 10:2* fire
Then set it empty upon the *Eze 24:11* c.
and burning c. went forth at *Hab 3:5* his
burning plague followed (A) *Hab 3:5*
burning fever follows (B) *Hab 3:5*
fiery bolts went forth at His *Hab 3:5* feet (E)
plague followed close behind *Hab 3:5* (R)
who had made a fire of c.; *Joh 18:18* for it
they saw a fire of c. there, *Joh 21:9* and fish
thou shalt heap c. of fire on *Ro 12:20* his

COAST

I bring the locusts into thy c. *Ex 10:4*
locusts into your country *Ex 10:4* (A)(R)
locusts in your territory (B) *Ex 10:4*
locusts in thy border (E) *Ex 10:4*
the sea, and by the c. of *Nu 13:29* Jordan
by the c. of the land of *Nu 20:23* Edom
Arnon, which is in the *Nu 22:36* utmost c.
shall come from the c. of *Nu 24:24* Chittim
of Zin along by the c. of *Nu 34:3* Edom
the outmost c. of the salt sea *Nu 34:3*
c. shall go down from *Nu 34:11* Shepham
through the c. of your brethren *De 2:4*
over through Ar, the c. of *De 2:18* Moab
Jordan, and the c. thereof *De 3:17*
uttermost sea shall your c. *De 11:24* be
your territory (A)(R) *De 11:24*
your frontiers shall be (B) *De 11:24*
your border, (E) *De 11:24;*
Jos 1:4; 18:5; J'g 11:20; 1Sa 6:9
seen with thee in all thy c. *De 16:4* seven
the Lord thy God enlarge thy *De 19:8* c.
enlarge your territory (A) *De 19:8*
your boundaries (B) *De 19:8*
enlarge thy border (E)(R) *De 19:8*

down of the sun, shall be your *Jos 1:4* c.
your territory (A)(B)(R) *Jos 1:4;* *18:5*
And the c. of Og king of *Jos 12:4* Bashan
The king of Dor in the c. *Jos 12:23* of Dor
their c. was from Aroer *Jos 13:16*
their c. was Jazer, and all *Jos 13:25*
And their c. was from *Jos 13:30* Mahanaim
uttermost part of the south c. *Jos 15:1*
out of that c. were at the sea *Jos 15:4*
this shall be your south c. *Jos 15:4*
the great sea, and the c. *Jos 15:12* thereof
is the c. of the children of *Jos 15:12* Judah
toward the c. of Edom *Jos 15:21* southward
to the c. of Japhleti, unto the *Jos 16:3* c.
the c. of Manasseh was from *Jos 17:7*
And the c. descended unto *Jos 17:9*
the c. of Manasseh also *Jos 17:9* was on
Judah shall abide in their c. *Jos 18:5*
and the c. of their lot came *Jos 18:11* forth
of Jordan: this was the *Jos 18:19* south c.
the c. reacheth to Tabor *Jos 19:22*
the c. turneth to Ramah, *Jos 19:29* and to
and the c. turneth to Hosah *Jos 19:29*
at the sea from the c. to *Jos 19:29* Achzib
their c. was from Heleph, *Jos 19:33* from
then the c. turneth westward *Jos 19:34* to
the c. of the inheritance was *Jos 19:41*
the c. of the children of *Jos 19:47* Dan went
Gaza with the c. thereof *J'g 1:18*
and Askelon with the c. *J'g 1:18* thereof
and Ekron with the c. thereof *J'g 1:18*
And the c. of the Amorites *J'g 1:36* was
not Israel to pass through his *J'g 11:20* c.
pass through his territory *J'g 11:20* (A)
pass through his country *J'g 11:20* (B)
by the way of his own c. to *1Sa 6:9*
its own land (A)(R) *1Sa 6:9*
his own territory (B) *1Sa 6:9*
no more into the c. of Israel *1Sa 7:13*
territory of Israel (A)(R) *1Sa 7:13*
Israel's boundaries (B) *1Sa 7:13*
border of Israel (E) *1Sa 7:13*
any more in any c. of Israel *1Sa 27:1*
the c. which belongeth to *1Sa 30:14* Judah
He restored the c. of Israel *2Ki 14:25* from
me indeed, and enlarge my *1Ch 4:10* c.
shall deliver the c. (S) *Job 22:30*
inhabitants of the c. *Isa 23:2;*
(A)(E)(R)(S) *23:6*
destroy the remnant of the *Eze 25:16* sea c.
which is by the c. of *Eze 47:16* Hauran
the c. of the way of *Eze 48:1* Hethlon, as
northward, to the c. of *Eze 48:1* Hamath
unto the inhabitants of the *Zep 2:5* sea c.
the sea c. shall be dwellings *Zep 2:6*
the c. shall be for the *Zep 2:7* remnant of
seacoast shall belong to Judah *Zep 2:7* (A)(R)
which is upon the sea c. *M't 4:13*
from the sea c. of Tyre and *Lu 6:17* Sidon

COASTLAND

the c. people spread (A)(R) *Ge 10:5*
the inhabitants of the c. *Isa 20:6* (A)(B)(E)(R)(S)
the c. across the sea (B)(R) *Jer 25:22*

COASTLANDS

c. of the Gentiles (A)(B)(R) Ge 105
c. of the sea (A)(R) Es 10:1
let the c. be glad (R) Ps 97:1
the c. of the sea (S) Isa 11:11
inhabitants of the c. (B) Isa 23:2; 23:6
the c. of the sea (R) Isa 24:15
keep silence O c. (S) Isa 41:1
the c. (A)(B)(R) Isa 41:5; Eze 26:15
the c. wait for his law (R) Isa 42:4
declare his praise in the c. Isa 42:12
(S)
I will make rivers c. (S) Isa 42:15
the c. wait for me (R) Isa 51:5
to the c. he will repay (S) Isa 59:18
the c. shake at the sound Eze 26:15
(S)
the c. tremble (S) Eze 26:18
people for many c. Eze 27:3
the c. of Elishah (B) Eze 27:7
many c. were the Eze 27:15
merchandise (S)
dwellers of the c. Eze 27:35
(B)(R)(S)
dwell securely in the c. Eze 39:6
(A)(B)(R)(S)
attention of the c. (B)(R) Da 11:18
the c. of the heathen (A) Zep 2:11

COASTS

and rested in all the c. of Ex 10:14
Egypt
one locust in all the c. of Ex 10:19
Egypt
out of the c. of the Amorites Nu 21:13
with the cities thereof in the Nu 32:33
c.
the land of Canaan with the Nu 34:2
c.
your land with the c. Nu 34:12
thereof
of Argob unto the c. of De 3:14
Geshuri
divide the c. of thy land De 19:3
olive trees throughout all thy De 28:40
c.
in all the c. of the great sea Jos 9:1
over
Joseph shall abide in their c. Jos 18:5
Benjamin by the c. thereof Jos 18:20
land for inheritance by their Jos 19:49
c.
all the c. of the Amorites J'g 11:22
that be along by the c. of J'g 11:26
Arnon
five men from their c. men of J'g 18:2
sent her into all the c. of J'g 19:29
Israel
even Ashdod and the c. 1Sa 5:6
thereof
and the c. thereof did Israel 1Sa 7:14
unto all the c. of Israel 1Sa 11:3
throughout all the c. of 1Sa 11:7
Israel
in any of the c. of Israel 1Sa 21:5
throughout all the c. of Israel 1Ki 1:3
smote them in all the c. of 2Ki 10:32
Israel
therein, and the c. thereof 2Ki 15:16
from
their castles in their c. 1Ch 6:54
had cities of their c. out of 1Ch 6:66
throughout all the c. of 1Ch 21:12
Israel
resorted to him out of all 2Ch 11:13
their c.
the c. of the sea (S) Es 10:1
the kings of the c. (A) Ps 72:10
flies, and lice in all their c. Ps 105:31
brake the trees of their c. Ps 105:33
the c. of the sea (S) Isa 24:15
he taketh up the c. as a (S) Isa 40:15
the c. saw it (S) Isa 41:5
the c. shall wait for his law Isa 42:4
(S)
the c. and the inhabitants Isa 42:10
(S)
Listen, O c. to me (S) Isa 49:1
the c. shall wait for me (S) Isa 51:5;
60:9
to the c. afar off (S) Isa 66:19;
Jer 31:10
pass over the c. of Chittim Jer 2:10
(A)(R)(S)
the kings of the c. (S) Jer 25:22
up from the c. of the earth Jer 25:32
them from the c. of the earth Jer 31:8

wild beasts of the c. shall be Jer 50:39
(S)
up from the c. of the earth Jer 50:41
the people of many c. Eze 27:3
(B)(S)
the c. of Cyprus (A)(B) Eze 27:3
the c. of Elishah (A)(R)(S) Eze 27:7
take a man of their c. and Eze 33:2
set
turn his face to the c. (S) Da 11:18
Zidon, and all the c. of Joe 3:4
Palestine
all the c. of the heathen (S) Zep 2:11
and in all the c. thereof, M't 2:16
from
he would depart out of their M't 8:34
c.
departed into the c. of Tyre M't 15:21
out of the same c. and M't 15:22
cried
came into the c. of M't 15:39
Magdala
Jesus came into the c. of Mt 16:13
Caesarea
and came into the c. of M't 19:1
Judæa
pray him to depart out of M'k 5:17
their c.
departing from the c. of M'k 7:31
Tyre
the midst of the c. of M'k 7:31
Decapolis
and cometh into the c. of M'k 10:1
Judæa
and expelled them out of Ac 13:50
their c.
passed through the upper c. Ac 19:1
throughout all the c. of Ac 26:20
Judæa
meaning to sail by the c. of Ac 27:2
Asia

COAT

like a hairy c. (B) Ge 25:25
made him c. of many Ge 37:3;
colours 37:23, 31-33
hold of his c. (B) Ge 39:12; 39:15
neighbor's c. (B) Ex 22:26; De 24:13
and a broidered c. a mitre, and Ex 28:4
undergarment of woven Ex 28:4
material (B)
c. of mail (S) Ex 28:32;
39:23; Jer 51:3
embroider the c. of fine Ex 28:39
linen
put upon Aaron the c. and the Ex 29:5
the tunic (B) Le 16:4
he put upon him the c. and Le 8:7
the undergarment (B) Le 8:7
He shall put on the holy linen Le 16:4
c.
his mother made him a little 1Sa 2:19
c.
little suit (B) 1Sa 2:19
little robe (E)(R) 1Sa 2:19
he was armed with a c. of 1Sa 17:5
mail
and the weight of the c. was 1Sa 17:5
mail
he armed him with a c. of 1Sa 17:38
mail
came to meet him with his 2Sa 15:32
c. rent
me about as the collar of Job 30:18
my c.
as with a c. (B)(R) Ps 109:18
I have put off my c.: how Ca 5:3
shall I
my garment (A)(E)(R) Ca 5:3
every c. rolled in blood (B) Isa 9:5
c. of mail (A)(B)(E)(R) Jer 51:3;
46:4
have your c. also (A)(B)(N) M't 5:4
at the law, and take away M't 5:40
thy
takes thy c. (B)(N)(P) M't 6:29
patch on an old c. M't 9:16
(B)(N)(P)
throwing off his c. (B) M'k 10:50
turn back to get his c. M'k 13:16
(B)(R)
forbid not to take thy c. also Lu 6:29
sell c. to buy one (B)(P) Lu 22:26
and also his c.: now the Joh 19:23
was
the tunic (A)(B)(N)(R) Joh 19:23
his shirt (P) Joh 19:23
cast lots for my c. (E) Joh 19:24

he girt his fisher's c. unto Joh 21:7
him
his work jacket (B) Joh 21:7
slipped on his clothes Joh 21:7
(P)(R)
put on c. and follow (B) Ac 12:8

COATS

did the Lord God make c. of Ge 3:21
skins
robes of skins (B) Ge 3:21
garments of skins (R) Ge 3:21
Aaron's sons thou shalt Ex 28:40
make c.
make tunics for Aaron's Ex 28:40;
sons (B) 29:8; Le 8:13; 10:5
his sons, and put c. upon them Ex 29:8
they made c. of fine linen of Ex 39:27
sons, and clothe them with Ex 40:14
the
put c. upon them, and girded Le 8:13
them
carried them in their c. out of Le 10:5
the
c. of mail (S) 2Ch 26:14;
Ne 4:16; Jer 46:4
bound in their c. their hosen Da 3:21
cloaks (A) Da 3:21
mantles (B)(E)(R) Da 3:21
neither were their c. changed Da 3:27
garments (A) Da 3:27
mantles (B)(R) Da 3:27
breeches (E) Da 3:27
neither two c. neither shoes M't 10:10
two undergarments (A)(B) M't 10:10
change of clothes (P) M't 10:10
two tunics (R) M't 10:10
sandals; and not put on two M'k 6:9
c.
two tunics (A)(R) M'k 6:9
two undergarments (B) M'k 6:9;
Lu 3:11
He that hath two c. let him Lu 3:11
two tunics (A) Lu 3:11
money; neither have two c. Lu 9:3
apiece
shewing the c. and garments Ac 9:39
under-shirts (A) Ac 9:39
undergarments (B) Ac 9:39
dresses and cloaks (P) Ac 9:39

COCK

this night, before the c. M't 26:34
crow, thou
rooster (A)(B) M't 26:34;
26:74; Joh 13:38
And immediately the c. crew M't 26:74
Before the c. crow, thou M't 26:75
shalt deny
before the c. crow twice, M'k 14:30
thou shalt
into the porch; and the c. M'k 14:68
crew
the second time the c. crew M'k 14:72
said unto him, Before the M'k 14:72
c. crow
the c. shall not crow this Lu 22:34
day
while he yet spake, the c. Lu 22:60
crew
Before the c. crow, thou Lu 22:61
shalt deny
The c. shall not crow, till Joh 13:38
thou hast
and immediately the c. crew Joh 18:27

COCKATRICE

shall come forth a c. and Isa 14:29
an adder (A)(B)(E)(R) Isa 14:29

COCKATRICE'

shall put his hand on the c. Isa 11:8
den
They hatch c. eggs, and Isa 59:5
weave the

COCKATRICES

I will send serpents, c. among Jer 8:17
adders (A)(B)(E)(R) Jer 8:17

COCKCROW

the c. (S) M'k 13:35

COCKCROWING

at midnight, or at the *c.* or   *M'k 13:35*
in the

COCKLE

instead of wheat, and *c.*   *Job 31:40*

COCK-SPARROW

this *c.* trying to say (N)   *Ac 17:18*

CODE

not under old *c.* of   *Ro 9:6*
(A)(N)(R)

CODICIL

no one add a *c.* (A)   *Ga 3:15*

COFFER

a trespass offering, in a *c.* by   *1Sa 6:8*
a box (A)(B)(R)   *1Sa 6:8; 6:11, 15*
the *c.* with the mice of gold   *1Sa 6:11*
and the *c.* that was with it,   *1Sa 6:15*
wherein

COFFIN

and he was put in a *c.* in   *Ge 50:26*
Egypt

COGITATIONS

my *c.* much troubled me, and   *Da 7:28*
my thoughts troubled   *Da 7:28*
(A)(B)(E)(R)

COHORT

the tribune of the *c.* (N)(R)   *Ac 21:31*

COIFFURE

with elaborate *c.* (P)   *1Pe 3:3*

COILING

the *c.* serpent (B)   *Isa 27:1*

COIN

find a *c.* (B)(N)(P)   *M't 17:27*
a silver *c.* a day (P)   *M't 20:2; 20:13*
show me the legal *c.* (B)   *M't 22:19*
pay her back in her *c.*   *Re 18:6*
(N)(P)

COLD

and *c.* and heat, and summer   *Ge 8:22*
they have no covering in the   *Job 24:7*
c.
whirlwind; and *c.* out of the   *Job 37:9*
north
c. by night (A)(B)(R)   *Job 38:29*
who can stand before his *c.*   *Ps 147:17*
will not plow by reason of the   *Pr 20:4*
c.
As the *c.* of snow in the   *Pr 25:13*
time of
away a garment in *c.*   *Pr 25:20*
weather
c. waters to a thirsty soul, so *Pr 25:25*
is
shall the *c.* flowing   *Jer 18:14*
waters that
camp in the hedges in the *c.*   *Na 3:17*
day
these little ones a cup of *c.*   *M't 10:42*
water
the love of many shall wax   *M't 24:12*
c.
made a fire of coals; for it   *Joh 18:18*
was *c.*
present rain, and because of   *Ac 28:2*
the *c.*
in fastings often, in *c.* and   *2Co 11:27*
that thou art neither *c.* nor   *Re 3:15*
hot
I would thou wert *c.* or hot   *Re 3:15*
and neither *c.* nor hot, I will   *Re 3:16*
spue

COL-HOZEH

repaired Shallum the son of   *Ne 3:15*
C.
the son of Baruch, the son of   *Ne 11:5*
C.

COLLAR

me about as the *c.* of my   *Job 30:18*
coat
the *c.* of his robe (R)   *Ps 133:2*

COLLARS

and *c.* and purple raiment   *J'g 8:26*

COLLEAGUE

Titus my *c.* (A)(P)   *2Co 8:23*

COLLEAGUES

your and your *c.* (A)   *Zec 3:8*

COLLECT

c. duties or tribute (A)(E)   *M't 17:25*
c. no more than appointed   *Lu 3:13*
(B)(R)

COLLECTION

out of Jerusalem the *c.*   *2Ch 24:6*
according
the tax of Moses   *2Ch 24:6*
(A)(E)(R)
the assessment (B)   *2Ch 24:6*
to the Lord the *c.* that   *2Ch 24:9*
Moses
concerning the *c.* for the   *1Co 16:1*
saints
money contributed (A)(R)   *1Co 16:1*
the fund for Christians (P)   *1Co 16:1*

COLLECTOR

tax *c.* (A)(B)(P)(R)(S)   *M't 10:3;*
18:17; Lu 5:27; 18:10, 11, 13

COLLECTORS

tax. *c.* (A)(B)(P)(R)(S)   *M't 5:46;*
9:10-11; 11:19; 21:31-32; M'k 2:15-16;
Lu 3:12; 5:29-30; 7:29, 34; 15:1; 19:2

COLLECTORS'

sitting at the *c.* office (A)(P)   *M't 9:9*

COLLEGE

she dwelt in Jerusalem in   *2Ki 22:14*
the *c.*
second quarter of Jerusalem   *2Ki 22:14*
(B)(E)(R)
she dwelt in Jerusalem in   *2Ch 34:22*
the *c.*

COLLOPS

maketh *c.* of fat on his   *Job 15:27*
flanks
layers of fat (A)(B)   *Job 15:27*
gathered fat (E)(R)   *Job 15:27*

COLONADES

with five *c.* (N)   *Joh 5:12*

COLONEL

the *c.* of the regiment (P)   *Ac 21:31*

COLONY

part of Macedonia, and a *c.*   *Ac 16:12*

COLOR

king's *c.* changed (R)   *Da 5:6; 5:9, 10*

COLOSSE

in Christ which are at C.   *Col 1:2*

COLOUR

plague have not changed his   *Le 13:55*
c.
c. thereof as the *c.* of   *Nu 11:7*
bdellium
when it giveth his *c.* in the   *Pr 23:31*
cup
midst thereof as the *c.* of   *Eze 1:4*
amber

like the *c.* of burnished brass   *Eze 1:7*
was like unto the *c.* of a   *Eze 1:16*
beryl
as the *c.* of the terrible   *Eze 1:22*
crystal
And I saw as *c.* of amber,   *Eze 1:27*
as
of brightness, as the *c.* of   *Eze 8:2*
amber
wheels was as the *c.* of a   *Eze 10:9*
beryl
feet like in *c.* to polished   *Da 10:6*
brass
under *c.* as though they   *Ac 27:30*
would
arrayed in purple and scarlet   *Re 17:4*
c.

COLOURED

sit upon a scarlet *c.* beast   *Re 17:3*

COLOURS

he made him a coat of many   *Ge 37:3*
c.
coat of many *c.* that was on   *Ge 37:23*
him
And they sent the coat of   *Ge 37:32*
many *c.*
to Sisera a prey of divers *c.*   *J'g 5:30*
a prey of divers *c.* of   *J'g 5:30*
needlework
of divers *c.* of needlework on *J'g 5:30*
both
a garment of divers *c.* upon   *2Sa 13:18*
her
rent her garment of divers   *2Sa 13:19*
c.
glistering stones, and of   *1Ch 29:2*
divers *c.*
I will lay thy stones with   *Isa 54:11*
fair *c.*
thy high places with divers   *Eze 16:16*
c.
of feathers, which had divers   *Eze 17:3*
c.

COLT

ass's *c.* unto the choice vine   *Ge 49:11*
man be born like a wild   *Job 11:12*
ass's *c.*
and upon a *c.* the foal of an   *Zec 9:9*
ass
find an ass tied and a *c.*   *M't 21:2;*
with her   *21:5, 7; M'k 11:2, 4-5, 7;*
          Lu 19:30, 33, 35
king cometh, sitting on an   *Joh 12:15*
ass's *c.*

COLTS

milch camels with their *c.*   *Ge 32:15*
forty
sons that rode on thirty ass *c.* *J'g 10:4*
rode on threescore and ten   *J'g 12:14*
ass *c.*

COLUMNS

read three or four *c.* (S)   *Jer 36:23*

COMBATIVE

not *c.*, but gentle (A)   *1Ti 3:3*

COME

the end of all flesh is *c.*   *Ge 6:13*
before me
two of every sort shall *c.*   *Ge 6:20*
unto thee
c. thou, and all thy house into *Ge 7:1*
the ark
And it shall *c.* to pass, when *Ge 9:14*
I bring
come (S)   *Ge 11:3;*
   11:4, 7; 38:16; Ec 2:1; Jas 4:13; 5:1
therefore are ye *c.* to your   *Ge 18:5*
servant
according to the cry which   *Ge 18:21*
is *c.* to me
c. let us make our father   *Ge 19:32*
drink wine
And let it *c.* to pass, that   *Ge 24:14*
the damsel
why *c.* to me seeing ye hate   *Ge 26:27*
me
c. let us make a covenant   *Ge 31:44*

c. let us slay him, and cast   *Ge 37:10*
him into
he said, whence *c.* ye   *Ge 42:7; J'g 9:8*
therefore is distress *c.* upon   *Ge 42:21*
us
take wagons, bring your   *Ge 45:19*
father and *c.*
sceptre not depart till Shiloh   *Ge 49:10*
c.
cry of children of Israel *c.* to   *Ex 3:9*
me
I *c.* to thee in a thick cloud   *Ex 19:9*
fear not, God is *c.* to prove   *Ex 20:20*
you
where I record my name I   *Ex 20:24*
will *c.*
destroy people to whom thou   *Ex 23:27*
shalt *c.*
c. with us, we will do thee   *Nu 10:29*
good
c. I pray thee curse this   *Nu 22:6*
people
there is a people *c.* out of   *Nu 22:11*
Egypt
out of Jacob shall *c.* he that   *Nu 24:19*
shall
if a Levite *c.* and *c.* with   *De 18:6*
desire
all these blessings shall *c.*   *De 28:2*
upon you
all these curses *c.* upon thee   *De 28:15*
when all Israel is *c.* to   *De 31:11*
appear before
as captain of host of Lord I   *Jos 5:14*
c.
no razor *c.* on his head   *J'g 13:5*
       1Sa 1:11
it was told, Samson is *c.*   *J'g 16:2*
hither
c. on thy two sons in one day   *1Sa 2:34*
God is *c.* into camp   *1Sa 4:7*
people will not eat till he *c.*   *1Sa 9:13*
looked on my people, their   *1Sa 9:16*
cry is *c.*
seven days tarry, till I *c.*   *1Sa 10:8*
I *c.* to thee in name of the   *1Sa 17:45*
Lord
c. what may (S)   *1Sa 18:22; 18:23*
c. thou, for there is peace   *1Sa 20:21*
to thee
slay me, for anguish is *c.*   *2Sa 1:9*
upon me
how shall the ark *c.* to me   *2Sa 6:9*
c. on him while weary and   *2Sa 17:2*
weak
speech of all Israel is *c.* to   *2Sa 19:11*
the king
c. with me and I will feed   *2Sa 19:33*
thee
the oath *c.* before thine altar   *1Ki 8:31*
whether any thing would *c.*   *1Ki 20:33*
from
feed this fellow until I *c.* in   *1Ki 22:27*
peace
creditor is *c.* to take my two   *2Ki 4:1*
sons
when this letter is *c.* unto   *2Ki 5:6*
thee
c. now to me, he shall know   *2Ki 5:8*
the man of God is *c.* hither   *2Ki 8:7*
till I *c.* and take you away   *2Ki 18:32;*
       Isa 36:17
Both riches and honour *c.*   *1Ch 29:12*
of these
all things *c.* of thee   *1Ch 29:14*
whereto is the ark of the   *2Ch 8:11*
Lord *c.*
after all that is *c.* upon us   *Ezr 9:13*
queen Vashti refused to *c.* at   *Es 1:12*
endure to see evil *c.* on my   *Es 8:6*
people
let no joyful voice *c.* therein   *Job 3:7*
the thing I greatly feared is   *Job 3:25;*
c.   *4:5*
that I may speak, let *c.*   *Job 13:13*
what will
all my time wait till my   *Job 14:14*
change *c.*
sons *c.* to honor, and he   *Job 14:21*
knoweth not
he caused it to *c.* for   *Job 37:13*
correction
Hitherto shalt thou *c.* but   *Job 38:11*
no further
then said I, lo, I *c.*   *Ps 40:7;*
       Heb 10:7, 9
when shall I *c.* and appear   *Ps 42:2*
before God
all this is *c.* upon us   *Ps 44:17*

God shall *c.* and not keep   *Ps 50:3*
silence
O that salvation of Israel   *Ps 53:6*
were *c.*
fearfulness and trembling are   *Ps 55:5*
c. upon
unto thee will all flesh *c.*   *Ps 65:2*
I am *c.* into deep waters,   *Ps 69:2*
floods
stir up strength, and *c.* save   *Ps 80:2*
us
all nations shall *c.* and   *Ps 86:9*
worship Thee
when wilt thou *c.* unto me? I   *Ps 101:2*
will
time to favour Zion is *c.*   *Ps 102:13*
as he loved cursing, so let it   *Ps 109:17*
c.
Let thy mercies *c.* also unto   *Ps 119:41*
me
so shall poverty *c.* as one that   *Pr 6:11*
fear of the wicked shall *c.*   *Pr 10:24*
upon him
the curse causeless shall not *c.*   *Pr 26:2*
all things *c.* alike to all   *Ec 9:2*
rise up, my love, *c.* away   *Ca 2:10;*
       2:13
C. with me from Lebanon, my   *Ca 4:8*
spouse
c. thou south wind, blow   *Ca 4:16*
upon my
let counsel of the Holy One   *Isa 5:19*
c.
he is *c.* to Aiath, he is passed   *Isa 10:28*
they *c.* from far country,   *Isa 13:5*
even the Lord
the day of the Lord *c.* with   *Isa 13:6*
destruction
if ye will inquire, inquire,   *Isa 21:12*
return, *c.*
C. my people, enter into   *Isa 26:20*
chambers
cause them that *c.* of Jacob   *Isa 27:6*
to take root
God will *c.* with vengeance,   *Isa 35:4*
he will *c.*
the Lord will *c.* with a   *Isa 40:10*
strong hand
I have raised up one, and he   *Isa 41:25*
c.
I appointed things coming,   *Isa 44:7*
and shall *c.*
assemble yourselves, and *c.*   *Isa 45:20*
draw near
even to him shall men *c.*   *Isa 45:24*
and all that are
the redeemed shall *c.* with   *Isa 51:11*
singing
c. to waters, *c.* ye, buy, *c.*   *Isa 55:1*
c. unto me, hear, your soul   *Isa 55:3*
shall live
my salvation is near to *c.*   *Isa 56:1*
the Redeemer shall *c.* to   *Isa 59:20*
Zion
Arise, shine, for thy light is   *Isa 60:1*
c.
Gentiles shall *c.* to thy light   *Isa 60:3;*
       60:5
the year of my redeemed is   *Isa 63:4*
c.
Lord will *c.* with fire and   *Isa 66:15*
chariots
why, say they, we will *c.* no   *Jer 2:31*
more
we *c.* to thee, thou art our   *Jer 3:22*
God
call mourning women, they   *Jer 9:17*
may *c.*
it shall *c.* to pass, after that   *Jer 12:15*
I have
And it shall *c.* to pass, if   *Jer 12:16*
they will
wherefore *c.* these things   *Jer 13:22*
upon me
where is the word of the   *Jer 17:15*
Lord? let it *c.*
serve him till time of his   *Jer 27:7*
land *c.*
they shall *c.* with weeping   *Jer 31:9*
if princes hear, and *c.* to   *Jer 38:25*
thee
sinned, therefore this is *c.*   *Jer 40:3*
upon us
if seem good to *c.*, if seem ill   *Jer 40:4*
as Carmel by the sea, so   *Jer 46:18*
shall he *c.*
baldness is *c.* on Gaza   *Jer 47:5*
trusted, saying, who shall *c.*   *Jer 49:4*
unto me

woe to them, for their day   *Jer 50:27*
is *c.*
thy day is *c.* that I will visit   *Jer 50:31*
you
dwellest on many waters,   *Jer 51:13*
the end is *c.*
none *c.* to the solemn feasts   *La 1:4*
Let their wickedness *c.* before   *La 1:22*
thee
our days are fulfilled, our end   *La 4:18*
is *c.*
remember, O Lord, what is *c.*   *La 5:1*
upon us
an end is *c.* upon the land   *Eze 7:2;*
       7:6
an evil, an only evil is *c.*   *Eze 7:5*
the time is *c.*, the day of   *Eze 7:7;*
trouble is *c.*   *7:10, 12*
will ye save souls alive that   *Eze 13:18*
c. to you
king of Babylon is *c.* to   *Eze 17:12*
Jerusalem
two ways sword may *c.*   *Eze 21:19;*
       21:20; 32:11
until he *c.* whose right it is   *Eze 21:27*
when he seeth sword *c.* on   *Eze 33:3;*
land   *33:6*
they *c.* to thee as the   *Eze 33:31*
people cometh
lo it will *c.* then shall know   *Eze 33:33*
a prophet
my people Israel, they are at   *Eze 36:8*
hand to *c.*
all this evil is *c.* upon us   *Da 9:13*
c. let us return to Lord for he   *Ho 6:1*
hath torn
and he shall *c.* to us, as the   *Ho 6:3*
rain to the earth
it is time to seek Lord till   *Ho 10:12*
he *c.*
day of Lord, as destruction   *Joe 1:15*
shall it *c.*
before the terrible day of the   *Joe 2:31*
Lord *c.*
the end is *c.* on my people   *Am 8:2*
Israel
c. let us cast lots, that we   *Jon 1:7*
may know
he is *c.* to the gate of my   *Mic 1:9*
people
to thee shall it *c.* the kingdom   *Mic 4:8*
shall *c.*
it will surely *c.* and not tarry   *Hab 2:3*
shame *c.* upon thee (S)   *Hab 2:16*
before fierce anger of Lord *c.*   *Zep 2:2*
on you
then said I, what *c.* these to   *Zec 1:21*
God shall *c.* and all saints   *Zec 14:5*
with thee
but it shall *c.* to pass, that   *Zec 14:7*
Lord ye seek shall *c.* to his   *Mal 3:1*
temple
lest I *c.* and smite earth with   *Mal 4:6*
a curse
for out of thee shall *c.* a   *M't 2:6*
Governor
who warned you to flee from   *M't 3:7*
wrath to *c.*
first be reconciled, *c.* and   *M't 5:24*
offer gift
kingdom *c.* thy will be done   *M't 6:10;*
       Lu 11:2
false prophets *c.* in sheep's   *M't 7:15*
clothing
Jesus saith to him, I will *c.*   *M't 8:7*
and heal him
not worthy thou shouldest *c.*   *M't 8:8*
under my roof
to another, *c.* and he cometh   *M't 8:9;*
       Lu 7:8
many *c.* from east and west,   *M't 8:11*
and sit down
art thou he that should *c.?*   *M't 11:3;*
       Lu 7:19, 20
c. all that labour and are   *M't 11:28*
heavy laden
if any man will *c.* after me,   *M't 16:24*
let him
Elias must first *c.*   *M't 17:10; 17:11*
Son of man *c.* to save the   *M't 18:11*
lost
sell that thou hast, and *c.*   *M't 19:21;*
       Lu 18:22
all things are ready *c.* unto   *M't 22:4*
marriage
gospel be preached, then   *M't 24:14*
shall end *c.*
ye know not what hour   *M't 24:42*
your Lord doth *c.*

c. blessed of My father, inherit kingdom   *M't 25:34*
art thou *c.* to destroy us   *M'k 1:24; Lu 4:34*
puts in sickle, because harvest is *c.*   *M'k 4:29*
if any will *c.* after me   *M'k 8:34; Lu 9:23; 14:27*
suffer little children to *c.* to me   *M'k 10:14; Lu 18:16*
c. take up the cross, and follow me   *M'k 10:21*
this is the heir, *c.* let us kill him   *M'k 12:7; Lu 20:14*
she is *c.* aforehand to anoint my body   *M'k 14:8*
sleep on now, it is enough, the hour is *c.*   *M'k 14:41*
Son of man is *c.* eating and drinking   *Lu 7:34*
every place where he would *c.*   *Lu 10:1*
three years I *c.* seeking fruit   *Lu 13:7*
six days, in them *c.* and be healed   *Lu 13:14*
brother is *c.,* father has killed the   *Lu 15:27*
when the kingdom of God should *c.*   *Lu 17:20*
this day is salvation *c.* to this house   *Lu 19:9*
Son of man *c.* to save the lost   *Lu 19:10*
he said, Occupy till I *c.*   *Lu 19:13*
shall *c.* and destroy husbandmen   *Lu 20:16*
fruit of vine, till kingdom of God *c.*   *Lu 22:18*
he saith unto them, *C.* and see   *Joh 1:39*
that light is *c.* into the world   *Joh 3:19*
same baptizeth, all men *c.* to him   *Joh 3:26*
when he is *c.* he will tell us   *Joh 4:25*
sin no more, lest a worse thing *c.* to thee   *Joh 5:14*
will not *c.* to me, that ye might have life   *Joh 5:40*
all that Father giveth me shall *c.*   *Joh 6:37*
no man can *c.* to me except Father draw him   *Joh 6:44; 6:65*
and, where I am, thither ye cannot *c.*   *Joh 7:34*
if any man thirst, let him *c.* to me and drink   *Joh 7:37*
cannot tell whence I *c.* and whither I go   *Joh 8:14*
the Master is *c.* and calleth for thee   *Joh 11:28*
the hour is *c.* that the Son of man be   *Joh 12:23*
I tell you before it *c.* to pass, when   *Joh 13:19*
not leave you comfortless, I will *c.*   *Joh 14:18*
we will *c.* unto him, and make our   *Joh 14:23*
when Comforter is *c.* whom I will send   *Joh 15:26*
when he is *c.* he will reprove world   *Joh 16:8*
when Spirit of truth is *c.* he will   *Joh 16:13*
woman hath sorrow because hour is *c.*   *Joh 16:21*
these are in world, I *c.* to thee   *Joh 17:11*
if I will he tarry till I *c.* what to thee   *Joh 21:22; 21:23*
shall so *c.* as ye have seen him go   *Ac 1:11*
before great and notable day of Lord *c.*   *Ac 2:20*
sins blotted out, when times of refreshing *c.*   *Ac 3:19*
and now *c.* I will send thee into Egypt   *Ac 7:34*
pray that none of these things *c.* upon me   *Ac 8:24*
that he would not delay to *c.* to them   *Ac 9:38*
lest that *c.* on you spoken in prophets   *Ac 13:40*
c. over into Macedonia, and help us   *Ac 16:9*
believe on him that should *c.* after him   *Ac 19:4*
forbid no acquaintance to *c.* to him   *Ac 24:23*

which promise our twelve tribes hope to *c.*   *Ac 26:7*
no other than prophets and Moses say should *c.*   *Ac 26:22*
we say, Let us do evil, that good *c.*   *Ro 3:8*
word of promise, at this time will I *c.*   *Ro 9:9*
salvation is *c.* unto the Gentiles   *Ro 11:11*
your obedience is *c.* abroad among   *Ro 16:19*
judge nothing till the Lord *c.*   *1Co 4:5*
do shew the Lord's death till he *c.*   *1Co 11:26*
rest will I set in order when I *c.*   *1Co 11:34*
when that which is perfect is *c.*   *1Co 13:10*
dead, and with what body do they *c.*   *1Co 15:35*
that there be no gatherings when I *c.*   *1Co 16:2*
if Timothy *c.* see he be without fear   *1Co 16:10*
as to Apollos, I desired him to *c.* to you   *1Co 16:12*
I was minded to *c.* to you before   *2Co 1:15*
I fear, lest when I *c.* I shall not find   *2Co 12:20*
if righteousness *c.* by the law, then   *Ga 2:21*
blessing of Abraham *c.* on Gentiles   *Ga 3:14*
it was added, till the seed should *c.*   *Ga 3:19*
after faith is *c.* we are no longer   *Ga 3:25*
gospel is *c.* to you, as in all world   *Col 1:6*
when he shall *c.* to be glorified   *2Th 1:10*
not *c.* except there *c.* falling away first   *2Th 2:3*
life that now is, and of that to *c.*   *1Ti 4:8*
till I *c.* give attendance to reading   *1Ti 4:13*
in last days perilous times shall *c.*   *2Ti 3:1*
time will *c.* not endure sound doctrine   *2Ti 4:3*
be diligent to *c.* to me to Nicopolis   *Tit 3:12*
let us *c.* boldly to throne of grace   *Heb 4:16*
able to save them that *c.* to God by him   *Heb 7:25*
those who *c.* to it (S)   *Heb 10:1*
he that shall *c.* will *c.* and not tarry   *Heb 10:37*
whence *c.* wars, *c.* they not of lusts   *Jas 4:1*
weep for miseries that shall *c.* on you   *Jas 5:1*
but all should *c.* to repentance   *2Pe 3:9*
day of Lord will *c.* as a thief   *2Pe 3:10; Re 3:3; 16:15*
ye have heard, antichrist shall *c.*   *1Jo 2:18*
that Jesus Christ is *c.* in the flesh   *1Jo 4:2*
spirit that confesseth not Jesus is *C.* in flesh   *1Jo 4:3; 2Jo 7*
know that the Son of God is *c.*   *1Jo 5:20*
if I *c.* I will remember his deeds   *3Jo 10*
repent, or else I will *c.* quickly   *Re 2:5*
have already, hold fast till I *c.*   *Re 2:25*
I *c.* quickly, hold that fast   *Re 3:11; 22:7,20*
one of four beasts, saying *c.*   *Re 6:1,3,5,7*
the great day of his wrath is *c.*   *Re 6:17*
thy wrath is *c.* and time of dead   *Re 11:18*
now is *c.* salvation and strength, and king   *Re 12:10*
fear God, for hour of judgment is *c.*   *Re 14:7*
for in one hour is thy judgment *c.*   *Re 18:10*
in one hour great riches *c.* to nought   *Re 18:17*
marriage of Lamb is *c.* and his wife   *Re 19:7*

let him that is athirst *c.* whosoever will   *Re 22:17*

COME *AGAIN*

that it *c. again* to my father's house   *Ge 28:21*
waters may *c. again* on Egyptians   *Ex 14:26*
if the plague *c. again* and break out   *Le 14:43*
when I *c. again* I will break down   *J'g 8:9*
let man of God *c. again* and teach us   *J'g 13:8*
Shimei had gone to Gath, and *c. again*   *1Ki 2:41*
depart 3 days, and *c. again*   *1Ki 12:5; 2Ch 10:5*
I pray, let this child's soul *c. again*   *1Ki 17:21*
children of Israel *c. again*   *Ezr 6:21; Ne 8:17*
he shall *c. again* with rejoicing   *Ps 126:6*
say not to neighbour, go and *c. again*   *Pr 3:28*
Chaldeans shall *c. again* and fight   *Jer 37:8*
when I *c. again* I will repay thee   *Lu 10:35*
will *c. again* and receive you to myself   *Joh 14:3*
have heard how I go away and *c. again*   *Joh 14:28*
I would not *c. again* in heaviness   *2Co 2:1*
lest, when I *c. again,* God will humble me   *2Co 12:21*
that if I *c. again* I will not spare   *2Co 13:2*

COME *DOWN*

thus saith Joseph, *c. down* to me   *Ge 45:9*
I am *c. down* to deliver and bring up   *Ex 3:8*
Lord will *c. down* on mount Sinai   *Ex 19:11*
I will *c. down* and talk with thee   *Nu 11:17*
from heaven it shall *c. down*   *De 28:24*
c. down against the Midianites   *J'g 7:24*
they said, we are *c. down* to bind thee   *J'g 15:12*
c. down and fetch ark up to you   *1Sa 6:21*
will Saul *c. down?* Lord said, he will *c. down*   *1Sa 23:11*
c. down, according to desire of thy soul   *1Sa 23:20*
shalt not *c. down* from that bed   *2Ki 1:4; 1:6, 16*
thou man of God, *c. down*   *2Ki 1:9*
let fire *c. down* and consume   *2Ki 1:10; 1:11, 12*
am doing great work, I cannot *c. down.*   *Ne 6:3*
his dealing shall *c. down* on own pate   *Ps 7:16*
He shall *c. down* like rain on mown grass   *Ps 72:6*
bow the heavens, O Lord, and *c. down*   *Ps 144:5*
my sword, shall *c. down* on Idumea   *Isa 34:5*
c. down, sit in dust, O virgin daughter   *Isa 47:1*
oh, that thou wouldest *c. down*   *Isa 64:1*
your principalities shall *c. down*   *Jer 13:18*
which say, who shall *c. down* against us   *Jer 21:13*
c. down from thy glory, sit in thirst   *Jer 48:18*
princes of the sea shall *c. down*   *Eze 26:16*
all pilots shall *c. down* from their ships   *Eze 27:29*
the pride of her power shall *c. down*   *Eze 30:6*
cause thy mighty ones to *c. down*   *Joe 3:11*
not *c. down* to take any thing of house   *M't 24:17*
c. down from cross   *M't 27:40; 27:42; M'k 15:30*

that we command fire *c.* *Lu 9:54*
down
Zaccheus, make haste and *c.* *Lu 19:5*
down
Sir, *c. down* ere my child die *Joh 4:49*
the gods are *c. down* to us *Ac 14:11*
like men
devil *c. down* to you, having *Re 12:12*
wrath
maketh fire *c. down* from *Re 13:13*
heaven on earth
angel *c. down.* having key of *Re 20:1*
bottomless pit

COME *FORTH*

shall *c. forth* out of thy *Ge 15:4*
bowels
Hebrews *c. forth* out of *1Sa 14:11*
their holes
Benaiah said, thus saith the *1Ki 2:30*
king *c. forth*
go slay them, let none *c.* *2Ki 10:25*
forth
when tried, I shall *c. forth* *Job 23:10*
as gold
let sentence *c. forth* from thy *Ps 17:2*
presence
I am shut up, and I cannot *c.* *Ps 88:8*
forth
that feareth God shall *c. forth* *Ec 7:18*
shall *c. forth* rod out of stem *Isa 11:1*
of Jesse
art *c. forth* out of waters of *Isa 48:1*
Judah
lest my fury *c. forth* like fire *Jer 4:4*
and burn
Pharaoh's army *c. forth* out *Jer 37:5;*
of Egypt *37:7*
let mighty men *c. forth,* the *Jer 46:9*
Ethiopians
a fire shall *c. forth.* out *Jer 48:45*
of Heshbon
both twain *c. forth* out of *Eze 21:19*
one land
servants of most high God, *c.* *Da 3:26*
forth
Daniel, I am *c. forth* to give *Da 9:22*
thee skill
fountain *c. forth* of house of *Joe 3:18*
Lord
out of thee *c. forth* that is to *Mic 5:2*
be ruler
c. forth and flee from land of *Zec 2:6*
north
angels *c. forth* and sever *M't 13:49*
wicked
c. forth from heart, and *M't 15:18*
defile the man
this kind *c. forth* by nothing *M'k 9:29*
but prayer
will *c. forth* and serve them *Lu 12:37*
shall *c. forth* they that have *Joh 5:29*
done good
cried with loud voice, *Joh 11:43*
Lazarus, *c. forth*
after that they shall *c. forth* *Ac 7:7*
and serve me

COME *HITHER*

in fourth generation shall *c.* *Ge 15:16*
hither
it was told Gazites, Samson *J'g 16:2*
is *c. hither*
at meal-time *c.* thou *hither* *Ru 2:14*
and eat
inquired if man should *c.* *1Sa 10:22*
hither
we will not sit down till he *1Sa 16:11*
c. hither
c. hither I may send thee to *2Sa 14:32*
king
Joab, *c. hither* that I may *2Sa 20:16*
speak with thee
told Ben-hadad, man of God, *2Ki 8:7*
is *c. hither*
better it be said to thee, *c. up* *Pr 25:7*
hither
ye servants of God *c.* forth *Da 3:26*
and *c. hither*
art *c. hither* to torment *M't 8:29*
before time
that I thirst not, neither *c.* *Joh 4:15*
hither to draw
Jesus saith, call thy husband *Joh 4:16*
and *c. hither*
that have turned world *c.* *Ac 17:6*
hither

voice said, *C. hither* *Re 4:1;*
11:12; 17:1; 21:9

COME *IN, INTO*

shalt *c. into* ark, and thy *Ge 6:18*
sons
not a man in earth to *c. in* *Ge 19:31*
to us
he said, *c. in* thou blessed *Ge 24:31*
of Lord
Lord not suffer destroyer to *Ex 12:23*
c. in
when they *c. in* unto the *Ex 28:43*
tabernacle
bathe his flesh, and *Le 16:26;*
afterward *c. into* camp *16:28;*
Nu 19:7; 31:24
at his word they shall *c. in* *Nu 27:21*
I can no more go out nor *c.* *De 31:2*
in
so is my strength to go out *Jos 14:11*
and *c. in*
I will *c. in* and confirm *1Ki 1:14*
I am child, know not how to *1Ki 3:7*
go out or *c. in*
he said *c. in* thou wife of *1Ki 14:6*
Jeroboam
might not suffer any to go *1Ki 15:17*
out or *c. in*
when *c. in* shut door upon *2Ki 4:4*
thee
took each his men to *c. in* *2Ki 11:9*
and go out
go out and *c. in* before this *2Ch 1:10*
people
might let none go out or *c.* *2Ch 16:1*
in to Asa
none *c. into* house of Lord *2Ch 23:6*
save priests
convey me over, till I *c. into* *Ne 2:7*
Judah
Esther let no man *c. in* with *Es 5:12*
king
the king said, let Haman *c. in* *Es 6:5*
the King of glory *c. in* *Ps 24:7; 24:9*
for waters are *c. in* unto my *Ps 69:1*
soul
bring an offering and *c. into* *Ps 96:8*
his courts
so let it *c. into* his bowels *Ps 109:18*
like water
let my beloved *c. into* his *Ca 4:16*
garden
the Lord shall *c into* Egypt *Isa 19:1*
Assyrian shall *c. into* Egypt *Isa 19:23*
every house shut up, that no *Isa 24:10*
man *c. in*
when enemy *c. in* like flood *Isa 59:19*
gate the kings of Judah *c. in* *Jer 17:19*
let Jerusalem *c. into* your *Jer 51:50*
mind
for strangers are *c. into* the *Jer 51:51*
sanctuaries
I know things that *c. into* *Eze 11:5*
mind
at same time things *c. into* *Eze 38:10*
mind
when Assyrian *c. into* land *Mic 5:5*
when ye *c. into* house, *M't 10:12*
salute it
Son of man *c. in* glory of *M't 16:27*
Father
many *c. in* my name, *M't 24:5;*
saying, I am Christ *M'k 13:6; Lu 21:8*
when Son of man *c. in* his *M't 25:31*
glory
they which *c. in* may see *Lu 11:33*
light
c. in second watch, or *c. in* *Lu 12:38*
third
c. in day when looketh not *Lu 12:46*
for him
go out, compel them to *c. in* *Lu 14:23*
lest they *c. into* this place of *Lu 16:28*
torment
I am *c. in* my Father's *Joh 5:43*
name, if another *c. in* his own name
prophet that should *c. into* *Joh 6:14;*
world *11:27*
Lydia, saying, *c. into* house, *Ac 16:15*
abide
till fulness of Gentiles *c. in* *Ro 11:25*
there *c. in* those unlearned *1Co 14:23*
if there *c. in* one that *1Co 14:24*
believeth not
c. in a poor man in vile *Jas 2:2*
raiment

I will *c. in* to him, and sup *Re 3:20*
with him

COME *NEAR*

Abram was *c. near* to enter *Ge 12:11*
Egypt
but Abimelech had not *c. near* *Ge 20:4*
her
then let him *c. near* and *Ex 12:48*
keep it
say unto Israel, *c. near* before *Ex 16:9*
the Lord
when they *c. near* to altar *Ex 28:43;*
30:20
will cause him to *c. near* *Nu 16:5*
no stranger *c. near* to offer *Nu 16:40*
incense
c. near, put feet on necks *Jos 10:24*
caused all tribes to *c. near* *1Sa 10:20*
be held in, lest *c. near* unto *Ps 32:9*
let my cry *c. near* before *Ps 119:169*
thee
let us *c. near* together to *Isa 41:1*
judgment
c. near unto me, hear ye this *Isa 48:16*
who is adversary? let him *c.* *Isa 50:8*
near
nor *c. near* to menstrous *Eze 18:6*
woman
which *c. near* to the Lord *Eze 40:46;*
to minister *44:15-16*
cause seat of violence to *c.* *Am 6:3*
near
I will *c. near* to you to *Mal 3:5*
judgment
when he was *c. near* beheld *Lu 19:41*
city
c. near, are ready to kill *Ac 23:15*
him

COME *NIGH*

they were afraid to *c. nigh* *Ex 34:30*
him
be sanctified in all that *c. nigh* *Le 10:3*
no man that hath blemish *c.* *Le 21:21;*
nigh *21:23*
stranger not *c. nigh* you *Nu 18:4*
when ye *c. nigh* to battle, the *De 20:2*
priest
kingdom of God *c. nigh* you *Lu 10:9;*
10:11

COME *NOT*

be ready, *c. not* at your *Ex 19:15*
wives
shall *not c.* nigh, nor the *Ex 24:2*
people
shall *not c.* into land I *Nu 14:30*
sware
Dathan, Abiram said, we *Nu 16:12;*
will *not c.* up *16:14*
unclean shall *not c.* within *De 23:10*
camp
c. not near unto ark, that ye *Jos 3:4*
may
that ye *c. not* among these *Jos 23:7*
nations
hath *not c.* razor on mine *J'g 16:17*
head
sent for Joab, but he would *2Sa 14:29*
not c.
carcase *not c.* to sepulchre *1Ki 13:22*
of fathers
king of Assyria *not c.* into *2Ki 19:32;*
this city *19:33; Isa 37:33, 34*
I *c. not* against thee this *2Ch 35:21*
day
whosoever *not c.* within *Ezr 10:8*
three days
Moabite *not c.* into *Ne 13:1*
congregation
let it *not c.* into number of *Job 3:6*
months
an hypocrite shall *not c.* *Job 13:16*
before him
in floods they shall *not c.* *Ps 32:6*
nigh
let them *not c.* into thy *Ps 69:27*
righteousness
thousand fall, but it shall *not* *Ps 91:7*
c. nigh thee
not c. into tabernacle of my *Ps 132:3*
house
c. not nigh the door of her *Pr 5:8*
house
Lord bring days that have *Isa 7:17*
not c.

shall *not* c. fear of briars and thorns	Isa 7:25
overflowing scourge *not* c. to me	Isa 28:15
vintage fail, gathering shall *not* c.	Isa 32:10
far from terror, it shall *not* c. near	Isa 54:14
say, stand by thyself, c. *not* near me	Isa 65:5
the king of Babylon shall *not* c.	Jer 37:19
like things shall *not* c. nor shall it be so	Eze 16:16
shall *not* c. near to Me to do office	Eze 44:13
c. *not* ye unto Gilgal, nor go	Ho 4:15
their soul *not* c. into house of Lord	Ho 9:4
if the family of Egypt c. *not*	Zec 14:18
sent to call and they would *not* c.	M't 22:3
could *not* c. nigh for press	M'k 2:4; Lu 8:19
I have married a wife, I *cannot* c.	Lu 14:20
shall *not* c. into condemnation	Joh 5:24
will *not* c. to Me that might have life	Joh 5:40
where I am, thither ye *cannot* c.	Joh 7:34; 7:36
think ye He will *not* c. to feast	Joh 11:56
if I had *not* c. they had not had sin	Joh 15:22
if I go not away, Comforter *not* c.	Joh 16:7
as though I would *not* c. to you	1Co 4:18

COME *OUT*

c. *out* with great substance	Ge 15:14
kings shall c. *out* of thee	Ge 17:6; 35:11
daughters of city c. *out* to draw water	Ge 24:13
till he c. *out* and made atonement	Le 16:17
eat till it c. *out* at your nostrils	Nu 11:20
c. *out* unto tabernacle of congregation	Nu 12:4
lest I c. *out* against thee with the sword	Nu 20:18
there is a people c. *out* of Egypt	Nu 22:5
Aaron died 40th year after Israel c. *out*	Nu 33:38
c. *out* one way, and flee seven ways	De 28:7
if not, let fire c. *out* of bramble	J'g 9:15
increase thine army and c. *out*	J'g 9:29
let not arrogancy c. *out* of mouth	1Sa 2:3
to-morrow we will c. *out* unto thee	1Sa 11:3; 11:10
after whom is king of Israel c. *out*	1Sa 24:14
C. *out*, c. *out*, thou bloody man	2Sa 16:7
in 480th year after Israel c. *out*	1Ki 6:1
saying, there are men c. *out* of Samaria	1Ki 20:17
he will c. *out* to me, lay hand	2Ki 5:11
make agreement and c. *out*	2Ki 18:31; Isa 36:16
he is c. *out* to fight against thee	2Ki 19:9
that salvation were c. *out* of Zion	Ps 14:7
princes shall c. *out* of Egypt	Ps 68:31
the just shall c. *out* of trouble	Pr 12:13
stink shall c. *out* of carcases	Isa 34:3
is one c. *out* that imagineth evil	Na 1:11
by no means c. *out* till hast paid	M't 5:26
c. *out* as against a thief with swords to take me	M't 26:55; M'k 14:48; Lu 22:52
hold peace, c. *out*	M'k 1:25; Lu 4:35

said, c. *out*, unclean spirit	M'k 5:8; Lu 8:29
can any good c. *out* of Nazareth	Joh 1:40
some said, shall Christ c. *out* of Galilee	Joh 7:41
in name of Jesus to c. *out* of her	Ac 16:18
shall c. *out* of Zion the Deliverer	Ro 11:26
wherefore c. *out* from among them	2Co 6:17
though c. *out* loins of Abraham	Heb 7:5
spirits c. *out* of mouth of dragon	Re 16:13
voice saying, C. *out* of her, my people	Re 18:4

COME *SHORT*

all sinned c. *short* of glory of God	Ro 3:23
lest any seem to c. *short* of it	Heb 4:1

COME *TO PASS*

c. *to pass* if they will not believe	Ex 4:8
whether my word c. *to pass* or not	Nu 11:23
c. *to pass* the man's rod blossom	Nu 17:5
c. *to pass* if ye hearken	De 7:12; 11:13; 28:1
the sign or the wonder c. *to pass*	De 13:2
all c. *to pass*, no thing failed	Jos 23:14
Manoah said, let words c. *to pass*	J'g 13:12
when sayings c. *to pass* may do honour	J'g 13:17
O Lord, why is this c. *to pass* in Israel	J'g 21:3
saying shall surely c. *to pass*	1Ki 13:32
it shall not stand, nor c. *to pass*	Isa 7:7
as I have thought, so shall it c. *to pass*	Isa 14:24
the former things are c. *to pass*	Isa 42:9
shall c. *to pass* if diligently hearken	Jer 17:24
what thou hast spoken is c. *to pass*	Jer 32:24
word that I speak shall c. *to pass*	Eze 12:25
I have spoken, it shall c. *to pass*	Eze 24:14
maketh known what shall c. *to pass*	Da 2:29
c. *to pass* I will break bow	Ho 1:5
c. *to pass* whosoever shall call on Lord	Joe 2:32
c. *to pass* cause sun go down at noon	Am 8:9
c. *to pass* if ye diligently obey	Zec 6:15
it is c. *to pass*, that as he cried	Zec 7:13
all these things c. *to pass*, end not	Mt 24:6
things he saith shall c. *to pass*	M'k 11:23
when see these c. *to pass*	M'k 13:29; Lu 21:31
see this thing which is c. *to pass*	Lu 2:15
what sign these things c. *to pass*	Lu 21:7; 21:28
wondering what was c. *to pass*	Lu 24:12
not known things which are c. *to pass*	Lu 24:18
when c. *to pass* may believe	Joh 13:19; 14:29
c. *to pass* every soul that will not hear	Ac 3:23
shew things shortly c. *to pass*	Re 1:1; 22:6

COME *TOGETHER*

we should c. *together* in judgment	Job 9:32
troops c. *together* against me	Job 19:12
c. *together* out of land of north	Jer 3:18

shall c. *together*, going and weeping	Jer 50:4
when they were c. *together*	Ac 1:6; 28:17
he found many that were c. *together*	Ac 10:27
knew not why they were c. *together*	Ac 19:32
the multitude must needs c. *together*	Ac 21:22
c. *together*, that Satan tempt not	1Co 7:5
c. *together*, not for better but worse	1Co 11:17
when c. *together* in church	1Co 11:18; 20:33; 14:26
that c. *not together* to condemnation	1Co 11:34
if whole church be c. *together*	1Co 14:23

COME *UP*

trumpet sound shall c. *up* to mount	Ex 19:13
c. *up*, thou and Aaron with thee	Ex 19:24
c. *up* to me into the mount, and be there	Ex 24:12
c. *up* into midst of thee in moment	Ex 33:5
c. *up* in the morning to mount Sinai	Ex 34:2
no man c. *up* with thee nor be seen	Ex 34:3
why made us c. *up* out Egypt	Nu 20:5
priests c. *up* out of Jordan	Jos 4:16; 4:17-18
c. *up* to me, and help me smite Gibeon	Jos 10:4
c. *up* quickly, save us, and help us	Jos 10:6
Judah said c. *up* into my lot	J'g 1:3
why are ye c. *up* against us	J'g 15:10
Delilah sent, saying, c. *up* this once	J'g 16:18
if say, c. *up* to us, we will go	1Sa 14:10
have ye seen this man that is c. *up*	1Sa 17:25
then ye shall c. *up* after him	1Ki 1:35
king of Syria will c. *up* against thee	1Ki 20:22
c. *up* save from king of Syria	2Ki 16:7
am I now c. *up* without Lord	2Ki 18:25; Isa 36:10
they c. *up* by the cliff of Ziz	2Ch 20:16
goeth to grave, shall c. *up* no more	Job 7:9
better that it be said, c. *up* hither	Pr 25:7
there shall c. *up* briers and thorns	Isa 5:6
he shall c. *up* over all his channels	Isa 8:7
since laid down no fellow is c. *up*	Isa 14:8
c. *up* with acceptance on mine altar	Isa 60:7
for death is c. *up* into our windows	Jer 9:21
he shall c. *up* like a lion	Jer 49:19; 50:44
he shall c. *up* and fly as eagle	Jer 49:22
cause horses to c. *up* as caterpillars	Jer 51:27
sea is c. *up* upon Babylon	Jer 51:42
wreathed, and c. *up* upon my neck	La 1:14
it might cause fury to c. *up*	Eze 24:8
cause you to c. *up* out of graves	Eze 37:12
shalt c. *up* against My people Israel	Eze 38:16
they shall c. *up* out of the land	Ho 1:11
thistle shall c. *up* on their altars	Ho 10:8
wind of Lord shall c. *up* from	Ho 13:15
his stink and ill savour shall c. *up*	Joe 2:20
men of war draw near, let them c. *up*	Joe 3:9
heathen c. *up* to valley of Jehoshaphat	Joe 3:12

made stink of your camps to   *Am 4:10*
c. up
saviours shall *c. up* on mount   *Ob 21*
Zion
wickedness is *c. up* before me   *Jon 1:2*
Lord made a gourd to *c. up*   *Jon 4:6*
breaker is *c. up* before them   *Mic 2:13*
he that dasheth in pieces is *c. Na 2:1*
up
it shall be whoso will not *c. up*   *Zec 14:17*
if family of Egypt go not   *Zec 14:18*
up, c. not
desired Philip to *c. up* sit with   *Ac 8:31*
him
when they were *c. up* out of   *Ac 8:39*
the water
Cornelius, thy alms are *c. up*   *Ac 10:4*
before God
c. up hither, I will shew thee   *Re 4:1;*
  11:12

I AM COME, AM I COME

I thy father-in-law *am c.* to   *Ex 18:6*
thee
Balaam said, lo *I am c.* to   *Nu 22:38*
thee
I am c. into country Lord   *De 26:3*
sware
I am c. to sacrifice to the   *1Sa 16:2;*
Lord   *16:5*
I am c. to speak of this   *2Sa 14:16*
thing
wherefore *am I c.* from   *2Sa 14:32*
Geshur
I am c. first to meet my   *2Sa 19:20*
lord the king
I am c. into deep waters   *Ps 69:2*
where floods
I communed, *I am c.* to great *Ec 1:16*
estate
I am c. into my garden my   *Ca 5:1*
sister
I am c. to shew thee   *Da 9:23; 10:14*
thy words were heard, *I am Da 10:12*
c. for
think not that *I am c.* to destroy *M't 5:17*
the law
I am not *c.* to call righteous   *M't 9:13*
but sinners
think not that *I am c.* to   *M't 10:34*
send peace
I am c. to set a man at   *M't 10:35*
variance against
suppose ye *I am c.* to give   *Lu 12:51*
peace
therefore *am I c.* baptizing   *Joh 1:31*
with water
I am c. in my Father's   *Joh 5:43*
name, ye receive
I am not *c.* of myself, He   *Joh 7:28*
that sent me
for judgment, *I am c.* into   *Joh 9:39*
world
I am c. that they might   *Joh 10:10*
have life
I am c. a light into world   *Joh 12:46*
I am c. into world, again I   *Joh 16:28*
leave

COME, with TIME

my righteous, answer in *time Ge 30:33*
to *c.*
when thy son asketh thee in   *Ex 13:14;*
time to *c.*   *De 6:20; Jos 4:6, 21*
in *time* to *c.* children speak *Jos 22:24;*
  22:28
time c. after Hannah   *1Sa 1:20*
conceived
time to favour Zion, set   *Ps 102:13*
time is *c.*
she shall rejoice in *time* to *c. Pr 31:25*
time of singing of birds is *c. Ca 2:12*
time is near to *c.* her days *Isa 13:22*
that it may be for *time* to *c. Isa 30:8*
who will hear for *time* to *c. Isa 42:23*
time is *c.* the day of trouble *Eze 7:7*
is near
time is not *c.* the Lord's   *Hag 1:2*
house be built
but when the fulness of *time*   *Ga 4:4*
was *c.*
good foundation against *time*   *1Ti 6:19*
to *c.*
time is *c.* judgment must   *1Pe 4:17*
begin

YET COME

ye are not as *yet c.* to rest   *De 12:9*
woman, My hour is not *yet c. Joh 2:4*
Jesus said, My time is not   *Joh 7:6;*
yet c.   *7:8*
because his hour was not   *Joh 7:30;*
yet c.   *8:20*
Jesus was not *yet c.* into   *Joh 11:30*
the town
five fallen, the other not *yet Re 17:10*
c.

COMELINESS

he hath no form nor *c.*; and   *Isa 53:2*
for it was perfect through   *Eze 16:14*
my *c.*
they set forth thy *c.*   *Eze 27:10*
for my *c.* was turned in me   *Da 10:8*
into
parts have more abundant   *1Co 12:23*
c.

COMELY

in matters, and a *c.* person   *1Sa 16:18*
his power, nor his *c.*   *Job 41:12*
proportion
for praise is *c.* for the upright *Ps 33:1*
for it is pleasant; and praise *Ps 147:1*
is *c.*
go well, yea, four are *c.* in   *Pr 30:29*
going
it is good and *c.* for one to   *Ec 5:18*
eat and
I am black, but *c.* O ye   *Ca 1:5*
daughters
Thy cheeks are *c.* with rows *Ca 1:10*
of
voice, and thy countenance is *Ca 2:14*
c.
thy speech is *c.*: thy temples   *Ca 4:3*
are
love, as Tirzah, *c.* as   *Ca 6:4*
Jerusalem
earth shall be excellent and *c. Isa 4:2*
daughter of Zion to a *c.* and   *Jer 6:2*
you, but for that which is *c. 1Co 7:35*
is it *c.* that a woman pray   *1Co 11:13*
unto
For our *c.* parts have no   *1Co 12:24*
need: but

COMERS

continually make the *c.*   *Heb 10:1*
thereunto

COMES

c. one the hills (A)(E)   *Ps 133:3*
before he *c.* (S)   *Ac 23:15*
c. down from above   *Jas 3:15*
(A)(B)(E)(N)(R)

COMEST

Sidon, as thou *c.* to Gerar,   *Ge 10:19*
unto
of Egypt, as thou *c.* unto Zoar *Ge 13:10*
this my oath, when thou *c. Ge 24:41*
to my
And when thou *c.* nigh over   *De 2:19*
When thou *c.* nigh unto a   *De 20:10*
city to
When thou *c.* into thy   *De 23:24*
neighbour's
When thou *c.* into the   *De 23:25*
standing corn
when thou *c.* in, and blessed *De 28:6*
shalt
when thou *c.* in, and cursed *De 28:19*
shalt
said unto him, Whence *c. J'g 17:9*
thou
that thou *c.* with such a   *J'g 18:23*
company
goest thou? and whence *c. J'g 19:17*
thou
thou *c.* to Shur, that is over *1Sa 15:7*
against
C. thou peaceably   *1Sa 16:4*
Am I a dog, that thou *c. 1Sa 17:43*
to me
Thou *c.* to me with a   *1Sa 17:45*
sword, and
unto him, From whence *c. 2Sa 1:3*
thou
when thou *c.* to see my face *2Sa 3:13*
she said, *C.* thou peaceably   *1Ki 2:13*

and when thou *c.* anoint   *1Ki 19:15*
Hazael to
Elisha said unto him,   *2Ki 5:25*
Whence *c.*
And when thou *c.* thither,   *2Ki 9:2*
look out
said unto Satan, Whence *c. Job 1:7*
thou
From whence *c.* thou? And   *Job 2:2*
Satan
When thou *c.* to Babylon,   *Jer 51:61*
and shalt
and whence *c.* thou? What is *Jon 1:8*
thy .
and *c.* thou to me   *M't 3:14*
remember me when thou *c. Lu 23:42*
into
when thou *c.* bring with thee *2Ti 4:13*

COMETH

they said, Behold this   *Ge 37:19*
dreamer *c.*
on which such water *c.* is   *Le 11:34*
unclean
beside what *c.* of sale of   *De 18:8*
patrimony
cover that which *c.* from thee *De 23:13*
when ark *c.* it may save us   *1Sa 4:3*
all that man of God saith *c. 1Sa 9:6*
to pass
wherefore *c.* not son of   *1Sa 20:27*
Jesse to meat
therefore he *c.* not to the   *1Sa 20:29*
king's table
when she *c.* in will feign   *1Ki 14:5*
herself
when the time *c.* (S)   *2Ki 4:16*
came, but he *c.* not again   *2Ki 9:18;*
  9:20
be with king as he *c.* in   *2Ki 11:8;*
  2Ch 23:7
which long for death, and it   *Job 3:21*
c. not
whence *c.* wisdom, where   *Job 28:20*
understanding
weeping for night, joy *c.* in   *Ps 30:5*
morning
soul wait on God, from Him *Ps 62:1*
c. my salvation
promotion *c.* not from east   *Ps 75:6*
nor west
before Lord, for he *c.* to   *Ps 96:13*
judge earth
blessed is he that *c.* in name *Ps 118:26*
of Lord
eyes to hills whence *c.* my   *Ps 121:1*
help
help *c.* from Lord who made *Ps 121:2*
heaven
I will mock when your fear *c. Pr 1:26*
when your destruction *c.* as   *Pr 1:27*
whirlwind
when pride *c.* then *c.* shame *Pr 11:2*
when the wicked *c.* then *c. Pr 18:3*
contempt
c. in vanity, departeth in   *Ec 6:4*
darkness
if man live many years, all *c. Ec 11:8*
is vanity
he *c.* leaping upon the   *Ca 2:8*
mountains
the day of the Lord *c.* with   *Isa 13:9*
wrath
breaking *c.* suddenly at an   *Isa 30:13*
instant
name of Lord *c.* from far,   *Isa 30:27*
burning
say to Zion, behold, thy   *Isa 62:11*
salvation *c.*
who is this *c.* from Bozra   *Isa 63:1*
he shall not see when good *c. Jer 17:6*
not see when heat *c.* but her *Jer 17:8*
leaf
when *c.* shall smite land of *Jer 43:11*
Egypt
A sound of a cry *c.* from   *Jer 51:54*
Babylon
who is he that saith, and it   *La 3:37*
c.
c. to a prophet to inquire   *Eze 14:4*
which *c.* in mind shall not   *Eze 20:32*
be
tidings, because it *c.* behold *Eze 21:7*
it *c.*
when this *c.* shall know I   *Eze 24:24*
am Lord
come to thee as people *c. Eze 33:31*
and sit

when this *c.* to pass, then shall know — *Eze 33:33*

every thing live whither rivers *c.* — *Eze 47:9*

c. against him shall do exploits — *Da 11:16*

blessed is he that *c.* to 1335 days — *Da 12:12*

thief *c.* in, and troop of robbers — *Ho 7:1*

day of Lord, *c.* — *Joe 2:1; Zec 14:1; 1Th 5:2*

deliver from Assyrian when he *c.* — *Mic 5:6*

day *c.* that shall burn, day that *c.* — *Mal 4:1*

that *c.* after me is mightier than I — *M't 3:11; M'k 1:7; Lu 3:16*

whatsoever is more than these *c.* of evil — *M't 5:37*

say to another, come, and he *c.* — *M't 8:9; Lu 7:8*

then *c.* wicked one, catcheth away — *M't 13:19*

thy king *c.* unto thee — *M't 21:5; Joh 12:15*

blessed is he that *c.* in name of Lord, *M'k 11:9; Lu 13:35; 19:38*

after long time lord of servants *c.* — *M't 25:19*

he *c.* to them walking on the sea — *M'k 6:48*

be ashamed when *c.* in glory of Father — *M'k 8:38*

Elias *c.* first, restoreth all things — *M'k 9:12*

while he spake *c.* Judas one of twelve — *M'k 14:43*

whosoever *c.* to me, and heareth — *Lu 6:47*

Lord when he *c.* find watching — *Lu 12:37*

Son of man *c.* at hour ye think not — *Lu 12:40*

his lord, when he *c.* shall find doing — *Lu 12:43*

ye say, there will be heat, and it *c.* to pass — *Lu 12:55*

kingdom of God *c.* not with observation — *Lu 17:20*

Son of man *c.* find faith on earth — *Lu 18:8*

but thou canst not tell whence it *c.* — *Joh 3:8*

nor *c.* to light, lest deeds be reproved — *Joh 3:20*

he that doth the truth, *c.* to the light — *Joh 3:21*

believe me, the hour *c.* — *Joh 4:21; 4:23; 16:32*

c. to me shall never hunger — *Joh 6:35; 6:37, 45*

when Christ *c.* no man knoweth — *Joh 7:27; 7:31*

said, that Christ *c.* of seed of David — *Joh 7:42*

night *c.* when no man can work — *Joh 9:4*

no man *c.* to the Father but by me — *Joh 14:6*

the time *c.* that whosoever killeth you — *Joh 16:2*

time *c.* I no more speak in proverbs — *Joh 16:25*

the hour *c.* that ye shall be scattered — *Joh 16:32*

who when he *c.* shall speak to thee — *Ac 10:32*

c. this blessedness on circumcision — *Ro 4:9*

faith *c.* by hearing, hearing by word — *Ro 10:17*

then *c.* end, when he shall have — *1Co 15:24*

besides that which *c.* on me daily — *2Co 11:28*

these things *c.* wrath of God — *Eph 5:6*

upon children of disobedience — *Col 3:6*

day of Lord *c.* as thief in night — *1Th 5:2*

c. to God must believe that he is — *Heb 11:6*

Christ *c.* in the flesh (S) — *2Jo 7*

Lord *c.* with 10,000 of his saints — *Jude 14*

c. with clouds, every eye see him — *Re 1:7*

he *c.* he must continue short space — *Re 17:10*

COMETH *DOWN*

as the rain *c. down* from heaven — *Isa 55:10*

bread of God is he which *c. down* — *Joh 6:33*

every good and perfect gift *c. down* — *Jas 1:17*

new Jerusalem *c. down* from God — *Re 3:12*

COMETH *FORTH*

when virgin *c. forth* to draw water — *Ge 24:43*

also he *c. forth* to meet thee — *Ex 4:14*

Pharaoh, lo, he *c. forth* to the water — *Ex 8:20*

whatsoever *c. forth* of the doors — *J'g 11:31*

whosoever *c.* not *forth* after Saul — *1Sa 11:7*

affliction *c.* not *forth* of dust — *Job 5:6*

c. forth like flower, is cut down — *Job 14:2*

this also *c. forth* from the Lord — *Isa 28:29*

hear what words *c. forth* from Lord — *Eze 33:30*

the Lord *c. forth* out of his place — *Mic 1:3*

COMETH *NIGH*

the stranger that *c. nigh* shall be put to death — *Nu 1:51; 3:10, 38; 18:7*

COMETH *OUT*

be heard when he *c. out* that — *Ex 28:35*

flesh half consumed when he *c. out* — *Nu 12:12*

eye evil toward young that *c. out* — *De 28:57*

stranger that *c. out* of far country — *1Ki 8:41*

it is drawn, and *c. out* of body — *Job 20:25*

fair weather *c. out* of north — *Job 37:22*

who is this that *c. out* of wilderness — *Ca 3:6*

Lord *c. out* of place to punish — *Isa 26:21*

spread forth earth, that *c. out* of it — *Isa 42:5*

destruction *c.* it *c. out* of north — *Jer 46:20*

bake with dung that *c. out* of man — *Eze 4:12*

but that which *c. out* of mouth defileth man — *M't 15:11; M'k 7:20*

for as the lightning *c. out* of the east — *M't 24:27*

COMETH *UP*

she said, an old man *c. up* covered — *1Sa 28:14*

this that *c. up* from wilderness — *Ca 8:5*

he that *c. up* out of midst of pit — *Isa 24:18*

who is this that *c. up* as a flood — *Jer 46:7*

out of north *c. up* nation against her — *Jer 50:3*

when he *c. up* to people, will invade — *Hab 3:16*

cast hook, take up fish first *c. up* — *M't 17:27*

COMFORT

shall *c.* us concerning our work — *Ge 5:29*

and *c.* ye your hearts; after that — *Ge 18:5*

c. himself, purposing to kill thee — *Ge 27:42*

all his daughters rose up to *c.* him — *Ge 37:35*

C. thine heart with a morsel of — *J'g 19:5*

said, *C.* thine heart, I pray thee — *J'g 19:8*

David sent to *c.* him by the hand — *2Sa 10:2*

and his brethren came to *c.* him — *1Ch 7:22*

David sent messengers to *c.* him — *1Ch 19:2*

to mourn with him and to *c.* him — *Job 2:11*

should I yet have *c.*; yea, I would — *Job 6:10*

My bed shall *c.* me, my couch — *Job 7:13*

my heaviness, and *c.* myself — *Job 9:27*

alone, that I may take *c.* a little — *Job 10:20*

How then *c.* ye me in vain, seeing — *Job 21:34*

thy rod and thy staff they *c.* me — *Ps 23:4*

and *c.* me on every side — *Ps 71:21*

This is my *c.* in my affliction: for — *Ps 119:50*

merciful kindness be for my *c.* — *Ps 119:76*

saying, When wilt thou *c.* me — *Ps 119:82*

with flagons, *c.* me with apples — *Ca 2:5*

to *c.* me, because of the spoiling — *Isa 22:4*

C. ye, *c.* ye my people, saith your — *Isa 40:1*

the Lord shall *c.* Zion — *Isa 51:3*

he will *c.* all her waste places — *Isa 51:3*

by whom shall I *c.* thee — *Isa 51:19*

Should I receive *c.* in these — *Isa 57:6*

to *c.* all that mourn — *Isa 61:2*

comforteth, so will I *c.* you — *Isa 66:13*

I would *c.* myself against sorrow — *Jer 8:18*

to *c.* them for the dead; neither — *Jer 16:7*

into joy, and will *c.* them — *Jer 31:13*

c., ease myself (A) — *Jer 42:10*

none to *c.* her: all her friends — *La 1:2*

is none to *c.*, her: the Lord hath — *La 1:17*

I sigh: there is none to *c.* me — *La 1:21*

I may *c.* thee, O virgin daughter — *La 2:13*

And they shall *c.* you, when ye see — *Eze 14:23*

in that thou art a *c.* unto them — *Eze 16:54*

and the Lord shall yet *c.* Zion — *Zec 1:17*

they *c.* in vain: therefore they — *Zec 10:2*

Daughter, be of good *c.*; thy faith — *M't 9:22; Lu 8:48*

of good *c.* rise; he calleth thee — *M'k 10:49*

to Martha and Mary, to *c.* them — *Joh 11:19*

son of *c.* (P) — *Ac 4:36*

and in the *c.* of the Holy Ghost — *Ac 9:31*

patience and *c.* of the scriptures — *Ro 15:4*

we bring *c.* (B) — *1Co 4:13*

and exhortation, and *c.* — *1Co 14:3*

of mercies, and the God of all *c.* — *2Co 1:3*

that we may be able to *c.* them — *2Co 1:4*

by the *c.* wherewith we ourselves — *2Co 1:4*

to forgive him. and *c.* him, lest — *2Co 2:7*

I am filled with *c.* I am exceeding — *2Co 7:4*

we were comforted in your *c.* — *2Co 7:13*

Be perfect, be of good *c.* be of — *2Co 13:11*

and that he might *c.* your hearts — *Eph 6:22*

if any *c.* of love, if any fellowship — *Ph'p 2:1*

that I also may be of good *c.* — *Ph'p 2:19*

your estate, and *c.* your hearts — *Col 4:8*

which have been a *c.* unto me — *Col 4:11*

to *c.* you concerning your faith — *1Th 3:2*

c. one another with these words — *1Th 4:18*

c. yourselves together, and edify — *1Th 5:11*

c. the feebleminded, support the — *1Th 5:14*

C. your hearts, and stablish you — *2Th 2:17*

COMFORTABLE

my lord the king shall now   *2Sa 14:17*
be *c.*
with good words and *c.*   *Zec 1:13*
words

COMFORTABLY

speak *c.* unto thy servants   *2Sa 19:7*
spake *c.* unto all the   *2Ch 30:22*
Levites
spake *c.* to them, saying   *2Ch 32:6*
Speak ye *c.* to Jerusalem   *Isa 40:2*
speak *c.* unto her   *Ho 2:14*

COMFORTED

Isaac was *c.* after his   *Ge 24:67*
mother's
he refused to be *c.; and he*   *Ge 37:35*
said
wife died; and Judah was *c.*   *Ge 38:12*
And he *c.* them, and spake   *Ge 50:21*
kindly
for that thou hast *c.* me, and   *Ru 2:13*
And David *c.* Bath-sheba   *2Sa 12:24*
his wife
he was *c.* concerning   *2Sa 13:39*
Amnon
they bemoaned him, and *c.*   *Job 42:11*
him
not: my soul refused to be *c.*   *Ps 77:2*
Lord, hast holpen me, and *c.*   *Ps 86:17*
me
of old, O Lord; and have *c.*   *Ps 119:52*
myself
the Lord hath *c.* his people,   *Isa 49:13*
and
the Lord hath *c.* his people   *Isa 52:9*
tossed with tempest, and not   *Isa 54:11*
c.
ye shall be *c.* in Jerusalem   *Isa 66:13*
children refused to be *c.* for   *Jer 31:15*
her
rest upon them, and I will   *Eze 5:13*
be *c.*
and ye shall be *c.*   *Eze 14:22*
concerning
shall be *c.* in the nether   *Eze 31:16*
parts
shall be *c.* over all his   *Eze 32:31*
multitude
would not be *c.* because they   *M't 2:18*
that mourn: for they shall be   *M't 5:4*
c.
but now he is *c.* and thou   *Lu 16:25*
art
in the house, and *c.* her   *Joh 11:31*
the brethren, they *c.* them   *Ac 16:40*
alive, and were not a little *c.*   *Ac 20:12*
that I may be *c.* together   *Ro 1:12*
with you
may learn, and all may be   *1Co 14:31*
c.
wherewith we ourselves are *c.*   *2Co 1:4*
or whether we be *c.* it is for   *2Co 1:6*
your
down, *c.* us by the coming of   *2Co 7:6*
Titus
wherewith he was *c.* in you   *2Co 7:7*
we were *c.* in your comfort   *2Co 7:13*
That their hearts might be *c.*   *Col 2:2*
ye know how we exhorted   *1Th 2:11*
and *c.*
we were *c.* over you in all   *1Th 3:7*
our

COMFORTEDST

is turned away, and thou *c.*   *Isa 12:1*
me

COMFORTER

oppressed, and they had no *c.*   *Ec 4:1*
was power; but they had no *c.*   *Ec 4:1*
down wonderfully: she had no   *La 1:9*
c.
the *c.* that should relieve my   *La 1:16*
soul
and he shall give you   *Joh 14:16*
another *C.*
your Advocate (N)   *Joh 14:16;*
   14:26; 15:26; 16:7
someone to stand by you   *Joh 14:16;*
(P)   *14:26*
another Counselor (R)   *Joh 14:16;*
   14:26; 15:26; 16:7

the *C.* which is the Holy   *Joh 14:26*
Ghost
But when the *C.* is come,   *Joh 15:26*
whom I
the *C.* will not come unto   *Joh 16:7*
you

COMFORTERS

that he hath sent *c.* unto   *2Sa 10:3*
thee
he hath sent *c.* unto thee?   *1Ch 19:3*
are not
miserable *c.* are ye all   *Job 16:2*
none; and for *c.* but I found   *Ps 69:20*
none
I looked for pity (A)(E)(R)   *Ps 69:20*
I looked for sympathy (B)   *Ps 69:20*
whence shall I seek *c.* for thee   *Na 3:7*

COMFORTETH

as one that *c.* the mourners   *Job 29:25*
I, even I, am he that *c.* you   *Isa 51:12*
As one whom his mother *c.*   *Isa 66:13*
so will
Who *c.* us in all our   *2Co 1:4*
tribulation
that *c.* those that are cast   *2Co 7:6*
down

COMFORTING

word of king be *c.* (S)   *2Sa 14:17*
good words, and *c.* (S)   *Zec 1:13*

COMFORTLESS

I will not leave you *c.:* I   *Joh 14:18*
will
leave you orphans (A)(B)   *Joh 14:18*
not leave you desolate   *Joh 14:18*
(E)(R)
not leave you bereft (N)   *Joh 14:18*
not leave you alone (P)   *Joh 14:18*

COMFORTS

within me thy *c.* delight my   *Ps 94:19*
soul
and restore *c.* unto him and   *Isa 57:18*

COMING

and, behold, the camels   *Ge 24:63*
were *c.*
hath blessed thee since my *c.*   *Ge 30:30*
for Joseph's *c.* (S)   *Ge 43:25*
they *c.* (S)   *Nu 10:21*
hinder them from *c.* unto   *Nu 22:16*
me
of the *c.* of the children of   *Nu 33:40*
Israel
Why is his chariot so long in   *J'g 5:28*
c.
a company of prophets *c.*   *1Sa 10:5*
down
of the town trembled at his   *1Sa 16:4*
c.
saw the son of Jesse *c.* to   *1Sa 22:9*
Nob
withholden thee from *c.* to   *1Sa 25:26*
shed
me this day from *c.* to shed   *1Sa 25:33*
blood
thy going out and thy *c.* in   *1Sa 29:6*
with me
of thy *c.* unto me unto this   *1Sa 29:6*
day
know thy going out and thy   *2Sa 3:25*
c. in
c. out of their forts (S)   *2Sa 22:46*
saw the king and his   *2Sa 24:20*
servants *c.*
son of Rechab *c.* to meet   *2Ki 10:15*
him
invaded the land at the *c.*   *2Ki 13:20*
in of the
and thy going out, and thy   *2Ki 19:27*
c. in
was of God by *c.* to Joram   *2Ch 22:7*
in the second year of their *c.*   *Ezr 3:8*
unto
bridegroom *c.* out of his   *Ps 19:5*
chamber
for he seeth that his day is   *Ps 37:13*
c.
and thy *c.* in from this time   *Ps 121:8*
forth

city, at the *c.* in at the doors   *Pr 8:3*
to meet thee at thy *c.:* it   *Isa 14:9*
stirreth
When it shall hail, *c.* down   *Isa 32:19*
on
and thy *c.* in, and thy rage   *Isa 37:28*
against
and the things that are *c.*   *Isa 44:7*
swallow observe the time of   *Jer 8:7*
their *c.*
watcher and an holy one *c.*   *Da 4:23*
down
According to the days of thy   *Mic 7:15*
c.
he had horns *c.* out of his   *Hab 3:4*
hand
who may abide the day of his   *Mal 3:2*
c.
before the *c.* of the great and   *Mal 4:5*
devils, *c.* out of the tombs   *M't 8:28*
the Son of man *c.* in his   *M't 16:28*
kingdom
what shall be the sign of thy   *M't 24:3*
c.
also the *c.* of the Son of   *M't 24:27*
man be
they shall see the Son of   *M't 24:30*
man *c.*
also the *c.* of the Son of   *M't 24:37;*
man   *24:39*
heart, My lord delayeth his   *M't 24:48*
c.
at my *c.* I should have   *M't 25:27*
received
and *c.* in the clouds of   *M't 26:64*
heaven
straightway *c.* up out of the   *M'k 1:10*
water
for there were many *c.* and   *M'k 6:31*
going
see the Son of man *c.* in   *M'k 13:26*
the clouds
c. suddenly he find you   *M'k 13:36*
sleeping
and *c.* in the clouds of   *M'k 14:62*
heaven
passed by *c.* out of the   *M'k 15:21*
country
she *c.* in that instant gave   *Lu 2:38*
thanks
And as he was yet a *c.* the   *Lu 9:42*
devil
My lord delayeth his *c.* and   *Lu 12:45*
by her continual *c.* she weary   *Lu 18:5*
me
at my *c.* I might have   *Lu 19:23*
required
things which are *c.* on the   *Lu 21:26*
earth
shall they see the Son of   *Lu 21:27*
man *c.*
a Cyrenian, *c.* out of the   *Lu 23:26*
country
behold, the days are *c.* in   *Lu 23:29*
the which
c. to him, and offering him   *Lu 23:36*
c. after me is preferred   *Joh 1:27*
before me
John seeth Jesus *c.* unto him   *Joh 1:29*
Jesus saw Nathanael *c.* to   *Joh 1:47*
him
but while I am *c.* another   *Joh 5:7*
steppeth
The hour is *c.* and now is,   *Joh 5:25*
when
for the hour is *c.* in the   *Joh 5:28*
which all
seeth the wolf *c.* and   *Joh 10:12*
leaveth the
as she heard that Jesus was   *Joh 11:20*
c.
that Jesus was *c.* to   *Joh 12:12*
Jerusalem
before the *c.* of the Just   *Ac 7:52*
One
a man named Ananias *c.* in   *Ac 9:12*
with them *c.* in and going out   *Ac 9:28*
an angel of God *c.* in to him   *Ac 10:3*
as Peter was *c.* in, Cornelius   *Ac 10:25*
met
c. down from heaven   *Ac 11:5*
(A)(B)(E)(N)(P)(R)
had first preached before his   *Ac 13:24*
c.
Berea: who *c.* thither went   *Ac 17:10*
into
while the day was *c.* on   *Ac 27:33*
much hindered from *c.* to   *Ro 15:22*
you

waiting for the *c.* of our Lord   *1Co 1:7*
they that are Christ's at his *c.*   *1Co 15:23*
glad of the *c.* of Stephanus   *1Co 16:17*
comforted us by the *c.* of Titus   *2Co 7:6*
And not by his *c.* only, but   *2Co 7:7*
This is the third time I am *c.*   *2Co 13:1*
for me by my *c.* to you again   *Ph'p 1:26*
our Lord Jesus Christ at his *c.*   *1Th 2:19*
at the *c.* of our Lord Jesus Christ   *1Th 3:13*
remain unto the *c.* of the Lord   *1Th 4:15*
the *c.* of our Lord Jesus Christ   *1Th 5:23*
by the *c.* of our Lord Jesus   *2Th 2:1*
with the brightness of his *c.*   *2Th 2:8*
him, whose *c.* is after the working   *2Th 2:9*
brethren, unto the *c.* of the Lord   *Jas 5:7*
the *c.* of the Lord draweth nigh   *Jas 5:8*
To whom *c.* as unto a living stone   *1Pe 2:4*
power and *c.* of our Lord Jesus   *2Pe 1:16*
Where is the promise of his *c.*   *2Pe 3:4*
unto the *c.* of the day of God   *2Pe 3:12*
be ashamed before him at his *c.*   *1Jo 2:28*
beast *c.* up out of the earth   *Re 13:11*
new Jerusalem, *c.* down from God   *Re 21:2*

COMINGS

and the *c.* in thereof and all   *Eze 43:11*

COMMAND

will *c.* his child, and household   *Ge 18:19*
C. me when I shall intreat (S)   *Ex 8:9*
sacrifice as God shall *c.* us   *Ex 8:27*
if thou do this thing, and God *c.* thee   *Ex 18:23*
I will hear what the Lord will *c.*   *Nu 9:8*
this is the thing which the Lord doth *c.*   *Nu 36:6*
Lord shall *c.* the blessing on thee   *De 28:8*
c. your children to observe to do   *De 32:46*
did Moses *c.* Joshua, and so he did   *Jos 11:15*
obeyed my *c.* (R)   *J'g 2:4*
under their *c.* (S)   *1Ch 12:32*
Lord will *c.* his lovingkindness   *Ps 42:8*
O God, *c.* deliverance for Jacob   *Ps 44:4*
will I *c.* (S)   *Isa 10:6; 1Ti 5:7; 6:13*
concerning work of my hands, *c.* me   *Isa 45:11*
c. them to say to their masters   *Jer 27:4*
c. not carried out (A)   *Jer 35:14*
didst *c.* they should not enter   *La 1:10*
c. stones be made bread   *M't 4:3; Lu 4:3*
why did Moses *c.* to give writing of   *M't 19:7*
I *c.* you by (P)   *M't 26:63*
c. that sepulchre be made sure   *M't 27:64*
what did Moses *c.* you   *M'k 10:3*
would not *c.* them to go into deep   *Lu 8:31*
wilt thou we *c.* fire to come down from heaven   *Lu 9:54*
saying, Did not we straitly *c.* you   *Ac 5:28*
to *c.* them to keep law of Moses   *Ac 15:5*
any conceivable *c.* (P)   *Eph 1:21*
do and will do things we *c.* you   *2Th 3:4*
we *c.* you in name of our Lord Jesus   *2Th 3:6*
we *c.* and exhort by our Lord Jesus   *2Th 3:12*
these things *c.* and teach   *1Ti 4:11*

I COMMAND

speak all that *I c.*   *Ex 7:2; Jer 1:7, 17*

observe what *I c.*   *Ex 34:11; De 12:28*
then *I* will *c.* blessing upon you   *Le 25:21*
shall not add to word *I c.* you   *De 4:2*
keep commandments *I c.* this day, to do them   *De 7:11; 8:11; 10:13; 11:8, 27; 13:18; 30:8*
I c. thee to do this thing   *De 24:18; 24:22*
I c. this day to love Lord God   *De 30:16*
I will *c.* clouds that they rain not   *Isa 5:6*
obey my voice, and do all which *I c.* you   *Jer 11:4*
I will *c.* saith the Lord, and thence will *I c.* serpent to bite them   *Jer 34:22; Am 9:3*
thence *I c.* the sword to slay them   *Am 9:4*
I will *c.* and sift house of Israel   *Am 9:9*
my friends, if ye do what *I c.* you   *Joh 15:14*
things *I c.* you, love one another   *Joh 15:17*
I c. thee in name of Jesus Christ   *Ac 16:18*
to married *I c.* yet not I, but Lord   *1Co 7:10*
I c. you to do (R)   *Ph'm 8*

COMMANDANT

the *c.* of the fortress (B)   *Ne 7:2*
the *c.* (A)(B)   *Ac 21:31; 21:32; 23:17; 24:7*

COMMANDANTS

the military *c.* (A)   *Ac 25:23*

COMMANDED

now thou art *c.,* take waggons   *Ge 45:19*
Joseph's sons did to him as he *c.* them   *Ge 50:12*
midwives did not as king of Egypt *c.*   *Ex 1:17*
eat in holy place, for so I am *c.*   *Le 10:13*
I c. you all things   *De 1:18; 3:18, 21*
children of Israel did as Joshua *c.*   *Jos 4:8*
set city on fire, see I have *c.* you   *Jos 8:8*
have obeyed my voice in all I *c.* you   *Jos 22:2*
all that I *c.* her, let her observe   *J'g 13:14*
my brother *c.* me to be there   *1Sa 20:29*
David said, The king *c.* me a business   *1Sa 21:2*
kill Amnon, have not I *c.* you   *2Sa 13:28*
they performed all that the king *c.*   *2Sa 21:14*
according to all that Jehoiada *c.*   *2Ki 11:9*
thus did according to all that king Ahaz *c.*   *2Ki 16:16*
I c. people to be numbered   *1Ch 21:17*
so had David the man of God *c.*   *2Ch 8:14*
c. Judah to seek Lord God   *2Ch 14:4; 32:12; 33:16*
I *c.* that the gates should be shut   *Ne 13:19*
I *c.* Levites to cleanse themselves   *Ne 13:22*
the king had *c.* concerning Haman   *Es 3:2*
written according to all Haman *c.*   *Es 3:12*
Mordecai did according as Esther *c.*   *Es 4:17*
written according to all Mordecai *c.*   *Es 8:9*
c. the morning since thy days   *Job 38:12*
my molten image hath *c.* them   *Isa 48:5*
Jonadab our father *c.* us   *Jer 35:6; 35:10, 14, 16, 18*
I did so as I was *c.*   *Eze 12:7; 37:7*
cried, To you it is *c.* O people   *Da 3:4*
he *c.* they should heat the furnace   *Da 3:19*
the king *c.* and they brought Daniel   *Da 6:16*
the king *c.* and they brought those men   *Da 6:24*

c. prophets, saying, Prophesy not   *Am 2:12*
c. it to be given her   *M't 14:9; M'k 6:27*
c. multitude sit down   *M't 14:19; 15:35; M'k 6:39*
his lord *c.* him to be sold   *M't 18:25*
disciples went and did as Jesus *c.*   *M't 21:6*
teaching to observe all things *I c.* you   *M't 28:20*
he *c.* to tell no man that thing   *Lu 9:21*
c. them to be baptized in the name   *Ac 10:48*
next day Festus *c.* Paul to be brought   *Ac 25:6*
the Lord has *c.* that (R)   *1Co 9:14*
but are *c.* to be under obedience   *1Co 14:34*
work with hands as we *c.*   *1Th 4:11*
c. that if any would not work   *2Th 3:10*
God *c.* you (A)(E)(R)   *Heb 9:20*
could not endure that which was *c.*   *Heb 12:20*
it was *c.* them not to hurt the grass   *Re 9:4*

GOD COMMANDED

God *c.* man to eat freely of every tree   *Ge 2:16*
according to all that God *c.* him   *Ge 6:22*
there went into the ark as God *c.*   *Ge 7:9*
had *c.* Noah   *7:16; 21:4; De 20:17; Jos 10:40*
God *c.* to keep the sabbath day   *De 5:15*
observe to do as Lord God *c.* you   *De 5:32*
walk in all ways God *c.* you   *De 5:33*
God *c.* to teach you   *De 6:1; 6:20; 13:5*
this day God *c.* thee to keep   *De 26:16*
hath not God *c.* to go to Tabor   *J'g 4:6*
David did as God *c.* him   *1Ch 14:16*
God *c.* me, make haste, forbear   *2Ch 35:21*
whatsoever is *c.* by God of heaven   *Ezr 7:23*
thy God hath *c.* thy strength   *Ps 68:28*
God *c.* saying, honour thy father   *M't 15:4*
hear all things *c.* thee of God   *Ac 10:33*
God *c.* light to shine out of darkness   *2Co 4:6*

LORD COMMANDED

Noah did according to all Lord *c.*   *Ge 7:5*
Moses and Aaron did as Lord *c.*   *Ex 7:6; 7:10, 20; 12:28, 50; Nu 17:11*
this is thing Lord *c.*   *Ex 16:16; 16:32; 35:4; Nu 30:1*
as Lord *c.* Moses   *Ex 16:34; 34:4; 39:1, 5, 7; 40:19; Le 8:9; 9:10*
Moses did as Lord *c.*   *Le 8:4; Nu 20:27; 27:11*
Lord *c.* to give land to Israel   *Nu 36:2*
Lord *c.* us to do all these statutes   *De 6:24*
turned aside out of way Lord *c.*   *De 9:16*
tables, there they be as Lord *c.*   *De 10:5*
Lord *c.* him be captain over people   *1Sa 13:14*
David went up, as the Lord *c.*   *2Sa 24:19*
Lord *c.* angel, he put up sword   *1Ch 21:27*
orderings as Lord God *c.* him   *1Ch 24:19*
concerning whom Lord *c.*   *Ps 106:34*
there Lord *c.* blessing, even life   *Ps 133:3*
I hid it by Euphrates, as Lord *c.*   *Jer 13:5*
Lord hath *c.* concerning Jacob   *La 1:17*
we turn to Gentiles, so Lord *c.*   *Ac 13:46; 13:47*

I, HE COMMANDED

eaten of tree *I c.* not to eat   *Ge 3:11; 3:17*
as *I c.* thee in time appointed   *Ex 23:15*
in day *he c.* children of Israel   *Le 7:38*

offered strange fire he *c.*   *Le 10:1*
them not
hath served other gods *I* have   *De 17:3;*
not *c.*   *18:20; Jer 19:5; 23:32; 29:23*
have not *I c.* thee? be strong   *Jos 1:9*
transgressed covenant *I c.*   *Jos 7:11;*
     J'g 2:20
divide it by lot, as *I c.* thee   *Jos 13:6*
I c. to feed my people   *2Sa 7:7;*
     1Ch 17:6
since time *I c.* judges   *2Sa 7:11;*
     1Ch 17:10
had *c.* him concerning this   *1Ki 11:10*
thing
I have *c.* ravens to feed thee   *1Ki 17:4*
I have *c.* widow woman to   *1Ki 17:9*
sustain thee
word he *c.* to thousand   *1Ch 16:15;*
generations   *Ps 105:8*
that is written in law he *c.*   *1Ch 16:40*
Israel
he *c.* and it stood fast   *Ps 33:9*
c. his covenant for ever   *Ps 111:9*
c. us to keep thy precepts   *Ps 119:4*
diligently
I have *c.* my sanctified ones   *Isa 13:3*
heavens and all their host   *Isa 45:12*
have *I c.*
this thing *c. I* them, obey my   *Jer 7:23*
voice
which *I c.* them not   *Jer 7:31;*
     19:5; 32:35
words of covenant which *I c.*   *Jer 11:8*
them
but hallow the sabbath, as *I*   *Jer 17:22*
c.
do according to all *I* have *c.*   *Jer 50:21*
his word he *c.* in days of old   *La 2:17*
I have done as thou hast *c.*   *Eze 9:11*
me
I did in morning as *c.*   *Eze 24:18;*
     37:10
my words *I c.* did they not   *Zec 1:6*
take
remember law which *I c.* in   *Mal 4:4*
Horeb
he *c.* us to preach to the   *Ac 10:42*
people

MOSES COMMANDED

Aaron took as *Moses* had *c.*   *Nu 16:47*
Moses c. us a law, even   *Nu 33:4*
inheritance
observe to do all *Moses c.*   *Jos 1:7*
ye have kept all that *Moses*   *Jos 22:2*
c. you
Moses c. according to word   *1Ch 15:15*
of Lord
offer gift *Moses c.* for   *M't 8:4*
testimony
offer things *Moses c.* for a   *M'k 1:44;*
testimony   *Lu 5:14*
Moses in law *c.* such be   *Joh 8:5*
stoned

COMMANDEDST

thou *c.* thy servant Moses   *Ne 1:7*
thou *c.* them precepts,   *Ne 9:14*
statutes, laws
have done nothing that thou   *Jer 32:23*
c.

COMMANDER

c. of all officers (B)   *1Ch 27:3*
the Persian *c.* (A)   *Ezr 4:8*
Rehum the *c.* (R)   *Ezr 4:8; 4:17*
given him for leader and *c.*   *Isa 55:4*

COMMANDER'S

the *c.* portion (B)(R)   *De 33:21*

COMMANDEST

all that thou *c.* us we will do   *Jos 1:16*
whoso will not hearken in all   *Jos 1:18*
thou *c.*
c. me be smitten contrary to   *Ac 23:3*
law

COMMANDETH

thy servants will do as my   *Nu 32:25*
lord *c.*
God, who *c.* sun, it riseth not   *Job 9:7*
he *c.* that they return from   *Job 36:10*
iniquity

---

he covereth the light, and *c.*   *Job 36:32*
it not to shine
that they may do whatever   *Job 37:12*
he *c.* them
he *c.* and raiseth the stormy   *Ps 107:25*
wind
who saith, it cometh, when   *La 3:37*
Lord *c.* it not
Lord *c.* and he will smite   *Am 6:11*
great horse
he *c.* the unclean spirits   *M'k 1:27;*
     Lu 4:36
he *c.* the winds, and they   *Lu 8:25*
obey him
now *c.* all men every where   *Ac 17:30*
to repent

COMMANDING

Jacob made an end of *c.* his   *Ge 49:33*
sons
Jesus made an end of *c.* his   *M't 11:1*
disciples
c. his accusers to come to   *Ac 24:8*
thee
c. to abstain from meats God   *1Ti 4:3*
created

COMMANDMENT

gave in *c.* all Lord had   *Ex 34:32*
spoken
broken his *c.* that soul be   *Nu 15:31*
cut off
broken his *c.* that soul be   *Nu 15:31*
bless
ye rebelled against my *c.* in   *Nu 27:14*
desert
this *c.* I command thee this   *De 30:11*
day
why hast thou not kept the   *1Ki 2:43*
c.
king's *c.* was, answered not   *2Ki 18:36;*
     Isa 36:21
their brethren were at their   *1Ch 12:32*
c.
people will be wholly at thy   *1Ch 28:21*
c.
offering according to *c.* of   *2Ch 8:13*
Moses
what cause come between   *2Ch 19:10*
law and *c.*
one heart to do *c.* of king   *2Ch 30:12*
as soon as *c.* came abroad,   *2Ch 31:5*
Israel
I sent them with *c.* to Iddo   *Ezr 8:17*
the chief
of those that tremble at the   *Ezr 10:3*
c. of God
it was king's *c.* concerning   *Ne 11:23*
them
Vashti refused to come at   *Es 1:12*
king's *c.*
Esther did the *c.* of   *Es 2:20*
Mordecai, like
why transgressest thou the   *Es 3:3*
king's *c.*
king's *c.* drew nigh to be in   *Es 9:1*
execution
nor gone back from the *c.*   *Job 23:12*
of his lips
but thy *c.* is exceeding   *Ps 119:96*
broad
he sendeth forth his *c.* upon   *Ps 147:15*
earth
c. is a lamp, and law is light   *Pr 6:23*
that the waters should not   *Pr 8:29*
pass his *c.*
he that feareth the *c.* shall   *Pr 13:13*
be rewarded
he that keepeth the *c.*   *Pr 19:16*
keepeth his soul
whoso keepeth *c.* shall feel no   *Ec 8:5*
evil
they obey their father   *Jer 35:14*
Jonadab's *c.*
because the king's *c.* was   *Da 3:22*
urgent
the *c.* came forth, and I am   *Da 9:23*
come
he willingly walked after *c.*   *Ho 5:11*
O ye priests, this *c.* is for   *Mal 2:1*
you
know that I sent this *c.* to   *Mal 2:4*
you
why do ye transgress *c.* of   *M't 15:3*
God

---

ye made *c.* of God of no   *M't 15:6*
effect
Master, which is great *c.* in   *M't 22:36*
law
this is first and great *c.*   *M't 22:38;*
     M'k 12:30
laying aside *c.* of God, ye   *M'k 7:8*
hold
full well ye reject the *c.* of   *M'k 7:9*
God
no other *c.* greater than these   *M'k 12:31*
nor transgressed I thy *c.*   *Lu 15:29*
rested sabbath day according   *Lu 23:56*
to *c.*
this *c.* I received of my   *Joh 10:18*
Father
he gave me a *c.* what I   *Joh 12:49*
should say
I know that his *c.* is life   *Joh 12:50*
everlasting
as Father gave me *c.* even   *Joh 14:31*
so I do
my *c.* love one another   *Joh 15:12;*
     1Jo 3:23
to whom we gave no such *c.*   *Ac 15:24*
receiving *c.* to Silas to come   *Ac 17:15*
to him
gave *c.* to accusers to say   *Ac 23:30*
at Festus' *c.* Paul was   *Ac 25:23*
brought forth
sin taking occasion by *c.*   *Ro 7:8; 7:11*
when *c.* came, sin revived, I   *Ro 7:9*
died
c. ordained to life, I found to   *Ro 7:10*
death
the *c.* is holy, and just, and   *Ro 7:12*
good
sin by *c.* become exceeding   *Ro 7:13*
sinful
if any other *c.* it is briefly in   *Ro 13:9*
this
according to the *c.* of the   *Ro 16:26*
everlasting God
I speak by permission, not of   *1Co 7:6*
c.
I speak not by *c.* but by   *2Co 8:8*
occasion of
which is the first *c.* with   *Eph 6:2*
promise
c. of God our Saviour   *1Ti 1:1; Tit 1:3*
end of *c.* is charity, out of   *1Ti 1:5*
pure heart
made not after law of a   *Heb 7:16*
carnal *c.*
a disannulling of *c.* going   *Heb 7:18*
before
Joseph gave *c.* concerning   *Heb 11:22*
his bones
they were not afraid of the   *Heb 11:23*
king's *c.*
turn from holy *c.* delivered   *2Pe 2:21*
to them
mindful of *c.* of apostles of   *2Pe 3:2*
Lord
but an old *c.* which ye have   *1Jo 2:7*
heard
this is his *c.* that we should   *1Jo 3:23*
believe on
this *c.* from him, he who   *1Jo 4:21*
loveth God
as we have received a *c.* from   *2Jo 4*
Father
this *c.* ye have heard from   *2Jo 6*
beginning

COMMANDMENT *OF LORD*

c. of Lord   *Ex 17:1; Nu 9:18, 20; 10:13*
Moses numbered at *c.* of   *Nu 3:39*
Lord
cannot go beyond *c.* of Lord   *Nu 24:13*
to do good
Aaron went to Hor at *c.* of   *Nu 33:38*
Lord and died
kept charge of *c.* of Lord   *Jos 22:3*
your God
not rebel against the *c.* of   *1Sa 12:14*
Lord
will not obey, but rebel   *1Sa 12:15*
against *c.* of Lord
thou hast not kept *c.* of   *1Sa 13:13*
Lord
Saul said, I have performed   *1Sa 15:13*
c. of Lord
I have transgressed *c,* of   *1Sa 15:24*
Lord
wherefore hast thou despised   *2Sa 12:9*
c. of Lord
at *c. of* Lord, came this on   *2Ki 24:3*
Judah

for so was *c. of Lord* by   2Ch 29:25
prophets
c. of Lord is pure, enlightening   Ps 19:8
concerning virgins I have no   1Co 7:25
c. of Lord

GIVE, GIVEN
COMMANDMENT

things which I will *give* thee   Ex 25:22
in *c.*
Lord had *given* in *c.* unto   De 1:3
them
give c. to cease till another   Ezr 4:21
commandment be given
given c. to save me, thou my   Ps 71:3
rock
Lord hath *given c.* against   Isa 23:11
the city
Lord hath *given c.* concerning Na 1:14
thee
given c. if any knew where   Joh 11:57
he were

NEW COMMANDMENT

new c. I give you, that ye   Joh 13:34
love
I write no *new c.* unto you   1Joh 2:7
a *new c.* I write unto you,   1Joh 2:8
which is true
not as though I wrote *new c.*   2Jo 5
to thee

REBELLED AGAINST
COMMANDMENT

rebelled against my *c.* in   Nu 27:14
desert of Zin
rebelled against c. of Lord   De 1:26;
                             1:43; 9:23
I have *rebelled against* his *c.*   La 1:18

COMMANDMENTS

because that Abraham kept   Ge 26:5
my *c.*
if thou wilt give ear to his   Ex 15:26
c.
wrote on tables ten *c.*   Ex 34:28;
                       De 4:13; 10:4
done somewhat against any of Le 4:13
the *c.*
commit sin forbidden by *c.*   Le 5:17
of Lord
these are *c.* the Lord   Le 27:34
commanded
remember all the *c.* of the Nu 15:39
Lord
not keeping *c.* I command   De 8:11
thee
if you shall hearken to *c.*   De 11:13;
                   28:13; J'g 3:4
if ye will obey *c.* of Lord   De 11:27
if ye will not obey *c.* of   De 11:28
Lord
Saul hath not performed   1Sa 15:11
my *c.*
because he hath kept my *c.* 1Ki 11:34
and statutes
David who kept my *c.* and   1Ki 14:8
followed me
ye have forsaken *c.* of Lord 1Ki 18:18
they left all *c.* of the Lord 2Ki 17:16
Judah kept not *c.* of Lord   2Ki 17:19
their God
kept his *c.* he commanded   2Ki 18:6
Moses
if ye forsake my *c.* I set   2Ch 7:19
before
why transgress *c.* of the   2Ch 24:20
Lord
for we have forsaken thy *c.*   Ezr 9:10
should we again break thy *c.* Ezr 9:14
and join
if keep not my *c.* then will I Ps 89:31
visit
works are verity, all his *c.*   Ps 111:7
are sure
blessed is he that delighteth   Ps 112:1
in his *c.*
let me not wander from thy Ps 119:10
c.
I am a stranger, hide not *c.* Ps 119:19
from me

make me to go in the path Ps 119:35
of thy *c.*
I will delight in thy *c.* I   Ps 119:47
have loved
teach me, for I have   Ps 119:66
believed thy *c.*
give understanding, that I Ps 119:73
may learn *c.*
all thy *c.* are faith   Ps 119:86
through *c.* hast made me   Ps 119:98
wiser than
I love thy *c.*   Ps 119:127
I longed for thy *c.*   Ps 119:131
thy *c.* are my delights   Ps 119:143
all thy *c.* are truth   Ps 119:151
I have done thy *c.*   Ps 119:166
all thy *c.* are righteousness Ps 119:172
I do not forget thy *c.*   Ps 119:176
if thou wilt hide my *c.* with   Pr 2:1
thee
keep my words and lay up my Pr 7:1
c.
the wise in heart will receive Pr 10:8
c.
that thou hadst hearkened Isa 48:18
to my *c.*
shall break one of these least M't 5:19
c.
teach for doctrines *c.* of   M't 15:9;
men   M'k 7:7
on two *c.* hang all law and M't 22:40
prophets
thou knowest the *c.*   M'k 10:19;
                           Lu 18:20
first of all *c.* is, hear O   M'k 12:29
Is. the Lord
walking in all *c.* of Lord   Lu 1:6
blameless
blamelessly in all *c.*   Lu 1:6
(A)(B)(P)
he that hath my *c.* and   Joh 14:21
keepeth them
if keep my *c.* as I kept   Joh 15:10
Father's *c.*
is nothing, but keeping *c.* of 1Co 7:19
God
things I write are *c.* of   1Co 14:37
Lord
after the *c.* and doctrines of Col 2:22
men
ye know what *c.* we gave you 1Th 4:2
by Lord
he that keepeth not his *c.* is 1Jo 2:4
a liar
he that keepeth his *c.*   1Jo 3:24
dwelleth in him
this is love, that we walk after 2Jo 6
His *c.*

DO COMMANDMENTS

do all *c.* and be holy to   Nu 15:40
God
to *do* all *c.*   De 6:25;
                  15:5; 28:1, 15; 30:8
if he be constant to *do* my *c.* 1Ch 28:7
that remember his *c.* to *do* Ps 103:18
them
understanding have they   Ps 111:10
that *do* his *c.*
blessed are they that *do* his *c.* Re 22:14

NOT DO COMMANDMENTS

but if ye will *not do* all   Le 26:14
these *c.*
so that ye will *not do* all my Le 26:15
c. but

COMMANDS

these are the *c.*   Nu 36:13
(A)(B)(E)(R)

COMMEND

into thy hands I *c.* my spirit Lu 23:46
now, brethren, I *c.* you to   Ac 20:32
God
if unrighteousness *c.*   Ro 3:5
righteousness
c. unto you Phebe our sister Ro 16:1
do we begin again to *c.*   2Co 3:1
ourselves
for we *c.* not ourselves again 2Co 5:12
to you
compare ourselves with   2Co 10:12
some that *c.*

COMMENDATION

need we, as some others,   2Co 3:1
epistles of *c.*

COMMENDED

the princes *c.* Sarai before Ge 12:15
Pharaoh
man shall be *c.* accord, to   Pr 12:8
wisdom
then I *c.* mirth, because a   Ec 8:15
man hath
Lord *c.* the unjust steward   Lu 16:8
c. them to Lord on whom   Ac 14:23
they believed
they were *c.* to the grace   Ac 14:26;
(S)   15:40
I ought to have been *c.* of   2Co 12:11
you

COMMENDETH

but God *c.* his love towards us Ro 5:8
but meat *c.* us not to God   1Co 8:8
not he that *c.* is approved, 2Co 10:18
but

COMMENDING

c. ourselves to every man's 2Co 4:2
conscience
c. ourselves as ministers (S) 2Co 6:4

COMMISSION

I went with *c.* from chief   Ac 26:12
priest
privileges of a *c.* (N)(P)   Ro 1:5
entrusted with a *c.* (R)   1Co 9:17
minister by a divine *c.* (P)   Col 1:25

COMMISSIONED

Lord *c.* ten others (B)(R)   Lu 10:1

COMMISSIONS

they delivered the kings *c.*   Ezr 8:36

COMMIT

thou shalt not *c.* adultery   Ex 20:14;
   De 5:18; M't 5:27; 19:18; Ro 13:9
if *c.* any of these things   Le 5:17
forbidden
not *c.* any of these   Le 18:26;
abominations   18:30
who shall *c.* any of these   Le 18:29
abominations
if *c.* any sin that men *c.*   Nu 5:6
c. no more any such evil   De 19:20
caused Jerusalem to *c.*   2Ch 21:11
fornication
unto God would I *c.* my cause Job 5:8
into thine hand I *c.* my spirit Ps 31:5
c. thy way to Lord, trust also Ps 37:5
in him
c. thy works unto the Lord   Pr 16:3
an abomination to kings to *c.* Pr 16:2
wickedness
will *c.* government into his Isa 22:21
hand
c. Jeremiah to the court of Jer 37:21
prison
why *c.* evil against your souls Jer 44:7
c. abominations which they Eze 8:17
c. here
thou shalt not *c.* this   Eze 16:43
lewdness
in the midst of thee they *c.* Eze 22:9
lewdness
shall *c.* against thee (S)   Eze 23:24
priests murder, they *c.*   Ho 6:9
lewdness
they *c.* falsehood, the thief Ho 7:1
cometh
did *c.* things worthy of   Lu 12:48
stripes
who will *c.* to your trust   Lu 16:11
true riches
Jesus did not *c.* himself to Joh 2:24
them
c. such things are worthy of Ro 1:32
death
is against them which *c.* such Ro 2:2
things
that abhorrest idols, dost   Ro 2:22
thou *c.* sacrilege

neither let us c. fornication	1Co 10:8
this charge I c. to thee, son Timothy	1Ti 1:18
the same c. thou to faithful men	2Ti 2:2
if ye respect persons ye c. sin	Jas 2:9
c. keeping of their souls to him	1Pe 4:19
whoso is born of God doth not c. sin	1Jo 3:9
who taught Israel to c. fornication	Re 2:14
seduce my servants to c. fornication	Re 2:20

COMMIT INIQUITY

if he c. iniquity I will chasten him	2Sa 7:14
Almighty, that he should c. iniquity	Job 34:10
they weary themselves to c. iniquity	Jer 9:5
turn from righteousness c. iniquity	Eze 3:20; 33:13

COMMIT TRESPASS

if soul c. trespass through ignorance	Le 5:15
if a man's wife c. trespass	Nu 5:12
caused Israel c. trespass against Lord	Nu 31:16
c. trespass in accursed thing	Jos 22:20

COMMIT WHOREDOM

cut off that c. whoredom with Molech	Le 20:5
c. whoredom with daughters of Moab	Nu 25:1
thou didst c. whoredom with images	Eze 16:17
none followeth thee to c. whoredoms	Eze 16:34
c. ye whoredom after their abominations	Eze 20:30
they c. whoredom with her, she with them	Eze 23:43
they shall c. whoredom and not increase	Ho 4:10
your daughters shall c. whoredom	Ho 4:13; 4:14

COMMITS

c. himself to you (A)	Isa 26:3

COMMITTED

hath c. all he hath to my hand	Ge 39:8
keeper c. to Joseph all the prisoners	Ge 39:22
priest make atonement for sin c.	Le 4:35
abominable customs which were c.	Le 18:30
c. these things, I abhorred them	Le 20:23
if aught be c. by ignorance	Nu 15:24
bring forth man or woman that c.	De 17:5
if man have c. sin worthy of death	De 21:22
c. a flagrant crime (B)	De 22:21
c. folly and lewdness in Israel	J'g 20:6
have sinned, have c. wickedness	1Ki 8:47
they provoked him with sins, they c.	1Ki 14:22
brasen shields c. to guard	1Ki 14:27; 2Ch 12:10
Saul died for transgression he c.	1Ch 10:13
for my people have c. two evils	Jer 2:13
wonderful and horrible thing is c.	Jer 5:30
she c. wicked acts (B)	Jer 11:15
what is our sin we c. against Lord	Jer 16:10
and have c. adultery with their	Jer 29:23
have c. to provoke to anger	Jer 44:3; 44:9
hast c. fornication with Egypt	Eze 16:26
nor hath Samaria c. half of thy sins	Eze 16:51

turn from his sins he c.	Eze 18:21; 18:22, 28
shall loathe yourselves for evils c.	Eze 20:43
c. whoredoms in Egypt in youth	Eze 23:3
thus she c. whoredoms with them	Eze 23:7
none of sins c. shall be mentioned	Eze 33:16
the land hath c. great whoredom	Ho 1:2
they have c. whoredom continually	Ho 4:18
who had c. murder in insurrection	M'k 15:7
to whom men c. much, of him	Lu 12:48
Father hath c. all judgment to Son	Joh 5:22
haling men and women, c. to prison	Ac 8:3
c. nothing worthy of (B)(N)(P)	Ac 25:8
if I c. any thing worthy of death	Ac 25:11
found he c. nothing worthy of death	Ac 25:25
c. themselves to the sea and loosed	Ac 27:40
though I have c. nothing against people	Ac 28:17
to them were c. oracles of God	Ro 3:2
dispensation of gospel c. to me	1Co 9:17; Tit 1:3
nor let us c. fornication as some c.	1Co 10:8
c. to us word of reconciliation	2Co 5:19
lasciviousness which they have c.	2Co 12:21
gospel of uncircumcision c. to me as	Ga 2:7; 1Ti 1:11
Timothy, keep what is c. to thee	1Ti 6:20
he is able to keep that which I c.	2Ti 1:12
if he c. sins, they shall be forgiven	Jas 5:15
c. himself to him that judgeth	1Pe 2:23
of all ungodly deeds they have c.	Jude 15
with whom kings c. fornication	Re 17:2; 18:3, 9

COMMITTED INIQUITY

c. iniquity we have done wickedly	Ps 106:6
for iniquity he c. shall die	Eze 33:13; 33:18
have c. iniquity and done foolishly	Da 9:5

COMMITTED TRESPASS

bring for trespass c. two turtle doves	Le 5:7
Israel c. trespass in accursed thing	Jos 7:1
what trespass is this ye have c. against God	Jos 22:16
ye have not c. trespass against Lord	Jos 22:31
because they c. trespass, I will	Eze 15:8
in that they c. a trespass against me	Eze 20:27

COMMITTEST

O Ephraim, thou c. whoredom	Ho 5:3

COMMITTETH

man that c. adultery with another	Le 20:10
c. adultery with his neighbour's	Le 20:10
the poor c. himself unto thee	Ps 10:14
whoso c. adultery with a woman	Pr 6:32
that the house of Israel c. here	Eze 8:6
But as a wife that c. adultery	Eze 16:32
c. iniquity, and doeth according	Eze 18:24

and c. iniquity, and dieth in them	Eze 18:26
and c. iniquity, he shall even die	Eze 33:18
her that is divorced c. adultery	M't 5:32
marry another, c. adultery	M't 19:9
another, c. adultery against her	M'k 10:11
married to another, she c. adultery	M'k 10:12
married another c. adultery	Lu 16:18
away from her husband c. adultery	Lu 16:18
c. sin is the servant of sin	Joh 8:34
but he that c. fornication sinneth	1Co 6:18
Whosoever c. sin transgresseth	1Jo 3:4
He that c. sin is of the devil	1Jo 3:8

COMMITTING

without c. iniquity; he shall	Eze 33:15
stealing, and c. adultery, they	Ho 4:2

COMMODIOUS

the haven was not c. to winter in	Ac 27:12

COMMON

c. people sin through ignorance	Le 4:27
If these men die the c. death of	Nu 16:29
is no c. bread under mine hand	1Sa 21:4
and the bread is in a manner c.	1Sa 21:5
gold as c. as stones (A)(B)(R)	2Ch 1:15
and it is c. among men	Ec 6:1
into the graves of the c. people	Jer 26:23
and shall eat them as c. things	Jer 31:5
men of the c. sort were brought	Eze 23:42
the c. place (S)	Eze 42:20; 44:23; 48:15
took Jesus into the c. hall	M't 27:27
the c. people heard him gladly	M'k 12:37
and had all things c.	Ac 2:44
c. men (R)	Ac 4:13
but they had all things c.	Ac 4:32
put them in the c. prison	Ac 5:18
any thing that is c. or unclean	Ac 10:14
cleansed, that call not thou c.	Ac 10:15
not call any man c. or unclean	Ac 10:28
for nothing c. or unclean hath at	Ac 11:8
cleansed, that call not thou c.	Ac 11:9
you but such as is c. to man	1Co 10:13
mine own son after the c. faith	Tit 1:4
c. and unhallowed (A)	Heb 10:29
write unto you of the c. salvation	Jude 3

COMMONLY

is c. reported among the Jews	M't 28:15
It is reported c. that there is	1Co 5:1

COMMONWEALTH

being aliens from the c. of Israel	Eph 2:12
rights of Israel as a nation (A)	Eph 2:12
Israel's citizenship (B)	Eph 2:12
the community of Israel (N)	Eph 2:12
God's chosen community, Israel (P)	Eph 2:12
our c. is in heaven (B)(R)	Ph'p 3:20

COMMOTION

great c. out of the north country	Jer 10:22
a great c. (B)	Jer 10:23
caused great c. (N)	Ac 17:8
this c. (P)(R)	Ac 19:40

COMMOTIONS

ye shall hear of wars and c.   Lu 21:9
insurrections, do not be   Lu 21:9
alarmed (A)(N)
disturbances, be not alarmed   Lu 21:9
(B)(P)
tumults, be not terrified   Lu 21:9
(E)(R)

COMMUNE

out unto Jacob to c. with   Ge 34:6
him
and I will c. with thee from   Ex 25:22
above
convey to you above (B)   Ex 25:22
C. with David secretly, and   1Sa 18:22
say
speak to David privately   1Sa 18:22
(A)
have a private chat with   1Sa 18:22
David (B)
speak to David in private   1Sa 18:22
(R)
I will c. with my father of   1Sa 19:3
thee
converse with my father   1Sa 19:3
about you (A)
talk about you (B)   1Sa 19:3
speak to my father about   1Sa 19:3
you (R)
we assay to c. with thee   Job 4:2
converse with you (A)   Job 4:2
venture a word with you   Job 4:2
(B)(R)
c. with your own heart upon   Ps 4:4
your bed
they c. of laying snares privily   Ps 64:5
they talk of laying snares   Ps 64:5
(A)(B)(R)
I c. with my own heart: and   Ps 77:6
with my heart I meditate   Ps 77:6
(A)(B)(R)

COMMUNED

he c. with them, saying, If it   Ge 23:8
told, conversed with,   Ge 23:8;
talked (B)   34:8, 20; 1Sa 9:25
And Hamor c. with them,   Ge 34:8
saying
and c. with the men of their   Ge 34:20
city
and c. with them, and   Ge 42:24
took from
and they c. with him at the   Ge 43:19
door
and c. with them, and with all   J'g 9:1
Samuel c. with Saul upon   1Sa 9:25
the top
David sent and c. with   1Sa 25:39
Abigail
she was come to Solomon,   1Ki 10:2
she c.
and they c. with her   2Ki 22:14
conferred with her (B)   2Ki 22:14
talked with her (R)   2Ki 22:14
she was come to Solomon,   2Ch 9:1
she c.
I c. with mine own heart,   Ec 1:16
saying
I entered into counsel with   Ec 1:16
(A)
I said to myself (B)(R)   Ec 1:16
the king c. with them; and   Da 1:19
none
king conversed with them   Da 1:19
(A)
king interviewed them (B)   Da 1:19
king spoke with them (R)   Da 1:19
that c. with me said unto me   Zec 1:14
angel who talked with me   Zec 1:14
(A)(E)(R)
angel who was speaking with   Zec 1:14
me (B)
c. one with another what they   Lu 6:11
discussed with   Lu 6:11
(A)(B)(N)(P)(R)
c. with the chief priests and   Lu 22:4
discussed with (A)(N)(P)   Lu 22:4
to confer with the chief   Lu 22:4
(B)(R)
they c. together, and   Lu 24:15
reasoned
conversing and discussing   Lu 24:15
(A)
conversation and   Lu 24:15
discussion (B)

discussed with one another   Lu 24:15
(N)
serious talk and discussion   Lu 24:15
(P)
talking and discussing   Lu 24:15
together (R)
him the oftener, and c. with   Ac 24:26
him
conversed with him often   Ac 24:26
(A)(R)
talked things over with him   Ac 24:26
(B)(N)
frequently summoned to talk   Ac 24:26
(P)

COMMUNICATE

did not c. (B)   Ga 1:16
c. unto him that teacheth in   Ga 6:6
all good
share in all good things   Ga 6:6
(A)(B)(N)(R)
contribute toward the livelihood   Ga 6:6
of (P)
ye did c. with my affliction   Ph'p 4:14
contribute for my needs   Ph'p 4:14
(A)
sharing as companions with   Ph'p 4:14
me (B)
fellowship with my affliction   Ph'p 4:14
(E)
share burden of my troubles   Ph'p 4:14
(N)
willing to share my troubles   Ph'p 4:14
(P)(R)
ready to distribute, willing to   1Ti 6:18
c.
ready to share with others   1Ti 6:18
(A)
to practice sharing (B)   1Ti 6:18
ready to distribute (E)   1Ti 6:18
be ready to give (N)(P)   1Ti 6:18
liberal and generous (R)   1Ti 6:18
to do good and c. forget   Heb 13:16
not
be generous, distribute, and   Heb 13:16
contribute to needy (A)
benevolences and   Heb 13:16
contributions (B)
show kindness and share   Heb 13:16
with (N)
do good and share what   Heb 13:16
you have (P)(R)

COMMUNICATED

c. unto them the gospel which   Ga 2:2
I put before them the gospel   Ga 2:2
(A)
laid before them gospel   Ga 2:2
(B)(E)(N)(R)
I gave full exposition of   Ga 2:2
gospel (P)
church c. with me as   Ph'p 4:15
concerning
partnership with me   Ph'p 4:15
(A)(B)
had fellowship with me (E)   Ph'p 4:15
partners in payments and   Ph'p 4:15
receipts (N)
fellowship of giving and   Ph'p 4:15
receiving (P)(R)
sent and c. it (A)   Re 1:1

COMMUNICATING

c. to necessities (E)   Ro 12:14

COMMUNICATION

And Abner had c. with the   2Sa 3:17
elders
Abner had consulted with   2Sa 3:17
(B)
Abner conferred with the   2Sa 3:17
elders (R)
Ye know the man, and his c.   2Ki 9:11
know the man and his talk   2Ki 9:11
(B)(E)(R)
your c. be, Yea, yea; Nay,   M't 5:37
nay
let your Yes be simply yes   M't 5:37
(A)(B)(P)(R)
let your speech be, Yea, yea;   M't 5:37
Nay, nay (E)
Plain Yes or No is all you   M't 5:37
need to say (N)
Let no corrupt c. proceed   Eph 4:29
out of mouth

no foul language   Eph 4:29;
(A)(B)(P)   Col 3:3
no corrupt speech proceed   Eph 4:29
(E)
no bad language pass your   Eph 4:29
lips (N)
no evil talk come out of   Eph 4:29
(R)
filthy c. out of your mouth   Col 3:8
The c. of thy faith may   Ph'm 6
become
participation in and sharing   Ph'm 6
faith (A)
sharing of faith (B)(P)(R)   Ph'm 6
fellowship of thy faith   Ph'm 6
(E)(N)
sent the c. (B)   Re 1:1

COMMUNICATIONS

What manner of c. are these   Lu 24:17
What is this   Lu 24:17
discussion (A)(P)
things you consider together   Lu 24:17
(B)
you are debating as you   Lu 24:17
walk (N)
what is this conversation   Lu 24:17
(R)
evil c. corrupt good   1Co 15:33
manners
evil companionships corrupt   1Co 15:33
(A)(E)
Bad associations corrupt   1Co 15:33
good morals (B)
Bad company is ruin of   1Co 15:33
good character (N)
Bad company ruins good   1Co 15:33
morals (R)

COMMUNION

not the c. of the blood of   1Co 10:16
Christ
is it not the c. of the body   1Co 10:16
of Christ
fellowship in the blood of   1Co 10:16
(A)(B)
sharing in blood of Christ   1Co 10:16
(N)(P)
participation in blood of   1Co 10:16
(R)
what c. hath light with   2Co 6:14
darkness
how can light fellowship   2Co 6:14
darkness (A)(B)
association between light   2Co 6:14
and darkness (B)
Can light consort with   2Co 6:14
darkness (N)
how can light and darkness   2Co 6:14
share together (P)
the c. of the Holy Ghost be   2Co 13:14
with you
fellowship of Holy Ghost   2Co 13:14
(A)(B)(N)(P)(R)

COMMUNING

as he had left off c. with   Ge 18:33
Abraham
he had made an end of c.   Ex 31:18
with him

COMMUNITIES

many Samaritan c. (B)   Ac 8:25

COMMUNITY

vanish from the c. (B)   Nu 16:33
the c. (B)   Nu 19:20; Jos 9:27
the building of the c. (N)   1Co 10:23
the c. of Israel (N)(P)   Eph 2:12

COMPACT

made a c. with (B)   2Sa 5:3
as a city that is c. together   Ps 122:3
a city bound together   Ps 122:3
(B)(R)

COMPACTED

and c. by that which every   Eph 4:16
joint
joined and firmly knit   Eph 4:16
together (A)(R)
harmoniously fitted together   Eph 4:16
and closely united (B)

fitly framed and knit together (E) — Eph 4:16

bonded and knit together (N) — Eph 4:16

harmonious structure knit together (P) — Eph 4:16

COMPANIED

these men which have c. with us — Ac 1:21

COMPANIES

three hundred men into three c. — J'g 7:16

the three c. blew the trumpets — J'g 7:20

wait against Shechem in four c. — J'g 9:34

divided them into three c. — J'g 9:43

other c. ran upon all the people — J'g 9:44

Saul put the people in three c. — 1Sa 11:11

camp of the Philistines in three c. — 1Sa 13:17

the Syrians had gone out by c. — 2Ki 5:2

they were porters in the c. of the — 1Ch 9:18

c. that ministered to the king by — 1Ch 28:1

two great c. of them that gave thanks — Ne 12:31

So stood the two c. of them that gave — Ne 12:40

the c. of Sheba waited for them — Job 6:19

O ye travelling c. of Dedanim — Isa 21:13

criest, let thy c. deliver thee — Isa 57:13

with horsemen, and c. and much — Eze 26:7

sat down by c. upon the green — M'k 6:39

COMPANION

will be a c. to me (A) — Ge 29:34

brother, and every man his c. — Ex 32:27

his brother (A)(B)(R) — Ex 32:27

Samson's wife was given to his c. — J'g 14:20

given to his c. (A)(B)(E)(R) — J'g 14:20

I gave her to thy c.: is not her — J'g 15:2

his wife, and given her to his c. — J'g 15:6

the Archite was the king's c. — 1Ch 27:33

Hushai was the king's confidant (B) — 1Ch 27:33

Hushai was the king's friend (E)(R) — 1Ch 27:33

brother to dragons, and a c. to owls — Job 30:29

am a c. of all them that fear thee — Ps 119:63

but a c. of fools shall be destroyed — Pr 13:20

but he that is a c. of riotous men — Pr 28:7

the same is the c. of a destroyer — Pr 28:24

in same class as a destroyer (A) — Pr 28:24

one lift up his c. (B) — Ec 4:10

yet is she thy c. and the wife of — Mal 2:14

my brother, and c. in labour — Ph'p 2:25

and c. in tribulation, and in — Re 1:9

COMPANIONS

I and my c. (A)(B)(E)(R)(S) — J'g 11:37

she went with her c. and bewailed — J'g 11:38

they brought thirty c. to be with — J'g 14:11

Tabeel, and the rest of their c. — Ezr 4:7

the rest of their c.; the Dinaites — Ezr 4:9

the rest of their c. that dwell in — Ezr 4:17

Shimshai the scribe, and their c. — Ezr 4:23

Shethar-boznai, and their c. — Ezr 5:3; 6:13

Shethar-boznai, and his c. the — Ezr 5:6

Shethar-boznai, and your c. — Ezr 6:6

will answer thee, and thy c. — Job 35:4

Shall the c. make a banquet of — Job 41:6

Will traders bargain over him (A)(B)(R) — Job 41:6

bands make traffic of him (E) — Job 41:6

the virgins her c. that follow her — Ps 45:14

aside by the flocks of thy c. — Ca 1:7

the c. hearken to thy voice — Ca 8:13

are rebellious, and c. of thieves — Isa 1:23

and for the children of Israel, his c. — Eze 37:16

for all the house of Israel his c. — Eze 37:16

tribes of Israel his c. (E) — Eze 37:19

Daniel and his c. — Da 2:13; 2:18

Mishael, and Azariah, his c. — Da 2:17

their own c. (B) — Ac 4:23

of Macedonia Paul's c. in travel — Ac 19:29

fellow travelers with Paul (A)(B) — Ac 19:29

be not their c. (B) — Eph 5:7

ye became c. of them that were so — Heb 10:33

making common cause with others (A)(B) — Heb 10:33

becoming partakers with them (E) — Heb 10:33

stood loyally by (N) — Heb 10:33

threw in your lot with those (P) — Heb 10:33

partners with those so treated (R) — Heb 10:33

COMPANIONS'

For my brethren and c. sakes — Ps 122:8

COMPANIONSHIP

into c. with (A)(B) — 1Co 1:9

COMPANY

If Esau come to the one c. — Ge 32:8

come upon one group (A) — Ge 32:8

come upon one camp (B) — Ge 32:8; 32:21

then the other c. which is left — Ge 32:8

himself lodged that night in the c. — Ge 32:21

a c. of nations shall be of thee — Ge 35:11

group of nations (B) — Ge 35:11

a c. of Ishmeelites came from — Ge 37:25

and it was a very great c. — Ge 50:9

making a formidable army (B) — Ge 50:9

they spake unto all the c. of — Nu 14:7

unto all his c. saying, Even — Nu 16:5

you censers, Korah, and all his c. — Nu 16:6

thou and all thy c. are gathered — Nu 16:11

and all thy c. before the Lord — Nu 16:16

he be not a Korah, and as his c. — Nu 16:40

Now shall this c. lick up all that — Nu 22:4

this multitude will now (A)(B)(E) — Nu 22:4

this horde will now lick (R) — Nu 22:4

in the c. of Korah, when they — Nu 26:9

when that c. died, what time the — Nu 26:10

in the c. of them that gathered — Nu 27:3

against the Lord in the c. of Korah — Nu 27:3

and another c. come along by the — J'g 9:37

Abimelech, and the c. that was — J'g 9:44

that thou comest with such a c. — J'g 18:23

such a large crowd (B) — J'g 18:23

thou shalt meet a c. of prophets — 1Sa 10:5

meet a group of prophets (B) — 1Sa 10:5; 19:20

meet a band of prophets (E)(R) — 1Sa 10:5

behold, a c. of prophets met him — 1Sa 10:10

one c. turned unto the way — 1Sa 13:17

And another c. turned the way to — 1Sa 13:18

Beth-horon: and another c. turned — 1Sa 13:18

they saw the c. of the prophets — 1Sa 19:20

thou bring me down to this c. — 1Sa 30:15

I will bring thee down to this c. — 1Sa 30:15

lead you to this band (A)(B)(R) — 1Sa 30:15

down to this troop (E) — 1Sa 30:15

he and all his c. and came — 2Ki 5:15

he spied the c. of Jehu as he came — 2Ki 9:17

and said, I see a c. And Joram — 2Ki 9:17

with a very great c. and camels — 2Ch 9:1

many attendants and camels (A) — 2Ch 9:1

had a large retinue (B)(R) — 2Ch 9:1

with a very great train (E) — 2Ch 9:1

have no might against this great c. — 2Ch 20:12

this huge array (B) — 2Ch 20:12

this great multitude (R) — 2Ch 20:12

And the other c. of them that — Ne 12:38

thou hast made desolate all my c. — Job 16:7

desolate all my family, associates (A) — Job 16:7

disbanded my whole family (B) — Job 16:7

Which goeth in c. with the — Job 34:8

unto the house of God in c. — Ps 55:14

great was the c. of those — Ps 68:11

are a great host (A)(B)(E)(R) — Ps 68:11

Rebuke the c. of spearmen — Ps 68:30

rebuke the wild beasts (A)(B)(E)(R) — Ps 68:30

and covered the c. of Abiram — Ps 106:17

And a fire was kindled in their c. — Ps 106:18

c. not with him (E) — Pr 20:19; 24:21

he that keepeth c. with — Pr 29:3

harlots associates with harlots (A)(B) — Pr 29:3

c. of horses in Pharaoh's chariots — Ca 1:9

to a mare in Pharaoh's chariots (A)(B)(R) — Ca 1:9

to a steed in Pharaoh's chariots (A) — Ca 1:9

As it were the c. of two armies — Ca 6:13

a dance before two armies (A)(R) — Ca 6:13

she dances the Mahanaim dance (B)(E) — Ca 6:13

a great c. shall return thither — Jer 31:8

They shall also bring up a c. — Eze 16:40

with his mighty army and great c. — Eze 17:17

I will bring up a c. upon them — Eze 23:46

bring up a host (A)(R) — Eze 23:46

bring up an assembly (B) — Eze 23:46

And the c. shall stone them — Eze 23:47

the c. of the Ashurites have made — Eze 27:6

in all thy c. which is in the midst — Eze 27:27

all thy c. in the midst of thee shall — Eze 27:34

my net over thee with a c. of many — Eze 32:3

Asshur is there and all her c. — Eze 32:22

and her c. is round about her — Eze 32:23

great c. with bucklers and shields — Eze 38:4

all thy c. that are assembled unto — Eze 38:7

hast thou gathered thy *c.* to *Eze 38:13*
take a
horses, a great *c.* and a *Eze 38:15*
mighty
c. of priests murder in the *Ho 6:9*
way
him to have been in the *c.* *Lu 2:44*
to be in the caravan (A)(B) *Lu 2:44*
with the party (N) *Lu 2:44*
c. of publicans and of others *Lu 5:29*
and the *c.* of his disciples *Lu 6:17*
great crowd of his disciples *Lu 6:17*
(A)(R)
large throng of disciples (B) *Lu 6:17*
great multitude of his *Lu 6:17*
disciples (E)
shall separate you from their *Lu 6:22*
c.
excommunicate you (A) *Lu 6:22*
exclude you (B)(R) *Lu 6:22*
outlaw you (N) *Lu 6:22*
them sit down by fifties in a *Lu 9:14*
c.
reclining in table-groups (A) *Lu 9:14*
recline in rows of about fifty *Lu 9:14*
(B)
sit down in groups of fifty *Lu 9:14*
(N)(P)
a man of the *c.* cried out, *Lu 9:38*
saying
man from crowd shouted *Lu 9:38*
(A)(B)(N)(P)(R)
man from the multitude cried *Lu 9:38*
(E)
certain woman of the *c.* *Lu 11:27*
lifted up
And one of the *c.* said unto *Lu 12:13*
him
great *c.* of people, and of *Lu 23:27*
women
certain women also of our *c.* *Lu 24:22*
mad
saw a great *c.* come unto him *Joh 6:5*
seeing a vast multitude *Joh 6:5*
(A)(E)(R)
a vast host (B) *Joh 6:5*
seeing a large crowd (N)(P) *Joh 6:5*
go, they went to their own *c.* *Ac 4:23*
resorted to their own *Ac 4:23*
companions (B)
went back to their friends *Ac 4:23*
(N)(P)(R)
and a great *c.* of the priests *Ac 6:7*
were
a large number of priests (A) *Ac 6:7*
a large group of priests (B) *Ac 6:7*
very many of the priests *Ac 6:7*
(N)(R)
considerable portion of *Ac 6:7*
priesthood (P)
is a Jew to keep *c.* or come *Ac 10:28*
unto
when Paul and his *c.* loosed *Ac 13:13*
chosen men of their own *c.* *Ac 15:22*
from among their number *Ac 15:22*
(A)
select some of their own *Ac 15:22*
men (B)
to choose representatives *Ac 15:22*
(N)(P)
choose men from among *Ac 15:22*
them (R)
gathered a *c.* and set all the *Ac 17:5*
city
gathered together a mob *Ac 17:5*
(A)(B)
gathering a crowd *Ac 17:5*
(E)(P)(R)
roused the rabble (N) *Ac 17:5*
day we that were of Paul's *c.* *Ac 21:8*
somewhat filled with your *c.* *Ro 15:24*
epistle not to *c.* with *1Co 5:9*
fornicators
written unto you not to keep *1Co 5:11*
c.
not to associate with *1Co 5:11;*
(A)(R) *5:9*
must not get intimate with *1Co 5:11*
(B)
have nothing to do with *1Co 5:11*
(N)
Don't mix with the immoral *1Co 5:11*
(P)
bad *c.* is the ruin of *1Co 15:33*
(N)(R)(S)
that man, and have no *c.* *2Th 3:14*
with him
do not associate with him *2Th 3:14*
A)(P)

do not get mixed up with *2Th 3:14*
him (B)
have no dealings with him *2Th 3:14*
(N)
have nothing to do with him *2Th 3:14*
(R)
to an innumerable *c.* of *Heb 12:22*
angels
countless multitudes of *Heb 12:22*
angels (A)
ten thousands of angels *Heb 12:22*
(B)
innumerable hosts of angels *Heb 12:22*
(E)
myriads of angels (N) *Heb 12:22*
the countless angelic army *Heb 12:22*
(P)
innumerable angels in *Heb 12:22*
festal (R)
ugly blot on your *c.* (N) *2Pe 2:13*
all the *c.* in ships, and *Re 18:17*
sailors

COMPARABLE

The precious sons of Zion, *c.* *La 4:2*
to

COMPARE

what likeness will ye *c.* unto *Isa 40:18*
him
and *c.* me, that we may be *Isa 46:5*
like
what comparison shall we *c.* *M'k 4:30*
shall I *c.* it (S) *Lu 13:18*
or *c.* ourselves with some *2Co 10:12*
that

COMPARED

c. with the loss (R) *Es 7:4*
Who in the heaven can be *c.* *Ps 89:6*
unto
thou canst desire are not to *Pr 3:15*
be *c.*
may be desired are not to be *Pr 8:11*
c. to
I have *c.* thee, O my love, to a *Ca 1:9*
not worthy to be *c.* with the *Ro 8:18*
glory

COMPARING

c. spiritual things with *1Co 2:13*
spiritual
c. themselves among *2Co 10:12*
themselves

COMPARISON

have I done now in *c.* of you *J'g 8:2*
what was I able to do in *c.* of *J'g 8:3*
you
is it not in your eyes in *c.* of *Hag 2:3*
or with what *c.* shall we *M'k 4:30*
compare

COMPASS

put it under the *c.* of the altar *Ex 27:5*
under the *c.* thereof beneath *Ex 38:4*
way of the Red sea, to *c.* the *Nu 21:4*
land
And the border shall fetch a *Nu 34:5*
c.
And ye shall *c.* the city, all ye *Jos 6:3*
men
ye shall *c.* the city seven times *Jos 6:4*
Pass on, and *c.* the city, and *Jos 6:7*
let him
and fetched a *c.* to Karkaa *Jos 15:3*
fetch a *c.* behind them, and *2Sa 5:23*
come
go around behind them (A) *2Sa 5:23*
circle them to the rear (B) *2Sa 5:23*
make a circuit behind them *2Sa 5:23*
(E)
line of twelve cubits did *c.* *1Ki 7:15*
either
of thirty cubits did *c.* it *1Ki 7:23*
round
was there a round *c.* of half *1Ki 7:35*
a cubit
they fetched a *c.* of seven *2Ki 3:9*
days'
made a circuit seven days *2Ki 3:9*
(A)(E)(R)
roundabout march of seven *2Ki 3:9*
days (B)

And ye shall *c.* the king *2Ki 11:8*
round
from brim to brim, round in *2Ch 4:2*
c.
a line of thirty cubits did *c.* *2Ch 4:2*
it
oven, which did *c.* it round *2Ch 4:3*
about
And the Levites shall *c.* the *2Ch 23:7*
king
His archers *c.* me round *Job 16:13*
about
willows of the brook *c.* him *Job 40:22*
about
with favour wilt thou *c.* him *Ps 5:12*
surround him with good will *Ps 5:12*
(A)(B)
congregation of the people *c.* *Ps 7:7*
thee
from my deadly enemies, who *c.* *Ps 17:9*
surround (A)(B)(R) *Ps 17:9;*
                  32:7; 49:5; 142:7
so will I *c.* thine altar, O *Ps 26:6*
Lord
thou shalt *c.* me about with *Ps 32:7*
songs
Lord, mercy shall *c.* him *Ps 32:10*
about
the iniquity of my heels shall *Ps 49:5*
c. me
for the head of those that *c.* *Ps 140:9*
me
the righteous shall *c.* me *Ps 142:7*
about
he set a *c.* upon the face of *Pr 8:27*
drew a circle upon the face *Pr 8:27*
(A)(B)(E)(R)
and he marketh it out with *Isa 44:13*
the *c.*
c. yourselves about with *Isa 50:11*
sparks
surround and gird yourselves *Isa 50:11*
(A)
earth, A woman shall *c.* a *Jer 31:22*
man
hill Gareb, and shall *c.* *Jer 31:39*
about to
a fillet of twelve cubits did *Jer 52:21*
c. it
for the wicked doth *c.* about *Hab 1:4*
the
wicked surrounds the *Hab 1:4*
righteous (A)(R)
wicked encircle the righteous *Hab 1:4*
(B)
for ye *c.* sea and land to *M't 23:15*
make one
travel over sea and land *M't 23:15*
(A)(N)
traverse sea and land *M't 23:15*
(B)(R)
scour sea and land (P) *M't 23:15*
a trench about thee, and *c.* *Lu 19:43*
thee
surround you (A)(R) *Lu 19:43*
encircle you (B)(N) *Lu 19:43*
surrounding, hemming you *Lu 19:43*
in (P)
thence we fetched a *c.* and *Ac 28:13*
came
made a circuit (A)(E)(R) *Ac 28:13*

COMPASSED

c. the house round, both old *Ge 19:4*
surrounded the house *Ge 19:4*
(A)(B)(R)
we *c.* mount Seir many days *De 2:1*
Journeyed around mount Seir *De 2:1*
(A)
circled round the hill country *De 2:1*
(B)
Ye have *c.* this mountain long *De 2:3*
enough
So the ark of the Lord *c.* *Jos 6:11*
the city
go round the city (A) *Jos 6:11*
moved around, encircling *Jos 6:11*
it (B)
the second day they *c.* the *Jos 6:14*
city once
c. the city after the same *Jos 6:15*
manner
And the border *c.* from *Jos 15:10*
Baalah
and *c.* the corner of the *Jos 18:14*
sea
and *c.* the land of Edom, *J'g 11:18*
and the

went around land of Edom *J'g 11:18* (A)
going round land of Edom *J'g 11:18* (B)(E)(R)
they *c.* him in, and laid wait *J'g 16:2*
they surrounded him *J'g 16:2* (A)(B)(R)
Saul and his men *c.* David *1Sa 23:26*
his men were surrounding *1Sa 23:26* him (A)
encircling and capturing *1Sa 23:26* David (B)
closing in upon David (R) *1Sa 23:26*
c. about and smote *2Sa 18:15* Absalom
surrounded and struck *2Sa 18:15* Absalom (A)
gathered around and struck *2Sa 18:15* (B)
surrounded Absalom (R) *2Sa 18:15*
waves of death *c.* me, the *2Sa 22:5* floods
sorrows of hell *c.* me about *2Sa 22:6;*
Ps 18:5
cords of Sheol entangling me *2Sa 22:6* (A)
cords of grave closed me in *2Sa 22:6* (B)
cords of Sheol closed me in *2Sa 22:6* (E)(R)
they came by night and *c.* *2Ki 6:14* the city
surrounded the city (A)(B)(R) *2Ki 6:14*
host *c.* the city both with *2Ki 6:15* horses
all around the city (A)(B) *2Ki 6:15*
was round about the city *2Ki 6:15* (E)(R)
smote Edomites which *c.* *2Ki 8:21;* him *2Ch 31:9*
Edomites around him *2Ki 8:21* together (B)
who had surrounded him *2Ki 8:21* (R)
Therefore they *c.* about *2Ch 18:31* him to
they turned about to fight *2Ch 18:31* (A)(E)(R)
encircled him to fight (B) *2Ch 18:31*
and *c.* about Ophel, and *2Ch 33:14* raised it
hath *c.* me with his net *Job 19:6*
closed his net about me *Job 19:6* (A)(R)
encircled me with his net *Job 19:6* (B)
hath *c.* the waters with *Job 26:10* bounds
placed an enclosing limit *Job 26:10* (A)
draws a circle over the deep *Job 26:10* (B)
described a boundary (E) *Job 26:10*
described a circle upon (R) *Job 26:10*
They have now *c.* us in our *Ps 17:11* steps
they surrounded us *Ps 17:11* (A)(B)(R)
sorrows of death *c.* me *Ps 18:4; 116:3*
Many bulls have *c.* me: *Ps 22:12* strong
bulls have surrounded me *Ps 22:12* (A)(B)
For dogs have *c.* me: the *Ps 22:16* assembly
innumerable evils have *c.* me *Ps 40:12*
evils have surrounded me *Ps 40:12* (B)
water; they *c.* me about *Ps 88:17* together
they surround me *Ps 88:17* (A)(B)(R)
came round about me (E) *Ps 88:17*
They *c.* me about also with *Ps 109:3* words
nations *c.* me about: but in *Ps 118:10;*
118:11-12
All nations encircled me *Ps 118:10* (B)
All nations surrounded me *Ps 118:10* (R)
and *c.* me with gall and travail *La 3:5*
surrounded me with bitterness *La 3:5* (A)(B)
enveloped me with bitterness *La 3:5* (R)
the floods *c.* me about *Jon 2:3; 2:5*
floods surrounded me (A) *Jon 2:3*
the current was engulfing me *Jon 2:3* (B)

the flood was round about me *Jon 2:3* (E)(R)
shall see Jerusalem *c.* with *Lu 21:20* armies
surrounded by armies *Lu 21:20* (A)(B)(P)(R)
encircled by armies (N) *Lu 21:20*
himself also is *c.* with *Heb 5:2* infirmity
is liable to moral weakness *Heb 5:2* and physical infirmity (A)(B)
beset by weakness (N)(R) *Heb 5:2*
prone to human weakness *Heb 5:2* (P)
they were *c.* about seven *Heb 11:30* days
encompassed seven days *Heb 11:30* (A)
circuited for seven days *Heb 11:30* (B)
encircled for seven days *Heb 11:30* (N)(P)(R)
are *c.* about with so great a *Heb 12:1* cloud
surrounded by a great cloud *Heb 12:1* (A)(P)(R)
encircled as we are with *Heb 12:1* (B)
around us like a cloud (N) *Heb 12:1*
and *c.* the camp of the *Re 20:9* saints about
encircled the fortress (A) *Re 20:9*
surrounded the encampment *Re 20:9* (B)(R)
encircled the army of the *Re 20:9* saints (P)

COMPASSEST

Thou *c.* my path and my *Ps 139:3* lying
sift and search out my path *Ps 139:3* (A)
traced my walking and *Ps 139:3* resting (B)
searchest out my path (E)(R) *Ps 139:3*

COMPASSETH

c. the whole land of Havilah *Ge 2:11*
flowing around the whole *Ge 2:11* land (A)
flows round all the land *Ge 2:11;*
(B)(R) *2:13*
the border *c.* it on the north *Jos 19:14* side
pride *c.* them about as a *Ps 73:6* chain
pride is about their neck *Ps 73:6* (A)(E)
pride encircles their neck (B) *Ps 73:6*
pride is their necklace (R) *Ps 73:6*
Ephraim *c.* me about with *Ho 11:12* lies
surrounds me with lies *Ho 11:12* (A)(B)
encompassed me with lies *Ho 11:12* (R)

COMPASSING

were knops *c.* it, ten in a *1Ki 7:24* cubit
c. the sea round about. Two *2Ch 4:3* rows

COMPASSION

Lord moved with *c.* (B) *J'g 2:18*
Israelites had *c.* on (B) *J'g 21:6*
Israelites had *c.* on (A)(R) *J'g 21:15*
motherly *c.* went out (B) *1Ki 3:26*
give them *c.* before them *1Ki 8:50* who carry
Lord felt *c.* (B) *1Ch 21:15*
your children shall find *c.* *2Ch 30:9* before them
gain favor with their captors *2Ch 30:9* (B)
greatness of thy *c.* (B) *Ps 51:1*
have *c.* on servants (B)(R) *Ps 135:14*
with great *c.* gather (B)(R) *Isa 54:7*
yearning pity and *c.* *Isa 63:15* (A)(B)(E)(R)
kindness and *c.* (B) *Jer 16:5*
I will grant you *c.* (B) *Jer 42:12*
find favor and *c.* *Da 1:9* (A)(E)(R)(S)
thy great *c.* (B) *Da 9:18*

my *c.* grows warm and *Ho 11:8* tender (R)
Lord had *c.* (B) *Am 7:3; 7:6*
Jesus moved with *c.* *M't 9:36;*
14:14; M'k 6:34
moved with pity and *M't 9:36* sympathy (A)(N)(P)
filled with pity over them *M't 9:36* (B)
lord of that servant was *M't 18:27* moved with *c.*
in pity for that agent *M't 18:27* (B)(N)(P)(R)
Jesus moved with *c.* put *M'k 1:41* forth his hand
moved with pity and *M'k 1:41* sympathy (A)
Deeply sympathetic (B) *M'k 1:41*
'n warm indignation (N) *M'k 1:41*
filled with pity for him *M'k 1:41* (P)(R)
warmth of *c.* (N) *Ph'p 2:1*
heart of *c.* (E) *Col 3:12*
be of one mind, having *c.* one *1Pe 3:8*
sympathizing with one *1Pe 3:8* another (A)
sympathetic (B)(R) *1Pe 3:8*
kindly and humble minded *1Pe 3:8* (N)
true love and sympathy (P) *1Pe 3:8*
shutteth up his bowels of *c.* *1Jo 3:17* from him
deep sympathies (B) *1Jo 3:17*
shuts up his heart against *1Jo 3:17* him (N)
shuts his eyes and his heart *1Jo 3:17* (P)
closes his heart against him *1Jo 3:17* (R)
shutteth up his *c.* (E) *1Jo 3:17*

FULL OF COMPASSION

being *full of c.* forgave their *Ps 78:38* iniquity
the merciful One forgave *Ps 78:38* (B)
being merciful, forgave (E) *Ps 78:38*
a God *full of c.* *111:4; 112:4; 145:8*
merciful and gracious *Ps 86:15* (A)(E)(R)

HAVE, HAD COMPASSION

babe wept, and she *had c.* on *Ex 2:6* him
she took pity on him (A) *Ex 2:6*
she pitied him (B)(R) *Ex 2:6*
Lord may turn and *have c.* *De 13:17* on thee
Lord will *have c.* on thee *De 30:3*
for ye *have c.* on me *1Sa 23:21*
having sympathy with me *1Sa 23:21*
that they may *have c.* on *1Ki 8:50* them
Lord was gracious and *had* *2Ki 13:23* *c.* on them
had mercy on them (B) *2Ki 13:23*
because he *had c.* on his *2Ch 36:15* people
had no *c.* on young men *2Ch 36:17* and maidens
did not spare young men *2Ch 36:17* (B)
that she should not *have c.* *Isa 49:15* on son
I will return and *have c.* on *Jer 12:15* them
yet ye will *have c.* *La 3:32; Mic 7:19*
I *have c.* on multitude *M't 15:32;*
M'k 8:2
pity, sympathy, deeply moved *M't 15:32* (A)
I feel deeply moved (B) *M't 15:32*
I feel sorry for all these *M't 15:32* people (N)
My heart goes out to this *M't 15:32* crowd (P)
also have *had c.* on *M't 18:33* fellow-servant
have *had* pity and mercy *M't 18:33* (A)(B)
also should have mercy *M't 18:33* (E)(R)
show fellow-servant same *M't 18:33* pity (N)

taken pity on fellow-servant   *M't 18:33* (P)
Jesus *had* c. on them,   *M't 20:34* touched eyes
Jesus in pity (A)(B)(R)   *M't 20:34*
Jesus was deeply moved (N)   *M't 20:34*
Jesus was deeply moved with pity (P)   *M't 20:34*
how the Lord *had* c. touched eyes   *M'k 5:19*
sympathy for you and mercy on you (A)(P)   *M'k 5:19*
the mercy he showed you (B)(E)   *M'k 5:19*
in mercy has done for you (N)   *M'k 5:19*
how kind he has been to you (P)   *M'k 5:19*
if thou canst, *have* c., and help us   *M'k 9:22*
do have pity on us (A)(B)(N)(P)(R)   *M'k 9:22*
when Lord saw her, he *had* c.   *Lu 7:13*
he felt sympathy for her (B)   *Lu 7:13*
his heart went out to her (N)(P)   *Lu 7:13*
Samaritan saw him, he *had* c. on him   *Lu 10:33*
moved with pity, sympathy (A)(B)(N)(P)   *Lu 10:33*
father *had* c. and ran and fell on neck   *Lu 15:20*
moved with pity and tenderness (A)   *Lu 15:20*
felt deeply moved for him (B)   *Lu 15:20*
his heart went out to him (N)(P)   *Lu 15:20*
I will *have* c. on whom I will *have* c.   *Ro 9:15*
pity on whom I will have pity (B)(N)   *Ro 9:15*
who can *have* c. on the ignorant   *Heb 5:2*
exercise gentleness and forbearance (A)   *Heb 5:2*
bear gently with the ignorant (B)(E)(R)   *Heb 5:2*
bear patiently with ignorant and erring (N)   *Heb 5:2*
deal sympathetically with ignorant (P)   *Heb 5:2*
for ye *had* c. of me in my bonds   *Heb 10:34*
did sympathize and suffer long (A)(B)(P)   *Heb 10:34*
shared sufferings of prisoners (N)   *Heb 10:34*
of some *have* c. making a difference   *Jude 22*
have mercy who waver and doubt (A)   *Jude 22*
doubting souls who need your pity (N)   *Jude 22*
you can feel pity (P)   *Jude 22*

COMPASSIONS

not consumed, because his c. fail not   *La 3:22*
Lord's mercies (B)(R)   *La 3:22*
my c. are bridled (A)(B)(E)(S)   *Ho 11:8*
shew mercy and c. every man to   *Zec 7:9*
show kindness and mercy (R)   *Zec 7:9*
any bowels and c. (S)   *Ph'p 2:1*
shut up c. (S)   *1Jo 3:17*

COMPEL

thou shalt not c. him to serve as   *Le 25:39*
do not make him serve (B)(E)(R)   *Le 25:39*
none did c. for so the king had   *Es 1:8*
no one was compelled (A)(R)   *Es 1:8*
no compulsion (B)   *Es 1:8*
shall c. thee to go a mile, go with   *M't 5:41*
forces you to go one mile (A)(B)(P)(R)   *M't 5:41*
makes you go one mile (N)   *M't 5:41*
they c. one Simon a Cyrenian   *M'k 15:21*
they forced a passerby to carry (A)(B)   *M'k 15:21*
they pressed him into service (N)   *M'k 15:21*

c. them to come in, that my house   *Lu 14:23*
urge and constrain them (A)   *Lu 14:23*
force them to come in (B)   *Lu 14:23*
constrain them to come in (E)   *Lu 14:23*
make them come in (N)(P)   *Lu 14:23*
try to c. you (A)   *Ga 6:12*

COMPELLED

together with the woman, c him   *1Sa 28:23*
urged him, he heeded their words (A)   *1Sa 28:23*
kept urging him (B)(R)   *1Sa 28:23*
constrained him (E)   *1Sa 28:23*
fornication, and c. Judah thereto   *2Ch 21:11*
led Judah away (A)   *2Ch 21:11*
causing the inhabitants (B)   *2Ch 21:11*
made the inhabitants (E)   *2Ch 21:11*
led the inhabitants (R)   *2Ch 21:11*
no one c. (A)(R)   *Es 1:8*
him they c. to bear his cross   *M't 27:32*
they forced to carry (A)(B)   *M't 27:32*
pressed him into service (N)   *M't 27:32*
felt c. to discuss (P)   *Ac 17:17*
and c. them to blaspheme   *M't 26:11*
to make them blaspheme (A)(R)   *Ac 26:11*
forced them by torture to (B)   *M't 26:11*
strove to make them blaspheme (E)   *Ac 26:11*
by repeated punishment to make them renounce their faith (N)   *Ac 26:11*
force them to deny their Lord (P)   *Ac 26:11*
I was c. to appeal to Caesar (R)   *Ac 28:19*
a fool in glorying: ye have c. me   *2Co 12:11*
you forced me to it (A)(B)(P)(R)   *2Co 12:11*
you drove me to it (N)   *2Co 12:11*
a Greek, was c. to be circumcised   *Ga 2:3*
not at all obliged to be (B)   *Ga 2:3*

COMPELLEST

why c. thou the Gentiles to live   *Ga 2:14*
urge and practically force (A)   *Ga 2:14*
impose Judaizing on Gentiles (B)   *Ga 2:14*
insist that the Gentiles (N)   *Ga 2:14*
try to make Gentiles (P)   *Ga 2:14*

COMPENSATE

cannot c. (B)(E)(S)   *Es 7:4*

COMPENSATION

glorious c. of (A)   *Heb 10:35*

COMPETES

c. for masteries (B)(R)   *2Ti 2:5*

COMPLACENT

c. daughters (R)   *Isa 32:9; 32:11*
c. or unproductive (P)   *2Pe 2:18*

COMPLAIN

you c. against him (B)   *Ex 16:11*
come unto us to c., that we will say   *J'g 21:22*
c. in the bitterness of my soul   *Job 7:11*
the furrows likewise thereof c.   *Job 31:38*
cried out against me (A)(B)(E)(R)   *Job 31:38*
why will you c. (A)(B)(R)   *Jer 2:9*
when I c. and contend (A)(B)(E)   *Jer 12:1*
Wherefore doth a living man c.   *La 3:39*
why does he still c. (B)   *Ro 9:19*
nor discontentedly c. (A)   *1Co 10:10*

COMPLAINED

the people c. (B)   *Ex 15:24*
when the people c. it displeased   *Nu 11:1*
I c. and my spirit was overwhelmed   *Ps 77:3*
I am disquieted and groan (A)   *Ps 77:3*
I was moaning (B)(R)   *Ps 77:3*
they c. in their tents (B)   *Ps 106:25*
c. to the disciples (N)   *Lu 5:30*
the Pharisees c. (N)   *Lu 15:2*
all who looked c. (B)   *Lu 19:7*
the Greeks c. (P)   *Ac 6:1*

COMPLAINERS

are murmurers, c., walking after   *Jude 16*

COMPLAINING

that there be no c. in our streets   *Ps 144:14*
no outcry in our streets (A)(E)   *Ps 144:14*
cry of distress in our streets (B)(R)   *Ps 144:14*
Who is c. (A)(E)(R)   *Pr 23:29*
his disciples c. (A)   *Joh 6:61*
without c. (A)   *Ph'p 2:14*

COMPLAINS

c. to God against Israel (B)(N)(R)   *Ro 11:2*

COMPLAINT

abundance of my c. and grief have   *1Sa 1:16*
provocation (A)   *1Sa 1:16*
my couch shall ease my c.   *Job 7:13*
I will forget my c., I will leave off   *Job 9:27*
I will leave my c. upon myself   *Job 10:1*
is my c. to man? And if it were so   *Job 21:4*
to-day is my c. bitter: my stroke is   *Job 23:2*
I mourn in my c. and make a   *Ps 55:2*
poureth out his c. before the Lord   *Ps 102 title*
I poured out my c. before him   *Ps 142:2*
against you a c. (B)   *Am 5:1*
c. made by (A)(B)   *Ac 6:1*
without c. and wrangling (N)   *Ph'p 2:14*
a cause of c. (N)   *Col 3:13*

COMPLAINTS

hearing your c. (B)   *Ex 16:8*
relieve myself of c. (B)   *Nu 17:5; 17:10*
who has c. (B)   *Pr 23:29*
and grievous c. against Paul   *Ac 25:7*
bringing many grave accusations (A)(N)   *Ac 25:7*
presented many charges (B)(R)   *Ac 25:7*
bringing many grievous charges (E)   *Ac 25:7*
bringing many serious accusations (P)   *Ac 25:7*

COMPLETE

seven sabbaths shall be c.   *Le 23:15*
put out in c. darkness (A)   *Pr 20:20*
if thou wilt be c. (B)   *M't 19:21*
third day c. my work (B)   *Lu 13:32*
when the c. comes (P)   *1Co 13:10*
c. our dedication (B)   *2Co 7:1*
c. gracious arrangement (B)   *2Co 8:6*
c. with the flesh (B)   *Ga 3:3*
c. being of God (N)   *Col 1:19*
present every man c. (B)   *Col 1:28*
full c. expression of (P)   *Col 2:9*
are c. in him, which is the head   *Col 2:10*
perfect and c. in all the will of God   *Col 4:12*
c. whatever is imperfect (P)   *1Th 3:10*
may be c. (A)(E)(R)   *2Ti 3:17*
will make you c. (A)   *1Pe 5:10*

COMPLETED

he has *c.* reconciling holy place (S)	Le 16:20
c. the tithing of tithes (S)	De 26:12
house of the Lord *c.* (A)(E)(R)	2Ch 8:16
Lord has *c.* his work (A)	Isa 10:12
c. the requirement of the Law (P)	Lu 2:39
c. my mission (A)(P)(R)	Ro 15:28
when the time was *c.* (B)(N)	Ga 4:4
his faith was *c.* (A)(R)	Jas 2:22
not found work *c.* (N)(P)	Re 3:2

COMPLETELY

c. closed the wombs (S)	Ge 20:18
passed *c.* over Jordan (S)	Jos 3:17; 4:1, 11
mercy *c.* gone for ever (S)	Ps 77:8
shall be *c.* confounded (S)	Jer 50:12
made it *c.* bare (S)	Joe 1:7
arm *c.* dried up (S)	Zec 11:17
were *c.* healed (B)(N)	M't 14:36
consecrating to him *c.* (P)	2Co 7:1

COMPLETENESS

all around *c.* (B)	2Co 13:9
c. of him who fills universe (B)(P)	Eph 1:23

COMPLETION

love is brought to *c.* (A)(B)	1Jo 4:17

COMPLEX

c. wisdom of God's plan (P)	Eph 3:10

COMPLEXITY

unfathomable *c.* of (P)	Ro 11:33

COMPLIMENTS

lose the *c.* (B)	Pr 23:8

COMPOSED

be on guard and *c.* (B)	1Th 5:6
be perfectly *c.* (B)	1Pe 1:13; 5:8

COMPOSITION

any other like it, after the *c.* of it	Ex 30:32
must not compound anything like it (B)	Ex 30:32
according to the *c.* thereof: it shall	Ex 30:37

COMPOSURE

c. may remedy serious mistakes (B)	Ec 10:4

COMPOUND

an ointment *c.* after the art of the	Ex 30:25
must not *c.* it (B)	Ex 30:32

COMPOUNDETH

Whosoever *c.* any like it, or	Ex 30:38

COMPREHEND

doeth he, which we cannot *c.*	Job 37:5
you *c.* the breadth (B)	Job 38:18
discern and *c.* words (A)	Pr 1:2
do not *c.* (A)	Isa 6:9
too deep to *c.* (A)(E)(R)	Isa 33:19
able to *c.* with all saints	Eph 3:18
apprehend and grasp with (A)(E)	Eph 3:18
understand fully with (B)	Eph 3:18
be strong to grasp (N)(P)	Eph 3:18

COMPREHENDED

and *c.* the dust of the earth	Isa 40:12
enclosed dust of earth in (A)(B)(R)	Isa 40:12
and the darkness *c.* it not	Joh 1:5
darkness never overpowered it (A)	Joh 1:5

darkness did not overtake it (B)	Joh 1:5
darkness never quenched it (N)	Joh 1:5
darkness has never put it out (P)	Joh 1:5
darkness has not overcome it (R)	Joh 1:5
it is briefly *c.* in this saying	Ro 13:9
summed up in a single command (A)(E)(P)	Ro 13:9
heads up in one word (B)	Ro 13:9
summed up in one rule (N)	Ro 13:9
summed up in one sentence (R)	Ro 13:9

COMPULSION

no *c.* (B)	Es 1:8

COMPUTE

priest *c.* the value (B)(R)	Le 27:18; 27:53

COMRADE

telling his *c.* (A)(B)(R)	J'g 7:13
every sword against his *c.* (A)	J'g 7:22

CONANIAH

C. also, and Shemaiah, and	2Ch 35:9

CONCEAL

slay our brother, and *c.* his blood	Ge 37:26
neither shalt thou *c.* him	De 13:8
c. me until (A)(B)(R)(S)	Job 14:13
is with the Almighty will I not *c.*	Job 27:11
I will not *c.* his parts, nor	Job 41:12
not keep silence concerning (A)(B)(E)(R)	Job 41:12
It is the glory of God to *c.* a thing	Pr 25:2
publish and *c.* not: say	Jer 50:2
c. greedy motives (P)	1Th 2:5

CONCEALED

not *c.* the words of the Holy One.	Job 6:10
I have not *c.* thy loving-kindness	Ps 40:10
not hid away in my heart (B)(E)(R)	Ps 40:10
better than love *c.* (B)	Pr 25:5
a *c.* tongue (B)	Pr 25:23
Jews *c.* true convictions (A)	Ga 2:13

CONCEALETH

is of a faithful spirit *c.* the matter	Pr 11:13
keeps the matter hidden (A)(B)(R)	Pr 11:13
A prudent man *c.* knowledge: but	Pr 12:23
reluctant to display his (A)	Pr 12:23

CONCEIT

and as an high wall in his own *c.*	Pr 18:11
lest he be wise in his own *c.*	Pr 26:5
thou a man wise in his own *c.*	Pr 26:12
The sluggard is wiser in his own *c.*	Pr 26:16
The rich man is wise in his own *c.*	Pr 28:11
knowledge breeds *c.* (N)	1Co 8:1
nothing prompted by *c.* (A)(R)	Ph'p 2:3
stupified with *c.* (A)(E)(R)	1Ti 6:4

CONCEITED

c. and arrogant (B)	Ps 101:5
c. men have hidden (R)	Ps 140:5
some are *c.* and arrogant (A)(P)	1Co 4:18
these *c.* persons (B)(P)	1Co 4:19
love is not *c.* or rude (N)	1Co 13:4
not *c.* and unmannerly (B)	1Co 13:5
being absurdly *c.* (P)	2Co 12:7
not be *c.* (N)(B)	Ga 5:26
he is *c.* (B)(P)	1Ti 6:4

CONCEITS

be wise in your own *c.*	Ro 11:25
Be not wise in your own *c.*	Ro 12:16
whisperings, *c.* (S)	2Co 12:20

CONCEIVABLE

any *c.* authority, power (P)	Eph 1:21

CONCEIVE

should *c.* when they came to drink	Ge 30:38
cattle did *c.* that Jacob laid	Ge 30:41
that they might *c.* among the rods	Ge 30:41
shall be free, and shall *c.* seed	Nu 5:28
but thou shalt *c.* and bear a son	J'g 13:3; 13:5, 7
They *c.* mischief, and bring forth	Job 15:35
c. words of deceit (R)	Ps 35:20
and in sin did my mother *c.* me	Ps 51:5
a virgin shall *c.* and bear a son	Isa 7:14
shall *c.* chaff, ye shall bring forth	Isa 33:11
c. mischief, and bring forth iniquity	Isa 59:4
c. and bear a son (B)	M't 1:23
thou shalt *c.* in thy womb	Lu 1:31
received strength to *c.* seed	Heb 11:11

CONCEIVED

and she *c.* and bare Cain, and	Ge 4:1
and she *s.* and bare Enoch	Ge 4:17
went in unto Hagar, and she *c.*	Ge 16:4
when she saw that she had *c.* her	Ge 16:4
when she saw that she had *c.*	Ge 16:5
Sarah *c.* and bare Abraham a son	Ge 21:2
and Rebekah his wife *c.*	Ge 25:21
And Leah *c.* and bare a son	Ge 29:32
she *c.* again, and bare a son	Ge 29:33; 29:34
And she *c.* again, and bare a son	Ge 29:35
Bilhah *c.* and bare Jacob a son.	Ge 30:5
And Bilhah Rachel's maid *c.* again	Ge 30:7
she *c.* and bare Jacob the fifth son	Ge 30:17
And Leah *c.* again, and bare	Ge 30:19
And she *c.* and bare a son	Ge 30:23
And the flocks *c.* before the rods	Ge 30:39
pass at the time that the cattle *c.*	Ge 31:10
And she *c.* and bare a son	Ge 38:3
and she *c.* again, and bare a son	Ge 38:4
And she yet again *c.* and bare	Ge 38:5
in unto her, and she *c.* by him	Ge 38:18
the woman *c.* and bare a son	Ex 2:2
If a woman have *c.* seed, and	Le 12:2
Have I *c.* all this people	Nu 11:12
after Hannah had *c.* that she bare	1Sa 1:20
that she *c.* and bare three sons	1Sa 2:21
And the woman *c.* and sent	2Sa 11:5
And the woman *c.* and bare a son	2Ki 4:17
she *c.* and bare a son, and he	1Ch 7:23
was said, There is a man child *c.*	Job 3:3
and hath *c.* mischief, and brought	Ps 7:14
devices they have *c.* (E)	Ps 10:2
they *c.* a mischievous plot (A)(E)	Pr 21:11
into the chamber of her that *c.* me	Ca 3:4
and she *c.* and bare a son	Isa 8:3
hath *c.* a purpose against you	Jer 49:30
which *c.* and bare him a son	Ho 1:3
she *c.* again, and bare a daughter	Ho 1:6

Lo-ruhamah, she c. and bare a   Ho 1:8
son
harlot: she that c. them hath   Ho 2:5
done
that which is c. in her is of   M't 1:20
his wife Elisabeth c. and hid   Lu 1:24
hath also c. a son in her old   Lu 1:36
age
before he was c. in the womb   Lu 2:21
why hast thou c. this thing in   Ac 5:4
when Rebecca also had c.   Ro 9:10
Then when lust hath c., it   Jas 1:15
bringeth

CONCEIVING

c. and uttering from the   Isa 59:13
heart

CONCENTRATE

c. on being devoted (P)   1Pe 3:15

CONCEPTION

multiply thy sorrow and thy   Ge 3:15
c.
multiply grief and suffering in Ge 3:16
pregnancy (A)
increase your pregnancy   Ge 3:16
troubles (B)
multiply pain and c. (E)   Ge 3:16
multiply pain in childbearing   Ge 3:16
(R)
the Lord gave her c. and she   Ru 4:13
bare
from the womb, and from   Ho 9:11
the c.
some people's c. of slowness   2Pe 3:9
(A)

CONCERN

things which c. the Lord   Ac 28:31
Jesus
same deep c. for you (P)   2Co 8:16
glory of the things which c.   2Co 11:30
mine

CONCERNETH

that which c. me: thy mercy   Ps 138:8
This burden c. the prince in   Eze 12:10

CONCERNING

commanded his men c. him   Ge 12:20
I have accepted thee c. this   Ge 19:21
thing
c. which I did swear Ex 6:8; Nu 14:30
priest make atonement c. sin   Le 4:26;
                                      5:6
found what was lost, lieth c. it Le 6:3
Lord hath spoken good c.   Nu 10:29
Israel
commanded him c. this   1Ki 11:10
thing
come to fight c. thee (S)   2Ki 19:9
Lord charged Moses with c.   1Ch 22:13
Israel
Iddo the seer c. Jeroboam   2Ch 9:29
(S)
I asked them c. Jews that   Ne 1:2
escaped
to proclaim c. thee (S)   Ne 6:7
repent thee c. thy servants   Ps 90:13;
                                     135:14
dost not inquire wisely c. this Ec 7:10
ask c. my sons, c. work of   Isa 45:11
hands
c. sons, c. daughters born in   Jer 16:3
this place, c. their mothers,
c. their fathers
c. pillars, c. sea, c. bases, c. Jer 27:19
vessels
shall be comforted c. evil,   Eze 14:22
c. all
thus saith Lord c. the   Eze 21:28
Ammonites
c. which I lifted up hand to   Eze 47:14
give
desire mercies of God c. this   Da 2:18
secret
purpose might not be   Da 6:17
changed c. Daniel
said he c. them (S)   M't 13:52
that I spake not to you c.   M't 16:11
bread
they that saw, told also c.   M'k 5:16
swine

he expounded things c.   Lu 24:27
himself
were perplexed c. (S)   Ac 5:24; 25:20
c. he raised him from dead   Ac 13:34
c. the resurrection (S)   Ac 24:21
c. all things I am accused   Ac 26:2
(S)
c. this sect, it is spoken   Ac 28:22
against
as c. flesh Christ came, who is Ro 9:5
God
c. the gospel, are enemies for   Ro 11:28
your sake
wise to what is good, and   Ro 16:19
simple c. evil
I speak as c. reproach, as   2Co 11:21
though
I speak c. Christ and the   Eph 5:32
church
c. giving and receiving, but   Ph'p 4:15
c. whom ye received (S)   Col 4:10
confidence in the Lord c. you   2Th 3:4
(S)
some professing have erred c.   1Ti 6:21
faith
who c. truth have erred   2Ti 2:18
minds, reprobates c. faith   2Ti 3:8
think it not strange c. fiery   1Pe 4:12
trial

CONCILIATE

we try to c. (R)   1Co 4:13

CONCISION

of evil workers, beware of   Ph'p 3:2
the c.
those who mutilate the flesh   Ph'p 3:2
(A)(R)
for the mutilation faction   Ph'p 3:2
(B)
those who insist on   Ph'p 3:2
mutilation (N)
would be mutilators of your   Ph'p 3:2
body (P)

CONCLUDE

we c. a man is justified by faith Ro 3:28

CONCLUDED

as touching Gentiles, we have   Ac 21:25
c.
letter with our decision   Ac 21:25
(A)(N)(P)
have issued the resolution   Ac 21:25
(B)
giving judgment (E)(R)   Ac 21:25
God hath c. them all in   Ro 11:32
unbelief
has consigned all men to   Ro 11:32
(A)(R)
confined them all under (B)   Ro 11:32
shut up all unto   Ro 11:32
disobedience (E)
making prisoners of   Ro 11:32
disobedience (N)
penned in prison of   Ro 11:32
disobedience (P)
the scripture hath c. all under Ga 3:22
sin
shut up and imprisoned by   Ga 3:22
sin (A)(B)
shut up all things under sin   Ga 3:22
(E)
prisoners in subjection to sin   Ga 3:22
(N)
all men imprisoned for their   Ga 3:22
sins (P)
consigned all things to sin   Ga 3:22
(R)

CONCLUSION

let us hear c. of the whole   Ec 12:13
matter
the end of the matter is this   Ec 12:13
(A)(E)(R)
to sum up the whole matter   Ec 12:13
(B)

CONCOCTED

scheme Haman c. (B)   Es 8:5
c. plots against me (B)   Jer 11:19
c. a plot to kill (B)(N)   M't 12:14

CONCORD

what c. hath Christ with   2Co 6:15
Belial
what harmony can there be   2Co 6:15
(A)(B)(P)
Can Christ agree with Belial   2Co 6:15
(N)
What accord has Christ with   2Co 6:15
Belial (R)

CONCOURSE

She crieth in the chief place   Pr 1:21
of c.
of the noisy intersections   Pr 1:21
(A)(B)
on the top of the walls (R)   Pr 1:21
we may give account of this c.   Ac 19:40
this disorder (A)   Ac 19:40
this uproar (N)   Ac 19:40
this commotion (P)(R)   Ac 19:40

CONCUBINE

And his c. whose name was   Ge 22:24
Bilhah his father's c.: and   Ge 35:22
Israel
Timna was c. to Eliphaz   Ge 36:12
Esau's son
And his c. that was in   J'g 8:31
Shechem
who took to him a c. out of   J'g 19:1
his c. played the whore   J'g 19:2
against
and his c. and his servant, his J'g 19:9
his c. also was with him   J'g 19:10
my daughter a maiden, and   J'g 19:24
his c.
so the man took his c. and   J'g 19:25
brought
the woman his c. was fallen   J'g 19:27
down
laid hold on his c. and   J'g 19:29
divided her
I and my c., to lodge   J'g 20:4
my c. have they forced, that   J'g 20:5
And I took my c. and cut her   J'g 20:6
in
And Saul had a c. whose   2Sa 3:7
name was
thou gone in unto my father's   2Sa 3:7
c.
the daughter of Aiah, the c.   2Sa 21:11
of Saul
the sons of Keturah,   1Ch 1:32
Abraham's c.
And Ephah, Caleb's c. bare   1Ch 2:46
Haran
Maachah, Caleb's c. bare   1Ch 2:48
Sheber
his c. the Aramitess bare   1Ch 7:14
Machir

CONCUBINES

the sons of the c. which   Ge 25:6
Abraham
David took him more c. and   2Sa 5:13
wives
ten women, which were c.   2Sa 15:16
to keep
Go in unto thy father's c.   2Sa 16:21
Absalom went in unto his   2Sa 16:22
father's c.
of thy wives, and the lives of   2Sa 19:5
thy c.
the ten women his c. whom   2Sa 20:3
he had
and three hundred c.: and   1Ki 11:3
beside the sons of the c. and   1Ch 3:9
above all his wives and his   2Ch 11:21
c.
and threescore c.; and   2Ch 11:21
begat
chamberlain, which kept the   Es 2:14
c.
and fourscore c. and virgins   Ca 6:8
the queens and the c. and they   Ca 6:8
his wives, and his c. might   Da 5:2
drink
his wives, and his c. drank in   Da 5:3
them
and thy c. have drunk wine   Da 5:23
in

CONCUPISCENCE

wrought in me all manner of   Ro 7:8
c.

all kinds of forbidden desires *Ro 7:8*
(A)
all sorts of covetousness *Ro 7:8*
(B)(E)(R)
all kinds of wrong desires (N) *Ro 7:8*
stimulated all my covetous *Ro 7:8*
desires (P)
evil *c.* and covetousness *Col 3:5*
unholy desires (A) *Col 3:5*
evil desire (B)(E)(P)(R) *Col 3:5*
foul cravings (N) *Col 3:5*
Not in the lust of *c.*, even as *1Th 4:5*
the passion of lust *1Th 4:5*
(A)(E)(R)
lustful passion (B) *1Th 4:5*
giving way to lust like pagans *1Th 4:5*
(N)
self-gratification (P) *1Th 4:5*

CONDEMN

whom judges shall *c.* they *Ex 22:9*
shall pay
judges pronounce guilty (B) *Ex 22:9*
the righteous, and *c.* the *De 25:1*
wicked
mine own mouth shall *c.* me *Job 9:20*
Do not *c.* me; shew me *Job 10:2*
wherefore
wilt thou *c.* him that is most *Job 34:17*
just
wilt thou *c.* me, that thou *Job 40:8*
mayest
wicked *c.* God (A) *Ps 10:13*
in his hand, nor *c.* him when *Ps 37:33*
he is
the righteous, and *c.* the *Ps 94:21*
innocent
him from those that *c.* his *Ps 109:31*
soul
a man of wicked devices will *Pr 12:2*
he *c.*
who is he that shall *c.* me? *Isa 50:9*
lo, they
in judgment thou shalt *c.* *Isa 54:17*
judge, criticize, *c.* (A) *M't 7:2*
shall *c.* it because *M't 12:41;*
                         12:42; Lu 11:32
they shall *c.* him to death *M't 20:18;*
                         M'k 10:33
sentence him to death *M't 20:18*
(A)(B)
c. not, and ye shall not be *Lu 6:37*
condemned
Judge not, not be judged *Lu 6:37*
(A)(B)(E)(N)(P)(R)
c. you out of your mouth *Lu 19:22*
(P)(R)
God sent not his Son to *c.* *Joh 3:17*
the world
to judge, pass sentence *Joh 3:17*
(A)(E)(N)(P)
does our law *c.* without *Joh 7:51*
(B)(P)
neither do I *c.* thee, sin no *Joh 8:11*
more
judge and *c.* those (A)(B)(R) *Ro 2:3*
I speak not this to *c.* you: for *2Co 7:3*
if our heart *c.* us, God is *1Jo 3:20*
greater
if our heart *c.* us not, then *1Jo 3:21*
we have
c. with insulting words *Jude 13*
(A)(P)

CONDEMNATION

greater *c.* heavier sentence *M't 23:14*
(A)
receive greater *c.* (S) *M'k 12:40;*
                         Lu 20:47
seeing thou art in the same *Lu 23:40*
c.
suffering the same *Lu 23:40*
punishment (B)(P)
under the same sentence *Lu 23:40*
(N)(P)
this is *c.* that light is come *Joh 3:19*
into world
this is the judgment *Joh 3:19*
(A)(E)(P)(R)
this is the verdict (B) *Joh 3:19*
here lies the test (N) *Joh 3:19*
shall not come into *c.;* but is *Joh 5:24*
does not come into judgment *Joh 5:24*
(A)(E)(N)(P)(R)
he comes under no sentence *Joh 5:24*
(B)
resurrected of *c.* (B) *Joh 5:29*

petitioning *c.* of him *Ac 25:15*
(A)(N)
c. is just (E)(R)(S) *Ro 3:8*
the judgment was by one to *Ro 5:16*
c.
For the sentence of one *Ro 5:16*
(A)(B)
for the judicial action (N) *Ro 5:16*
judgment came upon all men *Ro 5:18*
to *c.*
now no *c.* to them which are *Ro 8:1*
in Christ
drinks *c.* (B) *1Co 11:29*
ye come not together unto *1Co 11:34*
c.
to bring judgment *1Co 11:34*
(A)(B)(E)(N)(P)
For if the administration of *2Co 3:9*
c. be glorious
if the service that condemns *2Co 3:9*
(A)
administration that announces *2Co 3:9*
doom (B)
under which we are *2Co 3:9*
condemned (N)
he fall into the *c.* of the devil *1Ti 3:6*
fall under similar sentence *1Ti 3:6*
as (B)
judgment contrived by the *1Ti 3:6*
devil (N)
sharing the devil's downfall *1Ti 3:6*
(P)
they incur *c.* (A)(E)(R)(S) *1Ti 5:12*
we shall receive the greater *c.* *Jas 3:1*
assuming greater *Jas 3:1*
accountability (B)
receive heavier judgment (E) *Jas 3:1*
judged with greater strictness *Jas 3:1*
(N)(R)
judged with much higher *Jas 3:1*
standard (P)
your way, nay; lest ye fall *Jas 5:12*
into *c.*
so you may incur no *Jas 5:12*
judgment (B)(E)(N)
you cannot go wrong in the *Jas 5:12*
matter (P)
of old their *c.* has (R) *2Pe 2:3*
before of old ordained to this *Jude 4*
c.
their doom was predicted long *Jude 4*
ago (A)
long ago marked for doom *Jude 4*
incurred (N)

CONDEMNED

and *c.* the land in an *2Ch 36:3*
hundred talents of
fined the land (A)(E) *2Ch 36:3*
put the land under tribute *2Ch 36:3*
(B)(R)
no answer, and yet had *c.* *Job 32:3*
Job
declared him to be in the *Job 32:3*
wrong (A)(R)
pronounced Job wrong (B) *Job 32:3*
be judged, let him be *c.* *Ps 109:7*
drink the wine of the *c.* in *Am 2:8*
ye would not have *c.* the *M't 12:7*
guiltless
and by thy words thou shalt *M't 12:37*
be *c.*
c. to hell (N) *M't 23:33*
c. to the rubbish heap (P) *M't 23:33;*
                         5:30; M'k 9:43, 45, 47
when he saw that he was *c.* *M't 27:3*
they all *c.* him to be guilty *M'k 14:64*
of death
and ye shall not be *c.:* forgive *Lu 6:37*
delivered him to be *c.* to *Lu 24:20*
believeth on him is not *c.* *Joh 3:18*
that believeth not is *c.* *Joh 3:18*
already
hath no man *c.* thee *Joh 8:10*
base and *c.* mind (A) *Ro 1:28*
c. as a sinner (B)(N)(R) *Ro 3:7*
justly *c.* by them (A)(B) *Ro 3:8*
c. to frustration (A) *Ro 8:20*
c. sin in the flesh *Ro 8:3*
who doubts stands *c.* *Ro 14:23*
(A)(B)(E)(R)(S)
c. to death (N) *1Co 4:9*
that we should not be *c.* *1Co 11:32*
under which we are *c.* (N) *2Co 3:9*
be judged and *c.* *2Th 2:12*
(A)(E)(R)
stand *c.* (N) *1Ti 5:12*
Sound speech, that cannot be *Tit 2:8*
c.

and sinneth, being *c.* of *Tit 3:11*
himself
by the which he *c.* the *Heb 11:7*
world, and
passed judgment and *Heb 11:7*
sentence on (A)(B)
put the whole world in *Heb 11:7*
wrong (N)
Ye have *c.* and killed the just *Jas 5:6*
lest ye be *c.;* behold, the judge *Jas 5:9*
standeth
may not be judged *Jas 5:9*
(A)(E)(R)
come under judgment (B)(N) *Jas 5:9*
you may be one at fault (P) *Jas 5:9*
will be *c.* *2Pe 2:3*
(A)(B)(E)(N)(P)(R)
c. them with an overthrow *2Pe 2:6*

CONDEMNEST

judgest another, thou *c.* thyself *Ro 2:1*

CONDEMNETH

Thine own mouth *c.* thee *Job 15:6*
and he that *c.* the just, even *Pr 17:15*
they
Who is he that *c.?* It is *Ro 8:34*
Christ
Happy is he that *c.* not *Ro 14:22*
himself
no reason to judge himself *Ro 14:22*
(A)(R)
no qualms of conscience *Ro 14:22*
(B)(P)
judgeth not himself (E) *Ro 14:22*
make decision with clear *Ro 14:22*
conscience (N)

CONDEMNING

c. the wicked, to bring his *1Ki 8:32*
way
sentencing the wrongdoer *1Ki 8:32*
(B)
have fulfilled them in *c.* him *Ac 13:27*

CONDEMNS

the king *c.* himself (B)(R) *2Sa 14:13*
who judge and *c.* another *Ro 2:1*
(A)(R)
the service that *c.* (A) *2Co 3:9*

CONDESCEND

but *c.* to men of low estate *Ro 12:16*
give yourselves to humble *Ro 12:16*
tasks (A)
adjust yourselves to humble *Ro 12:16*
situations (B)
go about with humble folk *Ro 12:16*
(N)
take a real interest in *Ro 12:16*
ordinary people (P)
associate with the lowly (R) *Ro 12:16*

CONDITION

On this *c.* will I make a *1Sa 11:2*
covenant
looked healthier, better *c.* *Da 1:15*
(B)

CONDITIONS

containing terms and *c.* *Jer 32:11*
(A)(B)(R)
and desireth *c.* of peace *Lu 14:32*

CONDOLE

who shall *c.* thee (R) *Isa 51:19*

CONDUCT

king, to *c.* the king over *2Sa 19:15*
Jordan
the king, to *c.* him over *2Sa 19:31*
Jordan
c. yourselves in reverence (A) *Ne 5:9*
upright in *c.* (A) *Ps 37:14*
ordereth his *c.* right (S) *Ps 50:23*
c. a court case (B) *Eze 17:20*
break all rules of *c.* (N)(R) *Ro 1:28*
c. yourselves with honor *Ro 13:13*
(A)(R)
but *c.* him forth in peace, *1Co 16:11*
that he

c. yourselves carefully (B) *Eph 5:15*
c. as becometh the gospel *Ph'p 1:27*
(B)(N)(P)(S)
example in word, c. (S) *1Ti 4:12*
c. free from love of money *Heb 13:5*
(B)
his right c. give proof (N) *Jas 3:13*
c. and manner of living *1Pe 1:15*
(A)(B)(R)
c. yourselves properly, good, *1Pe 2:12*
right (A)(B)(E)(R)
by the c. of the wives (B) *1Pe 3:1*
behold your chaste c. (S) *1Pe 3:2*
accuse your good Christian *1Pe 3:16*
c. (B)(N)(P)

CONDUCTED

the people of Judah c. the *2Sa 19:40*
king
c. Paul brought him unto *Ac 17:15*
Athens
have c. ourselves (A) *2Co 1:12*

CONDUCTS

c. affairs with justice *Ps 112:5*
(A)(B)(R)

CONDUIT

stood by the c. of upper *2Ki 18:17;*
pool *Isa 36:2*
canal of the upper pool *2Ki 18:17*
(A)
stood at aqueduct (B) *2Ki 18:17;*
20:20; Isa 7:3

CONEY

c. because he cheweth the cud *Le 11:5*
camel, and the hare, and the *De 14:7*
c.

CONFECTION

c. after the art of the *Ex 30:35*
apothecary
perfume, an ointment *Ex 30:35*
(A)(B)
an incense, a perfume (E) *Ex 30:35*
incense blended by perfumer *Ex 30:35*
(R)

CONFECTIONARIES

take your daughters to be c. *1Sa 8:13*
perfumers, cooks, and bakers *1Sa 8:13*
(A)(B)(E)(R)

CONFEDERACY

Say ye not, A c., to all them *Isa 8:12*
to whom
conspiracy, conspiracy *Isa 8:12*
(A)(B)(E)(R)
all men of thy c. brought thee *Ob 7*
to the
all your allies have pushed *Ob 7*
(B)(R)

CONFEDERATE

these were c. with Abraham *Ge 14:13*
who were allies of Abraham *Ge 14:13*
(A)(B)(R)
they are c. against thee *Ps 83:5*
against you make a covenant *Ps 83:5*
(A)(E)(R)
they make an alliance (B) *Ps 83:5*
Syria is c. with Ephraim *Isa 7:2*
Syria is allied with Ephraim *Isa 7:2*
(A)(B)
Syria is in league with Ephraim *Isa 7:2*
(R)

CONFER

c. with the chief priests *Lu 22:4*
(B)(R)
did not c. with flesh (R) *Ga 1:16*

CONFERENCE

they in c. added nothing to me *Ga 2:6*
reputed to be something (A) *Ga 2:6*
who enjoyed reputation (B) *Ga 2:6*
reputed to somewhat (E) *Ga 2:6*
men of high reputation (N) *Ga 2:6*

CONFERRED

Abner c. with elders (B) *2Sa 3:17*
he c. with Joab the son of *1Ki 1:7*
Zeruiah
he consulted with Joab (B) *1Ki 1:7*
c. with her (B) *2Ki 22:14*
went his way and c. with (S) *Lu 22:4*
they c. among themselves *Ac 4:15*
what to do with
they consulted together (B) *Ac 4:15*
discussed matter among *Ac 4:15*
themselves (N)
hold a conference among *Ac 4:15*
themselves (P)
Festus, when he had c. with *Ac 25:12*
the council
consulted with the men (A) *Ac 25:12*
after a conference with the *Ac 25:12*
council (B)
after conferring with his *Ac 25:12*
advisers (N)(P)
I c. not with flesh and blood *Ga 1:16*
did not communicate with *Ga 1:16*
flesh (B)
without consulting any *Ga 1:16*
human being (N)(P)
did not confer with flesh and *Ga 1:16*
blood (R)

CONFERRING

after c. they bought (B)(N) *M't 27:7*
after c. together (N) *M't 28:12*

CONFESS

he shall c. that he hath sinned *Le 5:5*
and c. over him all the *Le 16:21*
iniquities
If they shall c. their iniquity *Le 26:40*
c. their sin which they have *Nu 5:7*
done
and c. thy name, and pray *1Ki 8:33*
and c. thy name, and turn *1Ki 8:35*
from
c. thy name, and pray and *2Ch 6:24*
make
toward this place, and c. thy *2Ch 6:26*
name
c. the sins of the children of *Ne 1:6*
Israel
Then will I also c. unto *Job 40:14*
thee that
acknowledge that your own *Job 40:14*
(A)(R)
praise you because your *Job 40:14*
own (B)
I will c. my transgressions *Ps 32:5*
unto
shall c. me before men, him *M't 10:32*
will I
acknowledges me *M't 10:32*
(B)(N)(P)(R)
will I c. also before my *M't 10:32*
Father
shall c. me before men, him *Lu 12:8*
shall the Son of man also c. *Lu 12:8*
before
any man did c. that he was *Joh 9:22*
Christ
acknowledge Jesus to be *Joh 9:22*
Christ (A)
confessor of Christ (B) *Joh 9:22*
acknowledge Jesus to be *Joh 9:22*
Messiah (N)
the Pharisees they did not *Joh 12:42*
c. him
but the Pharisees c. both *Ac 23:8*
acknowledge faith in both *Ac 23:8*
(A)
the Pharisees accept them *Ac 23:8*
(N)
Pharisees believe in all three *Ac 23:8*
(P)
Pharisees acknowledge them *Ac 23:8*
all (R)
But this I c. unto thee, that *Ac 24:14*
c. with thy mouth the Lord *Ro 10:9*
Jesus
and every tongue shall c. to *Ro 14:11*
God
acknowledge to God *Ro 14:11*
(B)(N)
give praise to God (R) *Ro 14:11*
c. to thee among the Gentiles *Ro 15:9*
praise you among Gentiles *Ro 15:9*
(A)(B)(E)(N)(R)
should c. that Jesus Christ *Ph'p 2:11*
is Lord

CONFERRED (right col top)

C. your faults one to *Jas 5:16*
another, and
If we c. our sins, he is *1Jo 1:9*
faithful and
c. that Jesus is the Son of *1Jo 4:15*
God
who c. not that Jesus Christ is *2Jo 7*
will c. his name before my *Re 3:5*
Father

CONFESSED

when he had c. weeping and *Ezr 10:1*
stood and c. their sins, and *Ne 9:2*
another fourth part they c. and *Ne 9:3*
he c. and denied not; but *Joh 1:20*
c. I am not the Christ *Joh 1:20*
and c. and showed their *Ac 19:18*
deeds
c. a good confession *1Ti 6:12*
(A)(B)(E)(R)
and c. that they were *Heb 11:13*
strangers

CONFESSETH

c. and forsaketh them shall *Pr 28:13*
have
he that c. that Jesus is (S) *1Jo 2:23*
Every spirit that c. that Jesus *1Jo 4:2*
every spirit that c. not that *1Jo 4:3*
Jesus

CONFESSING

praying, and c. my sin and *Da 9:20*
of him in Jordan, c. their sins *M't 3:6*
in the river of Jordan, c. *M'k 1:5*
their sins

CONFESSION

make c. unto him; and tell *Jos 7:19*
me
and making c. to the Lord *2Ch 30:22*
God of
make c. unto the Lord God *Ezr 10:11*
of
Lord my God, and made my *Da 9:4*
c.
mouth c. is made unto *Ro 10:10*
salvation
Pontius Pilate witnessed a *1Ti 6:13*
good c.
confessed a good c. *1Ti 6:13*
(A)(B)(E)(R)
high priest of our c. *Heb 3:1*
(B)(E)(R)
hold fast our c. *Heb 4:14*
(A)(B)(E)(R)

CONFESSOR

every c. of Christ should be *Joh 9:22*
(B)

CONFIDANT

David's c. (B) *2Sa 15:37;*
16:17
the king's c. (B) *1Ch 27:33*

CONFIDE

those in whom you c. (A) *Jer 2:37*
not c. in flesh (A) *Ph'p 3:3*

CONFIDENCE

men of Shechem put their c. *J'g 9:26*
in
put their trust in him (B)(E) *J'g 9:26*
hold c. in (B) *J'g 20:36*
c. is this wherein thou *2Ki 18:19*
trustest
put c. in (B) *2Ki 18:20;*
18:30; Job 4:18
not this thy fear, thy c. thy *Job 4:6*
hope
Whose c. shall be cut off (S) *Job 8:14*
His c. shall be rooted out *Job 18:14*
of his
dwelling place in which he *Job 18:14*
trusted (A)
dragged from safety of his *Job 18:14*
tent (B)
tent wherein he trusted *Job 18:14*
(E)(R)
they had no c. (S) *Job 29:24*
to the fine gold, Thou art *Job 31:24*
my c.

have *c.* (B) *Ps 56:3;*
    2Co 3:4; Ph'p 2:24; 3:4
the *c.* of all the ends of the *Ps 65:5*
earth
in the Lord than to put *c.* in *Ps 118:8*
man
the Lord than to put *c.* in *Ps 118:9*
princes
the Lord shall be thy *c.* and *Pr 3:26*
Lord will be your inward *Pr 3:26*
parts (B)
the upright are his. (R) *Pr 3:32*
the fear of the Lord is *Pr 14:26*
strong *c.*
the strength of the *c.* thereof *Pr 21:22*
stronghold in which they *Pr 21:22*
trust (A)(B)(R)
C. in an unfaithful man in *Pr 25:19*
time of
trust in a faithless man *Pr 25:19*
(B)(R)
and in *c.* shall be your *Isa 30:15*
strength
c. is this wherein thou *Isa 36:4*
trustest
was ashamed of Beth-el *Jer 48:13*
their *c.*
they shall dwell with *c.* *Eze 28:26*
when I
be no more the *c.* of the *Eze 29:16*
house
a friend, put ye not *c.* in a *Mic 7:5*
guide
have *c.* in (P) *Joh 5:45; 2Co 3:4;*
    Ph'p 3:4; 1Ti 6:17
with all *c.* no man *Ac 28:31*
forbidding
with boldness and quite *Ac 28:31*
openly (A)
altogether openly without *Ac 28:31*
hindrance (B)
with all boldness none *Ac 28:31*
forbidding (E)
quite openly without *Ac 28:31*
hindrance (N)(R)
utmost freedom without *Ac 28:31*
hindrance (P)
in this *c.* I was minded to *2Co 1:15*
come
it was with assurance *2Co 1:15*
(A)(B)
I felt so confident about all *2Co 1:15*
(N)
trusting you and believing (P) *2Co 1:15*
I was sure of this, I wanted *2Cor 1:15*
(R)
having *c.* in you all, that my *2Co 2:3*
joy
I have *c.* in you in all things *2Co 7:16*
the great *c.* which I have in *2Co 8:22*
you
c. wherewith I think to be *2Co 10:2*
bold
foolishly, in this *c.* of *2Co 11:17*
boasting
such reliance and *c.* *2Co 13:4*
(A)(E)(R)
have *c.* in you through the *Ga 5:10*
Lord
and access with *c.* by the *Eph 3:12*
faith
first put our *c.* (A) *Eph 3:12*
And having this *c.* I know *Ph'p 1:25*
that I
and have no *c.* in the flesh *Ph'p 3:3*
do not confide in the flesh *Ph'p 3:3*
(B)
might also have *c.* in the *Ph'p 3:4*
flesh
to rely on the flesh (A) *Ph'p 3:4*
have *c.* in the Lord touching *2Th 3:4*
Having *c.* in thy obedience I *Ph'm 21*
wrote
if we hold fast the *c.* and the *Heb 3:6*
if we hold the beginning of *Heb 3:14*
our *c.*
therefore your *c.* which *Heb 10:35*
hath
faith is the full *c.* (P) *Heb 11:1*
we may have *c.* and not be *1Jo 2:28*
then have we *c.* toward God *1Jo 3:21*
is the *c.* that we have in him *1Jo 5:14*
worthy of *c.* (A) *Re 22:6*

CONFIDENCES

the Lord hath rejected thy *c.* *Jer 2:37*
those in whom you confide *Jer 2:37*
(A)

those in whom thou trustest *Jer 2:37*
(E)(R)

CONFIDENT

he is *c.* (A)(B)(E)(R) *Job 40:28*
against me, in this will I be *c.* *Ps 27:3*
my heart is *c.* (B) *Ps 57:7*
but the fool rageth, and is *c.* *Pr 14:16*
c. and careless (A)(E) *Isa 32:9*
c. in own goodness (P) *Lu 18:9*
c. that thou thyself art a *Ro 2:19*
guide
felt so *c.* (N) *2Co 1:15*
Therefore we are always *c.* *2Co 5:6*
are *c.* I say, and willing *2Co 5:8*
rather
in this same *c.* boasting *2Co 9:4*
confident (A)(B) *2Co 10:7; Ph'p 2:4*
Being *c.* of this very thing, *Ph'p 1:6*
that
convinced and sure of *Ph'p 1:6*
(A)(B)
Of one thing I am certain *Ph'p 1:6*
(N)
I feel sure that the one (P) *Ph'p 1:6*
I am sure that he who began *Ph'p 1:6*
a good (R)
waxing *c.* by my bonds, are *Ph'p 1:14*
much

CONFIDENTLY

hopes *c.* in you (A) *Isa 26:3*
another *c.* affirmed, saying, *Lu 22:59*
Of a
emphatically insisted (A)(B) *Lu 22:59*
spoke more strongly still *Lu 22:59*
(N)
someone else insisted *Lu 22:59*
(P)(R)

CONFINEMENT

put them in *c.* (B) *Nu 15:34; 2Sa 20:3*
kept them in *c.* (S) *2Sa 20:3*

CONFIRM

changing, for to *c.* all things *Ru 4:7*
in after thee, and *c.* thy *1Ki 1:14*
words
support your words (B) *1Ki 1:14*
be with him to *c.* the *2Ki 15:19*
kingdom
support for himself in *2Ki 15:19*
holding (B)
to *c.* this second letter of *Es 9:29*
Purim
To *c.* these days of Purim in *Es 9:31*
their
thou didst *c.* thine inheritance *Ps 68:9*
restore heritage when *Ps 68:9*
exhausted (B)(R)
and *c.* the feeble knees *Isa 35:3*
make firm the feeble, *Isa 35:3*
tottering (A)(B)(R)
hope that they would *c.* the *Eze 13:6*
word
confirmation of their word *Eze 13:6*
see their message fulfilled *Eze 13:6*
(B)
expect him to fulfill their *Eze 13:6*
word (R)
c. the prophetic vision (B) *Da 9:24*
And he shall *c.* the covenant *Da 9:27*
enter strong and firm *Da 9:27*
covenant (A)
make the covenant prevail *Da 9:27*
for many (B)
make a firm covenant with *Da 9:27*
many (E)
make a strong covenant with *Da 9:27*
many (R)
stood to *c.* and to strengthen *Da 11:1*
him
support and strengthen (B) *Da 11:1*
to *c.* the promises made unto *Ro 15:8*
to verify the promises made *Ro 15:8*
(B)
by making good his promises *Ro 15:8*
(N)
he personally implemented *Ro 15:8*
promises (P)
Who shall also *c.* you unto *1Co 1:8*
the end
establish you to the end (A) *1Co 1:8*
establish you to the finish *1Co 1:8*
(B)

keep you firm to the end (N) *1Co 1:8*
keep you stedfast in faith to *1Co 1:8*
the end (P)
sustain you to the end (R) *1Co 1:8*
would *c.* your love toward *2Co 2:8*
him
assure him by your love for *2Co 2:8*
him (A)(N)
reinstate him in your *2Co 2:8*
affection (B)
reaffirm your love for him *2Co 2:8*
(R)

CONFIRMATION

c. of their word (A) *Eze 13:6*
in the defence and *c.* of the *Ph'p 1:7*
gospel
an oath for *c.* is to them an *Heb 6:16*
end of

CONFIRMED

thou hast *c.* to thyself thy *2Sa 7:24*
people
establish for thyself thy *2Sa 7:24*
people (B)(E)(R)
the kingdom was *c.* in his *2Ki 14:5*
hand
had a firm hold on the *2Ki 14:5*
kingdom (B)
kingdom established in his *2Ki 14:5*
hand (E)
royal power was firmly in *2Ki 14:5*
his hand (R)
Lord had *c.* him king over *1Ch 14:2*
Israel
established him as king *1Ch 14:2*
(B)(E)(R)
hath *c.* the same to Jacob *1Ch 16:17*
defined it for Jacob (B) *1Ch 16:17*
Esther *c.* these matters of *Es 9:32*
Purim
c. the same unto Jacob for *Ps 105:10*
law
And hath *c.* his words, which *Da 9:12*
carried out intact his words *Da 9:12*
(A)
with many words. and *c.* *Ac 15:32*
them
many words and *Ac 15:32*
strengthened (A)(B)(R)
much to encourage and *Ac 15:32*
strengthen (N)(P)
testimony of Christ was *c.* in *1Co 1:6*
you.
a man's covenant, yet if it be *Ga 3:15*
c.
has been ratified (B)(R) *Ga 3:15*
has been duly executed (N) *Ga 3:15*
properly drawn up and signed *Ga 3:15*
(P)
that was *c.* before of God in *Ga 3:17*
Christ
covenant previously *Ga 3:17*
established (A)
covenant has been ratified by *Ga 3:17*
God (B)
already been validated by *Ga 3:17*
God (N)
original contract which God *Ga 3:17*
has made (P)
covenant previously ratified *Ga 3:17*
by God (R)
c. unto us by them that *Heb 2:3*
heard him
of his counsel, *c.* it by an *Heb 6:17*
oath
intervened with an oath (A) *Heb 6:17*
gave surety with an oath *Heb 6:17*
(B)
interposed with an oath *Heb 6:17*
(E)(R)
guaranteed it with an oath *Heb 6:17*
(N)

CONFIRMETH

he *c.* them, because he held *Nu 30:14*
his
Cursed be he that *c.* not all *De 27:26*
That *c.* the word of his *Isa 44:26*
servant

CONFIRMING

c. the word with signs *M'k 16:20*
following
C. the souls of the disciples *Ac 14:22*
establishing and *Ac 14:22*
strengthening (A)(R)

reassuring and encouraging (B)(N) — Ac 14:22
urging them to stand firm in the (P) — Ac 14:22
Syria and Cilicia, c. the churches — Ac 15:41
establishing and strengthening (A) — Ac 15:41
he strengthened the churches (B)(P)(R) — Ac 15:41
bringing new strength to the (N) — Ac 15:41

CONFISCATED

goods were c. (P) — Heb 10:34

CONFISCATION

c. of goods, or to imprisonment — Ezr 7:26

CONFLICT

a c. between (B) — Ge 13:7; J'g 12:2
in c. with one another (N)(P) — Ga 5:17
the same c. which ye saw in me — Ph'p 1:30
knew what great c. I have for you — Col 2:1

CONFORMABLE

being made c. unto his death — Ph'p 3:10
so share his sufferings (A)(B)(N)(P)(R) — Ph'p 3:10
becoming conformed to his death (E) — Ph'p 3:10

CONFORMED

to be c. to the image of his Son — Ro 8:29
to be molded into the image (A) — Ro 8:29
share the likeness of his son (B) — Ro 8:29
shaped to the likeness of his son (N) — Ro 8:29
bear the family likeness of his son (P) — Ro 8:29
be not c. to this world: but be transformed — Ro 12:2
fashioned according to this world (E) — Ro 12:2
Adapt yourselves no longer to pattern of (N) — Ro 12:2
Don't let the world around you squeeze you into its own mold (P) — Ro 12:2

CONFOUND

and there c. their language — Ge 11:7; 11:9
confuse their speech (B)(R) — Ge 11:7
arrows and c. them (B) — Ps 144:6
c. omens of soothsayers (B) — Isa 44:25
lest I c. thee before them — Jer 1:17
lest I ruin you in their presence (B) — Jer 1:17
dismay you before them (E)(R) — Jer 1:17
things of world to c. wise, c. mighty — 1Co 1:27
put wise to shame, to put strong (A)(E) — 1Co 1:27
shame the wise, to shame (B)(N)(P)(R) — 1Co 1:27

CONFOUNDED

were c. (B) — Ge 45:3
they were dismayed and c. — 2Ki 19:26
sat down c. (B)(E) — Ezr 9:3; 9:4
were c. because they had hoped — Job 6:20
disappointed because they hoped (B)(R) — Job 6:20
put to shame because they hoped (E) — Job 6:20
trusted in thee, and were not c. — Ps 22:5
faces never c. (E) — Ps 34:5
Let them be c. — Ps 35:4; 40:14; 70:2; 129:5
be c. and ashamed (B) — Ps 35:4
let not those that seek thee be c. — Ps 69:6

not be put to shame through me (A)(B)(E)(R) — Ps 69:6
ashamed and c. (A)(B)(E) — Ps 70:2
Let them be c. and consumed — Ps 71:13
be put to shame and consumed (A)(B)(E)(R) — Ps 71:13
they are c., for they are brought to shame — Ps 71:24
shamed and disgraced (B)(R) — Ps 71:24
Let them be c. and troubled — Ps 83:17
be put to shame and dismayed (A)(E)(R) — Ps 83:17
be ashamed and terrified for ever (B) — Ps 83:17
C. be all they that serve graven images — Ps 97:7
put to shame (A)(B)(E)(R) — Ps 97:7; 129:5
ye shall be c. for the gardens — Isa 1:29
will be ashamed (A)(B)(E)(R) — Isa 1:29
that weave net works, shall be c. — Isa 19:9
will be humiliated (B) — Isa 19:9
will be in despair (R) — Isa 19:9
dismayed and c. (A)(B)(E)(R) — Isa 20:5
Then the moon shall be c. — Isa 24:23
be c. and cry (B) — Isa 29:9
Lebanon is c. (A)(E)(R) — Isa 33:9
they were dismayed and c. — Isa 37:27
shall be ashamed and c. — Isa 41:11
They shall be ashamed, and also c. — Isa 45:16
ye shall not be ashamed nor c. — Isa 45:17
me; therefore shall I not be c. — Isa 50:7
neither be thou c.; for thou shalt — Isa 54:4
we are greatly c. because we have — Jer 9:19
We are utterly ashamed (B)(R) — Jer 9:19
founder is c. by graven image — Jer 10:14; 51:17
brought to shame (A)(B)(E)(R) — Jer 10:14
they were ashamed and c. — Jer 14:3
she hath been ashamed and c. — Jer 15:9
them be c. that persecute me — Jer 17:18
put to shame (A)(B)(E)(R) — Jer 17:18
let not me be c.; let them be dismayed — Jer 17:18
then shalt thou be ashamed and c. — Jer 22:22
I was ashamed, yea, even c. — Jer 31:19
daughter of Egypt shall be c. — Jer 46:24
shall be disgraced (A) — Jer 46:24
put to shame (B)(E)(R) — Jer 46:24
Kiriathaim is c. and taken — Jer 48:1; 48:20
Hamath is c., and Arpad — Jer 49:23
put to shame (A)(B)(E) — Jer 49:23
Bel is c., her idols are c. — Jer 50:2
Your mother shall be sore c. — Jer 50:12
put to great shame (A)(E)(R) — Jer 50:12
utterly ashamed (B) — Jer 50:12
her whole land shall be c. — Jer 51:47
we are c., because we have — Jer 51:51
be thou c. Eze 16:52; 16:54; 63; 36:32
ashamed, and the diviners c. — Mic 3:7
nations shall see and be c. — Mic 7:16
nations shall be ashamed (A)(R) — Mic 7:16
let them despair (B) — Mic 7:16
the riders on horses shall be c. — Zec 10:5
put to shame (B) — Zec 10:5
came together, and were c. — Ac 2:6
astonished and bewildered (A) — Ac 2:6
Astounded and amazed (B) — Ac 2:6
Amazed and marvelled (E) — Ac 2:6
amazed and in their astonishment (N)(P) — Ac 2:6
amazed and wondered (R) — Ac 2:6
and c. the Jews which dwelt at Damascus — Ac 9:22
nonplused the Jews (B) — Ac 9:22
silenced the Jews (N) — Ac 9:22
reducing to confusion the Jews (P) — Ac 9:22
believeth on him shall not be c. — 1Pe 1:6

CONFRONT

c. him (A)(B)(E)(R) — Ps 17:13

CONFRONTING

no evil c. me (A) — 1Ki 5:4

CONFUSE

c. their speech (B)(R) — Ge 11:7
c. their speeches (B) — Ps 55:9
c. their tongues (S) — Ps 55:9

CONFUSED

c. them (B) — J'g 4:15; 1Sa 7:10
battle warrior is c. with noise — Isa 9:5
in the battle tumult (A)(E)(R) — Isa 9:5
of the battle turmoil (B) — Isa 9:5
like a man c. (A) — Jer 14:9
for the assembly was c. — Ac 19:32
gathering was in a tumult (A)(B) — Ac 19:32
assembly was in confusion (E)(N)(R) — Ac 19:32
assembly was at sixes and sevens (P) — Ac 19:32

CONFUSION

to lie down thereto: it is c. — Le 18:23
it is perversion (B)(R) — Le 18:23
they have wrought c. — Le 20:12
throw into c. (R) — De 7:23
send cursing and c. (A)(B)(R) — De 28:20
threw them into c. (R) — 1Sa 7:10
c. was terrible (A)(B)(R) — 1Sa 14:20
a very great c. (S) — 1Sa 14:20
to thine own c., and unto the c. of — 1Sa 20:30
own shame and shame of mother (A)(E)(R) — 1Sa 20:30
own dishonor, shame of mother (B) — 1Sa 20:30
Israel fell into c. (B) — 2Sa 4:1
and to c. of face, as it is this day — Ezr 9:7
to utter shame (A)(R) — Ezr 9:7
to our disgrace (B) — Ezr 9:7
I am full of c.; therefore see — Job 10:15
I am filled with disgrace (A)(B)(R) — Job 10:15
being filled with ignominy (E) — Job 10:15
be turned back and brought to c. — Ps 35:4; 35:26
be put to shame and dishonor (A)(E)(R) — Ps 35:4
be confounded and shamed (B) — Ps 35:4
My c. is continually before me — Ps 44:15
my dishonor is before me (A)(E) — Ps 44:15
my reproach faces me (B) — Ps 44:15
my disgrace is before me (R) — Ps 44:15
c. has covered our face (B) — Ps 69:7
and put to c. that desire my hurt — Ps 70:2
be put to shame and confounded (A)(B)(E) — Ps 70:2
let me never be put to c. — Ps 71:1
let me never be put to shame (B)(E)(R) — Ps 71:1
themselves with their own c. (R) — Ps 109:29
a spirit of c. (R) — Isa 19:14
a day of c. (B) — Isa 22:5
The city of c. is broken down — Isa 24:10
the city has become desolate (B) — Isa 24:10
the city is broken down (E)(R) — Isa 24:10
in the shadow of Egypt your c. — Isa 30:3
Egypt shall be to your reproach (B) — Isa 30:3
Egypt shall be to your humiliation (R) — Isa 30:3
stretch out upon it the line of c. — Isa 34:11
line of chaos (B) — Isa 34:11
molten images are wind and c. — Isa 41:29
images are wind and waste (B) — Isa 41:29
images are empty wind (R) — Isa 41:29

c. chaos, worthlessness (A) *Isa 44:9*
they shall go to c. together *Isa 45:16*
trusted in c. (B) *Isa 59:4*
and for c. they shall rejoice *Isa 61:7*
instead of dishonor and *Isa 61:7*
reproach (A)
instead of reproach they shall *Isa 61:7*
(B)
instead of dishonor they shall *Isa 61:7*
(E)(R)
our c. covereth us: for we *Jer 3:25*
have
let our dishonor cover us (R) *Jer 3:25*
to the c. of their own faces *Jer 7:19*
c. has overwhelmed (B) *Jer 8:21*
their everlasting c. shall *Jer 20:11*
never
eternal dishonor will never *Jer 20:11*
be (A)(B)(E)(R)
but unto us c. of faces, as at *Da 9:7;*
this day *9:8*
shamefacedness (B) *Da 9:7*
great c. from the Lord *Zec 14:13*
(A)(B)
covered with c. (N) *Lu 13:17*
reducing to c. (P) *Ac 9:22*
throwing you into c. (A) *Ac 15:24*
the whole city was filled *Ac 19:29*
with c.
city was agitated (B) *Ac 19:29*
whole city was in an uproar *Ac 19:29*
(P)
the assembly was in c. *Ac 19:32*
(E)(N)(R)(S)
For God is not the author *1Co 14:33*
of c.
He is not the God of *1Co 14:33*
disorder (B)(N)(P)
there is c. and every evil *Jas 3:16*
work
disorder and evil of every *Jas 3:16*
kind (N)(R)
disharmony and all kinds of *Jas 3:16*
evil (P)

CONFUTE

c. objectors (N)(P)(R) *Tit 1:9*
c. the gainsayers (S) *Tit 1:9*

CONFUTED

he powerfully c. the Jews *Ac 18:28*
(R)

CONGEALED

the depths were c. in the *Ex 15:8*
heart of sea

CONGENIAL

courageous, c., full of mercy *Jas 3:17*
(B)

CONGRATULATE

and to c. him, because he *1Ch 18:10*
had

CONGREGATION

it is a sin offering for the c. *Le 4:21*
God hath given to bear *Le 10:17*
iniquity of c.
the people (B)(E) *Le 10:17;*
Nu 14:27; 16:47
make an atonement for all *Le 16:33*
the c.
these were the renowned of *Nu 1:16*
the c.
when c. is gathered you shall *Nu 10:7*
blow
the assembly (B) *Nu 10:7;*
35:12; 1Ki 12:20; Ne 13:1; Ps 1:5;
89:5; Pr 21:16; Isa 14:13
how long shall I bear with *Nu 14:27*
this evil c.
one ordinance for c. and *Nu 15:15*
stranger
all residents (B) *Nu 15:15*
separate yourselves from c. *Nu 16:21*
that I may
gathering (B) *Nu 16:21;*
Job 15:34; Ps 26:5
get up from among c. that I *Nu 16:45*
may
Aaron ran into midst of the *Nu 16:47*
c.
that soul he cut off from *Nu 19:20*
among c.

the community (B) *Nu 19:20; Jos 9:27*
let the Lord set a man over *Nu 27:16*
the c.
stand before c. for *Nu 35:12;*
judgment *Jos 20:6*
made drawers of water for c. *Jos 9:27*
c. gathered as one man from *J'g 20:1*
Dan
they called Jeroboam to the c. *1Ki 12:20*
Hezekiah gave to c. 1000 *2Ch 30:24*
bullocks
himself separated from the c. *Ezr 10:8*
Moabite should not come into *Ne 13:1*
c.
c. of hypocrites shall be *Job 15:34*
desolate
I stood up and I cried in *Job 30:28*
the c.
nor sinners in c. of righteous *Ps 1:5*
in midst of c. will I praise *Ps 22:22*
thee
I have hated the c. of evil *Ps 26:5*
doers
do ye indeed speak *Ps 58:1*
righteousness, O c.
remember c. thou hast *Ps 74:2*
purchased of old
forget not the c. of thy poor *Ps 74:19*
for ever
life of your poor (A)(E)(R) *Ps 74:19*
life of afflicted ones (B) *Ps 74:19*
when I receive c. I will judge *Ps 75:2*
uprightly
God standeth in the c. of the *Ps 82:1*
mighty
thy faithfulness also in c. of *Ps 89:5*
the saints
let them exalt him in c. of *Ps 107:32*
people
praise the Lord in assembly *Ps 111:1*
and c.
almost in all evil in midst of *Pr 5:14*
c.
men shall remain in c. of *Pr 21:16*
dead
I will sit upon mount of c. *Isa 14:13*
know, O c. what is among *Jer 6:18*
them
their c. shall be established *Jer 30:20*
before me
they should not enter into c. *La 1:10*
I will chastise them as c. *Ho 7:12*
heard
gather the people, sanctify *Joe 2:16*
the c.
now when the c. was broken *Ac 13:43*
up

CONGREGATION *OF* ISRAEL

c. of Israel kill it in evening *Ex 12:6*
that soul be cut off from c. *Ex 12:19*
of Israel
all c. of Israel shall keep *Ex 12:47*
passover
if c. of Israel sin through *Le 4:13*
ignorance
Lord separated you from c. *Nu 16:9*
of Israel
c. of Israel sacrificed sheep *2Ch 5:6*
according to the *2Ch 24:6*
commandment of c. of Israel

CONGREGATION *OF* LORD

lift yourselves above c. of *Nu 16:3*
Lord
c. of Lord not as sheep *Nu 27:17*
without shepherd
plague among c. of Lord *Nu 31:16;*
Jos 22:17
not enter into c. of Lord *De 23:1;*
23:2-3
in sight of c. of Lord keep *1Ch 28:8*
cast a cord by lot in c. of *Mic 2:5*
Lord

ALL THE CONGREGATION

gather all the c. together to *Le 8:3*
door
make atonement for all the *Le 16:17*
c. of Israel
all the c. stone him *Le 24:14;*
24:16; Nu 14:10; 15:35
seeing all the c. are holy *Nu 16:3*
every one

one sin, wilt thou be wroth *Nu 16:22*
with all c.
went up in sight of all the *Nu 20:27;*
c. *25:6*
set him before all the c. *Nu 27:19;*
27:22
Joshua read not before all *Jos 8:35*
the c.
all the c. murmured against *Jos 9:18*
princes
wrath fell on all the c. of *Jos 22:20*
Israel
king blessed all the c. 1Ki 8:14; 8:55
all the c. blessed the Lord *1Ch 29:20*
God
all the c. made covenant *2Ch 23:3*
with
all the c. worshipped, *2Ch 29:28*
singers sang
all the c. said, Amen, and *Ne 5:13*
praised
all the c. made booths *Ne 8:17*

ELDERS OF THE CONGREGATION

elders of the c. shall lay their *Le 4:15*
hands
elders of c. said, How shall we *J'g 21:16*
do

GREAT CONGREGATION

Solomon held a feast for *1Ki 8:65;*
Israel, a great c. *2Ch 7:8; 30:13*
assembled to him a great c. *Ezr 10:1*
praise be of thee in great c. *Ps 22:25*
I will give thee thanks in *Ps 35:18*
great c.
preached righteousness in *Ps 40:9*
great c.
not concealed truth from *Ps 40:10*
great c.

TABERNACLE OF CONGREGATION

bullock before tabernacle of *Ex 29:10*
c.
meeting tent (A)(B) *Ex 29:10;*
29:44; 33:7; Le 3:8; 10:7; Nu 4:3; 8:9;
25:6; 2Ch 1:3
I will sanctify, anoint *Ex 29:44;*
tabernacle of c. *30:26*
called it tabernacle of c. went *Ex 33:7*
out to tabernacle of c.
kill it before tabernacle of c. *Le 3:8;*
3:13; 4:5
not go out from door of *Le 10:7*
tabernacle of c.
drink no wine when ye go *Le 10:9*
into tabernacle of c.
so do for tabernacle of c. *Le 16:16*
work of tabernacle of c. *Nu 4:3;*
4:23, 25, 30, 39, 43
thou shalt bring Levites before *Nu 8:9*
tabernacle of c.
Lord spake, Come out ye *Nu 12:4*
three to tabernacle of c.
tent of meeting (A)(B) *Nu 12:4;*
14:10; 17:4; De 31:14; 1Ki 8:4
glory of Lord appeared in *Nu 14:10*
tabernacle of c.
lay up in tabernacle of c. *Nu 17:4*
keep charge of tabernacle of c. *Nu 18:4*
Israel weeping before door of *Nu 25:6*
tabernacle of c.
present yourselves in *De 31:14*
tabernacle of c.
at Shiloh, and set up *Jos 18:1*
tabernacle of c.
they brought up tabernacle of *1Ki 8:4;*
c. *2Ch 5:5*
for there was tabernacle of c. *2Ch 1:3*
of God

TENT OF CONGREGATION

work of the tent of c. finished *Ex 39:32*
set up tent of c. *Ex 40:2*
the table in the tent of c. *Ex 40:22*
the candlestick in the tent *Ex 40:24*
of c.
and he put the golden altar *Ex 40:26*
in the tent of c.

then a cloud covered the *tent of c.* — Ex 40:34
Moses not able to enter into *tent of c.* — Ex 40:35

WHOLE CONGREGATION

the *whole c.* of Israel murmured — Ex 16:2
shall keep charge of *whole c.* — Nu 3:7
to-morrow he will be wroth with *whole c.* — Jos 22:18
whole c. sent to speak to Benjamin — J'g 21:13
king blessed *whole c.* of Israel — 2Ch 6:3
whole c. was 42,360 — Ezr 2:64; Ne 7:66
wickedness shewed *whole c.* — Pr 26:26

CONGREGATIONS

in the *c.* will I bless the Lord — Ps 26:12
Bless ye God in the *c.* even — Ps 68:26
roar in the midst of thy *c.* — Ps 74:4
in midst of holy place (A)(R) — Ps 74:4
in midst of thine assembly (E) — Ps 74:4

CONIAH

though *C.* the son of Jehoiakim — Jer 22:24
this man *C.* a despised broken idol — Jer 22:28
son of Josiah reigned instead of *C.* — Jer 37:1

CONIES

goats; and the rocks for the *c.* — Ps 104:18
The *c.* are but a feeble folk — Pr 30:26

CONNECTION

in *c.* with this god (B) — Da 6:5

CONONIAH

over which *C.* the Levite was ruler — 2Ch 31:12
overseers under the hand of *C.* — 2Ch 31:13

CONQUER

David did not *c.* Philistines (B) — 1Sa 17:50
could not *c.* it (A)(B)(R) — Isa 7:1
go against Judah and *c.* it (S) — Isa 7:6
active against him and *c.* (B) — Da 11:7
went forth conquering, and to *c.* — Re 6:2

CONQUERED

conquered (B) — Ge 14:5; Nu 32:4; De 2:33; 4:46; Jos 10:40; 1Sa 30:17
he *c.* them (B) — 1Sa 14:47
conquered (R) — 1Ki 15:20; 2Ki 3:25; 2Ch 16:4
by faith *c.* kingdoms (R) — Heb 11:33
I also *c.* (B)(R) — Re 3:21
has *c.* (A)(B)(R) — Re 5:5
they have *c.* him (B)(N)(P)(R) — Re 12:11

CONQUERING

he went forth *c.* and to conquer — Re 6:2

CONQUERORS

we are more than *c.* through him — Ro 8:37

CONSCIENCE

no pangs of *c.* (R) — 1Sa 25:31
David's *c.* accused him (B) — 2Sa 24:10
my *c.* does not accuse (R) — Job 27:6
I try the *c.* (S) — Jer 17:10
being convicted by their own *c.* — Joh 8:9

going out *c.* stricken (A)(B) — Joh 8:9
have lived in all good *c.* before God — Ac 23:1
to have always a *c.* void of offence — Ac 24:16
without *c.* (B)(N) — Ro 1:31
their *c.* also bearing witness — Ro 2:15
my *c.* also bearing me witness — Ro 9:1
for wrath, but also for *c.* sake — Ro 13:5
wrong to hurt the *c.* (A)(N)(R) — Ro 14:20
no qualms of *c.* (B)(P) — Ro 14:22
make decisions with clear *c.* (N) — Ro 14:22
for some with *c.* of the idol — 1Co 8:7
and their *c.* being weak is defiled — 1Co 8:7
shall not the *c.* of him which is weak — 1Co 8:10
and wound their weak *c.* ye sin — 1Co 8:12
eat, asking no question for *c.* sake — 1Co 10:25; 10:27
sake that showed it, and for *c.* sake — 1Co 10:28
C. I say, not thine own, but of the — 1Co 10:29
liberty judged of another man's *c.* — 1Co 10:29
is this, the testimony of our *c.* — 2Co 1:12
ourselves to every man's *c.* in — 2Co 4:2
a good *c.* and of faith unfeigned — 1Ti 1:5
Holding faith, and a good *c.* — 1Ti 1:19
mystery of the faith in a pure *c.* — 1Ti 3:9
their *c.* seared with a hot iron — 1Ti 4:2
from my forefathers with pure *c.* — 2Ti 1:3
even their mind and *c.* is defiled — Tit 1:15
perfect, as pertaining to the *c.* — Heb 9:9
purge your *c.* from dead works — Heb 9:14
should have had no more *c.* of sins — Heb 10:2
hearts sprinkled from an evil *c.* — Heb 10:22
we trust we have a good *c.* — Heb 13:18
if a man for *c.* toward God endure — 1Pe 2:19
Having a good *c.*; that whereas — 1Pe 3:16
answer of a good *c.* toward God — 1Pe 3:21

CONSCIENCELESS

c., faithless, heartless (A) — Ro 1:31

CONSCIENCES

also are made manifest in your *c.* — 2Co 5:11

CONSCIOUS

was not *c.* of (A) — Ac 12:9; 23:5
c. mind endorses (P) — Ro 7:22

CONSCIOUSLY

c. directing his hands (B) — Ge 44:14

CONSCIOUSNESS

no more *c.* of sins (S) — Heb 10:2

CONSCRIPT

batallion of *c.* laborers (B) — 1Ki 5:13; 5:14
c. for forced labor (S) — 1Ki 9:21

CONSCRIPTED

c. forced labor (S) — 1Ki 5:13; 9:15
c. the labor corps (B) — 1Ki 9:15

CONSECRATE

c., set apart (A)(R) — Ex 13:2
c. them today (B)(R) — Ex 19:10; 19:22-23; 28:41; 29:27
make Aaron's garments to *c.* him — Ex 28:3

garments to sanctify him (A)(E) — Ex 28:3
garments for dedication (B) — Ex 28:3
anoint them, and *c.* them — Ex 28:41
c. them to minister (A)(B) — Ex 29:1; Le 25:10
shalt *c.* Aaron and his sons — Ex 29:9
Ordain Aaron and his sons (A)(B)(R) — Ex 29:9
to *c.* and to sanctify them — Ex 29:33
seven days shalt thou *c.* them — Ex 29:35
seven days ordain them (A)(R) — Ex 29:35
seven days to installation (B) — Ex 29:35
anoint it and *c.* it (A) — Ex 29:36
c. the tent of meeting (R) — Ex 29:44
you shall *c.* them (R) — Ex 30:29
Aaron and his sons, and *c.* them — Ex 30:30
C. yourselves to day to the — Ex 32:29
you are installed today (B) — Ex 32:29
Today you ordained yourselves (R) — Ex 32:29
for seven days shall he *c.* you — Le 8:33
c. yourselves to be holy (A)(R) — Le 11:44
he shall *c.* to minister in — Le 16:32
And he shall *c.* unto the Lord the — Nu 6:12
He shall anew dedicate his head (B) — Nu 6:12
He shall separate unto Jehovah (E)(R) — Nu 6:12
all males you shall *c.* (B) — De 15:19
c. people, *c.* yourselves (B) — Jos 7:13; 1Ch 15:12
set apart to *c.* (R) — 1Ch 23:13
c. his service this day unto — 1Ch 29:5
to *c.* himself with a young — 2Ch 13:9
those who *c.* and cleanse (B) — Isa 66:17
set apart and *c.* (A) — Eze 37:28
and they shall *c.* themselves — Eze 43:26
and I will *c.* their gain unto the — Mic 4:13
devote their gain (A)(B)(E)(R) — Mic 4:13
c. them by the truth (N) — Joh 17:17
I *c.* myself (B)(N)(P)(R) — Joh 17:19
purify and *c.* (A)(N) — Heb 13:12

CONSECRATED

c. it (B)(R) — Ge 2:3; Ex 19:14; Le 8:10, 15
c. the sabbath (B) — Ex 20:11; 29:21
anointed therein, and to be *c.* — Ex 29:29
and that is *c.* to put on the — Le 21:10
whom he *c.* to minister in the — Nu 3:3
he ordained to minister (A)(R) — Nu 3:3
installed in the priestly office (B) — Nu 3:3
c. it (A)(B)(R) — Nu 7:1; 8:17; 1Sa 7:1; 16:5
the *c.* things (A)(R) — Nu 18:8
the *c.* portion (B) — Nu 26:13
of brass and iron, are *c.* unto the — Jos 6:19
set apart for the Lord (B) — Jos 6:19
are holy unto Jehovah (E) — Jos 6:19
are sacred to the Lord (R) — Jos 6:19
and *c.* one of his sons — J'g 17:5
And Micah *c.* the Levite — J'g 17:12
the *c.* bread (B) — 1Sa 21:4; 21:6
though it were *c.* (B)(R) — 1Sa 21:5; 1Ch 15:14; 2Ch 7:16
c. to the Lord (B) — 2Sa 8:11
c. middle of the court (A)(R) — 1Ki 8:64
c. this house (B)(R) — 1Ki 9:3
he *c.* him, and he became one — 1Ki 13:33
ordaining whom he wished (B) — 1Ki 13:33
Aaron, that are *c.* to burn incense — 2Ch 26:18
have *c.* yourselves unto the — 2Ch 29:31
the *c.* things were six hundred — 2Ch 29:33
c. things were 600 oxen, 3000 sheep — 2Ch 29:33
which were *c.* unto the Lord — 2Ch 31:6
he had *c.* (B) — 2Ch 36:14
set feasts of the Lord that were *c.* — Ezr 3:5
that were dedicated (B) — Ezr 3:5

c. the sheepgate (A)(R)	Ne 3:1
my c. ones (E)(R)	Isa 13:3
I c. you (R)	Jer 1:5
the c. priests (A)(R)	Eze 48:11
the Father c.	Joh 10:36
(A)(N)(P)(R)	
may be c. (B)(N)(R)	Joh 17:19
who are c. (P)	Ac 20:32
c. and made holy	Ro 15:16
(A)(B)(N)	
those c., made holy (A)	1Co 1:2
c. and set free (N)	1Co 1:30
you were c., set apart (A)	1Co 6:11
dedicated, c. (A)(P)(R)	1Co 7:14
you should be c. (A)	1Th 4:3
c. by the word (A)(B)(P)(R)	1Ti 4:5
c. and useful (R)	2Ti 2:21
the Son, who is c. for	Heb 7:28
evermore	
made perfect forever	Heb 7:28
(A)(B)(E)(N)(P)(R)	
those c. (R)	Heb 10:10
perfected those c. (A)(N)	Heb 10:14
way, which he hath c. for	Heb 10:20
us	
He initiated, dedicated (A)	Heb 10:20
way so recently made for	Heb 10:20
us (B)	
dedicated for us (E)	Heb 10:20
opened through the curtains	Heb 10:20
(N)(P)(R)	
blood by which he was c.	Heb 10:29
(A)(N)	
c. and holy behavior	2Pe 3:11
(A)(B)	

CONSECRATES

the Lord who c. you (B)	Ex 31:13
the Lord who c. you (A)	Le 22:32
those whom he c. (N)	Heb 2:11

CONSECRATING

c. to him completely (P)	2Co 7:1

CONSECRATION

for it is a ram of c.	Ex 29:22
breast of the ram of Aaron's	Ex 29:26
c.	
of the ram of the c., even of	Ex 29:27
that	
thou shalt take the ram of	Ex 29:31
the c.	
ordination ram (B)	Ex 29:31
ram of ordination (R)	Ex 29:31
the other ram, the ram of c.	Le 8:22
of the ram of c. it was Moses'	Le 8:29
part	
until the days of your c. be at	Le 8:33
live in c. to (B)(E)(R)	Nu 6:2
period of c. (B)	Nu 6:4;
	6:12-13, 19, 21
because the c. of his God is	Nu 6:7
upon	
he hath defiled the head of his	Nu 6:9
c.	
made our c. (A)	1Co 1:30
bring c. to completeness	2Co 7:1
(A)(N)	
possess body in c. and honor	1Th 4:4
(A)	
to c., purity (A)	1Th 4:7
continues in c. (B)	1Ti 2:15

CONSECRATIONS

And if ought of the flesh of	Ex 29:34
the c.	
and of the c. and of the	Le 7:37
sacrifice	
they were c. for a sweet	Le 8:28
savour	
an ordination offering	Le 8:28
(A)(B)(R)	
bread that is in the basket of	Le 8:31
c.	
basket of ordination offerings	Le 8:31
(B)	

CONSENT

But in this will we c. unto	Ge 34:15
you	
Only herein will the men c.	Ge 34:22
unto us	
only let us c. unto them	Ge 34:23
accept their condition (B)	Ge 34:23

let us agree with them (R)	Ge 34:23
Thou shalt not c. unto him	De 13:8
you must refuse him (B)	De 13:8
you shall not yield to him	De 13:8
(R)	
but he would not c.	J'g 11:17
and they came out with one	1Sa 11:7
c.	
him, Hearken not unto him,	1Ki 20:8
nor c.	
do not give in (B)	1Ki 20:8
consulted together with one c.	Ps 83:5
if sinners entice thee, c. thou	Pr 1:10
not	
priests murder in the way by	Ho 6:9
c.	
the Lord, to serve him with	Zep 3:9
one c.	
with one c. began to make	Lu 14:18
excuse	
I c. unto the law that it is	Ro 7:16
good	
I agree with the law	Ro 7:16
(A)(B)(N)(P)(R)	
except it be with c. for a	1Co 7:5
time	
and c. not to wholesome	1Ti 6:3
words	
assent to the sound and (A)	1Ti 6:3
does not adhere to the	1Ti 6:3
wholesome (B)	
will not give his mind to (N)	1Ti 6:3
teach some doctrinal novelty	1Ti 6:3
(P)	
does not agree with sound	1Ti 6:3
words (R)	

CONSENTED

the priests c. to receive no	2Ki 12:8
more	
priests agreed not to take	2Ki 12:8
(B)(R)	
So he c. to them in this	Da 1:14
matter	
he c. to (S)	M't 3:15
same had not c. to the	Lu 23:51
counsel and	
not agreed with or assented	Lu 23:51
to (A)(P)	
had not voted for council's	Lu 23:51
plan (B)	
dissented from their policy	Lu 23:51
(N)	
not c. to the purpose (R)	Lu 23:51
longer time with them, he c.	Ac 18:20
not	

CONSENTEDST

then thou c. with him, and	Ps 50:18
you associate with him	Ps 50:18
(A)(B)	
you are a friend of his (R)	Ps 50:18

CONSENTING

And Saul was c. unto his	Ac 8:1
death	
standing by, and c. unto his	Ac 22:20
death	

CONSIDER

and c. that this nation is thy	Ex 33:13
Then the priest shall c.: and	Le 13:13
Know therefore this day, and	De 4:39
Thou shalt also c. in thine	De 8:5
heart	
c. the years of many	De 32:7
generations	
that they would c. their	De 32:29
latter end	
now therefore c. what ye	J'g 18:14
have to	
c. of it, take advice, and	J'g 19:30
speak	
for c. how great things he	1Sa 12:24
hath	
therefore know and c. what	1Sa 25:17
thou	
c. and decide (B)(R)(S)	2Sa 24:13
wherefore c. I pray you, and	2Ki 5:7
see	
wickedness also; will he not	Job 11:11
then c.	
c. mean enemy (B)	Job 13:24
when I c. I am afraid of	Job 23:15
him	

and would not c. any of his	Job 34:27
ways	
and c. the wondrous works	Job 37:14
of God	
O Lord, c. my meditation	Ps 5:1
When I c. thy heavens, the	Ps 8:3
work	
c. my trouble which I suffer	Ps 9:13
of	
C. and hear me, O Lord my	Ps 13:3
God	
C. mine enemies; for they are	Ps 25:19
thou shalt diligently c. his	Ps 37:10
place	
Hearken, O daughter, and c.	Ps 45:10
well her bulwarks, c. her	Ps 48:13
palaces	
Now c. this, ye that forget	Ps 50:22
God	
they shall wisely c. of his	Ps 64:9
doing	
I will c. thy testimonies	Ps 119:95
C. mine affliction, and	Ps 119:153
deliver me	
C. how I love thy precepts	Ps 119:159
c. well the path of (E)	Pr 4:26
the ant, thou sluggard; c. her	Pr 6:6
ways	
c. diligently what is before	Pr 23:1
thee	
he that pondereth the heart	Pr 24:12
c. it	
for they c. not that they do	Ec 5:1
evil	
C. the work of God: for who	Ec 7:13
in the day of adversity c.:	Ec 7:14
God also	
not know, my people doth not	Isa 1:3
c.	
neither c. the operation of	Isa 5:12
his	
narrowly look upon thee,	Isa 14:16
and c. thee	
I will c. in my dwelling place	Isa 18:4
they may see, and know,	Isa 41:20
and c.	
that we may c. them, and	Isa 41:22
neither c. the things of old	Isa 43:18
they had not heard shall they	Isa 52:15
c.	
and c. diligently, and see if	Jer 2:10
there	
C. ye, and call for the	Jer 9:17
mourning	
in the latter days ye shall c.	Jer 23:20;
it	30:24
see, O Lord, and c.; for I am	La 1:11
Behold, O Lord, and c. to	La 2:20
whom	
c. and behold our reproach	La 5:1
may be they will c. though	Eze 12:3
they	
the matter, and c. the vision	Da 9:23
they c. not in their hearts that	Ho 7:2
I	
hosts; C. your ways	Hag 1:5;
	1:7
c. from this day and upward	Hag 2:15
C. now from this day and	Hag 2:18
Lord's temple was laid, c. it	Hag 2:18
c. the lilies of the field, how	M't 6:28
they	
C. the ravens: for they	Lu 12:24
neither	
C. the lilies how they grow:	Lu 12:27
they	
Nor c. that it is expedient for	Joh 11:50
us	
came together for to c. of	Ac 15:6
this	
if you c. me faithful (B)	Ac 16:15
c. my own life valuable (P)	Ac 20:24
I c. myself fortunate	Ac 26:2
(A)(B)(N)(P)(R)	
c. yourselves dead	Ro 6:11
(A)(B)(R)	
I c. the sufferings of this	Ro 8:18
(A)(R)	
I c. as loss (A)(B)(P)	Ph'p 3:7
C. what I say; and the Lord	2Ti 2:7
give	
c. the Apostle and High	Heb 3:1
Priest	
Now c. how great this man	Heb 7:4
was	
let us c. one another to	Heb 10:24
provoke	
For c. him that endured	Heb 12:3
such	
c. it wholly joyful (A)(B)	Jas 1:2

CONSIDERATELY

c. allowed (N)(P)   *Ac 27:3*

CONSIDERATENESS

known for *c.* (A)   *Ph'p 4:5*

CONSIDERED

will be *c.* criminals (B)   *1Ki 1:21*
but when I had *c.* it in the morning   *1Ki 3:21*
I have *c.* the things which thou   *1Ki 5:8*
not *c.* as anything (S)   *1Ki 10:21*
c. as anything (S)   *2Ch 9:20*
Hast thou *c.* my servant Job   *Job 1:8; 2:3*
thou hast *c.* my trouble; thou   *Ps 31:7*
have *c.* the days of old, the years   *Ps 77:5*
is *c.* intelligent (B)   *Pr 17:28*
I saw, and *c.* it well: I looked   *Pr 24:32*
and *c.* all the oppressions that   *Ec 4:1*
Again, I *c.* all travail, and every   *Ec 4:4*
I *c.* all the living which walk   *Ec 4:15*
I *c.* in my heart even to declare   *Ec 9:1*
c. an equal with clay (B)   *Isa 29:16*
ignorantly *c.* him stricken (A)   *Isa 53:4*
I *c.* the horns, and, behold, there   *Da 7:8*
c. him a prophet (B)   *M't 14:5*
For they *c.* not the miracle of the   *M'k 6:52*
c. in her mind (S)   *Lu 1:29*
c. worthy to obtain (A)(B)(P)   *Lu 20:35*
c. the greatest (A)(B)(P)   *Lu 22:24*
I *c.*, and saw fourfooted beasts   *Ac 11:6*
And when he had *c.* the thing   *Ac 12:12*
he *c.* not his own body now dead   *Ro 4:19*
c. worthy of honor (A)(P)(R)   *1Ti 5:17*
c. worthy of more glory (A)(P)   *Heb 3:3*
c. the covenant blood (A)(B)   *Heb 10:29*
c. God reliable (A)(R)   *Heb 11:11*
c. the contempt (A)(B)(N)(P)(R)   *Heb 11:26*

CONSIDEREST

that thou *c.* (B)   *Ps 143:3*
C. thou not what this people have   *Jer 33:24*
but *c.* not the beam that is in   *M't 7:3*

CONSIDERETH

hearts alike; he *c.* all their works   *Ps 33:15*
Blessed is he that *c.* the poor   *Ps 41:1*
wisely *c.* the house of the wicked   *Pr 21:12*
c. not that poverty shall come   *Pr 28:22*
The righteous *c.* the cause of   *Pr 29:7*
She *c.* a field, and buyeth it   *Pr 31:16*
none *c.* in his heart, neither   *Isa 44:19*
and *c.* and doeth not such like   *Eze 18:14*
Because he *c.* and turneth away   *Eze 18:28*

CONSIDERING

none *c.* that the righteous is taken   *Isa 57:1*
I was *c.*, behold, and he goat came   *Da 8:5*
c. thyself, lest thou also be   *Ga 6:1*
c. the end of their conversation   *Heb 13:7*
c. the issue of their life (E)   *Heb 13:7*

CONSIDERS

c. it unclean (B)(N)   *Ro 14:14*

CONSIGNED

c. all men to disobedience (A)(R)   *Ro 11:32*
c. all things to sin (R)   *Ga 3:22*

CONSIST

things, and by him all things *c.*   *Col 1:17*
all things are framed together (B)   *Col 1:17*
all things are held together (N)   *Col 1:17*
upholding principle of the whole scheme of creation (P)   *Col 1:17*
all things hold together (R)   *Col 1:17*

CONSISTENTLY

most cordially, *c.* love (B)   *1Pe 1:22*

CONSISTETH

man's life *c.* not in the abundance   *Lu 12:15*

CONSOLATION

give them the cup of *c.* to drink   *Jer 16:7*
an empty *c.* (R)   *Zec 10:2*
waiting for the *c.* of Israel   *Lu 2:25*
for ye have received your *c.*   *Lu 6:24*
being interpreted, The son of *c.*   *Ac 4:36*
Son of Encouragement (A)(R)   *Ac 4:36*
Son of Exhortation (E)(N)   *Ac 4:36*
son of comfort (P)   *Ac 4:36*
had read, they rejoiced for the *c.*   *Ac 15:31*
the God of patience and *c.* grant   *Ro 15:5*
who supplies encouragement (A)   *Ro 15:5*
source of all fortitude, encouragement (N)   *Ro 15:5*
who inspires men to endure (P)   *Ro 15:5*
God of stedfastness and encouragement (R)   *Ro 15:6*
for *c.* (A)(P)(R)   *1Co 14:3*
in us, so our *c.* also aboundeth   *2Co 1:5*
it is for your *c.* and salvation   *2Co 1:6*
we be comforted, it is for your *c.*   *2Co 1:6*
so shall ye be also of the *c.*   *2Co 1:7*
but by the *c.* wherewith he was   *2Co 7:7*
comfort which encouraged (A)(E)(P)(R)   *2Co 7:7*
by encouragement he received (B)   *2Co 7:7*
any *c.* in Christ, if any comfort   *Ph'p 2:1*
consoling and encouraging in him (A)   *Ph'p 2:1*
any encouragement (B)(P)(R)   *Ph'p 2:1*
given us everlasting *c.* and good   *2Th 2:16*
we have great joy and *c.* in   *Ph'm 7*
we might have a strong *c.*   *Heb 6:18*

CONSOLATIONS

Are the *c.* of God small with thee   *Job 15:11*
my speech, and let this be your *c.*   *Job 21:2*
satisfied with the breasts of her *c.*   *Isa 66:11*
satisfied consoling breasts (A)(B)(R)   *Isa 66:11*

CONSOLE

David sent to *c.* him (S)   *2Sa 10:2*
c. a delight ourselves (A)   *Pr 7:18*

CONSOLING

satisfied *c.* breasts (A)(B)(R)   *Isa 66:11*

CONSORT

light *c.* with darkness (N)   *2Co 6:14*

CONSORTED

believed, and *c.* with Paul   *Ac 17:4*
associated with (A)(B)   *Ac 17:4*
joined Paul and Silas (N)(R)   *Ac 17:4*
threw in their lot with Paul (P)   *Ac 17:4*

CONSPICUOUS

c., remarkable horn (A)(R)   *Da 8:5*
four *c.* horns (R)   *Da 8:8*
great and *c.* (B)   *Ac 2:20*

CONSPIRACY

the *c.* was strong; for the people   *2Sa 15:12*
his *c.* (B)(R)   *1Ki 16:20*
servants arose, and made a *c.* and   *2Ki 12:20*
contrived a plot (B)   *2Ki 12:20*
Now they made a *c.* against   *2Ki 14:19*
acts of Shallum, and his *c.*   *2Ki 15:15*
the son of Elah made a *c.*   *2Ki 15:30*
the king of Assyria found *c.* in   *2Ki 17:4*
found treachery in Hoshea (A)(R)   *2Ki 17:4*
was plotting rebellion (B)   *2Ki 17:4*
they made a *c.* against him   *2Ch 25:27*
c. of ungodly men (A)(B)   *Ps 64:2*
conspiracy, conspiracy (A)(B) (E)(R)   *Isa 8:12*
the Lord said unto me, A *c.*   *Jer 11:9*
There is a *c.* of her prophets   *Eze 22:25*
than forty which had made this *c.*   *Ac 23:13*

CONSPIRATORS

Ahithophel is among the *c.*   *2Sa 15:31*

CONSPIRED

they *c.* against him to slay him   *Ge 37:18*
all of you have *c.* against me   *1Sa 22:8*
Why have ye *c.* against me, thou   *1Sa 22:13*
c. against him; and Baasha smote   *1Ki 15:27*
c. against him, as he was in Tirzah   *1Ki 16:9*
Zimri hath *c.* and hath also slain   *1Ki 16:16*
Jehoshaphat the son of Nimshi *c.*   *2Ki 9:14*
I *c.* against my master, and slew   *2Ki 10:9*
And Shallum the son of Jabesh *c.*   *2Ki 15:10*
c. against him, and smote him in   *2Ki 15:25*
And the servants of Amon *c.*   *2Ki 21:23*
that had *c.* against king Amon   *2Ki 21:24*
And they *c.* against him   *2Ch 24:21*
his own servants *c.* against him for   *2Ch 24:25*
And these are they that *c.* against   *2Ch 24:26*
And his servants *c.* against him   *2Ch 33:24*
slew all them that had *c.* against   *2Ch 33:25*
c. all of them together to come   *Ne 4:8*
Amos hath *c.* against thee in   *Am 7:10*
the Jews *c.* to (A)(B)   *Ac 9:23*

CONSTABLES

magistrates and *c.* (P)   *Ac 16:35; 16:38*

CONSTANT

he be *c.* to do my commandments   *1Ch 28:7*

CONSTANTLY

man that heareth speaketh *c.*   *Pr 21:28*
she *c.* affirmed that it was even   *Ac 12:15*
things I will that thou affirm *c.*   *Tit 3:8*

CONSTELLATIONS

sun, moon, c. (A)(R)   2Ki 35:5
stars of heaven and the c.   Isa 13:10
thereof

CONSTERNATION

by reason of c. (S)   Job 41:25
and with c. (S)   Eze 4:16; 12:19

CONSTITUTED

divinely c. (B)   Ro 13:1
c. the body (B)   1Co 12:24

CONSTRAIN

c. them to come into (E)   M't 14:23
they c. you to be circumcised   Ga 6:12
try to compel you (A)   Ga 6:12
force circumcision on you   Ga 6:12
(B)(N)
urging you to be circumcised   Ga 6:12
(P)

CONSTRAINED

c. him (E)   1Sa 28:23
she c. him to eat bread. And   2Ki 4:8
so
insisted on his eating a meal   2Ki 4:8
(A)
persuaded him to stay for   2Ki 4:8
lunch (B)
urged him to eat some food   2Ki 4:8
(R)
Jesus c. his disciples to get   M't 14:22
into a
directed his disciples (A)   M't 14:22
urged the disciples to   M't 14:22
embark (B)
make disciples embark (N)   M't 14:22
insisted disciples get aboard   M't 14:22
(P)
made disciples get into boat   M't 14:22
(R)
straightway he c. his disciples   M'k 6:45
to
how am I c. (S)   Lu 12:50
But they c. him, saying,   Lu 24:29
Abide
they urged and insisted   Lu 24:29
(A)(B)
they pressed him (N)   Lu 24:29
stopped him with these   Lu 24:29
words (P)
And she c. us   Ac 16:15
earnestly entreated, induced   Ac 16:15
us (A)
she begged us (B)   Ac 16:15
she besought us (E)   Ac 16:15
she insisted on our going   Ac 16:15
(N)(P)
she prevailed upon us (R)   Ac 16:15
I was c. to appeal unto   Ac 28:19
Cæsar
I was forced to appeal to   Ac 28:19
(A)(B)(P)
I had no option but to   Ac 28:19
appeal (N)
I was compelled to appeal   Ac 28:19
to (R)

CONSTRAINETH

the spirit within me c. me   Job 32:18
the love of Christ c. us   2Co 5:14
controls, urges, and impels   2Co 5:14
us (A)(B)(R)
love leaves us no choice (N)   2Co 5:14
very spring of our action is   2Co 5:14
love (P)

CONSTRAINT

fostered lack of c. (B)   2Ch 28:19
thereof, not by c. but   1Pe 5:2
willingly

CONSTRUCTED

c. or invented (A)   Ac 17:29

CONSTRUCTION

explain the c. of temple (B)   Eze 43:11

CONSTRUCTIVE

all things are not c. (A)   1Co 10:23
for c. spiritual progress   1Co 14:3
(A)(B)
everything be c. (B)   1Co 14:26
for c. purposes (B)   2Co 13:10

CONSULT

They only c. to cast him   Ps 62:4
down
c. together (A)(B)(R)   Ps 71:10
c. together against   Ps 83:3
(A)(B)(E)(R)
c. mediums, wizards   Isa 8:19
(A)(B)(R)

CONSULTATION

Philistines after c. (B)   1Ch 12:19
hold a c. (A)   M't 12:14; M'k 3:6
after a c. they (A)(P)   M't 27:7
after c. together they (P)   M't 28:12
priests held a c. with the   M'k 15:1
elders

CONSULTED

Abner c. with elders (B)   2Sa 3:17
c. the word of God (A)(B)   2Sa 16:23
he c. with Joab (B)   1Ki 1:7
all the earth c. Solomon   1Ki 10:24
(S)
Rehoboam c. with the old   1Ki 12:6
men
and c. with the young men   1Ki 12:8
that
c. a medium (R)   1Ch 10:13
And David c. with the   1Ch 13:1
captains of
when he had c. with the   2Ch 20:21
people
Then I c. with myself, and I   Ne 5:7
and c. against thy hidden ones   Ps 83:3
have c. together with one   Ps 83:5
consent
he c. with images, he   Eze 21:21
looked in
have c. together to establish a   Da 6:7
now what Balak, king of   Mic 6:5
Moab c.
Thou hast c. shame to thy   Hab 2:10
house
c. that they might take Jesus   M't 26:4
they c. together (A)   M't 28:12
the chief priests c. that they   Joh 12:10
they c. together (B)   Ac 4:15
c. with the men (A)   Ac 25:12

CONSULTER

or a c. with familiar spirits   De 18:11
a medium (A)(B)(R)   De 18:11

CONSULTETH

c. whether he be able with   Lu 14:31
ten

CONSULTING

c. a medium (A)   1Ch 10:13
without c. any (N)(P)   Ga 1:16

CONSUME

will you c. the righteous   Ge 18:23;
(E)   18:24
and the famine shall c. the   Ge 41:30
land
shall exhaust the land   Ge 41:30
(A)(B)
Benjamin shall c. as a wolf   Ge 49:27
(S)
that I may c. them: and I   Ex 32:10
will
c. them from the face of the   Ex 32:12
earth
people: lest I c. thee in the   Ex 33:3
way
destroy you in the way   Ex 33:3
(A)(B)
in a moment, and c. thee   Ex 33:5
that shall c. the eyes, and   Le 26:16
cause
that destroys the eye (B)   Le 26:16
waste the eyes (A)(R)   Le 26:16
that I may c. them in a   Nu 16:21
moment

destroy them in a moment   Nu 16:21
(B)
that I may c. them as in a   Nu 16:45
moment
this great fire will c. us: if we   De 5:25
And thou shalt c. all the   De 7:16
people
completely annihilate nations   De 7:16
(B)
destroy all the peoples (R)   De 7:16
thou mayest not c. them at   De 7:22
once
for the locust shall c. it   De 28:38
worms shall devour grapes   De 28:38
(B)
of thy land shall the locust   De 28:42
c.
and shall c. the earth with   De 32:22
her
turn and do you hurt, and   Jos 24:20
c. you
destroy you (B)   Jos 24:20
to c. thine eyes, and to   1Sa 2:33
grieve thine
fire did c. (B)   2Sa 22:9
heaven, and c. thee and   2Ki 1:10;
thy fifty   1:12
thou didst not utterly c. them   Ne 9:31
did not forsake altogether   Ne 9:31
(B)(R)
did not make a full end of   Ne 9:31
(E)
to c. them, and to destroy   Es 9:24
them
shall c. the tabernacles of   Job 15:34
bribery
a fire not blown shall c.   Job 20:26
him; it
shall devour him   Job 20:26
(A)(E)(R)
and heat c. the snow waters   Job 24:19
fire c. them (A)(R)   Ps 21:9
c.; into smoke shall they c.   Ps 37:20
away
thou makest his beauty to c.   Ps 39:11
away
their beauty shall c. in the   Ps 49:14
grave
C. them in wrath, c. them   Ps 59:13
their days did he c. in vanity   Ps 78:33
and it shall also c. the beard   Isa 7:20
shall c. them (A)(B)(R)   Isa 10:17;
   33:11
shall c. the glory of his   Isa 10:18
forest
down, and c. the branches   Isa 27:10
thereof
surely c. them, saith the Lord   Jer 8:13
I will c. them by the sword   Jer 14:12
shall c. the palaces of   Jer 49:27
Ben-hadad
and c. away for their   Eze 4:17
iniquity
hailstones in my fury to c.   Eze 13:13
it
them in the wilderness, to   Eze 20:13
c. them
to c. because of the   Eze 21:28
glittering
will c. they filthiness out of   Eze 22:15
thee
kindle the fire, c. the flesh   Eze 24:10
has c. you (A)(R)   Eze 28:18
desolate, they are given us   Eze 35:12
to c.
and c. all these kingdoms   Da 2:44
completely destroy (B)   Da 2:44
bring them to an end (R)   Da 2:44
c. and to destroy it unto the   Da 7:26
end
and shall c. his branches   Ho 11:6
fire c. thy bars (A)(B)   Na 3:13
fire shall c. you (B)   Na 3:15
c. all things from off the land   Zep 1:2
I will c. man and beast   Zep 1:3
I will c. the fowls of heaven   Zep 1:3
and shall c. it with the timber   Zec 5:4
c. your cedars (B)   Zec 11:1
Their flesh shall c. away   Zec 14:12
eyes shall c. away in their   Zec 14:12
holes
and their tongue shall c.   Zec 14:12
away in
tongues decay away (A)(B)   Zec 14:12
tongue rot in mouths (R)   Zec 14:12
moth, rust, worm c.   M't 6:19
(A)(E)(R)
down from heaven, and c.   Lu 9:54
them

the Lord shall *c.* with the spirit   2Th 2:8

shall slay with the breath (A)(E)(R)   2Th 2:8

will remove with the breath (B)   2Th 2:8

will destroy with the breath (N)   2Th 2:8

truth spells his doom (P)   2Th 2:8

c. those in opposition (A)(N)(P)(R)   Heb 10:27

that ye may *c.* it upon your lusts   Jas 4:3

spend it in sensual pleasures (A)   Jas 4:3

spend it on dissolute pleasures (B)(E)(P)   Jas 4:3

to satisfy your own desires (P)   Jas 4:3

spend it on your passions (R)   Jas 4:3

CONSUMED

be *c.* in iniquity of the city   Ge 19:15

swept away in punishment (B)   Ge 19:15; 19:17

escape to mountain, lest thou be *c.*   Ge 19:17

in the day the drought *c.* me   Ge 31:40

the bush burned, and was not *c.*   Ex 3:2

sentest wrath, which *c.* them as stubble   Ex 15:7

if the corn or the field be *c.* therewith   Ex 22:6

c. upon altar the burnt-offering   Le 9:24

and *c.* them (B)   Nu 10:2; 26:10

c. them in uttermost parts of camp   Nu 11:1

not be as one of whom flesh is half *c.*   Nu 12:12

depart lest ye be *c.* in all their sins   Nu 16:26

there came out fire and *c.* 250 men   Nu 16:35

fire gone out, it hath *c.* Ar of Moab   Nu 21:28

that I *c.* not the children of Israel   Nu 25:11

till generation that had done evil was *c.*   Nu 32:13

when men of war were *c.*   De 2:16

rose fire out of rock and *c.* flesh   J'g 6:21

man that *c.* us, and devised against us   J'g 21:5

then fire of Lord fell and *c.* sacrifice, licked up water   1Ki 18:38; 2Ch 7:1

fire *c.* him and his fifty   2Ki 1:10; 1:12

whom children of Israel *c.* not   2Ch 8:8

gates thereof are *c.* with fire   Ne 2:3; 2:13

fire of God hath *c.* sheep and servants   Job 1:16

by breath of his nostrils are they *c.*   Job 4:9

snow and ice *c.* out of their place   Job 6:17

as the cloud is *c.* and vanisheth away   Job 7:9

my spirit is *c.* (E)   Job 17:1

my reins be *c.* within me   Job 19:27

his flesh is *c.* away   Job 33:12

Mine eye is *c.* because of grief   Ps 6:7; 31:9

let them be confounded and *c.* that   Ps 71:13

they are utterly *c.* with terrors   Ps 73:19

fire *c.* their young men   Ps 78:63

we are *c.* by thine anger and wrath   Ps 90:7

my days are *c.* like smoke   Ps 102:3

let sinners be *c.* out of the earth   Ps 104:35

they had almost *c.* me upon earth   Ps 119:87

my zeal hath *c.* me, because enemies   Ps 119:139

when thy flesh and body are *c.*   Pr 5:11

oppressors are *c.* out of land   Isa 16:4

scorner is *c.* and all that watch iniquity   Isa 29:20

c. us, because of our iniquities   Isa 64:7

c. them, but they refused correction   Jer 5:3

the lead is *c.* of the fire   Jer 6:29

the beasts are *c.* and the birds   Jer 12:4

that my days should be *c.* with shame   Jer 20:18

till all roll was *c.* in fire on hearth   Jer 36:23

been *c.* by sword and famine   Jer 44:18

those I swaddled hath mine enemy *c.*   La 2:22

it is Lord's mercies we are not *c.*   La 3:22

c. her foundations (A)(B)(R)   La 4:11

to be *c.* (B)   Eze 16:20

her rods broken, fire *c.* them   Eze 19:12; 22:31

c. fruit (B)(R)   Eze 19:14

on coals, that scum of it may be *c.*   Eze 24:11

I have *c.* them in mine anger   Eze 43:8

c. like stubble (A)(B)(E)(R)   Na 1:10

fire *c.* thy bars (B)   Na 3:13

c. by fire (A)(R)   Zep 1:18; 3:8

therefore sons of Jacob are not *c.*   Mal 3:6

take heed ye be not *c.* one of another   Ga 5:15

heaven and *c.* them (A)(B)(N)(P)(R)   Re 20:9

SHALL BE CONSUMED

in this wilderness *shall be c.*   Nu 14:35

shall die, *shall* we *be c.* with dying   Nu 17:13

shall be c. both ye and your kin   1Sa 12:25

they that forsake Lord *shall be c.*   Isa 1:28

eating swine's flesh, *shall be c.* together   Isa 66:17

by famine *shall* prophets *be c.*   Jer 14:15

they *shall be c.* by sword   Jer 16:4; 44:12, 27

with famine *shall they be c.*   Eze 5:12

ye *shall be c.* in the midst thereof   Eze 13:14

they *shall be* no more *c.* with hunger   Eze 34:29

leaf not fade, nor *shall* fruit *be c.*   Eze 47:12

land which his hand *shall be c.*   Da 11:16

CONSUMED, TILL, UNTIL

destroy, *until* they were *c.*   De 2:15; Jos 5:6

pestilence cleave *until* he have *c.* thee   De 28:21

end of slaying *till* they were *c.*   Jos 10:20

fight against them *until* they were *c.*   1Sa 15:18

turned not again *until*   2Sa 22:38; Ps 18:37

I *c.* them   Ps 18:37

shalt push Syrians *until c.* them   1Ki 22:11; 2Ki 13:17, 19; 2Ch 18:10

be angry *till* thou hadst *c.* us   Ezr 9:14

till I have *c.* them   Ps 9:16; 24:10; 27:8; 49:37

CONSUMES

consumes (B)   2Sa 11:25; Isa 5:24; La 2:3; Joe 2:3

c. both ends (A)(R)   Eze 15:4

c. their enemies (A)(B)(N)(P)(R)   Re 11:5

CONSUMETH

he, as a rotten thing, *c.* as   Job 13:28

the remnant of them the fire *c.*   Job 22:20

it is a fire that *c.* to destruction   Job 31:12

flame *c.* the chaff, so their root   Isa 5:24

CONSUMING

c. fire on the mountain (B)   Ex 24:17

the Lord thy God is a *c.* fire   De 4:24

as a *c.* fire he shall destroy them   De 9:3

c. all around (R)   La 2:3

his tongue is a *c.* fire (A)(B)   Isa 30:27

For our God is a *c.* fire   Heb 12:29

CONSUMMATED

all human history *c.* in Christ (P)   Eph 1:10

CONSUMMATION

until the *c.* and that determined   Da 9:27

the full determined end (A)(B)   Da 9:27

even until the full end (E)   Da 9:27

until the decreed end (R)   Da 9:27

CONSUMPTION

terror, *c.* and the burning ague   Le 26:16

tuberculosis (B)   Le 26:16; De 28:22

The Lord shall smite thee with a *c.*   De 28:22

the *c.* decreed shall overflow with   Isa 10:22

fully completed destruction (A)   Isa 10:22

Annihilation is determined (B)   Isa 10:22

destruction is determined (E)(R)   Isa 10:22

God of hosts shall make a *c.*   Isa 10:23

make a full end (A)(E)(R)   Isa 10:23

a full destruction (B)   Isa 10:23

a *c.* even determined upon   Isa 28:22

decree a destruction (A)(E)(R)   Isa 28:22

determined annihilation (B)   Isa 28:22

CONTACT

c. nothing holy (B)   Le 12:4

had *c.* with them (B)   1Sa 25:15

go *c.* that chariot (B)   Ac 8:29

CONTAIN

heaven of heavens cannot *c.* thee   1Ki 8:27

great as would *c.* two measures of   1Ki 18:32

heaven of heavens cannot *c.* him   2Ch 2:6

heaven of heavens cannot *c.* thee   2Ch 6:18

that the bath may *c.* the tenth   Eze 45:11

even the world itself could not *c.*   Joh 21:25

if they cannot *c.* let them marry   1Co 7:9

have not self-control (A)(R)   1Co 7:9

cannot restrain their passions (B)   1Co 7:9

have not continency (E)   1Co 7:9

cannot control themselves (N)   1Co 7:9

have not the gift of the self-control (P)   1Co 7:9

CONTAINED

of lilies: it *c.* two thousand baths   1Ki 7:26

of brass: one laver *c.* forty baths   1Ki 7:38

by nature the things *c.* in the law   Ro 2:14

of commandments *c.* in ordinances   Eph 2:15

also it is *c.* in the scripture   1Pe 2:6

CONTAINERS

in the *c.* (A)(B)   Ex 7:19

CONTAINETH

and had in derision; it *c.* much   Eze 23:32

CONTAINING

c. terms and conditions   *Jer 32:11*
(A)(B)(R)
of the Jews, c. two or three   *Joh 2:6*
firkins

CONTAMINATED

abstain from what is c.   *Ac 15:20*
(B)(P)
becomes c. (B)   *1Co 8:7;*
     Tit 1:15; Heb 12:15
c. with sensuality (N)   *Jude 23*
not c. with women (B)   *Re 14:4*

CONTAMINATES

everything that c. (A)   *2Co 7:1*

CONTAMINATING

c. and depraving (A)   *Jas 3:6*

CONTEMN

Wherefore doth the wicked   *Ps 10:13*
c. God
wicked condemn God (A)   *Ps 10:13*
wicked spurn God (B)   *Ps 10:13*
wicked renounce God (R)   *Ps 10:13*
what if the sword c. even   *Eze 21:13*
the rod

CONTEMNED

In whose eyes a vile person is   *Ps 15:4*
c.
vile person is despised   *Ps 15:4*
(A)(E)(R)
reprobate person is disdained   *Ps 15:4*
(B)
c. the council of the most   *Ps 107:11*
High
spurned the counsel of   *Ps 107:11*
(A)(R)
scorned the counsel of (B)   *Ps 107:11*
for love, it would utterly be c.   *Ca 8:7*
utterly scorned and despised   *Ca 8:7*
(A)(R)
would be scornfully refused   *Ca 8:7*
(B)
and the glory of Moab shall   *Isa 16:14*
be c.
be brought into contempt   *Isa 16:14*
(A)(B)(E)(R)

CONTEMNETH

it c. the rod of my son, as   *Eze 21:10*
views with contempt (A)   *Eze 21:10*
despised rod of my son   *Eze 21:10*
(B)(R)   *21:13*

CONTEMPT

looked with c. on (R)   *Ge 16:4; 16:5*
regarded with c. (B)   *Nu 15:31*
treated offering with c. (R)   *1Sa 2:17*
return c. upon their heads (B)   *Ne 4:4*
look with c. upon (S)   *Es 1:17*
shall there arise too much c.   *Es 1:18*
c. for misfortune   *Job 12:5*
(A)(B)(E)(R)
He poureth c. upon princes   *Job 12:21;*
     Ps 107:40
or did the c. of families   *Job 31:34*
terrify me
Remove from me reproach   *Ps 119:22*
and c.
for we are exceedingly filled   *Ps 123:3*
with c.
at ease, and with the c. of   *Ps 123:4*
the proud
wicked cometh then cometh   *Pr 18:3*
also c.
shown c. for the Holy One   *Isa 1:4*
(B)
brought to c.   *Isa 16:14*
(A)(B)(E)(R)
to bring into c. all the   *Isa 23:9*
honourable
views with c. (A)   *Eze 21:10*
with all c. (A)(B)(R)   *Eze 25:6; 36:5*
some to shame and   *Da 12:2*
everlasting c.
treated with c. (S)   *M'k 9:12; Lu 23:11*
treated him with c. (A)   *Lu 22:63*
as a speaker he is beneath   *2Co 10:10*
c. (N)(P)

---

showed c. for Moses (P)   *Heb 10:28*
he considered the c.   *Heb 11:26*
(A)(B)(N)(P)(R)
bearing the c. (A)   *Heb 13:13*

CONTEMPTIBLE

I will yet be more c. (S)   *2Sa 6:22*
base, c. fellow (A)   *2Sa 20:1*
contemptuous and c. person   *Da 11:21*
(A)(R)
ye say. The table of the Lord   *Mal 1:7*
is c.
the fruit thereof, even his   *Mal 1:12*
meat, is
have I also made you c. and   *Mal 2:9*
base
you c. slave B   *M't 18:32*
low born, c. (B)(N)   *1Co 1:28*
is weak, and his speech c.   *2Co 10:10*

CONTEMPTUOUS

c. and contemptible person   *Da 11:21*
(A)(R)

CONTEMPTUOUSLY

and c. against the righteous   *Ps 31:18*
others said c. (N)   *Ac 2:13*

CONTEND

if men c. (E)   *Ex 21:18*
if men c. with (A)   *Ex 21:22*
do not c. with them (E)(R)   *De 2:5*
neither c. with them in battle   *De 2:9*
possess it, and c. with him in   *De 2:24*
battle
do not c. for Baal   *J'g 6:31*
(A)(E)(R)
they did c. with him (S)   *J'g 8:1*
If he will c. with him, he   *Job 9:3*
cannot
his person? will ye c. for   *Job 13:8*
God
who will c. with me   *Job 13:19*
(E)(R)
c. with me (B)(E)(R)   *Job 23:6*
c. with me (R)   *Job 33:13;*
     Ps 35:1; Pr 3:30; Ho 4:4
c. with those who c. (B)(R)   *Ps 35:1*
such as keep the law c. with   *Pr 28:4*
them
neither may he c. with him   *Ec 6:10*
I will c. with him that   *Isa 49:25*
contendeth
who will c. with me? let us   *Isa 50:8*
stand
I will not c. for ever   *Isa 57:16*
how canst thou c. with horses   *Jer 12:5*
the voice of them that c.   *Jer 18:19*
with me
C. with your mother (S)   *Ho 2:2*
the Lord God called to c. by   *Am 7:4*
fire
c. thou before the mountains   *Mic 6:1*
he will c. with Israel (S)   *Mic 6:2*
ye should earnestly c. for the   *Jude 3*
faith

CONTENDED

they c. with (E)   *Ge 26:20*
Jacob c. with Laban (S)   *Ge 31:36*
the people c. with Moses (A)   *Ex 17:2*
the people c. with Moses (R)   *Nu 20:3*
Israel c. (A)(B)(R)   *Nu 20:13; 26:9*
has c. (A)   *De 33:8; Ps 35:1; Pr 3:30*
Then c. I with the rulers   *Ne 13:11*
Then I c. with the nobles of   *Ne 13:17*
Judah
I c. with them, and cursed   *Ne 13:25*
them
when they c. with me   *Job 31:13*
he c. with her (B)(E)(R)   *Isa 27:8*
them, even them that c.   *Isa 41:12*
with thee
of the circumcision c. with   *Ac 11:2*
him
part arose and c. sharply (S)   *Ac 23:9*

CONTENDEST

me wherefore thou c. with   *Job 10:2*
me

CONTENDETH

Shall he that c. with the   *Job 40:2*
Almighty
If a wise man c. with a   *Pr 29:9*
foolish
with him that c. with thee   *Isa 49:25*

CONTENDING

c. with at the waters (B)   *De 33:8*
when c. with the devil he   *Jude 9*
disputed

CONTENT

And his brethren were c.   *Ge 37:27*
And Moses was c. to dwell   *Ex 2:21*
with
Moses heard that, he was c.   *Le 10:20*
would to God we had been c.   *Jos 7:7*
And the Levite was c. to   *J'g 17:11*
dwell
Be c. I pray thee, and tarry   *J'g 19:6*
all
Naaman said, Be c. take two   *2Ki 5:23*
one said, Be c. I pray thee,   *2Ki 6:3*
and go
Now therefore be c. look   *Job 6:28*
upon
neither will he rest c. though   *Pr 6:35*
thou
Pilate, willing to c. the   *M'k 15:15*
and be c. with your wages   *Lu 3:14*
state I am, therewith to be   *Ph'p 4:11*
c.
raiment let us be therewith c.   *1Ti 6:8*
be c. with such things as ye   *Heb 13:5*
have
with malicious words: and not   *3Jo 10*
c.

CONTENTION

my eye gazes on their c. (B)   *Job 17:2*
contention (B)   *Ps 80:2;*
     Pr 22:10; 26:20
by pride cometh c.: but with   *Pr 13:10*
man stirs up c. (R)   *Pr 15:18*
leave off c. before it be   *Pr 17:14*
meddled
stop c. before it (A)(E)   *Pr 17:14*
A fool's lips enter into c. and   *Pr 18:6*
his
out the scorner, and c. shall   *Pr 22:10*
go out
fast for strife and c. (B)(E)   *Isa 58:4*
a man of c. to the whole   *Jer 15:10*
earth
there are that raise up strife   *Hab 1:3*
And the c. was so sharp   *Ac 15:39*
between
a sharp disagreement (A)   *Ac 15:39*
Irritation came to such a   *Ac 15:39*
pass (A)
dispute was so sharp (N)   *Ac 15:39*
sharp clash of opinion (P)   *Ac 15:39*
The one preach Christ of c.   *Ph'p 1:16*
the gospel of God with much   *1Th 2:2*
c.
perpetual c. (A)(B)   *1Ti 6:5*

CONTENTIONS

stirreth up c. (A)(B)   *Pr 10:2*
The lot causeth c. to cease   *Pr 18:18*
and their c. are like the bars   *Pr 18:19*
of a
the c. of a wife are a   *Pr 19:13*
continual
who hath c.? who hath   *Pr 23:29*
babbling
that there are c. among you   *1Co 1:11*
genealogies, and c. and   *Tit 3:9*
strivings

CONTENTIOUS

with a c. and an angry   *Pr 21:19*
woman
a c. woman (B)(E)(R)   *Pr 25:24*
so is a c. man to kindle   *Pr 26:21*
strife
rainy day and a c. woman   *Pr 27:15*
are alike
But unto them that are c.   *Ro 2:8*
self-seeking, and self-willed   *Ro 2:8*
(A)

like to be different (B)   *Ro 2:8*
that are factious (E)(R)   *Ro 2:8*
governed by selfish ambition (N)   *Ro 2:8*
rebel against God's plan of   *Ro 2:8*
life (P)
But if any man seem to be   *1Co 11:16*
c.

CONTENTIOUSNESS

nothing through c. (A)   *Ph'p 2:3*

CONTENTMENT

godliness with c. is great gain   *1Ti 6:6*

CONTINENCY

have not c. (E)   *1Co 7:9*

CONTINUAL

this shall be a c.   *Ex 29:42*
burnt-offering
the c. bread shall be thereon   *Nu 4:7*
I build an house for c.   *2Ch 2:4*
shew-bread
a merry heart hath a c. feast   *Pr 15:15*
who smote people with a c.   *Isa 14:6*
stroke
the going up c. weeping shall   *Isa 48:5*
go up
a c. diet given him   *Jer 52:34;*
  2Ki 25:30
sever out men of c.   *Eze 39:14*
employment
for the c. task of (S)   *Eze 39:14*
lest by her c. coming she   *Lu 18:5*
weary me
that I have c. sorrow in my   *Ro 9:2*
heart
insults, c. wrangling (P)   *1Ti 6:5*

CONTINUALLY

every imagination of heart evil   *Ge 6:5*
c.
upon his heart before Lord   *Ex 28:30*
c.
two lambs, day by day c.   *Ex 29:38*
oil olive to cause lamps burn   *Le 24:2*
c.
Saul became David's enemy   *1Sa 18:29*
c.
shalt eat bread at my table c.   *2Sa 9:7*
Jehoiachin eat bread, c.   *2Ki 25:29;*
  Jer 52:33
seek Lord, seek his face c.   *1Ch 16:11*
war between Jeroboam and   *2Ch 12:15*
Rehoboam c.
c. revolted (B)   *Ezr 4:15*
sanctified his sons, thus did   *Job 1:5*
Job c.
praise be c. in my mouth   *Ps 34:1;*
  71:6
say c. Lord be magnified   *Ps 35:27;*
  40:16; 70:4
my sorrow is c. before me   *Ps 38:17*
lovingkindness and truth c.   *Ps 40:11*
preserve
they c. say to me, Where is   *Ps 42:3*
thy God
my confusion is c. before me   *Ps 44:15*
burnt offerings been c. before   *Ps 50:8*
me
goodness of God endureth c.   *Ps 52:1*
my habitation, whereunto I   *Ps 71:3*
may c. resort
been holden up, my praise   *Ps 71:6*
shall be c.
hope c. and praise thee more   *Ps 71:14*
and more
c. with thee, thou hast holden   *Ps 73:23*
me
tumult of those that rise up   *Ps 74:23*
increaseth c.
let them be before Lord c.   *Ps 109:15*
to cut off
so shall I keep thy law c.   *Ps 119:44*
for ever
my soul is c. in my hand,   *Ps 119:109*
yet do I
I will have respect to thy   *Ps 119:117*
statutes c.
c. are they gathered together   *Ps 140:2*
for war
deviseth mischief c. he soweth   *Pr 6:14*
discord

bind them c. on thy heart,   *Pr 6:21*
and tie them
circles about c. (A)(E)   *Ec 1:6*
stand c. upon watch-tower in   *Isa 21:8*
day-time
hast feared c. every day   *Isa 51:13*
my name c. every day is   *Isa 52:5*
blasphemed
Lord shall guide thee c. and   *Isa 58:11*
satisfy
therefore thy gates shall be   *Isa 60:11*
open c.
people that provoketh me to   *Isa 65:3*
anger c.
before me c. is grief and   *Jer 6:7*
wounds
a meat-offering c. to the   *Eze 46:14*
Lord
thy God whom thou servest c.   *Da 6:16;*
  6:20
they have committed   *Ho 4:18*
whoredom c.
keep mercy, and wait on thy   *Ho 12:6*
God c.
so shall all the heathen drink c.   *Ob 16*
hath not thy wickedness   *Na 3:19*
passed c.
shall they not spare c. to slay   *Hab 1:17*
nations
c. in the temple, praising   *Lu 24:53*
God
we will give ourselves c. to   *Ac 6:4*
prayer
soldier that waited on   *Ac 10:7*
Cornelius c.
attending c. upon this very   *Ro 13:6*
thing
like Son of God, abideth a   *Heb 7:3*
priest c.
sacrifices offered year by   *Heb 10:1*
year c.
by him offer sacrifice of   *Heb 13:15*
praise c.

CONTINUANCE

to assure c. (B)   *Ge 45:7*
great plagues, and of long c.   *De 28:59*
and sore sicknesses, and of   *De 28:59*
long c.
which in c. were fashioned   *Ps 139:16*
in those is c., and we shall be   *Isa 64:5*
by patient c. in well doing seek   *Ro 2:7*
patient persistence in (A)   *Ro 2:7*
with insistent good behavior   *Ro 2:7*
(B)
by patience in well-doing   *Ro 2:7*
(E)(R)
steady persistence in   *Ro 2:7*
well-doing (N)
patiently doing good (P)   *Ro 2:7*

CONTINUE

if he c. a day or two, he   *Ex 21:21*
shall not
she shall then c. in the blood   *Le 12:4*
of
she shall c. in the blood of   *Le 12:5*
her
c. following the Lord your   *1Sa 12:14*
God
now thy kingdom shall not   *1Sa 13:14*
it may c. for ever before   *2Sa 7:29*
thee
That the Lord may c. his   *1Ki 2:4*
word
neither shall his substance   *Job 15:29*
c.
doth not mine eye c. in their   *Job 17:2*
c. thy lovingkindness unto   *Ps 36:10*
them
is, that their houses shall c.   *Ps 49:11*
children of thy servants   *Ps 102:28*
shall c.
They c. this day according   *Ps 119:91*
to
that c. until night, till wine   *Isa 5:11*
that they may c. many days   *Jer 32:14*
shall prosper and c. (S)   *Da 8:24*
shall c. more years than the   *Da 11:8*
king
c. many days (B)   *Ho 3:4*
they c. with me now three   *M't 15:32*
days
If ye c. in my word, then   *Joh 8:31*
are ye
c. in darkness (A)   *Joh 12:46*

I loved you: c. ye in my love   *Joh 15:9*
them to c. in the grace of   *Ac 13:43*
God
exhorting them to c. in the   *Ac 14:22*
faith
I c. unto this day, witnessing   *Ac 26:22*
Shall we c. in sin, that grace   *Ro 6:1*
if thou c. in his goodness   *Ro 11:22*
of the gospel might c. with   *Ga 2:5*
you
I shall abide and c. with you   *Ph'p 1:25*
all
If ye c. in the faith grounded   *Col 1:23*
C. in prayer, and watch in the   *Col 4:2*
if they c. in faith and charity   *1Ti 2:15*
c. in them: for in doing this   *1Ti 4:16*
c. thou in the things which   *2Ti 3:14*
suffered to c. by reason of   *Heb 7:23*
death
Let brotherly love c.   *Heb 13:1*
and c. there a year, and buy   *Jas 4:13*
all things c. as they were   *2Pe 3:4*
from
remain in you, ye also shall   *1Jo 2:24*
c.
him to c. forty and two   *Re 13:5*
months
cometh, he must c. a short   *Re 17:10*
space

CONTINUED

and they c. a season in ward   *Ge 40:4*
c. in custody (A)(R)   *Ge 40:4*
Asher c. on the seashore   *J'g 5:17*
country of Moab, and c. there   *Ru 1:2*
hath c. even from the morning   *Ru 2:7*
she c. praying before the   *1Sa 1:12*
Lord
ark of the Lord c. in the   *2Sa 6:11*
house
they c. three years without   *1Ki 22:1*
war
this c. until the burnt   *2Ch 29:28*
offering
also I c. in the work of this   *Ne 5:16*
wall
Moreover Job c. his parable,   *Job 27:1;*
and   *29:1*
shall be c. as long as the sun   *Ps 72:17*
And Daniel c. even unto the   *Da 1:21*
it c. and prospered (S)   *Da 8:12*
and c. all night in prayer to   *Lu 6:12*
God
c. with me in my   *Lu 22:28*
temptations
they c. there not many days   *Joh 2:12*
So when they c. asking him   *Joh 8:7*
and there c. with his   *Joh 11:54*
disciples
all c. with one accord in   *Ac 1:14*
prayer
they c. steadfastly in the   *Ac 2:42*
apostles
he c. with Philip, and   *Ac 8:13*
wondered
But Peter c. knocking, and   *Ac 12:16*
Paul also and Barnabas c. in   *Ac 15:35*
c. there a year and six   *Ac 18:11*
months
c. by the space of two years   *Ac 19:10*
and c. his speech until   *Ac 20:7*
midnight
c. fasting, having taken   *Ac 27:33*
nothing
they c. not in my covenant   *Heb 8:9*
would no doubt have c. with   *1Jo 2:19*
us

CONTINUETH

fleeth also as a shadow, and   *Job 14:2*
c. not
every one that c. not in all   *Gal 3:10*
things
c. in supplications and prayers   *1Ti 5:5*
this man, because he c. ever   *Heb 7:24*
law of liberty, and c. therein   *Jas 1:25*

CONTINUING

a c. whirlwind: it shall fall   *Jer 30:23*
And they, c. daily with one   *Ac 2:46*
accord
tribulations; c. instant in   *Ro 12:12*
prayer
here have we no c. city   *Heb 13:14*

CONTINUOUSLY

cursed *c.* as he came (S)   *2Sa 16:5*

CONTRADICT

c. nor withstand (S)   *Lu 21:15*
who *c.* and oppose (A)   *Tit 1:9*

CONTRADICTING

were spoken by Paul, *c.* and   *Ac 13:45*
c. people (A)(B)   *Ro 10:21*

CONTRADICTION

without all *c.* the less is blessed   *Heb 7:7*
c. of sinners against himself   *Heb 12:3*

CONTRADICTIONS

c. of so-called knowledge (A)(B)(N)   *1Ti 6:20*
godless chatter and *c.* (R)   *1Ti 6:20*

CONTRADICTORY

c. notions known as knowledge (P)   *1Ti 6:20*

CONTRARINESS

willful *c.* breaks (A)   *Pr 15:4*

CONTRARIWISE

that *c.* ye ought rather to forgive   *2Co 2:7*
But *c.* when they saw that the   *Ga 2:7*
railing for railing: but *c.* blessing   *1Pe 3:9*

CONTRARY

obstinate and *c.* (A)   *Nu 22:32*
if ye walk *c.* unto me and   *Le 26:21; 26:23, 27. 40*
Then will I also walk *c.* unto you   *Le 26:24; 26:28, 41*
though it was turned to the *c.*   *Es 9:1*
willful and *c.* talk (A)   *Pr 4:24*
nothing *c.* to truth (A)(B)(R)   *Pr 8:8*
c. and devious in his ways (A)   *Pr 14:2*
the *c.* tongue will (A)   *Pr 17:20*
the *c.* is in thee from other women   *Eze 16:34*
unto thee, therefore thou art *c.*   *Eze 16:34*
contrast, different (A)(B)(E)(R)   *Eze 16:34*
for the wind was *c.*   *M't 14:24*
wind was against them (A)(R)   *M't 14:24*
battling with a head-wind (N)   *M't 14:24*
the wind was dead against them (P)   *M't 14:24*
for the wind was *c.* unto them   *M'k 6:48*
these all do *c.* to the decrees of   *Ac 17:7*
men to worship God *c.* to the law   *Ac 18:13*
in violation of the law (A)   *Ac 18:13*
in an unlawful way (B)   *Ac 18:13*
in ways that are against the law (N)   *Ac 18:13*
commandest me to be smitten *c.* to   *Ac 23:3*
in defiance of the law (A)(N)   *Ac 23:3*
many things *c.* to the name of   *Ac 26:9*
Cyprus, because the winds were *c.*   *Ac 27:4*
c. people (A)(R)(S)   *Ro 10:21*
graffed *c.* to nature into a good   *Ro 11:24*
c. to the doctrine which ye have   *Ro 16:17*
on the *c.* (S) *2Co 2:7; Ga 2:7; 1Pe 3:9*
these are *c.* the one to the other   *Ga 5:17*
antagonistic to each other   *Ga 5:17*
in opposition to each other (B)(R)   *Ga 5:17*

in conflict with one another (N)(P)   *Ga 5:17*
which was *c.* to us, and took it out   *Col 2:14*
stood against us (A)(B)(N)(R)   *Col 2:14*
hung over our heads (P)   *Col 2:14*
not God, and are *c.* to all men   *1Th 2:15*
thing that is *c.* to sound doctrine   *1Ti 1:10*
is of the *c.* part may be ashamed   *Tit 2:8*

CONTRAST

c., different (A)(B)(E)(R)   *Eze 16:34*

CONTRIBUTE

c. to needs of saints (A)(B)(R)   *Ro 12:13*
c. to the material needs (N)   *Ro 15:27*
c. toward   *Ga 6:6; Ph'p 4:14*

CONTRIBUTION

to make a certain *c.* for the poor   *Ro 15:26*

CONTRIBUTIONS

apportion the *c.* (A)(B)(R)   *2Ch 31:14*
firstfruits of the *c.* (A)(B)(R)   *Eze 40:40*
send *c.* (B)(N)   *Ac 11:29*
liberal *c.* (B)(N)(R)   *2Co 9:13*

CONTRITE

saveth such as be of a *c.* spirit   *Ps 34:18*
crushed with sorrow for sin (A)   *Ps 34:18*
whose spirit is crushed (B)(R)   *Ps 34:18*
a broken and a *c.* heart, O God   *Ps 51:17*
a penitent heart (B)   *Ps 51:17*
also that is of a *c.* and humble   *Isa 57:15*
to revive the heart of the *c.* ones   *Isa 57:15*
penitent spirit (A)   *Isa 57:15*
him that is poor and of a *c.* spirit   *Isa 66:2*
broken or wounded spirit (A)   *Isa 66:2*
feels crushed in spirit (B)   *Isa 66:2*

CONTRIVE

c., dig up, cultivate (A)   *Pr 3:29*

CONTRIVED

c. a plot (B)   *2Ki 12:20*
c. by human art (P)(R)   *Ac 17:29*

CONTROL

could not *c.* himself (S)   *Ge 45:1*
Aaron let them get out of *c.*   *Ex 32:25*
under his *c.* the circle (B)   *Job 37:12*
c. of passions (A)   *Ac 14:25*
have *c.* over (A)(B)   *1Co 7:4*
cannot *c.* themselves (N)   *1Co 7:9*
any conceivable *c.* (P)   *Eph 1:21*
learn to *c.* his body (P)   *1Th 4:4*
out of *c.* (N)   *Tit 1:10; 1:6*
to *c.* themselves (R)   *Tit 2:6*

CONTROLLED

and *c.* himself (S)   *Ge 43:31; 1Sa 20:4]*
not possible to be *c.* (A)   *Ac 2:24*
men perfectly *c.* (N)   *1Pe 1:13*

CONTROLLER

blessed *c.* of all things (P)   *1Ti 6:15*

CONTROLS

c., urges, impels us (A)(B)(R)   *2Co 5:14*

CONTROVERSIES

judgment of the Lord, and for *c.*   *2Ch 19:8*

CONTROVERSY

being matters of *c.* within thy   *De 17:8*
disagreement (B)   *De 17:8*
the men, between whom the *c.* is   *De 19:17*
by their word shall every *c.*   *De 21:5*
If there be a *c.* between men   *De 25:1*
any man that had a *c.* came   *2Sa 15:2*
year of recompenses for the *c.* of   *Isa 34:8*
Lord hath a *c.* with the nations   *Jer 25:31*
in *c.* they shall stand in judgment   *Eze 44:24*
the Lord hath a *c.* with the Judah   *Ho 4:1*
Lord hath also a *c.* with Judah   *Ho 12:2*
Hear ye, O mountains, the Lord's *c.*   *Mic 6:2*
the Lord hath a *c.* with his people   *Mic 6:2*
has a *c.* with (E)(R)   *Mic 6:2*
also a *c.* (B)   *Lu 22:24*
there arose a *c.* (A)   *Lu 24:15*
dissension and *c.* (N)   *Ac 15:2*
without *c.* great is the mystery   *1Ti 3:16*
morbid fondness for *c.* (A)(B)(R)   *1Ti 6:4*

CONVENIENT

feed me with food *c.* for me   *Pr 30:8*
food needful for me (A)(E)(R)   *Pr 30:8*
feed me my portion of nourishment (B)   *Pr 30:8*
whither it seemeth good and *c.*   *Jer 40:4*
go wheresoever it seemeth *c.*   *Jer 40:5*
And when a *c.* day was come   *M'k 6:21*
when I have a *c.* season, I will call   *Ac 24:25*
do those things which are not *c.*   *Ro 1:28*
things not proper or decent (A)   *Ro 1:28*
what is not decent (B)   *Ro 1:28*
things which are not fitting (E)   *Ro 1:28*
break all rules of conduct (N)   *Ro 1:28*
perform unmentionable deeds (P)   *Ro 1:28*
base mind and improper conduct (R)   *Ro 1:28*
come when he shall have *c.* time   *1Co 16:12*
nor jesting, which are not *c.*   *Eph 5:4*
not fitting or becoming (A)(R)   *Eph 5:4*
which are not befitting (E)   *Eph 5:4*
these things are out of place (P)   *Eph 5:4*
to enjoin thee that which is *c.*   *Ph'm 8*

CONVENIENTLY

could not *c.* eat (B)   *M'k 6:31*
he sought how he might *c.* betray   *M'k 14:11*

CONVERSANT

the strangers that were *c.* among   *Jos 8:35*
foreigners who went with them (A)(B)   *Jos 8:35*
sojourners that were among them (E)(R)   *Jos 8:35*
as long as we were *c.* with them   *1Sa 25:15*
had contact with them (B)   *1Sa 25:15*
we were in the fields (E)(R)   *1Sa 25:15*

CONVERSATION

to slay such as be of upright *c.*   *Ps 37:14*
upright in conduct (A)   *Ps 37:14*
upright in the way (E)   *Ps 37:14*

who walk uprightly (R)	Ps 37:14
him that ordereth his *c.* aright	Ps 50:23
prepares his way (A)(B)	Ps 50:23
c. not discovered (A)	Jer 38:27
c. and discussion (B)	Lu 24:15
what is this *c.* (R)	Lu 24:17
we have had our *c.* in the world	2Co 1:12
have conducted ourselves (A)	2Co 1:12
we have behaved in the world (B)(E)(R)	2Co 1:12
our dealing with fellow men (N)	2Co 1:12
our activities in the world (P)	2Co 1:12
ye have heard of my *c.* in time	Ga 1:13
former manner of life (A)(E)(N)	Ga 1:13
previous career (B)(P)	Ga 1:13
my former life (R)	Ga 1:13
we all had our *c.* in times past	Eph 2:3
once lived, conducted ourselves (A)(E)(R)	Eph 2:3
we once walked (B)	Eph 2:3
put off concerning the former *c.*	Eph 4:22
former nature (A)	Eph 4:22
old nature with previous habits (B)	Eph 4:22
former manner of life (E)(R)	Eph 4:22
former way of life (N)	Eph 4:22
the old way of living (P)	Eph 4:22
c. not be nastiness, silliness, flippancy (P)	Eph 5:4
let your *c.* be as becometh the gospel	Ph'p 1:27
your manner of life (A)(E)(R)	Ph'p 1:27
conduct as citizens of Christ (B)	Ph'p 1:27
conduct be worthy of the gospel (N)(P)	Ph'p 1:27
our *c.* in heaven; from whence we look	Ph'p 3:20
citizens of a new state (A)	Ph'p 3:20
our commonwealth has its capitol (B)(R)	Ph'p 3:20
our citizenship is in heaven (E)	Ph'p 3:20
citizens of heaven (N)(P)	Ph'p 3:20
in word, in *c.*, in charity, in spirit	1Ti 4:12
in speech (A)(B)(N)(P)(R)	1Ti 4:12
your *c.* be without covetousness	Heb 13:5
character or moral disposition (A)	Heb 13:5
your conduct (B)	Heb 13:5
your lives free from money (P)(R)	Heb 13:5
considering the end of your *c.*	Heb 13:7
consider their manner of living (A)	Heb 13:7
copy their faith (B)	Heb 13:7
considering issue of their life (E)	Heb 13:7
follow the example of their faith (N)	Heb 13:7
imitate their faith (P)(R)	Heb 13:7
show out of a good *c.* his works with	Jas 3:13
by his noble living show (A)	Jas 3:13
by his good behaviour (B)	Jas 3:13
show by his good life (E)	Jas 3:13
Let his right conduct give proof (N)	Jas 3:13
show his works in meekness (R)	Jas 3:13
so be ye holy in all manner of *c.*	1Pe 1:15
conduct and manner of living (A)(E)	1Pe 1:15
in all your conduct (B)(R)	1Pe 1:15
holy in all your behaviour (N)	1Pe 1:15
holy in every department of your lives (P)	1Pe 1:15
from your vain *c.* received from fathers	1Pe 1:18
useless way of living (A)(B)	1Pe 1:18
vain manner of life (E)	1Pe 1:18
empty folly of traditional ways (N)	1Pe 1:18

the futile way of living (P)(R)	1Pe 1:18
Having your *c.* honest among Gentiles	1Pe 2:12
Conduct yourselves properly (A)	1Pe 2:12
Conduct yourselves honorably (B)	1Pe 2:12
having behaviour seemly among (E)(N)	1Pe 2:12
conduct be good and right (P)	1Pe 2:12
good conduct among Gentiles (R)	1Pe 2:12
be won by the *c.* of the wives	1Pe 3:1
by godly lives of their wives (A)	1Pe 3:1
by the conduct of their wives (B)	1Pe 3:1
by behaviour of their wives (E)(N)(P)(R)	1Pe 3:1
While they behold your chaste *c.*	1Pe 3:2
observe the pure and modest way (A)	1Pe 3:2
chaste respectful behaviour (B)(E)(N)(P)(R)	1Pe 3:2
falsely accuse your good *c.* in	1Pe 3:16
revile your right behaviour (A)(R)	1Pe 3:16
accuse your good Christian conduct (B)(N)	1Pe 3:16
revile your good manner of life (E)	1Pe 3:16
libeling your good Christian behaviour (P)	1Pe 3:16
with the filthy *c.* of the wicked	2Pe 2:7
by the wanton ways of the ungodly (A)	2Pe 2:7
by immoral behaviour of the lawless (B)	2Pe 2:7
by the lascivious life of the wicked (E)	2Pe 2:7
by dissolate habits of lawless society (N)	2Pe 2:7
by the filthy lives of the godless (P)	2Pe 2:7
by the licentiousness of the wicked (R)	2Pe 2:7
be in all holy *c.* and godliness	2Pe 3:11
consecrated and holy behaviour (A)(B)	2Pe 3:11
holy living and godliness (E)	2Pe 3:11
devout and dedicated lives (N)	2Pe 3:11
men of good and holy character (P)	2Pe 3:11
lives of holiness and godliness (R)	2Pe 3:11

CONVERSE

c. with my father (A)	1Sa 19:3; Job 4:21
hold sweet *c.* together (R)	Ps 55:14

CONVERSED

king *c.* with them (A)(S)	Da 1:19
he *c.* with him often (A)(R)	Ac 24:26

CONVERSING

c. and discussing (A)	Lu 24:15

CONVERSION

declaring the *c.* of the Gentiles	Ac 15:3

CONVERT

with their heart, and *c.* and be healed	Isa 6:10
turn again and be healed (A)(E)(R)	Isa 6:10
they repent and be healed (B)	Isa 6:10
win one *c.* (N)(P)	M't 23:15
to *c.* the rebellious (N)	Lu 1:17
a former *c.* to Judaism (N)(P)	Ac 6:5
a new *c.* (A)(B)(N)(R)	1Ti 3:6
from the truth, and one *c.* him	Jas 5:19

CONVERTED

and sinners shall be *c.* unto thee	Ps 51:13
of the sea shall be *c.* unto thee	Isa 60:5
Sea shall be turned to you (A)(B)(E)(R)	Isa 60:5
and should be *c.* and I should	M't 13:15
and turn and I should heal them (A)	M't 13:15
return and I would heal them (B)	M't 13:15
turn again, I should heal them (E)(N)(P)	M't 13:15
turn for me to heal them (R)	M't 13:15
Except ye be *c.* and become as	M't 18:3
unless you repent (A)	M't 18:3
Except you turn and become (E)(R)	M't 18:3
unless you turn around and become (N)	M't 18:3
unless you change your whole outlook (P)	M't 18:3
they should be *c.* and their sins	M'k 4:12
and when thou art *c.*, strengthen	Lu 22:32
have turned again (A)(E)(R)	Lu 22:32
when you return to me (B)	Lu 22:32
when you have come to yourself (N)	Lu 22:32
when you have turned back to me (P)	Lu 22:32
and be *c.* and I should heal them	Joh 12:40
repenting and turning to me to heal (A)	Joh 12:40
repent and I should heal them (B)	Joh 12:40
return and I should heal them (E)	Joh 12:40
turn to me to heal them (N)(R)	Joh 12:40
turn and I should heal them (P)	Joh 12:40
Repent ye therefore, and be *c.*	Ac 3:19
turn around and return to God (A)	Ac 3:19
repent and turn (B)	Ac 3:19
turn again (E)(R)	Ac 3:19
turn to God (N)(P)	Ac 3:19
should be *c.* and I should heal	Ac 28:27

CONVERTETH

he which *c.* the sinner from	Jas 5:20
whoever turns a sinner from his evil (A)	Jas 5:20
turns a sinner back from wandering (B)(N)	Jas 5:20
turning a man back from his wandering (P)	Jas 5:20
brings back a sinner from error of (R)	Jas 5:20

CONVERTING

of the Lord is perfect, *c.* the soul	Ps 19:7

CONVERTS

with judgment, and her *c.* with	Isa 1:27

CONVEY

will *c.* them by sea in floats unto	1Ki 5:9
river, that they may *c.* me over	Ne 2:7

CONVEYED

for Jesus had *c.* himself away	Joh 5:13

CONVICT

c. you from your own (P)	Lu 19:22
c. all ungodly (A)(B)(E)(N)(P)(R)(S)	Jude 15

CONVICTED

being c. by their own conscience | Joh 8:9
going out conscience-stricken (A)(B) | Joh 8:9
c., convinced of all (A)(B)(N)(P)(S) | 1Co 14:24
c. by the law (A)(B)(E)(N)(P)(S) | Jas 2:9
c. as violaters and offenders (A)(B) | Jas 2:9

CONVICTETH

c. me of sin (S) | Joh 8:46

CONVICTION

demand his c. (P) | Ac 25:15

CONVICTIONS

Jews concealed true c. (A) | Ga 2:13

CONVICTS

c. me of wrong (A)(B)(E)(R) | Joh 8:46

CONVINCE

exhort and to c. the gainsayers | Tit 1:9
to c. all that are ungodly among | Jude 15
convict all (A)(B)(E)(N)(P)(R) | Jude 15

CONVINCED

there was none of you that c. Job | Job 32:12
For he mightily c. the Jews | Ac 18:28
showing and proving by the (A)(B)(E) | Ac 18:28
demonstrating from the Scriptures (N) | Ac 18:28
publicly refuted the Jews (P) | Ac 18:28
powerfully confuted the Jews (R) | Ac 18:28
unlearned, he is c. of all | 1Co 14:24
c. and sure (A)(B) | Ph'p 1:6
c. of the law as trangressors | Jas 2:9
convicted by the law (A)(B)(E)(N)(R) | Jas 2:9

CONVINCETH

Which of you c. me of sin | Joh 8:46
convicts me of wrongdoing (A)(B)(E)(R) | Joh 8:46

CONVINCING

by many c. proofs (B)(E)(P)(R) | Ac 1:3

CONVOCATION

first day there shall be an holy c. | Ex 12:16
a holy assembly (A)(R) | Ex 12:16
a sacred gathering (B) | Ex 12:16
is the sabbath of rest, an holy c. | Le 23:3
first day ye shall have an holy c. | Le 23:7; 23:8
an holy calling together (A) | Le 23:7
have a sacred gathering (B) | Le 23:7
that it may be an holy c. | Le 23:21; 23:24, 35
An holy assembly (A) | Le 23:21
you will conduct an holy gathering (B) | Le 23:21
of atonement: it shall be an holy c. | Le 23:27
Day of Atonement; hold a holy meeting (B) | Le 23:27
the eighth day shall be an holy c. | Le 23:36
a solemn assembly (A) | Le 23:36
have a sacred gathering (B) | Le 23:36
In the first day shall be an holy c. | Nu 28:18; 28:25-26; 29:1, 7, 12
holy assembly (A) | Nu 28:18; 28:25-26; 29:1, 7, 12
set aside for a sacred meeting (B) | Nu 28:18; 28:25-26

the month, ye shall have an holy c. | Nu 29:1; 29:7, 12
have a sacred meeting (B) | Nu 29:1; 29:7, 12

CONVOCATIONS

ye shall proclaim to be holy c. | Le 23:2; 23:4, 37

CONVULSED

c. him greatly (S) | M'k 9:26; 9:20

COOK

Samuel said unto the c., Bring the | 1Sa 9:23
And the c. took up the shoulder | 1Sa 9:24
and c. pottage (A) | 2Ki 4:38

COOKED

c. with fire (B) | Ex 12:9; Le 6:28
c. holy offerings (A) | 2Ch 35:13

COOKS

to be confectionaries, and to be c. | 1Sa 8:13
perfumers, c., bakers (A)(E)(R) | 1Sa 8:13

COOL

in the garden in the c. of the day | Ge 3:8
finger in water, and c. my tongue | Lu 16:24

COOS

with a straight course unto C. | Ac 21:1

COPIED

Hezekiah king of Judah c. out | Pr 25:1

COPING

from the foundation unto thee c. | 1Ki 7:9

COPPER

two vessels of fine c. | Ezr 8:27
fine bright bronze (A)(R) | Ezr 8:27
fine bright brass (B)(E) | Ezr 8:27
and c. bowls (N) | M'k 7:4

COPPERSMITH

Alexander the c. did me much | 2Ti 4:14
Alexander the metalworker (B) | 2Ti 4:14

COPULATION

if any man's seed of c. go out | Le 15:16
has an emission of semen (A)(R) | Le 15:16; 15:17-18
has an emission of sperm (B) | Le 15:16; 15:17-18
whereon is the seed of c. shall be | Le 15:17
whom man shall lie with seed of c. | Le 15:18

COPY

he shall write him a c. of this law | De 17:18
a c. of the law of Moses, which he | Jos 8:32
This is the c. of the letter that | Ezr 4:11
when the c. of king Artaxerxes' | Ezr 4:23
The c. of the letter that Tatnai | Ezr 5:6
Now this the c. of the letter that | Ezr 7:11
The c. of the writing for a | Es 3:14
the c. of the writing of the decree | Es 4:8
the c. of the writing for a | Es 8:13
stir up to c. (A) | Ro 11:14
a c. of the real (A)(B)(R) | Heb 9:24
c. their faith (B) | Heb 13:7

COR

tenth part of a bath out of the c. | Eze 45:14

CORAL

No mention shall be made of c. | Job 28:18
and fine linen, and c. and agate | Eze 27:16

CORBAN

It is C., that is to say, a gift | M'k 7:11

CORD

a c. of blue (A)(E)(R)(S) | Nu 15:38
down by a c. through the window | Jos 2:15
with a rope (A)(B)(R) | Jos 2:15
hath loosed my c. and afflicted | Job 30:11
loosed my bowstring (A)(B) | Job 30:11
or his tongue with a c. | Job 41:1
threefold c. is not quickly broken | Ec 4:12
Or ever the silver c. be loosed, or | Ec 12:6
cast a c. by lot in the congregation | Mic 2:5
cast a line by lot (A)(B)(E)(R) | Mic 2:5

CORDIALLY

most c., consistently love (B) | 1Pe 1:22

CORDS

twisted like c. (A)(R) | Ex 28:14; 22:22; 39:17-18
the pins of the court, and their c. | Ex 35:18
his c. and his pins, and all the | Ex 39:40
c. of it for all the service thereof | Nu 3:26
sockets, their pins, and their c. | Nu 3:37
their c. and all the instruments of | Nu 4:26
their pins, and their c. with all | Nu 4:32
they bound him with two new c. | J'g 15:13
two new ropes (B)(E)(R) | J'g 15:13; 15:14
the c. that were upon his arms | J'g 15:14
seven fresh fiber c. (B)(S) | J'g 16:7
c. of Sheol (A)(B)(E)(R) | 2Sa 22:6
fastened with c. of fine linen | Es 1:6
and be holden in c. of affliction | Job 36:8
and cast away their c. from us | Ps 2:3
cast their shackles from us (B) | Ps 2:3
the c. of death (A)(B)(E) | Ps 18:4; 18:5
with c. even unto the horns | Ps 118:27
with woven strands (B) | Ps 118:27
Bind festal procession with | Ps 118:27
branches (R) |
cut asunder the c. of the wicked | Ps 129:4
have hid a snare for me, and c. | Ps 140:5
be holden with the c. of his sins | Pr 5:22
with ropes of his own sin (B) | Pr 5:22
the toils of his sin (R) | Pr 5:22
that draw iniquity with c. of vanity | Isa 5:18
any of the c. thereof be broken | Isa 33:20
lengthen thy c. and strengthen | Isa 54:2
is spoiled, all my c. are broken | Jer 10:20
they let down Jeremiah with c. | Jer 38:6
with ropes (A)(R) | Jer 38:6; 38:11-13
them down by c. into the dungeon | Jer 38:11
under thine armholes under the c. | Jer 38:12

they drew up Jeremiah with *c.* — Jer 38:13
shall put *c.* upon thee (S) — Eze 3:25
of rich apparel, bound with *c.* — Eze 27:24
I drew them with *c.* of a man, with — Ho 11:4
he had made a scourge of small *c.* — Joh 2:15
unfastening the *c.* of death (B) — Ac 2:24

CORE

perished in the gainsaying of *c.* — Jude 11

CORIANDER

and it was like *c.* seed, white — Ex 16:31
And the manna was as *c.* seed, and — Nu 11:7

CORINTH

from Athens, and came to C. — Ac 18:1
while Apollos was at C. Paul — Ac 19:1
the church of God which is at C. to — 1Co 1:2
church of God which is at C. with — 2Co 1:1
spare you I came not as yet unto C. — 2Co 1:23
Erastus abode at C.: but — 2Ti 4:20

CORINTHIANS

many of the C. hearing believed — Ac 18:8
O ye C. our mouth is open unto — 2Co 6:11

CORMORANT

the little owl, and the *c.* and — Le 11:17
and the gier eagle, and the *c.* — De 14:17
c. and the bittern shall possess — Isa 34:11
the pelican and porcupine (A)(B)(E) — Isa 34:11
the hawk and porcupine (R) — Isa 34:11
the *c.* and the bittern shall lodge — Zep 2:14
the pelican and hedgehog (A) — Zep 2:14
the pelican and porcupine (B)(E) — Zep 2:14
the vulture and hedgehog (R) — Zep 2:14

CORN

and lay up *c.* under the hand of — Ge 41:35
Joseph gathered *c.* as the sand — Ge 41:49
into Egypt to Joseph for to buy *c.* — Ge 41:57
grain (A)(B)(E)(R) — Ge 41:57; 42:1-5, 19, 25-26; 43:2; 44:2; 45:23; 47:14; Ex 22:6; Le 2:14, 16; 23:14; Nu 18:27; De 7:13; 11:14; 12:17; 16:9, 13; 18:4; 23:25; 25:4; 28:51; 33:28 Jos 5:11; J'g 15:5; Ru 2:2, 14; 3:7; 1Sa 17:17; 25:18; 2Sa 17:19, 28; 2Ki 18:32; 2Ch 31:5; 32:28; Ne 5:2-3, 10-11; 10:39; 13:5, 12
Jacob heard there was *c.* in Egypt — Ge 42:2; Ac 7:12
go carry *c.* for famine of your houses — Ge 42:19
so that stacks of *c.* be consumed — Ex 22:6
priest shall burn part of beaten *c.* — Le 2:16
eat neither bread nor parched *c.* — Le 23:14
as tho' it were *c.* of threshing floor — Nu 18:27
as thou beginnest to put sickle to *c.* — De 16:9
not muzzle the ox when he treadeth out the *c.* — De 25:4; 1Co 9:9; 1Ti 5:18
did eat of old *c.* of land — Jos 5:11; 5:12
reached her parched *c.* she did eat — Ru 2:14
went to lie down at end of heap of *c.* — Ru 3:7

take an ephah of parched *c.* — 1Sa 17:17
Abigail took five measures of parched *c.* — 1Sa 25:18
they brought parched *c.* and beans — 2Sa 17:28
they were as blasted *c.* — 2Ki 19:26; Isa 37:27
take up *c.* that we may eat — Ne 5:2
as a shock of *c.* cometh in in his season — Job 5:26
shock of grain (A)(B)(E)(R) — Job 5:26
reap every one his *c.* in the field — Job 24:6
reap his fodder in the field (A)(R) — Job 24:6
gather provender from the field (B)(E) — Job 24:6
their young ones they grow up with *c.* — Job 39:4
grow up in open field (A)(B)(E)(R) — Job 39:4
preparest them *c.* when thou providest — Ps 65:9
provideth grain (A)(B)(E)(R) — Ps 65:9
valleys also are covered over with *c.* — Ps 65:13
there shall be a handful of *c.* in earth — Ps 72:16
abundance of grain (A)(B)(E)(R) — Ps 72:16
had given them of *c.* of heaven — Ps 78:24
grain (A)(B)(E)(R) — Ps 78:24; Pr 11:26; Isa 17:5; 62:8; Eze 36:29; Ho 2:9; 7:14; 14:7; Joe 1:10; 2:19; Am 8:5; 9:9
that withholdeth *c.* people shall curse — Pr 11:26
when harvest-man gathereth *c.* — Isa 17:5
no more give thy *c.* to thine enemies — Isa 62:8
I will call for *c.* and will increase — Eze 36:29
take away my *c.* in time thereof — Ho 2:9
Ephraim loveth to tread out the *c.* — Ho 10:11
shall revive as *c.* and grow as vine — Ho 14:7
for *c.* is wasted, new wine is dried up — Joe 1:10
barns broken down, for *c.* is withered — Joe 1:17
new moon be gone that we may sell *c.* — Am 8:5
I will sift Israel like *c.* sifted in a sieve — Am 9:9
after that the full *c.* in the ear — M'k 4:28
grain (A)(B)(E)(R) — M'k 4:28; Jon 12:24
store my *c.* (N) — Joh 12:18
except *c.* of wheat fall into ground — Joh 12:24

EARS OF CORN

seven *ears of c.* came up on stalk — Ge 41:5
heads of full grain (B) — Ge 41:5
seven ears of grain (E)(R) — Ge 41:5
offer green *ears of c.* dried by fire — Le 2:14
heads of grain (B) — Le 2:14
first-fruit grain in the ear (E) — Le 2:14
crushed new grain (R) — Le 2:14
go and glean *ears of c.* after him — Ru 2:2
heads of grain (B) — Ru 2:2
the ears of grain (E)(R) — Ru 2:2
brought full *ears of c.* in husk — 2Ki 4:42
are cut off as tops of *ears of c.* — Job 24:24
ears of grain (A)(E) — Job 24:24
heads of grain (B)(R) — Job 24:24
to pluck *ears of c.* — M't 12:1; M'k 2:23; Lu 6:1
spikes of grain (A) — M't 12:1
pluck heads of grain (B) — M't 12:1
pluck ears of grain (E)(R) — M't 12:1
ears of wheat (P) — M't 12:1

CORN with FLOOR

O my threshing, and *c.* of my *floor* — Isa 21:10

my threshed and winnowed — Isa 21:10
one (A)(B)(R)
the grain of my floor (E) — Isa 21:10
hast loved a reward on every *c.* — Ho 9:1
every threshing-floor (A)(B)(R) — Ho 9:1
every grain-floor (E) — Ho 9:1

STANDING CORN

so that *standing c.* be consumed — Ex 22:6
standing grain (B)(E)(R) — Ex 22:6; J'g 15:5
come into *standing c.* of neighbour — De 23:25
grainfield (B) — De 23:25
standing grain (A)(E)(R) — De 23:25
foxes go into *standing c.* burn up *standing c.* — J'g 15:5

CORN AND WINE

God give plenty of *c.* and *wine* — Ge 27:28
grain and wine (A)(B)(E)(R) — Ge 27:28; De 7:13; 11:14; 12:17; 18:4; 28:51; 33:28; 2Ki 18:32; 2Ch 31:5; 32:28; Ne 5:11; 10:39; Ps 4:7; Zec 9:17
with *c.* and wine have I sustained him — Ge 27:37
he will also bless thy *c.* and *wine* — De 7:13
mayest gather in *c.* and wine — De 11:14
not eat tithe of *c.* and wine — De 12:17; 14:23
after thou gather in *c.* and *wine* — De 16:13
produce of threshing-floor (A)(B)(E)(R) — De 16:13
give him first-fruit of thy *c.* and *wine* — De 18:4
which shall not leave thee *c.* and wine — De 28:51
Jacob be upon land of *c.* and wine — De 33:28
to a land of *c.* and wine — 2Ki 18:32; Isa 36:17
brought first-fruits of *c.* and *wine* — 2Ch 31:5
store-houses for increase of *c.* wine — 2Ch 32:28
restore the 100th part of *c.* wine — Ne 5:11
bring offering of *c.* of new wine — Ne 10:39; 13:5, 12
in time their *c.* and wine increased — Ps 4:7
say to mothers, where is *c.* and wine — La 2:12
where is bread and wine (B)(R) — La 2:12
where is grain and wine (E) — La 2:12
she knew not that I gave her *c.* wine — Ho 2:8
grain (A)(B)(E)(R) — Ho 2:8; 2:22; 7:14; Joe 2:19; Hag 1:11
earth shall hear *c.* and wine — Ho 2:22
assemble themselves for *c.* and wine — Ho 7:14
I will send you *c.* and wine — Joe 2:19
called for drought on *c.* and new wine — Hag 1:11
c. make men cheerful, and wine — Zec 9:17
Cereals shall make young men (A) — Zec 9:17

CORN-FIELDS

he went through *c.* — M'k 2:23
on the sabbath-day — M't 12:1; Lu 6:1
fields of standing grain (A) — M'k 2:23; M't 12:1; Lu 6:1
through a wheat field (B) — M'k 2:23
through grain fields (E)(R) — M'k 2:23

CORNELIUS

C. a centurion of the band — Ac 10:1; 10:3, 7, 17, 21-22, 24-25, 30-31

CORNER

north *c.* he made twenty boards — Ex 36:25
shave off the *c.* of their beard — Le 21:5
edges of the beard (B)(R) — Le 21:5
the *c.* of the sea southward — Jos 18:14

from the right *c.* of the   *2Ki 11:11*
temple
to the left *c.* of the temple   *2Ki 11:11*
gate of Ephraim unto the *c.* *2Ki 14:13*
gate
gate of Ephraim to the *c.*   *2Ch 25:23*
gate
towers in Jerusalem at the *c.* *2Ch 26:9*
gate
altars in every *c.* of   *2Ch 28:24*
Jerusalem
of the wall, even unto the *c.*   *Ne 3:24*
and to the going up of the *c.*   *Ne 3:31*
between the going up of the   *Ne 3:32*
c.
or who laid the *c.* stone   *Job 38:6*
thereof
become the head stone of   *Ps 118:22*
the *c.*
daughters may be as *c.*   *Ps 144:12*
stones
through the street near her *c.*   *Pr 7:8*
and lieth in wait at every *c.*   *Pr 7:12*
to dwell in a *c.* of the   *Pr 21:9*
housetop
to dwell in the *c.* of the   *Pr 25:24*
housetop
precious *c.* stone, a sure   *Isa 28:16*
foundation
thy teachers be removed   *Isa 30:20*
into a *c.*
will not hide himself   *Isa 30:20*
(A)(B)(R)
teachers be hidden any more *Isa 30:20*
(E)
Hananeel unto the gate of   *Jer 31:38*
the *c.*
unto the *c.* of the horse gate *Jer 31:40*
shall devour the *c.* of Moab *Jer 48:45*
not take of thee a stone for *Jer 51:26*
a *c.*
behold, in every *c.* of the   *Eze 46:21*
court
in Samaria in the *c.* of a   *Am 3:12*
bed
Out of him came forth the *c.* *Zec 10:4*
come the corner-stone   *Zec 10:4*
(A)(B)(E)(R)
the *c.* gate, and from the   *Zec 14:10*
tower
same is become the head of *M't 21:42*
the *c.*
is become the head of the   *M'k 12:10*
c.
same is become the head of *Lu 20:17*
the *c.*
which is become the head of *Ac 4:11*
the *c.*
for this thing was not done *Ac 26:26*
in a *c.*
Christ himself being the   *Eph 2:20*
chief *c.*
I lay in Sion a chief *c.* stone, *1Pe 2:6*
elect
same is made the head of the *1Pe 2:7*
c.

CORNERS

put them in the four *c.*   *Ex 25:12;*
thereof   *25:26; 27:2, 4; 37:3, 13; 38:2*
make for the *c.* of the   *Ex 26:23;*
tabernacle   *36:28-29*
both; they shall be for the *Ex 26:24;*
two *c.*   *30:4; 37:27*
not wholly reap the *c.* of thy *Le 19:9*
field
shall not round the *c.* of   *Le 19:27*
your heads
shalt thou mar the *c.* of thy *Le 19:27*
beard
riddance of the *c.* of thy   *Le 23:22*
field
and shall smite the *c.* of   *Nu 24:17*
Moab
c. corners of Moab   *Nu 24:17*
(A)(B)(R)
said, I would scatter them   *De 32:26*
into *c.*
I will blow them away (B)   *De 32:26*
four *c.* thereof had   *1Ki 7:30*
undersetters
to the four *c.* of one base   *1Ki 7:34*
and didst divide them into *c.* *Ne 9:22*
smote the four *c.* of the   *Job 1:19*
house
from the four *c.* of the   *Isa 11:12*
earth
are in the utmost *c.* that *Jer 9:26*
dwell

all that are in the utmost   *Jer 25:23*
c.
them that are in the utmost *c.* *Jer 49:32*
come upon the four *c.* of the *Eze 7:2*
land
and the *c.* thereof, and the *Eze 41:22*
length
and on the four *c.* of the   *Eze 43:20*
settle
upon the four *c.* of the   *Eze 45:19*
settle of the
to pass by the four *c.* of   *Eze 46:21*
the court
in the four *c.* of the court *Eze 46:22*
bowls, and as the *c.* of the *Zec 9:15*
altar
in the *c.* of the streets, that *M't 6:5*
they
knit at the four *c.* and let *Ac 10:11*
down
let down from heaven by four *Ac 11:5*
c.
standing on the four *c.* of the *Re 7:1*
earth

CORNERSTONES

c. of the tribes   *Isa 19:13*
(A)(B)(E)(R)

CORNET

with sound of the *c.* and   *1Ch 15:28*
With trumpets and sound of *Ps 98:6*
c.
ye hear the sound of the *c.,*   *Da 3:5;*
flute   *3:15*
people heard the sound of the *Da 3:7*
c.
that shall hear the sound of *Da 3:10*
the *c.*
Blow ye the *c.* in Gibeah, and *Ho 5:8*

CORNETS

on timbrels, and on *c.* and on *2Sa 6:5*
and with trumpets, and   *2Ch 15:14*
with *c.*

CORPS

conscripted the labor (B)   *1Ki 9:15*
each *c.* of 24,000 (B)   *1Ch 27:1*

CORPSE

they came and took up his   *M'k 6:29*
c.
took John's body   *M'k 6:29*
(A)(B)(N)(P)(R)

CORPSES

behold, they were all dead *2Ki 19:35*
c.
behold, they were all dead *c. Isa 37:36*
dead bodies (A)   *2Ki 19:35; Isa 37:36*
c.; they stumble upon their *c.*   *Na 3:3*
masses of the slain (B)   *Na 3:3*
multitude of slain (E)   *Na 3:3*

CORRECT

c. discipline (A)   *De 4:36*
I will *c.* him (B)   *2Sa 7:14*
c. and discipline (B)(P)   *1Ch 9:34*
thou with rebukes dost *c.* man *Ps 39:11*
the heathen, shall not he *c.*   *Ps 94:10*
shall he not punish (A)   *Ps 94:10*
does he not chastise (R)   *Ps 94:10*
C. thy son, and he shall give *Pr 29:17*
thee
thine own wickedness shall *c. Jer 2:19*
thee
O Lord, *c.* me, but with   *Jer 10:24*
judgment
I will *c.* thee in measure,   *Jer 30:11*
but *c.* thee in measure; yet *Jer 46:28*
will I
c. his opponents (A)(P)   *2Ti 2:25*
train, *c.,* discipline (A)   *Heb 12:7*
to *c.* us (P)   *Heb 12:10*
c. and discipline (B)(P)   *Re 3:19*

CORRECTED

A servant will not be *c.* by *Pr 29:19*
words
fathers of our flesh which *c.* *Heb 12:9*
us
which disciplined us   *Heb 12:9*
(A)(N)(R)

CORRECTETH

happy is the man whom God *Job 5:17*
c.
whom God reproves (A)(R) *Job 5:17*
whom God disciplines (B) *Job 5:17*
For whom the Lord loveth he *Pr 3:12*
c.

CORRECTING

c. them that oppose (E)(R) *2Ti 2:25*

CORRECTION

do not despise *c.* (A)   *Job 5:17*
whether for *c.* or for his   *Job 37:13*
land
you hate *c.* (B)   *Ps 50:17*
neither be weary of his *c.*   *Pr 3:11*
his reproof (A)(B)(E)(R)   *Pr 3:11*
as a fool to the *c.* of the   *Pr 7:22*
stocks
whoso loveth *c.* loveth (E)   *Pr 12:1*
a wise son accepts *c.* (B)   *Pr 13:1*
C. is grievous unto him that *Pr 15:10*
severe discipline for him   *Pr 15:10*
(A)(B)(R)
who ignores *c.* (B)(E)   *Pr 15:32*
c. of fools is their (E)   *Pr 16:22*
rod of *c.* shall drive it far from *Pr 22:15*
him
discipline will drive   *Pr 22:15*
(A)(B)(R)
Withhold not *c.* from the   *Pr 23:13*
child
withhold not discipline   *Pr 23:13*
(A)(R)
they received no *c.:* your own *Jer 2:30*
they have refused to receive *c. Jer 5:3*
nor receiveth *c.:* truth is   *Jer 7:28*
perished
will you receive (B)   *Jer 35:13*
thou hast established them *Hab 1:12*
for *c.*
she received not *c.;* she   *Zep 3:2*
trusted
for reproof, for *c.* for   *2Ti 3:16*
instruction
exempt from *c.* (A)(B)(P) *Heb 12:8*

CORRECTLY

God instructs him *c.*   *Isa 28:26*
(A)(B)(E)

CORRECTS

c. and disciplines   *Heb 12:6*
(A)(B)(N)(R)

CORRESPOND

c. to one of the portions (S) *Eze 45:7*

CORRESPONDING

watch *c.* with watch (S)   *Ne 12:24*

CORRUPT

The earth also was *c.* before *Ge 6:11*
God
it was *c.;* for all flesh had   *Ge 6:12*
corrupted
Lest ye *c.* yourselves, and   *De 4:16*
make you
and shall *c.* yourselves, and *De 4:25*
make a
ye will utterly *c.* yourselves *De 31:29*
abominable *c.* (E)(R)   *Job 15:16*
breath is *c.* my days are   *Job 17:1*
extinct
my spirit is broken (A)(B) *Job 17:1*
my life is ruined (B)   *Job 17:1*
my spirit is consumed (E) *Job 17:1*
They are *c.* they have done *Ps 14:1*
all are *c.* (B)(N)   *Ps 14:3; 53:3*
My wounds stink and are *c.* *Ps 38:5*
C. are they, and have done *Ps 53:1*

They are *c.*, and speak wickedly   *Ps 73:8*
troubled fountain, and a *c.* spring   *Pr 25:26*
polluted spring (A)(B)(R)   *Pr 25:26*
heart is exceeding *c.* (A)(B)(E)(R)   *Jer 17:9*
according to your *c.* doings, O ye   *Eze 20:44*
was more *c.* in her inordinate love   *Eze 23:11*
have prepared lying and *c.* words   *Da 2:9*
shall he *c.* by flatteries: but the   *Da 11:32*
sacrificeth unto the Lord a *c.*   *Mal 1:14*
I will *c.* your seed, and spread   *Mal 2:3*
I will rebuke your seed (A)(E)(R)   *Mal 2:3*
I will denounce your offspring (B)   *Mal 2:3*
where moth and rust doth *c.*   *M't 6:19*
moth, rust, worm consume (A)(E)(R)   *M't 6:19*
moth and rust destroy (B)   *M't 6:19*
grows rusty and moth-eaten (N)   *M't 6:19*
moth and rust spoil them (P)   *M't 6:19*
neither moth nor rust doth *c.*   *M't 6:20*
a *c.* tree bring forth evil fruit   *M't 7:17; 7:18*
worthless tree bears bad (A)   *M't 7:17*
defective tree bears defective (B)   *M't 7:17*
a poor tree bad fruit (N)(P)(R)   *M't 7:17*
neither can a *c.* tree bring forth   *M't 7:18*
make the tree *c.* and his fruit *c.*   *M't 12:33*
tree rotten, its fruit rotten (A)(P)   *M't 12:33*
both tree and fruit bad (B)(N)(R)   *M't 12:33*
tree bringeth not forth *c.* fruit   *Lu 6:43*
neither doth a *c.* tree bring forth   *Lu 6:43*
evil communications *c.* good   *1Co 15:33*
many, which *c.* the word of God   *2Co 2:17*
old man, which is *c.* according to   *Eph 4:22*
discard your old unrenewed self (A)   *Eph 4:22*
rid yourself of the old nature (B)(R)   *Eph 4:22*
lay aside the old human nature (N)   *Eph 4:22*
were rotted through and through with lust's allusions (P)   *Eph 4:22*
Let no *c.* communication proceed   *Eph 4:29*
no foul, polluting language, nor evil word, unwholesome worthless talk (A)   *Eph 4:29*
no foul speech whatever (B)   *Eph 4:29*
no bad language (N)   *Eph 4:29*
no foul language (P)   *Eph 4:29*
no evil talk (R)   *Eph 4:29*
disputings of men of *c.* minds   *1Ti 6:5*
depraved minds (B)(R)   *1Ti 6:5; 2Ti 3:8*
reasoning powers become atrophied (N)   *1Ti 6:5*
warped minds (P)   *1Ti 6:5*
men of *c.* minds, reprobate   *2Ti 8:8*
c. the body (A)   *Jude 8*
those things they *c.* themselves   *Jude 10*
which did *c.* the earth with her   *Re 19:2*
the *c.* shall have their part (P)   *Re 21:8*

CORRUPTED

flesh had *c.* his way upon the earth   *Ge 6:12*
had perverted their way (B)   *Ge 6:12*
land was *c.* by reason of the swarm   *Ex 8:24*
being ruined by gadflies (B)(R)   *Ex 8:24*

out of Egypt, have *c.* themselves   *Ex 32:7*
have behaved wickedly (B)   *Ex 32:7*
out of Egypt have *c.* themselves   *De 9:12*
They have *c.* themselves, their   *De 32:5*
c. themselves more than their   *J'g 2:19*
behave worse than fathers (B)(R)   *J'g 2:19*
wast *c.* more than they in all thy   *Eze 16:47*
thou hast *c.* thy wisdom by reason   *Eze 28:17*
They have deeply *c.* themselves   *Ho 9:9*
rose early, and *c.* all their doings   *Zep 3:7*
ye have *c.* the covenant of Levi   *Mal 2:8*
we have *c.* no man, we have   *2Co 7:2*
c. no one (E)(R)   *2Co 7:2*
your minds should be *c.* from the   *2Co 11:3*
wranglings of men *c.* (E)   *1Ti 6:5*
is perverted and *c.* (A)   *Tit 3:11*
Your riches are *c.* and your   *Jas 5:2*
rotted and ruined (A)(B)(N)(P)(R)   *Jas 5:2*

CORRUPTERS

children that are *c.*: they have   *Isa 1:4*
brass and iron; they are all *c.*   *Jer 6:28*

CORRUPTETH

approacheth, neither moth *c.*   *Lu 12:33*
no moth destroys (A)(E)(N)(R)   *Lu 12:33*
no moth ruins (B)(P)   *Lu 12:33*

CORRUPTIBLE

into an image made like to *c.* man   *Ro 1:23*
resembling mortal man (A)(B)(N)(P)(R)   *Ro 1:23*
they do it to obtain a *c.* crown   *1Co 9:25*
win a wreath that will soon wither (A)(N)   *1Co 9:25*
receive a perishable crown (B)(R)   *1Co 9:25*
a fading crown of leaves (P)   *1Co 9:25*
this *c.* must put on incorruption   *1Cor 15:53*
this perishable nature (A)(B)(N)(P)(R)   *1Co 15:53*
So when this *c.* shall have put on   *1Co 15:54*
were not redeemed with *c.* things   *1Pe 1:18*
not with perishables (B)   *1Pe 1:18*
no perishable stuff (N)(R)   *1Pe 1:18*
money payment of transient value (P)   *1Pe 1:18*
not of *c.* seed, but of incorruptible   *1Pe 1:23*
not from a mortal origin (A)   *1Pe 1:23*
not from perishable sperm (B)   *1Pe 1:23*
not of mortal parentage (N)   *1Pe 1:23*
not of perishable seed (R)   *1Pe 1:23*
in that which is not *c.* even   *1Pe 3:4*
incorruptible, unfading spirit (A)(E)(N)   *1Pe 3:4*
imperishable qualities of spirit (B)   *1Pe 3:4*
imperishable jewel of quiet spirit (R)   *1Pe 3:4*

CORRUPTING

the daughter of women, *c.* her   *Da 11:17*
c. our people (P)   *Lu 23:2*

CORRUPTION

their *c.* is in them, and blemishes   *Le 22:25*
the right hand of the mount of *c.*   *2Ki 23:13*
mount of destruction (B)   *2Ki 23:13*
said to *c.*, Thou art my father   *Job 17:14*
suffer thine Holy One to see *c.*   *Ps 16:10*
still live for ever, and not see *c.*   *Ps 49:9*
turn man back to *c.* (B)   *Ps 90:3*
life from pit of *c.* (B)   *Ps 103:4*

delivered it from the pit of *c.*   *Isa 38:17*
was turned in me into *c.* and   *Da 10:8*
turned to pallor (B)   *Da 10:8*
thou brought up my life from *c.*   *Jon 2:6*
suffer thine Holy One to see *c.*   *Ac 2:27*
in hell, neither his flesh did see *c.*   *Ac 2:31*
to return to *c.* he said on this wise   *Ac 13:34*
not suffer thine Holy One to see *c.*   *Ac 13:35*
laid unto his fathers, and saw *c.*   *Ac 13:36*
whom God raised again, saw no *c.*   *Ac 13:37*
delivered from the bondage of *c.*   *Ro 8:21*
It is sown in *c.*; it is raised   *1Co 15:42*
is perishable and decays (A)   *1Co 15:42*
sown in decomposition (B)   *1Co 15:42*
sown in earth as perishable thing (R)   *1Co 15:42*
neither doth *c.* inherit incorruption   *1Co 15:50*
perishable inherit imperishable (A)(B)(R)   *1Co 15:50*
perishable cannot possess immortality (N)   *1Co 15:50*
transitory never possess the everlasting (P)   *1Co 15:50*
beyond reach of *c.* (P)   *1Co 15:53*
shall of the flesh reap *c.*; but   *Ga 6:8*
reap decay, ruin, and destruction (A)   *Ga 6:8*
harvest ruin of his flesh (B)   *Ga 6:8*
reap decay and death of his own nature (P)   *Ga 6:8*
escaped the *c.* that is in the world   *2Pe 1:4*
the moral decay in the world (A)   *2Pe 1:4*
inevitable disintegration lust produces (P)   *2Pe 1:4*
utterly perish in their own *c.*   *2Pe 2:12*
shall be destroyed (E)   *2Pe 2:12*
they will perish (N)   *2Pe 2:12*
destroyed in same destruction (R)   *2Pe 2:12*
themselves are the servants of *c.*   *2Pe 2:19*
slaves of depravity and defilement (A)   *2Pe 2:19*
bound hand and foot to utter depravity (P)   *2Pe 2:19*

CORRUPTLY

And the people did yet *c.*   *2Ch 27:2*
We have dealt very *c.* against thee   *Ne 1:7*
c. in her lusting (B)   *Eze 23:11*

CORRUPTS

c., destroys the temple (A)(N)(R)   *1Co 3:17*

COSAM

Addi, which was the son of C.   *Lu 3:28*

COSMETICS

supplied the *c.* (B)   *Es 2:9*

COSMIC

your *c.* powers (B)(N)   *Eph 6:12*
discarded *c.* powers (N)   *Col 2:15*
c. powers and authorities (N)   *Col 2:16*

COST

have we eaten at all of the king's *c.*   *2Sa 19:42*
of that which doth *c.* me nothing   *2Sa 24:24*
nor offer burnt offerings without *c.*   *1Ch 21:24*
not down first, and counteth the *c.*   *Lu 14:28*

COSTLINESS

ships in the sea by reason of her *c.*   *Re 18:19*

COSTLY

c. stones, and hewed stones   *1Ki 5:17*
All these were of *c.* stones   *1Ki 7:9*

COSTLY (cont.)

the foundation was of *c.* stones   *1Ki 7:10*
And above were *c.* stones   *1Ki 7:11*
the *c.* articles (S)   *2Ch 32:27*
of ointment of spikenard, very   *Joh 12:3* *c.*
or gold, or pearls, or *c.* array   *1Ti 2:9*

COTES

of beasts, and *c.* for flocks   *2Ch 32:28*
sheepfolds (A)(R)   *2Ch 32:28*
stalls for the flocks (B)   *2Ch 32:28*
folds for flocks (E)   *2Ch 32:28*

COTTAGE

daughter of Zion is left as a *c.*   *Isa 1:8*
and shall be removed like a *c.*   *Isa 24:20*

COTTAGES

c. for shepherds, and folds for   *Zep 2:6*

COTTON

weave *c.* cloth (S)   *Isa 19:9*

COUCH

thou it: he went up to my *c.*   *Ge 49:4*
upon the *c.* where Esther lay (S)   *Es 7:8*
my *c.* shall case my complaint   *Job 7:13*
When they *c.* in their dens   *Job 38:40*
I water my *c.* with my tears.   *Ps 6:6*
spread *c.* with rags (A)   *Pr 7:16*
of a bed, and in Damascus in   *Am 3:12* a *c.*
through the tiling with his *c.*   *Lu 5:19*
take up thy *c.* and go unto thine   *Lu 5:24*

COUCHED

he *c.* as a lion, and as an old   *Ge 49:9* lion
He *c.*, he lay down as a lion   *Nu 24:9*

COUCHES

c. as a lion (R)   *De 33:20*
the *c.* were of gold (S)   *Es 1:6*
stretch themselves upon their *c.*   *Am 6:4*
and laid them on beds and *c.*   *Ac 5:15*

COUCHETH

and for the deep that *c.*   *De 33:13* beneath

COUCHING

Issachar is a strong ass *c.*   *Ge 49:14* down

COUCHINGPLACE

and the Ammonites a *c.* for   *Eze 25:5* flocks

COULD

when Isaac was old he *c.* not   *Ge 27:1* see
did so to bring forth lice, but *c.*   *Ex 8:18* not
Eli's eyes wax dim, he *c.* not   *1Sa 3:2* see
c. not get warm (S)   *1Ki 1:1*
Ahijah *c.* not see his eyes were   *1Ki 14:4*
to break to king of Edom, but   *2Ki 3:26* *c.* not
but David *c.* not go before it   *1Ch 21:30*
Rehoboam *c.* not withstand   *2Ch 13:7* them
I sought him, but he *c.* not be   *Ps 37:36* found
what *c.* have been done to   *Isa 5:4* vineyard
my mind *c.* not be toward this   *Jer 15:1* people
rowed to bring to land, but *c.*   *Jon 1:13* not
would have killed him, but   *M'k 6:19* she *c.* not
cast him out, and they *c.* not   *M'k 9:18;*   *Lu 9:40*
she hath done what she *c.* she   *M'k 14:8*

the world *c.* not contain the   *Joh 21:25* books
from which *c.* not be justified   *Ac 13:39* by law

COULDEST

and done evil things as thou *c.*   *Jer 3:5*
and yet *c.* not be satisfied   *Eze 16:28*
seeing thou *c.* reveal this secret   *Da 2:47*
c. not thou watch one hour   *M'k 14:37*
Thou *c.* have no power at all   *Joh 19:11*

COULTER

every man his share, and his   *1Sa 13:20* *c.*

COULTERS

and for the *c.* and for the   *1Sa 13:21* forks

COUNCIL

come into their *c.* (E)(R)   *J'g 13:18*
listen to the *c.* of God (B)(R)   *Job 15:8*
the *c.* of God (A)   *Job 15:29*
princes of Judah and their *c.*   *Ps 68:27*
Raca, shall be in danger of the   *M't 5:22* *c.*
the Sanhedrin (A)(B)   *M't 5:22*
the supreme court (P)   *M't 5:22*
Pharisees went out, and held   *M't 12:14* a *c.*
and elders, and all the *c.*   *M't 26:59* sought
Sanhedrin (B)   *M't 26:59;*
   M'k 15:1; Lu 22:66; Joh 11:47; Ac 4:15;
   5:27, 34, 41; 6:12, 15; 22:30; 23:15; 24:20
chief priests and all the *c.*   *M'k 14:55* sought
and scribes and the whole *c.*   *M'k 15:1*
and led him into their *c.*   *Lu 22:66*
chief priests and the   *Joh 11:47* Pharisees a *c.*
to go aside out of the *c.* they   *Ac 4:15*
and called the *c.* together, and   *Ac 5:21*
they set them before the *c.*   *Ac 5:27*
Then stood there up one in the   *Ac 5:34* *c.*
from the presence of the *c.*   *Ac 5:41*
him, and brought him to the *c.*   *Ac 6:12*
And all that sat in the *c.*   *Ac 6:15* looking
all the *c.* of elders (S)   *Ac 22:5*
and all their *c.* to appear   *Ac 22:30*
Paul, earnestly beholding the *c.*   *Ac 23:1*
he cried out in the *c.*, Men and   *Ac 23:6*
Now therefore ye with the *c.*   *Ac 23:15* signify
down Paul to morrow into the   *Ac 23:20* *c.*
I brought him forth into their   *Ac 23:28* *c.*
while I stood before the *c.*   *Ac 24:20*
he had conferred with the *c.*   *Ac 25:12*

COUNCILS

they will deliver you up to   *M't 10:17* the *c.*
they shall deliver you up to *c.*   *M'k 13:9*

COUNSEL

I will give thee *c.* and God   *Ex 18:19* shall
the priest, who shall ask *c.*   *Nu 27:21* for
through the *c.* of Balaam, to   *Nu 31:16*
For they are a nation void of   *De 32:28* *c.*
of unsound mind (B)   *De 32:28*
and asked not *c.* at the mouth   *Jos 9:14* of
did not consult the Lord   *Jos 9:14* (A)(B)
ask direction from the Lord   *Jos 9:14* (R)
Ask *c.* we pray thee, of God   *J'g 18:5*
take *c.*, speak up (A)   *J'g 19:30*
give here your advice and *c.*   *J'g 20:7*
and asked *c.* of God, and said   *J'g 20:18*
and asked *c.* of the Lord,   *J'g 20:23* saying
And Saul asked *c.* of God,   *1Sa 14:37* Shall I

turn the *c.* of Ahithophel into   *2Sa 15:31*
advice into foolishness   *2Sa 15:31* (A)(B)
for me defeat the *c.* of   *2Sa 15:34* Ahithophel
Give *c.* among you what we   *2Sa 16:20* shall
And the *c.* of Ahithophel,   *2Sa 16:23* which he
Lord defeated good *c.* of   *2Sa 17:14* Ahithophel
they shall surely ask *c.* at   *2Sa 20:18* Abel
let me, I pray thee, give thee   *1Ki 1:12* *c.*
let me advise you (A)   *1Ki 1:12*
advice (B)   *1Ki 1:12;*
   12:8; 2Ki 18:20; 2Ch 22:5
forsook *c.* of old men   *1Ki 12:8*
   12:13; 2Ch 10:8, 13
king of Syria took *c.* with   *2Ki 6:8* servants
I have *c.* and strength for   *2Ki 18:20;* war   *Isa 36:5*
so Saul died for asking *c.* of   *1Ch 10:13* one
consulting a medium (A)(R)   *1Ch 10:13*
tried a medium's seance (B)   *1Ch 10:13*
Philistines took *c.* (R)   *1Ch 12:19*
Ahaziah walked after their *c.*   *2Ch 22:5*
king said, Art thou made of   *2Ch 25:16* king's *c.*
king of Judah took *c.* (A)   *2Ch 25:17*
king had taken *c.* to keep   *2Ch 30:2* passover
assembly took *c.* to keep   *2Ch 30:23* seven days
according to *c.* of my lord   *Ezr 10:3*
according to *c.* of princes and   *Ezr 10:8* elders
God brought their *c.* to nought   *Ne 4:15*
their plan frustrated (A)(B)   *Ne 4:15*
c. of the froward is carried   *Job 5:13* headlong
the plottings of the wily (B)   *Job 5:13*
the schemes of the wily (R)   *Job 5:13*
should shine upon *c.* of   *Job 10:3* wicked
favor schemes of the wicked   *Job 10:3* (A)
plottings of the wicked (B)   *Job 10:3*
designs of the wicked (R)   *Job 10:3*
wisdom and strength he hath   *Job 12:13* *c.*
c. of the wicked   *Job 21:16; 22:28*
ungodly far from my   *Job 21:16* comprehension (A)
planning of the wicked (B)   *Job 21:16*
this that darkeneth *c.* by   *Job 38:2* words
obscures purpose by words   *Job 38:2* (B)
he that hideth *c.* without   *Job 42:3* knowledge
walketh not in *c.* of ungodly   *Ps 1:1*
advice of the wicked (B)   *Ps 1:1*
you have shamed the *c.* of the   *Ps 14:6* poor
plans of the poor (A)(R)   *Ps 14:6*
planning of the afflicted (B)   *Ps 14:6*
bless the Lord, who hath given   *Ps 16:7* me *c.*
Lord grant thee, and fulfil all   *Ps 20:4* thy *c.*
fulfill all your plans (A)(B)(R)   *Ps 20:4*
they took *c.* together against   *Ps 31:13* me
they schemed together   *Ps 31:13* (A)(R)
they plotted together (B)   *Ps 31:13*
Lord brings *c.* of heathen to   *Ps 33:10* nought
took sweet *c.* together, and   *Ps 55:14* walked
had sweet fellowship together   *Ps 55:14* (A)(B)
hold sweet converse together   *Ps 55:14* (R)
hide me from the secret *c.* of   *Ps 64:2* the wicked
from secret *c.* of evildoers (E)   *Ps 64:2*
the princes of Judah and their   *Ps 68:27* *c.*
princes and their company   *Ps 68:27* (A)
princes of Judah in their   *Ps 68:27* crowd (B)
princes of Judah in their   *Ps 68:27* throng (R)

guide me with thy *c.* afterward *Ps 73:24*
receive me
taken crafty *c.* against thy *Ps 83:3*
people
consult together against *Ps 83:3*
(A)(B)(E)(R)
waited not for his *c.* but *Ps 106:13*
lusted
did not wait for his plans *Ps 106:13*
(A)
they provoked him with their *Ps 106:43*
c.
they contemned *c.* of Most *Ps 107:11*
High
sated with own *c.* (B) *Pr 1:31*
intimate *c.* is with God (B) *Pr 3:32*
c. is mine, sound wisdom, I am *Pr 8:14*
Where no *c.* is, the people fall *Pr 11:14*
where no guidance is *Pr 11:14*
(A)(E)(R)
Where there is no leadership *Pr 11:14*
(B)
but he that hearkeneth unto *c.* *Pr 12:15*
is wise
without *c.* purposes are *Pr 15:22*
disappointed
hear *c.* and receive instruction *Pr 19:20*
c. in the heart of man is like *Pr 20:5*
deep water
every purpose is established by *Pr 20:18*
c.
there is no wisdom nor *c.* *Pr 21:30*
against Lord
by wise *c.* thou shalt make war *Pr 24:6*
so doth sweetness of friend by *Pr 27:9*
c.
entered into *c.* with (A) *Ec 1:16*
let *c.* of Holy One draw nigh *Isa 5:19*
His prophesied vengeance (A) *Isa 5:19*
the purpose of the Holy One *Isa 5:19*
(B)
the work (R) *Isa 5:19*
they have taken evil *c.* against *Isa 7:5*
thee
have purposed evil against you *Isa 7:5*
(A)(E)
have plotted evil against you *Isa 7:5*
(B)
have devised evil against you *Isa 7:5*
(R)
spirit of *c.* and might rest upon *Isa 11:2*
him
I will destroy the *c.* of Egypt *Isa 19:3*
c. of counsellors of Pharaoh is *Isa 19:11*
brutish
who hath taken this *c.* against *Isa 23:8*
Tyre
from Lord, who is wonderful *Isa 28:29*
in *c.*
that seek deep to hide *c.* from *Isa 29:15*
Lord
with whom took he *c.*? who *Isa 40:14*
instructed him
performeth *c.* of his *Isa 44:26*
messengers
nor shall *c.* perish from the *Jer 18:18*
wise
thou knowest *c.* against me to *Jer 18:23*
slay me
know all their plotting *Jer 18:23*
(A)(R)
knowest all their scheming (B) *Jer 18:23*
I will make void *c.* of Judah *Jer 19:7*
God, great in *c.* mighty in *Jer 32:19*
work
if I give *c.* wilt thou hearken *Jer 38:15*
to me
is *c.* perished from prudent *Jer 49:7*
king of Babylon hath taken *c.* *Jer 49:30*
against you
c. shall perish from the *Eze 7:26*
ancients
that give wicked *c.* in this city *Eze 11:2*
answered with *c.* and wisdom *Da 2:14*
full of prudence and wisdom *Da 2:14*
(A)
answer with wisdom and tact *Da 2:14*
(B)
with prudence and discretion *Da 2:14*
(R)
thy people ask *c.* at stocks *Ho 4:12*
and staff
neither understand they his *c.* *Mic 4:12*
c. of peace shall be between *Zec 6:13*
them
Pharisees held a *c.* against *M't 12:14*
him
held a consultation (A) *M't 12:14*
concocted a plot to kill (B) *M't 12:14*

laid a plot to do away with *M't 12:14*
him (N)
discussed how to get rid of *M't 12:14*
him (P)
they took *c.* and bought *M't 27:7*
potter's field
after consultation they bought *M't 27:7*
(A)(P)
after conferring they bought *M't 27:7*
(B)(N)
when had taken *c.* they gave *M't 28:12*
money
consulted together (A) *M't 28:12*
deliberating in session (B) *M't 28:12*
conferring together (N) *M't 28:12*
after consultation together *M't 28:12*
(P)
they took *c.* against Jesus *M'k 3:6;*
Joh 11:53
held a consultation with the *M'k 3:6*
(A)
went out to plot against him *M'k 3:6*
(B)
began plotting against him *M'k 3:6*
(N)
walked straight out and *M'k 3:6*
discussed (P)
had not consented to *c.* of *Lu 23:51*
then
not agreed to purpose (A) *Lu 23:51*
the counsel's plan (B) *Lu 23:51*
their policy and action (N) *Lu 23:51*
nor voted for their decision *Lu 23:51*
(P)
not consented to purpose (R) *Lu 23:51*
now Caiaphas was he who *Joh 18:14*
gave *c.*
what thy *c.* determined before *Ac 4:28*
to be
your will and purpose *Ac 4:28*
predestined (A)
purpose preordained to take *Ac 4:28*
place (B)
under thy hand and decree (N) *Ac 4:28*
thy hand and will planned *Ac 4:28*
(P)(R)
when heard, they took *c.* to *Ac 5:33*
slay them
they wanted to kill them *Ac 5:33*
(A)(N)(P)(R)
they determined to kill them *Ac 5:33*
(B)
were minded to slay them (E) *Ac 5:33*
if this *c.* be of men, it will *Ac 5:38*
come to nought
after that the Jews took *c.* to *Ac 9:23*
kill him
Jews conspired to (A)(B) *Ac 9:23*
hatched a plot against his life *Ac 9:23*
(N)
made a plot to kill (P) *Ac 9:23*
plotted to kill him (R) *Ac 9:23*
soldiers' *c.* was to kill the *Ac 27:42*
prisoners
who worketh after *c.* of own *Eph 1:11*
will
design of his own will (B) *Eph 1:11*
decreed in his design (N) *Eph 1:11*
purpose in his sovereign will *Eph 1:11*
(P)
to shew immutability of his *c.* *Heb 6:17*
unchangeableness of purpose *Heb 6:17*
and plan (A)(B)
how unchanging was his *Heb 6:17*
purpose (N)
his plan was unchangeable *Heb 6:17*
(P)
unchangeable character of his *Heb 6:17*
purpose (R)
we have a *C.* for defense (B) *1Jo 2:1*
I *c.* thee buy of me gold *Re 3:18*
I advise you to buy (B)(N) *Re 3:18*
my advice to you is to buy (P) *Re 3:18*

COUNSEL *OF GOD, LORD*

ask *c.* we pray thee, *of God* *J'g 18:5*
inquire of (B)(R) *J'g 18:5;*
J'g 20:18; 1Sa 14:37
children of Israel asked *c.* of *J'g 20:18;*
God *20:23*
Saul asked *c. of God,* Shall I *1Sa 14:37*
go down
c. of the *Lord* standeth *Ps 33:11;*
Pr 19:21
because of the *c.* of the *Lord Isa 19:17*
of hosts
purpose of the Lord *Isa 19:17*
(A)(B)(E)(R)

who hath stood in the *c.* of *Jer 23:18*
the *Lord*
therefore hear the *c.* of Lord *Jer 49:20;*
50:45
the plan of the Lord (A)(R) *Jer 49:20*
the lawyers rejected the *c.* of *Lu 7:30*
God
brought to nothing God's *Lu 7:30*
purpose (A)(B)(N)(P)(R)
him delivered by determinate *Ac 2:23*
c. of God
settled plan and foreknowledge *Ac 2:23*
(A)
determined will and *Ac 2:23*
foreknowledge (B)
deliberate will and plan of God *Ac 2:23*
(N)
predetermined plan and *Ac 2:23*
foreknowledge (P)
definite plan and *Ac 2:23*
foreknowledge (R)
not ashamed to declare all *c.* *Ac 20:27*
of God
whole purpose of God *Ac 20:27*
(B)(N)
the complete will of God (P) *Ac 20:27*

MY COUNSEL

hast not hearkened to *my c.* *2Ch 25:16*
heed to my advice (B) *2Ch 25:16*
men waited and kept silence *Job 29:21*
at *my c.*
ye have set at nought all *my c.* *Pr 1:25*
they would none of *my c.* they *Pr 1:30*
despised
my c. shall stand, and I will *Isa 46:10*
do all
man that executeth *my c.* *Isa 46:11*
from a far country
but if they had stood in *my c.* *Jer 23:22*
O king, let *my c.* be acceptable *Da 4:27*

OWN COUNSEL

his *own c.* shall cast him down *Job 18:7*
Israel shall be ashamed of *own Ho 10:6*
c.*

TAKE COUNSEL

and let us *take c.* together *Ne 6:7*
rulers *take c.* against Lord and *Ps 2:2*
Anointed
how long shall I *take c.* in my *Ps 13:2*
soul
lay up cares within me (A) *Ps 13:2*
keep planning in my soul (B) *Ps 13:2*
bear pain in my soul (R) *Ps 13:2*
that wait for my soul, *take c.* *Ps 71:10*
together
consult together (A)(B)(R) *Ps 71:10*
take c. and it shall come to *Isa 8:10*
nought
take c., execute judgment *Isa 16:3*
woe to children that *take c.* *Isa 30:1*
tell ye, let them *take c.* *Isa 45:21*
together

COUNSELLED

which he *c.* in those days *2Sa 16:23*
and thus and thus have I *c.* *2Sa 17:15*
hath Ahithophel *c.* against *2Sa 17:21*
you
How hast thou *c.* him that *Job 26:3*
hath

COUNSELLER

David's *c.* from his city, even *2Sa 15:12*
for Zechariah his son, a wise *1Ch 26:14*
c.
Jonathan David's uncle was *1Ch 27:32*
a *c.*
Ahithophel was the king's *c.* *1Ch 27:33*
mother was his *c.* to do *2Ch 22:3*
wickedly
the *c.* and the cunning artificer *Isa 3:3*
shall be called Wonderful *C.* *Isa 9:6*
Who being his *c.* hath taught *Isa 40:13*
him
there was no *c.* that, when I *Isa 41:28*
asked
is thy *c.* perished? for pangs *Mic 4:9*
have
against the Lord, a wicked *c.* *Na 1:11*

COUNSELLERS

they were his *c.* after the death	2Ch 22:4
hired *c.* against them, to frustrate	Ezr 4:5
of the king, and of his seven *c.*	Ezr 7:14
king and his *c.* have freely offered	Ezr 7:15
me before the king, and his *c.*	Ezr 7:28
which the king, and his *c.*	Ezr 8:25
With kings and *c.* of the earth	Job 3:14
He leadeth *c.* away spoiled	Job 12:17
also are my delight and my *c.*	Ps 119:24
multitude of *c.* there is safety	Pr 11:14
but to the *c.* of peace is joy	Pr 12:20
in the multitude of *c.* they are	Pr 15:22
multitude of *c.* there is safety	Pr 24:6
and thy *c.* as at the beginning	Isa 1:26
counsel of the wise *c.* of Pharaoh	Isa 19:11
treasurers, the *c.* the sheriffs	Da 3:2; 2:3
said unto his *c.*, Did not we cast	Da 3:24
king's *c.* being gathered together	Da 3:27
c. and my lords sought unto me	Da 4:36
c. and the captains, have consulted	Da 6:7

COUNSELLOR

of Arimathaea, an honourable *c.*	M'k 15:43
was a man named Joseph, a *c.*	Lu 23:50
or who hath been his *c.*	Ro 11:34

COUNSELOR

another *C.* (R)	Joh 14:16; 14:26; 15:26; 16:7

COUNSELS

turned round about by his *c.*	Job 37:12
by their own guidance (A)(E)(B)	Job 37:12
Under his control the circle (B)	Job 37:12
let them fall by their own *c.*	Ps 5:10
fall by their own designs (B)	Ps 5:10
they walked in their own *c.*	Ps 81:12
walked in their own deliberations (B)	Ps 81:12
man of understanding shall attain to wise *c.*	Pr 1:5
attain to leadership (B)	Pr 1:5
will acquire skill (R)	Pr 1:5
but the *c.* of the wicked are deceit	Pr 12:5
suggestions of wicked are deceptive (B)	Pr 12:5
have not I written excellent things in *c.*	Pr 22:20
thy *c.* of old are faithfulness	Isa 25:1
purposes planned of old (A)	Isa 25:1
plans determined long ago (B)(R)	Isa 25:1
are wearied in the multitude of thy *c.*	Isa 47:13
exhausted due to your many plans (B)	Isa 47:13
walked in the *c.* of their evil heart	Jer 7:24
devour them, because of their own *c.*	Ho 11:6
we walked in the *c.* of the house of Ahab	Mic 6:16
will make manifest the *c.* of the heart	1Co 4:5
disclose, expose secret aims of the heart (A)	1Co 4:5
shall reveal the inner motives (B)	1Co 4:5
disclose men's inward motives (N)	1Co 4:5
disclose the purposes of the heart (R)	1Co 4:5

COUNT

c. the stars (S)	Ge 15:5
shall make your *c.* for the lamb	Ex 12:4
c. the fruit thereof as uncircumcised	Le 19:23
c. unto you from the morrow	Le 23:15
c. the years of the sale thereof	Le 25:27
then he shall *c.* with him	Le 25:52

priest *c.* the money (A)	Le 27:18
Who can *c.* the dust of Jacob	Nu 23:10
C. not thine handmaid for a	1Sa 1:16
bring them out by *c.* (S)	1Ch 9:28
c. me as an enemy (R)	Job 13:34
my maids, *c.* me for a stranger	Job 19:15
see my ways, and *c.* all my steps	Job 31:4
c. all my bones (S)	Ps 22:17
The Lord shall *c.* when he writeth	Ps 87:6
If I should *c.* them, they are	Ps 139:18
I *c.* them mine enemies	Ps 139:22
he shall *c.* seven days (R)	Eze 44:26
Shall I *c.* them pure with the	Mic 6:11
c. from the year (B)	Lu 25:50
neither *c.* I my life dear unto	Ac 20:24
esteem my life dear (A)	Ac 20:24
I set no store by life (N)	Ac 20:24
consider my own life valuable (P)	Ac 20:24
my life of any value (R)	Ac 20:24
Lord does not *c.* against (N)	Ro 4:8
c. for least, nothing (A)(N)(P)	1Co 6:4
I *c.* all things loss, and do *c.* them dung	Ph'p 3:8
regard as waste, consider as rubbish (B)(P)	Ph'p 3:8
I *c.* not my life to have apprehended, but	Ph'p 3:13
God would *c.* you worthy of this calling	2Th 1:11
c. him not as an enemy, but admonish him	2Th 3:15
c. their masters worthy of all honour	1Ti 6:1
esteem their masters worthy (A)	1Ti 6:1
regard masters as deserving (B)(R)	1Ti 6:1
treat their masters with respect (P)	1Ti 6:1
if thou *c.* me a partner, receive him	Ph'm 17
c. it all joy when ye fall into divers	Jas 1:2
Consider it wholly joyful (A)(B)	Jas 1:2
welcome trials as friends (P)	Jas 1:2
we *c.* them happy which endure	Jas 5:11
blessed who are stedfast (A)(B)(E)(P)	Jas 5:11
those happy who are stedfast (R)	Jas 5:11
they that *c.* it pleasure to riot	2Pe 2:13
as some men *c.* slackness; but	2Pe 3:9
some people's conception of slowness (A)	2Pe 3:9
some thing of dawdling (B)	2Pe 3:9
slow, as some men suppose (N)	2Pe 3:9
he is not dilatory (P)	2Pe 3:9
hath understanding *c.* the number	Re 13:18
calculate the number (A)(B)(P)	Re 13:18
work out the number of the beast (N)	Re 13:18
reckon the number of the beast (R)	Re 13:18

COUNTED

he *c.* it to him for righteousness	Ge 15:6
that shall be *c.* stolen with me	Ge 30:33
Are we not *c.* of him strangers	Ge 31:15
as it was *c.* according to the	Ex 38:21
shall be *c.* guilty (B)	Le 17:4
shall be *c.* as the fields of the	Le 25:31
it shall be *c.* unto the Levites	Nu 18:30
is *c.* to the Canaanite: five lords	Jos 13:3
son Solomon shall be *c.*	1Ki 1:21
be numbered nor *c.* for multitude	1Ki 3:8
not *c.* (S)	1Ki 8:5
c. the money	2Ki 12:10; 12:11
But Levi and Benjamin *c.* he not	1Ch 21:6
they were *c.* by number of names	1Ch 23:24
Solomon *c.* the men (S)	2Ch 2:2
could not be *c.* (S)	2Ch 5:6

they were *c.* faithful and their	Ne 13:13
Wherefore are we *c.* as beasts	Job 18:3
Darts are *c.* as stubble: he	Job 41:29
we are *c.* as sheep for the slaughter	Ps 44:22
I am *c.* with them that go down	Ps 88:4
was *c.* unto him for righteousness	Ps 106:31
he holdeth his peace, is *c.* wise	Pr 17:28
it shall be *c.* a curse to him	Pr 27:14
horses' hoofs shall be *c.* like flint	Isa 5:28
the fruitful field be *c.* for a forest	Isa 32:15
where is he that *c.* the towers	Isa 33:18
are *c.* as the small dust of the	Isa 40:15
are *c.* to him less than nothing	Isa 40:17
they were *c.* as a strange thing	Ho 8:12
because they *c.* him as a prophet	M't 14:5
regarded John as a prophet (A)	M't 14:5
considered him a prophet (B)	M't 14:5
in whose eyes John was a prophet (N)	M't 14:5
all thought John was a prophet (P)	M't 14:5
held him to be a prophet (R)	M't 14:5
men *c.* John that he was a prophet	M'k 11:32
c. and classed among (A)(N)	Lu 22:37
that they were *c.* worthy to suffer	Ac 5:41
happy to be thought worthy (B)(N)(P)	Ac 5:41
they *c.* the price of them	Ac 19:19
shall not his uncircumcision be *c.*	Ro 2:26
credited to (A)	Ro 2:26; 4:5
reckoned as circumcision (E)	Ro 2:26; 4:5
regarded as circumcision (R)	Ro 2:26
c. unto him for righteousness	Ro 4:3
c. as a favor or gift (A)(P)(R)	Ro 4:4
his faith is *c.* for righteousness	Ro 4:5
Abraham's faith *c.* for (N)(P)	Ro 4:9; 4:10
righteousness *c.* to them (N)	Ro 4:11
faith *c.* to him (N)	Ro 4:22; 4:23
be *c.* in the same way (N)	Ro 4:24
sin not *c.* where no law (N)	Ro 5:13
of the promise are *c.* for the seed	Ro 9:8
gain to me, those I *c.* loss for	Ph'p 3:7
consider as loss (A)(B)(P)	Ph'p 3:7
may be *c.* worthy of the kingdom	2Th 1:5
deemed deserving of the kingdom (A)	2Th 1:5
made worthy of the kingdom (B)(R)	2Th 1:5
prove you worthy of the kingdom (N)	2Th 1:5
make you worthy of his kingdom (P)	2Th 1:5
that he *c.* me faithful, putting me	1Ti 1:12
deemed me worthy and appointed me (A)	1Ti 1:12
judging me worthy of this trust (N)	1Ti 1:12
trusting me enough to appoint me (P)	1Ti 1:12
judge me faithful by appointing me (R)	1Ti 1:12
well be *c.* worthy of double honour	1Ti 5:17
considered worthy of double honor (A)	1Ti 5:17
reckoned worthy of double honor (N)	1Ti 5:17
be considered worthy of respect (P)(R)	1Ti 5:17
was *c.* worthy of more glory than	Heb 3:3
considered worthy of greater (A)(P)	Heb 3:3
entitled to greater honor (B)	Heb 3:3
deemed worthy of greater honor (N)	Heb 3:3
whose descent is not *c.* from them	Heb 7:6
hath *c.* the blood of the covenant	Heb 10:29
considered the covenant blood (A)(B)	Heb 10:29
profaned blood of the covenant (N)(R)	Heb 10:29

treated like dirt the blood (P) — *Heb 10:29*
she *c.* him faithful (A) — *Heb 11:11*

COUNTENANCE

Cain was very wroth, and his *c.* fell — *Ge 4:5*
he looked sad and depressed (A) — *Ge 4:5*
why is thy *c.* fallen — *Ge 4:6*
Why is your face downcast (B) — *Ge 4:6*
Jacob beheld the *c.* of Laban — *Ge 31:2; 31:5*
looked less favorably than before (A) — *Ge 31:2*
attitude not as used to be (B) — *Ge 31:2*
not regard with favor as before (R) — *Ge 31:2*
Neither shalt thou *c.* a poor man — *Ex 23:3*
The Lord lift up his *c.* upon thee — *Nu 6:26*
nation of fierce *c.* which shall not — *De 28:50*
of a fierce appearance (B) — *De 28:50*
his *c.* was like the *c.* of an angel — *J'g 13:6*
face like the angel of God (A) — *J'g 13:6*
appearance of an angel (B) — *J'g 13:6*
eat, and her *c.* was no more sad — *1Sa 1:18*
face showed no more sadness (B) — *1Sa 1:18*
Look not on his *c.* or on the — *1Sa 16:7*
Do not look on his appearance (A)(R) — *1Sa 16:7*
pay no attention to his looks (B) — *1Sa 16:7*
of a beautiful *c.* and goodly — *1Sa 16:12*
was fine looking (A) — *1Sa 16:12*
a handsome appearance (B)(R) — *1Sa 16:12*
youth, and ruddy, and of a fair *c.* — *1Sa 17:42*
and of a beautiful *c.* — *1Sa 25:3*
good understanding and beautiful (A)(R) — *1Sa 25:3*
intelligent and good-looking (B) — *1Sa 25:3*
she was a woman of a fair *c.* — *2Sa 14:27*
he settled his *c.* steadfastly — *2Ki 8:11*
Hazael was embarrassed (A) — *2Ki 8:11*
looked at him fixedly (B) — *2Ki 8:11*
fixed his gaze and stared at (R) — *2Ki 8:11*
Why is thy *c.* sad, seeing thou art — *Ne 2:2*
Why is your face sad (B)(R) — *Ne 2:2*
why should not my *c.* be sad — *Ne 2:3*
my face sad (A)(R) — *Ne 2:3*
my sad appearance (B) — *Ne 2:3*
thou changest his *c.,* and sendest — *Job 14:20*
you change his appearance (A) — *Job 14:20*
thou changest his looks (B) — *Job 14:20*
light of my *c.* they cast not down — *Job 29:24*
light of my face (B) — *Job 29:24*
lift thou up the light of thy *c.* — *Ps 4:6*
through the pride of his *c.* — *Ps 10:4*
his *c.* doth behold the upright — *Ps 11:7*
him exceeding glad with thy *c.* — *Ps 21:6*
joy by thy presence (A)(B)(E)(R) — *Ps 21:6*
praise him for the help of his *c.* — *Ps 42:5*
health of my *c.* and my God — *Ps 42:11*
my face-healer (B) — *Ps 42:11*
my help and my God (R) — *Ps 42:11; 43:5*
health of my *c.* and my God — *Ps 43:5*
my face-saver and my God (B) — *Ps 43:5*
light of thy *c.* because thou hadst — *Ps 44:3*
light of thy face (B) — *Ps 44:3*
they perish at the rebuke of thy *c.* — *Ps 80:16*
rebuke of thy appearance (B) — *Ps 80:16*
walk, O Lord, in the light of *c.* — *Ps 89:15*
secret sins in the light of thy *c.* — *Ps 90:8*
merry heart maketh a cheerful *c.* — *Pr 15:13*
makes the face look sunny (B) — *Pr 15:13*
the light of the king's *c.* is life — *Pr 16:15*
a king's face is life (B) — *Pr 16:15*
an angry *c.* a backbiting tongue — *Pr 25:23*

an angry face (B) — *Pr 25:23*
sharpeneth the *c.* of his friend — *Pr 27:17*
sharpens face of another (B) — *Pr 27:17*
by the sadness of the *c.* the heart — *Ec 7:3*
by facial sadness the heart (B) — *Ec 7:3*
let me see thy *c.* let me hear — *Ca 2:14*
let me see your face (A)(B)(R) — *Ca 2:14*
is thy voice, and thy *c.* is comely — *Ca 2:14*
his *c.* is as Lebanon, excellent as — *Ca 5:15*
appearance like Lebanon (A)(R) — *Ca 5:15*
his stature is like Lebanon (B) — *Ca 5:15*
his aspect is like Lebanon (E) — *Ca 5:15*
The shew of their *c.* doth witness — *Isa 3:9*
showing partiality witnesses against them (A)(R) — *Isa 3:9*
expression of faces witnesses (B) — *Isa 3:9*
they shall be troubled in their *c.* — *Eze 27:35*
their faces quiver (A) — *Eze 27:35*
their faces are convulsed (B)(R) — *Eze 27:35*
the king's *c.* was changed, and (A) — *Da 5:6*
the king's face was changed (A) — *Da 5:6*
the king's face paled (B) — *Da 5:6*
king's color changed (R) — *Da 5:6; 5:9-10*
his *c.* was changed in him, and — *Da 5:9*
nor let thy *c.* be changed — *Da 5:10*
and my *c.* changed in me: but — *Da 7:28*
a king of fierce *c.* and — *Da 8:23*
a hard-faced king (B) — *Da 8:23*
the hypocrites, of a sad *c.* — *M't 6:16*
put on a dismal *c.* (A) — *M't 6:16*
make their look unsightly (B) — *M't 6:16*
they disfigure their faces (R) — *M't 6:16*
His *c.* was like lightning, and — *M't 28:3*
appearance like lightning (A)(B)(E)(P)(R) — *M't 28:3*
face shone like lightning (N) — *M't 28:5*
his *c.* was altered, and — *Lu 9:29*
make me full of joy with thy *c.* — *Ac 2:28*
full of joy in your presence (A)(B)(N)(R) — *Ac 2:28*
of Moses for the glory of his *c.* — *2Co 3:7*
facial brilliance (A)(B) — *2Co 3:7*
the glory of his face (E) — *2Co 3:7*
face because of its brightness (R) — *2Co 3:7*
and his *c.* was as the sun shineth — *Re 1:16*
His face like the sun (A)(B)(N)(P)(R) — *Re 1:16*

COUNTENANCES

Then let our *c.* be looked upon — *Da 1:13*
our appearance (A)(R) — *Da 1:13*
our looks (B) — *Da 1:13*
their *c.* appeared fairer and — *Da 1:15*

COUNTERFEIT

men of *c.* faith (R) — *2Ti 3:8*

COUNTERFEITS

c. of the real (P) — *2Co 11:13*
unless you are *c.* (A)(B) — *2Co 13:5; 13:6-7*
c. as to faith (B) — *2Ti 3:8*

COUNTERVAIL

the enemy could not *c.* the king's — *Es 7:4*
not to be compared with the damage (A) — *Es 7:4*
cannot compensate (B)(E) — *Es 7:4*
compared with the loss (R) — *Es 7:4*

COUNTETH

he *c.* me unto him as one of his — *Job 19:11*
he *c.* me for his enemy — *Job 33:10*
hands of him that *c.* (S) — *Jer 33:13*
and *c.* the cost, whether he hath — *Lu 14:28*

COUNTING

saith the preacher, *c.* one by one — *Ec 7:27*
not *c.* up (A)(B)(R) — *2Co 5:19*
c. other better than (E)(R) — *Ph'p 2:3*

COUNTLESS

c. angelic army (A)(P) — *Heb 12:22*

COUNTRIES

after their tongues, in their *c.* — *Ge 10:20*
give all these *c.* and I will — *Ge 26:3*
all these lands (A)(E)(R) — *Ge 26:3*
all this territory (B) — *Ge 26:3*
give unto thy seed all these *c.* — *Ge 26:4*
all *c.* came into Egypt to Joseph — *Ge 41:57*
all nations (B) — *Ge 41:57*
all the earth (R) — *Ge 41:57*
These are the *c.* which Moses did — *Jos 13:32*
And these are the *c.* which the — *Jos 14:1*
and her towns, even three *c.* — *Jos 17:11*
gods of the *c.* that have delivered — *2Ki 18:35*
all the gods of the lands (B) — *2Ki 18:35*
and of glory throughout all *c.* — *1Ch 22:5*
glory through all lands (A)(B)(R) — *1Ch 22:5*
over all the kingdoms of the *c.* — *1Ch 29:30*
all the *c.* of Judah and Benjamin — *2Ch 11:23*
service of the kingdoms of the *c.* — *2Ch 12:8*
upon all the inhabitants of the *c.* — *2Ch 15:5*
on all the kingdoms of those *c.* — *2Ch 20:29*
kingdoms of all lands (B) — *2Ch 20:29*
out of all the *c.* that pertained — *2Ch 34:33*
because of the people of those *c.* — *Ezr 3:3*
the neighboring lands (B)(R) — *Ezr 3:3*
over all *c.* beyond the river — *Ezr 4:20*
wound the heads over many *c.* — *Ps 110:6*
all nations (B)(E)(R) — *Ps 110:6*
and give ear, all ye of far *c.* — *Isa 8:9*
c. bordering the Mediterranean (A) — *Isa 11:11*
waste all the nations and their *c.* — *Isa 37:18*
my flock out of all *c.* whither I have — *Jer 23:3*
all lands (B)(E) — *Jer 23:3; Eze 22:4*
from all *c.* whither I had driven — *Jer 23:8*
prophesied both against many *c.* — *Jer 28:8*
will gather them out of all *c.* — *Jer 32:37*
that were in all the *c.* heard that — *Jer 40:11*
the nations and *c.* that are round — *Eze 5:5*
the nations (B)(R) — *Eze 5:5; 6:8; 11:16-17; 25:7; 29:12; Zec 10:9*
the nations (E) — *Eze 5:5; Eze 5:6; 6:8; 11:16-17*
more than the *c.* that are round — *Eze 5:6*
be scattered throughout the *c.* — *Eze 6:8*
have scattered them among the *c.* — *Eze 11:16*
them as a little sanctuary in the *c.* — *Eze 11:16*
assemble you out of the *c.* — *Eze 11:17*
and disperse them in the *c.* — *Eze 12:15*
and disperse them through the *c.* — *Eze 20:23*
heathen, as the families of *c.* — *Eze 20:32*
gather you out of the *c.* wherein — *Eze 20:34*
c. wherein ye have been scattered — *Eze 20:41*
and a mocking to all *c.* — *Eze 22:4*
disperse thee in the *c.* and will — *Eze 22:15*
cause thee to perish out of the *c.* — *Eze 25:7*
midst of the *c.* that are desolate — *Eze 29:12*
will disperse them through the *c.* — *Eze 29:12*
midst of the *c.* that are desolate — *Eze 30:7*
disperse them through the *c.* — *Eze 30:23*
and disperse them among the *c.* — *Eze 30:26*
the *c.* which thou hast not known — *Eze 32:9*
and gather them from the *c.* — *Eze 34:13*
and these two *c.* shall be mine — *Eze 35:10*

two nations (B)(E)(R)	Eze 35:10
were dispersed through the c.	Eze 36:19
gather you out of all c. and	Eze 36:24
all the c. whither thou hast driven	Da 9:7
he shall enter in the c. and	Da 11:40
many c. shall be overthrown	Da 11:41
forth his hand also upon the c.	Da 11:42
they shall remember me in far c.	Zec 10:9
that are in the c. enter thereinto	Lu 21:21

COUNTRY

the whole c. (B)	Ge 13:9; 17:8
the smoke of the c. went up	Ge 19:28
shalt go to my c. and my kindred	Ge 24:4
it must not be so done in our c.	Ge 29:26
send me away, that I may go to my c.	Ge 30:25
Shechem the prince of the c. saw her	Ge 34:2
the Lord of the c. said unto us	Ge 42:33
locusts in the c. (A)(R)	Ex 10:4
all born in c. do these things	Nu 15:13
c. which Lord smote before Israel	Nu 32:4
come into c. Lord sware to give	De 26:3
there came men to search out c.	Jos 2:2
Joshua sent, saying, Go up and view c.	Jos 7:2
the hill c. (S)	J'g 2:9;
3:27; 1Sa 9:4; 1Ch 6:67; 2Ch 13:4; 15:8	
pass through his c. (B)	J'g 11:20
Israel possessed the land of that c.	J'g 11:21
our enemy and the destroyer of our c.	J'g 16:24
they came into the c. of Moab	Ru 1:2
who returned out of the c. of Moab	Ru 1:22
all thy c. wept with a loud voice	2Sa 15:23
bones of Saul buried in c. of Benjamin	2Sa 21:14
but the Syrians filled the c.	1Ki 20:27
the c. was filled with water	2Ki 3:20
your c. is desolate, your cities burnt	Isa 1:7
toss thee like a ball in a large c.	Isa 22:18
not return, nor see his native c.	Jer 22:10
I will bring them from the north c.	Jer 31:8
judgment is come upon the plain c.	Jer 48:21
cause an assembly to come from north c.	Jer 50:9
I will bring them forth out of c.	Eze 20:38
glory of c. Bethjeshi-moth, Baal-meon	Eze 25:9
they shall be to you as born in the c.	Eze 47:22
saying, when I was yet in my c.	Jon 4:2
spread abroad his fame in all c.	M't 9:31
he would not send them out of c.	M'k 5:10
told it in city, and in c.	M'k 5:14; Lu 8:34
joined himself to a citizen of c.	Lu 15:15
because their c. nourished by king's c.	Ac 12:20
shipmen deemed drew near some c.	Ac 27:27
sojourned in land as in strange c.	Heb 11:9
they declare plainly that they seek a c.	Heb 11:14
if they had been mindful of that c.	Heb 11:15
they desire a better c. an heavenly	Heb 11:16

FAR COUNTRY

we be come from a far c.	Jos 9:6; 9:9
out of far c. for thy sake	1Ki 8:41; 2Ch 6:32

they are come from a far c.	2Ki 20:14; Isa 39:3
so is good news from a far c.	Pr 25:25
from far c. to destroy whole land	Isa 13:5
man that executeth counsel from far c.	Isa 46:11
publish, that watchers come from far c.	Jer 4:16
because of them that dwell in a far c.	Jer 8:19
went into a far c.	M't 21:33; M'k 12:1
as man travelling into far c.	M't 25:14
younger son took journey into far c.	Lu 15:13

OWN COUNTRY

one of your own c.	Le 16:29; Le 17:15; 24:22
turned and went to her own c.	1Ki 10:13
I may go to my own c.	1Ki 11:21
proclamation every man to his own c.	1Ki 22:36
let us go every one into his own c.	Jer 51:9
they departed into their own c.	M't 2:12
save in his own c.	M't 13:57; M'k 6:4; Lu 4:24
went and came into his own c.	M'k 6:1
prophet no honour in his own c.	Joh 4:44

THY COUNTRY

get thee out of thy c.	Ge 12:1; Ac 7:3
return to thy c. and kindred	Ge 32:9
let us pass thro' thy c.	Nu 20:17
what is thy c.? of what people	Jon 1:8
heard done, do here in thy c.	Lu 4:23

COUNTRYMEN

in perils by mine own c. in perils	2Co 11:26
suffered like things of your own c.	1Th 2:14

COUNTS

c. iron as straw (A)(B)(E)(R)	Job 41:27
whom God c. as just (N)	Ro 4:6

COUPLE

and c. the curtains together with	Ex 26:6
c. five curtains by themselves	Ex 26:9
and c. the tent together, that	Ex 26:11
of brass to c. the tent together	Ex 36:18
shoulderpieces for it, to c. it	Ex 39:4
servant with him, and a c. of asses	J'g 19:3
make me a c. of cakes in my sight	2Sa 13:6
him, with a c. of asses saddled	2Sa 16:1
a chariot with a c. of horsemen	Isa 21:7
of men, with a c. of horsemen	Isa 9

COUPLED

five curtains shall be c.	Ex 26:3;
together	Ex 26:24; 36:10, 13, 16, 29
by the two edges was it c.	Ex 39:4
chaste coversation c. with fear	1Pe 3:2

COUPLETH

the edge of the curtain which c.	Ex 26:10
of the curtain which c. the second	Ex 36:17

COUPLING

from the selvedge in the c.	Ex 26:4; 36:11
curtain, in the c. of the second	Ex 26:4; 26:5; 36:11-12, 17
over against the other c.	Ex 28:27; 39:20

COUPLINGS

buy hewn stone, and timber for c.	2Cn 34:11

COURAGE

And be ye of good c. and bring	Nu 13:20
do your best and bring back (B)	Nu 13:20
Be strong and of a good c. fear not	De 31:6
be strong, courageous, and firm (A)	De 31:6
be resolute and strong (B)	De 31:6
Be strong and of a good c.	De 31:7; 31:23
Be strong, courageous and firm (A)	De 31:7
be very resolute and strong (B)	De 31:7
Be strong and of a good c.	Jos 1:6
Be strong and of a good c.; be not	Jos 1:9
only be strong and of a good c.	Jos 1:18
did there remain any more c.	Jos 2:11
Be strong and of a good c.	Jos 10:25
mighty men of c. (A)	J'g 6:12;
1Ki 11:28; 1Ch 12:21; 2Ch 14:8; 17:13	
Be of good c. and let us play	2Sa 10:12
Be of good c. and let us behave	1Ch 19:13
be strong, and of good c.; dread no	1Ch 22:13
mighty men of c. (A)	1Ch 26:6; 1Ch 26:20, 31-32
Be strong and of good c. and	1Ch 28:20
Oded the prophet, he took c.	2Ch 15:8
with thee: be of good c. and	Ps 27:14
Wait on the Lord: be of good	Ps 27:14
Be of good c. and he shall	Ps 31:24
said to his brother, Be of good c.	Isa 41:6
shall stir up his power and his c.	Da 11:25
saw, he thanked God, and took c.	Ac 28:15

COURAGEOUS

be strong, c. and firm (A)	De 31:6; 31:7
Only be thou strong and very c.	Jos 1:7
Be ye therefore very c. to keep	Jos 23:6
c. men (B)	J'g 18:2
mighty or c. man (A)	1Sa 14:52; J'g 3:29
I commanded you? be c. and	2Sa 13:28
Be strong and c. be not afraid	2Ch 32:7
And he that is c. among the	Am 2:16

COURAGEOUSLY

Deal c. and the Lord shall be	2Ch 19:11

COURSE

of every c. were twenty and four	1Ch 27:1; 27:2, 4-15
each division numbering 24,000 (A)(R)	1Ch 27:1
each corp consisted of 24,000 (B)	1Ch 27:1
Over the first c. for the first month	1Ch 27:2
that ministered to the king by c.	1Ch 28:1
and did not then wait by c.	2Ch 5:11
divisions (A)(R)	2Ch 5:11
priestly rotation (B)	2Ch 5:11
And they sang together by c.	Ezr 3:11
of the earth are out of c.	Ps 82:5
foundations are shaking (A)(B)	Ps 82:5
foundations are shaken (E)(R)	Ps 82:5
who takes a crooked c. (B)	Pr 10:9
every one turned to his c. as the	Jer 8:6
turns to his own devices (B)	Jer 8:6
their c. is evil, and their force	Jer 23:10
they pursue evil (B)	Jer 23:10
Zacharias, of the c. of Abia	Lu 1:5
daily service (division) of Abia (A)	Lu 1:5
Abia week of the series (B)	Lu 1:5
division of the priesthood of (N)(R)	Lu 1:5
Abijah section of the priesthood (P)	Lu 1:5
before God in the order of his c.	Lu 1:8
in the order of his division (A)(R)	Lu 1:8
in the sequence of his series (B)	Lu 1:8
as John fulfilled his c. he said	Ac 13:25

we came with a straight *c.* to   *Ac 16:11*
that I might finish my *c.* with   *Ac 20:24* joy
we came with a straight *c.* unto   *Ac 21:1*
when we had finished our *c.*   *Ac 21:7*
three, and that by *c.;* and let   *1Co 14:27* one
each one in turn   *1Co 14:27* (A)(B)(E)(R)
one at a time (N)   *1Co 14:27*
according to the *c.* or this   *Eph 2:2* world
no *c.* stupid, flippant talk (N)   *Eph 5:4*
word of the Lord may have   *2Th 3:1* free *c.*
I have finished my *c.* I have   *2Ti 4:7* kept
I have finished the race   *2Ti 4:7* (A)(B)(R)
I have run the great race (N)   *2Ti 4:7*
c. helmsman chooses (N)   *Jas 3:4*
setteth on fire the *c.* of nature   *Jas 3:6*
setting on fire the wheel of   *Jas 3:6* birth-the cycle of man's nature (A)
fire the whole machinery of   *Jas 3:6* existence (B)
fire the wheel of nature (E)   *Jas 3:6*
keeps wheel of existence red hot   *Jas 3:6* (N)
can make whole life a blazing   *Jas 3:6* hell (P)
setting on fire cycle of nature   *Jas 3:6* (R)

COURSES

stars in their *c.* fought against   *J'g 5:20*
ten thousand a month by *c.*   *1Ki 5:14*
divided them into *c.* among   *1Ch 23:6*
organized them into sections   *1Ch 23:6* (A)
into divisions (B)(R)   *1Ch 23:6;*
2Ch 8:14; 23:8; 31:2; 35:10; Ezr 6:18
the king in any matter of the   *1Ch 27:1* *c.*
Also for the *c.* of the priests   *1Ch 28:13*
the *c.* of the priests to their   *2Ch 8:14* service
the porters also by their *c.* at   *2Ch 8:14*
the priests dismissed not the   *2Ch 23:8* *c.*
appointed the *c.* of the priests   *2Ch 31:2*
and the Levites after their *c.*   *2Ch 31:2*
to give to their brethren by   *2Ch 31:15* *c.* as
their charges according to   *2Ch 31:16* their *c.*
in their charges by their *c.*   *2Ch 31:17*
fathers, after your *c.*   *2Ch 35:4* according to
the Levites in their *c.*   *2Ch 35:10* according to
and the Levites in their *c.* for   *Ezr 6:18*
as willows by the water *c.*   *Isa 44:4*
stray in godless *c.* (N)   *2Ti 2:16*

COURT

make the *c.* of the tabernacle   *Ex 27:9;*
Ex 35:17; 38:9; 39:40
breadth of the *c.*   *Ex 27:12; 7:13, 16-19*
the pins of the *c.*   *Ex 27:19;*
35:18; 38:20, 31
shalt set up the *c.* round about   *Ex 40:8*
in *c.* of tabernacle shall eat it   *Le 6:16;*
6:26
no unfairness of *c.* decision   *Le 19:15* (B)
man which had a well in his   *2Sa 17:18* *c.*
afore Isaiah was gone into   *2Ki 20:4* middle *c.*
Jehoshaphat stood before new   *2Ch 20:5* *c.*
stoned Zechariah in *c.* of   *2Ki 24:21* Lord's house
brought out uncleanness into   *2Ki 29:16* the *c.*
Esther stood in inner *c.* of king's   *Es 5:1* house
and the king said, Who is in the   *Es 6:4* *c.*
servants said, Haman standeth   *Es 6:5* in *c.*
come together in *c.* trial   *Job 9:2* (A)(B)
habitation of dragons, and *c.*   *Isa 34:13* for owls

abode of ostriches   *Isa 34:13* (A)(B)(R)
Jeremiah stood in *c.* of Lord's   *Jer 19:14* house
has a *c.* case against nation   *Jer 25:3* (B)
stand in *c.* of Lord's house and   *Jer 26:2* speak
shut up in *c.* of prison   *Jer 32:2;*
33:1; 39:15
cast Jeremiah into dungeon in   *Jer 38:6* *c.*
he brought me to door of *c.*   *Eze 8:7;*
8:16
man went in, cloud filled inner   *Eze 10:3* *c.*
brought me into outward *c.*   *Eze 40:17;*
42:1; 46:21
brought me to inner *c.* and   *Eze 40:28* measured
Spirit brought me into the   *Eze 43:5* inner *c.*
put blood upon the gate of   *Eze 45:19* the inner *c.*
in every corner of *c.* there   *Eze 46:21* was a *c.*
the *c.* took its seat (B)   *Da 7:22*
king's chapel, and it is king's   *Am 7:13* *c.*
escape punishment by the *c.*   *M't 5:21* (A)(B)
into the *c.* (S)   *M't 26:58;*
26:69; M'k 14:54, 66; Lu 22:55;
Joh 18:15
into the *c.* of the high priest   *M't 26:58* (E)
sitting without the *c.* (E)   *M't 26:69*
sitting in *c.* (N)   *M't 27:19*
guardeth his own *c.* (E)   *Lu 11:21*
led him into *c.* (B)(N)(P)   *Ac 18:12*
drove him from the *c.*   *Ac 18:16* (B)(N)(P)
in front of the *c.* (A)   *Ac 18:17*
standing before Caesar's *c.*   *Ac 25:10* (P)
seek judgment in a pagan *c.*   *1Co 6:1* (B)(P)
c. favor to gain ends (N)   *Jude 16*
the *c.* without the temple, leave   *Re 11:2* out

COURTEOUS

as brethren, be pitiful, be *c.*   *1Pe 3:8*

COURTEOUSLY

Julius *c.* entreated Paul   *Ac 27:3*
treated Paul in a man-loving   *Ac 27:3* way, with much consideration (A)
treated Paul kindly (E)(R)   *Ac 27:3*
very considerately allowed   *Ac 27:3* Paul (N)(P)
us, and lodged us three days *c.*   *Ac 28:7*
entertained us with hearty   *Ac 28:7* hospitality (A)
entertained us hospitably   *Ac 28:7* (N)(R)
entertained us most kindly (P)   *Ac 28:7*

COURTHOUSE

beat him in front of the *c.*   *Ac 18:17* (P)

COURTING

adulterously *c.* (B)   *Le 17:7*
the age of *c.* (B)   *Eze 16:8*

COURTS

two *c.* of the house of the   *2Ki 21:5* Lord
Manasseh had made in the   *2Ki 23:12* two *c.*
in the *c.* and in the chambers   *1Ch 23:28*
he shall build my house and   *1Ch 28:6* my *c.*
of the *c.* of the house of the   *1Ch 28:12* Lord
all the people shall be in the   *2Ch 23:5* *c.* of
two *c.* of the house of the   *2Ch 33:5* Lord
roof of his house, and in   *Ne 8:16* their *c.*
and in the *c.* of the house of   *Ne 8:16* God

preparing him a chamber in   *Ne 13:7* the *c.*
thee, that he may dwell in thy   *Ps 65:4* *c.*
even fainteth for the *c.* of the   *Ps 84:2* Lord
For a day in thy *c.* is better   *Ps 84:10* than
shall flourish in the *c.* of our   *Ps 92:13* God
courtyards of our God (B)   *Ps 92:13*
an offering, and come into his   *Ps 96:8* *c.*
into his *c.* with praise: be   *Ps 100:4* thankful
In the *c.* of the Lord's house   *Ps 116:19*
in the *c.* of the house of our   *Ps 135:2* God
this at your hand, to tread my   *Isa 1:12* *c.*
drink it in the *c.* of my   *Isa 62:9* holiness
and fill the *c.* with the slain   *Eze 9:7*
not pillars as the pillars of the   *Eze 42:6* *c.*
were *c.* joined of forty cubits   *Eze 46:22* long
and shalt also keep my *c.* and   *Zec 3:7*
live delicately, are in the king's   *Lu 7:25* *c.*
drag you into law *c.*   *Jas 2:6* (A)(B)(N)(R)

COURTYARD

sitting outside the *c.*   *M't 26:69* (A)(B)(N)(P)(R)

COURTYARDS

c. of our God (B)   *Ps 92:13*

COUSIN

And, behold, thy *c.* Elizabeth   *Lu 1:36*
your relative (A)   *Lu 1:36*
thy kinswoman (E)(N)(R)   *Lu 1:36*

COUSINS

her neighbours and her *c.*   *Lu 1:58* heard
relatives (A)(N)(P)   *Lu 1:58*
kin (B)   *Lu 1:58*
kinsfolk (E)(R)   *Lu 1:58*

COVENANT

this is token of *c.*   *Ge 9:12; 13:17; 17:11*
as for me, behold, my *c.* is   *Ge 17:4* with thee
my *c.* be in your flesh for   *Ge 17:13* everlasting *c.*
soul be cut off, he hath   *Ge 17:14* broken my *c.*
keep sabbath for a perpetual   *Ex 31:16* *c.*
wrote upon tables words of   *Ex 34:28* the *c.*
ye do not my commandments   *Le 26:15* but break my *c.*
I give to him my *c.* of peace   *Nu 25:12*
the *c.* of an everlasting   *Nu 25:13* priesthood
and he declared unto you his *c.*   *De 4:13*
lest ye forget *c.* of Lord your   *De 4:23* God
Lord will not forget *c.* of thy   *De 4:31* fathers
when I was gone to receive   *De 9:9* tables of *c.*
the Lord gave me the tables of   *De 9:11* the *c.*
two tables of *c.* were in my   *De 9:15* hands
are words of *c.* which Lord   *De 29:11* commanded
thou shouldest enter into *c.*   *De 29:12* with Lord
according to all curses of *c.* in   *De 29:21* this book
because ye have forsaken the   *De 29:25* *c.* of the Lord
will provoke me and break   *De 31:20* my *c.*
make a *c.* with us (A)(E)(R)   *Jos 9:6*
I will never break my *c.* with   *J'g 2:1* you
make a *c.* with (A)(B)(E)(R)   *J'g 2:2*

made a *c.* with (B)	*J'g* 22:8
brought thy servant into *c.* of	*1Sa* 20:8
Lord	
made a *c.* with (A)(E)(R)	*2Sa* 5:3
Israel have forsaken thy *c.*	*1Ki* 19:10;
	19:14
Ahab said, I will send away	*1Ki* 20:34
with *c.*	
because of his *c.* with	*2Ki* 13:23
Abraham	
perform words of *c.*	*2Ki* 23:3;
	2Ch 34:31
be mindful always of his *c.*	*1Ch* 16:15
they entered into *c.* to seek	*2Ch* 15:12
God	
they have defiled *c.* of	*Ne* 13:29
priesthood	
fear him, he will shew his *c.*	*Ps* 25:14
neither have we dealt falsely	*Ps* 44:17
in thy *c.*	
shouldest take my *c.* in thy	*Ps* 50:16
mouth	
put forth hands, he hath	*Ps* 55:20
broken *c.*	
respect to *c.* for dark places	*Ps* 74:20
of earth	
heart not right, nor stedfast in	*Ps* 78:37
c.	
c. shall stand fast with him	*Ps* 89:28
My *c.* will I not break, nor	*Ps* 89:34
alter the thing	
thou hast made void *c.* of thy	*Ps* 89:39
servant	
he will ever be mindful of his	*Ps* 111:5
c.	
commanded his *c.* for ever,	*Ps* 111:9
holy is his name	
and forgetteth the *c.* of her God	*Pr* 2:17
c. with death shall be	*Isa* 28:18
disannulled	
hath broken *c.* he hath	*Isa* 33:8
despised	
give thee for *c.* of people	*Isa* 42:6; 49:8
nor shall *c.* of peace be	*Isa* 54:10
removed	
eunuchs that take hold of my	*Isa* 56:4;
c.	56:6
as for me, this is my *c.* with	*Isa* 59:21
them	
hear ye the words of this *c.*	*Jer* 11:2;
	11:6
cursed be man that obeyeth	*Jer* 11:3
not words of *c.*	
remember, break not thy *c.*	*Jer* 14:21
with us	
because they have forsaken *c.*	*Jer* 22:9
of Lord	
which my *c.* they brake	*Jer* 31:32
if can break *c.* of day and *c.*	*Jer* 33:20;
of night then may *c.*	33:21, 25
be broken with David	
people which entered into *c.*	*Jer* 34:10
heard	
who have not performed	*Jer* 34:18
words of *c.*	
let us join to Lord in perpetual	*Jer* 50:5
c.	
I sware and entered into *c.*	*Eze* 16:8
with	
despised oath in breaking *c.*	*Eze* 16:59;
	17:18
give them for daughters, not	*Eze* 16:61
by *c.*	
shall he break *c.* and be	*Eze* 17:15
delivered	
oath he despised, whose *c.*	*Eze* 17:16;
he brake	17:19
I will bring you into the	*Eze* 20:37
bond of *c.*	
they have broken my *c.*	*Eze* 44:7
because of	
confirm *c.* with many for one	*Da* 9:27
week	
he broken, yea also prince of	*Da* 11:22
c.	
his heart shall be against holy	*Da* 11:28
c.	
have indignation against holy	*Da* 11:30
c.	
such as do wickedly against *c.*	*Da* 11:32
words, swearing falsely in	*Ho* 10:4
making *c.*	
I might break my *c.* I made	*Zec* 11:10
that my *c.* might be with Levi	*Mal* 2:4;
	2:5
ye have corrupted *c.* of Levi	*Mal* 2:8
by profaning the *c.* of our	*Mal* 2:10
fathers	

she is thy companion, and the	*Mal* 2:14
wife of thy *c.*	
messenger of *c.* whom ye	*Mal* 3:1
delight	
blood of the new *c.* (A)(B)	*M't* 26:28;
	M'k 14:24; *1Co* 11:25
are children of *c.* God made	*Ac* 3:25
with	
he gave him the *c.* of	*Ac* 7:8
circumcision	
this is my *c.* when I take	*Ac* 11:27
away sins	
ministers of the new *c.*	*2Co* 3:6
(A)(B)(E)(N)(R)	
read from the old *c.* (E)(N)	*2Co* 3:14
though man's *c.* yet if	*Ga* 3:15
confirmed	
the *c.* was confirmed before of	*Ga* 3:17
God	
surety of a better *c.* (B)(E)	*Heb* 7:22
a superior *c.* (N)	*Heb* 7:22; 9:18
Mediator of better *c.*	*Heb* 8:6
established	
if first *c.* had been faultless,	*Heb* 8:7
then no place	
they continued in my *c.* and I	*Heb* 8:9
regarded	
then the first *c.* had also	*Heb* 9:1
ordinances	
Aaron's rod that budded, and	*Heb* 9:4
tables of *c.*	
mediator of a better *c.*	*Heb* 9:15
(B)(E)(R)	
first *c.* inaugurated by blood	*Heb* 9:18
(E)(N)(R)	
ark of the *c.*	*Re* 11:19
(A)(B)(E)(N)(R)(S)	

BOOK OF COVENANT

Moses took *book of c.* and	*Ex* 24:7
read	
Josiah read in their ears all	*2Ki* 23:2;
the words of *book of c.*	*2Ch* 34:30
keep passover, as written in	*2Ki* 23:21
book of c.	

ESTABLISH COVENANT

with thee will I *establish* my	*Ge* 6:18
c.	
I will *establish* my *c.* between	*Ge* 17:7;
me and	9:9
establish c. with Isaac and	*Ge* 17:19;
his seed	17:21
I have *establish* my *c.* with	*Ex* 6:4
them to	
I will *establish* my *c.* with you	*Le* 26:9
he may *establish* his *c.* which	*De* 8:18
he sware	
establish to thee an	*Eze* 16:60
everlasting *c.*	
I will *establish* my *c.* with	*Eze* 16:62
thee	

EVERLASTING COVENANT

I may remember the *everlasting*	*Ge* 9:16
c.	
be in your flesh for an	*Ge* 17:13
everlasting c.	
establish my covenant with	*Ge* 17:19
Isaac for *everlasting c.*	
being taken from Israel by an	*Le* 24:8
everlasting c.	
yet he hath made with me an	*2 Sa* 23:5
everlasting c.	
confirmed the same to Israel	*1Ch* 16:17;
for an *everlasting c.*	*Ps* 105:10
because they have broken	*Isa* 24:5
everlasting c.	
make *everlasting c.* with you	*Isa* 55:3;
	61:8; *Jer* 32:40
it shall be *everlasting c.* with	*Eze* 37:26
them	
through the blood of the	*Heb* 13:20
everlasting c.	

KEEP COVENANT

keep my *c.* thou and thy seed	*Ge* 17:9
this my *c.* which ye shall	*Ge* 17:10
keep	
if ye *keep* my *c.*	*Ex* 19:5
faithful God, who *keepeth c.*	*De* 7:9;
7:12; *1Ki* 8:23; *2Ch* 6:14; *Ne* 1:5; 9:32	
keep words of this *c.* and do	*De* 29:9
them	
they observed thy word, *kept*	*De* 33:9
thy *c.*	

hast not *kept* my *c.*	*1Ki* 11:11;
	Ps 78:10
truth to such as *keep c.*	*Ps* 25:10;
	103:18
if thy children will *keep* my	*Ps* 132:12
c.	
keeping c. and mercy to them	*De* 9:4
that love	

MADE COVENANT

same day Lord *made c.* with	*Ge* 15:18
Abram	
Abraham and Abimelech	*Ge* 21:27;
made c.	21:32
I have *made c.* with thee and	*Ex* 34:27
Israel	
Lord *made c.* with us in Horeb	*De* 5:2
Lord *made* not this *c.* with our	*De* 5:3;
fathers	*Heb* 8:9
beside *c.* he *made* with them in	*De* 29:1
Horeb	
will break my *c.* I *made* with	*De* 31:16
them	
Joshua *made c.* with people	*Jos* 24:25
Jonathan and David *made c.*	*1Sa* 18:3;
	23:18
Jonathan *made c.* with house	*1Sa* 20:16
of David	
Lord *made c.* with Israel	*1Ki* 8:9;
	2Ch 6:11
ark wherein is *c.* of Lord	*1Ki* 8:21
which he *made*	
Ahab *made* a *c.* with	*1Ki* 20:34
Ben-hadad	
Jehoiada *made c.* with rulers	*2Ki* 11:4
made c. between Lord and	*2Ki* 11:17
the king	
Israel rejected *c.* he *made*	*2Ki* 17:15
with fathers	
with whom Lord *made c.*	*2Ki* 17:35
and charged	
c. made with you ye shall not	*2Ki* 17:38
forget	
Josiah *made c.* before Lord	*2Ki* 23:3;
	2Ch 34:31
David *made c.* with elders in	*1Ch* 11:3
Hebron	
c. made with Abraham	*1Ch* 16:16
	Ne 9:8; *Ps* 105:9
because of *c. made* with	*2Ch* 21:7
David	
congregation *made c.* with	*2Ch* 23:3
king Joash	
I *made c.* with mine eyes	*Job* 31:1
have *made c.* with me by	*Ps* 50:5
sacrifice	
have *made* a *c.* with my chosen	*Ps* 89:3
ye have *made* a *c.* with death	*Isa* 28:15
enlarged bed, and *made c.* with	*Isa* 57:8
them	
broke *c.* I *made* with their	*Jer* 11:10
fathers	
not according to *c. made* with	*Jer* 31:32
fathers	
Zedekiah *made* a *c.* with	*Jer* 34:8;
people	34:15
Lord, I *made* a *c.* with your	*Jer* 34:13
fathers	
made a *c.* before me in	*Jer* 34:15
house called	
performed not words of *c.* ye	*Jer* 34:18
had *made*	
made c. with him, and taken	*Eze* 17:13
oath	

MAKE COVENANT

make my *c.* between me and	*Ge* 17:2
thee	
make c. with thee	*Ge* 26:28
	31:44; *Ezr* 10:3
thou shalt *make* no *c.*	*Ex* 23:32; *De* 7:2
I *make c.* before all thy people	*Ex* 34:10
lest thou *make c.* with	*Ex* 34:12
inhabitants	
nor with you only do I *make*	*De* 29:14
c.	
make c. with us, we will serve	*1Sa* 11:1
on this condition will I *make*	*1Sa* 11:2
c. with you	
it is in my heart to *make c.*	*2Ch* 29:10
we make sure *c.* and write it	*Ne* 9:38
will he *make* a *c.* with thee	*Job* 41:4
this is *c.* I will *make*	*Jer* 31:33;
	Heb 8:10; 10:16
I will *make* with them a *c.*	*Eze* 34:25;
of peace	37:26

I will *make* c. for them with   *Ho 2:18*
beasts
they do *make* c. with the   *Ho 12:1*
Assyrians

NEW COVENANT

make *new* c. with Israel   *Jer 31:31;*
                             Heb 8:8
new c. he hath made the first   *Heb 8:13*
old
to Jesus the Mediator of   *Heb 12:24*
new c.

REMEMBER COVENANT

I will *remember* my c.   *Ge 9:15;*
              Le 26:42; Eze 16:60
I have *remembered* my c.   *Ex 6:5;*
                           6:6
for their sakes *remember* c. of   *Le 26:45*
ancestors
hath *remembered* his c. for   *Ps 105:8;*
ever   *106:45*
because they *remember* not   *Am 1:9*
brotherly c.
mercy promised, to *remember*   *Lu 1:72*
his holy c.

COVENANT *OF SALT*

salt of c. of God be lacking   *Le 2:13*
it is a c. *of salt* for ever   *Nu 18:19*
to David and sons by c. *of*   *2Ch 13:5*
salt

TRANGRESSED COVENANT

wrought wickedness in   *De 17:2*
transgressed his c.
they have also *transgressed*   *Jos 7:11*
my c.
he *transgressed* c. of Lord   *Jos 7:15;*
                       J'g 2:20; 2Ki 18:12
when ye have *transgressed* c.   *Jos 23:16*
of Lord
I will give men that   *Jer 34:18*
transgressed my c.
they like men have *transgressed*   *Ho 6:7*
c.
because they have *transgressed*   *Ho 8:1*
my c.

COVENANTBREAKERS

c., without natural affection   *Ro 1:31*
faithless   (A)(R)   *Ro 1:31*
without fidelity   (B)   *Ro 1:31*
no fidelity to plighted word   *Ro 1:31*
(N)
recognized no obligation to   *Ro 1:31*
honor (P)

COVENANTED

as I have c. with David thy   *2Ch 7:18*
father
I c. with you when ye came   *Hag 2:5*
out of
they c. with him for thirty   *M't 26:15*
pieces
my c. blood (B)   *M't 26:28;*
       M'k 14:24; Lu 22:20; 1Co 11:25;
                           Heb 9:20
glad, and c. to give him money   *Lu 22:5*

COVENANTS

glory, and the c. and the giving   *Ro 9:4*
for these are the two c.; the   *Ga 4:24*
one
strangers from the c. of   *Eph 2:12*
promise

COVER

locusts shall c. face of earth   *Ex 10:5*
if man shall dig a pit and not   *Ex 21:33*
c. it
make linen breeches to c.   *Ex 28:42*
nakedness
c. thee with my hand while I   *Ex 33:22*
pass
thou shalt c. the ark with the   *Ex 40:3*
veil
cloud of incense c. mercy-seat   *Le 16:13*
pour out blood, and c. it with   *Le 17:13*
dust
behold they c. face of the earth   *Nu 22:5*

c. that which cometh from   *De 23:13*
thee
Lord shall c. him all day long   *De 33:12*
and Saul went in to c. his feet   *1Sa 24:3*
under c. of the mountain (R)   *1Sa 25:20*
c. not their iniquity, let not their   *Ne 4:5*
sin
O earth, c. not my blood, let   *Job 16:18*
my cry
lie down in dust, worms shall   *Job 21:26*
c. them
the abundance of waters c.   *Job 22:11;*
thee   *38:34*
shady trees c. him with their   *Job 40:22*
shadow
he shall c. thee with his   *Ps 91:4*
feathers
that they turn not again to c.   *Ps 104:9*
the earth
c. themselves with their own   *Ps 109:29*
confusion
if I say, Surely darkness shall   *Ps 139:11*
c. me
let the mischief of their lips c.   *Ps 140:9*
them
as the waters c. the sea   *Isa 11:9;*
                         Hab 2:14
is spread under thee, the   *Isa 14:11*
worms c. thee
behold, the Lord will surely c.   *Isa 22:17*
thee
the earth shall no more c. her   *Isa 26:21*
slain
c. with covering, but not of my   *Isa 30:1*
Spirit
when thou seest the naked c.   *Isa 58:7*
him
neither c. themselves with their   *Isa 59:6*
works
for behold darkness shall c.   *Isa 60:2*
earth
multitude of camels shall c.   *Isa 60:6*
thee
I will go up, and c. the earth   *Jer 46:8*
horror c. them, shame on all   *Eze 7:18*
faces
thou shalt c. thy face that   *Eze 12:6*
thou see not
c. his face that he see not the   *Eze 12:12*
ground
poured it out on ground to c. it   *Eze 24:7*
with dust
c. not lips, eat not bread of   *Eze 24:17;*
men   *24:22*
their dust shall c. thee   *Eze 26:10*
when great waters shall c.   *Eze 26:19*
thee
as for her, a cloud shall c.   *Eze 30:18*
her
I will c. heaven, I will c. the   *Eze 32:7*
sun
c. you with skin, put breath in   *Eze 37:6*
you
be like a cloud to c. the land   *Eze 38:9;*
                         38:16
recover flax given to c. her   *Ho 2:9*
nakedness
say to mountains, C. us   *Ho 10:8;*
                         Lu 23:30
for thy violence shame shall c.   *Ob 10*
thee
they shall all c. their lips, no   *Mic 3:7*
answer
shame shall c. her that said to   *Mic 7:10*
me
violence of Lebanon shall c.   *Hab 2:17*
thee
began to spit on him and c.   *M'k 14:65*
his face
a man ought not to c. his   *1Co 11:7*
head
to c. up wickedness (B)   *1Pe 2:16*
charity shall c. multitude of   *1Pe 4:8*
sins

COVERED

mountains were c. with waters   *Ge 7:19;*
                         7:20
they c. the nakedness of their   *Ge 9:23*
father
Rebekah took a veil and c.   *Ge 24:65*
herself
Tamar c. with veil, sat in   *Ge 38:14*
open place
frogs came and c. land of Egypt   *Ex 8:6*
waters c. the chariots and   *Ex 14:28*
horsemen

depths c. them, they sank as a   *Ex 15:5*
stone
sea c. them, they sank as lead   *Ex 15:10;*
                         Jos 24:7
at even quails came up and c.   *Ex 16:13*
camp
Moses went up, cloud c.   *Ex 24:15*
mount
c. with their wings over the   *Ex 37:9*
mercy-seat
veil c. the ark of the testimony   *Ex 40:21*
cloud c. the tent of the   *Ex 40:34*
congregation
if leprosy have c. all his flesh   *Le 13:13*
to see when the holy things are   *Nu 4:20*
c.
cloud c. tabernacle   *Nu 9:15; 16:42*
waxen fat, thou art c. with   *De 32:15*
fatness
Jael c. him with a mantle   *J'g 4:18; 4:19*
Michal c. the pillow with a   *1Sa 19:13*
cloth
an old man cometh up c.   *1Sa 28:14*
with mantle
c. with shame (S)   *2Sa 19:5*
c. king David with clothes   *1Ki 1:1*
c. with gold (A)   *1Ki 6:35*
cherubims c. ark   *1Ki 8:7;*
              1Ch 28:18; 2Ch 5:8
c. place (S)   *1Ki 16:18*
c. himself with sackcloth   *2Ki 19:1;*
                         Isa 37:1
nor c. the darkness from my   *Job 23:17*
face
if I c. my transgressions as   *Job 31:33*
Adam
shame of my face hath c. me   *Ps 44:15*
hast c. us with the shadow of   *Ps 44:19*
death
valleys also are c. over with   *Ps 65:13*
corn
be as wings of a dove c. with   *Ps 68:13*
silver
confusion has c. our face (B)   *Ps 69:7*
let them be c. with reproach   *Ps 71:13*
that seek
enemies c. with the sea (B)   *Ps 78:53*
glory to cease, c. him with   *Ps 89:45*
shame
earth c. the company of   *Ps 106:17*
Abiram
hast c. me in my mother's   *Ps 139:13*
womb
like a potsherd c. with silver   *Pr 26:23*
dross
whose hatred is c. by deceit   *Pr 26:26*
his name shall be c. with   *Ec 6:4*
darkness
with twain c. his face, c. his feet   *Isa 6:2*
your rulers the seers hath be c.   *Isa 29:10*
c. thee in shadow of my hand   *Isa 51:16*
he c. me with robe of   *Isa 61:10*
righteousness
c. with the multitude of waves   *Jer 51:42*
c. daughter of Zion with a cloud   *La 2:1*
broken my teeth, he c. me with   *La 3:16*
ashes
c. with anger, and persecuted   *La 3:43*
us
c. thyself with a cloud, that   *La 3:44*
prayer
two wings c. their bodies   *Eze 1:11; 1:23*
I spread my skirt, and c. thy   *Eze 16:8*
nakedness
girded thee with linen, c. thee   *Eze 16:10*
with silk
hath c. naked with a garment   *Eze 18:7;*
                         24:16
that her blood should not be c.   *Eze 24:8*
blue and purple was that   *Eze 27:7*
which c. thee
I c. the deep for him, and I   *Eze 31:15*
restrained
flesh came up, and skin c.   *Eze 37:8*
them above
king of Nineveh c. with   *Jon 3:6*
sackcloth
let man and beast be c. with   *Jon 3:8*
sackcloth
God came, his glory c. the   *Hab 3:3*
heavens
the ship was c. with the waves   *M't 8:24*
nothing c. shall not be   *M't 10:26*
revealed
c. him with abuse (P)   *Lu 23:39*
if the woman be not c. let   *1Co 11:6;*
her be shorn   *Lu 12:2*

COVERED *FACE*

because Tamar had c. her face	Ge 38:15
the locusts c. the *face* of whole earth	Ex 10:15
but David c. his *face*, and cried	2Sa 19:4
as word went they c. Haman's face	Es 7:8
because shame hath c. my *face*	Ps 69:7
nettles had c. the *face* thereof	Pr 24:31
with twain he c. his *face*	Isa 6:2
heard reproach, shame c. our faces	Jer 51:51

COVERED *SIN, SINS*

blessed is he whose *sin* is c.	Ps 32:1; Ro 4:7
thou hast c. all their *sin*	Ps 85:2

HEAD COVERED

David and every man had head c.	2Sa 15:30
Haman went mourning, his head c.	Es 6:12
hast c. my *head* in day of battle	Ps 140:7
confounded, and c. their *head*	Jer 14:3; 14:4
every man praying, having head c.	1Co 11:4

COVEREDST

Thou c. it with the deep as with a	Ps 104:6
broidered garments, and c. them	Eze 16:18

COVEREST

vesture, wherewith thou c. thyself	De 22:12
Who c. thyself with light as with	Ps 104:2

COVERETH

all the fat that c. the inwards	Ex 29:13; 29:22; Le 3:3, 9, 14; 4:8; 7:3; 9:19
which c. the face of the earth	Nu 22:11
he c. his feet in his summer	J'g 3:24
he c. the faces of the judges	Job 9:24
Because he c. his face with his	Job 15:27
it, and c. the bottom of the sea	Job 36:30
With clouds he c. the light	Job 36:32
violence c. them as a garment	Ps 73:6
him as the garment which c. him	Ps 109:19
Who c. the heaven with clouds	Ps 147:8
but violence c. the mouth of the	Pr 10:6; 10:11
up strifes: but love c. all sins	Pr 10:12
but a prudent man c. shame	Pr 12:16
He that c. a transgression seeketh	Pr 17:9
that c. his sins shall not prosper	Pr 28:13
and our confusion c. us: for	Jer 3:25
art the anointed cherub that c.	Eze 28:14
cherub with overshadowing wings (A)(B)	Eze 28:14
anointed guardian cherub (R)	Eze 28:14
one c. violence with his garment	Mal 2:16
a candle, c. it with a vessel	Lu 8:16

COVERING

Noah removed the c. of the ark	Ge 8:13
he is to thee a c. of the eyes	Ge 20:16
For that is his c. only, it is his	Ex 22:27
c. the mercy seat with their wings	Ex 25:20
to be a c. upon the tabernacle	Ex 26:7
a c. for the tent of rams' skins	Ex 26:14
and a c. above of badgers' skins	Ex 26:14
tabernacle, his tent, and his c.	Ex 35:11

mercy seat, and the veil of the c.	Ex 35:12
a c. for the tent of rams' skins	Ex 36:19
a c. of badgers' skins above that	Ex 36:19
the c. of rams' skins dyed red	Ex 39:34
and the c. of badgers' skins	Ex 39:34
and the veil of the c.	Ex 39:34
the c. of the tent above upon it	Ex 40:19
set up the veil of the c. and	Ex 40:21
shall put a c. upon his upper lip	Le 13:45
the tent, the c. thereof, and the	Nu 3:25
they shall take down the c. veil	Nu 4:5
the c. of badgers' skins	Nu 4:6; 4:8, 10-12, 14-15, 25
plates for a c. of the altar	Nu 16:38; 16:39
no c. bound upon it, is unclean	Nu 19:15
spread a c. over the well's mouth	2Sa 17:19
Thick clouds are a c. to him, that	Job 22:14
that they have no c. in the cold	Job 24:7
him, and destruction hath no c.	Job 26:6
clothing, or any poor without c.	Job 31:19
made darkness his c. (B)(R)	Ps 18:11
He spread a cloud for a c.	Ps 105:39
the c. of it of purple, the midst	Ca 3:10
he discovered the c. of Judah	Isa 22:8
face of the c. cast over all people	Isa 25:7
and the c. narrower than that he	Isa 28:20
that cover with a c. but not of	Isa 30:1
c. of thy graven images of silver	Isa 30:22
and I make sackcloth their c.	Isa 50:3
every precious stone was thy c.	Eze 28:13
I will destroy thee, O c. cherub	Eze 28:16
the guardian cherub (A)(R)	Eze 28:16
overshadowing cherub (B)	Eze 28:16
c. the altar of the Lord with tears	Mal 2:13
for her hair is given her for a c.	1Co 11:15
having food and c. (B)	1Ti 6:8

COVERINGS

decked my bed with c. of tapestry	Pr 7:16
She maketh herself c. of tapestry	Pr 31:22

COVERS

and c. thereof, and bowls thereof	Ex 25:29
and his c. to cover withal, of pure	Ex 37:16
the bowls, and c. to cover withal	Nu 4:7

COVERT

came down by the c. of the hill	1Sa 25:20
down hidden by mountain (A)	1Sa 25:20
a mountain pass (B)	1Sa 25:20
under cover of the mountain (R)	1Sa 25:20
c. for the sabbath that they had	2Ki 16:18
and abide in the c. to lie in wait	Job 38:40
wait in hiding places (A)	Job 38:40
wait in the thicket (B)	Job 38:40
in the c. of the reed, and fens	Job 40:21
in the c. of his presence (E)(R)	Ps 31:20
I will trust in the c. of thy wings	Ps 61:4
the shelter of your wings (A)(R)	Ps 61:4
a c. from storm and from rain	Isa 4:6
for a shade in the day time (A)(R)	Isa 4:6
pavilion as a shade by day (B)(E)	Isa 4:6
be thou a c. to them from the face	Isa 16:4

a sheltered hiding place (A)	Isa 16:4
a hiding place in Moab (B)	Isa 16:4
be a refuge to them (R)	Isa 16:4
wind, and a c. from the tempest	Isa 32:2
a hiding place (A)(B)(E)	Isa 32:2
hath forsaken his c. as the lion	Jer 25:38
left his shelter as a lion (A)	Jer 25:38

COVET

shalt not c. thy neighbour's house	Ex 20:17
shalt not c. thy neighbour's wife	Ex 20:17
shalt thou c. thy neighbour's house	De 5:21
And they c. fields, and take them	Mic 2:2
law had said, Thou shalt not c.	Ro 7:7
Thou shalt not c.; and if there be	Ro 13:9
But c. earnestly the best gifts	1Co 12:31
earnestly desire, zealously cultivate (A)	1Co 12:31
aim hard for choicest graces (B)(N)	1Co 12:31
desire earnestly the greatest (E)(R)	1Co 12:31
set your hearts on the greatest (P)	1Co 12:31
c. to prophesy, and forbid not to	1Co 14:39
earnestly desire and set your hearts on prophesying (A)(E)(R)	1Co 14:39
set your mind to prophesy (B)	1Co 14:39
be eager to prophesy (P)	1Co 14:39

COVETED

then I c. them and took them	Jos 7:21
I have c. no man's silver, or gold	Ac 20:33
while some c. after, they have	1Ti 6:10

COVETETH

He c. greedily all the day long	Pr 21:26
him that c. an evil covetousness	Hab 2:9

COVETING

not be c. (S)	Ro 7:7
all manner of c. (S)	Ro 7:8

COVETOUS

blesseth the c. whom the Lord	Ps 10:3
the Pharisees also, who were c.	Lu 16:14
or with the c. or extortioners, or	1Co 5:10
greedy-graspers (A)	1Co 5:10; 6:10
the avaricious and grasping (B)	1Co 5:10; 6:10
grabbers and swindlers (N)	1Co 5:10; 6:10
cheats or thieves (P)	1Co 5:10
greedy and robbers (R)	1Co 5:10; 6:10
or c. or an idolator, or a railer, or	1Co 5:11
greed, greedy (A)(B)(R)	1Co 5:11
grasping (N)	1Co 5:11
swindler (P)	1Co 5:11
nor c., nor drunkards, nor revilers	1Co 6:10
nor c. man, who is an idolater	Eph 5:5
patient, not a brawler, not c.	1Ti 3:3
insatiable for wealth and ready to obtain it by questionable means (A)	1Ti 3:3
not after money (B)	1Ti 3:3
no lover of money (E)(N)(R)	1Ti 3:3
not fond of money-grabbing (P)	1Ti 3:3
lovers of their own selves, c.	2Ti 3:2
have exercised with c. practices	2Pe 2:14

COVETOUSNESS

fear God, men of truth, hating c.	Ex 18:21
hating unjust gain (A)(E)	Ex 18:21
who despise unfair profits (B)	Ex 18:21
who hate a bribe (R)	Ex 18:21
thy testimonies, and not to c.	Ps 119:36
hateth c. shall prolong his days	Pr 28:16
the iniquity of his c. was I wroth	Isa 57:17
them every one is given to c.	Jer 6:13
the greatest is given to c. from	Jer 8:10
are not but for c. and for to shed	Jer 22:17
is come, and the measure of thy c.	Jer 51:13
their heart goeth after their c.	Eze 33:31
coveteth an evil c. to his house	Hab 2:9
Thefts, c., wickedness, deceit	M'k 7:22
Take heed, and beware of c.	Lu 12:15
wickedness, c., maliciousness	Ro 1:29
all sorts of c. (B)(E)(R)	Ro 7:8
of bounty, and not as of c.	2Co 9:5
all uncleanness, or c., let it not be	Eph 5:3
greediness (A)(B)(N)	Eph 5:3
itch to get hands on what belongs to other people (P)	Eph 5:3
and c. which is idolatry	Col 3:5
as ye know, nor a cloke of c.	1Th 2:5
a cloak to conceal greedy motives (A)	1Th 2:5
under some pretext after money (B)	1Th 2:5
a cloak for greed (N)(R)	1Th 2:5
flattery to conceal greedy motives (P)	1Th 2:5
your conversation be without c.	Heb 13:5
moral disposition be free from love of money, greed, avarice, lust, and craving for earthly possessions (A)	Heb 13:5
conduct be free from love of money (B)	Heb 13:5
be free from the love of money (E)(P)(R)	Heb 13:5
do not live for money (N)	Heb 13:5
through c. shall they with feigned	2Pe 2:3

COW

And whether it be c. or ewe, ye	Le 22:28
But the firstling of a c. or	Nu 18:17
Their c. calveth, and casteth not	Job 21:10
is like a c. (B)	Pr 12:1
man shall nourish a young c.	Isa 7:21
And the c. and the bear shall feed	Isa 11:7
every c. at that which is before her	Am 4:3

COWS

cows (A)(B)(R)	Ge 32:15; 41:2-3, 26-27; 1Sa 6:7, 10, 14
cows (S)	Ge 32:15; 41:2-4, 18-20, 26-27; De 28:4, 18, 51; 32:14; 1Sa 6:7, 12, 14; 2Sa 27:29; Am 4:1
milk c. (S)	1Sa 6:7; 6:10
c. of Bashan (A)(R)	Am 4:1

COW'S

me, Lo, I have given thee c. dung	Eze 4:15

COZ

and C. begat Anub, and Zobebah	1Ch 4:8

COZBI

woman that was slain was C.	Nu 25:15
of Peor, and in the matter of C.	Nu 25:18

CRACKED

the ground is c. (A)(E)(S)	Jer 14:4

CRACKLING

as the c. of thorns under a pot	Ec 7:6

CRACKNELS

take with thee ten loaves and c.	1Ki 14:3
some cakes (A)(B)(E)(R)	1Ki 14:3

CRAFT

cause c. to prosper in his hand	Da 8:25
cause trickery to prosper (A)	Da 8:25
make treachery win out (B)	Da 8:25
make deceit prosper (R)	Da 8:25
how they might take him by c.	M'k 14:1
arrest Jesus by secrecy and deceit (A)	M'k 14:1
arrest, execute through treachery (B)	M'k 14:1
take him with subtilty (E)	M'k 14:1
devise some cunning plan to seize (N)	M'k 14:1
think of some trick by which they (P)	M'k 14:1
how to arrest him by stealth (R)	M'k 14:1
because he was of the same c.	Ac 18:3
was of the same occupation (A)(B)	Ac 18:3
by trade they were tent-makers (E)	Ac 18:3
he was of the same trade (N)(P)(R)	Ac 18:3
by this c. we have our wealth	Ac 19:25
occupation, trade (A)(B)(E)(R)	Ac 19:25; 19:27
business, industry (N)	Ac 19:25
not only this our c. is in danger	Ac 19:27
craftsman, of whatsoever c. he be	Re 18:22
skilled artisan (B)	Re 18:22
craftsman, craftsmen (E)(N)(P)(R)	Re 18:22

CRAFTILY

he sent messengers c. (S)	J'g 9:31
deals very c. (A) 1Sa 23:22; Ps 105:25	
they dealt c. with (B)(E)(S)	Ac 7:19
deal c. (A)	2Co 4:2

CRAFTINESS

taketh the wise in their own (R)	Job 5:13
catches wise in own trickiness (A)	Job 5:13
dark trickery and c. (A)	Da 8:23
But he perceived their c. and their cunning (A)	Lu 20:23
unscrupulousness (A)	Lu 20:23
aware of their trickery (B)	Lu 20:23
He saw through their trick (N)	Lu 20:23
saw through their cunning (P)	Lu 20:23
He taketh the wise in their own c.	1Co 3:19
not walking in c. nor handling the	2Co 4:2
deal craftily (A)	2Co 4:2
behave cunningly (B)	2Co 4:2
practice cunning (N)(R)	2Co 4:2
no hocus-pocus, no clever tricks (P)	2Co 4:2
beguiled Eve by c. (E)(S)	2Co 11:3
the sleight of men, and cunning c.	Eph 4:14
in every shifting form of trickery (A)	Eph 4:14
springs from human cunning, ingenuity (A)	Eph 4:14
dupes of crafty rogues (N)	Eph 4:14
teaching the jockeying men (P)	Eph 4:14
by the cunning of men (R)	Eph 4:14

CRAFTSMAN

the work of the hands of the c.	De 27:15
skillful c. (A)(B)(E)(S)	Isa 3:3
work of the c. (S)	Jer 10:9
no c. of whatsoever craft he be	Re 18:22
the c. (B)(E)(N)(P)(R)	Re 18:22

CRAFTSMEN

the c. (S)	Ge 4:22; 1Ch 29:5; 2Ch 34:11; Jer 24:1; 29:2
and all the c. and smiths: none	2Ki 24:14
and c. and smiths a thousand, all	2Ki 24:16
of Charashim; for they were c.	1Ch 4:14
they did engraving (B)	1Ch 4:14
Lod, and Ono, the valley of c.	Ne 11:35
the skilful c. (A)(R)	Jer 40:20
all of it the work of the c.	Ho 13:2
brought no small gain unto the c.	Ac 19:24
and the c. which are with him	Ac 19:38
his fellow tradesmen (A)	Ac 19:38
the c. (B)(E)(N)(P)(R)	Re 18:22

CRAFTY

came with c. cunning (A)	Ge 27:35
he was a very c. man (A)(B)	2Sa 13:3
disappointeth the devices of the c.	Job 5:12
thou choosest the tongue of the c.	Job 15:5
They have taken c. counsel against	Ps 83:3
c. of mind (R)	Pr 7:10
how c. the question was (N)	M'k 12:15
being c., I caught you with guile	2Co 12:16
dupes of c. rogues (N)(P)	Eph 4:14

CRAG

a rocky c. (A)(E)(R)	1Sa 4:4
the one c. was situated (S)	1Sa 14:5
upon the c. of the rock	Job 39:28
On the cliff he dwells (A)(E)	Job 39:28
perch on the craggy peak (B)	Job 39:28
On the rock he dwells (R)	Job 39:28

CRAGGY

perch on the c. peak (B)	Job 39:28

CRAMPED

c. and crushed (A)(B)(R)	2Co 4:8

CRANE

a c. or a swallow, so did I chatter	Isa 38:14
the c. and the swallow observe	Jer 8:7

CRASH

the c. of thy thunder (R)	Ps 77:18

CRASHING

and a great c. from the hills	Zep 1:10

CRAVED

Pilate, and c. the body of Jesus	M'k 15:43
asked the body of Jesus (A)(B)(E)(N)(P)(R)	M'k 15:43

CRAVES

appetites of sluggard c. (A)(B)(R)	Pr 13:4
life of the wicked c. (A)	Pr 21:10

CRAVETH

for his mouth c. it of him	Pr 16:26
his mouth urges him on (A)(B)(E)(R)	Pr 16:26

CRAVINGS

at opening were *c.* (A)(R)   1Ki 7:31
their animal *c.* (A)   Eze 7:19
foul *c.* (N)   Col 3:5
morbid *c.* (A)(P)   2Ti 3:6; Tit 3:3

CRAWLING

the *c.* locusts (R)   Joe 1:4

CREATE

C. in me a clean heart, O   Ps 51:10
God
Lord will *c.* upon every   Isa 4:5
dwelling
I form the light, and *c.*   Isa 45:7
darkness
I make peace, and *c.* evil   Isa 45:7
I *c.* the fruit of the lips;   Isa 57:19
Peace
I *c.* new heavens and a new   Isa 65:17
earth
rejoice for ever in that   Isa 65:18
which I *c.*
behold, I *c.* Jerusalem a   Isa 65:18
rejoicing

CREATED

God *c.* the heaven and the   Ge 1:1
earth
And God *c.* great whales,   Ge 1:21
and every
So God *c.* man in his own   Ge 1:27
image
in the image of God *c.* he   Ge 1:27
him
male and female *c.* he them   Ge 1:27
his work which God *c.* and   Ge 2:3
made
and of the earth, when they   Ge 2:4
were *c.*
In the day that God *c.* man   Ge 5:1
Male and female *c.* he them   Ge 5:2
in the day when they were *c.*   Ge 5:2
I will destroy man whom I   Ge 6:7
have *c.*
that God *c.* man upon the   De 4:32
earth
and the south thou hast *c.*   Ps 89:12
them
the people which shall be *c.*   Ps 102:18
shall
sendest forth thy spirit, they   Ps 104:30
are *c.*
he commanded, and they   Ps 148:5
were *c.*
behold who hath *c.* these   Isa 40:26
things
the Holy One of Israel hath   Isa 41:20
c. it
he that *c.* the heavens, and   Isa 42:5
thus saith the Lord that *c.*   Isa 43:1
thee
I have *c.* him for my glory, I   Isa 43:7
have
I the Lord have *c.* it   Isa 45:8
made the earth, and *c.* man   Isa 45:12
upon it
the Lord that *c.* the   Isa 45:18
heavens; God
he *c.* it not in vain, he   Isa 45:18
formed it to
he *c.* it not a chaos (R)   Isa 45:18;
                                 45:19
They are *c.* now, and not   Isa 48:7
from the
c. the smith that bloweth   Isa 54:16
the coals
I have *c.* the waster to   Isa 54:16
destroy
hath *c.* a new thing in the   Jer 31:22
earth
in the place where thou   Eze 21:30
wast *c.*
thee in the day that thou   Eze 28:13
wast *c.*
from the day that thou   Eze 28:15
wast *c.* till
hath not one God *c.* us?   Mal 2:10
why do we
which God *c.* unto this   M'k 13:19
time, neither
the *c.* universe waits (N)   Ro 8:19
was the man *c.* for the   1Co 11:9
woman; but
c. in Christ Jesus unto good   Eph 2:10
works

in God, who *c.* all things by   Eph 3:9
Jesus
Creator of all (B)   Eph 3:9
God the Creator of the   Eph 3:9
universe (N)
after God is *c.* in   Eph 4:24
righteousness
primacy over all *c.* things   Col 1:15
(N)
by him were things *c.* that   Col 1:16
are in
all things were *c.* by him,   Col 1:16
and for
after the image of him that   Col 3:10
c. him
which God hath *c.* to be   1Ti 4:3
received
everything *c.* is good   1Ti 4:4
(A)(N)(R)
since the world was *c.* (N)   Heb 4:3
for thou hast *c.* all things,   Re 4:11
and for
thy pleasure they are and   Re 4:11
were *c.*
who *c.* heaven, and the things   Re 10:6
that

CREATETH

and *c.* the wind, and   Am 4:13
declareth

CREATION

But from the beginning of   M'k 10:6
the *c.*
not from the beginning of   M'k 13:19
the *c.*
from the *c.* of the world are   Ro 1:20
clearly
whole *c.* on tiptoes (P)(S)   Ro 8:19;
                   8:20-21, 39; 2Co 5:17
that the whole *c.* groaneth   Ro 8:22
he is a new *c.* (A)(B)(R)   2Co 5:17
a new *c.* (A)(B)(N)(R)   Ga 6:15
firstborn of all *c.*   Col 1:15
(A)(B)(E)(R)(S)
existed before all *c.* began   Col 1:15
(P)
the whole *c.* is good (B)   1Ti 4:4
since the work of *c.* (P)   Heb 4:3
were from the beginning of   2Pe 3:4
the *c.*
the beginning of the *c.* of   Re 3:14
God

CREATIONS

earth full of well made *c.*   Ps 104:24
(B)

CREATOR

Remember now thy *C.* in the   Ec 12:1
days
the *C.* of the ends of the   Isa 40:28
earth
your Holy One, the *c.* of   Isa 43:15
Israel
more than the *C.* who is   Ro 1:25
blessed
The *C.* of all (B)(N)   Eph 3:9
well doing, as unto a faithful   1Pe 4:19
C.

CREATURE

the moving *c.* that hath life   Ge 1:20
every living *c.* that moveth   Ge 1:21
the earth bring forth the   Ge 1:24
living *c.*
called every living *c.* that was   Ge 2:19
every living *c.* that is with   Ge 9:10
you, of
me and you and every living   Ge 9:12
c.
and every living *c.* of all flesh   Ge 9:15
between God and every living   Ge 9:16
c.
every living *c.* that moveth   Le 11:46
in the
every *c.* that creepeth upon   Le 11:46
spirit of the living *c.* was   Eze 1:20;
                                 1:21
upon the heads of the living   Eze 1:22
c.
This is the living *c.* that I   Eze 10:15
saw by
spirit of the living *c.* was in   Eze 10:17
them

This is the living *c.* that I   Eze 10:20
saw by
and preach the gospel to   M'k 16:15
every *c.*
and served the *c.* more than   Ro 1:25
the earnest expectation of the   Ro 8:19
c.
expectation of *c.*   Ro 8:19;
                     8:20-21, 39; 2Co 5:17
For the *c.* was made subject   Ro 8:20
to
Because the *c.* itself also shall   Ro 8:21
be
nor any other *c.* shall be able   Ro 8:39
to
he is a new *c.*: old things   2Co 5:17
are
a new creation   2Co 5:17
(A)(B)(R)(S)
there is a new world (N)   2Co 5:17
becomes a new person   2Co 5:17
altogether (P)
uncircumcision, but a new *c.*   Ga 6:15
a new creation   Ga 6:15
(A)(B)(N)(R)
but the power of new birth   Ga 6:15
(P)
God, the firstborn of every *c.*   Col 1:15
the first-born of all creation   Col 1:15
(A)(B)(R)(S)
the firstborn before all   Col 1:15
creation (B)
his is primacy over all   Col 1:15
created things (N)
he existed before creation   Col 1:15
began (P)
which was preached to every   Col 1:23
c.
For every *c.* of God is good   1Ti 4:4
everything God has created is   1Ti 4:4
good (A)(N)(R)
the whole creation is good   1Ti 4:4
(B)
everything God made is good   1Ti 4:4
(P)
Neither is there any *c.* that   Heb 4:13
is not
the living *c.* (S)   Re 4:7; 6:3, 5, 7
And every *c.* which is in   Re 5:13
heaven
every living *c.* (B)   Re 16:5

CREATURES

earth is full of thy *c.* (R)   Ps 104:24
houses shall be full of   Isa 13:21
doleful *c.*
came the likeness of four   Eze 1:5;
living *c.*   1:13-15, 19; 3:13
c. watching with outstretched   Ro 8:19
(B)
be a kind of firstfruits of his   Jas 1:18
c.
living *c.* (S)   Re 4:6;
    4:8-9; 5:6, 8, 11, 14; 6:1, 6; 7:11;
                              14:3; 15:7; 19:4
third part of the *c.* which were   Re 8:9
in

CREDIT

do *c.* to the teaching (A)   Tit 2:10

CREDITED

it will be *c.* to him   Le 7:18
(A)(B)(R)
shall be *c.* to you (A)(B)   Nu 18:27
c. to (A)   Ro 2:26; 4:5
not *c.* as a favor (A)(P)(R)   Ro 4:4
faith *c.* to Abraham (A)   Ro 4:9; 4:10
faith *c.* to him (A)   Ro 4:22; 4:23

CREDITOR

as a *c.* (A)(B)(E)(R)   Ex 22:25
Every *c.* that lendeth   De 15:2
and the *c.* is come to take   2Ki 4:1
unto
as with the *c.* so   Isa 24:2
(A)(B)(E)(R)
There was a certain *c.* which   Lu 7:41
had

CREDITORS

c. seize all (B)(R)   Ps 109:11
which of my *c.* is it to whom   Isa 50:1
I

CREDITS

whom God c. righteousness (B)   *Ro 4:6*

CREDULITY

trade on your c. (N)   *2Pe 2:3*

CREEK

abode by his c. (A)(E)   *J'g 5:17*
they discovered a certain c.   *Ac 27:39*

CREEKS

abode in his c. (S)   *J'g 5:17*

CREEP

All fowls that c. going upon all   *Le 11:20*
the creeping things that c.   *Le 11:29; 11:31, 42; Eze 38:20*
the beasts of the forest do c. forth   *Ps 104:20*
are they which c. into houses   *2Ti 3:6*
worm their way into homes (A)(P)   *2Ti 3:6*
sneak into the homes (B)   *2Ti 3:6*
insinuate themselves into private homes (N)   *2Ti 3:6*
make their way into households (R)   *2Ti 3:6*

CREEPETH

and every thing that c. upon the   *Ge 1:25*
every creeping thing that c.   *Ge 1:26; 1:30; 7:8, 14, 21; 8:17, 19; Le 11:41, 43-44, 46; 20:25*
The likeness of any thing that c.   *De 4:18*

CREEPING

cattle, and c. thing, and beast of   *Ge 1:24*
over every c. thing that creepeth   *Ge 1:26*
the c. thing, and the fowls of the   *Ge 6:7; 7:14, 21, 23; 8:17; Le 11:41*
every c. thing of the earth after   *Ge 6:20*
Every beast, every c. thing   *Ge 8:19*
carcase of unclean c. things   *Le 5:2*
every flying c. thing that goeth   *Le 11:21*
among the winged insects (A)(B)(R)   *Le 11:21*
all other flying c. things   *Le 11:23*
among the c. things that creep   *Le 11:29; 11:42; Eze 38:20*
abominable with any c. thing that   *Le 11:43*
with any manner of c. thing that   *Le 11:44*
whosoever toucheth any c. thing   *Le 22:5*
every c. thing that flieth is unclean   *De 14:19*
cf fowl, and of c. things   *1Ki 4:33*
things c. innumerable, both small   *Ps 104:25*
c. things, and flying fowl   *Ps 148:10*
and behold every form of c. things   *Eze 8:10*
with the c. things of the ground   *Ho 2:18*
as the c. things, that have no ruler   *Hab 1:14*
and wild beasts, and c. things   *Ac 10:12; 11:6*
fourfooted beasts, and c. things   *Ro 1:23*
reptiles (A)(B)(R)   *Ro 1:23*

CREPT

For there are certain men c. in   *Jude 4*

CRESCENS

C. to Galatia, Titus unto   *2Ti 4:10*

CRESCENT

c. head ornaments (A)(B)(E)(R)   *Isa 3:18*

CRESCENTS

took c. from camels (B)(E)(R)   *J'g 8:21; J'g 8:26*
their c. like the moon (S)   *Isa 3:18*

CRESTFALLEN

turned away c. (P)   *M't 19:22*

CRETE

suffering us, we sailed under c.   *Ac 27:7; 27:12-13, 21*
For this cause left I thee in C.   *Tit 1:5*

CRETES

C. and Arabians, we do hear   *Ac 2:11*

CRETIANS

The C. are always liars, evil   *Tit 1:12*

CREW

And immediately the cock c.   *M't 26:74*
out into the porch; and the cock c.   *M'k 14:68*
And the second time the cock c.   *M'k 14:72*
while he yet spake, the cock c.   *Lu 22:60*
again: and immediately the cock c.   *Joh 18:27*

CRIB

to serve thee, or abide by thy c.   *Job 39:9*
remain beside the manger (A)   *Job 39:9*
Where no oxen are, the c. is clean   *Pr 14:4*
the stable is clean (B)   *Pr 14:4*
owner, and the ass his master's c.   *Isa 1:3*

CRIED

Esau c. with a great and bitter cry   *Ge 27:34*
I lifted up my voice and c.   *Ge 39:15*
and they c. before him, bow the knee   *Ge 41:43*
people c. to Pharaoh for bread   *Ge 41:55*
he c. cause every man to go out from me   *Ge 45:1*
officers came and c. to Pharaoh   *Ex 5:15*
people c. to Moses, and he prayed   *Nu 11:2*
stone damsel, because she c. not   *De 22:24*
damsel c. and there was none to save   *De 22:27*
Sisera's mother c. through lattice   *J'g 5:28*
all the host ran and c. and fled   *J'g 7:21*
and ye c. to me, and I delivered you   *J'g 10:12*
he stood and c. to the armies of Israel   *1Sa 17:8*
Jonathan c. after the lad   *1Sa 20:37; 20:38*
then c. wise woman out of city   *2Sa 20:16*
I c. to my God, and he did hear   *2Sa 22:7*
c. against altar in Beth-el   *1Ki 13:2; 4:32*
they c. aloud, and cut themselves   *1Ki 18:28*
Elisha saw it, and c., My father   *2Ki 2:12*
he c. Alas, master, for it was borrowed   *2Ki 6:5*
the woman c. to the king for her house   *2Ki 8:5*
and Athaliah c. Treason, treason   *2Ki 11:14*
they c. to God in the battle   *1Ch 5:20*
when they c. thou heardest from heaven   *Ne 9:27; 9:28*

because I delivered the poor that c.   *Job 29:12*
they c. after them, as after a thief   *Job 30:5*
in my distress I c. unto my God   *Ps 18:6*
they c. but there was none to save them   *Ps 18:41*
they c. to thee and were delivered   *Ps 22:5*
but when he c. unto him he heard   *Ps 22:24*
my God, I c. to thee, and hast healed   *Ps 30:2*
c. to thee and made supplication   *Ps 30:81*
heardest my supplications when I c.   *Ps 31:22*
this poor man c. and Lord heard him   *Ps 34:6*
I c. unto him with my mouth   *Ps 66:17; 77:1*
I have c. day and night before thee   *Ps 88:1*
unto thee have I c. O Lord, in morning   *Ps 88:13*
I c. with my whole heart, hear me   *Ps 119:145*
out of depths have I c., O Lord   *Ps 130:1*
in day I c. thou answeredst me   *Ps 138:3*
posts moved at voice of him that c.   *Isa 6:4*
therefore I c. concerning this is c.   *Isa 30:7*
destruction upon destruction   *Jer 4:20*
that I fell on my face and c.   *Eze 9:8*
c. to them in my hearing, O wheel   *Eze 10:13*
he c. with a lamentable voice   *Da 6:20*
have not c. to me with their heart   *Ho 7:14*
mariners c. every man to his god   *Jon 1:5*
I c. by reason of affliction, out of hell c. I   *Jon 2:2*
as he c. and they would not hear, so they c. and I would not   *Zec 7 13*
Peter c. saying, Lord save me   *M't 14:30*
c., have mercy   *M't 20:31; M'k 10:48; Lu 18:38*
the spirit c. and rent him sore   *M'k 9:26*
Jesus c., If any man thirst, let him come   *Joh 7:37*
some c. one thing, some another   *Ac 19:32; 21:34*
might know why they c. so against him   *Ac 22:24*
when he c. seven thunders uttered voices   *Re 10:3*
she being with child, c. travailing in   *Re 12:22*
c. loud to him that had sickle   *Re 14:18*
he c. mightily with a strong voice, saying   *Re 18:2*
c. when they saw smoke of her burning   *Re 18:18*
c. weeping and wailing Alas, alas   *Re 18:19*

CRIED *TO THE LORD*

Moses c. to the Lord   *Ex 8:12; 15:25; 17:4; Nu 12:13*
Israel c. to the Lord   *Ex 14:10; J'g 3:9; 4:3; 6:7; 10:10*
we c. to the Lord, he heard   *Nu 20:16*
they c. to the Lord, he put darkness   *De 26:7*
Samuel c. to the Lord   *Jos 24:7*
Elijah c. to the Lord for the widow   *1Sa 7:9; 15:11*
they c. to the Lord   *1Ki 17:20*
   2Ch 13:14; Ps 107:6, 13; Jon 1:14
I c. to the Lord   *Ps 3:4; 120:1; 142:1*
Their heart c. to the Lord, O daughter of   *La 2:18*

CRIED *OUT*

all the city c. out   *1Sa 4:13*
the Ekronites c. out. They have brought   *1Sa 5:10*

CRIED *OUT*

Jehoshaphat *c. out*   1Ki 22:32;
2Ch 18:31
c. out, there is death in the   2Ki 4:40
pot
I *c. out*, I cry violence and   Jer 20:8
spoil
the spirits *c. out*   M't 8:29; Lu 4:33
disciples *c. out* for fear   M't 14:26;
M'k 6:49
blind men *c. out*, Have   M't 20:30
mercy upon us
man with an unclean spirit   M'k 1:23
c. out
father of the child *c. out*   M'k 9:24;
Lu 9:38
they *c. out* again, Crucify   M'k 15:13;
him   M't 27:23; Lu 23:18; Joh 19:6

CRIED *WITH A LOUD VOICE*

woman at Endor *c. with a*   1Sa 28:12
loud voice
David *c. with a loud voice*,   2Sa 19:4
O Absalom
Rabshakeh *c. with a loud*   2Ki 18:28;
voice   Isa 36:13
Levites *c. with a loud voice*   Ne 9:4
unto the
about ninth hour Jesus *c.*   M't 27:46;
with a loud voice M't 27:50; M'k 15:34,
37; Lu 23:46
evil spirit *c. with a loud*   M'k 1:26
voice
Jesus *c. with a loud voice*,   Joh 11:43
Lazarus
Stephen's enemies *c. with a*   Ac 7:57
loud voice
Stephen *c. with a loud voice*,   Ac 7:60
Lord, lay
Paul *c. with a loud voice*,   Ac 16:28
Do thyself no
they *c. with a loud voice*,   Re 6:10
How long, O
angel *c. with a loud voice*   Re 7:2;
10:3; 19:17
the multitude *c. with a loud*   Re 7:10
voice, Salvation

CRIES

the *c.* of them which have   Jas 5:4
reaped

CRIEST

Wherefore *c.* thou unto me   Ex 14:15
Who art thou that *c.* to the   1Sa 26:14
king
Yea, if thou *c.* after   Pr 2:3
knowledge
When thou *c.* let thy   Isa 57:13
companies
Why *c.* thou for thine   Jer 30:15
affliction

CRIETH

the voice of thy brother's   Ge 4:10
blood *c.*
he *c.* unto me, that I will   Ex 22:27
hear
the soul of the wounded *c.*   Job 24:12
out
shall deliver the needy when   Ps 72:12
he *c.*
my heart and my flesh *c.* out   Ps 84:2
for
Wisdom *c.* without; she   Pr 1:20
uttereth
c. in the chief place of   Pr 1:21
concourse
She *c.* at the gates, at the entry   Pr 8:3
she *c.* upon the highest places   Pr 9:3
of
in pain, and *c.* out in her   Isa 26:17
pangs
of him that *c.* in the   Isa 40:3
wilderness
it *c.* out against me   Jer 12:8
The Lord's voice *c.* unto the   Mic 6:9
city
for she *c.* after us   M't 15:23
him, and he suddenly *c.* out   Lu 9:39
Esaias also *c.* concerning   Ro 9:27
Israel
is of you kept back by fraud,   Jas 5:4
c.

CRIME

this great *c.* (B)   Ge 39:9
your brother's *c.* (B)   Ge 50:17
committed a flagrant *c.* (B)   De 22:21
the *c.* of Abimelech (R)   J'g 9:56
the wanton *c.* (R)   J'g 20:10
For this is an heinous *c.*;   Job 31:11
yea
find no guilt or *c.* (A)(R)   Lu 23:4
the wages of *c.* (B)   Ac 1:18
c. or wrongdoing   Ac 18:14
(N)(P)(R)(S)
concerning the *c.* laid   Ac 25:16
against him
concerning the charge   Ac 25:16
(A)(B)(N)(P)(R)
defence concerning the   Ac 25:16
matter (E)

CRIMES

for the land is full of bloody   Eze 7:23
c.
city full of blood-guiltiness   Eze 7:23
(A)
signify the *c.* laid against   Ac 25:27
him
state the accusations (A)   Ac 25:27
signifying the charges   Ac 25:27
(B)(E)(N)(P)(R)

CRIMINAL

I find nothing *c.* (B)(P)   Lu 23:4
accuse as a *c.* (A)   Ac 25:5
I were a *c.* (P)   Ac 25:11

CRIMINALS

will be considered *c.* (B)   1Ki 1:21
made his grave with *c.* (B)   Isa 53:9
rated among the *c.* (B)   Lu 22:37

CRIMSON

a *c.* string (B)   Ge 38:30
in purple, and *c.*, and blue   2Ch 2:7
blue, and in fine linen, and   2Ch 2:14
in *c.*
purple, and *c.*, and fine linen   2Ch 3:14
though they be red like *c.*   Isa 1:18
thou clothest thyself with *c.*   Jer 4:30

CRIPPLE

a *c.* from his mother's womb   Ac 14:8

CRIPPLES

c. slandered (R)   Ps 35:15

CRISPING

the wimples, and the *c.* pins   Isa 3:22
handbags, purses (A)(R)   Isa 3:22
purses (B)   Isa 3:22
the satchels (E)   Isa 3:22

CRISPUS

And C. the chief ruler of the   Ac 18:8
I baptized none of you, but   1Co 1:14
C. and

CRITIC

Where is the *c.* (P)   1Co 1:20
becomes a *c.* of the law (P)   Jas 4:11

CRITICAL

stop turning a *c.* eye on (P)   Ro 14:13

CRITICISM

public behaviour above *c.*   Ro 12:17
(P)

CRITICISMS

do not bring insulting *c.* (P)   2Pe 2:11

CRITICIZE

Don't *c.* people (P)   M't 7:1
not *c.* his views (A)(B)   Ro 14:1
c. and pass judgment   Ro 14:3
(A)(P)(R)
c., blame, pass judgment   Ro 14:13
(A)

CRITICIZES

maligns, *c.* the law (B)   Jas 4:11

CROCODILE

a big *c.* (B)   Eze 29:3; 32:2

CROOKBACKED

Or *c.* or a dwarf, or that   Le 21:20
hath a

CROOKED

are a perverse and *c.*   De 32:5
generation
hand hath formed the *c.*   Job 26:13
serpent
swift, fleeing serpent   Job 26:13;
(A)(R)   Isa 27:1
the rushing serpent (B)   Job 26:13
the swift serpent (E)   Job 26:13;
Isa 27:1
turn aside unto their *c.* ways   Ps 125:5
Whose ways are *c.* and they   Pr 2:15
a *c.* mouth (S)   Pr 4:24; 8:8
who takes a *c.* way (A)(B)   Pr 10:9
a *c.* mind finds no good   Pr 17:20
(A)(B)(R)
is *c.* cannot be made straight   Ec 1:15
straight, which he hath made   Ec 7:13
c.
even leviathan that *c.* serpent   Isa 27:1
the coiling serpent (B)   Isa 27:1
and the *c.* shall be made   Isa 40:4
straight
them, and *c.* things straight   Isa 42:16
and make the *c.* places   Isa 45:2
straight
they have made them *c.* paths   Isa 59:8
he hath made my paths *c.*   La 3:9
with *c.* balances (B)   Mic 6:11
the *c.* shall be made straight   Lu 3:5
a *c.* generation   Ac 2:40
(A)(B)(E)(N)(R)(S)
making *c.* straight paths (R)   Ac 13:10
midst of a *c.* and perverse   Ph'p 2:15
nation

CROOKEDNESS

contrariness, *c.* (A)   Pr 11:2
trusted in oppression and *c.*   Isa 30:12
(B)
your *c.* passed (B)   Na 3:1
c., wicked unscrupulousness   Ac 18:14
(B)

CROON

who *c.* to the sound of (B)   Am 6:5

CROP

pluck away his *c.* with his   Le 1:16
feathers
I will *c.* off from the top of   Eze 17:22
his
produce no *c.* (P) M't 13:22; M'k 4:19
c. for eternal life (B)(N)   Joh 4:36
share the *c.* (B)(P)(R)   1Co 9:11
first claims the *c.* (N)   2Ti 2:6
precious *c.* land may yield   Jas 5:7
(N)

CROPPED

c. off the top of his young   Eze 17:4
twigs
have her hair *c.* (P)   1Co 11:6

CROPS

gather its *c.* (B)   Ex 23:10
according to *c.*   Le 25:15
(A)(B)(E)(R)
until the *c.* come in (A)   Le 25:22
store my *c.* (B)(R)(S)   Lu 12:17
share of *c.* (R)   2Ti 2:6
land produced its *c.* (A)(N)   Jas 5:18

CROSS

And he that taketh not his   M't 10:38
c.
deny himself, and take up   M't 16:24
his *c.*
him they compelled to bear   M't 27:32
his *c.*

Son of God, come down from the *c.*   *M't 27:40*
let him now come down from the *c.*   *M't 27:42*
deny himself, and take up his *c.*   *M'k 8:34*
take up the *c.*, and follow me   *M'k 10:21*
and Rufus, to bear his *c.*   *M'k 15:21*
and come down from the *c.*   *M'k 15:30*
descend now from the *c.* that we   *M'k 15:32*
himself, and take up his *c.* daily   *Lu 9:23*
whosoever doth not bear his *c.*   *Lu 14:27*
and on him they laid the *c.* that   *Lu 23:26*
And he bearing his *c.* went forth   *Joh 19:17*
wrote a title, and put it on the *c.*   *Joh 19:19*
stood by the *c.* of Jesus his mother   *Joh 19:25*
should not remain upon the *c.* on   *Joh 19:31*
lest the *c.* of Christ should be made   *1Co 1:17*
the preaching of the *c.* is to them   *1Co 1:18*
then is the offence of the *c.* ceased   *Ga 5:11*
should suffer persecution for the *c.*   *Ga 6:12*
save in the *c.* of our Lord Jesus   *Ga 6:14*
unto God in one body by the *c.*   *Eph 2:16*
death, even the death of the *c.*   *Ph'p 2:8*
are the enemies of the *c.* of Christ   *Ph'p 3:18*
peace through the blood of his *c.*   *Col 1:20*
out of the way, nailing it to his *c.*   *Col 2:14*
endured the *c.*, despising the shame   *Heb 12:2*

CROSSCURRENT

striking a *c.* (A)(B)(N)   *Ac 27:41*

CROSSING

c. his hands (A)(R)   *Ge 44:14*

CROSSWAY

shouldest thou have stood in the *c.*   *Ob 14*

CROUCH

c. to him for a piece of silver   *1Sa 2:36*
bow down for a mite (B)(E)   *1Sa 2:36*
they *c.* in their dens (S)   *Job 38:40*

CROUCHED

he *c.* as a lion (S)   *Ge 49:9; Nu 24:9*

CROUCHETH

He *c.* and humbleth himself   *Ps 10:10*

CROUCHING

as a strong ass *c.* down (S)   *Ge 49:14*

CROW

this night, before the cock *c.* thou   *M't 26:34*
Before the cock *c.* thou shalt deny   *M't 26:75*
before the cock *c.* twice, thou shalt   *M'k 14:30*
him, Before the cock *c.* twice, thou   *M'k 14:72*
the cock shall not *c.* this day, before   *Lu 22:34*
him, Before the cock *c.* thou shalt   *Lu 22:61*
The cock shall not *c.* till thou hast   *Joh 13:38*

CROWD

such a large *c.* (B)   *J'g 18:23*
perplexing cares *c.* me (B)(R)   *Ps 94:19*
for the *c.* (S)   *M'k 2:4; 3:9; 5:27, 30; Lu 8:19, 45; 19:3*
a great *c.* of disciples (A)(R)   *Lu 6:17*
man from the *c.* (A)(B)(N)(P)(R)   *Lu 9:38*
a large *c.* (N)(P)   *Joh 6:5*
gathering a *c.* (E)(P)(R)   *Ac 17:5*
without a *c.* or an uproar (A)   *Ac 24:18*

CROWDED

people *c.* him (S)   *M'k 5:24; Lu 8:42*

CROWDING

people *c.* him (S)   *M'k 5:31*

CROWED

the cock *c.* (S)   *M't 26:74; M'k 14:68, 72; Lu 22:60; Joh 18:27*

CROWN

and on the *c.* of the head of him   *Ge 49:26*
make upon it a *c.* of gold round   *Ex 25:11*
and make thereto a *c.* of gold   *Ex 25:24*
make a golden *c.* to the border   *Ex 25:25*
a golden molding (A)(B)(R)   *Ex 25:25*
put the holy *c.* upon the mitre   *Ex 29:6*
sacred diadem (B)   *Ex 29:6; 29:30; Le 8:9*
shalt make unto it a *c.* of gold   *Ex 30:3*
thou make to it under the *c.* of it   *Ex 30:4*
under the rim of it (A)   *Ex 30:4*
just below the molding (B)(R)   *Ex 30:4*
and made a *c.* of gold to it round   *Ex 37:2*
and made thereunto a *c.* of gold   *Ex 37:11*
made a *c.* of gold for the border   *Ex 37:12*
also he made unto it a *c.* of gold   *Ex 37:26*
of gold for it under the *c.* thereof   *Ex 37:27*
they made the plate of the holy *c.*   *Ex 39:30*
put the golden plate, the holy *c.*   *Le 8:9*
c. of the anointing oil of his God   *Le 21:12*
the arm with the *c.* of the head   *De 33:20*
took the *c.* that was upon his head   *2Sa 1:10*
And he took their king's *c.* from   *2Sa 12:30*
his foot even to the *c.* of his head   *2Sa 14:25*
and put the *c.* upon him   *2Ki 11:12*
David took the *c.* of their king   *1Ch 20:2*
son, and put upon him the *c.*   *2Ch 23:11*
queen before the king with the *c.*   *Es 1:11*
he set the royal *c.* upon her head   *Es 2:17*
c. royal which is set upon his head   *Es 6:8*
and with a great *c.* of gold   *Es 8:15*
the sole of his foot unto his *c.*   *Job 2:7*
and taken the *c.* from my head   *Job 19:9*
and bind it as a *c.* to me   *Job 31:36*
as a diadem (A)   *Job 31:36*
c. of pure gold on his head   *Ps 21:3*
hast profaned his *c.* by casting it   *Ps 89:39*
upon himself shall his *c.* flourish   *Ps 132:18*

a *c.* of glory shall she deliver to   *Pr 4:9*
woman is a *c.* to her husband   *Pr 12:4*
a crowning joy to her husband (A)   *Pr 12:4*
The *c.* of the wise is their riches   *Pr 14:24*
The hoary head is a *c.* of glory   *Ps 16:31*
Children's children are the *c.* of   *Pr 17:6*
the *c.* endure to every generation   *Pr 27:24*
behold king Solomon with the *c.*   *Ca 3:11*
Lord will smite with a scab the *c.*   *Isa 3:17*
the *c.* of pride, to the drunkards   *Isa 28:1*
The *c.* of pride, the drunkards of   *Isa 28:3*
Lord of hosts be for a *c.* of glory   *Isa 28:5*
Thou shalt also be a *c.* of glory   *Isa 62:3*
have broken the *c.* of thy head   *Jer 2:16*
down, even the *c.* of your glory   *Jer 13:18*
your beautiful *c.* (A)(B)(R)   *Jer 13:18*
c. of the head of the tumultuous   *Jer 48:45*
The *c.* is fallen from our head   *La 5:16*
and a beautiful *c.* upon thine head   *Eze 16:12*
the diadem, and take off the *c.*   *Eze 21:26*
shall be as the stones of a *c.*   *Zec 9:16*
they had platted a *c.* of thorns   *M't 27:29*
and platted a *c.* of thorns   *M'k 15:17*
the soldiers platted a *c.* of thorns   *Joh 19:2*
wearing the *c.* of thorns, and   *Joh 19:5*
to obtain a corruptible *c.*   *1Co 9:25*
win a wreath (A)(N)(R)   *1Co 9:25*
and longed for, my joy and *c.*   *Ph'p 4:1*
hope, or joy, or *c.* of rejoicing   *1Th 2:19*
victor's wreath (A)   *1Th 2:19*
our pride and joy (P)   *1Th 2:19*
up for me a *c.* of righteousness   *2Ti 4:8*
garland of righteousness (N)   *2Ti 4:8*
he shall receive the *c.* of life   *Jas 1:12*
the gift of life (N)   *Jas 1:12*
a *c.* of glory that fadeth not away   *1Pe 5:4*
the unfading garland of glory (N)   *1Pe 5:4*
and I will give thee a *c.* of life   *Re 2:10*
thou hast, that no man take thy *c.*   *Re 3:11*
and a *c.* was given unto him   *Re 6:2*
upon her head a *c.* of twelve stars   *Re 12:1*
a crownlike garland (tiara) of (A)   *Re 12:1*
having on his head a golden *c.*   *Re 14:14*

CROWNED

c. him with glory and honour   *Ps 8:5*
prudent are *c.* with knowledge   *Pr 14:18*
wherewith his mother *c.* him in   *Ca 3:11*
Thy *c.* are as the locusts   *Na 3:17*
yet is he not *c.* except he strive   *2Ti 2:5*
death, *c.* with glory and honour   *Heb 2:9*

CROWNEDST

thou *c.* him with glory and honour   *Heb 2:7*

CROWNEST

c. the year with thy goodness   *Ps 65:11*

CROWNETH

who *c.* thee with lovingkindness   *Ps 103:4*

CROWNING

counsel against Tyre, the *c.* *Isa 23:8*
city

CROWNS

and beautiful *c.* upon their *Eze 23:42*
heads
take silver and gold, and make *Zec 6:11*
c.
And the *c.* shall be to Helem *Zec 6:14*
they had on their heads *c.* of *Re 4:4*
gold
and cast their *c.* before the *Re 4:10*
throne
heads were as it were *c.* like *Re 9:7*
gold
and seven *c.* upon his heads *Re 12:3*
and upon his horns ten *c.* *Re 13:1*
and on his head were many *Re 19:12*
c.

CRUCIFIED

Son of man is betrayed to *M't 26:2*
be *c.*
all say unto him, Let him *M't 27:22*
be *c.*
out the more, saying, Let *M't 27:23*
him be *c.*
he delivered him to be *c.* *M't 27:26*
And they *c.* him, and *M't 27:35*
parted his
were there two thieves *c.* *M't 27:38*
with him
also, which were *c.* with *M't 27:44*
him
that ye seek Jesus, which *M't 28:5*
was *c.*
when he had scourged *M'k 15:15*
him, to be *c.*
when they had *c.* him, they *M'k 15:24*
parted
was the third hour, and *M'k 15:25*
they *c.* him
that were *c.* with him *M'k 15:32*
reviled him
Jesus of Nazareth, which *M'k 16:6*
was *c.*
requiring that he might be *c.* *Lu 23:23*
called Calvary, there they *c.* *Lu 23:33*
him
and be *c.* and the third day *Lu 24:7*
rise
to death, and have *c.* him *Lu 24:20*
him therefore unto them to *Joh 19:16*
be *c.*
Where they *c.* him, and two *Joh 19:18*
others
place where Jesus was *c.* *Joh 19:20*
was nigh
soldiers, when they had *c.* *Joh 19:23*
Jesus
the other which was *c.* with *Joh 19:32*
him
Now in the place where he *Joh 19:41*
was *c.*
wicked hands have *c.* and *Ac 2:23*
slain
same Jesus, whom ye have *c.* *Ac 2:36*
Christ of Nazareth, whom ye *Ac 4:10*
c.
that our old man is *c.* with *Ro 6:6*
him
old self nailed to cross (A) *Ro 6:6*
was Paul *c.* for you? or *1Co 1:13*
were ye
we preach Christ *c.* unto the *1Co 1:23*
Jews
you, save Jesus Christ, and *1Co 2:2*
him *c.*
would not have *c.* the Lord *1Co 2:8*
of glory
he was *c.* through weakness *2Co 13:4*
I am *c.* with Christ: *Ga 2:20*
nevertheless
evidently set forth, *c.* among *Ga 3:1*
you
have *c.* the flesh with the *Ga 5:24*
affections
by whom the world is *c.* unto *Ga 6:14*
me
Egypt, where also our Lord *Re 11:8*
was *c.*

CRUCIFY

and to scourge, and to *c.* *M't 20:19*
him
some of them ye shall kill *M't 23:34*
and *c.*
and led him away to *c.* him *M't 27:31*
they cried out again, C. him *M'k 15:13*
out the more exceedingly, *M'k 15:14*
C. him
and led him out to *c.* him *M'k 15:20*
And with him they *c.* two *M'k 15:27*
thieves
they cried, saying, C. him, *c.* *Lu 23:21*
him
cried out, saying, C. him, *c.* *Joh 19:6*
him
Take ye him, and *c.* him: for *Joh 19:6*
I find
not that I have power to *c.* *Joh 19:10*
thee
away with him, *c.* him. *Joh 19:15*
Pilate saith
Shall I *c.* your King? The *Joh 19:15*
chief
they *c.* to themselves the Son *Heb 6:6*
of God

CRUEL

and their wrath, for it was *c.* *Ge 49:7*
of spirit, and for *c.* bondage *Ex 6:9*
broken spirit, *c.* bondage (R) *Ex 6:9*
dragons, and the *c.* venom *De 32:33*
of asps
thou art become *c.* to me *Job 30:21*
and they hate me with *c.* *Ps 25:19*
hatred
of the unrighteous and *c.* man *Ps 71:4*
others, and thy years unto the *Pr 5:9*
c.
he that is *c.* troubleth his *Pr 11:17*
own flesh
tender mercies of the wicked *Pr 12:10*
are *c.*
a *c.* messenger shall be sent *Pr 17:11*
against
is *c.* and anger is outrageous *Pr 27:4*
jealousy is *c.* as the grave: *Ca 8:6*
the coals
Lord cometh, *c.* both with *Isa 13:9*
wrath
over into the hand of a *c.* *Isa 19:4*
lord
they are *c.* and have no *Jer 6:23*
mercy
the chastisement of a *c.* one *Jer 30:14*
they are *c.* and will not *Jer 50:42*
shew mercy
daughter of my people is *La 4:3*
become *c.*
what a *c.* punishment (S) *2Co 7:11*
others had trail of *c.* *Heb 11:36*
mockings

CRUELLY

father, because he *c.* *Eze 18:18*
oppressed
c. tormented by a demon *M't 15:22*
(A)

CRUELTY

instruments of *c.* are in their *Ge 49:5*
the *c.* done to the threescore *J'g 9:24*
dealt with reckless *c.* (A) *2Ch 28:19*
against me, and breathe out *Ps 27:12*
c.
are full of the habitations of *Ps 74:20*
c.
and with *c.* have ye ruled *Eze 34:4*
them
laid waste with *c.* (A) *Ac 8:3*

CRUMBS

casts ice like *c.* (A) *Ps 147:17*
dogs eat of the *c.* which *M't 15:27*
fall from
the table eat of the *M'k 7:28*
children's *c.*
to be fed with the *c.* which *Lu 16:21*
fell

CRUSE

and the *c.* of water, and let *1Sa 26:11*
us go

the bottle of water (A) *1Sa 26:11*
the water jug (B)(R) *1Sa 26:11;*
26:12
the *c.* of water from Saul's *1Sa 26:12*
bolster
and the *c.* of water that *1Sa 26:16*
was at his
and a *c.* of honey, and go to *1Ki 14:3*
him
a bottle of honey (A) *1Ki 14:3*
a jar of honey (B)(R) *1Ki 14:3*
in a barrel, and a little oil *1Ki 17:12*
in a *c.*
oil in a bottle (A) *1Ki 17:12*
oil in a jug (B) *1Ki 17:12; 17:14;*
16:6
waste, neither shall the *c.* *1Ki 17:14*
of oil fail
not, neither did the *c.* of *1Ki 17:16*
oil fail
and a *c.* of water at his *1Ki 19:6*
head
Bring me a new *c.* and put *2Ki 2:20*
salt

CRUSH

c. them utterly (B) *De 7:23*
I *c.* and heal (A) *De 32:29*
God to *c.* me (A)(E)(R) *Job 6:9*
that the foot may *c.* them *Job 39:15*
c. the chief heads (A) *Ps 110:6*
c. the fool (B)(R) *Pr 27:22*
against me to *c.* my young *La 1:15*
men
c. under his feet all the *La 3:34*
prisoners
which *c.* the needy, which say *Am 4:1*
to

CRUSHED

bruised, or, *c.*, or broken, or *Le 22:24*
cut
c. Balaam's foot against the *Nu 22:25*
wall
c. it and ground it small *De 9:21*
(A)(B)(R)
c. in his stones (B) *De 23:1*
be only oppressed and *c.* *De 28:33*
alway
they *c.* them (B) *J'g 2:18*
they *c.* and oppressed them *J'g 10:8*
(R)
c. them as mire (A)(E) *2Sa 22:43*
c. smashing them *2Ch 15:16*
(A)(B)(R)
which are *c.* before the moth *Job 4:19*
they are *c.* in the gate, neither *Job 5:4*
is
c. with sorrow for sin *Ps 34:18*
(A)(B)
utterly spent and *c.* (R) *Ps 38:8*
my heart is *c.* (B)(R) *Ps 102:4; 143:3*
is *c.* breaketh out into a *Isa 59:5*
viper
feels *c.* in spirit (B) *Isa 66:2*
Lord *c.* without pity (B) *Jer 20:16*
he hath *c.* me, he hath *Jer 51:34*
made me
c. and trampled (A) *Da 7:7; 7:19*
cramped and *c.* (A)(B)(R) *2Co 4:8*

CRUSHES

those it *c.* (B) *Pr 26:28*
c. justice to the earth (B) *Ho 5:11*

CRY

according to *c.* which is *Ge 18:21*
come up
their *c.* came up unto God *Ex 2:23;*
3:9
I have heard their *c.*, I know *Ex 3:7*
sorrows
they *c.* saying, Let us go and *Ex 5:8*
they *c.* unto me *Ex 22:23*
is it the voice of them that *Ex 32:18*
c.
shall I, Unclean, unclean *Le 13:45*
all Israel fled at *c.* of them *Nu 16:34*
Go and *c.* unto the gods *J'g 10:14*
which ye
c. of city went up to heaven *1Sa 5:12*
because their *c.* is come up *1Sa 9:16*
unto me
have I yet to *c.* any more *2Sa 19:28*
my *c.* did enter into his ears *2Sa 22:7*
to hearken to *c.* *1Ki 8:28; 2Ch 6:19*

she went forth to *c.* unto   *2Ki 8:3*
c. unto thee in our affliction *2Ch 20:9*
I was angry when I heard   *Ne 5:6*
their *c.*
thou heardest their *c.* by Red   *Ne 9:9*
sea
Mordecai cried loud and bitter *Es 4:1*
c.
matters of their fastings and   *Es 9:31*
c.
O earth, let my *c.* have no   *Job 16:18*
place
I *c.* unto thee, and thou   *Job 30:20*
dost
though they *c.* in his   *Job 30:24*
destruction
they make the oppressed to   *Job 35:9*
c.
they *c.* but none giveth   *Job 35:12*
answer
they *c.* not when he bindeth *Job 36:13*
them
when his young ones *c.*   *Job 38:41*
unto God
hearken to voice of my *c.* my *Ps 5:2*
King
he forgetteth not the *c.* of the *Ps 9:12*
humble
hear right, O Lord, attend   *Ps 17:1*
unto my *c.*
my *c.* came before him, into *Ps 18:6*
his ears
I *c.* in the day time   *Ps 22:2*
Hear, O Lord, when I *c.* with *Ps 27:7*
my
Unto thee will I *c.*, O. Lord *Ps 28:1*
and his ears are open to   *Ps 34:15*
their *c.*
The righteous *c.* and the   *Ps 34:17*
Lord
hear prayer, give ear to my *Ps 39:12*
c.
he inclined unto me, and   *Ps 40:1*
heard my *c.*
when I *c.* then shall mine   *Ps 56:9*
enemies turn
I will *c.* to God most high   *Ps 57:2*
from the end of the earth will *Ps 61:2*
I *c.*
Be merciful to me, for I *c.* to *Ps 86:3*
thee
God of my salvation incline   *Ps 88:2*
thine ear unto my *c.*
he shall *c.* unto me, thou art *Ps 89:26*
my
hear, Lord, let my *c.* come *Ps 102:1*
unto thee
he regarded, when he   *Ps 106:44*
heard their *c.*
let my *c.* come near before *Ps 119:169*
thee
I *c.* unto thee, make haste *Ps 141:1*
unto me
attend to my *c.*; I am   *Ps 142:6*
brought very low
he giveth food to young   *Ps 147:9*
ravens which *c.*
doth not wisdom *c.* and   *Pr 8:1*
understanding
he shall *c.* but shall not be *Pr 21:13*
heard
he stoppeth his ears at the *c.* *Pr 21:13*
more than *c.* of him that   *Ec 9:17*
ruleth
looked for righteousness,   *Isa 5:7*
behold a *c.*
before the child shall know to *Isa 8:4*
c. my
the wild beasts of the island *Isa 13:22*
shall *c.*
c. O city, thou Palestina, art *Isa 14:31*
dissolved
Heshbon shall *c.* and Elealeh *Isa 15:4*
they shall raise up a *c.* of   *Isa 15:5*
destruction
c. is gone round about   *Isa 15:8*
borders of Moab
will be gracious at voice of *Isa 30:19*
thy *c.*
their valiant ones shall *c.* *Isa 33:7*
without
the satyr shall *c.* to his   *Isa 34:14*
fellow
c. to Jerusalem, her warfare *Isa 40:2*
is
the voice said, C. And he said *Isa 40:6*
What shall I *c.*
He shall not *c.*, nor cause his *Isa 42:2*
voice to be

he shall *c.* yea, prevail   *Isa 42:13*
against his
now will I *c.* like travailing *Isa 42:14*
woman
Chaldeans, whose *c.* is in *Isa 43:14*
one shall *c.* to him, yet can *Isa 46:7*
he not
thou shalt *c.* and he shall *Isa 58:9*
say
but ye shall *c.* for sorrow of *Isa 65:14*
heart
go and *c.* in the ears of   *Jer 2:2*
Jerusalem
wilt thou not from this time *c.* *Jer 3:4*
blow the trumpet in the land, *Jer 4:5*
c. saying
nor lift up *c.* nor prayer for *Jer 7:16;*
them   *11:14*
behold the voice of the *c.* of *Jer 8:19*
my people
though they *c.* to me, I will *Jer 11:11*
not
c. to the gods to whom they *Jer 11:12*
offer
I will not hear when they *c.* *Jer 11:14;*
     Eze 8:18
and the *c.* of Jerusalem is *Jer 14:2*
gone up
let a *c.* be heard from their *Jer 18:22*
houses
go up, *c.* from the passages *Jer 22:20*
ye shepherds *c.*   *Jer 25:34;*
     48:20; Eze 21:12
the *c.* of the shepherds shall *Jer 25:36*
be heard
and thy *c.* hath filled the   *Jer 46:12*
land
her little ones caused *c.* to be *Jer 48:4*
heard
enemies have heard a *c.* of *Jer 48:5*
destruction
earth is moved at the *c.* of *Jer 49:21*
Edom
c. is heard at taking of   *Jer 50:46*
Babylon
sound of a *c.* cometh from *Jer 51:54*
Babylon
when I *c.* and shout, he   *La 3:8*
shutteth
hast heard, hide not thine ear *La 3:56*
at my *c.*
that *c.* for all the   *Eze 9:4*
abominations
forbear to *c.*, make no   *Eze 24:17*
mournful
the isles shake, when   *Eze 26:15*
wounded *c.*
the suburbs shake at the *c.* *Eze 27:28*
of
they shall *c.* bitterly for   *Eze 27:30*
Tyrus
Israel shall *c.* unto me, My *Ho 8:2*
God
O Lord, to thee will I *c.*: for *Joe 1:19*
beasts of the field *c.* also *Joe 1:20*
unto
and *c.* mightily unto God   *Jon 3:8*
with their teeth, and *c.* Peace *Mic 3:5*
Stand, stand, shall they *c.* but *Na 2:8*
none
mighty man shall *c.* there   *Zep 1:14*
bitterly
C. thou, saying, Thus saith *Zec 1:14*
the
He shall not strive, nor *c.* *M't 12:19*
at midnight there was a *c.* *M't 25:6*
made
own elect, which *c.* day and *Lu 18:7*
night
whereby we *c.* Abba, Father *Ro 8:15*
and *c.* thou that travailest   *Ga 4:27*
not

CRY AGAINST

he *c.* to Lord *against* thee   *De 15:9;*
     24:15
his priests to *c.* alarm   *2Ch 13:12*
against you
if my land *c. against* me   *Job 31:38*
go to Nineveh, and *c. against* *Jon 1:2*
it

CRY ALOUD

Elijah said, C. *aloud*, for he   *1Ki 18:27*
is god

I *c. aloud*, but there is no   *Job 19:7*
judgment
at noon will I pray and *c.* *Ps 55:17*
aloud
they shall *c. aloud* from the *Isa 24:14*
sea
sing, break forth into singing, *Isa 54:1*
c. aloud
c. aloud, spare not, lift up *Isa 58:1*
voice like
trumpet in Ramah, *c. aloud* at *Ho 5:8*
why dost thou *c. aloud*   *Mic 4:9*

CRY OUT

shall *c. out* because of your *1Sa 8:18*
king
I *c. out* of wrong, but I am *Job 19:7*
not heard
they *c. out* by reason of arm *1Sa 35:9*
of mighty
c. out and shout inhabitant *Isa 12:6*
of Zion
armed soldiers of Moab shall *Isa 15:4*
c. out
my heart shall *c. out* for   *Isa 15:5*
Moab
stay and wonder, *c. out* and *1Sa 29:9*
cry
I will howl and *c. out* for *Jer 48:31*
all Moab
arise, *c. out* in night, in   *La 2:19*
watches
will a young lion *c. out* of his *Am 3:4*
den
I *c. out* to thee, but thou   *Hab 1:2*
wilt not save
for the stone shall *c. out* of *Hab 2:11*
the wall
he began to *c. out*, have   *M'k 10:47*
mercy
stones would immediately *c.* *Lu 19:40*
out

CRY TO THE LORD

cease not to *c. unto the Lord* *1Sa 7:8*
for us
they *c. to the Lord* in   *Ps 107:19;*
trouble   *107:28*
shall *c. unto the Lord* because *Isa 19:20*
of oppressors
sanctify ye a fast, and *c. to* *Joe 1:14*
the Lord
c. to the Lord, but he will *Mic 3:4*
not hear

GREAT CRY

because *c.* of Sodom is   *Ge 18:20;*
great   *19:13*
Esau cried with a *great* and *Ge 27:34*
bitter *c.*
shall be a *great c.* through *Ex 11:6*
Egypt
there was a *great c.* in Egypt *Ex 12:30*
great c. of people and their *Ne 5:1*
wives
when he said, there arose   *Ac 23:9*
great c.

HEAR CRY

if they *c.* I will *hear* their *c.* *Ex 22:23*
will God *hear c.* when   *Job 27:9*
trouble comes
hear my *c.*, attend to my *Ps 61:1*
prayer
he will *hear* their *c.* and   *Ps 145:19*
save them
let him *hear* the *c.* in the *Jer 20:16*
morning

NOT HEAR CRY

when they fast, I will *not* *Jer 14:12*
hear c.

CRYING

when Eli heard the noise of *1Sa 4:14*
the *c.*
Tamar put ashes, and went *2Sa 13:19*
on *c.*
nor regardeth he the *c.* of *Job 39:7*
driver
let not thy soul spare for his *Pr 19:18*
c.

horse-leech hath two daughters c., Give | Pr 30:15
it is a day of c. to the mountains | Isa 22:5
there is a c. for wine in the streets | Isa 24:11
voice of c. be no more heard in her | Isa 65:19
a voice of c. shall be from Horonaim | Jer 48:3
shall bring forth head-stone with c. | Zec 4:7
covering the altar of the Lord with c. | Mal 2:13
voice of one c. in the wilderness, Prepare | M't 3:3; M'k 1:3; Lu 3:4; Joh 1:23
saw the children c. in the temple | M't 21:15
devils c., Thou art Christ, Son of God | Lu 4:41
for unclean spirits c. came out of many | Ac 8:7
they ran in among the people, c. out | Ac 14:14
laid hands on him, c. out, Men of Israel | Ac 21:28
multitude c., Away with him | Ac 21:36
Spirit into your hearts, c. Abba Father | Ga 4:6
he offered up prayers with strong c. | Heb 5:7
there will be no more death nor c. | Re 21:4

CRYPT

in a c. or a bushel (A) | Lu 11:33

CRYSTAL

The gold and the c. cannot equal | Job 28:17
the gold and glass (A)(B)(E)(R) | Job 28:17
as the colour of the terrible c. | Eze 1:22
was a sea of glass like unto c. | Re 4:6
like a jasper stone, clear as c. | Re 21:11
river of water of life, clear as c. | Re 22:1

CUB

like a lion's c. (A)(B) | Ge 49:9

CUBIT

in a c. shalt thou finish ark above | Ge 6:16
breadth of it, after c. of a man | De 3:11
knops compassing it, ten in a c. | 1Ki 7:24
ten in a c. compassing sea about | 2Ch 4:3
c. is a c. and an hand-breadth | Eze 43:13
add one c. to stature | M't 6:27; Lu 12:25

CUBITS

length of ark 300 c. breadth 50 c. | Ge 6:15
fifteen c. upward did waters prevail | Ge 7:20
two c. and a half length of ark | Ex 25:10
Goliath's height six c. and a span | 1Sa 17:4
length of the house 60 c. breadth 20 | 1Ki 6:2
each of the cherubims was ten c. high | 1Ki 6:23
every laver was four c. high | 1Ki 7:38
brake down wall 400 c. | 2Ki 14:13; 2Ch 25:23
the height 60 c. the breadth 60 c. | Ezr 6:3
let a gallows be made fifty c. high | Es 5:14; 7:9
measured from gate to gate 100 c. | Eze 40:23
court 100 c. | Eze 40:47
the breadth of the door was ten c. | Eze 41:2

the thickness of the wall was five c. | Eze 41:9
the altar shall be twelve c. long | Eze 43:16
height of the image was 60 c. | Da 3:1
length of the flying roll is 20 | Zec 5:2
they were from land as it were 200 c. | Joh 21:8
He measured wall of city 144 c. | Re 21:17

CUBS

robbed of her c. (B)(R) | 2Sa 17:8; Pr 17:12
she nourished her c. (A) | Eze 19:2; 19:3
robbed of her c. (A)(R) | Ho 13:8
where his c. were (A)(R) | Na 2:11

CUCKOW

the night hawk, and the c. | Le 11:16
the sea gull (A)(B)(R) | Le 11:16
the sea-mew (E) | Le 11:16
the night hawk, and the c. | De 14:15

CUCUMBERS

freely; the c. and the melons | Nu 11:5
as a lodge in a garden of c. | Isa 1:8

CUD

cheweth the c. among the beasts | Le 11:3; 11:4-7, 28; De 14:6-8

CUDGELS

multitude with c. (N) | M't 26:47; 25:55

CULTIVATE

contrive, dig up, c. (A) | Pr 3:29
c. these matters (B) | 1Ti 4:15
those who c. it (P) | Heb 6:7

CULTIVATED

ye are God's c. field (S) | 1Co 3:9
it is c. (A)(N)(R) | Heb 6:7

CULTIVATES

who c. the ground (B) | Zec 13:5

CUM

he said to her, Talitha c. (N) | M'k 5:41

CUMBERED

But Martha was c. about much | Lu 10:40
distracted about much serving (A)(R) | Lu 10:40
worried about much housework (B) | Lu 10:40
fretting and fussing about many (N) | Lu 10:40
worried and bothered about providing (P) | Lu 10:40

CUMBERETH

cut it down; why c. it the ground | Lu 13:7
use up the ground (A)(N)(R) | Lu 13:7
exhaust the soil (B) | Lu 13:7
use up valuable space (P) | Lu 13:7

CUMBRANCE

can I myself alone bear your c. | De 1:12
bear weariness, pressure, burden (A) | De 1:12
handle your troubles (B) | De 1:12
bear alone the weight (R) | De 1:12

CUMI

unto her, Talitha c.; which is | M'k 5:41

CUMMIN

and scatter the c. and cast | Isa 28:25
wheel turned about upon the c. | Isa 28:27
with a staff, and the c. with a rod | Isa 28:27
pay tithe of mint and anise and c. | M't 23:23

CUNNING

Esau was a c. hunter, a man of | Ge 25:27
an expert hunter (B) | Ge 25:27
skilful hunter (E)(R) | Ge 25:27
came with crafty c. (A) | Ge 27:35
cherubims of c. work shalt thou | Ex 26:1
cherubim skillfully embroidered (A) | Ex 26:1
cherubs skillfully wrought (B)(R) | Ex 26:1
work of skilful workmen (E) | Ex 26:1
and fine twined linen of c. work | Ex 26:31
fine twined linen, with c. work | Ex 28:6
breastplate of judgment with c. | Ex 28:15
in skilled work (A) | Ex 28:15
skilful (B)(E) | Ex 28:15; 38:23; 39:8
to devise c. works in gold and silver | Ex 31:4
Aholiab a c. workman and embroiderer | Ex 38:23
he made the breastplate of c. work | Ex 39:8
acted with c. (R) | Jos 9:4
man is a c. player on an harp | 1Sa 16:16
plays skilfully on the lyre (A) | 1Sa 16:16
skilful in playing (B)(E)(R) | 1Sa 16:16
seen a son of Jesse that is c. in playing | 1Sa 16:18
plays skilfully (A) | 1Sa 16:18
plays excellently (B) | 1Sa 16:18
skilful in playing (E)(R) | 1Sa 16:18
did it with c. (B) | 2Ki 10:19
all that were c. in songs, were 288 | 1Ch 25:7
send me a man c. to work in gold | 2Ch 2:7
I have sent a c. man of Huram my father's | 2Ch 2:13
a c. charmer (R) | Ps 58:5
if I forget, let my right hand forget her c. | Ps 137:5
c. of heart (A) | Pr 7:10
thy joints, the work of a c. workman | Ca 7:1
I will take away the c. artificer | Isa 3:3
expert craftsman (A) | Isa 3:3
skilful craftsman (B) | Isa 3:3
skilful magician (E) | Isa 3:3
he seeketh a c. workman to prepare | Isa 40:20
skilful craftsman (A)(R) | Isa 40:20
skilful carver (B) | Isa 40:20
skilful workman (E) | Isa 40:20
send for c. women that they may come | Jer 9:17
skilful women (A)(B)(E)(R) | Jer 9:17
they are all the work of c. men | Jer 10:9
skilful men (A)(E) | Jer 10:9
skilled men (B)(R) | Jer 10:9
children well favoured, c. in knowledge | Da 1:4
skilful in wisdom (A)(E)(R) | Da 1:4
c. and unscrupulousness (A)(P) | Lu 20:23
practice c. (N)(R) | 2Co 4:2
beguiled Eve through his c. (A)(B)(N)(R) | 2Co 11:3
carried about by c. craftiness | Eph 4:14

CUNNINGLY

they worked c. (A) | Jos 9:4
casting spells so c. (A)(B) | Ps 58:5
deal c. (B) | Ps 58:5
have not followed c. devised fables | 2Pe 1:16

cleverly devised stories, fables, myths (A)(B)(R)   2Pe 1:16
tales artfully spun (N)   2Pe 1:16
a cleverly written up story (P)   2Pe 1:16

CUP

Pharaoh's c. was in my hand   Ge 40:11; 40:13, 21
And put my c., the silver c. in   Ge 44:2
c. was found in Benjamin's sack   Ge 44:12
he also with whom the c. is found   Ge 44:16
man in whose hand the c. is found   Ge 44:17
and drank of his own c. and lay   2Sa 12:3
was wrought like the brim of a c.   1Ki 7:26
like the work of the brim of a c.   2Ch 4:5
this shall be the portion of their c.   Ps 11:6
of mine inheritance and of my c.   Ps 16:5
head with oil; my c. runneth over   Ps 23:5
and waters of a full c. are wrung out   Ps 73:10
hand of the Lord there is a c.   Ps 75:8
I will take the c. of salvation, and   Ps 116:13
when it giveth his colour in the c.   Pr 23:31
of the Lord the c. of his fury   Isa 51:17
the dregs of the c. of trembling   Isa 51:17
of thine hand the c. of trembling   Isa 51:22
even the dregs of the c. of my fury   Isa 51:22
the c. of consolation to drink for   Jer 16:7
the wine c. of this fury at my hand   Jer 25:15
took I the c. at the Lord's hand   Jer 25:17
take the c. at thine hand to drink   Jer 25:28
judgment was not to drink of the c.   Jer 49:12
Babylon hath been a golden c. in   Jer 51:7
the c. also shall pass through unto   La 4:21
will I give her c. into thine hand   Eze 23:31
of thy sister's c. deep and large   Eze 23:32
c. of astonishment and desolation   Eze 23:33
with the c. of thy sister Samaria   Eze 23:33
c. of the Lord's right hand shall be   Hab 2:16
make Jerusalem a c. of trembling   Zec 12:2
c. of cold water only in the name   M't 10:42
drink of the c. that I shall drink of   M't 20:22
Ye shall drink indeed of my c. and   M't 20:23
outside of the c. and of the platter   M't 23:25
first that which is within the c.   M't 23:26
he took the c. and gave thanks   M't 26:27
possible, let this c. pass from me   M't 26:39
this c. may not pass away from me   M't 26:42
give you a c. of water to drink   M'k 9:41
ye drink of the c. that I drink of   M'k 10:38
indeed drink of the c. that I drink   M'k 10:39
And he took the c. and when he   M'k 14:23
take away this c. from me   M'k 14:36
make clean the outside of the c.   Lu 11:39
he took the c. and gave thanks   Lu 22:17

Likewise also the c. after supper   Lu 22:20
This c. is the new testament in my   Lu 22:20
if thou be willing, remove this c.   Lu 22:42
c. which my Father hath given me   Joh 18:11
The c. of blessing which we bless   1Co 10:16
Ye cannot drink the c. of the Lord   1Co 10:21
and the c. of devils   1Co 10:21
same manner also he took the c.   1Co 11:25
This c. is the new testament in my   1Co 11:25
and drink this c. ye do show   1Co 11:26
drink this c. of the Lord, unworthily   1Co 11:27
of that bread, and drink of that c.   1Co 11:28
into the c. of his indignation   Re 14:10
the c. of the wine of the fierceness   Re 16:19
having a golden c. in her hand full   Re 17:4
in the c. which she hath filled, fill   Re 18:6

CUPBEARER

For I was the king's c.   Ne 1:11

CUPBEARERS

their apparel, and his c. and his   1Ki 10:5
their apparel; his c. also, and their   2Ch 9:4

CUPBOARD

in a c. or a bushel (P)   Lu 11:33

CUPS

and the bowls, and the c.   1Ch 28:17
the c. (A)   2Ch 24:14; Jer 52:19
brought forth the c. (B)   Ezr 1:7
from the vessels of c. even to all   Isa 22:24
pots full of wine, and c. and I   Jer 35:5
and the spoons, and the c.   Jer 52:19
as the washing of c. and pots   M'k 7:4
as the washing of pots and c.   M'k 7:8

CURDLED

as milk, and c. me like cheese   Job 10:10

CURE

c. the leprosy (S)   2Ki 5:3; 5:6, 7, 11
I will bring it health and c.   Jer 33:6
lay upon it health and healing (A)(R)   Jer 33:6
and I will c. them, and will reveal   Jer 33:6
bring restoration and health, I will heal them (B)   Jer 33:6
you, nor c. you of your wound   Ho 5:13
and they could not c. him   M't 17:16
over all devils, and to c. diseases   Lu 9:1

CURED

for thou shalt not be c.   Jer 46:11
there is no healing remedy (A)(B)(E)(R)   Jer 46:11
child was c. from that very hour   M't 17:18
boy c. instantly (A)(R)   M't 17:18
he c. many of their infirmities   Lu 7:21
healing many of sicknesses (A)   Lu 7:21
said unto him that was c. It is the   Joh 5:10

CURES

and I do c. to day and to morrow   Lu 13:32
perform healings (A)   Lu 13:32
I work healing today (B)   Lu 13:32

CURIOUS

the c. girdle of the ephod   Ex 28:8; 28:27-28; 29:5; 39:5, 20; Le 8:7
devise c. works, to work in gold   Ex 35:32
used c. arts brought their books   Ac 19:19

CURIOUSLY

c. wrought in the lowest parts   Ps 139:15

CURRENT

c. money with the merchant   Ge 23:16
the c. was engulfing me (B)(R)   Jon 2:3
symbol of the c. time (B)   Heb 9:9

CURSE

I will not again c. the ground any   Ge 8:21
and c. him that curseth thee   Ge 12:3
I shall bring a c. upon me, and not   Ge 27:12
Upon me be thy c. my son   Ge 27:13
gods, nor c. the ruler of thy people   Ex 22:28
Thou shalt not c. the deaf   Le 19:14
bitter water that causeth the c.   19:21-22, 24, 27
I pray thee, c. me this people   Nu 22:6
come now, c. me them   Nu 22:11
shalt not c. the people: for   Nu 22:12
I pray thee, c. me this people   Nu 22:17
Come, c. me Jacob, and   Nu 23:7
How shall I c. whom God hath not   Nu 23:8
I took thee to c. mine enemies   Nu 23:11
all: and c. me them from thence   Nu 23:13
c. them at all, nor bless them at all   Nu 23:25
mayest c. me them from thence   Nu 23:27
I called thee to c. mine enemies   Nu 24:10
you this day a blessing and a c.   De 11:26
a c. if ye will not obey the   De 11:28
and the c. upon mount Ebal   De 11:29
Pethor of Mesopotamia, to c. thee   De 23:4
God turned the c. into a blessing   De 23:5
shall stand upon mount Ebal to c.   De 27:13
he heareth the words of this c.   De 29:19
the blessing and the c. which I   De 30:1
and make the camp of Israel a c.   Jos 6:18
Balaam the son of Beor to c. you   Jos 24:9
C. ye Meroz, said the angel   J'g 5:23
c. ye bitterly the inhabitants   J'g 5:23
upon them came the c. of Jotham   J'g 9:57
bringing a c. upon themselves (A)(E)   1Sa 3:13
should this dead dog c. my lord   2Sa 16:9
let him c. because the Lord hath   2Sa 16:10
Lord hath said unto him, C. David   2Sa 16:10
let him alone, and let him c. for   2Sa 16:11
a grievous c. in the day when I   1Ki 2:8
should become a desolation and a c.   2Ki 22:19
entered into a c. and into an oath   Ne 10:29
against them, that he should c.   Ne 13:2
God turned the c. into a blessing   Ne 13:2
and he will c. thee to thy face   Job 1:11; 2:5
c. God, and die   Job 2:9
Let them c. it that   Job 3:8
that c. the day, who are   Job 3:8
to sin by wishing a c. to his soul   Job 31:30

their mouth, but they c. *Ps 62:4*
inwardly
Let them c. but bless thou *Ps 109:28*
The c. of the Lord is in the *Pr 3:33*
house
corn, the people shall c. him *Pr 11:26*
him shall the people c. *Pr 24:24*
nations
the c. causeless shall not *Pr 26:2*
come
morning, it shall be counted *Pr 27:14*
a c.
his eyes shall have many a c. *Pr 28:27*
lest he c. thee, and thou be *Pr 30:10*
found
lest thou hear thy servant c. *Ec 7:21*
thee
C. not the king, no not in *Ec 10:20*
thy
c. not the rich in *Ec 10:20*
thy bedchamber
and c. their king and their *Isa 8:21*
God
hath the c. devoured the *Isa 24:6*
earth
and upon the people of my c. *Isa 34:5*
given Jacob to the c. and *Isa 43:28*
Israel
ye shall leave your name for *Isa 65:15*
a c.
every one of them doth c. *Jer 15:10*
me
because of the c. of God *Jer 23:10*
(A)(B)(R)
and a proverb, a taunt, and a *Jer 24:9*
c.
astonishment, an hissing, *Jer 25:18*
and a c.
will make this city a c. to all *Jer 26:6*
to be a c. and an *Jer 29:18*
astonishment
them shall be taken up a c. *Jer 29:22*
by all
an astonishment, and a c. *Jer 42:18;*
44:12
ye might be a c. and a *Jer 44:8*
reproach
astonishment, and a c. *Jer 44:22*
without an
a reproach, a waste, and a *Jer 49:13*
c.; and
sorrow of heart, thy c. unto *La 3:65*
them
the c. is poured upon us, and *Da 9:11*
is the c. that goeth forth over *Zec 5:3*
the
ye were a c. among the *Zec 8:13*
heathen
I will even send a c. upon *Mal 2:2*
you
and I will c. your blessings *Mal 2:2*
are cursed with a c.: for ye *Mal 3:9*
have
come and smite the earth *Mal 4:6*
with a c.
bless them that c. you, do *M't 5:44*
good to
Then began he to c. and to *M't 26:74*
swear
But he began to c. and to *M'k 14:71*
swear
Bless them that c. you, and *Lu 6:28*
and bound themselves under *Ac 23:12*
a c.
bound ourselves under a *Ac 23:14*
great c.
persecute you: bless, and c. *Ro 12:14*
not
works of the law are under *Ga 3:10*
the c.
redeemed us from the c. of *Ga 3:13*
law, being made a c. for us *Ga 3:13*
therewith c. we men, which *Jas 3:9*
there shall be no more c.: but *Re 22:3*

CURSED

thou art c. above all cattle *Ge 3:14*
c. is the ground for thy sake *Ge 3:17*
now art thou c. from the *Ge 4:11*
earth
ground which the Lord hath *Ge 5:29*
c.
he said, C. be Canaan; a *Ge 9:25*
servant of
c. be every one that curseth *Ge 27:29*
thee
C. be their anger, for it was *Ge 49:7*
fierce

hath c. his father or his *Le 20:9*
mother
the name of the Lord, and c. *Le 24:11*
forth him that c. *Le 24:14*
without the
forth him that had c. out *Le 24:23*
of the
and he whom thou cursest is *Nu 22:6*
c.
I curse, whom God hath not *Nu 23:8*
c.
and c. is he that curseth thee *Nu 24:9*
lest thou be a c. thing like it *De 7:26*
abhor it; for it is a c. thing *De 7:26*
cleave nought of the c. thing *De 13:17*
C. be the man that maketh *De 27:15*
any
C. be he that setteth light by *De 27:16*
his
C. be he that removeth his *De 27:17*
C. be he that maketh the *De 27:18*
blind to
C. be he that perverteth the *De 27:19*
C. be he that lieth with his *De 27:20*
father's
C. be he that lieth with any *De 27:21*
manner
C. be he that lieth with his *De 27:22*
sister
C. be he that lieth with his *De 27:23*
mother
C. be he that smiteth his *De 27:24*
neighbour
C. be he that taketh reward *De 27:25*
to slay
C. be he that confirmeth not *De 27:26*
all the
C. shalt thou be in the city *De 28:16*
and c. shalt thou be in the *De 28:16*
field
C. shall be thy basket and *De 28:17*
thy store
C. shall be the fruit of thy *De 28:18*
body
C. shalt thou be when thou *De 28:19*
comest
c. shalt thou be when thou *De 28:19*
goest
C. be the man before the *Jos 6:26*
Lord, that
therefore ye are c. and there *Jos 9:23*
shall
eat and drink, and c. *J'g 9:27*
Abimelech
C. be he that giveth a wife *J'g 21:18*
to
C. be the man that eateth *1Sa 14:24;*
any *14:28*
Philistine c. David by his *1Sa 17:43*
gods
of men, c. be they before *1Sa 26:19*
the Lord
came forth, and c. still as he *2Sa 16:5*
came
said Shimei when he c., *2Sa 16:7*
Come out
and c. as he went, and *2Sa 16:13*
threw stones
because he c. the Lord's *2Sa 19:21*
anointed
which c. me with a grievous *1Ki 2:8*
curse
c. them in the name of the *2Ki 2:24*
Lord
now this c. woman, and *2Ki 9:34*
bury her
contended with them, and *Ne 13:25*
c. them
sinned, and c. God in their *Job 1:5*
hearts
Job his mouth, and c. his day *Job 3:1*
but suddenly I c. his *Job 5:3*
habitation
their portion is c. in the *Job 24:18*
earth: he
they that be c. of him shall *Ps 37:22*
be cut
hast rebuked the proud that *Ps 119:21*
are c.
he who is c. falls (B) *Pr 22:14*
thyself likewise hast c. others *Ec 7:22*
C. be the man that obeyeth *Jer 11:3*
not the
C. be the man that trusteth *Jer 17:5*
in man
C. be the day wherein I was *Jer 20:14*
born
C. be the man, who brought *Jer 20:15*
tidings
C. be he that doeth the work *Jer 48:10*

c. be he that keepeth back *Jer 48:10*
c. be the deceiver, which *Mal 1:14*
hath in
yea, I have c. them already *Mal 2:2*
Ye are c. with a curse: for *Mal 3:9*
ye have
Depart from me, ye c., into *M't 25:41*
who knoweth not the law *Joh 7:49*
are c.
C. is every one that *Ga 3:10*
continueth
c. is every one that hangeth *Ga 3:13*
on a
covetous practices; c. *2Pe 2:14*
children
full of c. offences (A) *Re 17:4*

CURSEDST

about which thou c. and *J'g 17:2*
spakest
behold, the fig tree which *M'k 11:21*
thou c.

CURSES

the priest shall write these c. *Nu 5:23*
in
these c. shall come upon *De 28:15;*
thee *28:45*
all the c. that are written in *De 29:20*
this
according to all the c. of the *De 29:21*
to bring upon it all the c. *De 29:27*
that are
put all these c. upon thine *De 30:7*
enemies
all the c. that are written *2Ch 34:24*
in the
c. from your lips (A) *Col 3:8*

CURSEST

and he whom thou c. is cursed *Nu 22:6*

CURSETH

and curse him that c. thee *Ge 12:3*
cursed be every one that c. *Ge 27:29*
thee
And he that c. his father, or *Ex 21:17*
his
every one that c. his father or *Le 20:9*
his
Whosoever c. his God shall *Le 24:15*
bear
thee, and cursed is he that c. *Nu 24:9*
thee
Whoso c. his father or his *Pr 20:20*
mother
There is a generation that c. *Pr 30:11*
their
He that c. father or mother, *M't 15:4*
let
Whoso c. father or mother, *M'k 7:10*
let him

CURSING

the woman with an oath of *Nu 5:21*
c.
The Lord shall send upon *De 28:20*
thee c.
life and death, blessing and *De 30:19*
c.
will requite me good for his *2Sa 16:12*
c.
His mouth is full of c. and *Ps 10:7*
deceit
for c. and lying which they *Ps 59:12*
speak
As he loved c. so let it *Ps 109:17*
come unto
he clothed himself with c. *Ps 109:18*
like as
he heareth c. and bewrayeth *Pr 29:24*
it
Whose mouth is full of c. *Ro 3:14*
nigh unto c.; whose end is to *Heb 6:8*
be
mouth proceedeth blessing *Jas 3:10*
and c.

CURSINGS

of the law, the blessings and *Jos 8:34*
c.

CURTAIN

c. of tabernacle   *Ex 26:2;*
26:4-5, 8-10, 12; 36:9, 11-12, 15, 17
c. for the door of the court   *Nu 3:26*
stretch out heavens like *c.*   *Ps 104:2;*
     Isa 40:22
the *c.* rent (A)(N)(P)(R)   *M't 27:51;*
     M'k 15:38; Lu 23:45
the second *c.* (B)(N)(P)(R)   *Heb 9:3*
through the *c.*   *Heb 10:20*
  (A)(B)(N)(P)(R)

CURTAINS

make tabernacle with ten   *Ex 26:1;*
c.   *26:2-3, 6-9, 12-13; 36:8-10, 13-16*
shall bear the *c.* of the   *Nu 4:25*
tabernacle
the ark of God dwelleth   *2Sa 7:2*
within *c.*
of the Lord remaineth under   *1Ch 17:1*
c.
of Kedar, as the *c.* of Solomon   *Ca 1:5*
and let them stretch forth the   *Isa 54:2*
c. of
spoiled, and my *c.* in a   *Jer 4:20*
moment
and to set up my *c.*   *Jer 10:20*
shall take to themselves   *Jer 49:29*
their *c.*
the *c.* of the land of Midian   *Hab 3:7*

CUSH

the sons of Ham; *C.* and   *Ge 10:6*
Mizraim
the sons of *C.*; Seba, and   *Ge 10:7*
Havilah
C. begat Nimrod: he began to   *Ge 10:8*
be
a woman of *C.* (S)   *Nu 12:1*
sons of Ham; *C.* and   *1Ch 1:8*
Mizraim
the sons of *C.*; Seba, and   *1Ch 1:9*
Havilah
C. begat Nimrod; he began   *1Ch 1:10*
to be
the words of *C.* the   *Ps 7 title*
Benjamite
from Pathros, and from *C.*   *Isa 11:11*
and
C. and Put (S)   *Jer 46:9; Eze 38:5*

CUSHAN

I saw the tents of *C.* in   *Hab 3:7*
affliction

CUSHI

said Joab to *C.*, Go tell the   *2Sa 18:21;*
king   *18:22-23, 31-32*
the son of *C.* unto Baruch,   *Jer 36:14*
saying
unto Zephaniah the son of *C.*   *Zep 1:1*

CUSHITE

the *C.* woman (S)   *Nu 12:1*

CUSTODIAN

gave it back to the *c.* (B)   *Lu 4:20*

CUSTODY

custody   (A)(R)   *Ge 40:3;*
40:4, 7; 41:10; 42:17; Le 24:12;
  Nu 15:34; Eze 19:9
continued in *c.* (A)(B)(R)   *Ge 40:4*
under the *c.* and charge of   *Nu 3:36*
the women, unto the *c.* of   *Es 2:3*
Hege the
the palace, to the *c.* of Hegai   *Es 2:8*
the king's house, to the *c.* of   *Es 2:8*
Hegai
the women, to the *c.* of   *Es 2:14*
Shaashgaz
in *c.* with rebels (N)   *M'k 15:7*
put them in *c.* (S)   *Ac 4:3*

CUSTOM

for the *c.* of women is upon   *Ge 31:35*
me
period of women is upon me   *Ge 31:35*
(A)
meeting with the   *Ge 31:35*
indisposition of (B)

manner of women is upon   *Ge 31:35*
me (E)
the way of women is upon   *Ge 31:35*
me (R)
according to the *c.* (S)   *Le 5:10;*
  9:16; 2Ki 11:14; 1Ch 24:19; 2Ch 30:16
And it was a *c.* in Israel   *J'g 11:39*
priest's *c.* with the people   *1Sa 2:13*
was
made them a standing *c.*   *2Ch 35:25*
(B)
according to the *c.* as the   *Ezr 3:4*
duty
according to the ordinance   *Ezr 3:4*
  (A)(E)(R)
as is prescribed (B)   *Ezr 3:4*
they not pay toll, tribute,   *Ezr 4:13*
and *c.*
and toll, tribute, and *c.* was   *Ezr 4:20*
paid
toll, tribute, or *c.* upon them   *Ezr 7:24*
sealed according to the law   *Jer 32:11*
and *c.*
sitting at the receipt of *c.*   *M't 9:9*
sitting at collector's office   *M't 9:9*
  (A)(P)
sitting at the tax office   *M't 9:9*
  (B)(R)
sitting at the place of toll (E)   *M't 9:9*
sitting in the custom-house   *M't 9:9*
  (N)
of the earth take *c.* or   *M't 17:25*
tribute
collect duties or tribute (A)   *M't 17:25*
receive toll or tribute   *M't 17:25*
  (E)(R)
collect tax or toll (N)   *M't 17:25*
their rates and taxes (P)   *M't 17:25*
sitting at the receipt or *c.*   *M'k 2:14*
as was his *c.* (S)   *M'k 10:1*
to the *c.* of the priest's office   *Lu 1:9*
do for him after the *c.* of the   *Lu 2:27*
law
Jerusalem after the *c.* of the   *Lu 2:42*
feast
as his *c.* was, he went into   *Lu 4:16*
Levi, sitting at the receipt of   *Lu 5:27*
ye have a *c.* that I should   *Joh 18:39*
release
is due; *c.* to whom *c.*; fear to   *Ro 13:7*
whom
revenue to whom revenue is   *Ro 13:7*
due (A)(R)
toll to whom toll is due (B)   *Ro 13:7*
pay tax and toll (N)   *Ro 13:7*
rates or taxes (P)   *Ro 13:7*
we have no such *c.* neither   *1Co 11:16*

CUSTOM-HOUSE

a seat in the *c.* (N)(P)   *M't 9:9*

CUSTOMS

any one of these abominable   *Le 18:30*
c.
c. of the heathen (A)(B)   *2Ki 17:8*
filled with *c.* from the east   *Isa 2:6*
  (A)(E)(S)
the *c.* of the people are vain   *Jer 10:3*
refuse to follow ancient *c.*   *M'k 7:5*
(P)
the *c.* which Moses delivered   *Ac 6:14*
us
institutions and usages which   *Ac 6:14*
Moses (A)
legal usages handed down by   *Ac 6:14*
Moses (B)
teach *c.* which are not   *Ac 16:21*
lawful for us
promulgating ways of   *Ac 16:21*
behaviour (B)
neither to walk after the *c.*   *Ac 21:21*
to be expert in all *c.* and   *Ac 26:3*
questions
the people, or *c.* of our   *Ac 28:17*
fathers

CUT

c. the wood (S)   *Ge 22:3*
c. down their Asherim   *Ex 34:13;*
  (A)(E)(R)   *2Ki 18:4; 23:14; 2Ch 14:3;*
  17:6
c. it in wires to work it in   *Ex 39:3*
the blue
c. the burnt-offering into   *Le 1:6;*
pieces   *1:12*

he *c.* the ram into pieces   *Le 8:20;*
  Ex 29:17
ye shall not offer to Lord   *Le 22:24*
what is *c.*
c. down, *c.* off (B)   *Nu 21:24;*
De 25:18; 2Ki 15:14, 25, 30; 25:21;
  M't 26:51
ye shall not *c.* yourselves nor   *De 14:1*
make
c. off (A)(R)   *De 25:18; M't 26:51*
my concubine *c.* her in   *J'g 20:6*
pieces
c. the hair of his head (S)   *2Sa 14:26*
c. down the image   *1Ki 15:13*
  (B)(E)(R)
and *c.* the bullock in pieces   *1Ki 18:23;*
  18:33
they *c.* themselves after   *1Ki 18:28*
their manner with
c. off images (B)   *2Ki 18:4; 23:14*
he *c.* in pieces all vessels   *2Ki 24:13;*
of gold Solomon had made   *2Ch 28:24*
the people, he *c.* them with   *1Ch 20:3*
saws
thy servants can skill to *c.*   *2Ch 2:8;*
timber   *2:10*
he bendeth, let them be as *c.*   *Ps 58:7*
in pieces
c. the bars of iron in   *Ps 107:16;*
sunder   *Isa 45:2*
art thou not it that hath *c.*   *Isa 51:9*
Rahab
nor lament, nor *c.* themselves   *Jer 16:6*
for them
they *c.* the calf in twain,   *Jer 34:18*
and passed
he *c.* the roll with penknife,   *Jer 36:23*
and cast
clothes rent, and having *c.*   *Jer 41:5*
themselves
how long wilt thou *c.* thyself   *Jer 47:5*
if ye will not, ye shall be *c.* in   *Da 2:5*
pieces
speak against God shall be *c.*   *Da 3:29*
in pieces
when born thy navel was not   *Eze 16:4*
c.
c. them down with swords   *Eze 23:47*
(A)
and *c.* them in the head, all   *Am 9:1*
of them
c. off the hair (S)   *Mic 1:16*
burden themselves with it   *Zec 12:3*
shall be *c.*
c. to the heart (N)(P)(R)   *Ac 2:37*
When they heard that, they   *Ac 5:33;*
were *c.*   *7:54*
c. her hair short   *Ac 18:18*
  (A)(B)(N)(P)(R)
she should *c.* her hair   *1Co 11:6*
  (A)(B)(N(R)

CUT *ASUNDER*

he hath *c. asunder* cords of   *Ps 129:4*
wicked
hammer of whole earth *c.*   *Jer 50:23*
asunder
I took staff Beauty, and *c.*   *Zec 11:10*
it *asunder*
I *c. asunder* my other staff,   *Zec 11:14*
even Bands
shall *c.* him *asunder*   *M't 24:51;*
  Lu 12:46

CUT *DOWN*

but ye shall *c. down* their   *Ex 34:13*
groves
I will *c. down* your images,   *Le 26:30*
and cast
c. down from thence a   *Nu 13:23;*
branch   *13:24*
c. down groves   *De 7:5; 2Ki 18:4; 23:14*
trees for meat thou shalt not   *De 20:19*
c. down
trees not for meat thou shalt   *De 20:20*
c. down
c. down the grove that is by   *J'g 6:25*
it
I will *c. down* cedars   *2Ki 19:23;*
  Isa 37:24
Asa *c. down* her idol, and   *2Ch 15:16*
stamped it
Josiah *c. down* all the idols   *2Ch 34:7*
in the land
while in his greenness, and   *Job 8:12*
not *c. down*.
cometh forth like a flower,   *Job 14:2*
and is *c. down*

there is hope of a tree if it　*Job 14:7*
be *c. down*
the wicked were *c. down*　*Job 22:16*
out of time
whereas our substance is　*Job 22:20*
not *c. down*
they shall soon be *c. down*　*Ps 37:2*
like grass
branch is burnt, it is *c.*　*Ps 80:16*
down, they perish
in evening it is *c. down*, and　*Ps 90:6*
withereth
sycamores are *c. down*, but　*Isa 9:10*
we will build
how art thou *c. down* to　*Isa 14:12*
the ground
the nail shall be removed　*Isa 22:25*
and *c. down*
they shall *c. down* thy choice　*Jer 22:7*
cedars
the peaceable habitations　*Jer 25:37*
are *c. down*
also thou shalt be *c. down*, O　*Jer 48:2*
madmen
that your images may be *c.*　*Eze 6:6*
down
though many, yet shall they　*Na 1:12*
be *c. down*
for all merchant people are　*Zep 1:11*
c. down
others *c. down* branches　*M't 21:8;*
　　　　　　　　　　　　　　　M'k 11:8
c. it *down* why cumbereth it　*Lu 13:7*
the ground
then after that thou shalt *c.* it　*Lu 13:9*
down

CUT *OFF*

neither shall all flesh be *c. off*　*Ge 9:11*
the uncircumcised child shall　*Ge 17:14*
be *c. off*
and *c. off* the fore skin of her　*Ex 4:25*
son
that soul shall be *c. off*　*Ex 12:15;*
from Israel　　*12:19; 31:14; Nu 15:30-31;*
　　　　　　　　　　　　　　　19:13
Angel go before, and I will　*Ex 23:23*
c. them *off*
shall be *c. off* from his　*Ex 30:33;*
people　　*30:38; Le 7:20-21, 25, 27; 17:4,*
　　　　　9; 19:8; 23:29; Nu 9:13
I will *c.* him *off* from his　*Le 17:10;*
among his people　　　*18:29; 20:3, 6, 18;*
　　　　　　　　　　　　　　Nu 19:20
whosoever eateth blood shall　*Le 17:14*
be *c. off*
shall be *c. off* in the sight of　*Le 20:17*
their people
that soul shall be *c. off* from　*Le 22:3*
my presence
c. ye not *off* the tribe of　*Nu 4:18*
Kohathites
that soul shall utterly be *c.*　*Nu 15:31*
off
when thy God shall *c. off*　*De 12:29*
nations
when God hath *c. off*　*De 19:1;*
nations　　　　　　　　　　　*Jos 23:4*
hath his privy member *c. off*　*De 23:1*
shall not
then thou shalt *c. off* her　*De 25:12*
hand, pity not
waters of Jordan be *c. off*　*Jos 3:13;*
　　　　　　　　　　　　　3:16; 4:7
shall *c. off* our name from the　*Jos 7:9*
earth
at that time Joshua *c. off*　*Jos 11:21*
the Anakims
c. off his thumbs, and great　*J'g 1:6*
toes
there is one tribe *c. off* from　*J'g 21:6*
Israel
that name of dead be not *c.*　*Ru 4:10*
off
days come I will *c. off* thine　*1Sa 2:31*
arm
man I shall not *c. off* from　*1Sa 2:33*
mine altar
the palms of Dagon's hands　*1Sa 5:4*
were *c. off*
David ran and *c. off*　*1Sa 17:51*
Goliath's head
not *c. off* thy kindness　*1Sa 20:15;*
　　　　　　　　　　　　　　24:21
David *c. off* the skirt of　*1Sa 24:5*
Saul's robe
for in that I *c. off* the skirt　*1Sa 24:11*
of thy robe

knowest how Saul hath *c. off*　*1Sa 28:9*
wizards
they *c. off* Saul's head, and　*1Sa 31:9*
stripped off
slew them and *c. off* their　*2Sa 4:12*
hands
c. off garments in middle　*2Sa 10:4;*
　　　　　　　　　　　　　　1Ch 19:4
and they *c. off* the head of　*2Sa 20:22*
Sheba
then will I *c. off* Israel out of　*1Ki 9:7*
the land
till he had *c. off* every male　*1Ki 11:16*
in Edom
even to *c. off* Jeroboam's　*1Ki 13:34;*
house　　　　　　　　　　　　*14:14*
c. off him that pisseth　*1Ki 14:10;*
　　　　　　　　　21:21; 2Ki 9:8
Jezebel *c. off* the prophets of　*1Ki 18:4*
the Lord from Ahab him that
Ahaz *c. off* the borders of　*2Ki 16:17*
the bases
Hezekiah *c. off* gold from　*2Ki 18:16*
doors
c. off thine enemies before　*1Ch 17:8*
thee
Lord anointed to *c. off*　*2Ch 22:7*
house of Ahab
angel of *c. off* mighty men　*2Ch 32:21*
of valour
or where were the righteous *c.*　*Job 4:7*
off
would let loose his hand, and　*Job 6:9*
c. me *off*
whose hope be *c. off*, and　*Job 8:14*
whose trust
if he *c. off*, then who can　*Job 11:10*
hinder him
above shall his branch be *c.*　*Job 18:16*
off
when number of months is　*Job 21:21*
c. off in midst
because I was not *c. off*　*Job 23:17*
before darkness
they are *c. off* as tops of　*Job 24:24*
ears of corn
when people are *c. off* in　*Job 36:20*
their place
Lord shall *c. off* all flattering　*Ps 12:3*
lips
I said, I am *c. off* from　*Ps 34:22*
before thine eyes
to *c. off* remembrance of　*Ps 34:16*
them from earth
evil doers shall be *c. off* but　*Ps 37:9*
those who
they that be cursed of him　*Ps 37:22*
shall be *c. off*
but the seed of the wicked　*Ps 37:28*
shall be *c. off*
when wicked are *c. off*, thou　*Ps 37:34*
shalt see it
the end of the wicked shall　*Ps 37:38*
be *c. off*
he shall reward, *c.* them *off* in　*Ps 54:5*
thy truth
all horns of the wicked will　*Ps 75:10*
I *c. off*
he shall *c. off* the spirit of　*Ps 76:12*
princes
they said, Come, and let us *c.*　*Ps 83:4*
them *off*
and they are *c. off* from thy　*Ps 88:5*
hand
wrath goeth over me, terrors　*Ps 88:16*
c. me *off*
he shall *c.* them *off* in their　*Ps 94:23*
wickedness
that slandereth neighbour　*Ps 101:5*
will I *c. off*
that I may *c. off* all wicked　*Ps 101:8*
doers
let posterity be *c. off* and　*Ps 109:13*
blotted out
that Lord may *c. off*　*Ps 109:15*
memory of them
of thy mercy *c. off* mine　*Ps 143:12*
enemies
the wicked shall be *c. off*　*Pr 2:22*
from earth
expectation shall not be *c.*　*Pr 23:18;*
off　　　　　　　　　　　　*24:14*
will *c. off* from Israel head　*Isa 9:14*
and tail
to destroy and *c. off* nations　*Isa 10:7*
not a few
the adversaries of Judah　*Isa 11:13*
shall be *c. off*
I will *c. off* from Babylon　*Isa 14:22*
the name

burden that was upon it　*Isa 22:25*
shall be *c. off*
all that watch for iniquity　*Isa 29:20*
are *c. off*
he will *c.* me *off* with pining　*Isa 38:12*
sickness
my praise will refrain, that I　*Isa 48:9*
c. not *off*
his name should not have　*Isa 48:19*
been *c. off*
he was *c. off* out of the land　*Isa 53:8*
of living
shall be for a sign that shall　*Isa 55:13*
not be *c. off*
that sacrificeth, as if he *c. off*　*Isa 66:3*
dog's neck
truth is perished and *c. off*　*Jer 7:28*
from mouth
c. off thine hair, O　*Jer 7:29*
Jerusalem, cast it away
to *c. off* children without,　*Jer 9:21*
and young men
let us *c.* him *off* from land　*Jer 11:19*
of living
to *c. off* from you man and　*Jer 44:7*
woman
ye might *c.* yourselves *off*　*Jer 44:8*
and be a curse
set my face against you to　*Jer 44:11*
c. off Judah
c. off from Tyrus and　*Jer 47:4;*
Ashkelon　　　　　　　　　　*47:7*
come, let us *c.* it *off* from　*Jer 48:2*
being a nation
horn of Moab is *c. off*, his　*Jer 48:25*
arm is broken
all men of war shall be *c.*　*Jer 49:26;*
off　　　　　　　　　　　　*50:30*
c. off sower from Babylon,　*Jer 50:16*
and him
flee out, and be not *c. off* in　*Jer 51:6*
her iniquity
hast spoken against this　*Jer 51:62*
place to *c.* if *off*
c. off in his anger the horn of　*La 2:3*
Israel
they have *c. off* my life in the　*La 3:53*
dungeon
I will *c.* him *off* from　*Eze 14:8*
my people
c. off man and beast　*Eze 14:13;*
　　　　14:17, 19, 21; 25:13; 29:8
shall not *c. off* fruit thereof,　*Eze 17:9*
that it wither
building forts to *c. off*　*Eze 17:17*
many persons
I will *c. off* righteous and　*Eze 21:3;*
wicked　　　　　　　　　　　*21:4*
I will *c.* thee *off* from the　*Eze 25:7*
people
I will *c. off* Cherethims,　*Eze 25:16*
and destroy
and I will *c. off* the　*Eze 30:15*
multitude of No
terrible of the nations have　*Eze 31:12*
c. him *off*
c. off from Seir him　*Eze 35:7*
that passeth out
our hope is lost, we are *c. off*　*Eze 37:11*
hew down tree, *c. off* his　*Da 4:14*
branches
Messiah be *c. off*, but not for　*Da 9:26*
himself
made idols, that they may be　*Ho 8:4*
c. off
Samaria, her king is *c. off* as　*Ho 10:7;*
foam　　　　　　　　　　　　*10:15*
new wine is *c. off* from your　*Joe 1:5;*
mouth　　　　　　　　　　　　*1:9*
is not the meat *c. off* before　*Joe 1:16*
our eyes
I will *c. off* the inhabitant　*Am 1:5*
from Aven
I will *c. off* the inhabitant　*Am 1:8*
from Ashdod
I will *c. off* the judge from　*Am 2:3*
midst thereof
the horns of the altar shall　*Am 3:14*
be *c. off*
if robbers by night, how art　*Ob 5*
thou *c. off*
every one of Esau may be *c. off*　*Ob 9*
by slaughter
and thou shalt be *c. off* for　*Ob 10*
ever
nor stand to *c. off* those that　*Ob 14*
did escape
all thine enemies shall be *c.*　*Mic 5:9*
off

horses, cities, witchcrafts *c.* | *Mic 5:10;*
off | *5:11-12*
thy graven images will I *c.* | *Mic 5:13;*
off | *Na 1:14*
for the wicked is utterly *c.* off | *Na 1:15*
I will *c.* off thy prey from | *Na 2:13*
the earth
the sword shall *c.* thee *off*, it | *Na 3:15*
shall eat
tho' flock shall be *c.* off | *Hab 3:17*
from fold
c. off man from off the land | *Zep 1:3;*
| *1:4, 11*
I have *c.* off nations, towers | *Zep 3:6*
are desolate
so their dwelling should not | *Zep 3:7*
be *c.* off
every one that sweareth, shall | *Zec 5:3*
be *c.* off
I will *c.* off the pride of the | *Zec 9:6*
Philistines
I will *c.* off the chariot from | *Zec 9:10*
Ephraim
three shepherds also I *c.* off | *Zec 11:8*
in one month
that, that is to be *c.* off, let it | *Zec 11:9*
be *c.* off
I will *c.* off names of idols | *Zec 13:2*
out of land
two parts in land shall be *c.* | *Zec 13:8*
off and die
residue of the people shall | *Zec 14:2*
not be *c.* off
Lord will *c.* off man that | *Ma 2:12*
doeth this
c. off hand *M't 5:30; 18:8; M'k 9:43-45*
c. off ear | *M'k 14:47;*
| *Lu 22:50; Joh 18:10, 26*
the soldiers *c.* off the ropes | *Ac 27:32*
of the boat
otherwise thou shalt also be | *Ro 11:22*
c. off
that I may *c.* off occasion | *2Co 11:12*
from them
I would they were *c.* off that | *Ga 5:12*
trouble you

CUT *OUT*

the forward tongue shall be | *Pr 10:31*
c. out
a stone was *c.* out without | *Da 2:34;*
hands | *2:45*
for if thou wert *c.* out of | *Ro 11:24*
the olive tree

CUT *SHORT*

the Lord began to *c.* Israel | *2Ki 10:32*
short
will finish and *c.* it *short* in | *Ro 9:28*
righteousness

CUT *UP*

who *c.* up mallows by the | *Job 30:4*
bushes
as thorns *c.* up shall they be | *Isa 33:12*
burnt

CUTH

and the men of *C.* made | *2Ki 17:30*
Nergal

CUTHAH

men from Babylon, and | *2Ki 17:24*
from *C.*

CUTTER

the hopper, destroyer, *c.* (R) | *Joe 2:25*

CUTTEST

thou *c.* down thine harvest | *De 24:19*
in

CUTTETH

c. out rivers among the | *Job 28:10*
rocks
bow, and *c.* the spear in | *Ps 46:9*
sunder
when one *c.* and cleaveth | *Ps 141:7*
wood
hand of the fool *c.* off the | *Pr 26:6*
feet
for one *c.* a tree out of the | *Jer 10:3*
forest
and *c.* him out windows | *Jer 22:14*

CUTTING

And in *c.* of stones, to set | *Ex 31:5;*
them | *35:33*
I said in the *c.* off of my | *Isa 38:10*
days
the *c.* locust (R) | *Joe 1:4*
thy house by *c.* off many | *Hab 2:10*
people
crying, and *c.* himself with | *M'k 5:5*
stones

CUTTINGS

not make any *c.* in your | *Le 19:28*
flesh for
nor make any *c.* in their flesh | *Le 21:5*
upon all the hands shall be | *Jer 48:37*
c.

CYMBAL

sounding brass, or a tinkling | *1Co 13:1*
c.

CYMBALS

and on cornets, and on *c.* | *2Sa 6:5*
with timbrels, and with *c.* | *1Ch 13:8*
psalteries and harps and *c.* | *1Ch 15:16*
to sound with *c.* of brass | *1Ch 15:19*
with trumpets, and with *c.* | *1Ch 15:28*
but Asaph made a sound | *1Ch 16:5*
with *c.*
with trumpets and *c.* for | *1Ch 16:42*
those
harps, with psalteries, and | *1Ch 25:1*
with *c.*
with *c.*, psalteries, and harps | *1Ch 25:6*
having *c.* and psalteries and | *2Ch 5:12*
harps
trumpets and *c.* and | *2Ch 5:13*
instruments
the Lord will *c.* with | *2Ch 29:25*
psalteries
the sons of Asaph with *c.* to | *Ezr 3:10*
praise
with singing, with *c.*, | *Ne 12:27*
psalteries
Praise him upon the loud *c.* | *Ps 150:5*
him upon the high sounding | *Ps 150:5*
c.

CYPRESS

and taketh the *c.* and the | *Isa 44:14*
oak

CYPRUS

the pines of *C.* (B) | *Eze 27:3*
Levite, and of the country of | *Ac 4:36*
C.
and *C.* and Antioch, | *Ac 11:19*
preaching
them were men of *C.* and | *Ac 11:20*
Cyrene
and from thence they sailed | *Ac 13:4*
to *C.*
took Mark, and sailed unto | *Ac 15:39*
C.
when we had discovered *C.*, | *Ac 21:3*
we left
with them one Mnason of | *Ac 21:16*
C.
we sailed under *C.* because | *Ac 27:4*

CYRENE

a man of *C.* Simon by | *M't 27:32*
name
of Libya about *C.* and | *Ac 2:10*
strangers
were men of Cyprus and *C.* | *Ac 11:20*
which
and Lucius of *C.* and Manaen | *Ac 13:1*

CYRENIAN

compel one Simon a *C.* | *M'k 15:21*
who
laid hold upon one Simon, a | *Lu 23:26*
C.

CYRENIANS

of the Libertines, and *C.* and | *Ac 6:9*

CYRENIUS

when *C.* was governor of | *Lu 2:2*
Syria

CYRUS

in first year of *C.* king of | *2Ch 36:22;*
Persia Lord stirred up | *Ezr 1:1*
spirit of *C.*
thus saith *C.* king of | *2Ch 36:23;*
Persia | *Ezr 1:2*
C. brought forth the vessels | *Ezr 1:7;*
| *1:8; 5:14*
according to the grant they | *Ezr 3:7*
had of *C.*
will build as *C.* hath | *Ezr 4:3*
commanded
C. made a decree to build | *Ezr 5:13;*
this house | *5:17*
that saith of *C.* he is my | *Isa 44:28*
shepherd
thus saith the Lord to his | *Isa 45:1*
anointed, to *C.*
Daniel continued to first year | *Da 1:21*
of *C.*
Daniel prospered in the reign | *Da 6:28*
of *C.*
in third year of *C.* a thing | *Da 10:1*
was revealed

D

DABAREH

D. with her suburbs | *Jos 21:28*

DABBASHETH

and reached to *D.* and | *Jos 19:11*
reached

DABERATH

and then goeth out to *D.* | *Jos 19:12*
D. with her suburbs | *1Ch 6:72*

DAGGER

Ehud made him a *d.* which | *J'g 3:16*
had two
took the *d.* from his right | *J'g 3:21*
thigh
he could not draw the *d.* out | *J'g 3:22*

DAGON

great sacrifice unto *D.* their | *J'g 16:23*
god
brought it into the house of | *1Sa 5:22;*
D. | *5:3-7*
his head in the temple of | *1Ch 10:10*
D.

DAGON'S

any that come into *D.* house | *1Sa 5:5*

DAILY

twice as much as they | *Ex 16:5*
gathered *d.*
the *d.* meat offering | *Nu 4:16;*
| *Eze 46:13*
after this manner ye shall | *Nu 38:24*
offer *d.*
beside the *d.* burnt offering | *Nu 29:6;*
| *Ezr 3:4*
when she pressed him *d.* with | *J'g 16:16*
words
allowance was *d.* rate for | *2Ki 25:30*
every day
that which was prepared for | *Nu 5:18*
me *d.*
when they spake *d.* hearkened | *Es 3:4*
not
having sorrow in my heart *d.* | *Ps 13:2*
while they said *d.* to me, | *Ps 42:10*
Where is God
be merciful, he fighting *d.* | *Ps 56:1*
oppresseth me
mine enemies would *d.* | *Ps 56:2*
swallow me up
I will sing, that I may *d.* | *Ps 61:8*
perform vows
blessed be the Lord who *d.* | *Ps 68:19*
loadeth us
he shall live and *d.* shall he | *Ps 72:15*
be praised
how the foolish man | *Ps 74:22*
reproacheth thee *d.*

I cry to thee d.   *Ps 86:3; 86:8*
they came round about me   *Ps 88:17*
d. like water
I was d. his delight, rejoicing   *Pr 8:30*
in
that heareth me, watching d.   *Pr 8:34*
at my gates
yet they seek me d. and   *Isa 58:2*
delight to know
d. rising up early and sending   *Jer 7:25*
them
I am in derision d. every one   *Jer 20:7;*
mocketh   *20:8*
Noph shall have distresses   *Eze 30:16*
d.
king appointed them a d.   *Da 1:5*
provision
d. sacrifice taken away   *Da 8:11;*
                  11:31; 12:11
Ephraim d. increaseth lies   *Ho 12:1*
and desolation
give us this day our d.   *M't 6:11;*
bread   *Lu 11:3*
I sat d. teaching in the   *M't 26:55;*
temple   *M'k 14:49; Lu 19:47; 22:53*
let him take up cross d.   *Lu 9:23*
follow me
continuing d. with one accord   *Ac 2:46*
in temple
Lord added to church d. such   *Ac 2:47*
to be saved
widows were neglected in d.   *Ac 6:1*
ministration
the churches increased in   *Ac 16:5*
number d.
noble Bereans searched   *Ac 17:11*
scriptures d.
I die d.   *1Co 15:31*
but exhort d.   *Heb 3:13*
who needeth not d. to offer   *Heb 7:27*
sacrifice
if sister be naked, destitute   *Jas 2:15*
of d. food

DAINTIES

fat, and he shall yield royal   *Ge 49:20*
d.
deliver royal d. (B)   *Ge 49:20*
and let me not eat of their   *Ps 141:4*
d.
words of a talebearer are as   *Pr 18:8*
d. (S)
not desirous of his d.: for   *Pr 23:3*
they
neither desire his d. (E)   *Pr 23:6*
feasted on d. (A)(B)(R)   *La 4:5*

DAINTY

abhorreth bread, and his   *Job 33:20*
soul d.
are d. morsels (A)(E)   *Pr 18:8;*
                  26:22
neither desire thou his d.   *Pr 23:6*
meats
d. foods (A)   *Pr 23:6*
called d. and delicate (A)   *Isa 47:1*
things which were d. and   *Re 18:14*
goodly

DALAIAH

Johanan, and D. and Anani   *1Ch 3:24*

DALE

of Shaveh, which is the   *Ge 14:17*
king's d.
a pillar, which is in the   *2Sa 18:18*
king's d.

DALMANUTHA

and came into the parts of D.   *M'k 8:10*

DALMATIA

Crescens to Galatia, Titus   *2Ti 4:10*
unto D.

DALPHON

Parshandatha, and D. and   *Es 9:7*

DAM

seven days it shall be with   *Ex 22:30*
his d.

---

shall be seven days under the   *Le 22:27*
d.
and the d. sitting upon the   *De 22:6*
young
shalt not take the d. with the   *De 22:6*
thou shalt in any wise let the   *De 22:7*
d. go

DAMAGE

d. of the house (B)   *2Ki 12:5;*
            12:8-12; 22:5
why should d. grow to the   *Ezr 4:22*
hurt
not countervail the king's d.   *Es 7:4*
return d. upon enemies (B)   *Ps 54:5*
off the feet, and drinketh d.   *Pr 26:6*
and the king should have no d.   *Da 6:2*
will be with hurt and much   *Ac 27:10*
d.
that ye might receive d. by us   *2Co 7:9*

DAMARIS

and a woman named D. and   *Ac 17:34*

DAMASCENES

the king kept the city of   *2Co 11:32*
the D.

DAMASCUS

steward of my house is   *Ge 15:2*
Eliezer of D.
garrisons in Syria of D.   *2Sa 8:6;*
               1Ch 18:6
Rezon went to D. and   *1Ki 11:24*
reigned in D.
return on way to wilderness   *1Ki 19:15*
of D.
thou shalt make streets for   *1Ki 20:34*
thee in D.
are not Abana, Pharpar,   *2Ki 5:12*
rivers of D.
Elisha came to D.   *2Ki 8:7*
king of Assyria went up   *2Ki 16:9*
against D.
king Ahaz saw an altar that   *2Ki 16:10*
was at D.
Syrians of D. came to help   *1Ch 18:5*
Hadarezer
sent spoil of them to king   *2Ch 24:23*
of D.
carried great multitude of   *2Ch 28:5*
captives to D.
for Ahaz sacrificed to the   *2Ch 28:23*
gods of D.
Lebanon, which looketh   *Ca 7:4*
toward D.
head of Syria is D. head of   *Isa 7:8*
D. Rezin
riches of D. shall be taken   *Isa 8:4*
away
for he saith, Is not Samaria   *Isa 10:9*
as D.
the burden of D. is taken   *Isa 17:1;*
               Jer 49:23
the kingdom shall cease from   *Isa 17:3*
D.
D. is waxed feeble   *Jer 49:24*
I will kindle a fire in the   *Jer 9:27*
wall of D.
D. thy merchant in wine   *Eze 27:18*
and wool
for three transgressions of D.   *Am 1:3*
and four
I will break also bar of D.   *Am 1:5*
and cut off
that dwell in D. in a couch   *Am 3:12*
cause you to go into   *Am 5:27*
captivity beyond D.
and D. shall be the rest   *Zec 9:1*
thereof
Saul desired of high priest   *Ac 9:2*
letters to D.
a disciple at D. named   *Ac 9:10*
Ananias
then was Saul with the   *Ac 9:19*
disciples at D.
Saul confounded Jews who   *Ac 9:22*
dwelt at D.
declared how he had   *Ac 9:27*
preached boldly at D.
as I was come nigh to D.   *Ac 22:6;*
about noon   *26:12*
Lord said to me, Arise, and   *Ac 22:10*
go into D.
in D. governor desirous to   *2Co 11:32*
apprehend
but I returned again unto D.   *Ga 1:17*

DAMNABLE

who privily shall bring in d.   *2Pe 2:1*
heresies
destructive heresies   *2Pe 2:1*
(A)(E)(R)
introduce ruinous heresies   *2Pe 2:1*
(B)
import disastrous heresies   *2Pe 2:1*
(N)
dangerous heresies (P)   *2Pe 2:1*

DAMNATION

receive greater d.   *M't 23:14;*
           M'k 12:40; Lu 20:47
greater condemnation,   *M't 23:14*
heavier sentence (A)
greater judgment (B)   *M't 23:14*
ye serpents, how can ye   *M't 23:33*
escape the d. of hell
escape the penalty suffered   *M't 23:33*
in hell (A)
escape the sentence of   *M't 23:33*
perdition (B)
escape the judgment of hell   *M't 23:33*
(E)
escape being condemned in   *M't 23:33*
hell (N)
avoid being condemned to   *M't 23:33*
rubbish heap (P)
escape being sentenced to   *M't 23:33*
hell (R)
but is in danger of eternal   *M'k 3:29*
d.
in the grasp of everlasting   *M'k 3:29*
trespass (A)
is guilty of eternal sin   *M'k 3:29*
(B)(E)(N)(P)(R)
have done evil to the   *Joh 5:29*
resurrection of d.
raised to meet their sentence   *Joh 5:29*
(A)
resurrection of condemnation   *Joh 5:29*
(B)
resurrection of judgment   *Joh 5:29*
(E)(R)
rise to hear their doom (N)   *Joh 5:29*
rise to face judgment (P)   *Joh 5:29*
evil, that good may come   *Ro 3:8*
whose d. is just
justly condemned by them (A)   *Ro 3:8*
Deservedly are such takers   *Ro 3:8*
condemned (B)
whose condemnation is just   *Ro 3:8*
(E)(R)
to condemn such men is no   *Ro 3:8*
injustice (N)
they shall receive to   *Ro 13:2*
themselves d.
receiving the penalty due   *Ro 13:2*
them (A)
draw sentence on themselves   *Ro 13:2*
(B)
receive to themselves   *Ro 13:2*
judgment (E)(R)
the punishment they will   *Ro 13:2*
receive (N)
bound to be punished (P)   *Ro 13:2*
he eateth and drinketh d.   *1Co 11:29*
to himself
drinks a verdict of   *1Co 11:29*
judgment (A)
drinks to his own   *1Co 11:29*
condemnation (B)
drinks judgment on himself   *1Co 11:29*
(E)(N)(P)(R)
having d. because have cast   *1Ti 5:12*
off first faith
they incur condemnation   *1Ti 5:12*
(A)(E)(R)
guilty of breaking prime   *1Ti 5:12*
engagement (B)
stand condemned for   *1Ti 5:12*
breaking truth with Christ (N)
proving unfaithful to their   *1Ti 5:12*
loyalty (P)
lingereth not, and their d.   *2Pe 2:3*
slumbereth not
their eternal misery has not   *2Pe 2:3*
been (A)
destruction has not been   *2Pe 2:3*
dormant (B)(E)(R)
judgment decreed has not   *2Pe 2:3*
been idle (N)

DAMNED

but he that believeth not   *M'k 16:16*
shall be d.

will be condemned   M'k 16:16
(A)(B)(E)(N)(P)(R)
and he that doubteth is d. if   Ro 14:23
he eat
who doubts stands   Ro 14:23
condemned (A)(B)(E)(R)
doubts is guilty if he eats   Ro 14:23
(N)
he is wrong to do it (P)   Ro 14:23
that all might be d. who   2Th 2:12
believed not
may be judged and   2Th 2:12
condemned (A)(E)(R)
may receive judgment (B)   2Th 2:12
all may be brought to   2Th 2:12
judgment (N)

DAMS

who build d. will be grieved   Isa 19:10
(A)

DAMSEL

the d. to whom I shall say   Ge 24:14;
     24:16, 28, 57
her mother said, Let the d.   Ge 24:55
the girl (B)   Ge 24:55;
34:3; 12; De 22:15, 20-21, 24, 26;
     J'g 5:30; 1Ki 1:4
the maiden (R)   Ge 24:55;
  34:3, 12; J'g 5:30; Ru 2:5-6; 1Ki 1:4
and he loved the d. and   Ge 34:3;
     34:4, 12
this girl (B)   Ge 34:3; 34:12
young woman (A)(R)   De 22:15;
    22:20-21, 24, 26
to every man a d. or two   J'g 5:30
the father of the d. saw him   J'g 19:3
over the reapers, Whose d. is   Ru 2:5
this
It is the Moabitish d. that   Ru 2:6
came
So they sought for a fair d.   1Ki 1:3
And the d. was very fair   1Ki 1:4
in a charger, and given to   M't 14:11
the d.
the little maid (A)   M't 14:11
the girl (B)(N)(P)(R)   M't 14:11
and a d. came unto him,   M't 26:69
saying
the d. is not dead, but   M'k 5:39
sleepeth
the little girl (A)   M'k 5:39; 5:40
the child (B)(N)(P)(R)   M'k 5:39;
     5:40
father and the mother of the   M'k 5:40
d.
and entereth in where the d.   M'k 5:40
was
he took the d. by the hand   M'k 5:41
interpreted, D. I say unto   M'k 5:41
thee
the d. arose, and walked,   M'k 5:42
for she
the king said unto the d.,   M'k 6:22
Ask of
and gave it to the d.: and   M'k 6:28
the d. gave it to her mother   M'k 6:28
Then saith the d. that kept   Joh 18:17
the
a d. came to hearken,   Ac 12:13
named
a maid (A)(N)(R)   Ac 12:13
a girl (B)   Ac 12:13
a certain d. possessed with a   Ac 16:16
a slave girl (A)(B)(N)(R)   Ac 16:16
a young girl (P)   Ac 16:16

DAMSELS

Rebekah arose, and her d.   Ge 24:61
with five d. of hers that   1Sa 25:42
went
were the d. playing with   Ps 68:25
timbrels

DAMSEL'S

bring forth the tokens of the   De 22:15
d.
the d. father, retained him   J'g 19:4

DAN a person

therefore called she his name   Ge 30:6
D.

son of Bilhah, D.   Ge 35:25;
     46:23; Nu 26:42
D. shall judge his people, as   Ge 49:16
one of tribes
D. shall be a serpent by the   Ge 49:17
way, an adder
of D. Ahiezer son of   Nu 1:12
Ammi-shaddai
standard of camp of D. on   Nu 2:25
north side
all numbered in camp of D.   Nu 2:31
were 157,600
of D. he said, D. is a lion's   De 33:22
whelp
after the name of D.   Jos 19:47;
     J'g 18:29
and why did D. remain in   J'g 5:17
ships
the Spirit moved him in the   J'g 13:25
camp of D.
a portion for D.   Eze 48:1; 48:32

DAN a place

Abraham pursued them unto   Ge 14:14
D.
Lord shewed Moses all   De 34:1
Gilead unto D.
they called Leshem, D.   Jos 19:47;
     J'g 18:29
from D. to Beer-sheba   J'g 20:1;
1Sa 3:20; 2Sa 3:10; 17:11; 24:2, 15;
    1Ki 4:25; 1Ch 21:2; 2Ch 30:5
other calf put he in D.   1Ki 12:29;
     2Ki 10:29
king of Syria smote D.   1Ki 15:20;
     2Ch 16:4
for a voice declareth from D.   Jer 4:15
snorting of horses was heard   Jer 8:16
from D.
D. and Javan occupied in   Eze 27:19
thy fairs
they that say, Thy God, O D.   Am 8:14
liveth

TRIBE OF DAN

Aholiab of the *tribe of* D.   Ex 31:6;
     35:34; 38:23
daughter of Dibri, of the   Le 24:11
tribe of D.
numbered of the *tribe of* D.   Nu 1:39
62,700
of *tribe of* D. to spy the   Nu 13:12
land, Ammiel
of *tribe of* D. to divide the   Nu 34:22
land, Bukki
lot came for the *tribe of* D.   Jos 19:40;
     19:48
out of the *tribe of* D. to the   Jos 21:5;
Levites   21:23
priests to *tribe of* D. till   J'g 18:30
captivity

DANCE

of Shiloh come out to d. in   J'g 21:21
dances
like a flock, and their   Job 21:11
children d.
praise his name in the d.: let   Ps 149:3
Praise him with the timbrel   Ps 150:4
and d.
a time to mourn, and a time   Ec 3:4
to d.
there, and satyrs shall d.   Isa 13:21
there
shall the virgin rejoice in   Jer 31:13
the d.
our d. is turned into   La 5:15
mourning

DANCED

to their number, of them   J'g 21:23
that d.
David d. before the Lord   2Sa 6:14
with all
unto you, and ye have not   M't 11:17;
d.   Lu 7:32
the daughter of Herodias d.   M't 14:6
before
the said Herodias came in,   M'k 6:22
and d.

DANCES

her with timbrels and with   Ex 15:20
d.
him with timbrels and with   J'g 11:34
d.

of Shiloh come out to dance   J'g 21:21
in d.
sing one to another of him   1Sa 21:11
in d.
they sang one to another   1Sa 29:5
in d.
shalt go forth in the d. of   Jer 31:4
them

DANCING

that he saw the calf, and the   Ex 32:19
d.
singing and d. to meet king   1Sa 18:6
Saul
eating and drinking, and d.   1Sa 30:16
saw king David leaping and   2Sa 6:16
saw king David d. and   1Ch 15:29
playing
for me my mourning into d.   Ps 30:11
the house, he heard musick   Lu 15:25
and d.

DANDLED

and be d. upon her knees   Isa 66:12
I have d. (E)(R)   La 2:22

DANGER

shall be in d. of the   M't 5:21;
judgment   5:22
shall be in d. of the council   M't 5:22
thou fool, shall be in d. of   M't 5:22
hell fire
is in d. of eternal damnation   M'k 3:29
not only this our craft is in   Ac 19:27
d.
we are in d. to be called in   Ac 19:40
question
d. to life and limb (P)   Ro 8:38
times full of d. (P)   2Ti 3:1

DANGEROUS

when sailing was no d.   Ac 27:9
d. heresies (P)   2Pe 2:1

DANGERS

in d. of rivers, among   2Co 11:26
sham brothers (B)(N)(P)(R)

DANIEL

David had D. of Abigail   1Ch 3:1
of Ithamar, D.   Ezr 8:2
tho' Noah, D. and Job   Eze 14:14;
were in it   14:20
thou art wiser than D. no   Eze 28:3
secret
D. of Judah   Da 1:6
he gave to D. the name of   Da 1:7
Belteshazzar
D. had understanding in   Da 1:19
visions   1:19
sought D. to be slain   Da 2:13;
     2:16; 4:8
the secret was revealed to D.   Da 2:19
in a vision
king Nebuchadnezzar   Da 2:46
worshipped D.
then the king made D. a   Da 2:48
great man
D. sat in the gate   Da 2:49
then D. was astonied for one   Da 4:19
hour
dissolving of doubts was   Da 5:12
found in D.
and they clothed D. with   Da 5:29
scarlet and put
D. was first   Da 6:2
we shall not find occasion   Da 6:5
against this D.
men found D. praying before   Da 6:11
his God
D. regardeth not thee, O   Da 6:13
king, nor the decree
that they should take up D.   Da 6:23
out of the den
that men tremble before the   Da 6:26
God of D.
who hath delivered D. from   Da 6:27
power of lions
so D. prospered in the reign   Da 6:28
of Darius
D. had a dream, and visions   Da 7:1
of his head
as for me D.   Da 7:28

vision appeared to me, even *Da 8:1;*
me *D.* 10:12
he said, Go thy way, *D.* *Da 12:9*
words are closed
desolation, spoken of by *D.* *M't 24:15;*
the prophet *M'k 13:14*

I DANIEL

I D. was grieved *Da 7:15; 8:27*
when *I*, even *I D.* had seen *Da 8:15*
the vision
I D. understood by books *Da 9:2*
number of years
I D. was mourning three full *Da 10:2*
weeks
I D. alone saw the vision *Da 10:7;*
12:5

O DANIEL

O D. servant of the living *Da 6:20*
God
O D. I am now come to give *Da 9:22*
thee skill
O D. a man greatly beloved *Da 10:11*
O D. shut up the words and *Da 12:4*
seal book

DANITES

of Zorah, of the fmily of the *J'g 13:2*
D.
the tribe of the *D.* sought *J'g 18:1*
them
from thence of the family of *J'g 18:11*
the *D.*
And of the *D.* expert in *1Ch 12:35*
war

DAN-JAAN

they came to *D.* and about *2Sa 24:6*
to

DANNAH

D. and Kirjath-sannah, *Jos 15:49*
which is

DAPPLED

d. horses (A)(B)(R)(S) *Zec 6:3; 6:6*

DARA

and Heman, and Calcol, and *1Ch 2:6*
D.

DARDA

Chalcol, and *D.* the son of *1Ki 4:31*
Mahol

DARE

None is so fierce that *d.* *Job 41:10*
stir him
did not *d.* to investigate (B) *Ac 7:32*
man some would even *d.* to *Ro 5:7*
die
For I will not *d.* to speak of *Ro 15:18*
not venture to speak *Ro 15:18*
(A)(E)(N)(R)
D. any of you, having a *1Co 6:1*
matter
For we *d.* not make *2Co 10:12*
ourselves
we venture to class *2Co 10:12*
(A)(B)(R)
not bold to number or *2Co 10:12*
compare (E)
d. to order you (P) *Ph'm 8*
d. not condemn (P) *Jude 9*

DARED

d. contemplate such (B) *Es 7:5*
d. not (A) *Job 32:6; Ac 5:13; Jude 9*
dared (S) *Job 32:6; M't 22:46;*
M'k 12:34; *Lu 20:40;* *Joh 21:12;*
Ac 5:13; 7:32; Jude 9
d. ask (B)(N)(P)(R) *M't 22:46;*
Joh 21:12
d. join (A)(B)(P)(R) *Ac 5:13*
d. not look (N)(R) *Ac 7:32*
d. not bring abusive (A) *Jude 9*

DARICS

ten thousand *d.* of gold *1Ch 29:7*
(E)(R)
Sixty-one thousand *d.* of gold *Ezr 2:69*
(E)
a thousand *d.* (A)(R) *Ezr 8:27;*
Ne 7:70
twenty thousand *d.* of gold *Ne 7:71;*
(A)(R) *7:72*

DARING

D. selfwilled (E) *2Pe 2:10*

DARIUS

to frustrate, till reign of *D.* *Ezr 4:5;*
4:24
not to cease, till the matter *Ezr 5:5*
came to *D.*
then *D.* the king made a *Ezr 6:1;*
decree *6:12*
house was finished in sixth *Ezr 6:15*
year of *D.*
also the priests to the reign *Ne 12:22*
of *D.*
D. the Median took the *Da 5:31*
kingdom
wherefore king *D.* signed the *Da 6:9*
writing
king *D.* wrote to all people *Da 6:25*
and nations
in the first year of *D.* the *Da 9:1;*
Mede *11:1*
in second year of *D.* *Hag 1:1;*
1:15; 2:10; Zec 1:7
in fourth year of *D.* the word *Zec 7:1*
came

DARK

the sun went down, and it *Ge 15:17*
was *d.*
if the plague be somewhat *d.* *Le 13:6*
the skin, but be somewhat *d.* *Le 13:21;*
13:28
other skin, but be somewhat *Le 13:26*
d.
the plague be somewhat *d.* *Le 13:56*
after
apparently, and not in *d.* *Nu 12:8*
speeches
when it was *d.* that the men *Jos 2:5*
went
round about him, *d.* waters *2Sa 22:12*
be *d.*
gates of Jerusalem began to *Ne 13:19*
be *d.*
stars of the twilight thereof *Job 3:9*
be *d.*
grope in the *d.* without *Job 12:25*
light
light shall be *d.* in his *Job 18:6*
tabernacle
he judge through the *d.* *Job 22:13*
cloud
In the *d.* they dig through *Job 24:16*
houses
round about him were *d.* *Ps 18:11*
waters
Let their way be *d.* and *Ps 35:6*
slippery
open my *d.* saying upon the *Ps 49:4*
harp
to a parable or proverb (A) *Ps 49:4*
disclose my riddle upon *Ps 49:4*
(B)(R)
the *d.* places of the earth are *Ps 74:20*
full
I will utter *d.* sayings of old *Ps 78:2*
thy wonders be known in the *Ps 88:12*
d.
He sent darkness, and made *Ps 105:28*
it *d.*
of the wise, and their *d.* *Pr 1:6*
sayings
evening, in the black and *d.* *Pr 7:9*
night
their works are in the *d.* *Isa 29:15*
and they
secret, in a *d.* place of the *Isa 45:19*
earth
d. cloud the nations (B) *Isa 60:2*
stumble upon the *d.* *Jer 13:16*
mountains
He hath sent me in *d.* places *La 3:6*
the house of Israel do in the *Eze 8:12*
d.
and make the stars thereof *Eze 32:7*
d.

of heaven will I make *d.* *Eze 32:8*
over thee
scattered in the cloudy and *Eze 34:12*
d. day
and understanding *d.* *Da 8:23*
sentences
the sun and the moon shall *Joe 2:10*
be *d.*
maketh the day *d.* with night *Am 5:8*
very *d.* and no brightness in *Am 5:20*
it
and it shall be *d.* unto you *Mic 3:6*
and the day shall be *d.* over *Mic 3:6*
them
light shall not be clear, nor *Zec 14:6*
d.
full of light, having no part *Lu 11:36*
d.
And it was now *d.* and Jesus *Joh 6:17*
was
spoken in *d.* sayings (E) *Joh 16:25*
speakest no *d.* saying (E) *Joh 16:29*
Magdalene early, when it *Joh 20:1*
was yet *d.*
men do in the *d.* (P) *Ro 13:13*
light that shineth in a *d.* *2Pe 1:19*
place
d. pits of hell (N)(P) *2Pe 2:4*

DARKEN

will *d.* the earth in the clear *Am 8:9*
day

DARKENED

earth, so that the land was *d.* *Ex 10:15*
Let their eyes be *d.* that they *Ps 69:23*
see
stars, be not *d.* nor the clouds *Ec 12:2*
that look out of the windows *Ec 12:3*
be *d.*
light is *d.* in the heavens *Isa 5:30*
thereof
the Lord of hosts is the land *Isa 9:19*
d.
sun shall be *d.* in his going *Isa 13:10*
forth
all joy is *d.* the mirth of the *Isa 24:11*
shall be *d.* when I shall *Eze 30:18*
break
sun and the moon shall be *d.* *Joe 3:15*
his right eye shall be utterly *Zec 11:17*
d.
of those days shall the sun *M't 24:29*
be *d.*
the sun shall be *d.* and the *M'k 13:24*
moon
And the sun was *d.* and the *Lu 23:45*
veil
and their foolish heart was *d.* *Ro 1:21*
Let their eyes be *d.* that they *Ro 11:10*
may
Having the understanding *d.* *Eph 4:18*
so as the third part of them *Re 8:12*
was *d.*
and the sun and the air were *Re 9:2*
d.

DARKENETH

Who is this that *d.* counsel *Job 38:2*
by

DARKISH

skin of their flesh be *d.* *Le 13:39*
white

DARKLY

we see through a glass, *d.* *1Co 13:12*
mirror that gives a dim *1Co 13:12*
reflection (A)
we see indistinctly in a *1Co 13:12*
mirror (B)
puzzling reflections in a *1Co 13:12*
mirror (N)(P)
see in a mirror dimly (R) *1Co 13:12*

DARKNESS

d. was upon the face of the *Ge 1:2*
deep
light day, and the *d.* he called *Ge 1:5*
night
God set them to divide light *Ge 1:18*
from *d.*
an horror of great *d.* fell *Ge 15:12*
upon Abram

that there may be *d.* over   *Ex 10:21*
Egypt
there was thick *d.* in all   *Ex 10:22*
Egypt three days
it was cloud and *d.* to them,   *Ex 14:20*
but light
Moses drew near unto thick   *Ex 20:21*
d.
the mountain burnt with   *De 4:11*
thick *d.*
these words Lord spake out   *De 5:22*
of thick *d.*
he put *d.* between you and   *Jos 24:7*
Egyptians
d. was under his feet   *2Sa 22:10;*
  Ps 18:9
he made *d.* his pavilions   *2Sa 22:12*
round about
Lord will enlighten my *d.*   *2Sa 22:29;*
  Ps 18:28
let *d.* and shadow of death   *Job 3:5*
stain it
as for that night, let *d.* seize   *Job 3:6*
upon it
they meet with *d.* in the day   *Job 5:14*
time
land of *d.* as *d.* itself,   *Job 10:22*
without order
and he hath set *d.* in my   *Job 19:8*
paths
all *d.* shall be hid in his   *Job 20:26*
secret places
or *d.* that thou canst not   *Job 22:11*
see
because I was not cut off   *Job 23:17*
before *d.*
he setteth an end to *d.* the   *Job 28:3*
stones of *d.*
no *d.* where workers of   *Job 34:22*
iniquity may hide
cannot order our speech by   *Job 37:19*
reason of *d.*
when I made thick *d.* a   *Job 38:9*
swaddling-band
as for *d.* where is the place   *Job 38:19*
thereof
he made *d.* his secret place   *Ps 18:11*
hast put mine acquaintance   *Ps 88:18*
into *d.*
clouds and *d.* are round about   *Ps 97:2*
him
thou makest *d.* and it is   *Ps 104:20*
night
he sent *d.* and made it dark   *Ps 105:28*
if I say, Surely *d.* shall   *Ps 139:11*
cover me
yea, the *d.* hideth not from   *Ps 139:12*
thee
leave paths to walk in ways   *Pr 2:13*
of *d.*
way of wicked is as *d.* they   *Pr 4:19*
know not
his name shall be covered with   *Ec 6:4*
d.
if one look to the land,   *Isa 5:30*
behold *d.*
shall look, behold trouble   *Isa 8:22*
and *d.*
blind see in spite of dimness   *Isa 29:13*
and *d.* (B)
I will give thee the treasures   *Isa 45:3*
of *d.*
get thee into *d.* O daughter   *Isa 47:5*
of Chaldeans
d. shall cover earth, and   *Isa 60:2*
gross *d.* the people, but
thick *d.* the people (R)   *Isa 60:2*
gross *d.*
before he cause *d.* and make   *Jer 13:16*
I will set *d.* upon thy land   *Eze 32:8*
a day of *d.* of clouds and of   *Joe 2:2*
thick *d.*
sun shall be turned into *d.*   *Joe 2:31;*
  Ac 2:20
he that maketh the morning   *Am 4:13*
d.
d. without divination (B)(R)   *Mic 3:6*
d. shall pursue his enemies   *Na 1:8*
thy whole body full of *d.*   *M't 6:23;*
  Lu 11:34
be cast out into outer *d.*   *M't 8:12;*
  22:13; 25:30
from sixth hour there was   *M't 27:45;*
d.   *M'k 15:33*
this is your hour and power   *Lu 22:53*
of *d.*
there was *d.* over all the   *Lu 23:44*
earth

there fell on him a mist and   *Ac 13:11*
a *d.*
minds plunged into *d.* (N)   *Ro 1:21*
have no fellowship with   *Eph 5:11*
works of *d.*
barren deeds of *d.* (A)(N)   *Eph 5:11*
against rulers of *d.* of this   *Eph 6:12*
world
who hath delivered us from   *Col 1:13*
power of *d.*
we are not of night nor of *d.*   *1Th 5:5*
ye are not come to   *Heb 12:18*
blackness and *d.*
delivered them into chains of   *2Pe 2:4*
d.
kept in pits of gloom (A)   *2Pe 2:4*
to black dungeons of Tartarus   *2Pe 2:4*
(B)
to pits of *d.* (E)   *2Pe 2:4*
dark pits of hell (N)   *2Pe 2:4*
the dark imprisonment of hell   *2Pe 2:4*
(P)
to pits of nether gloom (R)   *2Pe 2:4*
to whom mist of *d.* is   *2Pe 2:17*
reserved for ever
because *d.* hath blinded his   *1Jo 2:11*
eyes
reserved in everlasting chains   *Jude 6*
under *d.*
eternal chains in nether gloom   *Jude 6*
(R)
reserved blackness   *Jude 13*
of *d.* for ever
and his kingdom was full of   *Re 16:10*
d.

DARKNESS with *DAY*

let that *day* be *d.* let not God   *Job 3:4*
regard it
he knoweth that *day* of *d.* is   *Job 15:23*
at hand
let him remember the *days* of   *Ec 11:8*
d.
then shall thy *d.* be as   *Isa 58:10*
noon-*day*
a *day* of *d.* and gloominess   *Joe 2:2;*
  Zep 1:15
shall not the *day* of the Lord   *Am 5:20*
be *d.*

IN DARKNESS

thou shalt grope as blind *in*   *De 28:29*
d.
the wicked shall be silent *in*   *1Sa 2:9*
d.
the Lord said he would dwell   *1Ki 8:12;*
in thick *d.*   *2Ch 6:1*
I have made my bed *in* the   *Job 17:13*
d.
they know not, they walk on   *Ps 82:5*
in d.
thou hast laid me *in d.* in the   *Ps 88:6*
deeps
nor for pestilence that   *Ps 91:6*
walketh *in d.*
such as sin *in d.* and   *Ps 107:10*
shadow of death
enemy hath made me to   *Ps 143:3*
dwell *in d.*
his lamp be put out *in*   *Pr 20:20*
obscure *d.*
but the fool walketh *in d.*   *Ec 2:14*
he eateth *in d.*   *Ec 5:17*
bring them that sit *in d.* out   *Isa 42:7*
of prison
to them that are *in d.* shew   *Isa 49:9*
yourselves
we wait for light, but we   *Isa 59:9*
walk *in d.*
ways shall be as slippery   *Jer 23:12*
ways *in d.*
he knoweth what is *in d.* and   *Da 2:22*
light
that followeth me shall not   *Joh 8:12*
walk *in d.*
for he that walketh *in d.*   *Joh 12:35*
knoweth not
believeth me, should not   *Joh 12:46*
abide *in d.*
but ye, brethren, are not *in d.*   *1Th 5:4*
walk *in d.* we lie and do not   *1Jo 1:6*
truth
hateth his brother, is *in d.*   *1Jo 2:9*
even till now
hateth his brother, is *in d.*   *1Jo 2:11*
walketh *in d.*

LAND *OF* DARKNESS

before I go even to the   *Job 10:21*
land of d.
a *land of d.* as darkness   *Job 10:22*
itself, and shadow
have I been to Israel a *land*   *Jer 2:31*
of d.

DARKNESS with *LIGHT*

God divided the *light* from the   *Ge 1:4*
d.
two great lights to divide   *Ge 1:18*
light from *d.*
a land where the *light* is   *Job 10:22*
as *d.*
the *light* is short because of   *Job 17:12*
d.
he shall be driven from   *Job 18:18*
light into *d.*
when by his *light* I walked   *Job 29:3*
through *d.*
when I waited for *light*, there   *Job 30:26*
came *d.*
to upright there ariseth *light*   *Ps 112:4*
in *d.*
d. and *light* are both alike   *Ps 139:12*
to thee
wisdom excels as far as *light*   *Ec 2:13*
excelleth *d.*
that put *d.* for *light*, and   *Isa 5:20*
light for *d.*
people that walked in *d.* have   *Isa 9:2;*
seen a great *light*   *M't 4:16*
I will make *d.* *light* before   *Isa 42:16*
them
I form *light* and create *d.* I   *Isa 45:7*
that walketh in *d.* and hath   *Isa 50:10*
no *light*
ye look for *light*, he make   *Jer 13:16*
gross *d.*
brought me into *d.* but not   *La 3:2*
into *light*
day of the Lord is *d.* and   *Am 5:18*
not *light*
when I sit in *d.* Lord shall be   *Mic 7:8*
a *light*
light in thee be *d.* how great   *M't 6:23*
is that *d.*
what I tell in *d.* speak in   *M't 10:27;*
light   *Lu 12:3*
light to them that sit in *d.*   *Lu 1:79;*
  Ro 2:19
that the *light* which is in   *Lu 11:35*
thee be not *d.*
light sinneth in *d.*; *d.*   *Joh 1:5*
comprehended it not
and men loved *d.* rather than   *Joh 3:19*
light
walk while ye have *light*,   *Joh 12:35*
lest *d.* come
to turn them from *d.* to   *Ac 26:18*
light
cast off the works of *d.* put   *Ro 13:12*
on *light*
to bring to *light* hidden   *1Co 4:5*
things of *d.*
commanded *light* to shine out   *2Co 4:6*
of *d.*
what communion hath *light*   *2Co 6:14*
with *d.*
called out of *d.* into   *1Pe 2:9*
marvellous *light*
God is *light*, in him is no *d.*   *1Jo 1:5*
at all
d. is past, and the true *light*   *1Jo 2:8*
now shineth

OUT *OF* DARKNESS

when ye heard voice *out of*   *De 5:22*
d.
he discovereth deep things   *Job 12:22*
out of d.
believeth not he shall   *Job 15:22*
return *out of d.*
he shall not depart *out of*   *Job 15:30*
d.
brought them *out of d.* and   *Ps 107:14*
shadow
eyes of blind shall see *out*   *Isa 29:18*
of d.

DARKON

of Jaalah, the children of D.   *Ezr 2:56*
of Jaala, the children of D.   *Ne 7:58*

DARLING

my *d.* from the power of the dog	Ps 22:20
my dear life-my only one (A)(R)	Ps 22:20
my lonely self (B)	Ps 22:20
Lord, rescue my *d.* from the lions	Ps 35:17
my life (A)(R)	Ps 35:17
my only one (B)	Ps 35:17
he is a *d.* child (A)(B)(E)(R)	Jer 31:20

DARNEL

sowed *d.* (A)	M't 13:25; 13:26-27, 30, 36, 38, 40
sowed *d.* (B)	M't 13:25; 29:29

DART

spear, the *d.* nor the habergeon	Job 41:26
Till a *d.* strike through his liver	Pr 7:23
or thrust through with a *d.*	Heb 12:20

DARTS

he took three *d.* in his hand	2Sa 18:14
d. and shields in abundance	2Ch 32:5
D. are counted as stubble	Job 41:29
all the fiery *d.* of the wicked	Eph 6:16
flaming missles of the wicked (A)	Eph 6:16
flaming arrows of the wicked (N)	Eph 6:16
missle the enemy hurls (P)	Eph 6:16

DASH

d. the blood (A)	Ex 29:20; Le 1:11; 7:2; 17:6; 2Ki 16:15
wilt *d.* their children, and	2Ki 8:12
thou shalt *d.* them in pieces like	Ps 2:9
thou *d.* thy foot against a stone	Ps 91:12; M't 4:6; Lu 4:11
shall *d.* the young men to pieces	Isa 13:18
d. them one against another	Jer 13:14

DASHED

hand, O Lord, hath *d.* in pieces	Ex 15:6
nation *d.* against nation (B)	2Ch 15:6
children also shall be *d.* to pieces	Isa 13:16
the mother was *d.* in pieces upon	Ho 10:14
their infants shall be *d.* in pieces	Ho 13:16
children also were *d.* in pieces	Na 3:10

DASHETH

that taketh and *d.* thy little ones	Ps 137:9
He that *d.* in pieces is come	Na 2:1

DATHAN

D. and Abiram	Nu 16:1; 16:12, 24-25, 27; 26:9; De 11:6
earth opened and swallowed *D.*	Ps 106:17

DAUB

d. it with untempered mortar	Eze 13:11

DAUBED

d. it with slime and with pitch	Ex 2:3
d. it with untempered mortar	Eze 13:10; 13:12, 14-15
And her prophets have *d.* them	Eze 22:28

DAUBING

Where is the *d.* wherewith ye	Eze 13:12

DAUGHTER

d. of my father, not *d.* of my mother	Ge 20:12
whose *d.* art thou? tell me	Ge 24:23; 24:47
take my master's brother's *d.* to his son	Ge 24:48
wrought folly in lying with Jacob's *d.*	Ge 34:7
soul of Shechem longeth for your *d.*	Ge 34:8
then will we take our *d.* and be gone	Ge 34:17
because he had delight in Jacob's *d.*	Ge 34:19
but if it be a *d.* then she shall live	Ex 1:16
whether he have gored a son or a *d.*	Ex 21:31
when days are fulfilled for a	Le 12:6
nor shalt thou take her daughter's *d.*	Le 18:17
d. of priest, if she profane herself	Le 21:9
if priest's *d.* be married to a stranger	Le 22:12
if priest's *d.* be a widow or divorced	Le 22:13
if he have no *d.* give inheritance	Nu 27:9
every *d.* that possesseth an inheritance	Nu 36:8
cursed be he that lieth with sister, *d.* of father or *d.* of his mother	De 27:22
her eye shall be evil towards her *d.*	De 28:56
Jephthah's *d.* came out to meet him	J'g 11:34
lament Jephthah's *d.* four days in year	J'g 11:40
count not handmaid *d.* of Belial	1Sa 1:16
when Saul's *d.* should have been given	1Sa 18:19
little ewe lamb was unto him as a *d.*	2Sa 12:3
Solomon took Pharaoh's *d.*	1Ki 3:1
loved many women with *d.* of Pharaoh	1Ki 11:1
d. of Ahab was Jehoram's wife	2Ki 8:18
go bury Jezebel, for she is a king's *d.*	2Ki 9:34
the *d.* of Caleb was Achsah	1Ch 2:49
took uncle's *d.* for his own *d.*	Es 2:7
hearken, O *d.* and consider	Ps 45:10
the king's *d.* is all glorious within	Ps 45:13
how beautiful with shoes, prince's *d.*	Ca 7:1
how long go about, backsliding *d.*	Jer 31:22; 49:4
d. dwelling in Egypt, furnish thyself	Jer 46:19
d. that dost inhabit Dibon, come down	Jer 48:18
neither deliver son nor *d.*	Eze 14:16; 14:18, 20
as is the mother, so is her *d.*	Eze 16:44
thou art thy mother's *d.* that loatheth	Eze 16:45
for son or *d.* they may defile themselves	Eze 44:25
king's *d.* of the south shall come	Da 11:6
give him *d.* of women corrupting	Da 11:17
she conceived again, and bare a *d.*	Ho 1:6
gather in troops, O *d.* of troops	Mic 5:1
d. against mother	Mic 7:6; M't 10:35; Lu 12:53
the *d.* of my dispersed shall bring	Zep 3:10
hath married the *d.* of a strange god	Mal 2:11
D. be of good comfort thy faith	M't 9:22; M'k 5:34; Lu 8:48
he that loveth son or *d.* more than me	M't 10:37
d. of Herodias danced before them	M't 14:6
her *d.* was made whole from that hour	M't 15:28
would cast forth devil out of *d.*	M'k 7:26
he had one only *d.* 12 years of age	Lu 8:42
ought not this woman, being *d.* of Abraham	Lu 13:16
Pharaoh's *d.* took him and nourished	Ac 7:21
Moses refused to be son of Pharaoh's *d.*	Heb 11:24

DAUGHTER *OF BABYLON*

O *d. of* Babylon, art to be destroyed	Ps 137:8
O *d. of* Babylon, sit on the ground	Isa 47:1
battle against thee, O *d. of* Babylon	Jer 50:42
d. of Babylon is like a threshing floor	Jer 51:33
Zion, that dwellest with *d. of* Babylon	Zec 2:7

DAUGHTER *OF THE CHALDEANS*

there is no throne, O *d. of* the Chaldeans	Isa 47:1
get thee into darkness, O *d.* of the Chaldeans	Isa 47:5

DAUGHTER *OF EDOM*

rejoice and be glad, O *d. of* Edom	La 4:21
he will visit thine iniquity, O *d. of* Edom	La 4:22

DAUGHTER *OF EGYPT*

go into Gilead, O virgin, *d.* of Egypt	Jer 46:11
the *d.* of Egypt shall be confounded	Jer 46:24

DAUGHTER *OF GALLIM*

lift up thy voice, O *d. of* Gallim	Isa 10:30

DAUGHTER *OF JERUSALEM*

daughter of Zion, *d.* of Jerusalem hath shaken her head	2Ki 19:21; Isa 37:22
liken to thee, *d.* of Jerusalem	La 2:13
they wag their head at *d. of* Jerusalem	La 2:15
kingdom shall come to *d. of* Jerusalem	Mic 4:8
rejoice with all heart, *d. of* Jerusalem	Zep 3:14
shout, *d. of* Jerusalem, thy King cometh	Zec 9:9

DAUGHTER *OF JUDAH*

Lord hath trodden the *d.* of Judah	La 1:15
thrown down strong holds of *d. of* Judah	La 2:2
he hath increased in *d. of* Judah mourning	La 2:5

DAUGHTER *OF MY PEOPLE*

because of spoiling of *d. of* my people	Isa 22:4
dry wind toward *d. of* my people not to fan	Jer 4:11
healed heart of *d. of* my people slightly	Jer 6:14; 8:11
d. of my people, gird thee with sackcloth	Jer 6:26
voice of the cry of the *d. of* my people	Jer 8:19
for hurt of *d. of* my people am I hurt	Jer 8:21
why not health of *d. of* my people recovered	Jer 8:22
I might weep for slain of *d. of* my people	Jer 9:1
them, for how shall I do for *d. of* my people	Jer 9:7
virgin *d. of* my people broken with a breach	Jer 14:17
for destruction of *d. of* my people	La 2:11; 3:48

d. of my people become cruel,   *La 4:3*
like ostriches
iniquity of *d. of my people* is   *La 4:6*
greater than
their meat in destruction of   *La 4:10*
d. of my people

DAUGHTER *OF TARSHISH*

pass through as river, *d. of*   *Isa 23:10*
Tarshish

DAUGHTER *OF TYRE*

d. of Tyre shall be there   *Ps 45:12*
with gift

DAUGHTER *OF ZIDON*

thou oppressed virgin, *d. of*   *Isa 23:12*
Zidon

DAUGHTER *OF ZION*

d. of Zion hath despised   *2Ki 19:21;*
thee   *Isa 37:22*
praise in gates of *d. of Zion*   *Ps 9:14*
d. of Zion left as a cottage in   *Isa 1:8*
vineyard
washed away filth of the *d. of*   *Isa 4:4*
Zion
shake against mount of *d.*   *Isa 10:32;*
of Zion
loose thyself, O captive *d. of*   *Isa 52:2*
Zion
say to *d. of Zion,* Thy   *Isa 62:11*
salvation cometh
heard the voice of the *d. of*   *Jer 4:31*
Zion
likened *d. of Zion* to a comely   *Jer 6:2*
woman
as men of war against thee,   *Jer 6:23*
O *d. of Zion*
from *d. of Zion* beauty is   *La 1:6*
departed
Lord covereth *d. of Zion* with   *La 2:1*
a cloud
slew in the tabernacle of the *d.*   *La 2:4*
of Zion
Lord purposed to destroy wall   *La 2:8*
of *d. of Zion*
elders of *d. of Zion* sit on the   *La 2:10*
ground
what shall I equal to thee, O   *La 2:13*
d. of Zion
wall of *d. of Zion,* let tears   *La 2:18*
run down
punishment is accomplished,   *La 4:22*
O *d. of Zion*
beginning of sin to the *d. of*   *Mic 1:13*
Zion
tower, the strong hold of the   *Mic 4:8*
d. of Zion
be in pain, labour to bring   *Mic 4:10*
forth, O *d. of Zion*
arise and thresh, O *d. of*   *Mic 4:13*
Zion, I will make
sing, O *d. of Zion,* shout O   *Zep 3:14*
Israel
sing and rejoice, O *d. of*   *Zec 2:10;*
Zion   *9:9*
tell ye *d. of Zio*n, thy king   *M't 21:5*
cometh
fear not, *d. of Zio*n, thy   *Joh 12:15*
king cometh

DAUGHTER *OF ZUR*

the woman was Cozbi the *d.*   *Nu 25:15*
of Zur

HIS DAUGHTER

Rachael *his d.* cometh with   *Ge 29:6*
sheep
if a man sell *his d.* to be a   *Ex 21:7*
servant
for his son or *his d.* he may   *Le 21:2*
be defiled
cause inheritance to pass to   *Nu 27:8*
his d.
statutes between the father   *Nu 30:16*
and *his d.*
nor *his d.* shalt thou take to   *De 7:3*
thy son
maketh *his d.* pass through   *De 18:10;*
fire   *2Ki 23:10*

not any of us give *his d.* to   *J'g 21:1*
Benjamin
king will enrich and give   *1Sa 17:25*
him *his d.*

MY DAUGHTER

I gave *my d.* to this man to   *De 22:16*
wife
to him will I give *my d.*   *Jos 15:16;*
    J'g 1:12
alas, *my d.* thou hast   *J'g 11:35*
brought me low
behold, here is *my d.* a   *J'g 19:24*
maiden
and she said unto her, Go, *my*   *Ru 2:2*
d.
blessed be thou of the Lord,   *Ru 3:10*
my d.
her mother said, Who art   *Ru 3:16*
thou, *my d.*
sit still, *my d.* till thou know   *Ru 3:18*
the matter
ruler, saying, My *d.* is now   *M't 9:18*
dead
my d. is grievously vexed   *M't 15:22*
with a devil
my little *d.* lieth at the point   *M'k 5:23*
of death

THY DAUGHTER

I will serve 7 years for *thy*   *Ge 29:18*
d.
nor thy son, nor *thy d.*   *Ex 20:10;*
    De 5:14
nakedness of *thy* daughter's   *Le 18:10*
d.
do not prostitute *thy d.* to be   *Le 19:29*
a whore
thy d. shalt thou not give to   *De 7:3*
his son
shalt rejoice and *thy d.*   *De 12:18;*
    16:11, 14
if thy son or *thy d.* entice   *De 13:6*
thee, saying
saying, I found not *thy d.*   *De 22:17*
a maid
give *thy d.* to my son   *2Ki 14:9;*
    2Ch 25:18
certain who said, Thy *d.* is   *M'k 5:35;*
dead   *Lu 8:49*
go thy way, devil is gone   *M'k 7:29*
out of *thy d.*

DAUGHTER-IN-LAW

knew not that she was his   *Ge 38:16*
d.-in-law
Tamar thy *d.-in-law* hath   *Ge 38:24*
played harlot
not uncover nakedness of   *Le 18:15*
d.-in-law
if man lie with *d.-in-law*   *Le 20:12*
both die
Naomi returned, Ruth her   *Ru 1:22*
d-in-law
d-in-law which loveth thee,   *Ru 4:15*
hath born him
d-in-law Phinehas' wife with   *1Sa 4:19*
child
another lewdly defileth his   *Eze 22:11*
d.-in-law
d.-in-law riseth up against   *Mic 7:6;*
mother-in-law   *M't 10:35; Lu 12:53*

DAUGHTERS

and when *d.* were born to   *Ge 6:1*
them
sons of God saw *d.* of men,   *Ge 6:2*
and took
sons of God came in unto *d.*   *Ge 6:4*
of men
Lot spake to them which   *Ge 19:14*
married his *d.*
both *d.* of Lot with child by   *Ge 19:36*
their father
take not wife of *d.* of   *Ge 24:3*
Canaan   *24:37; 28:1, 6*
d. of the city came out to   *Ge 24:13*
draw water
weary of my life because of   *Ge 27:46*
d. of Heth
happy am I, for *d.* will call   *Ge 30:13*
me blessed
thou hast carried away my *d.*   *Ge 31:26*
captives

these *d.* are my *d.*   *Ge 31:43*
Dinah went out to see *d.* of   *Ge 34:1*
the land
give your *d.* to us, and take   *Ge 34:9*
our *d.*
then will we give *d.* to you,   *Ge 34:16*
and take *d.*
priest of Midian had seven *d.*   *Ex 2:16*
shall deal with her after   *Ex 21:9*
manner of *d.*
their *d.* go a whoring after   *Ex 34:16*
their gods
flesh of your *d.* shall ye eat   *Le 26:29*
names of *d.* of Zelophehad   *Nu 26:33;*
    27:1; Jos 17:3
the *d.* of Zelophehad speak   *Nu 27:7*
right
even so did the *d.* of   *Nu 36:10*
Zelophehad
be no whore of *d.* of Israel   *De 23:17*
took their *d.* to be their wives   *J'g 3:6*
will not give our *d.* to   *J'g 21:7*
wives
may not give them wives of   *J'g 21:18*
our *d.*
turn again, my *d.* why will ye   *Ru 1:11;*
go   *1:12*
my *d.* it grieveth me for   *Ru 1:13*
your sakes
take your *d.* to be   *1Sa 8:13*
confectionaries
were king's *d.* virgins   *2Sa 13:18*
apparelled
next repaired Shallum, he and   *Ne 3:12*
d.
our *d.* are brought into   *Ne 5:5*
bondage already
took one of *d.* of Barzillai   *Ne 7:63;*
to wife   *Ezr 2:61*
not give our *d.* to people of   *Ne 10:30*
land
no women so fair as *d.* of   *Job 42:15*
Job
king's *d.* among honourable   *Ps 45:9*
women
that our *d.* may be as   *Ps 144:12*
corner stones
many *d.* have done virtuously   *Pr 31:29*
as lily, so is my love among *d.*   *Ca 2:2*
the harem *d.* (B)   *Ca 6:8*
the *d.* saw her and blessed her   *Ca 6:9*
hear my voice, ye careless *d.*   *Isa 32:9*
give ear
confident and careless *d.*   *Isa 32:9*
(A)(B)(E)(R)
thy *d.* shall be nursed at thy   *Isa 60:4*
side
ye women, teach your *d.*   *Jer 9:20*
wailing
give *d.* to husbands, they may   *Jer 29:6*
bear
her *d.* shall be burnt with   *Jer 49:2*
fire
cry *d.* of Rabbah, gird with   *Jer 49:3*
sackcloth
because of all the *d.* of my   *La 3:51*
city
set face against *d.* of thy   *Eze 13:17*
people
sister Samaria, her *d.* Sodom,   *Eze 16:46*
her *d.*
abundance of idleness in   *Eze 16:49*
her and her *d.*
when I bring back the   *Eze 16:53*
captivity of her *d.*
when thy sister Sodom and   *Eze 16:55*
d. shall return
and I will give them unto   *Eze 16:61*
thee for *d.*
were two women, *d.* of one   *Eze 23:2*
mother
her *d.* shall be slain in the   *Eze 26:6;*
field   *26:8*
and her *d.* shall go into   *Eze 30:18*
captivity
the *d.* of the nations shall   *Eze 32:16*
lament her
your *d.* shall commit   *Ho 4:13*
whoredom
d. commit adultery   *Ho 4:13;*
(A)(B)(E)(R)   *4:14*
not punish your *d.* when they   *Ho 4:14*
commit
his wife was of the *d.* of   *Lu 1:5*
Aaron
the same man had four *d.*   *Ac 21:9*
virgins
whose *d.* ye are as long as do   *1Pe 3:6*
well

DAUGHTERS *OF ISRAEL*

be no whore of d. of Israel   De 23:17
d. of Israel went yearly to   J'g 11:40
lament
ye d. of Israel, weep over   2Sa 1:24
Saul

DAUGHTERS *OF JERUSALEM*

black, but comely, d. of   Ca 1:5
Jerusalem
I charge you, d. of Jerusalem   Ca 2:7;
    3:5; 5:8; 8:4
paved with love for d. of   Ca 3:10
Jerusalem
this is my beloved, d. of   Ca 5:16
Jerusalem
d. of Jerusalem, weep not   Lu 23:28
for me

DAUGHTERS *OF JUDAH*

let the d. of Judah be glad   Ps 48:11
Zion heard, and the d. of   Ps 97:8
Judah rejoiced

DAUGHTERS *OF MOAB*

Israel committed whoredom   Nu 25:1
with d. of Moab
so d. of Moab be at fords of   Isa 16:2
Arnon

DAUGHTERS *OF MUSIC*

d. of music shall be brought   Ec 12:4
low

DAUGHTERS *OF PHILISTINES*

Samson saw a woman of d.   J'g 14:1
of Philistines
I have seen a woman of d. of   J'g 14:2
Philistines
publish it not lest d. of   2Sa 1:20
Philistines
I have delivered thee to d.   Eze 16:27
of Philistines
d. of Philistines which   Eze 16:57
despise thee round about

DAUGHTERS *OF SHILOH*

if d. of Shiloh come out to   J'g 21:21
dance, catch every man a wife
of d. of Shiloh

DAUGHTERS with *SONS*

begat sons and d.   Ge 5:4;
    5:7, 10, 13, 16; 11:11
thy sons and d. bring out of   Ge 19:12
this place
not suffered me to kiss sons   Ge 31:28
and d.
kissed sons and d. and   Ge 31:55
blessed them
all his sons and d. rose to   Ge 37:35
comfort him
shall put them on your sons   Ex 3:22
and d.
with our sons and with our d.   Ex 10:9
will we go
and she have born him sons   Ex 21:4
or d.
earrings of your sons and d.   Ex 32:2
bring to me
and thou take of their d. to   Ex 34:16
thy sons
thou, thy sons and d. with   Le 10:14;
thee, shall eat   Nu 18:11, 19
given sons and d. into   Nu 21:29
captivity
Zelophehad had no sons, but   Nu 26:33;
d.   Jos 17:3
ye and your sons and d.   De 12:12
rejoice
their sons and d. they have   De 12:31;
burnt in fire 2Ki 17:17; Jer 7:31; 32:35
sons and d. given to another   De 28:32
people
beget sons and d. but shalt   De 28:41
not enjoy them

thou shalt eat the flesh of   De 28:53
thy sons and d.
because of provoking of his   De 32:19
sons and d.
they brought Achan, his sons   Jos 7:24
and d.
d. of Manasseh had   Jos 17:6
inheritance among sons
they gave their d. to their sons   J'g 3:6
Ibzan took in thirty d. for his   J'g 12:9
sons
gave Peninnah, her sons and   1Sa 1:4
d. portions
so Hannah bare three sons   1Sa 2:21
and two d.
their sons and d. were taken   1Sa 30:3
captives
grieved, every man for his   1Sa 30:6
sons and d.
nothing lacking, neither sons   1Sa 30:19
nor d.
d. born to David   2Sa 5:13; 1Ch 14:3
which saved lives of sons   2Sa 19:5
and d.
now Sheshan had no sons   1Ch 2:34
but d.
Shimei had sixteen sons and   1Ch 4:27
six d.
Eleazar died, and had no   1Ch 23:22
sons but d.
gave Heman fourteen sons   1Ch 25:5
and three d.
Rehoboam had 28 sons and   2Ch 11:21
60 d.
Abijah begat 22 sons and   2Ch 13:21
16 d.
Jehoiada took wives begat   2Ch 24:3
sons and d.
carried captive 200,000   2Ch 28:8
women, sons and d.
sons, d. and wives are in   2Ch 29:9
captivity
to the genealogy of their   2Ch 31:18
sons and d.
have taken of their d. for   Ezr 9:2
their sons
give not your d. to their   Ezr 9:12;
sons   Ne 13:25
fight for your sons, d. and   Ne 4:14
wives
said, we, our sons and our d.   Ne 5:2
are many
bring into bondage our sons   Ne 5:5
and our d.
sons and d. clave to their   Ne 10:28
brethren
born to Job 7 sons and 3 d.   Job 1:2;
    42:13
day when sons and d. were   Job 1:13;
eating   1:18
they sacrificed their sons and   Ps 106:37
d. to devils
shed even blood of their sons   Ps 106:38
and d.
bring my sons from far, my d.   Isa 43:6
from
bring sons in their arms,   Isa 49:22
and d.
will I give name better than   Isa 56:5
sons and d.
shame hath devoured sons   Jer 3:24
eat that which sons and d.   Jer 5:17
should eat
their sons and d. shall die by   Jer 11:22
famine
shall have none to bury sons   Jer 14:16
and d.
neither have sons nor d. in   Jer 16:2
this place
saith the Lord concerning   Jer 16:3
sons and d.
cause them eat flesh of sons   Jer 19:9
take ye wives and beget sons   Jer 29:6
and d.
we, our sons and our d.   Jer 35:8
drink no wine
thy sons and thy d. are   Jer 48:46
taken captives
shall deliver neither sons   Eze 14:16;
nor d.   14:18
remnant brought forth, both   Eze 14:22
sons and d.
taken sons and d. and   Eze 16:20
sacrificed them
were mine, and bare sons   Eze 23:4
and d.
took sons and d. and slew   Eze 23:10;
her   23:25

they shall slay their sons   Eze 23:47
and d.
your sons and d. fall by   Eze 24:21;
sword   Am 7:17
when I take from them   Eze 24:25
their sons and d.
your sons and d. prophesy   Joe 2:28;
    Ac 2:17
I will sell your sons and d. to   Joe 3:8
Judah
ye shall be my sons and d.   2Co 6:18
saith Lord

DAUGHTERS *OF SYRIA*

time of reproach of d. of   Eze 16:57
Syria

DAUGHTERS *OF THE UNCIRCUMCISED*

publish it not, lest d. of the   2Sa 1:20
uncircumcised triumph

DAUGHTERS *OF ZION*

go forth, O ye d. of Zion   Ca 3:11
because the d. of Zion re   Isa 3:16
haughty
smite with a scab head of d.   Isa 3:17
of Zion
have washed away filth of d.   Isa 4:4
of Zion

TWO DAUGHTERS

I have two d. let me bring   Ge 19:8
them out
take thy wife and two d.   Ge 19:15
which are here
Lot dwelt in a cave, he and   Ge 19:30
his two d.
Laban had two d. Leah and   Ge 29:16
Rachel
I served fourteen years for   Ge 31:41
two d.
Naomi went out with her two   Ru 1:7
d.
Hannah conceived and bare   1Sa 12:21
two d.
Saul's two d. were Merab   1Sa 14:49
and Michal
the horseleach hath two d.   Pr 30:15
crying

DAUGHTERS-IN-LAW

then she arose with her   Ru 1:6
d.-in-law
Naomi said to her two   Ru 1:8
d.-in-law

DAUGHTER'S

daughter, or thy d. daughter   Le 18:10
or her d. daughter, to   Le 18:17
uncover her
are the tokens of my d.   De 22:17
virginity

DAVID

Jesse begat D.   Ru 4:22;
    M't 1:6; Lu 3:31
Spirit of the Lord came   1Sa 16:13
upon D.
send me D. thy son   1Sa 16:19
D. came to Saul   1Sa 16:21; 17:15
D. played with his hand   1Sa 16:23;
    18:10; 19:9
D. was youngest   1Sa 17:14
and D. heard the words of   1Sa 17:23
Goliath
Eliab's anger was kindled   1Sa 17:28
against D.
Saul armed D.   1Sa 17:38
when Goliath saw D.   1Sa 17:42
the Philistine cursed D. by   1Sa 17:43
his gods
D. prevailed over the   1Sa 17:50
Philistine with a sling
as D. returned from the   1Sa 17:57
slaughter of Philistine
the soul of Jonathan was   1Sa 18:1
knit to D.
then Jonathan and D. made   1Sa 18:3
a covenant
D. went out whithersoever   1Sa 18:5
Saul sent him

D. hath slain his ten thousands 1Sa 18:7; 29:5
Saul eyed *D.* from that day 1Sa 18:9 and forward
D. behaved himself wisely 1Sa 18:14 in all his ways
but all Israel and Judah 1Sa 18:16 loved *D.*
the servants said, On this 1Sa 18:24 manner spake *D.*
Saul saw and knew that the 1Sa 18:28 Lord was with *D.*
Saul spake to his servants to 1Sa 19:1 kill *D.*
sin against innocent blood to 1Sa 19:5 slay *D.*
Saul sought to smite *D.* 1Sa 19:10; 19:18
but *D.* escaped
D. is at Naioth 1Sa 19:19
D. ask leave to run to 1Sa 20:6; Beth-lehem 20:28
Jonathan caused *D.* to 1Sa 20:17 swear again
D. hid himself 1Sa 20:24
Jonathan ate not, for he 1Sa 20:34 was grieved for *D.*
wept one with another, till 1Sa 20:41 *D.* exceeded
Ahimelech was afraid at the 1Sa 21:1 meeting of *D.*
D. arose, and fled to 1Sa 21:10 Achish for fear of Saul
is not this *D.* the king of 1Sa 21:11; the land 29:3
D. departed and escaped to 1Sa 22:1 cave Adullam
D. went thence to Mispeh of 1Sa 22:3 Moab
D. departed and came into 1Sa 22:5 forest of Hareth
who is faithful among thy 1Sa 22:14 servants as *D.*
because their hand also is 1Sa 22:17 with *D.*
therefore *D.* inquired of 1Sa 23:2; Lord 23:4; 30:8; 2Sa 2:1; 3:19, 22; 21:1
so *D.* and his men went to 1Sa 23:5 Keilah
D. knew that Saul practised 1Sa 23:9 mischief
D. was in wilderness of 1Sa 23:15 Ziph in a wood
D. and men were in 1Sa 23:24 wilderness of Maon
Saul returned from pursuing 1Sa 23:28 after *D.*
D. is in the wilderness of 1Sa 24:1 En-gedi
D. stayed his servants 1Sa 24:7
Saul said, Is this thy voice, 1Sa 24:16; my son *D.* 26:17
D. sware unto Saul 1Sa 24:22
D. went to Paran 1Sa 25:1
D. sent ten young men to 1Sa 25:5 Nabal
more also to God to 1Sa 25:22 enemies of *D.*
doth not *D.* hide in hill 1Sa 26:1 Hachilah
D. beheld the place where 1Sa 26:5 Saul lay
D. took the spear and curse 1Sa 26:12 of water
return, my son *D.* 1Sa 26:21
D. said, I shall perish by 1Sa 27:1 hand of Saul
D. was fled to Gath 1Sa 27:4
D. invaded the Geshurites 1Sa 27:8
so did *D.* and so will be his 1Sa 27:11 manner
Lord given it to neighbour, 1Sa 28:17 even *D.*
is not this *D.* 1Sa 29:3; 29:6
when *D.* and men were come 1Sa 30:1 to Ziklag
D. pursued 1Sa 30:10
D. smote them from twilight 1Sa 30:17
D. recovered all 1Sa 30:18; 30:19-20
D. took his clothes, and rent 2Sa 1:11
D. called one of young men 2Sa 1:15
D. lamented over Saul and 2Sa 1:17 Jonathan
D. sent messengers to men of 2Sa 2:5 Jabesh
but the house of Judah 2Sa 2:10 followed *D.*
but house of *D.* waxed 2Sa 3:1 stronger
unto *D.* were sons born in 2Sa 3:2 Hebron

except as Lord hath sworn to 2Sa 3:9 *D.* so I do
ye sought for *D.* in times 2Sa 3:17 past to be king
D. said, I and my kingdom 2Sa 3:28 are guiltless
then came all the tribes of 2Sa 5:1 Israel to *D.*
thinking *D.* cannot come in 2Sa 5:6 hither
D. took the strong hold of 2Sa 5:7 Zion
D. grew great 2Sa 5:10; 5:12, 17, 21
D. went to bring up the ark 2Sa 6:2; of God 6:5, 9, 14-15
what can *D.* say more 2Sa 7:20; 1Ch 17:18
D. smote the Philistines 2Sa 8:1; 8:3, 6-7, 13-15; 1Ch 18:14
D. sent to comfort Hanun 2Sa 10:2; 1Ch 19:2
thinkest *D.* doth honour thy 2Sa 10:3; father 1Ch 19:3
D. slew men of 700 chariots 2Sa 10:18 of Syrians
D. sent and inquired after 2Sa 11:3 the woman
D. sent for Uriah 2Sa 11:6
D. wrote a letter to Joab 2Sa 11:14
thing *D.* had done 2Sa 11:27 displeased the Lord
D. said, I have sinned 2Sa 12:13 against the Lord
D. besought God for the 2Sa 12:16 child, *D.* fasted
D. perceived that the child 2Sa 12:19 was dead
D. comforted Bath-sheba 2Sa 12:24 his wife
D. fought against Rabbah 2Sa 12:29 and took it
D. sent to Tamar 2Sa 13:7
D. went up by mount Olivet 2Sa 15:30
Shimei cast stones at *D.* 2Sa 16:6; 16:10
I will arise and pursue after 2Sa 17:1 *D.*
send quickly and tell *D.* 2Sa 17:16
D. was come to Mahanaim 2Sa 17:27
D. numbered people with 2Sa 18:1 him
D. sat between two gates 2Sa 18:24
we have also more right in 2Sa 19:43 *D.*
Sheba said, We have no part 2Sa 20:1 in *D.*
D. came to his house at 2Sa 20:3 Jerusalem
he that is for *D.* let him go 2Sa 20:11 after Joab
Ishbi-benob thought to 2Sa 21:16 have slain *D.*
he shewed mercy unto *D.* 2Sa 22:51; Ps 18:50
the last words of *D.* 2Sa 23:1
mighty men whom *D.* had 2Sa 23:8; 1Ch 11:10
D. built there an altar unto 2Sa 24:25 the Lord
D. our lord knoweth it not 1Ki 1:11
D. slept with fathers, and 1Ki 2:10 was buried
slew them, *D.* not knowing 1Ki 2:32
thou knowest what thou 1Ki 2:44 didst to *D.*
if thou wilt walk as thy 1Ki 3:14 father *D.*
given *D.* a wise son over this 1Ki 5:7 people
I chose *D.* to be over my 1Ki 8:16 people Israel
I am risen up in room of *D.* 1Ki 8:20 as I promised to *D.*
I will for this afflict the 1Ki 11:39 seed of *D.*
what portion have we in 1Ki 12:16; *D.* 2Ch 10:16
Lord turned the kingdom 1Ch 10:14 to *D.*
D. made covenant with them 1Ch 11:3 in Hebron
thine are we, *D.* Then *D.* 1Ch 12:18 received them
they helped *D.* against 1Ch 12:21 band of rovers
fame of *D.* went out into all 1Ch 14:17 lands
D. was clothed with robe 1Ch 15:27 of fine linen

they set ark in tent *D.* had 1Ch 16:1 pitched
D. returned to bless his 1Ch 16:43 house
Arnan saw *D.* and bowed 1Ch 21:21 himself to *D.*
so when *D.* was old and full 1Ch 23:1 of days
I made, said *D.*, to praise 1Ch 23:5 therewith
D. blessed Lord before 1Ch 29:10 congregation
shewed great mercy unto *D.* 2Ch 1:8
he began to seek after the 1Ch 34:3 God of *D.*
of sons of *D.* Hattush was Ezr 8:2 chief
place over against sepulchres Ne 3:16 of *D.*
with musical instruments of Ne 12:36 *D.*
prayers of *D.* son of Jesse Ps 72:20
I will not lie unto *D.* Ps 89:35; 89:49; 132:11
Lord, remember *D.* Ps 132:1
there will I make horn of Ps 132:17 *D.* to bud
thy neck is like the tower of *D.* Ca 4:4
on throne of *D.* and his Isa 9:7 kingdom
woe to Ariel, the city where Isa 29:1 *D.* dwelt
even sure mercies of *D.* Isa 55:3; Ac 13:34
kings and princes sitting on Jer 17:25 throne of *D.*
I will raise to *D.* a righteous Jer 23:5 branch
I will cause branch to grow Jer 33:15 up unto *D.*
D. never want a man to sit Jer 33:17 on throne
shall have none to sit on Jer 36:30 throne of *D.*
invent instruments of music Am 6:5 like *D.*
I raise up tabernacle of *D.* Am 9:11; that is fallen Ac 15:16
feeble be as *D.* and *D.* as Zec 12:8 God
thou Son of *D.* have mercy M't 9:27; 15:22; 20:30-31; M'k 10:47-48; Lu 18:38-39
have ye not read what *D.* M't 12:3; did when he M'k 2:25; Lu 6:3 was an hungered
people said, Is not this the M't 12:23 Son of *D.*
saying, Hosanna to the Son M't 21:9; of *D.* 21:15
Christ is the Son of *D.* M't 22:42; M'k 12:35
if *D.* then call him Lord, M't 22:45; how is he his son M'k 12:37; Lu 20:41, 44
blessed be kingdom of our M'k 11:10
that Christ cometh of seed Joh 7:42 of *D.*
let me freely speak of Ac 2:29 patriarch *D.*
for *D.* is not ascended into Ac 2:31 the heavens
he raised up to them *D.* to Ac 13:22 be king
for *D.* fell on sleep, and Ac 13:36 saw corruption
Christ, made of seed of *D.* Ro 1:3; 2Ti 2:8
even as *D.* also describeth Ro 4:6 blessedness
limiteth certain day, saying Heb 4:7 in *D.*
time would fail me to tell Heb 11:32 of *D.*
hath the key of *D.* Re 3:7
root of *D.* Re 5:5; 22:16

DAYS OF DAVID

there was famine in *days of* 2Sa 21:1 *D.*
days of *D.* drew nigh he 1Ki 2:1 should die
whose number was in *days of* 1Ch 7:2 *D.*

in the *days of D.* were chief   Ne 12:46
singers
God drave out unto the *days*   Ac 7:45
of D.

HAND OF DAVID

not delivered thee into *hand*   2Sa 3:8
of D.
by *hand of D.* I will save   2Sa 3:18
Israel
fell by the *hand of D.*   2Sa 21:22;
1Ch 20:8

HOUSE OF DAVID

Jonathan made covenant with   1Sa 20:16
house of D.
war between *house of* Saul   2Sa 3:1;
and *D.*   3:6
let *house of* servant *D.* be   2Sa 7:26
established
Israel rebelled against the   1Ki 12:19;
house of D. unto this day   2Ch 10:19
none followed *house of D.*   1Ki 12:20
but Judah
shall kingdom return to *house*   1Ki 12:26
of D.
child be born to *house of D.*   1Ki 13:2
Josiah
rent kingdom from *house*   1Ki 14:8;
of D.   2Ki 17:21
Lord would not destroy   2Ch 21:7
house of D.
the thrones of the *house of*   Ps 122:5
D.
it was told *house of D.*   Isa 7:2
hear ye now, O *house of D.*   Isa 7:13;
Jer 21:12
key of *house of D.* lay on   Isa 22:22
his shoulders
glory of *house of D.* do not   Zec 12:7
magnify
feeble as David and the *house*   Zec 12:8
of D. as God
pour on *house of D.* the   Zec 12:10
spirit of grace
family of *house of D.*   Zec 12:12
mourn apart
shall be a fountain opened   Zec 13:1
to *house of D.*
whose name was Joseph, of   Lu 1:27
house of D.
raised up horn of salvation   Lu 1:69
in *house of D.*
he was of *house* and lineage   Lu 2:4
of D.

DAVID with KING

is not this *D. king* of land   1Sa 21:11
they anointed *D. king* over   2Sa 2:4
Judah
time *D.* was *king* in Hebron   2Sa 2:11
over Judah
king D. himself followed the   2Sa 3:31
bier
king D. made league with   2Sa 5:3;
them, they anointed *D. king*   1Ch 11:3;
12:31, 38
king D. did dedicate   2Sa 8:11;
1Ch 6:26
lifted up hand against *king,*   2Sa 20:21
even *D.*
greater than throne of *king*   1Ki 1:37
D.
king's servants came to bless   1Ki 1:47
king D.
D. the *king* rejoiced with   1Ch 29:9
great joy
who hath given to *D.* the *king*   2Ch 2:12
ordained by *D. king* of   2Ch 29:27;
Israel   Ezr 3:10
shall serve Lord and *D.* their   Jer 30:9
king
shall seek Lord and *D.* their   Ho 3:5
king
Jesse begat *D.* the *king,* and   M't 1:6
D. the *king*
he raised up *D.* to be   Ac 13:22
their *king*

SERVANT DAVID

by hand of my *servant D.* I   2Sa 3:18
will have
go and tell my *servant D.*   2Sa 7:5; 7:8
house of *servant D.* be   2Sa 7:26;
established   1Ch 17:24
hast shewed *servant D.* great   1Ki 3:6
mercy

kept with thy *servant D.*   1Ki 8:24
thou promisedest
keep with thy *servant D.*   1Ki 8:25;
8:26; 2Ch 6:16
for goodness he had done   1Ki 8:66
for *D.* his *servant*
for *D.* my *servant's* sake   1Ki 11:13;
11:32, 34; Ps 132:10; Isa 37:35
that *D.* my *servant* may   1Ki 11:36
have a light
to keep my statutes, as my   1Ki 11:38;
servant   14:8
remember mercies of *D.* thy   2Ch 6:42
servant
chose *D.* also his *servant*   Ps 78:70
and took him
I have sworn unto *D.* my   Ps 89:3
servant
found *D.* my *servant,* I   Ps 89:20
anointed him
who delivered *D.* his   Ps 144:10
servant
my covenant broken with *D.*   Jer 33:21
my *servant*
I will multiply seed of *D.*   Jer 33:22
my *servant*
then will I cast away seed of   Jer 33:26
D. my *servant*
even my *servant D.* shall   Eze 34:23
feed them
my *servant D.* be prince   Eze 34:24
among them
D. my *servant* shall be king   Eze 37:24
over them
my *servant D.* be their   Eze 37:25
prince for ever
horn of salvation in house of   Lu 1:69
his *servant D.*
who by mouth of thy   Ac 4:25
servant D.

DAVID in Psalm titles

A Psalm of D.   Ps 3;
4-9, 11-32, 34-41, 51-65, 68-70, 86, 101,
103, 108-110, 122, 124, 131, 133, 138-144

DAVID mentioned in Psalms

18:50; 72:20; 79:70; 89:3, 20, 35, 49;
122:5; 132:1, 11, 17; 144:10

DAVID'S

became *D.* enemy   1Sa 18:29
continually
sent messengers unto *D.*   1Sa 19:11
house
Michal *D.* wife told him,   1Sa 19:11
saying,
require it at the hand of *D.*   1Sa 20:16
enemies
side, and *D.* place was   1Sa 20:25
empty
month, that *D.* place was   1Sa 20:27
empty
And *D.* men said unto him,   1Sa 23:3
Behold
afterward, that *D.* heart   1Sa 24:5
smote him
when *D.* young men came   1Sa 25:9
So *D.* young men turned   1Sa 25:12
their way
D. wife, to Phalti the son   1Sa 25:44
of Laish
Saul knew *D.* voice, and   1Sa 26:17
said, Is
D. two wives were taken   1Sa 30:5
captives
cattle, and said, This is *D.*   1Sa 30:20
spoil
lacked of *D.* servants,   2Sa 2:30
nineteen
sixth, Ithream, by Eglah *D.*   2Sa 3:5
wife
the blind that are hated of *D.*   2Sa 5:8
soul
the Moabites became *D.*   2Sa 8:2
servants
they of Edom became *D.*   2Sa 8:14
servants
D. sons were chief rulers   2Sa 8:18
D. servants came into the   2Sa 10:2
land of
D. servants, and shaved off   2Sa 10:4
the one
D. anger was greatly kindled   2Sa 12:5
stones: and it was set on *D.*   2Sa 12:30
head

son of Shimeah *D.* brother   2Sa 13:3
of Shimeah *D.* brother,   2Sa 13:32
answered
the Gilonite. *D.* counseller   2Sa 15:12
So Hushai *D.* friend came   2Sa 15:37
into the
Hushai the Archite, *D.*   2Sa 16:16
friend
all *D.* men with him, over   2Sa 19:41
Jordan
D. heart smote him after   2Sa 24:10
that he
unto the prophet Gad, *D.*   2Sa 24:11
seer
Solomon to ride upon king   1Ki 1:38
D. mule
one tribe for my servant *D.*   1Ki 11:32
sake
for *D.* sake did the Lord his   1Ki 15:4
God
give king *D.* spears and   2Ki 11:10
shields
sake, and for my servant *D.*   2Ki 19:34;
sake   2Ki 20:6
the Moabites became *D.*   1Ch 18:2
servants
the Syrians became *D.* servants 1Ch 18:6
the Edomites became *D.*   1Ch 18:13
servants
Wherefore Hanun took *D.*   1Ch 19:4
servants
in it: and it was set upon   1Ch 20:2
D. head
of Shimea *D.* brother slew him 1Ch 20:7
the Lord spake unto Gad,   1Ch 21:9
D. seer
the substance which was king 1Ch 27:31
D.
D. uncle was a counseller   1Ch 27:32
and shields, that had been   2Ch 23:9
king *D.*
For thy servant *D.* sake   Ps 132:10
turn not
D. Psalm of Praise   Ps 145 title
sake, and for my servant   Isa 37:35
D. sake
kings that sit upon *D.*   Jer 13:13
throne
say they that Christ is *D.*   Lu 20:41
son

DAWDLING

something of *d.* (B)   2Pe 3:9

DAWN

about *d.* (A)(B)(R)(S)   J'g 19:25
the *d.* of life (A)(B)(E)(R)   Ec 11:10
began to *d.* toward the first   M't 28:1
day
until the day *d.* and the day   2Pe 1:19
star

DAWNED

it *d.* upon Eli (B)   1Sa 3:8

DAWNING

rose early about the *d.* of the   Jos 6:15
day
at *d.* of the day (E)   J'g 19:25
the woman in the *d.* of the   J'g 19:26
day
neither let it see the *d.* of the   Job 3:9
day
to and fro unto the *d.* of the   Job 7:4
day
prevented the *d.* of the   Ps 119:147
morning

DAY

God called light *d.* and   Ge 1:5
darkness night
on the first *d.* of the month   Ge 8:5
the next *d.* (S)   Ge 19:34;
Ex 9:6; 32:6; Le 7:16; 19:6; 22:30;
23:11, 15-16; 32:6; Nu 16:41; 17:8;
22:41; 33:3; Jos 5:11-12; J'g 6:38; 9:42;
21:4; 1Sa 5:3; 11:11; 20:27; 31:8;
2Ki 8:15; 1Ch 10:8; Es 2:14; Jer 20:3;
M't 11:12; Lu 10:35; Ac 4:5; 10:9, 23,
34; 20:7; 22:30; 23:32; 25:17, 23;
Jas 4:14
he said, Let me go, for the   Ge 32:26
d. breaketh

if he continue a *d.* or two, *Ex 21:21* he shall
journeyed not, till the *d.* it *Ex 40:37* was taken up
feasts of Lord, every thing *Le 23:37* upon his *d.*
on the *d.* I smote the firstborn *Nu 3:13* in Egypt
each prince shall offer *Nu 7:11* offering on his *d.*
each *d.* for a year shall bear *Nu 14:34* iniquities
if husband disallow her on *Nu 30:8;* the *d.* *30:12*
d. thou stoodest before Lord *De 4:10* in Horeb
saw no manner of similitude *De 4:15* on the *d.*
from *d.* thou didst depart out *De 9:7* of Egypt
have been rebellious from *d.* I *De 9:24* knew you
at his *d.* thou shalt give him *De 24:15* his hire
till *d.* I bid you shout, then *Jos 6:10* shout
on the *d.* we came forth to *Jos 9:12* go to you
sun hasted not down about *Jos 10:13* whole *d.*
was no *d.* like that before *Jos 10:14* or after it
when it is *d.* we shall kill *J'g 16:2* Samson
from *d.* that Israel came out *J'g 16:30* of Egypt
what *d.* thou buyest field of *Ru 4:5* Naomi
Lord told Samuel a *d.* before *1Sa 9:15*
behold the *d.* of which the *1Sa 24:4* Lord said
smite him, or his *d.* shall *1Sa 26:10* come to die
while it was yet *d.* *2Sa 3:35; Jer 15:9*
from the *d.* he forced his *2Sa 13:32* sister Tamar
from the *d.* the king *2Sa 19:24* departed, till *d.*
that on the *d.* thou goest *1Ki 2:37;* out *2:42*
till the *d.* that Lord sendeth *1Ki 17:14* rain
it fell on *d.* Elisha passed *2Ki 4:8;* *4:11, 18*
month, in the tenth *d.* of the *2Ki 25:1* month
the feast *d.* (S) *1Ch 29:21*
will they make an end in a *d.* *Ne 4:2*
in night a guard, and labour *Ne 4:22* on *d.*
and made it a *d.* of feasting *Es 9:17;* *9:18-19*
feasted in their houses, every *Job 1:4* one his *d.*
there was a *d.* when the sons *Job 1:6;* of God *1:13; 2:1*
let the *d.* perish wherein I *Job 3:3* was born
rest, till he shall accomplish *Job 14:6* his *d.*
they shall be astonied at his *Job 18:20* *d.*
he shall stand at latter *d.* *Job 19:25* upon the earth
wicked is reserved to *d.* of *Job 21:30* destruction
d. unto *d.* uttereth speech, *Ps 19:2* and night
for he seeth that his *d.* is *Ps 37:13* coming
nor remembered *d.* when he *Ps 78:42* delivered
d. in thy courts is better *Ps 84:10* than a thousand
seven times a *d.* do I *Ps 119:164* praise thee
shineth more and more to *Pr 4:18* perfect *d.*
he will come home at the *d.* *Pr 7:20* appointed
knowest not what a *d.* may *Pr 27:1* bring forth
till *d.* break, and shadows flee *Ca 2:17;* *4:6*
from the *d.* that Ephraim *Isa 7:17* departed
yea, before the *d.* was, I am *Isa 43:13* he
a *d.* for man to afflict soul? *Isa 58:5* an acceptable *d.* to Lord

the *d.* of vengeance of our *Isa 61:2;* God *63:4*
prepare them for the *d.* of *Jer 12:3* slaughter
there shall they be till I *d.* *Jer 27:22* visit them
from *d.* they built it, even *Jer 32:31* to this *d.*
from *d.* I spake to thee, even *Jer 36:2* to *d.*
till the *d.* that Jerusalem *Jer 38:28* was taken
the ninth *d.* of the month, *Jer 39:2* the city was
because of the *d.* that cometh *Jer 47:4* to spoil
woe unto them, for their *d.* *Jer 50:27* is come
appointed thee each *d.* for a *Eze 4:6* year
behold the *d.* it is come, the *Eze 7:10* morning
wicked prince, whose *d.* is *Eze 21:25;* come *21:29*
from the *d.* that thou wast *Eze 28:15* created
at Tehaphnehes also the *d.* *Eze 30:18* shall be darkened
maketh petition three times *Da 6:10;* a *d.* *6:13*
what will ye do in the solemn *Ho 9:5* *d.*
a *d.* of darkness and of *Joe 2:2* gloominess
seek him that maketh *d.* dark *Am 5:8*
I will make end thereof a *Am 8:10* bitter *d.*
the *d.* shall be dark over *Mic 3:6* them
d. of thy watchmen, and *Mic 7:4* visitation
before the decree, the *d.* pass *Zep 2:2* as chaff
till the *d.* that I rise up to *Zep 3:8* the prey
who hath despised *d.* of *Zec 4:10* small things
who may abide the *d.* of his *Mal 3:2* coming
d. cometh that shall burn as *Mal 4:1* an oven
d. Noe entered into ark *M't 24:38;* *Lu 17:27*
in a *d.* looketh not for him *M't 24:50;* *Lu 12:46*
ye neither know the *d.* nor *M't 25:13* the hour
rising up great while before *M'k 1:35* *d.*
dumb till *d.* these things be *Lu 1:20* performed
child grew till *d.* of shewing *Lu 1:80* unto Israel
trespass seven times in a *d.* *Lu 17:4* and turn again
so shall also Son of man *Lu 17:24* be in his *d.*
but should raise it again at last *Joh 6:39* *d.*
I will raise him up at last *Joh 6:40;* *d.* *6:44, 54*
your father Abraham *Joh 8:56* rejoiced to see my *d.*
must work work of him *Joh 9:4* while it is *d.*
until *d.* in which he was *Ac 1:2* taken up
on set *d.* Herod sat upon his *Ac 12:21* throne
when it was *d.* *Ac 16:35; 23:12; 27:39*
he hath appointed a *d.* in *Ac 17:31* which
cast four anchors, and *Ac 27:29* wished for *d.*
treasurest wrath against *d.* of *Ro 2:5* wrath
d. is at hand, let us cast off *Ro 13:12* works
he that regardeth a *d.* *Ro 14:6* regardeth it to Lord
the *d.* shall declare it *1Co 3:13*
behold, now is the *d.* of *2Co 6:2* salvation
ye are sealed to the *d.* of *Eph 4:30* redemption
will perform it until *d.* of *Ph'p 1:6* Jesus Christ
a feast *d.* (S) *Col 2:16*
ye are all the children of the *1Th 5:5* *d.*

let us who are of *d.* be sober, *1Th 5:8* putting on
again he limiteth a certain *d.* *Heb 4:7*
would he not afterward *Heb 4:8* spoken of another *d.*
more as ye see the *d.* *Heb 10:25* approaching
till the *d.* dawn, and day star *2Pe 1:19* arise
hasting to coming of the *d.* *2Pe 3:12* of God
were prepared for an hour *Re 9:15* and a *d.*

ALL THE DAY

teach me, on thee do I wait *Ps 25:5* all the *d.*
mouth shew forth thy *Ps 71:15* salvation all the *d.*
in thy name shall they *Ps 89:16* rejoice all the *d.*
mine enemies reproach me *Ps 102:8* all the *d.*
thy law is my meditation *Ps 119:97* all the *d.*
ploughman plough all the *d.* *Isa 28:24* to sow
I have spread out my hands *Isa 65:2* all the *d.*
these are smoke, a fire that *Isa 65:5* burneth all the *d.*
made me desolate and faint *La 1:13* all the *d.*
he turneth his hand against *La 3:3* me all the *d.*
I was a derision to my people *La 3:14* all the *d.*
heard their device against me *La 3:62* all the *d.*
why stand ye here all the *d.* *M't 20:6* idle

ALL THE DAY LONG

fail with longing for them *De 28:32* all the *d.* long
Lord shall cover him all the *De 33:12* *d.* long
through my roaring all the *d.* *Ps 32:3* long
shall speak of thy praise all *Ps 35:28* the *d.* long
troubled, I go mourning all *Ps 38:6* the *d.* long
they imagine deceits all the *Ps 38:12* *d.* long
in God we boast all the *d.* *Ps 44:8* long
for thy sake we are killed all *Ps 44:22* the *d.* long
talk of thy righteousness all *Ps 71:24* the *d.* long
for all the *d.* long have I *Ps 73:14* been plagued
he coveteth greedily all the *Pr 21:26* *d.* long
be in fear of the Lord all *Pr 23:17* the *d.* long
all the *d.* long I stretched *Ro 10:21* forth hands

BY DAY, DAY BY DAY

as she spake to Joseph *d.* by *Ge 39:10* *d.*
the Lord went before them *Ex 13:21* by *d.*
took not away pillar of *Ex 13:22* cloud by *d.*
offer two lambs *d.* by *d.* *Ex 29:38* continually
cloud by *d.* fire by night *Ex 40:38;* *Nu 9:16*
cloud of the Lord was on *Nu 10:34;* them by *d.* *14:14; De 1:33; Ne 9:19*
because he could not do it by *J'g 6:27* *d.*
nor birds of air to rest on *1Sa 21:10* them by *d.*
d. by *d.* there came to help *1Ch 12:22* David
by reason of the sickness *d.* *2Ch 21:15* by *d.*
they did *d.* by *d.* and *2Ch 24:11* gathered money
the priests praised the Lord *2Ch 30:21* *d.* by *d.*
let it be given *d.* by *d.* *Ezr 6:9* without fail

d. by d. he read in the law   *Ne 8:18*
of God
nor the arrow that flieth *by d.*   *Ps 91:5*
the sun shall not smite thee   *Ps 121:6*
by d.
sun to rule *by d.* for his   *Ps 136:8*
mercy endureth
sun shall be no more thy   *Isa 60:19*
light *by d.*
who giveth sun for a light   *Jer 31:35*
by d.
and remove *by d.* in their   *Eze 12:3*
sight
did so, I brought forth my   *Eze 12:7*
stuff *by d.*
give us *d. by d.* our daily   *Lu 11:3*
bread
the inward man is renewed   *2Co 4:16*
d. by d.
gates of it shall not be shut   *Re 21:25*
by d.

EVERY DAY

go out gather a certain rate   *Ex 16:4*
every d.
thou shalt offer a bullock   *Ex 29:36*
every d.
and Saul sought David   *1Sa 23:14*
every d.
David mourned for his son   *2Sa 13:37*
every d.
given him a daily rate for   *2Ki 25:30*
every d.
even after a certain rate   *2Ch 8:13*
every d.
as duty of *every d.* required   *2Ch 8:14;*
                                  Ezr 3:4
portion for singers, due for   *Ne 11:23*
every d.
the porters *every d.* his   *Ne 12:47*
portion
Mordecai walked *every d.*   *Es 2:11*
before court
God is angry with wicked   *Ps 7:11*
every d.
every d. wrest my words, their   *Ps 56:5*
thoughts
every d. will I bless thee and   *Ps 145:2*
praise
hast feared continually *every   *Isa 51:13*
d.*
my name *every d.* is   *Isa 52:5*
blasphemed
seven days prepare *every d.*   *Eze 43:25*
a goat
rich man fared sumptuously   *Lu 16:19*
every d.
another esteemeth *every d.*   *Ro 14:5*
alike

FEAST DAY

blow trumpet on our solemn   *Ps 81:3*
feast d.
said, Not on *feast d.*   *M't 26:5;*
                          M'k 14:2
in *feast d.* many believed in   *Joh 2:23*
his name

FIRST DAY

evening and morning were *first*   *Ge 1:5*
d.
first d. of month mountains   *Ge 8:5;*
were seen   *8:13; Ex 40:2, 17; Le 23:24*
first d. put away leaven,   *Ex 12:15*
whoso eateth from *first d.* to
first d. shall be an holy   *Ex 12:16;*
convocation   *Le 23:7, 35; Nu 28:18;*
                                  29:1
on the *first d.* shall be a   *Le 23:39*
sabbath
take on *first d.* boughs of   *Le 23:40*
goodly trees
Lord spake to Moses on *first   *Nu 1:1*
d.*
assembled congregation on   *Nu 1:18*
the *first d.*
on *first d.* Aaron went up to   *Nu 33:38*
mount Hor
flesh sacrificed *first d.* not   *De 16:4*
remain
began of *first d.* to sanctify   *2Ch 29:17*
from the *first d.* began they to   *Ezr 3:6*
offer
first d. began he to go up   *Ezr 7:9*
from Babylon and on *first d.*
came he to Jerusalem

sat down on *first d.* of the   *Ezr 10:16*
tenth month
first d. of first month they   *Ezr 10:17*
made an end
Ezra brought law on *first d.*   *Neh 8:2*
of month
first unto last *d.* read law of   *Neh 8:18*
God
first d. the word of the   *Eze 26:1;*
Lord came   *29:17; 31:1; 32:1; Hag 1:1*
in *first d.* of month offer a   *Eze 45:18*
bullock
from *first d.* thou didst set   *Da 10:12*
heart
first d. of unleavened bread   *M't 26:17;*
                                  14:12
from *first d.* I came into   *Ac 20:18*
Asia
fellowship from *first d.* till   *Ph'p 1:5*
now

SECOND DAY

evening and morning were   *Ge 1:8*
second d.
when he went out the *second*   *Ex 2:13*
d.
on *second d.* Nethaneel did   *Nu 7:18*
offer
on *second d.* offer twelve   *Nu 29:17*
young bullocks
second d. they compassed   *Jos 6:14*
city once
took Lachish on *second d.*   *Jos 10:32*
and smite it
Israel came against   *J'g 20:24*
Benjamin *second d.*
Jonathan did eat no meat   *1Sa 20:34*
second d.
began to build *second d.* of   *2Ch 3:2*
month
on *second d.* were gathered   *Ne 8:13*
together
king said to Esther the *second   *Es 7:2*
d.*
second d. after he had slain   *Jer 41:4*
Gedaliah
on *second d.* thou shalt   *Eze 43:22*
offer a kid

THIRD DAY

evening and morning were   *Ge 1:13*
third d.
on *third d.* Abraham saw   *Ge 22:4*
place afar off
told Laban on *third d.*   *Ge 31:22*
Jacob was fled
on *third d.* when they were   *Ge 34:25*
sore
third d. for *third d.* Lord   *Ex 19:11;*
will come   *19:15*
third d. shall be burnt with   *Le 7:17;*
fire   *19:6*
purify himself on *third d.*   *Nu 19:12;*
                                  31:19
clean person sprinkle   *Nu 19:19*
unclean on *third d.*
third d. eleven bullocks, two   *Nu 29:20*
rams
Israel came to their cities on   *Jos 9:17*
third d.
Israel went against Benjamin   *J'g 20:30*
third d.
came to Rehoboam *third d.*   *1Ki 12:12;*
                                  2Ch 10:12
third d. go up to house of   *2Ki 20:5*
Lord   *20:8*
house was finished on *third   *Ezr 6:15*
d.*
third d. Esther put on royal   *Es 5:1*
apparel
third d. he will raise us up   *Ho 6:2*
and live
raised again *third d.*   *M't 16:21;*
                          17:23; Lu 9:22
third d. rise again   *M't 20:19;*
    M'k 9:31; 10:34; Lu 18:33; 24:7, 46
sepulchre be made sure till   *M't 27:64*
third d.
the *third d.* I shall be   *Lu 13:32*
perfected
to-day is *third d.* since all   *Lu 24:21*
these things
third d. there was a marriage   *Joh 2:1*
in Cana
third d. cast out tackling of   *Ac 27:19*
ship
that he rose again the *third*   *1Co 15:4*
d.

FOURTH DAY

evening and morning were   *Ge 1:19*
fourth d.
fourth d. ten bullocks, two   *Nu 29:23*
rams
on the *fourth d.* they   *2Ch 20:26*
assembled
fourth d. was silver and gold   *Ezr 8:33*
weighed
word came to Zechariah on   *Zec 7:1*
fourth d.

FIFTH DAY

evening and morning were   *Ge 1:23*
fifth d.
fifth d. nine bullocks, two   *Nu 29:26*
rams
fifth d. of the month   *Eze 1:1; 1:2; 8:1*
fifth d. one came unto me,   *Eze 33:21*
saying

SIXTH DAY

evening and morning were   *Ge 1:31*
sixth d.
sixth d. gather twice as much   *Ex 16:5;*
                                  16:22
giveth on *sixth d.* bread of   *Ex 16:29*
two days
on the *sixth d.* Eliasaph   *Nu 7:42*
offered
on *sixth d.* eight bullocks,   *Nu 29:29*
two rams

SEVENTH DAY

on *seventh d.* God ended his   *Ge 2:2*
work
God blessed the *seventh d.*   *Ge 2:3;*
                          Ex 20:11
eat leaven from first day to   *Ex 12:15*
seventh d.
on the *seventh d.* shall be   *Ex 12:16;*
an holy convocation   *Le 23:8; Nu 28:25*
and in the *seventh d.* shall   *Ex 13:6*
be a feast
six days gather it, but the   *Ex 16:26;*
seventh d.   *20:10; Le 23:3; De 5:14*
is the sabbath
there went out some on the   *Ex 16:27*
seventh d.
no man go out of place on   *Ex 16:29*
seventh d.
on the *seventh d.* he called   *Ex 24:16*
unto Moses
on the *seventh d.* God   *Ex 31:17;*
rested   *Heb 4:4*
on *seventh d.* thou shalt rest   *Ex 34:21*
seventh d. there shall be a   *Ex 35:2*
holy *d.*
the priest shall look on him   *Le 13:5;*
the *seventh d.*   *13:6, 27, 32, 34, 51;*
                                  14:39
seventh d. he shall shave it   *Le 14:9;*
                                  Nu 6:9
on the *seventh d.* he shall   *Nu 19:12*
be clean
on *seventh d.* purify himself   *Nu 19:19;*
                                  31:19
wash your clothes on the   *Nu 31:24*
seventh d.
on *seventh d.* a solomn   *De 16:8*
assembly
seventh d. compass city seven   *Jos 6:4;*
times   *6:15*
seventh d. said to Samson's   *J'g 14:15*
wife
the *seventh d.* he told her   *J'g 14:17*
on the *seventh d.* the child   *2Sa 12:18*
died
on the *seventh d.* battle was   *1Ki 20:29*
joined
on *seventh d.* came   *2Ki 25:8*
Nebuzar-adan
on *seventh d.* when Ahasuerus   *Es 1:10*
was merry
in the *seventh d.* the word   *Eze 30:20*
came
so do the *seventh d.* of the   *Eze 45:20*
month
spake of *seventh d.* on this   *Heb 4:4*
wise, God did rest *seventh d.*
from all works

EIGHTH DAY

eighth d. thou shalt give it   *Ex 22:30*
me

on the *eighth d*. Moses called   *Le 9:1*
Aaron
eighth d. flesh of foreskin be   *Le 12:3*
circumcised
eighth d. he shall take two   *Le 14:10*
he lambs
two turtles on *eighth d*.   *Le 14:23;*
    Le 15:14; Nu 6:10
from the *eighth d*. it shall be   *Le 22:27*
accepted
eighth d. be an holy   *Le 23:36*
convocation
on the *eighth d*. shall be a   *Le 23:39*
sabbath
eighth d. ye shall have a   *Nu 29:35;*
solemn assembly   *2Ch 7:9; Ne 8:18*
eighth d. priests make burnt   *Eze 43:27*
offerings
eighth d. they came to   *Lu 1:59;*
circumcise the child   *Ac 7:8; Ph'p 3:5*

NINTH DAY

shall afflict your souls in   *Le 23:32*
ninth d.
ninth d. famine was sore   *2Ki 25:3;*
    Jer 52:6
ninth d. the city was broken   *Jer 39:2*
up

TENTH DAY

tenth d. of this month take a   *Ex 12:3*
lamb
on *tenth d*. of month ye   *Le 16:29;*
shall afflict your souls   *23:27; Nu 29:7*
tenth d. trumpet of jubilee   *Le 25:9*
shall sound
people came out of Jordan   *Jos 4:19*
on *tenth d*.
tenth d. Nebuchadnezzar   *2Ki 25:1;*
came against   *Jer 52:4; Eze 24:1*
Jerusalem
tenth d. Nebuchadnezzar   *Jer 52:12*
burnt house of Lord
tenth d. elders came to   *Eze 20:1*
inquire
tenth d. hand of the Lord   *Eze 40:1*
was upon

ELEVENTH DAY

eleventh d. Pagiel of Asher   *Nu 7:72*
offered

TWELFTH DAY

twelfth d. Ahira of Naphtali   *Nu 7:78*
offered
departed on *twelfth d*. to   *Ezr 8:31*
Jerusalem
twelfth d. word came to   *Eze 29:1*
Ezekiel

THIRTEENTH DAY

king's scribes called *thirteenth*   *Es 3:12*
d.
destroy all Jews *thirteenth d*.   *Es 3:13;*
    8:12; 9:1
thirteenth d. of month Adar   *Es 9:17*
rested
Jews at Shushan assembled   *Es 9:18*
thirteenth d.

FOURTEENTH DAY

keep the lamb till *fourteenth*   *Ex 12:6*
d.
on *fourteenth d*. eat   *Ex 12:18*
unleavened bread
fourteenth d. is Lord's   *Le 23:5;*
passover   *Nu 9:3, 5; 28:16; Jos 5:10;*
2Ch 30:15; 35:1; Ezr 6:19; Eze 45:21
fourteenth d. at even shall   *Nu 9:11*
eat it
Jews gathered together   *Es 9:15*
fourteenth d.
on *fourteenth d*. of same   *Es 9:17*
rested they
this is *fourteenth d*.   *Ac 27:33*
continued fasting

FIFTEENTH DAY

came to wilderness of Sinai on   *Ex 16:1*
fifteenth d.
on *fifteenth d*. is feast   *Le 23:6;*
    Nu 28:17
fifteenth d. of the seventh   *Le 23:34;*

month   *23:39; Nu 29:12; Eze 45:25*
departed from Rameses on   *Nu 33:3*
fifteenth d.
ordained a feast on   *1Ki 12:32;*
fifteenth d.   *12:33*
Jews on *fifteenth d*. rested   *Es 9:18;*
yearly   *9:21*
fifteenth d. word of Lord   *Eze 32:17*
came to Ezekiel

SIXTEENTH DAY

in *sixteenth d*. they made   *2Ch 29:17*
an end

SEVENTEENTH DAY

seventeenth d. fountains   *Ge 7:11*
broken up
ark rested *seventeenth d*. on   *Ge 8:4*
mount Ararat

TWENTIETH DAY

twentieth d. cloud was taken   *Nu 10:11*
up
twentieth d. people sat in   *Ezr 10:9*
streets

TWENTY-FIRST DAY

eat unleavened bread till   *Ex 12:18*
twenty-first d.
twenty-first d. came word to   *Hag 2:1*
Haggai

TWENTY-THIRD DAY

twenty-third d. Solomon sent   *2Ch 7:10*
people to tents
twenty-third d. written as   *Es 8:9*
Mordecai commanded

TWENTY-FOURTH DAY

on *twenty-fourth d*. Israel   *Ne 9:1*
assembled with fasting
on *twenty-fourth d*. I was by   *Da 10:4*
river Hiddekel
in *twenty-fourth d*. Lord   *Hag 1:15*
stirred up Zerubbabel
twenty-fourth d. word came   *Hag 2:10;*
to Haggai   *2:20*
consider from *twenty-fourth*   *Hag 2:18*
d. of ninth month
on *twenty-fourth d*. came   *Zec 1:7*
word to Zechariah

TWENTY-FIFTH DAY

wall was finished in   *Ne 6:15*
twenty-fifth d.
on *twenty-fifth d*. Evil-   *Jer 52:31*
merodach lifted head

TWENTY-SEVENTH DAY

twenty-seventh d. was the   *Ge 8:14*
earth dried
twenty-seventh d. Evil-   *2Ki 25:27*
merodach lifted head

GOOD DAY

we come in *good d*. give to   *1Sa 25:8*
David
Jews had gladness *good d*.   *Es 8:17;*
    9:19
was turned from mourning   *Es 9:22*
into a *good d*.

GREAT DAY

alas, that *d*. is *great*, none is   *Jer 30:7*
like it
for *great* shall be the *d*. of   *Ho 1:11*
Jezreel
d. of the Lord is *great* and   *Joe 2:11*
terrible
the *great* and terrible *d*. of   *Joe 2:31;*
Lord   *Ac 2:20*
the *great d*. of the Lord is   *Zep 1:14*
near
before coming of *great d*. of   *Mal 4:5*
Lord
that *great d*. of feast, Jesus   *Joh 7:37*
cried
reserved unto judgment of   *Jude 6*
great d.

for the *great d*. of his wrath   *Re 6:17*
is come
to gather to the battle of the   *Re 16:14*
great d.

IN THE DAY

in the d. the Lord made the   *Ge 2:4*
earth
in the d. thou eatest thou   *Ge 2:17*
shalt die
in the d. ye eat, your eyes   *Ge 3:5*
shall be opened
in the d. drought consumed   *Ge 31:40*
me
answered me *in the d*. of   *Ge 35:3*
my distress
nevertheless *in the d*. when I   *Ex 32:34*
visit
in the d. of his   *Le 6:5*
trespass offering
offer *in the d*. when he is   *Le 6:20;*
anointed   *7:36*
in the d. he presented them to   *Le 7:35*
minister
law of leper *in the d*. of   *Le 14:2;*
cleansing   *Nu 6:9*
also *in the d*. of the   *Nu 28:26*
firstfruits
if father disallow *in the d*. he   *Nu 30:5*
heareth
husband held peace *in the d*.   *Nu 30:7*
he heard
in the d. Lord delivered up   *Jos 10:12*
Amorites
as strong as I was *in the d*.   *Jos 14:11*
Moses sent
put hot bread *in the d*. it   *1Sa 21:6*
was taken away
in the d. Lord had delivered   *2Sa 22:1*
him
who cursed me *in the d*. I   *1Ki 2:8*
fled
in the d. wherein they sold   *Ne 13:15*
victuals
in the d. enemies of Jews hoped   *Es 9:1*
goods flow away *in the d*.   *Job 20:28*
of wrath
as *in the d*. of temptation   *Ps 95:8;*
    Heb 3:8
in the d. of trouble, *in the d*.   *Ps 102:2*
when
people be willing *in the d*. of   *Ps 110:3*
thy power
strike through kings *in the d*.   *Ps 110:5*
of wrath
remember Edom *in the d*. of   *Ps 137:7*
Jerusalem
in the d. when I cried, thou   *Ps 138:3*
answeredst
will not spare *in the d*. of   *Pr 6:34*
vengeance
riches profit not *in the d*. of   *Pr 11:4*
wrath
if thou faint *in the d*. of   *Pr 24:10*
adversity
in the d. of prosperity be   *Ec 7:14*
joyful, but *in the d*. of adversity
consider
neither hath he power *in the*   *Ec 8:8*
d. of death
in the d. when the keepers   *Ec 12:3*
shall tremble
in the d. of espousals, *in the*   *Ca 3:11*
d. of
in the d. when she shall be   *Ca 8:8*
spoken for
broken yoke as *in the d*. of   *Isa 9:4*
Midian
what will ye do *in the d*. of   *Isa 10:3*
visitation
in the d. came out of Egypt   *Isa 11:16;*
    Ho 2:15
shall remove *in the d*. of   *Isa 13:13*
fierce anger
in the d. make plant grow   *Isa 17:11*
in the d.
in the d. of great slaughter,   *Isa 30:25*
when hewers
in the d. that Lord bindeth   *Isa 30:26*
up breach
in the d. of your fast you   *Isa 58:3*
find pleasure
Lord, my refuge *in the d*. of   *Jer 16:19*
affliction
thou art my hope *in the d*.   *Jer 17:17*
of evil
shew back and not face *in*   *Jer 18:17*
the d. of calamity

his dead body be cast out in *Jer 36:30* the *d.*
afflicted me in the *d.* of fierce *La 1:12* anger
remembered not footstool in *La 2:1* the *d.* of anger
thou drewest near in the *d.* I *La 3:57* called
gold not deliver in the *d.* of *Eze 7:19* wrath
thy nativity in the *d.* thou *Eze 16:4;* wast born *16:5*
Sodom not mentioned in *Eze 16:56* the *d.* of pride
they shall fall in the *d.* of *Ex 27:27* thy ruin
great pain came as in the *d. Eze 30:9* of Egypt
every man for his life in *Eze 32:10* the *d.* of thy fall
in the *d.* turneth from · his *Eze 33:12* wickedness, not able to live in the *d.* he sinneth
lest I set her as in the *d.* she *Ho 2:3* was born
therefore shalt thou fall in the *Ho 4:5* *d.*
with tempest in the *d.* of *Am 1:14* whirlwind
I will darken the earth in the *Am 8:9* clear *d.*
in the *d.* thou stoodest on *Ob 11* other side
nor rejoiced in the *d.* of their *Ob 12* destruction
those of his that did remain in *Ob 14* the *d.* of distress
in the *d.* I shall do this, saith *Mal 4:3* Lord
in the *d.* when the Son is *Lu 17:30* revealed
if any walk in the *d.* he *Joh 11:9* stumbleth not
in *d.* God shall judge secrets of *Ro 2:16* men
let us walk honestly as in *Ro 13:13* the *d.*
be blameless in the *d.* of our *1Co 1:8* Lord
in the *d.* of salvation I *2Co 6:2* succoured thee
I may rejoice in the *d.* of *Ph'p 2:16* Christ
in the *d.* when I took them *Heb 8:9* by hand
glorify God in the *d.* of *1Pe 2:12* visitation

ONE DAY

deprived of you both in *one Ge 27:45* *d.*
not kill it and her young in *Le 22:28* one *d.*
shall not eat *one d.* or two *Nu 11:19* days
in *one d.* shall die both of *1Sa 2:34* them
I shall *one d.* perish by the *1Sa 27:1* hand of Saul
Solomon's provision for *one 1Ki 4:22* *d.* was
Israel slew Syrians 100,000 *1Ki 20:29* in *one d.*
Pekah slew Judah 120,000 in *2Ch 28:6* *one d.*
neither is this the work of *Ezr 10:13* *one d.*
kill children and women in *Es 3:13;* one *d.* *8:12*
Lord cut off branch and rush *Isa 9:14* in *one d.*
devour thorns and briers in *Isa 10:17* *one d.*
two things shall come to thee *Isa 47:9* in *one d.*
earth be made to bring forth *Isa 66:8* in *one d.*
remove the iniquity of land in *Zec 3:9* *one d.*
it shall be *one d.* which shall be *Zec 14:7* known
we abode with the brethren *Ac 21:7* one *d.*
and after *one d.* the south *Ac 28:13* wind blew
one esteemeth *one d.* above *Ro 14:5* another
fell in *one d.* twenty-three *1Co 10:8* thousand

one *d.* with Lord as a *2Pe 3:8* thousand years
therefore her plagues come in *Re 18:8* one *d.*

SABBATH DAY

seventh *d.* is the *sabbath Ex 16:26;* *20:10*
remember *sabbath d.* holy *Ex 20:8;* *De 5:12*
Lord blessed *sabbath d. Ex 20:11* hallowed it
whosoever doth any work on *Ex 31:15* *sabbath d.*
kindle no fire on the *sabbath Ex 35:3* *d.*
man gathered sticks on *Nu 15:32* *sabbath d.*
offer on *sabbath d.* two *Nu 28:9* lambs of first year
God commanded to keep *De 5:15* *sabbath d.*
if people sell victuals on *Ne 10:31* *sabbath d.*
burdens brought to Jerusalem *Ne 13:15* on *sabbath d.*
evil that ye do, and profane *Ne 13:17* *sabbath d.*
no burden be brought in on *Ne 13:19* *sabbath d.*
Levites keep gates to *Ne 13:22* sanctify *sabbath d.*
bear no burden on the *Jer 17:21* *sabbath d.*
nor carry forth a burden on *Jer 17:22* the *sabbath d.*
prince shall offer in the *Eze 46:4* *sabbath d.*
sabbath d. through corn *M't 12:1;* *M'k 2:23*
the Son of man is Lord of *M't 12:8* *sabbath d.*
if it fall into a pit on *M't 12:11;* *sabbath d.* *Lu 14:5*
pray your flight be not on *M't 24:20* *sabbath d.*
why do on *sabbath d.* that *M'k 2:24* is not lawful
whether he would heal on *M'k 3:2;* *sabbath d.* *Lu 6:7*
went into synagogue on the *M'k 6:2;* *sabbath d.* *Lu 4:16; Ac 13:14*
loosed from this bond on *Lu 13:16* *sabbath d.*
as he went to eat bread on *Lu 14:1* *sabbath d.*
prepared spices, and rested *Lu 23:56* *sabbath d.*
it is *sabbath d.:* it is not *Joh 5:10* lawful to carry
because he had done these *Joh 5:16* on *sabbath d.*
ye on the *sabbath d. Joh 7:22* circumcise a man
it was *sabbath d.* when Jesus *Joh 9:14* made clay
bodies not remain on cross *Joh 19:31* on *sabbath d.*
which are read every *Ac 13:27;* *sabbath d.* *15:21*
next *sabbath d.* came almost *Ac 13:44* whole city

SAME DAY

same d. were fountains *Ge 7:11* broken up
self *same d.* entered Noah *Ge 7:13* into ark
in *same d.* Lord made a *Ge 15:18* covenant
same d. I brought your *Ex 12:17;* armies *12:51*
flesh eaten *same d. Le 7:15;* *7:16; 19:6; 22:30*
ye shall eat no parched corn *Le 23:14* till *same d.*
shall do no work in that *Le 23:28* *same d.*
shall not be afflicted in that *Le 23:29* *same d.*
priest hallow his head that *Nu 6:11* *same d.*
Lord spake to Moses that *De 32:48* *same d.*
same d. king hallowed *1Ki 8:64* middle court
he gave a sign the *same d. 1Ki 13:3*

defiled my sanctuary, *same Eze 23:38* *d.*
write name of this *same Eze 24:2* king
same d. also will I punish *Zep 1:9* those
take of them, and come the *Zec 6:10* *same d.*
the *same d.* Lot went out of *Lu 17:29* Sodom
same d. Pilate and Herod *Lu 23:12* made friends
on the *same d.* was the *Joh 5:9* sabbath
same d. at evening Jesus *Joh 20:19* stood in midst
unto *same d.* that he was *Ac 1:22* taken up
same d. were added to church *Ac 2:41* 3,000 souls

SINCE THE DAY

since the *d.* they were on *Ex 10:6* earth
since the *d.* that God created *De 4:32* man
since the *d.* that I brought *1Sa 8:8;* them up *1Ki 8:16; 1Ch 17:5* out of Egypt
since the *d.* that she left the *2Ki 8:6* land
since the *d.* your fathers *Jer 7:25* came forth
as in you, since the *d.* ye *Col 1:6* heard of it
since the *d.* we heard it, do *Col 1:9* not cease to pray

THAT DAY

I will sever in *that d.* land of *Ex 8:22* Goshen
Lord brought east wind on *Ex 10:13* land all *that d.*
that d. thou seest my face, *Ex 10:28* thou shalt die
thou shalt shew thy son in *Ex 13:8* *that d.*
Lord saved Israel *that d. Ex 14:30* out of hand
there fell of the people *that Ex 32:28* *d.* 3,000
that d. shall priest make *Le 16:30* atonement
could not keep passover *that Nu 9:6* *d.*
because he held his peace in *Nu 30:14* *that d.*
children in *that d.* had no *De 1:39* knowledge
shalt in any wise bury him *De 21:23* *that d.*
I will surely hide my face in *De 31:18* *that d.*
only *that d.* they compassed *Jos 6:15* city
heardest in *that d.* how *Jos 14:12* Anakims were
Israel fasted *that d. J'g 20:26; 1Sa 7:6*
ye shall cry out in *that d. 1Sa 8:18* and the Lord will not hear you in *that d.*
so Saul did eat with Samuel *1Sa 9:24* *that d.*
all those signs came to pass *1Sa 10:9* *that d.*
the Lord sent thunder and *1Sa 12:18* rain *that d.*
so the Lord saved Israel *1Sa 14:23* *that d.*
Saul asked, He answered *1Sa 14:37* not *that d.*
Spirit of Lord came on David *1Ki 16:13* from *that d.*
Saul eyed David from *that d. 1Sa 18:9*
David was afraid of Lord *2Sa 6:9* *that d.*
so Uriah abode in *2Sa 11:12* Jerusalem *that d.*
cut off house of Jeroboam *1Ki 14:14* *that d.*
behold, thou shalt see on *2Ch 18:24* *that d.*
to *that d.* Israel had not done *Ne 8:17* so
they should be ready against *Es 3:14;* *that d.* *8:13*
let *that d.* be darkness, let not *Job 3:4*

in *that* very *d.* his thoughts   *Ps 146:4*
perish
Lord alone be exalted in   *Isa 2:11;*
that d.   *2:17*
as yet shall he remain at   *Isa 10:32*
Nob *that d.*
Egyptians know the Lord in   *Isa 19:21*
that d.
in *that d.* Lord shall punish   *Isa 24:21*
host
in *that d.* this song be sung   *Isa 26:1*
in Judah
in *that d.* shall the deaf   *Isa 29:18*
hear the words
they shall know in *that d.*   *Isa 52:6*
that I am he
they shall be accomplished   *Jer 39:16*
in *that d.*
but I will deliver thee in   *Jer 39:17*
that d. saith Lord
in *that d.* Israel shall be   *Eze 29:21*
exalted
in *that d.* there shall be   *Eze 38:19*
great shaking
know I am Lord from *that*   *Eze 39:22*
d. forward
name of city from *that d.*   *Eze 48:35*
shall be
in *that d.* will I make a   *Ho 2:18*
covenant
in *that d.* mountains drop   *Joe 3:18*
new wine
he shall flee away naked in   *Am 2:16*
that d.
songs of temple be howlings   *Am 8:3*
in *that d.*
shall I not in *that d.* destroy   *Ob 8*
wise men
that d. is a day of wrath of   *Zep 1:15*
trouble
nations be joined to Lord in   *Zec 2:11*
that d.
Lord their God shall save   *Zec 9:16*
them in *that d.*
my covenant it was broken   *Zec 11:11*
in *that d.*
the feeble at *that d.* shall be   *Zec 12:8*
as David
in *that d.* shall be a great   *Zec 12:11*
mourning
in *that d.* shall be a fountain   *Zec 13:1*
opened
his feet shall stand *that d.*   *Zec 14:4*
on the mount
in *that d.* shall be one Lord,   *Zec 14:9*
his name
in *that d.* when I make up   *Mal 3:17*
my jewels
many will say to me in *that*   *M't 7:22*
d. Lord
but of *that d.* knoweth no   *M't 24:36;*
man   *M'k 13:32*
till *that d.* I drink it new   *M't 26:29;*
  M'k 14:25
rejoice ye in *that d.* and leap   *Lu 6:23*
for joy
be more tolerable in *that d.*   *Lu 10:12*
for Sodom
so *that d.* come on you   *Lu 21:34*
unawares
that d. was the preparation   *Lu 23:54*
and sabbath
they came and abode with   *Joh 1:39*
him *that d.*
from *that d.* they took   *Joh 11:53*
counsel together
at *that d.* ye shall know I   *Joh 14:20*
am in the Father
and in *that d.* ye shall ask   *Joh 16:23*
me nothing
at *that d.* ye shall ask in   *Joh 16:26*
my name
that d. overtake you as a   *1Th 5:4*
thief
our testimony believed in   *2Th 1:10*
that d.
that d. shall not come, except   *2Th 2:3*
there come
committed to him against   *2Ti 1:12*
that d.
he may find mercy of Lord   *2Ti 1:18*
in *that d.*
crown the Lord shall give me   *2Ti 4:8*
at *that d.*

THIS DAY

hast driven me out *this d.*   *Ge 4:14*
from earth

pray thee send me good   *Ge 24:12*
speed *this d.*
he said, Sell me *this d.* thy   *Ge 25:31*
birthright
swear to me *this d.* and he   *Ge 25:33*
sware unto him
I do remember my faults *this*   *Ge 41:9*
d.
God who fed me all my life   *Ge 48:15*
to *this d.*
this d. shall be for a   *Ex 12:14*
memorial
observe *this d.* in your   *Ex 12:17*
generations
remember *this d.* in which ye   *Ex 13:3;*
came out   *13:4*
you are *this d.* as stars of   *De 1:10*
heaven
this d. will I begin to put   *De 2:25*
dread of thee
are alive every one of you   *De 4:4;*
this d.   *5:3*
seen *this d.* God doth talk   *De 5:24*
with man
as it is at *this d.*   *De 6:24;*
  De 8:18; Ezr 9:7
statutes I commanded *this d.*   *De 7:11;*
  4:40; 6:6; 8:1, 11; 10:13; 30:2, 8
I testify against you *this d.*   *De 8:19*
commandments I command   *De 11:8;*
this d.   *11:13, 27-28; 13:18; 15:5; 19:9;*
  27:1, 4
statutes which I set before   *De 11:32*
you *this d.*
not do after all things ye do   *De 12:8*
here *this d.*
avouched *this d.* Lord to be   *De 26:17*
thy God
this d. thou art become   *De 27:9*
people of Lord
not given you ears to hear to   *De 29:4*
this d.
ye stand *this d.* all of you   *De 29:10*
before Lord
whose heart turneth away   *De 29:18*
this d. from Lord
I set before thee *this d.* life   *De 30:15;*
and death   *30:19*
I command thee *this d.* to   *De 30:16*
love Lord
while I am yet alive with   *De 31:27*
you *this d.*
no man knoweth his   *De 34:6*
sepulchre to *this d.*
this d. will I begin to magnify   *Jos 3:7*
thee
twelve stones are there unto   *Jos 4:9*
this d.
the Lord shall trouble thee   *Jos 7:25*
this d.
now I am *this d.* eighty-five   *Jos 14:10*
years old
I am as strong *this d.* as   *Jos 14:11*
when Moses sent
to turn away *this d.* from   *Jos 22:16*
following Lord
from which we are not   *Jos 22:17*
cleansed till *this d.*
if it be in rebellion, save us   *Jos 22:22*
not *this d.*
cleave to Lord as done   *Jos 23:8*
unto *this d.*
choose you *this d.* whom ye   *Jos 24:15*
will serve
Luz is the name unto *this d.*   *J'g 1:26*
deliver us only, we pray   *J'g 10:15*
thee, *this d.*
since Israel came out of   *J'g 19:30;*
Egypt to *this d.*   *1Sa 8:8; 2Sa 7:6;*
  2Ki 21:15; 1Ch 17:5; Jer 7:25
Boaz said, Ye are witnesses   *Ru 4:9;*
this d.   *4:10*
ye have *this d.* rejected God   *1Sa 10:10*
shall not man be put to   *1Sa 11:13*
death *this d.*
Jonathan hath wrought with   *1Sa 14:45*
God *this d.*
Lord rent kingdom from   *1Sa 15:28*
thee *this d.*
I defy the armies of Israel   *1Sa 17:10*
this d.
thou shalt *this d.* be my   *1Sa 18:21*
son-in-law
though it were sanctified *this*   *1Sa 21:5*
d. in
servant lie in wait as at *this*   *1Sa 22:8;*
d.   *22:13*
Lord which sent thee *this d.*   *1Sa 25:32*
to meet me

kept *this d.* from coming to   *1Sa 25:33*
shed blood
soul precious in thine eyes   *1Sa 26:21*
this d.
as thy life was much set by   *1Sa 26:24*
this d.
made an ordinance for   *1Sa 30:25*
israel to *this d.*
I am *this d.* weak, though   *2Sa 3:39*
anointed king
Beerothites were sojourners   *2Sa 4:3*
unto *this d.*
keep his commands as at   *1Ki 8:61*
this d.
this d. is a day of good   *2Ki 7:9*
tidings
unto *this d.* do after   *2Ki 17:34;*
former manners   *17:41*
there it is unto *this d.*   *2Ch 5:9*
I come not against thee   *2Ch 35:21*
this d. but against
behold, we are servants *this*   *Ne 9:36*
d.
Lord said, Thou art my Son,   *Ps 2:7;*
this d. have   *Ac 13:33; Heb 1:5*
I begotten thee
this is the *d.* which Lord   *Ps 118:24*
hath made
they continue *this d.*   *Ps 119:91*
according to thy
this d. have I paid my vows   *Pr 7:14*
I have made known to thee   *Pr 22:19*
this d.
living praise thee, as I do   *Isa 38:19*
this d.
to-morrow shall be as *this*   *Isa 56:12*
d.
hissing and a curse, as at   *Jer 25:18;*
this d.   *44:22*
to *this d.* they drink none   *Jer 35:14*
from the days of Josiah even   *Jer 36:2*
to *this d.*
they are not humbled even   *Jer 44:10*
unto *this d.*
this is the *d.* that we looked   *La 2:16*
for
this is the *d.* whereof I have   *Eze 39:8*
spoken
to us confusion of faces, as at   *Da 9:7*
this d.
consider from *this d.* and   *Hag 2:15;*
forward   *2:18*
from *this d.* will I bless you   *Hag 2:19*
give us *this d.* our daily   *M't 6:11*
bread
Sodom would have   *M't 11:23*
remained to *this d.*
was called the field of blood   *M't 27:8*
to *this d.*
suffered many things *this d.*   *M't 27:19*
in a dream
is reported among Jews to   *M't 28:15*
this d.
for to you is born *this d.*   *Lu 2:11*
a Saviour
this d. is this scripture   *Lu 4:21*
fulfilled
this d. is salvation come to   *Lu 19:9*
this house
if thou hadst known, at least   *Lu 19:42*
in *this d.*
cock not crow *this d.* before   *Lu 22:34*
thou deny
his sepulchre is with us to   *Ac 2:29*
this d.
zealous toward God, as ye   *Ac 22:3*
are all *this d.*
in good conscience before   *Ac 23:1*
God till *this d.*
I am called in question by   *Ac 24:21*
you *this d.*
continue to *this d.*   *Ac 26:22*
witnessing to small
would all that hear me *this*   *Ac 26:29*
d. were as I am
that they should not hear   *Ro 11:8*
unto *this d.*
till *this d.* remaineth the   *2Co 3:14;*
veil   *3:15*

TO DAY

neither yet heard I of it but   *Ge 21:26*
to *d.*
I will pass through all thy   *Ge 30:32*
flock to *d.*
wherefore look ye so sadly *to*   *Ge 40:7*
d.
how is it ye are come so   *Ex 2:18*
soon *to d.*

salvation which he will shew *Ex 14:13*
you *to d.*
bake that which you will *Ex 16:23*
bake *to d.*
consecrate yourselves *to d.* *Ex 32:29*
to Lord
for *to d.* Lord will appear to *Le 9:4*
you
I commanded thee this thing *De 15:15*
to d.
may establish thee *to d.* for *De 29:13*
a people
wherefore hath Lord smitten *1Sa 4:3*
us *to d.*
to d. Lord wrought *1Sa 11:13*
salvation in Israel
Lord delivered thee *to d.* *1Sa 24:10;*
into my hand *26:23*
how glorious was the king *to 2Sa 6:20*
d.
why art thou lean from day *2Sa 13:4*
to d.
to d. shall the house of *2Sa 16:3*
Israel restore me
I will shew myself to him *1Ki 18:15*
to d.
inquire at word of Lord *to 1Ki 22:5;*
d. *2Ch 18:4*
wherefore wilt thou go to *2Ki 4:23*
him *to d.*
give thy son that we may eat *2Ki 6:28*
him *to d.*
shew forth *to d.* *1Ch 16:23;*
his salvation *Ps 96:2*
they cast the lot from day *to Es 3:7*
d.
even *to d.* is my complaint *Job 23:2*
bitter
to d. if ye will hear *Ps 95:7;*
Heb 3:7, 15; 4:7
to d. do I declare, that I will *Zec 9:12*
render
grass *to d.* is, and *M't 6:30;*
to-morrow *Lu 12:28*
son, go work *to d.* in my *M't 21:28*
vineyard
we have seen strange things *Lu 5:26*
to d.
I do cures *to d.* and *Lu 13:32*
to-morrow
I must walk *to d.* and the *Lu 13:33*
day following
for *to d.* I must abide at thy *Lu 19:5*
house
to d. shalt thou be with me *Lu 23:43*
in paradise
besides all this, *to d.* is the *Lu 24:21*
third day
exhort daily, while it is *Heb 3:13*
called *to d.*
thou art my Son, *to d.* have *Heb 5:5*
I begotten thee
Christ, same yesterday *to d.* *Heb 13:8*
and for ever
say, *to d.* or to-morrow, we *Jas 4:13*
will go
Lot vexed righteous soul from *2Pe 2:8*
day *to d.*

DAY *OF DEATH*

I am old, I know not *d.* of *Ge 27:2*
death
child be a Nazarite *to d.* of *J'g 13:7*
death
Samuel came not to see Saul *1Sa 15:35*
till *d.* of death
Michal had no child till *d.* *2Sa 6:23*
of death
concubines were shut up to *2Sa 20:3*
d. of death
leper *to d.* of death *2Ki 15:5;*
2Ch 26:21
d. of death better than day of *Ec 7:1*
birth
neither hath he power in the *Ec 8:8*
d. of death
put him in prison till *d.* of *Jer 52:11*
death
every day a portion, till *d.* *Jer 52:34*
of death

DAY *OF JUDGMENT*

be more tolerable for *M't 10:15;*
Sodom in the *11:24; M'k 6:11*
d. of judgment
more tolerable for Tyre and *M't 11:22*
Sidon at *d. of judgment*

give account thereof in *d.* *M't 12:36*
of judgment
to reserve unjust to *d.* of *2Pe 2:9*
judgment
reserved unto fire against *d.* *2Pe 3:7*
of judgment
may have boldness in *d.* of *1Jo 4:17*
judgment

DAY *OF THE LORD*

d. of the Lord be on every *Isa 2:12*
one proud
d. of the Lord is at hand *Isa 13:6;*
Joe 1:15; Zep 1:7
d. of the Lord cometh *Isa 13:9;*
Joe 2:1; Zec 14:1
for it is *d.* of the Lord's *Isa 34:8*
vengeance
this is the *d.* of the Lord *Jer 46:10*
God
stand in battle in *d.* of the *Eze 13:5*
Lord
d. of the Lord is near *Eze 30:3;*
Joe 3:14; Ob 15
woe to you that desire *d.* of *Am 5:18*
the Lord
in *d.* of the Lord's sacrifice I *Zep 1:8*
will punish
deliver them in *d.* of the *Zep 1:18*
Lord's wrath
before *d.* of the Lord's anger *Zep 2:2*
come on you
be hid in the *d.* of the Lord's *Zep 2:3*
anger
before coming of *d.* of the *Mal 4:5*
Lord
spirit be saved in *d.* of the *1Co 5:5*
Lord
ye are ours in *d.* of the *2Co 1:14*
Lord
d. of Lord cometh as thief *1Th 5:2;*
2Pe 3:10

DAY *with NIGHT*

lights to divide *d.* from the *Ge 1:14*
night
to rule over the *d.* and over *Ge 1:18*
the *night*
cold and heat, *d.* and night, *Ge 8:22*
shall not cease
I bare loss, stolen by *d.* or *Ge 31:39*
night
Lord brought east wind *d.* *Ex 10:13*
and *night*
to give them light to go by *Ex 13:21*
d. and *night*
abide at door of tabernacle *d.* *Le 8:35*
and *night*
people stood up that *d.* and *Nu 11:32*
all *night*
and thou shalt fear *d.* and *De 28:66*
night
meditate therein *d.* and night *Jos 1:8;*
Ps 1:2
lay naked all that *d.* and *1Sa 19:24*
night
eyes open to house *night* *1Ki 8:29;*
and *d.* *2Ch 6:20*
which I pray before thee *d.* *Ne 1:6*
and *night*
set watch against them *d.* and *Ne 4:9*
night
neither eat nor drink *night* or *Es 4:16*
d.
they change the *night* into *Job 17:12*
d.
till *d.* and *night* come to an *Job 26:10*
end
d. and *night* hand was heavy *Ps 32:4*
on me
my tears have been my meat *Ps 42:3*
d. and *night*
d. and *night* they go about it *Ps 55:10*
on walls
d. is thine, the *night* also is *Ps 74:16*
thine
I have cried *d.* and *night* *Ps 88:1*
before thee
but the *night* shineth as the *Ps 139:12*
d.
neither *d.* nor *night* see sleep *Ec 8:16*
smoke by *d.* flaming fire by *Isa 4:5*
night
I the Lord will keep it *d.* *Isa 27:3*
and *night*
it shall not be quenched *d.* *Isa 34:10*
nor *night*

with pining sickness from *d.* *Isa 38:12*
to *night*
d. to *night* wilt make an *Isa 38:13*
end of me
gates, they shall not be shut *Isa 60:11*
d. nor *night*
watchmen never hold peace *Isa 62:6*
d. nor *night*
I might weep *d.* and *night* for *Jer 9:1*
slain
eyes run down tears *d.* and *Jer 14:17;*
night *La 2:18*
there serve other gods *d.* *Jer 16:13*
and *night*
that there should not be *d.* *Jer 33:20*
nor *night*
day known not *d.* nor *night* *Zec 14:7*
and should sleep and rise *M'k 4:27*
night and *d.*
d. and *night* he was in the *M'k 5:5*
mountains
this *d.* this *night*, before *M'k 14:30*
cock crow
with fastings and prayers *Lu 2:37*
night and *d.*
his elect, which cry *d.* and *Lu 18:7*
night to him
watched gates *night* and *d.* to *Ac 9:24*
kill
cease not to warn *night* and *Ac 20:31*
d.
tribes serving God *d.* and *Ac 26:7*
night
thrice I suffered shipwreck, *2Co 11:25*
a *d.* and *night*
labouring *d.* and *night* because *1Th 2:9*
would
night and *d.* praying *1Th 3:10;*
exceedingly *1Ti 5:5*
wrought with labour *night* *2Th 3:8*
and *d.*
remembrance in prayers *night* *2Ti 1:3*
and *d.*
they rest not *d.* and *night* *Re 4:8*
serve him *d.* and *night* in his *Re 7:15*
temple
accused them before God *d.* *Re 12:10*
and *night*
they have no rest *d.* nor *night* *Re 14:11*
be tormented *d.* and *night* *Re 20:10*
for ever

DAY *OF TROUBLE*

this day is a *d.* of trouble *2Ki 19:3;*
Isa 37:3
Lord hear thee in the *d.* of *Ps 20:1*
trouble
call upon me in the *d.* of *Ps 50:15*
trouble
hast been my refuge in the *Ps 59:16*
d. of trouble
in the *d.* of *trouble* I sought *Ps 77:2*
the Lord
in the *d.* of trouble I will call *Ps 86:7*
on thee
it is a *d.* of *trouble*, and of *Isa 22:5*
treading
in *d.* of *trouble* they shall be *Jer 51:2*
against her
the time is come, *d.* of *Eze 7:7*
trouble is near
Lord is a strong hold in *d.* of *Na 1:7*
trouble
that I might rest in the *d.* *Hab 3:16*
of trouble
that day is a *d.* of trouble *Zep 1:15*
and distress

DAYBREAK

at *d.* they let her go (B) *J'g 19:25*

DAYSPRING

caused the *d.* to *Job 38:12*
know his place
whereby *d.* from on high *Lu 1:78*
visited us

DAY STAR

D. *Star*, son of Dawn *Isa 14:12*
(A)(E)(R)
and the *d. star* arise in your *2Pe 1:19*
hearts

DAYTIME

they meet with darkness in *Job 5:14*
d.

dig thro' houses marked in *Job 24:16*
d.
I cry in d., thou hearest *Ps 22:2*
not
Lord command *Ps 42:8*
lovingkindness in d.
in d. also led them with *Ps 78:14*
cloud
be a tabernacle for a shadow *Isa 4:6*
in d.
I stand on watchtower in *Isa 21:8*
d.
in d. he was teaching in *Lu 21:37*
temple
count it pleasure to riot in *2Pe 2:13*
d.

DAYS

after 150 d. the waters were *Ge 8:3*
abated
d. of mourning for my *Ge 27:41*
father are at hand
the d. of my pilgrimage are *Ge 47:9*
130 years
when the d. of his mourning *Ge 50:4*
were past
after the number of d. ye *Nu 14:34*
searched land
for ask now of d. that are *De 4:32*
past
I stayed in the mount forty *De 10:10*
d.
Samuel came not within d. *1Sa 13:11*
appointed
the d. were not expired *1Sa 18:26*
which hath been with me *1Sa 29:3*
these d.
the d. David reigned over *1Ki 2:11*
Israel
no house was built to Lord *1Ki 3:2*
till those d.
d. that Jeroboam reigned *1Ki 14:20*
were 22 years
war all their d. *1Ki 14:30;*
15:16, 32; 2Ki 13:3
to those d. Israel did burn *2Ki 18:4*
incense to it
from d. of judges, not such *2Ki 23:22*
passover
when David was old and *1Ch 23:1*
full of d.
our d. are on earth as a *1Ch 29:15;*
shadow *Job 8:9*
he died full of d. riches *1Ch 29:28*
and honour
Jehoiada was old and full *2Ch 24:15*
of d.
since d. Esar-haddon brought *Ezr 4:2*
us up
since d. of our fathers been in *Ezr 9:7*
trespass
I wept and mourned certain d. *Ne 1:4*
since d. of Jeshua, son of *Ne 8:17*
Nun
as the d. whereon the Jews *Es 9:22*
rested
they called these d. Purim, *Es 9:26*
after Pur
these d. should be *Es 9:28*
remembered and kept
let it not be joined to d. of *Job 3:6*
the year
are not his d. also like d. of *Job 7:1*
an hireling
in length of d. *Job 12:12*
understanding
they spend their d. in *Job 21:13*
wealth
d. of affliction have taken *Job 21:16*
hold on me
the d. of affliction prevented *Job 21:27*
me
d. should speak, years teach *Job 32:7*
wisdom
he shall return to the d. of *Job 33:25*
his youth
they shall spend their d. in *Job 36:11*
prosperity
so Job died, being old and *Job 42:17*
full of d.
thou gavest him length of d. *Ps 21:4*
for ever
Lord knoweth d. of the *Ps 37:18*
upright
told us what work thou didst *Ps 44:1*
in their d.
deceitful men not live out *Ps 55:23*
half their d.
I have considered d. of old *Ps 77:5*

therefore their d. did he *Ps 78:33*
consume
his throne as the d. of *Ps 89:29*
heaven
d. of his youth hast thou *Ps 89:45*
shortened
all our d. are passed away in *Ps 90:9*
wrath
d. of our years are *Ps 90:10*
threescore and ten
teach us to number our d. *Ps 90:12*
that we may apply
we may rejoice and be glad *Ps 90:14*
all our d.
give him rest from d. of *Ps 94:13*
adversity
how many are the d. of thy *Ps 119:84*
servant
I remember the d. of old *Ps 143:5*
for length of d. shall they add *Pr 3:2*
to thee
length of d. is in her right *Pr 3:16*
hand
not much remember d. of his *Ec 5:20*
life
cause that former d. were *Ec 7:10*
better
shall abide with him all d. of *Ec 8:15*
life
let him remember of d. of *Ec 11:8*
darkness
while evil d. come not, nor *Ec 12:1*
years
whose antiquity is of ancient *Isa 23:7*
d.
seventy years, according to *Isa 23:15*
d. of one king
d. of thy mourning shall be *Isa 60:20*
ended
be no more thence an infant *Isa 65:20*
of d.
as d. of a tree are d. of my *Isa 65:22*
people
forgotten me d. without *Jer 2:32*
number
aged, with him that is full of *Jer 6:11*
d.
after those d. I will put my *Jer 31:33*
law in
from the d. of Josiah even to *Jer 36:2*
this day
our d. are fulfilled, our end is *La 4:18*
come
according to number of d. *Eze 4:4;*
5:9
d. are at hand, effect of *Eze 12:23*
every vision
not remembered d. of *Eze 16:22;*
youth *16:43*
unto 2300 d. sanctuary be *Da 8:14*
cleansed
abomination set up shall be *Da 12:1*
1290 d.
blessed is he that cometh to *Da 12:12*
1335 d.
I will visit on her the d. of *Ho 2:13*
Baalim
d. of visitation, d. of *Ho 9:7*
recompence come
thou hast sinned from the d. *Ho 10:9*
of Gibeah
according to the d. of thy *Mic 7:15*
coming out
since those d. were, when *Hag 2:16*
one came to
ye that hear in these d. these *Zec 8:9*
words
before these d. was no hire *Zec 8:10*
for man
I will not be as in former d. *Zec 8:11*
saith Lord
so have I thought in these d. *Zec 8:15*
to do well
from d. of our fathers are *Mal 3:7*
gone away
from d. of John the Baptist *M't 11:12*
till now
except those d. should be *M't 24:22;*
shortened, no flesh *M'k 13:20*
should be saved
as d. of Noe, so shall *M't 24:3*
coming of Son
after those d. Elisabeth *Lu 1:24*
conceived
for these be the d. of *Lu 21:22*
vengeance
have likewise foretold of *Ac 3:24*
these d.
for before these d. rose up *Ac 5:36*
Theudas

in these d. came prophets to *Ac 11:27*
Antioch
then were the d. of *Ac 12:3*
unleavened bread
sailed after d. of unleavened *Ac 20:6*
bread
before these d. made an *Ac 21:38*
uproar
ye observed d. and months *Ga 4:10*
and times
redeeming time, because d. *Eph 5:16*
are evil
neither beginning of d. nor *Heb 7:3*
end of life
but call to remembrance *Heb 10:32*
the former d.
he that would see good d. let *1Pe 3:10*
him refrain
shall prophesy 1260 d. in *Re 11:3*
sackcloth
that they should feed her *Re 12:6*
there 1260 d.

ALL THE DAYS

dust eat *all the* d. of thy life *Ge 3:14*
all the d. Adam lived were 930 *Ge 5:5*
years
all d. of Seth, Enos, Cainan, *Ge 5:8;*
Enoch, Methusaleh, *5:11, 14, 23, 27;*
and Noah were *9:29*
all the d. wherein plague *Le 13:46*
shall be
all the d. of her issue be *Le 15:25;*
unclean *15:26*
all the d. of his separation *Nu 6:4;*
6:5-6, 8
lest they depart from heart *De 4:9*
all the d.
to fear me *all the* d. they *De 4:10;*
live *1Ki 8:40*
possess it *all the* d. ye live on *De 12:1*
earth
Israel served Lord *all the* d. *Jos 24:31;*
d. of Joshua, *all the* *J'g 2:7*
d. of elders
delivered them *all the* d. of *J'g 2:18*
judge
I will give him to Lord *all* *1Sa 1:11*
d. of life
against Philistines *all the* d. *1Sa 7:13*
of Samuel
Samuel judged Israel *all the* *1Sa 7:15*
d. of life
dwelt safely *all the* d. of *1Ki 4:25*
Solomon
Rezon was adversary *all* *1Ki 11:25*
the d. of Solomon
Hazael oppressed Israel *all* *2Ki 13:22*
the d.
nor in *all the* d. of the *2Ki 23:22*
kings of Israel
all the d. of Jehoiada priest *2Ch 24:2;*
4:14
frustrate purposes *all* d. of *Ezr 4:5*
Cyrus
all the d. of appointed time *Job 14:14*
will I wait
mercy shall follow me *all* d. *Ps 23:6*
of my life
dwell in house of Lord *all the* *Ps 27:4*
d. of life
all the d. of the afflicted are *Pr 15:15*
evil
do him good, not evil, *all* *Pr 31:12*
the d. of life
in holiness before him *all the* *Lu 1:75*
d. of life

FEW DAYS

let damsel abide with us *few* *Ge 24:55*
d.
tarry *few* d. till brother's *Ge 27:44*
fury turn
they seemed to him but a *Ge 29:20*
few d.
few and evil are d. of my *Ge 47:9*
pilgrimage
when cloud was *few* d. on *Nu 9:20*
tabernacle
man that is born of woman *Job 14:1*
is of *few* d.
let his d. be *few*, and let *Ps 109:8*
another
within *few* d. he shall be *Da 11:20*
destroyed
they verily for a *few* d. *Heb 12:10*
chastened us

HIS DAYS

yet *his d.* shall be 120 years   Ge 6:3
in *his d.* was earth divided   Ge 10:25;
   1Ch 1:19
not put her away all *his d.*   De 22:19;
   22:29
Asa was perfect all *his d.*   1Ki 15:14;
   2Ch 15:17
in *his d.* did Hiel build   1Ki 16:34
Jericho
I will not bring the evil in   1Ki 21:29
his d.
in *his d.* Edom revolted   2Ki 8:20;
   2Ch 21:8
Jehoash did what was right   2Ki 12:2
all *his d.*
he departed not all *his d.*   2Ki 15:18
from the sins
quietness to Israel in *his d.*   1Ch 22:9
all *his d.* they departed not   2Ch 34:33
from
seeing *his d.* are determined   Job 14:5
wicked travaileth with pain   Job 15:20
all *his d.*
why do they that know him   Job 24:1
not see *his d.*
in *his d.* shall the righteous   Ps 72:7
flourish
as for man, *his d.* are as   Ps 103:15
grass
his d. are as shadow that   Ps 144:4
passeth away
hateth covetousness prolong   Pr 28:16
his d.
for all *his d.* are sorrows, his   Ec 2:23
travail
all *his d.* also he eateth in   Ec 5:17
darkness
though *his d.* be prolonged,   Ec 8:12
yet I know
wicked shall not prolong his   Ec 8:13
d.
old man that hath not filled   Isa 65:20
his d.
leave them in the midst of   Jer 17:11
his d.
a man that shall not prosper   Jer 22:30
in *his d.*
in *his d.* Judah shall be saved   Jer 23:6

IN THE DAYS

Reuben in *the d.* of   Ge 30:14
wheat harvest
in *the d.* of Shamgar, in *the d.*   J'g 5:6
of Jael
quietness 40 years in *the d.*   J'g 8:28
of Gideon
went for an old man in *the*   1Sa 17:12
d. of Saul
was famine in *the d.* of   2Sa 21:1
David
put to death in *the d.* of   2Sa 21:9
harvest
silver was nothing   1Ki 10:21;
accounted of in *the d.*   2Ch 9:20
of Solomon
Sodomites remained in *the*   1Ki 22:46
d. of Asa
these came in *the d.* of   1Ch 4:41
Hezekiah
we inquired not at it in *the*   1Ch 13:3
d. of Saul
sought God in *the d.* of   2Ch 26:5
Zechariah
came not on them in *the d.*   2Ch 32:26
of Hezekiah
as in *the d.* when God   Job 29:2
preserved me
as I was in *the d.* of my   Job 29:4
youth
in *the d.* of famine be   Ps 37:19
satisfied
wherefore should I fear in *the*   Ps 49:5
d. of evil
in *the d.* to come shall be   Ec 2:16
forgotten
let thy heart cheer thee in *the*   Ec 11:9
d. of youth
Remember thy Creator in *the*   Ec 12:1
d. of youth
Micah prophesied in *the d.*   Jer 26:18
of Hezekiah
Jerusalem remembered in *the d.*   La 1:7
of affliction
remember my covenant in *the*   Eze 16:60
d.
hands be strong in *the d.* I   Eze 22:14
deal

in *the d.* of these kings God   Da 2:44
set up
in *the d.* of father, light was   Da 5:11
found in him
she shall sing as in *the d.* of   Ho 2:15
her youth
deeply corrupted as in *the d.*   Ho 9:9
of Gibeah
to dwell, as in *the d.* of the   Ho 12:9
solemn feast
hath this been in *the d.* of   Joe 1:2
your fathers
when Jesus was born in *the d.*   M't 2:1
of Herod
if we had been in *the d.* of   M't 23:30
our fathers
for as in *the d.* that were   M't 24:38
before the flood
into house of God in *the d.* of   M'k 2:26
Abiathar
Lord dealt with me in *the d.*   Lu 1:25
many widows were in *the d.*   Lu 4:25
of Elias
in *d.* of Noe, in *d.* of Lot   Lu 17:26;
   17:28
rose up Judas in *the d.* of   Ac 5:37
taxing
came to pass in *the d.* of   Ac 11:28
Claudius Caesar
who in *the d.* of flesh, when   Heb 5:7
he offered
long-suffering of God   1Pe 3:20
waited in *the d.* of Noah
in *the d.* of voice of seventh   Re 10:7
angel
that it rain not in *the d.* of   Re 11:6
their prophecy

IN THOSE DAYS

were giants in the earth in   Ge 6:4
those d.
come to the judge in *those*   De 17:9;
d.   19:17
go to the priest that shall be   De 26:3
in *those d.*
in *those d.* no king   J'g 17:6; 18:1;
   21:25
for the ark of God was   J'g 20:27
there in *those d.*
word of Lord was precious in   Isa 3:1
those d.
which he counselled in   2Sa 16:23
those d.
in *those d.* was Hezekiah   2Ki 20:1;
sick unto death   2Ch 32:24; Isa 38:1
in *those d.* shall Judah be   Jer 33:16
saved
in *those d.* Israel shall go   Jer 50:4
and seek God
in *those d.* iniquity be sought   Jer 50:20
for, and none
in *those d.* pour out my   Joe 2:29;
Spirit on servants and   Ac 2:18
on handmaids
woe to them that give suck   M't 24:19;
in *those d.*   M'k 13:17; Lu 21:23
Mary arose in *those d.* and   Lu 1:39
went
on one of *those d.* as he   Lu 20:1
taught people
made a calf in *those d.* and   Ac 7:41
offered
hast not denied my faith in   Re 2:13
those d.
in *those d.* men seek death,   Re 9:6
not find it

LATTER DAYS

people do to thy people in   Nu 24:14
latter d.
in *latter d.* if thou turn to   De 4:30
the Lord
evil will befall you in the   De 31:29
latter d.
in *latter d.* consider it   Jer 23:20;
perfectly   30:24
bring captivity of Moab in   Jer 48:47
latter d.
captivity of Elam in the   Jer 49:39
latter d.
come against my people in   Eze 38:16
latter d.
maketh known what shall be   Da 2:28
in *latter d.*
what shall befall thy people   Da 10:14
in *latter d.*
shall fear the Lord in *latter*   Ho 3:5
d.

MANY DAYS

Israel mourned for son   Ge 37:34
many d.
nor left your brethren these   Jos 22:3
many d.
Shimei dwelt at Jerusalem   1Ki 2:38
many d.
she, and her house, did eat   1Ki 17:15
many d.
Ephraim mourned *many d.*   1Ch 7:22
what man is he that loveth   Ps 34:12
many d.
how *many* are the *d.* of thy   Ps 119:84
servant
so that the *d.* of his years be   Ec 6:3
many
for thou shalt find it after   Ec 11:1
many d.
after *many d.* shall they be   Isa 24:22;
visited   Eze 38:8
many d. and years shall ye   Isa 32:10
be troubled
they may continue *many d.*   Jer 32:14;
   35:7
Jeremiah had remained there   Jer 37:16
many d.
vision is for *many d.*   Eze 12:27;
   Da 8:26; 10:14
fall by captivity and spoil   Da 11:33
many d.
thou shalt abide for me *many*   Ho 3:3
d.
Israel shall abide *many d.*   Ho 3:4
without a king
not *many d.* after, younger   Lu 15:13
son
they continued there not   Joh 2:12
many d.
shall be baptized not *many d.*   Ac 1:5
hence
was seen *many d.* of them   Ac 13:31
which came
this did she *many d.* Paul   Ac 16:18
being grieved
nor sun nor stars in *many d.*   Ac 27:20
appeared

MY DAYS

give me my wife, for *my d.*   Ge 29:21
are fulfilled
good if peace and truth be   2Ki 20:19
in *my d.*
my d. are swifter than   Job 7:6
weaver's shuttle
let me alone, for *my d.* are   Job 7:16
vanity
now *my d.* are swifter than   Job 9:25
a post
are not *my d.* few, cease   Job 10:20
then
my d. are extinct, graves are   Job 17:1
ready for
my d. are past, my   Job 17:11
purposes are broken
I shall multiply *my d.* as   Job 29:18
the sand
know mine end, measure of   Ps 39:4
my d.
thou hast made *my d.* as an   Ps 39:5
handbreadth
for *my d.* are consumed like   Ps 102:3
smoke
my d. are like a shadow   Ps 102:11
that declineth
weakened my strength,   Ps 102:23
shortened *my d.*
take me not away in the   Ps 102:24
midst of *my d.*
I said, in the cutting off of   Isa 38:10
my d.
there shall be peace and truth   Isa 39:8
in *my d.*
my d. be consumed with   Jer 20:18
shame

NOW A DAYS

be many servants *now a d.*   1Sa 25:10
break away

PROLONG DAYS

shall not *prolong* your *d.*   De 4:26;
   30:18
that thou mayest *prolong d.*   De 4:40;
   22:7
that thy *d.* may be   De 5:16;
prolonged   6:2

that ye may *prolong* your *d.*   De 5:33; 11:9
to the end that he may *prolong* his *d.*   De 17:20
ye shall *prolong* your *d.* in the land   De 32:47
the fear of the Lord *prolongeth d.*   Pr 10:27
hateth covetousness, shall *prolong* his *d.*   Pr 28:16
though a sinner's *d.* be *prolonged*   Ec 8:12
neither shall the wicked *prolong* his *d.*   Ec 8:13
her *d.* shall not be *prolonged*   Isa 13:22
see his seed, he shall *prolong* his *d.*   Isa 53:10
d. are *prolonged,* vision faileth   Eze 12:22

SABBATH DAYS

how on *sabbath d.* priests profane   M't 12:5
is it lawful to heal on the *sabbath d.*   M't 12:10
it is lawful to do well on the *sabbath d.*   M't 12:12
lawful to do good on *sabbath d.*   M'k 3:4; Lu 6:9
he came and taught them on *sabbath d.*   Lu 4:31
which is not lawful to do on *sabbath d.*   Lu 6:2
three *sabbath d.* reasoned with them   Ac 17:2
judge you in respect of *sabbath d.*   Col 2:16

THY DAYS

that *thy d.* may be long   Ex 20:12
number of *thy d.* I will fulfil   Ex 23:26
not seek their prosperity all *thy d.*   De 23:6
that *thy d.* may be lengthened in land   De 25:15
he is thy life, and length of *thy d.*   De 30:20
thy d. approach that thou must die   De 31:14
as *thy d.* so shall thy strength be   De 33:25
evil not found with thee all *thy d.*   1Sa 25:28
and when *thy d.* be fulfilled   2Sa 7:12
not be any like thee all *thy d.*   1Ki 3:13
walk in my ways, then I will lengthen *thy d.*   1Ki 3:14
in *thy d.* I will not do it, for David's sake   1Ki 11:12
will add to *thy d.* 15 years   2Ki 20:6; Isa 38:5
when *thy d.* be expired   1Ch 17:11
are *thy d.* as days of man   Job 10:5
hast thou commanded morning since *thy d.*   Job 38:12
because the number of *thy d.* is great   Job 38:21
for by me *thy d.* be multiplied   Pr 9:11
hast caused *thy d.* to draw near   Eze 22:4

TWO DAYS

on sixth day bread of *two d.*   Ex 16:29
whether it were *two d.* or a month   Nu 9:22
not eat one, nor *two d.* nor five   Nu 11:19
David had abode *two d.* in Ziklag   2Sa 1:1
nor is this work of one or *two d.*   Eze 10:13
that they would keep these *two d.*   Es 9:27
after *two d.* will he revive us   Ho 6:2
after *two d.* is the feast   M't 26:2; M'k 14:1
and he abode there *two d.*   Joh 4:40
now after *two d.* he departed thence   Joh 4:43
he abode *two d.* still in the same place   Joh 11:6

THREE DAYS

Joseph said, Three branches are *three d.*   Ge 40:12

within *three d.* Pharaoh lift up thy head   Ge 40:13; 40:19
Joseph said, Three baskets are *three d.*   Ge 40:18
put them altogether into ward *three d.*   Ge 42:17
go *three d.* journey into wilderness to sacrifice   Ex 3:18; 5:3; 8:27; 15:22
a thick darkness in Egypt *three d.*   Ex 10:22
nor rose any from his place for *three d.*   Ex 10:23
within *three d.* pass over Jordan   Jos 1:11
hide yourselves there *three d.*   Jos 2:16; 2:22
he abode with him *three d.*   J'g 19:4
asses that were lost *three d.* ago   1Sa 9:20
women kept from us these *three d.*   1Sa 21:5
had eaten no bread *three d.* and nights   1Sa 30:12
master left me, because *three d.* ago I fell sick   1Sa 30:13
assemble the men of Judah in *three d.*   2Sa 20:4
depart for *three d.*   1Ki 12:5; 2Ch 10:5
sought him *three d.* but found him not   2Ki 2:17
were *three d.* gathering spoil   2Ch 20:25
there we abode in tents *three d.*   Ezr 8:15
whosoever would not come in *three d.*   Ezr 10:8; 10:9
neither eat nor drink *three d.*   Es 4:16
was in belly of fish *three d.*   Jon 1:17; M't 12:40
they continue with me *three d.*   M't 15:32; M'k 8:2
destroy temple of God, to build it in *three d.*   M't 26:61; 27:40; M'k 14:58; 15:29; Joh 2:19
after *thee d.* rise again   M't 27:63; M'k 8:31
after *three d.* found him in temple   Lu 2:46
Saul was *three d.* without sight   Ac 9:9
Publius lodged us *three d.* courteously   Ac 28:7
see dead bodies *three d.* and an half   Re 11:9
after *three d.* an half, spirit of life entered   Re 11:11

FOUR DAYS

lament daughter of Jephthah *four d.*   J'g 11:40
Lazarus had lain in grave *four d.*   Joh 11:17
he stinketh, for he hath been dead *four d.*   Joh 11:39
four d. ago I was fasting to this hour   Ac 10:30

FIVE DAYS

nor *five d.* nor ten days nor twenty days   Nu 11:19
we came to them to Troas in *five d.*   Ac 20:6
after *five d.* Ananias high priest descended   Ac 24:1

SIX DAYS

six d. gather it, but on sabbath   Ex 16:26
keep sabbath holy, *six d.*   Ex 20:9; 23:12; 34:21; De 5:13
labour and do all work
in *six d.* Lord made heaven and earth   Ex 20:11; 31:17
cloud covered mount Sinai *six d.*   Ex 24:16
six d. may work be done   Ex 31:15; 35:2; Le 23:3
six d. eat unleavened bread   De 16:8
go round city, thus do *six d.*   Jos 6:3
they compassed city once, so did *six d.*   Jos 6:14
gate shall be shut *six working d.*   Eze 46:1
six d. in which men ought to work   Lu 13:14
six d. before passover came to Bethany   Joh 12:1

SEVEN DAYS

yet *seven d.* I will cause it to rain   Ge 7:4
Noah stayed yet other *seven d.*   Ge 8:10; 8:12
Joseph mourned for his father *seven d.*   Ge 50:10
seven d. eat unleavened bread   Ex 12:15; 13:6-7; 23:15; 34:18; Le 23:6; Nu 28:17; De 16:3
seven d. no leaven be found   Ex 12:19; De 16:4
seven d. it shall be with dam   Ex 22:30; Le 22:27
the priest shall put them on *seven d.*   Ex 29:30
seven d. consecrate them   Ex 29:35; Le 8:33
seven d. make atonement for altar   Ex 29:37
man child, she shall be unclean *seven d.*   Le 12:2
shut him up *seven d.* more   Le 13:5; 21:26, 33, 50, 54
tarry abroad out of his tent *seven d.*   Le 14:8
an issue, she shall be put apart *seven d.*   Le 15:19
offer an offering by fire *seven d.*   Le 23:8
keep feast *seven d.*   Le 23:39; 23:40-41; Nu 29:12
Miriam be ashamed *seven d.*   Nu 12:14
all in tent shall be unclean *seven d.*   Nu 19:14
observe feast of tabernacles *seven d.*   De 16:13
if you can declare it within *seven d.*   J'g 14:12
she wept before him the *seven d.*   J'g 14:17
seven d. tarry till I come   1Sa 10:8
elders said, Give us *seven d.* respite   1Sa 11:3
he tarried *seven d.* according to the time   1Sa 13:8
they fasted *seven d.*   1Sa 31:13; 1Ch 10:12
Solomon held a feast *seven d.*   1Ki 8:65
Zimri did reign *seven d.* in Tirzah   1Ki 16:15
kept dedication of altar *seven d.*   2Ch 7:9
kept feast *seven d.*   2Ch 30:21; 2Ch 35:17; Ezr 6:22
took counsel to keep other *seven d.*   2Ch 30:23
feast to great and small *seven d.*   Es 1:5
light of sun, as light of *seven d.*   Isa 30:26
I remained there astonished *seven d.*   Eze 3:15
seven d. shall purge altar   Eze 43:26
fell, after compassed *seven d.*   Heb 11:30

EIGHT DAYS

eight d. old be circumcised   Ge 17:12; 21:4
sanctify house of Lord in *eight d.*   2Ch 29:17
when *eight d.* were accomplished for   Lu 2:21
after *eight d.* Jesus came and stood   Joh 20:26

TEN DAYS

shall not eat *ten d.* nor   Nu 11:19
ten d. after Lord smote Nabal   1Sa 25:38
once in *ten d.* store of all sorts   Ne 5:18
after *ten d.* the word of the Lord came   Jer 42:7
prove servants, I pray thee, *ten d.*   Da 1:12
at end of *ten d.* countenances fairer   Da 1:15
when he tarried more than *ten d.*   Ac 25:6
but ye shall have tribulation *ten d.*   Re 2:10

ELEVEN DAYS

eleven d. journey between Horeb and Kadesh   De 1:2

TWELVE DAYS

are but *twelve d.* since I   *Ac 24:11*
went up

FOURTEEN DAYS

Solomon held a feast   *1Ki 8:65*
fourteen d.

FIFTEEN DAYS

I abode with Peter *fifteen d.*   *Ga 1:18*

TWENTY DAYS

ye shall not eat flesh *twenty*   *Nu 11:19*
d.

TWENTY-ONE DAYS

prince of Persia withstood   *Da 10:13*
twenty-one d.

THIRTY DAYS

they mourned for Aaron   *Nu 20:29*
thirty d.
Israel wept for Moses *thirty*   *De 34:8*
d.
not been called to king *thirty*   *Es 4:11*
whosoever ask petition for   *Da 6:7;*
thirty d.   *6:12*

THIRTY-THREE DAYS

in blood of her purifying   *Le 12:4*
thirty-three d.

FORTY DAYS

cause it to rain on earth *forty*   *Ge 7:4*
d.
forty d. fulfilled for   *Ge 50:3*
embalming him
Moses in mount *forty d.*   *Ex 24:18;*
and forty nights   *34:28; De 9:9; 10:10*
they returned after *forty d.*   *Nu 13:25;*
      14:34
I fell down before Lord *forty*   *De 9:25*
d.
went in strength of meat   *1Ki 19:8*
forty d.
bear iniquity of Judah *forty*   *Eze 4:6*
d.
forty d. and Nineveh be   *Jon 3:4*
overthrown
he fasted *forty d.* and forty   *M't 4:2*
nights
Jesus *forty d.* in wilderness   *M'k 1:13;*
      Lu 4:2
seen of them *forty d.* and   *Ac 1:3*
speaking

FIFTY-TWO DAYS

the wall was finished in   *Ne 6:15*
fifty-two d.

YOUR DAYS

that *your d.* may be   *De 11:21*
multiplied
cause to cease in *your d.*   *Jer 16:9*
mirth
all *your d.* ye shall dwell in   *Jer 35:7*
tents
in *your d.* will I say word   *Eze 12:25*
hath been in *your d.* or days of   *Joe 1:2*
fathers
work a work in *your d.*   *Hab 1:5;*
      Ac 13:41

DAYS COME

bring on thee *d.* that have   *Isa 7:17*
not *come*
behold *d. come*   *Jer 23:5;*
   23:7; 30:3; 31:27, 31, 38
d. come that he will take you   *Am 4:2*
away
d. come when   *M't 9:15;*
bridegroom shall be *M'k 2:20; Lu 5:35*
d. come when ye shall desire   *Lu 17:22*
to see
d. come thy enemies shall   *Lu 19:43*
cast a trench
d. come in which there shall   *Lu 21:6*
not be left

d. come when I will make   *Heb 8:8*
new covenant

DAY'S

d. journey   *Nu 11:31;*
   1Ki 19:4; Jon 3:4; Lu 2:44
continually, as every *d.*   *1Ch 16:37*
work
according unto this *d.* decree   *Es 9:13*
a sabbath *d.* journey   *Ac 1:12*
in question for this *d.*   *Ac 19:40*
uproar

DAYS'

three *d.* journey   *Ge 30:36;*
   Ex 3:18; 5:3; 8:27; Nu 10:33; 33:8;
      Jon 3:3
pursued after him seven *d.*   *Ge 31:23*
journey
are eleven *d.* journey from   *De 1:2*
Horeb
Give us seven *d.* respite, that   *1Sa 11:3*
three *d.* pestilence in thy   *2Sa 24:13*
land
a compass of seven *d.* journey   *2Ki 3:9*

DAYSMAN

neither is there any *d.*   *Job 9:33*
betwixt us

DAZED

made us reel be *d.*   *Ps 60:3*
(A)(B)(R)
prophets astounded and *d.*   *Jer 4:9*
(A)

DAZZLED

bewildered and *d.* them (A)   *Ac 8:11*

DEACON

let them use the office of a   *1Ti 3:10*
d.
that have used the office of a   *1Ti 3:13*
d.

DEACONS

Philippi, with the bishops   *Ph'p 1:1*
and *d.*
Likewise must the *d.* be grave   *1Ti 3:8*
the *d.* be the husbands of   *1Ti 3:12*
one wife

DEAD

God said, Thou art but a *d.*   *Ge 20:3*
man
Abraham stood up from   *Ge 23:3*
before his *d.*
men are *d.* which sought thy   *Ex 4:19*
life
was not one of Israelites'   *Ex 9:7*
cattle *d.*
not house where was not one   *Ex 12:30*
d.
Egyptians said, We be all *d.*   *Ex 12:33*
men
Israel saw Egyptians *d.* on   *Ex 14:30*
shore
and the *d.* beast shall be his   *Ex 21:34;*
      21:36
the *d.* ox also they shall   *Ex 21:35*
divide
toucheth any thing unclean by   *Le 22:4*
d.
whosoever is defiled by the *d.*   *Nu 5:2*
let her not be as one *d.* of   *Nu 12:12*
he stood between *d.* and the   *Nu 16:48*
living
wife of the *d.* not marry a   *De 25:5*
stranger
their lord was fallen down *d.*   *J'g 3:25*
when he came in, Sisera lay   *J'g 4:22*
d.
d. Samson slew at his death   *J'g 16:30*
were more
as ye have dealt with *d.* and   *Ru 1:8*
to raise up name of *d.* on   *Ru 4:5*
inheritance
sons Hophni and Phinehas   *1Sa 4:17*
are *d.*
her father in law and   *1Sa 4:19*
husband were *d.*
dost thou pursue? after a *d.*   *1Sa 24:14*
dog

Saul and sons were *d.*   *1Sa 31:7;*
      1Ch 10:7
shouldest look on such *d.* dog   *2Sa 9:8*
as I am
to think that all the king's   *2Sa 13:33*
sons are *d.*
why should this *d.* dog curse   *2Sa 16:9*
my lord
all of father's house but *d.*   *2Sa 19:28*
men
living mine, and *d.* is thy   *1Ki 3:22*
son
when I am *d.* bury me in   *1Ki 13:31*
the sepulchre
arise, from Naboth is not   *1Ki 21:15*
alive but *d.*
d. bodies (A)   *2Ki 19:35; Isa 37:36*
house fell on young men,   *Job 1:19*
they are *d.*
d. things are formed from   *Job 26:5*
under waters
the shade below quake   *Job 26:5*
(B)(R)
they that are deceased   *Job 26:5*
tremble (E)
forgotten as *d.* man out of   *Ps 31:12*
mind
chariot and horse cast into *d.*   *Ps 76:6*
sleep
free among *d.* like slain lie in   *Ps 88:5*
grave
wilt thou show wonders to   *Ps 88:10*
the *d.*
they ate the sacrifices of the   *Ps 106:28*
d.
the *d.* praise not Lord   *Ps 115:17*
in darkness, as those been   *Ps 143:3*
long *d.*
inclineth, and her paths unto   *Pr 2:18*
d.
her paths to spirits of dead   *Pr 2:18*
(A)
her roads to the shades   *Pr 2:18*
(B)(R)
he knoweth not the *d.* are   *Pr 9:18*
there
shades of the dead are there   *Pr 9:18*
(A)
that ghosts are there (B)   *Pr 9:18*
shall remain in congregation   *Pr 21:16*
of *d.*
abide in congregation of   *Pr 21:16*
spirits (A)
I praised *d.* which are already   *Ec 4:2*
d.
after that they go to the *d.*   *Ec 9:3*
a living dog is better than a *d.*   *Ec 9:4*
lion
d. know not any thing, neither   *Ec 9:5*
have they
d. flies cause ointment of   *Ec 10:1*
apothecary
seek God, for living to the *d.*   *Isa 8:19*
stirreth up *d.* for thee   *Isa 14:9*
it rouses the shades to meet   *Isa 14:9*
you (R)
not slain with sword, nor *d.*   *Isa 22:2*
in battle
they are *d.* shall not live   *Isa 26:14*
they are *d.*, powerless ghosts   *Isa 26:14*
(B)
they are shades, they shall   *Isa 26:14*
not rise (R)
thy *d.* men shall live, with   *Isa 26:19*
my *d.* body
these were *d.* (S)   *Isa 37:36*
we are in desolate places as   *Isa 59:10*
d. men
in dark places, as they that be   *La 3:6*
d.
the realm of the *d.* (B)   *Eze 31:17*
shall come at no *d.* person   *Eze 44:25*
are *d.* that sought child's life   *M't 2:20*
follow me, and let the *d.*   *M't 8:22*
bury their *d.*
maid is not *d.*   *M't 9:24;*
      M'k 5:39; Lu 8:52
heal sick, raise the *d.*, cast   *M't 10:8*
out devils
deaf hear, *d.* are raised up   *M't 11:5;*
      Lu 7:22
wind was *d.* against them   *M't 14:24*
(P)
touching resurrection of *d.*   *M't 22:31;*
      M'k 12:26
not God of *d.*   *M't 22:32;*
   M'k 12:27; Lu 20:38
but are within full of *d.*   *M't 23:27*
men's bones

for fear keepers became as *M't 28:4*
d. men
was as one d. many said, He *M'k 9:26*
is d.
Pilate marvelled if he were *M'k 15:44*
already d.
there was a d. man carried *Lu 7:12*
out
departed, leaving him half d. *Lu 10:30*
why seek the living among *Lu 24:5*
the d.
for as the Father raiseth up *Joh 5:21*
the d.
d. shall hear voice of Son of *Joh 5:25*
God
those d. and buried (P) *Joh 5:28*
fathers did eat manna, and *Joh 6:49;*
are d.   *6:58*
that believeth, tho' he were *Joh 11:25*
d. shall he live
patriarch David is d. and *Ac 2:29*
buried
young men came in and *Ac 5:10*
found her d.
be judge of quick and d. *Ac 10:42;*
                                  2Ti 4:1
drew him out, supposing he *Ac 14:19*
had been d.
Eutychus fell down, and was *Ac 20:9*
taken up d.
why incredible God should *Ac 26:8*
raise d.
have swollen or fallen down *Ac 28:6*
d.
even God who quickeneth the *Ro 4:17*
d.
he considered not his own *Ro 4:19*
body now d.
through offence of one many *Ro 5:15*
be d.
we that are d. to sin, live *Ro 6:2*
therein
if we be d. with Christ, we *Ro 6:8*
reckon yourselves to be d. to *Ro 6:11*
sin
but if husband be d. *Ro 7:2;*
                      7:3; 1Co 7:39
ye are become d. to *Ro 7:4;*
law   *Ga 2:19*
be lord both of d. and living *Ro 14:9*
if so be that the d. rise not *1Co 15:15*
utterly d. and gone (P) *1Co 15:18*
will say, How are the d. *1Co 15:35*
raised
the d. shall be raised *1Co 15:52*
incorruptible
but trust in God who *2Co 1:9*
raiseth d.
if one died for all, then *2Co 5:14*
were all d.
d. in trespasses and sins *Eph 2:1;*
              2:5; Col 2:13
if ye be d. with Christ *Col 2:20;*
                           2Ti 2:11
ye are d. and life hid with *Col 3:3*
Christ
consider yourselves d. (P) *Col 3:5*
the d. in Christ shall rise *1Th 4:16*
first
foundation of repentance *Heb 6:1*
from d. works
blood of Christ purge *Heb 9:14*
conscience from d. works
testament is of force after *Heb 9:17*
men are d.
and by it he being d. yet *Heb 11:4*
speaketh
sprang even of one, and *Heb 11:12*
good as d.
women received d. raised *Heb 11:35*
to life again
we being d. to sin should *1Pe 2:24*
live
ready to judge quick and d. *1Pe 4:5*
gospel preached to them that *1Pe 4:6*
are d.
twice d. plucked up by the *Jude 12*
roots
Jesus, who is first begotten of *Re 1:5*
d.
when I saw him, I fell at his *Re 1:17*
feet as d.
hast name thou livest, and art *Re 3:1*
d.
Blessed are d. who die in the *Re 14:13*
Lord
sea became as blood of d. *Re 16:3*
man

but the rest of the d. lived *Re 20:5*
not again
saw d. stand before God; d. *Re 20:12*
were judged
sea gave up d. in it, death *Re 20:13*
and hell

FOR THE DEAD

shall not make cuttings for *Le 19:28*
the d.
there shall none be defiled for *Le 21:1*
the d.
shall not make baldness for *De 14:1*
the d.
I have not given ought *De 26:14*
thereof for the d.
as a woman mourned for the *2Sa 14:2*
d.
not tear to comfort them for *Jer 16:7*
the d.
weep ye not for the d. nor *Jer 22:10*
make no mourning for the *Eze 24:17*
d.
baptized for the d. *1Co 15:29*

FROM THE DEAD

John Baptist, he is risen from *M't 14:2*
the d.
what rising from the d. *M'k 9:10*
should mean
if one went to them from *Lu 16:30*
the d.
persuaded, though one rose *Lu 16:31*
from the d.
rise from the d. third day *Lu 24:46;*
                              Joh 20:9
drink with him after rose *Ac 10:41*
from the d.
be the first that should rise *Ac 26:23*
from the d.
as those that are alive from *Ro 6:13*
the d.
to bring up Christ again from *Ro 10:7*
the d.
receiving of them but life *Ro 11:15*
from d.
if Christ be preached that *1Co 15:12*
rose from d.
arise from d. Christ give *Eph 5:14*
light
who is the firstborn from *Col 1:18*
the d.
God able to raise from the *Heb 11:19*
d.
brought again from the d. *Heb 13:20*
our Lord

IS DEAD

his brother is d. *Ge 42:38; 44:20*
in the name of his brother *De 25:6*
that is d.
Moses my servant is d. arise *Jos 1:2*
my concubine they forced, *J'g 20:5*
she is d.
Saul, Uriah, Amnon, *2Sa 2:7;*
Absalom, and Naboth *4:10; 11:21, 24;*
is d.   *12:18-19; 13:32; 19:10; 1Ki 21:14*
I am a widow and my *2Sa 14:5*
husband is d.
no tidings because king's *2Sa 18:20*
son is d.
priests not eat that is d. of *Eze 44:31*
itself
my daughter is d. *M't 9:18;*
             M'k 5:35; Lu 8:49
insomuch that many said, He *M'k 9:26*
is d.
Abraham is d. and the *Joh 8:52*
prophets
then said Jesus plainly, *Joh 11:14*
Lazarus is d.
for he that is d. is freed from *Ro 6:7*
sin
if Christ be in you, body is *Ro 8:10*
d. because of sin
if righteousness by law, Christ *Ga 2:21*
is d. in vain
liveth in pleasure, is d. while *1Ti 5:6*
she liveth
faith, if hath not works is d. *Jas 2:17;*
                              2:20
as body without spirit is d. *Jas 2:26*

WAS DEAD

when judge was d. they *J'g 2:19*
returned

when Israel saw Abimelech *J'g 9:55*
was d.
Philistines saw champion *1Sa 17:51*
was d.
when David heard that *1Sa 25:39*
Nabal was d.
armour-bearer saw Saul was *1Sa 31:5;*
d.   *1Ch 10:5*
Saul's son heard that Abner *2Sa 4:1*
was d.
Bathsheba heard her *2Sa 11:26*
husband was d.
David perceived that the *2Sa 12:19*
child was d.
comforted for Amnon, *2Sa 13:39*
seeing he was d.
to give my child suck, it was *1Ki 3:21*
d.
when Hadad heard that *1Ki 11:21*
Joab was d.
when Jezebel heard that *1Ki 21:15*
Naboth was d.
when Ahab was d. Moab *2Ki 3:5*
rebelled
the child was d. and laid on *2Ki 4:32*
his bed
Athaliah saw her son was d. *2Ki 11:1;*
                          2Ch 22:10
when Herod was d. behold *M't 2:15*
an angel
he that was d. began to speak *Lu 7:15*
laughed to scorn, knowing *Lu 8:53*
she was d.
this my son was d. and is *Lu 15:24*
alive again
thy brother was d. and is *Lu 15:32*
alive again
Martha, the sister of him *Joh 11:39*
was d.
he that was d. came forth *Joh 11:44*
bound
saw Jesus was d. brake not *Joh 19:33*
his legs
questions of one Jesus who *Ac 25:19*
was d.
for without the law sin was d. *Ro 7:8*
I am he that liveth, and was *Re 1:18*
d.

DEADLY

was a d. destruction *1Sa 5:11*
throughout
d. discomfiture in city (E) *1Sa 5:11*
my d. enemies, who compass *Ps 17:9*
me
a d. thing has fastened (R) *Ps 41:8*
die of d. diseases (A)(R) *Jer 16:4*
groanings of a d. wounded *Eze 30:24*
man
mistress of d. charms (A) *Na 3:4*
and if they drink any d. *M'k 16:18*
thing
an unruly evil, full of d. *Jas 3:8*
poison
d. wound was healed: and all *Re 13:3*
whose d. wound was healed *Re 13:12*

DEADNESS

yet the d. of Sarah's womb *Ro 4:19*

DEAF

who maketh the dumb, or d. *Ex 4:11*
Thou shalt not curse the d. *Le 19:14*
But I, as a d. man, heard *Ps 38:13*
not
the d. adder that stoppeth her *Ps 58:4*
ear
in that day shall the d. hear *Isa 29:18*
ears of the d. shall be *Isa 35:5*
unstopped
Hear, ye d.; and look, ye *Isa 42:18*
blind
d. as my messenger that I *Isa 42:19*
sent
eyes, and the d. that have *Isa 43:8*
ears
their mouth, their ears shall *Mic 7:16*
be d.
and the d. hear, the dead are *M't 11:5*
was d. and had an *M'k 7:32*
impediment
he maketh both the d. to *M'k 7:37*
hear, and
Thou dumb and d. spirit, *M'k 9:25*
I charge
the d. hear, the dead are *Lu 7:22*
raised

DEAL

now will we d. worse with thee than	Ge 19:9
if you will d. truly with my master	Ge 24:49
return, and I will d. well with thee	Ge 32:9
should he d. with our sister as an harlot	Ge 34:31
come on, let us d. wisely with them	Ex 1:10
d. with her after manner of daughters	Ex 21:9
in like manner d. with thy vineyard	Ex 23:11
ye shall not steal, nor d. falsely	Le 19:11
if thou d. thus with me, kill me	Nu 11:15
but thus shall ye d. with them	De 7:5
as thou didst d. with David	2Ch 2:3
lest I d. with you after your folly	Job 42:8
I said to fools, D. not foolishly	Ps 75:4
d. bountifully with thy servant	Ps 119:17; 142:7
d. with thy servant according to mercy	Ps 119:124
they that d. truly are his delight	Pr 12:22
in land of uprightness he will d. unjustly	Isa 26:10
my servant shall d. prudently	Isa 52:13
is it not to d. thy bread to the hungry	Isa 58:7
d. thus with them in time of anger	Jer 18:23
if so be that the Lord d. with us according	Jer 21:2
therefore will I also d. in fury	Eze 8:18
I will d. with thee as thou hast done	Eze 16:59
hands be strong in days I d. with thee	Eze 22:14
they shall d. furiously with thee	Eze 23:25
mariners to d. in (A)(E)	Eze 27:9
he shall surely d. with him	Eze 31:11
as thou seest d. with thy servants	Da 1:13
shall d. against them and shall prevail	Da 11:7
d. out judgment for a bribe (B)(R)	Mic 3:11
with measure you d. out (A)(N)(P)(R)	M't 7:2
so much the more a great d.	M'k 7:36
he cried the more a great d.	M'k 10:48
d. craftily (A)	2Co 4:2

DEAL a measure

a tenth d. of flour mingled with oil	Ex 29:40; Le 14:21; Nu 15:4; 29:4
a tenth measure of fine flour (A)	Ex 29:40
six pints of fine flour (B)	Ex 29:40
tenth measure of fine flour (R)	Ex 29:40
a several tenth d.	Nu 28:13; 21:29; 29:10, 15
a tenth part of fine flour (A)	Nu 28:13
three quarts of fine flour (B)	Nu 28:13
a tenth of fine flour (R)	Nu 28:13

DEALER

the treacherous d. dealeth	Isa 21:2

DEALERS

the treacherous d. have dealt	Isa 24:16
yea, the treacherous d. have dealt	Isa 24:16
d. in merchandise (A)(E)(R)	Eze 27:27

DEALEST

d. thou thus with thy servants	Ex 5:15
d. treacherously, and they dealt	Isa 33:1

DEALETH

d. Micah with me, and hath told me that he d. very subtilly	J'g 18:4
	1Sa 23:22
He becometh poor that d. with	Pr 10:4
prudent man d. with knowledge	Pr 13:16
He that is soon angry d. foolishly	Pr 14:17
his name, who d. in proud wrath	Pr 21:24
treacherous dealer d. treacherously	Isa 21:2
the priest every one d. falsely	Jer 6:13
unto the priest every one d. falsely	Jer 8:10
God d. with you as with sons	Heb 12:7

DEALING

his violent d. shall come down	Ps 7:16
end of d. treacherously (S)	Isa 33:1
noblest ways of d. (B)	Ro 12:17
our d. with fellow men (N)	2Co 1:12

DEALINGS

of your evil d. by all this people	1Sa 2:23
his d. are just (B)	Da 4:37
had no d. with the Samaritans	Joh 4:9
have no d. with (N)	2Th 3:14

DEALS

three tenth d. of fine flour	Le 14:10
three tenths of an ephah (A)(R)	Le 14:10
six quarts of fine flour (B)	Le 14:10
two tenth d. of fine flour mingled	Le 23:13
two tenths of an ephah (A)	Le 23:13
fifth of a bushel of fine flour (B)	Le 23:13; 23:17; 24:5
two tenths part of an ephah (E)(R)	Le 23:13; 23:17; 24:5; Nu 15:6; 28:20, 28; 29:3, 9, 14
two wave loaves of two tenth d.	Le 23:17
two tenth d. shall be in one cake	Le 24:5
two tenth d. of flour mingled	Nu 15:6
two tenths of an ephah (A)	Nu 15:6
six quarts of fine flour (B)	Nu 15:6; 28:20; 29:3, 9, 14
three tenth d. to a bullock	Nu 28:20; 28:9, 12, 28; 29:3, 9, 14
three tenths of an ephah (A)(E)(R)	Nu 28:20; 28:28; 29:3, 9, 14
nine quarts with a bull (B)	Nu 28:20; 29:3, 9, 14

DEALT

when Sarai d. hardly with her	Ge 16:6
God hath d. graciously with me	Ge 33:11
Wherefore d. ye so ill with me	Ge 43:6
God d. well with the midwives	Ex 1:20
wherefore hast thou d. thus	Ex 14:11
the thing wherein they d. proudly	Ex 18:11
seeing he hath d. deceitfully	Ex 21:8
if ye have d. well with Jerubbaal	J'g 9:16
ye then have d. truly and sincerely	J'g 9:19
men of Shechem d. treacherously	J'g 9:23
as ye have d. with the dead	Ru 1:8
the Almighty hath d. very bitterly	Ru 1:20
thou hast d. well with me	1Sa 24:18
when the Lord shall have d. well	1Sa 25:31
And he d. among all the people	2Sa 6:19
we have d. wickedly (E)	1Ki 8:47
workmen: for they d. faithfully	2Ki 12:15
and d. with familiar spirits	2Ki 21:6
hand, because they d. faithfully	2Ki 22:7
And he d. to every one of Israel	1Ch 16:3
so d. David with all the cities	1Ch 20:3

done amiss, and have d. wickedly	2Ch 6:37
And he d. wisely, and dispersed of	2Ch 11:23
d. with a familiar spirit, and	2Ch 33:6
d. very corruptly against thee	Ne 1:7
that they d. proudly against them	Ne 9:10
they and our fathers d. proudly	Ne 9:16
yet they d. proudly and hearkened	Ne 9:29
My brethren have d. deceitfully as	Job 6:15
he hath d. bountifully with me	Ps 13:6
have we d. falsely in thy covenant	Ps 44:17
d. treacherously (A)(E)	Ps 73:15
d. unfaithfully like their fathers	Ps 78:57
hath not d. with us after our sins	Ps 103:10
hath d. bountifully with thee	Ps 116:7
hast d. well with thy servant	Ps 119:65
for they d. perversely with me	Ps 119:78
He hath not d. so with any nation	Ps 147:20
dealers have d. treacherously	Isa 24:16
have d. very treacherously	Isa 24:16
d. not treacherously with thee	Isa 33:1
have ye d. treacherously with	Jer 3:20
d. very treacherously against	Jer 5:11
have d. treacherously with thee	Jer 12:6
have d. treacherously with her	La 1:2
of these have they d. by oppression	Eze 22:7
d. against the house of Judah	Eze 25:12
the Philistines have d. by revenge	Eze 25:15
terror in all that d. in (S)	Eze 26:17
d. treacherously against the Lord	Ho 5:7
have d. treacherously against me	Ho 6:7
your God that hath d. wondrously	Joe 2:26
our doings, so hath he d. with us	Zec 1:6
Judah hath d. treacherously	Mal 2:11
hast d. treacherously: yet is she	Mal 2:14
Thus hath the Lord d. with me	Lu 1:25
why hast thou thus d. with us	Lu 2:48
The same d. subtilly with our	Lu 7:19
the Jews have d. with me	Ac 25:24
d. at length with (N)	Ac 28:23
as God hath d. to every man	Ro 12:3

DEAR

everything d. to you (B)	1Ki 20:6
Is Ephraim my d. son? is he	Jer 31:20
who was d. unto him, was sick	Lu 7:2
highly valued by him (A)(N)	Lu 7:2
who meant much to him (B)	Lu 7:2
thought very highly of him (P)	Lu 7:2
count I my life d. unto myself	Ac 20:24
followers of God, as d. children	Eph 5:1
as well-beloved children (A)	Eph 5:1
as his loved children (B)	Eph 5:1
as beloved children (E)(R)	Eph 5:1
our d. fellowservant, who is	Col 1:7
our beloved fellow servant (A)(E)(R)	Col 1:7
most beloved minister (P)	Col 1:7
into the kingdom of his d. Son	Col 1:13
kingdom of the Son of his love (A)(B)(E)	Col 1:13
kingdom of his beloved Son (P)(R)	Col 1:13
souls, because ye were d. unto us	1Th 2:8

DEARLY

the d. beloved of my soul	Jer 12:7
D. beloved, avenge not	Ro 12:19

Wherefore, my *d.* beloved, *1Co 10:14*
flee
these promises *d.* beloved, let *2Co 7:1*
us
do all things *d.* beloved for *2Co 12:19*
my brethren *d.* beloved and *Ph'p 4:1*
longed
fast in the Lord, my *d.* *Ph'p 4:1*
beloved
To Timothy my *d.* beloved *2Ti 1:2*
son
unto Philemon our *d.* beloved *Ph'm 1*
D. beloved, I beseech you as *1Pe 2:11*

DEARTH

seven years of *d.* began to *Ge 41:54*
come
said, and the *d.* was in all *Ge 41:54*
lands
seven years of scarcity began *Ge 41:54*
(B)
seven years of famine began *Ge 41:54*
(E)(R)
and there was a *d.* in the *2Ki 4:38*
land
there was a famine in the *2Ki 4:38*
land (B)(R)
If there be *d.* in the land *2Ch 6:28*
if there be famine in the *2Ch 6:28*
land (B)(E)(R)
might buy corn, because of the *Ne 5:3*
d.
because of the famine (R) *Ne 5:3*
to Jeremiah concerning the *d.* *Jer 14:1*
concerning the drought *Jer 14:1*
(A)(B)(E)(R)
there came a *d.* over all the *Ac 7:11*
land
there came a famine *Ac 7:11*
(A)(B)(E)(N)(P)(R)

DEATH

let me not see the *d.* of the *Ge 21:16*
child
Isaac was comforted after *Ge 24:67*
mother's *d.*
after *d.* of Abraham God *Ge 25:11*
blessed Isaac
eat, and bless thee before my *Ge 27:7*
d.
that he may bless thee *Ge 27:10*
before his *d.*
that he may take from me *Ex 10:17*
this *d.*
if these men die common *d.* *Nu 16:29*
of all men
let me die *d.* of righteous *Nu 23:10*
put the murderer to *d.* (R) *Nu 35:19*
surely be put to *d.* *Nu 35:21*
(A)(E)(R)
slayer shall abide in it unto *Nu 35:25;*
d. of the high priest *28:32; Jos 20:6*
no satisfaction for life of *Nu 35:31*
murderer guilty of *d.*
I have set before you this *De 30:15;*
day, *d.* and evil *Jer 21:8*
how much more will ye *De 31:27*
rebel after my *d.*
I know after my *d.* ye will *De 31:29*
corrupt yourselves
Moses blessed Israel before his *De 33:1*
d.
put them to *d.* (B) *Jos 11:17*
that jeoparded their lives to *J'g 5:18*
d.
she urged him that his soul was *J'g 16:16*
vexed to *d.*
dead which he slew at his *d.* *J'g 16:30*
Ruth said, If ought but *d.* *Ru 1:17*
part thee and me
all thou hast done since *d.* of *Ru 2:11*
thy husband
about time of her *d.* the *1Sa 4:20*
women said
Agag said, Surely bitterness *1Sa 15:32*
of *d.* is past
there is but a step between *1Sa 20:3*
me and *d.*
to put David to *d.* (E)(R) *1Sa 20:33*
I have occasioned *d.* of thy *1Sa 22:22*
father's house
in their *d.* they were not *2Sa 1:23*
divided
in *d.* or life, there will thy *2Sa 15:21*
servant be
waves of *d.* compassed me *2Sa 22:5;*
Ps 18:4; 116:3

snares of *d.* prevented me *2Sa 22:6;*
Ps 18:5
Jeroboam was in Egypt till *1Ki 11:40*
d. of Solomon
cause the *d.* of my son (R) *1Ki 17:18*
shall not be any more *d.* or *2Ki 2:21*
barren land
O thou man of God, *d.* is in *2Ki 4:40*
the pot
so David prepared before *1Ch 22:5*
his *d.*
his counsellors after *d.* of *2Ch 22:4*
his father
put to *d.* (A)(R) *2Ch 25:16*
all Judah did Hezekiah *2Ch 32:33*
honour at his *d.*
whether it be to *d.* or to *Ezr 7:26*
banishment
which long for *d.* but it *Job 3:21*
cometh not
my soul chooseth *d.* rather *Job 7:15*
than life
firstborn of *d.* shall devour *Job 18:13*
his strength
that remain of him shall be *Job 27:15*
buried in *d.*
destruction and *d.* say, We *Job 28:22*
have heard fame
I know that thou wilt bring *Job 30:23*
me to *d.*
in *d.* there is not remembrance *Ps 6:5*
of thee
prepared for him the *Ps 7:13*
instruments of *d.*
lighten eyes, lest I sleep sleep *Ps 13:3*
of *d.*
the snares of *d.* (A) *Ps 18:5*
thou hast brought me into *Ps 22:15*
dust of *d.*
seek to put him to *d.* *Ps 37:32*
(A)(B)
God will be our guide, even *Ps 48:14*
unto *d.*
laid in grave, *d.* shall feed *Ps 49:14*
on them
the terrors of *d.* are fallen *Ps 55:4*
upon me
let *d.* seize on them, and let *Ps 55:15*
them go down
there are no bands in their *Ps 73:4*
d. strength
what man that liveth, and *Ps 89:48*
shall not see *d.*
to loose those that are *Ps 102:20*
appointed to *d.*
precious in sight of Lord is *Ps 116:15*
d. of saints
but he hath not given me *Ps 118:18*
over unto *d.*
her house inclineth to *d.* *Pr 2:18*
feet go down to *d.* steps take *Pr 5:5*
hold on hell
to hell going down to the *Pr 7:27*
chambers of *d.*
all they that hate me love *d.* *Pr 8:36*
pursueth evil, pursueth it to *Pr 11:19*
his own *d.*
in pathways thereof there is *Pr 12:28*
no *d.*
to depart from the snares of *Pr 13:14;*
d. *14:27*
but the righteous hath hope *Pr 14:32*
in his *d.*
wrath of a king is as *Pr 16:14*
messengers of *d.*
d. and life are in the power *Pr 18:21*
of tongue
vanity tossed to and fro of *Pr 21:6*
them that seek *d.*
forbear to deliver them that *Pr 24:11*
are drawn to *d.*
as a mad man who casteth *Pr 26:18*
arrows and *d.*
I find more bitter than *d.* *Ec 17:26*
woman
love strong as *d.;* jealousy *Ca 8:6*
he will swallow up *d.* in *Isa 25:8*
victory
for *d.* cannot celebrate thee *Isa 38:18*
with the rich in his *d.* *Isa 53:9*
because
because he poured out his *Isa 53:12*
soul unto *d.*
d. shall be chosen rather than *Jer 8:3*
life
d. is come up to our *Jer 9:21*
windows
tell them such as are for *d.* *Jer 15:2;*
to *d.* *43:11*
D. has no cover (B) *Jer 26:6*

abroad the sword, at home *La 1:20*
there is as *d.*
no pleasure in *d.* of wicked *Eze 18:32;*
33:11
for they are all delivered *Eze 31:14*
unto *d.*
d. I will be thy plagues, O *Ho 13:14*
grave
I do well to be angry even *Jon 4:9*
unto *d.*
who is as *d.* and cannot be *Hab 2:5*
satisfied
was there till the *d.* of *M't 2:15*
Herod
brother deliver brother to *M't 10:21;*
d. *M'k 13:12*
curseth father or mother die *M't 15:4;*
d. *M'k 7:10*
the forces of *d.* (N)(P)(R) *M't 16:18*
not taste *d.* till see *M't 16:28;*
M'k 9:1; Lu 9:27
shall condemn him to *d.* *M't 20:18;*
M'k 10:33
my soul is sorrowful to *d.* *M't 26:38;*
M'k 14:34
he is guilty of *d.* *M't 26:66; M'k 14:64*
my daughter lieth at point *M'k 5:23*
of *d.*
should not see *d.* before he *Lu 2:26*
had seen
they will put to *d.* (A) *Lu 11:49*
I will go with thee both to *Lu 22:33*
prison and *d.*
I have found no cause of *d.* *Lu 23:22*
in him
heal son for he was at point *Joh 4:47*
of *d.*
man keep my saying never *Joh 8:51;*
8:52
Jesus said, This sickness is *Joh 11:4*
not unto *d.*
howbeit, Jesus spake of his *Joh 11:13*
signifying what *d.* should *Joh 12:33;*
die *18:32*
signifying what *d.* should *Joh 21:19*
glorify God
after his *d.* (N) *Ac 1:3*
raised up, having loosed *Ac 2:24*
pains of *d.*
wanted to put them to *d.* *Ac 5:33*
(N)
Saul was consenting to his *d.* *Ac 8:1;*
22:20
they found no cause of *d.* in *Ac 13:28*
him
I persecuted this way unto *Ac 22:4*
the *d.*
because there was no cause *Ac 28:18*
of *d.* in me
expiating sin by his sacrificial *Ro 3:25*
d. (N)
reconciled to God by *d.* of *Ro 5:10;*
his Son *Col 1:22*
d. by sin, and so *d.* passed *Ro 5:12*
upon all men
d. reigned from Adam to *Ro 5:14;*
Moses over *5:17*
as sin reigned to *d.* even so *Ro 5:21*
might grace
baptized into his *d.* *Ro 6:3*
buried with him by baptism *Ro 6:4*
into *d.*
have been planted in likeness *Ro 6:5*
of his *d.*
dieth no more, *d.* hath no *Ro 6:9*
dominion over him
his servants ye are, whether *Ro 6:16*
of sin unto *d.*
now ashamed, for end of *Ro 6:21*
those things is *d.*
for the wages of sin is *d.* but *Ro 6:23*
motions of sin did work to *Ro 7:5*
bring fruit to *d.*
the commandment of life I *Ro 7:10*
found to be to *d.*
was then that which is gold *Ro 7:13*
made *d.* unto me
who shall deliver me from *Ro 7:24*
body of this *d.*
made me free from law of sin *Ro 8:2*
and *d.*
to be carnally minded is *d.* *Ro 8:6*
habitually putting to *d.* *Ro 8:13*
(A)(B)(E)(N)(R)
nor *d.* nor life separate us *Ro 8:38*
from love of God
whether world, life, or *d.* all *1Co 3:22*
are yours

God set forth apostles, as it   1Co 4:9
were to d.
doomed to d. (E)   1Co 4:9
at the hand of the angel of   1Co 10:10
d. (P)
show the Lord's d. till he   1Co 11:26
come
since by man came d. by   1Co 15:21
last enemy be destroyed is   1Co 15:26
d.
d. is swallowed up in   1Co 15:54
victory
O d. where is thy sting!   1Co 15:55
sting of d. is sin   1Co 15:56
we had sentence of d. in   2Co 1:9
ourselves
delivered us from so great a   2Co 1:10
d.
who are heading for d. (P)   2Co 2:15
to one we are savour of d.   2Co 2:16
unto d.
if the ministration of d. was   2Co 3:7
glorious
we are always delivered to   2Co 4:11
d.
d. worketh in us, but life in   2Co 4:12
you
the sorrow of the world   2Co 7:10
worketh d.
reap decay and d. of nature   Ga 6:8
(P)
magnified, whether by life   Ph'p 1:20
or by d.
became obedient to d. even   Ph'p 2:8
d. of cross
Epaphroditus nigh to d. but   Ph'p 2:27
for work of Christ he was   Ph'p 2:30
nigh to d.
being made conformable to   Ph'p 3:10
his d.
put to d. your members   Col 3:5
(E)(N)(R)
our Lord, who hath   2Ti 1:10
abolished d.
see Jesus, for suffering of d.   Heb 2:9
should taste d. for every man
thro' d. might destroy him   Heb 2:14
that had power of d.
and deliver them who   Heb 2:15
through fear of d. were
not suffered to continue, by   Heb 7:23
reason of d.
by means of d. for   Heb 9:15
redemption
must of necessity be d. of   Heb 9:16
testator
Enoch translated, that he   Heb 11:5
not see d.
angel of d. killed firstborn   Heb 11:28
(P)
sin when finished bringeth   Jas 1:15
forth d.
loveth not brother abideth in   1Jo 3:14
d.
there is a sin unto d.   1Jo 5:16
a sin not unto d.   1Jo 5:17
I have keys of hell and d.   Re 1:18
keys of d. (A)(E)(N)(P)(R)   Re 1:18
be faithful unto d. give thee a   Re 2:10
crown
overcomes shall not be hurt of   Re 2:11
second d.
his name that sat on him was   Re 6:8
d.
d. and Hades   Re 6:8
(A)(B)(E)(N)(R)
d., and the grave followed (P)   Re 6:8
men seek d. and d. flee from   Re 9:6
them
they loved not their lives to   Re 12:11
d.
saw one of his heads   Re 13:3
wounded to d.
her plagues come one day, d.   Re 18:8
on such second d. hath no   Re 20:6
power
d. and hell delivered up   Re 20:13
dead in them
d. and Hades   Re 20:13
(A)(B)(E)(N)(R)
d. and hell cast into lake,   Re 20:14
this is second d.
there shall be no more d. nor   Re 21:4

FROM DEATH

deliver our lives from d.   Jos 2:13
in famine redeem thee from   Job 5:20
d.
to deliver soul from d.   Ps 33:19

delivered my soul from d.   Ps 56:13;
    116:8
to Lord belong issues from   Ps 68:20
d.
he spared not their soul   Ps 78:50
from d.
righteousness delivereth from   Pr 10:2;
d.   11:4
I will redeem from d. O   Ho 13:14
passed from d. to life   Joh 5:24;
    1Jo 3:14
to him able to save him   Heb 5:7
from d.
know he shall save a soul   Jas 5:20
from d.

GATES OF DEATH

have gates of d. been   Job 38:17
opened to thee
liftest me up from gates of d.   Ps 9:13
they draw near to the gates   Ps 107:18
of d.

PUT TO DEATH

toucheth this man shall be   Ge 26:11
put to d.
ox stoned, his owner be put   Ex 21:29
to d.
whosoever work on sabbath,   Ex 35:2
be put to d.
not be put to d. because not   Le 19:20
free
both shall surely be put to d.   Le 20:11
that killeth be put to d.   Le 24:21;
    Nu 35:30
stranger be put to d.   Nu 1:51;
    3:10, 38; 18:7
dreamer of dreams be put to   De 13:5
d.
thy hand be first to put to d.   De 13:9;
    17:7
at mouth of one witness not   De 17:6
put to d.
he be put to d. hang him on   De 21:22
a tree
fathers not be put to d. for   De 24:16;
children, nor children   2Ki 14:6
put to d. for fathers
rebel against commandment   Jos 1:18
put to d.
that pleadeth for Baal put to   J'g 6:31
d.
we may put them to d.   J'g 20:13;
    1Sa 11:12
not a man be put to d.   1Sa 11:13;
    2Sa 19:22
two lines measured to put to   2Sa 8:2
d.
shall not Shimei be put to   2Sa 19:21
d. for this
put to d. in days of barley   2Sa 21:9
harvest
I sware, I will not put thee to   1Ki 2:8
d.
Adonijah shall be put to d.   1Ki 2:24
this day
but I will not at this time   1Ki 2:26
put thee to d.
not seek Lord should be   2Ch 15:13
put to d.
cometh into house, shall be   2Ch 23:7
put to d.
there is one law of his to put   Es 4:11
him to d.
wives be widows, men be   Jer 18:21
put to d.
know that if ye put me to   Jer 26:15
d.
king and all Judah put him   Jer 26:19
to d.
Jehoiakim sought to put   Jer 26:21
Urijah to d.
beseech thee, let this man be   Jer 38:4
put to d.
said, Wilt thou not   Jer 38:15
surely put me to d.
king sware, I will not put   Jer 38:16;
to d.   38:25
hands of Chaldeans might put   Jer 43:3
us to d.
smote them and put them to   Jer 52:27
d.
rise up against parents   M't 10:21;
to be put to d.   M'k 13:12; Lu 21:16
when he would put him to   M't 14:5
d. he feared
Jesus to put him to d.   M't 26:59;
    27:1; M'k 11:55

take him by craft and   M'k 14:1
put to d.
shall scourge and put him to   Lu 18:33
d.
two malefactors led to be put   Lu 23:32
to d.
they took counsel to put   Joh 11:53
him to d.
they might put Lazarus also   Joh 12:10
to d.
not lawful to put any man   Joh 18:31
to d.
Herod commanded keepers to   Ac 12:19
be put to d.
when they were put to d. I   Ac 26:10
gave voice
put to d. in flesh, quickened   1Pe 3:18

SHADOW OF DEATH

let darkness and shadow of d.   Job 3:5
stain it
land of darkness and   Job 10:21;
shadow of d.   10:22
bringeth to light the shadow   Job 12:22
of d.
on my eye lids is the   Job 16:16
shadow of d.
morning is to them even as   Job 24:17
shadow of d.
searcheth out darkness and   Job 28:3
shadow of d.
no shadow of d. where   Job 34:22
sinners may hide
hast thou seen doors of   Job 38:17
shadow of d.
tho' I walk thro' valley of   Ps 23:4
shadow of d.
hast covered us with shadow   Ps 44:19
of d.
sit in darkness, and shadow   Ps 107:10
of d.
brought out of darkness and   Ps 107:14
shadow of d.
dwell in land of the shadow   Isa 9:2
of d.
brought us thro' land of   Jer 2:6
shadow of d.
light, he turn it into shadow   Jer 13:16
of d.
turneth shadow of d. into the   Am 5:8
morning
sat in region and shadow of   M't 4:16
d.
light to them that sit in   Lu 1:79
shadow of d.

WAYS OF DEATH

end thereof are ways of d.   Pr 14:12;
    16:25

WITH DEATH

we have made a covenant   Isa 28:15
with d.
covenant with d. shall be   Isa 28:18
disannulled
I will kill her children with d.   Re 2:23
power given to them to kill   Re 6:8
with d.

WORTHY OF DEATH

that is worthy of d. be put to   De 17:6
d.
slay him, he was not worthy   De 19:6
of d.
man have committed a sin   De 21:22
worthy of d.
there is in damsel no sin   De 22:26
worthy of d.
to Abiathar, thou art worthy   1Ki 2:26
of d.
nothing worthy of d. is done   Lu 23:15
nothing laid to his charge   Ac 23:29
worthy of d.
if I have committed any   Ac 25:11
thing worthy of d.
he had committed nothing   Ac 25:25
worthy of d.
this man doth nothing   Ac 26:31
worthy of d.
commit such things are   Ro 1:32
worthy of d.

DEATHLESS

d. and everlasting (A)(B)   2Co 4:18

DEATHS

They shall die of grievous *d.*   *Jer 16:4*
the *d.* of them that are slain   *Eze 28:8*
die the *d.* of the   *Eze 28:10*
uncircumcised
prisons more frequent in *d.*   *2Co 11:23*
oft

DEBASE

shall *d.* them (A)   *J'g 19:24*
didst *d.* thyself even unto hell   *Isa 57:9*
abased yourselves to Sheol   *Isa 57:9*
(B)
sent down even to hell (R)   *Isa 57:9*
do not dishonor, *d.*, lightly   *Jer 14:21*
esteem the throne (A)(R)

DEBASED

become *d.* (N)   *Ro 3:9*

DEBATE

D. thy cause with thy neighbour *Pr 25:9*
Argue your cause with   *Pr 25:9*
neighbor (A)(B)(R)
forth, thou wilt *d.* with it   *Isa 27:8*
you contended with them in   *Isa 27:8*
measure (A)
He contended with her   *Isa 27:8*
(B)(E)(R)
fast for strife and *d.* and to   *Isa 58:4*
smite
you fast for strife and   *Isa 58:4*
contention (B)(E)
you fast only to quarrel and *Isa 58:4*
fight (R)
murder, *d.*, deceit, malignity   *Ro 1:29*
full of envy, murder, strife   *Ro 1:29*
(A)(E)(R)
full of envy, murder,   *Ro 1:29*
quarreling (B)
envy, murder, rivalry (N)   *Ro 1:29*
steeped in envy, murder,   *Ro 1:29*
quarrelsomeness (P)
in a *d.* with the devil (N)   *Jude 9*

DEBATED

d. within themselves (R)   *M'k 2:8*

DEBATES

debates (A)(N)(R)   *1Co 1:20*
there be *d.* envyings, wraths *2Co 12:20*
factions, jealousy, temper *2Co 12:20*
(A)
strife, jealousy, ugly temper *2Co 12:20*
(B)(E)
quarreling and jealousy   *2Co 12:20*
(N)(R)
arguments, jealousies,   *2Co 12:20*
ill-feelings (P)

DEBATING

d. in minds (B)   *Lu 3:15*
you are *d.* as you walk (N)   *Lu 24:17*
talking and *d.* with (N)   *Ac 9:29*

DEBAUCHED

d. spiritually (A)   *2Ch 21:11*

DEBAUCHERY

not in immorality and *d.*   *Ro 13:13*
(A)(B)(R)
that is *d.* (A)(R)   *Eph 5:18*
lived in licence and *d.* (N)   *1Pe 4:3*

DEBIR

unto *D.* king of Eglon,   *Jos 10:3*
saying
and all Israel with him, to *Jos 10:38*
D.
did to *D.* and to the king *Jos 10:39*
thereof
from Hebron, from *D.* from *Jos 11:21*
king of *D.* one; the king of *Jos 12:13*
Geder
Mahanaim unto the border *Jos 13:26*
of *D.*
the border went up toward *Jos 15:7*
D.
up thence to the inhabitants *Jos 15:15*
of *D.*

of *D.* before was   *Jos 15:15*
Kirjath-sepher
and Kirjath-sannah, which *Jos 15:49*
is *D.*
Holon with her suburbs,   *Jos 21:15*
and *D.*
up against the inhabitants of *J'g 1:11*
D.
of *D.* before was   *J'g 1:11*
Kirjath-sepher
Hilen with her suburbs, *D.*   *1Ch 6:58*

DEBORAH

But *D.* Rebekah's nurse died   *Ge 35:8*
D. a prophetess, the wife of   *J'g 4:4*
dwelt under the palm tree of   *J'g 4:5*
D.
D. arose, and went with Barak *J'g 4:9*
and *D.* went up with him   *J'g 4:10*
D. said unto Barak, Up; for *J'g 4:14*
Then sang *D.* and Barak the   *J'g 5:1*
son of
until that I *D.* arose, that I   *J'g 5:7*
arose
Awake, awake, *D.*: awake   *J'g 5:12*
princes of Issachar were with *J'g 5:15*
D.

DEBT

every one that was in *d.* and *1Sa 22:2*
sell the oil, and pay thy *d.*   *2Ki 4:7*
and the exaction of every *d.* *Ne 10:31*
him, and forgave him the *d.* *M't 18:27*
prison, till he should pay *M't 18:30*
the *d.*
I forgave thee all that *d.* *M't 18:32*
not reckoned of grace, but of *Ro 4:4*
d.
something owed to him (A)   *Ro 4:4*
wages not favor but an   *Ro 4:4*
obligation (B)
wages not gift, but fair reward *Ro 4:4*
(P)
not reckoned as a gift, but as *Ro 4:4*
his due (R)

DEBTOR

so with the *d.*   *Isa 24:2*
(A)(B)(E)(R)
hath restored to the *d.* his   *Eze 18:7*
pledge
the gold of the temple, he *M't 23:16*
is a *d.*
I am *d.* both to the Greeks   *Ro 1:14*
I have a debt to repay (A)   *Ro 1:14*
I am under obligation to Greek *Ro 1:14*
(N)(R)
under universal obligation. I *Ro 1:14*
owe some-thing to all men (P)
he is a *d.* to do the whole law *Ga 5:3*
under obligation to practice   *Ga 5:3*
whole (A)(N)
ought to practice whole law   *Ga 5:3*
(B)
bound to obey rest of law   *Ga 5:3*
(P)(R)

DEBTORS

our debts, as we forgive our *M't 6:12*
d.
certain creditor which had   *Lu 7:41*
two *d.*
called every one of his lord's *Lu 16:5*
d.
we are *d.* not to the flesh   *Ro 8:12*
them verily; and their *d.*   *Ro 15:27*
they are

DEBTS

of them that are sureties for *Pr 22:26*
d.
forgive us our *d.* as we   *M't 6:12*
forgive

DECAMP

they would *d.* (B)   *Nu 9:20*

DECAPOLIS

and from *D.* and from   *M't 4:25*
Jerusalem
and began to publish in *D.*   *M'k 5:20*
the midst of the coasts of *M'k 7:31*
D.

DECAY

and fallen in *d.* with thee   *Le 25:35*
unable to support himself   *Le 25:35*
(A)
unable to meet his   *Le 25:35*
obligations (B)
his hand fail with thee (E)   *Le 25:35*
cannot maintain himself (R) *Le 25:35*
tongues *d.* away (A)(B)   *Zec 14:12*
outer nature suffers *d.*   *2Co 4:16*
(B)(N)
reap *d.* and death of nature   *Ga 6:8*
(A)(P)
fall into blight and *d.* (P)   *Jas 1:11*
the moral *d.* of the world   *2Pe 1:4*
(A)

DECAYED

of the bearers of burdens is *Ne 4:10*
d.
strength of burden-bearers is *Ne 4:10*
weakening (A)
weariness of the workers (B) *Ne 4:10*
strength failing (R)   *Ne 4:10*
and I will raise up the *d.*   *Isa 44:26*
places

DECAYETH

the flood *d.* and drieth up   *Job 14:11*
river drains and dries up   *Job 14:11*
(A)(B)
river wasteth and drieth up *Job 14:11*
(E)(R)
slothfulness the building *d.*   *Ec 10:18*
through neglect the ceiling   *Ec 10:18*
sinks (A)(R)
the roof sinketh in (E)   *Ec 10:18*
the body (E)   *Joh 11:39*
that which *d.* and waxeth   *Heb 8:13*
old
what is obsolete is ripe for   *Heb 8:13*
(A)
antiquated and obsolete   *Heb 8:13*
approaches (B)
that becoming old and   *Heb 8:13*
waxeth aged (E)(R)
growing old and   *Heb 8:13*
aging (N)
grows weak and out of   *Heb 8:13*
date (P)

DECAYING

he will be *d.* (P)   *Joh 11:39*
our outer man is *d.* (A)(E) *2Co 4:16*

DECEASE

spake of his *d.* which he   *Lu 9:31*
should
speaking of his exit from life *Lu 9:31*
(A)
his exodus was to   *Lu 9:31*
consummate at (B)
his departure, destiny he   *Lu 9:31*
was to (N)
way take and end fulfill at   *Lu 9:31*
Jerusalem (P)
his departure which he must *Lu 9:31*
accomplish (R)
may be able after my *d.* to *2Pe 1:15*
have
after my departure (A)(R)   *2Pe 1:15*
after I am gone (B)(N)(P)   *2Pe 1:15*

DECEASED

they are *d.* they shall not   *Isa 26:14*
rise
they are dead, powerless   *Isa 26:14*
ghosts (A)
dead do not live; ghosts do *Isa 26:14*
not (B)
they are shades, they will not *Isa 26:14*
arise (R)
when he had married a   *M't 22:25*
wife, *d.*
the first married and died   *M't 22:25*
(A)(B)(N)(P)(R)

DECEIT

and their belly prepareth *d.* *Job 15:35*
nor my tongue utter *d.*   *Job 27:4*
if my foot hath hasted to *d.*   *Job 31:5*
His mouth is full of cursing   *Ps 10:7*
and *d.*

of his mouth are iniquity and *Ps 36:3* d.
to evil, and thy tongue *Ps 50:19* frameth d.
d. and guile depart not from *Ps 55:11* her
shall redeem their soul from *Ps 72:14* d.
d. shall not dwell within my *Ps 101:7* statues: for their d. is *Ps 119:118* falsehood
mouth speaketh d. (A)(E) *Ps 144:8;* *144:11*
the counsels of the wicked are *Pr 12:5* d.
but a false witness d. *Pr 12:17* D. is in the heart of them *Pr 12:20* that
but the folly of fools is d. *Pr 14:8* Bread of d. is sweet to a *Pr 20:17* man
and layeth up d. within him *Pr 26:24* Whose hatred is covered by *Pr 26:26* d.
neither was any d. in his *Isa 53:9* mouth
their houses full of d.: *Jer 5:27* therefore
hold fast d. they refuse to *Jer 8:5* return
habitation is in the midst of *Jer 9:6* d.
through d. they refuse to *Jer 9:6* know me
it speaketh d.: one speaketh *Jer 9:8* nought, and the d. of their *Jer 14:14* heart
of the d. of their own heart *Jer 23:26* make d. prosper (R) *Da 8:25* and the house of Israel with *Ho 11:12* d.
the balances of d. are in his *Ho 12:7* hand
and falsifying the balances by *Am 8:5* d.
houses with violence and d. *Zep 1:9* wickedness, d., lasciviousness *M'k 7:22* arrest Jesus by d. (A) *M'k 14:1* no d. in him (B)(P) *Joh 7:18* full of all d. (B)(R)(S) *Ac 13:10* full of envy, murder, debate, *Ro 1:29* d.
their tongues they have used *Ro 3:13* d.
through philosophy and vain *Col 2:8* d.
our exhortation was not of d. *1Th 2:3* limitless d. (B)(E) *2Th 2:10* lay aside all d. (B)(P) *1Pe 2:1*

DECEITFUL

will abhor the bloody and d. *Ps 5:6* man
devise d. matters against *Ps 35:20* them
me from the d. and unjust *Ps 43:1* man
words, O thou d. tongue *Ps 52:4* bloody and d. men shall not *Ps 55:23* live
were turned aside like a d. *Ps 78:57* bow
of the d. are opened *Ps 109:2* against me
from lying lips, and from a *Ps 120:2* d.
The wicked worketh a d. *Pr 11:18* work
but a d. witness speaketh lies *Pr 14:25* his dainties: for they are d. *Pr 23:3* meat
but the kisses of an enemy *Pr 27:6* are d.
and the d. man meet *Pr 29:13* together
Favour is d. and beauty is *Pr 31:30* vain
The heart is d. above all *Jer 17:9* things
High: they are·like a d. bow *Ho 7:16* and with the bag of d. *Mic 6:11* weights
with d. weights (E) *Mic 6:11* their tongue is d. in their *Mic 6:12* mouth
d. tongue be found in their *Zep 3:13* mouth
to use d. wealth (B) *Lu 16:9* faithful in d. riches (B) *Lu 16:11*

false apostles, d. workers *2Co 11:13* d. schemes (N) *Eph 4:14* craftiness of d. wiles (R) *Eph 4:14* corrupt according to the d. *Eph 4:22* lusts
by d. spirits (R) *1Ti 4:1* d. men will go bad (P) *2Ti 3:13*

DECEITFULLY

Shechem and Hamor his *Ge 34:13* father d.
let not Pharaoh deal d. any *Ex 8:29* more
seeing he hath dealt d. with *Ex 21:8* her
thing which he hath d. gotten *Le 6:4* did it (R) *2Ki 10:19* brethren have dealt d. as a *Job 6:15* brook
for God? and talk d. for him *Job 13:7* his soul unto vanity, nor *Ps 24:4* sworn d.
like a sharp razor, working d. *Ps 52:2* distorted my cause d. (B) *Ps 119:78* dealt d. against own lives *Jer 42:20* (A)(E)
doeth the work of the Lord *Jer 48:10* d.
he shall work d.: for he *Da 11:23* shall
nor handling the word of *2Co 4:2* God d.
handle dishonestly Word of *2Co 4:2* God (A)(R)
nor do we falsify Word of *2Co 4:2* God (R)
nor distort the Word of God *2Co 4:2* (N)
tamper with God's Word (R) *2Co 4:2* teaches servants d. (B) *Re 2:20*

DECEITFULNESS

the d. of riches, choke the *M't 13:22* word
the d. of riches, and the *M'k 4:19* lusts of
by empty d. (B)(R) *Col 2:8* be hardened through the d. *Heb 3:13* of sin

DECEITS

and imagine d. all the day *Ps 38:12* long
meditate d. all day (A)(E) *Ps 38:12* us smooth things, prophesy *Isa 30:10* d.
strategies and d. of the devil *Eph 6:11* (A)

DECEIVABLENESS

with all d. of *2Th 2:10* unrighteousness in
all wicked deception (A)(R) *2Th 2:10* limitless deceit of wickedness *2Th 2:10* (B)(E)
all deception sinfulness can *2Th 2:10* impose (N)
with evil's undiluted power *2Th 2:10* to deceive (P)

DECEIVE

that he came to d. thee, and *2Sa 3:25* did I not say, Do not d. me *2Ki 4:28* Let not Hezekiah d. you: *2Ki 18:29* for he
God in whom thou trustest *2Ki 19:10* let not Hezekiah d. you *2Ch 32:15* cause; and d. not with thy *Pr 24:28* lips
the deceivers d. (B) *Isa 24:16* Let not Hezekiah d. you *Isa 36:14* God, in whom thou trustest, *Isa 37:10* d. thee
will d. every one his neighbour *Jer 9:5* that be in the midst of your d. *Jer 29:8* D. not yourselves, saying *Jer 37:9* they wear a rough garment *Zec 13:4* to d.
Take heed that no man d. *M't 24:4* you
I am Christ; and shall d. *M't 24:5* many

shall rise and shall d. many *M't 24:11* they shall d. the very elect *M't 24:24* Take heed lest any man d. *M'k 13:5* you
I am Christ: and shall d. *M'k 13:6* many
to d. men of God's choice *M'k 13:22* (P)
speeches d. the hearts of the *Ro 16:18* Let no man d. himself. If *1Co 3:18* whereby they lie in wait to *Eph 4:14* d.
inventing errors to mislead *Eph 4:14* (A)
for devising error (B) *Eph 4:14* after the wiles of error (E) *Eph 4:14* their deceitful schemes (N) *Eph 4:14* the crafty presentation of *Eph 4:14* lies (P)
by their craftiness in *Eph 4:14* deceitful wiles (R)
Let no man d. you with vain *Eph 5:6* words
Let no man d. you by any *2Th 2:3* means
we d. ourselves, and the truth *1Jo 1:8* that would d. you (R) *1Jo 2:26* let no man d. you: he that *1Jo 3:7* that he should d. the nations *Re 20:3* go out to d. the nations *Re 20:8* which are

DECEIVED

your father hath d. me, and *Ge 31:7* violence, or hath d. his *Le 6:2* neighbour
that your heart be not d. *De 11:16* You have d. me (B) *J'g 16:10* Why hast thou d. me so, *1Sa 19:17* and sent
Why hast thou d. me? for *1Sa 28:12* thou art
my servant d. me: for thy *2Sa 19:26* servant
the d. and the deceiver are *Job 12:16* his
not him that is d. trust in *Job 15:31* vanity
If mine heart have been d. *Job 31:9* by a
whosoever is d. thereby is not *Pr 20:1* the princes of Noph are d. *Isa 19:13* a d. heart had turned him *Isa 44:20* aside
thou hast greatly d. this *Jer 4:10* people
thou hast d. me, and I was *Jer 20:7* d.
Thy terribleness hath d. thee *Jer 49:16* I called for my lovers, but *La 1:19* they d.
if the prophet be d. when he *Eze 14:9* hath
I the Lord have d. that *Eze 14:9* prophet
pride of thine heart hath d. thee *Ob 3* at peace with thee hath d. thee *Ob 7* Take heed that ye be not d. *Lu 21:8* the Pharisees, Are ye also d. *Joh 7:47* d. me, and by it slew me *Ro 7:11* Be not d.: neither fornicators *1Co 6:9* Be not d.; evil *1Co 15:33* communications
Be not d.; God is not mocked *Ga 6:7* Adam was not d. but the *1Ti 2:14* woman
being d. was in the *1Ti 2:14* transgression
worse, deceiving, and being *2Ti 3:13* d.
d. serving divers lusts and *Tit 3:3* thy sorceries were all nations *Re 18:23* d.
with which he d. them that *Re 19:20* had
the devil that d. them was *Re 20:10* cast

DECEIVER

I shall seem to him as a d. *Ge 27:12* the deceived and the d. are *Job 12:16* his
cursed be the d. which hath *Mal 1:14* we remember that that d. *M't 27:63* said
This is a d. and an antichrist *2Jo 7*

DECEIVERS

the *d*. deceive (B)	*Isa 24:16*
good report: as *d*. and yet true	*2Co 6:8*
unruly and vain talkers and *d*.	*Tit 1:10*
For many *d*. are entered into	*2Jo 7*

DECEIVES

as one *d*. a man (A)(B)(E)(R)	*Job 13:9*
by her teaching *d*. (P)	*Re 2:20*

DECEIVETH

the man that *d*. his neighbour	*Pr 26:19*
said, Nay; but he *d*. the people	*Joh 7:12*
when he is nothing, he *d*. himself	*Ga 6:3*
his tongue, but *d*. his own heart	*Jas 1:26*
Satan, which *d*. the whole world	*Re 12:9*
d. them that dwell on the earth	*Re 13:14*

DECEIVING

worse and worse, *d*., and	*2Ti 3:13*
hearers only, *d*. your own selves	*Jas 1:22*

DECEIVINGS

their own *d*. while they feast	*2Pe 2:13*

DECENT

things not proper or *d*. (A)(B)	*Ro 1:28*

DECENTLY

let us behave *d*. (N)	*Ro 13:13*
all things be done *d*. and in order	*1Co 14:40*

DECEPTION

master of every form of *d*. (A)	*Ac 13:10*
similar piece of *d*. (P)	*Ga 2:13*
all wicked *d*. (A)(N)(R)	*2Th 2:10*

DECEPTIVE

sat with *d*. men (B)	*Ps 26:4*
seen *d*. visions (R)	*La 2:14*
bring down *d*. fantasy (P)	*2Co 10:5*

DECEPTIVELY

acted *d*. against Lord (B)	*Jer 15:12*

DECIDE

too difficult to *d*. (B)	*De 17:8*
competent to *d*. between (A)(B)(E)(P)(R)	*1Co 6:5*

DECIDED

definitely *d*. on evil (B)	*1Sa 20:7; 20:9*
judgment be; thyself hast *d*. it	*1Ki 20:40*
ruin has been *d*. (B)	*Es 7:7*
when he *d*. to set him free (B)(N)(P)	*Ac 3:13*
d. to send contribution (B)	*Ac 11:29*
d. that Paul (A)	*Ac 15:2*
d. upon by apostles (N)(P)(R)	*Ac 16:4*
d. and cleared up (A)	*Ac 19:39*
d. to know nothing (R)	*1Co 2:2*
d. in his own mind (N)	*1Co 7:37*

DECIDES

d. not to marry young (P)	*1Co 7:37*

DECIMATED

d. before enemies (B)	*Nu 14:42*

DECISION

no unfairness in court *d*. (B)	*Le 19:15*
the *d*. of the Urim (B)	*Nu 27:21*
requiring *d*. too difficult (R)	*De 17:8*
make clear the *d*.	*De 17:9;*
(A)(B)(R)	*17:10-11*
take case to court for judicial *d*.	*De 25:1*
heard about the *d*. (B)	*1Ki 3:28*
godly *d*. is on lips (B)	*Pr 16:10*
d. wholly with Lord (A)(B)(R)	*Pr 16:33*
relent and reverse my *d*. (A)(B)	*Jer 26:3*
multitudes in the valley of *d*.	*Joe 3:14*
the Lord is near in the valley of *d*.	*Joe 3:14*
my *d*. is to gather nations (R)	*Zep 3:8*
nor voted for their *d*. (P)	*Lu 23:51*
for *d*. of scruples (E)	*Ro 14:1*
give a *d*. in a cause (N)	*1Co 6:5*
disqualified by *d*. of people (N)	*Col 2:18*

DECISIONS

no partiality in *d*. (B)	*De 1:17*
because of thy just *d*. (B)	*Ps 48:11*
divinely directed *d*. (A)(R)	*Pr 16:10*
art just in his *d*. (A)(B)	*Re 16:5*

DECISIVE

full destruction, *d*. one (B)	*Isa 10:23*

DECK

D. thyself now with majesty	*Job 40:10*
d. it with silver and with gold	*Jer 10:4*

DECKED

I have *d*. my bed with coverings	*Pr 7:16*
I have spread my couch with rugs (A)	*Pr 7:16*
d. with gold, and precious stones	*Pr 18:16*
bedecked with gold (A)(P)(R)	*Pr 18:16*
gilded with gold (B)	*Pr 18:16*
bedizened with gold (N)	*Pr 18:16*
I *d*. thee also with ornaments	*Eze 16:11*
wast thou *d*. with gold and silver	*Eze 16:13*
she *d*. herself with her earrings	*Ho 2:13*
d. with gold and precious stones	*Re 17:4*
bedecked with gold (A)(R)	*Re 17:4*
gilded with gold (B)	*Re 17:4*
bedizened with gold (N)	*Re 17:4*
glittering with gold (P)	*Re 17:4*

DECKEDST

and *d*. thy high places with divers	*Eze 16:16*
decorated high places, shrines (A)	*Eze 16:16*
make more attractive high places (B)	*Eze 16:16*
make gaily decked shrines (R)	*Eze 16:16*
and *d*. thyself with ornaments	*Eze 23:40*

DECKEST

thou *d*. thee with ornaments of	*Jer 4:30*

DECKETH

as a bridegroom *d*. himself with	*Isa 61:10*

DECKS

lower, second and third *d*. (B)(R)	*Ge 6:16*

DECLARATION

d. of the greatness of Mordecai	*Es 10:2*
and my *d*. with your ears	*Job 13:17*

DECLARE

to set forth in order a *d*. of those	*Lu 1:1*
and *d*. of your ready mind	*2Co 8:19*

DECLARE

was none that could *d*. it to me	*Ge 41:24*
began Moses to *d*. this law, saying	*De 1:5*
I *d*. to the Lord (B) (R)	*De 26:3*
I *d*. unto you this day (S)	*De 30:18*
and shall *d*. his cause in the ears	*Jos 20:4*
d. it me within the seven days of	*J'g 14:12*
if ye cannot *d*. it me, then shall ye	*J'g 14:13*
that he may *d*. unto us the riddle	*J'g 14:15*
prophets *d*. good unto the king	*1Ki 22:13*
D. his glory among the heathen	*1Ch 16:24*
the words of the prophets *d*. good	*2Ch 18:12*
and to *d*. unto her, and to charge	*Es 4:8*
the fishes of the sea shall *d*. unto	*Job 12:8*
that which I have seen I will *d*.	*Job 15:17*
Who shall *d*. his way to his face	*Job 21:31*
Then did he see it, and *d*. it	*Job 28:27*
I would *d*. unto him the number	*Job 31:37*
d. if thou hast understanding	*Job 38:4*
earth? *d*. if thou knowest it all	*Job 38:18*
of thee, and *d*. thou unto me	*Job 40:7; 42:4*
I will *d*. the decree: the Lord	*Ps 2:7*
d. among the people his doings	*Ps 9:11*
The heavens *d*. the glory of God	*Ps 19:1*
d. they name unto my brethren	*Ps 22:22*
d. his righteousness unto a people	*Ps 22:31*
praise thee? shall it *d*. thy truth	*Ps 30:9*
For I will *d*. mine iniquity	*Ps 38:18*
if I would *d*. and speak of them	*Ps 40:5*
heavens shall *d*. his righteousness	*Ps 50:6*
hast thou to do to *d*. my statutes	*Ps 50:16*
and shall *d*. the work of God	*Ps 64:9*
and I will *d*. what he hath done	*Ps 66:16*
that I may *d*. all thy works	*Ps 73:28*
is near thy wondrous works	*Ps 75:1*
But I will *d*. for ever; I will	*Ps 75:9*
and *d*. them to their children	*Ps 78:6*
D. his glory among the heathen	*Ps 96:3*
The heavens *d*. his righteousness	*Ps 97:6*
To *d*. the name of the Lord	*Ps 102:21*
and *d*. his works with rejoicing	*Ps 107:22*
but live, and *d*. the works	*Ps 118:17*
and shall *d*. thy mighty acts	*Ps 145:4*
acts; and I will *d*. thy greatness	*Ps 145:6*
to *d*. all this, that the righteous	*Ec 9:1*
they *d*. their sin as Sodom	*Isa 3:9*
d. his doings among the people	*Isa 12:4*
let him *d*. what he seeth	*Isa 21:6*
or *d*. us things for to come	*Isa 41:22*
new things do I *d*.: before	*Isa 42:9*
unto the Lord, and *d*. his praise	*Isa 42:12*
who among them can *d*. this	*Isa 43:9*
d. thou, that thou mayest be	*Isa 43:26*
as I, shall call, and shall *d*. it	*Isa 44:7*
I *d*. things that are right	*Isa 45:19*
all this; and will not ye *d*. it	*Isa 48:6*
with a voice of singing *d*. ye	*Isa 48:20*
and who shall *d*. his generation	*Isa 53:8*
I will *d*. thy righteousness	*Isa 57:12*

and they shall *d.* my glory *Isa 66:19* among
D. ye in Judah, and publish in *Jer 4:5*
D. this in the house of Jacob *Jer 5:20*
d. it for what the land *Jer 9:12* perisheth
and *d.* it in the isles afar off *Jer 31:10*
If I *d.* it unto thee, wilt *Jer 38:15* thou not
D. unto us now what thou *Jer 38:25* hast
I will *d.* it unto you; I will *Jer 42:4* keep
d. unto us, and we will do *Jer 42:20* it
D. ye in Egypt, and publish *Jer 46:14* in
D. ye among the nations, and *Jer 50:2*
to *d.* in Zion the vengeance *Jer 50:28*
and let us *d.* in Zion the *Jer 51:10* work of
they may *d.* all their *Eze 12:16* abomination
d. unto them their *Eze 23:36* abomination
d. all that thou seest to the *Eze 40:4* house
d. the interpretation thereof *Da 4:18*
D. ye it not at Gath, weep *Mic 1:10* ye not
to *d.* unto Jacob his *Mic 3:8* transgression
even to day do I *d.* that I *Zec 9:12* will
I will *d.* to them (R) *M't 7:23*
D. unto us the parable of *M't 13:36*
unto him, *D.* unto us this *M't 15:15* parable
d. yourselves just and *Lu 16:15* upright (A)
them thy name, and will *d.* *Joh 17:29* it
and who shall *d.* his *Ac 8:33* generation
we *d.* unto you glad tidings *Ac 13:32*
though a man *d.* it unto you *Ac 13:41*
worship, him *d.* I unto you *Ac 17:23*
to *d.* unto you the counsel *Ac 20:27* of God
To *d.* his righteousness for the *Ro 3:25*
To *d.* I say, at this time his *Ro 3:26*
for the day shall *d.* it *1Co 3:13*
Now in this that I *d.* unto *1Co 11:17* you
brethren I *d.* unto you the *1Co 15:1* gospel
state shall Tychicus *d.* unto *Col 4:7* you
will *d.* thy name unto my *Heb 2:12* brethren
d. plainly that they seek a *Heb 11:14*
I *d.* this is true grace (A) *1Pe 5:12*
seen and heard *d.* we unto *1Jo 1:3* you
d. unto you, that God is light *1Jo 1:5*

DECLARED

my name may be *d.* *Ex 9:16* throughout
And Moses *d.* unto the *Le 23:44* children
and they *d.* their pedigrees *Nu 1:18* after
was not *d.* what should be *Nu 15:34* done
And he *d.* unto you his *De 4:13* covenant
thou hast *d.* this day, that *2Sa 19:6*
the words that were *d.* unto *Ne 8:12* them
hast thou plentifully *d.* the *Job 26:3* thing
I have *d.* thy faithfulness *Ps 40:10* and thy
have I *d.* thy wondrous *Ps 71:17* works
d. thy strength among the *Ps 77:14* people
Shall thy lovingkindness be *Ps 88:11* *d.*
With my lips have I *d.* all *Ps 119:13*
I have *d.* my ways, and *Ps 119:26* thou
A grievous vision is *d.* unto *Isa 21:2* me
of Israel, have I *d.* unto you *Isa 21:10*
Who hath *d.* from the *Isa 41:26* beginning

I have *d.* and have saved *Isa 43:12*
from that time, and have *d.* it *Isa 44:8*
who hath *d.* this from *Isa 45:21* ancient
I have *d.* the former things *Isa 48:3*
from the beginning *d.* it to *Isa 48:5* thee
among them hath *d.* these *Isa 48:14* things
Then Michaiah *d.* unto them *Jer 36:13*
And now I have this day *d.* *Jer 42:21* it
d. unto him before all the *Lu 8:47* people
the Father, he hath *d.* him *Joh 1:18*
Jesus himself *d.* (A)(N) *Joh 4:44*
I have *d.* unto them thy *Joh 17:26* name
d. unto them how he had *Ac 9:27* seen the
when he had *d.* all these *Ac 10:8* things
d. unto them how the Lord *Ac 12:17* had
d. all things that God had *Ac 15:4* done
Simeon hath *d.* how God at *Ac 15:14*
d. particularly what things *Ac 21:19* God
d. Paul's cause unto the king *Ac 25:14*
d. to be the Son of God with *Ro 1:4* power
righteousness been *d.* (P) *Ro 3:21*
my name might be *d.* *Ro 9:17* throughout
it hath been *d.* unto me of *1Co 1:11* you
manifestly *d.* to be the epistle *2Co 3:3* of
Who also *d.* unto us your love *Col 1:8*
d. to his servants the prophets *Re 10:7*

DECLARES

who *d.* me in the right (A) *Isa 50:8*

DECLARETH

there is none that *d.* yea *Isa 41:26*
For a voice *d.* from Dan *Jer 4:15*
and their staff *d.* unto them *Ho 4:12*
d. unto man what is his *Am 4:13* thought

DECLARING

D. the end from the *Isa 46:10* beginning
d. the conversion of the *Ac 15:3* Gentiles
d. what miracles and wonders *Ac 15:12*
d. unto you the testimony of *1Co 2:1* God

DECLINE

d. after many to wrest *Ex 23:2* judgment
nor side with a multitude to *Ex 23:2* pervert justice (A)
lean toward the majority (B) *Ex 23:2*
turn aside after the multitude *Ex 23:2* (E)(R)
shalt not *d.* from the *De 17:11* sentence
not depart from their *De 17:11* verdict (A)(B)(R)
turn aside from the sentence *De 17:11* (E)
do I not *d.* from thy *Ps 119:157* testimonies
not swerve from *Ps 119:157* testimonies (A)(R)
not deviated from *Ps 119:157* testimonies (B)
not swerved from thy *Ps 119:157* testimonies (E)
neither *d.* from the words of *Pr 4:5*
not turn back from words *Pr 4:5* (A)(B)(R)
Let not thine heart *d.* to her *Pr 7:25* ways
incline toward her ways *Pr 7:25* (A)(B)
turn aside to her ways (R) *Pr 7:25*

DECLINED

d. neither to the right hand, *2Ch 34:2* nor

turned aside to right or to *2Ch 34:2* (A)(E)(R)
not deviating to right or to *2Ch 34:2* (B)
his way have I kept and *Job 23:11* not *d.*
I have not turned aside *Job 23:11* (A)(E)(R)
have never swerved aside *Job 23:11* (B)
have our steps *d.* from thy *Ps 44:18* way
departed from thy way (R) *Ps 44:18*
yet have I not *d.* from thy *Ps 119:51* law

DECLINETH

days are like a shadow that *Ps 102:11* *d.*
gone like the shadow when *Ps 109:23* it *d.*

DECOMPOSE

work for food that must *d.* *Joh 6:27* (B)

DECOMPOSITION

sown in *d.* (B) *1Co 15:42*

DECORATED

decorated (B) *2Ch 3:6; M't 23:29*
swept, *d.* (A)(R) *M't 12:44*
d. with handsome stones (A) *Lu 21:5*

DECREASE

and suffereth not their *Ps 107:38* cattle to *d.*
He must increase, but I must *Joh 3:30* *d.*

DECREASED

the waters *d.* continually until *Ge 8:5*
waters continued to diminish *Ge 8:5* (A)
gradually waters kept lowering *Ge 8:5* (B)
the waters continued to abate *Ge 8:5* (R)

DECREE

an everlasting *d.* (B) *Le 6:18*
rulers *d.* what is just (B)(R) *2Sa 8:15*
So they established a *d.* to *2Ch 30:5* make
Cyrus made a *d.* to build *Ezr 5:13* this
that a *d.* was made of Cyrus *Ezr 5:17*
Darius the king made a *d.* *Ezr 6:1*
same Cyrus the king made a *Ezr 6:3* *d.*
I make a *d.* what ye shall do *Ezr 6:8*
I have made a *d.* that *Ezr 6:11* whosoever
I Darius have made a *d.*: let *Ezr 6:12*
I make a *d.* that all they of *Ezr 7:13*
I Artaxerxes the king, do *Ezr 7:21* make a *d.*
the king's *d.* which he shall *Es 1:20* make
and his *d.* was heard, and *Es 2:8*
and the *d.* was given in *Es 3:15* Shushan
commandment and his *d.* came *Es 4:3*
the copy of the writing of the *Es 4:8* *d.*
And the *d.* was given at *Es 8:14* Shushan
commandment and his *d.* *Es 8:17* came
and his *d.* drew near to be put *Es 9:1*
according unto this day's *d.* *Es 9:13* and let
the *d.* was given at Shushan *Es 9:14*
And the *d.* of Esther *Es 9:32* confirmed
Thou shalt also *d.* a thing *Job 22:28*
thou shalt also *d.* this thing *Job 22:28*
when he made a *d.* for the *Job 28:26* rain
I will declare the *d.*: the Lord *Ps 2:7* hath
made it a *d.* (R) *Ps 81:5*

confirmed to Jacob by a *d.* *Ps 105:10* (B)
according to righteous *d.* *Ps 119:149* (A)
made a *d.* which shall not pass *Ps 148:6*
reign, and princes *d.* justice *Pr 8:15*
When he gave to the sea his *d.* *Pr 8:29*
unto them that *d.* unrighteous *Isa 10:1*
d. a destruction (A)(E)(R) *Isa 28:22*
of the sea by a perpetual *d.* *Jer 5:22*
there is but one *d.* for you *Da 2:9*
there is but one sentence *Da 2:9* (A)(B)(R)
there is but one law for you *Da 2:9* (E)
And the *d.* went forth that wise men *Da 2:13*
is the *d.* so hasty from the king *Da 2:15*
Thou, O king, hast made a *d.* *Da 3:10*
I make a *d.*, That every people *Da 3:29*
Therefore made I a *d.* to bring in *Da 4:6*
by the *d.* of the watchers *Da 4:17*
and this is the *d.* of the most High *Da 4:24*
to make a firm *d.* that whosoever *Da 6:7*
O king, establish the *d.* and sign *Da 6:8*
signed the writing and the *d.* *Da 6:9*
king concerning the king's *d.* *Da 6:12*
Hast thou not signed a *d.* *Da 6:12*
nor the *d.* that thou hast signed *Da 6:13*
no *d.* nor statute which the king *Da 6:15*
I make a *d.*, That in every *Da 6:26*
the *d.* of the king and his nobles *Jon 3:7*
day shall the *d.* be far removed *Mic 7:11*
Before the *d.* bring forth *Zep 2:2*
there went out a *d.* from Cæsar *Lu 2:1*
under thy hand and *d.* (N) *Ac 4:28*
aware of God's righteous *d.* *Ro 1:32* (A)(N)(R)

DECREED

and what was *d.* against her *Es 2:1*
and as they had *d.* for themselves *Es 9:31*
brake up for it my *d.* place *Job 38:10*
forget what is *d.* (B)(R) *Pr 31:5*
the consumption *d.* shall overflow *Isa 10:22*
d. upon your people *Da 9:24* (A)(E)(R)
desolations are *d.* (A)(R) *Da 9:26*
the *d.* end (R) *Da 9:27*
it is *d.*, she shall be captive (S) *Na 2:7*
God *d.* before the ages (R) *1Co 2:7*
hath so *d.* in his heart that he *1Co 7:37*
resolved in his heart (A) *1Co 7:37*
determined in own heart *1Co 7:37* (B)(E)(R)
decided in his own mind (N) *1Co 7:37*
decides not to marry young (P) *1Co 7:37*
d. in his design (N) *Eph 1:11*

DECREES

teaching them *d.* (A) *Ex 18:20*
executed just *d.* (R) *De 33:21*
that decree unrighteous *d.* *Isa 10:1*
delivered them the *d.* for to keep *Ac 16:4*
all do contrary to the *d.* of Cæsar *Ac 17:7*

DEDAN

sons of Raamah; Sheba, and D. *Ge 10:7*
Jokshan begat Sheba and D. *Ge 25:3*
the sons of D. were Asshurim, and *Ge 25:3*
son of Raamah; Sheba, and D. *1Ch 1:9*
sons of Jokshan; Sheba, and D. *1Ch 1:32*

D. and Tema, and Buz, and *Jer 25:23*
dwell deep, O inhabitants of D. *Jer 49:8*
they of D. shall fall by the sword *Eze 25:13*
The men of D. were thy merchants *Eze 27:15*
D. was thy merchant in precious *Eze 27:20*
Sheba, and D. and the merchants *Eze 38:13*

DEDANIM

O ye travelling companies of D. *Isa 21:13*

DEDICATE

d. to me all firstborn (B) *Ex 13:2*
dedicate (A)(B)(R) *Ex 28:38; Le 22:2*
d. his head (B) *Nu 6:12*
firstborn males *d.* (B) *De 15:19*
battle, and another man *d.* it *De 20:5*
Which also king David did *d.* *2Sa 8:11*
which he consecrated to the Lord (B) *2Sa 8:11*
did they *d.* to maintain the house *1Ch 26:27*
to *d.* it to him, and to burn *2Ch 2:4*
to *d.* them (B) *Job 1:5*

DEDICATED

had been *d.* to the Lord (B) *Le 19:8*
new house, and hath not *d.* it *De 20:5*
wholly *d.* the silver unto the Lord *J'g 17:3*
the silver and gold that he had *d.* *2Sa 8:11*
which David his father had *d.* *1Ki 7:51*
and all the children of Israel *d.* *1Ki 8:63*
things which his father had *d.* *1Ki 15:15*
the things which himself had *d.* *1Ki 15:15*
money of the *d.* things that is *2Ki 12:4*
money of the sacred offerings (B) *2Ki 12:4*
money of the hallowed things (E) *2Ki 12:4*
money of the holy things (R) *2Ki 12:4*
kings of Judah, had *d.* and *2Ki 12:18*
priests *d.* themselves (B) *1Ch 5:11*
king David *d.* unto the Lord *1Ch 18:11*
over the treasures of the *d.* things *1Ch 26:20*
all the treasures of the *d.* things *1Ch 26:26*
the captains of the host, had *d.* *1Ch 26:26*
Joab the son of Jeruiah, had *d.* *1Ch 26:28*
and whosoever had *d.* any thing *1Ch 26:28*
of the treasuries of the *d.* things *1Ch 28:12*
things that David his father had *d.* *2Ch 5:1*
and all the people *d.* the house *2Ch 7:5*
the things that his father had *d.* *2Ch 15:18*
and that he himself had *d.* *2Ch 15:18*
d. things of the house of the Lord *2Ch 24:7*
and the *d.* things faithfully *2Ch 31:12*
that were *d.* (B) *Ezr 3:5*
they *d.* the sheep gate (B) *Ne 3:1*
those *d.* to me (B) *Isa 13:3*
be *d.* to the Lord (A)(R) *Isa 23:18*
I *d.* you (B) *Jer 1:5*
every *d.* thing in Israel shall be *Eze 44:29*
every thing devoted (B)(E)(R) *Eze 44:29*
Father *d.* (A)(B)(N)(P)(R) *Joh 10:36*
among all (N) *Ac 20:32*
people *d.* to him (N) *1Co 1:2*
d. consecrated (A)(P)(R) *1Co 1:2*
valued and *d.* (N) *2Ti 2:21*
testament was *d.* without blood *Heb 9:18*

inaugurated and ratified *Heb 9:18* (A)(B)(N)(R)
not put into force without (P) *Heb 9:18*
He initiated, *d.* (A)(E) *Heb 10:20*
devout and *d.* lives (N) *2Pe 3:11*

DEDICATES

if a man *d.* a field *Le 27:14* (A)(B)(R)
if he that *d.* it will (A)(R) *Le 27:15; 27:19*
no man *d.* it (A)(B)(R) *Le 27:26*

DEDICATING

princes offered for *d.* of the altar *Nu 7:10*
on his day, for the *d.* of the altar *Nu 7:11*

DEDICATION

garments for *d.* (B) *Ex 28:3*
the *d.* of the altar, in the day *Nu 7:84*
This was the *d.* of the altar *Nu 7:88*
they kept the *d.* of the altar *2Ch 7:9*
kept the *d.* of this house of God *Ezr 6:16*
And offered at the *d.* of this house *Ezr 6:17*
at the *d.* of the wall of Jerusalem *Ne 12:27*
to keep the *d.* with gladness *Ne 12:27*
at the *d.* of the house of David *Ps 30 title*
come to the *d.* of the image *Da 3:2*
together unto the *d.* of the image *Da 3:3*
at Jerusalem the feast of the *d.* *Joh 10:22*
complete our *d.* (B) *2Co 7:1*

DEED

a shameful *d.* committed (B) *Ge 34:7*
What *d.* is this that ye have done *Ge 44:15*
And in very *d.* for this cause *Ex 9:16*
There was no such *d.* done *J'g 19:30*
committed lewd and wanton *d.* (B) *J'g 20:6*
For in very *d.* as the Lord God of *1Sa 25:34*
that Saul was come in very *d.* *1Sa 26:4*
by this *d.* thou hast given great *2Sa 12:14*
But will God in very *d.* dwell with *2Ch 6:18*
For this *d.* of the queen shall *Es 1:17*
have heard of the *d.* of the queen *Es 1:18*
I took the *d.* (S) *Jer 32:11; 32:12, 14, 16*
I signed the *d.* (S) *Jer 32:44; 32:10*
to the counsel and *d.* of them *Lu 23:51*
had not agreed to purpose and action (A) *Lu 23:51*
had not voted for council's action (B) *Lu 23:51*
had dissented from policy and action (N) *Lu 23:51*
neither agreed with their plan (P) *Lu 23:51*
mighty in *d.* and word before God *Lu 24:19*
mighty in work and word (A) *Lu 24:19*
mighty in practice and preaching (B) *Lu 24:19*
powerful in speech and action (N) *Lu 24:19*
strong in what he did and said (P) *Lu 24:19*
good *d.* done to the impotent man *Ac 4:9*
Gentiles obedient, by word *Ro 15:18* and *d.*
hath done this *d.* might be taken *1Co 5:2*
him that hath so done this *d. 1Co 5:3*
also in *d.* when we are present *2Co 10:11*
releasing our *d.* of purchase *Eph 1:14* (B)

ye do in word or d. do all in Col 3:17
man shall be blessed in his d. Jas 1:25
tongue; but in d. and in 1Jo 3:18
truth

DEEDS

thou hast done d. unto me Ge 20:9
had done many d. (S) 2Sa 23:20; 1Ch 11:22
make known his d. among 1Ch 16:8
make known his doings 1Ch 16:8
among the (A)(E)
proclaim to nations his acts 1Ch 16:8
(B)
And his d. first and last hold 2Ch 35:27
his acts, first and last 2Ch 35:27
(A)(E)(R)
his affairs from first to last 2Ch 35:27
(B)
for our evil d. and for our Ezr 9:13
reported his good d. before Ne 6:19
him
his actions were good (B) Ne 6:19
wipe not out my good d. that Ne 13:14
the benevolent service I have Ne 13:14
(B)
Give them according to their Ps 28:4
d.
make known his d. among Ps 105:1
all his marvelous d. (A) Ps 105:2
According to their d. Isa 59:18
overpass the d. of the wicked Jer 5:28
she has done vile d. (R) Jer 11:15
them according to their d. Jer 25:14
take these d. (S) Jer 32:14
sign d. and seal them (S) Jer 32:44
good d. publicly (A)(B)(P) M't 6:1
wisdom is justified by d. M't 11:19
(A)(R)
ye allow the d. of your Lu 11:48
fathers
the due reward of our d. Lu 23:41
due reward for our actions Lu 23:41
(A)(R)
our deserts for our misdeeds Lu 23:41
(B)
paying the price for our Lu 23:41
misdeeds (N)
we only got what we deserve Lu 23:41
(P)
because their d. were evil Joh 3:19
lest his d. should be Joh 3:20
reproved
his activities would be Joh 3:20
exposed (B)
his works should be reproved Joh 3:20
(E)
practices would be shown up Joh 3:20
(N)
his d. may be made manifest Joh 3:21
his works may be plainly Joh 3:21
shown (A)
so that it will be perfectly Joh 3:21
clear (B)
works may be made manifest Joh 3:21
(E)
may be clearly seen that God Joh 3:21
is in (N)
to make it plain that all he Joh 3:21
has (P)
Ye do the d. of your father Joh 8:41
works of your father Joh 8:41
(A)(B)(E)(N)
was mighty in words and in Ac 7:22
d.
confessed, and shewed their Ac 19:18
d.
exposing their practices Ac 19:18
(A)(P)(R)
their magic practices (B) Ac 19:18
had been using magical Ac 19:18
spells (N)
and that very worthy d. are Ac 24:2
done
perform unmentionable d. Ro 1:28
(P)
to every man according to his Ro 2:6
d.
by the d. of the law there Ro 3:20
shall no
works prescribed by law Ro 3:20
(A)(E)(R)
through observance of the Ro 3:20
law (B)(N)(P)
faith without the d. of the Ro 3:28
law
do mortify the d. of the body Ro 8:13

and wonders, and mighty d. 2Co 12:12
miracles, signs, mighty 2Co 12:12
works (A)(P)
signs, miracles, and acts of 2Co 12:12
power (B)
signs, wonders, mighty 2Co 12:12
works (E)(R)
signs, marvels, miracles 2Co 12:12
(N)
barren d. of darkness Eph 5:11
(A)(N)
put off the old man with his Col 3:9
d.
old self with its evil practices Co 3:9
(A)
old nature with its evil Col 3:9
practices (B)(R)
the old man with his doings Col 3:9
(E)
to day with their unlawful d. 2Pe 2:8
speed is partaker of his evil d. 2Jo 11
partaker of his evil doings (A) 2Jo 11
makes himself a sharer of 2Jo 11
wicked works (B)(R)
partaketh in his evil works (E) 2Jo 11
share in the evil he is doing (P) 2Jo 11
of all their ungoldy d. which Jude 15
all their impious activities Jude 15
(B)
all their works of ungodliness Jude 15
(E)(P)
garments their d. defiled (P) Jude 23
hatest the d. of the Re 2:6
Nicolaitanes
detest the works of the Re 2:6
Nicolaitans (A)(E)(N)(P)(R)
hate the doings of the Re 2:6
Nicolaitans (B)
except they repent of their Re 2:22
d.
repent of their doings (A)(R) Re 2:22
unless they repent of their Re 2:22
practices (B)
repent of their works (E) Re 2:22
forswear what she is doing (N) Re 2:22
repented not of their d. Re 16:11
did not repent of their Re 16:11
practices (B)
repent of their works (E) Re 16:11
repent of what they had done Re 16:11
(N)(P)

DEEMED

is d. intelligent (R) Pr 17:28
shipmen d. that they drew Ac 27:27
near
d. deserving of kingdom (A) 2Th 1:5
d. me worthy (A) 1Ti 1:12
d. worthy (N) Heb 3:3

DEEP

was upon the face of the d. Ge 1:2
God caused a d. sleep to fall Ge 2:21
upon
fountains of the great d. Ge 7:11
broken
The fountains also of the d. Ge 8:2
down, a d. sleep fell upon Ge 15:12
Abram
blessings of the d. that lieth Ge 49:25
under
for the d. that coucheth De 33:13
beneath
d. sleep from the Lord was 1Sa 26:12
fallen
in d. distress (S) 2Sa 24:14
when d. sleep falleth on men Job 4:13
He discovereth d. things out Job 12:22
of
deep (A)(E)(R) Job 28:14; 38:16; Ps 33:7; Pr 8:27
when d. sleep falleth upon Job 33:15
men
deep (B) Job 38:16; Ps 33:7; Pr 8:27
and the face of the d. is Job 38:30
frozen
maketh the d. to boil like a Job 41:31
pot
would think the d. to be Job 41:32
hoary
thy judgments are a great d. Ps 36:6
D. calleth unto d. at the noise Ps 42:7
one of them, and the heart, is Ps 64:6
d.
I sink in d. mire, when there Ps 69:2
is no

I am come into d. waters Ps 69:2
hate me, and out of the d. Ps 69:14
waters
neither let the d. swallow me Ps 69:15
up
the d. (A)(B)(R) Ps 77:1; Ps 78:15; Pr 3:20
and didst cause it to take d. Ps 80:9
root
and thy thoughts are very d. Ps 92:5
In his hand are the d. places Ps 95:4
Thou coveredst it with the d. Ps 104:6
Lord, and his wonders in Ps 107:24
the d.
in the seas, and all d. places Ps 135:6
into the fire; into d. pits Ps 140:10
the fountains of the d. Pr 8:28
of a man's mouth are as d. Pr 18:4
waters
casteth into a d. sleep: and Pr 19:15
in the heart of man is like d. Pr 20:5
water
mouth of strange women is a Pr 22:14
d. pit
whore is a d. ditch; and a Pr 23:27
stranger
far off, and exceeding d. who Ec 7:24
can
the spirit of d. sleep, and Isa 29:10
Woe unto them that seek d. Isa 29:15
he hath made it d. and large Isa 30:33
That saith to the d., Be dry Isa 44:27
sea, the waters of the great Isa 51:10
d.
That led them through the Isa 63:13
d. as
dwell d. O inhabitants of Jer 49:8
Dedan
dwell d. O ye inhabitants of Jer 49:30
Hazor
shalt drink of thy sister's Eze 23:32
cup d.
when I shall bring up the d. Eze 26:19
upon
the d. set him up on high Eze 31:4
with her
I covered the d. for him Eze 31:15
Then will I make their Eze 32:14
waters d.
to have drunk of the d. Eze 34:18
waters
revealeth the d. and secret Da 2:22
things
I was in a d. sleep on my Da 8:18
face
then was I in a d. sleep on Da 10:9
my face
it devoured the great d. and Am 7:4
thou hadst cast me into the d. Jon 2:3
the d. was round about me Jon 2:5
(E)(R)
the d. uttered his voice, and Hab 3:10
lifted
Launch out into the d. and let Lu 5:4
built an house, and digged d. Lu 6:48
them to go out into the d. Lu 8:31
to draw with, and the well is Joh 4:11
d.
caused d. distress (P) Ac 15:24
being fallen into a d. sleep Ac 20:9
Who shall descend into the d. Ro 10:7
things, yea, the d. things of 1Co 2:10
God
their d. poverty abounded 2Co 8:2
unto the
same d. concern for you (P) 2Co 8:16
and a day I have seen in the 2Co 11:25
d.

DEEPER

plague in sight to be d. than Le 13:3; 13:4, 25, 30-32, 34
the skin
d. than hell; what canst thou Job 11:8
know
a people of d. speech than Isa 33:19
thou

DEEP-FELT

this is a d. mourning (B) Ge 50:11

DEEPLY

the queen was d. distressed Es 4:4
(B)(R)
children of Israel have d. Isa 31:6
revolted
ye may drink d. (S) Isa 66:11
gone d. into (S) Ho 5:2

They have *d.* corrupted themselves	*Ho 9:9*
d. moved (A)(B)	*M't 15:32*
Jesus was *d.* moved (N)(P)	*M't 20:34*
he sighed *d.* in his spirit, and saith	*M'k 8:12*
d. moved in spirit (A)(N)(P)(R)	*Joh 11:33*
d. indignant in spirit (B)	*Joh 11:33*
Peter was *d.* hurt (P)	*Joh 21:17*
so *d.* interested in you (B)	*2Co 8:17*

DEEPNESS

because they had no *d.* of earth	*M't 13:5*
not much soil (A)(N)(R)	*M't 13:5*
they had little earth (B)	*M't 13:5*
not much earth (E)	*M't 13:5*
very little soil (P)	*M't 13:5*

DEEPS

the *d.* were congealed (E)(R)	*Ex 15:8*
thou threwest into the *d.* as a	*Ne 9:11*
cast their pursuers into depths (B)	*Ne 9:11*
lowest pit, in darkness, in the *d.*	*Ps 88:6*
the earth, ye dragons, and all *d.*	*Ps 148:7*
all you ocean depths (B)	*Ps 148:7*
when there were no *d.* (A)	*Pr 8:24*
the *d.* of the river shall dry up	*Zec 10:11*
the depths of the Nile (A)(E)(R)	*Zec 10:11*

DEER

Naphtali is a *d.* (B)	*Ge 49:21; 2Sa 22:34*
as of the *d.* (B)	*De 12:15; 1Ki 4:23; Ps 42:1; Isa 35:6*
the roebuck, and the fallow *d.*	*De 14:5*
like a *d.* in the field (B)	*2Sa 2:18*
fast as a *d.* (B)	*1Ch 12:8*

DEFAME

exclude, denounce and *d.* (B)	*Lu 6:22*

DEFAMED

Being *d.* we intreat: we are made	*1Co 4:13*
be *d.* for the name of (B)	*1Pe 4:14*

DEFAMING

For I heard the *d.* of many	*Jer 20:10*
do not bring a *d.* charge (A)(B)	*2Pe 2:11*

DEFEAT

d. of Chedorlaomer (B)(R)	*Ge 14:17*
d. of them (B)	*Jos 10:10*
suffered a disastrous *d.* (B)	*1Sa 4:17*
d. the Philistines (B)	*1Sa 23:2*
me *d.* the counsel of Ahithophel	*2Sa 15:34*
d. the good counsel of Ahithophel	*2Sa 17:14*
cause *d.* to prosper (S)	*Da 8:25*
is a *d.* for you (B)	*1Co 6:7*
d. of the kings (B)(P)	*Heb 7:1*

DEFEATED

defeated (A)	*Ge 36:35; De 2:33; 28:7; 29:7; Jos 12:1, 7; 13:21; J'g 11:21; 20:36; 1Sa 7:10; 13:4; 2Sa 8:2-3; 10:15, 19; 2Ki 10:32; 1Ch 1:46; 18:3, 9-10; 2Ch 28:5, 23*
defeated (B)	*Ge 14:15; De 3:3; 29:7; Jos 10:26; 11:8; 12:1, 7; 13:21; J'g 3:13; 11:21; 12:4; 1Sa 14:48; 2Sa 8:3; 2Ki 10:32; 18:8; 1Ch 1:46; 18:3; 2Ch 13:15; 28:5; Jer 46:2*
defeated (R)	*Ge 36:35; Nu 14:45; De 1:42; 2:33; 4:46; 28:7, 25; 29:7; Jos 10:40; 12:1, 7; 13:21; J'g 2:13; 11:21; 20:35; 1Sa 4:2, 10; 13:3-4; 15:7; 2Sa 5:20; 8:1-3, 9-10; 10:15; 1Ki 8:33; 2Ki 10:32; 1Ch 1:46; 14:11; 18:1; 2Ch 13:15; 14:12; 28:5, 17, 23; Jer 37:10; 46:2*

d. Amalek (B)	*Ex 17:13*
d. them (B)(R)	*Nu 14:45; Jos 10:10*
Israel was *d.* (B)(R)	*1Sa 4:10*
he *d.* them (S)	*1Sa 14:47*
d. by (S)	*2Ki 14:12; 1Ch 19:16, 19; 2Ch 6:24; 25:22*
who *d.* him (A)(B)(R)	*2Ch 28:5*
they were *d.* (A)(R)	*Re 12:8*

DEFEATING

d. them with heavy losses (B)	*1Sa 19:8; 23:5*

DEFECT

or any *d.* (S)	*De 17:1*
is a *d.* in you (A)(E)	*1Co 6:7*
had been without *d.* (A)	*Heb 8:7*

DEFECTIVE

tree bears *d.* fruit (B)	*M't 7:17*

DEFENCE

their *d.* is departed from them	*Nu 14:9*
Jerusalem, and built cities for *d.*	*2Ch 11:5*
the Almighty shall be thy *d.*	*Job 22:25*
My *d.* is of God, which saveth	*Ps 7:10*
for an house of *d.* to save me	*Ps 31:2*
wait upon thee: for God is my *d.*	*Ps 59:9*
thou hast been my *d.* and refuge	*Ps 59:16*
God is my *d.* and the God of my	*Ps 59:17*
and my salvation; he is my *d.*	*Ps 62:2*
he is my *d.*; I shall not be moved	*Ps 62:6*
For the Lord is our *d.*; and	*Ps 89:18*
the Lord is my *d.*; and my God	*Ps 94:22*
wisdom is a *d.* and money is a *d.*	*Ec 7:12*
upon all the glory shall be a *d.*	*Isa 4:5*
the brooks of *d.* shall be emptied	*Isa 19:6*
place of *d.* shall be the munition	*Isa 33:16*
and the *d.* shall be prepared	*Na 2:5*
have made his *d.* unto the people	*Ac 19:33*
hear ye my *d.* which I make	*Ac 22:1*
d. and confirmation of the gospel	*Ph'p 1:7*
I am set for the *d.* of the gospel	*Ph'p 1:17*

DEFENCED

of a *d.* city a ruin: a palace	*Isa 25:2*
Yet the *d.* city shall be desolate	*Isa 27:10*
against all the *d.* cities of Judah	*Isa 36:1*
to lay waste *d.* cities into ruinous	*Isa 37:26*
have made thee this day a *d.* city	*Jer 1:18*
and let us go into the *d.* cities	*Jer 4:5*
and let us enter into the *d.* cities	*Jer 8:14*
for these *d.* cities remained	*Jer 34:7*
and to Judah in Jerusalem the *d.*	*Eze 21:20*

DEFEND

arose to *d.* Israel Tola the son of	*J'g 10:1*
For I will *d.* this city, to save it	*2Ki 19:34*
will *d.* this city for mine own sake	*2Ki 20:6*
d. their lives (S)	*Es 8:11*
I will *d.* my ways (S)	*Job 13:15*
name of the God of Jacob *d.* thee	*Ps 20:1*
d. me from them that rise up	*Ps 59:1*
D. the poor and fatherless: do	*Ps 82:3*

d. their cause (B)	*Pr 23:11*
d. the rights of the poor (B)	*Pr 31:9*
d. the widow (B)	*Isa 1:17*
d. the fatherless (A)(R)	*Isa 1:17*
d. the fatherless (R)	*Isa 1:23*
the Lord of hosts *d.*	*Isa 31:5*
Jerusalem	
For I will *d.* this city to save it	*Isa 37:35*
of Assyria: and I will *d.* this city	*Isa 38:6*
he will *d.* (B)	*Jer 50:34; 51:36*
The Lord of hosts shall *d.* them	*Zec 9:15*
In that day shall the Lord *d.*	*Zec 12:8*

DEFENDED

and *d.* it, and slew the Philistines	*2Sa 23:12*
suffer wrong, he *d.* him; and smote	*Ac 7:24*

DEFENDEST

because thou *d.* them: let them	*Ps 5:11*

DEFENDING

d. also he will deliver it; and	*Isa 31:5*

DEFENSE

d. of his anointed (B)	*Ps 28:8; 60:7*
Ephraim is my *d.* (E)	*Ps 60:7*
you have no *d.* (N)	*Ro 2:1*
at my first *d.* no man (S)	*2Ti 4:16*

DEFENSES

bring down your *d.* (A)(R)	*Am 3:11*

DEFER

d. not to pay it; for he hath no	*Ec 5:4*
Pay what you vow (A)(B)(R)	*Ec 5:4*
will I *d.* mine anger, and for my	*Isa 48:9*
I have postponed my anger (B)	*Isa 48:9*
d. not, for thine own sake	*Da 9:19*
Do not delay, for your own sake (A)	*Da 9:19*
take notice and take action (B)	*Da 9:19*
give heed and delay not (R)	*Da 9:19*

DEFERRED

young man *d.* not to do the thing	*Ge 34:19*
without delay the young man (A)(B)(R)	*Ge 34:19*
Hope *d.* maketh the heart sick	*Pr 13:12*
Hope drawn out makes the heart (B)	*Pr 13:12*
of that way, he *d.* them, and put them off (A)(R)	*Ac 24:22*
he adjourned the case (B)(N)(P)	*Ac 24:22*

DEFERRETH

discretion of a man *d.* his anger	*Pr 19:11*
restrain his anger (A)(B)	*Pr 19:11*
maketh him slow to anger (E)(R)	*Pr 19:11*

DEFIANCE

all in *d.* of its laws (P)	*M't 13:41*
in *d.* of the law (A)(N)	*Ac 23:3*

DEFIANT

d., rebellious (A)(B)(E)(R)	*Zep 3:1*

DEFIANTLY

who *d.* rebels (B)	*Nu 15:30*

DEFICIENT

d.; and impeded speech (A)	*Ex 6:12; Ro 6:30*

DEFIED

defy, whom the Lord hath *Nu 23:8*
not *d.*
seeing he hath *d.* the armies *1Sa 17:36*
of
armies of Israel, whom *1Sa 17:45*
thou hast *d.*
And when he *d.* Israel, *2Sa 21:21*
Jonathan
when they *d.* the Philistines *2Sa 23:9*
d. and blasphemed (E) *2Ki 19:22;*
19:23
But when he *d.* Israel, *1Ch 20:7*
Jonathan
d. and rebelled in *Ps 78:40*
(A)(E)(R)

DEFILE

neither shall ye *d.* yourselves *Le 11:4*
when they *d.* my tabernacle *Le 15:31*
that is
neighbour's wife, to *d.* *Le 18:20*
thyself with
thou lie with any beast to *d.* *Le 18:23*
thyself
D. not ye yourselves in any *Le 18:24*
of these
spue not you out also, when *Le 18:28*
ye *d.* it
that ye *d.* not yourselves *Le 18:30*
therein
to *d.* my sanctuary, and to *Le 20:3*
profane
shall not *d.* himself, being a *Le 21:4*
chief
nor *d.* himself for his father *Le 21:11*
not eat to *d.* himself therewith *Le 22:8*
that they *d.* not their camps *Nu 5:3*
D. not therefore the land *Nu 35:34*
which ye
children of Ammon, did the *2Ki 23:13*
king *d.*
my feet; how shall I *d.* them *Ca 5:3*
Ye shall *d.* also the covering *Isa 30:22*
of thy
my name to *d.* it *Jer 7:30*
(A)(B)(E)(R)
called by my name, to *d.* it *Jer 32:34*
they shall *d.* it (B) *Eze 7:21*
robbers shall enter into it, *Eze 7:22*
and *d.*
he said unto them, *D.* the *Eze 9:7*
house
neither *d.* themselves *Eze 14:11*
(A)(B)(E)(R)
d. not yourselves with the *Eze 20:7*
idols of
nor *d.* yourselves with their *Eze 20:18*
idols
d. yourselves after *Eze 20:30*
(A)(B)(R)
d. yourselves with idols *Eze 20:31*
(A)(B)(R)
maketh idols against herself *Eze 22:3*
to *d.*
and they shall *d.* thy *Eze 28:7*
brightness
ye *d.* every one his *Eze 33:26*
neighbour's
Neither shall they *d.* *Eze 37:23*
themselves
shall the house of Israel no *Eze 43:7*
more *d.*
no dead person to *d.* *Eze 44:25*
themselves
husband, they may *d.* *Eze 44:25*
themselves
he would not *d.* himself with *Da 1:8*
that he might not *d.* himself *Da 1:8*
the heart; and they *d.* the *M't 15:18*
man
are the things which *d.* a *M't 15:20*
man
entering into him can *d.* *M'k 7:15*
him: but
him, those are they that *d.* *M'k 7:15*
the man
into the man, it cannot *d.* *M'k 7:18*
him
come from within, and *d.* *M'k 7:23*
the man
desecrate, *d.* the temple *Ac 24:6*
(A)(B)
If any man *d.* the temple of *1Co 3:17*
God
corrupts, destroys temple *1Co 3:17*
(A)(N)(R)

ruins the temple of God (B) *1Co 3:17*
destroyeth the temple of *1Co 3:17*
God (E)
that *d.* themselves with *1Ti 1:10*
mankind
who abuse themselves with *1Ti 1:10*
men (A)
for sexual perverts (B)(N) *1Ti 1:10*
for abusers of themselves *1Ti 1:10*
with men (E)
sexually uncontrolled, or *1Ti 1:10*
perverted (P)
for immoral persons (R) *1Ti 1:10*
these filthy dreamers *d.* the *Jude 8*
flesh
corrupt the body (A) *Jude 8*
abandoned themselves to *Jude 8*
sexual immorality and bent
on perverted sensuality (B)
d. the body (N) *Jude 8*
gave themselves up to sexual *Jude 8*
immorality and perversion (P)

DEFILED

and lay with her, and *d.* her *Ge 34:2*
dishonored her (B) *Ge 34:2*
humbled her (E)(R) *Ge 34:2*
Jacob heard that he had *d.* *Ge 34:5*
Dinah
he had ravished her (B) *Ge 34:5*
he had *d.* Dinah their sister *Ge 34:13*
dishonored their sister (B) *Ge 34:13*
because they had *d.* their *Ge 34:27*
sister
that a man shall be *d.* withal *Le 5:3*
unclean (B) *Le 5:3;*
15:32; 18:25; 21:3; Nu 6:12; 9:6; 19:20;
Jer 19:13; Eze 23:38
them, that ye should be *d.* *Le 11:43*
thereby
shall be in him he shall be *Le 13:46*
d.
from him, and is *d.* *Le 15:32*
therewith
unclean (A) *Le 15:32*
all these the nations are *d.* *Le 18:24*
the land is *d.:* therefore I do *Le 18:25*
visit
before you, and the land is *Le 18:27*
d.
wizards, to be *d.* by them: I *Le 19:31*
am the
There shall none be *d.* for the *Le 21:1*
uncleanness (B) *Le 21:1*
no husband; for her may he *Le 21:3*
be *d.*
and whosoever is *d.* by the *Nu 5:2*
dead
kept close, and she be *d.,* and *Nu 5:13*
jealous of his wife, and she *Nu 5:14*
be *d.*
of his wife, and she be not *d.* *Nu 5:14*
if thou be *d.* and some man *Nu 5:20*
have
if she be *d.* and have done *Nu 5:27*
trespass
if the woman be not *d.* but *Nu 5:28*
instead of her husband, and *Nu 5:29*
is *d.*
and he hath *d.* the head of his *Nu 6:9*
lost, because his separation *Nu 6:12*
was *d.*
men, who were *d.* by the dead *Nu 9:6*
We are *d.* by the dead body *Nu 9:7*
of a
hath *d.* the sanctuary of the *Nu 19:20*
Lord
that thy land be not *d.* *De 21:23*
the fruit of thy vineyard, be *De 22:9*
forfeited to the sanctuary *De 22:9*
(A)
be confiscated to the *De 22:9*
sanctuary (B)
after that she is *d.;* for that *De 24:4*
the mighty is *d.* (A)(B)(R) *2Sa 1:21*
and *d.* the high places where *2Ki 23:8*
And he *d.* Topheth, which *2Ki 23:10*
forasmuch as he *d.* his *1Ch 5:1*
father's
polluted his father's couch *1Ch 5:1*
(A)(R)
violated his father's couch *1Ch 5:1*
(B)
they have *d.* the priesthood *Ne 13:29*
and *d.* my horn in the dust *Job 16:15*
laid my horn in dust *Job 16:15*
(B)(E)(R)
the godless and *d.* (A) *Job 20:5*

they have *d.* by casting down *Ps 74:7*
profaned dwelling place *Ps 74:7;*
(A)(B) *Eze 7:24*
desecrated dwelling place (R) *Ps 74:7*
thy holy temple have they *d.* *Ps 79:1*
d. his crown in dust (B)(R) *Ps 89:39*
Thus were they *d.* with *Ps 106:39*
their own
The earth also is *d.* under *Isa 24:5*
lies polluted by inhabitants *Isa 24:5*
(B)(E)(R)
your hands are *d.* with blood *Isa 59:3*
tainted with blood (B) *Isa 59:3*
when ye entered, ye *d.* my *Jer 2:7*
land
I am not *d.* (A)(E)(R) *Jer 2:23*
she *d.* the land, and *Jer 3:9*
committed
because they have *d.* my *Jer 16:18*
land
be *d.* as the place of Tophet *Jer 19:13*
Israel eat their *d.* bread *Eze 4:13*
among
I never *d.* myself *Eze 4:14*
(A)(B)(R)
thou hast *d.* my sanctuary *Eze 5:11*
and their holy places shall be *Eze 7:24*
d.
hath *d.* his neighbour's wife *Eze 18:6*
seduce his neighbor's wife *Eze 18:6*
(B)
and *d.* his neighbour's wife *Eze 18:11*
hath not *d.* his neighbour's *Eze 18:15*
wife
I *d.* them through gifts *Eze 20:26*
(B)(R)
wherein ye have been *d.* *Eze 20:43*
polluted (B)(E)(R) *Eze 20:43*
and hast *d.* thyself in thine *Eze 22:4*
idols
hath lewdly *d.* his daughter *Eze 22:11*
in law
with all their idols she *d.* *Eze 23:7*
herself
Then I saw that she was *d.* *Eze 23:13*
they *d.* her with their *Eze 23:17*
whoredom
they *d.* her (A)(B)(E)(R) *Eze 23:17*
d. yourself with idols (A) *Eze 23:30*
they have *d.* my sanctuary *Eze 23:38*
in the
Thou hast *d.* thy *Eze 28:18*
sanctuaries by
dwelt in their own land, *Eze 36:17*
they *d.* it
uncleaness of a *d.* woman *Eze 36:17*
(S)
they have even *d.* my holy *Eze 43:8*
name
profaned my holy name (A) *Eze 43:8*
sullied my holy name (B) *Eze 43:8*
whoredom, and Israel is *d.* *Ho 5:3*
whoredom of Ephraim, Israel *Ho 6:10*
is *d.*
shall be *d.* (A)(B)(R) *Ho 9:4*
die in a *d.* land (A) *Am 7:17*
that say, Let her be *d.* and *Mic 4:11*
rebellious and *d.* (R) *Zep 3:1*
priests *d.* the sanctuary (B) *Zep 3:4*
eat bread with *d.* that is to *M'k 7:2*
with unclean hands (B) *M'k 7:2*
lest they should be *d.* but *Joh 18:28*
hath *d.* his place (B)(E)(R) *Ac 21:28*
their conscience being weak *1Co 8:7*
is *d.*
becomes contaminated (B) *1Co 8:7;*
Tit 1:15; Heb 12:15
but unto them that are *d.* *Tit 1:15*
their mind and conscience is *Tit 1:15*
d.
you, and thereby many be *Heb 12:15*
d.
garments their deeds *d.* (P) *Jude 23*
which have not *d.* their *Re 3:4*
garments
soiled their clothes (A)(B)(R) *Re 3:4*
which were not *d.* with *Re 14:4*
women
not contaminated with women *Re 14:4*
(B)

DEFILEDST

then *d.* thou it: he went up *Ge 49:4*

DEFILEMENT

every *d.* of flesh *2Co 7:1*
(B)(E)(N)(R)

slaves of depravity and *d.* 2Pe 2:19 (A)

a remedy for the *d.* for our sins (N) 1Jo 2:2

DEFILEMENTS

d. of the world (E)(N)(R) 2Pe 2:20

DEFILES

she *d.* her father (B) Le 21:9
everything that *d.* (A) 2Co 7:1

DEFILETH

every one that *d.* it shall surely Ex 31:14
who profane it (A)(B)(E) Ex 31:14
d. the tabernacle of the Lord Nu 19:13
for blood it *d.* that land Nu 35:33
not pollute the land (A)(E)(R) Nu 35:33
not desecrate the land (B) Nu 35:33
into the mouth *d.* a man M't 15:11
does not pollute the person (B) M't 15:11; 15:20
makes him unclean (P) M't 15:11; 15:20
out of the mouth, this *d.* M't 15:11 a man
with unwashen hands *d.* not M't 15:20 a man
of the man, that *d.* the man M'k 7:20
unclean and unhallowed (A) M'k 7:20
common or unclean (P) M'k 7:20
members, that it *d.* the whole body Jas 3:6
contaminating and depraving the (A) Jas 3:6
taints the whole body (B) Jas 3:6
pollutes our whole being (N) Jas 3:6
it can poison the whole body (P) Jas 3:6
staining the whole body (R) Jas 3:6
enter into it anything that *d.* Re 21:27

DEFILING

d. the sabbath (B) Ne 13:17
lusts of *d.* passion (R) 2Pe 2:10
d. bodies by filthy fantasies (P) Jude 8

DEFINED

d. it for Jacob (B) 1Ch 16:17

DEFINITE

d. plan and foreknowledge (R) Ac 2:23

DEFRAUD

Thou shalt not *d.* thy neighbour Le 19:13
Neither use extortion (B) Le 19:13
not oppress neighbor (E)(R) Le 19:13
D. not, Honour thy father M'k 10:19
Do not cheat (B)(P) M'k 10:19
Nay, ye do wrong, and *d.* 1Co 6:8
rather let yourself be robbed (N) 1Co 6:8
be wronged or cheated (P) 1Co 6:8
D. ye not one the other, except it 1Co 7:5
Do not deprive each other (B) 1Co 7:5
not deny one another (N) 1Co 7:5
not cheat of normal sexual intercourse (P) 1Co 7:5
d. his brother in any matter 1Th 4:6
take advantage of his brother (B) 1Th 4:6
wrong his brother (E)(N)(R) 1Th 4:6
d. you of victory prize (B) Col 2:18

DEFRAUDED

I taken? of whom have I *d.* 1Sa 12:3
whom have I wronged (B) 1Sa 12:3
Thou hast not *d.* us, nor oppressed 1Sa 12:4
not mistreated us, not wronged us (B) 1Sa 12:4
d. our race (R) Ac 7:19

rather suffer yourselves to be *d.* 1Co 6:7
no man, we have *d.* no man 2Co 7:2
cheated or taken advantage of no one (A) 2Co 7:2
ruined no one; exploited no one (B) 2Co 7:2
corrupted no one; took advantage of no one (E)(R) 2Co 7:2
ruined no one; taken advantage of no one (N) 2Co 7:2
wronged or ruined or cheated by us (P) 2Co 7:2
d. of the truth (B) 1Ti 6:5

DEFY

me Jacob, and come, *d.* Nu 23:7 Israel
hath not cursed? or how shall I *d.* Nu 23:8
I *d.* the armies of Israel this day 1Sa 17:10
surely to *d.* Israel is he come up 1Sa 17:25
that he should *d.* the armies 1Sa 17:26
sent to *d.* living God (E) 2Ki 19:4

DEGENERATE

art thou turned into the *d.* Jer 2:21 plant
turn into bastard shoots of an alien vine (B) Jer 2:21
slaves to *d.* minds (P) Ro 1:28

DEGRADATION

d. of own bodies (N) Ro 1:24

DEGRADED

should seem *d.* (R) De 15:3

DEGREE

of the second *d.* Zechariah, Ben 1Ch 15:18
associates of second class (A)(B) 1Ch 15:18
brethren of second order (R) 1Ch 15:18
to the estate of a man of high *d.* 1Ch 17:17
standard of exalted men (B) 1Ch 17:17
d. are vanity, and men of high *d.* Ps 62:9
lowly man is but a breath (B) Ps 62:9
men of low estate are but breath (R) Ps 62:9
seats, and exalted them of low *d.* Lu 1:52
lifted up the lowly (B) Lu 1:52
the humble have been lifted high (N) Lu 1:52
lifted up the humble (P) Lu 1:52
purchase to themselves a good *d.* 1Ti 3:13
acquire a good standing (A)(E) 1Ti 3:13
worthwhile step upward for themselves (B) 1Ti 3:13
may claim a high standing (N) 1Ti 3:13
earn a certain legitimate standing (P) 1Ti 3:13
gain a good standing for themselves (R) 1Ti 3:13
Let the brother of low *d.* rejoice Jas 1:9
brother of humble circumstances glory (A)(N) Jas 1:9
Let the lowly brother be proud of (B)(R) Jas 1:9
brother who is poor be glad (P) Jas 1:9

DEGREES

the shadow go forward ten *d.* 2Ki 20:9;
2Ki 20:10-11; Isa 38:8
ten steps (A) 2Ki 20:9; 20:10-11
of *d.* Ps 120-134

DEHAVITES

the *D.* and the Elamites Ezr 4:9

DEJECT

do not *d.* the throne (B) Jer 14:21

DEJECTEDLY

went about *d.* (R) 1Ki 21:27

DEKAR

The son of *D.* in Makaz, and 1Ki 4:9

DELAIAH

The three and twentieth to *D.* 1Ch 24:18
The children of *D.* the children of Eze 2:60; Ne 7:62
house of Shemaiah the son of *D.* Ne 6:10
and *D.* the son of Shemaiah Jer 36:12
Nevertheless Elnathan and *D.* and Jer 36:25

DELAY

without *d.* (A)(B)(R) Ge 34:19
Thou shalt not *d.* to offer Ex 22:29
d. not, O Lord (B) Ps 40:17
not *d.* (A)(R) Da 9:19
that he would not *d.* to come Ac 9:38
without any *d.* on the morrow Ac 25:17
if I *d.* (P) 1Ti 3:15
and will not *d.* (P) Heb 10:37
that *d.* should be no longer (S) Re 10:6

DELAYED

Moses *d.* to come down out of the Ex 32:1
I made haste, and *d.* not to keep Ps 119:60
if I am *d.* (N)(R) 1Ti 3:15

DELAYETH

My lord *d.* his coming; and M't 24:48; Lu 12:45

DELECTABLE

their *d.* things shall not profit Isa 44:9
objects they delight in (A) Isa 44:9
precious productions are worthless (B) Isa 44:9
things they delight (E)(R) Isa 44:9

DELEGATION

he sends a *d.* (B) Lu 14:32

DELIBERATE

d. will and foreknowledge (N) Ac 2:23

DELIBERATELY

go on *d.* and willingly sinning (A)(P)(R) Heb 10:26

DELIBERATING

find knowledge through *d.* (B) Pr 8:12
d. in season (B) M't 28:12

DELIBERATIONS

great *d.* of heart (B) J'g 5:15
walked in their own *d.* (B) Ps 81:12

DELICACIES

baker's delicacies (B) Ge 40:17
are *d.* morsels (B)(R) Pr 18:8; 26:22
neither desire his *d.* (B)(R) Pr 23:6
filled belly with *d.* (A)(B)(E)(R)(S) Jer 51:34
I ate no *d.* (P) Da 10:3
through the abundance of her *d.* Re 18:3
rich with wealth of excessive luxury (A)(B) Re 18:3
rich by the power of her wantonness (E) Re 18:3
rich on her bloated wealth (N) Re 18:3

rich from extravagance of dissipation (P)   *Re 18:3*
rich with the wealth of her wantonness (R)   *Re 18:3*

DELICATE

is tender among you, and very *d.*   *De 28:54*
extremely particular and well-bred (A)   *De 28:54*
most refined, most kindly nature (B)   *De 28:54*
most tender and delicately bred (R)   *De 28:54*
The tender and *d.* woman among   *De 28:56*
no more be called tender and *d.*   *Isa 47:1*
called dainty and *d.* (A)   *Isa 47:1*
to a comely and *d.* woman   *Jer 6:2*
the comely and luxurious (B)   *Jer 6:2*
and poll thee for thy *d.* children   *Mic 1:16*
children of your delight (A)(E)(R)   *Mic 1:16*
your fondled children (B)   *Mic 1:16*

DELICATELY

And Agag came unto him *d.*   *1Sa 15:32*
cheerfully Agag approached (A)(B)(E)(R)   *1Sa 15:32*
He that *d.* bringeth up his servant   *Pr 29:21*
pampers his servant (A)(B)(R)   *Pr 29:21*
They that did feed *d.* are desolate   *La 4:5*
feasted on dainties (A)(B)(R)   *La 4:5*
and live *d.* are in kings' courts   *Lu 7:25*
live in luxury (A)(B)(N)(P)(R)   *Lu 7:25*

DELICATENESS

of her foot upon the ground for *d.*   *De 28:56*

DELICATES

he hath filled his belly with my *d.*   *Jer 51:34*
filled belly with delicacies (A)(B)(E)(R)   *Jer 51:34*

DELICIOUSLY

glorified herself, and lived *d.*   *Re 18:7*
waxed wanton (E)(R)   *Re 18:7*
flaunted herself (P)   *Re 18:7*
and lived *d.* with her, shall   *Re 18:9*

DELIGHT

he had *d.* in Jacob' daughter   *Ge 34:19*
If the Lord *d.* in us, then he   *Nu 14:8*
the Lord had a *d.* in thy fathers   *De 10:15*
if thou have no *d.* in her   *De 21:14*
Hath the Lord as great a *d.* in burnt   *1Sa 15:22*
the king hath *d.* in thee, and all   *1Sa 18:22*
I have no *d.* in thee; behold   *2Sa 15:26*
doth my lord the king *d.* in this   *2Sa 24:3*
who *d.* to fear thy name (S)   *Ne 1:11*
To whom would the king *d.* to do   *Es 6:6*
then shalt thou have thy *d.* in the   *Job 22:26*
Will he *d.* himself in the Almighty   *Job 27:10*
that he should *d.* himself with God   *Job 34:9*
But his *d.* is in the law of the Lord   *Ps 1:2*
excellent, in whom is all my *d.*   *Ps 16:3*
D. thyself also in the Lord; and   *Ps 37:4*
d. themselves in the abundance   *Ps 37:11*
I *d.* to do thy will, O my God   *Ps 40:8*
who *d.* in my hurt (E)   *Ps 40:14*
you *d.* not in (A)(R)   *Ps 51:16*
they *d.* in lies: they bless with   *Ps 62:4*
thou the people that *d.* in war   *Ps 68:30*

me thy comforts *d.* my soul   *Ps 94:19*
I will *d.* myself in thy statutes   *Ps 119:16*
Thy testimonies also are my *d.*   *Ps 119:24*
for therein do I *d.*   *Ps 119:35*
d. myself in thy commandments   *Ps 119:47*
fat as grease; but I *d.* in thy law   *Ps 119:70*
I may live: for thy law is my *d.*   *Ps 119:77*
O Lord; and thy law is my *d.*   *Ps 119:174*
the scorners *d.* in their scorning   *Pr 1:22*
and *d.* in the frowardness of   *Pr 2:14*
transported with *d.* in love (A)   *Pr 5:19*
console and *d.* ourselves (A)   *Pr 7:18*
I was daily his *d.* rejoicing always   *Pr 8:30*
but a just weight is his *d.*   *Pr 11:1*
but such as are upright are his *d.*   *Pr 11:20*
but they that deal truly are his *d.*   *Pr 12:22*
the prayer of the upright is his *d.*   *Pr 15:8*
Righteous lips are the *d.* of kings   *Pr 16:13*
fool hath no *d.* in understanding   *Pr 18:2*
D. is not seemly for a fool   *Pr 19:10*
them that rebuke him shall be *d.*   *Pr 24:25*
he shall give *d.* unto thy soul   *Pr 29:17*
under his shadow with great *d.*   *Ca 2:5*
I *d.* not in the blood of bullocks   *Isa 1:11*
as for gold, they shall not *d.* in it   *Isa 13:17*
objects, things *d.* in (A)(E)(R)   *Isa 44:9*
let your soul *d.* itself in fatness   *Isa 55:2*
me daily, and *d.* to know my ways   *Isa 58:2*
take *d.* in approaching to God   *Isa 58:2*
call the sabbath a *d.* the holy   *Isa 58:13*
shalt thou *d.* thyself in the Lord   *Isa 58:14*
reproach; they have no *d.* in it   *Jer 6:10*
these things I *d.* saith the Lord   *Jer 9:24*
children of *d.* (A)(E)(R)   *Mic 1:16*
of the covenant, whom ye *d.* in   *Mal 3:1*
For I *d.* in the law of God   *Ro 7:22*

DELIGHTED

Saul's son *d.* much in David   *1Sa 19:2*
delivered me, because he *d.* in me   *2Sa 22:20*
he delighted in me (A)   *2Sa 22:20*
for his favor is mine (B)   *2Sa 22:20*
which *d.* in thee, to set thee   *1Ki 10:9*
was pleased to give you (B)   *1Ki 10:9*
which *d.* in thee to set thee on his   *2Ch 9:8*
and *d.* themselves in thy great   *Ne 9:25*
they enjoyed life fully (B)   *Ne 9:25*
no more, except the king *d.* in her   *Es 2:14*
took a liking to her (B)   *Es 2:14*
delivered me, because he *d.* in me   *Ps 18:19*
deliver him, seeing he *d.* in him   *Ps 22:8*
as he *d.* not in blessing, so let it   *Ps 109:17*
did choose that wherein I *d.* not   *Isa 65:12*
and chose that in which I *d.* not   *Isa 66:4*
and be *d.* with the abundance   *Isa 66:11*

DELIGHTEST

thou *d.* not in burnt offering   *Ps 51:16*

DELIGHTETH

man whom the king *d.* to honour   *Es 6:6*
   Es 6:7, 9, 11
Lord: and he *d.* in his way   *Ps 37:23*

d. greatly in his commandments   *Ps 112:1*
d. not in the strength of the horse   *Ps 147:10*
a father the son in whom he *d.*   *Pr 3:12*
mine elect, in whom my soul *d.*   *Isa 42:1*
the Lord *d.* in thee, and thy land   *Isa 62:4*
their soul *d.* in their abominations   *Isa 66:3*
for ever, because he *d.* in mercy   *Mic 7:18*
and he *d.* in them; or, Where is the   *Mal 2:17*

DELIGHTFUL

d. to look at (A)(B)(E)(R)   *Ge 3:2*

DELIGHTS

you in scarlet, with other *d.*   *2Sa 1:24*
in which he *d.* (A)(E)(R)   *Job 20:20*
Unless thy law had been my *d.*   *Ps 119:92*
thy commandments are my *d.*   *Ps 119:143*
my *d.* were with the sons of men   *Pr 8:31*
and the *d.* of the sons of men   *Ec 2:8*
pleasant art thou, O love, for *d.*   *Ca 7:6*

DELIGHTSOME

for ye shall be a *d.* land   *Mal 3:12*

DELILAH

whose name was *D.*   *J'g 16:4*
   J'g 16:6, 10, 12-13, 18

DELIVER

d. Pharaoh's cup into his hand   *Ge 40:13*
d. royal dainties (B)   *Ge 49:20*
yet shall he *d.* the tale of bricks   *Ex 5:18*
if man *d.* unto his neighbour   *Ex 22:7; 22:10*
d. it by that the sun goeth down   *Ex 22:26*
I will *d.* the inhabitants of the land   *Ex 23:31*
if thou wilt indeed *d.* this people   *Nu 21:2*
congregation shall *d.* slayer out of   *Nu 35:25*
he shall *d.* their kings into thy hand   *De 7:24*
shalt not *d.* to his master the servant   *De 23:15*
to *d.* her husband out of the hand of him   *De 25:11*
any that can *d.* out of my hand   *De 32:39; Isa 43:13*
that ye will *d.* our lives from death   *Jos 2:13*
for your God will *d.* it into your hand   *Jos 8:7*
they shall not *d.* slayer into his hand   *Jos 20:5*
d. the Midianites into thine hand   *J'g 7:7*
to *d.* Israel (S)   *J'g 10:1*
if thou shalt without fail *d.* Ammonites   *J'g 11:30*
Samson shall begin to *d.* Israel from   *J'g 13:5*
coasts thereof did Israel *d.*   *1Sa 7:14*
he shall *d.* my people (B)   *1Sa 9:16*
after things which cannot profit nor *d.*   *1Sa 12:21*
I will *d.* the Philistines   *1Sa 23:4; 2Sa 5:19*
I will *d.* thine enemy into thine hand   *1Sa 24:4*
Lord will *d.* Israel to the Philistines   *1Sa 28:19*
king will hear to *d.* his handmaid   *2Sa 14:16*
you will *d.* (A)(R)   *2Sa 22:28*
wouldest *d.* thy servant to Ahab   *1Ki 18:9*
d. this multitude into thy hand   *1Ki 20:13; 20:28*

go up, for the Lord shall *d.* *1Ki 22:6;*
it into king's hand *12:15; 2Ch 18:5, 11*
will *d.* the Moabites into *2Ki 3:18*
your hand
but *d.* it for the breaches of *2Ki 12:7*
the house
Lord should *d.* Jerusalem *2Ki 18:35;*
Isa 36:20
let them *d.* it into hand of *2Ki 22:5*
workmen
who could not *d.* their own *2Ch 25:15*
people
now hear me and *d.* the *2Ch 28:11*
captives again
were gods of nations able *2Ch 32:13*
to *d.* their lands
your God should be able *2Ch 32:14;*
to *d.* you *32:17*
those *d.* thou before God of *Ezr 7:19*
Jerusalem
there is none can *d.* out of *Job 10:7*
thy hand
he shall *d.* the island of the *Job 22:30*
innocent
he will *d.* his soul from *Job 33:28*
going into pit
d. my soul *Ps 6:4;*
Ps 17:13; 22:20; 116:4; 120:2
rending it while none to *d.* *Ps 7:2;*
50:22
nor *d.* any by his great *Ps 33:17*
strength
d. soul from death, and to *Ps 33:19*
keep alive
d. for mercy's sake *Ps 44:26*
(A)(B)(R)
wilt not thou *d.* my feet *Ps 56:13*
from falling
he shall *d.* needy when he *Ps 72:12*
crieth
d. not the soul of thy *Ps 74:19*
turtle-dove
d. poor and needy out of *Ps 82:4*
hand of wicked
shall he *d.* his soul from *Ps 89:48*
hand of grave
crown of glory shall she *d.* to *Pr 4:9*
thee
do this now, my son, and *d.* *Pr 6:3*
thyself
beat him, thou shalt *d.* his *Pr 23:14*
soul from hell
d. his life from Sheol *Pr 23:14*
(A)(B)(E)(R)
nor wickedness *d.* those given *Ec 8:8*
to it
carry it away safe, and none *Isa 5:29*
d. it
which men *d.* to one that is *Isa 29:11*
learned
defending also he will *d.* it *Isa 31:5*
he cannot *d.* his soul, nor *Isa 44:20*
say, Is there not
they stoop, they could not *d.* *Isa 46:2*
the burden
they shall not *d.* themselves *Isa 47:14*
from flame
hand shortened? have I no *Isa 50:2*
power to *d.*
residue of them will I *d.* to *Jer 15:9*
sword
therefore *d.* up their *Jer 18:21*
children to famine
moreover I will *d.* strength of *Jer 20:5*
this city
afterwards I will *d.* Zedekiah *Jer 21:7*
from sword
d. the spoiled out of hand of *Jer 22:3*
oppressor
d. such as are for death to *Jer 43:11*
death
Babylon, *d.* every man his soul *Jer 51:6;*
51:45
I will *d.* my people *Eze 13:21; 13:23*
should *d.* their own souls *Eze 14:14;*
14:20
shall *d.* neither sons nor *Eze 14:16;*
daughters *18:20*
that taketh warning shall *d.* *Eze 33:6*
his soul
I will *d.* my flock from their *Eze 34:10*
mouth
no other god can *d.* after this *Da 3:29*
sort
nor was any that could *d.* *Da 8:4*
from ram
none that could *d.* ram out of *Da 8:7*
his hand
none shall *d.* her out of mine *Ho 2:10*
hand

neither shall mighty *d.* *Am 2:14*
himself
that is swift of foot shall not *Am 2:15*
d. himself
I will *d.* city with all that is *Am 6:8*
therein
teareth in pieces and none *Mic 5:8*
can *d.*
thou shalt take hold, but *Mic 6:14*
shalt not *d.*
d. thyself, O Zion, that *Zec 2:7*
dwellest with
I will *d.* every one into *Zec 11:6*
neighbour's hand
brother *d.* the brother to *M't 10:21*
death
who would *d.* Israel (B)(N) *Lu 24:21*
not manner of Romans to *d.* *Ac 25:16*
man to die
d. such one to Satan for *1Co 5:5*
destruction of
delivered us from death, and *2Co 1:10*
doth *d.*
Lord knoweth how to *d.* the *2Pe 2:9*
godly

DELIVER *HIM*

to *d.* him to his father again *Ge 37:22*
d. him into my hand, I will *Ge 42:37*
bring him
God will *d.* him into his *Ex 21:13*
hand
that he might *d.* him into thy *De 2:30*
hand
I will *d.* him into thy hand *De 3:2*
d. him into hand of avenger *De 19:12*
of blood
in any case thou shalt *d.* him *De 24:13*
pledge
draw Sisera and *d.* him into *J'g 4:7*
thy hand
our part be to *d.* him into *1Sa 23:20*
thy hand
said, *D.* him that smote his *2Sa 14:7*
brother
d. him and I will depart *2Sa 20:21*
from city
d. him from going down to *Job 33:24*
pit
that he would *d.* him, let him *Ps 22:8*
d. him
Lord will *d.* him in time of *Ps 41:1*
trouble
not *d.* him to the will of his *Ps 41:2*
enemies
take him, for there is none *Ps 71:11*
to *d.* him
set love on me, will I *d.* him *Ps 91:14*
I will be with him, will *d.* *Ps 91:15*
him
if *d.* him thou must do it *Pr 19:19*
again
d. him that is spoiled from *Jer 21:12*
oppressor
righteousness of righteous not *Eze 33:12*
d. him
king set heart on Daniel to *d.* *Da 6:14*
him
might be shadow to *d.* him *Jon 4:6*
from grief
shall *d.* him to Gentiles to *M't 20:19;*
crucify *M'k 10:33; Lu 20:20; Ac 21:11*
what will ye give, and I will *M'k 26:15*
d. him
let him *d.* him now, if he *M't 27:43*
will have him

DELIVER *ME*

d. me I pray thee from hand *Ge 32:11*
of Esau
will *d.* me out of hand of *1Sa 17:37*
Goliath
will men of Keilah *d.* me *1Sa 23:11;*
out of thy hand *23:12*
Lord be judge, and *d.* me *1Sa 24:15*
let him *d.* me out of all *1Sa 26:24*
tribulation
nor *d.* me into the hands of *1Sa 30:15*
my master
sent, saying, *D.* me my wife *2Sa 3:14*
Michal
d. me thy silver and gold *1Ki 20:5*
d. me from enemies *Job 6:23;*
Ps 31:15; 59:1
Lord, save me from them and *Ps 7:1*
d. me
keep my soul, and *d.* me. for *Ps 25:20*

d. me not over to will of *Ps 27:12*
enemies
bow down thine ear to me, *d.* *Ps 31:2*
me
d. me from my transgressions *Ps 39:8*
be pleased to *d.* me make *Ps 40:13*
haste to *d.* me
d. me from deceitful and *Ps 43:1*
unjust man
d. me from blood-guiltiness, *Ps 51:14*
O God
d. me from workers of *Ps 59:2*
iniquity
d. me out of mire, let me *Ps 69:14*
not
draw nigh to my soul, and *Ps 69:18*
redeem it, *d.* me
make haste to *d.* me *Ps 70:1*
d. me in righteousness, cause *Ps 71:2;*
31:1
d. me out of hand of the *Ps 71:4*
wicked
because thy mercy is good *Ps 109:21*
d. thou me
d. me from the oppression *Ps 119:134*
of man
consider mine affliction, *Ps 119:153*
and *d.* me
plead my cause, and *d.* me *Ps 119:154*
d. me according to thy *Ps 119:170*
word
d. me from evil man, *Ps 140:1*
preserve me
d. me from my persecutors *Ps 142:6*
d. me from mine enemies, I *Ps 143:9*
flee unto thee
rid me, and *d.* me out of *Ps 144:7*
great waters
d. me from the hand of *Ps 144:11*
strange children
he saith, *D.* me for thou art *Isa 44:17*
my God
afraid of Jews, lest they *d.* *Jer 38:19*
me
no man may *d.* me to them *Ac 25:11*
who shall *d.* me from body *Ro 7:24*
of death
shall *d.* me from every evil *2Ti 4:18*
work

DELIVER *THEE*

people which the Lord shall *De 7:16*
d. thee
walketh in midst of camp *De 23:14*
to *d.* thee
to bind thee, that we may *J'g 15:12;*
d. thee *15:13*
Lord will *d.* thee into mine *1Sa 17:46*
hand
the Lord said, They will *d.* *1Sa 23:12*
thee up
I will *d.* thee two thousand *2Ki 18:23*
horses
I will *d.* thee and this city *2Ki 20:6;*
Isa 38:6
he shall *d.* thee in six *Job 5:19*
troubles, in seven
beware, lest a great *Job 36:18*
ransom cannot *d.* thee
I will *d.* thee, thou shalt *Ps 50:15*
glorify me
he shall *d.* thee from the snare *Ps 91:3*
of fowler
to *d.* thee from way of evil *Pr 2:12*
man
to *d.* thee from the strange *Pr 2:16*
woman, the stranger
when thou criest, let thy *Isa 57:13*
companies *d.* thee
I am with thee to *d.* thee *Jer 1:8;*
Jer 1:19; 15:20-21
Jeremiah said, They shall not *Jer 38:20*
d. thee
I will *d.* thee in that day *Jer 39:17*
I will surely *d.* thee, thou *Jer 39:18*
shalt not fall by sword
d. thee into hand of brutish *Eze 21:31*
men
I will *d.* thee to them *Eze 23:28*
whom thou hatest
I will *d.* thee to men of east *Eze 25:4*
for possession
I will *d.* thee for a spoil to *Eze 25:7*
the heathen
God whom thou servest will *Da 6:16*
d. thee
is thy God able to *d.* thee *Da 6:20*
from lions

how shall I *d.* thee, Israel   *Ho 11:8*
judge *d.* thee to officer   *M't 5:25;*
                        Lu 12:58

DELIVER *THEM*

I am come down to *d.* them   *Ex 3:8;*
                        Ac 7:34
when Lord shall *d.* them   *De 7:2; 7:23*
to-morrow will I *d.* them up   *Jos 11:6*
all slain
if Lord *d.* them before me   *J'g 11:9*
to-morrow I will *d.* them   *J'g 20:28*
into thine hand
wilt thou *d.* them   *1Sa 14:37;*
        2Sa 5:19; 1Ch 14:10
d. them to enemy   *1Ki 8:46; 2Ki 21:14*
to *d.* them unto hand of   *2Ki 3:10*
Moab
Lord said, I will *d.* them into   *1Ch 14:10*
thy hand
and *d.* them over before their   *2Ch 6:36*
enemies
it came of God, that he   *2Ch 25:20*
might *d.* them
many times didst thou *d.*   *Ne 9:28*
them
crushed, neither is there any   *Job 5:4*
to *d.* them
they trusted, and thou didst *d.*   *Ps 22:4*
them
Lord shall help them, and *d.*   *Ps 37:40*
them
many times did *d.* them   *Ps 106:43*
they provoked
righteousness of upright *d.*   *Pr 11:6*
them
mouth of upright shall *d.*   *Pr 12:6*
them
forbear to *d.* them that are   *Pr 24:11*
drawn to death
shall send a Saviour and *d.*   *Isa 19:20*
them
I will *d.* them to be removed   *Jer 24:9;*
                         29:18
d. them into hand of   *Jer 29:21;*
Nebuchadrezzar   *46:26*
their gold shall not *d.* them   *Eze 7:19;*
                       Zep 1:18
will I seek and *d.* them out   *Eze 34:12*
of all places
carried away to *d.* them up to   *Am 1:6*
Edom
out of their hand I will not   *Zec 11:6*
d. them
that God by his hand would   *Ac 7:25*
d. them
d. them who through fear of   *Heb 2:15*
death

DELIVER *US*

d. us into hand of Amorites   *De 1:27;*
                       Jos 7:7
d. us only, we pray thee,   *J'g 10:15*
this day
d. us men, the children of   *J'g 20:13*
Belial
woe to us, who shall *d.* us   *1Sa 4:8*
out of hand
but now *d.* us out of hand   *1Sa 12:10*
of our enemies
Lord will *d.* us   *2Ki 18:30;*
       18:32; Isa 36:15, 18
save and *d.* us from heathen   *1Ch 16:35*
the Lord our God shall *d.* us   *2Ch 32:11*
d. us and purge away our   *Ps 79:9*
sins
to *d.* us into hand of   *Jer 43:3*
Chaldeans
none doth *d.* us out of their   *La 5:8*
hand
God is able to *d.* us and will   *Da 3:17*
d. us
thus shall he *d.* us from   *Mic 5:6*
Assyrians
but *d.* us from evil   *M't 6:13; Lu 11:4*
whom we trust that he will   *2Co 1:10*
d. us
that he might *d.* us from evil   *Ga 1:4*
world

DELIVER *YOU*

so will I *d.* you your brother   *Ge 42:34*
shall *d.* you your bread by   *Le 26:26*
weight
did not I *d.* you from   *J'g 10:11*
Egyptians

---

have forsaken me, I will *d.*   *J'g 10:13*
you no more
let them *d.* you in the time   *J'g 10:14*
of tribulation
he will *d.* you from the   *1Sa 7:3*
Philistines
he shall *d.* you from all   *2Ki 17:39*
enemies
not be able to *d.* you out   *2Ki 18:29*
of his hand
be able to *d.* you out of mine   *2Ch 32:14*
hand
Hezekiah not be able to *d.*   *Isa 36:14*
you
I will bear, I will carry, and   *Isa 46:4*
will *d.* you
I will *d.* you into hands of   *Eze 11:9*
strangers
who is that God that shall   *Da 3:15*
d. you
they will *d.* you up   *M't 10:17;*
                      M'k 13:9
when they *d.* you up   *M't 10:19;*
               24:9; M'k 13:11

DELIVERANCE

sent me to save lives by great   *Ge 45:7*
d.
thou hast given this great *d.*   *J'g 15:18*
wrought great *d.* (A)   *1Sa 14:45*
worked great *d.* (A)(B)   *1Sa 19:5*
great *d.* giveth he (E)   *1Sa 22:51*
insuring *d.* (B)   *2Sa 22:2*
by him Lord had given *d.* to   *2Ki 5:1*
Syria
arrow of Lord's *d.* from   *2Ki 13:17*
Syria
Lord saved them by a great   *1Ch 11:14*
d.
but I will grant them some   *2Ch 12:7*
d.
hast given us such *d.* as this   *Ezr 9:13*
then shall *d.* arise to Jews   *Es 4:14*
great *d.* giveth he to his   *Ps 18:50*
king
compass me about with songs   *Ps 32:7*
of *d.*
own arm gain *d.* (B)   *Ps 44:3*
we have not wrought any *d.*   *Isa 26:18*
in earth
in Zion and in Jerusalem shall   *Joe 2:32*
be *d.*
but upon mount Zion shall be   *Ob 17*
d.
brought *d.* to (A)(B)(R)   *Lu 1:68*
sent me to preach *d.* to   *Lu 4:18*
captives
your *d.* is near (B)   *Lu 21:28*
d. of sins under (N)   *Heb 9:15*
others tortured, not   *Heb 11:35*
accepting *d.*

DELIVERANCES

art my King, command *d.* for   *Ps 44:4*
Jacob

DELIVERED

on beast, into your hand are   *Ge 9:2*
they *d.*
God who *d.* thine enemies   *Ge 14:20*
into thy hand
when her days to be *d.* were   *Ge 25:24*
fulfilled
are *d.* ere midwives come to   *Ex 1:19*
them
neither hast thou *d.* thy   *Ex 5:23*
people at all
smote Egyptians, and *d.* our   *Ex 12:27*
houses
who hath *d.* people from   *Ex 18:10*
under Egypt
Lord our God *d.* all unto us   *De 2:36*
God *d.* into our hands king of   *De 3:3*
Bashan
d. out of bondage (B)   *De 7:8*
Lord *d.* me two tables of   *De 9:10*
stone
Moses *d.* the law unto the   *De 31:9*
priests
Lord *d.* enemies into their   *Jos 21:44*
hand
he *d.* the Canaanites into their   *J'g 1:4*
hand
after him Shamgar, he also *d.*   *J'g 3:31*
Israel
they that are *d.* from noise of   *J'g 5:11*
archers

---

when Lord hath *d.* Zebah and   *J'g 8:7*
Zalmunna
Lord *d.* Sihon into the hand   *J'g 11:21*
of Israel
our god hath *d.* Samson   *J'g 16:23,*
our enemy   *16:24*
Phinehas' wife was near to   *1Sa 4:19*
be *d.*
I smote him and *d.* it out   *1Sa 17:35*
of his mouth
who *d.* company that came   *1Sa 30:23*
against us
let seven of Saul's sons be *d.*   *2Sa 21:6*
to us
I was *d.* of a child with her   *1Ki 3:17*
third day after I was *d.* this   *1Ki 3:18*
woman was *d.*
shalt thou be *d.*   *2Ki 19:11; Isa 37:11*
d. that parcel and slew   *1Ch 11:14*
Philistines
then on that day David *d.*   *1Ch 16:7*
this psalm
Jehoiada *d.* to captains   *2Ch 23:9*
shields
d. money was brought into   *2Ch 34:9*
house of God
Hilkiah *d.* the book to   *2Ch 34:15*
Shaphan
the vessels were *d.* to   *Ezr 5:14*
Sheshbazzar
they *d.* the king's   *Ezr 8:36*
commissions
it is *d.* by pureness of thine   *Job 22:30*
hands
so should I be *d.* for ever   *Job 23:7*
from my judge
because I *d.* poor that   *Job 29:12*
cried, and fatherless
they cried to thee, and were   *Ps 22:5*
d.
mighty man is not *d.* by much   *Ps 33:16*
strength
d. my soul in peace from   *Ps 55:18*
battle
hast *d.* my soul from death   *Ps 56:13;*
                     86:13; 116:8
that thy beloved may be *d.*   *Ps 60:5;*
                     108:6
let me be *d.* from them that   *Ps 69:14*
hate me
d. his strength into captivity   *Ps 78:61*
the righteous is *d.* out of   *Pr 11:8*
trouble
but through knowledge shall   *Pr 11:9*
just be *d.*
but seed of righteous shall   *Pr 11:21*
be *d.*
but whoso walketh wisely   *Pr 28:26*
shall be *d.*
poor wise man by wisdom he   *Ec 9:15*
d. city
help to be *d.* from king of   *Isa 20:6*
Assyria
book is *d.* to him that is   *Isa 29:12*
not learned
have they *d.* Samaria out of   *Isa 36:19*
my hand
thou hast *d.* it from pit of   *Isa 38:17*
corruption
shall the lawful captive be   *Isa 49:24*
d.
the prey of the terrible shall   *Isa 49:25*
be *d.*
before pain came, she was *d.*   *Isa 66:7*
of man child
we are *d.* to do all these   *Jer 7:10*
abominations
for he hath *d.* the soul of   *Jer 20:13*
the poor
now when I had *d.* evidence   *Jer 32:16*
to Baruch
but thou hast *d.* thy soul   *Eze 13:19;*
                   3:21; 33:9
as I live, they only shall be   *Eze 14:16;*
d.   *14:18*
shall he break covenant and   *Eze 17:15*
be *d.*
for they are all *d.* unto   *Eze 31:14*
death to earth
she is *d.* to sword, draw   *Eze 32:20*
her multitudes
d. his servants that trusted in   *Da 3:28*
him
who *d.* Daniel from power of   *Da 6:27*
lions
at that time thy people shall   *Da 12:1*
be *d.*
shall call on name of Lord be   *Joe 2:32*
d.

he that escapeth shall not be *Am 9:1*
d.
go to Babylon, there shalt *Mic 4:10*
thou be d.
he may be d. from power of *Hab 2:9*
evil
they that tempt God are *Mal 3:15*
even d.
all things d. to me *M't 11:27;*
Lu 10:22
Pilate commanded the body *M't 27:58*
to be d.
thro' your tradition which *M'k 7:13*
ye have d.
Son of man shall be d. to *M'k 10:33*
chief priests
released Barabbas d. Jesus *M'k 15:15;*
Lu 23:25
time came she should be d. *Lu 1:57;*
2:6
d. to me, and to whom I will, *Lu 4:6*
I give it
there was d. to him the book *Lu 4:17*
of Esaias
send forth d. (A) *Lu 4:18*
Son of man be d. into hands *Lu 9:44*
of men
give diligence that thou mayest *Lu 12:58*
be d.
for he shall be d. unto the *Lu 18:32*
Gentiles
but as soon as she is d. of *Joh 16:21*
child
that I should not be d. to *Joh 18:36*
the Jews
him being d. by the counsel *Ac 2:23*
of God
Judas and Silas came and d. *Ac 15:30*
epistle
and they d. the epistle to the *Ac 23:33*
governor
d. Paul to one Julius, a *Ac 27:1*
centurion
was I d. prisoner from *Ac 28:17*
Jerusalem
d. for our offences and raised *Ro 4:25*
now we are d. from law, that *Ro 7:6*
creature itself shall be d. *Ro 8:21*
from corruption
be d. from them that do not *Ro 15:31*
believe
alway d. to death for Jesus' *2Co 4:11*
sake
be d. from unreasonable men *2Th 3:2*
I have d. to Satan, that they *1Ti 1:20*
learn
I was d. out of mouth of the *2Ti 4:17*
lion
by faith Sarah was d. of a *Heb 11:11*
child
d. just Lot, vexed with filthy *2Pe 2:7*
turn from commandment d. *2Pe 2:21*
to them
faith which was once d. to *Jude 3*
saints
travailing in birth, and pained *Re 12:2*
to be d.
woman which was ready to *Re 12:4*
be d.

DELIVERED HIM

Reuben d. him out of their *Ge 37:21*
hands
which was d. him to keep *Le 6:2;*
6:4
Lord our God d. him before *De 2:33*
us
therefore Lord d. him to lion *1Ki 13:26*
Elijah d. him unto his *1Ki 17:23*
mother
I have d. him that is mine *Ps 7:4*
enemy
his Lord d. him to *M't 18:34*
tormentors
d. him to Pontius Pilate *M't 27:2;*
M'k 15:1
for envy they d. him *M't 27:18;*
M'k 15:10
he d. him to be crucified *M't 27:26;*
Joh 19:16
Jesus d. him to his mother *Lu 7:15*
Jesus healed child, d. him to *Lu 9:42*
father
our rulers d. him to be *Lu 24:20*
condemned
we would not have d. him *Joh 18:30*
to thee

God d. him out of all *Ac 7:10*
afflictions
d. him to four quaternions *Ac 12:4*
of soldiers

DELIVERED ME

God d. me from sword of *Ex 18:4*
Pharaoh
when I saw that ye d. me not *J'g 12:3*
Lord that d. me from the *1Sa 17:37*
lion
he d. me from my strong *2Sa 22:18*
enemy
d. me because delighted in *2Sa 22:20;*
Ps 18:19
hast d. me from violent *2Sa 22:49;*
man *Ps 18:48*
Hilkiah the priest d. me a *2Ki 22:10*
book
God hath d. me to the *Job 16:11*
ungodly
he d. me from my strong *Ps 18:17*
enemies
hast d. me from strivings of *Ps 18:43*
people
Lord heard, and d. me from *Ps 34:4*
all my fears
for he hath d. me out of all *Ps 54:7*
trouble
he that d. me hath greater *Joh 19:11*
sin
out of them all Lord d. me *2Ti 3:11*

DELIVERED THEE

Lord d. thee to-day into my *1Sa 24:10*
hand
I d. thee out of hand of Saul *2Sa 12:7*
calledst in trouble, and I d. *Ps 81:7*
thee
I d. thee to will of them *Eze 16:27*
that hate thee
chief priests d. thee unto me *Joh 18:35*

DELIVERED THEM

Moses told how the Lord d. *Ex 18:8*
them
in tables of stone, and d. *De 5:22*
them to me
Lord raised up deliverer, who *J'g 3:9*
d. them
gods of nations d. them *2Ki 19:12;*
Isa 37:12
d. them to trouble, to *2Ch 29:8*
astonishment
when he d. them from the *Ps 78:42*
enemy
he d. them out of their *Ps 107:6*
distresses
he d. them from their *Ps 107:20*
destructions
he hath d. them to the *Isa 34:2*
slaughter
d. them to cause them to pass *Eze 16:21*
thro' fire
servants, and d. to them his *M't 25:14*
goods
they d. them to us as *Lu 1:2*
eyewitnesses
d. them ten pounds, said, *Lu 19:13*
Occupy till
they d. them decrees for to *Ac 16:4*
keep
keep ordinances, as d. them *1Co 11:2*
to you
d. them into chains of *2Pe 2:4*
darkness

DELIVERED UP

the Lord d. up the *Nu 21:3*
Canaanites
when the Lord d. up *Jos 10:12*
Amorites
d. up the men that lift up *2Sa 18:28*
their hand
they d. up the captivity to *Am 1:9*
Edom
nor have d. up those that *Ob 14*
remain
glorified his Son whom ye d. *Ac 3:13*
up
spared not Son, d. him up *Ro 8:32*
for us
when he shall have d. up *1Co 15:24*
kingdom
death and hell d. up dead *Re 20:13*
in them

DELIVERED US

and Egyptian d. us from *Ex 2:19*
shepherds
change customs Moses d. us *Ac 6:14*
who d. us from so great a *2Co 1:10*
death
d. us from the power of *Col 1:13*
darkness
Jesus d. us from wrath to *1Th 1:10*
come

DELIVERED YOU

obeyed doctrine which was d. *Ro 6:17*
you
I received that I d. you *1Co 11:23;*
15:3

DELIVEREDST

Therefore thou d. them into *Ne 9:27*
Lord, thou d. unto me five *M't 25:20*
talents
Lord, thou d. unto me two *M't 25:22*
talents

DELIVERER

the Lord raised up a d. to the *J'g 3:9*
raised up a savior (B)(E) *J'g 3:9*
the Lord raised them up a d. *J'g 3:15*
there was no d. because it *J'g 18:28*
no one delivered them (B) *J'g 18:28*
rock, and my fortress, and *2Sa 22:2*
my d.
insuring deliverance to me *2Sa 22:2*
(B)
my fortress, and my d.; my *Ps 18:2*
God
thou art my help and my d.; *Ps 40:17*
make
thou art my help and my d.; *Ps 70:5*
O Lord
God is my strong d. (R) *Ps 140:7*
my high tower, and my d.; my *Ps 144:2*
God send to be a ruler and a *Ac 7:35*
d. by
shall come out of Sion the *Ro 11:26*
D.

DELIVEREST

which d. the poor from him *Ps 35:10*
that
which thou d. will I give up *Mic 6:14*
to

DELIVERETH

He d. the poor in his *Job 36:15*
affliction
He d. me from mine enemies *Ps 18:48*
them that fear him, and d. *Ps 34:7*
them
d. them out of all their *Ps 34:17*
troubles
the Lord d. him out of them *Ps 34:19*
all
he d. them out of the hand *Ps 97:10*
of the
who d. David his servant *Ps 144:10*
from
but righteousness d. from *Pr 10:2;*
death *Pr 11:4*
A true witness d. souls: but *Pr 14:25*
a true witness saves lives *Pr 14:25*
(A)(R)
and d. girdles unto the *Pr 31:24*
merchant
for a prey, and none d.; for *Isa 42:22*
a spoil
He d. and rescueth, and he *Da 6:27*
He is a saviour and deliverer *Da 6:27*
(A)

DELIVERING

d. you up to the synagogues *Lu 21:12*
d. the message (A) *Ac 11:19*
and d. into prisons both men *Ac 22:4*
and
D. thee from the people, *Ac 26:17*
and from

DELIVERY

draweth near the time of *Isa 26:17*
her d.

DELUDED

d. dreamers (B)   *Jude 8*

DELUDES

hope never *d.* (A)(B)   *Ro 5:5*

DELUDING

giving heed to *d.* spirits (B)   *1Ti 4:1*

DELUGE

a water *d.* (B)   *Ge 6:17; 7:6, 10; 9:28*
a *d.* of words (B)   *Job 11:2*
washed out by a *d.* (B)(E)   *Job 22:16*

DELUGED

world was destroyed, *d.* with   *2Pe 3:6*
water (B)(N)(P)

DELUSION

a *d.* (R)   *Isa 41:29; 44:9; Eze 13:8*
seen falsehood and *d.* (A)   *La 2:14*
your faith is mere *d.* (A)   *1Co 15:17*
God shall send them strong   *2Th 2:11*
d.

DELUSIONS

I also will choose their *d.*   *Isa 66:4*

DELUSIVE

see *d.* vision (R)   *Eze 13:7*
false and *d.* words (A)   *Eze 13:8*
false, *d.* visions (A)(R)   *Eze 13:9;*
     13:23
by *d.* speculations (N)   *Col 2:8*

DEMAND

make no *d.* for repayment   *De 15:2*
(B)
for I will *d.* of thee, and   *Job 38:3*
answer
like a man: I will *d.* of thee   *Job 40:7*
will speak: I will *d.* of thee   *Job 42:4*
the *d.* by the word of the   *Da 4:17*
holy ones
never *d.* by terrifying (A)   *Lu 3:14*

DEMANDED

were beaten, and *d.*   *Ex 5:14*
Wherefore
the congregation *d.* to stone   *Nu 14:10*
(S)
David *d.* of him how Joab did   *2Sa 11:7*
The secret which the king hath   *Da 2:27*
d.
he *d.* of them where Christ   *M't 2:4*
should
soldiers likewise *d.* of him,   *Lu 3:14*
saying
when he was *d.* of the   *Lu 17:20*
Pharisees
Satan *d.* (R)   *Lu 22:31*
d. a murderer (A)   *Ac 3:14*
and *d.* who he was, and   *Ac 21:33*
what
d. his conviction (P)   *Ac 25:15*

DEMANDING

d. his condemnation (N)   *Ac 25:15*

DEMAS

the beloved physician, and   *Col 4:14*
D.
For *D.* hath forsaken me,   *2Ti 4:10*
having
Marcus, Aristarchus, *D.,*   *Ph'm 24*
Lucas

DEMENTED

pretended to be *d.* (B)   *1Sa 21:13*

DEMETRIUS

For a certain man named *D.*   *Ac 19:24*
Wherefore if *D.* and the   *Ac 19:38*
craftsmen
D. hath good report of all men   *3Jo 12*

DEMOLISH

d. all the high places (S)   *Nu 33:52*
he shall *d.* them (B)   *Ps 28:5*
we *d.* sophistries (N)   *2Co 10:5*

DEMOLISHES

the destroyer *d.* (B)   *Isa 21:2*

DEMOLISHING

not for *d.* you (A)   *2Co 10:8*

DEMON

demon (A)(B)(R)(S)   *M't 9:32;*
9:35; 11:18; 15:22; 17:18; M'k 7:26, 29-
30; Lu 4:33, 35; 7:33; 8:29; 9:42; 11:14;
Joh 7:20; 8:48-49, 52; 10:20-21

DEMONIAC

demoniac (B)(N)   *Jas 3:15*

DEMONIACAL

earthly, sensual, *d.* (S)   *Jas 3:15*

DEMONIACS

demoniacs (B)   *M't 4:24; 8:16, 28, 33;*
     Lu 8:36

DEMONS

shaggy he-goats, or *d.* (A)   *Le 17:7*
demons (A)(B)(E)(R)   *Ps 106:37*
demons (A)(E)(R)(S)   *M't 4:24;*
8:16, 28, 31, 33; M'k 1:32; 9:38; 16:17;
Lu 4:41; 8:2, 36; 9:1; 10:17; 13:32;
1Co 10:20; 1Ti 4:1; Jas 2:19; Re 9:20;
     16:14; 18:2
demons (B)   *M't 8:31;*
M'k 9:38; 16:17; Lu 4:41; 9:1; 10:17;
13:32; 1Co 10:20; Jas 2:19; Re 9:20;
     16:14; 18:2
d. believe and shudder   *Jas 2:19*
(B)(P)(R)

DEMONSTRATE

d. my holiness (A)(B)(R)   *Eze 38:23*

DEMONSTRATED

d. his power (P)   *Joh 2:11*

DEMONSTRATING

d. from scriptures (N)   *Ac 18:28*

DEMONSTRATION

in *d.* of the Spirit and of   *1Co 2:4*
power

DEMORALIZE

to frighten, *d.* (B)   *2Ch 32:18*

DEN

in wait secretly as a lion in   *Ps 10:9*
his *d.*
his hand on the cockatrice's *d.*   *Isa 11:8*
a *d.* of robbers in your eyes   *Jer 7:11*
heaps, and a *d.* of dragons   *Jer 9:11*
desolate, and a *d.* of   *Jer 10:22*
dragons
shall be cast into the *d.* of   *Da 6:7;*
lions   *6:12, 16-17, 19-20, 23-24*
will a young lion cry out of   *Am 3:4*
his *d.*
but ye have made it a *d.* of   *M't 21:13;*
thieves   *M'k 11:17; Lu 19:46*

DENARII

a hundred *d.*   *M't 18:28*
(A)(B)(R)(S)
two hundred *d.* (A)(R)   *M'k 6:37*
more than three hundred *d.*   *M'k 14:5;*
(A)(B)(E)(R)(S)   *Lu 7:41; 10:35;*
     Joh 12:5
owed him five hundred *d.* (S)   *Lu 7:41*
took out two *d.* (S)   *Lu 10:35*
for three hundred *d.* (S)   *Joh 12:5*

DENARIUS

for a *d.* a day (S)   *M't 20:2; 20:9, 13*
laborers for a *d.* (A)(R)   *M't 20:2;*
20:9-10, 13; 22:19; M'k 12:15; Lu 20:24
brought unto him a *d.* (S)   *M't 22:19*
     M'k 12:15
two hundred *d.* worth (S)   *M'k 6:37;*
     Joh 6:7
show me a *d.* (S)   *Lu 20:24*
a quart for a *d.* (A)(R)(S)   *Re 6:6*

DENIED

Sarah *d.* saying, I laughed   *Ge 18:15*
not
d. you children (A)   *Ge 30:2*
my gold, and I *d.* him not   *1Ki 20:7*
d. me justice (B)(E)(R)   *Job 27:2*
have *d.* the God that is   *Job 31:28*
above
they have *d.* the Lord (S)   *Jer 5:12*
have *d.* Jehovah (E)   *Jer 5:12*
he *d.* before them all,   *M't 26:70*
saying
again he *d.* with an oath, I   *M't 26:72*
do not
But he *d.* saying, I know   *M'k 14:68*
not
And he *d.* it again. And a   *M'k 14:70*
little after
When all *d.,* Peter and they   *Lu 8:45*
that
be *d.* before the angels of   *Lu 12:9*
God
he *d.* him, saying, Woman, I   *Lu 22:57*
know
he confessed, and *d.* not; but   *Joh 1:20*
crow, till thou hast *d.* me   *Joh 13:38*
thrice
He *d.* it, and said, I am not   *Joh 18:25*
Peter then *d.* again: and   *Joh 18:27*
d. him in the presence of   *Ac 3:13*
Pilate
ye *d.* the Holy One and the   *Ac 3:14*
Just
he hath *d.* the faith, and is   *1Ti 5:8*
worse
hast not *d.* my faith, even in   *Re 2:13*
those
word, and hast not *d.* my   *Re 3:8*
name

DENIETH

he that *d.* me before men   *Lu 12:9*
shall be
he that *d.* that Jesus is the   *1Jo 2:22*
Christ
that *d.* the Father and the   *1Jo 2:22*
Son
Whosoever *d.* the Son, the   *1Jo 2:23*
same

DENOUNCE

I *d.* unto you this day, that   *De 30:18*
ye
I wil *d.* your offspring (B)   *Mal 2:3*
exclude, *d.* and defame (B)   *Lu 6:22*

DENS

of Israel made them the *d.*   *J'g 6:2*
which
living quarters in mountain   *J'g 6:2*
caves (B)
Then the beasts go into *d.*   *Job 37:8*
When they couch in their *d.*   *Job 38:40*
and lay them down in their   *Ps 104:22*
d.
from the lions' *d.* from the   *Ca 4:8*
forts and towers shall be for   *Isa 32:14*
d.
with prey, and his *d.* with   *Na 2:12*
ravin
and in *d.* and caves of the   *Heb 11:38*
earth
hid themselves in the *d.* and   *Re 6:15*
in

DENSE

d. darkness all people (A)   *Isa 60:2*

DENY

unto you, lest ye *d.* your   *Jos 24:27*
God
one petition of thee, *d.* me   *1Ki 2:16*
not

then it shall *d.* him, saying, I *Job 8:18*
have
d. me them not before I die *Pr 30:7*
be full, and *d.* thee, and say, *Pr 30:9*
Who
whosoever shall *d.* me before *M't 10:33*
men.
him will I also *d.* before my *M't 10:33*
Father
come after me, let him *d.* *M't 16:24*
himself
cock crow, thou shalt *d.* me *M't 26:34;*
thrice   *26:75; M'k 14:30; Lu 22:61*
die with thee, yet will I not *M't 26:35*
d. thee
let him *d.* himself, and take *M'k 8:34*
up
I will not *d.* thee in any wise *M'k 14:31*
twice, thou shalt *d.* me thrice *M'k 14:72*
come after me, let him *d.* *Lu 9:23*
himself
d. that there is any *Lu 20:27*
resurrection
cock crow, thou shalt *d.* me *Lu 22:61*
thrice
Jerusalem; and we cannot *d.* *Ac 4:16*
it
if we *d.* him, he also will *d.* *2Ti 2:12*
us
faithful: he cannot *d.* himself *2Ti 2:13*
but in works they *d.* him, *Tit 1:16*
being

DENYING

working and *d.* myself (B) *Ec 4:8*
of godliness, but *d.* the power *2Ti 3:5*
d. ungodliness and worldly *Tit 2:12*
lusts
d. the Lord that bought them *2Pe 2:1*
d. the only Lord God, and our *Jude 4*
Lord

DEPART

or if thou *d.* to the right *Ge 13:9*
hand
sceptre shall not *d.* from *Ge 49:10*
Judah
And the frogs shall *d.* from *Ex 8:11*
that the swarms of flies may *Ex 8:29*
d.
And Moses let his father in *Ex 18:27*
law *d.*
so that her fruit *d.* from her *Ex 21:22*
D. and go up hence, thou and *Ex 33:1*
And then shall he *d.* from *Le 25:41*
thee
but I will *d.* to mine own *Nu 10:30*
land
D. I pray you, from the *Nu 16:26*
tents of
lest they *d.* from thy heart all *De 4:9*
from the day that thou didst *De 9:7*
d.
not *d.* from their verdict *De 17:11*
(A)(B)(R)
This book of the law shall not *Jos 1:8*
d.
So Joshua let the people *d.* *Jos 24:28*
D. not hence, I pray thee *J'g 6:18*
let him return and *d.* early *J'g 7:3*
from
he rose up to *d.*: and the *J'g 19:5*
damsel's
the man rose up to *d.* his *J'g 19:7*
father
the morning on the fifth day *J'g 19:8*
to *d.*
the man rose up to *d.* he, *J'g 19:9*
and his
d. get you down from among *1Sa 15:6*
d. and get thee into the land *1Sa 22:5*
of
in the morning, and have *1Sa 29:10*
light, *d.*
and his men rose up early *1Sa 29:11*
to *d.*
they may lead them away, *1Sa 30:22*
and *d.*
mercy shall not *d.* away from *2Sa 7:15*
him
and to morrow I will let *2Sa 11:12*
thee *d.*
shall never *d.* from thine *2Sa 12:10*
house
make speed to *d.* lest he *2Sa 15:14*
overtake
and I will *d.* from the city *2Sa 20:21*

statutes, I did not *d.* from *2Sa 22:23*
them
Let me *d.* that I may go to *1Ki 11:21*
mine
unto them, *D.* yet for three *1Ki 12:5*
days
returned to *d.* according to *1Ki 12:24*
king of Israel, that he may *1Ki 15:19;*
d. from *2Ch 16:3*
God moved them to *d.* *2Ch 18:31*
from him
might not *d.* from their *2Ch 35:15*
service
long wilt thou not *d.* from *Job 7:19*
He shall not *d.* out of *Job 15:30*
darkness
The increase of his house *Job 20:28*
shall *d.*
they say unto God, *D.* from *Job 21:14*
us
Which said unto God, *D.* *Job 22:17*
from us
to *d.* from evil is *Job 28:28*
understanding
D. from me, all ye workers of *Ps 6:8*
D. from evil, and do good *Ps 34:14;*
    37:27
before I *d.* (S) *Ps 39:13*
and guile *d.* not from her *Ps 55:11*
streets
froward heart shall *d.* from *Ps 101:4*
me
D. from me, ye evildoers: *Ps 119:115*
for I
d. from me therefore, ye *Ps 139:19*
bloody
fear the Lord, and *d.* from evil *Pr 3:7*
let not them *d.* from thine *Pr 3:21;*
eyes   *4:21*
d. not from the words of my *Pr 5:7*
to *d.* from the snares of *Pr 13:14*
death
abomination to fools to *d.* *Pr 13:19*
from
to *d.* from the snares of *Pr 14:27*
death
that he may *d.* from hell *Pr 15:24*
beneath
fear of the Lord men *d.* from *Pr 16:6*
evil
of the upright is to *d.* from *Pr 16:17*
evil
evil shall not *d.* from his *Pr 17:13*
house
he is old, he will not *d.* from *Pr 22:6*
it
not his foolishness *d.* from *Pr 27:22*
him
The envy also of Ephraim *Isa 11:13*
shall *d.*
shall his yoke *d.* from off *Isa 14:25*
them
burden *d.* from off their *Isa 14:25*
shoulders
D. ye, *d.* ye, go ye out *Isa 52:11*
from thence
the mountains shall *d.* and *Isa 54:10*
but my kindness shall not *d.* *Isa 54:10*
from
have I put in thy mouth, shall *Isa 59:21*
not *d.*
lest my soul *d.* from thee; lest *Jer 6:8*
and they that *d.* from me *Jer 17:13*
shall be
ordinances *d.* from before *Jer 31:36*
me
that they shall not *d.* from *Jer 32:40*
me
The Chaldeans shall surely *d.* *Jer 37:9*
from us: for they shall not *d.* *Jer 37:9*
they shall *d.* both man and *Jer 50:3*
beast
They cried unto them, *D.* ye *La 4:15*
it is unclean; *d.*, *d.* touch not *La 4:15*
my jealousy shall *d.* from *Eze 16:42*
thee
woe also to them when I *d.* *Ho 9:12*
from
Arise ye, and *d.*; for this is not *Mic 2:10*
sceptre of Egypt shall *d.* away *Zec 10:11*
d. from me, ye that work *M't 7:23*
iniquity
gave the commandment to *d.* *M't 8:18*
unto
he would *d.* out of their *M't 8:34*
coasts
ye *d.* out of that house or city *M't 10:14*
unto them. They need not *M't 14:16*
d.

D. from me, ye cursed, into *M't 25:41*
pray him to *d.* out of their *M'k 5:17*
coasts
abide till ye *d.* from that *M'k 6:10*
place
ye *d.* thence, shake off the *M'k 6:11*
dust
lettest thou thy servant *d.* in *Lu 2:29*
peace
that he should not *d.* from *Lu 4:42*
them
saying, *D.* from me; for I am *Lu 5:8*
besought him to *d.* from them *Lu 8:37*
into, there abide, and thence *Lu 9:4*
thou shalt not *d.* thence, till *Lu 12:59*
thou
d. from me, all ye workers *Lu 13:27*
of
Get thee out, and *d.* hence *Lu 13:31*
which are in the midst of it *Lu 21:21*
d. out
D. hence, and go into Judaea *Joh 7:3*
that he should *d.* out of this *Joh 13:1*
world
but if I *d.* I will send him *Joh 16:7*
unto
they should not *d.* from *Ac 1:4*
Jerusalem
therefore *d.* and go in peace *Ac 16:36*
desired them to *d.* out of *Ac 16:39*
the city
all Jews to *d.* from Rome *Ac 18:2*
them, ready to *d.* on the *Ac 20:7*
morrow
D.: for I will send thee far *Ac 22:21*
hence
then let the young man *d.* *Ac 23:22*
himself would *d.* shortly *Ac 25:4*
thither
part advised to *d.* thence *Ac 27:12*
also
not the wife *d.* from her *1Co 7:10*
husband
she *d.* let her remain *1Co 7:11*
unmarried
if the unbelieving *d.* let him *1Co 7:15*
d.
thrice, that it might *d.* from *2Co 12:8*
me
having a desire to *d.* and to *Ph'p 1:23*
be
some shall *d.* from the faith *1Ti 4:1*
name of Christ *d.* from *2Ti 2:19*
iniquity
say unto them, *D.* in peace *Jas 2:16*

DEPARTED

Abraham *d.* as Lord had *Ge 12:4*
spoken
they took Lot and *d.* *Ge 14:12*
Hagar, Eliezer, Isaac, *Ge 21:14;*
Laban *d.*   *24:10; 26:17; 31:55*
the man said, They are *d.* *Ge 37:17*
hence
they laded their asses with *Ge 42:26*
corn, and *d.*
he sent his brethren away, *Ge 45:24*
they *d.*
anger of Lord was kindled, he *Nu 12:9*
d.
the elders of Moab and *Nu 22:7*
Midian *d.*
she sent the spies away, they *Jos 2:21*
d.
d. every man to his place *J'g 9:55;*
    2Sa 6:19
then five men *d.* and came *J'g 18:7;*
to Laish   *18:21*
did they not let Israel go, *1Sa 6:6*
they *d.*
Samuel arose and *d.* (S) *1Sa 13:15*
nor washed from day the *2Sa 19:24*
king *d.*
the people *d.* *1Ki 12:5; 2Ch 10:5*
Jeroboam's wife arose and *1Ki 14:17*
d. to Tirza
Elijah *d.* and found Elisha *1Ki 19:19;*
    2Ki 1:4
messengers *d.* and brought *1Ki 20:9*
word again
prophet *d.* and waited for *1Ki 20:38*
the king
so Sennacherib *d.* and went *2Ki 19:36;*
    Isa 37:37
all people *d.* every man to *1Ch 16:43*
his house
Joab *d.* and went through *1Ch 21:4*
Israel

Jehoram *d.* without being desired	*2Ch 21:20*	

Jehoram *d.* without being *2Ch 21:20*
desired
d. from the way (R) *Ps 44:18*
Egypt was glad when they *Ps 105:38*
d.
mine age is *d.* and removed *Isa 38:12*
from me
Ishmael *d.* to go over to *Jer 41:10*
Ammonites
from daughter of Zion all her *La 1:6*
beauty is *d.*
when heard king, wise men *M't 2:9;*
d. *2:12*
Joseph and Mary arose, and *M't 2:14*
d. into Egypt
Jesus *d.* *M't 4:12;*
9:27; 11:1; 12:9; 13:53; 14:13; 15:21,
29; 16:4; M'k 1:35; 6:46; 8:13;
Lu 4:42 Joh 4:3, 43; 6:15; 12:36
Judas *d.* and hanged himself *M't 27:5*
Zacharias *d.* to his house *Lu 1:23*
d. to his own house, *Lu 5:25*
glorifying God
when the messengers of John *Lu 7:24*
were *d.*
man out of whom devils were *Lu 8:35*
d.
the thieves wounded him *Lu 10:30*
and *d.*
on the morrow when the *Lu 10:35*
Samaritan *d.*
man *d.* and told Jews it was *Joh 5:15*
Jesus
angel *d.* from *Ac 10:7; 12:10*
Barnabas *d.* to Tarsus to *Ac 11:25*
seek Paul
Paul and Barnabas *d.* *Ac 15:39*
asunder
Paul *d.* *Ac 15:40;*
17:33; 18:1, 7, 23; 20:1, 11
when he said these words, *Ac 28:29*
the Jews *d.*
Demas forsaken me, *d.* to *2Ti 4:10*
Thessalonica
for perhaps he therefore *d.* *Ph'm 15*
for a season
the heaven *d.* as a scroll *Re 6:14*
rolled

DEPARTED *FROM*

they arose and *d.* from Isaac *Ge 26:31*
thus was I, my sleep *d.* from *Ge 31:40*
mine eyes
they were *d.* from Rephidim *Ex 19:2;*
Nu 33:15
all Israel *d.* from the *Ex 35:20*
presence of Moses
if the plague be *d.* from *Le 13:58*
them, then
they *d.* from the mount of *Nu 10:33*
the Lord
cloud *d.* from off the *Nu 12:10*
tabernacle
their defence is *d.* from them, *Nu 14:9*
fear not
then *d.* from *Nu 33:3;*
33:6, 8, 13, 15, 17-20, 27, 30-31, 35,
41-45, 48
when we *d.* from Horeb, we *De 1:19*
went
he wist not that Lord was *d.* *J'g 16:20*
from him
the glory is *d.* from Israel *1Sa 4:21;*
4:22
when thou art *d.* from me, *1Sa 10:2*
thou shalt find
Kenites *d.* from among the *1Sa 15:6*
Amalekites
Spirit of the Lord *d.* from *1Sa 16:14;*
Saul *18:12*
refreshed, and evil Spirit *d.* *1Sa 16:23*
from him
God is *d.* from me, and *1Sa 28:15*
answereth me not
ask of me, seeing the Lord *1Sa 28:16*
is *d.* from thee
as soon as thou art *d.* from *1Ki 20:36*
me
they *d.* from him to their *2Ki 3:27*
own land
so he *d.* from Elisha a little *2Ki 5:19;*
way *8:14*
Sennacherib *d.* from Lachish *2Ki 19:8;*
Isa 37:8
when they were *d.* from *2Ch 24:25*
him
then we *d.* from the river of *Ezr 8:31*
Ahava

have not wickedly *d.* from *Ps 18:21*
my God
the day that Ephraim *d.* from *Isa 7:17*
Judah
the smiths were *d.* from *Jer 29:2*
Jerusalem
Chaldeans heard they *d.* from *Jer 37:5*
Jerusalem
whorish heart which hath *d.* *Eze 6:9*
from me
glory of Lord *d.* from *Eze 10:18*
threshold
O king, the kingdom is *d.* *Da 4:31*
from thee
for glory of Samaria is *d.* *Ho 10:5*
from it
Jesus *d.* from thence, and *M't 15:29*
came
finished these sayings, he *d.* *M't 19:1*
from Galilee
as they *d.* from Jericho, *M't 20:29*
multitude followed
Jesus went out and *d.* from *M't 24:1*
the temple
they *d.* quickly *from* the *M't 28:8*
sepulchre
leprosy *d. from* him *M'k 1:42; Lu 5:13*
and the angel *d. from* Mary *Lu 1:38*
the devil *d. from* him for a *Lu 4:13*
season
as they *d. from* him, Peter *Lu 9:33*
said to Jesus
d. from presence of the *Ac 5:41*
council
and forthwith the angel *d.* *Ac 12:10*
from him
they came when they had *d.* *Ac 13:14*
from Perga
John *d. from* them from *Ac 15:38*
Pamphylia
Paul *d. from* them *Ac 17:33;*
18:1; 19:9; Ph'p 4:15
diseases *d. from* them, and *Ac 19:12*
evil spirits
fruits soul lusted after are *d.* *Re 18:14*
from

DEPARTED *NOT FROM*

I have *not d. from* God *2Sa 22:22;*
Ps 18:21
he *d. not therefrom* *2Ki 3:3; 13:2*
d. not from sins of *2Ki 10:29;*
Jeroboam *10:31; 13:6, 11; 14:24; 15:9,*
18; 17:22
Hezekiah *d. not from* *2Ki 18:6*
following Lord
d. not from commandment *2Ch 8:15*
of king
Jehoshaphat *d. not from* *2Ch 20:32*
way of Asa
they *d. not from* following *2Ch 34:33*
the Lord
cloud *d. not from* them by *Ne 9:19*
day
I have *not d. from* thy *Ps 119:102*
judgments
d. not from temple but served *Lu 2:37*
God

DEPARTED *NOT OUT*

Joshua *d. not out* of the *Ex 33:11*
tabernacle
ark and Moses *d. not out* of *Nu 14:44*
camp

DEPARTED *OUT*

75 years old when *d. out* of *Ge 12:4*
Haran
when she is *d. out* of his *De 24:2*
house
angel of Lord *d. out* of his *J'g 6:21*
sight
Levite *d. out* of *J'g 17:8*
Beth-lehem-judah
David and his men *d. out* *1Sa 23:13*
of Keilah
Uriah *d. out* of the king's *2Sam 11:8*
house
d. out of the way, have *Mal 2:8*
corrupted
rebuked devil, he *d. out* of *M't 17:18*
him

DEPARTETH

carrieth him away, and he *Job 27:21*
d.
A wise man feareth, and *d.* *Pr 14:16*
from

avoids misfortune (B) *Pr 14:16*
turns away from evil (R) *Pr 14:16*
and *d.* in darkness, and his *Ec 6:4*
name
and he that *d.* from evil *Isa 59:15*
maketh
departs from evil (A)(R) *Isa 59:15*
turns from evil (B) *Isa 59:15*
a wife treacherously *d.* from *Jer 3:20*
her
and whose heart *d.* from the *Jer 17:5*
Lord
whose mind and heart turn *Jer 17:5*
aside (A)(R)
lies and robbery; the prey *d.* *Na 3:1*
not
bruising him hardly *d.* from *Lu 9:39*
him
scarcely leave him (A)(R) *Lu 9:39*
it hardly quits wounding him *Lu 9:39*
(B)
will hardly let him go (N) *Lu 9:39*

DEPARTING

her soul was in *d.* (for she *Ge 35:18*
died)
after their *d.* out of the land *Ex 16:1*
of
d. away from our God, *Isa 59:13*
speaking
even by *d.* from thy precepts *Da 9:5*
transgressed thy law, even by *Da 9:11*
d.
great whoredom, *d.* from the *Ho 1:2*
Lord
And the people saw them *d.* *M'k 6:33*
again *d.* from the coast of *M'k 7:31*
Tyre
John *d.* from them returned *Ac 13:13*
to
I know this, that after my *d.* *Ac 20:29*
unbelief, in *d.* from the living *Heb 3:12*
God
refuses to cleave to, trust in, *Heb 3:12*
rely on (A)
fall away from the living God *He 3:12*
(B)
falling away from the living *He 3:12*
God (E)
faithless heart of deserter *He 3:12*
from (N)
deserts the cause of the living *He 3:12*
(P)
leading you to fall away from *He 3:12*
God (R)
the *d.* of the children of *He 11:22*
Israel

DEPARTMENT

holy in every *d.* of your lives *1Pe 1:15*
(P)

DEPARTURE

the sea shall be troubled at *Eze 26:18*
thy *d.*
his *d.,* destiny (N)(R) *Lu 9:31;*
1Pe 1:15
and the time of my *d.* is at *2Ti 4:6*
hand

DEPEND

d. on Egypt (B) *2Ki 18:24*
will *d.* on him (R) *Job 39:11*

DEPENDED

on which he *d.* (B) *Lu 11:22*

DEPENDENT

he *d.* on nobody (R) *1Th 4:12*

DEPOSED

d. him at Jerusalem (S) *2Ch 36:3*
he was *d.* from his kingly *Da 5:20*
throne
thrust from kingly throne (B) *Da 5:20*

DEPOSIT

guard the *d.* (B) *1Ti 6:20*

DEPRAVED

become *d.* (B)(R) *Ps 14:3; 53:3*
up to *d.* reason (N) *Ro 1:28*
d. minds (B)(R) *2Ti 6:9; 3:8*

DEPRAVITY

your d. passed (A)	Na 3:19
bound to utter d. (A)(P)	2Pe 2:19

DEPRESSED

looked sad and d. (A)	Ge 4:5
with d. spots in (A)	Le 14:37
became d. in spirit (B)	Nu 21:4
grieved and d. (A)	Ne 8:10
began to be d. (S)	M't 26:37;
	M'k 14:33
hearts overburdened and d. (A)	Lu 21:34
am d. (P)	Ro 9:2
sore d. by filthy (E)(R)	2Pe 2:7

DEPRESSION

wickedly mention d. (B)	Ps 73:8

DEPRIVED

why should I be d. also of you	Ge 27:45
God hath d. her of wisdom	Job 39:17
I am d. of the residue of my years	Isa 38:10

DEPTH

The d. saith, It is not in me	Job 28:14
deep (A)(E)(R)	Job 28:14;
	38:16; Ps 33:7; Pr 8:27
the abyss says (B)	Job 28:14
walked in the search of the d.	Job 38:16
deep (B)	Job 38:16; Ps 33:7; Pr 8:27
layeth up the d. in storehouses	Ps 33:7
compass upon the face of the d.	Pr 8:27
for height, and the earth for d.	Pr 25:3
ask it either in the d. or in	Isa 7:11
the d. closed me round about	Jon 2:5
the abyss surrounding me (A)	Jon 2:5
the ocean surrounding me (B)	Jon 2:5
the deep was round about me (E)(R)	Jon 2:5
were drowned in the d. of the sea	M't 18:6
because it had no d. of earth	M'k 4:5
Nor height, nor d., nor any other	Ro 8:39
O the d. of the riches both of the	Ro 11:33
the breadth, and length, and d.	Eph 3:18

DEPTHS

The d. have covered them; they	Ex 15:5
d. were congealed in the heart	Ex 15:8
the waves were congealed (B)	Ex 15:8
the deeps were congealed (E)(R)	Ex 15:8
of fountains and d. that spring out	De 8:7
fountains and springs flowing (A)(B)	De 8:7
springs and lakes spring up (B)	De 8:7
springs flowing forth in valleys (E)	De 8:7
into d. (B)	Ne 9:11; Ps 148:7
again from the d. of the sea	Ps 68:22
up again from the d. of the earth	Ps 71:20
afraid: the d. also were troubled	Ps 77:16
the deep shuddered (A)(B)(R)	Ps 77:16
them drink as out of the great d.	Ps 78:15
drink abundantly as out of deep (A)(B)(R)	Ps 78:15
so he led them through the d.	Ps 106:9
they go down again to the d.	Ps 107:26
Out of the d. have I cried unto thee	Ps 130:1
By his knowledge the d. are	Pr 3:20
the deeps were broken up (A)(B)(R)	Pr 3:20
When there were no d. I was	Pr 8:24

when there were no deeps (A)	Pr 8:24
her guests are in the d. of hell	Pr 9:18
the d. of Sheol (A)(B)(E)(R)	Pr 9:18
that hath made the d. of the sea	Isa 51:10
by the seas in the d. of the waters	Eze 27:34
their sin into the d. of the sea	Mic 7:19
d. of the Nile (A)(E)(R)	Zec 10:11
brought down to the d. (N)	M't 11:23
brought down to d. (N)	Lu 10:15
have not known the d. of Satan	Re 2:24

DEPRIVE

d. righteous of justice (A)(B)(R)	Ps 18:5
d. me of ground of boasting (R)	1Co 9:15

DEPRIVED

d. you of fertility (B)	Ge 30:2

DEPRIVING

toiling, d. myself (R)	Ec 4:8

DEPUTED

there is no man d. of king to hear	2Sa 15:3

DEPUTIES

the d. and rulers of the provinces	Es 8:9
the d. and officers of the king	Es 9:3
the law is open, and there are d.	Ac 19:38

DEPUTY

no king in Edom: a d. was king	1Ki 22:47
was with the d. of the country	Ac 13:7
turn away the d. from the faith	Ac 13:8
Then the d. when he saw what	Ac 13:12
when Gallio was d. of Achaia	Ac 18:12

DERBE

and fled unto Lystra and D.	Ac 14:6
he departed with Barnabas to D.	Ac 14:20
Then came he to D. and Lystra	Ac 16:1
and Secundus; and Gaius of D. and	Ac 20:4

DERIDE

I will d. when terror (B)	Pr 1:26
they shall d. every strong hold	Hab 1:10
they ridicule every stronghold (A)	Hab 1:10
laughing at every stronghold (B)	Hab 1:10
laugh at every fortress (R)	Hab 1:10

DERIDED

ten times d. me (B)	Job 19:3
they d. him (R)	M't 27:39
they d. him (B)(R)	M'k 15:29
all these things: and they d. him	Lu 16:14
began to sneer, ridicule, scoff (A)	Lu 16:14
sneered at him (B)	Lu 16:14
they scoffed at him (E)(N)(R)	Lu 16:14
heard all this with a sneer (P)	Lu 16:14
the rulers also with them d. him	Lu 23:35
rulers scoffed and sneered (A)	Lu 23:35
the leaders sneered (B)	Lu 23:35
rulers also scoffed at him (E)(P)(R)	Lu 23:35
rulers jeered at him (N)	Lu 23:35

DERIDES

mouth d. my enemies (R)	1Sa 2:1

DERISION

are younger than I have me in d.	Job 30:1
the Lord shall have them in d.	Ps 2:4
a scorn and a d. to them	Ps 44:13
shalt have all the heathen in	Ps 59:8
a scorn and d. to them that are	Ps 79:4
proud have had me greatly in d.	Ps 119:51
am in d. daily, every one mocketh	Jer 20:7
a reproach unto me, and a d.	Jer 20:8
and he also shall be in d.	Jer 48:26
was not Israel a d. unto thee	Jer 48:27
a d. terror to all (A)(E)	Jer 48:39
so shall Moab be a d. and a	Jer 48:39
I was a d. to all my people	La 3:14
laughed to scorn and had in d.	Eze 23:32
which became a prey and d. to the	Eze 36:4
shall be their d. in the land of Egypt	Ho 7:16

DESCEND

and the border shall d. and	Nu 34:11
he shall d. into battle, and perish	1Sa 26:10
d. from the city of David (S)	Ne 3:15
his glory shall not d. after him	Ps 49:17
he that rejoiceth, shall d. into it	Isa 5:14
them that d. into the pit, with the	Eze 26:20
them that d. into the pit: and all	Eze 31:16
Let Christ the king of Israel d.	M'k 15:32
A certain vessel d. as it had been	Ac 11:5
coming down from heaven (A)(B)(E)	Ac 11:5
a thing was coming down (N)(P)	Ac 11:5
great sheet let down from heaven (R)	Ac 11:5
Or, Who shall d. into the deep	Ro 10:7
Lord himself shall d. from heaven	1Th 4:16

DESCENDANTS

descendants (A)	Ge 13:16;
17:7; 22:17; 25:12, 19; 26:24; 32:12;
46:6; Ex 48:23; Nu 14:24; 25:13; De 1:8;
4:37; 28:46, 59; 30:6, 19; 31:21;
1Sa 20:42; 1Ki 2:33; 11:39; 2Ki 11:1;
17:20; Ne 9:8; Es 9:27-28; Ps 106:27;
Isa 45:19; 48:19; 61:9; 65:23; Jer 33:26;
Ac 2:30; 7:5-6; 13:23; Ro 4:16; Re 12:17
descendens (B)	Ge 11:10;
13:16; 15:13; 17:7, 9; 22:17; 25:12, 19;
26:24; 32:12; 46:6; 48:19; Ex 28:43;
Nu 14:24; 15:23; Le 21:21; De 1:8; 4:37;
Jos 22:27-28; 1Sa 20:42; 24:21; 2Sa 4:8;
21:16; 1Ki 2:33; 11:39; 2Ki 5:27;
1Ch 16:13; 2Ch 20:6; Ne 9:8; Es 9:27-
28; Isa 1:4; 14:20; 45:19; 48:19; 54:3;
61:9; Jer 31:36; 33:26, 32; Eze 20:5;
Ac 2:30; 3:25; Ro 4:16
descendents (N)	Ac 2:30; 3:25
descendents (P)	Ac 2:30
descendents (R)	Ge 11:10;
12:7; 13:6; 15:5, 13; 17:7, 9. 19; 21:12;
22:17-18; 25:12, 19; 26:24; 32:12; 48:19;
Ex 28:43; 32:12; Le 21:17, 21; De 1:8;
Nu 14:24; 25:13; De 1:8; 4:37; 28:46,
59; 30:6; 31:21; 1Sa 20:42; 2Sa 4:8;
22:51; 1Ki 2:33; 11:39; 2Ki 5:27; 17:20;
Ne 9:8; Es 9:27-28; Job 5:25; Ps 89:4;
106:27; 112:2; Isa 14:20; 44:3; 48:19;
54:3; 61:9; 66:22; Jer 23:8; 29:32; 30:10;
31:36-37; 33:22, 26; Ac 2:30; Ro 4:16

DESCENDED

the Lord d. upon it in fire	Ex 19:18
came down (B)	Ex 19:18; 33:9

the cloudy pillar *d.* and stood *Ex 33:9*
And the Lord *d.* in the cloud *Ex 34:5*
the brook that *d.* out of the *De 9:21*
mount
flowing down the mountain *De 9:21*
(B)
returned, and *d.* from the *Jos 2:23*
mountain
came down from the *Jos 2:23*
mountain (B)
And the coast *d.* unto the *Jos 17:9*
river
the border *d.* to *Jos 18:13*
Ataroth-adar
and *d.* to the valley of *Jos 18:16*
Hinnom
south, and *d.* to En-rogel *Jos 18:16*
and *d.* to the stone of *Jos 18:17*
Bohan the
d. upon the mountains of *Ps 133:3*
Zion
comes down on hills of Zion *Ps 133:3*
(A)(E)
falls upon mountains of Zion *Ps 133:3*
(B)(R)
ascended up into heaven, or *Pr 30:4*
d.
And the rain *d.* and the *M't 7:25;*
floods *7:27*
rain fell, came down *M't 7:25*
(A)(B)(N)(P)(R)
for the angel of the Lord *d.* *M't 28:2*
from
the Holy Ghost *d.* in a bodily *Lu 3:22*
shape
the high priest *d.* with the *Ac 24:1*
elders
but that he also *d.* first into *Eph 4:9*
He that *d.* is the same also *Eph 4:10*
that

DESCENDETH

This wisdom *d.* not from *Jas 3:15*
above
comes down from above *Jas 3:15*
(A)(B)(E)(N)(R)
does not come from God (P) *Jas 3:15*

DESCENDING

angels of God ascending and *Ge 28:12;*
d. *Joh 1:51*
Spirit of God *d.* like a dove *M't 3:16*
the Spirit like a dove *d.* *M'k 1:10*
upon him
I saw the Spirit *d.* from the *Joh 1:32*
heaven
whom thou shalt see the *Joh 1:33*
Spirit *d.*
a certain vessel *d.* unto him *Ac 10:11*
Jerusalem, *d.* out of heaven *Re 21:10*
from

DESCENT

the royal *d.* (A) *1Ki 11:14*
d. of Horonaim (S) *Jer 48:5*
the *d.* of Jesus Christ (N) *M't 1:1*
at the *d.* of the mount of *Lu 19:37*
Olives
in natural *d.* (A)(N)(P) *Ro 9:5*
without mother, without *d.* *Heb 7:3*
without record of ancestral *Heb 7:3*
life (A)
without pedigree (B) *Heb 7:3*
without genealogy (E)(R) *Heb 7:3*
no lineage (N) *Heb 7:3*
no family tree (P) *Heb 7:3*
whose *d.* is not counted from *Heb 7:6*
who has not their Levitical *Heb 7:6*
ancestry (A)
without their pedigree (B) *Heb 7:6*
whose genealogy is not *Heb 7:6*
counted (E)
does not trace his descent *Heb 7:6*
from them (N)
quite independent of Levitic *Heb 7:6*
ancestry (P)
who has not their genealogy *Heb 7:6*
(R)

DESECRATE

d. the name of the Lord (B) *Le 21:6*
d. my holy name (B) *Le 22:2; 22:32*
d. the holy gifts (B) *Le 22:15*
not to *d.* holy (B) *Nu 18:32*
not to *d.* the land (B) *Nu 35:33*
d. my sanctuary (B) *Eze 24:21*
d., defile the temple (A)(B) *Ac 24:6*

DESECRATED

d. the temple (B) *2Ch 36:14*
d. dwelling place (R) *Ps 74:7*
they have *d.* this place (S) *Jer 19:4*
d. high places (A) *Eze 16:16*

DESCRIBE

and go through the land, *Jos 18:4;*
and *d.* it *18:6, 8*
write a description of it (A) *Jos 18:4*
make a description (B)(R) *Jos 18:4;*
18:8-9

DESCRIBED

and *d.* it by cities into seven *Jos 18:9*
parts
and he *d.* unto him the *J'g 8:14*
princes of

DESCRIBETH

as David also *d.* the *Ro 4:6*
blessedness
pronounces a blessing *Ro 4:6*
(A)(E)(R)
mentions, speaks of happiness *Ro 4:6*
(B)(N)
Moses *d.* the righteousness *Ro 10:5*
which
Moses writes *Ro 10:5*
(A)(E)(N)(P)(R)

DESCRIPTION

write a *d.* (A)(B)(R) *Jos 18:4;*
18:8-9
and bring the *d.* hither to me *Jos 18:6*

DESCRY

the house of Joseph sent to *J'g 1:23*
d.
sent to spy on Bethel *J'g 1:23*
(A)(B)(E)(R)

DESERT

desert (B) *Ge 14:6;*
16:7; 21:14, 20-21; 36:24; Ex 3:18;
4:27; 5:1; 7:16; 8:27-28; 13:18, 20;
14:3, 11-12; 15:22; 16:1-3, 10, 14,
32; 17:1; 18:5; 19:1-2; Nu 20:4; 21:5,
11, 13, 23; 24:1; 32:13; 33:6, 8;
De 1:19, 31, 40; 2:1, 7-8, 26; 4:43;
8:15; 9:7, 28; 11:5, 24; Jos 1:4; 5:5;
8:15, 24; 12:8; 15:51; 16:1; 18:12; 20:8;
24:7; J'g 11:18; 20:42, 45, 47;
1Sa 13:18; 17:28; 23:14, 24; 24:1;
25:1, 4, 14, 21; 26:2-3; 2Sa 2:24;
15:23, 28; 16:2; 17:16, 29; 1Ki 2:34;
9:18; 19:4, 15; 2Ki 3:8; 1Ch 5:9; 6:78;
12:8; 21:29; Job 1:19; 24:5; 38:26; 39:6;
Ps 55:7; 74:14; 78:52; 106:9, 14; 107:4,
33, 35; Ca 3:6; Isa 14:17; 16:1, 8;
32:15; 33:9; 42:11; 43:20; 50:2;
Jer 2:31; 4:11, 26; 9:10, 26; 13:24; 17:6;
50:12; Eze 6:14; 20:13, 17-18, 21, 23,
36; 23:42; Ho 2:3; 13:15; Joe 2:3;
Am 2:10; Zep 2:13; M't 3:3; 4:1;
M'k 1:3-4, 12; 8:14; Lu 3:2, 4; 4:1;
5:16; 7:24; Joh 1:23; 3:14; 6:49; 11:54;
Ac 7:36, 38, 42, 44; 13:18; 1Co 10:5;
Heb 3:8, 17; Re 12:14
the *d.* pit (B) *Ge 37:22*
to the backside of the *d.* and *Ex 3:1*
three days' journey into the *d.* *Ex 5:3*
were come to the *d.* of Sinai *Ex 19:2*
and from the *d.* unto the *Ex 23:31*
river
into the *d.* of Zin in the first *Nu 20:1*
wilderness (B)(E)(R) *Nu 20:1;*
27:14; 2Ch 26:10
in the *d.* of Zin, in the *Nu 27:14*
strife of
removed from the *d.* of *Nu 33:16*
Sinai, and
desert (B) *Le 16:21;*
16:22; Nu 32:15; Pr 21:19; Isa 32:16;
41:19; 43:19; Jer 2:2; 9:2; 48:6;
Eze 20:10, 13, 15; Ho 13:5; M't 3:1;
11:7; 15:33; Lu 8:29; Ac 7:30; 21:38;
2Co 11:26; Re 12:6; 17:3
He found him in a *d.* land *De 32:10*
in the *d.* land (A)(E)(R) *De 32:10*
do not urge me to *d.* you *Ru 1:16*
(A)(B)
he built towers in the *d.* *2Ch 26:10*

wild asses in the *d.* go they *Job 24:5*
forth
the wilderness *Job 24:5;*
(A)(B)(E)(R) *Ps 78:40; 102:6;*
106:14; Isa 40:3; 41:19; 51:3
hands; render to them their *d.* *Ps 28:4*
render to them what they *Ps 28:4*
deserve (A)
According to work, repay *Ps 28:4*
them (B)
render them their due reward *Ps 28:4*
(R)
and grieve him in the *d.* *Ps 78:40*
I am like an owl of the *d.* *Ps 102:6*
and tempted God in the *d.* *Ps 106:14*
beasts of the *d.* shall lie *Isa 13:21*
there
burden of the *d.* of the sea *Isa 21:1*
through; so it cometh from *Isa 21:1*
the *d.*
The wild beasts of the *d.* *Isa 34:14*
shall
wild beasts of the *d.* *Isa 34:14*
(A)(B)(E)
the *d.* shall rejoice, and *Isa 35:1*
blossom
break out, and streams in the *Isa 35:6*
d.
make straight in the *d.* a *Isa 40:3*
highway
I will set in the *d.* the fir *Isa 41:19*
tree
wilderness, and rivers in the *Isa 43:19*
d.
rivers in the *d.* to give drink *Isa 43:20*
to me
her *d.* like the garden of the *Isa 51:3*
Lord
like the heath in the *d.* and *Jer 17:6*
people that dwell in the *d.* *Jer 25:24*
wilderness, a dry land, and *Jer 50:12*
a *d.*
Therefore the wild beasts of *Jer 50:39*
the *d.*
wild beasts of the *d.* *Jer 50:39*
(A)(B)(E)
go down into the *d.* and go *Eze 47:8*
into
proclaiming in the *d.* (B) *M't 3:1*
he begins to distrust and *d.* *M't 13:21*
him whom (A)
by ship into a *d.* place *M't 14:13*
apart
This is a *d.* place, and the *M't 14:15*
time is
Behold, he is in the *d.* go *M't 24:26*
not
the wilderness (A)(E)(R) *M't 24:26;*
Joh 6:31
was without in *d.* places: *M'k 1:45*
and they
yourselves apart into a *d.* *M'k 6:31*
place
they departed into a *d.* place *M'k 6:32*
This is a *d.* place, and now *M'k 6:35*
departed and went into a *d.* *Lu 4:42*
place
into a *d.* place belonging to *Lu 9:10*
for we are here in a *d.* place *Lu 9:12*
fathers did eat manna in the *Joh 6:31*
d.
Jerusalem unto Gaza, which *Ac 8:26*
is *d.*

DESERTED

will cry in *d.* castles (A) *Isa 13:22*
went out to a *d.* place *M'k 1:35*
(A)(E)(R)

DESERTS

he led them through the *d.* *Isa 48:21*
a land of *d.* and of pits *Jer 2:6*
and according to their *d.* *Eze 7:27*
will I
according to their *d.* will I *Eze 7:27*
judge (B)
according to their way I will *Eze 7:27*
(R)
are like the foxes in the *d.* *Eze 13:4*
and was in the *d.* till the day *Lu 1:80*
of
getting *d.* for misdeeds (B) *Lu 23:41*
d. the cause of the living *Heb 3:12*
(P)
wandered in *d.* and in *Heb 11:38*
mountains

DESERVE

us less than our iniquities d.	Ezr 9:13
what they d. (A)	Ps 28:4
we got what we d. (P)	Lu 23:41

DESERVED

bring d. punishment (B)	Ro 13:4

DESERVES

d. his support (A)(B)	M't 10:10
worker d. his wage (B)(R)	1Ti 5:18

DESERVETH

of thee less than thine iniquity d.	Job 11:6

DESERVING

according to the d. of his hands	J'g 9:16
deemed d. of kingdom (A)	2Th 1:5

DESIGN

d. skillfully the work (S)	Ex 31:4
d. artistic work (B)	Ex 33:32
d. beautifully wrought (S)	Ex 35:35; 35:32
fall by their own d. (B)	Ps 5:10
to avert the evil d. (R)	Ec 8:3
decreed in his d. (N)	Eph 1:11
d. of his own will (B)	Eph 1:11

DESIGNATED

thou hast d. for (B)	Ge 24:14
my d. ones (A)	Isa 13:3
d. you a prophet (B)	Jer 1:5
Christ d. and appointed (A)(B)	Ac 3:20
d. by God as Judge (N)	Ac 10:42
good deeds God d. us (N)	Eph 2:10
d. for condemnation (R)	Jude 4

DESIGNS

plan d. of gold (B)	Ex 31:4
d. of the wicked (R)	Job 10:3
his d. (R)	2Co 2:11

DESIRABLE

tree d. to make wise (B)	Ge 3:6
spurned the d. land (B)	Ps 106:24
rulers, all of them d. young men	Eze 23:6; 23:12, 23
attractive young men (A)(B)	Eze 23:6; 23:12
d. vineyards (B)	Am 5:11

DESIRE

thy d. shall be to thy husband	Ge 3:16
unto thee shall be his d. and	Ge 4:7
serve the Lord; for that ye did d.	Ex 10:11
neither shall any man d. thy land	Ex 34:24
shalt thou d. thy neighbour's wife	De 5:21
shalt not d. the silver or gold	De 7:25
come with all the d. of his mind	De 18:6
and hast a d. unto her, that thou	De 21:11
if the man d. not (S)	De 25:7; 25:8; Ps 78:18, 30; 81:12
I would d. a request of you	J'g 8:24
on whom is all the d. of Israel	1Sa 9:20
according to all the d. of thy soul	1Sa 23:20
your hearts d. (R)	1Sa 23:20
all my salvation, and all my d.	2Sa 23:5
I d. one small petition of thee	1Ki 2:20
I will do all thy d. concerning	1Ki 5:8
thou shalt accomplish my d. in	1Ki 5:9
fir trees according to all his d.	1Ki 5:10
all Solomon's d. which he was	1Ki 9:1
according to all his d. that	1Ki 9:11

unto the queen of Sheba all her d.	1Ki 10:13
all the d. of your eyes (A)	1Ki 20:6
Did I d. a son of my lord	2Ki 4:28
to the queen of Sheba all her d.	2Ch 9:12
sought him with their whole d.	2Ch 15:15
who d. to fear thy name: and	Ne 1:11
and I d. to reason with God	Job 13:3
thou wilt have a d. to the work of	Job 14:15
we d. not the knowledge of thy	Job 21:14
withheld the poor from their d.	Job 31:16
my d. is, that the Almighty would	Job 31:35
speak, for I d. to justify thee	Job 33:32
My d. is that Job may be tried	Job 34:36
D. not the night, when people are	Job 36:20
wicked boasteth of his heart's d.	Ps 10:3
hast heard the d. of the humble	Ps 10:17
Thou hast given him his heart's d.	Ps 21:2
Lord, all my d. is before thee	Ps 38:9
and offering thou didst not d.	Ps 40:6
who d. my hurt (B)(R)	Ps 40:14
shall the king greatly d. thy beauty	Ps 45:11
mine eye hath seen his d. upon mine	Ps 54:7
let me see my d. upon mine enemies	Ps 59:10
put to confusion, that d. my hurt	Ps 70:2
upon earth that I d. beside thee	Ps 73:25
for he gave them their own d.	Ps 78:29
shall see my d. upon mine enemies	Ps 92:11
ears shall hear my d. of the wicked	Ps 92:11
he see his d. upon his enemies	Ps 112:8
the d. of the wicked shall perish	Ps 112:10
therefore shall I see my d. upon them	Ps 118:7
satisfiest the d. of every living	Ps 145:16
He will fulfil the d. of them that	Ps 145:19
all the things thou canst d.	Pr 3:15
but the d. of the righteous shall	Pr 10:24
The d. of the righteous is only good	Pr 11:23
when the d. cometh, it is a tree of	Pr 13:12
The d. accomplished is sweet	Pr 13:19
Through d. a man, having separated	Pr 18:1
The d. of a man is his kindness	Pr 19:22
The d. of the slothful killeth him	Pr 21:25
neither d. thou his dainty meats	Pr 23:6
men, neither d. to be with them	Pr 24:1
than the wandering of the d.	Ec 6:9
be a burden, and d. shall fail	Ec 12:5
beloved's, and his d. is toward me	Ca 7:10
the d. of our soul is to thy name	Isa 26:8
no beauty that we should d. him	Isa 53:2
whereunto they d. to return	Jer 22:27
the place whither ye d. to go	Jer 42:22
which they have a d. to return	Jer 44:14
away from thee the d. of thine	Eze 24:16
strength, the d. of your eyes	Eze 24:21
of their glory, the d. of their eyes	Eze 24:25
That they would d. mercies of the	Da 2:18
nor the d. of women, nor regard	Da 11:37

It is in my d. that I should chastise	Ho 10:10
Woe unto you that d. the day of	Am 5:18
he uttereth his mischievous d.	Mic 7:3
who enlargeth his d. as hell	Hab 2:5
the d. of all nations shall come	Hag 2:7
If any man d. to be first	M'k 9:35
do for us whatsoever we shall d.	M'k 10:35
What things soever ye d. when	M'k 11:24
began to d. him to do as he had	M'k 15:8
ye shall d. to see one of the days	Lu 17:22
the scribes, which d. to walk in	Lu 20:46
With d. I have desired to eat this	Lu 22:15
threatening and murderous d. (A)	Ac 9:1
The Jews have agreed to d. thee	Ac 23:20
we d. to hear of thee what thou	Ac 28:22
Brethren, my heart's d. and prayer	Ro 10:1
having a great d. these many	Ro 15:23
earnestly d. (A)(E)(R)	1Co 12:31; 14:39
and d. spiritual gifts, but rather	1Co 14:1
he told us your earnest d.	2Co 7:7
yea, what vehement d. yea	2Co 7:11
from them which d. occasion	2Co 11:12
For though I would d. to glory	2Co 12:6
ye d. again to be in bondage	Ga 4:9
I d. to be present with you now	Ga 4:20
Tell me, ye that d. to be under the	Ga 4:21
As many as d. to make a fair shew	Ga 6:12
but d. to have you circumcised	Ga 6:13
I d. that ye faint not at my	Eph 3:13
eager d., hope (A)(B)	Ph'p 1:20
having a d. to depart, and to be	Ph'p 1:23
Not because I d. a gift	Ph'p 4:17
but I d. fruit that may abound	Ph'p 4:17
and to d. that ye might be filled	Col 1:9
to see your face with great d.	1Th 2:17
If a man d. the office of a bishop	1Ti 3:1
And we d. that every one of you	Heb 6:11
But now they d. a better country	Heb 11:16
kill, and d. to have, and cannot	Jas 4:2
which things the angels d. to look	1Pe 1:12
d. the sincere milk of the word	1Pe 2:2
and shall d. to die, and death shall	Re 9:6

DESIRED

and a tree to be d. to make one	Ge 3:6
tree desirable to make wise (B)	Ge 3:6
chosen, and whom ye have d.	1Sa 12:13
king you asked for (A)(E)(R)	1Sa 12:13
king whom you wanted (B)	1Sa 12:13
that which Solomon d. to build in	1Ki 9:19
all that Solomon d. to build	2Ch 8:6
And he d. many wives	2Ch 11:23
sought many wives (A)	2Ch 11:23
seeking number of wives (B)(E)	2Ch 11:23
procured wives for sons (R)	2Ch 11:23
and departed without being d.	2Ch 21:20
whatsoever she d. was given her	Es 2:13

anything she wanted to take Es 2:13
(B)
shall not save of that which Job 20:20
he d.
in which he delights Job 20:20
(A)(E)(R)
More to be d. are they than Ps 19:10
gold
One thing have I d. of the Ps 27:4
Lord
bringeth them unto their d. Ps 107:30
haven
he hath d. it for his Ps 132:13
habitation
here will I dwell; for I have Ps 132:14
d. it
all the things that may be d. Pr 8:11
are
There is treasure to be d. Pr 21:20
and oil
whatsoever mine eyes d. I Ec 2:10
kept
the oaks which ye have d. Isa 1:29
and ye
With my soul have I d. thee Isa 26:9
neither have I d. the woeful Jer 17:16
day
Daniel went in, and d. of the Da 2:16
king
known unto me now what we Da 2:23
d.
For I d. mercy, and not Ho 6:6
sacrifice
my soul d. the first ripe fruit Mic 7:1
gather together, O nation not Zep 2:1
d.
righteous men have d. to M't 13:17
see those
d. him that he would shew M't 16:1
them
whatsoever they d. (S) M't 17:12;
M'k 9:13
one prisoner, whomsoever M'k 15:6
they d.
whom they requested M'k 15:6
(A)(B)(E)
at the people's request M'k 15:6
(N)(R)
And one of the Pharisees d. Lu 7:36
him
things? and he d. to see him Lu 9:9
prophets and kings have d. Lu 10:24
to see
longed to see (A)(B) Lu 10:24
wished to see (N) Lu 10:24
wanted to see (P) Lu 10:24
With desire I have d. to eat Lu 22:15
this
Satan hath d. to have you, Lu 22:31
that
Satan asked excessively Lu 22:31
(A)(B)(E)(P)
Satan demanded to have you Lu 22:31
(R)
into prison, whom they had Lu 23:25
d.
d. him, saying, Sir, we Joh 12:21
would see
the Just, and d. a murderer Ac 3:14
to
demanded a murderer (A) Ac 3:14
requested a murderer (B) Ac 3:14
asked for a murderer (E)(R) Ac 3:14
begged as a favor a murderer Ac 3:14
(N)(P)
d. to find a tabernacle for the Ac 7:46
God
prayed that he might find Ac 7:46
(A)(B)(P)
asked to find a habitation Ac 7:46
(E)(N)(R)
And he d. Philip that he Ac 8:31
would
requested Philip to come (A) Ac 8:31
invited Philip to come Ac 8:31
(B)(R)
besought Philip to come (E) Ac 8:31
d. of him letters to Damascus Ac 9:2
to
requested of him letters Ac 9:2
(A)(B)
asked of him letters (E)(R) Ac 9:2
applied for letters (N) Ac 9:2
begged him for letters (P) Ac 9:2
their friend, d. peace; Ac 12:20
because
asked for peace (A)(E)(R) Ac 12:20
they pleaded for peace (B) Ac 12:20
they sued for peace (N) Ac 12:20
begged him for peace (P) Ac 12:20

and d. to hear the word of Ac 13:7
God
sought to hear word of God Ac 13:7
(A)(E)(R)
seeking to hear the Word of Ac 13:7
God (B)
wanted to hear the word of Ac 13:7
God (N)
anxious to hear God's Ac 13:7
message (P)
afterward they d. a king Ac 13:21
asked for a king Ac 13:21
(A)(B)(E)(N)(R)
begged for a king (P) Ac 13:21
yet d. they Pilate that he Ac 13:28
should
them out, and d. them to Ac 16:39
depart
When they d. him to tarry Ac 18:20
longer
d. favour against him, that he Ac 25:3
and were d. to tarry with Ac 28:14
them
Apollos, I greatly d. him to 1Co 16:12
come
I urgently encouraged him 1Co 16:12
to (A)
I strongly appealed to him 1Co 16:12
to (B)
I besought him much to 1Co 16:12
(E)
I urged him strongly to 1Co 16:12
(N)(R)
Insomuch that we d. Titus, 2Co 8:6
that
we urged Titus (A)(R) 2Co 8:6;
12:18
call upon Titus (B) 2Co 8:6
we exhorted Titus (E) 2Co 8:6; 12:18
we asked Titus (N)(P) 2Co 8:6
I d. Titus, and with him I 2Co 12:18
sent
I summoned Titus (B) 2Co 12:18
I begged Titus (N) 2Co 12:18
I asked Titus (P) 2Co 12:18
the petitions that we d. of 1Jo 5:15
him
the requests made of him 1Jo 5:15
(A)(B)(R)
the petitions we asked (E) 1Jo 5:15
things we ask for (N) 1Jo 5:15
our prayers will be answered 1Jo 5:15
(P)

DESIREDST

According to all that thou d. De 18:16
of the
just as you requested (B) De 18:16
all that debt, because thou M't 18:32
d. me
because you begged me M't 18:32
(A)(B)(P)
because you besoughtest me M't 18:32
(E)(R)
because you appealed to me M't 18:32
(N)

DESIRES

give thee the d. of thine heart Ps 37:4
Grant not, O Lord, the d. of Ps 140:8
playthings of own d. (N)(P) Ro 1:24
all kinds of forbidden d. Ro 7:8
(A)(N)(P)
fulfilling the d. of the flesh Eph 2:3
and of
obeying impulses of the flesh Eph 2:3
(A)
obeyed promptings of own Eph 2:3
instincts (N)
followed impulses and Eph 2:3
imaginations of our evil nature (P)
unholy d. (A) Col 3:5
evil d. (B)(E)(P)(R) Col 3:5
various d. (A)(N) 2Ti 3:6
to satisfy own d. (P) Jas 4:3
keep clear of d. of lower 1Pe 2:11
nature (P)
the godless d. (N)(P) Jude 15;
Jude 18

DESIREST

thou d. truth in the inward Ps 51:6
parts
For thou d. not sacrifice; Ps 51:16
else
you delight not in (A)(R) Ps 51:16

DESIRETH

whatever thy soul d. (S) De 12:15;
De 12:20-21; 14:26
or for whatsoever thy soul De 14:26
d.
take as much as thy soul d. 1Sa 2:16
as much as you want 1Sa 2:16
(A)(B)
as much as you wish (R) 1Sa 2:16
The king d. not any dowry 1Sa 18:25
wants no dowry except 1Sa 18:25
(A)(B)
Whatsoever thy soul d. 1Sa 20:4
reign over all that thine 2Sa 3:21
heart d.
according to all that thy 1Ki 11:37
soul d.
As a servant earnestly d. the Job 7:2
who sighs for the shadow (B) Job 7:2
who longs for the shade Job 7:2
(A)(R)
what his soul d. even that Job 23:13
he
what he wants to do Job 23:13
(A)(B)
what man is he that d. life Ps 34:12
the hill which God d. to Ps 68:16
dwell in
The wicked d. the net of evil Pr 12:12
men
The soul of the sluggard d. Pr 13:4
appetite of sluggard craves Pr 13:4
(A)(B)(R)
The soul of the wicked d. evil Pr 21:10
life of wicked craves (A) Pr 21:10
for his soul of all that he d. Ec 6:2
lacks nothing for his soul Ec 6:2
(A)(R)
drunk old wine straightway d. Lu 5:39
new
and d. conditions of peace Lu 14:32
asks the terms of peace Lu 14:32
(A)(E)(N)(P)(R)
request for peace (B) Lu 14:32
of a bishop, he d. a good 1Ti 3:1
work

DESIRING

His brethren d. to speak M't 12:46;
with him 12:47
seeking to speak with him M't 12:46
(A)(E)
wanting to talk with him M't 12:46
(B)(N)(P)
asking to speak with him M't 12:46
(R)
worshipping and d. a M't 20:20
certain thing of him
ask a certain thing of him M't 20:20
(A)(E)
requesting something of M't 20:20
him (B)
begged of him a favor M't 20:20
(N)(P)
asked him for something M't 20:20
(R)
stand without, d. to see thee Lu 8:20
d. to justify himself (S) Lu 10:29
d. to be fed with the crumbs Lu 16:21
d. him that he would not Ac 9:38
delay
d. him that he would not Ac 19:31
d. to have judgment against Ac 25:15
him
earnestly d. to be clothed 2Co 5:2
upon
d. greatly to see us, as we 1Th 3:6
also
D. to be teachers of the law 1Ti 1:7
ambitious to be teachers of 1Ti 1:7
the law (A)
wanting to be law teachers 1Ti 1:7
(B)
set out to be teachers of 1Ti 1:7
moral law (N)
want a reputation as teachers 1Ti 1:7
(P)
Greatly d. to see thee, being 2Ti 1:4
I yearn to see you (A)(B) 2Ti 1:4
longing to see thee (E)(P) 2Ti 1:4
I long to see you again 2Ti 1:4
(N)(R)

DESIROUS

Be not d. of his dainties Pr 23:3
for he was d. to see him a Lu 23:8
long time

they were *d.* to ask him   *Joh 16:19*
they wanted to ask him   *Joh 16:19*
(A)(B)(P)(R)
they were wanting to   *Joh 16:19*
question him (N)
garrison, *d.* to apprehend   *2Co 11:32*
me
Let us not be *d.* of vain glory   *Ga 5:26*
not become vainglorious   *Ga 5:26*
(A)(B)(E)
let us have no self-conceit   *Ga 5:26*
(R)
So being affectionately *d.* of   *1Th 2:8*
you

DESOLATE

d. region, the desert (B)   *Le 16:22*
Tamar *d.* in Absalom's   *2Sa 13:20*
house
dwelleth in *d.* cities and   *Job 15:28*
houses
thou hast made *d.* all my   *Job 16:7*
company
wilderness in former time *d.*   *Job 30:3*
and waste
to satisfy the *d.* and waste   *Job 38:27*
ground
have mercy on me, for I am   *Ps 25:16*
d.
be *d.* for reward of shame   *Ps 40:15*
God gives the *d.* a home (R)   *Ps 68:6*
let habitation be *d.* let none   *Ps 69:25*
dwell
therefore my heart within me   *Ps 143:4*
is *d.*
who are left *d.*   *Pr 31:8*
(A)(B)(E)(R)
your country is *d.* your cities   *Isa 1:7*
burnt
she being *d.* shall sit upon   *Isa 3:26*
ground
they shall rest in *d.* valleys   *Isa 7:19*
beast shall cry in their *d.*   *Isa 13:21*
houses
they that dwell therein are *d.*   *Isa 24:6*
city become *d.* (B)   *Isa 24:10*
to cause to inherit the *d.*   *Isa 49:8*
heritages
I have lost my children, and   *Isa 49:21*
am *d.*
more are children of *d.*   *Isa 54:1;*
   Ga 4:27
make the *d.* cities to be   *Isa 54:3*
inhabited
be ye very *d.* saith the Lord   *Jer 2:12*
hand made *d.* (A)(E)   *Jer 4:20*
lest I make *d.* a land not   *Jer 6:8*
inhabited
make cities of Judah *d.*   *Jer 9:11;*
without an inhabitant   *10:22; 33:10;*
   44:6
they have made his   *Jer 10:25*
habitation *d.*
made it *d.,* being *d.* it   *Jer 12:11*
mourneth
I will make this city *d.* and   *Jer 19:8*
an hissing
d. without man or beast   *Jer 32:43;*
   33:12
Moab is made *d.* (A)   *Jer 48:15; 48:20*
make their habitations *d.*   *Jer 49:20;*
   50:45
all her gates are *d.* her priests   *La 1:4*
sigh
he hath made me *d.* all day   *La 1:13;*
   3:11
my children are *d.* the enemy   *La 1:16*
prevailed
they that did feed delicately   *La 4:5*
are *d.*
because of mountain of Zion   *La 5:18*
which is *d.*
that your altars may be made   *Eze 6:6*
d.
knew *d.* palaces, and laid   *Eze 19:7*
waste
I might make them *d.* to   *Eze 20:26*
the end
I will make Edom *d.* from   *Eze 25:13*
Teman
when I shall make thee a *d.*   *Eze 26:19*
city
in midst of countries that   *Eze 29:12*
are *d.*
I will make Pathros *d.* and   *Eze 30:14*
set fire
O mount Seir, I will make   *Eze 35:3;*
thee most *d.*   *35:7*

are *d.* they are given us to   *Eze 35:12*
consume
when earth rejoiceth, I will   *Eze 35:14*
make thee *d.*
as thou didst rejoice,   *Eze 35:15*
because it was *d.*
because they have made you   *Eze 36:3*
d.
thus saith Lord to hills and   *Eze 36:4*
d. wastes
d. cities become fenced and   *Eze 36:35*
inhabited
know that Lord plant that   *Eze 36:36*
that was *d.*
transgression makes *d.*   *Da 8:13*
(A)(E)(R)
shine on thy sanctuary that is   *Da 9:17*
d.
abominations he shall make   *Da 9:27*
it *d.*
abomination that maketh *d.*   *Da 11:31;*
   12:11
Samaria shall become *d.*   *Ho 13:16*
the fields are *d.* (B)   *Joe 1:10*
garners laid *d.* barns are   *Joe 1:17*
broken
the flocks of sheep are made   *Joe 1:18*
d.
be a *d.* wilderness (A)   *Joe 3:19*
all the idols thereof will I lay   *Mic 1:7*
d.
in making thee *d.* because of   *Mic 6:13*
thy sins
their towers are *d.* their   *Zep 3:6*
streets waste
your house is left *d.*   *M't 23:38;*
   Lu 13:35
it is written, Let his   *Ac 1:20*
habitation be *d.*
now she that is a widow   *1Ti 5:5*
indeed and *d.*
the real widow, left alone   *1Ti 5:5*
(B)(N)(R)
these hate whore, and make   *Re 17:16*
d.
make her cheerless (A)   *Re 17:16*
render her isolated (B)   *Re 17:16*
leave her deserted (P)   *Re 17:16*
for in one hour is she made   *Re 18:19*
d.
destroyed and become a   *Re 18:19*
desert (A)(B)
one hour laid waste (N)(R)   *Re 18:19*
in a single hour ruined (P)   *Re 18:19*

DESOLATE *PLACES*

which built *d. places* for   *Job 3:14*
themselves
let them seek bread out of   *Ps 109:10*
d. places
waste and *d. places* be too   *Isa 49:19*
narrow
we are in *d. places* as dead   *Isa 59:10*
men
cities laid waste, high *places*   *Eze 6:6*
d.
when I set thee in *places d.*   *Eze 26:20*
of old
to turn thine hand upon *d.*   *Eze 38:12*
places
high *places* of Isaac shall be   *Am 7:9*
d.
we will return, and build *d.*   *Mal 1:4*
places

DESOLATE *WILDERNESS*

made my pleasant portion *d.*   *Jer 12:10*
wilderness
behind them it is a *d.*   *Joe 2:3*
wilderness
Egypt and Edom shall be a   *Joe 3:19*
d. wilderness

LAND DESOLATE

give us seed that *land* be   *Ge 47:19*
not *d.*
lest *land* become *d.* beast   *Ex 23:29*
multiply
then *land* enjoy her sabbaths   *Le 26:34;*
as long as it lieth *d.*   *26:35, 43*
   2Ch 36:21
he said, until the *land* be   *Isa 6:11*
utterly *d.*
day of Lord cometh to lay   *Isa 13:9*
land d.
nor shall *land* any more be   *Isa 62:4*
termed *d.*

he is gone forth to make thy   *Jer 4:7*
land d.
Lord said, The whole *land*   *Jer 4:27*
shall be *d.*
cease voice of mirth, for *land*   *Jer 7:34*
shall be *d.*
they made it *d.* whole *land*   *Jer 12:11*
is made *d.*
make *land d.* and perpetual   *Jer 18:16*
hissing
for their *land* is *d.* because   *Jer 25:38*
of his anger
in this *land* whereof ye say   *Jer 32:43*
it is *d.*
a nation which shall make   *Jer 50:3*
her *land d.*
make the *land d.* yea more   *Eze 6:14*
land may be *d.* from all   *Eze 12:19*
that is therein
cities laid waste, and *land*   *Eze 12:20*
d.
but the *land* shall be *d.*   *Eze 14:16;*
   Mic 7:13
I will make *land d.* saith   *Eze 15:8*
Lord
land was *d.* and the fulness   *Eze 19:7*
thereof
land of Egypt *d.*   *Eze 29:9;*
   10:12; 30:7; 32:15
I will lay *land* most *d.*   *Eze 33:28*
pomp cease
when I have laid *land* most   *Eze 33:29*
d.
d. land be tilled, whereas it   *Eze 36:34*
lay *d.*
land that was *d.* is like   *Eze 36:35*
garden of Eden
drive him to a *land* barren   *Joe 2:20*
and *d.*
land was *d.* laid pleasant   *Zec 7:14*
land d.

SHALL BE, SHALT BE

DESOLATE

your highways *shall be d.*   *Le 26:22*
your land *shall be d.* and   *Le 26:33*
cities waste
congregation of hypocrites   *Job 15:31*
shall be d.
they that hate righteous *shall*   *Ps 34:21*
be d.
none of them that trust in   *Ps 34:22*
him *shall be d.*
of a truth many houses *shall*   *Isa 5:9*
be d.
waters of Nimrim *shall be d.*   *Isa 15:6;*
   Jer 48:34
defenced city *shall be d.* and   *Isa 27:10*
forsaken
this city *shall be d.* without   *Jer 26:9*
inhabitant
in this place which ye say   *Jer 33:10*
shall be d.
Noph *shall be d.* without an   *Jer 46:19*
inhabitant
Moab, for the cities thereof   *Jer 48:9*
shall be d.
Rabbah of Ammonites *shall*   *Jer 49:2*
be a d. heap
but Babylon *shall be* wholly   *Jer 50:13*
d.
thou *shalt be d.* for ever   *Jer 51:26*
your altars *shall be d.*   *Eze 6:4*
cities of Egypt *shall be d.*   *Eze 29:12*
forty years
the mountains of Israel   *Eze 33:28*
shall be d.
O mount Seir, thou *shalt be*   *Eze 35:4;*
d.   *35:15*
shall be d. in day of rebuke   *Ho 5:9*

DESOLATING

the *d.* transgression (B)   *Da 8:13*

DESOLATION

bring your sanctuaries unto *d.*   *Le 26:31*
lay waste (B)   *Le 26:31; 26:32*
And I will bring the land   *Le 26:32*
into *d.*
for ever, even a *d.* unto this   *Jos 8:28*
day
destruction (B)   *Jos 8:28*
a heap of ruins (R)   *Jos 8:28*
should become a *d.* and a   *2Ki 22:19*
curse

gave them up to d. as ye see 2Ch 30:7
in the d. they rolled Job 30:14
themselves
How are they brought into Ps 73:19
d.
When your fear cometh as Pr 1:27
neither of the d. of the Pr 3:25
wicked
the ruin of the wicked Pr 3:25
(A)(R)
stormy blast of the wicked Pr 3:25
(B)
and in the d. which shall Isa 10:3
come
of Israel: and there shall be Isa 17:9
d.
In the city is left d. and the Isa 24:12
gate
d. shall come upon thee Isa 47:11
suddenly
d. and destruction, and the Isa 51:19
is a wilderness, Jerusalem a Isa 64:10
d.
that this house shall become a Jer 22:5
d.
this whole land shall be a d. Jer 25:11
whole land be a waste (A) Jer 25:11
land a ruin and a waste Jer 25:11
(B)(R)
make them a d. an Jer 25:18
astonishment
became a d. (R) Jer 27:17
Judah a d. without an Jer 34:22
inhabitant
a d., curse, reproach (B) Jer 42:18
this day they are a d. and no Jer 44:2
man
therefore is your land a d. Jer 44:22
and an
became a d. (B)(E) Jer 46:19
Bozrah shall become a d. Jer 49:13
horror, reproach, waste Jer 49:13
(A)(B)(E)(R)
Edom shall be a d.: every Jer 49:17
one
an astonishment and a Jer 49:17
horror (A)(B)(E)(R)
for dragons, and a d. for Jer 49:33
ever
Babylon become a d. among Jer 50:23
Babylon a d. without an Jer 51:29
inhabitant
Her cities are a d. a dry Jer 51:43
land
come upon us, d. and La 3:47
destruction
make you a d. (A)(B)(E) Eze 5:14
prince shall be clothed with Eze 7:27
d.
the cup of astonishment Eze 23:33
and d.
transgression of d. to give Da 8:13
both
transgression that makes Da 8:13
desolate (A)(E)(R)
the desolating transgression Da 8:13
(B)
he daily increaseth lies and Ho 12:1
d.
increases lies and violence Ho 12:1
(A)(R)
Egypt shall be a d. and Joe 3:19
Edom
be a desolate wilderness (A) Joe 3:19
that I should make thee a d. Mic 6:16
a booty, and their houses a Zep 1:13
d.
a day of wasteness, and d. a Zep 1:15
day
day of ruin and devastation Zep 1:15
(A)(R)
be forsaken, and Ashkelon a Zep 2:4
d.
and salt pits, and a perpetual Zep 2:9
d.
will make Nineveh a d. and Zep 2:13
dry
d. shall be in the thresholds Zep 2:14
how is she become a d. a Zep 2:15
place
against itself is brought to d. M't 12:25
the abomination of d. spoken M't 24:15
of
see the appalling sacrilege M't 24:15
(A)
desolating abomination M't 24:15
(B)(R)
ye shall see the abomination M'k 13:14
of d.

against itself is brought to d. Lu 11:17
know that the d. thereof is Lu 21:20
nigh
her ruin is impending (B) Lu 21:20
her destruction is near (N) Lu 21:20
time of her devastation is Lu 21:20
near (P)

DESOLATIONS

to repair the d. thereof, and Ezr 9:9
what d. he hath made in the Ps 46:8
thy feet unto the perpetual d. Ps 74:3
they shall raise up the former Isa 61:4
d.
cities, the d. of many Isa 61:4
generations
and an hissing, and perpetual Jer 25:9
d.
and will make it perpetual Jer 25:12
d.
Chaldeans a perpetual waste Jer 25:12
(A)(B)(R)
make it desolate forever (E) Jer 25:12
I will make the perpetual d. Eze 35:9
years in the d. of Jerusalem Da 9:2
thine eyes, and behold our d. Da 9:18
end of the war d. are Da 9:26
determined
d. are decreed (A)(R) Da 9:26

DESOLATOR

shall the d. come (B) Da 9:27

DESPAIR

and Saul shall d. of me, to 1Sa 27:1
seek
about to faint and d. (A) Job 6:14
mocks at d. of innocent (B) Job 9:23
distress and d. come (B) Pr 1:27
my heart to d. of all the Ec 2:20
labour
will be in d. (R) Isa 19:9
let them d. (B) Mic 7:16
we are perplexed, but not in 2Co 4:8
d.

DESPAIRED

insomuch that we d. even of 2Co 1:8
life

DESPERATE

and speeches of one that is Job 6:26
d.
utterances of a d. man (B) Job 6:26
the day of grief and of d. Isa 17:11
sorrow

DESPERATELY

above all things, and d. Jer 17:9
wicked

DESPISE

who d. unfair profits (B) Ex 18:21
if ye shall d. my statutes, or Le 26:15
they d. me (A) Nu 14:11; De 31:20
and they that d. me shall be 1Sa 2:30
lightly
why then did ye d. us, 2Sa 19:43
that our
that they shall d. their ·Es 1:17
husbands
d. not thou the chastening of Job 5:17
my soul: I would d. my life Job 9:21
shouldst d. the work of thine Job 10:3
hands
did d. the cause of my Job 31:13
manservant
wicked d. God (S) Ps 10:13
heart, O God, thou wilt not Ps 51:17
d.
awakest, thou shalt d. their Ps 73:20
image
destitute, and not d. their Ps 102:17
prayer
fools d. wisdom and instruction Pr 1:7
d. not the chastening of the Pr 3:11
Lord
Men do not d. a thief, if he Pr 6:30
steal
he will d. the wisdom of thy Pr 23:9
words

d. not thy mother when she Pr 23:22
is old
Because ye d. this word, Isa 30:12
and trust
thy lovers will d. thee, they Jer 4:30
They say still unto them Jer 23:17
that d.
all that honoured her d. her La 1:8
of the Philistines, which d. Eze 16:57
thee
if the sword d. the rod (S) Eze 21:13
upon all those that d. them Eze 28:26
I hate. I d. your feast days Am 5:21
you, O priests, that d. my Mal 1:6
name
hold to the one, and d. the M't 6:24;
other Lu 16:13
ye d. not one of these little M't 18:10
ones
d. and underestimate (A) Ro 2:4
Let not him that eateth d. Ro 14:3
him
or d. ye the church of God 1Co 11:22
Let no man therefore d. 1Co 16:11
him
D. not prophesyings. Prove 1Th 5:20
all
Let no man d. thy youth; 1Ti 4:12
but be
masters, let them not d. them 1Ti 6:2
authority. Let no man d. thee Tit 2:15
d. not thou the chastening Heb 12:5
of
uncleanness, and d. 2Pe 2:10
government
d. authority 2Pe 2:10
(B)(E)(N)(P)(R)
d. dominion, and speak evil of Jude 8

DESPISED

her mistress was d. in her Ge 16:4
eyes
looked down upon (B) Ge 16:4; 16:5
looked with contempt on Ge 16:4;
16:5
conceived, I was d. in her Ge 16:5
eyes
way: thus Esau d. his Ge 25:34
birthright
scorned his birthright (A) Ge 25:34
lightly esteem his birthright Ge 25:34
(B)
because they d. my Le 26:43
judgments
ye have d. the Lord which Nu 11:20
is
have spurned the Lord (B) Nu 11:20
have rejected Jehovah Nu 11:20
(E)(R)
d., spurned me (B) Nu 14:23; 16:30
know the land which ye Nu 14:31
have d.
you have rejected (B)(E) Nu 14:31
he hath d. the word of the Nu 15:31
Lord
regarded with contempt the Nu 15:31
word (B)
this the people that thou hast J'g 9:38
d.
And they d. him, and 1Sa 10:27
brought him
scorned and d. him (A) 1Sa 17:42
and she d. him in her heart 2Sa 6:16
d. the commandment of the 2Sa 12:9
Lord
because thou hast d. me, 2Sa 12:10
and hast
the daughter of Zion hath 2Ki 19:21
d. thee
and she d. him in her heart 1Ch 15:29
and d. his words, and 2Ch 36:16
misused his
and d. us, and said, What is Ne 2:19
this
made light of us (B) Ne 2:19
Hear, O our God; for we are Ne 4:4
d.
Return contempt upon their Ne 4:4
(B)
a lamp d. in the thought of Job 12:5
him
contempt for misfortune Job 12:5
(A)(B)(E)(R)
young children, d. me; I Job 19:18
arose
vile person. (A)(E)(R) Ps 15:4
of men and d. of the people Ps 22:6
not d. nor abhorred the Ps 22:24
afflictions

because God hath *d.* them — Ps 53:5
God has rejected them — Ps 53:5
(A)(B)(E)(R)
d. the covenant (A) — Ps 89:39
Yea, they *d.* the pleasant — Ps 106:24
land
d. the counsel of Most High — Ps 107:11
(S)
I am small and *d.*: yet do — Ps 119:141
not I
counsel: they *d.* all my — Pr 1:30
reproof
and my heart *d.* reproof — Pr 5:12
is of a perverse heart shall be — Pr 12:8
d.
He that is *d.* and hath a — Pr 12:9
servant
the poor man's wisdom is *d.* — Ec 9:16
kiss thee; yea, I should not be — Ca 8:1
d.
utterly scorned and *d.* (A)(R) — Ca 8:7
d. Holy One of Israel (E)(R) — Isa 1:4
d. the word of the Holy One — Isa 5:24
of
shall be *d.* (S) — Isa 16:14
he hath *d.* the cities, he — Isa 33:8
regardeth
d. thee, and laughed thee to — Isa 37:22
scorn
He is *d.* and rejected of men — Isa 53:3
he was *d.* and we esteemed — Isa 53:3
him not
all they that *d.* thee shall — Isa 60:14
bow
Is this man Coniah a *d.* — Jer 22:28
broken idol
they have *d.* my people, that — Jer 33:24
the heathen, and *d.* among — Jer 49:15
men
I am become *d.* (R) — La 1:11
d. in the indignation of his — La 2:6
anger
hast *d.* the oath in breaking — Eze 16:59
oath he *d.* and whose — Eze 17:16
covenant
Seeing he *d.* the oath by — Eze 17:18
breaking
surely mine oath that he — Eze 17:19
hath *d.*
they *d.* my judgments, — Eze 20:13
which if
they *d.* my judgments, and — Eze 20:16
walked
d. my statutes, and had — Eze 20:24
polluted
d. rod of my son (B)(R) — Eze 21:10;
21:13
Thou hast *d.* mine holy — Eze 22:8
things
round about them, that *d.* — Eze 28:24
them
they have *d.* the law of the — Am 2:4
Lord
the heathen: thou art greatly *d.* — Ob 2
hath *d.* the day of small — Zec 4:10
things
Wherein have we *d.* thy name — Mal 1:6
d. and abased (A)(B)(R) — Mal 2:9
were righteous, and *d.* others — Lu 18:9
scorned, made nothing of rest — Lu 18:9
(A)
looking down on the rest — Lu 18:9
(B)(P)
set all others at nought (E) — Lu 18:9
looked down on everyone else — Lu 18:9
(N)
Diana should be *d.* — Ac 19:27
come into disrepute, count — Ac 19:27
for nothing (A)
lose all respect, her glory — Ac 19:27
end (B)
be made of no account (E) — Ac 19:27
cease to command respect — Ac 19:27
(N)
might come to be lightly — Ac 19:27
regarded (P)
may count for nothing (R) — Ac 19:27
things which are *d.*, hath — 1Co 1:28
God
the lowborn and insignificant — 1Co 1:28
(A)
lowborn, contemptibles, — 1Co 1:28
no-bodies (B)
low, contemptible, mere — 1Co 1:28
nothings (N)
little things and no repute — 1Co 1:28
(P)
low and *d.* (R) — 1Co 1:28

ye are honourable, but we — 1Co 4:10
are *d.*
in disrepute and contempt — 1Co 4:10
(A)
we have dishonor (E) — 1Co 4:10
we are in disgrace (N) — 1Co 4:10
we are in disrepute (R) — 1Co 4:10
in my flesh ye *d.* not, — Ga 4:14
nor rejected
did not regard with contempt — Ga 4:14
(A)
neither scorned nor spurned — Ga 4:14
me (B)
show scorn or disgust (N) — Ga 4:14
shrink or be revolted by (P) — Ga 4:14
He that *d.* Moses' law died — Heb 10:28
without
rejected and set at nought — Heb 10:28
(A)(B)(E)
disregards the laws of — Heb 10:28
Moses (N)
showed contempt for — Heb 10:28
Moses' law (P)
violated the law of Moses — Heb 10:28
(R)
But ye have *d.* the poor. Do — Jas 2:6
not
insulted, humiliated, — Jas 2:6
dishonored, and shown
contempt for poor (A)
dishonored the poor — Jas 2:6
(B)(E)(R)
insulted the poor man (N)(P) — Jas 2:6

DESPISERS

Behold, ye *d.* and wonder — Ac 13:41
you scoffers and scorners — Ac 13:41
(A)(B)(N)(R)
fierce, *d.* of those that are — 2Ti 3:3
good
haters of good (A)(R) — 2Ti 3:3
no love for the good (B)(E) — 2Ti 3:3
strangers to all goodness (N) — 2Ti 3:3

DESPISES

d. the Word is in debt to it — Pr 13:13
(B)

DESPISEST

d. thou the riches of his — Ro 2:4
goodness
trifle with, presume upon, — Ro 2:4
despise, and underestimate
the wealth (A)
underestimate his wealth (B) — Ro 2:4
think lightly of his wealth of — Ro 2:4
(N)
misinterpreting God's — Ro 2:4
generosity, and patient
mercy as weakness on his part (P)
presume upon the riches of his — Ro 2:4
kindness (R)

DESPISETH

God is mighty, and *d.* not — Job 36:5
any
regards nothing as trivial — Job 36:5
(B)
the poor, and *d.* not his — Ps 69:33
prisoners
void of wisdom *d.* his — Pr 11:12
neighbour
Whose *d.* the word shall be — Pr 13:13
that is perverse in his ways *d.* — Pr 14:2
him
He that *d.* his neighbour — Pr 14:21
sinneth
A fool *d.* his father's — Pr 15:5
instruction
but a foolish man *d.* his — Pr 15:20
mother
refuseth instruction *d.* his — Pr 15:32
own
but he that *d.* his ways shall — Pr 19:16
die
father, and *d.* to obey his — Pr 30:17
mother
scorns to obey mother — Pr 30:17
(A)(B)(R)
he that *d.* the gain of — Isa 33:15
oppressions
to him whom man *d.* to him — Isa 49:7
whom
it *d.* the rod of my son (S) — Eze 21:10
he that *d.* you *d.* me — Lu 10:16

slights, pays no attention to — Lu 10:16
(A)
rejects me, rejects you — Lu 10:16
(B)(E)(N)(R)
has no use for me (P) — Lu 10:16
and he that *d.* me *d.* him — Lu 10:16
that sent
He therefore that *d. d.* not — 1Th 4:8
man
disregards, sets aside and — 1Th 4:8
rejects this—disregards not man
but God (A)(R)
the slighter does not slight — 1Th 4:8
men but God (B)
rejecteth, rejecteth not man — 1Th 4:8
but God (E)
flouts these rules, flouts not — 1Th 4:8
man but God (P)

DESPISING

the cross *d.* the shame, and is — Heb 12:2

DESPITE

rejoiced in heart with all thy — Eze 25:6
d.
with all contempt, malice, — Eze 25:6
and spite (A)
with all malice within you — Eze 25:6
(B)(R)
and hath done *d.* unto the — Heb 10:29
Spirit
insulting and outraging — Heb 10:29
Holy Spirit (A)
has outraged the Spirit of — Heb 10:29
grace (B)(R)
affronted God's gracious — Heb 10:29
Spirit (N)
insulted the very Spirit of — Heb 10:29
grace (P)

DESPITEFUL

taken vengeance with a *d.* — Eze 25:15
heart
taken vengeance — Eze 25:15
contemptuously, with malice
and spite in their hearts (A)
wrecking malicious revenge — Eze 25:15
(B)
taken vengeance with — Eze 25:15
despite of soul destroy with
perpetual enmity (E)(R)
with *d.* minds, to cast it out — Eze 36:5
for
with uttermost contempt — Eze 36:5
(A)(B)(R)
with despite of soul (E) — Eze 36:5
Backbiters, haters of God, *d.* — Ro 1:30
full of insolence (A) — Ro 1:30
insolent (B)(E)(N)(R) — Ro 1:30
overflowed with insolent pride — Ro 1:30
(P)

DESPITEFULLY

pray for them which *d.* use — M't 5:44;
you — Lu 6:28
to use them *d.* and to stone — Ac 14:5
them
to insult, abuse, and molest — Ac 14:5
(A)
to abuse them (B) — Ac 14:5
to treat them shamefully (E) — Ac 14:5
to maltreat them (N) — Ac 14:5
to insult them (P) — Ac 14:5
molest them (R) — Ac 14:5

DESPOIL

despoil (R)(S) — Ex 3:22;
Pr 22:23; Isa 11:14; 17:14
despoil (R) — Ps 89:41;
Pr 22:23; Isa 17:14; Eze 39:10
d. the men (B) — Jer 49:28; Eze 39:10
they shall *d.* (A) — Eze 39:10

DESPOILED

despoiled (E)(R)(S) — Ex 12:36;
J'g 2:14, 16; 1Sa 14:48; 2Ch 14:14;
Pr 22:23; Col 2:15

DESPOILS

despoils (R) — Ps 35:10

DESPOTISMS

against *d.* (A) — Eph 6:12

DESTINED

d. to die (B)	Ps 102:20
as were d. to life (A)(P)	Ac 13:48
d. and appointed (B)(N)	Ac 17:31
d. and intended to (A)	Ro 7:10
he d. us (N)(R)	Eph 1:5
we were long ago d. (P)(R)	Eph 1:11
d. to be ruined by wear (B)	Col 2:22
not d. us to wrath (B)(N)(R)	1Th 5:9
d. before world (R)	1Pe 1:20

DESTINY

his departure, d. (N)(R)	Lu 9:31; 1Pe 1:15
whose d. he appointed (P)	Ro 11:2

DESTITUTE

not left d. my master of his mercy	Ge 24:27
not failed my master with mercy (B)	Ge 24:27
not forsaken his lovingkindness (E)	Ge 24:27
not forsaken his stedfast love (R)	Ge 24:27
will regard the prayer of the d.	Ps 102:17
is my trust; leave not my soul	Ps 141:8
joy to him that is d. of wisdom	Pr 15:21
who is without heart and sense (A)	Pr 15:21
who lacks sense (B)(R)	Pr 15:21
him that is void of wisdom (E)	Pr 15:21
and the country shall be d. of that	Eze 32:15
corrupt minds and d. of the truth	1Ti 6:5
bereft of the truth (A)(E)(R)	1Ti 6:5
defrauded of the truth (B)	1Ti 6:5
have lost grip of the truth (N)	1Ti 6:5
lost their real hold on the truth (P)	1Ti 6:5
being d. afflicted, tormented	Heb 11:37
utterly d., oppressed (A)(B)(N)	Heb 11:37
be naked, and d. of daily food	Jas 2:15
lacks food for each day (A)(B)(E)(N)(R)	Jas 2:15
nothing to eat (P)	Jas 2:15

DESTROY

wilt thou d. righteous with wicked	Ge 18:23
wipe out (B)	Ge18:23; 18:24
consume (E)	Ge 18:23; 18:24
wilt thou d. and not spare the place	Ge 18:24
wilt thou d. all the city for lack of five	Ge 18:28
we will d. this place	Ge 19:13; 19:14
on company and d. it (B)(R)	Ge 32:8
draw my sword, my hand d. them	Ex 15:9
d. you in the way (A)(B)	Ex 33:3; Le 26:16
but ye shall d. their altars	Ex 34:13 De 7:5
break down their altars (B)(E)	Ex 34:13
tear down their altars (R)	Ex 34:13
I will send beasts to d. your cattle	Le 26:22
d. with a plague (B)	Nu 14:12
d. them in a moment (B)	Nu 16:21
shall d. all children of Sheth	Nu 24:17
ye shall d. all this people	Nu 32:15
bring disaster to entire nation (N)	Nu 32:15
d. their pictures and molten images	Nu 33:52
smash all their stone idols (B)	Nu 33:52
lest anger of Lord God d. thee	De 6:15
wipe you off the face of earth (B)	De 6:15

d. all the peoples (R)	De 7:16
d. them with a mighty destruction	De 7:23
crush them utterly (B)	De 7:23
discomfit them with great discomfiture (E)	De 7:23
throw them into great confusion (R)	De 7:23
shalt d. their name from under heaven	De 7:24
he shall d. them, and bring them down	De 9:3
let me alone, I may d. them and blot	De 9:14
wipe them out (B)	De 9:14
the Lord had said he would d. you	De 9:25
the trees that are not for meat thou shalt d.	De 20:20
cut down and use (B)	De 20:20
Lord God will d. these nations	De 31:3
d. both young man and virgin	De 32:25
thrust out enemy, and say, D. them	De 33:27
except d. accursed among you	Jos 7:12
get rid of the devoted thing (B)	Jos 7:12
d. you (B)	Jos 24:20
depart, lest I d. you with them	1Sa 15:6
we will d. the heir also	2Sa 14:7
not suffer revengers to d. lest d. my son	2Sa 14:11
that would d. me and my son together	2Sa 14:16
far from me I should swallow or d.	2Sa 20:20
I might d. them that hate me	2Sa 22:41; Ps 18:40
thus did Zimri d. house of Baasha	1Ki 16:12
he might d. worshippers of Baal	2Ki 10:19
go against this land, and d. it	2Ki 18:25; Isa 36:10
to d. them (B)	2Ch 20:23
d. kings that shall put to their hand	Ezr 6:12
d. all Jews (B)	Es 3:13
if he d. him from his place	Job 8:18
snatches him from his property (A)	Job 8:18
pulled out from his place (B)	Job 8:18
hands made me, yet thou dost d. me	Job 10:8
though after skin, worms d. this body	Job 19:26
thou shalt d. them that speak leasing	Ps 5:6
d. them, let them fall by their counsels	Ps 5:10
Hold them guilty, O God (A)(B)(E)	Ps 5:10
make them bear their guilt (R)	Ps 5:10
their fruit shalt thou d. from the earth	Ps 21:10
he shall d. them, and not build them up	Ps 28:5
he will break them down (A)(E)(R)	Ps 28:5
he shall demolish them (B)	Ps 28:5
God shall likewise d. thee for ever	Ps 52:5
d. O Lord, and divide their tongues	Ps 55:9
they that would d. me are mighty	Ps 69:4
they said, Let us d. them together	Ps 74:8
make havoc of such places (A)(E)	Ps 74:8
let us subdue them completely (B)(R)	Ps 74:8
d. all them that afflict my soul	Ps 143:12
shoot out thine arrows and d. them	Ps 144:6
arrows and embarrass, frustrate them (A)	Ps 144:6
arrows and confound them (B)	Ps 144:6
arrows and discomfit them (E)	Ps 144:6
arrows and rout them (R)	Ps 144:6

but all the wicked will he d.	Ps 145:20
prosperity of fools shall d. them	Pr 1:32
perverseness of transgressors shall d. them	Pr 11:3
Lord will d. the house of the proud	Pr 15:25
tears down the house of proud (A)(B)(R)	Pr 15:25
root up the house of the proud (E)	Pr 15:25
the robberies of wicked shall d. them	Pr 21:7
shall sweep them away (A)(E)(R)	Pr 21:7
violence of the wicked snares them (B)	Pr 21:7
destroy (E)	Pr 24:15; Isa 33:1; Jer 5:6; 49:28
why should God d. work of thine hands	Ec 5:6
over wise, why shouldest thou d. thyself	Ec 7:16
they d. the way of thy paths	Isa 3:12
d. his thorn bushes (B)	Isa 10:17
nor d. in all my holy mountains	Isa 11:9; 65:25
he shall d. sinners thereof out of it	Isa 13:9
he will d. in this mountain the face	Isa 25:7
shall cease to d. (A)	Isa 33:1 Jer 5;6; 49:28; Eze 25:7; Ho 10:1
shall d. them (A)	Jer 5;6; Jer 47:4; 49:28; Ho 10:2
shall d. them (B)	Jer 5;6; Jer 47:4; Ho 10:2
go ye up upon her walls and d.	Jer 5:10
let us go by night and d. her palaces	Jer 6:5
let us d. tree with the fruit thereof	Jer 11:19
I will pluck up and d. that nation	Jer 12:17
not spare nor have mercy, and d. them	Jer 13:14
will stretch my hand against thee and d. thee	Jer 15:6
d. them with double destruction	Jer 17:18
woe to pastors that d. sheep of pasture	Jer 23:1
king of Babylon shall d. this land	Jer 36:29
he shall d. thy strong holds	Jer 48:18
if thieves by night d. till have	Jer 49:9
spare not, d. utterly all her host	Jer 51:3
persecute and d. them in anger	La 3:66
wilt thou d. all the residue of Israel	Eze 9:8
d. the remnant of the sea-coast	Eze 25:16
they shall d. the walls of Tyrus	Eze 26:4
they shall d. thy pleasant houses	Eze 26:12
completely d. (B)	Da 2:44
hew the tree down and d. it	Da 4:23
shall d. wonderfully, and d. mighty	Da 8:24
by peace shall he d. many	Da 8:25
people shall d. the city and the sanctuary	Da 9:26
they that feed on his meat shall d. him	Da 11:26
shall I not d. wise men out of Edom	Ob 8
because it is polluted, it shall d. you	Mic 2:10
stretch hand against north, and d. Assyria	Zep 2:13
moth and rust d. (B)	M't 6:19
they might d. him	M't 12:14; M'k 3:6; 11:18
might do away with him (A)(N)	M't 12:14
get rid of him altogether (P)	M't 12:14
miserably d. those wicked men	M't 21:41
put those miserable wretches to death (A)(B)(R)	M't 21:41
bring bad men to bad end (N)	M't 21:41
kill scoundrels without mercy (P)	M't 21:41
they should ask Barabbas, and d. Jesus	M't 27:20

put Jesus to death (A)(N) M't 27:20
demand Jesus' execution M't 27:20
(P)
he will d. the husbandmen M'k 12:9;
Lu 20:16
put an end to the tenants M'k 12:9
(B)
put the tenants to death (N) M'k 12:9
Jesus said to them, *D.* this Joh 2:19
temple
determined to d. them (B) Ac 5:33
Jesus of Nazareth shall d. Ac 6:14
this place
to d. carnal lusts (A) 1Co 5:5
but God shall d. both it and 1Co 6:13
them
d. with brightness of his 2Th 2:8
coming
end by his appearing at his 2Th 2:8
coming (A)
bring to an end by the 2Th 2:8
breaking forth of his coming (B)
bring to naught by the 2Th 2:8
manifestation of his coming (E)
the radiance of the coming of 2Th 2:8
d. with the breath (N)
the Lord Jesus will be his utter 2Th 2:8
destruction (P)
d. him that had power of Heb 2:14
death
bring to nought, make of no Heb 2:14
effect (A)(E)
neutralize the one who Heb 2:14
wields the power of death (B)
break the power of him who Heb 2:14
had death (N)
nothing can d., spoil, wither 1Pe 1:4
(B)
that he might d. works of 1Jo 3:8
devil
undo the works of the devil 1Jo 3:8
(A)(N)
break up the works of the 1Jo 3:8
devil (B)
liquidating the devil's 1Jo 3:8
activities (P)
to d. one third of men (A) Re 9:15
shouldest d. them which d. Re 11:18
earth

I WILL, WILL I DESTROY

I will d. man whom I have Ge 6:7
created
behold, *I will* d. them with Ge 6:13
earth
God will finally end both Ge 6:13
(A)(B)(N)
God shall bring to naught Ge 6:13
both (E)
God has no permanent Ge 6:13
purpose for both (P)
every living substance *will I* d. Ge 7:4
I will d. all people to whom Ex 23:27
same soul *will I* d. from Le 23:30
people
I will d. your high places Le 26:30;
Eze 6:3
I will early d. all wicked of Ps 101:8
land
in name of Lord *will I* d. Ps 118:10;
them 118:1, 12
I will d. the counsel therof Isa 19:3
I will cry, *I will* d. and Isa 42:14
devour at once
I will d. my people, since Jer 15:7
they return
I will d. city, and inhabitants Jer 46:8
thereof
I will d. king and princes Jer 49:38
my battle-axe *will I* d. Jer 51:20
kingdoms
I the Lord *will* d. that Eze 14:9
prophet
I will d. thee Eze 25:7; 28:16; Zep 2:5
thus saith Lord, *I will* d. Eze 30:13
idols
I will d. also all the beasts Eze 32:13
thereof
but *I will* d. the fat and the Eze 34:16
strong
I will d. her vines and fig Ho 2:12
trees
thou shalt fall, and *I will* d. Ho 4:5
thy mother
I will d. the sinful kingdom Am 9:8
I will d. thy chariots; d. thy Mic 5:10;
cities 5:14
I will d. strength of Hag 2:22
kingdoms

we heard him say, *I will* d. M'k 14:58
this temple
I will d. the wisdom of the 1Co 1:19
wise

NOT DESTROY

if I find forty-five I will *not* d. Ge 18:28
it
I will *not* d. it for twenty's Ge 18:31
sake
I will *not* d. Sodom for Ge 18:32
ten's sake
will not forsake thee, *not* d. De 4:31
thee
d. *not* thy people and thine De 9:26
inheritance
do not wipe out thy people De 9:26
(B)
the Lord would *not* d. thee De 10:10
thou shalt *not* d. the trees De 20:19
thereof
swear thou wilt *not* d. my 1Sa 24:21
name
David said to Abishai, *D.* 1Sa 26:9
him *not*
do not murder him (B) 1Sa 26:9
not d. Judah for David's 2Ki 8:19
sake
would *not* d. them, nor cast 2Ki 13:23
them out
therefore I will *not* d. them 2Ch 12:7
not bring them to ruin (B) 2Ch 12:7
Lord would *not* d. him 2Ch 12:12
altogether
not send total destruction 2Ki 12:12
(B)(R)
Lord would *not* d. house of 2Ki 21:7
David
forbear from God that he 2Ki 35:21
d. thee *not*
they did *not* d. nations of Ps 106:34
whom
d. it *not* for a blessing is in Isa 65:8
it
stand in gap, that I should Eze 20:30
not d. it
d. *not* wise men of Babylon Da 2:24
he shall *not* d. fruits of your Mal 3:11
ground
d. *not* him with thy meat Ro 14:15
for whom
cause the ruin of Ro 14:15
(A)(B)(P)(R)
bring disaster to (N) Ro 14:15
for meat d. *not* the work of Ro 14:20
God (N)
break down the work of Ro 14:20
God (B)
Overthrow not the work of Ro 14:20
God (E)
Do not ruin the work of God Ro 14:20
(N)
shouldn't want to undo Ro 14:20
God's work (P)

TO DESTROY

I bring flood of waters *to* d. Ge 6:17
exterminate from under Ge 6:17
heaven (B)
nor be any more a flood to Ge 9:11;
d. 9:15
be eliminated by a flood (B) Ge 9:11
cut off any more by waters Ge 9:11
(E)(R)
the Lord hath sent us *to* d. Ge 19:13
it
intreat for thee *to* d. the frogs Ex 8:9
have the frogs removed from Ex 8:9
you (B)
plague not be on you *to* d. Ex 12:13
you
No fatal plague shall attack Ex 12:13
you (B)
out of Egypt *to* d. us De 1:27;
Jos 7:7
to d. them from among the De 2:15
host
to exterminate them (A) De 2:15
snatch them away from camp De 2:15
(B)
repay them that hate him *to* De 7:10
d. them
Lord was wroth against you De 9:19
to d. you
Lord will rejoice over you *to* De 28:63
d. you
glory in your destruction De 28:63
(B)

to d. all inhabitants of the Jos 9:24
land
to d. land where Reubenites Jos 22:23
dwelt
Midianites entered *to* d. land J'g 6:5
Saul seeketh *to* d. city for 1Sa 23:10
my sake
came in one of people *to* d. 1Sa 26:15
king
not afraid *to* d. the Lord's 2Sa 1:14
anointed
not suffer the revengers of 2Sa 14:11
blood *to* d.
thou seekest *to* d. a city and 2Sa 20:19
a mother
stretched out hand on 2Sa 24:16
Jerusalem *to* d.
sin to the house of Jeroboam 1Ki 13:34
to d.
sent them against Judah *to* 2Ki 24:2
d.
God sent an angel to 1Ch 21:15
Jerusalem *to* d.
God hath determined *to* d. 2Ch 25:16
thee
Haman sought *to* d. Jews Es 3:6;
4:7-8; 9:24
moved me *to* d. him without Job 2:3
cause
even that it would please God Job 6:9
to d. me
God to crush me (A)(E)(R) Job 6:9
to cut me off (B) Job 6:9
seek after my soul *to* d. it Ps 40:14;
63:9
wicked waited for me *to* d. Ps 119:95
me
it is in his heart *to* d. and Isa 10:7
cut off
come from far *to* d. whole Isa 13:5
land
Lord hath given Isa 23:11
commandment *to* d.
he deviseth wicked devices *to* Isa 32:7
d. poor
as if the oppressor were Isa 51:13
ready *to* d.
behold, I have created the Isa 54:16
waster *to* d.
I have set thee *to* d. Jer 1:10;
18:7; 31:28
I will appoint beasts of earth Jer 15:3
to d.
his device is against Babylon Jer 51:11
to d. it
Lord hath purposed *to* d. wall La 2:8
famine, which I will send *to* Eze 5:16
d. you
to d. souls, to get dishonest Eze 22:27
gain
with a despiteful heart *to* d. Eze 25:15
it
nations be brought *to* d. Eze 30:11
the land
vision I saw when I came Eze 43:3
to d. city
to d. all wise men of Da 2:12;
Babylon 2:24
to d. his dominion unto the Da 7:26
end
shall go forth with great Da 11:44
fury *to* d.
I will not return *to* d. Ho 11:9
Ephraim
that I will seek *to* d. all Zec 12:9
nations
Herod will seek young child M't 2:13
to d. him
to murder him (B) M't 2:13
to do away with him (N) M't 2:13
seek young child, kill him M't 2:13
(P)
I am come *to* d. the law M't 5:17
undo the Law and the M't 5:17
prophets (A)
to annul the Law and M't 5:17
Prophets (B)
abolish Law and prophets M't 5:17
(N)(P)(R)
rather fear him who is able M't 10:28
to d. both
fellow said, I am able *to* d. M't 26:61
temple
tear down the temple (A) M't 26:61
pull down the temple of M't 26:61
God (N)(P)
art thou come *to* d. us M'k 1:24;
Lu 4:34

lawful on sabbath to save life or   *Lu 6:9*
to d.
Son of man not come *to d.*   *Lu 9:56*
men's lives
chief of people sought *to d.*   *Lu 19:47*
him
seeking to put him to death   *Lu 19:47*
(A)
bent on making an end of   *Lu 19:47*
him (N)
all time trying to get rid of   *Lu 19:47*
(P)
the thief cometh not but *to*   *Joh 10:10*
d.
to butcher and to spoil (B)   *Joh 10:10*
one law given able to save   *Jas 4:12*
and *to d.*

DESTROYED

before Lord *d.* Sodom and   *Ge 13:10*
Gomorrah
when God *d.* the cities of   *Ge 19:29*
the plain
knowest thou not yet that   *Ex 10:7*
Egypt is *d.*
eye of maid be *d.* (A)   *Ex 21:26*
Lord *d.* them before them   *De 2:21;*
     4:3; 11:4; 2Ki 21:9; 2Ch 33:9
with a mighty destruction, till   *De 7:23*
they be *d.*
no man be able to stand till   *De 7:24*
thou have *d.*
be *d.*, because (B)   *De 8:20*
Lord was angry to have *d.* you *De 9:8*
after that they be *d.* from   *De 12:30*
before thee
until thou be *d.*   *De 28:20;*
     28:24, 45, 51, 61
put yoke on thy neck till he   *De 28:48*
have *d.*
destroyed (B)   *Jos 11:11;*
   J'g 1:25; 1Ki 20:21; 2Ki 8:21; 15:16
I *d.* them from before you   *Jos 24:18*
Benjamin *d.* of Israel 22,000 *J'g 20:21;*
men   *20:25*
children of Israel *d.* 25,100   *J'g 20:35;*
of Benjamin   *20:42*
weapons of war *d.* (B)   *2Sa 1:27*
man devised we should be *d.* *2Sa 21:5*
he said to angel that *d.*   *2Sa 24:16;*
     1Ch 21:15
Asa *d.* her idol and burnt it   *1Ki 15:13*
cut down the image   *1Ki 15:13*
(B)(E)(R)
house of Ahab be *d.* (B)   *2Ki 9:8*
thus Jehu *d.* Baal out of   *2Ki 10:28*
Israel
eradicated Baal from Israel *2Ki 10:28*
(B)
wiped out Baal from Israel *2Ki 10:28*
(R)
Athaliah arose and *d.* all   *2Ki 11:1*
seed royal.
therefore they have *d.* them *2Ki 19:18;*
     Isa 37:19
d. tents (A)(R)   *1Ch 4:41; 4:43*
people whom God *d.* before *1Ch 5:25*
them
for they were *d.* before the *2Ch 14:13*
Lord
nation was *d.* of nation,   *2Ch 15:6*
city of city
broken in pieces, nation   *2Ch 15:6*
against nation (A)(E)(R)
nation dashed against nation *2Ch 15:6*
(B)
d. the Asherah's (R)   *2Ch 19:3; 33:3*
houses which kings of   *2Ch 34:11*
Judah had *d.*
kings had abandoned to   *2Ch 34:11*
ruin (B)(R)
for which cause was this city   *Ezr 4:15*
d.
let it be written, that they may *Es 3:9*
be *d.*
be *d.* from his place (S)   *Job 8:18*
he hath *d.* me on every side *Job 19:10*
broken me down on every   *Job 19:10*
side (A)(B)(E)
breaks me down on every   *Job 19:10*
side (R)
hast *d.* wicked; *d.* cities   *Ps 9:5; 9:6*
hast *d.* all them that go a   *Ps 73:27*
whoring
sent frogs among them,   *Ps 78:45*
which *d.* them
d. their vines with hail, and *Ps 78:47*
sycamore trees

were *d.* at En-dor (B)(R)   *Ps 83:10*
daughter of Babylon, who   *Ps 137:8*
art to be *d.*
there is that *d.* for want of   *Pr 13:23*
judgment
thou hast *d.* land, and slain *Isa 14:20*
people
gate battered and *d.* (A)   *Isa 24:12*
therefore hast thou visited *Isa 26:14*
and *d.* them
made an end of them (A)   *Isa 26:14*
visited them with   *Isa 26:14*
destruction (B)
not *d.* (A)   *Isa 33:1; Jer 4:13; 49:10*
not *d.* (E)(R)   *Isa 33:1;*
   Jer 10:20; 49:10; Ho 10:14
cities be *d.* (B)   *Jer 4:7;*
     Eze 6:6; Am 7:9
My tent is *d.*   *Jer 10:20*
many pastors have *d.* my   *Jer 12:10*
vineyard
laid waste my vineyard (B) *Jer 12:10*
Moab is *d.*; Babylon is *d.*   *Jer 48:4;*
     51:8
Lord *d.* out of Babylon   *Jer 51:55*
great voice
Lord is spoiling and laying *Jer 51:55*
waste (A)
devastating Babylon,   *Jer 51:55*
silencing her (B)
laying Babylon waste,   *Jer 51:55*
stilling her (R)
Lord hath *d.* his strong holds   *La 2:5*
he hath *d.* his places of the   *La 2:6*
assembly
hath *d.* and broken her bars   *La 2:9*
to be *d.* (A)   *Eze 16:20*
Tyrus, like the *d.* in midst *Eze 27:32*
of sea
beast was slain, and his body *Da 7:11*
d.
wasted and *d.* (A)(B)   *Ho 10:14*
thou hast *d.* thyself, but in   *Ho 13:9*
the help
d. I the Amorite, I *d.* his   *Am 2:9*
fruit
skins and *d.*   *M't 9:17*
he sent his armies and *d.*   *M't 22:7*
murderers
put those murderers to death *M't 22:7*
(A)
to kill those murderers (N)   *M't 22:7*
killed those murderers (P)   *M't 22:7*
be *d.* by the sword (B)   *M't 26:52*
the bottles will be *d.* (S)   *M'k 2:22*
flood came, and *d.* them all *Lu 17:27*
rained fire from heaven and *Lu 17:29*
d. them all
whole nation be *d.* (N)(P)   *Joh 11:50*
is not this he that *d.* them   *Ac 9:21*
that called
ravaging those in Jerusalem *Ac 9:21*
(B)
made havoc of them (E)   *Ac 9:21*
persecuted those who called *Ac 9:21*
upon (P)
had *d.* seven nations in   *Ac 13:19*
Chanaan
and her magnificence should *Ac 19:27*
be *d.*
come into disrepute, count *Ac 19:27*
for nothing (A)
that the body of sin might be *Ro 6:6*
d.
sin-controlled body be devitalized *Ro 6:6*
(B)
body of sin might be done   *Ro 6:6*
away (E)
for the destruction of sinful *Ro 6:6*
self (N)
that tyranny of sin might be *Ro 6:6*
broken (P)
weak man be *d.* (R)   *1Co 8:11*
d. of serpents   *1Co 10:9*
killed by poisonous serpents *1Co 10:9*
(A)
perished by serpents (E)   *1Co 10:9*
fell victims to poisonous   *1Co 10:9*
snakes (P)
put out of the way entirely *1Co 10:10*
by (A)(B)
perished by the destroyer   *1Co 10:10*
(E)
met their end at the hand *1Co 10:10*
of the angel of death (P)
now preacheth faith once he   *Ga 1:23*
d.
he once reviled, set out to   *Ga 1:23*
ruin (A)

preaches faith he once laid   *Ga 1:23*
waste (B)
faith of which he once made *Ga 1:23*
havoc (E)
if I build again the things   *Ga 2:18*
which I *d.*
what I tore down   *Ga 2:18*
(A)(B)(R)
a system I have pulled down *Ga 2:18*
shrink back and are *d.* (R) *Heb 10:39*
lest he that *d.* first born   *Heb 11:28*
touch them
destroyer of the firstborn   *Heb 11:28*
(A)(B)(E)(R)
destroying angel might not *Heb 11:28*
touch (N)
angel of death killed   *Heb 11:28*
firstborn (P)
was not *d.* along with (A) *Heb 11:31*
that lovely sight is *d.* (P)   *Jas 1:11*
judgment when godly are *d.*   *2Pe 2:7*
(N)
as natural brute beasts to   *2Pe 2:12*
be *d.*
shall surely be *d.* (E)(P)(R) *2Pe 2:12*
be *d.* by you in corruption *2Pe 2:12*
(B)
world was *d.*, deluged with *2Pe 3:6*
water (B)(N)(P)
not wish any be *d.* (P)   *2Pe 3:9*
Lord afterward *d.* them that   *Jude 5*
believed not
d. themselves by rebelling (P) *Jude 11*
the third part of ships were *d.* *Re 8:9*

ARE DESTROYED

the women *are d.* out of   *J'g 21:16*
Benjamin
women are killed (B)   *J'g 21:16*
they *are d.* from morning to *Job 4:20*
night
he overturneth them so that *Job 34:25*
they *are d.*
they that are led of them *are* *Isa 9:16*
d.
cry, for all thy lovers *are d.* *Jer 22:20*
my people *are d.* for lack of   *Ho 4:6*
knowledge
their cities *are d.* there is no *Zep 3:6*
inhabitant

NOT DESTROYED

but they *d.* them *not*   *2Ch 20:10;*
     Ps 78:38
his kingdom which shall *not* *Da 7:14*
be *d.*
not forsaken; cast down, *not* *2Co 4:9*
d.

SHALL BE DESTROYED

I *shall be d.* I and my   *Ge 34:30*
house
thou and father's house *shall* *Es 4:14*
be *d.*
but transgressors *shall be d.* *Ps 37:38*
together
it is that they *shall be d.* for *Ps 92:7*
ever
whoso despiseth word *shall*   *Pr 13:13*
be *d.*
brings destruction upon   *Pr 13:13*
himself (A)(E)(R)
despises the Word is in debt *Pr 13:13*
to it (B)
but a companion of fools   *Pr 13:20*
shall be d.
that hardeneth his neck *shall*   *Pr 29:1*
be *d.*
suddenly be broken beyond *Pr 29:1*
remedy (B)
suddenly be broken beyond *Pr 29:1*
healing (R)
yoke *shall* be *d.* because of *Isa 10:27*
anointing
valley shall perish, plain *shall* *Jer 48:8*
be *d.*
plain shall be devastated (A) *Jer 48:8*
when all her helpers *shall be* *Eze 30:8*
d.
kingdom *shall* never be *d.* *Da 2:44;*
     6:26
but within few days he *shall* *Da 11:20*
be *d.*
Aven, the sin of Israel *shall* *Ho 10:8*
be *d.*

he that will not hear *shall be* Ac 3:23
d.
be utterly exterminated (A)   Ac 3:23
must be extirpated from   Ac 3:23
Israel (N)
last enemy that *shall be* d. 1Co 15:26
is death
to be subdued and   1Co 15:26
abolished (A)(B)(E)(N)

UTTERLY DESTROYED

he shall be *utterly* d.   Ex 22:20
they *utterly* d. the Canaanites Nu 21:3
we *utterly* d. Sihon and his   De 2:34
people
we *utterly* d. cities of Og   De 3:6;
                                   Jos 2:10
corrupt yourselves, ye shall be De 4:26
utterly d.
Jericho; Ai; Makkedah;   Jos 6:21;
Eglon; Hebron; Debir; he   8:26; 10:1,
utterly d. all that breathed 28, 35, 37,
                                    39-40
Joshua *utterly* d. them with Jos 11:12;
cities   11:21
Judah and Simeon *utterly* d.   J'g 1:17
Zephath
Saul *utterly* d. all the people 1Sa 15:8
would not *utterly* d. best of   1Sa 15:9
sheep
to sacrifice, and rest we   1Sa 15:15
have *utterly* d.
I have *utterly* d. the   1Sa 15:20
Amalekites
things which should have   1Sa 15:21
been *utterly* d.
the inhabitants of Gedor   1Ch 4:41
utterly d.
Hezekiah *utterly* d. the   2Ch 31:1
images
gods those nations my   2Ch 32:14
father *utterly* d.
Lord hath *utterly* d. all   Isa 34:2
nations

DESTROYER

will not suffer d. to come   Ex 12:23
into houses
hath delivered the d. of our   J'g 16:24
country
in prosperity the d. shall   Job 15:21
come
I have kept me from paths of   Ps 17:4
the d.
the same is the companion   Pr 28:24
of a d.
destroyer (A)(E)(R)   Isa 16:4;
  21:2; Jer 6:26; 15:8; 48:18, 32; 51:56
destroyer (B)   Isa 21:2; Jer 6:26
d., destroyest (A)(E)(R)   Isa 33:1
the d. of the Gentiles is on his Jer 4:7
way
arouse spirit of d. (B)(R)   Jer 51:1
hopper, d., cutter (R)   Joe 2:25
d. and reconstructor (B)   M't 27:40
and were destroyed of the   1Co 10:10
d.
d. of firstborn   Heb 11:28
(A)(B)(E)(R)

DESTROYERS

and his life draweth near to   Job 33:22
the d.
thy d. shall go forth of thee   Isa 49:17
destroyers (E)(R)   Jer 12:12;
                                   51:48, 53
and I will prepare d. against   Jer 22:7
thee
because ye rejoiced, O d. of   Jer 50:11
my heritage
who plunder my heritage   Jer 50:11
(A)(B)(E)
plunderers of my heritage   Jer 50:11
(R)

DESTROYEST

earth: and thou d. the hope   Job 14:19
of man
destroyer, d. (A)(E)(R)   Isa 33:1
the Lord, which d. all the   Jer 51:25
earth
Thou that d. the temple   M't 27:40
tear down the temple (A)   M't 27:40
destroyer and reconstructor   M't 27:40
of (B)

you would pull the temple   M't 27:40
down (N)(P)
Ah, thou that d. the temple   M'k 5:29

DESTROYETH

As the nations which the   De 8:20
Lord d.
He d. the perfect and the   Job 9:22
wicked
increaseth the nations, and   Job 12:23
d. them
he that doeth it d. his own   Pr 6:32
soul
with his mouth d. his   Pr 11:9
neighbour
thy ways to that which d.   Pr 31:3
kings
man mad; and a gift d. the   Ec 7:7
heart
war: but one sinner d. much   Ec 9:18
good
d. the temple (E)   1Co 3:17

DESTROYING

of Heshbon, utterly d. the men   De 3:6
d. it utterly, and all that is   De 13:15
therein
edge of the sword, utterly d.   Jos 11:11
them
to all lands, by d. them   2Ki 19:11
utterly
angel of the Lord d.   1Ch 21:12
throughout
and as he was d. the Lord   1Ch 21:15
beheld
d. them utterly (R)   2Ch 20:23
a tempest of hail and a d.   Isa 28:2
storm
by d. them utterly; and shalt   Isa 37:11
thou
your prophets, like a d. lion   Jer 2:30
like a destructive lion (B)   Jer 2:30
like a ravening lion (R)   Jer 2:30
Lord is d. Philistines (R)   Jer 47:4
that rise up against me, a d.   Jer 51:1
wind
arouse spirit of destroyer   Jer 51:1
(B)(R)
I am against thee, O d.   Jer 51:25
mountain
not withdrawn his hand from   La 2:8
d.
withdrawn hand from   La 2:8
destruction (B)
every man with his d. weapon   Eze 9:1
his weapon of destruction (B)   Eze 9:1
eye spared them from d.   Eze 20:17
them
d. angel might not (N)   Heb 11:28

DESTROYS

eye and d. it (B)(E)(R)   Ex 21:26
the godless d. his   Pr 11:9
(A)(B)(E)(R)
destroys (A)(E)   Isa 21:2; Na 3:16
wicked d. him (A)   Hab 1:13
no moth (A)(E)(N)(R)   Lu 12:33

DESTRUCTION

a d. be made from thy   Le 27:18
valuation (S)
road leads into d. (B)   Nu 22:32
latter end come to d.   Nu 24:20;
(A)(B)(E)(R)   24:24
destroy them with a mighty   De 7:23
d.
crush them utterly, no longer   De 7:23
exist (B)
discomfit them with great   De 7:23
discomfiture until they are
destroyed (E)
throw into great confusion,   De 7:23
destroyed (R)
glory in your d. (B)   De 28:63
burning heat, and with bitter   De 32:24
d.
devoured with burning heat   De 32:24
and poisonous pestilence (A)(R)
devoured by burning fever   De 32:24
and deadly pestilence (B)
destruction (A)   Jos 8:28
the city with a very great d.   1Sa 5:9
causing a very great panic   1Sa 5:9
(A)(R)
city with resultant panic (B)   1Sa 5:9

city with great discomfiture   1Sa 5:9
(E)
there was a deadly d.   1Sa 5:11
throughout
deadly panic throughout   1Sa 5:11
whole city (A)(R)
fatal fear gripped the whole   1Sa 5:11
city (B)
deadly discomfiture in whole   1Sa 5:11
city (E)
more d. than sword (B)   2Sa 18:8
torrents of d. (A)   2Sa 22:5
whom I appointed to utter   1Ki 20:42
d.
mount of d. (B)   2Ki 23:13
not send total d. (B)(R)   2Ch 12:12
the death of his father to his   2Ch 22:4
d.
advisers, leading him to ruin   2Ch 22:4
(B)
the d. of Ahaziah was of   2Ch 22:7
God by
downfall of Ahaziah was of   2Ch 22:7
God (B)(R)
his heart was lifted up to   2Ch 26:16
his d.
how can I endure to see the d.   Es 8:6
of
the ruin of my race (B)   Es 8:6
slaughter, and d. and did what   Es 9:5
neither shalt thou be afraid   Job 5:21
of d.
At d. and famine thou shalt   Job 5:22
laugh
and d. shall be ready at his   Job 18:12
side
calamity ready at his side   Job 18:12
(A)(E)
ruin stands ready for his   Job 18:12
stumbling (B)
calamity is ready at his   Job 18:12
stumbling (R)
oft cometh their d. upon   Job 21:17
them
calamity comes upon them   Job 21:17
(A)(B)(E)(R)
His eyes shall see his d.   Job 21:20
and he
eyes see their calamity (B)   Job 21:20
is reserved to the day of d.   Job 21:30
in the day of their calamity   Job 21:30
(B)(E)(R)
him, and d. hath no covering   Job 26:6
Abaddon has no covering   Job 26:6
(A)(R)
Death has no cover (B)   Job 26:6
D. and death say, We have   Job 28:22
heard
Abaddon and Death say   Job 28:22
(A)(E)(R)
against me the ways of   Job 30:12
their d.
raise against me destructive   Job 30:12
paths (B)
grave, though they cry in   Job 30:24
his d.
in his calamity will he not   Job 30:24
(A)(B)(E)
in his disaster cry for help   Job 30:24
(R)
Is not d. to the wicked   Job 31:3
calamity befall unrighteous   Job 31:3
(A)(B)(E)(R)
it is a fire that consumeth   Job 31:12
to d.
d. from God was a terror   Job 31:23
to me
calamity from God was a   Job 31:23
terror (A)(B)(E)
I was in terror of calamity   Job 31:23
(R)
If I rejoiced at the d. of   Job 31:29
him that
happy at the calamity of   Job 31:29
him (B)
rejoiced at the ruin of him   Job 31:29
(R)
d. come upon him at   Ps 35:8
unawares
into that very d. let him fall   Ps 35:8
bring them down into the pit   Ps 55:23
of d.
thou castedst them down   Ps 73:18
into d.
grave? or thy faithfulness in   Ps 88:11
d.
turnest man to d.; and sayest   Ps 90:3
turn man back corruption   Ps 90:3
(A)(R)

turnest mortal man back to   Ps 90:3
dust (B)
the d. that wasteth at   Ps 91:6
noonday
Who redeemeth thy life from   Ps 103:4
d.
life from the pit of   Ps 103:4
corruption (A)
life from the grave (B)   Ps 103:4
life from the pit (R)   Ps 103:4
your d. cometh as a   Pr 1:27
whirlwind
calamity comes on as a   Pr 1:27
whirlwind (A)(B)(E)(R)
the mouth of the foolish is   Pr 10:14
near d.
the d. of the poor is their   Pr 10:15
poverty
poverty of poor is their ruin   Pr 10:15
(A)(B)(R)
but d. shall be to the   Pr 10:29
workers of
openeth wide his lips shall   Pr 13:3
have d.
ruin (A)(B)(R)   Pr 13:3; 14:28; 18:7
brings d. upon self   Pr 13:13
(A)(E)(R)
want of people is the d. of   Pr 14:28
the prince
lack of people is prince's   Pr 14:28
ruin (A)(B)
Hell and d. are before the   Pr 15:11
Lord
Sheol and Abaddon   Pr 15:11;
(A)(B)(E)(R)   27:20
Pride goeth before d. and an   Pr 16:18
that exalteth his gate seeketh   Pr 17:19
d.
A fool's mouth is his d. and   Pr 18:7
Before d. the heart of man is   Pr 18:12
before haughtiness comes   Pr 18:12
disaster (A)
but d. shall be to the   Pr 21:15
workers of
their heart studieth d. and   Pr 24:2
minds plot oppression, devise   Pr 24:2
violence (A)
minds devise violence (B)(R)   Pr 24:2
heart studieth oppression (E)   Pr 24:2
Hell and d. are never full   Pr 27:20
all such as are appointed to   Pr 31:8
d.
rights of desolate and   Pr 31:8
defenseless (A)
those who are left desolate   Pr 31:8
(B)(E)(R)
And the d. of the   Isa 1:28
transgressors
fully completed d.   Isa 10:22
(A)(E)(R)
full d., decisive one (B)   Isa 10:23
cease, and mine anger in   Isa 10:25
their d.
come as a d. from the   Isa 13:6
Almighty
will sweep it with the besom   Isa 14:23
of d.
they shall raise up a cry of   Isa 15:5
d.
one shall be called, The city   Isa 19:18
of d.
destruction (A)(E)(R)   Isa 22:4;
Jer 48:3; Hab 1:3
and the gate is smitten with   Isa 24:12
d.
gate battered and destroyed   Isa 24:12
(A)
gates battered into ruins   Isa 24:12
(B)(R)
decree a d. (A)(E)(R)(S)   Isa 28:22
sieve of d. (A)(B)(E)(R)   Isa 30:28
the land of thy d. shall even   Isa 49:19
now
desolation, and d. and the   Isa 51:19
famine
wasting and d. are in their   Isa 59:7
paths
wasting nor d. within thy   Isa 60:18
borders
evil from the north and a   Jer 4:6
great d.
D. upon d. is cried; for the   Jer 4:20
whole
out of the north, and great d.   Jer 6:1
d. is heard (A)(B)(E)(R)   Jer 6:7;
20:8; Hab 2:17
and destroy them with   Jer 17:18
double d.

but d. cometh; it cometh   Jer 46:20
out of
Horonaim, spoiling and great   Jer 48:3
d.
the enemies have heard a cry   Jer 48:5
of d.
battle is in the land and of   Jer 50:22
great d.
and great d. from the land   Jer 51:54
of the
withdrawn from d. (B)   La 2:8
d. of the daughter of my   La 2:11;
people   3:48; 4:10
come upon us, desolation and   La 3:47
d.
which shall be for their d.   Eze 5:16
D. cometh; and they shall   Eze 7:25
seek
his weapon of d. (B)   Eze 9:1
bring thy d. among the   Eze 32:9
nations
d. unto them! because they   Ho 7:13
have
lo, they are gone because of d.   Ho 9:6
enemy have been cut off   Ho 9:6
(A)(B)
enemy have come to an end   Ho 9:6
(E)
vanished in everlasting ruins   Ho 9:6
(R)
O grave, I will be thy d.   Ho 13:14
and as a d. from the   Joe 1:15
Almighty
destructive tempest from   Joe 1:15
Almighty (A)
destruction (A)(E)(R)   Am 5:9
of Judah in the day of their d.   Ob 12
the day of their ruin (A)(R)   Ob 12
the day when they perish (B)   Ob 12
the day of his disaster (E)   Ob 12
destroy you, even with a   Mic 2:10
sore d.
d. of beasts (E)   Hab 2:19
there shall be no more utter   Zec 14:11
d.
fire of d. (P)   M't 5:22; 10:29
broad is the way that   M't 7:13
leadeth to d.
twice as ripe for d. (P)   M't 23:15
thrown into d. (P)   Lu 12:5
d. is near (N)   Lu 21:20
except the son of d. (P)   Joh 17:12
d. overtake your money (A)   Ac 8:20
D. and misery are in their   Ro 3:16
ways
for the d. of sinful self (N)   Ro 6:6
vessels of wrath fitted to d.   Ro 9:22
those on way to d. (B)   1Co 1:18
unto Satan for the d. of the   1Co 5:5
flesh
to destroy carnal lusts (A)   1Co 5:5
for the ruin of the flesh (B)   1Co 5:5
body experience destructive   1Co 5:5
powers of sin (P)
utter d. to the weak   1Co 8:11
(N)(P)(R)
edification, and not for your   2Co 10:8
d.
not for demolishing you (A)   2Co 10:8
not for your ruin (B)   2Co 10:8
not for casting you down   2Co 10:8
(E)
not pull you down (N)   2Co 10:8
not to break you down (P)   2Co 10:8
me to edification and not   2Co 13:10
d.
reap decay, ruin, d. (A)   Ga 6:8
clear sign of d. (A)(B)(R)   Ph'p 1:28
Whose end is d. whose God   Ph'p 3:19
is
their fate is eternal misery   Ph'p 3:19
(A)
whose end is perdition (E)   Ph'p 3:19
sudden d. cometh upon them   1Th 5:3
at once calamity is upon   1Th 5:3
them (N)
catastrophe sweep down upon   1Th 5:3
them (P)
be punished with everlasting   2Th 1:9
d.
penalty of everlasting ruin   2Th 1:9
(B)
punishment of eternal ruin   2Th 1:9
eternal exclusion from   2Th 1:9
radiance of (P)
are going to d. (B)(N)   2Th 2:10
drown men in d. and   1Ti 6:9
perdition

into ruin, d. (A)(B)(R)   1Ti 6:9
bring upon themselves swift d.   2Pe 2:1
d. not dormant   2Pe 2:3
(B)(E)(R)(S)
day of judgment and d.   2Pe 2:7
(A)(B)(E)(P)(R)
shall be destroyed in same d.   2Pe 2:12
(R)
other scriptures, unto their   2Pe 3:16
own d.
abyss and go into d. (B)(P)   Re 17:8

DESTRUCTIONS

d. are come to a perpetual end   Ps 9:6
rescue my soul from their d.   Ps 35:17
and delivered them from   Ps 107:20
their d.

DESTRUCTIVE

raise against me d. paths   Job 30:12
(B)
like a d. lion (B)   Jer 2:30
d. tempest from Almighty   Joe 1:15
(A)
not d. purposes (B)   2Co 13:10
d. heresies (A)(E)(R)(S)   2Pe 2:1

DETAIL

expounded in greater d. (N)   Ac 18:26

DETAIN

I pray thee, let us d. thee   J'g 13:15
even though I stay with you   J'g 13:15
(B)
Though thou d. me, I will   J'g 13:16
not eat

DETAINED

girl's father d. him   J'g 19:4
(A)(B)(S)
there that day, d. before the   1Sa 21:7
Lord
if I am d. (A)   1Ti 3:15

DETERMINATE

delivered by the d. counsel   Ac 2:23
fixed purpose, settled plan   Ac 2:23
(A)
determined will of God (B)   Ac 2:23
deliberate will and plan of   Ac 2:23
God (N)
by the determined plan of   Ac 2:23
God (P)
definite plan of God (R)   Ac 2:23

DETERMINATION

for my d. is to gather the   Zep 3:8
nations
my verdict is to muster   Zep 3:8
nations (A)
my decision is to gather   Zep 3:8
nations (R)
d. to concentrate (P)   1Co 2:2

DETERMINE

and he shall pay as the   Ex 21:22
judges d.
d. your case (S)   Ac 24:22

DETERMINED

was stedfastly d. (S)   Ru 1:18
be sure that evil is d. by him   1Sa 20:7
definitely decided on evil   1Sa 20:7;
20:9
evil were d. by my father to   1Sa 20:9
come
Jonathan knew that it was   1Sa 20:33
d. of his
evil is d. against our master   1Sa 25:17
disaster has been decided   1Sa 25:17
upon (A)
this hath been d. from the   2Sa 13:32
day
this has been planned (B)   2Sa 13:32
Solomon d. to build an house   2Ch 2:1
for
know that God hath d. to   2Ch 25:16
destroy
there was evil d. against him   Es 7:7
by
ruin had been decided (B)   Es 7:7

Seeing his days are d. the number | Job 14:5
consumption, even d. in the midst | Isa 10:23
full destruction, decisive one (B) | Isa 10:23
a full end, as decreed (R) | Isa 10:23
hosts, which he hath d. against it | Isa 19:17
purposes against Egypt (A)(B)(E)(R) | Isa 19:17
plans d. long ago (B)(R) | Isa 25:1
a consumption even d. upon | Isa 28:22
d. annihilation (B) | Isa 28:22
Seventy weeks are d. upon thy | Da 9:24
are decreed upon your people (A)(E)(R) | Da 9:24
are settled on for your people (B) | Da 9:24
end of the war desolations are d. | Da 9:26
desolations are decreed (A)(R) | Da 9:26
that d. shall be poured upon | Da 9:27
the decreed end (R) | Da 9:27
for that that is d. shall be done | Da 11:36
Son of man goeth, as it was d. | Lu 22:22
d. plan and foreknowledge (A) | Ac 2:23
Pilate, when he was d. to let him | Ac 3:13
he decided to set him free (B)(N)(P)(R) | Ac 3:13
counsel d. before to be done | Ac 4:28
purpose preordained to take (A)(R) | Ac 4:28
purpose preordained to take place (B)(E) | Ac 4:28
they d. to kill them (B) | Ac 5:33
d. to send relief unto the brethren | Ac 11:29
decided to send contribution (B) | Ac 11:29
agreed to make a contribution (N) | Ac 11:29
they d. that Paul and Barnabas | Ac 15:2
decided that Paul and Barnabas (A) | Ac 15:2
arranged to have Paul (B)(N) | Ac 15:2
brethren appointed that Paul (E)(R) | Ac 15:2
agreed that Paul and Barnabas (P) | Ac 15:2
Barnabas d. to take with them | Ac 15:37
wanted to take with them (A)(B)(N)(P)(R) | Ac 15:37
was minded to take with them (E) | Ac 15:37
hath d. the times before appointed | Ac 17:26
definitely appointing the pre-established periods and boundaries (B) | Ac 17:26
fixed the epochs of their history and the limits of their territory (N) | Ac 17:26
shall be d. in a lawful assembly | Ac 19:39
decided and cleared up in (A) | Ac 19:39
straightened out in regular assembly (B) | Ac 19:39
be settled in regular assembly (E)(R) | Ac 19:39
dealt with in statutory assembly (N) | Ac 19:39
resolved in regular assembly (P) | Ac 19:39
Paul had d. to sail by Ephesus | Ac 20:16
decided to sail past Ephesus (B)(N)(P)(R) | Ac 20:16
Augustus, I have d. to send him | Ac 25:25
decided to send him (B)(N)(P)(R) | Ac 25:25
when it was d. that we should sail | Ac 27:1
decided that we should (B)(N)(P)(R) | Ac 27:1
For I d. not to know any thing | 1Co 2:2
resolved not to know (A)(N) | 1Co 2:2
I wanted to know nothing (B) | 1Co 2:2

my secret determination to concentrate entirely upon Jesus Christ (P) | 1Co 2:2
I decided to know nothing d. (R) | 1Co 2:2
d. in own heart (B)(E)(R) | 1Co 7:37
But I d. this with myself, that I | 2Co 2:1
I definitely made up my mind (A)(B)(N)(P)(R) | 2Co 2:1
for I have d. there to winter | Tit 3:12
I decided to spend the winter (A)(B)(R) | Tit 3:12
I have made up my mind to spend (P) | Tit 3:12

DETERMINES

where helmsman's whim d. (B) | Jas 3:4

DETEST

thou shalt utterly d. it, and | De 7:26
d. all you stand for (P) | Lu 6:22

DETESTABLE

their d. and abominable things | Jer 16:18
sanctuary with all thy d. things | Eze 5:11
and of their d. things therein | Eze 7:20
all the d. things thereof | Eze 11:18
loathsome, abominable impurities (B) | Eze 11:18
d. things and their abominations | Eze 11:21
idols, nor with their d. things | Eze 37:23
their sinful apostasies (B) | Eze 37:23

DEUEL

of Gad: Eliasaph the son of D. | Nu 1:14
sixth day Eliasaph the son of D. | Nu 7:42
offering of Eliasaph the son of D. | Nu 7:47
Gad was Eliasaph the son of D. | Nu 10:20

DEVASTATE

shall cease to d. (B) | Isa 33:1

DEVASTATED

not d. (B) | Isa 33:1; Zec 11:3
plain be d. (A) | Jer 48:8

DEVASTATING

d. Babylon (B) | Jer 51:55

DEVASTATION

because of the d. (B) | Isa 22:4
devastation (B) | Jer 15:8; 51:56
day of wreck and d. (A)(B)(R) | Zep 1:15
d. is near (P) | Lu 21:20

DEVASTATOR

d., pillager (B) | Isa 16:4; 33:1
I have created the d. (A)(R) | Isa 54:16

DEVELOPMENT

another's peace and d. (B) | Ro 14:19

DEVIATED

d. from testimonies (B) | Ps 119:157

DEVICE

to find out every d. which shall | 2Ch 2:14
his d. that he had devised against | Es 8:3
scheme he had framed against Jews (A)(B) | Es 8:3
by letters that his wicked d. which | Es 9:25

Haman's wicked scheme (A) | Es 9:25
wicked plot had schemed against Jews (B)(R) | Es 9:25
they imagined a mischievous d. | Ps 21:11
a mischievous plot (A) | Ps 21:11
devised a plot (B) | Ps 21:11
they devise mischief (R) | Ps 21:11
further not his wicked d.; lest | Ps 140:8
nor promote their schemes (B) | Ps 140:8
do not further his evil plot (R) | Ps 140:8
for there is no work, nor d. | Ec 9:10
neither work nor invention | Ec 9:10
no work or thought (R) | Ec 9:10
and devise a d. against | Jer 18:11
devising a plan against you (A)(B)(R) | Jer 18:11
for his d. is against Babylon | Jer 51:11
his purpose concerning Babylon (A)(E)(R) | Jer 51:11
his plan regarding Babylon (B) | Jer 51:11
their d. against me all the day | La 3:62
their lips and thoughts are against (A)(R) | La 3:62
their mutterings against me (B) | La 3:62
stone, graven by art and man's d. | Ac 17:29
anything constructed or invented (A) | Ac 17:29
anything manufactured or invented (B) | Ac 17:29
shaped by human craftsmanship and design (N) | Ac 17:29
contrived by human art or imagination (P)(R) | Ac 17:29

DEVICES

He disappointeth the d. of | Job 5:12
d. which ye wrongfully imagine | Job 21:27
let them be taken in the d. that | Ps 10:2
schemes they have devised (A)(B)(R) | Ps 10:2
he maketh the d. of the people | Ps 33:10
thoughts and plans of people no effect (A) | Ps 33:10
frustrated purposes of the people (B) | Ps 33:10
thoughts of peoples of no effect (E) | Ps 33:10
frustrates plans of the people (R) | Ps 33:10
who bringeth wicked d. to pass | Ps 37:7
man who carries out wicked plans (P) | Ps 37:7
and be filled with their own d. | Pr 1:31
sated with their own counsel (B) | Pr 1:31
man of wicked d. will he condemn | Pr 12:2
a man of wicked d. is hated | Pr 14:17
are many d. in a man's heart | Pr 19:21
Many plans in man's mind (A)(R) | Pr 19:21
Many schemes in man's mind (B) | Pr 19:21
many d. for evil (A)(B)(R)(S) | Ec 7:29
he deviseth wicked d. to destroy | Isa 32:7
they had devised d. against me | Jer 11:19
devised inventions and schemes (A) | Jer 11:19
concocted plots against me (B) | Jer 11:19
they devised schemes (R) | Jer 11:19
we will walk after our own d. | Jer 18:12
follow their own schemes (B) | Jer 18:12
follow their own plans (R) | Jer 18:12
let us devise d. against Jeremiah | Jer 18:18
devise schemes against Jeremiah (A)(B) | Jer 18:18
make plots against Jeremiah (R) | Jer 18:18

all their *d.* (A)(B)(E)(R) La 3:60; 3:61

forecast his *d.* against the strong Da 11:24

devise plans against strongholds (A)(R) Da 11:24

plan strategies against fortresses (B) Da 11:24

they shall forecast *d.* against him Da 11:25

schemes shall be devised (A)(B) Da 11:25

plots shall be devised against him (R) Da 11:25

we are not ignorant of his *d.* 2Co 2:11

of wiles and intentions (A) 2Co 2:11

his schemes (B) 2Co 2:11

his wiles as well (N) 2Co 2:11

his methods (P) 2Co 2:11

his designs (R) 2Co 2:11

the *d.* of the devil (N) Eph 6:11

DEVIL

wilderness to be tempted of the *d.* M't 4:1

d. taketh him up into the holy city M't 4:5

Again the *d.* taketh him up into M't 4:8

Then the *d.* leaveth him, and M't 4:11

a dumb man possessed with a *d.* M't 9:32

demon (A)(B)(R) M't 9:32; 9:33; 11:18; 15:22; 17:18; M'k 7:26, 29-30; Lu 4:33, 35; 7:33; 8:29; 9:42; 11:14; Joh 7:20; 8:48-49, 52; 10:20-21

when the *d.* was cast out M't 9:33

and they say, He hath a *d.* M't 11:18

one possessed with a *d.* blind M't 12:22

enemy that sowed them is the *d.* M't 13:39

is grievously vexed with a *d.* M't 15:22

Jesus rebuked the *d.*; and M't 17:18

prepared for the *d.* and his angels M't 25:41

was possessed with the *d.* M'k 5:15; 5:16

that had been possessed with a *d.* M'k 5:18

that he would cast forth the *d.* M'k 7:26

d. is gone out of thy daughter M'k 7:29

she found the *d.* gone out, and her M'k 7:30

Being forty days tempted of the *d.* Lu 4:2

the *d.* said unto him, If thou be Lu 4:3

d. taking him up into an high Lu 4:5

the *d.* said unto him, All this will Lu 4:6

d. had ended all the temptation Lu 4:13

had a spirit of an unclean *d.* Lu 4:33

when the *d.* had thrown him in Lu 4:35

wine; and ye say, He hath a *d.* Lu 7:33

cometh the *d.* and taketh away Lu 8:12

of the *d.* into the wilderness Lu 8:29

d. threw him down, and tare him Lu 9:42

casting out a *d.* and it was dumb Lu 11:14

to pass when the *d.* was gone out Lu 11:14

twelve, and one of you is a *d.* Joh 6:70

and said, Thou hast a *d.* Joh 7:20

Ye are of your father the *d.* Joh 8:44

art a Samaritan, and hast a *d.* Joh 8:48

Jesus answered, I have not Joh 8:49

Now we know that thou hast a *d.* Joh 8:52

many of them said, He hath a *d.* Joh 10:20

the words of him that hath a *d.* Joh 10:21

a *d.* open the eyes of the blind Joh 10:21

d. having now put into the heart Joh 13:2

all that were oppressed of the *d.* Ac 10:38

thou child of the *d.* thou enemy Ac 13:10

son of the *d.* Ac 13:10

(A)(B)(E)(N)(P)(R)

Neither give place to the *d.* Eph 4:27

stand against the wiles of the *d.* Eph 6:11

into the condemnation of the *d.* 1Ti 3:6

reproach and the snare of the *d.* 1Ti 3:7

out of the snare of the *d.* who 2Ti 2:26

power of death, that is, the *d.* Heb 2:14

even from the *d.* (P) Jas 3:15

Resist the *d.* and he will flee Jas 4:7

because your adversary the *d.* 1Pe 5:8

that committeth sin is of the *d.* 1Jo 3:8

d. sinneth from the beginning 1Jo 3:8

might destroy the works of the *d.* 1Jo 3:8

manifest, and the children of the *d.* 1Jo 3:10

when contending with the *d.* Jude 9

the *d.* shall cast some of you into Re 2:10

that old serpent, called the D. Re 12:9

the *d.* is come down unto you Re 12:12

that old serpent, which is the D. Re 20:2

the *d.* that deceived them was cast Re 20:10

DEVILISH

above, but is earthly, sensual, *d.* Jas 3:15

demonic (B)(N) Jas 3:15

even from the devil (P) Jas 3:15

DEVILS

offer their sacrifices unto *d.* after Le 17:7

shaggy he-goats, goat-like gods, or demons (A) Le 17:7

spirits (B) Le 17:7

he goats (E) Le 17:7

satyrs (R) Le 17:7

sacrificed unto *d.* not to God De 32:17

and for the *d.* and for the calves 2Ch 11:15

goat idols (B) 2Ch 11:15

he goats (E) 2Ch 11:15

satyrs (R) 2Ch 11:15

sons and their daughters unto *d.* Ps 106:37

demons (A)(B)(E)(R) Ps 106:37

which were possessed with *d.* M't 4:24

demons (A)(E)(R) M't 4:24; 8:16, 28, 31, 33; M'k 1:32; 9:38; 16:17; Lu 4:41; 8:2, 36; 9:1; 10:17; 13:32; 1Co 10:20; 1Ti 4:1; Jas 2:19; Re 9:20; 16:14; 18:2

demoniacs (B) M't 8:16, 28, 33; Lu 8:36

in thy name have cast out *d.* M't 7:22

that were possessed with *d.* M't 8:16

met him two possessed with *d.* M't 8:28

So the *d.* besought him, saying, If M't 8:31

demons (B) M't 8:31; M'k 9:38; 16:17; Lu 4:41; 9:1; 10:17; 13:32; 1Co 10:20; Jas 2:19; Re 9:20; 16:14; 18:2

befallen to the possessed of the *d.* M't 8:33

Pharisees said, He casteth out *d.* M't 9:34

through the prince of the *d.* M't 9:34

lepers, raise the dead, cast out *d.* M't 10:8

This fellow doth not cast out *d.* M't 12:24

by Beelzebub the prince of the *d.* M't 12:24

if I by Beelzebub cast out *d.* M't 12:27

If I cast out *d.* by the Spirit of M't 12:28

them that were possessed with *d.* M'k 1:32

diseases, and cast out many *d.* M'k 1:34

and suffered not the *d.* to speak M'k 1:34

all Galilee, and cast out *d.* M'k 1:39

sicknesses, and to cast out *d.* M'k 3:15

and by the prince of the *d.* M'k 3:22

casteth he out *d.* M'k 3:22

all the *d.* besought him, saying M'k 5:12

they cast out many *d.* and M'k 6:13

one casting out *d.* in thy name M'k 9:38

out of whom he had cast seven *d.* M'k 16:9

my name shall they cast out *d.* M'k 16:17

d. also came out of many, crying Lu 4:41

out of whom went seven *d.* Lu 8:2

a certain man, which had *d.* long Lu 8:27

because many *d.* were entered Lu 8:30

Then went the *d.* out of the man Lu 8:33

of whom the *d.* were departed Lu 8:35

possessed of the *d.* was healed Lu 8:36

the man out of whom the *d.* were Lu 8:38

power and authority over all *d.* Lu 9:1

Master, we saw one casting out *d.* Lu 9:49

even the *d.* are subject unto us Lu 10:17

casteth out *d.* through Beelzebub Lu 11:15

the chief of the *d.* Lu 11:15

I cast out *d.* through Beelzebub Lu 11:18

if I by Beelzebub cast out *d.* Lu 11:19

with the finger of God cast Lu 11:20

I cast out *d.* and I do cures Lu 13:32

sacrifice to *d.* and not to God 1Co 10:20

ye should have fellowship with *d.* 1Co 10:20

cup of the Lord, and the cup of *d.* 1Co 10:21

Lord's table, and of the table of *d.* 1Co 10:21

spirits, and doctrines of *d.* 1Ti 4:1

the *d.* also believe, and tremble Jas 2:19

that they should not worship *d.* Re 9:20

For they are the spirits of *d.* Re 16:14

is become the habitation of *d.* Re 18:2

DEVIL'S

sharing the *d.* downfall (P) 1Ti 3:6

DEVIOUS

put *d.* talk away (R) Pr 4:24

contrary and *d.* in his ways (A) Pr 14:2

way of man is *d.* and strange (S) Pr 21:8

DEVISE

To *d.* cunning works, to work in Ex 31:4

plan designs of gold, silver (B) Ex 31:4

And to *d.* curious works, to work in Ex 35:32

design artistic work (B) Ex 35:32

and of those that *d.* cunning work Ex 35:35

yet doth he *d.* means, that his 2Sa 14:14

takes measures so as not to (B) 2Sa 14:14

they conceived a *d.* (E) Ps 21:11

to confusion that *d.* my hurt Ps 35:4

plan my hurt (B) Ps 35:4

who intend my hurt (B) Ps 35:4

d. deceitful matters against them Ps 35:20

that plot treacheries (B) Ps 35:20

conceive words of deceit (R) Ps 35:20

against me do they *d.* my hurt Ps 41:7

plan harm against me (B) Ps 41:7

they imagine the worst for me   *Ps 41:7* (R)
d. mischiefs in heart (A)(E)   *Ps 140:2*
D. not evil against thy   *Pr 3:29* neighbour
Do not contrive, dig up,   *Pr 3:29* cultivate (A)
Do not plan evil against your   *Pr 3:29* (R)
who *d.* evil (A)(E)(R)   *Pr 12:20*
Do they not err that *d.* evil   *Pr 14:22*
plot mischief, plan good (B)   *Pr 14:22*
shall be to them that *d.* good   *Pr 14:22*
shutteth his eyes to *d.*   *Pr 16:30* froward
plan perverse things (B)(R)   *Pr 16:30*
and *d.* a device against you: *Jer 18:11* return
let us *d.* devices against   *Jer 18:18* Jeremiah
the men that *d.* mischief,   *Eze 11:2* and give
d. evil, mischief (A)(E)(R)   *Ho 7:15*
Woe to them that *d.* iniquity   *Mic 2:1*
against this family do I *d.* an   *Mic 2:3* evil
d. against Jehovah (E)   *Na 1:9*
d. evil against brother   *Zec 7:10* (E)(R)
people *d.* vain things (B)   *Ac 4:25*
d. every device (S)   *2Co 2:14*

DEVISED

that *d.* against us that we   *2Sa 21:5* should
planned to prevent us from   *2Sa 21:5* (A)
planned to exterminate us   *2Sa 21:5* (B)(R)
in the month which he had   *1Ki 12:33* *d.*
machines *d.* by inventors   *2Ch 26:15* (A)(B)
that he had *d.* against the Jews   *Es 8:3*
the scheme he framed against   *Es 8:3* (B)
reverse the letters *d.* by   *Es 8:5* Haman
scheme Haman concocted   *Es 8:5* (B)
had *d.* against the Jews to   *Es 9:24* destroy
which he *d.* against the Jews   *Es 9:25*
they *d.* a plot (B)   *Ps 21:11*
they *d.* to take away my life   *Ps 31:13*
plotted to take my life   *Ps 31:13* (A)(R)
schemed to take my life (B)   *Ps 31:13*
have *d.* evil (R)   *Isa 7:5*
they had *d.* devices against   *Jer 11:19* me
d. schemes (A)(R)   *Jer 11:19*
concocted plots against me   *Jer 11:19* (B)
in Heshbon they had *d.* evil   *Jer 48:2*
planned evil against her (A)(R)   *Jer 48:2*
the Lord hath both *d.* and   *Jer 51:12* done
purposed and done (A)   *Jer 51:12*
planned and done (R)   *Jer 51:12*
hath done that which he had   *La 2:17* *d.*
king of Moab *d.* (S)   *Mic 6:5*
not followed cunningly *d.*   *2Pe 1:16* fables

DEVISES

in hands are evil *d.* (R)   *Ps 26:10*
He *d.* mischief upon his bed   *Ps 36:4*
plans wrongdoing on his bed   *Ps 36:4* (A)
tongue *d.* mischiefs; like a   *Ps 52:2* sharp
heart, he *d.* mischief   *Pr 6:14* continually
d. trouble, vexation (A)   *Pr 6:14*
heart that *d.* wicked   *Pr 6:18* imaginations
heart that manufactures   *Pr 6:18* wicked thoughts and plans (A)
d. wicked plans (R)   *Pr 6:18*
A man's heart *d.* his ways   *Pr 16:9*
a man's mind plans his ways   *Pr 16:9* (A)(B)(R)
He that *d.* to do evil shall be   *Pr 24:8*
plans to do evil (A)(B)(R)   *Pr 24:8*
he *d.* wicked devices to   *Isa 32:7* destroy

But the liberal *d.* liberal   *Isa 32:8* things

DEVISETH

d. wicked schemes (B)(E)   *Pr 6:18*
d. evil against Jehovah (E)   *Na 1:11*

DEVISING

the *d.* of folly is sin (R)   *Pr 24:9*

DEVITALIZED

sin-controlled body be *d.* (B)   *Ro 6:6*

DEVOID

priest be *d.* of instruction   *Eze 7:26*

DEVOTE

that a man shall *d.* unto the   *Le 27:28* Lord
d. their gain (A)(B)(E)(R)   *Mic 4:13*

DEVOTED

unto the Lord, as a field *d.*   *Le 27:21;* 27:28-29
field set apart for him (B)   *Le 27:21*
Every thing *d.* in Israel shall   *Nu 18:14* be
violated *d.* portion (B)   *Jos 7:1*
the *d.* thing (S)   *1Ch 2:7*
preserve lives of *d.* ones (B)   *Ps 97:10*
servant, who is *d.* to thy   *Ps 119:38* fear
reverently fear, devotedly   *Ps 119:38* worship (A)
who revere thee (B)   *Ps 119:38*
in order unto the fear of   *Ps 119:38* thee (E)
those who fear thee (R)   *Ps 119:38*
everything *d.* (B)(E)(R)   *Eze 44:29*
they have *d.* themselves (S)   *1Co 16:15*
concentrate on being *d.* (P)   *1Pe 3:15*

DEVOTION

my *d.* to God's house (R)   *1Ch 29:3*
undistracted *d.* (A)(B)(R)   *1Co 7:35*
same *d.* for you (B)   *2Co 8:16*
sincere and pure *d.*   *2Co 11:3* (A)(N)(P)(R)

DEVOTIONS

I passed by, and beheld your   *Ac 17:23*
observed your objects of   *Ac 17:23* worship (A)(B)(E)(R)
I looked at your shrines (P)   *Ac 17:23*

DEVOUR

the morning he shall *d.* the   *Ge 49:27* prey
worms shall *d.* grapes (B)   *De 28:38*
blood, and my sword shall   *De 32:42* *d.* flesh
and *d.* the cedars of Lebanon   *Jg 9:15*
destroy the cedars (B)   *J'g 9:15; 9:20*
and *d.* the men of Shechem   *J'g 9:20*
house of Millo, and *d.*   *J'g 9:20* Abimelech
Shall the sword *d.* for ever   *2Sa 2:26*
consuming for ever (B)   *2Sa 2:26*
command the locusts to *d.*   *2Ch 7:13* the land
It shall *d.* the strength of   *Job 18:13* his skin
born of death shall *d.* his   *Job 18:13* strength
first-born of death eats   *Job 18:13* away limbs (A)
first-born of death consumes   *Job 18:13* limbs (R)
shall *d.* them (A)(E)(R)   *Job 20:26*
wrath, and the fire shall *d.*   *Ps 21:9* them
fire shall utterly consume   *Ps 21:9* them (A)(R)
silence: a fire shall *d.* before   *Ps 50:3* him
wild beasts of the field doth   *Ps 80:13* *d.* it
wild beasts feed on it   *Ps 80:13* (A)(B)(E)(R)

to *d.* the poor from off the   *Pr 30:14* earth
strangers *d.* it in your   *Isa 1:7* presence
shall *d.* Israel with open   *Isa 9:12* mouth
it shall *d.* the briers and   *Isa 9:18* thorns
and it shall burn and *d.* his   *Isa 10:17* thorns
destroy his thorn-bushes (B)   *Isa 10:17*
of thine enemies shall *d.*   *Isa 26:11* them
shall consume them   *Isa 26:11* (A)(B)(R)
not of a mean man, shall *d.*   *Isa 31:8* him
your breath, as fire, shall *d.*   *Isa 33:11* you
consume you (A)(B)(R)   *Isa 33:11*
I will destroy and *d.* at once   *Isa 42:14*
gasp and pant together   *Isa 42:14* (A)(B)(E)(R)
beasts of the field, come to *d.*   *Isa 56:9*
all that *d.* him shall offend   *Jer 2:3*
all who ate of it offended (A)   *Jer 2:3*
those devouring him be   *Jer 2:3* punished (B)
who ate of it became guilty   *Jer 2:3* (R)
people wood, and it shall *d.*   *Jer 5:14* them
the beasts of the field, come   *Jer 12:9* to *d.*
the sword of the Lord shall   *Jer 12:12* *d.*
of the earth, to *d.* and   *Jer 15:3* destroy
shall *d.* the palaces of   *Jer 17:27* Jerusalem
and it shall *d.* all things   *Jer 21:14* round
Therefore all they that *d.*   *Jer 30:16* shall be
and the sword shall *d.* and   *Jer 46:10* it shall
sword shall *d.* round about   *Jer 46:14* thee
and shall *d.* the corner of   *Jer 48:45* Moab
and it shall *d.* all round   *Jer 50:32* about him
famine and pestilence shall   *Eze 7:15* *d.* him
fire, and another fire shall *d.*   *Eze 15:7* them
it shall *d.* every green tree   *Eze 20:47* in thee
them through the fire to *d.*   *Eze 23:37* them
it shall *d.* thee, and I will   *Eze 28:18* bring
it has consumed you (A)   *Eze 28:18*
to burn you up (B)   *Eze 28:18*
it has consumed you (R)   *Eze 28:18*
the beast of the land *d.*   *Eze 34:28* them
thou shalt *d.* men no more,   *Eze 36:14* neither
thus unto it, Arise, *d.* much   *Da 7:5* flesh
and shall *d.* the whole earth   *Da 7:23*
now shall a month *d.* them   *Ho 5:7* with
and it shall *d.* the palaces   *Ho 8:14;*
thereof   *Am 1:7; 1:4*
and *d.* them, because of their   *Ho 11:6* own
and there will I *d.* them like   *Ho 13:8* a lion
shall *d.* the palaces of   *Am 1:4* Ben-hadad
of Tyrus, which shall *d.* the   *Am 1:10* palaces
shall *d.* the palaces of   *Am 1:12* Bozrah
Moab, and it shall *d.* the   *Am 2:2* Palaces
shall *d.* the palaces of   *Am 2:5* Jerusalem
in the house of Joseph, and   *Am 5:6* *d.* it
shall kindle in them, and *d.*   *Ob 18* them
the sword shall *d.* thy young   *Na 2:13* lions
enemies: the fire shall *d.* thy   *Na 3:13* bars
fire shall consume thy bars   *Na 3:13* (A)

fire has consumed your *Na 3:13*
lock-bars (B)
there shall the fire *d.* thee *Na 3:15*
fire will consume you (B) *Na 3:15*
was as to *d.* the poor *Hab 3:14*
secretly
and they shall *d.* and subdue *Zec 9:15*
with
that the fire may *d.* thy *Zec 11:1*
cedars
consume your cedars (B) *Zec 11:1*
and they shall *d.* all the *Zec 12:6*
people
ye *d.* widows' houses, and *M't 23:14;*
for *M'k 12:40; Lu 20:47*
swallow up widows' houses *M't 23:14*
(A)
became executives for *M't 23:14*
widows' properties (B)
if a man *d.* you, if a man *2Co 11:20*
take
if ye bite and *d.* one another *Ga 5:15*
which shall *d.* the *Heb 10:27*
adversaries
consume those in *Heb 10:27*
opposition (A)(N)(P)(R)
about, seeking whom he may *1Pe 5:8*
d.
for to *d.* her child as soon as *Re 12:4*

DEVOURED

and hath quite *d.* also our *Ge 31:15*
money
enjoyed profits of our dowry *Ge 31:15*
(B)
Some evil beast hath *d.* him *Ge 37:20*
and evil beast hath *d.* him: *Ge 37:33*
Joseph
And the seven thin ears *d.* the *Ge 41:7*
swallowed seven large ears *Ge 41:7*
(B)(E)(R)
And the thin ears *d.* the *Ge 41:24*
seven
and *d.* them, and they died *Le 10:2*
before
killed them (A) *Le 10:2*
consumed them (B) *Le 10:2; Nu 26:10*
the fire *d.* two hundred and *Nu 26:10*
fifty
and they shall be *d.* and *De 31:17*
many evils
and *d.* with burning heat *De 32:24*
the wood *d.* more people *2Sa 18:8*
more destruction than did *2Sa 18:8*
the sword (B)
that day than the sword *d.* *2Sa 18:8*
and fire out of his mouth *d.* *2Sa 22:9*
fire from his mouth did *2Sa 22:9*
consume (B)
and fire out of his mouth *d.* *Ps 18:8*
flies among them, which *d.* *Ps 78:45*
them
swarms of flies that ate them *Ps 78:45*
(B)
For they have *d.* Jacob, and *Ps 79:7*
laid
and *d.* the fruit of their *Ps 105:35*
ground
ye shall be *d.* with the sword *Isa 1:20*
hath the curse *d.* the earth *Isa 24:6*
own sword hath *d.* your *Jer 2:30*
prophets
shame hath *d.* the labour of *Jer 3:24*
our
they are come, and have *d.* *Jer 8:16*
the land
have eaten up Jacob, and *d.* *Jer 10:25*
him
they that devour thee shall *Jer 30:16*
be *d.*
All that found them have *d.* *Jer 50:7*
them
the king of Assyria hath *d.* *Jer 50:17*
him
the king of Babylon hath *Jer 51:34*
d. me
it hath *d.* the foundations *La 4:11*
thereof
consumed her foundations *La 4:11*
(A)(B)(R)
when the fire hath *d.* it, *Eze 15:5*
and it is
thou sacrificed unto them to *Eze 16:20*
be *d.*
to be destroyed (A) *Eze 16:20*
to be consumed (B) *Eze 16:20*
learned to catch the prey; it *Eze 19:3*
d. men

to catch the prey, and *d.* *Eze 19:6*
men
branches, which hath *d.* her *Eze 19:14*
fruit
consumed the vine's fruit *Eze 19:14*
(A)(R)
devouring her shoots and *Eze 19:14*
fruit (B)
they have *d.* souls; they *Eze 22:25*
have taken
thy residue shall be *d.* by *Eze 23:25*
the fire
will I give to the beasts to *Eze 33:27*
be *d.*
to the beasts of the field to *Eze 39:4*
be *d.*
teeth: it *d.* and brake in pieces *Da 7:7*
which *d.* brake in pieces, and *Da 7:19*
an oven, and have *d.* their *Ho 7:7*
judges
Strangers have *d.* his strength *Ho 7:9*
to thee will I cry for the fire *Joe 1:19*
hath *d.*
the fire hath *d.* the pastures *Joe 1:20*
of the
increased, the palmerworm, *d.* *Am 4:9*
them
and it *d.* the great deep, and *Am 7:4*
did eat
they shall be *d.* as stubble *Na 1:10*
fully
consumed like stubble *Na 1:10*
(A)(B)(E)(R)
shall be *d.* by the fire of his *Zep 1:18*
jealousy
consumed in the fire *Zep 1:18;*
(A)(R) *3:8*
be *d.* with the fire of my *Zep 3:8*
jealousy
and she shall be *d.* with fire *Zec 9:4*
the fowls came and *d.* them *M't 13:4*
up
ate them up (A)(B)(N) *M't 13:4*
gobbled them up (P) *M't 13:4*
fowls of the air came and *d.* *M'k 4:4*
it up
and the fowls of the air *d.* it *Lu 8:5*
hath *d.* thy living with *Lu 15:30*
harlots
squandering livelihood on *Lu 15:30*
prostitutes (B)
running through money with *Lu 15:30*
women (N)
spent all money on *Lu 15:30*
prostitutes (P)
out of heaven, and *d.* them *Re 20:9*
heaven and consumed them *Re 20:9*
(A)(B)(N)(P)(R)

DEVOURER

I will rebuke the *d.* for your *Mal 3:11*
sakes
rebuke the devouring locust *Mal 3:11*
(B)

DEVOUREST

Thou land *d.* up men, and *Eze 36:13*
hast

DEVOURETH

sword *d.* one as well as *2Sa 11:25*
another
consumes (B) *2Sa 11:25;*
Isa 5:24; La 2:3; Joe 2:3
mouth of the wicked *d.* *Pr 19:28*
iniquity
swallows iniquity (A)(B)(E) *Pr 19:28*
man who *d.* that which is *Pr 20:25*
holy
Therefore as the fire *d.* the *Isa 5:24*
stubble
a flaming fire, which *d.* round *La 2:3*
about
consuming all around (R) *La 2:3*
the fire *d.* both the ends of *Eze 15:4*
it
consumes both ends (A)(R) *Eze 15:4*
burns both ends (B) *Eze 15:4*
A fire *d.* before them; and *Joe 2:3*
behind
a flame of fire that *d.* the *Joe 2:5*
stubble
when the wicked *d.* the man *Hab 1:13*
that
wicked destroys him (A) *Hab 1:13*
wicked swallows up the man *Hab 1:13*
(B)(E)(R)

their mouth, and *d.* their *Re 11:5*
enemies
consumes their enemies *Re 11:5*
(A)(B)(N)(P)(R)

DEVOURING

like *d.* fire on the top of the *Ex 24:17*
mount
consuming fire on mountain *Ex 24:17*
(B)
Thou lovest all *d.* words, O *Ps 52:4*
thou
tempest, and the flame of *d.* *Isa 29:6*
fire
and his tongue as a *d.* fire *Isa 30:27*
his tongue is a consuming *Isa 30:27*
fire (A)(B)
and with the flame of a *d.* *Isa 30:30*
fire
us shall dwell with the *d.* fire *Isa 33:14*
those *d.* him be punished (B) *Jer 2:3*
d. shoots and fruit (B) *Eze 19:14*
rebuke the *d.* locust (B) *Mal 3:11*
inside they are *d.* wolves *M't 7:15*
(A)

DEVOUT

the same man was just and *d.* *Lu 2:25*
Jews, *d.* men, out of every *Ac 2:5*
nation
And *d.* men carried Stephen to *Ac 8:2*
his
A *d.* man, and one that *Ac 10:2*
feared God
a *d.* soldier of them that *Ac 10:7*
waited on
stirred up the *d.* and *Ac 13:50*
honourable
of the *d.* Greeks a great *Ac 17:4*
multitude
the Jews, and with the *d.* *Ac 17:17*
persons
a *d.* man according to the *Ac 22:12*
law

DEW

God give thee of the *d.* of *Ge 27:28*
heaven
and of the *d.* of heaven *Ge 27:39*
from above
the *d.* lay round about the *Ex 16:13*
host
when the *d.* that lay was *Ex 16:14*
gone
when the *d.* fell upon the *Nu 11:9*
camp
my speech shall distil us the *De 32:2*
d.
for the *d.* and for the deep *De 33:13*
also his heavens shall drop *De 33:28*
down *d.*
if the *d.* be on the fleece only *J'g 6:37*
wringed the *d.* out of the fleece *J'g 6:38*
upon all the ground let there *J'g 6:39*
be *d.*
there was *d.* on all the *J'g 6:40*
ground
Gilboa, let there be no *d.* *2Sa 1:21*
neither
light upon him as the *d.* *2Sa 17:12*
falleth
there shall not be *d.* nor rain *1Ki 17:1*
the *d.* lay all night upon my *Job 29:19*
branch
who hath begotten the *Job 38:28*
drops of *d.*
thou hast the *d.* of thy youth *Ps 110:3*
the *d.* of Hermon, and as *Ps 133:3*
the *d.*
and the clouds drop down the *Pr 3:20*
d.
his favour is as *d.* upon the *Pr 19:12*
grass
for my head is filled with *d.* *Ca 5:2*
like a cloud of *d.* in the heat *Isa 18:4*
of
for thy *d.* is as the *d.* of *Isa 26:19*
herbs
let it be wet with the *d.* of *Da 4:15*
heaven
d. or heaven, and let his *Da 4:23*
portion be
they shall wet thee with the *Da 4:25*
d. of
and his body was wet with *Da 4:33*
the *d.* of

body was wet with the *d.* of   *Da 5:21*
heaven
and as the early *d.* it goeth   *Ho 6:4*
away
and as the early *d.* that   *Ho 13:3*
passeth
I will be as the *d.* unto Israel   *Ho 14:5*
many people as a *d.* from the   *Mic 5:7*
Lord
heaven over you is stayed   *Hag 1:10*
from *d.*
the heavens shall give their   *Zec 8:12*
d.
how *d.,* just, blameless (N)   *1Th 2:10*
d. and dedicated lives (N)   *2Pe 3:11*

DEXTERITY

put *d.* and understanding (B)   *Ex 36:1*

DIABOLICAL

minds teemed with *d.*   *Ro 1:30*
invention (P)

DIADEM

sacred *d.* (B)   *Ex 29:6; 29:30; Le 8:9*
judgment was as a robe and   *Job 29:14*
a *d.*
dressed me as robe and   *Job 29:14*
turban (B)(R)
as a *d.* (A)   *Job 31:36*
and for a *d.* of beauty, unto   *Isa 28:5*
a royal *d.* in the hand of thy   *Isa 62:3*
God
Remove the *d.* and take off   *Eze 21:26*
remove the miter or   *Eze 21:26*
headband (A)(E)
Remove the turban (B)(R)   *Eze 21:26*

DIAL

which it had gone down in   *2Ki 20:11*
the *d.*
gone down on steps of   *2Ki 20:11*
Ahaz (B)
which is gone down in the   *Isa 38:8*
sun *d.*

DIALECT

their own *d.* (A)(B)   *Ac 1:19*
speak in his own *d.* (A)   *Ac 2:6*
in our own *d.* (A)   *Ac 2:8*
every *d.* (A)(B)   *Ac 13:7; 17:15*
the Hebrew *d.* (A)   *Ac 21:40*

DIALECTS

after their *d.* (B)   *Ge 10:31*

DIALOGUE

holding a *d.* (A)   *M't 2:6*

DIAMOND

an emerald, a sapphire, and   *Ex 28:18;*
a *d.*   *39:11*
and with the point of a *d.*   *Jer 17:1*
the sardius, topaz, and the   *Eze 28:13*
d.

DIANA

made silver shrines for D.   *Ac 19:24;*
  19:27-28, 34-35

DIBLAIM

took Gomer the daughter of   *Ho 1:3*
D.

DIBLATH

than the wilderness toward   *Eze 6:14*
D.

DIBON

Heshbon is perished even   *Nu 21:30*
unto D.
Ataroth, and D., and Jazer   *Nu 32:3*
And the children of Gad   *Nu 32:34*
built D.
all the plain of Medeba unto   *Jos 13:9*
D.

D. and Bamoth-baal, and   *Jos 13:17*
at D. and in the villages   *Ne 11:25*
thereof
He is gone up to Bajith, and   *Isa 15:2*
to D.
daughter that dost inhabit D.   *Jer 48:18*
And upon D. and upon   *Jer 48:22*
Nebo, and

DIBON-GAD

from Iim, and pitched in D.   *Nu 33:45*
removed from D. and   *Nu 33:46*
encamped

DIBRI

Shelomith, the daughter of   *Le 24:11*
D.

DICTATE

why let people *d.* to you (N)   *Col 2:20*

DICTATING

d. terms of your faith (N)   *2Co 1:24*

DID

D. not the Lord bring us up   *J'g 6:13*
from
or *d.* he ever fight against   *J'g 11:25*
them
her; therefore she wept, and   *1Sa 1:7*
d. not eat
besides the mischief that   *1Ki 11:25*
Hadad *d.*
d. right according to all   *2Ki 18:3*
David *d.*
of the Lord, *d.* the king   *2Ki 23:12*
beat down
neither *d.* all the kings of   *2Ch 35:18*
Israel keep
knew not whither' I went or   *Ne 2:16*
what I *d.*
Mordecai walked to know   *Es 2:11*
how Esther *d.*
and there they *d.* eat bread   *Jer 41:1*
together in
have ye not read what David   *M't 12:3*
d.
they saw wonderful things   *M't 21:15*
he *d.*
they heard what great things   *M'k 3:8*
he *d.*
they saw miracles which he   *Joh 2:23;*
d.   *6:2, 14*
told me all things that ever   *Joh 4:29;*
I *d.*   *4:34*
then said they, What *d.* he   *Joh 9:26*
to thee
done works none other   *Joh 15:24*
man *d.*
thro' ignorance *d.* it, as *d.*   *Ac 3:17*
your rulers
which thing I also *d.* in   *Ac 26:10*
Jerusalem
the saints *d.* I shut up in   *Ac 26:10*
prison
this they *d.* not as we hoped   *2Co 8:5*
who *d.* no sin, nor was guile   *1Pe 2:22*
found

DID AS

Lord *d.* to Sarah *as* he had   *Ge 21:1*
spoken
man *d.* as Joseph bade, and   *Ge 43:17*
brought men
his sons *d.* to him *as* he   *Ge 50:12*
commanded
d. as Lord commanded   *Ex 7:6;*
7:10, 20; 12:28, 50; 39:32; Le 8:4;
16:34; 24:23; Nu 1:54; 2:34; 20:27;
  27:22; 31:31
as he *d.* with the bullock   *Le 4:20;*
  16:15
Balak *d. as* Balaam had   *Nu 23:2;*
spoken   *2:30*
as Israel *d.* to land of his   *De 2:12*
possession
as he *d.* to children of Esau   *De 2:22*
waters flowed over banks, as   *Jos 4:18*
d. before
as Lord your God *d.* to Red   *Jos 4:23*
sea
d. to king of Makkedah, *as*   *Jos 10:28*
d. to Jericho

Joshua *d.* to them *as* Lord   *Jos 11:9*
bade him
Gideon *d. as* Lord said to   *J'g 6:27*
him
as they *d.* to me, so I have   *J'g 15:11*
done to them
as what the king *d.* pleased   *2Sa 3:36*
people
David *d.* so *as* Lord   *2Sa 5:25*
commanded him
elders *d. as* Jezebel had   *1Ki 21:11*
sent to them
Ahab *d.* according *as d.* the   *1Ki 21:26*
Amorites
Jehoram, *as d.* house of   *2Ki 8:18*
Ahab
as *d.* heathen which Lord   *2Ki 17:11*
carried
as *d.* their fathers, so do   *2Ki 17:41*
they to this day
David *d. as* God   *1Ch 14:16*
commanded him
d. as it is written in law of   *2Ch 25:4*
Moses
seek me *as* nation that *d.*   *Isa 58:2*
righteousness
Daniel gave thanks *as* he *d.*   *Da 6:10*
Joseph *d. as* angel had   *M't 1:24*
bidden him
d. as Jesus commanded   *M't 21:6;*
them   *26:19*
took money, so *d. as* were   *M't 28:15*
taught
consume them even *as* Elias   *Lu 9:54*
d.
thro' ignorance did it, *as d.*   *Ac 3:17*
rulers
resist Holy Ghost, *as* fathers   *Ac 7:51*
d. so do ye
God gave them like gift, *as*   *Ac 11:17*
d. to us
ceased from works, *as* God   *Heb 4:10*
d. from his

DID EVIL

he will requite us *evil* we *d.*   *Ge 50:15*
him
forgive brethren, for they *d.*   *Ge 50:17*
thee *evil*
d. evil in sight of the Lord   *J'g 2:11;*
3:7, 12; 4:1; 6:1; 10:6; 13:1; 1Ki 14:22;
15:26, 34; 16:7, 30; 2Ki 8:27; 13:2, 11;
14:24; 15:9, 18, 24, 28; 17:2; 2Ch 22:4
Solomon *d. evil* in sight of   *1Ki 11:6*
Lord
Manasseh *d. evil*   *2Ki 21:2; 2Ch 33:2*
Rehoboam, Jehoahaz,   *2Ki 23:32;*
Jehoiakim, Zedekiah   *2Ki 23:37;*
d. evil   *24:9, 19; 2Ch 12:14; 33:2, 22*
after they had rest, they *d.*   *Ne 9:28*
evil
understood *evil* that Eliashib *d.*   *Ne 13:7*
for Tobiah
d. evil before mine eyes   *Isa 65:12;*
  66:4
Alexander copper smith *d.*   *2Ti 4:14*
much *evil*

DID NOT

midwives *d. not* as king   *Ex 1:17*
commanded
Ahaz *d. not* what was right   *2Ki 16:2;*
  2Ch 28:1
d. not your fathers, *d. not*   *Ne 13:18*
our God
commanded to do, but they   *Jer 11:8*
d. not
God repented of evil, and *d.*   *Jon 3:10*
not
he *d. not* many mighty   *M't 13:58*
works there
d. it *not* to one of these, ye   *M't 25:45*
d. it *not* to me
ye seek to kill me, this *d.*   *Joh 8:40*
not Abraham
I *d.* it *not* for his cause had   *2Co 7:12*
done

DID SO

did Noah, as God commanded   *Ge 6:22*
so d. he
Jacob *d. so,* and fulfilled her   *Ge 29:28*
week
bring youngest brother, they   *Ge 42:20*
d. so
as Lord commanded *so d.*   *Ex 7:6;*

they	7:10; 12:28, 50; 39:32; 40:16;
	Nu 1:54
magicians d. so	Ex 7:22; 8:7, 18
Lord d. so	Ex 7:24; J'g 6:40
Moses and Joshua d. so	Ex 17:6;
	40:16
Aaron d. so	Nu 8:3
so d. the daughters of	Nu 36:10
Zelophehad	
compassed city, so they d. six	Jos 6:14
days	
so d. Moses command, so d.	Jos 11:15
Joshua	
they d. not so	J'g 2:17
as he d. so year by year	1Sa 1:7
so they d. in Shiloh to all	1Sa 2:14
Israelites	
so d. David, so will be his	1Sa 27:11
manner	
so d. he in Beth-el,	1Ki 12:32
sacrificing	
Jeroboam's wife d. so, went	1Ki 14:4
to Shiloh	
so they d.	Ezr 6:13
but so d. not I	Ne 5:15
Isaiah d. so, walking naked	Isa 20:2
and barefoot	
Jeremiah d. so	Jer 33:12; Eze 12:7
Jesus arose, and so d. his	M't 9:19
disciples	
stretch forth hand, and he d.	Lu 6:10
so	
so d. their fathers to the false	Lu 6:26
prophets	
followed Jesus, and so d.	Joh 18:15
another	
seven sons of Sceva who d.	Ac 19:14
so	

THUS DID

to fill their sacks, thus d. he	Ge 42:25
thus d. he to both of them	Ex 36:29
in corners	
thus d. your fathers when I	Nu 32:8
sent them	
thus d. he to all cities of	2Sa 12:31
Ammon	
thus d. Urijah the priest	2Ki 16:16
thus they d. day by day	2Ch 24:11
thus d. Hezekiah	2Ch 31:20
throughout all Judah	
d. not your fathers thus	Ne 13:18
sanctified them, thus d. Job	Job 1:5
continually	

DIDDEST

thou d. to the Egyptian	Ac 7:28

DIDST

thou d. this in integrity of	Ge 20:6
thy heart	
do as thou d. to Sihon	Nu 21:34;
	De 3:2
do as thou d. to Jericho and	Jos 8:2
her king	
and d. not call us to go with	J'g 12:1
thee	
man of God which thou d.	J'g 13:8
send come	
thou d. it secretly, but I	2Sa 12:12
will do	
greater than other thou d.	2Sa 13:16
to me	
that thou d. to David my	1Ki 2:44
father	
d. well that it was in thy	1Ki 8:18;
heart	2Ch 6:8
For thou d. separate them	1Ki 8:53
from among	
wonders that thou d. among	Ne 9:17
them	
I was dumb, because thou d.	Ps 39:9
it	
fathers told us what work	Ps 44:1
thou d. in their	
when d. terrible things not	Isa 64:3
looked for	
Sir, d. not thou sow good	M't 13:27
seed in thy	
wilt thou kill me as d.	Ac 7:28
Egyptian	

DIDYMUS

Thomas, who is called D.	Joh 11:16;
	20:24; 21:2

DIE

every thing in earth shall d.	Ge 6:17
if men over drive them, all	Ge 33:13
flock will d.	
fish that is in the river shall	Ex 7:18
d.	
nothing d. that is children's of	Ex 9:4
Israel	
day thou seest my face thou	Ex 10:28
shalt d.	
all first born in land of	Ex 11:5
Egypt shall d.	
if any beast of which ye	Le 11:39
may eat d.	
they shall bear sin, they shall	Le 20:20
d. childless	
not touch holy thing, lest	Nu 4:15
they d.	
when holy things are covered,	Nu 4:20
lest they d.	
if any man d. very suddenly by	Nu 6:9
him	
in this wilderness, and they	Nu 14:35
shall d.	
if these d. common death of	Nu 16:29
all men	
cometh near tabernacle	Nu 17:13;
shall d.	18:22
come near, neither they, nor	Nu 18:3
you also d.	
strip Aaron, he shall d. on	Nu 20:26
Hor	
let me d. the death of the	Nu 23:10
righteous	
if a man d. and have no son	Nu 27:8
shalt stone them that they d.	De 17:5;
	22:21, 24
that man shall d.	De 17:12;
18:20; 22:22, 25; 24:3,	7; 25:5;
	M'k 12:19
to Moses, thy days approach	De 31:14
that thou d.	
behold land of Canaan, and	De 32:50
d. in the mount	
d. alone because of	Jos 22:20
wickedness (B)	
Samson said, Let me d. with	J'g 16:30
Philistines	
all increase of thy house	1Sa 2:33
shall d.	
two sons, in one day they	1Sa 2:34
shall d. both	
people said to Saul, Shall	1Sa 14:45
Jonathan d.	
nor if half of us d. will they	2Sa 18:3
care	
when feet enter city, child	1Ki 14:12
shall d.	
thou shalt d. and not live	2Ki 20:1;
	Isa 38:1
fathers not d. for children,	2Ch 25:4;
but every man d. for his own	Jer 31:30
sin	
his wife said, Curse God and	Job 2:9
d.	
excellency goeth away, d.	Job 4:21
without wisdom	
ye are the people, wisdom d.	Job 12:2
with you	
though the stock thereof d.	Job 14:8
in ground	
man d. shall he live again	Job 14:14
in a moment shall d. people	Job 34:20
be troubled	
if obey not, d. without	Job 36:12
knowledge	
they d. in youth, life is	Job 36:14
among unclean	
he seeth that wise men d.	Ps 49:10
also fool	
takest away their breath,	Ps 104:29
they d.	
but fools d. for want of	Pr 10:21
wisdom	
why shouldest thou d. before	Ec 7:17
time	
living know they shall d. but	Ec 9:5
dead know	
ball in large country, there	Isa 22:18
shalt d.	
they that dwell therein d. in	Isa 51:6
like manner	
should be afraid of a man	Isa 51:12
that shall d.	
the child shall d. a hundred	Ec 65:20
years old	
punish them, young men d.	Jer 11:22

by sword, sons and daughters	
d. by famine	
d. of grievous deaths, not	Jer 16:4
lamented	
both great and small d. in	Jer 16:6
this land	
thus saith Lord, This year	Jer 28:16
thou shalt d.	
shalt d. in peace, and with	Jer 34:5
burnings	
soul that sinneth, it shall d.	Eze 18:4;
	18:20
d. deaths of them that are	Eze 28:8
slain	
thou shalt d. deaths of	Eze 28:10
uncircumcised	
that wicked man shall d. in	Eze 33:8
his iniquity	
they in caves shall d. of	Eze 33:27
pestilence	
Moab shall d. with tumult	Am 2:2
if ten men in one house they	Am 6:9
shall d.	
Amos saith, Jeroboam shall d.	Am 7:11
by sword	
thou shalt d. in a polluted	Am 7:17
land	
sinners of my people shall d.	Am 9:10
by sword	
then said I, that that dieth,	Zec 11:9
let it d.	
two parts shall be cut off	Zec 13:8
and d.	
d. in the water (A)	M't 8:32
he that curseth, let him d.	M't 15:4;
the death	M'k 7:10
if man d. having no seed	M't 22:24;
	Lu 20:28
will d. by the sword	M't 26:52
(A)(N)(P)	
nor can they d. any more	Lu 20:36
may not d. (N)	Joh 3:16
Sir, come down ere my child	Joh 4:49
d.	
they shall never d. (P)	Joh 10:28
that one man d. for the	Joh 11:50;
people	18:14
prophesied Jesus should d.	Joh 11:51
for that nation	
except corn of wheat d. but	Joh 12:24
if it d. it	
d. without reference to law	Ro 2:12
(P)	
scarcely for righteous man	Ro 5:7
will one d.	
as in Adam all d. so in	1Co 15:22
Christ	
what sowest is not	1Co 15:36
quickened except it d.	
here men that d. receive	Heb 7:8
tithes	
blessed are dead that d. in	Re 14:13
Lord	

HE DIE

he said, Lest he d. as	Ge 38:11
brethren did	
when he seeth lad not with	Ge 44:31
us he will d.	
he that smiteth a man that	Ex 21:12
he d.	
take him from mine altar,	Ex 21:14
that he may d.	
smite his servant, he d.	Ex 21:20
under his hand	
if thief be found and smitten	Ex 22:2
that he d.	
if he smite him so that he	Nu 35:16;
d. 35:20-21, 23; De 13:10;	19:5, 11;
	21:21
wherewith he may d.	Nu 35:17;
	18:23; De 19:12
let him return, lest he d.	De 20:5;
	20:6-7
bring out thy son that he	J'g 6:30
may d.	
retire from him that he may	2Sa 11:15
d.	
if wickedness be in him, he	1Ki 1:52
shall d.	
days of David drew nigh he	1Ki 2:1
should d.	
Elijah requested for himself	1Ki 19:4
he might d.	
carry out and stone him	1Ki 21:10
that he may d.	
when shall he d. and his	Ps 41:5
name perish	

he shall *d.* without instruction *Pr 5:23*
he that hateth reproof shall *Pr 15:10*
d.
but *he* that despiseth his *Pr 19:16*
ways shall *d.*
he shall *d.* whither they led *Jer 22:12*
him captive
take Jeremiah out of *Jer 38:10*
dungeon before *he d.*
if thou warn wicked, *he* *Eze 3:19;*
shall *d.* in his iniquity *3:20; 18:18, 24,*
       26; 33:9, 13, 18
shall not see it, though *he* *Eze 12:13*
shall *d.* there
in the midst of Babylon *he* *Eze 17:16*
shall *d.*
signifying what death *he* *Joh 12:33;*
should *d.* *18:32*

I DIE

lest some evil take me, and *Ge 19:19*
I d.
Isaac said, Lest *I d.* for her *Ge 26:9*
that my soul may bless thee *Ge 27:4*
before *I d.*
Rachel said, Give me children, *Ge 30:1*
or else *I d.*
I will go and see him before *Ge 45:28*
I d.
Israel said, to Joseph, Behold, *Ge 48:21*
I d.
Joseph said to his brethren, *I* *Ge 50:5;*
d. *50:24*
but *I* must *d.* in this land *De 4:22*
now *I d.* for thirst, and fall *J'g 15:18*
into
where thou diest will *I d.* *Ru 1:17*
I did but taste, and lo, *I* *1Sa 14:43*
must *d.*
that *I* may *d.* in mine own *2Sa 19:37*
city
here said, Nay, but *I* will *d.* *1Ki 2:30*
here
I said, *I* shall *d.* in my nest *Job 29:18*
and multiply
two things, deny me not *Pr 30:7*
before *I d.*
cause me not to return, lest *Jer 37:20*
I d.
I should *d.* with thee *M't 26:35;*
       M'k 14:31
I protest by rejoicing, *I d.* *1Co 15:31*
daily

NOT DIE

we may live and *not d.* *Ge 42:2;*
       43:8; 47:19
your words be verified, ye *Ge 42:20*
shall *not d.*
he *d. not,* but keepeth his *Ex 21:18*
bed
his sound shall be heard, *Ex 28:35*
that he *d. not*
wash with water, that they *Ex 30:20;*
d. not *30:21*
keep charge of Lord that ye *Le 8:35*
d. not
that they *d. not* *Le 15:31;*
       Nu 4:19; 17:10
come not at all times, that he *Le 16:2*
d. not
cloud cover mercy seat, that *Le 16:13*
he *d. not*
that the manslayer, *d. not* *Nu 35:12;*
       Jos 20:9
nor let me see this fire, that *De 18:16*
I d. not
let Reuben live and *not d.* let *De 33:6*
not his men
fear, not, thou shalt *not d.* *J'g 6:23;*
1Sa 20:2; 2Sa 12:13; 19:23; Jer 38:24
pray to Lord that we *d. not* *1Sa 12:19*
shew me kindness of Lord *1Sa 20:14*
that I *d. not*
take you, that ye live and *2Ki 18:32*
not d.
fathers shall *not d.* for *2Ch 25:4*
children
I shall *not d.* but live, and *Ps 118:17*
declare
if beatest him with rod, he *Pr 23:13;*
shall *not d.* *Eze 18:17, 21, 28; 33:15;*
       Joh 21:23
that he should *not d.* in the *Isa 51:14*
pit
worm *not d.* nor fire *Isa 66:24*
quenched

that thou *d. not* by our *Jer 11:21*
hand
Zedekiah, thou shalt *not d.* *Jer 34:4*
by sword
to slay souls that should *Eze 13:19*
not d.
we shall *not d.* Lord thou *Hab 1:12*
hast ordained
man may eat thereof, and *Joh 6:50*
not d.
saying that that disciple *Joh 21:23*
should *not d.*

SURELY DIE

thou shalt *surely d.* *Ge 2:17;*
20:7; 1Sa 14:44; 22:16; 1Ki 2:37, 42;
      Jer 26:8; Eze 3:18; 33:8, 14
the serpent said, Ye shall not *Ge 3:4*
surely d.
the Lord had said, They shall *Nu 26:65*
surely d.
surely d. because we have *J'g 13:22*
seen
he shall *surely d.* *1Sa 14:39;*
20:31; 2Sa 12:5; 2Ki 8:10; Eze 18:13
child born to thee shall *2Sa 12:14*
surely d.
not come down, but *surely d.* *2Ki 1:4*
       1:6, 16

TO DIE

Esau said, I am at the point *Ge 25:32*
to d.
to d. in the wilderness *Ex 14:11;*
       Nu 21:5
not testify against any, to *Nu 35:30*
cause *to d.*
Lord smite him, or his day *1Sa 26:10*
come *to d.*
ye are worthy *to d.* *1Sa 26:16*
because ye kept not
layest snare for my life, to *1Sa 28:9*
cause me *to d.*
to give yourselves *to d.* by *2Ch 32:11*
famine
preserve those that are *Ps 79:11*
appointed *to d.*
I am afflicted and ready *to d.* *Ps 88:15*
time to be born, and a time *to* *Ec 3:2*
d.
worthy *to d.* *Jer 26:11; 26:16*
he is like *to d.* for hunger in *Jer 38:9*
the place
to return to Jonathan's house *Jer 38:26*
to d. there
it is better for me *to d.* than *Jon 4:3;*
live *4:8*
Jonah fainted, and wished in *Jon 4:8*
himself *to d.*
centurion's servant ready *to d.* *Lu 7:2*
have a law, by our law *Joh 19:7*
ought *to d.*
I am ready also *to d.* at *Ac 21:13*
Jerusalem
if worthy of death I refuse *Ac 25:11*
not *to d.*
not manner of Romans to *Ac 25:16*
deliver *to d.*
for good man some would *Ro 5:7*
dare *to d.*
for it were better for me *to* *1Co 9:15*
d. than
you are in our hearts *to d.* *2Co 7:3*
and live
for me *to* live is Christ, *to* *Ph'p 1:21*
d. is gain
it is appointed to men once *Heb 9:27*
to d.
things that remain, ready *to d.* *Re 3:2*
men desire *to d.,* and death *Re 9:6*
shall flee

WE DIE

why should *we d.* in thy *Ge 47:15;*
presence *47:19*
than that *we* should *d.* in *Ex 14:12*
wilderness
let not God speak, lest *we* *Ex 20:19;*
d. *De 5:25*
we d. we perish, we all *Nu 17:12*
perish
that *we* and our cattle should *Nu 20:4*
d. there
pray for servants, that *we* *1Sa 12:19*
d. not
we must needs *d.* and are *2Sa 14:14*
as water

I dress it, that *we* may eat *1Ki 17:12*
it and *d.*
why sit we here till *we d.* *2Ki 7:3; 7:4*
if they kill us, *we* shall but *d.* *2Ki 7:4*
for to-morrow *we* shall *d.* *Isa 22:13;*
       1Co 15:32
let us go that *we* may *d.* *Joh 11:16*
with him
whether *we d. we d.* unto the *Ro 14:8*
Lord

YE DIE

neither touch it, lest *ye d.* *Ge 3:3*
neither rend clothes, lest *ye* *Le 10:6*
shall not go out from door, *Le 10:7*
lest *ye d.*
nor pollute holy things, lest *Nu 18:32*
ye d.
but *ye* shall *d.* like men, and *Ps 82:7*
fall
this iniquity not be purged *Isa 22:14*
till *ye d.*
country, there shall *ye d.* *Jer 22:26;*
       42:16
for why will *ye d.* *Jer 27:13;*
       Eze 18:31; 33:11
know that *ye* shall *d.* by the *Jer 42:22*
sword
seek me, and *ye* shall *d.* in *Joh 8:21;*
sins *8:24*
if ye live after the flesh *ye* *Ro 8:13*
shall *d.*

DIED

all flesh *d.* *Ge 7:21; 7:22*
died (S) *Ge 25:8;*
25:17; 35:29; 49:33; Job 10:18; 13:19;
La 1:19; Jer 15:9; M't 22:25; Ac 5:5, 10
the king of Egypt *d.* *Ex 2:23*
would to God we had *d.* by *Ex 16:3;*
hand of Lord in Egypt *Nu 14:2; 20:3;*
       26:10
Nadab and Abihu *d.* before *Le 10:2;*
the Lord *16:1; Nu 3:4; 26:61; 1Ch 24:2*
searchers of the land *d.* by *Nu 14:37*
plague
now they that *d.* beside *Nu 16:49*
them that *d.*
Miriam *d.;* much people of *Nu 20:1;*
Israel *d.* *21:6*
Aaron *d.* *Nu 20:28;*
       33:38-39; De 10:6; 32:50
those that *d.* in the plague *Nu 25:9*
were 24,000
the children of Korah *d.* not *Nu 26:11*
our father *d.* in his own sin *Nu 27:3*
Moses *d.,* was 120 years *De 34:5;*
when he *d.* *34:7*
all the men of war *d.* by the *Jos 5:4*
way
they were more which *d.* *Jos 10:11*
with hailstones
Joshua the son of Nun *d.* *Jos 24:29;*
       J'g 2:8
Eleazar son of Aaron *d.* *Jos 24:33;*
       1Ch 23:22
Adonibezek Othniel, Gibeon, *J'g 1:7;*
Tola, Jair *d.* *3:11; 8:32; 10:2, 5*
all the men of the tower of *J'g 9:49*
Shechem *d.*
Jephthah judged Israel six *J'g 12:7*
years, then *d.*
Ibzan, Elon, Abdon, *J'g 12:12;*
Elimelech, Mahlon, Chilion *12:11-15;*
d. *Ru 1:2*
that *d.* not were smitten with *1Sa 5:12*
the emerods
Nabal's heart *d.* within him *1Sa 25:1*
there he *d.* before the Lord *2Sa 6:7;*
       1Ch 13:10
king of children of Ammon *2Sa 10:1;*
d. *1Ch 19:1*
seventh day child *d.* feared *2Sa 12:18*
to tell David
Ahithophel hanged himself *2Sa 17:23*
and *d.*
would to God I had *d.* for *2Sa 18:33*
thee
we had *d.* this day, it had *2Sa 19:6*
pleased thee
d. of people from Dan to *2Sa 24:15*
Beersheba
this woman's child *d.* in the *1Ki 3:19*
night
when she came to threshold *1Ki 14:17*
child *d.*

Zimri, Tibni, Ahab d.   1Ki 16:18
                              16:22; 22:35, 37
he sat on her knees till noon   2Ki 4:20
and d.
Ahaziah fled to Megiddo and   2Ki 9:27
d. there
Elisha, Hazael king of   2Ki 13:14;
Syria d.   13:20, 24
Jehoahaz came to Egypt   2Ki 23:34
and d. there
but Seled d. without children   1Ch 2:30
Jether, Asa d.   1Ch 2:32;
                                  2Ch 16:13
armour-bearer fell on his   1Ch 10:5;
sword and d.   10:13
Jehoiada was full of days   2Ch 24:15
when he d.
when he d. he said, The   2Ch 24:22
Lord look on it
why d. I not from the womb   Job 3:11
so Job d. being old and full   Job 42:17
of days
in year that king Uzziah d. I   Isa 6:1
saw Lord
in year king Ahaz d. was   Isa 14:28
this burden
Hananiah, Pelatiah d.   Jer 28:17;
                                  Eze 11:13
I spake in morning at even   Eze 24:18
my wife d.
but when he offended in   Ho 13:1
Baal, he d.
married and d.   M't 22:25
(A)(B)(N)(P)(R)
woman d.   M't 22:27;
                         M'k 12:22; Lu 20:32
d. between altar and   Lu 11:51
sanctuary (P)
beggar d. rich man also d.   Lu 16:22
had been here, my brother   Joh 11:21;
not d.   11:32
caused that this man should   Joh 11:37
not have d.
in those days Dorcas was   Ac 9:37
sick and d.
in due time Christ d. for   Ro 5:6;
ungodly   5:8
sin revived and I d.   Ro 7:9
it is Christ that d.   Ro 8:34
to this end Christ d. rose and   Ro 14:9
revived
brother for whom Christ d.   Ro 14:15;
                                  1Co 8:11
how that Christ d. for our   1Co 15:3
sins
those who have d.   1Co 15:18
(A)(N)(P)
if one d. for all, then were   2Co 5:14
all dead
live to him who d. for them   2Co 5:15
if we believe Jesus d. and   1Th 4:14
rose again
who d. for us that we   1Th 5:10
should live
he that despised Moses'   Heb 10:28
law d.
these d. in faith, not   Heb 11:13
having received
by faith Joseph when d.   Heb 11:22
made mention
third part of creatures which   Re 8:9
had life d.
many men d. of waters made   Re 8:11
bitter
every living soul d. in the sea Re 16:3

AND HE, SO HE,
THAT HE DIED

days of Adam 930 years and   Ge 5:5
he d.
Noah's days were 950 years,   Ge 9:29
and he d.
Jael smote nail into temple,   J'g 4:21
so he d.
Eli's neck brake and he d.   1Sa 4:18
people rescued Jonathan   1Sa 14:45
that he d. not
that the Lord smote Nabal   1Sa 25:38
that he d.
smote Abimelech that he d.   2Sa 11:21
stoned Adoram that he d.   1Ki 12:18;
                                 2Ch 10:18
so he d. according to the word   2Ki 1:17
of Lord
trod on him in gate and he   2Ki 7:17;
d.   7:20
spread cloth on his face, so   2Ki 8:15
that he d.

Lord struck Jeroboam and   2Ch 13:20
he d.
Jehoram's bowels fell out,   2Ch 21:19
so he d.
and he d. without children   Lu 20:29;
                                   20:30
Jacob d. in Egypt, he and   Ac 7:15
our fathers
for in that he d. he d. unto   Ro 6:10
sin once
that he d. for all, that they   2Co 5:15
who live

DIEST

where thou d. will I die and   Ru 1:17
be buried

DIET

for d. there was a continual   Jer 52:34
d. given him

DIETH

fat of beast that d. of itself   Le 7:24
not eat
what d. of itself shall not eat Le 22:8;
                                  De 14:21
when man d. in a tent all   Nu 19:14
be unclean
king said, Died Abner as a   2Sa 3:33
fool d.
him that d. in city shall   1Ki 14:11
dogs eat
d. in field fowls of air eat   1Ki 16:4;
                                   21:24
man d., wasteth away, gives   Job 14:10
up ghost
one d. in his full strength,   Job 21:23
being at ease
another d. in the bitterness   Job 21:25
of his soul
when he d. shall carry   Ps 49:17
nothing away
when wicked man d. his   Pr 11:7
expectation
how d. wise man? as the fool   Ec 2:16
as one d. so d. other, all one   Ec 3:19
breath
their fish stinketh and d. for   Isa 50:2
thirst
eateth of their eggs d. what   Isa 59:5
is crushed
nor eaten that which d. of   Eze 4:14
itself
committeth iniquity, and d.   Eze 18:26
in them
no pleasure in death of him   Eze 18:32
that d.
then said I, That that d. let it Zec 11:9
die
where their worm d. not   M'k 9:44;
                                  9:46, 48
Christ raised from dead d. no   Ro 6:9
more
none of us liveth and d. to   Ro 14:7
himself

DIFFER

maketh thee to d. from   1Co 4:7
another
who makes you superior (A)   1Co 4:7
who has made you   1Co 4:7
distinguished (B)
who makes you so important   1Co 4:7
(N)
makes you different from   1Co 4:7
everybody (P)
who sees anything different in   1Co 4:7
you (R)

DIFFERENCE

the Lord doth put a d.   Ex 11:7
between
distinguishes (B)   Ex 11:7
distinction between (E)(R)   Ex 11:7;
                          Le 10:10; 11:47; 20:25
And that ye may put d.   Le 10:10
between holy
make a distinction between   Le 10:10
(A)
distinguish between (B)   Le 10:10;
                                   20:25
d. between the unclean and   Le 11:47
the clean
discriminate between (B)   Le 11:47
shall therefore put d. between   Le 20:25

they have put no d.   Eze 22:26
between the
have they showed d.   Eze 22:26
between
the d. between the holy and   Eze 44:23
no d. between us and them   Ac 15:9
did not discriminate between   Ac 15:9
us (B)(E)
no distinction between us   Ac 15:9
(E)(R)
that believe: for there is no   Ro 3:22
d.
there is no distinction   Ro 3:22
(A)(B)(E)(N)(P)(R)
no d. between the Jew and   Ro 10:12
no distinction between Jew   Ro 10:12
and Greek (A)(B)(E)(N)(P)(R)
There is d. also between a   1Co 7:34
wife
have compassion, making a   Jude 22
d.

DIFFERENCES

there are d. of administrations 1Co 12:5
distinctive varieties of   1Co 12:5
service and ministration (A)
are distinctive ministries (B)   1Co 12:5
diversities of ministrations   1Co 12:5
(E)
varieties of service (N)(R)   1Co 12:5
different ways of serving   1Co 12:5
God (P)

DIFFERENT

d. kinds (A)(B)(R)   Le 19:19;
                          Es 1:7; Da 7:3, 7, 19, 24
different (S)   De 22:11;
                          25:13, 14; Es 1:7; 3:8; Lu 21:11
in every d. city (S)   2Ch 31:19
contrast. (S)   Eze 16:34
(A)(B)(E)(R)(S)
like to be d. (B)   Ro 2:8
who makes you d. (P)(R)   1Co 4:7
d. gifts (P)   1Co 12:4
d. ways of serving God (P)   1Co 12:5
d. men in different ways (P)   1Co 12:6
d. tongues (A)   1Co 12:28
d. ways God spoke (A)   Heb 1:1
d. washings (A)(P)   Heb 9:10
d., varied, alien teachings   Heb 13:9
(A)

DIFFERETH

for one star d. from   1Co 15:41
another star
a child, d. nothing from a   Ga 4:1
servant

DIFFERING

gifts d. according to the   Ro 12:6
grace

DIFFICULT

unbelieving and d. people   M't 17:17
(P)
live when things are d. (P)   Ph'p 4:12

DIFFICULTIES

those in d. (B)   1Sa 22:2
keep an eye on those who   Ro 16:17
make d. (P)(R)

DIFFICULTY

with d. (S)   M't 19:23; Ac 27:16
had d. in speaking (A)   M'k 7:32
with what d. (S)   M'k 10:23; Lu 18:24

DIG

if a man shall d. a pit, and   Ex 21:33
whose hills thou mayest d.   De 8:9
brass
thou shalt d. therewith, and   De 23:13
d. for it more than for hid   Job 3:21
treasures
and ye d. pit for your   Job 6:27
friend
yea, thou shalt d. about thee   Job 11:18
the dark they d. through   Job 24:16
houses
Son of man, d. now in the   Eze 8:8
wall

D. thou through the wall in   *Eze 12:5*
their
d. through the wall to carry   *Eze 12:12*
out
Though they *d.* into hell   *Am 9:2*
till I shall *d.* about it, and   *Lu 13:8*
dung it
I cannot *d.*; to beg I am   *Lu 16:3*
ashamed

DIGGED

unto me, that I have *d.* this   *Ge 21:30*
well
had *d.* in the days of   *Ge 26:15;*
Abraham   *26:18-19, 21-22, 25, 32*
their selfwill they *d.* down a   *Ge 49:6*
wall
in my grave which I have *d.*   *Ge 50:5*
for
the Egyptians *d.* round about   *Ex 7:24*
The princes *d.* the well   *Nu 21:18*
the nobles of the people *d.*   *Nu 21:18*
it
wells *d.* which thou diggedst   *De 6:11*
not
d. and drunk strange waters   *2Ki 19:24*
in the desert, and *d.* many   *2Ch 26:10*
wells
houses full of all goods, wells   *Ne 9:25*
d.
He made a pit, and *d.* it, and   *Ps 7:15*
cause they have *d.* for my   *Ps 35:7*
soul
they have *d.* a pit before me   *Ps 57:6*
until the pit be *d.* for the   *Ps 94:13*
wicked
The proud have *d.* pits for   *Ps 119:85*
me
it shall not be pruned, nor *d.*   *Isa 5:6*
on all hills that shall be *d.*   *Isa 7:25*
with
I have *d.* and drunk water   *Isa 37:25*
hole of the pit whence ye are   *Isa 51:1*
d.
Then I went to Euphrates,   *Jer 13:7*
and *d.*
they have *d.* a pit for my   *Jer 18:20*
soul
they have *d.* a pit to take   *Jer 18:22*
me
and when I had *d.* in the wall   *Eze 8:8*
in the even I *d.* through the   *Eze 12:7*
wall
and *d.* a winepress in it,   *M't 21:33*
and built
and *d.* in the earth, and hid   *M't 25:18*
and *d.* a place for the   *M'k 12:1*
winevat
d. deep, and laid the   *Lu 6:48*
foundation
and *d.* down thine altars   *Ro 11:3*

DIGGEDST

wells digged, which thou *d.*   *De 6:11*
not

DIGGETH

An ungodly man *d.* up evil   *Pr 16:27*
Whoso *d.* a pit shall fall   *Pr 26:27*
therein
He that *d.* a pit shall fall into   *Ec 10:8*
it

DIGNITARIES

revile *d.* (A)   *2Pe 2:10*

DIGNITIES

are not afraid to speak evil   *2Pe 2:10*
of *d.*
dominion, and speak evil of *d.*   *Jude 8*

DIGNITY

the excellency of *d.* and the   *Ge 49:3*
What honour and *d.* has been   *Es 6:3*
done
what honor or distinction has   *Es 6:3*
been (A)(B)
Folly is set in great *d.* and   *Ec 10:6*
d. shall proceed of themselves   *Hab 1:7*
stripped himself of all   *Ph'p 2:7*
privileges and rightful *d.* (A)(P)
under control with true *d.*   *1Ti 3:4*
(A)(B)

DIKLAH

And Hadoram, and Uzal,   *Ge 10:27*
and *D.*
Hadoram also, and Uzal,   *1Ch 1:21*
and *D.*

DILATORY

he is not *d.* (P)   *2Pe 3:9*

DILEAN

and *D.* and Mizpeh, and   *Jos 15:38*
Joktheel

DILIGENCE

Keep thy heart with all *d.*;   *Pr 4:23*
for out
keep heart with all vigilance   *Pr 4:23*
(A)(R)
Above all that you guard,   *Pr 4:23*
watch over your heart (B)
way, give *d.* that thou   *Lu 12:58*
mayest be
make diligent effort to settle   *Lu 12:58*
(A)(N)(R)
give him on way there his   *Lu 12:58*
earned profit (B)
do your best to come to   *Lu 12:58*
terms with him (P)
he that ruleth, with *d.*; he   *Ro 12:8*
that
gives aid and superintends   *Ro 12:8*
with zeal and singleness of mind
(A)
the leader in his deep interest   *Ro 12:8*
(B)
exert yourself to lead (N)   *Ro 12:8*
who wields authority think of   *Ro 12:8*
his responsibility (P)
he who gives aid, with zeal   *Ro 12:8*
(R)
and knowledge, and in all *d.*   *2Co 8:7*
thy *d.* to come shortly unto   *2Ti 4:9*
me
Make every effort to come to   *2Ti 4:9*
me (A)
Make haste to visit me soon   *2Ti 4:9*
(B)
Do your best to join me   *2Ti 4:9*
soon (N)(P)(R)
Do thy *d.* to come before   *2Ti 4:21*
winter
the same *d.* to the full   *Heb 6:11*
assurance
evidence the same   *Heb 6:11*
earnestness (B)(R)
show the same eager   *Heb 6:11*
concern (N)
show a similar keenness to   *Heb 6:11*
grasp (P)
giving all *d.* add to your faith   *2Pe 1:5*
give *d.* to make your calling   *2Pe 1:10*
be all the more solicitous   *2Pe 1:10*
and eager (A)
exert yourselves the more   *2Pe 1:10*
(B)(N)
Set your minds on endorsing   *2Pe 1:10*
by conduct (P)
be zealous to confirm your   *2Pe 1:10*
call (R)
when I gave all *d.* to write   *Jude 3*
unto
my whole cncern was to write   *Jude 3*
to you (A)
I am making every effort to   *Jude 3*
write to you (B)
I was fully engaged in writing   *Jude 3*
(N)
I fully intended to write (P)   *Jude 3*
being very eager to write (R)   *Jude 3*

DILIGENT

judges shall make *d.*   *De 19:18*
inquisition
judges make careful inquiry   *De 19:18*
(B)
d. heed to do the   *Jos 22:5*
commandment
be very careful to obey (B)   *Jos 22:5*
take good care to observe   *Jos 22:5*
(R)
they accomplish a *d.* search   *Ps 64:6*
accomplished a   *Ps 64:6*
well-devised plan (A)(B)
thought out cunningly   *Ps 64:6*
conceived plot (R)

heart: and my spirit made *d.*   *Ps 77:6*
search
the hand of the *d.*   *Pr 10:4*
maketh rich
The hand of the *d.* shall   *Pr 12:24*
bear rule
substance of a *d.* man is   *Pr 12:27*
precious
the soul of the *d.* shall be   *Pr 13:4*
made fat
d. to discipline (R)   *Pr 13:24*
The thoughts of the *d.* tend   *Pr 21:5*
only to
thou a man *d.* in his   *Pr 22:29*
business
Be thou *d.* to know the state   *Pr 27:23*
of
make *d.* effort (A)(N)(R)   *Lu 12:58*
often proved *d.* in many   *2Co 8:22*
things
but now much more *d.* upon   *2Co 8:22*
I also was *d.* to do (S)   *Ga 2:10;*
  2Co 8:17
be *d.* in season (S)   *2Ti 4:2*
d. to come unto me to   *Tit 3:12*
Nicopolis
d. that ye may be found of   *2Pe 3:14*
him in
be eager to be found by   *2Pe 3:14*
him at peace (A)
do your utmost to be found   *2Pe 3:14*
at peace (B)(N)
make certain that such a day   *2Pe 3:14*
would find you at peace with
God and man (P)
be zealous to be found by   *2Pe 3:14*
him at peace (R)

DILIGENTLY

If thou wilt *d.* hearken to   *Ex 15:26*
the voice
if you will carefully listen   *Ex 15:26*
(B)
And Moses *d.* sought the   *Le 10:16*
goat of
Moses searched and searched   *Le 10:16*
(B)
keep thy soul *d.* lest thou   *De 4:9*
forget
be on guard and watch your   *De 4:9*
step (B)
teach them *d.* unto thy   *De 6:7*
children
shall impress them deeply   *De 6:7*
upon children (B)
Ye shall *d.* keep the   *De 6:17*
commandments
obey strictly the   *De 6:17*
commandments (B)
hearken *d.* unto my   *De 11:13*
commandments
For if ye shall *d.* keep all   *De 11:22*
these
make search, and ask *d.*   *De 13:14*
investigate and make   *De 13:14*
thorough inquiry (B)
hast heard of it, and   *De 17:4*
enquired *d.*
of leprosy, that thou observe   *De 24:8*
d.
exceedingly concerned to do   *De 24:8*
exactly (B)
be very careful to do   *De 24:8*
according to all (R)
if thou shalt hearken *d.* unto   *De 28:1*
did *d.* observe whether any   *1Ki 20:33*
thing
quickly catching his word   *1Ki 20:33*
(B)
quickly took it up from   *1Ki 20:33*
him (R)
let it be *d.* done for the   *Ezr 7:23*
house of
be completely provided for   *Ezr 7:23*
the house (B)
let it be done exactly for the   *Er 7:23*
house (E)
let it be done in full for the   *Ezr 7:23*
house (R)
seek *d.* (A)(B)(E)   *Job 8:5*
Hear *d.* my speech, and my   *Job 13:17*
listen attentively to what I   *Job 13:17*
say (B)
listen carefully to my words   *Job 13:17*
(R)
Hear *d.* my speech, and let   *Job 21:2*
this be
thou shalt *d.* consider his   *Ps 37:10*
place

look with care where he used to be (A)	Ps 37:10	See to it that no one fail to obtain (R)	Heb 12:15	**DIMLY**		
look for his location, it shall be gone (B)	Ps 37:10	have enquired and searched d.	1Pe 1:10	see in a mirror d. (R)	1Co 13:12	

DILIGENTLY

look with care where he used to be (A)	Ps 37:10
look for his location, it shall be gone (B)	Ps 37:10
look well at his place, he will not be (R)	Ps 37:10
us to keep thy precepts d.	Ps 119:4
d. to seek thy face, and I have	Pr 7:15
He that d. seeketh good procureth	Pr 11:27
ruler, consider d. what is before thee	Pr 23:1
he hearkened d. with much heed	Isa 21:7
hearken d. unto me, and eat ye that	Isa 55:2
Listen carefully to me (B)	Isa 55:2
and consider d. and see if there	Jer 2:10
carefully consider (A)(B)	Jer 2:10
examine with care (R)	Jer 2:10
if they will d. learn the ways	Jer 12:16
if ye d. hearken unto me, saith	Jer 17:24
will d. obey the voice of the Lord	Zec 6:15
of them d. what time the star	M't 2:7
accurately to the last point (A)	M't 2:7
ascertained from them just when (B)(N)(R)	M't 2:7
learned of them exactly what time (E)	M't 2:7
found out from them the exact time (P)	M't 2:7
search d. for the young child	M't 2:8
find out every particular about (B)	M't 2:8
search out exactly concerning (E)	M't 2:8
make a careful inquiry of the child (N)	M't 2:8
search with utmost care (P)	M't 2:8
had d. enquired of the wise men	M't 2:16
ascertained from the wise men (B)(N)(R)	M't 2:16
exactly learned of the wise men (E)	M't 2:16
careful questioning of the wise men (P)	M't 2:16
house, and seek d. till she find it	Lu 15:8
search carefully until she find it (B)	Lu 15:8
look in every corner till she found it (N)	Lu 15:8
search house from top to bottom (P)	Lu 15:8
he spake and taught d. the things	Ac 18:25
accurately things of (A)(B)(N)(P)(R)	Ac 18:25
d. in prayer (S)	Ro 12:12
d. followed every good work	1Ti 5:10
devoted to all kinds of good (B)(R)	1Ti 5:10
taken every opportunity doing good (N)	1Ti 5:10
conscientiously done all good (P)	1Ti 5:10
Rome, he sought me out very d.	2Ti 1:17
eagerly searched for and found me (B)(R)	2Ti 1:17
took pains to search me out (N)	2Ti 1:17
great deal of trouble to find me (P)	2Ti 1:17
and Apollos on their journey d.	Tit 3:13
reward of them that d. seek him	Heb 11:6
worth a man's while to seek him (P)	Heb 11:6
Looking d. lest any man fail of	Heb 12:15
see that no one falls back from and fails to secure God's grace (A)	Heb 12:15
See to it that no one falls short of divine grace (B)	Heb 12:15
See to it that no one forfeits grace (N)	Heb 12:15
Be careful that none of you fails to respond to the grace (P)	Heb 12:15
See to it that no one fail to obtain (R)	Heb 12:15
have enquired and searched d.	1Pe 1:10
searched and inquired earnestly (A)(R)	1Pe 1:10
pondered and explored grace (N)	1Pe 1:10
did their utmost to obtain this (P)	1Pe 1:10

DILL

scatter d. (A)(B)(R)	Eze 28:25; 28:27
mint, d., cummin (A)(B)(N)(R)	M't 23:23

DIM

was old, and his eyes were d.	Ge 27:1
the eyes of Israel were d. for age	Ge 48:10
his eye was not d. nor his	De 34:7
his eyes began to wax d. that	1Sa 3:2
his eyes were d. that he could	1Sa 4:15
his eyes were d. (S)	1Ki 14:4
eye also is d. by reason of sorrow	Job 17:7
of them that see shall not be d.	Isa 32:3
How is the gold become d.	La 4:1
for these things our eyes are d.	La 5:17

DIMINISH

waters continued to d. (A)	Ge 8:5
ye shall not d. ought thereof	Ex 5:8
not one less (B)	Ex 5:8
by no means lessen it (R)	Ex 5:8
d. your bricks (A)(E)(S)	Ex 5:19
duty of marriage, shall he not d.	Ex 21:10
marriage rights shall lessen (B)	Ex 21:10
thou shalt d. the price of it	Le 25:16
neither shall ye d. ought from it	De 4:2
nor take from it (B)(R)	De 4:2
not add thereto, nor d. from it	De 12:32
speak unto them; d. not a word	Jer 26:2
do not restrain one word (B)	Jer 26:2
do not hold back a word (R)	Jer 26:2
therefore will I also d. thee	Eze 5:11
cut you down without mercy (B)(R)	Eze 5:11
for I will d. them, that they shall	Eze 29:15

DIMINISHED

ought of your work shall be d.	Ex 5:11
output will not be reduced (B)	Ex 5:11
not be lessened in the least (R)	Ex 5:11
they were d. (A)(E)(R)	Ps 107:39
gotten by vanity shall be d.	Pr 13:11
will dwindle away (A)(B)(R)	Pr 13:11
children of Kedar, shall be d.	Isa 21:17
may be increased there, and not d.	Jer 29:6
multiply and do not decrease (B)(R)	Jer 29:6
and have d. thine ordinary food	Eze 16:27

DIMINISHING

and the d. of them the riches of	Ro 11:12
their stumbling, lapse, transgression enriched the world (A)	Ro 11:12
their misdemeanor means the world's enrichment (B)	Ro 11:12
their fall is the riches of world (E)	Ro 11:12
their offence means enrichment (N)	Ro 11:12
their failure enriched the world (P)	Ro 11:12
their trespass means riches of world (R)	Ro 11:12
never d. love (B)	Eph 6:24

DIMLY

see in a mirror d. (R)	1Co 13:12

DIMNAH

D. with her suburbs, Nahalal	Jos 21:35

DIMNESS

and darkness, d. of anguish	Isa 8:22
Gloom of anguish (A)(B)(E)(R)	Isa 8:22
the d. shall not be such as was	Isa 9:1
no gloom for her (A)(B)(E)(R)	Isa 9:1
blind see in spite of d. and darkness (B)	Isa 29:13

DIMON

waters of D. shall be full of blood	Isa 15:9
I will bring more upon D.	Isa 15:9

DIMONAH

Kinah, and D. and Adadah	Jos 15:22

DINAH

daughter, and called her name D.	Ge 30:21
D. the daughter of Leah	Ge 34:1; Ge 34:3, 5, 13, 26
Padan-aram, with his daughter D.	Ge 46:15

DINAH'S

Simeon, and Levi, D. brethren	Ge 34:25

DINAITES

the D., the Apharsathchites	Ezr 4:9

DINE

these men shall d. with me at noon	Ge 43:16
besought him to d. with him	Lu 11:37
invited him to take dinner (A)(N)(P)	Lu 11:37
them that d. (S)	Lu 14:10
saith unto them, Come and d.	Joh 21:12
Come and have breakfast (A)(B)(N)(P)(R)	Joh 21:12
come and break your fast (E)	Joh 21:12
d. with him (B)(P)	Re 3:20

DINED

So when they had d. Jesus saith	Joh 21:15
when they had eaten (A)	Joh 21:15
when they had breakfasted (B)	Joh 21:15
when they had broken fast (E)	Joh 21:15
when they had breakfast (P)(R)	Joh 21:15

DINETH

he that d. (S)	Lu 22:27

DINHABAH

and the name of his city was D.	Ge 36:32; 1Ch 1:43

DINING

d. with him (S)	M't 14:9

DINNER

dinner (A)(B)	Ge 19:3; 2Sa 3:20
made a d. (A)	Ge 26:30
is a d. of herbs where love is	Pr 15:17
Behold, I have prepared my d.	M't 22:4
invite him to take d. (A)(N)(P)	Lu 11:37

had not first washed before *Lu 11:38* d.

When thou makest a *d.* or a *Lu 14:12* supper

made a *d.* (N) *Lu 14:12; 14:16-17*

give a *d.* (B) *Lu 14:13*

DIONYSIUS

the which was *D.* the *Ac 17:34* Areopagite

DIOTREPHES

I wrote unto the church: but *D. 3Jo 9*

DIP

d. it in the blood that is in *Ex 12:22*

shall *d.* his finger in the blood *Le 4:6*

d. his finger in some of the *Le 4:17* blood

shall *d.* them and the living *Le 14:6* bird

the priest shall *d.* his right *Le 14:16* finger

d. them in the blood of the *Le 14:51* slain

and *d.* it in the water, and *Nu 19:18* sprinkle

and let him *d.* his foot in *De 33:24* oil

and *d.* thy morsel in the *Ru 2:14* vinegar

that he may *d.* the tip of his *Lu 16:24* finger

DIPPED

and *d.* the coat in the blood *Ge 37:31*

and he *d.* his finger in the *Le 9:9* blood

were *d.* in the brim of the *Jos 3:15* water

and *d.* it in an honeycomb, *1Sa 14:27* and put

d. himself seven times in *2Ki 5:14* Jordan

and *d.* it in water, and *2Ki 8:15* spread it on

thy foot may be *d.* in the *Ps 68:23* blood

give a sop when I have *d. Joh 13:26* it

had *d.* the sop, he gave it to *Joh 13:26* Judas

with a vesture *d.* in blood *Re 19:13*

DIPPETH

He that *d.* his hand with *M't 26:23* me in

that *d.* with me in the dish *M'k 14:20*

DIRECT

to *d.* his face unto Goshen *Ge 46:28*

will I *d.* my prayer unto thee *Ps 5:3*

him, and he shall *d.* thy paths *Pr 3:6*

of the perfect shall *d.* his way *Pr 11:5*

shall rectify, make plain his *Pr 11:5* way, and keep it straight (A)

maketh straight his way (B) *Pr 11:5*

keeps his way straight (R) *Pr 11:5*

but wisdom is profitable to *Ec 10:10* d.

wisdom helps him to succeed *Ec 10:10* (A)(R)

wisdom is advantage for *Ec 10:10* gaining success (B)

and I will *d.* all his ways *Isa 45:13*

and I will *d.* their work in *Isa 61:8* truth

give them their recompense *Isa 61:8* (A)(B)(E)(R)

man that walketh to *d.* his *Jer 10:23* steps

Christ, *d.* our way unto you *1Th 3:11*

guide our steps to you *1Th 3:11* (A)(P)

prepare our way to you (B) *1Th 3:11*

d. your hearts into the love *2Th 3:5* of God

DIRECTED

hath not *d.* his words *Job 32:14* against me

Who hath *d.* him (S) *Job 36:23*

ways were *d.* to keep thy *Ps 119:5* statutes

divinely *d.* decisions are (A) *Pr 16:10*

Who hath *d.* the spirit of *Isa 40:13* the Lord

I *d.* ancient people (B) *Isa 44:7*

our rulers who *d.* us (B) *Da 9:12*

d. his disciples (A) *M't 14:22*

as the Lord *d.* *M't 27:10* (A)(B)(N)(R)

Lord *d.* that (A)(B) *1Co 9:14*

DIRECTETH

He *d.* it under the whole *Job 37:3* heaven

way: but the Lord *d.* his steps *Pr 16:9*

as for the upright, he *d.* his *Pr 21:29* way

DIRECTION

it, by the *d.* of the lawgiver *Nu 21:18*

DIRECTIONS

I will give you *d.* (A)(R) *1Co 11:34*

give *d.* as to your duty (B) *Ph'm 8*

DIRECTLY

blood *d.* before the *Nu 19:4* tabernacle

even the way *d.* before the *Eze 42:12* wall

DIRECTS

where will of pilot *d.* (R) *Jas 3:4*

DIRGE

a *d.* of the desert (B) *Jer 9:10*

take up a *d.* (B) *Eze 19:1;* *Eze 19:14; 28:12; 32:2; Am 8:10*

DIRT

his belly; and the *d.* came out *J'g 3:22*

them out as the *d.* in the *Ps 18:42* streets

whose waters cast up mire *Isa 57:20* and *d.*

DIRTY

fling off *d.* clothes of (P) *Eph 4:22*

DIRTYMINDEDNESS

dirtymindedness (P) *Col 3:5*

a *d.* between those (N) *Ac 6:1*

DISAGREEING

d., quarrelsome (A) *Pr 25:24*

DISAGREEMENT

matters of *d.* (B) *De 17:8*

d. and discussion (A) *Ac 15:2*

a sharp *d.* (A) *Ac 15:39*

DISALLOW

if her father *d.* her in the *Nu 30:5* day that

DISALLOWED

her, because her father *d.* her *Nu 30:5*

forbidden by her father (B) *Nu 30:5;* *30:8*

her husband *d.* her on the *Nu 30:8* day that

her peace at her, and *d.* her *Nu 30:11* not

d. indeed of men, but chosen *1Pe 2:4* of

men tried to throw it away *1Pe 2:4* (A)

rejected by men *1Pe 2:4* (B)(E)(N)(P)(R)

the stone which the builders *1Pe 2:7* *d.*

builders rejected *1Pe 2:7* (A)(B)(E)(N)(P)(R)

DISANNUL

Wilt thou also *d.* my *Job 40:8* judgment

annul, set aside, render void *Job 40:8* (A)

discredit my justice (B) *Job 40:8*

annul my judgment (E) *Job 40:8*

will you even put me in the *Job 40:8* wrong (R)

purposed, and who shall *d. Isa 14:27* it

who will annul it *Isa 14:27* (A)(B)(E)(R)

years after, cannot *d.* that it *Ga 3:17*

cannot annul the covenant *Ga 3:17* (A)(B)(R)

it cannot be invalidated (N) *Ga 3:17*

cannot render null and void *Ga 3:17* (P)

DISANNULLED

covenant with death shall be *Isa 28:18* *d.*

covenant with death *Isa 28:18* annulled (A)(B)(E)(R)

DISANNULLETH

no man *d.* or addeth thereto *Ga 3:15*

no one sets it aside, makes it *Ga 3:15* void, or adds to it (A)(B)

no one maketh it void, or *Ga 3:15* addeth thereto (E)

no one can set it aside or *Ga 3:15* add a codicil (N)

can neither be disregarded *Ga 3:15* nor modified by a third party (P)

no one annuls or adds to it *Ga 3:15* (R)

DISANNULLING

verily a *d.* of the *Heb 7:18* commandment

command is cancelled (A) *Heb 7:18*

previous regulation is set *Heb 7:18* aside (B)(R)

earlier rules are cancelled *Heb 7:18* (N)

a definite cancellation of *Heb 7:18* previous commandment (P)

DISAPPEARS

cloud dissolves and *d.* (B) *Job 7:9*

it *d.* (A)(B) *Jas 4:14*

DISAPPOINT

Arise, O Lord, *d.* him, cast *Ps 17:13* him

Confront and forestall him *Ps 17:13* (A)

confront him (B)(E)(R) *Ps 17:13*

DISAPPOINTED

were bitterly *d.* (A)(B)(R) *Job 6:20*

Without counsel purposes are *Pr 15:22* *d.*

purposes are frustrated (A) *Pr 15:22*

plans go wrong (B)(R) *Pr 15:22*

d., put to shame (A)(E) *2Co 7:14*

DISAPPOINTETH

He *d.* the devices of the *Job 5:12* crafty

frustrates devices of crafty *Job 5:12* (A)(E)(R)

thwarts schemes of crafty *Job 5:12* (B)

DISAPPOINTS

hope never *d.* (A)(B)(P)(R) *Ro 5:5*

DISARMED

d. principalities and powers *Col 2:15* (R)

DISARMING

d. in wilderness (B) *Ps 78:40*

not *d.* your orders *Lu 15:29* (A)(N)(P)(R)

d. princes and authorities *Col 2:15* (B)

DISASTER

bring *d.* to nation (B)	Nu 32:15
d. has been decided upon	1Sa 25:17
(B)	
in his *d.* cry for help (R)	Job 30:24
I felt it (B)	Ps 40:7
the end sudden *d.* (B)	Ps 78:33
before haughtiness come *d.*	Pr 18:12
(A)	
d. shall come upon you (B)	Isa 47:11
d. upon *d.* (B)(R)	Eze 7:26
the day of his *d.* (E)	Ob 12
bring *d.* to (N)	Ro 14:15

DISASTROUS

suffered a *d.* defeat (B)	1Sa 4:17
impart *d.* heresies (N)	2Pe 2:1

DISBELIEVE

for those who *d.* (A)(E)	1Pe 2:7
they disobey and *d.*	1Pe 2:8
(A)(B)(N)	

DISCARD

d. old unrenewed self (A)	Eph 4:22

DISCARDED

d. cosmic powers (N).	Col 2:15

DISCERN

d. thou what is thine with me	Ge 31:32
search for what is yours (B)	Ge 31:32
point out what I have that is yours (R)	Ge 31:32
D. I pray thee, whose are these	Ge 38:25
look well, whose are the signet (B)(R)	Ge 38:25
lord the king to *d.* good and bad	2Sa 14:17
can I *d.* between good and evil	2Sa 19:35
distinguish (B)	2Sa 19:35; 1Ki 3:9; Job 4:16
I may *d.* between good and bad	1Ki 3:9
understanding to *d.* judgment	1Ki 3:11
the people could not *d.* the noise	Ezr 3:13
distinguish (B)(R)	Ezr 3:13; Eze 44:23; Mal 3:18
I could not *d.* the form thereof	Job 4:16
cannot my taste *d.* perverse things	Job 6:30
d. and comprehend words (A)(B)(E)	Pr 1:2
them to *d.* between the unclean	Eze 44:23
that cannot *d.* between their right	Jon 4:11
discriminate between (B)	Jon 4:11
do not know right hand from left (R)	Jon 4:11
and *d.* between the righteous	Mal 3:18
ye can *d.* the face of the sky	M't 16:3
interpret appearance of sky (A)(P)(R)	M't 16:3
distinguish looks of the sky (B)	M't 16:3
but can ye not *d.* the signs of the	M't 16:3
do you not *d.* (A)	M'k 7:18; 8:17
ye can *d.* the face of the sky	Lu 12:56
is it that ye do not *d.* this time	Lu 12:56
let others *d.* (E)	1Co 14:29
exercised to *d.* both good and evil	Heb 5:14
to discriminate and distinguish (A)	Heb 5:14
to distinguish between good and evil (B)(R)	Heb 5:14
to discriminate between good and evil (N)(P)	Heb 5:14

DISCERNED

he *d.* him not, because his hands	Ge 27:23
did not identify him (B)	Ge 27:23

did not recognize him (R)	Ge 27:23
and the king of Israel *d.*	1Ki 20:41
him that	
king of Israel recognized him (B)(R)	1Ki 20:41
I *d.* God had not sent (E)	Ne 6:12
I *d.* among the youths, a young	Pr 7:7
I perceived among the youths	Pr 7:7
(A)(B)(R)	
because they are spiritually *d.*	1Co 2:14
because they are estimated from a spiritual standpoint (B)	1Co 2:14
because they are spiritually judged (E)	1Co 2:14
to be judged in light of the Spirit (N)	1Co 2:14
the former is sharing God's wisdom (P)	1Co 2:14
if we *d.* ourselves (E)	1Co 11:31

DISCERNER

and is a *d.* of the thoughts	Heb 4:12
exposing, sifting, analyzing, and judging thoughts and purposes of heart (A)	Heb 4:12
skilled in judging the heart's ponderings and meditations (B)	Heb 4:12
sifts thoughts and purposes of heart (N)	Heb 4:12

DISCERNETH

and a wise man's heart *d.* both	Ec 8:5
wise man's mind will know both when and what to do (A)	Ec 8:5
wise man knows time and procedure (B)	Ec 8:5
will know the time and way (R)	Ec 8:5

DISCERNING

none as *d.* and wise (B)	Ge 41:39
a *d.* mind (A)(R)	1Ki 3:12
understand *d.* words (B)	Pr 1:2
the discernment of the *d.* (A)(E)	1Co 1:19
himself, not *d.* the Lord's body	1Co 11:29
without discriminating, recognizing with due appreciation Christ's body (A)	1Co 11:29
without due appreciation of the body (B)	1Co 11:29
blind to presence of Lord's body (N)	1Co 11:29
eats without *d.* (R)	1Co 11:29
to another *d.* of spirits; to another	1Co 12:10
ability to discern and distinguish between utterances of true and false spirits (A)(N)	1Co 12:10
discrimination between spirits (B)	1Co 12:10
to discriminate in spiritual matters (E)	1Co 12:10
distinguish between spirits (R)	1Co 12:10

DISCERNMENT

the *d.* of the discerning (A)(E)	1Co 1:19

DISCHARGE

and there is not *d.* in that war	Ec 8:8
no furlough during battle (B)	Ec 8:8

DISCHARGED

and will cause them to be *d.* there	1Ki 5:9
have them taken apart (B)	1Ki 5:9
be broken up there (E)(R)	1Ki 5:9

DISCHARGING

I am simply *d.* a trust (N)	1Pe 9:17

DISCIPLE

The *d.* is not above his master	M't 10:24; Lu 6:40
pupil (B)(N)	M't 10:24; 10:25
enough for *d.* that he be as his master	M't 10:25

give a cup of cold water to a *d.*	M't 10:42
made a *d.* (E)(P)	M't 13:52
Joseph of Arimathea himself was *d.*	M't 27:57
thou art his *d.* we are Moses' disciples	Joh 9:28
so did another *d.* that *d.* was known	Joh 18:15
then went out other *d.* that was known	Joh 18:16
d. standing by, whom Jesus loved	Joh 19:26
saith he to that *d.*, Behold, thy mother, that *d.* took	Joh 19:27
her to his own home	
being a *d.* but secretly, for fear of Jews	Joh 19:38
other *d.* whom Jesus loved	Joh 20:2; 21:7, 20
Peter went forth, and that other *d.* and came	Joh 20:3
the other *d.* did outrun Peter, and came first	Joh 20:4
then went in also that other *d.* and he saw	Joh 20:8
this saying, that that *d.* should not die	Joh 21:23
this is the *d.* which testifieth these things	Joh 21:24
there was a certain *d.* at Damascus	Ac 9:10
but they believed not that he was a *d.*	Ac 9:26
there was at Joppa a *d.* named Tabitha	Ac 9:36
certain *d.* was there, named Timotheus	Ac 16:1
an old *d.* with whom we should lodge	Ac 21:16

MY DISCIPLE

if hate not his life, cannot be *my d.*	Lu 14:26
doth not bear cross, cannot be *my d.*	Lu 14:27
forsaketh not all, cannot be *my d.*	Lu 14:33

DISCIPLES

then came to him the *d.* of John	M't 9:14
when he called his twelve *d.*	M't 10:1
made an end of commanding his *d.*	M't 11:1
when *d.* saw him walking on the sea	M't 14:26
when *d.* heard it, they fell on their face	M't 17:6
the *d.* rebuked them	M't 19:13; M'k 10:13
Jesus took twelve *d.* apart in way	M't 20:17
Jesus sent two *d.* saying, Go into village	M't 21:1
the Pharisees sent unto him their *d.*	M't 22:16
Jesus took bread, and gave it to *d.*	M't 26:26
I will not deny thee, likewise also said the *d.*	M't 26:35
then all the *d.* forsook them, and fled	M't 26:56
why do *d.* of John fast, but thy *d.* fast not	M'k 2:18; Lu 5:33
now *d.* had forgotten to take bread	M'k 8:14
d. began to rejoice and praise God	Lu 19:37
between John's *d.* and Jews	Joh 3:25
that Jesus baptized more *d.* than John	Joh 4:1
thou art his disciple, but we are Moses' *d.*	Joh 9:28
art not thou also one of this man's *d.*	Joh 18:25
Mary told *d.* that she had seen Lord	Joh 20:18
Saul breathing out slaughter against *d.*	Ac 9:1
Saul essayed to join himself to the *d.*	Ac 9:26
d. were called Christians first in Antioch	Ac 11:26
Paul came to Ephesus, finding certain *d.*	Ac 19:1

Paul would enter, *d.* suffered *Ac 19:30*
him not
first day of week *d.* came *Ac 20:7*
together break
men speaking, to draw away *Ac 20:30*
d. after them

HIS DISCIPLES

his d. came and awoke him *M't 8:25*
Jesus arose, followed, so did *M't 9:19*
his d.
go, and tell *his d.* He is *M't 28:7*
risen from dead
say *his d.* came by night *M't 28:13*
and stole him
in house *his d.* asked him *M'k 10:10*
again
Pharisees murmured against *Lu 5:30*
his d.
he lifted up eyes on *his d.* *Lu 6:20*
and said
teach us to pray, as John *Lu 11:1*
taught *his d.*
his glory, and *his d.* *Joh 2:11*
believed on him
Jesus himself baptized not, *Joh 4:2*
but *his d.*
upon this came *his d.* and *Joh 4:27*
marvelled
up to a mountain, there he *Joh 6:3*
sat with *his d.*
but that *his d.* were gone *Joh 6:22*
away alone
why hear it again? will ye be *Joh 9:27*
his d.
then said *his d.* If he sleep *Joh 11:12*
shall do well
went with *his d.* over brook *Joh 18:1*
Cedron
for Jesus often resorted *Joh 18:2*
thither with *his d.*
again, *his d.* were within, *Joh 20:26*
Thomas with

OF HIS DISCIPLES

John heard works of Christ, *M't 11:2;*
he sent two *of his d.* *M'k 11:1; 14:13;*
Lu 19:29
some *of his d.* eat with *M'k 7:2*
unwashen hands
that time many *of his d.* *Joh 6:66*
went back
the high priest asked Jesus *Joh 18:19*
of his d.
art not thou also one of *Joh 18:25*
his d.? he denied
none *of his d.* durst ask, *Joh 21:12*
Who art thou

TO HIS DISCIPLES

blessed, and gave loaves *to* *M't 14:19*
his d.
expounded all things *to his* *M'k 4:34*
d.
turned himself *to his d.* *Lu 10:23*
and said
third time Jesus shewed *Joh 21:14*
himself *to his d.*

MY DISCIPLES

bind up testimony, seal law *Isa 8:16*
among *my d.*
master saith, I will keep *M't 26:18;*
passover with *my d.* *M'k 14:14;*
Lu 22:11
then are ye *my d.* indeed *Joh 8:31;*
13:35
bear much fruit, so shall ye *Joh 15:8*
be *my d.*

THY DISCIPLES

why do we fast, *thy d.* fast *M't 9:14;*
not *M'k 2:18*
thy d. do which is not lawful *M't 12:2*
on sabbath
why do *thy d.* transgress the *M't 15:2*
tradition
I brought him to *thy d.* *M't 17:16*
could not cure
why walk not *thy d.* *M'k 7:5*
according to
I spake to *thy d.* to cast *M'k 9:18;*
him out *Lu 9:40*
Pharisees said, Master, *Lu 19:39*
rebuke *thy d.*

that *thy d.* may see works *Joh 7:3*
thou doest

DISCIPLES'

to wash the *d.* feet, and to *Joh 13:5*
wipe

DISCIPLINE

know my *d.* (R) *Nu 14:34*
correct, *d.* (A)(B)(R) *De 4:36*
d. of the Lord (R) *De 11:2*
then *d.* him (B) *De 21:18*
I have felt *d.* (B) *De 34:31*
He openeth also their ear *Job 36:10*
to *d.*
d. me (B) *Ps 6:1*
you hate *d.* (R) *Ps 50:17*
you *d.* and instruct (A)(B) *Ps 94:12*
I hated *d.* (B)(R) *Pr 5:12*
dies for lack of *d.* (B)(R) *Pr 5:23*
reproofs of *d.* (A)(B)(R) *Pr 6:23*
whoever loves *d.* loves *Pr 12:1*
(B)(R)
diligent to *d.* (R) *Pr 13:24*
severe *d.* (A)(B)(R) *Pr 15:10; 22:15*
d. your son (A)(B)(R) *Pr 19:18*
withhold not *d.* (A)(R) *Pr 23:13*
power, love *d.* (E)(N) *2Ti 1:7*
d. those in opposition *2Ti 2:25*
(B)(N)
train, correct, *d.* (A)(B)(R) *Heb 12:7*
left without *d.* (A)(N)(R) *Heb 12:8*
no *d.* brings joy *Heb 12:11*
(A)(B)(N)(R)
I *d.* and instruct *Re 3:19*
(A)(B)(N)(P)

DISCIPLINED

hast *d.* me (B) *Jer 31:18*
d. but not to death (B)(N) *2Co 6:9*
not *d.* by father (N) *Heb 12:7*
which *d.* us (A)(N)(R) *Heb 12:9*
d. us (A)(B)(N)(R) *Heb 12:10*

DISCIPLINES

d. his son (A)(B)(R) *De 8:5*
whom God *d.* (B) *Job 5:17*
d. and instructs (A)(B) *Ps 94:10*
d. and punishes (A) *Pr 13:24*
d. with (A)(B)(N)(P)(R) *Lu 6:11*
d. with (A)(N)(P)' *Lu 22:4*
he *d.* us (P) *1Co 11:32*
corrects and *d.* *Heb 12:6*
(A)(B)(N)(R)

DISCIPLINING

he is *d.* us (N) *1Co 11:32*

DISCLOSE

d. ourselves to them (E) *1Sa 14:8*
d. themselves (E) *1Sa 14:11*
d. secret to another (S) *Pr 25:9*
the earth also shall *d.* her *Isa 26:21*
blood
d. myself to him (N) *Joh 14:21; 14:22*
d. and expose aims *1Co 4:5*
(A)(N)(P)(R)

DISCLOSED

d. themselves to the *1Sa 14:11*
garrison (S)
nothing hid but shall be *d.* *Lu 8:17*
(A)(B)(E)(N)(P)(R)
God *d.* it to them (P) *Ro 1:19*
his love was *d.* (N) *1Jo 4:9*

DISCOMFIT

d. them with great *De 7:23*
discomfiture (E)
arrows *d.* them (E) *Ps 144:6*

DISCOMFITED

d. the host (A)(R) *Ex 14:24*
And Joshua *d.* Amalek and *Ex 17:13*
his
defeated Amalek (B) *Ex 17:13*
mowed down Amalek and *Ex 17:13*
his people (R)
smote them, and *d.* them, *Nu 14:45*
even

defeat (B) *Nu 14:45; Jos 10:10*
smote them and beat them *Nu 14:45*
down (E)
defeated them (R) *Nu 14:45*
And the Lord *d.* them *Jos 10:10*
before
And the Lord *d.* Sisera, and *J'g 4:15*
all his
confused them (B) *J'g 4:15*
routed Sisera (R) *J'g 4:15*
and Zalmunna, and *d.* all the *J'g 8:12*
host
routed the entire army (B) *J'g 8:12*
threw all the army into panic *J'g 8:12*
(R)
the Philistines, and *d.* them *1Sa 7:10*
confused them (B) *1Sa 7:10*
threw them into confusion *1Sa 7:10*
(R)
them: lightning, and *d.* *2Sa 22:15*
them
put them to flight (B) *2Sa 22:15*
routed them (R) *2Sa 22:15*
they were *d.* (R) *Job 32:15*
shot out lightnings, and *d.* *Ps 18:14*
them
and his young men shall be *Isa 31:8*
d.
young men put to bond *Isa 31:8*
service (B)
become subject to taskwork *Isa 31:8*
(E)
put to forced labor (R) *Isa 31:8*

DISCOMFITURE

discomfit them with great *d.* *De 7:23*
(E)
send *d.* (E) *De 28:20*
city of great *d.* (E) *1Sa 5:9*
deadly *d.* in city (E) *1Sa 5:11*
and there was a very great *1Sa 14:20*
d.
the confusion was terrible *1Sa 14:20*
(A)(B)(R)

DISCONTENTED

every one that was *d.* *1Sa 22:2*
those with grievances (B) *1Sa 22:2*

DISCONTINUE

And thou, even thyself, shalt *Jer 17:4*
d.
abandon your heritage (B) *Jer 17:4*
loosen your hand from *Jer 17:4*
heritage (R)

DISCORD

continually; he soweth *d.* *Pr 6:14*
that soweth *d.* among *Pr 6:19*
brethren
d. grew so bitter (B) *Ac 23:10*
a fomenter of *d.* (N) *Ac 24:5*
no division or *d.* *1Co 12:25*
(A)(B)(N)(R)

DISCOURAGE

d. ye the heart of the *Nu 32:7*
children of
turn the heart of Israelites *Nu 32:7*
(B)

DISCOURAGED

the soul of the people was *Nu 21:4*
much *d.*
became depressed in spirit *Nu 21:4*
(B)
became impatient (R) *Nu 21:4*
they *d.* the heart of the *Nu 32:9*
children
spread fear in hearts of (B) *Nu 32:9*
thee: fear not, neither be *d.* *De 1:21*
our brethren have *d.* our *De 1:28*
heart
made our hearts melt *De 1:28*
(B)(E)(R)
d. Judah (R) *Ezr 4:4*
He shall not fail nor be *d.,* *Isa 42:4*
till
not fail nor be suppressed *Isa 42:4*
(B)
children to anger, lest they *Col 3:21*
be *d.*
so they may not lose heart *Col 3:21*
(B)

for fear they grow   Col 3:21
disheartened (N)
grow up feeling inferior and   Col 3:21
frustrated (P)

DISCOURSE

Balaam began his. (B)(R)   Nu 23:7
took up his figurative d.   Nu 23:18;
(A)   23:3, 15
Balaam announced his d.   Nu 23:18
(B)(R)
he took up his d. (B)(R)   Nu 24:15;
                                   24:20, 23
took up his d. (A)(B)(R)   Job 27:1;
                                   29:1

DISCOURSED

d. with Jews (B)   Ac 17:17
d. and argued (A)(B)(R)   Ac 18:4
d. with them (A)(B)(E)   Ac 20:7
Paul d. longer (E)   Ac 20:9

DISCOVER

would unquestionably d. (B)   Ge 44:15
wife, nor d. his father's skirt   De 22:30
and we will d. ourselves unto   1Sa 14:8
them
show ourselves to them   1Sa 14:8
(B)(R)
disclose ourselves to them   1Sa 14:8
(E)
can d. the face of his   Job 41:13
garment
strip off the outer garment   Job 41:13
(A)(E)(R)
stripped off his coat of mail   Job 41:13
(B)
but that his heart may d.   Pr 18:2
itself
revealing personal opinions   Pr 18:2
(A)(B)(R)
his heart may reveal itself (E)   Pr 18:2
and d. not a secret to another   Pr 25:9
Lord will d. their secret parts   Isa 3:17
cause them to be stripped   Isa 3:17
naked (A)
expose their secret parts (B)   Isa 3:17
lay bare their secret parts   Isa 3:17
(E)(R)
Therefore will I d. thy   Jer 13:26
skirts
throwing skirts over your   Jer 13:26
face (A)(R)
strip off your skirts up to   Jer 13:26
face (B)
uncover thy skirts (E)   Jer 13:26
of Edom; he will d. thy sins   La 4:22
uncover your sins   La 4:22
(A)(B)(E)(R)
will d. thy nakedness unto   Eze 16:37
them
uncover your nakedness   Eze 16:37
(A)(E)(R)
expose your nakedness (B)   Eze 16:37
now will I d. her lewdness in   Ho 2:10
uncover her lewdness   Ho 2:10
(A)(E)(R)
show her in her shame (B)   Ho 2:10
I will d. the foundations   Mic 1:6
thereof
lay bare her foundations   Mic 1:6
(A)(B)
uncover the foundations   Mic 1:6
(E)(R)
will d. thy skirts upon thy face   Na 3:5

DISCOVERED

he d. his money (S)   Ge 42:27
that thy nakedness be not d.   Ex 20:26
nakedness be not exposed on   Ex 20:26
it (A)(R)
lest on it your nudity be   Ex 20:26
exposed (B)
nakedness be not uncovered   Ex 20:26
thereon (E)
he hath d. her fountain, and   Le 20:18
she
uncovered fountain of her   Le 20:18
blood (A)(E)(R)
exposed her fountain (B)   Le 20:18
And both of them d.   1Sa 14:11
themselves
coming out of the holes   1Sa 14:11
(A)
both showed themselves to   1Sa 14:11
the (B)(R)

disclosed themselves to the   1Sa 14:11
(E)
Saul heard that David was d.   1Sa 22:6
foundations of the world   2Sa 22:16
were d.
and d. the evil (S)   Ne 13:7
foundations of the world   Ps 18:15
were d.
And he d. the covering of   Isa 22:8
Judah
removed protecting cover of   Isa 22:8
Judah (A)
removed covering of Judah   Isa 22:8
(B)(E)(R)
thou hast d. thyself to   Isa 57:8
another
deserting me you uncovered   Isa 57:8
your bed (A)(B)(R)
uncovered thyself to another   Isa 57:8
beside me (E)
thine iniquity are thy skirts   Jer 13:22
d.
your long robe pulled aside   Jer 13:22
(A)
your skirts are lifted   Jer 13:22
(B)(R)
thy skirts uncovered (E)   Jer 13:22
conversation not d. (A)   Jer 38:27
they have not d. thine iniquity   La 2:14
not exposed your iniquity and   La 2:14
guilt (A)(R)
not shown you your iniquity   La 2:14
(B)
not uncovered thine iniquity   La 2:14
(E)
foundation thereof shall be   Eze 13:14
d.
its foundations shall be   Eze 13:14
exposed (A)
its foundations shall be laid   Eze 13:14
bare (B)(R)
foundations shall be   Eze 13:14
uncovered (E)
thy nakedness d. through   Eze 16:36
thy
nakedness uncovered   Eze 16:36
through harlotries (A)(E)(R)
exposure of your nakedness   Eze 16:36
(B)
thy wickedness was d. as at   Eze 16:57
uncovered (A)(B)(E)(R)   Eze 16:57;
                                   21:24; 22:10; 23:10
that your transgressions are   Eze 21:24
d.
In thee have they d. their   Eze 22:10
fathers
These d. her nakedness: Eze 23:10
they
she d. her whoredoms, and   Eze 23:18
d. her
thy whoredoms shall be d.   Eze 23:29
both
the iniquity of Ephraim was   Ho 7:1
d.
when we had d. Cyprus, we   Ac 21:3
left
sighted Cyprus   Ac 21:3
(A)(B)(E)(N)(P)(R)
they d. a certain creek with   Ac 27:39
noticed a bay with a beach   Ac 27:39
(A)(N)(R)
noticed an inlet with a   Ac 27:39
beach (B)
perceived a certain bay with   Ac 27:39
a beach (E)
made out a beach with a   Ac 27:39
sandy shore (P)

DISCOVERETH

He d. deep things out of   Job 12:22
darkness
uncovers deep things out of   Job 12:22
(A)(B)(E)(R)
and d. the forests: and in his   Ps 29:9
it strips bare the forest   Ps 29:9
(A)(B)(E)(R)

DISCOVERING

d. the foundation unto the   Hab 3:13
neck
laying bare foundation to   Heb 3:13
the neck (A)(B)(E)
laying bare from thigh to   Hab 3:13
neck (R)

DISCREDIT

d. my justice (B)   Job 40:8

DISCREDITED

unless you are d. (S)   2Co 13:5
we are not d. (S)   2Co 13:6
appear as d. (S)   2Co 13:7

DISCREET

look out a man d. and wise   Ge 41:33
an intelligent and prudent   Ge 41:33
man (B)
none so d. and wise as thou   Ge 41:39
art
none as discerning and wise   Ge 41:39
(B)
temperate, d. (B)   1Ti 3:2
To be d. chaste, keepers at   Tit 2:5
home
to be self-controlled (A)   Tit 2:5
to be sensible (B)(P)(R)   Tit 2:5
to be sober-minded (E)   Tit 2:5
to be temperate (N)   Tit 2:5

DISCREETLY

saw that he answered d. he   M'k 12:34
said

DISCRETION

d. and understanding (E)(R)   1Ch 22:12
he will guide his affairs with   Ps 112:5
d.
conducts affairs with justice   Ps 112:5
(A)(R)
conducts business with   Ps 112:5
fairness (B)
maintain his cause in   Ps 112:5
judgment (E)
the young man knowledge and   Pr 1:4
d.
D. shall preserve thee   Pr 2:11
eyes: keep sound wisdom and   Pr 3:21
d.
That thou mayest regard d.   Pr 5:2
find knowledge and d.   Pr 8:12
(A)(E)(R)
a fair woman which is   Pr 11:22
without d.
beautiful woman who   Pr 11:22
neglects good taste (B)
d. of a man deferreth his   Pr 19:11
anger
Good sense makes man   Pr 19:11
restrain (A)(R)
prudent for man to restrain   Pr 19:11
(B)
his God doth instruct him   Isa 28:26
to d.
God instructs him correctly   Isa 28:26
(A)(B)(E)
his God teaches him aright   Isa 28:26
(R)
out the heavens by his d.   Jer 10:12
by understanding and skill   Jer 10:12
(A)(B)(E)(R)

DISCRIMINATE

d. between (B)   Le 11:47
d. words (A)   Job 12:11
d. between (B)   Jon 4:11
d. between us (B)(E)   Ac 15:9
to d. and distinguish   Heb 5:14
between (A)(N)(P)

DISCRIMINATING

without d. Christ's body   1Co 11:29
(A)
d. in spiritual matters (E)   1Co 12:10
not d. among (A)(B)   Jas 2:4

DISCRIMINATION

d. between spirits (B)   1Co 12:10
things without d. (B)   1Ti 5:21

DISCUSS

felt compelled to d. (P)   Ac 17:17

DISCUSSED

d. how to get rid of (P)   M't 12:14
d. it among themselves (R)   M't 16:7;
                                   Lu 20:5
walked out and d. (P)   M'k 3:6
d. with one another (A)(R)   M'k 9:34
d. with one another (S)   Lu 6:11

d. with one another (N)   Lu 24:15
d. the matter (N)   Ac 4:15
talked and d. (B)   Ac 9:29
d. out of scriptures (B)   Ac 17:2
d. purity of life (B)   Ac 24:25

DISCUSSING

d. among yourselves   M't 16:8
(A)(B)(R)
d. and arguing (B)(R)   M'k 9:33
inwardly d. (P)   Lu 3:15
conversing and d. (A)(R)   Lu 24:15
d. the kingdom (B)   Ac 19:8

DISCUSSION

took up his d. (A)   Job 29:1
there came a d. (B)   Lu 9:46
conversation and d. (B)(P)   Lu 24:15
what is this d. (A)(P)   Lu 24:17
much whispered d. and   Joh 7:12
(A)(P)
disagreement and d. (A)(P)   Ac 15:2
had considerable d. (B)   Ac 28:29
wearing d. (A)   1Ti 6:5

DISCUSSIONS

listened to the d.   M't 12:28
(B)(N)(P)
held d. in synagogue (P)   Ac 18:4
perplex him with d. (A)   Ro 14:1
d., purposeless talk   1Ti 1:6
empty d. (B)(E)   1Ti 6:20
empty d. (A)(B)   2Ti 2:16
uncultural d. (B)   2Ti 2:23

DISDAIN

with d. brings reproof (B)   Pr 18:3
became a d. (B)   Da 9:16

DISDAINED

and saw David, he d. him   1Sa 17:42
he scorned and despised   1Sa 17:42
him (A)
he d. to lay hands on (S)   Es 3:6
whose fathers I would have   Job 30:1
d. to
reprobate person d. (B)   Ps 15:4

DISDAINFUL

nor my eyes d. (B)   Ps 131:1

DISEASE

if the d. spread (A)   Le 13:5;
    13:30, 44, 50, 57-58
whether I shall recover of this   2Ki 1:2
d.
recover from this injury (B)   2Ki 1:2
recover of this sickness   2Ki 1:2
(E)(R)
Shall I recover of this d.   2Ki 8:8; 8:9
recover from this illness (B)   2Ki 8:8
recover of this sickness   2Ki 8:8
(E)(R)
until his d. was exceeding   2Ch 16:12
great
this illness grew severe; yet   2Ch 16:12
in his sickness, he did not seek
(B)
yet in his d. he sought not   2Ch 16:12
to the
sickness by d. of thy   2Ch 21:15
bowels, until
his bowels with an   2Ch 21:18
incurable d.
By the great force of my d.   Job 30:18
is my
I wrestle with my torments   Job 30:18
(B)
are filled with a loathsome d.   Ps 38:7
are charged with inflamation   Ps 38:7
(B)
are filled with burning   Ps 38:7
(E)(R)
An evil d. say they, cleaveth   Ps 41:8
fast
fatal plague is poured out (B)   Ps 41:8
A deadly thing has fastened   Ps 41:8
upon (R)
this is vanity, and it is an evil d.   Ec 6:2
it is a sore affliction (A)(R)   Ec 6:2
a hurtful d. (B)   Ec 6:2
all manner of d. among the   M't 4:23
people

and every d. among the   M't 9:35
people
of sickness and all manner   M't 10:1
of d.
healed of her d. (A)(R)   M'k 5:34
whole of whatsoever d. he   Joh 5:4
had
of what ailment he suffered   Joh 5:4
(B)

DISEASED

his old age he was d. in his   1Ki 15:23
feet
year of his reign was d. in   2Ch 16:12
his feet
as d. meat (A)   Job 6:7
they that are d. tremble (E)   Job 26:5
The d. have ye not   Eze 34:4
strengthened
nor healed the sick   Eze 34:4
(A)(B)(R)
pushed all the d. with your   Eze 34:21
horns
the weak with your horns   Eze 34:21
(B)(R)
was d. with an issue of   M't 9:20
blood
suffered from a flow of   M't 9:20
blood (A)
suffered from hemorrhages   M't 9:20
(B)(N)(R)
had a hemorrhage for 12   M't 9:20
years (P)
unto him all that were d.   M't 14:35;
    M'k 1:32
all that were sick   M't 14:35
(A)(E)(R)
all who suffered ailments   M't 14:35
(B)
all who were ill (N)   M't 14:35
did on them that were d.   Joh 6:2
performed on the sick   Joh 6:2
(A)(B)(E)(N)(P)
warped and d. world (P)   Ph'p 2:15

DISEASES

put none of these d. upon   Ex 15:26
thee
put none of the evil d. of   De 7:15
Egypt
bring upon thee all the d. of   De 28:60
Egypt
his sickness: so he died of   2Ch 21:19
sore d.
because of sickness (B)   2Ch 21:19
(for they left him in great   2Ch 24:25
d.) his
leaving him very ill (A)   2Ch 24:25
leave him with many   2Ch 24:25
wounds (B)
they left him very sick (E)   2Ch 24:25
leaving him severely   2Ch 24:25
wounded (R)
iniquities: who healeth all   Ps 103:3
thy d.
die of deadly d. (A)(R)   Jer 16:4
that were taken with divers   M't 4:24
d.
many that were sick of   M'k 1:34
divers d.
any sick with divers d.   Lu 4:40
brought
healed of d. (B)(P)   Lu 5:15; 7:21
him; and to be healed of   Lu 6:17
their d.
cured of d., plagues (N)(R)   Lu 7:21
over all devils, and to cure d.   Lu 9:1
and the d. departed from   Ac 19:12
them
their illnesses were removed   Ac 19:12
(B)
which had d. in the island,   Ac 28:9
came

DISFIGURE

for they d. their faces, that   M't 6:16
put on a dismal countenance   M't 6:16
(A)
make their looks unsightly   M't 6:16
(B)(N)
d. faces to be seen   M't 6:16
(E)(P)(R)

DISGRACE

were a d. (A)(B)(R)   Ge 34:14
    1Sa 11:2; Isa 30:5

returned in d. (B)   2Ch 32:21;
    Ps 89:45
to our d. (B)   Ezr 9:7
I am filled with d. (A)(B)(R)   Job 10:15
my d. is before me (R)   Ps 44:15
caused unending d. (B)   Ps 78:66
his d. not wiped away (B)(R)   Pr 6:33
a d. of master's palace (A)(B)   Isa 22:18
do not d. the throne of thy   Jer 14:21
glory
do not dishonor, debase,   Jer 14:21
and lightly esteem your glorious
throne (A)
do not deject the throne of   Jer 14:21
(B)
do not dishonor the throne   Jer 14:21
of (R)
d. of the peoples (R)   Eze 36:15
to suffer d. (B)   Ac 5:41
we have disrepute, d.   1Co 4:10
(A)(E)(N)(R)
it is a d. to (B)   Eph 5:12
exposing him to d. (B)   Heb 6:6
bearing the d. (B)   Heb 13:13
foam up own d. (B)   Jude 13

DISGRACED

shamed and d. (B)(R)   Ps 71:24
shall be d. (A)   Jer 46:24
not want her d. (P)   M't 1:19

DISGRACEFUL

done a d. thing (B)   Jos 7:15
this d. act (B)   2Sa 13:12
a d. thing (B)   Jer 29:23
d. passions (P)   Ro 1:26
it is d. for   1Co 11:6
(A)(B)(N)(P)(R)
it is d. for (A)   1Co 14:35
renounce d. (A)   2Co 4:2

DISGRACEFULLY

acts d. (B)   Pr 12:4; 19:26
treated them d. (P)   M't 22:6

DISGUISE

Arise, I pray thee, and d.   1Ki 14:2
thyself
I will d. myself and enter   1Ki 22:30
into the
I will d. myself and will go   2Ch 18:29
to the
d. as servants (R)   2Co 11:15

DISGUISED

And Saul d. himself, and put   1Sa 28:8
on
and d. himself with ashes   1Ki 20:38
upon
And the king of Israel d.   1Ki 22:30
himself
So the king of Israel d.   2Ch 18:29
himself
but d. himself, that he   2Ch 35:22
might fight

DISGUISES

d. himself as an angel (R)   2Co 11:14

DISGUISETH

shall see me: and d. his   Job 24:15
face

DISGUISING

d. themselves as apostles   2Co 11:13
(R)

DISGUST

show scorn or d. (N)   Ga 4:14

DISGUSTED

d. and angry (B)   Ge 34:7
the refrain d. him (B)   1Sa 18:8
I was d. (B)   Ps 95:10

DISGUSTING

was d. to Samuel (B)   1Sa 8:6

DISH

dish (R)   *Nu 7:14;*
7:20, 26, 32, 38, 44, 50, 56, 62, 68, 74,
                             80
brought forth butter in a   *J'g 5:25*
lordly *d.*
in a lordly bowl (B)(R)   *J'g 5:25*
as a man wipeth a *d.*   *2Ki 21:13*
wiping it
hideth his hand in his *d.* (S)   *Pr 19:24*
cup and *d.* (N)(P)   *M't 23:45*
dippeth his hand with me   *M't 26:23*
in the *d.*
that dippeth with me in the   *M'k 14:20*
d.
cup and *d.* (R)   *Lu 11:29*

DISHAN

And Dishon, and Ezer, and   *Ge 36:21*
D.
The children of *D.* are these;   *Ge 36:28*
Uz
Duke Dishon, duke Ezer,   *Ge 36:30*
duke *D.*
and Dishon, and Ezar, and   *1Ch 1:38*
D.
The sons of *D.* Uz, and   *1Ch 1:42*
Aran

DISHARMONY

d. and evil (P)   *Jas 3:16*

DISHEARTENED

d. the people (B)   *Jos 14:8*
for fear they grow *d.* (N)   *Col 3:21*

DISHES

thou shalt make the *d.*   *Ex 25:29*
thereof
the plates (B)   *Ex 25:29*
the table, his *d.* and his   *Ex 37:16*
spoons
put thereon the *d.* and the   *Nu 4:7*
spoons
dishes (E)   *Nu 7:84; 7:86;*
2Ki 25:14; 2Ch 4:23; 24:14; Jer 52:18-19
dishes (A)   *2Ki 25:14; 2Ch 4:12*
cups and *d.* (P)   *Lu 11:29*

DISHON

And *D.* and Ezer, and   *Ge 36:21*
Dishan
D. and Aholibamah the   *Ge 36:25*
daughter
are the children of *D.;*   *Ge 36:26*
Hemdan
Duke *D.* duke Ezar, duke   *Ge 36:30*
Dishan
and *D.* and Ezar, and   *1Ch 1:38*
Dishan
The sons of Anah *D.* And   *1Ch 1:41*
sons of *D.* Amram, and   *1Ch 1:41*
Eshban

DISHONEST

smitten mine hand at thy *d.*   *Eze 22:13*
gain
to destroy souls, to get *d.*   *Eze 22:27*
gain
rain on the *d.* (N)(P)   *M't 5:45;*
                     Lu 18:6, 10
the *d.* manager (A)(B)(P)   *Lu 16:8*
I am not *d.* (N)(P)   *Lu 18:11*
d. people (B)   *1Co 6:9*
we use no *d.* manipulation   *2Co 4:2*
(P)
not greedy of *d.* gain (B)   *Tit 1:7*
d. gain (B)(N)   *Tit 1:11*

DISHONESTLY

all who act *d.* (R)   *De 25:16*
handle *d.* (A)(R)   *2Co 4:2*

DISHONESTY

renounced the hidden things   *2Co 4:2*
of *d.*
renounced disgraceful way,   *2Co 4:2*
secret thoughts, feelings,
desires, underhandedness (A)
we do eliminate underhanded   *2Co 4:2*
ways (B)

renounced hidden ways of   *2Co 4:2*
shame (E)
renounced deeds men hide for   *2Co 4:2*
shame (N)
We use no hocus-pocus, no   *2Co 4:2*
clever tricks, no dishonest
manipulation (P)
renounced disgraceful   *2Co 4:2*
underhanded ways (R)

DISHONOR

d. the name of God (B)   *Le 19:12;*
                         20:3
not *d.* his offspring (B)   *Le 21:15*
own *d.* (B)   *1Sa 20:30*
be put to shame and *d.*   *Ps 35:4*
(A)(E)(R)
my *d.* is before me (A)(E)   *Ps 44:15*
with *d.* comes disgrace (R)   *Pr 18:3*
instead of *d.* (A)(E)(R)   *Isa 61:7*
let our *d.* cover us (R)   *Jer 3:25*
do not *d.,* debase, lightly   *Jer 14:21*
esteem the throne (A)(R)
eternal *d.* will   *Jer 20:11*
(A)(B)(E)(R)
to suffer *d.* (E)(R)   *Ac 5:4*
we have disrepute *d.*   *1Co 4:10*
(A)(E)(N)(R)

DISHONORABLE

d. over honorable (B)   *Isa 3:5*
d. passions (R)   *Ro 1:26*

DISHONORED

d. her (B)   *Ge 34:2; 34:13*
d., shame, contempt for poor *Jas 2:6*
(A)(B)

DISHONORETH

that *d.* father or mother   *De 27:16*
(S)

DISHONOUR

meet for us to see the king's   *Ezr 4:14*
d.
be clothed with shame and   *Ps 35:26*
d. that
and my shame, and my *d.:*   *Ps 69:19*
mine
be covered with reproach   *Ps 71:13*
and *d.*
A wound and *d.* shall he get   *Pr 6:33*
honour my Father, and ye   *Joh 8:49*
do *d.* me
to *d.* their own bodies   *Ro 1:24*
between
unto honour, and another   *Ro 9:21*
unto *d.*
one for noble use, one for   *Ro 9:21*
ignoble (A)(B)
one to be treasured, the other   *Ro 9:21*
for common use (N)
one a lovely vase, another a   *Ro 9:21*
pipe for sewage (P)
one for beauty, one for   *Ro 9:21*
menial use (R)
It is sown in *d.;* it is raised   *1Co 15:43*
in
By honour and *d.* by evil   *2Co 6:8*
report
through honor and shame   *2Co 6:8*
(B)
some to honour, and some to   *2Ti 2:20*
d.
some menial and ignoble   *2Ti 2:20*
(A)(B)(R)
some for lowest purposes   *2Ti 2:20*
(P)

DISHONOUREST

breaking the law *d.* thou God *Ro 2:23*

DISHONOURETH

son *d.* the father, the   *Mic 7:6*
daughter
his head covered, *d.* his   *1Co 11:4*
head
her head uncovered *d.* her   *1Co 11:5*
head

DISINHERIT

with the pestilence, and *d.*   *Nu 14:12*
them

DISINTEGRATION

inevitable *d.* lust produces   *2Pe 1:4*
(P)

DISLIKED

he *d.* it (B)   *Ge 48:17*

DISLOCATED

Jacob's highways *d.* (B)   *Ge 32:25*

DISLOYAL

children of sin, *d.* brood (B)   *Isa 57:4*

DISLOYALTY

because of *d.* (B)   *Da 9:7*

DISMAY

d. you before them (E)(R)   *Jer 1:17*
d. has taken hold   *Jer 8:21*
(A)(E)(R)(S)
drink water in *d.*   *Eze 4:16*
(A)(B)(E)(R)
in anguish and *d.* (N)   *M't 26:37*
horror and *d.* came (N)   *M'k 14:33*
in horror and *d.* (N)   *M'k 14:34*

DISMAYED

distressingly disturbed and *d.*   *Ge 45:3*
(A)
were *d.* (R)   *Ge 45:3;*
         Ps 30:7; 83:17; 104:29
thee: fear not, neither be *d.*   *De 31:8*
neither be thou *d.* for the   *Jos 1:9*
Lord
neither be thou *d.* take all the   *Jos 8:1*
Fear not, nor be *d.* be   *Jos 10:25*
strong and
men were *d.* (E)(R)   *J'g 28:41*
Philistine, they were *d.* and   *1Sa 17:11*
greatly
they were alarmed (B)   *1Sa 17:11*
Israel was *d.* (R)   *2Sa 4:1*
they were *d.* and   *2Ki 19:26*
confounded
courage; dread not, nor be   *1Ch 22:13*
fear not, nor be *d.:* for the   *1Ch 28:20*
Lord
Be not afraid nor *d.* by   *2Ch 20:15*
reason of
fear not, nor be *d.;* to   *2Ch 20:17*
morrow go
be not afraid nor *d.* for the   *2Ch 32:7*
king of
you grow *d.* (B)   *Job 4:5*
D. they stand (B)   *Job 32:15*
not *d.* or terrified   *Job 39:22*
(A)(B)(R)(S)
enemies greatly *d.* (B)   *Ps 6:10*
shame and *d.* (A)(E)(R)   *Ps 83:17*
d. and confounded   *Isa 20:5*
(A)(B)(E)(R)
of it; I was *d.* at the seeing   *Isa 21:3*
of it
I am terrified (B)   *Isa 21:3*
they were *d.* and   *Isa 37:27*
confounded
be not *d.;* for I am thy God   *Isa 41:10*
that we may be *d.* and   *Isa 41:23*
behold it
that we may be astonished   *Isa 41:23*
(B)
be not *d.* at their faces, lest I   *Jer 1:17*
ashamed, they are *d.* and   *Jer 8:9*
taken
wise men are dumbfounded and *Jer 8:9*
trapped (B)
be not *d.* at the signs of   *Jer 10:2*
heaven
for the heathen are *d.* at   *Jer 10:2*
them
be confounded: let them be   *Jer 17:18*
d.
but let not me be *d.:* bring   *Jer 17:18*
upon
they shall fear no more, nor   *Jer 23:4*
be *d.*
neither be *d.* O Israel: for   *Jer 30:10*
Wherefore have I seen them   *Jer 46:5*
d.
be not *d.* O Israel: for,   *Jer 46:27*
behold
Misgab is confounded and *d.*   *Jer 48:1*

Misgab is put to shame (A)(B)(E)   *Jer 48:1*
the fortress is put to shame (R)   *Jer 48:1*
For I will cause Elam to be d.   *Jer 49:37*
mighty men; and they shall be d.   *Jer 50:36*
of their words, nor be d. at their   *Eze 2:6*
neither be d. at their looks   *Eze 3:9*
the lands are d. (R)   *Eze 26:18*
look d. (A)(B)(E)(S)   *Eze 4:17*
was d. (R)   *Da 4:19*
mighty men, O Teman, shall be d.   *Ob 9*
to be d. (N)   *M'k 14:19*

DISMAYING

a derision and a d. to all them   *Jer 48:39*
become derision, terror to all (A)(E)   *Jer 48:39*
become a derision and a horror (B)(R)   *Jer 48:39*

DISMEMBERED

is Christ d. (B)   *1Co 1:13*

DISMISSED

Jehoiada the priest d. not   *2Ch 23:8*
d. sentence against you (B)   *Zep 3:15*
So when they were d. they came   *Ac 15:30*
when they were sent off (A)(N)(P)(R)   *Ac 15:30*
those who were dispatched (B)   *Ac 15:30*
thus spoken, he d. the assembly   *Ac 19:41*

DISOBEDIENCE

by one man's d. many were made   *Ro 5:19*
all in d. (A)(B)(E)(N)(P)(R)   *Ro 11:32*
to revenge all d. when your   *2Co 10:6*
now worketh in the children of d.   *Eph 2:2*
of God upon the children of d.   *Eph 5:6*
of God cometh on the children of d.   *Col 3:6*
transgression and d. received a.   *Heb 2:2*
same sort of d. (B)(R)   *Heb 4:11*

DISOBEDIENT

the man of God, who was d. unto   *1Ki 13:26*
Nevertheless they were d. and   *Ne 9:26*
the d. to the wisdom of the just   *Lu 1:17*
obstinate to the wisdom (B)   *Lu 1:17*
to convert the rebellious (N)   *Lu 1:17*
was not d. unto the heavenly vision   *Ac 26:19*
of evil things, d. to parents   *Ro 1:30*
parent-despisers (B)   *Ro 1:30*
no loyalty to parents (N)   *Ro 1:30*
scoffed at duty to parents (P)   *Ro 1:30*
unto a d. and gainsaying people   *Ro 10:21*
but for the lawless and d. for   *1Ti 1:9*
for the lawless and unruly (A)(E)(N)   *1Ti 1:9*
for the lawless and refractory (B)   *1Ti 1:9*
for the man who has neither principles nor self-control (P)   *1Ti 1:9*
blasphemers, d. to parents   *2Ti 3:2*
being abominable, and d. and   *Tit 1:16*
sometimes foolish, d. deceived   *Tit 3:3*
did not share fate of d. (P)   *Heb 11:31*
but unto them which be d.   *1Pe 2:7*
for those who disbelieve (A)(E)   *1Pe 2:7*
to the unbelieving (B)   *1Pe 2:7*
for those who have no faith (N)   *1Pe 2:7*
to those who disobey God (P)   *1Pe 2:7*
for those who do not believe (R)   *1Pe 2:7*

stumble at the word, being d.   *1Pe 2:8*
they disobey and disbelieve (A)   *1Pe 2:8*
because they disbelieve (B)(N)   *1Pe 2:8*
because they disobey (P)(R)   *1Pe 2:8*
Which sometime were d. when   *1Pe 3:20*

DISOBEY

those who d. God (P)   *1Pe 2:7*
they d. and disbelieve (A)(P)(R)   *1Pe 2:8*

DISOBEYED

hast d. the mouth of the Lord   *1Ki 13:21*
because thou hast rebelled (B)   *1Ki 13:21*

DISORDER

this d. (A)   *Ac 19:40*
not the God of d. (B)(N)(P)   *1Co 14:33*
d. and evil (N)(R)   *Jas 3:16*

DISORDERLY

warn the d. (B)(E)   *1Th 5:14*
every brother that walketh d.   *2Th 3:6*
behaved not ourselves d. among   *2Th 3:7*
some which walk among you d.   *2Th 3:11*

DISORDERS

swellings, d. (S)   *2Co 12:20*

DISPARAGES

d. and judges the law (N)   *Jas 4:11*

DISPATCH

that I may d. him (B)   *1Sa 19:15*
you yourself d. me (B)   *1Sa 20:8*
and d. them with their swords   *Eze 23:47*
cut them down with swords (A)   *Eze 23:47*

DISPATCHED

those who were d. (B)   *Ac 15:30*

DISPENSATION

a d. of the gospel is committed   *1Co 9:17*
entrusted with sacred trusteeship and commission (A)   *1Co 9:17*
an office with which I am entrusted (B)   *1Co 9:17*
a stewardship entrusted to me (E)   *1Co 9:17*
I am simply discharging a trust (N)   *1Co 9:17*
a sacred responsibility (P)   *1Co 9:17*
entrusted with a commission (R)   *1Co 9:17*
the d. of death (A)(R)   *2Co 3:7*
the d. of the Spirit (A)(N)(R)   *2Co 3:8*
That in the d. of the fulness of   *Eph 1:10*
the maturity of times and the climax of the ages (A)   *Eph 1:10*
the times should reach maturity (B)   *Eph 1:10*
when the time was ripe (N)   *Eph 1:10*
plan for the fulness of time (R)   *Eph 1:10*
heard of the d. of the grace of God   *Eph 3:2*
stewardship of God's grace (A)(R)   *Eph 3:2*
administration of divine grace (B)   *Eph 3:2*
assigned gift of grace to me (N)   *Eph 3:2*
according to the d. of God which   *Col 1:25*
the divine stewardship (A)   *Col 1:25*
by divine appointment (B)   *Col 1:25*
task assigned to me (N)   *Col 1:25*
minister by divine commission (P)   *Col 1:25*
minister according to divine office (R)   *Col 1:25*

DISPENSE

d. with threatening (B)   *Eph 6:9*

DISPERSE

D. yourselves among the people   *1Sa 14:34*
The lips of the wise d. knowledge   *Pr 15:7*
and d. them in the countries   *Eze 12:15; 22:15*
and d. them through the countries   *Eze 20:23; 30:23*
and d. them among the countries   *Eze 30:26*

DISPERSED

d. of all his children throughout   *2Ch 11:23*
and d. among the people in all   *Es 3:8*
He hath d., he hath given to   *Ps 112:9*
Let thy fountains be d.   *Pr 5:16*
offspring be d. (A)   *Pr 5:16*
your springs be d. (B)(E)(R)   *Pr 5:16*
gather together the d. of Judah   *Isa 11:12*
scattered of Judah (B)   *Isa 11:12*
were d. through the countries   *Eze 36:19*
the daughter of my d. shall bring   *Zep 3:10*
unto the d. among the Gentiles   *Joh 7:35*
the Dispersion (A)(B)(E)(N)(R)   *Joh 7:35*
refugees among the Greeks (P)   *Joh 7:35*
as many as obeyed him, were d.   *Ac 5:37*
adherents were scattered (A)(B)(E)(N)(R)   *Ac 5:37*
He hath d. abroad; he hath given   *2Co 9:9*

DISPERSION

the D. (A)(B)(E)(N)(R)   *Joh 7:35*

DISPERSIONS

of your slaughter and of your d.   *Jer 25:34*
your days to be slaughtered are (B)   *Jer 25:34*

DISPLAY

reluctant to d. knowledge (A)   *Pr 12:23*
does not come with visible d. (A)   *Lu 17:20*
no d. of fine words (N)   *1Co 2:1*
does not d. itself haughtily (A)   *1Co 13:4*
love is not out for d. (B)   *1Co 13:4*

DISPLAYED

he d. wisdom (B)   *2Ch 11:23*
may be d. because of the truth   *Ps 60:4*
d. his greatness and power (A)   *Joh 2:11*

DISPLAYING

d. his greatness (B)   *Joh 2:11*

DISPLEASE

Let it not d. my lord that I cannot   *Ge 31:35*
object to my being unable (B)   *Ge 31:35*
let not my lord be angry (E)(R)   *Ge 31:35*
d. thee, I will get me back   *Nu 22:34*
thou d. not the lords of   *1Sa 29:7*
Let not this thing d. thee   *2Sa 11:25*
do not let this worry you (B)   *2Sa 11:25*
the Lord see it, and it d. him   *Pr 24:18*

DISPLEASED

Do not be d. (R)   *Ge 21:12*
which he did d. the Lord   *Ge 38:10*

And when Joseph, it *d.*   *Ge 48:17*
him
he disliked it (B)   *Ge 48:17*
complained, it *d.* the Lord   *Nu 11:1;*
  11:10
greatly; Moses also was *d.*   *Nu 11:10*
But the thing *d.* Samuel   *1Sa 8:6*
was disgusting to Samuel (B)   *1Sa 8:6*
and the saying *d.* him; and   *1Sa 18:8*
he
the refrain disgusted him   *1Sa 18:8*
(B)
And David was *d.* because the   *2Sa 6:8*
thing that David had done   *2Sa 11:27*
d.
his father had not *d.* him at   *1Ki 1:6*
any
went to his house heavy   *1Ki 20:43*
and *d.*
came into his house heavy   *1Ki 21:4*
and *d.*
And David was *d.* because   *1Ch 13:11*
God was *d.* with this thing   *1Ch 21:7*
were much *d.* (B)(R)   *Ne 2:10*
thou hast been *d.*; O turn   *Ps 60:1*
thyself
thou hast been angry   *Ps 60:1*
(A)(B)(E)(R)
it *d.* him that there was no   *Isa 59:15*
was sore *d.* with himself, and   *Da 6:14*
set
greatly distressed (B)(R)   *Da 6:14*
But it *d.* Jonah exceedingly   *Jon 4:1*
the Lord *d.* against the rivers   *Hab 3:8*
The Lord hath been sore *d.*   *Zec 1:2*
with
Lord was very angry   *Zec 1:2*
(A)(B)(R)
I am very sore *d.* with the   *Zec 1:15*
heathen
I am very angry (A)(R)   *Zec 1:15*
at ease: for I was but a little   *Zec 1:15*
d.
son of David; they were   *M't 21:15*
sore *d.*
they were indignant (A)   *M't 21:15*
they were chagrined (B)   *M't 21:15*
they were moved with   *M't 21:15*
indignation (E)
they asked him indignantly   *M't 21:15*
(N)
they were highly indignant   *M't 21:15*
(P)(R)
Jesus saw it, he was much   *M'k 10:14*
d.
he was indignant   *M'k 10:14*
(A)(B)(N)(P)(R)
he was moved with   *M'k 10:14*
indignation (E)
began to be much *d.* with   *M'k 10:41*
James
began to be indignant with   *M'k 10:41*
(A)(B)(N)(P)(R)
began to be moved with   *M'k 10:41*
indignation (E)
does it *d.* you (A)   *Joh 6:61*
Herod was highly *d.* with   *Ac 12:20*
them of
cherished bitter animosity,   *Ac 12:20*
hostility (A)
he felt ugly toward the   *Ac 12:20*
Tyrians (B)
angry with people of Tyre   *Ac 12:20*
(N)(P)(R)
sorely *d.* with (B)(E)(P)   *Heb 3:10*

DISPLEASING

thing was very *d.* (R)   *Ge 21:11*

DISPLEASURE

know my *d.* (A)   *Nu 14:34*
was afraid of the anger and   *De 9:19*
hot *d.*
the awful indignation of Lord   *De 9:19*
(B)
though I do them a *d.*   *J'g 15:3*
when I do them evil (A)   *J'g 15:3*
when I harm the Philistines   *J'g 15:3*
(B)
when I do them mischief (R)   *J'g 15:3*
and vex them in his sore *d.*   *Ps 2:5*
speaks in his sore indignation   *Ps 2:5*
(B)
terrify them in his fury (R)   *Ps 2:5*
neither chasten me in thy hot *d.*   *Ps 6:1;*
  38:1

DISPOSE

d. of all I possess (P)   *1Co 13:3*

DISPOSED

who hath *d.* the whole   *Job 34:13*
world
laid on him whole world   *Job 34:13*
(A)(R)
established the whole world   *Job 34:13*
(B)
thou know when God *d.*   *Job 37:15*
them
lays his command upon   *Job 37:15*
them (A)(R)
how God controls these (B)   *Job 37:15*
layeth charge upon them   *Job 37:15*
(E)
he was *d.* to pass into   *Ac 18:27*
Achaia
you to a feast, and ye be *d.*   *1Co 10:27*
to go
you want to go (A)(P)   *1Co 10:27*
you wish to go (B)   *1Co 10:27*
you care to go (N)   *1Co 10:27*

DISPOSING

the whole *d.* thereof is of the   *Pr 16:33*
Lord
decision wholly with Lord   *Pr 16:33*
(A)(B)(R)

DISPOSITION

the law by the *d.* of angels   *Ac 7:53*
ordained, set in order,   *Ac 7:53*
delivered (A)
through mediation of angels   *Ac 7:53*
(B)
ordained by angels (E)   *Ac 7:53*
angels gave it to you (N)   *Ac 7:53*
by the hand of angels (P)   *Ac 7:53*
delivered by angels (R)   *Ac 7:53*
character or moral *d.* (A)   *Heb 13:5*

DISPOSITIONS

knows the *d.* of all (R)   *Nu 27:16*

DISPOSSESS

And ye shall *d.* the   *Nu 33:53*
inhabitants
more than I; how can I *d.*   *De 7:17*
them

DISPOSSESSED

and *d.* the Amorite which   *Nu 32:39*
was
driving out Amorites (B)   *Nu 32:39;*
  De 7:17; J'g 11:23
God of Israel hath *d.* the   *J'g 11:23*
Amorites
d. every man from his   *Eze 46:18*
possession (S)

DISPUTATION

no small dissension and *d.*   *Ac 15:2*
with
disagreement and discussion   *Ac 15:2*
(A)
dissension and debate (B)(R)   *Ac 15:2*
dissension and questioning   *Ac 15:2*
(E)
dissension and controversy   *Ac 15:2*
(N)
much earnest discussion (P)   *Ac 15:2*

DISPUTATIONS

receive ye, but not to   *Ro 14:1*
doubtful *d.*
perplex him with discussions   *Ro 14:1*
(A)
do not criticize his views (B)   *Ro 14:1*
not for decision of scruples   *Ro 14:1*
(E)
without attempting to settle   *Ro 14:1*
doubtful points (N)
not arguing over his   *Ro 14:1*
principles (P)
not for disputes over   *Ro 14:1*
opinions (R)

DISPUTE

the righteous might *d.* with   *Job 23:7*
him
a *d.* arose (P)   *Lu 9:46*
also a *d.* (N)(P)(R)   *Lu 22:22*
considerable *d.* about him   *Joh 7:12*
(N)
d. was so sharp (N)   *Ac 15:39*
d. between (A)(B)   *Ac 23:7*
beyond all *d.* (B)(N)(R)   *Heb 6:16*

DISPUTED

d. with herdmen (B)   *Ge 26:20*
that ye *d.* among yourselves   *M'k 9:33*
by
discussing and arguing (A)   *M'k 9:33*
arguing on the road (B)(N)   *M'k 9:33*
reasoning on the way (E)   *M'k 9:33*
discussing as we came along   *M'k 9:33*
(P)(R)
they had *d.* among   *M'k 9:34*
themselves
discussed and disputed (A)   *M'k 9:34*
argued with one another   *M'k 9:34*
(B)
disputed one with another   *M'k 9:34*
(E)
arguing about on the way   *M'k 9:34*
(N)(P)
discussed with one another   *M'k 9:34*
(R)
and *d.* against the Grecians   *Ac 9:29*
talked and discussed (B)   *Ac 9:29*
talking and debating with the   *Ac 9:29*
(N)
talk and aruge with the Jews   *Ac 9:29*
(P)
d. he in the synagogue with   *Ac 17:17*
reasoned and argued with   *Ac 17:17*
Jews (A)
discoursed with the Jews   *Ac 17:17*
(B)
reasoned in the synagogues   *Ac 17:17*
with (E)
argued with the Jews in the   *Ac 17:17*
(N)(R)
felt compelled to discuss (P)   *Ac 17:17*
he *d.* about the body of Moses   *Jude 9*
argued about the body of   *Jude 9*
Moses (A)(B)
was in a debate with the devil   *Jude 9*
(N)

DISPUTER

where is the *d.* of this world   *1Co 1:20*
the investigator, logician,   *1Co 1:20*
debater (A)
the philosopher, scholar,   *1Co 1:20*
investigator (B)
man of learning, subtle   *1Co 1:20*
debater (N)
philosopher, writer, critic   *1Co 1:20*
(P)
the debater of this age (R)   *1Co 1:20*

DISPUTES

d. over opinions (R)   *Ro 14:1*
furnish *d.* (B)   *1Ti 1:4*
d. about words (R)(S)   *1Ti 6:4*

DISPUTING

no *d.* between (B)   *Ge 13:8*
d. with one another (R)   *M't 12:28*
listened to them *d.* (A)   *M't 12:28*
hot *d.* about him (A)(P)   *Joh 7:12*
and of Asia, *d.* with Stephen   *Ac 6:9*
when there had been much *d.*   *Ac 15:7*
after there had been long   *Ac 15:7*
debate (A)(B)(N)(R)
when there had been much   *Ac 15:7*
questioning (E)
after an exhaustive inquiry   *Ac 15:7*
(P)
three months, *d.* and   *Ac 19:8*
persuading
spoke boldly, persuading,   *Ac 19:8*
arguing, pleading (A)
persuasively discussing the   *Ac 19:8*
kingdom (B)
reasoning and persuading (E)   *Ac 19:8*
using argument and   *Ac 19:8*
persuasion (N)(P)
arguing and pleading (R)   *Ac 19:8*
d. daily in the school of one   *Ac 19:9*
Tyrannus

me in the temple *d.* with | *Ac 24:12*
any man
arguing and *d.* (A)(S) | *Ac 28:29*
without *d.* (B)(E) | *1Ti 2:8*

DISPUTINGS

without murmurings and *d.* | *Ph'p 2:14*
without grumbling, | *Ph'p 2:14*
faultfinding, complaining,
questioning, and doubting (A)
without grumblings and | *Ph'p 2:14*
objections (B)
without murmurings and | *Ph'p 2:14*
questionings (E)
without complaint or | *Ph'p 2:14*
wrangling (N)
without grumbling and | *Ph'p 2:14*
arguing (P)
without grumbling or | *Ph'p 2:14*
questioning (R)
Perverse *d.* of men of corrupt | *1Ti 6:5*
minds
protracted wrangling, wearing | *1Ti 6:5*
discussion, and perpetual
contention among men (A)
perpetual contention between | *1Ti 6:5*
people (B)
wranglings of men corrupted | *1Ti 6:5*
in mind (E)
endless wrangles (P)(R) | *1Ti 6:5*

DISQUALIFIED

d. by decision of people (N) | *Col 2:18*

DISQUALIFIES

detestable obstinancy *d.* them | *Tit 1:16*
(N)

DISQUALIFY

let no one *d.* you (R) | *Col 2:18*

DISQUALIFYING

d. you for the prize (A) | *Col 2:18*

DISQUIET

d. the inhabitants of | *Jer 50:34*
Babylon
unrest to inhabitants of | *Jer 50:34*
Babylon (A)(R)

DISQUIETED

Why hast thou *d.* me, to | *1Sa 28:15*
bring me up
disturbed me to bring me | *1Sa 28:15*
up (A)(B)(R)
surely they are *d.* in vain | *Ps 39:6*
why art thou *d.* in me | *Ps 42:5;*
| *42:11; 43:5*
why so restless within me (B) | *Ps 42:5*
I am *d.* and groan (A) | *Ps 77:3*
For three things the earth is | *Pr 30:21*
d.
the earth trembles | *Pr 30:21*
(B)(E)(R)
was *d.* (B) | *Joh 11:33*
less *d.* (A) | *Ph'p 2:28*

DISQUIETNESS

I have roared by reason of | *Ps 38:8*
the *d.*
groan because of heart | *Ps 38:8*
murmurings (B)
groan because of tumult of | *Ps 38:8*
my heart (R)

DISREGARD

he will *d.* no right (A) | *Job 37:23*

DISREGARDED

d. the statutes | *Isa 24:5*
(A)(B)(E)(R)
my right is *d.* by God (R) | *Isa 40:27*
he is *d.* (A)(B) | *1Co 14:38*

DISREGARDS

if anyone *d.* (A)(B) | *1Co 14:38*
d., sets aside (A)(R) | *1Th 4:8*
d. laws of Moses (N) | *Heb 10:28*

DISREPUTE

come into *d.* (A) | *Ac 19:17*
we have *d.*, dishonor | *1Co 4:10*
(A)(E)(N)(R)

DISREPUTABLE

senseless, *d.* brood (R) | *Job 30:8*
a *d.* person (B) | *Da 11:21*
for *d.* gain (A) | *Tit 1:11*

DISSEMBLED

and have also stolen, and *d.* | *Jos 7:11*
also
For ye *d.* in your hearts, | *Jer 42:20*
when ye
dealt deceitfully against own | *Jer 42:20*
lives (A)(E)
gone astray at cost of own | *Jer 42:20*
lives (B)(R)
other Jews *d.* likewise with | *Ga 2:13*
him
rest of Jews also concealed | *Ga 2:13*
their true convictions, acted
insincerely (A)
rest of Jews played the | *Ga 2:13*
hypocrite (B)
other Jewish Christians | *Ga 2:13*
showed the same lack of
principle (N)
carried out similar piece of | *Ga 2:13*
deception (P)
rest of Jews acted insincerely | *Ga 2:13*
(R)

DISSEMBLERS

neither will I go in with *d.* | *Ps 26:4*
nor fellowship with pretenders | *Ps 26:4*
(A)(B)

DISSEMBLETH

he that hateth *d.* with his | *Pr 26:24*
lips
pretends with his lips | *Pr 26:24*
(A)(B)

DISSENSION

had no small *d.* and | *Ac 15:2*
disputation
no small disagreement and | *Ac 15:2*
discussion (A)
d. and debate (B)(R) | *Ac 15:2*
much earnest discussion (P) | *Ac 15:2*
a *d.* between the Pharisees | *Ac 23:7*
and the
dispute between Pharisees, | *Ac 23:7*
Sadducees (A)(B)
Pharisees and Sadducees fell | *Ac 23:7*
out among themselves (N)
tension between Pharisees | *Ac 23:7*
and (P)
And when there arose a | *Ac 23:10*
great *d.*
strife became more and | *Ac 23:10*
more tense and violent (A)
discord grew so bitter (B) | *Ac 23:10*
As the tension mounted (P) | *Ac 23:10*
quarrels, *d.*, abuse (A)(R) | *1Ti 6:4*

DISSENSIONS

take note of those who | *Ro 16:17*
create *d.* (A)
have to be *d.* (B)(N) | *1Co 11:19*
d., factional spirit (B)(N) | *Ga 5:20*
d., party spirit (R) | *Ga 5:20*

DISSENTED

d. from policy and action | *Lu 23:51*
(B)(N)

DISSIMULATION

Let love be without *d.* Abhor | *Ro 12:9*
Let love be sincere-a real | *Ro 12:9*
thing (A)
love be perfectly sincere (B) | *Ro 12:9*
love be without hypocrisy | *Ro 12:9*
(E)
Love in all sincerity (N) | *Ro 12:9*
have no imitation Christian | *Ro 12:9*
love (P)
Let love be genuine (R) | *Ro 12:9*

was carried away with their | *Ga 2:13*
d.
carried away with their | *Ga 2:13*
hypocrisy (A)(B)
played false like the rest (N) | *Ga 2:13*
Barnabas was affected by it | *Ga 2:13*
(P)
carried away by their | *Ga 2:13*
insincerity (R)

DISSIPATION

overcharged with *d.* | *Lu 21:34*
(B)(N)(P)(R)
d. that goes with it (N) | *Eph 5:18*

DISSOLUTE

shocked by *d.* habits (N) | *2Pe 2:7*

DISSOLVE

interpretations, and *d.* doubts | *Da 5:16*
you can make interpretations | *Da 5:16*
(A)(E)
you can give explanations | *Da 5:16*
(B)
give interpretations, solve | *Da 5:16*
problems (R)

DISSOLVED

the inhabitants therefore are | *Ps 75:3*
d.
thou, whole Palestina, art *d.* | *Isa 14:31*
the earth is clean *d.* the | *Isa 24:19*
earth
all the host of heaven shall | *Isa 34:4*
be *d.*
and the palace shall be *d.* | *Na 2:6*
house of this tabernacle were | *2Co 5:1*
d.
that all these things shall be | *2Pe 3:11*
d.
heavens being on fire shall | *2Pe 3:12*
be *d.*

DISSOLVES

cloud *d.* and disappears (B) | *Job 7:9*

DISSOLVEST

upon it, and *d.* my | *Job 30:22*
substance

DISSOLVING

hard sentences, and *d.* of | *Da 5:12*
doubts

DISTAFF

and her hands hold the *d.* | *Pr 31:19*

DISTANT

equally *d.* one from another | *Ex 36:22*
even *d.* Sinai (S) | *J'g 5:5*

DISTIL

my speech shall *d.* as the dew | *De 32:2*
clouds do drop and *d.* upon | *Job 36:28*
man

DISTINCT

give *d.* tones (A)(B)(R) | *1Co 14:7*

DISTINCTION

make a *d.* between (B) | *Ex 8:23*
a *d.* between (E)(R) | *Ex 11:7;*
| *Le 11:10; 11:47; 20:25*
make a *d.* between (A) | *Le 10:10*
honor or *d.* (A)(B) | *Es 6:3*
make no *d.* (E) | *Ac 11:12*
no *d.* between us (E)(R) | *Ac 15:9*
there is no *d.* | *Ro 3:22;*
(A)(B)(E)(N)(P)(R) | *10:12*
no *d.* of eloquence (B) | *1Co 2:1*
they give a *d.* in the sounds | *1Co 14:7*
makes no *d.* between (P) | *Eph 6:9*
once you allow any *d.* (P) | *Jas 2:9*
d. between the children (N) | *1Jo 3:10*

DISTINCTIONS

brag of earthly *d.* (N) | *2Co 11:18*
make *d.* among (E)(P)(R) | *Jas 2:4*

DISTINCTIVE

d. varieties and distributions of endowments (A)	*1Co 12:4*
d. gifts of grace (B)	*1Co 12:4*
d. varieties of service, ministries (A)(B)(E)	*1Co 12:5*
d. varieties of operations (A)	*1Co 12:6*

DISTINCTLY

in the book in the law of God *d.*	*Ne 8:8*
the Spirit says *d.* (B)	*1Ti 4:1*

DISTINGUISH

distinguish (B)	*Isa 19:35; Ezr 3:13; 1Ki 3:9; Job 4:16; Eze 44:23; Mal 3:18*
d. looks of sky (B)	*M't 16:3*
d. between spirits (R)	*1Co 12:10*
d. between good and evil (B)(R)	*Heb 5:14*

DISTINGUISHED

who made you *d.* (B)	*1Co 4:7*
children of God *d.* (B)	*1Jo 3:10*

DISTINGUISHES

distinguishes (B)	*Ex 11:7*

DISTORT

turn aside after a multitude to *d.* (S)	*Ex 23:2*
not *d.* word of God (N)	*2Co 4:2*
d. the gospel (B)(N)	*Ga 1:7*

DISTORTED

d. my cause deceitfully (B)	*Ps 119:78*
they have *d.* their way (B)	*Jer 3:21*
his face was *d.* with rage (B)	*Da 3:19*
teach *d.* things (B)(N)	*Ac 20:30*
crooked and *d.* generation (B)	*Ph'p 2:15*
their minds *d.* (P)	*2Ti 3:8*
such a person is *d.* (B)(N)	*Tit 3:11*

DISTRACTED

while I suffer thy terrors I am *d.*	*Ps 88:15*
d. about much serving (A)(R)	*Lu 10:40*

DISTRACTION

attended upon the Lord without *d.*	*1Co 7:35*
undistracted, undivided devotion (A)(R)	*1Co 7:35*
choice behaviour, undisturbed devotion (B)	*1Co 7:35*

DISTRESS

brought great *d.* (B)	*Ge 26:35*
answered me in the day of my *d.*	*Ge 35:3*
therefore is this *d.* come upon us	*Ge 42:21*
this agony is come upon us (B)	*Ge 42:21*
saw *d.* of his soul (E)(R)	*Ge 42:21*
cause *d.* (B)	*Ex 22:22; 22:23*
D. not the Moabites, neither	*De 2:9*
Ammon, *d.* them not, nor meddle	*De 2:19*
thine enemies shall *d.* thee	*De 28:53*
thine enemies shall *d.* thee in all	*De 28:55*
enemy shall *d.* thee in thy gates	*De 28:57*
time of your *d.* (A)(B)(E)(R)	*J'g 10:14*
unto me now when ye are in *d.*	*J'g 11:7*
stress of provocation, *d.* (B)	*1Sa 1:16*
it was *d.* to him (B)	*1Sa 20:3*
And every one that was in *d.*	*1Sa 22:2*
those in difficulties (B)	*1Sa 22:2*
In my *d.* I called upon the Lord	*2Sa 22:7*
in my anguish I cried (A)	*2Sa 22:7*

in deep *d.* (S)	*2Sa 24:14*
redeemed my soul out of all *d.*	*1Ki 1:29*
redeemed from all adversity (B)(E)(R)	*1Ki 1:29*
soul in bitter *d.* (R)	*2Ki 4:27*
distress (A)	*2Ki 19:3;*
	Job 15:24; Ps 59:16; 66:14; 69:17; 78:49; 81:7; 102:2; Isa 8:22; 46:7
distress (B)	*2Ki 19:3;*
	Job 38:23; Ps 31:7; 54:7; 59:16; 66:14; 77:2; 78:49; 81:7; 107:19, 28; 119:143; 143:11; Isa 8:22; 26:16; 46:7; Jer 30:7; 2Ti 2:9
distress (R)	*2Ki 19:3;*
	2Ch 15:4; Job 15:24; Ps 31:9; 59:16; 69:17; 78:49; 81:7; Isa 8:22; 26:16; 37:3; Jer 30:7
distress (E)	*2Ch 15:4;*
	Job 15:24; Ps 31:9; 59:16; 66:14; 69:17; 102:2; Isa 8:22
And in the time of his *d.* did he	*2Ch 28:22*
Ye see the *d.* that we are in	*Ne 2:17*
pleasure, and we are in great *d.*	*Ne 9:37*
through *d.* opens ears (B)	*Job 36:15*
out of *d.* (B)(E)(R)(S)	*Job 36:16*
enlarged me when I was in *d.*	*Ps 4:1*
In my *d.* I called upon the Lord	*Ps 18:6*
d. was stirred (A)(B)(R)	*Ps 39:2; Isa 5:30*
security in days of *d.* (B)	*Ps 94:13*
called upon the Lord in *d.*	*Ps 118:5*
In my *d.* I cried unto the Lord	*Ps 120:1*
cry of *d.* in our streets (B)(R)	*Ps 144:14*
d. and anguish cometh upon you	*Pr 1:27*
d. as an harlot (A)(R)	*Pr 7:10*
increases *d.* (B)	*Ec 1:18; Isa 5:30; Ro 9:2*
darkness and *d.* (R)	*Isa 5:30*
a strength to the needy in his *d.*	*Isa 25:4*
Yet I will *d.* Ariel, and there shall	*Isa 29:2*
and her munition, and that *d.* her	*Isa 29:7*
borne our *d.* (A)	*Isa 53:4*
the cry of *d.* (A)	*Isa 65:19*
My *d.*, my *d.* (S)	*Jer 4:19*
and will *d.* them, that they may	*Jer 10:18*
in the siege and *d.* (S)	*Jer 19:9; De 28:53, 55, 57*
O Lord; for I am in *d.*: my bowels	*La 1:20*
compassed with *d.* (B)	*La 3:5*
spoken proudly in the day of *d.* (B)(R)	*Ob 12*
in the day of his misfortune (B)	*Ob 12*
in the day of his disaster (E)	*Ob 12*
that did remain in the day of *d.*	*Ob 14*
a day of trouble and *d.* a day of	*Zep 1:15*
And I will bring *d.* upon men	*Zep 1:17*
in terrible *d.* (R)	*M't 8:6*
great *d.* (N)	*M't 24:21; 24:29; M'k 13:24*
after the great *d.* (B)	*M't 24:29*
in great *d.* (N)(P)	*M't 26:22*
in terrible *d.* and misery (P)	*M't 26:37*
went away in deep *d.* (P)	*M'k 10:22*
d. as never been (N)	*M'k 13:19*
there shall be great *d.* in the land	*Lu 21:23*
and upon the earth *d.* of nations	*Lu 21:25*
caused deep *d.* (P)	*Ac 15:24*
tribulation and *d.* (R)	*Ro 2:9*
tribulations, or *d.* or persecution	*Ro 8:35*
this is good for the present *d.*	*1Co 7:26*
encourages in *d.* (A)(B)(N)(P)	*2Co 1:4*
if *d.* is our lot (N)	*2Co 1:6*
great sorrow and *d.* (A)	*2Co 2:4*
our affliction and *d.* by your faith	*1Th 3:7*
pay with *d.* and affliction (A)(B)	*2Th 1:6*
widows in *d.* (N)(P)	*Jas 1:27*

sharer in the *d.* (B)(P)	*Re 1:9*
I know your *d.* (B)	*Re 2:9*
d. last ten days (P)	*Re 2:10*
down to pressing *d.* (A)(B)	*Re 2:22*

DISTRESSED

Jacob was greatly afraid and *d.*	*Ge 32:7*
and Moab was *d.* because of them: and they were greatly *d.*	*Nu 22:3*
	J'g 2:15
so that Israel was sore *d.*	*J'g 10:9*
(for the people were *d.*)	*1Sa 13:6*
then the the men of Israel were *d.* that day	*1Sa 14:24*
And Saul answered, I am sore *d.*	*1Sa 28:15*
he was sore *d.* (B)	*1Sa 28:21*
And David was greatly *d.* for the	*1Sa 30:6*
I am *d.* for thee, my brother	*2Sa 1:26*
d. him, but strengthened him not	*2Ch 28:20*
d. them (A)	*Ne 2:10*
soul *d.* (A)(E)	*Ne 9:27; 2Pe 2:7*
the queen was deeply *d.* (R)	*Es 4:4*
would it *d.* you (B)	*Job 4:2*
My heart is *d.* (B)	*Ps 55:4; 29:19*
greatly *d.* (S)	*Isa 8:21*
greatly *d.* (B)(R)	*Da 6:14*
my spirit was *d.* (B)	*Da 7:15*
king was *d.* (B)	*M't 14:9; 17:23; 18:31*
deeply *d.* (N)	*M't 14:9; 18:31; M'k 6:26*
deeply *d.* (A)(P)(R)	*M't 17:23*
was greatly *d.* (A)	*M't 18:31*
greatly *d.* (B)	*M't 26:22; 26:37; Lu 18:23*
shocked and *d.* (P)	*M'k 14:19*
d. and troubled (B)(R)	*M'k 14:33*
d. and tormented (B)	*Lu 2:48*
greatly *d.* (P)	*M'k 18:23*
not be *d.* (P)	*Joh 14:1; 14:27*
they were *d.* (P)	*Joh 16:6*
be greatly *d.* (P)	*Joh 16:20*
Peter felt *d.* (B)	*Joh 21:17*
d. and sorrowful (A)(N)	*Ac 20:38*
troubled on every side, yet not *d.*	*2Co 4:8*
hedged in, troubled, oppressed in every way; but not cramped, crushed (A)	*2Co 4:8*
hedged in, but live no cramped lives (B)	*2Co 4:8*
pressed down, but not straitened (E)	*2Co 4:8*
hard-pressed, never hemmed in (N)	*2Co 4:8*
handicapped, never frustrated (P)	*2Co 4:8*
afflicted in every way, not crushed (R)	*2Co 4:8*
who are *d.* (A)	*2Th 1:7*
helped relieve *d.* (A)(B)(N)(P)	*1Ti 5:10*

DISTRESSFUL

I am in a *d.* day (B)	*Ps 102:2*

DISTRESSES

your troubles and *d.* (A)(E)	*1Sa 10:19*
O bring thou me out of my *d.* (E)	*Ps 25:17*
my life in *d.* (A)	*Ps 31:7*
he delivered them out of their *d.*	*Ps 107:6*
he saved them out of their *d.*	*Ps 107:13*
he saveth them out of their *d.*	*Ps 107:19*
he bringeth them out of their *d.*	*Ps 107:28*
d., wearies him (A)	*Pr 26:15*
and Noph shall have *d.* daily	*Eze 30:16*
Noph shall have adversaries (A)(E)	*Eze 30:16*
in afflictions, in necessities, in *d.*	*2Co 6:4*
persecutions, in *d.* for Christ's sake	*2Co 12:10*
crushing *d.* and afflictions (A)(B)(R)	*2Th 1:4*

DISTRESSINGLY

d. disturbed and dismayed (A)	*Ge 45:3*
d. tormented by a demon (A)	*M't 15:22*

DISTRIBUTE

Moses did *d.* for inheritance in	*Jos 13:32*
allocations Moses made in Moab (B)	*Jos 13:32*
to *d.* the oblations of the Lord	*2Ch 31:14*
d. them into corners (S)	*Ne 9:22*
was to *d.* unto their brethren	*Ne 13:13*
d. unto the poor, and thou shalt	*Lu 18:22*
divide among the poor (A)	*Lu 18:22*
donate to the poor (B)	*Lu 18:22*
give money away to poor (P)	*Lu 18:22*
works, ready to *d.* willing to	*1Ti 6:18*
ready to share (A)(B)(N)	*1Ti 6:18*
ready to give to others and to sympathize with those in distress (P)	*1Ti 6:18*
rich in good deeds, liberal, generous (R)	*1Ti 6:18*
ready to *d.* (E)	*1Ti 6:18*
be generous, *d.* to needy (A)	*Heb 13:16*

DISTRIBUTED

Israel, *d.* for inheritance to them	*Jos 14:1*
allotted to them (B)	*Jos 14:1*
he *d.* among all people (S)	*2Sa 6:19*
David *d.* them, both Zadok of	*1Ch 24:3*
d. all his countries (S)	*2Ch 11:23*
whom David had *d.* in the house of	*2Ch 23:18*
He hath *d.* to poor (S)	*Ps 112:9*
he *d.* to the disciples, and	*Joh 6:11*
as God hath *d.* to every man	*1Co 7:17*
allotted (A)	*1Co 7:17; 2Co 10:13*
God has given each his calling (B)	*1Co 7:17*
life the Lord assigned to him (R)	*1Co 7:17*
rule which God hath *d.* to us	*2Co 10:13*
God has allotted (B)	*2Co 10:13*
God has apportioned a measure (E)	*2Co 10:13*
limit God laid down for us (N)	*2Co 10:13*
limits God has apportioned (R)	*2Co 10:13*

DISTRIBUTES

d. to each (P)	*1Co 12:11*

DISTRIBUTETH

God *d.* sorrows in his anger	*Job 21:17*

DISTRIBUTING

D. to the necessity of saints	*Ro 12:13*
Contribute to needs of saints (A)(B)(R)	*Ro 12:13*
communicating to necessities of (E)	*Ro 12:13*
give freely to fellow Christians in want (P)	*Ro 12:13*
d. to each (B)(N)	*1Co 12:11*

DISTRIBUTION

feet: and *d.* was made unto every	*Ac 4:35*
and for your liberal *d.* unto them	*2Co 9:13*
for your generous-hearted liberality (A)	*2Co 9:13*
for liberality of your contribution (B)(E)	*2Co 9:13*
liberal contribution to their need (N)	*2Co 9:13*
generosity of your contribution (R)	*2Co 9:13*

DISTRIBUTIONS

d. of endowments (A)	*1Co 12:4*

DISTRIBUTOR

judge and *d.* over (B)	*Lu 12:14*

DISTRICT

ruler of the *d.* (S)	*Ne 3:14; 3:15, 17*

DISTRUST

he begins to *d.* and desert	*M't 13:21*
him whom he ought to trust and obey (A)	
though all *d.* and desert you I will never (A)	*M't 26:33*

DISTURBANCE

a source of *d.* (A)	*Ac 24:5*
no mob or *d.* (P)	*Ac 24:18*
cause a *d.* (B)	*Heb 12:15*

DISTURBANCES

d., be not alarmed (B)(P)	*Lu 21:9*

DISTURBED

spirit was *d.* (B)	*Ge 41:8; 1Sa 14:29; 2Ki 6:11; Ps 77:4*
distressingly *d.* and dismayed (A)	*Ge 45:3*
d. me to bring me up (B)(R)	*1Sa 28:15*
was *d.* (B)	*Da 2:1; M't 2:3; Joh 5:7; 12:27; 13:21; 2Th 2:2*
d. you (N)	*Ac 15:24*
to be *d.* (B)	*M'k 14:19*
have *d.* you (A)	*Joh 15:24; 2Th 2:2; 1Pe 3:14*
have *d.* you (N)	*Joh 15:24*

DISTURBER

a pestilential *d.* of peace (P)	*Ac 24:5*

DISUSE

fall into *d.* (S)	*Es 9:28*

DITCH

Yet shalt thou plunge me in the *d.*	*Job 9:31*
plunge me into a slough (B)	*Job 9:31*
plunge me into a pit (R)	*Job 9:31*
is fallen into the *d.* which he (A)(B)(R)	*Ps 7:15*
fallen into the hole he made (A)(B)(R)	*Ps 7:15*
For a whore is a deep *d.*; and a	*Pr 23:27*
harlot is a deep pit (B)(R)	*Pr 23:27*
Ye made also a *d.* between reservoir between two walls (A)(B)(E)(R)	*Isa 22:11*
blind, both shall fall into the *d.*	*M't 15:14*
fall into a pit (B)(E)(R)	*M't 15:14*
they not both fall into the *d.*	*Lu 6:39*

DITCHES

Make this valley full of *d.*	*2Ki 3:16*

DIVERS

sow thy vineyard with *d.* seeds	*De 22:9*
two kinds (A)(B)(E)(R)	*De 22:9; J'g 5:30*
a garment of *d.* sorts, as of	*De 22:11*
shalt not have in thy bag *d.* weights	*De 25:13*
not have in thine house *d.* measures	*De 25:14*
to Sisera a prey of *d.* colours	*J'g 5:30*
she had a garment of *d.* colours	*2Sa 13:18*
rent her garment of *d.* colours	*2Sa 13:19*
glistering stones, and of *d.* colours	*1Ch 29:2*
filled with sweet odours and *d.* kinds	*2Ch 16:14*
various kinds (A)(B)(R)	*2Ch 16:14*

and *d.* also of the princes of Israel	*2Ch 21:4*
d. of Asher and Manasseh	*2Ch 30:11*
sent *d.* sorts of flies among them	*Ps 78:45*
came *d.* sort of flies, and lice	*Ps 105:31*
D. weights, and *d.* measures	*Pr 20:10*
diverse weights (A)(B)(E)(R)	*Pr 20:10, 20:23*
D. weights are an abomination	*Pr 20:23*
words there are also *d.* vanities	*Ec 5:7*
thy high places with *d.* colours	*Eze 16:16*
diverse colors (B)	*Eze 16:16*
of feathers, which had *d.* colours	*Eze 17:3*
various or many colors (A)(B)(R)	*Eze 17:3*
with *d.* diseases and torments	*M't 4:24*
various diseases (A)(B)(R)	*M't 4:24*
and earthquakes, in *d.* places	*M't 24:7*
place after place (A)	*M't 24:7*
various places (B)(R)	*M't 24:7*
many that were sick of *d.* diseases	*M'k 1:34*
for *d.* of them came from far	*M'k 8:3*
shall be earthquakes in *d.* places	*M'k 13:8*
sick with *d.* diseases brought	*Lu 4:40*
great earthquakes shall be in *d.*	*Lu 21:11*
But when *d.* were hardened	*Ac 19:9*
to another *d.* kind of tongues	*1Co 12:10*
various kinds of tongues (A)(B)(R)	*1Co 12:10*
d. kinds of tongues (E)	*1Co 12:28*
with sins, led away with *d.* lusts	*2Ti 3:6*
various evil desires (A)	*2Ti 3:6*
all sorts of impulses (B)	*2Ti 3:6*
all kinds of desires (N)	*2Ti 3:6*
morbid cravings (P)	*2Ti 3:6*
various impulses (R)	*2Ti 3:6*
serving *d.* lusts and pleasures	*Tit 3:3*
all sorts of cravings (A)	*Tit 3:3*
passions of all sorts (B)(N)	*Tit 3:3*
various desires and pleasant feelings (P)	*Tit 3:3*
various passions (R)	*Tit 3:3*
times and in *d.* manners spake in	*Heb 1:1*
different ways God spoke (A)	*Heb 1:1*
various times and many ways (B)	*Heb 1:1*
fragmentary and varied fashion (P)	*Heb 1:1*
in many and various ways God spoke (R)	*Heb 1:1*
and with *d.* miracles, and gifts of	*Heb 2:4*
variety of miraculous powers (B)	*Heb 2:4*
by manifold powers and by gifts (E)	*Heb 2:4*
manifold works of power (N)	*Heb 2:4*
all kinds of spiritual power (P)	*Heb 2:4*
various miracles, gifts of the Spirit (R)	*Heb 2:4*
meats and drinks, and *d.* washings	*Heb 9:10*
different washings (A)	*Heb 9:10*
various ablutions (B)(R)	*Heb 9:10*
various rites of cleansing (N)	*Heb 9:10*
various washings, rules for body (P)	*Heb 9:10*
divers and strange doctrines	*Heb 13:9*
different, varied, alien teachings (A)	*Heb 13:9*
all sorts of strange teachings (B)	*Heb 13:9*
all sorts of outlandish teachings (N)	*Heb 13:9*
various peculiar teachings (P)	*Heb 13:9*
diverse and strange teachings (R)	*Heb 13:9*
when ye fall into *d.* temptations	*Jas 1:2*
various temptations (A)	*Jas 1:2*
all sorts of trials (B)	*Jas 1:2*
manifold temptations (E)	*Jas 1:2*

trials of many kinds (N)   *Jas 1:2*
all kinds of trials and   *Jas 1:2*
temptations (P)
various trials (R)   *Jas 1:2*

DIVERSE

cattle gender with a *d*. kind   *Le 19:19*
cattle breed with a different   *Le 19:19;*
kind (A)(B)(R) *Es 1:7; Da 7:3, 7, 19,*
                        24
vessels being *d*. one from   *Es 1:7*
another
their laws are *d*. from all   *Es 3:8*
people
d. weights   *Pr 20:10;*
(A)(B)(E)(R)(S)   *20:23*
d. colors (B)   *Eze 16:16*
the sea, *d*. one from another *Da 7:3*
and it was *d*. from all the   *Da 7:7*
beasts
which was *d*. from all the   *Da 7:19*
others
which shall be *d*. from all   *Da 7:23*
kingdoms
and he shall be *d*. from the *Da 7:24*
first

DIVERSITIES

Now there are *d*. of gifts,   *1Co 12:4*
but the
distinctive varieties and   *1Co 12:4*
distributions of endowments (A)
distinctive gifts of grace (B) *1Co 12:4*
varieties of gifts (N)(R)   *1Co 12:4*
Men have different gifts (P) *1Co 12:4*
there are *d*. of operations, *1Co 12:6*
but it
distinctive varieties of   *1Co 12:6*
operations (A)
varieties of things   *1Co 12:6*
accomplished (B)
There are many forms of   *1Co 12:6*
work (N)
God works in different men *1Co 12:6*
in different ways (P)
varieties of workings (R)   *1Co 12:6*
helps, governments, *d*. of *1Co 12:28*
tongues
different (unknown)   *1Co 12:28*
tongues (A)
speaking in tongues (B)   *1Co 12:28*
divers kinds of tongues (E) *1Co 12:28*
gift of ecstatic utterance of *1Co 12:28*
various kinds (N)
the gift of speaking in   *1Co 12:28*
tongues (P)
various kinds of tongues   *1Co 12:28*
(R)

DIVERTED

his anger is *d*. (A)   *Ge 27:45*

DIVIDE

let it *d*. the waters from the *Ge 1:6*
waters
to *d*. the day from the night *Ge 1:14*
to *d*. the light from the   *Ge 1:18*
darkness
will *d*. them in Jacob, and *Ge 49:7*
scatter
at night he shall *d*. the spoil *Ge 49:27*
thine hand over the sea and *Ex 14:16*
d. it
I will overtake, I will *d*. the *Ex 15:9*
spoil
the live ox, and *d*. the   *Ex 21:35*
money of it
the dead ox also they shall *Ex 21:35*
d.
the veil shall *d*. unto you *Ex 26:33*
between
thereof, but shall not *d*. it   *Le 1:17*
asunder
neck, but shall not *d*. it   *Le 5:8*
asunder
cud, or of them that *d*. the *Le 11:4*
hoof
the swine, though he *d*. the *Le 11:7*
hoof
And *d*. the prey into two *Nu 31:27*
parts
And ye shall *d*. the land by *Nu 33:54*
lot for
which shall *d*. the land unto *Nu 34:17*
you

tribe, to *d*. the land by   *Nu 34:18*
inheritance
Lord commanded to *d*. the *Nu 34:29*
inheritance
or of them that *d*. the cloven *De 14:7*
hoof
chew the cud, but *d*. not the *De 14:7*
hoof
d. the coasts, into three   *De 19:3*
parts
shalt thou *d*. for an   *Jos 1:6*
inheritance
d. thou it by lot unto the *Jos 13:6*
Israelites
d. this land for an   *Jos 13:7*
inheritance
And they shall *d*. it into *Jos 18:5*
seven
the spoil of your enemies   *Jos 22:8*
with
they shall *d*. alike (S)   *1Sa 30:24*
said, Thou and Ziba *d*. the *2Sa 19:29*
land
D. the living child in two *1Ki 3:25*
be neither mine nor thine, *1Ki 3:26*
but *d*.
thou didst *d*. the sea before *Ne 9:11*
them
and didst *d*. them into   *Ne 9:22*
corners
and the innocent shall *d*. *Job 27:17*
the silver
Destroy, O Lord, and *d*. their *Ps 55:9*
I will *d*. Shechem, and mete *Ps 60:6*
out
Thou didst *d*. the sea by thy *Ps 74:13*
will rejoice, I will *d*.   *Ps 108:7*
Shechem, and
than to *d*. the spoil with the *Pr 16:19*
proud
rejoice when they *d*. the spoil *Isa 9:3*
divide (A)(B)(E)(R) *Isa 18:2; 18:7*
Therefore will I *d*. him a *Isa 53:12*
portion
he shall *d*. the spoil with *Isa 53:12*
the strong
balances to weigh, and *d*. the *Eze 5:1*
hair
Moreover, when ye shall *d*. *Eze 45:1*
by lot
So shall ye *d*. this land   *Eze 47:21*
unto you
shall *d*. it by lot for an *Eze 47:22*
inheritance
ye shall *d*. by lot unto the *Eze 48:29*
tribes
and shall *d*. the land for *Da 11:39*
gain
that he *d*. the inheritance *Lu 12:13*
with me
d. the poor (A)   *Lu 18:22*
Take this, and *d*. it among *Lu 22:17*

DIVIDED

God *d*. the light from the *Ge 1:4*
darkness
and *d*. the waters which were *Ge 1:7*
under
were the isles of the Gentiles *Ge 10:5*
d.
in his days was the earth *d*. *Ge 10:25*
by these were the nations *d*. *Ge 10:32*
And he *d*. himself against *Ge 14:15*
them
and *d*. them in the midst, and *Ge 15:10*
laid
another: but the birds he *d*. *Ge 15:10*
not
and he *d*. the people that was *Ge 32:7*
with
And he *d*. the children unto *Ge 33:1*
Leah
dry land, and the waters *Ex 14:21*
were *d*.
Unto these the land shall be *Nu 26:53*
d.
the land shall be *d*. by lot *Nu 26:55*
shall the possession thereof *Nu 26:56*
be *d*.
which Moses *d*. from the *Nu 31:42*
men that
which the Lord thy God hath *De 4:19*
d.
d. to the nations their   *De 32:8*
inheritance
Israel did, and they *d*. the *Jos 14:5*
land
there Joshua *d*. the land *Jos 18:10*
unto the

d. for an inheritance by lot *Jos 19:51*
I have *d*. unto you by lot *Jos 23:4*
have they not *d*. the prey; to *J'g 5:30*
And he *d*. the three hundred *J'g 7:16*
men
and *d*. them into three   *J'g 9:43*
companies
and *d*. her, together with her *J'g 19:29*
in their death they were not *2Sa 1:23*
d.
Then were the people of *1Ki 16:21*
Israel *d*.
So they *d*. the land between *1Ki 18:6*
them
they were *d*. hither and *2Ki 2:8*
thither
in his days the earth was *d*. *1Ch 1:19*
And David *d*. them into *1Ch 23:6*
courses
of Ithamar; and thus were *1Ch 24:4*
they *d*.
Thus were they *d*. by lot, *1Ch 24:5*
one sort
and *d*. them speedily   *2Ch 35:13*
among all
Who hath *d*. a watercourse *Job 38:25*
for the
that tarried at home *d*. the *Ps 68:12*
spoil
He *d*. the sea, and caused *Ps 78:13*
them
and *d*. them an inheritance *Ps 78:55*
by
To him which *d*. the Red *Ps 136:13*
sea into
is the prey of a great spoil *Isa 33:23*
d.
his hand hath *d*. it unto *Isa 34:17*
them by
the Lord thy God, that *d*. *Isa 51:15*
the sea
anger of the Lord hath *d*. *La 4:16*
them
neither shall they be *d*. into *Eze 37:22*
two
of iron, the kingdom shall be *Da 2:41*
d.
Thy kingdom is *d*. and given *Da 5:28*
and shall be *d*. toward the *Da 11:4*
four
Their heart is *d*.; now shall *Ho 10:2*
they
and thy land shall be *d*. by *Am 7:17*
line
away he hath *d*. our field *Mic 2:4*
and thy spoil shall be *d*. in *Zec 14:1*
Every kingdom be *d*.   *M't 12:25*
against itself is
city or house *d*. against *M't 12:25*
itself
Satan, he is *d*. against   *M't 12:26*
himself
if a kingdom be *d*. against *M'k 3:24*
itself
if a house be *d*. against *M'k 3:25*
itself
and be *d*. he cannot stand, *M'k 3:26*
but hath
the two fishes *d*. he among *M'k 6:41*
them all
Every kingdom *d*. against *Lu 11:17*
itself is
house *d*. against a house *Lu 11:17*
falleth
If Satan also be *d*. against *Lu 11:18*
himself
there shall be five in one *Lu 12:52*
house *d*.
father shall be *d*. against the *Lu 12:53*
son
And he *d*. unto them his *Lu 15:12*
living
he *d*. their land to them by *Ac 13:19*
lot
the multitude of the city was *Ac 14:4*
d.
and the multitude was *d*. *Ac 23:7*
Is Christ *d*.? was Paul   *1Co 1:13*
crucified
Is Christ dismembered (B) *1Co 1:13*
Is there more than one   *1Co 1:13*
Christ (P)
the great city was *d*. into *Re 16:19*
three
broken into three parts (A) *Re 16:19*
split into three parts   *Re 16:19*
(B)(N)(P)(R)

DIVIDER

made me a judge or a d. over you	Lu 12:14
judge, empire, divider over you (A)	Lu 12:14
judge and distributor over (B)	Lu 12:14
to judge or arbitrate (N)	Lu 12:14
a judge or arbitrator (P)	Lu 12:14

DIVIDETH

the cud; but d. not the hoof	Le 11:4; 11:5-6
part the hoof (B)(E)(R)	Le 11:4
every beast which d. the hoof	Le 11:26
parts the hoof (A)(R)	Le 11:26
with parted hoof (B)	Le 11:26
which parteth the hoof (E)	Le 11:26
the swine, because it d. the hoof	De 14:8
He d. the sea with his power	Job 26:12
stills or stirs up the sea by his (A)	Job 26:12
By his power the sea is stilled (B)(E)(R)	Job 26:12
the Lord d. the flames of fire	Ps 29:7
splits and flashes forth forked lightning (A)	Ps 29:7
splits flames of fire (B)	Ps 29:7
cleaveth the flames of fire (E)	Ps 29:7
flashes forth flames of fire (R)	Ps 29:7
which d. the sea when the waves	Jer 31:35
stirs up the sea's roaring billows or stills the waves when they roar (A)	Jer 31:35
stirs up the sea so that waves roar (B)	Jer 31:35
stirreth up the sea so waves roar (E)(R)	Jer 31:35
as a shepherd d. his sheep from goats	M't 25:32
separates sheep from the goats (A)(E)(R)	M't 25:32
parts sheep from the goats (B)	M't 25:32
he trusted, and d. his spoils	Lu 11:22

DIVIDING

end of d. the land for inheritance	Jos 19:49
made an end of d. the country	Jos 19:51
d. the water before them, to	Isa 63:12
a time and times and the d. of	Da 7:25
d. to every man severally as he	1Co 12:11
apportions each person individually (A)(R)	1Co 12:11
distributing to each individual (B)(N)	1Co 12:11
distributes to each individual (P)	1Co 12:11
abolished the hostile d. wall (A)	Eph 2:14
rightly d. the word of truth	2Ti 2:15
correctly analyzing message of truth (B)	2Ti 2:15
handling aright the word of truth (E)(R)	2Ti 2:15
driving a straight furrow, in proclamation of truth (N)	2Ti 2:15
knows how to use the work of truth to the best advantage (P)	2Ti 2:15
even to the d. asunder of soul and	Heb 4:12
piercing as far as the place where life and spirit, joints and marrow divide (N)	Heb 4:12
piercing to the division of soul and (R)	Heb 4:12

DIVINATION

have learned by d. (R)	Ge 30:27
use it for d. (B)	Ge 44:5
with the rewards of d. in their	Nu 22:7
with rewards of foretelling (A)	Nu 22:7

with fees of sorcery in hand (B) — Nu 22:7

is there any d. against Israel	Nu 23:23
neither is witchcraft found in (B)	Nu 23:23
or that useth d. or an observer	De 18:10
sin of d. (R)	1Sa 15:23
used d. and enchantments	2Ki 17:17
a false vision and d. and a thing	Jer 14:14
vain vision nor flattering d. within	Eze 12:24
vanity and lying d. saying	Eze 13:6
have ye not spoken a lying d.	Eze 13:7
practice d. (B)	Eze 13:23
head of the two ways, to use d.	Eze 21:21
hand was the d. for Jerusalem	Eze 21:22
the lot marked for Jerusalem (A)(B)(R)	Eze 21:22
be unto them as a false d. in their	Eze 21:23
darkness without d. (B)(R)	Mic 3:6
possessed with a spirit of d. met us	Ac 16:16
possessed of a clairvoyant spirit (B)(P)	Ac 16:16
possessed by an oracular spirit (N)	Ac 16:16

DIVINATIONS

see no more vanity, nor divine d.	Eze 13:23
lying d. (R)	Eze 13:23

DIVINE

such a man as I can certainly d.	Ge 44:15
would unquestionably discover (B)	Ge 44:15
d. unto me by the familiar spirit	1Sa 28:8
inquire for me as a medium (B)	1Sa 28:8
A d. sentence is in the lips of the	Pr 16:10
Divinely directed decisions are (A)	Pr 16:10
godly decision is on lips of (B)	Pr 16:10
Inspired decisions are on lips (R)	Pr 16:10
that see vanity, and that d. lies	Eze 13:9
who see empty, false and delusive visions, and give lying prophecies (A)	Eze 13:9
who see vain visions and pronounce lying divinations (B)(R)	Eze 13:9
no more vanity, nor d. divinations	Eze 13:23
nor practice divination (B)	Eze 13:23
give lying divinations (R)	Eze 13:23
whiles they d. a lie unto thee	Eze 21:29
unto you, that ye shall not d.	Mic 3:6
darkness without divination (B)(R)	Mic 3:6
the prophets thereof d. for money	Mic 3:11
take part in d. service (N)	Lu 1:8
place to d. retribution (B)	Ro 12:19
worthy of d. calling (A)(B)(E)(N)(R)	Eph 4:1
d. nature was his (N)	Ph'p 2:6
the d. stewardship (A)(B)(P)(R)	Col 1:25
had also ordinances of d. service	Heb 9:1
According as his d. power hath	2Pe 1:3
might be partakers of the d. nature	2Pe 1:4

DIVINED

I have d. that the Lord (B)(E)	Ge 30:27

DIVINELY

d. directed decisions are (A)	Pr 16:10
time d. visited (B)	Lu 19:44

DIVINER

Balaam the d. (B)	Jos 13:2

DIVINERS

observers of times, and unto d.	De 18:14
called for the priests and the d.	1Sa 6:2
fall of d. from the east (R)	Isa 2:6
of the liars, and maketh d. mad	Isa 44:25
to your d. nor to your dreamers	Jer 27:9
Let not your prophets and your d.	Jer 29:8
ashamed, and the d. confounded	Mic 3:7
and the d. have seen a lie	Zec 10:2

DIVINETH

and whereby indeed he d.	Ge 44:5
use it for divination (B)	Ge 44:5

DIVINING

seeing vanity, and d. lies unto	Eze 22:28
their divinations for them (B)	Eze 22:28

DIVISION

I will put a d. between my people	Ex 8:23
make distinction between (B)	Ex 8:23
each d. 24,000 (A)(R)	1Ch 27:1
and after the d. of the families	2Ch 35:5
to bring d. (B)	M't 10:35
d. of Abia (A)(N)(R)	Lu 1:5
order of the d. (A)(R)	Lu 1:8
I tell you, Nay; but rather d.	Lu 12:51
there was a d. among the people	Joh 7:43
there was a d. among them	Joh 9:16
There was a d. therefore again	Joh 10:19
no d. or discord (A)(B)(N)(R)	1Co 12:25

DIVISIONS

to their d. by their tribes	Jos 11:23
a possession according to their d.	Jos 12:7
of Israel according to their d.	Jos 18:10
For the d. of Reuben, thoughts	J'g 5:15
the d. of Reuben, searchings	J'g 5:16
into d. (B)(R)(S)	1Ch 23:6; 2Ch 8:14; 23:8; 31:2; 35:10; Ezr 6:18
are the d. of the sons of Aaron	1Ch 24:1
Concerning the d. of the porters	1Ch 26:1
these were the d. of the porters	1Ch 26:12
These are the d. of the porters	1Ch 26:19
d. of priests (A)(R)	2Ch 5:11
according to the d. of the families	2Ch 35:5; 35:12
they set the priests in their d.	Ezr 6:18
of the Levites were d. in Judah	Ne 11:36
them which cause d. and offences	Ro 16:17
mark them causing d. (E)	Ro 16:17
that there be no d. among you	1Co 1:10
you envying, and strife, and d.	1Co 3:3
factions among you (A)	1Co 3:3
jealousy and quarreling (B)	1Co 3:3
jealousy and strife (E)(N)(R)	1Co 3:3
jealousy and squabbling (P)	1Co 3:3
hear that there be d. among you	1Co 11:18
factions among you (B)	1Co 11:18
fall into sharply divided groups (N)	1Co 11:18
split up into small groups (P)	1Co 11:18
d., party spirit (A)	Ga 5:20

DIVORCE

a bill of d. (A)(B)(R)   De 24:1
away, and given her a bill of   Jer 3:8
d.
bill of divorcement (A)(E)   Jer 3:8

DIVORCED

widow, or a d. woman, or   Le 21:14
profane
priest's daughter be a   Le 22:13
widow, or d.
of a widow, and of her that   Nu 30:9
is d.
a divorcee (B)   Nu 30:9
her that is d. committeth   M't 5:32
adultery
marries a divorcee (B)   M't 5:32
when she is put away (E)   M't 5:32

DIVORCEE

a d. (B)   Nu 30:9
marries a d. (B)   M't 5:32

DIVORCEMENT

then let him write her a bill   De 24:1
of d.
a bill of divorce (A)(B)(R)   De 24:1
hate her, and write her a bill   De 24:3
of d.
Where is the bill of your   Isa 50:1
mother's d.
bill of your mother's divorce   Isa 50:1
(A)(R)
let him give her a writing of   M't 5:31
d.
command to give a writing   M't 19:7
of d.
Moses suffered to write a   M'k 10:4
bill of d.

DIZAHAB

and Laban, and Hazeroth, and   De 1:1
D.

DO

Abram said, Do to her as it   Ge 16:6
pleaseth
shall not Judge of all earth   Ge 18:25
do right
what God hath said to thee,   Ge 31:16
do
thou saidst, I will surely do   Ge 32:12
thee good
God shewed what he is   Ge 41:25;
about to do   41:28
I will teach you what ye shall   Ex 4:15
do
if thou wilt do that which is   Ex 15:26;
right   De 6:18; 12:25; 13:18; 21:9
shew them work that they   Ex 18:20
must do
all that Lord hath spoken we   Ex 19:8
will do
six days do all thy work   Ex 20:9;
          23:12; De 5:13
shalt thou do to Aaron and   Ex 29:35
his sons
ye shall do my judgments,   Le 18:4;
and keep my ordinances   19:37; 20:22;
          Eze 36:27
which if man do   Le 18:5;
   Ne 9:29; Eze 20:11, 13, 21
do my statutes and keep my   Le 25:18
judgments   20:8; 22:31; De 17:19; 26:16
word I say to thee, shalt   Nu 22:20
thou do
what this people shall do to   Nu 24:14
thy people
servants will do as my lord   Nu 32:25
commandeth
keep commandments to do   De 7:11;
them   11:22
shalt do according to   De 17:10;
sentence   17:11
and these statutes, to do   De 17:19
them
then shall do to him as he   De 19:19
thought to do
thus shalt thou do to all the   De 20:15
cities
all the words of this law to   De 27:26
do them
that we may hear it and do   De 30:12;
          30:13

Lord do to them as he did to   De 31:4
Sihon
do thus requite Lord O foolish   De 32:6
people
round city, thus do six days   Jos 6:3
what wilt thou do to thy great   Jos 7:9
name
thus shall the Lord do to your   Jos 10:25
enemies
what have ye to do with God   Jos 22:24
of Israel
to do all written in book of   Jos 23:6;
the law   1Ch 16:40; 2Ch 34:21
it shall be, as I do so shall   J'g 7:17
ye do
what was I able to do in   J'g 8:3
comparison of you
do to us whatsoever seemeth   J'g 10:15
good to thee
consider therefore what ye   J'g 18:14
have to do
then said the priest unto   J'g 18:18
them, What do ye
he will tell thee what thou   Ru 3:4
shalt do
I will shew thee what thou   1Sa 16:3
shalt do
till I know what God will do   1Sa 22:3
for me
shalt do great things, and   1Sa 26:25
still prevail
now then do it, Lord hath   2Sa 3:18
spoken
oh that I were judge, I   2Sa 15:4
would do justice
let him do to me as   2Sa 15:26
seemeth good
that I may do it to thee   2Sa 24:12;
          1Ch 21:10
do according to thy wisdom   1Ki 2:6
do as he hath said, and fall   1Ki 2:31
upon him
hear, and do, and judge thy   1Ki 8:32
servants
hear in heaven, forgive, and   1Ki 8:39;
do   2Ch 6:23
do that is right in mine   1Ki 11:33;
eyes   11:38; 14:8
do it second time, do it   1Ki 18:34
third time
what hast thou to do with   2Ki 9:18;
peace   9:19
to this day they do after   2Ki 17:34
former manners
the Lord will do as he hath   2Ki 20:9
spoken
Nathan said, Do all that is   1Ch 17:2
in thine heart
let thing be established and   1Ch 17:23
do as said
do away the iniquity of thy   1Ch 21:8
servant
thee king, to do judgment   2Ch 9:8
and justice
said to the judges, take heed   2Ch 19:6
what ye do
wherefore now take heed   2Ch 19:7
and do it
thus shall ye do in the fear   2Ch 19:9
of the Lord
have no might, nor know   2Ch 20:12
what to do
if thou wilt go, do it, be   2Ch 25:8
strong for battle
for we seek your God, as ye   Ezr 4:2
do
to seek the law of the Lord,   Ezr 7:10
and do it
that do after the will of your   Ezr 7:18
God
what God put in my heart to   Ne 2:12
do
they should do according to   Ne 5:12
this promise
they might do with them as   Ne 9:24
they would
I have sinned, what shall I   Job 7:20
do to thee
it is high as heaven, what   Job 11:8
canst thou do
only do not two things unto   Job 13:20
me
In thee, O Lord, do I put my   Ps 31:1
trust; let
young lions do lack, and   Ps 34:10
suffer hunger
I delight to do thy will, O God   Ps 40:8
what hast thou to do to   Ps 50:16
declare statutes

which pass by the way do   Ps 80:12
pluck her
do unto them as unto the   Ps 83:9
Midianites
but do thou for me, O God   Ps 109:21
the Lord
teach me to do thy will   Ps 143:10
thou art God
it is in power of thy hand to   Pr 3:27
do it
do it with thy might, there is   Ec 9:10
no work
what will ye do in day of   Isa 10:3
visitation
he may do his work, his   Isa 28:21
strange work
I the Lord do all these things   Isa 45:7
what hast thou to do in way   Jer 2:18
of Egypt in way of Assyria
when thou art spoiled, what   Jer 4:30
wilt thou do
what will ye do in the end   Jer 5:31
thereof
seest what they do in cities   Jer 7:17
of Judah
saying, Obey my voice, and   Jer 11:4
do them
what hath my beloved to   Jer 11:15
do in mine house
how wilt thou do in swelling   Jer 12:5
of Jordan
O Lord, do thou it for thy   Jer 14:7
name's sake
and do tell them, and cause   Jer 23:32
my people
do to him, even as he shall   Jer 39:12
say to thee
may shew the thing that we   Jer 42:3
may do
as she hath done, do unto   Jer 50:15;
her   50:29
do to them as thou hast done   La 1:22
to me
son of man, seest thou what   Eze 8:6
they do
no eye pitied thee, to do any   Eze 16:5
of these to thee
but if a man be just, and   Eze 18:5;
do that which is   18:21; 33:14, 19
I will do these things unto   Eze 23:30
thee
and ye shall do as I have   Eze 24:22;
done   24:24
I will be inquired of to do   Eze 36:37
it for them
O Lord, hearken and do,   Da 9:19
defer not
he shall do according to his   Da 11:3;
will   11:16, 36
thus shall he do in most   Da 11:39
strong holds
what will ye do in the solemn   Ho 9:5
day
what then should a king do   Ho 10:3
to us
what have ye to do with me,   Joe 3:4
O Tyre
the Lord will do nothing, but   Am 3:7
he revealeth
I do well to be angry, even   Jon 4:9
unto death
but to do justly, and to love   Mic 6:8
mercy
then said I, What come these   Zec 1:21
to do
these are the things that ye   Zec 8:16
shall do
whosoever shall do and teach   M't 5:19
them
brethren only, what do ye   M't 5:47
more than others
cried out, saying, What have,   M't 8:29;
we to do with thee   M'k 1:24; Lu 4:34
for whosoever shall do the   M't 12:50;
will of my Father who   M'k 3:35
is in heaven
In vain they do worship me,   M't 15:9
teaching
lawful to do what I will   M't 20:15
with mine own
what will ye that I shall do   M't 20:32;
to you   M'k 10:36
if ye tell me, I will tell   M't 21:24;
you by what authority I do   M'k 11:29
these things
he said, Neither tell I you   M't 21:27;
by what authority I do   M'k 11:33:

these things	Lu 20:8
when lord of vineyard	M't 21:40;
cometh, what will he	M'k 12:9; Lu 20:15
do to husbandmen	
all their works *do* to be seen	M't 23:5
of men	
have nothing to *do* with	M't 27:19
that just man	
many other such like things,	M'k 7:8
ye *do*	
suffer him no more to *do*	M'k 7:12
for father or	
who gave thee authority to	M'k 11:28
do these things	
neither *do* I tell you by	M'k 11:33
what authority	
what heard done, *do* in thy	Lu 4:23
country	
why *do* ye that which is not	Lu 6:2
lawful to *do*	
commune what they might	Lu 6:11
do to Jesus	
as ye would men should *do*	Lu 6:31
to you, *do* ye	
these who hear word of God	Lu 8:21
and *do* it	
I am resolved what to *do*	Lu 16:4
when I am put	
done that which was our	Lu 17:10
duty to *do*	
could not find what they might	Lu 19:48
do	
if they *do* these things in a	Lu 23:3
green tree	
forgive them, they know not	Lu 23:34
what they *do*	
whatsoever he saith to you,	Joh 2:5
do it	
meat is to *do* will of him	Joh 4:34
that sent	
I can of mine own self *do*	Joh 5:30
nothing	
the works that I *do* bear	Joh 5:36
witness of me	
for he himself knew what	Joh 6:6
he would *do*	
what shall we *do*	Joh 6:28;
	Ac 2:37; 16:30
if *do* these things shew self to	Joh 7:4
world	
if any man will *do* his will,	Joh 7:17
he shall know	
I *do* always those things that	Joh 8:29
please him	
ye would *do* the works of	Joh 8:39
Abraham	
if he were not of God, he	Joh 9:33
could *do* nothing	
works that I *do* in my	Joh 10:25
Father's name	
chief priests and Pharisees	Joh 11:47
said, What *do* we	
what I *do* thou knowest not	Joh 13:7
now	
that ye should *do* as I have	Joh 13:15
done to you	
if know these, happy are ye	Joh 13:17
if *do* them	
the works that I *do* shall he	Joh 14:12
do also	
if ask any thing in my	Joh 14:14
name, I will *do* it	
friends, if ye *do* whatever I	Joh 15:14
command you	
these things will they *do*	Joh 15:21;
unto you	Joh 16:3
the work which thou gavest	Joh 17:4
me to *do*	
Lord, and what shall this	Joh 21:21
man *do*	
of all Jesus began to *do* and	Ac 1:1
teach	
to *do* whatsoever thy counsel	Ac 4:28
determined	
ye *do* always resist the Holy	Ac 7:51
Ghost	
said, Lord, what wilt thou	Ac 9:6
have me to *do*	
tell thee what thou oughtest	Ac 10:6
to *do*	
sirs, why *do* ye these things	Ac 14:15
visit our brethren, and see	Ac 15:36
how they *do*	
do thyself no harm, we are	Ac 16:28
all here	
do contrary to the decrees of	Ac 17:7
Caesar	
not only *do* same but have	Ro 1:32
pleasure	

do by nature things contained	Ro 2:14
in law	
that which I *do* I allow not,	Ro 7:15
what I would that *do* I not,	
but what I hate that *do* I	
if I *do* that which I would	Ro 7:16
not, I consent	
then it is no more I that *do*	Ro 7:17;
it, but sin	7:20
that giveth, let him *do* it with	Ro 12:8
simplicity	
let him *do* what he will, he	1Co 7:36
sinneth not	
whatsoever ye *do*, *do* all to	1Co 10:31
glory of God	
worketh work of Lord as I	1Co 16:10
also *do*	
not only to *do* but also be	2Co 8:10
forward	
that ye should *do* that which	2Co 13:7
is honest	
same which I also was	Ga 2:10
forward to *do*	
not as do the Jews, to live as	Ga 2:14
do the Jews	
written in book of law to *do*	Ga 3:10
them	
which *do* such things shall	Ga 5:21
not inherit	
masters, *do* same things to	Eph 6:9
servants	
ye may know my affairs,	Eph 6:21
and how I *do*	
God worketh both to will	Ph'p 2:13
and to *do*	
things ye have heard and	Ph'p 4:9
seen in me, *do*	
whatsoever ye *do* in word or	Col 3:17
deed, *do* all in name of	
whatsoever ye *do*, *do* it	Col 3:23
heartily, as to Lord	
in love, even as we *do*	1Th 3:12
towards you	
indeed ye *do* it towards all	1Th 4:10
the brethren	
therefore let us not sleep as	1Th 5:6
do others	
edify one another, even as	1Th 5:11
also ye *do*	
faithful is he that calleth,	1Th 5:24
who will *do* it	
that ye both *do* and will *do*	2Th 3:4
things	
do work of an evangelist,	2Ti 4:5
make proof	
do thy diligence to come	2Th 4:9;
shortly	4:21
albeit I *do* not say to thee	Ph'm 19
knowing thou wilt *do* more	Ph'm 21
than I say	
to eyes of him with whom	Heb 4:13
we have to *do*	
said I, Lo, I come to *do* thy	Heb 10:7;
will	10:9
I will not fear what man	Heb 13:6
shall *do* to me	
make perfect in every	Heb 13:21
work, to *do* his will	
let him *do* it as of ability	1Pe 4:11
God giveth	
if ye *do* these, ye shall never	2Pe 1:10
fall	
wrest, as they *do* also other	2Pe 3:16
scriptures	
we lie, and *do* not the truth	1Jo 1:6
do things that are pleasing in	1Jo 3:22
his sight	
repent, and *do* the first works	Re 2:5

CAN, CANST DO

what *can* I *do* to my	Ge 31:43
daughters	
none *can do* according to thy	De 3:24
works	
know what thy servant *can*	1Sa 28:2
do	
speeches wherewith he *can*	Job 15:3
do no good	
what *can* the Almighty *do*	Job 22:17
for them	
I know that thou *canst do*	Job 42:2
everything	
found, destroyed, what *can*	Ps 11:3
righteous *do*	
not fear what flesh *can do* to	Ps 56:4;
me	56:11
I will not fear what man *can*	Ps 118:6
do to me	

what *can* man *do* that cometh	Ec 2:12
after king	
that *can do* any thing against	Jer 38:5
you	
if *canst do* any thing, have	M'k 9:22
after that have no more they	Lu 12:4
can do	
no man *can do* miracles thou	Joh 3:2
dost	
the Son *can do* nothing	Joh 5:19;
of himself	5:30
for without me ye *can do*	Joh 15:5
nothing	
we *can do* nothing against	2Co 13:8
truth	
can do all things through	Ph'p 4:13
Christ	

HAVE I TO DO

what *have I to do* with	2Sa 16:10;
you	19:22
what *have I to do* with	1Ki 17:18;
thee 2Ki 3:13; 2Ch 35:21; M'k 5:7;	
Lu 8:28; Joh 2:4	
what *have I to do* with idols	Ho 14:8
what *have I to do* to judge	1Co 5:12
them	

I WILL, SHALL DO

what *shall I do* now to thee	Ge 27:37
said, I *will do* as thou hast	Ge 47:30
said	
which I *will do* in midst	Ex 3:20
thereof	
shalt see what I *will do* to	Ex 6:1
Pharaoh	
Moses cried, What *shall I do*	Ex 17:4
to this people	
I *will do* marvels, I *will do*	Ex 34:10
with thee	
I *will do* it to this	Nu 14:35
congregation	
I *will do* whatsoever thou	Nu 22:17
sayest to me	
I *shall do* to you as I	Nu 33:56
thought to *do*	
said, All thou sayest to me I	Ru 3:5
will do	
I *will do* to thee all that thou	Ru 3:11
requirest	
will I *do* part of a kinsman	Ru 3:13
to thee	
I *will do* a thing in Israel	1Sa 3:11
saying, What *shall I do* for	1Sa 10:2
my son	
thy soul desireth, I *will do* it	1Sa 20:4
for thee	
make known to me what I	1Sa 28:15
shall do	
I *will do* this thing before	2Sa 12:12
Israel	
what seemeth best I *will do*	2Sa 18:4;
	19:38
Gibeonites, what *shall I do*	2Sa 21:3
for you	
what you say, that *will I do*	2Sa 21:4
for you	
I *will do* all thy desire for	1Ki 5:8
timber	
all thou didst send for at	1Ki 20:9
first, I *will do*	
Elijah said, Ask what I *shall*	2Ki 2:9
do for thee	
Elisha said to her, What *shall*	2Ki 4:2
I *do* for thee	
I *will do* to-morrow as king	Es 5:8
hath said	
what *shall I do* to thee, O	Job 7:20
preserver	
what *shall I do* when God	Job 31:14
riseth up	
if done iniquity, I *will do*	Job 34:32
no *more*	
I *will do* to him as he hath	Pr 24:29
done	
tell what I *will do* to my	Isa 5:5
vineyard	
these things *will I do*, and	Isa 42:16
not forsake	
I *will do* a new thing, it	Isa 43:19
shall spring	
I *will do* all my pleasure	Isa 46:10
I have purposed it, I *will*	Isa 46:11
also *do* it	
even for mine own sake *will*	Isa 48:11
I *do* it	
therefore *will I do* unto this	Jer 7:14
house	

how *shall I do* for daughter of   *Jer 9:7*
my people
thus *will I do* to this place   *Jer 19:12*
provoke me not, *I will do*   *Jer 25:6*
you no hurt
good that *I will do* for my   *Jer 29:32*
people
I will do judgment on   *Jer 51:47*
graven images
I will do what I have not done   *Eze 5:9*
I will do unto them after   *Eze 7:27*
their way
I have spoken, and *will do*   *Eze 22:14;*
it   *24:14; 36:36*
I will even *do* according to   *Eze 35:11*
thine anger
I will do better than at   *Eze 36:11*
beginning
Ephraim, what *shall I do* to   *Ho 6:4*
thee
thus *will I do* unto thee, O   *Am 4:12*
Israel
Master, what good thing   *M't 19:16*
shall I do
Pilate saith, What *shall I do*   *M't 27:22*
with Jesus
what *shall I do*, I have no   *Lu 12:17*
room
what *shall I do*   *Lu 16:3;*
    20:13; Ac 22:10
whatever shall ask, that *will*   *Joh 14:13*
I do
if ask any thing in my   *Joh 14:14*
name *I will do*
but what I do, that *I will*   *2Co 11:12*
do
without thy mind *would I do*   *Ph'm 14*
nothing

MUST DO

shalt shew work that they   *Ex 18:20*
must do
all Lord speaketh, that I   *Nu 23:26*
must do
if deliver, thou *must do* it   *Pr 19:19*
again
jailer said, What *must* I do   *Ac 16:30*
to be saved

OBSERVE with DO

ye shall *observe to do* as Lord   *De 5:32;*
commanded you *8:1; 11:32; 12:1; 24:8;*
    2Ki 17:37
observe to do   *De 6:3;*
12:32; 28:13, 15, 58; 31:12; 32:46
if we *observe to do* these   *De 6:25*
commandments
to *observe to do* all these   *De 15:5*
commandments
thou shalt *observe* and *do*   *De 16:12*
these statutes
shalt *observe to do* as they   *De 17:10*
inform thee
thou mayest *observe to do* all   *Jos 1:7*
the law
if they *observe to do*   *2Ki 21:8*
according to
entered into oath to *observe*   *Ne 10:29*
and *do*
they shall *observe* and *do*   *Eze 37:24*
them
what they bid you, that   *M't 23:3*
observe and *do*

SHALL WE DO,
WE SHALL DO

teach us what *we shall do* to   *J'g 13:8*
child
how shall order, how *shall*   *J'g 13:12*
we do unto him
how *shall we do* for wives   *J'g 21:7*
for them
what *shall we do* with ark of   *1Sa 5:8*
God
what *shall we do* to the ark   *1Sa 6:2*
of the Lord
among you what *we shall do*   *2Sa 16:20*
shall we do after his saying?   *2Sa 17:6*
speak thou
alas my master, how *shall*   *2Ki 6:15*
we do
what *shall we do* for the 100   *2Ch 25:9*
talents
what *shall we do* to queen   *Es 1:15*

---

thro' God *we shall do*   *Ps 60:12;*
    108:13
valiantly
what *shall we do* for our sister   *Ca 8:8*
in the day
they said, What *shall we do*   *Jon 1:11*
to thee
people asked, What *shall we*   *Lu 3:10;*
do   *12:14*
What *shall we do* that we   *Joh 6:28*
might work
Men and brethren, what *shall*   *Ac 2:37*
we do
saying, What *shall we do* to   *Ac 4:16*
these men

SO DO, DO SO

they said, *So do* as thou hast   *Ge 18:5*
said
pray you, *do* not *so* wickedly   *Ge 19:7;*
    J'g 19:23
Joseph said, God forbid that   *Ge 44:17*
I should *do so*
Moses said, It is not meet *so*   *Ex 8:26*
so shall he *do*   *Le 4:20;*
    16:16; Nu 9:14; 15:14
so the Lord hath commanded   *Le 8:34*
to *do*
so will I do   *Nu 14:28;*
    32:31; Isa 65:8; Eze 35:15
so shall he *do* to every one   *Nu 15:12*
according to number
was I ever wont to *do so*   *Nu 22:30*
unto thee
if ye will not *do so* ye have   *Nu 32:23*
sinned
so shall the Lord *do* to all   *De 3:21*
the kings
ye shall not *do so* to Lord   *De 12:4;*
your God   *12:31*
how did these nations serve   *De 12:30*
their gods *so I do*
Lord God hath not suffered   *De 18:14*
thee *so to do*
and *so* shalt thou *do* with his   *De 22:3*
raiment
all that *do so* are   *De 22:5*
abomination to Lord
it shall be, that as I do, *so*   *J'g 7:17*
shall ye *do*
if we *do* not *so* according to   *J'g 11:10*
thy words
for *so* used the young men   *J'g 14:10*
to *do*
but to this man *do* not *so*   *J'g 19:24*
vile thing
Lord *do so* to me   *Ru 1:17; 1Sa 14:44*
God *do so* to thee and more   *1Sa 3:17*
also
served other gods, *so do* to   *1Sa 8:8*
thee
Lord *do so* and much more   *1Sa 20:13*
to Jonathan
so and more also *do* God to   *1Sa 25:22*
enemies of David
David said, Ye shall not   *1Sa 30:23*
do so
so do God to Abner, even *so*   *2Sa 3:9*
I do to him
God *do so* to me, and more   *2Sa 3:35;*
also   *19:13; 1Ki 2:23; 20:10; 2Ki 6:31*
then said Ziba, *So* shall thy   *2Sa 9:11*
servant *do*
even *so* will I certainly *do*   *1Ki 1:30*
this day
as the king said, *so* will thy   *1Ki 2:38*
servant *do*
so let the gods *do* to me,   *1Ki 19:2*
and more also
he said, Go forth, and *do*   *1Ki 22:22;*
so   *2Ch 18:21*
as did their fathers, *so do*   *2Ki 17:41*
they to-day
all congregation said they   *1Ch 13:4*
would *do so*
as thou hast said, *so* must   *Ezr 10:12*
we *do*
they said, *So* will we *do* as   *Ne 5:12*
thou sayest
that I should be afraid, and   *Ne 6:13*
do so, and sin
if ye *do so*, I will lay hands   *Ne 13:21*
on you
and *do* even *so* to Mordecai   *Es 6:10*
the Jew
who and where is he durst   *Es 7:5*
presume to *do so*

---

as one man mocketh, *do* ye   *Joh 13:9*
so mock him
so do stripes the inward   *Pr 20:30*
parts of belly
say not, I will *do so* to him   *Pr 24:29*
as he hath done
shall I *so do* to Jerusalem   *Isa 10:11*
and her idols
the Lord *do so*, the Lord   *Jer 28:6*
perform words
so thou shalt *do* seventh   *Eze 45:20*
day of month
so shall he *do*, he shall even   *Da 11:30*
return
so shall Beth-el *do* to you,   *Ho 10:15*
because of your
do not even the publicans *so*   *M't 5:47*
men *do* to you, *do* ye even   *M't 7:12*
so to them
so shall my heavenly Father   *M't 18:35*
do unto you
as Father gave   *Joh 14:31*
commandment, *so* I *do*
as your fathers did, *so do* ye   *Ac 7:51*
as I have given order, even   *1Co 16:1*
so do ye
even as Christ forgave you,   *Col 3:13*
so do ye
than edifying, which is in faith,   *1Ti 1:4*
so do
so do ye, as they that shall   *Jas 2:12*
be judged

WILL WE DO, WE WILL DO

all Lord hath said *we will do*   *Ex 19:8;*
    24:3, 7
same goodness *will we do* to   *Nu 10:32*
thee
and *we will* hear it and *do* it   *De 5:27*
all thou commandest us *we*   *Jos 1:16*
will do
the thing which *we will do* to   *J'g 20:9*
Gibeah
we will do all that thou bid   *2Ki 10:5*
us
we will every one *do* the   *Jer 18:12*
imagination
so declare unto us, and *we*   *Jer 42:20*
will do it
we will certainly *do*   *Jer 44:17*
whatever proceedeth

DO EVIL

not follow a multitude to *do*   *Ex 23:2*
evil
if a soul swear to *do evil* or   *Le 5:4*
good
shall *do evil* in sight of the   *De 4:25*
Lord
ye will *do evil* in sight of   *De 31:29*
the Lord
if it please father to *do*   *1Sa 20:13*
thee *evil*
why despised Lord to *do evil*   *2Sa 12:9*
in sight
because I know *evil* thou   *2Ki 8:12*
wilt *do*
sold themselves to *do evil*   *2Ki 17:17*
in sight of Lord
Manasseh seduced them to   *2Ki 21:9*
do more evil
face of Lord against them   *Ps 34:16*
that *do evil*
fret not thyself in any wise to   *Ps 37:8*
do evil
rejoice to *do evil*, and delight   *Pr 2:14*
in
he that deviseth to *do evil*   *Pr 24:8*
shall be called
they consider not that they *do*   *Ec 5:1*
evil
heart of men fully set to *do*   *Ec 8:11*
evil
though a sinner *do evil* an   *Ec 8:12*
hundred times
wash, make clean, cease to   *Isa 1:16*
do evil
do good or *evil*, we may be   *Isa 41:23*
dismayed
my people are wise to *do evil*   *Jer 4:22*
be not afraid, for they   *Jer 10:5*
cannot *do evil*
may ye that are accustomed   *Jer 13:23*
to *do evil*
if it *do evil* in my sight,   *Jer 18:10*
that it obey not
that I would *do* this *evil*   *Eze 6:10*
unto them

they may *do evil* with both hands   *Mic 7:3*

Lord not do good, nor will he *do evil*   *Zep 1:12*

lawful to do good or *do evil*   *M'k 3:4; Lu 6:9*

let us *do evil* that good may   *Ro 3:8*

but if thou *do* that which is *evil*   *Ro 13:4*

now I pray to God ye *do* no *evil*   *2Co 13:5*

Lord is against them that *do evil*   *1Pe 3:12*

DO GOOD

do to them as is *good* in your eyes   *Ge 19:8*

said, What *good* shall my life *do* me   *Ge 27:46*

if swear, pronouncing to *do good*   *Le 5:4*

come with us, we will *do* thee *good*   *Nu 10:29*

to *do* either *good* or bad of my mind   *Nu 24:13*

thing spoken is *good* for us to *do*   *De 1:14*

prove thee, to *do good* at latter end   *De 8:16*

Lord rejoiced to *do* you *good*   *De 28:63*

he will *do* thee *good* and multiply thee   *De 30:5*

now know I the Lord will *do good*   *J'g 17:13*

do with them what seemeth *good* to you   *J'g 19:24*

Elkanah said to Hannah, Do what seemeth *good*   *1Sa 1:23; 14:36, 40; 2Sa 19:27, 37*

Eli said, It is the Lord; let him *do* what seemeth *good*   *1Sa 3:18; 2Sa 10:12*

do that which is *good* in thine eyes   *2Ki 10:5*

let Lord *do* what is *good* in his sight   *1Ch 19:13*

lest king *do* that which is *good* in his eyes   *1Ch 21:23*

also I said, It is not *good* that ye *do*   *Ne 5:9*

do good   *Ps 34:14; 37:3, 27; 51:18; 125:4; M't 5:44; Lu 6:9, 35*

hath left off to be wise and to *do good*   *Ps 36:3*

she will *do* him *good* and not evil   *Pr 31:12*

for a man to *do good* in his life   *Ec 3:12*

do good or do evil, that we may   *Isa 41:23*

to *do good* they have no knowledge   *Jer 4:22*

cannot do evil, nor is it in them to *do good*   *Jer 10:5*

then may ye *do good* that are accustomed   *Jer 13:23*

do with me as seemeth *good* and meet   *Jer 26:14*

nor behold the *good* I will *do* for my people   *Jer 29:32*

not turn away from them to *do* them *good*   *Jer 32:40*

I will rejoice over them to *do* them *good*   *Jer 32:41*

which shall hear all the *good* I *do*   *Jer 33:9*

do not my words *do good* to upright   *Mic 2:7*

that say, The Lord will not *do good*   *Zep 1:12*

is it lawful to *do good* on sabbath days, or to *do* evil   *M'k 3:4; Lu 6:9*

poor, when ye will, ye may *do* them *good*   *M'k 14:7*

if *do good* to them that *do good* to you   *Lu 6:33*

for the *good* that I would, I *do* not   *Ro 7:19*

when I would *do good* evil is present   *Ro 7:21*

do what is *good*, and have praise   *Ro 13:3*

let us *do good* to all men, especially to   *Ga 6:10*

charge the rich, that they do *good*   *1Ti 6:18*

do good and communicate, forget not   *Heb 13:16*

---

knoweth to *do good,* and doth it not   *Jas 4:17*

let him eschew evil, and *do good*   *1Pe 3:11*

DO NOT, NOT DO, DO NO

I will *not do* it for forty's sake   *Ge 18:29*

I will *not do* if I find thirty there   *Ge 18:30*

young man deferred *not* to *do* the thing   *Ge 34:19*

not do any work   *Ex 20:10; Le 23:31; Nu 29:7*

if he *do not* these three unto her   *Ex 21:11*

thou shalt *not do* after their works   *Ex 23:24*

do no work   *Le 16:29; 23:3, 28; De 15:19; Jer 17:24*

after their doings ye shall *not do*   *Le 18:3*

do no unrighteousness in judgment   *Le 19:15; 19:35*

do no servile work therein   *Le 23:7; 23:8, 21, 25, 35-36; Nu 28:18, 25-26*

if ye will *not do* my commandments   *Le 26:14; 26:15; Nu 29:7; De 5:14; 16:8*

from age of fifty years *do no* service   *Nu 8:26*

hath he said, and shall he *not do* it   *Nu 23:19*

not do after all things we do here   *De 12:8*

shall *do no* more any such wickedness   *De 13:11*

fear and *do no* more presumptuously   *De 17:13*

feared he could *not do* it by day   *J'g 6:27*

my brethren, I pray you, *do not* this folly   *J'g 19:23*

but to this man *do not* so vile a thing   *J'g 19:24*

if he will *not do* part of a kinsman   *Ru 3:13*

I will *no* more *do* thee harm   *1Sa 26:21*

in thy days I will *not do* it for David   *1Ki 11:12*

lepers said, We *do not* well   *2Ki 7:9*

charged they should *not do* like them   *2Ki 17:15*

would *not* hear them, nor *do* them   *2Ki 18:12*

whoso will *not do* law of God   *Ezr 7:26*

only *do not* two things unto me   *Job 13:20*

yea, surely God will *not do* wickedly   *Job 34:12*

remember the battle, *do no* more   *Job 41:8*

they *do no* iniquity, they walk   *Ps 19:3*

do no wrong, *do no* violence to stranger   *Jer 22:3*

Lord be a true witness, if we *do not*   *Jer 42:5*

I will *not do* any more the like   *Eze 5:9*

be taught *not* to *do* after lewdness   *Eze 23:48*

hear thy words, but will *not do* them   *Eze 33:31*

hear thy words, but they *do* them *not*   *Eze 33:32*

the just Lord, he will *not do* iniquity   *Zep 3:5*

remnant of Israel shall *not do* iniquity   *Zep 3:13*

do not even publicans the same   *M't 5:46; 5:47*

do not your alms before men   *M't 6:1*

Jesus said, Thou shalt *do no* murder   *M't 19:18*

he said, Friend, I *do* thee *no* wrong   *M't 20:13*

do not their works, they say and *do not*   *M't 23:3*

he could there *do no* mighty work   *M'k 6:5*

do not the things which I say   *Lu 6:46*

I came down *not* to *do* own will   *Joh 6:38*

If I *do not* the works of my Father   *Joh 10:37*

for what I would, that *do* I *not*   *Ro 7:15; 7:19*

for what the law could *not do*   *Ro 8:3*

---

ye *cannot do* things that ye would   *Ga 5:17*

we lie, and *do not* the truth   *1Jo 1:6*

he said, see thou *do* it *not*   *Re 19:10; 22:9*

DO THIS, THIS DO

people is one, and *this* begin to *do*   *Ge 11:6*

can I *do this* great sin against God   *Ge 39:9*

let Pharaoh *do this,* appoint officers   *Ge 41:34*

Joseph said, *This do* and live, I fear God   *Ge 42:18*

if it must be so now, *do this*   *Ge 43:11; 45:17, 19*

I will *do this* to you, I will appoint terror   *Le 26:16*

this do, take censers, Korah and all   *Nu 16:6*

this we will *do* to the Gibeonites   *Jos 9:20*

brethren, I pray, *do not this* folly   *J'g 19:23*

my brother, *do* not thou *this* folly   *2Sa 13:12*

be it far from me that I should *do this*   *2Sa 23:17*

zeal of Lord shall *do this*   *2Ki 19:31; Isa 37:32*

this do, and ye shall not trespass   *2Ch 19:10*

take heed that ye fail not to *do this*   *Ezr 4:2*

do this now, my son, deliver thyself   *Pr 6:3*

living praise thee, as I *do this* day   *Isa 38:19*

that they should *do this* abomination   *Jer 32:35*

that I would *do this* evil to them   *Eze 6:10*

I *do not this* for your sakes   *Eze 36:22; 36:32*

and because I will *do this* to thee   *Am 4:12*

in day that I shall *do this,* saith Lord   *Mal 4:3*

to my servant, *do this* he doeth   *M't 8:9; Lu 7:8*

believe ye that I am able to *do this*   *M't 9:28*

if ye have faith, ye shall not only *do this*   *M't 21:21*

if any say to you, Why do ye *this*   *M'k 11:3*

was worthy for whom he should *do this*   *Lu 7:4*

said to him, *This do,* and thou shalt live   *Lu 10:28*

said, *This* will I *do,* I will pull down   *Lu 12:18*

this do in remembrance of me   *Lu 22:19; 1Co 11:24-25*

do therefore *this* that we say to thee   *Ac 21:23*

if I *do this* thing willingly, have reward   *1Co 9:17*

and *this* I *do* for the gospel's sake   *1Co 9:23*

and *this* will we *do* if God permit   *Heb 6:3*

but I beseech you the rather to *do this*   *Heb 13:19*

if Lord will, we will *do this* or that   *Jas 4:15*

DO WELL

learn to *do well,* seek judgment   *Isa 1:17*

I *do well* to be angry, even to death   *Jon 4:9*

to *do well* to Jerusalem and Judah   *Zec 8:15*

it is lawful to *do well* on sabbath days   *M't 12:12*

Lord, if he sleep, he shall *do well*   *Joh 11:12*

if ye keep yourselves, ye shall *do well*   *Ac 15:29*

if ye fulfil the royal law, ye *do well*   *Jas 2:8*

for the praise of them that *do well*   *1Pe 2:14*

but if when ye *do well* and suffer for it   *1Pe 2:20*

daughters ye are as long as ye *1Pe 3:6*
do well
whereto ye *do well* that ye take *2Pe 1:19*
heed
whom if thou bring, thou shalt *3Jo 6*
do well

DOCTOR

then stood up Gamaliel, a *d.* *Ac 5:34*
of the law
teacher of the law *Ac 5:34*
(A)(B)(N)(P)(R)

DOCTORS

they found Jesus sitting in *Lu 2:46*
midst of the *d.*
sitting among teachers *Lu 2:46*
(A)(B)(E)(N)(P)(R)
there were Pharisees and *d.* *Lu 5:17*
of law sitting by
teachers of the law *Lu 5:17*
(A)(B)(N)(R)
experts in the law (P) *Lu 5:17*

DOCTRINAL

teach some *d.* novelty (R) *1Ti 6:3*

DOCTRINE

whom shall he make to *Isa 28:9*
understand *d.*
and they that murmured *Isa 29:24*
shall learn *d.*
brutish, the stock is a *d.* of *Jer 10:8*
vanities
the people were astonished *M't 7:28;*
at his *d.*   *22:33; M'k 1:22; 11:18;*
                                      Lu 4:32
beware of the *d.* of the *M'k 16:12*
Pharisees
people amazed, saying, What *M'k 1:27*
new *d.*
taught and said to them in *M'k 4:2;*
his *d.*   *12:38*
if do his will, he shall know *Joh 7:17*
of the *d.*
high priest then asked Jesus *Joh 18:19*
of his *d.*
they continued in the *Ac 2:42*
apostles' *d.*
ye have filled Jerusalem with *Ac 5:28*
your *d.*
being astonished at the *d.* of *Ac 13:12*
the Lord
saying, May we know what *Ac 17:19*
this new *d.* is
but ye have obeyed that form *Ro 6:17*
of *d.*
contrary to the *d.* which ye *Ro 16:17*
have learned
the *d.* of the cross (N) *1Co 1:18*
except I shall speak to you *1Co 14:6*
by *d.*
every one of you hath a *d.* *1Co 14:26*
a tongue
carried about with every *Eph 4:14*
wind of *d.*
charge that they teach no *1Ti 1:3*
other *d.*
till I come, give attendance *1Ti 4:13*
to reading, to *d.*
take heed to thyself, and to *1Ti 4:16*
thy *d.*
especially they who labour in *1Ti 5:17*
the word and *d.*
name of God and his *d.* be not *1Ti 6:1*
blasphemed
to the *d.* which is according *1Ti 6:3*
to godliness
all scripture is profitable for *2Ti 3:16*
d.
rebuke with all long suffering *2 Ti 4:2*
and *d.*
in *d.* shewing incorruptness, *Tit 2:7*
gravity
they may adorn the *d.* of God *Tit 2:10*
our Saviour
leaving principles of *d.* of *Heb 6:1*
Christ
of the *d.* of baptisms, and of *Heb 6:2*
laying on of hands
whose abideth not in *d.* of *2Jo 9*
Christ
hast them that hold *d.* of *Re 2:14*
Balaam
hold *d.* of Nicolaitans, which *Re 2:15*
I hate

GOOD DOCTRINE

I give you *good.* forsake not *Pr 4:2*
my law
nourished up in the words of *1Ti 4:6*
good d.

MY DOCTRINE

my d. shall drop as the rain *De 32:2*
my d. is pure, and I am *Job 11:4*
clean
my d. is not mine, but his *Joh 7:16*
but thou hast fully known *2Ti 3:10*
my d.

SOUND DOCTRINE

any thing contrary to *sound* *1Ti 1:10*
d.
when they will not endure *2Ti 4:3*
sound d.
by *sound. d.* to exhort and *Tit 1:9*
convince
but speak things which *Tit 2:1*
become *sound d.*

THIS DOCTRINE

if there come any and bring *2Jo 10*
not *this d.*
and to as many as have not *Re 2:24*
this d.

DOCTRINES

for *d.* commandments of men *M't 15:9;*
                                              M'k 7:7
after commandments and *d.* *Col 2:22*
of men
erroneous *d.* (N) *1Ti 1:4*
from faith, giving heed to *d.* *1Ti 4:1*
of devils
be not carried about with *Heb 13:9*
strange *d.*

DOCUMENT

make the second *d.* (B) *Es 9:29*

DODAI

second month was *D.* an *1Ch 27:4*
Ahohite

DODANIM

and Tarshish, Kittim, and *D.* *Ge 10:4;*
                                              1Ch 1:7

DODAVAH

Then Eliezer the son of *D.* *2Ch 20:37*
of

DODO

the son of *D.* a man of *J'g 10:1*
Issachar
Eleazar the son of *D.* the *2Sa 23:9*
Ahohite
Elhanan the son of *D.* of *2Sa 23:24*
Beth-lehem
him was Eleazar the son of *1Ch 11:12*
D.
Elhanan the son of *D.* of *1Ch 11:26*
Beth-lehem

DOE

loving hind and pleasant *d.* *Pr 5:19*
(A)(B)(E)(R)

DOEG

his name was *D.* an Edomite *1Sa 21:7*
Then answered *D.* the *1Sa 22:9*
Edomite
the king said to *D.,* Turn *1Sa 22:18*
thou
D. the Edomite turned, and *1Sa 22:18*
he fell
when *D.* the Edomite was *1Sa 22:22*
there
when *D.* the Edomite came *Ps 52 title*

DOER

did there, he was the *d.* of *Ge 39:22*
it

Lord shall reward the *d.* of *2Sa 3:39*
evil
plentifully rewardeth the *Ps 31:23*
proud *d.*
wicked *d.* giveth heed to false *Pr 17:4*
lips
as an evil *d.* even unto bonds *2Ti 2:9*
hearer of the word, and not *Jas 1:23*
a *d.*
hearer, but a *d.* of the work *Jas 1:25*
not a *d.* of the law, but a *Jas 4:11*
judge

DOERS

the hand of the *d.* of the *2Ki 22:5*
work
them give it to the *d.* of the *2Ki 22:5*
work
neither will he help the evil *Job 8:20*
d.
hated the congregation of evil *Ps 26:5*
d.
that I may cut off all wicked *Ps 101:8*
d.
d. of the law shall be justified *Ro 2:13*
be ye *d.* of the word, and *Jas 1:22*
not

DOEST

if thou *d.* well, if thou *d.* not *Ge 4:7*
well
God is with thee in all that *Ge 21:22*
thou *d.*
thing that thou *d.* is not *Ex 18:17*
good
when thou *d.* good and right *De 12:28*
God shall bless thee in all *De 15:18*
that thou *d.*
Abner came to know all that *2Sa 3:25*
thou *d.*
that thou mayest prosper in *1Ki 2:3*
all thou *d.*
he said, What *d.* thou here, *1Ki 19:9;*
Elijah   *19:13*
go, and mark, and see what *1Ki 20:22*
thou *d.*
who will say to him, What *d.* *Job 9:12*
thou
if thou sinnest, what *d.* thou *Job 35:6*
against him
praise thee, when thou *d.* *Ps 49:18*
well to thyself
thou art the God that *d.* *Ps 77:14*
wonders
thou art great, and *d.* *Ps 86:10*
wondrous things
thou art good, and *d.* good *Ps 119:68*
say to him, What *d.* thou *Ec 8:4;*
                                              Da 4:35
when thou *d.* evil, then *Jer 11:15*
rejoicest
who shall go aside to ask *Jer 15:5*
how thou *d.*
rebellious house said, What *Eze 12:9*
d. thou
weak heart, seeing thou *d.* *Eze 16:30*
all these things
tell what these are to us, *Eze 24:19*
that thou *d.* so
Lord said, *D.* thou well to be *Jon 4:4;*
angry   *4:9*
therefore when thou *d.* thine *M't 6:2;*
alms   *6:3*
elders said, By what *M't 21:23;*
authority *d.* thou *M'k 11:28; Lu 20:2*
these things
what sign seeing that thou *d.* *Joh 2:18*
these things
no man can do these miracles *Joh 3:2*
that thou *d.*
that disciples may see works *Joh 7:3*
thou *d.*
Jesus said, That thou *d.* do *Joh 13:27*
quickly
saying, Take heed what thou *Ac 22:26*
d.
thou that judgest, *d.* same *Ro 2:1;*
things   *2:3*
thou believest on God, thou *Jas 2:19*
d. well
thou *d.* faithfully what thou *d.* *3Jo 5*
to

DOETH

I have seen all that Laban *Ge 31:12*
d. to thee
whosoever *d.* any work *Ex 31:14;*

therein shall be cut off *31:15; Le 23:30*
in any of these that man *d.* *Le 6:3*
sinning
who shall live when God *d.* *Nu 24:23*
this
to God who *d.* great things *Job 5:9;*
and unsearchable *5:10; 37:5;*
Ps 72:18; 136:4
what his soul desireth, even *Job 23:13*
that he *d.*
leaf not wither, whatsoever he *Ps 1:3*
d. prosper
there is none *d.* good *Ps 14:1;*
14:3; 53:1; Ro 3:12
he that *d.* these things, shall *Ps 15:5*
never be moved
blessed is he that *d.* *Ps 106:3*
righteous at all times
right hand of Lord *d.* *Ps 118:15;*
valiantly *118:16*
he that *d.* it, destroyeth his *Pr 6:32*
own soul
merciful man *d.* good to own *Pr 11:17*
soul
a merry heart *d.* good like a *Pr 17:22*
medicine
and I said of mirth, What *d.* it *Ec 2:2*
whatsoever God *d.* shall be *Ec 3:14*
for ever, and God *d.* it
not a man *d.* good and *Ec 7:20*
sinneth not
for he *d.* whatsoever pleaseth *Ec 8:3*
him
blessed is the man *d.* this *Isa 56:2*
shall he escape that *d.* such *Eze 17:15*
things
that *d.* the like to any one *Eze 18:10*
of these things
that *d.* not any of those *Eze 18:11*
duties
d. that which is lawful and *Eze 18:27*
right
d. according to will in heaven *Da 4:35*
and earth
Lord is righteous in all he *d.* *Da 9:14*
are called, saith Lord that *d.* *Am 9:12*
this
Lord will cut off man that *Mal 2:12*
d. this
let not left hand know what *M't 6:3*
right *d.*
but he that *d.* will of Father *M't 7:21*
in heaven
whoso heareth these sayings, *M't 7:24*
and *d.* them
every one that heareth and *M't 7:26;*
d. not *Lu 6:49*
to my servant, do this, and *M't 8:9;*
he *d.* it *Lu 7:8*
every one that *d.* evil, hateth *Joh 3:20*
light
but he that *d.* truth cometh *Joh 3:21*
to the light
what things soever he *d.* *Joh 5:19*
these *d.* the Son
before it hear him and know *Joh 7:51*
what he *d.*
but if any man *d.* his will, *Joh 9:31*
him he heareth
servant knoweth not what *Joh 15:15*
his lord *d.*
killeth you, will think he *d.* *Joh 16:2*
God service
anguish upon every soul that *Ro 2:9*
d. evil
righteousness of law, the *Ro 10:5;*
man that *d.* these things *Ga 3:12*
shall live by them
to execute wrath upon him *Ro 13:4*
that *d.* evil
every sin a man *d.* is *1Co 6:18*
without body
decreed he will keep his *1Co 7:37*
virgin, *d.* well
so then he that giveth her in *1Co 7:38*
marriage *d.* well
d. he it by works of law, or *Ga 3:5*
by faith
whatsoever good thing any *Eph 6:8*
man *d.*
bringeth forth fruit, as it *d.* *Col 1:6*
also in you
but he that *d.* wrong, shall *Col 3:25*
receive for wrong
exhorted as a father *d.* his *1Th 2:11*
children
that knoweth to do good, *Jas 4:17*
and *d.* it not
he that *d.* will of God *1Jo 2:17*
abideth for ever

that *d.* righteousness is born *1Jo 2:29;*
of him *3:7*
remember his deeds which he *3Jo 10*
d.
but he that *d.* evil hath not *3Jo 11*
seen God
and he *d.* great wonders, he *Re 13:13*
maketh fire

DOG

shall not a *d.* move his *Ex 11:7*
tongue
the price of a *d.* into the *De 23:18*
house
with his tongue, as a *d.* *J'g 7:5*
lappeth
Am I a *d.* that thou comest *1Sa 17:43*
to me
after a dead *d.* after a flea *1Sa 24:14*
look upon such a dead *d.* as I *2Sa 9:8*
am
Why should this dead *d.* *2Sa 16:9*
curse my
is thy servant a *d.* that he *2Ki 8:13*
should
darling from the power of *Ps 22:20*
the *d.*
they make a noise like a *d.* *Ps 59:6*
and go
let them make a noise like a *Ps 59:14*
d.
As a *d.* returneth to his *Pr 26:11*
vomit
one that taketh a *d.* by the *Pr 26:17*
ears
living *d.* is better than a dead *Ec 9:4*
lion
The *d.* is turned to his own *2Pe 2:22*
vomit

DOGS

the field; ye shall cast it to *Ex 22:31*
the *d.*
in the city shall the *d.* eat *1Ki 14:11*
Baasha in the city shall the *1Ki 16:4*
d. eat
place where *d.* licked the *1Ki 21:19*
blood of
Naboth shall *d.* lick thy *1Ki 21:19*
blood
The *d.* shall eat Jezebel by *1Ki 21:23*
the wall
Ahab in the city, the *d.* *1Ki 21:24*
shall eat
and the *d.* licked up his *1Ki 22:38*
blood
the *d.* shall eat Jezebel in the *2Ki 9:10*
shall *d.* eat the flesh of *2Ki 9:36*
Jezebel
to have set with the *d.* of *Job 30:1*
my flock
For *d.* have compassed me *Ps 22:16*
and the tongue of thy *d.* in *Ps 68:23*
all ignorant, they are all dumb *Isa 56:10*
d.
Yea, they are greedy *d.* *Isa 56:11*
which can
and the *d.* to tear, and the *Jer 15:3*
fowls
not that which is holy unto *M't 7:6*
the *d.*
bread, and to cast it to *d.* *M't 15:26*
yet the *d.* eat of the crumbs *M't 15:27*
which
little pups eat crumbs *M't 15:27*
(A)(B)
bread, and to cast it unto *M'k 7:27*
the *d.*
yet the *d.* under the table *M'k 7:28*
eat of the
the *d.* came and licked his *Lu 16:21*
sores
Beware of *d.* beware of evil *Ph'p 3:2*
For without are *d.* and *Re 22:15*
sorcerers

DOG'S

Am I a *d.* head, which *2Sa 3:8*
against
a lamb, as if he cut off a *d.* *Isa 66:3*
neck

DOING

thou hast done foolishly in *Ge 31:28*
so *d.*

is not this it? ye have done *Ge 44:5*
evil in so *d.*
like thee, fearful in praises, *Ex 15:11*
d. wonders
I will only, without *d.* any *Nu 20:19*
thing else
because ye sinned in *d.* *De 9:18*
wickedly
he sinned in *d.* evil *1Ki 16:19;*
2Ki 21:16
d. that which was right *1Ki 22:43;*
2Ch 20:32
arise, and be *d.*, Lord be *1Ch 22:16*
with thee
d. a great work, I cannot *Ne 6:3*
come down
in so *d.* my Maker would *Job 32:22*
take me away
they shall wisely consider of *Ps 64:9*
his *d.*
he is terrible in *d.* toward *Ps 66:5*
children of men
this is the Lord's *d.* it is *Ps 118:23;*
marvellous *M't 21:42; M'k 12:11*
keepeth his hand from *d.* any *Isa 56:2*
evil
from *d.* thy pleasure on my *Isa 58:13*
holy day
his Lord shall find so *d.* *M't 24:46;*
Lu 12:43
Jesus, who went about *d.* *Ac 10:38*
good
if they have found any evil *Ac 24:20*
d. in me
for in so *d.* thou shalt heap *Ro 12:20*
coals of fire
now therefore perform the *2Co 8:11*
d. of it
d. the will of God from the *Eph 6:6*
heart
in *d.* this thou shalt save *1Ti 4:16*
thyself
observe things, *d.* nothing by *1Ti 5:21*
partiality

WELL-DOING

by patient continuance in *Ro 2:7*
well-*d.*
let us not be weary in well-*d.* *Ga 6:9;*
2Th 3:13
with well-*d.* ye may put to *1Pe 2:15*
silence
for it is better that ye suffer *1Pe 3:17*
for well-*d.*
commit their souls unto him in *1Pe 4:19*
well-*d.*

DOINGS

after the *d.* of Egypt, and after *Le 18:3*
the *d.* of Canaan shall ye not do
because of the wickedness of *De 28:20*
thy *d.*
they ceased not from their *J'g 2:19*
own *d.*
Nabal was churlish and evil *1Sa 25:3*
make known his *d.* (A)(E) *1Ch 16:8*
walked not after the *d.* of *2Ch 17:4*
'srael
declare among people his *d.* *Ps 9:11;*
Isa 12:4
meditate of thy works, talk *Ps 77:12*
of thy *d.*
even a child is known by his *Pr 20:11*
d.
vengeance on their *d.* (E) *Ps 99:8*
provoke Lord with *d.* *Ps 106:29*
(E)(R)
played harlot with *d.* *Ps 106:39*
(E)(R)(S)
wash ye, put away evil of *Isa 1:16*
your *d.*
because their tongue and *d.* are *Isa 3:8*
against Lord
for they shall eat the fruit of *Isa 3:10*
their *d.*
lest my fury come and burn, *Jer 4:4;*
because of evil of your *d.* *21:12; 26:3;*
44:22
thy *d.* have procured these *Jer 4:18*
things to thee
amend your ways and *d.* *Jer 7:3;*
7:5; 26:13; 35:15
then thou shewedst me their *Jer 11:18*
d.
according to the fruit of his *Jer 17:10;*
d. *21:14*

return, make your ways and *Jer 18:11*
d. good
I will visit upon you evil of *Jer 23:2*
your *d.*
from evil of their *d.* *Jer 23:22;*
25:5; Zec 1:4
to give according to the *Jer 32:19*
fruit of his *d.*
ye shall see their way and *Eze 14:22*
their *d.*
there shall ye remember *Eze 20:43*
your *d.*
nor according to wicked *Eze 20:44*
ways, corrupt *d.*
so that in all your *d.* your *Eze 21:24*
sins do appear
according to thy *d.* shall *Eze 24:14*
they judge
they defiled it by their own *Eze 36:17*
way and *d.*
according to their *d.* I *Eze 36:19*
judged them
shall remember your *d.* that *Eze 36:31*
were not good
I will punish and reward their *Ho 4:9*
d.
they will not frame their *d.* to *Ho 5:4*
turn to their God
now their own *d.* have set *Ho 7:2*
them about
for wickedness of their *d.* I *Ho 9:15*
will drive
according to his *d.* will he *Ho 12:2*
recompense
O house of Jacob, are these *Mic 2:7*
his *d.*
behaved themselves ill in their *Mic 3:4*
d.
land be desolate for fruit of *Mic 7:13*
their *d.*
but they rose early, corrupted *Zep 3:7*
all their *d.*
shalt thou not be ashamed *Zep 3:11*
for all thy *d.*
according to our *d.* dealt with *Zec 1:6*
us
d. of the flesh are of man's *Ga 5:19*
(A)
the old man with his *d.* (E) *Col 3:9*
partaker of evil *d.* (A)(P) *2Jo 11*
repent of their *d.* (A)(R) *Re 2:22*

DOLE

d. out all I have *1Co 13:3*
(A)(N)(R)

DOLEFUL

their houses full of *d.* *Isa 13:21*
creatures
dolefully howling creatures *Isa 13:21*
(A)
howling creatures (B)(R) *Isa 13:21*
in that day shall lament with *Mic 2:4*
d. lamentation

DOLLAR

sold for a *d.* (B) *2Ki 7:1; 7:16, 18*
a half a *d.* (B) *Eze 30:13*
fifty *d.* worth of bread (B) *M'k 6:37;*
Joh 6:7
spend ten *d.* (P) *M'k 6:37; Joh 6:7*

DOLLARS

land worth 250 *d.* (B) *Ge 23:15*
250 *d.* of myrrh (B) *Ex 21:32*
fine him one hundred *d.* (B) *De 22:19*
must pay 50 *d.* (B) *De 22:29*
with 200 *d.* (B) *Jos 7:21*
fifty silver *d.* (B) *2Sa 24:24*
6,000 *d.* of gold (B) *1Ki 10:16;*
1Ch 21:25
a thousand *d.* (B) *Isa 7:23*
owed him a few *d.* (P) *M't 18:28*

DOMINATE

d. you or your faith (P) *2Co 1:24*

DOMINATED

Philistines *d.* Israel (B) *J'g 14:4*

DOMINEER

to *d.* over the man (B)(N) *1Ti 2:12*

DOMINEERING

bold, *d.* harlot (A) *Eze 16:30*
d. over those in your charge *1Pe 5:3*
(A)

DOMINION

have *d.* over the fish of the *Ge 1:26;*
sea *1:28*
have complete authority over *Ge 1:26*
(A)
rule over (B) *Ge 1:26*
when thou shalt have the *d.* *Ge 27:40*
shalt break
when thou shalt break loose *Ge 27:40*
(A)(E)(R)
when you exert your power *Ge 27:40*
(B)
or shalt thou indeed have *d.* *Ge 37:8*
over us
are you going to dominate us *Ge 37:8*
(A)(B)
are you to reign over us (R) *Ge 37:8*
out of Jacob come he that *Nu 24:19*
shall have *d.*
he made him have *d.* over *J'g 5:13*
nobles
at that time Philistines had *d.* *J'g 14:4*
over Israel
Philistines dominated Israel *J'g 14:4*
(B)
Philistines had rule over *J'g 14:4*
Israel (E)
Solomon had *d.* over all the *1Ki 4:24*
region
to build in land of his *d.* *1Ki 9:19;*
2Ch 8:6
nothing in his house or all *2Ki 20:13;*
his *d.* that *Isa 39:2*
in all his realm (A)(R) *2Ki 20:13*
in all his kingdom (B) *2Ki 20:13*
men of Chozeba who had *d.* *1Ch 4:22*
in Moab
who ruled in Moab (A)(R) *1Ch 4:22*
who were leaders in Moab *1Ch 4:22*
(B)
as he went to stablish his *d.* *1Ch 18:3*
by the river
his power by the river *1Ch 18:3*
Euphrates (B)
set up his monument at the *1Ch 18:3*
river (R)
Edomites from under *2Ch 21:8*
Judah's *d.*
revolted from the rule of *2Ch 21:8*
Judah (A)(R)
from under Judah's control *2Ch 21:8*
(B)
revolted from under the *2Ch 21:8*
hand of (E)
so that they had fine *d.* over *Ne 9:28*
them
again held control over them *Ne 9:28*
(B)
they have *d.* over our bodies *Ne 9:37*
and cattle
they have power over our *Ne 9:37*
bodies (A)(E)(R)
exercised authority over our *Ne 9:37*
bodies (B)
d. and fear are with him, he *Job 25:2*
maketh
canst thou set *d.* thereof in *Job 38:33*
earth
establish their rule in earth *Job 38:33*
(A)(B)(R)
to have *d.* over works of thy *Ps 8:6*
hands
from sins, let them not have *Ps 19:13*
d. over me
the upright shall have *d.* *Ps 49:14*
over them
he shall have *d.* also from *Ps 72:8*
sea to sea
bless the Lord in all places *Ps 103:22*
of his *d.*
Judah was his sanctuary, and *Ps 114:2*
Israel his *d.*
let not any iniquity have *Ps 119:133*
d. over me
thy *d.* endureth through all *Ps 145:13*
generations
other lords besides thee had *Isa 26:13*
d. over us
have ruled us (A)(R) *Isa 26:13*
d. is from generation to *Da 4:3*
generation
thy *d.* reacheth to the end of *Da 4:22*
the earth

most High, whose *d.* is an *Da 4:34;*
everlasting *d.* *7:14*
in every *d.* men tremble *Da 6:26*
before God, and his *d.* shall
beast had four heads, and *d.* *Da 7:6*
was given to it
rest of beasts had their *d.* *Da 7:12*
taken away
was given him *d.* and glory, *Da 7:14*
a kingdom
they shall take away his *d.* to *Da 7:26*
consume it
d. shall be given to saints of *Da 7:27*
most High
mighty king that shall rule *Da 11:3;*
with great *d.* *11:5*
not according to his *d.* which *Da 11:4*
he ruled
to thee shall it come even the *Mic 4:8*
first *d.*
his *d.* shall be from sea to *Zec 9:10*
sea
the princes of Gentiles *M't 20:25*
exercise *d.*
lord it over them *M't 20:25*
(A)(B)(E)(N)(P)(R)
from *d.* of Satan (N) *Ac 26:18*
raised, death hath no more *d.* *Ro 6:9*
over him
death no longer has power *Ro 6:9*
(A)
death hold lordship over (B) *Ro 6:9*
death's power to touch him *Ro 6:9*
(P)
sin shall not have *d.* over you *Ro 6:14*
Sin not be your master *Ro 6:14*
(B)(N)(P)
law hath *d.* over man as long *Ro 7:1*
as he liveth
legal claims have power over a *Ro 7:1*
person (A)
the law lords it over a person *Ro 7:1*
(B)
a person is subject to the law *Ro 7:1*
(N)
law exercises authority over a *Ro 7:1*
man (P)
law is binding over a person *Ro 7:1*
(R)
not that we have *d.* over *2Co 1:24*
your faith
lord it over your faith *2Co 1:24*
(B)(R)
lordship over your faith (E) *2Co 1:24*
not dictating terms of your *2Co 1:24*
faith (N)
dominate you or your faith *2Co 1:24*
(P)
above all power, might, and *Eph 1:21*
d.
all government, authority, *Eph 1:21*
power, and lordship (B)
any conceivable command, *Eph 1:21*
authority, power, or control (P)
have *d.* over the man (E) *1Ti 2:12*
to him be honor and *d.* *1Ti 6:16*
(B)(R)
d. for ever and ever *1Pe 4:11;*
5:11; Re 1:6
to the only wise God be *d.* *Jude 25*
and power
glory, honor, and *d.* (A)(B) *Re 4:11*
glory, honor, and *d.* (B)(E) *Re 5:13*

DOMINIONS

and all *d.* shall serve and *Da 7:27*
obey him
whether they be thrones, or *Col 1:16*
d. or powers
thrones or lordships or rulers *Col 1:16*
or authorities (B)
thrones, sovereignties, *Col 1:16*
authorities, and powers (N)

DONATE

d. to the poor (B) *Lu 18:22*

DONATIONS

give *d.* to the poor (A) *Lu 11:41;*
12:33

DONE

Noah knew what his younger *Ge 9:24*
son had *d.*
they have *d.* according to *Ge 18:21*
the cry of it

the servant told Isaac all | Ge 24:66
that he had d.
as we have d. to thee | Ge 26:29
nothing but good
Laban said, It must not be | Ge 29:26
d. in our country
wrought folly, which ought | Ge 34:7
not to be d.
ye have d. evil in so doing | Ge 44:5
Joseph said, What deed is | Ge 44:15
this ye have d.
he said, Why have ye d. this | Ex 1:18
thing
sister witness what would be d. | Ex 2:4
to him
no manner of work be d. in | Ex 12:16
them
this is d. because the Lord | Ex 13:8
did to me
Jethro heard all that God had | Ex 18:1
d. for Moses
goodness which the Lord had | Ex 18:9
d. to Israel
according to this judgment | Ex 21:31
shall it be d.
six days work be d. | Ex 31:15;
| 35:2; Le 23:3
had d. as the Lord | Ex 39:43
commanded, they d. it
and commit things forbidden | Le 5:17
to be d.
Lord commanded to be d. | Le 8:5;
| De 26:14
what vessel it be, wherein | Le 11:32
any work is d.
these abominations have the | Le 18:27
men of land d.
eye for eye, so shall it be d. | Le 24:20
to him again
they shall confess sin they | Nu 5:7
have d.
we have d. foolishly and | Nu 12:11
sinned
not declared what should be | Nu 15:34
d. to him
Balak saw all that Israel had | Nu 22:2
d. to Amorites
why should name of our | Nu 27:4
father be d. away
all that had d. evil in sight | Nu 32:13
of Lord were
he is thy God that hath d. | De 10:21
for thee
be d. to that man who will | De 25:9
not build up
say, Wherefore hath Lord d. | De 29:24;
thus to this land | 1Ki 9:8; 2Ch 7:21
as he had d. also to Libnah | Jos 10:32;
| 10:39
he had d. to Lachish, d. to | Jos 10:35;
Eglon | 10:37
if we have not d. for fear | Jos 22:24
of this
had known all that he had | Jos 24:31
d. for Israel
knew not works he had d. | J'g 2:10
for Israel
they had d. evil in sight of | J'g 3:12
Lord
if d. truly and sincerely, and | J'g 9:16
have d. to Jerubbaal
cruelty d. to the seventy sons | J'g 9:24
of Jerubbaal
there was no such deed d. | J'g 19:30
nor seen
told her all the man had d. | Ru 3:16
to her
he said, What is there d. my | 1Sa 4:16
son
cometh not forth, so shall be | 1Sa 11:7
d. to his oxen
what shall be d. to man | 1Sa 17:26
that killeth him
so shall it be d. to man | 1Sa 17:27
that killeth him
when the Lord shall have d. | 1Sa 25:30
to my lord
Lord hath d. as he spake | 1Sa 28:17;
| Eze 12:28
thing David had d. | 2Sa 11:27
displeased the Lord
no such thing ought to be | 2Sa 13:12
d. in 'srael
what have they d. | 2Sa 24:17;
| 1Ch 21:17
goodness Lord hath d. for | 1Ki 8:66
David
above all that their fathers | 1Ki 14:22
had d.

Ahab told Jezebel all that | 1Ki 19:1
Elijah had d.
provoked Lord according | 1Ki 22:53;
to all that his father had d. | 2Ki 15:3,
| 9, 34; 23:32
he said, What is to be d. for | 2Ki 4:13
thee
tell me all the great things | 2Ki 8:4
Elisha hath d.
Lord hath d. that which | 2Ki 10:10;
he spake by | Isa 38:15; Jer 40:3
thou hast heard what the | 2Ki 19:11;
kings of Assyria have d. to | 2Ch 32:13;
all lands | Isa 37:11
because they have d. evil | 2Ki 21:15;
| 2Ch 29:6
all the acts that he had d. | 2Ki 23:19
in Bethel
because he had d. good in | 2Ch 24:16
Israel
rejoiced, for the thing was | 2Ch 29:36
d. suddenly
rendered not according to | 2Ch 32:25
benefit d. to him
sent to inquire of wonder | 2Ch 32:31
that was d.
made a decree, let it be d. | Ezr 6:12
with speed
when these things were d. | Ezr 9:1
princes came
no such things d. as thou | Ne 6:8
sayest
we have d. wickedly | Ne 9:33;
| Ps 106:6; Da 9:5, 15
remember Vashti, and what she | Es 2:1
had d.
Mordecai perceived all d., rent | Es 4:1
clothes
king said, What shall be d. to | Es 6:6
the man
shall it be d. to man the king | Es 6:9
honours
who shall repay what he | Job 21:31
hath d.
whether it be d. against | Job 34:29
nation or man only
he spake and it was d. he | Ps 33:9
commanded
he hath d. great things | Ps 71:19;
| 106:21; 126:2-3
what shall be d. to thee, | Ps 120:3
false tongue
strive not if he have d. thee | Pr 3:30
no harm
sleep not, except they have d. | Pr 4:16
mischief
that which is d. is that which | Ec 1:9
shall be d.
have seen works d. under sun | Ec 1:14;
| 4:1, 3
even that which hath been | Ec 2:12
already d.
who hath wrought and d. it | Isa 41:4
sing, O heavens, for the | Isa 44:23
Lord hath d. it
lest shouldest say, My idol | Isa 48:5
hath d. them
seen what backsliding Israel | Jer 3:6
hath d.
neither shall that be d. any | Jer 3:16
more
prophets wind, thus shall it | Jer 5:13
be d. unto
because ye have d. all these | Jer 7:13
works
children of Judah have d. evil | Jer 7:30
in my sight
turned, and had d. right in | Jer 34:15
my sight
have d. all that Jonadab | Jer 35:10;
commanded | 35:18
these men have d. evil to | Jer 38:9
Jeremiah
as we have d. we and our | Jer 44:17
fathers, kings
ask him that fleeth, and say, | Jer 48:19
What is d.
vengeance as she hath d. do | Jer 50:15;
unto her | 50:29
the violence d. to me and to | Jer 51:35
my flesh
Lord hath d. that which he | La 2:17
devised
thus have d. in midst of my | Eze 23:39
house
it is come, it is d., saith the | Eze 39:8
Lord God
if they be ashamed of all | Eze 43:11
they have d.

and for all that shall be d. | Eze 44:14
therein
that that is determined shall | Da 11:36
be d.
priests have d. violence to the | Zep 3:4
law
thy will be d. | M't 6:10;
| 26:42; Lu 11:2; 22:42
as thou hast believed, so be | M't 8:13
it d. to thee
if mighty works d. in you | M't 11:21;
had been d. in Tyre and | Lu 10:13
any thing they ask, it shall | M't 18:19
be d. for them
when his fellow-servants | M't 18:34
saw what was d.
be thou cast into the sea, it | M't 21:21
shall be d.
these ought ye to have d. | M't 23:23;
| Lu 11:42
well d. good and faithful | M't 25:21;
servant | 25:23
inasmuch as ye have d. it | M't 25:40
to one of the least of these my
brethren, ye have d. it to me
saw those things that were | M't 27:54;
d. | 28:11
went out to see what was | M'k 5:14;
d. | Lu 8:35
tell what great things Lord | M'k 5:19;
hath d. | 5:20; Lu 8:39
woman knowing what was | M'k 5:33
d. in her
told him what they had d. | M'k 6:30
and taught
have d. to him whatsoever | M'k 9:13
they listed
shall not pass till all these | M'k 13:30
things be d.
desire him to do, as he had | M'k 15:8
ever d.
he that is mighty hath d. | Lu 1:49
great things
being reproved for evils | Lu 3:19
Herod had d.
charged them to tell no man | Lu 8:56
what was d.
apostles told him all they | Lu 9:10
had d.
Lord, it is d. as thou hast | Lu 14:22
commanded
when ye have d. all those | Lu 17:10
things, we have d. that which
if in green tree, what shall | Lu 23:31
be d. in dry
now when the centurion saw | Lu 23:47
what was d.
the third day since these | Lu 24:21
things were d.
that have d. good to | Joh 5:29
resurrection of life; have d. evil
ask what ye will, it shall be | Joh 15:7
d. unto you
these things were d. that | Joh 19:36
the Scripture be
many signs were d. by the | Ac 2:43
apostles
of the good deed d. to the | Ac 4:9
impotent man
a notable miracle hath been | Ac 4:16
d. by them
all glorified God for that | Ac 4:21
which was d.
what thy counsel determined | Ac 4:28
before to be d.
his wife, not knowing what | Ac 5:7
was d. came in
he wist not that it was true | Ac 12:9
which was d.
they rehearsed all that God | Ac 14:27;
had d. | 15:4
saying, The will of the Lord | Ac 21:14
be d.
chief captain demanded | Ac 21:33
what he had d.
neither having d. any good or | Ro 9:11
evil
nor that it should be d. unto | 1Co 9:15
me
that which is in part shall | 1Co 13:10
be d. away
let all things be d. to | 1Co 14:26
edifying
be d. decently; be d. with | 1Co 14:40;
charity | 16:14
which glory was to be d. | 2Co 3:7
away
old testament, which veil is | 2Co 3:14
d. away in Christ

receive things *d.* in body,   2Co 5:10
according to that he hath *d.*
things which are *d.* of them   Eph 5:12
in secret
able to withstand, having *d.*   Eph 6:13
all to stand
let nothing be *d.* thro' strife   Ph'p 2:3
or vainglory
have well *d.* that ye did   Ph'p 4:14
communicate
will make known all things   Col 4:9
that are *d.*
not by works of righteousness   Tit 3:5
we have *d.*
hath *d.* despite to the   Heb 10:29
Spirit of grace
came a voice, saying, It is   Re 16:17;
d.   21:6
to shew things which must   Re 22:6
shortly be *d.*

HAVE I DONE

in innocency of my hands   Ge 20:5
have I *d.* this
here also *have I d.* nothing   Ge 40:15
to put me
what *have I d.*   Nu 22:28;
       1Ki 19:20; Mic 6:3
I have sinned, thus and thus
have I d.
he said, What *have I* now *d.*   J'g 8:2;
       1Sa 17:29
what *have I d.*   1Sa 20:1;
    26:18; 29:8; Jer 8:6
according to their   Eze 39:24
transgressions *have I d.*
to the Jews *have I d.* no   Ac 25:10
wrong

HE HATH DONE,
HATH HE DONE

he hath d. evil to this people   Ex 5:23
make amends for harm *he*   Le 5:16
hath d.
as *he hath d.* so Lord   Le 8:34
commanded to do
atonement for his sin which   Le 19:21
he hath d.
as *he hath d.* so shall it be   Le 24:19
done to him
consume you, after *he hath*   Jos 24:20
d. good
to do to him as *he hath d.*   J'g 15:10
to us
then *he hath d.* us this great   1Sa 6:9
evil
consider how great things   1Sa 12:24
he hath d.
why shall he be slain? what   1Sa 20:32
hath he d.
remember his marvellous   1Ch 16:12;
works that *he hath d.*   Ps 78:4; 98:1;
              105:5
I will declare what *he hath*   Ps 66:16
d.
our God *hath d.* whatsoever   Ps 115:3
he pleased
I will do so to him as *he*   Pr 24:29
hath d.
sing to Lord *he hath d.*   Isa 12:5
excellent things
righteousness which *he hath*   Eze 3:20;
d.   18:24
he hath d. these things, he   Eze 17:18
shall not escape
he hath d. all these   Eze 18:13
abominations
that seeth his father's sins   Eze 18:14
which *he hath d.*
in righteousness that *he*   Eze 18:22
hath d. he shall live
according to all *he hath d.*   Eze 24:24
shall ye do
he hath d. that which is   Eze 33:16
lawful and right
because *he hath d.* great   Joe 2:20
things
the governor said, Why,   M't 27:23;
what evil *hath he d.*   M'k 15:14;
              Lu 23:22
saying, He *hath d.* all things   M'k 7:37
well
much evil *hath he d.* to thy   Ac 9:13
saints
may receive according to   2Co 5:10
that *he hath d.*

receive for the wrong which   Col 3:25
he hath d.

I HAVE DONE

nor will I smite every thing   Ge 8:21
as *I have d.*
according to the kindness *I*   Ge 21:23
have d. thee
I am Esau, *I have d.* as   Ge 27:19
thou badest me
till *I have d.* that which I   Ge 28:15
have spoken
thou knowest my service *I*   Ge 30:26
have d. thee
my signs *I have d.* among   Ex 10:2
them
your eyes have seen what *I*   Jos 24:7
have d.
as *I have d.* so God hath   J'g 1:7
requited me
as they did to me, so *have I*   J'g 15:11
d. to them
behold now *I have d.* this   2Sa 14:21
thing
I have d. I have d. very   2Sa 24:10;
foolishly   1Ch 21:8
I have sinned, and *I have*   2Sa 24:17
d. wickedly
I have d. according to thy   1Ki 3:12
word
hast thou not heard, how *I*   2Ki 19:25
have d. it
that *I have d.* for the   Neh 13:14
house of my God
if *I have d.* iniquity, I will   Job 34:32
do no more
O Lord, my God, if *I have d.*   Ps 7:3
this
I have d. judgment and   Ps 119:121
justice, leave not
saith, *I have d.* no wickedness   Pr 30:20
shall I not, as *I have d.* to   Isa 10:11
Samaria, so do
by the strength of my hand   Isa 10:13
I have d. it
hear ye that are far off   Isa 33:13
what *I have d.*
hath thou not heard how *I*   Isa 37:26
have d. it
I repent of the evil *I have*   Jer 42:10
d. to you
I have d. as thou hast   Eze 9:11
commanded
as *I have d.* so shall it be   Eze 12:11
done to them
I have not *d.* without cause,   Eze 14:23
all *I have d.* in it
ye shall do as *I have d.* ye   Eze 24:22
shall not cover
before thee *have I d.* no hurt   Da 6:22
weep, as *I have d.* these so   Zec 7:3
many years
I have d. one work, and ye   Joh 7:21
all marvel
know ye what *I have d.* to   Joh 13:12
you
that ye should do as *I have*   Joh 13:15
d. to you

HAST THOU DONE

he said, What *hast thou d.*   Ge 4:10;
31:26; Nu 23:11; 1Sa 13:11; 2Sa 3:24;
                 Joh 18:35
what *hast thou d.* to us   Ge 20:9;
              J'g 15:11
according to thy heart *hast*   2Sa 7:21
thou d.
who shall say, Wherefore   2Sa 16:10
hast thou d. so
in saying, Why *hast thou d.*   1Ki 1:6
so
O Lord, *hast thou d.* all   1Ch 17:19
this greatness
these things *hast thou d.* I   Ps 50:21
kept silence
the men said, why *hast thou*   Jon 1:10
d. this

THOU HAST DONE

what is this that *thou hast d.*   Ge 3:13;
12:18; 26:10; 29:25; J'g 15:11; 2Sa 12:21
because *thou hast d.* this   Ge 3:14;
        22:16; 2Ch 25:16
thou hast d. deeds which   Ge 20:9
ought not be done

he forget that which *thou*   Ge 27:45
hast d. to him
thou hast now *d.* foolishly   Ge 31:28;
in so doing   1Sa 13:13; 2Ch 16:9
tell me what *thou hast d.*   Jos 7:19;
             1Sa 14:43
it hath been shewed all *thou*   Ru 2:11
hast d.
that *thou hast d.* to me this   1Sa 24:19
day
thing is not good that *thou*   1Sa 26:16
hast d.
but *thou hast d.* evil above   1Ki 14:9
all
because *thou hast d.* well in   2Ki 10:30
executing
thou hast d. against the   2Ki 23:17
altar of Beth-el
for *thou hast d.* right, but we   Ne 9:33
wickedly
wonderful works which *thou*   Ps 40:5
hast d.
I will praise thee, because   Ps 52:9
thou hast d. it
that they may know that   Ps 109:27
thou hast d. it
if *thou hast d.* foolishly in   Pr 30:32
lifting up
thou hast d. wonderful works   Isa 25:1
see thy way, know what *thou*   Jer 2:23
hast d.
thou hast spoken and *d.* evil   Jer 3:5
things
they are glad that *thou hast*   La 1:21
d. it
do unto them as *thou hast d.*   La 1:22
unto me
Lord, consider to whom *thou*   La 2:20
hast d. this
Sodom hath not done as   Eze 16:48
thou hast d.
in all thy abominations   Eze 16:51
which *thou hast d.*
I will even deal with thee   Eze 16:59
as *thou hast d.*
when I am pacified for all   Eze 16:63
thou hast d.
as *thou hast d.* it shall be done   Ob 15
to thee
Lord, *thou hast d.* as it   Jon 1:14
pleaseth thee
thou hast d. well that thou   Ac 10:33
art come

NOT DONE

done deeds that ought *not* be   Ge 20:9
d.
which thing ought *not* to be   Ge 34:7
d.
marvels, such as have *not*   Ex 34:10
been *d.*
concerning things which ought   Le 4:2;
not to be *d.*   4:13
I have *not d.* them of mine   Nu 16:28
own mind
lest they say, Lord hath *not*   De 32:27
d. all this
wouldest thou *not* have *d.* it   2Ki 5:13
they had *not d.* it of a long   2Ch 30:5
time
weakened from work, that it   Ne 6:9
be *not d.*
from days of Joshua, Israel   Ne 8:17
had *not d.* so
Vashti had *not d.* wrong to   Es 1:16
king only
what could been done, that I   Isa 5:4
have *not d.*
declaring the things that are   Isa 46:10
not yet *d.*
I will do in thee that I have   Eze 5:9
not d.
under whole heaven hath *not*   Da 9:12
been *d.* as done upon Jerusalem
do that which his fathers   Da 11:24
have *not d.*
shall evil be in city, and Lord   Am 3:6
hath *not d.* it
if I had *not d.* among them   Joh 15:24
the works
scarce restrained they had *not*   Ac 14:18
for this thing was *not d.* in   Ac 26:26
a corner

DONE *THIS*

I wot not who hath *d. this*   Ge 21:26
thing

what is *this* that God hath   *Ge 42:28*
d. to us
what deed is *this* that ye   *Ge 44:15*
have d.
why have ye d. *this* thing, and   *Ex 1:18*
this is d. because of that   *Ex 13:8*
which the Lord did
they said, Why have we d.   *Ex 14:5*
this
we were sore afraid, and   *Jos 9:24*
have d. *this*
but cleave to Lord, as ye   *Jos 23:8*
have d. to *this* day
have not obeyed, why have ye   *J'g 2:2*
d. *this*
they said, Who hath d. *this*   *J'g 6:29;*
thing   *15:6*
she said, Let *this* thing be d.   *J'g 11:37*
for me
though ye have d. *this*, yet   *J'g 15:7*
will I be avenged
what wickedness is *this* that   *J'g 20:12*
is d. among you
ye have d. all *this*   *1Sa 12:20*
wickedness
therefore hath the Lord d.   *1Sa 28:18*
this thing
because ye have d. *this* thing   *2Sa 2:6*
man that hath d. *this* thing   *2Sa 12:5*
shall die
hath thy servant Joab d.   *2Sa 14:20*
this thing
king said, I have d. *this*   *2Sa 14:21*
thing
is *this* thing d. by my Lord   *1Ki 1:27*
king
Lord said, Forasmuch as   *1Ki 11:11*
this is d. of thee
return, for *this* thing is d. of   *2Ch 11:4*
men
Lord, my God, if I have d.   *Ps 7:3*
this
they shall declare that he   *Ps 22:31*
hath d. *this*
I have sinned, and d. *this* evil   *Ps 51:4*
in thy sight
the hand of Lord hath d. *this*   *Isa 41:20*
moreover, *this* they have d.   *Eze 23:38*
unto me
this have ye d. again,   *Mal 2:13*
covering altar
now all *this* was d.   *M't 1:22;*
        21:4; 26:56
he said, An enemy hath d.   *M't 13:28*
this
not only do *this* which is d.   *M't 21:21*
to fig tree
that this woman hath d.   *M't 26:13;*
        M'k 14:9
to see her that had d. *this*   *M'k 5:32*
thing
when they had d. *this* they   *Lu 5:6*
inclosed
but *this* man hath d. nothing *Lu 23:41*
amiss
miracles than these *this* man *Joh 7:31*
hath d.
for they heard he had d. *this* *Joh 12:18*
miracle
by what power or name have   *Ac 4:7*
ye d. *this*
this was d. thrice, vessel   *Ac 10:16;*
received   *11:10*
so when *this* was d. others   *Ac 28:9*
also came
not mourned that he hath d.   *1Co 5:2;*
this deed   *5:3*

DONKEY

saddled his d. (B)   *Ge 23:3; 22:5*
Issachar is a big-boned d.   *Ge 49:14*
(B)
a wild d. (A)(B)   *Job 6:5; Jer 2:24*
a d. (A)(B)   *Job 24:3;*
Pr 26:3; Isa 1:3; 32:20; Jer 2:24; 22:19;
        Zec 9:9; 14:15
the swift d. (A)(B)   *Job 39:5*

DONKEYS

d., she-d. (B)   *Ge 12:16; 30:43;*
36:24; 47:17; J'g 5:10; 1Sa 8:16; 9:3,
20; 2Sa 16:2; 1Ch 27:30; 2Ch 28:15;
     Job 42:12; Isa 21:7; Eze 23:20
wild d. (B)   *Job 24:5;*
     Ps 104:11; Isa 32:14; Da 5:21

DONKEY'S

d. foal (B)   *Ge 49:11*
sitting on a d. colt (A)   *Joh 12:15*

DOOM

rise to hear their d. (N)   *Joh 5:29*
administration announces d.   *2Co 3:9*
(B)
sign their d. is sealed (N)   *Ph'p 1:28*
the son of d. (A)(B)   *2Th 2:3*
escaped d. of unbelievers   *Heb 11:31*
(N)
their d. was predicted long ago *Jude 4*
(A)(N)
share his d. (N)   *Jude 11*
d. of the great whore (A)(B)   *Re 17:1*

DOOMED

best that was d. (B)(R)   *1Sa 15:21*
d. to die (R)   *Ps 102:20*

DOOR

if dost not well, sin lieth at d. *Ge 4:7*
pressed, and came near to   *Ge 19:9*
break d.
Lord also will pass over d.   *Ex 12:23*
his master shall bring him to *Ex 21:6*
the d.
thrust it through his ear to *De 15:17*
d.
put her from me, bolt d.   *2Sa 13:17*
after her
brought her out, and bolted *2Sa 13:18*
d. after her
when he called, she stood in *2Ki 4:15*
d.
then open d. and flee, and   *2Ki 9:3*
tarry not
of those which kept the d.   *Es 2:21;*
        6:2
if I have laid wait at   *Job 31:9*
neighbour's d.
did I fear, that I went not *Job 31:34*
out of d.
O Lord, keep the d. of my   *Ps 141:3*
lips
as d. turneth upon his hinges *Pr 26:14*
he put in hand by hole of d.   *Ca 5:4*
if she be d. we will inclose her *Ca 8:9*
with boards
brought me to d. of inner   *Eze 8:3;*
gate   *8:7*
when I had digged in the   *Eze 8:8*
wall, behold a d.
every one stood at d. of   *Eze 10:19*
east gate
at d. of the gate, twenty-five *Eze 11:1*
men
the breadth of the d. was ten *Eze 41:2*
cubits
people shall worship at d. of *Eze 46:3*
this gate
give valley of Achor for d. of *Ho 2:15*
hope
he said, Smite the lintel of the   *Am 9:1*
d.
rolled stone to d. of   *M't 27:60;*
sepulchre   *M'k 15:46*
angel rolled the stone from *M't 28:2*
the d.
all the city was gathered at *M'k 1:33*
the d.
was no room, no not so   *M'k 2:2*
much as about d.
who shall roll us the stone *M'k 16:3*
from the d.
he that entereth not by d. is *Joh 10:1*
a thief
that entereth in by the d.   *Joh 10:2*
I am the d.   *Joh 10:7*
but Peter stood at the d.   *Joh 18:16*
without
then saith damsel that kept *Joh 18:17*
d. to Peter
feet of them are at d. to carry *Ac 5:9*
thee out
as Peter knocked at the d.   *Ac 12:13*
of the gate
when they opened d. and   *Ac 12:16*
saw him
how he opened d. of faith   *Ac 14:27*
to Gentiles
a great d. and effectual is   *1Co 16:9*
opened
a d. was opened to me of   *2Co 2:12*
the Lord

that God would open a d. of   *Col 4:3*
utterance
the judge standeth before the   *Jas 5:9*
d.
set before thee open d. none   *Re 3:8*
can shut
I stand at d. and knock, if   *Re 3:20*
any man open d.
I looked, a d. was open in   *Re 4:1*
heaven

DOOR with *HOUSE*

smote them at d. of *house*   *Ge 19:11*
they communed at the d. of   *Ge 43:19*
the *house*
none of you go out at d. of *Ex 12:22*
house
the priest shall go to the d. *Le 14:38*
of the *house*
bring damsel to d. of   *De 22:21*
father's *house*
fell down at d. of the man's *J'g 19:26;*
house   *19:27*
Uriah slept at d. of the   *2Sa 11:9*
king's *house*
Naaman stood at d. of *house* *2Ki 5:9*
of Elisha
unto d. of the *house* of   *Ne 3:20*
Eliashib
Merimoth repaired from d. of *Ne 3:21*
the *house*
come not nigh d. of her *house* *Pr 5:8*
she sitteth at d. of her *house* *Pr 9:14*
on a seat
he brought me to d. of   *Eze 8:14;*
Lord's *house*   *47:1*

DOOR with *SHUT*

shut the d.   *Ge 19:6; 19:10*
when come in *shut* d. upon   *2Ki 4:4*
thee
she *shut* d.   *2Ki 4:5; 4:21*
he went in, and *shut* the d. *2Ki 4:33*
on them
shut the d. and hold him   *2Ki 6:32*
fast as the d.
when thou hast *shut* thy d.   *M't 6:6*
pray to
the d. was shut   *M't 25:10; Lu 11:7*
master risen, and hath *shut* *Lu 13:25*
to d.
set before thee open d. no   *Re 3:8*
man can *shut*

DOOR *OF TABERNACLE*

bring to d. of *tabernacle*   *Ex 29:4;*
    40:12; Le 4:4; 8:3-4; 12:6; Nu 6:10
kill bullock by d. of   *Ex 29:11;*
tabernacle   33:9-10; 40:28; Le 1:3; 3:2;
burnt-offering at the d. of   *Ex 29:42;*
tabernacle   33:9-10; 40:28; Le 1:3; 3:2;
        4:7, 18
before d. of *tabernacle*   *Ex 40:6;*
        Nu 25:6
at the d. of *tabernacle*   *Le 8:31;*
8:35; 14:11; 16:7; 17:6; Nu 6:18; 10:3;
        Jos 19:51
ye shall not go out of d. of   *Le 8:33*
tabernacle
not go out from d. of *tabernacle Le 10:7*
unto d. of *tabernacle*   *Le 14:23;*
   15:14, 29; 19:21; Nu 16:18-19, 50; 20:6
bringeth it not to d. of   *Le 17:4;*
tabernacle   *17:9*
stood in d. of *tabernacle*   *Nu 12:5;*
        16:18
cloud stood over d. of   *De 31:15*
tabernacle
Zechariah porter of d. of   *1Ch 9:21*
tabernacle

TENT DOOR

Abraham sat in *tent* d. in   *Ge 18:1*
heat of
ran to meet them from *tent* *Ge 18:2*
d. and bowed
Sarah heard it in *tent* d.   *Ge 18:10*
behind him
people stood every man at   *Ex 33:8*
tent d.
people worshipped, every   *Ex 33:10*
man in *tent* d.
weeping, every man in d. of *Nu 11:10*
tent

Dathan and Abiram stood   *Nu 16:27*
in *d.* of *tents*
he said, Stand in *d.* of the   *J'g 4:20*
tent

DOORKEEPER

rather be *d.* in house of God   *Ps 84:10*
the *d.* opens   *Joh 10:3*
(A)(B)(N)(P)(R)

DOORKEEPERS

gatekeepers, *d.* (A)(B)(R)   *1Ch 9:18;*
9:22, 24, 26; 15:18; 16:38; 2Ch 23:4;
              34:13
Berechiah, Elkanah, were   *1Ch 15:23*
d.
Obed-edom and Jehiah   *1Ch 15:24*
d. for ark
the *d.* at (B)   *2Ch 35:15*
gatekeepers, *d.* (A)(B)(R)   *Ezr 2:70;*
7:7, 24; 10:24; Ne 7:1, 73; 10:28, 39;
11:19; 12:25, 45, 47; 13:5

DOOR *POST*

his master shall bring him to   *Ex 21:6*
d. post
he measured *post* of *d.* two   *Eze 41:3*
cubits

DOOR *POSTS*

strike blood on upper *d. posts*   *Ex 12:7*
of houses
write them on *d. posts* of   *De 11:20*
thy house
posts of the *d.* moved at the   *Isa 6:4*
voice
doors and *d.* (S)   *Isa 57:8*
he measured *d. posts* and   *Eze 41:16*
windows

DOORS

whosoever shall go out of the   *Jos 2:19*
d.
the *d.* of the parlour were   *J'g 3:24*
locked
he opened not the *d.* of the   *J'g 3:24*
parlour
what cometh forth of *d.* I   *J'g 11:31*
will offer it
Samson took the *d.* of the   *J'g 16:3*
gate of city
her lord rose up, and   *J'g 19:27*
opened the *d.*
Samuel opened the *d.* of   *1Sa 3:15*
house
David scrabbled on the *d.*   *1Sa 21:13*
of gate
Hezekiah cut off the gold   *2Ki 18:16*
from *d.*
of the Levites be porters of   *2Ch 23:4*
d.
Hezekiah opened the *d.* of   *2Ch 29:3*
the house
they set up *d.* of it   *Ne 3:1; 3:3; 7:1*
but I opened my *d.* to   *Job 31:32*
traveller
when I set bars and *d.* to   *Job 38:10*
the sea
hast thou seen *d.* of shadow   *Job 38:17*
of death
who can open the *d.* of his   *Job 41:14*
face
be ye lifted up, ye everlasting   *Ps 24:7;*
d.   *24:9*
though he had opened the *d.*   *Ps 78:23*
of heaven
Wisdom crieth at coming in at   *Pr 8:3*
d.
heareth me, waiting at the   *Pr 8:34*
posts of my *d.*
behind *d.* set up   *Isa 57:8*
remembrance
still talking in the *d.* of the   *Eze 33:30*
houses
keep the *d.* of thy mouth   *Mic 7:5*
from her
open thy *d.* O Lebanon, that   *Zec 11:1*
know it is near, at the *d.*   *M't 24:33;*
       M'k 13:29
behind closed *d.* (A)(N)   *Lu 12:3*
angel by night opened prison   *Ac 5:19*
d.
and the keepers standing   *Ac 5:23*
before the *d.*

immediately all the *d.* were   *Ac 16:26*
opened
keeper awaking, and seeing   *Ac 16:27*
prison *d.* open

SHUT DOORS

Ehud *shut* the *d.* of the   *J'g 3:23*
parlour
Ahaz *shut* up *d.* of Lord's   *2Ch 28:24*
house
our fathers have *shut* the *d.*   *2Ch 29:7*
of porch
and let us *shut* the *d.* of the   *Ne 6:10*
temple
let them *shut* the *d.* and bar   *Ne 7:3*
them
shut not up *d.* of mother's   *Job 3:10*
womb
or who *shut* up the sea with   *Job 38:8*
d.
the *d.* shall be *shut* in the   *Ec 12:4*
streets
enter, and *shut* thy *d.* about   *Isa 26:20*
thee
who that would *shut* the *d.*   *Mal 1:10*
for nought
when the *d.* were *shut*   *Joh 20:19;*
Jesus came   *20:26*
and forthwith the *d.* were   *Ac 21:30*
shut

DOPHKAH

of Sin, and encamped in D.   *Nu 33:12*
And they departed from D.   *Nu 33:13*

DOR

the borders of D. on the   *Jos 11:2*
west
The king of D. in the coast   *Jos 12:23*
of D.
the inhabitants of D. and   *Jos 17:11;*
her towns   *J'g 1:27*
of Abinadab, in all the   *1Ki 4:11*
region of D.
and her towns, D. and her   *1Ch 7:29*
towns

DORCAS

by interpretation is called D.   *Ac 9:36*
D. made while she was with   *Ac 9:39*
them

DORMANT

destruction not *d.* (B)(E)(R)   *2Pe 2:3*

DOST

is it that thou *d.* ask after   *Ge 32:29*
my name
thou *d.* overtake them, say   *Ge 44:4*
unto them
d. thou go to possess their   *De 9:5*
land
thou *d.* lend thy brother any   *De 24:10*
thing
the man to whom thou *d.*   *De 24:11*
lend shall
Thou *d.* but hate me, and   *J'g 14:16*
lovest me
after whom *d.* thou   *1Sa 24:14*
pursue? after
Wherefore then *d.* thou ask   *1Sa 28:16*
of me
d. thou ask Abishag the   *1Ki 2:22*
Shunammite
D. thou now govern the   *1Ki 21:7*
kingdom of
Now on whom *d.* thou   *2Ki 18:20*
trust, that
their sin, when thou *d.*   *2Ch 6:26*
afflict them
For what *d.* thou make   *Ne 2:4*
request
D. thou still retain thine   *Job 2:9*
integrity
d. thou not pardon my   *Job 7:21*
transgression
round about; yet thou *d.*   *Job 10:8*
destroy
And *d.* thou open thine eyes   *Job 14:3*
upon
d. thou not watch over my   *Job 14:16*
sin

d. thou restrain wisdom for   *Job 15:8*
thyself
unto thee, and thou *d.* not   *Job 30:20*
hear me
Why *d.* thou strive against   *Job 33:13*
him
D. thou know when God   *Job 37:5*
disposed
D. thou know the   *Job 37:16*
balancings of
thou with rebukes *d.* correct   *Ps 39:11*
man for
why *d.* thou cast me off? why   *Ps 43:2*
and *d.* not increase thy   *Ps 44:12*
wealth
thou *d.* establish equity, thou   *Ps 99:4*
executest
to honour, when thou *d.*   *Pr 4:8*
embrace her
d. not enquire wisely   *Ec 7:10*
concerning this
that thou *d.* so charge us   *Ca 5:9*
most upright, *d.* weigh the   *Isa 26:7*
path of the
now on whom *d.* thou trust   *Isa 36:5*
Wherefore *d.* thou prophesy,   *Jer 32:3*
and say
D. thou certainly know that   *Jer 40:14*
Baalis
daughter that *d.* inhabit   *Jer 48:18*
Dibon
Wherefore *d.* thou forget us   *La 5:20*
for ever
and thou *d.* dwell among   *Eze 2:6*
scorpions
Whom *d.* thou pass in   *Eze 32:19*
beauty
if thou *d.* not speak to warn   *Eze 33:8*
why *d.* thou cry out aloud? is   *Mic 4:9*
there
Why *d.* thou shew me   *Hab 1:3*
iniquity, and
Lord, *d.* thou not care that   *Lu 10:40*
my sister
D. not thou fear God, seeing   *Lu 23:40*
thou art
believe thee? what *d.* thou   *Joh 6:30*
work
and *d.* thou teach us? And   *Joh 9:34*
they cast
D. thou believe on the Son   *Joh 9:35*
of God
How long *d.* thou make us   *Joh 10:24*
to doubt
Lord, *d.* thou wash my feet   *Joh 13:6*
man should not steal, *d.* thou   *Ro 2:21*
steal
d. thou commit adultery?   *Ro 2:22*
thou that
idols, *d.* thou commit   *Ro 2:22*
sacrilege
and circumcision *d.* transgress   *Ro 2:27*
But why *d.* thou judge thy   *Ro 14:10*
brother
or why *d.* thou set at   *Ro 14:10*
nought thy
why *d.* thou glory, as if thou   *1Co 4:7*
hadst
Lord, holy and true, *d.* thou   *Re 6:10*
not judge

DOT

not one *d.* (A)(N)(P)(R)   *M't 5:18;*
       Lu 16:17

DOTE

and they shall *d.*: a sword is   *Jer 50:36*
upon
that they may become fools   *Jer 50:36*
(A)(E)(R)

DOTED

and she *d.* on her lovers on   *Eze 23:5*
with all on whom she *d.*   *Eze 23:7*
of the Assyrians, upon whom   *Eze 23:9*
she *d.*
She *d.* upon the Assyrians   *Eze 23:12*
she saw them with her eyes,   *Eze 23:16*
she *d.*
For she *d.* upon their   *Eze 23:20*
paramours

DOTH

God *d.* know that in the day   *Ge 3:5*
ye eat
Esau, as touching thee, *d.*   *Ge 27:42*
comfort

d. my father yet live   *Ge 45:3*
how that the Lord *d.* put a   *Ex 11:7*
difference
am the Lord that *d.* sanctify   *Ex 31:13*
you
why *d.* thy wrath wax hot   *Ex 32:11*
against thy
when they are dead, *d.* fall,   *Ex 32:31*
it shall be
d. touch them, when they be   *Le 11:32*
dead
years of the fruits *d.* he sell   *Le 25:16*
unto thee
the Lord *d.* make thy thigh   *Nu 5:21*
to rot
the man whom the Lord *d.*   *Nu 16:7*
choose
thing which the Lord *d.*   *Nu 36:6*
command
Lord our God *d.* give unto   *De 1:20;*
us   *1:25; 20:16*
God bare thee, as a man *d.*   *De 1:31*
bear his
this day that God *d.* talk   *De 5:24*
with man
that man *d.* not live by bread   *De 8:3*
only
of the mouth of the Lord *d.*   *De 8:3*
man live
the Lord *d.* drive them out   *De 9:4;*
from before   *9:5; 18:12*
d. the Lord thy God require   *De 11:10*
of thee
He *d.* execute the judgment   *De 11:18*
of the
a gift *d.* blind the eyes of   *De 16:19*
the wise
thy God, he it is that *d.* go   *De 31:6*
with thee
Lord, he it is that *d.* go   *De 31:8*
before thee
Whosoever he be that *d.*   *Jos 1:18*
rebel
when he that *d.* flee unto one   *Jos 20:4*
of
any man *d.* come and   *J'g 4:20*
enquire of thee
for all the city of my people   *Ru 3:11*
d. know
because he *d.* bless the   *1Sa 9:13*
sacrifice; and
D. not David hide himself   *1Sa 23:19*
with us
D. not David hide himself in   *1Sa 26:1*
the hill
Wherefore *d.* my lord thus   *1Sa 26:18*
pursue
flea, as when one *d.* hunt a   *1Sa 26:20*
partridge
Thinkest thou that David *d.*   *2Sa 10:3*
honour
for the king *d.* speak this   *2Sa 14:13*
thing
in that the king *d.* not fetch   *2Sa 14:13*
home
d. God respect any person: *2Sa 14:14*
yet a
Behold, the king *d.* sit in the   *2Sa 19:8*
gate
servant *d.* know that I have   *2Sa 19:20*
sinned
but why *d.* my lord the king   *2Sa 24:3*
delight
that which *d.* cost me   *2Sa 24:24*
nothing
Adonijah the son of Haggith   *1Ki 1:11*
d. reign
throne? why then *d.*   *1Ki 1:13*
Adonijah reign
d. not prophesy good   *1Ki 22:8*
concerning me
The spirit of Elijah *d.* rest   *2Ki 2:15*
on Elisha
this man *d.* send unto me to   *2Ki 5:7*
recover
thou that David *d.* honour   *1Ch 19:3*
thy father
then *d.* my lord require this   *1Ch 21:3*
thing
and fear thee, as *d.* thy   *2Ch 6:33*
people Israel
D. not Hezekiah persuade   *2Ch 32:11*
you to give
said, *D.* Job fear God for   *Job 1:9*
nought
D. not their excellency which   *Job 4:21*
d. trouble spring out of the   *Job 5:6*
ground

D. the wild ass bray when he   *Job 6:5*
hath
but what *d.* your arguing   *Job 6:25*
reprove
D. God pervert judgment? or   *Job 8:3*
d. the
D. not the ear try words   *Job 12:11*
Why *d.* thine heart carry   *Job 15:12*
thee away
my reins asunder, and *d.*   *Job 16:13*
not spare
d. not mine eye continue in   *Job 17:2*
their
How *d.* God know? can he   *Job 22:13*
judge
On the left hand, where he   *Job 23:9*
d. work
d. the grave those which   *Job 24:19*
have sinned
upon whom *d.* not his light   *Job 25:3*
arise
D. not he see my ways, and   *Job 31:4*
count all
d. Job open his mouth in   *Job 35:16*
vain
he *d.* establish them for ever   *Job 36:7*
D. the hawk fly by thy   *Job 39:26*
wisdom, and
D. the eagle mount up at   *Job 39:27*
thy
By his neesings a light *d.*   *Job 41:18*
shine
and in his law *d.* he meditate   *Ps 1:2*
day and
his pride *d.* persecute the   *Ps 10:2*
poor
in the secret places *d.* he   *Ps 10:8*
murder the
d. catch the poor, when he   *Ps 10:9*
draweth
Wherefore *d.* the wicked   *Ps 10:13*
contemn
his countenance *d.* behold the   *Ps 11:7*
in his temple *d.* every one   *Ps 29:9*
speak
because mine enemy *d.* not   *Ps 41:11*
triumph
D. not David hide himself   *Ps 54 title*
with us
their lips: for who, say they,   *Ps 59:7*
d. hear
lo, he *d.* send out his voice   *Ps 68:33*
How *d.* God know? and is   *Ps 73:11*
there
why *d.* thine anger smoke   *Ps 74:1*
against
d. his promise fail for   *Ps 77:8*
evermore
boar out of the wood *d.*   *Ps 80:13*
waste it
wild beast of the field *d.*   *Ps 80:13*
devour it
neither *d.* a fool understand   *Ps 92:6*
this
therefore *d.* my soul keep   *Ps 119:129*
them
d. wait, and in his word do   *Ps 130:5*
I hope
The Lord *d.* build up   *Ps 147:2*
Jerusalem
These six things *d.* the Lord   *Pr 6:16*
hate
D. not wisdom cry? and   *Pr 8:1*
understanding
stranger *d.* not intermeddle   *Pr 14:10*
with his
d. keep his soul shall be far   *Pr 22:5*
from
d. not he that pondereth the   *Pr 24:12*
heart
keepeth thy soul, *d.* not he   *Pr 24:12*
know it
so *d.* an angry countenance a   *Pr 25:23*
upon his hinges, so *d.* the   *Pr 26:14*
slothful
so *d.* the sweetness of a man's   *Pr 27:9*
friend
and *d.* the crown endure to   *Pr 27:24*
every
but the righteous *d.* sing and   *Pr 29:6*
rejoice
and *d.* not bless their mother   *Pr 30:11*
husband *d.* safely trust in her   *Pr 31:11*
so *d.* a little folly him that is   *Ec 10:1*
and his right hand *d.* embrace   *Ca 2:6*
me
but Israel *d.* not know   *Isa 1:3*
my people *d.* not consider   *Isa 1:3*

d. the cause of the widow   *Isa 1:23*
come unto
the Lord of hosts, *d.* take   *Isa 3:1*
away from
shew of their countenance *d.*   *Isa 3:9*
witness
neither *d.* his heart think so   *Isa 10:7*
D. the plowman plow all   *Isa 28:24*
day to sow
d. he open and break the   *Isa 28:24*
clods of his
d. he not cast abroad the   *Isa 28:25*
fitches
d. instruct him to discretion,   *Isa 28:26*
and *d.*
a stream of brimstone, *d.*   *Isa 30:33*
kindle it
the villages that Kedar *d.*   *Isa 42:11*
inhabit
an ash, and the rain *d.*   *Isa 44:14*
nourish it
that day that I am he that *d.*   *Isa 52:6*
speak
us, neither *d.* judgment   *Isa 59:9*
overtake us
glory for that which *d.* not   *Jer 2:11*
profit
for to thee *d.* it appertain   *Jer 10:7*
d. the way of the wicked   *Jer 12:1*
prosper
therefore the Lord *d.* not   *Jer 14:10*
accept them
yet every one of them *d.*   *Jer 15:10*
curse me
none *d.* return from his   *Jer 23:14*
wickedness
whether a man *d.* travail   *Jer 30:6*
with child
keep him, as a shepherd *d.*   *Jer 31:10*
his flock
why then *d.* their king inherit   *Jer 49:1*
Gad
d. any son of man pass   *Jer 51:43*
thereby
How *d.* the city sit solitary   *La 1:1*
For he *d.* not afflict willingly   *La 3:33*
Wherefore *d.* a living man   *La 3:39*
complain
d. deliver us out of their hand   *La 5:8*
When a righteous man *d.*   *Eze 3:18*
turn from
and he *d.* not sin, he shall   *Eze 3:21*
surely live
Why? *d.* not the son bear   *Eze 18:19*
the iniquity
me, *D.* he not speak in   *Eze 20:49*
parables
the people that *d.* not   *Ho 4:14*
understand
pride of Israel *d.* testify to his   *Ho 5:5*
face
and what *d.* the Lord require   *Mic 6:8*
of thee
and judgment *d.* never go   *Hab 1:4*
forth: for
d. compass about the   *Hab 1:4*
righteous
morning *d.* he bring his   *Zep 3:5*
judgment
where moth and rust *d.*   *M't 6:19*
corrupt
neither moth nor rust *d.*   *M't 6:20*
corrupt
This fellow *d.* not cast out   *M't 12:24*
devils
D. not your master pay   *M't 17:24*
tribute
d. he not leave the ninety   *M't 18:12*
and nine
is put away *d.* commit   *M't 19:9*
adultery
then *d.* David in spirit call   *M't 22:43*
him Lord
not what hour your Lord *d.*   *M't 24:42*
come
he is at hand that *d.* betray   *M't 26:46*
me
d. this man thus speak   *M'k 2:7*
blasphemies
new wine *d.* burst the   *M'k 2:22*
bottles
d. this generation seek after a   *M'k 8:12*
sign
My soul *d.* magnify the Lord   *Lu 1:46*
neither *d.* a corrupt tree   *Lu 6:43*
bring
a candle *d.* give thee light   *Lu 11:36*
Thou hypocrite, *d.* not each   *Lu 13:15*
one of

a hen *d.* gather her brood *Lu 13:34* under
And whosoever *d.* not bear *Lu 14:27* his cross
if he lose one of them, *d.* not *Lu 15:4* leave the
lose one piece, *d.* not light a *Lu 15:8* candle
D. he thank that servant *Lu 17:9* because he
that is chief, as he that *d. Lu 22:26* serve
beginning *d.* set forth good *Joh 2:10* wine
said unto them, *D.* this *Joh 6:61* offend you
D. our law judge any man, *Joh 7:51* before
born blind? how then *d.* he *Joh 9:19* now see
Therefore *d.* my Father love *Joh 10:17* me
even by him *d.* this man *Ac 4:10* stand here
what *d.* hinder me to be *Ac 8:36* baptized
the high priest *d.* bear me *Ac 22:5* witness
much learning *d.* make thee *Ac 26:24* mad
seeth, why *d.* he yet hope for *Ro 8:24* Why *d.* he yet find fault? For *Ro 9:19* to the Lord he *d.* not regard *Ro 14:6* it
D. God take care for oxen *1Co 9:9*
D. not even nature itself *1Co 11:14* teach you
D. not behave itself *1Co 13:5* unseemly
d. corruption inherit *1Co 15:50* incorruption
so great a death, and *d. 2Co 1:10* deliver
d. the ministration of *2Co 3:9* righteousness
d. make manifest is light *Eph 5:13*
d. also in you, since the day *Col 1:6* ye heard
you, as a father *d.* his *1Th 2:11* children
mystery of iniquity *d.* already *2Th 2:7* work
their word will eat as *d.* a *2Ti 2:17* canker
all shall wax old as *d.* a *Heb 1:11* garment
the sin which *d.* so easily *Heb 12:1* beset us
What *d.* it profit, my *Jas 2:14* brethren, though
to the body; what *d.* it profit *Jas 2:16*
D. a fountain send forth at *Jas 3:11* the same
killed the just; and he *d.* not *Jas 5:6* resist
even baptism *d.* also now *1Pe 3:21* save us
you; and so *d.* Marcus my *1Pe 5:13* son
and it *d.* not yet appear what *1Jo 3:2* we
is born of God *d.* not commit *1Jo 3:9* sin
d. he himself receive the *3Jo 10* brethren
righteousness he *d.* judge and *Re 19:11* make

DOTHAN

I heard them say, Let us go *Ge 37:17* to *D.*
his brethren, and found *Ge 37:17* them in *D.*
him, saying, Behold, he is in *2Ki 6:13* *D.*

DOTING

corrupt in her *d.* (E)(R) *Eze 23:11*
but *d.* about questions and *1Ti 6:4* strifes
morbid fondness for *1Ti 6:4* controversy (A)(B)(R)
morbidly keen on mere verbal *1Ti 6:4* questions (N)
a conceited idiot. His mind is *1Ti 6:4* a morbid jumble of disputation (P)

DOUBLE

take *d.* money in your hand *Ge 43:12*
they took *d.* money in their *Ge 43:15* hand
or sheep; and he shall restore *Ex 22:4* *d.*
the thief be found, let him *Ex 22:7* pay *d.*
shall pay *d.* unto his *Ex 22:9* neighbour
and shalt *d.* the sixth curtain *Ex 26:9*
they made the breastplate *d. Ex 39:9*
worth a *d.* hired servant to *De 15:18* thee
by giving him a *d.* portion *De 21:17* of all
d. portion of thy spirit be *2Ki 2:9* upon me
they were not of *d.* heart *1Ch 12:33*
of wisdom, that they are *d. Job 11:6*
who can come to him with *Job 41:13* his *d.*
and with a *d.* heart do they *Ps 12:2* speak
d. minded people *Ps 119:113* (A)(E)(R)
wilfully goes in *d.* and wrong *Pr 28:6* ways (A)
received of the Lord's hand *Isa 40:2* *d.* for
shall have *d.;* and for *Isa 61:7* confusion
they shall possess the *d. Isa 61:7*
their iniquity and their sin *Jer 16:18* *d.*
destroy them with *d. Jer 17:18* destruction
that I will render *d.* unto *Zec 9:12* thee
be counted worthy of *d. 1Ti 5:17* honour
A *d.* minded man is unstable *Jas 1:8* in all
purify your hearts, ye *d. Jas 4:8* minded
wavering individuals with *Jas 4:8* divided interests (A)(B)
rewarded you, and *d.* unto *Re 18:6* her
d. according to her works *Re 18:6* which she hath filled fill to *Re 18:6* her *d.*

DOUBLED

for that the dream was *d. Ge 41:32* unto
Foursquare it shall be being *Ex 28:16* *d.*
Foursquare and *d.* (S) *Ex 28:16*
the breadth thereof, being *d. Ex 39:9*
and let the sword be *d.* the *Eze 21:14* third

DOUBLE-TONGUED

not *d.,* not given to much wine *1Ti 3:8*

DOUBT

Joseph is without *d.* rent in *Ge 37:33* pieces
life shall hang in *d.* before *De 28:66* thee
your life in suspense (B) *De 28:66*
be in dread, have no *De 28:66* assurance of live (R)
No *d.* but ye are the people *Job 12:2*
faith, wherefore didst thou *M't 14:31* *d.*
If ye have faith, and *d.* not *M't 21:21*
shall not *d.* in his heart *M'k 11:23*
no *d.* the kingdom of God is *Lu 11:20* come
dost thou make us to *d. Joh 10:24*
were all amazed, and were in *Ac 2:12* *d.*
No *d.* this man is a murderer *Ac 28:4*
our sakes, no *d.* this is *1Co 9:10* written
voice; for I stand in *d.* of *Ga 4:20* you
never a *d.* (B)(N) *Jas 1:6*
they would no *d.* have *1Jo 2:19* continued

DOUBTED

worshipped him: but some *M't 28:17* *d.*
they *d.* of them whereunto *Ac 5:24* this
while Peter *d.* in himself *Ac 10:17* what
d. of such manner of *Ac 25:20* questions

DOUBTER

the *d.* is like (N) *Jas 1:6*

DOUBTETH

he that *d.* is damned if he *Ro 14:23* eat

DOUBTFUL

drink, neither be ye of *d. Lu 12:29* mind
anxious (troubled) mind— *Lu 12:29* unsettled, excited, worried, in suspense (A)
neither be anxious (B) *Lu 12:29*
you are not to worry (N) *Lu 12:29*
nor live in a state of anxiety *Lu 12:29* (P)
nor be of anxious mind (R) *Lu 12:29*
ye, but not to *d.* disputations *Ro 14:1*
but not to criticize his *Ro 14:1* opinions or pass judgment on his scruples or perplex him with discussions (A)
but not to criticize his views *Ro 14:1* (B)
yet not for decision of scruples *Ro 14:1* (E)(P)
to settle *d.* points (N) *Ro 14:1*
not for disputes over opinions *Ro 14:1* (R)

DOUBTING

on another, *d.* of whom we *Joh 13:22* spake
puzzled as to whom he *Joh 13:22* could mean (A)
undecided to whom he *Joh 13:22* referred (B)
looked in bewilderment (N) *Joh 13:22*
completely mystified as to *Joh 13:22* whom (P)
uncertain of whom he *Joh 13:22* spoke (R)
and go with them, *d.* nothing *Ac 10:20*
go unhesitatingly (B) *Ac 10:20*
go without any misgivings *Ac 10:20* (N)(P)
accompany them without *Ac 10:20* hesitation (R)
bade me go with them, *Ac 11:12* nothing *d.*
without hesitation or *Ac 11:12* misgivings or discrimination (A)
without any hesitation *Ac 11:12* (B)(R)
making no distinction (E) *Ac 11:12*
without any misgiving (P) *Ac 11:12*
without *d.* (A) *Ph'p 2:14*
holy hands, without wrath and *1Ti 2:8* *d.*
without anger or quarreling or *1Ti 2:8* resentment or doubts in their minds (A)
without anger and disputing *1Ti 2:8* (B)
without wrath and disputing *1Ti 2:8* (E)
with pure intention, excluding *1Ti 2:8* angry or quarrelsome thoughts (N)
without resentment or doubt *1Ti 2:8* in minds (P)
without anger or quarreling *1Ti 2:8* (R)
nothing *d.* (E)(R) *Jas 1:6*
d. souls need pity (N) *Jude 22*

DOUBTLESS

D. ye shall not come into *Nu 14:30*
I will *d.* deliver the *2Sa 5:19* Philistines
I will certainly deliver *2Sa 5:19* (B)(E)(R)

d. come again with rejoicing *Ps 126:6*
D. thou art our Father, *Isa 63:16*
though
unto others, yet d. I am to *1Co 9:2*
you
at least I am to you *1Co 9:2*
(A)(E)(R)
I certainly am to you (B) *1Co 9:2*
not expedient for me d. to *2Co 12:1*
glory
nothing is to be gained by it *2Co 12:1*
(A)(B)(R)
it does no good (N) *2Co 12:1*
I don't thing it's really good *2Co 12:1*
(P)
Yea d. and I count all things *Ph'p 3:8*
without d. (A)(P) *1Ti 2:8*

DOUBTS

and dissolving of d. were *Da 5:12*
found
interpretations, and dissolve *Da 5:16*
d.
d. and qualms of others (P) *Ro 15:1*
one who d. (B)(P)(R) *Jas 1:6*

DOUGH

the people took their d. *Ex 12:34*
before it
baked unleavened cakes of *Ex 12:39*
the d.
a cake of the first of your *Nu 15:20*
d. for an
the first of your d. ye shall *Nu 15:21*
give
the firstfruits of your d. *Ne 10:37*
and our
the women knead their d. to *Jer 7:18*
the first of your d. that he *Eze 44:30*
may
after he hath kneaded the d. *Ho 7:4*
leavens all the d. (N) *1Co 5:6*
that you may be a fresh d. *1Co 5:7*
(A)(R)

DOVE

he sent forth a d. from him *Ge 8:8*
the d. found no rest for the *Ge 8:9*
sole of
again he sent forth the d. out *Ge 8:10*
of
d. came in to him in the *Ge 8:11*
evening
seven days; and sent forth *Ge 8:12*
the d.
O that I had wings like a d. *Ps 55:6*
ye be as the wings of a d. *Ps 68:13*
covered
O my d. that art in the clefts *Ca 2:14*
of
to me, my sister, my love, my *Ca 5:2*
d.
My d. my undefiled is but one *Ca 6:9*
I did mourn as a d.: mine *Isa 38:14*
eyes fail
be like the d. that maketh *Jer 48:28*
her nest
Ephraim also is like a silly d. *Ho 7:11*
as a d. out of the land of *Ho 11:11*
Assyria
Spirit of God descending like *M't 3:16*
a d.
and the Spirit like a d. *M'k 1:10*
descending
in a bodily shape like a d. *Lu 3:22*
upon
descending from heaven like *Joh 1:32*
a d.

DOVES

His eyes are as the eyes of d. *Ca 5:12*
like bears, and mourn sore *Isa 59:11*
like d.
and as the d. to their *Isa 60:8*
windows
shall be on the mountains *Eze 7:16*
like d.
lead her as with the voice of *Na 2:7*
d.
as serpents, and harmless as *M't 10:16*
d.
the seats of them that sold *M't 21:12;*
d.   *M'k 11:15*

that sold oxen and sheep and *Joh 2:14*
d.
said unto them that sold d. *Joh 2:16*
Take

DOVE'S

fourth part of a cab of d. *2Ki 6:25*
dung

DOVES'

thou art fair; thou hast d. *Ca 1:15*
eyes
thou hast d. eyes within thy *Ca 4:1*
locks

DOVETAILING

d. and fitting together (A) *Ex 26:17*

DOWN

when the sun is d. *Le 22:7; De 23:11*
the border shall go d. to *Nu 34:12*
Jordan
as soon as sun was d. Joshua *Jos 8:29*
commanded to take king of Ai's
carcase d.
if I taste aught till the sun *2Sa 3:35*
be d.
from walking up and d. in it *Job 1:7;*
                                 2:2
let them wander up and d. *Ps 59:15*
for meat
I am tossed up and d. as *Ps 109:23*
the locust
walked up and d. in midst *Eze 28:14*
of stones
they shall walk up and d. in *Zec 10:12*
his name
the multitude to sit d. on *M't 14:19*
the grass
as we were driven up and d. *Ac 27:27*
in Adria
sat d. on the right hand of *Heb 10:12*
God
sit d. at the right hand of *Heb 12:2*
the throne
clothed with a garment d. to *Re 1:13*

DOWNCAST

why is your face d. (B) *Ge 4:6*

DOWNFALL

d. of Ahaziah (B)(R) *2Ch 22:7*
causes brother's d. (N) *Ro 14:21*
if food be d. of my brother *1Co 8:13*
(N)
sharing the devil's d. (P) *1Ti 3:6*

DOWNHEARTED

why so d. (B) *1Sa 1:8*

DOWNSITTING

thou knowest my d. and *Ps 139:2*
uprising

DOWNTRODDEN

those d., bruised (A)(B) *Lu 4:18*

DOWNWARD

shall again take root d. *2Ki 19:30;*
                              Isa 37:31
spirit of the beast that goeth *Ec 3:21*
d.
the appearance of his loins *Eze 1:27;*
d.   *8:2*

DOWRY

God hath endued me with a *Ge 30:20*
good d.
presented with rich d. (B) *Ge 30:20*
enjoyed profits of our d. *Ge 31:15*
(B)
ask me never so much d. *Ge 34:12*
and gift
pay her a d. (A)(B)(E) *Ex 22:16*
pay according to the d. of *Ex 22:17*
virgins
the king desireth not any d. *1Sa 18:25*

DRAG

gather them in their d. *Hab 1:15*
collects them in their seine *Hab 1:15*
(B)
burn incense to their d. *Hab 1:16*
burn incense to their seine *Hab 1:16*
(B)(R)
d. men and women *Ac 8:3*
(A)(B)(E)(P)(R)
d. you into law courts *Jas 2:6*
(A)(B)(E)(N)(P)(R)

DRAGGING

cubits, d. the net with fishes *Joh 21:8*
hauling in the net of fish *Joh 21:8*
(B)
towing the net full of fish *Joh 21:8*
(N)

DRAGNET

like a d. (A) *M't 13:47*

DRAGON

even before the d. well, and *Ne 2:13*
a d. (B) *Job 7:12*
the young lion and the d. *Ps 91:13*
shalt
serpent trample under *Ps 91:13*
(A)(E)(R)
tread on the snake (B) *Ps 91:13*
he shall slay the d. that is in *Isa 27:1*
slay the monster in sea *Isa 27:1*
(A)(E)
cut Rahab, and wounded the *Isa 51:9*
d.
pierce the monster (E) *Isa 51:9*
hath swallowed me up like a *Jer 51:34*
d.
the great d. that lieth in the *Eze 29:3*
midst
the great monster (A)(E) *Eze 29:3*
a big crocodile (B) *Eze 29:3*
like a d. in the seas (A)(R) *Eze 32:2*
behold a great red d. having *Re 12:3*
the d. stood before the *Re 12:4*
woman
his angels fought against the *Re 12:7*
d.
and the d. fought and his *Re 12:7*
angels
the great d. was cast out, that *Re 12:9*
when the d. saw that he was *Re 12:13*
cast
out
the flood which the d. cast *Re 12:16*
out
the d. was wroth with the *Re 12:17*
woman
and the d. gave him his *Re 13:2*
power
they worshipped the d. which *Re 13:4*
gave
like a lamb, and he spake as *Re 13:11*
a d.
out of the mouth of the d. *Re 16:13*
he laid hold on the d. that *Re 20:2*
old

DRAGONS

Their wine is the poison of *De 32:33*
d.
The venom of serpents *De 32:33*
(B)(E)(R)
I am a brother to d. and a *Job 30:29*
brother to jackals *Job 30:29*
(A)(B)(E)(R)
sore broken us in the place *Ps 44:19*
of d.
place of jackals (A)(E)(R) *Ps 44:19*
in the wild-dogs region (B) *Ps 44:19*
thou breakest the heads of *Ps 74:13*
the d.
heads of the sea-monsters *Ps 74:13*
(E)
the earth, ye d. and all deeps *Ps 148:7*
sea monsters (A)(B)(E)(R) *Ps 148:7*
and d. in their pleasant *Isa 13:22*
palaces
jackals (A)(E)(R) *Isa 13:22;*
34:13; 35:7; 43:20; Jer 9:11; 10:22; 14:6;
49:33; 51:37; Mic 1:8; Mal 1:3
it shall be an habitation of *Isa 34:13*
d.
in the habitation of d. where *Isa 35:7*
honour me, the d. and the *Isa 43:20*
owls

Jerusalem heaps, and a den *Jer 9:11* of *d.*
Judah desolate, and a den *Jer 10:22* of *d.*
they snuffed up the wind like *Jer 14:6* *d.*
jackals (B) *Jer 14:6; Mic 1:8; Mal 1:3*
Hazor shall be a dwelling *Jer 49:33* for *d.*
wild dogs (B) *Jer 49:33; 51:37*
a dwelling place or *d.* an *Jer 51:37*
make a wailing like the *d.* *Mic 1:8*
waste for the *d.* of the *Mal 1:3* wilderness

DRAIN

d. them out and drink them *Ps 75:8* (S)

DRAINS

river *d.*, wasteth *Job 14:11* (A)(B)(E)(R)

DRAMS

talents and ten thousand *d.* *1Ch 29:7*
ten thousand darics of gold *1Ch 29:7* (A)(E)(R)
and one thousand *d.* of gold *Ezr 2:69*
sixty one thousand darics of *Ezr 2:69* gold (E)
of gold, of a thousand *d.* *Ezr 8:27*
a thousand darics (A)(R) *Ezr 8:27; Ne 7:70*
thousand *d.* of gold, fifty *Ne 7:70* basons
twenty thousand *d.* of gold *Ne 7:71*
twenty thousand darics *Ne 7:71; 7:72* (A)(R)
gave was twenty thousand *d.* *Ne 7:72*

DRANK

And he *d.* of the wine, and *Ge 9:21*
I *d.* and she made the *Ge 24:46* camels drink
he brought him wine, and *Ge 27:25* he *d.*
they *d.* and were merry with *Ge 43:34* him
and the congregation *d.* and *Nu 20:11*
d. the wine of their drink *De 32:38* offerings
d. water three days and *1Sa 30:12* three nights
eat own meat, and *d.* own *2Sa 12:3* cup
eat bread in his house, and *1Ki 13:19* *d.* water
brought bread and flesh, and *1Ki 17:6* *d.* of brook
the king appointed of the wine *Da 1:5* which he *d.*
he would not defile himself *Da 1:8* with wine he *d.*
Belshazzar *d.* wine before the *Da 5:1* thousand
his wives and his concubines *Da 5:3* *d.* in them
they *d.* wine, and praised the *Da 5:4* gods of gold
he gave to them, and they *M'k 14:23* all *d.* of it
they eat, they *d.* they *Lu 17:27; 17:28* married
than our father Jacob who *Joh 4:12* *d.* thereof
for they *d.* of that spiritual *1Co 10:4* rock

DRAUGHT

made Baal's house a *d.* to *2Ki 10:27* this
house of Baal a privy (A) *2Ki 10:27*
is cast out in the *d.* *M't 15:17; M'k 7:19*
launch out, let down nets for a *Lu 5:4* *d.*
for he was astonished at the *d.* *Lu 5:9* of fishes

DRAVE

chariot-wheels, *d.* them *Ex 14:25* heavily
they *d.* not out Canaanites *Jos 16:10* in Gezer

and *d.* them out from *Jos 24:12;* before you *J'g 6:9*
Lord *d.* out before us all *Jos 24:18* the people
Judah *d.* out inhabitants of *J'g 1:19* mountain
which they *d.* before other *1Sa 30:20* cattle
Uzzah and Ahio *d.* cart *2Sa 6:3; 1Ch 13:7*
at that time Rezin *d.* Jews *2Ki 16:6* from Elath
Jeroboam *d.* Israel from *2Ki 18:21* following Lord
whom God *d.* out before our *Ac 7:45* fathers
Gallio *d.* them from the *Ac 18:16* judgment seat

DRAW

I will also *d.* for thy camels *Ge 24:44*
enemy said, I will *d.* my *Ex 15:9* sword
d. toward mount Tabor, and *J'g 4:6* take with thee
will *d.* to thee Sisera, *J'g 4:7* captain of Jabin's army
Abimelech said, D. thy sword *J'g 9:54;* and slay me *1Sa 31:4; 1Ch 10:4*
d. them from the city to the *J'g 20:32* highways
we will *d.* that city into the *2Sa 17:13* river
and every man shall *d.* after *Job 21:33* him
d. me not away with the *Ps 28:3* wicked
d. me, we will run after thee *Ca 1:4*
woe to those *d.* iniquity with *Isa 5:18*
send those to the nations *Isa 66:19* that *d.* the bow
I will *d.* my sword out of *Eze 21:3* his sheath
and strangers shall *d.* their *Eze 28:7* swords
they shall *d.* their swords *Eze 30:11* against Egypt
d. her, and all her *Eze 32:20* multitudes
thou hast nothing to *d.* with *Joh 4:11*
water that I thirst not, nor *Joh 4:15* come to *d.*
except Father which hath *Joh 6:44* sent me *d.* him
d. all men to me *Joh 12:32*
and now they were not able *Joh 21:6* to *d.* it
to *d.* away disciples after *Ac 20:30* them
you *d.* me to it (N) *2Co 12:11*
d. you before the *Jas 2:6* judgment seats
drag you into law courts *Jas 2:6* (A)(B)(E)(N)(P)(R)

DRAW BACK

just shall live by faith, but *Heb 10:38* if any *d. back*
we are not of them who *d.* *Heb 10:39* *back* to perdition

DRAW NEAR

let us *d. near* to one of *J'g 19:13* these cities
said the priest, Let us *d.* *1Sa 14:36* *near* to God
Saul said, D. ye *near* hither *1Sa 14:38* all the chief
it is good for me to *d. near* *Ps 73:28* to God
they *d. near* to the gates of *Ps 107:18* death
this people *d. near* with lips *Isa 29:13* but heart
d. near, ye that are escaped *Isa 45:20* of nations
d. near hither, ye sons of the *Isa 57:3* sorceress
I will cause him to *d. near* *Jer 30:21* to me
order the buckler, and *d.* *Jer 46:3* *near* to battle
that have charge over city to *Eze 9:1* *d. near*
thou hast caused thy days to *Eze 22:4* *d. near*

wake up, let all men of war *Joe 3:9* *d. near*
let us *d. near* with true *Heb 10:22* heart, in full

DRAW NIGH

he said, D. not *nigh* hither, put *Ex 3:5* off shoes
d. nigh to my soul, and *Ps 69:18* redeem it
they *d. nigh* that follow *Ps 119:150* mischief
nor years *d. nigh* when thou *Ec 12:1* shalt say
let counsel of holy One *Isa 5:19* *d. nigh*
by the which we *d. nigh* *Heb 7:19* unto God
d. nigh to God, he will *d.* *Jas 4:8* *nigh* to you

DRAW OUT

d. out and take lamb and *Ex 12:21*
I will *d. out* a sword after *Le 26:33* you
he could not *d.* dagger *out* of *J'g 3:22* belly
canst thou *d. out* leviathan *Job 41:1* with hook
d. out also spear, and stop *Ps 35:3* the way
wilt *d. out* anger to all *Ps 85:5* generations
man of understanding will *d.* *Pr 20:5* it *out*
against whom do ye *d. out* *Isa 57:4* tongue
if thou *d. out* thy soul to *Isa 58:10* the hungry
least of flock *d.* them *out* *Jer 49:20; 50:45*
even sea monsters *d. out* breast *La 4:3*
third part scatter in wind *Eze 5:2;*
and I will *d. out* a sword *5:12; 12:14* after them
when one came to *d. out* *Hag 2:16* fifty vessels
d. out now, and bear to the *Joh 2:8* governor

DRAW UP

he trusteth that he can *d.* *Job 40:23* *up* Jordan

DRAW WATER

time that women go out to *Ge 24:11; 24:43* *d. water*
the daughters come out to *d.* *Ge 24:13* water
Rebekah ran again to well *Ge 24:20* to *d. water*
found young maidens going *1Sa 9:11* to *d. water*
with joy *d. water* of wells of *Isa 12:3*
d. waters for the siege, *Na 3:14* fortify
cometh woman of Samaria to *Joh 4:7* *d. water*

DRAWER

from hewer of wood to *d.* *De 29:11* of water

DRAWERS

be *d.* of water to *Jos 9:21; 9:27* congregation
d. of water for the house of *Jos 9:23* God

DRAWETH

wife of the one *d. near* to *De 25:11* deliver
now the day *d.* towards *J'g 19:9* evening
he *d.* also the mighty with *Job 24:22* his power
yea his soul *d. near* to the *Job 33:22* grave
catch poor when he *d.* him *Ps 10:9* into his net
my life *d. nigh* unto the grave *Ps 88:3*

that *d*. near the time of her   *Isa 26:17*
delivery
the time is come, the day *d*.   *Eze 7:12*
near
this people *d*. nigh with their   *M't 15:8*
lips
I am Christ, and the time *d*.   *Lu 21:8*
near
then look up, for redemption   *Lu 21:28*
d. nigh
for the coming of the Lord *d*.   *Jas 5:8*
nigh

DRAWING

are delivered in places of *d*.   *J'g 5:11*
water
they see Jesus *d*. nigh to the   *Joh 6:19*
ship

DRAWN

ass saw angel, and his   *Nu 22:23*
sword *d*.   22:31; *Jos 5:13; 1Ch 21:16*
an heifer, which hath not *d*.   *De 21:3*
in yoke
but shalt be *d*. away, and   *De 30:17*
worship gods
till we have *d*. them from the   *Jos 8:6*
city
they were *d*. away from city   *Jos 8:16;*
                    J'g 20:31
drank that which young men   *Ru 2:9*
have *d*.
it is *d*. and cometh out of   *Job 20:25*
the body
wicked have *d*. out the   *Ps 37:14*
sword
words softer than oil yet   *Ps 55:21*
were *d*. swords
Hope *d*. out makes (B)   *Pr 13:12*
to deliver them that are *d*. to   *Pr 24:11*
death
for they fled from the *d*.   *Isa 21:15*
swords
them that are *d*. from the   *Isa 28:9*
breasts
d. and cast forth beyond the   *Jer 22:19*
gates
with lovingkindness have I   *Jer 31:3*
d. thee
he hath *d*. back his right hand   *La 2:3*
I the Lord have *d*. my   *Eze 21:5;*
sword   *21:28*
all were *d*. up again to   *Ac 11:10*
heaven
when he is *d*. away of his   *Jas 1:14*
own lusts

DREAD

d. of you shall be on every   *Ge 9:2*
beast
were in *d*. because (R)   *Ex 1:12*
fear and *d*. shall fall upon   *Ex 15:16*
them
I said to you *d*. not   *De 1:29*
this day will I begin to put   *De 2:25;*
d. and fear of thee upon   *11:25*
do not *d*. them (A)(B)(R)   *De 7:21*
be in *d*., have no assurance   *De 28:66*
(R)
be strong, *d*. not, nor be   *1Ch 22:13*
shall not his *d*. fall upon   *Job 13:11*
you
let not thy *d*. make me   *Job 13:21*
afraid
let him be your fear, your *d*.   *Isa 8:13*
seized with profound *d*. (A)   *Lu 8:25*

DREADFUL

Jacob said, How *d*. is this   *Ge 28:17*
place
a *d*. plague (B)   *Ex 9:3*
great and *d*. (B)   *Ne 4:14*
d. sound in his ears, in   *Job 15:21*
prosperity
who is *d*. to kings (B)   *Ps 76:12*
d. and awesome things (A)   *Ps 106:22*
as for their rings, they were   *Eze 1:18*
d.
a fourth beast, *d*. and terrible   *Da 7:7;*
                        7:19
I said, O Lord, the great and   *Da 9:4*
d. God
the Chaldeans are terrible   *Hab 1:7*
and *d*.
my name is *d*. among the   *Mal 1:14*
heathen

coming of the great and *d*.   *Mal 4:5*
day of Lord
more *d*. punishment (P)   *Heb 10:29*

DREAM

God came to Abimelech in   *Ge 20:3;*
d.   *20:6*
Jacob saw in *d*. rams which   *Ge 31:10*
leaped
angel of God spake to Jacob   *Ge 31:11*
in a *d*.
God came to Laban the   *Ge 31:24*
Syrian in a *d*.
Joseph dreamed a *d*. and   *Ge 37:5;*
told it   *37:9-10*
butler and baker dreamed a   *Ge 40:5*
d. both of them
awoke, and it was a *d*.   *Ge 41:7;*
                     1Ki 3:15
interpret to each man   *Ge 41:12*
according to *d*.
Joseph said, The *d*. of   *Ge 41:25;*
Pharaoh is one   *41:26*
for that *d*. was doubled unto   *Ge 41:32*
Pharaoh
I the Lord will speak to him   *Nu 12:6*
in *d*.
a man that told a *d*. to his   *J'g 7:13*
fellow
when Gideon heard the   *J'g 7:15*
telling of the *d*.
Lord appeared to Solomon in   *1Ki 3:5*
a *d*.
fly away as *d*. and not be   *Job 20:8*
found
in a *d*. he openeth the ears   *Job 33:15*
of men
as a *d*. when one awaketh   *Ps 73:20*
we were like them that *d*.   *Ps 126:1*
a *d*. cometh through much   *Ec 5:3*
business
nations that fight against   *Isa 29:7*
Ariel be as *d*.
prophet that hath *d*. let him   *Jer 23:28*
tell *d*.
my spirit was troubled to   *Da 2:3*
know *d*.
tell thy servants the *d*.;   *Da 2:4;*
if ye shew the *d*.   *2:6*
this is *d*. and interpretation   *Da 2:36*
the *d*. be to them that hate   *Da 4:19*
thee
Daniel had a *d*. then he wrote   *Da 7:1*
the *d*.
old men shall *d*. dreams   *Joe 2:28;*
                     Ac 2:17
angel of Lord appeared to   *M't 1:20;*
Joseph in *d*. saying   *2:13, 19*
being warned of God in a *d*.   *M't 2:12;*
                     2:22
I have suffered many things   *M't 27:19*
in a *d*.

DREAMED

Jacob, Joseph *d*. a dream   *Ge 28:12;*
                     37:5
the officers, Pharaoh *d*.   *Ge 40:5;*
                41:1, 15
Joseph remembered dreams   *Ge 42:9*
he *d*.
prophets said, I have *d*. I   *Jer 23:25*
have *d*.
to your dreams which you   *Jer 29:8*
cause to be *d*.
Nebuchadnezzar *d*. dreams,   *Da 2:1*
spirit troubled
king said to them, I have *d*. a   *Da 2:3*
dream

DREAMER

they said, Behold, this *d*.   *Ge 37:19*
cometh
this master of dreams   *Ge 37:19*
(A)(B)
if a *d*. of dreams arise among   *De 13:1*
you
thou shalt not hearken to   *De 13:3*
that *d*. of dreams
that prophet or *d*. of dreams   *De 13:5*
be put to death

DREAMERS

hearken not to diviners nor   *Jer 27:9*
d.
those filthy *d*. defile flesh   *Jude 8*
deluded *d*. (B)   *Jude 8*

DREAMETH

when a hungry man *d*. a   *Isa 29:8*
thirsty man *d*.

DREAMS

hated Joseph the more for his   *Ge 37:8*
d.
this master of *d*. (A)(B)   *Ge 37:19*
we shall see what will   *Ge 37:20*
become of his *d*.
an Hebrew, and he   *Ge 41:12*
interpreted our *d*.
Joseph remembered the *d*. he   *Ge 42:9*
dreamed
the Lord answered him not   *1Sa 28:6*
by *d*.
thou scarest me with *d*. and   *Job 7:14*
in multitude of *d*. are divers   *Ec 5:7*
vanities
to forget my name with   *Jer 23:27*
their *d*.
I am against them that   *Jer 23:32*
prophesy false *d*.
Daniel had understanding in   *Da 1:17;*
d.   *5:12*
the diviners have told false   *Zec 10:2*
d.

DREGS

d. thereof the wicked shall   *Ps 75:8*
drink out
thou hast drunken *d*. of   *Isa 51:17;*
cup   *51:22*

DRESS

God put man into garden to   *Ge 2:15*
d. it
gave to young man, he hasted   *Ge 18:7*
to *d*. it
widow's *d*. to pledge (B)   *De 24:17*
thou shalt plant vineyards,   *De 28:39*
and *d*. them
to *d*. of his own for   *2Sa 12:4*
wayfaring man
let Tamar *d*. the meat in my   *2Sa 13:5*
sight
go to Amnon's house, and *d*.   *2Sa 13:7*
him meat
long sleeved *d*. (B)   *2Sa 13:18; 13:19*
that I may *d*. it for me and   *1Ki 17:12*
my son
I will *d*. bullock and lay it   *1Ki 18:23*
on wood
Elijah said, *D*. it first, for   *1Ki 18:25*
ye are many
d. modestly (B)(N)(P)   *1Ti 2:9*

DRESSED

Abraham took calf which he   *Ge 18:8*
had *d*.
all that is *d*. in fryingpan be   *Le 7:9*
priest's
Abigail took five sheep   *1Sa 25:18*
ready *d*.
but took poor man's lamb   *2Sa 12:4*
and *d*. it
Mephibosheth had not *d*.   *2Sa 19:24*
his feet
they *d*. it and called on   *1Ki 18:26*
Baal
d. like one of these (B)   *M't 6:29*
not *d*. in robe (B)(N)(P)   *M't 22:11*
stylishly *d*. (B)   *Lu 7:24*
d. in gorgeous robe (N)   *Lu 23:11*
bringeth herbs for them by   *Heb 6:7*
whom it is *d*.
whose benefit it is cultivated   *Heb 6:7*
(A)(N)(R)
for whom it is tilled (B)(E)   *Heb 6:7*
to those who cultivate it (P)   *Heb 6:7*
d. in a robe (A)(B)(P)(R)   *Re 1:13*
d. in white robes (P)   *Re 7:13*
d. in fine linen   *Re 19:8*
(A)(B)(N)(P)
d. in beauty for her (P)   *Re 21:2*

DRESSER

then said he to the *d*. of the   *Lu 13:7*
vineyard

DRESSERS

vine *d*. in the mountains   *2Ch 26:10*

DRESSETH

when he *d.* lamps, he shall   *Ex 30:7*
burn

DRESSING

d. him up in bright (A)(P)   *Lu 23:11*

DREW

Rebekah *d.* water for   *Ge 24:20;*
camels   *24:45*
they *d.* up Joseph out of pit   *Ge 37:28*
it came to pass, Zarah *d.*   *Ge 38:29*
back his hand
because I *d.* him out of the   *Ex 2:10*
water
Jethro's daughters came and   *Ex 2:16*
d. water
an Egyptian *d.* water enough   *Ex 2:19*
for us
for Joshua *d.* not his hand   *Jos 8:26*
back
there fell 120,000 men that *d.*   *J'g 8:10*
sword
youth *d.* not his sword, for   *J'g 8:20*
chief of Israel 400,000 that   *J'g 20:2*
d. sword
of Benjamin numbered   *J'g 20:15*
26,000 that *d.* sword
all these *d.* the sword   *J'g 20:25*
liers in wait *d.* themselves   *J'g 20:37*
along
fell of Benjamin 25,000 that *d.*   *J'g 20:46*
sword
buy it for thee, so he *d.* off   *Ru 4:8*
his shoe
Israel gathered to Mizpeh,   *1Sa 7:6*
and *d.* water
David *d.* Goliath's sword   *1Sa 17:51*
out of the sheath
d. me out of waters   *2Sa 22:17;*
   Ps 18:16
mighty men *d.* water   *2Sa 23:16;*
   1Ch 11:18
were in Israel 800,000 that   *2Sa 24:9*
d. sword
certain man *d.* bow   *1Ki 22:34;*
   2Ch 18:33
king of Moab took 700 that   *2Ki 3:26*
d. sword
Jehu *d.* bow with his full   *2Ki 9:24*
strength
they sent and *d.* forth   *1Ch 19:16*
Syrians
d. sword, Judah 470,000 that   *1Ch 21:5*
d. sword
d. out staves of the ark   *2Ch 5:9;*
   1Ki 8:8
of Benjamin that *d.* bows,   *2Ch 14:8*
280,000
they *d.* up Jeremiah with   *Jer 38:13*
cords
I *d.* them with cords of a   *Ho 11:4*
man
when full, they *d.* to shore   *M't 13:48;*
   M'k 6:53
Peter *d.* his sword   *M't 26:51;*
   M'k 14:47; Joh 18:10
preparation, and sabbath *d.*   *Lu 23:54*
servants which *d.* the water   *Joh 2:9*
knew
d. the net to land full of   *Joh 21:11*
fishes
d. away much people after   *Ac 5:37*
him
stoned Paul and *d.* him out   *Ac 14:19*
of city
d. Paul and Silas into   *Ac 16:19*
market-place
jailer *d.* sword, and would   *Ac 16:27*
have killed
they *d.* Jason and certain   *Ac 17:6*
brethren
they *d.* Alexander out of   *Ac 19:33*
multitude
took Paul and *d.* him out of   *Ac 21:30*
temple
his tail *d.* the third part of   *Re 12:4*
the stars

DREW *NEAR, NIGH*

Abraham *d. near* and said   *Ge 18:23*
time *d. nigh* that Israel must   *Ge 47:29*
die
when Pharaoh *d. nigh* Israel   *Ex 14:10*
Moses *d. near* to thick   *Ex 20:21*
darkness

congregation *d. near* before   *Le 9:5*
Lord
all the people *d. nigh* before   *Jos 8:11*
Ai
the Philistines *d. near* to   *1Sa 7:10*
battle
Saul *d. near* to Samuel in the   *1Sa 9:18*
gate
Goliath *d. near* morning and   *1Sa 17:16;*
evening   *17:41, 48*
David *d. near* to Goliath   *1Sa 17:40*
the Philistine
Joab *d. nigh* against Syrians   *2Sa 10:13*
Ahimaaz came apace and *d.*   *2Sa 18:25*
near
Esther *d. near* and touched   *Es 5:2*
sceptre
king's decree *d. near* to be put   *Es 9:1*
in execution
she trusted not, she *d.* not   *Zep 3:2*
near to God
when they *d. nigh* to   *M't 21:1*
Jerusalem
when time of fruit *d. near,*   *M't 21:34*
he sent
then *d. near* publicans to   *Lu 15:1*
hear him
elder son came, and as he *d.*   *Lu 15:25*
nigh to house
now feast of unleavened   *Lu 22:1*
bread *d. nigh*
Judas *d. near* to Jesus to   *Lu 22:47*
kiss him
Jesus himself *d. near,* went   *Lu 24:15*
with them
d. nigh to village where they   *Lu 24:28*
went
when time of promise *d. nigh*   *Ac 7:17*
he *d. near* to behold it, the   *Ac 7:31*
voice came
as they *d. nigh* to city, Peter   *Ac 10:9*
went
deemed that they *d. near*   *Ac 27:27*
some country

DREWEST

thou *d. near* in day that I   *La 3:57*
called

DRIED

until waters were *d.* up from   *Ge 8:7;*
earth   *8:13*
on twenty-seventh day was   *Ge 8:14*
earth *d.*
offer green ears of corn *d.* by   *Le 2:14*
fire
nor shall he eat moist grapes   *Nu 6:3*
or *d.*
our soul is *d.* away, there is   *Nu 11:6*
nothing at all
have heard how Lord *d.* up   *Jos 2:10*
Red sea
d. up waters of Jordan   *Jos 4:23*
heard Lord had *d.* up waters   *Jos 5:1*
of Jordan
bind him with withs never *d.*   *J'g 16:7*
Jeroboam's hand *d.* up   *1Ki 13:4*
brook *d.* because been no   *1Ki 17:7*
rain
I *d.* all the rivers   *2Ki 19:24; Isa 37:25*
his roots shall be *d.* up   *Job 18:16*
beneath
they are *d.* up, they are gone   *Job 28:4*
away
strength is *d.* up like   *Ps 22:15*
potsherd
throat is *d.* mine eyes fail   *Ps 69:3*
he rebuked Red sea, and it   *Ps 106:9*
d. up
their multitude *d.* up with   *Isa 5:13*
thirst
river shall be wasted and *d.*   *Isa 19:5*
up
brooks of defence shall be *d.*   *Isa 19:6*
up
art thou not it which hath   *Isa 51:10*
d. the sea
pleasant places of wilderness   *Jer 23:10*
d. up
upon her waters and they   *Jer 50:38*
shall be *d.* up
know that I have *d.* up   *Eze 17:24*
green tree
the east wind *d.* up her   *Eze 19:12*
fruit
say, Our bones are *d.* and   *Eze 37:11*
hope is lost

their root is *d.* up, shall   *Ho 9:16*
bear no fruit
his fountain shall be *d.* up   *Ho 13:15*
new wine is *d.* up, oil   *Joe 1:10*
vine is *d.* up; rivers of   *Joe 1:12;*
water *d.* up   *1:20*
his arm shall be clean *d.* up   *Zec 11:17*
fountain of her blood was *d.*   *M'k 5:29*
up
they saw fig tree *d.* up   *M'k 11:20*
from roots
the water of Euphrates was   *Re 16:12*
d. up

DRIEDST

flood, thou *d.* up mighty   *Ps 74:15*
rivers

DRIETH

as the flood decayeth and *d.*   *Job 14:11*
up
but a broken spirit *d.* the   *Pr 17:22*
bones
makes sea dry, and *d.* up all   *Na 1:4*
rivers

DRILLED

d. into his forehead (B)   *1Sa 17:49*

DRINK

Hagar filled bottle, gave lad   *Ge 21:19*
d.
I will give camels *d.* also   *Ge 24:14;*
   24:46
he set rods when flocks   *Ge 30:38*
came to *d.*
people murmured, What shall   *Ex 15:24*
we *d.*
Moses made children of   *Ex 32:20*
Israel *d.* of it
do not *d.* wine nor strong *d.*   *Le 10:9*
neither shall he *d.* liquor of   *Nu 6:3*
grapes
thou shalt give congregation   *Nu 20:8*
d.
she gave Sisera *d.* and   *J'g 4:19*
covered man
that boweth down on his   *J'g 7:5*
knees to *d.*
when athirst, go to vessels and   *Ru 2:9*
d.
three mighty men drew   *2Sa 23:16;*
water, David   *23:17; 1Ch 11:18-19*
would not *d.*
that thou shalt *d.* of the   *1Ki 17:4*
brook
gave meat and *d.* to them of   *Ezr 3:7*
Zidon
they gave them *d.* in vessels of   *Es 1:7*
gold
king and Haman sat down to   *Es 3:15*
d.
he shall *d.* the wrath of   *Job 21:20*
Almighty
make them *d.* of river of   *Ps 36:8*
pleasures
made us to *d.* the wine of   *Ps 60:3*
astonishment
in thirst they gave me   *Ps 69:21*
vinegar to *d.*
the wicked of the earth shall   *Ps 75:8*
d. them
he gave them *d.* as out of   *Ps 78:15*
great depths
rivers into blood, they could   *Ps 78:44*
not *d.*
thou gavest them tears to *d.*   *Ps 80:5*
for I have mingled *d.* with   *Ps 102:9*
weeping
they gave *d.* to every beast   *Ps 104:11*
of field
he shall *d.* of the brook in   *Ps 110:7*
the way
for they *d.* the wine of   *Pr 4:17*
violence
lest they *d.* and forget law   *Pr 31:5*
let him *d.* and forget his   *Pr 31:7*
poverty
d. yea, *d.* abundantly, O   *Ca 5:1*
beloved
strong drink bitter to them   *Isa 24:9*
that *d.* it
will cause *d.* of the thirsty to   *Isa 32:6*
fail

rivers, to give *d.* to my Isa 43:20
people
thou shalt no more *d.* it Isa 51:22
again
shall *d.* it in courts of my Isa 62:9
holiness
servants *d.* but ye shall be Isa 65:13
thirsty
ye may *d.* deeply (S) Isa 66:11
nor give cup of consolation Jer 16:7
to *d.*
make them *d.* the water of Jer 23:15
gall
nations, to whom I send Jer 25:15
thee, to *d.* it
shall *d.* and be moved, and Jer 25:16
I took cup, and made all Jer 25:17
nations to *d.*
d. ye, and be drunken, and Jer 25:27
spue, and fall
thus saith Lord, Ye shall Jer 25:28
certainly *d.*
to this day they *d.* none, but Jer 35:14
obey father's
they whose judgment was Jer 49:12
not to *d.* of the cup shalt
surely *d.* of it
d. by measure, time to time Eze 4:11
shalt *d.*
d. of sister's cup deep and Eze 23:32
large
they *d.* that which ye have Eze 34:19
fouled
that his concubines might Da 5:2
therein
go after lovers that give *d.* Ho 2:5
their *d.* is sour, they have Ho 4:18
committed
say to masters, Let us *d.* Am 4:1
heathen *d.,* shall *d.* and Ob 16
swallow
woe to him that giveth Hab 2:15
neighbour *d.*
d. thou, let foreskin be Hab 2:16
uncovered
d. but ye are not filled with Hag 1:6
drink
they shall *d.* and make a Zec 9:15
noise
whoso shall give to *d.* to M't 10:42
one of these
able to *d.* of cup I shall *d.* M't 20:22;
of M'k 10:38
shall *d.* indeed of my cup M't 20:23;
M'k 10:39
I was thirsty, ye gave me *d.* M't 25:35
thirsty, and ye gave me no M't 25:42
d.
he gave cup, saying, D. ye M't 26:27
all of it
I will not *d.* till that day I M't 26:29;
d. it new M'k 14:25; Lu 22:18
if cup not pass except I *d.,* M't 26:42
thy will be
gave him vinegar to *d.* M't 27:34
mingled
vinegar, and gave him to *d.* M't 27:48;
M'k 15:36
if *d.* any deadly thing, not M'k 16:18
hurt
that thou, being a Jew, askest Joh 4:9
d.
who it is that saith Give me Joh 4:10
to *d.*
my flesh is meat, my blood Joh 6:55
is *d.*
if any man thirst, come to Joh 7:37
me and *d.*
cup my father hath given, Joh 18:11
shall I not *d.*
if thine enemy thirst, give Ro 12:20
him *d.*
kingdom of God is not meat Ro 14:17
and *d.*
did all drink the same 1Co 10:4
spiritual *d.*
cannot *d.* cup of Lord and 1Co 10:21
devils
this do, as oft as ye *d.* in 1Co 11:25
remembrance
been all made to *d.* into 1Co 12:13
one spirit
let no man judge in meat or Col 2:16
d.

STRONG DRINK

do not drink strong *d.* when Le 10:9
ye go

Nazarite separate from *strong* Nu 6:3
d.
bestow that money for De 14:26
strong d.
nor have drunk strong *d.* De 29:6
forty years
Manoah's wife not drink J'g 13:4;
strong *d.* 7:14
I drunk neither wine nor 1Sa 1:15
strong *d.*
wine is mocker, *strong d.* Pr 20:1
raging
not for princes to drink Pr 31:4
strong d.
give strong *d.* to him ready to Pr 31:6
perish
that they may follow strong Isa 5:11
d.
woe to men of strength to Isa 5:22
mingle strong *d.*
strong *d.* be bitter to them Isa 24:9
that drink it
erred through strong *d.* Isa 28:7
they stagger, but not with Isa 29:9
strong *d.*
we will fill ourselves with Isa 56:12
strong *d.*
will prophesy of wine and Mic 2:11
strong *d.*
John shall not drink wine nor Lu 1:15
strong *d.*

DRINK *OFFERING*

Jacob poured *d. offering* on Ge 35:14
pillar
wine for a *d. offering* Ex 29:40;
Nu 15:5
shalt do thereto according to Ex 29:41
d. offering
nor shall ye pour *d. offering* Ex 30:9
thereon
the *d. offering* shall be of Le 23:13
wine
priest shall offer also *d.* Nu 6:17
offering
for *d. offering* a third part of Nu 15:7
hin of wine
bring for *d. offering* half hin Nu 15:10
of wine
his *d. offering* according to Nu 15:24
the manner
besides continual *d. offering* Nu 28:10;
28:15, 24; 29:16
to them hast poured *d.* Isa 57:6
offering
furnish *d. offering* to that Isa 65:11
number
d. offering cut off from house Joe 1:9
of Lord
d. offering withholden from Joe 1:13
house of God
if he will return and leave *d.* Joe 2:14
offering

DRINK *OFFERINGS*

d. offerings Le 23:18;
Nu 6:15; 28:31; 29:11, 18-19, 21, 24,
30, 33, 37, 39
d. offerings be half an hin of Nu 28:14
wine
drank wine of their *d.* De 32:38
offerings
offered with their *d.* 1Ch 29:21;
offerings 2Ch 29:35
buy speedily meat offerings Ezr 7:17
and *d. offerings*
their *d. offerings* of blood will Ps 16:4
I not offer
d. offerings to other gods Jer 7:18;
19:13; 32:29
d. offerings to queen of Jer 44:17;
heaven 47:18-19, 25
47:18, 19, 25
they poured out their *d.* Eze 20:28
offerings
prince's part to give *d.* Eze 45:17
offerings in feasts

DRINK *WATER, WATERS*

give me little *water* of Ge 24:43
pitcher to *d.*
shall lothe to *d. water* of the Ex 7:18;
river 7:21
digged round about river for Ex 7:24
water to *d.*
the could not *d.* of *waters* Ex 15:23
of Marah

there was no *water* for the Ex 17:1
people to *d.*
come *water* out of it, that Ex 17:6
they may *d.*
cause woman to *d.* bitter Nu 5:24;
water 5:26-27
neither is there any *water* to Nu 20:5;
d. 33:14
nor will we *d.* of *water* of Nu 20:17;
wells 21:22
buy *water* for money, that ye De 2:6;
may *d.* 2:28
give me little *water* to *d.* I J'g 4:19
am thirsty
rest bowed upon knees to *d.* J'g 7:6
water
they made the Egyptian *d.* 1Sa 30:11
water
David said, Give me to *d.* 2Sa 23:15;
of *water* of 1Ch 11:17
nor will I eat bread, nor *d.* 1Ki 13:8;
water 13:9
fetch little *water* in vessel 1Ki 17:10
that I may *d.*
valley filled with *water* ye 2Ki 3:17
may *d.*
d. every one *waters* of his 2Ki 18:31;
cistern Isa 36:16
not given *water* to weary to Job 22:7
d.
d. waters out of own cistern Pr 5:15
if enemy be thirsty, give him Pr 25:21
water to *d.*
to *d. waters* of Sihor, waters Jer 2:18
of river
Lord hath given *water* of Jer 8:14;
gall to *d.* 9:15
shalt *d. water* by measure Eze 4:11;
4:16
son of man, *d. water* with Eze 12:18
trembling
shall *d. water* with Eze 12:19
astonishment
all their trees that *d. water* Eze 31:14;
31:16
give us pulse to eat, and Da 1:12
water to *d.*
wandered to *d. water,* were Am 4:8
not satisfied
let them not feed nor *d. water* Jon 3:7
shall give you cup of *water* M'k 9:41
to *d.*
Jesus saith to her, Give me Joh 4:7
water to *d.*
d. no longer *water,* but use 1Ti 5:23
little wine

DRINK *WINE*

let us make our father *d.* Ge 19:32;
wine 19:34
they made their father *d.* Ge 19:33;
wine 19:35
nor *d. wine* when go into Le 10:9
tabernacle
Nazarite shall *d.* no vinegar of Nu 6:3
wine
after that the Nazarite may Nu 6:20
d. wine
vineyards, but not *d. wine* De 28:39;
Am 5:11
Manoah's wife might *d.* no J'g 13:4;
wine 16:7,14
wine, that such as be faint 2Sa 16:2
may *d.*
made us *d.* the *wine* of Ps 60:3
astonishment
for they *d.* the *wine* of Pr 4:17
violence
d. of the *wine* ·which I have Pr 9:5
mingled
it is not for kings, O Lemuel, Pr 31:4
to *d. wine*
go and *d. wine* with merry Ec 9:7
heart
I would cause thee to *d.* Ca 8:2
spiced *wine*
woe to them that are mighty Isa 5:22
to *d. wine*
they shall not *d. wine* with a Isa 24:9
song
the sons of the stranger shall Isa 62:8
not *d.* thy *wine*
go and give the Rechabites Jer 35:2
wine to *d.*
we will *d.* no *wine,* ye shall Jer 35:6
d. no *wine*

neither shall any priest d.   *Eze 44:21*
wine
took away *wine* they should   *Da 1:16*
d.
they have sold girl for *wine* to *Joe 3:3*
d.
they d. the *wine* of the   *Am 2:8*
condemned
but ye gave the Nazarites   *Am 2:12*
wine to d.
that d. *wine* in bowls, and   *Am 6:6*
anoint themselves
plant vineyards, and d. *wine* *Am 9:14*
thereof
but shall not d. *wine*   *Mic 6:15;*
                    Zep 1:13
gave him d. *wine*, mingled *M'k 15:23*
with myrrh
John shall d. neither *wine* nor *Lu 1:15*
strong
not good to eat flesh or d. *Ro 14:21*
wine
she made all nations d. of the *Re 14:8*
wine
same shall d. *wine* of wrath *Re 14:10*
of God

DRINKER

a *wine* d.   *M't 11:19*
(A)(B)(N)(P)(R)

DRINKERS

awake, and howl, all ye d. of *Joe 1:5*
wine

DRINKETH

is not this it in which my   *Ge 44:5*
lord d.
land d. water of rain of   *De 11:11*
heaven
poison whereof d. up my   *Job 6:4*
spirit
how filthy is man, who d. *Job 15:16*
iniquities like water
like Job who d. up scorning *Job 34:7*
like water
he d. up a river, and   *Job 40:23*
hasteth not
he that sendeth by a fool d. *Pr 26:6*
damage
he d. but he awaketh, and he *Isa 29:8*
is faint
smith, he d. no water and is *Isa 44:12*
faint
how is it that he d. with   *M'k 2:16*
publicans
whosoever d. of this water   *Joh 4:13*
shall thirst
whosoever d. of water that I *Joh 4:14*
shall give him
whoso d. my blood, hath   *Joh 6:54*
eternal life
d. my blood dwelleth in me *Joh 6:56*
he that d. unworthily d. *1Co 11:29*
damnation
for the earth which d. in the *Heb 6:7*
rain

DRINKING

water camels till they have *Ge 24:19*
done d.
as camels had done d. he   *Ge 24:22*
took an earring
till Boaz have done eating and *Ru 3:3*
d.
were eating and d. and   *1Sa 30:16*
dancing
Judah and Israel were many, *1Ki 4:20*
d.
Solomon's d. vessels of gold *1Ki 10:21;*
                     2Ch 9:20
Elah was d.; Benhadad was *1Ki 16:9;*
d.   *20:12, 16*
with David three days   *1Ch 12:39*
eating and d.
d. according to law, none   *Es 1:8*
compel
his sons and daughters were *Job 1:13;*
d.   *1:18*
behold, eating flesh, and d. *Isa 22:13*
wine
John came neither eating *M't 11:18;*
nor d.   *Lu 7:33*
Son of man came eating *M't 11:19;*
and d.   *Lu 7:34*

they were eating and d. till *M't 24:38*
flood came
eating and d. such things as *Lu 10:7*
they give
in eating and d. (B)(E)(N) *Ro 14:17*

DRINKS

which stood only in meats, *Heb 9:10*
and d.

DRIPPED

my hands d. with myrrh (S)   *Ca 5:5*

DRIVE

with strong hand d. them out *Ex 6:1*
send hornets, which shall d. *Ex 23:28*
out Hivite
not d. them out before thee *Ex 23:29*
in one year
by little and little I will d. *Ex 23:30*
them out before
thou shalt d. them out   *Ex 23:31*
before thee
I will d. out Canaanite, the *Ex 33:2*
Amorite
I d. out before thee the   *Ex 34:11*
Amorite
that I may d. them out of *Nu 22:6*
the land
be able to overcome and d. *Ex 22:11*
them out
then shall ye d. out all   *Nu 33:52*
inhabitants
but if ye will not d. out   *Nu 33:55*
the inhabitants
d. out nations before thee *De 4:38;*
greater   *9:4-5; Jos 3:10*
thou d. them out and destroy *De 9:3*
them
then will the Lord d. out *De 11:23*
these nations
Lord thy God doth d. them *De 18:12*
out before thee
no man d. them away (S) *De 28:26*
them will I d. out from   *Jos 13:6*
before Israel
I shall be able to d. them *Jos 14:12*
out
children of Judah could not *Jos 15:63*
d. them out
children of Manasseh could *Jos 17:12*
not d. out
did not utterly d. them out *Jos 17:13;*
                      J'g 1:28
for thou shalt d. out the *Jos 17:18*
Canaanites
Lord shall d. them out of *Jos 23:5*
your sight
Lord will no more d. out *Jos 23:13;*
                   J'g 2:3, 21
Judah could not d.   *J'g 1:19*
inhabitants of mount
Benjamin did not d. out *J'g 1:21*
Jebusites
Manasseh, Ephraim,   *J'g 1:27;*
Zebulun, Naphtali   *1:29-31, 33*
did not d. out
whom the Lord our God *J'g 11:24*
shall d. out
d. go forward, slack not *2Ki 4:24*
riding
who didst d. out the   *2Ch 20:7*
inhabitants
terrors shall make afraid, *Job 18:11*
and d. to feet
they d. away the ass of the *Job 24:3*
fatherless
how thou didst d. out the *Ps 44:2*
heathen
as smoke is driven away, so *Ps 68:2*
d. them
but rod of correction d. it *Pr 22:15*
away
I will d. thee from thy   *Isa 22:19*
station
to be a curse whither I shall *Jer 24:9*
d. them
I should d. you out, and ye *Jer 27:10;*
perish   *27:15*
stood not, because Lord did *Jer 46:15*
d. them
among Gentiles, whither I *Eze 4:13*
will d. them
they shall d. thee from men *Da 4:25;*
                      4:32

I will d. them out of my house *Ho 9:15*
I will d. northern army into *Joe 2:20*
a land
they shall d. out Ashdod at *Zep 2:4*
noon day
ship was caught, we let her d. *Ac 27:15*

DRIVEN

thou hast d. me out this day *Ge 4:14*
they were d. from Pharaoh's *Ex 10:11*
presence
beast be d. away, no man *Ex 22:10*
seeing it
till he have d. out enemies *Nu 32:21*
before him
lest thou be d. to worship *De 4:19*
them
whither the Lord thy God *De 30:1*
hath d. thee
if any of them be d. out to *De 30:4*
utmost parts
Lord hath d. out great   *Jos 23:9*
nations
they have d. me out this day *1Sa 26:19*
had d. mediums (B)(R) *1Sa 28:3;*
                      28:9
is wisdom d. quite from me *Job 6:13*
wilt thou break leaf d. to *Job 13:25*
and fro
he shall be d. from light *Job 18:18*
into darkness
they were d. forth from *Job 30:5*
among men
let them be d. backward that *Ps 40:14*
wish
as smoke is d. away, so drive *Ps 68:2*
sea saw it and fled, Jordan *Ps 114:3*
d. back   *114:5*
wicked is d. away in   *Pr 14:32*
wickedness
and they shall be d. to   *Isa 8:22*
darkness
every thing sown by brooks be *Isa 19:7*
d. away
he gave them as d. stubble to *Isa 41:2*
his bow
who remain in all places   *Jer 8:3;*
whither I have d. them   *23:3, 8; 29:14,*
                  18; 32:37
from all lands whither he *Jer 16:15*
had d. them
have d. them away, have not *Jer 23:2*
visited
they shall be d. on and fall *Jer 23:12*
therein
out of all places whither   *Jer 40:12;*
they were d.   *43:5*
full end of nations whither I *Jer 46:28*
have d. thee
ye shall be d. out every man *Jer 49:5*
right forth
Israel, the lions have d. him *Jer 50:17*
away
I have d. him out for his *Eze 31:11*
wickedness
nor brought again, which *Eze 34:4;*
was d. away   *34:16*
he was d. from men *Da 4:33; 5:21*
thro' all countries whither *Da 9:7*
thou hast d.
as chaff that is d. with   *Ho 13:3*
whirlwind
I will gather her that was d. *Mic 4:6;*
                     Zep 3:19
he was d. of devil into   *Lu 8:29*
wilderness
they strake sail, and so were *Ac 27:17*
d.
we were d. up and down in *Ac 27:27*
Adria
is like a wave of sea d. with *Jas 1:6*
wind
ships though great are d. of *Jas 3:4*
fierce winds

DRIVER

Ahab said to the d. of his *1Ki 22:34*
chariot
nor regardeth the crying of *Job 39:7*
the d.

DRIVERS

by reason of slave d. (B) *Ex 3:7;*
                   5:10, 13-14

DRIVETH

driving is like Jehu, for he   *2Ki 9:20*
d. furiously
ungodly like chaff which wind   *Ps 1:4*
d. away
the north wind d. away rain   *Pr 25:23*
spirit d. him into the   *M'k 1:12*
wilderness

DRIVING

d. out Amorites (B)   *Nu 32:39;*
   De 7:17; J'g 11:23
Lord left without d. them out   *J'g 2:23*
hastily
and the d. is like the d. of   *2Ki 9:20*
Jehu
by d. out nations before   *1Ch 17:21*
people
d. straight furrow in   *2Ti 2:15*
proclamation (N)

DROMEDARIES

and d. brought they unto the   *1Ki 4:28*
mules, camels, and young d.   *Es 8:10*
the d. of Midian and Ephah   *Isa 60:6*

DROMEDARY

a swift d. traversing her ways   *Jer 2:23*

DROOLED

d. on his beard (A)   *1Sa 21:13*

DROP

My doctrine shall d. as the   *De 32:2*
rain
also his heaven shall d.   *De 33:28*
down dew
the clouds do d. and distil   *Job 36:28*
goodness; and thy paths d.   *Ps 65:11*
fatness
They d. upon the pastures of   *Ps 65:12*
and the clouds d. down the   *Pr 3:20*
dew
woman d. as an honeycomb   *Pr 5:3*
my spouse, d. as the   *Ca 4:11*
honeycomb
a d. of a bucket, and are   *Isa 40:15*
counted
D. down, ye heavens, from   *Isa 45:8*
above
and d. thy word toward the   *Eze 20:46*
south
and d. thy word toward the   *Eze 21:2*
holy
the mountains shall d. down   *Joe 3:18*
new
d. not thy word against the   *Am 7:16*
house
and the mountains shall d.   *Am 9:13*
sweet

DROPPED

the heavens d. the clouds also   *J'g 5:4*
d.
behold, the honey d.; but   *1Sa 14:26*
no man
until water d. upon them   *2Sa 21:10*
out of
and my speech d. upon   *Job 29:22*
them
heavens also d. at the   *Ps 68:8*
presence of
my hands d. with myrrh, and   *Ca 5:5*

DROPPETH

the hands the house d.   *Ec 10:18*
through

DROPPING

of a wife are a continual d.   *Pr 19:13*
A continual d. in a very   *Pr 27:15*
rainy day
lilies, d. sweet smelling myrrh   *Ca 5:13*

DROPS

he maketh small that d. of   *Job 36:27*
water
who hath begotten the d. of   *Job 38:28*
dew

my locks with the d. of the   *Ca 5:2*
night
as it were great d. of blood   *Lu 22:44*
falling

DROPSY

man before him which had   *Lu 14:2*
the d.

DROSS

all the wicked of the earth   *Ps 119:119*
like d.
Take away the d. from the   *Pr 25:4*
silver
a potsherd covered with   *Pr 26:23*
silver d.
Thy silver is become d. thy   *Isa 1:22*
purely purge away thy d. and   *Isa 1:25*
house of Israel is to me   *Eze 22:18*
become d.
they are even the d. of   *Eze 22:18*
silver
all become d. behold   *Eze 22:19*

DROUGHT

in the day the d. consumed   *Ge 31:40*
me
serpents, and scorpions, and   *De 8:15*
d.
D. and heat consume the   *Job 24:19*
snow
is turned into the d. of   *Ps 32:4*
summer
and satisfy thy soul in d.   *Isa 58:11*
through a land of d. and of   *Jer 2:6*
concerning the d.   *Jer 14:1*
(A)(B)(E)(R)
not be careful in the year of   *Jer 17:8*
d.
A d. is upon her waters;   *Jer 50:38*
and they
wilderness, in the land of   *Ho 13:5*
great d.
I called for a d. upon the   *Hag 1:11*
land

DROVE

So he d. out the man; and he   *Ge 3:24*
carcases, Abram d. them   *Ge 15:11*
away
every d. by themselves; and   *Ge 32:16*
put a space betwixt d. and   *Ge 32:16*
What meanest thou by all   *Ge 33:8*
this d.
came and d. them away: but   *Ex 2:17*
and d. out the Amorites   *Nu 21:32*
that were
Caleb d. thence the three   *Jos 15:14*
sons of
who d. away the inhabitants   *1Ch 8:13*
of
I d. him from me (S)   *Ne 13:28*
who d. him away, and he   *Ps 34 title*
and d. asunder the nations   *Hab 3:6*
he d. them all out of the   *Joh 2:15*
temple

DROVES

all that followed the d.   *Ge 32:19*
saying

DROWN

neither can the floods d. it: if   *Ca 8:7*
which d. men in destruction   *1Ti 6:9*

DROWNED

his chosen captains also are   *Ex 15:4*
d.
and it shall be cast out and   *Am 8:8*
d. as
and shall be d. as by the   *Am 9:5*
flood of
into the lake and were d.   *M't 8:32*
(P)
he were d. in the depth of   *M't 18:6*
the sea
Egyptians assaying to do   *Heb 11:29*
were d.

DROWNING

we are d. (P)   *M't 8:25*

DROWSINESS

d. shall clothe a man with   *Pr 23:21*
rags

DRUGGED

offered d. wine (N)(P)   *M'k 15:23*

DRUNK

Noah was d. in his tent (S)   *Ge 9:21*
all drink that may be d. in   *Le 11:34*
every
neither have ye d. wine or   *De 29:6*
strong
make mine arrows d. with   *De 32:42*
blood
and when he had d. his   *J'g 15:19*
spirit
when Boaz had eaten and d.   *Ru 3:7*
in Shiloh, and after they had   *1Sa 1:9*
d.
thought she had been d. (S)   *1Sa 1:13*
I have d. neither wine nor   *1Sa 1:15*
strong
eaten no bread, nor d. any   *1Sa 30:12*
water
and he made him d.: and at   *2Sa 11:13*
even
and d. water in the place,   *1Ki 13:22*
of the
after he had d. that he   *1Ki 13:23*
saddled
drinking himself d. in the   *1Ki 16:9*
house of
drinking himself d. in the   *1Ki 20:16*
pavilions
when they had eaten and d.   *2Ki 6:23*
digged and d. strange   *2Ki 19:24*
waters, and
I have d. my wine with my   *Ca 5:1*
milk
I have digged, and d. water   *Isa 37:25*
which hast d. at the hand of   *Isa 51:17*
and make them d. in my fury   *Isa 63:6*
Drink and be d. (S)   *Jer 25:27*
and made d. with their   *Jer 46:10*
blood
And I will make d. her   *Jer 51:57*
princes
to have d. of the deep   *Eze 34:18*
waters
drink blood till ye be d.   *Eze 39:19*
(S)
have d. wine in them; and   *Da 5:23*
have d. upon my holy   *Ob 16*
mountain
maketh neighbor d. (S)   *Hab 2:15*
No man also having d. old   *Lu 5:39*
wine
have eaten and d. in thy   *Lu 13:26*
presence
when men have well d. then   *Joh 2:10*
these are not d. (S)   *Ac 2:15*
and another is d. (S)   *1Co 11:21*
And be not d. with wine   *Eph 5:18*
are d. in the night (S)   *1Th 5:7*
have been made d. with the   *Re 17:2*
wine
d. with the blood of saints   *Re 17:6*
(S)
all nations have d. of the   *Re 18:3*
wine

DRUNKARD

voice; he is a glutton, and a   *De 21:20*
the d. and the glutton shall   *Pr 23:21*
come
goeth up into the hand of a   *Pr 26:9*
shall reel to and fro like a   *Isa 24:20*
a d. (B)(P)(R)   *M't 11:19; Lu 7:34*
railer, or a d. or an   *1Co 5:11*

DRUNKARDS

and I was the song of the d.   *Ps 69:12*
of pride, to the d. of   *Isa 28:1*
Ephraim
crown of pride, the d. of   *Isa 28:3*
Ephraim
Awake, ye d. and weep; and   *Joe 1:5*
howl
while they are drunken as d.   *Na 1:10*
drink with the d. (S)   *M't 24:49*
nor d. nor revilers, nor   *1Co 6:10*

DRUNKEN

he drank of the wine, and was *d*.   *Ge 9:21*
Eli thought she had been *d*.   *1Sa 1:13*
How long wilt thou be *d*.   *1Sa 1:14*
within him, for he was very *d*.   *1Sa 25:36*
them to stagger like a *d*. man   *Job 12:25*
and stagger like a *d*. man   *Ps 107:27*
a *d*. man staggereth in his vomit   *Isa 19:14*
they are *d*. but not with wine   *Isa 29:9*
shall be *d*. with their own blood   *Isa 49:26*
thou hast *d*. the dregs of the cup   *Isa 51:17*
and *d*. but not with wine   *Isa 51:21*
I am like a *d*. man, and like   *Jer 23:9*
Drink ye, and be *d*. and spue   *Jer 25:27*
Make ye him *d*.: for he magnified   *Jer 48:26*
of the cup have assuredly *d*.   *Jer 49:12*
that made all the earth *d*.   *Jer 51:7*
the nations have *d*. of her wine   *Jer 51:7*
feasts, and I will make them *d*.   *Jer 51:39*
hath made me *d*. with wormwood   *La 3:15*
thou shalt be *d*. and shalt make   *La 4:21*
We have *d*. our water for money   *La 5:4*
and drink blood till ye be *d*.   *Eze 39:19*
while they are *d*. as drunkards   *Na 1:10*
Thou also shalt be *d*.: thou shalt   *Na 3:11*
to him, and makest him *d*. also   *Hab 2:15*
and to eat and drink with the *d*.   *M't 24:49*
eat and drink, and to be *d*.   *Lu 12:45*
till I have eaten and *d*.: and   *Lu 17:8*
these are not *d*. as ye suppose   *Ac 2:15*
one is hungry, and another is *d*.   *1Co 11:21*
they that be *d*. are *d*. in the night   *1Th 5:7*
d. with the blood of the saints   *Re 17:6*

DRUNKENNESS

mine heart, to add *d*. to thirst   *De 29:19*
for strength, and not for *d*.   *Ec 10:17*
inhabitants of Jerusalem, with *d*.   *Jer 13:13*
shalt be filled with *d*. and sorrow   *Eze 23:33*
and *d*. and cares of this life   *Lu 21:34*
rioting and *d*. not in chambering   *Ro 13:13*
Envyings, murders, *d*., revellings   *Ga 5:21*

DRUSILLA

when Felix came with his wife *D*.   *Ac 24:24*

DRY

let the *d*. land appear: and it   *Ge 1:9*
And God called the *d*. land Earth   *Ge 1:10*
of all that was in the *d*. land, died   *Ge 7:22*
the face of the ground was *d*.   *Ge 8:13*
pour it upon the *d*. land: and   *Ex 4:9*
become blood upon the *d*. land   *Ex 4:9*
of Israel shall go on *d*. ground   *Ex 14:16*
the sea *d*. land, and the waters   *Ex 14:21*
of the sea upon the *d*. ground   *Ex 14:22*
of Israel walked upon *d*. land   *Ex 14:29*
children of Israel went on *d*. land   *Ex 15:19*
offering mingled with oil, and *d*.   *Le 7:10*
it is a *d*. scall, even a leprosy upon   *Le 13:30*

stood firm on *d*. ground in the   *Jos 3:17*
Israelites passed over on *d*. ground   *Jos 3:17*
were lifted up unto the *d*. land   *Jos 4:18*
came over this Jordan on *d*. land   *Jos 4:22*
their provision was *d*. and mouldy   *Jos 9:5*
behold, it is *d*. and it is mouldy   *Jos 9:12*
be *d*. upon all the earth beside   *J'g 6:37*
it now be *d*. only upon the fleece   *J'g 6:39*
for it was *d*. upon the fleece only   *J'g 6:40*
they two went over on *d*. ground   *2Ki 2:8*
midst of the sea on the *d*. land   *Ne 9:11*
the waters, and they *d*. up   *Job 12:15*
wilt thou pursue the *d*. stubble   *Job 13:25*
the flame shall *d*. up his branches   *Job 15:30*
for thee in a *d*. and thirsty land   *Ps 63:1*
He turned the sea into *d*. land   *Ps 66:6*
the rebellious dwell in a *d*. land   *Ps 68:6*
and his hands formed the *d*. land   *Ps 95:5*
ran in the *d*. places like a river   *Ps 105:41*
the watersprings into *d*. ground   *Ps 107:33*
and *d*. ground into watersprings   *Ps 107:35*
is a *d*. morsel, and quietness   *Pr 17:1*
strangers, as the heat in a *d*. place   *Isa 25:5*
as rivers of water in a *d*. place   *Isa 32:2*
and the *d*. land springs of water   *Isa 41:18*
and *d*. up all their herbs   *Isa 42:15*
islands, and I will *d*. up the pools   *Isa 42:15*
and floods upon the *d*. ground   *Isa 44:3*
saith to the deep, Be *d*.   *Isa 44:27*
and I will *d*. up thy rivers   *Isa 44:27*
at my rebuke I *d*. up the sea   *Isa 50:2*
as a root out of a *d*. ground   *Isa 53:2*
say, Behold, I am a *d*. tree   *Isa 56:3*
A *d*. wind of the high places   *Jer 4:11*
a *d*. land and a desert   *Jer 50:12*
I will *d*. up her sea, and make   *Jer 51:36*
and make her springs *d*.   *Jer 51:36*
a *d*. land, and a wilderness   *Jer 51:43*
have made the *d*. tree to flourish   *Eze 17:24*
in a *d*. and thirsty ground   *Eze 19:13*
tree in thee, and every *d*. tree   *Eze 20:47*
I will make the rivers *d*. and sell   *Eze 30:12*
valley; and lo, they were very *d*.   *Eze 37:2*
O ye *d*. bones, hear the word of   *Eze 37:4*
set her like a *d*. land, and slay   *Ho 2:3*
miscarrying womb and *d*. breasts   *Ho 9:14*
and his spring shall become *d*.   *Ho 13:15*
hath made the sea and the *d*. land   *Jon 1:9*
vomited out Jonah upon the *d*. land   *Jon 2:10*
rebuketh the sea, and maketh it *d*.   *Na 1:4*
be devoured as stubble fully *d*.   *Na 1:10*
desolation, and *d*. like a wilderness   *Zep 2:13*
and the sea, and the *d*. land   *Hag 2:6*
the deeps of the river shall *d*. up   *Zec 10:11*
he walketh through *d*. places   *M't 12:43; Lu 11:24*
what shall be done in the *d*.   *Lu 23:31*
through the Red sea as by *d*. land   *Heb 11:29*

DRYSHOD

streams, and make men go over *d*.   *Isa 11:15*

DUCTS

seven *d*. (B)   *Zec 4:2*

DUE

justice *d*. (S)   *Ex 23:6; De 27:19; 40:27; 49:4*
it is thy *d*. and thy sons'   *Le 10:13*
they be thy *d*. and thy sons'   *Le 10:14*
I will give thee rain in *d*. season   *Le 26:4*
offer unto me in their *d*. season   *Nu 28:2*
rain of your land in his *d*. season   *De 11:14*
be the priest's *d*. from the people   *De 18:3*
their foot shall slide in *d*. time   *De 32:35*
sought him not after the *d*. order   *1Ch 15:13*
Give unto the Lord the glory *d*.   *1Ch 16:29*
for the singers, *d*. for every day   *Ne 11:23*
Lord the glory *d*. unto his name   *Ps 29:2; 96:8*
give them their meat in *d*. season   *Ps 104:27; 145:15; M't 24:45*
good for them to whom it is *d*.   *Pr 3:27*
a word spoken in *d*. season   *Pr 15:23*
princes eat in *d*. season, for strength   *Ec 10:17*
pay all that was *d*. unto him   *M't 18:34*
their portion of meat in *d*. season   *Lu 12:42*
receive the *d*. reward of our deeds   *Lu 23:41*
in *d*. time Christ died for the ungodly   *Ro 5:6*
dues: tribute to whom tribute is *d*.   *Ro 13:7*
unto the wife *d*. benevolence   *1Co 7:3*
as of one born out of *d*. time   *1Co 15:8*
for in *d*. season we shall reap   *Ga 6:9*
for all, to be testified in *d*. time   *1Ti 2:6*
in *d*. time manifested his word   *Tit 1:3*
that he may exalt you in *d*. time   *1Pe 5:6*

DUES

Render therefore to all their *d*.   *Ro 13:7*

DUG

the pit be *d*. (S)   *Ps 94:13; 119:85; Isa 5:2; M't 21:33; 25:18; M'k 12:1; Lu 6:48*
d. down thine altars (S)   *Ro 11:3*

DUKE

d. Teman, *d*. Omar, *d*. Zepho, *d*. Kenaz   *Ge 36:15*
D. Korah, *d*. Gatam, and *d*. Amalek   *Ge 36:16*
d. Nahath, *d*. Zerah, *d*. Shammah, *d*. Mizzah   *Ge 36:17*
d. Jeush, *d*. Jaalam, *d*. Korah   *Ge 36:18*
d. Lotan, *d*. Shobal, *d*. Zibeon, *d*. Anah   *Ge 36:29*
D. Dishon, *d*. Ezer, *d*. Dishan   *Ge 36:30*
d. Timnah, *d*. Alvah, *d*. Jetheth   *Ge 36:40*
D. Aholibamah, *d*. Elah, *d*. Pinon   *Ge 36:41; 1Ch 1:52*
D. Kenaz, *d*. Teman, *d*. Mibzar   *Ge 36:42; 1Ch 1:53*
D. Magdiel, *d*. Iram   *Ge 36:43; 1Ch 1:54*
d. Timnah, *d*. Aliah, *d*. Jetheth   *1Ch 1:51*

DUKES

These were *d.* of the sons   Ge 36:15
are the *d.* that came of   Ge 36:16
Eliphaz
are the *d.* that came of   Ge 36:17
Reuel
the *d.* that came of   Ge 36:18
Aholibamah
is Edom, and these are their   Ge 36:19
d.
these are the *d.* of the   Ge 36:21
Horites
the *d.* that came of the   Ge 36:29
Horites
are the *d.* that came of Hori   Ge 36:30
among their *d.* in the land of   Ge 36:30
Seir
of the *d.* that came of Esau   Ge 36:40
these be the *d.* of Edom   Ge 36:43
the *d.* of Edom shall be   Ex 15:15
amazed
were *d.* of Sihon, dwelling   Jos 13:21
in the
And the *d.* of Edom were   1Ch 1:51;
                               1:54

DULCIMER

d. and all kinds of   Da 3:5; 3:10, 15
musick

DULL

the *d.* man cannot know (A)   Ps 92:6
their ears are *d.* of hearing   M't 13:15
heart has grown *d.* (B)(R)   M't 13:15
their ears are *d.* of hearing   Ac 28:27
seeing ye are *d.* of hearing   Heb 5:11

DULLNESS

d. of heart (B)   La 3:65
reproached for incredulity   M'k 16:14
and *d.* (N)

DUMAH

Mishma, and *D.* and Massa   Ge 25:14
Arab, and *D.* and Eshean   Jos 15:52
and *D.*, Massa, Hadad, and   1Ch 1:30
Tema
The burden of *D.* He calleth   Isa 21:11
to

DUMB

or who maketh the *d.* or deaf   Ex 4:11
and I was as a *d.* man that   Ps 38:13
openeth
I was *d.* with silence, I held   Ps 39:2
my
I was *d.* I opened not my   Ps 39:9
mouth
Open thy mouth for the *d.* in   Pr 31:8
and the tongue of the *d.* sing   Isa 35:6
a sheep before her shearers is   Isa 53:7
d.
they are all *d.* dogs, they   Isa 56:10
thou shalt be *d.* and shalt   Eze 3:26
not be
shalt speak, and be no   Eze 24:27
more *d.*
was opened, and I was no   Eze 33:22
more *d.*
toward the ground, and I   Da 10:15
became *d.*
trusteth therein, to make *d.*   Hab 2:18
idols
Awake; to the *d.* stone   Hab 2:19
brought to him a *d.* man   M't 9:32
possessed
devil was cast out, the *d.*   M't 9:33
spake
with a devil, blind, and *d.*   M't 12:22
that the blind and *d.* both   M't 12:22
spake
blind, *d.*, maimed, and many   M't 15:30
others
when they saw the *d.* to   M't 15:31
speak
deaf to hear, and the *d.* to   M'k 7:37
speak
my son, which hath a *d.*   M'k 9:17
spirit
Thou *d.* and deaf spirit, I   M'k 9:25
charge
shalt be *d.* and not able to   Lu 1:20
speak

casting out a devil, and it   Lu 11:14
was *d.*
devil was gone out, the *d.*   Lu 11:14
spake
like a lamb *d.* before his   Ac 8:32
shearer
carried away unto these *d.*   1Co 12:2
idols
d. ass speaking with man's   2Pe 2:16
voice

DUMBFOUNDED

wise men *d.* and trapped (B)   Jer 8:9
a man *d.* (S)   Jer 14:9
were utterly *d.* (B)   Eze 19:25
multitude was *d.* (N)   M'k 6:51
they were *d.* (N)   M'k 16:5

DUNG

bullock, and his skin, and   Ex 29:14
his *d.*
his legs, and his inwards, and   Le 4:11
his *d.*
and his hide, his flesh, and   Le 8:17
his *d.*
skins, their flesh, and their   Le 16:27
d.
flesh, and her blood, with her   Nu 19:5
d.
as a man taketh away *d.*   1Ki 14:10
till it be
fourth part of a cab of   2Ki 6:25
dove's *d.*
Jezebel shall be as *d.* upon   2Ki 9:37
the face
they may eat their own *d.*   2Ki 18:27;
                          Isa 36:12
and to the *d.* port, and viewed   Ne 2:13
cubits on the wall unto the *d.*   Ne 3:13
gate
But the *d.* gate repaired   Ne 3:14
Malchiah
upon the wall toward the *d.*   Ne 12:31
gate
shall perish for ever like his   Job 20:7
own *d.*
they became as *d.* for the   Ps 83:10
earth
they shall be for *d.* upon the   Jer 8:2
face
shall fall as *d.* upon the open   Jer 9:22
field
they shall be as *d.* upon the   Jer 16:4
face of
they shall be *d.* upon the   Jer 25:33
ground
and thou shalt bake it with   Eze 4:12
d. that
Lo I have given thee cow's   Eze 4:15
d.
for man's *d.* and thou shalt   Eze 4:15
as dust, and their flesh as the   Zep 1:17
d.
spread *d.* upon your faces,   Mal 2:3
even
even the *d.* of your solemn   Mal 2:3
feasts
I shall dig about it, and *d.* it   Lu 13:8
and do count them but *d.*   Ph'p 3:8
that I

DUNGEON

that they should put me into   Ge 40:15
the *d.*
brought him hastily out of   Ge 41:14
the *d.*
the captive that was in the *d.*   Ex 12:29
was entered into the *d.*   Jer 37:16
cast him into the *d.* of   Jer 38:6
Malchiah the
cistern (A)(B)(R)   Jer 38:6;
                      38:10-11, 13
And in the *d.* there was no   Jer 38:6
water, but
they had put Jeremiah into   Jer 38:7
the *d.*
whom they have cast into the   Jer 38:9
d. and
Jeremiah the prophet out of   Jer 38:10
the *d.*
let them down by cords into   Jer 38:11
the *d.* to
cords, and took him up out   Jer 38:13
of the *d.*
They have cut off my life in   La 3:53
the *d.*

pit (B)(R)   La 3:53; 3:55
thy name, O Lord, out of the   La 3:55
low *d.*
d. of loathsome spirit (A)   Re 18:2

DUNGEONS

to black *d.* of Tartarus (B)   2Pe 2:4

DUNGHILL

lifted up the beggar from the   1Sa 2:8
d.
his house be made a *d.* for   Ezr 6:11
and lifteth the needy out of the   Ps 113:7
d.
as straw is trodden down   Isa 25:10
for the *d.*
your houses shall be made a   Da 2:5
d.
their houses shall be made a   Da 3:29
d.
for the land, nor yet for the   Lu 14:35
d.

DUNGHILLS

brought up in scarlet embrace   La 4:5
d.

DUPES

d., crafty rogues (N)   Eph 4:14

DURA

he set it up in the plain of *D.*   Da 3:1

DURABLE

yea, *d.* riches and   Pr 8:18
righteousness
sufficiently, and for *d.*   Isa 23:18
clothing

DURETH

root in himself, but *d.* for a   M't 13:21
while

DURST

that *d.* presume in his heart to   Es 7:5
do so
dared contemplate such a thing   Es 7:5
(B)
and *d.* not shew you mine   Job 32:6
opinion
dared not declare my   Job 32:6
opinion (A)(B)
afraid to show you my   Job 32:6
opinion (R)
neither *d.* any man from   M't 22:46
that day
venture or dare to ask (A)   M't 22:46
anyone presume to ask him   M't 22:46
any (B)
dared ask him any more   M't 22:46
question (N)(P)(R)
no man after that *d.* ask   M'k 12:34
him any
they *d.* not ask him any   Lu 20:40
question
none of the disciples *d.* ask   Joh 21:12
him
dared ask him   Joh 21:12
(B)(N)(P)(R)
And of the rest *d.* no man   Ac 5:13
join
dared join or associate with   Ac 5:13
them (A)(B)
venturing to join with them   Ac 5:13
(N)
dared to associate with them   Ac 5:13
(P)
dared join them (R)   Ac 5:13
Moses trembled, and *d.* not   Ac 7:32
behold
did not venture to look (A)   Ac 7:32
did not dare to investigate   Ac 7:32
(B)
dared not look (N)(R)   Ac 7:32
afraid to look any more (P)   Ac 7:32
d. not bring against him a railing   Jude 9
he dared not bring an abusive   Jude 9
(A)
did not venture to pronounce   Jude 9
sentence (B)

DUST

did not presume to condemn *Jude 9*
him (N)(R)
did not dare to condemn him *Jude 9*
(P)

DUST

d. shalt thou eat all days of *Ge 3:14*
life
d. thou art, and unto d. shalt *Ge 3:19*
thou return
if a man can number the d. *Ge 13:16*
of earth
to speak to Lord, who am *Ge 18:27*
but d. and ashes
say to Aaron, Smite d. of *Ex 8:16*
land
for Aaron smote the d. of the *Ex 8:17*
earth
it shall become small d. in all *Ex 9:9*
the land
shall pour out d. they scrape *Le 14:41*
off
pour out blood, and cover it *Le 17:13*
with d.
who can count the d. of *Nu 23:10*
Jacob
I cast d. into brook *De 9:21;*
2Ki 23:12
Lord shall make rain of thy *De 28:24*
land d.
the elders put d. on their *Jos 7:6*
heads
Shimei cursed David, and *2Sa 16:13*
cast d.
like d. (A)(B)(E)(R) *2Sa 22:43*
fire of the Lord consumed *1Ki 18:38*
d.
if d. of Samaria shall *1Ki 20:10*
suffice for handfuls
Josiah made d. of the *2Ch 34:4*
images
they sprinkled d. upon their *Job 2:12*
heads
flesh clothed with worms and *Job 7:5*
clods of d.
wilt thou bring me into d. *Job 10:9*
again
as for the earth, it hath d. *Job 28:6*
of gold
all flesh perish, man shall *Job 34:15*
turn again to d.
when the d. groweth into *Job 38:38*
hardness
I abhor myself, and repent *Job 42:6*
in d. and ashes
thou hast brought me into *Ps 22:15*
the d.
shall d. praise thee, shall it *Ps 30:9*
declare truth
his enemies shall lick the d. *Ps 72:9*
he rained flesh also upon *Ps 78:27*
them as d.
thy servants favour the d. *Ps 102:14*
thereof
he remembereth that we are *Ps 103:14*
d.
then shall the d. return to the *Ec 12:7*
earth
their d. shall be made fat *Isa 34:7*
with fatness
d. thereof shall be turned into *Isa 34:9*
brimstone
who hath comprehended d. *Isa 40:12*
of earth
they shall lick up the d. of *Isa 49:23*
thy feet
shake thyself from the d. O *Isa 52:2*
Jerusalem
d. shall be the serpent's *Isa 65:25*
meat
cast d. on their heads *La 2:10;*
Eze 27:30
she poured it not, to cover it *Eze 24:7*
with d.
I will also scrape her d. *Eze 26:4*
from her
by his horses, their d. shall *Eze 26:10*
cover thee
that pant after the d. of the *Am 2:7*
earth
they shall lick the d. like a *Mic 7:17*
serpent
and the clouds are the d. of *Na 1:3*
his feet
for they shall heap d. and *Hab 1:10*
take it
like d. of the streets (R) *Zec 9:3*
when ye depart out of that *M't 10:14;*

city, shake off d. of feet *M'k 6:11;*
Lu 9:5
even the d. of your city we *Lu 10:11*
do wipe off
they shook off the d. of *Ac 13:51*
their feet
as they threw d. into the air *Ac 22:23*
they cast d. on their heads, *Re 18:19*
and cried

AS THE DUST

and make thy seed *as the d.* *Ge 13:16;*
of earth *28:14; 2Ch 1:9*
I stamped the calf small *as* *De 9:21*
the d.
I beat them as small *as d.* *2Sa 22:43;*
Ps 18:42
then shalt thou lay up gold *Job 22:24*
as the d.
though he heap up silver *as* *Job 27:16*
the d.
and their blossom shall go up *Isa 5:24*
as d.
the nations *as the* small *d.* *Isa 40:15*
of the balance
he gave them *as the d.* to his *Isa 41:2*
sword
their blood shall be poured *Zep 1:17*
out *as d.*
Tyrus heaped up silver *as the* *Zec 9:3*
d.

IN THE DUST

them, whose foundation is *in* *Job 4:19*
the d.
now shall I sleep *in the d.* *Job 7:21*
thou shalt
and I have defiled my horn *in* *Job 16:15*
in the d.
when our rest together is *in* *Job 17:16*
the d.
which shall lie down with *Job 20:11*
him *in the d.*
they shall lie down alike *in* *Job 21:26*
the d.
leaveth eggs, and warmeth *Job 39:14*
them *in the d.*
hide them *in the d.* *Job 40:13*
together, and bind
let enemy lay mine honour *in* *Ps 7:5*
the d.
hide thee *in the d.* for fear *Isa 2:10*
of Lord
awake and sing, ye that *Isa 26:19*
dwell *in the d.*
come down and sit *in the d.* *Isa 47:1*
putteth his mouth *in the d.* if *La 3:29*
so be
many that sleep *in the d.* *Da 12:2*
shall awake
weep not at all, roll thyself *Mic 1:10*
in the d.
thy nobles shall dwell *in the* *Na 3:18*
d.

LIKE THE DUST

make them *like the d.* by *2Ki 13:7*
threshing
multitude of thy strangers be *Isa 29:5*
like d.

OF THE DUST

Lord formed man *of the d.* of *Ge 2:7*
ground
priest shall take *of the d.* in *Nu 5:17*
tabernacle
I will send poison of *De 32:24*
serpents *of the d.*
raiseth poor out *of the d.* *1Sa 2:8;*
Ps 113:7
exalted thee out *of the d.* *1Ki 16:2*
affliction cometh not forth *of* *Job 5:6*
the d.
washest away things that *Job 14:19*
grow out *of the d.*
nor highest part *of the d.* of *Pr 8:26*
the world
all go to one place, all are *of* *Ec 3:20*
the d.
thy speech shall be low out *Isa 29:4*
of the d.

TO THE DUST

all that go down *to the d.* *Ps 22:29*
shall bow

for our soul is bowed down *Ps 44:25*
to the d.
they die and return *to* their *Ps 104:29*
d.
my soul cleaveth *to the d.* *Ps 119:25*
quicken me
all are of the dust and turn *Ec 3:20*
to d. again
he shall bring the fortress *to* *Isa 25:12*
the d.
he bringeth the lofty city *Isa 26:5*
even *to the d.*

DUTIES

for their d. (S) *1Ch 25:8;*
26:12; Ne 13:30
if he beget a son that doth *Eze 18:11*
not these d.

DUTY

her d. of marriage shall not *Ex 21:10*
diminish
privilege as a wife shall he *Ex 21:10*
not diminish (A)
her marriage rights shall not *Ex 21:10*
(B)
her marital rights (R) *Ex 21:10*
perform d. of a husband's *De 25:5*
brother
will not perform d. of *De 25:7*
husband's brother
as d. of every day required *2Ch 8:14;*
Ezr 3:4
for this is the whole d. of man *Ec 12:13*
done that which was our d. *Lu 17:10*
to do
d. is to minister in carnal *Ro 15:27*
things
owe service in material *Ro 15:27*
things (A)(B)
contribute to their material *Ro 15:27*
needs (N)
service to them in material *Ro 15:27*
things (R)
give directions as to your d. *Ph'm 8*
(B)(N)

DWARF

a d. shall not come nigh to *Le 21:20*
offer offerings

DWELL

Japhet shall d. in the tents of *Ge 9:27*
Shem
shall d. in presence of his *Ge 16:12*
brethren
live on the borders of his *Ge 16:12*
kinsmen (A)
live over against his kindred *Ge 16:12*
(B)
Lot went up, for he feared *Ge 19:30*
to d. in Zoar
afraid to stay in Zoar *Ge 19:30*
(A)(B)
behold my land, d. where it *Ge 20:15*
pleaseth thee
settle (B) *Ge 20:15;*
34:10, 16; 35:1; Jos 24:13; Job 3:5
daughters of Canaan, *Ge 24:3*
amongst whom I d.
among whom I have settled *Ge 24:3*
(A)
among whom I am living (B) *Ge 24:3*
land before you, d. and *Ge 34:10*
trade therein
we will d. with you, become *Ge 34:16*
one people
arise, go up to Beth-el, and *Ge 35:1*
d. there
Moses was content to d. with *Ex 2:21*
man
stay (B) *Ex 2:21;*
J'g 17:10; 1Ki 17:9; Ps 15:1
that I may d. amongst them *Ex 25:8;*
29:46
I will d. amongst the *Ex 29:45*
children of Israel
the unclean shall d. alone *Le 13:46*
he shall live alone (A) *Le 13:46*
be isolated (B) *Le 13:46*
ye shall d. in booths *Le 23:42; 23:43;*
Ne 8:14
live in (B) *Le 23:42;*
9:7; 2Ki 4:13; 17:27
their camps, in midst whereof *Nu 5:3*
I d.

people shall *d.* alone, not be   *Nu 23:9*
reckoned
live by themselves (B)   *Nu 23:9*
our little ones shall *d.* in   *Nu 32:17*
fenced cities
cities to *d.* in   *Nu 35:2;*
     35:3; Jos 14:4; 21:2
I the Lord *d.* among the   *Nu 35:34*
children of Israel
to cause his name *d.* there   *De 12:11;*
     Ezr 6:12
servant escaped shall *d.* with   *De 23:16*
thee
remain among you (B)   *De 23:16*
he shall *d.* between his   *De 33:12*
shoulders
peradventure ye *d.* among us   *Jos 9:7;*
     9:22
perhaps you live among us (A)   *Jos 9:7*
perhaps you live nearby (B)   *Jos 9:7*
d. in that city, till he stand   *Jos 20:6*
before
cities ye built not, and ye *d.*   *Jos 24:13*
in them
that Gaal should not *d.* in   *J'g 9:41*
Shechem
Micah said to the Levite, D.   *J'g 17:10*
with me
that I may *d.* there, for why   *1Sa 27:5*
I will *d.* among children of   *1Ki 6:13*
Israel
abide with (B)   *1Ki 6:13*
he would *d.* in thick   *1Ki 8:12;*
darkness   *2Ch 6:1*
get thee to Zarephath, and *d.*   *1Ki 17:9*
there
I *d.* among mine own people   *2Ki 4:13*
let them go and *d.* there, let   *2Ki 17:27*
him teach
let cloud *d.* upon it, let   *Job 3:5*
blackness of day
let not wickedness *d.* in thy   *Job 11:14*
tabernacle
d. in his tabernacle, because   *Job 18:15*
none of his
to *d.* in the clifts of the   *Job 30:6*
valleys, in caves
neither shall evil *d.* with thee   *Ps 5:4*
Lord, who shall *d.* in thy holy   *Ps 15:1*
hill
his soul shall *d.* at ease, and   *Ps 25:13*
depart from evil, and *d.* for   *Ps 37:27*
evermore
abide for evermore (B)   *Ps 37:27*
to approach, that he may *d.*   *Ps 65:4*
in thy courts
they also that *d.* in the   *Ps 65:8*
uttermost parts of earth
live (B)   *Ps 65:8;*
84:10; 107:36; Pr 21:19; Isa 11:6; 13:21;
16:4; 40:22; 49:20; Jer 40:5, 10;
Ho 12:9; 14:7; Mic 4:10; 7:14; Zec 9:6
this is hill God desireth to *d.*   *Ps 68:16*
in, the Lord will *d.* in it
that the Lord might *d.* among   *Ps 68:18*
them
will build Judah that they   *Ps 69:35*
may *d.* there
they that *d.* in the wilderness   *Ps 72:9*
shall bow
and made Israel to *d.* in   *Ps 78:55*
their tents
settled tribes of Israel in   *Ps 78:55*
tents (B)
than to *d.* in the tents of   *Ps 84:10*
wickedness
on faithful, that they may *d.*   *Ps 101:6*
with me
be my associates (B)   *Ps 101:6*
shall not *d.* in (A)   *Ps 101:7*
wandered, they found no   *Ps 107:4*
city to *d.* in
no road to a residence city   *Ps 107:4*
(A)(B)
and there he maketh the   *Ps 107:36*
hungry to *d.*
woe is me, that I *d.* in tents   *Ps 120:5*
of Kedar
here will I *d.* for I have   *Ps 132:14*
desired it
if I *d.* in uttermost parts of   *Ps 139:9*
the sea
the upright shall *d.* in thy   *Ps 140:13*
presence
he hath made me to *d.* in   *Ps 143:3*
darkness
whoso hearkeneth to me *d.*   *Pr 1:33*
safely

I wisdom *d.* with prudence   *Pr 8:12*
and find out
it is better to *d.* in   *Pr 21:19*
wilderness, than with
I *d.* in midst of people of   *Isa 6:5*
unclean lips
living among (B)   *Isa 6:5; Jer 29:32*
the wolf also shall *d.* with   *Isa 11:6*
the lamb
owls *d.* there, satyrs shall   *Isa 13:21*
dance there
let mine outcasts *d.* with   *Isa 16:4*
thee, Moab
merchandise for them that   *Isa 23:18*
d. before Lord
they that *d.* therein are desolate   *Isa 24:6*
he bringeth down them that   *Isa 26:5*
d. on high
awake and sing, ye that *d.*   *Isa 26:19*
in the dust
people shall *d.* in Zion at   *Isa 30:19*
Jerusalem
then judgment shall *d.* in   *Isa 32:16*
wilderness
my people *d.* in a peaceful   *Isa 32:18*
habitation
who shall *d.* with devouring   *Isa 33:14*
fire who shall *d.* with everlasting
burnings
he shall *d.* on high, his   *Isa 33:16*
place of defence
people that *d.* therein shall   *Isa 33:24*
be forgiven
living there (B)   *Isa 33:24*
the owl and the raven shall   *Isa 34:11*
d. in it
he spreadeth them out as a   *Isa 40:22*
tent to *d.* in
give place to me that I may   *Isa 49:20*
d.
be called the restorer of   *Isa 58:12*
paths to *d.* in
and my servants shall *d.*   *Isa 65:9*
there
Shemaiah shall not have a   *Jer 29:32*
man to *d.*
there shall *d.* in Judah   *Jer 31:24*
husbandmen
but all your days ye shall *d.*   *Jer 35:7*
in tents
and *d.* with him among the   *Jer 40:5*
people
I will *d.* at Mizpeh to serve   *Jer 40:10*
Chaldeans
we will go into Egypt, and   *Jer 42:14*
there will we *d.*
they have a desire to return   *Jer 44:14*
to *d.* there
flee ye, *d.* deep, O   *Jer 49:8*
inhabitants of Dedan
nor shall a son of man *d.*   *Jer 49:18;*
in it   *49:33; 50:40*
which *d.* alone   *Jer 49:31*
that *d.* in midst of them   *Jer 51:1*
thou dost *d.* among scorpions   *Eze 2:6*
she and her daughters *d.* at   *Eze 16:46*
thy left hand
where I will *d.* in the midst   *Eze 43:7;*
of Israel for ever   *43:9; Zec 2:10, 11*
I will make thee to *d.* in   *Ho 12:9*
tabernacles
they that *d.* under his   *Ho 14:7*
shadow shall return
Judah shall *d.* for ever, and   *Joe 3:20*
shall be inhabited for ever   *Joe 3:20*
(A)(B)
Israel shall be taken out that   *Am 3:12*
d. in Samaria
who sit on corner of bed   *Am 3:12*
(B)
thou shalt *d.* in field, go to   *Mic 4:10*
Babylon
the flock which *d.* solitarily   *Mic 7:14*
in the wood
O Assyria, thy nobles shall *d.*   *Na 3:18*
in dust
is it time to *d.* in your ceiled   *Hag 1:4*
houses
old men and women *d.* in   *Zec 8:4*
Jerusalem
shall yet sit in streets of   *Zec 8:4*
Jerusalem (B)
and a bastard shall *d.* in   *Zec 9:6*
Ashdod
shall be inhabited, and men   *Zec 14:11*
shall *d.* in it
they enter in and *d.* there   *M't 12:45;*
     Lu 11:26
make their home there (A)   *M't 12:45*

enter and live there (B)   *M't 12:45*
all come in and settle down   *M't 12:45*
(N)
go in and make themselves   *M't 12:45*
at home (P)
all them that *d.* on face of   *Lu 21:35;*
the whole earth   *Ac 17:26*
live upon face of the earth   *Lu 21:35*
(A)
every inhabitant of whole   *Lu 21:35*
earth (P)
he removed into land wherein   *Ac 7:4*
ye now *d.*
Paul was suffered to *d.* by   *Ac 28:16*
himself
permitted to live by himself   *Ac 28:16*
(A)(B)
permitted to abide by   *Ac 28:16*
himself (E)
allowed to lodge by himself   *Ac 28:16*
(N)(R)
permission to live alone (P)   *Ac 28:16*
if so be the Spirit of God *d.*   *Ro 8:9;*
in you   *8:11*
is at home with you (B)   *Ro 8:9*
finds a home with you (P)   *Ro 8:9*
and she be pleased to *d.*   *1Co 7:12*
with him
consents to live with him   *1Co 7:12*
(A)(R)
enjoys living with him (B)   *1Co 7:12*
she is willing to live with   *1Co 7:12*
him (N)(P)
as God hath said, I will *d.*   *2Co 6:16*
in them
Christ may *d.* in your hearts   *Eph 3:17*
by faith
Father that in him should all   *Col 1:19*
fulness *d.*
let the word of Christ *d.* in   *Col 3:16*
you richly
likewise, ye husbands, *d.* with   *1Pe 3:7*
them
hereby know we that we *d.*   *1Jo 4:13*
in him
that we abide in him   *1Jo 4:13*
(A)(E)(R)
we remain in him (B)   *1Jo 4:13*
guarantee of our living in   *1Jo 4:13*
him (P)
he that sitteth on the throne   *Re 7:15*
shall *d.*
spread his tabernacle over   *Re 7:15*
and shelter them with his
presence (A)(E)
spreads his tent over them   *Re 7:15*
(B)
will be their shelter (P)   *Re 7:15*
will shelter them with his   *Re 7:15*
presence (R)
rejoice, ye heavens, and ye   *Re 12:12*
that *d.* in them
you who live in heaven (P)   *Re 12:12*
and against them that *d.* in   *Re 13:6*
heaven
those who live in heaven   *Re 13:6*
(A)(P)
is with men, and he will *d.*   *Re 21:3*
with them
he will live among them   *Re 21:3*
(A)(P)
at last God has his dwelling   *Re 21:3*
among men (N)

DWELL with *EARTH*

will God *d.* on earth   *1Ki 8:27;*
     2Ch 6:18
languages that *d.* in all the   *Da 4:1;*
earth   *6:25*
to try them that *d.* on the   *Re 3:10*
earth
avenge our blood on them   *Re 6:10*
that *d.* on earth
they that *d.* on the *earth*   *Re 11:10*
shall rejoice
all that *d.* on the *earth* shall   *Re 13:8*
worship
deceiveth them that *d.* on   *Re 13:14*
earth
to preach to them that *d.* on   *Re 14:6*
the earth
they that *d.* on the *earth* shall   *Re 17:8*
wonder

DWELL with *HOUSE*

build an *house*, shalt not *d.*   *De 28:30*
therein   *Am 5:11*

I *d.* in a *house* of cedar — 2Sa 7:2; 1Ch 17:1
build me an *house* to *d.* in — 2Sa 7:5; 1Ch 17:1
build *house* in Jerusalem and *d.* there — 1Ki 2:36
my lord, I and this woman *d.* in one *house* — 1Ki 3:17
I have surely built thee an *house* to *d.* in — 1Ki 8:13
my wife shall not *d.* in *house* of David — 2Ch 8:11
much less them that *d.* in *houses* of clay — Job 4:19
they that *d.* in my *house* count me stranger — Job 19:15
I will *d.* in *house* of the Lord for ever — Ps 23:6
that I may *d.* in the *house* of the Lord — Ps 27:4
blessed are they that *d.* in thy *house* — Ps 84:4
worketh deceit, shall not *d.* in my *house* — Ps 101:7
better *d.* in corner of a *house* — Pr 21:9; 25:24
all that *d.* in thy *house* go to captivity — Jer 20:6
build ye *houses,* and *d.* in them — Jer 29:5; 29:28
not to build *houses* for us to *d.* in — Jer 35:9

DWELL with *JERUSALEM*

ye may *d.* in *Jerusalem* for ever — 1Ch 23:25
bring one of ten to *d.* in *Jerusalem* — Ne 11:1
willingly offered themselves to *d.* at *Jerusalem* — Ne 11:2
Judah saved, *Jerusalem* shall *d.* safe — Jer 33:16
fear of Chaldeans we *d.* at *Jerusalem* — Jer 35:11
I will *d.* in the midst of *Jerusalem* — Zec 8:3
they shall *d.* in the midst of *Jerusalem* — Zec 8:8
and all ye that *d.* at *Jerusalem* — Ac 2:14
manifest to all that *d.* in *Jerusalem* — Ac 4:16
they that *d.* at *Jerusalem* have condemned him — Ac 13:27

DWELL with *LAND*

of the Canaanites in whose *land* I *d.* — Ge 24:37
d. in the *land* which I shall tell thee of — Ge 26:2
let them *d.* in *land,* and trade therein — Ge 34:21
and thou shalt *d.* in the *land* of Goshen — Ge 45:10
that ye may *d.* in the *land* of Goshen — Ge 46:34
in the *land* of Goshen let them *d.* — Ge 47:6
land of Goshen people *d.* — Ex 8:22
they shall not *d.* in thy *land* — Ex 23:33
ye shall *d.* in your *land* in safety — Le 25:18
ye shall eat and *d.* in your *land* safely — Le 26:5
what the *land* is that they *d.* in — Nu 13:19
defile not the *land* wherein I *d.* — Nu 35:34
d. in the land which Lord giveth you — De 12:10
may *d.* in *land* Lord sware — De 30:20
Canaanites would *d.* in *land* — Jos 17:12; J'g 1:27
gods in whose *land* ye *d.* — Jos 24:15; J'g 6:10
fear not, *d.* in *land* — 2Ki 25:24; Jer 25:5; 40:9
do good, so shalt thou *d.* in *land* — Ps 37:3
but the rebellious *d.* in a dry *land* — Ps 68:6
salvation near, that glory may *d.* in *land* — Ps 85:9
for upright shall *d.* in *land* — Pr 2:21
that *d.* in *land* of the shadow of death — Isa 9:2
they shall *d.* in own *land* — Jer 23:8; 27:11

that *d.* in *land* of Egypt — Jer 24:8; 44:1, 8, 13, 26
ye shall *d.* in *land* — Jer 35:15; Eze 36:28; 37:25
if ye say, We will not *d.* in this *land* — Jer 42:13
obeyed not Lord to *d.* in *land* of Judah — Jer 43:4; 43:5
make *land* desolate, none *d.* therein — Jer 50:3
then shall they *d.* in their *land* — Eze 28:25
people that *d.* in midst of *land* — Eze 38:12
they shall not *d.* in Lord's *land* — Ho 9:3
for violence of *land,* and all that *d.* — Hab 2:8; 2:17
make riddance of all that *d.* in *land* — Zep 1:18

DWELL with *PLACE*

in *place* thou hast made to *d.* in — Ex 15:17
made them to *d.* in this *place* — 1Sa 12:8
they may *d.* in *place* of their own — 2Sa 7:10
behold *place* where we *d.* is strait — 2Ki 6:1
let us make us a *place* where we may *d.* — 2Ki 6:2
they shall *d.* in their *place* — 1Ch 17:9
I *d.* in the high and holy *place* — Isa 57:15
I will cause you to *d.* in this *place* — Jer 7:3; 7:7

DWELL *IN SAFETY*

and *d.* in land *in safety* — Le 25:19; De 12:10
beloved of Lord shall *d.* in *safety* — De 33:12
Israel then shall *d.* in *safety* alone — De 33:28
thou, Lord, makest me *d.* in *safety* — Ps 4:8

DWELL *SAFELY*

whoso hearkeneth to me shall *d. safely* — Pr 1:33
in his days Judah be saved — Jer 23:6;
and Israel *d. safely* — Eze 28:26; 34:25; 28; 38:8
I will cause them to *d. safely* — Jer 32:37
go to them at rest that *d. safely* — Eze 38:11

DWELL *THEREIN*

enemies which *d. therein* be astonished — Le 27:32
land I sware to make you *d. therein* — Nu 14:30
ye shall *d. therein* — Nu 33:53; De 11:31
the world and they that *d. therein* — Ps 24:1
the righteous shall *d. therein* for ever — Ps 37:29
they that love his name shall *d. therein* — Ps 69:36
wickedness of them that *d. therein* — Ps 107:34; Jer 12:4
they that *d. therein* are desolate — Isa 24:6; Am 9:5
people that *d. therein* forgiven iniquity — Isa 33:24
generation to generation shall *d. therein* — Isa 34:17
that *d. therein* shall die in like manner — Isa 51:6
city forsaken, and not a man *d. therein* — Jer 4:29
devoured city, and all that *d. therein* — Jer 8:16
wickedness of them that *d. therein* — Jer 12:4
overflow land and them that *d. therein* — Jer 47:2
cities desolate without any to *d. therein* — Jer 48:9
wild beasts and owls shall *d. therein* — Jer 50:39
violence of them that *d. therein* — Eze 12:19

when I shall smite them that *d. therein* — Eze 32:15
they and their children shall *d. therein* — Eze 37:25
desolate, because of them that *d. therein* — Mic 7:13
world is burnt, and all that *d. therein* — Na 1:5
his habitation, let no man *d. therein* — Ac 1:20

DWELL *TOGETHER*

they might *d. together,* so they could not *d. together* — Ge 13:6
riches more than that they might *d. together* — Ge 36:7
if brethren *d. together,* and one die — De 25:5
for brethren to *d. together* in unity — Ps 133:1

DWELLED

the Perizzite *d.* then in the land — Ge 13:7
living in the land (B) — Ge 13:7
Abram *d.* in Canaan, Lot *d.* in cities of plain — Ge 13:12
Abraham living in the Canaan country (B) — Ge 13:12
Abraham *d.* between Kadesh and Shur — Ge 20:1
lived for a time in Gerar (B) — Ge 20:1
they *d.* there about ten years — Ru 1:4
they had lived there (B)(R) — Ru 1:4
God delivered you, and ye *d.* safe — 1Sa 12:11
lived in safety (B) — 1Sa 12:11

DWELLERS

d. of Canaan (B) — Ex 15:15
d. on earth, see when he lifteth up — Isa 18:3
d. of Saphir (B) — Mic 1:11; 1:12-13, 15
it was known to the *d.* at Jerusalem — Ac 1:19
residents of Jerusalem (A) — Ac 1:19
the whole Jerusalem population (B) — Ac 1:19
the inhabitants of Jerusalem (R) — Ac 1:19
d. in Mesopotamia, we do hear them speak — Ac 2:9
inhabitants of Mesopotamia (A)(N) — Ac 2:9
residents of Mesopotamia (R) — Ac 2:9

DWELLEST

succeedest them and *d.* in their land — De 12:29
Lord God, which *d.* between the cherubims — 2Ki 19:15; Ps 80:1; Isa 37:16
O thou that *d.* in the heavens — Ps 123:1
enthroned in heaven (A)(B)(R) — Ps 123:1
sittest in the heavens (E) — Ps 123:1
thou that *d.* in the gardens — Ca 8:13
my people that *d.* in Zion, be not afraid — Isa 10:24
hear now this, thou that *d.* carelessly — Isa 47:8
thou that *d.* in the clefts — Jer 49:16; Ob 3
thou that *d.* upon many waters — Jer 51:13
Edom, that *d.* in land of Uz — La 4:21
thou that *d.* in the land, time — Eze 7:7
thou *d.* in the midst of a rebellious house — Eze 12:2
that *d.* with daughter of Babylon — Zec 2:7
they said, Master, where *d.* thou — Joh 1:38
I know thy works, and where *d.* thou — Re 2:13

DWELLETH

the stranger that *d.* with you — Le 19:34
And if thy brother that *d.* by thee — Le 25:39
and thy brother that *d.* by him — Le 25:47

people that *d.* therein | Nu 13:18
he *d.* as a lion, and teareth | De 33:20
the arm
lurks as a lion (B) | De 33:20
couches as a lion (R) | De 33:20
and she *d.* in Israel even | Jos 6:25
unto
wherein the Lord's tabernacle | Jos 22:19
d.
which *d.* between the | 1Sa 4:4
cherubims
throned above the cherubim | 1Sa 4:4
(B)(R)
sitteth above the cherubim | 1Sa 4:4
(E)
while he *d.* in the country | 1Sa 27:11
that *d.* between the cherubims | 2Sa 6:2
the ark of God *d.* within | 2Sa 7:2
curtains
that *d.* between the | 1Ch 13:6
cherubims
And he *d.* in desolate cities | Job 15:28
Where is the way where | Job 38:19
light *d.*
She *d.* and abideth on the | Job 39:28
rock
to the Lord, which *d.* in Zion | Ps 9:11
the place where thine honour | Ps 26:8
d.
He that *d.* in the secret place | Ps 91:1
the Lord our God, who *d.* | Ps 113:5
on high
of Zion, which *d.* at | Ps 135:21
Jerusalem
seeing he *d.* securely by thee | Pr 3:29
of hosts, which *d.* in mount | Isa 8:18
Zion
for he *d.* on high: he hath | Isa 33:5
filled
of all the people that *d.* in | Jer 29:16
this
desolation, and no man *d.* | Jer 44:2
therein
nation that *d.* without care | Jer 49:31
a land wherein no man *d.* | Jer 51:43
she *d.* among the heathen, she | La 1:3
that *d.* at thy right hand, | Eze 16:46
is Sodom
the place where the king *d.* | Eze 17:16
when my people of Israel *d.* | Eze 38:14
safely
darkness, and the light *d.* | Da 2:22
with
every one that *d.* herein shall | Ho 4:3
cleansed: for the Lord *d.* in | Joe 3:21
Zion
every one mourn that *d.* | Am 8:8
therein
by it, and by him that *d.* | M't 23:21
therein
my blood, *d.* in me, and I in | Joh 6:56
him
the Father that *d.* in me, | Joh 14:10
he doeth
lives continually in me | Joh 14:10
(A)(P)
Father abiding in me doeth | Joh 14:10
the works (E)
for he *d.* with you, and | Joh 14:17
shall be
he lives with you (A) | Joh 14:17
he remains with you (B) | Joh 14:17
he abideth with you (E) | Joh 14:17
he is with you now (P) | Joh 14:17
the most High *d.* not in | Ac 7:48
temples
of heaven and earth, *d.* not | Ac 17:24
in temple
that do it, but sin that *d.* in | Ro 7:17
me
sin which is at home in me | Ro 7:17
and has possession of me (A)(B)
sin that lodges in me (N) | Ro 7:17
Sin that has made its home | Ro 7:17
in my nature (P)
is, in my flesh, *d.* no good | Ro 7:18
thing
in my flesh, what is good is | Ro 7:18
not at home (B)
nothing good lodges in me | Ro 7:18
(N)
my being can scarcely be | Ro 7:18
called the home of good (P)
I that do it, but sin that *d.* | Ro 7:20
in me
bodies by his Spirit that *d.* in | Ro 8:11
your
and that the Spirit of God | 1Co 3:16
d. in you
in him *d.* all the fulness of | Col 2:9

the Holy Ghost which *d.* in | 2Ti 1:14
us
The spirit that *d.* in us lusteth | Jas 4:5
earth, wherein *d.* | 2Pe 3:13
righteousness
how *d.* the love of God in | 1Jo 3:17
him
how can love of God live | 1Jo 3:17
and remain in (A)
how is the love of God | 1Jo 3:17
lodging in him (B)
how does love of God abide | 1Jo 3:17
in him (E)(R)
the love of God lives in him | 1Jo 3:17
(P)
his commandments *d.* in | 1Jo 3:24
him
God *d.* in us, and his love is | 1Jo 4:12
God abides in us | 1Jo 4:12
(A)(E)(R)
God remains in us (B) | 1Jo 4:12
God does actually live in us | 1Jo 4:12
(P)
God *d.* in him, and he in | 1Jo 4:15
God
he that *d.* in love *d.* in God | 1Jo 4:16
the truth's sake, which *d.* in us | 2Jo 2
slain among you, where Satan | Re 2:13
d.

DWELLING

their *d.* was from Mesha, as | Ge 10:30
thou
Jacob was a plain man, *d.* | Ge 25:27
in tents
thy *d.* shall be the fatness of | Ge 27:39
thy holy *d.* place (B) | Ex 15:13
out of camp be his *d.* (E) | Le 13:46
if a man sell a *d.* house in a | Le 25:29
walled
that goeth down to the *d.* of | Nu 21:15
Ar
De 12:5; | De 12:5;
2Ch 29:6; Job 8:6; Ps 33:14; | 69:25;
 | 132:13
dukes of Sihon, *d.* in the | Jos 13:21
country
and hear thou in heaven thy | 1Ki 8:30
d.
Then hear thou in heaven | 1Ki 8:39
thy *d.*
Hear thou in heaven thy *d.* | 1Ki 8:43
place
supplication in heaven thy *d.* | 1Ki 8:49
place
were in his city, *d.* with | 1Ki 21:8
Naboth
the beginning of their *d.* | 2Ki 17:25
there, that
they ministered before the *d.* | 1Ch 6:32
are their *d.* places | 1Ch 6:54
throughout
a place for thy *d.* for ever | 2Ch 6:2
hear thou from thy *d.* place | 2Ch 6:21
hear thou from heaven thy *d.* | 2Ch 6:30
place
even from thy *d.* place, and | 2Ch 6:33
even from thy *d.* place, their | 2Ch 6:39
prayer
came up to his holy *d.* | 2Ch 30:27
place
his people, and on his *d.* | 2Ch 36:15
place
whose *d.* in Jerusalem (A) | Ezr 7:15
and the *d.* place of the | Job 8:22
wicked
are the *d.* places of the | Job 21:28
wicked
their *d.* places to all | Ps 49:11
generations
consume in the grave from | Ps 49:14
their *d.*
pluck thee out of thy *d.* place | Ps 52:5
down the *d.* place of thy | Ps 74:7
name
and his *d.* place in Zion | Ps 76:2
Jacob, and laid waste his *d.* | Ps 79:7
place
Lord, thou hast been our *d.* | Ps 90:1
place
Most High your *d.* place (A) | Ps 91:9
shall any plague come nigh | Ps 91:10
thy *d.*
the *d.* of the righteous (B) | Pr 3:33
and oil in the *d.* of the wise | Pr 21:20
against the *d.* of the | Pr 24:15
righteous
every *d.* place of mount Zion | Isa 4:5
I will consider in my *d.* place | Isa 18:4

carves out a *d.* (A)(B) | Isa 22:16
d. place of your holiness | Isa 63:15
(A)
O thou daughter *d.* in Egypt | Jer 46:19
Hazor shall be a *d.* for | Jer 49:33
dragons
all of them *d.* without walls | Eze 38:11
the city, for *d.* and for | Eze 48:15
suburbs
gods, whose *d.* is not with | Da 2:11
flesh
thy *d.* shall be with the | Da 4:25; 4:32
beasts
and his *d.* was with the wild | Da 5:21
asses
the Lord your God *d.* in Zion | Joe 3:17
Where is the *d.* of the lions | Na 2:11
so their *d.* should not be cut | Zep 3:7
off
Who had his *d.* among the | M'k 5:3
tombs
guards his own *d.* (A) | Lu 11:21
let his *d.* be desolate (B) | Ac 1:20
And there were *d.* at Jerusalem | Ac 2:5
Greeks also *d.* at Ephesus | Ac 19:17
d. of God (B)(N)(R) | Eph 2:22
d. in the light which no man | 1Ti 6:16
can
d. in tabernacles with Isaac | Heb 11:9
righteous man *d.* among them | 2Pe 2:8
abandoned proper *d.* place | Jude 6
(A)(B)(R)
d. place of demons | Re 18:2
(A)(N)(R)

DWELLINGPLACE

Strong is thy *d.* and thou | Nu 24:21
puttest
Babylon shall become heaps, | Jer 51:37
a *d.*
are buffeted, have no certain | 1Co 4:11
d.

DWELLINGPLACES

tents, and have mercy on his | Jer 30:18
d.
women: they have burned | Jer 51:30
her *d.*
In all your *d.* the cities shall | Eze 6:6
be
I will save them out of all | Eze 37:23
their *d.*
possess the *d.* that are not | Hab 1:6
theirs

DWELLINGS

of Israel had light in their *d.* | Ex 10:23
throughout all your *d.* that ye | Le 3:17
fowl, or of beast, in any of | Le 7:26
your *d.*
sabbath of the Lord in all | Le 23:3
your *d.*
your generations in all your | Le 23:14
d.
for ever in all your *d.* | Le 23:21
throughout

DWELLS

who *d.* in Jerusalem (B)(R) | Ezr 7:15;
 | 2Ch 6:2

DWELT

and they *d.* there | Ge 11:2;
11:31; 26:17; 2Ki 16:6; | 2Ch 28:18
there they settled (B)(R) | Ge 11:2
Ephron *d.* among children | Ge 23:10
of Heth
Ephron present among sons | Ge 23:10
of Heth (A)
sitting among sons of Heth | Ge 23:10
(B)(E)(R)
doings of Egypt wherein ye *d.* | Le 18:3
not do
lived (B) | Le 18:3; Nu 31:10; Jer 39:14
wherein they *d.* | Nu 31:10; 2Ki 17:29
d. and old prophet in | 1Ki 13:11;
Beth-el | 13:25
old prophet was living (B) | 1Ki 13:11
and I *d.* as a king in the | Job 29:25
army
sitting among (B) | Job 29:25
mount Zion wherein thou hast | Ps 74:2
d.

woe to Ariel, city where David d. | Isa 29:1
where David encamped (A)(B)(E)(R) | Isa 29:1
and returned, and d. at Nineveh | Isa 37:37
led us through land where no man d. | Jer 2:6
no man passes through our inhabits (B) | Jer 2:6
so Jeremiah d. among the people | Jer 39:14
that d. by the river of Chebar | Eze 3:15
under his shadow d. great nations | Eze 31:6; 31:17
the land wherein your fathers have d. | Eze 37:25
under which the beasts of the field d. | Da 4:21
this is the rejoicing city that d. carelessly | Zep 2:15
fear came on all that d. round about | Lu 1:65
fear came upon neighbors (A)(B)(N)(P)(R) | Lu 1:65
Word was made flesh and d. among us | Joh 1:14
tabernacled-fixed his tent of flesh, lived awhile-among us (A) | Joh 1:14
tented among us (B) | Joh 1:14
lived among us (P) | Joh 1:14
they came and saw where he d. and abode | Joh 1:39
where he was staying (A)(B)(N)(P)(R) | Joh 1:39
where he abode (E) | Joh 1:39
when they d. as strangers in Egypt | Ac 13:17
lived as strangers in Egypt (B) | Ac 13:17
sojourned in the land of Egypt (E) | Ac 13:17
living as aliens in Egypt (N) | Ac 13:17
were exiles in the land of Egypt (P) | Ac 13:17
their stay in Egypt (R) | Ac 13:17
Ananias having good report of all that d. | Ac 22:12
Jews who resided there (A) | Ac 22:12
Jews who lived there (B)(P)(R) | Ac 22:12
Jews of that place (N) | Ac 22:12
Paul d. two years in his own hired house | Ac 28:30
Paul lived there two years (A)(R) | Ac 28:30
remained for two whole years (B) | Ac 28:30
abode two whole years (E) | Ac 28:30
stayed there two whole years (N)(P) | Ac 28:30
tormented them that d. on the earth | Re 11:10
torment to all dwellers of earth (A) | Re 11:10
torment to the whole earth (N) | Re 11:10
misery to inhabitants of earth (P) | Re 11:10

DWELT AT

and Abraham d. at Beer-sheba | Ge 22:19
Amor, which d. at Heshbon | Nu 21:34; De 3:2
and Abimelech d. at Arumah | J'g 9:41
Benhadad d. at Damascus | 1Ki 15:18; 2Ch 16:2
Sennacherib d. at Nineveh | 2Ki 19:36; Isa 37:37
families of scribes which d. at Jabez | 1Ch 2:55
these fathers of Levites d. at Jerusalem | 1Ch 9:34
Saul confounded Jews that d. at Damascus | Ac 9:22
Peter came to the saints who d. at Lydda | Ac 9:32

DWELT IN

we have d. in Egypt a long time | Nu 20:15
thus Israel d. in land of Amorites | Nu 21:31
d. in their stead | De 2:12; 2:21-23; 1Ch 5:22
good will of him that d. in the bush | De 33:16

by the way of them that d. in J'g 18:11 tents | J'g 18:11
Jerubbaal went and d. in his own house | J'g 8:29
David and Samuel d. in Naioth | 1Sa 19:18
Philistines came and d. in them | 1Sa 31:7; 1Ch 10:7
I have not d. in any house | 2Sa 7:6; 1Ch 17:5
all that d. in the house of Ziba were servants | 2Sa 9:12
Absalom d. two full years in Jerusalem | 2Sa 14:28
Shimei d. in Jerusalem many days | 1Ki 2:38
Jeroboam was fled from Solomon, d. in Egypt | 1Ki 12:2
Israel d. in their tents as aforetime | 2Ki 13:5
Ahaziah d. in a several house | 2Ki 15:5; 2Ch 26:21
Huldah the prophetess d. in Jerusalem, in the college | 2Ki 22:14; 2Ch 34:22
these came and d. in their rooms | 1Ch 4:41
Hagarites fell, and they d. in their tents | 1Ch 5:10
were chief men, these d. in Jerusalem | 1Ch 8:28
David d. in the castles | 1Ch 11:7; 2Sa 5:9
priests, Levites, and Nethinims | Ezr 2:70; Ne 3:26; 11:21
d. in their cities
Nethinims and all Israel d. in Ne 7:73 cities | Ne 7:73
the honourable men d. in it | Job 22:8
my soul had almost d. in silence | Ps 94:17
never be inhabited, nor be d. in from | Isa 13:20; Jer 50:39
but we have d. in tents, and obeyed | Jer 35:10
they d. in the habitation of Chimham | Jer 41:17
when Israel d. in their own land | Eze 36:17
when d. safely in their land | Eze 39:26
fowls of heaven d. in boughs | Da 4:12
Joseph d. in a city called Nazareth | M't 2:23
Jesus came and d. in Capernaum | M't 4:13
were sinners above all that d. in Jerusalem | Lu 13:4
before Abraham d. in Charran | Ac 7:2; 7:4
all who d. in Asia heard word of Jesus | Ac 19:10
which d. first in thy grandmother Lois | 2Ti 1:5

DWELT THEREIN

gave Gilead to Machir, he d. therein | Nu 32:40
Emims giants d. therein in old time | De 2:10; 2:20
Rezon went to Damascus and d. therein | 1Ki 11:24
Jeroboam built Shechem, and d. therein | 1Ki 12:25
there d. men of Tyre also therein | Ne 13:16
thy congregation hath d. therein | Ps 68:10

DWELT WITH

Ruth d. with her mother in law | Ru 2:23
father and mother d. with Moab | 1Sa 22:4
there they d. with king for his work | 1Ch 4:23
these also d. with their brethren | 1Ch 8:32; 9:38
my soul hath long d. with him that | Ps 120:6
Jeremiah d. with him among the people | Jer 40:6

DYED

rams' skins d. red | Ex 25:5; 26:14; 35:7; 36:19; 39:34
d. garments red | J'g 5:30
with d. garments from Bozrah | Isa 63:1
exceeding in d. attire upon | Eze 23:15

DYING

shall we be consumed with d. | Nu 17:13
one d. (S) | Job 11:20
and the first took a wife, and d. | M'k 12:20
years of age, and she lay a d. | Lu 8:42
I am d. of hunger (P) | Lu 15:17
nonsense to d. world (P) | 1Co 1:18
bearing about in the body the d. | 2Co 4:10
known; as d. and behold, we live | 2Co 6:9
those involved in d. (P) | 2Th 2:10
Jacob, when he was a d. blessed | Heb 11:21

DYSENTERY

fever and d. (A)(B)(E)(N)(P)(R) | Ac 28:8

E

EACH

Abraham laid e. piece against another | Ge 15:10
Simeon and Levi took e. man his sword | Ge 34:25
e. man his dream | Ge 40:5
and they asked e. other of their welfare | Ex 18:7
of e. shall there be a like weight | Ex 30:34
e. one was for house of fathers | Nu 1:44
they brought for e. one an ox | Nu 7:3
thou also and Aaron e. of you his censer | Nu 16:17
put pure frankincense upon e. row | Le 24:7
of e. chief house a prince, | Jos 22:14
e. one was head | J'g 8:18
e. one resembled the children of a king | J'g 8:18
because we reserved not to e. man his wife | J'g 21:22
grant that they may find rest e. of you | Ru 1:9
e. man his month in a year | 1Ki 4:7
the kings e. sat on his throne | 1Ki 22:10
he exacted of e. man fifty shekels | 2Ki 15:20
righteousness and peace kissed e. other | Ps 58:10
they made e. one for himself to worship | Isa 2:20
stood seraphims, e. one had six wings | Isa 6:2
where he lay, shall be grass | Isa 35:7
e. one walking in his uprightness | Isa 57:2
appointed thee e. day for a year | Eze 4:6
doth not e. on sabbath loose ox or ass | Lu 13:15
cloven tongues sat upon e. of them | Ac 2:3
let e. esteem other better than himself | Ph'p 2:3
charity toward e. other aboundeth | 2Th 1:3
four beasts had e. six wings | Re 4:8

EAGER

be e. to prophesy (P) | 1Co 14:39
how e. you are (N) | 2Co 7:7
he is so e. that by (N) | 2Co 8:17
I know how e. you are (N) | 2Co 9:2
I was also e. to do (A)(B)(R) | Ga 2:10

EAGERLY

the more e. (S) | Ph'p 2:28

EAGERNESS

your e. to help (P) | 2Co 7:7
of e. to help (P) | 2Co 8:8
your e. (A) | 2Co 9:2

EAGLE

the *e*. and the ossifrage, and *Le 11:13*
the black *e*. (B) *Le 11:13*
and the pelican and the gier *Le 11:18* *e*.
not eat: the *e*. and the *De 14:12* ossifrage
the gier *e*. and the *De 14:17* cormorant
the earth, as swift as the *e*. *De 28:49* flieth
swooping down like a *De 28:49* vulture (B)
As an *e*. stirreth up her nest *De 32:11*
as the *e*. that hasteth to the *Job 9:26* prey
Doth the *e*. mount up at *Job 39:27*
fly away as an *e*. toward *Pr 23:5* heaven
The way of an *e*. in the air *Pr 30:19*
Behold, he shall fly as an *e*. *Jer 48:40*
make thy nest as high as the *Jer 49:16* *e*.
and fly as the *e*. and spread *Jer 49:22* his
they four also had the face *Eze 1:10* of an *e*.
and the fourth the face of *Eze 10:14* an *e*.
A great *e*. with great wings *Eze 17:3*
There was also another great *Eze 17:7* *e*.
He shall come as an *e*. against *Ho 8:1*
Though thou exalt thyself as the *Ob 4* *e*.
enlarge thy baldness as the *Mic 1:16* *e*.
they shall fly as the *e*. that *Hab 1:8* hasteth
the fourth beast was like a *Re 4:7* flying *e*.
were given two wings of a *Re 12:14* great *e*.

EAGLES

they were swifter than *e*. *2Sa 1:23*
the *e*. eye (B) *Job 28:7*
and the young *e*. shall eat it *Pr 30:17*
shall mount up with wings *Isa 40:31* as *e*.
his horses are swifter than *e*. *Jer 4:13*
swifter than the *e*. of the *La 4:19* heaven
is, there will the *e*. be *M't 24:28* gathered
is, thither will the *e*. be *Lu 17:37* gathered

EAGLE'S

thy youth is renewed like the *Ps 103:5* *e*.
was like a lion, and had *e*. *Da 7:4* wings

EAGLES'

and how I bare you on *e*. *Ex 19:4* wings
his hairs were grown like *e*. *Da 4:33*

EAR

for barley was in the *e*. and *Ex 9:31* flax bolled
his master shall bore his *e*. *Ex 21:6;* *De 15:17*
the king will set them to *e*. *1Sa 8:12* the ground
Lord hath told Samuel in his *1Sa 9:15* *e*.
bow down thine *e*. *2Ki 19:16;* *Ps 31:2; 86:1*
let thine *e*. be attentive, eyes *Ne 1:6;* open *1:11*
and mine *e*. received a little *Job 4:12* thereof
doth not the *e*. try words *Job 12:11;* *34:3*
mine *e*. hath heard and *Job 13:1* understood it
when the *e*. heard me, then *Job 29:11* it blessed me
to me men gave *e*. waited, *Job 29:21* and kept silence
behold, I gave *e*. to your *Job 32:11* reasons

he openeth also their *e*. to *Job 36:10* discipline
I have heard of thee by *Job 42:5* hearing of *e*.
thou wilt cause thine *e*. to *Ps 10:17* hear
bow down thine *e*. to me, *Ps 31:2* deliver me speedily
like the deaf adder that *Ps 58:4* stoppeth her *e*.
I cried unto God, and he *Ps 77:1* gave *e*. unto me
he that planted the *e*. shall he *Ps 94:9* not hear
because he hath inclined his *Ps 116:2* *e*. unto me
and bow thine *e*. to my *Pr 5:1* understanding
nor inclined my *e*. to them *Pr 5:13* that instructed
e. that heareth the reproof *Pr 15:31* of life
a liar giveth *e*. to a naughty *Pr 17:4* tongue
the *e*. of the wise seeketh *Pr 18:15* knowledge
hearing *e*. the seeing eye, Lord *Pr 20:12* made both
bow thine *e*. hear the words *Pr 22:17* of the wise
so is a wise reprover on an *Pr 25:12* obedient *e*.
he that turneth away his *e*. *Pr 28:9* from hearing
nor is the *e*. filled with hearing *Ec 1:8*
the oxen that *e*. the ground *Isa 30:24* shall eat
from that time thine *e*. was *Isa 48:8* not opened
he wakeneth my *e*. to hear as *Isa 50:4* learned
Lord hath opened mine *e*. *Isa 50:5* and I was not rebellious
nor is his *e*. heavy that it *Isa 59:1* cannot hear
men have not heard, nor *Isa 64:4* perceived by *e*.
behold their *e*. is *Jer 6:10* uncircumcised
they hearkened not, nor *Jer 7:24;* inclined their *e*. *7:26; 11:8; 17:23;* *25:4; 34:14; 44:5*
let your *e*. receive word of *Jer 9:20* Lord
but ye have not inclined *Jer 35:15* your *e*.
hide not thine *e*. at my *La 3:56* breathing
taketh from the lion a piece *Am 3:12* of an *e*.
what ye hear in the *e*. that *M't 10:27* preach
smote off his *e*. *M't 26:51; M'k 14:47*
that which ye have spoken in *Lu 12:3* *e*.
he touched his *e*. and healed *Lu 22:51* him
servant whose *e*. Peter cut *Joh 18:26* off
eye hath not seen, nor *e*. *1Co 2:9* heard
if *e*. shall say, Because I *1Co 12:16* am not the eye
he that hath an *e*. let him *Re 2:7;* hear what Spirit saith *2:11, 17, 29; 3:6,* to churches *13, 22; 13:9*

INCLINE EAR

incline thine *e*. to me, and *Ps 17:6;* hear my speech *71:2; 88:2; Isa 37:17;* *Da 9:18*
daughter, consider, and *Ps 45:10* *incline* thine *e*.
I will *incline* mine *e*. to a *Ps 49:4* parable
so that thou *incline* thine *e*. to *Pr 2:2* wisdom
my son, *incline* thine *e*. to my *Pr 4:20* sayings
incline your *e*. and come unto *Isa 55:3* me

GIVE EAR

if wilt *give e*. to his *Ex 15:26* commandments
but Lord would not hearken *De 1:45*
nor *give e*. to your voice *2Ch 24:19;* *Ne 9:30*

give e. O heavens, and I will *De 32:1* speak
hear, O ye kings, *give e*. O *J'g 5:3* princes
give e. to me, ye that have *Job 34:2* knowledge
give e. to my words, O *Ps 5:1;* Lord *54:2*
give e. unto my prayer *Ps 17:1* *55:1; 86:6*
hear my prayer, *give e*. to *Ps 39:12;* my cry *141:1*
give e. all ye inhabitants of *Ps 49:1* the world
give e. my people; *give e*. *Ps 78:1;* shepherd *80:1*
hear my prayer, *give e*. O *Ps 84:8* God
O Lord, *give e*. to my *Ps 143:1* supplication
give e., O earth, for the Lord *Isa 1:2* hath spoken
give e. to law of our God, ye *Isa 1:10* people
give e. far countries, gird *Isa 8:9* yourselves
give ye *e*. and hear my voice *Isa 28:23*
careless daughters, *give e*. to *Isa 32:9* my speech
who among you will *give e*. *Isa 42:23* to this
hearken and *give e*. to me, O *Isa 51:4* my nation
give e. be not proud, Lord *Jer 13:15* hath spoken
give e. O house of the king *Ho 5:1*
give e. all ye inhabitants of *Joe 1:2* the land

RIGHT EAR

upon the tip of the *right e*. *Ex 29:20;* *Le 8:23-24; 14:14, 17, 25, 28*
one cut off his *right e*. *Lu 22:50;* *Joh 18:10*

EARED

to a rough valley neither *e*. *De 21:4* nor sown

EARING

in which shall be neither *e*. *Ge 45:6* nor harvest
in *e*. time and harvest rest *Ex 34:21*

EARLY

ye shall rise *e*. and go on *Ge 19:2* your way
early (S) *Ge 26:31; 2Ch 26:31;* *2Ch 36:15; Job 8:5; 24:5; Pr 13:24*
whoso is fearful, let him *J'g 7:3* depart *e*.
to-morrow get you *e*. on your *J'g 19:9* way
servant of man of God was *2Ki 6:15* risen *e*.
God shall help her, and that *Ps 46:5* right *e*.
awake up, I myself will *Ps 57:8;* awake *e*. *108:2*
thou art my God, *e*. will I *Ps 63:1* seek thee
returned and enquired *e*. *Ps 78:34* after God
satisfy us *e*. with mercy that *Ps 90:14* we may
I will *e*. destroy all wicked *Ps 101:8* of land
they shall seek me *e*. but not *Pr 1:28* find me
those that seek me *e*. shall *Pr 8:17* find me
let us get up *e*. to the *Ca 7:12* vineyards
with my spirit will I seek *Isa 26:9* thee *e*.
as the *e*. fruit (S) *Isa 28:4*
in affliction they will seek me *Ho 5:15* *e*.
as the *e*. dew it goeth away *Ho 6:4;* *13:3*
women who were *e*. at *Lu 24:22* sepulchre
led Jesus to the hall, it was *Joh 18:28* *e*.
first day cometh Mary *Joh 20:1* Magdalene *e*.

an *e.* disciple (S)   Ac 21:16
till he receive *e.* and latter   Jas 5:7
rain

EARNEST

the *e.* expectation of the   Ro 8:19
creature
longs earnestly for God's sons   Ro 8:19
(A)
creature's watching with   Ro 8:19
outstretched head in expectancy (B)
created universe waits with   Ro 8:19
eager expectation for God's
sons to be revealed (N)
the whole creation is on tip   Ro 8:19
toe to see (P)
waits with eager longing for the   Ro 8:19
revealing of the sons of God (R)
the *e.* of the Spirit in our   2Co 1:22
hearts
the security deposit and   2Co 1:22
guarantee of fulfillment of
promise (P)
the Spirit's security deposit   2Co 1:22
(B)
a pledge of what is to come   2Co 1:22
(N)
living guarantee of the Spirit   2Co 1:22
(P)
Spirit in our hearts as a   2Co 1:22
guarantee (R)
given unto us the *e.* of the   2Co 5:5
Spirit
he told us your *e.* desire   2Co 7:7
your yearning affection (A)   2Co 7:7
how you are longing for us   2Co 7:7
(B)(E)(N)(R)
your eagerness to help (P)   2Co 7:7
put the same *e.* care into   2Co 8:16
the heart
same devotion for you (B)   2Co 8:16
same deep concern for you   2Co 8:16
(P)
being very *e.* (E)(R)   2Co 8:17
Which is the *e.* of our   Eph 1:14
inheritance
Spirit is guarantee of our   Eph 1:14
inheritance (A)
pledge-deposit of our legacy   Eph 1:14
for releasing of our deed of
purchase (B)
pledge we shall enter   Eph 1:14
heritage (N)
a guarantee of purchase (P)   Eph 1:14
guarantee of our inheritance   Eph 1:14
(R)
to my *e.* expectation and   Ph'p 1:20
my hope
eager desire, persistent   Ph'p 1:20
expectation, hope (A)
I eagerly desire and have   Ph'p 1:20
hope (B)
I passionately hope (N)   Ph'p 1:20
eager expectation and hope   Ph'p 1:20
(R)
we ought to give the more *e.*   Heb 2:1
heed
closer attention than ever   Heb 2:1
(A)(R)
more careful attention (B)   Heb 2:1
pay the greatest attention to   Heb 2:1
truth (P)
the *e.* prayer (A)(B)(P)   Jas 5:16

EARNESTLY

Did I not *e.* send unto thee   Nu 22:37
to call thee
say, David *e.* asked leave of   1Sa 20:6
me that
David *e.* asked leave of me   1Sa 20:28
to go to
the son of Zabbai *e.* repaired   Ne 3:20
As a servant *e.* desireth the   Job 7:2
shadow
For I *e.* protested unto your   Jer 11:7
fathers
him, I do *e.* remember him   Jer 31:20
still
may do evil with both hands   Mic 7:3
e.
besought him *e.* (S)   Lu 7:4
in an agony he prayed more   Lu 22:44
e.
and *e.* looked upon him, and   Lu 22:56
why look ye so *e.* on us   Ac 3:12
Paul, *e.* beholding the council   Ac 23:1
e. serving God day and night   Ac 26:7
(S)

longs *e.* for God's sons (A)   Ro 8:19
But covet *e.* the best gifts   1Co 12:31
e. desiring to be clothed upon   2Co 5:2
prayed *e.* that it might not   Jas 5:17
rain
love *e.* from the heart (R)   1Pe 1:22
ye should *e.* contend for the   Jude 3
faith

EARNESTNESS

through *e.* of others   2Co 8:8
(E)(R)(S)

EARNETH

he that *e.* wages, *e.* wages to   Hag 1:6
put it

EARNS

worker *e.* his pay (N)   1Ti 5:18

EARRING

golden *e.* of half a shekel   Ge 24:22
weight
ring   (B)(R)   Ge 24:22;
     24:30, 47; Job 42:11; Pr 25:12
came to pass, when saw the   Ge 24:30
e.
I put the *e.* upon her face   Ge 24:47
and every one an *e.* of gold   Job 42:11
an *e.* of gold, and an   Pr 25:12
ornament of
nose ring of gold (A)   Pr 25:12
earring (E)   Pr 25:12

EARRINGS

their *e.* which were in their   Ge 35:4
ears
Break off the golden *e.* which   Ex 32:2
people brake off the golden *e.*   Ex 32:3
e. and rings, and tablets, all   Ex 35:22
jewels
chains, and bracelets, rings,   Nu 31:50
e.
me every man the *e.* of his   J'g 8:24
prey
For they had golden *e.*   J'g 8:24
because they
every man the *e.* of his prey   J'g 8:25
And the weight of the golden   J'g 8:26
e.
and the tablets, and the *e.*   Isa 3:20
e. in thine ears, and a   Eze 16:12
beautiful
herself with her *e.* and her   Ho 2:13
jewels

EARS

behold, seven *e.* of corn   Ge 41:5;
came up   41:22
let me speak a word in my   Ge 44:18
lord's *e.*
speak, I pray in the *e.* of   Ge 50:4
Pharaoh
thou mayest tell it in the *e.*   Ex 10:2
and rehearse it in the *e.* of   Ex 17:14
Joshua
offer for a meat offering   Le 2:14
green *e.*
not eat green *e.* till bring an   Le 23:14
offering
for you have wept in *e.* of   Nu 11:18
the Lord
mayest pluck *e.* with thine   De 23:25
hand
spake in *e.* of congregation   De 31:30
declare his cause in *e.* of   Jos 20:4
elders
in the *e.* of the men of   J'g 9:2;
Shechem   9:3
e. of every one that heareth   1Sa 3:11;
shall tingle   2Ki 21:12; Jer 19:3
he rehearseth them in the *e.*   1Sa 8:21
of Lord
according to all that we   2Sa 7:22;
have heard with our *e.*   1Ch 17:20
and my cry did enter into   2Sa 22:7
his *e.*
let me go and glean *e.* of corn   Ru 2:2
after him
brought the man of God full   2Ki 4:42
e. of corn
dreadful sound is in his *e.*   Job 15:21
in prosperity

wicked cut off as tops of *e.*   Job 24:24
of corn
we have heard fame thereof   Job 28:22
with our *e.*
then he openeth *e.* of men,   Job 33:16
and sealeth
and my cry came even into   Ps 18:6
his *e.*
and his *e.* are opened to   Ps 34:15
their cry
we have heard with our *e.* O   Ps 44:1
God
they have *e.* but hear not   Ps 115:6;
     135:17
whoso stoppeth his *e.* at cry   Pr 21:13
of the poor
speak not in *e.* of a fool, he   Pr 23:9
will despise
like one that taketh a dog by   Pr 26:17
the *e.*
nor reprove after the hearing   Isa 11:3
of his *e.*
glory of Jacob, as when one   Isa 17:5
reapeth *e.*
the *e.* of them that hear shall   Isa 32:3
hearken
stoppeth his *e.* from hearing   Isa 33:15
of blood
the *e.* of the deaf shall be   Isa 35:5
unstopped
opening the *e.* but he   Isa 42:20
heareth not
bring forth blind and deaf   Isa 43:8
that have *e.*
go, and cry in the *e.* of   Jer 2:2
Jerusalem
O people, which have *e.* and   Jer 5:21
hear not
Zephaniah read in the *e.* of   Jer 29:29
Jeremiah
sit down now, and read it   Jer 36:15
in our *e.*
Jehudi read it in *e.* of king   Jer 36:21
and princes
hungered, and began to   M't 12:1;
pluck the *e.* of corn   M'k 2:23; Lu 6:1
if this come to the   M't 28:14
governor's *e.*
he put his fingers into his *e.*   M'k 7:33
and spit
and straightway his *e.* were   M'k 7:35
opened
having *e.* hear ye not? do ye   M'k 8:18
not
in the *e.* of the people (E)   Lu 7:1
ye uncircumcised in heart and   Ac 7:51
e. resist
tidings came to the *e.* of the   Ac 11:22
church
thou bringest strange things   Ac 17:20
to our *e.*
hath given *e.* that they should   Ro 11:8
not hear
they heap teachers, having   2Ti 4:3
itching *e.*
are entered into *e.* of Lord of   Jas 5:4
sabaoth
his *e.* are open to their   1Pe 3:12
prayers

EARS *OF THE PEOPLE*

speak now in the *e. of the*   Ex 11:2
people
Moses spake in the *e. of the*   De 32:44
people
go to, proclaim in the *e. of*   J'g 7:3
the people
told the tidings in the *e. of*   1Sa 11:4
the people
talk not in the *e. of people*   2Ki 18:26;
     Isa 36:11
e. of the people were attentive   Ne 8:3
to the law

EARS *TO HEAR*

the Lord hath not given you   De 29:4
e. to hear
they have *e. to hear*, and hear   Eze 12:2
not
he that hath *e. to hear*, let   M't 11:15;
him hear   13:9, 43; M'k 4:9, 23; 7:16;
     Lu 8:8; 14:35

MINE EARS

as ye have spoken in *mine*   Nu 14:28
e. I will do

the silver thou spakest of in *J'g 17:2*
mine *e.*
this bleating of sheep in *1Sa 15:14*
mine *e.*
tumult come into *mine e.* *2Ki 19:28;*
Isa 37:29
and *mine e.* attent to the *2Ch 7:15*
prayer
mine e. hast thou opened, *Ps 40:6*
burnt offering
mine e. shall hear my desire *Ps 92:11*
of the wicked
in *mine e.* said the Lord of *Isa 5:9*
hosts
it was revealed in *mine e.* *Isa 22:14*
by the Lord
tho' they cry in *mine e.* with *Eze 8:18*
loud voice
he cried also in *mine e.* with *Eze 9:1*
a loud voice
thy salutation sounded in *Lu 1:44*
mine *e.*

THEIR EARS

Abimelech told these things *Ge 20:8*
in *their e.*
gave Jacob earrings which *Ge 35:4*
were in *their e.*
people brake off the earrings *Ex 32:3*
in *their e.*
I may speak these words in *De 31:28*
their e.
read in *their e.* *2Ki 23:2;*
2Ch 34:30; Jer 36:15
he openeth *their e.* in *Job 36:15*
oppression
make heart fat, *their e.* *Isa 6:10;*
heavy, lest they hear with *M't 13:15;*
their e. *Ac 28:27*
the nations shall see, *their e.* *Mic 7:16*
shall be deaf
but they stopped *their e.* *Zec 7:11;*
Ac 7:57
they shall turn away *their e.* *2Ti 4:4*
from truth

THINE EARS

let *thine e.* be attent to the *2Ch 6:40*
prayer
thou wilt cause *thine e.* to *Ps 10:17*
hear
let *thine e.* be attentive to *Ps 130:2*
the voice
apply *thine e.* to words of *Pr 23:12*
knowledge
thine e. shall hear a word *Isa 30:21*
behind thee
children shall say again in *Isa 49:20*
thine e.
hear this word that I speak *Jer 28:7*
in *thine e.*
and hear with *thine e.* *Eze 3:10;*
40:4; 44:5
I put earrings in *thine e.* *Eze 16:12*
and a crown
they shall take away thy *Eze 23:25*
nose and *thine e.*
to cause thee to hear with *Eze 24:26*
thine e.

YOUR EARS

hear statutes which I speak in *De 5:1*
your e.
hear my declaration with *Job 13:17*
your e.
incline *your e.* to words of *Ps 78:1*
my mouth
as ye have heard with *your* *Jer 26:11*
e.
Lord sent me to speak these *Jer 26:15*
words in *your e.*
but blessed are *your e.* for *M't 13:16*
they hear
this scripture is fulfilled in *Lu 4:21*
your e.
let these sayings sink down in *Lu 9:44*
your e.

EARTH

the *e.* was without form and *Ge 1:2*
void
and God called the dry land *e.* *Ge 1:10*
and God said, Let the *e.* *Ge 1:11;*
bring forth grass *1:24*
and the *e.* brought forth grass *Ge 1:12*
and herb

be fruitful, replenish the *e.* *Ge 1:28;*
and subdue it *9:1*
the *e.* also was corrupt before *Ge 6:11*
God
and the ark was lifted up *Ge 7:17*
above the *e.*
in the second month was the *Ge 8:14*
e. dried
while *e.* remaineth, seedtime *Ge 8:22*
not cease
for a token of covenant *Ge 9:13*
between me and *e.*
in his days was *e.* divided *Ge 10:25;*
1Ch 1:19
all nations of *e.* shall be *Ge 18:18;*
blessed in him *22:18; 26:4; 28:14*
God give thee of the fatness *Ge 27:28*
of the *e.*
in plenteous years *e.* brought *Ge 41:47*
forth
all the *e.* (R) *Ge 41:57*
I am the Lord in midst of *e.* *Ex 8:22*
thou mayest know that *e.* is *Ex 9:29;*
Lord's *De 10:14; Ps 24:1; 1Co 10:26*
that one cannot be able to *Ex 10:5*
see the *e.*
stretchest thy hand, *e.* *Ex 15:12*
swallowed them
an altar of *e.* make unto me *Ex 20:24*
if *e.* open her mouth and *Nu 16:30*
swallow
and the *e.* opened her *Nu 16:32;*
mouth and swallowed them up *26:10;*
Ps 106:17
they said, Lest the *e.* swallow *Nu 16:34*
us up also
Lord set thee above all *De 28:1*
nations of *e.*
e. that is under thee shall be *De 28:23*
iron
hear, O *e.* the words of my *De 32:1*
mouth
he made him ride on high *De 32:13*
places of *e.*
fire shall consume *e.* with *De 32:22*
her increase
for pillars of the *e.* are the *1Sa 2:8*
Lord's
Israel shouted, so that the *e.* *1Sa 4:5*
rang again
they trembled, and the *e.* *1Sa 14:15*
quaked
man came with *e.* on his head *2Sa 1:2;*
15:32
then *e.* shook and trembled *2Sa 22:8;*
Ps 18:7
so that *e.* rent with the *1Ki 1:40*
sound
to servant two mules' burden *2Ki 5:17*
of *e.*
let the *e.* rejoice *1Ch 16:31; Ps 96:11*
because God cometh to *1Ch 16:33;*
judge *e.* *Ps 96:13; 98:9*
servants of God of heaven *Ezr 5:11*
and *e.*
thou hast made the *e.* *Ne 9:6;*
Isa 45:12
offspring as the grass of the *Job 5:25*
e.
which shaketh the *e.* out of *Job 9:6*
her place
e. is given into the hand of *Job 9:24*
wicked
measure thereof is longer *Job 11:9*
than *e.*
sendeth waters and they *Job 12:15*
overturn the *e.*
to whom alone the *e.* was *Job 15:19*
given
e. cover not my blood, let *Job 16:18*
my cry
shall the *e.* be forsaken for *Job 18:4*
thee
the *e.* shall rise up against *Job 20:27*
him
but as for the mighty man, *Job 22:8*
he had the *e.*
the poor of the *e.* hide *Job 24:4*
themselves
he hangeth the *e.* upon *Job 26:7*
nothing
to dwell in caves of *e.* and *Job 30:6*
in rocks
children of base men were *Job 30:8*
viler than *e.*
who hath given him charge *Job 34:13*
over *e.*
when he quieteth *e.* by *Job 37:17*
south wind

when I laid the foundations *Job 38:4*
of the *e.*
hast thou perceived breadth *Job 38:18*
of *e.*
give thee uttermost parts of *e.* *Ps 2:8*
be instructed, ye judges of *Ps 2:10*
the *e.*
that man of *e.* may no *Ps 10:18*
more oppress
pure words, as silver tried in *Ps 12:6*
furnace of *e.*
his seed shall inherit the *e.* *Ps 25:13*
e. is full of goodness of the *Ps 33:5*
Lord
he looketh on all inhabitants *Ps 33:14*
of *e.*
that wait on Lord shall *Ps 37:9;*
inherit *e.* *37:11, 22*
we will not fear though *e.* be *Ps 46:2*
removed
he uttered his voice, the *e.* *Ps 46:6*
melted
for the shields of the *e.* *Ps 47:9*
belong unto God
the joy of the whole *e.* is *Ps 48:2*
mount Zion
thou hast made the *e.* to *Ps 60:2*
tremble
shall go into the lower parts *Ps 63:9*
of the *e.*
that dwell in the uttermost *Ps 65:8*
parts of *e.*
thou visitest the *e.* and *Ps 65:9*
waterest it
then shall *e.* yield increase *Ps 67:6;*
Eze 34:27
the *e.* shook, the heavens also *Ps 68:8*
dropped
sing unto God, ye kingdoms *Ps 68:32*
of the *e.*
shalt bring me up from *Ps 71:20*
depths of *e.*
come down as showers that *Ps 72:6*
water *e.*
their tongue walketh through *Ps 73:9*
the *e.*
the *e.* and all the inhabitants *Ps 75:3;*
thereof are dissolved *Isa 24:19*
wicked of the *e.* shall wring *Ps 75:8*
them out
the *e.* feared, the *e.* trembled *Ps 76:8;*
77:18; 97:4
when God arose to save meek *Ps 76:9*
of the *e.*
like *e.* which he hath *Ps 78:69*
established for ever
arise, judge the *e.* thou shalt *Ps 82:8*
inherit
ever thou hadst formed the *e.* *Ps 90:2*
the Lord reigneth, let the *e.* *Ps 97:1*
rejoice
the Lord reigneth, let the *e.* be *Ps 99:1*
moved
of old hast thou laid *Ps 102:25;*
foundation of *e.* *104:5; Pr 8:29;*
Isa 48:13
e. is satisfied with fruit of *Ps 104:13*
thy works
O Lord, the *e.* is full of thy *Ps 104:24*
riches
tremble, O *e.* at the presence *Ps 114:7*
of Lord
e. hath he given to children *Ps 115:16*
of men
the *e.* O Lord, is full of thy *Ps 119:64*
mercy
thou hast established *e.* and *Ps 119:90*
it abideth
who prepareth rain for the *e.* *Ps 147:8*
his glory is above *e.* and *Ps 148:13*
heaven
Lord hath founded *e.* *Pr 3:19; Isa 24:1*
I was set up from everlasting, *Pr 8:23*
or ever *e.* was
as yet he had not made the *e.* *Pr 8:26*
nor fields
e. for depth, heart of kings *Pr 25:3*
unsearchable
the *e.* that is not filled with *Pr 30:16*
water
for three things *e.* is *Pr 30:21*
disquieted, for four
but the *e.* abideth for ever *Ec 1:4*
moreover, the profit of the *e.* *Ec 5:9*
is for all
the fruit of *e.* shall be excellent *Isa 4:2*
that smiteth *e.* with rod of *Isa 11:4*
his mouth
e. be full of knowledge of *Isa 11:9*
Lord

the *e.* shall remove out of | Isa 13:13
her place
is this the man that made *e.* | Isa 14:16
to tremble
the *e.* mourneth and fadeth | Isa 24:4;
away | 33:9
e. is defiled under inhabitants | Isa 24:5
thereof
e. is utterly broken down, *e.* | Isa 24:19
is dissolved
e. shall reel; *e.* shall cast out | Isa 24:20;
dead | 26:19
the *e.* also shall disclose her | Isa 26:21
blood
let the *e.* hear, and all that is | Isa 34:1
therein
it is he that sitteth on the | Isa 40:22
circle of *e.*
Creator of ends of *e.* | Isa 40:28
fainteth not
that spread abroad the *e.* by | Isa 44:24
myself
let *e.* open; I have made *e.* | Isa 45:8;
| 45:12
look to me and be saved, | Isa 45:22
all ends of *e.*
sing, O heavens, and be | Isa 49:13
joyful, O *e.*
look on the *e.* the *e.* shall | Isa 51:6
wax old
unto the end of the *e.* (S) | Isa 62:11
thus saith Lord, *e.* is my | Isa 66:1
footstool
shall *e.* be made to bring | Isa 66:8
forth in one day
I behold the *e.* it was | Jer 4:23
without form
for this shall the *e.* mourn, | Jer 4:28
heavens be black
hear, O *e.* I will bring evil | Jer 6:19
on people
at his wrath the *e.* shall | Jer 10:10
tremble
e. e. e. hear word of Lord | Jer 22:29;
| Mic 1:2
Egypt saith, I will go up and | Jer 46:8
cover *e.*
the *e.* is moved at the noise | Jer 49:21;
| 50:46
he hath made the *e.* by his | Jer 51:15
power
I will give it to wicked of *e.* | Eze 7:21
they say, The Lord hath | Eze 9:9
forsaken *e.*
and the *e.* shined with his | Eze 43:2
glory
the *e.* shall hear corn and | Ho 2:22
wine
the *e.* shall quake before them | Joe 2:10
I will darken *e.* in clear day | Am 8:9
e. with her bars was about | Jon 2:6
me
hear, ye strong foundations | Mic 6:2
of *e.*
they shall move out like | Mic 7:17
worms of *e.*
e. is burnt up at his presence | Na 1:5
e. filled with knowledge of | Hab 2:14
Lord
and the *e.* was full of his | Hab 3:3
praise
thou didst cleave the *e.* with | Hab 3:9
rivers
the *e.* is stayed from her | Hag 1:10
fruit
sent to walk to and fro thro' | Zec 1:10;
e. | 6:7
eyes of Lord which run | Zec 4:10
thro' *e.*
lest I smite the *e.* with a | Mal 4:6
curse
blessed are meek, they shall | M't 5:5
inherit *e.*
swear not by *e.* it is God's | M't 5:35
footstool
where they had not much *e.* | M't 13:5;
| M'k 4:5
e. bringeth forth fruit of | M'k 4:28
herself
founding of the *e.* (B) | Lu 11:50
he that is of *e.* is earthly, | Joh 3:31
and speaketh of *e.*
the first man is of *e.* earthy | 1Co 15:47
but also vessels of wood and | 2Ti 2:20
of *e.*
the *e.* which drinketh in the | Heb 6:7
rain
whose voice then shook *e.* | Heb 12:26
waiteth for precious fruit of *e.* | Jas 5:7

the *e.* brought forth her fruit | Jas 5:18
e. and works shall be burnt | 2Pe 3:10
up
hurt not *e.* nor sea, nor trees | Re 7:3
olive trees standing before | Re 11:4
God of *e.*
have power to smite *e.* with | Re 11:6
all plagues
e. opened and swallowed up | Re 12:16
flood
causeth *e.* to worship first | Re 13:12
beast
e. was lightened with his | Re 18:1
glory
great whore, which did | Re 19:2
corrupt *e.*
from whose face the *e.* fled | Re 20:11
away

ALL THE EARTH

have dominion over *all the e.* | Ge 1:26
to keep seed alive on *all the e.* | Ge 7:3
there confound language of | Ge 11:9
all the e.
shall not Judge of *all the e.* | Ge 18:25
do right
come in to us after manner | Ge 19:31
of *all the e.*
there is none like me in *all* | Ex 9:14
the e.
my name declared thro' *all* | Ex 9:16;
the e. | Ro 9:17
peculiar treasure; for *all the* | Ex 19:5
e.
as have not been done in | Ex 34:10
all the e.
all the e. shall be filled | Nu 14:21
with glory
Lord of *all the e.* | Jos 3:11;
| 3:13; Zec 6:5
going way of *all the e.* | Jos 23:14;
| 1Ki 2:2
if it be dry on *all the e.* | J'g 6:37
beside
all the e. may know there is | 1Sa 17:46
a God
all the e. sought Solomon | 1Ki 10:24
to hear
no God in *all the e.* but in | 2Ki 5:15
Israel
judgments are in *all the e.* | 1Ch 16:14;
| Ps 105:7
sing to the Lord, *all the e.* | 1Ch 16:23;
| Ps 96:1
fear before him, *all the e.* | 1Ch 16:30;
| Ps 33:8; 96:9
excellent is thy name in *all the* | Ps 8:1;
e. | 8:9
whom make princes in *all* | Ps 45:16
e.
Lord is great king over *all the* | Ps 47:2;
e. | 47:7; Zec 14:9
let thy glory be above *all the* | Ps 57:5;
e. | 57:11; 108:5
all the e. shall worship thee, | Ps 66:4
and sing
thou art most high over *all* | Ps 83:18;
the e. | 97:9
so have I gathered *all the e.* | Isa 10:14
done excellent things, known | Isa 12:5
in *all e.*
take rebuke of people, from | Isa 25:8
all the e.
make this city a curse to *all* | Jer 26:6
the e.
it shall be an honour before | Jer 33:9
all the e.
golden cup that made *all the* | Jer 51:7
e. drunken
O mountain, which | Jer 51:25
destrovest *all the e.*
at Babylon shall fall slain of | Jer 51:49
all the e.
a kingdom shall bear rule | Da 2:39
over *all the e.*
let *all the e.* keep silence | Hab 2:20
before him
all the e. shall be devoured | Zep 3:8
with fire
all the e. sitteth still and is | Zec 1:11
at rest
was a darkness over *all the e.* | Lu 23:44
their sound went into *all the* | Ro 10:18
e.
Spirits of God sent forth into | Re 5:6
all e.

FROM THE EARTH

but there went up a mist *from* | Ge 2:6
the e.
and now art thou cursed | Ge 4:11
from the e.
they were destroyed *from the* | Ge 7:23
e.
Noah knew waters were | Ge 8:11
abated *from the e.*
thou shalt be cut off *from* | Ex 9:15;
the *e.* | Jos 7:9; Ps 109:15; Pr 2:22;
| Na 2:13
Saul arose *from the e.* and | 1Sa 28:23
sat on bed
shall I not take you away | 2Sa 4:11
from the e.
elders went to raise him | 2Sa 12:17
from the e.
David arose *from the e.* | 2Sa 12:20
and washed himself
his remembrance shall | Job 18:17
perish *from the e.*
shalt destroy their fruit *from* | Ps 21:10
the *e.*
cut off remembrance of them | Ps 34:16
from the e.
praise Lord *from the e.* ye | Ps 148:7
dragons and deeps
as knives to devour poor | Pr 30:14
from the e.
even they shall perish *from* | Jer 10:11
the *e.*
living creatures were lift up | Eze 1:19;
from e. | 1:21
and it was lifted up *from the* | Da 7:4
e.
shall one take up a snare | Am 3:5
from the e.
and I, if I be lifted up | Joh 12:32
from the e.
for his life is taken *from the* | Ac 8:33
e.
Saul arose *from the e.* and he | Ac 9:8
saw no man
said, Away with such a | Ac 22:22
fellow *from the e.*
power given him to take peace | Re 6:4
from the e.
but 144,000 which were | Re 14:3
redeemed *from the e.*

IN THE EARTH

and let fowl multiply *in the e.* | Ge 1:22
a vagabond shalt thou be *in* | Ge 4:12;
the *e.* | 4:14
the wickedness of man was | Ge 6:5
great *in the e.*
Nimrod began to be a mighty | Ge 10:8
one *in the e.*
not a man *in the e.* to come | Ge 19:31
in unto us
sent me, to preserve a | Ge 45:7
posterity *in the e.*
or that is *in the e.* beneath | Ex 20:4
and behold they are hid *in* | Jos 7:21
the e.
no want of any thing that is | J'g 18:10
in the e.
great name, like the name | 2Sa 7:9;
of great men that are *in the e.* | 1Ch 17:8
what nation *in e.* like Israel | 2Sa 7:23;
| 1Ch 17:21
to know all things that are | 2Sa 14:20
in the e.
for all that is *in the e.* is | 1Ch 29:11
thine
there is no God like thee *in* | 2Ch 6:14
the e.
from going to and fro *in the* | Job 1:7;
e. | 2:2
that there is none like him *in* | Job 1:8;
the e. | 2:3
though root thereof wax old | Job 14:8
in the e.
their portion is cursed *in* | Job 24:18
the e.
ostrich, which leaveth her | Job 39:14
eggs *in the e.*
but to the saints that are *in* | Ps 16:3
the e.
what desolations he hath | Ps 46:8
made *in the e.*
be still, I will be exalted *in* | Ps 46:10
the e.
verily he is a God that | Ps 58:11
judgeth *in the e.*
there shall be a handful of | Ps 72:16
corn *in the e.*

I am a stranger *in the e.*   *Ps 119:19*
hide not thy
let not an evil speaker be   *Ps 140:11*
established *in e.*
righteous be recompensed *in*   *Pr 11:31*
the e.
for when thy judgments are   *Isa 26:9*
in the e.
we have not wrought   *Isa 26:18*
deliverance *in the e.*
their stock shall not take   *Isa 40:24*
root *in the e.*
till he have set judgment *in*   *Isa 42:4*
the e.
till he make Jerusalem a   *Isa 62:7*
praise *in the e.*
blesseth himself *in the e.* and   *Isa 65:16*
sweareth *in the e.*
that forsake thee, be written   *Jer 17:13*
in the e.
Lord hath created a new   *Jer 31:22*
thing *in the e.*
I will sow her unto me *in*   *Ho 2:23*
the e.
and I will shew wonders *in*   *Joe 2:30*
the e.
who leave off righteousness *in*   *Am 5:7*
the e.
he went and digged *in the*   *M't 25:18*
e. and hid
I was afraid, and hid thy   *M't 25:25*
talent *in the e.*
when sown *in the e.* is less   *M'k 4:31*
than all seeds that be
there are three that bear   *1Jo 5:8*
witness *in the e.*

ON, UPON THE EARTH

repented he had made man *on*   *Ge 6:6*
the e.
looked *upon the e.* behold it   *Ge 6:12*
was corrupt
cause it to rain *upon the e.*   *Ge 7:4*
forty days
the rain was *upon the e.*   *Ge 7:12;*
forty days   *7:17*
be fruitful and multiply *upon*   *Ge 8:17*
the e.
sun was risen *upon the e.*   *Ge 19:23*
when Lot
behold a ladder set *upon the*   *Ge 28:12*
e.
since the day they were *upon*   *Ex 10:6*
the e.
things that creep *upon the*   *Le 11:29;*
e.   *11:42, 44*
all days they live *upon the*   *De 4:10;*
e.   *12:1, 19*
upon the e. he shewed thee   *De 4:36*
his great fire
ye shall pour it *upon the e.*   *De 12:16;*
as water   *12:24*
David lay all night *upon*   *2Sa 12:16*
the e.
not leave name nor   *2Sa 14:7*
remainder *upon the e.*
will God indeed dwell *on*   *1Ki 8:27;*
the e. heaven cannot   *2Ch 6:18*
till the day the Lord sends   *1Ki 17:14*
rain *upon the e.*
our days *on e.* as a   *1Ch 29:15;*
shadow   *Job 8:9*
is there not an appointed time   *Job 7:1*
to man *on e.*
he shall stand at the latter   *Job 19:25*
day *upon the e.*
knowest not since man was   *Job 20:4*
placed *on the e.*
for he saith to the snow, Be   *Job 37:6*
thou *on the e.*
on e. there is not his like,   *Job 41:33*
leviathan made
let enemy tread down life *on*   *Ps 7:5*
the e.
he shall be blessed *upon the*   *Ps 41:2*
e.
that thy way may be known   *Ps 67:2*
upon the e.
none *upon e.* I desire besides   *Ps 73:25*
thee
his seed shall be mighty   *Ps 112:2*
upon the e.
four things that are little   *Pr 30:24*
upon the e.
there is not a just man *upon*   *Ec 7:20*
the e.
princes walking as servants   *Ec 10:7*
upon the e.

knowest not what evil shall   *Ec 11:2*
be done *upon e.*
clouds empty themselves *upon*   *Ec 11:3*
the e.
flowers appear *on the e.* time   *Ca 2:12*
of singing
consumption determined   *Isa 28:22*
upon the e.
lift up your eyes, and look   *Isa 51:6*
upon the e.
are not valiant for the truth   *Jer 9:3*
upon the e.
eyes fail, my liver is poured   *La 2:11*
upon the e.
not man *on the e.* can shew   *Da 2:10*
the matter
can a bird fall in a snare   *Am 3:5*
upon the e.
shall not the least grain fall   *Am 9:9*
upon the e.
lay not up for yourselves   *M't 6:19*
treasures *upon e.*
may know that Son of man   *M't 9:6;*
e. hath power *on e.* to *M'k 2:10; Lu 5:24*
think not I am come to send   *M't 10:34*
peace *on e.*
whatsoever thou shalt bind   *M't 16:19;*
on e.   *18:18*
if two of you shall agree *on e.*   *M't 18:19*
call no man your father   *M't 23:9*
upon the e.
all the righteous blood shed   *M't 23:35*
upon the e.
so as no fuller *on e.* can   *M'k 9:3*
white them
glory to God in the highest,   *Lu 2:14*
on e. peace
like a man that built an   *Lu 6:49*
house *upon the e.*
I am come to send fire *on*   *Lu 12:49*
the e.
suppose that I am come to   *Lu 12:51*
give peace *on e.*
Son cometh, shall he find   *Lu 18:8*
faith *on e.*
for the things which are   *Lu 21:26*
coming *on the e.*
I have glorified thee *on the*   *Joh 17:4*
e.
short work will Lord make   *Ro 9:28*
on the e.
set affection not on things *on*   *Col 3:2*
the e.
mortify members which are   *Col 3:5*
upon the e.
if he were *on e.* he should   *Heb 8:4*
not be a priest
confessed they were   *Heb 11:13*
strangers *on the e.*
who refused him that   *Heb 12:25*
spake *on e.*
ve have lived in pleasure *on*   *Jas 5:5*
the e.
it rained not *on the e.* for   *Jas 5:17*
three years
to try them that dwell *upon*   *Re 3:10*
the e.
made us kings and priests, we   *Re 5:10*
shall reign *on e.*
avenge blood on them that   *Re 6:10*
dwell *on the e.*
that the wind should not blow   *Re 7:1*
on the e.
hail, and fire, and they were   *Re 8:7*
cast *upon the e.*
in hand of angel which   *Re 10:8*
standeth *upon the e.*
dwell *on the e.*   *Re 11:10;*
          13:8, 14; 14:6; 17:8
he thrust in his sickle *on the*   *Re 14:16*
e.
first poured out his vial *upon*   *Re 16:2*
the e.
blood of all that were slain   *Re 18:24*
upon the e.

OUT OF THE EARTH

I saw gods ascending *out of*   *1Sa 28:13*
the e.
as tender grass springing *out*   *2Sa 23:4*
of the e.
and *out of the e.* shall others   *Job 8:19*
grow
iron is taken *out of the e.*   *Job 28:2*
and brass molten
as for the *e. out of it*   *Job 28:5*
cometh bread

truth shall spring *out of the*   *Ps 85:11*
e.
that he may bring food   *Ps 104:14*
out of the e.
let the sinners be consumed   *Ps 104:35*
out of the e.
four kings shall arise *out of*   *Da 7:17*
e.
I will break the battle *out of*   *Ho 2:18*
the e.
the good man is perished *out*   *Mic 7:2*
of the e.
another beast coming up *out*   *Re 13:11*
of the e.

TO, UNTO THE EARTH

worshipped, bowing himself   *Ge 24:52*
to the e.
to bow down ourselves to   *Ge 37:10*
thee, *to the e.*
they bowed themselves *to the*   *Ge 42:6;*
e.   *43:26*
he bowed himself with his   *Ge 48:12*
face *to the e.*
Joshua fell on his face *to*   *Jos 5:14;*
the e.   *7:6*
Dagon was fallen on his face   *1Sa 5:3*
to the e.
Goliath fell on his face *to*   *1Sa 17:49*
the e.
David stooped with his face   *1Sa 24:8*
to the e.
she bowed herself *to the e.*   *1Sa 25:41;*
          1Ki 1:31
let me smite him, I pray   *1Sa 26:8*
thee, *to the e.*
therefore let not my blood   *1Sa 26:20*
fall *to the e.*
he came to David he fell *to*   *2Sa 1:2*
the e.
not one hair shall fall *to*   *2Sa 14:11;*
the e.   *1Ki 1:52*
fall *to the e.* nothing of the   *2Ki 10:10*
word of Lord
were dead bodies fallen *to*   *2Ch 20:24*
the e.
or speak *to the e.* it shall   *Job 12:8*
teach thee
set eyes, bowing down *to the*   *Ps 17:11*
e.
for our belly cleaveth *unto*   *Ps 44:25*
the e.
he shall call *to the e.* that he   *Ps 50:4*
may judge
breath goeth forth, he   *Ps 146:4*
returneth *to the e.*
spirit of beast that goeth *to*   *Ec 3:21*
the e.
then shall the dust return *to*   *Ec 12:7*
the e.
and they shall look *unto the*   *Isa 8:22*
e.
I will bring down their   *Isa 63:6*
strength *to the e.*
man of contention *to the*   *Jer 15:10*
whole *e.*
as latter and former rain *to*   *Ho 6:3*
the e.
bowed down their faces *to*   *Lu 24:5*
the e.
Saul fell *to the e.* and heard a   *Ac 9:4*
voice
a great sheet, and let down   *Ac 10:11*
to the e.
and when we were all fallen   *Ac 26:14*
to the e.
and the stars of heaven fell   *Re 6:13*
to the e.
drew stars, did not cast them   *Re 12:4*
to the e.
when the dragon saw he was   *Re 12:13*
cast *unto the e.*

EARTH'S

e. filthiness (P)   *Re 17:4*

EARTHEN

the *e.* vessel wherein it was   *Le 6:28*
sodden
e. vessel whereinto any of   *Le 11:33*
them falleth
one of the birds killed in an   *Le 14:5;*
e. vessel   *14:50*
priest shall take holy water   *Nu 5:17*
in *e.* vessel
brought beds, basins, and *e.*   *2Sa 17:28*
vessels

like an *e.* vessel with scum   *Pr 26:26*
(A)(R)
go and get a potter's *e.* bottle   *Jer 19:1*
put these evidences in an *e.*   *Jer 32:14*
vessel
how are they esteemed as *e.*   *La 4:2*
pitchers
we have this treasure in *e.*   *2Co 4:7*
vessels
as *e.* pots are broken (A)(R)   *Re 2:27*

EARTHENWARE

pots of *e.* (N)(P)   *2Co 4:7; Re 2:7*

EARTHLY

an *e.* sanctuary (S)   *Hab 9:1*
if I have told you *e.* things   *Joh 3:12*
he that is of earth is *e.*   *Joh 3:31*
speaks of earth
not to our *e.* nature (B)   *Ro 8:12*
e. bodies (A)(B)(E)(P)   *1Co 15:40*
not with *e.* wisdom (R)   *2Co 1:12*
if our *e.* house of tabernacle   *2Co 5:1*
were dissolved
brag of *e.* distinctions (N)   *2Co 11:18*
many walk, who mind *e.*   *Ph'p 3:19*
things
this wisdom is *e.* sensual,   *Jas 3:15*
devilish

EARTHQUAKE

and after the wind an *e.*   *1Ki 19:11*
but the Lord was not in the   *1Ki 19:11*
e.
after the fire; but   *1Ki 19:12*
and with *e.* and great noise   *Isa 29:6*
two years before the *e.*   *Am 1:1*
the *e.* in the days of Uzziah   *Zec 14:5*
saw the *e.* and those things   *M't 27:54*
behold, there was a great *e.*   *M't 28:2*
And suddenly there was a   *Ac 16:26*
great *e.*
lo, there was a great *e.*   *Re 6:12*
and lightnings, and an *e.*   *Re 8:5*
same hour was there a great   *Re 11:13*
e.
and in the *e.* were slain of   *Re 11:13*
men
and an *e.* and great hail   *Re 11:19*
and there was a great *e.*   *Re 16:18*
so mighty an *e.* and so great   *Re 16:18*

EARTHQUAKES

and *e.* in divers places   *M't 24:7*
there shall be *e.* in divers   *M'k 13:8*
places
great *e.* shall be in divers   *Lu 21:11*
places

EARTHY

The first man is of the   *1Co 15:47*
earth, *e.*
As is the *e.* such are they   *1Co 15:48*
also
such are they also that are   *1Co 15:48*
e.
we have born the image of   *1Co 15:49*
the *e.*

EASE

when thou wilt *e.* thyself   *De 23:13*
abroad
these nations shalt thou find   *De 28:65*
no *e.*
and trode them down with   *J'g 20:43*
e.
e. thou somewhat the   *2Ch 10:4*
grievous
E. somewhat the yoke that   *2Ch 10:9*
my couch shall *e.* my   *Job 7:13*
complaint
help bear my grievance (B)   *Job 7:13*
the thought of him that is at   *Job 12:5*
e.
I was at *e.* but he hath   *Job 16:12*
broken
being wholly at *e.* and quiet   *Job 21:23*
His soul shall dwell at *e.*   *Ps 25:13*
scorning of those that are at   *Ps 123:4*
e.
will *e.* me of mine   *Isa 1:24*
adversaries
I will appease myself of my   *Isa 1:24*
adversaries (A)

I will vent my wrath on my   *Isa 1:24*
foes (B)
I will vent my wrath on my   *Isa 1:24*
enemies (R)
Rise up, ye women that are   *Isa 32:9*
at *e.*
you confident and careless   *Isa 32:9*
daughters (A)(E)
you irresponsible daughters   *Isa 32:9;*
(B)   *32:11*
you complacent daughters   *Isa 32:9;*
(R)   *32:11*
Tremble, ye women that are   *Isa 32:11*
at *e.*
and be in rest and at *e.*   *Jer 46:27*
Moab hath been at *e.* from   *Jer 48:11*
a voice of a multitude   *Eze 23:42*
being at *e.*
Woe to them that are at *e.* in   *Am 6:1*
Zion
with the heathen that are at   *Zec 1:15*
e.
take thine *e.* eat, drink, and   *Lu 12:19*

EASED

though I forbear, what am I   *Job 16:6*
e.
I mean not that other men   *2Co 8:13*
be *e.*

EASIER

so shall it be *e.* for thyself   *Ex 18:22*
whether is *e.* to say, Thy sins   *M't 9:5*
be
It is *e.* for a camel to go   *M't 19:24;*
through   *M'k 10:25; Lu 18:25*
Whether it is *e.* to say to the   *M'k 2:9*
sick
Whether is *e.* to say, Thy sins   *Lu 5:23*
be
it is *e.* for heaven and earth   *Lu 16:17*
to pass

EASILY

not *e.* provoked, thinketh no   *1Co 13:5*
evil
the sin which doth so *e.*   *Heb 12:1*
beset us

EAST

God placed at *e.* of garden of   *Ge 3:24*
Eden
Abraham removed to a   *Ge 12:8*
mountain on *e.*
Lot chose the plain, and   *Ge 13:11*
journeyed *e.*
thou shalt spread abroad to   *Ge 28:14*
west and *e.*
came into the land of the   *Ge 29:1*
people of the *e.*
but those that encamp   *Nu 3:38*
toward the *e.*
Balak hath brought me out   *Nu 23:7*
of the *e.*
to the *e.* (A)(B)(R)   *De 4:41; 4:47*
toward the *e.* (B)   *Jos 1:15;*
    19:34; J'g 20:43
children of the *e.* came up   *J'g 6:3;*
against them *6:33; 7:12; 8:10; 1Ki 4:30*
three looking toward the *e.*   *1Ki 7:25;*
    2Ch 4:4
porters toward the *e.* west   *1Ch 9:24*
they put to flight them   *1Ch 12:15*
toward the *e.*
the greatest of all the men of   *Job 1:3*
the *e.*
promotion cometh not from *e.*   *Ps 75:6*
nor west
as far as the *e.* is from the   *Ps 103:12*
west
he gathered them from the *e.*   *Ps 107:3*
and west
because they be replenished   *Isa 2:6*
from *e.*
shall spoil them of the *e.*   *Isa 11:14;*
    Jer 49:28
glorify Jehovah in the *e.*   *Isa 24:15*
(E)(R)
who raised up righteous man   *Isa 41:2*
from *e.*
I will bring thy seed from   *Isa 43:5;*
the *e.*   *Zec 8:7*
calling a ravenous bird from   *Isa 46:11*
the *e.*
men 25, with their faces   *Eze 8:16*
towards the *e.*

I will deliver thee to men of   *Eze 25:4;*
e.   *25:10*
came he to gate which   *Eze 40:6;*
looketh toward the *e.*   *40:22; 43:1;*
    44:1; 46:1, 12
glory of God came from way   *Eze 43:2*
of *e.*
these waters issue out   *Eze 47:8*
toward *e.* country
toward the *e.* ten thousand   *Eze 48:10*
in breadth
suburbs of the city toward   *Eze 48:17*
the *e.*
the horn waxed great toward   *Da 8:9*
the *e.*
tidings out of the *e.* shall   *Da 11:44*
trouble him
I will drive him toward the   *Joe 2:20*
e. sea
they shall wander from north   *Am 8:12*
to *e.*
the mount shall cleave   *Zec 14:4*
toward the *e.*
there came wise men from the   *M't 2:1*
e.
for we have seen his star in   *M't 2:2;*
the *e.*   *2:9*
many come from *e.* and west   *M't 8:11;*
    Lu 13:29
as lightning cometh out of   *M't 24:27*
the *e.*
another angel ascending from   *Re 7:2*
the *e.*
way of kings of *e.* might be   *Re 16:12*
prepared
on the *e.* three gates, on the   *Re 21:13*
north three

EAST *BORDER*

ye shall point out your *e.*   *Nu 34:10*
border
encamped in *e. border* of   *Jos 4:19*
Jericho
e. border was salt sea to end   *Jos 15:5*
of Jordan
from west border to *e.*   *Eze 45:7*
border
of the oblation toward the   *Eze 48:21*
e. border

EAST *GATE*

Shemaiah, the keeper of the   *Ne 3:29*
e. gate
which is by the entry of the   *Jer 19:2*
e. gate
every one stood at the door   *Eze 10:19*
of the *e. gate*
the Spirit brought me unto   *Eze 11:1*
the *e. gate*

EAST *SIDE*

the breadth of the court on   *Ex 27:13*
the *e. side*
and on the *e. side* shall Judah   *Nu 2:3*
pitch
to Ai, which is on the *e. side*   *Jos 7:2*
of Bethel
the border of their   *Jos 16:5*
inheritance on the *e. side*
came by *e. side* of the land   *J'g 11:18*
of Moab
the mountain on the *e. side*   *Eze 11:23*
of the city
he measured the *e. side*   *Eze 42:16*
with the reed
from the *e. side* even unto   *Eze 48:2;*
the west side   *48:3-8, 23-27*
    25, 26, 27
Jonah sat on the *e. side* of   *Jon 4:5*
the city

EAST *WIND*

thin ears, blasted with *e.*   *Ge 41:6;*
wind   *41:23, 27*
Lord brought an *e. wind*   *Ex 10:13;*
    14:21
fill his belly with the *e. wind*   *Job 15:2*
e. wind carrieth him away,   *Job 27:21*
he departeth
which scattereth *e. wind*   *Job 38:24*
upon earth
thou breakest ships with an *e.*   *Ps 48:7*
wind
he caused an *e. wind* to blow   *Ps 78:26*
in heaven

he stayeth his rough wind in   *Isa 27:8*
day of *e.* wind
scatter them as with an *e.*   *Jer 18:17*
wind
wither, when *e.* wind   *Eze 17:10*
toucheth it
and the *e.* wind drieth up   *Eze 19:12*
her fruit
e. wind hath broken thee in   *Eze 27:26*
the seas
Ephraim followeth after *e.*   *Ho 12:1*
wind
though he be fruitful, an *e.*   *Ho 13:15*
wind shall
God prepared a vehement *e.*   *Jon 4:8*
wind
their faces shall sup up as *e.*   *Hab 1:9*
wind

EASTER

intending after *E.* to bring   *Ac 12:4*
him

EASTERN

on the *e.* border (B)   *Nu 21:1; 34:15*
the *e.* sea (S)   *Joe 2:20*

EASTWARD

God planted a garden *e.* of   *Ge 2:8*
Eden
southward, and *e.* and   *Ge 13:14*
yet lived, *e.* unto the east   *Ge 25:6*
country
east side *e.* shall be fifty   *Ex 27:13*
cubits
the east side *e.* fifty cubits   *Ex 38:13*
his finger upon the mercy   *Le 16:14*
seat *e.*
e. shall be Moses, and Aaron   *Nu 3:38*
fallen to us on this side   *Nu 32:19*
Jordan *e.*
outmost coast of the salt sea   *Nu 34:3*
e.
side of the sea of   *Nu 34:11*
Chinnereth *e.*
Jericho *e.* toward the   *Nu 34:15*
sunrising
sea, under Ashdoth-pisgah *e.*   *De 3:17*
northward, and southward, and   *De 3:27*
e.
the plain on this side Jordan *e.*   *De 4:49*
eastward (A)(B)(R)   *Jos 1:15; 13:5; 19:12*
and unto the valley of   *Jos 11:8*
Mizpeh *e.*
gave them, beyond Jordan *e.*   *Jos 13:8*
on the other side Jordan *e.*   *Jos 13:27*
other side Jordan, by   *Jos 13:32*
Jericho, *e.*
about *e.* unto Taanath-shiloh   *Jos 16:6*
from Sarid *e.* toward the   *Jos 19:12*
other side Jordan by Jericho   *Jos 20:8*
e.
in Michmash, *e.* from   *1Sa 13:5*
Beth-aven
on the right side of the   *1Ki 7:39*
house *e.*
Get thee hence, and turn   *1Ki 17:3*
thee *e.*
Jordan *e.* all, land of   *2Ki 10:33*
Gilead
And he said, Open the   *2Ki 13:17*
window *e.*
And *e.* he inhabited unto the   *1Ch 5:9*
E. Naaran, and westward   *1Ch 7:28*
Gezer
waited in the king's gate *e.*   *1Ch 9:18*
the lot *e.* fell to Shelemiah   *1Ch 26:14*
E. were six Levites,   *1Ch 26:17*
northward four
even unto the water gate *e.*   *Ne 12:37*
Lord's house, which looketh   *Eze 11:1*
e.
little chambers of the gate *e.*   *Eze 40:10*
hundred cubits *e.* and   *Eze 40:19*
northward
and from the east side *e.*   *Eze 45:7*
the threshold of the house *e.*   *Eze 47:1*
gate by the way that looketh   *Eze 47:2*
e.
the line in his hand went   *Eze 47:3*
forth *e.*
residue, shall be ten   *Eze 48:18*
thousand *e.*

EASY

knowledge is *e.* unto him that   *Pr 14:6*
For my yoke is *e.* and my   *M't 11:30*
burden
tongue words *e.* to be   *1Co 14:9*
understood
e. to be intreated, full of   *Jas 3:17*
mercy

EAT

of every tree thou mayest   *Ge 2:16*
freely *e.*
in day ye *e.* your eyes shall be   *Ge 3:5*
opened
Eve took and did *e.*; I did *e.*   *Ge 3:6;*
                    3:13
dust shalt thou *e.* all days of   *Ge 3:14*
thy life
in sorrow *e.* of it all days of   *Ge 3:17*
thy life
he stood by angels, they did   *Ge 18:8;*
e.   *19:3*
savoury meat, bring me, that   *Ge 27:4*
I may *e.*
they did *e.* there upon the   *Ge 31:46*
heap
the birds did *e.* them out of   *Ge 40:17*
the basket
for the Egyptians did *e.* by   *Ge 40:32*
themselves
locusts shall *e.* every tree that   *Ex 10:5*
grow
locusts may *e.* every herb of   *Ex 10:12*
land
roast with fire, with bitter   *Ex 12:8*
herbs *e.* it
no work done, save which   *Ex 12:16*
every man *e.*
no stranger *e.* thereof   *Ex 12:43;*
               12:48; Le 22:13
when circumcised, then shall   *Ex 12:44*
he *e.* thereof
e. to-day, for to-day is   *Ex 16:25*
sabbath to Lord
Israel did *e.* manna forty   *Ex 16:35;*
years   *Joh 6:31, 49, 58*
that the poor of thy people   *Ex 23:11*
may *e.*
Aaron and sons shall *e.*   *Ex 29:32;*
              Le 6:16; 8:31
one call thee, and thou *e.* of   *Ex 34:15*
sacrifice
males shall *e.* it   *Le 6:18;*
         6:29; 7:6; Nu 18:10
priest that offereth it for sin   *Le 6:26*
shall *e.* it
all that be clean *e.* thereof   *Le 7:19;*
                  Nu 18:11
any other use, ye shall in no   *Le 7:24*
wise *e.* of it
e. it without leaven beside   *Le 10:12*
the altar
yet these ye may *e.*   *Le 11:21;*
              11:22; De 14:20
Aaron and sons shall *e.* in   *Le 24:9*
holy place
if ye say, What shall we *e.*   *Le 25:20*
seventh year
sow in vain, your enemies   *Le 26:16*
shall *e.* it
we remember fish we did *e.*   *Nu 11:5*
freely
saying, Give us flesh, that we   *Nu 11:13*
may *e.*
he shall not lie down till he   *Nu 23:24*
e. cf prev
people did *e.* of sacrifices,   *Nu 25:2*
and bowed
buy meat of them that ye may   *De 2:6*
e. in thy gates   *De 12:15;*
      12:21; 15:22; 26:12
the unclean and clean may *e.*   *De 12:15,*
                12:22; 15:22
thou must *e.* before the   *De 12:18;*
Lord   *14:26; 15:20*
shalt say, I will *e.* flesh,   *De 12:20*
thou mayest *e.* flesh
give it to the stranger that   *De 14:21*
he may *e.*
and the clean person shall *e.*   *De 15:22*
it alike
lest he die, and another man   *De 20:6*
e. of it
then thou mayest *e.* grapes   *De 23:24*
thy fill
not gather grapes, for worms   *De 28:39*
shall *e.* them

shall *e.* fruit of thine own   *De 28:53;*
body   *La 2:20*
which did *e.* fat of their   *De 32:38*
sacrifices
they did *e.* of old corn of   *Jos 5:11*
land
of vineyards ye planted not   *Jos 24:13*
do ye *e.*
they tarried, and did *e.* both   *J'g 19:8*
of them
Hannah did *e.* and was no   *1Sa 1:18*
more sad
afterwards they *e.* that be   *1Sa 9:13*
bidden
e. and sin not against the   *1Sa 14:34*
Lord
Jonathan did *e.* no meat   *1Sa 20:34*
second day
and *e.* that thou mayest   *1Sa 28:22*
have strength
he shall *e.* at my table   *2Sa 9:11;*
                   1Ki 2:7
him that dieth of   *1Ki 14:11;*
Jeroboam shall the dogs *e.*   *16:4; 21:23;*
              2Ki 9:10, 36
for me and my son, we   *1Ki 17:12*
may *e.* and die
angel said, Arise and *e.*   *1Ki 19:5;*
            Ac 10:13; 11:7
they shall *e.* and leave   *2Ki 4:43*
thereof
did *e.* and left thereof,   *2Ki 4:44*
according to word
son that we may *e.* him to-day,   *2Ki 6:28*
we will *e.* my son to-morrow
so we boiled my son, and   *2Ki 6:29*
did *e.* him
e. every man of own vine   *2Ki 18:31;*
                 Isa 36:16
yet did they *e.* the passover   *2Ch 30:18*
the children of Israel did *e.*   *Ezr 6:21*
take up corn, that we may   *Ne 5:2*
and live
they did *e.* and were filled   *Ne 9:25;*
                 Ps 78:29
for my sighing cometh   *Job 3:24*
before I *e.*
then let me sow, and let   *Job 31:8*
another *e.*
the meek shall *e.* and be   *Ps 22:26*
satisfied
all they that be fat on earth   *Ps 22:29*
shall *e.*
will I *e.* flesh of bulls, or   *Ps 50:13*
drink blood
man did *e.* angels' food, he   *Ps 78:25*
sent them meat
thou shalt *e.* the labour of   *Ps 128:2*
thine hands
e. fruit of their own way   *Pr 1:31;*
                 Isa 3:10
the soul of transgressors shall   *Pr 13:2*
e. violence
they that love it shall *e.* the   *Pr 18:21*
fruit
my son, *e.* thou honey,   *Pr 24:13*
because it is good
whoso keepeth fig tree shall   *Pr 27:18*
e. fruit thereof
eye, and the young eagles   *Pr 30:17*
shall *e.* it
who can *e.* or hasten more   *Ec 2:25*
than I
goods increase they are   *Ec 5:11*
increased that *e.*
sleep is sweet, whether he *e.*   *Ec 5:12*
little or much
thy princes *e.* in the morning   *Ec 10:16*
blessed, when thy princes *e.*   *Ec 10:17*
in due season
come into his garden and *e.*   *Ca 4:16*
his pleasant fruits
we will *e.* our own bread   *Isa 4:1*
butter and honey shall he *e.*   *Isa 7:15*
that he may
butter and honey shall every   *Isa 7:22*
one *e.* that
e. on left hand, *e.* flesh of his   *Isa 9:20*
arm
lion shall *e.* straw like the   *Isa 11:7;*
ox   *65:25*
oxen and asses shall *e.* clean   *Isa 30:24*
provender
sow ye and reap, plant   *Isa 37:30;*
vineyards, and *e.*   *65:21; Jer 29:5, 28*
and the worm shall *e.* them   *Isa 51:8*
like wool
come ye, buy and *e.* yea   *Isa 55:1*
hearken to me, and *e.* that   *Isa 55:2*
which is good

they that have gathered it   *Isa 62:9*
shall *e.* it
people which *e.* swine's flesh   *Isa 65:4*
servants shall *e.* but ye shall   *Isa 65:13*
be hungry
they shall not plant and   *Isa 65:22*
another *e.*
words were found, and I did   *Jer 15:16*
e. them
e. every one the flesh of his   *Jer 19:9*
friend
open mouth and *e.* that I give   *Eze 2:8*
son of man, *e.* that thou   *Eze 3:1*
findest, *e.* this roll
e. by weight; fathers shall *e.*   *Eze 4:10;*
sons   *5:16*
thou didst *e.* fine flour, and   *Eze 16:13*
honey, and oil
in thee they *e.* upon the   *Eze 22:9*
mountains
ye *e.* fat, and clothe you   *Eze 34:3*
with wool
Nebuchadnezzar did *e.* grass   *Da 4:33*
as oxen
shall *e.* and not have   *Ho 4:10;*
enough   *Mic 6:14; Hag 1:6*
they shall *e.* unclean things in   *Ho 9:3*
Assyria
all that *e.* thereof shall be   *Ho 9:4*
polluted
that *e.* the lambs out of the   *Am 6:4*
flock
who also *e.* the flesh of my   *Mic 3:3*
people
let rest *e.* flesh of another   *Zec 11:9*
he shall *e.* flesh of fat and   *Zec 11:16*
tear
how David did *e.* the   *M't 12:4*
shewbread
did all *e.* and were filled   *M't 14:20;*
  15:37; M'k 6:42; 8:8; Lu 9:17
yet the dogs *e.* of the   *M't 15:27;*
crumbs   *M'k 7:28*
they that did *e.* were 4000,   *M't 15:38*
beside women
as they did *e.* he said   *M't 26:21;*
  M'k 14:18, 22
said, Take,' *e.*, this is my   *M't 26:26;*
body   *M'k 14:22; 1Co 11:24*
they saw him *e.* with   *M'k 2:16*
publicans
they that did *e.* were above   *M'k 6:44*
5,000 men
no man *e.* fruit of thee   *M'k 11:14*
hereafter for ever
where go and prepare   *M'k 14:12;*
mayest *e.* the passover   *14:14; Lu 22:8,*
  11; Joh 18:28
did *e.* rubbing them in their   *Lu 6:1*
hands
one desired he would *e.* with   *Lu 7:36*
him
eat (S)   *Lu 7:36; 11:37; 12:37; 17:7*
e. such things as are set   *Lu 10:8*
before you
kill fatted calf, let us *e.* and   *Lu 15:23*
be merry
he took it, and did *e.* before   *Lu 24:43*
them
disciples prayed him, saying,   *Joh 4:31*
Master, *e.*
ye did *e.* of loaves and were   *Joh 6:26*
filled
that a man may *e.* thereof   *Joh 6:50*
and not die
except he *e.* the flesh of the   *Joh 6:53*
Son of man
they did *e.* their meat with   *Ac 2:46*
gladness
thou wentest in and didst *e.*   *Ac 11:3*
with them
e. nothing till we have slain   *Ac 23:14*
Paul
one believeth he may *e.* all   *Ro 14:2*
things
he that doubteth is damned   *Ro 14:23*
if he *e.*
some *e.* as a thing offered to   *1Co 8:7*
an idol
if we *e.* are we the better, if   *1Co 8:8*
we *e.* not
I will *e.* no flesh while the   *1Co 8:13*
world standeth
and did all *e.* the same   *1Co 10:3*
spiritual meat
who *e.* of sacrifices,   *1Co 10:18*
partakers of altar

whatsoever is sold in the   *1Co 10:25*
shambles, that *e.*
e. asking no question for   *1Co 10:27*
conscience sake
if any man hunger, let him   *1Co 11:34*
e. at home
if any work not, neither   *2Th 3:10*
should he *e.*
their word will *e.* as doth a   *2Ti 2:17*
canker
shall *e.* your flesh as it were   *Jas 5:3*
fire
e. with him (A)(R)   *Re 3:20*
e. her flesh, and burn her   *Re 17:16*
with fire
ye may *e.* flesh of kings and   *Re 19:18*
captains

EAT with DRINK

they did *e.* and *drink*   *Ge 24:54;*
  26:30; Ex 24:11; J'g 9:27; 19:4
sat down to *e.* and *drink*   *Ex 32:6;*
  1Co 10:7
nor *e.* bread, nor *drink*   *Ex 34:28;*
water   *De 9:9, 18*
Egyptians did *e.* bread and   *1Sa 30:11*
drink water
shall I go to my house to *e.*   *2Sa 11:11*
and *drink*
it did *e.* of his meat and   *2Sa 12:3*
drink of his cup
can thy servant taste what I   *2Sa 19:35*
e. or *drink*
they *e.* and *drink* before   *1Ki 1:25*
Adonijah
I will not *e.* bread nor   *1Ki 13:8;*
drink water   *13:9, 17, 22*
neither will I *e.* bread nor   *1Ki 13:16*
drink water
Elijah said, Get thee up, *e.*   *1Ki 18:41*
and *drink*
set bread, *e.* and *drink*   *2Ki 6:22*
went into one tent and did   *2Ki 7:8*
e. and *drink*
e. own dung and *drink* piss   *2Ki 18:27;*
  Isa 36:12
did *e.* and *drink* before   *1Ch 29:22*
Lord
and gave them to *e.* and to   *2Ch 28:15*
drink
Ezra did *e.* no bread nor   *Ezr 10:6*
drink water
go your way, *e.* fat and *drink*   *Ne 8:10*
sweet
fast for me, nor *e.* nor *drink*   *Es 4:16*
three days
called sisters to *e.* and *drink*   *Job 1:4*
with them
so is he, *e.* and *drink* saith he   *Pr 23:7*
to thee
is nothing better than that he   *Ec 2:24;*
should *e.* and *drink*   *3:13; 5:18; 8:15*
e. O friends, yea, *drink*   *Ca 5:1*
abundantly
e. *drink*, ye princes, anoint   *Isa 21:5*
the shield
let us *e.* and *drink*, for   *Isa 22:13;*
to-morrow we shall die   *1Co 15:32*
did not thy father *e.* and   *Jer 22:15*
drink
shall *e.* thy fruit and *drink*   *Eze 25:4*
thy milk
that ye may *e.* flesh and   *Eze 39:17*
drink blood
give us pulse to *e.* and water   *Da 1:12*
to *drink*
when ye did *e.* and when ye   *Zec 7:6*
did *drink*
what shall *e.* or *drink*   *M't 6:25;*
  6:31; Lu 12:29
to *e.* and *drink* with   *M't 24:49;*
drunken   *Lu 12:45*
why do ye *e.* and *drink* with   *Lu 5:30*
publicans
John's disciples fast, but thy   *Lu 5:33*
disciples *e.* and *drink*
take thine ease, *e.*, *drink*,   *Lu 12:19*
and be merry
and afterward thou shalt *e.*   *Lu 17:8*
and *drink*
they did *e.* they *drank*, they   *Lu 17:27*
married
that ye may *e.* and *drink* at   *Lu 22:30*
my table
Saul three days did neither *e.*   *Ac 9:9*
nor *drink*
e. nor *drink* till they had   *Ac 23:12;*
killed Paul   *23:21*

neither to *e.* flesh nor *drink*   *Ro 14:21*
wine
have we not power to *e.* and   *1Co 9:4*
to *drink*
whether therefore ye *e.* or   *1Co 10:31*
drink, or whatever
have ye not houses to *e.* and   *1Co 11:22*
drink in
as oft as ye *e.* this bread   *1Co 11:26*
and *drink* this cup
whosoever shall *e.* and   *1Co 11:27*
drink unworthily
and so let him *e.* and *drink*   *1Co 11:28*
of that cup

EAT NOT

but of the tree of the   *Ge 2:17;*
knowledge of good and evil,   *3:1, 3*
thou shalt *not e.* of it
whereof I commanded thee   *Ge 3:11;*
not to *e.*   *3:17*
blood thereof shall you *not e.*   *Ge 9:4;*
  Le 19:26; De 12:16, 23-25; 15:23
I will *not e.* till I have told   *Ge 24:33*
my errand
children of Israel *e.* *not* of   *Ge 32:32*
the sinew
Egyptians might *not e.* with   *Ge 43:32*
Hebrews
e. *not* of it raw, nor sodden   *Ex 12:9*
foreigner shall *not e.*   *Ex 12:45*
thereof   *29:33*
these shall ye *not e.*   *Le 11:40*
  De 14:3, 7
leper *not e.* of holy things   *Le 22:4;*
  2:26, 10, 12
that torn he shall *not e.* to   *Le 22:8*
defile himself
not e. one day, or two days   *Nu 11:19*
not e. of any thing that   *De 14:21;*
dieth of itself   *Eze 44:31*
ox be slain, and thou shalt   *De 28:31*
not e. thereof
e. *not* any unclean thing   *J'g 13:4;*
  13:7, 14
therefore she wept, and did   *1Sa 1:7*
not e.
for the people will *not e.* till   *1Sa 9:13*
he come
Saul refused, and said, I   *1Sa 28:23*
will *not e.*
and they could *not e.* thereof   *2Ki 4:40*
see it with thy eyes, but *not*   *2Ki 7:2;*
e. thereof   *7:19*
not e. of most holy things   *Ezr 2:63;*
  Ne 7:65
let me *not e.* of their   *Ps 141:4*
dainties
e. *not* bread of him that hath   *Pr 23:6*
evil eye
cover not lips, and *e.* *not*   *Eze 24:17*
bread of men
Jews, except they wash, they   *M'k 7:3;*
e. *not*   *7:4*
I will *not e.* thereof, until   *Lu 22:16*
fulfilled
with such an one no *not* to   *1Co 5:11*
e.
neither if we *e.* *not* are we   *1Co 8:8*
the worse
e. *not*, for his sake that   *1Co 10:28*
shewed it

EAT UP

lean did *e.* *up* the seven fat   *Ge 41:4;*
kine   *41:20*
land of your enemies shall *e.*   *Le 26:38*
you *up*
he shall *e.* *up* the nations his   *Nu 24:8*
enemies
nations thou knowest not   *De 28:33*
shall *e.* *up*
my enemies came on me to *e.*   *Ps 27:2*
up my flesh
did *e.* *up* all the herbs in   *Ps 105:35*
their land
the moth shall *e.* them *up*   *Isa 50:9;*
  51:8
shall *e.* *up* harvest, *e.* *up* thy   *Jer 5:17*
flocks, *e.* *up* thy vines and fig trees
the wind shall *e.* *up* all thy   *Jer 22:22*
pastures
they *e.* *up* the sin of my   *Ho 4:8*
people
devoured the deep, and did *e.*   *Am 7:4*
up a part

it shall *e*. thee *up* like the   *Na 3:15*
cankerworm
angel said to me, Take it, and   *Re 10:9*
e. it *up*

HE DID EAT

Eve gave to her husband, and   *Ge 3:6*
he did e.
loved Esau, because *he did*   *Ge 25:28*
e. of venison
he brought it near to Isaac,   *Ge 27:25*
and *he did e*.
he knew not ought, save   *Ge 39:6*
bread *he did e*.
gave Egyptian bread, and   *1Sa 30:11*
he did e.
he did e. continually at his   *2Sa 9:13*
table
they set bread before him,   *2Sa 12:20*
and *he did e*.
John *did e*. locusts and wild   *M'k 1:6*
honey
and in those days *he did e*.   *Lu 4:2*
nothing
for before *he did e*. with the   *Ga 2:12*
Gentiles

SHALL YE EAT

thus *shall ye e*. it, with loins *Ex 12:11*
girded
seven days *shall ye e*.   *Ex 12:15;*
unleavened bread   *12:20*
nor *shall ye e*. any flesh torn *Ex 22:31*
of beasts
wave breast *shall ye e*. in   *Le 10:14*
clean place
cheweth the cud, that *shall*   *Le 11:3;*
ye e.   *De 14:4, 6*
these *shall ye e*. of all that   *Le 11:9*
are in the waters
in the fifth year *shall ye e*.   *Le 19:25*
of the fruit
the flesh of your daughters   *Le 26:29*
shall ye e.
all that have fins and scales   *De 14:9*
shall ye e.

TO EAT

Lord shall give you flesh *to e*. *Ex 16:8*
who shall give us flesh *to e*.   *Nu 11:4;*
     11:18
because thy soul longeth *to*   *De 12:20*
e. flesh
they shall have like portions   *De 18:8*
to e.
before he go to the high   *1Sa 9:13*
place *to e*.
the king sat him down *to e*. *1Sa 20:24*
meat
people came to cause David *2Sa 3:35*
to e.
that thy master's son may   *2Sa 9:10*
have food *to e*.
poured before him, but he   *2Sa 13:9*
refused *to e*.
summer fruit for the young   *2Sa 16:2*
men *to e*.
for the people that were   *2Sa 17:29*
with him *to e*.
so they poured out for   *2Ki 4:40*
men *to e*.
we have had enough *to e*. *2Ch 31:10*
and left
land thou gavest, *to e*. the   *Ne 9:36*
fruit thereof
had rained manna on them   *Ps 78:24*
to e.
when thou sittest *to e*. with a *Pr 23:1*
ruler
it is not good to *e*. much   *Pr 25:27*
honey
hath given him power *to e*.   *Ec 5:19*
thereof
God giveth him not power *to e*. *Ec 6:2*
thereof
shall be for them *to e*.   *Isa 23:18*
sufficiently
cause them *to e*. flesh of   *Jer 19:9*
their sons
he caused me *to e*. that roll   *Eze 3:2*
he said, Son of man, cause   *Eze 3:3*
thy belly *to e*.
they shall make thee *to e*.   *Da 4:25;*
grass   *4:32*
woe is me, there is no cluster *Mic 7:1*
to e.

they shall flee as eagle that   *Hab 1:8*
hasteth *to e*.
began to pluck ears of corn, *M't 12:1*
and *to e*.
not lawful for him *to e*.   *M't 12:4;*
   M'k 2:26; Lu 6:4
give ye them *to e*.   *M't 14:16;*
   M'k 6:37; Lu 9:13
to e. with unwashen hands *M't 15:20*
defileth not
multitude have nothing *to*   *M't 15:32;*
e.   *M'k 8:1-2*
where wilt that we prepare *M't 26:17*
to e. passover
something should be given   *M'k 5:43*
her *to e*.
they had no leisure so much *M'k 6:31*
as *to e*.
! have desired *to e*. this   *Lu 22:15*
passover
I have meat *to e*. that ye   *Joh 4:32*
know not of
hath any man brought him   *Joh 4:33*
aught *to e*.
how can this man give us his *Joh 6:52*
flesh *to e*.
when he had broken it, he   *Ac 27:35*
began *to e*.
emboldened *to e*. things   *1Co 8:10*
offered to idols
when ye come, this is not   *1Co 11:20*
to e. Lord's supper
brethren, when ye come   *Ac 11:33*
together *to e*.
an altar whereof they have   *Heb 13:10*
no right *to e*.
will I give *to e*. of tree of life *Re 2:7*
in midst
to e. things sacrificed unto   *Re 2:14;*
idols   *2:20*
give *to e*. of hidden manna, a *Re 2:17*
white stone

YE SHALL EAT

ye shall e. the fat of the   *Ge 45:18*
land
ye shall e. it in haste   *Ex 12:11*
first month at even *ye shall* *Ex 12:18*
e. unleavened bread
at even *ye shall e*. flesh, and *Ex 16:12*
in morning
ye shall e. no manner of fat   *Le 7:23;*
     7:24
ye shall e. no manner of blood *Le 7:26;*
     17:14
ye shall e. it in the holy   *Le 10:13*
place
ye shall e. neither bread nor *Le 23:14*
parched corn
ye shall e. increase thereof *Le 25:12*
out of field
ye shall e. your fill, and   *Le 25:19*
dwell in safety
ye shall e. of the old store   *Le 25:22;*
     26:10
and *ye shall e*. and not be   *Le 26:26*
satisfied
ye shall e. flesh of your sons *Le 26:29*
and daughters
Lord will give flesh, and *ye* *Nu 11:18*
shall e.
ye shall e. in every place,   *Nu 18:31*
and households
there *ye shall e*. before Lord *De 12:7*
your God
of all clean birds *ye shall e*. *De 14:11*
go up, for *ye shall e*. with   *1Sa 9:19*
me to-day
ye shall e. this year such   *2Ki 19:29;*
things as grow themselves   *Isa 37:30*
if obedient, *ye shall e*. good *Isa 1:19*
of the land
ye shall e. the riches of the *Isa 61:6*
ye shall e. fat till ye be full *Eze 39:19*
ye shall e. in plenty, and be *Joe 2:26*
satisfied
take no thought what *ye*   *Lu 12:22*
shall e.

EATEN

hast thou *e*. of tree whereof *Ge 3:11*
shouldest not
save that which the young   *Ge 14:24*
men have *e*.
the rams of thy flock have I *Ge 31:38*
not *e*.

when they had *e*. them up,   *Ge 41:21*
it could not be known
they had *e*. them
in one house shall it be *e*.   *Ex 12:46*
there shall no leavened bread *Ex 13:3;*
be *e*.   *13:7*
ox be stoned, his flesh shall *Ex 21:28*
not be *e*.
if man cause field or vineyard *Ex 22:5*
to be *e*.
it shall not be *e*. because it *Ex 29:34*
is holy
it shall be *e*. in the holy   *Le 6:16;*
place   *6:26; 7:6*
it shall be wholly burnt, not *Le 6:23;*
be *e*.   *7:19*
no sin offering shall be *e*. it *Le 6:30*
shall be burnt
shall be *e*. the same day it is *Le 7:15;*
offered   *7:16*
if the sacrifice of peace   *Le 7:18*
offering be *e*.
why have ye not *e*. the sin *Le 10:17*
offering
ye should indeed have *e*. it *Le 10:18*
in holy place
if I had *e*. the sin offering to *Le 10:19*
day
they shall not be *e*.   *Le 11:13;*
    11:41; De 14:19
it shall be *e*. same day ye   *Le 19:6;*
offer   *22:30*
if it be *e*. at all on the third *Le 19:7*
day
unleavened bread be *e*.   *Nu 28:17;*
     Eze 45:21
when have *e*. and be full   *De 6:11;*
     8:10, 12
even as the roebuck and the *De 12:22*
hart is *e*.
planted a vineyard, and hath *De 20:6*
not *e*. of it
I have not *e*. thereof in my *De 26:14*
mourning
ye have not *e*. bread nor   *De 29:6*
drunk wine
when they shall have *e*. and *De 31:20*
be filled
after they had *e*. of the old *Jos 5:12*
corn
when Boaz had *e*. and drunk, *Ru 3:7*
he went
if haply the people had *e*. *1Sa 14:30*
freely
for he had *e*. no bread all *1Sa 28:20*
the day
when he had *e*. his spirit *1Sa 30:12*
came again
have *e*. at all of king's   *2Sa 19:42*
cost
but camest back, and.   *1Ki 13:22*
bread
lion had not *e*. carcase, nor *1Ki 13:28*
torn the ass
have not *e*. bread of governor *Ne 5:14*
that is unsavoury be *e*.   *Job 6:6*
without salt
or have *e*. my morsel myself *Job 31:17*
alone
if I have *e*. fruits without *Job 31:39*
money
zeal of thine house *e*. me up *Ps 69:9;*
     Joh 2:17
e. ashes like bread, mingled *Ps 102:9*
my drink
bread *e*. in secret is pleasant *Pr 9:17*
morsel thou hast *e*. shalt   *Pr 23:8*
vomit
I have *e*. my honeycomb with *Ca 5:1*
honey
ye have *e*. up vineyard spoil *Isa 3:14*
of poor
have *e*. up Jacob, and   *Jer 10:25*
devoured him
figs which could not be *e*.   *Jer 24:2;*
    24:3, 8; 29:17
fathers *e*. sour grapes   *Jer 31:29;*
     Eze 18:2
have not *e*. that which dieth *Eze 4:14*
of itself
hath not *e*. upon the   *Eze 18:6;*
mountains   *18:15*
but even hath *e*. upon the *Eze 18:11*
mountains
ye have *e*. the fruit of lies *Ho 10:13*
locust hath left, cankerworm *Joe 1:4;*
e.   *2:25*
and they that had *e*.   *M't 14:21;*
     M'k 8:9

EATEN

have e. and drunk in thy presence · Lu 13:26
til I have e. afterward thou shalt e. · Lu 17:8
which remained to them that had e. · Joh 6:13
when they had e. (A) · Joh 21:15
became hungry, and would have e. · Ac 10:10
I have never e. any thing common · Ac 10:14
he was e. of worms, and gave up ghost · Ac 12:23
when he had broken bread and e. · Ac 20:11
when they had e. enough they lightened · Ac 27:38
as soon as I had e. it, my belly was bitter · Re 10:10

EATER

he said, Out of the e. came forth meat · J'g 14:14
that it may give bread to the e. · Isa 55:10
they shall fall into mouth of e. · Na 3:12

EATERS

be not among riotous e. of flesh · Pr 23:20

EATEST

in day thou e. thou shalt surely die · Ge 2:17
said Elkanah, Why e. thou not · 1Sa 1:8
why spirit so sad thou e. no bread · 1Ki 21:5

EATETH

who e. leavened bread be cut off · Ex 12:15; 12:19
soul that e. · Le 7:18; 7:20, 25, 27; 17:10, 15
every one that e. shall bear his iniquity · Le 19:8
a land that e. up the inhabitants · Nu 13:32
cursed be the man that e. · 1Sa 14:24; 14:28
whose harvest the hungry e. up · Job 5:5
and another never e. with pleasure · Job 21:25
behemoth I made, he e. grass as an ox · Job 40:15
the similitude of an ox that e. grass · Ps 106:20
righteous e. to satisfying of soul · Pr 13:25
she e. and wipeth her mouth, and saith · Pr 30:20
and she e. not the bread of idleness · Pr 31:27
fool foldeth hands and e. own flesh · Ec 4:5
all his days also he e. in darkness · Ec 5:17
stranger e. it, this is vanity, evil disease · Ec 6:2
while it is yet in his hand he e. it up · Isa 28:4
behold, he e. but awaketh, and is hungry · Isa 29:8
with part thereof he e. flesh, roasteth · Isa 44:16
he that e. of their eggs dieth · Isa 59:5
every man that e. the sour grape · Jer 31:30
why e. your master with publicans and · M't 9:11; M'k 2:16; Lu 15:2
you who e. with me, shall betray me · M'k 14:18; Joh 13:18
whoso e. my flesh hath eternal life · Joh 6:54
he that e. my flesh dwelleth in me, I in him · Joh 6:56
so he that e. me, even he shall live by me · Joh 6:57
he that e. of this bread, shall live for ever · Joh 6:58
another who is weak e. herbs · Ro 14:2
let not him that e. despise him that e. not · Ro 14:3

that e. to Lord, that e. not, to Lord e. not · Ro 14:6
it is evil for that man who e. with offence · Ro 14:20
damned if he eat, because e. not of faith · Ro 14:23
planteth vineyard, and e. not fruit thereof and e. not of · 1Co 9:7
e. unworthily, e. damnation to himself · 1Co 11:29

EATING

man according to his e. · Ex 12:4; 16:16, 18, 21
Samson took thereof, and went on e. · J'g 14:9
sin not against Lord in e. with blood · 1Sa 14:34
they were spread abroad on all earth e. · 1Sa 30:16
Adonijah's guests made an end of e. · 1Ki 1:41
as they were e. of pottage, cried out · 2Ki 4:40
shall rain it upon him while he is e. · Job 20:23
e. swine's flesh, and the abomination · Isa 66:17
when they had made an end of e. grass · Am 7:2
eating (S) · M't 9:10; 14:3; 16:14; 26:7; M'k 2:15; Lu 7:37, 49; 14:15; 24:30
as they were e. Jesus took bread · M't 26:26
in e. and drinking (B)(E)(N) · Ro 14:17
concerning e. of things sacrificed to idols · 1Co 8:4
in e. every one taketh his own supper · 1Co 11:21

EBAL

Alvan, and Manaheth, and E. · Ge 36:23
and the curse upon mount E. · De 11:29
command you this day, in mount E. · De 27:4
shall stand upon mount E. to curse · De 27:13
Lord God of Israel in mount E. · Jos 8:30
half of them over against mount E. · Jos 8:33
And E. and Abimael, and Sheba · 1Ch 1:22
Alian, and Manahath, and E. · 1Ch 1:40

EBED

Gaal the son of E. · J'g 9:26; 9:28, 30-31, 35
E. the son of Jonathan, and · Ezr 8:6

EBED-MELECH

Now when E. the Ethiopian · Jer 38:7 38:8, 10-12; 39:16

EBENEZER

to battle, and pitched beside E. · 1Sa 4:1
and brought it from E. unto Ashdod · 1Sa 5:1
and called the name of it E. · 1Sa 7:12

EBER

the father of all the children of E. · Ge 10:21
begat Salah; and Salah begat E. · Ge 10:24
And unto E. were born two sons · Ge 10:25; 1Ch 1:19
lived thirty years, and begat E. · Ge 11:14
Salah lived after he begat E. · Ge 11:15
And E. lived four and thirty years · Ge 11:16
and E. lived after he begat Peleg · Ge 11:17
shall afflict E. and he also shall · Nu 24:24
begat Shelah, and Shelah begat E. · 1Ch 1:18

E. Peleg, Reu · 1Ch 1:25
E. and Misham, and Shamed, who · 1Ch 8:12
of Sallai, Kallai; of Amok, E. · Ne 12:20

EBIASAPH

Elkanah his son, and E. his son · 1Ch 6:23
the son of Assir, the son of E. · 1Ch 6:37
the son of Kore, the son of E. · 1Ch 9:19

EBONY

a present horns of ivory and e. · Eze 27:15

EBRONAH

Jotbathah, and encamped at E. · Nu 33:34
And they departed from E. · Nu 33:35

ECSTATIC

gift of e. utterance (N) · 1Co 12:10; 12:28; 14:9, 18, 26-27, 39
e. language (N) · 1Co 14:6

ECSTASY

a language of e. (N) · 1Co 14:2; 14:4, 13, 19, 27

ED

children of Gad called the altar E. · Jos 22:34

EDAR

his tent beyond the tower of E. · Ge 35:21

EDEN

planted a garden eastward in E. · Ge 2:8
went out of E. to water the garden · Ge 2:10
him into the garden of E. to dress it · Ge 2:15
him forth from the garden of E. · Ge 3:23
east of the garden of E. Cherubims · Ge 3:24
the land of Nod, on the east of E. · Ge 4:16
of E. which were in · 2Ki 19:12
of Zimnah, and E. the son of Joah · 2Ch 29:12
next him were E. and Miniamin · 2Ch 31:15
of E. which were in Telassar · Isa 37:12
will make her wilderness like E. · Isa 51:3
Haran, and Canneh, and E. · Eze 27:23
hast been in E. the garden of God · Eze 28:13
trees of E. that were in the garden · Eze 31:9
the trees of E. the choice and best · Eze 31:16
greatness among the trees of E. · Eze 31:18
brought down with the trees of E. · Eze 31:18
is become like the garden of E. · Eze 36:35
is as the garden of E. before them · Joe 2:3
the sceptre from the house of E. · Am 1:5

EDER

were Kabzeel, and E. and Jagur · Jos 15:21
Mahli, and E. and Jeremoth, three · 1Ch 23:23
Mahli, and E. and Jerimoth · 1Ch 24:30

EDGE

with the *e.* of the sword — Ge 34:26
Etham, in the *e.* of the — Ex 13:20
wilderness
people with the *e.* of the — Ex 17:13
sword
upon the *e.* of the one — Ex 26:4;
curtain — 26:5, 10
of blue on the *e.* of one — Ex 36:11;
curtain — 36:12, 17
by the *e.* of Jordan (S) — Nu 13:29
smote him with the *e.* of the — Nu 21:24
sword
Etham, which is in the *e.* of — Nu 33:6
Hor, in the *e.* of the land — Nu 33:37
of Edom
with the *e.* of the sword — De 13:15;
20:13; Jos 6:21; 8:24; 10:28, 30, 32, 39;
11:11-12, 14; 13:27; 19:47; J'g 1:8, 25;
4:15-16; 18:27; 20:37, 48; 21:10;
1Sa 15:8; 22:19; 2Sa 15:14; 2Ki 10:25;
Job 1:15, 17
also turned the *e.* of his — Ps 89:43
sword
and he do not whet the *e.* — Ec 10:10
them with the *e.* of the sword — Jer 21:7
the children's teeth are set — Jer 31:29;
on *e.* — Eze 18:2
his teeth shall be set on *e.* — Jer 31:30
by the *e.* thereof round — Eze 43:13
about shall
touched *e.* of cloak (N)(P) — M't 9:20
shall fall by the *e.* of the — Lu 21:24
sword
escaped the *e.* of the — Heb 11:34
sword, out of

EDGED

and a two-*e.* sword in their — Ps 149:6
hand
but her end is sharp as a — Pr 5:4
two-*e.* sword
word of God sharper than — Heb 4:12
two-*e.* sword
out of mouth went a sharp — Re 1:16
two-*e.* sword

EDGES

joined at the two *e.* thereof — Ex 28:7
two *e.* was it coupled together — Ex 39:4
e. of the beard (B)(N) — Le 21:5
a dagger which had two *e.* — J'g 3:16
hath the sharp sword with — Re 2:12
two *e.*

EDIBLE

all *e.* food (A)(B)(E)(R) — Le 11:34;
22:11, 13; 25:6
left nothing *e.* for (B) — J'g 6:4

EDIFICATION

his neighbour for his good to — Ro 15:2
e.
to strengthen, build him up — Ro 15:2
spiritually (A)
to strengthen him (B) — Ro 15:2
for that which is good to — Ro 15:2
edifying (E)
for his good, build up the — Ro 15:2
common life (N)
help them build up their — Ro 15:2
characters (P)
for his good to edify him — Ro 15:2
(R)
speaketh unto men to *e.* — 1Co 14:3
for their upbuilding, — 1Co 14:3
constructive spiritual progress,
encouragement, and consolation
(A)
give people a constructive, — 1Co 14:3
encouraging, and comforting
message (B)
they stimulate and encourage — 1Co 14:3
(N)
building up faith, — 1Co 14:3
encouraging, consolation (P)
upbuilding, encouragement, — 1Co 14:3
consolation (R)
done to *e.* (R) — 1Co 14:26
the Lord hath given us for — 2Co 10:8
e.
for upbuilding (A) — 2Co 10:8
for your establishment (B) — 2Co 10:8
for building you up (E) — 2Co 10:8

to build you up (N)(P)(R) — 2Co 10:8
the Lord hath given me to — 2Co 13:10
e.
for building you up (A) — 2Co 13:10
for constructive, not — 2Co 13:10
destructive purposes (B)
for building up, not casting — 2Co 13:10
down (E)(N)(P)(R)

EDIFICE

the *e.* is not for man (B) — 1Ch 29:1

EDIFIED

the churches rest, and were — Ac 9:31
e.
thanks well, but the other — 1Co 14:17
is not *e.*

EDIFIETH

puffeth up, but charity *e.* — 1Co 8:1
an unknown tongue *e.* — 1Co 14:4
himself
he that propesieth *e.* the — 1Co 14:4
church

EDIFY

wherewith one may *e.* — Ro 14:19
another
for mutual building up — Ro 14:19
(A)(R)
one another's peace and — Ro 14:19
development (B)
for peace, build up common — Ro 14:19
life (N)
for growth of one another's — Ro 14:19
character (P)
good to *e.* him (R) — Ro 15:2
lawful for me, but all — 1Co 10:23
things *e.* not
all things not constructive, — 1Co 10:23
edifying (A)
not everything is helpful — 1Co 10:23
(B)(R)
not all things edify (E) — 1Co 10:23
does everything help the — 1Co 10:23
building of the community (N)
everything is not useful (P) — 1Co 10:23
together, and *e.* one another — 1Th 5:11
build up one the other — 1Th 5:11
(B)(E)(R)
hearten, fortify one another — 1Th 5:11
(N)
cheering and strengthening — 1Th 5:11
one another (P)

EDIFYING

good to *e.* (E) — Ro 15:2
all things not *e.* (A) — 1Co 10:23
that the church may receive — 1Co 14:5
e.
may excel to the *e.* of the — 1Co 14:12
church
in ways that will build up — 1Co 14:12
(A)
for the upbuilding of the — 1Co 14:12
church (B)(R)
that will build up the — 1Co 14:12
church (N)
for the real growth of the — 1Co 14:12
church (P)
Let all things be done unto — 1Co 14:26
e.
everything shall be — 1Co 14:26
constructive (B)
to build up the church (N) — 1Co 14:26
make your church strong in — 1Co 14:26
faith (P)
done to edification (R) — 1Co 14:26
things, dearly beloved, for — 2Co 12:19
your *e.*
in order to build you up — 2Co 12:19
(A)(N)
for your upbuilding — 2Co 12:19
(B)(R)
to help you in your — 2Co 12:19
spiritual life (P)
for the *e.* of the body of — Eph 4:12
Christ
building up the body of — Eph 4:12
Christ (A)(B)(E)(N)(R)
that the whole body might — Eph 4:12
be built up (P)
unto the *e.* of itself in love — Eph 4:16
building itself up in love — Eph 4:16
(A)(E)(N)(R)

body for its upbuilding in — Eph 4:16
love (B)
which is good to the use of — Eph 4:29
e.
good and beneficial to — Eph 4:29
spiritual progress (A)
serves well to improve the — Eph 4:29
occasion (B)(N)
words suitable to the — Eph 4:29
occasion (P)
than godly *e.* which is in faith — 1Ti 1:4
which foster, promote useless — 1Ti 1:4
speculations and questioning (A)
furnish disputes (B) — 1Ti 1:4
which minister questionings — 1Ti 1:4
(E)
which issue in mere — 1Ti 1:4
speculation (N)
lead men to speculation — 1Ti 1:4
(P)(R)

EDOM

therefore was his name — Ge 25:30;
called *E.* — 36:1
dukes of *E.* amazed — Ex 15:15
Moses sent messengers from — Nu 20:14;
Kedesh to the king of *E.* — J'g 11:17
E. refused to give Israel — Nu 20:21
passage thro' border
E. shall be a possession for — Nu 24:18
his enemies
thou marchedst out of the field — J'g 5:4
of *E.*
Saul fought against Moab — 1Sa 14:47
and *E.*
David put garrisons in *E.* — 2Sa 8:14;
1Ch 18:13
Hadad was of the king's — 1Ki 11:14
seed in *E.*
till he had cut off every — 1Ki 11:16
male in *E.*
there was then no king in — 1Ki 22:47
E.
there came water by the way — 2Ki 3:20
of *E.*
in his days *E.* revolted from — 2Ki 8:20
under Judah
thou hast indeed smitten *E.* — 2Ki 14:10
glory of this
they sought after the gods — 2Ch 25:20
of *E.*
over *E.* will I cast out my — Ps 60:8;
shoe — 108:9
who will lead me into *E.* — Ps 60:9;
108:10
the tabernacles of *E.* are — Ps 83:6
confederate
remember, O Lord, the — Ps 137:7
children of *E.*
they shall lay their hand on — Isa 11:14
E.
who is this that cometh — Isa 63:1
from *E.*
Judah and *E.* I will punish — Jer 9:26;
25:21
send bonds and yokes to the — Jer 27:3
king of *E.*
concerning *E.* saith the Lord — Jer 49:7;
Ob 1
E. be a desolation, every — Jer 49:17
one astonished
the counsel he hath taken — Jer 49:20
against *E.*
because *E.* hath dealt — Eze 25:12
against Judah
and I will lay my vengeance — Eze 25:14
upon *E.*
there is *E.* her kings and all — Eze 32:29
her princes
E. shall escape out of his — Da 11:41
hand
E. shall be a desolate — Joe 3:19
wilderness
captivity to deliver them up — Am 1:6;
to *E.* — 1:9
he burnt the bones of the — Am 2:1
king of *E.*
that they may possess the — Am 9:12
remnant of *E.*
I will destroy the wise men — Ob 8
out of *E.*
whereas *E.* saith, We are — Mal 1:4
impoverished

EDOMITE

Thou shalt not abhor an *E.* — De 23:7
his name was Doeg, an *E.* — 1Sa 21:7;
22:9, 18, 22

EDOMITE

unto Solomon, Hadad the *E.* — *1Ki 11:14*
Doeg the *E.* came and told Saul — *Ps 52 title*

EDOMITES

Esau the father of the *E.* — *Ge 36:9;*
36:43
E. Zidonians, and Hittites — *1Ki 11:1*
Hadad fled, he and certain *E.* — *1Ki 11:17*
smote the *E.* which compassed him — *2Ki 8:21*
the son Zeruiah slew of the *E.* — *1Ch 18:12*
all the *E.* became David's servants — *1Ch 18:13*
In his days the *E.* revolted — *2Ch 21:8*
smote the *E.* which compassed him — *2Ch 21:9*
So the *E.* revolted from under the — *2Ch 21:10*
come from the slaughter of the *E.* — *2Ch 25:14*
sayest, Lo, thou hast smitten the *E.* — *2Ch 25:19*
E. had come and smitten Judah — *2Ch 28:17*

EDREI

all his people, to the battle at *E.* — *Nu 21:33*
which dwelt at Astaroth in *E.* — *De 1:4*
and all his people, to battle at *E.* — *De 3:1*
all Bashan, unto Salchah and *E.* — *De 3:10*
that dwelt at Ashtaroth and at *E.* — *Jos 12:4*
reigned in Ashtaroth and in *E.* — *Jos 13:12*
half Gilead, and Ashtaroth, and *E.* — *Jos 13:31*
And Kedesh, and *E.* and En-hazor — *Jos 19:37*

EDUCATE

e. a child according (B) — *Pr 22:6*

EFFECT

shall make her vow of none *e.* — *Nu 30:8*
make void and annul her vow (A) — *Nu 30:8*
by annulling her vow (B) — *Nu 30:8*
make void her vow (E)(R) — *Nu 30:8*
and they spake to her to that *e.* — *2Ch 34:22*
spoke to her as instructed (B) — *2Ch 34:22*
devices of the people of none *e.* — *Ps 33:10*
the *e.* of righteousness quietness — *Isa 32:17*
his lies shall not so *e.* it — *Jer 48:30*
hand, and the *e.* of every vision — *Eze 12:23*
commandment of God of none *e.* — *M't 15:6*
the word of God of none *e.* — *M'k 7:13*
make the faith of God without *e.* — *Ro 3:3*
and the promise made of none *e.* — *Ro 4:14*
word of God hath taken none *e.* — *Ro 9:6*
Christ should be made of none *e.* — *1Co 1:17*
make the promise of none *e.* — *Ga 3:17*
Christ is become of no *e.* unto — *Ga 5:4*

EFFECTED

own house, he prosperously *e.* — *2Ch 7:11*

EFFECTS

wisdom is justified by *e.* (B) — *M't 11:19*

EFFECTUAL

a great door and *e.* is opened — *1Co 16:9*

which is *e.* in the enduring of — *2Co 1:6*
by the *e.* working of his power — *Eph 3:7*
the *e.* working in the measure of — *Eph 4:16*
become *e.* by the acknowledging — *Ph'm 6*
e. fervent prayer of a righteous — *Jas 5:16*

EFFECTUALLY

(For he that wrought *e.* in Peter — *Ga 2:8*
which *e.* worketh also in you — *1Th 2:13*

EFFEMINATE

adulterers, nor *e.,* nor abusers of — *1Co 6:9*
who participate in homosexuality (A)(B) — *1Co 6:9*
guilty of homosexual perversion (N) — *1Co 6:9*
nor homosexuals (R) — *1Co 6:9*

EFFICIENT

man of God may be *e.* (N) — *2Ti 3:17*

EGG

any taste in the white of an *e.* — *Job 6:6*
Or if he shall ask an *e.* will he — *Lu 11:12*

EGGS

whether they be young ones, or *e.* — *De 22:6*
upon the young, or upon the *e.* — *De 22:6*
Which leaveth her *e.* in the earth — *Job 39:14*
as one gathereth *e.* that are left — *Isa 10:14*
They hatch cockatrice's *e.* and — *Isa 59:5*
he that eateth of their *e.* dieth — *Isa 59:5*
As the partridge sitteth on *e.* — *Jer 17:11*

EGLAH

Ithream, by *E.* David's wife — *2Sa 3:5*
the sixth, Ithream by *E.* his wife — *1Ch 3:3*

EGLAIM

the howling thereof unto *E.* — *Isa 15:8*

EGLATH-SHELISHIYAH

Eglath-shelishiyah (A)(E)(R)(S) — *Isa 15:5*

EGLON

king of *E.* — *Jos 10:3;*
10:5, 23, 34, 36-37; 12:12
Lachish, Bozkath, and *E.* — *Jos 15:39*
Lord strengthened *E.* the king — *J'g 3:12*
children of Israel served *E.* — *J'g 3:14*
Israel sent a present unto *E.* — *J'g 3:15*
brought the present unto *E.* — *J'g 3:17*
And *E.* was a very fat man — *J'g 3:17*

EGRESS

with every *e.* from the sanctuary (S) — *Eze 44:5*

EGRESSES

the *e.* (S) — *Eze 43:11; 48:30*

EGYPT

from the river of *E.* to Euphrates — *Ge 15:18*
God made me lord of all *E.* — *Ge 45:9*
I will smite *E.* — *Ex 3:20;*
Jer 9:26; 46:25
not hearken, that I may lay my hand on *E.* — *Ex 7:4*
Aaron's stretched his hand over waters of *E.* — *Ex 8:6*
sever between the cattle of Israel and of *E.* — *Ex 9:4*

knowest thou not that *E.* is destroyed — *Ex 10:7*
for in it thou camest out of *E.* — *Ex 23:15;*
34:18
thou hast forgiven this people from *E.* — *Nu 14:19*
behold, there is a people come out of *E.* — *Nu 22:5*
the Lord shewed great signs upon *E.* — *De 6:22*
will put none of the diseases of *E.* on thee — *De 7:15*
and what he did unto the army of *E.* — *De 11:4*
Lord will smite thee with the botch of *E.* — *De 28:27*
he will bring on thee all diseases of *E.* — *De 28:60*
I have rolled away the reproach of *E.* — *Jos 5:9*
I sent Moses and Aaron, and I plagued *E.* — *Jos 24:5*
he said, I am a young man of *E.* — *1Sa 30:13*
Solomon's wisdom excelled wisdom of *E.* — *1Ki 4:30*
thou trustest on *E.* — *2Ki 18:21;*
18:24; Isa 36:6, 9
E. was glad when they departed — *Ps 105:38*
who smote firstborn of *E.* of man — *Ps 135:8*
who sent wonders into midst of thee, O *E.* — *Ps 135:9*
to him that smote *E.* in their firstborn — *Ps 136:10*
decked my bed with fine linen of *E.* — *Pr 7:16*
after the manner of *E.* — *Isa 10:24;*
Am 4:10
to recover the remnant of people from *E.* — *Isa 11:11*
burden of *E.* the idols of *E.* shall be moved — *Isa 19:1*
the spirit of *E.* shall fail in midst thereof — *Isa 19:3*
in that day shall *E.* be like unto women — *Isa 19:16*
in that day shall Israel be the third with *E.* — *Isa 19:24*
bless, saying, Blessed be ye *E.* my people — *Isa 19:25*
they shall be ashamed of *E.* their glory — *Isa 20:5*
as at the report concerning *E.* so of Tyre — *Isa 23:5*
Lord shall beat off from the stream of *E.* — *Isa 27:12*
they trust in shadow of *E.* your confusion — *Isa 30:3*
I gave *E.* for thy ransom, Seba for thee — *Isa 43:3*
the labour of *E.* shall come over to thee — *Isa 45:14*
what hast thou to do in the way of *E.* — *Jer 2:18*
thou shalt be ashamed of *E.* as of Assyria — *Jer 2:36*
word of the Lord which came against *E.* — *Jer 46:2*
E. is like a fair heifer, but destruction comes — *Jer 46:20*
defile not yourselves with the idols of *E.* — *Eze 20:7*
nor left she her idols brought from *E.* — *Eze 23:8*
thou shalt not remember *E.* any more — *Eze 23:27*
fine linen with broidered work from *E.* — *Eze 27:7*
prophesy against him and against all *E.* — *Eze 29:2*
I will bring again the captivity of *E.* — *Eze 29:14*
they also that uphold *E.* shall fall — *Eze 30:6*
pain come on them, as in day of *E.* — *Eze 30:9*
pour my fury on Sin the strength of *E.* — *Eze 30:15*
they shall spoil the pomp of *E.* and all — *Eze 32:12*
they shall lament for her, even for *E.* — *Eze 32:16*
son of man, wail for the multitude of *E.* — *Eze 32:18*
have power over precious things of *E.* — *Da 11:43*
they are gone, *E.* shall gather them up — *Ho 9:6*

E. shall be a desolation, and *Joe 3:19*
be drowned, as by the flood *Am 8:8;*
of *E.*   *9:5*
Ethiopia and *E.* were her *Na 3:9*
strength
the sceptre of *E.* shall *Zec 10:11*
depart away
if family of *E.* go not up *Zec 14:18*
and come not
he made him governor over *Ac 7:10*
E. and his
by faith he forsook *E.* not *Heb 11:27*
fearing
which spiritually is called *Re 11:8*
Sodom and *E.*

IN EGYPT

tell my father of all my *Ge 45:13*
glory *in E.*
Jacob said, Bury me not, I *Ge 47:29*
pray thee, *in E.*
I have seen affliction of my *Ex 3:7*
people *in E.*
I have seen that which is *Ex 3:16*
done to you *in E.*
grievous hail, such as hath *Ex 9:18*
not been *in E.*
what things I wrought *in E.* *Ex 10:2;*
          Jos 24:7
great cry *in E.;* no graves *Ex 12:30;*
in E.   *14:11*
for it was well with us *in E.* *Nu 11:18*
and we have dwelt *in E.* a *Nu 20:15*
long time
all that he did for you *in E.* *De 1:30;*
          4:34
we have heard all that he did *Jos 9:9*
in E.
how he had wrought his *Ps 78:43*
signs *in E.*
he smote all the firstborn in *Ps 78:51*
E.
they understood not thy *Ps 106:7*
wonders *in E.*
forgat God, who had done *Ps 106:21*
great things *in E.*
famine shall follow close *Jer 42:16*
after you *in E.*
declare ye *in E.* and publish *Jer 46:14*
it in Migdol
they committed whoredoms *Eze 23:3*
in E.
shall know, when I have set *Eze 30:8*
a fire *in E.*   *30:16*
thus will I execute *Eze 30:19*
judgments *in E.*
an angel appeared to Joseph *M't 2:19*
in E.
the dwellers *in E.* we do hear *Ac 2:10*
them speak
greater riches than the *Heb 11:26*
treasures *in E.*

INTO EGYPT

all countries came *into E.* to *Ge 41:57*
buy corn
I will go down with thee *into* *Ge 46:4*
E.
all the souls that came with *Ge 46:26*
Jacob *into E.*
better for us to return *into* *Nu 14:3;*
E.   *14:4*
behold, the Lord shall come *Isa 19:1*
into E.
walk to go down *into E.* to *Isa 30:2*
strengthen
Urijah afraid, fled and went *Jer 26:21*
into E.
if ye set your faces to go *Jer 41:17;*
into E.   *42:15*
Lord said, Go ye not *into E.* *Jer 42:19;*
          43:2
sending his ambassadors *Eze 17:15*
into E.
he shall also carry captives *Da 11:8*
into E.
with Assyrians, and oil is *Ho 12:1*
carried *into E.*
flee *into E.;* he departed *M't 2:13;*
into E.   *2:14*
the patriarchs sold Joseph *into* *Ac 7:9*
E.
and now come, I will send *Ac 7:34*
thee *into E.*
in their hearts turned back *Ac 7:39*
again *into E.*

LAND OF EGYPT

Sodom was like the *land of* *Ge 13:10*
E.
Ishmael's wife out of the *Ge 21:21*
land of E.
such as I never saw in all *Ge 41:19*
the *land of E.*
seven years plenty, thro' all *Ge 41:29;*
land of E.   *41:30, 53*
set thee over all the *land of* *Ge 41:41;*
E.   *45:8, 26*
but in all the *land of E.* was *Ge 41:54*
bread
I will give you the good of *Ge 45:18;*
the *land of E.*   *45:20*
the *land of E.* is before thee, *Ge 47:6*
in best of land
when money failed in the *Ge 47:15*
land of E.
Joseph bought all the *land* *Ge 47:20*
of *E.* for Pharaoh
Joseph made it a law over *Ge 47:26*
the *land of E.*
all the elders of the *land of* *Ge 50:7*
E. went up
that there may be blood in all *Ex 7:19*
land of E.
frogs blains, hail, locusts in *Ex 8:6;*
land of E. *8:16, 24; 9:9, 22; 10:14*
may be darkness over all the *Ex 10:21*
land of E.
Moses was very great in the *Ex 11:3*
land of E.
Lord smote firstborn in *Ex 12:29;*
land of E.   *13:15*
would God we had died in *Ex 16:3;*
land of E.   *Nu 14:2*
brought you out of *land of E.* *Ex 16:6;*
        20:2; 29:46
were strangers in the *land* *Ex 22:21;*
of E. *23:9; Le 19:34; Ac 13:17*
these be thy gods which *Ex 32:4;*
brought thee out of *1Ki 12:28; Ne 9:18*
land of E.
after doings of *land of E.* *Le 18:3*
shall ye not do
God, who brought you out *Le 19:36;*
of *land of E.* *26:13; Nu 15:41; De 5:6;*
 13:5, 10; 20:1; J'g 2:12; 1Sa 12:6
from day thou didst depart *De 9:7;*
out of *land of E.* *J'g 19:30; Isa 11:16;*
 Jer 7:22; 11:7; 34:13; Mic 7:15
land whither thou goest is *De 11:10*
not *land of E.*
camest out of *land of E.* in *De 16:3*
haste
marvellous things did he in *Ps 78:12*
the *land of E.*
when he went out through the *Ps 81:5*
land of E.
in *land of E.* speak language *Isa 19:18*
of Canaan
altar to Lord for a witness *Isa 19:19;*
land of E.   *19:20*
outcasts in the *land of E.* *Isa 27:13*
shall come
go into the *land of E.* *Jer 42:14*
sword shall overtake you in *Jer 42:16*
land of E.
so they came into the *land of* *Jer 43:7*
E.
he shall array himself with *Jer 43:12*
the *land of E.*
shall return out of *land of* *Jer 44:28*
E. into Judah
myself known to them in *Eze 20:5*
land of E.
played the harlot in the *Eze 23:19*
land of E.
whoredom brought from *Eze 23:27*
land of E.
land of E. desolate, utterly *Eze 29:9;*
waste   *29:10*
given him *land of E.* for his *Eze 29:20*
labour
be no more a prince of *Eze 30:13*
land of E.
the *land of E.* shall not *Da 11:42*
escape
this be their derision in *land* *Ho 7:16*
of *E.*
Lord God from *land of E.* *Ho 12:9;*
         13:4
bring them out of *land of* *Zec 10:10*
E.
to lead them out of *land of* *Heb 8:9*
E.
saved people out of *land of E.* *Jude 5*

OUT OF EGYPT

Abraham *out of E.* *Ge 13:1; 47:30*
that I should bring Israel *out* *Ex 3:11*
of *E.*
because they were thrust *out* *Ex 12:39*
of *E.*
Lord brought thee *out of E.* *Ex 13:9;*
          13:16
saying, Why came we forth *Nu 11:20*
out of E.
behold there is a people *Nu 22:11*
come *out of E.*
none of men that came *out* *Nu 32:11*
of *E.*
at season camest forth *out of* *De 16:6*
E.
dried up Red sea, when *Jos 2:10*
came *out of E.*
till all that came *out of E.* *Jos 5:6*
were consumed
I made you go *out of E.* *J'g 2:1;*
      1Sa 10:18
shewed kindness when Israel *1Sa 15:6*
came *out of E.*
whom thou hast redeemed *1Ch 17:21*
out of *E.*
people that came with him *2Ch 12:3*
out of E.
princes shall come *out of E.* *Ps 68:31*
thou hast brought a vine *out* *Ps 80:8*
of *E.*
when Israel went *out of E.* *Ps 114:1*
house of Jacob
there shall be a highway *Isa 19:23*
out of E.
they set forth Urijah *out of* *Jer 26:23*
E.
Pharaoh's army was come *Jer 37:5*
out of E.
I called my son *out of E.* *Ho 11:1;*
        M't 2:15
they shall tremble as a bird *Ho 11:11*
out of E.
by prophet Lord brought *Ho 12:13*
Israel *out of E.*
I covenanted, when ye came *Hag 2:5*
out of E.
howbeit not all that came *Heb 3:16*
out of E.

TO EGYPT

Hadad and the Edomites *1Ki 11:18*
came *to E.*
Jehoahaz came *to E.* *2Ki 23:34;*
      2Ch 36:4
land of Judah be a terror *to* *Isa 19:17*
E.
the Lord shall be known *to* *Isa 19:21*
E.
woe to them that go down *to* *Isa 31:1*
E. for help
they call *to E.* they go to *Ho 7:11*
Assyria

EGYPTIAN

Sarai had an handmaid an *Ge 16:1;*
E.   *16:3; 21:9*
an *E.* bought Joseph of the *Ge 39:1*
Ishmaelites
Hebrews are not as the *E.* *Ex 1:19*
women
Moses spied an *E.* smiting an *Ex 2:11*
Hebrew
he slew the *E.* and hid him *Ex 2:12;*
        Ac 7:24
an *E.* delivered us from *Ex 2:19*
shepherds
whose father was an *E.* went *Le 24:10*
out
thou shalt not abhor an *E.* *De 23:7*
they found an *E.* in the *1Sa 30:11*
field
Sheshan had a servant an *E.* *1Ch 2:34*
Jarha
Lord shall destroy tongue of *Isa 11:15*
E. sea
the *E.* shall come into *Isa 19:23*
Assyria
art not thou that *E.* who *Ac 21:38*
made uproar

EGYPTIANS

Pharaoh said to *E.,* Go to *Ge 41:55*
Joseph
that is abomination to the *Ge 43:32;*
E.   *46:34*

E. mourned for Jacob   *Ge 50:39*
seventy days
ye shall spoil the E.   *Ex 3:22; 12:36*
shall we sacrifice abomination *Ex 8:26*
of E.
Lord put difference between *Ex 11:7*
E. and Israel
they borrowed of the E.   *Ex 12:35*
jewels of gold
but the E. pursued after   *Ex 14:9;*
them   *14:10*
E. whom ye have seen see *Ex 14:13*
no more
E. said, Lord fighteth for *Ex 14:25*
them against E.
Lord overthrew E. in midst *Ex 14:27*
of sea
ye have seen what I did to E. *Ex 19:4*
wherefore should the E.   *Ex 32:12*
speak and say
Moses said, E. shall hear it *Nu 14:13*
E. vexed us and our fathers *Nu 20:15*
E. evil entreated and afflicted *De 26:6*
us
he put darkness between you *Jos 24:7*
and E.
did not I deliver you from *J'g 10:11*
E.
these are the gods that smote *1Sa 4:8*
E.
why do you harden hearts, as *1Sa 6:6*
E. did
according to abominations of *Ezr 9:1*
the E.
I will set the E. against the *Isa 19:2*
E.
E. will I give into hand of a *Isa 19:4*
cruel lord
the E. shall know the Lord in *Isa 19:21*
that day
the E. shall serve with the *Isa 19:23*
Assyrians
king of Assyria shall lead E. *Isa 20:4*
prisoners
E. shall help in vain and to *Isa 30:7*
no purpose
now E. are men and not   *Isa 31:3*
God, their horses
houses of gods of E. shall *Jer 43:13*
he burn
we have given the hand to the *La 5:6*
E.
hast committed fornication *Eze 16:26*
with E.
in bruising thy teats by E. *Eze 23:21*
for paps
I will scatter the E.   *Eze 29:12;*
    30:23, 26
I will gather the E. from *Eze 29:13*
the people
Moses was learned in wisdom *Ac 7:22*
of E.
which E. assaying to do, *Heb 11:29*
were drowned

EGYPTIAN'S

Lord blessed the E. house   *Ge 39:5*
plucked the spear out of the *2Sa 23:21*
E.
E. hand was a spear like a *1Ch 11:23*
out of the E. hand and *1Ch 11:23*
slew him

EHI

Gera, Naaman, E.   *Ge 46:21*

EHUD

raised up E. son of Gera a *J'g 3:15*
Benjamite
E. made him a dagger *J'g 3:16; 3:23*
E. escaped while they tarried *J'g 3:26*
and passed
Israel again did evil, when E. *J'g 4:1*
was dead
sons of Bilham, E.   *1Ch 7:10*
the sons of E.   *1Ch 8:6*

EIGHT

he that is e. days old shall *Ge 17:12;*
be circumcised   *21:4; Lu 2:21*
these e. Milcah did bear to *Ge 22:23*
Nahor
they shall be e. boards, and *Ex 26:25*
sockets silver
Moses gave 4 wagons, e.   *Nu 7:8*
oxen to Merari

on sixth day e. bullocks, *Nu 29:29*
two rams
Israel served   *J'g 3:8*
Chushan-rishathaim e. years
Abdon, son of Hillel, judged *J'g 12:14*
Israel e. years
Jesse the Ephrathite had e. *1Sa 17:12*
sons
foundation was of stones of *1Ki 7:10*
e. cubits
Jehoram reigned e. years in *2Ki 8:17*
Jerusalem
Josiah e. years old when   *2Ki 22:1;*
began to reign   *2Ch 34:1*
e. among the sons of Ithamar *1Ch 24:4*
they sanctified house of Lord *2Ch 29:17*
in e. days
give portion to seven, and   *Ec 11:2*
also to e.
but Ishmael escaped with e. *Jer 41:15*
men
going up had e. steps   *Eze 40:31;*
    40:34, 37
e. tables, whereon they slew *Eze 40:41*
their sacrifices
raise against him 7 shepherds, *Mic 5:5*
e. principal men
about e. days after these *Lu 9:28*
sayings, Peter
after e. days his disciples *Joh 20:26*
were within
Aeneas, who had kept his bed *Ac 9:33*
e. years
wherein e. souls were saved *1Pe 3:20*
by water

EIGHT *HUNDRED*

Adam lived after he begat   *Ge 5:4*
Seth e. *hundred* years
Jared lived after he begat *Ge 5:19*
Enoch e. *hundred* years
Adino slew e. *hundred* at *2Sa 23:8*
one time
Jeroboam set in array e. *2Ch 13:3*
hundred thousand

EIGHTEEN

Israel served Eglon king of *J'g 3:14*
Moab e. years
Ammon vexed and oppressed *J'g 10:8*
Israel e. years
for he cast two pillars of   *1Ki 7:15;*
brass e. cubits high apiece *2Ki 25:17;*
    Jer 52:21
Meshelemiah had sons and *1Ch 26:9*
brethren e.
for Rehoboam took e. *2Ch 11:21*
wives
those e. on whom tower in *Lu 13:4*
Siloam fell
Satan hath bound, lo, these *Lu 13:16*
e. years

EIGHTEEN *THOUSAND*

Benjamin destroyed of Israel *J'g 20:25*
e. *thousand*
there fell of Benjamin *J'g 20:44*
e. *thousand* men
of half tribe of Manasseh, *1Ch 12:31*
e. *thousand*
Abishai slew of Edomites *1Ch 18:12*
e. *thousand*
princes gave of brass e. *1Ch 29:7*
thousand talents
city round was e. *thousand* *Eze 48:35*
measures

EIGHTEENTH

in e. year of Jeroboam   *1Ki 15:1;*
    2Ch 13:1
Jehoram reigned the e. year *2Ki 3:1*
of Jehoshaphat
in e. year of king   *2Ki 22:3;*
Josiah, king sent *23:23; 2Ch 34:8; 35:19*
the e. lot came forth to *1Ch 24:15*
Aphses
e. to Hanani, he, his sons *1Ch 25:25*
was e. year of   *Jer 32:1;*
Nebuchadnezzar   *52:29*

EIGHTH

ye shall sow the e. year and *Le 25:22*
eat

in Bul, which is e. month, *1Ki 6:38*
house finished
Jeroboam ordained a feast *1Ki 12:32*
in e. month
the e. lot came forth to *1Ch 24:10*
Abijah
e. to Jeshaiah; Peulthaia *1Ch 25:15;*
the e.   *26:5*
e. captain for e. month, *1Ch 27:11*
Sibbecai
in e. month word came to *Zec 1:1*
Zechariah
but saved Noah the e. person *2Pe 2:5*
beast that was, is not, even *Re 17:11*
he is the e.
e. foundation was a beryl *Re 21:20*

EIGHTIETH

in the four hundred and e. year *1Ki 6:1*

EIGHTY

an hundred and e. and seven *Ge 5:25*
years
seven hundred e. and two *Ge 5:26*
years
an hundred e. and two years *Ge 5:28*

EITHER

speak not to Jacob e. good *Ge 31:24;*
or bad   *31:29*
Nadab and Abihu took e. of *Le 10:1*
them his censer
hath worship, other gods, e. *De 17:3*
sun or moon
nation shall not leave thee e. *De 28:51*
corn or wine
e. he is talking, or   *1Ki 18:27*
pursuing, or in
whether shall prosper, e. this *Ec 11:6*
or that
ask a sign e. in depth or *Isa 7:11*
height above
masters, for e. he will hate *M't 6:24;*
one   *Lu 16:13*
e. make the tree good, and *M't 12:33*
his fruit good
e. how canst thou say to thy *Lu 6:42*
brother
e. what woman having ten *Lu 15:8*
pieces of silver
crucified, on e. side one, *Joh 19:18*
Jesus in midst
except I speak to you e. by *1Co 14:6*
revelation
e. can a vine, my brethren, *Jas 3:12*
bear figs
of e. side river there was tree *Re 22:2*
of life

EJECTS

e. from the stomach (B) *Job 20:15*

EKER

Maaz, and Jamin, and E. *1Ch 2:27*

EKRON

Egypt, even unto the borders *Jos 13:3*
of E.
unto the side of E.   *Jos 15:11*
northward
E. with her towns and her *Jos 15:45*
villages
From E. even unto the sea *Jos 15:46*
Elon, and Thimnathah, and *Jos 19:43*
E.
with the coast thereof, and E. *J'g 1:18*
they sent the ark of God to *1Sa 5:10*
E.
pass, as the ark of God *1Sa 5:10*
came to E.
had seen it, they returned to *1Sa 6:16*
E.
one, for Gath one, for E. *1Sa 6:17*
one
to Israel, from E. even unto *1Sa 7:14*
Gath
the valley, and to the gates *1Sa 17:52*
of E.
even unto Gath, and unto *1Sa 17:52*
E.
enquire of Baal-zebub the god *2Ki 1:2*
of E.

of Baal-zebub the god of *E.* 2Ki 1:3; 1:6
enquire of Baal-zebub the 2Ki 1:16
god of *E.*
and *E.* and the remnant of Jer 25:20
Ashdod
I will turn mine hand against Am 1:8
E.
and *E.* shall be rooted up Zep 2:4
and *E.;* for her expectation Zec 9:5
shall
in Judah, and *E.* as a Jebusite Zec 9:7

EKRONITES

the Gittites, and the *E.;* also Jos 13:3
that the *E.* cried out, saying, 1Sa 5:10
They

EL

E., the God of Israel (B) Ge 33:20

ELABORATE

with *e.* coiffure (P) 1Pe 3:3

ELADAH

E. his son, and Tahath his 1Ch 7:20
son

ELAH

Duke Aholibamah, duke *E.* Ge 36:41;
1Ch 1:52
and pitched by the valley of 1Sa 17:2
E.
were in the valley of *E.* 1Sa 17:19
fighting
thou slewest in the valley of 1Sa 21:9
E.
Shimei the son of *E.* in 1Ki 4:18
Benjamin
E. his son reigned in his stead 1Ki 16:6
E. the son of Baasha to 1Ki 16:8
reign
sins of Baasha, and the sins 1Ki 16:13
of *E.*
the rest of the acts of *E.* 1Ki 16:14
the son of *E.* made a 2Ki 15:30
conspiracy
began Hoshea the son of 2Ki 17:1
to reign
the third year of Hoshea son 2Ki 18:1
of *E.*
seventh year of Hoshea son 2Ki 18:9
of *E.*
Jephunneh; Iru, *E.* and 1Ch 4:15
Naam
and the sons of *E.* even 1Ch 4:15
Kenaz
the son of Jeroham, and *E.* 1Ch 9:8

ELAM

children of Shem; *E.* and Ge 10:22
Ashur
Chedorlaomer king of *E.* and Ge 14:1
With Chedorlaomer the king Ge 14:9
of *E.*
The sons of Shem; *E.* and 1Ch 1:17
Asshur
Hananiah, and *E.* and 1Ch 8:24
Antothijah
E. the fifth, Jehohanan the 1Ch 26:3
sixth
The children of *E.* a thousand Ezr 2:7
two
The children of the other *E.* Ezr 2:31
And of the sons of *E.;* Ezr 8:7
Jeshaiah
son of Jehiel, one of the Ezr 10:2
sons of *E.*
sons of *E.;* Mattaniah, Ezr 10:26
Zechariah
children of *E.* a thousand two Ne 7:12
The children of the other *E.* Ne 7:34
people; Parosh, Ne 10:14
Pahath-moab, *E.*
and Malchijah and *E.* and Ne 12:42
Ezer
and from Cush, and from *E.* Isa 11:11
Go up, O *E.:* besiege, O Isa 21:2
Media
E. bare the quiver with Isa 22:6
chariots
and all the kings of *E.* and Jer 25:25
Jeremiah the prophet Jer 49:34;
against *E.* 49:35-39

is *E.* and all her multitude Eze 32:24
round
which is in the province of *E.* Da 8:2

ELAMITES

the Dehavites, and the *E.* Ezr 4:9
Parthians, and Medes, and *E.* Ac 2:9

ELASAH

Nethaneel, Jozabad, *E.* Ezr 10:22
hand of *E.* the son of Jer 29:3
Shaphan

ELATED

unduly *e.* (N) 2Co 12:7

ELATH

the way of the plain from *E.* De 2:8
built *E.* and restored it to 2Ki 14:22
Judah
king of Syria recovered *E.* to 2Ki 16:6
Syria

EL-BETH-EL

an altar, and called the place Ge 35:7
E.

ELDAAH

and Hanoch, and Abida, Ge 25:4
and *E.*
and Henoch, and Abida, and 1Ch 1:33
E.

ELDAD

the name of the one was *E.* Nu 11:26
E. and Medad do prophesy Nu 11:27
in the

ELDER

the brother of Japheth the *e.* Ge 10:21
Japheth and the ancestor of Ge 10:21
Eber (A)
and the *e.* shall serve the Ge 25:23
younger
the older shall serve (R) Ge 25:23;
1Sa 18:17; 1Ki 2:22
these words of Esau her *e.* Ge 27:42
son
the name of the *e.* was Leah Ge 29:16
Behold my *e.* daughter 1Sa 18:17
Merah
for he is mine *e.* brother 1Ki 2:22
men, much *e.* than thy Job 15:10
father
the older (A)(B)(R) Job 15:10; 32:4
because they were *e.* than he Job 32:4
thine *e.* sister is Samaria, Eze 16:46
she and
sisters, thine *e.* and thy Eze 16:61
younger
names of them were Aholah Eze 23:4
the *e.*
Now his *e.* son was in the Lu 15:25
field
the older (A)(B) Lu 15:25; 1Ti 5:2
The *e.* shall serve the Ro 9:12
younger
Rebuke not an *e.* but entreat 1Ti 5:1
him
e. woman as mothers; the 1Ti 5:2
younger
an *e.* receive not an 1Ti 5:19
accusation
I exhort, who am also an *e.* 1Pe 5:1
submit yourselves unto the *e.* 1Pe 5:5
The *e.* unto the elect lady and 2Jo 1
The *e.* unto the well beloved 3Jo 1
Gaius

ELDERS

e. of his house went up with Ge 50:7
him
senators (B) Ge 50:7
e. of congregation shall lay Le 4:15
their hands
Lord gave of the Spirit to Nu 11:25
seventy *e.*
go up to the gate to the *e.* De 25:7
and say
ye stand before Lord your *e.* De 29:10
and officers

gather to me all *e.* of your De 31:28
tribes and officers
ask thy father and *e.* and De 32:7
they will tell thee
of *e.* that overlived Joshua Jos 24:31;
J'g 2:7
he described to him the *e.* of J'g 8:14
Succoth
e. of the town trembled at 1Sa 16:4
his coming
he sent of the spoil to the 1Sa 30:26
e. of Judah
the *e.* of Judah (B) 1Sa 30:26
all the *e.* said to him, 1Ki 20:8
Hearken not
the *e.* did as Jezebel had 1Ki 21:11
sent to them
Elisha sat in house, and *e.* 2Ki 6:32
sat with him
Jehu wrote letters and sent 2Ki 10:1
to *e.* of Jezreel
Hezekiah sent *e.* of priests 2Ki 19:2;
Isa 37:2
the eye of their God was Ezr 5:5
upon the *e.*
e. of Jews builded and Ezr 6:14
prospered
according to counsel of Ezr 10:8
princes and *e.*
teach *e.* wisdom Ps 105:22
(A)(B)(E)(R)(S)
praise him in the assembly Ps 107:32
of *e.*
her husband is known among Pr 31:23
the *e.*
my priests and *e.* gave up La 1:19
ghost
e. of Zion sit upon ground La 2:10
and keep silence
respected not priests, La 4:16;
favoured not *e.* 5:12
e. have ceased from gate, La 5:14
young men from music
the *e.* of Judah sat before me Eze 8:1
sanctify a fast, gather the *e.* Joe 1:14;
2:16
why transgress the tradition M't 15:2
of the *e.*
must suffer many things of M't 16:21;
e. 27:12
e. sought false witness M't 26:59
against Jesus
chief priests and *e.* M't 27:20
persuaded multitude
chief priests mocking with M't 27:41
e. said
when they were assembled M't 28:12
with *e.*
Jews holding the tradition of M'k 7:3
e.
must suffer and be rejected M'k 8:31;
of *e.* Lu 9:22
with Judas a great M'k 14:43
multitude from *e.*
chief priests held a M't 15:1
consultation with *e.*
Jesus said unto the captains Lu 22:52
and *e.*
their rulers and *e.* were Ac 4:5
gathered together
they reported all that *e.* had Ac 4:23
said
they stirred up the people Ac 6:12
and the *e.*
sent it to the *e.* by Barnabas Ac 11:30
and Saul
when they ordained *e.* in Ac 14:23
every church
they were received of church Ac 15:4
and of *e.*
apostles and *e.* came together Ac 15:6
to consider
apostles, *e.* and brethren, Ac 15:23
send greeting
they delivered decrees Ac 16:4
ordained of *e.*
he sent and called the *e.* of Ac 20:17
the church
all the estate of the *e.* bear Ac 22:5
me witness
Ananias the priest descended Ac 24:1
with the *e.*
about whom *e.* of Jews Ac 25:15
informed me
e. laid hands on you 1Ti 4:14
(A)(N)(P)(R)
let *e.* that rule well be 1Ti 5:17
counted worthy
thou shouldest ordain *e.* in Tit 1:5
every city

by faith the *e.* obtained a   *Heb 11:2*
good report
let him call for the *e.* of the   *Jas 5:14*
church
the *e.* which are among you,   *1Pe 5:1*
I exhort
upon seats I saw 24 *e.* sitting   *Re 4:4*
the 24 *e.* fall before him   *Re 4:10;*
                        5:8, 14; 11:16; 19:4
and one of the *e.* saith unto   *Re 5:5*
me, Weep not
and lo, in the midst of the *e.*   *Re 5:6*
stood a Lamb
I heard the voice of many   *Re 5:11*
angels about *e.*
all angels stood about *e.* and   *Re 7:11*
four beasts
one of *e.* answered saying to   *Re 7:13*
me, What are these
they sung a new song before   *Re 14:3*
throne and *e.*

ELDERS *OF CITY*

e. of his *city* shall fetch him   *De 19:12*
thence
e. of that *city* shall take and   *De 21:3*
bring heifer
e. of that *city* shall wash   *De 21:6*
hands over heifer
shall bring their son to the   *De 21:19*
e. of his *city*
bring tokens of virginity to   *De 22:15*
e. of *city*
e. of his *city* call and speak   *De 25:8*
to him
shall declare his cause to *e.*   *Jos 20:4*
of that *city*
he took the *e.* of the *city* and   *J'g 8:16*
thorns
Boaz took ten men of the *e.*   *Ru 4:2*
of the *city*
and with them the *e.* of   *Ezr 10:14*
every *city*

ELDERS *OF ISRAEL*

go and gather *e.* of *Israel*   *Ex 3:16*
together
Moses called for all the *e.* of   *Ex 12:21*
Israel
take with thee of the *e.* of   *Ex 17:5*
Israel
e. of *Israel* came to eat with   *Ex 18:12*
Jethro
seventy of *e.* of *Israel*   *Ex 24:1;*
                        24:9; Nu 11:16
e. of *Israel* commanded   *De 27:1*
people
Moses delivered this law to *e.*   *De 31:9*
of *Israel*
e. of *Israel* put dust on their   *Jos 7:6*
heads
so all *e.* of *Israel* came to   *2Sa 5:3;*
king at Hebron   *1Ki 8:3; 2Ch 5:4*
saying pleased all the *e.* of   *2Sa 17:4*
Israel
thus did Ahithophel counsel   *2Sa 17:15*
e. of *Israel*
e. of *Israel* came to king to   *1Ch 11:3*
Hebron
David and *e.* of *Israel* fell   *1Ch 21:16*
upon faces
then came the *e.* of *Israel*   *Eze 14:1*
unto me
e. of *Israel* came to inquire   *Eze 20:1*
of Lord
ye rulers of people, and *e.* of   *Ac 4:8*
Israel

ELDERS *with PEOPLE*

Moses called for *e.* of   *Ex 19:7*
people
whom knowest to be *e.* of   *Nu 11:16*
people
Moses gathered 70 men of   *Nu 11:24*
the *e.* of *people*
buy it before the *e.* of my   *Ru 4:4*
people
honour me before *e.* of my   *1Sa 15:30*
people
e. of the *people* came   *M't 21:23;*
                        Lu 22:66
with a multitude from *e.* of   *M't 26:47*
people
e. of *people* took counsel   *M't 27:1*
against Jesus

they stirred up the *people*   *Ac 6:12*
and *e.*

ELDEST

Abraham said to his *e.*   *Ge 24:2*
servant
oldest (B)   *Ge 24:2;*
        44:12; 1Sa 17:28; 2Ch 22:1
Isaac called Esau his *e.* son,   *Ge 27:1*
and said
he searched, and began at   *Ge 44:12*
the *e.*
Reuben, Israel's *e.* son   *Nu 1:20; 26:5*
the three *e.* sons of Jesse   *1Sa 17:13;*
followed   *17:14*
Eliab his *e.* brother heard   *1Sa 17:28*
he took his *e.* son and   *2Ki 3:27*
offered him
for band of men had slain   *2Ch 22:1*
all *e.*
drinking in their *e.* brother's   *Job 1:13;*
house   *1:18*
went out one by one,   *Joh 8:9*
beginning at *e.*

ELEAD

and Ezer, and *E.* whom the   *1Ch 7:21*
men

ELEALEH

Heshbon, and *E.* and Shebam   *Nu 32:3*
of Reuben built Heshbon,   *Nu 32:37*
and *E.*
And Heshbon shall cry, and   *Isa 15:4*
E.
with my tears, O Heshbon,   *Isa 16:9*
and *E.*
the cry of Heshbon even   *Jer 48:34*
unto *E.*

ELEASAH

begat Helez, and Helez   *1Ch 2:39*
begat *E.*
E. begat Sisamai, and   *1Ch 2:40*
Rapha was his son, *E.* his   *1Ch 8:37*
son
Rephaiah his son, *E.* his son   *1Ch 9:43*

ELEAZAR

Aaron's son *E.*   *Ex 6:25;*
28:1; Nu 3:2; 26:60; 1Ch 6:3; 24:1;
                        Ezr 8:33
Moses was angry with *E.* and   *Le 10:16*
Ithamar
E. ministered in the priest's   *Nu 3:4*
office
E. son of Aaron shall be   *Nu 3:32*
chief over the Levites
to the office of *E.* pertaineth   *Nu 4:16*
the oil
E. the priest took the brasen   *Nu 16:39*
censers
and put his garments upon   *Nu 20:26*
E. his son
Moses and *E.* came down   *Nu 20:28*
from the mount
that were numbered by   *Nu 26:63*
Moses and *E.*
he set Joshua before *E.* the   *Nu 27:22*
priest
they brought the spoil to   *Nu 31:12*
Moses and *E.*
take the sum of prey thou   *Nu 31:26*
and *E.* the priest
and Moses gave tribute unto   *Nu 31:41*
E.
E. and Joshua shall divide   *Nu 34:17*
the land
came near before *E.*   *Jos 17:4*
E. son of Aaron died   *Jos 24:33*
they sanctified *E.* to keep the   *1Sa 7:1*
ark
after him *E.* son of Dodo   *2Sa 23:9;*
                        1Ch 11:12
the son of *E.* was ruler over   *1Ch 9:20*
them
the sons of Mahli, *E.* and   *1Ch 23:21;*
Kish   *24:28*
E. died, and had no sons,   *1Ch 23:22*
but daughters
more chief men of sons of   *1Ch 24:4*
E. than Ithamar
the governors were of the   *1Ch 24:5*
sons of *E.*

Shemaiah and *E.* were   *Ne 12:42*
priests
Eliud begat *E.* and *E.* begat   *M't 1:15*
Matthan

ELECT

e. in whom my soul   *Isa 42:1*
delighteth
sake, and Israel mine *e.*   *Isa 45:4*
chosen (A)(B)(E)(R)   *Isa 45:4*
mine *e.* shall inherit it, and   *Isa 65:9*
mine *e.* shall long enjoy the   *Isa 65:22*
work
they shall deceive the very   *M't 24:24*
e.
and shall gather together   *M't 24:31*
his *e.*
chosen (B)(N)(P)   *M't 24:31;*
                Lu 18:7; Ro 8:33
if it were possible, even the   *M'k 13:22*
e.
and shall gather together   *M'k 13:27*
his *e.*
shall not God avenge his own   *Lu 18:7*
e.
anything to the charge of   *Ro 8:33*
God's *e.*
Put on therefore, as the *e.* of   *Col 3:12*
God
chosen ones (A)(B)(N)(R)   *Col 3:12;*
                1Pe 1:2; 2:6
picked representatives (P)   *Col 3:12*
Lord Jesus Christ, and the *e.*   *1Ti 5:21*
angels
according to the faith of   *Tit 1:1*
God's *e.*
E. according to the   *1Pe 1:2*
foreknowledge
a chief corner stone, *e.*,   *1Pe 2:6*
precious
The elder unto the *e.* lady and   *2Jo 1*
The children of thy *e.* sister   *2Jo 13*
greet

ELECTED

e. together with you, saluteth   *1Pe 5:13*
you

ELECTION

the purpose of God according   *Ro 9:11*
to *e.*
selection (A)   *Ro 9:11;*
                11:5, 28; 1Th 1:4
God's choice (B)   *Ro 9:11;*
                11:5; 1Th 1:4
according to the *e.* of grace   *Ro 11:5*
the *e.* hath obtained it, and   *Ro 11:7*
as touching the *e.* they are   *Ro 11:28*
beloved
brethren beloved, your *e.* of   *1Th 1:4*
God
make your calling and *e.*   *2Pe 1:10*
sure

ELECT'S

for the *e.* sake those days   *M't 24:22*
shall be
for the *e.* sake, whom he   *M'k 13:20*
hath
endure all things for the *e.*   *2Ti 2:10*
sakes

EL-ELOHE-ISRAEL

there an altar, and called it   *Ge 33:20*
E.
El, the God of Israel (B)   *Ge 33:20*

ELEMENTAL

e. spirits of the world (N)(R)   *Ga 4:3*
e. spirits of the universe   *Col 2:8*
(A)(N)(R)

ELEMENTARY

the *e.* teachings (A)(B)   *Ga 4:3*
worthless *e.* things (A)(R)   *Ga 4:9*
world's *e.* principles (B)   *Ga 4:9*
the *e.* beginnings (B)   *Heb 5:12*
the *e.* stage (A)(B)(P)(R)   *Heb 6:1*

ELEMENTS

in bondage under the *e.* of the   *Ga 4:3*
the elementary teachings of a   *Ga 4:3*
system of external observations
and regulations (A)
world's elementary teachings   *Ga 4:3*
(B)
rudiments of the world (E)   *Ga 4:3*
slaves to elemental spirits of   *Ga 4:3*
world (N)(R)
under authority of basic moral   *Ga 4:3*
principles (P)
to the weak and beggarly *e.*   *Ga 4:9*
worthless elementary things   *Ga 4:9*
(A)
beggarly rudiments (B)(E)   *Ga 4:9*
beggarly spirits of the elements   *Ga 4:9*
(N)
dead and sterile principles (P)   *Ga 4:9*
beggarly elementary spirits   *Ga 4:9*
(R)
the *e.* shall melt with fervent   *2Pe 3:10;*
heat   *3:12*

ELEPH

And Zelah, *E.* and Jebusi   *Jos 18:28*
which is

ELEVATED

shall be *e.* (B)   *M't 23:12*

ELEVEN

took his *e.* sons, and passed   *Ge 32:22*
and the moon and the *e.*   *Ge 37:9*
stars
e. curtains shalt thou make   *Ex 26:7*
e. curtains shall be all of one   *Ex 26:8*
e. curtains he made them   *Ex 36:14*
the *e.* curtains were of one   *Ex 36:15*
on the third day *e.* bullocks   *Nu 29:20*
e. days' journey from Horeb   *De 1:2*
e. cities with their villages   *Jos 15:51*
one of us *e.* hundred pieces   *J'g 16:5*
of
e. hundred shekels of silver   *J'g 17:2*
restored the *e.* hundred   *J'g 17:3*
shekels
reign; and he reigned *e.*   *2Ki 23:36;*
years   *24:18*
and he reigned *e.* years *2Ch 36:5; 36:11*
in
reigned *e.* years in Jerusalem   *Jer 52:1*
and the breadth *e.* cubits   *Eze 40:49*
Then the *e.* disciples went   *M't 28:16*
away
he appeared unto the *e.* as   *M'k 16:14*
they
told all these things unto the   *Lu 24:9*
e.
found the *e.* gathered   *Lu 24:33*
together
was numbered with the *e.*   *Ac 1:26*
apostles
Peter, standing up with the *e.*   *Ac 2:14*

ELEVENTH

the *e.* day Pagiel, offered   *Nu 7:72*
in the fortieth year, in the *e.*   *De 1:3*
in the *e.* year, in the month   *1Ki 6:38*
in the *e.* year of Joram the   *2Ki 9:29*
the *e.* year of Zedekiah   *2Ki 25:2*
the tenth, Machbanai the *e.*   *1Ch 12:13*
The *e.* to Eliashib, the   *1Ch 24:12*
twelfth
The *e.* to Azareel, he, his   *1Ch 25:18*
sons
The *e.* captain for the *e.*   *1Ch 27:14*
month
of the *e.* year of Zedekiah the   *Jer 1:3*
in the *e.* year of Zedekiah, in   *Jer 39:2*
was besieged unto the *e.* year   *Jer 52:5*
in the *e.* year, in the first   *Eze 26:1*
day
came to pass in the *e.* year   *Eze 30:20*
the *e.* year, in the third   *Eze 31:1*
month
twentieth day of, *e.* month   *Zec 1:7*
about the *e.* hour he went   *M't 20:6*
out
that were hired about the *e.*   *M't 20:9*
hour
the *e.* a jacinth; the twelfth   *Re 21:20*

ELHANAN

where *E.* the son of   *2Sa 21:19*
Jaare-oregim
E. the son of Dodo of   *2Sa 23:24*
Bethlehem
brother of Joab, *E.* the son   *1Ch 11:26*
of Dodo
E. the son of Jair slew   *1Ch 20:5*
Lahmi

ELI

they brought the child to *E.*   *1Sa 1:25*
child did minister to Lord   *1Sa 2:11;*
before *E.*   *3:1*
now the sons of *E.* were sons   *1Sa 2:12*
of Belial
there came a man of God to   *1Sa 2:27*
E. and said
Samuel ran to *E.* and said,   *1Sa 3:5;*
Here am I   *3:6, 8*
in that day I will perform   *1Sa 3:12*
against *E.* all things
the man came in hastily and   *1Sa 4:14*
told *E.*
which he spake concerning   *1Ki 2:27*
E.

ELI, ELI, *LAMA SABACHTHANI*

Jesus cried *E. E. lama*   *M't 27:46;*
sabachthani   *M'k 15:34*

ELIAB

of the tribe of Zebulun, *E.*   *Nu 1:9;*
the son of Helon   *2:7; 7:24, 29; 10:16*
Dathan and Abiram sons of   *Nu 16:1;*
E.   *16:12; 26:9*
sons of Pallu, *E.*   *Nu 26:8*
what he did to the sons of *E.*   *De 11:6*
E. and said
looked on *E.*   *1Sa 16:6*
E. heard, and his anger was   *1Sa 17:28*
kindled
and Jesse begat his firstborn   *1Ch 2:13*
E.
E. the son of Nahath, the   *1Ch 6:27*
son of Zophai
E. captain of the Gadites   *1Ch 12:9*
came to David
E. porter   *1Ch 15:18; 15:20; 16:5*
Rehoboam took the   *2Ch 11:18*
daughter of *E.*

ELIAB'S

E. anger was kindled   *1Sa 17:28*
against

ELIADA

Elishama, and *E.* and   *2Sa 5:16*
Eliphalet
E. and Eliphelet, nine   *1Ch 3:8*
E. a mighty man of valour   *2Ch 17:17*

ELIADAH

Rezon the son of *E.* which   *1Ki 11:23*
fled

ELIAH

Jaresiah, and *E.* and Zichri   *1Ch 8:27*
and Abdi, and Jeremoth,   *Ezr 10:26*
and *E.*

ELIAHBA

E. the Shaalbonite, of the   *2Sa 23:32*
sons of
the Baharumite, *E.* the   *1Ch 11:33*
Shaalbonite

ELIAKIM

there came out to them *E.*   *2Ki 18:18;*
the son   *18:26, 37*
And he sent *E.* which was   *2Ki 19:2*
over
Pharaoh-nechoh made *E.*   *2Ki 23:34*
the son of
of Egypt made *E.* his   *2Ch 36:4*
brother king

the priests; *E.*, Maaseiah,   *Ne 12:41*
Miniamin
I will call my servant *E.* the   *Isa 22:20*
son of
Then came forth unto him   *Isa 36:3;*
E.   *36:11, 22*
And he sent *E.* who was over   *Isa 37:2*
Abiud begat *E.;* and *E.*   *M't 1:13*
begat Azor
Jonan, which was the son of   *Lu 3:30*
E.

ELIAM

Bath-sheba, the daughter of   *2Sa 11:3*
E.
E. the son of Ahithophel   *2Sa 23:34*

ELIAS

is *E.* which was for to   *M't 11:14*
come
some, *E.;* and others,   *M't 16:14*
Jeremias
Moses and *E.* talking with   *M't 17:3;*
him   *17:4, 10-12*
This man calleth for *E.*   *M't 27:47*
whether *E.* will come to   *M't 27:49*
save him
Others said, That it is *E.*   *M'k 6:15*
but some say, *E.;* and others   *M'k 8:28*
unto them *E.* with Moses   *M'k 9:4;*
  9:5, 11-13
Behold, he calleth *E.*   *M'k 15:35*
whether *E.* will come to   *M'k 15:36*
take him
in the spirit and power of *E.*   *Lu 1:17*
were in Israel in the days of   *Lu 4:25*
E.
But unto none of them was   *Lu 4:26*
E.
of some, that *E.* had appeared   *Lu 9:8;*
  9:19, 30, 33
consume them, even as *E.* did   *Lu 9:54*
What then? Art thou *E.*   *Joh 1:21*
nor *E.* neither that prophet   *Joh 1:25*
what the scripture saith of *E.*   *Ro 11:2*
E. was a man subject to like   *Jas 5:17*

ELIASAPH

Of Gad; *E.* the son of Deuel   *Nu 1:14*
of the sons of Gad shall be *E.*   *Nu 2:14*
Gershonites shall be *E.* the   *Nu 3:24*
son of
the sixth day *E.* the son of   *Nu 7:42*
Deuel
the offering of *E.* the son of   *Nu 7:47*
Deuel
tribe of the children of Gad   *Nu 10:20*
was *E.*

ELIASHIB

Hodaiah, and *E.* and   *1Ch 3:24*
Pelaiah
eleventh to *E.*, the twelfth   *1Ch 24:12*
to Jakim
chamber of Johanan the son   *Ezr 10:6;*
of *E.*   *10:24, 27, 36*
Then *E.* the high priest rose   *Ne 3:1;*
up   *3:20-21*
Joiakim also begat *E.*   *Ne 12:10*
  12:22-23
E. the priest, having the   *Ne 13:4;*
oversight   *13:7, 28*

ELIATHAH

Hanani, *E.*, Giddalti   *1Ch 25:4*
The twentieth to *E.* he, his   *1Ch 25:27*
sons

ELIDAD

of Benjamin, *E.* the son of   *Nu 34:21*
Chislon

ELIEL

Epher, and Ishi, and *E.* and   *1Ch 5:24*
Azriel
the son of Jeroham, the son   *1Ch 6:34*
of *E.*
And Elienai, and Zilthai,   *1Ch 8:20*
and *E.*
And Ishpan, and Heber, and   *1Ch 8:22*
E.

ELIEL (continued)

E. the Mahavite, and Jeribai — 1Ch 11:46
E. and Obed, and Jasiel the — 1Ch 11:47
Attai the sixth, E. the seventh — 1Ch 12:11
E. the chief, and his brethren — 1Ch 15:9
Shemaiah, and E. and Amminadab — 1Ch 15:11
Jozabad, and E. and Ismachiah — 2Ch 31:13

ELIENAI

E. and Zilthai and Eliel — 1Ch 8:20

ELIEZER

the steward of my house is this E. — Ge 15:2
the name of the other was E. — Ex 18:4
Zemira, and Joash, and E. — 1Ch 7:8
Benaiah, and E. the priests, did — 1Ch 15:24
of Moses were, Gershom, and E. — 1Ch 23:15
sons of E. were, Rehabiah the chief — 1Ch 23:17
And E. had none other sons — 1Ch 23:17
brethren by E.; Rehabiah his son — 1Ch 26:25
the ruler of the Reubenites was E. — 1Ch 27:16
Then E. the son of Dodavah of — 2Ch 20:37
Then sent I for E., of Ariel — Ezr 8:16
Maaseiah, and E. and Jarib — Ezr 10:18
Pethahiah, Judah, and E. — Ezr 10:23
of the sons of Harim, E. Ishijah — Ezr 10:31
which was the son of E. — Lu 3:29

ELIHOENAI

E. the son of Zerahiah, and — Ezr 8:4

ELIHOREPH

E. and Ahiah, the sons of Shisha — 1Ki 4:3

ELIHU

the son of E., the son of Tohu — 1Sa 1:1
Jozabad, and E. and Zilthai — 1Ch 12:20
strong men, E. and Semachiah — 1Ch 26:7
E. one of the brethren of David — 1Ch 27:18
Then was kindled the wrath of E. — Job 32:2
E. had waited till Job had spoken — Job 32:4
E. saw that there was no answer — Job 32:5
E. the son of Barachel the Buzite — Job 32:6
E. answered and said — Job 34:1
E. spake moreover, and said — Job 35:1
E. also proceeded, and said — Job 36:1

ELIJAH

E. the Tishbite — 1Ki 17:1; 17:13, 15-16. 18
the Lord heard the voice of E.; and — 1Ki 17:22
E. took the child, and brought him — 1Ki 17:23
the woman said to E., Now by this — 1Ki 17:24
Lord came to E. in the third year — 1Ki 18:1
E. went to shew himself unto Ahab — 1Ki 18:2; 18:7-8, 11, 14-17, 21-22
E. said unto the prophets of Baal — 1Ki 18:25
E. mocked them, and said, Cry — 1Ki 18:27
E. said unto all the people, Come — 1Ki 18:30; 18:31, 36, 40
E. said unto Ahab, Get thee up, eat — 1Ki 18:41
E. went up to the top of Carmel — 1Ki 18:42
the hand of the Lord was on E. — 1Ki 18:46
told Jezebel all that E. had done — 1Ki 19:1
Jezebel sent a messenger unto E. — 1Ki 19:2
unto him, What doest thou here, E. — 1Ki 19:9
it was so, when E. heard it, that he — 1Ki 19:13
and said, What doest thou here, E. — 1Ki 19:13
and E. passed by him, and cast his — 1Ki 19:19
he left the oxen, and ran after E. — 1Ki 19:20
Then he arose, and went after E. — 1Ki 19:21
the Lord came to E. the Tishbite — 1Ki 21:17
Ahab said to E., Hast thou found — 1Ki 21:20
word of the Lord came to E. the — 1Ki 21:28
said to E. the Tishbite, Arise, go up — 2Ki 1:3
shalt surely die. And E. departed — 2Ki 1:4
And he said, It is E. the Tishbite — 2Ki 1:8
E. answered and said to the captain — 2Ki 1:10
E. answered and said unto them — 2Ki 1:12
came and fell on his knees before E. — 2Ki 1:13
the angel of the Lord said unto E. — 2Ki 1:15
of the Lord which E. had spoken — 2Ki 1:17
Lord would take up E. into heaven — 2Ki 2:1
E. went with Elisha from Gilgal — 2Ki 2:1
E. said unto Elisha, Tarry here, I — 2Ki 2:2
E. said unto him, Elisha, tarry here — 2Ki 2:4
E. said unto him, Tarry, I pray thee — 2Ki 2:6
E. took his mantle, and wrapped it — 2Ki 2:8
E. said unto Elisha, Ask what I — 2Ki 2:9
E. went up by a whirlwind into — 2Ki 2:11
He took up also the mantle of E. — 2Ki 2:13
And he took the mantle of E. that — 2Ki 2:14
Where is the Lord God of E. — 2Ki 2:14
The spirit of E. doth rest on Elisha — 2Ki 2:15
poured water on the hand of E. — 2Ki 3:11
which he spake by his servant E. the — 2Ki 9:36
which he spake by his servant E. the — 2Ki 10:10
of the Lord, which he spake to E. — 2Ki 10:17
there came a writing to him from E. — 2Ch 21:12
Maaseiah, and E. and Shemaiah — Ezr 10:21
I will send you E. the prophet — Mal 4:5

ELIKA

the Harodite, E. the Harodite — 2Sa 23:25

ELIM

they came to E. where were twelve — Ex 15:27
they took their journey from E. — Ex 16:1
Sin, which is between E. and Sinai — Ex 16:1
from Marah, and came unto E. — Nu 33:9
in E. were twelve fountains of water — Nu 33:9
And they removed from E. — Nu 33:10

ELIMELECH

And the name of the man was E. — Ru 1:2
And E. Naomi's husband died — Ru 1:3
man of wealth, of the family of E. — Ru 2:1
Boaz, who was of the kindred of E. — Ru 2:3

ELIMELECH'S

of land, which was our brother E. — Ru 4:3
that I have bought all that was E. — Ru 4:9

ELIMINATE

e. you from countries (B) — Eze 25:7

ELIMINATED

e. by a flood (B) — Ge 9:11

ELIOENAI

sons of Neariah: E. and Hezekiah — 1Ch 3:23
the sons of E. were, Hodaiah, and — 1Ch 3:24
E. and Jaakobah, and Jeshohaiah — 1Ch 4:36
Eliezer, and E. and Omri — 1Ch 7:8
Jehohanan the sixth, E. the — 1Ch 26:3
the sons of Pashur; E. Maaseiah — Ezr 10:22
of the sons of Zattu; E., Eliashib — Ezr 10:27
Michaiah, E., Zechariah — Ne 12:41

ELIPHAL

Sacar the Hararite, E. the son of Ur — 1Ch 11:35

ELIPHALET

Elishama, and Eliada, and E. — 2Sa 5:16
Elishama, and Beeliada, and E. — 1Ch 14:7

ELIPHAZ

And Adah bare to Esau E. — Ge 36:4; 36:10
the sons of E. were Teman, Omar — Ge 36:11; 1Ch 1:36
Timna was concubine to E. Esau's — Ge 36:12
and she bare to E. Amalek — Ge 36:12
sons of E. the firstborn son of Esau — Ge 36:15
these are the dukes that came of E. — Ge 36:16
the sons of Esau; E. Reuel — 1Ch 1:35
E. the Temanite, and Bildad — Job 2:11
E. the Temanite answered and said — Job 4:1; 22:1
Then answered E. the Temanite — Job 15:1
the Lord said to E. the Temanite — Job 42:7
So E. the Temanite and Bildad the — Job 42:9

ELIPHELEH

Mattithiah, and E. and Mikneiah — 1Ch 15:18
E. and Mikneiah, and Obed-edom — 1Ch 15:21

ELIPHELET

E. the son of Ahasbai, the son of — 2Sa 23:34
Ibhar also, and Elishama, and E. — 1Ch 3:6
Elishama, and Eliada, and E. — 1Ch 3:8
Jehush the second, and E. the third — 1Ch 8:39
whose names are these, E., Jeiel — Ezr 8:13
Zabad, E., Jeremai, Manasseh — Ezr 10:33

ELI'S

the iniquity of E. house shall not — 1Sa 3:14

ELISABETH

of Aaron, and her name was E.   Lu 1:5

child, because that E. was barren   Lu 1:7

thy wife E. shall bear thee a son   Lu 1:13

those days his wife E. conceived   Lu 1:24

behold, thy cousin E. she hath also   Lu 1:36

house of Zacharias, and saluted E.   Lu 1:40

E. heard the salutation of Mary   Lu 1:41

E. was filled with the Holy Ghost   Lu 1:41

ELISABETH'S

Now E. full time came that she   Lu 1:57

ELISEUS

in the time of E. the prophet   Lu 4:27

ELISHA

E. the son Shaphat of Abel-meholah   1Ki 19:16

from the sword of Jehu shall E. slay   1Ki 19:17

he departed thence, and found E.   1Ki 19:19

Elijah went with E. from Gilgal   2Ki 2:1

Elijah said unto E., Tarry here   2Ki 2:2

E. said unto him, As the Lord   2Ki 2:2

were at Beth-el came forth to E.   2Ki 2:3

Elijah said unto him, E. tarry here   2Ki 2:4

that were at Jericho came to E.   2Ki 2:5

Elijah said unto E., Ask what I   2Ki 2:9

E. said, I pray thee, let a double   2Ki 2:9

E. saw it, and he cried, My father   2Ki 2:12

and thither: and E. went over   2Ki 2:14

The spirit of Elijah doth rest on E.   2Ki 2:15

the men of the city said unto E.   2Ki 2:19

to the saying of E. which he spake   2Ki 2:22

Here is E. the son of Shaphat   2Ki 3:11

E. said unto the king of Israel, What   2Ki 3:13

E. said, As the Lord of hosts liveth   2Ki 3:14

of the sons of the prophets unto E.   2Ki 4:1

E. said unto her, What shall I do   2Ki 4:2

on a day, that E. passed to Shunem   2Ki 4:8

season that E. had said unto her   2Ki 4:17

when E. was come into the house   2Ki 4:32

E. came again to Gilgal: and   2Ki 4:38

when E. the man of God had heard   2Ki 5:8

stood at the door of the house of E.   2Ki 5:9

E. sent a messenger unto him   2Ki 5:10

Gehazi, the servant of E. the man   2Ki 5:20

E. said unto him, Whence comest   2Ki 5:25

sons of the prophets said unto E.   2Ki 6:1

but E. the prophet that is in Israel   2Ki 6:12

E. prayed, and said, Lord, I pray   2Ki 6:17

and chariots of fire round about E.   2Ki 6:17

E. prayed unto the Lord, and said   2Ki 6:18

according to the word of E.   2Ki 6:18

E. said unto them, This is not the   2Ki 6:19

E. said, Lord, open the eyes of these   2Ki 6:20

the king of Israel said unto E.   2Ki 6:21

the head of E. the son of Shaphat   2Ki 6:31

E. sat in his house, and the elders   2Ki 6:32

E. said, Hear ye the word of the Lord   2Ki 7:1

Then spake E. unto the woman   2Ki 8:1

the great things that E. hath done   2Ki 8:4

is her son, whom E. restored to life   2Ki 8:5

And E. came to Damascus   2Ki 8:7

E. said unto him, Go, say unto him   2Ki 8:10

E. answered, The Lord hath shewed   2Ki 8:13

So he departed from E. and came   2Ki 8:14

said to him, What said E. to thee   2Ki 8:14

E. the prophet called one of   2Ki 9:1

E. was fallen sick of his sickness   2Ki 13:14

E. said unto him, Take bow   2Ki 13:15

E. put his hands upon the king's   2Ki 13:16

Then E. said, Shoot. And he shot   2Ki 13:17

And E. died, and they buried him   2Ki 13:20

the man into the sepulchre of E.   2Ki 13:21

down, and touched the bones of E.   2Ki 13:21

ELISHAH

the sons of Javan; E. and Tarshish   Ge 10:4; 1Ch 1:7

blue and purple from the isles of E.   Eze 27:7

ELISHAMA

Ephraim; E. the son of Ammihud   Nu 1:10

of the sons of Ephraim shall be E.   Nu 2:18

seventh day E. the son of Ammihud   Nu 7:48

this was the offering of E. the sons of   Nu 7:53

over his host was E. the son of   Nu 10:22

E. and Eliada, and Eliphalet   2Sa 5:16

the son of E. of the seed royal   2Ki 25:25

Jekamiah, and Jekamiah begat E.   1Ch 2:41

Ibhar also, and E. and Eliphalet   1Ch 3:6

E. and Eliada, and Eliphelet, nine   1Ch 3:8

Ammihud his son, E. his son   1Ch 7:26

E. and Beeliada, and Eliphalet   1Ch 14:7

and with them E. and Jehoram   2Ch 17:8

even E. the scribe, and Delaiah   Jer 36:12

in the chamber of E. the scribe   Jer 36:20

out of E. the scribe's chamber   Jer 36:21

the son of Nethaniah the son of E.   Jer 41:1

ELISHAPHAT

and E. the son of Zichri, into   2Ch 23:1

ELISHEBA

Aaron took him E., daughter of   Ex 6:23

ELISHUA

Ibhar also, and E. and Nepheg   2Sa 5:15

And Ibhar, and E. and Elpalet   1Ch 14:5

ELIUD

begat Achim; and Achim begat E.   M't 1:14

And E. begat Eleazar; and   M't 1:15

ELIZAPHAN

of the Kohathites shall be E.   Nu 3:30

of Zebulun, E. the son of Parnach   Nu 34:25

the sons of E., Shemaiah the chief   1Ch 15:8

of the sons of E.; Shimri, and Jeiel   2Ch 29:13

ELIZUR

of Reuben; E. the son of Shedeur   Nu 1:5

the children of Reuben shall be E.   Nu 2:10

fourth day E. the son of Shedeur   Nu 7:30

this was the offering of E. the son   Nu 7:35

host was E. the son of Shedeur   Nu 10:18

ELKANAH

the sons of Korah; Assir, and E.   Ex 6:24

and his name was E. the son of   1Sa 1:1

when the time was that E. offered   1Sa 1:4

Then said E. her husband to her   1Sa 1:8

and E. knew Hannah his wife   1Sa 1:19

the man E. and all his house, went   1Sa 1:21

E. her husband said unto her, Do   1Sa 1:23

And E. went to Ramah to his house   1Sa 1:11

And Eli blessed E. and his wife   1Sa 2:20

E. his son, and Ebiasaph his son   1Ch 6:23

sons of E.; Amasai, and Ahimoth   1Ch 6:25

As for E.: the sons of E.; Zophai   1Ch 6:26

Jeroham his son, E. his son   1Ch 6:27

The son of E., the son of Jeroham   1Ch 6:34

The son of Zuph, the son of E.   1Ch 6:35

The son of E. the son of Joel   1Ch 6:36

the son of E. that dwelt in the   1Ch 9:16

E. and Jesiah, and Azareel   1Ch 12:6

Berechiah and E. were door keepers   1Ch 15:23

and E. that was next to the king   2Ch 28:7

ELKOHSHITE

book of the vision of Nahum the E.   Na 1:1

ELLASAR

Arioch king of E. Chedorlaomer   Ge 14:1

and Arioch king of E.; four kings   Ge 14:9

ELMODAM

which was the son of E.   Lu 3:28

ELMS

under oaks and poplars and e.   Ho 4:13

ELNAAM

and Joshaviah, the sons of E.   1Ch 11:46

ELNATHAN

the daughter of *E.* of Jerusalem — *2Ki 24:8*
for *E.* and for Jarib, and for *E.* — *Ezr 8:16*
and for *E.* men of understanding — *Ezr 8:16*
E. the son of Achbor, and certain — *Jer 26:22*
E. the son of Achbor, and Gemariah — *Jer 36:12*
Nevertheless *E.* and Delaiah — *Jer 36:25*

ELOI

E. E. lama sabacthani — *M'k 15:34*

ELON

Bashemath the daughter of *E.* the — *Ge 26:34*
Adah the daughter of *E.* the — *Ge 36:2*
sons of Zebulun; Sered, and *E.* — *Ge 46:14*
of *E.* the family of the Elonites — *Nu 26:26*
E. and Thimnathah, and Ekron — *Jos 19:43*
And after him *E.* a Zebulonite — *J'g 12:11*
And *E.* the Zebulonite died, and was — *J'g 12:12*

ELON-BETH-HANAN

and Beth-shemesh, and *E.* — *1Ki 4:9*

ELONITES

of Elon, the family of the *E.* — *Nu 26:26*

ELOQUENCE

words of *e.* (A)(B) — *1Co 2:1*

ELOQUENT

O my Lord, I am not *e.* — *Ex 4:10*
I am no orator (B) — *Ex 4:10*
artificer, and the *e.* orator — *Isa 3:3*
the skillful enchanter (A)(E) — *Isa 3:3*
the expert charmer (B) — *Isa 3:3*
expert in charms (R) — *Isa 3:3*
an *e.* man, and mighty in — *Ac 18:24*
a man of learning (B) — *Ac 18:24*
a gifted speaker (P) — *Ac 18:24*

ELOTH

Ezion-geber, which is beside *E.* — *1Ki 9:26*
E. at the sea side in the land of — *2Ch 8:17*
He built *E.* and restored it to Judah — *2Ch 26:2*

ELPAAL

Hushim he begat Abitub, and *E.* — *1Ch 8:11*
The sons of *E.*, Eber, and Misham — *1Ch 8:12*
Jezliah, and Jobab, the sons of *E.* — *1Ch 8:18*

ELPALET

Ibhar, and Elishua, and *E.* — *1Ch 1:15; 14:5*

EL-PARAN

unto *E.* which is by the wilderness — *Ge 14:6*

ELSE

she said, Give me children or *e.* I die — *Ge 30:1*
I will without doing any thing *e.* go — *Nu 20:19*
the Lord he is God, there is none *e.* — *De 4:35; 4:39; 1Ki 8:60; Isa 45:5-6, 14, 18, 21-22; 46:9; Joe 2:27*
e. if ye do in any wise go back and cleave — *Jos 23:12*
this is nothing *e.* save sword of Gideon — *J'g 7:14*

if I taste ought *e.* till the sun be down — *2Sa 3:35*
or *e.* thou shalt pay a talent of silver — *1Ki 20:39*
or *e.*, if it please thee, I will give thee — *1Ki 21:6*
or *e.* three days sword of the Lord — *1Ch 21:12*
whoso *e.* cometh in, shall be put to death — *2Ch 23:7*
this is nothing *e.* but sorrow of heart — *Ne 2:2*
desirest not sacrifice, *e.* would I give it — *Ps 51:16*
who *e.* can hasten hereunto more than I — *Ec 2:25*
that sayest, I am, none *e.* besides me — *Isa 47:8*
or *e.* believe me for the work's sake — *Joh 14:11*
spent time in nothing *e.* but tell or hear — *Ac 17:21*
accusing or *e.* excusing one another — *Ro 2:15*
e. were your children unclean, but now holy — *1Co 7:14*
e. when thou shalt bless with the Spirit — *1Co 14:16*
repent, or *e.* I will come to thee quickly — *Re 2:5; 2:16*

ELTEKEH

And *E.* and Gibbethon, and Baalath — *Jos 19:44*
out of the tribe of Dan, *E.* with her — *Jos 21:23*

ELTEKON

Maarath, and Beth-anoth, and *E.* — *Jos 15:59*

ELTOLAD

And *E.* and Chesil, and Hormah — *Jos 15:30*
And *E.* and Bethul, and Hormah — *Jos 19:4*

ELUL

and fifth day of the month *E.* — *Ne 6:15*

ELUZAI

E. and Jerimoth, and Bealiah — *1Ch 12:5*

ELYMAS

But *E.* the sorcerer (for so is his — *Ac 13:8*

ELZABAD

Johanan the eighth, *E.* the ninth — *1Ch 12:12*
E. whose brethren were strong — *1Ch 26:7*

ELZAPHAN

the sons of Uzziel; Mishael, and *E.* — *Ex 6:22*
Moses called Mishael and *E.* — *Le 10:4*

EMBALM

the physicians to *e.* his father — *Ge 50:2*

EMBALMED

and the physicians *e.* Israel — *Ge 50:2*
the days of those which are *e.* — *Ge 50:3*
and they *e.* him, and he was put in — *Ge 50:26*

EMBARRASS

might *e.* them (B) — *J'g 18:7*
why *e.* the woman (B) — *M't 26:10; M'k 14:6*

EMBARRASSED

they were *e.* (B) — *J'g 3:25*
Hazael was *e.* (A) — *2Ki 8:11*
feeling deeply *e.* (B)(P) — *Lu 14:9*

EMBASSY

he sends an *e.* (R)(S) — *Lu 14:32*

EMBITTER

e. your stomach (A)(B)(N)(R) — *Re 10:9*

EMBITTERED

e. men knock you down (B) — *J'g 18:25*
e. in minds (A)(B) — *2Sa 17:8*
e. my soul (B) — *Job 27:2*
my heart was *e.* (R) — *Ps 73:21*
provoked, irritated, *e.* God (A) — *Heb 3:15*

EMBODIMENT

e. of knowledge (A)(B)(R) — *Ro 2:20*

EMBOLDENED

of him which is weak be *e.* to eat — *1Co 8:10*

EMBOLDENETH

what *e.* thee that thou answerest — *Job 16:3*

EMBOSSED

his heavily *e.* shield (S) — *Job 15:26*

EMBRACE

time of life, thou shalt *e.* a son — *2Ki 4:16*
e. the rock for want of a shelter — *Job 24:8*
to honour when thou dost *e.* her — *Pr 4:8*
and *e.* the bosom of a stranger — *Pr 5:20*
a time to *e.* and a time to refrain — *Ec 3:5*
and his right hand doth *e.* me — *Ca 2:6*
and his right hand should *e.* me — *Ca 8:3*
that were brought up in scarlet *e.* — *La 4:5*

EMBRACED

he ran to meet him, and *e.* him — *Ge 29:13*
Esau ran to meet him, and *e.* him — *Ge 33:4*
he kissed them, and *e.* them — *Ge 48:10*
unto him the disciples, and *e.* — *Ac 20:1*
e. them, and confessed that they — *Heb 11:13*

EMBRACING

a time to refrain from *e.* — *Ec 3:5*
and fell on him, and *e.* him said — *Ac 20:10*

EMBROIDER

And thou shalt *e.* the coat of fine — *Ex 28:39*

EMBROIDERED

'cherubim skillfully *e.* (A) — *Ex 26:1*
'embroidered (S) — *Ex 28:4; Pr 7:16; Eze 16:10, 13, 18; 26:16; 27:7, 16, 24*
e. work (A)(B)(R) — *Eze 16:10; 16:13, 18; 26:16; 27:16, 24*

EMBROIDERER

manner of work. and of the *e.* — *Ex 35:35*
and an *e.* in blue, and in purple — *Ex 38:23*

EMERALD

And the second row shall be an *e.* — *Ex 28:18*
an *e.* a sapphire, and a diamond — *Ex 39:11*
sapphire, *e.* and the carbuncle — *Eze 28:13*

EMERALD

in sight like unto an *e.*   *Re 4:3*
a chalcedony; the fourth,   *Re 21:19*
an *e.*

EMERALDS

they occupied in thy fairs   *Eze 27:16*
with *e.*

EMERODS

and with the *e.* and with the   *De 28:27*
scab
with tumors (A)(B)   *De 28:27*
with the ulcers (R)   *De 28:27*
smote them with *e.* even   *1Sa 5:6*
Ashdod
with tumors or boils (A)   *1Sa 5:6*
with hemorrhoids (B)   *1Sa 5:6;*
                                    5:9, 12; 6:4-5
with tumors (E)(R)   *1Sa 5:6;*
                                    5:9, 12; 6:4-5
they had *e.* in their secret   *1Sa 5:9*
parts
died not were smitten with   *1Sa 5:12*
the *e.*
Five golden *e.* and five golden   *1Sa 6:4*
ye shall make images of your   *1Sa 6:5*
e.
and the images of their *e.*   *1Sa 6:11*
these are the golden *e.* which   *1Sa 6:17*
the

EMIMS

and the *E.* in Shaveh   *Ge 14:5*
Kiriathaim
E. dwelt therein in times past   *De 2:10*
but the Moabites call them *E.*   *De 2:11*

EMINENT

also built unto thee an *e.*   *Eze 16:24*
place
(brothel) vaulted place   *Eze 16:24;*
(A)(B)(E)(R)   *16:31, 39*
thou buildest thine *e.* place   *Eze 16:31*
in the
shall throw down thine *e.*   *Eze 16:39*
place
upon an high mountain and   *Eze 17:22*
e.
mountain high and exalted   *Eze 17:22*
(A)
a lofty mountain height (B)   *Eze 17:22*
a high and lofty mountain   *Eze 17:22*
(E)(R)
most *e.* apostles (B)   *2Co 11:5*

EMMANUEL

they shall call his name *E.*   *M't 1:23*

EMMAUS

to a village called *E.* which   *Lu 24:13*
was

EMMOR

of the sons of *E.* the father   *Ac 7:16*
of

EMOTIONS

who try hearts and *e.* (A)(B)   *Ps 7:9*
my *e.* admonish me (B)   *Ps 16:7*
my *e.* stir (B)   *Jer 31:20; La 2:11*
my *e.* are disturbed (A)   *La 2:11*
human, with *e.* as yourselves   *Ac 14:15*
(B)
aroused the *e.* (B)   *Ac 17:8*

EMPIRE

published throughout all his   *Es 1:20*
e.

EMPLOY

to *e.* them in the seige   *De 20:19*
do not *e.* insults in (N)   *2Pe 2:11*

EMPLOYED

for they were *e.* in that   *1Ch 9:33*
work day
Tikvah were *e.* about this   *Ezr 10:15*
matter

EMPLOYMENT

shall sever out men of   *Eze 39:14*
continual *e.*
standing without *e.* (B)   *M't 20:3*

EMPOWERED

e. to take peace from the earth   *Re 6:4*
(A)(B)

EMPTIED

she hasted, and *e.* her   *Ge 24:20*
pitcher
to pass as they *e.* their sacks   *Ge 42:35*
officer came and *e.* the   *2Ch 24:11*
chest
thus be he shaken out, and *e.*   *Ne 5:13*
defence shall be *e.* and dried   *Isa 19:6*
up
The land shall be utterly *e.*   *Isa 24:3*
hath not been *e.* from vessel   *Jer 48:11*
for the emptiers have *e.* them   *Na 2:2*
out
e. himself (B)(E)(R)   *Ph'p 2:7*

EMPTIERS

for the *e.* have emptied them   *Na 2:2*
out

EMPTINESS

went after *e.* (B)   *2Ki 17:15*
months of *e.* (R)   *Job 7:3*
trust in *e.* (R)   *Job 15:31*
they are *e.* (A)   *Ps 62:9*
they are *e.* (B)   *Ps 62:9; Ec 2:23; 7:6*
e. falsity, futility (A)(B)   *Ps 89:47*
increase *e.* (A)   *Ec 6:9*
all is *e.* (A)   *Ec 12:8*
offerings of vanity, *e.* (A)   *Isa 1:13*
of confusion, and the stones   *Isa 34:11*
of *e.*
e., waste, futility (A)   *Isa 40:17*
e., falsity (A)   *Isa 40:23;*
                                    41:29; Jer 2:5; Hab 2:13
e., worthlessness (A)   *Isa 59:4*
e., futility (A)   *Jer 16:10*
e., falsity, futility (A)   *Jer 51:18*

EMPTY

an *e.* waste (A)(B)   *Ge 1:2; Jer 4:23*
thou hadst sent me away   *Ge 31:42*
now *e.*
the pit was *e.*; there was no   *Ge 37:24*
water
the seven *e.* ears blasted   *Ge 41:27*
with the
when ye go, ye shall not go *e.*   *Ex 3:21*
and none shall appear before   *Ex 23:15;*
me *e.*   *34:20*
command that they *e.* the   *Le 14:36*
house
thou shalt not let him go   *De 15:13*
away *e.*
shall not appear before the   *De 16:16*
Lord *e.*
e. and worthless trifle (A)   *De 32:47*
e. pitchers, and lamps within   *J'g 7:16*
hath brought me home again   *Ru 1:21*
e.
Go not *e.* unto thy mother in   *Ru 3:17*
law
send it not *e.*; but in any wise   *1Sa 6:3*
missed because thy seat will   *1Sa 20:18*
be *e.*
side, and David's place was   *1Sa 20:25*
e.
that David's place was *e.*:   *1Sa 20:27*
and Saul
the sword of Saul returned   *2Sa 1:22*
not *e.*
barrel not be *e.* (B)   *1Ki 17:10*
borrow thee vessels, *e.*   *2Ki 4:3*
vessels
e. words (A)   *2Ki 18:20; Ps 2:1*
Thou hast sent widows away   *Job 22:9*
e.
out the north over the *e.*   *Job 26:7*
place
not hear an *e.* cry (E)(R)   *Job 35:13*
e. talk (R)   *Job 35:16*
an *e.* scheme (B)   *Ps 2:1*
he speaketh *e.* words (R)   *Ps 41:6*
his *e.* life (B)   *Ec 6:12*
they *e.* themselves upon the   *Ec 11:3*
earth

the Lord maketh the earth *e.*   *Isa 24:1*
he awaketh, and his soul is *e.*   *Isa 29:8*
worthless and *e.* (R)   *Isa 30:7*
to make *e.* the soul of the   *Isa 32:6*
hungry
return to me *e.* (R)   *Isa 55:11*
rely on *e.* pleas (R)   *Isa 59:4*
returned with their vessels *e.*   *Jer 14:3*
shall *e.* his vessels, and   *Jer 48:12*
break
returns not *e.* (B)(R)   *Jer 50:9*
shall fan her, and shall *e.* her   *Jer 51:2*
land
he hath made me an *e.*   *Jer 51:34*
vessel
seen an *e.* vision (B)   *La 2:14;*
                                    Eze 12:24
e., delusive visions (A)   *Eze 13:9*
e. visions (B)   *Eze 22:28*
set it *e.* upon the coals   *Eze 24:11*
thereof
Israel is an *e.* vine, he   *Ho 10:1*
bringeth
She is *e.* and void, and waste   *Na 2:10*
Shall they therefore *e.* their   *Hab 1:17*
net
through the two golden pipes   *Zec 4:12*
e.
an *e.* consolation (R)   *Zec 10:2*
heap up *e.* phrases (R)   *M't 6:7*
he findeth it *e.* swept, and   *M'k 12:44*
beat him, and sent him   *M'k 12:3;*
away *e.*   *Lu 20:10*
the rich he hath sent *e.* away   *Lu 1:53*
shamefully, and sent him   *Lu 20:11*
away *e.*
faith is *e.* (N)   *Ro 4:14*
an *e.* boast (A)(B)(N)   *2Co 9:3*
e. excuses (A)(E)(R)   *Eph 5:6*
by *e.* deceitfulness (B)(R)   *Col 2:8*
aside to *e.* talk (N)   *1Ti 1:6*
unholy, *e.* discussions (A)   *1Ti 2:16*
irreligious and *e.* discussions   *1Ti 6:20*
(B)
e. worldly chatter (N)(R)   *1Ti 6:20;*
                                    2Ti 2:16
e. talkers and deceivers (R)   *Tit 1:10*
e. folly of traditional ways   *1Pe 1:18*
(N)
utter big, *e.* words (N)   *2Pe 2:18*

EMULATION

to stir Israel to *e.* (N)   *Ro 11:11;*
                                    11:14
I may provoke to *e.* them   *Ro 11:14*
which
to stir them up to imitate,   *Ro 11:14*
copy and appropriate (A)
to arouse my kin to jealousy   *Ro 11:14*
(B)
may provoke to jealousy   *Ro 11:14*
(E)
make my kinfolk jealous   *Ro 11:14*
(P)(R)

EMULATIONS

hatred, variance, *e.*, wrath,   *Ga 5:20*
strife

ENABLED

Jesus our Lord, who hath *e.*   *1Ti 1:12*
me

ENAM

and En-gannim, Tappuah,   *Jos 15:34*
and *E.*

ENAN

Of Naphtali; Ahira the son   *Nu 1:15*
of *E.*
shall be Ahirah the son of *E.*   *Nu 2:29*
the twelfth day Ahira the son   *Nu 7:78*
of *E.*
the offering of Ahira the son   *Nu 7:83*
of *E.*
Naphtali was Ahira the son   *Nu 10:27*
of *E.*

ENCAMP

turn and *e.* before Pi-hahiroth   *Ex 14:2*
before it shall ye *e.* by the   *Ex 14:2*
sea
shall minister unto it, and   *Nu 1:50*
shall *e.*

ENCAMP

encamp (S) *Nu 2:3; 2:5; 3:23, 29, 35*
as they *e.* so shall they set *Nu 2:17*
forward
And those that *e.* by him *Nu 2:27*
shall be
But those that *e.* before the *Nu 3:38*
how we are to *e.* in the *Nu 10:31*
wilderness
and *e.* against the city, and *2Sa 12:28*
take it
and *e.* round about my *Job 19:12*
tabernacle
Though an host should *e.* *Ps 27:3*
against
will *e.* against thee (S) *Isa 29:3*
And I will *e.* about mine *Zec 9:8*
house

ENCAMPED

encamped (S) *Ge 31:25;*
Ex 17:1; 19:2; Nu 2:34; 9:18; 12:16;
21:10-13; 22:1; 33:5-9, 15-16, 18-23, 25,
27-29, 31, 33, 36-37, 41-45, 47-49;
Jos 9:11; 11:5; J'g 6:33; 7:1; 11:18, 20;
15:9; 18:12; 1Sa 4:1; 13:5; 17:1-2; 26:3,
5; 28:4; 29:1; 2Sa 17:26; 23:13; 24:5;
1Ki 20:27, 29; 2Ki 25:1; 1Ch 9:7;
Jer 52:4
and *e.* in Etham, in the edge *Ex 13:20*
of the
and they *e.* there by the *Ex 15:27*
waters
where he *e.* at the mount of *Ex 18:5*
God
e. by the Red sea *Nu 33:10;*
33:11-14, 24, 26, 30, 32, 34-35, 46
they *e.* there (B) *Jos 3:1*
and *e.* in Gilgal, in the east *Jos 4:19*
border
And the children of Israel *e.* *Jos 5:10*
in
and *e.* before Gibeon, and *Jos 10:5*
made war
and *e.* against it, and fought *Jos 10:31;*
10:34
And they *e.* against them, and *J'g 6:4*
and *e.* against Thebez, and *J'g 9:50*
took it
gathered together, and *e.* in *J'g 10:17*
Gilead
together, and *e.* in Mizpeh *J'g 10:17*
morning, and *e.* against *J'g 20:19*
Gibeah
and *e.* against Jabesh-gilead *1Sa 11:1*
but the Philistines *e.* in *1Sa 13:16*
Michmash
my lord, are *e.* in the open *2Sa 11:11*
fields
And the people were *e.* *1Ki 16:15*
against
the people that were *e.* *1Ki 16:16*
heard say
the Philistines *e.* in the *1Ch 11:15*
valley of
and *e.* against the fenced *2Ch 32:1*
cities
where David *e.* *Isa 29:1*
(A)(B)(E)(R)

ENCAMPETH

The angel of the Lord *e.* *Ps 34:7*
round
the bones of him that *e.* *Ps 53:5*
against

ENCAMPING

and overtook them *e.* by the *Ex 14:9*
sea

ENCAMPMENT

the *e.* (S) *Ge 25:16; Nu 31:10*
the *e.* of Kedar (B) *Isa 42:11*

ENCHANTER

spirits, or an *e.* or a witch *De 18:10*

ENCHANTERS

your *e.* nor to your sorcerers *Jer 27:9*
the skillful *e.* (A)(E) *Ac 3:3*

ENCHANTMENT

neither shall ye use *e.* *Le 19:26*
there is no *e.* against Jacob *Nu 23:23*

the serpent will bite without *Ec 10:11*
e.

ENCHANTMENTS

did in like manner with their *Ex 7:11*
e.
of Egypt did so with their *e.* *Ex 7:22*
the magicians did so with their *Ex 8:7*
e.
did so with their *e.* to bring *Ex 8:18*
forth
to seek for *e.* but he set his *Nu 24:1*
face
and used divination and *e.* *2Ki 17:17*
and observed times, and *2Ki 21:6*
used *e.*
also he observed times, and *2Ch 33:6*
used *e.*
through her *e.* (A) *Ne 3:4*
the great abundance of thine *Isa 47:9*
e.
Stand now with thine *e.* and *Isa 47:12*
your many *e.* (B) *Isa 47:12*

ENCIRCLE

wicked *e.* the rightous (B) *Hab 1:4*
e. you (B)(N) *Lu 19:43*

ENCIRCLED

e. him to fight (B) *2Ch 18:31; Job 19:6*
all nations *e.* me (B) *Ps 118:10*
e. by armies (N) *Lu 21:20*
e. for seven days *Heb 11:30*
(N)(P)(R)
e. as we are with (A)(P) *Heb 12:1*
e. the fortress (A)(P) *Re 20:9*

ENCIRCLES

pride *e.* their neck (B) *Ps 73:6*

ENCIRCLING

moved round, *e.* it (B) *Jos 6:11*
e. and capturing David (B) *1Sa 23:26*

ENCLOSING

placed in *e.* limit (A) *Job 26:10*

ENCOMPASSED

e. me with lies (R)(S) *Ho 11:12*
e. seven days (A) *Heb 11:30*

ENCOUNTERED

and of the Stoicks, *e.* him *Ac 17:18*

ENCOUNTERETH

right hand *e.* on (E) *Pr 27:16*

ENCOURAGE

he shall go in thither: *e.* him *De 1:38*
charge Joshua, and *e.* him *De 3:28*
and overthrow it: and *e.* *2Sa 11:25*
thou him
They *e.* themselves in an evil *Ps 64:5*
to *e.* and strengthen (N)(P) *Ac 15:32*
they stimulate and *e.* (N) *1Co 14:3*
e. the feebleminded (S) *1Th 5:14*
e. one another to love (P) *Heb 10:24*

ENCOURAGED

the men of Israel *e.* *J'g 20:22*
themselves
but David *e.* himself in the *1Sa 30:6*
Lord
that they might be *e.* in the *2Ch 31:4*
law of
and *e.* them to the service *2Ch 35:2*
of the
So the carpenter *e.* the *Isa 41:7*
goldsmith
comfort which *e.* *2Co 7:7*
(A)(E)(P)(R)
exhorted, *e.* and charged (S) *2Th 2:11*

ENCOURAGEMENT

son of *e.* (A)(R) *Ac 4:36*
who supplies *e.* (A)(N)(R) *Ro 15:5*

God of stedfastness and *e.* *Ro 15:5*
(A)
for *e.* (A)(R) *1Co 14:3*
by *e.* received (B) *2Co 7:7*
any *e.* (B)(P)(R) *Ph'p 2:1*

ENCOURAGES

e. in trouble (A)(B) *2Co 1:4*

ENCOURAGING

e. words (S) *2Ch 30:22*
e. mediums and wizards *Isa 33:6*
(A)(B)(R)
give *e.* message (B) *1Co 14:3*
consoling, *e.* (A) *Ph'p 2:1*

ENCOURAGINGLY

spake *e.* to them (S) *2Ch 32:6*

END

the *e.* of all flesh is come *Ge 6:13*
before me
from one *e.* of Egypt to the *Ge 47:21*
other *e.*
feast of ingathering in *e.* of *Ex 23:16;*
year *34:22*
make one cherub on one *e.* *Ex 25:19*
and other cherub on other *e.* of
mercy seat
the far *e.* of Jordan (S) *Nu 34:3*
the *e.* of the border (S) *Nu 34:8;*
34:12; Jos 15:4, 7, 11; 16:3, 8; 18:12,
14
Lord scatter from one *e.* of *De 28:64*
earth
Lord said, I will see what *e.* *De 32:20*
shall be
the *e.* (S) *Jos 17:9;*
18:19; 19:14, 22, 29, 33
angel put forth the *e.* of his *J'g 6:21*
staff
the day groweth to an *e.* *J'g 19:9*
lodge here
Jonathan put forth *e.* of *1Sa 14:27*
rod
house of Baal was full from *2Ki 10:21*
one *e.*
filled Jerusalem with blood *2Ki 21:16*
from one *e.*
after *e.* of two years, his *2Ch 21:19*
bowels
filled with unclean from one *Ezr 9:11*
e. to another
what is my *e.* that I should *Job 6:11*
prolong my life
shall vain words have *e.*? *Job 16:3*
what emboldens
no *e.* to iniquities *Job 22:5*
(A)(B)(E)(R)
till the day and night come *Job 26:10*
to an *e.*
he setteth an *e.* to darkness, *Job 28:3*
and searcheth
wickedness of wicked come to *Ps 7:9*
an *e.*
destructions are come to a *Ps 9:6*
perpetual *e.*
his going forth is from *e.* of *Ps 19:6*
heaven
upright man, for *e.* of that *Ps 37:37*
man is peace
e. of the wicked shall be cut *Ps 37:38*
off
make me know my *e.* *Ps 39:4*
from *e.* of earth will I cry to *Ps 61:2*
thee
I understood their *e.* *Ps 73:17*
thou art same, and thy *Ps 102:27*
years have no *e.*
I have seen an *e.* of all *Ps 119:96*
perfection
her *e.* is bitter *Pr 5:4*
but *e.* thereof are ways of *Pr 14:12*
death
lest thou know not what to *Pr 25:8*
do in *e.*
there is no *e.* of all his labour *Ec 4:8*
there is no *e.* of all the *Ec 4:16*
people before them
the *e.* of all men *Ec 7:2*
e. of his talk is mischievous *Ec 10:13*
madness
of making many books there *Ec 12:12*
is no *e.*
e. of the matter is this *Ec 12:13*
(A)(E)(R)

nor is there any *e.* of their   *Isa 2:7*
treasures, nor is there any *e.*
of their chariots
of his government there shall   *Isa 9:7*
be no *e.*
a full *e.,* as decreed (R)(S)   *Isa 10:23*
they come from *e.* of heaven   *Isa 13:5*
to destroy
for extortioner is at an *e.*   *Isa 16:4*
spoiler ceaseth
after *e.* of 70 years Tyre   *Isa 23:15;*
shall sing   *23:17*
made an *e.* of them (A)   *Isa 26:14*
sing his praise from the *e.*   *Isa 42:10*
of the earth
shall not be confounded   *Isa 45:17*
world without *e.*
declaring the *e.* from the   *Isa 46:10*
beginning
what will you do in the *e.*   *Jer 5:31*
thereof
devour from one *e.* to other   *Jer 12:12;*
e. of land   *25:33*
gets riches, and at his *e.* he   *Jer 17:11*
shall be a fool
I think to give you an   *Jer 29:11*
expected *e.*
there is hope in thine *e.*   *Jer 31:17*
saith the Lord
be consumed, till there be   *Jer 44:27*
an *e.* of them
O thou that dwellest, thine   *Jer 51:13*
e. is come
to shew that his city is   *Jer 51:31*
taken at one *e.*
our *e.* is near, for our *e.* is   *La 4:18*
come
an *e.* the *e.* is come on the   *Eze 7:2;*
land   *7:3, 6*
when iniquity shall have an   *Eze 21:25;*
e.   *21:29; 35:5*
hitherto is the *e.* of the   *Da 7:28*
matter
at the time of *e.* shall be the   *Da 8:17*
vision
at time appointed the *e.*   *Da 8:19;*
shall be   *11:27*
e. thereof shall be with a   *Da 9:26*
flood, and to *e.*
in the *e.* of years they shall   *Da 11:6*
join
to purge them even to the   *Da 11:35*
time of the *e.*
at time of *e.* king of south   *Da 11:40*
shall push him
yet he shall come to his *e.*   *Da 11:45*
and none help
seal the book even to the   *Da 12:4*
time of the *e.*
O Lord, what shall be *e.* of   *Da 12:8*
these things
words are closed up, till the   *Da 12:9*
time of the *e.*
but go thou thy way till the   *Da 12:13*
e. be, shalt rest
the great houses shall have   *Am 3:15*
an *e.*
to what *e.* is it for you to   *Am 5:18*
desire the day
e. is come upon my people of   *Am 8:2*
Israel
I will make *e.* thereof as a   *Am 8:10*
bitter day
for there is none *e.* of the   *Na 2:9*
store
there is none *e.* of their   *Na 3:3*
corpses
the harvest is the *e.* of the   *M't 13:39*
world
what shall be sign of *e.* of   *M't 24:3*
the world
gospel be preached, then   *M't 24:14*
shall *e.* come
gather from one *e.* of   *M't 24:31*
heaven to the other
but Peter went in and sat   *M't 26:58*
to see the *e.*
in the *e.* of sabbath came   *M't 28:1*
Mary to see
he cannot stand, but hath   *M'k 3:26*
an *e.*
of his kingdom there shall be   *Lu 1:33*
no *e.*
he spake a parable to them,   *Lu 18:1*
to this *e.*
the things concerning me   *Lu 22:37*
have an *e.*
sayest I am a king, to this   *Joh 18:37*
e. was I born

for the *e.* of those things is   *Ro 6:21*
death
have fruit to holiness, *e.*   *Ro 6:22*
everlasting life
Christ is *e.* of the law for   *Ro 10:4*
righteousness
to this *e.* Christ both died,   *Ro 14:9*
rose, and revived
to this *e.* also did I write to   *2Co 2:9*
know
whose *e.* shall be according   *2Co 11:15*
to works
to him be glory world   *Eph 3:21*
without *e.*
many walk, whose *e.* is   *Ph'p 3:19*
destruction
e. of the commandment is   *1Ti 1:5*
charity
bring to an *e.* to nought   *2Th 2:8*
(A)(B)(E)
nigh to cursing, whose *e.* is   *Heb 6:8*
to be burned
an oath is to them an *e.* of   *Heb 6:16*
all strife
having neither beginning nor   *Heb 7:3*
e. of life
but now once in the *e.* hath   *Heb 9:26*
he appeared
considering the *e.* of their   *Heb 13:7*
conversation
and ye have seen the *e.* of   *Jas 5:11*
the Lord
receiving *e.* of your faith,   *1Pe 1:9*
even salvation
what shall be *e.* of them   *1Pe 4:17*
obey not gospel
I am Alpha and Omega, the   *Re 21:6;*
beginning and the *e.*   *22:13*

AT THE END

at the *e.* of forty days Noah   *Ge 8:6*
opened window
at the *e.* of two years   *Ge 41:1*
Pharaoh dreamed
at the *e.* of 430 years, Lord's   *Ex 12:41*
hosts
days of consecration be at an   *Le 8:33*
e. of life
at the *e.* of 40 days and 40   *De 9:11*
nights
at the *e.* of three years bring   *De 14:28*
the tithe
at the *e.* of every seventh   *De 15:1*
year a release
at the *e.* of every seventh   *De 31:10*
year read this law
at the *e.* of three days after   *Jos 9:16*
league
at the *e.* of two months she   *J'g 11:39*
returned
Boaz lay down at the *e.* of   *Ru 3:7*
heap
at the *e.* of every year he   *2Sa 14:26*
polled it
Joab came to Jerusalem at the   *2Sa 24:8*
e. of nine months
at the *e.* of 3 years two of   *1Ki 2:39*
Shimei's servants
at the *e.* of 7 years the woman   *2Ki 8:3*
returned
at the *e.* of three years they   *2Ki 18:10*
took Samaria
ye shall find them at the *e.*   *2Ch 20:16*
of the brook
at the *e.* of year host of   *2Ch 24:23*
Syria came
stagger, and are at wit's *e.*   *Ps 107:27*
go to meet Ahaz at the *e.* of   *Isa 7:3*
conduit
at the *e.* of seven years let   *Jer 34:14*
go every servant
at the *e.* of seven days word   *Eze 3:16*
of Lord
at the *e.* they might stand   *Da 1:5*
before the king
at the *e.* of 12 months he   *Da 4:29*
walked in palace
stand in lot at the *e.* of   *Da 12:13*
days
at the *e.* it shall speak, and   *Hab 2:3*
not lie
so shall it be in the *e.* of   *M't 13:40*
this world

BUT THE END

way that seems right to   *Pr 14:12;*
man, *but the e.* are ways of   *16:25*

but the *e.* thereof shall not   *Pr 20:21*
be blessed
but the *e.* is not yet   *M't 24:6;*
  M'k 13:7; Lu 21:9
but the *e.* of all things is at   *1Pe 4:7*
hand

LAST END

and let my *last e.* be like his   *Nu 23:10*
they said, He shall not see   *Jer 12:4*
our *last e.*
she remembereth not her *last*   *La 1:9*
e.
make thee know what shall   *Da 8:19*
be *last e.*

LATTER END

his *latter e.* shall be that he   *Nu 24:20*
perish
to do thee good at thy *latter*   *De 8:16*
e.
that they would consider   *De 32:29*
their *latter e.*
shewed more kindness in   *Ru 3:10*
latter e.
it will be bitterness in *latter*   *2Sa 2:26*
e.
yet thy *latter e.* should greatly   *Job 8:7*
increase
Lord blessed *latter e.* of   *Job 42:12*
Job more
thou mayest be wise in   *Pr 19:20*
latter e.
consider them, and know   *Isa 41:22*
latter e.
neither didst remember *latter*   *Isa 47:7*
e. of it
the *latter e.* is worse than   *2Pe 2:20*
beginning

MADE AN END

as Isaac had *made an e.* of   *Ge 27:30*
blessing
Jacob *made an e.*   *Ge 49:33*
commanding sons
made an e. of reconciling   *Le 16:20*
holy place
made an e. of covering the   *Nu 4:15*
sanctuary
made an e. of speaking   *Nu 16:31;*
  De 20:9
hast *made an e.* of tithing   *De 26:12*
tithes
when Moses had *made an e.*   *De 31:24*
of writing
made an e. of speaking   *De 32:45;*
J'g 15:17; 1Sa 18:1; 24:16; 2Sa 13:36;
  1Ki 1:41; 3:1; Jer 26:8; 43:1; 51:63
Israel *made an e.* of slaying   *Jos 8:24;*
  10:20
made an e. of dividing the   *Jos 19:49;*
land
made an e. to offer   *J'g 3:18; 1Sa 13:10*
he had *made an e.* of   *1Sa 10:13*
prophesying
when thou hast *made an e.*   *2Sa 11:19*
of telling
Hiram *made an e.* of doing   *1Ki 7:40*
the work
Solomon *made an e.* of   *1Ki 8:54;*
praying   *2Ch 7:1*
as soon as *made an e.* of   *2Ki 10:25;*
offering   *1Ch 16:2; 2Ch 29:29*
made an e. of inhabitants   *2Ch 20:23*
of Seir
cast into chest, till *made*   *2Ch 24:10*
an e.
made an e. with all that   *Ezr 10:17*
had strange wives
made an e. of measuring   *Eze 42:15*
inner house
when thou hast *made an e.*   *Eze 43:23*
of cleansing it
they *made an e.* of eating   *Am 7:2*
grass
made an e. of commanding   *M't 11:1*
disciples

MAKE AN END

when I begin, I will *make an*   *1Sa 3:12*
e.
feeble Jews, will they *make an*   *Ne 4:2*
e. in a day
how long you *make an e.* of   *Job 18:2*
words

shalt *make an e.* to deal   *Isa 33:1*
treacherously
to-night wilt thou *make an*   *Isa 38:12;*
e. of me   *38:13*
eye spared, nor did I *make*   *Eze 20:17*
an e.
seventy weeks, to *make an e.*   *Da 9:24*
of sins
he will *make an* utter *e.* of   *Na 1:8;*
the place   *1:9*

MAKE A FULL END

will I not *make a full e.*   *Jer 4:27;*
     5:18; 30:11; 46:28
go ye up and destroy, but   *Jer 5:10*
make not *a full e.*
ah Lord, wilt thou *make a*   *Eze 11:13*
full e.

TO THE END

Goshen, *to the e.* thou mayest   *Ex 8:22;*
know   *Eze 20:26*
to the e. Israel may bring   *Le 17:5*
sacrifices
to the e. that he should   *De 17:16*
multiply horses
to the e. that he may   *De 17:20*
prolong his days
their words *to the e.* of the   *Ps 19:4*
world
to the e. my glory may sing   *Ps 30:12*
praise
to perform thy statutes   *Ps 119:112*
even *to the e.*
can find out from beginning   *Ec 3:11*
to the e.
to the e. man find nothing   *Ec 7:14*
after him
utter it even *to the e.* of the   *Isa 48:20*
earth
mayest be my salvation *to*   *Isa 49:6*
the e. of earth
his anger, will he keep it *to*   *Jer 3:5*
the e.
to the e. that none of trees   *Eze 31:14*
exalt
sight thereof *to the e.* of all   *Da 4:11*
earth
dominion reacheth *to the e.*   *Da 4:22*
of earth
how long be *to the e.* of   *Da 12:6*
these wonders
to the e. every one may be cut   *Ob 9*
off
he that endureth *to the e.*   *M't 10:22;*
shall be saved   *24:13; M'k 13:13*
cast out, *to the e.* they might   *Ac 7:19*
not live
to the e. you may be   *Ro 1:11*
established
to the e. the promise be sure   *Ro 4:16*
to seed
I trust you acknowledge *to*   *2Co 1:13*
the e.
look *to the e.* of that which   *2Co 3:13*
is abolished
to the e. he may establish   *1Th 3:13*
hearts
wherefore be sober, and   *1Pe 1:13*
hope *to the e.*

UNTO THE END

from beginning *unto the e.*   *De 11:12*
of year
east border was *unto the e.*   *Jos 15:5*
of Jordan
to glean *unto the e.* of barley   *Ru 2:23*
harvest
desire is Job may be tried   *Job 34:36*
unto the e.
maketh wars to cease *unto*   *Ps 46:9*
the e. of earth
teach me, and I shall keep   *Ps 119:33*
it *unto the e.*
Lord hath proclaimed *unto the*   *Isa 62:11*
e. of earth
it came *unto the e.* of eleventh   *Jer 1:3*
year
dominion shall be even *unto*   *Da 6:26*
the e.
to destroy his dominion *unto*   *Da 7:26*
the e.
unto the e. of the war   *Da 9:26*
desolations
I am with you alway, even   *M't 28:20*
unto the e.

having loved, he loved them   *Joh 13:1*
unto the e.
who shall confirm you *unto*   *1Co 1:8*
the e.
if we hold fast the confidence   *Heb 3:6*
unto the e.
if we hold the beginning   *Heb 3:14*
stedfast *unto the e.*
to the full assurance of   *Heb 6:11*
hope *unto the e.*
he that keepeth my works   *Re 2:26*
unto the e.

ENDAMAGE

so thou shalt *e.* the revenue   *Ezr 4:13*
of

ENDANGER

then shall ye make me *e.*   *Da 1:10*
my head

ENDANGERED

he that cleaveth wood shall   *Ec 10:9*
be *e.*

ENDEARING

speak *e.* words (B)   *J'g 19:3*

ENDEAVOUR

I will *e.* that ye may be able   *2Pe 1:15*
after

ENDEAVOURED

we *e.* to go into Macedonia   *Ac 16:10*
e. the more abundantly to   *1Th 2:17*
see

ENDEAVOURING

E. to keep the unity of the   *Eph 4:3*
Spirit

ENDEAVOURS

to the wickedness of their *e.*   *Ps 28:4*

ENDED

And on the seventh day God   *Ge 2:2*
e.
years of plenteousness, were *e.*   *Ge 41:53*
When that year was *e.* they   *Ge 47:18*
came
of this song, until they were   *De 31:30*
e.
and mourning for Moses were   *De 34:8*
e.
until they have *e.* all my   *Ru 2:21*
harvest
ended (S)   *2Sa 11:1*
     1Ch 20:1; 17:11; 2Ch 36:10; Re 20:7
so they *e.* the matter   *2Sa 20:18*
So was *e.* all the work that   *1Ki 7:51*
king
till the work was *e.* and   *2Ch 29:34*
until
The words of Job are *e.*   *Job 31:40*
of David the son of Jesse   *Ps 72:20*
are *e.*
deliverance never be *e.* (R)   *Isa 51:6*
days of thy mourning shall   *Isa 60:20*
be *e.*
the summer is *e.* and we are   *Jer 8:20*
not
till thou hast *e.* the days of   *Eze 4:8*
thy
evil-doings. (B)   *Eze 6:6*
when Jesus had *e.* these   *M't 7:28*
sayings
and when they were *e.* he   *Lu 4:2*
And when the devil had *e.* all   *Lu 4:13*
when he had *e.* all his sayings   *Lu 7:1*
supper being *e.* the devil   *Joh 13:2*
having
After these things were *e.*   *Ac 19:21*
Paul
the seven days were almost   *Ac 21:27*
e.

ENDETH

the noise of them that rejoice   *Isa 24:8*
e.

ENDING

Omega, the beginning and the   *Re 1:8*
e.

ENDLESS

thine iniquities *e.* (S)   *Job 22:5*
to fables and *e.* genealogies   *1Ti 1:4*
which
legends and *e.* genealogies   *1Ti 1:4*
(A)
lost in *e.* words (P)   *1Ti 1:6*
e. wrangles (N)(R)   *1Ti 6:5*
but after the power of an *e.*   *Heb 7:16*
life

EN-DOR

and the inhabitants of *E.*   *Jos 17:11*
and her
that hath a familiar spirit at   *1Sa 28:7*
E.
Which perished at *E.*: they   *Ps 83:10*

ENDOW

he shall surely *e.* her to be   *Ex 22:16*
pay her dowry (A)(B)(E)   *Ex 22:16*
give marriage present (R)   *Ex 22:16*

ENDOWED

e. with marriage gift   *Ge 30:20*
(A)(E)(R)
e. with skill (A)(B)(R)   *Ex 28:3*

ENDOWMENT

spiritual *e.* (A)   *1Co 1:7*

ENDOWMENTS

about spiritual *e.* (B)   *1Co 12:1*
distributions of *e.* (A)   *1Co 12:4*

ENDS

shall push people to *e.* of   *De 33:17*
earth
Lord shall judge the *e.* of   *1Sa 2:10*
earth
e. of staves were seen   *1Ki 8:8;*
     2Ch 5:9
for he looketh to *e.* of the   *Job 28:24*
earth
directeth his lightning to *e.*   *Job 37:3*
of earth
it might take hold of the *e.*   *Job 38:13*
of earth
and his circuit to the *e.* of it   *Ps 19:6*
all the *e.* of the world shall   *Ps 22:27*
remember
so is thy praise to the *e.* of   *Ps 48:10*
the earth
God ruleth in Jacob to *e.* of   *Ps 59:13*
earth
the confidence of all the *e.* of   *Ps 65:5*
the earth
all the *e.* of the earth shall   *Ps 67:7*
fear him
the *e.* of earth have seen the   *Ps 98:3*
salvation of God
Lord causeth vapours to   *Ps 135:7;*
ascend from *e.* of earth   *Jer 10:13; 51:16*
eyes of a fool are in *e.* of   *Pr 17:24*
earth
who hath established all *e.* of   *Pr 30:4*
earth
Lord, the creator of *e.* of   *Isa 40:28*
earth
e. of earth were afraid, drew   *Isa 41:5*
near
whom I have taken from *e.*   *Isa 41:9*
of earth
bring my daughters from *e.*   *Isa 43:6*
of earth
look to me and be saved, all   *Isa 45:22*
e. of earth
all *e.* shall see the salvation   *Isa 52:10*
of God
Gentiles shall come from *e.*   *Jer 16:19*
of earth
a noise shall come to *e.* of   *Jer 25:31*
earth
fire devoureth both *e.* of it   *Eze 15:4*
now shall he be great to *e.* of   *Mic 5:4*
earth
his dominion to *e.* of the   *Zec 9:10*
earth

thou be for salvation to *e.*   *Ac 13:47*
of earth
their words to the *e.* of   *Ro 10:18*
world
on whom *e.* of the world   *1Co 10:11*
are come

ENDUED

God hath *e.* me with a good   *Ge 30:20*
dowry
endowed with marriage gift   *Ge 30:20*
(A)(E)(R)
presented me with a rich   *Ge 30:20*
dowry (B)
David a wise son, *e.* with   *2Ch 2:12*
prudence
sent a cunning man, *e.* with   *2Ch 2:13*
understanding
till ye be *e.* with power from   *Lu 24:49*
on high
clothed with power from on   *Lu 24:49*
high (A)(B)(E)(P)(R)
armed with power from   *Lu 24:49*
above (N)
e. you with Spirit (B)   *1Co 3:5*
who is wise and *e.* with   *Jas 3:13*
knowledge

ENDURABLE

more *e.* (A)(B)   *M't 11:22;*
   11:24; M'k 6:11; Lu 10:12, 14

ENDURANCE

e. brings proof (N)   *Ro 5:4*

ENDURE

and as the children be able   *Ge 33:14*
to *e.*
then thou shalt be able to *e.*   *Ex 18:23*
how can I *e.* to see evil and   *Es 8:6*
destruction
he shall hold it fast, but it   *Job 8:15*
shall not *e.*
by reason of highness I   *Job 31:23*
could not *e.*
Lord *e.* for ever   *Ps 9:7;*
   102:12, 26; 104:31
weeping may *e.* for night, but   *Ps 30:5*
joy cometh
fear thee as long as sun   *Ps 72:5*
moon *e.*
name shall *e.* for ever, as   *Ps 72:17*
long as sun
his seed will I make to *e.*   *Ps 89:29;*
for ever   *89:36*
proud heart I will not *e.* (R)   *Ps 101:5*
doth crown *e.* to every   *Pr 27:24*
generation
can thy heart *e.* or hands   *Eze 22:14*
be strong
e. day of coming (A)(B)(R)   *Mal 3:2*
endure (N)   *M't 17:17;*
   M'k 9:19; Lu 9:41
he that shall *e.* to end   *M't 24:13;*
   M'k 13:13
no human being *e.*   *M't 24:22*
(A)(P)(R)
having no root, and so *e.*   *M'k 4:17*
for a time
how long shall I *e.* you (S)   *M'k 9:19*
and *e.* you (B)   *Lu 9:41*
suffering trains us to *e.* (N)   *Ro 5:4*
persecuted, we *e.* it (S)   *1Co 4:12*
you *e.* it (A)   *2Co 11:20*
in all your tribulations that   *2Th 1:4*
ye *e.*
therefore *e.* hardness as a   *2Ti 2:3*
soldier
I *e.* all things for elects' sake   *2Th 2:10*
when they will not *e.* sound   *2Th 4:3*
doctrine
but watch thou in all things,   *2Th 4:5*
e. afflictions
if ye *e.* chastening, God   *Heb 12:7*
dealeth with
they could not *e.* what was   *Heb 12:20*
commanded
we count them happy who *e.*   *Jas 5:11*
if a man for conscience *e.*   *1Pe 2:19*
grief

ENDURED

their time should have *e.* for   *Ps 81:15*
ever

if God *e.* with much   *Ro 9:22*
longsuffering
hast known what   *2Ti 3:11*
persecutions I *e.*
after patiently *e.* he   *Heb 6:15*
obtained promise
ye *e.* a great fight of   *Heb 10:32*
afflictions
Moses *e.* as seeing him   *Heb 11:27*
who is invisible
he *e.* the cross; *e.* such   *Heb 12:2;*
contradiction   *12:3*

ENDURETH

for his anger *e.* but a moment   *Ps 30:5*
the goodness of God *e.*   *Ps 52:1*
continually
abundance of peace so long   *Ps 72:7*
as moon *e.*
his truth *e.* to all generations   *Ps 100:5*
dominion *e.* through all   *Ps 145:13*
generations
he that *e.* to end shall be   *M't 10:22*
saved
e. for a while (S)   *M't 13:21*
but for that meat which *e.*   *Joh 6:27*
unto life
hopeth all things, *e.* all   *1Co 13:7*
things
blessed is the man that *e.*   *Jas 1:12*
temptation

ENDURETH *FOR EVER*

for his mercy *e. for ever*   *1Ch 16:34;*
   16:41; 2Ch 5:13; 7:3, 6; 20:21;
   Ezr 3:11; Ps 106:1; 107:1; 118:1-4;
   136:1-3; 138:8; Jer 33:11
his righteousness *e. for ever*   *Ps 111:3;*
   112:3, 9
his praise *e. for ever;* his   *Ps 111:10;*
truth   *117:2*
every one of thy judgments   *Ps 119:160*
e. for ever
thy name, O Lord, *e.* for   *Ps 135:13*
ever
the word of the Lord *e. for*   *1Pe 1:25*
ever

ENDURING

fear of the Lord is clean, *e.*   *Ps 19:9*
for ever
is effectual in *e.* the same   *2Co 1:6*
sufferings
have in heaven better and   *Heb 10:34*
e. substance

EN-EGLAIM

fishers shall stand from   *Eze 47:10*
En-gedi to E.

ENEMIES

to be avenged of the king's   *1Sa 18:25*
e.
when Lord hath cut off *e.*   *1Sa 20:15*
of David
the Lord require it at hand   *2Sa 20:16*
of David's *e.*
so and more do God to *e.*   *2Sa 25:22*
of David
behold a present of spoil of   *2Sa 30:26*
e. of Lord
given occasion to *e.* to   *2Sa 12:14*
blaspheme
e. of my lord be as that   *2Sa 18:32*
young man's
Lord fought against *e.* of   *2Ch 20:29*
Israel
e. of the Jews hoped to have   *Es 9:1*
power
hide me from deadly *e.* who   *Ps 17:9*
compass
e. of the Lord shall be as fat   *Ps 37:20*
of lambs
thine arrows are sharp in   *Ps 45:5*
heart of king's *e.*
he delivered his glory into   *Ps 78:61*
the *e.* hand
they shall speak with the *e.*   *Ps 127:5*
in the gate
given beloved into hands of   *Jer 12:7*
her *e.*
the *e.* have heard a cry of   *Jer 48:5*
destruction

all her friends are become her   *La 1:2*
e.
her adversaries are chief, her   *La 1:5*
e. prosper
man's *e.* are men of his own   *Mic 7:6*
house
if when *e.* we were reconciled   *Ro 5:10*
as concerning the gospel,   *Ro 11:28*
they are *e.*
till he hath put all *e.* under   *1Co 15:25*
feet
they are *e.* of cross of   *Ph'p 3:18*
Christ
were *e.* in mind by wicked   *Col 1:21*
works

HIS ENEMIES

thy seed possess gate of *his*   *Ge 22:17*
e.
he shall eat up the nations   *Nu 24:8*
his e.
till he hath driven out *his e.*   *Nu 32:21*
before him
be an help to him from *his e.*   *De 33:7*
Lord hath given him rest   *2Sa 7:1*
from *his e.*
how Lord hath avenged him   *2Sa 18:19*
of *his e.*
delivered him out of hand of   *2Sa 22:1*
all *his e.*
I will give him rest from all   *1Ch 22:9*
his e.
he counteth me as one of   *Job 19:11*
his e.
as for all *his e.* he puffeth at   *Ps 10:5*
them
wilt not deliver him to will of   *Ps 41:2*
his e.
let God arise, let *his e.* be   *Ps 68:1*
scattered
but God shall wound the   *Ps 68:21*
head of *his e.*
and *his e.* shall lick the dust   *Ps 72:9*
he smote *his e.* in the hinder   *Ps 78:66*
parts
thou hast made all *his e.* to   *Ps 89:42*
rejoice
a fire burneth up *his e.* round   *Ps 97:3*
about
until he see his desire upon   *Ps 112:8*
his e.
his e. will I clothe with   *Ps 132:18*
shame
he maketh *his e.* to be at   *Pr 16:7*
peace
the Lord shall join *his e.*   *Isa 9:11*
together
he shall prevail against *his*   *Isa 42:13*
e.
he will repay recompence to   *Isa 59:18*
his e.
voice that rendereth   *Isa 66:6*
recompence to *his e.*
his indignation be known   *Isa 66:14*
towards *his e.*
will give Pharaoh into hand   *Jer 44:30*
of *his e.*
and he reserveth wrath for *his*   *Na 1:2*
e.
and darkness shall pursue *his*   *Na 1:8*
e.
expecting till *his e.* be   *Heb 10:13*
made footstool

MINE ENEMIES

I took thee to curse *mine*   *Nu 23:11;*
e.   *24:10*
I will render vengeance to   *De 32:41*
mine e.
my mouth is enlarged over   *1Sa 2:1*
mine e.
that I may be avenged on   *1Sa 14:24*
mine e.
Lord hath broken forth   *2Sa 5:20;*
upon *mine e.* as breach of   *1Ch 14:11*
waters
so shall I be saved from   *2Sa 22:4;*
mine e.   *Ps 18:3*
I have pursued *mine e.*   *2Sa 22:38;*
   Ps 18:37
hast given me the necks of   *2Sa 22:41;*
mine e.   *Ps 18:40*
and that bringeth me forth   *2Sa 22:49*
from *mine e.*
if ye be come to betray me   *1Ch 12:17*
to *mine e.*
save me, hast smitten all *mine*   *Ps 3:7*
e.

lead me, O Lord, because of *mine e.* — *Ps 5:8*

mine eye waxeth old because of all *mine e.* — *Ps 6:7*

let all *mine e.* be ashamed and sore vexed — *Ps 6:10*

arise, O Lord, because of the rage of *mine e.* — *Ps 7:6*

when *mine e.* are turned, they shall fall — *Ps 9:3*

he delivereth me from *mine e.* — *Ps 18:48*

thou preparest a table in presence of *mine e.* — *Ps 23:5*

let not *mine e.* triumph over me — *Ps 25:2; 35:19*

consider *mine e.* for they are many — *Ps 25:19*

when *mine e.* came upon me to eat my flesh — *Ps 27:2*

now shall mine head be lifted up above *mine e.* — *Ps 27:6*

lead me in a plain path, because of *mine e.* — *Ps 27:11*

deliver me not over to the will of *mine e.* — *Ps 27:12*

I was a reproach among all *mine e.* — *Ps 31:11*

deliver me from the hand of *mine e.* — *Ps 31:15*

but *mine e.* are lively, and they are strong — *Ps 38:19*

mine e. speak evil of me; when shall he die — *Ps 41:5*

mine e. reproach me all the day — *Ps 42:10; 102:8*

he shall reward evil to *mine e.* cut them off — *Ps 54:5*

eye hath seen his desire upon *mine e.* — *Ps 54:7; 59:10*

mine e. would swallow me up, they be many — *Ps 56:2*

when I cry, then shall *mine e.* turn back — *Ps 56:9*

deliver me from *mine e.* O my God — *Ps 59:1; 143:9*

they being *mine e.* wrongfully are mighty — *Ps 69:4*

draw nigh, deliver me because of *mine e.* — *Ps 69:18*

mine e. speak against me, they lay wait — *Ps 71:10*

mine eye shall see my desire on *mine e.* — *Ps 92:11*

thou hast made me wiser than *mine e.* — *Ps 119:98*

because *mine e.* have forgotten thy word — *Ps 119:139*

many are *mine e.* yet do I not decline — *Ps 119:157*

stretch forth thy hand against *mine e.* — *Ps 138:7*

I hate them, I count them *mine e.* — *Ps 139:22*

of thy mercy cut off *mine e.* and destroy — *Ps 143:12*

saith the Lord, I will avenge me of *mine e.* — *Isa 1:24*

all *mine e.* have heard of my trouble — *La 1:21*

mine e. chased me sore like a bird without — *La 3:52*

those *mine e.* bring hither and slay them — *Lu 19:27*

OUR ENEMIES

they join also to *our e.* and fight — *Ex 1:10*

our e. themselves being judges — *De 32:31*

it may save us out of hand of *our e.* — *1Sa 4:3*

but deliver us out of the hand of *our e.* — *1Sa 12:10*

saved us out of hand of *our e.* — *2Sa 19:9; Ps 44:7*

because of the reproach of *our e.* — *Ne 5:9*

when rest of *our e.* heard I had builded — *Ne 6:1; 6:16*

through thee will we push down *our e.* — *Ps 44:5*

he it is shall tread down *our e.* — *Ps 60:12; 108:13*

and *our e.* laugh among themselves — *Ps 80:6*

and hath redeemed us from *our e.* — *Ps 136:24*

our e. have opened their mouths — *La 3:46*

that we should be saved from *our e.* — *Lu 1:71*

being delivered out of the hands of *our e.* — *Lu 1:74*

THEIR ENEMIES

had made them naked amongst *their e.* — *Ex 32:25*

send faintness in amongst *their e.* — *Le 26:36*

when they be in land of *their e.* — *Le 26:44*

Israel turneth backs before *their e.* — *Jos 7:8; 7:12*

stood not man of *their e.* — *Jos 21:44*

Lord delivered all *their e.* into their hand — *Jos 21:44*

had given rest from *their e.* — *Jos 23:1; Es 9:16*

sold them into the hand of *their e.* — *J'g 2:14*

delivered out of hand of *their e.* — *J'g 2:18; 8:34*

deliver them into the hand of *their e.* — *2Ki 21:14; 2Ch 6:36; 25:20; Ne 9:27*

but the sea overwhelmed *their e.* — *Ps 78:53*

I should soon have subdued *their e.* — *Ps 81:14*

and made them stronger than *their e.* — *Ps 105:24*

the waters covered *their e.* not one was left — *Ps 106:11*

their e. oppressed them, he delivered — *Ps 106:42*

I will deliver to the sword before *their e.* — *Jer 15:9*

to fall by the sword before *their e.* — *Jer 19:7; 20:4*

wherewith *their e.* shall straiten them — *Jer 19:9*

all treasures of Judah will give into hands of *their e.* — *Jer 20:5; 34:20-21; 21:7; Eze 39:23*

tho they go into captivity before *their e.* — *Am 9:4*

mighty men, which tread down *their e.* — *Zec 10:5*

if any hurt, fire devoureth *their e.* — *Re 11:5*

they ascended, and *their e.* beheld them — *Re 11:12*

THINE ENEMIES

who delivered *thine e.* into thy hand — *Ge 14:20*

thy hand shall be in the neck of *thine e.* — *Ge 49:8*

then I will be an enemy to *thine e.* — *Ex 23:22*

I will make *thine e.* to turn their backs to thee — *Ex 23:27*

raise, Lord, let *thine e.* be scattered — *Nu 10:35*

to cast out all *thine e.* from before thee — *De 6:19*

when thou goest against *thine e.* — *De 20:1; 21:10*

wherewith *thine e.* shall distress thee — *De 28:53; 28:55, 57*

thine e. shall be found liars to thee — *De 33:29*

thou canst not stand before *thine e.* — *Jos 7:13*

so let all *thine e.* perish, O Lord — *J'g 5:31*

hath taken vengeance for thee of *thine e.* — *J'g 11:36*

now let *thine e.* be as Nabal — *1Sa 25:26*

the souls of *thine e.* shall he sling out — *1Sa 25:29*

I have cut off all *thine e.* — *2Sa 7:9; 1Ch 17:8*

in that lovest *thine e.* and hatest thy friends — *2Sa 19:6*

or flee, three months before *thine e.* — *2Sa 24:13*

nor asked life of *thine e.* — *1Ki 3:11; 2Ch 1:11; 1Ch 21:12*

sword of *thine e.* overtaketh — *1Ch 21:12*

hast ordained strength because of *thine e.* — *Ps 8:2*

thine hand shall find out all *thine e.* — *Ps 21:8*

through thy power shall *thine e.* submit — *Ps 66:3*

thy foot may be dipped in blood of *thine e.* — *Ps 68:23*

thine e. roar — *Ps 74:4*

forget not the voice of *thine e.* the tumult — *Ps 74:23*

thine e. make a tumult — *Ps 83:2*

thou hast scattered *thine e.* with thy arm — *Ps 89:10*

wherewith *thine e.* have reproached, O Lord — *Ps 89:51*

lo, *thine e.* O Lord, *thine e.* shall perish — *Ps 92:9*

till I make *thine e.* thy footstool — *Ps 110:1; M't 22:44; M'k 12:36; Lu 20:43; Heb 1:13*

rule thou in the midst of *thine e.* — *Ps 110:2*

and *thine e.* take thy name in vain — *Ps 139:20*

the fire of *thine e.* shall devour them — *Isa 26:11*

no more give thy corn to be meat for *thine e.* — *Isa 62:8*

I will make thee to pass with *thine e.* — *Jer 15:14*

thine e. have opened their mouth — *La 2:16*

and the interpretation be to *thine e.* — *Da 4:19*

Lord shall redeem thee from *thine e.* — *Mic 4:10*

and all *thine e.* shall be cut off — *Mic 5:9*

thy gate shall be set open to *thine e.* — *Na 3:13*

thine e. shall cast a trench about thee — *Lu 19:43*

YOUR ENEMIES

ye shall chase *your e.* they shall fall — *Le 26:7*

your e. shall fall before you by the sword — *Le 26:8*

ye shall sow in vain, for *your e.* shall eat it — *Le 26:16*

and ye shall be slain before *your e.* — *Le 26:17*

shall have no power to stand before *your e.* — *Le 26:37*

ye shall be saved from *your e.* — *Nu 10:9*

be not smitten before *your e.* — *Nu 14:42; De 1:42*

he giveth you rest from all *your e.* — *De 12:10*

ye approach to battle against *your e.* — *De 20:3*

Lord goeth to fight for you against *your e.* — *De 20:3*

and there ye shall be sold to *your e.* — *De 28:68*

thus shall the Lord do to all *your e.* — *Jos 10:25*

divide spoil of *your e.* with brethren — *Jos 22:8*

the Lord delivered you out of hand of *your e.* — *1Sa 12:11; 2Ki 17:39*

but I say, love *your e.* — *M't 5:44; Lu 6:27, 35*

ENEMIES'

ye be in your *e.* land — *Le 26:34*

their iniquity in your *e.* lands — *Le 26:39*

gathered them out of their *e.* lands — *Eze 39:27*

ENEMY

thy right hand hath dashed in pieces *e.* — *Ex 15:6*

the *e.* said, I will pursue, I will overtake — *Ex 15:9*

then I will be an *e.* to thine enemies — *Ex 23:22*

e. to your enemies (E)(R) — *Ex 23:22*

and if you go to war against the *e.* — *Nu 10:9*

and was not his *e.* nor sought his harm — *Nu 35:23*

were it not I feared wrath of *e.* — *De 32:27*

from the beginning of revenges upon the *e.* — *De 32:42*

he shall thrust out the *e.*   *De 33:27*
before thee
our god hath delivered our   *J'g 16:23;*
e. into   *16:24*
thou shalt see an *e.* in my   *1Sa 2:32*
habitation
Saul became David's *e.*   *1Sa 18:29*
continually
if a man find his *e.* will he   *1Sa 24:19*
let him go
when people be smitten   *1Ki 8:33;*
down before *e.* because   *2Ch 6:24*
sinned
if they sin, and thou deliver   *1Ki 8:46*
them to *e.*
God shall make thee fall   *2Ch 25:8*
before *e.*
e. could not countervail   *Es 7:4*
damage
Esther said, The *e.* is this   *Es 7:6*
wicked Haman
Haman is an *e.* (B)(R)   *Es 7:6*
behold, he counteth me for   *Job 33:10*
his *e.*
let *e.* persecute my soul and   *Ps 7:5*
take it
thou mightest still the *e.* and   *Ps 8:2*
the avenger
O thou *e.* destructions are   *Ps 9:6*
come to an end
why go I mourning because   *Ps 42:9;*
c f *e.*   *43:2*
thou makest us to turn back   *Ps 44:10*
from *e.*
I mourn, because of the voice   *Ps 55:3*
of the *e.*
for it was not an *e.* that   *Ps 55:12*
reproached me
thou hast been a strong tower   *Ps 61:3*
from *e.*
preserve my life from fear of   *Ps 64:1*
the *e.*
even all that *e.* hath done   *Ps 74:3*
wickedly
shall *e.* blaspheme thy name   *Ps 74:10*
for ever
remember *e.* hath   *Ps 74:18*
reproached, O Lord
remembered not when he   *Ps 78:42*
delivered from *e.*
the *e.* shall not exact upon   *Ps 89:22*
him
for the *e.* hath persecuted   *Ps 143:3*
my soul
but kisses of an *e.* are   *Pr 27:6*
deceitful
when *e.* shall come in like a   *Isa 59:19*
flood
therefore he was turned to   *Isa 63:10*
be their *e.*
the sword of the *e.* is on   *Jer 6:25*
every side
I will cause the *e.* to entreat   *Jer 15:11*
thee well
scatter them with east-wind   *Jer 18:17*
before *e.*
I have wounded thee with   *Jer 30:14*
wound of an *e.*
are gone into captivity before   *La 1:5*
the *e.*
behold, for the *e.* hath   *La 1:9*
magnified himself
children are desolate, because   *La 1:16*
e. prevailed
he hath drawn back his hand   *La 2:3*
before the *e.*
he hath bent his bow like an   *La 2:4*
e. he stood
the Lord was as an *e.* he hath   *La 2:5*
swallowed up
that the *e.* should have   *La 4:12*
entered the gates
because *e.* had said against   *Eze 36:2*
you, Aha
Israel, the *e.* shall pursue him   *Ho 8:3*
My people is risen up as an   *Mic 2:8*
e.
shalt seek strength because of   *Na 3:11*
e.
his *e.* came, sowed tares,   *M't 13:25*
went way
he said unto them, An *e.*   *M't 13:28*
hath done this
the *e.* that sowed them is   *M't 13:39*
the devil
to tread over all the power   *Lu 10:19*
of the *e.*
child of devil, thou *e.* of all   *Ac 13:10*
righteousness

the last *e.* to be destroyed   *1Co 15:26*
is death
am I become your *e.* because   *Ga 4:16*
I tell truth
count him not as an *e.* but   *2Th 3:15*
admonish
give *e.* no occasion (P)(R)   *1Ti 5:14*
e. the devil (A)(N)(P)   *1Pe 5:8*
a friend of the world is the *e.*   *Jas 4:4*
of God
being world's friend is being   *Jas 4:4*
God's *e.* (A)(P)(R)

HAND OF THE ENEMY

be delivered into *hand* of   *Le 26:25;*
the *e.*   *Ne 9:27*
he delivered us from *hand* of   *Ezr 8:31*
the *e.*
hast not shut me up into   *Ps 31:8*
hand of the *e.*
redeemed from *hand* of the   *Ps 106:10;*
e.   *107:2*
her people fell into *hand* of   *La 1:7*
the *e.*
hath given into the *hand* of   *La 2:7*
the *e.*

MINE ENEMY

why hast thou sent away   *1Sa 19:17*
mine e.
delivered me from *my e.*   *2Sa 22:18;*
  Ps 18:17
hast thou found me, O   *1Ki 21:20*
mine e.
mine e. sharpeneth his eyes   *Job 16:9*
upon me
let *mine e.* be as wicked, he   *Job 27:7*
that riseth
I delivered him that is *mine e.*   *Ps 7:4*
how long shall *mine e.* be   *Ps 13:2*
exalted over me
lest *mine e.* say, I have   *Ps 13:4*
prevailed
because *mine e.* doth not   *Ps 41:11*
triumph over me
those I swaddled *mine e.*   *La 2:22*
consumed
rejoice not against me, O   *Mic 7:8*
mine e.
then she that is *mine e.* shall   *Mic 7:10*
see it

THINE ENEMY

if thou meet *thine e.* ox or   *Ex 23:4*
his ass
thine e. shall distress thee in   *De 28:57*
gates
deliver *thine e.* into thy   *1Sa 24:4;*
hand   *26:8*
seeing the Lord is become   *1Sa 28:16*
thine e.
behold head of Ish-bosheth   *2Sa 4:8*
thine e.
wherefore holdest thou me   *Job 13:24*
for *thine e.*
rejoice not when *thine e.*   *Pr 24:17*
falleth
if *thine e.* hunger, give   *Pr 25:21;*
bread   *Ro 12:20*
hath caused *thine e.* to   *La 2:17*
rejoice over thee
the Lord hath cast out *thine*   *Zep 3:15*
e.
it hath been said, thou shalt   *M't 5:43*
hate *thine e.*

ENEMY'S

If thou meet thine *e.* ox   *Ex 23:4*
Deliver me from the *e.* hand   *Job 6:23*
his glory into the *e.* hand   *Ps 78:61*

ENERGY

with unflogging *e.* (N)   *Ro 12:11*

ENFLAMING

E. yourselves with idols   *Isa 57:5*
under

ENFOLD

to *e.* her (P)   *Eph 5:29*

ENFORCE

never *e.* by terrifying (A)   *Lu 3:14*

ENGAGE

e. in lusts of defiling (R)   *2Pe 2:10*

ENGAGED

for who is this that *e.* his   *Jer 30:21*
heart

EN-GANNIM

Zanoah, and *E.*, Tappuah   *Jos 15:34*
Remeth, and *E.*, and   *Jos 19:21*
En-haddah
Jarmuth with her suburbs,   *Jos 21:29*
E. with

EN-GEDI

and the city of Salt, and *E.*   *Jos 15:62*
and dwelt in strong holds at   *1Sa 23:29*
E.
David is in the wilderness of   *1Sa 24:1*
E.
be in Hazaon-tamar, which   *2Ch 20:2*
is *E.*
camphire in the vineyards of   *Ca 1:14*
E.
fishers shall stand upon it   *Eze 47:10*
from *E.*

ENGINES

And he made in Jerusalem   *2Ch 26:15*
e.
made machines devised by   *2Ch 26:15*
inventors (A)(B)
he shall set *e.* of war against   *Eze 26:9*
thy
his battering rams shall   *Eze 26:9*
pound (B)(R)

ENGRAFTED

with meekness the *e.* word   *Jas 1:21*
implanted and rooted (A)   *Jas 1:21*
word implanted (B)(E)(R)   *Jas 1:21*
message planted in your   *Jas 1:21*
hearts (N)
message God has sown in   *Jas 1:21*
hearts (P)

ENGRAVE

e. on them (S)   *Ex 28:9;*
  28:36; 2Ch 2:7, 14
shalt thou *e.* the two stones   *Ex 28:11*
e. any engraving (A)   *2Ch 2:14*
behold, I will *e.* the graving   *Zec 3:9*
thereof

ENGRAVED

engraved (S)   *Ex 32:16;*
39:6; Job 19:24; Isa 49:16; Jer 10:14;
  17:1; 51:17; Hab 2:18
e. (B)(R)   *Ex 32:16; 39:6; Job 19:24*
an *e.* image (B)   *J'g 17:3;*
  17:4; 18:14, 17
e. cherubims (A)   *2Ch 3:7*
e. on tablet of heart   *Jer 17:1*
(A)(B)(R)

ENGRAVEN

written and *e.* in stones, was   *2Co 3:7*

ENGRAVER

With the work of an *e.* in   *Ex 28:11*
stone
all manner of work, of the   *Ex 35:35*
e.
an *e.* and a cunning   *Ex 38:23*
workman

ENGRAVING

engraving (S)   *Ex 32:4;*
  2Ch 2:14; Zec 3:9
engrave any *e.* (A)(B)(R)   *2Ch 2:14*
they did *e.* (B)   *2Ch 4:14*
e. its inscriptions (B)(R)   *Zec 3:9*

ENGRAVINGS

in stone, like the *e.* of a signet	Ex 28:11
names, like the *e.* of a signet	Ex 28:21
upon it, like the *e.* of a signet	Ex 28:36
names, like the *e.* of a signet	Ex 39:14
writing, like to the *e.* of a signet	Ex 39:30
upon the mouth were *e.* (B)	1Ki 7:21

ENGULFING

current *e.* me (B)	Jon 2:3

EN-HADDAH

and *E.* and Beth-pazzez	Jos 19:21

EN-HAKKORE

he called the name thereof *E.*	J'g 15:19

EN-HAZOR

And Kedesh, and Edrei, and *E.*	Jos 19:37

ENJOIN

I *e.* youth's day (R)	De 32:46
much bold in Christ to *e.* thee	Ph'm 8
charge you to do what is fitting(A)	Ph'm 8
give you directions as to your duty (B)	Ph'm 8
point out your duty (N)	Ph'm 8
dare to order you to do (P)	Ph'm 8
to command you to do (R)	Ph'm 8

ENJOINED

and Esther the queen had *e.* them	Es 9:31
had ordained for themselves (A)	Es 9:31
Esther had appointed them (B)	Es 9:31
Who hath *e.* him his way	Job 36:23
Who has appointed God his way (A)	Job 36:23
Who would assign to him his way (B)	Job 36:23
Who has prescribed to him his way (P)	Job 36:23
which God hath *e.* unto you	Heb 9:20
God commanded you (A)(E)(R)	Heb 9:20
agreement God makes with you (P)	Heb 9:20

ENJOY

shall the land *e.* her sabbaths	Le 26:34
the land rest, and *e.* her sabbaths	Le 26:34
shall *e.* her sabbaths, while	Le 26:43
children of Israel may *e.* every	Nu 36:8
daughters, but thou shalt not *e.*	De 28:41
land of your possession, and *e.* it	Jos 1:15
with mirth, therefore *e.* pleasure	Ec 2:1
he should make his soul *e.* good in	Ec 2:24
and *e.* the good of all his labour	Ec 3:13
eat and to drink, and to *e.* the good	Ec 5:18
long *e.* the work of their hands	Isa 65:22
eat, drink, *e.* thyself (A)(B)(N)	Lu 12:19
Seeing that by thee we *e.* great	Ac 24:2
know how to *e.* plenty (A)	Ph'p 4:12
giveth us richly all things to *e.*	1Ti 6:17
than to *e.* the pleasures of sin	Heb 11:25

ENJOYABLE

waters were made *e.* (B)	Ex 15:25

ENJOYED

ate, drank, *e.* life (B)	1Ki 4:20
until the land had *e.* her sabbaths	2Ch 36:21

ENJOYMENT

prohibit *e.* of foods (B)(N)(P)(R)	1Ti 4:3

ENLARGE

God shall *e.* Japheth, and he shall	Ge 9:27
before thee, and *e.* thy borders	Ex 34:24
When the Lord thy God shall *e.* thy	De 12:20
if the Lord thy God *e.* thy coast	De 19:8
wouldest bless, and *e.* my coast	1Ch 4:10
when thou shalt *e.* my heart	Ps 119:32
E. the place of thy tent, and let	Isa 54:2
that they might *e.* their border	Am 1:13
e. thy baldness as the eagle	Mic 1:16
e. the borders of their garments	M't 23:5

ENLARGED

my mouth is *e.* over mine enemies	1Sa 2:1
my mouth is no longer silent (A)	1Sa 2:1
my mouth is freely opened (B)	1Sa 2:1
my mouth derides my enemies (R)	1Sa 2:1
Thou hast *e.* my steps under me	2Sa 22:37
Thou stretchest my stride (B)	2Sa 22:37
give a wide place for my steps (R)	2Sa 22:37
thou hast *e.* me when I was in	Ps 4:1
given relief when in distress (B)	Ps 4:1
set me at large when in distress (E)	Ps 4:1
given me room when in distress (R)	Ps 4:1
Thou hast *e.* my steps under me	Ps 18:36
The troubles of my heart are *e.*	Ps 25:17
troubles are multiplied (A)	Ps 25:17
Relieve the trouble of my heart (R)	Ps 25:17
Therefore hell hath *e.* herself	Isa 5:14
gone up; thou hast *e.* thy bed	Isa 57:8
widened thy bed (B)(R)	Isa 57:8
thine heart shall fear, and be *e.*	Isa 60:5
hearts be filled with awe and swell (B)	Isa 60:5
heart shall thrill and rejoice (R)	Isa 60:5
is open unto you, our heart is *e.*	2Co 6:11
our heart is expanded wide (A)	2Co 6:11
with wide-open hearts (B)	2Co 6:11
we have opened our heart wide (N)(R)	2Co 6:11
our hearts are absolutely open (P)	2Co 6:11
unto my children, be ye also *e.*	2Co 6:13
open wide your hearts (A)(B)(N)	2Co 6:13
with the same complete candor (P)	2Co 6:13
widen your hearts also (R)	2Co 6:13
that we shall be *e.* by you	2Co 10:15
be magnified in you (E)	2Co 10:15

ENLARGEMENT

shall there *e.* and deliverance	Es 4:14
relief and deliverance (A)	Es 4:14
deliverance rescue from (B)	Es 4:14
deliverance arise from another (E)(R)	Es 4:14

ENLARGEST

e. thine eyes with paint (S)	Jer 4:30

ENLARGETH

Blessed be he that *e.* Gad	De 33:20
he *e.* the nations, and straiteneth	Job 12:23
who *e.* his desire as hell	Hab 2:5

ENLARGING

there was an *e.* and a winding	Eze 41:7

ENLIGHTEN

Lord my God will *e.* my darkness	Ps 18:28

ENLIGHTENED

his mouth; and his eyes were *e.*	1Sa 14:27
his eyes brightened (A)(B)	1Sa 14:27
his eyes became bright (R)	1Sa 14:27
mine eyes have been *e.* because	1Sa 14:29
to be *e.* with the light of the living	Job 33:30
that he may see the light of life (B)(R)	Job 33:30
His lightnings *e.* the world	Ps 97:4
lightnings illuminate the world (A)(B)	Ps 97:4
lightnings lighten the world (R)	Ps 97:4
of your understanding being *e.*	Eph 1:18
eyes of your heart flooded with light (A)	Eph 1:18
granting you illumined eyes of heart (B)	Eph 1:18
inward eyes may be illumined (N)	Eph 1:18
inner illumination of the spirit (P)	Eph 1:18
those who were once *e.* and have	Heb 6:4
have once for all been illumined (B)	Heb 6:4
were first spiritually *e.* (A)(E)(N)(R)	Heb 10:32

ENLIGHTENING

of the Lord is pure, *e.* the eyes	Ps 19:8

EN-MISHPAT

they returned, and came to *E.*	Ge 14:7

ENMITY

put *e.* between thee and the woman	Ge 3:15
Or in *e.* smite him with his hand	Nu 35:21
if from animosity he strikes (B)	Nu 35:21
thrust him suddenly without *e.*	Nu 35:22
without ill will (B)	Nu 35:22
were at *e.* between themselves	Lu 23:12
the carnal mind is *e.* against God	Ro 8:7
hostile to God (A)(B)(R)	Ro 8:7
inevitably opposed to purpose of God (P)	Ro 8:7
broke down the *e.* (N)	Eph 2:14
abolished in his flesh the *e.*	Eph 2:15
end the feud (B)	Eph 2:15
removed hostility of law (P)	Eph 2:15
having slain the *e.* thereby	Eph 2:16
killing the feud (B)	Eph 2:16
made utterly irrelevant the antagonism (P)	Eph 2:16
bringing hostility to an end (R)	Eph 2:16
friendship of the world is *e.* with	Jas 4:4
being world's friend is being God's enemy (A)(P)(R)	Jas 4:4

ENOCH

and she conceived, and bare *E. Ge 4:17;*
　　　　　　　　　　　　　　　　　4:18
and two years, and he begat *E. Ge 5:18*
which was the son of *E.* which *Lu 3:37;*
　　　　　　　　　　　　　　　　5:19, 21-24
By faith *E.* was translated *Heb 11:3*
E. also, the seventh from *Jude 14*
Adam

ENOS

called his name *E.* then began *Ge 4:26*
and five years, and begat *E. Ge 5:6;*
　　　　　　　　　　　　　　5:7, 9-11
Which was the son of *E.* which *Lu 3:38*

ENOSH

Adam, Sheth, *E.*　　　　　　　*1Ch 1:1*

ENOUGH

have both straw and　　　　　*Ge 24:25*
provender *e.*
Esau said, I have *e.* my brother *Ge 33:9*
with me, and because I have *Ge 33:11*
e.
behold, it is large *e.* for them *Ge 34:21*
Israel said, It is *e.;* Joseph my *Ge 45:28*
and also drew water *e.* for us *Ex 2:19*
Intreat the Lord (for it is *e.*) *Ex 9:28*
much more than *e.* for the *Ex 36:5*
service
Ye have dwelt long *e.* in this *De 1:6*
mountain
compassed this mountain long *e. De 2:3*
The hill is not *e.* for us *Jos 17:16*
It is *e.:* stay now thine hand *2Sa 24:16*
It is *e.;* now, O Lord, take *1Ki 19:4*
away
It is *e.* stay now thine hand *1Ch 21:15*
we have had *e.* to eat, and *2Ch 31:10*
have
have goats' milk *e.* for thy *Pr 27:27*
food
persons shall have poverty *e. Pr 28:19*
yea, four things say not, It is *e Pr 30:15*
and the fire that saith not, It *Pr 30:16*
is *e.*
dogs which can never have *e. Isa 56:11*
they will destroy till they have *Jer 49:9*
e.
they shall eat, and not have *e. Ho 4:10*
not have stolen till they had *e. Ob 5*
did tear in pieces *e.* for his *Na 2:12*
whelps
little; ye eat, but ye have not *e. Hag 1:6*
that there shall not be room *e. Mal 3:10*
It is *e.* for the disciple that *M't 10:25*
he be
lest there be not *e.* for us and *M't 25:9*
you
your rest: it is *e.* the hour is *M'k 14:41*
come
have bread *e.* and to spare *Lu 15:17*
he said unto them, It is *e. Lu 22:38*
they had eaten *e.* they *Ac 27:38*
lightened

ENQUIRE

We will call the damsel, and *Ge 24:57*
e. at
And she went to *e.* of the *Ge 25:22*
Lord
people come unto me to *e.* of *Ex 18:15*
God
that thou *e.* not after their *De 12:30*
gods
shalt thou *e.* and make search *De 13:14*
and *e.;* and they shall shew *De 17:9*
thee
man doth come and *e.* of thee *J'g 4:20*
when a man went to *e.* of God *1Sa 9:9*
E. thou whose son the *1Sa 17:56*
stripling is
Did I then begin to *e.* of God *1Sa 22:15*
that I may go to her, and *e.* of *1Sa 28:7*
her
E. I pray thee, at the word of *1Ki 22:5*
the
besides, that we might *e.* of *1Ki 22:7*
him
by whom we may *e.* of the *1Ki 22:8*
Lord
e. of Baal-zebub the god of *2Ki 1:2*
Ekron

that ye go to *e.* of Baal-zebub *2Ki 1:3*
thou sendest to *e.* of Baal-zebub *2Ki 1:6*
e. of Baal-zebub the god of *2Ki 1:16*
Ekron
no God in Israel to *e.* of his *2Ki 1:16*
word
that we may *e.* of the Lord by *2Ki 3:11*
him
and *e.* of the Lord by him *2Ki 8:8*
altar shall be for me to *e.* by *2Ki 16:15*
Go ye, *e.* of the Lord for me *2Ki 22:13*
which sent you to *e.* of the *2Ki 22:18*
Lord
had a familiar spirit, to *e.* of *1Ch 10:13*
it
his son to king David, to *e. 1Ch 18:10*
of his
could not go before it to *e. 1Ch 21:30*
of God
E. I pray thee, at the word of *2Ch 18:4*
the
besides, that we might *e.* of *2Ch 18:6*
him
by whom we may *e.* of the *2Ch 18:7*
Lord
sent unto him to *e.* of the *2Ch 32:31*
wonder
Go, *e.* of the Lord for me, *2Ch 34:21*
and for
who sent you to *e.* of the *2Ch 34:26*
Lord
to *e.* concerning Judah and *Ezr 7:14*
e. I pray thee, of the former *Job 8:8*
age
the Lord, and to *e.* in his *Ps 27:4*
temple
dost not *e.* wisely concerning *Ec 7:10*
this
if ye will *e., e.* ye: return, *Isa 21:12*
come
E. I pray thee, of the Lord for *Jer 21:2*
us
that sent you unto me to *e.* of *Jer 37:7*
me
prophet to *e.* of him *Eze 14:7*
concerning
of Israel came to *e.* of the *Eze 20:1*
Lord
Are ye come to *e.* of me *Eze 20:3*
e. who in it is worthy; and *M't 10:11*
there
began to *e.* among themselves *Lu 22:23*
Do ye *e.* among yourselves of *Joh 16:19*
that
e. in the house of Judas for one *Ac 9:11*
But if ye *e.* any thing *Ac 19:39*
concerning
as though ye would *e. Ac 23:15*
something
as though they would *e. Ac 23:20*
somewhat
e. more closely (P)(R) *Ac 23:20*
Whether any do *e.* of Titus, *2Co 8:23*
he is

ENQUIRED

e. diligently, and, behold, it be *De 17:4*
And when they *e.* and asked *J'g 6:29*
a young man, and *e.* of him *J'g 8:14*
children of Israel *e.* of the *J'g 20:27*
Lord
they *e.* of the Lord further, if *1Sa 10:22*
And he *e.* of the Lord for *1Sa 22:10*
him
and hast *e.* of God for him *1Sa 22:13*
Therefore David *e.* of the *1Sa 23:2*
Lord
David *e.* of the Lord yet again *1Sa 23:4*
And when Saul *e.* of the Lord *1Sa 28:6*
And David *e.* at the Lord, *1Sa 30:8*
saying
that David *e.* of the Lord, *2Sa 2:1*
saying
And David *e.* of the Lord, *2Sa 5:19*
saying
when David *e.* of the Lord, he *2Sa 5:23*
said
David sent and *e.* after the *2Sa 11:3*
woman
as if a man had *e.* at the *2Sa 16:23*
oracle
year; and David *e.* of the Lord *2Sa 21:1*
And *e.* not of the Lord: *1Ch 10:14*
therefore
we *e.* not at it in the days of *1Ch 13:3*
Saul
And David *e.* of God, saying *1Ch 14:10*

Therefore David *e.* again of *1Ch 14:14*
God
returned and *e.* early after *Ps 78:34*
God
should I be *e.* of at all by *Eze 14:3*
them
Lord God, I will not be *e.* of *Eze 20:3*
by you
and shall I be *e.* of by you, *Eze 20:31*
O house
Lord God, I will not be *e.* of *Eze 20:31*
by you
I will yet for this be *e.* of by *Eze 36:37*
king *e.* of them, he found them *Da 1:20*
sought the Lord, nor *e.* for him *Zep 1:6*
e. of them diligently what time *M't 2:7*
had diligenlty *e.* of the wise *M't 2:16*
men
Then *e.* he of them the hour *Joh 4:52*
or our brethren be *e.* of, they *2Co 8:23*
have *e.* and searched diligently *1Pe 1:10*

ENQUIREST

That thou *e.* after mine *Job 10:6*
iniquity

ENQUIRY

and after vows to make *e. Pr 20:25*
had made *e.* for Simon's *Ac 10:17*
house

ENRAGED

they are *e.* (R) *2Sa 17:8*
angry and greatly *e.* (R) *Ne 4:1*
the king was *e.* (S) *Es 1:12*
was *e.* against him (R) *Da 8:7*
e., shall march forth (B) *Da 11:11*
e. to take action (R) *Da 11:30*

ENRICH

king will *e.* him with great *1Sa 17:25*
riches
will richly reward the one *1Sa 17:25*
(B)
thou didst *e.* the kings of the *Eze 27:33*
earth
making kings rich (B) *Eze 27:33*

ENRICHED

in every thing ye are *e.* by him *1Co 1:5*
e. in every thing to all *2Co 9:11*
bountifulness

ENRICHEST

greatly *e.* it with the river of *Ps 65:9*
God

EN-RIMMON

And at *E.* and at Zareah, and *Ne 11:29*

EN-ROGEL

the goings out thereof were at *Jos 15:7*
E.
on the south, and descended *Jos 18:16*
to *E.*
and Ahimaaz stayed by *E. 2Sa 17:17*
stone of Zoheleth, which is by *1Ki 1:9*
E.

ENSAMPLE

walk as ye have us for an *e. Ph'p 3:17*
to make ourselves an *e.* unto *2Th 3:9*
you
making them an *e.* unto those *2Pe 2:6*

ENSAMPLES

things happened unto them *1Co 10:11*
for *e.*
that ye were *e.* to all that *1Th 1:7*
believe
but being *e.* to the flock *1Pe 5:3*

EN-SHEMESH

passed toward the waters of *E. Jos 15:7*
and went forth to *E.* and *Jos 18:17*

ENSIGN

the *e.* of their father's house	*Nu 2:2*
he will lift up an *e.* to the nations	*Isa 5:26*
shall stand for an *e.* of the people	*Isa 11:10*
he shall set up an *e.* for the nations	*Isa 11:12*
lifteth up an *e.* on the mountains	*Isa 18:3*
and as an *e.* on an hill	*Isa 30:17*
his princes shall be afraid of the *e.*	*Isa 31:9*
I will set up in *e.* (E)	*Isa 49:22*
lift up as *e.* (E)(R)	*Isa 62:10*
lifted up as an *e.* upon his land	*Zec 9:16*

ENSIGNS

they set up their *e.* for signs	*Ps 74:4*

ENSLAVE

sell for money or *e.* (B)(E)(R)	*De 21:7*
none should *e.* himself (S)	*Jer 34:9; 27:7; 30:8; 34:10*

ENSLAVED

e. the sons of Israel (B)	*Ex 1:13*
those that *e.* themselves (S)	*Eze 34:27*
the *e.* (S)	*Re 13:16; 19:18*

ENSNARED

reign not, lest the people be *e.*	*Job 34:30*

ENSUE

let him seek peace, and *e.* it	*1Pe 3:11*

ENTANGLE

how they might *e.* him in his talk	*M't 22:15*

ENTANGLED

of Israel, They are *e.* in the land	*Ex 14:3*
while they are *e.* (S)	*Na 1:10*
e. again with the yoke of bondage	*Ga 5:1*
they are again *e.* therein, and	*2Pe 2:20*

ENTANGLETH

e. himself with the affairs of this	*2Ti 2:4*

ENTANGLING

cord of sheol *e.* me (A)	*2Sa 22:6*

EN-TAPPUAH

hand, unto the inhabitants of E.	*Jos 17:7*

ENTER

not slothful to *e.* to possess the land	*J'g 18:9*
e. into judgment with (S)	*Eze 17:20; 20:35-36; 38:22*
prince shall *e.* by the porch	*Eze 44:3; 46:2, 8*
shall also set his face to *e.* with strength	*Da 11:17*
he shall *e.* peaceably on the fattest places	*Da 11:24*
it remaineth that some must *e.* therein	*Heb 4:6*

ENTER *IN, INTO*

Abram was come near to *e. into* Egypt	*Ge 12:11*
Moses was not able to *e. into* the tent	*Ex 40:35*
all that *e. in* to perform the service	*Nu 4:23*
water that causeth curse shall *e. into* the woman	*Nu 5:24; 5:27*
children shall *e. into* the congregation	*De 23:8*
thou shouldest *e. into* covenant with Lord	*De 29:12*
suffer them not to *e. into* their cities	*Jos 10:19*
and my cry did *e. into* his ears	*2Sa 22:7*
when thy feet *e. into* city, child die	*1Ki 14:12*
disguise myself and *e. into* battle	*1Ki 22:30*
if we *e. into* city, then famine	*2Ki 7:4*
third part of you that *e. in* on sabbath	*2Ki 11:5*
I will *e. into* lodgings of his borders	*2Ki 19:23; Isa 37:24*
that none unclean should *e. in*	*2Ch 23:19*
e. into his sanctuary, which he sanctified	*2Ch 30:8*
for the house that I shall *e. into*	*Ne 2:8*
for none might *e. into* king's gate	*Es 4:2*
will he *e.* with thee *into* judgment	*Job 22:4*
that he should *e. into* judgment with God	*Job 34:23*
sword shall *e. into* their own heart	*Ps 37:15*
they shall *e. into* the king's palace	*Ps 45:15*
e. into his gates with thanksgiving	*Ps 100:4*
the gate *into* which righteous shall *e.*	*Ps 118:20*
a fool's lips *e. into* contention	*Pr 18:6*
e. into rock, and hide thee in dust	*Isa 2:10*
Lord will *e. into* judgment with ancients	*Isa 3:14*
that the righteous nation may *e. in*	*Isa 26:2*
come, my people, *e.* thou *into* thy chambers	*Isa 26:20*
he shall *e. into* peace, rest in beds	*Isa 57:2*
e. in at these gates	*Jer 7:2; 7:20; 22:2*
let us *e. into* the defenced cities	*Jer 8:14*
if I *e. into* the city, behold famine	*Jer 14:18*
there shall *e. into* gates	*Jer 17:25; 22:4*
or who shall *e. into* our habitations	*Jer 21:13*
they departed to go to *e. into* Egypt	*Jer 41:17*
if ye set your faces to *e. into* Egypt	*Jer 42:15*
caused arrows to *e. into* my reins	*La 3:13*
robbers shall *e. into* it and defile it	*Eze 7:22*
nor shall they *e. into* the land of Israel	*Eze 13:9*
he shall *e. into* gates, as men *into* a city	*Eze 26:10*
I will cause breath to *e. into* you	*Eze 37:5*
when priests *e. therein,* then not go out	*Eze 42:14*
gate be shut, no man *e. in* by it	*Eze 44:2*
they shall *e. into* my sanctuary, and come	*Eze 44:16*
when *e. in* at gates of inner court	*Eze 44:17*
shall *e. into* fortress of king of north	*Da 11:7*
he shall *e. into* the countries and overflow	*Da 11:40*
he shall *e.* also *into* the glorious land	*Da 11:41*
like a thief they shall *e. in* at windows	*Joe 2:9*
seek not Beth-el, nor *e. into* Gilgal	*Am 5:5*
and Jonah began to *e. into* the	*Jon 3:4*
flying roll shall *e. into* house of thief	*Zec 5:4*
in no case *e. into* kingdom of heaven	*M't 5:20*
when thou prayest, *e. into* thy closet	*M't 6:6*
e. in at the strait gate	*M't 7:13; Lu 13:24*
not every one that saith, Lord, shall *e. in.*	*M't 7:21*
into what city ye shall *e.*	*M't 10:11; Lu 10:8, 10*
e. into a strong man's house	*M't 12:29; M'k 3:27*
they *e. in* and dwell there	*M't 12:45; Lu 11:26*
better *e. into* life halt rather than into everlasting fire	*M't 18:8; M'k 9:43, 45, 47*
if thou wilt *e. into* life, keep commands	*M't 19:17*
rich man shall hardly *e. into* kingdom	*M't 19:23*
than for a rich man to *e.*	*M't 19:24*
into kingdom of God	*M'k 10:25; Lu 18:25*
well done, *e. into* the joy of thy Lord	*M't 25:21*
could no more openly *e. into* city	*M'k 1:45*
that we may *e. into* swine	*M'k 5:12; Lu 8:32*
what house ye *e. into*	*M'k 6:10; Lu 9:4; 10:5*
come out of him, *e.* no more *into* him	*M'k 9:25*
lest ye *e. into* temptation	*M'k 14:38; Lu 22:46*
that they which *e. in* may see light	*Lu 8:16*
many seek to *e. in* and not be able	*Lu 13:24*
to have suffered, and to *e. into* his glory	*Lu 24:26*
can he *e. into* mother's womb again	*Joh 3:4*
he cannot *e. into* the kingdom of God	*Joh 3:5*
by me if any man *e. in,* he shall be saved	*Joh 10:9*
through tribulation *e. into* kingdom	*Ac 14:22*
grievous wolves *e. in* among you	*Ac 20:29*
do *e. into* rest, shall *e. into* rest	*Heb 4:3; 4:5*
let us labour to *e. into* that rest	*Heb 4:11*
boldness to *e. into* holiest by blood	*Heb 10:19*
no man able to *e. into* temple	*Re 15:8*
no wise *e. into* it any thing that defileth	*Re 21:27*
may *e. in* through gates into city	*Re 22:14*

ENTER *NOT*

e. not into judgment with thy servant	*Ps 143:2*
e. not into the path of the wicked	*Pr 4:14*
e. not into the fields of the fatherless	*Pr 23:10*
e. not into the house of mourning	*Jer 16:5*
into any city of Samaritans *e. not*	*M't 10:5*
ye *e. not* into temptation	*M't 26:41; Lu 22:40*

NOT ENTER

for Aaron shall *not e.* into the land	*Nu 20:24*
shall *not e.* into congregation	*De 23:1; 23:2-3*
priests could *not e.* into house	*2Ch 7:2*
that they should *not e.* into my rest	*Ps 95:11*
truth is fallen, and equity cannot *e.*	*Isa 59:14*
they should *not e.* into congregation	*La 1:10*
they shall *not e.* into the land	*Eze 20:38*
nor uncircumcised *e.* into my sanctuary	*Eze 44:9*
I will *not e.* into the city	*Ho 11:9*
shall *not e.* into kingdom of heaven	*M't 18:3*
he shall *not e.* therein	*M'k 10:15; Lu 18:17*
they shall *not e.* into my rest	*Heb 3:11; 3:18*
they could *not e.* because of unbelief	*Heb 3:19*

ENTERED

self-same day *e.* Noah and sons   *Ge 7:13*
angels turned in, and *e.* into   *Ge 19:3*
house
sun was risen when Lot *e.*   *Ge 19:23*
into Zoar
Joseph *e.* into chamber and   *Ge 43:30*
wept
as Moses *e.* into the tabernacle   *Ex 33:9*
bring men that are *e.* into house   *Jos 2:3*
they *e.* into land to destroy it   *J'g 6:5*
they *e.* into an hold of the god   *J'g 9:46*
Berith
e. into another tent, and took   *2Ki 7:8*
as Jehu *e.* in at the gate,   *2Ki 9:31*
Jezebel said
when the king *e.* into house   *2Ch 12:11*
e. into covenant to seek Lord   *2Ch 15:12*
Jotham *e.* not into temple of   *2Ch 27:2*
Lord
they *e.* into curse, and an   *Ne 10:29*
oath
Hast thou *e.* into springs of   *Job 38:16*
sea
hast thou *e.* into treasures of   *Job 38:22*
snow
but when ye *e.* ye defiled my   *Jer 2:7*
land
for death is *e.* into our   *Jer 9:21*
windows and
people which had *e.* into   *Jer 34:10*
covenant
when Jeremiah was *e.* into   *Jer 37:16*
dungeon
heathen *e.* into her sanctuary   *La 1:10*
that enemy should have *e.* gates   *La 4:12*
spirit *e.* into me when he   *Eze 2:2;*
  13:24
I sware and *e.* into covenant   *Eze 16:18*
with
e. into judgment with (S)   *Eze 20:36*
and when they *e.* unto the   *Eze 36:20*
heathen
because God of Israel hath *e.*   *Eze 44:2*
in by it
in day that foreigners *e.* into   *Ob 11*
gates
thou shouldest not have *e.* into   *Ob 13*
the gate
rottenness *e.* into my bones   *Hab 3:16*
when Jesus was *e.* into   *M't 8:5*
Capernaum
he *e.* into a ship and passed   *M't 9:1*
over
how he *e.* into house of God   *M't 12:4*
day that Noah *e.* into ark   *M't 24:38;*
  Lu 17:27
unclean spirits went out and   *M'k 5:13;*
e. into the swine   *Lu 8:33*
whithersoever he *e.* they laid   *M't 6:56*
the sick
Mary *e.* into house of   *Lu 1:40*
Zacharias
e. thine house, thou gavest me   *Lu 7:44*
no water
they feared as they *e.* into   *Lu 9:34*
cloud
woe to lawyers, ye *e.* not in   *Lu 11:52*
yourselves
then *e.* Satan into Judas   *Lu 22:3;*
  Joh 13:27
when *e.* city there shall meet   *Lu 22:10*
you
and ye *e.* into their   *Joh 4:38*
labours
where was a garden, into   *Joh 18:1*
which he *e.*
then Pilate *e.* into the   *Joh 18:33*
judgment hall
Ananias *e.* putting hands on   *Ac 9:17*
Saul
nothing unclean hath *e.* into   *Ac 11:8*
my mouth
he *e.* into castle and told Paul   *Ac 23:10*
Agrippa was *e.* into place of   *Ac 25:23*
hearing
to whom Paul *e.* in, and prayed   *Ac 28:8*
sin *e.* into world; law *e.*   *Ro 5:12;*
  5:20
neither have *e.* into heart of   *1Co 2:9*
man
they *e.* not in because of   *Heb 4:6*
unbelief
he that is *e.* into his rest,   *Heb 4:10*
hath ceased
whither forerunner is for us *e.*   *Heb 6:20*
e. on our behalf (B)(P)   *Heb 6:20*
he *e.* in once into the holy   *Heb 9:12;*
place   *9:24*

are *e.* into ears of Lord of   *Jas 5:4*
sabaoth
sojourners *e.* (A)(R)   *1Pe 2:11*
many deceivers are *e.* into world   *2Jo 7*
Spirit of life from God *e.* into   *Re 11:11*
them

ENTERETH

number every one that *e.* into   *Nu 4:30;*
service of tabernacle   *4:35, 39, 43*
to every one that *e.* house of   *2Ch 31:16*
Lord
when wisdom *e.* into thine   *Pr 2:10*
heart
reproof *e.* more into wise man   *Pr 17:10*
than
sword *e.* into their privy   *Eze 21:14*
chambers
he that *e.* in by way of north   *Eze 46:9*
gate
whatsoever *e.* in at mouth,   *M't 15:17;*
goeth into belly   *M'k 7:18*
e. in where damsel was lying   *M'k 5:40*
follow into house where he *e.*   *Lu 22:10*
e. not by door into sheepfold   *Joh 10:1*
he that *e.* in by door, is the   *Joh 10:2*
shepherd
which *e.* into that within the   *Heb 6:19*
veil
as high priest *e.* every year   *Heb 9:25*
with blood

ENTERING

cast it at *e.* of the gate of city   *Jos 8:29*
shall stand at *e.* of gate of the   *Jos 20:4*
city
Gaal stood in *e.* of gate of city   *J'g 9:35*
Abimelech stood in *e.* of gate   *J'g 9:44*
of city
600 men of Dan stood by *e.* of   *J'g 18:16*
gate
the priest stood in the *e.* of   *J'g 18:17*
the gate
by *e.* into town that hath gates   *1Sa 23:7*
put battle in array at *e.* of   *2Sa 10:8*
gate
the *e.* of oracle he made doors   *1Ki 6:31*
Elijah stood in the *e.* in of   *1Ki 19:13*
the cave
four leprous men at *e.* of gate   *2Ki 7:3*
lay heads in two heaps at *e.* of   *2Ki 10:8*
gate
e. of Hamath unto the sea of   *2Ki 14:25*
the plain
that were in *e.* of the gate of   *2Ki 23:8*
Joshua
kings sat at *e.* of gate of   *2Ch 18:9*
Samaria
so that there is no house, no *e.*   *Isa 23:1*
in
set thrones at *e.* of gates   *Jer 1:15; 17:27*
mark well the *e.* in of the   *Eze 44:5*
house
neither go in yourselves, nor   *M't 23:13;*
suffer them that are *e.* to go in   *Lu 11:52*
lusts of other things *e.* in   *M'k 4:19*
choke
nothing without *e.* into him   *M'k 7:15*
can defile him
e. into sepulchre they saw   *M'k 16:5*
young man
at your *e.* ye shall find a colt   *Lu 19:30*
tied
Saul *e.* into every house, haling   *Ac 8:3*
men
what manner of *e.* in we had to   *1Th 1:9*
you
promise left us of *e.* into his   *Heb 4:1*
rest

ENTERPRISE

their hands cannot perform   *Job 5:12*
their *e.*
complete the *e.* (B)   *2Co 8:11*
unfit for any good *e.* (B)(R)   *Tit 1:16*

ENTERTAIN

be not forgetful to *e.*   *Heb 13:2*
strangers

ENTERTAINED

e. us (A)(N)(P)(R)   *Ac 28:7*
for thereby some have *e.*   *Heb 13:2*
angels

ENTHUSIASM

keen in *e.* (A)(P)   *2Co 8:17*
your *e.* stimulated the majority   *2Co 9:2*
(A)(P)

ENTICE

if a man *e.* a maid that is not   *Ex 22:16*
e. thee secretly, saying, Let us   *De 13:6*
go
E. thy husband, that he may   *J'g 14:15*
E. him, and see wherein his   *J'g 16:5*
great
Who shall *e.* Ahab king of   *2Ch 18:19*
Israel
before the Lord, and said, I   *2Ch 18:20*
will *e.*
Thou shalt *e.* him, and thou   *2Ch 18:21*
shalt
My son, if sinners *e.* thee,   *Pr 1:10*
consent
e. to immoral passions   *2Pe 2:18*
(B)(E)(R)

ENTICED

Satan *e.* David (S)   *1Ch 21:1*
my heart hath been secretly   *Job 31:27*
e.
Peradventure he will be *e.*   *Jer 20:10*
drawn away of his own lust,   *Jas 1:14*
and *e.*

ENTICETH

A violent man *e.* his neighbour   *Pr 16:29*

ENTICING

with *e.* words of man's wisdom   *1Co 2:4*
should beguile you with *e.*   *Col 2:4*
words

ENTIRE

that ye may be perfect and *e.*   *Jas 1:4*

ENTIRELY

made a man *e.* well (S)   *Joh 7:23*
but is *e.* clean (S)   *Joh 13:10*

ENTITLED

e. to greater honor (B)   *Heb 3:3*

ENTOMBED

to be *e.* (B)   *Re 11:9*

ENTRAILS

his *e.* poured out (N)   *Ac 1:18*

ENTRANCE

border unto the *e.* of Hamath   *Nu 34:8*
entrance (S)   *Jos 8:29;*
13:5; 20:4; J'g 3:3; 9:35, 40, 44; 18:16,
17; 2Sa 10:8; 11:23; 1Ki 6:31; 8:65;
19:13; 2Ki 7:3; 10:8; 23:8, 11; 16:18;
1Ch 5:9; 9:19; 13:5; 2Ch 4:22; 7:8; 18:9;
23:13, 15; 26:8; 33:14; Es 5:1; Pr 8:3;
Jer 1:15; 19:2; 26:10; 36:10; 38:14; 43:9;
Eze 8:5; 27:3; 40:11, 40; 42:9; 44:5;
46:19; Am 6:14
Shew us, the *e.* into the city   *J'g 1:24*
when he shewed them the *e.*   *J'g 1:25*
into
ran before Ahab to the *e.* of   *1Ki 18:46*
Jezreel
in the *e.* of the gate of   *1Ki 22:10*
Samaria
they went to the *e.* of Gedor   *1Ch 4:39*
that kept the *e.* of the king's   *2Ch 12:10*
The *e.* of thy words giveth   *Ps 119:130*
light
the face of the gate of the *e.*   *Eze 40:15*
know our *e.* in unto you, that it   *1Th 2:1*
an *e.* shall be ministered unto   *2Pe 1:11*
you

ENTRANCES

entrances (S)   *Eze 40:38; 43:11*
land of Nimrod in the *e.*   *Mic 5:6*
thereof
with five *e.* (B)   *Joh 5:2*

ENTREAT

cause the enemy to *e.* thee well   *Jer 15:11*
and *e.* them evil four hundred   *Ac 7:6*

ENTREATED

he *e.* Abram well for her sake   *Ge 12:16*
hast thou so evil *e.* this people   *Ex 5:22*
And the Egyptians evil *e.* us   *De 26:6*
I have *e.* (E)(R)   *1Sa 13:12*
e. them spitefully, and slew them   *M't 22:6*
shall be mocked, and spitefully *e.*   *Lu 18:32*
e. him shamefully, and sent him   *Lu 20:11*
evil *e.* our fathers, so that they   *Ac 7:19*
e., induced us (A)   *Ac 16:15*
Julius courteously *e.* Paul, and   *Ac 20:3*
before, and were shamefully *e.*   *1Th 2:2*

ENTREATETH

He evil *e.* the barren that beareth   *Job 24:21*

ENTREATIES

listen to their *e.* (A)   *Isa 19:22*

ENTREATY

listened to their *e.* (A)(R)   *Ezr 8:23*
all *e.*, interceding (A)(B)(N)   *Eph 6:18*

ENTRIES

the chambers and the *e.* thereof   *Eze 40:38*

ENTRUSTED

e. with sacred trusteeship (A)(B)(E)(R)   *1Co 9:17*
being *e.* by God (P)   *1Th 2:4*
authority to act as judges and pass sentence was *e.* (A)(B)   *Re 20:4*

ENTRY

king's *e.* without, turned he from   *2Ki 16:18*
of the Lord, were keepers of the *e.*   *1Ch 9:19*
e. of the house, the inner doors   *2Ch 4:22*
at the *e.* of the city, at the coming   *Pr 8:3*
which is by the *e.* of the east gate   *Jer 19:2*
sat down in the *e.* of the new gate   *Jer 26:10*
court, at the *e.* of the new gate   *Jer 36:10*
prophet unto him into the third *e.*   *Jer 38:14*
is at the *e.* of Pharaoh's house   *Jer 43:9*
this image of jealousy in the *e.*   *Eze 8:5*
art situate at the *e.* of the sea   *Eze 27:3*
the breadth of the *e.* of the gate   *Eze 40:11*
goeth up to the *e.* of the north gate   *Eze 40:40*
was the *e.* on the east side   *Eze 42:9*
he brought me through the *e.*   *Eze 46:19*

ENVELOPED

e. me with bitterness (R)   *La 3:5*

ENVIED

and the Philistines *e.* him   *Ge 26:14*
no children, Rachel, *e.* her sister   *Ge 30:1*
his brethren *e.* him; but his father   *Ge 37:11*
They *e.* Moses also in the camp   *Ps 106:16*
this a man is *e.* of his neighbour   *Ec 4:4*
that all the trees of Eden, *e.* him   *Eze 31:9*

ENVIES

guile, and hypocrisies, and *e.*   *1Pe 2:1*

ENVIEST

unto him, *E.* thou for my sake   *Nu 11:29*

ENVIETH

charity *e.* not; charity vaunteth   *1Co 13:4*

ENVIOUS

all the *e.* (B)   *Ne 11:25; 11:27-28, 30-31; 12:28-29*
neither be thou *e.* against the   *Ps 37:1*
For I was *e.* at the foolish   *Ps 73:3*
Be not thou *e.* against evil men   *Pr 24:1*
neither be thou *e.* at the wicked   *Pr 24:19*
e. of you (N)   *Ga 4:17*

ENVIRON

shall *e.* us round, and cut off   *Jos 7:9*

ENVIRONS

the *e.* of them (S)   *Nu 35:3; 35:7*

ENVOY

he sends an *e.* (A)(N)   *Lu 14:32*

ENVY

and *e.* slayeth the silly one   *Job 5:2*
E. thou not the oppressor, and   *Pr 3:31*
do not resentfully *e.* (A)   *Pr 3:31*
do not *e.* a violent man (B)   *Pr 3:31*
e. not a man of violence (E)(R)   *Pr 3:31*
but *e.* the rottenness of the bones   *Pr 14:30*
Let not thine heart *e.* sinners   *Pr 23:17*
who is able to stand before *e.*   *Pr 27:4*
their hatred, and their *e.* is now   *Ec 9:6*
The *e.* also of Ephraim shall depart   *Isa 11:13*
Ephraim shall not *e.* Judah   *Isa 11:13*
for they *e.* at the people; yea   *Isa 26:11*
according to thine *e.* which thou   *Eze 35:11*
that for *e.* they had delivered him   *M't 27:18*
priests had delivered him for *e.*   *M'k 15:10*
patriarchs, moved with *e.* sold   *Ac 7:9*
were filled with *e.* and spake   *Ac 13:45*
which believed not, moved with *e.*   *Ac 17:5*
full of *e.* murder, debate, deceit,   *Ro 1:29*
preach Christ even of *e.* and strife   *Ph'p 1:15*
whereof cometh *e.* strife, railings   *1Ti 6:4*
result in *e.* (B)(R)   *1Ti 6:4*
living in malice and *e.* hateful   *Tit 3:3*
that dwelleth in us lusteth to *e.*   *Jas 4:5*

ENVYING

wantonness, not in strife and *e.*   *Ro 13:13*
e. and strife, and divisions, are   *1Co 3:3*
one another, *e.* one another   *Ga 5:26*
But if ye have bitter *e.* and strife   *Jas 3:14*
For where *e.* and strife is, there   *Jas 3:16*

ENVYINGS

e. wraths, strifes, backbitings   *2Co 12:20*
E. murders, drunkenness   *Ga 5:21*

EPAENETUS

Salute my well beloved *E.* who   *Ro 16:5*

EPAPHRAS

As ye also learned of *E.* our dear   *Col 1:7*
E. who is one of you, a servant of   *Col 4:12*
salute thee *E.* my fellowprisoner   *Ph'm 23*

EPAPHRODITUS

it necessary to send to you *E.*   *Ph'p 2:25*
having received of *E.* the things   *Ph'p 4:18*

EPHAH

an omer is the tenth part of an *e.*   *Ex 16:36*
the tenth part of an *e.* of fine flour   *Le 5:11; 6:20*
just weights, a just *e.* and a just   *Le 19:36*
tenth part of an *e.* of barley meal   *Nu 5:15*
And a tenth part of an *e.* of flour   *Nu 28:5*
unleavened cakes of an *e.* of flour   *J'g 6:19*
and it was about an *e.* of barley   *Ru 2:17*
one *e.* of flour, and a bottle of wine   *1Sa 1:24*
brethren an *e.* of this parched corn   *1Sa 17:17*
seed of an homer shall yield an *e.*   *Isa 5:10*
and a just *e.* and a just bath   *Eze 45:10*
The *e.* and the bath shall be of one   *Eze 45:11*
the *e.* the tenth part of an homer   *Eze 45:11*
part of an *e.* of an homer of wheat   *Eze 45:13*
an *e.* for a bullock, and an *e.*   *Eze 45:24*
a ram, and an hin of oil for an *e.*   *Eze 45:24*
offering shall be an *e.* for a ram   *Eze 46:5*
to give, and an hin of oil to an *e.*   *Eze 46:5*
an *e.* for a bullock, and an *e.*   *Eze 46:7*
unto, and an hin of oil to an *e.*   *Eze 46:7*
an *e.* to a bullock, and an *e.*   *Eze 46:11*
to a ram
to give, and an hin of oil to an *e.*   *Eze 46:11*
morning, the sixth part of an *e.*   *Eze 46:14*
making the *e.* small, and the shekel   *Am 8:5*
This is an *e.* that goeth forth.   *Zec 5:6*
sitteth in the midst of the *e.*   *Zec 5:7*
he cast it into the midst of the *e.*   *Zec 5:8*
they lifted up the *e.* between the   *Zec 5:9*
Whither do these bear the *e.*   *Zec 5:10*

EPHAH, a person

And the sons of Midian; *E.*   *Ge 25:4*
E. and Epher, and Henoch   *1Ch 1:33*
E. Caleb's concubine, bare Haran   *1Ch 2:46*
And Pelet, and *E.* and Shaaph   *1Ch 2:47*
the dromedaries of Midian and *E.*   *Isa 60:6*

EPHAI

the sons of *E.* the Netophathite   *Jer 40:8*

EPHER

sons of Midian; Ephah, and *E.*   *Ge 25:4*
Ephah, and *E.* and Henoch   *1Ch 1:33*
were, Jether, and Mered, and *E.*   *1Ch 4:17*
the house of their fathers, even *E.*   *1Ch 5:24*

EPHES-DAMMIN

Shochoh and Azekah, in *E.*   *1Sa 17:1*

EPHESIAN

him in the city Trophimus an *E.*   *Ac 21:29*

EPHESIANS

saying, Great is Diana of the *E.*   *Ac 19:28*
cried out, Great is Diana of the *E.*   *Ac 19:34*
the city of the *E.* is a worshipper   *Ac 19:35*

EPHESUS

And he came to *E*. and left them | Ac 18:19
God will. And he sailed from *E*. | Ac 18:21
mighty in the scriptures, came to *E*. | Ac 18:24
through the upper coasts came to *E*. | Ac 19:1
and Greeks also dwelling at *E*. | Ac 19:17
that not alone at *E*. but almost | Ac 19:26
Ye men of *E*. what man is there | Ac 19:35
Paul had determined to sail by *E*. | Ac 20:16
And from Miletus he sent to *E*. | Ac 20:17
I have fought with beasts at *E*. | 1Co 15:32
I will tarry at *E*. until Pentecost | 1Co 16:8
to the saints which are at *E*. | Eph 1:1
besought thee to abide still at *E*. | 1Ti 1:3
he ministered unto me at *E*. | 2Ti 1:18
And Tychicus have I sent to *E*. | 2Ti 4:12
unto *E*. and unto Smyrna, and | Re 1:11
angel of the church of *E*. write | Re 2:1

EPHLAL

Zabad begat *E*. and *E*. begat | 1Ch 2:37

EPHOD

and stones to be set in the *e*. | Ex 25:7
a breastplate, and an *e*. and a robe | Ex 28:4; 28:6, 8, 12, 15, 25-28, 31
and the robe of the *e*. and the *e*. | Ex 29:5
with the curious girdle of the *e*. | Ex 29:5
and stones to be set for the *e*. | Ex 35:9; 35:27
he made the *e*. of gold | Ex 39:2; 39:5, 7-8, 18-22
put the *e*. upon him, and he girded | Le 8:7
with the curious girdle of the *e*. | Le 8:7
And Gideon made an *e*. thereof | J'g 8:27
made an *e*. and teraphim, and | J'g 17:5
there is in these houses an *e*. | J'g 18:14
took the graven image, and the *e*. | J'g 18:17
fetched the carved image, the *e*. | J'g 18:18
he took the *e*. and the teraphim | J'g 18:20
being a child, girded with a linen *e*. | 1Sa 2:18
to wear an *e*. before me? and did | 1Sa 2:28
priest in Shiloh, wearing an *e*. | 1Sa 14:3
wrapped in a cloth behind the *e*. | 1Sa 21:9
persons that did wear a linen *e*. | 1Sa 22:18
came down with an *e*. in his hand | 1Sa 23:6
the priest, Bring hither the *e*. | 1Sa 23:9
I pray thee, bring me hither the *e*. | 1Sa 30:7
And Abiathar brought thither the *e*. | 1Sa 30:7
David was girded with a linen *e*. | 2Sa 6:14
David also had upon him an *e*. of | 1Ch 15:27
without an *e*. and without teraphim | Ho 3:4

EPHOD, a person

Manasseh, Hanniel the son of *E*. | Nu 34:23

EPHPHATHA

unto him, *E*. that is, Be opened | M'k 7:34

EPHRAIM, a person, people

name of Joseph's second son was *E*. | Ge 41:52

God make thee as *E*. and he set *E*. before Manasseh | Ge 48:20
the prince of *E*. was Elishama | Nu 1:10; 7:48
on west side shall be standard of *E*. | Nu 2:18
standard of camp of *E*. set forward | Nu 10:22
these are the sons of *E*. | Nu 26:35; 1Ch 7:20
they are ten thousands of *E*. | De 33:17
cities for children of *E*. | Jos 16:9; 17:9
nor did *E*. drive out Canaanites | J'g 1:29
out of *E*. a root against Amalek | J'g 5:14
is not gleaning of grapes of *E*. better | J'g 8:2
then Jephthah fought with *E*. | J'g 12:4
smote *E*. |
Abner made Ish-bosheth king over *E*. | 2Sa 2:9
E. their father mourned many days | 1Ch 7:22
in Jerusalem dwelt of children of *E*. | 1Ch 9:3
strangers out of *E*. fell to Asa | 2Ch 15:9
Jehoshaphat set garrisons in cities of *E*. | 2Ch 17:2
Amasiah separated army out of *E*. | 2Ch 25:10
Zichri a mighty man of *E*. slew Maaseiah | 2Ch 28:7
many of *E*. had not cleansed themselves | 2Ch 30:18
all Israel brake images in *E*. and Manasseh | 2Ch 31:1
children of *E*. being armed, turned | Ps 78:9
before *E*. stir up thy strength and save us | Ps 80:2
saying, Syria is confederate with *E*. | Isa 7:2
E. hath taken evil counsel against thee | Isa 7:5
within sixty-five years shall *E*. be broken | Isa 7:8
head of *E*. is Samaria, and head of Samaria | Isa 7:9
from day that *E*. departed from Judah | Isa 7:17
E. that say in pride and stoutness of heart | Isa 9:9
Manasseh shall eat *E*. and *E*. Manasseh | Isa 9:21
envy of *E*. depart; *E*. not envy Judah, Judah not vex *E*. | Isa 11:13
the fortress also shall cease from *E*. | Isa 17:3
woe to drunkards of *E*. whose beauty | Isa 28:1
drunkards of *E*. be trodden under feet | Isa 28:3
as I have cast out the whole seed of *E*. | Jer 7:15
I have heard *E*. bemoaning himself | Jer 31:18
the stick of *E*. | Eze 37:16
take stick of Joseph in hand of *E*. | Eze 37:19
I know *E*., O *E*. committest whoredom | Ho 5:3
Israel and *E*. shall fall in their iniquity | Ho 5:5
E. shall be desolate | Ho 5:9
be to *E*. as a moth | Ho 5:12
E. saw his sickness, *E*. went to Assyria | Ho 5:13
E. as a lion | Ho 5:14
there is whoredom of *E*. | Ho 6:10
then iniquity of *E*. was discovered | Ho 7:1
E. hath mixed himself among people | Ho 7:8
E. hired lovers | Ho 8:9
E. eat unclean things in Assyria | Ho 9:3
watchman of *E*. was with my God | Ho 9:8
E. made altars to sin | Ho 9:11
as for *E*. their glory shall fly away | Ho 9:11
E. bring forth children to murderer | Ho 9:13
E. receive shame, Israel be ashamed | Ho 10:6
make *E*. to ride; Judah shall plow | Ho 10:11

I taught *E*. to go | Ho 11:3
how shall I give thee up *E*. | Ho 11:8
I will not return to destroy *E*. for I am God | Ho 11:9
E. compasseth me about with lies | Ho 11:12
E. feedeth on wind; *E*. said, I am rich | Ho 12:1; 12:8
E. provoked him to anger most bitterly | Ho 12:14
E. spake trembling, he exalted himself | Ho 13:1
iniquity of *E*. is bound up, his sin is hid | Ho 13:12
E. say, what have I to do with idols | Ho 14:8
they shall possess the fields of *E*. | Ob 19
I will cut off the chariot from *E*. | Zec 9:10
when I have filled the bow with *E*. | Zec 9:13
they of *E*. shall be like mighty man | Zec 10:7

EPHRAIM, a place

Absalom had sheep-shearers beside *E*. | 2Sa 13:23
Abijah took *E*. and towns thereof | 2Ch 13:19
Jesus went into a city called *E*. | Joh 11:54

EPHRAIM *IS*

E. is the strength of my head | Ps 60:7; 108:8
father to Israel, *E*. is my first born | Jer 31:9
is *E*. my dear son? is he pleasant child | Jer 31:20
E. is joined to idols, let him alone | Ho 4:17
E. is oppressed | Ho 5:11
E. is a cake not turned | Ho 7:8
E. is like a silly dove | Ho 7:11
E. is as an heifer taught and loveth | Ho 10:11

EPHRAIM, *TRIBE*

numbered of the *tribe of E*. 40,500 | Nu 1:33
of the *tribe of E*. to spy the land | Nu 13:8
of *tribe of E*. to divide land, Kemuel | Nu 34:24
the inheritance of the *tribe of E*. | Jos 16:8
Kohathites had cities the *tribe of E*. Dan and Manasseh | Jos 21:5; 21:20; 1Ch 6:66
and he chose not the *tribe of E*. | Ps 78:67

MOUNT EPHRAIM

if *mount E*. be too narrow for thee | Jos 17:15
Shechem in *mount E*. a city of refuge | Jos 20:7; 21:21
they buried Joshua in the *mount of E*. | J'g 2:9
Gideon sent messengers through *mount E*. | J'g 7:24
Micah of *mount E*. | J'g 17:1; 17:8; 2Sa 20:21
the Danites passed unto *mount E*. | J'g 18:13
Levite sojourning on side of *mount E*. | J'g 19:1
Elkanah of *mount E*. | 1Sa 1:1
Saul passed through *mount E*. | 1Sa 9:4
two men be come to me from *mount E*. | 2Ki 5:22
publisheth affliction from *mount E*. | Jer 4:15
the watchman upon *mount E*. shall cry | Jer 31:6
Israel shall be satisfied on *mount E*. | Jer 50:19

EPHRAIMITE

said unto him, Art thou an *E*. | J'g 12:5

EPHRAIMITES

Canaanites dwell among the *E*. | Jos 16:10

EPHRAIMITES (continued)

fugitives of Ephraim among the E. — J'g 12:4

passages of Jordan before the E. — J'g 12:5

those E. which were escaped said — J'g 12:5

there fell at that time of the E. — J'g 12:6

EPHRAIM'S

and laid it upon E. head, who was — Ge 48:14

to remove it from E. head unto — Ge 48:17

Joseph saw E. children of the third — Ge 50:23

Southward it was E. and northward — Jos 17:10

EPHRAIN

and E. with the towns thereof — 2Ch 13:19

EPHRATAH

and do thou worthily in E. — Ru 4:11

the son of Hur, the firstborn of E. — 1Ch 2:50

E. the father of Beth-lehem — 1Ch 4:4

Lo, we heard of it at E.: we found — Ps 132:6

But thou Beth-lehem E. though — Mic 5:2

EPHRATH

was but a little way to come to E. — Ge 35:16

and was buried in the way to E. — Ge 35:19

but a little way to come unto E. — Ge 48:7

I buried her there in the way of E. — Ge 48:7

Caleb took unto him E. which bare — 1Ch 2:19

EPHRATHITE

of John, the son of Zuph, an E. — 1Sa 1:1

Now David was the son of that E. — 1Sa 17:12

Jeroboam the son of Nebat, an E. — 1Ki 11:26

EPHRATHITES

E. of Beth-lehem-judah — Ru 1:2

EPHRON

for me to E. the son of Zohar — Ge 23:8; 23:10, 13-14, 16-17

of E. the son of Zohar the Hittite — Ge 25:9

that is in the field of E. the Hittite — Ge 49:29

with the field of E. the Hittie for a — Ge 49:30

of a burying place of E. the Hittite — Ge 50:13

went out to the cities of mount E. — Jos 15:9

EPICUREANS

certain philosophers of the E. — Ac 17:18

EPILEPTIC

he is an e. (S) — M't 17:15

EPILEPTICS

which were e. (A)(B)(E)(N)(P)(R)(S) — M't 4:24; 17:15

EPISTLE

together, they delivered the e. — Ac 15:30

delivered the e. to the governor — Ac 23:33

I Tertius, who wrote this e. — Ro 16:22

letter (A)(N)(R) — 1Co 5:9; 2Co 3:2-3; 7:8; 1Th 5:27; 2Th 2:15; 3:14, 17; 2Pe 3:1

letter (A)(N)(R) — Ro 16:22; 1Co 5:9; 2Co 7:8; 2Th 2:15; 2Pe 3:1

I wrote unto you in an e. — 1Co 5:9

letter (P) — 1Co 5:9; 2Co 3:2; 7:8; Col 4:16; 1Th 5:27; 2Th 3:17; 2Pe 3:1

are our e. written in our hearts — 2Co 3:2

the e. of Christ ministered by us — 2Co 3:3

I perceive that the same e. hath — 2Co 7:8

when this e. is read among you — Col 4:16

that ye likewise read the e. from — Col 4:16

this e. be read unto all the holy — 1Th 5:27

whether my word, or our e. — 2Th 2:15

our writings (P) — 2Th 2:15

our word by this e. note that man — 2Th 3:14

which is the token in every e. — 2Th 3:17

second e. beloved, I now write — 2Pe 3:1

EPISTLES

e. of commendation to you, or — 2Co 3:1

letters (A)(B)(N)(R) — 2Co 3:1; 2Pe 3:16

As also in all his e. speaking — 2Pe 3:16

EPOCHS

fixed the e. of history (N) — Ac 17:26

EQUAL

gold and the crystal cannot e. — Job 28:17

topaz of Ethiopia shall not e. — Job 28:19

behold the things that are e. — Ps 17:2

it was thou, a man mine e. — Ps 55:13

The legs of the lame are not e. — Pr 26:7

will ye liken me, or shall I be e. — Isa 40:25

will ye liken me, and make me e. — Isa 46:5

what shall I e. to thee, that I may — La 2:13

The way of the Lord is not e. — Eze 18:25

house of Israel; Is not my way e. — Eze 18:25

The way of the Lord is not e. — Eze 18:29

of Israel, are not my ways e. — Eze 18:29

The way of the Lord is not e. but — Eze 33:17

as for them, their way is not e. — Eze 33:17

The way of the Lord is not e. — Eze 33:20

thou hast made them e. unto us — M't 20:12

for they are e. unto the angels — Lu 20:36

making himself e. with God — Joh 5:18

e. heirs (P) — Eph 3:6

it not robbery to be e. with God — Ph'p 2:6

servants that which is just and e. — Col 4:1

breadth and the height of it are e. — Re 21:6

EQUALITY

But by an e. that now at this time — 2Co 8:14

your want: that there may be e. — 2Co 8:14

EQUALLY

e. distant one from another — Ex 36:22

EQUALS

many my e. in mine own nation — Ga 1:14

EQUIP

to e. God's people (N) — Eph 4:12

personally e., stabilize (B) — 1Pe 5:10

EQUIPMENT

e. (B) — Nu 4:16; 1Ch 22:19; 23:26; 28:13

with all its e. (B) — Isa 29:17

necessary e. (B) — Eze 12:3

much substance and e. (A)(B) — Da 11:13

e. of foolish shepherd (B) — Zec 11:15

carry any household e. (A) — M'k 11:16

for e. of saints (R) — Eph 4:12

EQUIPPED

army amply e. (B) — Da 11:13

Christians properly e. (P) — Eph 4:12

EQUITY

judge with e. (R) — Ps 75:2

the world, and the people with e. — Ps 98:9

justice (B) — Ps 98:9; Pr 1:3; 2:9; Isa 11:4; Mic 3:9

dost establish e. thou executest — Ps 99:4

justice, and judgment, and e. — Pr 1:3

justice (A) — Pr 1:3; 2:9; Isa 11:4

and judgment, and e.; yea, every — Pr 2:9

good, nor to strike princes for e. — Pr 17:26

for their uprightness (A)(B) — Pr 17:26

and in knowledge, and in e. — Ec 2:21

with e. for the meek of the earth — Isa 11:4

in the street, and e. cannot enter — Isa 59:14

justice cannot enter (A) — Isa 59:14

honesty cannot enter (B) — Isa 59:14

abhor judgment, pervert all e. — Mic 3:9

walked with me in peace and e. — Mal 2:6

peace and uprightness (A)(B) — Mal 2:6

EQUIVALENT

side e. to the length of gates (S) — Eze 40:18

ER

a son; and he called his name E. — Ge 38:3

And Judah took a wife for E. his — Ge 38:6

E. Judah's firstborn, was wicked — Ge 38:7

the sons of Judah; E. and Onan — Ge 46:12

but E. and Onan died in the land — Ge 46:12

sons of Judah were E. and Onan — Nu 26:19

and E. and Onan died in the land — Nu 26:19

The sons of Judah; E. and Onan — 1Ch 2:3

And E. the firstborn of Judah — 1Ch 2:3

son of Judah were, E. the father — 1Ch 4:21

Elmodam, which was the son of E. — Lu 3:28

ERADICATED

e. Baal (B) — 2Ki 10:28

ERAN

of E. the family of the Eranites — Nu 26:36

ERANITES

of Eran, the family of the E. — Nu 26:36

ERASTUS

Timotheus and E.; but he himself — Ac 19:22

E. the chamberlain of the city — Ro 16:23

E. abode at Corinth: but Trophimus — 2Ti 4:20

ERE

delivered e. the midwives come — Ex 1:19

their teeth, e. it was chewed — Nu 11:33

how long will it be e. they believe — Nu 14:11

And e. the lamp of God went out — 1Sa 3:3

it be then, e. thou bid the people — 2Sa 2:26

but e. the messenger came to him — 2Ki 6:32

How long will it be e. ye make — Job 18:2

how long will it be e. thou be quiet — Jer 47:6

how long will it be e. they attain — Ho 8:5

Sir, come down e. my child die — Joh 4:49

ERECH

Babel, and *E.*, and Accad, and *Ge 10:10*

ERECT

make you go *e.* (A)(B)(R)   *Le 26:13*
e. a statue (B)(P)   *Re 13:14;*
  13:15; 15:9, 11; 16:2; 19:20; 20:4

ERECTED

And he *e.* there an altar   *Ge 33:20*

ERI

Ezbon, *E.* and Arodi, and   *Ge 46:16*
Areli
of *E.* the family of the Erites   *Nu 26:16*

ERITES

of Eri, the family of the *E.*   *Nu 26:16*

ERR

whole of Israel *e.* (E)   *Le 4:13*
So Manasseh made   *2Ch 33:9*
Judah to *e.*
is a people that do *e.* in their   *Ps 95:10*
heart
rebuked the proud, which   *Ps 119:21*
do *e.*
hast trodden down all them   *Ps 119:118*
that *e.*
wicked causeth them to *e.* (E)   *Pr 12:26*
Do they not *e.* that devise evil   *Pr 14:22*
the instruction that causeth to   *Pr 19:27*
e.
which lead thee cause thee to   *Isa 3:12*
e.
of this people cause them to *e.*   *Isa 9:16*
they have caused Egypt to *e.*   *Isa 19:14*
they *e.* in vision, they stumble   *Isa 28:7*
of the people, causing them   *Isa 30:28*
to *e.*
men, though fools, shall not *e.*   *Isa 35:8*
why hast thou made us to *e.*   *Isa 63:17*
and caused my people Israel   *Jer 23:13*
to *e.*
cause my people to *e.* by their   *Jer 23:32*
lies
whoredoms hath caused them   *Ho 4:12*
to *e.*
and their lies caused them to *e.*   *Am 2:4*
prophets that make my people   *Mic 3:5*
e.
Ye do *e.* not knowing the   *M't 22:29*
Do ye not therefore *e.*   *M'k 12:24*
because ye
ye therefore do greatly *e.*   *M'k 12:27*
They do alway *e.* in their   *Heb 3:10*
heart
Do not *e.* my beloved brethren   *Jas 1:16*
Brethren, if any of you do *e.*   *Jas 5:19*

ERRAND

not eat, until I have told mine   *Ge 24:33*
e.
I have a secret *e.* unto thee   *J'g 3:19*
I have an *e.* to thee, O captain   *2Ki 9:5*

ERRED

his ignorance wherein he *e.* and   *Le 5:18*
if ye have *e.* and not observed   *Nu 15:22*
the fool, and have *e.*   *1Sa 26:21*
exceedingly
me to understand wherein I   *Job 6:24*
have *e.*
And be it indeed that I have *e.*   *Job 19:4*
I have *e.* not from thy   *Ps 119:110*
precepts
they also have *e.* through wine   *Isa 28:7*
priest and the prophet have *e.*   *Isa 28:7*
They also that *e.* in spirit   *Isa 29:24*
shall
they have *e.* from the faith   *1Ti 6:10*
have *e.* concerning the faith   *1Ti 6:21*
Who concerning the truth   *2Ti 2:18*
have *e.*

ERRETH

but he that refuseth reproof *e.*   *Pr 10:17*
every one that *e.* and for him   *Eze 45:20*

ERRING

bear with ignorant and *e.* (N)   *Heb 5:2*

ERRONEOUS

e. doctrines (N)   *1Ti 1:4*

ERROR

it was an *e.* (A)(E)(R)   *Nu 15:25*
God smote him there for his *e.*   *2Sa 6:7*
angels he charges with *e.*   *Job 4:18*
(B)(R)
mine *e.* remaineth with myself   *Job 19:4*
neither say thou it was an *e.*   *Ec 5:6*
as an *e.* which proceedeth from   *Ec 10:5*
mingled a spirit of *e.* (B)   *Isa 19:14*
and to utter *e.* against the   *Isa 32:6*
Lord
neither was there any *e.* or fault   *Da 6:4*
so the last *e.* shall be worse   *M't 27:64*
than
that recompence of their *e.*   *Ro 1:27*
which
devising *e.* (B)(E)   *Eph 4:14*
the sinner from the *e.* of his   *Jas 5:20*
way
escape from them who live in   *2Pe 2:18*
e.
being led away with the *e.* of   *2Pe 3:17*
the
spirit of truth, and the spirit of   *1Jo 4:6*
e.
ran greedily after the *e.* of   *Jude 11*
Balaam

ERRORS

Who can understand his *e.*   *Ps 19:12*
are vanity, and the work of *e.*   *Jer 10:15*
They are vanity, the work of   *Jer 51:18*
e.
inventing *e.* to deceive (A)   *Eph 4:14*
himself, and for the *e.* of the   *Heb 9:7*
people

ERUPTION

scabby *e.* (S)   *Le 13:30;*
  13:31-37; 14:54

ESAIAS

spoken of by the prophet *E.*   *M't 3:3*
was spoken by *E.* the   *M't 4:14*
prophet
fulfilled which was spoken by   *M't 8:17*
E.
fulfilled which was spoken by   *M't 12:17*
E.
fulfilled the prophecy of *E.*   *M't 13:14*
hypocrites, well did *E.*   *M't 15:7*
prophesy
Well hath *E.* prophesied of you   *M'k 7:6*
in the book of the words of *E.*   *Lu 3:4*
him the book of the prophet *E.*   *Lu 4:17*
the Lord, as said the prophet   *Joh 1:23*
E.
That the saying of *E.* the   *Joh 12:38*
prophet
could not believe, because   *Joh 12:39*
that *E.*
These things said *E.* when he   *Joh 12:41*
sitting in his chariot read *E.*   *Ac 8:28*
heard him read the prophet *E.*   *Ac 8:30*
Well spake the Holy Ghost by   *Ac 28:25*
E.
E. also crieth concerning Israel   *Ro 9:27*
and as *E.* said before, Except   *Ro 9:29*
E. saith, Lord, who hath   *Ro 10:16*
believed
But *E.* is very bold, and saith   *Ro 10:20*
And again, *E.* saith, There   *Ro 15:12*
shall

ESAR-HADDON

E. his son reigned in his   *2Ki 19:37*
stead
since the days of *E.* king of   *Ezr 4:2*
Assur
E. his son reigned in his stead   *Isa 37:38*

ESAU

they called his name *E.*   *Ge 25:25;*
  25:27-30, 32, 34
And *E.* was forty years old   *Ge 26:34*
when he
he called *E.* his eldest son, and   *Ge 27:1;*
said   *27:5-6, 11, 15, 19, 21-22, 24, 30,*
  32, 34, 37-38, 41-42

When *E.* saw that Isaac had   *Ge 28:6*
blessed
And *E.* seeing that the   *Ge 28:8*
daughters of
Then went *E.* unto Ishmael   *Ge 28:9*
sent messengers before him to   *Ge 32:3;*
E.   *32:4, 6, 8, 11, 13, 17-19*
and, behold, *E.* came, and with   *Ge 33:1*
him
And *E.* ran to meet him, and   *Ge 33:4*
E. said, I have enough, my   *Ge 33:9*
brother
And *E.* said, Let me not leave   *Ge 33:15*
So *E.* returned that day on his   *Ge 33:16*
way
from the face of *E.* thy brother   *Ge 35:1*
his sons *E.* and Jacob buried   *Ge 35:29*
him
generations of *E.* who is   *Ge 36:1;*
Edom   *36:2, 4-6, 8-10, 14-15, 19, 40, 43*
children of *E.* which dwell in   *De 2:4*
Seir
Seir unto *E.* for a possession   *De 2:5*
children of *E.* which dwelt in   *De 2:8*
Seir
the children of *E.* succeeded   *De 2:12*
them
As he did to the children of *E.*   *De 2:22*
children of *E.* which dwelt in   *De 2:29*
Seir
I gave unto Isaac Jacob and *E.*   *Jos 24:4*
and I gave unto *E.* mount Seir   *Jos 24:4*
The sons of Isaac; *E.* and   *1Ch 1:34*
Israel
The sons of *E.*; Eliphaz,   *1Ch 1:35*
Reuel
bring the calamity of *E.* upon   *Jer 49:8*
him
But I have made *E.* bare, I   *Jer 49:10*
have
are the things of *E.* searched out   *Ob 6*
the wise men out of the mount of   *Ob 8*
E.
every one of the mount of *E.* may   *Ob 9*
and the house of *E.* for stubble   *Ob 18*
any remaining of the house of *E.*   *Ob 18*
shall possess the mount of *E.*   *Ob 19*
Zion to judge the mount of *E.*   *Ob 21*
Was not *E.* Jacob's brother   *Mal 1:2*
mountains
I hated *E.* and laid his   *Mal 1:3*
I loved, *E.* have I hated   *Ro 9:13*
By faith Isaac blessed Jacob   *Heb 11:20*
and *E.*
fornicator, or profane   *Heb 12:16*
person, as *E.*

ESAU'S

his hand took hold on *E.* heel   *Ge 25:26*
hairy, as his brother *E.* hands   *Ge 27:23*
Rebekah, Jacob's and *E.*   *Ge 28:5*
mother
names of *E.* sons; Eliphaz   *Ge 36:10;*
  36:12-14, 17-18

ESCAPE

E. for thy life; look not   *Ge 19:17*
behind
e. to the mountain, lest thou   *Ge 19:17*
be
I cannot *e.* to the mountain,   *Ge 19:19*
lest
Oh, let me *e.* thither, (is it not   *Ge 19:20*
Haste thee, *e.* thither; for I   *Ge 19:20*
can not
company which is left shall *e.*   *Ge 32:8*
let none of them remain or *e.*   *Jos 8:22*
I should speedily *e.* into the   *1Sa 27:1*
land
so shall I *e.* out of his hand   *1Sa 27:1*
we shall not else *e.* from   *2Sa 15:14*
Absalom
lest he get him fenced cities,   *2Sa 20:6*
and *e.*
let not one of them *e.*   *1Ki 18:40*
then let none go forth nor *e.*   *2Ki 9:15*
If any of the men *e.*   *2Ki 10:24*
and they that *e.* out of mount   *2Ki 19:31*
Zion
to leave us a remnant to *e.*   *Ezr 9:8*
thou shalt *e.* in the king's house   *Es 4:13*
they shall not *e.* and their   *Job 11:20*
hope
my *e.* from the windy storm   *Ps 55:8*
and
Shall they *e.* by iniquity   *Ps 56:7*

cause me to *e.:* incline thine ear *Ps 71:2*
own nets, whilst that I withal *Ps 141:10*
e.
he that speaketh lies shall not *Pr 19:5*
e.
pleaseth God shall *e.* from her *Ec 7:26*
of Assyria: and how shall we *e.* *Isa 20:6*
and they that *e.* out of mount *Isa 37:32*
Zion
I will send those that *e.* of *Isa 66:19*
them
they shall not be able to *e.* *Jer 11:11*
nor the principal of the flock *Jer 25:35*
to *e.*
shall not *e.* out of the hand of *Jer 32:4*
thou shalt not *e.* out of his *Jer 34:3*
hand
shalt not *e.* out of their *Jer 38:18;*
hand *38:23*
none of them shall remain or *Jer 42:17*
e.
of Egypt to sojourn there, *Jer 44:14*
shall *e.*
shall return but such as shall *Jer 44:14*
e.
a small number that *e.* the *Jer 44:28*
sword
flee away, nor the mighty man *Jer 46:6*
e.
no city shall *e.;* the valley also *Jer 48:8*
The voice of them that flee *Jer 50:28*
and *e.*
let none thereof *e.:* *Jer 50:29*
recompense
ye may have some that shall *e.* *Eze 6:8*
they that *e.* of you shall *Eze 6:9*
remember
But they that *e.* of them shall *Eze 7:16*
e.
shall he *e.* that doeth such *Eze 17:15*
things
all these things, he shall not *Eze 17:18*
e.
But these shall *e.* out of his *Da 11:41*
hand
and the land of Egypt shall *Da 11:42*
not *e.*
yea, and nothing shall *e.* them *Joe 2:3*
to cut off those of his that did *e.* *Ob 14*
ye *e.* the damnation of hell *M't 23:33*
worthy to *e.* all these things *Lu 21:36*
of them should swim out, and *Ac 27:42*
e.
thou shalt *e.* the judgment of *Ro 2:3*
God
temptation also make a way *1Co 10:13*
to *e.*
with child; and they shall not *1Th 5:3*
e.
How shall we *e.* if we neglect *Heb 2:3*
earth, much more shall not *Heb 12:25*
we *e.*

ESCAPED

And there came one that had *Ge 14:13*
e.
the residue of that which is *e.* *Ex 10:5*
he hath given his sons that *e.* *Nu 21:29*
servant which is *e.* from his *De 23:15*
master
Ehud *e.* while they tarried, and *J'g 3:26*
quarries, and *e.* unto Seirath *J'g 3:26*
of valour; and there *e.* not a *J'g 3:29*
man
those Ephraimites which were *J'g 12:5*
e.
for them that be *e.* of *J'g 21:17*
Benjamin
were taken: but the people *e.* *1Sa 14:41*
and David fled, and *e.* that *1Sa 19:10*
night
and he went, and fled, and *e.* *1Sa 19:12*
away mine enemy, that he is *1Sa 19:17*
e.
David fled, and *e.* and came *1Sa 19:18*
thence, and *e.* to the cave *1Sa 22:1*
Adullam
sons of Ahimelech, *e.* and *1Sa 22:20*
fled
that David was *e.* from *1Sa 23:13*
Keilah
and there *e.* not a man of *1Sa 30:17*
them
Out of the camp of Israel am *2Sa 1:3*
I *e.*
Rechab and Baanah his brother *2Sa 4:6*

Ben-hadad the king of Syria *1Ki 20:20*
e.
that is *e.* of the house of *2Ki 19:30*
Judah
they *e.* into the land of *2Ki 19:37*
Armenia
of the Amalekites that were *e.* *1Ch 4:43*
the host of the king of Syria *2Ch 16:7*
e.
fallen to the earth, and none *2Ch 20:24*
e.
the remnant of you, that are *2Ch 30:6*
e.
them that had *e.* from the *2Ch 36:20*
sword
we remain yet *e.* as it is this *Ezr 9:15*
day
concerning the Jews that had *e.* *Ne 1:2*
I only am *e.* alone to tell *Job 1:15;*
1:16-17. 19
I am *e.* with the skin of my *Job 19:20*
teeth
Our soul is *e.* as a bird out of *Ps 124:7*
the snare is broken and we *Ps 124:7*
are *e.*
for them that are *e.* of Israel *Isa 4:2*
such as are *e.* of the house of *Isa 10:20*
Jacob
that is *e.* of the house of *Isa 37:31*
Judah
and they *e.* into the land of *Isa 37:38*
ye that are *e.* of the nations *Isa 45:20*
Ishmael the son of Nethaniah *Jer 41:15*
e.
Ye that have *e.* the sword *Jer 51:50*
the day of the Lord's anger *La 2:22*
none *e.*
mouth be opened to him *Eze 24:27*
which is *e.*
one that had *e.* out of *Eze 33:21*
Jerusalem
evening, afore he that was *e.* *Eze 33:22*
came
him: but he *e.* out of their *Joh 10:39*
hand
pass, that they *e.* all safe to *Ac 27:44*
land
when they were *e.* then they *Ac 28:1*
knew
whom, though he hath *e.* the *Ac 28:4*
sea
was I let down by the wall, *2Co 11:33*
and *e.*
e. doom of unbelievers (N) *Heb 11:3*
of fire, *e.* the edge of the *Heb 11:34*
sword
For if they *e.* not who *Heb 12:25*
refused him
having *e.* the corruption that is *2Pe 1:4*
those that were clean *e.* from *2Pe 2:18*
them
For if after they have *e.* the *2Pe 2:20*

ESCAPETH

him that *e.* the sword of *1Ki 19:17*
Hazael
him that *e.* from the sword *1Ki 19:17*
of Jehu
lions upon him that *e.* of *Isa 15:9*
Moab
him that fleeth, and her that *Jer 48:19*
e.
he that *e.* in that day shall *Eze 24:26*
come
he that *e.* of them shall not be *Am 9:1*

ESCAPING

should be no remnant nor *e.* *Ezr 9:14*
are just *e.* (S) *2Pe 2:18*

ESCHEW

Let him *e.* evil, and do good *1Pe 3:11*

ESCHEWED

one that feared God, and *e.* evil *Job 1:1*

ESCHEWETH

one that feareth God and *e.* evil *Job 1:8*
one that feareth God, and *e.* *Job 2:3*
evil

ESEK

he called the name of the well *Ge 26:20*
E.

ESH-BAAL

Malchi-shua, and Abinadab, *1Ch 8:33*
and *E.*
Malchi-shua, and Abinadab, *1Ch 9:39*
and *E.*

ESH-BAN

Hemdan, and *E.* and Ithran *Ge 36:26*
Amram, and *E.* and Ithran *1Ch 1:41*

ESHCOL

brother of *E.* and brother of *Ge 14:13*
Aner
men which went with me, *Ge 14:24*
Aner, *E.*
they came unto the brook of *Nu 13:23*
E.
The place was called the *Nu 13:24*
brook *E.*
they went up unto the valley of *Nu 32:9*
E.
came unto the valley of *E.* and *De 1:24*

ESHEAN

Arab, and Dumah, and *E.* *Jos 15:52*

ESHEK

And the sons of *E.* his brother *1Ch 8:39*

ESHKALONITES

Ashdothites, the *E.* the *Jos 13:3*
Gittites

ESHTAOL

in the valley *E.* and Zoreah *Jos 15:33*
Zorah, and *E.* and *Jos 19:41*
Ir-shemesh
camp of Dan between Zorah *J'g 13:25*
and *E.*
buried him between Zorah *J'g 16:31*
and *E.*
of valour, from Zorah, and *J'g 18:2*
from *E.*
unto their brethren to Zorah *J'g 18:8*
and *E.*
out of Zorah and out of *E.* *J'g 18:11*

ESHTAULITES

the Zareathites, and the *E.* *1Ch 2:53*

ESHTEMOA

and *E.* with her suburbs *Jos 21:14*
and to them which were in *E.* *1Sa 30:28*
and Ishbah the father of *E.* *1Ch 4:17*
Garmite, and *E.* the *1Ch 4:19*
Maachathite
Jattir, and *E.* with their *1Ch 6:57*
suburbs

ESHTEMOH

Anab, and *E.* and Anim *Jos 15:50*

ESHTON

Mehir, which was the father *1Ch 4:11*
of *E.*
E. begat Beth-rapha, and *1Ch 4:12*
Paseah

ESLI

which was the son of *E.* which *Lu 3:25*

ESPECIALLY

but *e.* among my neighbours *Ps 31:11*
E. because I know thee to be *Ac 26:3*
men, *e.* unto them who are of *Ga 6:10*
e. they who labour in the word *1Ti 5:17*
the books, but *e.* the *2Ti 4:13*
parchments

ESPIED

of them opened his sack he *Ge 42:27*
e.
into a land that I have *e.* for *Eze 20:6*
them

ESPOUSALS

crowned him in the day of his   *Ca 3:11* e.
of thy youth, the love of thine e.   *Jer 2:2*

ESPOUSED

my wife Michal, which I e. to   *2Sa 3:14* me
When as his mother Mary was   *M't 1:18* e.
To a virgin e. to a man whose   *Lu 1:27*
To be taxed with Mary his e.   *Lu 2:5* wife
For I have e. you to one   *2Co 11:2* husband

ESPY

sent, from Kadesh-barnea to   *Jos 14:7* e.
stand by the way, and e.; ask   *Jer 48:19* him

ESROM

Phares begat E.; and E. begat   *M't 1:3*
which was the son of E. which   *Lu 3:33*

ESTABLISH

with thee will I e. my covenant   *Ge 6:18*
behold, I e. my covenant with   *Ge 9:9* you
And I will e. my covenant with   *Ge 9:11* you
And I will e. my covenant   *Ge 17:7* between
and I will e. my covenant   *Ge 17:19* with him
my covenant will I e. with   *Ge 17:21* Isaac
you, and e. my covenant with   *Le 26:9* you
her husband may e. it or her   *Nu 30:13*
that he may e. his covenant   *De 8:18* which
The Lord shall e. thee an holy   *De 28:9* people
That he may e. thee to day   *De 29:13*
only the Lord e. his word   *1Sa 1:23*
e. a place (B)   *2Sa 7:10*
and I will e. his kingdom   *2Sa 7:12*
e. thy people (B)(E)(R)   *2Sa 7:24*
concerning his house, e. it for   *2Sa 7:25*
Then I will e. the throne of thy   *1Ki 9:5*
after him, and to e. Jerusalem   *1Ki 15:4*
e. him as king (B)(E)(R)   *1Ch 14:2*
and I will e. his kingdom   *1Ch 17:11*
and I will e. the throne of   *1Ch 22:10* his
Moreover I will e. his   *1Ch 28:7* kingdom
loved Israel, to e. them for ever   *2Ch 9:8*
yea, he doth e. them for ever   *Job 36:7*
but e. the just: for the righteous   *Ps 7:9*
e. his throne for judging (B)   *Ps 9:7*
God will e. it for ever   *Ps 48:8*
and the highest himself shall e.   *Ps 87:5* her
thy faithfulness shalt thou e. in   *Ps 89:2*
Thy seed will I e. for ever   *Ps 89:4*
and e. thou the work of our   *Ps 90:17* hands
the work of our hands e. thou   *Ps 90:17* it
thou dost e. equity, thou   *Ps 99:4* executest
E. thy word unto thy servant   *Ps 119:38* (S)
he will e. the border of the   *Pr 15:25* widow
and to e. it with judgment and   *Isa 9:7*
thou wilt e. peace (B)   *Isa 26:12*
e. people of antiquity (A)(P)   *Isa 44:7*
of the people, to e. the earth to   *Isa 49:8*
And give him no rest, till he e.   *Isa 62:7*
the Lord that formed it, to e.   *Jer 33:2*
I will e. unto thee an   *Eze 16:60* everlasting
And I will e. my covenant   *Eze 16:62* with thee
together to e. a royal statute   *Da 6:7*
Now, O king, e. the decree   *Da 6:8*
exalt themselves to e. the   *Da 11:14* vision
and e. judgment in the gate   *Am 5:15*
e. a city by iniquity (S)   *Hab 2:12*

God forbid: yea, we e. the law   *Ro 3:31*
about to e. their own   *Ro 10:3* righteousness
able to e. (A)(B)(E)(N)(R)   *Ro 16:25*
e. you (A)(B)   *1Co 1:8*
he which e. us in God (S)   *2Co 1:21*
to e. you, and to comfort you   *1Th 3:2*
the first, that he may e. the   *Heb 10:9* second
restore, e. (N)(R)   *1Pe 5:10*

ESTABLISHED

the covenant, which I have e.   *Ge 9:17*
because the thing is e. by God   *Ge 41:32*
I have also e. my covenant with   *Ex 6:4*
O Lord, which thy hands have e   *Ex 15:17*
then the house shall be e.   *Le 25:30*
Sihon be built and e. (S)   *Nu 21:27*
witnesses, shall the matter be   *De 19:15* e.
hath he not made thee, and e.   *De 32:6* thee
knew that Samuel was e. to   *1Sa 3:20* be a
the Lord have e. thy kingdom   *1Sa 13:13*
shalt not be e. nor thy   *1Sa 20:31* kingdom
the kingdom of Israel shall   *1Sa 24:20* be e.
Lord had e. him king over   *2Sa 5:12* Israel
thy kingdom shall be e. for   *2Sa 7:16* ever
thy throne shall be e. for ever   *2Sa 7:16*
house of thy servant David be   *2Sa 7:26* e.
and his kingdom was e.   *1Ki 2:12* greatly
the Lord liveth, which hath e.   *1Ki 2:24* me
throne of David shall be e.   *1Ki 2:45* before
the kingdom was e. in the   *1Ki 2:46* hand of
hath e. his word (E)   *1Ki 8:20*
kingdom e. in his hand (E)   *2Ki 14:5*
the seer had e. (A)(R)   *1Ch 9:22*
I have e. a place (B)   *1Ch 17:9*
his throne shall be e. for   *1Ch 17:14* evermore
let the thing be e. for ever   *1Ch 17:23*
Let it even be e. that thy   *1Ch 17:24* name be
let the house of David, be   *1Ch 17:24* e.
went to e. his dominion (S)   *1Ch 18:3*
unto David my father be e.   *2Ch 1:9*
when Rehoboam had e. the   *2Ch 12:1*
so shall ye be e.; believe his   *2Ch 20:20*
when the kingdom was e. to   *2Ch 25:3* him
So they e. a decree to make   *2Ch 30:5*
to e. this among them (S)   *Es 9:21*
Their seed is e. in their sight   *Job 21:8*
and it shall be e. unto thee   *Job 22:28*
e. strength because (A)(E)   *Ps 8:2*
stars hast e. (B)(R)   *Ps 8:2*
and e. it upon the floods   *Ps 24:2*
feet upon a rock, and e. my   *Ps 40:2* goings
For he e. a testimony in Jacob   *Ps 78:5*
earth which he hath e. for ever   *Ps 78:69*
with whom my hand shall be   *Ps 89:21* e.
It shall be e. for ever as the   *Ps 89:37* moon
the world is e. (S)   *Ps 93:1; 148:6*
Thy throne is e. of old: thou art   *Ps 93:2*
the world also shall be e. that   *Ps 96:10*
their seed shall be e. before   *Ps 102:28* thee
His heart is e. he shall not be   *Ps 112:8*
thou hast e. the earth, and it   *Ps 119:90*
Let not an evil speaker be e.   *Ps 140:11*
by understanding hath he e. the   *Pr 3:19*
and let all thy ways be e.   *Pr 4:26*
when he e. the clouds above   *Pr 8:28*
man shall not be e. by   *Pr 12:3* wickedness
The lip of truth shall be e.   *Pr 12:19* for ever
of counsellors they are e.   *Pr 15:22*
and thy thoughts shall be e.   *Pr 16:3*
the throne is e. by   *Pr 16:12* righteousness
Every purpose is e. by counsel   *Pr 20:18*
and by understanding it is e.   *Pr 24:3*
and his throne shall be e. in   *Pr 25:5*

his throne shall be e. for ever   *Pr 29:14*
hath e. all the ends of the earth   *Pr 30:4*
of the Lord's house shall be e.   *Isa 2:2*
believe, surely ye shall not be e.   *Isa 7:9*
in mercy shall the throne be e.   *Isa 16:5*
he hath e. it, he created it   *Isa 45:18*
In righteousness shalt thou be   *Isa 54:14* e.
hath e. the world by his   *Jer 10:12* wisdom
their congregation shall be e.   *Jer 30:20*
by his power, he hath e. the   *Jer 51:15* world
I was e. in my kingdom   *Da 4:36*
be e. in the top of the   *Mic 4:1* mountains
thou hast e. them for   *Hab 1:12* correction
and it shall be e. and set there   *Zec 5:11*
witnesses every word may be   *M't 18:16* e.
were the churches e. in the   *Ac 16:5* faith
to the end ye may be e.   *Ro 1:11*
e. according to the gospel (S)   *Ro 16:25*
witnesses shall every word be   *2Co 13:1* e.
covenant previously e. (A)   *Ga 3:17*
e. in the faith (S)   *1Th 3:13*
e. your hearts unblameable   *1Th 3:13* (S)
e. you in every good work (S)   *2Th 2:17*
e. and keep you (S)   *2Th 3:3*
was e. upon better promises   *Heb 8:6*
that the heart be e. with grace   *Heb 13:9*
e. your hearts (S)   *Jas 5:8*
e. strengthen, settle you (S)   *1Pe 5:10*
and be e. in the present truth   *2Pe 1:12*

ESTABLISHETH

then he e. all her vows, or   *Nu 30:14* all her
The king by judgment e. the   *Pr 29:4* land
nor statute which the king e.   *Da 6:15*

ESTABLISHING

time of e. all God spoke (R)   *Ac 3:21*
e. and strengthening (A)(R)   *Ac 14:22*
e. and strengthening (A)   *Ac 15:41*

ESTABLISHMENT

After these things, and the e.   *2Ch 32:1*
for your e. (B)   *2Co 10:8*

ESTATE

inheritance in father's e. (B)   *J'g 11:2*
regarded me according to   *1Ch 17:17* the e.
give her royal e. unto   *Es 1:19* another
Who remembered us in our   *Ps 136:23* low e.
Lo, I am come to great e.   *Ec 1:16*
concerning the e. of the sons of   *Ec 3:18*
shall return to their   *Eze 16:55* former e.
shall return to your former   *Eze 16:55* e.
shall one stand up in his e.   *Da 11:7*
Then shall stand up in his e.   *Da 11:20*
And in his e. shall stand up a   *Da 11:21* vile
in his e. shall he honour the   *Da 11:38* God
and all the e. of the elders   *Ac 22:5*
the low e. of his handmaiden   *Lu 1:48*
condescend to men of low e.   *Ro 12:16*
he might know your e. and   *Col 4:8*
which kept not their first e.   *Jude 6*

ESTATES

I will settle you after your   *Eze 36:11* old e.
captains, and chief e. of   *M'k 6:21* Galilee

ESTEEM

lightly e. his birthright (B)   *Ge 25:34*
Will he e. thy riches? no, not   *Job 36:19*
I e. all thy precepts, to be   *Ps 119:128* right
yet we did e. him stricken   *Isa 53:4*

ignorantly considered him stricken (A) — *Isa 53:4*
regarded him as stricken (B) — *Isa 53:4*
lightly e. the throne (A) — *Jer 14:21*
e. other better than themselves — *Ph'p 2:3*
regard others as better, superior (A)(B) — *Ph'p 2:3*
counting other better than himself (E)(R) — *Ph'p 2:3*
reckon other better than themselves (B) — *Ph'p 2:3*
think more of one another than you do of yourselves (P) — *Ph'p 2:3*
And to e. them very highly in love — *1Th 5:13*
hold them lovingly in highest regard (B) — *1Th 5:13*
hold them in the highest honor (P) — *1Th 5:13*

ESTEEMED

lightly e. the Rock of his salvation — *De 32:15*
treated with scorn the Rock (B) — *De 32:15*
scoffed at the Rock of his salvation (R) — *De 32:15*
despise me shall be lightly e — *1Sa 2:30*
I am a poor man, and lightly e. — *1Sa 18:23*
poor and insignificant as I am (B) — *1Sa 18:23*
poor man of no repute (R) — *1Sa 18:23*
life was much e. (S) — *1Sa 18:30*
I have e. the words of his mouth — *Job 23:12*
treasured words of his mouth (B)(E)(R) — *Job 23:12*
shutteth his lips is e. a man of — *Pr 17:28*
closed is considered intelligent (B) — *Pr 17:28*
is deemed intelligent (P) — *Pr 17:28*
shall be e. as the potter's clay — *Isa 29:16*
considered on an equal with clay (B) — *Isa 29:16*
potter be regarded as clay (R) — *Isa 29:16*
fruitful field shall be e. as a forest — *Isa 29:17*
be considered a forest (B) — *Isa 29:17*
be regarded as a forest (R) — *Isa 29:17*
was despised, and we e. him not — *Isa 53:3*
are they e. as earthen pitchers — *La 4:2*
which is highly e. among men — *Lu 16:15*
exalted and highly thought of (A) — *Lu 16:15*
what to men seems outstanding (B) — *Lu 16:15*
what is exalted among men (E)(R) — *Lu 16:15*
sets itself up to be admired by men (N) — *Lu 16:15*
things men consider perfectly splendid (P) — *Lu 16:15*
them to judge who are least e. — *1Co 6:4*
count for least, without standing (A) — *1Co 6:4*
who have no standing (B) — *1Co 6:4*
who are of no account in the church (E) — *1Co 6:4*
men who count for nothing (N)(P) — *1Co 6:4*

ESTEEMETH

He e. iron as straw, and brass — *Job 41:27*
counts iron as straw (A)(E)(R) — *Job 41:27*
To him iron is as straw (B) — *Job 41:27*
One man e. one day above another — *Ro 14:5*
rates one day greater than another (B) — *Ro 14:5*
regards one day more highly than (N) — *Ro 14:5*
thinks some days of more importance (P) — *Ro 14:5*
another e. every day alike — *Ro 14:5*
but to him that e. any thing to be — *Ro 14:14*
who thinks it is unclean (A)(P)(R) — *Ro 14:14*
who considers it unclean (B) — *Ro 14:14*
accounteth anything to be unclean (E) — *Ro 14:14*
considers a thing to be impure (N) — *Ro 14:14*

ESTEEMING

E. the reproach of Christ greater — *Heb 11:26*
considered the contempt (A)(B)(N)(P)(R) — *Heb 11:26*
accounting the reproach of Christ (E) — *Heb 11:26*

ESTHER

he brought up Hadassah, that is E. — *Es 2:7*
the king loved E. — *Es 2:17*
the king made E. a feast — *Es 2:18*
told it to E. — *Es 2:22*
E. maids came, she sent raiment to Mordecai — *Es 4:4*
Mordecai did all that E. had commanded — *Es 4:17*
king held out to E. the golden sceptre — *Es 5:2; 8:4*
what wilt thou, queen E. — *Es 5:3*
E. let no man come with king but myself — *Es 5:12*
king said, what is thy petition, queen E. — *Es 7:2*
Haman stood up to make request for life to E. — *Es 7:7*
and E. spake yet again before the king — *Es 8:3*
I have given E. the house of Haman — *Es 8:7*
E. the queen wrote with all authority — *Es 9:29*
decree of E. confirmed these matters of Purim — *Es 9:32*

ESTHER'S

and his servants, even E. feast — *Es 2:18*
E. maids and her chamberlains — *Es 4:4*
they told to Mordecai E. words — *Es 4:12*

ESTIMATE

than the priest shall e. it, whether — *Le 27:14*
as the priest shall e. it, so shall — *Le 27:14*
the priest shall appraise it (A) — *Le 27:14*
priest shall evaluate it (B) — *Le 27:14*
priest shall value it (R) — *Le 27:14*

ESTIMATION

with thy e. by shekels of silver — *Le 5:15*
valued in silver shekels (A)(R) — *Le 5:15*
evaluated in silver coin (B) — *Le 5:15*
with thy e. for a trespass offering — *Le 5:18;*
shall be for the Lord by thy e. — *Le 6:6*
— *Le 27:2; 27:3-8, 13, 15-19, 23, 27*
at your valuation (A)(R) — *Le 27:2; 27:3 (B)*
involves evaluating of a person — *Le 27:2*
according to thine e. for the money — *Nu 18:16*

ESTIMATIONS

thy e. shall be according to the — *Le 27:25*

ESTRANGED

mine acquaintance are verily e. — *Job 19:13*
The wicked are e. from the womb — *Ps 58:3*
They were not e. from their lust — *Ps 78:30*
and have e. this place, and have — *Jer 19:4*
they are all e. from me through — *Eze 14:5*

ESTRANGEMENT

know my e. (A) — *Nu 14:34*

ETAM

dwelt in the top of the rock E. — *J'g 15:8*
went to the top of the rock E. — *J'g 15:11*
And these were of the father of E. — *1Ch 4:3*
their villages were, E. and Ain — *1Ch 4:32*
He built even Bethlehem, and E. — *2Ch 11:6*

ETERNAL

blessings of e. mountains (R) — *Ge 49:26*
The e. God is thy refuge, and — *De 33:27*
I will make thee an e. excellency — *Isa 60:15*
an everlasting majesty (B) — *Isa 60:15*
make you majestic for ever (R) — *Isa 60:15*
but is in danger of e. damnation — *M'k 3:29*
in grasp of everlasting trespass (A) — *M'k 3:29*
guilty of e. sin (B)(E)(N)(P)(R) — *M'k 3:29*
that are made, even his e. power and — *Ro 1:20*
crown of e. blessedness (A) — *1Co 9:25*
an e. crown (P) — *1Co 9:25*
worketh for us an e. weight of glory — *2Co 4:17*
everlasting weight of glory (A)(B) — *2Co 4:17*
permanent, glorious, solid reward (P) — *2Co 4:17*
according to the e. purpose in Christ — *Eph 3:11*
fate in e. misery (A) — *Ph'p 3:19*
unto the King e. be honour and glory — *1Ti 1:17*
King of eternity (A) — *1Ti 1:17*
King of the ages (B)(P)(R) — *1Ti 1:17*
King of all worlds (N) — *1Ti 1:17*
God who is e. felicity alone (N) — *1Ti 6:15*
may obtain salvation with e. glory — *2Ti 2:10*
but the things which are not seen are e. — *Heb 4:18*
are deathless and everlasting (A)(B) — *Heb 4:18*
are really permanent (P) — *Heb 4:18*
we have an house e. in the heavens — *Heb 5:1*
that will last for ever (B) — *Heb 5:1*
permanent house in heaven (P) — *Heb 5:1*
he became the author of e. salvation — *Heb 5:9*
doctrine of baptisms, and of e. judgment — *Heb 6:2*
having obtained e. redemption for us — *Heb 9:12*
who thro' e. Spirit offered himself to God — *Heb 9:14*
might receive the promise of e. inheritance — *Heb 9:15*
draw back to e. misery (A) — *Heb 10:39*
God calls us unto his e. glory by Christ Jesus — *1Pe 5:10*
an example, suffering vengeance of e. fire — *Jude 7*

ETERNAL *LIFE*

what shall I do that I may have e. life — *M't 19:16*
but the righteous shall go into life e. — *M't 25:46*
good Master, what shall I — *M'k 10:17;*
do, that I may inherit e. life — *Lu 10:25; 18:18*
he shall receive in the world to come e. life — *M'k 10:17*
believeth in him should have e. life — *Joh 3:15*
and gathereth fruit unto life e. — *Joh 4:36*
search scriptures, in them ye have e. life — *Joh 5:39*
whoso drinketh my blood hath e. life — *Joh 6:54*
to whom shall we go? thou hast words of e. life — *Joh 6:68*
I give them e. life never perish — *Joh 10:28*
that hateth his life, shall keep it to e. life — *Joh 12:25*
he should give e. life to as many as given him — *Joh 17:2*
this is life e. that they might know thee — *Joh 17:3*
many as were ordained to e. life believed — *Ac 13:48*
to them who seek for glory and — *Ro 2:7*
e. life
so might grace reign to e. life by Jesus — *Ro 5:21*
gift of God is e. life thro' Jesus Christ — *Ro 6:23*

O man of God, lay hold on *e.*   1Ti 6:12
life   6:19
in hope of *e. life,* which God   Tit 1:2
promised
be made heirs according to   Tit 3:7
hope of *e. life*
e. life which was with the   1Jo 1:2
Father
this is promise he promised,   1Jo 2:25
even *e. life*
no murderer hath *e. life*   1Jo 3:15
abiding in him
record that God hath given to   1Jo 5:11
us *e. life*
that ye may know that ye have   1Jo 5:13
e. life
this is the true God, and *e. life*   1Jo 5:20
looking for mercy of Lord unto   Jude 21
e. life

ETERNITY

and lofty One that inhabiteth   Isa 57:15
e.
king of *e.* (A)   1Ti 1:17

ETHAM

and encamped in *E.* in the   Ex 13:20
edge of
and pitched in *E.* which is in   Nu 33:6
they removed from *E.* and   Nu 33:7
turned
journey in the wilderness of *E*   Nu 33:8

ETHAN

than *E.* the Ezrahite, and   1Ki 4:31
Heman
And the sons of Zera; Zimri,   1Ch 2:6
and *E.*
And the sons of *E.;* Azariah   1Ch 2:8
The son of *E.* the son of   1Ch 6:42
Zimmah
E. the son of Kishi, the son of   1Ch 6:44
Abdi
of Merari their brethren, *E.*   1Ch 15:17
the son
the singers, Heman, Asaph,   1Ch 15:19
and *E.*
Maschil of *E.* the Ezrahite   Ps 89 title

ETHANIM

at the feast in the month *E.*   1Ki 8:2

ETHBAAL

to wife Jezebel the daughter   1Ki 16:31
of *E.*

ETHER

Libnah, and *E.* and Ashan   Jos 15:42
Ain, Remmon, and *E.* and   Jos 19:7
Ashan

ETHIOPIA

compasseth the whole land of   Ge 2:13
E.
heard say of Tirhakah king of   2Ki 19:9
E.
reigned from India even unto *E.*   Es 1:1
which are from India unto *E.*   Es 8:9
The topaz of *E.* shall not   Job 28:19
equal it
E. shall soon stretch out her   Ps 68:31
hands
behold Philistia, and Tyre, with   Ps 87:4
E.
which is beyond the rivers of   Isa 18:1
E.
wonder upon Egypt and upon   Isa 20:3
E.
afraid and ashamed of *E.* their   Isa 20:5
concerning Tirhakah king of   Isa 37:9
E.
thy ransom, *E.* and Seba for   Isa 43:3
thee
of Egypt, and merchandise of   Isa 45:14
E.
even unto the borders of *E.*   Eze 29:10
and great pain shall be in *E.*   Eze 30:4
E. and Libya, and Lydia, and   Eze 30:5
all
Persia, and Libya with them   Isa 38:5
E. and Egypt were her strength   Na 3:9
From beyond the rivers of *E.*   Zep 3:10
and, behold, a man of *E.*   Ac 8:27

ETHIOPIAN

against Moses because of the   Nu 12:1
E.
for he had married an *E.*   Nu 12:1
woman
out against them Zerah the *E.*   2Ch 14:9
Can the *E.* change his skin, or   Jer 13:23
Now when Ebed-melech the *E.*   Jer 38:7
commanded Ebed-melech the   Jer 38:10
E.
Ebed-melech the *E.* said unto   Jer 38:12
and speak to Ebed-melech the   Jer 39:16
E.

ETHIOPIANS

Lubims, the Sukkiims, and   2Ch 12:3
the *E.*
the Lord smote the *E.* before   2Ch 14:12
Asa
before Judah; and the *E.*   2Ch 14:12
fled
and the *E.* were overthrown   2Ch 14:13
Were not the *E.* and the   2Ch 16:8
Lubims
Arabians, that were near the   2Ch 21:16
E.
Egyptians prisoners, and the *E.*   Isa 20:4
E. and the Libyans, that   Jer 46:9
handle
to make the careless *E.* afraid   Eze 30:9
and the *E.* shall be at his   Da 11:43
steps
not as children of the *E.* unto   Am 9:7
me
Ye *E.* also ye shall be slain   Zep 2:12
under Candace queen of the *E.*   Ac 8:27

ETHNAN

Zereth, and Jezoar, and *E.*   1Ch 4:7

ETHNI

The son of *E.* the son of   1Ch 6:41
Zerah

EUBULUS

E. greeteth thee, and Pudens   2Ti 4:21

EUNICE

Lois and thy mother *E.;* and I   2Ti 1:5
am

EUNUCH

has been made a *e.* (A)   De 23:1
the *e.*   2Ki 23:11; Es 1:10; 2:15, 21
neither let the *e.* say, Behold, I   Isa 56:3
e. which had the charge of the   Jer 52:25
an *e.* of great authority under   Ac 8:27
the *e.* answered Philip and said   Ac 8:34
the *e.* said, See, here is water   Ac 8:36
the water, both Philip and the   Ac 8:38
e.
that the *e.* saw him no more   Ac 8:39

EUNUCHS

looked out to him two or   2Ki 9:32
three *e.*
and they shall be *e.* in the   2Ki 20:18
palace of
and they shall be *e.* in the   Isa 39:7
palace of
thus saith the Lord unto the *e.*   Isa 56:4
and the queen, and the *e.*   Jer 29:2
the princes of Jerusalem, and   Jer 34:19
e.
Ethiopian, one of the *e.* which   Jer 38:7
the children, and the *e.* whom   Jer 41:16
Ashpenaz the master of his *e.*   Da 1:3;
                          1:7-11, 18
For there are some *e.* which   M't 19:12
were made *e.* of men, and
made themselves *e.*

EUODIAS

beseech *E.* and beseech   Ph'p 4:2
Syntyche

EUPHRATES

Assyria, And the fourth river is   Ge 2:14
E.

unto the great river, the river   Ge 15:18
E.
unto the great river, the river *E.*   De 1:7
from the river, the river *E.*   De 11:24
unto the great river, the river *E.*   Jos 1:4
beyond the *E.* (R)   Jos 24:2
recover his border at the river   2Sa 8:3
E.
the king of Assyria to the   2Ki 23:29
river *E.*
river of Egypt unto the river   2Ki 24:7
E.
his dominion by the river *E.*   1Ch 5:9
the wilderness from the river   1Ch 5:9
E.
his dominion by the river *E.*   1Ch 18:3
to fight against Carchemish   2Ch 35:20
by *E.*
upon thy loins, and arise, go to   Jer 13:4
E.
went, and hid it by *E.* as the   Jer 13:5
Lord
Arise, go to *E.* and take the   Jer 13:6
girdle
Then I went to *E.* and digged   Jer 13:7
of Egypt, which was by the   Jer 46:2
river *E.*
towards the north by the river   Jer 46:6
E.
the north country by the river   Jer 46:10
E.
it, and cast it into the midst   Jer 51:63
of *E.*
are bound in the great river *E.*   Re 9:14
his vial upon the great river   Re 16:12
E.

EUROCLYDON

a tempestuous wind, called *E.*   Ac 27:14

EUTYCHUS

a certain young man named *E.*   Ac 20:9

EVALUATE

priest *e.* it (B)   Le 27:14

EVALUATED

e. in silver coin (B)   Le 5:15

EVALUATING

involves *e.* a person (B)   Le 27:2

EVANGELIST

entered the house of Philip the   Ac 21:8
e.
afflictions, do the work of an *e.*   2Ti 4:5

EVANGELISTS

and some, *e.;* and some,   Eph 4:11
pastors

EVANGELIZE

to *e.* there (B)   Ac 16:10; 2Co 10:16

EVANGELIZED

poor are *e.* (B)   M't 11:5

EVANGELIZES

e. with the gospel (B)   Ga 1:9

EVAPORATE

waters *e.* (A)(B)   Job 14:11

EVE

Adam called his wife's name *E.*   Ge 3:20
And Adam knew *E.* his wife   Ge 4:1
the serpent beguiled *E.*   2Co 11:3
through
Adam was first formed, then   1Ti 2:13
E.

EVEN

there came two angels to   Ge 19:1
Sodom at *e.*
e. of all that went in at the   Ge 23:10
gate of the
on fourteenth day of month at   Ex 12:18
e.

Moses said, At *e.* then shall ye *Ex 16:6*
know that Lord
at *e.* eat flesh *Ex 16:12; 16:13*
people stand by from morning *Ex 18:14*
to *e.*
when Aaron lighteth the lamps *Ex 30:8*
at *e.*
shall be unclean until *e.* *Le 11:24;*
11:25, 27-28, 31, 39-40; 14:46; 15:5, 7;
17:15; 22:6; Nu 19:7-8, 10, 21-22
I will *e.* set my face against *Le 20:6*
that soul
fourteenth day of first month, *Le 23:5;*
at *e.* is Lord's passover *Nu 9:3; De 16:6*
14th day of second month at *e.* *Nu 9:11*
when the cloud abode from *e.* *Nu 9:21*
to morning
bathe himself in water, shall *Nu 19:19*
be clean at *e.*
unto the judge, *e.* that man *De 17:12*
shall die
thou shalt say, would God it *De 28:67*
were *e.*
they wept before the Lord till *J'g 20:23*
e.
they wept and fasted till *e.* *J'g 20:26;*
2Sa 1:12
people abode till *e.* before *J'g 21:2*
God, and wept
so Ruth gleaned in the field *Ru 2:17*
until *e.*
hide myself unto third day at *1Sa 20:5*
e.
he *e.* took away all: and he *1Ki 14:26*
took away
Ahab died at *e.* *1Ki 22:35; 2Ch 18:34*
city round about, *e.* from *1Ch 11:8*
Milo
praise Lord every morning *1Ch 23:30*
and *e.*
e. as their brethren (S) *1Ch 24:31*
let me be weighed in an *e.* *Job 31:6*
balance
my foot standeth in an *e.* *Ps 26:12*
place
I made known to thee, *e.* to *Pr 22:19*
thee
teeth like a flock of sheep that *Ca 4:2*
are *e.* shorn
e. saying to Jerusalem thou *Isa 44:28*
shalt be built
e. to them will I give a name *Isa 56:5*
better than
e. the great abominations that *Eze 8:6*
thou shalt go forth at *e.* in *Eze 12:4*
their sight
in *e.* I digged thro' wall with *Eze 12:7*
my hand
which if a man do, he shall *e.* *Eze 20:11*
live
what if sword contemn *e.* the *Eze 21:13*
rod
I spake to people, and at *e.* *Eze 24:18*
my wife died
when the *e.* was come *M't 8:16*
20:8; 26:20; 27:57; M'k 4:35; 6:47;
11:19; 15:42
at *e.* they brought to him the *M'k 1:32*
diseased
at *e.* at midnight, or at *M'k 13:35*
cock-crowing
enemies shall lay thee *e.* with *Lu 19:44*
ground
when *e.* was come, disciples *Joh 6:16*
went down
e. we ourselves groan within *Ro 8:23*
ourselves
doth not *e.* nature itself *1Co 11:14*
teach you
deliver, up kingdom to God, *1Co 15:24*
e. Father
blessed be God, *e.* Father of *2Co 1:3*
our Lord.
hath distributed a measure *2Co 10:13*
to reach *e.* to you
which are on earth; *e.* in him *Eph 1:10*
obedient to death, *e.* death of *Ph'p 2:8*
cross
God, *e.* thy God, hath *Heb 1:9*
anointed
e. to the dividing asunder of *Heb 4:12*
soul
of full age, *e.* those who by *Heb 5:14*
reason
for us entered, *e.* Jesus made *Heb 6:20*
whom *e.* the patriarch *Heb 7:4*
Abraham
sprang there *e.* of one *Heb 11:12*

to raise him up, *e.* from the *Heb 11:19*
dead
E. so faith, if it hath not *Jas 2:17*
works
E. so the tongue is a little *Jas 3:5*
member
bless we God, *e.* the Father *Jas 3:9*
E. as Sodom and Gomorrha *Jude 7*
hating *e.* the garment spotted *Jude 23*
because of him. E. so, Amen *Re 1:7*
thou dwellest, *e.* where Satan's *Re 2:13*
e. unto the horse bridles *Re 14:20*
E. so, Lord God Almighty, true *Re 16:7*
e. he is the eighth, *Re 17:11*
Reward her *e.* as she rewarded *Re 18:6*
you
e. like a jasper stone, clear as *Re 21:11*
E. so, come, Lord Jesus *Re 22:20*

EVENING

the dove came in to him in the *Ge 8:11*
e.
Jacob came out of the field in *Ge 30:16*
the *e.*
assembly of Israel shall kill it *Ex 12:6*
in *e.*
when *e.* cometh, shall wash *De 23:11*
himself
they were hanging on trees *Jos 10:26*
until *e.*
now the day draweth towards *e.* *J'g 19:9*
evening (S) *J'g 19:16;*
20:23, 26; 21:2; Isa 17:14; Eze 12:4, 7;
24:18; M't 8:16; 20:8; 26:20; 27:57;
M'k 1:32; 4:35; 6:47; 11:11, 19; 13:35;
15:42; Joh 6:16
cursed be the man that eateth *1Sa 14:24*
till *e.*
David smote them to *e.* of *1Sa 30:17*
next day
they prophesied till the *e.* *1Ki 18:29*
sacrifice
at the time of the offering of *1Ki 18:36*
the *e.* sacrifice
on great altar burn *e.* *2Ki 16:15*
meat-offering
I sat astonished until the *e.* *Ezr 9:4*
sacrifice
at *e.* sacrifice I arose from my *Ezr 9:5*
heaviness
they return at *e.* they make a *Ps 59:6*
at *e.* let them return and *Ps 59:14*
make a noise
in the *e.* it is cut down and *Ps 90:6*
withereth
man goeth forth to his labour *Ps 104:23*
until the *e.*
let my prayer be as the *e.* *Ps 141:2*
sacrifice
he went the way to her house in *Pr 7:9*
the *e.*
in the *e.* withhold not thine *Ec 11:6*
hand
the shadows of the *e.* are *Jer 6:4*
stretched out
the hand of the Lord was on *Eze 33:22*
me in the *e.*
but the gate shall not be shut *Eze 46:2*
till the *e.*
touched me about the time of *e.* *Da 9:21*
oblation
and are more fierce than the *e.* *Hab 1:8*
wolves
in Ashkelon shall they lie down *Zep 2:7*
in *e.*
her judges are *e.* wolves, they *Zep 3:3*
gnaw not
come to pass, that at *e.* time *Zec 14:7*
shall be light
when *e.* was come, he was *M't 14:23*
there alone
when it is *e.* ye say, It will be *M't 16:2*
fair weather
in the *e.* he cometh with the *M'k 14:17*
twelve
abide with us, for it is *Lu 24:29*
towards *e.*
the same day at *e.* came *Joh 20:19*
Jesus and stood

EVENING, with *MORNING*

e. and *morning* were the first *Ge 1:5*
day
e. and *morning* were second day *Ge 1:8*
e. and *morning* were third day *Ge 1:13*
e and *morning* were fourth day *Ge 1:19*

e. and *morning* were the fifth *Ge 1:23*
day
e. and *morning* were the sixth *Ge 1:31*
day
people stood by Moses from *Ex 18:13*
morning to *e.*
shall order it from *e.* to *Ex 27:21;*
morning *Le 24:3*
Philistine drew near *morning* *1Sa 17:16*
and *e.*
brought him bread *morning* *1Ki 17:6*
and *e.*
to offer burnt-offerings *1Ch 16:40;*
morning and *e.* *2Ch 2:4; 13:11; 31:3;*
Ezr 3:3
they are destroyed from *Job 4:20*
morning to *e.*
e. and *morning,* and at noon, *Ps 55:17*
will I pray
out-goings of *morning* and *e.* to *Ps 65:8*
rejoice
vision of the *e.* and *morning* is *Da 8:26*
true
toward *e.* and the day is far *Lu 24:29*
spent
same day at *e.* being the first *Joh 20:19*
the prophets, from morning *Ac 28:23*
till *e.*

EVENINGS

a wolf of the *e.* shall spoil them *Jer 5:6*

EVENINGTIDE

it came to pass in an *e.* *2Sa 11:2*
And behold at *e.* trouble *Isa 17:14*

EVENT

one *e.* happeneth to them all *Ec 2:14*
one *e.* to the righteous, and *Ec 9:2*
to the
that there is one *e.* unto all *Ec 9:3*

EVENTIDE

Isaac went out, at the *e.* *Ge 24:63*
the ark of the Lord until the *e.* *Jos 7:6*
he hanged on a tree until *e.* *Jos 8:29*
and now the *e.* was come *M'k 11:11*
the next day: for it was now *e.* *Ac 4:3*

EVER

fire shall *e.* be burning on the *Le 6:13*
altar
hast ridden on, *e.* since I was *Nu 22:30*
thine
did *e.* people hear the voice of *De 4:33*
God
to love God, and to walk *e.* in *De 19:9*
his ways
did *e.* fight against Israel *J'g 11:25*
for Hiram was *e.* a lover of *1Ki 5:1*
David
remember, who *e.* perished, *Job 4:7*
being innocent
those that trust, let them *e.* *Ps 5:11*
shout for joy
thy tender mercies have been *e.* *Ps 25:6*
of old
mine eyes are *e.* towards Lord, *Ps 25:15*
shall pluck
he is *e.* merciful, and lendeth *Ps 37:26*
my transgressions; and my sin *Ps 51:3*
is *e.* before me
or *e.* thou hadst formed earth *Ps 90:2;*
Pr 8:23
he will *e.* be mindful of his *Ps 111:5*
covenant
thy commandments are *e.* *Ps 119:98*
with me
or *e.* I was aware, my soul *Ca 6:12*
made me like
because he will not *e.* be *Isa 28:28*
threshing it
not one of the stakes shall *e.* *Isa 33:20*
be removed
or *e.* they came at the bottom *Da 6:24*
of the den
hath not been *e.* the like nor *Joe 2:2*
any more
such as was not, no, nor *e.* *M't 24:21*
shall be
to desire him to do as he had *M'k 15:8*
e. done
and he said, Son, thou art *e.* *Lu 15:31*
with me

man told me all things that *e.* Joh 4:29; 4:39
I did
servant abideth not, but Son Joh 8:35 abideth *e.*
all that *e.* came before me are Joh 10:8 thieves
I *e.* taught in synagogue and Joh 18:20 temple
we, or *e.* he come, are ready Ac 23:15 to kill him
for *e.* and ever (P) Eph 3:21
no man *e.* yet hated his own Eph 5:29 flesh
and so shall we *e.* be with 1Th 4:17 Lord
but *e.* follow that which is 1Th 5:15 good
e. learning, and never able to 2Ti 3:7 come
but this man, because he Heb 7:24 continueth *e.*
e. liveth to make intercession Heb 7:25 for them
to God our Saviour be glory, Jude 25 now and *e.*

FOR EVER

to thee I give it and thy seed Ge 13:15 for *e.*
then let me bear the blame for Ge 43:9; *e.* 44:32
this is my name *for e.* my Ex 3:15 memorial
keep it a feast by an Ex 12:14; ordinance *for e.* 12:17
an ordinance to thee, and to Ex 12:24 thy sons *for e.*
ye shall see them again no Ex 14:13 more *for e.*
that the people may believe Ex 19:9 thee *for e.*
bore his ear, and he shall Ex 21:6 serve him *for e.*
it is a sign between me and Ex 31:17 Israel *for e.*
give this land, and they shall Ex 32:13 inherit it *for e.*
land shall not be sold *for e.* is Le 25:23 mine
the house shall be established Le 25:30 *for e.* to him
they shall be your bondmen Le 25:46 *for e.*
for an ordinance *for e.* Nu 10:8; 15:15; 18:8
it is a covenant of salt *for e.* Nu 18:19 unto thee
he said, Amalek shall perish Nu 24:20 *for e.*
shall afflict Eber, he also shall Nu 24:24 perish *for e.*
earth which God giveth thee De 4:40 *for e.*
it might be well with them for De 5:29; *e.* 12:28
it shall be an heap *for e.* not De 13:16 built again
he shall be thy servant *for e.* De 15:17
God hath chosen him and his De 18:5 sons *for e.*
thou shalt not seek their peace De 23:6 *for e.*
they shall be upon thee for a De 28:46 sign *for e.*
those things revealed belong De 29:29 to us *for e.*
these stones shall be for a Jos 4:7 memorial *for e.*
that ye might fear the Lord Jos 4:24 your God *for e.*
Joshua burnt Ai, and made it Jos 8:28 an heap *for e.*
land shall be thine inheritance Jos 14:9 *for e.*
appear before the Lord and 1Sa 1:22 abide *for e.*
thy house should walk before 1Sa 2:30 me *for e.*
not be an old man in house 1Sa 2:32 *for e.*
walk before mine Anointed 1Sa 2:35 *for e.*
I will judge his house *for e.* 1Sa 3:13 for iniquity
iniquity of Eli's house shall 1Sa 3:14 not be purged *for e.*
shalt not cut off thy kindness 1Sa 20:15 *for e.*

the Lord be between thee 1Sa 20:23; and me *for e.* 20:42
he shall be my servant *for e.* 1Sa 27:12
make thee keeper of mine 1Sa 28:2 head *for e.*
Abner said, Shall the sword 2Sa 2:26 devour *for e.*
I and my kingdom guiltless 2Sa 3:28 before Lord *for e.*
thou hast confirmed Israel to 2Sa 7:24 thee *for e.*
let thy name be magnified for 2Sa 7:26 *e.*
his house may continue *for e.* 2Sa 7:29 before thee
settled place to abide in *for e.* 1Ki 8:13
house built, to put name there 1Ki 9:3 *for e.*
because Lord loved Israel for 1Ki 10:9 *e.*
afflict David's seed, but not 1Ki 11:39 *for e.*
will be thy servants *for e.* 1Ki 12:7; 2Ch 10:7
leprosy cleave to thee and 2Ki 5:27 seed *for e.*
didst thou make thine own 1Ch 17:22 *for e.*
he and sons *for e.* to burn 1Ch 23:13 incense before Lord
if forsake him, he will cast 1Ch 28:9 thee off *for e.*
Lord God of Israel, keep 1Ch 29:18 this *for e.*
that my name may be there 2Ch 7:16 *for e.*
he promised to give light to 2Ch 21:7 sons *for e.*
sanctuary which he hath 2Ch 30:8 sanctified *for e.*
in Jerusalem shall my name 2Ch 33:4 be *for e.*
not come into congregation of Ne 13:1 God *for e.*
they perish *for e.* without any Job 4:20 regarding it
thou prevailest *for e.* against Job 14:20 him, and he passeth
graven with iron pen in the Job 19:24 rock *for e.*
yet he shall perish *for e.* like Job 20:7 his own dung
so should I be delivered *for e.* Job 23:7 from my judge
yea, he doth establish them Job 36:7 *for e.*
but the Lord shall endure *for e.* Ps 9:7
expectation of poor shall not Ps 9:18 perish *for e.*
O Lord, thou shalt preserve Ps 12:7 them *for e.*
how long wilt thou forget me, Ps 13:1 *for e.*
fear of the Lord is clean, Ps 19:9 enduring *for e.*
thou hast made him most Ps 21:6 blessed *for e.*
I will dwell in the house of the Ps 23:6 Lord *for e.*
feed them also, and lift them Ps 28:9 up *for e.*
yea, the Lord sitteth king for Ps 29:10 *e.*
I will give thanks to thee for Ps 30:12; *e.* 79:13
the counsel of the Lord Ps 33:11 standeth *for e.*
and their inheritance shall be Ps 37:18 *for e.*
and his saints are preserved Ps 37:28 *for e.*
the righteous shall dwell in the Ps 37:29 land *for e.*
thou settest me before thy face Ps 41:12 *for e.*
and we praise thy name *for e.* Ps 44:8 Selah
awake, O Lord, arise, cast us Ps 44:23 not off *for e.*
therefore God hath blessed thee Ps 45:2 *for e.*
redemption of their soul Ps 49:8 ceaseth *for e.*
thought is, that their houses Ps 49:11 continue *for e.*
God shall likewise destroy thee Ps 52:5 *for e.*
I will praise thee *for e.* I will Ps 52:9 wait on

I will abide in thy tabernacle Ps 61:4 *for e.*
he shall abide before God *for e.* Ps 61:7
I will sing praise unto thy name Ps 61:8 *for e.*
he ruleth by his power *for e.* Ps 66:7
yea, the Lord will dwell in it Ps 68:16 *for e.*
His name shall endure *for e.* Ps 72:17
blessed be his glorious name Ps 72:19 *for e.*
God is my strength and Ps 73:26 portion *for e.*
O God, why hast thou cast us Ps 74:1 off *for e.*
shall enemy blaspheme thy Ps 74:10 name *for e.*
forget not congregation of Ps 74:19 poor *for e.*
I will declare *for e.* I will sing Ps 75:9 praises
will Lord cast off *for e.?* Ps 77:7 favourable no more
is mercy clean gone *for e.?* doth Ps 77:8 promise fail
how long wilt thou be angry? Ps 79:5 *for e.*
but their time should have Ps 81:15 endured *for e.*
let them be confounded and Ps 83:17 troubled *for e.*
wilt thou be angry with us for Ps 85:5 *e.*
I will sing of the mercies of Ps 89:1 Lord *for e.*
I have said, Mercy shall be Ps 89:2 built up *for e.*
his seed will I make to endure Ps 89:29; *for e.* 89:36
how long wilt thou hide Ps 89:46 thyself? *for e.*
it is that they shall be destroyed Ps 92:7 *for e.*
holiness becometh thine house, Ps 93:5 *for e.*
neither will he keep his anger Ps 103:9 *for e.*
he hath remembered his Ps 105:8 covenant *for e.*
thou art a priest *for e.* after Ps 110:4; order of Melchizedek Heb 5:6; 6:20; 7:17, 21
he hath commanded his Ps 111:9 covenant *for e.*
surely he shall not be moved Ps 112:6 *for e.*
for e. Thy word is settled in Ps 119:89 heaven
from henceforth even *for e.* Ps 125:2; 131:3; Isa 9:7
this is my rest *for e.* here will Ps 132:14 I dwell
the Lord who keepeth truth Ps 146:6 *for e.*
Lord shall reign *for e.* even Ps 146:10 thy God
for riches are not *for e.* Pr 27:24
no remembrance of wise more Ec 2:16 than fool *for e.*
whatsoever God doth, it shall Ec 3:14 be *for e.*
they more a portion *for e.* in Ec 9:6 any thing
trust ye in Lord *for e.* for in Isa 26:4 Lord
of righteousness, quietness, Isa 32:17 and assurance *for e.*
the smoke thereof shall go up Isa 34:10 *for e.*
possess it *for e.* from Isa 34:17 generation to generation
but the word of our God shall Isa 40:8 stand *for e.*
and thou saidst, I shall be a Isa 47:7 lady *for e.*
my salvation shall be *for e.* Isa 51:6
my righteousness shall be *for e.* Isa 51:8
not contend *for e.* nor be Isa 57:16 always wroth
and my words shall not depart Isa 59:21 *for e.*
thy people shall inherit the Isa 60:21 land *for e.*
be not wroth nor remember Isa 64:9 iniquity *for e.*
be glad *for e.* in what I create Ps 65:18
will he reserve his anger *for e.* Jer 3:5
I am merciful, I will not keep Jer 3:12 anger *for e.*

ye kindled a fire which shall   *Jer 17:4*
burn *for e.*
Jerusalem and this city shall   *Jer 17:25*
remain *for e.*
not be plucked up any more   *Jer 31:40*
for e.
one heart that they may fear   *Jer 32:39*
for e.
Jonadab said, Ye shall drink   *Jer 35:6*
no wine *for e.*
Jonadab not want man before   *Jer 35:19*
me *for e.*
Hazor be for dragons and   *Jer 49:33*
desolation *for e.*
shall be no more inhabited   *Jer 50:39;*
for e.   *51:26, 62*
the Lord will not cast off *for e.*   *La 3:31*
thou, O Lord remainest *for e.*   *La 5:19*
thy throne
wherefore dost thou forget us   *La 5:20*
for e.
they and children dwell *for e.*   *Eze 37:25*
and David shall be prince *for e.*
I will dwell in the midst of   *Eze 43:7*
Israel *for e.*
but his kingdom shall stand *for*   *Da 2:44*
e.
I praised him that liveth   *Da 4:34*
for e.
he is living God and stedfast   *Da 6:26*
for e.
saints of most High possess   *Da 7:18*
kingdom *for e.*
sware by him that liveth *for*   *Da 12:7*
e.
I will betroth thee unto me *for*   *Ho 2:19*
e.
Judah dwell *for e.* and   *Joe 3:20*
Jerusalem
Edom cast off pity and kept   *Am 1:11*
wrath *for e.*
Edom, thou shalt be cut off *for*   *Ob 10*
e.
earth with her bars about me   *Jon 2:6*
for e.
ye have taken away my glory   *Mic 2:9*
for e.
Lord shall reign over them *for*   *Mic 4:7*
e.
retaineth not anger *for e.*   *Mic 7:18*
against whom Lord hath   *Mal 1:4*
indignation *for e.*
for thine is power and glory   *M't 6:13*
for e.
no fruit grow on thee *for e.*   *M't 21:19;*
       M'k 11:14
he shall reign over Jacob *for e.*   *Lu 1:33*
spake to Abraham and seed *for*   *Lu 1:55*
e.
servant abideth not in house   *Joh 8:35*
for e.
have heard that Christ   *Joh 12:34*
abideth *for e.*
Comforter may abide with   *Joh 14:16*
you *for e.*
more than Creator, who is   *Ro 1:25*
blessed *for e.*
Christ, who is over all, God   *Ro 9:5*
blessed *for e.*
to whom be glory *for e.*   *Ro 11:36;*
amen   *16:27*
his righteousness remaineth *for*   *2Co 9:9*
e.
thou shouldest receive him *for*   *Ph'm 15*
e.
for e. sat down on right   *Heb 10:12*
hand of God
perfected *for e.* them that   *Heb 10:14*
are sanctified
Jesus Christ, same to-day and   *Heb 13:8*
for e.
word of God, which liveth *for*   *1Pe 1:23*
e.
the word of the Lord endureth   *1Pe 1:25*
for e.
mist of darkness reserved *for*   *2Pe 2:17*
       Jude 13
truth's sake which shall be with   *2Jo 2*
us *for e.*

LIVE FOR EVER

lest he eat of tree of life and   *Ge 3:22*
live *for e.*
I lift up my hand and say, I   *De 32:40*
live *for e.*
let my lord king David live *for*   *1Ki 1:31*
e.
I said to the king, Let the king   *Ne 2:3*
live *for e.*

---

your hearts shall live *for e.*   *Ps 22:26*
that he should still live *for e.*   *Ps 49:9*
O king, live *for e.*   *Da 2:4;*
       3:9; 5:10; 6:6, 21
the prophets, do they live *for e.*   *Zec 1:5*
eat of this bread live   *Joh 6:51; 6:58*
for e.

FOR EVER *AND* EVER

the Lord shall reign *for e.*   *Ex 15:18*
and e.
blessed be God *for e.* and *e.*   *1Ch 16:36;*
       29:10; Da 2:20
bless Lord your God *for e.*   *Ne 9:5*
and e.
put out their name *for e.* and *e.*   *Ps 9:5*
Lord is King *for e.* and *e.* the   *Ps 10:16*
heathen
gavest him length of days *for e.*   *Ps 21:4*
and e.
thy throne, O God, is *for e.* and   *Ps 45:6*
e.
the people shall praise thee *for*   *Ps 45:17*
e. and e.
for this God is our God *for e.*   *Ps 48:14*
and e.
I trust in the mercy of God *for*   *Ps 52:8*
e. and e.
they stand fast *for e.* and *e.*   *Ps 111:8*
so shall I keep thy law *for e.*   *Ps 119:44*
and e.
I will bless thy name *for e.*   *Ps 145:1*
I will praise Thy name *for e.*   *Ps 145:2;*
and e.   *145:21*
He hath stablished them *for*   *Ps 148:6*
e. and e.
it may be for time to come, *for*   *Isa 30:8*
e. and e.
none shall pass through it *for*   *Isa 34:10*
e. and e.
dwell in land that I gave   *Jer 7:7*
for e. and e.
Lord given to you and fathers   *Jer 25:5*
for e. and e.
possess the kingdom *for e.* and   *Da 7:18*
e.
shall shine as stars *for e.* and   *Da 12:3*
e.
walk in name of God *for e.* and   *Mic 4:5*
e.
of God, to whom be glory *for*   *Ga 1:5;*
e. and e.   *Ph'p 4:20; 1Ti 1:17;*
       2Ti 4:18; Heb 13:21
thy throne, O God, is *for e.*   *Heb 1:8*
and e.
Him that sat on throne, who   *Re 4:9;*
liveth *for e.* and *e.* 4:10; 5:14; 10:6; 15:7
honour be to the Lamb *for*   *Re 5:13*
e. and e.
power be unto our God *for*   *Re 7:12*
e. and e.
Christ shall reign *for e.* and *e.*   *Re 11:15*
smoke ascendeth *for e.* and *e.*   *Re 14:11;*
       19:3
be tormented day and night   *Re 20:10*
for e. and e.
and they shall reign *for e.* and   *Re 22:5*
e.

STATUTE FOR EVER

it shall be a *statute for e.*   *Ex 27:21;*
28:43; 30:21; Le 6:18; 10:9; 17:7; 23:14,
       21, 31; 24:3; Nu 18:23
it shall be by a *statute for e.*   *Ex 29:28;*
Le 7:34, 36; 10:15; 16:31; Nu 18:11, 19
it is a *statute for e.* unto the   *Le 6:22*
Lord
to the stranger for a *statue*   *Nu 19:10*
for e.

EVERLASTING

land of Canaan for an *e.*   *Ge 17:8;*
possession   *18:4*
the *e.* God   *Ge 21:33;*
       Isa 40:28; Ro 16:26
to the utmost bound of the *e.*   *Ge 49:26*
hills
an *e.* institution (B)   *Ex 27:21*
an *e.* priesthood   *Ex 40:15; Nu 25:13*
e. decree (B)   *Le 6:18*
e. statute; *e.* arms   *Le 16:34; De 33:27*
an *e.* regulation (B)   *Le 24:3;*
       Nu 19:10; 19:21
abundance of *e.* hills (A)   *De 33:15*
be lift up, ye *e.* doors; mercy *e.*   *Ps 24:7;*
       Ps 24:9; 100:5

---

put them to *e.* shame (R)   *Ps 78:66*
righteous shall be in *e.*   *Ps 112:6*
remembrance
righteousness is an *e.*   *Ps 119:142;*
righteousness   *119:144*
search me, and lead me in   *Ps 139:24*
way *e.*
kingdom is an *e.* kingdom   *Ps 145:13;*
thro all generation   *Da 4:3; 7:27;*
       2Pe 1:11
but the righteous is an *e.*   *Pr 10:25*
foundation
His name shall be called the *e.*   *Isa 9:6*
Father
in the Lord Jehovah is *e.*   *Isa 26:4*
strength
who among us shall dwell   *Isa 33:14*
with *e.* burnings
they shall come with *e.* joy   *Isa 35:10*
       51:11; 61:7
e. salvation; *e.* kindness   *Isa 45:17; 54:8*
e. sign; *e.* name   *Isa 55:13; 56:5; 63:12*
an *e.* majesty (B)   *Isa 60:15*
Lord be unto thee an *e.* light   *Isa 60:19;*
       60:20
an *e.* King *e.* confusion   *Jer 10:10; 20:11*
I will bring an *e.* reproach   *Jer 23:40*
upon you
an *e.* reproach (A)(B)   *Jer 23:40*
yea I have loved thee with an   *Jer 31:3*
e. love
dominion is an *e.* dominion   *Da 4:34;*
       7:14
the *e.* mountains were scattered   *Hab 3:6*
to be cast into *e.* fire   *M't 18:8; 18:25, 41*
go away into *e.* punishment   *M't 25:46*
grasp of *e.* trespass (A)   *M'k 3:29*
may receive you into *e.*   *Lu 16:9*
habitations
e. weight of glory (A)(B)   *2Co 4:17*
deathless and *e.* (A)(B)   *2Co 4:18*
be punished with *e.* destruction   *2Th 1:9*
penalty of *e.* ruin (B)   *2Th 1:9*
loved us, and hath given us *e.*   *2Th 2:16*
consolation
to whom be honour and power   *1Ti 6:16*
e.
angels he hath reserved in *e.*   *Jude 6*
chains
having *e.* gospel to preach to   *Re 14:6*
them

EVERLASTING *LIFE*

awake, some to *e.* life   *Da 12:2*
shall inherit *e.* life   *M't 19:29*
and in the world to come *e.*   *Lu 18:30*
life
whoso believeth should have   *Joh 3:16;*
e. life   *3:36*
well of water springing up to   *Joh 4:14*
e. life
he that heareth my words hath   *Joh 5:24*
e. life
labour for meat which   *Joh 6:27*
endureth to *e.* life
every one who seeth the Son   *Joh 6:40*
may have *e.* life
he that believeth on me hath   *Joh 6:47*
e. life
I know that his   *Joh 12:50*
commandment is life *e.*
judge yourselves unworthy of   *Ac 13:46*
e. life
being free from sin, the end *e.*   *Ro 6:22*
life
soweth to Spirit, of Spirit reap   *Ga 6:8*
life *e.*
hereafter believe on him to life   *1Ti 1:16*
e.

FROM EVERLASTING

blessed be God *from e.* to   *Ps 41:13;*
everlasting   *106:48*
from e. to everlasting thou art   *Ps 90:2*
God
thy throne is of old, thou art   *Ps 93:2*
from e.
mercy of Lord is *from e.* to   *Ps 103:17*
everlasting
I was set up *from e.* or ever   *Pr 8:23*
earth was
O Lord, thy name is *from e.*   *Isa 63:16*
whose goings forth have been   *Mic 5:2*
from e.
art thou not *from e.* O Lord   *Hab 1:12*

EVERMORE

shalt be oppressed and spoiled *e.*   *De 28:29*
he sheweth mercy unto David *e.*   *2Sa 22:51*
ye shall observe to do for *e.*   *2Ki 17:37*
throne shall be established for *e.*   *1Ch 17:14*
at right hand are pleasures for *e.*   *Ps 16:11*
sheweth mercy to David and seed for *e.*   *Ps 18:50*
depart from evil, do good, and dwell for *e.*   *Ps 37:27*
is mercy gone? doth his promise fail for *e.*   *Ps 77:8*
praise and glorify Thy name for *e.*   *Ps 86:12*
my mercy will I keep for him for *e.*   *Ps 89:28*
blessed be Lord for *e.* amen and amen   *Ps 89:52*
but thou, Lord, art most high for *e.*   *Ps 92:8*
seek the Lord, seek his face *e.*   *Ps 105:4*
was counted for *e.*   *Ps 106:31*
righteousness for *e.*
blessed be name of Lord for *e.*   *Ps 113:2*
but we will bless the Lord for *e.*   *Ps 115:18*
preserve going out and coming in *e.*   *Ps 121:8*
their children sit upon throne for *e.*   *Ps 132:12*
Lord commanded blessing, life for *e.*   *Ps 133:3*
make covenant and set my sanctuary in midst of them for *e.*   *Eze 37:26; 37:28*
Lord, *e.* give us this bread   *Joh 6:34*
Father of our Lord blessed for *e.*   *2Co 11:31*
rejoice *e.* pray without ceasing   *1Th 5:16*
maketh the Son, who is consecrated for *e.*   *Heb 7:28*
was dead, behold, I am alive for *e.*   *Re 1:18*

EVERY

Adam called *e.* living creature that was   *Ge 2:19*
e. imagination of his heart was evil   *Ge 6:5*
and upon *e.* fowl of the air, upon   *Ge 9:2*
of the ark, to *e.* beast of the earth   *Ge 9:10*
e. man child shall be circumcised   *Ge 17:10*
all the people from *e.* quarter   *Ge 19:4*
But *e.* man's servant that is bought   *Ex 12:44*
and the breadth fifty *e.* where   *Ex 27:18*
E. raven after his kind   *Le 11:15*
e. thing, whereon he sitteth, shall   *Le 15:4*
nor gather *e.* grape of thy vineyard   *Le 19:10*
that they put out of camp *e.* leper   *Nu 15:2*
e. daughter, that possesseth an   *Nu 36:8*
Samuel told him *e.* whit, hid nothing   *1Sa 3:18*
silver by weight for *e.* bason of silver   *1Ch 28:17*
and to *e.* governor in all Israel   *2Ch 1:2*
porters also by their courses at *e.* gate   *2Ch 8:14*
I have refrained from *e.* evil way   *Ps 119:101*
therefore I hate *e.* false way   *Ps 119:104; 119:128*
shalt thou understand *e.* good path   *Pr 2:9*
in streets, she lieth in wait at *e.* corner   *Pr 7:12*
simple believeth *e.* word, but prudent man   *Pr 14:15*
eyes of Lord are in *e.* place, beholding   *Pr 15:3*
cease from strife, but *e.* fool will be meddling   *Pr 20:3*
e. word of God is pure, he is a shield   *Pr 30:5*
e. knee shall bow, *e.* tongue swear   *Isa 45:23*
e. one that goeth out thence shall   *Jer 5:6*

e. purpose of Lord be performed   *Jer 51:29*
days at hand, and effect of *e.* vision   *Eze 12:23*
magnify himself above *e.* god   *Da 11:36*
land shall mourn, *e.* family apart   *Zec 12:12*
in *e.* place incense be offered to my name   *Mal 1:11*
but by *e.* word that proceedeth from God   *M't 4:4*
man to put away his wife for *e.* cause   *M't 19:3*
they came to him from *e.* quarter   *M'k 1:45*
the fame of him went into *e.* place   *Lu 4:37*
for *e.* tree is known by his own fruit   *Lu 6:44*
fear came upon *e.* soul, wonders done   *Ac 2:43*
Moses hath in *e.* city them that preach him   *Ac 15:21*
e. knee shall bow, *e.* tongue confess   *Ro 14:11*
as I teach *e.* where in *e.* church   *1Co 4:17*
bringing into captivity *e.* thought   *2Co 10:5*
far above *e.* name named   *Eph 1:21; Ph'p 2:9*
e. joint supplieth, in measure of *e.* part   *Eph 4:16*
salute *e.* saint in Christ Jesus   *Ph'p 4:21*
for *e.* creature of God is good if   *1Ti 4:4*
prepared unto *e.* good work   *2Ti 2:21*
let us lay aside *e.* weight, and   *Heb 12:1*
e. good and perfect gift is from above   *Jas 1:17*
submit to *e.* ordinance of man for   *1Pe 2:13*
believe not *e.* spirit, but try spirit   *1Jo 4:1*

EVERY ONE

e. one that findeth me shall slay me   *Ge 4:14*
cursed be *e.* one that curseth thee   *Ge 27:29*
all congregation are holy, *e.* one of them   *Nu 16:3*
ye are alive *e.* one of you this day   *De 4:4*
hearken, O people, *e.* one of you   *1Ki 22:28*
and then eat ye *e.* one of his fig tree   *2Ki 18:31*
saying, The good Lord pardon *e.* one   *2Ch 30:18*
of *e.* one that willingly offered an offering   *Ezr 3:5*
were assembled to me *e.* one that trembled   *Ezr 9:4*
e. one that is proud, and abase him   *Job 40:11*
look on *e.* one proud, and bring him low   *Job 40:12*
in temple of *e.* one doth speak of his glory   *Ps 29:9*
for this shall *e.* one that is godly pray   *Ps 32:6*
e. one that sweareth by him shall glory   *Ps 63:11*
till *e.* one submit himself with silver   *Ps 68:30*
and thy power to *e.* one that is to come   *Ps 71:18*
so is *e.* one that trusteth in them   *Ps 115:8; 135:18*
e. one of judgments endureth for ever   *Ps 119:100*
blessed is *e.* one that fear the Lord   *Ps 128:1*
he saith to *e.* one that he is a fool   *Ec 10:3*
whereof *e.* one bear twins   *Ca 4:2; 6:6*
honey *e.* one eat left in land   *Isa 7:22*
for *e.* one is an hypocrite and an evil doer   *Isa 9:17*
vultures be gathered, *e.* one with her mate   *Isa 34:15*
even *e.* one that is called by my name   *Isa 43:7*
ho, *e.* one that thirsteth, come to waters   *Isa 55:1*
e. one goeth out shall be torn in pieces   *Jer 5:6*

e. one neighed after his neighbour's wife   *Jer 5:8*
for *e.* one is given to covetousness   *Jer 6:13*
I am in derision daily, *e.* one mocketh me   *Jer 20:7*
turn ye now *e.* one from his evil way   *Jer 25:5*
them mourning, *e.* one for iniquity   *Eze 7:16*
opened feet to *e.* one that passed by   *Eze 16:25*
behold *e.* one were in thee to shed blood   *Eze 22:6*
e. one that be found written in book   *Da 12:1*
they shall march *e.* one on his ways   *Joe 2:7*
for *e.* one that stealeth shall be cut off   *Zec 5:3*
e. one that asketh, receiveth   *M't 7:8; Lu 11:10*
said to them, Hearken, *e.* one of you   *M'k 7:14*
to *e.* one which hath, shall be given   *Lu 19:26*
so is *e.* one that is born of the Spirit   *Joh 3:8*
e. one that is of truth heareth my voice   *Joh 18:37*
repent, be baptized, *e.* one of you   *Ac 2:38*
though he be not far from *e.* one of us   *Ac 17:27*
ceased not to warn *e.* one night and day   *Ac 20:31*
e. one shall give account of himself to God   *Ro 14:12*
as Lord called *e.* one, so walk   *1Co 7:17*
cursed is *e.* one that continueth not   *Ga 3:10*
e. one that nameth name of Christ   *2Ti 2:19*
e. one that loveth is born of God   *1Jo 4:7*
white robes given to *e.* one of them   *Re 6:11*

EVERYTHING

Samuel told him *e.* (S)   *1Sa 3:18*

EVERY WHERE

send abroad to our brethren *e.* where   *1Ch 13:2*
they went forth and preached *e.* where   *M'k 16:20*
preaching the gospel *e.* where   *Lu 9:6; Ac 8:4*
commanding all men *e.* where to repent   *Ac 17:30*
we know it is *e.* where spoken against   *Ac 28:22*
as I teach *e.* where in every church   *1Co 4:17*
e. where, and in all things instructed   *Ph'p 4:12*
I will therefore that men pray *e.* where   *1Ti 2:8*

EVI

E. and Rekem, and Zur   *Nu 31:8*
with the princes of Midian, *E.*   *Jos 13:21*

EVIDENCE

e. of her chastity (B)   *De 22:17*
do not know your *e.* (S)   *Job 21:29*
I subscribed the *e.* and sealed it   *Jer 32:10; 32:12*
so I took the *e.*   *Jer 32:11*
this *e.* both which is sealed, and this *e.* open   *Jer 32:14*
when I delivered the *e.* of the purchase   *Jer 32:16*
your *e.* is not valid (P)   *Joh 8:13*
my *e.* is valid (P)   *Joh 8:14*
the *e.* of two persons (B)   *Joh 8:17*
whose *e.* is to be trusted (N)   *Joh 19:35*
e. of the truth (N)   *1Co 1:6*
to each is granted *e.* (B)   *1Co 12:7*
e. that he is excepted (A)(B)(E)(P)(R)   *1Co 15:27*
works of flesh are in *e.* (B)   *Ga 5:19*
faith is the *e.* of things not seen   *Heb 11:1*

EVIDENCES

e. of her virginity (A)(B)   *De 22:17;*
                         22:20
thus saith the Lord, Take   *Jer 32:14*
these *e.*
men buy fields for money and   *Jer 32:44*
subscribe *e.*

EVIDENT

look upon me, for it is *e.* to   *Job 6:28*
you if I lie
that no man is justified by the   *Ga 3:11*
law is *e.*
which is to them an *e.* token   *Ph'p 1:28*
of perdition
it is *e.* our Lord sprang out of   *Heb 7:14*
Judah
it is yet far more *e.* for that   *Heb 7:15*
after Melchisedec

EVIDENTLY

Cornelius saw in a vision *e.* an   *Ac 10:3*
angel
Jesus Christ hath been *e.* set   *Ga 3:1*
forth crucified

EVIL

thoughts of his heart were only   *Ge 6:5;*
e.   *8:21*
e. minded from youth (B)   *Ge 8:21*
lest some *e.* take me and I die   *Ge 19:19*
some *e.* beast hath devoured   *Ge 37:20;*
him   *37:33*
ye have done *e.* in so doing   *Ge 44:5*
lest I see *e.* come on my   *Ge 44:34*
father
as for you, ye thought *e.*   *Ge 50:20*
against me
Israel did see that they were in   *Ex 5:19*
e. case
since I came, he hath done *e.*   *Ex 5:23*
to people
look to it, for *e.* is before you   *Ex 10:10*
Lord repented of *e.* He   *Ex 32:14;*
thought to do to people   *2Sa 24:16;*
                   1Ch 21:15
they are set on *e.* (A)(E)(R)   *Ex 32:22*
people heard these *e.* tidings   *Ex 33:4*
they mourned
how long bear this *e.*   *Nu 14:27*
congregation
bringing an *e.* report (E)(R)   *Nu 14:36*
to bring us in unto this *e.* place *Nu 20:5*
e. those men (B)   *Nu 25:5*
e. the murderer (B)   *Nu 35:19*
this great. (B)   *Nu 39:9*
not one of this *e.* generation   *De 1:35*
shall see land
evil (B)   *De 13:11;*
   17:2; 1Sa 12:17; 12:20; 1Ki 1:52
evil (R)   *De 17:2;*
   28:20; 1Sa 12:20; 1Ki 2:44; 21:25;
   2Ki 21:6; Ps 7:9; 28:4; 1Co 5:9
evil (E)   *De 17:5;*
   23:9; Job 21:30; Pr 14:19; Eze 20:44;
             M't 12:45; Col 1:21
and bring up an *e.* name upon *De 22:14;*
her   *22:19*
evil (A)   *De 23:9;*
   Job 21:30; Ps 101:4; Eze 20:44
evil (B)   *De 23:9; 17:11;*
2Ch 7:14; Job 21:30; Pr 11:21; 12:2;
              13; Col 1:21
evil (E)   *De 28:20; 1Sa 12:20; 2Ki 21:6*
his eye shall be *e.* toward his   *De 28:54*
brother
her eye shall be *e.* toward her   *De 28:56*
husband
Lord shall separate him to *e.*   *De 29:21*
out of tribes
I have set before thee death   *De 30:15*
and *e.*
e. will befall you in the latter   *De 31:29*
days
if it seem *e.* to you to serve   *Jos 24:15*
Lord
the hand of the Lord against   *J'g 2:15*
them for *e.*
the *e.* of the men of Shechem   *J'g 9:57*
did God render
when I do them *e.* (A)(S)   *J'g 15:3*
but they knew not that *e.* was   *J'g 20:34*
near them
the *e.* of your heart (R)   *1Sa 17:28*
be sure that *e.* is determined   *1Sa 20:7*
by him

if I knew certainly that *e.*   *1Sa 20:9*
were determined
e. the Lord's priests (B)   *1Sa 22:17*
Saul was planning *e.*   *1Sa 23:9*
(A)(B)(R)
nor is *e.* nor transgression in *1Sa 24:11*
mine hand
me good, whereas, I have   *1Sa 24:17*
rewarded thee *e.*
for *e.* is determined against   *1Sa 25:17*
our master
they that seek *e.* to my lord, *1Sa 25:26*
be as Nabal
e. hath not been found in   *1Sa 25:28*
thee all thy days
what have I done? what *e.* is *1Sa 26:18*
in my hand
I have not found *e.* since thy   *1Sa 29:6*
coming
Lord shall reward the doer of *2Sa 3:39*
e.
behold I will raise up *e.*   *2Sa 12:11*
against thee
be worse than all *e.* that befell *2Sa 19:7*
thee
hast done *e.* above all before *1Ki 14:9*
thee
Omri wrought *e.* in eyes of *1Ki 16:25*
the Lord
spoken *e.* concerning thee   *1Ki 22:23;*
              2Ch 18:22
I am bringing such *e.* on   *2Ki 21:2*
Jerusalem
eyes shall not see all *e.* on   *2Ki 22:20*
this place
I have sinned and done *e.*   *1Ch 21:17*
indeed
if when *e.* cometh on us, as *2Ch 20:9*
the sword
he saw that there was *e.*   *Es 7:7*
determined
avert the *e.* plot (A)(R)   *Es 8:3*
for how can I endure to see *e.* to *Es 8:6*
my people
feared God and eschewed *e.*   *Job 1:1*
in seven there shall no *e.*   *Job 5:19*
touch thee
let not *e.* dwell (A)   *Job 11:14; Ps 55:15*
lift up myself when *e.* found *Job 31:29*
him
they comforted him over all   *Job 42:11*
e. on him
neither shall *e.* dwell with thee *Ps 5:4*
if I have rewarded *e.* to him at *Ps 7:4*
peace
plan *e.* things (B)(R)   *Ps 14:2*
nor doth *e.* to his neighbour, *Ps 15:3*
nor taketh up
for they intended *e.* against *Ps 21:11*
thee
I will fear no *e.* for thou art *Ps 23:4*
with me
in hands are *e.* devices (R) *Ps 26:10*
e. shall slay wicked, those hate *Ps 34:21*
righteous
he deviseth mischief, he   *Ps 37:4*
abhorreth not *e.*
let them be put to shame that *Ps 40:14*
wish me *e.*
wherefore should I fear in days *Ps 49:5*
of *e.*
thou givest thy mouth to *e.* *Ps 50:19*
and thy tongue
he shall reward *e.* unto mine *Ps 54:5*
enemies
all their thoughts are against *Ps 56:5*
me for *e.*
they encourage themselves in *Ps 64:5*
an *e.* matter
trouble, by sending *e.* angels *Ps 78:49*
among them
and the years wherein we have *Ps 90:15*
seen *e.*
there shall no *e.* befall thee   *Ps 91:10;*
              Jer 23:17
ye that love the Lord, hate *e.* *Ps 97:10*
of them that speak *e.* against *Ps 109:20*
my soul
he shall not be afraid of *e.* *Ps 112:7*
tidings
let not an *e.* speaker be   *Ps 140:11*
established in earth
for their feet run to *e.* *Pr 1:16; Isa 59:7*
dwell safely, shall be quiet from *Pr 1:33*
fear of *e.*
devise not *e.* against thy   *Pr 3:29*
neighbour
I was almost in all *e.* in midst *Pr 5:14*
of congregation

swift in running to *e.*   *Pr 6:18*
(A)(B)(R)
to keep thee from the *e.* woman *Pr 6:24*
he that pursueth *e.* pursueth it *Pr 11:19*
to his death
the *e.* man go unpunished   *Pr 11:21;*
(E)(R)   *12:13*
deceit in heart of them that   *Pr 12:20*
imagine *e.*
who devise *e.* (A)(E)(R)   *Pr 12:20*
who plan *e.* (B)   *Pr 12:20*
there shall no *e.* happen to   *Pr 12:21*
the just
e. pursueth sinners; that   *Pr 13:21;*
devise *e.*   *14:22*
e. bow before the good, the *Pr 14:19*
wicked
yea, even the wicked for the   *Pr 16:4*
day of *e.*
an ungodly man diggeth up *e.* *Pr 16:27*
fire in his lips
moving his lips he bringeth *e.* *Pr 16:30*
to pass
he shall not be visited with *e.* *Pr 19:23*
king scattereth away all *e.* with *Pr 20:8*
his eyes
say not thou, I will   *Pr 20:22*
recompense *e.* wait on Lord
the soul of the wicked   *Pr 21:10*
desireth *e.*
a prudent man forseeth the *e.* *Pr 22:3;*
              27:12
if thou hast thought *e.* lay   *Pr 30:32*
thine hand
this also is vanity, and a great *Ec 2:21*
e.
there is a sore *e.* which I have *Ec 5:13;*
seen   *5:16*
many devices for *e.*   *Ec 7:29*
(A)(B)(R)
this is an *e.* among things none *Ec 9:3*
under sun, the heart of sons of men is
full of *e.*
an *e.* odor (S)   *Ec 10:1*
knowest not what *e.* shall be on *Ec 11:2*
earth
for they have rewarded *e.* to   *Isa 3:9*
themselves
I will punish the world for   *Isa 13:11*
their *e.*
the instruments also of the   *Isa 32:7*
churl are *e.*
and shutteth his eyes from   *Isa 33:15*
seeing *e.*
I make peace and create *e.*   *Isa 45:7*
therefore shall *e.* come upon *Isa 47:11*
thee
shall *e.* come upon you   *Isa 47:11*
(A)(E)(R)
and keepeth his hand from   *Isa 56:2*
doing any *e.*
that righteous is taken away   *Isa 57:1*
from *e.*
out of the north an *e.* break   *Jer 1:14*
forth   *6:1*
e. shall come upon them, saith *Jer 2:3*
the Lord
fire, because of *e.* of your   *Jer 4:4;*
doings   *23:2; 26:3; 44:22*
it is not he, neither shall *e.*   *Jer 5:12*
come upon us
children of Judah have done *e.* *Jer 7:30*
in my sight
by them that remain of this *e.* *Jer 8:3*
family
when thou doest *e.* then thou *Jer 11:15*
rejoicest
pronounced *e.* against thee   *Jer 11:17*
for *e.* of Israel
thus saith against all mine *e.* *Jer 12:14*
neighbours
this *e.* people refuse to hear   *Jer 13:10*
my words
ye shall be comforted   *Jer 14:22*
concerning the *e.*
will cause to entreat thee well *Jer 15:11*
in time of *e.*
thou art my hope in the day of *Jer 17:17*
e.
bring on them day of *e.* and   *Jer 17:18*
destroy them
if nation turn from their *e.* I   *Jer 18:8;*
will repent of *e.*   *26:3, 13, 19; 42:10*
behold, I frame *e.* against you *Jer 18:11*
and devise
I will bring all *e.* that I have   *Jer 19:15*
pronounced
I set my face against this city *Jer 21:10*
for *e.*

their course is *e.* their force   *Jer 23:10*
not right
e. figs, very *e.* they are so *e.*   *Jer 24:3;*
24:8; 29:17
e. shall go forth from nation   *Jer 25:32*
to nation
the prophets prophesied of war   *Jer 28:8*
and of *e.*
I think thoughts of peace,   *Jer 29:11*
and not of *e.*
the children of Judah have   *Jer 32:30*
only done *e.*
because of all the *e.* of   *Jer 32:32*
children of Israel
I will bring on Judah all *e.* I   *Jer 35:17;*
have pronounced against them   *36:31*
men have done *e.* in all they   *Jer 38:9*
have done
I will set my face against you   *Jer 44:11*
for *e.*
had plenty, were well, and saw   *Jer 44:17*
no *e.*
watch over them for *e.* and   *Jer 44:27*
not for good
my words shall stand against   *Jer 44:29*
you for *e.*
in Heshbon they have devised   *Jer 48:2*
e. against it
they have heard *e.* tidings,   *Jer 49:23*
fainthearted
render to Babylon all *e.* done   *Jer 51:24*
in Zion
wrote all *e.* that should come   *Jer 51:60*
on Babylon
I will send on them *e.* arrows   *Eze 5:16*
of famine
so will I send on you famine   *Eze 5:17*
and *e.* beasts
alas, for all the *e.*   *Eze 6:11*
abominations of Israel
an *e.* an only *e.* behold it is   *Eze 7:5*
come
e. beasts (S)   *Eze 14:15; 14:21*
the hand of *e.* men (A)(E)   *Eze 30:12*
I will cause the *e.* beasts to   *Eze 34:25*
cease from land
the *e.* report of (E)   *Eze 36:3*
and thou shalt think an *e.*   *Eze 38:10*
thought
taught *e.* women (B)   *Jer 2:33*
e. thoughts (R)   *Jer 4:14*
the Lord hath watched upon   *Da 9:14*
the *e.*
remember their *e.* works (R)   *Ho 7:2*
devise *e.* against me (A)(R)   *Ho 7:15*
Lord your God repenteth him   *Joe 2:13*
of the *e.*
shall there be *e.* in a city, Lord   *Am 3:6*
who say, *e.* shall not overtake   *Am 9:10*
nor prevent us
God repented of *e.* he said   *Jon 3:10;*
4:2
e. came down from Lord to   *Mic 1:12*
Jerusalem
woe to them that work *e.* upon   *Mic 2:1*
their beds
against this family do I devise   *Mic 2:3*
an *e.*
made deeds *e.* (A)(B)(E)(R)   *Mic 3:4*
is not Lord among us no *e.*   *Mic 3:11*
can come
that imagineth *e.* against the   *Na 1:11*
Lord
thou art of purer eyes than to   *Hab 1:13*
behold *e.*
he may be delivered from the   *Hab 2:9*
power of *e.*
thou shalt not see *e.* any more   *Zep 3:15*
let none of you imagine *e.*   *Zec 7:10;*
8:17
ye offer the lame and sick, is it   *Mal 1:8*
not *e.*
when ye say, Every one that   *Mal 2:17*
doeth *e.* is good
say all manner of *e.* against   *M't 5:11*
you
whatsoever is more than these,   *M't 5:37*
cometh of *e.*
but I say unto you, that ye   *M't 5:39*
resist not *e.*
he maketh his sun to rise on *e.*   *M't 5:45*
and good
sufficient unto the day is the *e.*   *M't 6:34*
thereof
if ye then being *e.*   *M't 7:11; Lu 11:13*
a good tree cannot bring forth   *M't 7:18*
e. fruit
wherefore think ye *e.* in your   *M't 9:4*
hearts

how can ye being *e.* speak   *M't 12:34*
good things
an *e.* generation seeketh a   *M't 12:39;*
sign   *Lu 11:29*
an *e.* generation (P)(R)   *M't 12:45;*
13:49
out of heart proceed *e.*   *M't 15:19;*
thoughts, murders, adulteries,   *M'k 7:21*
if that *e.* servant shall say in   *M't 24:48*
his heart
Pilate said to them, Why,   *M't 27:23;*
what *e.* hath he done?   *M'k 15:14;*
Lu 23:22
spoke sharply to *e.* spirit (P)   *M'k 9:25*
that can lightly speak *e.* of me   *M'k 9:30*
and shall cast out your name   *Lu 6:22*
as *e.*
he is kind to the unthankful   *Lu 6:35*
and to the *e.*
an evil man bringeth forth   *Lu 6:45*
what is *e.*
e. them in my presence   *Lu 19:27*
(B)(P)
loved darkness, for their deeds   *Joh 3:19*
were *e.*
every one that doeth *e.* hateth   *Joh 3:20*
the light
they that have done *e.* to the   *Joh 5:29*
resurrection of
if I have spoken *e.* bear   *Joh 18:23*
witness
they should entreat them *e.* 400   *Ac 7:6*
years
the same *e.* entreated our   *Ac 7:19*
fathers
how much *e.* he hath done to   *Ac 9:13*
thy saints
their minds *e.* affected against   *Ac 14:2*
the brethren
but spake *e.* of that way before   *Ac 19:9*
the multitude
shall not speak *e.* of the ruler   *Ac 23:5*
of thy people
a great cry, saying, We find no   *Ac 23:9*
e. in this man
if they have found any *e.*   *Ac 24:20*
doing in me
anguish on every soul of man   *Ro 2:9*
that doeth *e.*
but the *e.* which I would not,   *Ro 7:19*
that I do
abhor that which is *e.* cleave to   *Ro 12:9*
what is good
recompense to no man *e.* for   *Ro 12:17*
e. provide things
be not overcome of *e.*   *Ro 12:21*
overcome *e.* with good
a revenger to execute wrath on   *Ro 13:4*
him doeth *e.*
let not your good be *e.* spoken   *Ro 14:16*
of
it is *e.* for that man who   *Ro 14:20*
eateth with offence
I would have you simple   *Ro 16:19*
concerning *e.*
why am I *e.* spoken of   *1Co 10:30*
charity not provoked,   *1Co 13:5*
thinketh no *e.*
e. communications corrupt   *1Co 15:33*
good manners
e. companionships corrupt   *1Co 15:33*
(A)(E)
that he might deliver us from   *Ga 1:4*
this *e.* world
no *e.* talk (R)   *Eph 4:29*
let *e.* speaking be put away   *Eph 4:31*
from you
darts of the *e.* one   *Eph 6:16*
(B)(E)(N)(R)
beware of dogs, beware of *e.*   *Ph'p 3:2*
workers
mortify therefore *e.*   *Col 3:5*
concupiscence
see that none render *e.* for *e.*   *1Th 5:15*
to any
abstain from all appearance   *1Th 5:22*
of *e.*
whereof cometh *e.* surmisings   *1Ti 6:4*
the love of money is the root   *1Ti 6:10*
of all *e.*
the Cretians are *e.* beasts, slow   *Tit 1:12*
bellies
put them in mind to speak *e.* of   *Tit 3:2*
no man
your hearts sprinkled from   *Heb 10:22*
e. conscience
and are become judges of *e.*   *Jas 2:4*
thoughts

the tongue is an unruly *e.* full of   *Jas 3:8*
poison
speak not *e.* one of another,   *Jas 4:11*
he that speaks, *e.* of brother,
speaks *e.* of law
ye rejoice in boastings, all   *Jas 4:16*
such rejoicing is *e.*
laying aside all malice and *e.*   *1Pe 2:1*
speakings
not rendering *e.* for *e.* or   *1Pe 3:9*
railing, but blessing
that whereas they speak *e.* of   *1Pe 3:16*
you
better ye suffer for well-doing   *1Pe 3:17*
than for *e.* doing
they think it strange, speaking   *1Pe 4:4*
e. of you
their part he is *e.* spoken of,   *1Pe 4:14*
but on your part
the way of truth shall be *e.*   *2Pe 2:2*
spoken of
are not afraid to speak *e.* of   *2Pe 2:10;*
dignities   *Jude 8*
speak *e.* of things that they   *2Pe 2:12;*
understand not   *Jude 10*
he that doeth *e.* hath not seen   *2Jo 11*
God
how thou canst not bear them   *Re 2:2*
who are *e.*

EVIL *DAY, DAYS*

few and *e.* have *days* of life   *Ge 47:9*
been
all the *days* of the afflicted are   *Pr 15:15*
e.
in youth, while the *e.* *days*   *Ec 12:1*
come not
ye that put far away the *e.* *day*   *Am 6:3*
redeeming time, because *days*   *Eph 5:16*
are *e.*
ye may be able to withstand   *Eph 6:13*
in *e.* *day*

EVIL with *GOOD*

tree of knowledge of *good* and   *Ge 2:9;*
e.   *2:17*
be as gods knowing *good* and *e.*   *Ge 3:5;*
3:22
wherefore have ye rewarded *e.*   *Ge 44:4*
for *good*
no knowledge between *good*   *De 1:39*
and *e.*
he hath requited me for *e.*   *1Sa 25:21*
good
can I discern between *good*   *2Sa 19:35*
and *e.*
not prophesy *good* concerning   *1Ki 22:8;*
me, but *e.*   *22:18*
never prophesieth *good* to me,   *2Ch 18:7*
but *e.*
he would not prophesy *good*   *2Ch 18:17*
to me, but *e.*
shall we receive *good*, and not   *Job 2:10*
receive *e.*
I looked for *good*, then *e.*   *Job 30:26*
came unto me
they rewarded me *e.* for *good*   *Ps 35:12;*
109:5
that render *e.* for *good* are my   *Ps 38:20*
adversaries
thou lovest *e.* more than *good*,   *Ps 52:3*
and lying
eyes of Lord beholding *e.* and   *Pr 15:3*
good
whoso rewardeth *e.* for *good*   *Pr 17:13*
will do him *good* and not *e.* all   *Pr 31:12*
her days
woe to them that call *e.* *good*,   *Isa 5:20*
and *good* *e.*
may know to refuse *e.* and   *Isa 7:15;*
choose *good*   *7:16*
shall *e.* be recompensed for   *Jer 18:20*
good
whether it be *good* or *e.* we   *Jer 42:6*
will obey
of most High proceedeth not *e.*   *La 3:38*
and *good*
seek *good* and not *e.* that ye   *Am 5:14*
may live
set mine eyes on them for *e.*   *Am 9:4*
not for *good*
who hate the *good* and love the   *Mic 3:2*
e.
when I would do *good*,   *Ro 7:21*
present
not born, neither having done   *Ro 9:11*
good or *e.*

senses exercised to discern   Heb 5:14
good and e.
follow not what is e. but what   3Jo 11
is good

EVIL *HEART*

imagination of man's *heart* e.   Ge 8:21
from youth
nor walk after imagination of   Jer 3:17
e. hearts
walked in the imagination of   Jer 7:24
their e. heart
every one in imagination of   Jer 11:8
their e. heart
every one after imagination of   Jer 16:12
their e. heart
every one do the imagination   Jer 18:12
of his e. heart
lest there be in any an e.   Heb 3:12
heart of unbelief

EVIL *IN THE SIGHT*
OF THE LORD

done e. *in the sight* of Lord   Nu 32:13;
                        J'g 3:12
Israel did e. *in sight* of Lord   J'g 2:11;
3:7, 12; 4:1; 6:1; 10:6; 13:1; 1Ki 11:6;
14:22; 15:26, 34; 16:7, 30; 22:52;
2Ki 8:18, 27; 13:2, 11; 14:24; 15:9, 18,
24, 28; 17:2; 21:2, 20; 2Ch 22:4; 33:2,
                          22; 36:5, 9, 12
thou didst e. *in sight* of Lord   1Sa 15:19
in doing e. *in sight* of   1Ki 16:19
Lord
sold to work e. *in sight* of   1Ki 21:20
Lord
he wrought e. *in sight* of Lord   2Ki 3:2
sold themselves to do e. in   2Ki 17:17
sight of Lord
to sin, in doing that which   2Ki 21:16;
was e. *in sight* of Lord   23:32, 37; 24:9
Er was e. *in sight* of Lord   1Ch 2:3
he wrought much e. *in sight*   2Ch 33:6
of Lord

EVIL *MAN, MEN*

none answer because of pride   Job 35:12
of e. men
break thou the arm of the e.   Ps 10:15
man
deliver me, O Lord, from the   Ps 140:1
e. man
to deliver thee from way of the   Pr 2:12
e. man
and go not in the way of e. men   Pr 4:14
the wicked desireth the net of   Pr 12:12
e. men
an e. *man* seeketh only   Pr 17:11
rebellion
be not thou envious against   Pr 24:1
e. men
fret not thyself because of e.   Pr 24:19
men
for there shall be no reward to   Pr 24:20
the e. man
e. men understand not judgment   Pr 28:5
in transgression of an e. man   Pr 29:6
there is a snare
an e. *man* out of evil treasure   M't 12:35;
bringeth forth evil things   Lu 6:45
but e. men shall wax worse   2Ti 3:13
and worse

EVIL *SPIRIT, SPIRITS*

sent e. *spirit* between   J'g 9:23
Abimelech and men
an e. *spirit* from the Lord   1Sa 16:14
troubled him
when the e. *spirit* from God is   1Sa 16:16
upon thee
and the e. *spirit* departed from   1Sa 16:23
him
e. *spirit* from God came on   1Sa 18:10;
Saul   19:9
that hour he cured many of e.   Lu 7:21
spirits
woman which had been healed   Lu 8:2
of e. spirits
and the e. spirits went out of   Ac 19:12
them
to call over them which had e.   Ac 19:13
spirits
e. spirit said, Jesus I know,   Ac 19:15
Paul I know
man in whom the e. spirit   Ac 19:16
was, leaped

EVIL *THING*

what e. *thing* is this that ye do   Ne 13:17
incline not my heart to any e.   Ps 141:4
thing
stand not in an e. thing, doth   Ec 8:3
what pleases
keepeth commandment, shall   Ec 8:5
feel no e. thing
every secret *thing*, whether it   Ec 12:14
be good or e.
know that it is an e. *thing* and   Jer 2:19
bitter
having no e. *thing* to say of you   Tit 2:8

EVIL *THINGS*

the Lord shall bring on you all   Jos 23:15
e. things
mouth of wicked poureth out   Pr 15:28
e. things
thou hast done e. things as thou   Jer 3:5
couldest
an evil man bringeth forth e.   M't 12:35
things
all these e. things come from   M'k 7:23
within
and likewise Lazarus e. things   Lu 16:25
proud, boasters, inventors of e.   Ro 1:30
things
we should not lust after e.   1Co 10:6
things

EVIL *TIMES*

not be ashamed in the e. time   Ps 37:19
so sons of men are snared in e.   Ec 9:12
time
prudent keep silence, for it is   Am 5:13
an e. time
nor go haughtily, for this time   Mic 2:3
is e.

EVIL *WAY*

Jeroboam returned not from   1Ki 13:33
e. way
I refrained my feet from   Ps 119:101
every e. way
fear of the Lord is to hate the   Pr 8:13
e. way
who causeth righteous to go   Pr 28:10
astray in e. way
return ye now every one   Jer 18:11;
from his e.   25:5; 26:3; 35:15; 36:3, 7
way
should have turned them   Jer 23:22
from their e. way
let them turn every one from e.   Jon 3:8
way
saw that they turned from   Jon 3:10
their e. way

EVIL *WAYS*

turn from your e. ways   2Ki 17:13;
                          Eze 33:11
then shall ye remember your   Eze 36:31
own e. ways
turn from your e. ways and   Zec 1:4
doings

EVIL *WORK, WORKS*

who hath not seen e. *work* that   Ec 4:3
is done
because sentence against an e.   Ec 8:11
work is not
I testify that the *works* thereof   Joh 7:7
are e.
are not a terror to good *works*   Ro 13:3
but e.
Lord shall deliver me from   2Ti 4:18
every e. work
there is confusion, and every   Jas 3:16
e. work
because his own *works* were e.   1Jo 3:12

BRING, BROUGHT EVIL

the Lord shall *bring* on you   Jos 23:15
all e. things
lest he overtake and bring e.   2Sa 15:14
on us
that the Lord might *bring* e.   2Sa 17:14
upon Absalom
I will *bring* e. on the house   1Ki 14:10
of Jeroboam
he said, Hast thou also   1Ki 17:20
brought e. on widow

behold, I will *bring* e. upon   1Ki 21:21
thee
not *bring* e. in his days, but   1Ki 21:29
in son's days
thus saith the Lord, Behold,   2Ki 22:16;
I will *bring* e. upon this place   2Ch 34:24
nor eyes see all the e. I will   2Ch 34:28
bring
bring e. and not call back his   Isa 31:2
word
for I will *bring* e. from the   Jer 4:6
north
behold, I will *bring* e. upon   Jer 6:19
this people
behold, I will *bring* e. upon   Jer 11:11
them
I will *bring* e. upon the men   Jer 11:23
of Anathoth
behold, I will *bring* e. on this   Jer 19:3;
place   19:15
I will *bring* e. even year of   Jer 23:12
their visitation
for lo, I begin to *bring* e. on   Jer 25:29
the city
I will *bring* on Judah e.   Jer 35:17;
pronounced   36:31
I will *bring* my words on this   Jer 39:16
city for e.
I will *bring* e. upon all flesh   Jer 45:5

FROM EVIL

Angel who redeemed me *from*   Ge 48:16
all e.
and hath kept his servant   1Sa 25:39
from e.
that thou wouldest keep me   1Ch 4:10
from e.
to depart *from* e. is   Job 28:28
understanding
keep tongue *from* e. lips from   Ps 34:13
guile
depart *from* e. do good   Ps 34:14
                     37:27; Pr 3:7
Lord shall preserve thee *from*   Ps 121:7
all e.
turn not, remove thy foot *from*   Pr 4:27
e.
it is abomination to fools to   Pr 13:19
depart *from* e.
wise man feareth, and   Pr 14:16
departeth *from* e.
by fear of Lord men depart   Pr 16:6
from e.
highway of upright is to   Pr 16:17
depart *from* e.
that departeth *from* e. makes   Isa 59:15
himself a prey
they proceed *from* e. to evil, and   Jer 9:3
know
should have turned *from* their   Jer 23:22
e. ways, and *from* e. of their
doings
Babylon not rise *from* e. I   Jer 51:64
will bring
but deliver us *from* e.   M't 6:13;
                          Lu 11:4
but that thou shouldest keep   Joh 17:15
them *from* e.
stablish you, and keep you   2Th 3:3
from e.
let him refrain his tongue   1Pe 3:10
from e.

PUT *AWAY* EVIL

put e. *away* from midst of thee   De 13:5
so thou shalt *put* e. *away* from   De 17:7;
among you   19:19; 21:21; 22:21, 24; 24:7
put e. *away* from Israel   De 17:12
                 21:22; J'g 20:13
and *put away* e. from thy   Ec 11:10
flesh
wash ye, *put away* e. of your   Isa 1:16
doings

THIS EVIL

repent of *this* e. against   Ex 32:12
people
then he hath done us *this* great   1Sa 6:9
e.
we have added *this* e. to ask a   1Sa 12:19
king
this e. sending me away is   2Sa 13:16
greater
Lord brought on them all *this*   1Ki 9:9
e.
he said, Behold, *this* e. is of   2Ki 6:33
Lord

therefore he brought *this e.*   2Ch 7:22
on them
did not our God bring *this*   Ne 13:18
e. on us
we hearken to you to do all   Ne 13:27
this e.
when Job's three friends heard   Job 2:11
of *this e.*
I have done *this e.* in thy sight   Ps 51:4
Lord pronounced all *this e.*   Jer 16:10
against us
therefore thou hast caused all   Jer 32:23
this e.
like as I have brought all *this*   Jer 32:42
e.
God pronounced *this e.* on this   Jer 40:2
place
why commit ye *this* great. *e.*   Jer 44:7
against souls
therefore *this e.* is happened   Jer 44:23
unto you
all *this e.* is come upon us   Da 9:13
for whose cause *this e.* is on us   Jon 1:7;
   1:8

EVILDOER

every one is a hypocrite and an   Isa 9:17
e.
put away that *e.* (N)   1Co 5:13
or as an *e.* or as a busybody   1Pe 4:15
the *e.* (N)   Re 22:11

EVILDOERS

when *e.* came (E)(R)   Ps 27:2; Pr 17:4
assembly of *e.* (E)(R)   Ps 27:2;
   64:2; 92:11
Fret not thyself because of *e.*   Ps 37:1
e. shall be cut off: but those   Ps 37:9
that
e. shall be no more (B)   Ps 37:10;
   37:14, 16, 35, 40; 39:1; Ec 8:13
seed of *e.* (B)   Ps 37:28; 37:38
desire of *e.* (A)   Ps 92:11
will rise up for me against the   Ps 94:16
e.
Depart from me, ye *e.*: for I   Ps 119:115
will
a seed of *e.* children that are   Isa 1:4
seed of *e.* shall never be   Isa 14:20
renowned
arise against the house of the *e.*   Isa 31:2
soul of the poor from the   Jer 20:13
hand of *e.*
strengthen also the hands of   Jer 23:14
e.
they speak against you as *e.*   1Pe 2:12
by him for the punishment of   1Pe 2:14
e.
speak evil of you, as of *e.*   1Pe 3:16

EVIL-DOING

e. of Nabal (E)(R)   1Sa 25:39;
   Pr 14:32; Ec 7:15
his life in *e.* (A)   Ec 7:15

EVIL-DOINGS

avenging *e.* (A)   Ps 99:8
the *e.* of Samaria (B)   Ho 7:1
remember their *e.* (B)   Ho 7:2; 7:3

EVILFAVOUREDNESS

wherein is blemish, or any *e.*   De 17:1

EVIL-MERODACH

that *E.* king of Babylon in   2Ki 25:27
the year
E. king of Babylon in the first   Jer 52:31
year

EVILNESS

presumption and *e.* (B)   1Sa 17:28

EVILS

e. and troubles shall befall   De 31:17
them
Are not these *e.* come upon us   De 31:17
e. which they shall have   De 31:18
wrought
e. and troubles are befallen   De 31:21
them
I will heap *e.* upon   De 32:23
(A)(E)(R)

innumerable *e.* have   Ps 40:12
compassed me
my people have committed two   Jer 2:13
e.
the *e.* which they have   Eze 6:9
committed
all these *e.* (B)   Eze 18:13
all your *e.* that ye have   Eze 20:43
committed
all the *e.* which Herod had   Lu 3:19
done

EWE

Abraham set seven *e.* lambs   Ge 21:28
of
What mean these seven *e.*   Ge 21:29
lambs
seven *e.* lambs shalt thou take   Ge 21:30
and one *e.* lamb of the first   Le 14:10
year
cow or *e.* ye shall not kill it   Le 22:28
and
and one *e.* lamb of the first   Nu 6:14
year
one little *e.* lamb, which he   2Sa 12:3
had

EWES

thy *e.* and thy she goats have   Ge 31:38
not
two hundred *e.* and twenty   Ge 32:14
rams
following the *e.* great with   Ps 78:71
young

EXACT

shall not *e.* it of his neighbour   De 15:2
make no demand for   De 15:2
repayment (B)
foreigner thou mayest *e.* it   De 15:3
again
foreigner you may press for   De 15:3
payment (B)
Ye *e.* usury, every one of his   Ne 5:7
and my brethren, might *e.*   Ne 5:10
the corn, that ye *e.* of them   Ne 5:11
The enemy shall not *e.* upon   Ps 89:22
him
pleasure, and *e.* all your   Isa 58:3
labours
you extort from hired servants   Isa 58:3
(A)
oppress all your employees   Isa 58:3
(B)(R)
E. no more than that which is   Lu 3:13
collect no more than appointed   Lu 3:13
rate (B)(R)
Extort no more than appointed   Lu 3:13
(E)
not demand more than entitled   Lu 3:13
(P)

EXACTED

Menahem *e.* the money of   2Ki 15:20
Israel
he *e.* the silver and the gold   2Ki 23:35
of

EXACTETH

God *e.* of thee less than thine   Job 11:6
he that *e.* gifts overthroweth it   Pr 29:4
(S)

EXACTING

cease this *e.* of interest (S)   Ne 5:10

EXACTION

year, and the *e.* of every debt   Ne 10:31

EXACTIONS

take away your *e.* from my   Eze 45:9
people

EXACTLY

examine more *e.* (A)(E)   Ac 23:20

EXACTORS

peace, and thine *e.*   Isa 60:17
righteousness

righteousness your   Isa 60:17
taskmasters (A)(R)
justice your ruler (B)   Isa 60:17

EXALT

my father's God, and I will *e.*   Ex 15:2
him
began to *e.* you (B)   Jos 3:7
and *e.* the horn of his   1Sa 2:10
anointed
therefore shalt thou not *e.*   Job 17:4
them
and let us *e.* his name together   Ps 34:3
shall *e.* thee to inherit the land   Ps 37:34
let not the rebellious *e.*   Ps 66:7
themselves
But my horn shalt thou *e.* like   Ps 92:10
E. ye the Lord our God, and   Ps 99:5
E. the Lord our God, and   Ps 99:9
worship
e. him also in the   Ps 107:32
congregation
thou art my God, I will *e.*   Ps 118:28
thee
device; lest they *e.* themselves   Ps 140:8
E. her, and she shall promote   Pr 4:8
thee
e. the voice unto them, shake   Isa 13:2
I will *e.* my throne above the   Isa 14:13
stars
thou art my God; I will *e.* thee   Isa 25:1
e. him that is low, and abase   Eze 21:26
him
neither shall it *e.* itself any   Eze 29:15
more
e. themselves for their height   Eze 31:14
the robbers of thy people   Da 11:14
shall *e.*
shall *e.* himself and magnify   Da 11:36
he shall *e.* himself above all   Da 11:37
(B)
most High, none at all would   Ho 11:7
e. him
Though thou *e.* thyself as the   Ob 4
And whosoever shall *e.*   M't 23:12
himself
a man *e.* himself, if a man   2Co 11:20
smite
that he may *e.* you in due time   1Pe 5:6

EXALTED

and his kingdom shall be *e.*   Nu 24:7
mine horn is *e.* in the Lord   1Sa 2:1
had *e.* his kingdom for his   2Sa 5:12
people
and *e.* be the God, of the   2Sa 22:47
rock of
the son of Haggith *e.* himself   1Ki 1:5
I *e.* thee from among the   1Ki 14:7
people
Forasmuch as I *e.* thee out of   1Ki 16:2
against whom hast thou *e.*   2Ki 19:22
thy
thou art *e.* as head above all   1Ch 29:11
e. in the eyes of many   2Ch 32:23
nations (B)
name, which is *e.* above all   Ne 9:5
which mourn may be *e.* to   Job 5:11
safety
They are *e.* for a little while   Job 24:24
them forever, and they are *e.*   Job 36:7
when the vilest men are *e.*   Ps 12:8
how long shall mine enemy be   Ps 13:2
e.
let the God of my salvation be   Ps 18:46
e.
Be thou *e.* Lord, in thine own   Ps 21:13
I will be *e.* among the heathen   Ps 46:10
I will be *e.* in the earth   Ps 46:10
belong unto God; he is greatly   Ps 47:9
e.
thou *e.* O God, above the   Ps 57:5
heavens
thou *e.* O God, above the   Ps 57:11
heavens
horns of the righteous shall be   Ps 75:10
e.
thy righteousness shall they be   Ps 89:16
e.
in thy favour our horn shall be   Ps 89:17
e.
e. one chosen out of the   Ps 89:19
people
in my name shall his horn be   Ps 89:24
e.
thou art *e.* far above all gods   Ps 97:9
thou *e.* O God, above the   Ps 108:5
heavens

EXALTED   407   EXCEEDING

his horn shall be *e.* with honour *Ps 112:9*
The right hand of the Lord is *e.* *Ps 118:16*
of the upright the city is *e.* *Pr 11:11*
and shall be *e.* above the hills *Isa 2:2*
raised above the hills (B)(R) *Isa 2:2*
Lord alone shall be *e.* in that *Isa 2:11; 2:17*
But the Lord of hosts shall be *e.* *Isa 5:16*
make mention that his name is *e.* *Isa 12:4*
and therefore he will be *e.* *Isa 30:18*
The Lord is *e.* for he dwelleth on *Isa 33:5*
now will I be *e.;* now will I lift up *Isa 33:10*
against whom hast thou *e.* thy voice *Isa 37:23*
Every valley shall be *e.* and *Isa 40:4*
and my highways shall be *e.* *Isa 49:11*
he shall be *e.* and extolled, and be *Isa 52:13*
have *e.* the low tree, have dried *Eze 17:24*
was *e.* among the thick branches *Eze 19:11*
Therefore his height was *e.* above *Eze 31:5*
Ephraim *e.* himself in Israel *Ho 13:1*
filled, and their heart was *e.* *Ho 13:6*
and it shall be *e.* above the hills *Mic 4:1*
e. themselves against (B) *Zep 2:8*
be not *e.* over Judah (B) *Zec 12:7*
a mountain high and *e.* (A) *Zec 17:22*
which art *e.* unto heaven, shalt be *M't 11:23*
shall humble himself, shalt be *M't 23:12 e.*
shall be raised to honor (A) *M't 23:12*
shall be elevated (B) *M't 23:12*
will find promotion (P) *M't 23:12*
seats, and *e.* them of low degree *Lu 1:52*
lifted up the lowly (B) *Lu 1:52*
humble have been lifted high (N) *Lu 1:52*
lifted up the humble (P) *Lu 1:52*
which art *e.* to heaven, shalt be *Lu 10:15*
that humbleth himself shall be *Lu 14:11 e.*
e. among men (A)(E)(R) *Lu 16:15*
that humbleth himself shall be *Lu 18:14 e.*
being by the right hand of God *Ac 2:33 e.*
lifted high by the right hand (A)(B) *Ac 2:33*
being raised to the right hand (P) *Ac 2:33*
Him hath God *e.* with his right *Ac 5:31*
e. the people when they dwelt *Ac 13:17*
abasing myself that ye might *2Co 11:7* be *e.*
lest I should be *e.* above measure *2Co 12:7*
puffed up and too much elated (A) *2Co 12:7*
might not swell with pride (B) *2Co 12:7*
being unduly elated (N) *2Co 12:7*
prevent my being absurdly conceited (P) *2Co 12:7*
lest I should be *e.* above measure *2Co 12:7*
God also hath highly *e.* him *Ph'p 2:9*
low degree rejoice in that he is *Jas 1:9 e.*

EXALTEST
e. thou thyself against my people *Ex 9:17*

EXALTETH
Behold, God *e.* by his power *Job 36:22*
also *e.* the horn of his people *Ps 148:14*
he that is hasty of spirit *e.* folly *Pr 14:29*
Righteousness *e.* a nation: but sin *Pr 14:34*
e. his gate seeketh destruction *Pr 17:19*
e. himself shall be abased *Lu 14:11*
one that *e.* himself shall be abased *Lu 18:14*

every high thing that *e.* itself *2Co 10:5*
Who opposeth and *e.* himself *2Th 2:4*

EXALTING
e. one teacher above another *1Co 4:6* (P)

EXAMINATION
that, after *e.* had, I might have *Ac 25:26*

EXAMINE
the tenth month to *e.* the matter *Ezr 10:16*
E. me, O Lord, and prove me *Ps 26:2*
let a man *e.* himself, and so let *Ps 11:28*
more exactly (A)(E) *Ac 23:20*
to them that do *e.* me in this *1Co 9:3*
E. yourselves, whether ye be *2Co 13:5*

EXAMINED
I, having *e.* him before you *Lu 23:14*
If we this day be *e.* of the good *Ac 4:9* deed
found him not, he *e.* the keepers *Ac 12:19*
he should be *e.* by scourging *Ac 22:24*
him, which should have *e.* *Ac 22:29* him
Who, when they had *e.* me *Ac 28:18*
if we *e.* ourselves *1Co 11:31* (A)(N)(P)

EXAMINING
e. of whom thyself mayest take *Ac 24:8*

EXAMPLE
make her a public *e.* was minded *M't 1:19*
expose, disgrace her publicly *M't 1:19* (A)(B)
wanting to save her from exposure *M't 1:19*
not see her disgraced (P) *M't 1:19*
to put her to shame (R) *M't 1:19*
For I have given you an *e.* that *Joh 13:15*
follow the *e.* of faith (R) *Ro 4:12*
example (S) *1Co 10:11; Ph'p 3:17; 1Th 1:7; 2Th 3:9; 1Pe 5:3; 2Pe 2:6*
be thou an *e.* of the believers *1Ti 4:12*
after the same *e.* of unbelief *Heb 4:11*
by the same kind of unbelief *Heb 4:11* (A)(P)
disobedience as they exemplified (B) *Heb 4:11*
same sort of disobedience (R) *Heb 4:11*
serve unto the *e.* and shadow *Heb 8:5*
pattern, foreshadowing of heavenly (A) *Heb 8:5*
copy and shadow of heavenly *Heb 8:5* (B)(E)(N)(R)
pattern or reproduction of things (P) *Heb 8:5*
follow *e.* of their faith (N) *Heb 13:7*
for an *e.* of suffering affliction *Jas 5:10*
leaving us an *e.* that ye should *1Pe 2:21*
for an *e.* suffering the vengeance *Jude 7*
as an exhibit of perpetual punishment (A) *Jude 7*
as a warning by suffering punishment of (B) *Jude 7*
as a permanent warning of fire of *Jude 7* judgment (P)

EXAMPLES
Now these things were our *e.* *1Co 10:6*

EXASPERATE
do not *e.* your children (N) *Col 3:21*

EXASPERATED
e. at teaching (N) *Ac 4:2*

EXCEED
he may give him, and not *e.* *De 25:3*
lest, if he should *e.* and beat *De 25:3* him
your righteousness shall *e.* the *M't 5:20*
of righteousness *e.* in glory *2Co 3:9*

EXCEEDED
one with another, until David *e.* *1Sa 20:41*
So king Solomon *e.* all the kings *1Ki 10:23*
transgressions that they have *e.* *Job 36:9*
mostly *e.* by grace (N) *Ro 5:15*

EXCEEDEST
thou *e.* the fame that I heard *2Ch 9:6*

EXCEEDETH
thy wisdom and prosperity *e.* the *1Ki 10:7*

EXCEEDING
shield, and thy *e.* great reward *Ge 15:1*
And I will make thee *e.* fruitful *Ge 17:6*
with a great and *e.* bitter cry *Ge 27:34*
Multiplied, and waxed *e.* mighty *Ex 1:7*
the voice of the trumpet *e.* loud *Ex 19:16*
to search it, is an *e.* good land *Nu 14:7*
it is *e.* bitter (A)(R) *Ru 1:13*
Talk no more so *e.* proudly *1Sa 2:3*
king David took *e.* much brass *2Sa 8:8*
The rich man had *e.* many flocks *2Sa 12:2*
wisdom and understanding *e.* *1Ki 4:29* much
because they were *e.* many *1Ki 7:47*
also *e.* much spoil out of the *1Ch 20:2* city
the Lord must be *e.* magnifical *1Ch 22:5*
and made them *e.* strong *2Ch 11:12*
for there was *e.* much spoil *2Ch 14:14*
until his disease was *e.* great *2Ch 16:12*
Hezekiah had *e.* much riches *2Ch 32:27*
him *e.* glad with thy countenance *Ps 21:6*
altar of God, unto God my *e.* joy *Ps 43:4*
thy commandment is *e.* broad *Ps 119:96*
the earth, but they are *e.* wise *Pr 30:24*
That which is far off, and *e.* deep *Ec 7:24*
e. angry (S) *Isa 64:9*
pride of Moab, (he is *e.* proud) *Jer 48:29*
Israel and Judah is *e.* great *Eze 9:9*
and thou wast *e.* beautiful *Eze 16:13*
e. in dyed attire upon their heads *Eze 23:15*
upon their feet, and *e.* great army *Eze 37:10*
fish of the great sea, *e.* many *Eze 47:10*
and the furnace *e.* hot, the flame *Da 3:22*
was the king *e.* glad for him *Da 6:23*
e. dreadful, whose teeth were of *Da 7:19*
waxed *e.* great, toward the south *Da 8:9*
Nineveh was an *e.* great city *Jon 3:3*
Jonah was *e.* glad of the gourd *Jon 4:6*
they rejoiced with *e.* great joy *M't 2:10*
of the wise men, was *e.* wroth *M't 2:16*
him up into an *e.* high mountain *M't 4:8*
Rejoice, and be *e.* glad: for great *M't 5:12*
coming out of the tombs, *e.* fierce *M't 8:28*
And they were *e.* sorry *M't 17:23*
And they were *e.* sorrowful *M't 26:22*
soul is *e.* sorrowful, even unto *M't 26:38*
And the king was *e.* sorry; yet for *M'k 6:26*
became shining, *e.* white as snow *M'k 9:3*
soul is *e.* sorrowful unto death *M'k 14:34*
Herod saw Jesus he was *e.* glad *Lu 23:8*
and was *e.* fair, and nourished *Ac 7:20*
sin, might become *e.* sinful *Ro 7:13*
e. greatness of power (A)(E) *2Co 4:7*
a far more *e.* and eternal *2Co 4:17*
am *e.* joyful in all our tribulation *2Co 7:4*
for the *e.* grace of God in you *2Co 9:14*
And what is the *e.* greatness of *Eph 1:19*
shew the *e.* riches of his grace *Eph 2:7*

EXCEEDING

e. abundantly above all that we | Eph 3:20
Lord was e. abundant with faith | 1Ti 1:14
ye may be glad also with e. joy | 1Pe 4:13
us e. great and precious promises | 2Pe 1:4
the presence of his glory with e. joy | Jude 24
the plague thereof was e. great | Re 16:21

EXCEEDINGLY

prevailed e. upon the earth | Ge 7:19
and sinners before the Lord e. | Ge 13:13
I will multiply thy seed e. | Ge 16:10; 17:2
multiply him e.; twelve princes | Ge 17:20
And Isaac trembled very e. | Ge 27:33
And the man increased e. and | Ge 30:43
and grew, and multiplied e. | Ge 47:27
the fool, and have erred e. | 1Sa 26:21
Then Amnon hated her e. | 2Sa 13:15
But they were e. afraid, and said | 2Ki 10:4
the Lord magnified Solomon e. | 1Ch 29:25
was with him, and magnified him e. | 2Ch 1:1
great e.; and he built in Judah | 2Ch 17:12
for he strengthened himself e. | 2Ch 26:8
it grieved them e. that there was | Ne 2:10
distressed them e. (A) | Ne 2:10
Then was the queen e. grieved | Es 4:4
Which rejoice e. and are glad | Job 3:22
yea, let them e. rejoice | Ps 68:3
But lusted e. in the wilderness | Ps 106:14
testimonies; and I love them e. | Ps 119:167
for we are e. filled with contempt | Ps 123:3
soul is e. filled with the scorning | Ps 123:4
dissolved, the earth is moved e. | Isa 24:19
strong e.; and it had great iron | Da 7:7
Then were the men e. afraid, and | Jon 1:10
Then the men feared the Lord e. | Jon 1:16
it displeased Jonah e. and he was | Jon 4:1
they were e. amazed, saying, Who | M't 19:25
they feared e. and said one | M'k 4:41
they cried out the more e. Crucify | M'k 15:14
being Jews, do e. trouble our city | Ac 16:20
and being e. mad against them | Ac 26:11
we being e. tossed with a tempest | Ac 27:18
e. the more joyed we for the joy of | 2Co 7:13
more e. zealous of the traditions | Ga 1:14
Night and day praying e. | 1Th 3:10
your faith groweth e. and the charity | 2Th 1:3
Moses said, I e. fear and quake | Heb 12:21

EXCEL

as water, thou shalt not e. | Ge 49:4
will not retain pre-eminence (B)(E)(R) | Ge 49:4
with harps on the Sheminith to e. | 1Ch 15:21
were to lead with lyres (A)(R) | 1Ch 15:21
harps for leading off (B)(E) | 1Ch 15:21
that e. in strength, that do his | Ps 103:20
his angels—you mighty ones (A)(R) | Ps 103:20
angels who abound in strength (B) | Ps 103:20
angels, mighty in strength (E) | Ps 103:20
whose graven images did e. them | Isa 10:10
images more to be feared and dreaded (A) | Isa 10:10

were greater than those in Jerusalem (R) | Isa 10:10
that ye may e. to the edifying of | 1Co 14:12

EXCELL

you e. in every thing (R) | 2Co 8:7
e., overflow with love (A) | 1Th 3:12

EXCELLED

Solomon's wisdom e. the wisdom | 1Ki 4:30
superior to the wisdom of Easterners (B) | 1Ki 4:30
surpassed the wisdom of the east (R) | 1Ki 4:30

EXCELLENCE

called you to e. (A)(R) | 2Pe 1:3

EXCELLENCY

e. of dignity, and the e. of power | Ge 49:3
the greatness of thine e. thou hast | Ex 15:7
and in his e. on the sky | De 33:26
and who is the sword of thy e. | De 33:29
Doth not their e. which is in them | Job 4:21
Shall not his e. make you afraid | Job 13:11
Though his e. mount up to the | Job 20:6
with the voice of his e.; and he will | Job 37:4
thyself now with majesty and e. | Job 40:10
the e. of Jacob whom he loved | Ps 47:4
to cast him down from his e. | Ps 62:4
his e. is over Israel and his | Ps 68:34
but the e. of knowledge is, that | Ec 7:12
the beauty of the Chaldees' e. | Isa 13:19
the e. of Carmel and Sharon | Isa 35:2
of the Lord, and the e. of our God | Isa 35:2
I will make thee an eternal e. | Isa 60:15
the e. of your strength, the desire | Eze 24:21
I abhor the e. of Jacob, and hate | Am 6:8
hath sworn by the e. of Jacob | Am 8:7
turned away the e. of Jacob | Na 2:2
as the e. of Israel | Na 2:2
you, came not with e. of speech | 1Co 2:1
lofty words of eloquence (A) | 1Co 2:1
came with no distinction of eloquence (B) | 1Co 2:1
without display of fine words (N) | 1Co 2:1
with any brilliance of speech (P) | 1Co 2:1
in lofty words (R) | 1Co 2:1
the e. of the power may be of God | 2Co 4:7
grandeur, exceeding greatness of power (A) | 2Co 4:7
unparalled power (B) | 2Co 4:7
exceeding greatness of power (E) | 2Co 4:7
such transcendent power (N)(R) | 2Co 4:7
the splended power (P) | 2Co 4:7
the e. of the knowledge of Christ | Ph'p 3:8
for his sake I lost everything (A)(B)(P) | Ph'p 3:8
surpassing worth of knowing Christ (R) | Ph'p 3:8

EXCELLENT

location of city is e. (B) | 2Ki 2:19
the honour of his e. majesty | Es 1:4
he is e. in power, and in judgment | Job 37:23
e. is thy name in all the earth | Ps 8:1; 8:9
to the e. in whom is all my delight | Ps 16:3
e. is thy loving kindness, O God | Ps 36:7
Thou art more glorious and e. than | Ps 76:4
it shall be an e. oil, which shall | Ps 141:5
his name alone is e.; his glory | Ps 148:13
him according to his e. greatness | Ps 150:2

for I will speak of e. things | Pr 8:6
The righteous is more e. than his | Pr 12:26
E. speech becometh not a fool | Pr 17:7
of understanding is of an e. spirit | Pr 17:27
not I written to thee e. things in | Pr 22:20
Lebanon, e. as the cedars | Ca 5:15
the fruit of the earth shall be e. | Isa 4:2
for he hath done e. things | Isa 12:5
in counsel and e. in working | Isa 28:29
thou art come to e. ornaments | Eze 16:7
image, whose brightness was e. | Da 2:31
and e. majesty was added unto me | Da 4:36
Forasmuch as an e. spirit, and | Da 5:12
and e. wisdom is found in thee | Da 5:14
because an e. spirit was in him | Da 6:3
in order, most e. Theophilus | Lu 1:3
unto the most e. governor Felix | Ac 23:26
the things that are more e. being | Ro 2:18
shew I unto you a more e. way | 1Co 12:31
ye may approve things that | Ph'p 1:10
e. and admirable (N) | Ph'p 4:8
obtained a more e. name than they | Heb 1:4
hath he obtained a more e. ministry | Heb 8:6
a more e. sacrifice than Cain | Heb 11:4
a voice to him from the e. glory | 2Pe 1:17

EXCELLENTLY

plays e. (B) | 1Sa 16:18
daughters have done e. (R) | Pr 31:29

EXCELLEST

virtuously, but thou e. them all | Pr 31:29

EXCELLETH

Then I saw that wisdom e. folly | Ec 2:13
wisdom better than folly (A)(B) | Ec 2:13
as far as light e. darkness | Ec 2:13
by reason of the glory that e. | 2Co 3:10

EXCEPT

E. the God of my father, the God | Ge 31:42
let thee go, e. thou bless me | Ge 32:26
e. your youngest brother come | Ge 42:15
e. your brother be with you | Ge 43:3
not see my face, e. your brother | Ge 43:5
e. we had lingered, surely now we | Ge 43:10
E. your youngest brother | Ge 44:23
e. our youngest brother be with | Ge 44:26
e. the land of the priests only | Ge 47:26
e. thou make thyself altogether | Nu 16:13
except (S) De 1:36; 15:4; Jos 11:13; 14:4;
J'g 7:14; 1Sa 21:9; 30:22; 2Sa 22:32;
1Ki 3:18; 8:9; 15:5; 22:31; 2Ki 4:2;
2Ki 15:4; 24:14; 2Ch 2:6; 5:10; 18:30;
21:17; 23:6; Ne 2:12; Da 6:7, 12;
Am 9:8; M't 5:32; 11:27; 13:57; 17:8;
19:11; M'k 5:37; 6:5, 8; 9:8; Lu 8:51;
17:18; 18:19; Joh 6:22, 46; 13:10;
Ac 20:23; 21:25; 1Co 2:2, 11; Ga 1:19;
6:14; Re 2:17; 13:17
e. their Rock had sold | De 32:30
e. ye destroy the accursed | Jos 7:12
e. thou hadst hasted and | 1Sa 25:34
God to Abner, and more also | 2Sa 3:9
not see my face, e. thou first | 2Sa 3:13
E. thou take away the blind | 2Sa 5:6
not thy riding for me, e. I bid | 2Ki 4:24
e. the king delighted in her | Es 2:14
e. such to whom the king shall | Es 4:11
E. the Lord build the house | Ps 127:1
e. the Lord keep the city, the | Ps 127:1
sleep not, e. they have done | Pr 4:16
E. the Lord of hosts had left unto | Isa 1:9
e. the gods, whose dwelling is not | Da 2:11
nor any god, e their own God | Da 3:28
Daniel, e. we find it against him | Da 6:5
walk together, e. they be agreed | Am 3:3
e. your righteousness shall exceed | M't 5:20

e. he first bind the strong man	M't 12:29
E. ye be converted, and become as	M't 18:3
e. it be for fornication, and shall	M't 19:9
e. those days should be shortened	M't 24:22
e. I drink it, thy will be done	M't 26:42
e. he will first bind the strong man	M'k 3:27
e. they wash their hands oft	M'k 7:3
e. they wash, they eat not	M'k 7:4
e. that the Lord had shortened	M'k 13:20
e. we should go and buy meat for	Lu 9:13
e. ye repent, ye shall all likewise	Lu 13:3
that thou doest, e. God be with him	Joh 3:2
E. a man be born again, he cannot	Joh 3:3
E. a man be born of water and of	Joh 3:5
e. it be given him from heaven	Joh 3:27
E. ye see signs and wonders	Joh 4:48
e. the Father which hath sent me	Joh 6:44
E. ye eat the flesh of the Son of	Joh 6:53
e. it were given unto him of my	Joh 6:65
E. a corn of wheat fall into	Joh 12:24
e. it abide in the vine; no more can	Joh 15:4
no more can ye, e. ye abide in me	Joh 15:4
e. it were given thee from above	Joh 19:11
E. I shall see in his hands the print	Joh 20:25
were all scattered, e. the apostles	Ac 8:1
How can I, e. some man should	Ac 8:31
E. ye be circumcised after the	Ac 15:1
E. it be for this one voice, that I	Ac 24:21
such as I am, e. these bonds	Ac 26:29
E. these abide in the ship, ye	Ac 27:31
e. the law had said, Thou shalt not	Ro 7:7
E. the Lord of Sabbaoth had left us	Ro 9:29
e. they be sent, as it is written	Ro 10:15
e. it be with consent for a time	1Co 7:5
tongues, e. he interpret, that	1Co 14:5
e. I shall speak to you either by	1Co 14:6
e. they give a distinction in	1Co 14:7
e. ye utter by the tongue words	1Co 14:9
sowest is not quickened, e. it die	1Co 15:36
e. it be that I myself was not	2Co 12:13
is in you, e. ye be reprobates	2Co 13:5
e. there come a falling away first	2Th 2:3
not crowned, e. he strive lawfully	2Ti 2:5
out of his place, e. thou repent	Re 2:5
e. they repent of their deeds	Re 2:22

EXCEPTED

that he is e. which did put	1Co 15:27

EXCEPTIONAL

he received e. help (B)	2Ch 26:15
are you doing anything e. (P)	M't 5:46

EXCESS

they are full of extortion and e.	M't 23:25
grasping self-indulgence (A)	M't 23:25
intemperance (B)	M't 23:25
self-indulgence (N)(P)	M't 23:25
rapacity (R)	M't 23:25
drunk with wine, wherein is e.	Eph 5:18
with wine, for that is debauchery (A)(R)	Eph 5:18
wine, which brings incorrigibleness (B)	Eph 5:18
wine, wherein is riot (E)	Eph 5:18
the dissipation that goes with it (N)	Eph 5:18

malice that hurries e. (N)	Jas 1:21
e. of wine, revellings	1Pe 4:3
e. of riot, speaking evil of you	1Pe 4:4

EXCESSIVE

e. lawlessness (B)	M't 24:12
e. luxury (A)(B)	Re 18:3

EXCHANGE

them bread in e. for horses	Ge 47:17
and the e. thereof shall be holy	Le 27:10
and the e. of it shall not be	Job 28:17
e. thy merchandise (S)	Eze 27:9
e. nor alienate the first fruits	Eze 48:14
shall a man give in e. for his soul	M't 16:26
shall a man give in e. for his soul	M'k 8:37
women did e. (S)	Ro 1:26

EXCHANGED

who e. the truth of God (S)	Ro 1:25

EXCHANGERS

to have put my money to the e.	M't 25:27

EXCITED

anxious mind unsettled e., worried, in suspense (A)	Lu 12:29
kept them e. (B)	Ac 8:11

EXCITING

e. his ardent anger (B)	1Ki 14:22

EXCLAIMED

amazed the men e. (B)	M't 8:27
Jesus e. in deep agitation (N)	Joh 13:21

EXCLUDE

e., excommunicate you (A)(B)(R)	Lu 6:22
it means to e. God (N)	1Co 15:27
yea, they would e. you, that ye	Ga 4:17

EXCLUDED

Where is boasting then? It is e.	Ro 3:27

EXCLUSION

eternal e. from radiance of (P)	2Th 1:9

EXCLUSIVE

have e. control over (A)(B)	1Co 7:4

EXCOMMUNICATE

exclude, e. you (A)(B)(R)	Lu 6:22

EXCUSE

no e. for sin (A)(B)(E)(N)(P)(R)	Lu 6:29
with one consent began to make e.	Lu 14:18
so that they are without e.	Ro 1:20
no e., defense (A)(B)(E)(R)	Ro 2:1
that we e. ourselves unto you	2Co 12:19
an e. for doing wrong (P)	1Pe 2:16

EXCUSED

and see it: I pray thee have me e.	Lu 14:18
prove them: I pray thee have me e.	Lu 14:19

EXCUSING

accusing or else e. one another	Ro 2:15

EXECRATION

be an e. and an astonishment	Jer 42:18
shall be an e. and an astonishment	Jer 44:12

EXECUTE

will e. judgment: I am the Lord	Ex 12:12
e. vengeance (A)(E)(R)	Le 26:25
priest shall e. upon her all this law	Nu 5:30
deal with her according to entire law (B)	Nu 5:30
may e. the service of the Lord	Nu 8:11
e. the judgment of the fatherless	De 10:18
secure justice for the widow (B)	De 10:18
and e. my judgments, and keep all	1Ki 6:12
carry out my judgments (B)	1Ki 6:12
when wilt thou e. judgment on	Ps 119:84
To e. vengeance upon the heathen	Ps 149:7
To e. upon them the judgment	Ps 149:9
Take counsel, e. judgment; make	Isa 16:3
Lord will e. judgment (A)(B)(E)(R)	Isa 66:16
thoroughly e. judgment between	Jer 7:5
E. judgment in the morning	Jer 21:12
practice judgment in the morning (B)	Jer 21:12
saith the Lord; E. ye judgment	Jer 22:3
and prosper, and shall e. judgment	Jer 23:5
and he shall e. judgment and	Jer 33:15
I will e. judgment (S)	Jer 51:47; 51:52
and will e. judgments in the midst	Eze 5:8
and I will e. judgments in thee	Eze 5:10
when I shall e. judgments in thee	Eze 5:15
and will e. judgments among you	Eze 11:9
and e. judgments upon thee in the	Eze 16:41
I will e. judgments upon Moab	Eze 25:11
will e. great vengeance upon them	Eze 25:17
I will carry out my punishments (S)	Eze 25:17
and will e. judgments in No	Eze 30:14
Thus will I e. judgments in Egypt	Eze 30:19
e. judgment and justice, take away	Eze 45:9
do justice and righteousness (A)	Eze 45:9
Practice justice (B)	Eze 45:9
not e. the fierceness of mine anger	Ho 11:9
And I will e. vengeance in anger	Mic 5:15
my cause, and e. judgment for me	Mic 7:9
render true judgment (B)(R)	Mic 7:9
E. true judgment, and shew	Zec 7:9
e. the judgment of truth and peace	Zec 8:16
render the truth (A)	Zec 8:16
judge with truth (B)	Zec 8:16
speak the truth (R)	Zec 8:16
authority to e. judgment also	Joh 5:27
to act as judge (B)	Joh 5:27
given the right to pass judgment (N)	Joh 5:27
authority to judge (P)	Joh 5:27
a revenger to e. wrath upon him	Ro 13:4
to bring deserved punishment on (B)	Ro 13:4
an avenger of wrath on him that (E)	Ro 13:4
for retribution on the offender (N)	Ro 13:4
to inflict God's punishment upon (P)	Ro 13:4
To e. judgment upon all, and to	Jude 15

EXECUTED

gods also the Lord e. judgments	Nu 33:4
shall be e. (B)	Nu 35:21
he e. the justice of the Lord	De 33:21
David e. judgment and justice	2Sa 8:15
(he it is that e. the priest's office in	1Ch 6:10
e. judgment and justice among	1Ch 18:14

and Ithamar *e.* the priest's   1Ch 24:2
office
they *e.* judgment against   2Ch 24:24
Joash
judgment be *e.* speedily upon   Ezr 7:26
him
stood up Phinehas, and *e.*   Ps 106:30
judgment
an evil work is not *e.* speedily   Ec 8:11
until he have *e.* and till he   Jer 23:20
have
neither *e.* my judgments, but   Eze 11:12
have
hath *e.* true judgment between   Eze 18:8
practices true judgment   Eze 18:8
between (B)
hath *e.* my judgments, hath   Eze 18:17
walked
they had not *e.* my judgments   Eze 20:24
for they had *e.* judgment   Eze 23:10
upon her
I shall have *e.* judgments in   Eze 28:22
her
when I have *e.* judgments   Eze 28:26
upon all
see my judgment that I have   Eze 39:21
e.
that while he *e.* the priest's   Lu 1:8
office
serving as priest (A)   Lu 1:8
administering the priest's office Lu 1:8
(B)
to take part in divine service   Lu 1:8
(N)
performing his priestly function Lu 1:8
(P)
has been duly *e.* (N)   Ga 3:15

EXECUTEDST

e. his fierce wrath upon   1Sa 28:18
Amalek

EXECUTEST

e. judgment and righteousness   Ps 99:4

EXECUTETH

by the judgment which he *e.*   Ps 9:16
The Lord *e.* righteousness and   Ps 103:6
e. judgment for the oppressed   Ps 146:7
the man that *e.* my counsel   Isa 46:11
from
if there be any that *e.* judgment Jer 5:1
for he is strong that *e.* his   Joe 2:11
word

EXECUTING

thou hast done well in *e.* that 2Ki 10:30
them off from *e.* the priest's   2Ch 11:14
office
when Jehu was *e.* judgment   2Ch 22:8
upon

EXECUTION

there is one penalty, *e.* (B)   Es 4:11
decree drew near to be put in *e.* Es 9:1
demand Jesus' *e.* (P)   M't 27:20

EXECUTIONER

king sent an *e.* and   M'k 6:27
commanded

EXEMPTED

none was *e.*: and they took   1Ki 15:22
away

EXERCISE

e. kingship over Israel (B)   1Ki 21:7
do I *e.* myself in great matters Ps 131:1
the Lord which *e.*   Jer 9:24
lovingkindness
Gentiles *e.* dominion   M't 20:25
over them
are great *e.* authority upon   M't 20:25
them
the Gentiles *e.* lordship over   M'k 10:42
them
great ones *e.* authority upon   M'k 10:42
them
kings of the earth *e.* lordship Lu 22:25
they that *e.* authority upon   Lu 22:25
them

herein do I *e.* myself, to have Ac 24:16
alway
e. thyself rather unto godliness 1Ti 4:7
For bodily *e.* profiteth little: but 1Ti 4:8

EXERCISED

sons of man to be *e.* therewith Ec 1:13
to the sons of men to be *e.* in it Ec 3:10
and *e.* robbery, and have   Eze 22:29
vexed
e. to discern both good and   Heb 5:14
evil
unto them which are *e.*   Heb 12:11
thereby
have *e.* with covetous   2Pe 2:14
practices

EXERCISETH

e. all the power of the first   Re 13:12
beast

EXERT

when you *e.* your power (B)   Ge 27:40
e. yourselves more (B)   2Pe 1:10

EXHAUST

shall *e.* the land (A)(B)   Ge 41:30
e. the soil (B)   Lu 13:7

EXHAUSTED

weary and *e.* (B)   De 25:18
e. with want (B)   Job 30:3
e. due to many plans (B)(R)   Isa 47:13
you were not *e.* (B)   Isa 57:10
uselessly *e.* themselves (B)   Jer 12:13

EXHAUSTIVE

after an *e.* inquiry (P)   Ac 15:7

EXHAUSTLESS

the *e.* riches of Christ (A)   Eph 3:8

EXHIBIT

an *e.* of perpetual punishment   Jude 7
(A)

EXHIBITION

an *e.* to the universe (B)   1Co 4:9

EXHORT

did he testify and *e.* saying,   Ac 2:40
Save
now I *e.* you to be of good   Ac 27:22
cheer
it necessary to *e.* the brethren 2Co 9:5
I *e.* you too (A)   Ph'p 4:3
and *e.* you by the Lord Jesus   1Th 4:1
we *e.* you, brethren, warn   1Th 5:14
them
and *e.* by our Lord Jesus   2Th 3:12
Christ
I *e.* therefore, that, first of all 1Ti 2:1
e. him as a father (E)(R)(S)   1Ti 5:1
These things teach and *e.*   1Ti 6:2
rebuke, *e.* with all long   2Ti 4:2
suffering
to *e.* and to convince the   Tit 1:9
gainsayers
likewise *e.* to be sober minded Tit 2:6
E. servants to be obedient unto   Tit 2:9
speak, and *e.* and rebuke with   Tit 2:15
all
But *e.* one another daily,   Heb 3:13
while it
I *e.* who am also an elder   1Pe 5:1
me to write unto you, and *e.* you Jude 3

EXHORTATION

e. preached he unto the people Lu 3:18
son of *e.* (E)(N)   Ac 4:36
any word of *e.* for the people   Ac 13:15
and had given them much *e.*   Ac 20:2
Or he that exhorteth, on *e.*   Ro 12:8
edification, and *e.* and   1Co 14:3
comfort
For indeed he accepted the *e.*   2Co 8:17
For our *e.* was not of deceit   1Th 2:3
to reading, to *e.* to doctrine   1Ti 4:13

forgotten the *e.* which   Heb 12:5
speaketh
brethren, suffer the word of   Heb 13:22
e.

EXHORTED

and *e.* them all, that with   Ac 11:23
purpose
e. the brethren with many   Ac 15:32
words
I *e.* Titus (S)   2Co 12:18
As ye know how we *e.* and   1Th 2:11

EXHORTETH

Or he that *e.* on exhortation   Ro 12:8

EXHORTING

e. them to continue in the faith Ac 14:22
e. the disciples to receive him Ac 18:27
but *e.* one another: and so   Heb 10:25
much
written briefly, *e.* and   1Pe 5:12
testifying

EXILE

art a stranger, and also an *e.* 2Sa 15:19
The captive *e.* hasteneth that   Isa 51:14
he
an *e.* and an alien   Ac 7:29
(A)(B)(P)(R)

EXILED

gathers the *e.* of Israel (B)   Isa 56:8

EXILES

gathering together the *e.*   Ps 147:2
(A)(B)
were *e.* in Egypt (P)   Ac 13:17
outsiders, *e.*, migrants (A)   Eph 2:19
temporary residents, *e.*   Heb 11:13
(A)(P)(R)
e. scattered abroad (A)(P)(R)   1Pe 1:1
aliens and *e.* (A)   1Pe 2:11

EXITS

the *e.* (S)   Eze 42:11

EXODUS

your *e.* from Egypt (B)(R)   De 16:6
his *e.* was to consummate (B)   Lu 9:31

EXORCISTS

vagabond Jews, *e.* took upon   Ac 19:13
them

EXPANDED

our heart is *e.* (A)   2Co 6:11

EXPECTANCY

watching with outstretched   Ro 8:19
head is in *e.* (B)

EXPECTANTLY

waiting *e.* (A)   Lu 3:15

EXPECTATION

the *e.* of the poor shall not   Ps 9:18
perish
my *e.* is from him   Ps 62:5
the *e.* of the wicked shall   Pr 10:28
perish
man dieth, his *e.* shall perish Pr 11:7
the *e.* of the wicked is wrath   Pr 11:23
and thine *e.* shall not be cut   Pr 23:18
off
and thy *e.* shall not be cut off Pr 24:14
Ethiopia their *e.* and of Egypt Isa 20:5
such is our *e.* whither we flee Isa 20:6
Ekron; for her *e.* shall be   Zec 9:5
ashamed
as the people were in *e.*   Lu 3:15
on tiptoe of *e.* (N)(P)(B)   Lu 3:15
all the *e.* of the people of the Ac 12:11
Jews
the earnest *e.* of the creature Ro 8:19
waits with eager *e.* (N)   Ro 8:19
to my earnest *e.* and my hope   Ph'p 1:20
eager *e.* and hope (R)   Ph'p 1:20

EXPECTED

not of evil, to give you an *e.* end   *Jer 29:11*

EXPECTING

e. to receive something of them   *Ac 3:5*
e. till his enemies be made his   *Heb 10:13*

EXPEDIENT

Nor consider that it is *e.* for us   *Joh 11:50*
It is *e.* for you that I go away   *Joh 16:7*
e.
it was *e.* that one man should die   *Joh 18:14*
unto me, but all things are not *e.*   *1Co 6:12*
but all things are not *e.*   *1Co 10:23*
this is *e.* of you, who have begun   *2Co 8:10*
not *e.* for me doubtless to glory   *2Co 12:1*

EXPEL

shall *e.* them from before you   *Jos 23:5*
Did not ye hate me, and *e.* me   *J'g 11:7*

EXPELLED

of Israel *e.* not the Geshurites   *Jos 13:13*
e. thence the three sons of Anak   *J'g 1:20*
his banished be not *e.* from him   *2Sa 14:14*
and *e.* them out of their coasts   *Ac 13:50*

EXPENCES

and let the *e.* be given out of   *Ezr 6:4*
forthwith *e.* be given unto these   *Ezr 6:8*

EXPENSES

be at *e.* with them (S)   *Ac 21:24*

EXPERIENCE

by *e.* that the Lord hath blessed   *Ge 30:27*
I have divined that the Lord (B)(E)   *Ge 30:27*
I have learned by divination (R)   *Ge 30:27*
my heart had great *e.* of wisdom   *Ec 1:16*
my heart observed abundance (B)   *Ec 1:16*
And patience, *e.;* and *e.* hope   *Ro 5:4*
develops maturity of character, character produces hope (A)(B)(P)(R)   *Ro 5:4*
stedfastness approvedness, approvedness hope (E)   *Ro 5:4*
suffering trains us to endure, endurance brings proof we have stood the test, and this proof is the ground of hope (N)   *Ro 5:4*
e. richly the sufferings (B)   *2Co 1:5*
without *e.* (E)   *Heb 5:13*

EXPERIMENT

by the *e.* of this ministration   *2Co 9:13*

EXPERT

an *e.* hunter (B)   *Ge 25:27*
e. in war, with all instruments of   *1Ch 12:33*
of the Danites *e.* in war twenty   *1Ch 12:35*
battle *e.* in war, forty thousand   *1Ch 12:36*
being *e.* in war: every man hath   *Ca 3:8*
e. craftsman (A)(E)   *Isa 3:3*
skilful craftsman and *e.* charmer (B)(R)   *Isa 3:3*
shall be as of a mighty *e.* man   *Jer 50:9*
the *e.* charmer (B)(R)   *Ac 3:3*
be *e.* in all customs and questions   *Ac 26:3*

EXPERTS

e. in evil (B)(R)   *Jer 4:22*
e. in forjoining (B)   *Eze 27:27*
e. of the law (B)   *Lu 5:17*
e. in goodness (N)   *Ro 16:19*

EXPIATE

to *e.* sins of people (N)   *Heb 2:17*

EXPIATING

e. sin by his sacrificial death (N)   *Ro 3:25*

EXPIATION

on *e.* by his blood (R)   *Ro 3:25*
make *e.* for sins (R)   *Heb 2:17*
an *e.* for our sins (R)   *1Jo 2:2*

EXPIRE

why did I not *e.* (S)   *Job 3:11*

EXPIRED

and the days were not *e.*   *1Sa 18:26*
after the year was *e.* at the time   *2Sa 11:1*
when thy days be *e.* that thou   *1Ch 17:11*
after the year was *e.* at the time   *1Ch 20:1*
was *e.* king Nebuchadnezzar   *2Ch 36:10*
And when these days were *e.*   *Es 1:5*
these days are *e.* it shall be   *Eze 43:27*
And when forty years were *e.*   *Ac 7:30*
when the thousand years are *e.*   *Re 20:7*

EXPIRETH

man *e.* (S)   *Job 14:10*

EXPLAIN

explain (S)   *Es 4:8; M't 13:36; 15:15*
e. situation (P)   *Ac 11:4*

EXPLAINED

e. everything (A)(B)(N)(P)(R)   *M'k 4:34*
e. the scriptures (B)(N)(P)   *Lu 24:27*
e. the kingdom (B)(P)   *Ac 8:25; 28:23*
narrated and *e.* (A)   *Ac 11:4*
e. way of God (B)(P)   *Ac 18:26*
e. the matter (A))(B)(P)   *Ac 28:23*

EXPLAINING

e. and interpreting (A)   *Lu 24:27*

EXPLANATIONS

give *e.* and solve problems (B)   *Da 5:16*

EXPLOIT

see how far we can *e.* grace (P)   *Ro 6:1*
e. with false arguments (A)(B)(P)(R)   *2Pe 2:3*

EXPLOITED

e. no one (A)   *2Co 7:2*

EXPLOITS

and he shall do *e.* and return to   *Da 11:28*
God shall be strong, and do *e.*   *Da 11:32*

EXPOSE

e. secret parts (B)(E)(R)   *Isa 3:17*
e. nakedness (B)   *Eze 16:37*
e. disgrace her publicly (A)(B)   *M't 1:19*
e. my life dear (A)   *Ac 20:24*
disclose and *e.* aims (A)   *1Co 4:5*
e. secret motives (P)   *1Co 4:5*

EXPOSED

land lies *e.* (B)   *Ge 42:9*
lest nudity be *e.* (A)(B)(R)(S)   *Ex 20:26*

e. her fountain (B)   *Le 20:18*
nakedness be *e.* (B)   *Jer 13:26*
foundation *e.* (A)   *Eze 13:14*
bare and *e.* before him (B)   *Heb 4:13*

EXPOSITION

gave full *e.* of (P)   *Ga 2:2*

EXPOSURE

e. of nakedness (B)   *Eze 16:36*
wanted to save her from *e.* (N)   *M't 1:19*

EXPOUND

they could not in three days *e.*   *J'g 14:14*
could not solve riddle (A) (B)   *J'g 14:14; 14:19*
could not declare riddle (E)   *J'g 14:14; 14:19*
could not tell riddle (R)   *J'g 14:14; 14:19*

EXPOUNDED

unto them which *e.* the riddle   *J'g 14:19*
he *e.* all things to his disciples   *M'k 4:34*
explained everything (A)(B)(N)(P)(R)   *M'k 4:34*
he *e.* unto them in all the   *Lu 24:27*
explaining and interpreting (A)   *Lu 24:27*
explained to them in scriptures (B)(N)(P)   *Lu 24:27*
interpreted to them all scriptures (E)(R)   *Lu 24:27*
e. it by order unto them, saying   *Ac 11:4*
narrated and explained to them (A)   *Ac 11:4*
put the whole matter plainly (B)   *Ac 11:4*
laying before them the facts (N)   *Ac 11:4*
explain how situation had arisen (P)   *Ac 11:4*
explained them in order (R)   *Ac 11:4*
and *e.* unto him the way of God   *Ac 18:26*
explained the way of God (B)(P)   *Ac 18:26*
to whom he *e.* and testified the   *Ac 28:23*
explained the matter (A)(B)(P)   *Ac 28:23*
dealt at length with the matter (N)   *Ac 28:23*

EXPRESS

and the *e.* image of his person   *Heb 1:3*

EXPRESSED

men which are *e.* by their names   *Nu 1:17*
which were *e.* by name, to come   *1Ch 12:31*
were *e.* by name, to give thanks   *1Ch 16:41*
which were *e.* by name rose up   *2Ch 28:15*
the men that were *e.* by name, to   *2Ch 31:19*
all of them were *e.* by name   *Ezr 8:20*

EXPRESSION

e. of face changed (R)   *Da 3:19*
astonish beyond *e.* (B)   *M'k 5:42*
complete *e.* of himself (P)   *Col 2:9*
true *e.* of his being (B)(P)   *Heb 1:3*
faith reaches supreme *e.* (B)   *Jas 2:22*

EXPRESSLY

If I *e.* say unto the lad, Behold   *1Sa 20:21*
word of the Lord came *e.* unto Ezekiel   *Eze 1:3*
Now the Spirit speaketh *e.*   *1Ti 4:1*
the Spirit says distinctly (B)   *1Ti 4:1*
God's Spirit specifically tells (P)   *1Ti 4:1*

EXPUNGE

do not *e.* benevolent service (B)   *Ne 13:14*

EXTEND

Let there be none to *e.* mercy   Ps 109:12
I will *e.* peace to her like a   Isa 66:12
river
word of Lord *e.* (B)   Ac 19:20

EXTENDED

the border *e.* (S)   Jos 15:9;
           15:11; 18:14, 17
e. mercy unto me before the   Ezr 7:28
king.
hath *e.* mercy unto us in the   Ezr 9:9
sight

EXTENDETH

my goodness *e.* not to thee   Ps 16:2

EXTERMINATE

e. from under heaven (B)   Ge 6:7
e. them (A)   De 2:15

EXTERMINATED

e. necromancers (B)   2Ki 23:24
be utterly *e.* (A)   Ac 3:23

EXTERNAL

e. observations (A)   Ga 4:3
e. rules and regulations (A)   Heb 9:10

EXTERNALISM

world's teaching of *e.* (A)   Col 2:20

EXTINCT

breath is corrupt, my days are   Job 17:1
e.
my days are snuffed out (A)   Job 17:1
my days are extinguished (B)   Job 17:1
they are *e.* they are quenched   Isa 43:17
as
they are extinguished   Isa 43:17
(A)(B)(R)

EXTINGUISHED

my days are *e.* (B)   Job 17:1
they are *e.* (A)(B)(R)   Isa 43:17

EXTIRPATED

must be *e.* (N)   Ac 3:23

EXISTENCE

whole machinery of *e.* (B)(N)   Jas 3:6

EXTOL

to *e.* his works (R)   Job 36:24
I will *e.* thee, O Lord; for thou   Ps 30:1
e. him that rideth upon the   Ps 68:4
I will *e.* thee, my God, O king   Ps 145:1
I Nebuchadnezzar praise and   Da 4:37
e.

EXTOLLED

and he was *e.* with my tongue   Ps 66:17
he shall be exalted and *e.* and   Isa 52:13
Jesus was highly *e.* (R)   Ac 19:17

EXTOLLING

e. and magnifying God   Ac 10:46
(A)(R)

EXTORT

you *e.* from hired servants (A)   Isa 58:3
e. no more than appointed (E)   Lu 3:13
do not *e.* (B)   Lu 3:14

EXTORTION

neither use *e.* (B)   Le 19:13
e. maddens wisemen (B)(E)   Ec 7:7
foreigner suffers *e.* (B)(R)   Jer 22:17;
           22:29
gained of thy neighbours by   Eze 22:12
e.
they are full of *e.* and excess   M't 23:25
full of *e.* and wickedness   Lu 11:39
(S)

EXTORTIONER

Let the *e.* catch all that he   Ps 109:11
hath
creditors seize all he has   Ps 109:11
(B)(R)
the *e.* is at an end, the spoiler   Isa 16:4
the oppressor has met his end   Isa 16:4
(B)(R)
a railer, or a drunkard, or an   1Co 5:11
e.
a swindler (A)(N)   1Co 5:11
a robber (B)(R)   1Co 5:11
a thief (P)   1Co 5:11

EXTORTIONERS

not as other men are *e.* unjust   Lu 18:11
thieves, cheats (B)   Lu 18:11
greedy, dishonest (N)(P)   Lu 18:11
covetous, or *e.* or with   1Co 5:10
idolaters
cheats (A)(P)   1Co 5:10
avaricious and grasping (B)   1Co 5:10
swindlers (N)   1Co 5:10
greedy and robbers (R)   1Co 5:10
revilers, nor *e.* shall inherit   1Co 6:10
nor robbers (B)(R)   1Co 6:10
or swindlers (N)(P)   1Co 6:10

EXTRAORDINARY

what an *e.* thing (N)(P)   Joh 9:30

EXTRA-SPECIAL

e. messengers (P)   2Co 11:5

EXTRA-SUPER

e. apostles (A)   2Co 11:5

EXTREME

an *e.* burning, and with the   De 28:22
sword

EXTREMITY

he knoweth it not in great *e.*   Job 35:15

EYE

e. for *e.*   Ex 21:24;
       Le 24:20; De 19:21; M't 5:38
if a man smite the *e.* of his   Ex 21:26
servant, or the *e.*
or that hath a blemish in his   Le 21:20
his *e.* shall be evil toward his   De 28:54
brother
cruel and grudging of food   De 28:54
(A)
grudgingly toward brother   De 28:54;
(B)   28:56
grudge food to his brother   De 28:54;
(R)   28:56
her *e.* shall be evil towards   De 28:56
her husband
he kept him as the apple of   De 32:10
his *e.*
his *e.* was not dim, nor his   De 34:7
force abated
the *e.* of their God was on the   Ezr 5:5
elders
e. that hath seen me, shall see   Job 7:8
me no more
given up ghost, and no *e.* had   Job 10:18
seen me
e. which saw him, shall see   Job 20:9
him no more
e. of adulterer waiteth for   Job 24:15
twilight, saying, No *e.* shall
see me
path which the vulture's *e.*   Job 28:7
hath not seen
and his *e.* seeth every   Job 28:10
precious thing
when *e.* saw me, it gave   Job 29:11
witness to me
e. of Lord is on them that fear   Ps 33:18
him
neither let them wink with the   Ps 35:19
e.
they said, Aha, aha, our *e.*   Ps 35:21
hath seen it
he that formed the *e.* shall he   Ps 94:9
not see
that winketh with *e.* causeth   Pr 10:10
sorrow

seeing *e.* hearing ear, Lord   Pr 20:12
hath made
he that hath a bountiful *e.* shall   Pr 22:9
be blessed
e. that mocketh at his father   Pr 30:17
the *e.* is not satisfied with seeing   Ec 1:8
neither is his *e.* satisfied with   Ec 4:8
riches
their *e.* shall not spare   Isa 13:18
children
watchmen sing, for they shall   Isa 52:8
see *e.* to *e.*
neither hath the *e.* seen   Isa 64:4;
           1Co 2:9
slew all that were pleasant to *e.*   La 2:4
let not your *e.* spare, neither   Eze 9:5
have pity
none *e.* pitied, to do any of   Eze 16:5
these to thee
be defiled, and let our *e.* look   Mic 4:11
on Zion
if *e.* entice you to sin (B)   M't 5:29;
           5:30
light of the body is the *e.*   M't 6:22;
           Lu 11:34
brother's *e.* and not beam in   M't 7:3;
thine own *e.*   Lu 6:41-42
if thine *e.* offend thee, pluck   M't 18:9
it out
easier for camel to go   M't 19:24;
through *e.* of   M'k 10:25; Lu 18:25
needle than rich man
does not come with *e.* appeal   Lu 17:20
(B)
because I am not *e.* I am not   1Co 12:16
of body
if whole body were an *e.,* *e.*   1Co 12:17;
cannot say   12:21
in twinkling of an *e.* at the   1Co 15:52
last trump
he cometh, and every *e.* shall see   Re 1:7
him

EYEBROWS

shave all his hair off his   Le 14:9
e.

EYED

Leah was tender *e.*   Ge 29:17
Saul *e.* David from that day   1Sa 18:9

EYELIDS

on mine *e.* is the shadow of   Job 16:16
death
his eyes are like the *e.* of   Job 41:18
morning
his *e.* try the children of men   Ps 11:4
sleep to mine eyes, or slumber   Ps 132:4
to mine *e.*
let thine *e.* look straight before   Pr 4:25
thee
sleep to thine eyes, or slumber to   Pr 6:4
thine *e.*
neither let her take thee with   Pr 6:25
her *e.*
how lofty their eyes, their *e.*   Pr 30:16
are lifted up
that our *e.* may gush out with   Jer 9:18
waters

EYE-SALVE

anoint thine eyes with *e.* to see   Re 3:18

EYE-SERVICE

not with *e.* as men-pleasers,   Eph 6:6;
but as the servants of Christ   Col 3:22

EYESIGHT

recompensed according to   2Sa 22:25;
my cleanness in his *e.*   Ps 18:24

EYEWITNESSES

who from beginning were *e.*   Lu 1:2
but were *e.* of his majesty   2Pe 1:16

EVIL EYE

bread of him that hath an *evil*   Pr 23:6
e.

he that hasteth to be rich hath *Pr 28:22*
an *evil* e.
but if thine e. be *evil M't 6:23; Lu 11:34*
is thine e. *evil* because I am *M't 20:15*
good
out of heart proceedeth an *M'k 7:22*
evil e.

MINE EYE

bade kill thee, but *mine.* e. *1Sa 24:10*
spared
mine e. shall no more see good *Job 7:7*
mine e. hath seen all this, *Job 13:1*
mine ear heard
but *mine* e. poureth out tears *Job 16:20*
to God
doth *mine* e. continue in their *Job 17:2*
provocation
mine e. also is dim by reason *Job 17:7*
of sorrow
heard of thee, now *mine* e. *Job 42:5*
seeth thee
mine e. is consumed with grief *Ps 6:7;*
31:9
I will guide thee with *mine* e. *Ps 32:8*
mine e. seen his desire on mine *Ps 54:7*
enemies
mine e. mourneth by reason of *Ps 88:9*
affliction
mine e. see my desire on mine *Ps 92:11*
enemies
mine e. *mine* e. runneth down *La 1:16;*
3:48
mine e. trickleth down and *La 3:49*
ceaseth not
mine e. affecteth my heart, *La 3:51*
because of all daughters
neither *mine* e. spare, nor will *Eze 5:11;*
I have any pity *7:4, 9; 8:18; 9:10*
nevertheless *mine* e. spared *Eze 20:17*
them

THINE EYE

thine e. shall not pity, nor *De 7:16;*
serve their gods *13:8; 19:13, 21; 25:12*
thine e. be evil against poor *De 15:9*
brother
if *thine* e. be single *M't 6:22; Lu 11:34*
beam that is in *thine* own e. *M't 7:3;*
Lu 6:41
if *thine* e. offend pluck it out *M't 18:9;*
M'k 9:47

RIGHT EYE

his *right* e., his *right* e. *Zec 11:17*
be utterly darkened
if thy *right* e. offend thee, *M't 5:29*
pluck it out

EYES

was good for food, pleasant *Ge 3:6*
to e.
the e. of them both were *Ge 3:7*
opened
her mistress was despised in *Ge 16:4*
her e.
she had conceived, I was *Ge 16:5*
despised in her e.
he is to thee a covering of *Ge 20:16*
the e.
God opened Hagar's e. she *Ge 21:19*
saw a well
Jacob laid the rods before the *Ge 30:41*
e. of the cattle
his master's wife cast her e. *Ge 39:7*
on Joseph
was good in the e. of Pharaoh *Ge 41:37*
now the e. of Israel were dim *Ge 48:10*
for age
to be abhorred in e. of *Ex 5:21*
Pharaoh
glory of Lord was like fire in e. *Ex 24:17*
of Israel
thing be hid from e. of the *Le 4:13*
assembly
the burning ague shall *Le 26:16*
consume the e.
be hid from the e. of her *Nu 5:13*
husband
thou mayest be to us instead *Nu 10:31*
of e.
wilt thou put out the e. of *Nu 16:14*
these men
to sanctify me in the e. of *Nu 20:12*
Israel

then the Lord opened the e. *Nu 22:31*
of Balaam
the man whose e. are open *Nu 24:3;*
hath said *24:1*
a gift doth blind the e. of the *De 16:19*
wise
the Lord shall give thee *De 28:65*
failing of e.
the Lord hath not given you e. *De 29:4*
to see
that I may be avenged for my *J'g 16:28*
e.
uncovered himself in e. of *2Sa 6:20*
handmaids
that the e. of my lord king may *2Sa 24:3*
see it
the e. of all Israel are upon *1Ki 1:20*
thee
Lord opened e. of young man *2Ki 6:17*
Elisha said, Lord, open e. of *2Ki 6:20*
these men
put out e. of Zedekiah *2Ki 25:7;*
Jer 39:7; 52:11
was right in e. of all the *1Ch 13:4*
people
hast thou e. of flesh? or seest *Job 10:4*
as man
but the e. of the wicked shall *Job 11:20*
fail
even the e. of his children *Job 17:5*
shall fail
seeing it is hid from the e. *Job 28:21*
of all living
I was e. to the blind, and feet *Job 29:15*
to the lame
or have caused the e. of the *Job 31:16*
window to fail
seeketh prey, and her e. *Job 39:29*
behold afar off
in whose e. vile person *Ps 15:4*
contemned
commandment is pure, *Ps 19:8*
enlightening e.
e. have they, but they see not *Ps 115:5;*
135:16
as the e. of servants, the e. *Ps 123:2*
of a maiden
e. of all wait upon thee *Ps 145:15*
Lord openeth e. of the *Ps 146:8*
blind
as smoke to e., so is the *Pr 10:26*
sluggard
light of the e. rejoiceth the *Pr 15:30*
heart
gift is as precious stone in e. *Pr 17:8*
of him
e. of a fool are in the ends *Pr 17:24*
of earth
who hath wounds? who hath *Pr 23:29*
redness of e.
so the e. of man are never *Pr 27:20*
satisfied
the wise man's e. are in his *Ec 2:14*
head
better sight of e. than wandering *Ec 6:9*
desire
it is pleasant for e. to behold *Ec 11:7*
sun
thou art fair, thou hast dove's *Ca 1:15;*
e. *4:1*
against Lord, to provoke e. *Isa 3:8*
of glory
daughters of Zion walk with *Isa 3:16*
wanton e.
the e. of the lofty shall be *Isa 5:15*
humbled
e. of blind shall see out of *Isa 29:18*
obscurity
the e. of them that see shall *Isa 32:3*
not be dim
then the e. of the blind shall *Isa 35:5*
be opened
to open blind e., to bring out *Isa 42:7*
prisoners
bring forth blind people that *Isa 43:8*
have e.
Lord made bare His arm in e. *Isa 52:10*
of all nations
like blind we grope as if we *Isa 59:10*
had no e.
which have e. and see not *Jer 5:21;*
Eze 12:2
their rings were full of e. *Eze 1:18*
wheels were full of e. round *Eze 10:12*
about
as soon as she saw them with *Eze 23:16*
her e.
I will be known in e. of many *Eze 38:23*
nations
in this horn were e. like a *Dan 7:8*
of man

even of that horn that had *Dan 7:20*
e. and a mouth
art of purer e. than to behold *Hab 1:13*
evil
upon one stone shall be seven e. *Zec 3:9*
if it be marvellous in e. of *Zec 8:6*
remnant
when e. of man shall be towards *Zec 9:1*
Lord
better to enter with one eye *M't 18:9;*
rather than having two e. to be *M'k 9:47*
cast into hell fire
having e. see ye not? and *M'k 8:18*
ears, hear not
the e. of all were fastened on *Lu 4:20*
him
blessed are the e. which see the *Lu 10:23*
things
he anointed the e. of the blind *Joh 9:6*
man
that any opened e. of one born *Joh 9:32*
can a devil open the e. of the *Joh 10:21*
blind
could not this man, which *Joh 11:37*
opened e.
Dorcas opened her e. and sat *Ac 9:40*
up
given them e. they should *Ro 11:8*
not see
before whose e. Christ been set *Ga 3:1*
crucified
e. of your understanding *Eph 1:18*
enlightened
but all things are naked and *Heb 4:13*
open to e. of him with whom
having e. full of adultery *2Pe 2:14*
the lust of the e. and pride of *1Jo 2:16*
life
shuts e. and heart (P) *1Jo 3:17*
in midst of throne four beasts *Re 4:6*
full of e.
each six wings, and full of e. *Re 4:8*
within
Lamb, as it had been slain, *Re 5:6*
having seven e.

EYES OF THE LORD

Noah found grace in e. *of the Ge 6:8*
Lord
e. *of the Lord* are always on it *De 11:12*
to do what is right in e. *of the De 13:18*
Lord
my life much set by in e. of *1Sa 26:24*
the Lord
if I find favour in the e. of *2Sa 15:25*
the Lord
David did right in e. *of the 1Ki 15:5;*
Lord *1Ki 15:11; 22:43; 2Ch 14:2*
e. *of the Lord* run to and *2Ch 16:9;*
fro through whole earth *Zec 4:10*
e. *of the Lord* are upon *Ps 34:15;*
righteous, his ears are open *1Pe 3:12*
ways of man are before e. of *Pr 5:21*
the Lord
e. *of the Lord* are in every *Pr 15:3*
place
e. *of the Lord* preserve *Pr 22:12*
knowledge
shall I be glorious in e. of the *Isa 49:5*
Lord
e. *of the Lord* are on the sinful *Am 9:8*
kingdom

HIS EYES

Isaac was old, and *his* e. were *Ge 27:1*
dim
his e. shall be red with wine, *Ge 49:12*
teeth white
into a trance, having *his* e. *Nu 24:4;*
open *24:16*
that if she find no favour in *his De 24:1*
e.
Philistines took him and put *J'g 16:21*
out *his* e.
Eli, *his* e. began to wax dim *1Sa 3:2;*
4:15
he tasted, and *his* e. were *1Sa 14:27*
enlightened
Ahijah could not see, for *his 1Ki 14:4*
e. were set
lay on child, put *his* e. on *his 2Ki 4:34*
e.
child sneezed seven times, *2Ki 4:35*
opened *his* e.
I pray thee, open *his* e. that *2Ki 6:17*
he may see

slew sons of Zedekiah before *2Ki 25:7;*
his e. put out eyes of   *Jer 39:6; 52:10*
Zedekiah
let king do what is good in   *1Ch 21:23*
his e.
if things seem right, and   *Es 8:5*
pleasing in *his e.*
mine enemy sharpeneth *his e.*   *Job 16:9*
on me
his e. shall see his   *Job 21:20*
destruction, and drink
he resteth, yet *his e.* are on   *Job 24:23*
their ways
the rich man openeth *his e.*   *Job 27:19*
and he is not
his e. are on the ways of man, *Job 34:21*
and he seeth
he withdraweth not *his e.*   *Job 36:7*
from the righteous
he taketh it with *his e.:* his *Job 40:24*
nose pierceth
his e. are like eyelids of   *Job 41:18*
morning
his e. are privily set against *Ps 10:8*
poor
his e. behold the children of *Ps 11:4*
men
there is no fear of God before *Ps 36:1*
his e.
ruleth by power, *his e.* behold *Ps 66:7*
nations
he winketh with *his e.* he   *Pr 6:13*
speaketh
shutteth *his e.* to devise   *Pr 16:30*
froward things
king scattereth away evil with *Pr 20:8*
his e.
neighbour findeth no favour in *Pr 21:10*
his e.
that hideth *his e.* shall have *Pr 28:27*
many curse
day nor night sleepeth with *his Ec 8:16*
e.
his e. are as the eyes of doves *Ca 5:12*
I was in *his e.* as one that found *Ca 8:10*
favour
shall not judge after sight of *Isa 11:3*
his e.
his e. shall have respect to holy *Isa 17:7*
One
shutteth *his e.* to devise   *Pr 16:30*
evil
his e. shall behold *his e.*   *Jer 32:4*
that he see not ground with *Eze 12:12*
his e.
cast ye away the abomination *Eze 20:7*
of *his e.*
had notable horn between *his Da 8:5;*
e.   *8:21*
his e. were as lamps of fire   *Da 10:6*
when He had spit on *his e.*   *M'k 8:23*
put hands
after He put His hands again *M'k 8:25*
on *his e.*
Jesus made clay, and opened *Joh 9:14*
his e.
who hath opened *his e.* we *Joh 9:21*
know not
Peter fastening *his e.* upon him, *Ac 3:4*
said
when *his e.* were opened he saw *Ac 9:8*
no man
there fell from *his e.* as it had *Ac 9:18*
been scales
then Saul set *his e.* on him, and *Ac 13:9*
said
because darkness hath blinded *1Jo 2:11*
his e.
his e. were as flame of fire   *Re 1:14;*
                                2:18; 19:12

LIFT, LIFTED UP EYES

Lot *lifted up e.* and beheld *Ge 13:10*
Jordan
lift up now thine *e.* and look *Ge 13:14;*
31:12; De 3:27; 2Ki 19:22; Isa 49:18;
          60:4; Jer 3:2; Eze 8:5; Zec 5:5
lift up his *e.* Ge *18:2; 22:4, 13; 24:63-*
           64; 31:10; 33:1; 43:29
lift up their *e.*   *Ex 14:10*
marched
Balaam *lift up* his *e.* and saw *Nu 24:2*
Israel
lest thou *lift up* thine *e.* unto *De 4:19*
heaven
Joshua *lifted up* his *e.* and *Jos 5:13*
looked
old man *lift up e.* and saw man *J'g 19:17*

lifted up their *e.* and saw   *1Sa 6:13*
the ark
the watchman *lift up* his *e.* *2Sa 13:34;*
                            18:24
David *lift up* his *e.* and saw *1Ch 21:16*
angel
lift up their *e.* and knew him *Job 2:12*
not
I will *lift up* mine *e.*   *Ps 121:1*
to hills
to thee *lift* I *up* mine *e.*   *Ps 123:1*
against whom hast thou *lifted Isa 37:23*
up e.
lift up your *e.*   *Isa 51:6;*
            Eze 33:25; Joh 4:35
nor hath *lift up* his *e.* to idols *Eze 18:6;*
                           18:15
hath spoiled, hath *lift up e.* *Eze 18:12*
to idols
thou shalt not *lift up* thine *e.* *Eze 23:27*
I Nebuchadnezzar *lift up* mine *Da 4:34*
e.
I *lifted up* mine *e.* and saw   *Da 8:3;*
   10:5; Zec 1:18; 2:1; 5:1, 5, 9; 6:1
had *lift up* their *e.* they saw *M't 17:8*
no man
Jesus lifted up his *e.*   *Lu 6:20;*
       Joh 6:5; 11:41; 17:1
in hell he *lift up e.* being in *Lu 16:23*
torments
would not *lift up* so much as *Lu 18:13*
e. to heaven

MINE EYES

my sleep departed from *mine Ge 31:40*
e.
bring him, that I may set *mine Ge 44:21*
e. upon
received any bribe to blind *1Sa 12:3*
mine e.
see how *mine e.* have been *1Sa 14:29*
enlightened
thy life much set by this day *1Sa 26:24*
in *mine e.*
hath given one to sit, *mine e.* *1Ki 1:48*
seeing it
hallowed this house, *mine e.* *1Ki 9:3;*
and mine heart shall be there *2Ch 7:16*
perpetually
until *mine e.* had seen it   *1Ki 10:7;*
                         2Ch 9:6
not walked in My ways, to do *1Ki 11:33;*
right in *mine e.*   *14:8; 2Ki 10:30*
now *mine e.* shall be open   *2Ch 7:15*
because it hid not sorrow from *Job 3:10*
mine e.
it stood still, an image was *Job 4:16*
before *mine e.*
mine e. shall behold, and not *Job 19:27*
another
made covenant with *mine e.* *Job 31:1*
why then
and mine heart walked after *Job 31:7*
mine e.
lighten *mine e.* lest I sleep sleep *Ps 13:3*
of death
mine e. are ever toward the *Ps 25:15*
Lord
for thy loving-kindness is   *Ps 26:3*
before *mine e.*
as for light of *mine e.* it is *Ps 38:10*
gone from me
mine e. fail, whilst I wait for *Ps 69:3*
my God
holdest *mine e.* waking, I am *Ps 77:4*
troubled
I will set no evil thing before *Ps 101:3*
mine e.
mine e. shall be on the faithful *Ps 101:6*
of the land
thou hast delivered *mine e.* *Ps 116:8*
from tears
open *mine e.;* turn away   *Ps 119:18;*
mine e.   *119:37*
mine e. fail for thy word,   *Ps 119:82*
saying, Comfort me
mine e. fail for thy   *Ps 119:123*
salvation, and for the word
rivers of waters run down *Ps 119:136*
mine e.
mine e. prevent the   *Ps 119:148*
night watches
heart is not haughty, nor *mine Ps 131:1*
e. lofty
I will not give sleep to *mine e.* *Ps 132:4*
but *mine e.* are unto thee, O *Ps 141:8*
God
whatsoever *mine e.* desired, I *Ec 2:10*
kept not

I will hide *mine e.* from you *Isa 1:15*
put away evil doings from *Isa 1:16*
mine e.
mine e. have seen King, Lord *Isa 6:5*
of hosts
mine e. fail with looking *Isa 38:14*
upward
but did evil before *mine e.* *Isa 65:12;*
                             66:4
and because they are hid *Isa 65:16*
from *mine e.*
O that *mine e.* were a fountain *Jer 9:1*
of tears
mine e. shall weep sore, and *Jer 13:17*
run down
let *mine e.* run down with *Jer 14:17*
tears
mine e. are on their ways *Jer 16:17*
their iniquity hid from *mine e.*
I will set *mine e.* upon them *Jer 24:6*
for good
mine e. do fail with tears   *La 2:11*
repentance be hid from *mine Ho 13:14*
e.
I will set *mine e.* on them for *Am 9:4*
evil
mine e. behold her, be   *Mic 7:10*
trodden down
should it also be marvellous in *Zec 8:6*
mine e.
for now have I seen with *mine Zec 9:8*
e.
I will open *mine e.* on house *Zec 12:4*
of Judah
for *mine e.* have seen thy   *Lu 2:30*
salvation
Jesus made clay, anointed *Joh 9:11;*
mine e.   *9:15*
whence he is, yet he hath *Joh 9:30*
opened *mine e.*
on which when I had fastened *Ac 11:6*
mine e.

OUR EYES

nothing but this manna before *Nu 11:6*
our e.
the Lord shewed signs before *De 6:22*
our e.
not shed this blood, nor have *De 21:7*
our e. seen it
O God, *our e.* are upon thee *2Ch 20:12*
that our God may lighten *our e.* *Ezr 9:8*
doing, it is marvellous   *Ps 118:23;*
in *our e.*   *M't 21:42; M'k 12:11*
so *our e.* wait upon the Lord *Ps 123:2*
our God
that *our e.* may run down with *Jer 9:18*
tears
our e. as yet failed for our vain *La 4:17*
help
heart faint, for these things *our La 5:17*
e. dim
is not the meat cut off before *Joe 1:16*
our e.
Lord, that *our e.* may be   *M't 20:33*
opened
that which we have seen with *1Jo 1:1*
our e.

OWN EYES

that ye seek not after your *Nu 15:39*
own e.
every man whatsoever is right *De 12:8;*
in his *own e.*   *J'g 17:6; 21:25*
enemies cast down in their *Ne 6:16*
own e.
because he was righteous in *Job 32:1*
his *own e.*
he flattereth himself in his *own Ps 36:2*
e.
be not wise in thine *own e.* fear *Pr 3:7*
God
way of a fool is right in his *Pr 12:15*
own e.
all ways of man are clean in *Pr 16:2*
own e.
every way of man is right in his *Pr 21:2*
own e.
generation that are pure in *Pr 30:12*
own e.
woe to them that are wise in *Isa 5:21*
own e.
ye would have plucked out *Ga 4:15*
own e.

RIGHT EYES

that I may thrust out all your 1Sa 11:2
right e.

THEIR EYES

took and bound Simeon Ge 42:24
before their e.
abomination of Egyptians Ex 8:26
before their e.
do any ways hide their e. from Le 20:4
man
speak to the rock before their Nu 20:8
e.
to sanctify me at water before Nu 27:14
their e.
Lord opened their e. and they 2Ki 6:20
saw
foundation was laid before Ezr 3:12
their e.
despise their husbands in their Es 1:17
e.
and their offspring before Job 21:8
their e.
they have set their e. bowing Ps 17:11
down
let their e. be darkened, that Ps 69:23
they see not
their e. stand out with fatness, Ps 73:7
have more
the Lord lighteneth both their Pr 29:13
e.
a generation, O how lofty are Pr 30:13
their e.
saving beholding them with Ec 5:11
their e.
make ears heavy, shut their e. Isa 6:10;
lest they see with their e. M't 13:15;
  Ac 28:27
children be dashed to pieces Isa 13:16
before their e.
for he hath shut their e. they Isa 44:18
cannot see
their e. did fail, because no Jer 14:6
grass
and with their e. which go a Eze 6:9
whoring
not cast away abominations Eze 20:8
of their e.
their e. were after their Eze 20:24
father's idols
with bitterness sigh before Eze 21:6
their e.
have hid their e. from my Eze 22:26
sabbaths
when I take from them desire Eze 24:25
of their e.
I shall be sanctified in you Eze 36:23
before their e.
sticks shall be in thy hand Eze 37:20
before their e.
sanctified in thee, O Gog, Eze 38:16
before their e.
and their e. shall consume Zec 14:12
away
then touched he their e. saying M't 9:29
their e. were opened, Jesus M't 9:30
charged them
their e. they have closed, lest M't 13:15
at any time
Jesus touched their e., M't 20:34
their e. received sight
for their e. were heavy M't 26:43;
  M'k 14:40
but their e. were holden, that Lu 24:16
they
their e. were opened, and they Lu 24:31
knew him
he hath blinded their e. and Joh 12:40
hardened
to open their e. and to turn Ac 26:18
them
there is no fear of God before Ro 3:18
their e.
let their e. be darkened, that Ro 11:10
they see not
God shall wipe away all Re 7:17;
tears from their e. 21:4

THINE EYES

if I have found favour in Ge 30:27
thine e. tarry
Joseph shall put his hand on Ge 46:4
thine e.
wherefore shall we die before Ge 47:19
thine e.
for a memorial between thine Ex 13:9
e.

for frontlets between thine e. Ex 13:16;
  De 6:8
thine e. have seen all that the De 3:21
Lord
lift up thine e., behold it De 3:27
with thine e.
forget the things which thine e. De 4:9
have seen
great temptations thine e. saw De 7:19;
  29:3
terrible things which thine e. De 10:21
have seen
thine ox shall be slain before De 28:31
thine e.
thine e. shall look, and fail De 28:32
with longing
shalt be mad for sight of De 28:34;
thine e. 28:67
caused thee to see it with De 34:4
thine e.
let thine e. be on field they reap Ru 2:9
why have I found grace in Ru 2:10
thine e.
shall be to consume thine e. 1Sa 2:33
I have found grace in thine e. 1Sa 20:3
now if I have found favour in 1Sa 20:29
thine e.
thine e. have seen how Lord 1Sa 24:10
delivered
let the young men find favour 1Sa 25:8
in thine e.
my soul was precious in thine 1Sa 26:21
e. this day
if I have found grace in thine 1Sa 27:5
e. give me
I will take thy wives before 2Sa 12:11
thine e.
do therefore what is good in 2Sa 19:27
thine e.
thine e. are upon haughty to 2Sa 22:28
bring down
thine e. be open toward this 1Ki 8:29;
house night and day 8:52; 2Ch 6:20, 40
whatsoever is pleasant in 1Ki 20:6
thine e.
thou shalt see it with thine e. 2Ki 7:2
open, Lord, thine e. and see 2Ki 19:16;
  Isa 37:17
thine e. shall not see all evil 2Ki 22:20
this was a small thing in 1Ch 17:17
thine e.
nor shall thine e. see all evil 2Ch 34:28
let ear be attentive, thine e. Ne 1:6
open
thine e. are upon me, and I am Job 7:8
not
my doctrine is pure, I am Job 11:4
clean in thine e.
dost thou open thine e. upon Job 14:3
such an one
and what do thine e. wink at Job 15:12
I said, I am cut off from Ps 31:22
before thine e.
and set them in order before Ps 50:21
thine e.
only with thine e. shalt thou see Ps 91:8
thine e. did see my substance Ps 139:16
unperfect
let them not depart from thine Pr 3:21;
e. 4:21
let thine e. look right on, and Pr 4:25
eyelids
give not sleep to thine e. nor Pr 6:4
slumber to
open thine e. and thou shalt Pr 20:13
be satisfied
wilt set thine e. on that which Pr 23:5
is not
give me heart, let thine e. Pr 23:26
observe my ways
thine e. shall behold strange Pr 23:33
women
of the prince whom thine e. Pr 25:7
have seen
O young man, walk in sight of Ec 11:9
thine e.
hast ravished my heart with Ca 4:9
thine e.
turn away thine e. from me, Ca 6:5
they overcome
thine e. like the fishpools in Ca 7:4
Heshbon
but thine e. shall see thy Isa 30:20
teachers
thine e. shall see king in his Isa 33:17
beauty
thine e. see Jerusalem a quiet Isa 33:20
habitation

O Lord, are not thine e. Jer 5:3
upon the truth
fall by sword, thine e. shall Jer 20:4
behold it
thine e. are not but for thy Jer 22:17
covetousness
refrain weeping, and thine e. Jer 31:16
from tears
thine e. are open on all ways Jer 32:19
of men
thine e. shall behold king of Jer 34:3
Babylon
we are but few, as thine e. do Jer 42:2
behold
let not apple of thine e. cease La 2:18
for whom thou paintedst Eze 23:40
I take from thee the desire of Eze 24:16
thine e.
son of man, behold with Eze 40:4;
thine e. 44:5
open thine e. and behold our Da 9:18
but now they are hid from Lu 19:42
thine e.
how were thine e. opened Joh 9:10
sayest thou that He hath Joh 9:17
opened thine e.
anoint thine e. with eye-salve Re 3:18

YOUR EYES

in day ye eat your e. be opened Ge 3:5
do ye to them as is good in Ge 19:8
your e.
let me find grace in your e. Ge 34:11
your e. and eyes of my Ge 34:12
brother Benjamin
if now I have found grace in Ge 50:4
your e.
those which ye let remain Nu 33:55;
shall be pricks in your e. Jos 23:13
that he did before your e. De 1:30;
  4:34; 29:2
your e. have seen what Lord De 4:3;
did because of 11:7; Jos 24:7
I brake the two tables before De 9:17
your e.
they may be as frontlets De 11:18
between your e.
not make any baldness De 14:1
between your e.
what Lord will do before 1Sa 12:16
your e.
to hissing, as ye see with your 2Ch 29:8
e.
for the Lord hath closed your Isa 29:10
e.
lift up your e. on high Isa 40:26;
  Jer 13:20
this house den of robbers in Jer 7:11
your e.
cause to cease out of this place Jer 16:9
in your e.
he shall slay them before your Jer 29:21
e.
the desire of your e. and Eze 24:21
what you pity
when I turn your captivity Zep 3:20
before your e.
in your e. in comparison is Hag 2:3
nothing
your e. shall see, the Lord will Mal 1:5
be magnified
but blessed are your e. for M't 13:16
they see

EYE'S

let him go for his e. sake Ex 21:26

EZAR

and Dishon, and E. and 1Ch 1:38
Dishan

EZBAI

Carmelite, Naarai the son of 1Ch 11:37
E.

EZBON

Haggi, Shuni, and E. Eri Ge 46:16
the sons of Bela; E. and Uzzi 1Ch 7:7

EZEKIAS

Achaz; and Achaz begat E. M't 1:9
And E. begat Manasses; and M't 1:10

EZEKIEL

the Lord came expressly unto E.   *Eze 1:3*

Thus E. is unto you a sign   *Eze 24:24*

EZEL

and shalt remain by the stone E.   *1Sa 20:19*

EZEM

Bilhah, and at E. and at Tolad   *1Ch 4:29*

EZER

And Dishon, and E. and Dishan   *Ge 36:21*

The children of E. are these; Bilhan   *Ge 36:27*

Dishon, duke E. duke Dishan   *Ge 36:30*

The sons of E.; Bilhan, and Zavan   *1Ch 1:42*

and E. the father of Hushah   *1Ch 4:4*

and E. and Elead, whom the men   *1Ch 7:21*

E. the first, Obadiah the second   *1Ch 12:9*

next to him repaired E. the son   *Ne 3:19*

and Malchijah, and Elam, and E.   *Ne 12:42*

EZION-GABER

Ebronah, and encamped at E.   *Nu 33:35*

And they removed from E.   *Nu 33:36*

from E we turned and passed   *De 2:8*

and they made the ships in E.   *2Ch 20:36*

EZION-GEBER

made a navy of ships in E.   *1Ki 9:26*

for the ships were broken at E.   *1Ki 22:48*

went Solomon to E. and to Eloth   *2Ch 8:17*

EZNITE

the same was Adino the E.: he   *2Sa 23:8*

EZRA

of E. were, Jether, and Mered   *1Ch 4:17*

E. the son of Seraiah, the son   *Ezr 7:1*

This E. went up from Babylon   *Ezr 7:6*

E. had prepared his heart to seek   *Ezr 7:10*

Artaxerxes gave unto E. the priest   *Ezr 7:11; 7:12, 21; 10:10, 16; Ne 8:2, 9*

E. after the wisdom of thy God   *Ezr 7:25*

Now when E. had prayed, and said unto E. We have trespassed   *Ezr 10:1 Ezr 10:2*

Then arose E. and made the chief   *Ezr 10:5; 10:6*

and they spake unto E. the scribe   *Ne 8:1; 8:4, 13; 12:36*

E. opened the book in the sight of   *Ne 8:5*

E. blessed the Lord, the great God   *Ne 8:6*

Seraiah, Jeremiah, E.   *Ne 12:1*

Of E., Meshullam; of Amariah   *Ne 12:13*

and of E. the priest, the scribe   *Ne 12:26*

And Azariah, E., Meshullam   *Ne 12:33*

EZRAHITE

than Ethan the E. and Heman   *1Ki 4:31*

Maschil of Heman the E.   *Ps 88 title*

Maschil of Ethan the E.   *Ps 89 title*

EZRI

ground was E. the son of Chelub   *1Ch 27:26*

F

FABLES

nor give heed to f. and genealogies   *1Ti 1:4*

legends and endless genealogies (A)   *1Ti 1:4*

invented stories, interminable genealogies (B)   *1Ti 1:4*

erroneous doctrines, interminable myths (N)   *1Ti 1:4*

new doctrines, hoary old myths (P)(R)   *1Ti 1:4*

but refuse profane and old wives' f.   *1Ti 4:7*

avoid irreverent legends, profane and impure godless fictions, grandmothers' tales, and silly myths (A)   *1Ti 4:7*

unholy and old-womanish tales (B)   *1Ti 4:7*

godless myths, fit only for old women (N)   *1Ti 4:7*

all these godless fictions (P)   *1Ti 4:7*

nothing to do with godless, silly myths (R)   *1Ti 4:7*

and they shall be turned unto f.   *2Ti 4:4*

myths and man-made fictions (A)(B)(P)(R)   *2Ti 4:4*

turn to mythology (N)   *2Ti 4:4*

not giving heed to Jewish f. and commandments   *Tit 1:14*

Jewish myths (N)(R)   *Tit 1:14*

Jewish fairy tales (P)   *Tit 1:14*

have not followed cunningly devised f.   *2Pe 1:16*

cleverly devised stories (A)   *2Pe 1:16*

tales artfully spun (N)   *2Pe 1:16*

a cleverly written-up story (P)   *2Pe 1:16*

cleverly devised myths (R)   *2Pe 1:16*

FABRICATION

f. of own heart (B)   *Ne 6:8*

made it a f. (B)   *Jer 8:8*

with sheer f. (N)   *2Pe 2:3*

FACE

in the sweat of thy f. shalt thou eat bread   *Ge 3:19*

sweat of your brow (B)   *Ge 3:19*

I flee from the f. of my mistress Sarai   *Ge 16:8*

and I put the earrings upon her f.   *Ge 24:47*

when thou fleddest from f. of Esau   *Ge 35:1; 35:7*

Esau went from f. of his brother Jacob   *Ge 36:6*

he sent to Joseph to direct his f. to Goshen   *Ge 46:28*

Joseph bowed with his f. to the earth   *Ge 48:12*

Moses fled from the f. of Pharaoh   *Ex 2:15*

said, Let us flee from the f. of Israel   *Ex 14:25*

skin of his f. shone   *Ex 34:29; 34:30, 35*

till he had done speaking, he put a veil on his f.   *Ex 34:33*

that hath his hair fallen towards his f.   *Le 13:41*

thou shalt honour the f. of the old man   *Le 19:32*

if her father had but spit in her f.   *Nu 12:14*

one shall slay the red heifer before his f.   *Nu 19:3*

ye shall not be afraid of f. of man   *De 1:17*

repayeth them that hate him to their f.   *De 7:10*

nations the Lord destroyeth before your f.   *De 8:20*

cause wicked man be beaten before his f.   *De 25:2*

loose his shoe, and spit in his f. and say   *De 25:9*

thine ass shall be taken before thy f.   *De 28:31*

Lord shall give them up before your f.   *De 31:5*

wherefore liest thou upon thy f.   *Jos 7:10*

f. like the angel of God (A)   *J'g 13:6*

f. showed no more sadness (B)   *1Sa 1:18*

behold, Dagon was fallen on his f.   *1Sa 5:3*

David stooped with his f. to the earth   *1Sa 24:8*

Abigail bowed on her f. and said   *1Sa 25:41*

Saul stooped with his f. to the ground   *1Sa 28:14*

how should I hold up my f. to Joab   *2Sa 2:22*

Absalom bowed on his f. to ground   *2Sa 14:33*

Araunah went out and bowed himself before king on his f.   *2Sa 24:20; 1Ch 21:21*

Nathan bowed himself with his f.   *1Ki 1:23*

Bath-sheba bowed with her f. to earth   *1Ki 1:31*

king turned his f. about   *1Ki 8:14; 2Ch 6:3*

Elijah put his f. between his knees   *1Ki 18:42*

that he wrapped his f. in his mantle   *1Ki 19:13*

prophet disguised with ashes on his f.   *1Ki 20:38*

Ahab turned away f. and would not eat   *1Ki 21:4*

lay my staff upon f. of child   *2Ki 4:29*

Gehazi laid his staff on f. of child   *2Ki 4:31*

Hazael spread it on his f. so that he died   *2Ki 8:15*

Jezebel painted her f. and tired her head   *2Ki 9:30*

Jehu lift up his f. to window, and said   *2Ki 9:32*

Joash wept over his f. said, O my father   *2Ki 13:14*

how wilt thou turn away f. of one   *2Ki 18:24; Isa 36:9*

Hezekiah turned his f. to wall   *2Ki 20:2; Isa 38:2*

O Lord God, turn not away the f. of thine anointed   *2Ch 6:42; Ps 132:10*

Lord will not turn away f. from you   *2Ch 30:9*

returned with shame of f. to own land   *2Ch 30:21*

Josiah would not turn his f. from him   *2Ch 35:22*

I blush to lift up f. to thee, my God   *Ezr 9:6*

to confusion of f. as it is this day   *Ezr 9:7; 9:8*

he will curse thee to thy f.   *Job 1:11; 2:5*

then a spirit passed before my f.   *Job 4:15*

then thou lift up thy f. without spot   *Job 11:15*

my leanness beareth witness to my f.   *Job 16:8*

f. is foul with weeping, on my eyelids   *Job 16:16*

who shall declare his way to his f.   *Job 21:31*

and thou shalt lift up thy f. unto God   *Job 22:26*

no eye shall see me; and disguiseth his f.   *Job 24:15*

he holdeth back the f. of his throne   *Job 26:9*

and they spare not to spit in my f.   *Job 30:10*

who can discover the f. of his garment   *Job 41:13*

who can open the doors of his f.   *Job 41:14*

make thy way straight before my f.   *Ps 5:8*

I will behold thy f. in righteousness   *Ps 17:15*

make ready arrows against f. of them   *Ps 21:12*

thou settest me before thy f. for ever   *Ps 41:12*

and look upon the f. of thine anointed   *Ps 84:9*

mercy and truth shall go before thy f.   *Ps 89:14*

I will beat down his foes before his f.   *Ps 89:23*

and with an impudent f. said unto him   *Pr 7:13*

a wicked man hardeneth his f.   *Pr 21:29*

boldness of his f. shall be changed   *Ec 8:1*

be a covert from the f. of the spoiler   *Isa 16:4*

he will destroy the f. of the covering   *Isa 25:7*

when he hath made plain f. thereof   *Isa 28:25*

neither shall his f. now wax pale   *Isa 29:22*

shall bow down to thee with their f.   *Isa 49:23*

that provoketh me continually *Isa 65:3*
to my *f.*
let me see your *f.* (A)(B)(R)　*Ca 2:14*
turned their back, and not the　*Jer 2:27;*
f.　　　　　　　　　　　　　*32:33*
though thou rentest thy *f.* with　*Jer 4:30*
painting
will I discover thy skirts　*Jer 13:26;*
upon thy *f.*　　　　　　　　*Na 3:5*
I will shew them back, and　*Jer 18:17*
not the *f.*
from hand of them whose *f.*　*Jer 22:25*
thou fearest
I should remove it from　*Jer 32:31*
before my *f.*
the right of man before *f.* of　*La 3:35*
most High
they four had *f.* of a man, *f.*　*Eze 1:10*
of a lion, *f.* of an ox, *f.* of eagle
I made thy *f.* strong against　*Eze 3:8*
their faces
my *f.* will I turn also from　*Eze 7:22*
them
f. of a man, *f.* of a lion, *f.* of *Eze 10:14;*
an eagle　　　　　　　　　　*41:19*
put stumblingblock before　*Eze 14:3*
their *f.*
that my fury shall come up in *Eze 38:18*
my *f.*
I was in a deep sleep on my *f.*　*Da 8:18;*
　　　　　　　　　　　　　　10:9
his *f.* as the appearance of　*Da 10:6*
lightning
he shall turn his *f.* unto the　*Da 11:18*
isles
pride of Israel testifieth to　*Ho 5:5;*
his *f.*　　　　　　　　　　　*7:10*
now their own doings, they are *Ho 7:2*
before my *f.*
before their *f.* people be much *Joe 2:6*
pained
will drive him with *f.* toward　*Joe 2:20*
east sea
that dasheth in pieces, come　*Na 2:1*
before thy *f.*
anoint thine head, and wash　*M't 6:17*
thy *f.*
I send my messenger before　*M't 11:10;*
thy *f.*　　　*M'k 1:2; Lu 7:27*
their angels behold *f.* of my　*M't 18:10*
Father
then did they spit in his *f.*　*M't 26:67*
and buffeted
thou hast prepared before *f.* of *Lu 2:31*
all people
he sent messengers before his *Lu 9:52;*
f.　　　　　　　　　　　　　*10:1*
His *f.* was as though He would *Lu 9:53*
go to Jerusalem
they struck him on the *f.* and　*Lu 22:64*
asked him
his *f.* was bound about with　*Joh 11:44*
a napkin
I foresaw the Lord always　*Ac 2:25*
before my *f.*
God drave out before *f.* of our *Ac 7:45*
fathers
so falling down on his *f.* will *1Co 14:25*
worship
could not stedfastly behold the *2Co 3:7*
f. of Moses
not as Moses, who put a veil *2Co 3:13*
over his *f.*
but we all with open *f.*　*2Co 3:18*
beholding the glory
the glory of God, in the *f.* of　*2Co 4:6*
Jesus Christ
suffer, if a man smite you on *2Co 11:20*
f.
I was unknown by *f.* to　*Ga 1:22*
churches
I withstood him to the *f.*　*Ga 2:11*
because he was
beholding his natural *f.* in a　*Jas 1:23*
glass
the third beast had a *f.* as a man *Re 4:7*
and his *f.* was as it were the sun *Re 10:1*
where nourished from *f.* of　*Re 12:14*
serpent
from whose *f.* earth and　*Re 20:11*
heaven fled

FACE *COVER, COVERED*

an harlot, because she　*Ge 38:15*
covered her *f.*
locusts shall *cover* the *f.* of the *Ex 10:5;*
earth　　　　　　　　　　　*10:15*
behold, they *cover* the *f.* of the *Nu 22:5*
earth

the king *covered* his *f.* and　*2Sa 19:4*
cried
word went out, they *covered*　*Es 7:8*
Haman's *f.*
he *covereth* his *f.* with his　*Job 15:27*
fatness
nor hath he *covered* darkness *Job 23:17*
from my *f.*
the shame of my *f.* hath　*Ps 44:15*
covered me
for thy sake shame hath　*Ps 69:7*
covered my *f.*
nettles had *covered* the *f.*　*Pr 24:31*
thereof
with twain he *covered* his *f.* and *Isa 6:2*
his feet
thou shalt *cover* thy *f.* that　*Eze 12:6*
thou see not
the prince shall *cover* his *f.*　*Eze 12:12*
that he see not
began to spit on him, and　*M'k 14:65*
cover his *f.*

FACE with *LOOK, LOOKED*

Come, let us *look* one another *2Ki 14:8;*
in the *f.*　　　　　*2Ch 25:17*
and they *looked* one another *2Ki 14:11*
in the *f.*

FACE *OF THE COUNTRY*

battle was scattered over *f.* of *2Sa 18:8*
the country

FACE *OF THE DEEP*

darkness was upon the *f.* of the *Ge 1:2*
deep
and the *f.* of the *deep* is　*Job 38:30*
frozen
he set a compass on the *f.* of　*Pr 8:27*
the depth

FACE *OF THE EARTH*

every herb upon the *f.* of the *Ge 1:29*
earth
thou hast driven me from the *f. Ge 4:14*
of the earth
men began to multiply on the *f. Ge 6:1*
of the earth
to keep seed alive on the *f.* of　*Ge 7:3*
all *the earth*
I will destroy from off the *f.* of *Ge 7:4;*
the earth　*De 6:15; 1Ki 13:34; Am 9:8*
the waters were on the *f.* of the *Ge 8:9*
whole *earth*
lest we be scattered on the *f.* of *Ge 11:4*
the earth
the famine was over all the *f.* *Ge 41:56*
of the earth
to consume them from *f.* of　*Ex 32:12*
the earth
from all people unto the *f.* of *Ex 33:16*
the earth
meek above all men on *f.* of the *Nu 12:3*
earth
above all people on the *f.* of the *De 7:6*
earth
cut off every one 'from *f.* of　*1Sa 20:15*
the earth
thou renewest the *f.* of the　*Ps 104:30*
earth
with all kingdoms on the *f.* of *Isa 23:17*
earth
be for dung on the *f.* of the　*Jer 8:2;*
earth　　　　　　　　　　　*16:4*
I will cast thee from the *f.* of *Jer 28:16*
the earth
all men on the *f.* of the earth *Eze 38:20*
shake
an he-goat came on the *f.* of the *Da 8:5*
earth
poureth them on the *f.* of the　*Am 5:8;*
earth　　　　　　　　　　　*9:6*
curse that goeth over the *f.* of *Zec 5:3*
earth
ye can discern the *f.* of the　*Lu 12:56*
earth
that dwell on the *f.* of the　*Lu 21:35*
whole *earth*
to dwell on all the *f.* of the　*Ac 17:26*
earth

FACE *OF THE FIELD*

Jezebel as dung on the *f.* of　*2Ki 9:37*
the field

FACE *OF THE GATE*

from the *f.* of the gate of the *Eze 40:15*
entrance

FACE *OF THE GROUND*

a mist watered the whole *f.* of *Ge 2:6*
the ground
destroyed, that was on the *f.* of *Ge 7:23*
the ground
were abated from off the *f.* of　*Ge 8:8*
the ground
and behold, the *f.* of the　*Ge 8:13*
ground was dry

FACE *OF THE HOUSE*

the breadth of the *f.* of the　*Eze 41:14*
house

FACE *OF THE LORD*

the cry great before the *f.* of　*Ge 19:13*
the Lord
let not my blood 'fall before *f. 1Sa 26:20*
of Lord
entreat now the *f.* of the Lord *1Ki 13:6*
the *f.* of the Lord is against *Ps 34:16;*
them that do evil　　　　*1Pe 3:12*
pour out thy heart before *f.* of *La 2:19*
the Lord
thou shalt go before the *f.* of *Lu 1:76*
the Lord

FACE *OF THE PORCH*

to the *f.* of the porch were　*Eze 40:15*
fifty cubits
were thick planks on the *f.* of *Eze 41:25*
the porch

FACE *OF THE SKY*

discern the *f.* of the sky　*M't 16:3;*
　　　　　　　　　　　　　Lu 12:56

FACE *OF THE WATERS*

Spirit of God moved on the *f.* of *Ge 1:2*
the waters
the ark went upon the *f.* of the *Ge 7:18*
waters

FACE *OF THE WILDERNESS*

on the *f.* of the wilderness lay *Ex 16:14*
manna

FACE *OF THE WORLD*

do what he commandeth on　*Job 37:12*
f. of the world
nor fill the *f.* of the world　*Isa 14:21*
with cities
Israel shall fill the *f.* of the　*Isa 27:6*
world with fruit

FACE with *SEE, SAW, SEEN*

and afterward I will *see* his *f. Ge 32:20*
for therefore I have *seen* thy *Ge 33:10*
f. as though
ye shall not *see* my *f.* except *Ge 43:3;*
　　　　　　　　　　43:5; 44:23
for we may not *see* the man's *Ge 44:26*
f. except
now let me die, since I have　*Ge 46:30*
seen thy *f.*
I had not thought to *see* thy *f. Ge 48:11*
and lo
Pharaoh said to him, *See* my *Ex 10:28*
f. no more
Moses said, I will *see* thy *f.*　*Ex 10:29*
again no more
and he said, Thou canst not　*Ex 33:20*
see my *f.*
see back parts, but my *f.* shall *Ex 33:23*
not be *seen*
children of Israel *saw* the *f.* of *Ex 34:35*
Moses
not *see* my *f.* except thou　*2Sa 3:13*
bring Michal
the king said, Let him not　*2Sa 14:24*
see my *f.*
Absalom dwelt two years and *2Sa 14:28*
saw not king's *f.*
now therefore let me *see*　*2Sa 14:32*
the king's *f.*

the seven princes who *saw* the   *Es 1:14*
king's *f.*
and he shall *see* his *f.* with   *Job 33:26*
joy
saw his *f.* as it had been face   *Ac 6:15*
of an angel
I know that ye shall *see* my *f.*   *Ac 20:25;*
no more   *20:38*
as many as have not *seen* my *f.*   *Col 2:1*
in the flesh
endeavoured to *see* your *f.*   *1Th 2:17*
with desire
praying, that we might *see*   *1Th 3:10'*
your *f.*
and they shall *see* his *f.* and his   *Re 22:4*
name

FACE *SHINE*

the Lord make his *f.* to *shine*   *Nu 6:25*
upon thee
make thy *f.* to *shine* on thy   *Ps 31:16;*
servant   *119:135*
God bless us, and cause his *f.*   *Ps 67:1*
to *shine* on us
cause thy *f. shine*, we shall be   *Ps 80:3;*
saved   *80:7, 19*
and oil to make his *f.* to   *Ps 104:15*
shine
a man's wisdom maketh his *f.* to   *Ec 8:1*
shine
cause thy *f.* to *shine* on thy   *Da 9:17'*
sanctuary
and his *f.* did *shine* as the sun   *M't 17:2*

FACE *TO* FACE

Peniel; for I have seen God *f.*   *Ge 32:30*
to f.
and the Lord spake to Moses *f.*   *Ex 33:11*
to f.
that thou, Lord, art seen *f. to*   *Nu 14:14*
f.
the Lord talked with you *f. to f.*   *De 5:4*
like Moses, whom the Lord   *De 34:10*
knew *f. to f.*
because I have seen an angel *f.*   *J'g 6:22*
to f.
as in water *f.* answereth *to f.*   *Pr 27:19*
there I will plead with you *f.*   *Eze 20:35*
to f.
before he have the accusers *f.*   *Ac 25:16*
to f.
we see thro' a glass, but then   *1Co 13:12*
f. to f.
I trust to come to you, and   *2Jo 12*
speak *f. to f.*
I trust to see thee and speak *f.*   *3Jo 14*
to f.

FELL *ON* FACE, FACES

Joseph *fell on* his father's *f.*   *Ge 50:1*
and wept
his brethren *fell down* before   *Ge 50:18*
his *f.*
when the people saw, they *fell*   *Le 9:24*
on their *f.*
Moses and Aaron *fell on f.*   *Nu 14:5;*
           16:4, 22, 45
Balaam *fell* flat *on* his *f.*   *Nu 22:31*
Joshua *fell on* his *f.* to the   *Jos 5:14;*
earth   *7:6*
Manoah and his wife *fell on*   *J'g 13:20*
their *f.*
then she *fell on* her *f.* to the   *Ru 2:10*
ground
Goliath *fell on* his *f.*   *1Sa 17:49*
David *fell on* his *f.*   *1Sa 20:41*
Abigail *fell on* her *f.*   *1Sa 25:23*
Mephibosheth *fell on* his *f.*   *2Sa 9:6*
the woman *fell on* her *f.*   *2Sa 14:4*
Joab *fell on* his *f.*   *2Sa 14:22*
Ahimaaz *fell on* his *f.*   *2Sa 18:28*
Obadiah *fell on* his *f.*   *1Ki 18:7*
the people *fell on* their *f.*   *1Ki 18:39*
David and elders *fell on* their   *1Ch 21:16*
f.
when I saw it I *fell upon* my   *Eze 1:28;*
f. 3:23; 9:8; 11:13; 43:3; 44:4; Da 8:17'
Nebuchadnezzar *fell upon* his   *Da 2:46*
f.
the disciples *fell on* their *f.*   *M't 17:6*
Jesus *fell on* his *f.*   *M't 26:39*
the leper *fell on* his *f.*   *Lu 5:12*
the Samaritan *fell on* his *f.*   *Lu 17:16*
the twenty four elders *fell on*   *Re 11:16*
their *f.*

HIDE, HIDETH, HID FACE

and from thy *f.* shall I be *hid*   *Ge 4:14*
and Moses *hid* his *f.* for he was   *Ex 3:6*
afraid
will *hide* my *f.* from them   *De 31:17;*
           31:18; 32:20
wherefore *hidest* thou *thy f.*   *Job 13:24;*
and   *Ps 44:24; 88:14*
when he *hideth* his *f.* who   *Job 34:29*
can behold
he *hideth* his *f.* he will never   *Ps 10:11*
see it
how long wilt thou *hide* thy *f.*   *Ps 13:1*
from me
neither hath he *hid* his *f.* from   *Ps 22:24*
him
hide not thy *f.*   *Ps 27:9;*
       69:17; 102:2; 143:7
didst *hide* thy *f.* and I was   *Ps 30:7;*
troubled   *104:29*
hide thy *f.* from my sins, and   *Ps 51:9*
blot out all
hideth his *f.* from the house of   *Isa 8:17*
Jacob
I *hid* not my *f.* from shame   *Isa 50:6*
and spitting
in a little wrath I *hid* my *f.*   *Isa 54:8*
from thee
your sins have *hid* his *f.* from   *Isa 59:2*
you
thou hast *hid* thy *f.* from us   *Isa 64:7*
and consumed
thy ways are not *hid* from my   *Jer 16:17*
f.
I have *hid* my *f.* from this city   *Jer 33:5*
therefore *hid* I my *f.* from   *Eze 39:23;*
them   *39:24*
nor will I *hide* my *f.* any   *Eze 39:29*
more from them
he will even *hide* his *f.* at that   *Mic 3:4*
time
hide us from the *f.* of him that   *Re 6:16*
sitteth

SEEK FACE

seek his *f.* continually   *1Ch 16:11;*
           Ps 105:4
if my people shall pray and   *2Ch 7:14*
seek my *f.*
a generation that *seek* thy *f.* O   *Ps 24:6*
Jacob
seek ye my *f.,* thy *f.* Lord   *Ps 27:8*
will I *seek*
I came diligently to *seek* thy *f.*   *Pr 7:15*
return to my place, till they   *Ho 5:15*
seek my *f.*

SET FACE

Jacob *set* his *f.* toward mount   *Ge 31:21*
Gilead
I will *set* my *f.* against that   *Le 17:10;*
soul   *20:6*
set my *f.* against that man   *Le 20:3;*
       20:5; Eze 14:8
I will *set* my *f.* against you   *Le 26:17;*
           Jer 44:11
Balaam *set* his *f.* toward   *Nu 24:1*
wilderness
Hazael *set* his *f.* to Jerusalem   *2Ki 12:17*
I have *set* my *f.* like a flint, not   *Isa 50:7*
be ashamed
I have *set* my *f.* against this   *Jer 21:10*
city
set thy *f.* against it, it shall be   *Eze 4:3*
besieged
thou shalt *set* thy *f.* towards the   *Eze 4:7*
siege at Jerusalem
set thy *f.* towards the   *Eze 6:2*
mountains of Israel
set thy *f.* against the   *Eze 13:17*
daughters of my people
and I will *set* my *f.* against   *Eze 15:7*
them
son of man, *set* thy *f.* toward   *Eze 20:46*
the south
son of man, *set* thy *f.* toward   *Eze 21:2*
Jerusalem
go thee whithersoever thy *f.*   *Eze 21:16*
is *set*
son of man, *set* thy *f.* against   *Eze 25:2*
the Ammonites
set f. against Zidon   *Eze 28:21*
set f. against Pharaoh   *Eze 29:2*
set f. against mount Seir   *Eze 35:2*
set f. against Gog   *Eze 38:2*
and I *set* my *f.* unto the Lord   *Da 9:3*
God

I *set* my *f.* toward ground and   *Da 10:15*
became dumb
he shall *set* his *f.* to enter   *Da 11:17*
with strength
he stedfastly *set* his *f.* to go to   *Lu 9:51*
Jerusalem

FACES

and their *f.* were backward   *Ge 9:23*
their *f.* from thence, and went   *Ge 18:22*
and set the *f.* of the flocks   *Ge 30:40*
with their *f.* to the earth   *Ge 42:6*
before their *f.* all these words   *Ex 19:7*
his fear may be before your *f.*   *Ex 20:20*
their *f.* shall look one to   *Ex 25:20*
another
shall the *f.* of the cherubims   *Ex 25:20*
be
with their *f.* one to another   *Ex 37:9*
were the *f.* of the cherubims   *Ex 37:9*
they shouted, and fell on their   *Le 9:24*
f.
Moses and Aaron fell on their   *Nu 14:5*
f.
they fell upon their *f.* and   *Nu 16:22*
said
And they fell upon their *f.*   *Nu 16:45*
they fell upon their *f.:* and the   *Nu 20:6*
and fell on their *f.* to the   *J'g 13:20*
ground
turned their *f.* and said unto   *J'g 18:23*
Micah
this day the *f.* of all thy   *2Sa 19:5*
servants
all Israel set their *f.* on me   *1Ki 2:15*
they fell on their *f.:* and they   *1Ki 18:39*
said
whose *f.* were like the *f.* of   *1Ch 12:8*
lions
in sackcloth, fell upon their   *1Ch 21:16*
f.
feet, and their *f.* were inward   *2Ch 3:13*
with their *f.* to the ground upon   *2Ch 7:3*
have turned away their *f.*   *2Ch 29:6*
from
Lord with their *f.* to the ground   *Ne 8:6*
he covereth the *f.* of the   *Job 9:24*
judges
and bind their *f.* in secret   *Job 40:13*
and their *f.* were not ashamed   *Ps 34:5*
Fill their *f.* with shame; that   *Ps 83:16*
they
expression of *f.* witnesses (B)   *Isa 3:9*
and grind the *f.* of the poor   *Isa 3:15*
their *f.* shall be as flames   *Isa 13:8*
wipe away tears from off all *f.*   *Isa 25:8*
we hid as it were our *f.* from   *Isa 53:3*
him
Be not afraid of their *f.* for I   *Jer 1:8*
be not dismayed at their *f.*   *Jer 1:17*
made their *f.* harder than a rock   *Jer 5:3*
to the confusion of their own   *Jer 7:19*
f.
all *f.* are turned into paleness   *Jer 30:6*
If ye wholly set your *f.* to   *Jer 42:15*
enter
all the men that set their *f.* to   *Jer 42:17*
that have set their *f.* to go   *Jer 44:12*
into
to Zion with their *f.*   *Jer 50:5*
thitherward
shame hath covered our *f.*   *Jer 51:51*
f. of elders were not honoured   *La 5:12*
And every one had four *f.*   *Eze 1:6*
four had their *f.* and their   *Eze 1:8*
wings
As for the likeness of their *f.*   *Eze 1:10*
Thus were their *f.:* and their   *Eze 1:11*
wings
living creatures, with his four   *Eze 1:15*
f.
thy face strong against their *f.*   *Eze 3:8*
and shame shall be upon all *f.*   *Eze 7:18*
and their *f.* toward the east   *Eze 8:16*
And every one had four *f.*   *Eze 10:14*
Every one had four *f.* apiece   *Eze 10:21*
and the likeness of their *f.*   *Eze 10:22*
was
was the same *f.* which I saw   *Eze 10:22*
f. from all your abominations   *Eze 14:6*
all *f.* from the south to the   *Eze 20:47*
north
their *f.* quiver (A)(B)(R)   *Eze 27:35*
and every cherub had two *f.*   *Eze 41:18*
gate which *f.* east   *Eze 42:15;*
(A)(B)(R)   *43:4*
why should he see your *f.;*   *Da 1:10*
worse
us confusion of *f.* as at this day   *Da 9:7*

all *f.* shall gather blackness   *Joe 2:6*
f. of them shall gather   *Na 2:10*
blackness
f. shall sup up as the east wind   *Hab 1:9*
and spread dung upon your *f.*   *Mal 2:3*
they disfigure their *f.* (R)   *M't 5:6*
for they disfigure their *f.* that   *M't 6:16*
bowed down their *f.* to the   *Lu 24:5*
earth
fell before the throne on their   *Re 7:11*
f.
and their *f.* were as the *f.* of   *Re 9:7*
men
upon their *f.* and worshipped   *Re 11:16*
God

FACIAL

by *f.* sadness the heart (B)   *Ec 7:3*
his *f.* expression (A)   *Da 3:19*
f. brilliance (A)(B)   *2Co 3:7*

FACING

f. the street (S)   *Ne 8:3*
f., looking toward   *Eze 40:44*
(A)(B)(R)
chamber *f.* south (B)(R)   *Eze 40:45;*
  40:46
facing (S)   *Eze 42:3; M'k 15:39*

FACTION

the mutilation *f.* (B)   *Ph'p 3:2*

FACTIONAL

dissensions, *f.* spirit (B)(N)   *Ga 5:20*
nothing from *f.* motives (A)   *Ph'p 2:3*

FACTIONS

that are *f.* (E)(R)   *Ro 2:8*
f. among you (A)   *1Co 3:3*
f. among you (B)   *1Co 11:18*
have to be *f.* (A)(E)(R)   *1Co 11:19*
f., divisions (E)(P)(S)   *Ga 5:20*
f., a heretical sectarian (A)   *Tit 3:10*

FACTIOUS

a *f.* person (B)(E)(R)   *Tit 3:10*

FACTS

laying before them the *f.* (N)   *Ac 11:4*
two unalterable *f.* (B)(N)   *Heb 6:18*

FADE

Stranger shall *f.* away, and   *2Sa 22:46*
they
Foreigners faded away (A)   *2Sa 22:46*
foreigners shrink in despair   *2Sa 22:46*
(B)
foreigners lost heart (R)   *2Sa 22:46*
strangers shall *f.* away, and be   *Ps 18:45*
and we all do *f.* as a leaf   *Isa 64:6*
the fig tree, and the leaf shall *f.*   *Jer 8:13*
whose leaf shall not *f.* neither   *Eze 47:12*
so also shall the rich man *f.*   *Jas 1:11*
away
rich man wither and die   *Jas 1:11*
(A)(N)
wealthy waste away (B)   *Jas 1:11*
fall into the blight of decay   *Jas 1:11*
(P)

FADED

foreigners *f.* away (A)   *2Sa 22:46*
finishing of something *f.* (B)   *2Co 3:13*

FADES

its beauty *f.* away (A)   *Jas 1:11*

FADETH

shall be as an oak whose leaf *f.*   *Isa 1:30*
whose leaf withers (A)(R)   *Isa 1:30*
oak shedding her withering   *Isa 1:30*
leaves (P)
The earth mourneth and *f.*   *Isa 24:4*
away
wither (A)(R)   *Isa 24:4; 40:7*
the world languisheth and *f.*   *Isa 24:4*
away

the flower *f.*: because the spirit   *Isa 40:7*
withers   (B)(E)   *Isa 40:7*
the flower *f.*: but the word of   *Isa 40:8*
undefiled, and that *f.* not away   *1Pe 1:4*
a crown of glory that *f.* not   *1Pe 5:4*
away

FADING

glorious beauty is a *f.* flower   *Isa 28:1*
shall be a *f.* flower, and as the   *Isa 28:4*

FAIL

you for your cattle, if money   *Ge 47:16*
f.
thine eyes shall look, and *f.*   *De 28:32*
with
he will not *f.* thee, nor forsake   *De 31:6*
he will not *f.* thee, neither   *De 31:8*
forsake
I will not *f.* thee, nor forsake   *Jos 1:5*
thee
that he will without *f.* drive   *Jos 3:10*
out from
without *f.* deliver the children   *J'g 11:30*
Let them not *f.* to burn the fat   *1Sa 2:16*
no man's heart *f.* because of   *1Sa 17:32*
him
f. to sit with the king at meat   *1Sa 20:5*
overtake them, and without *f.*   *1Sa 30:8*
recover
not *f.* from the house of Joab   *2Sa 3:29*
there shall not *f.* thee (said he)   *1Ki 2:4*
in
There shall not *f.* thee a man   *1Ki 8:25*
in
There shall not *f.* thee a man   *1Ki 9:5*
upon
neither shall the cruse of oil   *1Ki 17:14*
f.
neither did the cruse of oil *f.*   *1Ki 17:16*
will not *f.* thee, nor forsake   *1Ch 28:20*
thee
There shall not *f.* thee a man   *2Ch 6:16*
in
There shall not *f.* thee a man   *2Ch 7:18*
to be
now that ye *f.* not to do this   *Ezr 4:22*
given them day by day without   *Ezr 6:9*
f.
let nothing *f.* of all that thou   *Es 6:10*
so as it should not *f.* that they   *Es 9:27*
should not *f.* from among the   *Es 9:28*
Jews
Purim not *f.* among Jews (E)   *Es 9:28*
the eyes of the wicked shall *f.*   *Job 11:20*
As the waters *f.* from the sea   *Job 14:11*
waters *f.* from the sea   *Job 14:11*
(E)(R)
the eyes of his children shall *f.*   *Job 17:5*
caused the eyes of the widow   *Job 31:16*
to *f.*
f. from among the children of   *Ps 12:1*
men
eyes *f.* while I wait for my God   *Ps 69:3*
doth his promise *f.* for   *Ps 77:8*
evermore
nor suffer my faithfulness to *f.*   *Ps 89:33*
Mine eyes *f.* for thy word   *Ps 119:82*
Mine eyes *f.* for thy   *Ps 119:123*
salvation
and the rod of his anger shall *f.*   *Pr 22:8*
and desire shall *f.*: because   *Ec 12:5*
man
And the spirit of Egypt shall *f.*   *Isa 19:3*
the waters shall *f.* from the sea   *Isa 19:5*
and all the glory of Kedar   *Isa 21:16*
shall *f.*
and they shall *f.*: together   *Isa 31:3*
cause the drink of the thirsty   *Isa 32:6*
to *f.*
the vintage shall *f.* the   *Isa 32:10*
gathering
no one of these shall *f.* none   *Isa 34:16*
mine eyes *f.* with looking   *Isa 38:14*
upward
shall not *f.* nor be discouraged   *Isa 42:4*
not *f.* nor be suppressed (B)   *Isa 42:4*
nor that his bread should *f.*   *Isa 51:14*
the spirit should *f.* before me   *Isa 57:16*
spring of water, whose waters   *Isa 58:11*
f.
their eyes did *f.* because there   *Jer 14:6*
and as waters that *f.*   *Jer 15:18*
and I have caused wine to *f.*   *Jer 48:33*
from
Mine eyes do *f.* with tears, my   *La 2:11*
because his compassions *f.* not   *La 3:22*
and the new wine shall *f.* in her   *Ho 9:2*

to make the poor of the land to   *Am 8:4*
f.
the labour of the olive shall *f.*   *Hab 3:17*
when ye *f.* they may receive   *Lu 16:9*
you
than one tittle of the law to *f.*   *Lu 16:17*
for thee, that thy faith *f.* not   *Lu 22:32*
a *f.* crown of leaves (P)   *1Co 9:25*
there be prophecies, they shall   *1Co 13:8*
f.
end of *f.* splendor (R)   *2Co 2:13*
same, and thy years shall not   *Heb 1:12*
f.
time would *f.* me to tell of   *Heb 11:32*
Gedeon
any man *f.* of the grace of   *Heb 12:15*
God

FAILED

not *f.* my master (B)   *Ge 24:27*
and their heart *f.* them, and   *Ge 42:28*
they
And when money *f.* in the   *Ge 47:15*
land
the plain, even the salt sea, *f.*   *Jos 3:16*
f. not ought of any good   *Jos 21:45*
thing
thing hath *f.* of all the good   *Jos 23:14*
things
and not one thing hath *f.*   *Jos 23:14*
thereof
there hath not *f.* one word of   *1Ki 8:56*
all his
f. to carry out orders (B)   *Es 1:15*
My kinsfolk have *f.* and my   *Job 19:14*
refuge *f.* me; no man cared for   *Ps 142:4*
my
my soul *f.* when he spake   *Ca 5:6*
their might hath *f.*; they   *Jer 51:30*
became
eyes as yet *f.* for our vain help   *La 4:17*

FAILETH

thy presence? for the money *f.*   *Ge 47:15*
Their bull gendereth, and *f.*   *Job 21:10*
not
my strength *f.* because of mine   *Ps 31:10*
heart panteth, my strength *f.*   *Ps 38:10*
me
therefore my heart *f.* me   *Ps 40:12*
me not when my strength *f.*   *Ps 71:9*
My flesh and my heart *f.*   *Ps 73:26*
and my flesh *f.* of fatness   *Ps 109:24*
O Lord; my spirit *f.*: hide not   *Ps 143:7*
his wisdom *f.* him, and he saith   *Ec 10:3*
grass *f.* there is no green thing   *Isa 15:6*
he is strong in power; not one   *Isa 40:26*
f.
and their tongue *f.* for thirst, I   *Isa 41:17*
the
he is hungry, and his strength   *Isa 44:12*
f.
truth *f.*; and he that departeth   *Isa 59:15*
prolonged, and every vision *f.*   *Eze 12:22*
his judgment to light, he *f.* not   *Zep 3:5*
treasure in the heavens that *f.*   *Lu 12:33*
not
Charity never *f.*: but whether   *1Co 13:8*

FAILING

a trembling heart, and *f.* of   *De 28:65*
eyes
strength *f.* (R)   *Ne 4:10*
Men's hearts *f.* them for fear   *Lu 21:26*

FAILINGS

forgive *f.* (A)   *M'k 11:25; 11:26*
the *f.* of the weak (R)   *Ro 15:1*

FAILS

when it *f.* (S)   *Lu 16:9*
f. in one point (R)   *Jas 2:10*

FAILURE

their *f.* enriched world (P)   *Ro 11:12*
every *f.* to obey is sin (P)   *1Jo 5:17*

FAILURES

forgive *f.* (P)   *M't 6:14; 6:15*

FAIN

he would *f*. flee out of his hand	*Job 27:22*
he would *f*. have filled his belly	*Lu 15:16*
would gladly have fed (A)(R)	*Lu 15:16*
aimed to get his stomach filled (B)	*Lu 15:16*
would have been glad to fill his (N)	*Lu 15:16*
longing to stuff himself with (P)	*Lu 15:16*

FAINT

came from the field, and he was *f*.	*Ge 25:29*
that same red pottage; for I am *f*.	*Ge 25:30*
let not your hearts *f*., fear not	*De 20:3*
lest his brethren's heart *f*. as well	*De 20:8*
when thou wast *f*. and weary	*De 25:18*
inhabitants of the land *f*. because	*Jos 2:9*
inhabitants of the country do *f*.	*Jos 2:24*
men that were with him *f*. yet	*J'g 8:4*
that follow me; for they be *f*.	*J'g 8:5*
And the people were *f*.	*1Sa 14:28*
and the people were very *f*.	*1Sa 14:31*
were so *f*. that they could not go	*1Sa 30:10*
two hundred men, which were so *f*.	*1Sa 30:21*
such as be *f*. in the wilderness	*2Sa 16:2*
Philistines: and David waxed *f*.	*2Sa 21:15*
about to *f*. and despair (A)	*Job 6:14*
made heart *f*. (A)(B)(E)(R)	*Job 23:16*
I am *f*. (A)	*Ps 6:2*
I am *f*. and bruised (A)	*Ps 38:8*
my spirit was *f*. (B)(R)	*Ps 77:3*
my spirit is *f*. (R)	*Ps 143:3*
If thou *f*. in the day of adversity	*Pr 24:10*
is sick, and the whole heart *f*.	*Isa 1:5*
neither let heart be *f*. (E)(R)	*Isa 7:4*
Therefore shall all hands be *f*.	*Isa 13:7*
he awaketh, and, behold, he is *f*.	*Isa 29:8*
He giveth power to the *f*.	*Isa 40:29*
Even the youths shall *f*. and be	*Isa 40:30*
and they shall walk, and not *f*.	*Isa 40:31*
he drinketh no water, and is *f*.	*Isa 44:12*
not *f*. or heartsick (A)(R)	*Isa 57:10*
sorrow, my heart is *f*. in me	*Jer 8:18*
lest your heart *f*. and ye fear	*Jer 51:46*
me desolate and *f*. all the day	*La 1:13*
sighs are many, and my heart is *f*.	*La 1:22*
f. in the streets (A)(R)	*La 2:11; 2:12*
young children, that *f*. for hunger	*La 2:19*
For this our heart is *f*. for these	*La 5:17*
and every spirit shall *f*. and all	*Eze 21:7*
that their heart may *f*. and their	*Eze 21:15*
the fair virgins and young men *f*.	*Am 8:13*
f. believers (B)	*M't 6:30; 8:26; 14:31; Lu 12:28*
they were *f*. (S)	*M't 9:36*
lest they *f*. in the way	*M't 15:32*
they will *f*. by the way	*M'k 8:3*
always to pray, and not to *f*.	*Lu 18:1*
we have received mercy, we *f*. not	*2Co 4:1*
For which cause we *f*. not; but	*2Co 4:16*
we shall reap, if we *f*. not.	*Ga 6:9*
Wherefore I desire that ye *f*. not	*Eph 3:13*
be wearied and *f*. in your minds	*Heb 12:3*
f. when thou art rebuked of him	*Heb 12:5*

FAINTED

Jacob's heart *f*. for he believed	*Ge 45:26*
all the land of Canaan *f*. by reason	*Ge 47:13*
I had *f*. unless I had believed	*Ps 27:13*
thirsty, their soul *f*. in them	*Ps 107:5*
Thy sons have *f*. they lie at the	*Isa 51:20*
I *f*. in my sighing, and I find no	*Jer 45:3*
the trees of the field *f*. for him	*Eze 31:15*
And I Daniel *f*. and was sick	*Da 8:27*
When my soul *f*. within me I	*Jon 2:7*
upon the head of Jonah, that he *f*.	*Jon 4:8*
they *f*. and were scattered	*M't 9:36*
hast laboured, and hast not *f*.	*Re 2:3*

FAINTEST

it is come upon thee, and thou *f*.	*Job 4:5*

FAINTETH

My soul longeth, yea, even *f*.	*Ps 84:2*
My soul *f*. for thy salvation	*Ps 119:81*
be as when a standardbearer *f*.	*Isa 10:18*
of the ends of the earth, *f*. not	*Isa 40:28*

FAINTHEARTED

there that is fearful and *f*.	*De 20:8*
weakhearted (B)	*De 20:8*
immature and *f*. (B)	*2Ch 13:7*
quiet; fear not, neither be *f*.	*Isa 7:4*
be not afraid or timid of heart (B)	*Isa 7:4*
neither let thy heart be faint (E)(R)	*Isa 7:4*
they are *f*.; there is sorrow on	*Jer 49:23*
they melted in fear (B)	*Jer 49:23*
they are melted away (E)	*Jer 49:23*
they melt in fear (R)	*Jer 49:23*
comfort the *f*. (S)	*1Th 5:14*

FAINTING

f. of mind (A)	*De 28:65*
my spirit *f*. (R)	*Ps 77:3*

FAINTNESS

I will send a *f*. into their hearts	*Le 26:36*

FAINTS

my spirit *f*. (R)	*Ps 143:4*

FAIR

daughters of men that they were *f*.	*Ge 6:2*
admired their looks (B)	*Ge 6:2*
I know that thou art a *f*. woman	*Ge 12:11*
beautiful (A)	*Ge 12:14; 26:7; 1Ki 1:4; Es 2:2-3; Ca 1:15; Eze 31:7; Ac 7:20*
beautiful (B)	*Ge 12:14; 26:7; 2Sa 13:1; 1Ki 1:4; Es 2:2, 3; Job 42:15; Pr 11:22; Ca 1:15; Eze 31:7; Ac 7:20*
beautiful (R)	*Ge 12:14; 2Sa 13:1; 1Ki 1:4; Es 2:2-3; Pr 11:22; Ca 1:15; Ac 7:20*
doing what is right and *f*. (B)	*Ge 18:19*
damsel was very *f*. to look upon	*Ge 24:16*
because she was *f*. to look upon	*Ge 26:7*
ruddy, and of a *f*. countenance	*1Sa 17:42*
the son of David had a *f*. sister	*2Sa 13:1*
was a woman of a *f*. countenance	*2Sa 14:27*
So they sought for a *f*. damsel	*1Ki 1:3*
damsel was very *f*. and cherished	*1Ki 1:4*
for she was *f*. to look on	*Es 1:11*
f. young virgins sought for	*Es 2:2*
together all the *f*. young virgins	*Es 2:3*
maid was *f*. and beautiful	*Es 2:7*
by wind heavens made *f*. (R)	*Job 26:13*
in this claim you are not *f*. (B)	*Job 33:12*
F. weather cometh out of the	*Job 37:22*
so *f*. as the daughters of Job	*Job 42:15*
render *f*. judgments (B)	*Ps 75:2*
thy judgments *f*. (B)	*Ps 119:137*
With her much *f*. speech she	*Pr 7:21*
so is a *f*. woman which is without	*Pr 11:22*
When he speaketh *f*. believe him	*Pr 26:25*
Behold, thou art *f*.; my love	*Ca 1:15*
beautiful (A)	*Ca 1:15; Ac 7:20*
behold, thou art *f*.; thou hast dove's	*Ca 1:15*
Behold, thou art *f*. my beloved	*Ca 1:16*
Rise up, my love, my *f*. one	*Ca 2:10*
my love, my *f*. one, and come	*Ca 2:13*
Behold, thou art *f*. my love	*Ca 4:1*
behold, thou art *f*.; thou hast dove's	*Ca 4:1*
Thou art all *f*. my love	*Ca 4:7*
How *f*. is thy love, my sister	*Ca 4:10*
f. as the moon, clear as the sun	*Ca 6:10*
How *f*. and how pleasant art thou	*Ca 7:6*
be desolate, even great and *f*.	*Isa 5:9*
will lay thy stones with *f*. colours	*Isa 54:11*
in vain shalt thou make thyself *f*.	*Jer 4:30*
olive tree *f*. and of goodly fruit	*Jer 11:16*
they speak *f*. words unto thee	*Jer 12:6*
Egypt is like a very *f*. heifer	*Jer 46:20*
Thou hast also taken thy *f*. jewels	*Eze 16:17*
and shall take thy *f*. jewels	*Eze 16:39*
Lord is not *f*. (B)	*Eze 18:25; 18:29*
and take away thy *f*. jewels	*Eze 23:26*
cedar in Lebanon wtih *f*. branches	*Eze 31:3*
Thus was he *f*. in his greatness	*Eze 31:7*
made him *f*. by the multitude	*Eze 31:9*
The leaves thereof were *f*. and	*Da 4:12*
Whose leaves were *f*. and the fruit	*Da 4:21*
passed over upon her *f*. neck	*Ho 10:11*
In that day shall the *f*. virgins	*Am 8:13*
them set a *f*. mitre upon his head	*Zec 3:5*
they set a *f*. mitre upon his head	*Zec 3:5*
Joseph was *f*. minded (B)	*M't 1:19*
ye say, It will be *f*. weather	*M't 16:2*
was born, and was exceeding *f*.	*Ac 7:20*
which is called The *f*. havens	*Ac 27:8*
by good words and *f*. speeches	*Ro 16:18*
by *f*. and flattering words (R)	*Ro 16:18*
intend to do the *f*. thing (B)	*2Co 8:21*
to make a *f*. shew in the flesh	*Ga 6:12*
upright and *f*. minded (A)(P)	*Tit 1:8*
must be *f*., of holy life (B)	*Tit 1:8*

FAIRER

her younger sister *f*. than she	*J'g 15:2*
better looking (B)	*J'g 15:2*
f. than I am (B)	*1Sa 24:17*
art *f*. than the children of men	*Ps 45:2*
appeared *f*. and fatter in flesh	*Da 1:15*
better looking (A)	*Da 1:15*
looked healthier, better condition (B)	*Da 1:15*
better in appearance (R)	*Da 1:15*

FAIREST

the *f*. are mine (S)	*1Ki 20:3*
O thou *f*. among women, go thy	*Ca 1:8*
thou *f*. among women? what is thy	*Ca 5:9*
O thou *f*. among women? whither	*Ca 6:1*

FAIRLY

treat my master *f*. (B)	*Ge 24:49*

FAIRMINDED

Joseph was *f*. (B)	*M't 1:19*

FAIRNESS

my *f*. dressed me (B)	*Job 29:14*
conducts business with *f*. (B)	*Ps 112:5*
refuse to act with *f*. (B)	*Pr 21:7*
rests in all *f*. (B)	*Ro 2:2*

FAIRS

and lead, they traded in thy *f*.	*Eze 27:12; 27:14, 16, 19, 22, 27*
they traded for your wares (A)(B)(E)(R)	*Eze 27:12; 27:14, 16, 19, 22, 27*

FAIRY

Jewish *f*. tales (P)   *Tit 1:14*

FAITH

they are children in whom is   *De 32:20*
no *f*.
who know nothing of loyalty   *De 32:20*
(B)
in whom is no faithfulness   *De 32:20*
(A)(E)(R)
you broke *f*. (A)(B)(R)   *De 32:51;*
    29:6
acted in good *f*. and honor (R)   *J'g 9:19*
if in good *f*. (A)   *J'g 9:15*
broken *f*. (A)(R)   *Ezr 10:2*
keep *f*. forever (B)(R)   *Ps 146:6*
keep *f*. and troth with God   *Isa 26:2*
(A)(E)(R)
O ye of little *f*. therefore take   *M't 6:30;*
no thought   *8:26; 14:31; 16:8; Lu 12:28*
faint believers (B)   *M't 6:30;*
   8:26; 14:31; Lu 12:28
you "little-faiths" (P)   *M't 6:30;*
   8:26; 14:31; Lu 12:28
found so great *f*. no not in   *M't 8:10;*
Israel   *Lu 7:9*
who never loses *f*. in me (P)   *M't 11:6*
he gives up *f*. at once (P)   *M't 13:21*
if ye have *f*. as a grain of   *M't 17:20*
mustard seed
if ye have *f*. ye shall not only   *M't 21:21*
do this
and have omitted judgment,   *M't 23:23*
mercy, and *f*.
fidelity (A)(B)   *M't 23:23*
(N)(P)
many will lose their *f*.   *M't 24:10*
(N)(P)
everyone shall lose *f*. (N)(P)   *M't 26:31*
even if everyone should lose   *M't 26:33*
f. in you (P)
said to them, How is it ye   *M'k 4:40*
have no *f*.
Jesus saith unto them, have   *M'k 11:22*
f. in God
he pinned his *f*. (P)   *Lu 11:22*
apostles said to the Lord,   *Lu 17:5*
Increase our *f*.
if had *f*. ye might say to   *Lu 17:6*
sycamine tree
when Son of man cometh, shall   *Lu 18:8*
He find *f*.
guard against breakdown of   *Joh 16:1*
your *f*. (N)(P)
f. which is by him, hath given   *Ac 3:16*
they chose Stephen, a man full   *Ac 6:5;*
of *f*.   *6:8*
great company of priests   *Ac 6:7*
obedient to *f*.
Barnabas was a good man,   *Ac 11:24*
full of *f*.
seeking to turn the deputy   *Ac 13:8*
from the *f*.
perceiving he had *f*. to be   *Ac 14:9*
healed
and exhorting them to   *Ac 14:22*
continue in the *f*.
how he had opened door of *f*.   *Ac 14:27*
to Gentiles
the churches were established   *Ac 16:5*
in the *f*.
and *f*. toward our Lord Jesus   *Ac 20:21*
Christ
Felix heard Paul concerning   *Ac 24:24*
the *f*.
we have received grace for   *Ro 1:5*
obedience to *f*.
the righteousness of God   *Ro 1:17*
revealed from *f*. to *f*.
unbelief make the *f*. of God   *Ro 3:3*
without effect
where boasting? It is excluded   *Ro 3:27*
by law of *f*.
his *f*. is counted for   *Ro 4:5;*
righteousness   *4:9*
circumcision a seal of the   *Ro 4:11*
righteousness of *f*.
but also walk in steps of that *f*.   *Ro 4:12*
of Abraham
but was through the   *Ro 4:13*
righteousness of *f*.
if they of law be heirs, *f*. is   *Ro 4:14*
made void
it is of *f*. which is of the *f*. of   *Ro 4:16*
Abraham
even the righteousness, which   *Ro 9:3;*
is of *f*.   *10:6*

that is the word of *f*. which   *Ro 10:8*
we preach
f. cometh by hearing, hearing   *Ro 10:17*
by word of God
according as God hath dealt   *Ro 12:3*
measure of *f*.
prophesy according to   *Ro 12:6*
proportion of *f*.
hast thou *f*.? have it to thyself   *Ro 14:22*
before God
he eateth not of *f*. what is not   *Ro 14:23*
of *f*. is sin
to all nations for the   *Ro 16:26*
obedience of *f*.
to another *f*. by the same   *1Co 12:9*
Spirit
though I have all *f*. and have   *1Co 13:2*
no charity
now abideth *f*. hope, charity,   *1Co 13:13*
these three
we having the same Spirit of *f*.   *2Co 4:13*
have his *f*. hurt (A)(R)   *2Co 11:29*
upsetting you *f*. (P)   *Ga 1:7*
now preached *f*. which once he   *Ga 1:23*
destroyed
by the works of law, or by the   *Ga 3:2;*
hearing of *f*.   *3:5*
know ye, that they which are   *Ga 3:7;*
of *f*.   *3:9*
law is not of *f*. but the man   *Ga 3:12*
that doeth them
before *f*. came; after that *f*. is   *Ga 3:23;*
come   *3:25*
but *f*. which worketh by love   *Ga 5:6*
but the fruit of the Spirit is   *Ga 5:22*
love, joy, *f*.
unto them who are of the   *Ga 6:10*
household of *f*.
one Lord, one *f*., one baptism   *Eph 4:5*
till we all come in the unity of   *Eph 4:13*
the *f*.
above all, taking the shield of   *Eph 6:16*
f.
peace be to the brethren, with   *Eph 6:23*
f. from God
for your furtherance and joy   *Ph'p 1:25*
of *f*.
striving together for the *f*. of   *Ph'p 1:27*
the gospel
remembering your work of *f*.   *1Th 1:3*
putting on breastplate of *f*.   *1Th 5:8*
and love
we glory for your patience and   *2Th 1:4*
f.
would fulfil the work of *f*.   *2Th 1:11*
with power
may be delivered, for all men   *2Th 3:2*
have not *f*.
f. unfeigned   *1Ti 1:14*
grace of our Lord exceeding   *1Ti 1:14*
abundant with *f*.
holding *f*. and good   *1Ti 1:19*
conscience; which some put away
concerning *f*. made shipwreck
holding mystery of *f*. in a pure   *1Ti 3:9*
conscience
in latter times, some shall   *1Ti 4:1*
depart from *f*.
nourished up in words of *f*. and   *1Ti 4:6*
good doctrine
he hath denied the *f*.   *1Ti 5:8*
because they have cast off their   *1Ti 5:12*
first *f*.
they have erred from the *f*.   *1Ti 6:10;*
   6:21
follow *f*.   *1Ti 6:11*
fight the good fight of *f*.   *1Ti 6:12*
confessed your *f*. nobly (N)   *1Ti 6:12*
the unfeigned *f*. that is in thee   *2Ti 1:5*
and overthrow the *f*. of some   *2Ti 2:18*
follow *f*.   *2Ti 2:22*
reprobate concerning the *f*.   *2Ti 3:8*
but thou hast fully known my   *2Ti 3:10*
f. charity
I have finished my course, I   *2Ti 4:7*
have kept the *f*.
according to the *f*. of God's   *Tit 1:1*
elect
to Titus mine own son, after the   *Tit 1:4*
common *f*.
hearing of *f*. toward the Lord   *Ph'm 5*
Jesus
high priest of *f*. we hold (P)   *Heb 3:1*
word did not profit, not mixed   *Heb 4:2*
with *f*.
hold firmly to our *f*. (P)   *Heb 4:14*
not laying again the   *Heb 6:1*
foundation of *f*.
with a true heart in full   *Heb 10:22*
assurance of *f*.

let us hold fast the   *Heb 10:23*
profession of our *f*.
f. is the substance of things   *Heb 11:1*
hoped for
without *f*. it is impossible to   *Heb 11:6*
please God
Jesus, the author and finisher   *Heb 12:2*
of our *f*.
whose *f*. follow, considering   *Heb 13:7*
the end
follow example of their *f*.   *Heb 13:7*
(A)(B)(N)(P)(R)
have not *f*. with respect of   *Jas 2:1*
persons
though a man say he hath *f*.   *Jas 2:14*
can *f*. save him
even so *f*. without works is   *Jas 2:17;*
dead   *20:26*
man may say, thou hast *f*. and   *Jas 2:18*
I have works
seest thou how *f*. wrought with   *Jas 2:22*
his works, and by works was
f. made perfect
and the prayer of *f*. shall save   *Jas 5:15*
the sick
that have obtained like precious   *2Pe 1:1*
f.
that overcometh the world,   *1Jo 5:4*
even our *f*.
ye should earnestly contend   *Jude 3*
for the *f*.
building up yourselves on   *Jude 20*
your most holy *f*.
thou holdest fast and hast not   *Re 2:13*
denied my *f*.
I know thy works, and *f*. and   *Re 2:19*
thy patience
here is the patience and *f*. of   *Re 13:10*
the saints
here are they that keep *f*. of   *Re 14:12*
Jesus

BY FAITH

the just shall live *by* his *f*.   *Hab 2:4;*
   Ro 1:17; Ga 3:11; Heb 10:38
purifying their hearts *by f*.   *Ac 15:9*
who are sanctified *by f*. that is   *Ac 26:18*
in me
may be comforted *by* the   *Ro 1:12*
mutual *f*.
the righteousness of God *by f*.   *Ro 3:22*
of Jesus Christ
a man is justified *by f*.   *Ro 3:28;*
   5:1; Ga 2:16; 3:24
which shall justify the   *Ro 3:30*
circumcision *by f*.
by whom we have access *by f*. to   *Ro 5:2*
this grace
because they sought it not *by f*.   *Ro 9:32*
thou standest *by f*.   *Ro 11:20; 2Co 1:24*
for we walk *by f*. not by sight   *2Co 5:7*
I live *by* the *f*. of the Son of   *Ga 2:20*
God
that the promise *by f*. might be   *Ga 3:22*
given
ye are children of God *by f*. in   *Ga 3:26*
Christ
we wait for the hope of   *Ga 5:5*
righteousness *by f*.
in whom we have access *by f*.   *Eph 3:12*
of him
that Christ may dwell in your   *Eph 3:17*
hearts *by f*.
the righteousness which is of   *Ph'p 3:9*
God *by f*.
by f. Abel, Enoch, Noah,   *Heb 11:4;*
Abraham, Sarah, Isaac, Jacob,   *11:5,*
Joseph, Moses, *7-9, 17, 20-21, 23, 27, 31*
Rahab
by f. they passed through the   *Heb 11:29*
Red sea
by f. the walls of Jericho fell   *Heb 11:30*
down
by works man is justified, not   *Jas 2:24*
by f. only

IN FAITH

being not weak *in f*. he   *Ro 4:19*
considered not
he staggered not, but was   *Ro 4:20*
strong *in f*.
him that is weak *in* the *f*.   *Ro 14:1*
receive you
watch, stand fast *in* the *f*. be   *1Co 16:13*
strong
as ye abound *in f*. and   *2Co 8:7*
utterance

examine yourselves whether   *2Co 13:5*
ye be *in* the *f.*
if ye continue *in* the *f.*   *Col 1:23*
grounded
rooted in him, and stablished *in*   *Col 2:7*
the *f.*
unto Timothy my own son *in f.*   *1Ti 1:2*
rather than godly edifying   *1Ti 1:4*
which is *in f.*
teacher of Gentiles *in f.* and   *1Ti 2:7*
verity
be saved, if continue *in f.* and   *1Ti 2:15*
charity
they purchase great boldness   *1Ti 3:13*
in f.
be thou an example of believers   *1Ti 4:12*
in f.
hold fast form *in f.* and love   *2Ti 1:13*
that they may be found *in f.*   *Tit 1:13;*
       2:2
greet them that love us *in f.*   *Tit 3:15*
grace be
these all died *in f.* not   *Heb 11:13*
having received
but let them ask *in f.* not   *Jas 1:6*
wavering
God chosen the poor of this   *Jas 2:5*
world, rich *in f.*
whom resist, stedfast *in* the *f.*   *1Pe 5:9*

THEIR FAITH

Jesus seeing *their f.*   *M't 9:2;*
       M'k 2:5; Lu 5:20

THROUGH FAITH

through f. in his name this   *Ac 3:16*
man strong
a propitiation *through f.* in his   *Ro 3:25*
blood
justify the uncircumcision   *Ro 3:30*
through f.
do we make void law *through*   *Ro 3:31*
f.? God forbid
God would justify the heathen   *Ga 3:8*
through f.
might receive the promise of   *Ga 3:14*
Spirit *through f.*
for by grace are ye saved   *Eph 2:8*
through f.
but that righteousness which   *Ph'p 3:9*
is *through f.*
risen *through* the *f.* of   *Col 2:12*
operation of God
make thee wise to salvation   *2Ti 3:15*
through f.
who *through f.* inherit the   *Heb 6:12*
promises
through f. we understand   *Heb 11:3*
worlds framed
through f. Sara received   *Heb 11:11*
strength to conceive
through f. he kept the   *Heb 11:28*
passover, and sprinkling
who *through f.* subdued   *Heb 11:33*
kingdoms
having obtained a good   *Heb 11:39*
report *through f.*
kept by power of God *through f.*   *1Pe 1:5*
to salvation

THY FAITH

thy f. hath made thee whole   *M't 9:22;*
       M'k 5:34; 10:52; Lu 8:48; 17:19
Jesus said, O woman, great is   *M't 15:28*
thy f.
thy f. saved thee, go in peace   *Lu 7:50;*
       18:42
I prayed for thee, that *thy f.*   *Lu 22:32*
fail not
communication of *thy f.*   *Ph'm 6*
effectual
shew me *thy f.* without thy   *Jas 2:18*
works

YOUR FAITH

according to *your f.* be it unto   *M't 9:29*
you
he said unto them, Where is   *Lu 8:25*
your f.
your f. is spoken of through the   *Ro 1:8*
world
your f. not stand in wisdom of   *1Co 2:5*
men
and *your f.* is also vain   *1Co 15:14;*
       15:17
not have dominion over *your*   *2Co 1:24*
f.

having hope when *your f.* is   *2Co 10:15*
increased
after I heard of *your f.* in   *Eph 1:15*
the Lord
if I be offered on service of   *Ph'p 2:17*
your f.
since we heard of *your f.* in   *Col 1:4*
Christ Jesus
beholding the stedfastness of   *Col 2:5*
your f. in Christ
your f. to God-ward is spread   *1Th 1:8*
abroad
and to comfort you concerning   *1Th 3:2*
your f.
I sent to know *your f.* lest the   *1Th 3:5*
tempter
Timothy brought us good   *1Th 3:6*
tidings of *your f.*
we were comforted over you by   *1Th 3:7*
your f.
and might perfect what is   *1Th 3:10*
lacking in *your f.*
that *your f.* groweth   *2Th 1:3*
exceedingly
the trying of *your f.* worketh   *Jas 1:3*
patience
trial of *your f.* being more   *1Pe 1:7*
precious
receiving the end of *your f.*   *1Pe 1:9*
even salvation
that *your f.* and hope might be   *1Pe 1:21*
in God
add to *your f.* virtue, to virtue   *2Pe 1:5*

FAITHFUL

Moses is *f.* in mine house   *Nu 12:7;*
       Heb 3:2, 5
the *f.* God who keepeth   *De 7:9*
covenant
guard feet of *f.* ones (R)   *1Sa 2:9*
I will raise me up a *f.* priest   *1Sa 2:35*
Ahimelech said, Who is so *f.*   *1Sa 22:14*
as David
I am one of them that are *f.*   *2Sa 20:19*
in Israel
f. in keeping themselves holy   *2Ch 31:18*
(R)
Hananiah was a *f.* man and   *Ne 7:2*
feared God
and foundest his heart *f.*   *Ne 9:8*
before thee
for they were counted *f.* to   *Ne 13:13*
distribute
for the *f.* fail from among men   *Ps 12:1*
the *f.* God (R)   *Ps 31:5*
love the Lord, for Lord   *Ps 31:23*
preserveth *f.*
gather all my *f.* ones (R)   *Ps 50:5*
and as a *f.* witness in heaven   *Ps 89:37*
mine eyes shall be on the *f.* of   *Ps 101:6*
the land
f. and right (A)(B)(R)   *Ps 111:7*
all thy commandments are *f.*   *Ps 119:86*
thy testimonies are   *Ps 119:138*
righteous and very *f.*
assembly of *f.* (R)   *Ps 149:1; 149:5, 9*
a *f.* spirit concealeth the   *Pr 11:13*
matter
but a *f.* ambassador is health   *Pr 13:17*
a *f.* witness will not lie, but a   *Pr 14:5*
false utter lies
a *f.* witness delivers souls (B)   *Pr 14:25*
but a *f.* man who can find?   *Pr 20:6*
as snow in harvest, so is a *f.*   *Pr 25:13*
messenger
f. are the wounds of a friend,   *Pr 27:6*
but kisses
a *f.* man shall abound with   *Pr 28:20*
blessings
how is the *f.* city become an   *Isa 1:21*
harlot
afterwards thou shalt be called   *Isa 1:26*
f. city
I took unto me *f.* witnesses to   *Isa 8:2*
record
kings shall see, because of   *Isa 49:7*
Lord that is *f.*
the Lord be a *f.* witness   *Jer 42:5*
between us
works are *f.* and right (A)   *Da 4:37*
could find none, forasmuch as   *Da 6:4*
he was *f.*
but Judah is *f.* with the saints   *Ho 11:12*
with *f.* Holy One   *Ho 11:12*
(A)(B)(E)(R)
the *f.* city (R)   *Zec 8:3*
who then is a *f.* and wise   *M't 24:45*
servant

well done, thou good and *f.*   *M't 25:21*
servant
thou hast been *f.* in a few   *M't 25:23;*
things   *Lu 19:17*
who then is that *f.* and wise   *Lu 12:42*
steward
he that is *f.* in the least is *f.*   *Lu 16:10*
also in much
have not been *f.* in   *Lu 16:11*
unrighteous mammon
have not been *f.* in what is   *Lu 16:12*
another man's
if ye have judged me *f.* to the   *Ac 16:15*
Lord
many *f.* holy ones (A)   *Ac 26:10*
God is *f.* by whom ye were   *1Co 1:9;*
called   *10:13*
it is required in stewards, that   *1Co 4:2*
a man be *f.*
I have sent you Timothy *f.* in   *1Co 4:17*
the Lord
that hath obtained mercy of   *1Co 7:25*
Lord to be *f.*
God is *f.* (A)(P)(R)   *2Co 1:18*
they are blessed with *f.*   *Ga 3:9*
Abraham
to the saints and *f.* in Christ   *Eph 1:1*
Jesus
Tychicus a. *f.* minister in the   *Eph 6:21*
Lord
to the saints and *f.* brethren in   *Col 1:2*
Christ
Epaphras, who is for you a *f.*   *Col 1:7;*
minister   *4:7*
Onesimus, a *f.* brother, who is   *Col 4:9*
one of you
f. is he that calleth you, who   *1Th 5:24*
will do it
the Lord is *f.* who shall   *2Th 3:3*
stablish you
I thank Christ, that he   *1Ti 1:12*
counted me *f.*
this is a *f.* saying   *2Ti 1:15;*
       4:9; Tit 3:8
their wives must be sober, and   *1Ti 3:11*
f. in all things
rather do them service because   *1Ti 6:2*
they are *f.*
the same commit thou to *f.* men   *2Ti 2:2*
it is a *f.* saying; yet he abideth   *2Ti 2:11;*
       2:13
if any be blameless, having *f.*   *Tit 1:6*
children
holding fast the *f.* word, as he   *Tit 1:9*
was taught
reliable and *f.* (A)   *Tit 2:10*
that he might be a *f.*   *Heb 2:17*
high priest
who was *f.* to him that   *Heb 3:2*
appointed him
for he is *f.* that promised   *Heb 10:23;*
       11:11
commit their souls, as unto a   *1Pe 4:19*
f. Creator
I have written by Silvanus a *f.*   *1Pe 5:12*
brother
if we confess, he is *f.* to   *1Jo 1:9*
forgive us
Christ who is the *f.* witness   *Re 1:5; 3:14*
be *f.* to death, I will give thee a   *Re 2:10*
crown of life
those days wherein Antipas my   *Re 2:13*
f. martyr
they that are with him, are   *Re 17:14*
called, and *f.*
and he that sat upon him   *Re 19:11*
was called *f.*
these words are true and *f.*   *Re 21:5;*
       22:6

FAITHFULLY

deal loyally, *f.* (A)   *Ge 47:29; Jos 2:14*
serve him *f.* (A)(B)(R)   *1Sa 12:24*
for they dealt *f.*   *2Ki 12:15; 22:7*
thus do in the fear of the   *2Ch 19:9*
Lord *f.*
and they brought in the   *2Ch 31:12*
offerings *f.*
and the men did the work *f.*   *2Ch 34:12*
the king that *f.* judgeth the   *Pr 29:14*
poor
hath my word, let him speak   *Jer 23:28*
my word *f.*
teach way of God *f.* (P)   *M't 22:16*
doest *f.* whatsoever do to   *3Jo 5*
brethren

FAITHFULNESS

faithfulness (R)	Ge 24:27;
32:10; Ex 34:6; De 32:4; Jos 24:14;	
2Sa 2:6; 15:20; 1Ki 2:4; 3:6; 2Ki 20:3;	
Ps 25:10; 26:3; 30:9; 33:4; 40:10-11;	
54:5; 57:3, 10; 61:7; 71:22; 85:10-11;	
86:15 89:14, 49; 91:4; 98:3; 100:5; 108:4;	
111:8; 117:2; 119:30; 138:2; Pr 3:3;	
14:22; 16:6; 20:28; Isa 16:5; 38:3, 18-19;	
Ho 4:1; Mi 7:20; Zec 8:8	
faithfulness (B)	De 13:14;
Ps 33:4; 40:10; 54:5; 57:10; 71:22; 89:14,	
49; 91:4; 96:13; 98:3; 100:5; 108:4;	
111:9; 119:30; 138:2; Pr 3:3; 16:6;	
20:28; Isa 16:5; 38:18-19; Mic 7:20;	
9:27; Lu 12:44; 21:3	
God of f. (A)(E)	De 32:4
in whom is no f. (A)(E)(R)	De 32:20
Lord render to every man	1Sa 26:23;
his f.	
faithfulness (A)	2Sa 2:6;
15:20; Ps 33:4; 54:5; 61:7; 89:49;	
Pr 12:22; Isa 38:18; 39:8; Ho 4:1	
for there is no f. in their mouth	Ps 5:9
and thy f. reacheth unto the	Ps 36:5
clouds	
I have declared thy f. and thy	Ps 40:10
salvation	
shall thy f. be declared in	Ps 88:11
destruction	
I will make known f. to all	Ps 89:1
generations	
thy f. shalt thou establish in	Ps 89:2
the heavens	
thy f. also in the congregation	Ps 89:5
of the saints	
who is like thee, or to thy f.	Ps 89:8
round about thee	
but my f. and my mercy shall	Ps 89:24
be with them	
nor will I suffer my f. to fail	Ps 89:33
it is good to shew forth thy f.	Ps 92:2
every night	
and that thou in f. hast	Ps 119:75
afflicted me	
thy f. is unto all generations	Ps 119:90
hear my prayer; in thy f.	Ps 143:1
answer me	
and f. shall be the girdle of his	Isa 11:5
reins	
thy counsels of old are f. and	Isa 25:1
truth	
thy mercies are new, great is	La 3:23
thy f.	
I will betroth thee unto me in	Ho 2:20
f.	
shall unbelief make the f. of	Ro 3:3
God (S)	

FAITHLESS

had been f. to God (R)	2Ch 28:19
became more f. (R)	2Ch 28:22
who were f. (R)	2Ch 30:7
the f. (R)	Ps 119:158; Pr 13:15; 23:28
the f. (R)	Pr 21:18; 22:12
f. sister Judah (B)	Jer 3:8; 3:10-11
acted f.	Eze 15:8
Judah hath been f. (B)(R)	Mal 2:11;
	2:14-16
O f. generation	M't 17:17;
	M'k 9:19; Lu 9:41
you unbelieving and	M't 17:17
(A)(B)(N)(P)	
and be not f. but believing	Joh 20:27
f., heartless, loveless (A)(R)	Ro 1:31
f. heart of deserter from (N)	Heb 3:12

FAITHLESSNESS

his f. (R)	2Ch 33:19; Ezr 9:2
because of f. (R)	Ezr 9:4; 10:6
the exile's f. (R)	Ezr 10:6
their f. (A)(R)	Ho 14:4

FALCON

whole species of f.	Le 11:14
(A)(E)(R)(S)	
the f. (E)	De 14:13
the f. eye (A)(E)(R)(S)	Job 28:7

FALL

God caused deep sleep to f.	Ge 2:21
upon Adam	
may seek occasion against us,	Ge 43:18
and f. on us	

see that ye f. not out by the	Ge 45:24
way	
so that his rider shall f.	Ge 49:17
backward	
fear and dread shall f. upon	Ex 15:16
them	
if a man dig a pit, and an ox	Ex 21:33
or ass f. therein	
on whatsoever any of them	Le 11:32
doth f.	
if their carcase f. on any	Le 11:37;
sowing seed	11:38
lest land f. to whoredom and	Le 19:29
become wicked	
they shall f. before you by the	Le 26:7;
sword	26:8
they shall f. when none	Le 26:36
pursueth	
they shall f. one upon another	Le 26:37
let them f. by camp round	Nu 11:31
about	
your carcases shall f. in the	Nu 14:29;
wilderness	14:32
this is the land that shall f. to	Nu 34:2
you	
if any man f. from thence	De 22:8
they said, Rise thou, and f.	J'g 8:21
upon us	
Samson said, Swear ye will	J'g 15:12
not f. upon me	
f. into the hand of the	J'g 15:18
uncircumcised	
let f. some handfuls of purpose	Ru 2:16
for her	
until thou know how the	Ru 3:18
matter will f.	
let none of his words f. to	1Sa 3:19
ground	
not one hair of head f. to	1Sa 14:45
ground 2Sa 14:11; 1Ki 1:52; Ac 27:34	
Saul sought to make David	1Sa 18:25
f. by Philistines	
would not f. on the priests of	1Sa 22:17
the Lord	
king said, Turn thou, and f.	1Sa 22:18
on priests	
therefore let not my blood f.	1Sa 26:20
to earth	
go near and f. on him	2Sa 1:15;
	1Ki 2:29, 31
so thou didst f. (E)	2Sa 3:34
let us f. into hand of God,	2Sa 24:14;
let me not f. into	1Ch 21:13
hand of man	
who shall persuade Ahab to	1Ki 22:20;
go up and f. at	2Ch 18:19
Ramoth-gilead	
let us f. unto the host of	2Ki 7:4
Syrians	
shall f. nothing of word of	2Ki 10:10
the Lord	
why shouldst meddle, that	2Ki 14:10
thou shouldst f.	
he will f. to his master Saul	1Ch 12:19
have sickness, till bowels f.	2Ch 21:15
out	
God shall make thee f. before	2Ch 25:8
enemy	
that thou shouldest f. and	2Ch 25:19
Judah with thee	
before whom begun to f. shall	Es 6:13
not prevail against him, but	
shalt surely f. before him	
Purim never f. into disuse	Es 9:28
(R)(S)	
shall not his dread f. upon	Job 13:11
you	
let mine arm f. from	Job 31:22
shoulder blade	
let them f. by their own	Ps 5:10
counsels	
enemies shall f. and perish at thy	Ps 9:3
presence	
that the poor may f. by his	Ps 10:10
strong ones	
into that very destruction let	Ps 35:8
him f.	
tho' he f. shall not be utterly	Ps 37:24
cast down	
arrows, whereby the people f.	Ps 45:5
under thee	
make their tongue to f. on	Ps 64:8
themselves	
he let it f. in midst of their	Ps 78:28
camp	
but ye shall f. like one of the	Ps 82:7
princes	
thousand shall f. at thy side,	Ps 91:7
and 10,000	

thou hast thrust at me that I	Ps 118:13
might f.	
let burning coals f. upon	Ps 140:10
them	
let the wicked f. into their	Ps 141:10
own nets	
the Lord upholdeth all that f.	Ps 145:14
unless they cause some to f.	Pr 4:16
but a prating fool shall f.	Pr 10:8; 10:10
wicked shall f. by his own	Pr 11:5
wickedness	
where no counsel is the people	Pr 11:14
f.	
he that trusteth in his riches	Pr 11:28
shall f.	
an haughty spirit before a f.	Pr 16:18
he that is abhorred of Lord	Pr 22:14
shall f. therein	
but the wicked shall f. into	Pr 24:16
mischief	
diggeth pit shall f. therein	Pr 26:27;
	Ec 10:8
causeth to go astray shall f. in	Pr 28:10
own pit	
but he that hardeneth his	Pr 28:14
heart shall f.	
but he that is perverse shall f.	Pr 28:18
at once	
righteous shall see their f.	Pr 29:16
if they f. one will lift up his	Ec 4:10
fellow	
if the tree f. toward the south	Ec 11:3
or north	
many among them shall	Isa 8:15
stumble and f.	
they shall f. under the slain	Isa 10:4
Lebanon shall f. by a mighty	Isa 10:34
nail fastened in the sure place	Isa 22:25
shall f.	
who fleeth from fear shall f.	Isa 24:18
into pit	
the earth shall f. and not rise	Isa 24:20
again	
that they might go and f.	Isa 28:13
backward	
iniquity shall be as a breach	Isa 30:13
ready to f.	
in day of slaughter, when	Isa 30:25
towers f.	
the young men shall utterly f.	Isa 40:30
therefore mischiefs shall f.	Isa 47:11
upon thee	
whoso shall gather shall f. for	Isa 54:15
thy sake	
I will not cause mine anger to	Jer 3:12
f.	
they shall f. among them that	Jer 6:15;
f.	8:12
the fathers and sons shall f.	Jer 6:21
upon them	
saith Lord, shall they f. and not	Jer 8:4
arise	
even carcases of men shall f. as	Jer 9:22
dung	
I have caused him to f. upon it	Jer 15:8
suddenly	
my f. (B)(E)(R)(S)	Jer 20:10
they shall be driven on, and f.	Jer 23:12
therein	
whirlwind f. on head of	Jer 23:19;
wicked	30:23
drink ye, and be drunken, and	Jer 25:27
spue, and f.	
ye shall f. like a pleasant	Jer 25:34
vessel	
it is false, I f. not away to	Jer 37:14
Chaldeans	
they shall all f. in the land of	Jer 44:12
Egypt	
they shall stumble and f.	Jer 46:6
toward north	
he made many to f. one fell	Jer 46:16
on another	
he that fleeth shall f. into the	Jer 48:44
pit	
earth moved at noise of their	Jer 49:21
f.	
her young men f. in her	Jer 49:26;
streets	50:30
the most proud shall stumble	Jer 50:32
and f.	
slain shall f. in land of	Jer 51:4;
Chaldeans	51:47, 49
the wall of Babylon shall f.	Jer 51:44
as Babylon caused slain of	Jer 51:49
Israel to f.	
he hath made my strength to f.	La 1:14

the slain shall *f.* in the midst of   *Eze 6:7* you
say that it shall *f.* and great   *Eze 13:11* hailstones shall *f.* and
foundation be discovered,   *Eze 13:14* and it shall *f.*
bring out piece by piece, let   *Eze 24:6* no lot *f.* on it
isles shake at noise of their *f.*   *Eze 26:15*
isles tremble in day of thy *f.*   *Eze 26:18*
all thy company shall *f.* into   *Eze 27:27;* seas   *27:34*
shalt *f.* upon open fields   *Eze 29:5; 39:5*
great pain, when slain shall *f.*   *Eze 30:4* in Egypt
they also that uphold Egypt   *Eze 30:6* shall *f.*
cause sword to *f.* out of his   *Eze 30:22* hand
every man for his life in day   *Eze 31:16* of thy *f.*
by swords will I cause   *Eze 32:12* multitude to *f.*
not *f.* thereby in day that he   *Eze 33:12* turneth
and in all thy rivers shall they   *Eze 35:8* *f.*
steep places shall *f.* every   *Eze 38:20* wall shall *f.*
arrows to *f.; f.* on mountains   *Eze 39:3; 39:4*
they caused Israel to *f.* into   *Eze 44:12* iniquity
thus land shall *f.* to you for   *Eze 47:14* inheritance
also robbers of thy people   *Da 11:14* shall *f.*
he shall stumble and *f.* and   *Da 11:19* not be found
when they shall *f.; some f.* to   *Da 11:34;* try them   *11:35*
shalt thou *f.* in day, the prophet   *Ho 4:5* also shall *f.* in night
people that doth not   *Ho 4:14* understand shall *f.*
Israel and Ephraim shall *f.*   *Ho 5:5* Judah shall *f.*
they shall say to the hills, *F.*   *Ho 10:8* on us
but the transgressors shall *f.*   *Ho 14:9* therein
can a bird *f.* in snare where no   *Am 3:5* gin is
horns of altar shall *f.* to   *Am 3:14* ground
even they shall *f.* and never   *Am 8:14* rise again
yet shall not least grain *f.* to   *Am 9:9* earth
rejoice not, O mine enemy,   *Mic 7:8* when I *f.*
they shall *f.* into mouth of   *Na 3:12* eater
house fell, great was *f.* of it   *M't 7:27*
not one sparrow *f.* to ground   *M't 10:29* without
if it *f.* into a pit on the   *M't 12:11* sabbath day
both shall *f.* into the ditch   *M't 15:14; Lu 6:39*
eat crumbs which *f.* from   *M't 15:27* masters' table
whoso *f.* on stone be   *M't 21:44;*
broken, on whom it shall *f.* it   *Lu 20:18*
many then shall *f.* away   *M't 24:10* (B)(R)
sun shall be darkened, and   *M't 24:29;*
stars *f.* from heaven   *M'k 13:25*
all *f.* away because of me   *M't 26:31* (N)(R)
though all stumble and *f.*   *M't 26:33* away (A)(N)(P)(R)
child set for *f.* and rising of   *Lu 2:34*
I beheld Satan as lightning *f.*   *Lu 10:18* from heaven
shall begin to say to   *Lu 23:30* mountains, *F.* on us
except a corn *f.* into ground   *Joh 12:24* and die
fearing lest they should *f.* into   *Ac 27:17* quicksands
then soldiers cut ropes and let   *Ac 27:32* her *f.* off
not an hair *f.* from head of   *Ac 27:34* any of you
due to one person's *f.* (B)   *Ro 5:17*
a Rock that will make them *f.*   *Ro 9:33* (A)(R)
have they stumbled that they   *Ro 11:11* should *f.*

through *f.* salvation is come to   *Ro 11:11* Gentiles
f. of them be riches of the   *Ro 11:12* world
put an occasion to *f.* in   *Ro 14:13* brother's way
him that standeth take heed   *1Co 1:12* lest he *f.*
made to stumble and *f.* (A)   *2Co 11:29*
he *f.* into condemnation of the   *1Ti 3:6* devil
have good report, lest he *f.* into   *1Ti 3:7* reproach
they that will be rich *f.* into   *1Ti 6:9* temptation
f. away from living God (B)   *Heb 3:12*
lest any *f.* after the same   *Heb 4:11* example
it is fearful to *f.* into hands   *Heb 10:31* of living God
count it joy, when ye *f.* into   *Jas 1:2* temptation
swear not, lest ye *f.* into   *Jas 5:12* condemnation
a Rock that will make them *f.*   *1Pe 2:8* (R)
if ye do these things ye shall   *2Pe 1:10* never *f.*
beware lest ye *f.* from your   *2Pe 3:17* stedfastness
said to mountains and rocks,   *Re 6:16* *F.* on us
I saw a star *f.* from heaven unto   *Re 9:1* earth

FALL *AWAY*

in time of temptation *f. away*   *Lu 8:13*
if they *f. away* to renew them   *Heb 6:6* again

FALL *BY SWORD*

lest he *f.* on us with pestilence   *Ex 5:3* or *sword*
brought us to this land to *f.* by   *Nu 14:3* *sword*
ye shall *f.* by the *sword*   *Nu 14:43*
Sennacherib *f.* by *sword*   *2Ki 19:7*
they shall *f.* by *sword*   *Ps 63:10; Eze 6:11*
thy men shall *f.* by the *sword*   *Isa 3:25*
and every one shall *f.* by the   *Isa 13:15* *sword*
then shall Assyrian *f.* with the   *Isa 31:8* *sword*
cause to *f.* by *sword*   *Isa 37:7; Jer 19:7*
Pashur's friends shall *f.* by   *Jer 20:4* *sword*
and thou shalt not *f.* by the   *Jer 39:18* *sword*
a third part shall *f.* by the   *Eze 5:12* *sword*
he that is near shall *f.* by the   *Eze 6:12* *sword*
ye shall *f.* by *sword*, I will   *Eze 11:10* judge you
his fugitives shall *f.* by the   *Eze 17:21* *sword*
thy remnant shall *f.* by the   *Eze 23:25* *sword*
sons and daughters shall *f.* by   *Eze 24:21* *sword*
they of Dedan shall *f.* by the   *Eze 25:13* *sword*
men in the league shall *f.* by   *Eze 30:5* *sword*
from tower of Syene, shall *f.*   *Eze 30:6* by *sword*
young men shall *f.* by the   *Eze 30:17* *sword*
I will cause *sword* to *f.* out   *Eze 30:22* of hand
they in wastes shall *f.* by   *Eze 33:27* *sword*
they that understand shall *f.*   *Da 11:33* by *sword*
their princes shall *f.* by *sword*   *Ho 7:16*
Samaria shall *f.* by the *sword*   *Ho 13:16*
when they *f.* on *sword* not be   *Joe 2:8* wounded
thy sons and daughters *f.* by   *Am 7:17* *sword*
they shall *f.* by edge of *sword*   *Lu 21:24*

FALL *DOWN*

see brother's ass *f. down* by   *De 22:4* way
wall of the city shall *f. down*   *Jos 6:5* flat

David let his spittle *f. down*   *1Sa 21:13*
all kings shall *f. down* before   *Ps 72:11* him
he that is holpen shall *f. down*   *Isa 31:3*
their host shall *f. down* as   *Isa 34:4* leaf falleth
shall I *f. down* to the stock of   *Isa 44:19* a tree
the Sabeans shall *f. down*   *Isa 45:14* unto thee
they *f. down*, yea, they worship   *Isa 46:6*
the arms of Pharaoh shall *f.*   *Eze 30:25* down
ye *f. down* and worship image   *Da 3:15; 3:10*
if ye *f. down* and worship the   *Da 3:15* image, well
and many shall *f. down* slain   *Da 11:26*
things will I give thee, if thou   *M't 4:9;* wilt *f. down.*   *Lu 4:7;*
twenty-four elders *f. down*   *Re 4:10* before him

FALLEN

Lord said to Cain, Why is thy   *Ge 4:6* countenance *f.*
why is your face downcast (B)   *Ge 4:6*
that hath his hair *f.* off from   *Le 13:41* his head
if thy brother be *f.* in decay   *Le 25:35*
all Ai were *f.* on the edge of   *Jos 8:24* sword
behold, their lord was *f.* down   *J'g 3:25* dead
their inheritance had not *f.*   *J'g 18:1* unto them
behold, the woman was *f.* at   *J'g 19:27* the door
Dagon was *f.;* a deep sleep *f.*   *1Sa 5:3; 26:12*
they found Saul and sons *f.*   *1Sa 31:8; 1Ch 10:8*
sure he could not live after he   *2Sa 1:10* was *f.*
they mourned, because they   *2Sa 1:12* were *f.*
you have *f.* (B)(R)   *2Sa 3:34*
there is a great man *f.* this day   *2Sa 3:38* in Israel
now Elisha was *f.* sick of his   *2Ki 13:14* sickness
became ill of the illness (A)   *2Ki 13:14*
was confined with the illness   *2Ki 13:14* (B)
were dead bodies *f.* to earth   *2Ch 20:24*
for lo, our fathers have *f.* by   *2Ch 29:9* sword
Haman was *f.* on bed where   *Es 7:8* Esther
they are brought down and *f.*   *Ps 20:8*
there are the workers of   *Ps 36:12* iniquity *f.*
how art thou *f.* from heaven,   *Isa 14:12* O Lucifer!
nor have the inhabitants of   *Isa 26:18* the world *f.*
f. gods of the nations (B)   *Jer 14:22*
all of them *f.* by the sword   *Eze 32:22; 32:23-24*
for thou hast *f.* by thine   *Ho 14:1* iniquity
which of you have ox *f.* into a   *Lu 14:5* pit
Holy Ghost was *f.* on none of   *Ac 8:16* them
Eutychus being *f.* into deep   *Ac 20:9* sleep fell down
when we were all *f.* I heard a   *Ac 26:14* voice
fearing lest they should have   *Ac 27:29* *f.* on rocks
looked when Paul should have   *Ac 28:6* *f.* down dead
f. out to furtherance of the   *Ph'p 1:12* gospel
remember from whence thou art   *Re 2:5* *f.*

ARE FALLEN

many of people *are f.* and dead   *2Sa 1:4*
how *are* the mighty *f.*   *2Sa 1:19; 1:25, 27*
they *are f.* under my feet   *2Sa 22:39; Ps 18:38*
lines *are f.* to me in pleasant   *Ps 16:6* places
the terrors of death *are f.* upon   *Ps 55:4* me

into midst whereof they are *f.* Ps 57:6
themselves
reproaches of them are *f.* upon Ps 69:9
me
bricks are *f.* down, but we will Isa 9:10
build
Jews that are *f.* to the Jer 38:19
Chaldeans
the mighty men, they are *f.* Jer 46:12
both together
Babylon's foundations are *f.* Jer 50:15
walls down
my virgins are *f.* by the sword La 2:21
his branches are *f.* boughs Eze 31:12
broken
shall not lie with mighty that Eze 32:27
are *f.*
all their kings are *f.* none calleth Ho 7:7
to me
part remain, some are *f.* 1Co 15:6;
asleep 15:18
justified by law, ye are *f.* from Ga 5:4
grace
are seven kings, five are *f.* and Re 17:10
one is

IS FALLEN

man whose hair *is f.* off his Le 13:40
head
our lot *is f.* on this side Nu 32:19
Jordan
I know that your terror *is f.* Jos 2:9
upon us
the fire of God *is f.* from Job 1:16
heaven
is f. into the ditch which he Ps 7:15
made
Jerusalem is ruined, and Judah Isa 3:8
is f.
shouting for thy summer fruits Isa 16:9
is f.
Babylon *is f., is f.* Isa 21:9;
 Re 14:8; 18:2
for truth *is f.* in streets, Isa 59:14
equity cannot
spoilers *is f.* on thy summer Jer 48:32
fruits
Babylon *is* suddenly *f.* and Jer 51:8
destroyed
crown *is f.* from our heads, La 5:16
woe to us
when wall *is f.* shall it not be Eze 13:12
said
virgin of Israel *is f.* shall no Am 5:2
more rise
I will raise up the tabernacle Am 9:11
that *is f.*
Howl, fir tree, for the cedar *is* Zec 11:2
f.
build tabernacle of David Ac 15:16
which *is f.*

FALLEST

thou *f.* away to the Chaldeans Jer 37:13

FALLETH

when there *f.* out any war, they Ex 1:10
join
every vessel whereinto any of Le 11:33
them *f.*
every thing whereupon their Le 11:35
carcase *f.*
inheritance be where his lot *f.* Nu 33:54
not fail one that *f.* on the 2Sa 3:29
sword
as man *f.* before wicked men, 2Sa 3:34
so fellest
will light on him as dew *f.* on 2Sa 17:12
ground
when deep sleep *f.* on men Job 4:13;
 33:15
a wicked messenger *f.* into Pr 13:17
mischief
a perverse tongue *f.* into Pr 17:20
mischief
just man *f.* seven times, riseth Pr 24:16
up again
rejoice not when thine enemy Pr 24:17
f.
woe to him that is alone when Ec 4:10
he *f.*
sons of men are snared when it Ec 9:12
f. on
where the tree *f.* there shall it Ec 11:3
be
as the leaf *f.* off from the vine Isa 34:4

maketh an image, and *f.* Isa 44:15
down
he that *f.* to Chaldeans shall Jer 21:9
live
whoso *f.* not down, and Da 3:6;
worshippeth 3:11
for ofttimes he *f.* into the M't 17:15
fire
a house divided against a Lu 11:17
house *f.*
give me the portion of goods Lu 15:12
that *f.* to me
to his own master he standeth Ro 14:4
or *f.*
the flower thereof *f.* Jas 1:11; 1Pe 1:24

FALLING

f. into a trance, but his eyes Nu 24:4;
open 24:16
thy words have upholden him Job 4:4
that was *f.*
the mountain *f.* cometh to Job 14:18
nought
wilt not deliver my feet from Ps 56:13;
f. 116:8
a righteous man *f.* before the Pr 25:26
wicked
and as a *f.* fig from the fig- Isa 34:4
tree
came trembling and *f.* down Lu 8:47
before him
as it were great drops of blood Lu 22:44
f. down
to keep you from *f.* away (R) Joh 16:1
and Judas *f.* headlong, burst Ac 1:18
asunder
and *f.* into a place where two Ac 27:41
seas met
striking a crosscurrent Ac 27:41
(A)(B)(N)
they struck a shoal (P)(R) Ac 27:41
their *f.*-off means enrichment Ro 11:12
(N)
if eating cause brother's *f.* 1Co 8:13
(A)(R)
and so *f.* down, he will 1Co 14:25
worship God
except there come a *f.* away 2Th 2:3
first
apostasy is to come first (B) 2Th 2:3
final rebellion against God (N) 2Th 2:3
a definite rejection of God (P) 2Th 2:3
the rebellion comes first (R) 2Th 2:3
f. away from living God Heb 3:12
(E)(R)
to him that is able to keep you Jude 24
from *f.*
keep you from stumbling (A) Jude 24

FALLS

f. down upon mountains Ps 133:3
(B)(R)
he *f.* away (A)(N)(R) M't 13:21

FALLOW

and the roebuck and the *f.* deer De 14:5
the *f.* ground (S) Pr 13:23
Break up your *f.* ground, and Jer 4:3
sow
break up your *f.* ground: for Ho 10:12
it is
my intellect is *f.* (N) 1Co 14:14

FALLOWDEER

harts, and roebucks, and *f.* 1Ki 4:23

FALSE

thou shalt not raise a *f.* report Ex 23:1
keep thee far from a *f.* matter Ex 23:7
they said, It is *f.* tell us now 2Ki 9:12
went after *f.* idols and 2Ki 17:15
became *f.* (A)(R)
he was *f.* to his God (R) 2Ch 26:16
f. men (E) Job 11:11
for truly my words shall not Job 36:4
be *f.*
played *f.* to thy children (B) Ps 73:15
play thee (B)(R) Ps 73:27
I hate every *f.* way Ps 119:104; 119:128
what shall be done to thee, *f.* Ps 120:3
tongue
f. balance is an abomination to Pr 11:1
the Lord
a wicked doer giveth heed to *f.* Pr 17:4
lips

and a *f.* balance is not good Pr 20:23
whoso boasteth of a *f.* gift, is Pr 25:14
like wind
f., harsh, wicked speaking (A) Isa 58:9
f. sister Judah (R) Jer 3:7; 3:8, 10-11
are *f.,* empty and futile Jer 10:3
(B)(R)
they prophecy unto you a *f.* Jer 14:14
vision
f. gods of the nations (A) Jer 14:23
to *f.* gods (A)(B)(E)(R) Jer 18:15
I am against them that Jer 23:32
prophesy *f.* dreams
then said Jeremiah, It is *f.* I Jer 37:14
fall not away
but have seen for thee *f.* La 2:14
burdens
seen *f.* visions (B) Eze 13:7
f. and delusive words (A) Eze 13:8
f. visions (E) Eze 13:8;
 Eze 13:23; 21:29; 22:28
f. visions (A) Eze 13:23; 21:29; 22:28
it shall be to them as a *f.* Eze 21:23
divination
let none imagine evil, love no Zec 8:17
f. oath
the diviners have told *f.* Zec 10:2
dreams
I will be swift witness against Mal 3:5
f. swearers
f. Christs M't 24:24; M'k 13:22
don't bring *f.* charges (P) Lu 3:14
have taken any thing by *f.* Lu 19:8
accusation
nothing *f.* in him (N) Joh 7:18
for such are *f.* apostles, 2Co 11:13
deceitful
I have been in perils among 2Co 11:26
f. brethren
because of *f.* brethren unawares Ga 2:4
brought in
played *f.* like the rest (N) Ga 2:13
without natural affection, *f.* 2Ti 3:3
accusers
aged women, that they be not *f.* Tit 2:3
accusers
heart *f.* (R) Heb 10:2
there shall be *f.* teachers among 2Pe 2:1
you
exploit with *f.* arguments 2Pe 2:3
(A)(B)(P)(R)

FALSE *PROPHET*

sorcerer, a *f.* prophet, a Jew Ac 13:6
out of the mouth of the *f.* Re 16:13
prophet
f. prophet that wrought Re 19:20
miracles
the beast and *f.* prophet are Re 20:10

FALSE *PROPHETS*

beware of *f.* prophets in M't 7:15
sheep's clothing
many *f.* prophets shall rise M't 24:11;
 24:24
f. prophets shall rise, and M'k 13:22
shew signs
so did their fathers to the *f.* Lu 6:26
prophets
there were *f.* prophets among 2Pe 2:1
people
f. prophets are gone out into 1Jo 4:1
world

FALSE *WITNESS*

not bear *f.* witness against Ex 20:16;
neighbour De 5:20; M't 19:18
if a *f.* witness rise up against De 19:16
any man
behold, if the witness be a *f.* De 19:18
witness
a *f.* witness that speaketh lies Pr 6:19
a *f.* witness sheweth forth Pr 12:17;
deceit 14:5
a *f.* witness shall not be Pr 19:5;
unpunished 19:9
a *f.* witness shall perish Pr 21:28
a man that beareth *f.* witness Pr 25:18
is a maul
for out of the heart proceed M't 15:19
f. witness
the elders sought *f.* witness M't 26:59
against Jesus
many bare *f.* witness M'k 14:56;
against him 14:57

FALSE *WITNESSES*

f. witnesses are risen up   Ps 27:12
against me
f. witnesses did rise, they laid Ps 35:11
to my charge
many *f. witnesses* came, at   M't 26:60
the last came two *f. witnesses*
set up *f. witnesses*, who said   Ac 6:13
we are found *f. witnesses* of 1Co 15:15
God

FALSEHOOD

should have wrought *f.*   2Sa 18:13
against my life
I had dealt falsely (A)(E)   2Sa 18:13
I have acted treacherously   2Sa 18:13
(B)(R)
in your answers there   Job 21:34
remaineth *f.*
lips speak *f.* (R)   Job 27:4
walked in *f. Job 31:5; Pr 30:8; Eze 13:6*
pursue *f.* (B)(E)(S)   Ps 4:2
behold, he hath brought forth *f.* Ps 7:14
gives birth to lies (A)(R)   Ps 7:14
they speak *f.*   Ps 10:7; 24:4; 41:6
lifted soul to *f.* (A)   Ps 24:4; 41:6;
  Pr 30:8; Eze 13:6
sat with men of *f.* (E)   Ps 26:4
hast trodden them down, for Ps 119:118
deceit is *f.*
I despise *f.*   Ps 119:163
their hand is a right hand of *f.* Ps 144:8
(B)   144:11; Pr 30:8
cords of *f.* (A)(E)(R)   Isa 5:18
and under *f.* have we hid   Isa 28:15
ourselves
are ye not a seed of *f.*; words Isa 57:4;
of *f.*   59:13
children of sin, a disloyal   Isa 57:4
brood (B)
children of transgression,   Isa 57:4
offspring of deceit (R)
made the law of *f.* (A)   Jer 8:8
for his molten image is *f.*   Jer 10:14;
  51:17
thou hast forgotten me, and   Jer 13:25
trusted in *f.*
see *f.* and delusion (A)   La 2:14
they commit *f.* and thief cometh Ho 7:1
in
if a man walking in the spirit Mic 2:11
and *f.*
in him is no *f.* (R)   Joh 7:18

FALSEHOODS

walked with *f.* (E)   Job 31:5;
Ps 12:2; 24:4; 41:6; Pr 30:8; Jer 13:6, 8
through specious *f.* (N)   1Ti 4:2

FALSELY

swear to me that thou wilt   Ge 21:23
not deal *f.*
have found what was lost, and Le 6:3
sweareth *f.*
all that about which he hath   Le 6:5
sworn *f.*
neither deal *f.* nor lie one to   Le 19:11
another
ye shall not swear by my name Le 19:12
f.
if the witness have testified *f.* De 19:18
nor have we dealt *f.* in thy   Ps 44:17
covenant
they say, The Lord liveth, they Jer 5:2
swear *f.*
prophets prophesy *f.* unto you Jer 5:31;
  29:9
prophet, priest, every one   Jer 6:13;
dealeth *f.*   8:10
will ye steal, murder, and swear Jer 7:9
f.
for thou speakest *f.* of   Jer 40:16
Ishmael
thou speakest *f.* the Lord hath Jer 43:2
not sent
swearing *f.* in making a   Ho 10:4
covenant
curse enter his house that   Zec 5:4
sweareth *f.*
say evil against you *f.* for my M't 5:11
sake
nor accuse any *f.* be content   Lu 3:14
with wages
oppositions of science, *f.* so   1Ti 6:20
called

f. accuse your good   1Pe 3:16
conversation in Christ

FALSIFYING

and *f.* the balances by deceit   Am 8:5
f. straight ways of the Lord   Ac 13:10
(N)

FALSITY

my days are *f.*, futility (A)   Job 7:16
emptiness, *f.*, futility, frailty Ps 89:47
(A)
increase *f.*, futility (A)   Ec 6:11
all is futility, *f.* (A)   Ec 12:8
offerings of vanity, *f.*, futility Isa 1:13
(A)
f., futility (A)   Isa 40:23;
  41:29; Jer 2:5; Hab 2:13
emptiness, *f.*, futility (A)   Jer 51:18
f. word of God (B)   2Co 4:2

FALSELY

I dealt *f.* (A)(E)   2Sa 18:13
spoken *f.* of the Lord (R)   Jer 5:12

FAME

f. was heard in Pharaoh's   Ge 45:16
house
nations that have heard *f.* of Nu 14:15
thee
Joshua's *f.* was noised thro'   Jos 6:27
country
we heard the *f.* of God, what he Jos 9:9
did in Egypt
his *f.* was in all nations round 1Ki 4:31
about
queen heard *f.* of Solomon   1Ki 10:1;
  2Ch 9:1
thy wisdom exceedeth *f.*   1Ki 10:7;
  2Ch 9:6
f. of David went to all lands 1Ch 14:17
the house must be of *f.* and of 1Ch 22:5
glory
Mordecai's *f.* went through   Es 9:4
provinces
we have heard the *f.* with our Job 28:22
ears
to isles that have not heard   Isa 66:19
my *f.*
we have heard *f.* our hands   Jer 6:24
wax feeble
and I will get them *f.* in every Zep 3:19
land
f. of Jesus   M't 4:24;
  M'k 1:28; Lu 4:14, 37; 5:15
the *f.* thereof went abroad   M't 9:26
into all that land
they, when departed, spread   M't 9:31
abroad his *f.*
Herod the tetrarch heard of   M't 14:1
the *f.* of Jesus

FAMILIAR

f. friends (S)   2Ki 10:11
my *f.* friends have forgotten Job 19:14
me
my *f.* friends abhor me   Job 19:19
(A)(E)
my *f.* friend hath lift up his   Ps 41:9
heel against me
separates *f.* friends (B)   Pr 16:28

FAMILIAR *SPIRIT*

man or woman of a *f. spirit*   Le 20:27
put to death
a medium or fortune teller   Le 20:27
(B)
medium or a wizard (R)   Le 20:27
seek woman that hath *f.*   1Sa 28:7
spirit to inquire of her; a *f.*
spirit at Endor
who is a medium (A)   1Sa 28:7
a woman who contacts   1Sa 28:7
spirits, there is a medium at
Endor (B)(R)
divine by the *f. spirit* and   1Sa 28:8
bring him up
Saul inquired of one that   1Ch 10:13
had *f. spirit*
for consulting a medium (A)   1Ch 10:13
tried a medium seance (B)   1Ch 10:13
consulted a medium (R)   1Ch 10:13
Manasseh dealt with a *f.*   2Ch 33:6
spirit

encouraging mediums and   2Ch 33:6
wizards (A)(B)(R)
thy voice as of one that hath a Isa 29:4
f. spirit
voice like that of a ghost   Isa 29:4
(A)(R)
as the spirit of one dead (B)   Isa 29:4

FAMILIAR *SPIRITS*

regard not them that have *f.* Le 19:31
spirits
do not turn to mediums,   Le 19:31
wizards (B)(R)
against soul that turneth after Le 20:6
f. spirits
who turns to spirits and   Le 20:6
wizards (A)
turns to mediums and wizards Le 20:6
(R)
nor a consulter with *f. spirits* De 18:11
a medium (B)(R)   De 18:11
Saul put away those that had 1Sa 28:3
f. spirits
had driven mediums (B)(R) 1Sa 28:3;
  28:9
how he hath cut off those that 1Sa 28:9
have *f. spirits*
Manasseh dealt with *f. spirits* 2Ki 21:6
provided necromancers and   2Ki 21:6
wizards (B)
dealt with mediums and   2Ki 21:6
wizards (R)
workers with *f. spirits* Josiah 2Ki 23:24
put away
exterminated necromancers, 2Ki 23:24
wizards (B)
put away mediums and   2Ki 23:24
wizards (R)
when they say to you, Seek *f.* Isa 8:19
spirits
consult mediums and wizards Isa 8:19
(A)(R)
consult necromancers,   Isa 8:19
fortunetellers (B)
they shall seek to them that   Isa 19:3
have *f. spirits*
to wizards and fortunetellers Isa 19:3
(B)
to mediums and wizards (R)   Isa 19:3

FAMILIARS

all my *f.* watched for my   Jer 20:10
halting

FAMILIES

creepeth on the earth, after   Ge 8:19
their *f.*
the isles of Gentiles divided   Ge 10:5
after their *f.*
tribes, clans (B)   Ge 10:5; 10:20
were *f.* of the Canaanites   Ge 10:18
spread abroad
the sons of Ham after their *f.* Ge 10:20
the *f.* of Shem   Ge 10:31
in thee all the *f.* of earth be   Ge 12:3;
blessed   28:14
the dukes of Esau according   Ge 36:40
to their *f.*
Joseph nourished his brethren Ge 47:12
with their *f.*
these be the *f.* of Reuben. the Ex 6:14;
firstborn of Israel   Nu 26:7; Jos 13:15,
  23
these are the *f.* of Simeon   Ex 6:15;
  Nu 26:12, 14; Jos 19:1, 8
the *f.* of Gershon   Ex 6:17;
  Nu 3:18, 21; 4:22, 24, 38, 40-41;
  Jos 21:33
these are the *f.* of Levi   Ex 6:19;
6:25; Nu 4:46; 26:57-58; Jos 21:27;
  1Ch 6:19
take you a lamb according to Ex 12:21
your *f.*
of the *f.* of strangers shall ye Le 25:45
buy
take the sum of Israel after   Nu 1:2
their *f.*
and the sons of Kohath by   Nu 3:19;
their *f.*   3:27, 29-30; 4:37; Jos 21:4, 10
the sons of Merari, by their *f.* Nu 3:20;
3:33, 35; 4:33, 42, 44-45; Jos 21:34, 40;
  1Ch 6:63
cut not off the tribe of the *f.* of Nu 4:18
Kohathites
Moses heard them weep   Nu 11:10
through their *f.*

the f. of Gad   *Nu 26:15; 26:18;*
        Jos 13:24, 28
the f. of Judah   *Nu 26:20;*
  26:22; Jos 15:1, 12, 20
the sons of Issachar after   *Nu 26:23*
their f.   *Nu 26:25; Jos 19:17, 23; 21:6;*
        1Ch 6:62; 7:5
the f. of Zebulun   *Nu 26:26;*
  Nu 26:27; Jos 19:10, 16
the sons of Joseph after their *Nu 26:28;*
f.   *36:1*
the f. of Manasseh   *Nu 26:34;*
  36:12; Jos 13:29; 17:2
these are sons of Ephraim   *Nu 26:35;*
after their f. *26:37; Jos 16:5, 8; 21:5, 20;*
               1Ch 6:66
the sons of Benjamin after *Nu 26:38;*
their f.   *26:41; Jos 18:11, 20-21;*
               1Sa 10:21
the sons of Dan after their *Nu 26:42;*
          Jos 19:40, 48
sons of Asher after their f. *Nu 26:44;*
          Jos 19:24, 31
sons of Naphtali after their f. *Nu 26:48;*
    26:50; Jos 19:32
daughters of Zelophehad of   *Nu 27:1*
Manesseh's f.
divide your land by lot among *Nu 33:54*
your f.
the chief fathers of the f. of   *Nu 36:1*
Gilead
tribe the Lord taketh come   *Jos 7:14*
according to f.
to half the children of   *Jos 13:31*
Machir, by their f.
the tribe of Dan according   *Jos 19:40;*
to their f.   *19:48*
the least of all the f. of   *1Sa 9:21*
Benjamin
the f. of Kirjath-jearim, the *1Ch 2:53*
Puhites
f. of the scribes which dwelt *1Ch 2:55*
at Jabez
these are the f. of the   *1Ch 4:2*
Zorathites
the f. of them that wrought fine *1Ch 4:21*
linen
these mentioned were princes *1Ch 4:38*
in their f.
according to divisions of f. *2Ch 35:5;*
                 35:12
I set the people after their f. *Ne 4:13*
did the contempt of f. terrify *Job 31:34*
me?
God setteth the solitary in f. *Ps 68:6*
and maketh him f. like a *Ps 107:41*
flock
I will call all the f. of the north *Jer 1:15*
hear all the f. of the house of *Jer 2:4*
Israel
fury on the f. that call not on *Jer 10:25*
thy name
behold, I will take all the f. of *Jer 25:9*
the north
I will be the God of all the f. *Jer 31:1*
of Israel
the two f. which the Lord   *Jer 33:24*
hath chosen
we will be as the f. of the *Eze 20:32*
countries
you have I known of all f. of *Am 3:2*
the earth
that selleth f. through her *Na 3:4*
witchcrafts
all the f. that remain, every *Zec 12:14*
family apart
whoso will not come up of all *Zec 14:17*
the f.

FAMILY

the f. of Bethuel (B)   *Ge 28:2*
family (B)   *Ge 38:8;*
     1Ki 11:14; Eze 43:19; Da 1:3
his father's f. (B)   *Ge 50:22*
I will set my face against his f. *Le 20:5*
as a f. man (B)   *Le 21:4*
ye shall return every man to *Le 25:10;*
his f.   *25:41*
sell himself to the stock of the *Le 25:47*
stranger's f.
his uncle or any of his f.   *Le 25:49*
may redeem him
of Gershon was the f. of the *Nu 3:21*
Libnites
of Kohath was the f. of the *Nu 3:27*
Amramites
f. of the Hanochites, f. of the *Nu 26:5;*
Palluites   *25:6, 12-13, 15-17, 20:21;*

23-24, 26, 29-32, 35-36, 38-40, 42, 44-45,
                      48-49, 57-58
why our father's name done *Nu 27:4*
away from f.
give his inheritance to the *Nu 27:11*
next of his f.
marry to f. of their father's *Nu 36:6;*
tribe   *36:8, 12*
lest a f. turn away from Lord *De 29:18*
our God
f. which the Lord taketh shall *Jos 7:14*
come
and he took the f. of the   *Jos 7:17*
Zarhites
but they let go the man and all *J'g 1:25*
his f.
behold, my f. is poor in   *J'g 6:15*
Manasseh
communed with f. of his   *J'g 9:1*
mother's father
Manoah a man of the f. of the *J'g 13:2*
Danites
kinsmen of tribal f. (A)   *J'g 16:31*
a young man, a Levite of the f. *J'g 17:7*
of Judah
Danites sent of their f. five *J'g 18:2*
men to spy
that thou be a priest to a f. *J'g 18:19*
in Israel
Israel departed, every man to *J'g 21:24*
his f.
she had a kinsman of the f. of *Ru 2:1*
Elimelech
f. of your fathers walk (B) *1Sa 2:30*
my f. the least of tribe of *1Sa 9:21*
Benjamin
f. of Matri was taken, and *1Sa 10:21*
Saul was taken
his father's f. (B)   *1Sa 17:25*
what is my life, or my   *1Sa 18:18*
father's f. in Israel?
a yearly sacrifice there for all *1Sa 20:6;*
every f.   *20:29*
his whole f. (B)   *1Sa 22:11; 22:16*
my father's f.   *1Sa 24:21*
whole f. is risen against thine *2Sa 14:7*
handmaid
man of f. of Saul, his name *2Sa 16:5*
Shimei
family (R)   *2Ki 11:1;*
     25:25; Eze 43:19; Da 1:3
neither did all their f. multiply *1Ch 4:27*
to the f. of Kohath were   *1Ch 6:61;*
cities given   *6:70*
the ark remained with the f. *1Ch 13:14*
of Obed-edom
these days of Purim kept by *Es 9:28*
every f.
all my f. (A)(B)   *Job 16:7*
I will take one of a city, and *Jer 3:14*
two of a f.
death shall be chosen by residue *Jer 8:3*
of this evil f.
against the f. I brought out of *Am 3:1*
Egypt
every f. shall mourn apart *Zec 12:12;*
                12:13-14
if f. of Egypt go not up, and *Zec 14:18*
come not
his f. heard of this (N)   *M'k 3:21*
whole f. in heaven and earth *Eph 3:15*
is named
no f. tree (P)   *Heb 7:3*

FAMINE

for the f. was grievous in the *Ge 12:10*
land
there was a f. in the land,   *Ge 26:1*
besides first f.
seven empty ears shall be *Ge 41:27*
seven years of f.
and the f. shall consume the *Ge 41:30*
land
seven years of f. (E)(R)   *Ge 41:30*
plenty not be known by reason *Ge 41:31*
of f.
to Joseph were born two sons *Ge 41:50*
before f.
famine (S)   *Ge 41:54;*
2Ki 4:38; 2Ch 6:28; Ne 5:3; Ac 7:11;
                   11:28
the f. was over all the face of *Ge 41:56*
the earth
the land fainted by reason of *Ge 47:13*
the f.
when the judges ruled there was *Ru 1:1*
a f.
there was a f. in days of David *2Sa 21:1*

shall seven years of f. come *2Sa 24:13*
to land
if there be in the land f.   *1Ki 8:37;*
                 2Ch 20:9
was a sore f. in Samaria   *1Ki 18:2;*
                 2Ki 6:25
a f. in the land (B)(R)   *2Ki 4:38*
then f. is in the city, we shall *2Ki 7:4*
die
Lord hath called for a f. it shall *2Ki 8:1*
come
f. prevailed in Jerusalem, no *2Ki 25:3*
bread
if there be f. (B)(E)(R)   *2Ch 6:28*
Hezekiah persuadeth you to *2Ch 32:11*
die by f.
because of f. (R)   *Ne 5:3*
in f. he shall redeem thee from *Job 5:20*
death
at destruction and f. thou   *Job 5:22*
shalt laugh
for want and f. they were   *Job 30:3*
solitary
and to keep them alive in f. *Ps 33:19*
in days of f. they shall be   *Ps 37:19*
satisfied
moreover, he called for a f. *Ps 105:16*
on land
and I will kill thy root with f. *Isa 14:30*
destruction, f. and sword, are *Isa 51:19*
come on thee
nor shall we see sword, nor f. *Jer 5:12;*
                14:13, 15
by sword and f. shall   *Jer 14:15*
prophets be consumed
people shall be cast out,   *Jer 14:16*
because of f.
then behold them that are   *Jer 14:18*
sick with f.
and such as are for the f. to *Jer 15:2*
the f.
deliver up their children to *Jer 18:21*
the f.
deliver from the f. to   *Jer 21:7*
Nebuchadnezzar
I will send the f. among them *Jer 24:10;*
                 29:17
that nation will I punish with *Jer 27:8*
the f.
I will persecute with sword *Jer 29:18*
and f.
city is given to Chaldeans *Jer 32:24*
because of f.
I proclaim a liberty for you *Jer 34:17*
to f.
die of the f. (E)   *Jer 38:9*
the f. shall follow close after *Jer 42:16*
you
f. was sore in the city, there *Jer 52:6*
was no bread
our skin was black because of *La 5:10*
f.
third part shall be consumed *Eze 5:12*
with f.
when I send on them evil *Eze 5:16*
arrows of f.
so will I send on you f. *Eze 5:17; 14:13*
f. within, f. and pestilence *Eze 7:15*
shall devour
I will leave a few men from *Eze 12:16*
f.
subjected to f. (B)(E)   *Eze 34:29*
and I will lay no f. upon you *Eze 36:29*
ye shall receive no more   *Eze 36:30*
reproach of f.
I will send a f. not of bread, *Am 8:11*
but of word
when great f. was thro' all the *Lu 4:25*
land
there arose a mighty f. in that *Lu 15:14*
land
there came a f.   *Ac 7:11*
(A)(B)(E)(N)(P)(R)
shall f. separate us from love *Ro 8:35*
of Christ
kill with f.   *Re 6:8*
(A)(B)(E)(N)(P)(R)
her plagues come in one day, *Re 18:8*
death, f.

BY THE FAMINE

sons and daughters shall die *Jer 11:22*
by the f.
I will consume them by the f. *Jer 14:12;*
                 14:15
they shall be consumed by f. *Jer 16:4;*
            44:12, 18, 27
he that abideth in city shall die *Jer 21:9*
by the f.

why will ye die by the f. and   Jer 27:13
pestilence
be delivered to king of   Jer 32:36
Babylon by the f.
remaineth in city shall die by   Jer 38:2;
f.   Eze 6:12
they shall die by the f. and   Jer 42:17
pestilence
know certainly that ye shall   Jer 42:22
die by the f.
as I have punished Jerusalem   Jer 44:13
by the f.
they shall fall by the f. and   Eze 6:11
pestilence

FAMINES

there shall be f. and   M't 24:7
pestilences
and there shall be f. and   M'k 13:8
troubles
and f. and pestilences: and   Lu 21:11
fearful

FAMISH

the soul of the righteous to f.   Pr 10:3
will f. all the gods of the earth   Zep 2:11

FAMISHED

when all the land of Egypt   Ge 41:55
was f.
and their honourable men are   Isa 5:13
f.
he was f. (N)   M't 4:2

FAMOUS

assembly, f. in the   Nu 16:2
congregation
which were f. in the   Nu 26:9
congregation
Ephratah, f. in Beth-lehem   Ru 4:11
that his name may be f. in   Ru 4:14
Israel
mighty men of valour, f. men   1Ch 5:24
f. throughout the house of   1Ch 12:30
their
A man was f. according as he   Ps 74:5
had
And slew f. kings: for his   Ps 136:18
she became f. among women   Eze 23:10
the daughters of the f.   Eze 32:18
nations

FAN

with the shovel and with   Isa 30:24
the f.
Thou shalt f. them, and the   Isa 41:16
wind
not to f. or to cleanse   Jer 4:11
And I will f. them with the f.   Jer 15:7
in the gates
Babylon fanners, that shall f.   Jer 51:2
her
whose f. is in his hand, and   M't 3:12
he
The winnower in his hand (B)   M't 3:12
His shovel in his hand (N)   M't 3:12
His winnowing-fork in hand   M't 3:12
(R)
Whose f. is in his hand, and he   Lu 3:17
will

FANNERS

Babylon f. that shall fan her   Jer 51:2

FANTASIES

defiling bodies by filthy f. (P)   Jude 8

FANTASY

bring down deceptive f. (P)   2Co 10:5

FAR

that be f. from thee to slay   Ge 18:25
righteous
only you shall not go very f.   Ex 8:28
away
keep thee f. from a false matter   Ex 23:7
the f. end (S)   Nu 34:3
if the place be too f. from   De 12:21;
thee   14:24

the stranger that shall come   De 29:22
from a f. land
waters stood f. from city   Jos 3:16
Adam
go not very f. from city, but be   Jos 8:4
ready
saying, We are f. from you,   Jos 9:22
when ye dwell
my father adventured his life f.   J'g 9:17
they were f. from the   J'g 18:7; 18:28
Zidonians
they were by Jebus, day was f.   J'g 19:11
spent
Jonathan said, F. be it from   1Sa 20:9
thee
thus f. (S)   2Sa 7:18;
   1Ch 17:16; Job 38:11; Ro 1:13
they carry them away f. or   1Ki 8:46
near
his name was spread f.   2Ch 26:15
abroad
now therefore be yet f. from   Ezr 6:6
thence
we are separated one f. from   Ne 4:19
another
to all the Jews both nigh and f.   Es 9:20
his children are f. from safety   Job 5:4
put iniquity f. away   Job 11:14; 22:23
f. be it from God to do   Job 34:10
wickedness
thy judgments are f. out of   Ps 10:5
sight
why art thou so f. from helping   Ps 22:1
me
they that are f. from thee shall   Ps 73:27
perish
Lord, thou art exalted f. above   Ps 97:9
all gods
as f. as east is from west, so   Ps 103:12
f. hath he removed
so let blessing be f. from him   Ps 109:17
that follow mischief are f.   Ps 119:150
from thy law
salvation is f. from the   Ps 119:155
wicked
perverse lips put f. from thee   Pr 4:24
remove thy way f. from her,   Pr 5:8
come not nigh
the Lord is f. from the wicked   Pr 15:29
much more do his friends go f.   Pr 19:7
from him
doth keep his soul shall be f.   Pr 22:5
from them
rod of correction drive it f.   Pr 22:15
from him
for her price is f. above rubies   Pr 31:10
folly, as f. as light excelleth   Ec 2:13
darkness
Lord have removed men f.   Isa 6:12
away
they shall turn the rivers f.   Isa 19:6
away
thou hast removed the   Isa 26:15
nations f.
hear ye that are f. from   Isa 46:12
righteousness
that swallowed thee shall be   Isa 49:19
f. away
thou shalt be f. from   Isa 54:14
oppression
therefore is judgment f. from   Isa 59:9
us
thou art f. from their reins   Jer 12:2
all the kings of the north f. and   Jer 25:26
near
to remove you f. from your   Jer 27:10
land
upon all the cities of Moab f.   Jer 48:24
or near
thus f. is the judgment of   Jer 48:47
Moab
thus f. are the words of   Jer 51:64
Jeremiah
hast removed my soul f. from   La 3:17
peace
therefore have I set it f. from   Eze 7:20
them
they have said, Get ye f.   Eze 11:15
from the Lord
the fourth king f. richer than   Da 11:2
they all
ye might remove them f. from   Joe 3:6
border
ye that put f. away the evil day   Am 6:3
in that day shall decree be f.   Mic 7:11
removed
Peter said, Be it f. from thee,   M't 16:22
Lord
and when the day was now f.   M'k 6:35
spent

thou art not f. from the   M'k 12:34
kingdom of God
Son of man is as a man   M'k 13:34
taking a f. journey
when he was not f. from the   Lu 7:6
house
Jesus said, Suffer ye thus f.   Lu 22:51
he healed him
abide with us, for the day is f.   Lu 24:29
spent
and he led them out as f. as to   Lu 24:50
Bethany
for they were not f. from land   Joh 21:8
they travelled as f. as Phenice   Ac 11:19
that Barnabas should go as f.   Ac 11:22
as Antioch
though he be not f. from   Ac 17:27
every one of us
I will send thee f. hence to   Ac 22:21
Gentiles
they came to meet us as f. as   Ac 28:15
Appii-forum
night is f. spent, the day is at   Ro 13:12
hand
worketh a f. more exceeding   2Co 4:17
weight of glory
for we are come as f. as to   2Co 10:14
you also
f. above all principality and   Eph 1:21
power
that ascended up f. above all   Eph 4:10
heavens
to be with Christ, which is f.   Ph'p 1:23
better
it is yet f. more evident, after   Heb 7:15
Melchisedec

FAR *FROM ME*

but now the Lord saith, Be it   1Sa 2:30;
f. from me   22:15; 2Sa 20:20; 23:17
withdraw thine hand f. from   Job 13:21
me
he hath put my brethren f.   Job 19:13
from me
the counsel of wicked is f.   Job 21:16;
from me   22:18
they flee f. from me, and   Job 30:10
spare not to spit
O Lord, be not f. from me,   Ps 22:11;
for trouble is near   22:19; 35:22; 38:21;
   71:12
hide not thy face f. from me,   Ps 27:9
leave me not
thou hast put mine acquaintance   Ps 88:8
f. from me
lover and friend hast thou put   Ps 88:18
f. from me
remove f. from me vanity and   Pr 30:8
lies
I will be wise, but it was f.   Ec 7:23
from me
but have removed their heart   Isa 29:13
f. from me
they are gone f. from me, and   Jer 2:5
become vain
because the comforter is f.   La 1:16
from me
the carcases of their kings f.   Eze 43:9
from me
the Levites that are gone f.   Eze 44:10
from me
their heart is f. from me   M't 15:8;
   M'k 7:6

FAR *OFF*

when they were gone, and not   Ge 44:4
yet f. off
shall pitch f. off about the   Nu 2:2
tabernacle
not consent to serve gods of   De 13:7
people f. off
thus do to all the cities very f.   De 20:15
off
neither is the commandment   De 30:11
f. off
the king tarried in a place f.   2Sa 15:17
off
carry their captives to a land   2Ch 6:36
f. off
lo, then I would wander f. off   Ps 55:7
is better than a brother f. off   Pr 27:10
that which is f. off who can   Ec 7:24
find out
they shall flee f. off and be   Isa 17:13
chased
hear, ye that are f. off what I   Isa 33:13
have done

they shall behold the land that is *f. off*	Isa 33:17
my righteousness shall not be *f. off*	Isa 46:13
and thou didst send thy messengers *f. off*	Isa 57:9
peace to him that is *f. off* and that is near	Isa 57:19
we look for salvation, but it is *f. off*	Isa 59:11
he that is *f. off* shall die of pestilence	Eze 6:12
that I should go *f. off* from my sanctuary	Eze 8:6
although I have cast them *f. off*	Eze 11:16
he prophesieth of times that are *f. off*	Eze 12:27
those that be *f. off* from thee shall mock	Eze 22:5
confusion to Israel that are near and *f. off*	Da 9:7
I will remove *f. off* northern army	Joe 2:20
they shall sell them to the Sabeans *f. off*	Joe 3:8
make her that was cast *f. off* a nation	Mic 4:7
they *f. off* shall come and build in temple	Zec 6:15
ye who were *f. off* made nigh by Christ	Eph 2:13

FROM FAR

a nation against thee *from f.*	De 28:49; Jer 5:15
I will fetch my knowledge *from f.*	Job 36:3
he will lift up an ensign *from f.*	Isa 5:26
desolation which shall come *from f.*	Isa 10:3
they are bound which are fled *from f.*	Isa 22:3
the name of the Lord cometh *from f.*	Isa 30:27
bring my sons *from f.* and daughters	Isa 43:6; 60:9
listen, O isles, hearken, ye people, *from f.*	Isa 49:1
behold, these shall come *from f.*	Isa 49:12
thy sons shall come *from f.* and daughters	Isa 60:4
for lo, I will save thee *from f.*	Jer 30:10
that ye sent for men to come *from f.*	Eze 23:40
and their horsemen shall come *from f.*	Hab 1:8
for divers of them came *from f.*	M'k 8:3

FARE

and look how thy brethren *f.*	1Sa 17:18
he paid the *f.* thereof, and went	Jon 1:3
ye shall do well. *F.* ye well	Ac 15:29

FARED

How hast thou *f.* (S)	Ru 3:16
and *f.* sumptuously every day	Lu 16:19

FAREWELL

but let me first go bid them *f.*	Lu 9:61
But bade them *f.* saying, I must	Ac 18:21
what they had against him, *f.*	Ac 23:30
Finally, brethren, *f.* Be perfect	2Co 13:11

FARM

f. was before my eyes (A)(B)(E)(R)	De 4:16
farm workers (P)	M't 21:33; 21:34, 38-41; M'k 12:1
and went their ways, one to his *f.*	M'k 22:5

FARMER

farmer (S)	Ge 9:20; Jer 51:23; Am 5:16; 2Ti 2:6; Jas 5:7
I will scatter the *f.* (B)(R)	Jer 51:23
the hard-working *f.* (A)(B)(N)(R)	2Ti 2:6
the *f.* waits (A)(B)(N)(P)(R)	Jas 5:7

FARMERS

vinedressers and *f.* (B)	2Ki 25:12
f. and vinedressers (A)(R)	2Ch 26:10
f. (B)	Jer 31:24; Joe 1:11
farmers (S)	Jer 31:24; 52:16; Joe 1:11; M't 21:33-35, 38, 40-41
call the *f.* to mourning (R)	Am 5:16

FARMING

Noah began his *f.* (B)	Ge 9:20
he loved *f.* (A)	2Ch 26:10

FARMLAND

God's *f.* (B)	1Co 3:9

FARTHER

yea *f.*; though a wise man think	Ec 8:17
And he went a little *f.* and fell	M't 26:39
And when he had gone a little *f.*	M'k 1:19
by the *f.* side of Jordan	M'k 10:1

FARTHEREST

fartherest (S)	Jer 25:32; 31:8

FARTHEST

the *f.* part of the coast	Jos 15:1; 15:5
tarried in the *f.* part of (S)	1Sa 14:2
the *f.* part of the earth (S)	M't 12:42; Lu 11:31

FARTHING

thou hast paid the uttermost *f.*	M't 5:26
not two sparrows sold for a *f.*	M't 10:29
in two mites, which make a *f.*	M'k 12:42

FARTHINGS

not five sparrows sold for two *f.*	Lu 12:6

FASHION

f. which thou shalt make it of	Ge 6:15
according to the *f.* thereof which	Ex 26:30
made after the *f.* of almonds	Ex 37:19
according to all the *f.* of it	1Ki 6:38
the *f.* of the altar, and the pattern	2Ki 16:10
did not one *f.* us in the womb	Job 31:15
the house, and the *f.* thereof	Eze 43:11
We never saw it on this *f.*	M'k 2:12
the *f.* of his countenance was	Lu 9:29
to the *f.* that he had seen	Ac 7:44
for the *f.* of this world passeth	1Co 7:31
in an orderly *f.* (A)(B)	1Co 11:40
his ministers *f.* themselves	2Co 11:15
And being found in *f.* as a man	Ph'p 2:8
the grace of the *f.* of it perisheth	Jas 1:11

FASHIONED

and *f.* it with a graving tool	Ex 32:4
hands have made me and *f.* me	Job 10:8
hands have made me and *f.* me	Ps 119:73
which in continuance were *f.*	Ps 139:16
had respect unto him that *f.* it	Isa 22:11
thy breasts are *f.* and thine hair	Eze 16:7
f. to this world (E)	Ro 12:2
be *f.* like unto his glorious body	Ph'p 3:21
f. out of every kind (P)	Re 21:19

FASHIONETH

He *f.* their hearts alike: he	Ps 33:15
the coals, and *f.* it with hammers	Isa 44:12
Shall the clay say to him that *f.* it	Isa 45:9
Satan *f.* himself (E)	2Co 11:14

FASHIONING

f. themselves as apostles (E)	2Co 11:13
not *f.* yourselves according to	1Pe 1:14

FASHIONS

f. it with planes (A)(R)	Isa 44:13
out were both according to their *f.*	Eze 42:11

FAST

Lord had *f.* closed up all the wombs	Ge 20:18
for he was *f.* asleep and weary	J'g 4:21
No, but we will bind thee *f.*	J'g 15:13
they bind me *f.* with new ropes	J'g 16:11
but abide here *f.* by my maidens	Ru 2:8
Thou shalt keep *f.* by my young men	Ru 2:21
So she kept *f.* by the maidens of Boaz	Ru 2:23
didst *f.* and weep for the child	2Sa 12:21
he is dead, wherefore should I *f.*	2Sa 12:23
held *f.* to them in love (B)	1Ki 11:2
Proclaim a *f.* and set Naboth	1Ki 21:9
proclaimed a *f.* and set Naboth	1Ki 21:12
and hold him *f.* at the door	2Ki 6:32
held *f.* to the Lord (R)	2Ki 18:6
proclaimed a *f.* throughout all	2Ch 20:3
and this work goeth *f.* on	Ezr 5:8
Then I proclaimed a *f.* there	Ezr 8:21
and *f.* ye for me, and neither eat	Es 4:16
and my maidens will *f.* likewise	Es 4:16
and still he holdeth *f.* his integrity	Job 2:3
do you still hold *f.* (A)(B)(E)(R)	Job 2:9
he shall hold it *f.* but it shall not	Job 8:15
My righteousness I hold *f.* and will	Job 27:6
my heart beats *f.* (B)	Job 38:10
and the clods cleave *f.* together	Job 38:38
he commanded, and it stood *f.*	Ps 33:9
For thine arrows stick *f.* in me	Ps 38:2
disease, say they, cleaveth *f.* unto him	Ps 41:8
his strength setteth *f.* the mountains	Ps 65:6
my covenant shall stand *f.* with him	Ps 89:28
They stand *f.* for ever and ever	Ps 111:8
eyeryone who holds her *f.* (A)(B)(R)	Pr 3:18
heart hold *f.* my words (A)(B)(R)	Pr 4:4
Take *f.* hold of instruction; let her not	Pr 4:13
Behold, in the day of your *f.* ye	Isa 58:3
ye *f.* for strife and debate	Isa 58:4
ye shall not *f.* as ye do this day	Isa 58:4
Is it such a *f.* that I have chosen	Isa 58:5
wilt thou call this a *f.* and an	Isa 58:6
not this the *f.* that I have chosen	Isa 58:6
they hold *f.* deceit, they refuse to	Jer 8:5
When they *f.* I will not hear	Jer 14:12
upon the *f.* day (S)	Jer 36:6
proclaimed a *f.* before the Lord	Jer 36:9
Stand *f.* and prepare thee; for	Jer 46:14
and his affliction hasteth *f.*	Jer 48:16
took them captives held them *f.*	Jer 50:33
Sanctify ye a *f.* call a solemn	Joe 1:14
sanctify a *f.* call a solemn assembly	Joe 2:15
and he lay, and was *f.* asleep	Jon 1:5
and proclaimed a *f.* and put on	Jon 3:5
did ye all *f.* unto me, even to me	Zec 7:5
The *f.* of the fourth month	Zec 8:19
and the *f.* of the fifth	Zec 8:19
and the *f.* of the seventh	Zec 8:19
and the *f.* of the tenth	Zec 8:19
Moreover when ye *f.* be not, as	M't 6:16
they may appear unto men to *f.*	M't 6:16

thou appear not unto men to   *M't 6:18*
f.
Why do we and the Pharisees *M't 9:14*
f. oft
but thy disciples *f.* not   *M't 9:14*
from them, and then shall they *M't 9:15*
f.
that same is he: hold him *f.* *M't 26:48*
of the Pharisees used to *f.*   *M'k 2:18*
of John and of the Pharisees *M'k 2:18*
f.
but thy disciples *f.* not   *M'k 2:18*
children of the bridechamber *M'k 2:19*
f.
bridegroom with, they   *M'k 2:19*
cannot *f.*
then shall they *f.* in those   *M'k 2:20*
days
do the disciples of John *f.*   *Lu 5:33*
often
children of the bridechamber *f. Lu 5:34*
then shall they *f.* in those days *Lu 5:35*
I *f.* twice in the week   *Lu 18:12*
come break your *f.* (E)   *Joh 21:12*
when they had broken *f.* (E) *Joh 21:15*
made their feet *f.* in the stocks *Ac 16:24*
because the *f.* was now already *Ac 27:9*
forepart stuck *f.* and   *Ac 27:41*
remained
Watch ye, stand *f.* in the   *1Co 16:13*
faith, quit
Stand *f.* therefore in the liberty *Ga 5:1*
that ye stand *f.* in one spirit, *Ph'p 1:27*
with one
so stand *f.* in the Lord, my   *Ph'p 4:1*
dearly
now we live, if ye stand *f.* in   *1Ti 3:8*
the Lord
hold *f.* that which is good   *1Th 5:21*
brethren, stand *f.* and hold   *2Th 2:15*
Hold *f.* the form of sound   *2Ti 1:13*
words
Holding *f.* the faithful word as *Tit 1:9*
he
if we hold *f.* the confidence   *Heb 3:6*
and
let us hold *f.* our profession   *Heb 4:14*
Let us hold *f.* the profession *Heb 10:23*
of our
and thou holdest *f.* my name   *Re 2:13*
ye have already, hold *f.* till I   *Re 2:25*
come
and hold *f.* and repent   *Re 3:3*
hold that *f.* which thou hast,   *Re 3:11*
that no

FASTED

f. that day until even, and   *J'g 20:26*
offered
and *f.* on that day, and said   *1Sa 27:6*
there
tree at Jabesh, and *f.* seven   *1Sa 31:13*
days
and *f.* until even, for Saul   *2Sa 1:12*
and David *f.* and went in   *2Sa 12:16*
child was yet alive, I *f.* and   *2Sa 12:22*
wept
and *f.* and lay in sackcloth   *1Ki 21:27*
oak in Jabesh, and *f.* seven   *1Ch 10:12*
days
So we *f.* and besought our   *Ezr 8:23*
God
and *f.* and prayed before the   *Ne 1:4*
God of
Wherefore have we *f.* say they *Isa 58:3*
when ye *f.* and mourned in the *Zec 7:5*
when he had *f.* forty days   *M't 4:2*
they ministered to the Lord,   *Ac 13:2*
and *f.*
when they had *f.* and prayed   *Ac 13:3*

FASTEN

and *f.* the wreathen chains to   *Ex 28:14*
thou shalt *f.* in the two ouches *Ex 28:25*
to *f.* it on high upon the mitre *Ex 39:31*
And I will *f.* him as a nail   *Isa 22:23*
they *f.* it with nails and with   *Jer 10:4*

FASTENED

chains they *f.* in the two   *Ex 39:18*
ouches
and *f.* his sockets, and set up *Ex 40:18*
the
and *f.* it into the ground   *J'g 4:21*
And she *f.* it with the pin   *J'g 16:14*
and they *f.* his body to the   *1Sa 31:10*
wall of

with a sword *f.* upon his loins *2Sa 20:8*
beams should not be *f.* in the   *1Ki 6:6*
and *f.* his head in the temple *1Ch 10:10*
which were *f.* to the throne   *2Ch 9:18*
f. with cords of fine linen and   *Es 1:6*
purple
are the foundations thereof *f. Job 38:6*
f. by the masters of assemblies *Ec 12:11*
shall the nail that is *f.* in the *Isa 22:25*
sure
f. it with nails, that it should   *Isa 41:7*
not
a hand broad, *f.* round about *Eze 40:43*
in the synagogue were *f.* on   *Lu 4:20*
him
which when I had *f.* mine eyes, *Ac 11:6*
I
out of the heat, and *f.* on his   *Ac 28:3*
hand

FASTENING

Peter, *f.* his eyes upon him with *Ac 3:4*

FASTEST

when thou *f.* anoint thine head *M't 6:17*

FASTING

of Israel were assembled with *f.* *Ne 9:1*
and *f.* and weeping, and wailing *Es 4:3*
I humbled my soul with *f.*   *Ps 35:13*
and chastened my soul with *f Ps 69:10*
My knees are weak through *f. Ps 109:24*
the Lord's house upon the *f.*   *Jer 36:6*
day
palace, and passed the night *f.* *Da 6:18*
with *f.* and sackcloth, and ashes *Da 9:3*
f. and with and with weeping   *Joe 2:12*
f. for many years (B)   *Zec 7:3*
I will not send them away *f. M't 15:32*
lest
not out but by prayer and *f.*   *M't 17:21*
And if I send them away *f.* to   *M'k 8:3*
by nothing, but by prayer and *M'k 9:29*
f.
Four days ago I was *f.* until   *Ac 10:30*
this
prayed with *f.* they   *Ac 14:23*
commended
ye have tarried and continued *Ac 27:33*
f.
give yourselves to *f.* and prayer *1Co 7:5*

FASTINGS

the matters of the *f.* and their   *Es 9:31*
cry
with *f.* and prayers night and   *Lu 2:37*
day
in labours, in watchings, in *f.*   *2Co 6:5*
in *f.* often, in cold and   *2Co 11:27*
nakedness

FAT

his flock and of the *f.* thereof   *Ge 4:4*
seven well favoured and *f.* kine *Ge 41:4*
seven *f.* and full ears (S)   *Ge 41:7*
did eat up the first seven *f.*   *Ge 41:20*
kine
ye shall eat the *f.* of the land *Ge 45:18*
Out of Asher his bread shall *Ge 49:20*
be *f.*
shall the *f.* of my sacrifice   *Ex 23:18*
remain
shalt take all the *f.* that   *Ex 29:13*
covereth
the *f.* (S)   *Ex 29:13;*
    29:22; Le 3:4, 10, 15; 4:9; 7:4; 8:16, 25;
               9:10, 19
kidneys, and the *f.* that is   *Ex 29:13*
upon
thou shalt take of the ram the *Ex 29:22*
f.
the *f.* that covereth the   *Ex 29:22*
inwards
and the *f.* that is upon them   *Ex 29:22*
f. tail   (A)(B)(E)(R)   *Ex 29:22;*
     Le 3:9; 7:3; 8:25; 9:19
the head, and the *f.* in order   *Le 1:8;*
  upon   *1:12; 3:3-4, 9-10, 14-17; 4:8-9,*
  19, 26, 31, 35; 6:12; 7:3-4, 23-25, 30-31,
      33; 8:16, 20, 25-26; 9:10, 19-20, 24
the offerings made by fire of *Le 10:15*
the *f.*
And the *f.* of the sin offering *Le 16:25*
shall

and burn the *f.* for a sweet   *Le 17:6*
savour
land is, whether it be *f.* or   *Nu 13:20*
lean
shalt burn their *f.* for an   *Nu 18:17*
offering
filled themselves, and waxen *f. De 31:20*
with *f.* of lambs, and rams of *De 32:14*
with the *f.* of kidneys of   *De 32:14*
wheat
Jeshurun waxed *f.* and kicked *De 32:15*
art waxen *f.* thou art grown *De 32:15*
thick
did eat the *f.* of their sacrifices *De 32:38*
and Eglon was a very *f.* man   *J'g 3:17*
and the *f.* closed upon the   *J'g 3:22*
blade
Also before they burnt the *f.* *1Sa 2:15*
Let them not fail to burn the   *1Sa 2:16*
f.
yourselves *f.* with the chiefest *1Sa 2:29*
of
and to hearken than the *f.* of *1Sa 15:22*
rams
And the woman had a *f.* calf *1Sa 28:24*
from the *f.* of the mighty, the *2Sa 1:22*
bow
slew sheep and oxen and *f.*   *1Ki 1:9*
cattle
he hath slain oxen and *f.* cattle *1Ki 1:19*
slain oxen and *f.* cattle and   *1Ki 1:25*
sheep
Ten *f.* oxen, and twenty oxen *1Ki 4:23*
and the *f.* of the peace   *1Ki 8:64;*
offerings   *2Ch 7:7*
they found *f.* pasture and good *1Ch 4:40*
the meat offerings, and the *f.* *2Ch 7:7*
with the *f.* of the peace   *2Ch 29:35*
offerings
offerings and the *f.* until   *2Ch 35:14*
night
eat the *f.* and drink the sweet *Ne 8:10*
took strong cities, and a *f.* land *Ne 9:25*
and were filled, and became   *Ne 9:25*
f.
and in the large and *f.* land   *Ne 9:35*
which
layers of *f.* (A)(B)(E)(R)   *Job 13:27*
maketh collops of *f.* on his   *Job 15:27*
flanks
They are inclosed in their own *Ps 17:10*
f.
All they that be *f.* upon earth *Ps 22:29*
shall
Lord shall be as the *f.* of   *Ps 37:20*
lambs
they shall be *f.* and flourishing *Ps 92:14*
Their heart is as *f.* as grease *Ps 119:70*
The liberal soul shall be made *Pr 11:25*
f.
soul of the diligent shall be   *Pr 13:4*
made *f.*
a good report maketh the   *Pr 15:30*
bones *f.*
trust in the Lord shall be   *Pr 28:25*
made *f.*
rams, and the *f.* of fed beasts *Isa 1:11*
the waste places of the *f.* ones *Isa 5:17*
Make the heart of this people *Isa 6:10*
f.
send among his *f.* ones   *Isa 10:16*
leanness
unto all people a feast of *f.*   *Isa 25:6*
things
of *f.* things full of marrow   *Isa 25:6*
are on the head of the *f.* valleys *Isa 28:1*
of
which is on the head of the *f.* *Isa 28:4*
valley
and it shall be *f.* and   *Isa 30:23*
plenteous
it is made *f.* with fatness   *Isa 34:6*
with the *f.* of the kidneys of *Isa 34:6*
rams
their dust made *f.* with fatness *Isa 34:7*
hast thou filled me with the *f.* *Isa 43:24*
of
drought, and make *f.* thy   *Isa 58:11*
bones
They are waxen, *f.* they shine *Jer 5:28*
ye are grown *f.* as the heifer *Jer 50:11*
Ye eat the *f.* and ye clothe you *Eze 34:3*
in a *f.* pasture shall they feed *Eze 34:14*
will destroy the *f.* and the   *Eze 34:16*
strong
I will judge between the *f.*   *Eze 34:20*
cattle
And ye shall eat *f.* till ye be *Eze 39:19*
full

my bread, the *f.* and the blood *Eze 44:7*
offer unto me the *f.* and the *Eze 44:15*
blood
out of the *f.* pastures of *Eze 45:15*
Israel
peace offerings of your *f.* *Am 5:22*
beasts
by them their portion is *f.* *Hab 1:16*
but he shall eat the flesh of *Zec 11:16*
the *f.*

FATAL

a *f.* fear gripped the city (B) *1Sa 5:11*

FATE

did not share *f.* of *Heb 11:31*
disobedient (P)

FATFLESHED

seven well favoured kine and *f.* *Ge 41:2*
seven kine, *f.* and well *Ge 41:18*
favoured

FATHER

Jabal was *f.* of such as dwell in *Ge 4:20*
tents
Jubal was *f.* of all such as *Ge 4:21*
handle harp
went out of ark, and Ham is *f.* *Ge 9:18*
of Canaan
be the *f.* of many nations *Ge 17:4;*
17:5; Ro 4:17-18
have ye a *f.* *Ge 44:19; 44:20*
God made me *f.* to Pharaoh, *Ge 45:8*
lord of house
whose *f.* was an Egyptian, he *Le 24:10*
went out
as a nursing *f.* beareth *Nu 11:12*
sucking child
are statutes between *f.* and his *Nu 30:16*
daughter
f. shall bring forth tokens of *De 22:15*
virginity
man shall give the damsel's *f.* *De 22:29*
fifty shekels
family of house of his mother's *f.* *J'g 9:1*
dwell with me, and be to me a *J'g 17:10*
f. and priest
go with us, and be to us a *f.* *J'g 18:19*
and a priest
f. of damsel saw him, he *J'g 19:3*
rejoiced
damsel's *f.* retained him, he *J'g 19:4*
abode three days
Kish was *f.* of Saul *1Sa 9:3; 14:51*
Salma the *f.* of Bethlehem *1Ch 2:51*
of Hemath, the *f.* of the house *1Ch 2:55*
of Rechab
Joab the *f.* of the valley of *1Ch 4:14*
Charashim
at Gibeon dwelt the *f.* of *1Ch 8:29;*
Gibeon *9:35*
Esther had neither *f.* nor mother *Es 2:7*
I was a *f.* to poor, and *Job 29:16*
searched out
he was brought up with me, *Job 31:18*
as with a *f.*
hath the rain a *f.?* or who *Job 38:28*
begat the dew
f. of fatherless, judge of *Ps 68:5*
widows
as a *f.* pitieth his children, so *Ps 103:13*
Lord pities
Lord correcteth, even as a *f.* *Pr 3:12*
the son
hear, ye children, the instruction *Pr 4:1*
of a *f.*
a wise son maketh a glad *f.* *Pr 10:1;*
15:20
and the *f.* of a fool hath no *Pr 17:21*
joy
the *f.* of the righteous shall *Pr 23:24*
rejoice
his name called, everlasting *F.* *Isa 9:6*
Eliakim shall be a *f.* to *Isa 22:21*
inhabitants of Jerusalem
f. to children shall make *Isa 38:19*
known thy truth

I will lead them, for I am a *f.* *Jer 31:9*
to Israel
as soul of *f.* so of son, is mine *Eze 18:4*
doth not the son bear *Eze 18:19*
iniquity of *f.*
son shall not bear the iniquity *Eze 18:20*
of the *f.*
in thee they set light by *f.* and *Eze 22:7*
mother
for *f.* or mother they may *Eze 44:25*
defile themselves
for the son dishonoureth the *f.* *Mic 7:6*
if I be a *f.* where is mine *Mal 1:6*
honour
have we not all one *f.?* one *Mal 2:10*
God created us
f. deliver up the child *M't 10:21;*
M'k 13:12
he that loveth *f.* or mother *M't 10:37*
more than me
Jesus said, I thank thee, O *F.* *M't 11:25*
so *F.* it seemed good *M't 11:26*
Lu 10:21; Joh 11:41
no man knoweth the Son but *M't 11:27*
the *F.*
he that curseth *f.* let him die *M't 15:4;*
M'k 7:10
leave *f.* and mother, and *M't 19:5*
cleave to his wife
hath forsaken *f.* mother, or *M't 19:29;*
wife, for my name's sake *M'k 10:29*
baptizing them in name of *M't 28:19*
the *F.*
he taketh *f.* of the damsel *M'k 5:40;*
Lu 8:51
the *f.* of the child cried, Lord, *M'k 9:24*
I believe
of that day knoweth no man, *M'k 13:32*
but the *F.*
Abba, *F.* all things are *M'k 14:36*
possible to thee
Simon, *f.* of Alexander, to *M'k 15:21*
bear his cross
no man knows who *F.* is but *Lu 10:22*
Son
if a son shall ask bread of any *Lu 11:11*
that is a *f.*
f. shall be divided against son, *Lu 12:53*
and son against *f.*
son said, *F.* I have sinned *Lu 15:21*
against heaven
the *f.* said, Bring forth the *Lu 15:22*
best robe
I pray thee, *f.* send to my *Lu 16:27*
father's house
F. if thou be willing, remove *Lu 22:42*
this cup
F. forgive them, for they *Lu 23:34*
know not
F. into thy hands I commend *Lu 23:46*
my spirit
glory as of the only begotten *Joh 1:14*
of the *F.*
the Son which is in the bosom *Joh 1:18*
of the *F.*
F. loveth the Son, and hath *Joh 3:35;*
given *5:20*
nor yet at Jerusalem worship *Joh 4:21*
the *F.*
worship the *F.* in spirit and in *Joh 4:23*
truth
the *f.* knew that it was at the *Joh 4:53*
same hour
do nothing but what he seeth *Joh 5:19*
the *F.* do
for as *F.* raiseth up dead, so *Joh 5:21*
the Son
F. judgeth no man, but hath *Joh 5:22*
committed all
honour Son, even as they *Joh 5:23*
honour the *F.* he that honours
not Son, honours not *F.*
as *F.* hath life in himself, so *Joh 5:26*
hath given
I seek not mine own, but will *Joh 5:30*
of *F.*
works which the *F.* hath given *Joh 5:36*
me bear witness that *F.* hath
F. which hath sent me, hath *Joh 5:37;*
borne witness of me *8:16; 12:49; 14:24;*
1Jo 4:14
think not that I will accuse *Joh 5:45*
you to the *F.*

for him hath God the *F.* *Joh 6:27*
sealed
all that *F.* giveth me shall *Joh 6:37*
come to me
this is the *F.'s* will, that I lose *Joh 6:39*
nothing
is not this Jesus, whose *f.* and *Joh 6:42*
mother we know
no man can come, except *F.* *Joh 6:44*
draw him
that hath learned of the *F.* *Joh 6:45*
cometh to me
not that any hath seen *F.* he *Joh 6:46*
hath seen *F.*
as *F.* hath sent me, and I live *Joh 6:57*
by the *F.*
I am not alone, but I and *F.* *Joh 8:16*
that sent me
F. that sent me beareth witness *Joh 8:18*
of me
understood not he spake to *Joh 8:27*
them of *F.*
F. hath not left me alone, I do *Joh 8:29*
those things
then said they, We have one *F.* *Joh 8:41*
even God
the devil is a liar, and the *f.* of *Joh 8:44*
it
as *F.* knoweth me, even so *Joh 10:15*
know I the *F.*
say ye of him whom the *F.* *Joh 10:36*
hath sanctified
believe that the *F.* is in me, *Joh 10:38*
and I in him
what shall I say? *F.* save me *Joh 12:27*
from this hour
F. glorify thy name; then *Joh 12:28*
came there a voice
even as the *F.* said unto me, *Joh 12:50*
so I speak
Jesus knew that he should *Joh 13:1*
depart unto *F.*
knowing that the *F.* had given *Joh 13:3*
all things
no man cometh to *F.* but by *Joh 14:6*
me
Lord, shew us the *F.* and it *Joh 14:8*
sufficeth us
Philip, he that hath seen me, *Joh 14:9*
hath seen the *F.*
that I am in the *F.* and the *F.* *Joh 14:11;*
in me *17:21*
that the *F.* may be glorified *Joh 14:13*
in the Son
and I will pray the *F.* for you *Joh 14:16;*
16:26
but the Comforter whom the *Joh 14:26*
F. will send
I love the *F.* as the *F.* gave *Joh 14:31*
me commandment
as the *F.* hath loved me, so *Joh 15:9*
have I loved you
that whatsoever ye shall ask *Joh 15:16;*
of the *F.* in my name *16:23*
Comforter whom I will send *Joh 15:26*
you from *F.* the Spirit who
proceedeth from *F.*
they have not known the *F.* *Joh 16:3*
nor me
all things that the *F.* hath, *Joh 16:15*
are mine
ye shall see me, because I go *Joh 16:16;*
to the *F.* *16:17*
but I shall shew you plainly *Joh 16:25*
of the *F.*
F. loveth you, because ye *Joh 16:27*
have loved me
I came forth from the *F.* and *Joh 16:28*
go to the *F.*
I am not alone, because the *Joh 16:32*
F. is with me
F. the hour is come, glorify *Joh 17:1*
thy Son
F. glorify thou me with thine *Joh 17:5*
ownself
Holy *F.* keep those whom *Joh 17:11*
thou hast given
F. I will that they given me *Joh 17:24*
be where I am
O righteous *F.* the world *Joh 17:25*
hath not known thee
but wait for the promise of the *Ac 1:4*
F.

the seasons, the *F.* hath put in *Ac 1:7*
his own power
received of *F.* the promise of *Ac 2:33*
the Holy Ghost
he might be *f.* of all them that *Ro 4:11*
believe
the *f.* of circumcision to them *Ro 4:12*
who are not
faith of Abraham, who is the *Ro 4:16*
f. of us all
as Christ was raised from the *Ro 6:4*
dead by the *F.*
Spirit of adoption, whereby we *Ro 8:15*
cry, Abba, *F.*
glorify God the *F.* of Lord *Ro 15:6;*
Jesus Christ *2Co 1:3; 11:31; Eph 1:3;*
 1Pe 1:3
but to us there is but one God, *1Co 8:6*
the *F.*
have delivered up the *1Co 15:24*
kingdom to God the *F.*
F. of mercies, the God of all *2Co 1:3*
comfort
I will be a *F.* unto you, ye *2Co 6:18*
shall be my sons
an apostle by Jesus Christ and *Ga 1:1*
God the *F.*
peace from God the *F.* *Ga 1:3;*
 2Ti 1:2; Tit 1:4
according to the will of God and *Ga 1:4*
our *F.*
until the time appointed of the *Ga 4:2*
F.
sent Spirit into hearts, crying, *Ga 4:6*
Abba *F.*
God of our Lord Jesus the *F.* *Eph 1:17*
of glory
have access by one Spirit to *Eph 2:18*
the *F.*
I bow my knees unto the *F.* *Eph 3:14*
one God and *F.* of all, who is *Eph 4:6*
giving thanks to the *F.* *Eph 5:20;*
 Col 1:3; 3:17
love with faith from God the *Eph 6:23*
F.
that Jesus is Lord to glory of *Ph'p 2:11*
the *F.*
as son with *f.* hath served *Ph'p 2:22*
with me
pleased *F.* that in him all *Col 1:19*
fulness dwell
acknowledgment of the mystery *Col 2:2*
of the *F.*
unto church which is in God *1Th 1:1*
the *F.*
we charged you, as a *f.* doth *1Th 2:11*
his children
rebuke not an elder, entreat *1Ti 5:1*
him as a *f.*
be to him a *F.* he shall be to *Heb 1:5*
me Son
Melchisedec without *f.* without *Heb 7:3*
mother
what son whom the *F.* *Heb 12:7*
chasteneth not
be in subjection to *F.* of *Heb 12:9*
spirits, and live
every good gift cometh from *Jas 1:17*
F. of lights
pure undefiled religion before *Jas 1:27*
God and *F.*
therewith bless we God, even *Jas 3:9*
the *F.*
to the foreknowledge of God *1Pe 1:2*
the *F.*
if ye call on the *F.* who *1Pe 1:17*
judgeth man's work
he received from God the *F.* *2Pe 1:17*
honour
we shew eternal life, which was *1Jo 1:2*
with *F.*
our fellowship is with the *F.* *1Jo 1:3*
and his Son
we have an Advocate with the *1Jo 2:1*
F.
I write to you, because ye *1Jo 2:13*
have known the *F.*
if any love world, the love of *1Jo 2:15*
F. is not in him

pride of life is not of the *F.* *1Jo 2:16*
but of world
he is antichrist that denieth *1Jo 2:22*
the *F.* and Son
denieth Son, hath not *F.* he *1Jo 2:23*
that acknowledgeth Son hath *F.*
ye shall continue in the Son *1Jo 2:24*
and in the *F.*
what manner of love *F.* hath *1Jo 3:1*
bestowed on us
three bear record, the *F.* Word, *1Jo 5:7*
and Spirit
peace from God the *F.*, from the *2Jo 3*
Lord Jesus Christ, Son of the *F.*
as we received commandment *2Jo 4*
from the *F.*
he that abideth in Christ hath *F.* *2Jo 9*
and Son
to them that are sanctified by *Jude 1*
God the *F.*

HER FATHER

firstborn went in and lay *Ge 19:33*
with *her f.*
he was her father's brother, *Ge 29:12*
she ran and told *her f.*
if *her f.* utterly refuse to give *Ex 22:17*
her
she profaneth *her f.* she shall *Le 21:9*
be burnt
if *her f.* had but spit in her *Nu 12:14*
face
her f. hear her, and shall hold *Nu 30:4*
his peace
if *her f.* disallow her in the day *Nu 30:5*
he heareth
shall be wife to one of the *Nu 36:8*
tribe of *her f.*
bewail *her f.* and mother a *De 21:13*
month
spies brought out Rahab and *Jos 6:23*
her f.
to ask of *her f.* a field *Jos 15:18;*
 J'g 1:14
in two months she returned to *J'g 11:39*
her f.
but *her f.* would not suffer him *J'g 15:1*
to go in
the Philistines burnt her and *J'g 15:6*
her f. with fire
when *her f.* and mother were *Es 2:7*
dead

HIS FATHER

a man leave *his f.* and mother, *Ge 2:24;*
and cleave to wife *M'k 10:7; Eph 5:31*
Ham saw the nakedness of his *Ge 9:22*
f. and told
Haran died before *his f.* *Ge 11:28*
Terah
blessing wherewith *his f.* *Ge 27:41*
blessed him
Jacob obeyed *his f.* and *Ge 28:7*
mother, was gone
Jacob sware by the fear of his *Ge 31:53*
f. Isaac
in land wherein *his f.* was a *Ge 37:1*
stranger
Joseph brought to *his f.* their *Ge 37:2*
evil report
he told dream to *his f. his f.* *Ge 37:10*
rebuked him
brethren envied, but *his f.* *Ge 37:11*
observed the saying
he might rid him, to deliver *Ge 37:22*
him to *his f.*
and we said, The lad cannot *Ge 44:22*
leave *his f.*
he offered sacrifices to the God *Ge 46:1*
of *his f.*
and Joseph went up to meet *Ge 46:29*
Israel *his f.*
Joseph nourished *his f.* and *Ge 47:12*
brethren
he made a mourning for *his f.* *Ge 50:10*
seven days
he that smiteth *his f.* shall be *Ex 21:15*
put to death

he that curseth *his f.* shall die *Ex 21:17;*
 Le 20:9
shall fear every man his mother *Le 19:3*
and *his f.*
a son of Aaron may be defiled *Le 21:2*
for *his f.*
the high priest not defile *Le 21:11*
himself for *his f.*
a Nazarite not make unclean *Nu 6:7*
for *his f.*
if *his f.* have no brethren, to *Nu 27:11*
his kinsman
which will not obey *his f.* and *De 21:18*
mother
then shall *his f.* bring him to *De 21:19*
the elders
cursed be he that setteth light *De 27:16*
by *his f.*
cursed be he that lieth with *De 27:22*
daughter of *his f.*
who said to *his f.* I have not *De 33:9*
seen him
Gideon buried in sepulchre of *J'g 8:32*
his f.
God rendered wickedness he *J'g 9:56*
did to *his f.*
his f. knew not that it was of *J'g 14:4*
the Lord
but Jonathan told not *his f.* *1Sa 14:1*
heard not when *his f.* *1Sa 14:27*
charged the people
Jonathan spake good of David *1Sa 19:4*
to *his f.*
it was determined of *his f.* to *1Sa 20:33*
slay David
because *his f.* had done him *1Sa 20:34*
shame
Asahel buried in sepulchre of *2Sa 2:32*
his f.
I will be *his f.* and he shall be *1Sa 7:14*
my son
as *his f.* shewed kindness to *2Sa 10:2;*
me *1Ch 19:2*
Ahithophel buried in *2Sa 17:23*
sepulchre of *his f.*
Saul buried in sepulchre of *2Sa 21:14*
Kish *his f.*
his f. was a man of Tyre *1Ki 7:14;*
 2Ch 2:14
which *his f.* had dedicated *1Ki 7:51*
 15:15; 2Ch 15:18
not perfect, as the heart of *1Ki 11:4*
David *his f.*
not as did David *his f.* *1Ki 11:6;*
 15:11; 2Ki 18:3; 2Ch 28:1; 29:2
not as did David *his f.* *1Ki 11:6;*
 2Ki 14:3; 16:2
and he walked in all the sins *1Ki 15:3*
cf *his f.*
Nadab did evil and walked in *1Ki 15:26;*
way of *his f.* *22:43, 52; 2Ki 21:21*
Jehoram did evil, but not like *2Ki 3:2*
his f.
and thou rode together after *2Ki 9:25*
Ahab *his f.*
the cities taken out of the *2Ki 13:25*
hand of *his f.*
Amaziah slew servants who *2Ki 14:5;*
had slain king *his f.* *2Ch 25:3*
him king instead of *his f.* *2Ki 14:21;*
 23:30, 34
I will be *his f.* he shall be *1Ch 17:13;*
my son *28:6*
not firstborn, yet *his f.* made *1Ch 26:10*
him chief
the Lord appeared to David *2Ch 3:1*
his f.
according to the order of *2Ch 8:14*
David *his f.*
he walked in the first ways of *2Ch 17:3*
his f. David
Jehoshaphat sought Lord God *2Ch 17:4*
of *his f.*
he walked in the way of Asa *2Ch 20:32*
his f.
his counsellors after the death *2Ch 22:4*
of *his f.*
he walked in the ways of *2Ch 34:2;*
David *his f.* *34:3*
wise son heareth instruction of *Pr 13:1*
his f.

foolish son is a grief to *his f.*   Pr 17:25
foolish son is the calamity of   Pr 19:13
his f.
he that wasteth *his f.* causeth   Pr 19:26
shame
whoso curseth *his f.* his lamp   Pr 20:20
shall be put out
companion of riotous men   Pr 28:7
shameth *his f.*
whoso robbeth *his f.* or   Pr 28:24
mother, and saith
whoso loveth wisdom, rejoiceth   Pr 29:3
his f.
ravens pick out eye that   Pr 30:17
mocketh *his f.*
woe to him that saith to *his f.,*   Isa 45:10
What begettest
he shall not die for the   Eze 18:17
iniquity of *his f.*
as for *his f.* because he   Eze 18:18
cruelly oppressed
to bring the golden vessels *his f.*   Da 5:2
had taken
man and *his f.* go in to the   Am 2:7
same maid
his f. and mother shall thrust   Zec 13:3
him thro'
son honours *his f.* a servant his   Mal 1:6
master
to set a man at variance   M't 10:35
against *his f.*
whoso shall say to *his f.,* It is   M't 15:5;
a gift   M'k 7:11
honour not *his f.* or mother, he   M't 15:6
shall be free
Son of man come in glory of   M't 16:27;
his F. with angels   M'k 8:38; Lu 9:26
whether of them did the will   M't 21:31
of *his f.*
he asked *his f.* how long ago   M'k 9:21
it is since
Lord shall give him the throne   Lu 1:32
of *his f.*
they called him after the name   Lu 1:59
of *his f.*
they made signs unto *his f.*   Lu 1:62
how to call him
his f. Zacharias was filled with   Lu 1:67
Holy Ghost
Jesus delivered him again to   Lu 9:42
his f.
if any man come to me, and   Lu 14:26
hate not *his f.*
the younger of them said to   Lu 15:12
his f.
arose and came to *his f. his f.*   Lu 15:20
saw him
therefore came *his f.* and   Lu 15:28
entreated him
because he said, that God was   Joh 5:18
his f.
son of a Jewess, *his f.* was a   Ac 16:1
Greek
for he was yet in the loins of   Heb 7:10
his f.
made us kings and priests to   Re 1:6
God and *his F.*

MY FATHER

I lay yesternight with *my f.*   Ge 19:34
she is daughter of *my f.* not   Ge 20:12
of my mother
my f. peradventure will feel   Ge 27:12
me, I shall
Esau cried, Bless me, even me   Ge 27:34
also, O *my f.*
the God of *my f.*   Ge 31:5;
  31:42; 32:9; Ex 18:4
when we came to thy servant   Ge 44:24;
my f.   44:27, 30
for I became surety for the   Ge 44:32
lad to *my f.*
my f. yet live; go up to *my f.*   Ge 45:3;
  45:9
tell *my f.; my f.* and brethren   Ge 45:13;
come   47:1
not so, *my f.* for this is the   Ge 48:18
firstborn
a Syrian ready to perish was   De 26:5
my f.
ye will save alive *my f.* and   Jos 2:13
mother
my f. fought for you, and   J'g 9:17
delivered
my f. if thou hast opened thy   J'g 11:36
mouth

I have not told it *my f.* nor   J'g 14:16
my mother
lest *my f.* leave caring for the   1Sa 9:5
asses
Jonathan said, My *f.* troubled   1Sa 14:29
the land
saying, Saul *my f.* seeketh to   1Sa 19:2
kill thee
I will commune with *my f.* of   1sa 19:3
thee
my f. will do nothing, he will   1Sa 20:2
shew me
Lord be with thee, as been   1Sa 20:13
with *my f.*
let *my f.* and my mother be   1Sa 22:3
with you
hand of Saul *my f.* shall not   1Sa 23:17
find thee
restore me the kingdom of *my*   2Sa 16:3
f.
that I may be buried by the   2Sa 19:37
grave of *my f.*
thou barest ark of the Lord   1Ki 2:26
before David *my f.* in all
my f. was afflicted
my f. David not knowing   1Ki 2:32
thereof
wickedness that thou didst to   1Ki 2:44
David *my f.*
hast shewed to David *my f.*   1Ki 3:6
great mercy
made thy servant king instead   1Ki 3:7
of *my f.*
David *my f.* could not build an   1Ki 5:3
house
as Lord spake to David my   1Ki 5:5
f. saying
it was in heart of David *my f.*   1Ki 8:17
to build
who hast kept with thy   1Ki 8:24
servant David *my f.*
let my word be verified to *my*   1Ki 8:26;
f.   2Ch 6:16
my f. lade you with a heavy   1Ki 12:11;
yoke   2Ch 10:11
my f. chastised you with   1Ki 12:14;
whips   2Ch 10:14
league between *my f.* and   1Ki 15:19;
thy father   2Ch 16:3
let me, I pray thee, kiss *my f.*   1Ki 19:20
and mother
the cities *my f.* took I will   1Ki 20:34
restore
Elisha saw it, and he cried,   2Ki 2:12
My *f. my f.*
my f. shall I smite them? shall   2Ki 6:21
I smite them
my f. my f. the chariot of   2Ki 13:14
Israel
Lord chose me before all   1Ch 28:4
house of *my f.* and among sons
of *my f.*
as thou didst deal with *my f.*   2Ch 2:3
so deal
I said to corruption, Thou art   Job 17:14
my f.
when *my f.* and my mother   Ps 27:10
forsake me
he shall cry, thou art *my F.*   Ps 89:26
my God
child have knowledge to cry, My   Isa 8:4
f.
saying to a stock, Thou art *my*   Jer 2:27
f.
wilt thou not cry unto me, My   Jer 3:4;
F.   3:19
cursed be man who brought   Jer 20:15
tidings to *my f.*
whom *my f.* brought out of   Da 5:13
Jewry
he that doeth will of *my F.*   M't 7:21;
  12:50
suffer me to go and bury my   M't 8:21;
f.   Lu 9:59
him will I confess before *my*   M't 10:32
F. in heaven
will I deny before *my F.* in   M't 10:33
heaven
are delivered to me of *my F.*   M't 11:27;
  Lu 10:22
plant *my* heavenly *F.* hath   M't 15:13
not planted
but *my F.* who is in heaven   M't 16:17
revealed it
their angels behold face of   M't 18:10
my F.

it shall be done of *my F.* who   M't 18:19
is in heaven
so shall *my* heavenly *F.* also   M't 18:35
do unto you
for whom it is prepared of   M't 20:23
my F.
that day knoweth no man but   M't 24:36
my F. only
King shall say, Come ye   M't 25:34
blessed of *my F.*
my F. if it be possible, let   M't 26:39
this cup pass from me
my F. if this cup may not   M't 26:42
pass, thy will be done
thinkest thou that I cannot   M't 26:53
pray to *my F.*
how many hired servants of   Lu 15:17
my f. have bread
I will arise, and go to *my f.*   Lu 15:18
and will say,
as *my f.* hath appointed unto   Lu 22:29
me
I send the promise of *my F.*   Lu 24:49
upon you
my F. worketh hitherto, and I   Joh 5:17
work
but *my F.* giveth you the true   Joh 6:32
bread
none come to me, except it be   Joh 6:65
given of *my F.*
Jesus said, Ye neither know   Joh 8:19
me, nor *my F.*
as *my F.* hath taught me, I   Joh 8:28
speak these things
I speak that which I have seen   Joh 8:38
with *my F.*
but I honour *my F.* and ye   Joh 8:49
dishonour me
it is *my F.* that honoureth me,   Joh 8:54
of whom ye say
therefore doth *my F.* love   Joh 10:17
me, because
this commandment have I   Joh 10:18
received of *my F.*
my F. is greater than all   Joh 10:29
I and *my F.* are one   Joh 10:30
many good works have I   Joh 10:32
shewed from *my F.*
if I do not works of *my F.*   Joh 10:37
believe me not
if any serve me, him will *my*   Joh 12:26
F. honour
if known me, should have   Joh 14:7
known *my F.* also
greater works, because I go   Joh 14:12;
to *my F.*   16:10
at that day ye shall know   Joh 14:20
that I am in *my F.*
he that loveth me, shall be   Joh 14:21
loved of *my F.*
I go to the Father, *my F.* is   Joh 14:28
greater than I
I am the vine, *my F.* is the   Joh 15:1
husbandman
herein is *my F.* glorified, that   Joh 15:8
ye bear fruit
all that I heard of *my F.* I   Joh 15:15
have made known
he that hateth me, hateth *my*   Joh 15:23;
F. also   15:24
cup *my F.* hath given, shall I   Joh 18:11
not drink it
touch not, for I am not yet   Joh 20:17
ascended to *my F.* I ascend
to *my F.*
as *my F.* hath sent me, so   Joh 20:21
send I you
even as I received of *my F.*   Re 2:27
I will confess his name before   Re 3:5
my F.

OUR FATHER

our *f.* is old; make *our f.*   Ge 19:31;
drink wine   19:32
Jacob hath taken away all   Ge 31:1;
that is *our f.*   31:16
youngest is this day with *our*   Ge 42:13;
f.   42:32
thy servant *our f.* is in good   Ge 43:28
health
bring *our f.* with sorrow to   Ge 44:31
the grave
our *f.* died in the wilderness,   Nu 27:3
had no sons

why should name of *our f.* be   *Nu 27:4*
done away
blessed be thou, Lord God of   *1Ch 29:10*
Israel *our* F.
thou art *our* F. Abraham   *Isa 63:16*
ignorant
Lord, thou art *our* F. we are   *Isa 64:8*
the clay
our f. commanded us to drink   *Jer 35:6*
no wine
we have obeyed the voice of   *Jer 35:8;*
our f.   *35:10*
our F. which art in heaven   *M't 6:9;*
     Lu 11:2
blessed be kingdom of *our f.*   *M'k 11:10*
David
the oath which he sware to *our*   *Lu 1:73*
f. Abraham
begin not to say, We have   *Lu 3:8*
Abraham to *our f.*
art thou greater than *our f.*   *Joh 4:12;*
     8:53
the God of glory appeared to   *Ac 7:2*
our f.
peace from God *our* F.   *Ro 1:7;*
1Co 1:3;   *2Co 1:2;*   *Eph 1:2;*   *Ph'p 1:2;*
Col 1:2;   *1Th 1:1;*   *2Th 1:2;*   *1Ti 1:2;*
     Ph'm 3
conceived by one, even by *our*   *Ro 9:10*
f. Isaac
according to will of God, and   *Ga 1:4*
our F.
unto God *our* F. be glory for   *Ph'p 4:20*
ever
in the sight of God and *our* F.   *1Th 1:3*
God *our* F. direct our way   *1Th 3:11*
unto you
stablish you in holiness before   *1Th 3:13*
God *our* F.
Paul unto church in God *our*   *2Th 1:1*
F.
now God, even *our* F.   *2Th 2:16*
comfort your hearts

THEIR FATHER

Shem and Japhet covered   *Ge 9:23*
nakedness of *their f.* and
saw not nakedness of *their f.*
they made *their f.* drink wine   *Ge 19:33*
that night
both Lot's daughters with   *Ge 19:36*
child by *their f.*
anoint them as thou didst   *Ex 40:15*
anoint *their f.*
to tribe of *their f.* shall they   *Nu 36:6*
marry
after Dan *their f.*   *Jos 19:47; J'g 18:29*
hearkened not to voice of   *1Sa 2:25*
their f.
one of same place said, Who   *1Sa 10:12*
is *their f.*
the prophet's sons told *their*   *1Ki 13:11*
f.
their f. mourned many days   *1Ch 7:22*
Nadab and Abihu died before   *1Ch 24:2*
their f.
under the hands of *their f.*   *1Ch 25:3;*
Jeduthun   *25:6*
their f. gave them great gifts   *2Ch 21:3*
their f. gave them inheritance   *Job 42:15*
there is generation that   *Pr 30:11*
curseth *their f.*
cup of consolation to drink for   *Jer 16:7*
their f.
in a ship with Zebedee *their f.*   *M't 4:21*
left ship and *their f.* and   *M't 4:22*
followed him
righteous shine in kingdom   *M't 13:43*
of *their f.*

THY FATHER

I heard *thy f.* speak to Esau   *Ge 27:6*
thy brother
thou shalt bring it to *thy f.*   *Ge 27:10*
that he eat
I am the God of *thy f.* fear not   *Ge 46:3*
to go down

by the God of *thy f.* who shall   *Ge 49:25*
help thee
the blessings of *thy f.* have   *Ge 49:26*
prevailed above
thy f. commanded before he   *Ge 50:16*
died, saying
forgive the servants of the   *Ge 50:17*
God of *thy f.*
honour *thy f.* and thy mother   *Ex 20:12;*
     De 5:16; M't 15:4; 19:19
thy brethren of the tribe of *thy*   *Nu 18:2*
f. bring
as the God of *thy f.* promised   *De 6:3*
thee
is not he *thy f.* that bought   *De 32:6*
thee
ask *thy f.* and he will shew thee   *De 32:7*
elders
how thou hast left *thy f.* and   *Ru 2:11*
mother
and what is my sin before *thy*   *1Sa 20:1*
f.
if *thy f.* at all miss me say,   *1Sa 20:6*
David asked
the Lord which chose me   *2Sa 6:21*
before *thy f.*
think David doth honour *thy f.*   *2Sa 10:3;*
     1Ch 19:3
thy f. made yoke grievous   *1Ki 12:4;*
     12:10; 2Ch 10:4
there is a league between my   *1Ki 15:19*
father and *thy f.*
cities which my father took   *1Ki 20:34*
from *thy f.*
get thee to prophets of *thy f.*   *2Ki 3:13*
God of David *thy f.*   *2Ki 20:5;*
     2Ch 21:12; Isa 38:5
my son, know thou God of   *1Ch 28:9*
thy f.
if thou wilt walk before me as   *2Ch 7:17*
thy f.
are aged men much elder   *Job 15:10*
than *thy f.*
hear instruction of *thy f.*   *Pr 1:8; 23:22*
thy f. and mother shall be glad   *Pr 23:25*
thy first *f.* hath sinned   *Isa 43:27*
against me
feed thee with the heritage of   *Isa 58:14*
Jacob *thy f.*
house of *thy f.* dealt   *Jer 12:6*
treacherously with thee
did not *thy f.* eat, drink, and   *Jer 22:15*
do judgment
thy f. was an Amorite, mother   *Eze 16:3*
an Hittite
in days of *thy f.* the king, I say   *Da 5:11*
thy f.
God gave *thy f.* a kingdom and   *Da 5:18*
glory
thy F. which seeth in secret   *M't 6:4;*
     6:18
shut thy door, pray to *thy* F.   *M't 6:6*
who is in secret
honour *thy f.* and mother   *M'k 7:10;*
     10:19; Lu 18:20; Eph 6:2
thy f. and I sought thee   *Lu 2:48*
sorrowing
and *thy f.* hath killed the   *Lu 15:27*
fatted calf
then said they unto him,   *Joh 8:19*
Where is *thy f.*

YOUR FATHER

with all my power I have   *Ge 31:6*
served *your f.*
your f. deceived me, changed   *Ge 31:7*
my wages
is *your f.* alive? have ye   *Ge 43:7*
another brother
as for you, get you up in   *Ge 44:17*
peace to *your f.*
take you wagons, bring *your*   *Ge 45:19*
f.
sons of Jacob, hearken unto   *Ge 49:2*
Israel *your f.*
because ye obeyed Jonadab   *Jer 35:18*
your f.
mother an Hittite, *your f.* an   *Eze 16:45*
Amorite
may glorify *your* F. who is in   *M't 5:16*
heaven
may be children of *your* F. in   *M't 5:45*
heaven
be ye perfect, as *your* F. in   *M't 5:48*
heaven is perfect

otherwise ye have no reward of   *M't 6:1*
your F.
your F. knoweth what things ye   *M't 6:8;*
have need of   *6:32; Lu 12:30*
if ye forgive, *your* heavenly F.   *M't 6:14*
will forgive you
if ye forgive not, neither will   *M't 6:15;*
your F. forgive   *M'k 11:25-26*
your trespasses
not one sparrow shall fall   *M't 10:29*
without *your* F.
it is not will of *your* F. that   *M't 18:14*
one perish
call no man *your f.* upon   *M't 23:9*
earth, for one is *your* F.
be ye merciful, as *your* F. also is   *Lu 6:36*
merciful
ye do what ye have seen with   *Joh 8:38*
your f.
ye do deeds of *your f.* then   *Joh 8:41*
said they to him
if God were *your* F. ye would   *Joh 8:42*
love me
ye are of *your f.* the devil, and   *Joh 8:44*
lusts of *your f.* ye will do
I ascend to my Father and   *Joh 20:17*
your F. to my God

FATHER *IN LAW*

behold, thy *f. in law* goeth to   *Ge 38:13*
Timnath
when brought forth, she went   *Ge 38:25*
to her *f. in law*
flock of Jethro his *f. in law*   *Ex 3:1; 4:18*
Moses' *f. in law*   *Ex 18:1;*
     18:8, 14, 17; J'g 1:16; 4:11
Moses let his *f. in law* depart,   *Ex 18:27*
and he went
Raguel the Midianite, Moses'   *Nu 10:29*
f. in law
his *f. in law* retained him, and   *J'g 19:4*
he abode
when he rose to depart, his   *J'g 19:7*
f. in law urged him
when she heard *f. in law* was   *1Sa 4:19;*
dead   *4:21*
Annas was *f. in law* to   *Joh 18:13*
Caiaphas

FATHERLESS

ye shall not afflict any *f.* child   *Ex 22:22*
your wives shall be widows,   *Ex 22:24*
and children *f.*
he doth execute the judgment   *De 10:18;*
of the *f.* and widow   *Ps 82:3; Isa 1:17*
ye overwhelm the *f.* and dig a   *Job 6:27*
pit
the arms of the *f.* have been   *Job 22:9*
broken
they drive away the ass of the   *Job 24:3*
f.
they pluck the *f.* from the   *Job 24:9*
breast
because I delivered the poor   *Job 29:12*
and the *f.*
eaten alone, and *f.* hath not   *Job 31:17*
eaten thereof
if I have lifted up my hand   *Job 31:21*
against the *f.*
thou art the helper of the *f.*   *Ps 10:14*
to judge the *f.* and the   *Ps 10:18*
oppressed
a father of the *f.* a judge of the   *Ps 68:5*
widows
let his children be *f.* his wife   *Ps 109:9*
a widow
nor let any favour his *f.*   *Ps 109:12*
children
enter not into the fields of the   *Pr 23:10*
f.
they judge not the *f.*   *Isa 1:23; Jer 5:28*
the Lord shall not have mercy   *Isa 9:17*
on their *f.*
widows their prey, that they   *Isa 10:21*
may rob the *f.*
leave thy *f.* children, I will   *Jer 49:11*
preserve
we are orphans and *f.* our   *La 5:3*
mothers widows
in thee have they vexed the *f.*   *Eze 22:7*
and widow

for in thee the *f.* findeth mercy   Ho 14:3
a witness against those that   Mal 3:5
oppress the *f.*
pure religion is to visit the *f.*   Jas 1:27
and widows

FATHERLESS with
STRANGER

the *stranger, f.* and the widow   De 14:29;
shall come and eat   24:19-21;
  26:12-13
the *stranger* and *f.* rejoice   De 16:11;
with thee   16:14
nor pervert judgment of   De 24:17
stranger nor *f.*
cursed that perverts judgment   De 27:19
of *stranger* and *f.*
they slay the *stranger* and   Ps 94:6
murder the *f.*
Lord preserveth the *strangers*   Ps 146:9
and *f.*
if ye oppress not the *siranger,*   Jer 7:6;
f. and the widow   22:3; Zec 7:10

FATHERS

these are the heads of the *f.*   Ex 6:25;
  Jos 14:1; 19:51; 21:1;
  1Ch 8:10, 13, 28
which neither thy *f.*   Ex 10:6
visiting the iniquity of *f.* upon   Ex 20:5;
children   34:7; Nu 14:18; De 5:9
by the house of their *f.*   Nu 1:42
according
f. shall not be put to death   De 24:16;
for children, nor children for *f.*   2Ki 14:6
family of your *f.* walk (B)   1Sa 2:30
whose *f.* I would have   Job 30:1
disdained to set
house and riches are   Pr 19:14
inheritance of *f.*
kings be thy nursing *f.* and   Isa 49:23
f. and sons shall fall on them   Jer 6:21;
children gather wood, *f.* kindle   Jer 7:18
the fire
f. have eaten sour grapes   Jer 31:29;
  Eze 18:2
recompensest iniquity of *f.* on   Jer 32:18
children
f. shall not look back to their   Jer 47:3
children
f. shall eat the sons in midst   Eze 5:10
of these
he shall turn heart of *f.* to   Mal 4:6;
children, and children to *f.*   Lu 1:17
not because it is of Moses, but   Joh 7:22
of the *f.*
men, brethren, and *f.* hearken   Ac 7:2;
  22:1
promise which was made unto   Ac 13:32
f.
perfect manner of the law of the   Ac 22:3
f.
whose are the *f.* of whom Christ   Ro 9:5
came
though instructors, yet not   1Co 4:15
many *f.*
f. provoke not your children   Eph 6:4;
  Col 3:21
God who spake in times past   Heb 1:1
to the *f.*
we had *f.* of our flesh who   Heb 12:9
corrected us
since the *f.* fell asleep, all   2Pe 3:4
things continue
I write unto you *f.* ye have   1Jo 2:13;
known   2:14

HIS FATHERS

he removed the idols *his f.*   1Ki 15:12
made
took the things *his f.* had   2Ki 12:18
dedicated
he did what was evil as *his f.*   2Ki 15:9
had done
he forsook Lord God of his   2Ki 21:22;
f.   2Ch 21:10
according to all *his f.* had   2Ki 23:32;
done   23:37; 24:9
no burning like the burning   2Ch 21:19
of *his f.*

Ahaz provoked the Lord   2Ch 28:25
God of *his f.*
prepareth his heart to seek   2Ch 30:19
the god of *his f.*
he humbled himself before   2Ch 33:12
God of *his f.*
he shall go to the generation   Ps 49:19
of *his f.*
let the iniquity of *his f.* be   Ps 109:14
remembered
shall do what *his f.* have not   Da 11:24
done
neither shall he regard the   Da 11:37
God of *his f.*
a god whom *his f.* knew not   Da 11:38
shall honour
David was laid to *his f.* saw   Ac 13:36
corruption

MY FATHERS

not attained to the years of *my*   Ge 47:9
f.
I will lie with *my f.* carry me   Ge 47:30
out of Egypt
the name of *my f.* be named   Ge 48:16
on them
bury me with *my f.* in cave in   Ge 49:29
field
for I am no better than *my f.*   1Ki 19:4
give the inheritance of *my f.*   1Ki 21:3
to thee   21:4
have gods of nations *my f.*   2Ki 19:12;
destroyed   2Ch 32:14; Isa 37:12
know not what I and *my f.*   2Ch 32:13
have done
for I am a sojourner, as all *my*   Ps 39:12
f. were
I thank and praise thee, O   Da 2:23
God of *my f.*
so worship I the God of *my f.*   Ac 24:14
being zealous of the traditions   Ga 1:14
of *my f.*

OUR FATHERS

till now both we and also *our*   Ge 46:34;
f.   47:3
how *our f.* went down into   Nu 20:15
Egypt
Lord made not this covenant   De 5:3
with *our f.*
land which he sware to *our f.*   De 6:23;
  26:3, 15
cried to the God of *our f.*   De 26:7
the Lord heard
the pattern of the altar *our f.*   Jos 22:28
made
brought *our f.* out of the land   Jos 24:17
of Egypt
where be miracles which *our f.*   J'g 6:13
told of
God be with us, as he was   1Ki 8:57
with *our f.*
his statutes, which he   1Ki 8:58
commanded *our f.*
because *our f.* have not   2Ki 22:13
hearkened
the God of *our f.* look and   1Ch 12:17
rebuke it
for we are sojourners, as were   1Ch 29:15
all *our f.*
God of *our f.* keep for ever   1Ch 29:18;
  2Ch 20:6
which thou gavest *our f.*   2Ch 6:31;
  Ne 9:36
our f. have trespassed and   2Ch 29:6
done evil
for lo, *our f.* have fallen by   2Ch 29:9
the sword
our f. have not kept word of   2Ch 34:21
Lord
but after *our f.* had provoked   Ezr 5:12
God
blessed be the Lord God of our   Ezr 7:27
f.
since the days of *our f.* in a   Ezr 9:7
great trespass
did see affliction of *our f.* in   Ne 9:9
Egypt
our f. dealt proudly, and   Ne 9:16
hardened necks
our f. trusted in thee, they   Ps 22:4
trusted
our f. have told us what thou   Ps 44:1;
didst   78:3

we have sinned with *our f.*   Ps 106:6
and committed
our f. understood not thy   Ps 106:7
wonders in Egypt
house where *our f.*   Isa 64:11
praised thee
shame devoured labour of *our*   Jer 3:24
f.
we and *our f.* have not obeyed   Jer 3:25
the voice
surely *our f.* have inherited   Jer 16:19
lies
we have done, we and *our f.*   Jer 44:17
our kings
our f. have sinned, and are not   La 5:7
confusion of face belongeth   Da 9:8
to *our f.*
for our sins and the iniquities   Da 9:16
of *our f.*
sworn to *our f.* from days of   Mic 7:20
old
by profaning the covenant of   Mal 2:10
our f.
if we had been in days of *our*   M't 23:30
f.
as he spake to *our f.* to   Lu 1:55
Abraham
to perform the mercy promised   Lu 1:72
to *our f.*
our f. worshipped in this   Joh 4:20
mountain
our f. did eat manna in the   Joh 6:31
desert
God of *our f.* hath glorified his   Ac 3:13
Son Jesus
of covenant which God made   Ac 3:25
with *our f.*
God of *our f.* raised up Jesus,   Ac 5:30
whom ye slew
came dearth, *our f.* found no   Ac 7:11
sustenance
Jacob went down and died, he   Ac 7:15
and *our f.*
evil entreated *our f.* and cast   Ac 7:19
out children
this is he which spake in Sinai   Ac 7:38
and with *our f.*
to whom *our f.* would not   Ac 7:39
obey, but thrust
our f. had tabernacle of witness   Ac 7:44
God of this people of Israel   Ac 13:17
chose *our f.*
a yoke which *our f.* nor we   Ac 15:10
were able to bear
for hope of the promise made   Ac 26:6
to *our f.*
well spake Holy Ghost by   Ac 28:25
Esaias to *our f.*
all *our f.* were under the cloud   1Co 10:1

SLEPT WITH FATHERS

so David *slept with* his *f.*	1Ki 2:10; 11:21
Solomon *slept with* his *f.*	1Ki 2:43; 2Ch 9:31
Jeroboam *slept with* his *f.*	1Ki 14:20; 2Ki 14:29
Rehoboam *slept with* his *f.*	1Ki 14:31; 2Ch 12:16
Abijam *slept with* his *f.*	1Ki 15:8; 2Ch 14:1
and Asa *slept with* his *f.*	1Ki 15:24; 2Ch 16:13
Baasha, Omri *slept with f.*	1Ki 16:6; 16:28
Ahab, Jehoshaphat *slept with* his *f.*	1Ki 22:40; 22:50; 2Ch 21:1
Joram, Jehu *slept with* his *f.*	2Ki 8:24; 10:35
Jehoahaz, Joash *slept with* his *f.*	2Ki 13:9; 13:13; 14:16
after that the king *slept with* *f.*	2Ki 14:22; 2Ch 26:2
Azariah, Menahem *slept with* his *f.*	2Ki 15:7; 15:22
Jotham *slept with* his *f.*	2Ki 15:38; 2Ch 27:9
Ahaz *slept with* his *f.*	2Ki 16:20; 2Ch 28:27
Hezekiah *slept with* his *f.*	2Ki 20:21; 2Ch 32:33
Manasseh *slept with* his *f.*	2Ki 21:18; 2Ch 33:20
Jehoiakim *slept with* his *f.*	2Ki 24:6
Uzziah *slept with* his *f.*	2Ch 26:23

THEIR FATHERS

that the God of *their f.* hath   Ex 4:5
appeared
heads of *their f.*   Ex 6:14;
6:25; Jos 14:1; 19:51; 21:1; 1Ch 5:24
     7:2, 7; 8:6; 9:9, 13
in iniquity of *their f.* shall   Le 26:39
pine away
if they confess the iniquity of   Le 26:40
their f.
land thou swarest to give to   Nu 11:12;
their f. 14:23; De 10:11; 31:20; Jos 1:6;
     5:6; 21:43-44; Jer 32:22
have forsaken the covenant of   De 29:25
their f.
when your children ask *their f.*   Jos 4:6;
     4:21
each one a head of the house   Jos 22:14
of *their f.*
that generation gathered to   J'g 2:10
their f.
they forsook the Lord God of   J'g 2:12
their f.
turned out of way *their f.*   J'g 2:17
walked in
corrupted themselves more   J'g 2:19
than *their f.*
my covenant which I   J'g 2:20
commanded *their f.*
if they keep way of Lord, as   J'g 2:22
their f. kept it
which he commanded *their f.* by   J'g 3:4
Moses
bring them again to land   1Ki 8:34;
thou gavest *their f.*   8:48; 2Ch 6:25, 38
who brought forth *their f.* out   1Ki 9:9
of Egypt
out of land which he gave to   1Ki 14:15;
their f.   2Ki 21:8; Jer 16:15; 24:10
provoked above all that *their*   1Ki 14:22
f. had done
since day *their f.* came out of   2Ki 21:15
Egypt
house of *their f.* increased   1Ch 4:38
greatly
transgressed against the God   1Ch 5:25
of *their f.*
blessed the God of *their f.*   1Ch 29:20
and bowed down
forsook God of *their f.*   2Ch 7:22;
     24:24; 28:6
came to sacrifice to the God   2Ch 11:16
of *their f.*
they relied on the Lord God   2Ch 13:18
of *their f.*
commanded to seek God of   2Ch 14:4;
their f.   15:12
brought them back to the   2Ch 19:4
God of *their f.*
not prepared their hearts to   2Ch 20:33
God of *their f.*
which trespassed against the   2Ch 30:7
God of *their f.*
making confession to the   2Ch 30:22
God of *their f.*
according to covenant of   2Ch 34:32
God of *their f.*
following Lord the God of   2Ch 34:33
their f.
God of *their f.* sent by his   2Ch 36:15
messengers
confessed sins and iniquities of   Ne 9:2
their f.
into the land thou promisedst   Ne 9:23
to *their f.*
prepare thyself to the search of   Job 8:8
their f.
which wise men have told   Job 15:18
from *their f.*
might not be as *their f.* a   Ps 78:8
stubborn
marvellous things did he in   Ps 78:12
sight of *their f.*
they dealt unfaithfully like   Ps 78:57
their f.
the glory of children are *their f.*   Pr 17:6
slaughter for iniquity of *their*   Isa 14:21
f.
they did worse than *their f.*   Jer 7:26
after Baalim, which *their f.*   Jer 9:14
taught them
whom they nor *their f.* have   Jer 9:16;
known   19:4
as *their f.* have forgotten my   Jer 23:27
name
make new covenant, not   Jer 31:32;
according to covenant   11:10; Heb 8:9
with *their f.*

sinned against Lord, hope of   Jer 50:7
their f.
they and *their f.* have   Eze 2:3
transgressed
fathers eat sons, and sons eat   Eze 5:10
their f.
cause them to know   Eze 20:4
abominations of *their f.*
their lies, after which *their f.*   Am 2:4
walked
turn the heart of children to   Mal 4:6
their f.
for in like mnner did *their f.*   Lu 6:23
for so did *their f.* to the false   Lu 6:26
prophets

THY FATHERS

thou shalt go to *thy f.* in   Ge 15:15
peace
into land which he sware to   Ex 13:5;
thy f. 13:11; De 6:10, 18; 7:12-13; 8:18;
     9:5; 13:17; 19:8; 28:11; 29:13; 30:20
go up, possess it, as God of *thy*   De 1:21
f. said
nor forget the covenant of *thy*   De 4:31
f. he sware
and because he loved *thy f.*   De 4:37;
     10:15
manna neither did *thy f.* know   De 8:3;
     8:16
thy f. went into Egypt with   De 10:22
seventy persons
land which the God of *thy f.*   De 12:1
giveth thee
other gods thou nor *thy f.*   De 13:6;
known   28:64
give land which he promised   De 19:8;
thy f.   27:3
to a nation thou nor *thy f.*   De 28:36
have known
do thee good and multiply thee   De 30:5
above *thy f.*
rejoice over thee, as he   De 30:9
rejoiced over *thy f.*
thou shalt sleep with *thy f.*   De 31:16;
     2Sa 7:12
shall not come to sepulchre   1Ki 13:22
of *thy f.*
what *thy f.* laid up be carried   2Ki 20:17
away
I will gather thee to *thy f.*   2Ki 22:20;
     2Ch 34:28
thou must go to be with *thy*   1Ch 17:11
f.
search the book of the records   Ezr 4:15
of *thy f.*
instead of *thy f.* be thy   Ps 45:16
children
remove not the landmark *thy*   Pr 22:28
f. set
burned with the burnings of   Jer 34:5
thy f.
I am God of *thy f.* the God of   Ac 7:32
Abraham

YOUR FATHERS

shall bring you to the land of   Ge 48:21
your f.
the God of *your f.* hath sent   Ex 3:13;
me De 1:11; 4:1; Jos 18:3; 2Ch 28:9;
     29:5
thus did *your f.*   Nu 32:8; Ne 13:18
possess land Lord sware to   De 1:8;
your f. 1:35; 7:8; 8:1; 11:9, 21; J'g 2:1
sacrificed to gods whom *your*   De 32:17
f. feared not
your f. dwelt on the other side   Jos 24:2
the flood
I brought *your f.* out of Egypt,   Jos 24:6
Egypt pursued
put away the gods which *your*   Jos 24:14
f. served
whether the gods which *your*   Jos 24:15
f. served
acts the Lord did to you and   1Sa 12:7
your f.
your f. cried, The Lord   1Sa 12:8
brought forth *your f.*
hand of Lord against you as   1Sa 12:15
against *your f.*
law which I commanded   2Ki 17:13
your f.

fight ye not against the God   2Ch 13:12
of *your f.*
be not like *your f.* and   2Ch 30:7;
brethren   30:8; Zec 1:4
remove out of the land   2Ch 33:8
appointed for *your f.*
freewill offering to the God of   Ezr 8:28
your f.
make confession to the God   Ezr 10:11
of *your f.*
when *your f.* tempted me   Ps 95:9;
     Heb 3:9
your and the iniquities of *your*   Isa 65:7
f. together
what iniquity have *your f.*   Jer 2:5
found in me
shall come to land I have given   Jer 3:18
to *your f.*
dwell in the land I gave to *your* Jer 7:7;
f. 23:39; 25:5; 35:15; Eze 20:42; 36:28;
     47:14
I spake not to *your f.* in day I   Jer 7:22
brought
since day *your f.* came forth   Jer 7:25
out of Egypt
which I commanded *your f.*   Jer 11:4;
     17:22
for I earnestly protested unto   Jer 11:7
your f.
because *your f.* have forsaken   Jer 16:11
me
done worse than *your f.*   Jer 16:12;
     16:13
I made a covenant with *your*   Jer 34:13
f. in day
but *your f.* hearkened not   Jer 34:14
unto me
whom they knew not, neither   Jer 44:3
they nor *your f.*
have ye forgotten the   Jer 44:9
wickedness of *your f.*
in my statutes I set before   Jer 44:10
you and *your f.*
the incense ye, *your f.* and   Jer 44:21
kings, your
walk ye not in the statutes   Eze 20:18
of *your f.*
in this *your f.* have   Eze 20:27
blasphemed me
are ye polluted after manner   Eze 20:30
of *your f.*
like as I pleaded with *your f.*   Eze 20:36
so with you
shall dwell in land wherein   Eze 37:25
your f. dwelt
I saw *your f.* as first ripe of   Ho 9:10
fig tree
hath this been in days of *your f.*   Joe 1:2
Lord hath been displeased with   Zec 1:2
your f.
be not as *your f.*   Zec 1:4; 1:5
did not my words take hold of   Zec 1:6
your f.
when *your f.* provoked me to   Zec 8:14
wrath
from days of *your f.* ye are   Mal 3:7
gone away
fill ye up then the measure of   M't 23:32
your f.
of prophets, and *your f.* killed   Lu 11:47
them
ye witness that ye allow the   Lu 11:48
deeds of *your f.*
your f. did eat manna and are   Joh 6:49
dead
not as *your f.* did eat manna   Joh 6:58
and are dead
ye resist Holy Ghost as *your f.*   Ac 7:51
did, so ye
who of prophets have not *your*   Ac 7:52
f. persecuted
received by tradition from   1Pe 1:18
your f.

FATHER'S

and they saw not their *f.*   Ge 9:23
nakedness
thy kindred, and from thy *f.*   Ge 12:1
house
me to wander from my *f.*   Ge 20:13
house
which took me from my *f.*   Ge 24:7
house
is there room in thy *f.* house   Ge 24:23
for us to
But thou shalt go unto my *f.*   Ge 24:38
house
of my kindred, and of my *f.*   Ge 24:40
house

which his *f.* servants had digged in | Ge 26:15
So that I come again to my *f.* house | Ge 28:21
Rachel came with her *f.* sheep | Ge 29:9
told Rachel that he was her *f.* brother | Ge 29:12
taken away all that was our *f.* | Ge 31:1
that which was our *f.* hath he gotten | Ge 31:1
I see your *f.* countenance, that | Ge 31:5
inheritance for us in our *f.* house | Ge 31:14
stolen the images that were her *f.* | Ge 31:19
thou sore longedst after thy *f.* house | Ge 31:30
and lay with Bilhah his *f.* concubine | Ge 35:22
with the sons of Zilpah, his *f.* wives | Ge 37:2
brethren went to feed their *f.* flock | Ge 37:12
Remain a widow at thy *f.* house | Ge 38:11
Tamar went and dwelt in her *f.* house | Ge 38:11
forget all my toil, and all my *f.* house | Ge 41:51
his brethren, and unto his *f.* house | Ge 46:31
My brethren, and my *f.* house | Ge 46:31
brethren, and all his *f.* household | Ge 47:12
and he held up his *f.* hand | Ge 48:17
thou wentest up to thy *f.* bed | Ge 49:4
thy *f.* children shall bow down before | Ge 49:8
And Joseph fell upon his *f.* face | Ge 50:1
and his brethren, and his *f.* house | Ge 50:8
dwelt in Egypt, he, and his *f.* house | Ge 50:22
the troughs to water their *f.* flock | Ex 2:16
him Jochebed his *f.* sister to wife | Ex 6:20
my *f.* God, and I will exalt him | Ex 15:2
in the priest's office in his *f.* stead | Le 16:32
The nakedness of thy *f.* wife shalt | Le 18:8
not uncover: it is thy *f.* nakedness | Le 18:8
nakedness of thy *f.* wife's daughter | Le 18:11
uncover the nakedness of thy *f.* sister | Le 18:12
she is thy *f.* near kinswoman | Le 18:12
the nakedness of thy *f.* brother | Le 18:14
the man that lieth with his *f.* wife | Le 20:11
hath uncovered his *f.* nakedness | Le 20:11
shall take his sister, his *f.* daughter | Le 20:17
mother's sister, nor of thy *f.* sister | Le 20:19
and is returned unto her *f.* house | Le 22:13
she shall eat of her *f.* meat | Le 22:13
with the ensign of their *f.* house | Nu 2:2
and thy sons and thy *f.* house | Nu 18:1
inheritance among their *f.* brethren | Nu 27:7
his inheritance unto his *f.* brethren | Nu 27:10
being in her *f.* house in her youth | Nu 30:3
yet in her youth in her *f.* house | Nu 30:16
unto their *f.* brothers' sons | Nu 36:11
damsel to the door of her *f.* house | De 22:21
to play the whore in her *f.* house | De 22:21
A man shall not take his *f.* wife | De 22:30
nor discover his *f.* skirt | De 22:30
be he that lieth with his *f.* wife | De 27:20
because he uncovereth his *f.* skirt | De 27:20
shew kindness unto my *f.* house | Jos 2:12
all thy *f.* household, home unto thee | Jos 2:18
the harlot alive, and her *f.* household | Jos 6:25

and I am the least in my *f.* house | J'g 6:15
Take thy *f.* young bullock, even | J'g 6:25
because he feared his *f.* household | J'g 6:27
he went unto his *f.* house at Ophrah | J'g 9:5
ye are risen up against my *f.* house | J'g 9:18
Thou shalt not inherit our *f.* house | J'g 11:2
and expel me out of my *f.* house | J'g 11:7
lest we burn thee and thy *f.* house | J'g 14:15
and he went up to his *f.* house | J'g 14:19
away from him unto her *f.* house | J'g 19:2
she brought him into her *f.* house | J'g 19:3
thine arm, and the arm of thy *f.* house | 1Sa 2:31
not on thee, and on all thy *f.* house | 1Sa 9:20
to feed his *f.* sheep at Beth-lehem | 1Sa 17:15
and make his *f.* house free in Israel | 1Sa 17:25
his *f.* family (B) | 1Sa 17:25
Thy servant kept his *f.* sheep | 1Sa 17:34
him go no more home to his *f.* house | 1Sa 18:2
is my life, or my *f.* family in Israel | 1Sa 18:18
when his brethren and all his *f.* house | 1Sa 22:1
son of Ahitub, and all his *f.* house | 1Sa 22:11
Ahimelech, thou, and all thy *f.* house | 1Sa 22:16
of all the persons of thy *f.* house | 1Sa 22:22
destroy my name out of my *f.* house | 1Sa 24:21
thou gone in unto my *f.* concubine | 2Sa 3:7
head of Joab, and on all his *f.* house | 2Sa 3:29
kindness for Jonathan thy *f.* sake | 2Sa 9:7
be on me, and on my *f.* house | 2Sa 14:9
as I have been thy *f.* servant hitherto | 2Sa 15:34
as I have served in thy *f.* presence | 2Sa 16:19
Go in unto thy *f.* concubines | 2Sa 16:21
went in unto his *f.* concubines | 2Sa 16:22
of my *f.* house were but dead men | 2Sa 19:28
against me, and against my *f.* house | 2Sa 24:17
will not do it for David thy *f.* sake | 1Ki 11:12
certain Edomites of his *f.* servants | 1Ki 11:17
shall be thicker than my *f.* loins | 1Ki 12:10; 2Ch 10:10
Israel; but thou and thy *f.* house | 1Ki 18:18
and set him on his *f.* throne | 2Ki 10:3
and made him king in his *f.* stead | 2Ki 23:30
made Mattaniah his *f.* brother | 2Ki 24:17
forasmuch as he defiled his *f.* bed | 1Ch 5:1
Shemuel, heads of their *f.* house | 1Ch 7:2
heads of their *f.* house, choice | 1Ch 7:40
his *f.* house twenty and two captains | 1Ch 12:28
be on me, and on my *f.* house | 1Ch 21:17
according to their *f.* house | 1Ch 23:11
understanding, of Huram my *f.* | 2Ch 2:13
slain thy brethren of thy *f.* house | 2Ch 21:13
made him king in his *f.* stead | 2Ch 36:1
they could not shew their *f.* house | Ezr 2:59; Ne 7:61
both I and my *f.* house have sinned | Ne 1:6
and thy *f.* house shall be destroyed | Es 4:14
thine own people, and thy *f.* house | Ps 45:10
I was my *f.* son, tender and only | Pr 4:3
My son, keep thy *f.* commandment | Pr 6:20

A wise son heareth his *f.* instruction | Pr 13:1
A fool despiseth his *f.* instruction | Pr 15:5
and thy *f.* friend forsake not | Pr 27:10
thy people, and upon thy *f.* house | Isa 7:17
for a glorious throne to his *f.* house | Isa 22:23
upon him all the glory of his *f.* house | Isa 22:24
but obey their *f.* commandment | Jer 35:14
a son, that seeth all his *f.* sins | Eze 18:14
humbled his sister, his *f.* daughter | Eze 22:11
new with you in my *F.* kingdom | M't 26:29
I must be about my *F.* business | Lu 2:49
in his *F.* and of the holy angels | Lu 9:26
it is your *F.* good pleasure to give | Lu 12:32
hired servants of my *f.* have bread | Lu 15:17
wouldest send him to my *f.* house | Lu 16:27
make not my *F.* house an house of | Joh 2:16
I am come in my *F.* name, and ye | Joh 5:43
And this is the *F.* will which hath | Joh 6:39
that I do in my *F.* name, they bear | Joh 10:25
to pluck them out of my *F.* hand | Joh 10:29
In my *F.* house are many mansions | Joh 14:2
not mine, but the *F.* which sent me | Joh 14:24
I have kept my *F.* commandments | Joh 15:10
was nourished up in his *f.* house | Ac 7:20
that one should have his *f.* wife | 1Co 5:1
having his *F.* name written in | Re 14:1

FATHERS'

These be the heads of their *f.* houses | Ex 6:14
fathers, or thy *f.* fathers have seen | Ex 10:6
according to their *f.* houses | Nu 17:6
upward, throughout their *f.* house | Nu 26:2
ye are risen up in your *f.* stead, an | Nu 32:14
the place of my *f.* sepulchres, lieth | Ne 2:3
the city of my *f.* sepulchres, that I | Ne 2:5
their eyes were after their *f.* idols | Eze 20:24
they discovered their *f.* nakedness | Eze 22:10
they are beloved for the *f.* sakes | Ro 11:28

FATHOMLESS

the *f.* riches of Christ (A)(B) | Eph 3:8

FATHOMS

sounded, and found it twenty *f.* | Ac 27:28
again, and found it fifteen *f.* | Ac 27:28

FATLING

young lion and the *f.* together | Isa 11:6

FATLINGS

and of the *f.* and the lambs | 1Sa 15:9
he sacrificed oxen and *f.* | 2Sa 6:13
unto thee burnt sacrifices of *f.* | Ps 66:15
bullocks, all of them *f.* of Bashan | Eze 39:18
my oxen and my *f.* are killed | M't 22:4

FATNESS

of heaven, and the *f.* of the earth | Ge 27:28
dwelling shall be the *f.* of the earth | Ge 27:39

FATNESS

thick, thou art covered with f.   *De 32:15*
Should I leave my f. wherewith   *J'g 9:9*
he covereth his face with his   *Job 15:27*
f.
thy table should be full of f.   *Job 36:16*
satisfied with the f. of thy   *Ps 36:8*
house
be satisfied as with marrow and   *Ps 63:5*
f.
goodness; and thy paths drop   *Ps 65:11*
f.
Their eyes stand out with f.   *Ps 73:7*
and my flesh faileth of f.   *Ps 109:24*
the f. of his flesh shall wax   *Isa 17:4*
lean
it is made fat with f. and   *Isa 34:6*
and their dust made fat with f.   *Isa 34:7*
let your soul delight itself in f   *Isa 55:2*
the soul of the priests with f.   *Jer 31:14*
the root and f. of the olive   *Ro 11:17*
tree

FATS

the f. shall overflow with wine   *Joe 2:24*
the press is full, the f. overflow   *Joe 3:13*

FATTED

and fallowdeer, and f. fowl   *1Ki 4:23*
the midst of her like f.   *Jer 46:21*
bullocks
And bring hither the f. calf   *Lu 15:23*
thy father hath killed the f.   *Lu 15:27*
calf
thou hast killed for him the f.   *Lu 15:30*
calf

FATTER

appeared fairer and f. in flesh   *Da 1:15*

FATTEST

upon them, and slew the f. of   *Ps 78:31*
them
upon the f. places of the   *Da 11:24*
province

FAULT

but the f. is in thine own   *Ex 5:16*
people
your people are unfair (B)   *Ex 5:16*
found f. with Moses (R)   *Ex 17:2*
f.-findings of Israel (R)   *Ex 17:7*
before his face, according to   *De 25:2*
his f.
stripes in proportion to the   *De 25:2*
offense (A)(R)
receive number of stripes he   *De 25:2*
deserves (B)
according to his wickedness,   *De 25:2*
by number (E)
I have found no f. in him   *1Sa 29:3*
found nothing wrong with him   *1Sa 29:3*
(B)
with a f. concerning this   *2Sa 3:8*
woman
brought up a misstep with a   *2Sa 3:8*
woman (B)
find f. with Almighty (A)   *Job 40:2*
prepare themselves without my   *Ps 59:4*
without any wrong of mine   *Ps 59:4*
they run (B)
apart from any f. of mine (S)   *Ps 59:4*
could find none occasion nor f.   *Da 6:4*
there any error or f. found in   *Da 6:4*
him
and tell him his f. between   *M't 18:15*
thee
show him his f.   *M't 18:15*
(A)(B)(E)(R)
unwashen, hands, they found f.   *M'k 7:2*
I find no f. in this man   *Lu 23:4*
I find no guilt or crime in   *Lu 23:4*
(A)(R)
I find nothing criminal (B)(P)   *Lu 23:4*
I find no case for this man (N)   *Lu 23:4*
have found no f. in this man   *Lu 23:14*
I find in him no f. at all   *Joh 18:38*
know that I find no f. in him   *Joh 19:4*
for I find no f. in him   *Joh 19:6*
Why doth he yet find f.? For   *Ro 9:19*
who
Why does he still complain (B)   *Ro 9:19*
why does God blame a man   *Ro 9:19*
(N)

f.-finding people (A)   *Ro 10:21*
there is utterly a f. among you   *1Co 6:7*
is a defect in you (A)(E)   *1Co 6:7*
it means loss to you at every   *1Co 6:7*
point (B)
fall below your standard (N)   *1Co 6:7*
must be seriously wrong in   *1Co 6:7*
your church (P)
is a defeat for you (R)   *1Co 6:7*
if a man be overtaken in a f.   *Ga 6:1*
overtaken in a misconduct or   *Ga 6:1*
sin (A)(B)
overtaken in any trespass   *Ga 6:1*
(E)(R)
do something wrong on sudden   *Ga 6:1*
impulse (N)
be detected in some sin (P)   *Ga 6:1*
irreproachable, without f. (N)   *1Ti 6:14*
For finding f. with them, he   *Heb 8:8*
saith
you may be one at f. (P)   *Jas 5:9*
without f. (P)   *Jude 24*
are without f. before the throne   *Re 14:5*
without blemish before the   *Re 14:5*
throne (A)(E)
they are faultless (B)(N)   *Re 14:5*
they are beyond reproach (P)   *Re 14:5*
they are spotless (R)   *Re 14:5*

FAULTFINDER

will f. contend with (B)(R)   *Job 40:2*

FAULTFINDING

without f. (A)   *Ph'p 2:14*
without reproach and f. finding   *Jas 1:5*
(A)
without reserve, f. (B)   *Jas 1:5*

FAULTLESS

was also f. (B)   *Ps 18:23*
present you f. (A)   *Col 1:22*
establish you f. (N)   *1Th 3:13*
if that first covenant had been   *Heb 8:7*
f.
had been without defect (A)   *Heb 8:7*
had been flawless (B)   *Heb 8:7*
had proved satisfactory (P)   *Heb 8:7*
and to present you f. before the   *Jude 24*
present you unblemished (A)   *Jude 24*
without blemish (E)(R)   *Jude 24*
jubilant and above reproach   *Jude 24*
(N)
without fault with unspeakable   *Jude 24*
joy (P)
they are f. (B)(N)   *Re 14:5*

FAULTS

I do remember my f. this day   *Ge 41:9*
I am reminded of my offences   *Ge 41:9*
cleanse thou me from secret f.   *Ps 19:12*
secret sins (B)   *Ps 19:12*
Confess your f. one to another   *Jas 5:16*
confess your sins to each other   *Jas 5:16*
(B)(E)(N)(P)(R)
if, when ye be buffeted for   *1Pe 2:20*
your f.
if you do wrong and are   *1Pe 2:20*
punished (A)(N)(R)
standing for a beating for doing   *1Pe 2:20*
wrong (B)
when ye sin and are buffeted   *1Pe 2:20*
for it (E)

FAULTY

this thing as one which is f.   *2Sa 14:13*
as one that is guilty (A)(E)   *2Sa 14:13*
the king condemns himself   *2Sa 14:13*
(B)
the king convicts himself (R)   *2Sa 14:13*
now shall they be found (A)   *Ho 10:2*
found guilty and suffer   *Ho 10:2*
punishment (A)(E)
heart slippery, must suffer for   *Ho 10:2*
it (B)
heart false, must bear their   *Ho 10:2*
guilt (R)

FAVOR

his f. is mine (B)   *2Sa 22:20*
gain f. with their captors (B)   *2Ch 30:9*
obtained f. and kindness (E)   *Es 2:17*
sue your f. with gifts (R)   *Ps 45:12*

bestows f. and honor (R)   *Ps 84:11*
take into f. his servants A)   *Ps 135:14*
find f. and compassion (A)(R)   *Da 1:9*
grant f. and sympathy (B)   *Da 1:9*
show a f. (S)   *Ac 24:27; 25:9*
counted a f. or gift   *Ro 4:4*
(A)(B)(N)(P)(R)
double f. (A)   *2Co 1:15*
seek thee f. of (S)   *Ga 1:10*
have a f. to give (P)   *Ph'm 14*

FAVORABLY

no longer looks f. upon (B)   *La 4:16*

FAVORITES

God has no f. (N)   *Ac 10:34;*
Ro 2:11; Eph 6:9; Col 3:25

FAVORITISM

God shows no f. (B)   *Ro 2:11*
judges without slightest f. (P)   *1Pe 1:17*

FAVOUR

now I have found f. in thy   *Ge 18:3*
sight
if I have found f. in thine eyes   *Ge 30:27*
him f. in the sight of the   *Ge 39:21*
keeper
will give his people f. in the   *Ex 3:21*
sight
And the Lord gave the people   *Ex 11:3*
f. in
Lord gave the people f. in the   *Ex 12:36*
sight
have I not found f. in thy   *Nu 11:11*
sight
if I have found f. in they sight   *Nu 11:15;*
Es 7:3
pass that she find no f. in his   *De 24:1*
eyes
the old, nor shew f. to the   *De 28:50*
young
O Naphtali, satisfied with f.   *De 33:23*
and that they might have no   *Jos 11:20*
f.
Let me find f. in thy sight   *Ru 2:13*
and was in f. both with the   *1Sa 2:26*
Lord
for he hath found f. in my   *1Sa 16:22*
sight
if I have found f. in thine   *1Sa 20:29*
eyes
young men find f. in thine eyes   *1Sa 25:8*
the lords f. thee not   *1Sa 29:6*
if I shall find f. in the eyes of   *2Sa 15:25*
Hadad found great f. in the   *1Ki 11:19*
sight
if thy servant have found f. in   *Ne 2:5*
Esther obtained f. in the sight   *Es 2:15*
of
she obtained grace and f. in his   *Es 2:17*
that she obtained f. in his sight   *Es 5:2*
If I have found f. in the sight of   *Es 5:8*
and if I have found f. in his   *Es 8:5*
sight
Thou hast granted me life   *Job 10:12*
and f.
with f. wilt thou compass him   *Ps 5:12*
his f. is life: weeping may   *Ps 30:5*
endure
f. thou hast made my mountain   *Ps 30:7*
glad, that f. my righteous   *Ps 35:27*
cause
because thou hadst a f. unto   *Ps 44:3*
the people shall intreat thy f.   *Ps 45:12*
thy f. our horn shall be exalted   *Ps 89:17*
for the time to f. her, yea, the   *Ps 102:13*
set
stones, and f. the dust thereof   *Ps 102:14*
with the f. that thou bearest   *Ps 106:4*
unto
neither let there be any to f.   *Ps 109:12*
his
man sheweth f. and lendeth   *Ps 112:5*
I intreated thy f. with my   *Ps 119:58*
So shalt thou find f. and good   *Pr 3:4*
and shall obtain f. of the Lord   *Pr 8:35*
seeketh good procureth f: but   *Pr 11:27*
good man obtaineth f. of the   *Pr 12:2*
Lord
Good understanding giveth f.   *Pr 13:15*
among the righteous there is f.   *Pr 14:9*
king's f. is toward a wise   *Pr 14:35*
servant

f. is as a cloud of the latter rain — Pr 16:15
thing, and obtaineth *f.* of the Lord — Pr 18:22
will intreat the *f.* of the prince — Pr 19:6
his *f.* is as dew upon the grass — Pr 19:12
neighbour findeth no *f.* in his eyes — Pr 21:10
f. rather than silver and gold — Pr 22:1
find more *f.* than he that flattereth — Pr 28:23
Many seek the ruler's *f.* — Pr 29:26
F. is deceitful, and beauty is vain — Pr 31:30
nor yet *f.* to men of skill — Ec 9:11
I in his eyes as one that found *f.* — Ca 8:10
Let *f.* be shewed to the wicked — Isa 26:10
formed them will shew them no *f.* — Isa 27:11
but in my *f.* have I had mercy on — Isa 60:10
where I will not shew you *f.* — Jer 16:13
God had brought Daniel into *f.* — Da 1:9
for thou hast found *f.* with God — Lu 1:30
and in *f.* with God and man — Lu 2:52
and having *f.* with all the people — Ac 2:47
him *f.* and wisdom in the sight of — Ac 7:10
Who found *f.* before God, and — Ac 7:46
And desired *f.* against him — Ac 25:3

FAVOURABLE

Be *f.* unto them for our sakes — J'g 21:22
and he will be *f.* unto him — Job 33:26
and will he be *f.* no more — Ps 77:7
thou hast been *f.* unto thy land — Ps 85:1

FAVOURED

Rachel was beautiful and well *f.* — Ge 29:17
was a goodly person, and well *f.* — Ge 39:6
out of the river seven well *f.* kine — Ge 41:2
seven other kine, ill *f.* and — Ge 41:3
the ill *f.* kine did eat up the seven — Ge 41:4
kine did eat up the seven well *f.* — Ge 41:4
kine, fatfleshed and well *f.* — Ge 41:18
poor and very ill *f.* and leanfleshed — Ge 41:19
the lean and the ill *f.* kine did eat — Ge 41:20
were still ill *f.* as at the beginning — Ge 41:21
And the seven thin and ill *f.* kine — Ge 41:27
priests, they *f.* not the elders — La 4:16
was no blemish, but well *f.* — Da 1:4
Hail, thou that art highly *f.* — Lu 1:28

FAVOUREST

By this I know that thou *f.* me — Ps 41:11

FAVOURETH

He that *f.* Joab, and he that is for — 2Sa 20:11

FEAR

the *f.* of you and the dread of you — Ge 9:2
and the *f.* of Isaac, had been with — Ge 31:42
Jacob sware by the *f.* of his father — Ge 31:53
in great *f.* (S) — Ex 14:10
F. and dread shall fall upon them — Ex 15:16
I will send my *f.* before thee — Ex 23:27
Ye shall *f.* every man his mother — Le 19:3
neither *f.* ye the people or the land — Nu 14:9
the dread of thee and the *f.* of thee — De 2:25
that they may learn to *f.* me — De 4:10
f. this glorious name — De 28:58
thou shalt *f.* day and night — De 28:66
f. of heart that thou shalt *f.* — De 28:67
spread *f.* in hearts (B) — De 32:9
if thou *f.* to go down — J'g 7:10

fatal *f.* gripped city (B) — 1Sa 5:11
that they may *f.* thee — 1Ki 8:40; 2Ch 6:31
know that name to *f.* thee — 1Ki 8:43; 2Ch 6:33
neither shall ye *f.* other gods — 2Ki 17:38
your God ye shall *f.* — 2Ki 17:39
Lord brought *f.* of him on nations — 1Ch 14:17
f. before him all earth — 1Ch 16:30; Ps 96:9
f. not, nor be dismayed (S) — 1Ch 22:13
f. was on them because of the people — Ezr 3:3
servants who desire to *f.* thy name — Ne 1:11
think on them that put me in *f.* — Ne 6:14; 6:19
the *f.* of the Jews fell upon them — Es 8:17; 9:2
because the *f.* of Mordecai fell on them — Es 9:3
is not this thy *f.* thy confidence, thy hope — Job 4:6
f. came upon me and trembling — Job 4:14
he forsaketh the *f.* of the Almighty — Job 6:14
and let not his *f.* terrify me — Job 9:34
yea, thou castest off *f.* and restrainest prayer — Job 15:4
houses safe from *f.* nor rod of God on them — Job 21:9
snares round about, sudden *f.* troubleth thee — Job 22:10
dominion and *f.* are with him, makes peace — Job 25:2
did I *f.* a great multitude — Job 31:34
he mocketh at *f.* and is not affrighted — Job 39:22
in thy *f.* will I worship toward thy temple — Ps 5:7
put them in *f.* O Lord, that nations may — Ps 9:20
there were they in great *f.*: God is in generation — Ps 14:5
I will *f.* no evil, for thou art with me — Ps 23:4
my salvation, whom shall I *f.* — Ps 27:1
and I was a *f.* to mine acquaintance — Ps 31:11
f. was on every side, they took counsel against me — Ps 31:13
laid up for them that *f.* thee — Ps 31:19
many shall see it and *f.* — Ps 40:3
f. took hold upon them there, and pain — Ps 48:6
wherefore should I *f.* days of evil — Ps 49:5
righteous shall see and *f.* — Ps 52:6
there were they in *f.* where no *f.* was — Ps 53:5
a banner to them that *f.* thee — Ps 60:4
heritage of those that *f.* thy name — Ps 61:5
preserve my life from *f.* of the enemy — Ps 64:1
all shall *f.* and declare the work of — Ps 64:9
they shall be in *f.* (E)(R) — Ps 64:9
f. thee as long as the sun endureth — Ps 72:5
unite my heart to *f.* thy name — Ps 86:11
according to thy *f.* so is thy wrath — Ps 90:11
the heathen shall *f.* thy name — Ps 102:15
for the *f.* of them fell upon them — Ps 105:38
thy servant, who is devoted to thy *f.* — Ps 119:38
turn away my reproach which I *f.* — Ps 119:39
companion of all them that *f.* thee — Ps 119:63
they that *f.* thee will be glad — Ps 119:74
let those that *f.* thee turn unto me — Ps 119:79
I will mock when your *f.* cometh — Pr 1:26
when your *f.* cometh as desolation and destruction — Pr 1:27
and shall be quiet from *f.* of evil — Pr 1:33
be not afraid of sudden *f.* nor desolation — Pr 3:25
the *f.* of the wicked shall come upon him — Pr 10:24

the *f.* of a king is as the roaring of a lion — Pr 20:2
the *f.* of man bringeth a snare — Pr 29:25
men should *f.* before him — Ec 3:14
hath his sword because of *f.* in the night — Ca 3:8
there shall not come the *f.* of briers — Isa 7:25
neither fear ye their *f.* nor be afraid — Isa 8:12
the Lord, let him be your *f.* and your dread — Isa 8:13
the Lord shall give thee rest from thy *f.* — Isa 14:3
Egypt shall be afraid and *f.* — Isa 19:16
the night of pleasure be turned into *f.* to me — Isa 21:4
f. and the pit, and the snare are upon thee — Isa 24:17
that fleeth from *f.* shall fall — Isa 24:38; Jer 48:44
terrible nations shall *f.* thee — Isa 25:3
their *f.* toward me is taught by men — Isa 29:13
the workmen shall *f.* and be ashamed — Isa 44:11
so shall they *f.* the name of Lord — Isa 59:19
thine heart shall *f.* and be enlarged — Isa 60:5
and hardened our heart from thy *f.* — Isa 63:17
an evil thing, that my *f.* is not in thee — Jer 2:19
the sword and *f.* is on every side — Jer 6:25; 20:10
who would *f.* thee, O King of nations — Jer 10:7
a *f.* inspiring warrior (B) — Jer 20:11
they shall *f.* no more, nor be dismayed — Jer 23:4
we have heard a voice of *f.* nor of peace — Jer 30:5
give them one heart that they may *f.* — Jer 32:39
but I will put my *f.* in their hearts — Jer 32:40
they shall *f.* and tremble for all — Jer 33:9
turned in *f.* one to another (S) — Jer 36:16
f. and the pit shall be upon thee, O Moab — Jer 48:43
behold, I will bring a *f.* upon thee, saith Lord — Jer 49:5
they melted in *f.* (B)(R) — Jer 49:23
f. hath seized on Damascus, anguish and sorrow — Jer 49:24
they shall cry to them, *f.* is on every side — Jer 49:29
your heart faint, and ye *f.* for — Jer 51:46
f. and a snare is come upon us — La 3:47
I will put a *f.* in the land of Egypt — Eze 30:13
if *f.* my lord the king — Da 1:10
that men may *f.* the God of Daniel — Da 6:26
inhabitants of Samaria shall *f.* — Ho 10:5
and *f.* because of thee — Mic 7:17
surely thou wilt *f.* me — Zep 3:7
the people did *f.* before the Lord — Hag 1:12
Ashkelon shall see an *f.* — Zec 9:5
if I be a master, where is my *f.* — Mal 1:6
to you that *f.* my name shall — Mal 4:2
of men, we *f.* the people for — M't 21:26
f. nothing (E) — M'k 16:6
when Zacharias saw him, *f.* fell upon him — Lu 1:12
f. came on all that dwelt round about them — Lu 1:65; 7:16; Ac 2:43; 5:5, 11; 19:17; Re 11:11
forewarn you whom ye shall *f.* — Lu 12:5
not received spirit of bondage to *f.* — Ro 8:15
be not highminded, but *f.* — Ro 11:20
render *f.* to whom *f.* is due — Ro 13:7
I was with you in weakness — 1Co 2:3
what *f.*! what vehement desire — 2Co 7:11
I *f.* lest the serpent beguiled Eve — 2Co 11:3
I *f.* lest I shall not find you such — 2Co 12:20
see that she *f.* her husband (E) — Eph 5:33
for *f.* they grow disheartened (N) — Col 3:21
rebuke before all, that others *f.* — 1Ti 5:20

God hath not given us the spirit *2Ti 1:7*
of *f.*
let us *f.* lest a promise being left *2Ti 4:1*
us
deliver them who thro *f.* or   *Heb 2:15*
death
I exceedingly *f.* and quake   *Heb 12:21*
may serve God with   *Heb 12:28*
reverence and godly *f.*
pass the time of your sojourn *1Pe 1:17*
here in *f.*
give an answer with meekness *1Pe 3:15*
and *f.*
no *f.* in love, but love casteth *1Jo 4:18*
out *f.*
f. none of those things thou   *Re 2:10*
must
give reward to them that *f.*   *Re 11:18*
thy

FEAR *GOD*

this do, and live, for I *f.* God *Ge 42:18*
provide able men, such as *f.*   *Ex 18:21*
God
but shalt *f.* thy God, I am   *Le 19:14;*
Lord   *19:32*
but thou shalt *f.* thy God   *Le 25:17;*
                  25:36, 43
Satan said, Doth Job *f.* God   *Job 1:9*
for nought
come and hear, all ye that *f.*   *Ps 66:16*
God
in words are vanities, but *f.* thou *Ec 5:7*
God
it shall be well with them that *f. Ec 8:12*
God
f. God, and keep his   *Ec 12:13*
commandments
and they shall *f.* the God of   *Isa 29:23*
Israel
rebuked him, saying, Dost not *Lu 23:40*
f. God
and ye that *f.* God give   *Ac 13:16*
audience
honour men, *f.* God, honour   *1Pe 2:17*
the king
f. God and give glory to him   *Re 14:7*

FEAR *HIM*

deliver me from Esau, for I   *Ge 32:11*
f. him
ye shall walk after God, and *f.* *De 13:4*
him
him shall ye *f.* him shall ye   *2Ki 17:36*
worship
men therefore *f. him,* he   *Job 37:24*
respecteth not
and *f. him* all ye seed of Israel *Ps 22:23*
I will pay my vows before   *Ps 22:25*
them that *f. him*
secret of Lord is with them that *Ps 25:14*
f. him
the eye of the Lord is on them *Ps 33:18*
that *f. him*
angel encampeth about them   *Ps 34:7*
that *f.him*
for there is no want to them   *Ps 34:9*
that *f. him*
all the ends of the earth shall *f. Ps 67:7*
him
surely his salvation is nigh   *Ps 85:9*
them that *f. him*
great is his mercy to them   *Ps 103:11*
that *f. him*
so the Lord pitieth them that *Ps 103:13*
f. him
the mercy of the Lord is on *Ps 103:17*
them that *f. him*
he hath given meat to them   *Ps 111:5*
that *f. him*
he will fulfil the desire of   *Ps 145:19*
them that *f. him*
Lord taketh pleasure in them *Ps 147:11*
that *f. him*
f. him who is able to destroy *M't 10:28;*
                    Lu 12:5
his mercy is on them that *f. him Lu 1:50*
praise God, ye that *f. him,*   *Re 19:5*
small and great

FEAR *NOT*

f. not, Abram, I am thy shield *Ge 15:1*
f. not, God hath heard voice   *Ge 21:17*
of the lad
f. not, I am with thee, and will *Ge 26:24*
bless thee

the midwife said to Rachel, *F.   Ge 35:17*
not
and he said, Peace be to you, *Ge 43:23*
f. not
he said, *F. not* to go down into *Ge 46:3*
Egypt
Joseph said, *F. not,* for am I in *Ge 50:19*
place of God
f. not, I will nourish you and *Ge 50:21*
your little ones
f. not, stand and see salvation *Ex 14:13*
of Lord
Moses said, *F. not,* God is   *Ex 20:20*
come to prove
the Lord is with us, *f.* them *not Nu 14:9*
Lord said to Moses, *F.* him *Nu 21:34*
not
go up and possess the land, *f. De 1:21*
not
f. not Og; *f. not* your enemies *De 3:2;*
                     3:22
f. not the Canaanites   *De 31:6;*
             Jos 10:8, 25
Lord go before thee, not   *De 31:8;*
forsake thee, *f. not*   *Jos 8:1; 1Ch 28:20*
turn in, my lord, turn in to me, *J'g 4:18*
F. not
I said, *F. not* the gods of the *J'g 6:10*
Amorites
peace be to thee, *f. not,* thou *J'g 6:23*
shalt not die
and now, my daughter, *f. not Ru 3:11*
women that stood by said to *1Sa 4:20*
her, *F. not*
and Samuel said to the people, *1Sa 12:20*
F. not
abide thou with me, *f. not,* *1Sa 22:23*
he that seeketh
Jonathan said unto David, *1Sa 23:17*
F. not
David said to Mephibosheth,   *2Sa 9:7*
F. not
he said to his servants, Kill *2Sa 13:28*
Amnon, *f. not*
Elijah said to the widow, *F.   1Ki 17:13*
not
f. not more with us than with *2Ki 6:16*
them
unto this day, they *f. not*   *2Ki 17:34*
Lord
f. not to serve Chaldees   *2Ki 25:24;*
                     Jer 40:9
Lord will be with you, *f. not 2Ch 20:17*
no changes, therefore they *f.   Ps 55:19*
not God
suddenly do they shoot at him, *Ps 64:4*
and *f. not*
f. not the tails of smoking   *Isa 7:4*
firebrands
say to them that are of a   *Isa 35:4*
fearful heart, *F. not*
f. thou *not,* for I am with   *Isa 41:10;*
thee   *43:5*
f. not, I will help thee   *Isa 41:13*
f. not, thou worm Jacob, and *Isa 41:14*
ye men of Israel
f. not, I have redeemed thee, *Isa 43:1*
thou art mine
f. not, O Jacob my servant, *Isa 44:2;*
and Jeshurun   *Jer 30:10; 46:27-28*
f. ye *not,* nor be afraid, have *Isa 44:8*
not I told
hearken to me, *f. not* reproach *Isa 51:7*
of men
f. not, for thou shalt not be   *Isa 54:4*
ashamed
f. ye *not* me, saith the Lord *Jer 5:22*
thou drewedst near, thou   *La 3:57*
saidst, *F. not*
f. not, nor be dismayed at their *Eze 3:9*
looks
then said he to me *F. not,*   *Da 10:12;*
Daniel   *10:19*
f. not, O land, be glad and   *Joe 2:21*
rejoice
it shall be said to ʰerusalem, *F. Zep 3:16*
not
my Spirit remaineth among   *Hag 2:5*
you, *f. not*
and ye shall be a blessing, *f.   Zec 8:13*
not
again I will do well to Judah, *Zec 8:15*
f. ye *not*
swift witness against them that *Mal 3:5*
f. not me
f. not to take to thee Mary thy *M't 1:20*
wife
f. them *not,* there is nothing *M't 10:26*
covered

f. not them which kill the   *M't 10:28*
body
f. not, ye are of more value *M't 10:31;*
                     Lu 12:7
the angel said to the women, *M't 28:5*
F. not
f. not, Zacharias; *f. not,* Mary *Lu 1:13;*
                     1:30
to shepherds, *F. not*   *Lu 2:10*
said to Simon, *F. not*   *Lu 5:10*
Jairus, *F. not*   *Lu 8:50*
F. not, little flock   *Lu 12:32*
though I *f. not* God, nor regard *Lu 18:4*
man
f. not, daughter of Sion,   *Joh 12:15*
behold
f. not, Paul, thou must be   *Ac 27:24*
before Cæsar
f. not, I am the first and the   *Re 1:17*
last

FEAR *OF GOD*

surely the *f. of* God is not in *Ge 20:11*
this place
must be just, ruling in the *f. of 2Sa 23:3*
God
the *f. of* God was on all   *2Ch 20:29*
kingdoms
ought ye not to walk in the *f. of Ne 5:9*
God
but so did not I, because of *f.   Ne 5:15*
of God
there is no *f. of* God before his *Ps 36:1*
eyes
there is no *f. of* God before   *Ro 3:18*
their eyes
perfecting holiness in the *f. of 2Co 7:1*
God
submitting one to another in *Eph 5:21*
f. of God

FEAR *OF THE LORD*

f. of Lord fell on people   *1Sa 11:7;*
                    2Ch 17:10
f. of the Lord came upon   *2Ch 14:14*
them
let *f. of* the Lord be upon you *2Ch 19:7*
thus shall ye do, in the *f. of   2Ch 19:9*
the Lord
to man he said *F. of* Lord is *Job 28:28*
wisdom
f. of Lord is clean, enduring *Ps 19:9*
for ever
children, I will teach you *f. of Ps 34:11*
the Lord
f. of the Lord is beginning of *Ps 111:10*
wisdom
f. of Lord beginning of   *Pr 1:7;*
knowledge   *9:10*
did not choose the *f. of* the *Pr 1:29*
Lord
then shalt understand the *f. of Pr 2:5*
Lord
the *f. of* the Lord is to hate evil *Pr 8:13*
the *f. of* the Lord prolongeth *Pr 10:27*
days
in *f. of* the Lord is strong   *Pr 14:26*
confidence
the *f. of* the Lord is a fountain *Pr 14:27*
of life
better is a little with the *f. of Pr 15:16*
the Lord
f. of the Lord is instruction of *Pr 15:33*
wisdom
by the *f. of* the Lord men depart *Pr 16:6*
from evil
the *f. of* the Lord tendeth to *Pr 19:23*
life
by *f. of* the Lord are riches and *Pr 22:4*
honour
be thou in *f. of* the Lord all   *Pr 23:17*
day long
hide thee in dust for *f. of* the *Isa 2:10*
Lord
they shall go into caves for *f.   Isa 2:19*
of the Lord
to go into clefts of rocks for *f. Isa 2:21*
of the Lord
spirit of knowledge, and of the *Isa 11:2*
f. of the Lord
of quick understanding in the *Isa 11:3*
f. of the Lord
the *f. of* the Lord is his   *Isa 33:6*
treasure
walking in *f. of* the Lord and *Ac 9:31*
comfort

FEAR *THE LORD*

that thou mightest *f. the Lord*	De 6:2

that thou mightest *f. the Lord*   De 6:2
thy God
thou shalt *f. Lord* thy God   De 6:13;
     De 10:20; 2Ki 17:39
to *f. the Lord* our God for our De 6:24
good always
f. the Lord, walk in his ways, De 10:12
and love him
learn to *f. the Lord*   De 14:23;
     De 17:19; 31:12-13
that ye might *f. the Lord* your Jos 4:24
God
now therefore *f. the Lord*,   Jos 24:14
and serve him
if ye will *f. the Lord*, and   1Sa 12:14
serve him
only *f. the Lord*, and serve   1Sa 12:24
him in truth
I thy servant *f. the Lord*   1Ki 18:12;
     2Ki 4:1
taught them how they should 2Ki 17:28
f. the Lord
he honoureth them that *f. the* Ps 15:4
Lord
ye that *f. the Lord*, praise him Ps 22:23
let all earth *f. the Lord*, and Ps 33:8
stand in awe
O *f. the Lord*, ye his saints, Ps 34:9
there is no want
ye that *f. the Lord*, trust in Ps 115:11
the Lord
he will bless them that *f. the* Ps 115:13
Lord
that *f. the Lord*, say, His mercy Ps 118:4
endureth
ye that *f. the Lord*, bless the Ps 135:20
Lord
f. the Lord, and depart from evil Pr 3:7
my son, *f.* thou *the Lord*, and Pr 24:21
the king
neither say they, Let us *f. the* Jer 5:24
Lord
he not *f. the Lord*, and   Jer 26:19
besought Lord
afterward shall Israel *f. the*   Ho 3:5
Lord
I *f. the Lord*, the God of   Jon 1:9
heaven

FOR FEAR

for the *f.* wherewith thou   De 28:67
shalt fear
have not rather done it *for f.* Jos 22:24
of thing
dwelt *for f.* of Abimelech his J'g 9:21
brother
David arose, fled that day *for f.* 1Sa 21:10
of Saul
David made haste to get   1Sa 23:26
away *for f.* of Saul
will he reprove thee *for f.* of Job 22:4
thee
he shall pass over his strong Isa 31:9
hold *for f.*
for f. of the army of Chaldeans Jer 35:11
army broken up *for f.* of   Jer 37:11
Pharaoh's army
which Asa had made *for f.* of Jer 41:9
Baasha
for f. was round about, saith Jer 46:5
the Lord
for f. of oppressing sword   Jer 50:16
they return
for the *f.* wherewith he feared Mal 2:5
me
the disciples cried out *for f.* M't 14:26
for f. of him the keepers did M't 28:4
shake
men's hearts failing them *for* Lu 21:26
f.
no man spake openly *for f.* of Joh 7:13
Jews
a disciple, but secretly *for f.* Joh 19:38
of Jews
disciples were assembled *for* Joh 20:19
f. of Jews
afar off *for f.* of her torment; Re 18:20;
     18:15

HEAR AND FEAR

all Israel shall *hear and f.*   De 13:11;
     21:21
and all the people shall *hear* De 17:13
and f.
those which remain shall *hear* De 19:20
and f.

NOT FEAR

I know ye will *not f.* yet the Ex 9:30
Lord
ye shall *not f.* other gods   2Ki 17:35;
     17:37
then would I speak, and *not f.* Job 9:35
him
shalt be steadfast, and shalt Job 11:15
not f.
tho' an host encamp, my heart Ps 27:3
shall *not f.*
we will *not f.* though the earth Ps 46:2
be removed
I will *not f.* what flesh can do Ps 56:4;
     118:6
far from oppression, thou   Isa 54:14
shalt *not f.*
who would *not f.* thee, O King Jer 10:7
of nations
the lion hath roared, who will Am 3:8
not f.
the other said, Dost *not* thou Lu 23:40
f. God
I will *not f.* what man shall Heb 13:6
do to me
who shall *not f.* thee, O Lord Re 15:4
and glorify

WITH FEAR

Serve the Lord *with f.* and   Ps 2:11
rejoice
they departed *with f.* and   M't 28:8
great joy
they were all filled *with f.*   Lu 5:26
Gadarenes were taken *with*   Lu 8:37
great *f.*
how *with f.* you received him 2Co 7:15
obedient to masters *with f.* and Eph 6:5
trembling
work out salvation *with f.*   Ph'p 2:12
and trembling
Noah moved *with f.* prepared Heb 11:7
an ark
servants, be subject to masters 1Pe 2:18
your chaste conversation   1Pe 3:2
coupled *with f.*
others save *with f.* pulling them Jude 23
out

WITHOUT FEAR

her labour is in vain *without* Job 39:16
f.
there is not his like, who is Job 41:33
made *without f.*
that we might serve him *without* Lu 1:74
f.
that he may be with you   1Co 16:10
without f.
are bold to speak the word Ph'p 1:14
without f.
they feast, feeding themselves Jude 12
without f.

FEARED

Lot *f.* to dwell in Zoar, dwelt Ge 19:30
in cave
Isaac *f.* to say of Rebekah, She Ge 26:7
is my wife
Moses *f.* and said, This thing is Ex 2:14
known
he that *f.* word of the Lord Ex 9:20
made servants
Amalek smote thee, and *f.* not De 25:18
God
to new gods whom your   De 32:17
fathers *f.* not
were it not that I *f.* the wrath De 32:27
of enemy
they *f.* Joshua as they did   Jos 4:14
Moses
Gideon *f.* Jether *f.* to slay   J'g 6:27;
them   8:20
Samuel *f.* to shew Eli the   1Sa 3:15
vision
honey dropped, for the   1Sa 14:26
people *f.* the oath
because I *f.* the people, and 1Sa 15:24
obeyed them
Ish-bosheth not answer, he *f.* 2Sa 3:11
Abner

the Syrians *f.* to help Ammon 2Sa 10:19
any more
David's servant *f.* to tell him 2Sa 12:18
child was dead
Adonijah *f.* because of   1Ki 1:50
Solomon
all Israel heard the judgment, 1Ki 3:28
and *f.* the king
f. other gods and *f.* not Lord 2Ki 17:7;
     17:25
to be *f.* above all gods   1Ch 16:25;
     Ps 96:4
Jehoshaphat *f.* and   2Ch 20:3
proclaimed a fast
thou art to be *f.*   Ps 76:7
the earth *f.*   Ps 76:8
bring presents to him that Ps 76:11
ought to be *f.*
he led them safely, so that Ps 78:53
they *f.* not
to be *f.* above all (E)(R)   Ps 89:7
there is forgiveness, thou Ps 130:4
mayest be *f.*
a people *f.* (R)   Isa 18:2; 18:7
isles saw it and *f.* the ends of Isa 41:5
earth
hast *f.* continually every day Isa 51:13
whom hast thou *f.* that thou Isa 57:11
hast lied
her treacherous sister Judah *f.* Jer 3:8
not
sword which ye *f.* shall   Jer 42:16
overtake you
they are not humbled, nor   Jer 44:10
have they *f.*
ye have *f.* the sword, I will Eze 11:8
bring it
all people and nations *f.* before Da 5:19
him
for the fear wherewith he *f.* me Mal 2:5
Herod *f.* the multitude   M't 14:5; 21:46
they *f.* exceedingly, and said M'k 4:41
Herod *f.* John, knowing he M'k 6:20
was just
scribes and the chief priests M'k 11:18
f. Jesus
if we shall say, Of men,   M'k 11:32;
they *f.* the people   12:12; Lu 20:19;
     22:2; Ac 5:26
they *f.* as they entered into Lu 9:34
cloud
they *f.* to ask him of that   Lu 9:45
saying
was in a city a judge which *f.* Lu 18:2
not God
I *f.* because thou art an   Lu 19:21
austere man
spake thus, because they *f.* the Joh 9:22
Jews
magistrates *f.* when they   Ac 16:38
heard
Christ was heard in that he *f.* Heb 5:7

FEARED *GOD*

but midwives *f. God*, saved Ex 1:17
children
they *f. God*, he made them Ex 1:21
houses
was faithful, and *f. God* above Ne 7:2
many
Job *f. God* and eschewed evil Job 1:1
Cornelius *f. God* with his Ac 10:2
house

FEARED *GREATLY*

the Canaanites *f. greatly*   Jos 10:2
all the people *greatly f.* the 1Sa 12:18
Lord
nor Obadiah *f.* the Lord   1Ki 18:3
greatly
thing I *greatly f.* is come upon Job 3:25
me
God is *greatly* to be *f.* in   Ps 89:7
assembly
centurion and they with him M't 27:54
f. greatly

FEARED *THE LORD*

people *f. the Lord* and   Ex 14:31
believed Moses
so they *f. the Lord* 2Ki 17:32; 17:33, 41
no king, because we *f.* not *the* Ho 10:3
Lord
the men *f. the Lord*   Jon 1:16
exceedingly
they that *f. the Lord* spake Mal 3:16
oft one to another

FEAREST

now I know that thou *f.* God   *Ge 22:12*
even of old, and thou *f.* me *Isa 57:11*
not
hand of them whose face thou *Jer 22:25*
f.

FEARETH

Behold, Adonijah *f.* king   *1Ki 1:51*
Solomon
an upright man, one that *f.*   *Job 1:8;*
God   *2:3*
What man is he that *f.* the Lord *Ps 25:12*
Blessed is the man that *f.* the *Ps 112:1*
Lord
is every one that *f.* the Lord *Ps 128:1*
shall the man be blessed that *Ps 128:4*
f. the
but he that *f.* the   *Pr 13:13*
commandment
in his uprightness *f.* the Lord *Pr 14:2*
A wise man *f.* and departeth *Pr 14:16*
from
Happy is the man that *f.*   *Pr 28:14*
alway
but a woman that *f.* the Lord *Pr 31:30*
he that *f.* God shall come forth *Ec 7:18*
because he *f.* not before God *Ec 8:13*
as he that *f.* an oath   *Ec 9:2*
Who is among you that *f.* the *Isa 50:10*
Lord
a just man, and one that *f.*   *Ac 10:22*
God
But in every nation he that *f.* *Ac 10:35*
him
whosoever among you *f.* God *Ac 13:26*
He that *f.* is not made perfect *1Jo 4:18*
in

FEARFUL

f. in praises, doing wonders *Ex 15:11*
What man is there that is *f.* *De 20:8*
fear this glorious and *f.* name *De 28:58*
Whosoever is *f.* and afraid, let *J'g 7:3*
f. and glorious things (A) *Ps 65:5*
Say to them that are of a *f.* *Isa 35:4*
heart
Why are ye *f.* O ye of little *M't 8:26*
faith
said unto them, Why are ye *M'k 4:40*
so *f.*
f. sights and great signs shall *Lu 21:11*
certain *f.* looking for of   *Heb 10:27*
judgment
It is a *f.* thing to fall into the *Heb 10:31*
hands
the f. and unbelieving, and the *Re 21:8*

FEARFULLY

awesome and *f.* glorious (A) *Ps 66:3*
I am *f.* and wonderfully   *Ps 139:14*
made

FEARFULNESS

F. and trembling are come   *Ps 55:5*
upon
heart panted, *f.* affrighted me *Isa 21:4*
f. hath surprised the   *Isa 33:14*
hypocrites

FEARING

children cease from *f.* the   *Jos 22:25*
Lord
But the woman *f.* and   *M'k 5:33*
trembling
the chief captain, *f.* lest Paul *Ac 23:10*
and, *f.* lest they should fall *Ac 27:17*
into
f. lest we should have fallen *Ac 27:29*
upon
himself, *f.* them which were of *Ga 2:12*
but in singleness of heart, *f.* *Col 3:22*
God
not *f.* the wrath of the king *Heb 11:27*

FEARLESSLY

we speak freely, openly, *f.*   *2Co 3:12*
(A)

FEARS

and delivered me from all my *f. Ps 34:4*
and *f.* shall be in the way   *Ec 12:5*

and will bring their *f.* upon   *Isa 66:4*
them
were fightings, within were *f.*   *2Co 7:5*

FEARSOME

he is *f.* to the kings (S)   *Ps 76:12*

FEAST

Lot made a *f.*   *Ge 19:3*
dinner (A)(B)   *Ge 19:3; 2Sa 3:20*
Abraham made a *f.*   *Ge 21:8*
Isaac made a *f.*   *Ge 26:30*
made them a dinner (A)   *Ge 26:30*
banquet (B)   *Ge 26:30;*
   29:22; 40:20; Es 1:9; 2:18; Ec 10:19
Laban made a *f.*   *Ge 29:22*
Pharaoh made a *f.* unto his *Ge 40:20*
servants
that they may hold a *f.* unto me *Ex 5:1;*
   10:9
you shall keep it a *f.*   *Ex 12:14;*
   Le 23:39, 41
seventh day shall be a *f.* to the *Ex 13:6*
Lord
three times thou shalt keep a *Ex 23:14*
f. in year
f. of harvest, firstfruits of thy *Ex 23:16*
labours
Aaron said, To-morrow is a *f.* *Ex 32:5*
to Lord
fifteenth day of this month is *Nu 28:17*
a *f.*
ye shall keep a *f.* to the Lord *Nu 29:12*
seven days
and thou shalt rejoice in thy *f. De 16:14*
and Samson made there a *f.*   *J'g 14:10*
declare it within the seven *J'g 14:12*
days of the *f.*
she wept before him while *J'g 14:17*
their *f.* lasted
Nabal held a *f.* in his house *1Sa 25:36*
like a king
banqueting in his house (B) *1Sa 25:36*
David made Abner and his   *2Sa 3:20*
men a *f.*
Solomon made a *f.* to his   *1Ki 3:15;*
servants   *8:65*
all men of Israel assembled at *1Ki 8:2*
the *f.*
Jeroboam ordained a *f.* like *1Ki 12:32*
to *f.* that is in Judah
Jeroboam set a festival (B)   *1Ki 12:32;*
   12:33
he ordained a *f.* to the   *1Ki 12:33*
children of Israel
the *f.* in the seventh month *2Ch 5:3;*
   Ne 8:14
Solomon kept the *f.* seven days, *2Ch 7:8;*
and all Israel with him   *7:9; 30:22;*
   Ne 8:18; Eze 45:25
Ahasuerus made a *f.*   *Es 1:3; 1:5; 2:18*
gave a banquet (R)   *Es 1:3; 1:5, 9; 2:18*
Vashti made a *f.*   *Es 1:9*
the Jews had a *f.*   *Es 8:17*
a merry heart hath a continual *Pr 15:15*
f.
f. is made for laughter, wine *Ec 10:19*
makes merry
Lord shall make to all people *Isa 25:6*
a *f.*
when a holy *f.* is kept   *Isa 30:29*
(A)(E)(R)
f. soul of the priests (B)(R) *Jer 31:14*
seven days of *f.* he shall   *Eze 45:23*
prepare
Belshazzar the king made a   *Da 5:1*
great *f.*
prepared a marriage *f.*   *M't 22:2*
(N)(R)
come to the wedding *f.*   *M't 22:4*
(A)(R)
went into marriage *f.*   *M't 25:10*
(A)(E)(R)
at that *f.* governor was wont *M't 27:15;*
to release to people   *M'k 15:6*
they went up after the custom *Lu 2:42*
of the *f.*
Levi made him a great *f.* in his *Lu 5:29*
house
made him a great banquet   *Lu 5:29*
(A)(B)
big reception in his house   *Lu 5:29*
(N)(P)
but when thou makest a *f.* call *Lu 14:13*
the poor
when you give a banquet (A) *Lu 14:13*

when you give dinner (B)   *Lu 14:13*
when you give a party (N)   *Lu 14:13*
when you give a luncheon (P) *Lu 14:13*
he must release one unto them *Lu 23:17*
at the *f.*
draw, and hear to the governor *Joh 2:8*
of *f.*
when ruler of the *f.* tasted the *Joh 2:9*
water
Galileans having seen all he *Joh 4:45*
did at *f.* at Jerusalem, for
they also went to *f.*
after this there was a *f.* of the *Joh 5:1*
Jews
the passover, a *f.* of the Jews, *Joh 6:4*
was nigh
go ye up to this *f.* I go not up *Joh 7:8*
yet to this *f.*
then went he also up to the *f.* *Joh 7:10*
not openly
then the Jews sought him at *Joh 7:11*
the *f.* and said
now about the midst of the *f.* *Joh 7:14*
Jesus taught
in the last day, that great day *Joh 7:37*
of the *f.*
it was at Jerusalem the *f.* of *Joh 10:22*
dedication
what think ye, that he will   *Joh 11:56*
not come to *f.*
next day much people that   *Joh 12:12*
were come to *f.*
certain Greeks among them *Joh 12:20*
that came to *f.*
buy what we have need of   *Joh 13:29*
against the *f.*
I must by all means keep this *Ac 18:21*
f.
let us keep the *f.* not with old *1Co 5:8*
leaven
if any that believe not bid   *1Co 10:27*
you to a *f.*
a *f.* day (S)   *Col 2:16*
deceiving while they *f.* with *2Pe 2:13*
you
of charity, when they *f.* with *Jude 12*
you
your *f.* (P)(S)   *Jude 12*

FEAST *DAY, DAYS*

I will also cause her *f. days* to *Ho 2:11*
cease
what will ye do in *day* of *f.* of *Ho 9:5*
Lord
I hate, I despise your *f. days Am 5:21*
they said, Not on the *f. day M'k 14:2*
   M't 14:2
in *f. day* many believed in   *Joh 2:23*
his name

FEAST *OF PASSOVER*

nor sacrifice of *f. of passover Ex 34:25*
be left
after two days is *f. of passover M't 26:2;*
   M'k 14:1
every year at *f. of passover* his *Lu 2:41*
parents went
before *f. of passover* Jesus   *Joh 13:1*
knew his hour

FEAST *OF TABERNACLES*

the fifteenth day shall be   *Le 23:34*
f. of tabernacles
thou shalt observe *f.* of   *De 16:13*
tabernacles seven days
three times appear in *f.* of   *De 16:16;*
tabernacles   *31:10; 2Ch 8:13*
they kept *f. of tabernacles* as *Ezr 3:4*
it is written
shall even go up to keep *f.* of *Zec 14:16*
tabernacles
heathen that come not to   *Zec 14:18;*
keep *f. of tabernacles*   *14:19*
now Jews' *f. of tabernacles*   *Jch 7:2*
was at hand

FEAST *OF UNLEAVENED BREAD*

ye shall observe *f.* of   *Ex 12:17;*
unleavened bread   *23:15; 34:18*
and on fifteenth day is *f.* of *Le 23:6*
unleavened bread
appear in *f. of unleavened De 16:16;*
bread   *2Ch 8:13*

people assembled to keep f.　2Ch 30:13
of unleavened bread
children of Israel kept f. of　2Ch 30:21
unleavened bread seven days
f. of unleavened bread　2Ch 35:17;
seven days　Ezr 6:22; Eze 45:21
first day of f. of unleavened　M't 26:17
bread disciples came
after two days was f. of　M'k 14:1;
unleavened bread　Lu 22:1

FEAST OF WEEKS

thou shalt observe f. of weeks　Ex 34:22;
　De 16:10
all thy males appear in the f.　De 16:16
of weeks
Solomon offered burnt　2Ch 18:13
offering in f. of weeks

SOLEMN FEAST

seven days shalt thou keep a　De 16:15
solemn f.
blow the trumpet on our　Ps 81:3
solemn f. day
made a noise as in the solemn　La 2:7
f. day

FEASTED

his sons went and f. in their　Job 1:4

FEASTING

and made it a day of f. and　Es 9:17;
　9:18
Adar a day of gladness and f.　Es 9:19
they should make them days of　Es 9:22
f.
when the days of their f. were　Job 1:5
than to go to the house of f.　Ec 7:2
not also go into the house of f.　Jer 16:8

FEASTS

even these are my f.　Le 23:2 23:4, 37, 44
with hypocritical mockers in f.　Ps 35:16
the harp, pipe, and wine are in　Isa 5:12
their f.
the city of appointed. (R)　Isa 33:20
in their heat I will make their　Jer 51:39
f.
the princes part to give　Eze 45:17
offerings in f.
all the appointed f.　Eze 45:17
(A)(B)(E)(R)
in f. the meat offering shall　Eze 46:11
be an ephah
I will turn your f. into　Am 8:10
mourning
shall be joy, gladness, and　Zec 8:19
cheerful f.
uppermost rooms at f.　M't 23:6;
　M'k 12:39; Lu 20:46
these are spots in your f. of　Jude 12
charity

APPOINTED FEASTS

your appointed f. my soul　Isa 1:14
hateth

SET FEASTS

these things do in your set f.　Nu 29:39
to offer on the set f. 1Ch 23:31; Ezr 3:5
the king's portion for the set　2Ch 31:3
f.
we charged for offerings in　Ne 10:33
the set f.

SOLEMN FEASTS

when you make offering in　Nu 15:3
your solemn f.
build an house for offering on　2Ch 2:4
solemn f.
offering on solemn f. three　2Ch 8:13
times in a year
because none come to the　La 1:4
solemn f.
hath caused solemn f. to be　La 2:6
forgotten
as flock of Jerusalem in　Eze 36:38
solemn f.
when people come before　Eze 46:9
Lord in solemn f.

I will cause to cease her　Ho 2:11
solemn f.
make thee dwell as in days of　Ho 12:9
solemn f.
O Judah, keep thy solemn f.　Na 1:15
perform vows
even the dung of your solemn f.　M't 2:3

FEATHERED

and f. fowls like as the sand　Ps 78:27
Speak unto every f. fowl, and　Eze 39:17

FEATHERS

pluck away his crop with his f.　Le 1:16
wings and f. unto the ostrich　Job 39:13
and her f. with yellow gold　Ps 68:13
He shall cover thee with his f.　Ps 91:4
great wings, long winged, full　Eze 17:3
of f.
with great wings and many f.　Eze 17:7
hairs were grown like eagles' f.　Da 4:33

FED

Jacob f. the rest of Laban's　Ge 30:36
flocks
as he f. the asses of Zibeon　Ge 36:24
fatfleshed; and they f. in a　Ge 41:2
meadow
favoured; and they f. in a　Ge 41:18
meadow
and he f. them with bread for　Ge 47:17
all
the God which f. me all my　Ge 48:15
life
I have f. you in the wilderness　Ex 16:32
to hunger, and f. thee with　De 8:3
manna
Who f. thee in the wilderness　De 8:16
with
put them in ward, and f. them　2Sa 20:3
and f. them with bread and　1Ki 18:4;
water　18:13
over the herds that f. in　1Ch 27:29
Sharon
and verily thou shalt be f.　Ps 37:3
f. them according to the　Ps 78:72
integrity
He should have f. them also　Ps 81:16
of rams, and the fat of f.　Isa 1:11
beasts
when I had f. them to the full　Jer 5:7
They were as f. horses in the　Jer 5:8
and honey, wherewith I f.　Eze 16:19
thee
ye kill them that are f. but ye　Eze 34:3
but the shepherds f.　Eze 34:8
themselves
and f. not my flock　Eze 34:8
and all flesh was f. of it　Da 4:12
they f. him with grass like oxen　Da 5:21
called Bands; and I f. the flock　Zec 11:7
thee an hungered, and f. thee　M't 25:37
they that f. the swine fled, and　M'k 5:14
they that f. them saw what was　Lu 8:34
desiring to be f. with the　Lu 16:21
crumbs
I have f. you with milk, and　1Co 3:2
not

FEEBLE

But when the cattle were f. he　Ge 30:42
the weaker (B)　Ge 30:42
even all that were f. behind　De 25:18
thee
weary and exhausted (B)　De 25:18
faint and weary (E)(R)　De 25:18
hath many children is waxed f.　1Sa 2:5
his hand f. and all the　2Sa 4:1
and carried all the f. of them　2Ch 28:15
upon
What do these f. Jews? will　Ne 4:2
they
decrepit Jews do (B)　Ne 4:2
hast strengthened the f. knees　Job 4:4
I am f. and sore broken　Ps 38:8
I am faint and sorely bruised　Ps 38:8
(A)
I am benumbed and sorely　Ps 38:8
bruised (B)
utterly spent and crushed (R)　Ps 38:8
and there was not one f.　Ps 105:37
person
no invalids among them (B)　Ps 105:37
none among tribes who　Ps 105:37
stumbled (R)

The conies are but a f. folk　Pr 30:26
the remnant shall be very f.　Isa 16:14
hands, and confirm the f. knees　Isa 35:3
our hands wax f.: anguish hath　Jer 6:24
Damascus is waxed f. and　Jer 49:24
turneth
and his hands waxed f.:　Jer 50:43
anguish
All hands shall be f. and all　Eze 7:17
knees
and all hands shall be f.　Eze 21:7
and he that is f. among them　Zec 12:8
f. and sick (N)(P)　1Co 11:30
which seem to be more f. are　1Co 12:22
so f. when face to face (N)　2Co 10:1
hand down, and the f. knees　Heb 12:12

FEEBLEMINDED

comfort the f. support the　1Th 5:14
weak

FEEBLENESS

to their children for f. of hands　Jer 47:3

FEEBLER

so the f. were Laban's, and　Ge 30:42

FEED

F. me, I pray thee, with that　Ge 25:30
same
ye the sheep, and go and f.　Ge 29:7
them
I will against f. and keep thy　Ge 30:31
flock
went to f. their father's flock　Ge 37:12
Do not thy brethren f. the　Ge 37:13
flock in
tell me, I pray thee, were they　Ge 37:16
their trade hath been to f.　Ge 46:32
cattle
shall f. in another man's field　Ex 22:5
neither let the flocks nor herds　Ex 34:3
f.
from Saul to f. his father's　1Sa 17:15
sheep
Thou shalt f. my people Israel　2Sa 5:2
to f. my people Israel, saying　2Sa 7:7
and I will f. thee with me in　2Sa 19:33
commanded the ravens to f.　1Ki 17:4
thee
woman f. thee (B)　1Ki 17:9
and f. him with bread of　1Ki 22:27;
affliction　2Ch 18:26
Thou shalt f. my people Israel　1Ch 11:2
I commanded to f. my people　1Ch 17:6
take away flocks, and f.　Job 24:2
thereof
the worm shall f. sweetly on　Job 24:20
him
f. them also, and lift them up　Ps 28:9
death shall f. on them; and the　Ps 49:14
brought him to f. Jacob his　Ps 78:71
people
The lips of the righteous f.　Pr 10:21
many
f. me with food convenient for　Pr 30:8
me
f. thy kids beside the shepherds　Ca 1:8
twins, which f. among the lilies　Ca 4:5
bed of spices, to f. in the　Ca 6:2
gardens
the lambs f. after their manner　Isa 5:17
And the cow and the bear shall　Isa 11:7
f.
And the first born of the poor　Isa 14:30
shall f.
there shall the calf f. and　Isa 27:10
shall thy cattle f. in large　Isa 30:23
pastures
shall f. his flock like a　Isa 40:11
shepherd
They shall f. in the ways, and　Isa 49:9
I will f. them that oppress thee　Isa 49:26
f. thee with the heritage of　Isa 58:14
Jacob
strangers shall stand and f.　Isa 61:5
your
wolf and the lamb shall f.　Isa 65:25
together
which shall f. you with　Jer 3:15
knowledge
they shall f. every one in his　Jer 6:3
place

I will *f.* them, even this people *Jer 9:15*
the pastors that *f.* my people *Jer 23:2*
over them which shall *f.* them *Jer 23:4*
I will *f.* them with *Jer 23:15*
wormwood, and
he shall *f.* on Carmel and *Jer 50:19*
Bashan
They that did *f.* delicately are *La 4:5*
the shepherds of Israel that do *Eze 34:2*
f.
not the shepherds *f.* the flocks *Eze 34:2*
that are fed; but ye *f.* not the *Eze 34:3*
flock
shall the shepherds *f.* *Eze 34:10*
themselves
and *f.* them upon the *Eze 34:13*
mountains of
I will *f.* them in a good *Eze 34:14*
pasture
in a fat pasture they shall *f.* *Eze 34:14*
upon
I will *f.* my flock, and I will *Eze 34:15*
cause
I will *f.* them with judgment *Eze 34:16*
he shall *f.* them, even my *Eze 34:23*
servant
he shall *f.* them, and he shall *Eze 34:23*
be
that *f.* of the portion of his *Da 11:26*
meat
the Lord will *f.* them as a lamb *Ho 4:16*
and the winepress shall not *f.* *Ho 9:2*
them
let them not *f.* nor drink water *Jon 3:7*
and *f.* in the strength of the *Mic 5:4*
Lord
F. thy people with thy rod *Mic 7:14*
let them *f.* in Bashan and *Mic 7:14*
Gilead
they shall *f.* thereupon: in the *Zep 2:7*
for they shall *f.* and lie down *Zep 3:13*
F. the flock of the slaughter *Zec 11:4*
And I will *f.* the flock of *Zec 11:7*
slaughter
Then said I, I will not *f.* you *Zec 11:9*
nor *f.* that that standeth still *Zec 11:16*
him into his fields to *f.* swine *Lu 15:15*
He saith unto him, *F.* my *Joh 21:15*
lambs
He saith unto him, *F.* my *Joh 21:16*
sheep
Jesus saith unto him, *F.* my *Joh 21:17*
sheep
overseers, to *f.* the church of *Ac 20:28*
God
if thine enemy hunger, *f.* him *Ro 12:20*
bestow all my goods to *f.* the *1Co 13:3*
poor
F. the flock of God which is *1Pe 5:2*
midst of the throne shall *f.* *Re 7:17*
them
that they should *f.* her there a *Re 12:6*

FEEDEST

f. them with the bread of tears *Ps 80:5*
my soul loveth, where thou *f.* *Ca 1:7*

FEEDETH

mouth of fools *f.* on *Pr 15:14*
foolishness
I am his: he *f.* among the lilies *Ca 2:16*
is mine: he *f.* among the lilies *Ca 6:3*
He *f.* on ashes: a deceived *Isa 44:20*
heart
Ephraim *f.* on wind, and *Ho 12:1*
followeth
yet your heavenly Father *f.* *M't 6:26*
them
and God *f.* them: how much *Lu 12:24*
more
who *f.* a flock, and eateth not *1Co 9:7*

FEEDING

was *f.* the flock with his *Ge 37:2*
brethren
oxen were plowing, and the *Job 1:14*
asses *f.*
f. on wind (A) *Ec 1:14*
them to cease from *f.* the *Eze 34:10*
flock
them an herd of many swine *f.* *M't 8:30*
mountains a great herd of *M'k 5:11*
swine *f.*
many swine *f.* on the mountain *Lu 8:32*
a servant plowing or *f.* cattle *Lu 17:7*
you *f.* themselves without fear *Jude 12*

FEEDINGPLACE

and the *f.* of the young lions *Na 2:11*

FEEDS

wild beast *f.* on it (A)(B)(R) *Ps 80:13*

FEEL

will *f.* me, and I shall seem to *Ge 27:12*
him
I pray thee, that I may *f.* thee *Ge 27:21*
Suffer me that I may *f.* the *J'g 16:26*
pillars
shall not *f.* quietness in his *Job 20:20*
belly
Before your pots can *f.* the *Ps 58:9*
thorns
the commandments shall *f.* no *Ec 8:5*
evil
did not Lord *f.* grief (B) *Jer 26:19*
if haply they might *f.* after *Ac 17:27*
him
who gives generously without *Jas 1:5*
making them *f.* foolish or guilty
(P)
you can *f.* pity (P) *Jude 22*

FEELING

Who being past *f.* have given *Eph 4:19*
sung with a lovely *f.* (B) *Col 3:16*
cannot be touched with the *f.* *Heb 4:15*
of our
anyone *f.* cheerful (B)(E)(R) *Jas 5:13*

FEELINGS

f. moved like a harp (B) *Isa 16:11*
my *f.* are moved (E) *Isa 16:11*
my *f.*, my *f.* (B) *Jer 4:19*
human beings with *f.* like *Ac 14:15*
yours (P)
his *f.* go out to you (B) *2Co 7:15*
various desires and pleasant *f.* *Tit 3:3*
(P)

FEELS

f. grieved over punishment *Joe 2:13*
(B)
at once he *f.* scandalized (B) *M't 13:21*

FEES

with *f.* of sorcery in hand (B) *Nu 22:7*

FEET

nor a lawgiver from between *Ge 49:10*
his *f.* till
Jacob gathered *f.* in bed, *Ge 49:33*
yielded ghost
put shoes from off *f.* *Ex 3:5; Ac 7:33*
shall eat passover with shoes *Ex 12:11*
on *f.*
have legs above their *f.* ye *Le 11:21*
may eat
only I will pass through on my *De 2:28*
f.
young one cometh from *De 28:57*
between her *f.*
and they sat down at thy *f.* *De 33:3*
every one
f. of priests were dipped in *Jos 3:15*
Jordan
old shoes, and clouted upon *Jos 9:5*
their *f.*
put your *f.* on the necks of *Jos 10:24*
these kings
the land whereon thy *f.* have *Jos 14:9*
trodden
surely he covereth his *f.* in his *J'g 3:24*
chamber
so that Sisera fled away on his *J'g 4:15;*
f. *4:17*
bowed at her *f.* he fell down *J'g 4:27*
dead
go in, uncover his *f.* and lay *Ru 3:4*
down
be turned, behold a woman lay *Ru 3:8*
at his *f.*
he will keep the *f.* of his saints *1Sa 2:9*
Jonathan climbed on his *1Sa 14:13*
hands and *f.*
and Saul went in to cover his *1Sa 24:3*
f.
Abigail rode with five *1Sa 24:42*
damsels at her *f.*

hands not bound, nor *f.* put *2Sa 3:34*
into fetters
Jonathan's son was lame of his *2Sa 4:4;*
f. *9:3, 13*
they cut off their hands and *2Sa 4:12*
their *f.*
Mephibosheth had not *2Sa 19:24*
dressed his *f.*
maketh my *f.* like hinds' *f.* *2Sa 22:34;*
Ps 18:33; Hab 3:19
so that my *f.* did not slip *2Sa 22:37;*
Ps 18:36
put blood of war in shoes on *1Ki 2:5*
his *f.*
when Ahijah heard sound of *1Ki 14:6*
her *f.*
when thy *f.* enter city, child *1Ki 14:12*
shall die
Asa was diseased in his *f.* *1Ki 15:23;*
2Ch 16:12
when she came, she caught *2Ki 4:27*
him by the *f.*
is not sound of master's *f.* *2Ki 6:32*
behind him
but they found no more of her *2Ki 9:35*
than the *f.*
dead man revived, and stood *2Ki 13:21*
upon *f.*
nor make *f.* of Israel move *2Ki 21:8*
any more
then David the king stood on *1Ch 28:2*
his *f.*
clothes waxed not old, their *f.* *Ne 9:21*
swelled not
he that is ready to slip with *Job 12:5*
his *f.*
thou puttest my *f.* in the *Job 13:27*
stocks
for he is cast into a net by his *Job 18:8*
own *f.*
terrors make afraid, and *Job 18:11*
drive him to his *f.*
I was eyes to blind, *f.* was I *Job 29:15*
to lame
the youth rise, they push *Job 30:12*
away my *f.*
thou settest a print upon *Job 33:11*
heels of my *f.*
they pierced my hands and my *Ps 22:16*
f.
he shall pluck my *f.* out of net *Ps 25:15*
thou hast see my *f.* in a large *Ps 31:8*
room
set *f.* on rock, and established *Ps 40:2*
my goings
wilt thou not deliver my *f.* *Ps 56:13*
from falling
suffereth not our *f.* to be moved *Ps 66:9*
but as for me, my *f.* were *Ps 73:2*
almost gone
lift up thy *f.* to the perpetual *Ps 74:3*
desolations
whose *f.* they hurt with *Ps 105:18*
fetters
f. have they, but they walk *Ps 115:7*
not, nor speak
thou hast delivered my *f.* from *Ps 116:8*
falling
I turned my *f.* unto thy *Ps 119:59*
testimonies
I refrained my *f.* from every *Ps 119:101*
evil way
thy word is lamp to my *f.* *Ps 119:105*
light to path
our *f.* shall stand within thy *Ps 122:2*
gates
their *f.* run to evil *Pr 1:16;*
6:18; Isa 59:7
ponder path of thy *f.* ways be *Pr 4:26*
established
her *f.* go down to death, steps *Pr 5:5*
take hold
wicked man speaketh with his *Pr 6:13*
f.
can one go on coals, and *f.* not *Pr 6:28*
be burnt
she is loud, her *f.* abide not in *Pr 7:11*
house
and he that hasteth with his *f.* *Pr 19:2*
sinneth
cutteth off the *f.* and drinketh *Pr 26:6*
damage
a flatterer spreadeth a net for *Pr 29:5*
his *f.*
how beautiful are *f.* with shoes *Ca 7:1*
making a tinkling with their *f.* *Isa 3:16*
Lord take away the ornaments *Isa 3:18*
about their *f.*

with twain covered *f.* with twain   *Isa 6:2* did fly ..
Lord shall shave the hair of   *Isa 7:20* the *f.*
her own *f.* shall carry he afar   *Isa 23:7* off
the *f.* of the poor shall tread it   *Isa 26:6* down
that send forth the *f.* of ox   *Isa 32:20* and ass
by way that he had not gone   *Isa 41:3* with his *f.*
they shall lick up the dust of   *Isa 49:23* thy *f.*
the *f.* of him that bringeth   *Isa 52:7* good tidings
I will make the place of my *f.*   *Isa 60:13* glorious
before your *f.* stumble on   *Jer 13:16* mountains
loved to wander, have not   *Jer 14:10* refrained *f.*
digged a pit, and hid snares   *Jer 18:22* for my *f.*
thy *f.* are sunk in the mire,   *Jer 38:22* and are turned
he hath spread a net for my *f.*   *La 1:13*
and their *f.* were straight *f.*   *Eze 1:7*
he said to me, Son of man,   *Eze 2:1* stand upon *f.*
and the Spirit set me upon my   *Eze 2:2;* *f.*   *3:24*
opened thy *f.* to every one   *Eze 16:25* that passed by
and put on thy shoes upon thy   *Eze 24:17* *f.*
tires be on heads, shoes on   *Eze 24:23* your *f.*
because thou hast stamped   *Eze 25:6* with the *f.*
thou troubledst the waters   *Eze 32:2* with thy *f.*
but ye must foul the residue   *Eze 34:18* with your *f.*
what ye have trodden and   *Eze 34:19* fouled with your *f.*
they lived, and stood up   *Eze 37:10* upon their *f.*
his *f.* part of iron, and part   *Da 2:33;* clay   *2:42*
a stone smote the image upon   *Da 2:34* his *f.*
thou sawest the *f.* and toes   *Da 2:41* part of clay
and stamped the residue with   *Da 7:7;* the *f.* of it   *17:19*
his *f.* like polished brass   *Da 10:6;*   *Re 1:15; 2:18*
and the clouds are the dust of   *Na 1:3* his *f.*
the *f.* of him that bringeth   *Na 1:15* good tidings
and *f.* shall stand upon mount   *Zec 14:4* of Olives
city, shake off dust of your *f.*   *M't 10:14;*   *M'k 6:11; Lu 9:5*
cast lame and blind down at   *M't 15:30* Jesus' *f.*
rather than having two *f.* to   *M't 18:8* be cast into fire
they held him by *f.* and   *M't 28:9* worshipped him
to guide our *f.* into the way of   *Lu 1:79* peace
she kissed his *f.* and anointed   *Lu 7:38* them
this woman hath not ceased to   *Lu 7:45* kiss my *f.*
they found a man sitting at *f.*   *Lu 8:35* of Jesus
Jairus fell down at Jesus' *f.*   *Lu 8:41* and besought him
Mary, who sat at Jesus' *f.*   *Lu 10:39* heard his word
put a ring on his hand, and   *Lu 15:22* shoes on his *f.*
behold my hands and my *f.*   *Lu 24:39* that it is I
he shewed them his hands and   *Lu 24:40* his *f.*
wiped his *f.* with her hair   *Joh 11:2;*   *12:3*
Mary anointed the *f.* of Jesus   *Joh 12:3*
one angel at the head, the   *Joh 20:12* other at the *f.*
immediately his *f.* received   *Ac 3:7* strength
laid them down at apostles' *f.*   *Ac 4:35;*   *4:37; 5:2*

f. of them who have buried thy   *Ac 5:9* husband
laid their clothes at a young   *Ac 7:58* man's *f.*
shoes of his *f.* I am not   *Ac 13:25* worthy to loose
they shook off dust of *f.*   *Ac 13:51* against them
at Lystra a man impotent in   *Ac 14:8* his *f.*
Paul said, Stand upright on   *Ac 14:10* thy *f.* he leaped
who made their *f.* fast in   *Ac 16:24* stocks
Agabus bound his own hands   *Ac 21:11* and *f.*
yet brought up at *f.* of   *Ac 22:3* Gamaliel
but rise, and stand upon thy *f.*   *Ac 26:16*
their *f.* are swift to shed blood   *Ro 3:15*
the *f.* of them that preach the   *Ro 10:15* gospel
nor head to the *f.* I have no   *1Co 12:21* need of you
your *f.* shod with the   *Eph 6:15* preparation of gospel
make straight paths for your   *Heb 12:13* *f.*
make them come worship before   *Re 3:9* thy *f.*
another mighty angel, his *f.* as   *Re 10:1* pillars of fire
the two witnesses stood upon   *Re 11:11* their *f.*
his *f.* were as *f.* of a bear,   *Re 13:2* mouth of a lion
I fell down to worship before   *Re 22:8* his *f.*

FEET with SOLE, SOLES

soles of your *f.* tread shall be   *De 11:24* yours
as soon as *soles* of the priests'   *Jos 3:13;* *f.*   *4:18*
till Lord put them under the   *1Ki 5:3* *soles* of his *f.*
with *sole* of my *f.* have dried   *2Ki 19:24;*   *Isa 37:26*
shall bow down at the *soles*   *Isa 60:14* of thy *f.*
the *sole* of their *f.* was like   *Eze 1:7* a calf's foot
place of *soles* of my *f.* no more   *Eze 43:7* defiled
wicked shall be ashes under   *Mal 4:3* *soles* of your *f.*

FEET WASH, WASHED

let water be fetched, and *wash*   *Ge 18:4* your *f.*
turn in, tarry all night, and   *Ge 19:2* *wash* your *f.*
and Laban gave water to   *Ge 24:32* *wash* his *f.*
gave them water, and   *Ge 43:24* *washed* their *f.*
Aaron and his sons shall   *Ex 30:19;* *wash* their hands and *f.*   *30:21; 40:31*
Levite and concubine *washed*   *J'g 19:21* their *f.*
to *wash* the *f.* of servants of   *1Sa 25:41* my lord
Uriah, go to thy house, *wash*   *2Sa 11:8* thy *f.*
shall *wash* his *f.* in blood of   *Ps 58:10* wicked
have *washed* my *f.* how shall I   *Ca 5:3* defile them
she began to *wash* his *f.* with   *Lu 7:38* tears
but she hath *washed* my *f.* with   *Lu 7:44* tears
he began to *wash* the   *Joh 13:5* disciples' *f.*
Peter saith, Lord, dost thou   *Joh 13:6* *wash* my *f.*
Peter saith, Thou shalt never   *Joh 13:8* *wash* my *f.*
needeth not save to *wash* his   *Joh 13:10* *f.* but is clean
so after he had *washed* their   *Joh 13:12* *f.* he said to them
if I your Lord and Master   *Joh 13:14* have *washed* your *f.*
if she have *washed* the saints'   *1Ti 5:10* *f.*

AT HIS FEET

Zipporah cast the foreskin *at*   *Ex 4:25* *his f.*
Barak went with ten thousand   *J'g 4:10* *at his f.*
she lay *at his f.* until the   *Ru 3:14* morning
Abigail fell *at his f.* and said   *1Sa 25:24*
the woman of Shunem fell *at*   *2Ki 4:37* *his f.*
Esther fell down *at his f.* and   *Es 8:3* besought
and burning coals went forth   *Hab 3:5* *at his f.*
his fellow-servant fell down   *M't 18:29* *at his f.*
Jairus, when he saw him, fell   *M'k 5:22* *at his f.*
Syrophenician woman came,   *M'k 7:25* fell *at his f.*
she stood *at his f.* behind him   *Lu 7:38* weeping
Mary fell down *at his f.*   *Joh 11:32* saying
Sapphira fell *at his f.* and   *Ac 5:10* yielded up ghost
Cornelius met him, fell down   *Ac 10:25* *at his f.*
when I saw him, I fell *at his f.*   *Re 1:17* as dead
and I fell *at his f.* to worship   *Re 19:10* him

UNDER FEET

under f. as it were sapphire   *Ex 24:10* stone
darkness was *under* his *f.*   *2Sa 22:10;*   *Ps 18:9*
yea, they are fallen *under* my   *2Sa 22:39* *f.*
thou hast put all things *under*   *Ps 8:6;* his *f.*   *1Co 15:27; Eph 1:22*
he shall subdue the nations   *Ps 47:3* *under* our *f.*
the dragon shalt thou trample   *Ps 91:13* *under f.*
as a carcase trodden *under f.*   *Isa 14:19*
drunkards of Ephraim be   *Isa 28:3* trodden *under f.*
to crush *under* his *f.* all   *La 3:34* prisoners
lest they trample them *under*   *M't 7:6* their *f.*
God shall bruise Satan *under*   *Ro 16:20* your *f.*
till he hath put all enemies   *1Co 15:25* *under* his *f.*
he put all in subjection *under*   *Heb 2:8* his *f.*
clothed with the sun, moon   *Re 12:1* *under* her *f.*

FEIGN

thee, *f.* thyself to be a   *2Sa 14:2* mourner
Pretend to be a mourner   *2Sa 14:2* (A)(R)
play the part of a mourner   *2Sa 14:2* (B)
f. herself to be another   *1Ki 14:5* woman
she pretended to be another   *1Ki 14:5* woman (A)(R)
pretend to be another woman   *1Ki 14:5* (B)
sent forth spies which would   *Lu 20:20*
pretended to be upright   *Lu 20:20* (A)(B)(P)(R)
agents in the guise of honest   *Lu 20:20* men (N)

FEIGNED

and *f.* himself mad in their   *1Sa 21:13* hands
pretended to be insane (A)   *1Sa 21:13*
pretended to be demented   *1Sa 21:13* (B)
that goeth not out of *f.* lips   *Ps 17:1*
with *f.* words make   *2Pe 2:3* merchandise
exploit with false arguemnts   *2Pe 2:3* (A)(B)(P)(R)
trade on your credulity with   *2Pe 2:3* sheer fabrications (N)

FEIGNEDLY

me with her whole heart, but *f.*   *Jer 3:10*
in sheer hypocrisy (A)   *Jer 3:10*
returned to me, but in pretense *Jer 3:10*
(B)(R)

FEIGNEST

why *f.* thou thyself to be   *1Ki 14:6*
another
why pretend to be another   *1Ki 14:6*
(A)(B)(R)
thou *f.* them out of thine own   *Ne 6:8*
heart
inventing them of own mind   *Ne 6:8*
(A)(R)
being fabrications of own heart *Ne 6:8*
(B)

FELICITY

God who is eternal *f.* alone   *1Ti 6:15*
(N)

FELIX

him safe unto *F.* the governor *Ac 23:24*
unto the most excellent   *Ac 23:26*
governor *F.*
and in all places, most noble *F.* *Ac 24:3*
And when *F.* heard these   *Ac 24:22*
things
F. came with his wife Drusilla *Ac 24:24*
F. trembled, and answered,   *Ac 24:25*
Go thy
and *F.* willing to shew the   *Ac 24:27*
Jews a
a certain man left in bonds by *Ac 25:14*
F.

FELIX'

Porcius Festus came into *F.*   *Ac 24:27*
room

FELL

Cain was wroth, and his   *Ge 4:5*
countenance *f.*
the kings of Sodom and   *Ge 14:10*
Gomorrah *f.*
a deep sleep *f.* on Abram, and *Ge 15:12*
lo, and horror
Esau ran, and *f.* on his   *Ge 33:4*
brother's neck
Joseph's brethren *f.* before   *Ge 44:14*
him on ground
Joseph *f.* on Benjamin's neck *Ge 45:14*
and wept
Jacob *f.* on Joseph's neck and *Ge 46:29*
wept
there *f.* of the people 3000   *Ex 32:28*
men
the goat on which the Lord's   *Le 16:9;*
lot *f.*   *16:10*
the mixt multitude *f.* a lusting *Nu 11:4*
the dew *f.* on the camp, the   *Nu 11:9*
manna *f.* upon it
Moses and Aaron *f.*   *Nu 14:5;*
  16:22, 45; 20:6
that all that *f.* that day, were *Jos 8:25*
12,000
so Joshua came and *f.* upon *Jos 11:7*
them
and wrath *f.* on all the   *Jos 22:20*
congregation
Sisera's host *f.* on edge of   *J'g 4:16*
sword
Sisera *f.;* there *f.* 120,000 men *J'g 5:27;*
  8:10
a cake of bread smote the tent *J'g 7:13*
that it *f.*
f. of Ephraimites at that time *J'g 12:6*
42,000
house *f.* on the lords and on *J'g 16:30*
the people
there *f.* of Benjamin 18,000 *J'g 20:44*
men
there *f.* of Israel 30,000   *1Sa 4:10*
footmen
Eli *f.* from his seat backward *1Sa 4:18*
by gate
the fear of the Lord *f.* on the *1Sa 11:7*
people
the Philistines *f.* before   *1Sa 14:13*
Jonathan
Doeg turned, and *f.* upon the *1Sa 22:18*
priests

Abigail *f.* at David's feet,   *1Sa 25:24*
and said
Saul *f.* straightway along on *1Sa 28:20*
the earth
I found no fault in him since *1Sa 29:3*
he *f.* on me
because three days agone I *f.* *1Sa 30:13*
sick
Saul took a sword and *f.* upon *1Sa 31:4*
it
his armour-bearer *f.* likewise   *1Sa 31:5;*
  1Ch 10:4-5
so you *f.* (A)   *2Sa 3:34*
Mephibosheth *f.* and became *2Sa 4:4*
lame
there *f.* some of the people of *2Sa 11:17*
David
Amnon *f.* sick for his sister *2Sa 13:2*
Tamar
Joab's sword *f.* out as he went *2Sa 20:8*
forth
they *f.* all seven in days of   *2Sa 21:9*
harvest
they *f.* by the hand of David *2Sa 21:22;*
  1Ch 20:8
f. upon knees, did homage   *1Ki 1:16*
(B)
Benaiah *f.* on Adonijah that *1Ki 2:25*
he died
who *f.* upon two men more   *1Ki 2:32*
righteous than he
Benaiah *f.* on Joab; Benaiah *1Ki 2:34;*
f. on Shimei   *2:46*
Abijah the son of Jeroboam *1Ki 14:1*
f. sick
son of woman *f.* sick, it was *1Ki 17:17*
so sore
fire of Lord *f.* and consumed *1Ki 18:38*
the sacrifice
wall *f.* on 27,000 men that   *1Ki 20:30*
were left
third captain *f.* on knees   *2Ki 1:13*
before Elijah
he took mantle of Elijah that *2Ki 2:13*
f. from him
it *f.* on a day Elisha passed to *2Ki 4:8;*
Shunem   *4:11*
if *f.* on a day the child went to *2Ki 4:18*
reapers
Shunammite *f.* at his feet   *2Ki 4:37*
bowed herself
axe head *f.* into the water, and *2Ki 6:5*
he cried
the man of God said, Where *f.* *2Ki 6:6*
it
so it *f.* out to him, people   *2Ki 7:20*
trode on him
the fugitives that *f.* away to *2Ki 25:11*
the king
there *f.* some of Manasseh to *1Ch 12:19*
David
and there *f.* of Israel 70,000 *1Ch 21:14*
men
because here *f.* wrath for it *1Ch 27:24*
against Israel
for they *f.* to David out of   *2Ch 15:9*
Israel
fear of Lord *f.* on all   *2Ch 17:10*
kingdoms of lands
inhabitants of Jerusalem *f.*   *2Ch 20:18*
before Lord
his bowels *f.* out by reason *2Ch 21:19*
of sickness
soldiers of Israel *f.* on cities *2Ch 25:13*
of Judah
I *f.* on knees and spread my   *Ezr 9:5*
hands
for fear of the Jews *f.* on them *Es 8:17;*
  9:2
because the fear of Mordecai *f.* *Es 9:3*
upon them
Sabeans *f.* on the asses, and *Job 1:15*
took them
Chaldeans *f.* on camels, and *Job 1:17*
carried them away
house *f.* on young men, they *Job 1:19*
are dead
wicked came to eat up my flesh, *Ps 27:2*
they *f.*
their priests *f.* by sword,   *Ps 78:64*
widows not lament
for the fear of Israel *f.* on *Ps 105:38*
Egypt
those that *f.* away, that *f.* to *Jer 39:9;*
him   *52:15*
one *f.* upon another, and they *Jer 46:16*
said, Arise
her people *f.* into hand of enemy *La 1:7*

and the children *f.* under the   *La 5:13*
wood
hand of Lord *f.* upon me   *Eze 8:1; 11:5*
so *f.* they all by the sword   *Eze 39:23*
there *f.* a voice from heaven, *Da 4:31*
saying
other which came up, before *Da 7:20*
whom three *f.*
but a great quaking *f.* upon *Da 10:7*
them
cast lots, the lot *f.* on Jonah *Jon 1:7*
house *f.* not; it *f.*   *M't 7:25;*
  7:27; Lu 6:49
rain *f.,* came down   *M't 7:25*
(A)(B)(N)(P)(R)
seed *f.* by way side   *M't 13:4;*
  M'k 4:4; Lu 8:5
some *f.* upon stony places   *M't 13:5;*
  M'k 4:5; Lu 8:6
some *f.* among thorns   *M't 13:7;*
  M'k 4:7; Lu 8:7
other *f.* into good ground   *M't 13:8;*
  M'k 4:8; Lu 8:8
so they *f.* foul of him (N)   *M't 13:57*
Jairus saw him, *f.* at his feet *M'k 5:22*
Syrophenician woman *f.* at   *M'k 7:25*
his feet
he *f.* on ground and wallowed *M'k 9:20*
foaming
Jesus *f.* on the ground and *M'k 14:35*
prayed
and fear *f.* upon Zacharias   *Lu 1:12*
but as they sailed, Jesus *f.*   *Lu 8:23*
asleep
a certain man *f.* among   *Lu 10:30;*
thieves   *10:36*
upon whom the tower in   *M'k 13:4*
Siloam *f.*
his father *f.* on his neck and *M'k 15:20*
kissed him
crumbs which *f.* from rich *M'k 16:21*
man's table
went backward and *f.* to the   *Joh 18:6*
ground
from which Judas by   *Ac 1:25*
transgression *f.*
gave forth lots, and lot *f.* upon *Ac 1:26*
Matthias
when he had said this, he *f.*   *Ac 7:60*
asleep
Saul *f.* to the earth and heard a *Ac 9:4*
voice
there *f.* from his eyes as it had *Ac 9:18*
been scales
Peter became hungry, and *f.* *Ac 10:10*
into a trance
the Holy Ghost *f.* on them all *Ac 10:44;*
  11:15
the chains *f.* off from Peter's *Ac 12:7*
hands
there *f.* on him a mist and a *Ac 13:11*
darkness
David *f.* on sleep and saw   *Ac 13:36*
corruption
and fear *f.* on all the Jews at *Ac 19:17*
Ephesus
Paul went down, and *f.* on   *Ac 20:10*
Eutychus
they all *f.* on Paul's neck, and *Ac 20:37*
kissed him
I *f.* unto the ground, and heard *Ac 22:7*
a voice
on them which *f.* severity   *Ro 11:22*
reproaches of them reproached *Ro 15:3*
thee *f.* on me
and *f.* in one day 23,000   *1Co 10:8*
whose carcases *f.* in the   *Heb 3:17*
wilderness
since fathers *f.* asleep all   *2Pe 3:4*
things continue
I saw him, I *f.* at his feet   *Re 1:17*
as dead
the stars of heaven *f.* unto the *Re 6:13*
earth
there *f.* a great star from heaven *Re 8:10*
great fear *f.* on them who saw *Re 11:11*
them
tenth part of the city *f.* by   *Re 11:13*
earthquake
there *f.* a noisome and grievous *Re 16:2*
sore
city was divided, and cities of *Re 16:19*
nations *f.*
there *f.* on men, great hail out *Re 16:21*
of heaven
and I *f.* at his feet to worship *Re 19:10*
him

FELL *DOWN*

when the ass saw the angel,   *Nu 22:27*
she *f. down*
I *f. down* before the Lord   *De 9:18; 9:25*
people shouted, the wall *f.*   *Jos 6:20*
down flat
where he bowed there he *f.*   *J'g 3:27*
down dead
concubine *f. down* at door of   *J'g 19:26*
the house
Philistines *f. down* by the   *1Sa 17:52*
way
men of Israel *f. down* in   *1Sa 31:1;*
Gilboa   *1Ch 10:1*
so they *f. down* together   *2Sa 2:16*
Asahel *f. down* there, died in   *2Sa 2:23*
the place
Ahimaaz *f. down*   *2Sa 18:28*
Shimei *f. down*   *2Sa 19:18*
Ahaziah *f. down* through a   *2Ki 1:2*
lattice
there *f. down* many slain, war   *1Ch 5:22*
was of God
there *f. down* of Israel   *2Ch 13:17*
500,000 men
Esther *f. down* at Ahasuerus'   *Es 8:3*
feet
Job *f. down* on ground and   *Job 1:20*
worshipped
they *f. down* there was one to   *Ps 107:12*
help
all nations *f. down* and   *Da 3:7*
worshipped image
these three *f. down* bound in   *Da 3:23*
the furnace
wise men *f. down* and   *M't 2:11*
worshipped him
servant therefore *f. down*   *M't 18:26;*
saying   *18:29*
and unclean spirits *f. down*   *M'k 3:11*
before him
woman with the issue of   *M'k 5:33*
blood, *f. down*
Simon Peter *f. down* at Jesus'   *Lu 5:8*
knees
man which had devils *f. down*   *Lu 8:28*
before Jesus
Jairus *f. down*   *Lu 8:41*
the Samaritan *f. down*   *Lu 17:16*
Mary *f. down* at his feet,   *Job 11:32*
saying
Ananias *f. down*   *Ac 5:5*
Sapphira *f. down*   *Ac 5:10*
Cornelius *f. down*   *Ac 10:25*
jailer *f. down*   *Ac 16:29*
the image which *f. down* from   *Ac 19:35*
Jupiter
Eutychus *f. down* from the   *Ac 20:9*
third loft
by faith walls of Jericho   *Heb 11:30*
f. down
elders *f. down* before Lamb   *Re 5:8;*
  5:14; 19:4
John *f. down* to worship before   *Re 22:8*
the angel

FELLED

and *f.* all the good trees: only   *2Ki 3:25*

FELLER

no *f.* is come up against us   *1Sa 14:8*
no woodcutter comes up   *1Sa 14:8*
(A)(B)
no hewer is come up (E)(R)   *1Sa 14:8*

FELLEST

before wicked men, so *f.* thou   *2Sa 3:34*
so you fell (A)   *2Sa 3:34*
you have fallen (B)(R)   *2Sa 3:34*
so thou didst fall (E)   *2Sa 3:34*

FELLING

But as one was *f.* a beam   *2Ki 6:5*

FELLOES

and their *f.* and their spokes   *1Ki 7:33*
spokes and hubs were all cast   *1Ki 7:33*
(A)(B)(R)

FELLOW

This one *f.* came in to sojourn   *Ge 19:9*
Wherefore smitest thou thy *f.*   *Ex 2:13*

Why are you striking your   *Ex 2:13*
comrade (A)
Why strike neighbor (B)   *Ex 2:13*
man that told a dream unto his   *J'g 7:13*
f.
telling his comrade a dream   *J'g 7:13*
(A)(B)(R)
his *f.* answered and said, This   *J'g 7:14*
is
every man's sword against his   *J'g 7:22*
f.
every sword against his   *J'g 7:22*
comrade (A)
every man fighting man next to   *J'g 7:22*
him (B)
ye have brought this *f.* to   *1Sa 21:15*
play madman; shall *f.* come
worthless *f.* (S)   *1Sa 25:17*
in vain have I kept all that   *1Sa 25:21*
this *f.* hath
make this *f.* return, he may go   *1Sa 29:4*
to his place
You dismiss this man (B)   *1Sa 29:4*
Make this man return (E)   *1Sa 29:4*
Send this man back (R)   *1Sa 29:4*
caught every one his *f.* by the   *2Sa 2:16*
head
caught his opponent (A)   *2Sa 2:16*
caught hold of opponent's   *2Sa 2:16*
head (B)(R)
put this *f.* in prison   *1Ki 22:27;*
  2Ch 18:26
wherefore came this mad *f.* to   *2Ki 9:11*
thee
Why did this madman come   *2Ki 9:11*
to thee (B)
if they fall, one will lift up his   *Ec 4:10*
f.
one will lift up his companion   *Ec 4:10*
(B)
the satyr shall cry to his *f.*   *Isa 34:14*
they said every one to his *f.,*   *Jon 1:7*
cast lots
the man that is my *f.*   *Zec 13:7*
man who is my associate   *Zec 13:7*
(A)(B)
man who stands next to me   *Zec 13:7*
(R)
this *f.* doth not cast out   *M't 12:24*
devils but by
This man drives out demons   *M't 12:24*
(A)(E)(N)(P)(R)
this *f.* said, I am able to   *M't 26:61*
destroy the temple
this *f.* was also with Jesus   *M't 26:71;*
  Lu 22:59
we found this *f.* perverting the   *Lu 23:2*
nation
This man perverting   *Lu 23:2*
(A)(E)(N)(P)(R)
as for this *f.* we know not   *Joh 9:29*
whence he is
Didymus said to his *f.*   *Joh 11:16*
disciples, Let us go
this *f.* persuadeth men to   *Ac 18:13*
worship God
f. travelers with Paul (A)(B)   *Ac 19:29*
away with such a *f.* from the   *Ac 22:22*
earth
we have found this man a   *Ac 24:5*
pestilent *f.*
man to be a perfect pest   *Ac 24:5*
(A)(N)
man to be a veritable plague   *Ac 24:5*
(B)
a pestilential disturber of peace   *Ac 24:5*
(P)
f. heirs with Christ   *Ro 8:17*
(A)(R)(N)
dealing with *f.* men (N)   *2Co 1:12*
my *f.* workers (S)   *Ph'p 4:3; Ph'm 24*
our *f.* worker in the gospel   *1Th 3:2;*
(S)   *Ph'm 1*

FELLOW-CITIZENS

but *f.-citizens* with saints and   *Eph 2:19*
household
share citizenship with the   *Eph 2:19*
saints (A)

FELLOWDISCIPLES

Didymus, unto his *f.,* Let us   *Joh 11:16*
also

FELLOW-HEIRS

that the Gentiles should be   *Eph 3:6*
f.-heirs

---

joint-inheritors (B)   *Eph 3:6*
equal heirs (P)   *Eph 3:6*

FELLOW-HELPER,

HELPERS

Titus my *f.-helper* concerning   *2Co 8:23*
you
Titus my colleague (A)(P)   *2Co 8:23*
Titus is my associate (B)   *2Co 8:23*
Titus my partner and associate   *2Co 8:23*
(N)(R)
that we might be *f.-helpers*   *3Jo 8*
to the truth

FELLOW-LABOURER,

LABOURERS

Clement, with other my   *Ph'p 4:3*
f.-labourers
we sent Timotheus our   *1Th 3:2*
f.-labourer
Paul to Philemon our   *Ph'm 1*
f.-labourer
Marcus, Demas, Lucas, my   *Ph'm 24*
f.-labourers

FELLOWMEN

blameless among *f.* (B)   *Ge 6:9*

FELLOW-PRISONER,

PRISONERS,

Andronicus and Junia my   *Ro 16:7*
f.-prisoners
Aristarchus my *f.-prisoner*   *Col 4:10*
saluteth you
Epaphras my *f.-prisoner* in   *Ph'm 23*
Christ

FELLOW-SERVANT,

SERVANTS

found one of his *f.-servants*   *M't 18:28*
who owed him
his *f.-servant* fell down at his   *M't 18:29*
feet, saying
so when his *f.-servants* saw   *M't 18:31*
what was done
have had compassion on   *M't 18:33*
f.-servant as I on thee
and shall begin to smite his   *M't 24:49*
f.-servants
ye learned of Epaphras our   *Col 1:7*
f.-servant
Tychicus, who is *f.-servant* in   *Col 4:7*
the Lord
till their *f.-servants* should be   *Re 6:11*
fulfilled
see thou do it not, I am thy   *Re 19:10;*
f.-servant   *22:9*

FELLOW-SOLDIER

to send Epaphroditus my   *Ph'p 2:25*
f.-soldier
Paul to Archippus our *f.-soldier*   *Ph'm 2*

FELLOW-WORKER,

WORKERS

my partner, and *f.* (S)   *2Co 8:23*
these only are my *f.-workers*   *Col 4:11*
to kingdom

FELLOWS

base *f.* are gone (A)(E)(R)   *De 13:13*
worthless, base *f.* (S)   *De 13:13;*
  J'g 19:22; 20:13; 1Sa 2:12; 10:27; 25:17,
  25; 30:22; 2Sa 16:7; 20:1; 23:6;
  1Ki 21:10, 13; 2Ch 13:7
the *f.* of Belial (S)   *De 13:13; J'g 20:13;*
  1Sa 10:27; 1Ki 21:13; 2Ch 13:7
bewail my integrity, I and my   *J'g 11:37*
f.
I and my companions   *J'g 11:37*
(A)(B)(E)(R)
lest angry *f.* run upon thee   *J'g 18:25*
embittered men knock you   *J'g 18:25*
down (B)
certain worthless *f.* (A)   *J'g 19:22*
certain base *f.* (E)(R)   *J'g 19:22*

base, perverted *f.*   J'g 20:13;
(A)(B)(E)(R)   1Sa 10:27;   1Ki 21:13
as cne of the vain *f.*   2Sa 6:20
shamelessly
the oil of gladness above thy *f.* Ps 45:7
Behold, all his *f.* shall be   Isa 44:11
ashamed
all his associates shall be (B)   Isa 44:11
and the tribes of Israel his *f.*   Eze 37:19
tribes of Israel associated   Eze 37:19
with him (B)
tribes of Israel his   Eze 37:19
companions (E)
they sought Daniel and his *f.*   Da 2:13
Daniel and his companions   Da 2:13;
(A)(B)(E)(R)   2:18
that Daniel and his *f.* should   Da 2:18
look was more stout than his *f.*   Da 7:20
looked greater than the others   Da 7:20
(A)
the high priest, thou, and thy *f.* Zec 3:8
you and your colleagues (A)   Zec 3:8
you and your friends (B)(R)   Zec 3:8
markets, and calling unto   M't 11:16
their *f.*
who call to their playmates   M't 11:16
(A)(B)(R)
calling out to their friends   M't 11:16
(P)
certain lewd *f.* of the baser sort Ac 17:5
loungers in the market place   Ac 17:5
(A)(B)(P)
the oil of gladness above thy   Heb 1:9
f.

FELLOW'S

thrust his sword in his *f.* side   2Sa 2:16

FELLOWSHIP

or in *f.* or in a thing taken   Le 6:2
nor *f.* with pretenders (A)(B)   Ps 26:4
had sweet *f.* together (A)(B)   Ps 55:14
of iniquity have *f.* with thee   Ps 94:20
corrupt government be allied   Ps 94:20
with (B)(R)
and *f.* and in breaking of   Ac 2:42
bread
were called unto the *f.* of his   1Co 1:9
Son
into companionship with (A)(B)   1Co 1:9
to share in the life of his Son   1Co 1:9
(N)
f. in the blood of (A)(B)   1Co 10:16
that ye should have *f.* with   1Co 10:20
devils
what *f.* hath righteousnes with   2Co 6:14
what partnership have right   2Co 6:14
living with (A)(R)
common ground between (B)   2Co 6:14
common interest between (P)   2Co 6:14
upon us the *f.* of the   2Co 8:4
ministering
part in this service to saints   2Co 8:4
(B)
share in this generous service   2Co 8:4
(N)
taking part in relief of saints   2Co 8:4
(R)
f. of Holy Ghost   2Co 13:14
(A)(B)(N)(P)(R)
and Barnabas the right hand of   Ga 2:9
f.
see what is the *f.* of the   Eph 3:9
mystery
And have no *f.* with the   Eph 5:11
unfruitful
Do not participate in (B)   Eph 5:11
take no part in (N)(R)   Eph 5:11
have nothing to do with (P)   Eph 5:11
your *f.* in the gospel from the   Ph'p 1:5
first
of love, if any *f.* of the Spirit Ph'p 2:1
and the *f.* of his sufferings   Ph'p 3:10
sharing of his sufferings   Ph'p 3:10
(A)(B)(N)(P)(R)
f. with affliction (E)   Ph'p 4:14
f. with me (E)(P)(R)   Ph'p 4:15
f. of thy faith (E)(N)(S)   Ph'm 6
ye also may have *f* with us; and   1Jo 1:3
truly our *f.* is with the Father   1Jo 1:3
If we say that we have *f.* with   1Jo 1:6
him
light, we have *f.* one with   1Jo 1:7
another

FELT

and he *f.* him, and said, The   Ge 27:22
voice
even darkness which may be *f.*   Ex 10:21
Israelites *f.* grieved (B)   J'g 21:6
Lord *f.* grieved (B)   J'g 24:15
Amnon *f.* frustrated (B)   2Sa 13:2
Lord *f.* compassion (B)   1Ch 21:15
f. more love for Esther (B)   Es 2:17
and *f.* great indignation (S)   Ne 4:1
f. grieved according to (B)   Ps 106:45
I *f.* it not: when shall I awake   Pr 23:35
f. in her body that she was   M'k 5:29
healed
Peter *f.* distressed (B)   Joh 21:17
f. ugly toward Tyrians (B)   Ac 12:20
beast into the fire, and *f.* no   Ac 28:5
harm

FEMALE

male and *f.* created he them   Ge 1:27;
                                        5:2
two of every sort, they shall be   Ge 6:19
male and *f.*
take to thee by sevens, male   Ge 7:2;
and *f.*   7:3
there went in two and two, male   Ge 7:9
and *f.*
they that went in, went in male   Ge 7:16
and *f.*
if he offer it, whether it be   Le 3:1
male or *f.*
if his offering be of the flock,   Le 3:6
male or *f.*
offering a *f.* without blemish   Le 4:28;
                                   4:32; 5:6
if she bear a *f.* (S)   Le 12:5; Nu 31:18
law for her that hath born   Le 12:7
a male or *f.*
if it be a *f.* thy estimation be 30 Le 27:4
shekels
thy estimation for the *f.* ten   Le 27:5;
shekels   27:7
for the *f.* from a month old,   Le 27:6
three shekels
both male and *f.* shall ye   Nu 5:3
put out
graven image, the likeness of   De 4:16
male or *f.*
shall not be a male or *f.* barren De 7:14
among you
made them male and *f.*   M't 19:4;
                                    M'k 10:6
in Christ there is neither male   Ga 3:28
nor *f.*

FENCE

ye be as a bowing wall and a   Ps 62:3
tottering *f.*

FENCED

till thy high and *f.* walls come   De 28:52
down
men that shall touch them must   2Sa 23:7
be *f.*
and ye shall smite every *f.* city 2Ki 3:19
there are with you a *f.* city   2Ki 10:2
and armour
from the tower to the *f.* city   2Ki 17:9;
                                        18:8
he hath *f.* me with bones and   Job 10:11
sinews
he hath *f.* up my way that I   Job 19:8
cannot
the day of the Lord on every *f.*   Isa 2:15
wall
my beloved hath a vineyard,   Isa 5:2
and he *f.*
I will make thee a *f.* brazen   Jer 15:20
wall
waste and ruined cities are   Eze 36:35
become *f.*

FENCED *CITIES*

our little ones shall dwell in *f.* Nu 32:17
cities
all these *cities* were *f.* with   De 3:5
walls
to possess *cities* great and *f.* up De 9:1
to heaven
rest of them entered into *f.*   Jos 10:20
cities
and that the *cities* were great   Jos 14:12
and *f.*

golden mice, according to *f.*   1Sa 6:18
cities
pursue, lest he get *f.* cities and 2Sa 20:6
escape
f. cities and took them   2Ki 18:13;
                                    2Ch 12:4
shouldest be to lay waste *f.*   2Ki 19:25
cities
Solomon built *f.* cities with   2Ch 8:5
walls
Shishak took the *f.* cities of   2Ch 12:4
Judah
Asa built *f.* cities in Judah,   2Ch 14:6
land had rest
Jehoshaphat placed forces in   2Ch 17:2;
the *f.* cities   17:19
set judges throughout all *f.*   2Ch 19:5
cities of Judah
Jehoshaphat gave them *f.*   2Ch 21:3
cities in Judah
Manasseh put captains of   2Ch 33:14
war in *f.* cities
they shall impoverish thy *f.*   Jer 5:17
cities
king of north shall take most   Da 11:15
f. cities
Judah hath multiplied *f.* cities   Ho 8:14
day of alarm against *f.* cities   Zep 1:16

FENS

in the covert of the reed, and   Job 40:21
f.
covert of reeds and marshes   Job 40:21
(A)(R)

FEROCIOUS

f. wolves will (A)   Ac 20:29

FERRET

And the *f.* and the chameleon   Le 11:30

FERRY

And there went over a *f.* boat   2Sa 19:18

FERTILIZE

and *f.* it (S)   Lu 13:8

FERVENT

being *f.* in the spirit, he spake Ac 18:25
burning with spiritual zeal   Ac 18:25
(A)
with a burning spirit (B)   Ac 18:25
full of spiritual fervor (N)   Ac 18:25
spoke with burning zeal (P)   Ac 18:25
f. in spirit; serving the Lord   Ro 12:11
burning with the Spirit (A)   Ro 12:11
keeping spiritually aglow   Ro 12:11
(B)(R)
in ardour of spirit (N)   Ro 12:11
keep fires of the spirit burning   Ro 12:11
(P)
your *f.* mind toward me; so that   2Co 7:7
told us your yearning affection   2Co 7:7
(A)
related your zeal for me   2Co 7:7
(B)(E)(R)
how eager you are to take my   2Co 7:7
side (N)
keen interest on my behalf (P)   2Co 7:7
f. prayer of a righteous man   Jas 5:16
the earnest prayer (A)(B)(P)   Jas 5:16
the supplication of a righteous   Jas 5:16
(E)
A good man's prayer is   Jas 5:16
powerful (N)
have *f.* charity among   1Pe 4:8
yourselves
have intense and unfailing love   1Pe 4:8
(A)(B)(R)
keep your love at full strength   1Pe 4:8
(N)
have real deep love (P)   1Pe 4:8
the elements shall melt with *f.*   2Pe 3:10;
heat   3:12

FERVENTLY

labouring *f.* for you in prayers   Col 4:12
striving for you earnestly (A)   Col 4:12
wrestling for you in prayers   Col 4:12
(B)
striving for you in prayers (E)   Col 4:12
prays hard for you at all time   Col 4:12
(N)

he prays constantly and *Col 4:12*
earnestly (R)
one another with a pure heart *1Pe 1:22*
f.
most cordially consistently *1Pe 1:22*
love (B)
love one another *1Pe 1:22*
wholeheartedly (N)
love earnestly from the heart *1Pe 1:22*
(R)

FESTAL

bind *f.* procession with *Ps 118:27*
branches (R)

FESTER

wounds grow foul and *f.* (R) *Ps 38:5*

FESTERING

festering (S) *Le 13:51; 13:52; 14:44*
f. because of my folly (B) *Ps 38:5*

FESTIVAL

Jeroboam at a *f.* (B) *1Ki 12:32; 12:33*
the closing *f.* (B) *Ne 8:18*
the *f.* robes (S) *Isa 3:22*
the great appointed *f.* (R) *Ho 9:5*
the harvest *f.* (B) *Ho 12:9*

FESTIVALS

the city of our *f.* (B) *Isa 33:20*
the appointed *f.* (B) *Eze 46:11*

FESTIVE

it is a *f.* gathering (B) *Le 23:36*

FESTIVITIES

went to the *f.* (P) *M't 25:10*

FESTUS

Porcius *F.* came into Felix' *Ac 24:27*
room
F. was come into the province *Ac 25:1;*
25:4, 9, 12-14, 22, 24
F. said with a loud voice, *Ac 26:24*
Paul
I am not mad, most noble *F. Ac 26:25;*
26:32

FESTUS'

at *F.* commandment Paul was *Ac 25:23*

FETCH

And I will *f.* a morsel of bread *Ge 18:5*
f. me from thence two good *Ge 27:9*
kids
obey my voice, and go *f.* me *Ge 27:13*
them
will send, and *f.* thee from *Ge 27:45*
thence
and let him *f.* your brother, *Ge 42:16*
and ye
she sent her maid to *f.* it *Ex 2:5*
we *f.* you water out of this *Nu 20:10*
rock
the border shall *f.* a compass *Nu 34:5*
of his city shall send and *f. De 19:12*
him
into his house to *f.* his pledge *De 24:10*
thou shalt not go again to *f.* it *De 24:19*
and from thence will he *f.* thee *De 30:4*
elders of Gilead went to *f. J'g 11:5*
Jephthah
to *f.* victual for the people *J'g 20:10*
Let us *f.* the ark of the *1Sa 4:3*
covenant
come ye down, and *f.* it up to *1Sa 6:21*
you
Send and *f.* him: for we will *1Sa 16:11*
not
now send and *f.* him unto *1Sa 20:31*
me, for
the young men come over *1Sa 26:22*
and *f.* it
but *f.* a compass behind them *2Sa 5:23*
the king doth not *f.* home *2Sa 14:13*
again
To *f.* about this form of *2Sa 14:20*
speech

F. me, I pray thee, a little *1Ki 17:10*
water
And as she was going to *f.* it *1Ki 17:11*
that I may send and *f.* him *2Ki 6:13*
F. quickly Micaiah the son of *2Ch 18:8*
Imla
and *f.* olive branches, and pine *Ne 8:15*
I will *f.* my knowledge from *Job 36:3*
afar
I will *f.* wine, and we will fill *Isa 56:12*
the king sent Jehudi to *f.* the *Jer 36:21*
roll
come themselves and *f.* us out *Ac 16:37*

FETCHED

Let a little water, I pray you, *Ge 18:4*
be *f.*
he went, and *f.* and brought *Ge 27:14*
them
and *f.* a compass to Karkaa *Jos 15:3*
f. the carved image, the ephod *J'g 18:18*
and *f.* up the ark of the Lord *1Sa 7:1*
And they ran and *f.* him *1Sa 10:23*
thence
though they would have *f. 2Sa 4:6*
wheat
king David sent, and *f.* him out *2Sa 9:5*
sent and *f.* her to his house *2Sa 11:27*
and *f.* thence a wise woman *2Sa 14:2*
king Solomon sent and *f. 1Ki 7:13*
Hiram
to Ophir, and *f.* from thence *1Ki 9:28*
gold
they *f.* a compass of seven days' *2Ki 3:9*
Jehoiada sent and *f.* the rulers *2Ki 11:4*
And they *f.* up, and brought *2Ch 1:17*
forth
the guard came and *f.* them *2Ch 12:11*
they *f.* forth Urijah out of *Jer 26:23*
Egypt
from thence we *f.* a compass *Ac 28:13*

FETCHETH

his hand *f.* a stroke with the *De 19:5*
axe

FETCHT

and *f.* a calf tender and good *Ge 18:7*

FETTERS

and bound him with *f.* of *J'g 16:21*
brass
bronze chains (B) *J'g 16:21*
not bound, nor thy feet put *2Sa 3:34*
into *f.*
and bound him with *f.* of brass *2Ki 25:7*
chains (B) *2Ki 25:7; 2Ch 36:6*
and bound him with *f.* and *2Ch 33:11*
and bound him in *f.* to carry *2Ch 36:6*
him
And if they be bound in *f. Job 36:8*
Whose feet they hurt with *f. Ps 105:18*
irons (B) *Ps 105:18*
to bind their nobles with *f.* of *Ps 149:8*
iron
being often bound with *f. M'k 5:4;*
Lu 8:29

FEUD

had a great *f.* (R) *J'g 12:2*
end the *f.* (B) *Eph 2:15; 2:16*

FEVER

the burning *f.* (B)(E)(R) *Le 26:16*
the Lord shall smite thee with *De 28:22*
a *f.*
sick with the *f.* of wine (B) *Ho 7:5*
burning *f.* follows (B) *Hab 3:5*
Jesus was come, he saw *M't 8:14;*
Peter's wife's *M'k 1:30; Lu 4:38*
mother sick of a *f.*
yesterday at seventh hour *f. Joh 4:52*
left him
father of Publius lay sick of a *Ac 28:8*
f.

FEW

let damsel abide with us a *f. Ge 24:55*
days
tarry *f.* days till brother's fury *Ge 27:44*
turn

I being *f.* in number, they will *Ge 34:30*
slay me
f. and evil have days of my life *Ge 47:9*
been
I will make you *f. Le 26:22;*
De 4:27; 28:62
cloud was a *f.* days on *Nu 9:20*
tabernacle
see people whether they be *f. Nu 13:18*
or many
to *f.* shall give less *Nu 26:54;*
inheritance *35:8*
possession divided between *Nu 26:56*
many and *f.*
my father sojourned there a *f. De 26:5*
let Reuben live, let not his men *De 33:6*
be *f.*
no restraint, to save by many *1Sa 14:6*
or *f.*
with whom hast thou left *f. 1Sa 17:28*
sheep
but the priests were too *f. 2Ch 29:34*
I arose, I and some *f.* men *Ne 2:12*
with me
city large, but people were *f. Ne 7:4*
therein
are not my days *f.?* let alone *Job 10:20*
man is of *f.* days, and full of *Job 14:1*
trouble
when a *f.* years are come, *Job 16:22*
then I shall go
let his days be *f.* and let *Ps 109:8*
another take
God is in heaven, let words be *f. Ec 5:2*
there was a little city, and *f. Ec 9:14*
men in it
grinders cease, because they are *Ec 12:3*
f.
rest of the trees of forest shall *Isa 10:19*
be *f.*
inhabitants are burned, and *f. Isa 24:6*
men left
thou shalt also take a *f.* in *Eze 5:3*
number
I will leave a *f.* men from the *Eze 12:16*
sword
within *f.* days he shall be *Da 11:20*
destroyed
strait is gate, and *f.* there be *M't 7:14*
that find it
but the labourers are *f. M't 9:37;*
Lu 10:2
seven, and a *f.* little fishes *M't 15:34;*
M'k 8:7
many be called, but *f. M't 20:16;*
chosen *22:14*
thou hast been faithful in *f. M't 25:21;*
things *25:23*
laid hands on *f.* sick folk, *M'k 6:5*
healed them
shall be beaten with *f.* stripes *Lu 12:48*
one said, Lord, are there *f. Lu 13:23*
that be saved
that thou wouldest hear us a *f. Ac 24:4*
words
mystery as I wrote afore in *f. Eph 3:3*
words
for they verily for a *f.* days *Heb 12:10*
chastened us
for I have written unto you *Heb 13:22*
in *f.* words
wherein *f.* that is, eight souls *1Pe 3:20*
were saved
I have a *f.* things against thee *Re 2:14;*
2:20
thou hast a *f.* names even in *Re 3:4*
Sardis

BUT A FEW

they seemed to him *but a f. Ge 29:20*
days
if there remain *but f.* years to *Le 25:52*
jubilee
the men of Ai are *but f. Jos 7:3*
when ye were *but f. 1Ch 16:19;*
Ps 105:12
for we are left *but a f.* of many *Jer 42:2*

NOT A FEW

borrow empty vessels, borrow *2Ki 4:3*
not a f.
to destroy, and cut off nations *Isa 10:7*
not a f.
multiply them, and they shall *Jer 30:19*
not be f.
chief women *not a f. Ac 17:4*
of men *not a f. Ac 17:12*

FEWER

to *f.* ye shall give the less inheritance	*Nu 33:54*

FEWEST

for ye were the *f.* of all people	*De 7:7*

FEWNESS

according to *f.* of years diminish pride	*Le 25:16*

FIBER

seven fresh *f.* cords (B)	*J'g 16:7*

FICTIONS

godless *f.* (A)(P)	*1Ti 4:7*
myths, man-made *f.* (A)(B)(P)(R)	*2Ti 4:4*

FIDELITY

fidelity (A)(B)	*M't 23:23*
without conscience, *f.* (B)(N)	*Ro 1:31*
servants not purloining, shewing good *f.*	*Tit 2:10*
truly loyal, entirely reliable, and faithful throughout (A)	*Tit 2:10*
to evidence such complete reliableness (B)	*Tit 2:10*
strictly honest and trustworthy (N)(P)	*Tit 2:10*

FIELD

f. give I thee, and cave therein	*Ge 23:11*
f. and cave were made sure to Abraham	*Ge 23:20*
smell of my son is as smell of a *f.*	*Ge 27:27*
Jacob called Rachel and Leah to the *f.*	*Ge 31:4*
in the *f.* which Abraham bought	*Ge 49:30; 50:13*
if a man shall cause a *f.* to be eaten	*Ex 22:5*
so that corn or *f.* be consumed therewith	*Ex 22:6*
shalt not sow thy *f.* with mingled seed	*Le 19:19*
six years shalt sow *f.* and prune vineyard	*Le 25:3*
in the seventh year thou shalt not sow thy *f.*	*Le 25:4*
if he sanctify his *f.* from year of jubilee	*Le 27:17; 27:18*
if he will not redeem *f.* or if he sold *f.*	*Le 27:20*
nor shalt thou covet thy neighbour's *f.*	*De 5:21*
to ask of her father a *f.*	*Jos 15:18; J'g 1:14*
go not to glean in another *f.* but abide	*Ru 2:8*
Boaz said, What day thou buyest *f.* of Naomi	*Ru 4:5*
Joab's *f.* is near mine, and he hath barely	*2Sa 14:30*
why have thy servants set my *f.* on fire	*2Sa 14:31*
stood by upper pool, which is in highway of fuller's *f.*	*2Ki 18:17; Isa 7:3; 36:2*
the Levites fled every one to his *f.*	*Ne 13:10*
let the *f.* be joyful and all therein	*Ps 96:12*
I went by the *f.* of the slothful	*Pr 24:30*
lambs for clothing, and goats price of *f.*	*Pr 27:26*
she considereth a *f.* and buyeth it	*Pr 31:16*
the king himself is served by the *f.*	*Ec 5:9*
woe to them that lay *f.* to *f.* till no place	*Isa 5:8*
and joy is taken out of the plentiful *f.*	*Isa 16:10*
how long shall herbs of every *f.* wither	*Jer 12:4*
Zion shall be plowed like a *f.*	*Jer 26:18; Mic 3:12*
buy thee my *f.* that is in Anathoth	*Jer 32:7; 32:8, 25*

neither have we vineyard, nor *f.* nor seed	*Jer 35:9*
joy and gladness is taken from plentiful *f.*	*Jer 48:33*
the *f.* is wasted, the land mourneth	*Joe 1:10*
that soweth good seed in his *f.*	*M't 13:24; 13:31*
the *f.* is the world, good seed children of kingdom	*M't 13:38*
treasure hid in a *f.* he selleth all, and buyeth that *f.*	*M't 13:44*
they bought with them potter's *f.*	*M't 27:7; 27:10*
the *f.* was called the *f.* of blood	*M't 27:8; Ac 1:19*
will say to him, when come from *f.*	*Lu 17:7*
the *f.* that Jacob gave (R)	*Joh 4:5*
this man purchased *f.* with reward of	*Ac 1:18*
a *f.* under God's cultivation (P)(R)(S)	*1Co 3:9*

FRUITFUL FIELD

shall consume glory of his *fruitful f.*	*Isa 10:18*
Lebanon shall be turned into *fruitful f.*	*Isa 29:17*
wilderness be *fruitful f.;* *fruitful f.* be a forest	*Isa 32:15*
and righteousness in the *fruitful f.*	*Isa 32:16*
he planted the seed in a *fruitful f.*	*Eze 17:5*

IN THE FIELD

it came to pass when they were *in the f.*	*Ge 4:8*
Isaac went out to meditate *in the f.*	*Ge 24:63*
he looked, and behold a well *in the f.*	*Ge 29:2*
Joseph was wandering *in the f.*	*Ge 37:15*
send and gather all thou hast *in f.*	*Ex 9:19*
hail smote in Egypt all that was *in the f.*	*Ex 9:25*
to-day ye shall not find it *in f.*	*Ex 16:25*
if one be found slain, lying *in the f.*	*De 21:1*
if man find betrothed damsel *in the f.*	*De 22:25*
blessed in city and *in the f.*	*De 28:3*
cursed in city and *in the f.*	*De 28:16*
angel came to woman as she sat *in the f.*	*J'g 13:9*
which stone remaineth *in f.* of Joshua	*1Sa 6:18*
I will stand beside my father *in the f.*	*1Sa 19:3*
they found an Egyptian *in the f.*	*1Sa 30:11*
two sons, they two strove *in the f.*	*2Sa 14:6*
they two were alone *in the f.*	*1Ki 11:29*
him that dieth of Jeroboam *in the f.*	*1Ki 14:11*
him that dieth of Ahab *in the f.*	*1Ki 21:24*
kings were by themselves *in the f.*	*1Ch 19:9*
over them that did the work *in the f.*	*1Ch 27:26*
they reap every one his corn *in the f.*	*Job 24:6*
marvellous things *in the f.* of Zoan	*Ps 78:12; 78:43*
make it for thyself *in the f.*	*Pr 24:27*
yea, the hind calved *in the f.*	*Jer 14:5*
my mountain *in the f.* give to spoil	*Jer 17:3*
for we have treasures *in the f.* of wheat	*Jer 41:8*
he that is *in the f.* shall die by sword	*Eze 7:15*
he shall slay daughters *in the f.*	*Eze 26:6; 26:8*
shalt dwell *in the f.* and go to Babylon	*Mic 4:10*
shall give to every one grass *in f.*	*Zec 10:1*
nor shall your vine cast her fruit *in the f.*	*Mal 3:11*
neither let him who is *in the f.*	*M't 24:18;*

f. return	*M'k 13:16; Lu 17:31*
then shall two be *in the f.*	*M't 24:40; Lu 17:36*
there were shepherds abiding *in the f.*	*Lu 2:8*
clothe the grass which is to-day *in the f.*	*Lu 12:28*
elder son was *in the f.* heard music	*Lu 15:25*

INTO THE FIELD

ass turned aside, and went *into the f.*	*Nu 22:23*
the people went out *into the f.*	*J'g 9:42*
the cart came *into the f.* of Joshua	*1Sa 6:14*
Jonathan said, Come let us go *into the f.*	*1Sa 20:11*
men came out unto us *into the f.*	*2Sa 11:23*
removed Amasa out of way *into the f.*	*2Sa 20:12*
one went *into f.* and gathered gourds	*2Ki 4:39*
my beloved, let us go forth *into the f.*	*Ca 7:11*
go not forth *into f.* nor walk by way	*Jer 6:25*
if I go forth *into the f.* behold the slain	*Jer 14:18*

OF THE FIELD

every plant and herb *of the f.*	*Ge 2:5*
the sons of Jacob came out *of the f.*	*Ge 34:7*
four parts your own, for seed *of the f.*	*Ge 47:24*
the trees *of the f.* yield fruit	*Le 26:4*
no devoted thing *of the f.* shall be sold	*Le 27:28*
for tree *of the f.* is man's life	*De 20:19*
when thou marchedst out *of the f.*	*J'g 5:4*
came an old man from work out *of the f.*	*J'g 19:16*
on a part *of the f.* belonging to Boaz	*Ru 2:3*
Saul came after the herd out *of the f.*	*1Sa 11:5*
cast him in portion *of the f.* of Naboth	*2Ki 9:25*
carcase shall be as dung upon face *of the f.*	*2Ki 9:37*
shall be in league with stones *of the f.*	*Job 5:23*
as a flower *of the f.* he flourisheth	*Ps 103:15*
I charge you by roes *of the f.*	*Ca 2:7; 3:5*
inhabitants were as grass *of the f.*	*Isa 37:27*
all flesh is grass, and as flower *of the f.*	*Isa 40:6*
the beast *of the f.* shall honour me	*Isa 43:20*
all trees *of the f.* shall clap their hands	*Isa 55:12*
as keepers *of the f.* are they against her	*Jer 4:17*
snow of Lebanon from rock *of the f.*	*Jer 18:14*
stricken for want of fruits *of the f.*	*La 4:9*
caused thee to multiply as bud *of the f.*	*Eze 16:7*
all trees *of the f.* shall know that I Lord	*Eze 17:24*
the tree *of the f.* shall yield her fruit	*Eze 34:27*
I will multiply the increase *of the f.*	*Eze 36:30*
they shall take no wood out *of the f.*	*Eze 39:10*
in tender grass *of the f.* and wet with dew	*Da 4:15*
as hemlock in the furrows *of the f.*	*Ho 10:4*
their altars as heaps in furrows *of the f.*	*Ho 12:11*
because the harvest *of the f.* is perished	*Joe 1:11*
even all the trees *of the f.* are withered	*Joe 1:12*
flame hath burnt all the trees *of the f.*	*Joe 1:19*
I will make Samaria as an heap *of the f.*	*Mic 1:6*

consider lilies *of the f.* how they grow	*M't 6:28*
wherefore, if God so clothe the grass *of the f.*	*M't 6:30*
declare the parable of the tares *of the f.*	*M't 13:36*

OPEN FIELD

shall let living bird loose into the *open f.*	*Le 14:7*
bring sacrifices which they offer in the *open f.*	*Le 17:5*
men's carcases as dung upon the *open f.*	*Jer 9:22*
but thou wast cast out in the *open f.*	*Eze 16:5*
I will cast thee forth upon the *open f.*	*Eze 32:4*
him that is in the *open f.* I will give to beasts	*Eze 33:2*
thou shalt fall upon the *open f.* saith Lord God	*Eze 39:5*

FIELDS

frogs died out of the houses and *f.*	*Ex 8:13*
shall be counted as the *f.* of the country	*Le 25:31*
which is not of the *f.* of his possession	*Le 27:22*
thou hast not given us inheritance of *f.*	*Nu 16:14*
we will not pass thro' *f.* or vineyards	*Nu 20:17; 21:22*
and I will send grass into thy *f.*	*De 11:15*
that he might eat the increase of the *f.*	*De 32:13*
their vine is as the vine of the *f.* of Gomorrah	*De 32:32*
but the *f.* and villages gave they to Caleb	*Jos 21:12*
he will take your *f.* and vineyards	*1Sa 8:14*
will the son of Jesse give each of you *f.*	*1Sa 22:7*
they were a wall to us when we were in *f.*	*1Sa 25:15*
get thee to Anathoth, to thine own *f.*	*1Ki 2:26*
dieth of Baasha in *f.* shall fowls eat	*1Ki 16:4*
let the *f.* rejoice and all therein	*1Ch 16:32*
over the storehouses in the *f.* in cities	*1Ch 27:25*
and who sendeth waters upon the *f.*	*Job 5:10*
sow the *f.* and plant vineyards	*Ps 107:37*
we found it in the *f.* of the wood	*Ps 132:6*
while as yet he had not made the *f.*	*Pr 8:26*
enter not into the *f.* of the fatherless	*Pr 23:10*
for *f.* of Heshbon languish and vine of	*Isa 16:8*
they shall lament for teats, pleasant *f.*	*Isa 32:12*
their *f.* shall be turned to others	*Jer 6:12; 8:10*
I have seen thine abominations in the *f.*	*Jer 13:27*
f. shall be possessed again in this land	*Jer 32:15*
f. bought, men shall buy *f.* for money	*Jer 32:43; 32:44*
Nebuzar-adan gave them *f.* at same time	*Jer 39:10*
captains of forces which were in *f.*	*Jer 40:7; 40:13*
they shall possess the *f.* of Ephraim	*Ob 19*
covet *f.* and take them by violence	*Mic 2:2*
turning away, he hath divided our *f.*	*Mic 2:4*
although the *f.* shall yield no meat	*Hab 3:17*
he went through the corn *f.*	*M'k 2:23; Lu 6:1*
lift up your eyes, and look on the *f.*	*Joh 4:35*
the labourers, which reaped down your *f.*	*Jas 5:4*

OPEN FIELDS

he shall let go the living bird into *open f.*	*Le 14:53*
one slain with a sword in the *open f.*	*Nu 19:16*
servants are encamped in the *open f.*	*2Sa 11:11*
thou shalt fall upon the *open f.*	*Eze 29:5*

FIERCE

Cursed be their anger, for it was *f.*	*Ge 49:7*
Turn from thy *f.* wrath, and repent	*Ex 32:12*
f. anger of the Lord may be turned	*Nu 25:4*
augment yet the *f.* anger of	*Nu 32:14*
A nation of *f.* countenance, which	*De 28:50*
arose from the table in *f.* anger	*1Sa 20:34*
nor executedst his *f.* wrath upon	*1Sa 28:18*
f. wrath of the Lord is upon you	*2Ch 28:11*
and there is *f.* wrath against Israel	*2Ch 28:13*
that his *f.* wrath may turn away	*2Ch 29:10*
until the *f.* wrath of our God for this	*Ezr 10:14*
voice of the *f.* lion, and the teeth	*Job 4:10*
Thou huntest me as a *f.* lion	*Job 10:16*
nor the *f.* lion passed by it	*Job 28:8*
None is so *f.* that dare stir him up	*Job 41:10*
Thy *f.* wrath goeth over me	*Ps 88:16*
the *f.* anger of Rezin with Syria	*Isa 7:4*
with wrath and *f.* anger, to lay	*Isa 13:9*
and in the day of his *f.* anger	*Isa 13:13*
and a *f.* king shall rule over them	*Isa 19:4*
Thou shalt not see a *f.* people	*Isa 33:19*
f. anger of the Lord is not turned	*Jer 4:8*
of the Lord, and by his *f.* anger	*Jer 4:26*
revenues because of the *f.* anger of	*Jer 12:13*
cut down because of the *f.* anger of	*Jer 25:37*
and because of his *f.* anger	*Jer 25:38*
The *f.* anger of the Lord shall not	*Jer 30:24*
evil upon them, even my *f.* anger	*Jer 49:37*
man his soul from the *f.* anger of	*Jer 51:45*
me in the day of his *f.* anger	*La 1:12*
He hath cut off in his *f.* anger	*La 2:3*
he hath poured out his *f.* anger	*La 4:11*
a king of *f.* countenance, and	*Da 8:23*
and turn away from his *f.* anger	*Jon 3:9*
more *f.* than the evening wolves	*Hab 1:8*
the *f.* anger of the Lord come upon	*Zep 2:2*
indignation, even all my *f.* anger	*Zep 3:8*
exceeding *f.* so that no man might	*M't 8:28*
they were the more *f.* saying	*Lu 23:5*
f. wolves will come (R)	*Ac 20:29*
false accusers, incontinent, *f.*	*2Ti 3:3*
a *f.* fire (N)	*Heb 10:27*
driven of *f.* winds, yet are they	*Jas 3:4*

FIERCENESS

turn from the *f.* of his anger	*De 13:17*
turned from the *f.* of his anger	*Jos 7:26*
not from the *f.* of his great wrath	*2Ki 23:26*
the *f.* of his wrath may turn away	*2Ch 30:8*
He swalloweth the ground with *f.*	*Job 39:24*
cast upon them the *f.* of his anger	*Ps 78:49*
thyself from the *f.* of thine anger	*Ps 85:3*
because of the *f.* of the oppressor	*Jer 25:38*
not execute the *f.* of mine anger	*Ho 11:9*

can abide in the *f.* of his anger	*Na 1:6*
f. of fire (E)	*Heb 10:27*
of the wine of the *f.* of his wrath	*Re 16:19*
the *f.* and wrath of Almighty God	*Re 19:15*

FIERCER

words of the men of Judah were *f.*	*2Sa 19:43*
more violent than the charges of (A)(B)	*2Sa 19:43*

FIERY

the Lord sent *f.* serpents among	*Nu 21:6*
stinging serpents (B)	*Nu 21:6; 21:8*
a *f.* serpent, and set it upon a pole	*Nu 21:8*
were *f.* serpents, and scorpions	*De 8:15*
right hand went a *f.* law for them	*De 33:2*
a flaming fire, a law (A)	*De 33:2*
flames of fire at his right hand (B)(R)	*De 33:2*
Thou shalt make them as a *f.* oven	*Ps 21:9*
like a blazing furnace (A)(B)(R)	*Ps 21:9*
fruit shall be a *f.* flying serpent	*Isa 14:29*
the viper and *f.* flying serpent	*Isa 30:6*
midst of the burning *f.* furnace	*Da 3:6; 3:11, 15*
us from the burning *f.* furnace	*Da 3:17*
to cast them into the burning *f.*	*Da 3:20*
into the midst of the burning *f.*	*Da 3:21; 3:23*
the mouth of the burning *f.* furnace	*Da 3:26*
his throne was like the *f.* flame	*Da 7:9*
like a blaze of flames (B)	*Da 7:9*
A *f.* stream issued and came forth	*Da 7:10*
all the *f.* darts of the wicked	*Eph 6:16*
flaming missles of the wicked one (A)	*Eph 6:16*
flaming arrows of the evil one (N)	*Eph 6:16*
every burning missile of the enemy (P)	*Eph 6:16*
and *f.* indignation, which shall	*Heb 10:27*
fury of burning wrath, indignation (A)	*Heb 10:27*
burning indignation (B)	*Heb 10:27*
fierceness of fire (E)	*Heb 10:27*
a fierce fire (N)	*Heb 10:27*
fire of God's indignation (P)	*Heb 10:27*
fury of fire (R)	*Heb 10:27*
the *f.* trial which is to try you	*1Pe 4:12*

FIFTEEN

eight hundred and *f.* years	*Ge 5:10*
F. cubits upward did the	*Ge 7:20*
an hundred threescore and *f.*	*Ge 25:7*
of the gate shall be *f.* cubits	*Ex 27:14*
shall be hangings *f.* cubits	*Ex 27:15*
side of the gate were *f.* cubits	*Ex 38:14*
were hangings of *f.* cubits	*Ex 38:15*
threescore and *f.* shekels	*Ex 38:25*
estimation shall be *f.* shekels	*Le 27:7*
and threescore and *f.*	*Nu 31:37*
about *f.* thousand men, all	*J'g 8:10*
Ziba had *f.* sons and twenty	*2Sa 9:10*
house of Saul, and his *f.* sons	*2Sa 19:17*
forty five pillars, *f.* in a row	*1Ki 7:3*
Jehoahaz king of Israel *f.* years	*2Ki 14:17; 2Ch 25:25*
will add unto thy days *f.* years	*2Ki 20:6*
will add unto thy days *f.* years	*Isa 38:5*
f. shekels, shall be your	*Eze 45:12*
to me for *f.* pieces of silver	*Ho 3:2*
unto Jerusalem, about *f.* furlongs	*Joh 11:18*
threescore and *f.* souls	*Ac 7:14*
again, and found it *f.* fathoms	*Ac 27:28*
Peter, and abode with him *f.* days	*Ga 1:18*

FIFTEENTH

f. day of the second month	*Ex 16:1*
the *f.* day of the same month	*Le 23:6*

f. day of this seventh month *Le 23:34*
the f. day of the seventh month *Le 23:39*
in the f. day of this month is *Nu 28:17*
f. day of the seventh month *Nu 29:12*
ye
the f. day of the first month *Nu 33:3*
the eighth month, on the f. *1Ki 12:32*
day
the f. day of the eighth *1Ki 12:33*
month
In the f. year of Amaziah the *2Ki 14:23*
The f. to Bilgah, the *1Ch 24:14*
sixteenth
f. to Jeremoth, he, his sons *1Ch 25:22*
the f. year of the reign of *2Ch 15:10*
Asa
f. day of the same they rested *Es 9:18*
and the f. day of the same *Es 9:21*
in the f. day of the month *Eze 32:17*
seventh month, in the f. day *Eze 45:25*
Now in the f. year of the reign *Lu 3:1*

FIFTH

and the morning were the f. day *Ge 1:23*
conceived, and bare Jacob the *Ge 30:17*
f.
and take up the f. part of the *Ge 41:34*
land
that ye shall give the f. part *Ge 47:24*
unto
that Pharaoh should have the *Ge 47:26*
f.
and shall add the f. part thereto *Le 5:16*
add the f. part more thereto, and *Le 6:5*
And in the f. year shall ye eat *Le 19:25*
of the
then he shall put the f. part *Le 22:14*
thereof
then he shall add a f. part *Le 27:13*
thereof
shall add the f. part of the *Le 27:15;*
money *27:19*
and shall add a f. part of it *Le 27:27*
thereto
shall add thereto the f. part *Le 27:31*
thereof
and add unto it the f. part *Nu 5:7*
thereof
On the f. day Shelumiel the *Nu 7:36*
son of
And on the f. day nine *Nu 29:26*
bullocks
in the first day of the f. *Nu 33:38*
month
the f. lot came out for the *Jos 19:24*
tribe
morning on the f. day to depart *J'g 19:8*
spear smote him under the f. *2Sa 2:23*
rib
and the f. Shephatiah the son *2Sa 3:4*
of
smote him there under the f. *2Sa 3:27*
rib
they smote him under the f. rib *2Sa 4:6*
smote him therewith in the f. *2Sa 20:10*
rib
lintel and side posts were a f. *1Ki 6:31*
part
in the f. year of king *1Ki 14:25*
Rehoboam
in the f. year of Joram the son *2Ki 8:16*
of
the f. month, on the seventh *2Ki 25:8*
day
Nethaneel the fourth, *1Ch 2:14*
Raddai the f.
The f. Shephatiah of Abital *1Ch 3:3*
Nohah the fourth, and Rapha *1Ch 8:2*
the f.
the fourth, Jeremiah the f. *1Ch 12:10*
The f. to Malchijah, the sixth *1Ch 24:9*
The f. to Nethaniah, he, his *1Ch 25:12*
sons
Elam the f. Jehohanan the *1Ch 26:3*
sixth
Sacar the fourth, Nethaneel *1Ch 26:4*
the f.
The f. captain for the *1Ch 27:8*
month
in the f. year of king *2Ch 12:2*
Rehoboam
came to Jerusalem in the f. *Ezr 7:8*
month
on the first day of the f. month *Ezr 7:9*
the f. time with an open letter *Ne 6:5*
finished in the twenty and f. day *Ne 6:15*
Jerusalem captive in the f. *Jer 1:3*
month

fourth year, and in the f. *Jer 28:1*
month
to pass in the f. year of *Jer 36:9*
Jehoiakim
in the f. month, in the tenth *Jer 52:12*
day
in the f. day of the month, *Eze 1:1*
as I was
In the f. day of the month *Eze 1:2*
the f. year of king Jehoiachin's *Eze 1:2*
in the f. day of the month, as I *Eze 8:1*
sat
the seventh year, in the f. *Eze 20:1*
month
in the f. day of the month, *Eze 33:21*
that one
Should I weep in the f. month *Zec 7:3*
mourned in the f. and seventh *Zec 7:5*
of the f. and the fast of the *Zec 8:19*
seventh
when he had opened the f. seal *Re 6:9*
And the f. angel sounded, and I *Re 9:1*
saw
And the f. angel poured out *Re 16:10*
his vial
The f., sardonyx; the sixth, *Re 21:20*
sardius

FIFTIES

rulers of f. and rulers of tens *Ex 18:21*
rulers of hundreds, rulers of f. *Ex 18:25*
captains over f. and captains *De 1:15*
over
captains over f.; and will set *1Sa 8:12*
them
captains of the former f. with *2Ki 1:14*
their
in ranks, by hundreds, and by *M'k 6:40*
f.
them sit down by f. in a *Lu 9:14*
company

FIFTIETH

And ye shall hallow the f. year *Le 25:10*
A jubile shall that f. year be *Le 25:11*
unto
In the f. year of Azariah king *2Ki 15:23*
of
In the two and f. year of *2Ki 15:27*
Azariah

FIFTY

breadth of ark shall be f. *Ge 6:15*
cubits
not spare place for f. *Ge 18:24;*
righteous *18:26*
f. loops shalt thou make *Ex 26:5;*
26:10; 36:12, 17
shalt make f. taches of gold *Ex 26:6;*
26:11; 36:13, 18
shall be hangings of f. cubits *Ex 27:12;*
38:12
cinnamon two hundred and f. *Ex 30:23*
shekels, sweet calamus two
hundred and f. shekels
after the seventh sabbath, *Le 23:16*
number f. days
of males thy estimation f. *Le 27:3*
shekels of silver
an homer of barley be valued *Le 27:16*
at f. shekels
thirty to f. years old *Nu 4:3;*
4:23, 30, 35, 39
from age of f. they shall serve *Nu 8:25*
no more
two hundred and f. princes of *Nu 16:2*
assembly
and bring two hundred and f. *Nu 16:17*
censers
fire devoured two hundred *Nu 26:10*
and f. men
thou shalt take one portion of *Nu 31:30*
f. for Levites
Moses took one portion of f. *Nu 31:47*
of man and beast
shall give to damsel's father f. *De 22:29*
shekels
I took a wedge of gold of f. *Jos 7:21*
shekels
Absalom had f. men to run *2Sa 15:1*
before him
Adonijah had f. men to run *1Ki 1:5*
before him
breadth of the house of the *1Ki 7:2*
forest f. cubits

hid them by f. in a cave, and *1Ki 18:4;*
fed them *18:13*
a captain of f. with his f. *2Ki 1:9;*
1:11, 13
then let fire consume thee and *2Ki 1:10;*
thy f. *1:12*
f. men of sons of prophets *2Ki 2:7*
stood to view
they sent therefore f. men to *2Ki 2:17*
seek Elijah
he left to Jehoahaz but f. *2Ki 13:7*
horsemen
Menahem exacted of each f. *2Ki 15:20*
shekels
but Pekah slew f. men of the *2Ki 15:25*
Gileadites
weight of nails was f. shekels *2Ch 3:9*
of gold
Ebed son of Jonathan went up *Ezr 8:6*
with f. males
Tirshatha gave to treasure f. *Ne 7:70*
basins
let a gallows be made f. cubits *Es 5:14;*
high *7:9*
the Lord will take away the *Isa 3:3*
captain of f.
to the face of the porch *Eze 40:15*
were f. cubits
the length f. cubits *Eze 40:21*
40:25, 29, 33, 36
the breadth of the north door *Eze 42:2*
was f. cubits
when one came to draw out f. *Hag 2:16*
vessels
f. dollars worth of bread (E) *M'k 6:37;*
Joh 6:7
the one owed 500 pence, the *Lu 7:41*
other f.
he said, Sit down quickly, and *Lu 16:6*
write f.
thou art not yet f. years old, *Joh 8:57*
hast thou

FIFTY *AND TWO*

Azariah reigned f. and two *2Ki 15:2*
years
children of Nebo f. and two *Ezr 2:29;*
Ne 7:33
the wall was finished in f. and *Ne 6:15*
two days

FIFTY *AND SIX*

the men of Netophah, f. and *Ezr 2:22*
six

FIFTY *THOUSAND*

he smote of the people f. *1Sa 6:19*
thousand
they took of their camels f. *1Ch 5:21*
thousand
of Zebulun f. thousand could *1Ch 12:33*
keep rank
books burn f. thousand *Ac 19:19*
pieces of silver

FIFTY *AND THREE*
THOUSAND

of Naphtali numbered f. *Nu 1:43;*
and three thousand *2:30; 26:47*

FIFTY *AND FOUR*
THOUSAND

of Issachar f. and four *Nu 1:29;*
thousand four hundred *2:6*

FIFTY *AND SEVEN*
THOUSAND

of Zebulun f. and seven *Nu 1:31;*
thousand four hundred *2:8*

FIFTY *AND NINE*
THOUSAND

of Simeon numbered f. and *Nu 1:23*
nine thousand three

FIG

and they sewed f. leaves *Ge 3:7*
together

FIG 453 FIGS

barley, and vines, and f. trees | De 8:8
the trees said to the f. tree | J'g 9:10
But the f. tree said unto them | J'g 9:11
his vine and under his f. tree | 1Ki 4:25
and every one of his f. tree | 2Ki 18:31
their vines also and their f. | Ps 105:33
trees
Whoso keepeth the f. tree | Pr 27:18
shall eat
f. tree putteth forth her green | Ca 2:13
figs
as a falling f. from the f. tree | Isa 34:4
vine, and every one of his f. | Isa 36:16
tree
eat up thy vines and thy f. | Jer 5:17
trees
nor figs on the f. tree, and the | Jer 8:13
leaf
destroy her vines and her f. | Ho 2:12
trees
as the firstripe in the f. tree | Ho 9:10
vine waste, and barked my f. | Joe 1:7
tree
and the f. tree languisheth; the | Joe 1:12
the f. tree and the vine do | Joe 2:22
yield
your vineyards and your f. trees | Am 4:9
under his f. tree; and none | Mic 4:4
shall
strong holds shall be like f. | Na 3:12
trees
the f. tree shall not blossom | Hab 3:17
as yet the vine, and the f. tree | Hag 2:19
the vine and under the f. tree | Zec 3:10
when he saw a f. tree in the | M't 21:19
way
presently the f. tree withered | M't 21:19
away
soon is the f. tree withered | M't 21:20
away
do this which is done to the | M't 21:21
f. tree
learn a parable of the f. tree | M't 24:32;
| M'k 13:28
a f. tree afar off having | M'k 11:13
leaves
they saw the f. tree dried | M'k 11:20
up
the f. tree which thou | M'k 11:21
cursedst
A certain man had a f. tree | Lu 13:6
planted
come seeking fruit in this f. | Lu 13:7
tree
the f. tree (P) | Lu 17:6
Behold the f. tree, and all the | Lu 21:29
trees
when thou wast under the f. | Joh 1:48
tree
I saw thee under the f. tree | Joh 1:50
Can the f. tree, my brethren, | Jas 3:12
bear
a f. tree casteth her untimely | Re 6:13
figs

FIGHT

then ye said, We will go up | De 1:41
and f.
go not up, nor f. for I am | De 1:42
not among you
Sihon and his people came to | De 2:32
f. at Jahaz
men f. each other (R) | De 25:11
thou art come against me to | J'g 11:12
f. in my land
quit yourselves like men, and | 1Sa 4:9
f.
give me a man that we may | 1Sa 17:10
f. together
as the host was going forth | 1Sa 17:20
to f.
why went ye so nigh when | 2Sa 11:20
ye did f.
f. not small nor great | 1Ki 22:31;
| 2Ch 18:30
Do not bother to attack | 1Ki 22:31
anyone (B)
compassed about | 2Ch 18:31
Jehoshaphat to f.
ye shall not need to f. in | 2Ch 20:17
this battle
which teacheth my fingers to | Ps 144:1
f.
teaches my hands to wage | Ps 144:1
war (B)(E)(R)
the mighty men have | Jer 51:30
forborn to f.
shall f. because the Lord is | Zec 10:5
with them

and Judah also shall f. at | Zec 14:14
Jerusalem
Judah also shall wage war | Zec 14:14
(B)
if kingdom, then would my | Joh 18:36
servants f.
my servants would have | Joh 18:36
struggled (B)
would have fought (P) | Joh 18:36
so f. I, not as one that | 1Co 9:26
beateth the air
I do not box as one beating | 1Co 9:26
(A)(B)(R)
I am like a boxer who does | 1Co 9:26
not (N)
I am no shadowboxer. I | 1Co 9:26
really fight (P)
put up a splendid f. (B) | 1Ti 1:18
not f. wordy battles (P) | 1Ti 2:14
f. the good fight of faith, lay | 1Ti 6:12
hold on
I have fought a good f. | 2Ti 4:7
endured a great f. of | Heb 10:32
afflictions
made strong, waxed valiant | Heb 11:34
in f.
f. against sin (P) | Heb 12:4
ye kill, ye f. and war, yet ye | Jas 4:2
have not

FIGHT AGAINST

lest they join our enemies and | Ex 1:10
f. against us
when come nigh to a city to | De 20:10
f. against it
so do to enemies against | Jos 10:25
whom ye f.
they came and pitched to f. | Jos 11:5
against Israel
the Danites went up to f. | Jos 19:47
against Leshem
who shall go up first to f. | J'g 1:1
against the Canaanites
that we may f. against the | J'g 1:3
Canaanites
Ammon passed over Jordan | J'g 10:9
to f. against Judah
Jephthah f. against | J'g 11:8;
Ammon | 11:9
did he ever strive against | J'g 11:25
Israel, or f. against them
why come ye this day to f. | J'g 12:3
against me
Israel set themselves to f. | J'g 20:20
against Benjamin
f. against Amalekites till | 1Sa 15:18
consumed
behold, the Philistines f. | 1Sa 23:1
that I may not f. against | 1Sa 29:8
enemies of king
assembled Judah with | 1Ki 12:21;
Benjamin to f. against Israel | 2Ch 11:1
shall not f. against | 1Ki 12:24
brethren | 2Ch 11:4
but let us f. against them | 1Ki 20:23;
in the plain | 20:25
they turned to f. against | 1Ki 22:32
Jehoshaphat
kings were come to f. | 2Ki 3:21
against them
he is come out to f. against | 2Ki 19:9
thee
O Israel, f. ye not against | 2Ch 13:12
the Lord
Sennacherib purposed to f. | 2Ch 32:2
against Jerusalem
Necho came to f. against | 2Ch 35:20
Carchemish
conspired to come and f. | Ne 4:8
against Jerusalem
f. against them that f. against | Ps 35:1
me
they be many that f. against | Ps 36:2
me
f. every one against his | Isa 19:2
brother
all the nations that f. against | Isa 29:7
Ariel
nations that f. against mount | Isa 29:8
Zion
shall f. against thee, but not | Jer 1:19;
prevail | 15:20
wherewith ye f. against the | Jer 21:4
king of Babylon
I myself will f. against you | Jer 21:5
with strong arm

Chaldeans that f. against it | Jer 32:24;
| 34:22; 37:8
had smitten Chaldeans that | Jer 37:10
f. against you
Lord shall f. against those | Zec 14:3
nations
lest ye be found to f. against | Ac 5:39
God
if angel hath spoken, let us | Ac 23:9
not f. against God
f. against them with the | Re 2:16
sword of my mouth

FIGHT FOR

Lord, f. for you | Ex 14:14;
| De 1:30; 3:22; 20:4
and f. for your master's | 2Ki 10:3
house
f. for your brethren, sons, | Ne 4:14
and wives
resort ye thither to us, our | Ne 4:20
God shall f. for us
Lord shall come to f. for | Isa 31:4
mount Zion

FIGHT WITH

choose men, go out f. with | Ex 17:9
Amalek
Canaanites gathered to f. with | Jos 9:2
Joshua
when wentest to f. with the | J'g 8:1
Midianites
go out now and f. with | J'g 9:38
Abimelech
that we may f. with the | J'g 11:6
children of Ammon
Philistines gathered to f. with | 1Sa 13:5;
Israel | 28:1
if he be able to f. with me, | 1Sa 17:9
and to kill me
thy servant will go and f. | 1Sa 17:32
with this Philistine
Josiah disguised himself to f. | 2Ch 35:22
with him
in battles of shaking will he | Isa 30:32
f. with it
though ye f. with Chaldeans, | Jer 32:5
not prosper
they came to f. with the | Jer 33:5
Chaldeans
they took men, and went to | Jer 41:12
f. with Ishmael
I will return to f. with | Da 10:20
prince of Persia
the king of the south come | Da 11:11
and f. with him

FIGHTER

not a fist f. (B) | 1Ti 3:3

FIGHTETH

Lord f. for them against | Ex 14:25
Egyptians
Lord God, he it is that f. | Jos 23:10
for you
my lord f. the battles of the | 1Sa 25:28
Lord

FIGHTING

the f. men (B) | De 2:14; 2:16; Joe 3:9
the f. men (R) | De 8:1
there was hard f. (S) | 1Sa 14:52
Israel were f. with the | 1Sa 17:19
Philistines
Uzziah had an host of f. | 2Ch 26:11
men
be merciful, O God, he f. | Ps 56:1
oppresseth me

FIGHTINGS

without were f. within were | 2Co 7:5
fears
whence come wars and f. | Jas 4:1
among you

FIGS

the pomegranates, and of | Nu 13:23
the f.
it is no place of seed, or of | Nu 20:5
f.
two hundred cakes of f. | 1Sa 25:18
and laid

they gave him a piece of a *1Sa 30:12*
cake of *f.*
Isaiah said, Take a lump of *2Ki 20:7*
f.
oxen, and meat, meal, *1Ch 12:40*
cake of *f.*
also wine, grapes, and *f.* *Ne 13:15*
fig tree putteth forth her *Ca 2:13*
green *f.*
Let them take a lump of *f.* *Isa 38:21*
nor *f.* on the fig tree, and the *Jer 8:13*
leaf
two baskets of *f.* were set *Jer 24:1;*
before *1:2-3, 5, 8*
I will make them like vile *f.* *Jer 29:17*
like fig trees with the firstripe *Na 3:12*
f.
grapes of thorns, or *f.* of *M't 7:16*
thistles
for the time of *f.* was not *M'k 11:13*
yet
of thorns men do not gather *Lu 6:44*
either a vine *f.?* so can no *Jas 3:12*
fountain
a fig tree casteth her untimely *Re 6:13*
f.

FIGURATIVE

Balaam took up *f.* speech *Nu 23:7;*
(A) *23:3, 15, 18*

FIGURATIVELY

was *f.* dead (A)(R) *Heb 11:19*

FIGURE

image, the similitude of any *De 4:16*
f.
shape of any statue *De 4:16*
resembling (B)
maketh it after the *f.* of a *Isa 44:13*
man
is the *f.* of him that was to *Ro 5:14*
come
Adam was a type of the One *Ro 5:14*
to come (A)(R)
who foreshadowed the *Ro 5:14*
Coming One (B)(N)
corresponds in some degree *Ro 5:14*
to the man (P)
I have in a *f.* transferred to *1Co 4:6*
myself
applied to myself (A)(B)(R) *1Co 4:6*
used as an illustration (P) *1Co 4:6*
was a *f.* for the time then *Heb 9:9*
present
a visible symbol, type, or *Heb 9:9*
picture of the present age (A)
a symbol of that current time *Heb 9:9*
(B)
symbolic pointing to present *Heb 9:9*
time (N)(R)
a picture of the present time *Heb 9:9*
(P)
also he received him in a *f.* *Heb 11:19*
was figuratively dead (A) *Heb 11:19*
in a sense receive him back *Heb 11:19*
(N)
in a manner of speaking *Heb 11:19*
did receive (P)
figuratively speaking he did *Heb 11:19*
receive (R)
like *f.* whereunto even *1Pe 3:21*
baptism

FIGUREHEAD

as its *f.* (A)(B)(P)(R) *Ac 28:11*

FIGURES

the *f.* of gold (A)(R) *1Sa 6:8*
carved *f.* of cherubims and *2Ki 6:29*
palm
f. of oxen (A)(B) *2Ch 4:3*
f. like those of (A) *Eze 23:14*
using *f.* of speech (N)(R) *Joh 16:25*
speaking not in *f.* *Joh 16:29*
(B)(N)(R)
f. which ye made to worship *Ac 7:43*
which are the *f.* of the true *Heb 9:24*
copy, pattern, type of the
true (A)
a copy of the real (B)(R) *Heb 9:24*
in pattern of the true (E) *Heb 9:24*
a symbol of the reality (N) *Heb 9:24*

FILE

had a *f.* for the mattocks *1Sa 13:21*

FILIGREE

in settings of gold *f.* (R) *Ex 39:13*
settings of gold *f.* (A)(R) *Ex 39:16*
two settings of *f.* (R) *Ex 39:18*

FILL

and *f.* the waters in the seas *Ge 1:22*
multiply and *f.* (S) *Ge 1:28; 9:1*
Joseph commanded to *f.* *Ge 42:25*
their sack
F. the men's sacks with food *Ge 44:1*
And they shall *f.* thy houses *Ex 10:6*
F. an omer of it to be kept *Ex 16:32*
eat your *f.* and dwell therein *Le 25:19*
thou mayest eat grapes thy *De 23:24*
f. at
f. thine horn with oil, and *1Sa 16:1*
go
F. four barrels with water *1Ki 18:33*
Till he *f.* thy mouth with *Job 8:21*
laughing
and *f.* his belly with the east *Job 15:2*
wind
When he is about to *f.* his *Job 20:23*
belly
and *f.* my mouth with *Job 23:4*
arguments
f. the appetite of the young *Job 38:39*
lions
thou *f.* his skin with barbed *Job 41:7*
irons
open mouth wide, I will *f.* it *Ps 81:10*
f. their faces with shame to *Ps 83:16*
seek thee
he shall *f.* the places with *Ps 110:6*
dead bodies
we shall *f.* our houses with *Pr 1:13*
spoil
let us take our *f.* of love *Pr 7:18*
to inherit substance, I will *f.* *Pr 8:21*
their treasures
his wings shall *f.* breadth of *Isa 8:8*
thy land
nor *f.* the face of the world *Isa 14:21*
with cities
Israel *f.* face of world with *Isa 27:6*
fruit
we will *f.* ourselves with *Isa 56:12*
strong drink
I will *f.* inhabitants with *Jer 13:13*
drunkenness
do not I *f.* heaven and earth *Jer 23:24*
f. to the full (S) *Jer 31:14;*
31:25; 46:10
it is to *f.* them with dead *Jer 33:5*
bodies of men
surely I will *f.* thee with *Jer 51:14*
men as caterpillars
son of man *f.* thy bowels with *Eze 3:3*
this roll
shall not satisfy their souls *Eze 7:19*
nor *f.* their bowels
f. the courts with the slain, *Eze 9:7*
go ye forth
go in, *f.* thine hand with *Eze 10:2*
coals of fire
gather the pieces, *f.* it with *Eze 24:4*
choice bones
they shall *f.* the land with *Eze 30:11*
the slain
I will *f.* beasts of the whole *Eze 32:4*
earth with fire
I will *f.* the valleys with thy *Eze 35:1*
height
I will *f.* his mountains with *Eze 35:8*
the slain
who *f.* their masters' houses *Zep 1:9*
with violence
I will *f.* this house with glory *Hag 2:7*
for that which is put in to *f.* *M't 9:16*
it up
whence have bread to *f.* *M't 15:33*
such a multitude
f. ye up then the measure *M't 23:32*
of your fathers
f. the waterpots with water *Joh 2:7*
God of hope *f.* you with all *Ro 15:13*
joy and peace
he ascended, that he might *f.* *Eph 4:10*
all things
f. up what is behind of *Col 1:24*
sufferings of Christ

the Jews, to *f.* up their sins *1Th 2:16*
alway
cup she hath filled, *f.* *Re 18:6*
her double

FILLED

earth *f.* with violence through *Ge 6:13*
men
Hagar went and *f.* the bottle *Ge 21:19*
with water
Rebekah *f.* her pitcher and *Ge 24:16*
came up
Philistines had *f.* the wells *Ge 26:15*
with earth
the children of Israel *f.* the *Ex 1:7*
land
they *f.* the troughs to water *Ex 2:16*
their flock
whom I have *f.* with wisdom *Ex 28:3;*
35:35
I have *f.* him with the Spirit *Ex 31:3*
of God *35:31*
glory of the Lord *f.* the *Ex 40:34;*
tabernacle *40:35*
they may eat within thy *De 26:12*
gates and be *f.*
when they have eaten and *f.* *De 31:20*
themselves
these bottles we *f.* were new *Jos 9:13*
and are rent
the cloud *f.* the house of the *1Ki 8:10*
Lord
glory of Lord *f.* the house *1Ki 8:11;*
2Ch 5:14; 17:1-3
and he *f.* the trench also *1Ki 18:35*
with water
but the Syrians *f.* the *1Ki 20:27*
country
they cast every man his *2Ki 3:25*
stone and *f.* it
Manasseh *f.* Jerusalem *2Ki 21:16;*
with blood *24:4*
Josiah *f.* their places with *2Ki 23:14*
bones of men
which have *f.* it from one *Ezr 9:11*
end to another
was *f.* with wrath (A)(E)(R) *Es 5:9*
with princes who *f.* their *Job 3:15*
houses with silver
and thou hast *f.* me with *Job 16:8*
wrinkles
yet he *f.* their houses with *Job 22:18*
good things
for my loins are *f.* with *Ps 38:7*
loathsome disease
let my mouth be *f.* with thy *Ps 71:8*
praise
let the whole earth be *f.* with *Ps 72:19*
his glory
cause it to take deep root, it *Ps 80:9*
f. the land
thou openest thine hand, *Ps 104:28*
are *f.* with good
for we are exceedingly *f.* *Ps 123:3*
with contempt
our soul is exceedingly *f.* *Ps 123:4*
with scorning
lest strangers be *f.* with thy *Pr 5:10*
wealth
lest thou be *f.* with honey *Pr 25:16*
and vomit it
the earth that is not *f.* with *Pr 30:16*
water
and for a fool when he is *f.* *Pr 30:22*
with meat
nor is the ear *f.* with hearing *Ec 1:8*
and his soul be not *f.* with *Ec 6:3*
good
and yet the appetite is not *f.* *Ec 6:7*
open to me, my head is *f.* *Ca 5:2*
with dew
f. with customs from the east *Isa 2:6*
(A)(E)(S)
high and lifted up, and his *Isa 6:1*
train *f.* temple
therefore are my loins *f.* with *Isa 21:3*
pain
lips are *f.* with fury (B) *Isa 30:27*
the Lord hath *f.* Zion with *Isa 33:5*
judgment
the sword of the Lord is *f.* *Isa 34:6*
with blood
nor *f.* me with the fat of *Isa 43:24*
thy sacrifices
nor an old man that hath *Isa 65:20*
not *f.* his days
for thou hast *f.* me with *Jer 15:17*
indignation

they *f.* mine inheritance   *Jer 16:18*
with carcases
f. this place with blood of   *Jer 19:4*
innocents
Ishmael *f.* the pit with them   *Jer 41:9*
that were slain
and thy cry hath *f.* the land   *Jer 46:12*
he hath *f.* his belly with my   *Jer 51:34*
delicates
he hath *f.* me with bitterness   *La 3:15*
he is *f.* full with reproach   *La 3:30*
they have *f.* land with   *Eze 8:17*
violence
and the cloud *f.* the inner   *Eze 10:3*
court
ye have *f.* the streets with   *Eze 11:6*
the slain
they *f.* the midst of thee   *Eze 28:16*
with violence
waste cities shall be *f.* with   *Eze 36:38*
flocks of men
glory of the Lord *f.* the   *Eze 43:5;*
house   *44:4*
the stone cut out *f.* the whole   *Da 2:35*
earth
the lion *f.* his holes with prey   *Na 2:12*
thou art *f.* with shame for   *Hab 2:16*
glory
ye drink, but ye are not *f.*   *Hag 1:6*
with drink
I have *f.* the bow with   *Zec 9:13*
Ephraim
were *f.* with astonishment   *M't 8:27*
(P)
ran, and *f.* a sponge with   *M't 27:48;*
vinegar   *M'k 15:36; Joh 19:29*
new piece that *f.* it up   *M'k 2:21*
taketh from old
Jesus said, Let the children   *M'k 7:27*
first be *f.*
he hath *f.* hungry with good   *Lu 1:53*
things
Jesus waxed strong in spirit,   *Lu 2:40*
f. with wisdom
and they came and *f.* both the   *Lu 5:7*
ships
compel them to come, that   *Lu 14:23*
my house be *f.*
would fain have *f.* his belly   *Lu 15:16*
with husks
and they *f.* them up to the   *Joh 2:7*
brim
they *f.* twelve baskets with   *Joh 6:13*
fragments
I said these things, sorrow   *Joh 16:6*
hath *f.* your heart
as of a rushing mighty wind, *f.*   *Ac 2:2*
house
Peter *f.* with the Holy Ghost   *Ac 4:8*
said
why hath Satan *f.* thine heart   *Ac 5:3*
to lie to Holy Ghost
ye have *f.* Jerusalem with   *Ac 5:28*
your doctrine
that thou mightest be *f.* with   *Ac 9:17*
the Holy Ghost
Paul, *f.* with the Holy Ghost   *Ac 13:9*
set his eyes
being *f.* with all   *Ro 1:29*
unrighteousness
that ye also are *f.* with all   *Ro 15:14*
knowledge
if first I be *f.* with your   *Ro 15:24*
company
I am *f.* with comfort, I   *2Co 7:4*
am joyful
might be *f.* with all the   *Eph 3:19*
fulness of God
be not drunk with wine, but   *Eph 5:18*
f. with Spirit
being *f.* with the fruits of   *Ph'p 1:11*
righteousness
might be *f.* with the   *Col 1:9*
knowledge of his will
that I may be *f.* with joy   *2Ti 1:4*
depart in peace, be ye   *Jas 2:16*
warmed and *f.*
angel *f.* the censer with fire of   *Re 8:5*
altar
for them is *f.* up the wrath   *Re 15:1*
of God
in cup which she *f.* fill to her   *Re 18:6*
double

SHALL BE FILLED

in morning ye *shall be f.*   *Ex 16:12*
with bread

earth *shall be f.* with glory   *Nu 14:21*
of Lord
that valley *shall be f.* with   *2Ki 3:17*
water
they *shall be f.* with own   *Pr 1:31*
devices
so *shall* thy barns be *f.* with   *Pr 3:10*
plenty
the wicked *shall be f.* with   *Pr 12:21*
mischief
backslider *shall be f.* with   *Pr 14:14*
own ways
with increase of his lips *shall*   *Pr 18:20*
he *be f.*
his mouth *shall be f.* with   *Pr 20:17*
gravel
by knowledge *shall* chambers *Pr 24:4*
be *f.*
every bottle *shall be f.* with   *Jer 13:12*
wine
thou *shalt be f.* with   *Eze 23:33*
drunkenness
ye *shall be f.* at my table   *Eze 39:20*
with horses
earth *shall be f.* with   *Hab 2:14*
knowledge of Lord
and they *shall be f.* like   *Zec 9:15*
bowls
blessed are they that hunger,   *M't 5:6*
they *shall be f.*
John *shall be f.* with the   *Lu 1:15*
Holy Ghost
every valley *shall be f.*   *Lu 3:5*
mountain brought low
blessed ye that hunger now,   *Lu 6:21*
ye *shall be f.*

WAS FILLED

and the earth *was f.* with   *Ge 6:11*
violence
and Hiram *was f.* with   *1Ki 7:14*
wisdom
the country *was f.* with   *2Ki 3:20*
water
then the house *was f.* with a   *2Ch 5:13*
cloud
bed which *was f.* with   *2Ch 16:14*
sweet odours
then our mouth *was f.* with   *Ps 126:2*
laughter
and the house *was f.* with   *Isa 6:4*
smoke
their land *was f.* with sin   *Jer 51:5*
against Holy One
and the house *was f.* with   *Eze 10:4*
the cloud
Elisabeth *was f.* with Holy   *Lu 1:41*
Ghost
Zacharias *was f.* with the   *Lu 1:67*
Holy Ghost
house *was f.* with odour of   *Joh 12:3*
ointment
whole city *was f.* with   *Ac 19:29*
confusion
and the temple *was f.* with   *Re 15:8*
smoke

WERE FILLED

they *were f.* and heart was   *Ho 13:6*
exalted
when heard, they *were f.* with *Lu 4:28*
wrath
they glorified God, and *were*   *Lu 5:26*
f. with fear
they *were f.* with madness,   *Lu 6:11*
and communed
they *were f.* with water, and   *Lu 8:23*
in jeopardy
when they *were f.* he said,   *Joh 6:12*
Gather up
because ye did eat of the   *Joh 6:26*
loaves, and *were f.*
they *were* all *f.* with the Holy *Ac 2:4;*
Ghost   *4:31*
they *were f.* with wonder and   *Ac 3:10*
amazement
rose up, and *were f.* with   *Ac 5:17*
indignation
the Jews *were f.* with envy,   *Ac 13:45*
and spake
disciples *were f.* with joy   *Ac 13:52*
and Holy Ghost
all the fowls *were f.* with   *Re 19:21*
their flesh

FILLEDST

and houses full, which thou *f.*   *De 6:11*
not
when wares went forth, *f.*   *Eze 27:33*
many people

FILLEST

whose belly thou *f.* with thy   *Ps 17:14*
hid treasure

FILLET

f. of twelve cubits did   *Jer 52:21*
compass it
ornamental molding of   *Jer 52:21*
twelve cubits (A)

FILLETED

round about the court shall   *Ex 27:17*
be *f.*
all the pillars of the court   *Ex 38:17*
were *f.*
overlaid their chapiters, and   *Ex 38:28*
f.

FILLETH

but *f.* me with bitterness   *Job 9:18*
the rain also *f.* the pools   *Ps 84:6*
f. the hungry soul with   *Ps 107:9*
goodness
Wherewith the mower *f.* not   *Ps 129:7*
his
f. thee with the finest of the *Ps 147:14*
wheat
the fulness of him that *f.* all   *Eph 1:23*
in all

FILLETS

their *f.* shall be of silver   *Ex 27:10*
their joinings (A)   *Ex 27:10*
     36:38; 38:10-12, 17, 19, 28
their bands (B)   *Ex 27:10;*
     36:38; 38:10-12, 17, 19, 28
the pillars and their *f.* of   *Ex 27:11*
silver
chapiters and their *f.* with   *Ex 36:38*
gold
and their *f.* were of silver   *Ex 38:10;*
                38:11
of the pillars and their *f.* of   *Ex 38:12;*
silver   *38:17*
their chapiters and their *f.*   *Ex 38:19*
of silver.

FILLING

f. our hearts with food and   *Ac 14:17*

FILLS

who *f.* the universe   *Eph 1:23*
(B)(P)

FILTH

the *f.* of the daughters of Zion   *Isa 4:4*
I will cast abominable *f.* upon   *Na 3:6*
thee
all kinds of *f.* (N)   *M't 23:27*
putting away of the *f.* of the   *1Co 3:21*
flesh
bodily pollution (N)   *1Co 3:21*
washing of a dirty body (P)   *1Co 3:21*
removal of dirt from the   *1Co 3:21*
body (R)
are made as the *f.* of the   *1Co 4:13*
world
considered scum of earth   *1Co 4:13*
(B)(N)(P)
the refuse of the world (R)   *1Co 4:13*
godless myths, *f.* for old   *1Ti 4:7*
women (N)
f. of her lewdness and vice   *Re 17:4*
(A)

FILTHINESS

forth the *f.* out of the holy   *2Ch 29:5*
place
taking away unclean things   *2Ch 29:5*
(B)
them from the *f.* of the   *Ezr 6:21*
heathen of
pollutions of the people   *Ezr 6:21*
(A)(R)

the sin of the nations (B)   *Ezr 6:21*
an unclean land with the *f.*   *Ezr 9:11*
of the
pollutions of the people   *Ezr 9:11*
(A)(R)
wicked practices of the people *Ezr 9:11*
(B)
uncleanness of the people   *Ezr 9:11*
(E)
yet is not washed from their *Pr 30:12*
f.
all tables are full of vomit   *Isa 28:8*
and *f.*
Her *f.* is in her skirts; she   *La 1:9*
Because thy *f.* was poured   *Eze 16:36*
out
throwing away your virtue   *Eze 16:36*
(B)
shame was laid bare and   *Eze 16:36*
your nakedness uncovered in
harlotries (R)
will consume thy *f.* out of   *Eze 22:15*
thee
purge you of moral foulness   *Eze 22:15*
(B)
that the *f.* of it may be   *Eze 24:11*
molten in it
all its impurities be burned   *Eze 24:11*
up (B)
In thy *f.* is lewdness: because *Eze 24:13*
shalt not be purged from   *Eze 24:13*
thy *f.*
ye shall be clean: from all   *Eze 36:25*
your *f.*
clean from all uncleanness   *Eze 36:25*
(A)(R)
cleansed from all impurities   *Eze 36:25*
(B)
from all *f.* of the flesh and   *2Co 7:1*
spirit
everything that contaminates *2Co 7:1*
and defiles (A)
every defilement of flesh and *2Co 7:1*
(B)(E)(N)(R)
anything that smirches soul   *2Co 7:1*
and body (P)
Neither *f.* nor foolish talking, *Eph 5:4*
nor
indecency (B)   *Eph 5:4*
no coarse talk (N)   *Eph 5:4*
no *f.,* no silly talk (R)   *Eph 5:4*
lay apart all *f.* and   *Jas 1:21*
superfluity
all uncleanness (A)   *Jas 1:21*
everything vile (B)   *Jas 1:21*
all *f.,* overflowing of   *Jas 1:21*
wickedness (E)(R)
wine of her *f.* (P)   *Re 17:2*
full of abominations and *f.* of *Re 17:4*
her
full of cursed offenses and   *Re 17:4*
filth of her lewdness and vice (A)
full of offenses, impurities,   *Re 17:4*
lewdness (B)
full of abominations, unclean *Re 17:4*
things (E)
full of obscenities, foulness of *Re 17:4*
fornication (N)
full of *f.,* impurity (P)   *Re 17:4*
full of abominations and   *Re 17:4*
impurities of (R)

FILTHY

more abominable and *f.* is   *Job 15:16*
man
loathsome and foul (B)   *Job 15:16*
abominable and corrupt   *Job 15:16*
(E)(R)
aside, they are altogether   *Ps 14:3*
become *f.*
have become corrupt,   *Ps 14:3;*
depraved (B)(R)   *53:3*
back: they are altogether   *Ps 53:3*
become *f.*
righteousnesses are as *f.* rags *Isa 64:6*
Woe to her that is *f.* and   *Zep 3:1*
polluted
defiant, rebellious   *Zep 3:1*
(A)(B)(E)(R)
was clothed with *f.* garments *Zec 3:3*
soiled garments (B)   *Zec 3:3; 3:4*
Take away the *f.* garments   *Zec 3:4*
from
f. communication out of your *2Co 3:8*
curses, slander, foulmouthed *2Co 3:8*
abuse, and shameful utterances
from your lips (N)
slander, shameful language   *2Co 3:8*
(B)(E)

cursing, filthy talk (N)   *2Co 3:8*
slander, foul talk (R)   *2Co 3:8*
f. talk (N)   *2Co 3:8*
no striker, not greedy of *f.*   *1Ti 3:3*
lucre
not lover of money-insatiable *1Ti 3:3*
for wealth (A)
not after money (B)   *1Ti 3:3*
no lover of money   *1Ti 3:3*
(E)(N)(R)
not fond of money-grabbing *1Ti 3:3*
(P)
much wine, not greedy of *f.* *1Ti 3:8*
lucre
no striker, not given to *f.*   *Tit 1:7*
lucre
or greedy of dishonest gain   *Tit 1:7*
(B)
no money-grabber (N)   *Tit 1:7*
greedy of financial gain   *Tit 1:7*
(P)(R)
they ought not, for *f.* lucre's *Tit 1:11*
sake
disreputable gain (A)   *Tit 1:11*
for dishonest gain (B)   *Tit 1:11*
all for sordid gain (N)   *Tit 1:11*
for base gain (R)   *Tit 1:11*
not for *f.* lucre, but of a   *1Pe 5:2*
ready mind
vexed with the *f.* conversation *2Pe 2:7*
of
by wanton ways of ungodly   *2Pe 2:7*
and lawless (A)
by immoral behavior of   *2Pe 2:7*
lawless (B)
by lascivious life of wicked   *2Pe 2:7*
(E)
by dissolate habits of lawless *2Pe 2:7*
society (N)
f. lives of godless (P)   *2Pe 2:7*
by licentiousness of wicked   *2Pe 2:7*
(R)
also these *f.* dreamers defile   *Jude 8*
deluded dreamers (B)   *Jude 8*
defiling bodies by *f.* fantasies (P) *Jude 8*
he which is *f.* let him be *f.*   *Re 22:11*
still

FINALLY

F. brethren, farewell. Be   *2Co 13:11*
perfect
F. my brethren, be strong in *Eph 6:10*
the Lord
F. my brethren, rejoice in   *Ph'p 3:1*
the Lord
F. brethren, whatsoever   *Ph'p 4:8*
things are
F. brethren, pray for us, that *2Th 3:1*
F. be ye all of one mind,   *1Pe 3:8*
having

FIND

wearied themselves to *f.* the *Ge 19:11*
door
shall speak to Esau, when   *Ge 32:19*
you *f.* him
be sure your sin shall *f.* you *Nu 32:23*
out
revenger of blood *f.* him   *Nu 35:27*
without city
a man *f.* a damsel and lie   *De 22:25;*
with her   *22:28*
to sojourn where he could *f.*   *J'g 17:8;*
a place   *17:9*
Lord grant ye may *f.* rest   *Ru 1:9*
saying, Go, *f.* out the arrows *1Sa 20:21;*
   20:36
if a man *f.* his enemy, will   *1Sa 24:19*
he let him go
peradventure we may *f.* grass *1Ki 18:5*
to save horses
when thou comest, *f.* Jehu   *2Ki 9:2*
(S)
to *f.* out every device be put *2Ch 2:14*
to him
why should Assyria come   *2Ch 32:4*
and *f.* much water
O that I knew where I might *Job 23:3*
f. him
cause every man to *f.*   *Job 34:11*
according to his ways
seek out his wickedness till   *Ps 10:15*
thou *f.* none
thou shalt *f.* the knowledge of *Pr 2:5*
God
my words are life to those   *Pr 4:22*
that *f.* them
they are right to them that *f.* *Pr 8:9*
knowledge

I *f.* out knowledge of witty *Pr 8:12*
inventions
a man should *f.* nothing for *Ec 7:14*
him
counting one by one, to *f.* out *Ec 7:27*
the account
he sought to *f.* out   *Ec 12:10*
acceptable words
if *f.* my beloved, tell him I am *Ca 5:8*
sick of love
screech owl shall *f.* place of *Isa 34:14*
rest
in the day of your fast you *f.* *Isa 58:3*
pleasure
distress them, that they may *Jer 10:18*
f. it so
are become like harts that *f.* *La 1:6*
no pasture
her prophets also *f.* no vision *La 2:9*
from God
princes sought to *f.* occasion *Da 6:4*
against Daniel, but could *f.* none
not *f.* except we *f.* concerning *Da 6:5*
law of God
strait is gate; few there be   *M't 7:14*
that *f.* it
if so be that he *f.* it, he   *M't 18:13*
rejoiceth more
if haply might *f.* any thing *M'k 11:13*
thereon
lest coming suddenly *f.* you *M'k 13:36*
sleeping
that they might *f.* an   *Lu 6:7*
accusation against him
f. them so, blessed are those *Lu 12:38*
servants
he said I come seeking fruit *Lu 13:7*
and *f.* none
go after that which is lost,   *Lu 15:4*
till he *f.* it
doth she not seek diligently *Lu 15:8*
till she *f.* it
shall go in and out, and *f.*   *Joh 10:9*
pasture
desired to *f.* a tabernacle for *Ac 7:46*
God of Jacob
they might feel after him   *Ac 17:27*
and *f.* him
scribes, saying, We *f.* no evil *Ac 23:9*
in this man
thou wilt say, Why doth he   *Ro 9:19*
yet *f.* fault
they come with me, and *f.*   *2Co 9:4*
you unprepared
he may *f.* mercy of Lord in *2Ti 1:18*
that day

FIND *GRACE*

may *f. grace* in thy   *Ge 32:5;*
sight   *Ex 33:13*
these are. to *f. grace* in sight *Ge 33:8*
of my lord
let me *f. grace*   *Ge 33:15; 34:11*
let us *f. grace* in the sight of *Ge 47:25*
my lord
in whose sight I shall *f. grace* *Ru 2:2*
let thy handmaid *f. grace* in *1Sa 1:18*
thy sight
that I may *f. grace* in thy   *2Sa 16:4*
sight
we may *f. grace* to help in   *Heb 4:16*
time of need

CAN, CANST FIND

can we *f.* such a one as this *Ge 41:38*
go, get straw where you *can* *Ex 5:11*
f. it
all the silver and gold thou *Ezr 7:16*
canst f.
are glad when they *can f.*   *Job 3:22*
the grave
canst thou by searching *f.*   *Job 11:7*
out God? *canst* thou *f.* out
but a faithful man who *can f.* *Pr 20:6*
who *can f.* virtuous woman *Pr 31:10*
price above rubies
no man *can f.* out the work *Ec 3:11*
God maketh
that which is exceeding deep, *Ec 7:24*
who *can f.* it
if ye *can f.* a man that   *Jer 5:1*
seeketh truth

CANNOT FIND

he returned, and said, I   *Ge 38:22*
cannot f. her

if he *cannot f.* thee, he will   *1Ki 18:12*
slay me
I *cannot f.* one wise man   *Job 17:10*
among you
touching Almighty, we   *Job 37:23*
cannot f. him out
a man *cannot f.* out work   *Ec 8:17*
under sun

I FIND

if I *f.* in Sodom fifty   *Ge 18:26*
righteous
if I *f.* there forty-five; if I *f.*   *Ge 18:28;*
thirty   *18:30*
till I *f.* out a place for the   *Ps 132:5*
Lord
I *f.* more bitter than death the   *Ec 7:26*
woman
when I *f.* thee, I would kiss   *Ca 8:1*
thee
I fainted in my sighing, I *f.*   *Jer 45:3*
no rest
I *f.* no fault in this man   *Lu 23:4;*
           Joh 18:38; 19:4, 6
to perform that which is   *Ro 7:18*
good I *f.* not
I *f.* then a law, that when I   *Ro 7:21*
would do good

NOT FIND, FIND NOT

to-day ye shall *not f.* it in   *Ex 16:25*
the field
Saul my father shall *not f.*   *1Sa 23:17*
thee
had sought, and could *not*   *2Sa 17:20*
f. them
they shall seek me early, but   *Pr 1:28;*
they shall *not f.* me   *Ho 5:6;*
          Joh 7:34, 36
which my soul seeketh, but I   *Ec 7:28*
f. not
I sought him, but I could *not*   *Ca 5:6*
f. him
them, but shalt *not f.* them   *Isa 41:12;*
              Ho 2:7
not f. any occasion against   *Da 6:5*
Daniel
make wall that she shall *not f.*   *Ho 2:6*
her paths
shall run to seek word, and   *Am 8:12*
not f. it
not f. what way they might   *Lu 5:19*
bring him
could *not f.* what they   *Lu 19:48*
might do to Jesus
whither go, that we shall *not*   *Joh 7:35*
f. him
how to do that which is   *Ro 7:18*
good, I *f. not*
I shall *not f.* you such as I   *2Co 12:20*
would
shall men seek death, and shall   *Re 9:6*
not f. it

SHALL, SHALT FIND

if thence thou seek Lord, *shalt f.*   *De 4:29*
him
thou *shalt f.* no ease among   *De 28:65*
nations
then do as thou *shalt f.*   *J'g 9:33*
occasion
shall f. him before he go up   *1Sa 9:13*
to eat
shall f. two men by Rachel's   *1Sa 10:2*
sepulchre
shall f. them at end of the   *2Ch 20:16*
brook
brethren and children *shall f.*   *2Ch 30:9*
compassion
thou *shalt f.* in the book of   *Ezr 4:15*
records
hast tried me, and *shalt f.*   *Ps 17:3*
nothing
thy hand *shall f.* out all thine   *Ps 21:8*
enemies
we *shall f.* all precious   *Pr 1:13*
substance
that seek me early *shall f.* me   *Pr 8:17;*
           Jer 29:13
handleth matter wisely, shall   *Pr 16:20*
f. good
that keepeth understanding   *Pr 19:8*
shall f. good
for thou *shalt f.* it after many   *Ec 11:1*
days
in her month they *shall f.* her   *Jer 2:24*

ye *shall f.* rest to your souls   *Jer 6:16;*
              M't 11:29
in labours they *shall f.* none   *Ho 12:8*
iniquity
seek and ye *shall f.*   *M't 7:7; Lu 11:9*
that loseth life for my sake   *M't 10:39*
shall f. it
thou *shalt f.* a piece of money   *M't 17:27*
shall f. an ass tied, and a   *M't 21:2;*
colt   *M'k 11:2*
as many as ye *shall f.* bid to   *M't 22:9*
marriage
when cometh, *shall f.* so   *M't 24:46;*
doing   *Lu 12:37, 43*
shall f. babe wrapped in   *Lu 2:12*
swaddling clothes
Son of man cometh, *shall f.*   *Lu 18:8*
faith on earth
cast net on right side, ye   *Joh 21:6*
shall f. it
thou *shalt f.* them no more   *Re 18:14*
at all

FINDEST

with whomsoever thou *f.* thy   *Ge 31:32*
gods
scorner seeketh wisdom, and   *Pr 14:6*
f. it not
eat that thou *f.* eat this roll,   *Eze 3:1*
and go

FINDETH

every one that *f.* me shall   *Ge 4:14*
slay me
he *f.* occasions against me   *Job 33:10*
I rejoice as one that *f.*   *Ps 119:162*
spoil
happy is the man that *f.*   *Pr 3:13*
wisdom
whoso *f.* me, *f.* life, shall   *Pr 8:35*
obtain favour
scorner seeketh wisdom, and   *Pr 14:6*
f. it not
he that hath froward heart,   *Pr 17:20*
f. no good
whoso *f.* a wife, *f.* good thing   *Pr 18:22*
his neighbour *f.* no favour in   *Pr 21:10*
his eyes
followeth after mercy, *f.* life   *Pr 21:21*
and honour
whatsoever thy hand *f.* to do,   *Ec 9:10*
do it
dwells among heathen, she *f.*   *La 1:3*
no rest
for in thee the fatherless *f.*   *Ho 14:3*
mercy
and he that seeketh *f.*   *M't 7:8;*
           Lu 11:10
he that *f.* his life shall lose   *M't 10:39*
it
walk thro' dry places,   *M't 12:43*
seeking rest, *f.* none
f. it empty, swept,   *M't 12:44;*
garnished   *Lu 11:25*
he *f.* his disciples asleep   *M't 26:40;*
          M'k 14:37
he first *f.* his own brother   *Joh 1:41*
Simon
Jesus *f.* Philip   *Joh 1:43*
Philip *f.* Nathaniel   *Joh 1:45*
afterward Jesus *f.* him in the   *Joh 5:14*
temple

FINDING

lest any *f.* Cain should kill   *Ge 4:15*
him
who doeth things past *f.* out   *Job 9:10*
f. own pleasure nor speaking   *Isa 58:13*
words
unclean spirit seeking rest, *f.*   *Lu 11:24*
none
f. nothing how they might   *Ac 4:21*
punish
Paul *f.* certain disciples   *Ac 19:1;*
           21:4
f. ship sailing over to   *Ac 21:2*
Phenicia
unsearchable, and his ways   *Ro 11:33*
past *f.* out
for *f.* fault with them, he   *Heb 8:8*
saith

FINE

f. him one hundred shekels   *De 22:19*
(S)
laid a *f.* on the land (B)   *2Ki 23:33*

and two vessels of *f.* copper,   *Ezr 8:27*
as gold
is a place for gold where   *Job 28:1*
they *f.* it
they that work in *f.* flax be   *Isa 19:9*
confounded
dressed in *f.* clothes (P)   *M't 11:8;*
          Lu 7:25
f. pearls (S)   *M't 13:45; Jas 2:2*
look *f.* on the outside (P)   *M't 23:26*
with *f.* clothes (S)   *Jas 2:3*
his feet like unto *f.* brass   *Re 1:15;*
              2:18

FINE FLOUR

his offering shall be of *f. flour*   *Le 2:1;*
               24:5
cakes of *f. flour* mingled with   *Le 2:4;*
oil   *5:7; 7:12; 14:10, 21; 23:13;*
Nu 6:15; 7:13, 19, 25, 31, 37, 43, 49,
              55, 61; 8:8
tenth part of an ephah of   *Le 5:11;*
f. flour   *6:20*
thirty measures of *f. flour* in   *1Ki 4:22*
one day
measure *f. flour* sold for   *2Ki 7:1;*
shekel   *7:16, 18*
were appointed to oversee   *1Ch 9:29;*
f. flour   *23:29*
thou didst eat *f. flour*,   *Eze 16:13*
honey, and oil
I gave thee *f. flour*, and oil,   *Eze 16:19*
and honey
an hin of oil to temper   *Eze 46:14*
with the *f. flour*
none buyeth merchandise of   *Re 18:13*
f. flour

FINE GOLD

ceiling overlaid with *f. gold*   *2Ch 3:5*
the most holy he overlaid   *2Ch 3:8*
with *f. gold*
exchange shall not be for   *Job 28:17*
jewels of *f. gold*
or said to *f. gold*, Thou art   *Job 31:24*
my confidence
more to be desired than *f.*   *Ps 19:10*
gold
I love thy commandments   *Ps 119:127*
above *f. gold*
the gain of wisdom than *f.*   *Pr 3:14*
gold
my fruit is better than gold,   *Pr 8:19*
than *f. gold*
as ornament of *f. gold*, so is a   *Pr 25:12*
reprover
his head is as most *f. gold*   *Ca 5:11*
locks bushy
legs are as pillars set on   *Ca 5:15*
sockets of *f. gold*
make a man more precious   *Isa 13:12*
than *f. gold*
how is the most *f. gold*   *La 4:1*
changed
the precious sons of Zion   *La 4:2*
comparable to *f. gold*
image's head *f. gold*, breast   *Da 2:32*
of silver
loins girded with *f. gold* of   *Da 10:5*
Uphaz
Tyrus heaped *f. gold* as mire   *Zec 9:3*
of streets

FINE LINEN

Pharaoh arrayed him in   *Ge 41:42*
vestures of *f. linen*
this is the offering ye shall   *Ex 25:4*
take, *f. linen*
with ten curtains of *f.* twined   *Ex 26:1*
linen
veil of *f. linen*   *Ex 26:31;*
         36:35; 2Ch 3:14
make an hanging of *f.*   *Ex 26:36;*
twined *linen*   *27:9, 16, 18; 36:37; 38:9,*
               16, 18
take gold and *f. linen* to   *Ex 28:5*
make garments
shall make the ephod of *f.*   *Ex 28:6;*
linen   *39:2*
girdle *f. linen*   *Ex 28:8; 39:5, 29*
breastplate of *f.* twined *linen*   *Ex 39:8;*
              39:15
embroider the coat of *f.*   *Ex 28:39*
linen, and thou shalt make
the mitre of *f. linen*
let him bring an offering of *f.*   *Ex 35:6*
linen

every man with whom was   *Ex 35:23*
found *f. linen*
the women brought of   *Ex 35:25*
scarlet and *f. linen*
to work all manner of work   *Ex 35:35;*
and *f. linen*   *38:23; 2Ch 2:14*
that wrought curtains of *f.*   *Ex 36:8*
linen and blue
they made coats of *f. linen*   *Ex 39:27*
for Aaron
made mitre of *f. linen,*   *Ex 39:28*
bonnets of *f. linen*
families for them that   *1Ch 4:21*
wrought *f. linen*
David clothed with robe of   *1Ch 15:27*
f. linen
hangings fastened with cords of   *Es 1:6*
f. linen
Mordecai went with a   *Es 8:15*
garment of *f. linen*
I have decked my bed with *f.*   *Pr 7:16*
linen
she maketh *f. linen,* and   *Pr 31:24*
selleth it
the Lord will take away the   *Isa 3:23*
f. linen
I girded thee about with *f.*   *Eze 16:10*
linen
thy raiment was of *f. linen*   *Eze 16:13*
and silk
f. linen from Egypt was to   *Eze 27:7*
be thy sail
Syria occupied in thy fairs   *Eze 27:16*
with *f. linen*
Joseph bought *f. linen* and   *M'k 15:46*
wrapped
rich man clothed in purple   *Lu 16:19*
and *f. linen*
merchandise of *f. linen*   *Re 18:12*
departed from thee
that city clothed in *f. linen*   *Re 18:16*
is come to nought
to her was granted to be   *Re 19:8*
arrayed in *f.*
the armies in heaven were   *Re 19:14*
clothed in *f. linen*

FINE MEAL

make ready three measures of   *Ge 18:6*
f. meal

FINED

f. the land (E)(S)   *2Ch 36:3*

FINER

there shall come forth a vessel   *Pr 25:4*
for the *f.*

FINEST

have fed thee with the *f.* of   *Ps 81:16*
the wheat
he filleth thee with the *f.* of   *Ps 147:14*
the wheat

FINGER

Pharaoh, This is the *f.* of   *Ex 8:19*
God
the horns of the altar with   *Ex 29:12*
thy *f.*
stone, written with the *f.* of   *Ex 31:18*
God
priest shall dip his *f.* in the   *Le 4:6*
blood
the priest shall dip his *f.* in   *Le 4:17*
some
blood of the sin offering with   *Le 4:25*
his *f.*
take of the blood thereof with   *Le 4:30*
his *f.*
blood of the sin offering with   *Le 4:34*
his *f.*
of the altar round about with   *Le 8:15*
his *f.*
he dipped his *f.* in the blood   *Le 9:9*
the priest shall dip his right *Le 14:16*
f. in
sprinkle of the oil with his *f.*   *Le 14:16*
seven
shall sprinkle with his right   *Le 14:27*
f. some
and sprinkle it with his *f.*   *Le 16:14*
seven
of the blood with his *f.*   *Le 16:14*
seven times

blood upon it with his *f.*   *Le 16:19*
seven times
shall take of her blood with   *Nu 19:4*
his *f.*
them was written with the *f.*   *De 9:10*
of God
My little *f.* shall be thicker   *1Ki 12:10;*
than   *2Ch 10:10*
the putting forth of the *f.*   *Isa 58:9*
with the *f.* of God cast out   *Lu 11:20*
devils
may dip the tip of his *f.* in   *Lu 16:24*
water
with his *f.* wrote on the   *Joh 8:6*
ground
put my *f.* into the print of   *Joh 20:25*
the nails
Reach hither thy *f.* and   *Joh 20:27*
behold my

FINGERS

that had on every hand six   *2Sa 21:20*
f.
f. and toes were four and   *1Ch 20:6*
twenty
thy heavens, the work of thy *f.*   *Ps 8:3*
my hands to war, and my *f.*   *Ps 144:1*
to fight
his feet, he teacheth with his   *Pr 6:13*
f.
Bind them upon thy *f.* write   *Pr 7:3*
them
my *f.* with sweet smelling   *Ca 5:5*
myrrh
that which their own *f.* have   *Isa 2:8*
made
that which his *f.* have made   *Isa 17:8*
and your *f.* with iniquity;   *Isa 59:3*
your lips
the thickness thereof was   *Jer 52:21*
four *f.*
In the same hour came forth   *Da 5:5*
f. of
move them with one of their   *M't 23:4*
f.
put his *f.* into his ears, and   *M'k 7:33*
he spit
the burdens with one of   *Lu 11:46*
your *f.*

FINING

The *f.* pot is for silver, and   *Pr 17:3*
As the *f.* pot for silver, and   *Pr 27:21*

FINISH

in a cubit shalt thou *f.* it   *Ge 6:16*
above
to *f.* the transgression, and to   *Da 9:24*
his hands shall also *f.* it   *Zec 4:9*
whether he have sufficient to   *Lu 14:28*
f. it
foundation, and is not able   *Lu 14:29*
to *f.* it
to build, and was not able   *Lu 14:30*
to *f.*
that sent me, and to *f.* his   *Joh 4:34*
work
the Father hath given me to   *Joh 5:36*
f.
I might *f.* my course with   *Ac 20:24*
joy
will *f.* the work, and cut it   *Ro 9:28*
short
he would also *f.* in you the   *2Co 8:6*
same

FINISHED

the heavens and the earth   *Ge 2:1*
were *f.*
finished (S)   *Ge 24:15;*
24:19, 22, 45; 27:30; Ex 34:33; Nu 4:15;
16:31; De 20:9; 32:45; Jos 19:49, 51;
J'g 3:18; 15:17; Ru 3:3; 2Sa 6:18; 11:19;
1Ki 3:1;   7:40;   8:54; 1Ch 16:2;
2Ch 24:10;   29:17,   29; Ezr 10:17;
   Job 1:5; Jer 51:63; Eze 42:15; 43:23
of the tent of the   *Ex 39:32*
congregation (.)
So Moses *f.* the work   *Ex 40:33*
law in a book, until they   *De 31:24*
were *f.*
until every thing was *f.* that   *Jos 4:10*
f. offering the tribute (S)   *J'g 3:18*
until he have *f.* the thing this   *Ru 3:18*
day

he built the house, and *f.* it   *1Ki 6:9*
Solomon built the house, and   *1Ki 6:14*
f. it
until he had *f.* all the house   *1Ki 6:22*
eighth month, was the house   *1Ki 6:38*
f.
and he *f.* all his house   *1Ki 7:1*
so was the work of the pillars *1Ki 7:22*
f.
when Solomon had *f.* the   *1Ki 9:1*
building
the Lord. So he *f.* the house *1Ki 9:25*
Zeruiah began to number,   *1Ch 27:24*
but he *f.*
until thou hast *f.* all the   *1Ch 28:20*
work for
Huram *f.* the work that he   *2Ch 4:11*
was
for the house of the Lord   *2Ch 5:1*
was *f.*
Solomon *f.* the house of the   *2Ch 7:11*
Lord
of the Lord, and until it was   *2Ch 8:16*
f.
house of Lord was *f.* (B)   *2Ch 8:16*
when they had *f.* it, they   *2Ch 24:14*
brought
until the burnt offering was   *2Ch 29:28*
f.
Now when all this was *f.*   *2Ch 31:1*
all Israel
and *f.* them in the seventh   *2Ch 31:7*
month
building, and yet it is not *f.*   *Ezr 5:16*
And they builded, and *f.* it   *Ezr 6:14*
this house was *f.* on the   *Ezr 6:15*
third day
will they *f.* it in a day (S)   *Ne 4:2*
So the wall was *f.* in the   *Ne 6:15*
twenty
Lord has *f.* his work   *Isa 10:12*
(B)(R)
numbered thy kingdom, and   *Da 5:26*
f. it
all these things shall be *f.*   *Da 12:7*
when Jesus had *f.* these   *M't 13:53*
parables
when Jesus had *f.* these   *M't 19:1*
sayings
when Jesus had *f.* all these   *M't 26:1*
sayings
f. everything according to law *Lu 2:39*
(B)
third day *f.* my course   *Lu 13:32*
(A)(R)
third day work be *f.* (P)   *Lu 13:32*
I shall have *f.* (S)   *Lu 13:32*
I have *f.* the work which   *Joh 17:4*
thou
he said, It is *f.*: and he   *Joh 19:30*
bowed
And when we had *f.* our   *Ac 21:7*
course
I have *f.* this business (N)   *Ro 15:28*
go on and *f.* it (N)(P)   *2Co 8:11*
I have *f.* my course, I have   *2Ti 4:7*
kept
works were *f.* from the   *Heb 4:3*
foundation
sin, when it is *f.* bringeth   *Jas 1:15*
forth
the mystery of God should be   *Re 10:7*
f.
they shall have *f.* their   *Re 11:7*
testimony
until the thousand years were   *Re 20:5*
f.

FINISHER

Jesus the author and *f.* of   *Heb 12:2*
our

FINEST

the *f.* spices (R)   *Ex 30:23*
anoint with *f.* oils (A)(R)   *Am 6:6*

FINS

hath *f.* and scales in the   *Le 11:9;*
waters   *11:10, 12; De 14:9-10*

FIR

of instruments made of *f.*   *2Sa 6:5*
wood
and concerning timber of *f.*   *1Ki 5:8*
gave Solomon cedar trees   *1Ki 5:10*
and *f.*

of the house with planks of *f.* *1Ki 6:15*

the two doors were of *f.* tree *1Ki 6:34*
with cedar trees and *f.* trees *1Ki 9:11*
and the choice *f.* trees *2Ki 19:23*
thereof
Send me also cedar trees, *f.* *2Ch 2:8*
trees
greater house he ceiled with *2Ch 3:5*
f. tree
stork, the *f.* trees are her *Ps 104:17*
house
are cedar, and our rafters of *Ca 1:17*
f.
Yea, the *f.* trees rejoice at *Isa 14:8*
thee
and the choice *f.* trees *Isa 37:24*
thereof
I will set in the desert the *f* *Isa 41:19*
tree
the thorn shall come up the *Isa 55:13*
f. tree
f. tree, the pine tree, and *Isa 60:13*
the box
thy ship boards of *f.* trees of *Eze 27:5*
Senir
f. trees were not like his *Eze 31:8*
boughs
I am like a green *f.* tree *Ho 14:8*
f. trees shall be terribly shaken *Na 2:3*
f. tree; for the cedar is fallen *Zec 11:2*

FIRE

smoking *f.* pot, flaming *Ge 15:17*
torch (R)
Abraham took *f.* in hand, a *Ge 22:6*
knife
behold the *f.* and the wood, *Ge 22:7*
but where
and behold, the bush burned *Ex 3:2*
with *f.*
Lord sent hail and *f.* along *Ex 9:23*
on ground
there was hail, and *f.* mingled *Ex 9:24*
with hail
shall eat flesh in that night *Ex 12:8;*
roast with *f.* *12:9*
Lord descended upon mount *Ex 19:18*
Sinai in *f.*
if *f.* break out, and catch in *Ex 22:6*
thorns
I cast gold into *f.* and came *Ex 32:24*
this calf
f. was on tabernacle by *Ex 40:38;*
night through all *Nu 9:16; De 1:33*
sons of priest put *f.* on the *Le 1:7*
altar, lay wood in order upon *f.*
upon wood that is in the *f.* *Le 1:8;*
1:12, 17; 3:5
offer green ears of corn dried *Le 2:14*
by the *f.*
the *f.* of the altar be burning *Le 6:9;*
in it *6:10, 12-13*
there came *f.* out from before *Le 9:24*
the Lord
sons of Aaron put *f.* in their *Le 10:1*
censers
went out *f.* from Lord and *Le 10:2*
devoured them
he shall put the incense upon *Le 16:13*
the *f.*
not let any of thy seed pass *Le 18:21;*
thro' *f.* to Molech *De 18:10;*
2Ki 17:17; 23:10
take the hair, and put it in *Nu 6:18*
the *f.*
when Moses prayed the *f.* *Nu 11:2*
was quenched
take ye censers, and put *f.* *Nu 16:7;*
therein *16:18*
he take censers, and scatter *Nu 16:37*
f. yonder
take censer, and put *f.* therein *Nu 16:46*
from off altar
thine of most holy things *Nu 18:9*
reserved from *f.*
for there is a *f.* gone out *Nu 21:28*
from Heshbon
every thing that may abide *Nu 31:23*
f. go thro' *f.*
the mountain burnt with *f.* *De 4:11;*
9:15
upon earth he shewed thee *De 4:36*
his great *f.*
for ye were afraid by reason *De 5:5*
of the *f.*
nor let me see this great *f.* *De 18:16*
any more

flames of *f.* at right hand *De 33:2*
(B)(R)
all Israel burned Achan with *Jos 7:25*
f.
there rose up *f.* out of the *J'g 6:21*
rock
let *f.* come out of bramble *J'g 9:15*
and devour cedars
as a thread of tow when it *J'g 16:9*
toucheth the *f.*
lay it on wood, put no *f.* *1Ki 18:23;*
under *18:25*
God that answereth by *f.* *1Ki 18:24*
let him be God
then *f.* of the Lord fell *1Ki 18:38;*
2Ch 7:1, 3
after earthquake *f.* but *1Ki 19:12*
Lord was not in *f.* after the
f. a still small voice
then let *f.* come down from *2Ki 1:10*
heaven
f. of God came down *2Ki 1:12*
from heaven
there appeared a chariot and *2Ki 2:11*
horses of *f.*
the mountain was full of *2Ki 6:17*
chariots of *f.*
Ahaz made his son to pass *2Ki 16:3*
through *f.*
and have cast their gods *2Ki 19:18*
into the *f.*
Manasseh made son pass *2Ki 21:6;*
thro' *f.* *2Ch 33:6*
no man might make son *2Ki 23:10*
pass thro' *f.*
Lord answered from heaven *1Ch 21:26*
by *f.*
they roasted the passover *2Ch 35:13*
with *f.*
gates thereof are consumed *Ne 2:3;*
with *f.* *2:13*
f. of God is fallen from *Job 1:16*
heaven
the spark of his *f.* shall not *Job 18:5*
shine
under it is turned up as it *Job 28:5*
were *f.*
burning lamps, and sparks *Job 41:19*
of *f.* leap out
while I was musing the *f.* *Ps 39:3*
burned
he burneth the chariot in the *Ps 46:9*
f.
we went through *f.* and *Ps 66:12*
through water
as wax melteth before *f.* so *Ps 68:2*
let wicked perish
they have cast *f.* into thy *Ps 74:7*
sanctuary
all the night with a light of *Ps 78:14;*
f. *105:39*
as *f.* burneth wood, and as *Ps 83:14*
flame
a *f.* goeth before him and *Ps 97:3*
burneth up enemies
he gave hail and flaming *Ps 105:32*
f. in their land
they are quenched as the *f.* *Ps 118:12*
of thorns
let them be cast into *f.* into *Ps 140:10*
deep pits
f. and hail, stormy wind *Ps 148:8*
fulfilling his word
can a man take *f.* in his *Pr 6:27*
bosom
and in his lips there is as a *Pr 16:27*
burning *f.*
where no wood is, the *f.* goeth *Pr 26:20*
out
as wood to *f.* so is *Pr 26:21*
contentious man to kindle
grave and the *f.* saith not, It *Pr 30:16*
is enough
shall be with burning and fuel *Isa 9:5*
of *f.*
for wickedness burneth as the *Isa 9:18*
f.
the people shall be as the *Isa 9:19*
fuel of the *f.*
kindle a burning like *Isa 10:16*
burning of *f.*
the light of Israel shall be *Isa 10:17*
for a *f.*
not be found a sherd to *Isa 30:14*
take *f.* from hearth
the pile thereof is *f.* and *Isa 30:33*
much wood
saith the Lord, whose *f.* is in *Isa 31:9*
Zion

kings of Assyria have cast *Isa 37:19*
gods into *f.*
when thou walkest through *f.* *Isa 43:2*
not be burnt
he burneth part in *f.* he *Isa 44:16*
saith, Aha, I have seen *f.*
they shall be as stubble, the *Isa 47:14*
f. shall burn them
walk in light of your *f.* and *Isa 50:11*
in sparks
as when melting *f.* burneth, *Isa 64:2*
causeth waters to boil
these are a *f.* that burneth all *Isa 65:5*
the day'
for behold, the Lord will *Isa 66:15*
come with *f.*
by *f.* will the Lord plead *Isa 66:16*
with all flesh
worm not die, neither their *Isa 66:24*
f. be quenched
lest my fury come forth like *f.* *Jer 4:4*
and burn
I will make my words in thy *Jer 5:14*
mouth *f.*
his word was as a *f.* shut up *Jer 20:9*
in my bones
lest my fury go out like *f.* *Jer 21:12*
and burn
shall cut down cast choice *Jer 22:7*
cedars in *f.*
whom king of Babylon *Jer 29:22*
roasted in *f.*
to cause their sons pass thro' *Jer 32:35;*
f. to Molech *Eze 16:21; 20:26, 31*
their daughters to pass *Jer 32:35*
through the *f.*
there was a *f.* on the hearth *Jer 36:22*
burning
Jehudi cut the roll, and cast *Jer 36:23*
it into the *f.*
but a *f.* shall come forth out *Jer 48:45*
of Heshbon
folk shall labour in vain and *Jer 51:58*
in the *f.*
burned against Jacob like *La 2:3*
flaming *f.*
bent bow, he poured out his *La 2:4*
fury like *f.*
I looked, behold, a *f.* *Eze 1:4*
infolding itself
f. was bright, and out of *f.* *Eze 1:13*
lightning
take *f.* from between the *Eze 10:6*
wheels
one cherub stretched forth *Eze 10:7*
hand to the *f.*
I will blow against thee in *Eze 21:31;*
the *f.* *22:21*
shalt be for fuel to *f.* *Eze 21:32*
no more remembered
to blow *f.* upon it, to melt *Eze 22:20*
it
Lord, I will even make pile *Eze 24:9*
for *f.* great
her scum be in *f.* in *Eze 24:12*
filthiness is lewdness
will bring forth a *f.* from *Eze 28:18*
midst of thee
in the *f.* of my jealousy *Eze 36:5;*
have I spoken *38:19*
upon whose bodies *f.* had no *Da 3:27*
power, nor smell of *f.*
his throne like flames, wheels *Da 7:9*
like burning *f.*
his face as lightning, his eyes *Da 10:6*
as lamps of *f.*
in the morning it burneth as a *Ho 7:6*
flaming *f.*
blood *f.* and pillars of *Joe 2:30;*
smoke *Ac 2:19*
lest he break out like *f.* in *Am 5:6*
house of Joseph
the Lord God called to *Am 7:4*
contend by *f.*
and the house of Jacob shall *Ob 18*
be a *f.*
be molten under him as wax *Mic 1:4*
before *f.*
fury poured out like *f.* rocks *Nah 1:6*
thrown down
people shall labour in the *Hab 2:13*
very *f.*
only for *f.* (S) *Hab 2:13*
will be unto her a wall of *f.* *Zec 2:5*
round about
is not this a brand plucked *Zec 3:2*
out of the *f.*

like hearth of *f.* and like   *Zec 12:6*
torch of *f.* in sheaf
I will bring the third part   *Zec 13:9*
through the *f.*
he is like a refiner's *f.* and   *M't 3:2*
fuller's soap
every tree that bringeth not   *M't 3:10;*
forth good fruit   *7:19; Lu 3:9; Joh 15:6*
is cast into *f.*
baptize with Holy Ghost,   *M't 3:11;*
and *f.*   *Lu 3:16*
f. of destruction (P)   *M't 5:22; 10:28*
shall cast them into a   *M't 13:42;*
furnace of *f.*   *13:50*
ofttimes he falleth into   *M't 17:15;*
the *f.*   *M'k 9:22*
having two hands or two   *M't 18:8;*
feet, be cast into everlasting   *M'k 9:43;*
f.   *46*
thrown into everlasting *f.*   *M't 18:9*
(P)
depart from me, ye cursed,   *M't 25:41*
into everlasting *f.*
where *f.* is not quenched   *M'k 9:44;*
   9:45
Peter warmed himself at   *M'k 14:54*
the *f.*
wilt thou that we command *f.*   *Lu 9:54*
to come
in agony in this *f.* (N)(P)   *Lu 16:24;*
   16:25
same day it rained *f.* and   *Lu 17:29*
brimstone
a maid beheld him as he sat *Lu 22:56*
by the *f.*
appeared to them cloven   *Ac 2:3*
tongues, like as *f.*
when Paul had laid sticks on *Ac 28:3*
the *f.*
he shook off the beast into *f.* *Ac 28:5*
felt no harm
it shall be revealed by *f.*   *1Co 3:13*
and *f.* shall try work
he himself shall be saved,   *1Co 3:15*
yet so as by *f.*
in flaming *f.* taking vengeance *2Th 1:8*
on them
who maketh his ministers   *Heb 1:7*
flame of *f.*
f. of God's indignation   *Heb 10:27*
(E)(N)(P)(R)
who thro' faith quenched   *Heb 11:34*
violence of *f.*
come to mount that burned *Heb 12:18*
with *f.*
how great a matter a little *f.* *Jas 3:5*
kindleth
the tongue is a *f.* a world of *Jas 3:6*
iniquity
shall eat your flesh as it were *Jas 5:3*
f.
than of gold, tho' it be tried *1Pe 1:7*
with *f.*
reserved unto *f.* against day *2Pe 3:7*
of judgment
the heavens being on *f.* shall *2Pe 3:12*
be dissolved
suffering the vengeance of   *Jude 7*
eternal *f.*
others save pulling them out *Jude 23*
of the *f.*
thee to buy of me gold tried *Re 3:18*
in *f.*
seven lamps of *f.* burning   *Re 4:5*
before the throne
angel filled censer with *f.* of *Re 8:5*
altar
there followed hail and *f.*   *Re 8:7*
mingled with blood
as it were a great mountain   *Re 8:8*
burning with *f.*
out of their mouths issued   *Re 9:17;*
f.   *11:5*
third part of men was killed *Re 9:18*
by the *f.*
he maketh *f.* come down   *Re 13:13*
from heaven
another angel which had   *Re 14:18*
power over *f.*
I saw as it were a sea of   *Re 15:2*
glass mingled with *f.*
power was given him to   *Re 16:8*
scorch men with *f*
f. came down from God out *Re 20:9*
of heaven
devil was cast into lake of *f.* *Re 20:10*
and brimstone
death and hell were cast into *Re 20:14*
the lake of *f.*

whoso not written in book   *Re 20:15*
of life, cast into *f.*
have part in the lake which   *Re 21:8*
burneth with *f.*

KINDLE, KINDLED FIRE

he that *kindled* the *f.* make   *Ex 22:6*
restitution
ye shall *kindle* no *f.* on the   *Ex 35:3*
sabbath day
a *f.* is *kindled* in my anger   *De 32:22;*
   Jer 15:14; 17:4
before him were coals of *f.* *2Sa 22:13*
kindled
so a *f.* was *kindled* against *Ps 78:21*
Jacob
a *f.* was *kindled* in their   *Ps 106:18*
company
he shall *kindle* a burning   *Isa 10:16*
like a *f.*
all ye that *kindle* a *f.* that   *Isa 50:11*
compass
children gathered wood,   *Jer 7:18*
fathers *kindled f.*
he hath *kindled f.* on the   *Jer 11:16*
green olive
then will I *kindle* a *f.* in the *Jer 17:27*
gates thereof
I will *kindle* a *f.* in the   *Jer 21:14*
forest thereof
I will *kindle* a *f.* in the   *Jer 43:12*
houses of gods
I will *kindle* a *f.* in wall of *Jer 49:27*
Damascus
and I will *kindle* a *f.* in his *Jer 50:32*
cities
the Lord hath *kindled* a *f.* in *La 4:11*
Zion
I will *kindle* a *f.* in the   *Eze 20:47*
forest
heap on wood, *kindle* the *f.* *Eze 24:10*
consume flesh
I will *kindle* a *f.* in wall of *Am 1:14*
Rabbah
nor do ye *kindle f.* on altar *M'l 1:10*
for nought
to send *f.* and what if   *Lu 12:49*
already *kindled*
when they had *kindled* a *f.* *Lu 22:55*
in the hall
barbarians *kindled* a *f.* and   *Ac 28:2*
received us

MADE BY FIRE

an offering *made by f.* unto *Ex 29:18;*
the Lord   *25, 41; Le 1:9, 13, 17; 2:2, 9,*
16; 3:3, 5, 9, 11, 14, 16; 7:5, 25; 8:21,
28; 21:6; 22:27; 23:8, 13, 18, 25, 27,
36-37; 24:7; Nu 15:3, 10, 13-14; 18:17;
   28:3
offerings of the Lord *made by* *Le 2:3;*
  f. 2:10; 4:35; 5:12; 6:17-18; 7:30, 35;
10-12, 15; 21:21; 24:9; De 18:1;
   1Sa 2:28
sacrifices *made by f.*   *Le 10:13;*
   Nu 28:2; Jos 13:14
bring their sacrifice *made* *Nu 15:25;*
by f. unto the Lord *28:6, 8, 13, 19, 24;*
   29:6, 13, 36

PILLAR OF FIRE

the Lord looked thro' the   *Ex 14:24*
pillar of f.
face as the sun, and his feet *Re 10:1*
as *pillars of f.*

SEND, SENT FIRE

from above he *sent f.* into my *La 1:13*
bones
and I will *send* a *f.* on   *Eze 39:6*
Magog
but I will *send* a *f.* upon his *Ho 8:14*
cities
I will *send* a *f.* into the house *Am 1:4*
of Hazael
I will *send* a *f.* on the wall of *Am 1:7*
Gaza
I will *send* a *f.* on wall of   *Am 1:10;*
Tyrus; on Teman   *1:12*
I will *send a f.* on Moab; on *Am 2:2;*
Judah   *2:5*
I am come to *send f.* on the *Lu 12:49*
earth

SET FIRE

set on *f.* foundations of   *De 32:22*
mountains
ye shall *set* the city of Ai on *Jos 8:8*
f.
they hasted, and *set* the city *Jos 8:19*
on *f.*
now Judah had *set* Jerusalem *J'g 1:8*
on *f.*
the people *set* the hold on *f.* *J'g 9:49*
upon them
had *set* the brands on *f.* and *J'g 15:5*
burnt the corn
they *set* on *f.* all the cities *J'g 20:48*
of Benjamin
servants *set* Joab's field on *2Sa 14:30*
f.
why have thy servants *set* my *2Sa 14:31*
field on *f.*
Hazael will *set* strong holds *2Ki 8:12*
on *f.*
I lie among them that are *set* *Ps 57:4*
on *f.*
the women come and *set*   *Isa 27:11*
them on *f.*
he hath *set* him on *f.* round *Isa 42:25*
about
set up a sign of *f.* in   *Jer 6:1*
Beth-haccerem
the Chaldeans shall *set* on *f.* *Jer 32:29*
this city
when I have *set* a *f.* in   *Eze 30:8*
Egypt
I will *set f.* in Zoan; *f.* in   *Eze 30:14;*
Egypt   *30:16*
set on *f.* and burn the   *Eze 39:9*
weapons of Gog
tongue is a fire, and setteth on *Jas 3:6*
fire it is *set* on *f.*

STRANGE FIRE

Nadab and Abihu offered   *Le 10:1*
strange f.
died when they offered   *Nu 3:4;*
strange f.   *26:61*

FIREBRAND

turned tail to tail, and put a *J'g 15:4*
f.
ye were as a *f.* plucked out *Am 4:11*
of the

FIREBRANDS

and took *f.* and turned tail to *J'g 15:4*
tail
As a mad man who casteth *f.* *Pr 26:18*
for the two tails of these   *Isa 7:4*
smoking *f.*

FIREPANS

and his fleshhooks, and his *f.* *Ex 27:3*
and the fleshhooks, and the *f.* *Ex 38:3*
And the *f.* and the bowls,   *2Ki 25:15*
and such
the basons, and the *f.* and   *Jer 52:19*
the bowls

FIRED

most have been *f.* by zeal   *2Co 9:2*
(N)

FIRES

glorify ye the Lord in the *f.* *Isa 24:15*
even
in the regions of the sunrise *Isa 24:15*
(B)
glorify Jehovah in the east   *Isa 24:15*
(E)(R)

FIRKINS

containing two or three *f.*   *Joh 2:6*
apiece
twenty to thirty gallons apiece *Joh 2:6*
(A)(N)(P)(R)
eighteen to twenty-four   *Joh 2:6*
gallons (B)

FIRM

the covenant of the Lord   *Jos 3:17*
stood *f.*

where the priests' feet stood *f.*   *Jos 4:3*
had *f.* hold on kingdom (B)   *2Ki 14:5*
they are *f.* in themselves;   *Job 41:23*
they
His heart is as *f.* as a   *Job 41:24*
stone; they
but their strength is *f.*   *Ps 73:4*
his heart will remain *f.*   *Ps 112:7*
(B)(R)
and to make a *f.* decree   *Da 6:7*
keep you *f.* to the end (N)   *1Co 1:8*
rejoicing of the hope *f.* unto   *Heb 3:6*
the end
be *f.* in the faith   *1Pe 5:9*
(A)(B)(N)(P)(R)

FIRMAMENT

Let there be a *f.* in the midst   *Ge 1:6*
of
God made the *f.* and divided   *Ge 1:7; 1:8*
Let there be lights in the *f.*   *Ge 1:14*
of the
for lights in the *f.* of heaven   *Ge 1:15*
to give
God set them in the *f.* of   *Ge 1:17*
heaven to
earth in the open *f.* of   *Ge 1:20*
heaven
and the *f.* sheweth his   *Ps 19:1*
handiwork
praise him in the *f.* of his   *Ps 150:1*
power
the likeness of the *f.* upon   *Eze 1:22*
the heads
an expanse (B)   *Eze 1:22; 10:1*
And under the *f.* were their   *Eze 1:23*
wings
And there was a voice from   *Eze 1:25*
the *f.*
And above the *f.* that was   *Eze 1:26*
over their
in the *f.* that was above the   *Eze 10:1*
head
shine as the brightness of the   *Da 12:3*
f.

FIRMLY

hold *f.* to our faith (P)   *Heb 4:14*

FIRMNESS

f. of iron (B)(R)   *Da 2:41*
f. of your faith (B)(R)   *Col 2:5*

FIRST

the *f.* came out red all over   *Ge 25:25*
there was a famine beside the   *Ge 26:1*
f. famine
the midwife said, This came   *Ge 38:28*
out *f.*
if they will not hearken to the   *Ex 4:8*
f. sign
the *f.* of the firstfruits bring   *Ex 23:19*
to the Lord
the *f.* row shall be a sardius   *Ex 28:17; 39:10*
two tables like to the *f.*   *Ex 34:1; 34:4; De 10:1, 3*
shall offer what is for the   *Le 5:8*
sin offering *f.*
camp of Judah, these shall *f.*   *Nu 2:9*
set forth
and they *f.* took their   *Nu 10:13*
journey
it was the time of the *f.*   *Nu 13:20*
ripe grapes
offer up a cake of the *f.* of   *Nu 15:20*
your dough   *15:21; Eze 44:30*
whatsoever is *f.* ripe shall   *Nu 18:13*
be thine
Amalek was the *f.* of the   *Nu 24:20*
nations
according to *f.* time, forty   *De 10:10*
days
I will give thee *f.* rain and   *De 11:14*
latter rain
thine hand shall be *f.* upon   *De 13:9*
him
hands of witnesses shall be *f.*   *De 17:7*
upon him
f. of the fleece of thy sheep   *De 18:4*
give him
he provided the *f.* part for   *De 33:21*
himself
theirs was *f.* lot   *Jos 21:10; 1Ch 24:7; 25:9*

who shall go up *f.* to   *J'g 1:1; 20:18*
fight
Israel are smitten as in the   *J'g 20:39*
f. battle
that *f.* slaughter was twenty   *1Sa 14:14*
men
same was *f.* altar Saul built   *1Sa 14:35*
to Lord
except thou *f.* bring Michal   *2Sa 3:13*
Saul's
I am come *f.* this day to   *2Sa 19:20*
meet my lord
advice should not be *f.* had   *2Sa 19:43*
in bringing
he attained not unto the   *2Sa 23:19;*
f. three   *23:23; 1Ch 11:21, 25*
but make thereof a little   *1Ki 17:13*
cake *f.*
and dress it *f.* for ye are   *1Ki 18:25*
many
young men of the princes   *1Ki 20:17*
went out *f.*
now the *f.* inhabitants that   *1Ch 9:2*
dwelt
whosoever smiteth the   *1Ch 11:6*
Jebusites *f.*
that day David delivered f.   *1Ch 16:7*
this psalm
length by cubits after *f.*   *2Ch 3:3*
measure
that had seen the glory of *f.*   *Ezr 3:12*
house
f. in the trespass (S)   *Ezr 9:2*
which sat the *f.* in the   *Es 1:14*
kingdom
art thou the *f.* man that was   *Job 15:7*
born
that is *f.* in his own cause   *Pr 18:17*
seemeth just
the *f.* shall say to Zion,   *Isa 41:27*
Behold them
thy *f.* father hath sinned   *Isa 43:27*
against me
went down at the *f.* (S)   *Isa 52:4*
ships of Tarshish *f.* to bring   *Isa 60:9*
thy sons
her that bringeth forth her *f.*   *Jer 4:31*
child
f. I will recompense their   *Jer 16:18*
iniquity
good figs, even like figs that   *Jer 24:2*
are *f.* ripe
write the words that were in   *Jer 36:28*
f. roll
f. the king of Assyria hath   *Jer 50:17*
devoured him
Daniel was *f.* president, of an   *Da 6:2*
excellent
the *f.* beast was like a lion   *Da 7:4; Re 4:7*
and another shall be diverse   *Da 7:24*
from the *f.*
great horn between his eyes   *Da 8:21*
is the *f.* king
I will go and return to my *f.*   *Ho 2:7*
husband
f. ripe in the fig tree at her   *Ho 9:10*
time
shall go captive with the *f.*   *Am 6:7*
that go
to thee shall come the *f.*   *Mic 4:8*
dominion
like fig trees with the *f.* ripe   *Na 3:12*
figs
who is left that saw house in   *Hag 2:3*
f. glory
in the *f.* chariot were red   *Zec 6:2*
horses
the Lord shall save the tents   *Zec 12:7*
of Judah *f.*
f. be reconciled to brother,   *M't 5:24*
and come
seek *f.* kingdom of God and   *M't 6:33*
righteousness
f. cast beam out of thine eye   *M't 7:5; Lu 6:42*
f. to go and bury my father   *M't 8:21; Lu 9:59*
except he *f.* bind the   *M't 12:29;*
strong man   *M'k 3:27*
latter state worse than the   *M't 12:45;*
f.   *Lu 11:26*
gather together *f.* tares,   *M't 13:30*
bind them
Elias must *f.* come   *M't 17:10; 17:11; M'k 9:12*
take up the fish that *f.*   *M't 17:27*
cometh up

but when the *f.* came, they   *M't 20:10*
supposed
came to *f.* and said, Son, go   *M't 21:28*
work
who of twain, they say unto   *M't 21:31*
him, The *f.*
he sent other servants more   *M't 21:36*
than the *f.*
f. when married   *M't 22:25; M'k 12:20; Lu 20:29*
f. commandment   *M't 22:38; M'k 12:28-30*
Pharisee, cleanse *f.* that   *M't 23:26*
which is within
f. the blade, then ear, after   *M'k 4:28*
that corn
Jesus said to her, Let   *M'k 7:27*
children *f.* be filled
if any desire to be *f.* he   *M'k 9:35*
shall be last
and the gospel must *f.* be   *M'k 13:10*
published
he appeared *f.* to Mary   *M'k 16:9*
Magdalene
had perfect understanding   *Lu 1:3*
from the *f.*
was *f.* made when Cyrenius   *Lu 2:2*
was governor
on second sabbath after the *f.*   *Lu 6:1*
he went
f. say, Peace be to this house   *Lu 10:5*
he had not *f.* washed before   *Lu 11:38*
dinner
sitteth not down *f.* and   *Lu 14:28*
counteth cost
but *f.* must he suffer many   *Lu 17:25*
things
for these things must *f.* come   *Lu 21:9*
to pass
he *f.* findeth his brother   *Joh 1:41*
Simon
whosoever *f.* stepped in, was   *Joh 5:4*
made whole
without sin, let him *f.* cast a   *Joh 8:7*
stone at her
into place where John at *f.*   *Joh 10:40*
baptized
and led him away to Annas   *Joh 18:13*
f.
soldiers came, and brake   *Joh 19:32*
legs of *f.*
disciple came *f.* to sepulchre   *Joh 20:4; 20:8*
to you *f.* God sent him to   *Ac 3:26*
bless you in
Jacob sent out our fathers *f.*   *Ac 7:12*
were called Christians *f.* at   *Ac 11:26*
Antioch
they were past the *f.* and   *Ac 12:10*
second ward
when John had *f.* preached   *Ac 13:24*
baptism
necessary it should *f.* been   *Ac 13:46*
spoken to you
but shewed *f.* unto them of   *Ac 26:20*
Damascus
Christ be *f.* that should rise   *Ac 26:23*
from dead
should cast themselves *f.*   *Ac 27:43*
into the sea
f. I thank my God through   *Ro 1:8*
Jesus Christ
of the Jew *f.* and also of the   *Ro 2:9; 2:10*
Gentile
or who hath *f.* given to him   *Ro 11:35*
if *f.* I be somewhat filled   *Ro 15:24*
with company
f. apostles, secondarily   *1Co 12:28*
prophets
let the *f.* hold his peace   *1Co 14:30*
I delivered *f.* of all that   *1Co 15:3*
which I received
f. man Adam was made a   *1Co 15:45*
living soul
howbeit that was not *f.*   *1Co 15:46*
which is spiritual
the *f.* man is of the earth,   *1Co 15:47*
earthy
f. gave their own selves to   *2Co 8:5*
the Lord
if there be *f.* a willing mind,   *2Co 8:12*
it is accepted
who *f.* trusted in Christ   *Eph 1:12*
descended *f.* into lower parts   *Eph 4:9*
of earth
which is *f.* commandment   *Eph 6:2*
with promise
he might have *f.* place (B)   *Col 1:18*

the dead in Christ shall rise *1Th 4:16*
f.
except there come a falling *2Th 2:3*
away *f.*
in me *f.* Christ Jesus might *1Ti 1:16*
shew
for Adam was *f.* formed, *1Ti 2:13*
then Eve
let their *f.* be proved, then *1Ti 3:10*
let them use
let them learn *f.* to shew piety *1Ti 5:4*
at home
because they have cast off *1Ti 5:12*
their *f.* faith
faith dwelt *f.* in grandmother *2Ti 1:5*
Lois
husbandman must be *f.* *2Ti 2:6*
partaker of fruits
at my *f.* answer no man *2Ti 4:16*
stood with me
after *f.* and second *Tit 3:10*
admonition, reject
to whom it was *f.* preached, *Heb 4:6*
entered not
one teach you which be the *Heb 5:12*
f. principles
f. by interpretation, king of *Heb 7:2*
righteousness
offer *f.* for his own sins, *Heb 7:27*
then for people's
the *f.* covenant *Heb 8:7;*
8:13; 9:1, 15, 18
f. tabernacle, wherein was *Heb 9:2;*
shewbread *9:6, 8*
he taketh away *f.* that he *Heb 10:9*
may establish
wisdom that is from above, *Jas 3:17*
is *f.* pure
if judgment *f.* begin at us, *1Pe 4:17*
what end
knowing this *f.* that no *2Pe 1:20;*
prophecy *3:3*
we love him, because he *f.* *1Jo 4:19*
loved us
the angels who kept not their *Jude 6*
f. estate
because thou hast left thy *f.* *Re 2:4*
love
repent, and do *f.* works, else I *Re 2:5*
will come
he exerciseth all the power *Re 13:12*
of *f.* beast
this is the *f.* resurrection *Re 20:5*
f. heaven and *f.* earth were *Re 21:1*
passed away
f. foundation was jasper, *Re 21:19*
second sapphire

FIRST BEGOTTEN

bringeth in the *f.* begotten into *Heb 1:6*
world

FIRST MONTH

in the *f.* month, the first day *Ge 8:13*
of month
shall be the *f.* month of the *Ex 12:2*
year to you
in *f.* month eat unleavened *Ex 12:18;*
bread *Le 23:5*
first day of *f.* month set up *Ex 40:2;*
tabernacle *40:17*
in the *f.* month keep the *Nu 9:1;*
passover *28:16; 2Ch 35:1; Ezr 6:19;*
Eze 45:21
came into desert of Zin in *Nu 20:1*
the *f.* month
departed from Rameses in *Nu 33:3*
the *f.* month
people came out of Jordan in *Jos 4:19*
f. month
went over Jordan in *f.* *1Ch 12:15*
month
the captain that served the *1Ch 27:2;*
f. month *27:3*
in the *f.* month opened the *2Ch 29:3*
doors
began on first day of *f.* *2Ch 29:17*
month to sanctify, in sixteenth
day of *f.* month made an end
f. month began he to go from *Ezr 7:9*
Babylon
the *f.* month we departed *Ezr 8:31*
from Ahava
they made an end with *Ezr 10:17*
them by *f.* month
in the *f.* month they cast Pur, *Es 3:7*
the thirteenth day of the *f.* month

in the *f. month* take young *Eze 45:18*
bullock
cause former and latter rain *Joe 2:23*
in *f.* month

FIRST YEAR

your lambs shall be male of *Ex 12:5*
f. year
offer two lambs of the *f.* *Ex 29:38;*
year day by *Le 23:19; Nu 28:3, 9*
take a kid of the *f.* year *Le 9:3*
without blemish
he shall bring a lamb of the *Le 12:6;*
f. year *Nu 6:12; 7:15, 21, 27, 33, 39,*
45, 51, 57, 63, 69, 75, 81; Eze 46:13
take an ewe lamb of *f.* year *Le 14:10;*
Nu 6:14
offer an he lamb of *f.* year *Le 23:12;*
Nu 6:14
offer seven lambs of *f.* year *Le 23:18;*
without blemish *Nu 28:11, 19, 27;*
29:2, 8, 36
for a peace offering five *Nu 7:17;*
lambs of *f.* year *7:23, 29, 35, 41, 47,*
53, 59
lambs of *f.* year twelve for *Nu 7:87*
burnt offering
lambs of *f.* year sixty for a *Nu 7:88*
peace offering
then he shall bring a *Nu 15:27*
she goat of *f.* year
offer a burnt offering, *Nu 29:13;*
fourteen lambs of *f.* year *29:17, 20, 23,*
26, 29, 32
Hezekiah in *f.* year of his *2Ch 29:3*
reign
in *f.* year of Cyrus *2Ch 36:22;*
Ezr 1:1; 5:13; 6:3
that was *f.* year of *Jer 25:1*
Nebuchadnezzar
in the *f.* year of reign of *Jer 52:31*
Evil-merodach
Daniel continued to *f.* year *Da 1:21*
of Cyrus
in the *f.* year of Belshazzar *Da 7:1*
Daniel dreamed
in *f.* year of Darius I *Da 9:1;*
understand by books *9:2*
in the *f.* year of Darius I *Da 11:1*
stood to confirm

AT THE FIRST

where Abram made altar *at* *Ge 13:4*
the f.
the city was called Luz *at* *Ge 28:19*
the f.
because of the money *Ge 43:18*
returned *at the f.*
we came down indeed *at the* *Ge 43:20*
f. to buy food
I fell down before Lord as *De 9:18;*
at the f. *9:25*
when they come against us *at* *Jos 8:5*
the f.
will say, They flee before us as *Jos 8:6*
at the f.
name of city, was Laish *at* *J'g 18:29*
the f.
are smitten down before us *J'g 20:32*
as *at the f.*
some of them be overthrown *2Sa 17:9*
at the f.
thou didst send for to thy *1Ki 20:9*
servant *at f.*
because ye did it not *at the* *1Ch 15:13*
f.
register of them which came *Ne 7:5*
up *at the f.*
I will restore thy judges as *at* *Isa 1:26*
the f.
when *at the f.* he lightly *Isa 9:1*
afflicted the land
place where I set my name *at* *Jer 7:12*
the f.
I will build them as *at the f.* *Jer 33:7*
return captivity of the land, *Jer 33:11*
as *at the f.*
after that which appeared to *Da 8:1*
me *at the f.*
his disciples understood not *Joh 12:16*
at the f.
which *at the f.* came to *Joh 19:39*
Jesus by night
God *at the f.* did visit the *Ac 15:14*
Gentiles
was *at the f.* among mine *Ac 26:4*
own nation

¶ preached gospel unto you, *Ga 4:13*
at the f.
at the f. began to be spoken *Heb 2:3*
by Lord

FIRSTBORN

the *f.* said to the younger *Ge 19:31;*
19:34
f. went in, and lay with her *Ge 19:33*
father
f. bare a son, and called his *Ge 19:37*
name Moab
and Jacob said, I am Esau, *Ge 27:19;*
thy *f.* *27:32*
not done to give the younger *Ge 29:26*
before the *f.*
the *f.* according to his *Ge 43:33*
birthright
not so my father, for this is *Ge 48:18*
the *f.*
Israel is my son, even my *f.* *Ex 4:22*
I will slay thy son, even thy *f.* *Ex 4:23*
all *f.* in the land of Egypt *Ex 11:5*
shall die
I will smite all the *f.* in the *Ex 12:12*
land
the Lord smote all *f.* in *Ex 12:29;*
Egypt *13:15*
sanctify unto me all the *f.* it *Ex 13:2*
is mine
f. of thy sons shalt thou give *Ex 22:29*
to me
f. of thy sons shalt redeem *Ex 34:20;*
Nu 18:15
instead of all the *f.* *Nu 3:12;*
3:41, 45; 8:17-18
because all the *f.* of Israel *Nu 3:13*
are mine, I hallowed all the *f.*
of Israel
number all the *f.* of the *Nu 3:40*
males of Israel
Moses numbered all the *f.* of *Nu 3:42*
Israel
of the *f.* of Israel took he *Nu 3:50*
the money
for the Egyptians buried all *Nu 33:4*
their *f.*
if the *f.* son be hers that *De 21:15*
was hated
beginning of strength, for *De 21:17*
right of *f.* is his
f. which she beareth, succeed *De 25:6*
in name
shall lay the foundation in *Jos 6:26*
his *f.*
laid foundation in Abiram *1Ki 16:34*
his *f.*
sons of Reuben the *f.* for *1Ch 5:1*
he was *f.*
though he was not the *f.* *1Ch 26:10*
yet his father
Jehoram, because he was the *2Ch 21:3*
f.
to bring the *f.* to the house *Ne 10:36*
of God
f. of death shall devour his *Job 18:13*
strength
he smote all *f.* in Egypt, *Ps 78:51;*
chief of their strength *105:36; 135:8;*
136:10
will make him my *f.* higher *Ps 89:27*
than kings
and the *f.* of the poor shall *Isa 14:30*
feed
I am father to Israel, *Jer 31:9*
Ephraim is my *f.*
all their *f.* (S) *Eze 20:26*
I give my *f.* for my *Mic 6:7*
transgression
as one in bitterness for his *Zec 12:10*
f.
Mary brought forth her *f.* *M't 1:25;*
son *Lu 2:7*
might be *f.* among many *Ro 8:29*
brethren
who is the *f.* of every *Col 1:15*
creature
who is the beginning, the *f.* *Col 1:18*
from the dead
lest he that destroyed *f.* *Heb 11:28*
touch them
ye are come to the church *Heb 12:23*
of the *f.*

FIRSTFRUIT

f. also of thy corn, of thy *De 18:4*
wine
if the *f.* be holy, the lump is *Ro 11:16*
also

FIRSTFRUITS

the f. of thy labours, which thou	Ex 23:16
The first of the f. of thy land thou	Ex 23:19
f. of wheat harvest, and the feast	Ex 34:22
first of the f. of thy land thou shalt	Ex 34:26
the oblation of the f. ye shall offer	Le 2:12
offer a meat offering of thy f.	Le 2:14
offer for the meat offering of thy f.	Le 2:14
of grain (E)	Le 2:14
ye shall bring a sheaf of the f. of	Le 23:10
they are the f. unto the Lord	Le 23:17
wave them with the bread of the f.	Le 23:20
f. of them which they shall offer	Nu 18:12
Also in the day of the f. when ye	Nu 28:26
I have brought the f. of the land	De 26:10
bread, of the f. twenty loaves of	2Ki 4:42
the f. of corn, wine, and oil	2Ch 31:5
And to bring the f. of our ground	Ne 10:35
and the f. of all fruit trees, yearly	Ne 10:35
should bring the f. of our dough	Ne 10:37
for the f. and for the tithes	Ne 12:44
at times appointed, and for the f.	Ne 13:31
with the f. of all thine increase	Pr 3:9
the Lord, and the f. of his increase	Jer 2:3
and the f. of your oblations	Eze 20:40
the first of all the f. of all things	Eze 44:30
nor alienate the f. of the land	Eze 48:14
which have the f. of the Spirit	Ro 8:23
who is the f. of Achaia unto Christ	Ro 16:5
and become the f. of them that slept	1Co 15:20
Christ the f.; afterward they that	1Co 15:23
Stephanas, that it is the f. of Achaia	1Co 16:15
be a kind of f. of his creatures	Jas 1:18
the f. unto God and to the Lamb	Re 14:4

FIRSTLING

every f. that cometh of a beast	Ex 13:12
every f. of an ass thou shalt redeem	Ex 13:13
and every f. among thy cattle	Ex 34:19
the f. of an ass thou shalt redeem	Ex 34:20
Only the f. of the beasts	Le 27:26
which should be the Lord's f. no	Le 27:26
the f. of unclean beasts shalt thou	Nu 18:15
But the f. of a cow, or the f. of a	Nu 18:17
a sheep, or the f. of a goat	Nu 18:17
All the f. males that come of thy	De 15:19
no work with the f. of thy bullock	De 15:19
nor shear the f. of thy sheep	De 15:19
glory is like the f. of his bullock	De 33:17

FIRSTLINGS

also brought of the f. of his flock	Ge 4:4
instead of all the f. among	Nu 3:41
and the f. of your herds	De 12:6
the f. of thy herds or of thy flock	De 12:17
the f. of your herds and of your	De 14:23
f. of our herds and of our flocks	Ne 10:36

FIRSTRIPE

was the time of the f. grapes	Nu 13:20
I saw your fathers as the f.	Ho 9:10
eat: my soul desired the f. fruit	Mic 7:1
be like fig trees with the f. figs	Na 3:12

FISH

let them have dominion over f. of sea	Ge 1:26; 1:28
the f. in the river shall die	Ex 7:18; 7:21
the f. hawk (B)	Le 11:13
we remember f. we did eat in Egypt	Nu 11:5
shall all f. of the sea be gathered together	Nu 11:22
nor likeness of any f. in the water	De 4:18
men of Tyre also, which brought f.	Ne 13:16
thou hast put the f. under his feet	Ps 8:8
turned waters into blood, and slew their f.	Ps 105:29
all that make sluices and ponds for f.	Isa 19:10
their f. stinketh because there is no water	Isa 50:2
I will cause the f. to stick to thy scales	Eze 29:4
I will leave thee, and all the f. of thy rivers	Eze 29:5
and there shall be as a very great multitude of f.	Eze 47:9
their f. shall be as the f. of the great sea	Eze 47:10
Lord prepared a great f. to swallow up Jonah, he was in	Jon 1:17
belly of f. three days	
Lord spake to f. and it vomited out Jonah	Jon 2:10
if he ask a f. will he give him a serpent	M't 7:10
the belly of the great f. (S)	M't 12:40
cast a hook, take up the f. that first cometh	M't 17:27
they gave him a piece of a broiled f.	Lu 24:42
they saw f. laid thereon, and bread	Joh 21:9
bring of the f. which ye have now caught	Joh 21:10
Jesus taketh bread, giveth them, and f.	Joh 21:13

FISH *GATE*

Manasseh built to entering of f. gate	2Ch 33:14
the f. gate did sons of Hassenaah build	Ne 3:3
I after them from above the f. gate	Ne 12:39
the noise of a cry from the f. gate	Zep 1:10

FISH *SPEARS*

canst thou fill his head with f. spears	Job 41:7

FISHERMEN

but the f. were gone out of them	Lu 5:2

FISHERS

The f. also shall mourn, and	Isa 19:8
Behold, I will send for many f.	Jer 16:16
that the f. shall stand upon it	Eze 47:10
a net into the sea: for they were f.	M't 4:18
I will make you f. of men	M't 4:19
a net into the sea: for they were f.	M'k 1:16
I will make you to become f. of men	M'k 1:17

FISHER'S

he girt his f. coat unto him	Joh 21:7

FISHES

shall be upon all the f. of the sea	Ge 9:2
and of creeping things, and of f.	1Ki 4:33
the f. of the sea shall declare unto	Job 12:8
the f. that are taken in an evil net	Ec 9:12
So that the f. of the sea	Eze 38:20
the f. of the sea shall be taken	Ho 4:3
makest men as the f. of the sea	Hab 1:14
and the f. of the sea, and the	Zep 1:3
here but five loaves, and two f.	M't 14:17
took the five loaves, and the two f.	M't 14:19; Lu 9:16
said, Seven, and a few little f.	M't 15:34
took the seven loaves and the f.	M't 15:36
they say, Five, and two f.	M'k 6:38
taken the five loaves and the two f.	M'k 6:41
the two f. divided he among them	M'k 6:41
full of the fragments, and of the f.	M'k 6:43
And they had a few small f.	M'k 8:7
inclosed a great multitude of f.	Lu 5:6
draught of the f. which they had	Lu 5:9
no more but five loaves and two f.	Lu 9:13
barley loaves, and two small f.	Joh 6:9
and likewise of the f. as much as	Joh 6:11
to draw it for the multitude of f.	Joh 21:6
dragging the net with f.	Joh 21:8
drew the net to land full of great f.	Joh 21:11
another of f. and another of birds	1Co 15:39

FISHHOOKS

and your posterity with f.	Am 4:2

FISHING

Peter saith unto them, I go a f.	Joh 21:3

FISHPOOLS

thine eyes like the f. in Heshbon	Ca 7:4

FISH'S

Lord his God out of the f. belly	Jon 2:1

FISSURE

caused a f. in (B)	J'g 15:19

FIST

or with his f. and he die not	Ex 21:18
to smite with the f. of wickedness	Isa 58:4

FIST-FIGHTER

not a f. (B)	1Ti 3:3

FISTS

hath gathered the wind in his f.	Pr 30:4

FIT

fit (S)	Ge 2:18; 2:20; De 3:18; Eze 15:4-5; Ac 26:20; 1Co 15:9; Col 1:12; 2Ti 2:21; Heb 6:7
by the hand of a f. man into	Le 16:21
most f. (S)	2Ki 10:3
soldiers, f. to go out for war	1Ch 7:11
and men of war f. for the battle	1Ch 12:8

Is it *f.* to say to a king,   *Job 34:18*
Thou art
make it *f.* for thyself in the   *Pr 24:27*
field
back, is *f.* for the kingdom of   *Lu 9:62*
God
It is neither *f.* for the land,   *Lu 14:35*
nor yet
it is not *f.* that he should   *Ac 22:22*
live
husbands, as it is *f.* in the   *Col 3:18*
Lord

FITCHES

cast abroad the *f.* and   *Isa 28:25*
scatter the
scatter dill (A)(B)(R)   *Isa 28:25;*
                              28:27
For the *f.* are not threshed   *Isa 28:27*
with a
the *f.* are beaten out with a   *Isa 28:27*
staff
and lentiles, and millet, and *f.*   *Eze 4:9*
and spelt (A)(B)(E)(R)   *Eze 4:9*

FITLY

word *f.* spoken is like apples   *Pr 25:11*
word spoken in the right   *Pr 25:11*
moment (B)
washed with milk, and *f.* set   *Ca 5:12*
all the building *f.* framed   *Eph 2:21*
together
joined (bound, welded)   *Eph 2:21*
together (A)(R)
harmoniously framed   *Eph 2:21*
together (B)
bonded together and grows   *Eph 2:21*
(N)
each separate piece of the   *Eph 2:21*
building properly fitting
into its neighbor (P)
the whole body *f.* joined   *Eph 4:16*
together
joined and firmly knit   *Eph 4:16*
together (A)(R)
harmoniously fitted together   *Eph 4:16*
and closely united by every
contributing (B)
f. framed together (E)   *Eph 4:16*
bonded and knit together by   *Eph 4:16*
(N)(P)

FITS

has bad *f.* (N)   *M't 17:15*

FITTED

with gold *f.* upon the carved   *1Ki 6:35*
work
covered with gold (A)   *1Ki 6:35*
spread over the carved work   *1Ki 6:35*
(B)
overlaid them with gold (R)   *1Ki 6:35*
they shall withal be *f.* in thy   *Pr 22:18*
lips
lips accustomed to confessing   *Pr 22:18*
them (A)
ready upon your lips (B)(R)   *Pr 22:18*
established upon thy lips (E)   *Pr 22:18*
vessels of wrath, *f.* to   *Ro 9:22*
destruction
ripe for destruction (A)   *Ro 9:22*
maturing for destruction (B)   *Ro 9:22*
objects of retribution due for   *Ro 9:22*
destruction (N)
made for destruction (R)   *Ro 9:22*
f. together, closely united   *Eph 4:16*
(B)

FITTETH

he *f.* it with planes, and he   *Isa 44:13*
fashions it with planes   *Isa 44:13*
(A)(R)
shapes it with chisels (B)   *Isa 44:13*
shapeth it with planes (E)   *Isa 44:13*

FITTING

dovetailing and *f.* together   *Ex 26:17*
(A)(R)
fitting (S)   *Ezr 4:14;*
Job 34:31; Pr 11:24; Lu 15:32; Ro 1:27;
2Th 1:3; 2Pe 1:13
praise is *f.* (S)   *Ps 147:1; Ec 5:18*
is not *f.* (S)   *Pr 19:10; 26:1*
toward thee it is *f.* (B)   *Jer 10:7*

it is not *f.* to leave (S)   *Ac 6:2*
things not *f.* (E)   *Ro 1:28*
not *f.* or becoming (A)(R)   *Eph 5:4*
which is not *f.* (S)   *Eph 5:4*
enjoin thee that which is *f.*   *Ph'm 8*
(S)
an high priest *f.* us (S)   *Heb 7:26*

FIVE

battle in vale of Siddim, four   *Ge 14:9*
kings with
wilt thou destroy all for lack   *Ge 18:28*
of *f.*
Benjamin's mess was *f.*   *Ge 43:34*
times so much
f. years in which no earing   *Ge 45:6;*
or harvest   *46:11*
to Benjamin he gave *f.*   *Ge 45:22*
changes of raiment
he presented *f.* of his   *Ge 47:2*
brethren to Pharaoh
the thief shall restore *f.* oxen   *Ex 22:1*
for an ox
other *f.* curtains coupled   *Ex 26:3;*
26:9; 36:10, 16
make *f.* bars for the boards   *Ex 26:26;*
26:27; 36:31-32
f. pillars *f.* sockets of brass   *Ex 26:37;*
36:38
an altar *f.* cubits long, *f.*   *Ex 27:1*
cubits broad
the height of the hangings   *Ex 27:18;*
f. cubits   *38:18*
f. cubits the breadth, and *f.*   *Ex 38:1*
the length
f. of you shall chase an   *Le 26:8*
hundred
if thy estimation be from *f.*   *Le 27:5*
years old
if it be from a month old to   *Le 27:6*
f. years old
even take *f.* shekels apiece   *Nu 3:47;*
18:16
peace offerings, *f.* rams, *f.*   *Nu 7:17;*
goats, *f.* lambs   *7:23, 29, 35, 41, 47, 53*
slew *f.* kings of Midian,   *Nu 31:8*
Balaam son of Beor
f. kings of Amorites went   *Jos 10:5*
against Gibeon
these *f.* kings fled and hid   *Jos 10:16*
themselves
f. kings hid; bring out the   *Jos 10:17;*
f. kings   *10:22*
they brought out these *f.*   *Jos 10:23*
kings unto him
he slew them and hanged   *Jos 10:26*
them on *f.* trees
f. lords of the Philistines   *Jos 13:3;*
J'g 3:3
children of Dan sent *f.* men   *J'g 18:2*
from coasts
f. golden emerods, *f.* golden   *1Sa 6:4*
mice
when *f.* lords of the   *1Sa 6:16*
Philistines had seen it
David chose him *f.* smooth   *1Sa 17:40*
stones
give me *f.* loaves of bread in   *1Sa 21:3*
my hand
she brought *f.* sheep, *f.*   *1Sa 25:18*
measures of corn
Abigail rode on an ass with   *1Sa 25:42*
f. damsels
Mephibosheth was *f.* years old   *2Sa 4:4*
when tidings of Saul's death
but David took the *f.* sons   *2Sa 21:8*
of Michal
f. bases on right, *f.* on left   *1Ki 7:39*
side
candlesticks *f.* on the   *1Ki 7:49;*
right side, and *f.* on the left   *2Ch 4:7*
part of cab of dove's dung   *2Ki 6:25*
sold *f.* pieces
let some take *f.* of the   *2Ki 7:13*
horses that remain
shouldest have smitten *f.* or   *2Ki 13:19*
six times
f. men that were in the   *2Ki 25:19*
king's presence
the sons of Zera, *f.* of them   *1Ch 2:6*
in all
Benaiah slew an Egyptian,   *1Ch 11:23*
f. cubits high
four or *f.* in utmost fruitful   *Isa 17:6*
branches
f. cities in Egypt speak   *Isa 19:18*
language of Canaan
at the rebuke of *f.* shall ye   *Isa 30:17*
flee

f. loaves   *M't 14:17; M'k 6:38; Lu 9:13*
f. loaves of *f.* thousand   *M't 16:9;*
M'k 8:19
f. of them were wise, and *f.*   *M't 25:2*
were foolish
and unto one he gave *f.*   *M't 25:15;*
talents   *25:16*
are not *f.* sparrows sold for   *Lu 12:6*
two farthings
there shall be *f.* in one   *Lu 12:52*
house divided
another said, I have bought *f.*   *Lu 14:19*
yoke of oxen
send him to my father's, I   *Lu 16:28*
have *f.* brethren
Lord, thy pound hath gained   *Lu 19:18*
f. pounds
be thou also over *f.* cities   *Lu 19:19*
for thou hast had *f.*   *Joh 4:18*
husbands
there is a pool Bethesda   *Joh 5:2*
having *f.* porches
there is a lad which hath *f.*   *Joh 6:9*
barley loaves
with the fragments of the *f.*   *Joh 6:13*
barley loaves
I had rather speak *f.* words   *1Co 14:19*
with understanding
f. times received I forty   *2Co 11:24*
stripes
there are seven kings, *f.* are   *Re 17:10*
fallen

FIXED

f. number of bricks   *Ex 5:8;*
(A)(B)(E)(R)   *5:18*
My heart is *f.* O God   *Ps 57:7; 108:1*
my heart is confident (B)   *Ps 57:7*
my heart is stedfast (R)   *Ps 57:7*
his heart is *f.* trusting in the   *Ps 112:7*
Lord
his heart will remain firm   *Ps 112:7*
(B)(R)
us and you there is a great   *Lu 16:26*
gulf *f.*

FLAG

can the *f.* grow without   *Job 8:11*
water
reed grass grow without   *Job 8:11*
water (B)(R)
must I set the *f.* (A)   *Jer 4:21*
never *f.* in zeal (R)   *Ro 12:11*

FLAGON

piece of flesh, and a *f.* of   *2Sa 6:19;*
wine   *1Ch 16:3*

FLAGONS

its *f.* with which to pour (S)   *Ex 37:16*
Stay me with *f.* comfort me   *Ca 2:5*
with apples
sustain me with raisins   *Ca 2:5*
(A)(E)(R)
sustain me with dainties (B)   *Ca 2:5*
even to all the vessels of *f.*   *Isa 22:24*
all flasks and bulging   *Isa 22:24*
bottles (A)
from bowls to pitchers (B)   *Isa 22:24*
to other gods, and love *f.*   *Ho 3:1*
of wine
love raisin cakes (A)(B)(E)(R)   *Ho 3:1*

FLAGRANT

committed a *f.* crime (B)   *De 22:21*

FLAGS

laid it in the *f.* by the river's   *Ex 2:3*
brink
set it among the rushes (A)   *Ex 2:3*
set it among the reeds (B)(R)   *Ex 2:3;*
2:5
when she saw the ark among   *Ex 2:5*
the *f.*
the reeds and *f.* shall wither   *Isa 19:6*
reeds and rushes shall wither   *Isa 19:6*
(A)(B)(R)

FLAKES

f. of his flesh are joined   *Job 41:23*
together
folds of his flesh cleave   *Job 41:23*
(A)(B)(R)

FLAME

the Lord appeared unto him in   *Ex 3:2* a *f.*
a *f.* from the city of Sihon   *Nu 21:28*
when the *f.* went up toward   *J'g 13:20* heaven
of the Lord ascended in the   *J'g 13:20* *f.* of
make a great *f.* with smoke   *J'g 20:38* rise
But when the *f.* began to   *J'g 20:40* rise
the *f.* of the city ascended   *J'g 20:40* up
the *f.* shall dry up his   *Job 15:30* branches
the *f.* of his fire (A)(R)   *Job 18:5*
and a *f.* goeth out of his   *Job 41:21* mouth
as the *f.* setteth the   *Ps 83:14* mountains
the *f.* burned up the wicked   *Ps 106:18*
which hath a most vehement *f.*   *Ca 8:6*
and the *f.* consumeth the   *Isa 5:24* chaff, so
and his Holy One for a *f.*   *Isa 10:17*
and the *f.* of devouring fire   *Isa 29:6*
and with the *f.* of a   *Isa 30:30* devouring fire
neither shall the *f.* kindle   *Isa 43:2* upon
themselves from the power   *Isa 47:14* of the *f.*
a *f.* from the midst of Sihon   *Jer 48:45*
flaming *f.* shall not be   *Eze 20:47* quenched
the *f.* of the fire slew those   *Da 3:22* men
his throne was like the fiery *f.*   *Da 7:9*
and given to the burning *f.*   *Da 7:11*
shall fall by the sword, and   *Da 11:33* by *f.*
the *f.* hath burned all the   *Joe 1:19* trees
behind them a *f.* burneth   *Joe 2:3*
like the noise of a *f.* of fire   *Joe 2:5*
and the house of Joseph a *f.*   *Ob 18*
or I am tormented in this *f.*   *Lu 16:24*
in a *f.* of fire in a bush   *Ac 7:30*
and his ministers a *f.* of fire   *Heb 1:7*
furious *f.* of fire (P)   *Heb 11:34*
and his eyes were as a *f.* of   *Re 1:14* fire
hath his eyes like unto a *f.* of   *Re 2:18* fire
His eyes were as a *f.* of fire   *Re 19:12*

FLAMES

f. of fire at right hand   *De 33:2* (B)(R)
voice of the Lord divideth the   *Ps 29:7* *f.*
their faces shall be as *f.*   *Isa 13:8*
and his rebuke with *f.* of   *Isa 66:15* fire

FLAMING

f. sword which turned every   *Ge 3:24* way
smoking furnace, *f.* torch   *Ge 15:17* (E)(R)
a *f.* fire (A)   *De 33:2*
and his ministers a *f.* fire   *Ps 104:4*
and *f.* fire in their land   *Ps 105:32*
the shining of a *f.* fire by   *Isa 4:5* night
burned against Jacob like a *f.*   *La 2:3* fire
the *f.* flame shall not be   *Eze 20:47* quenched
the morning it burneth as a *f.*   *Ho 7:6* fire
shall be with *f.* torches in the   *Na 2:3* day
f. missiles of wicked one   *Eph 6:16* (A)
In *f.* fire taking vengeance on   *2Th 1:8*

FLANKS

is on them, which is by the *f.*   *Le 3:4*
on them at the loins   *Le 3:4* (A)(B)(E)(R)
upon them which is by the *f.*   *Le 3:10; 3:15; 4:9; 7:4*
maketh collops of fat on   *Job 15:27* his *f.*

layers of fat on loins   *Job 15:27* (A)(B)(E)(R)

FLARED

Lord's anger *f.* up (B)   *Nu 11:33*

FLASH

your eyes *f.* (A)(B)(E)(R)   *Job 15:12*
the appearance of a *f.* of   *Eze 1:14* lightning
chariots *f.* with steel (E)(R)   *Na 2:3*

FLASK

took a *f.* of oil (B)   *1Sa 10:1*
take this *f.* of oil (S)   *2Ki 9:1; 9:3*
a potter's earthen *f.* (R)(S)   *Jer 19:1*

FLASKS

f. and bulging bottles (A)   *Isa 22:24*
took *f.* of oil (B)(N)(P)(R)   *M't 25:4*

FLAT

or he that hath a *f.* nose   *Le 21:18*
bowed down his head, and   *Nu 22:31* fell *f.*
wall of the city shall fall   *Jos 6:5* down *f.*
that the wall fell down *f.* so   *Jos 6:20* that
the tent lay *f.* (S)   *J'g 7:13*

FLATTER

they *f.* with their tongue   *Ps 5:9*
Nevertheless they did *f.* him   *Ps 78:36*

FLATTERETH

For he *f.* himself in his own   *Ps 36:2* eyes
stranger which *f.* with her   *Pr 2:16; 7:5* words
meddle not with him, that *f.*   *Pr 20:19*
do not associate with him   *Pr 20:19* (B)(E)
that opens wide his lips (B)(E)
one who speaks foolishly   *Pr 20:19* (R)
than he that *f.* with the   *Pr 28:23* tongue
A man that *f.* his neighbour   *Pr 29:5*

FLATTERIES

and obtain the kingdom by   *Da 11:21* *f.*
acquire royalty by devious   *Da 11:21* intrigues (B)
covenant shall he corrupt by   *Da 11:32* *f.*
many shall cleave to them   *Da 11:34* with *f.*

FLATTERING

let me give *f.* titles unto   *Job 32:21* man
I know not to give *f.* titles   *Job 32:22*
f. lips and with a double   *Ps 12:2* heart
The Lord shall cut off all *f.*   *Ps 12:3* lips
the *f.* of her lips she forced   *Pr 7:21* him
and a *f.* mouth worketh ruin   *Pr 26:28*
any vain vision nor *f.*   *Eze 12:24* divination
by fair and *f.* words (R)   *Ro 16:18*
used we *f.* words, as ye know   *1Th 2:5*

FLATTERY

that speaketh *f.* to his   *Job 17:5* friends
from the *f.* of the tongue of a   *Pr 6:24*
with her *f.* (B)   *Pr 7:21*
ingratiating words of *f.* (B)   *Ro 16:18*

FLAUNTED

f. herself (P)   *Re 18:7*

FLAW

there is no *f.* in you (A)(R)   *Ca 4:7*

FLAWLESS

it must be *f.* (B)   *Le 22:21*
f. yearlings (B)   *Nu 28:3; Nu 28:9, 11; 29:17*
f. and without blame (N)   *Ph'p 1:10*
unsullied, *f.*, irreproachable   *1Ti 6:14* (A)(B)
f. expression of nature (P)   *Heb 1:3*
had been *f.* (B)   *Heb 8:7*
offered himself a *f.* sacrifice   *Heb 9:14* (B)
looks into the *f.* law (A)   *Jas 1:25*
f. and spotless (B)   *1Pe 1:19*

FLAX

the *f.* and the barley was   *Ex 9:31* smitten
in the ear, and the *f.* was   *Ex 9:31* bolled
and hid them with the stalks   *Jos 2:6* of *f.*
were upon his arms became   *J'g 15:14* of *f.*
seeketh wool, and *f.* and   *Pr 31:13* worketh
Moreover they that work in   *Isa 19:9* fine *f.*
smoking *f.* shall he not   *Isa 42:3;* quench   *M't 12:20*
with a line of *f.* in his hand   *Eze 40:3*
my wool and my *f.*, mine oil   *Ho 2:5*
wool and my *f.* given to   *Ho 2:9* cover her

FLAY

And he shall *f.* the burnt   *Le 1:6* offering
could not *f.* all the burnt   *2Ch 29:34* offerings
and *f.* their skin from off   *Mic 3:3* them
strip skin from off them   *Mic 3:3* (A)(B)

FLAYED

hands, and the Levites *f.*   *2Ch 35:11* them
Levites did the skinning   *2Ch 35:11* (A)(B)

FLEA

after a dead dog, after a *f.*   *2Sa 24:14*
of Israel is come out to   *1Sa 26:20* seek a *f.*

FLED

the kings of Sodom and   *Ge 14:10* Gomorrah *f.*
Hagar *f.*; Jacob *f.*   *Ge 16:6; 31:22; Ho 12:12*
Moses *f.* from Pharaoh   *Ex 2:15; 4:3; Ac 7:29*
it was told king of Egypt   *Ex 14:5* that the people *f.*
and the Egyptians *f.* against   *Ex 14:27* the sea
Israel round about *f.* at cry   *Nu 16:34* of them
Israel *f.* by the way of the   *Jos 8:15* wilderness
these five kings *f.* and hid   *Jos 10:16* themselves
Adoni-bezek *f.*; Sisera *f.*   *J'g 1:6; 4:15*
all the host ran and cried,   *J'g 7:21;* and *f.*   *7:22*
Zalmunna *f.*; Jotham *f.*   *J'g 8:12; 9:21*
to the tower *f.* all the men   *J'g 9:51* and women
Jephthah *f.*; the Benjamites   *J'g 11:2;* *f.*   *11:45, 47*
I *f.* to-day out of the army   *1Sa 4:16*
when they heard that the   *1Sa 14:22* Philistines *f.*
the men of Israel *f.* from   *1Sa 17:24* Goliath
David *f.* and escaped   *1Sa 19:10; 19:12, 18; 20:1; 21:10*
Abiathar escaped and *f.*   *1Sa 22:20;* after David   *23:6*
save four hundred which   *1Sa 30:17* rode and *f.*
Israel *f.* from the Philistines   *1Sa 31:1; 31:7; 2Sa 19:8*

Beerothites *f.* to Gittaim and   *2Sa 4:3*
sojourned

his nurse *f.*; the Syrians *f.*   *2Sa 4:4;*
     10:14, 18

Absalom and the king's   *2Sa 13:29;*
sons *f.*   *34:37-38*

all Israel *f.* every one to his   *2Sa 18:17*
tent

for so they came to me when   *1Ki 2:7*
I *f.*

Joab *f.* to tabernacle;   *1Ki 2:28;*
Hadad *f.*   *11:17*

Rezon *f.*; Jeroboam *f.*   *1Ki 11:23;*
     11:40

the Syrians *f.*   *1Ki 20:20;*
   2Ki 7:7; 1Ch 19:18

and the people *f.* to their   *2Ki 8:21*
tents

prophet *f.*; Joram *f.*   *2Ki 9:10; 9:23*

all the men of war *f.* by   *2Ki 25:4;*
night   *Jer 52:7*

the men of Israel *f.*   *1Ch 10:1;*
   11:13; 2Ch 13:16

Lord smote Ethiopians and   *2Ch 14:12*
they *f.*

Levites *f.* every one to his   *Ne 13:10*
field

they that did see me *f.* from   *Ps 31:11*
me

sea saw it and *f.* Jordan was   *Ps 114:3*
driven

were we *f.* (S)   *Isa 20:6*

they prevented with bread   *Isa 21:14*
him that *f.*

all thy rulers are *f.* together,   *Isa 22:3*
they are

at the noise of the tumult the   *Isa 33:3*
people *f.*

all the birds of the heavens   *Jer 4:25*
were *f.*

the fowl and beast are *f.* they   *Jer 9:10*
are gone

Urijah *f.*; Egyptians *f.*   *Jer 26:21; 46:5*

also her hired men are *f.*   *Jer 46:21*
away together

therefore I *f.* before to   *Jon 4:2*
Tarshish

flee as ye *f.* before the   *Zec 14:5*
earthquake

they that kept them *f.* and   *M't 8:33*
went away

disciples forsook him and   *M't 26:56;*
f.   *M'k 14:50*

they went out and *f.* from   *M'k 16:8*
the sepulchre

supposing the prisoners had   *Ac 16:27*
been *f.*

f. for refuge to lay hold on   *Heb 6:18*
the hope

the woman *f.*; every island *f.*   *Re 12:6;*
away   *16:20*

from whose face earth and   *Re 20:11*
heaven *f.* away

HE FLED

in that he told him not that   *Ge 31:20*
he *f.*

so he *f.*; he *f.* from his   *Ge 31:21;*
brother   *35:7*

he left his garment and *f.*   *Ge 39:12;*
   39:13, 15, 18

house, to city from   *Jos 20:6;*
whence he *f.*   *Nu 35:25*

Abimelech chased Gaal, and   *J'g 9:40*
he *f.*

because they knew when he   *1Sa 22:17*
f.

Ahaziah fled, and he *f.* to   *2Ki 9:27*
Megiddo

and he *f.* to Lachish   *2Ki 14:19;*
     2Ch 25:27

and he *f.* from the presence   *Jon 1:10*
of the Lord

he left the linen cloth, and   *M'k 14:52*
f. naked

IS FLED

take no satisfaction for him   *Nu 35:32*
that *is f.*

Israel *is f.* before the   *1Sa 4:17*
Philistines

David *is f.* out of the land for   *2Sa 19:9*
Absalom

Ramah is afraid, Gibeah of   *Isa 10:29*
Saul *is f.*

THEY FLED

they that remained *f.* to the   *Ge 14:10*
mountains

they *f.* from before the men   *Jos 7:4*
of Ai

as *they f.* the Lord cast   *Jos 10:11*
down great stones

Israel was smitten, and they   *1Sa 4:10;*
f. every man to his tent   *2Ki 14:12*

when saw their champion   *1Sa 17:51*
was dead they *f.*

David slew Philistines, and   *1Sa 19:8*
they *f.* from him

Joab drew nigh, they *f.*   *2Sa 10:13;*
     1Ch 19:14

smote Moabites, they *f.*   *2Ki 3:24*
before them

when all Israel saw that   *1Ch 10:7*
they *f.*

at thy rebuke *they f.* they   *Ps 104:7*
hasted away

for *they f.* from the swords,   *Isa 21:15*
and bent bow

then *they f.* and went forth   *Jer 39:4*
of the city

when *they f.* away, and   *La 4:15*
wandered

so that *they f.* to save   *Da 10:7*
themselves

woe unto them, for *they* have   *Ho 7:13*
f. from me

when they saw what was   *Lu 8:34*
done, *they f.*

so that *they f.* out of that   *Ac 19:16*
house wounded

FLEDDEST

when thou *f.* from the face   *Ge 35:1*
of Esau

what ailed thee, O sea, that   *Ps 114:5*
thou *f.*

FLEE

I *f.* from the face of my   *Ge 16:8*
mistress Sarai

behold this city is near to *f.*   *Ge 19:20*
unto

arise, *f.* to Laban my   *Ge 27:43*
brother to Haran

let us *f.* from the face of   *Ex 14:25*
Israel

appoint a place whither he   *Ex 21:13*
shall *f.*

ye shall *f.* when none   *Le 26:17;*
pursueth   *26:36*

that hate thee *f.* before thee   *Nu 10:35;*
     Ps 68:1

therefore now *f.* thou to thy   *Nu 24:11*
place

six cities, that the man   *Nu 35:6;*
slayer may *f.* thither   *35:11, 15;*
   De 4:42; 19:3-5; Jos 20:3-4, 9

and *f.* before thee seven   *De 28:7*
ways

as at first we will *f.* before   *Jos 8:5;*
them   *8:6*

had no power to *f.* this way   *Jos 8:20*
or that way

let us *f.* and draw them   *J'g 20:32*
from the city

as his nurse made haste to *f.*   *2Sa 4:4*
she fell

f. else we shall not escape   *2Sa 15:14*
from Absalom

as men steal away when they   *2Sa 19:3*
f. in battle

wilt thou *f.* three months   *2Sa 24:13*
before enemies

Rehoboam made speed and   *1Ki 12:18;*
f. to Jerusalem   *2Ch 10:18*

then open the door, and *f.*   *2Ki 9:3*
tarry not

I said, Should such a man as   *Ne 6:11*
I *f.*

he shall *f.* from the iron   *Job 20:24*
weapon

he would fain *f.* out of his   *Job 27:22*
hand

they abhor me, they *f.* far   *Job 30:10*
from me

the arrow cannot make him   *Job 41:28*
f.

how say ye, *F.* as bird to your   *Ps 11:1*
mountain

kings of armies *f.* apace, she   *Ps 68:12*
that tarried

whither shall I *f.* from thy   *Ps 139:7*
presence

deliver me, O Lord, I *f.* to   *Ps 143:9*
thee to hide me

the wicked *f.* when no man   *Pr 28:1*
pursueth

he shall *f.* to the pit, let no   *Pr 28:17*
man stay him

to whom will ye *f.* for help   *Isa 10:3*

and *f.* every one into his   *Isa 13:14*
own land

his fugitives shall *f.* unto   *Isa 15:5*
Zoar

they shall *f.* far off, and   *Isa 17:13*
shall be chased

such our expectation whither   *Isa 20:6*
we *f.* for help

but ye said No, for we will   *Isa 30:16*
f. on horses

at the rebuke of five shall   *Isa 30:17*
ye *f.*

go from Babylon, *f.* ye from   *Isa 48:20*
the Chaldeans

the city shall *f.* for noise of   *Jer 4:29*
horsemen

gather yourselves to *f.* out of   *Jer 6:1*
Jerusalem

the shepherds shall have no   *Jer 25:35*
way to *f.*

f. save your lives, and be like   *Jer 48:6*
the heath

give wings to Moab, that it   *Jer 48:9*
may *f.* and get away

Edom shall *f.*; Damascus   *Jer 49:8;*
turned to *f.*   *49:24*

f. dwell deep, O ye   *Jer 49:30*
inhabitants of Hazor

F. out of the midst of   *Jer 50:8*
Babylon (S)

they shall *f.* every one to his   *Jer 50:16*
own land

voice of them that *f.* and   *Jer 50:28*
escape from Babylon

f. out of the midst of   *Jer 51:6;*
Babylon   *Zec 2:6*

as if a man did *f.* from a   *Am 5:19*
lion, and bear

Jonah rose up to *f.* to   *Jon 1:3*
Tarshish

all they that look on, shall *f.*   *Na 3:7*
from thee

arise, take the young child   *M't 2:13*
and *f.*

hath warned you *f.* from   *M't 3:7;*
wrath   *Lu 3:7*

when persecute you in city   *M't 10:23*
f. to another

let them which be in Judea   *M't 24:16;*
f. to the mountains   *M'k 13:14;*
     Lu 21:21

a stranger will not follow,   *Joh 10:5*
but *f.* from

as the shipmen were about   *Ac 27:30*
to *f.*

f. fornication, *f.* from   *1Co 6:18;*
idolatry   *10:14*

but thou, O man of God *f.*   *1Ti 6:11*
these things

f. also youthful lusts, follow   *2Ti 2:22*
faith

resist the devil, and he will *f.*   *Jas 4:7*
from you

in those days death shall *f.*   *Re 9:6*
from them

that the woman might *f.*   *Re 12:14*
into wilderness

FLEE *AWAY*

wherefore didst thou *f. away*   *Ge 31:27*
secretly

if we *f. away* they will not   *2Sa 18:3*
care for us

my days *f. away*, they see no   *Job 9:25*
good

f. away as a dream, and   *Job 20:8*
shall not be found

all that see them, shall *f.*   *Ps 64:8*
away

till day break, and shadows   *Ca 2:17;*
f. away   *4:6*

sorrow and sighing shall *f.*   *Isa 35:10;*
away   *51:11*

let not the swift *f. away*, nor   *Jer 46:6*
escape

he that is courageous shall *f.*   *Am 2:16*
away

O thou seer, go *f. away* into   *Am 7:12*
the land of Judah

he that fleeth of them, shall *Am 9:1*
not *f. away*

Ninevah shall *f. away*, they *Na 2:8*
shall cry

as great grasshoppers in *Na 3:17*
hedges they *f. away*

FLEECE

the first of the *f.* of thy sheep *De 18:4*

I will put a *f.* of wool in the *J'g 6:37*
floor

and if the dew be on the *f.* *J'g 6:37*
only

thrust the *f.* together, and *J'g 6:38*
wringed

and wringed the dew out of *J'g 6:38*
the *f.*

I pray thee, but this once *J'g 6:39*
with the *f.*

let it now be dry only upon *J'g 6:39*
the *f.*

for it was dry upon the *f.* *J'g 6:40*
only

if he were not warmed with *Job 31:20*
the *f.*

FLEEING

they shall flee, as *f.* from a *Le 26:36*
sword

and that *f.* unto one of these *De 4:42*
cities

f. into the wilderness in *Job 30:3*
former

FLEET

built a *f.* (A)(B)(R) *1Ki 9:26;*
9:27; 10:11, 22

FLEETH

and *f.* into one of these *De 19:11*
cities

he *f.* also as a shadow, and *Job 14:2*

who *f.* from the noise of the *Isa 24:18*
fear

ask him that *f.* and her that *Jer 48:19*

he that *f.* from the fear *Jer 48:44*
shall fall

he that *f.* of them shall not *Am 9:1*
flee

cankerworm spoileth, and *f.* *Na 3:16*
away

leaveth the sheep, and *f.* *Joh 10:12*

The hireling *f.* because he *Joh 10:13*
is an

FLEETING

my days are *f.* (B) *Job 7:16*

FLESH

God closed up the *f.* instead *Ge 2:21*
thereof

shall cleave to his wife, and *Ge 2:24*
be one *f.*

shall not strive with man, for *Ge 6:3*
that he is *f.*

ye shall circumcise the *f.* of *Ge 17:11*
your foreskin

whose *f.* is not circumcised *Ge 17:14*
shall be cut off

Abraham circumcised the *f.* *Ge 17:23*
of their foreskin

for he is our brother and *Ge 37:27*
our *f.*

his hand was turned again as *Ex 4:7*
his other *f.*

burn the *f.* *Ex 29:14;*
Le 9:11; 16:27; Nu 19:5

upon man's *f.* shall it not be *Ex 30:32*
poured

what shall touch *f.* thereof *Le 6:27*
shall be holy

as for *f.* all that are clean *Le 7:19*
shall eat thereof

boil the *f.* at the door of the *Le 8:31*
tabernacle

if there be quick raw *f.* *Le 13:10;*
13:14-16, 24

if in the skin of their *f.* *Le 13:38;*
13:39

have bright spots

that toucheth the *f.* of him *Le 15:7*
that hath an issue

if her issue in her *f.* be *Le 15:19*
blood, she is put apart

nor shall make any cuttings *Le 21:5*
in their *f.*

while the *f.* was between *Nu 11:33*
their teeth

as dead, of whom the *f.* is *Nu 12:12*
half consumed

and the *f.* of them shall be *Nu 18:18*
thine

and my sword shall devour *De 32:42*
f.

take the *f.* and the *J'g 6:20*
unleavened cakes

there rose up fire out of rock, *J'g 6:21*
and consumed the *f.*

servant came, while *f.* was *1Sa 2:13*
in seething

he said, Give *f.* to roast for *1Sa 2:15*
the priest

David dealt to each *f.* *2Sa 6:19;*
1Ch 16:3

ravens brought bread and *f.* *1Ki 17:6*
in the morning, and bread
and *f.* in the evening

boiled their *f.* with the *1Ki 19:21*
instruments of oxen

and the *f.* of the child waxed *2Ki 4:34*
warm

with him is an arm of *f.* *2Ch 32:8*
with us is God

yet our *f.* is as the *f.* of our *Ne 5:5*
brethren

hast thou eyes of *f.*? or *Job 10:4*
seest as man

thou hast clothed me with *Job 10:11*
skin and *f.*

I will not fear what *f.* can do *Ps 56:4*

can he provide *f.* for his *Ps 78:20*
people

he rained *f.* also upon them *Ps 78:27*
as dust

for he remembered that they *Ps 78:39*
were but *f.*

f. of thy saints given to beasts *Ps 79:2*
of earth

healing to your *f.* (R) *Pr 3:8*

my sayings are health to their *Pr 4:22*
f.

be not among riotous eaters *Pr 23:20*
of *f.*

and their horses are *f.* and *Isa 31:3*
not spirit

I will feed them with their *Isa 49:26*
own *f.*

and the holy *f.* is passed *Jer 11:15*
from thee

spoilers are come, no *f.* shall *Jer 12:12*
have peace

cursed be the man that *Jer 17:5*
maketh *f.* his arm

nor came abominable *f.* into *Eze 4:14*
my mouth

this city is the caldron, and *Eze 11:3*
we be the *f.*

your slain in midst of it, *Eze 11:7*
they are the *f.*

nor shall ye be the *f.* in the *Eze 11:11*
midst thereof

and I will give them a *Eze 11:19;*
heart of *f.* *36:26*

great of *f.* and hast *Eze 16:26*
increased whoredoms

paramours, whose *f.* is as *f.* *Eze 23:20*
of asses

heap on wood, consume the *Eze 24:10*
f. spice it well

and I will bring up *f.* upon *Eze 37:6;*
you *37:8*

gods, whose dwelling is not *Da 2:11*
with *f.*

they said to it, Arise, devour *Da 7:5*
much *f.*

neither came *f.* nor wine in *Da 10:3*
my mouth

they sacrifice *f.* for sacrifices *Ho 8:13*
of offerings

who pluck the *f.* from off *Mic 3:2*
their bones

dens with torn *f.* (R)(S) *Na 2:12*

their *f.* shall be poured out *Zep 1:17*
as dung

if one bear holy *f.* in skirt *Hag 2:12*
of his garment

their *f.* shall consume away *Zec 14:12*

f. and blood hath not *M't 16:17*
revealed it

cleave to his wife, and be *M't 19:5;*
one *f.* *19:6; M'k 10:8; 1Co 6:16;*
Eph 5:31

there should no *f.* be saved *M't 24:22;*
M'k 13:20

no human being would *M't 24:22*
endure, survive (A)(P)(R)

not a mortal could survive *M't 24:22*
(B)

no living thing could *M't 24:22*
survive (N)

spirit willing, but *f.* is *M't 26:41;*
weak *M'k 14:38*

spirit hath not *f.* and bones, *Lu 24:39*
as ye see me

the Word was made *f.* and *Joh 1:14*
dwelt

the Spirit quickeneth, the *f.* *Joh 6:63*
profiteth nothing

the seed of David according *Ac 2:30;*
to *f.* *Ro 1:3*

there shall no *f.* be justified *Ro 3:20*
in his sight

no person will be justified *Ro 3:20*
(A)

no human being be *Ro 3:20*
(B)(N)(R)

No man can justify himself *Ro 3:20*
(P)

Abraham as pertaining to the *Ro 4:1*
f. found

our forefather humanly *Ro 4:1*
speaking (A)

our human ancestor *Ro 4:1*
(B)(N)(P)

but with the *f.* I serve the *Ro 7:25*
law of sin

human nature under sin's *Ro 7:25*
control (B)

unspiritual nature, a slave to *Ro 7:25*
(N)

in my own nature I am *Ro 7:25*
bound fast (P)

law was weak through *f.* God *Ro 8:3*
sent Son in likeness of sinful *f.*

for my brethren and kinsmen *Ro 9:3*
according to *f.*

of whom as concerning the *f.* *Ro 9:5*
Christ came

from them, in natural descent *Ro 9:5*
(A)(N)

from them in human lineage *Ro 9:5*
sprang Christ (B)

as far as human descent goes *Ro 9:5*
(P)

make not provision for the *Ro 13:14*
f. to fulfil

satisfying bodily appetites *Ro 13:14*
(N)

that no *f.* should glory in *1Co 1:29*
his presence

no mortal man should boast *1Co 1:29*
(A)

that all humanity may be *1Co 1:29*
boastless (B)

there is no place for human *1Co 1:29*
pride (N)

that no man may boast (P) *1Co 1:29*

no human being may *1Co 1:29*
boast (R)

there is one *f.* of men, *1Co 15:39*
another of beasts

f. and blood cannot inherit *1Co 15:50*
the kingdom of God

do I purpose according to the *2Co 1:7*
f.

that life of Jesus be made *2Co 4:11*
manifest in our *f.*

our *f.* had no rest, but we *2Co 7:5*
were troubled

as if we walked according to *2Co 10:2*
the *f.*

I conferred not with *f.* and *Ga 1:16*
blood

by works of the law shall no *Ga 2:16*
f. be justified

are ye now made perfect by *Ga 3:3*
the *f.*

use not liberty for an *Ga 5:13*
occasion to the *f.*

f. lusteth against the Spirit, *Ga 5:17*
Spirit against *f.*

they that are Christ's have *Ga 5:24*
crucified the *f.*

we all had our conversation *Eph 2:3*
in lusts of our *f.*

your masters according to *Eph 6:5;*
the *f.* *Col 3:22*

for we wrestle not against *f.* *Eph 6:12*
and blood

children are partakers of *f.*   *Heb 2:14*
and blood
we had fathers of our *f.*   *Heb 12:9*
who corrected us
abstain from passions of the   *1Pe 2:11*
f. (R)
going after strange *f.* are in   *Jude 7*
example
gave themselves over to   *Jude 7*
impurity, indulged in unnatural
vice, sexual perversity (A)
abandoned themselves to   *Jude 7*
sexual immorality, bent on
perverted sensuality (B)
followed unnatural lusts (N)   *Jude 7*
up to sexual immorality and   *Jude 7*
perversion (P)
acted immorally, indulged in   *Jude 7*
unnatural lust (R)
likewise these filthy dreamers   *Jude 8*
defile the *f.*
corrupt the body (A)   *Jude 8*
besmut the body (B)   *Jude 8*
defile the body (N)   *Jude 8*
defiling bodies by filthy   *Jude 8*
fantasies (P)
hating even the garment   *Jude 23*
spotted by the *f.*
clothing polluted by sensuality   *Jude 23*
(B)(N)
garments their deeds defiled   *Jude 23*
(P)
may eat *f.* of captains *f.* of   *Re 19:18*
mighty men
and all the fowls were filled   *Re 19:21*
with their *f.*

AFTER THE FLESH

ye judge *after the f.* I judge   *Joh 8:15*
no man
You judge by human   *Joh 8:15*
standards (B)(P)
You judge by worldly   *Joh 8:15*
standards (N)
are in Christ, who walk not   *Ro 8:1;*
after the f.   *8:4*
they that are *after the f.* mind   *Ro 8:5*
things of the flesh
not debtors to the flesh to   *Ro 8:12*
live *after the f.*
not to our earthly nature (B)   *Ro 8:12*
lower nature has no claim on   *Ro 8:12*
us (N)
no reason to feel grateful to   *Ro 8:12*
sensual nature, live on level
of instincts (P)
for if ye live *after the f.* ye   *Ro 8:13*
shall die
not many wise men *after the*   *1Co 1:26*
f. are called
behold Israel *after the f.*   *1Co 10:18*
know no man *after the f.*   *2Co 5:16*
though we have known Christ
after f. yet know him no more
tho' walk in flesh, we do not   *2Co 10:3*
war *after the f.*
seeing that many glory   *2Co 11:18*
after the f. I also
boast of worldly things   *2Co 11:18*
(A)(B)(R)
brag of earthly distinctions   *2Co 11:18*
(N)
Ishmael was born *after the*   *Ga 4:23;*
f.   *4:22, 29*
chiefly them that walk *after*   *2Pe 2:10*
the f.
who yield to the sensual (B)   *2Pe 2:10*
who follow their abominable   *2Pe 2:10*
lusts (N)
indulged all foulness of   *2Pe 2:10*
lower nature (P)
engage lusts of defiling   *2Pe 2:10*
passion (R)

ALL FLESH

for *all f.* had corrupted his   *Ge 6:12*
way on earth
God said, The end of *all f.* is   *Ge 6:13*
come before me
of *all f.* two of every sort   *Ge 6:19;*
bring into the ark to keep alive   *7:15*
all f. died that moved upon   *Ge 7:21*
the earth
bring forth of *all f.* both of   *Ge 8:17*
fowl and cattle
nor shall *all f.* be cut off any   *Ge 9:11;*
more   *9:15*

covenant between me and *all*   *Ge 9:16;*
f. on earth   *9:17*
for the life of *all f.* is the   *Le 17:14*
blood
let them shave *all* their *f.* and   *Nu 8:7*
wash clothes
the God of the spirits of *all*   *Nu 16:22;*
f.   *27:16*
every thing that openeth the   *Nu 18:15*
matrix of *all f.*
who of *all f.* heard the word   *De 5:26*
of God
all f. shall perish together,   *Job 34:15*
man turn to dust
thou hearest prayer, to thee   *Ps 65:2*
shall *all f.* come
who giveth food to *all f.* his   *Ps 136:25*
mercy for ever
let *all f.* bless his holy name   *Ps 145:21*
for ever
and *all f.* shall see it together   *Isa 40:5*
all f. is grass, as flower of   *Isa 40:6;*
the field   *1Pe 1:24*
all f. shall know I am thy   *Isa 49:26;*
Saviour   *Eze 21:5*
for by fire will the Lord   *Isa 66:16*
plead with *all f.*
all f. shall come to worship   *Isa 66:23*
before me, saith Lord
they shall be an abhorring   *Isa 66:24*
to *all f.*
he will plead with *all f.*   *Jer 25:31*
saith the Lord
behold, I am the Lord the   *Jer 32:27*
God of *all f.*
for behold, I will bring evil   *Jer 45:5*
on *all f.* saith Lord
all f. shall see that I have   *Eze 20:48*
kindled it
shall my sword go forth   *Eze 21:4*
against *all f.* from south
fowls dwelt, and *all f.* was   *Da 4:12*
fed of it
will pour out my Spirit on   *Joe 2:28;*
all f.   *Ac 2:17*
be silent, O all *f.* before the   *Zec 2:13*
Lord
and *all f.* shall see the   *Lu 3:6*
salvation of God
thou hast given him power   *Joh 17:2*
over *all f.*
all f. is not the same flesh,   *1Co 15:39*
one of men

HIS FLESH

and *his f.* shall not be eaten   *Ex 21:28*
and seethe *his f.* in the holy   *Ex 29:31*
place
burn all *his f.* with his head   *Le 4:11;*
     8:17
he shall put linen breeches   *Le 6:10;*
on *his f.*   *16:4*
shall have a rising in the skin   *Le 13:2*
of *his f.*
priest look on the plague in   *Le 13:3*
the skin of *his f.*
if bright spot be white in the   *Le 13:4*
skin of *his f.*
it is an old leprosy in the   *Le 13:11;*
skin of *his f.*   *13:13*
he shall wash his clothes,   *Le 14:9;*
also wash *his f.* in water   *15:16; 16:24,*
     28; Nu 19:7
any man hath a running issue   *Le 15:2*
out of *his f.*
whether *his f.* run with his   *Le 15:3*
issue, or be stopped
but if he wash them not, nor   *Le 17:16*
bathe *his f.*
be unclean, unless he wash   *Le 22:6*
his f. with water
Ahab put sackcloth on *his*   *1Ki 21:27*
f.
his f. came again, and he   *2Ki 5:14*
was clean
behold Joram had sackcloth   *2Ki 6:30*
on *his f.*
touch his bone and *his f.* he   *Job 2:5*
will curse thee
but *his f.* upon him shall   *Job 14:22*
have pain
if men said not, O that we   *Job 31:31*
had of *his f.*
his f. is consumed away, it   *Job 33:21*
cannot be seen
his f. shall be fresher than   *Job 33:25*
a child's
the flakes of *his f.* are   *Job 41:23*
joined together

he that is cruel troubleth *his*   *Pr 11:17*
f.
the fool foldeth his hands, and   *Ec 4:5*
eateth *his f.*
the fatness of *his f.* shall wax   *Isa 17:4*
lean
can this man give us *his f.*   *Joh 6:52*
to eat
neither *his f.* did see   *Ac 2:31*
corruption
he that soweth to *his f.* shall   *Ga 6:8*
reap corruption
having abolished in *his f.*   *Eph 2:15*
the enmity
no man ever yet hated his   *Eph 5:29*
own *f.*
for we are members of *his f.*   *Eph 5:30*
now hath reconciled in the   *Col 1:22*
body of *his f.*
in days of *his f.* when   *Heb 5:7*
offered prayers
consecrated thro' veil, that   *Heb 10:20*
is to say, *his f.*

IN, IN THE FLESH

Abraham was circumcised   *Ge 17:24*
in the *f.*
Ishmael circumcised in the *f.*   *Ge 17:25*
of his foreskin
brought in uncircumcised in   *Eze 44:7*
the *f.*
uncircumcised in the *f.* not   *Eze 44:9*
enter the sanctuary
countenances appeared fairer   *Da 1:15*
and fatter in *f.*
circumcision which is   *Ro 2:28*
outward in the *f.*
for when we were in the *f.* the   *Ro 7:5*
motions of sin
and for sin condemned sin in   *Ro 8:3*
the *f.*
they that are in the *f.* cannot   *Ro 8:8*
please God
but ye are not in the *f.* but in   *Ro 8:9*
the Spirit
such shall have trouble in   *1Co 7:28*
the *f.*
though we walk in the *f.* not   *2Co 10:3*
war after flesh
there was given to me a   *2Co 12:7*
thorn in the *f.*
life which I now live in the   *Ga 2:20*
f. is by faith
as desire to make a fair   *Ga 6:12*
show in the *f.*
in time past Gentiles in the   *Eph 2:11*
f. called circumcision in
the *f.* made by hands
if I live in the *f.* this is the   *Ph'p 1:22*
fruit of labour
to abide in the *f.* is more   *Ph'p 1:24*
needful for you
and have no confidence in   *Ph'p 3:3*
the *f.*
though I might have   *Ph'p 3:4*
confidence in the *f.*
as many as have not seen my   *Col 2:1*
face in the *f.*
tho' I be absent in the *f.* I   *Col 2:5*
am with you in spirit
God was manifest in the *f.*   *1Ti 3:16*
justified
how much more to thee,   *Ph'm 16*
both in the *f.*
Christ being put to death in   *1Pe 3:18*
the *f.*
Christ suffered for us in the *f.*   *1Pe 4:1*
he that hath suffered in
the *f.* hath ceased from sin
no longer live the rest of his   *1Pe 4:2*
time in the *f.*
might be judged according to   *1Pe 4:6*
men in the *f.*
denieth that Christ is come   *1Jo 4:2;*
in the *f.*   *4:3*
confess not that Christ is come   *2Jo 7*
in the *f.*

MY FLESH

shall I then take my bread   *1Sa 25:11*
and *my f.*
the hair of *my f.* stood up   *Job 4:15*
is my strength of stones? or   *Job 6:12*
is *my f.* brass
my f. is clothed with worms   *Job 7:5*
and dust
wherefore do I take *my f.*   *Job 13:14*
in my teeth

my bone cleaveth to my   *Job 19:20*
skin, and *my f.*
why persecute, and not   *Job 19:22*
satisfied with *my f.*
worms destroy body, yet in   *Job 19:26*
my f. shall I see God
and trembling taketh hold of   *Job 21:6*
my f.
my f. shall rest in hope   *Ps 16:9;*
                    Ac 2:26
there is no soundness in my   *Ps 38:3;*
f.   *38:7*
my f. longeth for thee in a   *Ps 63:1*
dry thirsty land
my f. faileth, but God is my   *Ps 73:26*
portion
my heart and *my f.* crieth out   *Ps 84:2*
for God
knees are weak, *my f.*   *Ps 109:24*
faileth of fatness
my f. trembleth for fear of   *Ps 119:120*
thee
violence done to me, and to   *Jer 51:35*
my f.
my f. and my skin hath he   *La 3:4*
made old
the bread that I will give, is   *Joh 6:51*
my f.
whoso eateth *my f.* hath   *Joh 6:54;*
eternal life   *6:56*
my f. is meat indeed, my   *Joh 6:55*
blood drink indeed
in *my f.* dwelleth no good   *Ro 7:18*
thing
if I may provoke them   *Ro 11:14*
which are *my f.*
my temptation which was in   *Ga 4:14*
my f.
of the afflictions of Christ in   *Col 1:24*
my f.

OF THE FLESH

shall not carry forth ought   *Ex 12:46*
of the f.
if ought *of the f.* remain   *Ex 29:34*
unto morning
nor give *of the f.* of his   *De 28:55*
children
a sound heart is the life *of*   *Pr 14:30*
the f.
much study is a weariness *of*   *Ec 12:12*
the f.
born, not of the will *of the*   *Joh 1:13*
f. but of God
that which is born *of the f.* is   *Joh 3:6*
flesh
that after flesh do mind the   *Ro 8:5*
things *of the f.*
that is, they which are the   *Ro 9:8*
children *of the f.*
to Satan for the destruction   *1Co 5:5*
of the f.
let us cleanse from all   *2Co 7:1*
filthiness *of the f.*
through infirmity *of the f.* I   *Ga 4:13*
preached
ye shall not fulfil the lusts *of*   *Ga 5:16*
the f.
now the works *of the f.* are   *Ga 5:19*
manifest, adultery
that soweth to *f.* shall *of the*   *Ga 6:8*
f. reap corruption
walked in lusts *of the f.*   *Eph 2:3*
desires *of the f.*
putting off the body of sins   *Col 2:11*
of the f.
not in honour to the   *Col 2:23*
satisfying *of the f.*
sanctifieth to the purging *of*   *Heb 9:13*
the f.
not the putting away the   *1Pe 3:21*
filth *of the f.*
they allure through the lusts   *2Pe 2:18*
of the f.
the lust *of the f.* the lust of   *1Jo 2:16*
the eyes

THY FLESH

the birds shall eat *thy f.*   *Ge 40:19*
from off thee
I will give *thy f.* unto fowls   *1Sa 17:44*
of the air
we are thy bone and *thy f.*   *2Sa 5:1;*
              1Ch 11:1
wash, and *thy f.* shall come   *2Ki 5:10*
again
mourn at last, when *thy f.* is   *Pr 5:11*
consumed

suffer not thy mouth to cause   *Ec 5:6*
thy f. to sin
therefore put away evil from   *Ec 11:10*
thy f.
that thou hide not thyself   *Isa 58:7*
from *thy* own *f.*
I will lay *thy f.* on the   *Eze 32:5*
mountains

YOUR FLESH

ye shall not make cuttings in   *Le 19:28*
your f.
then I will tear *your f.* with   *J'g 8:7*
the thorns
I will take stony heart out   *Eze 36:26*
of *your f.*
because of the infirmity of   *Ro 6:19*
your f.
that they may glory in *your*   *Ga 6:13*
f.
being dead in uncircumcision   *Col 2:13*
of *your f.*
rust shall eat *your f.* as it   *Jas 5:3*
were fire

FLESH-HOOK

the priest's servant came   *1Sa 2:13*
with a *f.*
all that the *f.* brought up, the   *1Sa 2:14*
priest took

FLESH-HOOKS

shalt make his *f.* and his   *Ex 27:3*
fire-pans
he made all the vessels and   *Ex 38:3*
the *f.*
put upon the purple cloth the   *Nu 4:14*
f.
David gave pure gold for   *1Ch 28:17*
the *f.*
he made also the pots and   *2Ch 4:16*
the *f.*

FLESH-POTS

when we sat by the *f.*   *Ex 16:3*
and did eat

FLESHY

not with *f.* wisdom, but by   *2Co 1:12*
not with worldly wisdom   *2Co 1:12*
(B)(N)(P)
not with earthly wisdom   *2Co 1:12*
(R)
but in *f.* tables of the heart   *2Co 3:3*
tablets of human hearts   *2Co 3:3*
(A)(R)
but on human tablets (B)   *2Co 3:3*
in tables that are hearts (E)   *2Co 3:3*
on pages of the human heart   *2Co 3:3*
(N)
in living men and women (P)   *2Co 3:3*
vainly puffed up by his *f.*   *Col 2:18*
mind
inflated by his worldly mind   *Col 2:18*
(B)
try to enter some vision of   *Col 2:18*
their own (N)
inflated by unspiritual   *Col 2:18*
imaginations (P)
puffed up by his sensuous   *Col 2:18*
mind (R)
abstain from *f.* lusts, which   *1Pe 2:11*
war
refrain from sensual urges   *1Pe 2:11*
(B)
keep clear of desires of   *1Pe 2:11*
lower nature (P)
abstain from passions of the   *1Pe 2:11*
flesh (R)

FLEW

And the people *f.* upon the   *1Sa 14:32*
spoil
threw themselves on the   *1Sa 14:32*
loot (B)
Then *f.* one of the seraphims   *Isa 6:6*
unto

FLIES

I will send swarms of *f.* upon   *Ex 8:21*
thee, and
swarms of gadflies (B)   *Ex 8:21; 8:31*

shall be full of swarms of *f.*   *Ex 8:21*
and also
that no swarms of *f.* shall be   *Ex 8:22*
there
there came a grievous swarm   *Ex 8:24*
of *f.* into
corrupted by reason of the   *Ex 8:24*
swarm of *f.*
that the swarms of *f.* may   *Ex 8:29*
depart from
and he removed the swarms   *Ex 8:31*
of *f.* from
He sent divers sorts of *f.*   *Ps 78:45*
among
there came divers sorts of *f.*   *Ps 105:31*
and
Dead *f.* cause the ointment of   *Ec 10:1*
the

FLIETH

likeness of any winged fowl   *De 4:17*
that *f.*
creeping thing that *f.* is   *De 14:19*
unclean
the earth as swift as the   *De 28:49*
eagle *f.*
nor for the arrow that *f.* by   *Ps 91:5*
day

FLIGHT

you shall put ten thousand to   *Le 26:8*
f.
and two put ten thousand to   *De 32:30*
f.
put them to *f.* (B)   *2Sa 22:15*
and they put to *f.* all them   *1Ch 12:15*
of the
not to go out with haste,   *Isa 52:12*
nor go by *f.*
the *f.* shall perish from the   *Am 2:14*
swift
But pray ye that your *f.* be   *M't 24:20*
not in
And pray ye that your *f.* be   *M'k 13:18*
not in
turned to *f.* the armies of   *Heb 11:34*
the alien

FLING

f. off dirty clothes of old   *Eph 4:22*
way (P)

FLINT

took a *f.* knife   *Ex 4:24*
(A)(B)(E)(R)
forth water out of the rock   *De 8:15*
of *f.*
make knives of *f.* (A)(E)(R)   *Jos 5:2*
the *f.* into a fountain of   *Ps 114:8*
waters
hoofs shall be counted like *f.*   *Isa 5:28*
have I set my face like *f.*   *Isa 50:7*
As an adamant harder than *f.*   *Eze 3:9*
have
tear out and *f.* away (N)   *M't 5:29*

FLINTY

and oil out of the *f.* rock   *De 32:13*

FLIPPANCY

conversation not be nastiness,   *Eph 5:4*
silliness, (P)

FLIPPANT

no course, stupid, *f.* talk (N)   *Eph 5:4*

FLIRTATIOUS

f., alluring eyes (A)   *1Sa 3:16*

FLOATS

and I will convey them by sea   *1Ki 5:9*
in *f.*

FLOCK

Abel brought of the firstlings   *Ge 4:4*
of his *f.*
Abraham set ewe-lambs of *f.*   *Ge 21:28*
by themselves
go now to the *f.* and fetch   *Ge 27:9*
two good kids

Jacob watered the *f.* of   Ge 29:10
Laban's *f.*
I will again feed and keep   Ge 30:31
thy *f.*
I will pass through all thy *f.*   Ge 30:32
today
and Jacob fed the rest of   Ge 30:36
Laban's *f.*
Jacob did separate all the   Ge 30:40
brown in the *f.*
Jacob called Rachel and Leah   Ge 31:4
to his *f.*
the rams of thy *f.* have I   Ge 31:38
not eaten
if men overdrive them, the *f.*   Ge 33:13
will die
Joseph was feeding the *f.*   Ge 37:2
with his brethren
his brethren went to feed   Ge 37:12;
their *f.*   37:13
I will send thee a kid from   Ge 38:17
the *f.*
the troughs to water their   Ex 2:16
father's *f.*
Moses helped, and watered   Ex 2:17;
their *f.*   2:19
Moses led *f.* to back-side of   Ex 3:1
the desert
bring of your offering of the   Le 1:2
herd or *f.*
he shall bring a female from   Le 5:6
the *f.*
bring a ram without blemish   Le 5:18;
out of the *f.*   6:6; Ezr 10:19;
  Eze 43:23, 25
concerning the tithe of the   Le 27:32
herd or of the *f.*
make a sweet savour of the   Nu 15:3
herd or *f.*
then thou shalt kill of thy   De 12:21
herd and *f.*
furnish him liberally out of   De 15:14
thy *f.*
all the firstling males of thy   De 15:19
f. shalt sanctify
shalt sacrifice to the Lord thy   De 16:2
God of the *f.*
a lion took a lamb out of   1Sa 17:34
the *f.*
he spared to take of his own   2Sa 12:4
f.
Josiah gave to the people of   2Ch 35:7
the *f.*
I disdained to set with the   Job 30:1
dogs of my *f.*
where thou makest thy *f.* to   Ca 1:7
rest at noon
go thy way forth by the   Ca 1:8
footsteps of the *f.*
thy hair is as a *f.* of goats   Ca 4:1; 6:5
thy teeth are like a *f.* of   Ca 4:2;
sheep   6:6
he shall feed his *f.* like a   Isa 40:11
shepherd
brought them with the   Isa 63:11
shepherd of his *f.*
because Lord's *f.* is carried   Jer 13:17
captive
where is *f.* was given thee,   Jer 13:20
thy beautiful *f.*
ye have scattered my *f.* and   Jer 23:2
driven them
I will gather the remnant of   Jer 23:3
my *f.*
cry and wallow, ye principal   Jer 25:34
of the *f.*
nor the principal of the *f.* to   Jer 25:35
escape
an howling of the principal   Jer 26:36
of the *f.* be heard
and keep him as a shepherd   Jer 31:10
doth his *f.*
they shall sing for the young   Jer 31:12
of the *f.*
least of the *f.* shall draw   Jer 49:20;
them out   50:45
will break in pieces the   Jer 51:23
shepherd and his *f.*
take the choice of the *f.*   Eze 24:5
burn the bones
ye eat the fat, but ye feed   Eze 34:3
not the *f.*
my *f.* was scattered on the   Eze 34:6
face of the earth
surely because my f. became   Eze 34:8
a prey, my *f.* meat
I will require my *f.* I will   Eze 34:10
deliver my *f.*

as a shepherd seeketh out   Eze 34:12
his *f.* in the day
I will feed my *f.* as for   Eze 34:15;
you, O my *f.*   34:17
therefore will I save my *f.*   Eze 34:22
no more a prey
ye my *f.,* the *f.* of my   Eze 34:31
pasture, are men
as the holy *f.* as the *f.* of   Eze 36:38
Jerusalem
ye shall offer one lamb out   Eze 45:15
of the *f.*
and eat the lambs out of the   Am 6:4
f.
the Lord took me as I   Am 7:15
followed the *f.*
let not herd nor *f.* taste any   Jon 3:7
thing
as the *f.* in the midst of   Mic 2:12
their fold
thou, O tower of the *f.* the   Mic 4:8
strong hold
feed thy people, the *f.* of   Mic 7:14
thine heritage
tho' the *f.* shall be cut off   Hab 3:17
from the fold
save them as the *f.* of his   Zec 9:16
people
therefore they went their way   Zec 10:2
as a *f.*
for the Lord of hosts hath   Zec 10:3
visited his *f.*
saith the Lord, will feed the   Zec 11:4
f. of slaughter
the poor of the *f.* that   Zec 11:7;
waited on me   11:11
woe to the idol shepherd,   Zec 11:17
that leaveth the *f.*
deceiver which hath in his *f.*   Mal 1:14
a male
sheep of the *f.* shall be   M't 26:31
scattered
keeping watch over *f.* by night   Lu 2:8
fear not little *f.* it is   Lu 12:32
Father's pleasure
take heed therefore to all   Ac 20:28
the *f.*
grievous wolves shall enter,   Ac 20:29
not sparing the *f.*
who feedeth a *f.* and eateth   1Co 9:7
not of milk
feed the *f.* of God which is   1Pe 5:2
among you
not being lords, but being   1Pe 5:3
ensamples to *f.*

LIKE A FLOCK

send forth their little ones   Job 21:11
like a *f.*
thou leddest thy people like   Ps 77:20
a *f.*
he guided them in the   Ps 78:52
wilderness like a *f.*
thou that leadest Joseph like   Ps 80:1
a *f.*
and maketh him families   Ps 107:41
like a *f.*
I will increase them with   Eze 36:37
men like a *f.*

FLOCKS

three *f.* of sheep lying by the   Ge 29:2
well, for out of that
they watered the *f.*
and thither were all the *f.*   Ge 29:3
gathered
we cannot, till all the *f.* be   Ge 29:8
gathered together
Jacob set the rods he pilled   Ge 30:38
before the *f.*
and the *f.* conceived before   Ge 30:39
the rods
set faces of the *f.* towards   Ge 30:40
the ring-straked, he put
his own *f.* by themselves
I have oxen, asses, *f.* and   Ge 32:5
men-servants
he divided the *f.* and herds,   Ge 32:7
and camels
go, see whether it be well   Ge 37:14
with the *f.*
tell me, I pray thee, where   Ge 37:16
they feed their *f.*
thy servants have no pasture   Ge 47:4
for their *f.*
Joseph gave bread in exchange   Ge 47:17
for horses and *f.*

if his offering be of the *f.* of   Le 1:10
the sheep
bring a ram without blemish   Le 5:15
out of the *f.*
Israel took spoil of all their   Nu 31:9
f. and goods
thou shalt take one portion   Nu 31:30
of the *f.*
our wives, our *f.* and cattle,   Nu 32:26
shall be there
he will also bless the *f.* of   De 7:13
thy sheep
blessed shall be the *f.* of thy   De 28:4
sheep
cursed shall be the *f.* of thy   De 28:18
sheep
who shall not leave the *f.* of   De 28:51
thy sheep
to hear the bleatings of the *f.*   J'g 5:16
pitched like two little *f.* of   1Ki 20:27
kids
they went to seek pasture   1Ch 4:39
for their *f.*
because there was pasture   1Ch 4:41
for their *f.*
and over the *f.* was Jaziz   1Ch 27:31
the Hagarite
the Arabians brought him   2Ch 17:11
f.
stalk for *f.* **(B)**   2Ch 32:28
folds for *f.* **(E)**   2Ch 32:28
violently take away *f.* and   Job 24:2
feed thereof
the pastures are clothed with   Ps 65:13
f.
he gave their *f.* to hot   Ps 78:48
thunderbolts
and *f.* above all at Jerusalem   Ec 2:7
(S)
turn aside by the *f.* of thy   Ca 1:7
companions
cities of Aroer are forsaken,   Isa 17:2
shall be for *f.*
the palaces shall be a   Isa 32:14
pasture of *f.*
all *f.* of Kedar shall be   Isa 60:7
gathered together
and strangers shall stand and   Isa 61:5
feed your *f.*
Sharon shall be a fold for *f.*   Isa 65:10
valley of Achor
shepherds with their *f.* shall   Jer 6:3
come to her
shall not prosper, all *f.* shall   Jer 10:21
be scattered
dwell in Judah they that go   Jer 31:24
forth with *f.*
shepherds causing their *f.* to   Jer 33:12
lie down
the *f.* shall pass again under   Jer 33:13
the rod
their tents and *f.* shall they   Jer 49:29
take away
and be as the he-goats before   Jer 50:8
the *f.*
Ammonites a couching-place   Eze 25:5
for *f.*
should not the shepherds   Eze 34:2
feed the *f.*
the waste cities shall be   Eze 36:38
filled with *f.* of men
the *f.* of sheep are made   Joe 1:18
desolate
as a young lion among the *f.*   Mic 5:8
of sheep
and the sea-coast shall be   Zep 2:6
folds for *f.*
f. shall lie down in the midst   Zep 2:14
of Nineveh

FLOCKS with *HERDS*

Lot also had *f.* and *herds,*   Ge 13:5
and tents
the Lord hath given   Ge 24:35
Abraham *f.* and *herds*
Isaac had possession of *f.*   Ge 26:14
and *herds*
Jacob divided *f.* and *herds*   Ge 32:7
into two bands
the *f.* and *herds* with young   Ge 33:13
are with me
thou shalt be near me, thou,   Ge 45:10
thy *f.* and *herds*
my brethren, their *f.* and   Ge 47:1
herds are come
their *f.* and *herds* left they in   Ge 50:8
land of Goshen
we will go with our *f.* and   Ex 10:9
our *herds*

only let your *f.* and your | *Ex 10:24*
herds be stayed
also take your *f.* and *herds* | *Ex 12:32*
and be gone
neither let *f.* nor *herds* | *Ex 34:3*
feed before the mount
shall the *f.* and *herds* be | *Nu 11:22*
slain for them
when thy *herds* and thy *f.* | *De 8:13*
multiply
firstlings of *herds* and *f.* | *De 12:6;*
12:17; 14:23; Ne 10:36
David took all the *f.* and | *1Sa 30:20*
the *herds*
rich man had exceeding | *2Sa 12:2*
many *f.* and *herds*
provided possessions of *f.* | *2Ch 32:29*
and *herds*
know thy *f.* look well to thy | *Pr 27:23*
herds
shame had devoured their *f.* | *Jer 3:24*
and *herds*
an ancient nation shall eat | *Jer 5:17*
thy *f.* and *herds*
they shall go with *f.* and | *Ho 5:6*
herds to seek Lord

FLOG

f. with scorpions (B) | *1Ki 12:11; 12:14*
f. noble men (B)(R) | *Pr 17:26*

FLOGGED

f. you with whips (B) | *1Ki 12:11;*
12:14
officials ordered them *f.* (B) | *Ac 16:22*

FLOGGING

let him off with a *f.* (N) | *Lu 23:16;*
23:22

FLOOD

I, even I, bring a *f.* of water | *Ge 6:17*
on the earth
a water-deluge (B) | *Ge 6:17;*
7:6; 10; 9:28
when the *f.* of waters was | *Ge 7:6*
upon the earth
Noah went in, because of the | *Ge 7:7*
waters of the *f.*
after seven days the *f.* was | *Ge 7:10*
on the earth
the *f.* was forty days on the | *Ge 7:17*
earth
nor shall be any more a *f.* to | *Ge 9:11*
destroy the earth
Noah lived after the *f.* 350 | *Ge 9:28*
years
to them were sons born after | *Ge 10:1*
the *f.*
the nations were divided in | *Ge 10:32*
the earth after *f.*
your fathers on either side | *Jos 24:2;*
of *f.* | *3:14-15*
beyond the river Euphrates | *Jos 24:2*
(A)
lived beyond the river | *Jos 24:2*
(B)(E)
beyond the Euphrates (R) | *Jos 24:2*
like a bursting *f.* (R) | *2Sa 5:20*
as the *f.* decayeth and | *Job 14:11*
drieth up
waters evaporate (A)(B) | *Job 14:11*
waters fail from the sea | *Job 14:11*
(E)(R)
whose foundation was | *Job 22:16*
overthrown with a *f.*
poured out as a stream (A) | *Job 22:16*
washed out by a deluge | *Job 22:16*
(B)(E)
foundation was wasted | *Job 22:16*
away (R)
the *f.* breaketh out from the | *Job 28:4*
inhabitant
the Lord sitteth upon the *f.* | *Ps 29:10*
he is king
they went thro' the *f.* on foot, | *Ps 66:6*
we rejoice
passed through river on foot | *Ps 66:6*
(A)(B)(E)(R)
thou didst cleave the | *Ps 74:15*
fountain and the *f.*
cleave open fountains and | *Ps 74:15*
streams (A)
break open the fountain and | *Ps 74:15*
brook (R)

cleave open springs and | *Ps 74:15*
brooks (R)
thou carriest them away as | *Ps 90:5*
with a *f.*
anger is an overwhelming *f.* | *Pr 27:4*
(A)(B)(E)(R)
a strong one, which as a *f.* | *Isa 28:2*
shall cast down
the enemy shall come in like | *Isa 59:19*
a *f.*
like a rushing stream | *Isa 59:19*
(B)(E)(R)
who is this that cometh up | *Jer 46:7;*
as a *f.* | *46:8*
rises up like the Nile | *Jer 46:7;*
(A)(B)(E)(R) | *46:8*
waters shall be an overflowing | *Jer 47:2*
f.
shall be an overflowing | *Jer 47:2*
stream (A)(E)
become an overflowing | *Jer 47:2*
torrent (B)(R)
the end thereof shall be with | *Da 9:26*
a *f.*
end shall come | *Da 9:26*
overwhelmingly (A)
with arms of a *f.* shall be | *Da 11:22*
overflown
be broken and utterly swept | *Da 11:22*
away (A)(B)(R)
be overwhelmed before him | *Da 11:22*
(E)
it shall rise up wholly as a *f.* | *Am 8:8;*
9:5
rise up like the Nile | *Am 8:8;*
(A)(B)(E)(R) | *9:5*
shall be drowned as by *f.* of | *Am 9:5*
Egypt
with an overrunning *f.* make | *Na 1:8*
an end
in days before *f.* were | *M't 24:38*
eating
and knew not till the *f.* | *M't 24:39;*
came | *Lu 17:27*
when the *f.* arose the stream | *Lu 6:48*
beat
bringing in *f.* on world of | *2Pe 2:5*
ungodly
dragon poured out water as | *Re 12:15*
a *f.*
water like a river | *Re 12:15*
(B)(E)(P)(R)
the earth helped, and | *Re 12:16*
swallowed up the *f.*
swallowed up stream of | *Re 12:16*
water (A)(B)(E)(N)(P)(R)

FLOODED

eyes *f.* with light (A) | *Eph 1:18*

FLOODS

the *f.* stood upright as an | *Ex 15:8*
heap
streams stood like a wall (B) | *Ex 15:8*
f. of ungodly made me | *2Sa 22:5;*
afraid | *Ps 18:4*
he shall not see the rivers | *Job 20:17*
and *f.*
rivers and flowing streams | *Job 20:17*
(A)(E)(R)
streams and brooks (B) | *Job 20:17*
he bindeth the *f.* from | *Job 28:11*
overflowing
Man binds the streams | *Job 28:11*
(A)(B)(E)(R)
he hath established it upon | *Ps 24:2*
the *f.*
founded it upon the seas | *Ps 24:2*
(A)(B)(E)(R)
surely in *f.* of great waters | *Ps 32:6*
not come nigh
into deep waters, where *f.* | *Ps 69:2*
overflow me
and had turned their *f.* into | *Ps 78:44*
blood
rivers to blood | *Ps 78:44*
(A)(B)(E)(R)
f. have lifted up, O Lord, *f.* | *Ps 93:3*
have lifted up
let *f.* clap their hands, let hills | *Ps 98:8*
be joyful
rivers clap their hands | *Ps 98:8*
(A)(B)
neither can the *f.* drown love | *Ca 8:7*
nor can rivers drown it (B) | *Ca 8:7*
for I will pour *f.* upon dry | *Isa 44:3*
ground

streams upon the dry ground | *Isa 44:3*
(B)(E)(R)
I restrained the *f.* thereof, | *Eze 31:15*
waters stayed
f. compassed me about, thy | *Jon 2:3*
billows
the current was engulfing me | *Jon 2:3*
(B)
f. came, winds blew, and | *M't 7:25;*
beat | *7:27*

FLOOR

they came to the threshing *f.* | *Ge 50:10*
of Atad
when inhabitants saw | *Ge 50:11*
mourning in *f.* of Atad
in the threshing *f.* of Atad | *Ge 50:11*
(S)
the priests shall take dust | *Nu 15:17*
that is in *f.*
as ye do the heave-offering | *Nu 15:20*
of threshing *f.*
as tho' it were the corn of | *Nu 18:27*
the threshing *f.*
be counted as the increase | *Nu 18:30*
of the threshing *f.*
thou shalt furnish him out | *De 15:14*
of thy *f.*
I will put a fleece of wool in | *J'g 6:37*
the *f.*
he winnoweth in the threshing | *Ru 3:2*
f.
came to Nachon's threshing *f.* | *2Sa 6:6;*
1Ch 13:9
the threshing *f.* (S) | *2Sa 24:16;*
1Ki 22:10
rear an altar in the | *2Sa 24:18*
threshing *f.* of Araunas
David said, To buy the | *2Sa 24:21*
threshing *f.* of thee
he overlaid the *f.* of house | *1Ki 6:30*
with gold
with cedar from one side of | *1Ki 7:7*
the *f.* to the other
out of the barn *f.* or the | *2Ki 6:27*
wine-press
Lord had answered in the | *1Ch 21:28*
threshing *f.*
prepared in threshing *f.* of | *2Ch 3:1*
Ornan
O my threshing, and the | *Isa 21:10*
corn of my *f.*
daughter of Babylon is like a | *Jer 51:33*
threshing *f.*
thou hast loved a reward on | *Ho 9:1*
every corn *f.*
the threshing *f.* (S) | *Ho 9:1*
the *f.* and winepress shall | *Ho 9:2*
not feed them
as the chaff that is driven | *Ho 13:3*
out of the *f.*
shall gather them as sheaves | *Mic 4:12*
into the *f.*
he will thoroughly purge his | *M't 3:12;*
f. | *Lu 3:17*

FLOORS

and they rob the threshing *f.* | *1Sa 23:1*
like chaff of the summer | *Da 2:35*
threshing *f.*
and the *f.* shall be full of | *Joe 2:24*
wheat

FLOTES

we will bring it to thee in *f.* | *2Ch 2:16*

FLOUR

of wheaten *f.* shalt thou make | *Ex 29:2*
them
f. mingled with oil | *Ex 29:40;*
Nu 6:15; 29:3, 9, 14
he shall take his handful of the | *Le 2:2;*
f. | *6:13*
fine *f.* | *Le 2:4;*
2:5, 7; 5:11; 6:20; 7:12; 14:10, 21;
23:13, 17; 24:5; Nu 7:13, 19, 25, 31, 37,
43, 49, 55, 61, 67, 73, 79; 8:8; 1Ki 4:22;
2Ki 7:1, 16, 18; 1Ch 9:29; 23:29;
Eze 16:13, 19; 46:14; Re 18:13
and a tenth part of an | *Nu 28:5;*
ephah of *f.* for a meat offering | *28:20,*
28; 29:3, 9, 14
cakes of an ephah of *f.* | *J'g 6:19;*
1Sa 1:24; 28:24
she took *f.* and kneaded it | *1Sa 28:24;*
2Sa 13:8

brought *f.* parched corn, *2Sa 17:28*
and beans
half hundred weight of *f.* *M't 13:33*
(N)

FLOURISH

made all to *f.* (A) *Ge 39:3*
in his days shall the righteous *Ps 72:7*
f.
they of the city shall *f.* like *Ps 72:16*
grass of the earth
when all the workers of *Ps 92:7*
iniquity *f.*
the righteous shall *f.* like the *Ps 92:12*
palm tree
they shall *f.* in the courts of *Ps 92:13*
our God
but upon himself shall his *Ps 132:18*
crown *f.*
the righteous shall *f.* as a *Pr 11:28*
branch
the tabernacle of the upright *Pr 14:11*
shall *f.*
when the almond tree shall *f.* *Ec 12:5*
let us get up, let us see if the *Ca 7:12*
vine *f.*
in morning make thy seed *Isa 17:11*
to *f.*
your bones shall *f.* like an *Isa 66:14*
herb
I the Lord have made the dry *Eze 17:24*
tree to *f.*

FLOURISHED

I went down to see whether *Ca 6:11*
the vine *f.*
your care of me hath *f.* *Ph'p 4:10*
again

FLOURISHETH

in the morning it *f.* and *Ps 90:6*
groweth up
as a flower of the field, so *Ps 103:15*
he *f.*

FLOURISHING

in old age, they shall be fat *Ps 92:14*
and *f.*
I was at rest, and *f.* in my *Da 4:4*
palace
if anyone is *f.* (P) *Jas 5:13*

FLOW

his goods shall *f.* away in *Job 20:28*
day of his wrath
he causeth the wind blow, *Ps 147:18*
and waters *f.*
that the spices thereof may *f.* *Ca 4:10*
out
and all nations shall *f.* unto it *Isa 2:2*
he caused waters to *f.* out *Isa 48:21*
of the rock
then thou shalt see and *f.* *Isa 60:5*
together
mountains might *f.* down at *Isa 64:1*
thy presence
shall *f.* to the goodness of *Jer 31:12*
the Lord
nations shall not *f.* together *Jer 51:44*
any more to him
in that day hills shall *f.* with *Joe 3:18*
milk, and rivers of Judah
f. with waters
the people shall *f.* to the *Mic 4:1*
mountain of Jehovah
suffered from a *f.* of blood *M't 9:20*
(A)
out of his belly shall *f.* living *Joh 7:38*
water

FLOWED

f. over all his banks, as they *Jos 4:18*
mountains *f.* down at thy *Isa 64:3*
presence
Waters *f.* over mine head *La 3:54*

FLOWER

a knop and a *f.* in one *Ex 25:33;*
branch *37:19*
shall die in the *f.* of their *1Sa 2:33*
age
like the *f.* of a lily (S) *2Ch 4:5*

He cometh forth like a *f.* *Job 14:2*
and is cut
shall cast off his *f.* as the *Job 15:33*
olive
casts off his blossoms *Job 15:33*
(A)(B)(R)
a *f.* of the field, so he *Ps 103:15*
flourisheth
sour grapes is ripening in the *Isa 18:5*
f.
f. a ripening grape *Isa 18:5*
(A)(B)(E)(R)
glorious beauty is a fading *f.* *Isa 28:1*
shall be a fading *f.* and as *Isa 28:4*
thereof is as the *f.* of the *Isa 40:6*
field
the *f.* fadeth: because the *Isa 40:7*
spirit
f. fadeth: but the word of *Isa 40:8*
our God
the *f.* of Lebanon languisheth *Na 1:4*
if she pass the *f.* of her age *1Co 7:36*
bloom of her youth (A)(B) *1Co 7:36*
because as the *f.* of the grass *Jas 1:10*
the grass, and the f. thereof *Jas 1:11*
falleth
the glory of man as the *f.* of *1Pe 1:24*
grass
and the *f.* thereof falleth *1Pe 1:24*
away

FLOWERS

his bowls, his knops, and *Ex 25:31;*
his *f.* *25:34; 37:17, 20*
her *f.* be upon him, he shall *Le 15:24*
And of her that is sick of *Le 15:33*
her *f.*
the *f.* thereof, was beaten *Nu 8:4*
work
knops and open *f.* all was *1Ki 6:18*
cedar
palm trees and open *f.* *1Ki 6:29*
within and
palm trees and open *f.* and *1Ki 6:32*
overlaid
palm trees and open *f.* and *1Ki 6:35*
covered
the brim of a cup, with *f.* of *1Ki 7:26*
lilies
with the *f.* and the lamps *1Ki 7:49*
brim of a cup, with *f.* of *2Ch 4:5*
lilies
And the *f.* and the lamps *2Ch 4:21*
The *f.* appear on the earth *Ca 2:12*
as a bed of spices, as sweet *Ca 5:13*

FLOWETH

land that *f.* with milk and *Le 20:24;*
honey *Nu 13:27; 14:8; 16:13-14;*
De 6:3; 11:9; 26:9, 15; 27:3; 31:20;
Jos 5:6

FLOWING

a land *f.* with milk and honey *Ex 3:8;*
3:17; 13:5; 33:3; Jer 11:5; 32:22;
Eze 20:6, 15
f. down the mountain (B) *De 9:21;*
stopped *f.* (S) *2Ki 4:6*
wellspring of wisdom as a *f.* *Pr 18:4*
brook
the glory of the Gentiles *Isa 66:12*
like a *f.*
the cold *f.* waters that come *Jer 18:14*

FLUTE

players on harp and *f.* (B) *Ge 4:21*
a *f.* (A)(B)(R) *1Sa 10:5;*
Isa 5:12; 30:29; 1Co 14:7
make merry at sound of *f.* *Job 21:12*
(B)
flute (S) *Job 21:12; 30:31*
my *f.* to bitter lamentation *Job 30:31*
(B)
the *f.* (S) *Isa 5:12; 30:29; 1Co 14:7*
flute (A)(R) *Jer 48:36*
ye hear the sound of the *Da 3:5;*
cornet. *f.* *3:7, 10, 15*
the pipe (A)(B)(R) *Da 3:5; 3:7, 10, 15*
f. players *Re 18:22*
(A)(B)(E)(N)(P)(R)(S)

FLUTES

playing *f.* (B) *1Ki 1:40;*
Jer 48:36; M't 11:17; Lu 7:32; 1Co 14:7

played on the *f.* (S) *1Ki 1:40*
wind instruments or *f.* *Ps 150:4*
(A)(B)
praise him with *f.* (S) *Ps 150:4*
the *f.* (S) *Jer 48:36;*
1Sa 10:5; Eze 28:13

FLUTTERETH

up her nest, *f.* over her *De 32:11*
young
my heart *f.* (E) *Isa 21:4*

FLUX

sick of a fever and of a *Ac 28:8*
bloody *f.*
fever and dysentery *Ac 28:8*
(A)(B)(E)(N)(P)(R)

FLY

fowl that may *f.* above the *Ge 1:20*
earth
but didst *f.* upon the spoil, *1Sa 15:19*
and
he rode upon a cherub, and *2Sa 22:11*
did *f.*
trouble, as the sparks *f.* *Job 5:7*
upward
He shall *f.* away as a dream *Job 20:8*
Doth the hawk *f.* by thy *Job 39:26*
wisdom
rode upon a cherub, and did *Ps 18:10*
f.
yea, he did *f.* upon the wings *Ps 18:10*
would I *f.* away, and be at *Ps 55:6*
rest
it is soon cut off, and we *f.* *Ps 90:10*
away
they *f.* away as an eagle *Pr 23:5*
toward
his feet, and with twain he *Isa 6:2*
did *f.*
shall hiss for the *f.* that is in *Isa 7:18*
they shall *f.* upon the *Isa 11:14*
shoulders
Who are these that *f.* as a *Isa 60:8*
cloud
Behold, he shall *f.* as an *Jer 48:40*
eagle
shall come up and *f.* as the *Jer 49:22*
eagle
hunt the souls to make *Eze 13:20*
them *f.*
souls that ye hunt to make *Eze 13:20*
them *f.*
being caused to *f.* swiftly, *Da 9:21*
touched
glory shall *f.* away like a *Ho 9:11*
bird
shall *f.* as the eagle that *Hab 1:8*
hasteth
she might *f.* into the *Re 12:14*
wilderness
saw another angel *f.* in the *Re 14:6*
midst
to all the fowls that *f.* in the *Re 19:17*
midst

FLYING

ye eat of every *f.* creeping *Le 11:21*
thing
But all other *f.* creeping *Le 11:23*
things
creeping things, and *f.* fowl *Ps 148:10*
as the swallow by *f.* so the *Pr 26:2*
curse
his fruit shall be a fiery *f.* *Isa 14:29*
serpent
the viper and fiery *f.* serpent *Isa 30:6*
birds *f.* so will the Lord of *Isa 31:5*
hosts
and looked, and behold a *f.* *Zec 5:1*
roll
And I answered, I see a *f.* *Zec 5:2*
roll
fourth beast was like a *f.* eagle *Re 4:7*
f. through the midst of *Re 8:13*
heaven

FOAL

Binding his *f.* unto the vine *Ge 49:11*
and upon a colt the *f.* of an *Zec 9:9*
ass
and a colt the *f.* of an ass *M't 21:5*

FOALS

bulls, twenty she asses, and   Ge 32:15
ten *f.*

FOAM

waters roar and *f.* (A)   Ps 46:3
cut off as the *f.* upon the   Ho 10:7
water
as a chip on surface of   Ho 10:7
waters (B)(R)

FOAMETH

he *f.* and gnasheth with his   M'k 9:18
teeth
and it teareth him that he *f.* Lu 9:39
again

FOAMING

on the ground, and wallowed   M'k 9:20
f.
of the sea *f.* out their own   Jude 13
shame

FODDER

straw and *f.* (B)   Ge 24:25; 24:32
fodder (S)   Ge 24:25;
     24:32; 42:27; 43:24; J'g 19:19, 21
give his ass *f.* (A)   Ge 42:27
straw and *f.* for donkeys (B)   J'g 19:19;
                                       19:21
or loweth the ox over his *f.*   Job 6:5
reap *f.* in the field (A)(R)   Job 24:6

FODDERED

f. their donkeys (B)   Ge 43:24

FOE

Haman is a *f.* and an enemy   Es 7:6
(R)

FOES

to be destroyed before thy   1Ch 21:12
f.
their *f.* seventy and five   Es 9:16
thousand
many are my *f.* (R)   Ps 3:1
even mine enemies and my *f.*   Ps 27:2
and hast not made my *f.* to   Ps 30:1
rejoice
beat down his *f.* before his   Ps 89:23
face
And a man's *f.* shall be   M't 10:36
they of his
Until I make thy *f.* thy   Ac 2:35
footstool

FOG

days disappear like *f.* (B)   Ps 78:33

FOGS

whirl-wind-driven *f.* (B)   2Pe 2:17

FOLD

shall the shepherds make   Isa 13:20
their *f.*
And Sharon shall be a *f.* of   Isa 65:10
flocks
mountains of Israel shall their Eze 34:14
f.
there shall they lie in a   Eze 34:14
good *f.*
the flock in the midst of   Mic 2:12
their *f.*
flock shall be cut off from   Hab 3:17
the *f.*
I have, which are not of   Joh 10:16
this *f.*
shall be one *f.* and one   Joh 10:16
shepherd
as a vesture shalt thou *f.*   Heb 1:12
them up

FOLDEN

they be *f.* together as thorns Na 1:10

FOLDETH

The fool *f.* his hands together Ec 4:5

FOLDING

two leaves of the one door   1Ki 6:34
were *f.*
two leaves of the other door   1Ki 6:34
were *f.*
a little *f.* of the hands to   Pr 6:10
sleep
a little *f.* of the hands to   Pr 24:33
sleep

FOLDS

and *f.* for your sheep: and   Nu 32:24
do that
fenced cities: and *f.* for   Nu 32:36
sheep
f. for flocks (E)   2Ch 32:28
f. of his flesh cleave   Job 41:23
(A)(B)(R)
nor he goats out of thy *f.*   Ps 50:9
will bring them again to their   Jer 23:3
f.
for shepherds, and *f.* for   Zep 2:6
flocks

FOLIAGE

put forth *f.* (B)(R)   Eze 17:6

FOLK

now leave with thee some of   Ge 33:15
the *f.*
The conies are but a feeble   Pr 30:26
f.
and the *f.* in the fire, and   Jer 51:58
they
laid his hands upon a few   M'k 6:5
sick *f.*
a great multitude of impotent   Joh 5:3
f.

FOLKS

bringing sick *f.* and them   Ac 5:16
which

FOLLOW

if woman will not be willing   Ge 24:8
to *f.* thee
Joseph said, Up, *f.* after the Ge 44:4
men
get thee out, and people that   Ex 11:8
f. thee
I will harden Pharaoh that he   Ex 14:4
shall *f.* them
and the Egyptians shall *f.*   Ex 14:17
them
if hurt a woman, and yet no   Ex 21:22
mischief *f.*
and if any mischief *f.* then   Ex 21:23
life for life
thou shalt not *f.* a multitude Ex 23:2
to do evil
f. after (B)   De 8:19;
13:4-5;   1Ki 11:38;   16:31;   2Ki 23:3;
Ec 11:9;   Jer 3:17;   7:6;   13:10;   16:12;
          18:12; Eze 11:20; 33:15; 37:24
what is altogether just shalt   De 16:20
thou *f.*
if the thing *f.* not, nor come De 18:22
to pass
their hearts inclined to *f.*   J'g 9:3
Abimelech
it be given young men, who   1Sa 25:27
f. my lord
so faint that they could not   1Sa 30:21
f. David
among the people that *f.*   2Sa 17:9
Absalom
let me kiss father, then I   1Ki 19:20
will *f.* thee
because I *f.* the thing that   Ps 38:20
good is
the virgins her companions   Ps 45:14
that *f.* her
all the upright in heart shall   Ps 94:15
f. it
they draw nigh that *f.*   Ps 119:150
after mischief
that they may *f.* strong drink Isa 5:11
hearken, ye that *f.* after   Isa 51:1
righteousness
f. the heart (R)   Jer 3:17;
          13:10; 18:12; Eze 37:24
I hastened from being a   Jer 17:16
pastor to *f.* thee
f. own schemes (B)(R)   Jer 18:12

the famine shall *f.* close   Jer 42:16
after you
the prophets that *f.* their   Eze 13:3
own spirit
f. his laws (R)   Da 9:10
and she shall *f.* after her   Ho 2:7
lovers
shall know, if we *f.* on to   Ho 6:3
know Lord
Master, I will *f.* thee   M't 8:19;
                            Lu 9:57, 61
these signs *f.* them that   M'k 16:17
believe
go not after them, nor *f.*   Lu 17:23
them
when they about him saw   Lu 22:49
what would *f.*
and a stranger will they not   Joh 10:5
f.
Peter said, Lord, why   Joh 13:37
cannot I *f.* thee now
all the prophets from Samuel,   Ac 3:24
and that *f.*
f. example of faith (R)   Ro 4:12
let us *f.* things that make   Ro 14:19
for peace
f. after charity, desire   1Co 14:1
spiritual gifts
but I *f.* after, if that I may Ph'p 3:12
apprehend
but ever *f.* that which is   1Th 5:15
good
for yourselves know how ye   2Th 3:7
ought to *f.* us
to make ourselves an   2Th 3:9
ensample to you to *f.* us
and some men they *f.* after   1Ti 5:24
O man of God, *f.*   1Ti 6:11;
righteousness   2Ti 2:22
f. peace with all men, and   Heb 12:14
holiness
whose faith *f.* considering   Heb 13:7
the end
when it testified the glory   1Pe 1:11
that should *f.*
an example, that ye should *f.* 1Pe 2:21
his steps
many shall *f.* their pernicious 2Pe 2:2
ways
f. their abominable lusts (N) 2Pe 2:10
f. not that which is evil, but 3Jo 11
what is good
these are they that *f.* the   Re 14:4
Lamb
blessed are dead in Lord, and   Re 14:13
their works do *f.* them

FOLLOW *HIM*

if the Lord be God, *f. him*   1Ki 18:21
and he suffered no man to *f.*   M'k 5:37
him
he went out thence, and his   M'k 6:1
disciples *f. him*
f. him into the house   Lu 22:10;
                             M'k 14:13
he goeth before, and the   Joh 10:4
sheep *f. him*

FOLLOW *ME*

woman will not be willing to   Ge 24:5;
f. me   24:39
Ehud said unto them, *F.* after J'g 3:28
me
give bread, I pray, to the   J'g 8:5
people that *f. me*
for handfuls for people that   1Ki 20:10
f. me
f. me I will bring you to   2Ki 6:19
man ye seek
goodness and mercy shall *f.*   Ps 23:6
me all my life
f. me and I will make you   M't 4:19;
fishers of men   8:22; 9:9; M'k 2:14;
                                 Lu 5:27
deny himself and take up   M't 16:24;
his cross and *f. me*   M'k 8:34; 10:21;
                                 Lu 9:23
sell that thou hast, *f. me*   M't 19:21;
                                 Lu 18:22
he said, *F. me* Lu 9:59; Joh 1:43; 21:22
my sheep hear my voice   Joh 10:27
and *f. me*
if any man will serve me,   Joh 12:26
let him *f. me*
thou canst not *f. me* now,   Joh 13:36
but afterwards
cast thy garment about thee,   Ac 12:8
and *f. me*

FOLLOWED

Rebekah and her damsels *f.*   *Ge 24:61*
the man
so commanded he all that *f.*   *Ge 32:19*
the droves
they have wholly *f.* the Lord   *Nu 32:12;*
  De 1:36
for all the men that *f.*   *De 4:3*
Baal-peor
the ark of the covenant *f.*   *Jos 6:8*
them
I wholly *f.* the Lord my   *Jos 14:8;*
God   *9:14*
they forsook the Lord and *f.*   *J'g 2:12*
other gods
cut down his bough and *f.*   *J'g 9:49*
Abimelech
they *f.* hard after the   *1Sa 14:22*
Philistines
Jesse's three sons *f.* Saul to   *1Sa 17:13*
battle,
Philistines *f.* Saul   *1Sa 31:2;*
  2Sa 1:6; 1Ch 10:2
but the house of Judah *f.*   *2Sa 2:10*
David
and king David himself *f.*   *2Sa 3:31*
the bier
Ahithophel saw his counsel   *2Sa 17:23*
was not *f.*
Israel *f.* Sheba the son of   *2Sa 20:2*
Bichri
none that *f.* house of David   *1Ki 12:20*
half of the people *f.* Tibni,   *1Ki 16:21;*
half *f.* Omri   *16:22*
forsaken the Lord, thou   *1Ki 18:18*
hast *f.* Baalim
came out, and the army   *1Ki 20:19*
which *f.* them
was no water for cattle that   *2Ki 3:9*
f. them
Elisha arose and *f.* her   *2Ki 4:30*
so Gehazi *f.* after Naaman,   *2Ki 5:21*
is all well
Jehu *f.* after Ahaziah, and   *2Ki 9:27*
said, Smite him
Jehoahaz *f.* sins of Jeroboam   *2Ki 13:2*
son of Nebat
and they *f.* vanity, and   *2Ki 17:15*
became vain
the players on instruments *f.*   *Ps 68:25*
after
whither the head looked,   *Eze 10:11*
they *f.* it
the Lord took me as I *f.* the   *Am 7:15*
flock
many women which *f.* Jesus   *M't 27:55*
from Galilee
we left all and *f.* thee   *M'k 10:28;*
  Lu 18:28
were amazed, and as they *f.*   *M'k 10:32*
they were afraid
they took him, and Peter *f.*   *Lu 22:54*
afar off
religious proselytes *f.* Paul   *Ac 13:43*
and Barnabas
the same *f.* Paul and us, and   *Ac 16:17*
cried
Gentiles who *f.* not after   *Ro 9:30*
righteousness
who *f.* after the law of   *Ro 9:31*
righteousness
they drank of that rock that   *1Co 10:4*
f. them
if she have diligently *f.* every   *1Ti 5:10*
good work
we have not *f.* cunningly   *2Pe 1:16*
devised fables
f. unnatural lusts (N)   *Jude 7*
his name was Death, and Hell   *Re 6:8*
f. with him
there *f.* hail and fire mingled   *Re 8:7*
with blood
there *f.* another angel, saying,   *Re 14:8*
Babylon is
third angel *f.* them, saying, If   *Re 4:9*
any man

FOLLOWED HIM

Moses rose up, the elders of   *Nu 16:25*
Israel *f.* him
hired vain and light persons   *J'g 9:4*
who *f.* him
and all the people *f.* him   *1Sa 13:7*
trembling
there *f.* him a mess of meat   *2Sa 11:8*
from the king
they left their nets and *f.*   *M't 4:20;*
him   *M'k 1:18*

they immediately left the   *M't 4:22*
ship and *f.* him
and there *f.* him great   *M't 4:25;*
multitudes of people   *8:1; 12:15; 19:2;*
  20:29; M'k 2:15; 5:24; Lu 23:27; Joh 6:2
when entered, his disciples   *M't 8:23;*
f. him   *Lu 22:39*
two blind men *f.* him,   *M't 9:27*
crying, and saying
but Peter *f.* him afar off   *M't 26:58;*
  M'k 14:54
there *f.* him a certain   *M'k 14:51*
young man
they forsook all and *f.* him   *Lu 5:11;*
  5:28
Jesus said to the people that *f.*   *Lu 7:9*
him, not found
Peter went out and *f.* him   *Ac 12:9*
and wist not
the armies *f.* him on white   *Re 19:14*
horses

FOLLOWED ME

my servant Caleb hath *f.* me   *Nu 14:24*
fully
because they have not   *Nu 32:11*
wholly *f.* me
David who *f.* me with all his   *1Ki 14:8*
heart
nor the men of the guard   *Ne 4:23*
which *f.* me
ye that *f.* me in the   *M't 19:28*
regeneration

FOLLOWEDST

thou *f.* not young men, poor   *Ru 3:10*
or rich

FOLLOWERS

presence of thy *f.* (B)   *Ps 52:9*
have begotten you through   *1Co 4:16;*
gospel be *f.* of me   *11:1; Ph'p 3:17*
be ye *f.* of God as dear   *Eph 5:1*
children
ye became *f.* of us and of the   *1Th 1:6*
Lord
for ye became *f.* of the   *1Th 2:14*
churches of God
be *f.* of them who thro'   *Heb 6:12*
faith inherit promises
if ye be *f.* of that which is   *1Pe 3:13*
good

FOLLOWETH

him that *f.* her be killed   *2Ki 11:15;*
  2Ch 23:14
my soul *f.* hard after thee,   *Ps 63:8*
hand upholds
but he that *f.* vain persons   *Pr 12:11;*
  28:19
he loveth him that *f.*   *Pr 15:9;*
righteousness   *21:21*
every one loveth gifts and *f.*   *Isa 1:23*
after rewards
none *f.* thee to commit   *Eze 16:34*
whoredoms
Ephraim feeds on wind, *f.*   *Ho 12:1*
after east wind
he that taketh not up his   *M't 10:38*
cross and *f.* me
because he *f.* not us   *M'k 9:38; Lu 9:49*
he that *f.* me shall not walk   *Joh 8:12*
in darkness

FOLLOWING

plenty not known by reason   *Ge 41:31*
of famine *f.*
they will turn away thy son   *De 7:4*
from *f.* me
take heed thou be not   *De 12:30*
snared by *f.* them
from *f.* the Lord   *Jos 22:16;*
  22:18, 23, 29; 1Sa 12:20; 2Ki 17:21;
  2Ch 25:27; 34:33
corrupted in *f.* other gods to   *J'g 2:19*
serve them
or to return from *f.* after   *Ru 1:16*
thee
if ye continue *f.* the Lord   *1Sa 12:14*
your God
Saul went up from *f.* the   *1Sa 14:46*
Philistines
Saul is turned back from *f.*   *1Sa 15:11*
me
when Saul was returned   *1Sa 24:1*
from *f.* Philistines

Asahel turned not from *f.*   *2Sa 2:19;*
Abner   *2:30*
bid the people return from *f.*   *2Sa 2:26*
their brethren
I took thee from *f.* the   *2Sa 7:8;*
sheep, to be ruler   *1Ch 17:7; Ps 78:71*
went up from *f.* David (S)   *2Sa 20:2*
and they *f.* Adonijah, helped   *1Ki 1:7*
him
but if you shall at all turn   *1Ki 9:6*
from *f.* me
Ahab did very abominably   *1Ki 21:26*
in *f.* idols
the day *f.* (S)   *2Ch 29:21*
that ye may tell it to the   *Ps 48:13*
generation *f.*
in generation *f.* let their name   *Ps 109:13*
be blotted out
and confirming the word   *M'k 16:20*
with signs *f.*
I must walk to-morrow, and   *Lu 13:33*
the day *f.*
then Jesus turned and saw   *Joh 1:38*
them *f.*
the day *f.* the day *f.* when   *Joh 1:43;*
people saw   *6:22*
Peter seeth the disciple   *Joh 21:20*
whom Jesus loved *f.*
we came the day *f.* unto   *Ac 21:1;*
Rhodes   *21:18*
and the night *f.* the Lord   *Ac 23:11*
stood by him
are gone astray, *f.* the way   *2Pe 2:15*
of Balaam

FOLLOWS

burning fever *f.* (B)   *Hab 3:5*

FOLLY

because Shechem had   *Ge 34:7*
wrought *f.* in Israel
done a vile thing in Israel   *Ge 34:7*
(A)
a shameful deed had been   *Ge 34:7*
committed (B)
she wrought *f.* by playing   *De 22:21*
the whore
playing the harlot (A)   *De 22:21*
committed a flagrant crime   *De 22:21*
(B)
because Achan wrought *f.* in   *Jos 7:15*
Israel
done a disgraceful thing (B)   *Jos 7:15*
done a shameful thing   *Jos 7:15*
(A)(R)
nay, I pray you, do not this   *J'g 19:23*
f.
do not commit such wicked   *J'g 19:23*
act (B)
do not do this vile thing   *J'g 19:23*
(R)
do not such *f.* (A)   *J'g 19:24*
they have committed lewdness   *J'g 20:6*
and *f.*
committed a lewd and   *J'g 20:6*
wanton deed (B)
abomination and wantonness   *J'g 20:6*
in Israel (R)
according to the *f.* that they   *J'g 20:10*
wrought in
all lewdness committed in   *J'g 20:10*
Israel (B)
all the wanton crime in   *J'g 20:10*
Israel (R)
Nabal is his name, and *f.* is   *1Sa 25:25*
with
he is a fool (B)   *1Sa 25:25*
my brother, do not thou   *2Sa 13:12*
this *f.*
foolhardy, scandalous thing   *2Sa 13:12*
(A)
this disgraceful act (B)   *2Sa 13:12*
his angels he charged with *f.*   *Job 4:18*
angels he charges with error   *Job 4:18*
(B)(R)
yet God layeth not *f.* to   *Job 24:12*
them
God regards not wrong   *Job 24:12*
done them (A)
God does not hear their   *Job 24:12*
petitions (R)
God pays no attention to   *Job 24:12*
their prayers (R)
lest I deal with you after   *Job 42:8*
your *f.*
deal according to your   *Job 42:8*
misdemeanor (B)

nor charged God with *f.* (S)   *Job 1:22*
festering because of my *f.* (B)   *Ps 38:5*
this their way is their *f.* yet   *Ps 49:13*
posterity
know my *f.* and blundering   *Ps 69:5*
(A)(B)(R)
but let them not turn again to   *Ps 85:8*
f.
in greatness of *f.* he shall go   *Pr 5:23*
astray
but a fool layeth open his *f.*   *Pr 13:16*
but the *f.* of fools is deceitful   *Pr 14:8*
simple inherit *f.* but prudent   *Pr 14:18*
are crowned
crown of wise is riches,   *Pr 14:24*
foolishness of fools is *f.*
f. of fools is still *f.*   *Pr 14:24*
(B)(E)(R)
but he that is hasty of spirit   *Pr 14:29*
exalteth *f.*
pours out *f.* (A)(B)(E)(R)   *Pr 15:2*
feeds on *f.* (A)(B)(E)(R)   *Pr 15:14*
f. is joy to him that is   *Pr 15:21*
destitute of wisdom
but the instruction of fools   *Pr 16:22*
is *f.*
let a bear meet rather than a   *Pr 17:12*
fool in his *f.*
before he heareth it, ·it is *f.*   *Pr 18:13*
and shame to him
F. schemes are sin (B)   *Pr 24:9*
the devising of *f.* is sin (R)   *Pr 24:9*
answer not a fool according to   *Pr 26:4*
his *f.* lest like him
fool according to his *f.* lest wise   *Pr 26:5*
in conceit
as dog to vomit, so a fool   *Pr 26:11*
returneth to his *f.*
I gave my heart to know   *Ec 1:17*
wisdom and *f.*
I sought in my heart to lay   *Ec 2:3*
hold on *f.*
to lay hold on frivolity (B)   *Ec 2:3*
turned to behold *f.*; wisdom   *Ec 2:12;*
excelleth *f.*   *2:13*
I applied to know the   *Ec 7:25*
wickedness of *f.*
so doth a little *f.* him that is   *Ec 10:1*
in reputation
f. is set in great dignity, rich   *Ec 10:6*
sit in low place
words of his mouth are *f.*   *Ec 10:13*
(B)
an evil doer, and every   *Isa 9:17*
mouth speaketh *f.*
will speak *f.* (A)(B)(E)(R)   *Isa 32:6;*
  Jer 29:23
I have seen *f.* in the prophets   *Jer 23:13*
or Samaria
I saw something unsavory   *Jer 23:13*
(B)(R)
folly (N)(P)   *M'k 7:22*
absurdity and *f.*   *1Co 1:18*
(A)(B)(N)(R)
through *f.* of proclamation   *1Co 1:21*
(B)(E)(N)
by the *f.* of the gospel   *1Co 1:21*
(N)(R)
f. of the Gentiles   *1Co 1:23*
(B)(N)(R)
the *f.* that has source in   *1Co 1:25*
God (B)
divine *f.* is wiser (N)   *1Co 1:25*
are *f.* to him   *1Co 2:14*
(A)(B)(N)(R)
wisdom of world is *f.*   *1Co 3:19*
(B)(N)(R)
ye could bear with me a   *2Co 11:1*
little in my *f.*
little foolishness   *2Co 11:1*
(A)(B)(E)(P)(R)
their *f.* shall be made   *2Ti 3:9*
manifest to all men
their shallowness will be   *2Ti 3:9*
obvious (B)
will be recognized as fools   *2Ti 3:9*
(N)
empty *f.* of traditional ways   *1Pe 1:18*
(N)
loud boasts of *f.* (A)   *2Pe 2:18*

FOMENTOR

a *f.* of discord (N)   *Ac 24:5*

FOND

not *f.* of money-grabbing (P)   *1Ti 3:3*
not *f.* of money-grabbing (P)   *Tit 1:7*

FONDLED

f. children (B)   *1Sa 15:32*
I have *f.* (B)   *La 2:22*

FONDLING

Isaac *f.* Rebekah (R)   *Ge 26:8*

FONDLY

caring *f.* for (N)   *1Th 2:7*

FONDNESS

corrupt in foolish *f.* (A)   *Eze 23:11*

FOOD

food (S)   *Ge 1:29;*
1:30; 9:3; 27:4, 7, 9, 14, 17, 31; 39:6;
45:23; Le 11:34; 22:11, 13; 25:6, 7;
Nu 7:43; 28:24; De 2:4, 6, 28; 20:20;
28:26; J'g 14:14; Ru 1:6; 1Sa 20:34;
2Sa 3:35; 12:3, 20; 13:5, 10; 1Ki 10:5;
19:8; 21:4, 5, 7; 2Ch 9:4; 28:15;
Ezr 3:7; Ne 5:14, 15, 18; Job 12:11;
20:14, 21; 30:4; 33:20; 34:3; 36:31;
38:41; Ps 42:3; 44:11; 59:15; 69:21;
74:14; 78:18, 25, 30; 79:2; 104:21, 27;
107:18; 111:5; 145:15; Pr 6:8; 23:3;
30:22, 25; 31:15; Isa 65:25; Jer 7:33;
16:4; 19:7, 34:20; La 1:11, 19; 4:10;
Eze 4:10; 16:19; 29:5; 34:5, 10; 47:12;
Da 1:5, 8, 10, 13, 15, 16; 4:12, 21;
11:26; Ho 1:17; Joe 1:16; Hab 1:16;
3:17; Hag 2:12; Mal 1:12; 3:10; M't 3:4;
6:25; 10:10; 24:45; 25:35, 42; Lu 3:11;
8:55; 9:13; 12:23, 42; Joh 4:8, 32,
34; 6:27, 55; 21:5; Ac 2:46; 9:19; 16:34;
27:21, 33, 34, 36; Ro 14:15, 17, 20;
1Co 8:8, 13; 10:3; Col 2:16; Heb 12:16
it shall be for *f.*   *Ge 1:29;*
(A)(B)(E)(R)   *1:30; 9:3*
to the sight, and good for *f.*   *Ge 2:9*
saw that the tree was good for   *Ge 3:6*
f.
unto thee of all *f.* that is   *Ge 6:21*
eaten
and it shall be for *f.* for thee   *Ge 6:21*
f. supplies (S)   *Ge 14:11;*
Le 25:37; Jos 1:11; J'g 20:10; 1Ki 4:7,
27; 11:18; M't 14:15
there was set *f.* before him   *Ge 24:33*
(S)
And let them gather all the   *Ge 41:35*
f.
and let them keep *f.* in the   *Ge 41:35*
cities
And that *f.* shall be for   *Ge 41:36*
store to the
And he gathered up all the   *Ge 41:48*
f. of the
laid up the *f.* in the cities: *Ge 41:48*
the *f.* of
From the land of Canaan to   *Ge 42:7*
buy *f.*
but to buy *f.* are thy servants   *Ge 42:10*
come
and take *f.* for the famine   *Ge 42:33*
of your
Go again, buy us a little *f.*   *Ge 43:2*
we will go down and buy   *Ge 43:4*
thee *f.*
down at the first time to   *Ge 43:20*
buy *f.*
down in our hands to buy *f.*   *Ge 43:22*
I fill the men's sacks with *f.*   *Ge 44:1*
Go again, and buy us a   *Ge 44:25*
little *f.*
f. for his father (S)   *Ge 45:23*
seed of the field, and for   *Ge 47:24*
your *f.*
and for *f.* for your little   *Ge 47:24*
ones
prepared *f.* (A)   *Ex 12:39;*
  1Ki 4:27; 2Ch 11:11
prepared *f.* (B)   *Ex 12:39;*
J'g 20:10; 1Ki 4:27; 2Ch 11:11, 23
f. offering (B)   *Le 2:1;*
2:3; 6:14; 14:10; Nu 28:26
f. offering from the master (B)   *Le 2:7*
it is the *f.* of the offering   *Le 3:11;*
made   *3:16*
planted all manner of trees   *Le 19:23*
for *f.*
holy things because it is his   *Le 22:7*
f.
food (A)   *Le 25:37; Jos 9:14*
food (B)   *Le 25:37;*

De 23:19; 1Ki 4:7; Ne 13:15; Jer 40:5;
  44:17; M't 14:15; Lu 9:12
food (R)   *Le 25:37;*
1Ki 11:18; Ne 13:15; Jer 40:5; 44:17;
  M't 14:15
food (A)(B)(E)(R)   *De 2:6; 2:28;*
1Ki 10:5; Job 6:7; 12:11; 20:14; 30:4;
33:20; 34:3; 36:31; 38:41; Ps 42:3; 59:15;
69:21; 74:14; 78:25, 30; 79:2; 104:27;
107:18; 145:15; Pr 6:8; 23:3; 30:22, 25;
31:15; Isa 62:8; 65:25; La 1:11, 19; 4:10;
Eze 4:10; 16:19; 29:5; 34:10; 47:12;
Da 1:10; 4:12; Joe 1:16; Hab 1:16; 3:17;
  Hag 2:12; Mal 1:12; 3:10
in giving him *f.* and raiment   *De 10:18*
f. offerings (B)   *Jos 22:29*
scraps of *f.* (S)   *J'g 1:7*
be the man that eateth any   *1Sa 14:24*
f. until
So none of the people   *1Sa 14:24*
tasted any *f.*
be the man that eateth any   *1Sa 14:28*
f. this
master's son may have *f.* to   *2Sa 9:10*
eat
prepare the *f.* (S)   *2Sa 13:5*
desire, in giving *f.* for my   *1Ki 5:9*
household
thousand measures of wheat   *1Ki 5:11*
for *f.*
his *f.* regularly (S)   *2Ki 25:29*
store of *f.* (R)   *2Ch 11:11*
loathsome *f.* to me (S)   *Job 6:7*
mouth more than my   *Job 23:12*
necessary *f.*
wilderness yieldeth *f.* for   *Job 24:5*
them
provideth for the raven his   *Job 38:41*
f.
the mountains bring him   *Job 40:20*
forth *f.*
Man did eat angels' *f.*; he   *Ps 78:25*
sent
bring forth *f.* out of the   *Ps 104:14*
earth
Who giveth *f.* to all flesh: *Ps 136:25*
for his
which giveth *f.* to the hungry   *Ps 146:7*
He giveth to the beast his *f.*   *Ps 147:9*
gathereth her *f.* in the harvest   *Pr 6:8*
Much *f.* is in the tillage of   *Pr 13:23*
the poor
have goats' milk enough for   *Pr 27:27*
thy *f.*
for the *f.* of thy household,   *Pr 27:27*
and for
sweeping rain which leaveth   *Pr 28:3*
no *f.*
feed me with *f.* convenient for   *Pr 30:8*
me
she bringeth her *f.* from afar   *Pr 31:14*
and have diminished thine   *Eze 16:27*
ordinary *f.*
f. unto them that serve the   *Eze 48:18*
city
life greater than *f.*   *M't 6:25*
(A)(E)(N)(P)(R)
deserves his *f.* (A)(E)(R)   *M't 10:10*
buy *f.* (E)(N)(P)   *M't 14:15; Lu 9:12*
give to the others *f.*   *M't 24:45*
(A)(E)(P)(R)
gone off to buy *f.*   *Joh 4:8*
(A)(B)(E)(N)(P)(R)
I have *f.* of (A)(N)(P)(R)   *Joh 4:32;*
  4:34
labor not for *f.*   *Joh 6:27*
(A)(B)(E)(N)(P)(R)
my flesh is genuine *f.*   *Joh 6:55*
(A)(B)(N)(P)(R)
our hearts with *f.* and   *Ac 14:17*
gladness
abstain from *f.* offered (B)   *Ac 15:29*
a matter of *f.* and drink   *Ro 14:17*
(A)(R)
solid *f.* (S)   *1Co 3:2; Heb 5:12, 14*
f. does not commend us   *1Co 8:8;*
(A)(B)(E)(N)(R)   *8:10, 13*
same spiritual *f.*   *1Co 10:3*
(A)(B)(E)(N)(P)(R)
both minister bread for your   *2Co 9:10*
f.
abstain from certain *f.* (A)   *1Ti 4:3*
having *f.* and raiment let us   *1Ti 6:8*
be
solid *f.*   *Heb 5:12;*
(A)(B)(E)(N)(P)(R)   *5:14*
f. and drink (B)(N)(P)(R)   *Heb 9:10*
be naked, and destitute of   *Jas 2:15*
daily *f.*

FOODS

there was all manner of *f.*   *Ge 40:17*
(S)
dainty *f.* (A)   *Pr 23:6*
foods (S)   *Pr 23:6;*
M'k 7:19; 1Co 6:13; 1Ti 4:5; Heb 9:10;
  13:9
prohibit enjoyment of *f.*   *1Ti 4:3*
(B)(N)(P)(R)

FOOL

he is a *f.* (B)   *1Sa 25:25*
I have played the *f.* and   *1Sa 26:21*
erred
the *f.* hath said in his heart   *Ps 14:1;*
  53:1
scorn to the *f.* (R)   *Ps 39:8*
likewise the *f.* and brutish   *Ps 49:10*
person perish
neither doth a *f.* understand   *Ps 92:6*
but a prating *f.* shall fall   *Pr 10:8;*
  10:10
it is a sport to a *f.* to do   *Pr 10:23*
mischief
the *f.* shall be servant to the   *Pr 11:29*
wise of heart
the foolish (A)(E)   *Pr 11:29*
the foolish (B)   *Pr 11:29;*
  12:15, 16; 15:5; 20:3; Ec 2:19
the way of a *f.* is right in   *Pr 12:15*
his own eyes
wise man feareth, but *f.*   *Pr 13:16*
layeth open his folly
but the *f.* rageth and is   *Pr 14:16*
confident
a *f.* despiseth his father's   *Pr 15:5*
instruction
excellent speech becometh not   *Ps 17:7*
a *f.*
a reproof more than a   *Pr 17:10*
hundred stripes into a *f.*
let a bear meet a man rather   *Pr 17:12*
than *f.* in his folly
why is a price in hand of a   *Pr 17:16*
f. to get wisdom
he that begetteth a *f.* doth it   *Pr 17:21*
to his sorrow
a *f.* when he holdeth his   *Pr 17:28*
peace is counted wise
a *f.* hath no delight in   *Pr 18:2*
understanding
but every *f.* will be meddling   *Pr 20:3*
answer not a *f.*   *Pr 26:4*
answer a *f.*   *Pr 26:5*
so is he that giveth honour to   *Pr 26:8*
a *f.*
the great God rewardeth the   *Pr 26:10*
f. and transgressors
as a dog so a *f.* returneth to   *Pr 26:11*
his folly
but a *f.* wrath is heavier than   *Pr 27:3*
them both
though thou shouldest bray a   *Pr 27:22*
f. in a mortar
f. uttereth all his mind, but   *Pr 29:11*
a wise man keeps
but the *f.* walketh in darkness   *Ec 2:14*
as it happeneth to the *f.* so   *Ec 2:15*
even to me
is no remembrance of wise   *Ec 2:16*
man more than of *f.*
who knoweth whether he be   *Ec 2:19*
wise or a *f.*
the *f.* foldeth his hands   *Ec 4:5*
together, eats his flesh
for what hath the wise more   *Ec 6:8*
than the *f.*
f. is full of words, man   *Ec 10:14*
cannot tell what to be
a *f.* shall (A)(B)(E)(R)   *Isa 32:5;*
  32:6
and at his end he shall be a   *Jer 17:11*
f.
whosoever shall say, Thou *f.*   *M't 5:22*
be in danger
f. this night thy soul shall be   *Lu 12:20*
required
simpleton (B)   *Lu 12:20; 1Co 15:36*
let him become a *f.* that he   *1Co 3:18*
may be wise
thou *f.* that thou sowest is   *1Co 15:36*
not quickened
I say again, Let no man   *2Co 11:16*
think me a *f.*
tho' I would desire to glory,   *2Co 12:6*
shall not be a *f.*

I am become a *f.* in   *2Co 12:11*
glorying, ye compelled me
you cannot make a *f.* of God   *Ga 6:7*
(P)

AS A FOOL

David said, Died Abner, *as a*   *2Sa 3:33*
f. dieth
as a f. to the correction of   *Pr 7:22*
the stocks
how dieth the wise man? *as*   *Ec 2:16*
the f.
if otherwise, yet *as a f.*   *2Co 11:16*
receive me
are they ministers? I speak   *2Co 11:23*
as a f. I am more

FOR A FOOL

delight not seemly *for a f.*   *Pr 19:10*
wisdom is too high *for a f.*   *Pr 24:7*
opens not mouth
so honour is not seemly *for a*   *Pr 26:1*
f.
for a f. when he is filled   *Pr 30:22*
with meat

IS A FOOL

he that uttereth a slander *is*   *Pr 10:18*
a f.
than he that is perverse in his   *Pr 19:1*
lips, and *is a f.*
he that trusteth in his own   *Pr 28:26*
heart *is a f.*
when he that *is a f.* walketh,   *Ec 10:3*
he saith to everyone that he *is a f.*
prophet *is a f.* the spiritual   *Ho 9:7*
man is mad

OF A FOOL

the way *of a f.* is right in   *Pr 12:15*
his own eyes
and the father *of a f.* hath   *Pr 17:21*
no joy
the eyes *of a f.* are in the   *Pr 17:24*
ends of the earth
speak not in the ears *of a f.*   *Pr 23:9*
he will despise
he that sendeth a message by   *Pr 26:6*
the hand *of a f.*
there is more hope *of a f.*   *Pr 26:12;*
than of him   *29:20*
as crackling of thorns, so   *Ec 7:6*
laughter *of the f.*
but the lips *of a f.* will   *Ec 10:12*
swallow up himself

FOOLED

had been *f.* by wise men (P)   *M't 2:16*
God is not to be *f.* (N)   *Ga 6:7*

FOOLHARDY

worthless and *f.* men (A)(B)   *J'g 9:4*
f. scandalous thing (A)   *2Sa 13:12*

FOOLISH

do ye thus requite the Lord   *De 32:6*
O *f.* people
will provoke them with a *f.*   *De 32:21;*
nation   *Re 10:19*
thou speakest as one of *f.*   *Job 2:10*
women speaketh
for wrath killeth the *f.* man,   *Job 5:2*
envy slays
I have seen the *f.* taking root,   *Job 5:3*
but I cursed
the *f.* shall not stand in thy   *Ps 5:5*
sight
make me not the reproach of   *Ps 39:8*
the *f.*
I was envious at *f.* when I   *Ps 73:3*
saw prosperity
so *f.* was I and ignorant, I   *Ps 73:22*
was as a beast
the *f.* people have   *Ps 74:18*
blasphemed thy name
remember how *f.* man   *Ps 74:22*
reproacheth thee daily
f. men despise wisdom (B)(E)   *Pr 1:7*
forsake the *f.* and live, go in   *Pr 9:6*
way understanding
a *f.* woman is clamorous: is   *Pr 9:13*
simple, known

but a *f.* son is the heaviness   *Pr 10:1*
of his mother
but the mouth of the *f.* is   *Pr 10:14*
near destruction
the *f.* (B)   *Pr 10:21; 15:14; Isa 19:11*
the *f.* (A)(E)   *Pr 11:29;*
  12:15, 16; 15:5; 20:3; 11:29
but the *f.* plucketh it down   *Pr 14:1*
with her hands
in the mouth of the *f.* is a   *Pr 14:3*
rod of pride
go from the presence of a *f.*   *Pr 14:7*
man
but the heart of the *f.* doeth   *Pr 15:7*
not so
but a *f.* man despiseth his   *Pr 15:20*
mother
a *f.* son is a grief to his   *Pr 17:25*
father, and bitter
a *f.* son is the calamity of   *Pr 19:13*
his father
a *f.* man spendeth a treasure   *Pr 21:20*
if a wise man contendeth   *Pr 29:9*
with a *f.* man
better is a wise child than a   *Ec 4:13*
f. king
be not overmuch wicked,   *Ec 7:17*
neither be thou *f.*
labour of the *f.* wearieth   *Ec 10:15*
every one of them
he maketh their knowledge   *Isa 44:25*
f.
for my people are *f.* they are   *Jer 4:22*
sottish children
f., experts in evil (B)(R)   *Jer 4:22*
I said. Surely these are poor,   *Jer 5:4*
they are *f.*
hear now this, O *f.* people,   *Jer 5:21*
who see not
but they are altogether   *Jer 10:8*
brutish and *f.*
thy prophets have seen vain   *La 2:14*
and *f.* things
empty, *f.* vision (A)   *Eze 12:24*
thus saith the Lord; Woe to   *Eze 13:3*
the *f.* prophets
corrupt in *f.* fondness (A)   *Eze 23:11*
f. son (B)   *Ho 13:13*
take the instruments of a *f.*   *Zec 11:15*
shepherd
shall be likened unto a *f.*   *M't 7:26*
man who built
five of the virgins were wise,   *M't 25:2*
and five *f.*
you will look *f.* (N)   *Lu 14:9*
you *f.* ones (A)(S)   *Lu 24:25*
wise and *f.* (A)(E)(R)   *Ro 1:14;*
  Eph 5:17
and their *f.* heart was darkened   *Ro 1:21*
f. faithless, heartless (R)   *Ro 1:31*
an instructor of the *f.* a   *Ro 2:20*
teacher of babes
hath not God made *f.*   *1Co 1:20*
wisdom of this world
f. thing (A)   *1Co 1:25*
O *f.* Galatians, who hath   *Ga 3:1*
bewitched you
are ye so *f.* having begun in   *Ga 3:3*
the spirit
neither filthiness, nor *f.*   *Eph 5:4*
talking
the *f.* (B)   *Eph 5:15*
they that will be rich fall into   *1Ti 6:9*
f. lusts
but *f.* questions avoid   *2Ti 2:23;*
  Tit 3:9
we ourselves were sometimes   *Tit 3:3*
f. deceived
steer clear of *f.* speculations   *Tit 3:9*
(N)
without making them *f.* or   *Jas 1:5*
guilty (P)
may put to silence the   *1Pe 2:15*
ignorance of *f.* men

FOOLISHLY

thou hast now done *f.* in so   *Ge 31:28;*
doing   *1Sa 13:13; 2Ch 16:9*
the sin on us wherein we   *Nu 12:11*
have done *f.*
Thou hast done *f.*   *1Sa 13:13*
I have done very *f.*   *2Sa 24:10; 1Ch 21:8*
I have sinned greatly   *2Sa 24:10*
(B)(E)(R)
in all this Job sinned not,   *Job 1:22*
nor charged God *f.*
charged God of doing wrong   *Job 1:22*
(B)(R)

I said to the fools, Deal not *f.*   Ps 75:4
Deal not arrogantly-do not   Ps 75:4
boast (A)
Do not boast (B)(R)   Ps 75:4
Deal not arrogantly (E)   Ps 75:4
he that is soon angry dealeth   Pr 14:17
f.
one who speaks *f.* (R)   Pr 20:19
if thou hast done *f.* in lifting   Pr 30:32
thyself
I speak it as it were *f.* in   2Co 11:17
this boasting
I speak *f.* I am bold also,   2Co 11:21
are they Hebrews

FOOLISHNESS

turn the counsel of   2Sa 15:31
Ahithophel into *f.*
my wounds stink because of   Ps 38:5
my *f.*
festering because of my folly   Ps 38:5
(B)
O God, thou knowest my *f.;*   Ps 69:5
sins are not hid
you know my folly and   Ps 69:5
blundering (A)(B)(R)
but the heart of fools   Pr 12:23
proclaimeth *f.*
but the *f.* of fools is folly   Pr 14:24
folly of fools is still folly   Pr 14:24
(B)(E)(R)
but the mouth of fools   Pr 15:2
poureth out *f.*
pours out folly   Pr 15:2
(A)(B)(E)(R)
but the mouth of fools   Pr 15:14
feedeth on *f.*
feeds on folly   Pr 15:14
(A)(B)(E)(R)
the *f.* of man perverteth his   Pr 19:3
way
f. is bound in the heart of a   Pr 22:15
child
the thought of *f.* is sin, the   Pr 24:9
scorner abomination
Folly's schemes are sin (B)   Pr 24:9
the devising of folly is sin   Pr 24:9
(R)
yet will not his *f.* depart   Pr 27:22
from him
to know the wickedness of *f.*   Ec 7:25
madness
beginning of the words of   Ec 10:13
his mouth is *f.*
words of his mouth are folly   Ec 10:13
(B)
thefts, pride, *f.,* come from   M'k 7:22
within
thoughtlessness (B)   M'k 7:22
folly (N)(P)   M'k 7:22
preaching of cross to them   1Co 1:18
that perish *f.*
absurdity and folly   1Co 1:18
(A)(B)(N)(R)
nonsense to dying world (P)   1Co 1:18
it pleased God by the *f.* of   1Co 1:21
preaching to save
through folly of its   1Co 1:21
proclamation (B)
by the folly of the gospel   1Co 1:21
(N)(R)
by simplemindedness of   1Co 1:21
gospel message (P)
we preach Christ crucified, to   1Co 1:23
the Greeks *f.*
absurd, utterly   1Co 1:23
unphilosophical nonsense (A)
folly to the Gentiles   1Co 1:23
(B)(N)(R)
sheer nonsense to Gentiles   1Co 1:23
(P)
because the *f.* of God is   1Co 1:25
wiser than men
foolish thing (A)   1Co 1:25
folly that has its source in   1Co 1:25
God (B)
divine folly is wiser than   1Co 1:25
(N)
the things of the Spirit of   1Co 2:14
God are *f.* to him
are folly to him   1Co 2:14
(A)(B)(N)(R)
they just don't make sense   1Co 2:14
to him (P)
the wisdom of this world is   1Co 3:19
f. with God
wisdom of world is folly   1Co 3:19
(B)(N)(R)

world's cleverness is   1Co 3:19
stupidity (P)
little *f.* (A)(B)(E)(P)(R)   2Co 11:1
f. of thoughtless people   1Pe 2:15
(A)(B)(R)

FOOLS

thou shalt be as one of the   2Sa 13:13
f. in Israel
like the immoral pack in   2Sa 13:13
Israel (B)
and he maketh the judges *f.*   Job 12:17
they were children of *f.*   Job 30:8
children of base men
sons of the worthless   Job 30:8
(A)(B)
children of base men (E)   Job 30:8
A senseless, disreputable   Job 30:8
brood (R)
I said to the *f.* Deal not   Ps 75:4
foolishly
said to the boastful   Ps 75:4
(A)(B)(R)
said to the arrogant (E)   Ps 75:4
ye *f.* when will ye be wise   Ps 94:8
f. because of their   Ps 107:17
transgression are afflicted
but *f.* despise wisdom and   Pr 1:7
instruction
foolish men despise wisdom   Pr 1:7
(B)(E)
how long, ye *f.* will ye hate   Pr 1:22
knowledge
and the prosperity of *f.* shall   Pr 1:32
destroy them
but shame shall be the   Pr 3:35
promotion of *f.*
and ye *f.* be ye of an   Pr 8:5
understanding heart
but *f.* die for want of   Pr 10:21
wisdom
the foolish (B)   Pr 10:21;
      15:14; Isa 19:11
but the heart of *f.*   Pr 12:23
proclaimeth foolishness
but it is abomination to *f.* to   Pr 13:19
depart from evil
but a companion of *f.* shall   Pr 13:20
be destroyed
folly of *f.* is deceit; *f.* make   Pr 14:8;
a mock at sin   14:9
crown of wise is riches,   Pr 14:24
foolishness of *f.* is folly
what is in the midst of *f.* is   Pr 14:33
made known
the mouth of *f.* poureth out   Pr 15:2
foolishness
the mouth of *f.* feedeth on   Pr 15:14
foolishness
but the instruction of *f.* is   Pr 16:22
folly
stripes are prepared for the   Pr 19:29
back of *f.*
so is a parable in the mouth   Pr 26:7;
of *f.*   26:9
more ready to hear, than give   Ec 5:1
sacrifice of *f.*
he hath no pleasure in *f.* pay   Ec 5:4
what hast vowed
but the heart of *f.* is in the   Ec 7:4
house of mirth
than for a man to hear the   Ec 7:5
song of *f.*
be not hasty, for anger resteth   Ec 7:9
in the bosom of *f.*
more than cry of him that   Ec 9:17
ruleth among *f.*
surely the princes of Zoan   Isa 19:11;
are *f.*   19:13
wayfaring men, tho' *f.* shall   Isa 35:8
not err therein
become (S)   Jer 50:36
ye *f.* and blind, whether is   M't 23:17;
greater   23:19
ye *f.* did not he that made   Lu 11:40
that without
Simpletons (B)   Lu 11:40; 24:25
senseless ones (A)   Lu 11:40
f. and slow of heart to   Lu 24:25
believe the prophets
you foolish ones (A)   Lu 24:25
professing to be wise, they   Ro 1:22
become *f.*
we are *f.* for Christ's sake,   1Co 4:10
seeing ye are wise
for ye suffer *f.* gladly,   2Co 11:19
seeing ye are wise
see than that ye walk not as   Eph 5:15
f. but as wise

the unwise and witless   Eph 5:15
(A)(E)(R)
the foolish (B)   Eph 5:15
like sensible men, not like   Eph 5:15
simpletons (N)
be not *f.* (N)   Eph 5:15
be regarded as *f.* (N)   2Ti 3:9

FOOL'S

A *f.* wrath is presently   Pr 12:16
known: but
A *f.* lips enter into contention   Pr 18:6
A *f.* mouth is his destruction   Pr 18:7
the ass, and a rod for the *f.*   Pr 26:3
back
A *f.* wrath is heavier than   Pr 27:3
them
a *f.* voice is known by   Ec 5:3
multitude
but a *f.* heart at his left   Ec 10:2

FOOT

found no rest for the sole of   Ge 8:9
her *f.*
shall no man lift up his   Ge 41:44
hand or *f.*
about six hundred thousand   Ex 12:37
on *f.*
for tooth, hand for hand, *f.*   Ex 21:24
for *f.*
upon the great toe of their   Ex 29:20;
right *f.*   Le 8:23; 13:12; 14:14, 17, 25, 28
a laver of brass, and his *f.*   Ex 30:18;
also   30:28; 31:9; 35:16; 38:8; 39:39;
      40:11; Le 8:11
crushed Balaam's *f.* against   Nu 22:25
no, not so much as a *f.*   De 2:5
breadth
did thy *f.* swell, these forty   De 8:4
years
wateredst it with thy *f.* as a   De 11:10
garden
for tooth, hand for hand, *f.*   De 19:21
for *f.*
and loose his shoe from off   De 25:9
his *f.*
from the sole of thy *f.* unto   De 28:35
the top
the sole of her *f.* upon the   De 28:56
ground
shall the sole of thy *f.* have   De 28:65
rest
shoe is not waxen old upon   De 29:5
thy *f.*
their *f.* shall slide in due   De 32:35
time
and let him dip his *f.* in oil   De 33:24
the sole of your *f.* shall tread   Jos 1:3
upon
Loose thy shoe from off thy   Jos 5:15
f.
he was sent on *f.* into the   J'g 5:15
valley
was as light of *f.* as a wild   2Sa 2:18
roe
the sole of his *f.* even to   2Sa 14:25
the crown
and on every *f.* six toes,   2Sa 21:20
four and
the horses: and he trode her   2Ki 9:33
under *f.*
on each hand, and six on   1Ch 20:6
each *f.*
any more remove the *f.* of   2Ch 33:8
Israel
the sole of his *f.* unto his   Job 2:7
crown
My *f.* hath held his steps,   Job 23:11
his way
the waters forgotten of the *f.*   Job 28:4
if my *f.* hath hasted to   Job 31:5
deceit
forgetteth that the *f.* may   Job 39:15
crush
which they hid is their own *f.*   Ps 9:15
taken
My *f.* standeth in an even   Ps 26:12
place
Let not the *f.* of pride come   Ps 36:11
against
when my *f.* slippeth, they   Ps 38:16
magnify
they went through the flood   Ps 66:6
on *f.*
thy *f.* may be dipped in the   Ps 68:23
blood of
thou dash thy *f.* against a   Ps 91:12
stone

I said, My *f.* slippeth; thy mercy	*Ps 94:18*
will not suffer thy *f.* to be moved	*Ps 121:3*
refrain thy *f.* from their path	*Pr 1:15*
and thy *f.* shall not stumble	*Pr 3:23*
shall keep thy *f.* from being taken	*Pr 3:26*
to the left: remove thy *f.* from evil	*Pr 4:27*
thy *f.* from thy neighbour's house	*Pr 25:17*
broken tooth, and a *f.* out of joint	*Pr 25:19*
Keep thy *f.* when thou goest to	*Ec 5:1*
From the sole of the *f.* even unto	*Isa 1:6*
my mountains tread him under *f.*	*Isa 14:25*
meted out and trodden under *f.*	*Isa 18:7*
and put off thy shoe from thy *f.*	*Isa 20:2*
The *f.* shall tread it down, even the	*Isa 26:6*
from the east, called him to his *f.*	*Isa 41:2*
turn away thy *f.* from the sabbath	*Isa 58:13*
Withhold thy *f.* from being unshod	*Jer 2:25*
have trodden my portion under *f.*	*Jer 12:10*
Lord hath trodden under *f.*	*La 1:15*
was like the sole of a calf's *f.*	*Eze 1:7*
and stamp with thy *f.* and say	*Eze 6:11*
No *f.* of man shall pass through it	*Eze 29:11*
nor *f.* of beast shall pass through it	*Eze 29:11*
shall the *f.* of man trouble them	*Eze 32:13*
the host to be trodden under *f.*	*Da 8:13*
that is swift of *f.* shall not deliver	*Am 2:15*
lest at any time thou dash thy *f.*	*M't 4:6*
and to be trodden under *f.* of men	*M't 5:13*
followed him on *f.* out of the cities	*M't 14:13*
if thy hand or thy *f.* offend thee	*M't 18:8*
Bind him hand and *f.* and take him	*M't 22:13*
And if thy *f.* offend thee, cut it off	*M'k 9:45*
thou dash thy *f.* against a stone	*Lu 4:11*
hand and *f.* with gravec018thes	*Joh 11:44*
not so much as to set his *f.* on	*Ac 7:5*
If the *f.* shall say, Because I am not	*1Co 12:15*
trodden under *f.* the Son of God	*Heb 10:29*
with a garment down to the *f.*	*Re 1:13*
and he set his right *f.* upon	*Re 10:2*
sea, and his left *f.* on the earth	*Re 10:2*
the holy city shall they tread under *f.*	*Re 11:2*

FOOTED

whatsoever is cloven *f.* that ye shall eat	*Le 11:3*
and the swine though he be cloven *f.* is unclean	*Le 11:7*
man that is broken *f.* shall not approach	*Le 21:19*
all manner of four *f.* beasts	*Ac 10:12; 11:6*
image made like birds and four *f.* beasts	*Ro 1:23*

FOOTHILLS

the *f.* (B)	*De 1:7; Jos 10:40*
the *f.* (B)	*Jos 10:40; 12:8*

FOOTHOLD

f. washed out by deluge (B)	*Job 22:16*
lose own proper *f.* (N)(P)	*2Pe 3:17*

FOOTMEN

are six hundred thousand *f.*	*Nu 11:21*
thousand *f.* that drew sword	*J'g 20:2*
fell of Israel thirty thousand	*1Sa 4:10*
two hundred thousand *f.* and ten	*1Sa 15:4*
king said unto the *f.* that stood	*1Sa 22:17*
and twenty thousand *f.*: and	*2Sa 8:4*
twenty thousand *f.* and of king	*2Sa 10:6*
hundred thousand *f.* in one day	*1Ki 20:29*
and ten thousand *f.*; for the king	*2Ki 13:7*
and twenty thousand *f.*:	*1Ch 18:4*
forty thousand *f.* and killed	*1Ch 19:18*
If thou hast run with the *f.*	*Jer 12:5*

FOOTSTEPS

in thy paths, that my *f.* slip not	*Ps 17:5*
and thy *f.* are not known	*Ps 77:19*
reproached the *f.* of thine anointed	*Ps 89:51*
thy way forth by the *f.* of the flock	*Ca 1:8*

FOOTSTOOL

and for the *f.* of our God	*1Ch 28:2*
to the throne, with a *f.* of gold	*2Ch 9:18*
and worship at his *f.*; for he	*Ps 99:5*
I make thine enemies thy *f.*	*Ps 110:1*
we will worship at his *f.*	*Ps 132:7*
and the earth is my *f.* where	*Isa 66:1*
remembered not his *f.* in the	*La 2:1*
earth; for it is his *f.*	*M't 5:35*
thine enemies thy *f.*	*M't 22:44; M'k 12:36; Lu 20:43*
make thy foes thy *f.*	*Ac 2:35*
and earth is my *f.*	*Ac 7:49*
thine enemies thy *f.*	*Heb 1:13*
enemies be made his *f.*	*Heb 10:13*
or sit here under my *f.*	*Jas 2:3*

FOR

so nigh in all things that we call on him *f.*	*De 4:7*
shewed David all Joab had sent him *f.*	*2Sa 11:22*
f. piece of bread that man will transgress	*Pr 28:21*
f. maketh his sun to rise on evil and good	*M't 5:45*
they think to be heard *f.* their much speaking	*M't 6:7*
f. I was hungry, ye gave me meat	*M't 25:35; 25:42*
of his fulness we received grace *f.* grace	*Joh 1:16*
f. f. this cause ye pay tribute also	*Ro 13:6*
f. we know, if this house were dissolved	*2Co 5:1*
f. we can do nothing against but *f.* the truth	*2Co 13:8*
looking for the coming of the day of God	*2Pe 3:12*

FORASMUCH

f. as God hath shewed thee all this	*Ge 41:39*
f. as he hath no inheritance with you	*De 12:12*
f. as the Lord hath taken vengeance	*J'g 11:36*
f. as we have sworn both of us	*1Sa 20:42*
f. as my lord is come again in peace	*2Sa 19:30*
f. as thou hast disobeyed the Lord	*1Ki 13:21*
f. as Reuben defiled his father's bed	*1Ch 5:1*
f. as this people draw near with their mouth	*Isa 29:13*
f. as there is none like to thee, O Lord	*Jer 10:6*
f. among all wise men of nations none like thee	*Jer 10:7*
f. as iron break, and subdueth all things	*Da 2:40*

f. as he also is the son of Abraham	*Lu 19:9*
f. then as God gave them the like gift	*Ac 11:17*
f. then as we are the offspring of God	*Ac 17:29*
f. as I know that thou hast been a judge	*Ac 24:10*
f. as he is the image and glory of God	*1Co 11:7*
f. as ye are zealous of spiritual gifts	*1Co 14:12*
f. as ye know your labour is not in vain	*1Co 15:58*
f. as ye know ye were not redeemed	*1Pe 1:18*
f. then as Christ hath suffered for us	*1Pe 4:1*

FORBADE

nor unto whatsoever the Lord *f.* us	*De 2:37*
but John *f.* him, saying, I have need	*M't 3:14*
one casting out devils, we *f.* him	*M'k 9:38; Lu 9:49*
ass *f.* madness of the prophet	*2Pe 2:16*

FORBARE

David escaped, and Saul *f.* to go forth	*1Sa 23:13*
then the prophet *f.* and said, I know	*2Ch 25:16*
so Ishmael *f.* and slew them not	*Jer 41:8*

FORBEAR

if see his ass, and would *f.* to help him	*Ex 23:5*
hesitate lending a hand (B)	*Ex 23:5*
refrain from leaving him with it (A)(R)	*Ex 23:5*
if *f.* to vow, it shall be no sin	*De 23:22*
refrain from vowing (A)	*De 23:22*
refrain from making a vow (B)(R)	*De 23:22*
shall I go, or *f.*	*1Ki 22:6; 2Ch 18:5, 14*
shall I hold back (A)	*1Ki 22:6;*
shall I let it alone (B)	*1Ki 22:6; 1Ki 22:15*
f. why shouldest thou be smitten	*2Ch 25:16*
Stop! should you be put to death (A)(R)	*2Ch 25:16*
Quiet! should you be killed (B)	*2Ch 25:16*
f. thee from meddling with God	*2Ch 35:21*
Refrain from opposing God (A)	*2Ch 35:21*
Quit interferring with God (B)	*2Ch 35:21*
Cease opposing God (R)	*2Ch 35:21*
yet many years didst thou *f.* them	*Ne 9:30*
you bore with them many years (A)	*Ne 9:30*
didst bear with them (B)(E)(R)	*Ne 9:30*
and though I *f.* what am I eased	*Job 16:6*
if I refrain from speaking (A)	*Job 16:6*
if I do not speak (B)	*Job 16:6*
thou *f.* to deliver them drawn to death	*Pr 24:11*
but if it seem ill to thee to come, *f.*	*Jer 40:4*
whether they will hear or *f.*	*Eze 2:5; 2:7; 3:11*
whether hear or refuse (A)(B)(R)	*Eze 2:5; 2:7; 3:11*
and he that forbeareth, let him *f.*	*Eze 3:27*
let him decline who will (B)	*Eze 3:27*
let him refuse (R)	*Eze 3:27*
f. to cry, make no mourning for the dead	*Eze 24:17*
I said, Give me my price, if not *f.*	*Zec 11:12*
but if not, withhold them (A)	*Zec 11:12*
if not, let it go (B)	*Zec 11:12*
but if not, keep them (R)	*Zec 11:12*

FORBEAR

have not we power to f. working	1Co 9:6
refrained from doing manual labor (A)	1Co 9:6
entitled to freedom from manual labor (B)	1Co 9:6
bound to work for our living (N)	1Co 9:6
allowed to leave ordinary work (P)	1Co 9:6
refrain from working for living (R)	1Co 9:6
f. lest any should think of me above what	2Co 12:6
I abstain so that no one (A)	2Co 12:6
I will refrain (B)(N)(R)	2Co 12:6
I am not going to do so (P)	2Co 12:6
f. threatening (E)(R)	Eph 6:9
wherefore when we could no longer f.	2Th 3:1

FORBEARANCE

the riches of his goodness and f.	Ro 2:4
and tolerance (B)(N)	Ro 2:4
God's generosity and patient mercy (P)	Ro 2:4
that are past, through the f. of God	Ro 3:25
your f. be known (E)(R)	Ph'p 4:5

FORBEARETH

that f. keep the passover shall be cut off	Nu 9:13
and he that f. let him forbear	Eze 3:27

FORBEARING

by long f. is a prince persuaded	Pr 25:15
I was weary with f. I could not stay	Jer 20:9
enduring and holding it in (A)(B)(R)	Jer 20:9
f. one another in love	Eph 4:2; Col 3:13
bearing with one another (A)	Eph 4:2
bear with one another (B)	Eph 4:2
making allowances for one another (P)	Eph 4:2
masters, do the same things, f. threatening	Eph 6:9
give up threatening, using violent and abusive words (A)	Eph 6:9
dispense with threatening (B)	Eph 6:9
forbear threatening (E)(R)	Eph 6:9
give up using threats (N)	Eph 6:9
misusing power over others (P)	Eph 6:9
known your f. spirit (A)	Ph'p 4:5
exercise gentleness and f. (A)	Heb 5:2

FOREBEARS

blessings of our f. (B)	Ge 49:26

FORBID

Joshua said, My lord Moses, f.	Nu 11:28
the Lord f. I should do this thing	1Sa 24:6
Lord f. I should stretch forth mine hand	1Sa 26:11
Naboth said to Ahab, The Lord f. it me	1Ki 21:3
my God f. it me, that I should do this	1Ch 11:19
but Jesus said, F. him not	M'k 9:39; Lu 9:50
suffer little children f. them not	M'k 10:14; Lu 18:16
taketh thy cloke, f. not to take coat also	Lu 6:29
Peter answered, Can any f. water, that these	Ac 10:47
should f. none of his acquaintance to come	Ac 24:23
and f. not to speak with tongues	1Co 14:39

GOD FORBID

God f.	Ge 44:7; 44:17; Jos 22:29; 24:16; 1Sa 12:23; 14:45; 20:2; Job 27:5;

	Lu 20:16; Ro 3:4, 6, 31; 6:2, 15; 7:7, 13; 9:14; 11:1, 11; 1Co 6:15; Ga 2:17; 3:21; 6:14

FORBIDDEN

if a soul commit any of these things f.	Le 5:17
f. by father (B)	Nu 30:5; 30:8
or the likeness of what the Lord hath f.	De 4:23
and were f. to preach the word in Asia	Ac 16:6

FORBIDDETH

f. them that would, and casteth	3Jo 10

FORBIDDING

f. to give tribute to Caesar, saying	Lu 23:2
all confidence, no man f. him	Ac 28:31
F. us to speak to the Gentiles	1Th 2:16
F. to marry, and commanding	1Ti 4:3

FORBORN

men of Babylon have f. to fight	Jer 51:30

FORCE

wouldest take by f. thy daughters	Ge 31:31
the man f. her, and lie with her	De 22:25
not dim, nor his natural f. abated	De 34:7
and if not, I will take it by f.	1Sa 2:16
Nay, my brother, do not f. me	2Sa 13:12
f. to pay tribute (S)	2Ch 8:8
them to cease by f. and power	Ezr 4:23
he f. the queen also before me	Es 7:8
By the great f. of my disease	Job 30:18
and his f. is in the navel of his	Job 40:16
their blood by the f. of the sword	Jer 18:21
is evil, and their f. is not right	Jer 23:10
of Heshbon because of the f.	Jer 48:45
but with f. and with cruelty have	Eze 34:4
by the f. of the sword in the time	Eze 35:5
strong shall not strengthen his f.	Am 2:14
and the violent take it by f.	M't 11:12
f. them to come in (B)	Lu 14:23
take him by f. to make him a king	Joh 6:15
by f. (B)	Ac 5:26; 24:7; 27:41
take him by f. from among them	Ac 23:10
f. them to deny their Lord (P)	Ac 26:11
a testament is of f. after men are	Heb 9:17

FORCED

f. labor (S)	Ge 49:15; Jos 17:13; J'g 1:28; 2Sa 20:24; 1Ki 4:6; 5:13, 14; 9:15; 12:18; 2Ch 10:18
f. them by harsh treatment (B)	Ex 1:14
become slaves to do f. labor (S)	Jos 16:10
subject to f. labor (S)	J'g 1:30
subjects of f. labor	J'g 1:33; 1:35
Amorites f. the children of Dan	J'g 1:34
have they f. that she is dead	J'g 20:5
I f. myself therefore, and offered	1Sa 13:12
than she, f. her, and lay with her	2Sa 13:14
because he had f. his sister	2Sa 15:22
from the day that he f. his sister	2Sa 15:32

conscript for f. labor (S)	1Ki 9:21
the flattering of her lips she f. him	Pr 7:21
put to f. labor (S)	Pr 12:24
put to f. labor (R)	Isa 31:8
they f. to carry (A)(B)	M't 27:32
they f. a passerby to (A)(B)	M'k 15:21
f. them by torture to (B)	Ac 26:11
I was f. to appeal (A)(B)(P)	Ac 28:19
you f. me to it (A)(B)(P)(R)	2Co 12:11

FORCES

he placed f. in all the fenced cities	2Ch 17:2
nor all the f. of strength	Job 36:19
the f. of the Gentiles shall come	Isa 60:5
unto thee the f. of the Gentiles	Isa 60:11
when all the captains of the f. which	Jer 40:7
and all the captains of the f. that	Jer 40:13
the f. that were with him	Jer 41:11; 41:13, 16
Then all the captains of the f. and	Jer 42:1
the f. which were with him, and all	Jer 42:8
captains of the f. and all the people	Jer 43:4
all the captains of the f. took all	Jer 43:5
assemble a multitude of great f.	Da 11:10
f. shall stand on his part (S)	Da 11:31
shall he honour the God of f.	Da 11:38
carried away captive his f. and	Ob 11
f. you to go one mile (A)(B)(P)(R)	M't 5:21
the f. of death (N)(P)(R)	M't 16:18
f. of heaven be shaken (B)	M't 24:29
everyone f. into it (B)(N)	Lu 16:16
spiritual f. of evil (B)	Eph 6:12

FORCIBLE

How f. are right words! but what	Job 6:25

FORCIBLY

f. removed (S)	2Ki 17:21

FORCING

destroy the trees thereof by f. an	De 20:19
f. of wrath bringeth forth strife	Pr 30:33
men are f. their way (P)	Lu 16:16

FORD

and passed over the f. Jabbok	Ge 32:22

FORDS

the way to Jordan unto the f.	Jos 2:7
the f. of Jordan toward Moab	J'g 3:28
at the f. (S)	J'g 12:5; 12:6
Moab shall be at the f. of Arnon	Isa 16:2
the f. were seized (S)	Jer 51:32

FORECAST

f. his devices against the strong	Da 11:24
they shall f. devices against him	Da 11:25

FOREFATHER

our f. humanly speaking (A)	Ro 4:1

FOREFATHERS

blessings of our f. (A)	Ge 49:26
back to the iniquities of their f.	Jer 11:10
whom I serve from my f. with pure	2Ti 1:3

FOREFRONT

in the *f.* of the tabernacle	Ex 26:9
upon the *f.* of the mitre it shall	Ex 28:37
upon his *f.* did he put the	Le 8:9
The *f.* of the one was situate	1Sa 14:5
in the *f.* of the hottest battle	2Sa 11:15
f. of hardest fighting (R)	2Sa 11:15
the *f.* of the house, from between	2Ki 16:14
Jehoshaphat in the *f.* of them	2Ch 20:27
from the *f.* of the lower gate unto	Eze 40:19
the *f.* of the inner court without	Eze 40:19
f. of the house stood toward	Eze 47:1

FOREGO

f. the seventh year (S)	Ne 10:31

FOREHEAD

And it shall be upon Aaron's *f.*	Ex 28:38
and it shall be always upon his *f.*	Ex 29:38
he is *f.* bald: yet is he clean	Le 13:41
or bald *f.* a white reddish sore	Le 13:42
in his bald head, or his bald *f.*	Le 13:42
or in his bald *f.* as the leprosy	Le 13:43
and smote the Philistine in his *f.*	1Sa 17:49
that the stone sunk into his *f.*	1Sa 17:49
the leprosy even rose up in his *f.*	2Ch 26:19
behold, he was leprous in his *f.*	2Ch 26:20
and thou hadst a whore's *f.*	Jer 3:3
f. strong against their foreheads	Eze 3:8
harder than flint have I made thy *f.*	Eze 3:9
And I put a jewel on thy *f.*	Eze 16:12
and receive his mark in his *f.*	Re 14:9
upon her *f.* was a name written	Re 17:5

FOREHEADS

forehead strong against their *f.*	Eze 3:8
set a mark upon the *f.* of the men	Eze 9:4
servants of our God in their *f.*	Re 7:3
have not the seal of God in their *f.*	Re 9:4
in their right hand, or in their *f.*	Re 13:16
Father's name written in their *f.*	Re 14:1
received his mark upon their *f.*	Re 20:4
and his name shall be in their *f.*	Re 22:4

FOREIGN

f. gods (B)	Ge 35:2; 35:4; Jos 24:20; J'g 10:16; 1Sa 7:3; 2Ch 33:15; Jer 5:19
f. gods (E)	Ge 35:2; 35:4; Jos 24:20, 23; J'g 10:16; 1Sa 7:3; 2Ch 33:15
foreign (S)	Ge 35:2; 35:4; Ex 2:22; 18:3; 21:8; De 32:12; Jos 24:20, 23; J'g 10:16; 1Sa 7:3; 1Ki 11:1, 8; 2Ch 14:3; 33:15; Ezr 10:10, 11; Ps 81:9; 137:4; Pr 6:24; 27:13; Jer 5:19; 8:19; Da 11:39; Zep 1:8; Mal 2:11; Ac 26:11; Heb 11:9
f. land (B)	Ex 2:22; 18:3; Ps 137:4; Heb 11:9
f. land (E)	Ex 2:22; 18:3; Ps 137:4
f. land (R)	Ex 2:22; 18:3
f. people (A)(B)(E)(R)	Ex 21:8
f. god, gods (A)	De 32:12; Jos 24:23; J'g 10:16; 1Sa 7:2; 2Ch 33:15; Da 11:39; Mal 2:11
f. god (B)(E)	De 32:12; Da 11:39; Mal 2:11
f. women (A)	1Ki 11:1; Ne 13:27
f. women (B)	1Ki 11:1; Ezr 10:2, 10, 17-18, 44; Ne 13:27
f. women (E)	1Ki 11:1; Ezr 10:2, 10, 14, 17, 18; Ne 13:27; Pr 23:27; 27:13
f. women (R)	1Ki 11:1; Ezr 10:2, 10, 14, 17-18, 44; Ne 13:27
f. wives (A)	1Ki 11:8; Ezr 10:2, 10, 14, 17, 44
f. wives (B)	1Ki 11:8; Ezr 10:11, 14
f. wives (E)	1Ki 11:8; Ezr 10:44
f. wives (R)	1Ki 11:8
f. waters (A)(B)	2Ki 19:24
f. altars (A)(B)(E)(R)	2Ch 14:3
f. residents (B)	2Ch 30:25
f. gods (R)	2Ch 33:15; Jer 5:19
married *f.* women (S)	Ezr 10:2; 2:14, 17-18, 44
f. women caused sin (B)(E)(R)(S)	Ne 13:26
God is our *f.* (B)	Ps 46:1
f. vine (E)	Jer 2:21
f. idols (A)(B)(R)	Jer 8:19
f. vanities (E)	Jer 8:19
followed *f.* gods (B)(R)	Jer 16:11
the mixed, *f.* population (A)(R)	Jer 25:20
all the *f.* troops (B)(R)	Jer 50:37
f. speech (A)(B)(R)	Eze 3:5; 3:6
f. tongue (R)	Eze 3:6
f. apparel (A)(B)(E)(R)	Zep 1:8
went off to a *f.* land (P)	Lu 16:13
speak in *f.* languages (B)	Ac 2:4
f. land (B)(N)(R)	Ac 7:6
f. deities (A)(B)(N)	Ac 17:18
f. residents (A)(N)(P)	Ac 17:21
spoke in *f.* languages (A)	Ac 19:6
f. cities (A)(B)(E)(N)(R)	Ac 26:11
seem a *f.* (A)(B)(P)(R)	1Co 14:11
f. or savage (P)	Col 3:11
f. country (R)	Heb 11:9
as aliens in a *f.* land (N)	1Pe 2:11

FOREIGNER

foreigner (S)	Ge 17:12; 17:27; Ex 12:43; 22:21; 23:9; De 77:15; 23:20; 29:22; J'g 19:12; Ru 2:10; 2Sa 15:19; 1Ki 8:41, 43; 2Ch 6:32; Pr 2:16; 5:10, 20; Isa 56:3, 6; 62:8; Eze 14:7; 44:9
A *f.* and an hired servant shall	Ex 12:45
a *f.* (B)	Le 25:35; Le 35:15
Of a *f.* thou mayest exact it again	De 15:3
the *f.* resides (A)	Eze 47:23

FOREIGNERS

foreigners (S)	Ge 31:15; 2Sa 22:45, 46; 2Ch 6:32, 33; Ne 9:2; 13:30; Ps 18:44, 45; Pr 20:16; 27:13; Isa 1:7; 2:6; 25:2; 60:10; 61:5; Jer 51:51; Eze 11:9; 28:10; 30:12; 44:7
from a *f.* hand (S)	Le 22:25
stock of a *f.* family (S)	Le 25:47
f. faded away (A)(B)(R)	2Sa 22:46
castle of, is (B)	Isa 25:2
and *f.* entered into his gates	Ob 11
perils from *f.* (N)	2Co 11:26
ye are no more strangers and *f.*	Eph 2:19
outsiders—exiles, migrants, aliens (A)	Eph 2:19
strangers and immigrants (B)	Eph 2:19
strangers and sojourners (E)(R)	Eph 2:19
aliens in a foreign land (N)	Eph 2:19
outsiders or aliens (P)	Eph 2:19
lived as exiles, *f.* (P)	Heb 11:13

FOREKNEW

f. loved beforehand (A)	Ro 8:29
cast away his people which he *f.*	Ro 11:2
marked out, appointed and foreknown (A)	Ro 11:2
whom beforehand he had in mind (B)	Ro 11:2
acknowledged of old as his own (N)	Ro 11:2
whose destiny he himself appointed (P)	Ro 11:2

FOREKNOW

For whom he did *f.* he also	Ro 8:29
foreknew-loved beforehand (A)	Ro 8:29

He knew beforehand (B)	Ro 8:29
knew his own before ever they were (N)	Ro 8:29
in his foreknowledge chose them (P)	Ro 8:29

FOREKNOWLEDGE

and *f.* of God, ye have taken	Ac 2:23
settled plan and *f.* (A)	Ac 2:23
determined will and *f.* (B)	Ac 2:23
predetermined plan and *f.* (P)	Ac 2:23
definite plan and *f.* (R)	Ac 2:23
in his *f.* chose (P)	Ro 8:29
Elect according to the *f.* of God	1Pe 1:2
chosen and foreknown by God (A)	1Pe 1:2
chosen of old in the purpose of God (N)	1Pe 1:2
knew and chose long ago (P)	1Pe 1:2
chosen and destined by God (R)	1Pe 1:2

FOREKNOWN

appointed and *f.* (A)	Ro 11:2
chosen and *f.* by God (A)	1Pe 1:2

FOREMAN

set over them gang *f.* (B)	Ex 1:11; 5:6
3,600 *f.* (B)	2Ch 2:2; 2:18; 34:18

FOREMOST

And he commanded the *f.* saying	Ge 32:17
handmaids and their children *f.*	Ge 33:2
the running of the *f.* is like	2Sa 18:27
first, *f.* of ways of God (A)(B)(R)	Job 40:19
I am *f.* (A)(B)(R)	1Ti 1:15

FORENSIC

a certain *f.* advocate (A)	Ac 24:1

FOREORDAINED

God *f.* before the world (E)	1Co 2:7
he *f.* us to be (A)(E)	Eph 1:5
been *f.* in (A)(B)(E)	Eph 1:11
Who verily was *f.* before the foundation of world (N)	1Pe 1:20
predestined before foundation of world (N)	1Pe 1:20
chose him to fulfill his part before world was founded (P)	1Pe 1:20
destined before foundation of the world (R)	1Pe 1:20

FOREPART

toward the *f.* thereof, over against	Ex 28:27
ephod underneath, toward the *f.*	Ex 39:20
oracle in the *f.* was twenty cubits	1Ki 6:20
court on the *f.* of the chambers	Eze 42:7
the *f.* stuck fast, and remained	Ac 27:41

FORERUNNER

Whither the *f.* is for us entered	Heb 6:20
entered in for us in advance (B)	Heb 6:20
already entered on our behalf (P)	Heb 6:20

FORESAW

I *f.* the Lord always before my	Ac 2:25

FORESEEING

the scripture, *f.* that God would	Ga 3:8

FORESEETH

A prudent man *f.* the evil	Pr 22:3; 27:12

FORESHADOW

a *f.* of the coming one   *Ro 5:14*
(B)(N)

FORESHADOWING

f. of heavenly (A)   *Heb 8:5*

FORESHIP

have cast anchors out of the   *Ac 27:30*
f.

FORESKIN

circumcise the flesh of your   *Ge 17:11*
f.
flesh of his *f.* is not   *Ge 17:14*
circumcised
circumcised the flesh of their   *Ge 17:23*
f.
circumcised in the flesh of   *Ge 17:24;*
his *f.*   *17:25*
stone, and cut off the *f.* of   *Ex 4:25*
her son
flesh of his *f.* shall be   *Le 12:3*
circumcised
Circumcise therefore the *f.*   *De 10:16*
of your
and let thy *f.* be uncovered   *Hab 2:16*

FORESKINS

of Israel at the hill of the *f.*   *Jos 5:3*
an hundred *f.* of the   *1Sa 18:25*
Philistines
David brought their *f.* and   *1Sa 18:27*
they
an hundred *f.* of the   *2Sa 3:14*
Philistines
and take away the *f.* of your   *Jer 4:4*
heart

FOREST

forest (S)   *De 19:5;*
Jos 17:18; 1Sa 14:25-26; 23:15-16, 18-
19; 2Sa 18:6, 8, 17; Ps 80:13; 83:14;
    96:12; Isa 7:2; Mic 7:14
get thee up into the *f.* (S)   *Jos 17:15*
and came into the *f.* of   *1Sa 22:5*
Hareth
Hereth woods (B)   *1Sa 22:5*
also the house of the *f.* of   *1Ki 7:2*
Lebanon
of Lebanese lumber (B)   *1Ki 7:2*
in the house of the *f.* of   *1Ki 10:17*
Lebanon
of the house of the *f.* of   *1Ki 10:21*
Lebanon
and into the *f.* of his   *1Ki 19:23*
Carmel
in the house of the *f.* of   *2Ch 9:16*
Lebanon
of the house of the *f.* of   *2Ch 9:20*
Lebanon
Asaph the keeper of the king's   *Ne 2:8*
f.
king's forester (B)   *Ne 2:8*
For every beast of the *f.* is   *Ps 50:10*
mine
all the beasts of the *f.* do   *Ps 104:20*
creep
kindle in the thickets of the   *Isa 9:18*
f.
shall consume the glory of   *Isa 10:18*
his *f.*
And the trees of his *f.* shall   *Isa 10:19*
be few
shall cut down the thickets   *Isa 10:34*
of the *f.*
In the *f.* in Arabia shall ye   *Isa 21:13*
lodge
thickets of Arabian desert   *Isa 21:13*
(B)
the armour of the house of   *Isa 22:8*
the *f.*
field shall be esteemed as a   *Isa 29:17*
f.
fruitful field be counted for   *Isa 32:15*
a *f.*
shall hail, coming down on   *Isa 32:19*
the *f.*
border, and the *f.* of his   *Isa 37:24*
Carmel
himself among the trees of   *Isa 44:14*
the *f.*
O *f.* and every tree therein   *Isa 44:23*
yea, all ye beasts in the *f.*   *Isa 56:9*

a lion out of the *f.* shall slay   *Jer 5:6*
them
one cutteth a tree out of the   *Jer 10:3*
f.
is unto me as a lion in the *f.*   *Jer 12:8*
I will kindle a fire in the *f.*   *Jer 21:14*
thereof
the house as the high places   *Jer 26:18*
of a *f.*
They shall cut down her *f.*   *Jer 46:23*
saith
which is among the trees of   *Eze 15:2*
the *f.*
vine tree among the trees of   *Eze 15:6*
the *f.*
prophesy against the *f.* of   *Eze 20:46*
the south
And say to the *f.* of the   *Eze 20:47*
south
and I will make them a *f.*   *Ho 2:12*
Will a lion roar in the *f.*   *Am 3:4*
when he
the house as the high places   *Mic 3:12*
of the *f.*
as a lion among the beasts of   *Mic 5:8*
the *f.*
the *f.* of the vintage is come   *Zec 11:2*
down

FORESTS

and in the *f.* he built castles   *2Ch 27:4*
to calve, and discovereth the   *Ps 29:9*
f.
neither cut down any out of   *Eze 39:10*
the *f.*

FORESTER

king's *f.* (B)   *Ne 2:8*

FORESTALL

f. him (A)   *Ps 17:13*
f. those who died (N)   *1Th 4:16*

FORESTALLED

Jesus *f.* him (B)(N)   *M't 17:25*

FORETELL

and *f.* you, as if I were   *2Co 13:2*
present

FORETELLING

rewards of *f.* foretold (A)   *Nu 22:7*
behold, I have *f.* you all   *M'k 13:23*
things
told everything beforehand   *M'k 13:23*
(A)(E)(R)
forewarning you of it all   *M'k 13:23*
(B)(N)
giving warning before it   *M'k 13:23*
happens (P)
have likewise *f.* of these days   *Ac 3:24*
prophets successively   *Ac 3:24*
announced these times (B)
predicted this present time   *Ac 3:24*
(N)
have foretold these days (P)   *Ac 3:24*
proclaimed these days (R)   *Ac 3:24*
f. by the Spirit (P)(R)   *Ac 11:28*

FOREVER

will last *f.* (B)   *2Co 5:1*

FOREWARN

I will *f.* you whom ye shall   *Lu 12:5*
fear
warn you whom you should   *Lu 12:5*
fear (A)(E)(N)(R)
I will show you whom to fear   *Lu 12:5*
(B)(P)

FOREWARNED

all such as we also have *f.*   *1Th 4:6*
you

FOREWARNING

f. of it all (B)(N)   *M'k 13:23*

FORFEITED

all his substance should be *f.*   *Ezr 10:8*

FORGAT

remember Joseph, but *f.* him   *Ge 40:23*
and *f.* the Lord their God, and   *J'g 3:7*
when they *f.* the Lord their   *1Sa 12:9*
God
And *f.* his works, and   *Ps 78:11*
his wonders
They soon *f.* his works;   *Ps 106:13*
they
They *f.* God their saviour,   *Ps 106:21*
which
far off from peace: I *f.*   *La 3:17*
prosperity
went after her lovers, and *f.*   *Ho 2:13*
me

FORGAVE

f. their iniquity, and   *Ps 78:38*
destroyed
loosed him, and *f.* him the   *M't 18:27*
debt
I *f.* thee all that debt,   *M't 18:32*
because thou
to pay, he frankly *f.* them   *Lu 7:42*
both
that he, to whom he *f.* most   *Lu 7:43*
if I *f.* any thing, to whom I *f.*   *2Co 2:10*
it
for your sakes *f.* I it in the   *2Co 2:10*
person
even as Christ *f.* you, so also   *Col 3:13*
do ye

FORGAVEST

and thou *f.* the iniquity of my   *Ps 32:5*
sin
thou wast a God that *f.* them   *Ps 99:8*

FORGED

the proud have *f.* a lie   *Ps 119:69*
against me
put together a lie (A)(B)   *Ps 119:69*
besmear me with lies (R)   *Ps 119:69*

FORGERS

But ye are *f.* of lies, ye are   *Job 13:4*
all

FORGET

and he *f.* that which thou   *Ge 27:45*
hast
hath made me *f.* all my toil   *Ge 41:51*
lest thou *f.* the things which   *De 4:9*
thine
lest ye *f.* the covenant of the   *De 4:23*
Lord
nor *f.* the covenant of thy   *De 4:31*
fathers
Then beware lest thou *f.* the   *De 6:12*
Lord
Beware that thou *f.* not the   *De 8:11*
Lord
and thou *f.* the Lord thy God   *De 8:14*
if thou do at all *f.* the Lord   *De 8:19*
thy God
Remember, and *f.* not, how   *De 9:7*
thou
under heaven; thou shalt not   *De 25:19*
f. it
and not *f.* thine handmaid   *1Sa 1:11*
have made with you ye   *2Ki 17:38*
shall not *f.*
So are the paths of all that   *Job 8:13*
f. God
If I say, I will *f.* my   *Job 9:27*
complaint
Because thou shalt *f.* thy   *Job 11:16*
misery
The womb shall *f.* him; the   *Job 24:20*
worm
and all the nations that *f.*   *Ps 9:17*
God
thine hand; *f.* not the   *Ps 10:12*
humble
How long wilt thou *f.* me, O   *Ps 13:1*
Lord
f. also thine own people, and   *Ps 45:10*
thy
ye that *f.* God, lest I tear   *Ps 50:22*
you in

slay them not, lest my   *Ps 59:11*
people *f.*
f. not the congregation of   *Ps 74:19*
thy poor
F. not the voice of thine   *Ps 74:23*
enemies
and not *f.* the works of God   *Ps 78:7*
so that I *f.* to eat my bread   *Ps 102:4*
my soul, and *f.* not all his   *Ps 103:2*
benefits
thy statutes: I will not *f.* thy   *Ps 119:16*
word
yet do I not *f.* thy statutes   *Ps 119:83*
I will never *f.* thy precepts: *Ps 119:93*
for
in my hand; yet do I not   *Ps 119:109*
f. thy law
yet do not I *f.* thy precepts   *Ps 119:141*
deliver me: for I do not *f.*   *Ps 119:153*
thy law
I do not *f.* thy   *Ps 119:176*
commandments
If I *f.* thee, O Jerusalem   *Ps 137:5*
let my right hand *f.* her   *Ps 137:5*
cunning
My son, *f.* not my law; but let   *Pr 3:1*
thine
get understanding: *f.* it not   *Pr 4:5*
Lest they drink, and *f.* the   *Pr 31:5*
law
Let him drink, and *f.* his   *Pr 31:7*
poverty
Can a woman *f.* her sucking   *Isa 49:15*
child
son of her womb? yea, they   *Isa 49:15*
may *f.*
yet will I not *f.* thee   *Isa 49:15*
shalt *f.* the shame of thy   *Isa 54:4*
youth
forsake the Lord, that *f.* my   *Isa 65:11*
holy
Can a maid *f.* her ornaments   *Jer 2:32*
to cause my people to *f.* my   *Jer 23:27*
name
I, even I, will utterly *f.* you   *Jer 23:39*
Wherefore dost thou *f.* us for   *La 5:20*
ever
thy God, I will also *f.* thy   *Ho 4:6*
children
I will never *f.* any of their   *Am 8:7*
works
to *f.* your work and labour   *Heb 6:10*
of love
do good and to   *Heb 13:16*
communicate *f.* not

FORGETFUL

Be not *f.* to entertain   *Heb 13:2*
strangers
being not a *f.* hearer, but a   *Jas 1:25*
doer

FORGETFULNESS

righteousness in the land of   *Ps 88:12*
f.

FORGETTEST

and *f.* our affliction and our   *Ps 44:24*
And *f.* the Lord thy maker   *Isa 51:13*

FORGETTETH

And *f.* that the foot may   *Job 39:15*
crush
he *f.* not the cry of the   *Ps 9:12*
humble
and *f.* the covenant of her   *Pr 2:17*
God
f. what manner of man he   *Jas 1:24*
was

FORGETTING

f. those things which are   *Ph'p 3:13*
behind

FORGIVE

F. I pray thee now the   *Ge 50:17*
trespass
f. the trespass of the   *Ge 50:17*
servants of the
Now therefore *f.* I pray   *Ex 10:17*
thee, my
Yet now, if thou wilt *f.* their   *Ex 32:32*
sin

the Lord shall *f.* her, because   *Nu 30:5*
her
effect: and the Lord shall *f.*   *Nu 30:8*
her
void; and the Lord shall *f.*   *Nu 30:12*
her
he will not *f.* your   *Jos 24:19*
transgressions
I pray thee, *f.* the trespass   *1Sa 25:28*
of thine
and when thou hearest *f.*   *1Ki 8:30*
and *f.* the sin of thy people   *1Ki 8:34*
Israel
and *f.* the sin of thy servants   *1Ki 8:36*
heaven thy dwelling place,   *1Ki 8:39*
and *f.*
And *f.* thy people that have   *1Ki 8:50*
sinned
f. your servant (B)   *2Ki 5:18*
heaven; and when thou   *2Ch 6:21*
hearest *f.*
hear thou from the heavens,   *2Ch 6:25*
and *f.*
hear thou from heaven, and   *2Ch 6:27*
f.
heaven, thy dwelling place,   *2Ch 6:30*
and *f.*
and *f.* thy people which   *2Ch 6:39*
have
and will *f.* their sin, and   *2Ch 7:14*
will heal
my pain; and *f.* all my sins   *Ps 25:18*
Lord, art good and ready to   *Ps 86:5*
f.
himself; therefore *f.* them not   *Isa 2:9*
f. not their iniquity, neither   *Jer 18:23*
blot
I will *f.* their iniquity, and I   *Jer 31:34*
will
that I may *f.* their iniquity   *Jer 36:3*
and
O Lord, hear; O Lord, *f.*   *Da 9:19*
O Lord God, *f.* I beseech thee   *Am 7:2*
f. us our debts, as we *f.* our   *M't 6:12*
For if ye *f.* men their   *M't 6:14*
trespasses
your heavenly Father will   *M't 6:14*
also *f.*
if ye *f.* not men their   *M't 6:15*
trespasses
will your Father *f.* your   *M't 6:15*
trespasses
hath power on earth to *f.* sins   *M't 9:6*
my brother sin against me   *M't 18:21*
and I *f.*
f. not every one his brother   *M't 18:35*
their
who can *f.* sins but God only   *M'k 2:7*
man hath power on earth to   *M'k 2:10*
f. sins
f. if ye have ought against   *M'k 11:25*
any
may *f.* you your trespasses   *M'k 11:25*
if ye do not *f.* neither will   *M'k 11:26*
your
in heaven *f.* your trespasses   *M'k 11:26*
Who can *f.* sins, but God   *Lu 5:21*
alone
hath power upon earth to *f.*   *Lu 5:24*
sins
f. and ye shall be forgiven   *Lu 6:37*
f. us our sins; for we also *f.*   *Lu 11:4*
every
and if he repent, *f.* him   *Lu 17:3*
saying, I repent; thou shalt *f.*   *Lu 17:4*
him
Then said Jesus, Father, *f.*   *Lu 23:34*
them
if you *f.* sins of any   *Joh 20:23*
(A)(B)(N)(P)(R)
ought rather to *f.* him, and   *2Co 2:7*
comfort
To whom ye *f.* anything, I *f.*   *2Co 2:10*
also
to you? *f.* me this wrong   *2Co 12:13*
faithful and just to *f.* us our   *1Jo 1:9*
sins

FORGIVEN

make atonement, and it shall   *Le 4:20;*
be *f.* them *26:31, 35; 5:10, 13, 16, 18;*
   6:7; 19:22; Nu 15:25, 26, 28; De 21:8
pardon, as thou hast *f.* from   *Nu 14:19*
Egypt
blessed, whose transgression is   *Ps 32:1;*
f.   *Ro 4:7*
thou hast *f.* the iniquity of   *Ps 85:2*
thy people

the people shall be *f.* their   *Isa 33:24*
iniquity
son, be of good cheer, thy   *M't 9:2;*
sins be *f.* thee *9:5; M'k 2:5, 9; Lu 5:20,*
   23; 7:48
all sin and blasphemy shall   *M't 12:31;*
be *f.* but *12:32; M'k 3:28; Lu 12:10*
against Holy Ghost shall not be *f.*
and their sins should be *f.*   *M'k 4:12*
them
forgive, and ye shall be *f.*   *Lu 6:37*
her many sins are *f.* but to   *Lu 7:47*
whom little is *f.*
have your sins *f.* (P)   *Ac 2:38*
the thought of thy heart may   *Ac 8:22*
be *f.* thee
as God for Christ's sake   *Eph 4:32*
hath *f.* you
he quickened, having *f.* you   *Col 2:13*
all trespasses
where sins have been *f.*   *Heb 10:18*
(B)(N)
if committed sins they shall   *Jas 5:15*
be *f.* him
I write to you, because your   *1Jo 2:12*
sins are *f.*

FORGIVENESS

there is *f.* with thee that   *Ps 130:4*
mayest be feared
f. of sins (A)(B)(N)(R)   *M't 26:28;*
   M'k 1:4; Lu 3:3; 24:47; Ac 2:38; 10:43
hath never *f.* but is in   *M'k 3:29*
danger of hell
him hath God exalted to give   *Ac 5:31*
f. of sins
thro' him is preached unto   *Ac 13:38*
you *f.* of sins
to God, that they may   *Ac 26:18*
receive *f.* of sins
in whom we have *f.* of sins   *Eph 1:7;*
   Col 1:14
no *f.* of sins (B)(N)(R)   *Heb 9:22*
where there is *f.* (R)   *Heb 10:18*

FORGIVENESSES

to Lord our God belong   *Da 9:9*
mercies and *f.*

FORGIVETH

heals thy diseases, who *f.* all   *Ps 103:3*
iniquities
they began to say, Who is this   *Lu 7:49*
f. sins also

FORGIVING

f. iniquity, transgression   *Ex 34:7;*
   Nu 14:8
in *f.* sins (B)   *Ro 3:25*
forbearing *f.* one another   *Eph 4:32;*
   Col 3:13

FORGOT

and hast *f.* a sheaf in the   *De 24:19*
field

FORGOTTEN

and all the plenty shall be *f.*   *Ge 41:30*
not transgressed   *De 26:13*
commandments nor *f.* them
it shall not be *f.* out of   *De 31:21*
mouths of their seed
thou hast *f.* God that   *De 32:18*
formed thee
my familiar friends have *f.*   *Job 19:14*
me
flood breaks out, even waters   *Job 28:4*
f. of the foot
for the needy shall not alway   *Ps 9:18*
be *f.*
he hath said in his heart,   *Ps 10:11*
God hath *f.*
I am *f.* as a dead man out   *Ps 31:12*
of mind
I will say, my rock, why hast   *Ps 42:9*
thou *f.* me
all this is come on us, yet   *Ps 44:17*
have we not *f.* thee
if we have *f.* name of our   *Ps 44:20*
God, or stretched out
hath God *f.* to be gracious   *Ps 77:9*
but I have not *f.* thy law   *Ps 119:61*

because mine enemies have *Ps 119:139*
f. thy words
in the days to come shall all *Ec 2:16*
be *f.*
and the wicked were *f.* in the *Ec 8:10*
city
for the memory of them is *f.* *Ec 9:5*
thou hast *f.* the God of thy *Isa 17:10*
salvation
that Tyre shall be *f.* seventy *Isa 23:15*
years
take an harp, thou harlot *Isa 23:16*
that hast been *f.*
O Israel, thou shalt not be *Isa 44:21*
f. of me
but Zion said, My Lord hath *Isa 49:14*
f. me
because the former troubles *Isa 65:16*
are *f.*
my people have *f.* me *Jer 2:32;*
13:25; 18:15
they have *f.* the Lord their *Jer 3:21*
God
their confusion shall never *Jer 20:11;*
be *f.* *23:40*
to forget, as their fathers *Jer 23:27*
have *f.* my name
all thy lovers have *f.* thee, *Jer 30:14*
they seek thee not
have ye *f.* the wickedness of *Jer 44:9*
your fathers
let us join in a covenant that *Jer 50:5*
shall not be *f.*
they turned away, have *f.* *Jer 50:6*
their restingplace
Lord caused the sabbath to be *La 2:6*
f. in Zion
thou hast *f.* me, saith the *Eze 22:12*
Lord
saith the Lord, because *Eze 23:35*
thou hast *f.* me
seeing thou hast *f.* the law of *Ho 4:6*
thy God
for Israel hath *f.* Maker, *Ho 8:14*
and builds temples
their heart exalted, therefore *Ho 13:6*
have *f.* me
they had *f.* to take bread *M't 16:5;*
M'k 8:14
and not one of them is *f.* *Lu 12:6*
before God
and ye have *f.* the *Heb 12:5*
exhortation that speaks
f. that he was purged from *2Pe 1:9*
his old sins

FORKS

yet they had a file for the *f.* *1Sa 13:21*
and axes

FORLORN

my soul is *f.* (R) *Ps 35:12*

FORM

the earth was without *f.* and *Ge 1:2*
void
earth formless and empty (B) *Ge 1:2*
earth was waste and void (E) *Ge 1:2*
the *f.* of the Lord *Nu 12:8*
(A)(B)(E)(R)
saw no *f.* (A)(B)(E)(R) *De 4:12;*
4:15
he said unto her, What *f.* is *1Sa 28:14*
he of
of what appearance is he *1Sa 28:14*
(B)(R)
To fetch about this *f.* of *2Sa 14:20*
speech
of gold according to their *f.* *2Ch 4:7*
I could not discern the *f.* *Job 4:16*
thereof
discern the appearance *Job 4:16*
(A)(B)(E)(R)
f. the light, and create *Isa 45:7*
darkness
his *f.* more than the sons of *Isa 52:14*
men
his whole appearance *Isa 52:14*
(A)(B)(R)
he hath no *f.* nor comeliness *Isa 53:2*
earth, and, lo, it was without *Jer 4:23*
f.
a waste and a vacant void *Jer 4:23*
(A)
earth formless and empty (B) *Jer 4:23*
earth a waste and void *Jer 4:23*
(E)(R)

he put forth the *f.* of an hand *Eze 8:3*
behold every *f.* of creeping *Eze 8:10*
thing
the *f.* of a man's hand under *Eze 10:8*
their
shew them the *f.* of the *Eze 43:11*
house
explain the construction of *Eze 43:11*
temple (B)
may keep the whole *f.* *Eze 43:11*
thereof
and the *f.* thereof was *Da 2:31*
terrible
the *f.* of his visage was *Da 3:19*
changed
his facial visage was changed *Da 3:19*
(A)
his face was distorted with *Da 3:19*
rage (B)
expression of his face was *Da 3:19*
changed (R)
f. of the fourth is like the *Da 3:25*
Son of
the appearance of the fourth *Da 3:25*
(B)(R)
the aspect of the fourth (E) *Da 3:25*
he appeared in another *f.* *M'k 16:12*
unto
bodily *f.* like a dove *Lu 3:22;*
(A)(E)(N)(R) *Joh 5:37*
which hast the *f.* of *Ro 2:20*
knowledge
embodiment of knowledge *Ro 2:20*
(A)(B)(R)
the very shape of knowledge *Ro 2:20*
(N)
the basis of true knowledge *Ro 2:20*
(P)
that *f.* of doctrine which was *Ro 6:17*
the standard of teaching *Ro 6:17*
(A)(B)(R)
the pattern of teaching (N) *Ro 6:17*
responded to the impact of *Ro 6:17*
teaching (P)
Who, being in the *f.* of God *Ph'p 2:6*
divine nature was his from *Ph'p 2:6*
first (N)
had always been God by *Ph'p 2:6*
nature (P)
took upon him the *f.* of a *Ph'p 2:7*
servant
assume the guise of a *Ph'p 2:7*
servant (A)
bearing human likeness, *Ph'p 2:7*
revealed in human shape (N)
consenting to be a slave by *Ph'p 2:7*
nature (P)
Hold fast the *f.* of sound *2Ti 1:13*
words
pattern of wholesome *2Ti 1:13*
teaching (A)(B)(E)(R)
an outline of sound teaching *2Ti 1:13*
(N)
Having a *f.* of godliness, but *2Ti 3:5*

FORMED

And the Lord God *f.* man of *Ge 2:7*
the
he put the man whom he had *Ge 2:8*
f.
the ground the Lord *f.* every *Ge 2:19*
beast
hast forgotten God that *f.* *De 32:18*
thee
of ancient times that I have *2Ki 19:25*
f. it
Dead things are *f.* from *Job 26:5*
under
hand hath *f.* the crooked *Job 26:13*
serpent
I also am *f.* out of the clay *Job 33:6*
or ever thou hadst *f.* the earth *Ps 90:2*
that *f.* the eye, shall he not *Ps 94:9*
see
and his hands *f.* the dry land *Ps 95:5*
The great God that *f.* all *Pr 26:10*
things
he that *f.* them will shew *Isa 27:11*
them
thing *f.* say to him that *f.* it *Isa 29:16*
(S)
of ancient times, that I have *Isa 37:26*
f. it
and he that *f.* thee, O Israel *Isa 43:1*
I have *f.* him; yea, I have *Isa 43:7*
made
before me there was no God *Isa 43:10*
f.

This people have I *f.* for *Isa 43:21*
myself
and *f.* thee from the womb *Isa 44:2*
Who hath *f.* a god, or *Isa 44:10*
molten a
have *f.* thee; thou art my *Isa 44:21*
servant
and he that *f.* thee from the *Isa 44:24*
womb
God himself that *f.* the *Isa 45:18*
earth and
he *f.* it to be inhabited: I *Isa 45:18*
am the
the Lord that *f.* me from the *Isa 49:5*
womb
No weapon that is *f.* against *Isa 54:17*
thee
Before I *f.* thee in the belly *Jer 1:5*
the Lord that *f.* it to *Jer 33:2*
establish it
one who *f.* (S) *Jer 51:19*
f. grasshoppers in the *Am 7:1*
beginning
the thing *f.* say to him that *f.* *Ro 9:20*
it
until Christ be *f.* in you *Ga 4:19*
Adam was first *f.* then Eve *1Ti 2:13*

FORMER

after the *f.* manner when *Ge 40:13*
thou
fought against the *f.* king of *Nu 21:26*
Moab
Her *f.* husband, which sent *De 24:4*
her
this was the manner in *f.* time *Ru 4:7*
answered him again after *1Sa 17:30*
the *f.*
two captains of the *f.* fifties *2Ki 1:14*
they do after the *f.* manners *2Ki 17:34*
but they did after their *f.* *2Ki 17:40*
manner
the *f.* governors that had *Ne 5:15*
been
enquire, I pray thee, of the *f.* *Job 8:8*
age
in *f.* time desolate and waste *Job 30:3*
not against us *f.* iniquities *Ps 79:8*
where are thy *f.* loving *Ps 89:49*
kindnesses
is no remembrance of *f.* *Ec 1:11*
things
the *f.* days were better than *Ec 7:10*
these
let them shew the *f.* things, *Isa 41:22*
what
the *f.* things are come to pass *Isa 42:9*
declare this, and shew us *f.* *Isa 43:9*
things
Remember ye not the *f.* *Isa 43:18*
things
Remember the *f.* things of *Isa 46:9*
old
I have declared the *f.* things *Isa 48:3*
from
shall raise up the *f.* *Isa 61:4*
desolations
will I measure their *f.* work *Isa 65:7*
into
the *f.* troubles are forgotten *Isa 65:16*
and the *f.* shall not be *Isa 65:17*
remembered
rain, both the *f.* and the *Jer 5:24*
latter
for he is the *f.* of all things *Jer 10:16*
f. kings which were before *Jer 34:5*
thee
f. words that were in the *Jer 36:28*
first roll
for he is the *f.* of all things *Jer 51:19*
shall return to their *f.* *Eze 16:55*
estate, and
shall return to their *f.* *Eze 16:55*
estate, then
shall return to your *f.* estate *Eze 16:55*
a multitude greater than the *Da 11:13*
f.
but it shall not be as the *f.* *Da 11:29*
latter and *f.* rain unto the *Ho 6:3*
earth
given you the *f.* rain *Joe 2:23*
moderately
the *f.* rain, and the latter *Joe 2:23*
rain
shall be greater than of the *Hag 2:9*
f.
unto whom the *f.* prophets *Zec 1:4*
have

Lord hath cried by the *f.* prophets   Zec 7:7
sent in his spirit by the *f.* prophets   Zec 7:12
of this people as in the *f.* days   Zec 8:11
half of them toward the *f.* sea   Zec 14:8
the days of old, and as in *f.* years   Mal 3:4
The *f.* treatise have I made, O   Ac 1:1
f. life (A)(E)(N)(R)   Ga 1:13
concerning the *f.* conversation   Eph 4:22
f. nature (A)(E)(N)(R)   Eph 4:22
in *f.* times God (N)   Heb 1:1
call to remembrance the *f.* days   Heb 10:32
according to the *f.* lusts in your   1Pe 1:14
for the *f.* things are passed away   Re 21:4

FORMERLY

formerly (S)   De 2:12; 1Sa 9:9; 2Sa 7:10
giants dwelt there *f.* (S)   De 2:20
that *f.* was blind (S)   Joh 9:13

FORMETH

For, lo, he that *f.* the mountains   Am 4:13
and *f.* the spirit of man within him   Zec 12:1

FORMLESS

earth *f.* and empty (B)   Ge 1:2; Jer 4:23

FORMS

f. thereof, and all the ordinances   Eze 43:11
all the *f.* thereof, and all the laws   Eze 43:11

FORNICATION

of Jerusalem to commit *f.*   2Ch 21:11
debauched spiritually (A)   2Ch 21:11
to become unfaithful (B)   2Ch 21:11
to play the harlot (E)   2Ch 21:11
and shall commit *f.* with all   Isa 23:17
Tyre will play harlot (A)(B)(E)(R)   Isa 23:17
f. and wickedness (B)   Jer 3:2
Thou hast also committed *f.*   Eze 16:26
with
hast moreover multiplied thy *f.*   Eze 16:29
multiply your harlotry (A)(B)(R)   Eze 16:29
multiplied your whoredom (E)   Eze 16:29
his wife, saving for the cause of *f.*   M't 5:32
except for unfaithfulness (A)(B)(R)   M't 5:32
other than unchastity (N)   M't 5:32
away his wife, except it be for *f.*   M't 19:9
We be not born of *f.* we have one   Joh 8:41
We are not illegitimate children (A)(P)   Joh 8:41
We are not born illegitimately (B)   Joh 8:41
We are not base-born (N)   Joh 8:41
from *f.* and from things strangled   Ac 15:20
abstain from all sexual impurity (A)   Ac 15:20
abstain from unchastity (B)(R)   Ac 15:20
abstain from sexual immorality (P)   Ac 15:20
from things strangled, and from *f.*   Ac 15:29
and from strangled, and from *f.*   Ac 21:25
f. wickedness, covetousness   Ro 1:29
immorality (B)   Ro 1:29
that there is *f.* among you, and   1Co 5:1
sexual immorality (A)(B)(N)(P)(R)   1Co 5:1

such *f.* as is not so much as   1Co 5:1
Now the body is not for *f.*   1Co 6:13
sexual immorality (A)(R)   1Co 6:13; 6:18; 7:2
not for lust (B)(N)   1Co 6:13
sexual promiscuity (P)   1Co 6:13
Flee *f.* Every sin that a man doeth   1Co 6:18
but he that committeth *f.* sinneth   1Co 6:18
to avoid *f.* let every man have   1Co 7:2
Neither let us commit *f.* as some   1Co 10:8
and *f.* and lasciviousness which   2Co 12:21
sexual vice (A)   2Co 12:21
unchastity (B)   2Co 12:21
immorality (P)(R)   2Co 12:21
Adultery, *f.* uncleanness   Ga 5:19
But *f.* and all uncleanness, or   Eph 5:3
immorality, sexual vice (A)(P)(R)   Eph 5:3
unchastity (B)   Eph 5:3
given to *f.* (N)   Eph 5:5
f., uncleanness, inordinate   Col 3:5
that ye should abstain from *f.*   1Th 4:3
abstain, shrink from all   1Th 4:3
sexual vice (A)
keep yourselves from   1Th 4:3
lewdness (B)
clean cut from sexual   1Th 4:3
immorality (P)(R)
giving themselves over to *f.*   Jude 7
impurity, unnatural vice,   Jude 7
sexual perversity (A)
sexual immorality, perverted   Jude 7
sensuality (B)
sexual immorality and   Jude 7
perversion (P)
acted immorally, indulged in   Jude 7
unnatural lust (R)
unto idols, and to commit *f.*   Re 2:14
to commit *f.* and to eat   Re 2:20
things
gave her space to repent of   Re 2:21
her *f.*
her immorality (A)(P)(R)   Re 2:21
her unchastity (B)   Re 2:21
nor of their *f.* nor of their   Re 9:21
thefts
the wine of the wrath of her   Re 14:8
f.
wine of her passionate   Re 14:8
unchastity (A)(B)
wine of passionate   Re 14:8
unfaithfulness (P)
wine of her impure passion   Re 14:8
(R)
of the earth have committed   Re 17:2
f.
wine of immorality (A)   Re 17:2
wine of unchastity (B)   Re 17:2
wine of her filthiness (P)   Re 17:2
drunk with the wine of her *f.*   Re 17:2
and filthiness of her *f.*   Re 17:4
full of accursed offenses, filth   Re 17:4
of her lewdness and vice (A)
offenses, impurities, lewdness   Re 17:4
(B)
earth's filthiness, foul   Re 17:4
impurity (P)
of the wine of the wrath of   Re 18:3
her *f.*
wine of her passionate   Re 18:3
unchastity (B)
wine of her passionate   Re 18:3
unfaithfulness (P)
wine of her impure passion   Re 18:3
(R)
have committed *f.* with her   Re 18:3
who have committed *f.* and   Re 18:9
lived
did corrupt the earth with her   Re 19:2
f.
poisoned earth with her   Re 19:2
lewdness and adultery (A)
corrupted earth with lewdness   Re 19:2
(B)
corrupted earth with   Re 19:2
wickedness (P)

FORNICATIONS

pouredst out thy *f.* on every   Eze 16:15
one
harlotries (B)(R)   Eze 16:15
thoughts, murders   M't 15:19
adulteries *f.*
evil thoughts, adulteries *f.*   M'k 7:21

FORNICATOR

Man that is called a brother   1Co 5:11
be a *f.*
guilty of immorality   1Co 5:11
(A)(P)(R)
brother is lewd (B)   1Co 5:11
who leads a loose life (N)   1Co 5:11
no *f.*, nor (E)(S)   Eph 5:5
Lest there be any *f.* or   Heb 12:16
profane
a profane, godless,   Heb 12:16
sacrilegious person (A)
unchaste or profane (B)   Heb 12:16
immoral and worldly   Heb 12:16
minded (N)
immoral or irreligious (R)   Heb 12:16

FORNICATORS

an epistle not to company   1Co 5:9
with *f.*
altogether with the *f.* of this   1Co 5:10
world
neither *f.* nor idolaters nor   1Co 6:9
for *f.* (E)(N)   1Ti 1:10
fornicators (S)   1Ti 1:10; Heb 13:4; Re 21:8; 22:15
f. and sorcerers (E)(N)(R)   Re 21:8

FORSAKE

people will *f.* me and break   De 31:16
covenant
I will *f.* them and hide my   De 31:17
face
God forbid we should *f.* the   Jos 24:16
Lord
if ye *f.* the Lord and serve   Jos 24:20
strange gods
should I *f.* my sweetness and   J'g 9:11
my fruit
I will *f.* remnant of my   2Ki 21:14
inheritance
if thou *f.* him, will cast thee   1Ch 28:9
off for ever
if ye turn away, and *f.* my   2Ch 7:19
statutes
but if ye *f.* him, he will *f.*   2Ch 15:2
you
his wrath is against them   Ezr 8:22
that *f.* him
did not *f.* altogether (B)(R)   Ne 9:31
when my father and mother   Ps 27:10
f. me
cease from anger and *f.*   Ps 37:8
wrath, fret not
if his children *f.* my law and   Ps 89:30
walk not
neither will he *f.* his   Ps 94:14
inheritance
horror taken hold, because   Ps 119:53
wicked *f.* law
let not mercy and truth *f.* thee,   Pr 3:3
bind them
f. the foolish, and live, go in   Pr 9:6
way of understanding
they that *f.* the law praise   Pr 28:4
the wicked
they that *f.* the Lord shall be   Isa 1:28
consumed
let wicked *f.* his way,   Isa 55:7
unrighteous his thoughts
ye are they that *f.* Lord   Isa 65:11
forget my holy mountain
all that *f.* the Lord shall be   Jer 17:13
ashamed
I will even *f.* you saith the   Jer 23:33; 23:39
Lord
f. her and let us go every   Jer 51:9
one to his country
wherefore dost thou *f.* us so   La 5:20
long time
with them that *f.* the holy   Da 11:30
covenant
observe lying vanities *f.* their   Jon 2:8
own mercy
thou teachest the Jews to *f.*   Ac 21:21
Moses

FORSAKE *NOT*

take heed that thou *f. not*   De 12:19
the Levite
though he spare wickedness   Job 20:13
and *f.* it *not*
f. me *not*, O Lord my God   Ps 38:21; 71:9, 18
I will keep thy statutes, O *f.*   Ps 119:8
me *not* utterly

f. not the works of thine   *Ps 138:8*
own hands
and *f. not* the law of thy   *Pr 1:8;*
mother   *6:20*
I give you good doctrine, *f.* ye *Pr 4:2*
not my law
f. her *not* and she shall   *Pr 4:6*
preserve thee
thine own friend and father's *Pr 27:10*
friend *f. not*

NOT FORSAKE

he will *not f.* thee   *De 4:31;*
           31:6, 8; 1Ch 28:20
and the Levite, thou shalt *De 14:27*
not f. him
I will *not* fail nor *f.* thee   *Jos 1:5;*
              Heb 13:5
Lord will *not f.* his people *1Sa 12:22;*
             1Ki 6:13
let him *not* leave us, nor *f.* *1Ki 8:57*
us
thou didst *not* consume, nor   *Ne 9:31*
f. them
we will *not f.* the house of *Ne 10:39*
our God
neither *f.* me, O God of my *Ps 27:9*
salvation
I, the God of Israel, will   *Isa 41:17*
not f. them
these things will I do, and *Isa 42:16*
not f. them
nor did they *f.* the idols of *Eze 20:8*
Egypt

FORSAKEN

not forsaken (E)(R)   *Ge 24:27*
because he had *f.* the Lord *2Ch 21:10;*
          24:24; 28:6
I said, Why is the house of *Ne 13:11*
God *f.*
shall the earth be *f.* for thee *Job 18:4*
yet have I not seen the   *Ps 37:25*
righteous *f.*
the land shall be *f.* of both *Isa 7:16*
her kings
the cities of Aroer are *f.*   *Isa 17:2*
shall be for flocks
shall be as a *f.* bough, and *Isa 17:9*
an uppermost branch
and the habitation shall be *f.* *Isa 27:10*
and left
because the palaces shall be *Isa 32:14*
f. city left
the Lord hath called thee as *Isa 54:6*
a woman *f.*
thou shalt no more be termed *Isa 62:4*
f.
every city shall be *f.* no man *Jer 4:20*
dwell therein
shall cold waters from   *Jer 18:14*
another place be *f.*
thus saith the Lord to the   *Eze 36:4*
cities *f.*
the virgin of Israel is *f.* on   *Am 5:2*
her land
for Gaza shall be *f.* and   *Zep 2:4*
Ashkelon desolate

HAVE, HAST, HATH
FORSAKEN

thy doings, whereby thou   *De 28:20*
hast f. me
because they *have f.* the   *De 29:25;*
Lord   *J'g 10:10*
but now the Lord *hath f.* us *J'g 6:13*
yet ye *have f.* me, and   *J'g 10:13*
served other gods
the works wherewith they   *1Sa 8:8*
have f. me
we have sinned, because we *1Sa 12:10*
have f. the Lord
because that they *have f.*   *1Ki 11:33*
me
ye *have f.* the   *1Ki 18:18*
commandments of the Lord
for Israel *have f.* thy   *1Ki 19:10;*
covenant   *19:14*
have f. me and burnt   *2Ki 22:17;*
incense to gods *2Ch 34:25; Jer 16:11;*
             19:4
ye *have f.* me, and I have   *2Ch 12:5*
left you
we keep charge of the Lord *2Ch 13:11*
but ye *have f.* him

because ye *have f.* the   *2Ch 24:20*
Lord, he *hath f.* you
for fathers have done evil,   *2Ch 29:6*
and *have f.* him
for we *have f.* thy   *Ezr 9:10*
commandments
because he *hath* oppressed *Job 20:19*
and *f.* the poor
my God, my God, why *hast* *Ps 22:1;*
thou *f.* me   *M't 27:46; M'k 15:34*
they take counsel, saying, *Ps 71:11*
God *hath f.* him
they *have f.* the Lord and   *Isa 1:4*
provoked Holy One
for a small moment *have* I *Isa 54:7;*
f. thee   *49:14*
have f. me, burnt incense to *Jer 1:16*
other gods
they *have f.* me the fountain *Jer 2:13*
of living waters
in that thou *hast f.* the Lord *Jer 2:17;*
thy God   *2:19*
how shall I pardon thee? thy *Jer 5:7*
children *have f.* me
thou shalt answer, like as ye *Jer 5:19*
have f. me
the Lord saith, Because they *Jer 9:13*
have f. my law
are confounded, because ye *Jer 9:19*
have f. the land
I *have f.* my house, I have *Jer 12:7*
left my heritage
thou *hast f.* me, saith the *Jer 15:6*
Lord
they *have f.* the fountain of *Jer 17:13*
living waters
because they *have f.* the *Jer 22:9*
covenant of God
he *hath f.* his covert as the *Jer 25:38*
lion
the Lord *hath f.* the earth   *Eze 8:12;*
              M't 9:9
we *have f.* all and followed *M't 19:27*
thee
every one that *hath f.*   *M't 19:29*
houses or brethren
Demas *hath f.* me, having *2Ti 4:10*
loved world
which *have f.* the right way, *2Pe 2:15*
gone astray

NOT FORSAKEN

as for us, the Lord is our *2Ch 13:10*
God. we have *not f.* him
yet God hath *not f.* us in our *Ezr 9:9*
bondage
thou hast *not f.* them that   *Ps 9:10*
seek thee
shall be called, sought out, a *Isa 62:12*
city *not f.*
Israel hath *not* been *f.* nor   *Jer 51:5*
Judah of his God
we are persecuted, but *not f.* *2Co 4:9*
cast down

FORSAKETH

but he *f.* the fear of the *Job 6:14*
Almighty
for the Lord *f.* not his saints *Ps 37:28*
from her who *f.* the guide of *Pr 2:17*
her youth
correction grievous to him *Pr 15:10*
that *f.* the way
whoso confesseth and *f.* shall *Pr 28:13*
have mercy
whoso *f.* not all that he   *Lu 14:33*
hath cannot

FORSAKING

until there be a great *f.* in *Isa 6:12*
the land
not *f.* the assembling of   *Heb 10:25*
ourselves together

FORSOMUCH

f. as he also is a son of *Lu 19:9*
Abraham

FORSOOK

then he *f.* God which made *De 32:15*
him
f. the Lord God of their *J'g 2:12*
fathers
they *f.* the Lord, and served *J'g 2:13*
Baal

f. the Lord, and served not *J'g 10:6*
him
they *f.* the cities, and fled; *1Sa 31:7*
and the
Because they *f.* the Lord their *1Ki 9:9*
God
he *f.* the counsel of the old *1Ki 12:8*
men
and *f.* the old men's   *1Ki 12:13*
counsel that
he *f.* the Lord God of his *2Ki 21:22*
fathers
then they *f.* their cities, and *1Ch 10:7*
fled
they *f.* the Lord God of   *2Ch 7:22*
their fathers
he *f.* the counsel which the *2Ch 10:8*
old men
Rehoboam *f.* the counsel of *2Ch 10:13*
the old
he *f.* the law of the Lord,   *2Ch 12:1*
and all
he *f.* the tabernacle of Shiloh *Ps 78:60*
earth; but I *f.* not thy   *Ps 119:87*
precepts
f. not the ordinance of their *Isa 58:2*
God
also calved in the field, and *Jer 14:5*
f. it
all the disciples *f.* him, and *M't 26:56*
fled
they *f.* their nets, and   *M'k 1:18*
followed
And they all *f.* him and   *M'k 14:50*
fled
land, they *f.* all, and followed *Lu 5:11*
him
stood with me, but all men *f.* *2Ti 4:16*
me
By faith he *f.* Egypt, not *Heb 11:27*
fearing

FORSOOKEST

great kindness, and *f.* them *Ne 9:17*
not
thy manifold mercies *f.* them *Ne 9:19*
not

FORSWEAR

Thou shalt not *f.* thyself, but *M't 5:33*

FORT

David dwelt in the *f.* and *2Sa 5:9*
called
my *f.* (B)   *2Sa 22:3*
fortress of the high *f* of thy *Isa 25:12*
walls
and build a *f.* against it, and *Eze 4:2*
cast
to cast a mount, and to   *Eze 21:22*
build a *f.*
he shall make a *f.* against *Eze 26:8*
thee
shall turn his face toward *Da 11:19*
the *f.*
f. for unclean spirit   *Re 18:2*
(B)(E)(N)(P)

FORTH

and they both came *f.*   *Nu 12:5*
I brought *f.* my people Israel *1Ki 8:16*
out
forth (S)   *1Ch 13:11; 15:13; 2Sa 6:8*
set *f.* in the Aramaic language *Ezr 4:7*
(S)
and so *f.* (S)   *Ezr 4:10; 4:17; 7:12*
from that time *f.* my servants *Ne 4:16*
wrought
from that time *f.* came they *Ne 13:21*
no more
blessed be name of Lord, *Ps 113:2;*
from this time *f.* for ever *115:18;*
             121:8
ye shall be driven out every *Jer 49:5*
man right *f.*
justice goeth *f.* perverted (S) *Hab 1:4*
from that time *f.* began   *M't 16:21*
Jesus to shew
nor durst from that day *f.* *M't 22:46*
ask him questions
from that day *f.* they took *Joh 11:53*
counsel
sent *f.* to minister for them *Heb 1:14*
who

FORTHWITH

f. expences be given unto these   *Ezr 6:8*
f. they sprung up, because they   *M't 13:5*
f. he came to Jesus, and said   *M't 26:49*
f. when they were come out of   *M'k 1:29*
charged him, and *f.* sent him away   *M'k 1:43*
And *f.* Jesus gave them leave   *M'k 5:13*
f. came thereout blood and water   *Joh 19:34*
he received sight *f.* and arose   *Ac 9:18*
f. the angel departed from him   *Ac 12:10*
and *f.* the doors were shut   *Ac 21:30*

FORTIETH

and died there, in the *f.* year after   *Nu 33:38*
and it came to pass in the *f.* year   *De 1:3*
In the *f.* year of the reign of David   *1Ch 26:31*
and died in the one and *f.* year of   *2Ch 16:13*

FORTIFIED

fortified (S)   *Nu 32:17;*
32:36; De 3:5; 9:1; 28:52; Jos 10:20;
14:12; 19:35; 1Sa 6:18; 2Sa 20:6;
2Ki 3:19; 10:2; 17:9; 18:8, 13; 19:25;
2Ch 8:5; 11:10, 23; 12:4; 14:6; 17:2, 19;
19:5; 21:3; 32:1; 33:14; Isa 2:15; 25:2;
27:10; 36:1; 37:26; Jer 1:18; 4:5; 5:17;
8:14; 15:20; 34:7; Eze 21:20; 36:35;
   Da 11:15; Ho 8:14; Zep 1:16
And he *f.* the strong holds   *2Ch 11:11*
turning of the wall, and *f.* them   *2Ch 26:9*
f. Jerusalem unto the broad wall   *Ne 3:8*
Assyria, and from the *f.* cities   *Mic 7:12*

FORTIFY

they *f.* the city against thee   *J'g 9:31*
Jews? will they *f.* themselves   *Ne 4:2*
ye broken down to *f.* the wall   *Isa 22:10*
should *f.* the height of her strength   *Jer 51:53*
loins strong, *f.* thy power mightily   *Na 2:1*
f. thy strong holds: go into clay   *Na 3:14*
f. one another (N)   *1Th 5:11*

FORTITUDE

source of *f.*, encouragement (N)   *Ro 15:5*

FORTRESS

The Lord is my rock, and my *f.*   *2Sa 22:2*
the gates of the *f.* (A)(B)(R)   *Ne 2:8*
the command out of the *f.* (B)   *Ne 7:2*
rock, and my *f.* and my deliverer   *Ps 18:2*
For thou art my rock and my *f.*   *Ps 31:3*
he is their *f.* (B)   *Ps 37:39; 73:4*
for thou art my rock and my *f.*   *Ps 71:3*
He is my refuge and my *f.*   *Ps 91:2*
My goodness, and my *f.*; my high   *Ps 144:2*
f. also shall cease from Ephraim   *Isa 17:3*
And the *f.* of the high fort of thy   *Isa 25:12*
a tower and a *f.* among my people   *Jer 6:27*
the land, O inhabitant of the *f.*   *Jer 10:17*
O Lord, my strength, and my *f.*   *Jer 16:19*
the *f.* is put to shame (R)   *Jer 48:1*

shall enter into the *f.* of the king   *Da 11:7*
and be stirred up, even to his *f.*   *Da 11:10*
driven to the *f.* (B)   *Am 4:3*
spoiled shall come against the *f.*   *Am 5:9*
and from the *f.* even to the river   *Mic 7:12*
keep the *f.* (A)(E)(S)   *Na 2:1*

FORTRESSES

he built *f.* (S)   *2Ch 17:12; 27:4*
will be *f.* of rocks   *Isa 33:16*
(A)(B)(R)
and brambles in the *f.* thereof   *Isa 34:13*
toward the *f.* of his own land (S)   *Da 11:19*
the god of *f.* (S)   *Da 11:38*
the strongest *f.* (S)   *Da 11:39*
and all thy *f.* shall be spoiled   *Ho 10:14*

FORTS

they built *f.* against it round about   *2Ki 25:1*
and I will raise *f.* against thee   *Isa 29:3*
f. and towers shall be for dens   *Isa 32:14*
and built *f.* against it round about   *Jer 52:4*
casting up mounts, and building   *Eze 17:17*
that be in the *f.* and in the caves   *Eze 33:27*

FORTUNATE

I am *f.* (B)(E)(R)   *Ge 30:11*
f. are your men (B)   *1Ki 10:8*
consider myself *f.*   *Ac 26:2*
(A)(B)(N)(P)(R)

FORTUNATUS

the coming of Stephanas and F.   *1Co 16:17*

FORTUNE

Good *f.* (S)   *Ge 30:11*
a medium or *f.* teller (B)   *Le 20:27*
wasted his *f.* (A)   *Lu 15:13*

FORTUNETELLER

medium or *f.* (B)   *Le 20:27;*
1Sa 28:3, 9; 2Ch 33:6; Isa 8:19; 19:3

FORTUNETELLERS

that are *f.* (B)   *Isa 19:3*

FORTUNETELLING

sin of *f.* (B)   *1Sa 15:23*
f. and sorcery (B)   *2Ch 33:6*
much gain by *f.*   *Ac 16:16*
(A)(B)(N)(P)

FORTY

upon the earth *f.* days and *f.* nights   *Ge 7:12*
peradventure there be *f.* found: ¹   *Ge 18:29*
thou shalt make *f.* sockets of silver   *Ex 26:19*
and their *f.* sockets of silver   *Ex 26:21;*
   36:24, 26
Abdon had *f.* sons and thirty daughters   *J'g 12:14*
so Hazael took *f.* camels' burden   *2Ki 8:9*
the governors had taken *f.* shekels   *Ne 5:15*
more than *f.* made this conspiracy   *Ac 23:13;*
   23:21

FORTY *BATHS*

made ten layers. one contained *f.* baths   *1Ki 7:38*

FORTY *CUBITS*

the house before it was *f.* cubits long   *1Ki 6:17*
he measured the length thereof *f.* cubits   *Eze 41:2*
there were courts joined of *f.* cubits   *Eze 46:22*

FORTY *KINE*

f. kine, ten bulls, a present to Esau   *Ge 32:15*

FORTY *STRIPES*

f. stripes he may give him, and not exceed   *De 25:3*
of Jews I received *f.* stripes save one   *2Co 11:24*

FORTY *YEARS*

Isaac was *f.* years when he took Rebekah   *Ge 25:20*
Esau *f.* years when he took to wife Judith   *Ge 26:34*
Israel did eat manna *f.* years   *Ex 16:35;*
   Ne 9:21
shall wander in wilderness *f.* years   *Nu 14:33;*
   32:13
ye shall bear your iniquities *f.* years   *Nu 14:34*
he knoweth thy walking these *f.* years   *De 2:7*
the way which God led thee *f.* years   *De 8:2;*
   29:5
neither did thy foot swell these *f.* years   *De 8:4*
Israel walked *f.* years in the wilderness   *Jos 5:6*
f. years old was I when Moses sent me   *Jos 14:7*
the land had rest *f.* years   *J'g 3:11;*
   5:31; 8:28
Israel into the hand of Philistines *f.* years   *J'g 13:1*
Eli had judged Israel *f.* years   *1Sa 4:18*
Ish-bosheth *f.* years old when he began   *2Sa 2:10*
David reigned *f.* years   *2Sa 5:4;*
   1Ki 2:11
after *f.* years Absalom said to the king   *2Sa 15:7*
time Solomon reigned was *f.* years   *1Ki 11:42*
Jehoash reigned *f.* years in Jerusalem   *2Ki 12:1*
Joash reigned *f.* years in Jerusalem   *2Ch 24:1*
f. years was I grieved with this generation   *Ps 95:10*
nor shall it be inhabited *f.* years   *Eze 29:11*
and her cities shall be desolate *f.* years   *Eze 29:12*
at the end of *f.* years I will gather the Egyptians   *Eze 29:13*
I led you *f.* years in the wilderness   *Am 2:10*
ye offered sacrifices *f.* years   *Am 5:25;*
   Ac 7:42
for the man healed was above *f.* years old   *Ac 4:22*
Moses was *f.* years old, he visited his brethren   *Ac 7:23*
when *f.* years expired, there appeared an angel   *Ac 7:30*
had shewed wonders in the wilderness *f.* years   *Ac 7:36*
the time of *f.* years suffered he their manners   *Ac 13:18*
God gave them Saul by space of *f.* years   *Ac 13:21*
when your fathers saw my works *f.* years   *Heb 3:9*
but with whom was he grieved *f.* years   *Heb 3:17*

FORTY-ONE *YEARS*

Rehoboam was *f.*-one years old when he began to reign   *1Ki 14:21;*
   2Ch 12:13
Asa reigned *f.*-one years in Jerusalem   *1Ki 15:10*
Jeroboam reigned *f.*-one years Samaria   *2Ki 14:23*

FORTY-TWO

to cities of refuge add *f.-two*   *Nu 35:6*
cities
two bears tare *f.* and *two*   *2Ki 2:24*
children
Jehu took them alive, even   *2Ki 10:14*
f. and *two* men
f.-two years old Ahaz, when   *2Ch 22:2*
he began
the children of Azmaveth *f.*   *Ezr 2:24*
and *two*
the men of Beth-azmaveth *f.*   *Ne 7:28*
and *two*
holy city they tread *f.-two*   *Re 11:2*
months
power was given him to   *Re 13:5*
continue *f.-two* months

FORTY-FIVE

if I find *f.-five,* I will not   *Ge 18:28*
destroy it
Lord kept me alive these   *Jos 14:10*
f.-five years
upon the beams that lay on   *1Ki 7:3*
f.-five pillars

FORTY-SIX

f.-six years was this temple   *Joh 2:20*
in building

FORTY-EIGHT

cities of Levites *f.-eight*   *Nu 35:7;*
                      Jos 21:41

FORTY-NINE

space shall be to thee *f.-nine*   *Le 25:8*
years

FORTY THOUSAND

numbered of tribe of   *Nu 1:33;*
Ephraim *f. thousand* five   *2:19; 26:18*
hundred
about *f. thousand* prepared   *Jos 4:13*
for war
was a shield or spear seen   *J'g 5:8*
among *f. thousand*
David slew *f. thousand*   *2Sa 10:18;*
horsemen   *1Ch 19:18*
Solomon had *f. thousand*   *1Ki 4:26*
stalls of horses
of Asher expert in war *f.*   *1Ch 12:36*
thousand

FORTY-ONE THOUSAND

of Asher were *f.* and *one*   *Nu 1:41;*
thousand   *2:28*

FORTY-TWO THOUSAND

there fell of Ephraimites   *J'g 12:6*
f.-two thousand
whole congregation was 42,360 *Ezr 2:64;*
                         Ne 7:66

FORTY-THREE THOUSAND

families of the Reubenites   *Nu 26:7*
was 43,730

FORTY-FOUR THOUSAND

the children of Reuben were *1Ch 5:18*
44,760

FORTY-FIVE THOUSAND

that were numbered of Gad *Nu 1:25*
45,650
that were numbered of   *Nu 26:41*
Benjamin 45,600
of Naphtali were numbered *Nu 26:50*
45,400

FORTY-SIX THOUSAND

of Reuben were 46,500   *Nu 1:21; 2:11*

FORTY'S

he said, I will not do it for   *Ge 18:29*
f. sake

FORUM

came to meet us as far as   *Ac 28:15*
Appii *f.*

FORWARD

we will not inherit on   *Nu 32:19*
yonder side or *f.*
walls of Jerusalem went *f.* (S) *Ne 4:7*
and they went backward and *Jer 7:24*
not *f.*
it shall be upon the eighth *Eze 43:27*
day and so *f.*
the set of the faces is *f.* (S) *Hab 1:9*
and they helped *f.* the   *Zec 1:15*
affliction
not only to do, but also to *2Co 8:10*
be *f.* year ago
being more *f.* of his own   *2Co 8:17*
accord he went
so keen in enthusiasm and *2Co 8:17*
interest (A)(P)
so deeply interested in you *2Co 8:17*
(B)
being himself very earnest *2Co 8:17*
(E)(R)
he is so eager that by his *2Co 8:17*
own desire (N)
the same which I also was *f.* *Ga 2:10*
to do
I was also eager to do   *Ga 2:10*
(A)(B)(R)
I was also zealous to do (E) *Ga 2:10*
I made it my business to do *Ga 2:10*
(N)
only too ready to agree (P) *Ga 2:10*
whom if thou bring *f.* on their *3Jo 6*
journey

FORWARDNESS

but by occasion of the *f.* of *2Co 8:8*
others
by the zeal of others (A)   *2Co 8:8*
by the readiness of others *2Co 8:8*
(B)
through the earnestness of *2Co 8:8*
others (E)(R)
telling you how keen others *2Co 8:8*
are (N)
seen in others of eagerness to *2Co 8:8*
help (P)
for I know *f.* of your mind, *2Co 9:2*
for which I boast
your willingness, readiness, *2Co 9:2*
eagerness (A)
I know of your willingness *2Co 9:2*
(B)
I know your readiness   *2Co 9:2*
(E)(R)
I know how eager you are to *2Co 9:2*
help (N)
I know how willing you are *2Co 9:2*
(P)

FOSTER

f. fathers and guardians   *Isa 49:23*
(A)(B)(R)
f. useless speculations (A)   *1Ti 1:4*
possess and *f.* them (N)   *2Pe 1:8*

FOSTERING

tenderly *f.* (B)   *1Th 2:7*

FOUGHT

then came Amalek and *f.*   *Ex 17:8*
with Israel
so Joshua *f.* with Amalek,   *Ex 17:10*
Moses went up
then king Arad *f.* against   *Nu 21:1*
Israel and took some
Sihon came and *f.* against *Nu 21:23;*
Israel   *J'g 11:20*
Sihon *f.* against the former *Nu 21:26*
king of Moab
for the Lord *f.* for Israel   *Jos 10:14;*
              10:42; 23:3
Joshua and all Israel *f.*
against Libnah
f. against Lachish   *Jos 10:31; 10:34, 36*
the Amorites on the other   *Jos 24:8*
side *f.* with you
and the men of Jericho *f.*   *Jos 24:11*
against you
they found Adoni-bezek and *f.* *J'g 1:5*
against him

Judah had *f.* against   *J'g 1:8*
Jerusalem, and taken it
the kings came, then *f.* the *J'g 5:19*
kings of Canaan
they *f.* from heaven, the stars *J'g 5:20*
in courses (S)
my father *f.* for you and   *J'g 9:17*
delivered you
Gaal went out and *f.* with *J'g 9:39*
Abimelech
all the men of Gilead *f.* with *J'g 12:4*
Ephraim
the Philistines *f.*   *1Sa 4:10; 1Ch 10:1*
Saul *f.* against all his   *1Sa 14:47*
enemies on every side
so David *f.* with the   *1Sa 19:8;*
Philistines   *23:5*
people stood still, nor *f.* they *2Sa 2:28*
any more
he had *f.* against Hadadezer *2Sa 8:10;*
                1Ch 18:10
the Syrians *f.* against   *2Sa 10:17;*
David   *1Ch 19:17*
David *f.* against Rabbah   *2Sa 12:29*
and took it
Joram *f.* against Hazael *2Ki 8:29; 9:15*
then Hazael went and *f.*   *2Ki 12:17*
against Gath
Joash *f.* against Amaziah   *2Ki 13:12;*
                14:15
Lord *f.* against the enemies *2Ch 20:29*
of Israel
they *f.* against me without a *Ps 109:3*
cause
Tartan *f.* against Ashdod and *Isa 20:1*
took it
he was turned their enemy *Isa 63:10*
and *f.* against them
the people *f.* against   *Jer 34:1;*
Jerusalem   *34:7*
as when he *f.* in the day of *Zec 14:3*
battle
Lord will smite them that *f.* *Zec 14:12*
against Jerusalem
would have *f.* (P)   *Joh 18:36*
I have *f.* with beasts at   *1Co 15:32*
Ephesus
I have *f.* a good fight, finished *2Ti 4:7*
my course
Michael and his angels *f.*   *Re 12:7*
against dragon

FOUL

river become *f.* smelling   *Ex 7:18*
(A)(B)(E)
did not become *f.*   *Ex 16:25*
(A)(B)(E)
my face is *f.* with weeping, *Job 16:16*
on my eyelids
red, swollen with weeping *Job 16:16*
(A)(B)(E)(R)
wounds grow *f.* and fester   *Ps 38:5*
(B)
so they fell *f.* of him (N) *M't 13:47*
ye say, it will be *f.* weather *M't 16:3*
to-day
It will be stormy today   *M't 16:3*
(A)(R)
there will be a storm today *M't 16:3*
(P)
he rebuked the *f.* spirit,   *M'k 9:25*
saying to him
rebuked unclean spirit   *M'k 9:25*
(A)(B)(E)(N)(R)
spoke sharply to the evil   *M'k 9:25*
spirit (P)
person with a *f.* tongue   *1Co 5:11*
(A)(P)
no *f.* polluting language   *Eph 4:29*
(A)(B)(P)
f. mouthed abuse (A)(R)   *Col 3:8*
f. and painful ulcers   *Re 16:2*
(A)(N)(R)(S)
f. impurity (P)   *Re 17:4*
Babylon the hold of every *f.* *Re 18:2*
spirit and cage
dungeon of every loathsome *Re 18:2*
spirit (A)
fort for every unclean spirit *Re 18:2*
(B)(E)(N)(P)

FOULED

they drink that ye have *f.*   *Eze 34:19*
with your feet
befouled with your feet (B) *Eze 34:19*
garments their deeds have   *Jude 23*
f. (P)

FOULEDST

thou troubledst waters and *f.*   *Eze 32:2*
their rivers

FOULNESS

purge you of moral *f.* (B)   *Eze 22:15*
indulged all *f.* (P)   *2Pe 2:10*
full of *f.* of fornication (N)   *Re 17:4*

FOUND

for Adam there was not *f.* an   *Ge 2:20*
help meet
the dove *f.* no rest for the sole   *Ge 8:9*
of her foot
Isaac's servants digged and *f.*   *Ge 8:19*
a well of water
Isaac's servants said to him,   *Ge 8:32*
We have *f.* water
how is it that thou hast *f.* it   *Ge 27:20*
so quickly
Reuben went and *f.*   *Ge 30:14*
mandrakes in the field
Laban went into tents, but *f.*   *Ge 31:33*
not images
what hast thou *f.* of all thy   *Ge 31:37*
household stuff
Anah that *f.* the mules in   *Ge 36:24*
the wilderness
brought the coat, and said,   *Ge 37:32*
This have we *f.*
I sent this kid, and thou   *Ge 38:23*
hast not *f.* her
money which we *f.* in our   *Ge 44:8*
sacks we brought
God hath *f.* out the iniquity   *Ge 44:16*
of his servants
they went three days and *f.*   *Ex 15:22*
no water
they went to gather manna   *Ex 16:27*
and *f.* none
or if he have *f.* that which was   *Le 6:3*
lost
f. a man that gathered   *Nu 15:32*
sticks on sabbath
they that *f.* him brought   *Nu 15:33*
him to Moses
with what thou hast *f.* shall   *De 22:3*
do likewise
when I came to her I *f.* her   *De 22:14;*
not a maid   *22:17*
he *f.* her in the field, and   *De 22:27*
the damsel cried
because he hath *f.* some   *De 24:1*
uncleanness in her
he *f.* him in a desert land,   *De 32:10*
he led him about
the pursuers sought, but *f.*   *Jos 2:22*
them not
he will *f.* it at price of (B)   *Jos 6:26*
five kings are *f.* hid in a   *Jos 10:17*
cave at Makkedah
they *f.* Adoni-bezek and fought   *J'g 1:5*
against him
if not plowed with heifer,   *J'g 14:18*
not *f.* out my riddle
and he *f.* a new jawbone of   *J'g 15:15*
an ass
and they *f.* four hundred   *J'g 21:12*
young virgins
passed thro' Shalisha, but   *1Sa 9:4*
they *f.* not asses
they *f.* young maidens going   *1Sa 9:11*
to draw water
as for thine asses they are *f.*   *1Sa 9:20;*
   10:2, 16
is witness ye have not *f.*   *1Sa 12:5*
ought in my hand
now there was no smith *f.*   *1Sa 13:19*
in Israel
no sword nor spear *f.* in   *1Sa 13:22*
hand of the people
and evil hath not been *f.*   *1Sa 25:28*
with thee
I have *f.* no fault in him,   *1Sa 29:3*
since he fell to me
and they *f.* an Egyptian in   *1Sa 30:11*
the field
f. Saul and his three sons   *1Sa 31:8*
fallen in Gilboa
therefore thy servant *f.* in   *2Sa 7:27;*
his heart to pray   *1Ch 17:25*
nor was the weight of the   *1Ki 7:47*
brass *f.* out
the prophet Ahijah *f.*   *1Ki 11:29*
Jeroboam in the way
he went and *f.* his carcase   *1Ki 13:28*
cast in the way

he took an oath that they *f.*   *1Ki 18:10*
thee not
Elijah departed thence and   *1Ki 19:19*
f. Elisha
behold, a lion *f.* him and   *1Ki 20:36*
slew him
hast thou *f.* me, O mine   *1Ki 21:20*
enemy have *f.* thee
they sought Elijah but *f.*   *2Ki 2:17*
him not
they *f.* no more of her than   *2Ki 2:35*
the skull
I *f.* the book of the law in   *2Ki 22:8*
house of the Lord
he took sixty men that were   *2Ki 25:19*
f. in the city
they *f.* fat pasture and good   *1Ch 4:40*
they with whom precious   *1Ch 29:8*
stones were *f.*
there are good things *f.* in   *2Ch 19:3*
thee
sought their register by   *Ezr 2:62;*
genealogy, but they were   *Ne 7:64*
not *f.*
and I *f.* there none of the   *Ezr 8:15*
sons of Levi
then they *f.* nothing to answer   *Ne 5:8*
they *f.* written in the law of   *Ne 8:14*
Lord by Moses
nor is wisdom *f.* in the land   *Job 28:13*
of the living
or lift up myself when evil   *Job 28:29*
f. mine enemy
wrath kindled, because they   *Job 32:3*
had *f.* no answer
lest ye should say, we have   *Job 32:13*
f. out wisdom
deliver from the pit, I have   *Job 33:24*
f. a ransom
no women *f.* so fair as the   *Job 42:15*
daughters of Job
I looked for comforters, but   *Ps 69:20*
f. none
none of the men of might   *Ps 76:5*
have *f.* their hands
yea, sparrow hath *f.* an house,   *Ps 84:3*
and swallow
I have *f.* David my servant,   *Ps 89:20*
I anointed him
did *f.* earth   *Ps 102:25; Isa 48:13;*
(B)   *Heb 1:10*
they wandered and *f.* no city   *Ps 107:4*
to dwell in
we *f.* it in the fields of the   *Ps 132:6*
wood
to seek thy face, and I have   *Pr 7:15*
f. thee
so shall wisdom be when   *Pr 24:14*
thou hast *f.* it
hast thou *f.* honey? eat so   *Pr 25:16*
much as is sufficient
behold, this have I *f.* saith   *Ec 7:27*
the preacher
one man among a thousand   *Ec 7:28*
have I *f.* but a woman
among all those have I not *f.*
this only have I *f.* that God   *Ec 7:29*
made man upright
I sought him, but I *f.* him not   *Ca 3:1;*
   3:2
the watchmen *f.* me, to whom   *Ca 3:3;*
I said   *5:7*
but I *f.* him whom my soul   *Ca 3:4*
loveth
as my hand hath *f.*   *Isa 10:10*
kingdoms of idols
my hand hath *f.* the riches   *Isa 10:14*
of the people
all that are *f.* in thee are   *Isa 22:3*
bound together
thou hast *f.* the life of thine   *Isa 57:10*
hand
I am *f.* of them that sought   *Isa 65:1*
me not
what iniquity have your   *Jer 2:5*
fathers *f.* in me
in thy skirts is *f.* the blood   *Jer 2:34*
of poor innocents
for among my people are *f.*   *Jer 5:26*
wicked men
they came to the pits and *f.*   *Jer 14:3*
no water
thy words were *f.* and I did   *Jer 15:16*
eat them
in my house have I *f.* their   *Jer 23:11*
wickedness
ten men were *f.* that said,   *Jer 41:8*
Slay us not

all that *f.* them have   *Jer 50:7*
devoured them
this is the day, we have *f.* we   *La 2:16*
have seen
I sought for a man, but I *f.*   *Eze 22:30*
none
an excellent spirit was *f.* in   *Da 5:12*
Daniel
thou art weighed, and art *f.*   *Da 5:27*
wanting
nor was there any fault *f.* in   *Da 6:4*
Daniel
these men *f.* Daniel praying   *Da 6:11*
before his God
I *f.* Israel like grapes in the   *Ho 9:10*
wilderness
he *f.* him in Beth-el, and   *Ho 12:4*
there spake with us
Ephraim said, I have *f.* me   *Ho 12:8*
out substance
I am like a tree. From me is   *Ho 14:8*
thy fruit *f.*
he *f.* a ship for Tarshish, so   *Jon 1:3*
he paid fare
the transgressions of Israel   *Mic 1:13*
were *f.* in thee
when ye have *f.* him bring me   *M't 2:8*
word
I have not *f.* so great faith   *M't 8:10;*
in Israel   *Lu 7:9*
which when a man hath *f.*   *M't 13:44*
he hideth in
when he had *f.* one pearl of   *M't 13:46*
great price
and *f.* one of his   *M't 18:28*
fellow-servants who owed
he went out and *f.* others   *M't 20:6*
standing idle
f. nothing thereon   *M't 21:19;*
   M'k 11:13; Lu 13:6
they gathered all as many   *M't 22:10*
as they *f.*
he *f.* them asleep   *M't 26:43;*
   M'k 14:40; Lu 22:45
sought witnesses, yet *f.*   *M't 26:60;*
they none   *M'k 14:55*
they *f.* a man of Cyrene,   *M't 27:32*
Simon by name
when they had *f.* him, they   *M'k 1:37*
said to him
some ate with defiled hands,   *M'k 7:2*
they *f.* fault
when she was come, she *f.*   *M'k 7:30*
the devil gone out
they *f.* the colt tied by the   *M'k 11:4*
door without
they *f.* the babe lying in a   *Lu 2:16*
manger
after three days they *f.* him   *Lu 2:46*
in the temple
he *f.* the place where it was   *Lu 4:17*
written
they returning *f.* the servant   *Lu 7:10*
whole
they *f.* man clothed and in   *Lu 8:35*
his right mind
when he hath *f.* the sheep, he   *Lu 15:5*
layeth it
rejoice, for I have *f.* my   *Lu 15:6*
sheep which was lost
when she hath *f.* the piece,   *Lu 15:9*
she calleth friends
are not any *f.* that returned   *Lu 17:18*
to give glory
they *f.* even as he had said   *Lu 19:32;*
to them   *22:13*
we *f.* this fellow perverting   *Lu 23:2*
the nation
behold, I have *f.* no fault in   *Lu 23:14*
this man
and they *f.* the stone rolled   *Lu 24:2*
away
they *f.* not the body of the   *Lu 24:3*
Lord Jesus
when they *f.* not his body,   *Lu 24:23*
they came, saying
and they *f.* the eleven   *Lu 24:33*
gathered together
and saith, We have *f.* the   *Joh 1:41;*
Messias   *1:45*
Jesus *f.* in the temple those   *Joh 2:14*
that sold oxen
the young men came in, and   *Ac 5:10*
f. her dead
when the officers *f.* them not   *Ac 5:22*
in the prison
and our fathers *f.* no   *Ac 7:11*
sustenance

that if he *f.* any of this way,   *Ac 9:2*
whether men
Peter *f.* many that were   *Ac 10:27*
come together
Herod sought for Peter, and   *Ac 12:19*
f. him not
they *f.* a certain sorcerer, a   *Ac 13:6*
false prophet
I have *f.* David, a man after   *Ac 13:22*
mine own heart
I *f.* an altar with this   *Ac 17:23*
inscription
we have *f.* this man a   *Ac 24:5*
pestilent fellow
if they have *f.* any evil   *Ac 24:20*
doing in me
I *f.* he hath done nothing   *Ac 25:25*
worthy of death
we came to Puteoli, where   *Ac 28:14*
we *f.* brethren
what Abraham our father hath   *Ro 4:1*
f.
which was ordained to life, I   *Ro 7:10*
f. to be to death
yea, we are *f.* false   *1Co 15:15*
witnesses of God
because I *f.* not Titus my   *2Co 2:13*
brother
we ourselves also are *f.*   *Gal 2:17*
sinners
and being *f.* in fashion as a   *Ph'p 2:8*
man
use the office, being *f.*   *1Ti 3:10*
blameless
Onesiphorus sought me and   *2Ti 1:17*
f. me
for he *f.* no place of   *Heb 12:17*
repentance
that your faith might be *f.* to   *1Pe 1:7*
praise
f. of thy children walking in   *2Jo 4:1*
truth
thou hast tried them, and hast   *Re 2:2*
f. them liars
I have not *f.* thy works perfect   *Re 3:2*
before God
nor was their place *f.* any   *Re 12:8*
more in heaven
and the mountains were not   *Re 16:20*
f.

BE FOUND

peradventure there shall be   *Ge 18:29*
forty *f.*
with whomsoever of thy   *Ge 44:9*
servants it be *f.*
seven days no leaven shall be   *Ex 12:19*
f. in houses
that stealeth a man, if he be   *Ex 21:16*
f. in his hand
if a thief be *f.* breaking up   *Ge 22:2;*
       22:7
if the theft be certainly *f.* in   *Ex 22:4*
his hand
if a man lie with her, and   *De 22:28*
they be *f.*
they sought him, he could not   *1Sa 10:21*
be *f.*
shall come on him where he   *2Sa 17:12*
shall be *f.*
if wickedness be *f.* in him he   *1Ki 1:52*
shall die
if seek him, will *f.* of   *1Ch 28:9;*
thee   *2Ch 15:2*
he shall fly away, and shall   *Job 20:8*
not be *f.*
but where shall wisdom be   *Job 28:12*
f.
shall pray in time when thou   *Ps 32:6*
mayest be *f.*
till his iniquity be *f.* to be   *Ps 36:2*
hateful
I sought him, but he could   *Ps 37:36*
not be *f.*
if he be *f.* he shall restore   *Pr 6:31*
sevenfold
if it be *f.* in the way of   *Pr 16:31*
righteousness
lest he reprove thee and thou   *Pr 30:6*
be *f.* a liar
lest he curse thee, and thou   *Pr 30:10*
be *f.* guilty
there shall not be *f.* a sherd   *Isa 30:14*
to take fire
no lion, nor any beast shall   *Isa 35:9*
be *f.* thereon
joy and gladness shall be *f.*   *Isa 51:3*
therein

seek ye the Lord while he   *Isa 55:6*
may be *f.*
I will be *f.* of you, saith the   *Jer 29:14*
Lord
sins of Judah be sought for,   *Jer 50:20*
shall not be *f.*
yet shalt thou never be *f.*   *Eze 26:21*
again
he shall stumble and fall,   *Da 11:19*
and not be *f.*
every one that shall be *f.*   *Da 12:1*
written in the book
now shall they be *f.* faulty   *Ho 10:2*
nor a deceitful tongue be *f.*   *Zep 3:13*
in mouth
and place shall not be *f.* for   *Zec 10:10*
lest ye be *f.* to fight against   *Ac 5:39*
God
it is required that a steward   *1Co 4:2*
be *f.* faithful
if clothed, we shall not be *f.*   *2Co 5:3*
naked
wherein glory, they may be   *2Co 11:12*
f. even as we
that I shall be *f.* such as ye   *2Co 12:20*
would not
be *f.* in him, not having my   *Ph'p 3:9*
own righteousness
that ye may be *f.* of him in   *2Pe 3:14*
peace
the city of Babylon be *f.* no   *Re 18:21*
more at all
no craftsman shall be. *f.* any   *Re 18:22*
more in thee

IS FOUND

he with whom it *is f.* be   *Ge 44:10;*
       44:16
my servant
people that *is f.* shall be   *De 20:11*
tributaries
in him there *is f.* some   *1Ki 14:13*
good thing
this book that *is f.*   *2Ki 22:13;*
       2Ch 34:21
it *is f.* this city hath been   *Ezr 4:19*
rebellious
seeing the root of the   *Job 19:28*
matter *is f.*
in the lips of him wisdom *is*   *Pr 10:13*
f.
every one that *is f.* shall be   *Isa 13:15*
thrust thro'
as the new wine *is f.* in the   *Isa 65:8*
cluster
as the thief is ashamed when   *Jer 2:26*
he is *f.*
in thy skirts *is f.* the blood   *Jer 2:34*
of innocents
a conspiracy *is f.* among the   *Jer 11:9*
men of Judah
excellent wisdom *is f.* in thee   *Da 5:12;*
       5:14
I am like a tree, from me is   *Ho 14:8*
thy fruit *f.*
this my son was lost and *is*   *Lu 15:24;*
f.   *15:32*
our boasting I made *is f.* a   *2Co 7:14*
truth

WAS FOUND

the cup was *f.* in Benjamin's   *Ge 44:12*
sack
Joseph gathered the money   *Ge 47:14*
that was *f.*
every man with whom was *f.*   *Ex 35:23*
purple
every man with whom was *f.*   *Ex 35:24*
shittim wood
with Saul and Jonathan   *1Sa 13:22*
there was *f.*
high priest told the money   *2Ki 12:10*
that was *f.*
shewed all that was *f.* in   *2Ki 20:13;*
treasury   *Isa 39:2*
gathered the money that   *2Ki 22:9;*
was *f.*   *2Ch 34:17*
read book which was *f.*   *2Ki 23:2;*
       2Ch 34:30
sought him, he was *f.* of   *2Ch 15:4*
them
carried away the substance   *2Ch 21:17*
that was *f.*
there was *f.* at Achmetha a   *Ezr 6:2*
roll
there was *f.* in it a poor wise   *Ec 9:15*
man

was Israel a derision? was he   *Jer 48:27*
f. among thieves
perfect till iniquity was *f.*   *Eze 28:15*
in thee
among all none was *f.* like   *Da 1:19*
Daniel
iron, clay broken, no place   *Da 2:35*
was *f.* for them
like the wisdom of the gods   *Da 5:11*
was *f.* in him
because before him innocency   *Da 6:22*
was *f.* in me
she was *f.* with child of the   *M't 1:18*
Holy Ghost
when voice was past, Jesus   *Lu 9:36*
was *f.* alone
but Philip was *f.* at Azotus,   *Ac 8:40*
he preached
I was *f.* of them that sought   *Ro 10:20*
me not
neither was guile *f.* in his   *1Pe 2:22*
mouth
no man was *f.* worthy to open   *Re 5:4*
the book
and in their mouth was *f.* no   *Re 14:5*
guile
in her was *f.* the blood of   *Re 18:24*
the prophets
and there was *f.* no place   *Re 20:11*
for them

WAS NOT FOUND

and iniquity was not *f.* in his   *Mal 2:6*
lips
Enoch was not *f.* because   *Heb 11:5*
God translated
whoso was not *f.* written in   *Re 20:15*
book of life

FOUND *GRACE*

Noah *f.* *grace* in the eyes of   *Ge 6:8*
the Lord
thy servant hath *f.* *grace* in   *Ge 19:19*
thy sight
if I have *f.* *grace* in thy   *Ge 33:10;*
sight   *47:29; 50:4*
Joseph *f.* *grace* in his sight,   *Ge 39:4*
he served him
thou hast also *f.* *grace* in   *Ex 33:12*
my sight   *33:17*
if I have *f.* *grace* in thy sight   *Ex 33:13;*
       34:9; J'g 6:17; 1Sa 27:5
how known that I and thy   *Ex 33:16*
people have *f.* *grace*
if we have *f.* *grace* in thy   *Nu 32:5*
sight
why have I *f.* *grace* in thine   *Ru 2:10*
eyes
thy father knoweth I have *f.*   *1Sa 20:3*
grace
thy servant knoweth I have   *2Sa 14:22*
f. *grace*
the people *f.* *grace* in the   *Jer 31:2*
wilderness

FOUNDATION

as hath not been in Egypt   *Ex 9:18*
since the *f.*
from its founding (A)(B)   *Ex 9:18*
since day it was founded   *Ex 9:18*
(E)(R)
he shall lay the *f.* in his   *Jos 6:26*
firstborn
He will found it at price of   *Jos 6:26*
(B)
his *f.* is in the holy mountains   *Ps 87:1*
f. of thy throne   *Ps 89:14*
(A)(B)(E)(R)
of old thou hast laid the *f.*   *Ps 102:25*
of the earth
did found earth (B)   *Ps 102:25;*
       Isa 48:13; Heb 1:10
they brought hewn stones to   *1Ki 5:17*
lay the *f.*
in the fourth year was *f.* of   *1Ki 6:37*
house of Lord laid
were of costly stones even   *1Ki 7:9;*
from the *f.*   *7:10*
he laid the *f.* of Jericho in   *1Ki 16:34*
his firstborn
work was prepared to-day of   *2Ch 8:16*
the *f.*
they began to lay the *f.* of   *2Ch 31:7*
the heaps
the *f.* of the temple was not   *Ezr 3:6*
yet laid

when the builders laid the *f.* Ezr 3:10;
of temple 3:12
Sheshbazzar laid the *f.* of the Ezr 5:16
house
how much less in them Job 4:19
whose *f.* is in dust
whose *f.* was overflown Job 22:16
with a flood
foothold washed out by Job 22:16
deluge (B)
Rase it, rase it, even to the Ps 137:7
f. thereof
the righteous is an Pr 10:25
everlasting *f.*
I lay in Zion for a *f.* tried a Isa 28:16
stone
saying to the temple, Thy *f.* Isa 44:28
shall be laid
my hand hath laid the *f.* of Isa 48:13
the earth
the *f.* thereof shall be Eze 13:14
discovered
by discovering the *f.* to the Hab 3:13
neck
from the day that the *f.* was Hag 2:18
laid
Zerubbabel hath laid *f.* and Zec 4:9
shall finish
prophets which were when the Zec 8:9
f. was laid
the Lord, which layeth the *f.* Zec 12:1
of the earth
digged deep, and laid the *f.* Lu 6:48
on a rock
like a man that without a *f.* Lu 6:49
built an house
lest haply after he hath laid Lu 14:29
the *f.*
lest I should build on Ro 15:20
another man's *f.*
as a wise master-builder I 1Co 3:10
laid the *f.*
for other *f.* can no man lay 1Co 3:11
than is laid
if any man build on this *f.* 1Co 3:12
gold, silver, wood
are built on the *f.* of the Eph 2:20
prophets
laying up in store for 1Ti 6:19
themselves a good *f.*
laying good *f.* 1Ti 6:19
(A)(B)(N)(R)
nevertheless *f.* of God 2Ti 2:19
standeth sure
thou, Lord, hast laid the *f.* Heb 1:10
of the earth
not laying the *f.* of repentance Heb 6:1
and faith
the first *f.* jasper; second Re 21:19
sapphire

FOUNDATION *OF*
THE *WORLD*

kept secret from the *f.* of M't 13:35
the world
kingdom prepared from the M't 25:34
f. of the world
the blood shed from the *f.* Lu 11:50
of the world
the founding of the world Lu 11:50;
(B) Heb 4:3; Re 13:8; 17:8
the foundation of the earth Lu 11:50
(P)
thou lovedst me before the Joh 17:24
f. of the world
before the world began Joh 17:24
(N)(P)
chosen us in him before the Eph 1:4
f. of the world
before the world was founded Eph 1:4
(B)(N)
works were finished from the Heb 4:3
f. of the world
since the world was created Heb 4:3
(N)
since work of creation was Heb 4:3
finished (P)
must have oft suffered since Heb 9:26
f. of the world
since the world began (B) Heb 9:26
since the world was made Heb 9:26
(N)
from beginning of the world Heb 9:26
(P)
foreordained before the *f.* of 1Pe 1:20
the world

before the world was 1Pe 1:20
founded (P)
Lamb slain from the *f. of the* Re 13:8
world
since the world was made Re 13:8;
(N) 17:8
names not written from the *f.* Re 17:8
of the world

FOUNDATIONS

and set on fire the *f.* of the De 32:22
mountains
scorching bases of the hills De 32:22
(B)
the *f.* of heaven moved and 2Sa 22:8
shook
f. of the world were 2Sa 22:16;
discovered Ps 18:7, 15
have set up the walls and Ezr 4:12
joined the *f.*
and let the *f.* thereof be Ezr 6:3
strongly laid
where wast thou when I laid Job 38:4
f. of earth
when I founded the earth Job 38:4
(B)
whereupon are the *f.* thereof Job 38:6
fastened
if *f.* be destroyed, what can Ps 11:3
righteous do
all the *f.* of the earth are out Ps 82:5
of course
who laid the *f.* of earth not Ps 104:5
to be removed
when he appointed the *f.* of Pr 8:29
the earth
for the *f.* of Kir-hareseth Isa 16:7
shall ye mourn
and the *f.* of the earth do Isa 24:18
shake
have ye not understood Isa 40:21
from *f.* of earth
the Lord that laid the *f.* of Isa 51:13
the earth
that I may lay the *f.* of the Isa 51:16
earth
I will lay thy *f.* with Isa 54:11
sapphires
thou shalt raise up *f.* of Isa 58:12
many generations
if the *f.* of the earth can be Jer 31:37
searched
her *f.* are fallen, her walls Jer 50:15
are thrown down
they shall not take of thee a Jer 51:26
stone for *f.*
and it hath devoured the *f.* La 4:11
thereof
Egypt's *f.* shall be broken Eze 30:4
down
the *f.* of the side chambers Eze 41:8
were a full reed
and I will discover the *f.* Mic 1:6
thereof
hear, O mountains, and ye Mic 6:2
strong *f.* of earth
the *f.* of the prison were Ac 16:26
shaken
for he looked for a city Heb 11:10
that hath *f.*
the walls of the city had Re 21:14
twelve *f.*
the *f.* were garnished with Re 21:19
precious stones

FOUNDED

since day it was *f.* (E)(R) Ex 9:18
when I *f.* the earth (B) Job 38:4
f. a bulwark because (R) Ps 8:2
For he hath *f.* it upon the Ps 24:2
seas
fulness thereof, thou hast *f.* Ps 89:11
them
place which thou hast *f.* for Ps 104:8
them
that thou hast *f.* them for Ps 119:152
ever
Lord by wisdom hath *f.* the Pr 3:19
earth
the Lord hath *f.* Zion, and Isa 14:32
the poor
Assyrian *f.* it for them that Isa 23:13
dwell
and hath *f.* his troop in the Am 9:6
earth
fell not: for it was *f.* upon a M't 7:25
rock

shake it: for it was *f.* upon a Lu 6:48
rock
before world was *f.* (B)(N) Eph 1:4
before world was *f.* (P) 1Pe 1:20

FOUNDER

and gave them to the *f.* who J'g 17:4
made
f. melteth in vain: for the Jer 6:29
wicked
hands of the *f.*: blue and Jer 10:9
purple
every *f.* is confounded by Jer 10:14;
51:17

FOUNDEST

f. his heart faithful before thee Ne 9:8

FOUNDING

from its *f.* (A)(B) Ex 9:18
f. of the world (B) Lu 11:50;
Heb 4:30; Re 13:8; 17:8
f. of the earth (P) Lu 11:50

FOUNTAIN

found her by a *f.* of water in Ge 16:7
the
a spring of water (A)(B)(R) Ge 16:7
by the *f.* in the way to Shur Ge 16:7
Nevertheless a *f.* or pit, Le 11:36
wherein
he hath discovered her *f.* Le 20:18
and she
she hath uncovered the *f.* of Le 20:18
her
f. of Jacob shall be upon a De 33:28
land
the *f.* of the water of Jos 15:9
Nephtoah
Israelites pitched by a *f.* 1Sa 29:1
which
I went on to the gate of the Ne 2:14
f.
the gate of the *f.* repaired Ne 3:15
Shallun
And at the *f.* gate, which Ne 12:37
was over
For with thee is the *f.* of life Ps 36:9
the Lord, from the *f.* of Ps 68:26
Israel
Thou didst cleave the *f.* and the Ps 74:15
water, the flint into a *f.* of Ps 114:8
waters
Let thy *f.* be blessed: and Pr 5:18
rejoice
a *f.* of life (B) Pr 10:11
The law of the wise is a *f.* Pr 13:14
of life
The fear of the Lord is a *f.* Pr 14:27
of life
f. of life (B)(R) Pr 16:22
f. of wisdom (A)(B)(R) Pr 18:4
troubled *f.* and a corrupt Pr 25:26
spring
or the pitcher be broken at Ec 12:6
the *f.*
a spring shut up, a *f.* sealed Ca 4:12
a *f.* of gardens, a well of Ca 4:15
living
forsaken me the *f.* of living Jer 2:13
waters
As a *f.* casteth out her waters Jer 6:7
waters, and mine eyes a *f.* of Jer 9:1
tears
forsaken the Lord, the *f.* of Jer 17:13
living
and his *f.* shall be dried Ho 13:15
up
a *f.* shall come forth of the Joe 3:18
house
that day there shall be a *f.* Zec 13:1
opened
straightway the *f.* of her M'k 5:29
blood
Doth a *f.* send forth at the Jas 3:11
same
so can no *f.* both yield salt Jas 3:12
water
that is athirst of the *f.* of the Re 21:6
water

FOUNTAINS

were all the *f.* of the great Ge 7:11
deep
f. also of the deep and the Ge 8:2
windows

in Elim were twelve *f.* of Nu 33:9
water
of *f.* and depths that spring De 8:7
out of
unto all *f.* of water, and 1Ki 18:5
unto all
all the springs (B)(R) 1Ki 18:5
to stop the waters of the *f.* 2Ch 32:3
which
the waters of the springs 2Ch 32:3;
(B)(R) 32:4
stopped all the *f.* and the 2Ch 32:4
brook
f. of the sea (B) Job 38:16
my *f.* are in the (B)(E) Ps 87:7
the *f.* of waters (B) Ps 107:33
Let thy *f.* be dispersed abroad Pr 5:16
should offspring be dispersed Pr 5:16
(A)
your springs be dispersed Pr 5:16
(B)(E)(R)
when there were no *f.* Pr 8:24
abounding
when there were no springs Pr 8:24
(B)(R)
he strengthened the *f.* of the Pr 8:28
deep
and *f.* in the midst of the Isa 41:18
valleys
shall lead them unto living *f.* Re 7:17
of
springs of living waters Re 7:17
(A)(B)(N)(P)(R)
rivers, and upon the *f.* of Re 8:10
waters
springs of water Re 8:10;
(A)(B)(N)(P) 14:7; 16:4
the sea, and the *f.* of waters Re 14:7
upon the rivers and *f.* of Re 16:4
waters

FOUR

a river parted, and became *f.* Ge 2:10
heads
f. kings joined battle with five Ge 14:9
and *f.* parts shall be your Ge 47:24
own for seed
he shall restore *f.* sheep for a Ex 22:1
sheep
thou shalt make for it *f.* Ex 25:26
rings of gold
shall be *f.* bowls made like Ex 25:34
unto almonds
the breadth of one curtain *f.* Ex 26:2;
cubits 26:8
their pillars *f.* their sockets Ex 27:16;
f. 38:19
and in the candlestick were Ex 37:20
f. bowls
he cast *f.* rings for the *f.* ends Ex 38:5
of the grate
f. rows of stones set in the Ex 39:10
breastplate
all fowls that creep going on Le 11:20
all *f.*
of beasts that go on all *f.* Le 11:27;
unclean 11:42
two wagons *f.* oxen to sons Nu 7:7
of Gershon
f. wagons, eight oxen to the Nu 7:8
sons of Merari
make thee fringes on the *f.* De 22:12
quarters
a custom to lament *f.* days J'g 11:40
in a year
these *f.* were born to the 2Sa 21:22
giant
in *f.* hundred and eightieth 1Ki 6:1
year after
he said, Fill *f.* barrels with 1Ki 18:33
water
there were *f.* leprous men at 2Ki 7:3
the entry
saw his son's sons, even *f.* Job 42:16
generations
yea, *f.* things say not, It is Pr 30:15
enough
yea, there be *f.* things which Pr 30:18
I know not
and for *f.* which it Pr 30:21
cannot bear
there be *f.* things which are Pr 30:24
little on earth
yea *f.* things are comely in Pr 30:29
going
f. or five in the utmost Isa 17:6
fruitful branches

I will appoint over them *f.* Jer 15:3
kinds
when Jehudi had read three Jer 36:23
or *f.* leaves
the likeness of *f.* living Eze 1:5
creatures
and every one had *f.* faces Eze 1:6;
1:15; 10:14
and every one had *f.* wings Eze 1:6;
10:21
and they *f.* had one likeness Eze 1:16;
10:10
they went upon their *f.* sides Eze 1:17;
10:11
when I send my *f.* sore Eze 14:21
judgments on Jerusalem
and say, Come from the *f.* Eze 37:9
winds, O breath
f. tables were on this side, Eze 40:41
f. on that
the altar *f.* cubits, and Eze 43:15
upward *f.* horns
these *f.* children God gave Da 1:17
knowledge
I see *f.* men loose, walking in Da 3:25
the fire
the *f.* winds of heaven strove Da 7:2
on the sea
and *f.* great beasts came up Da 7:3
from the sea
these *f.* beasts are *f.* kings Da 7:17
who shall arise
came *f.* notable horns towards Da 8:8
the *f.* winds
whereas *f.* stood up, *f.* Da 8:22
kingdoms shall stand
his kingdom divided towards Da 11:4
the *f.* winds
and for *f.* I will not turn Am 1:3;
away the punishment thereof 6:9, 11,
13; 2:1,4, 6
I saw, and behold *f.* horns Zec 1:18
and the Lord shewed me *f.* Zec 1:20
carpenters
and behold, there came *f.* Zec 6:1
chariots out
from the *f.* winds M't 24:31; M'k 13:27
one sick of the palsy who M'k 2:3
was borne of *f.*
are yet *f.* months, then Joh 4:35
cometh harvest
Lazarus had lain in the Joh 11:17
grave *f.* days
the soldiers made *f.* parts Joh 19:23
of his garment
f. days ago I was fasting to Ac 10:30
this hour
Philip had *f.* daughters, Ac 21:9
virgins, who prophesy
we have *f.* men which have Ac 21:23
a vow on them
they cast *f.* anchors out of Ac 27:29
the stern
round about the throne were *f.* Re 4:6
beasts
the *f.* beasts had each of them Re 4:8
six wings
the *f.* beasts said, Amen, and Re 5:14
the elders fell
I heard a voice in the midst of Re 6:6
the *f.* beasts
I saw *f.* angels, on *f.* corners, Re 7:1
holding *f.* winds
a voice from the *f.* horns of Re 9:13
the golden altar
loose the *f.* angels who are Re 9:14
bound in Euphrates
they sung a new song before Re 14:3
the *f.* beasts
one of the *f.* beasts gave Re 15:7
seven vials
the 24 elders and the *f.* beasts Re 19:4
fell down

FOUR *TIMES*

yet they sent to me *f.* times Ne 6:4
after this sort

FOURFOLD

and he shall restore the 2Sa 12:6
lamb *f.*
if I have taken any thing, I Lu 19:8
restore *f.*

FOURSCORE

Moses was *f.* years old, and Ex 7:7
Aaron *f.* and three years old

and the land had rest *f.* years J'g 3:30
Barzillai was *f.* years old 2Sa 19:32;
19:35
an ass's head was sold for *f.* 2Ki 6:25
pieces
Jehu appointed *f.* men 2Ki 10:24
without, and said
Eliel the chief, and his 1Ch 15:9
brethren *f.*
with him *f.* priests, valiant 2Ch 26:17
men
Zebadiah, and with him *f.* Ezr 8:8
males
and if by strength they be *f.* Ps 90:10
years
are threescore queens and *f.* Ca 6:8
concubines
there came from Samaria, *f.* Jer 41:5
men
she was a widow about *f.* Lu 2:37
and four years
he said to him, Take thy bill, Lu 16:7
and write *f.*

FOURSCORE *AND FIVE*

lo, I am this day *f.* and five Jos 14:10
years old
Doeg slew that day *f.* and 1Sa 22:18
five persons

FOURSCORE *AND SIX*

Abraham was *f.* and six when Ge 16:16
Hagar bare

FOURSCORE *THOUSAND*

f. thousand hewers in mount 1Ki 5:15;
2Ch 2:18

FOURSCORE *AND*
SEVEN THOUSAND

Issachar reckoned in all *f.* 1Ch 7:5
and seven thousand

FOURSQUARE

altar shall be *f.* Ex 27:1;
30:2; 37:25; 38:1
the breastplate *f.* Ex 28:16;
39:9
their borders *f.* 1Ki 7:31
he measured the court *f.* Eze 40:47
ye shall offer the holy Eze 48:20
oblation *f.*
and the city lieth *f.* Re 21:16

FOURTEEN

I served *f.* years for thy Ge 31:41
daughters
who were born to Jacob, all Ge 46:22
the souls were *f.*
ye shall offer for Nu 29:13;
burnt offering *f.* 17:20, 23, 26, 29, 32
lambs of the first year
the tribe of Judah had in Jos 15:36;
the valley *f.* cities 18:28
Solomon and Israel held a 1Ki 8:65
feast *f.* days
God gave to Heman *f.* sons, 1Ch 25:5
three daughters
Abijah waxed mighty, 2Ch 13:21
married *f.* wives
the settle shall be *f.* cubits long Eze 43:17
from Abraham to David *f.* M't 1:17
from David to carrying to
Babylon *f.* to Christ *f.* generations
I knew a man above *f.* years 2Co 12:2
ago
then *f.* years after I went up Ga 2:1
to Jerusalem

FOURTEEN *THOUSAND*

Job had *f.* thousand sheep, Job 42:12
and 6,000 camels

FOURTEEN *THOUSAND*
SEVEN HUNDRED

that died in plague were *f.* Nu 16:49
thousand seven hundred

FOURTEENTH

in the f. year came Ge 14:5
Chedorlaomer
in the f. year of Hezekiah 2Ki 18:13;
Isa 36:1
the f. lot came forth to 1Ch 24:13
Jeshebeab
the f. lot came forth to 1Ch 25:21
Mattithiah
in the f. year after the city Eze 40:1
was smitten
but when the f. night was Ac 27:27
come

FOURTH

and the f. river is Euphrates Ge 2:14
in f. generation they shall Ge 15:16
come hither
visiting iniquity of fathers to Ex 20:5;
the f. generation 34:7; Nu 14:18;
De 5:9
and the f. row shall be a Ex 28:20;
beryl 39:13
in the f. year the fruit shall Le 19:24
be holy
the f. lot came out to Jos 19:17
Issachar
David's f. son, Adonijah 2Sa 3:4;
1Ch 3:2
thy children of f. generation 2Ki 10:30;
15:12
the f. had the face of an Eze 10:14
eagle
the f. kingdom shall be Da 2:40
strong as iron
the form of the f. is like the Da 3:25
Son of God
behold, a f. beast dreadful and Da 7:7
strong
then I would know the truth Da 7:19
of the f. beast
the f. beast shall be the f. Da 7:23
kingdom on earth
the f. shall be far richer than Da 11:2
they all
in the f. chariot were grisled Zec 6:3
horses
Jesus came in the f. watch M't 14:25
of the night
the f. beast was like a flying Re 4:7
eagle
when he had opened the f. Re 6:7
seal, I heard
the f. angel sounded, the sun Re 8:12
was smitten
the f. angel poured out his Re 16:8
vial on the sun
the third, a chalcedony; the Re 21:19
f. an emerald

FOURTH YEAR

in f. year of Solomon's 1Ki 6:1;
reign he began to build 6:37; 2Ch 3:2
Jehoshaphat began to reign 1Ki 22:41
in f. year of Ahab
in the f. year of Hezekiah 2Ki 18:9
Shalmaneser came up against
word came to Jeremiah in f. Jer 25:1
year of Jehoiakim
in the f. year of Zedekiah, Jer 28:1
Hannaniah spake
in the f. year of Jehoiakim Jer 36:1;
this word came to Jeremiah 45:1; 46:2
commanded Seraiah in f. year Jer 51:59
of Zedekiah
in f. year of Darius word Zec 7:1
came to Zechariah

FOWL

let them have dominion over Ge 1:26;
the f. 1:28
and over the f. of the air Ge 1:28
out of the ground God Ge 2:19
formed every f. of air
the f. of the heaven was Ge 7:23
destroyed
bring forth of all flesh, of f. Ge 8:17
of cattle
the fear of you shall be on Ge 9:2
every f. of the air
behold, I establish my Ge 9:10
covenant with the f.
eat no blood, whether of f. or Le 7:26
beast
this is the law of the beasts Le 11:46
and f.

the likeness of any winged f. De 4:17
in the air
there is a path which no f. Job 28:7
knoweth
to have dominion over the f. Ps 8:8
of the air
beasts and flying f. praise Ps 148:10
the Lord
the f. of the heavens and Jer 9:10
beast are fled
and under it shall dwell all Eze 17:23
f.
son of man, speak to every Eze 39:17
feathered f.
priest shall not eat any Eze 44:31
thing torn f. or beast
had on the back of it four Da 7:6
wings of a f.

FOWLER

thee from the snare of the f. Ps 91:3
as a bird from the hand of the Pr 6:5
f.
but the prophet is a snare of Heb 9:8
a f.

FOWLERS

as a bird out of the snare of Ps 124:7
the f.

FOWLS

take of f. also of the air by Ge 7:3
sevens
when the f. came down on Ge 11:15
the carcases
if the burnt sacrifice to Lord Le 1:14
be of f.
these f. ye shall have in Le 11:13
abomination
but of all clean f. ye may De 14:20
eat
thy carcase shall be meat to De 28:26
all f. of the air
I will give thy flesh to the 1Sa 17:44;
f. 17:46
Solomon spake of beasts and 1Ki 4:33
of f.
that dieth in fields, f. eat 1Ki 14:11;
16:4; 21:24
also f. were prepared for me, Ne 5:18
store of wine
ask the f. and they shall tell Job 12:7
thee
I know all the f. of the Ps 50:11
mountains
he rained f. like as the sand Ps 78:27
of the sea
shall be left to f. of Isa 18:6
mountains, and f. shall
summer upon them
let the f. get from his Da 4:14
branches
the f. they sow not, neither M't 6:26
reap
the f. devoured the seed M't 13:4
M'k 4:4; Lu 8:5
that f. may lodge under it M'k 4:32;
Lu 13:19
how much more are ye Lu 12:24
better than f.
a sheet wherein were f. Ac 10:12;
Ac 11:6
an angel cried to all the f. Re 19:17
that fly
and all the f. were filled Re 19:21
with their flesh

FOWLS OF HEAVEN

who maketh us wiser than Job 35:11
the f. of heaven
bodies of thy servants meat to Ps 79:2
f. of heaven
by them the f. of heaven have Ps 104:12
their habitation
carcases of people shall be Jer 7:33;
meat for f. of the heaven 16:4;
19:7; 34:20
I will appoint the f. of the Jer 15:3
heaven to destroy
given Pharaoh for meat to f. Eze 29:5
of heaven
the f. of heaven made their Eze 31:6
nests in Assyria
on his ruin shall all the f. Eze 31:13
of heaven remain

will cause all f. of heaven to Eze 32:4
remain on thee
the f. of heaven shall shake Eze 38:20
at my presence
the f. of heaven given to Da 2:38
Nebuchadnezzar
made a covenant for them Ho 2:18
with f. of heaven
every one shall languish with Ho 4:3
f. of heaven
I will bring them down as Ho 7:12
the f. of heaven
I will consume the f. of the Zep 1:3
heaven
the f. of heaven lodged in Lu 13:19
the branches

FOX

if a f. go up, he shall even Ne 4:3
break
Go ye, and tell that f. Lu 13:32
Behold, I

FOXES

went and caught three J'g 15:4
hundred f.
they shall be a portion for f. Ps 63:10
Take us the f. the little f. that Ca 2:15
is desolate, the f. walk upon La 5:18
are like the f. in the deserts Eze 13:4
The f. have holes, and the M't 8:20
birds of
F. have holes, and birds of Lu 9:58
the air

FRACTURE

f. for f. (A)(B)(R) Le 24:20

FRAGMENTARY

f. and varied fashion (P) Heb 1:1

FRAGMENTS

hurls ice in f. (B) Ps 147:11
smitten into f. (R) Am 6:11
took up of the f. that M't 14:20
remained
up twelve baskets full of the M'k 6:43
f.
20 baskets full of f. took ye M'k 8:19
up
taken up of f. that remained Lu 9:17
to
Gather up the f. that remain Joh 6:12
filled twelve baskets with the Joh 6:13
f.

FRAGRANCE

Lord discerned f. (B) Ge 8:21
an acceptable f. (B) Ex 29:25; 29:41
f. cinnamon (B) Ex 30:23; 37:29; 40:27;
Le 16:12; Nu 4:16; 2Ch 2:4
a pleasing f. (B) Le 1:9;
2:9, 12; 3:5; 17:6; 23:13, 18; Nu 15:3,
7, 10, 14, 24; 18:17; 28:2, 6, 8, 13, 36
27; 29:2, 6, 8, 13, 36
an agreeable f. (B) Le 2:2;
3:16; 4:31; 6:15, 21; 8:28
fragrance (A)(B)(E)(R) Ca 1:12;
2:13; 4:10
spikenard sends forth a f. Ca 1:12;
(S) 2:13
the f. of thine ointments (S) Ca 4:10;
4:11
f. of garments (B) Ca 4:11
f. of breath like apples (B)(S) Ca 7:8
mandrakes give f. Ca 7:13
(A)(B)(E)(R)(S)
the f. (S) Isa 3:24; Ca 1:12; 4:10-11;
7:13; Ho 14:6
f. like Lebanon Ho 14:6
(A)(B)(R)(S)
filled with f. of perfume Joh 12:3
(A)(B)
makes evident the f. (A)(R) 2Co 2:14
a sweet f. (A)(N) Eph 5:2
a lovely f. (P) Ph'p 4:18
Christ's f. (B) 2Pe 2:15

FRAGRANT

f. incense (R) Ex 25:6
30:7; 31:11; 35:8, 15, 28; 37:29; 39:38;
30:27; Le 4:7; Nu 4:16
like a f. of pottery (A) Ps 22:15

FRAGRANT

f. odor of an offering (A)(B)(N)(R)	*Ph'p 4:18*
a *f.* odor (B)(R)	*Eph 5:2*

FRAIL

children were *f.* (B)(R)	*Ge 33:13*
that I may know how *f.* I am	*Ps 39:4*

FRAILTIES

bear the *f.* of (A)	*Ro 15:1*

FRAILTY

emptiness, falsity, futility, *f.* (A)	*Ps 89:47*
subject to *f.*, futility (A)	*Ro 8:20*

FRAME

imagination which they *f.* (S)	*De 31:21*
could not *f.* to pronounce it right	*J'g 12:6*
For he knoweth our *f.*; he	*Ps 103:14*
my *f.* not hid (A)(E)(R)	*Ps 139:15*
I *f.* evil against you, and devise	*Jer 18:11*
by which was as the *f.* of a city on	*Eze 40:2*
They will not *f.* their doings	*Ho 5:4*

FRAMED

or shall the thing *f.* say of him	*Isa 29:16*
say of him that *f.* it, He had no	*Isa 29:16*
f. from the beginning (N)	*1Co 2:7*
In whom all the building fitly *f.*	*Eph 2:21*
fitly *f.* together (B)	*Eph 4:16*
all things are *f.* together (B)	*Col 1:17*
the worlds were *f.* by the word of	*Heb 11:3*

FRAMES

borders between the *f.* (B)	*1Ki 7:28; 7:35-36*
between the *f.* (S)	*1Ki 7:28; 7:29, 35-36*

FRAMETH

evil, and thy tongue *f.* deceit	*Ps 50:19*
which *f.* mischief by a law	*Ps 94:20*

FRANK

we speak quite *f.* and open (P)	*2Co 3:12*
I am perfectly *f.* with you (N)	*2Co 7:4*

FRANKINCENSE

these sweet spices with pure *f.*	*Ex 30:34*
oil upon it, and put *f.* thereon	*Le 2:1*
with all the *f.* thereof; and the	*Le 2:2*
and lay *f.* thereon it is a meat	*Le 2:15*
with all the *f.* thereof: it is	*Le 2:16*
neither shall he put any *f.* thereon	*Le 5:11*
all the *f.* which is upon the meat	*Le 6:15*
shalt put pure *f.* upon each row	*Le 24:7*
put *f.* thereon; for it is an offering	*Nu 5:15*
the oil, and the *f.* and the spices	*1Ch 9:29*
the *f.* and the vessels, and the	*Ne 13:5*
with the meat offering and the *f.*	*Ne 13:9*
perfumed with myrrh and *f.*	*Ca 3:6*
of myrrh, and to the hill of *f.*	*Ca 4:6*
with all trees of *f.*; myrrh	*Ca 4:14*
gifts; gold, and *f.* and myrrh	*M't 2:11*
f. and wine, and oil, and fine flour	*Re 18:13*

FRANKLY

I will *f.* say to them (B)	*M't 7:23*
to pay, he *f.* forgave them both	*Lu 7:42*

FRAUD

full of cursing and deceit and *f.*	*Ps 10:7*

FRAUDS

they are palpable *f.* (P)	*Tit 1:16*
which is of you kept back by *f.*	*Jas 5:4*

FRAY

and no man shall *f.* them away	*De 28:26*
none to frighten them away (B)(E)(R)	*De 28:26*
and none shall *f.* them away	*Jer 7:33*
but these are come to *f.* them	*Zec 1:21*
have come to terrorize and cause them to be panic-stricken (A)	*Zec 1:21*
have come to rout them and cast down (B)	*Zec 1:21*
have come to terrify them (E)(R)	*Zec 1:21*

FRECKLED

it is a *f.* spot that groweth	*Le 13:39*

FREE

in the seventh he shall go out *f.*	*Ex 21:2*
my children; I will not go out *f.*	*Ex 21:5*
shall she go out *f.* without money	*Ex 21:11*
let him go *f.* for his eye's sake	*Ex 21:26*
let him go *f.* for his tooth's sake	*Ex 21:27*
brought yet unto him *f.* offerings	*Ex 36:3*
to death, because she was not *f.*	*Le 19:20*
be thou *f.* from this bitter water	*Nu 5:19*
then she shall be *f.* and shall	*Nu 5:28*
thou shalt let him go *f.* from thee	*De 15:12*
thou sendest him out *f.* from thee	*De 15:13*
sendest him away *f.* from thee	*De 15:18*
he shall be *f.* at home one year	*De 24:5*
we will be *f.* of thine oath (S)	*Jos 2:20*
his father's house *f.* in Israel	*1Sa 17:25*
every male bond and *f.* (S)	*2Ki 15:20*
in the chambers were *f.*: for they	*1Ch 9:33*
and as many as were of a *f.* heart	*2Ch 29:31*
the servant is *f.* from his master	*Job 3:19*
man full of talk *f.* from guilt	*Job 11:2*
Who hath sent out the wild ass *f.*	*Job 39:5*
and uphold me with thy *f.* spirit	*Ps 51:12*
F. among the dead, like the slain	*Ps 88:5*
of the people, and let him go *f.*	*Ps 105:20*
and to let the oppressed go *f.*	*Isa 58:6*
an Hebrew or an Hebrewess, go *f.*	*Jer 34:9*
every one his maidservant, go *f.*	*Jer 34:10*
whom they had let go *f.* to return	*Jer 34:11*
thou shalt let him go *f.* from thee	*Jer 34:14*
and publish the *f.* offerings	*Am 4:5*
or his mother, he shall be *f.*	*M't 15:6*
unto him, Then are the children *f.*	*M't 17:26*
set many *f.* from sins (P)	*M't 26:28*
be profited by me; he shall be *f.*	*M'k 7:11*
set *f.* the downtrodden	*Lu 4:18*
and the truth shall make you *f.*	*Joh 8:32*
sayest thou, Ye shall be made *f.*	*Joh 8:33*
Son therefore shall make you *f.*	*Joh 8:36*
ye shall be *f.* indeed	*Joh 8:36*
And Paul said, But I was *f.* born	*Ac 22:28*
the offence, so also is the *f.* gift	*Ro 5:15*
but the *f.* gift is of many offences	*Ro 5:16*
the *f.* gift came upon all men unto	*Ro 5:18*
Being then made *f.* from sin, ye	*Ro 6:18*
ye were *f.* from righteousness	*Ro 6:20*
But now being made *f.* from sin	*Ro 6:22*
she is *f.* from that law, so that	*Ro 7:3*
hath made me *f.* from the law of	*Ro 8:2*
if thou mayest be made *f.* use it	*1Co 7:21*
that is called, being *f.* is Christ's	*1Co 7:22*
Am I not an apostle? am I not *f.*	*1Co 9:1*
For though I be *f.* from all men	*1Co 9:19*
whether we be bond or *f.*; and have	*1Co 12:13*
bought us *f.* from the curse (B)	*Ga 3:13*
Greek, there is neither bond nor *f.*	*Ga 3:28*
But Jerusalem which is above is *f.*	*Ga 4:26*
of the bondwoman, but of the *f.*	*Ga 4:31*
wherewith Christ hath made us *f.*	*Ga 5:1*
freedom Christ made *f.* (A)(B)(E)(P)	*Ga 5:1*
Christ set *f.* to be *f.* men (N)	*Ga 5:1*
whether he be bond or *f.*	*Eph 6:8*
Barbarian, Scythian, bond nor *f.*	*Col 3:11*
of the Lord may have *f.* course	*2Th 3:1*
As *f.* and not using your liberty	*1Pe 2:16*
set us *f.* from our sins (P)	*Re 1:5*
every bondman, and every *f.* man	*Re 6:15*
rich and poor, *f.* and bond, to	*Re 13:16*
all men, both *f.* and bond	*Re 19:18*

FREED

there shall none of you be *f.* from	*Jos 9:23*
f. us from adversaries (B)	*Ps 136:24*
is *f.* from everything (R)	*Ac 13:39*
For he that is dead is *f.* from sin	*Ro 6:7*
loosed and *f.* from sins (A)(N)(P)	*Re 1:5*

FREEDOM

at all redeemed, nor *f.* given her	*Le 19:20*
I walk with *f.* (B)	*Ps 119:34*
a great sum obtained I this *f.*	*Ac 22:28*
utmost *f.* (A)	*Ac 28:31*
Christ purchased our *f.* (A)(N)	*Ga 3:13*
purchase *f.* of those (A)(N)	*Ga 4:5*
f. Christ made free (A)(B)(E)(P)	*Ga 5:1*

FREELY

tree of the garden thou mayest *f.* eat	*Ge 2:16*
which we did eat in Egypt *f.*	*Nu 11:5*
mouth *f.* opened (B)	*1Sa 2:1*
if haply the people had eaten *f.* to day	*1Sa 14:30*
offered *f.* for the house of God	*Ezr 2:68*
and his counsellors have *f.* offered unto	*Ezr 7:15*
I will *f.* sacrifice unto thee: I	*Ps 54:6*
I will love them *f.*: for mine anger	*Ho 14:4*
f. ye have received, *f.* give	*M't 10:8*
let me *f.* speak unto you of	*Ac 2:29*
before whom also I speak *f.*	*Ac 26:26*
Being justified *f.* by his grace	*Ro 3:24*

FREELY

shall he not with him also *f.*   *Ro 8:32*
give us
give *f.* to fellow Christians   *Ro 12:13*
in want (P)
we might know the things   *1Co 2:12*
that are *f.*
we speak *f.*, openly,   *2Co 3:12*
fearlessly (A)
to you the gospel of God *f.*   *2Co 11:7*
the fountain of the water of   *Re 21:6*
life *f.*
let him take the water of   *Re 22:17*
life *f.*

FREEMAN

being a servant, is the   *1Co 7:22*
Lord's *f.*

FREEWILL

all his *f.* offerings, which   *Le 22:18*
they
a *f.* offering in beeves or sheep   *Le 2:21*
mayest thou offer for a *f.*   *Le 22:23*
offering
all your *f.* offerings, which   *Le 23:38*
ye give
a vow, or in a *f.* offering, or   *Nu 15:3*
in your
your vows, and your *f.*   *Nu 29:39*
offerings, for
your vows, and your *f.*   *De 12:6*
offerings, and
thy *f.* offerings, or heave   *De 12:17*
offering of
of a *f.* offering of thine   *De 16:10*
hand, which
a *f.* offering, according as   *De 23:23*
thou hast
the *f.* offerings of God, to   *2Ch 31:14*
distribute
the *f.* offering for the house   *Ezr 1:4*
of God
offered a *f.* offering unto the   *Ezr 3:5*
Lord
which are minded of their   *Ezr 7:13*
own *f.*
with the *f.* offering of the   *Ezr 7:16*
people
a *f.* offering unto the Lord   *Ezr 8:28*
God of
the *f.* offerings of my   *Ps 119:108*
mouth, O
the *f.* offering   *Eze 46:12;*
(A)(B)(E)(R)   *Le 7:16*

FREEWOMAN

by a bondmaid, the other by   *Ga 4:22*
a *f.*
but he of the *f.* was by   *Ga 4:23*
promise
not be heir with the son of   *Ga 4:30*
the *f.*

FREIGHT

buys *f.*, cargo   *Re 18:11*
(A)(B)(N)(P)(R)

FREQUENT

no *f.* vision (S)   *1Sa 3:1*
in prisons more *f.* in deaths   *2Co 11:23*
oft
thy *f.* infirmities (S)   *1Ti 5:23*

FRESH

eat *f.* or dried grapes   *Nu 6:3*
(A)(B)(E)(R)
taste of it was as the taste of   *Nu 11:8*
f. oil
f. gutstrings (A)(B,((R)   *J'g 16:7*
with seven *f.* cords (S)   *J'g 16:8*
My glory was *f.* in me, and   *Job 29:20*
my
I shall be anointed with *f.*   *Ps 92:10*
oil
f. and bleeding stripes (A)(E)   *Isa 1:6*
a *f.* unspoiled girl (P)   *2Co 11:2*
both yield salt water and *f.*   *Jas 3:12*

FRESHER

His flesh shall be *f.* than a   *Job 33:25*
child's

FRET

burn it in the fire; it is *f.*   *Le 13:55*
inward
sore, for to make her *f.*   *1Sa 1:6*
because
F. not thyself because of   *Ps 37:1*
f. not thyself because of him   *Ps 37:7*
who
f. not thyself in any wise to   *Ps 37:8*
do evil
F. not thyself because of evil   *Pr 24:19*
men
hungry, they shall *f.*   *Isa 8:21*
themselves

FRETTED

hast *f.* me in all these   *Eze 16:43*
things; but

FRETTETH

and his heart *f.* against the   *Pr 19:3*
Lord

FRETTING

the plague is a *f.* leprosy; it   *Le 13:51*
it is a *f.* leprosy; it shall be   *Le 13:52*
burnt
it is a *f.* leprosy in the   *Le 14:44*
house: it is
f. and fussing about (N)   *Lu 10:20*
f. and fussing about (N)   *Lu 10:41*

FRIED

mingled with oil, of fine flour   *Le 7:12*
f.
and for that which is *f.*   *1Ch 23:29*
and for

FRIEND

and his *f.* Hirah the   *Ge 38:12*
Adullamite
sent the kid by the hand of   *Ge 38:20*
his *f.*
face, as a man speaketh   *Ex 33:11*
unto his *f.*
or the wife of thy bosom, or   *De 13:6*
thy *f.*
whom he had used as his *f.*   *J'g 14:20*
given to his companion   *J'g 14:20*
(A)(B)(E)(R)
Amnon had a *f.* whose name   *2Sa 13:3*
was
Hushai David's *f.* came into   *2Sa 15:37*
David's confidant (B)   *2Sa 15:37;*
   16:17
Hushai the Archite, David's   *2Sa 16:16*
f.
Is this thy kindness to thy   *2Sa 16:17*
f.
why wentest thou not with   *2Sa 16:17*
thy *f.*
principal officer, and the   *1Ki 4:5*
king's *f.*
the king's *f.* (E)(R)   *1Ch 27:33*
seed of Abraham thy *f.* for   *2Ch 20:7*
ever
pity should be shewed from   *Job 6:14*
his *f.*
and ye dig a pit for your *f.*   *Job 6:27*
as though he had been my *f.*   *Ps 35:14*
mine own familiar *f.* in whom   *Ps 41:9*
I trusted
you are a *f.* of his (R)   *Ps 50:18*
Lover and *f.* hast thou put   *Ps 88:18*
far
son, if thou be surety for thy *f.*   *Pr 6:1*
surety for thy neighbor   *Pr 6:1*
(A)(B)(E)(R)
art come into the hand of thy   *Pr 6:3*
f.
thyself, and make sure thy *f.*   *Pr 6:3*
alienates a close *f.* (B)(R)   *Pr 17:9*
A *f.* loveth at all times, and   *Pr 17:17*
a
surety in the presence of his   *Pr 17:18*
f.
neighbor (A)(B)(E)(R)   *Pr 17:18; 27:14*
and there is *f.* that sticketh   *Pr 18:24*
closer
man is a *f.* to him that giveth   *Pr 19:6*
gifts
of his lips the king shall be   *Pr 22:11*
his *f.*

FRIENDS

Faithful are the wounds of a   *Pr 27:6*
f.
doth the sweetness of a man's   *Pr 27:9*
f. by
Thine own *f.* and thy   *Pr 27:10*
father's *f.*
blesseth his *f.* with a loud   *Pr 27:14*
voice
a man, the countenance   *Pr 27:17*
of his *f.*
my *f.* O daughters of   *Ca 5:16*
Jerusalem
chosen, the seed of Abraham   *Isa 41:8*
my *f.*
neighbour and his *f.* shall   *Jer 6:21*
perish
eat every one the flesh of his   *Jer 19:9*
f. in
yet, love a woman beloved of   *Ho 3:1*
her *f.*
beloved of a paramour   *Ho 3:1*
(A)(B)(R)
Trust ye not in a *f.* put ye   *Mic 7:5*
not
a *f.* of publicans and   *M't 11:19*
sinners
F. I do thee no wrong: *M't 20:13*
didst not
F. how camest thou in   *M't 22:12*
hither not
F. wherefore art thou come   *M't 26:50*
a *f.* of publicans and sinners   *Lu 7:34*
Which of you shall have a *f.*   *Lu 11:5*
unto him, F. lend me three   *Lu 11:5*
loaves
For a *f.* of mine in his   *Lu 11:6*
journey is
and give him, because he is   *Lu 11:8*
his *f.*
F. go up higher: then shalt   *Lu 14:10*
thou
but the *f.* of the bridegroom,   *Joh 3:29*
which
Our *f.* Lazarus sleepeth; but   *Joh 11:11*
I go
thou art not Caesar's *f.*:   *Joh 19:12*
whosoever
and having made Blastus   *Ac 12:20*
their *f.*
has been a *f.* to many (N)   *Ro 16:2*
and he was called the *F.* of   *Jas 2:23*
God
f. of the world is the enemy   *Jas 4:4*
of God
being world's *f.* (A)   *Jas 4:4*

FRIENDLY

to speak *f.* unto her, and to   *J'g 19:3*
bring
speak kindly unto her   *J'g 19:3*
(A)(E)(R)
speak endearing words to her   *J'g 19:3*
(B)
spoken *f.* unto thine   *Ru 2:13*
handmaid
spoken to the heart of your   *Ru 2:13*
maidservant (A)
spoken so kindly to me   *Ru 2:13*
(B)(E)(R)
friends must shew himself *f.*   *Pr 18:24*
became mutually *f.* (B)   *Pr 23:24*

FRIENDS

and Ahuzzath one of his *f.*   *Ge 26:26*
to his *f.* saying, Behold a   *1Sa 30:26*
present
to the elders of Judah (B)   *1Sa 30:26*
to his brethren, and to his *f.*   *2Sa 3:8*
and
thine enemies, and hatest thy   *2Sa 19:6*
f.
hate those who love you   *2Sa 19:6*
(A)(B)(E)(R)
of his kinsfolks, nor of his   *1Ki 16:11*
f. and
familiar (S)   *2Ki 10:11; Ps 55:13*
he sent and called for his *f.*   *Es 5:10*
said Zeresh his wife and all   *Es 5:14*
his *f.*
told Zeresh his wife and all   *Es 6:13*
his *f.*
when Job's three *f.* heard of   *Job 2:11*
all
My *f.* scorn me; but mine   *Job 16:20*
eye
He that speaketh flattery to   *Job 17:5*
his *f.*

and my familiar *f.* have   *Job 19:14*
forgotten me
All my inward *f.* abhorred   *Job 19:19*
me
have pity upon me, O ye   *Job 19:21*
my *f.*
against his three *f.* was his   *Job 32:3*
wrath
thee, and against thy two *f.*:   *Job 42:7*
for ye
when he prayed for his *f.*:   *Job 42:10*
also the
My lovers and my *f.* stand   *Ps 38:11*
aloof
but the rich hath many *f.*   *Pr 14:20*
and a whisperer separateth   *Pr 16:28*
chief *f.*
he that, a matter separateth   *Pr 17:9*
very *f.*
A man that hath *f.* must   *Pr 18:24*
shew
Wealth maketh many *f.*; but   *Pr 19:4*
more do his *f.* go far from   *Pr 19:7*
him
eat, O *f.*; drink, yea, drink   *Ca 5:1*
terror to thyself, and to all   *Jer 20:4*
thy *f.*
be buried there, thou, and all   *Jer 20:6*
thy
say, Thy *f.* have set thee on   *Jer 38:22*
her *f.* have dealt treacherously   *La 1:2*
you and your *f.* (B)(R)   *Zec 3:8*
was wounded in the house of   *Zec 13:6*
my *f.*
bridegroom's *f.* (N)   *M't 9:15*
calling to *f.* (P)   *M't 11:16*
when his *f.* heard of it, they   *M'k 3:21*
when his relatives heard of   *M'k 3:21*
it (A)(B)(P)
When his family heard of   *M'k 3:21*
this (N)
Go home to thy *f.* and tell   *M'k 5:19*
them
centurion sent *f.* to him,   *Lu 7:6*
saying
And I say unto you my *f.* Be   *Lu 12:4*
not
call not thy *f.* nor thy   *Lu 14:12*
brethren
he calleth together his *f.* and   *Lu 15:6*
calleth her *f.* and her   *Lu 15:9*
neighbours
I might make merry with my   *Lu 15:29*
f.
to yourselves *f.* of the   *Lu 16:9*
mammon of
brethren, and kinsfolks, and   *Lu 21:16*
f.
day Pilate and Herod were   *Lu 23:12*
made *f.*
became mutually friendly   *Lu 23:12*
(B)
a man lay down his life for   *Joh 15:13*
his *f.*
Ye are my *f.* if ye do   *Joh 15:14*
whatsoever
I have called you *f.* for all   *Joh 15:15*
things
their own *f.* (N)(P)(R)   *Ac 4:23*
together his kinsmen and   *Ac 10:24*
near *f.*
the chief of Asia, which   *Ac 19:31*
were his *f.*
to go unto his *f.* to refresh   *Ac 27:3*
himself
welcome trials as *f.* (P)   *Jas 1:2*
Our *f.* salute thee   *3Jo 14*
Greet the *f.* by name   *3Jo 14*

FRIENDSHIP

f. of God (A)(B)(E)(R)   *Job 29:4*
f. of Jehovah is with (E)(R)   *Ps 25:14*
f. is with upright (E)   *Pr 3:32*
Make no *f.* with an angry   *Pr 22:24*
man
do not associate with one *f.*   *Pr 22:24*
(B)
f. of the world is emmity with   *Jas 4:4*
God
being world's friend is being   *Jas 4:4*
God's enemy (A)
love of world is enmity to   *Jas 4:4*
God (N)
being world's lover means   *Jas 4:4*
enemy of God (P)
love and *f.* (A)(B)   *3Jo 6*

FRIGHTEN

none to *f.* them away   *De 28:26*
(B)(E)(R)
to *f.* them (A)(B)(S)   *2Ch 32:18*
none shall *f.* them away (S)   *Jer 7:33*

FRIGHTENED

became *f.* (B)   *Ex 1:12*
frightened (S)   *De 7:21;*
   Job 18:20; Lu 24:37
men of war *f.* (A)   *Jer 51:32*
they were *f.* (B)(P)   *M'k 6:50*
f. and bewildered (P)   *Lu 8:25*

FRINGE

put upon the *f.* of the   *Nu 15:38*
borders a
tassels (B)(R)   *Nu 15:38;*
   15:39; De 22:12
And it shall be unto you for   *Nu 15:39*
a *f.*
touched *f.* of robe (B)   *M't 9:20*

FRINGES

may make them *f.* in the   *Nu 15:38*
borders
thee *f.* upon the four   *De 22:12*
quarters

FRIVOLITY

to lay hold on *f.* (B)   *Ec 2:3*

FRO

raven, which went forth to   *Ge 8:7*
and *f.*
walked in the house to and   *2Ki 4:35*
f.
the eyes of the Lord run to   *2Ch 16:9*
and *f.*
From going to and *f.* in the   *Job 1:7;*
earth   *2:2*
I am full of tossings to and *f.*   *Job 7:4*
break a leaf driven to and   *Job 13:25*
f.
They reel to and *f.* and   *Ps 107:27*
stagger
a vanity tossed to and *f.* of   *Pr 21:6*
them
shall reel to and *f.* like a   *Isa 24:20*
drunkard
as the running to and *f.* of   *Isa 33:4*
locusts
a captive, and removing to   *Isa 49:21*
and *f.*
ye to and *f.* through the   *Jer 5:1*
streets
and run to and *f.* by the   *Jer 49:3*
hedges
Dan also and Javan going   *Eze 27:19*
to and *f.*
many shall run to and *f.* and   *Da 12:4*
shall run to and *f.* in the city   *Joe 2:9*
they shall run to and *f.* to   *Am 8:12*
seek the
to walk to and *f.* through   *Zec 1:10*
the earth
We have walked to and *f.*   *Zec 1:11*
through the
of the Lord, which run to   *Zec 4:10*
and *f.*
might walk to and *f.* through   *Zec 6:7*
the earth
Get you hence, walk to and *f.*   *Zec 6:7*
through
So they walked to and *f.*   *Zec 6:7*
through the
tossed to and *f.* and carried   *Eph 4:14*
about

FROGS

will smite all thy borders with   *Ex 8:2*
f.
And the river shall bring forth   *Ex 8:3*
f.
the *f.* shall come up both on   *Ex 8:4*
thee
and cause *f.* to come upon the   *Ex 8:5*
land
the *f.* came up, and covered   *Ex 8:6*
the land
and brought up *f.* upon the   *Ex 8:7*
land of

that he may take away the *f.*   *Ex 8:8*
from
the *f.* from thee and thy   *Ex 8:9*
houses
And the *f.* shall depart from   *Ex 8:11*
thee
of the *f.* which he had   *Ex 8:12*
brought
and the *f.* died out of the   *Ex 8:13*
houses
and *f.* which destroyed them   *Ps 78:45*
land brought forth *f.* in   *Ps 105:30*
abundance
I saw three unclean spirits   *Re 16:13*
like *f.*

FRONT

upon the mitre in *f.* (S)   *Le 8:9*
Joab saw that the *f.* of the   *2Sa 10:9*
battle
f. line of fighting (A)(B)   *2Sa 11:15*
that was in the *f.* of the   *2Ch 3:4*
house
in *f.* of (S)   *Eze 42:10; 48:21*
f. seats (B)   *M't 23:6*
in *f.* of the throne (S)   *Re 4:6*

FRONTIERS

your *f.* shall be (B)   *De 11:24*
at the *f.* of (S)   *Jos 22:11*
from his cities which are on   *Eze 25:9*
his *f.*

FRONTLETS

and for *f.* between thine eyes   *Ex 13:16*
sign on your forehead (B)   *Ex 13:16*
shall be as *f.* between thine   *De 6:8*
eyes
on forehead as a badge (B)   *De 6:8*
they may be as *f.* between   *De 11:18*
your eyes

FROST

consumed me, and the *f.* by   *Ge 31:40*
night
cold by night (A)(B)(R)   *Ge 31:40*
small as the hoar *f.* on the   *Ex 16:14*
ground
By the breath of God *f.* is   *Job 37:10*
given
breath of God ice is given   *Job 37:10*
(A)(B)(E)(R)
and the hoary *f.* of heaven   *Job 38:29*
came the ice (A)(B)(R)   *Job 38:29*
and their sycamore trees   *Ps 78:47*
with *f.*
with sleet their sycamores   *Ps 78:47*
(B)
hail, snow, and *f.*   *Ps 148:8*
(A)(B)(R)
the heat, and in the night to   *Jer 36:30*
the *f.*

FROWARD

for they are a very *f.*   *De 32:20*
generation
with the *f.* thou wilt shew   *2Sa 22:27*
thyself
counsel of the *f.* is carried   *Job 5:13*
and with the *f.* thou wilt   *Ps 18:26*
shew
with, thou wilt show   *Ps 18:26*
thyself *f.*
A *f.* heart shall depart from   *Ps 101:4*
me
the man that speaketh *f.*   *Pr 2:12*
things
and they *f.* in their paths   *Pr 2:15*
the *f.* is abomination to the   *Pr 3:32*
Lord
Put away from thee a *f.*   *Pr 4:24*
mouth
man. walketh with a *f.* mouth   *Pr 6:12*
nothing *f.* or perverse in them   *Pr 8:8*
and the *f.* mouth, do I hate   *Pr 8:13*
but the *f.* tongue shall be cut   *Pr 10:31*
out
are of a *f.* heart are   *Pr 11:20*
abomination
A *f.* man soweth strife: and   *Pr 16:28*
his eyes to devise *f.* things   *Pr 16:30*
hath a *f.* heart findeth no   *Pr 17:20*
good
way of man is *f.* and strange   *Pr 21:8*

snares are in the way of the　*Pr 22:5*
f.

good and gentle, but also to　*1Pe 2:18*
the *f.*

FROWARDLY

he went on *f.* in the way of　*Isa 57:17*
his

FROWARDNESS

delight in the *f.* of the wicked　*Pr 2:14*
F. is in his heart, he deviseth　*Pr 6:14*
mouth of the wicked　　　　*Pr 10:32*
speaketh *f.*

FROZEN

and the face of the deep is　*Job 38:30*
f.

FRUIT

given you every tree wherein　*Ge 1:29*
is *f.*
Cain brought of the *f.* of the　*Ge 4:3*
ground
produce of ground (B)　　　*Ge 4:3;*
　　　　　　　　　　　Le 25:3; Ps 105:35
hath withheld from thee the　*Ge 30:2*
f. of the womb
denied you of children (A)　*Ge 30:2*
deprived you of fertility (B)　*Ge 30:2*
so that her *f.* depart from　*Ex 21:22*
her
so that there is a　　　　　*Ex 21:22*
miscarriage (A)(R)
so that she miscarries (B)　*Ex 21:22*
ye shall count the *f.*　　　*Le 19:23*
uncircumcised
in the fourth year the *f.*　*Le 19:24*
shall be holy
six years thou shalt gather in　*Le 25:3*
the *f.*
the tithe of the *f.* is the　*Le 27:30*
Lord's, it is holy
they shewed them the *f.* of　*Nu 13:26*
the land
we came to the land, and　*Nu 13:27*
this is the *f.* of it
they took of the *f.* in their　*De 1:25*
hands
he will also bless the *f.* of　*De 7:13*
thy land
lest of thy seed, *f.* of thy　*De 22:9*
vineyard be defiled
thou shalt take of the first of　*De 26:2*
all the *f.*
blessed shall be the *f.* of thy　*De 28:4*
body and ground
make thee plenteous in *f.* of　*De 28:11;*
thy body　　　　　　　　　　　　*30:9*
cursed shall be the *f.* of thy　*De 28:18*
body and of land
for thine olive shall cast his　*De 28:40*
f.
all thy trees and *f.* shall the　*De 28:42*
locust consume
should I forsake my　　　　*J'g 9:11*
sweetness and *f.*
summer *f.* for the young men　*2Sa 16:2*
to eat
their *f.* shalt thou destroy　*Ps 21:10*
from the earth
their offspring you will　　*Ps 21:10*
destroy (A)(B)(R)
the *f.* thereof shall shake like　*Ps 72:16*
Lebanon
the earth is satisfied with *f.*　*Ps 104:13*
of thy works
the locusts devoured the *f.*　*Ps 105:35*
of their ground
the *f.* of the womb is his　*Ps 127:3*
reward
of *f.* of thy body will I set　*Ps 132:11*
on thy throne
my *f.* is better than fine gold　*Pr 8:19*
the *f.* of the wicked tendeth　*Pr 10:16*
to sin
profit of wicked is for　　　*Pr 10:16*
further sin (A)
increase of wicked is for sin　*Pr 10:16*
(B)(E)
gain of the wicked to sin　*Pr 10:16*
(R)
the *f.* of the righteous is a　*Pr 11:30*
tree of life
a man is satisfied by the *f.*　*Pr 12:14*
of his mouth

shall be satisfied with the *f.*　*Pr 18:20*
of his mouth
with the *f.* of her hand she　*Pr 31:16*
planteth
give her of the *f.* of her　*Pr 31:31*
hands
the product of her hands　*Pr 31:31*
(B)
and his *f.* was sweet to my　*Ca 2:3*
taste
those that keep the *f.* thereof　*Ca 8:12*
two hundred
they shall eat the *f.* of their　*Isa 3:10*
doings
the *f.* of the earth shall be　*Isa 4:2*
excellent
I will punish the *f.* of the　*Isa 10:12*
stout heart
they shall have no pity on　*Isa 13:18*
the *f.* of the womb
his *f.* shall be a fiery flying　*Isa 14:29*
serpent
and fill the face of the world　*Isa 27:6*
with *f.*
cover face of earth with　*Isa 27:6*
produce (B)
this is all the *f.* to take away　*Isa 27:9*
his sin
as the hasty *f.* before the　*Isa 28:4*
summer
I create the *f.* of the lips,　*Isa 57:19*
peace, peace
shall plant vineyards, and　*Isa 65:21*
eat *f.* of them
I will bring the *f.* of their　*Jer 6:19*
thoughts
my fury shall be on the *f.* of　*Jer 7:20*
the ground
a green olive tree, fair, and　*Jer 11:16*
of goodly *f.*
let us destroy the tree with　*Jer 11:19*
the *f.* thereof
according to *f.* of his　　　*Jer 17:10;*
doings　　　　　　　　*21:14; 32:19*
cut off the *f.* thereof that it　*Eze 17:9*
wither
and the east wind dried up　*Eze 19:12*
her *f.*
fire is gone which hath　*Eze 19:14*
devoured her *f.*
they shall eat thy *f.* and　*Eze 25:4*
drink thy milk
I will multiply the *f.* of the　*Eze 36:30*
tree
nor shall the *f.* thereof be　*Eze 47:12*
consumed
the leaves fair and the *f.*　*Da 4:12;*
thereof much　　　　　　　　*4:21*
he cried, and said thus,　*Da 4:14*
Scatter his *f.*
ye have eaten the *f.* of lies　*Ho 10:13*
I like a green fir tree, from　*Ho 14:8*
me is thy *f.* found
I destroyed his *f.* from above　*Am 2:9*
have turned *f.* of　　　　　*Am 6:12*
righteousness into hemlock
I was an herdman, a　　　*Am 7:14*
gatherer of sycamore *f.*
and behold a basket of　*Am 8:1;*
summer *f.*　　　　　　　　　*8:2*
shall I give *f.* of body for sin　*Mic 6:7*
of my soul
the land desolate, for the *f.*　*Mic 7:13*
of their doings
neither shall *f.* be in their　*Hab 3:17*
vines
the earth is stayed from her　*Hag 1:10*
f.
the vine shall give her *f.*　*Zec 8:12*
the table is polluted, and the　*Mal 1:12*
f. thereof
nor shall your vine cast her　*Mal 3:11*
f. before time
make tree good, and his *f.*　*M't 12:33*
good, tree corrupt, *f.* corrupt, for
the tree is known by his *f.*
he said, Let no *f.* grow on　*M't 21:19*
thee for ever
when the time of the *f.*　*M't 21:34*
drew near he sent
not drink of *f.* of vine, till　*M't 26:29;*
I drink it new　　　　　　*M'k 14:25*
product of the vine (B)　*M't 26:29*
might receive the *f.* of the　*M'k 12:2*
vineyard
and blesed is the *f.* of thy　*Lu 1:42*
womb
he sought *f.* thereon, and　*Lu 13:6*
found none

behold, I come seeking *f.* on　*Lu 13:7*
this fig tree
lo that they should give him　*Lu 20:10*
of the *f.*
and gathereth *f.* to life　*Joh 4:36*
eternal
crop for eternal life (B)(N)　*Joh 4:36*
harvest for eternal life (P)　*Joh 4:36*
of the *f.* of his loins he　*Ac 2:30*
would raise
one of his descendants　*Ac 2:30*
(A)(B)(N)(P)(R)
that I might have some *f.*　*Ro 1:13*
among you
reap some harvest among you　*Ro 1:13*
(B)(R)
achieving something among　*Ro 1:13*
you (N)
some results among you (P)　*Ro 1:13*
what *f.* had ye then in those　*Ro 6:21*
things whereof
what benefit did you get　*Ro 6:21*
(A)(B)
what was the gain (N)　*Ro 6:21*
what harvest did you reap　*Ro 6:21*
(P)
what return did you get (R)　*Ro 6:21*
being free, ye have your *f.*　*Ro 6:22*
unto holiness
when I have sealed to them　*Ro 15:28*
this *f.*
but the *f.* of the Spirit is　*Ga 5:22*
love, joy, peace
the Spirit's fruition is (B)　*Ga 5:22;*
　　　　　　　　　　　　　Eph 5:9
the harvest of the Spirit is　*Ga 5:22*
(N)
the *f.* of the Spirit is in all　*Eph 5:9*
goodness
if I live, this is the *f.* of　*Ph'p 1:22*
my labour
I desire *f.* that may abound　*Ph'p 4:17*
to your account
by him let us offer the *f.*　*Heb 13:15*
of our lips
the *f.* of righteousness is　*Jas 3:18*
sown in peace
harvest of righteousness　*Jas 3:18*
(A)(B)(P)(R)
the husbandman waiteth for the　*Jas 5:7*
precious *f.*
waits for precious harvest (A)(P)　*Jas 5:7*
awaits the precious produce (B)　*Jas 5:7*
precious crop land may yield (N)　*Jas 5:7*
trees whose *f.* withereth, without　*Jude 12*
f.

BEAR, BEARETH FRUIT

shall *bear f.* upward　　　*2Ki 19:30;*
　　　　　　　　　　　　　Isa 37:31
in a good soil, that it might　*Eze 17:8*
bear f.
in the height of Israel it　*Eze 17:23*
shall *bear f.*
their root is dried up, they　*Ho 9:16*
shall *bear* no *f.*
be not afraid, the tree　*Joe 2:22*
beareth her *f.*
in good ground, is he who　*M't 13:23*
beareth f.
other fell on good ground, and　*Lu 8:8*
bare f.
if it *bear f.* well, if not, cut it　*Lu 13:9*
down
every branch in me that　*Joh 15:2*
beareth not *f.* every branch that
beareth f. he purgeth it
as the branch cannot *bear f.*　*Joh 15:4*
of itself, except it
that ye *bear* much *f.* so shall　*Joh 15:8*
ye be my disciples

BRING, BRINGETH BROUGHT FORTH FRUIT

it shall *bring forth f.* for　*Le 25:21*
three years
and *bring* of the *f.* of the　*Nu 13:20*
land
to *bring* the *f.* of all trees　*Ne 10:35;*
　　　　　　　　　　　　　10:37
that *bringeth forth f.* in his　*Ps 1:3*
season
they shall still *bring forth f.*　*Ps 92:14*
in old age
every one for the *f.* was to　*Ca 8:11*
bring silver

the wicked grow, they *bring*   *Jer 12:2*
forth f.
they shall increase, and   *Eze 36:11*
bring forth f.
it shall *bring forth* new f.   *Eze 47:12*
for meat
Israel *bringeth forth* f. to   *Ho 10:1*
himself
bringeth not *forth* good f.   *M't 3:10;*
                                    7:19; Lu 3:9
every good tree *bringeth*   *M't 7:17*
forth good f.
a good tree cannot *bring*   *M't 7:18*
forth evil f.
but when the blade *brought*   *M't 13:26*
forth f.
such as hear the word and   *M'k 4:20*
bring forth f.
for the earth *bringeth forth*   *M'k 4:28*
f. of herself
and *bring* no f. to perfection   *Lu 8:14*
they keep it and *bring forth*   *Lu 8:15*
f. with patience
if it die, it *bringeth forth*   *Joh 12:24*
much f.
yields a rich harvest   *Joh 12:24*
(A)(B)(N)(P)
purgeth it, that it may *bring*   *Joh 15:2*
forth more f.
abideth in me, the same   *Joh 15:5*
bringeth forth much f.
I ordained that you should   *Joh 15:16*
bring forth f.
that we should *bring forth* f.   *Ro 7:4*
to God
might yield God a harvest (B)   *Ro 7:4*
may be productive for God   *Ro 7:4*
(P)
motions did work to *bring*   *Ro 7:5*
forth f. unto death
yield death a harvest (B)   *Ro 7:5*
became productive for death   *Ro 7:5*
(P)
the gospel *bringeth forth* f. in   *Col 1:6*
you
Elijah prayed, the earth   *Jas 5:18*
brought forth f.
the land produced its crops (A)   *Jas 5:18*
the soil yielded its produce   *Jas 5:18*
(B)
the land bore crops once   *Jas 5:18*
more (N)
earth sprouted vegetation (P)   *Jas 5:18*

YIELD, YIELDETH,
YIELDING FRUIT

and the fruit tree *yielding* f.   *Ge 1:11;*
                                    1:12
and the land shall *yield* her   *Le 25:19*
f.
the trees of the field shall   *Le 26:4*
yield their f.
and that the land *yield* not her   *De 11:17*
f.
the root of the righteous   *Pr 12:12*
yieldeth f.
neither shall cease from   *Jer 17:8*
yielding f.
the tree of the field shall   *Eze 34:27*
yield her f.
yield your f. to my people   *Eze 36:8*
Israel
the thorns choked it, it   *M'k 4:7*
yielded no f.
other fell on good ground   *M'k 4:8*
and did *yield* f.
yieldeth peaceable f. of   *Heb 12:11*
righteousness
the tree *yielded* her f. every   *Re 22:2*
month

FRUIT TREES

possessed f. *trees* in   *Ne 9:25*
abundance

FRUITFUL

God blessed them, saying, Be   *Ge 1:22;*
f. and multiply   *1:28; 8:17; 9:7; 35:11*
and I will make thee   *Ge 17:6*
exceeding f.
I will make Ishmael f.   *Ge 17:20*
God hath made room for   *Ge 26:22*
us, we shall be f.
God Almighty bless thee, and   *Ge 28:3*
make thee f.

make Jacob f.   *Ge 48:4*
Joseph is a f. bough, even a   *Ge 49:22*
f. bough
and the children of Israel were   *Ex 1:7*
f.
I will make you f. and   *Le 26:9*
multiply you
he turneth a f. land into   *Ps 107:34*
barrenness
thy wife shall be as a f. vine   *Ps 128:3*
mountains and f. trees,   *Ps 148:9*
praise the Lord
my beloved hath a vineyard in   *Isa 5:1*
a f. hill
four or five in the outmost f.   *Isa 17:6*
branches thereof
they shall lament for the f.   *Isa 32:12*
vine
lo, the f. place was a   *Jer 4:26*
wilderness
and they shall be f. and   *Jer 23:3*
increase
she was f. and full of   *Eze 19:10*
branches
though he be f. an east   *Ho 13:15*
wind shall come
and gave us rain and f.   *Ac 14:17*
seasons
being f. in every good work,   *Col 1:10*
increasing

FRUITION

the Spirit's f. is (B)   *Ga 5:22; Eph 5:9*

FRUITLESS

all is f (B)   *Ec 2:17*
it becomes f. (A)(B)   *M'k 4:19*
f., without effect (A)(B)   *1Co 15:10*
faith is f. (A)   *1Co 15:17*
f. deeds of darkness (A)(B)   *Eph 5:11*
not useless and f. (A)(N)   *1Th 2:1;*
                                    8:5

FRUITLESSNESS

f., hurtful disease (B)   *Ec 6:2*
there is f. (B)   *Ec 8:14*

FRUITS

take of the best f. in land in   *Ge 43:11*
vessels
products of the land (A)(B)   *Ge 43:11*
not delay to offer the first of   *Ex 22:29*
thy ripe f.
offerings of grains and vines   *Ex 22:29*
(B)
thy harvest and presses   *Ex 22:29*
(E)(R)
six years shalt gather in the   *Ex 23:10*
f. thereof
gather in its yield (A)(R)   *Ex 23:10*
six years gather its crops   *Ex 23:10*
(B)
gather the increase (E)   *Ex 23:10*
according to the years of   *Le 25:15;*
f.   *25:16*
according to years and crop   *Le 25:15*
(A)(B)(E)(R)
until her f. come in eat the   *Le 25:22*
old store
until crops of ninth year   *Le 25:22*
come in (A)
till its harvest comes in (B)   *Le 25:22*
when the produce comes in   *Le 25:22*
(R)
neither shall the trees yield   *Le 26:20*
their f.
for precious f. brought forth   *De 33:14*
by the sun
thou and thy sons shall bring   *2Sa 9:10*
in f.
restore to her all the f. of the   *2Ki 8:6*
field
plant vineyards, and eat the   *2Ki 19:29*
f. thereof
if I have eaten the f.   *Job 31:39*
without money
sow fields, which may yield   *Ps 107:37*
f. of increase
I planted trees of all kind of f.   *Ec 2:5*
the plants are an orchard   *Ca 4:13*
with pleasant f.
let my beloved eat his pleasant   *Ca 4:16*
f.
I went down to see the f. of   *Ca 6:11*
the valley

at our gates are all manner   *Ca 7:13*
of pleasant f.
Bashan and Carmel shake off   *Isa 33:9*
their f.
pine away for want of the f.   *La 4:9*
of the earth
he shall not destroy the f. of   *Mal 3:11*
your ground
bring f. meet for repentance   *M't 3:8;*
                                    Lu 3:8
ye shall know them by their   *M't 7:16;*
f.   *7:20*
that they might receive the   *M't 21:34*
f. of it
who shall render him the f.   *M't 21:41*
in their seasons
kingdom given to a nation   *M't 21:43*
bringing forth f.
I have no room where to   *Lu 12:17*
bestow my f.
to gather together my   *Lu 12:17*
harvest (A)(P)
to store my crops (B)(R)   *Lu 12:17*
to store my produce (N)   *Lu 12:17*
and there will I bestow all   *Lu 12:18*
my f.
store all my grain, goods   *Lu 12:18*
(A)(E)(P)(R)
store all my produce (B)   *Lu 12:18*
store all my corn and other   *Lu 12:18*
goods (N)
increase the f. of your   *2Co 9:10*
righteousness
filled with the f. of   *Ph'p 1:11*
righteousness
the husbandman first partaker   *2Ti 2:6*
of the f.
the first share of the produce   *2Ti 2:6*
(B)(P)
has first claim on the crop   *2Ti 2:6*
(N)
the first share of the crops   *1Ti 2:6*
(R)
wisdom from above is full of   *Jas 3:17*
good f.
f. thy soul lusted after   *Re 18:14*
departed from
the tree of life bare twelve   *Re 22:2*
manner of f.

SUMMER FRUITS

Ziba with an hundred of   *2Sa 16:1*
summer f.
thy summer f. and harvest   *Isa 16:9*
are fallen
but gather ye wine and   *Jer 40:10*
summer f.
Jews gathered wine and   *Jer 40:12*
summer f. very much
the spoiler is fallen on thy   *Jer 48:32*
summer f.
as when they gathered the   *Mic 7:1*
summer f.

FRUSTRATE

and hired counsellors to f.   *Ezr 4:5*
their purpose
arrows embarrass, f. them   *Ps 144:6*
(A)
I do not f. the grace of God   *Ga 2:21*
I do not slight the grace of   *Ga 2:21*
God (B)
do not make void the grace   *Ga 2:21*
of God (E)
I will not nullify the grace   *Ga 2:21*
of God (N)(R)
I refuse to stultify the grace   *Ga 2:21*
of God (P)

FRUSTRATED

Amnon felt f. (B)   *2Sa 13:2*
their plan f. (A)(B)   *Ne 4:15*
f. purposes of people (B)   *Ps 33:10*
f. your Lord (A)   *Ps 119:126*
purposes f. (A)   *Pr 15:22*
handicapped, never f. (P)   *2Co 4:8*
grow up feeling inferior and   *Col 3:21*
f. (P)

FRUSTRATETH

that f. the tokens of the   *Isa 44:25*
liars
confounds omens of   *Isa 44:25*
soothsayers (B)

FRUSTRATES

f. devices of crafty (A)(E)(R) *Job 5:12*
f. plans of people (R) *Ps 33:10*

FRUSTRATION

condemned to f. (A)(N) *Ro 8:20*

FRYINGPAN

if oblation be a meat offering in the f. *Le 2:7*
food offering from the roaster (B) *Le 2:7*
all that is dressed in the f. shall be the priest's *Le 7:9*

FUEL

this shall be with burning and f. of fire *Isa 9:5*
the people shall be as the f. of the fire *Isa 9:19*
the vine tree is cast into the fire for f. *Eze 15:4; 15:6*
thou shalt be for f. to the fire *Eze 21:32*

FUGITIVE

a f. and a vagabond shalt thou be *Ge 4:12*
a vagrant and a wanderer (B) *Ge 4:12*
I shall be a f. and a vagabond in the earth *Ge 4:14*
meet the f. with bread (A)(B)(E)(R) *Isa 21:14*

FUGITIVES

ye Gileadites are f. of Ephraim *J'g 12:4*
and the f. that fell away to the king *2Ki 25:11*
shall cry for Moab, his f. shall flee to Zoar *Isa 15:5*
all his f. shall fall by the sword *Eze 17:21*

FULFIL

f. her week, and we will give thee this *Ge 29:27*
f. your works, your daily task *Ex 5:13*
the number of thy days I will f. *Ex 23:26*
that he might f. the word of the Lord *1Ki 2:27*
if thou takest heed to f. statutes of Lord *1Ch 22:13*
to f. threescore and ten years *2Ch 36:21*
canst thou number months that they f. *Job 39:2*
the Lord grant thee to f. all thy counsel *Ps 20:4*
the Lord f. all thy petitions *Ps 20:5*
he will f. the desire of them that fear him *Ps 145:19*
it becometh us to f. all righteousness *M't 3:15*
I am not come to destroy, but to f. *M't 5:17*
found David, who shall f. all my will *Ac 13:22*
uncircumcision, if it f. the law *Ro 2:27*
for the flesh, to f. the lusts thereof *Ro 13:14*
ye shall not f. the lusts of the flesh *Ga 5:16*
bear burdens, and so f. the law of Christ *Ga 6:2*
f. ye my joy, that ye be like-minded *Ph'p 2:2*
is given to me, to f. the word of God *Col 1:25*
take heed thou f. the ministry *Col 4:17*
f. all the good pleasure of his will *2Th 1:11*
if ye f. the royal law, ye do well *Jas 2:8*
for God put in their hearts to f. his will *Re 17:17*

FULFILL

to f. a special vow (B) *Nu 15:3; 15:8*
to f. their word (R) *Eze 13:6*

FULFILLED

when her days to be delivered were f. *Ge 25:24*
give me my wife, for my days are f. *Ge 29:21*
forty days were f. for so are f. the days *Ge 50:3*
wherefore have ye not f. your task *Ex 5:14*
seven days f. after Lord hath smitten river *Ex 7:25*
till the days of purification be f. *Le 12:4; 12:6*
when the days of his separation are f. *Nu 6:13*
when days be f. and thou shalt sleep *2Sa 7:12*
in that the king f. the request of servant *2Sa 14:22*
and hath with his hand f. it *1Ki 8:15*
and hast f. it with thy hand *1Ki 8:24; 2Ch 6:15*
the Lord hath f. that which he spake *2Ch 6:4*
that the word of the Lord might be f. *Ezr 1:1*
fulfilled (S) *Es 1:5; Eze 43:27*
it shall be f. (R) *Es 5:6*
thou hast f. the judgment of the wicked *Job 36:17*
vow shall be f. (B) *Ps 65:1*
wives have f. with your hands *Jer 44:25*
he hath f. his word he had commanded *La 2:17*
our days are f. for our end is come *La 4:18*
when the days of the siege are f. *Eze 5:2*
their message f. (A) *Eze 13:6*
the same hour was the thing f. *Da 4:33*
till three whole weeks were f. *Da 10:3*
that it might be f. *M't 1:22; 2:15, 23; 8:17; 12:17; 13:35; 21:4; 27:35; Joh 12:38; 15:25; 17:12; 18:9, 32; 19:24, 28, 36*
then was f. that which was spoken *M't 2:17; 27:9*
shall in no wise pass from the law till all be f. *M't 5:18*
in them is f. the prophecy of Esaias *M't 13:14*
shall not pass till all these things be f. *M't 24:34*
time is f. kingdom of God is at hand *M'k 1:15*
what sign when all these things shall be f. *M'k 13:4*
my words which shall be f. in their season *Lu 1:20*
Lord's promise be f. (N) *Lu 1:45*
when they had f. the days, they returned *Lu 2:43*
that all things which are written may be f. *Lu 21:22*
until the times of the Gentiles be f. *Lu 21:24*
not eat till it be f. in the kingdom of God *Lu 22:16*
all things must be f. spoken by Moses *Lu 24:44*
this is my joy therefore is f. *Joh 3:29*
they might have my joy f. in themselves *Joh 17:13*
what God had shewed, he hath so f. *Ac 3:18*
after many days were f. Jews took counsel *Ac 9:23*
Paul and Barnabas f. their ministry *Ac 12:25*
and as John f. his course, he said *Ac 13:25*
they have f. them in condemning him *Ac 13:27*
when they had f. all that was written of him *Ac 13:29*
God hath f. the same to us their children *Ac 13:33*
to grace of God for the work which they f. *Ac 14:26*
the righteousness of law might be f. in us *Ro 8:4*
he that loveth another hath f. the law *Ro 13:8*
when your obedience is f. *2Co 10:6*
the law is f. in one word, even in this *Ga 5:14*

FULFILLING

fire, hail, stormy wind f. his word *Ps 148:8*
their f. of God's plan (P) *Ro 11:12*
therefore love is the f. of the law *Ro 13:10*
f. the desires of the flesh and of the mind *Eph 2:3*

FULFILLMENT

a f. of things (A)(E)(R) *Lu 1:45*
concerning me have a f. (S) *Lu 22:37*

FULL

the vale of Siddim was f. of slimepits *Ge 14:10*
the iniquity of the Amorites is not yet f. *Ge 15:16*
Abraham an old man, and f. of years *Ge 25:8*
Isaac being old and f. of days, died *Ge 35:29*
at the end of two f. years, Pharaoh dreamed *Ge 41:1*
seven ears, f. and good (S) *Ge 41:5*
the thin ears devoured the seven f. ears *Ge 41:7; 41:22*
every man's money in his sack f. weight *Ge 43:21*
the houses shall be f. of swarms of flies *Ex 8:21*
and put an homer f. of manna therein *Ex 16:33*
for he should make f. restitution *Ex 22:3*
shalt offer even corn beaten out of f. ears *Le 2:14*
restore it in f. (A)(B)(E)(R) *Le 6:5*
censer f. of coals, hands f. of incense *Le 16:12*
and the land became f. of wickedness *Le 19:29*
within a f. year may he redeem it *Le 25:29*
if not redeemed in a f. year, then the house *Le 25:30*
make restitution in f. (A)(B)(R) *Nu 5:7*
both of them were f. of fine flour *Nu 7:13; 7:19, 25, 31, 37, 43, 49, 55, 61, 67, 73, 79*
one spoon of ten shekels f. of incense *Nu 7:14; 7:20, 26, 32, 38, 44, 50, 56, 62, 68, 74, 80, 86*
Balak give me house f. of silver *Nu 22:18; 22:24*
houses f. of all good things *De 6:11*
and ye be f. *De 8:10, 12*
will send grass, that thou mayest eat and be f. *De 11:15*
she shall bewail her father a f. month *De 21:13*
Naphtali f. with the blessing of the Lord *De 33:23*
Joshua was f. of the Spirit of wisdom *De 34:9*
wringed the dew, a bowl f. of water *J'g 6:38*
now the house was f. of men and women *J'g 16:27*
I went out f. and the Lord hath brought *Ru 1:21*
and a f. reward be given thee of the Lord *Ru 2:12*
they that were f. hired out themselves *1Sa 2:5*
they gave them in f. tale to the king *1Sa 18:27*
the f. number (A)(B)(E)(R) *1Sa 18:27*
David dwelt in country of Philistines a f. year *1Sa 27:7*
and with one f. line to keep alive *2Sa 8:2*
make this valley f. of ditches *2Ki 3:16*
when vessels were f. she said to her son *2Ki 4:6*

till killing of their brethren *Re 6:11*
should be f.
till the seven plagues of seven *Re 15:8*
angels were f.
till the words of God shall *Re 17:17*
be f.
should deceive no more, till *Re 20:3*
1,000 years be f.

behold, the mountain was *f.*   *2Ki 6:17*
of horses
and lo, all the way was *f.* of   *2Ki 7:15*
garments
house of Baal was *f.* from   *2Ki 10:21*
one end to another
shall grant it me for the *f.*   *1Ch 21:22*
price
nay, but I will verily buy it   *1Ch 21:24*
for a *f.* price
when David was old and *f.*   *1Ch 23:1;*
of days   *29:28*
then was Haman *f.* of wrath   *Es 3:5*
Haman *f.* of fury (R))   *Es 3:5*
he was *f.* of indignation   *Es 5:9*
against Mordecai
thou shalt come to thy grave   *Job 5:26*
in a *f.* age
I am *f.* of tossings to and fro   *Job 7:4*
to dawning of day
I am *f.* of confusion, see   *Job 10:15*
mine affliction
and should a man *f.* of talk   *Job 11:2*
be justified
man *f.* of talk be vindicated   *Job 11:2*
(R)
man is of few days and *f.* of   *Job 14:1*
trouble
his bones are *f.* of the sins   *Job 20:11*
of his youth
one dieth in his *f.* strength,   *Job 21:23*
being at ease
his breasts are *f.* of milk,   *Job 21:24*
his bones moistened
I am *f.* of matter, the Spirit   *Job 32:18*
constraineth me
that on thy table should be   *Job 36:16*
f. of fatness
so Job died, being old and   *Job 42:17*
f. of days
they are *f.* of children, and   *Ps 17:14*
leave rest
hath broken my heart, I am   *Ps 69:20*
f. of heaviness
waters of a *f.* cup are wrung   *Ps 73:10*
out to them
dark places are *f.* of   *Ps 74:20*
habitations of cruelty
man did eat angels' food,   *Ps 78:25*
sent meat to the *f.*
the trees of the Lord are *f.*   *Ps 104:16*
of sap
happy that hath his quiver *f.*   *Ps 127:5*
of them
that our garners may be *f.*   *Ps 144:13*
affording store
until the *f.*-orbed day (B)   *Pr 4:18*
than a house *f.* of sacrifice with   *Pr 17:1*
strife
the *f.* soul loatheth an   *Pr 27:7*
honeycomb
hell and destruction are   *Pr 27:20*
never *f.*
lest I be *f.* and deny thee,   *Pr 30:9*
and say, Who is Lord
run into the sea, yet the sea is   *Ec 1:7*
not *f.*
all things are *f.* of labour, man   *Ec 1:8*
cannot utter
than both hands *f.* with travail   *Ec 4:6*
and vexation
if the clouds be *f.* of rain,   *Ec 11:3*
they empty
I am *f.* of the burnt offerings   *Isa 1:11*
of rams
I will not hear, your hands   *Isa 1:15*
are *f.* of blood
the faithful city, it was *f.* of   *Isa 1:21*
judgment
f. of diviners from the east   *Isa 2:6*
(R)
the earth shall be *f.* of   *Isa 11:9*
knowledge of the Lord
their houses shall be *f.* of   *Isa 13:21*
doleful creatures
the waters of Dimon shall be   *Isa 15:9*
f. of blood
f. of stirs   *Isa 22:2*
valleys shall be *f.* of chariots   *Isa 22:7*
a feast of fat things, a feast   *Isa 25:6*
f. of marrow
for all tables are *f.* of vomit   *Isa 28:8*
and filthiness
his lips are *f.* of   *Isa 30:27*
indignation, and his tongue
come in *f.* measure   *Isa 47:9*
(A)(B)(E)(R)
they are *f.* of the fury of   *Isa 51:20*
the Lord

a *f.* wind from those places   *Jer 4:12*
shall come
when I had fed them to the *f.*   *Jer 5:7*
they committed
therefore I am *f.* of the fury   *Jer 6:11*
of the Lord
within two *f.* years will I   *Jer 28:3;*
bring   *28:11*
I set before the Rechabites   *Jer 35:5*
pots *f.* of wine
how city sit solitary that was   *La 1:1*
f. of people
he is filled *f.* with reproach   *La 3:30*
and their wings were *f.* of   *Eze 1:18*
eyes
court was *f.* of the   *Eze 10:4*
brightness of Lord's glory
the wheels were *f.* of eyes   *Eze 10:12*
round about
a great eagle with wings *f.*   *Eze 17:3*
of feathers
she was fruitful and *f.* of   *Eze 19:10*
branches
the sum *f.* of wisdom and   *Eze 28:12*
perfect in beauty
and the rivers shall be *f.* of   *Eze 32:6*
thee
in midst of the valley which   *Eze 37:1*
was *f.* of bones
ye shall eat fat till ye be *f.*   *Eze 39:19*
and drink blood
then was Nebuchadnezzar *f.*   *Da 3:19*
of fury
when the transgressors are   *Da 8:23*
come to the *f.*
in those days Daniel mourned   *Da 10:2*
three *f.* weeks
the floors shall be *f.* of   *Joe 2:24*
wheat
but truly I am *f.* of power by   *Mic 3:8*
the Spirit
the rich men thereof are *f.*   *Mic 6:12*
of violence
and the earth was *f.* of his   *Hab 3:3*
praise
the streets shall be *f.* of boys   *Zec 8:5*
and girls
thy body shall be *f.* of light   *M't 6:22;*
          Lu 11:36
which when it was *f.* they   *M't 13:48*
drew to shore
of fragments twelve baskets   *M't 14:20;*
f.   *M'k 6:43*
they took up that was left   *M't 15:37*
seven baskets *f.*
but within are *f.* of   *M't 23:25*
extortion and excess
but within are *f.* of dead   *M't 23:27*
men's bones
within ye are *f.* of hypocrisy   *M't 23:28*
and iniquity
f. will ye reject   *M'k 7:9*
commandment of God
one ran and filled a spunge   *M'k 15:36*
f. of vinegar
now Elizabeth's *f.* time came to   *Lu 1:57*
be delivered
were I *f.* of wonder (N)   *Lu 2:33*
Jesus being *f.* of the Holy   *Lu 4:1*
Ghost, was led
behold a man *f.* of leprosy,   *Lu 5:12*
fell on his face
woe unto you that are *f.* ye   *Lu 6:25*
shall hunger
Lazarus was laid at his gate   *Lu 16:20*
f. of sores
dwelt among us *f.* of grace   *Joh 1:14*
and truth
I go not up, for my time is   *Joh 7:8*
not yet *f.* come
and that your joy might be   *Joh 15:11;*
f.   *16:24*
there was set a vessel *f.* of   *Joh 19:29*
vinegar
others said, These men are *f.*   *Ac 2:13*
of new wine
shalt make me *f.* of joy with   *Ac 2:28*
thy countenance
look ye out men *f.* of the Holy   *Ac 6:3*
Ghost
Stephen *f.* of faith and the   *Ac 6:5;*
Holy Ghost   *7:55*
when Moses was *f.* forty   *Ac 7:23*
years old
Dorcas *f.* of good works and   *Ac 9:36*
alms deeds
Barnabas *f.* of the Holy   *Ac 11:24*
Ghost and faith

and said, O *f.* of all subtilty   *Ac 13:10*
and mischief
they were *f.* of wrath, and   *Ac 19:28*
cried out
being *f.* of envy, murder,   *Ro 1:29*
debate, deceit
their *f.* inclusion   *Ro 11:12*
(B)(N)(R)
f. number of ingathering   *Ro 11:25*
(A)(B)(P)(R)
I am persuaded that ye also   *Ro 15:14*
are *f.* of goodness
f. measure of blessing   *Ro 15:29*
(N)(P)
in *f.* agreement (A)   *1Co 1:10*
the *f.* grown (A)   *1Co 2:6*
now ye are *f.* now ye are rich   *1Co 4:8*
for he longed and was *f.* of   *Ph'p 2:26*
heaviness
I am instructed to be *f.* and   *Ph'p 4:12*
to be hungry
but I have all, and abound,   *Ph'p 4:18*
I am *f.*
the *f.* nature of God (P)   *Col 1:19*
every man to *f.* maturity (P)   *Col 1:28*
f. complete expression of (P)   *Col 2:9*
make *f.* proof of thy ministry   *2Ti 4:5*
but strong meat to them   *Heb 5:14*
that are of *f.* age
tongue an unruly evil, *f.* of   *Jas 3:8*
deadly poison
wisdom from above is pure, *f.*   *Jas 3:17*
of mercy
ye rejoice with joy unspeakable   *1Pe 1:8*
and *f.* of glory
eyes *f.* of adultery, not cease   *2Pe 2:14*
from sin
we write to you, that your joy   *1Jo 1:4*
may be *f.*
but that we receive a *f.* reward   *2Jo 8*
speak face to face, that our   *2Jo 12*
joy may be *f.*
there are four beasts *f.* of   *Re 4:6;*
eyes   *4:8*
having every one golden vials   *Re 5:8*
f. of odours
seven golden vials *f.* of the   *Re 15:7*
wrath of God
and his kingdom was *f.* of   *Re 16:10*
darkness
I saw a woman *f.* of names   *Re 17:3*
of blasphemy
a golden cup *f.* of   *Re 17:4*
abominations and filthiness
the seven vials *f.* of the seven   *Re 21:9*
last plagues

IS FULL

thou shalt set aside that   *2Ki 4:4*
which *is f.*
his mouth *is f.* of cursing   *Ps 10:7;*
          Ro 3:14
and their right hand *is f.* of   *Ps 26:10*
bribes
the voice of the Lord *is f.* of   *Ps 29:4*
majesty
the earth *is f.* of the goodness   *Ps 33:5*
of the Lord
thy right hand *is f.* of   *Ps 48:10*
righteousness
with the river of God, which   *Ps 65:9*
is f. of water
and the wine is red, it *is f.* of   *Ps 75:8*
mixture
my soul *is f.* of troubles, and   *Ps 88:3*
my life
O Lord, the earth *is f.* of   *Ps 104:24*
thy riches
the earth, O Lord, *is f.* of   *Ps 119:64*
thy mercy
the heart of the sons of men *is*   *Ec 9:3*
f. of evil
a fool *is f.* of words, man   *Ec 10:14*
not tell what to be
their land *is f.* of silver, *is f.*   *Isa 2:7*
of horses
their land also *is f.* of idols,   *Isa 2:8*
they worship
holy is Lord, the whole earth   *Isa 6:3*
is f. of his glory
as a cage *is f.* of birds,   *Jer 5:27*
houses full of deceit
the aged, with him that *is f.*   *Jer 6:11*
of days
for the land *is f.* of   *Jer 23:10*
adulterers
land *is f.* of crimes, city *is f.*   *Eze 7:23*
of violence

land *is f.* of blood, city *is f.* Eze 9:9
of perverseness
for the press *is f.* the fats Joe 3:13
overflow
a cart is pressed, that *is f.* Am 2:13
of sheaves
it *is* all *f.* of lies and robberies Na 3:1
body *is f.* of light, *is f.* of Lu 11:34
darkness
but your inward part *is f.* of Lu 11:39
ravening

TO THE FULL

when we sat and did eat Ex 16:3
bread *to the f.*
when Lord shall give in the Ex 16:8
morning bread *to the f.*
ye shall eat your bread *to the* Le 26:5
f.

FULLER

as no *f.* on earth can white M'k 9:3
them
any bleacher could bleach M'k 9:3
(B)(N)
whiter than earthly bleach M'k 9:3
(P)

FULLER'S

is in the highway of the *f.* 2Ki 18:17
field
pool in the highway of the *f.* Isa 7:3
field
pool in the highway of the *f.* Isa 36:2
field

FULLERS'

like a refiner's fire, and like Mal 3:2
f. sope

FULLY

had *f.* set up the tabernacle Nu 7:1
and hath followed me *f.* him Nu 14:24
will
It hath *f.* been shewed me, Ru 2:11
all
went not *f.* after the Lord, 1Ki 11:6
as did
heart of the sons of men is *f.* Ec 8:11
set
f. mixed (S) Ps 75:8
be devoured as stubble *f.* dry Na 1:10
the day of Pentecost was *f.* Ac 2:1
come
And being *f.* persuaded that, Ro 4:21
what
Let every man be *f.* Ro 14:5
persuaded
I have *f.* preached the Ro 15:19
gospel of
thou hast *f.* known my 2Ti 3:10
doctrine
the preaching might be *f.* 2Ti 4:17
known
for her grapes are *f.* ripe Re 14:18

FULNESS

and as the *f.* of the Nu 18:27
winepress
things of the earth and *f.* De 33:16
thereof
Let the sea roar, and the *f.* 1Ch 16:32
thereof
In the *f.* of his sufficiency Job 20:22
he shall
in thy presence is *f.* of joy Ps 16:11
is the Lord's, and the *f.* Ps 24:1
thereof
world is mine, and the *f.* Ps 50:12
thereof
the world and the *f.* thereof, Ps 89:11
thou
let the sea roar, and the *f.* Ps 96:11
thereof
Let the sea roar, and the *f.* Ps 98:7
thereof
f. of bread, and abundance Eze 16:49
of
was desolate, and the *f.* Eze 19:7
thereof
of his *f.* have all we received Joh 1:16
from his abundance all have Joh 1:16
received (B)

of his full store all received Joh 1:16
(N)
shared in his riches (P) Joh 1:16
Gentiles: how much more Ro 11:12
their *f.*
their full reinstatement (A) Ro 11:12
how much more their full Ro 11:12
number (B)
their coming to full strength Ro 11:12
(N)
their fulfilling of God's plan Ro 11:12
(P)
their full inclusion (R) Ro 11:12
the *f.* of the Gentiles be Ro 11:25
come
full number of ingathering Ro 11:25
of Gentiles has come in (A)(P)(R)
full number of Gentiles be Ro 11:25
entered in (B)
Gentiles admitted in full Ro 11:25
strength (N)
come in the *f.* of the Ro 15:29
blessing
abundant blessing of the Ro 15:29
gospel (A)(B)
full measure of the blessing Ro 15:29
of (N)
the full blessing of Christ Ro 15:29
(P)
is the Lord's and the *f.* 1Co 10:26;
thereof 10:28
when the *f.* of the time was Ga 4:4
come
when the proper time had Ga 4:4
fully come (A)(P)
when the time was completed Ga 4:4
(B)
when the time was completed Ga 4:4
(N)
when the time had fully come Ga 4:4
(R)
dispensation of the *f.* of Eph 1:10
times
the maturity of times and Eph 1:10
the climax of the ages to
unify all things (A)
times should reach their Eph 1:10
maturity (B)
when the time was ripe (N) Eph 1:10
all human history shall be Eph 1:10
consummated in Christ (P)
the *f.* of him that filleth all Eph 1:23
in all
the completeness of him Eph 1:23
who fills the universe at all
points (B)
who fills the whole wide Eph 1:23
universe (P)
be filled with all the *f.* of Eph 3:19
God
the stature of the *f.* of Christ Eph 4:13
that in him should all *f.* Col 1:19
dwell
in him the complete being of Col 1:19
God came to dwell (N)
the full nature of God chose Col 1:19
to live (P)
all the *f.* of the Godhead Col 2:9
bodily
the complete being of Col 2:9
Godhead dwells (N)
full and complete expression Col 2:9
of himself (P)

FUN

made *f.* of him (P) M'k 15:29

FUNCTION

performing Priestly *f.* (P) Lu 1:8

FURBISH

f. the spears, and put on the Jer 46:4

FURBISHED

sword is sharpened, and Eze 21:9;
also *f.* 21:10, 11, 28

FURIOUS

he was *f.* and insulted (B) Ne 4:7
with a *f.* man thou shalt not Pr 22:24
go
wrathful man (A)(B)(E)(R) Pr 22:24;
29:22
and a *f.* man aboundeth in Pr 29:22

descending in *f.* anger Isa 30:30
(B)(R)
and in fury, and in *f.* Eze 5:15
rebukes
upon them with *f.* rebukes Eze 25:17
the king was angry and very Da 2:12
f.
Lord revengeth, and is *f.* Na 1:2
Herodias was *f.* (P) M'k 6:19
f. flame of fire (P) Heb 11:34

FURIOUSLY

son of Nimshi; for he 2Ki 9:20
driveth *f.*
they turned on him *f.* (P) Jer 9:28
and they shall deal *f.* with Eze 23:25
thee

FURLONGS

Jerusalem about threescore *f.* Lu 24:13
about seven miles Lu 24:13
(A)(B)(N)(P)(R)
about five and twenty or Joh 6:19
thirty *f.*
rowed three of four miles Joh 6:19
(A)(B)(N)(P)(R)
unto Jerusalem, about Joh 11:18
fifteen *f.* off
only about two miles away Joh 11:18
(A)(B)(N)(P)(R)
a thousand and six hundred Re 14:20
f.
about two hundred miles Re 14:20
(A)(B)(N)(P)
the reed, twelve thousand *f.* Re 21:16
about fifteen hundred miles Re 21:16
(A)(B)

FURLOUGH

no *f.* during battle (B) Ec 8:8

FURNACE

behold a smoking *f.* and a Ge 15:17
a smoking oven and burning Ge 15:17
torch (A)
smoking *f.*, flaming torch Ge 15:17
(E)
smoking fire pot and flaming Ge 15:17
torch (R)
went up as the smoke of a Ge 19:28
f.
to you handfuls of ashes of Ex 9:8
the *f.*
And they took ashes of the *f.* Ex 9:10
ascended as the smoke of a *f.* Ex 19:18
you forth out of the iron *f.* of De 4:20
from the midst of the *f.* of 1Ki 8:51
iron
as silver tried in a *f.* of earth Ps 12:6
like a blazing *f.* (A)(B)(R) Ps 21:9
and the *f.* for gold: but the Pr 17:3
Lord
and the *f.* for gold: so is a Pr 27:21
man
and his *f.* in Jerusalem Isa 31:9
I have chosen thee in the *f.* Isa 48:10
of
from the iron *f.* saying, Obey Jer 11:4
and lead, in the midst of Eze 22:18
the *f.*
into the midst of the *f.* Eze 22:20
is melted in the midst of Eze 22:22
the *f.*
the midst of a burning fiery Da 3:6
f. 3:11, 15, 17, 19, 20, 21, 22, 23, 26
shall cast them into a *f.* of M't 13:42
fire
shall cast them into the *f.* M't 13:50
of fire
as if they burned in a *f.* Re 1:15
as the smoke of a great *f.* Re 9:2

FURNACES

other piece, and the tower of Ne 3:11
the *f.*
of the *f.* even unto the Ne 12:38
broad wall

FURNISH

f. him liberally out of thy De 15:14
flock
God *f.* a table in the Ps 78:19
wilderness
f. the drink offering unto Isa 65:11
f. thyself to go into captivity Jer 46:19

FURNISHED

Hiram the king of Tyre had *f.*	*1Ki 9:11*
she hath also *f.* her table	*Pr 9:2*
the wedding was *f.* with guests	*M't 22:10*
large upper room *f.* and prepared	*M'k 14:15*
shew you a large upper room *f.*	*Lu 22:12*
thoroughly *f.* unto all good works	*2Ti 3:17*

FURNISHINGS

all the *f.* thereof (S)	*Ex 25:9*
the *f.* (R)	*Nu 1:50; 19:18*
all the *f.* (B)(R)	*Nu 3:8*
the house *f.* (A)	*Ne 13:8*

FURNITURE

the camel's *f.* and sat upon them	*Ge 31:34*
regard not your *f.* (B)	*Ge 45:20*
all the *f.* (A)(B)(E)(R)	*Ex 25:9*
and all the *f.* of the tabernacle	*Ex 31:7*
the table and his *f.* and the pure candlestick with all his *f.*	*Ex 31:8* *Ex 31:8*
of burnt offering with all his *f.*	*Ex 31:9*
also for the light, and his *f.*	*Ex 35:14*
all his *f.* his taches, his boards	*Ex 39:33*
the *f.* thereof (A)(B)	*Ex 40:9;* *Nu 4:15, 16; 7:1; 1Ch 9:29*
the *f.* thereof (E)	*Nu 1:50;* *4:15, 16; 7:1*
upon all the *f.* (B)	*Nu 19:18*
the household *f.* (R)	*Ne 13:8*
glory that of all the pleasant *f.*	*Na 2:9*

FURORE

because of *f.* (A)	*Ac 21:34*

FURROW

unicorn with his band in the *f.*	*Job 39:10*
driving a straight *f.* (A)	*2Ti 2:15*

FURROWS

the *f.* likewise thereof complain	*Job 31:38*
settlest the *f.* thereof: thou makest	*Ps 65:10*
they made long their *f.*	*Ps 129:3*
it by the *f.* of her plantation	*Eze 17:7*
wither in the *f.* where it grew	*Eze 17:10*
as hemlock in the *f.* of the field	*Ho 10:4*
bind themselves in their two *f.*	*Ho 10:10*
are as heaps in the *f.* of the fields	*Ho 12:11*

FURTHER

the angel of the Lord went *f.*	*Nu 22:26*
shall speak *f.* unto the people	*De 20:8*
enquired of the Lord *f.* if the man	*1Sa 10:22*
is thy request *f.*? and it shall	*Es 9:12*
shalt thou come, but no *f.*	*Job 38:11*
yea, twice; but I will proceed no *f.*	*Job 40:5*
f. not his wicked device; lest they	*Ps 140:8*
profit of wicked is for *f.* sin (B)(E)	*Pr 10:16*
And *f.* by these, my son, be	*Ec 12:12*
what *f.* need have we of witnesses	*M't 26:65*
troublest thou the Master any *f.*	*M'k 5:35*
What need we any *f.* witnesses	*M'k 14:63*
What need we any *f.* witness	*Lu 22:71*
as though he would have gone *f.*	*Lu 24:28*
spread no *f.* among the people	*Ac 4:17*
when they had *f.* threatened them	*Ac 4:21*
he proceeded *f.* to take Peter	*Ac 12:3*
f. brought Greeks also into	*Ac 21:28*
I be not *f.* tedious unto thee	*Ac 24:4*
when they had gone a little *f.*	*Ac 27:28*
proceed no *f.*: for their folly	*2Ti 3:9*
f. need was there that another	*Heb 7:11*

FURTHERANCE

rather unto the *f.* of the gospel	*Ph'p 1:12*
for your *f.* and joy of faith	*Ph'p 1:25*

FURTHERED

they *f.* the people, and the house	*Ezr 8:36*

FURTHERMORE

And the Lord said *f.* unto him	*Ex 4:6*
F. the Lord was angry with me	*De 4:21*
F. the Lord spake unto me	*De 9:13*
David said *f.* As the Lord liveth	*1Sa 26:10*
F. I tell thee that the Lord will	*1Ch 17:10*
F. over the tribes of Israel	*1Ch 27:16*
F. David the king said unto	*1Ch 29:1*
F. he made the court of the	*2Ch 4:9*
F. Elihu answered and said	*Job 34:1*
He said *f.* unto me, Son of man	*Eze 8:6*
And *f.* that ye have sent for men	*Eze 23:40*
F. when I came to Troas to	*2Co 2:12*
F. then we beseech you, brethren	*1Th 4:1*
F. we have had fathers of our	*Heb 12:9*

FURY

until thy brother's *f.* turn away	*Ge 27:44*
walk contrary unto you also in *f.*	*Le 26:28*
Haman full of *f.* (R)	*Es 3:5*
God shall cast the *f.* of his wrath	*Job 20:23*
terrify them in his *f.* (R)	*Ps 2:5*
F. is not in me: who would set	*Isa 27:4*
lips are filled with *f.* (B)	*Isa 30:27*
and his *f.* upon all their armies	*Isa 34:2*
upon him the *f.* of his anger	*Isa 42:25*
because of the *f.* of the oppressor	*Isa 51:13*
where is the *f.* of the oppressor	*Isa 51:13*
of the Lord the cup of his *f.*	*Isa 51:17*
they are full of the *f.* of the Lord	*Isa 51:20*
the dregs of the cup of my *f.*	*Isa 51:22*
f. to his adversaries, recompence	*Isa 59:18*
anger, and trample them in my *f.*	*Isa 63:3*
and my *f.* it upheld me	*Isa 63:5*
and make them drunk in my *f.*	*Isa 63:6*
to render his anger with *f.*	*Isa 66:15*
lest my *f.* come forth like fire	*Jer 4:4*
I am full of the *f.* of the Lord	*Jer 6:11*
mine anger and my *f.* shall be	*Jer 7:20*
Pour out thy *f.* upon the heathen	*Jer 10:25*
and in *f.* and in great wrath	*Jer 21:5*
my *f.* go out like fire, and burn	*Jer 21:12*
the Lord is gone forth in *f.*	*Jer 23:19*
Take the wine cup of this *f.* at my	*Jer 25:15*
of the Lord goeth forth with *f.*	*Jer 30:23*
of mine anger and of my *f.*	*Jer 32:31*
and in my *f.* and in great wrath	*Jer 32:37*
in mine anger and in my *f.*	*Jer 33:5*
that the Lord hath pronounced	*Jer 36:7*
and my *f.* hath been poured forth	*Jer 42:18*
my *f.* be poured forth upon you	*Jer 42:18*
f. and mine anger was poured	*Jer 44:6*
he poured out his *f.* like fire	*La 2:4*
Lord hath accomplished his *f.*	*La 4:11*
cause my *f.* to rest upon them,	*Eze 5:13*
have accomplished my *f.* in them	*Eze 5:13*
in *f.* and in furious rebukes	*Eze 5:15*
I accomplish my *f.* upon them	*Eze 6:12*
Now will I shortly pour out my *f.*	*Eze 7:8*
Therefore will I also deal in *f.*	*Eze 8:18*
in thy pouring out of thy *f.*	*Eze 9:8*
with a stormy wind in my *f.*	*Eze 13:13*
hailstones in my *f.* to consume it	*Eze 13:13*
pour out my *f.* upon it in blood	*Eze 14:19*
I will give thee blood in *f.*	*Eze 16:38*
I make my *f.* toward thee to rest	*Eze 16:42*
plucked up in *f.* she was cast	*Eze 19:12*
I will pour out my *f.* upon them	*Eze 20:8*
I would pour out my *f.* upon them	*Eze 20:13; 21*
and with *f.* poured out, will I rule	*Eze 20:33*
stretched out arm, and with *f.*	*Eze 20:34*
and I will cause my *f.* to rest	*Eze 21:17*
in mine anger and in my *f.*	*Eze 22:20*
have poured out my *f.* upon you	*Eze 22:22*
That it might cause *f.* to come up	*Eze 24:8*
caused my *f.* to rest upon thee	*Eze 24:13*
anger and according to my *f.*	*Eze 25:14*
I will pour my *f.* upon Sin	*Eze 30:15*
pour out my *f.* on sin (B)	*Eze 30:16*
in my jealousy and in my *f.*	*Eze 36:6*
my *f.* upon them for the blood	*Eze 36:18*
my *f.* shall come up in my face	*Eze 38:18*
rage and *f.* commanded to bring	*Da 3:13*
Then was Nebuchadnezzar full of *f.*	*Da 3:19*
unto him in the *f.* of his power	*Da 8:6*
thine anger and thy *f.* be turned	*Da 9:16*
go forth with great *f.* to destroy	*Da 11:44*
in anger and *f.* upon the heathen	*Mic 5:15*
f. is poured out like fire, and	*Na 1:6*
I was jealous for her with great *f.*	*Zec 8:2*
sow *f.* of the wind (P)	*M't 14:30*
were filled with *f.* (S)	*Lu 6:11*
in *f.* of jealousy (P)	*Ac 5:17*
f. of fire (R)	*Heb 10:27*
quenched *f.* of fire (N)	*Heb 11:34*
nations full of *f.* (P)	*Re 11:18*

FUSSING

fretting and *f.* about (N)	*Lu 10:20; 10:41*

FUTILE

months of *f.* suffering (A)	*Job 7:3*
f. words (A)	*Job 16:3; 21:34;* *1Co 3:20; Tit 3:9*
they are *f.* (B)	*Ps 94:11*
man is *f.* (B)	*Ps 127:1; 1Co 3:20;* *15:14, 17, 58; 1Th 2:1*
all is *f.* (B)	*Ec 1:2; 2:15; 12:8*
and striving after wind (B)	*Ec 6:9*
became *f.* in thinking (R)	*Ro 1:21*
faith is *f.* (B)	*Ro 4:14*
arguments of this are *f.* (N)(R)	*1Co 3:20*
faith is *f.* (A)(P)	*1Co 15:17*
labor is *f.* (A)	*1Co 15:58*
bursting with *f.* conceit (N)(P)	*Col 2:18*
this man's religion is *f.* (N)	*Jas 1:26*

are *f*. and purposeless (B)(R) *Tit 3:9*
ransomed from *f*. ways *1Pe 1:18*
(P)(R)

FUTILITIES

futility of *f*. (A)(B) *Ec 1:2; 12:8*

FUTILITY

my days are falsity, *f*. (A) *Job 7:16*
trust in *f*. (B) *Job 15:31;*
Ps 4:2; 119:37; Ec 5:10; 8:14; Jer 2:5
they are *f*. (A) *Ps 62:9; 78:33; 94:11*
emptiness, falsity, *f*., frailty *Ps 89:47*
(A)
reap calamity and *f*. (A) *Pr 22:8*
f. of futilities (A)(B) *Ec 1:2; 12:8*
f. and chasing of wind (B) *Ec 4:4;*
4:16
comes to *f*. (A) *Ec 6:4*
increase falsity, *f*. (A) *Ec 6:11*
all the days of *f*. (A) *Ec 9:9*
all is *f*., falsity (A) *Ec 12:8*
offerings of vanity, falsity, *f*. *Isa 1:13*
(A)
emptiness waste *f*. (A) *Isa 40:17*
falsity, *f*. (A) *Isa 40:23;*
41:29; Jer 2:5; Hab 2:13
emptiness, *f*. (A) *Isa 59:4; Jer 16:19*
emptiness, falsity, *f*. (A) *Jer 51:18*
thinking ended in *f*. (N)(R) *Ro 1:21*
subject to frailty, *f*. (A) (R) *Ro 8:20*
f. of their minds (R) *Eph 4:17*
f. and purposeless (B) *Tit 3:9*

FUTURE

careful of his own *f*. (P) *Lu 16:8*

G

GAAL

Zebul thrust out *G*. and his *J'g 9:41;*
brethren *9:26, 28, 30-31, 35-37, 39*

GAASH

on the north side of the hill *Jos 24:30*
of *G*.
on the north side of the hill *J'g 2:9*
G.
Hiddai of the brooks of *G*. *2Sa 23:30*
Hurai of the brooks of *G*. *1Ch 11:32*
Abiel

GABA

and Ophni, and *G*.: twelve *Jos 18:24*
cities
The children of Ramah and *Ezr 2:26*
G.
The men of Ramah and *G*. *Ne 7:30*

GABBAI

And after him *G*. Sallai, nine *Ne 11:8*

GABBATHA

but in the Hebrew, *G*. *Joh 19:13*

GABRIEL

G. make this man to *Da 8:16*
understand
even the man *G*. whom I had *Da 9:21*
seen
I am *G*. that stand in the *Lu 1:19*
sixth month the angel *G*. was *Lu 1:26*
sent

GAD

a troop cometh, she called *Ge 30:11*
his name *G*.
the sons of Zilpah, *G*. and *Ge 35:26*
Asher
sons *G*. *Ge 46:16;*
Nu 1:24; 26:15, 18; 1Ch 12:14
G. a troop shall overcome *Ge 49:19*
the prince of *G*. Eliasaph *Nu 1:14;*
2:14; 7:42
children of *G*. had a *Nu 32:1*
multitude of cattle

the children of *G*. came and *Nu 32:2*
spake to Moses
if the children of *G*. will *Nu 32:29*
pass over Jordan
Moses gave to *G*. the *Nu 32:33*
kingdom of Sihon
the tribe of the children of *Nu 34:14;*
G. have received their *Jos 13:28; 18:7*
on mount Ebal to curse *G*. *De 27:13*
and Asher
and of *G*. blessed be he that *De 33:20*
enlargeth *G*.
the children of *G*. passed over *Jos 4:12*
armed
the children of *G*. returned *Jos 22:9*
out of Shiloh
some Hebrews went to the *1Sa 13:7*
land of *G*.
that lieth in the midst of the *2Sa 24:5*
river of *G*.
word of the Lord came to *2Sa 24:11;*
the prophet *G*. David's *1Ch 21:9, 18*
seer, saying
David said unto *G*. I am in *2Sa 24:14*
a great strait
David did according to the *2Sa 24:19*
saying of *G*.
acts of David are in the *1Ch 29:29*
book of *G*.
Levites according to *2Ch 29:25*
command of *G*.
why then doth their king *Jer 49:1*
inherit *G*.
a portion for *G*. one gate *Eze 48:27;*
of *G*. *48:34*

TRIBE OF GAD

that were numbered of *tribe Nu 1:25*
of G. 45,650
tribe of G. shall set forward, *Nu 2:14;*
captain of Gad shall be *10:20*
of the *tribe of G*. to spy the *Nu 13:15*
land, Geuel
the *tribe of* the children of *Nu 34:14;*
G. *Jos 13:24*
out of the *tribe of G*. *Jos 20:8;*
assigned Ramoth-Gilead *21:7; 38;*
to the Levites *1Ch 6:63, 80*
of the *tribe of G*. were sealed *Re 7:5*
12,000

GADARENES

they came over to the other *M'k 5:1;*
side of the sea into the *Lu 8:26*
country of the *G*.
country of *G*. besought him *Lu 8:37*
to depart

GADDEST

why *g*. thou about to change *Jer 2:36*
thy way
Why do you roam about (B) *Jer 2:36*

GADDI

tribe of Manasseh. *G*. the *Nu 13:11*
son of

GADDIEL

of Zebulun *G*. the son of *Nu 13:10*
Sodi

GADI

Menahem the son of *G*. *2Ki 15:14*
went up
Menahem the son of *G*. to *2Ki 15:17*
reign

GADITE

of Zobah, Bani the *G*. *2Sa 23:36*

GADITES

the Reubenites and to the *G*. *De 3:12*
unto the *G*. I gave from *De 3:16*
Gilead even
Gilead, of the *G*.; and Golan *De 4:43*
and to the *G*. and to the half *De 29:8*
tribe
and to the *G*. and to half the *Jos 1:12*
tribe
unto the Reubenites, and the *Jos 12:6*
G.

the Reubenites and the *G*. *Jos 13:8*
have
and the *G*. and the half tribe *Jos 22:1*
land of Gilead, the *G*. and *2Ki 10:33*
and the *G*. and half the *1Ch 5:18*
tribe of
and the *G*. and the half *1Ch 5:26*
tribe of
And of the *G*. there *1Ch 12:8*
separated
and the *G*. and of the half *1Ch 12:37*
tribe of
the *G*. and the half tribe of *1Ch 26:32*

GADFLIES

swarms of *g*. (B) *Ex 8:2; 8:31*
being ruined by *g*. (B)(R) *Ex 8:24*

GAHAM

bare also Tebah, and *G*. and *Ge 22:24*

GAHAR

of Giddel, the children of *G*. *Ezr 2:47*
of Giddel, the children of *G*. *Ne 7:49*

GAIETY

fools in the house of *g*. (B) *Ec 7:4*
an end to all her *g*. (B) *Ho 2:11*

GAIN

all his *g*. (A) *Ge 31:18*
hating unjust *g*. (A)(E) *Ex 18:21*
they took no *g*. of money *J'g 5:19*
turned aside after *g*. (R) *1Sa 8:3*
or is it *g*. to him, that thou *Job 22:3*
makest
every one that is greedy of *g*. *Pr 1:19*
and the *g*. thereof than fine *Pr 3:14*
gold
g. of the wicked to sin (R) *Pr 10:16*
He that is greedy of *g*. *Pr 15:27*
troubleth
by usury and unjust *g*. *Pr 28:8*
increaseth
never lack profit, *g*. *Pr 31:11*
(B)(E)(R)
despiseth the *g*. of *Isa 33:15*
oppressions
one for his *g*. from his *Isa 56:11*
quarter
mine hand at thy dishonest *Eze 22:13*
g.
destroy souls, to get *Eze 22:27*
dishonest *g*.
certainty that ye would *g*. the *Da 2:8*
time
cause many to *g*. insight *Da 11:33*
(B)
and shall divide the land for *Da 11:39*
g.
consecrate their *g*. unto the *Mic 4:13*
Lord
if he shall *g*. the whole *M't 16:26*
world, and
saw nothing being *g*. (N) *M't 27:24*
if he shall *g*. the whole *M'k 8:36*
world, and
if he *g*. the whole world, *Lu 9:25*
and lose
what will a man *g*. (A)(N) *Lu 9:25;*
1Co 15:32
what will a man *g*. (P) *Lu 9:25*
brought her masters much *g*. *Ac 16:16*
brought no small *g*. unto the *Ac 19:24*
what was the *g*. (N) *Ro 6:21*
unto all, that I might *g*. the *1Co 9:19*
more
that I might *g*. the Jews *1Co 9:20*
that I might *g*. them that *1Co 9:20*
are under
might *g*. them that are *1Co 9:21*
without law
that I might *g*. the weak *1Co 9:22*
what do I *g*. if the dead *1Co 15:32*
(A)(N)(R)
Did I make a *g*. of you by *2Co 12:17*
any
Did Titus make a *g*. of you *2Co 12:18*
to live is Christ, and to die *Ph'p 1:21*
is *g*.
But what things were *g*. to *Ph'p 3:7*
me
learn to *g*. mastery over body *1Th 4:4*
(N)
supposing that *g*. is godliness *1Ti 6:5*

with contentment is great *g.*	*1Ti 6:6*
not greedy of *g.* (B)(P)(R)	*Tit 1:7*
for base *g.* (A)(B)(N)(R)	*Tit 1:11*
and buy and sell, and get *g.*	*Jas 4:13*
not out for greedy *g.* (B)(R)	*1Pe 5:2*
for the sake of *g.* (A)(R)	*Jude 11*

GAINED

though he hath *g.* when God	*Job 27:8*
and thou hast greedily *g.* of thy	*Eze 22:12*
thee, thou hast *g.* thy brother	*M't 18:15*
received two, he also *g.* other two	*M't 25:17*
I have *g.* beside them five talents	*M't 25:20*
g. two other talents beside them	*M't 25:22*
every man had *g.* by trading	*Lu 19:15*
thy pound hath *g.* ten pounds	*Lu 19:16*
thy pound hath *g.* five pounds	*Lu 19:18*
to have *g.* this harm and loss	*Ac 27:21*

GAINS

the hope of their *g.* was gone	*Ac 16:19*

GAINSAY

shall not be able to *g.* nor resist	*Lu 21:15*

GAINSAYERS

to exhort and to convince the *g.*	*Tit 1:9*
those who contradict and oppose it (A)	*Tit 1:9*
refute those who raise objections (B)	*Tit 1:9*
to confute objectors (N)	*Tit 1:9*
confute opposition (P)(R)	*Tit 1:9*

GAINSAYING

came I unto you without *g.*	*Ac 10:29*
a disobedient, unruly people	*Ro 10:21*
unyielding, disobedient,	*Ro 10:21*
self-willed. fault-finding, contrary, contradicting people (A)	
an unyielding, contradicting people (B)	*Ro 10:21*
an unruly, recalcitrant people (N)	*Ro 10:21*
a disobedient and contrary people (R)	*Ro 10:21*
and perished in the *g.* of Core	*Jude 11*
rebellion of Korah (A)(N)(P)(R)	*Jude 11*
the Korah revolt (B)	*Jude 11*

GAIUS

caught *G.* and Aristarchus	*Ac 19:29*
and *G.* of Derbe, and Timotheus	*Ac 20:4*
G. mine host and of the whole	*Ro 16:23*
none of you, but Crispus and *G.*	*1Co 1:14*
The elder unto the wellbeloved *G.*	*3Jo 1*

GALAL

Heresh, and *G.* and Mattaniah	*1Ch 9:15*
the son of *G.* the son of Jeduthun	*1Ch 9:16*
Shammua, the son of *G.* the son of	*Ne 11:17*

GALATIA

Phrygia and the region of *G.*	*Ac 16:6*
country of *G.* and Phyrgia in order	*Ac 18:23*
given order to the churches of *G.*	*1Co 16:1*
with me unto the churches of *G.*	*Ga 1:2*
Crescens to *G.* Titus unto	*2Ti 4:10*
Pontus, *G.* Cappadocia, Asia	*1Pe 1:1*

GALATIANS

O foolish *G.* who hath bewitched	*Ga 3:1*

GALBANUM

onycha, and *g.* these sweet spices	*Ex 30:34*

GALE

saw strength of the *g.* (N)	*M't 14:30*

GALEED

but Jacob called it *G.*	*Ge 31:47*
was the name of it called *G.*	*Ge 31:48*

GALILAEAN

for thou art a *G.* and thy speech	*M'k 14:70*
also was with him: for he is a *G.*	*Lu 22:59*
asked whether the man were a *G.*	*Lu 23:6*

GALILAEANS

some that told him of the *G.*	*Lu 13:1*
Suppose ye that these *G.* were	*Lu 13:2*
sinners above all the *G.*	*Lu 13:2*
the *G.* received him, having seen	*Joh 4:45*
are not all these which speak *G.*	*Ac 2:7*

GALILEE

Kedesh in *G.* for a city of refuge	*Jos 20:7*
Kedesh in *G.* to the Levites	*Jos 21:32; 1Ch 6:76*
Solomon gave Hiram 20 cities in *G.*	*1Ki 9:11*
Tiglath-pileser took Ijon and *G.*	*2Ki 15:29*
did more grievously afflict her in *G.*	*Isa 9:1*
Joseph turned into the parts of *G.*	*M't 2:22*
then cometh Jesus from *G.* to John	*M't 3:13; M'k 1:9*
G. of the Gentiles; Jesus of *G.*	*M't 4:15; 21:11*
Jesus walking by the sea of *G.*	*M't 4:18; M'k 1:16*
there followed multitudes from *G.*	*M't 4:25; M'k 3:7*
Jesus came nigh unto the sea of *G.*	*M't 15:29*
I will go before you into *G.*	*M't 26:32; M'k 14:28*
many women which followed Jesus from *G.*	*M't 27:55; M'k 15:41; Lu 23:49, 55*
he goeth before you into *G.*	*M't 28:7; M'k 16:7*
he preached throughout all *G.*	*M'k 1:39*
Jesus returned in power of Spirit into *G.*	*Lu 4:14*
he preached in synagogues of *G.*	*Lu 4:44*
beginning from *G.* to this place	*Lu 23:5*
when Pilate heard of *G.* he asked whether Galilaean	*Lu 23:6*
how he spake to you when he was in *G.*	*Lu 24:6*
some said, Shall Christ come out of *G.*	*Joh 7:41*
art thou of *G.*? out of *G.* ariseth no prophet	*Joh 7:52*
Philip who was of Bethsaida in *G.*	*Joh 12:21*
ye men of *G.*; Judas of *G.* rose up	*Ac 1:1; 5:37*
then had the churches rest through all *G.*	*Ac 9:31*
the word you know which began from *G.*	*Ac 10:37*
he was seen of them that came from *G.*	*Ac 13:31*

GALL

that beareth *g.* and wormwood	*Pr 29:18*

such poison and wormwood (B)	*Pr 29:18*
bearing poisonous and bitter fruit (R)	*Pr 29:18*
their grapes are grapes of *g.*	*Pr 32:32*
grapes are grapes of poison (B)(R)	*Pr 32:32*
out my *g.* upon the ground	*Job 16:13*
it is the *g.* of asps within him	*Job 20:14*
sword cometh out of his *g.*	*Job 20:25*
arrow goes through his back (B)	*Job 20:25*
gave me also *g.* for my meat	*Ps 69:21*
given us water of *g.* to drink	*Jer 8:14*
has given us a poisonous drink (B)(R)	*Jer 8:14*
give them water of *g.* to drink	*Jer 9:15*
give them poisonous water (B)(R)	*Jer 9:15*
make them drink the water of *g.*	*Jer 23:15*
compassed me with *g.* and travel	*La 3:5*
misery, the wormwood and the *g.*	*La 3:19*
ye have turned judgment into *g.*	*Am 6:12*
turned justice into wormwood (B)	*Am 6:12*
justice into poison (R)	*Am 6:12*
vinegar to drink mingled with *g.*	*M't 27:34*
thou art in the *g.* of bitterness	*Ac 8:23*

GALLANT

neither shall *g.* ship pass thereby	*Isa 32:21*

GALLANTLY

fight *g.* (N)	*1Ti 1:18*

GALLON

an honest *g.* (B)	*Le 19:36*
half a *g.* of oil (B)	*Eze 46:14*

GALLONS

1½ *g.* of oil (B)	*Eze 45:24*
a thousand *g.* of oil (N)	*Lu 16:6*

GALLERIES

the king is held in the *g.*	*Ca 7:5*
and the *g.* thereof on the one side	*Eze 41:15*
windows, and the *g.* round about	*Eze 41:16*
for the *g.* were higher than these	*Eze 42:5*

GALLERY

g. against *g.* in three stories	*Eze 42:3*

GALLEY

wherein shall go no *g.* with oars	*Isa 33:21*

GALLIM

son of Laish, which was of *G.*	*1Sa 25:44*
Lift up thy voice, O daughter of *G.*	*Isa 10:30*

GALLIO

G. was the deputy of Achaia	*Ac 18:12*
G. said unto the Jews, If it were a	*Ac 18:14*
And *G.* cared for none of those	*Ac 18:17*

GALLOWS

a *g.* be made of fifty cubits high	*Es 5:14*
he caused the *g.* to be made	*Es 5:14*
to hang Mordecai on the *g.* that he	*Es 6:4*
Behold also, the *g.* fifty cubits high	*Es 7:9*

So they hanged Haman on the *g.* — *Es 7:10*

they have hanged upon the *g.* — *Es 8:7*

ten sons be hanged upon the *g.* — *Es 9:13*

his sons should be hanged on the *g.* — *Es 9:25*

GAMALIEL

Manasseh; *G.* the son of Pedahzur — *Nu 1:10*

of Manasseh shall be *G.* the son of — *Nu 2:20*

offered *G.* the son of Pedahzur — *Nu 7:54*

this was the offering of *G.* the son — *Nu 7:59*

of the children of Manasseh was *G.* — *Nu 10:23*

a Pharisee, named *G.* a doctor of — *Ac 5:34*

in this city at the feet of *G.* — *Ac 22:3*

GAME

did eat of his *g.* (A)(B)(R) — *Ge 25:28; 27:3, 5, 7, 19, 25, 31, 33*

made great *g.* of knocking him about (P) — *Lu 22:63*

GAMMADIMS

and the *G.* were in thy towers — *Eze 27:11*

GAMUL

the two and twentieth to *G.* — *1Ch 24:17*

GANG

set over them *g.* foreman (B) — *Ex 1:11*

GANGRENE

spread like *g.* (A)(B)(E)(N)(R) — *2Ti 2:17*

GAP

and stand in the *g.* before me — *Eze 22:30*

GAPED

g. upon me with their mouth — *Job 16:10*

g. upon me with their mouths — *Ps 22:13*

GAPS

Ye have not gone up into the *g.* — *Eze 13:5*

GARDEN

God took the man and put him in the *g.* — *Ge 2:15*

Lord sent him forth from the *g.* of Eden — *Ge 3:23*

the plain of Jordan was as the *g.* of the Lord — *Ge 13:10*

and waterest it as a *g.* of herbs — *De 11:10*

that I may have it for a *g.* of herbs — *1Ki 21:2*

his branch shooteth forth in his *g.* — *Job 8:16*

a *g.* inclosed is my sister, my spouse — *Ca 4:12*

blow upon my *g.* let him come into his *g.* — *Ca 4:16*

I am come into my *g.* my sister, my spouse — *Ca 5:1*

my beloved is gone down into his *g.* — *Ca 6:2; 6:11*

the daughter of Zion is as a lodge in a *g.* — *Isa 1:8*

ye shall be as a *g.* which hath no water — *Isa 4:30*

he will make her desert like the *g.* of God — *Isa 51:3*

and thou shalt be like a watered *g.* — *Isa 58:11*

as the *g.* causeth things sown to spring — *Isa 61:11*

their souls shall be as a watered *g.* — *Jer 31:12*

taken away his tabernacle as it were of a *g.* — *La 2:6*

thou hast been in Eden the *g.* of God — *Eze 28:13*

cedars in *g.* of God could not hide him — *Eze 31:8*

all the trees in the *g.* of God envied him — *Eze 31:9*

desolate land is become like the *g.* of Eden — *Eze 36:35*

land is as the *g.* of Eden before them — *Joe 2:3*

which a man took and cast into his *g.* — *Lu 13:19*

over the brook Cedron, where was a *g.* — *Joh 18:1*

did not I see thee in the *g.* with him — *Joh 18:26*

there was a *g.* and in the *g.* a sepulchre — *Joh 19:41*

God's *g.*, vineyard (A)(N) — *1Co 3:9*

GARDENER

my Father is the *g.* (N) — *Joh 15:1*

She, supposing him to be the *g.* — *Joh 20:15*

GARDENS

forth, as *g.* by the river's side — *Nu 24:6*

I made me *g.* and orchards — *Ec 2:5*

I laid out *g.* and parks (B)(E)(R) — *Ec 2:5*

of *g.* a well of living waters — *Ca 4:15*

in the *g.* and to gather lilies — *Ca 6:2*

Thou that dwellest in the *g.* — *Ca 8:13*

for the *g.* that ye have chosen — *Isa 1:29*

that sacrificeth in *g.* and burneth — *Isa 65:3*

the *g.* behind one tree in the midst — *Isa 66:17*

plant *g.* and eat the fruit of them — *Jer 29:5*

plant *g.* and eat the fruit of them — *Jer 29:28*

when your *g.* and your vineyards — *Am 4:9*

make *g.* and eat the fruit of them — *Am 9:14*

GAREB

Ira an Ithrite, *G.* an Ithrite — *2Sa 23:38*

Ira the Ithrite, *G.* the Ithrite — *1Ch 11:40*

upon the hill *G.* and shall compass — *Jer 31:39*

GARLAND

a fair *g.* upon head (B)(R) — *Pr 1:9; 4:9*

deck with a *g.* (A)(E)(R) — *Isa 61:10*

g. of righteousness (N) — *2Ti 4:8*

unfading *g.* of glory (N) — *1Pe 5:4*

a crown like *g.* (A) — *Re 12:1*

GARLANDS

brought oxen and *g.* unto the gates — *Ac 14:13*

GARLICK

leeks, and the onions, and the *g.* — *Nu 11:5*

GARMENT

Shem and Japheth took a *g.* and laid it — *Ge 9:23*

got a robe and laid it on (B) — *Ge 9:23*

the first came out red, like a hairy *g.* — *Ge 25:25*

like a hairy coat (B) — *Ge 25:25*

like a hairy mantle (R) — *Ge 25:25*

she caught Joseph by his *g.* he left his *g.* — *Ge 39:12*

caught hold of his coat (B) — *Ge 39:12*

he left his *g.* with me and fled out — *Ge 39:15; 39:18*

she laid up his *g.* till her lord came home — *Ge 39:16*

sprinkled of the blood thereof on any *g.* — *Le 6:27*

g. wherein is the plague of leprosy — *Le 13:47; 13:49*

if plague be spread in the *g.* in warp or woof — *Le 13:51*

the law of the plague of leprosy in a *g.* — *Le 13:59; 14:55*

every *g.* whereon is the seed of copulation — *Le 15:17*

nor *g.* mingled come on thee — *Le 19:19; De 22:11*

a man shall not put on a woman's *g.* — *De 22:5*

when I saw a goodly Babylonish *g.* — *Jos 7:21*

an attractive mantle (A) — *Jos 7:21*

a beautiful robe (B) — *Jos 7:21*

a goodly Babylonish mantle (E)(R) — *Jos 7:21; 7:24*

Joshua took Achan, the silver, and the *g.* — *Jos 7:24*

they spread a *g.* and cast earrings — *J'g 8:25*

Lamar had a *g.* of divers colours on her — *2Sa 13:18*

long robe with sleeves (A)(R) — *2Sa 13:18; 13:19*

long-sleeved dress (B) — *2Sa 13:18; 13:19*

she rent her *g.* and went on crying — *2Sa 13:19*

Jeroboam clad himself with a new *g.* — *1Ki 11:29*

a new robe (B) — *1Ki 11:29*

took every man his *g.* and put under him — *2Ki 9:13*

when I heard this I rent my *g.* and mantle — *Ezr 9:3*

having rent my *g.* and mantle I fell on knees — *Ezr 9:5*

Mordecai went with a *g.* of purple — *Es 8:15*

consumeth, as a *g.* that is moth-eaten — *Job 13:28*

by force of my disease is my *g.* changed — *Job 30:18*

when I made the cloud the *g.* thereof — *Job 38:9*

made the clouds its clothes (B) — *Job 38:9*

it is turned as clay to the seal, they stand as a — *Job 38:14*

who can discover the face of his *g.* — *Job 41:13*

I made sackcloth also my *g.* — *Ps 69:11*

sackcloth for clothing (A)(B)(E)(R) — *Ps 69:11*

pride compasseth, violence covereth them as a *g.* — *Ps 73:6*

they shall perish, yea, all of them shall wax old like a *g.* — *Ps 102:26; 51:6; Heb 1:11*

as a *g.* (A)(E) — *Ps 102:26; Re 19:16*

thou coverest thyself with light, as with a *g.* — *Ps 104:2*

as with a robe (B) — *Ps 104:2*

thou coveredst it with the deep as with a *g.* — *Ps 104:6*

he clothed himself with cursing as a *g.* — *Ps 109:18*

as with a coat (B)(R) — *Ps 109:18*

let it be to him as the *g.* which covereth him — *Ps 109:19*

be as robe he wraps around (B) — *Ps 109:19*

as raiment he covereth (E) — *Ps 109:19*

take his *g.* that is surety — *Pr 20:16; 27:13*

as he that taketh away a *g.* in cold weather — *Pr 25:20*

who hath bound the waters in a *g.* — *Pr 30:4*

my *g.* (A)(E)(R) — *Ca 5:3*

the moth shall eat them up like a *g.* — *Isa 51:8*

to give a *g.* of praise for the spirit of heaviness — *Isa 61:3*

a mantle of praise (B)(R) — *Isa 61:3*

as a shepherd putteth on his *g.* — *Jer 43:12*

hath covered the naked with a *g.* — *Eze 18:7; 18:16*

clothes naked with a robe (B) — *Eze 18:7*

whose *g.* was white as snow — *Da 7:9*

clothing was as white as snow (B) — *Da 7:9*

raiment was as white as snow (E)(R) — *Da 7:9*

ye pull off the robe with the *g.* from them — *Mic 2:8*

if one bear holy flesh in the   *Hag 2:12*
skirt of his *g.*
neither shall wear a rough *g.*   *Zec 13:4*
to deceive
mantle of hair to deceive   *Zec 13:4*
(B)(E)(R)
for one covereth violence with *Mal 2:16*
his *g.*
covers his clothing with   *Mal 2:16*
cruelty (B)
takes your outer *g.* (A)   *M't 8:29*
new cloth to old *g.*   *M't 9:16;*
       M'k 2:21; Lu 5:36
patch on an old coat   *M't 9:16*
(B)(N)(P)
a woman diseased touched   *M'k 9:20;*
the hem of his *g.* *21; 14:36; M'k 5:27;*
       Lu 8:44
touched fringe of robe (B)   *M't 9:20*
touched edge of his cloak   *M't 9:20*
(N)(P)
saw a man who had not   *M't 22:11;*
on a wedding *g.*   *22:12*
not dressed in wedding robe *M't 22:11*
(B)
not dressed for the wedding *M't 22:11*
(N)(P)
not turn back again to take   *M'k 13:16*
up his *g.*
turn back to get his mantle *M'k 13:16*
(A)(R)
turn back to pick up his   *M'k 13:16*
coat (B)(P)
turn back to get his cloak   *M'k 13:16*
(E)(P)
young man clothed with   *M'k 16:5*
long white *g.*
clothed in robe of white   *M'k 16:5*
(A)(B)(E)(N)(P)(R)
let him sell his *g.* and buy   *Lu 22:36*
one
sell his mantle and buy   *Lu 22:36*
sword (A)(R)
sell his coat and buy one   *Lu 22:36*
(B)(P)
sell his cloak and buy a   *Lu 22:36*
sword (E)(N)
cast thy *g.* about thee and   *Ac 12:8*
follow me
put on your coat and follow *Ac 12:8*
me (B)
wrap your cloak around you *Ac 12:8*
(N)(P)
Wrap your mantle around   *Ac 12:8*
you (R)
hating even the *g.* spotted by the *Jude 23*
flesh
loathing even the clothing   *Jude 23*
polluted (B)(N)
Son of man clothed with a *g.* *Re 1:13*
down to foot
dressed in a robe   *Re 1:13*
(A)(B)(P)(R)
robed down to the feet (N)   *Re 1:13*
clothed in a *g.* (N)   *Re 19:13*

GARMENTS

g. of skins (R)   *Ge 3:21*
g. and gave (A)   *Ge 24:53*
and be clean, and change   *Ge 35:2*
your *g.*
clothes (B)   *Ge 35:2; Nu 15:38;*
2Sa 13:31; 2Ki 7:15; 25:29; Job 37:17;
Ec 9:8; Eze 42:14; 44:19; Da 3:21
Tamar put her widow's *g.*   *Ge 38:14*
off from her
widow's weeds (B)   *Ge 38:14*
fine line *g.* (B)(R)   *Ge 41:42*
washed his *g.* in wine, his   *Ge 49:11*
clothes in grapes
may make Aaron's *g.* to   *Ex 28:3*
consecrate him
sprinkled the blood on   *Ex 29:21;*
Aaron's *g.*   *Le 8:30*
I have given them wisdom   *Ex 31:10*
to make *g.*
put off his *g.* put on other *g.* *Le 6:11;*
       16:23, 24
make fringes in the borders *Nu 15:38*
of their *g.*
strip Aaron of his *g.* put   *Nu 20:26*
them on Eleazar
robes (B)   *Nu 20:26;*
20:28; 1Sa 18:4; 2Sa 10:4; Ps 45:8;
       Isa 59:17; 61:10
Moses stript Aaron of *g.*   *Nu 20:28*
put them on Eleazar
Gibeonites brought old *g.*   *Jos 9:5*
mouldy bread

garments (B)   *Jos 22:8;*
   2Ki 7:8; Job 27:16; Zec 3:4
I will give you thirty change *J'g 14:12*
of *g.*
thirty changes of raiment   *J'g 14:12*
(A)
thirty linen tunics (B)   *J'g 14:12*
linen *g.* (S)   *J'g 14:12; 14:13*
Jonathan gave David his *g.*   *1Sa 18:4*
cut off their *g.* in the middle *2Sa 10:4;*
       1Ch 19:4
David tare his *g.* and lay   *2Sa 13:31*
on the earth
is it a time to receive money *2Ki 5:26*
and *g.*
to take money and suits (B) *2Ki 5:26*
all the way was full of *g.*   *2Ki 7:15*
and vessels
he changed Jehoiakim's *g.*   *2Ki 25:29;*
       Jer 52:33
they gave one hundred   *Ezr 2:69*
priests' *g.*
the Tirshatha gave 530   *Ne 7:70*
priests' *g.*
the people gave sixty-seven *Ne 7:72*
priests' *g.*
how thy *g.* are warm, when *Job 37:17*
he quieteth
they part my *g.* among them, *Ps 22:18*
cast lots
all thy *g.* smell of myrrh,   *Ps 45:8*
aloes, and cassia
ointment that went down to *Ps 133:2*
skirts of his *g.*
let thy *g.* be always white, and *Ec 9:8*
thy head
smell of thy *g.* is like smell   *Ca 4:11*
of Lebanon
every battle is with *g.* rolled   *Isa 9:5*
in blood
every coat rolled in blood (B) *Isa 9:5*
put on thy beautiful *g.* O   *Isa 52:1*
Jerusalem
apparel (B)   *Isa 52:1; 63:1*
their webs shall not become *g.* *Isa 59:6*
clothing (B)   *Isa 59:6; 63:3; Lu 24:4*
he put on the *g.* of   *Isa 59:17*
vengeance for clothing
he hath clothed me with the *Isa 61:10*
g. of salvation
that cometh with dyed *g.*   *Isa 63:1*
from Bozrah
their blood shall be sprinkled *Isa 63:3*
upon my *g.*
yet they were not afraid,   *Jer 36:24*
nor rent *g.*
rags and worn-out *g.* (S)   *Jer 38:11;*
       38:12
so that men could not touch *La 4:14*
their *g.*
tookest thy broidered *g.* and *Eze 16:18*
covered them
there shall lay their *g.* they *Eze 42:14*
ministered in
they shall not sanctify   *Eze 44:19*
people with their *g.*
were bound in their coats   *Da 3:21*
and other *g.*
wore their *g.* (A)   *Da 5:27*
rend your heart, and not   *Joe 2:13*
your *g.*
Joshua was clothed with filthy *Zec 3:3*
g.
saying, Take away the filthy *Zec 3:4*
g. from him
garments (A)   *Zec 3:4;*
11:8; 27:31; 28:3; M'k 9:3; Lu 7:25;
   23:34; Joh 19:4; Ac 22:20; Re 3:5
spread their *g.* in the way   *M't 21:8;*
       M'k 11:8
clothes (B)   *M't 21:8;*
   M'k 11:7; Jas 5:2; Re 3:4; 16:15
they enlarge the borders of *M't 23:5*
their *g.*
enlarge their law-reminding *M't 23:5*
tassels (B)
they parted his *g.* casting   *M't 27:35;*
lots   *M'k 15:24*
cast lots for my *g.* (R)   *M't 27:35*
Bartimaeus casting away his *M'k 10:50*
g. arose
throwing off his coat (B)   *M'k 10:50*
they cast their *g.* on the   *M'k 11:7;*
colt   *Lu 19:35*
spread *g.* on road   *M'k 11:8*
(A)(B)(E)(R)
two men stood by them in   *Lu 24:4*
shining *g.*

he laid aside his *g.* and took *Joh 13:4*
a towel
laid aside his robe (B)   *Joh 13:4*
cast lots for my *g.* (N)(P) *Joh 19:24*
shewing coats and *g.* which *Ac 9:39*
Dorcas made
undergarments (B)   *Ac 9:39*
he shook his *g.* (B)   *Ac 18:6*
and your *g.* are moth-eaten *Jas 5:2*
g. their deeds defiled (P)   *Jude 23*
few names which have not   *Re 3:4*
defiled their *g.*
blessed that watcheth and   *Re 16:15*
keepeth his *g.*

HOLY GARMENTS

thou shalt make *holy g.* for *Ex 28:2;*
Aaron   *28:4*
I have put wisdom to make *Ex 31:10*
holy g.
these are *holy g.* he shall   *Le 16:4;*
wash   *16:32*
lay their *holy g.* wherein   *Eze 42:14*
they minister

GARMITE

Keilah the G. and Eshtemoa *1Ch 4:19*

GARNER

gather his wheat into the *g.* *M't 3:12;*
       Lu 3:17
gather wheat into his barn   *M't 3:12*
(A)
store in the granary   *M't 3:12*
(B)(N)(P)(R)

GARNERS

our *g.* may be full,   *Ps 144:13*
affording store
our granaries filled (B)(R)   *Ps 144:13;*
       Joe 1:17
the *g.* are laid desolate,   *Joe 1:17*
barns broken down

GARNISH

and *g.* the sepulchres of the *M't 23:29*

GARNISHED

And he *g.* the house with   *2Ch 3:6*
precious
adorned the house (A)   *2Ch 3:6*
decorated (B)   *2Ch 3:6; M't 23:29*
his spirit he hath *g.* the   *Job 26:13*
heavens
breath skies are cleared   *Job 26:13*
(A)(B)
by wind are heavens made *Job 26:13*
fair (R)
he findeth it empty, swept, *M't 12:44*
and *g.*
swept, put in order,   *M't 12:44*
decorated (A)(R)
cleaned and orderly (B)(P) *M't 12:44*
swept clean and tidy (N)   *M't 12:44*
he findeth it swept and *g.*   *Lu 11:25*
of the wall of the city were *Re 21:19*
g.
ornamented with (A)(B)   *Re 21:19*
adorned with all manner   *Re 21:19*
(E)(N)(R)
fashioned out of every kind *Re 21:19*
(P)

GARRISON

where is the *g.* of the   *1Sa 10:5*
Philistines
Jonathan smote the *g.* of the *1Sa 13:3*
had smitten a *g.* of the   *1Sa 13:4*
Philistines
the *g.* of the Philistines   *1Sa 13:23*
went out
let us go over to the   *1Sa 14:1*
Philistines' *g.*
to go over unto the   *1Sa 14:4*
Philistines' *g.*
Come, and let us go over   *1Sa 14:6*
unto the *g.*
unto the *g.* of the   *1Sa 14:11*
Philistines: and
men of the *g.* answered   *1Sa 14:12*
Jonathan
people, the *g.* and the   *1Sa 14:15*
spoilers

and the *g.* of the Philistines   *2Sa 23:14*
the Philistines' *g.* was then   *1Ch 11:16*
king kept the city of,   *2Co 11:32*
with a *g.*

GARRISONS

Then David put *g.* in Syria of   *2Sa 8:6*
And he put *g.* in Edom   *2Sa 8:14*
throughout all Edom put he   *2Sa 8:14*
g.
Then David put *g.* in   *1Ch 18:6*
Syria-damascus
And he put *g.* in Edom   *1Ch 18:13*
and set *g.* in the land of   *2Ch 17:2*
Judah
and thy strong *g.* shall go   *Eze 26:11*
down

GASHES

upon all hands shall be *g.*   *Jer 48:37*
(S)

GASHMU

and *G.* saith it, that thou and   *Ne 6:6*

GASP

g. and pant together   *Isa 42:14*
(A)(B)(E)(R)

GAT

And Abraham *g.* up early in   *Ge 19:27*
and *g.* him up into the   *Ex 24:18*
mount
And Moses *g.* him into the   *Nu 11:30*
camp
and *g.* them up into the top   *Nu 14:40*
so they *g.* up from the   *Nu 16:27*
tabernacle
Abimelech *g.* him up to mount   *J'g 9:48*
and *g.* them up to the top of   *J'g 9:51*
the man rose up, and *g.* him   *J'g 19:28*
unto
And Samuel arose, and *g.*   *1Sa 13:15*
him up
David and his men *g.* them   *1Sa 24:22*
up unto
and they *g.* them away, and   *1Sa 26:12*
and *g.* them away through the   *2Sa 4:7*
And David *g.* him a name   *2Sa 8:13*
when
every man *g.* him up upon   *2Sa 13:29*
and *g.* him home to his   *2Sa 17:23*
house
And the people *g.* them by   *2Sa 19:3*
stealth
him with clothes, but he *g.* no   *1Ki 1:1*
heat
the pains of hell *g.* hold   *Ps 116:3*
upon me
I *g.* me men singers and   *Ec 2:8*
women
We *g.* our bread with the peril   *La 5:9*

GATAM

Omar, Zepho, and *G.* and   *Ge 36:11*
Kenaz
Duke Korah, duke *G.* and   *Ge 36:16*
duke
Omar, Zephi, and *G.*, Kenaz   *1Ch 1:36*

GATE

thy seed possess the *g.* of   *Ge 22:17;*
enemies   *24:60*
Jacob said, This is the *g.* of   *Ge 28:17*
heaven
go in and out from *g.* to *g.*   *Ex 32:27*
throughout camp
his father shall bring him to   *De 21:19*
the *g.*
bring them both out to the   *De 22:24*
g. of the city
let his brother's wife go up   *De 25:7*
to the *g.*
they were gone out, they shut   *Jos 2:7*
the *g.*
Samson took the doors of the   *J'g 16:3*
g.
then went Boaz to the *g.* and   *Ru 4:1*
sat down
the name of the dead be not   *Ru 4:10*
cut off from the *g.*

Eli fell backward by the side   *1Sa 4:18*
of the *g.*
Absalom stood beside the   *2Sa 15:2*
way of the *g.*
watchman called to the *g.* (R)   *2Sa 18:26*
the king went up to the   *2Sa 18:33*
chamber over the *g.*
water of Beth-lehem, by *g.*   *2Sa 23:15;*
  1Ch 11:18
when Elijah came to the *g.*   *1Ki 17:10*
of the city
a lord to have the charge of   *2Ki 7:17*
the *g.*
and they cast lots for every   *1Ch 26:13*
g.
he appointed the porters at   *2Ch 8:14*
every *g.*
Dragon's well, and Dung *G.*   *Ne 2:13*
(A)(B)(E)(R)
I commanded the *g.* should   *Ne 13:19*
be shut
Mordecai came before the   *Es 4:2;*
king's *g.*   *6:12*
when I went out to the *g.*   *Job 29:7*
and prepared
this *g.* of the Lord, the   *Ps 118:20*
righteous enter
thine eyes like the fish-pools   *Ca 7:4*
by the *g.*
howl, O *g.* cry, O city, shall   *Isa 14:31*
come smoke
the *g.* is smitten with   *Isa 24:12*
destruction
to them that turn the battle   *Isa 28:6*
to the *g.*
Baruch read at the entry of   *Jer 36:10*
new *g.*
the elders have ceased from   *La 5:14*
the *g.*
brought me to the door of the   *Eze 8:3*
inner *g.*
at the door of the *g.*   *Eze 11:1*
twenty-five men
the glory of the Lord came   *Eze 43:4*
by way of the *g.*
this *g.* shall be shut, none   *Eze 44:2*
shall enter
prince shall enter by the   *Eze 44:3;*
way of the *g.*   *46:2, 8*
put the blood on the posts   *Eze 45:19*
of the *g.*
the *g.* of the inner court   *Eze 46:1*
shall be shut
but the *g.* shall not be shut   *Eze 46:2*
till evening
one shall open him the *g.*   *Eze 46:12*
one shall shut the *g.*
one *g.* of Reuben, one *g.* of   *Eze 48:31*
Judah, of Levi
not entered into the *g.* of my   *Ob 13*
people
he is come into the *g.* of my   *Mic 1:9*
people to Jerusalem
evil came down from Lord   *Mic 1:12*
to the *g.* of Jerusalem
they have passed through the   *Mic 2:13*
g.
enter in at the strait *g.* wide   *M't 7:13;*
is the *g.* and broad is the   *7:14;*
  Lu 13:24
when he came nigh the *g.* of   *Lu 7:12*
the city
a beggar Lazarus laid at his   *Lu 16:20*
g. full of sores
near the sheep *g.*   *Joh 5:2*
(A)(B)(E)(P)(R)
men from Cornelius stood   *Ac 10:17*
before the *g.*
they came to the iron *g.*   *Ac 12:10*
which opened
Rhoda opened not the *g.* for   *Ac 12:14*
gladness
Jesus also suffered without   *Heb 13:12*
the *g.*
every several *g.* was of one   *Re 21:21*
pearl

AT THE GATE

of all that went in at the *g.*   *Ge 23:10;*
of city   *23:18*
as Jehu entered in *at the g.*   *2Ki 9:31*
she said
third part be *at the g.* of   *2Ki 11:6;*
Sur. and third *at the g.*   *2Ch 23:5*
behind the guard
which were on a man's left   *2Ki 23:8*
hand *at the g.*
set a chest *at the g.* of the   *2Ch 24:8*
house of Lord

I see Mordecai sitting *at the*   *Es 5:13*
king's *g.*
horsemen set themselves in   *Isa 22:7*
array *at the g.*
they laid daily *at the g.* of the   *Ac 3:2*
temple
who sat for alms *at beautiful*   *Ac 3:10*
g. of the temple

HIGH GATE

they came through the *high*   *2Ch 23:20*
g.
Jotham built the *high g.* of   *2Ch 27:3*
the house
put Jeremiah in the stocks in   *Jer 20:2*
the *high g.*

IN THE GATE

and Lot sat *in the g.* of   *Ge 19:1*
Sodom
Moses stood *in the g.* of the   *Ex 32:26*
camp
bring tokens of virginity to   *De 22:15*
elders *in g.*
they laid wait for Samson *in*   *J'g 16:2*
the *g.*
people *in the g.* said, We are   *Ru 4:11*
witnesses
Saul drew near to Samuel *in*   *1Sa 9:18*
the *g.*
Joab took Abner aside *in the*   *2Sa 3:27*
g.
king sat *in the g.* they told   *2Sa 19:8*
all the people
two measures for a shekel *in*   *2Ki 7:1;*
the *g.*   *7:18*
the people trod on him *in*   *2Ki 7:20*
the *g.* and he died
Mordecai sat *in the* king's *g.*   *Es 2:19;*
  2:21
when Haman saw him *in the*   *Es 5:9*
king's *g.*
his children are crushed *in*   *Job 5:4*
the *g.*
when I saw my help *in the*   *Job 31:21*
g.
they that sit *in the g.* speak   *Ps 69:12*
against me
they shall speak with the   *Ps 127:5*
enemies *in g.*
nor oppress the afflicted *in*   *Pr 22:22*
the *g.*
he openeth not his mouth *in*   *Pr 24:7*
the *g.*
lay a snare for him that   *Isa 29:21*
reproveth *in g.*
stand *in the g.* of the Lord's   *Jer 7:2*
house
stand *in the g.* of the   *Jer 17:19*
children of people
when he was *in the g.* of   *Jer 37:13*
Benjamin
the king then sitting *in the g.*   *Jer 38:7*
of Benjamin
all the princes of Babylon sat   *Jer 39:3*
in the g.
but Daniel sat *in the g.* of   *Da 2:49*
the king
they hate him that rebuketh   *Am 5:10*
in the g.
they turn aside the poor *in*   *Am 5:12*
the *g.*
hate evil, and establish   *Am 5:15*
judgment *in the g.*

OLD GATE

the *old g.* repaired Jehoiada   *Ne 3:6*
son of Paseah
the priests went above the   *Ne 12:39*
old g. and fish-gate

PRISON GATE

and they stood still in the   *Ne 12:39*
prison g.

SHEEP GATE

they went even unto the   *Ne 12:39*
sheep g.

VALLEY GATE

Uzziah built towers at the   *2Ch 26:9*
valley g.
and I went out by the *g.* of   *Ne 2:13*
the *valley*

and I entered by the *g.* of the   Ne 2:15
valley
the *valley g.* repaired Hanun   Ne 3:13

WATER GATE

Nethinims dwelt over against   Ne 3:26
water g.
gathered into the street before   Ne 8:1
the *water g.*
he read in the law before the   Ne 8:3
water g.
made booths in the street of   Ne 8:16
the *water g.*
priests went even to the   Ne 12:37
water g. eastward

GATEKEEPER

watchman called to *g.*   2Sa 18:26
(A)(B)
g., doorkeeper (A)(B)(R)   2Ki 7:10;
   1Ch 9:21; 2Ch 31:14
the *g.* opens (R)   Joh 10:3

GATEKEEPERS

the *g.* were called   2Ki 7:11
(A)(B)(R)
the *g.* were (A)(B)(R)   1Ch 9:17;
   23:5
the *g.*, doorkeepers   1Ch 9:18;
(A)(B)(R) 9:22, 24, 26; 15:18; 16:38;
   2Ch 23:4; 34:13
divisions of *g.* (A)(B)(R)   1Ch 26:1;
   26:12, 19; 2Ch 8:14
the *g.* at (A)   2Ch 35:15
set *g.* at (A)(B)(R) 2Ch 23:19; 35:15
g., doorkeepers (A)(B)(R)   Ezr 2:7;
7:7, 24; 10:24; Ne 7:1, 73; 10:28, 39;
   11:19; 12:25, 45, 47; 13:5

GATES

rejoice, ye and Levite,   De 12:12
within your *g.*
in his youngest son set up *g.*   Jos 6:26;
   1Ki 16:34
chose new gods, then was war *J'g* 5:8
in the *g.*
the people of the Lord shall *J'g* 5:11
go to the *g.*
Hezekiah appointed to   2Ch 31:2
praise in the *g.*
the *g.* are burnt with fire   Ne 1:3;
   1:2-3, 13, 17
let not the *g.* of Jerusalem be Ne 7:3
opened
the priests and Levites   Ne 12:30
purified the *g.*
some of my servants set I at   Ne 13:19
the *g.*
I commanded the Levites to   Ne 13:22
keep the *g.*
may shew forth thy praise in   Ps 9:14
the *g.*
lift up your heads, O ye *g.*   Ps 24:7
and be ye lift up
the Lord loveth the *g.* of   Ps 87:2;
Zion, more than   87:9
enter into his *g.* with   Ps 100:4
thanksgiving
for he hath broken the *g.*   Ps 107:16
of brass
open to me the *g.* of   Ps 118:19
righteousness
wisdom crieth in the   Pr 1:21;
openings of *g.*   Pr 8:3
that heareth me, watching   Pr 8:34
daily at my *g.*
the wicked at the *g.* of the   Pr 14:19
righteous
her husband is known in the   Pr 31:23
g.
let her own works praise her   Pr 31:31
in the *g.*
at our *g.* are all manner of   Pr 7:13
pleasant fruits
and her *g.* shall lament and   Isa 3:26
mourn
they may go into the *g.* of   Isa 13:2
the nobles
open ye the *g.* that the   Isa 26:2
righteous may enter
I shall go to the *g.* of the   Isa 38:10
grave
to open before him the   Isa 45:1
two-leaved *g.*
I will break in pieces the *g.*   Isa 45:2
of brass

go thro', go thro' the *g.*   Isa 62:10
prepare the way
hear, ye that enter in at the   Jer 7:2;
g.   17:20; 22:2
Judah mourneth, and the *g.*   Jer 14:2
languish
I will fan them with a fan in   Jer 15:7
g. of the land
go and stand in all the *g.* of   Jer 17:19
Jerusalem
bear no burden on the   Jer 17:21;
sabbath by the *g.*   17:24
then shall there enter into   Jer 17:25;
the *g.*   22:4
I will kindle a fire in the *g.* Jer 17:27;
of Jerusalem
shall be drawn and cast   Jer 22:19
forth beyond the *g.*
Zion's *g.* are desolate, her   La 1:4
priests sigh
her *g.* are sunk into the   La 2:9
ground, bars broken
the adversary should have   La 4:12
entered the *g.*
I have set point of sword   Eze 21:15
against their *g.*
to appoint battering rams   Eze 21:22
against the *g.*
she is broken that was the *g.* Eze 26:2
of the people
at the east side three *g.* one Eze 48:32
of Joseph
in the day that foreigners   Ob 11
entered his *g.*
the *g.* of the rivers shall be   Na 2:6
opened
the *g.* of thy land shall be set Na 3:13
wide open
execute the judgment of truth   Zec 8:16
and peace in your *g.*
the *g.* of hell shall not   M't 16:18
prevail against it
and they watched the *g.* to   Ac 9:24
kill Paul
Jupiter's priests brought   Ac 14:13
oxen to the *g.*
the city had twelve *g.* at *g.*   Re 21:12
twelve angels
on the east three *g.* on the   Re 21:13
north, three *g.*
the twelve *g.* were twelve   Re 21:21
pearls
each one of the *g.* (S)   Re 21:21
g. of it shall not be shut Re 21:25
at all by day

THY GATES

thy stranger within *thy g.*   Ex 20:10;
   De 5:14
thou shalt write them on *thy* De 6:9;
g.   11:20
thou mayest eat flesh in *thy* De 12:15;
g.   12:21
thou mayest not eat within   De 12:17
thy g. the tithe
thou must eat, thou and   De 12:18
Levite in *thy g.*
give it to the stranger that is De 14:21
in *thy g.*
Levite within *thy g.* thou   De 14:27
shalt not forsake
thou shalt lay up the tithe   De 14:28
within *thy g.*
the widow within *thy g.*   De 14:29
shall come and eat
if there be a poor man   De 15:7
within any of *thy g.*
thou shalt eat the firstling   De 15:22
within *thy g.*
not sacrifice the passover   De 16:5
within *thy g.*
shalt rejoice, and Levite in De 16:11;
thy g.   16:14; 26:12
judges and officers shalt   De 16:18
thou make in all *thy g.*
bring forth that man or   De 17:5
woman to *thy g.*
if a Levite come from any of De 18:6
thy g.
servant escaped dwell in one De 23:16
of *thy g.*
thou shalt not oppress   De 24:14
within *thy g.*
he shall besiege thee in all   De 28:52
thy g.
thine enemies shall distress De 28:55
thee in all *thy g.*

gather the people within *thy* De 31:12
g. to hear
our feet shall stand within   Ps 122:2
thy g. O Jerusalem
I will make *thy g.* of   Isa 54:12
carbuncles
therefore *thy g.* shall be   Isa 60:11
open continually
call thy walls salvation, and Isa 60:18
thy g. praise
when he shall enter *thy g.*   Eze 26:10
as men

GATH

let the ark be carried about   1Sa 5:8
to *G.*
these are the golden   1Sa 6:17
emerods, for *G.* one
it was told Saul, that David 1Sa 27:4
was fled to *G.*
tell it not in *G.* publish it   2Sa 1:20
not in Ashkelon
these four were born to 2Sa 21:22;
giant in *G.* and fell by   1Ch 20:8
hand of David
two servants of Shimei ran 1Ki 2:39
to *G.*
Shimei went to *G.* to seek   1Ki 2:40
his servants
Hazael went and fought   2Ki 12:17
against *G.*
Beraiah drove away   1Ch 8:13
inhabitants of *G.*
David took *G.* from the   1Ch 18:1
Philistines
Uzziah brake down the wall 2Ch 26:6
of *G.*
then go down to *G.* of the   Am 6:2
Philistines
declare ye it not at *G.* weep Mic 1:10
not at all

GATHER

he said, *G.* stones, and they   Ge 31:46
took stones
let them *g.* all the food of   Ge 41:35
those years
let them go and *g.* straw; *g.* Ex 5:7;
stubble   5:12
g. thy cattle; shall *g.* a   Ex 9:19;
certain rate   16:4
g. twice as much; six days *g.* Ex 16:5;
it   16:26
six years sow thy land and Ex 23:10;
g.   Le 25:3
shalt not *g.* the gleanings   Le 19:9;
   23:22
thou shalt not *g.* every grape Le 19:10
of thy vineyard
nor *g.* grapes of the vine   Le 25:5;
undressed   25:11
we shall not sow, nor *g.* in Le 25:20
our increase
if with one trumpet, then   Nu 10:4
princes *g.*
g. seventy men of the elders Nu 11:16
of Israel
a man that is clean shall *g.*   Nu 19:9
the ashes
I will give rain that thou   De 11:14
mayest *g.*
thou shalt *g.* all the spoil of De 13:16
it into street
plant a vineyard and not *g.* De 28:30;
grapes   28:39
carry much seed out, and *g.* De 28:38
but little in
he will *g.* thee from all   De 30:3;
nations   Eze 36:24
one went into the field to *g.* 2Ki 4:39
herbs
I will *g.* thee to thy fathers 2Ki 22:20;
   2Ch 34:28
send to brethren and Levites 1Ch 13:2
to *g.*
g. money to repair house of 2Ch 24:5
the Lord
yet will I *g.* them from thence Ne 1:9
some appointed to *g.* for the Ne 12:44
priests
they *g.* the vintage of the   Job 24:6
wicked
if he *g.* to himself his spirit Job 34:14
and his breath
will he bring seed, and *g.* it Job 39:12
into thy barn

g. not my soul with sinners, *Ps 26:9*
nor life
and knoweth not who shall g. *Ps 39:6*
that thou givest them they *Ps 104:28*
g.
save us, and g. us from *Ps 106:47*
among the heathen
shall g. for him that will pity *Pr 28:8*
the poor
to sinner travel to g. and *Ec 2:26*
heap up
my beloved is gone down to g. *Ca 6:2*
lilies
there the owl g. under her *Isa 34:15*
shadow
he shall g. the lambs with *Isa 40:11*
his arms
fear not, I will g. thee from *Isa 43:5*
the west
but with great mercies will I *Isa 54:7*
g. thee
yet will I g. others to him, *Isa 56:8*
besides those
cast up the highway, g. out *Isa 62:10*
the stones
I will g. all nations and *Isa 66:18*
tongues
g. to flee; the children g. *Jer 6:1;*
wood *7:18*
none shall g. them; g. up thy *Jer 9:22;*
wares *10:17*
I will g. the remnant of my *Jer 23:3*
flock
I will g. you from all the *Jer 29:14*
nations
I will g. them from the *Jer 31:8;*
coasts of the earth *32:37; Eze 20:34,*
41; 34:13
he that scattered Israel will *Jer 31:10*
g. him
g. ye wine, and *Jer 40:10*
summer fruits, and oil
and none shall g. up him that *Jer 49:5*
wandereth
I will even g. you from my *Eze 11:17*
people
I will g. all thy lovers *Eze 16:37*
against thee
I will g. you into the midst *Eze 22:19*
of Jerusalem
as they g. silver, so will I *Eze 22:20;*
g. you in fury *22:21*
g. the pieces; I will g. the *Eze 24:4;*
Egyptians *29:13*
I will g. them on every *Eze 37:21;*
side *39:17*
though hired among the *Ho 8:10*
nations, I will g.
Egypt shall g. them up, *Ho 9:6*
Memphis bury them
g. the elders and the *Joe 1:14*
inhabitants of land
people much pained, all faces *Joe 2:6*
shall g. blackness
g. the people, g. the children *Joe 2:16*
that suck
I will g. all nations, and bring *Joe 3:2*
them down
I will surely g. the remnant *Mic 2:12*
of Israel
I will g. her that was driven *Mic :6*
out *Zep 3:19*
he shall g. them as sheaves into *Mic 4:12*
the floor
g. thyself in troops, O *Mic 5:1*
daughter of troops
the faces of them all g. *Na 2:10*
blackness
they shall g. the captivity as *Hab 1:9*
the sand
they catch them, and g. *Hab 1:15*
them in their drag
for my determination is to g. *Zep 3:8*
the nations
I will g. them that are *Zep 3:18*
sorrowful for assembly
bring you even in the time *Zep 3:20*
that I g. you
I will hiss for them and g. *Zec 10:8*
them
and I will g. them out of *Zec 10:10*
Assyria
I will g. all nations against *Zec 14:2*
Jerusalem
g. his wheat into his garner *M't 3:12;*
Lu 3:17
they sow not, nor do they g. *M't 6:26*
into barns

do men g. grapes of thorns *M't 7:16;*
Lu 6:44
wilt thou that we go and g. *M't 13:28*
them up
he said, Nay, lest while ye *M't 13:29*
g. up the tares
burn tares, but g. the wheat *M't 13:30*
into my barn
shall g. out of his kingdom all *M't 13:41*
things that offend
and that I g. where I have *M't 25:26*
not strawed
as a hen doth g. her brood *Lu 13:34*
under wings
g. up the fragments that *Joh 6:12*
remain
men g. them and cast them *Joh 15:6*
into the fire
g. the clusters of the vine of *Re 14:18*
the earth
g. them to the battle of that *Re 16:14*
day of God

GATHER *TOGETHER*

I being few they shall g. *Ge 34:30*
together against me
g. yourselves *together*, ye *Ge 49:1;*
sons of Jacob *49:2*
go g. the elders of Israel *Ex 3:16*
together
g. congregation of Israel *Le 8:3;*
together *Nu 8:9*
and g. thou the assembly *Nu 20:8*
together
g. the people *together* *Nu 21:16;*
De 4:10; 31:12
g. the rest *together* and *2Sa 12:28*
encamp
save us, O God, and g. us *1Ch 16:35*
together
David commanded to g. *1Ch 22:2*
together the strangers
God put in my heart to g. *Ne 7:5*
together nobles
may g. *together* all the fair *Es 2:3*
virgins
g. *together* the Jews present *Es 4:16*
in Shushan
if he g. *together*, who can *Job 11:10*
hinder him
g. my saints *together* unto me *Ps 50:5*
they g. themselves *together* to *Ps 56:6*
mark my steps
they g. *together* against the *Ps 94:21*
righteous
the sun ariseth, they g. *Ps 104:22*
themselves *together*
there is a time to g. stones *Ec 3:5*
together
he shall g. *together* the *Isa 11:12*
dispersed of Judah
these g. *together* and come *Isa 49:18;*
to me *60:4*
they shall surely g. *together*, *Isa 54:15*
but not by me
blow the trumpet, cry, g. *Jer 4:5*
together
g. ye *together* and come *Jer 49:14*
against Edom
the king sent to g. *together* *Da 3:2*
the princes
g. yourselves *together* round *Joe 3:11*
about
g. *together*, yea, g. *together* *Zep 2:1*
O nation not desired
g. *together* first the tares, *M't 13:30*
and bind
they shall g. *together* his *M't 24:31;*
elect *M'k 13:27*
he should g. *together* in *Joh 11:52;*
one *Eph 1:10*
g. *together* to the supper of the *Re 19:17*
great God
to g. Gog and Magog *Re 20:8*
together to battle

GATHERED

Abraham died and was g. to *Ge 25:8*
his people
Ishmael was g.; Isaac was *Ge 25:17;*
g. to people *35:29*
Jacob was g. to his *Ge 49:29;*
people *49:33*
and they g. some more, *Ex 16:17*
some less
he that g. much, he that g. *Ex 16:18;*
little *2Co 8:15*

they g. it every morning, *Ex 16:21*
every man according
when thou hast g. in thy *Ex 23:16*
labours out of field
when ye have g. in the fruits *Le 23:39*
of the land
the people g. quails; g. *Nu 11:32;*
sticks *15:32*
Korah g. congregation *Nu 16:19;*
against Moses *16:42*
Aaron shall be g. to his *Nu 20:24;*
people *20:26*
Moses g. to his people *Nu 27:13;*
31:2; De 32:50
kings g. their meat under my *J'g 1:7*
table
that generation was g. to *J'g 2:10*
their fathers
and Abiezer was g. after him *J'g 6:34*
there were g. vain men to *J'g 11:3*
Jephthah
they g. all the lords of the *1Sa 5:8*
Philistines
every one that was in *1Sa 22:2*
distress g. to David
as water spilt which cannot *2Sa 14:14*
be g. up
they g. all able to put on *2Ki 3:21*
armour
Josiah be g. to grave in *2Ki 22:20;*
peace *2Ch 34:28*
all my servants were g. to the *Ne 5:16*
work
rich man lie down, but *Job 27:19*
shall not be g.
the mighty are g. against me *Ps 59:3*
he g. them out of the lands *Ps 107:3*
and herbs of the mountains *Pr 27:25*
are g.
who hath g. the wind in his *Pr 30:4*
fists
I g. me also silver and gold *Ec 2:8*
and treasure
I have g. my myrrh with my *Ca 5:1*
spice
he fenced it, and g. out the *Isa 5:2*
stones
as one gathereth eggs, have *Isa 10:14*
I g. the earth
ye shall be g. one by one, O *Isa 27:12*
Israel
vultures be g.; his Spirit g. *Isa 34:15;*
them *34:16*
though Israel be not g. yet shall *Isa 49:5*
I be glorious
I will gather others, besides *Isa 56:8*
those that are g.
but they that have g. it shall *Isa 62:9*
eat it
and all nations shall be g. *Jer 3:17*
unto it
they shall not be g. nor *Jer 8:2;*
buried *25:33*
all people g. against Jeremiah *Jer 26:9*
in house of Lord
all the Jews g. to thee *Jer 40:15*
should be scattered
when I shall have g. the *Eze 28:25*
house of Israel
thou shalt not be brought *Eze 29:5*
together nor g.
hast thou g. thy company *Eze 38:13*
to take a prey
have g. them out of their *Eze 39:27*
enemies' lands
but I have g. them to their *Eze 39:28*
own land
the people shall be g. *Ho 10:10*
against them
I am as when they g. the *Mic 7:1*
summer fruits
as tares are g. and burnt in *M't 13:40*
the fire
net cast into the sea, and g. *M't 13:47*
of every kind
before him shall be g. all *M't 25:32*
nations
and g. to him the whole *M't 27:27*
band of soldiers
then g. chief priests a *Joh 11:47*
council, and said
g. a company, set the city on *Ac 17:5*
an uproar
when Paul had g. a bundle of *Ac 28:3*
sticks
the angel g. the vine of the *Re 14:19*
earth

GATHERED *TOGETHER*

they *g.* them *together* upon Ex 8:14
heaps
when the congregation is to Nu 10:7
be *g. together*
shall all the fish of the sea Nu 11:22
be *g. together*
the congregation was *g.* J'g 20:1;
together as one man 20:11;
Ezr 3:1; Ne 8:1
Judah *g. together* to ask 2Ch 20:4
help of Lord
they *g.* themselves *together* Job 16:10
against me
under the nettles were they Job 30:7
g. together
the abjects *g.* themselves Ps 35:15
together against me
the princes of the people are Ps 47:9
g. together
when people are *g. together* Ps 102:22
to serve the Lord
continually are they *g.* Ps 140:2
together for war
then shall children of Judah Ho 1:11
be *g. together*
many nations are *g. together* Mic 4:11
against thee
tho' all people be *g. together* Zec 12:3
against it
where two or three are *g.* M't 18:20
together
how often would I have *g.* M't 23:37;
thy children *together* Lu 13:34
there will eagles be *g.* M't 24:28;
together Lu 17:37
all the city was *g. together* M'k 1:33
at the door
the younger son *g.* all Lu 15:13
together
they found the eleven *g.* Lu 24:33
together
rulers were *g. together* against Ac 4:26
the Lord
where many were *g. together* Ac 12:12
praying
when they had *g.* the church Ac 14:27
together
when ye are *g. together* and 1Co 5:4
my spirit
g. together into a place called Re 16:16
Armageddon
beast and his army *g.* Re 19:19
together to make war

GATHERER

and a *g.* of sycomore Am 7:14
fruit
tax *g.* (N) M't 10:3;
18:17; Lu 5:27; 18:10-11, 13

GATHERERS

tax *g.* (N) M't 5:46;
9:10, 11; 11:19; 21:31, 32; M'k 2:15,
16; Lu 3:12; 5:29, 30; 7:29, 34; 15:1;
19:2

GATHEREST

When thou *g.* the grapes of De 24:21
thy

GATHERETH

he that *g.* the ashes of the Nu 19:10
heifer
he *g.* the waters of the sea Ps 33:7
his heart *g.* iniquity to itself Ps 41:6
g. together the outcasts of Ps 147:2
Israel
and *g.* her food in the harvest Pr 6:8
He that *g.* in summer is a Pr 10:5
wise son
but he that *g.* by labour shall Pr 13:11
and as one *g.* eggs that are Isa 10:14
left
when the harvestman *g.* the Isa 17:5
corn
as he that *g.* ears in the Isa 17:5
valley
which *g.* the outcasts of Isa 56:8
Israel
mountains, and no man *g.* Na 3:18
them
but *g.* unto him all nations Hab 2:5
he that *g.* not with me M't 12:30;
scattereth Lu 11:23

even as a hen *g.* her M't 23:37
chickens
and *g.* fruit unto life eternal Joh 4:36

GATHERING

and the *g.* together of the Ge 1:10
waters
him shall the *g.* of the Ge 49:10
people be
a sacred *g.* (B) Ex 12:16;
23:7; Le 23:7, 36
an holy *g.* (B) Le 23:21
it is a festive *g.* (B) Le 23:36
they that found him *g.* Nu 15:33
sticks
the *g.* (B) Nu 16:21;
Job 15:34; Ps 26:5
widow woman was there *g.* 1Ki 17:10
of sticks
and, behold, I am *g.* two 1Ki 17:12
sticks
were three days in *g.* of the 2Ch 20:25
spoil
shall fail, the *g.* shall not Isa 32:10
come
the *g.* of the caterpiller Isa 33:4
g. where thou hast not M't 25:24
strawed
assuredly *g.* that the Lord Ac 16:10
had
by our *g.* together unto him 2Th 2:1

GATHERINGS

that there be no *g.* when I 1Co 16:2
come

GATH-HEPHER

the prophet, which was of 2Ki 14:25
G.

GATH-RIMMON

Jehud, and Bene-berak, and Jos 19:45
G.
her suburbs, G. with her Jos 21:24
suburbs
suburbs, and G. with her Jos 21:25;
suburbs 1Ch 6:69

GAUNT

g. and thin (R) Ge 41:3
g. with want (A)(E) Job 30:3

GAVE

Adam *g.* names to all cattle Ge 2:20
and to fowl
the woman *g.* me of the tree, Ge 3:12
and I did eat
and he *g.* him tithes of all Ge 14:20;
Heb 7:2, 4
and Abraham *g.* all that he Ge 25:5
had to Isaac
the land which God *g.* to Ge 28:4;
Abraham 35:12
g. him families (S) Ex 1:21
the Lord *g.* the people Ex 11:3;
favour 12:36
they *g.* unto them (S) Ex 12:36
the cloud *g.* light by night to Ex 14:20
these
Lord took of the Spirit and Nu 11:25
g. to seventy
I *g.* my daughter to this De 22:16
man to wife
they *g.* him the city which Jos 19:50
he asked
the Lord *g.* to Israel all the Jos 21:43
land
the Lord *g.* them rest Jos 21:44;
2Ch 15:15; 20:30
I drave them out, and *g.* you J'g 6:9
their land
the Lord *g.* her conception, Ru 4:13
and she bare
God *g.* to Saul another heart 1Sa 10:9
and I *g.* thee thy master's 2Sa 12:8
house
the Lord *g.* Solomon 1Ki 4:29;
wisdom 5:12
and the Lord *g.* Israel a 2Ki 13:5
saviour
God *g.* to Heman fourteen 1Ch 25:5
sons
and God *g.* Hezekiah a 2Ch 32:24
sign

read in book of the law, and Ne 8:8
g. the sense
Lord *g.* and the Lord hath Job 1:21
taken away
God *g.* Job twice as much Job 42:10
as he had before
and the Highest *g.* his voice Ps 18:13
the Lord *g.* the word, great Ps 68:11
was the company
they *g.* me also gall, they *g.* Ps 69:21
me vinegar
for he *g.* them their own Ps 78:29;
desire 106:15
the spirit shall return to God Ec 12:7
that *g.* it
who *g.* Jacob for a spoil, Isa 42:24
and Israel
I *g.* Egypt for thy ransom, Isa 43:3
Seba for thee
I *g.* my back to the smiters, Isa 50:6
and my cheeks
my meat also which I *g.* Eze 16:19
thee
I *g.* them my statutes, and Eze 20:11
shewed them
moreover also, I *g.* them Eze 20:12
my sabbaths
I *g.* them also statutes that Eze 20:25
were not good
God *g.* these four children Da 1:17
knowledge
Daniel prayed and *g.* thanks Da 6:10
before God
for she did not know that I *g.* Ho 2:8
her corn
I *g.* thee a king in mine Ho 13:11
anger
ye *g.* the Nazarites wine to Am 2:12
drink
I *g.* my covenant to Levi of Mal 2:5
life
Jesus *g.* them power against M't 10:1;
unclean spirits M'k 6:7; Lu 9:1
he brake and *g.* the loaves M't 14:19;
to his disciples 15:36; 26:16; M'k 6:41;
8:6; 14:22; Lu 9:16; 22:19
who *g.* thee author M't 21:23;
M'k 11:28; Lu 20:2
ye *g.* me meat, ye *g.* me M't 25:35
drink, took me in
ye *g.* me no meat, and ye *g.* M't 25:42
me no drink
a certain man *g.* a feast (S) Lu 14:16
with husks, and no man *g.* Lu 15:16
unto him
to them *g.* he power to Joh 1:12
become sons of God
God so loved world that he Joh 3:16
g. his only Son
he *g.* them bread from Joh 6:31
heaven to eat
my Father who *g.* them me Joh 10:29
is greater than all
as the Father *g.* me Joh 14:31
commandment, so I do
to speak as the Spirit *g.* them Ac 2:4
utterance
and he *g.* them no inheritance Ac 7:5
in it
God *g.* Joseph favour and Ac 7:10
wisdom before Pharaoh
Cornelius *g.* much alms to Ac 10:2
the people
g. generously to help (N) Ac 10:2
as God *g.* them the like gift Ac 11:17
he did to us
smote him, because he *g.* Ac 12:23
not God the glory
afterward God *g.* them Saul Ac 13:21
forty years
he did good, and *g.* us rain Ac 14:17
from heaven
to whom we *g.* no such Ac 15:24
commandment
when put to death, I *g.* my Ac 26:10
voice against them
God *g.* them over to a Ro 2:28
reprobate mind
even as the Lord *g.* to every 1Co 3:5
man
Apollos watered, but God *g.* 1Co 3:6
the increase
but first *g.* their own selves 2Co 8:5
to the Lord
who *g.* himself for our sins Ga 1:4;
Tit 2:14
who loved me, and *g.* himself Ga 2:20
for me

but God g. it to Abraham by   Ga 3:18
promise
and g. him to be head over   Eph 1:22
all things
he led captivity captive and   Eph 4:8
g. gifts to men
and he g. some apostles;   Eph 4:11
some prophets
Christ loved the church, and   Eph 5:25
g. himself for it
ye know what commandment   1Th 4:2
we g. you
who g. himself a ransom for   1Ti 2:6
all
who corrected us, we g.   Heb 12:9
them reverence
he prayed, and the heavens g.   Jas 5:18
rain
love one another, as he g. us   1Jo 3:23
command.
he believeth not the record   1Jo 5:10
God g. of his Son
the revelation of Jesus Christ   Re 1:1
which God g.
I g. her space to repent of   Re 2:21
her fornication
the dragon g. him his power   Re 13:2
and his seat

GAVE UP

Abraham g. up the ghost and   Ge 25:8
died
Ishmael g. up ghost and died   Ge 25:17
Isaac g. up the ghost and died   Ge 35:29
Joab g. up the sum of the   2Sa 24:9
number
who g. them up to   2Ch 30:7
desolation, as ye see
he g. up their cattle also to   Ps 78:48
the hail
I g. them up to their own   Ps 81:12
heart's lust
my elders g. up the ghost in   La 1:19
the city
Jesus cried with a loud   M'k 15:37;
voice, and g. up the ghost   15:39;
     Lu 23:46; Joh 19:30
Ananias g. up the ghost   Ac 5:5
God g. them up to worship   Ac 7:42
the host of heaven
Herod g. up the ghost   Ac 12:23
God also g. them up to   Ro 1:24
uncleanness
God for this cause g. them up   Ro 1:26
to vile affections
the sea g. up the dead that   Re 20:13
were in it

GAVEST

the woman whom thou g. to   Ge 3:12
be with me
the land which thou g. to   1Ki 8:34;
their fathers   8:40, 48; 2Ch 6:25, 31, 38;
     Ne 9:35
thou g. him the name of   Ne 9:7
Abraham
thou g. them right judgments,   Ne 9:13
true laws
g. them bread from heaven   Ne 9:15
for their hunger
thou g. also thy good Spirit,   Ne 9:20
g. water for thirst
thou g. them kingdoms and   Ne 9:22
nations
thou g. them saviours who   Ne 9:27
saved them
g. thou the goodly wings to   Job 39:13
the peacocks
he asked life of thee; thou g.   Ps 21:4
it him
thou g. him to be meat to   Ps 74:14
the people
thou g. me no water for my   Lu 7:44
feet
thou g. me no kiss, but this   Lu 7:45
woman not ceased
yet thou never g. me a kid,   Lu 15:29
to make merry
finished work thou g. me to   Joh 17:4
do; manifested to men whom
thou g. me and thou g. them
I have given them the words   Joh 17:8
which thou g. me
those that thou g. me I   Joh 17:12
have kept, none lost
the glory which thou g. me,   Joh 17:22
I have given

of them whom thou g. me   Joh 18:9
have I lost none

GAY

respect to him that weareth g.   Jas 2:3
clothing

GAZA

Samson went to G. and saw   J'g 16:1
an harlot
the Philistines brought   J'g 16:21
Samson down to G.
before that Pharaoh smote G.   Jer 47:1
baldness is come upon G.   Jer 47:5
Ashkelon is cut off
for three transgressions of G.   Am 1:6
and for four
but I will send a fire on the   Am 1:7
wall of G.
G. shall be forsaken and   Zep 2:4
Ashkelon a desolation
G. shall see it, king shall   Zec 9:5
perish from G.
way that goeth from   Ac 8:26
Jerusalem to G.

GAZATHITES

lords of the Philistines; the   Jos 13:3
G.

GAZE

break through unto the Lord   Ex 19:21
to g.
fixed his g. and stared (B)   2Ki 8:11
g. with envious hostility (B)   Ps 68:16

GAZELLE

the g. and the hart   De 12:15;
(A)(R)(S)   12:22; 15:22
the g. (S)   De 12:15;
     12:22; 14:5; 15:22; 1Ki 4:23
like a wild g. (R)   2Sa 2:18
swift as g. (A)(R)   1Ch 12:8
deliver as a captured g.   Pr 6:5
(B)(R)
by the g. (A)(B)(R)   Ca 2:7;
     3:5; 4:5; 7:3
like a g. (A)(B)(R)   Ca 2:9;
     2:17; 8:14
as a chased g. (B)(R)   Isa 13:24
Tabitha (means) Gazelle   Ac 9:36
(A)(P)(R)

GAZER

from Geba until thou come   2Sa 5:25
to G.
Philistines from Gibeon   1Ch 14:16
even to G.

GAZEZ

Moza, and G. and Haran   1Ch 2:46
begat G.

GAZING

g. through the lattice (S)   Ca 2:9
g. intently (A)(B)   Ac 1:10; 6:15; 14:9

GAZING

why stand ye g. up into   Ac 1:11
heaven

GAZINGSTOCK

and will set thee as a g.   Na 3:6
render you a g. (A)(B)(R)   Na 3:6
whilst ye were made a g.   Heb 10:33
both by

GAZITES

it was told the G. saying,   J'g 16:2
Samson

GAZZAM

of Nekoda, the children of   Ezr 2:48
G.
The children of G. the   Ne 7:51
children of

GEAR

lowered the g.   Ac 27:17
(A)(B)(E)(R)

GEBA

her suburbs, G. with her   Jos 21:17
suburbs
of the Philistines that was in   1Sa 13:3
G.
Philistines from G. until   2Sa 5:25
thou come
built with them G. of   1Ki 15:22
Benjamin
incense, from G. to   2Ki 23:8
Beer-sheba, and
Benjamin; G. with her   1Ch 6:60
suburbs
fathers of the inhabitants of   1Ch 8:6
he built therewith G. and   2Ch 16:6
Mizpah
of Benjamin from G. dwelt   Ne 11:31
Gilgal, and out of the fields   Ne 12:29
of G.
have taken up their lodging   Isa 10:29
at G.
turned as a plain from G.   Zec 14:10

GEBAL

men of G. (S)   1Sa 5:18
G. and Ammon, and Amalek   Ps 83:7
The ancients of G. and the   Eze 27:9
wise

GEBER

The son of G. in   1Ki 4:13
Ramoth-gilead
G. the son Uri was in the   1Ki 4:19
country

GEBIM

the inhabitants of G. gather   Isa 10:31

GEDALIAH

G. the son of Ahikam, the   2Ki 25:22
son of
G. governor, there came to   2Ki 25:23
G. to
G. sware to them, and to   2Ki 25:24
their men
smote G. that he died, and   2Ki 25:25
sons of Jeduthun; G. and   1Ch 25:3
Zeri
the second to G. who with   1Ch 25:9
his
and Eliezer, and Jarib, and   Ezr 10:18
G.
G. the son of Pashur, and   Jer 38:1
Jucal the
committed him unto G. the   Jer 39:14
son of
Go back to G. the son of   Jer 40:5;
Ahikam   40:6-9, 11-16; 41:1-4, 6, 9-10,
     16, 18
guard had left with G. the   Jer 43:6
son of
Cushi, the son of G. the son   Zep 1:1

GEDEON

time would fail me to tell of   Heb 11:32
G.

GEDER

Debir, one; the king of G.   Jos 12:13
one

GEDERAH

and Adithaim, and G. and   Jos 15:36

GEDERATHITE

Johanan, and Josabad the   1Ch 12:4
G.

GEDERITE

low plains was Baal-hanan   1Ch 27:28
the G.

GEDEROTH

And G. Beth-dagon, and Naamah　　　　*Jos 15:41*
Ajalon, and G. and Shocho with the　　　*2Ch 28:18*

GEDEROTHAIM

Adithaim, and Gederah, and G.　　　*Jos 15:36*

GEDOR

Halhul, Beth-zur, and G.　　　*Jos 15:58*
Penuel the father of G. Ezer　　　*1Ch 4:4*
Jered the father of G. and Heber　　　*1Ch 4:18*
entrance of G. even unto the east　　　*1Ch 4:39*
and G. and Ahio, and Zacher　　　*1Ch 8:31*
G. and Ahio, and Zechariah　　　*1Ch 9:37*
the sons of Jeroham of G.　　　*1Ch 12:7*

GEHAZI

said to G. his servant. Call this　　　*2Ki 4:12; 4:14, 25, 27, 29, 31, 36*
But G. the servant of Elisha　　　*2Ki 5:20*
so G. followed after Naaman　　　*2Ki 5:21*
Whence comest thou G.　　　*2Ki 5:25*
G. the servant of the man of God　　　*2Ki 8:4*
G. said, My lord, O king, this is the　　　*2Ki 8:5*

GEHENNA

unable to escape G. of fire (A)　　　*M't 5:22*
thrown in G. fire (B)　　　*M'k 9:45; 9:47*
kindled by G. (B)　　　*Jas 3:6*

GELILOTH

went forth toward G. which　　　*Jos 18:17*

GEMALLI

of Dan, Ammiel the son of G.　　　*Nu 13:12*

GEMARIAH

and G. the son of Hilkiah　　　*Jer 29:3*
in the chamber of G. the son of　　　*Jer 36:10*
Michaiah the son of G. the son of　　　*Jer 36:11*
Elnathan the son of Achbor, and G.　　　*Jer 36:12*
Elnathan and Delaiah and G. had　　　*Jer 36:25*

GENDER

Thou shalt not let thy cattle g.　　　*Le 19:19*
knowing that they do g. strifes　　　*2Ti 2:23*

GENDERED

frost of heaven, who hath g. it　　　*Job 38:29*

GENDERETH

Their bull g. and faileth not　　　*Job 21:10*
g. to bondage, which is Agar　　　*Ga 4:24*

GENEALOGIES

All these were reckoned by g. in　　　*1Ch 5:7*
reckoned in all by their g.　　　*1Ch 7:5*
and were reckoned by their g.　　　*1Ch 7:7*
all Israel were reckoned by g.　　　*1Ch 9:1*
and of Iddo the seer concerning g.　　　*2Ch 12:15*
to all that were reckoned by g.　　　*2Ch 31:19*
give heed to fables and endless g.　　　*1Ti 1:4*
But avoid foolish questions, and g.　　　*Tit 3:9*

GENEALOGY

the roll of Adam's g. (B)(R)　　　*Ge 5:1*
their habitations, and their g.　　　*1Ch 4:33*
and the g. is not to be reckoned　　　*1Ch 5:1*
when the g. of their generations　　　*1Ch 5:7*
after their g. by their generations　　　*1Ch 7:9*
throughout the g. of them　　　*1Ch 7:40*
These were reckoned by their g. in　　　*1Ch 9:22*
Beside their g. of males, from three　　　*2Ch 31:16*
the g. of the priests by the house　　　*2Ch 31:17*
And to the g. of all their little ones　　　*2Ch 31:18*
those that were reckoned by　　　*Ezr 2:62*
and this is the g. of them that went　　　*Ezr 8:1*
were reckoned by g. of the males　　　*Ezr 8:3*
that they might be reckoned by g.　　　*Ne 7:5*
And I found a register of the g. of　　　*Ne 7:5*
those that were reckoned by g.　　　*Ne 7:64*
the g. of Jesus Christ (B)(R)(S)　　　*M't 1:1*
without g. (E)(R)　　　*Heb 7:3; 7:6*

GENERAL

and the g. of the king's army　　　*1Ch 27:34*
To the g. assembly and church of　　　*Heb 12:23*

GENERALLY

that all Israel be g. gathered　　　*2Sa 17:11*
There shall be lamentation g.　　　*Jer 48:38*

GENERALISSIMO

shall be g. (B)　　　*1Ch 11:6*

GENERALS

the g. (B)(R)　　　*Re 6:15*

GENERATION

thee have I seen righteous in this g.　　　*Ge 7:1*
Joseph died, and all that g.　　　*Ex 1:6*
will have war with Amalek from g. to g.　　　*Ex 17:16*
till that g. was consumed　　　*Nu 32:13; De 2:14*
not one of this evil g. shall see that land　　　*De 1:35*
a bastard shall not enter even to his tenth g.　　　*De 23:2*
an Ammonite to tenth g. shall not enter　　　*De 23:3*
Edomite and Egyptian in the third g. shall enter　　　*De 23:8*
so that the g. to come shall rise up and say　　　*De 29:22*
they are a perverse and crooked g.　　　*De 32:5; 32:20*
a twisted and crooked race (B)　　　*De 32:5*
all that g. were gathered to their fathers, and another g. after them　　　*J'g 2:10*
these days should be remembered in every g.　　　*Es 9:28*
preserve them from this g. for ever　　　*Ps 12:7*
for God is in the g. of the righteous　　　*Ps 14:5*
it shall be accounted to the Lord for a g.　　　*Ps 22:30*
this is the g. of them that seek him　　　*Ps 24:6*
that ye may tell it to the g. following　　　*Ps 48:13*
he shall go to the g. of his fathers　　　*Ps 49:19*
till I have shewed thy strength to this g.　　　*Ps 71:18*
I should offend against the g. of thy children　　　*Ps 73:15*
shewing to the g. to come the praises of Lord　　　*Ps 78:4*
that the g. to come might know them　　　*Ps 78:6*
might not be a stubborn and rebellious g.　　　*Ps 78:8*
forty years grieved with this g.　　　*Ps 95:10; Heb 3:10*
this shall be written for the g. to come　　　*Ps 102:18*
in g. following let their name be blotted out　　　*Ps 109:13*
the g. of the upright shall be blessed　　　*Ps 112:2*
the race of the upright (B)　　　*Ps 112:2*
one g. shall praise thy works to another　　　*Ps 145:4*
doth the crown endure to every g.　　　*Pr 27:24*
there is a g. that curseth their father　　　*Pr 30:11*
there is a g. that are pure in their own eyes　　　*Pr 30:12*
a g. lofty　　　*Pr 30:13*
a g. whose teeth are swords　　　*Pr 30:14*
one g. passeth away, another g. cometh　　　*Ec 1:4*
not dwelt in from g. to g.　　　*Isa 13:20; Jer 50:39*
from g. to g. it shall lie waste　　　*Isa 34:10*
from g. to g. they shall dwell therein　　　*Isa 34:17*
but my salvation shall be from g. to g.　　　*Isa 51:8*
who shall declare his g.　　　*Isa 53:8; Ac 8:33*
O g. see ye the word of the Lord　　　*Jer 2:31*
the Lord hath rejected the g. of his wrath　　　*Jer 7:29*
thy throne, O Lord remains from g. to g.　　　*La 5:19*
and his dominion is from g. to g.　　　*Da 4:3*
and let their children tell another g.　　　*Joe 1:3*
Jerusalem shall dwell from g. to g.　　　*Joe 3:20*
the book of the g. of Jesus Christ　　　*M't 1:1*
the ancestry of Jesus Christ (A)(P)　　　*M't 1:1*
the genealogy of Jesus Christ (B)(R)　　　*M't 1:1*
the descent of Jesus Christ (N)　　　*M't 1:1*
O g. of vipers　　　*M't 3:7; 12:34; 23:33; Lu 3:7*
you viper brood (A)(B)(N)(R)　　　*M't 3:7*
you offspring of vipers (E)　　　*M't 3:7*
you serpent's brood (P)　　　*M't 3:7*
whereto shall I liken this g.　　　*M't 11:16; Lu 7:31*
evil and adulterous g.　　　*M't 12:39*
seeketh after a sign　　　*16:4; M'k 8:12; Lu 11:29*
shall rise in judgment with this g.　　　*M't 12:41; Lu 11:32*
queen of the south rise up with g.　　　*M't 12:42; Lu 11:31*
even so shall it be also to this wicked g.　　　*M't 12:45*
O perverse g.　　　*M't 17:17; M'k 9:19; Lu 9:41*
all these things shall come on this g.　　　*M't 23:36*
this g. shall not pass　　　*M't 24:34; M'k 13:30; Lu 21:32*
shall be ashamed of me in this sinful g.　　　*M'k 8:38*
his mercy is on them from g. to g.　　　*Lu 1:50*
so shall the Son of man be to this g.　　　*Lu 11:30*
the blood of the prophets required of this g.　　　*Lu 11:50; 11:51*
children of this world in their g. are wiser　　　*Lu 16:8*
the Son of man must be rejected of this g.　　　*Lu 17:25*
save you from this untoward g.　　　*Ac 2:40*
David, after he had served his own g.　　　*Ac 13:36*

crooked and wicked *g.*   *Ph'p 2:15*
(A)(B)(E)(N)(R)
ye are a chosen *g.* a royal   *1Pe 2:9*
priesthood
a chosen race (A)(B)(N)(R)   *1Pe 2:9*
an elect race (E)   *1Pe 2:9*

GENERATIONS

these are *g.* of the heavens   *Ge 2:4*
and earth
the *g.* of Adam   *Ge 5:1*
the roll of Adam's genealogy   *Ge 5:1*
(B)
the *g.* of Noah *Ge 6:9; 10:1; 6:9, 10:1*
Noah was a just man, and   *Ge 6:9*
perfect in his *g.*
blameless among his fellowmen   *Ge 6:9*
(B)
of the covenant I make for   *Ge 9:12*
perpetual *g.*
These are the *g.* of Shem   *Ge 11:10*
g. of Terah   *Ge 11:27*
these are Shem's descendents   *Ge 11:10*
(B)(R)
covenant between me and thy   *Ge 17:7*
seed in their *g.*
thou and thy seed after thee   *Ge 17:9*
in their *g.*
man child in your *g.* be   *Ge 17:12*
circumcised
these are the *g.* of Ishmael   *Ge 25:12;*
   25:13; 1Ch 1:29
these are descendents of   *Ge 25:12*
Ishmael (A)(B)(R)
these are the *g.* of Isaac   *Ge 25:19*
these are descendents of   *Ge 25:19*
Isaac (A)(B)(R)
the *g.* of Esau   *Ge 36:1; 25:9*
these are the *g.* of Jacob,   *Ge 37:2*
Joseph 17 years old
this is Jacob's line (A)   *Ge 37:2*
This is Jacob's family record   *Ge 37:2*
(B)
This is the history of Jacob's   *Ge 37:2*
family (R)
this is my memorial unto all   *Ex 3:15*
g.
the sons of Levi according to   *Ex 6:16;*
their *g.*   *6:19*
in the order of their birth   *Ex 6:16*
(A)(B)
a feast to the Lord   *Ex 12:14*
throughout your *g.*
ye shall observe this day in   *Ex 12:17*
your *g.*
a night to be much observed   *Ex 12:42*
by Israel in their *g.*
fill an homer to be kept for   *Ex 16:32;*
your *g.*   *16:33*
it shall be a statute for ever   *Ex 27:21;*
to their *g.* *30:21; Le 3:17; 6:18; 7:36;*
   10:9; 17:7; 23:14, 21, 31, 41
a continuous burnt offering   *Ex 29:42*
throughout your *g.*
burn incense; oil throughout   *Ex 30:8;*
your *g.*   *30:31*
my sabbaths a sign   *Ex 31:13;*
throughout your *g.*   *31:16*
an everlasting priesthood   *Ex 40:15*
through their *g.*
of thy seed in their *g.* that   *Le 21:17*
hath blemish
your *g.* may know that I   *Le 23:43*
made Israel dwell
a statute for ever in *g.*   *Le 24:3;*
   Nu 10:8; 18:23
Lord keepeth covenant to a   *De 7:9*
thousand *g.*
consider the years of many *g. De 32:7*
a witness between you and   *Jos 22:27*
our *g.*
to our descendents (B)   *Jos 22:27;*
   22:28
when they should say to our   *Jos 22:28*
g. in time to come
the *g.* of Israel might teach   *J'g 3:2*
them war
now these are the *g.* of   *Ru 4:18*
Pharez
of his covenant, the word   *1Ch 16:15;*
which he commanded to   *Ps 105:8*
a thousand *g.*
Job saw his sons' sons,   *Job 42:16*
even four *g.*
the thoughts of his heart to   *Ps 33:11*
all *g.*
make thy name to be   *Ps 45:17*
remembered in all *g.*

their dwelling places continue   *Ps 49:11*
to all *g.*
thou wilt prolong the king's   *Ps 61:6*
years as many *g.*
they shall fear thee   *Ps 72:5*
throughout all *g.*
we will shew forth thy praise *Ps 79:13*
to all *g.*
wilt thou draw out thine   *Ps 85:5*
anger to all *g.*
I will make known thy   *Ps 89:1*
faithfulness to all *g.*
and I will build up thy throne *Ps 89:4*
to all *g.*
thou hast been our   *Ps 90:1*
dwelling place in all *g.*
and his truth endureth to all *Ps 100:5*
g.
and thy remembrance unto *Ps 102:12*
all *g.*
thy years are throughout all *Ps 102:24*
g.
was counted to him for   *Ps 106:31*
righteousness to all *g.*
thy faithfulness is unto all *Ps 119:90*
g.
and thy memorial   *Ps 135:13*
throughout all *g.*
and thy dominion   *Ps 145:13*
throughout all *g.*
thy God, O Zion, shall   *Ps 146:10*
reign to all *g.*
calling the *g.* from the   *Isa 41:4*
beginning
awake, arm of the Lord, as in *Isa 51:9*
g. of old
as in times long past (B)   *Isa 51:9*
shalt raise up the   *Isa 58:12*
foundations of many *g.*
I will make thee a joy of   *Isa 60:15*
many *g.*
they shall repair the   *Isa 61:4*
desolations of many *g.*
even to the years of many *g. Joe 2:2*
the *g.* from Abraham to   *M't 1:17*
David are 14 *g.*
behold, all *g.* shall call me   *Lu 1:48*
blessed
in past *g.*   *Eph 3:5*
(A)(B)(E)(N)(P)(R)
throughout all *g.*   *Eph 3:21*
(A)(B)(E)(N)(P)(R)
mystery hath been hid from *Col 1:26*
ages and *g.*

GENEROSITY

God's *g.,* patient mercy (P)   *Ro 2:4*
in a wealth of lavish *g.*   *2Co 8:2*
(A)(B)
work of *g.* (N)(P)   *2Co 8:6*
g. of contribution (R)   *2Co 9:13*
his inexpressible *g.* (P)   *2Co 9:15*

GENEROUS

glad and *g.* hearts (R)   *Ac 2:46*
liberal and *g.* (R)   *1Ti 6:18*
be *g.* contribute to needy   *Heb 13:16*
(A)
God is a *g.* giver who neither *Jas 1:5*
refuses nor reproaches (N)

GENEROUS-HEARTED

g. liberality (A)(R)   *2Co 9:13*

GENEROUSLY

gave *g.* to help (N)   *Ac 10:2*
who gives *g.* without making *Jas 1:5*
them foolish and guilty (P)

GENNESARET

they came into the land of   *M't 14:34*
G.
into the land of *G.* and   *M'k 6:53*
drew to
he stood by the lake of *G.*   *Lu 5:1*

GENTILE

the *G.* nations (A)   *Ps 79:6;*
   79:10, Jer 49:14
the *G.* nations (A)   *Ps 79:10*
as a *G.* and a (R)   *M't 18:17*
the Jew first, and also to the *Ro 2:9*
G.

to the Greek as well   *Ro 2:9*
(A)(B)(E)(N)(P)(R)
the Jew first, and also to the *Ro 2:10*
G.

GENTILES

By these were the isles of the *Ge 10:5*
G.
the coastland people spread *Ge 10:5*
(A)(R)
the isles of the nations   *Ge 10:5*
divided (E)
dwelt in Harosheth of the *G.*   *J'g 4:2*
from Harosheth of the *G.*   *J'g 4:13*
unto the
the host, unto Harosheth of   *J'g 4:16*
the *G.*
sold to the *G.* (B)   *Ne 5:8*
to it shall the *G.* seek: and *Isa 11:10*
the nations seek   *Isa 11:10*
(A)(B)(E)(R)
bring forth judgment to the *G. Isa 42:1*
truth to the nations   *Isa 42:1*
(A)(B)(R)
of the people, for a light of   *Isa 42:6*
the *G.*
light to the nations (A)(R)   *Isa 42:6*
give thee for a light to the   *Isa 49:6*
G.
I will lift up mine hand to   *Isa 49:22*
the *G.*
lift up my hand to nations   *Isa 49:22*
(B)(E)(R)
and thy seed shall inherit the *Isa 54:3*
G.
offspring possess the nations *Isa 54:3*
(A)(B)(E)(R)
the *G.* shall come to thy light *Isa 60:3*
nations come to light   *Isa 60:3*
(A)(B)(E)(R)
the forces of the *G.* shall   *Isa 60:5*
come
unto thee the forces of the   *Isa 60:11*
G.
shalt also suck the milk of   *Isa 60:16*
the *G.*
milk the nations (B)(E((R) *Isa 60:16*
ye shall eat the riches of the *Isa 61:6*
G.
eat wealth of the nations   *Isa 61:6*
(A)(B)(E)(R)
shall be known among the *G. Isa 61:9*
known among the nations   *Isa 61:9*
(A)(B)(E)(R)
G. shall see thy righteousness *Isa 62:2*
the nations (A)(B)(E)(R)   *Isa 62:2;*
66:12, 19; Jer 4:7; 14:22; 16:19; Eze 4:13;
Ho 8:8; Joe 3:9; Mic 5:8; Zec 1:21;
   Mal 1:11
of the *G.* like a flowing   *Isa 66:12*
stream
declare my glory among the *Isa 66:19*
G.
destroyer of the *G.* is on his *Jer 4:7*
way
among the vanities of the *G. Jer 14:22*
the *G.* shall come unto thee *Jer 16:19*
the prophet against the *G.*   *Jer 46:1*
her princes are among the *G. La 2:9*
their defiled bread among the *Eze 4:13*
G.
shall they be among the *G.* as *Ho 8:8*
Proclaim ye this among the *Joe 3:9*
G.
of Jacob shall be among the *Mic 5:8*
G.
to cast out the horns of the *Zec 1:21*
G.
name shall be great among   *Mal 1:11*
the *G.*
beyond Jordan, Galilee of   *M't 4:15*
the *G.*
the nations (B)   *M't 4:15; 12:21;*
   Ac 9:15
the *G.* (A)(E)   *M't 6:7;*
   2Co 11:26; Ga 2:9; 3:8
all these things do the *G.*   *M't 6:32*
seek
Go not into the way of the   *M't 10:5*
G.
testimony against them and   *M't 10:18*
the *G.*
he shall shew judgment to   *M't 12:18*
the *G.*
in his name shall the *G.* trust *M't 12:21*
they shall deliver him to the *M't 20:19*
G.
the princes of the *G.*   *M't 20:25*
exercise

and shall deliver him to the *M'k 10:33* G.
are accounted to rule over *M'k 10:42* the G.
A light to lighten the G. and *Lu 2:32*
he shall be delivered unto *Lu 18:32* the G.
shall be trodden down of the *Lu 21:24* G.
the times of the G. be *Lu 21:24* fulfilled
kings of the G. exercise *Lu 22:25* lordship
the dispersed among the *Joh 7:35*
the Greeks (B) *Joh 7:35*
and teach the G. *Joh 7:35*
the G. and the people of *Ac 4:27* Israel
into the possession of the G. *Ac 7:45*
to bear my name before the *Ac 9:15* G.
on the G. also was poured *Ac 10:45*
the G. had also received the *Ac 11:1* word
hath God also to the G. *Ac 11:18* granted
the G. besought that these *Ac 13:42* words
the people begged (B) *Ac 13:42*
lo, we turn to the G. *Ac 13:46*
set thee to be a light of the *Ac 13:47* G.
the G. heard this, they were *Ac 13:48* glad
Jews stirred up the G. *Ac 14:2*
of the G. and also of the *Ac 14:5* Jews
the door of faith unto the *Ac 14:27* G.
declaring the conversion of *Ac 15:3* the G.
the G. by my mouth should *Ac 15:7* hear
wrought among the G. by *Ac 15:12* them
did visit the G. to take out *Ac 15:14* of them
all the G. upon whom my *Ac 15:17* name
from among the G. are *Ac 15:19* turned
the brethren which are of *Ac 15:23* the G.
henceforth I will go unto the *Ac 18:6* G.
him into the hands of the G. *Ac 21:11*
God had wrought among the *Ac 21:19* G.
the Jews which are among *Ac 21:21* the G.
as touching the G. which *Ac 21:25* believe
send thee far hence unto the *Ac 22:21* G.
from the people, and from *Ac 26:17* the G.
to the G. that they should *Ac 26:20* repent
light unto the people, and *Ac 26:23* to the G.
salvation of God is sent *Ac 28:28* unto the G.
you also, even as among *Ro 1:13* other G.
among other nations (B) *Ro 1:13*
the G. which have not the *Ro 2:14* law
God is blasphemed among *Ro 2:24* the G.
before proved both Jews and *Ro 3:9* G.
of the G.? Yes, of the G. *Ro 3:29* also
the Jews only, but also of the *Ro 9:24* G.
That the G. which followed *Ro 9:30* not
salvation is come unto the *Ro 11:11* G.
of them the riches of the G. *Ro 11:12*
For I speak to you G. *Ro 11:13* inasmuch as
I am the apostle of the G. *Ro 11:13*
until the fulness of the G. *Ro 11:25* be come
And that the G. might glorify *Ro 15:9* God
I will confess to thee among *Ro 15:9* the G.

he saith, Rejoice, ye G. with *Ro 15:10* his
Praise the Lord, all ye G. *Ro 15:11*
shall rise to reign over the *Ro 15:12* G.
in him shall the G. trust *Ro 15:12*
minister of Jesus Christ to *Ro 15:16* the G.
the offering up of the G. *Ro 15:16* might be
to make the G. obedient, by *Ro 15:18* word
if the G. have been made *Ro 15:27* partakers
but also all the churches of *Ro 16:4* the G.
folly to G. *1Co 1:23* (B)(N)(P)(R)(S)
so much as named among the *1Co 5:1* G.
the things which the G. *1Co 10:20* sacrifice
neither to the Jews, nor to *1Co 10:32* the G.
Ye know that ye were G. *1Co 12:2* carried
whether we be Jews or G. *1Co 12:13*
perils by the G. *2Co 11:26;* (B)(R)(S) *Ga 2:9; 3:8*
among the G. *Ga 1:16* (A)(B)(E)(N)(R)
which I preach among the G. *Ga 2:2*
was mighty in me toward the *Ga 2:8* G.
should go to the G. (P) *Ga 2:9; 3:8*
he did eat with the G.: but *Ga 2:12* when
livest after the manner of G. *Ga 2:14*
the G. to live as do the Jews *Ga 2:14*
nature, and not sinners of the *Ga 2:15* G.
come on the G. through Jesus *Ga 3:14*
being in time past G. in the *Eph 2:11* flesh
prisoner of Jesus Christ for *Eph 3:1* you G.
That the G. should be *Eph 3:6* fellow-heirs
that I should preach among *Eph 3:8* the G.
walk not as other G. walk, *Eph 4:17* in the
of this mystery among the G. *Col 1:27*
Forbidding us to speak to *1Th 2:16* the G.
as the G. which know not *1Th 4:5* God
a teacher of the G. in faith *1Ti 2:7*
preached unto the G. *1Ti 3:16* believed
apostle, and a teacher of the *2Ti 1:11* G.
and that all the G. might hear *2Ti 4:17*
conversation honest among *1Pe 2:12* the G.
to have wrought the will of *1Pe 4:3* the G.
forth, taking nothing of the G. *3Jo 7*
for it is given unto the G. *Re 11:2*

GENTLE

But we were g. among you *1Th 2:7*
not violent, but g. (A)(P)(R) *1Ti 3:3*
not strive; but be g. unto all *2Ti 2:24* men
to be no brawlers, but g. *Tit 3:2* shewing
g. and easy to be intreated *Jas 3:17*
not only to the good and g. *1Pe 2:18* but also

GENTLENESS

and thy g. hath made me *2Sa 22:36;* great *Ps 18:35*
by the meekness and g. of *2Co 10:1* Christ
longsuffering, g., goodness, *Ga 5:22* faith
have a reputation for g. (P) *Ph'p 4:5*
exercise g. and forbearance *Heb 5:2* (A)

GENTLY

Deal g. for my sake with the *2Sa 18:5*
g. lead those that are with *Isa 40:11* young
bear g. with ignorant *Heb 5:2* (B)(E)(R)

GENUBATH

Tahpenes bare him G. his *1Ki 11:20* son
and G. was in Pharaoh's *1Ki 11:20* household

GENUINE

g. worshippers (B) *Joh 4:23;*   *Eph 4:24; Ph'p 4:3*
with g. cheerfulness *Ro 12:8* (A)(B)(E)(N)(R)
let love be g. (P)(R) *Ro 12:9*
with g. love (P)(R) *2Co 6:6*
g. yokefellow (A)(B) *Ph'p 4:3*
faith that is g. (N)(P) *1Ti 1:5*

GENUINENESS

test the g. of love (B)(R) *2Co 8:8*

GERA

and Becher, and Ashbel, G. *Ge 46:21*
Ehud the son of G. a *J'g 3:15* Benjamite
name was Shimei, the son of *2Sa 16:5* G.
Shimei the son of G. a *2Sa 19:16* Benjamite
Shimei the son of G. fell *2Sa 19:18* down
hast with thee Shimei the son *1Ki 2:8* of G.
Addar, and G. and Abihud *1Ch 8:3*
G. and Shephuphan, and *1Ch 8:5* Huram
Ahiah, and G. he removed *1Ch 8:7* them

GERAHS

shekel is twenty g.:) an half *Ex 30:13* shekel
twenty g. shall be the shekel *Le 27:25*
take them: (the shekel is *Nu 3:47* twenty g.
the sanctuary, which is *Nu 18:16* twenty g.
the shekel shall be twenty g. *Eze 45:12*

GERAR

as thou comest to G. unto *Ge 10:19* Gaza
and Shur, and sojourned in *Ge 20:1*
and Abimelech king of G. *Ge 20:2* sent
king of the Philistines unto *Ge 26:1* G.
And Isaac dwelt in G. *Ge 26:6*
pitched his tent in the valley *Ge 26:17* of G.
herdmen of G. did strive *Ge 26:20*
Abimelech went to him from *Ge 26:26* G.
with him pursued them *2Ch 14:13* unto G.
smote all the cities round *2Ch 14:14* about G.

GERGESENES

side into the country of the *M't 8:28* G.

GERIZIM

put the blessing upon mount *De 11:29* G.
upon mount G. to bless the *De 27:12* people
against mount G. and half of *Jos 8:33* them
in the top of mount G. and *J'g 9:7* lifted

GERMINATE

does not g. (P) *1Co 15:36*

GERSHOM

son, and he called his name *Ex 2:22* G.
which the name of the one *Ex 18:3* was G.
and Jonathan, the son of G. *J'g 18:30*

The sons of Levi; _G._,   1Ch 6:16
Kohath, and
the sons of _G._; Libni, and   1Ch 6:17
Shimei
_G._; Libni his son, Jahath his   1Ch 6:20
son
The son of Jahath, the son   1Ch 6:43
of _G._
of _G._ throughout their   1Ch 6:62
families
the sons of _G._ were given   1Ch 6:71
Of the sons of _G._; Joel the   1Ch 15:7
chief
sons of Moses were _G._ and   1Ch 23:15
Eliezer
sons of _G._, Shebuel was the   1Ch 23:16
chief
And Shebuel the son of _G._   2Ch 26:24
the son
Of the sons of Phinehas; _G._: Ezr 8:2
of the

GERSHON

sons of Levi; _G._, Kohath   Ge 46:11
_G._ and Kohath, and Merari   Ex 6:16
sons of _G._; Libni, and Shimi   Ex 6:17
by their names; _G._ and   Nu 3:17
Kohath
the sons of _G._ by their   Nu 3:18
families
of _G._ was the family of the   Nu 3:21
Libnites
charge of the sons of _G._ in   Nu 3:25
sum of the sons of _G._   Nu 4:22
throughout
the sons of _G._ in the   Nu 4:28
tabernacle
were numbered of the sons   Nu 4:38
of _G._
of the families of the sons of   Nu 4:41
_G._
oxen he gave unto the sons of   Nu 7:7
_G._
sons of _G._ and the sons of   Nu 10:17
Merari
_G._ the family of the   Nu 26:57
Gershonites
_G._ had by lot out of the   Jos 21:6
families
unto the children of _G._ of   Jos 21:27
the sons of Levi; _G._, Kohath   1Ch 6:1
sons of Levi, namely _G._,   1Ch 23:6
Kohath

GERSHONITE

the sons of the _G._ Laadan,   1Ch 26:21
chief
even of Laadan the _G._   1Ch 26:21
were
Lord, by the hand of Jehiel   1Ch 29:8
the _G._

GERSHONITES

these are the families of the   Nu 3:21
_G._
The families of the _G._ shall   Nu 3:23
pitch
father of the _G._ shall be   Nu 3:24
Eliasaph
service of the families of the   Nu 4:24
_G._
service of the sons of the _G._   Nu 4:27
in all
of Gershon, the family of   Nu 26:57
the _G._
the cities of the _G._   Jos 21:33
according to
Of the _G._ were, Laadan, and   1Ch 23:7
and of the _G._; Joah the   2Ch 29:12
son of

GESHAM

Regem, and Jotham, and _G._   1Ch 2:47

GESHEM

and _G._ the Arabian, heard it   Ne 2:19
Tobiah, and _G._ the Arabian   Ne 6:1
Sanballat and _G._ sent unto me   Ne 6:2

GESHUR

the daughter of Talmai king   2Sa 3:3
of _G._
the son of Ammihud, king   2Sa 13:37
of _G._

Absalom fled, and went to   2Sa 13:38
_G._
Joab arose and went to _G._   2Sa 14:23
Wherefore am I come from   2Sa 14:32
_G._
vow while I abode at _G._ in   2Sa 15:8
Syria
And he took _G._ and Aram   1Ch 2:23
daughter of Talmai king of   1Ch 3:2
_G._

GESHURI

the coasts of _G._ and   De 3:14
Maachathi
of the Philistines, and all _G._   Jos 13:2

GESHURITES

of the _G._ and the   Jos 12:5
Maachathites
border of the _G._ and   Jos 13:11
Maachathites
Israel expelled not the _G._   Jos 13:13
nor the
the _G._ and the Maachathites   Jos 13:13
dwell
invaded the _G._ and the   1Sa 27:8
Gezrites

GET

saying, _G._ me this damsel to   Ge 34:4
wife
and so _g._ them up out of the   Ex 1:10
land
and I will _g._ me honour   Ex 14:17
upon Pharaoh
if he be poor and cannot _g._   Le 14:21
so much
two pigeons, such as he is   Le 14:22;
able to _g._   14:30-31
the law of him whose hand is   Le 14:32
not able to _g._
besides that that his hand   Nu 6:21
shall _g._
now therefore I will _g._ me   Nu 22:34
back again
it is he giveth thee power to   De 8:18
_g._ wealth
the strangers shall _g._ up   De 28:43
above thee
therefore _g._ her for me to   J'g 14:2;
wife   14:3
let me _g._ away and see my   1Sa 20:29
brethren
David made haste to _g._   1Sa 23:26
away for fear
lest Sheba _g._ fenced cities   2Sa 20:6
and escape
that my lord the king may   1Ki 1:2
heat
king Rehoboam made   1Ki 12:18;
speed to _g._ up to his chariot   2Ch 10:18
shall _g._ catch them alive, and   2Ki 7:12
_g._ the city
thro' the precepts I _g._   Ps 119:104
understanding
_g._ wisdom, _g._ understanding   Pr 4:5;
    4:7
a wound and dishonour shall   Pr 6:33
he _g._
much better it is to _g._   Pr 16:16
wisdom than gold, _g._
understanding rather than silver
a price in the hand of a fool   Pr 17:16
to _g._ wisdom
lest thou learn his ways and   Pr 22:25
_g._ a snare
there is a time to _g._ and a   Ec 3:6
time to lose
I will _g._ me to the mountains   Ca 4:6
of myrrh
let us _g._ up early to the   Ca 7:12
vineyards and see if
I will _g._ me to great men, and   Jer 5:5
will speak
and _g._ a potter's earthen   Jer 19:1
bottle
harness the horses, and _g._ up,   Jer 46:4
ye horseman
give wings to Moab, that it   Jer 48:9
may _g._ away
he hath hedged me about, I   La 3:7
cannot _g._ out
to destroy souls, to _g._   Eze 22:27
dishonest gain
let the beasts _g._ away from   Da 4:14
under it

I will _g._ their praise from   Zep 3:19
every land
constrain them to _g._ into ship M't 14:22;
    M'k 6:45
that they may lodge and _g._   Lu 9:12
vituals
cast themselves into sea, and   Ac 27:43
_g._ to land
lest Satan should _g._ the   2Co 2:11
advantage of us
continue there, buy, sell, and   Jas 4:13
_g._ gain

GET THEE

g. thee out of thy country   Ge 12:1;
    Ac 7:3
he said, _G. thee_ into the land   Ge 22:2
of Moriah
g. thee out from this land,   Ge 31:13
and return
g. thee to Pharaoh in the   Ex 7:15
morning
g. thee from me, take heed   Ex 10:28
to thyself
g. thee out, and all the people   Ex 11:8
that follow thee
Lord said to Moses, _G. thee_   Ex 19:24;
down and thou shalt   32:7; De 9:12
g. thee to mount Abarim   Nu 27:12;
    De 32:49
g. thee up to the top of   De 3:27
Pisgah
g. thee up to the place the   De 17:8
Lord shall choose
g. thee up, wherefore liest   Jos 7:10
thou thus
then _g. thee_ up to the wood   Jos 17:5
country
arise, _g. thee_ down unto the   J'g 7:9
host
wash thyself, _g. thee_ down to   Ru 3:3
the floor
depart, _g. thee_ into the land   1Sa 22:5
of Judah
go, _g. thee_ in to king David,   1Ki 1:13
and say
g. thee to Anathoth to thine   1Ki 2:26
own fields
g. thee to Shiloh, behold   1Ki 14:2
there is Ahijah
arise therefore, _g. thee_ to   1Ki 14:12
thine own house
g. thee hence   1Ki 17:3
g. thee to Zarephath   1Ki 17:9
Elijah said, _G. thee_ up, eat   1Ki 18:41
and drink
g. thee down, that the rain   1Ki 18:44
stop thee not
g. thee to the prophets of   2Ki 3:13
thy father
so didst thou _g. thee_ a name   Ne 9:10
as this day
g. thee to this treasurer, to   Isa 22:15
Shebnah
thou shalt say unto it, _G._   Isa 30:22
thee hence
O Zion, _g. thee_ up into the   Isa 40:9
high mountain
sit thou silent, and _g. thee_   Isa 47:5
into darkness
g. thee a linen girdle, put it   Jer 13:1
on thy loins
son of man, _g. thee_ to the   Eze 3:4
house of Israel
and go, _g. thee_ to them of   Eze 3:11
the captivity
Jesus saith to him, _G. thee_   M't 4:10
hence, Satan
he turned, and said to   M't 16:23;
Peter, _G. thee_ behind M'k 8:33; Lu 4:8
me, Satan
g. thee out, for Herod will   Lu 13:31
kill thee
arise, _g. thee_ down, go with   Ac 10:20
them
g. thee quickly out of   Ac 22:18
Jerusalem, will not

GET YE

Lot said, Up, _g. ye_ out of   Ge 19:14
this place
_g. ye_ out of the way, turn   Isa 30:11
aside from path
arise, _g. ye_ up to the   Jer 49:31
wealthy nation
have said, _G. ye_ far from   Eze 11:15
the Lord

come, g. ye down, for the press is full   Joe 3:13
he said, G. ye hence, walk to and fro   Zec 6:7

GET YOU

dwell and trade, g. you possessions therein   Ge 34:10
g. you down thither and buy for us thence   Ge 42:2
rise up, g. you up in peace unto your father   Ge 44:17
the king said, G. you to your burdens   Ex 5:4
go you, g. you straw where you can find it   Ex 5:11
rise up, g. you forth from among my people   Ex 12:31
turn you, g. you into the wilderness   Nu 14:25
g. you up from about tabernacle of Korah   Nu 16:24
Balaam said, G. you into your land   Nu 22:13
g. you into your tents again   De 5:30; Jos 22:4
g. you to the mountain, lest pursuers meet   Jos 2:16
to-morrow, g. you early on your way   J'g 19:9
g. you up, for ye shall find him   1Sa 9:13
g. you down from among the Amalekites   1Sa 15:6
g. you up to Carmel, and go to Nabal   1Sa 25:5
Flee, g. you far off, dwell deep, ye of Hazor   Jer 49:30

GETHER

of Aram; Uz, and Hul, and G.   Ge 10:23
Aram, and Uz, and Hul, and G.   1Ch 1:17

GETHSEMANE

with them unto a place called G.   M't 26:36
to a place which was named G.   M'k 14:32

GETTETH

Whosoever g. up to the gutter   2Sa 5:8
the man that g. understanding   Pr 3:13
a scorner g. to himself shame   Pr 9:7
rebuketh a wicked man g. himself   Pr 9:7
heareth reproof g. understanding   Pr 15:32
heart of the prudent g. knowledge   Pr 18:15
He that g. wisdom loveth his own   Pr 19:8
he that g. riches, and not by right   Jer 17:11
and he that g. up out of the pit   Jer 48:44

GETTING

the cattle of his g. which he had   Ge 31:18
with all thy g. get understanding   Pr 4:7
g. of treasures by a lying tongue   Pr 21:6

GEUEL

Of the tribe of Gad, G. the son of   Nu 13:15

GEZER

Horam king of G. came up to   Jos 10:33
Eglon, one; the king of G.   Jos 12:12
Beth-horon the nether, and to G.   Jos 16:3
Canaanites that dwelt in G.; but   Jos 16:10
of refuge for the slayer; and G.   Jos 21:21
G.; but the Canaanites dwelt in G.   J'g 1:29

and Hazor, and Megiddo, and G.   1Ki 9:15
gone up, and taken G. and burnt   1Ki 9:16
Solomon built G., and Beth-horon   1Ki 9:17
they gave also G. with her suburbs   1Ch 6:67
eastward Naaran, and westward G.   1Ch 7:28
a war at G. with the Philistines   1Ch 20:4

GEZRITES

Geshurites, and the G. and   1Sa 27:8

GHOST

Then Abraham gave up the g.   Ge 25:8
and he gave up the g. and died   Ge 25:17
And Isaac gave up the g. and died   Ge 35:29
and yielded up the g. and   Ge 49:33
why did I not give up the g.   Job 3:11
Oh that I had given up the g. when   Job 10:18
shall be as the giving up of the g.   Job 11:20
tongue, I shall give up the g.   Job 13:19
yea, man giveth up the g.   Job 14:10
voice like a g. (A)(R)   Isa 29:4
she hath given up the g.; her sun   Jer 15:9
mine elders gave up the g. in the   La 1:19
found with child of the Holy G.   M't 1:18
in her is of the Holy G.   M't 1:20
with the Holy G. and with fire   M't 3:11
blasphemy against the Holy G.   M't 12:31
speaketh against the Holy G.   M't 12:32
yielded up the g.   M't 27:50
of the Son, and of the Holy G.   M't 28:19
baptize you with the Holy G.   M'k 1:8
blaspheme against the Holy G.   M'k 3:29
himself said by the Holy G.   M'k 12:36
ye that speak, but the Holy G.   M'k 13:11
a loud voice, and gave up the g.   M'k 15:37
so cried out, and gave up the g.   M'k 15:39
be filled with the Holy G.   Lu 1:15
Holy G. shall come upon thee   Lu 1:35
was filled with the Holy G.   Lu 1:41, 67
and the Holy G. was upon him   Lu 2:25
unto him by the Holy G.   Lu 2:26
baptize you with the Holy G.   Lu 3:16
And the Holy G. descended   Lu 3:22
Jesus being full of the Holy G.   Lu 4:1
against the Holy G.   Lu 12:10
For the Holy G. shall teach   Lu 12:12
said, thus, he gave up the g.   Lu 23:46
baptizeth with the Holy G.   Joh 1:33
for the Holy G. was not yet   Joh 7:39
Holy G. whom the Father   Joh 14:26
his head, and gave up the g.   Joh 19:30
them, Receive ye the Holy G.   Joh 20:22
he through the Holy G. had   Ac 1:2
be baptized with the Holy G.   Ac 1:5
after that the Holy G. is come   Ac 1:8
which the Holy G. by the mouth   Ac 1:16
were all filled with the Holy G.   Ac 2:4
the promise of the Holy G.   Ac 2:33
receive the gift of the Holy G.   Ac 2:38
Peter, filled with the Holy G.   Ac 4:8
were all filled with the Holy G.   Ac 4:31
to lie to the Holy G. and to keep   Ac 5:3
fell down, and gave up the g.   Ac 5:5
at his feet and yielded up the g.   Ac 5:10
and so is also the Holy G.   Ac 5:32

full of the Holy G. and wisdom   Ac 6:3
of faith and of the Holy G.   Ac 6:5
do always resist the Holy G.   Ac 7:51
he, being full of the Holy G.   Ac 7:55
they might receive the Holy G.   Ac 8:15
they received the Holy G.   Ac 8:17
Holy G. was given, he offered   Ac 8:18
he may receive the Holy G.   Ac 8:19
and be filled with the Holy G.   Ac 9:17
in the comfort of the Holy G.   Ac 9:31
the Holy G. and with power   Ac 10:38
the Holy G. fell on all them   Ac 10:44
out the gift of the Holy G.   Ac 10:45
have received the Holy G. as   Ac 10:47
the Holy G. fell on them, as   Ac 11:15
be baptized with the Holy G.   Ac 11:16
man, and full of the Holy G.   Ac 11:24
of worms and gave up the g.   Ac 12:23
the Holy G. said, Separate   Ac 13:2
being sent forth by the Holy G.   Ac 13:4
Paul, filled with the Holy G.   Ac 13:9
with joy, and with the Holy G.   Ac 13:52
giving them the Holy G. even   Ac 15:8
it seemed good to the Holy G.   Ac 15:8
were forbidden of the Holy G.   Ac 16:6
Have ye received the Holy G.   Ac 19:2
whether there be any Holy G.   Ac 19:2
the Holy G. came on them   Ac 19:6
that the Holy G. witnesseth   Ac 20:23
Holy G. hath made you overseers   Ac 20:28
Thus saith the Holy G., So   Ac 21:11
spake the Holy G. by Esaias   Ac 28:25
by the Holy G. which is given   Ro 5:5
me witness in the Holy G.   Ro 9:1
peace, and joy in the Holy G.   Ro 14:17
the power of the Holy G.   Ro 15:13
being sanctified by the Holy G.   Ro 15:16
the Holy G. teacheth   1Co 2:13
the temple of the Holy G.   1Co 6:19
the Lord, but by the Holy G.   1Co 12:3
the Holy G. by love unfeigned   2Co 6:6
the communion of the Holy G.   2Co 13:14
in power, and in the Holy G.   1Th 1:5
with joy of the Holy G.   1Th 1:6
by the Holy G. which dwelleth   2Ti 1:14
and renewing of the Holy G.   Tit 3:5
gifts of the Holy G. according   Heb 2:4
(as the Holy G. saith, To day if   Heb 3:7
made partakers of the Holy G.   Heb 6:4
The Holy G. this signifying   Heb 9:8
Holy G. also is a witness to us   Heb 10:15
Holy G. sent down from heaven   1Pe 1:12
were moved by the Holy G.   2Pe 1:21
Holy G.: and these three are one   1Jo 5:7
praying in the Holy G.   Jude 20

GHOSTS

that g. are there (B)   Pr 9:18

GIAH

G. by the way of the wilderness   2Sa 2:24

GIANT

which was of the sons of the g.   2Sa 21:16
among the descendents of Raphah (B)   2Sa 21:16
which was of the sons of the g.   2Sa 21:18
and he also was born to the g.   2Sa 21:20
four were born to the g. in Gath   2Sa 21:22

GIANT

that was of the children of the g.   1Ch 20:4
and he also was the son of the g.   1Ch 20:6
of the descendents of the Rephaim (B)   1Ch 20:6
were born unto the g. in Gath   1Ch 20:8
he runneth upon me like a g.   Job 16:14
like a warrior (B)(R)   Job 16:14

GIANTS

were g. in the earth in those days   Ge 6:4
And there we saw the g. the sons   Nu 13:33
of Anak, which come of the g.   Nu 13:33
accounted g. as the Anakims   De 2:11
used to be regarded as Rephaim (B)(E)(R)   De 2:11
accounted a land of g.: g. dwelt   De 2:20
remained of the remnant of g.   De 3:11
last survivor of the Rephaim (B)(E)(R)   De 3:11
which was called the land of g.   De 3:13
called the land of the Rephaim (B)(E)(R)   De 3:13
was of the remnants of the g.   Jos 12:4
of the surviving Rephaim (B)(E)(R)   Jos 12:4
remained of the remnant of the g.   Jos 13:12
at the end of the valley of the g.   Jos 15:8
the valley of the Rephaim (B)(E)(R)   Jos 15:8; 18:16
of the Perizzites and of the g.   Jos 17:15
of the Perizzites and Rephaim (B)(E)(R)   Jos 17:15
which is in the valley of the g.   Jos 18:16

GIBBAR

children of G., ninety and five   Ezr 2:20

GIBBERISH

will be g. (N)   1Co 14:11

GIBBETHON

Eltekeh, and G., and Baalath   Jos 19:44
Eltekeh with her suburbs, G. with   Jos 21:23
and Baasha smote him at G.   1Ki 15:27
and all Israel laid siege to G.   1Ki 15:27
encamped against G. which   1Ki 16:15
Omri went up from G. and   1Ki 16:17

GIBEA

Machbenah, and the father of G.   1Ch 2:49

GIBEAH

Cain, G., and Timnah; ten cities   Jos 15:57
of Israel; we will pass over to G.   J'g 19:12
lodge all night, in G., or in Ramah   J'g 19:13
G. which belongeth to Benjamin   J'g 19:14
thither, to go in and to lodge in G.   J'g 19:15
he sojourned in G.: but the men   J'g 19:16
answered and said, I came into G.   J'g 20:4; 5, 9, 10, 13, 15, 19-21, 25, 29-31, 33-34, 36-37, 43
Saul also went home to G.   1Sa 10:26
came the messengers to G. of Saul   1Sa 11:4
thousand were with Jonathan in G.   1Sa 13:2
and gat him up from Gilgal unto G.   1Sa 13:15
them, abode in G. of Benjamin   1Sa 13:16

tarried in the uttermost part of G.   1Sa 14:2
other southward over against G.   1Sa 14:5
of Saul in G. of Benjamin looked   1Sa 14:16
went up to his house to G. of Saul   1Sa 15:34
in G. under a tree in Ramah   1Sa 22:6
came up the Ziphites to Saul to G.   1Sa 23:19
the Ziphites came unto Saul to G.   1Sa 26:1
of Abinadab that was in G.   2Sa 6:3
of Abinadab which was at G.   2Sa 6:4
unto the Lord in G. of Saul, whom   2Sa 21:6
of G. of the children of Benjamin   2Sa 23:29
Ithai the son of Ribai of G. that   1Ch 11:31
the daughter of Uriel of G.   2Ch 13:2
Ramah is afraid; G. of Saul is fled   Isa 10:29
Blow ye the cornet in G. and the   Ho 5:8
themselves, as in the days of G.   Ho 9:9
hast sinned from the days of G.   Ho 10:9
battle in G. against the children of   Ho 10:9

GIBEATH

Jebusi, which is in Jerusalem, G.   Jos 18:28

GIBEATHITE

of Shemaah the G.; and Jeziel   1Ch 12:3

GIBEON

G. heard what Joshua had done   Jos 9:3
cities were g. and Chephirah   Jos 9:17
inhabitants of G. had made peace   Jos 10:1; 2-6, 10, 12, 41
the Hivites the inhabitants of G.   Jos 11:19
G. and Ramah, and Beeroth   Jos 18:25
of Benjamin, G. with her suburbs   Jos 21:17
went out from Mahanaim to G.   2Sa 2:12
and met together by the pool of G.   2Sa 2:13
Helkath-hazzurim, which is in G.   2Sa 2:16
by the way of the wilderness of G.   2Sa 2:24
brother Asahel at G. in the battle   2Sa 3:30
at the great stone which is in G.   2Sa 20:8
king went to G. to sacrifice there   1Ki 3:4
In G. the Lord appeared to   1Ki 3:5
as he had appeared unto him at G.   1Ki 9:2
And at G. dwelt the father of G.; whose   1Ch 8:29
And in G. dwelt Jehiel, whose   1Ch 9:35
And dwelt the father of G. Jehiel   1Ch 9:35
Philistines from G. even to   1Ch 14:16
in the high place that was at G.   1Ch 16:39
that season in the high place at G.   1Ch 21:29
to the high place that was at G.   2Ch 1:3
from the high place that was at G.   2Ch 1:13
the men of G. and of Mizpah   Ne 3:7
The children of G. ninety and five   Ne 7:25
shall be wroth as in the valley of G.   Isa 28:21
Azur the prophet, which was of G.   Jer 28:1

by the great waters that are in G.   Jer 41:12
he had brought again from G.   Jer 41:16

GIBEONITE

Ismaiah the G. a mighty man   1Ch 12:4
Melatiah the G. and Jadon the   Ne 3:7

GIBEONITES

house, because he slew the G.   2Sa 21:1
G. and said unto them: (now the G.   2Sa 21:2
David said unto the G., What shall   2Sa 21:3
the G. said unto him, We will have   2Sa 21:4
them into the hands of the G.   2Sa 21:9

GIBLITES

And the land of the G.   Jos 13:5

GIDDALTI

Hanani, Eliathah, G. and   1Ch 25:4
and twentieth to G. he, his sons   1Ch 25:29

GIDDEL

The children of G., the children   Ezr 2:47
of Darkon, the children of G.   Ezr 2:56; Ne 7:58
of Hanan, the children of G.   Ne 7:49

GIDDINESS

overcharged with g. (A)   Lu 21:24

GIDEON

his son G. threshed wheat by   J'g 6:11
G. said unto him, O my Lord, if the   J'g 6:13; 6:36, 39
G. went in, and made ready a kid   J'g 6:19
G. perceived that he was an angel   J'g 6:22
G. built an altar there unto   J'g 6:24
G. took ten men of his servants   J'g 6:27
G. the son of Joash hath done this   J'g 6:29
Spirit of the Lord came upon G.   J'g 6:34
who is G. and all the people   J'g 7:1
said unto G. The people that   J'g 7:2
The sword of the Lord, and of G.   J'g 7:4-5, 7, 20
So G. and the hundred men that   J'g 7:19; 7:13-15
G. sent messengers throughout all   J'g 7:24
to G. on the other side Jordan   J'g 7:25
G. came to Jordan, and passed   J'g 8:4
G. said, Therefore when the Lord   J'g 8:7
And G. went up by the way of them   J'g 8:11
G. the son of Joash returned   J'g 8:13
G. arose, and slew Zebah and   J'g 8:21
Israel said unto G., Rule thou over   J'g 8:22
G. said unto them, I will not rule   J'g 8:23
G. said unto them, I would desire   J'g 8:24
G. made an ephod thereof   J'g 8:27
thing became a snare unto G.   J'g 8:27
forty years in the days of G.   J'g 8:28
G. had threescore and ten sons of   J'g 8:30
G. the son of Joash died in a good   J'g 8:32
as G. was dead, that the children of   J'g 8:33
house of Jerubbaal, namely, G.   J'g 8:35

GIDEONI

Benjamin; Abidan, the son of *Nu 1:11*
G.
shall be Abidan the son of *Nu 2:22*
G.
Abidan the son of G. prince *Nu 7:60*
offering of Abidan the son of *Nu 7:65*
G.
Benjamin was Abidan the *Nu 10:24*
son of G.

GIDOM

pursued hard after them *J'g 20:45*
unto G.

GIER

the pelican, and the g. eagle *Le 11:18;*
De 14:17

GIFT

endowed with marriage g. *Ge 30:20*
(A)(E)(R)
me never so much dowry *Ge 34:12*
and g.
And thou shalt take no g. *Ex 23:8*
for the g. blindeth the wise *Ex 23:8*
I have given the Levites as a *Nu 8:19*
g.
are given as a g. for the *Nu 18:6*
Lord
office unto you as a service *Nu 18:7*
of g.
the heave offering of their g. *Nu 18:11*
neither take a g.: for a g. *De 16:19*
or hath he *2Sa 19:42*
given us any g.
of Tyre shall be there with a *Ps 45:12*
g.
A g. is as a precious stone in *Pr 17:8*
A wicked man taketh a g. *Pr 17:23*
out of
A man's g. maketh room for *Pr 18:16*
him
A g. in secret pacifieth anger *Pr 21:14*
boasteth himself of a false g. *Pr 25:14*
of all his labour, it is the g. *Ec 3:13*
of God
in his labour; this is the g. of *Ec 5:19*
God
a g. destroyeth the heart *Ec 7:7*
prince give a g. unto any of *Eze 46:16*
his sons
if he give a g. of his *Eze 46:17*
inheritance
if thou bring thy g. to the *M't 5:23*
altar
Leave there thy g. before the *M't 5:24*
altar
and then come and offer thy *M't 5:24*
g.
offer the g. that Moses *M' 8:4*
commanded
It is a g. by whatsoever thou *M't 15:5*
swearest by the g. that is *M't 23:18*
upon it
for whether is greater, the *M't 23:19*
g. or
or the altar that sanctifieth *M't 23:19*
the g.
Corban, that is to say, a g. *M'k 7:11*
If thou knewest the g. of *Joh 4:10*
God
receive the g. of the Holy *Ac 2:38*
Ghost
hast thought that the g. of *Ac 8:20*
God
poured out the g. of the *Ac 10:45*
Holy Ghost
God gave them the like g. as *Ac 11:17*
he did
impart unto you some *Ro 1:11*
spiritual g.
as the offence, so also is the *Ro 5:15*
free g.
grace of God, and the g. by *Ro 5:15*
grace
by one that sinned, so is the *Ro 5:16*
g.
the free g. is of many *Ro 5:16*
offences
the g. of righteousness shall *Ro 5:17*
reign
the free g. came upon all *Ro 5:18*
men unto
but the g. of God is eternal *Ro 6:23*
life

So that ye come behind in no *1Co 1:7*
spiritual endowment or *1Co 1:7*
Christian grace (A)
every man hath his proper g. *1Co 7:7*
of God
though I have the g. of *1Co 13:2*
prophecy
for the g. bestowed upon us *2Co 1:11*
that we would receive the g. *2Co 8:4*
unto God for his *2Co 9:15*
unspeakable g.
of yourselves: it is the g. of *Eph 2:8*
God
according to the g. of the *Eph 3:7*
grace of
the measure of the g. of *Eph 4:7*
Christ
Not because I desire a g. *Ph'p 4:17*
but I
Neglect not the g. that is in *1Ti 4:14*
thee
stir up the g. of God, which *2Ti 1:6*
is in
have tasted of the heavenly g. *Heb 6:4*
the g. of life (N) *Jas 1:12*
Every good g. and every *Jas 1:17*
perfect g.
As every man hath received *1Pe 4:10*
the g.

GIFTED

a g. speaker (P) *Isa 18:24*
g. in knowledge (S) *Da 1:4*

GIFTS

all sorts of choice g. (R) *Ge 24:10*
Abraham gave g. and sent *Ge 25:6*
them
Israel shall hallow all their *Ex 28:38*
holy g.
beside your g. and beside all *Le 23:38*
your
Out of all your g. ye shall *Nu 18:29*
offer
David's servants, and brought *2Sa 8:2*
g.
to David, and brought g. *2Sa 8:6*
servants and brought g. *1Ch 18:2, 6*
of persons, nor taking of g. *2Ch 19:7*
their father gave them great *2Ch 21:3*
g.
Ammonites gave g. to *2Ch 26:8*
Uzziah
many brought g. unto the *2Ch 32:23*
Lord
to the provinces, and gave g. *Es 2:18*
portions one to another, and *Es 9:22*
g.
thou hast received g. for men *Ps 68:18*
of Sheba and Seba shall *Ps 72:10*
offer g.
though thou givest many g. *Pr 6:35*
but he that hateth g. shall *Pr 15:27*
live
is a friend to him that giveth *Pr 19:6*
g.
that receiveth g. overthroweth *Pr 29:4*
every one loveth g. and *Isa 1:23*
followeth
They give g. to all whores *Eze 16:33*
but thou givest thy g. to all *Eze 16:33*
I polluted them in their *Eze 20:26*
own g.
when ye offer your g. when *Eze 20:31*
holy name no more with *Eze 20:39*
your g.
have they taken g. to shed *Eze 22:12*
blood
shall receive of me g. and *Da 2:6*
rewards
and gave him many great g. *Da 2:48*
Let thy g. be to thyself, *Da 5:17*
and give
they presented unto him g.; *M't 2:11*
gold
give good g. unto your *M't 7:11;*
children *Lu 11:13*
casting their g. into the *Lu 21:1*
treasury
with goodly stones and g. *Lu 21:5*
For the g. and calling of *Ro 11:29*
God are
Having then g. differing *Ro 12:6*
according
concerning spiritual g. *1Co 12:1*
brethren

about the spiritual *1Co 12:1*
endowments (B)
information in spiritual *1Co 12:1*
matters (P)
there are diversities of g. *1Co 12:4*
varieties, distributions of *1Co 12:4*
endowments (A)
to another the g. of healing *1Co 12:9*
extraordinary powers of *1Co 12:9*
healing (A)
graces of healing (B) *1Co 12:9*
the ability to heal (P) *1Co 12:9*
g. of healings, helps, *1Co 12:28*
governments
Have all the g. of healing? *1Co 12:30*
do all
covet earnestly the best g. *1Co 12:31*
the choicest graces (B) *1Co 12:31*
desire spiritual g. but rather *1Co 14:1*
as ye are zealous of *1Co 14:12*
spiritual g.
captive, and gave g. unto *Eph 4:8*
men
miracles, and g. of the Holy *Heb 2:4*
Ghost
variety of miraculous powers *Heb 2:4*
(B)
may offer both g. and *Heb 5:1*
sacrifices
ordained to offer g. and *Heb 8:3*
sacrifices
that there are priests that *Heb 8:4*
offer g.
were offered both g. and *Heb 9:9*
sacrifices
God testifying of his g. and *Heb 11:4*
by it
shall send g. one to another *Re 11:10*

GIHON

the name of the second river *Ge 2:13*
is G.
mule, and bring him down *1Ki 1:33*
to G.
mule, and brought him to G. *1Ki 1:38*
have anointed him king in *1Ki 1:45*
G.
the upper watercourse of *2Ch 32:30*
G.
of David, on the west side *2Ch 33:14*
of G.

GILALAI

Milalai, G., Maai, Nethaneel *Ne 12:36*

GILBOA

together, and they pitched in *1Sa 28:4*
G.
and fell down slain in mount *1Sa 31:1*
G.
his three sons fallen in *1Sa 31:8*
mount G.
happened by chance upon *2Sa 1:6*
mount G.
Ye mountains of G. let there *2Sa 1:21*
Philistines had slain Saul in *2Sa 21:12*
G.
and fell down slain in *1Ch 10:1*
mount G.
and his sons fallen in mount *1Ch 10:8*
G.

GILDED

g. with gold (B) *Pr 18:16; Re 17:4*

GILEAD

saw the land of G. was a *Nu 32:1*
place for cattle
Moses gave G. to Machir *Nu 32:40;*
De 3:15
the Lord shewed him the *De 34:1*
land of G.
Machir, being a man of war, *Jos 17:1*
had G.
Israel sent Phinehas into the *Jos 22:13*
land of G.
be head over the inhabitants *J'g 10:18*
of G.
then Jephthah went with the *J'g 11:11*
elders of G.
Abner made Ishbosheth king *2Sa 2:9*
over G.
Israel and Absalom pitched *2Sa 17:26*
in land of G.

Elijah the Tishbite, who was *1Ki 17:1*
of *G.*
G. is mine, Manasseh is mine *Ps 60:7;*
 108:8
thy hair as a flock of goats *Ca 4:1;*
from *G.* *6:5*
is there no balm in *G.*, no *Jer 8:22*
physician there
thou art *G.* to me *Jer 22:6*
his soul shall be satisfied on *Jer 50:19*
mount *G.*
G. is the city of them that *Ho 6:8*
work iniquity
is there iniquity in *G.*? they *Ho 12:11*
are vanity
they have threshed *G.* with *Am 1:3*
instruments
they have ripped up women *Am 1:13*
with child of *G.*
and Benjamin shall possess *G.* *Ob 19*
let them feed in Bashan and *Mic 7:14*
G.
I will bring thee into the *Zec 10:10*
land of *G.*

GILEADITE

after him arose Jair, a *G.* *J'g 10:3*
Jephthah the *G.* was a mighty *J'g 11:1*
the daughter of Jephthah the *J'g 11:40*
G.
Then died Jephthah the *G.* *J'g 12:7*
and Barzillai the *G.* of *2Sa 17:27*
Rogelim
And Barzillai the *G.* came *2Sa 19:31*
down
of Gilead by Barzillai the *G.* and let *1Ki 2:7*
them be
daughters of Barzillai the *G.* *Ezr 2:61*
daughters of Barzillai the *G.* *Ne 7:63*
to

GILEADITES

Gilead come the family of *Nu 26:29*
the *G.*
Ye *G.* are fugitives of *J'g 12:4*
Ephraim
the *G.* took the passages of *J'g 12:5*
Jordan
and with him fifty men of *2Ki 15:25*
the *G.*

GILEAD'S

And *G.* wife bare him sons *J'g 11:2*

GILGAL

people came up and *Jos 4:19*
encamped in *G.*
they went to Joshua unto the *Jos 9:6*
camp at *G.*
the men of *G.* sent to the *Jos 10:6*
camp at Gibeon
an angel came up from *G.* to *J'g 2:1*
Bochim
Samuel went in circuit to *G.* *1Sa 7:16*
and thou shalt go down *1Sa 10:8*
before me to *G.*
let us go to *G.* and renew *1Sa 11:14*
the kingdom
Saul was in *G.* *1Sa 13:7*
Samuel came not to *G.* *1Sa 13:8*
Samuel hewed Agag in *J'g 15:33*
pieces in *G.*
come not ye to *G.* nor go to *Ho 4:15*
Beth-aven
their wickedness is in *G.* *Ho 9:15*
there I hated them
they sacrifice bullocks in *G.* *Ho 12:11*
their altars
at *G.* multiply transgression *Am 4:4*
and bring
enter not into *G.* for *G.* shall *Am 5:5*
go into captivity
Balaam answered him from *Mic 6:5*
Shittim to *G.*

GILOH

Goshen and Holon, and *G.* *Jos 15:51*
city, even from *G.* while he *2Sa 15:12*
offered

GILONITE

Ahithophel the *G.* David's *2Sa 15:12*
Eliam the son of Ahithophel
the *G.*

GIMEL

Gimel *Ps 119:17 title*

GIMZO

G. also and the villages *2Ch 28:18*
thereof

GIN

The *g.* shall take him by the *Job 18:9*
heel
for a *g.* and for a snare to *Isa 8:14*
for a trap and a snare *Isa 8:14*
(A)(B)(R)
where no *g.* is for him? shall *Am 3:5*
where there is no trap for *Am 3:5*
him (A)(R)
where there is no bait in it (B) *Am 3:5*

GINATH

Tibni the son of *G.* to *1Ki 16:21*
make him
Tibni the son of *G.*: so *1Ki 16:22*
Tibni died

GINNETHO

Iddo, *G.*, Abijah *Ne 12:4*

GINNETHON

Daniel, *G.*, Baruch *Ne 10:6*
Iddo, Zechariah; of *G.*, *Ne 12:16*
Meshullam

GINS

wayside; they have set *g.* for *Ps 140:5*
me
they have set traps for me *Ps 140:5*
(A)(B)(R)
g. of the workers of iniquity *Ps 141:9*
laid snares for evildoers *Ps 141:9*
(A)(B)(R)
the *g.* of the workers of *Ps 141:9*
iniquity

GIRD

and *g.* him with the curious *Ex 29:5*
girdle
thou shalt *g.* them with *Ex 29:9*
girdles
he did *g.* it under his raiment *J'g 3:16*
G. ye on every man his *1Sa 25:13*
sword
g. you with sackcloth, and *2Sa 3:31*
mourn
G. up thy loins, and take my *2Ki 4:29*
staff
G. up thy loins, and take this *2Ki 9:1*
box
G. up now thy loins like a *Job 38:3*
man
G. up thy loins now like a *Job 40:7*
man
G. thy sword upon thy thigh *Ps 45:3*
g. yourselves, and ye shall be *Isa 8:9*
g. themselves with sackcloth *Isa 15:3*
and *g.* sackcloth upon your *Isa 32:11*
loins
Thou therefore *g.* up thy *Jer 1:17*
loins
For this *g.* you with sackcloth *Jer 4:8*
g. thee with sackcloth, and *Jer 6:26*
wallow
g. you with sackcloth; *Jer 49:3*
lament, and
They shall also *g.* themselves *Eze 7:18*
and *g.* them with sackcloth *Eze 27:31*
they shall not *g.* themselves *Eze 44:18*
with
G. yourselves, and lament, ye *Joe 1:13*
that he shall *g.* himself, and *Lu 12:37*
make
and *g.* thyself, and serve me *Lu 17:8*
another shall *g.* thee and *Joh 21:18*
carry
G. thyself, and bind on thy *Ac 12:8*
Wherefore *g.* up the loins of *1Pe 1:13*
your

GIRDED

shall ye eat it; with your *Ex 12:11*
loins *g.*
and *g.* him with the girdle, and *Le 8:7*

he *g.* him with the curious *Le 8:7*
girdle
them, and *g.* them with *Le 8:13*
girdles
and shall be *g.* with a linen *Le 16:4*
girdle
And when ye had *g.* on every *De 1:41*
man
stumbled are *g.* with *1Sa 2:4*
strength
a child, *g.* with a linen *1Sa 2:18*
ephod
And David *g.* his sword *1Sa 17:39*
upon his
they *g.* on every man his *1Sa 25:13*
sword
and David also *g.* on his *1Sa 25:13*
sword
David was *g.* with a linen *2Sa 6:14*
ephod
garment that he had put on *2Sa 20:8*
was *g.*
he being *g.* with a new *2Sa 21:16*
sword
For thou hast *g.* me with *2Sa 22:40*
strength
and he *g.* up his loins, and *1Ki 18:46*
ran
So they *g.* sackcloth on *1Ki 20:32*
their loins
one had his sword *g.* by his *Ne 4:18*
side
For thou hast *g.* me with *Ps 18:39*
strength
sackcloth, and *g.* me with *Ps 30:11*
gladness
mountains; being *g.* with *Ps 65:6*
power
wherewith he hath *g.* himself *Ps 93:1*
wherewith he is *g.* continually *Ps 109:19*
I *g.* thee, though thou hast *Isa 45:5*
not
they have *g.* themselves with *La 2:10*
and I *g.* thee about with *Eze 16:10*
fine linen
G. with girdles upon their *Eze 23:15*
loins
whose loins were *g.* with fine *Da 10:5*
gold
like a virgin *g.* with sackcloth *Joe 1:8*
Let your loins be *g.* about *Lu 12:35*
and took a towel, and *g.* *Joh 13:4*
himself
the towel wherewith he was *Joh 13:5*
g.
g. with a golden girdle (B) *Re 1:13*
breasts *g.* with golden girdles *Re 15:6*

GIRDEDST

thou wast young, thou *g.* *Joh 21:18*
thyself

GIRDETH

Let not him that *g.* on his *1Ki 20:11*
harness
and *g.* their loins with a *Job 12:18*
girdle
It is God that *g.* me with *Ps 18:32*
strength
She *g.* her loins with strength *Pr 31:17*

GIRDING

of a stomacher a *g.* of *Isa 3:24*
sackcloth
baldness, and to *g.* with *Isa 22:12*
sackcloth

GIRDLE

broidered coat, a mitre, and a *Ex 28:4*
g.
And the curious *g.* of the *Ex 28:8*
ephod
above the curious *g.* of the *Ex 28:27;*
ephod *28:28; 39:20, 21*
shalt make the *g.* of *Ex 28:39*
needlework
with the curious *g.* of the *Ex 29:5*
ephod
And the curious *g.* of the *Ex 39:5*
ephod
a *g.* of fine twined linen, *Ex 39:29*
and blue
and girded him with the *g.* and *Le 8:7*
with the curious *g.* of the *Le 8:7*
ephod

GIRDLE (continued)

and shall be girded with a linen g. — Le 16:4

sword, and to his bow, and to his g. — 1Sa 18:4

ten shekels of silver, and a g. — 2Sa 18:11

upon it a g. with a sword fastened — 2Sa 20:8

put the blood of war upon his g. — 1Ki 2:5

girt with a g. of leather about his — 2Ki 1:8

and girdeth their loins with a g. — Job 12:18

and for a g. wherewith he is girded — Ps 109:19

and instead of a g. a rent — Isa 3:24

shall the g. of their loins be loosed — Isa 5:27

righteousness shall be the g. of his — Isa 11:5

loins, and faithfulness the g. of his — Isa 11:5

strengthen him with thy g. — Isa 22:21

a bride her marriage g. (A) — Jer 2:32

Go and get thee a linen g. and put — Jer 13:1

So I got a g. according to the word — Jer 13:2

Take the g. that thou hast got — Jer 13:4

take the g. from thence, which I — Jer 13:6

took the g. from the place where I — Jer 13:7

g. was marred, it was profitable for — Jer 13:7

even be as this g. which is good for — Jer 13:10

For, as the g. cleaveth to the loins — Jer 13:11

and a leathern g. about his loins — M't 3:4

with a g. of a skin about his loins — M'k 1:6

he took Paul's g. and bound his — Ac 21:11

bind the man that owneth this g. — Ac 21:11

about the paps with a golden g. — Re 1:13

GIRDLES

shalt make for them g. and bonnets — Ex 28:40

And thou shalt gird them with g. — Ex 29:9

girded them with g. and put — Le 8:13

delivereth g. unto the merchant — Pr 31:24

with g. upon their loins, exceeding — Eze 23:15

breasts girded with golden g. — Re 15:6

GIRGASHITE

also, and the Amorite, and the G. — 1Ch 1:14

GIRGASHITES

the Canaanites, and the G. — Ge 15:21

the Hittites, and the G. and — De 7:1

the Perizzites, and the G. — Jos 3:10

and the G., the Hivites, and — Jos 24:11

Jebusites, and the G. to give it — Ne 9:8

GIRGASITE

and the Amorite, and the G. — Ge 10:16

GIRL

the g. was (B) — Ge 24:43

the g. (B) — Ge 24:55; 34:3, 12; De 22:15, 20-21, 24, 26; J'g 5:30; 1Ki 1:4

the g. (B) — Ge 34:3; 34:12

and sold a g. for wine, that they — Joe 3:3

the g. (B)(N)(P)(R)(S) — M't 14:11

the little g. (A) — M'k 5:39; 5:40

to a g. espoused (N) — Lu 1:27

a g. (B) — Ac 12:13

a slave girl (A)(B)(N)(P)(R) — Ac 16:16

if a g. marry (R) — 1Co 7:28; 7:34

as an unspoiled g. (P) — 2Co 11:2

GIRLS

more than all the g. (B) — Es 2:17

boys and g. playing in the streets — Zec 8:5

like ten g. (N) — M't 25:1; 25:7

GIRL'S

the g. name was Mary (N)(P) — Lu 1:27

GIRLHOOD

after her g. (B) — Lu 2:36

GIRLISH

handled her g. bosom (A)(B) — Eze 23:8

g. breasts (A)(B)(E) — Eze 23:21

GIRT

and g. with a girdle of leather about — 2Ki 1:8

he g. his fisher's coat unto him — Joh 21:7

wrapped his work jacket about him (B)(N) — Joh 21:7

slipped on his clothes (P) — Joh 21:7

put on his clothes (R) — Joh 21:7

your loins g. about with truth — Eph 6:14

tightened the belt of truth (A)(B) — Eph 6:14

Buckle on the belt of truth (N) — Eph 6:14

with truth as your belt (P) — Eph 6:14

having girded your loins with truth (R) — Eph 6:14

and g. about the paps with a golden — Re 1:13

a girdle of gold about his breast (A) — Re 1:13

girded with a golden girdle (B) — Re 1:13

golden girdle around his breast (N)(P)(R) — Re 1:13

GISPA

and Ziha and G. were over — Ne 11:21

GITTAH-HEPHER

on the east to G. to Ittah-kazin — Jos 19:13

GITTAIM

Beerothites fled to G. and were — 2Sa 4:3

Hazor, Ramah, G. — Ne 11:33

GITTITE

the house of Obed-edom the G. — 2Sa 6:10

house of Obed-edom the G. three — 2Sa 6:11

the king to Ittai the G. — 2Sa 15:19

Ittai the G. passed over, and all his — 2Sa 15:22

under the hand of Ittai the G. — 2Sa 18:2

slew the brother of Goliath the G. — 2Sa 21:19

the house of Obed-edom the G. — 1Ch 13:13

the brother of Goliath the G. — 1Ch 20:5

GITTITES

the G. and the Ekronites; also the — Jos 13:3

and all the G. six hundred men — 2Sa 15:18

GITTITH

To the chief Musician upon G. — Ps 8, 81, 84 title

GIVE

g. me the persons, and take the goods — Ge 14:21

what g. me, seeing I go childless — Ge 15:2

the field I g. thee, and the cave therein — Ge 23:11

therefore God g. thee of the dew of heaven — Ge 27:28

of all thou shalt g. me, I will g. tenth — Ge 28:22

better I g. her thee, than g. her to another — Ge 29:19

g. me my wife; g. children — Ge 29:21; 30:1

g. me my wives and my children — Ge 30:26

then will we g. our daughters to you — Ge 34:16

thou must g. us also sacrifices — Ex 10:25

if her father utterly refuse to g. her to him — Ex 22:17

on the eighth day thou shalt g. it me — Ex 22:30

then they shall g. every man a ransom — Ex 30:12

this they shall g. every one half a shekel — Ex 30:13

thou shalt g. the Levites unto Aaron — Nu 3:9

and the Lord g. thee peace — Nu 6:26

they said, Who shall g. us flesh to eat — Nu 11:4

if Balak would g. me his house full — Nu 22:18; 24:13

I g. to Phinehas my covenant of peace — Nu 25:12

to many g. more inheritance, to few g. less inheritance — Nu 26:54; 33:54

ye shall g. to Levites suburbs for the cities — Nu 35:2

thou shalt g. him thine heart — De 15:10; 15:1

every man g. as he is able — De 16:17; Eze 46:5, 11

at his day thou shalt g. him his hire — De 24:15

forty stripes he may g. him, and not exceed — De 25:3

swear to me, and g. me a true token — Jos 2:12

now therefore g. me this mountain — Jos 14:12

g. me a blessing, g. springs — Jos 15:19; J'g 1:15

that fleeth, they shall g. him a place — Jos 20:4

g. hearts to the Lord (B) — Jos 24:23

to g. the Midianites into their hands — J'g 7:2

they answered, We will willingly g. them — J'g 8:25

nay, but thou shalt g. it me — 1Sa 2:16

in all the wealth which God shall g. Israel — 1Sa 2:32

when they said, G. us a king to judge us — 1Sa 8:6

g. me a man that we may fight together — 1Sa 17:10

the king will g. him his daughter — 1Sa 17:25

David said, None like that, g. it me — 1Sa 21:9

will the son of Jesse g. every one fields — 1Sa 22:7

shall I then g. it to men whom I know not — 1Sa 25:11

oh that one would g. me drink of water of well of Beth-lehem — 2Sa 23:15; 1Ch 11:17

all these did Araunah g. — 2Sa 24:23; 1Ch 21:23

g. thy servant an understanding heart — 1Ki 3:9

O my lord, g. her the living child — 1Ki 3:26; 3:27

g. every man according to his ways — 1Ki 8:39

if thou wilt g. me half thine house — 1Ki 13:8

he said, G. me thy son, and he took him — 1Ki 17:19

I said, G. thy son, that we may eat him — 2Ki 6:29

if it be, g. me thine hand and he gave it — 2Ki 10:15

saying, G. thy daughter to my son to wife — 2Ki 14:9

g. to Lord glory and strength — 1Ch 16:28; Ps 29:1-2; 96:7-8

the Lord g. thee wisdom and understanding — 1Ch 22:12

g. me now wisdom and knowledge — 2Ch 1:10

the hand of God was to *g.*   *2Ch 30:12*
them one heart
and to *g.* us a nail in his holy   *Ezr 9:8*
place
to *g.* us a reviving, to *g.* us a   *Ezr 9:9*
wall in Judah
and *g.* them for a prey in land   *Ne 4:4*
of captivity
all that a man hath will he *g.*   *Job 2:4*
for his life
nor let me *g.* flattering titles   *Job 32:21*
to man
ask of me, and I shall *g.* thee   *Ps 2:8*
the heathen
g. them according to their   *Ps 28:4*
deeds
he shall *g.* thee the desires of   *Ps 37:4*
thine heart
none can *g.* to God a ransom   *Ps 49:7*
for him
thou desirest not sacrifice,   *Ps 51:16*
else would I *g.* it
g. us help from trouble   *Ps 60:11;*
     108:12
can he *g.* bread also? can he   *Ps 78:20*
provide flesh
O turn, *g.* thy strength to thy   *Ps 86:16*
servant
he shall *g.* his angels charge   *Ps 91:11;*
     M't 4:6
but I *g.* myself unto prayer   *Ps 109:4*
g. me understanding   *Ps 119:34;*
     119:73; 125, 144, 169
g. me life (S)   *Ps 119:40*
g. instruction to a wise man he   *Pr 9:9*
will be wiser
my son, *g.* me thine heart,   *Pr 23:26*
observe my
if enemy hunger, *g.* him   *Pr 25:21;*
bread   *Ro 12:20*
the rod and reproof *g.*   *Pr 29:15*
wisdom
be shall *g.* thee rest, shall *g.*   *Pr 29:17*
delight to thy soul
g. me neither poverty nor   *Pr 30:8*
riches, feed me
horseleach hath two   *Pr 30:15*
daughters, crying, G. g.
that he may *g.* to him that is   *Ec 2:26*
good
g. a portion to seven, also to   *Ec 11:2*
eight
if a man would *g.* substance   *Ca 8:7*
of his house
then he shall *g.* the rain of   *Isa 30:23*
thy seed
g. place to me, that I may   *Isa 49:20*
dwell
that it may *g.* seed to the   *Isa 55:10*
sower, and bread
to *g.* unto them beauty for   *Isa 61:3*
ashes
g. him no rest till he   *Isa 62:7*
establish Jerusalem
how shall I *g.* thee a   *Jer 3:19*
pleasant land
to whom shall I speak and *g.*   *Jer 6:10*
warning
to *g.* man according to his   *Jer 17:10;*
ways   *32:19*
g. heed to me, O Lord, and   *Jer 18:19*
hearken
I think to *g.* you an   *Jer 29:11*
expected end
bring them, and *g.* them wine   *Jer 35:2*
to drink
let tears run down, *g.* thyself   *La 2:18*
no rest
g. them sorrow of heart, thy   *La 3:65*
curse to them
open thy mouth, eat that I *g.*   *Eze 2:8*
thee
fill thy bowels with this roll   *Eze 3:3*
that I *g.* thee
and *g.* them warning from   *Eze 3:17*
me
by blood of children which   *Eze 16:36*
didst *g.* them
I had brought them to   *Eze 20:28;*
land, I lifted up hand to   *20:42; 47:14*
g. them
if wicked *g.* again that he   *Eze 33:15*
had robbed
if the prince *g.* a gift to his   *Eze 46:16*
sons
and *g.* thy rewards to another   *Da 5:17*
I am come forth to *g.* thee   *Da 9:22*
skill

her rulers with shame do   *Ho 4:18*
love, *g.* ye
g. them, O Lord, what wilt   *Ho 9:14*
thou *g.*
thou saidst, G. me a king   *Ho 13:10*
and princes
shall I *g.* my firstborn for my   *Mic 6:7*
transgression
vine *g.* her fruit, ground *g.*   *Zec 8:12*
increase, and heavens *g.* dew
g. me my price, if not   *Zec 11:12*
forbear
g. to him that asketh thee   *M't 5:42*
g. us this day our daily   *M't 6:11;*
bread   *Lu 11:3*
if he ask bread, will he *g.*   *M't 7:9*
him a stone
if he ask fish, will he *g.* a   *M't 7:10;*
serpent   *Lu 11:11*
g. gifts to your children, so   *M't 7:11;*
your Father *g.* them that   *Lu 11:13*
ask him
g. place   *M't 9:24*
freely ye received, freely *g.*   *M't 10:8*
whoso shall *g.* to drink a   *M't 10:42*
cup of cold water
he promised to *g.* her what   *M't 14:7*
she would ask
g. ye them to eat   *M't 14:16;*
     M'k 6:37; Lu 9:13
g. in exchange for his soul   *M't 16:26;*
     M'k 8:37
that take, and *g.* to them   *M't 17:27*
for me and thee
why command to *g.* a   *M't 19:7*
writing of divorcement
go sell, and *g.* to the poor   *M't 19:21;*
     M'k 10:21
call the labourers, and *g.*   *M't 20:8*
them their hire
sit on hand is not mine to   *M't 20:23;*
g.   *M'k 10:40*
g. us of your oil, for our   *M't 25:8*
lamps are gone out
what will ye *g.* me, and I   *M't 26:15*
will deliver him
I will that thou *g.* me the   *M'k 6:25*
head of John
and he will *g.* the vineyard   *M'k 12:9*
unto others
and to whomsoever I will, I *g.*   *Lu 4:6*
it
g. and it shall be given unto   *Lu 6:38*
you
good measure shall men *g.*   *Lu 6:38*
into your bosom
he will *g.* him as many as he   *Lu 11:8*
needeth
g. alms of such things as ye   *Lu 11:41;*
have   *12:33*
he that bade thee say, G. this   *Lu 14:9*
man place
the younger said, G. me the   *Lu 15:12*
portion of goods
who shall *g.* you that which   *Lu 16:12*
is your own
Jesus saith to her, G. me to   *Joh 4:7;*
drink   *4:10*
whoso drinketh the water I   *Joh 4:14*
shall *g.* him
meat which the Son of man   *Joh 6:27*
shall *g.* you
they said, Lord, evermore *g.*   *Joh 6:34*
us this bread
how can this man *g.* us his   *Joh 6:52*
flesh to eat
g. God the praise, this man   *Joh 9:24*
is a sinner
I *g.* to them eternal life,   *Joh 10:28*
never perish
what thou wilt ask, God   *Joh 11:22*
will *g.* it thee
that he should *g.* something   *Joh 13:29*
to the poor
he shall *g.* you another   *Joh 14:16*
Comforter to abide
my peace I *g.* to you not as   *Joh 14:27*
world giveth *g.* I to you
whatsoever ye shall ask, he   *Joh 15:16*
may *g.* it
whatsoever ye ask he will *g.*   *Joh 16:23*
it you
that he should *g.* eternal life   *Joh 17:2*
to as many
such as I have *g.* I thee, rise   *Ac 3:6*
and walk
but we will *g.* ourselves to   *Ac 6:4*
prayer

promised he would *g.* it for a   *Ac 7:5*
possession
Simon said, G. me also this   *Ac 8:19*
power
it is more blessed to *g.* than   *Ac 20:35*
to receive
g. life to mortal body (S)   *Ro 8:11*
with him also freely *g.* us all   *Ro 8:32*
things
avenge not, but rather *g.*   *Ro 12:19*
place to wrath
that ye may *g.* yourselves to   *1Co 7:5*
fasting
g. none offence, neither to   *1Co 10:32*
the Jews
so let him *g.* not grudgingly   *2Co 9:7*
or of necessity
God may *g.* you the spirit   *Eph 1:17*
of wisdom
that he may have to *g.* to   *Eph 4:28*
him that needeth
g. to your servants that which   *Col 4:1*
is just
g. attendance to reading, to   *1Ti 4:13*
doctrine
meditate, *g.* thyself wholly to   *1Ti 4:15*
them
which the righteous Judge   *2Ti 4:8*
shall *g.* me
we ought to *g.* the more   *Heb 2:1*
earnest heed
g. life for them that sin not   *1Jo 5:16*
to death
g. me the little book, he said,   *Re 10:9*
Take it
he had power to *g.* life to   *Re 13:15*
image
to *g.* her the cup of wine of   *Re 16:19*
his wrath
so much torment and sorrow   *Re 18:7*
g. her
to *g.* every man according to   *Re 22:12*
his work

GIVE *THANKS*

I will *g.* thanks to thee   *2Sa 22:50;*
     Ps 18:49
g. thanks to Lord   *1Ch 16:8;*
Ps 105:1;   106:1;   107:1;   118:1,   29;
     136:1, 3
save us that we may *g.*   *1Ch 16:35;*
thanks to thy holy name   *Ps 106:47*
who were expressed by   *1Ch 16:41*
name, to *g. thanks*
sons of Jeduthun with a   *1Ch 25:3*
harp to *g. thanks*
Hezekiah appointed Levites   *2Ch 31:2*
to *g. thanks*
in the grave who shall *g.* thee   *Ps 6:5*
thanks
g. thanks at remembrance of   *Ps 30:4;*
his holiness   *97:12*
I will *g. thanks* to thee for   *Ps 30:12*
ever
I will *g. thanks* in the great   *Ps 35:18*
congregation
to thee, O God, do we *g.*   *Ps 75:1*
thanks, do *g. thanks*
so we thy people will *g.* thee   *Ps 79:13*
thanks
it is a good thing to *g. thanks*   *Ps 92:1*
to the Lord
save us to *g. thanks* to thy   *Ps 106:47*
holy name
at midnight I will rise to *g.*   *Ps 119:62*
thanks
whither the tribes go up to   *Ps 122:4*
g. thanks
O *g. thanks* unto the God   *Ps 136:2*
of gods
O *g. thanks* unto the God of   *Ps 136:26*
heaven
righteous shall *g. thanks* to   *Ps 140:13*
thy name
to whom not only I *g. thanks*   *Ro 16:4*
for that for which I *g.*   *1Co 10:30*
thanks
I cease not to *g. thanks* for   *Eph 1:16*
you
we *g. thanks* to God and   *Col 1:3*
the Father
we *g. thanks* to God always   *1Th 1:2*
for you
in every thing *g. thanks,* this   *1Th 5:18*
is the will of God
we are bound to *g. thanks*   *2Th 2:13*
for you
we *g.* thee *thanks,* Lord God   *Re 11:17*
Almighty

GIVE *UP*

Lord walketh to *g. up* thine   De 23:14;
enemies   31:5
he shall *g.* Israel *up*, because   1Ki 14:16
of sins
why did not I *g. up* the   Job 3:11
ghost
if I hold my tongue, I shall   Job 13:19
g. up the ghost
I will say to north, *G. up,*   Isa 43:6
and to south
how shall I *g.* thee *up,*   Ho 11:8
Ephraim
therefore will he *g.* them *up*   Mic 5:3
that which thou deliverest   Mic 6:14
will I *g. up*

I *WILL* GIVE

I will g. thee and seed the   Ge 17:8;
land wherein thou art a   48:4; De 34:4
I will g. thee a son also of   Ge 17:16
her, and bless her
I will surely *g.* the tenth to   Ge 28:22
thee
what ye shall say to me *I*   Ge 34:11;
will g.   34:12
and *I will g.* this people   Ex 3:21
favour
my presence with thee, and   Ex 33:14
I will g. thee rest
I will g. you rain in season   Le 26:4;
  De 11:14
I will g. peace in the land, ye   Le 26:6
shall lie down
I will g. him to the Lord all   1Sa 1:11
his life
I will g. her, that she may   1Sa 18:21
be a snare to him
I will g. thy wives to thy   2Sa 12:11
neighbour
not rend all, but *I will g.*   1Ki 11:13
one tribe
I will g. ten tribes to thee   1Ki 11:31
come home, and *I will g.*   1Ki 13:7
thee a reward
I will g. thee for it a better   1Ki 21:2
vineyard
I will g. thee the vineyard of   1Ki 21:7
Naboth
I will g. him rest, *I will g.*   1Ch 22:9
peace to Israel
I will g. thee riches, wealth,   2Ch 1:12
honour
O Lord, *I will g.* thanks to   Ps 30:12
thee
I will sing and *g.* praise   Ps 57:7;
  108:1
to-morrow *I will g.* when thou   Pr 3:28
hast it
I will g. them children to be   Isa 3:4
princes
I will g. to Jerusalem one   Isa 41:27
that bringeth good tidings
I will g. thee for covenant   Isa 42:6;
of the people   49:8
I will g. thee the treasures of   Isa 45:3
darkness
I will g. thee for a light to   Isa 49:6
the Gentiles
I will g. them an everlasting   Isa 56:5
name
I will g. pastors according to   Jer 3:15
my heart
I will g. them waters of gall   Jer 9:15
to drink
I will g. you assured peace   Jer 14:13
in this land
I will g. thy substance to the   Jer 17:3
spoil
I will g. them an heart to   Jer 24:7
know me
I will g. them one heart   Jer 32:39;
  Eze 11:19
I will g. the men that have   Jer 34:18
transgressed
I will g. it into the hand of   Eze 7:21
strangers
and *I will g.* you the land   Eze 11:17
of Israel
I will g. thee blood in fury,   Eze 16:38
and jealousy
I will also *g.* thee into their   Eze 16:39
hand
I will g. them to thee for   Eze 16:61
daughters
he come whose right it is, *I*   Eze 21:27
will g. it him

I will g. them to be   Eze 23:46
removed and spoiled
I will g. land of Egypt to   Eze 29:19
Nebuchadnezzar
I will g. thee the opening of   Eze 29:21
the mouth
and *I will g.* you an heart of   Eze 36:26
flesh
I will g. her vineyards from   Ho 2:15
thence
come unto me, and *I will g.*   M't 11:28
you rest
I will g. to thee the keys of   M't 16:19
the kingdom
and whatsoever is right, *I*   M't 20:4
will g. you
I will g. to this last even as   M't 20:14
unto thee
ask what thou wilt, *I will g.*   M'k 6:22
it thee
for *I will g.* you a mouth   Lu 21:15
and wisdom
the bread *I will g.* is my   Joh 6:51
flesh, which *I will g.* for
the life of the world
I will g. you the sure   Ac 13:34
mercies of David
be faithful, and *I will g.* thee a   Re 2:10
crown of life
I will g. him a white stone   Re 2:17
and a new name
I will g. to every one according   Re 2:23
to your works
and *I will g.* him the morning   Re 2:28
star
and *I will g.* power to my   Re 11:3
two witnesses
I will g. to him that is athirst   Re 21:6
water of life

LORD GIVE

when come to land *Lord* will   Ex 12:25;
g. you   Le 14:34; 23:10; 25:2; Nu.15:2
when the *Lord* shall *g.* you   Ex 16:8
flesh to eat
therefore the *Lord* will *g.*   Nu 11:18
you flesh
if the *Lord* delight in us, he   Nu 14:8
will *g.* it us
the *Lord* refuseth to *g.* me   Nu 22:13
leave to go
the *Lord* commanded to *g.*   Nu 34:13
the nine tribes
the *Lord* commanded to *g.*   Nu 36:2
the land by lot
it is a good land the *Lord*   De 1:25
doth *g.*
the *Lord* shall *g.* thee a   De 28:65
trembling heart
the *Lord* commanded Moses   Jos 9:24
to *g.* the land
the *Lord* commanded to *g.* us   Jos 17:4
inheritance
the *Lord* commanded to *g.* us   Jos 21:2
cities
which the *Lord* shall *g.* thee of   Ru 4:12
this woman
the *Lord* his God did *g.* him   1Ki 15:4
a lamp
the *Lord* is able to *g.* thee   2Ch 25:9
much
the *Lord* will *g.* strength to   Ps 29:11
his people
the *Lord* will *g.* grace and   Ps 84:11
glory
the *Lord* shall *g.* that which   Ps 85:12
is good
the *Lord* himself shall *g.* you   Isa 7:14
a sign
the *Lord* shall *g.* thee rest   Isa 14:3
from sorrow
though the *Lord g.* you   Isa 30:20
bread of adversity
the Lord shall *g.* them   Zec 10:1
showers of rain
Lord shall *g.* him the throne   Lu 1:32
of his Father
Lord g. mercy to house of   2Ti 1:16
Onesiphorus

NOT GIVE, GIVE *NOT*

Jacob said, Thou shalt *not g.*   Ge 30:31
me anything
I will *not g.* you straw, go,   Ex 5:10
get straw
the rich shall *not g.* more,   Ex 30:15
poor *not g.* less

thou shalt *not g.* thy money   Le 25:37
on usury
I will *not g.* you of their land   De 2:5;
  2:9, 19
thy daughter thou shalt *not g.*   De 7:3
to his son
he will *not g.* of the flesh of   De 28:55
his children
shall *not* any of us *g.* his   J'g 21:1
daughter to Benjamin
we have sworn we will *not g.*   J'g 21:7
them wives
we will *not g.* them ought   1Sa 30:22
of the spoil
I will *not g.* inheritance of   1Ki 21:4
my fathers
g. not your daughters   Ezr 9:12;
  Ne 10:30; 13:25
I will *not g.* sleep to mine   Ps 132:4
eyes
g. not sleep to thine eyes, nor   Pr 6:4
slumber
g. not thy strength unto   Pr 31:3
women
constellations shall *not g.*   Isa 13:10
their light
my glory will *I not g.* to   Isa 42:8;
another   48:11
I will *no* more *g.* thy corn to   Isa 62:8
enemies
let us *not g.* heed to any of   Jer 18:18
his words
not g. Jeremiah into the   Jer 26:24
hand of the people
cover sun with cloud, moon   Eze 32:7;
shall *not g.* her light   M't 24:29;
  M'k 13:24
to whom *not g.* honour of   Da 11:21
kingdom
g. not thine heritage to   Joe 2:17
reproach
g. not that which is holy to   M't 7:6
the dogs
shall we give or shall we *not*   M'k 12:15
g.
neither *g.* place to the devil   Eph 4:27
and *g. not* those things they   Jas 2:16
need

WILL I GIVE

to thy seed *will I g.* this   Ge 12:7;
land   13:15; 24:7; 28:13; 35:12;
  Ex 32:13; 33:1
save Caleb, to him *will I g.*   De 1:36
the land
they shall go in thither, to   De 1:39
them *will I g.* it
to him *will I g.* Achsah   Jos 15:16;
  J'g 1:12
that *will I g.* to the man of   1Sa 9:8
God to tell
my daughter Merab, her   1Sa 18:17
will I g. thee
to thee *will I g.* land   1Ch 16:18;
  Ps 105:11
therefore *will I g.* thanks to   Ps 18:49
thee
there *will I g.* thee my loves   Ca 7:12
therefore *will I g.* men for   Isa 43:4
thee
to them *will I g.* in mine   Isa 56:5
house a place
so *will I g.* Zedekiah king of   Jer 24:8
Judah
thy life *will I g.* to thee for a   Jer 45:5
prey
so *will I g.* inhabitants of   Eze 15:6
Jerusalem
new heart also *will I g.*   Eze 36:26
you, and new spirit
and in this place *will I g.*   Hag 2:9
peace
devil said, All these things *will*   M't 4:9
I g. thee
all this power *will I g.* thee,   Lu 4:6
and glory
to him that overcometh *will I*   Re 2:7;
g.   2:17, 26

GIVEN

Sarah should have *g.* children   Ge 21:7
suck
because he hath *g.* his seed to   Le 20:3
Molech
they are *g.* as a gift for the   Nu 18:6
Lord
according to the blessing *g.*   De 12:15;
  16:17

full reward be *g.* thee of the *Ru 2:12*
Lord
who thought I would have *g.* *2Sa 4:10*
a reward
I would have *g.* thee such *2Sa 12:8*
and such things
I would have *g.* thee ten *2Sa 18:11*
shekels of silver
or hath the king *g.* us any *2Sa 19:42*
gift
the sign which the man of *1Ki 13:5*
God had *g.*
and of thine own have we *1Ch 29:14*
g. thee
let it be *g.* them day by day *Ezr 6:9*
without fail
the silver is *g.* to thee, the *Es 3:11*
people also
let my life be *g.* me at *Es 7:3*
my petition and people
why is light *g.* to him that is *Job 3:20*
in misery
why is light *g.* to a man *Job 3:23*
whose way is hid
to whom alone the earth *Job 15:19*
was *g.*
Who hath *g.* to me (S) *Job 41:11*
dead bodies of thy servants *g.* *Ps 79:2*
to be meat
he hath *g.* to the poor *Ps 112:9;*
 2Co 9:9
the earth hath he *g.* to the *Ps 115:16*
children of men
g. me life (S) *Ps 119:50; 119:93*
that which he hath *g.* will he *Pr 19:17*
pay him
nor wickedness deliver those that *Ec 8:8*
are *g.* to it
which are *g.* from one *Ec 12:11*
shepherd
for to us a Child is born, to *Isa 9:6*
us a Son is *g.*
therefore hear, thou that art *Isa 47:8*
g. to pleasures
every one is *g.* to *Jer 6:13;*
covetousness *8:10*
he said to all who had *g.* *Jer 44:20*
him that answer
we have *g.* the hand to the *La 5:6*
Egyptians
unto us is this land *g.* *Eze 11:15;*
 33:24
they are desolate, they are *Eze 35:12*
g. to consume
beasts, fowls hath he *g.* into *Da 2:38*
thine hand
like a lion, and a man's heart *Da 7:4*
was *g.* to it
she shall be *g.* up, and they *Da 11:6*
that brought her
it is *g.* to you to know the *M't 13:11;*
mysteries of the kingdom *M'k 4:11;*
 Lu 8:10
all cannot receive, save they *M't 19:11*
to whom it is *g.*
be *g.* to a nation bringing *M't 21:43*
forth fruits
are *g.* in marriage *M't 22:30;*
 M'k 12:25; Lu 20:35
sold for much and *g.* to the *M't 26:9;*
poor *M'k 14:5*
all power is *g.* to me in *M't 28:18*
heaven and earth
unto you that hear more *M'k 4:24*
shall be *g.*
to whom much *g.* of him *Lu 12:48*
much required
can receive nothing, except it *Joh 3:27*
be *g.*
he hath *g.* to the Son to *Joh 5:26*
have life in himself
of all he hath *g.* me, I *Joh 6:39*
should lose nothing
no man can come to me, *Joh 6:65*
except it were *g.* him
except it were *g.* thee from *Joh 19:11*
above
there is none other name *g.* *Ac 4:12*
among men
he hoped that money should *Ac 24:26*
be *g.* him
by the Holy Ghost which is *g.* *Ro 5:5*
to us
or who hath first *g.* to him, *Ro 11:35*
and recompensed
because of the grace that is *Ro 15:15*
g. me of God
might know things freely *g.* *1Co 2:12*
us of God

that thanks may be *g.* by *2Co 1:11*
many
been a law *g.* which could *Ga 3:21*
have *g.* life
dispensation, which is *g.* me *Eph 3:2*
to you-ward
to me who am the least is *Eph 3:8*
this grace *g.*
g. themselves over to *Eph 4:19*
lasciviousness
Christ hath loved us, and *g.* *Eph 5:2*
himself for us
to you it is *g.* in behalf of *Ph'p 1:29*
Christ
and hath *g.* him a name *Ph'p 2:9*
above every name
for if Jesus had *g.* them rest, *Heb 4:8*
then not spoken
by the Spirit which he hath *1Jo 3:24*
g. us
because he hath *g.* us of his *1Jo 4:13*
Spirit
white robes were *g.* to every *Re 6:11*
one of them
power was *g.* him to continue *Re 13:5*
42 months
it was *g.* to him to make war *Re 13:7*
with the saints

GOD, LORD HATH, HAD GIVEN

the Lord hath *g.* Abraham *Ge 24:35*
flocks and herds
and Rachel said, *God hath* *Ge 30:6*
g. me a son
Leah said, *God hath g.* me *Ge 30:18*
mine hire
thus *God hath g.* me your *Ge 31:9*
father's cattle
the children which *God hath* *Ge 33:5*
graciously *g.* me
God hath g. you treasure in *Ge 43:23*
your sacks
the children *God hath g.* me *Ge 48:9*
in this place
the bread which the *Lord* *Ex 16:15*
hath g. you
for that the *Lord hath g.* *Ex 16:29*
you the sabbath
land which the *Lord hath g.* *Nu 32:7;*
them *32:9; De 3:18; 28:52; Jos 2:9, 14;*
 23:13, 15; Jer 25:5
shout, for the *Lord hath g.* *Jos 6:16*
you the city
to possess land which the *Jos 18:3*
Lord hath g. you
Lord hath g. me my petition *1Sa 1:27*
I asked
Lord hath g. it to a *1Sa 15:28;*
neighbour of thine *28:17*
not to do so with what the *1Sa 30:23*
Lord hath g.
kingdoms *hath God g.* me *2Ch 36:23;*
 Ezr 1:2
every man to whom *God hath* *Ec 5:19*
g. riches
I and the children *Lord hath g.* *Isa 8:18;*
 Heb 2:13
the *Lord hath g.* a *Isa 23:11*
commandment against
the *Lord hath g.* me the tongue *Isa 50:4*
of the learned
the *Lord hath g.* me *Jer 11:18*
knowledge of it
seeing the *Lord hath g.* it a *Jer 47:7*
charge
after that the *Lord had g.* *Joh 6:23*
thanks
whom *God hath g.* to them *Ac 5:32*
that obey him
God hath g. thee all that *Ac 27:24*
sail with thee
God hath g. them the spirit *Ro 11:8*
of slumber
the *Lord hath g.* us for *2Co 10:8;*
edification *13:10*
but *God who hath g.* us his *1Th 4:8*
Holy Spirit
this is the record *God hath* *1Jo 5:11*
g. to us

I HAVE, HAVE I GIVEN

brethren *have I g.* him for *Ge 27:37*
servants
I have g. thee that thou hast *1Ki 3:13*
not asked

therefore *I have g.* Jacob to *Isa 43:28*
the curse
I have g. him for a witness *Isa 55:4*
to the people
things *I have g.* shall pass *Jer 8:13*
from them
I have g. it to whom it *Jer 27:5*
seemed meet to me
I have g. thee cow's dung *Eze 4:15*
for man's dung
I have g. him the land of *Eze 29:20*
Egypt for labour
I also *have g.* you cleanness *Am 4:6*
of teeth
no more be pulled out of *Am 9:15*
land *I have g.*
I have g. you an example, *Joh 13:15*
that ye do
I have g. them words thou *Joh 17:8;*
gavest *17:14*
the glory thou gavest me, *I* *Joh 17:22*
have g. them
as *I have g.* order to the *1Co 16:1*
churches

NOT GIVEN

she was *not g.* unto him to *Ge 38:14*
wife
I have *not g.* ought thereof *De 26:14*
for the dead
yet Lord hath *not g.* you an *De 29:4*
heart to perceive
hath he *not g.* you rest on *1Ch 22:18*
every side
portion of Levites had *not* *Ne 13:10*
been *g.*
thou hast *not g.* water to the *Job 22:7*
weary
maidens were *not g.* to *Ps 78:63*
marriage
but he hath *not g.* me over *Ps 118:18*
to death
hath *not g.* us a prey to *Ps 124:6*
their teeth
Jerusalem *not* be *g.* into the *Isa 37:10*
hand of Assyria
shalt *not* be *g.* into hand of *Jer 39:17*
the men
because thou hast *not g.* him *Eze 3:20*
warning
he that hath *not g.* forth *Eze 18:8*
upon usury
it is given to you, to them *M't 13:11*
it is *not g.*
for the Holy Ghost was *not* *Joh 7:39*
yet *g.*
bishop *not g.* to wine, *1Ti 3:3;*
no striker *Tit 1:7*
deacons *not g.* to much wine, *1Ti 3:8*
not greedy
God hath *not g.* us the spirit *2Ti 1:7*
of fear
aged women likewise *not g.* to *Tit 2:3*
wine

SHALL BE GIVEN

to every one *shall* *Nu 26:54*
inheritance *be g.*
thy sheep *shall* be *g.* to *De 28:31*
enemies
thy sons *shall* be *g.* to *De 28:32*
another people
till another commandment *Ezr 4:21*
shall be g.
it *shall* be *g.* to half of the *Es 5:3*
kingdom
to him *shall* be *g.* of gold of *Ps.72:15*
Sheba
what *shall* be *g.* to thee, *Ps 120:3*
thou false tongue
the reward of his hands *shall* *Isa 3:11*
be *g.* him
bread *shall* be *g.* him, *Isa 33:16*
waters shall be sure
the glory of Lebanon *shall be* *Isa 35:2*
g. to it
this city *shall be g.* into the *Jer 21:10;*
hand of king of Babylon *38:3, 18*
marishes, they *shall be g.* to *Eze 47:11*
salt
the saints *shall be g.* into his *Da 7:25*
hand
the kingdom *shall be g.* to *Da 7:27*
the saints
ask, and it *shall be g.* you *M't 7:7;*
 Lu 11:9
it *shall be g.* you in same *M't 10:19;*
hour *M'k 13:11*

no sign *shall be* g.   *M't* 12:39
      M'k 8:12; *Lu* 11:29
for whosoever hath to him, *M't* 13:12;
shall be g.   25:29; *M'k* 4:25; *Lu* 8:18
it *shall be* g. them for   *M't* 20:23
whom it is prepared
the kingdom of God *shall*   *M't* 21:43
be g. to a nation
give, and it *shall be* g. you   *Lu* 6:38
thro' your prayers *I shall be Ph'm* 22
g. you
let him ask of God, it *shall be Jas* 1:5
g. him

THOU HAST,
HAST THOU GIVEN

Abram said, To me *thou*   *Ge* 15:3
hast g. no seed
bless the land which *thou*   *De* 26:15
hast g. us
thou hast g. me south land *Jos* 15:19;
      J'g 1:15
why *hast thou* g. me but   *Jos* 17:14
one lot to inherit
thou hast g. this great   *J'g* 15:18
deliverance
thou hast g. him bread and *1Sa* 22:13
a sword
by this deed *thou hast* g. *2Sa* 12:14
occasion
thou hast g. me shield of   2Sa 22:36;
salvation   *Ps* 18:35
thou hast g. me the necks *2Sa* 22:41;
of enemies   *Ps* 18:40
thou hast g. him a son to sit *1Ki* 3:6
on throne
rain on thy land *thou hast 1Ki* 8:36;
g.   *2Ch* 6:27
what cities are these *thou*   *1Ki* 9:13
hast g. me
cast us out of possession *2Ch* 20:11
thou hast g.
thou hast g. us such   *Ezr* 9:13
deliverance as this
thou hast g. him his heart's *Ps* 21:2
desire
thou hast g. us like sheep for *Ps* 44:11
meat
thou hast g. a banner to them *Ps* 60:4
that fear thee
thou hast g. me the heritage of *Ps* 61:5
those that fear
thou hast g. commandment to *Ps* 71:3
save me
as *thou hast* g. him power   *Joh* 17:2
over all flesh
that all things *thou hast* g. *Joh* 17:7
me. are of thee
I pray not but for them *thou Joh* 17:9
hast g. me
keep those *thou hast* g. me *Joh* 17:11
thou hast g. them blood to *Re* 16:6
drink

GIVER

as with taker of usury, so   *Isa* 24:2
with g.
not grudgingly, God loveth *2Co* 9:7
cheerful g.
God is a generous g. who   *Jas* 1:5
neither refuses nor reproaches (N)

GIVEST

g. him nought, he cry to Lord *De* 15:9
thy heart not be grieved   *De* 15:10
when thou g. him
if thou be righteous, what g. *Job* 35:7
thou him
thou g. thy mouth to evil, *Ps* 50:19
thy tongue
g. them tears to drink in great *Ps* 80:5
measure
that thou g. them, they   *Ps* 104:28
gather
thou g. them their meat in *Ps* 145:15
due season
nor rest content, though g.   *Pr* 6:35
many gifts
thou g. not warning, to save *Eze* 3:18
his life
but thou g. thy gifts to all *Eze* 16:33
thy lovers
thou g. a reward, and none *Eze* 16:34
is given
when thou g. a dinner (S)   *Lu* 14:12;
      14:13

for thou verily g. thanks   *1Co* 14:17
well

GIVETH

he g. you on sixth day   *Ex* 16:29
bread of two
days may be long in the   *Eze* 20:12;
land which God g. thee *De* 4:40; 5:16;
      25:15
every man that g. it willingly *Ex* 25:2
with heart
all that any man g. of such *Le* 27:9
shall be holy
into the land which Lord   *De* 2:29;
our God g. thee   4:1, 21; 11:17, 31;
12:1, 10; 15:4, 7; 16:20; 17:14; 18:9;
19:1-2, 10, 14, 21:1, 23; 24:4; 26:1-2;
   27:2-3; 28:8; *Jos* 1:11, 15
it is he that g. thee power to *De* 8:18
get wealth
God g. not this land for thy *De* 9:6
righteousness
when he g. rest from   *De* 12:10;
enemies   25:19
if a prophet g. thee a sign or *De* 13:1
a wonder
in thy gates which Lord g.   *De* 16:5;
thee   16:18; 17:2
who g. rain upon earth and *Job* 5:10
field
he g. no account of any of *Job* 33:13
his ways
when he g. quietness   *Job* 34:29
who g. songs in the night *Job* 35:10
but g. right to the poor   *Job* 36:6
he g. meat in abundance *Job* 36:31
great deliverance g. he to his *Ps* 18:50
king
but the righteous sheweth *Ps* 37:21
mercy and g.
the God of Israel is he that *Ps* 68:35
g. strength
the entrance of thy words *Ps* 119:130
g. light
for so he g. his beloved sleep *Ps* 127:2
who g. food to all flesh   *Ps* 136:25;
     146:7; 147:9
g. salvation to kings   *Ps* 144:10
he g. snow like wool   *Ps* 147:16
the lord g. wisdom out of his *Pr* 2:6
mouth
he g. grace to the lowly   *Pr* 3:34;
    Jas 4:6; *1Pe* 5:5
good understanding g. favour *Pr* 13:15
the righteous g. and spareth *Pr* 21:26;
not   22:9
he that g. to the poor shall *Pr* 28:27
not lack
God g. to a man that is   *Ec* 2:26
good, wisdom and knowledge
sinner he g. travail
yet God g. him not power to *Ec* 6:2
eat thereof
he g. power to the faint   *Isa* 40:29
he g. breath unto the people *Isa* 42:5
g. rain; g. sun for a light   *Jer* 5:24;
      31:35
woe to him that g. him not *Jer* 22:13
for his work
g. his cheek to him that   *La* 3:30
smiteth him
g. wisdom to the wise, and *Da* 2:21
knowledge
g. it to whomsoever he will *Da* 4:17;
     4:25. 32
woe to him that g.   *Hab* 2:15
neighbour drink
it g. light to all that are in *M't* 5:15
the house
God g. not Spirit by measure *Joh* 3:34
to him
but my Father g. you the   *Joh* 6:32
true bread
who cometh down and g. life *Joh* 6:33
to the world
all that Father g. me shall *Joh* 6:37
come to me
good shepherd g. his life *Joh* 10:11
for the sheep
not as the world g. give I *Joh* 14:27
unto you
g. to all life, breath, all   *Ac* 17:25
things
he that g. do it with   *Ro* 12:8
simplicity
he eateth to the Lord, he g. *Ro* 14:6
God thanks
but God that g. the increase *1Co* 3:7

he that g. her in marriage   *1Co* 7:38
doth well
God g. it a body as it hath *1Co* 15:38
pleased him
thanks be to God who g. *1Co* 15:57
us victory
the letter killeth, but the   *2Co* 3:6
Spirit g. life
who g. us richly all things to *1Ti* 6:17
enjoy
ask of God, that g. to all men *Jas* 1:5
liberally
g. more grace, God g. grace to *Jas* 4:6
the humble
let him do it as of ability *1Pe* 4:11
God g.
for the Lord God g. them   *Re* 22:5
light

GIVING

he loveth stranger in g. him *De* 10:18
food
by g. him a double portion *De* 21:17
of all he hath
Lord visited his people in g. *Ru* 1:6
bread
accomplish my desire, in g. *1Ki* 5:9
food
by g. him according to   *2Ch* 6:23
righteousness
their hope be as the g. up *Job* 11:20
of the ghost
were marrying and g. in   *M't* 24:38
marriage
g. out that himself was some *Ac* 8:9
great one
g. them the Holy Ghost, as *Ac* 15:8
he did to us
was strong in faith, g. glory *Ro* 4:20
to God
the g. of the law, and the   *Ro* 9:4
service of God
things g. sound; g. of   *1Co* 14:7;
thanks   14:16
g. no offence in any thing *2Co* 6:3
concerning g. and receiving *Ph'p* 4:15
g. heed to seducing spirits and *1Ti* 4:1
doctrines
g. honour to the wife as to *1Pe* 3:7
weaker vessel
g. all diligence, add to faith *2Pe* 1:5
virtue
g. themselves over to   *Jude* 7
fornication

GIZONITE

sons of Hashem the G.   *1Ch* 11:34

GLAD

when he seeth thee, he will be *Ex* 4:14
g.
and the priest's heart was g. *J'g* 18:20
and the men of Jabesh were g. *1Sa* 11:9
Israel went to tents g.   *1Ki* 8:66;
      2Ch 7:10
joyful and g.-hearted (B)   *2Ch* 7:10
Haman g. city; Shushan was *Es* 5:9;
      8:15
are g. when they can find the *Job* 3:22
grave
righteous see it and are g. *Job* 22:19;
      Ps 64:10
therefore my heart is g.   *Ps* 16:9
made him g. with thy   *Ps* 21:6
countenance
the humble shall hear and be *Ps* 34:2;
g.   69:32
them be g. that favour   *Ps* 35:27
righteous cause
proclaimed g. tidings   *Ps* 40:9
(A)(B)(E)
seek thee rejoice and be g. *Ps* 40:16
in thee
whereby they have made   *Ps* 45:8
thee g.
the streams shall make g. the *Ps* 46:4
city of God
let the nations be g. and sing *Ps* 67:4
for joy
make us g.; made me g. *Ps* 90:15; 92:4
let isles be g.; Zion heard, *Ps* 97:1;
and was g.   97:8
wine that maketh g. the *Ps* 104:15
heart of man
I will be g. in the Lord *Ps* 104:34
Egypt was g.   *Ps* 105:38

then are they g. because they be quiet | Ps 107:30
they that fear thee will be g. when | Ps 119:74
I was g. when they said to me, Let us go | Ps 122:1
done great things for us, whereof we are g. | Ps 126:3
a wise son maketh a g. father | Pr 10:1; 15:20
but a good word maketh it g. | Pr 12:25
g. heart has continual feast (B) | Pr 15:15
is g. at calamities, not be unpunished | Pr 17:5
thy father and thy mother shall be g. | Pr 23:25
not heart be g. when he stumbleth | Pr 24:17
my son, be wise, and make my heart g. | Pr 27:11
the wilderness shall be g. for them | Isa 35:1
Hezekiah was g. of them, shewed them | Isa 39:2
a child is born, making him very g. | Jer 20:15
because ye were g. O ye destroyers | Jer 50:11
they are g. that thou hast done it | La 1:21
then was the king exceeding g. | Da 6:23
make the king g. with their wickedness | Ho 7:3
Jonah was g. because of the gourd | Jon 4:6
their children shall see it and be g. | Zec 10:7
were g. and promised money | M'k 14:11; Lu 22:5
I am sent to shew thee these g. tidings | Lu 1:19
shewing the g. tidings of the kingdom | Lu 8:1
would have been g. to fill his stomach (N) | Lu 15:16
was meet we should make merry and be g. | Lu 15:32
Abraham saw my day and was g. | Joh 8:56
I am g. for your sakes that I was not | Joh 11:15
g. and generous hearts (R) | Ac 2:46
when had seen grace of God he was g. | Ac 11:23
the Gentiles heard this, they were g. | Ac 13:48
proclaim g. tidings (A) | Ac 10:10
I am g. therefore on your behalf | Ro 16:19
I am g. of the coming of Stephanas | 1Co 16:17
who is he then that maketh me g. | 2Co 2:2
we are g. when we are weak, and ye strong | 2Co 13:9
proclaimed g. tidings (A)(N) | 1Th 2:9
g. tidings proclaimed (A) | Heb 4:2
Is any g. at heart (A)(N) | Jas 5:13
his glory revealed, ye may be g. also | 1Pe 4:13

GLAD with REJOICE

let the heavens be g. and let the earth rejoice | 1Ch 16:31; Ps 96:11
I will be g. and rejoice in thee | Ps 9:2
Jacob shall rejoice, Israel shall be g. | Ps 14:7; 53:6
I will be g. and rejoice in thy mercy | Ps 31:7
be g. and rejoice, ye righteous | Ps 32:11; 68:3
that seek thee, be g. and rejoice | Ps 40:16; 70:4
let Zion rejoice, daughters of Judah be g. | Ps 48:11
may be g. and rejoice all our days | Ps 90:14
this is the day, we will rejoice and be g. | Ps 118:24
we will be g. and rejoice in thee | Ca 1:4
rejoice and be g. in his salvation | Isa 25:9
but be you g. and rejoice for ever | Isa 65:18

rejoice ye with Jerusalem, and be g. with her | Isa 66:10
rejoice and be g. daughter of Edom | La 4:21
fear not, O land, be g. and rejoice | Joe 2:21
be g. ye children of Zion, and rejoice | Joe 2:23
therefore they rejoice and are g. | Hab 1:15
be g. and rejoice daughter of Jerusalem | Zep 3:14
rejoice and be g. great is your reward | M't 5:12
heart did rejoice, my tongue was g. | Ac 2:26
be g. and rejoice the marriage is come | Re 19:7

GLADLY

Herod feared John, heard him g. | M'k 6:20
the common people heard Christ g. | M'k 12:37
would g. have fed (A)(R) | Lu 15:16
that g. received word were baptized | Ac 2:41
when come, the brethren received us g. | Ac 21:17
ye suffer fools g. seeing ye are wise | 2Co 11:19
most g. therefore will I rather glory | 2Co 12:9
I will very g. spend and be spent for you | 2Co 12:15

GLADNESS

in the day of your g. ye shall blow | Nu 10:10
servedst not the Lord with g. of heart | De 28:47
David brought up the ark with g. | 2Sa 6:12
strength and g. are in his place | 1Ch 16:27
did eat and drink that day with great g. | 1Ch 29:22
and they sang praises with g. | 2Ch 29:30
Israel kept feast of unleavened bread with g. | 2Ch 30:21
and they kept other seven days with g. | 2Ch 30:23
and there was very great g. | Ne 8:17
Levites, to keep the dedication with g. | Ne 12:27
Jews had light, and g. and joy | Es 8:16; 8:17
they made it a day of feasting and g. | Es 9:17; 18:19
thou hast put g. in my heart more than | Ps 4:7
and thou hast girded me with g. | Ps 30:11
hath anointed thee with oil of g. | Ps 45:7; Heb 1:9
with g. and rejoicing shall they be brought | Ps 45:15
make me to hear joy and g. that bones | Ps 51:8
and g. is sown for the upright in heart | Ps 97:11
serve the Lord with g. come with singing | Ps 100:2
he brought forth his chosen with g. | Ps 105:43
that I may rejoice in the g. of thy nation | Ps 106:5
the hope of the righteous shall be g. | Pr 10:28
test you with g. (B) | Ec 2:1
and in the day of the g. of his heart | Ca 3:11
joy and g. taken away out of field | Isa 16:10
and, behold, joy and g. slaying oxen | Isa 22:13
ye shall have a song and g. of heart | Isa 30:29
they shall obtain joy and g. | Isa 35:10; 51:11
joy and g. shall be found therein | Isa 51:3
cease voice of mirth and g. | Jer 7:34; 16:9; 25:10
sing with g. for Jacob, shout among nations | Jer 31:7

there shall be heard a voice of joy and g. | Jer 33:11
joy and g. taken from the plentiful field | Jer 48:33
joy and g. from the house of our God | Joe 1:16
shall be to house of Judah joy and g. | Zec 8:19
who immediately receive it with g. | M'k 4:16
shalt have joy and g. and many rejoice | Lu 1:14
did eat their meat with g. of heart | Ac 2:46
she opened not the gate for g. but ran | Ac 12:14
filling our hearts with food and g. | Ac 14:17
receive him in the Lord with all g. | Ph'p 2:29

GLASS

gold and g. (A)(B)(E)(R) | Job 26:17
for now we see through a g. darkly | 1Co 13:12
with open face, beholding as in a g. | 2Co 3:18
a man beholding his natural face in a g. | Jas 1:23
there was a sea of g. like unto crystal | Re 4:6
and I saw a sea of g. mingled with fire | Re 15:2
city was pure gold, like clear g. | Re 21:18; 21:21

GLASSES

the Lord will take away the g. and veils | Isa 3:23

GLEAN

thou shalt not g. vineyard | Le 19:10; De 24:21
go to the field and g. ears | Ru 2:2; 2:7-8, 15-16, 23
they shall thoroughly g. the remnant | Jer 6:9

GLEANED

they g. of them in the highways | J'g 20:45
she came and g. after reapers | Ru 2:3; 2:17-19

GLEANING

not gather the g. of harvest | Le 23:22
is not the g. of the grapes of Ephraim | J'g 8:2
yet g. grapes shall be left in it as shaking | Isa 17:6
as the g. grapes when vintage is done | Isa 24:13
would they not leave some g. | Jer 49:9

GLEANINGS

shalt thou gather the g. of thy | Le 19:9

GLEDE

And the g. and the kite, and | De 14:13

GLIB

must a g. talker be right (B) | Job 11:2

GLISTENING

g. stones (S) | 1Ch 29:2
raiment white and g. (S) | Lu 9:29

GLISTERING

g. stones, and of divers colours | 1Ch 29:2
his raiment was white and g. | Lu 9:29

GLITTER

it is furbished that it may g. | Eze 21:10

GLITTERING

If I whet my g. sword, and mine | De 32:41

yea, the g. sword cometh   *Job 20:25*
out of
the g. spear and the shield   *Job 39:23*
to consume because of the   *Eze 21:28*
g.
the bright sword and the g.   *Na 3:3*
spear
at the shining of thy g.   *Hab 3:11*
spear
g. with gold (P)   *Re 17:4*

GLOOM

g. of anguish (A)(B)(E)(R)   *Isa 8:22*
no g. for her (A)(B)(E)(R)   *Isa 9:1*
out of g. and darkness (R)   *Isa 58:10*
kept in pits of g. (A)(R)   *2Pe 2:4*

GLOOMINESS

A day of darkness and of g. a   *Joe 2:2*
day
a day of darkness and g. a   *Zep 1:15*
day of

GLOOMY

a g. threatening look (A)   *M't 16:3*

GLORIES

a hint of the g. of heaven   *1Pe 1:8*
(P)

GLORIEST

Wherefore g. thou in the   *Jer 49:4*
valleys

GLORIETH

But let him that g. glory in   *Jer 9:24*
this
that g. let him glory in the   *1Co 1:31;*
Lord   *2Co 10:17*

GLORIFIED

before all the people I will be   *Le 10:3*
g.
increased the nation: thou   *Isa 26:15*
art g.
Jacob, and g. himself in   *Isa 44:23*
Israel
O Israel, in whom I will be   *Isa 49:3*
g.
One of Israel; for he hath g.   *Isa 55:5*
thee
of Israel, because he hath g.   *Isa 60:9*
thee
of my hands, that I may be   *Isa 60:21*
g.
of the Lord, that he might be   *Isa 61:3*
g.
Let the Lord be g.: but he   *Isa 66:5*
shall
I will be g. in the midst of   *Eze 28:22*
thee
that I shall be g. saith the   *Eze 39:13*
Lord
are all thy ways hast thou not   *Da 5:23*
g.
and I will be g. saith the   *Hag 1:8*
Lord
they marvelled, and g. God   *M't 9:8*
and they g. the God of   *M't 15:31*
Israel
then were all amazed, and g.   *M'k 2:12*
God
their synagogues, being g. of   *Lu 4:15*
all
were all amazed, and they g.   *Lu 5:26*
God
they g. God, saying, That a   *Lu 7:16*
great
she was made straight, and   *Lu 13:13*
g. God
and with a loud voice g.   *Lu 17:15*
God
saw what was done, he g.   *Lu 23:47*
God
because that Jesus was not   *Joh 7:39*
yet g.
Son of God might be g.   *Joh 11:4*
thereby
but when Jesus was g. then   *Joh 12:16*
that the Son of man should   *Joh 12:23*
be g.
I have both g. it, and will   *Joh 12:28*
glorify
Now is the Son of man g.   *Joh 13:31*

and God is g. in him   *Joh 13:31*
If God be g. in him, God   *Joh 13:32*
shall
the Father may be g. in the   *Joh 14:13*
Son
Herein is my Father g. that   *Joh 15:8*
ye bear
I have g. thee on the earth   *Joh 17:4*
and am g. in them   *Joh 17:10*
hath g. his Son Jesus   *Ac 3:13*
for all men g. God for that   *Ac 4:21*
which
they held their peace, and g.   *Ac 11:18*
God
and g. the word of the   *Ac 13:48*
Lord: and
they g. the Lord, and said   *Ac 21:20*
unto him
they g. him not as God   *Ro 1:21*
neither
that we may also be g.   *Ro 8:17*
together
whom he justified, them he   *Ro 8:30*
also g.
And they g. God in me   *Ga 1:24*
shall come to be g. in his   *2Th 1:10*
saints
of our Lord Jesus Christ   *2Th 1:12*
may be g.
may have free course and be   *2Th 3:1*
g.
Christ g. not himself to be   *Heb 5:5*
made
may be g. through Jesus   *1Pe 4:11*
Christ
but on your part he is g.   *1Pe 4:14*
How much she hath g. herself   *Re 18:7*

GLORIFIES

g. his neighbor (A)   *Pr 27:14*

GLORIFIETH

Whoso offereth praise g. me   *Ps 50:23*

GLORIFY

to g. his works (B)   *Job 36:24*
all ye the seed of Jacob g.   *Ps 22:23*
him
deliver thee, and thou shalt   *Ps 50:15*
g. me
O Lord; and shall g. thy   *Ps 86:9*
name
I will g. thy name for   *Ps 86:12*
evermore
Wherefore g. ye the Lord in   *Isa 24:15*
shall the strong people g. thee   *Isa 25:3*
I will g. the house of my   *Isa 60:7*
glory
I will also g. them, and they   *Jer 30:19*
shall
see your good works, and g.   *M't 5:16*
your
Father, g. thy name. Then   *Joh 12:28*
came
have both glorified it, and   *Joh 12:28*
will g. it
God shall also g. him in   *Joh 13:32*
himself
and shall straightway g. him   *Joh 13:32*
He shall g. me: for he shall   *Joh 16:14*
receive
g. thy Son, that thy Son also   *Joh 17:1*
that thy Son also may g.   *Joh 17:1*
O Father, g. thou me with   *Joh 17:5*
thine
by what death he should g.   *Joh 21:19*
God
I g. my ministry (E)   *Ro 11:13*
one mind and one mouth g.   *Ro 15:6*
God
the Gentiles might g. God for   *Ro 15:9*
his
therefore g. God in your   *1Co 6:20*
body
they g. God for your   *2Co 9:13*
professed
g. God in the day of   *1Pe 2:12*
visitation
let him g. God on this   *1Pe 4:16*
behalf
fear thee, O Lord, and g. thy   *Re 15:4*
name

GLORIFYING

g. and praising God for all   *Lu 2:20*
things

departed to his own house g.   *Lu 5:25*
God
and followed him, g. God   *Lu 18:43*
foreign languages g. God   *Ac 10:46*
(P)

GLORIOUS

O Lord, is become g. in   *Ex 15:6*
power
who is like thee, g. in   *Ex 15:11*
holiness
fear this g. and fearful name   *De 28:58*
How g. was the king of   *2Sa 6:20*
Israel to-day
thank thee, and praise thy   *1Ch 29:13*
g. name
blessed be thy g. name, which   *Ne 9:5*
shewed the riches of his g.   *Es 1:4*
kingdom
king's daughter is all g.   *Ps 45:13*
fearful and g. things (A)   *Ps 65:5*
of his name: make his praise   *Ps 66:2*
g.
awesome and fearfully g. (A)   *Ps 66:3*
And blessed be his g. name   *Ps 72:19*
for ever
Thou art more g. and   *Ps 76:4*
excellent
G. things are spoken of thee   *Ps 87:3*
His work is honourable and   *Ps 111:3*
g.
I will speak of the g. honour   *Ps 145:5*
of thy
and the g. majesty of his   *Ps 145:12*
kingdom
of the Lord be beautiful and   *Isa 4:2*
g.
and his rest shall be g.   *Isa 11:10*
and he shall be for a g.   *Isa 22:23*
throne
whose g. beauty is a fading   *Isa 28:1*
flower
the g. beauty which is on the   *Isa 28:4*
head
the Lord shall cause his g.   *Isa 30:30*
voice
But there the g. Lord will   *Isa 33:21*
be
I be g. in the eyes of the   *Isa 49:5*
Lord
I will make the place of my   *Isa 60:13*
feet g.
g. in his apparel, travelling in   *Isa 63:1*
with his g. arm, dividing the   *Isa 63:12*
water
people, to make thyself a g.   *Isa 63:14*
name
A g. high throne from the   *Jer 17:12*
wast replenished, and made   *Eze 27:25*
very g.
the g. land (E)(R)   *Da 8:9*
and he shall stand in the g.   *Da 11:16*
land
He shall enter also into the   *Da 11:41*
g. land
the seas in the g. holy   *Da 11:45*
mountain
g. things that were done by   *Lu 13:17*
him
g. liberty of the children of   *Ro 8:21*
God
engraven in stones, was g.   *2Co 3:7*
of the spirit be rather g.   *2Co 3:8*
which was made g. had no   *2Co 3:10*
glory
which is done away was g.   *2Co 3:11*
that which remaineth is g.   *2Co 3:11*
the light of the g. gospel of   *2Co 4:4*
Christ
permanent, g., solid reward (P)   *2Co 4:17*
present it to himself a g.   *Eph 5:27*
church
fashioned like unto his g.   *Ph'p 3:21*
body
according to his g. power,   *Col 1:11*
unto
the g. gospel of the blessed   *1Ti 1:11*
God
the g. appearing of the great   *Tit 2:13*
God
inexpressible g. joy (A)   *1Pe 1:8*

GLORIOUSLY

the Lord, for he hath   *Ex 15:1;*
triumphed g.   *15:21*
and before his ancients g.   *Isa 24:23*

GLORY

hath he gotten all this g.   Ge 31:1
Moses said unto Pharaoh, G.   Ex 8:9
over
thy brother for g. and for   Ex 28:2
beauty
make them inherit the throne   1Sa 2:8
of g.
The g. is departed from   1Sa 4:21;
Israel   4:22
the g. of Israel is slain (S)   2Sa 1:19
the g. of Israel (R)   2Sa 15:29
g. of this, and tarry at   2Ki 14:10
home
G. ye in his holy name: 1Ch 16:10;
let the   16:24, 27-29, 35
and of g. throughout all   1Ch 22:5
countries
and the power, and the g.   1Ch 29:11
Haman told them of the g. of   Es 5:11
the g. of his nostrils is   Job 39:20
terrible
array thyself with g. and   Job 40:10
beauty
and the King of g. shall   Ps 24:7;
come in   24:8-10
one that sweareth by him   Ps 63:11
shall g.
all the upright in heart shall   Ps 64:10
g.
thou shalt afterward receive   Ps 73:24
me to g.
help us, O God, for the g. of   Ps 79:9
thy name
that g. may dwell in our land   Ps 85:9
for thou art the g. of their   Ps 89:17
strength
that I may g. with thine   Ps 106:5
inheritance
they changed their g. into   Ps 106:20
similitude
speak of the g. of thy   Ps 145:11
kingdom
let the saints be joyful in g.   Ps 149:5
the wise shall inherit g.   Pr 3:35
the g. of children are their   Pr 17:6
fathers
the g. of young men is their   Pr 20:29
strength
so for men to search their   Pr 25:27
own g. is not g.
when the righteous men   Pr 28:12
rejoice there is g.
hide thee for the g. of his   Isa 2:10;
majesty   19:21
for upon all the g. shall be a   Isa 4:5
defence
their g. and pomp shall   Isa 5:14
descend unto it
and where will ye leave your   Isa 10:3
g.
I will punish the g. of his   Isa 10:12
high looks
and shall consume the g. of   Isa 10:12
his forest
Babylon the g. of kingdom be   Isa 13:19
as Sodom
all of them lie in g. each in   Isa 14:18
his house
the g. of Moab shall be   Isa 16:14
contemned
they shall be as the g. of the   Isa 17:3
children of Israel
that the g. of Jacob shall be   Isa 17:4
made thin
they shall be ashamed of   Isa 20:5
Egypt their g.
and all the g. of Kedar shall   Isa 21:16
fail
shall hang on him g. of his   Isa 22:24
Father's house
hath purposed to stain the   Isa 23:9
pride of all g.
we heard songs, even g. to   Isa 24:16
the righteous
the g. of Lebanon shall be   Isa 35:2
given to it
shalt g. in the holy One of   Isa 41:16
Israel
shall all the seed of Israel g.   Isa 45:23
in their g. ye shall boast   Isa 61:6
yourselves
be delighted with the   Isa 66:11
abundance of her g.
the g. of the Gentiles as a   Isa 66:12
flowing stream
but my people have changed   Jer 2:11
their g.

in him shall they g.   Jer 4:2
let not rich man g. in riches   Jer 9:23
let him g. that he knoweth me   Jer 9:24
that they might be to me for a   Jer 13:11
g.
shall come down, even the   Jer 13:18
crown of your g.
which is the g. of all   Eze 20:6;
lands   20:15
when I take from them the   Eze 24:25
joy of their g.
I will open the g. of the   Eze 25:9
country
I shall set g. in the land of   Eze 26:20
the living
to whom art thou thus like in   Eze 31:18
g.
God hath given power and g.   Da 2:37;
  7:14
the g. of my kingdom   Da 4:36
returned to me
the G.-land (B)   Da 8:9
shall acknowledge, and   Da 11:39
increase with g.
I will change their g. into shame   Ho 4:7
love shame more than g. (S)   Ho 4:18
as for Ephraim, their g. shall   Ho 9:11
fly away
priests that rejoiced for the g.   Ho 10:5
thereof
he shall come to Adullam the   Mic 1:15
g. of Israel
there is none end of the store   Na 2:9
and g.
thou art filled with shame for   Hab 2:16
g.
who saw this house in her first   Hag 2:3
g.
I will fill this house with g.   Hag 2:7
saith the Lord
g. of this latter house greater   Hag 2:9
than former
I will be the g. in the midst of   Zec 2:5
her
after the g. hath he sent me to   Zec 2:8
the nations
he shall build temple, he shall   Zec 6:13
bear the g.
their g. is spoiled, a voice of   Zec 11:3
roaring of lions
g. of the house of David, g. of   Zec 12:7
Jerusalem
kingdoms of the world, and g.   M't 4:8
of them
sound trumpet, that they may   M't 6:2
have g. of men
shall come in the g. of his   M't 16:27;
Father   M'k 8:38
shall see Son of Man coming   M't 24:30;
with power and great g.   M'k 13:26;
  Lu 21:27
saying, G. to God in the highest   Lu 2:14;
  19:38
light to Gentiles, and g. of   Lu 2:32
Israel
all this power will I give thee,   Lu 4:6
and the g.
appeared in g. and spake of his   Lu 9:31
decease
with the g. which I had with   Joh 17:5
thee
the g. thou gavest me, I have   Joh 17:22
given them
the God of g. appeared to our   Ac 7:2
father
because he gave not God the   Ac 12:23
g.
when I could not see for the   Ac 22:11
g. of light
he hath whereof to g. but not   Ro 4:2
was strong in faith, giving g. to   Ro 4:20
God
but we g. in tribulations also   Ro 5:3
raised from the dead by the g.   Ro 6:4
of the Father
are not worthy to be compared   Ro 8:18
with the g.
to whom pertaineth the g. and   Ro 9:4
covenants
which he had afore prepared   Ro 9:23
unto g.
to whom be g. for ever   Ro 11:36;
  Ga 1:5; 2Ti 4:18; Heb 13:21; 1Pe 5:11
I have whereof I may g.   Ro 15:17
to God only wise be g.   Ro 16:27;
  1Ti 1:17
that no flesh should g. in his   1Co 1:29
he that glorieth g. in the Lord   1Co 1:31

which God hath ordained to   1Co 2:7
our g.
they would not have crucified   1Co 2:8
the Lord of g.
let no man g. in men   1Co 3:21
why dost g. as if thou hadst   1Co 4:7
though I preach, I have   1Co 9:16
nothing to g.
but the woman is the g. of the   1Co 11:7
man
if a woman have long hair, it   1Co 11:15
is a g. to her
g. of celestial is one, the g.   1Co 15:40
of the terrestrial
one g. of the sun, another g.   1Co 15:41
of the moon
it is sown in dishonour, it is   1Co 15:43
raised in g.
for the g. of his countenance,   2Co 3:7
which g.
ministration of   2Co 3:9
condemnation be g. ministration
exceed in g.
had no g. by reason of the g.   2Co 3:10
that excelleth
but we all are changed from   2Co 3:18
g. to g.
worketh for us an eternal   2Co 4:17
weight of g.
give occasion to g. on our   2Co 5:12
behalf
answer them who g. in   2Co 5:12
appearance
administered to us to the g. of   2Co 8:19
the same Lord
they are messengers, and the   2Co 8:23
g. of Christ
wherein they g. they may be   2Co 11:12
found
seeing many g. after flesh, I   2Co 11:18
will g.
if I must needs g. I will g. in   2Co 11:30
not expedient for me   2Co 12:1
doubtless to g.
of such an one will I g. of   2Co 12:5
myself
though I would desire to g.   2Co 12:6
I will rather g. in mine   2Co 12:9
infirmities
that they may g. in the flesh   Ga 6:13
forbid I should g. save in the   Ga 6:14
cross
to the praise of the g. of his   Eph 1:6
grace
the Father of g. may give you   Eph 1:17
the Spirit
ye may know what is the   Eph 1:18
riches of the g.
my tribulations for you,   Eph 3:13
which is your g.
to him be g. in the church by   Eph 3:21
Christ Jesus
fruits, which are by Christ to   Ph'p 1:11
g. of God
and whose g. is in their   Ph'p 3:19
shame
according to his riches in g.   Ph'p 4:19
by Christ
now to God and our Father   Ph'p 4:20
be g. for ever
the riches of the g. of this   Col 1:27
mystery, Christ in you
the hope of g.
then shall ye appear with him   Col 3:4
in g.
nor of men sought we g. nor of   1Th 2:6
you
who hath called you to his   1Th 2:12
kingdom and g.
for ye are our g. and joy   1Th 2:20
we ourselves g. in you   2Th 1:4
punished from the g. of his   2Th 1:9
power
to the obtaining of the g. of   2Th 2:14
our Lord
seen of angels, received up   1Ti 3:16
into g.
salvation in Christ, with   2Ti 2:10
eternal g.
in bringing many sons to   Heb 2:10
g. to make
this man was counted worthy   Heb 3:3
of more g.
over it the cherubims of g.   Heb 9:5
shadowing
the faith of our Lord Jesus, the   Jas 2:1
Lord of g.
if ye have envying in hearts, g.   Jas 3:14
not

rejoice with joy unspeakable, *1Pe 1:8*
full of *g.*
it testified the *g.* that should *1Pe 1:11*
follow
that God raised him up, and *1Pe 1:21*
gave him *g.*
and all the *g.* of man, as the *1Pe 1:24*
flower of grass
for what *g.* is it, if when ye be *1Pe 2:20*
buffeted
the Spirit of *g.* and of God *1Pe 4:14*
resteth on you
a partaker of the *g.* that shall *1Pe 5:1*
be revealed
hath called us to eternal *g.* *1Pe 5:10*
by Christ Jesus
that hath called us to *g.* *2Pe 1:3*
and virtue
came such a voice to him from *2Pe 1:17*
excellent *g.*
to him be *g.* both now and *2Pe 3:18;*
ever *Re 1:6*
to the only wise God our *Jude 25*
Saviour be *g.*
thou art worthy to receive *g.* *Re 4:11;*
5:12
blessing and *g.* and wisdom be *Re 7:12*
to our God
remnant were affrighted, and *Re 11:13*
gave *g.* to God

GIVE GLORY

my son, *give g.* to the God of *Jos 7:19*
Israel
ye shall *give g.* to the God of *1Sa 6:5*
Israel
give to the Lord *g. give* to *1Ch 16:28;*
Lord *g.* and strength *16:29; Ps 29:1-2;*
96:7-8; Jer 13:16
the Lord will *give* grace and *g.* *Ps 84:11*
not to us, but to thy name *give Ps 115:1*
the *g.*
let them *give g.* unto the Lord *Isa 42:12*
if ye will not lay it to heart to *Mal 2:2*
give g.
that returned to *give g.* to *Lu 17:18*
God
when those beasts *give g.* and *Re 4:9*
honour
fear God, and *give g.* to him, *Re 14:7*
worship him
were scorched, and repented *Re 16:9*
not to *give g.*

HIS GLORY

the Lord our God hath shewed *De 5:24*
us *his g.*
his g. like the firstling of a *De 33:17*
bullock
declare *his g.* among *1Ch 16:24;*
heathen *Ps 96:3*
his g. is great in thy salvation *Ps 21:5*
in his temple doth every one *Ps 29:9*
speak of *his g.*
his g. shall not descend after *Ps 49:17*
him
let the whole earth be filled *Ps 72:19*
with *his g.*
delivered *his g.* into the *Ps 78:61*
enemies' hand
thou hast made *his g.* to cease *Ps 89:44*
and all the people see *his g.* *Ps 97:6*
when Lord build Zion, shall *Ps 102:16*
appear in *his g.*
and *his g.* above the heavens *Ps 113:4;*
148:13
it is *his g.* to pass over *Pr 19:11*
transgression
to provoke the eyes of *his g.* *Isa 3:8*
one cried, the whole earth is full *Isa 6:3*
of *his g.*
king of Assyria and *his g.* shall *Isa 8:7*
come up
under *his g.* he shall kindle a *Isa 10:16*
burning
shall fear *his g.* from rising of *Isa 59:19*
the sun
and *his g.* shall be seen upon *Isa 60:2*
thee
not lament, saying, Ah lord, *Jer 22:18*
or, Ah *his g.*
and the earth shined with *his* *Eze 43:2*
g.
and they took *his g.* from him *Da 5:20*
God came, *his g.* covered the *Hab 3:3*
heavens
Solomon in all *his g.* *M't 6:29; Lu 12:27*

Son of man shall sit in *his g.* *M't 19:28;*
Lu 9:26
when they were awake, they *Lu 9:32*
saw *his g.*
to have suffered, and to enter *Lu 24:26*
into *his g.*
we beheld *his g.* the glory as *Joh 1:14*
of the only
thus did Jesus, and manifested *Joh 2:11*
forth *his g.*
but he that seeketh *his g.* that *Joh 7:18*
sent him
these things said Esaias, *Joh 12:41*
when he saw *his g.*
hath abounded through my lie *Ro 3:7*
unto *his g.*
might make known the riches *Ro 9:23*
of *his g.*
should be to the praise of *his Eph 1:12;*
g. *1:14*
grant you according to the *Eph 3:16*
riches of *his g.*
who being the brightness of his *Heb 1:3*
g.
that when *his g.* shall be *1Pe 4:13*
revealed
present you before the presence *Jude 24*
of *his g.*
the earth was lightened with *Re 18:1*
his g.

MY GLORY

tell my father of all *my g.* in *Ge 45:13*
Egypt
tabernacle shall be sanctified *Ex 29:43*
by *my g.*
while *my g.* passeth by, I will *Ex 33:22*
put thee
those men which have seen *Nu 14:22*
my g.
he hath stripped me of *my g.* *Job 19:9*
and taken
my g. was fresh in me, my *Job 29:20*
bow renewed
thou art *my g.* and lifter up of *Ps 3:3*
my head
how long will ye turn *my g.* into *Ps 4:2*
shame
my g. rejoiceth *Ps 16:9*
my g. may sing *Ps 30:12*
awake up *my g.* *Ps 57:8*
in God is *my g.* *Ps 62:7*
I will sing and give praise with *Ps 108:1*
my g.
my g. will I not give to *Isa 42:8;*
another *48:11*
for I have created him for *my Isa 43:7*
g.
I will place salvation for *Isa 46:13*
Israel, *my g.*
and they shall come and see *Isa 66:18*
my g.
have not seen *my g.* they shall *Isa 66:19*
declare *my g.*
I will set *my g.* among the *Eze 39:21*
heathen
from children have ye taken *Mic 2:9*
away *my g.*
and I seek not *mine* own *g.* *Joh 8:50*
one seeks
be with me, that they may *Joh 17:24*
behold *my g.*

THY GLORY

said, I beseech thee shew me *Ex 33:18*
thy g.
who hast set *thy g.* above *Ps 8:1*
heavens
gird thy sword on thy thigh *Ps 45:3*
with *thy g.*
let *thy g.* be above all earth *Ps 57:5;*
57:11; 108:5
to see thy power *thy g.* as I *Ps 63:2*
have seen
let *thy g.* appear unto their *Ps 90:16*
children
and all the kings of the earth *Ps 102:15*
thy g.
chariots of *thy g.* shall be the *Isa 22:18*
shame
thy God *thy g.* *Isa 60:19*
kings shall see *thy g.* *Isa 62:2*
behold from the habitation of *Isa 63:15*
thy g.
do not disgrace the throne of *Jer 14:21*
thy g.

come down from *thy g.* and *Jer 48:18*
sit in thirst
shameful spewing shall be on *Hab 2:16*
thy g.
other on thy left hand in *thy M'k 10:37*
g.

GLORY *OF GOD*

the heavens declare the *g.* of *Ps 19:1*
God
it is the *g.* of God to conceal a *Pr 25:2*
thing
the *g.* of the *God* of Israel was *Eze 8:4*
there
the *g.* of *God* was gone up *Eze 9:3*
from the cherub
the *g.* of *God* was over them *Eze 10:19;*
above *11:22*
the *g.* of *God* came from the *Eze 43:2*
way of the east
this sickness is for the *g.* of *Joh 11:4*
God
if thou wouldest, thou shouldest see *Joh 11:40*
the *g.* of *God*
Stephen looked up and saw the *Ac 7:55*
g. of *God*
all sinned and come short of *Ro 3:23*
the *g.* of *God*
we rejoice in hope of the *g.* of *Ro 5:2*
God
as Christ also received us to *Ro 15:7*
ye eat or drink, do all to the *1Co 10:31*
g. of *God*
for a man is the image and *g.* *1Co 11:7*
of *God*
promises in him yea and *2Co 1:20*
amen, to *g.* of *God*
the light of the knowledge of *2Co 4:6*
the *g.* of *God*
thanksgiving of many redound *2Co 4:15*
to *g.* of *God*
which are by Christ to the *g.* *Ph'p 1:11*
of *God*
confess that Jesus is Lord to *Ph'p 2:11*
the *g.* of *God*
temple filled with smoke from *Re 15:8*
g. of *God*
the holy Jerusalem, having the *Re 21:11*
g. of *God*
no need of the sun, *g.* of *God Re 21:23*
did lighten it

GLORY *OF THE LORD*

in the morning ye shall see *g.* *Ex 16:7*
of the Lord
g. of the *Lord* appeared in *Ex 16:10;*
the cloud *Le 9:23; Nu 14:10; 16:19, 42;*
20:6
the *g.* of the *Lord* abode on *Ex 24:16*
mount Sinai
the *g.* of the *Lord* was like *Ex 24:17*
devouring fire
the *g.* of the *Lord* filled the *Ex 40:34;*
tabernacle *40:35*
g. of the *Lord* shall appear unto *Le 9:6*
you
earth shall be filled with *g.* of *Nu 14:21*
the Lord
g. of the *Lord* filled the *1Ki 8:11;*
house *2Ch 5:14; 7:1-3; Eze 43:5; 44:4*
g. of the *Lord* shall endure *Ps 104:31*
for ever
for great is the *g.* of the *Lord Ps 138:5*
they shall see the *g.* of the *Isa 35:2*
Lord
and the *g.* of the *Lord* shall be *Isa 40:5*
revealed
the *g.* of the *Lord* shall be thy *Isa 58:8*
rereward
and the *g.* of the *Lord* is risen *Isa 60:1*
upon thee
appearance of likeness of *g.* of *Eze 1:28*
Lord
blessed be *g.* of the *Lord* from *Eze 3:12*
his place
and behold, the *g.* of the *Lord Eze 3:23*
stood there
g. of the *Lord* went up from *Eze 10:4*
the cherub
g. of the *Lord* departed from *Eze 10:18*
the threshold
the *g.* of the *Lord* went up *Eze 11:23*
from the city
the *g.* of the *Lord* came into *Eze 43:4*
the house
filled with knowledge of *g.* of *Hab 2:14*
the Lord

g. *of the Lord* shone round about them   *Lu 2:9*

beholding as in glass g. *of the Lord*   *2Co 3:18*

GLORYING

your g. is not good, a little leaven   *1Co 5:6*

than that any man should make my g. void   *1Co 9:15*

great is my boldness, great my g. of you   *2Co 7:4*

I am become a fool in g. ye compelled me   *2Co 12:11*

GLOW

the g. of his fire (B)   *Job 18:5*

GLUED

forced (g.) himself upon (A)   *Lu 15:15*

GLUTTED

land g. with blood (B)   *Isa 34:7*

GLUTTON

he is a g. and a drunkard   *De 21:20*

a spendthrift and a drunkard (B)   *De 21:20*

the drunkard and the g. shall come   *Pr 23:21*

a g. (A)(B)(N)(P)(R)   *M't 11:19*

GLUTTONOUS

among g. eaters of the flesh (S)   *Pr 23:20; 28:7*

a man g. and a winebibber, a   *M't 11:19*

glutton and wine drinker (A)(B)(N)(P)(R)   *M't 11:19*

Behold a g. man, and a winebibber   *Lu 7:34*

GLUTTONS

lazy g. (S)   *Tit 1:2*

GNASH

he shall g. with his teeth, and   *Ps 112:10*

they hiss and g. the teeth: they   *La 2:16*

GNASHED

they g. upon me with their teeth   *Ps 35:16*

they g. on him with their teeth   *Ac 7:54*

GNASHETH

he g. upon me with his teeth   *Job 16:9*

and g. upon him with his teeth   *Ps 37:12*

foameth, and g. with his teeth   *M'k 9:18*

grinds his teeth (B)(E)(N)(P)(R)   *M'k 9:18*

GNASHING

shall be weeping and g. of teeth   *M't 8:12; 13:42, 50; 22:13; 24:51; 25:30; Lu 13:28*

grinding of teeth (A)(B)   *M't 8:12; 13:42, 50; 22:13; 24:51; 25:30*

GNAT

which strain at a g. and swallow   *M't 23:24*

GNAW

they g. not the bones till the   *Zep 3:3*

GNAWED

and they g. their tongues for pain   *Re 16:10*

GO

on thy belly shalt thou go, and eat dust   *Ge 3:14*

whence camest thou? whither wilt thou go   *Ge 16:8*

if now thou do prosper my way which I go   *Ge 24:42*

abide a few days, after that Rebekah shall go   *Ge 24:55*

send me away, that I may go to my master   *Ge 24:56*

wilt thou go with this man? she said, I will go   *Ge 24:58*

and Abimelech said to Isaac, Go from us   *Ge 26:16*

if God will keep me in this way that I go   *Ge 28:20*

send me away that I may go to my place   *Ge 30:25*

let me go, for the day breaketh; I will not let thee go   *Ge 32:26*

the child is not, and I, whither shall I go   *Ge 37:30*

send lad with me, and we will arise, and go   *Ge 43:8*

king of Egypt will not let you go   *Ex 3:19; 4:21*

and after that he will let you go   *Ex 3:20; 11:1*

that when ye go, ye shall not go empty   *Ex 3:21*

let my son go; if thou refuse to let him go, I will slay   *Ex 4:23; 8:2, 21; 9:2; 10:4*

so he let him go, then she said, a bloody husband   *Ex 4:26*

thus saith the Lord God of Israel, Let my people go   *Ex 5:1; 7:16; 8:1, 20; 9:1-13; 10:3*

I know not the Lord, nor will I let Israel go   *Ex 5:2*

I will let thy people go   *Ex 8:8; 8:28*

Pharaoh hardened his heart, neither would he let the people go   *Ex 8:32; 7:14; 9:35; 10:26-27*

let men go; who are they that shall go   *Ex 10:7*

we will go with our young and with our old   *Ex 10:9*

light to go by day and night   *Ex 13:21; Ne 9:12, 19*

that we have let Israel go from serving us   *Ex 14:5*

Lord said to Moses, Go on before people   *Ex 17:5*

mine Angel shall go before thee   *Ex 23:23; 32:34*

make us gods to go before us   *Ex 32:23; Ac 7:40*

he said, My presence shall go with thee   *Ex 33:14*

if I have found grace in sight, go among us   *Ex 34:9*

and it shall be, if thou go with us   *Nu 10:32*

we will go by the king's highway   *Nu 20:17; 20:19*

the Lord refuseth to give me leave to go   *Nu 22:13*

if men call thee, rise up, and go with them   *Nu 22:20; 22:35*

and now behold, I go unto my people   *Nu 24:14*

make it go through fire and water   *Nu 31:23*

shall brethren go to war, and ye sit here   *Nu 32:6*

but we will go ready armed before Israel   *Nu 32:17*

to shew you by what way ye should go   *De 1:33*

in land whither ye go   *De 4:5; 4:26; 11:8, 11; 30:18*

that it may go well with thee   *De 5:16; 19:13*

a curse, if ye go after other gods   *De 11:28; 28:14*

let him go and return to his house   *De 20:5; 20:6-8*

then thou shalt let her go whither she will   *De 21:14*

thou shalt in anywise let the dam go   *De 22:7*

she may go and be another man's wife   *De 24:2*

thy God, he it is that doth go with thee   *De 31:6*

for thou must go with this people to the land   *De 31:7*

the Lord, he it is that doth go before thee   *De 31:8*

land whither they go to be amongst them   *De 31:16*

I know their imagination they go about   *De 31:21*

whither thou sendest us we will go   *Jos 1:16*

ye may know the way by which ye must go   *Jos 3:4*

but they let go the man and his family   *J'g 1:25*

if thou wilt go with me, then I will go   *J'g 4:8*

the Lord said to him, Go in this thy might   *J'g 6:14*

of whom I say, This shall go, the same shall go   *J'g 7:4*

we turn to thee, that thou mayest go with us   *J'g 11:8*

if I be shaven, then my strength will go   *J'g 16:17*

whether our way we go shall be prosperous   *J'g 18:5*

before the Lord is your way wherein ye go   *J'g 18:6*

be not slothful to go to possess the land   *J'g 18:9*

when ye go; hold thy peace, go with us   *J'g 18:10; 18:19*

when day began, they let her go   *J'g 19:25*

will go up by lot against it   *J'g 20:9*

turn again, why will ye go with   *Ru 1:11*

she saw she was stedfastly minded to go   *Ru 1:11*

let me go to field and glean, go my daughter   *Ru 2:2*

let it go again to its own place   *1Sa 5:11*

did they not let people go? and they departed   *1Sa 6:6*

take the ark, send it away, that it may go   *1Sa 6:8*

let us go thither, he can shew us our way   *1Sa 9:6*

if we go what shall we bring the man   *1Sa 9:7*

go up before me, to-morrow I will let thee go   *1Sa 9:19*

when he turned his back to go from Samuel   *1Sa 10:9*

for then should ye go after vain things   *1Sa 12:21*

how can I go? if Saul hear it he will kill me   *1Sa 16:2*

thou art not able to go against this Philistine   *1Sa 17:33*

Saul would let him go no more home   *1Sa 18:2*

he said, Let me go, why should I kill thee   *1Sa 19:17*

but let me go, that I may hide myself in field   *1Sa 20:5*

David and men went whither could go   *1Sa 23:13*

driven me out, saying, Go serve other gods   *1Sa 26:19*

woman, that I may go and inquire of her   *1Sa 28:7*

I shall go to him, he shall not return   *2Sa 12:23*

whither shall I cause my shame to go   *2Sa 13:13*

Absalom said, Let me go and pay my vow   *2Sa 15:7*

seeing I go whither I may, return thou   *2Sa 15:20*

that thou go to battle in thy person   *2Sa 17:11*

thy servant will go a little way over   *2Sa 19:36*

that is for David, let him go after Joab   *2Sa 20:11*

I go way of all the earth, be strong   *1Ki 2:2*

depart, that I may go to my country   *1Ki 11:21*

nothing, howbeit, let me go in any wise   *1Ki 11:22*

shall kill me, and go to Rehoboam   *1Ki 12:27*

nor turn to go by the way thou camest   *1Ki 13:17*

because thou hast let go a man appointed   *1Ki 20:42*

wilt thou go with me to battle   *1Ki 22:4; 2Ch 18:3*

wilt thou go with me against Moab   *2Ki 3:7*

wherefore wilt thou go to him to-day   *2Ki 4:23*

set bread and water, that they may go   *2Ki 6:22*

he that letteth him *go* his life *2Ki 10:24*
be for him
it will *go* into hand pierce it *2Ki 18:21;*
Isa 36:6
in thy name we *go* against *2Ch 14:11*
this multitude
let not the army of Israel *go* *2Ch 25:7*
with thee
if thou wilt *go*, do it, be *2Ch 25:8*
strong for battle
they *go* to nothing and perish *Job 6:18*
before I *go* whence shall not *Job 10:21;*
return *16:22*
it shall *go* ill with him that is *Job 20:26*
left
have ye not asked them that *Job 21:29*
go by way
my righteousness I will not let *Job 27:6*
go
teach thee in the way thou shalt *Ps 32:8*
go
before I *go* hence, and be no *Ps 39:13*
more
I will say to God, Why *go* I *Ps 42:9;*
mourning *43:2*
he shall *go* to the generation *Ps 49:19*
of his fathers
they *go* from strength to *Ps 84:7*
strength
righteousness shall *go* before *Ps 85:13*
him
mercy and truth shall *go* *Ps 89:14*
before thy face
that they might *go* to a city of *Ps 107:7*
habitation
we will *go* into his tabernacles *Ps 132:7*
whither shall I *go* from thy *Ps 139:7*
presence
none that *go* unto her return *Pr 2:19*
again
go and come again, to-morrow *Pr 3:28*
I will give
can one *go* on hot coals, and *Pr 6:28*
not be burnt
to call passengers who *go* right *Pr 9:15*
on way
go from the presence of a *Pr 14:7*
foolish man
neither will the scorner *go* to *Pr 15:12*
the wise
much more do his friends *go* *Pr 19:7*
far from him
train up a child in the way he *Pr 22:6*
should *go*
they that *go* to seek mixed wine *Pr 23:30*
there be three things which *go* *Pr 30:29*
well
rivers come, thither they return *Ec 1:7*
to *go*
all *go* unto one place, all are of *Ec 3:20*
the dust
naked shall he return to *go* as *Ec 5:15;*
he came *5:16*
seen no good, do not all *go* to *Ec 6:6*
one place
it is better to *go* to the house of *Ec 7:2*
mourning
and after that, they *go* to the *Ec 9:3*
dead
because he knoweth not how *Ec 10:15*
to *go* to city
and the mourners *go* about the *Ec 12:5*
streets
I held him, I would not let him *Ca 3:4*
go
walking and mincing as they *Isa 3:16*
go
whom shall I send, and who *Isa 6:8*
will *go* for us
he said, *Go* and tell this people *Isa 6:9;*
Ac 28:26
I will *go* through them, I *Isa 27:4*
would burn them
that they might *go* and fall *Isa 28:13*
backward
he shall let *go* my captives, *Isa 45:13*
not for price
leadth thee by way thou *Isa 48:17*
shouldest *go*
thy righteousness shall *go* *Isa 58:8*
before thee
go thro', *go* thro' the gates, *Isa 62:10*
prepare way
thou shalt *go* to all that I send *Jer 1:7*
thee
might leave my people, and *go* *Jer 9:2*
go from them
ye shall *go* and pray to me, I *Jer 29:12*
will

how long wilt thou *go* about, *Jer 31:22*
O daughter
thou shalt *go* to Babylon *Jer 34:3;*
Mic 4:10
whither it seemeth good to *go*, *Jer 40:4;*
there *go* *40:5*
he gave him reward, and let *Jer 40:5*
him *go*
saying, Let me *go*, and I will *Jer 40:15*
slay Ishmael
ye shall die, in place whither *Jer 42:22*
ye desire to *go*
furnish thyself to *go* into *Jer 46:19*
captivity
the voice thereof shall *go* like *Jer 46:22*
a serpent
they shall *go* and seek the Lord *Jer 50:4*
their God
held them fast, they refused *Jer 50:33*
to let them *go*
whither the Spirit was to *go* *Eze 1:12;*
1:20
that I should *go* far from my *Eze 8:6*
sanctuary
go through the midst of the *Eze 9:4;*
city *9:5*
or if I say, Sword, *go* through *Eze 14:17*
the land
what is the high place *Eze 20:29*
whereto ye *go*
go thee one way or other, *Eze 21:16*
either on right
shall *go* with flocks to seek the *Ho 5:6*
Lord
they call to Egypt, they *go* to *Ho 7:11*
Assyria
when they shall *go* will spread *Ho 7:12*
my net
I taught Ephraim also to *go* *Ho 11:3*
if he *go* through, both treadeth *Mic 5:8*
down
the bay went forth, and sought *Zec 6:7*
to *go*
these *go* towards north, have *Zec 6:8*
quieted my spirit
inhabitants of one city shall *Zec 8:21*
go to another
we will *go* with you, for we *Zec 8:23*
have heard
and shall *go* with whirlwinds *Zec 9:14*
of the south
Joseph was afraid to *go* *M't 2:22*
thither
compel thee to *go* a mile, *go* *M't 5:41;*
twain *Lu 7:8*
and I say to this man, *Go*, and *M't 8:9*
he goeth
he said to them, *Go*, they went *M't 8:32*
into the herd
but *go* ye and learn what that *M't 9:13*
meaneth
go rather to lost sheep of *M't 10:6*
house of Israel
he answered, I *go*, sir, and *M't 21:30*
went not
but *go* rather to them that sell, *M't 25:9*
and buy
sit ye here, while I *go* and *M't 26:36*
pray yonder
go, tell my brethren that they *M't 28:10*
go to
go ye therefore and teach all *M't 28:19*
nations
go and see *M'k 6:38*
and they let them *go* *M'k 11:6*
shall *go* before him in the *Lu 1:17*
power of Elias
stedfastly set his face to *go* to *Lu 9:51*
Jerusalem
go thou and preach the *Lu 9:60*
kingdom of God
then said Jesus, *Go*, and do *Lu 10:37*
likewise
I bought ground and must *Lu 14:18*
go and see
I am ready to *go* with thee to *Lu 22:33*
prison
you will not answer me, nor *Lu 22:68*
let me *go*
I will chastise him, and let *Lu 23:22*
him *go*
Peter said, Lord, to whom *Joh 6:68*
shall we *go*
and then I *go* unto him that *Joh 7:33*
sent me
but I know whence I came *Joh 8:14*
and whither I *go*
I *go* my way, whither I *go* ye *Joh 8:21*
cannot come

Jesus saith, Loose him, and *Joh 11:44*
let him *go*
whither I *go* thou canst not *Joh 13:36*
follow now
I *go* to prepare a place for you *Joh 14:2*
whither I *go* ye know, the way *Joh 14:4*
ye know
because I *go* unto my Father *Joh 14:12;*
16:10
because I said, I *go* to the *Joh 14:28;*
Father *16:17, 28*
the Jews cried, If thou let this *Joh 19:12*
man *go*
I *go* a fishing, they say, we *Joh 21:3*
also *go*
that he might *go* to his own *Ac 1:25*
place
when he was determined to let *Ac 3:13*
him *go*
had threatened them, they let *Ac 4:21*
them *go*
being let *go* they went to their *Ac 4:23*
company
they should not speak, and let *Ac 5:40*
them *go*
Barnabas should *go* as far as *Ac 11:22*
Antioch
essayed to *go* into Bithynia, *Ac 16:7*
but Spirit
magistrates sent, saying, Let *Ac 16:35*
those men *go*
taken security of Jason, they *Ac 17:9*
let them *go*
I *go* bound in the Spirit to *Ac 20:22*
Jerusalem
appealed to Caesar, to Caesar *Ac 25:12*
shalt thou *go*
had examined me, would have *Ac 28:18*
let me *go*
now I *go* to Jerusalem to *Ro 15:25*
minister
dare you *go* to law before the *1Co 6:1*
unjust
if any bid you and ye be *1Co 10:27*
disposed to *go*
if it be meet that I *go* also, *1Co 16:4*
they shall *go*
exhort brethren that they *go* *2Co 9:5*
before
as I shall see how it will *go* *Ph'p 2:23*
with me
we will *go* into such a city and *Jas 4:13*
buy

GO A WHORING

lest they *go a whoring* after *Ex 34:15*
their gods
and thy sons *go a whoring* *Ex 34:16*
after their gods
I will cut off all that *go a* *Le 20:5*
whoring after him
I will cut off such as *go a* *Le 20:6*
whoring after wizards
ways, after which ye use to *Nu 15:39*
go a whoring
this people will *go a whoring* *De 31:16*
after gods
Jehoram made Judah *go a* *2Ch 21:13*
whoring
destroyed all that *go a whoring* *Ps 73:27*
from thee
eyes which *go a whoring* after *Eze 6:9*
idols

GO ASIDE

if any man's wife *go aside* *Nu 5:12*
and commit
thou shalt not *go aside* from *De 28:14*
words
shall *go aside* to ask how *Jer 15:5*
thou dost
they commanded them to *go* *Ac 4:15*
aside

GO ASTRAY

shalt not see brother's ox *go* *De 22:1*
astray
go astray as soon as they be *Ps 58:3*
born
in greatness of folly he shall *Pr 5:23*
go astray
decline not to her ways, *go* *Pr 7:25*
not *astray*
whoso causeth the righteous *Pr 28:10*
to *go astray*
shepherds caused them to *go* *Jer 50:6*
astray

house of Israel may *go* no   *Eze 14:11*
more *astray*

GO *AWAY*

only you shall not *go* very far   *Ex 8:28*
away
shalt not let him *go away*   *De 15:13*
empty
if he say, I will not *go away*   *De 15:16*
from thee
as Samuel turned about to   *1Sa 15:27*
go away
find his enemy, will he let   *1Sa 24:19*
him *go away*
doth not their excellency *go*   *Job 4:21*
away
by breath of his mouth   *Job 15:30*
shall he *go away*
ye that escaped the sword,   *Jer 51:50*
go away
I, even I, will tear and *go*   *Ho 5:14*
away
suffer us to *go away* into the   *M't 8:31*
swine
these *go away* into   *M't 25:46*
everlasting punishment
then said Jesus, Will ye also   *Joh 6:67*
go away
ye have heard how I said,   *Joh 14:28;*
I *go away*   *16:7*

GO BACK

the Lord caused the sea to   *Ex 14:21*
go back
else if ye do in any wise *go*   *Jos 23:12*
back
I opened my mouth, I   *J'g 11:35*
cannot *go back*
go back again, what have I   *1Ki 19:20*
done to thee
shall the shadow *go back* ten   *2Ki 20:9*
degrees
so will not we *go back* from   *Ps 80:18*
thee
go back to Gedaliah, son of   *Jer 40:5*
Ahikam
I will not *go back*, nor will   *Eze 24:14*
I spare

GO DOWN

let us *go down* and confound   *Ge 11:7*
language
I will *go down* now, and see   *Ge 18:21*
whether
the Lord said, Go not *down*   *Ge 26:2*
into Egypt
if thou wilt not send him, we   *Ge 43:5*
will not *go down*
we cannot *go down*, then   *Ge 44:26*
will we *go down*
fear not, Jacob, to *go down*   *Ge 46:3*
into Egypt
Lord said, *Go down*, charge   *Ex 19:21*
the people
and they *go down* quick   *Nu 16:30*
into the pit
nor shall the sun *go down*   *De 24:15*
on his hire
sun hasted not to *go down*   *Jos 10:13*
about a day
if thou fear to *go down*, go   *J'g 7:10*
with Phurah
thou shalt *go down* before   *1Sa 10:8*
me to Gilgal
let us *go down* after   *1Sa 14:36*
Philistines by night
go down to Keilah, I will   *1Sa 23:4*
deliver Philistines
who will *go down* with me   *1Sa 26:6*
to Saul
let him not *go down* with us   *1Sa 29:4*
to battle
David said, *Go down* to thy   *2Sa 11:8*
house
why didst thou not *go*   *2Sa 11:10*
down to thine house
should I this day make thee   *2Sa 15:20*
go up and *down*
go down to meet Ahab king   *1Ki 21:18*
of Israel
go down with him, be not   *2Ki 1:15*
afraid
for the shadow to *go down*   *2Ki 20:10*
ten degrees
to-morrow *go down* against   *2Ch 20:16*
him

in a moment *go down* to   *Job 21:13*
the grave
all that *go down* to the dust   *Ps 22:29*
shall bow
I become like them that *go*   *Ps 28:1*
down to the pit
and let them *go down* quick   *Ps 55:15*
into hell
they that *go down* to the   *Ps 107:23*
sea in ships
neither any that *go down*   *Ps 115:17*
into silence
lest I be like them that *go*   *Ps 143:7*
down to the pit
her feet *go down* to death, her   *Pr 5:5*
steps take
thou art cast out, as those   *Isa 14:19*
that *go down*
woe to them that walk to *go*   *Isa 30:2;*
down to Egypt   *31:1*
they that *go down* into pit   *Isa 38:18*
cannot hope
sun shall not *go down* nor   *Isa 60:20*
moon withdraw
let them *go down* to the   *Jer 50:27*
slaughter
and thy strong garrisons   *Eze 26:11*
shall *go down*
I shall set thee with them   *Eze 26:20;*
that *go down* to the pit   *31:14; 32:18,*
  24-25; 29-30
these waters *go down* into   *Eze 47:8*
the desert
then *go down* to Gath of the   *Am 6:2*
Philistines
I will cause the sun to *go*   *Am 8:9*
down at noon
the sun shall *go down* over   *Mic 3:6*
the prophets
let him that is on   *M'k 13:15*
housetop not *go down*
which are able to *go down*   *Ac 25:5*
with me
let not sun *go down* on your   *Eph 4:26*
wrath

GO FORTH

go forth of the ark, thou and   *Ge 8:16*
thy wife
not *go forth* hence, except   *Ge 42:15*
brother come
the priest shall *go forth* of   *Le 14:3*
the camp
all able to *go forth* to war   *Nu 1:3;*
  2Ch 25:5
thou shalt have a place to   *De 23:12*
go forth
and he forbare to *go forth*   *1Sa 23:13*
at time when kings *go forth*   *2Sa 11:1*
to battle
I will surely *go forth* with   *2Sa 18:2*
you myself
if thou *go* not *forth*, there   *2Sa 19:7*
will not tarry
and *go* not *forth* thence any   *1Ki 2:36*
whither
he said, I will *go forth*: go   *1Ki 22:22*
forth and do so
if it be your minds, let none   *2Ki 9:15*
go forth
out of Jerusalem shall *go*   *2Ki 19:31;*
forth a remnant they   *Isa 37:32*
as wild asses go they *forth*   *Job 24:5*
to their work
he made his own people to   *Ps 78:52*
go forth
wilt not thou *go forth* with   *Ps 108:11*
our hosts
go not *forth* hastily to strive   *Pr 25:8*
lest thou
have no king, yet *go* they   *Pr 30:27*
forth by bands
go forth, O ye daughters of   *Ca 3:11*
Zion
come, let us *go forth* into the   *Ca 7:11*
villages
out of Zion shall *go forth* the   *Isa 2:3;*
law   *Mic 4:2*
the Lord shall *go forth* as a   *Isa 42:13*
mighty man
go forth of Babylon, flee ye   *Isa 48:20;*
  Jer 50:8
that thou mayest say to   *Isa 49:9*
prisoners, Go *forth*
they that made thee waste   *Isa 49:17*
shall *go forth*
till the righteousness thereof   *Isa 62:1*
go forth

go not *forth* into the field,   *Jer 6:25*
nor walk
if I *go forth* into the field,   *Jer 14:18*
then the slain
let them *go forth*; whither   *Jer 15:1;*
shall we *go forth*   *15:2*
evil shall *go forth* from   *Jer 25:32*
nation to nation
O Israel, thou shalt *go forth*   *Jer 31:4*
in the dances
the measuring line shall yet   *Jer 31:39*
go forth
if thou wilt *go forth* to king   *Jer 38:17*
of Babylon
if thou will not *go forth* to   *Jer 38:18;*
princes   *38:21*
he shall *go forth* from   *Jer 43:12*
thence in peace
go forth as they that *go*   *Eze 12:4*
forth into captivity
prince *go forth*; my sword   *Eze 12:12;*
shall *go forth*   *21:4*
in that day messengers shall   *Eze 30:9*
go forth
and he shall *go forth* by the   *Eze 46:8*
way thereof
but he shall *go forth* over   *Eze 46:9*
against it
he shall *go forth* with great   *Da 11:44*
fury
let the bridegroom *go forth* of   *Joe 2:16*
his chamber
and judgment doth never *go*   *Hab 1:4*
forth
these are the four spirits   *Zec 6:5*
which *go forth*
black horses *go forth* into the   *Zec 6:6*
north country
then shall the Lord *go forth*   *Zec 14:3*
and fight
go forth and grow up as   *Mal 4:2*
calves
he is in the desert, *go* not   *M't 24:26*
forth
him would Paul have to *go*   *Ac 16:3*
forth
let us *go forth* to him   *Heb 13:13*
without camp
the spirits of devils which *go*   *Re 16:14*
forth

GO *FORWARD*

speak to Israel that they *go*   *Ex 14:15*
forward
shall *go forward* in the third   *Nu 2:24*
rank
shall shadow *go forward* ten   *2Ki 20:9*
degrees
behold, I *go forward*, but he   *Job 23:8*
is not there

GO HIS WAY

her lord rose up and went   *J'g 19:27*
to *go his way*

GO IN, INTO,
NOT GO IN

from Ur, to *go into* land of   *Ge 11:31;*
Canaan   *12:5*
Sarai said, I pray thee, *go in*   *Ge 16:2*
unto my maid
make him drink wine, and   *Ge 19:34*
go thou in
behold my maid Bilhah, *go in*   *Ge 30:3*
unto her
go in unto thy brother's wife,   *Ge 38:8*
and marry her
when *go into* tabernacle,   *Ex 30:20*
shall wash
go in and out from gate to   *Ex 32:27*
gate thro' camp
do not drink wine, when ye   *Le 10:9*
go into tabernacle
empty the house, before the   *Le 14:36*
priest *go in*
neither shall he *go in* to any   *Le 21:11*
dead body
only he shall not *go in* to   *Le 21:23*
the veil or near altar
Aaron and his sons shall *go in*   *Nu 4:19*
in and
they shall not *go in* to see   *Nu 4:20*
when holy things
and after that shall the   *Nu 8:15*
Levites *go in*

which may go out, and go *Nu 27:17*
in before them
that they should not go into *Nu 32:9*
the land
thou also shalt not go in *De 1:37;*
thither   *4:21*
Joshua son of Nun he shall *De 1:38*
go in thither
that ye may live, and go in *De 4:1;*
and possess   *8:1*
that thou mayest go in and *De 6:18;*
possess   *10:11*
that ye may be strong, and *De 11:8*
go in and
after that thou shalt go in *De 21:13*
unto her
if take a wife, and go in *De 22:13*
unto her, hate her
not go into his house to *De 24:10*
fetch his pledge
her husband's brother shall *De 25:5*
go in unto her
make marriages, and go in *Jos 23:12*
unto them
I will go in to my wife into *J'g 15:1*
the chamber
they turned aside to go in *J'g 19:15*
and lodge
thou shalt go in, and uncover *Ru 3:4*
his feet
shall I then go into mine *2Sa 11:11*
house to eat
go in unto thy father's *2Sa 16:21*
concubines
ye shall not go in to them, *1Ki 11:2*
nor they
I will not go in, nor eat *1Ki 13:8*
with thee
I may not return, nor go in *1Ki 13:16*
with thee
may go in, and dress it for *1Ki 17:12*
me and my son
look out Jehu, and go in, *2Ki 9:2*
make him arise
go in and slay them, let *2Ki 10:25*
none come forth
thou shalt go into an inner *2Ch 18:24*
chamber
they that minister of the *2Ch 23:6*
Levites shall go in
would go into the temple to *Ne 6:11*
save his life? I will not go in
when Esther's turn was come *Es 2:15*
to go in
and to charge her that she *Es 4:8*
should go in
and so will I go in unto the *Es 4:16*
king, if I perish
then go thou in merrily unto *Es 5:14*
the king
nor will I go in with *Ps 26:4*
dissemblers
open the gates, I will go in *Ps 118:19*
to them
make me go into path of *Ps 119:35*
commandment
we will go into his *Ps 132:7*
tabernacle and worship
nor go into thy brother's *Pr 27:10*
house
they shall go into the holes *Isa 2:19*
of the rocks
and let us go into the *Jer 4:5*
defenced cities
I cannot go into the house of *Jer 36:5*
the Lord
no, but we will go into the *Jer 42:14*
land of Egypt
the Lord hath said, Go ye *Jer 42:19*
not into Egypt
went to her as they go in *Eze 23:44*
to a woman
the prince when they go in *Eze 46:10*
shall go in
man and his father go in to *Am 2:7*
same maid
go into clay, and tread the *Na 3:14*
mortar
go into house of Josiah son *Zec 6:10*
of Zephaniah
take the young child, and go *M't 2:20*
into Israel
and many there be that go *M't 7:13*
in thereat
go into the vineyard, and *M't 20:4;*
they went   *20:7*
go into village over against *M't 21:2;*
you   *Lu 19:30*

harlots go into kingdom of *M't 21:31*
God before you
go into the highways, as *M't 22:9*
many as ye find, bid
ye neither go in, nor suffer *M't 23:13*
others to go in
go into the city, to such a *M't 26:18;*
man   *M'k 14:13*
that they may go into the *M'k 6:36*
country
nor go into the town, nor *M'k 8:26*
tell it to any
go into all the world, *M'k 16:15*
preach the gospel
he suffered no man to go in, *Lu 8:51*
save Peter
and he was angry, and *Lu 15:28*
would not go in
he shall go in and out, and *Joh 10:9*
find pasture
shall so come, as ye see him *Ac 1:11*
go into heaven
the beast was, is not, shall go *Re 17:8*
into perdition

GO IN PEACE

thou shalt go to thy fathers *Ge 15:15*
in peace
Jethro said to Moses, Go in *Ex 4:18*
peace
this people shall go to their *Ex 18:23*
place in peace
the priest said to Danites, Go *J'g 18:6*
in peace
Eli said to Hannah, Go in *1Sa 1:17*
peace
Jonathan said to David, Go *1Sa 20:42*
in peace
David said to Abigail, Go *1Sa 25:35*
up in peace
Achish said to David, Go in *1Sa 29:7*
peace
the king said to Absalom, Go *2Sa 15:9*
in peace
let not his hoary head go *1Ki 2:6*
down in peace
Elisha said to Naaman, Go *2Ki 5:19*
in peace
go in peace, and be whole *M'k 5:34*
of thy plague
faith hath saved thee, go in *Lu 7:50;*
peace   *8:48*
they were let go in peace *Ac 15:33*
from brethren

GO NEAR

go near, and hear all the *De 5:27*
Lord says
David said, Go near, and fall *2Sa 1:15*
on him
as a prince would I go near *Job 31:37*
unto him
go near, join thyself to this *Ac 8:29*
chariot

GO NOT, NOT GO, CANNOT GO

if thy presence go not with *Ex 33:15*
me
Hobab said, I will not go, *Nu 10:30*
but depart
and he said, Thou shalt not *Nu 20:20*
go through
God said to Balaam, Shalt *Nu 22:12*
not go with them
I cannot go beyond the *Nu 22:18;*
word of Lord   *24:13*
thou shalt not go over this *De 3:27*
Jordan
ye shall not go after other *De 6:14;*
gods   *1Ki 11:10*
if he say, I will not go away *De 15:16*
from thee
thou shalt not go again to *De 24:19*
fetch it
but thou shalt not go thither *De 32:52*
to the land
go not far from the city, but *Jos 8:4*
be ready
if thou wilt not go with me, I *J'g 4:8*
will not go
I say, this shall not go, the *J'g 7:4*
same shall not go
we will not any of us go to *J'g 20:8*
his tent

go not empty to thy *Ru 3:17*
mother in law
David said, I cannot go *1Sa 17:39*
with these
that I may not go fight against *1Sa 29:8*
enemies of the king
let not all go, howbeit he *2Sa 13:25*
would not go
he said, Did I not say to *2Ki 2:18*
you, Go not
but David could not go *1Ch 21:30*
before it
soldiers that should not go *2Ch 25:13*
to battle
take hold of instruction, let *Pr 4:13*
her not go
and go not into the way of *Pr 4:14*
evil men
with a furious man thou *Pr 22:24*
shalt not go
for ye shall not go out with *Isa 52:12*
haste
must be borne, because they *Jer 10:5*
cannot go
shalt not go into the house *Jer 16:8*
of feasting
go not after other gods to *Jer 25:6;*
serve them   *35:15*
that the vessels left go not *Jer 27:18*
to Babylon
go not into Egypt to sojourn *Jer 43:2;*
there   *42:19*
shalt not go unpunished, but *Jer 49:12*
drink of it
hunt steps, that we cannot go *La 4:18*
in our streets
when the priests enter, shall *Eze 42:14*
not go out
go not into the way of the *M't 10:5*
Gentiles
go not from house to house *Lu 10:7*
see here or there, go not *Lu 17:23;*
after them   *21:8*

GO OVER

I pray thee let me go over *De 3:25*
and see land
Joshua shall go over before *De 3:28;*
the people   *31:3*
land whither ye go over *De 4:14;*
      4:26; 31:13; 32:47
I must not go over Jordan, *De 4:22*
ye shall go over
thou shalt not go over the *De 24:20*
boughs again
who shall go over sea for us *De 30:13*
and bring it
the Lord thy God will go *De 31:3*
over before thee
but thou shalt not go over *De 34:4*
thither
therefore arise, go over this *Jos 1:2*
Jordan
the Ephraimites said, Let me *J'g 12:5*
go over
come, let us go over to the *1Sa 14:1;*
Philistines   *14:6*
so faint, they could not go *1Sa 30:10*
over the brook
let me go over and take off *2Sa 16:9*
his head
thy servant Chimham, let *2Sa 19:37*
him go over
shall come and go over all his *Isa 8:7*
banks
he shall make men go over *Isa 11:15*
dryshod
said, Bow down, that we *Isa 51:23*
may go over
waters of Noah should no *Isa 54:9*
more go over
Ishmael departed to go over *Jer 41:10*
to Ammonites
let us go over to the other *Lu 8:22*
side

GO OUT

from all that go out of the *Ge 9:10*
ark
time that women go out to *Ge 24:11*
draw water
cried, Cause every man to go *Ge 45:1*
out from me
that he let children of Israel *Ex 6:11*
go out
behold, I go out from thee, I *Ex 8:29*
will entreat

after that I will *go out,* and *Ex 11:8*
he went out
would not let the children of *Ex 11:10*
Israel *go out*
none of you shall *go out* at *Ex 12:22*
door of house
people *go out* and gather a rate *Ex 16:4*
every day
let no man *go out* of place *Ex 16:29*
on seventh day
in the seventh year he shall *Ex 21:2*
go out free
himself, shall *go out* by *Ex 21:3*
himself; if married, wife shall
go out with him
her master's, and he shall *go* *Ex 21:4*
out by himself
if the servant say, I will not *Ex 21:5*
go out free
a maidservant not *go out* as *Ex 21:7*
menservants do
then shall she *go out* free *Ex 21:11*
without money
the fire on the altar shall *Le 6:13*
never *go out*
not *go out* of tabernacle in *Le 8:33*
seven days
ye shall not *go out* at the *Le 10:7*
door, lest ye die
then the priest shall *go out* *Le 14:38*
of the house
if any man's seed of *Le 15:16*
copulation *go out*
shall *go out* to altar before *Le 16:18*
the Lord
nor shall he *go out* of the *Le 21:12*
sanctuary
in the jubilee it shall *go out* *Le 25:28*
it shall not *go out* in jubile *Le 25:30;*
25:31, 33, 54
taken a wife, he shall not *go* *De 24:5*
out to war
shalt *go out* one way, flee *De 28:25*
seven ways
who shall *go out,* his blood *Jos 2:19*
be on his
go out and fight with them *J'g 9:38*
he said, I will *go out* as at *J'g 16:20*
other times
shall I yet again *go out* to *J'g 20:28*
battle against Benjamin
it is good thou *go out* with *Ru 2:22*
his maidens
I will *go out* and stand *1Sa 19:3*
beside my father
come, let us *go out* into the *1Sa 20:11*
field
Achish said, Thou shalt *go* *1Sa 28:1*
out with me
then the Lord shall *go out* *2Sa 5:24*
before thee
go no more *out* with us to *2Sa 21:17*
battle
that he might not suffer *1Ki 15:17;*
any to *go out,* or come in *2Ch 16:1*
put ropes on heads, and *go* *1Ki 20:31*
out to king
at the time kings *go out* to *1Ch 20:1*
battle
go out and be a lying *2Ch 18:21*
spirit, *go out*
fear not, to-morrow *go out* *2Ch 20:17*
against them
go out of sanctuary, for *2Ch 26:18*
thou hast trespassed
yea, himself hasted also to *2Ch 26:20*
go out
lettest such words *go out* of *Job 15:13*
thy mouth
which didst not *go out* with *Ps 60:10*
our armies
cast out the scorner, *Pr 22:10*
contention *go out*
be not hasty to *go out* of his *Ec 8:3*
sight
depart ye, *go* ye *out* from *Isa 52:11*
thence
shall *go out* with joy, and *Isa 55:12*
be led forth
lest my fury *go out* like fire *Jer 21:12*
and burn
my people, *go* ye *out* of the *Jer 51:45*
midst of her
they shall *go out* from one *Eze 15:7*
fire
the prince shall *go out* *Eze 44:3*
same way
entered by north, shall *go out* *Eze 46:9*
by south gate

and ye shall *go out* at the *Am 4:3*
breaches
that living waters *go out* *Zec 14:8*
from Jerusalem
bridegroom cometh, *go* ye *M't 25:6*
out to meet him
when ye *go out* of the city *Lu 9:5*
shake off dust
go out quickly into the *Lu 14:21*
streets and lanes
go out into the highways *Lu 14:23*
and hedges
then must ye needs *go out* *1Co 5:10*
of the world
Abraham, when he was *Heb 11:8*
called to *go out*
he that overcometh, shall *go* *Re 3:12*
no more *out*
and shall *go out* to deceive *Re 20:8*
the nations

GO THEIR WAY

if ye seek me, let these *go* *Joh 18:8*
their way

GO THY WAY

thy wife, take her, *go thy* *Ge 12:19*
way
go thy way, the Lord hath *1Sa 20:22*
sent thee
he said, Take my staff, and *2Ki 4:29*
go thy way
go thy way, eat thy bread with *Ec 9:7*
joy
go thy way forth by footsteps *Ca 1:8*
of the flock
go thy way, for words are *Da 12:9*
closed up
go thy way till the end be, *Da 12:13*
for thou shalt rest
go thy way, be reconciled to *M't 5:24*
brother
go thy way, shew thyself to *M't 8:4*
the priest
take that thine is, and *go* *M't 20:14*
thy way
he said, For this saying, *go* *M'k 7:29*
thy way
go thy way, sell whatsoever *M'k 10:21*
thou hast
go thy way faith made thee *M'k 10:52;*
whole *Lu 17:19*
Jesus saith, *Go thy way,* thy *Joh 4:50*
son liveth
go thy way, for he is a *Ac 9:15*
chosen vessel
Felix answered, *Go thy way* *Ac 24:25*
for this time

GO TO

go to, let us make brick, and *Ge 11:3*
burn them
go to, let us build; *go to,* let *Ge 11:4;*
us confound *11:7*
go to now, I will prove thee *Ec 2:1*
with mirth
go to, I will tell you what I *Isa 5:5*
will do
go to now, ye that say, *Jas 4:13*
to-day, or to-morrow
go to now, ye rich men, weep *Jas 5:1*
and howl

GO UP

arise, *go up* to Bethel, dwell *Ge 35:1;*
there *35:3*
and let the lad *go up* with *Ge 44:33*
his brethren
how shall I *go up* to my *Ge 44:34;*
father *45:9*
Pharaoh said, *Go up* and bury *Ge 50:6*
thy father
frogs shall *go up* and come *Ex 8:3*
into thy house
take heed ye *go* not *up* into *Ex 19:12*
the mount
nor shalt thou *go up* by *Ex 20:26*
steps to my altar
neither shall the people *go up* *Ex 24:2*
with him
ye have sinned a great sin, I *Ex 32:30*
will *go up*
depart and *go up,* thou and *Ex 33:1*
the people
for I will not *go up* in the *Ex 33:3*
midst of thee

not desire thy land. when *Ex 34:24*
thou shalt *go up*
not *go up* and down as *Le 19:16*
talebearer
let us *go up* at once and *Nu 13:30*
possess it
we be not able to *go up* *Nu 13:31*
against this people
lo, we be here, and will *go* *Nu 14:40;*
up *De 1:41*
go not *up;* but they presumed *Nu 14:42;*
to *go up* *14:44*
let his brother's wife *go up* *De 25:7*
to the gate
who shall *go up* for us to *De 30:12*
heaven, and bring
let not all *go up,* let 3,000 men *Jos 7:3*
go up
did not intend to *go up* *Jos 22:33*
against them in battle
who shall *go up* for us to fight *J'g 1:1*
them
the Lord said, Judah shall *go* *J'g 1:2;*
up *20:18*
angel said, I made you *go up* *J'g 2:1*
out of Egypt
that I may *go up* and down *J'g 11:37*
on mountains
arise, that we may *go up* *J'g 18:9*
against them
we will *go up* by lot against *J'g 20:9*
Gibeah
which of us shall *go up* first *J'g 20:18*
to battle
shall I *go up* again; *go up* *J'g 20:23;*
against him *20:28*
I will not *go up* till the child *1Sa 1:22*
be weaned
if it *go up* by the way of his *1Sa 6:9*
own coast
and to whom shall he *go up* *1Sa 6:20*
from us
ye shall find him before he *1Sa 9:13*
go up to eat
Samuel came to *go up* to *1Sa 9:14;*
the high place *9:19*
if they say, Tarry, we will *1Sa 14:9*
not *go up*
if they say, Come up unto *1Sa 14:10*
us, we will *go up*
shall I *go up* to any of cities *2Sa 2:1*
of Judah? the Lord said, Go
up to Hebron
shall I *go up* against the *2Sa 5:19*
Philistines
should I make thee *go up* *2Sa 15:20*
and down with us
how long have I to live, that *2Sa 19:34*
I should *go up*
go up, rear an altar in *2Sa 24:18;*
floor *1Ch 21:18*
ye shall not *go up* *1Ki 12:24;* *2Ch 11:4*
if this people *go up* to do *1Ki 12:27*
sacrifice at Jerusalem
it is too much for you to *1Ki 12:28*
go up to Jerusalem
go up, look towards the *1Ki 18:43*
sea, and he went
go up, for the Lord shall *1Ki 22:6;*
deliver it into hand of *22:12;*
2Ch 18:11, 14
may *go up* and fall at *1Ki 22:20;*
Ramoth *2Ch 18:19*
go up, meet the messengers of *2Ki 1:3*
the king
go up thou bald head, *go up* *2Ki 2:23*
thou bald head
wilt thou *go up* with me *2Ki 3:7*
against Moab
and he said, Which way shall *2Ki 3:8*
we *go up*
Hazael set his face to *go* *2Ki 12:17*
up to Jerusalem
Lord said, *Go up* against *2Ki 18:25;*
the land *Isa 36:10*
on third day thou shalt *go* *2Ki 20:5*
up to the house
what the sign that I shall *2Ki 20:8;*
go up *Isa 38:22*
go up to Hilkiah high priest *2Ki 22:4*
to sum silver
shall I *go up;* *go* not *up* *1Ch 14:10;*
after them *14:14*
shall we *go up* to *2Ch 18:5*
Ramoth-gilead
God be with him, let him *2Ch 36:23;*
go up *Ezr 1:3*
he began to *go up* from *Ezr 7:9*
Babylon

GO UP

all which are minded to *go* | *Ezr 7:13*
up go with me
if a fox *go up* he shall even | *Ne 4:3*
break down
they *go up* by the mountains | *Ps 104:8*
surely I will not *go up* into | *Ps 132:3*
my bed
as a flock of sheep that *go up* | *Ca 6:6*
from washing
I said, I will *go up* to the | *Ca 7:8*
palm tree
let us *go up* to mountain of | *Isa 2:3;*
Lord | *Mic 4:2*
let us *go up* against Judah | *Isa 7:6*
and vex it
with weeping shall they *go* it | *Isa 15:5*
up
go up, O Elam; the smoke | *Isa 21:2;*
shall *go up* | *34:10*
nor any ravenous beast shall | *Isa 35:9*
go up there
go up against this land, and | *Isa 36:10*
destroy it
go ye up upon her walls and | *Jer 5:10*
destroy
arise, and let us *go up* at | *Jer 6:4*
noon, woe unto us
that Nebuchadnezzar may *go* | *Jer 21:2*
up from us
go up to Lebanon, and cry, | *Jer 22:20*
lift up thy voice
let us *go up* to Zion, to the | *Jer 31:6*
Lord our God
he saith, I will *go up* and | *Jer 46:8*
cover the earth
go up into Gilead, and take | *Jer 46:11*
balm, O virgin
continual weeping shall *go* | *Jer 48:5*
go up to Kedar, and spoil | *Jer 49:28*
men of the east
go up against the land of | *Jer 50:21*
Merathaim
I will *go up* to land of | *Eze 38:11*
unwalled villages
there were seven steps to *go* | *Eze 40:26*
up to it
neither *go up* to Beth-aven, | *Ho 4:15*
nor swear
go up to the mountain, and | *Hag 1:8*
bring wood
go up from year to year to | *Zec 14:16*
worship
we *go up* to Jerusalem, | *M't 20:18;*
Son of man | *M'k 10:33; Lu 18:31*
he may say to thee, Friend, | *Lu 14:10*
go up higher
go ye up to this feast, I *go* | *Joh 7:8*
not *up* yet
go up to Jerusalem about | *Ac 15:2*
this question
that Paul should not *go up* to | *Ac 21:4*
Jerusalem
we besought him not to *go* | *Ac 21:12*
up to Jerusalem
wilt thou *go up* to Jerusalem | *Ac 25:9*
and be judged

GO YOUR WAY, WAYS

ye shall rise up and *go* on | *Ge 19:2*
your ways
afterward *go your way* | *Jos 2:16;*
| *J'g 19:5*
turn again my daughters, *go* | *Ru 1:12*
your way
go your way, eat the fat, drink | *Ne 8:10*
the sweet
go your way make it as sure | *M't 27:65*
as you can
go your way into village | *M'k 11:2*
over against
go your way, tell his | *M'k 16:7*
disciples that he goeth
go your way, tell John what | *Lu 7:22*
things ye heard
go your ways, I send you as | *Lu 10:3*
lambs among wolves
they receive you not, *go your* | *Lu 10:10*
ways to streets
go your ways, pour out the | *Re 16:1*
vials of wrath

I WILL GO

I will go to the right, I will | *Ge 13:9*
go to the left
wilt thou *go* with this man? | *Ge 24:58*
I will go
let us go, *I will go* before | *Ge 33:12;*
thee | *Isa 45:2*

my son is alive, *I will go* | *Ge 45:28*
see him before I die
I will only *go* through on | *Nu 20:19*
my feet
stand by the burnt offering, | *Nu 23:3*
and *I will go*
I will go along by the | *De 2:27*
highway
I will go likewise with thee | *J'g 1:3*
into thy lot
if thou wilt *go* with me, then | *J'g 4:8*
will I go
she said, *I will* surely *go* with | *J'g 4:9*
thee
I will go out as at other | *J'g 16:20*
times before
Ruth said, Whither thou goest, | *Ru 1:16*
I will go
go with servant, he answered, | *2Ki 6:3*
I will go
he said, *I will go* to the | *2Ch 18:29*
battle
then *will I go* to the altar of | *Ps 43:4*
God
I will go into thy house with | *Ps 66:13*
burnt offering
I will go in the strength of | *Ps 71:16*
the Lord God
open the gates of | *Ps 118:19*
righteousness, *I will go* in
I loved strangers, after them | *Jer 2:25*
I will go
I will go to them that are | *Eze 38:11*
at rest
for she said, *I will go* after | *Ho 2:5*
my lovers
I will go and return to my | *Ho 2:7*
first husband
I will go to my place, till | *Ho 5:15*
they seek my face
I will wail, *I will go* stripped | *Mic 1:8*
and naked
go to seek the Lord; *I will* | *Zec 8:21*
go also
I will go before into | *M't 26:32;*
Galilee | *M'k 14:28*
I will arise and *go* to my | *Lu 15:18*
father
henceforth *I will go* to the | *Ac 18:6*
Gentiles

LET US GO

I heard them say, *Let us go* | *Ge 37:17*
to Dothan
now *let us go* three days' | *Ex 3:18;*
journey | *5:3*
therefore they say, *Let us go* | *Ex 5:8;*
sacrifice | *5:17*
when Pharaoh would hardly | *Ex 13:15*
let us go
let us go after other gods | *De 13:2;*
| *13:6, 13*
thus he spake, *Let us go* to | *1Sa 9:9;*
the seer | *9:10*
let us go to Gilgal, and | *1Sa 11:14*
renew the kingdom
let us go over to the | *1Sa 14:1;*
Philistines' garrison | *14:6*
let us go to Jordan, take | *2Ki 6:2*
thence a beam
let us go into the house of | *Ps 122:1*
the Lord
let us go up to the mountain | *Isa 2:3*
of the Lord
let us go into the defenced | *Jer 4:5*
cities
let us go by night, and destroy | *Jer 6:5*
her palaces
let us go to Jerusalem for | *Jer 35:11*
fear of Chaldeans
arise, *let us go* again to our | *Jer 46:16*
own people
let us go, every one to his | *Jer 51:9*
own country
let us go to pray before the | *Zec 8:21*
Lord
he said, *Let us go* into the | *M'k 1:38*
next towns
rise up, *let us go*, he that | *M'k 14:42*
betrayeth is at hand
let us go to Bethlehem, see | *Lu 2:15*
then saith he, *Let us go* to | *Joh 11:7*
Judaea again
let us go to him; *let us go*, | *Joh 11:15;*
that we may die | *11:16*
even so *I* do; arise, *let us* | *Joh 14:31*
go hence

let us go again, and visit | *Ac 15:36*
our brethren
let us go on to perfection, | *Heb 6:1*
not laying again

GO-BETWEEN

a *g.* (A)(B) | *Ga 3:19;*
| *3:20; 1Ti 2:5*

GOAD

six hundred men with an ox | *J'g 3:31*
g.
kicking against the *g.* (A) | *Ac 9:5;*
| *26:14*

GOADED

g. into action by jealousy | *Ac 5:17*
(N)

GOADS

for the axes, and to sharpen | *1Sa 13:21*
the *g.*
The words of the wise are | *Ec 12:11*
as *g.*
kick against the *g.* (S) | *Ac 9:5; 26:14*

GOAL

third day reach my *g.* (N) | *Lu 13:32*

GOAT

and a she *g.* of three years | *Ge 15:9*
old
if his offering be a *g.* then he | *Le 3:12*
shall
his hand upon the head of | *Le 4:24*
the *g.*
fat, of ox, or of sheep, or of | *Le 7:23*
g.
and took the *g.* which was | *Le 9:15*
the sin
Moses diligently sought the | *Le 10:16*
g. of
Aaron shall bring the *g.* upon | *Le 16:9*
which
But the *g.* on which the lot | *Le 16:10*
fell to be
Then shall he kill the *g.* of | *Le 16:15*
the sin
and of the blood of the *g.* | *Le 16:18*
and put it
he shall bring the live *g.* | *Le 16:20*
hands upon the head of the | *Le 16:21*
live *g.*
the *g.* shall bear upon him | *Le 16:22*
all their
shall let go the *g.* in the | *Le 16:22*
wilderness
that let go the *g.* for the | *Le 16:26*
scapegoat
and the *g.* for the sin | *Le 16:27*
offering
that killeth an ox, or lamb, or | *Le 17:3*
g.
When a bullock, or a sheep, | *Le 22:27*
or a *g.*
he shall bring a she *g.* of | *Nu 15:27*
the first
or the firstling of a *g.* thou | *Nu 18:17*
shalt
And one *g.* for a sin | *Nu 28:22;*
offering | *29:22, 28, 31, 34, 38*
eat: the ox, the sheep, and | *De 14:4*
the *g.*
and the wild *g.* and the | *De 14:5*
pygarg
A greyhound; an he *g.* also | *Pr 30:31*
the wild *g.* (S) | *Isa 34:14*
every day a *g.* for a sin | *Eze 45:25*
offering
an he *g.* came from the west | *Da 8:5*
and the *g.* had a notable horn | *Da 8:5*
Therefore the he *g.* waxed | *Da 8:8*
very
the rough *g.* is the king of | *Da 8:21*
Grecia

GOAT-IDOLS

goat-idols (B) | *2Ch 11:15*

GOAT-LIKE

shagg he goats, *g.* gods | *Le 17:7*
(A)(E)

GOATH

and shall compass about to *Jer 31:39*
G.

GOATS

thence two good kids of the *Ge 27:9*
g.
put the skins of the kids of *Ge 27:16*
the g.
spotted and speckled among *Ge 30:32*
the g.
speckled and spotted among *Ge 30:33*
the g.
he removed that day the he *Ge 30:35*
g.
the she g. that were speckled *Ge 30:35*
thy ewes and thy she g. have *Ge 31:38*
not
Two hundred she g. and *Ge 32:14*
twenty
and twenty he g. two *Ge 32:14*
hundred
killed a kid of the g. and *Ge 37:31*
dipped
ye shall take it out from *Ex 12:5*
sheep or g.
if his offering be of the sheep *Le 1:10*
or g.
he shall bring his offering, *Le 4:23;*
a kid of g.   *4:28; 5:6*
take a kid of the g. for a *Le 9:3*
sin offering
two kids of the g. *Le 16:5; 16:7*
ye shall offer a male of the *Le 22:19*
sheep or g.
then ye shall sacrifice one *Le 23:19;*
kid of the g. for *Nu 7:16; 15:24*
five rams, five he g., five *Nu 7:17;*
lambs *7:23, 29, 35, 41, 47, 53, 59, 65,*
71, 77, 83
kids of the g. for a sin *Nu 7:87*
offering, twelve
the he g. sixty, the lambs of *Nu 7:88*
first year sixty
rams and he g. of the breed *De 32:14*
of Bashan
Nabal had a thousand g. was *1Sa 25:2*
shearing
the Arabians brought *2Ch 17:11*
7,700 he g.
they brought seven he g. *2Ch 29:21*
for a sin offering
offered at the dedication *Ezr 6:17*
twelve he g.
children out of captivity *Ezr 8:35*
offered 12 he g.
I will take no he g. out of thy *Ps 50:9*
fold
or will I drink the blood of *Ps 50:13*
g.
I will offer to thee bullocks *Ps 66:15*
with g.
the g. are the price of thy *Pr 27:26*
field
thou shalt have g. milk *Pr 27:27*
enough for food
thy hair is as a flock of g. *Ca 4:1; 6:5*
I delight not in the blood of *Isa 1:11*
he g.
the he-g. (S) *Isa 13:21*
sword of the Lord fat with *Isa 34:6*
the blood of g.
and be as the he g. before *Jer 50:8*
the flocks
Arabia occupied with thee *Eze 27:21*
in g.
I judge between the rams *Eze 34:17*
and he g.
ye shall drink the blood of *Eze 39:18*
lambs and g.
on the second day offer a *Eze 43:22*
kid of the g.
a kid of the g. daily for a *Eze 45:23*
sin offering
my anger was kindled, I *Zec 10:3*
punished the g.
a shepherd divideth the *M't 25:32*
sheep from the g.
he shall set the g. on his *M't 25:33*
left hand
nor entered by blood of g. *Heb 9:12*
and calves
if the blood of bulls and g. *Heb 9:13*
sanctifieth
he took the blood of g. and *Heb 9:19*
sprinkled the book
is not possible blood of g. *Heb 10:4*
take away sins

GOATS'

scarlet, and fine linen, and g. *Ex 25:4;*
hair *35:6; 35:23*
thou shalt make curtains of g. *Ex 26:7*
hair
them up in wisdom spun g. *Ex 35:26*
hair
And he made curtains of g. *Ex 36:14*
hair
all work of g. hair, and all *Nu 31:20*
things
put a pillow of g. hair for *1Sa 19:13*
his bolster
with a pillow of g. hair for *1Sa 19:16*
his bolster
thou shalt have g. milk *Pr 27:27*
enough for

GOATSKINS

about in sheepskins and g. *Heb 11:37*

GOB

a battle with the Philistines *2Sa 21:18*
at G.
a battle in G. with the *2Sa 21:19*
Philistines

GOBBLED

g. them up (P) *M't 13:4*

GOBLET

Thy navel is like a round g. *Ca 7:2*

GOBLETS

brought forth the g. (A)(R) *Ezr 1:7*

GOD

ye shall be as G. (S) *Ge 3:5*
called name of Lord, thou *Ge 16:13*
G. seest me
to be a G. to thee and thy *Ge 17:7*
seed after thee
I am the G. of Beth-el, *Ge 31:13*
where thou vowedst
what is this that G. hath *Ge 42:28*
done to us
it was not you that sent me *Ge 45:8*
hither, but G.
behold, I die, but G. shall *Ge 48:21*
be with you
I will take you to me, and be *Ex 6:7*
to you a G.
give thee counsel, and G. *Ex 18:19*
shall be with thee
thou shalt not revile G. (S) *Ex 22:28*
said of Jacob, What hath G. *Nu 23:23*
wrought
alas, who shall live when G. *Nu 24:23*
doth this
what nation which hath G. so *De 4:7*
nigh
put the Lord your G. to the *De 6:16;*
test (S) *M't 4:7; Lu 4:12; Ac 15:10*
that he may be to thee a G. *De 29:13*
as he said
G. do so and more also *1Sa 3:17;*
14:44; 25:22; 2Sa 3:9, 35; 19:13;
1Ki 2:23; 2Ki 6:31
all may know that there is *1Sa 17:46*
a G. in Israel
till I know what G. will do *1Sa 22:3*
for me
who is G. save the Lord *2Sa 22:32;*
Ps 18:31
the name of the Lord G. of *1Ki 8:20*
Israel
if the Lord be G. follow *1Ki 18:21*
him
the Lord, he is the G. the *1Ki 18:39*
Lord, he is the G.
thou art the G. even thou *2Ki 19:15*
alone
O Lord G. art not thou G. *2Ch 20:6*
in heaven
his G. be with him, he *Eze 1:3*
is the G.
art a G. ready to pardon, *Neh 9:17*
slow to anger
sayest, How doth G. know *Job 22:13;*
Ps 73:11
art not a G. that hast pleasure *Ps 5:4*
in wickedness

the man that made not G. his *Ps 52:7*
strength
thou art great, thou art G. *Ps 86:10;*
alone *Isa 37:16*
O G. the Lord, the strength *Ps 140:7*
of my
behold, G. is my salvation, I *Isa 12:2*
will trust
in the Lord G. is everlasting *Isa 26:4*
strength (S)
is there a G. besides me? *Isa 44:8*
yea, there is no G.
look unto me, I am G. there *Isa 45:22*
is none else
I am G. there is none else, *Isa 46:9*
none like me
I will be their G. they my *Jer 31:33;*
people *32:38*
hast said, I am a god, I sit *Eze 28:2*
I am a g. (S) *Eze 28:2; 28:9*
petition to any g. (S) *Da 6:7*
but thou shalt be a man, and *Eze 28:9*
no g.
petition to any g. (S) *Da 6:7*
g. of fortresses (S) *Da 11:38*
workman made it, therefore it *Ho 8:6*
is not G.
for I am G. and not man, the *Ho 11:9*
holy One
who is a G. like to thee, *Mic 7:18*
that pardons
name Immanuel, which is G. *M't 1:23*
with us
serve G. and mammon *M't 6:24;*
Lu 16:13
none good but G. *M't 19:17;*
M'k 10:18; Lu 18:19
there is one G. and none *M'k 12:32*
other but he
the Word was with G. and *Joh 1:1*
Word was G.
can do miracles, except G. be *Joh 3:2*
with him
they said, We have one *Joh 8:41*
Father, even G.
for I proceeded forth, and *Joh 8:42*
came from G.
they might know thee, the *Joh 17:3*
only true G.
by wonders, which G. did by *Ac 2:22*
him
we ought to obey G. rather *Ac 5:29*
than men
patriarchs sold Joseph, but G. *Ac 7:9*
was with him
I perceive G. is no *Ac 10:34*
respecter of persons
let G. be true, and every man *Ro 3:4*
a liar
if G. be for us, who can be *Ro 8:31*
against us
now the G. of patience and *Ro 15:5*
consolation
to us there is but one G. the *1Co 8:6*
Father
that G. may be all in all *1Co 15:28*
he which hath anointed us, *2Co 1:21*
is G.
the g. of this world hath *2Co 4:4*
blinded minds
G. of love and peace shall *2Co 13:11*
be with you
above all called G. so that he *2Th 2:4*
as G.
G. was manifest in the flesh *1Ti 3:16*
they profess that they know *Tit 1:16*
G.
but he that built all things is *Heb 3:4*
G.
ceased from his works, as *Heb 4:10*
G. did from his
I will be to them a G. *Heb 8:10*
they to me a people
G. is light, in him is no *1Jo 1:5*
darkness at all
no man hath seen G. at any *1Jo 4:12*
time
and G. himself shall be with *Re 21:3*
them
G. shall wipe away all tears *Re 21:4*
I will be his G. and he shall *Re 21:7*
be my son

GOD for idol

moved me with that which *De 32:21*
is not g.
if he be a g. let him plead for *J'g 6:31*
himself

they made Baal-berith their *g.*   *J'g 8:33*
they went into the house of   *J'g 9:27*
their *g.* and eat
possess that which Chemosh   *J'g 11:24*
thy *g.* giveth
the Philistines' *g.* was   *J'g 16:23;*
Dagon   *16:24*
his hand is sore on us, and   *1Sa 5:7*
our *g.*
Israel worshipped the *g.* of   *1Ki 11:33*
Moabites
he is a *g.* either talking, or   *1Ki 18:27*
pursuing
Baal-zebub the *g.* of Ekron   *2Ki 1:2;*
    1:3, 6, 16
of Nisroch his *g.* smote   *2Ki 19:37;*
with sword   *2Ch 32:21; Isa 37:38*
sorrows multiplied, hasten   *Ps 16:4*
after other *g.*
who hath formed a *g.* or   *Isa 44:10*
molten image
he maketh a *g.* and   *Isa 44:15;*
worshippeth it   *44:17*
and that pray to a *g.* that   *Isa 45:20*
cannot save
he maketh it a *g.* they fall   *Isa 46:6*
down, they worship
he carried the vessels into   *Da 1:2*
house of his *g.*
Belteshazzar according to the   *Da 4:8*
name of my *g.*
and magnify himself above   *Da 11:36*
every *g.*
the star of your *g.* ye made   *Am 5:26;*
    Ac 7:43
that swear, and say, Thy *g.* O   *Am 8:14*
Dan, liveth
the mariners cried, Every man   *Jon 1:5*
to his *g.*
all people will walk in the   *Mic 4:5*
name of his *g.*
inputing this his power to   *Hab 1:11*
his *g.*
it is the voice of a *g.* not of   *Ac 12:22*
a man

GOD referred to man

thou shalt be to Aaron   *Ex 4:16*
instead of *g.*
I have made thee a *g.* to   *Ex 7:1*
Pharaoh

GOD *IS*

G. is with thee in all that   *Ge 21:22*
thou doest
see, *G. is* witness betwixt me   *Ge 31:50*
and thee
fear not, for *G. is* come to   *Ex 20:20*
prove you
G. is not a man, that he   *Nu 23:19*
should lie
what *G. is* there in heaven who   *De 3:24*
can do
the eternal *G. is* thy refuge,   *De 33:27*
and underneath
our holy *G. is* a jealous   *Jos 24:19;*
God   *Na 1:2*
G. is come into the camp,   *1Sa 4:7*
woe unto us
for *G. is* come with thee   *1Sa 10:7;*
    1Ch 17:2
G. is departed from me, he   *1Sa 28:15*
answereth not
G. is my strength and   *2Sa 22:33*
power
G. is gone forth before   *1Ch 14:15*
thee to smite
G. himself *is* with us for our   *2Ch 13:12*
captain
I answer thee, *G. is* greater   *Job 33:12*
than man
G. is mighty and despiseth   *Job 36:5*
not any
G. is great, and we know   *Job 36:26*
him not
G. is angry with wicked every   *Ps 7:11*
day
G. is not in all his thoughts,   *Ps 10:4*
not seek after *G.*
for *G. is* in the generation of   *Ps 14:5*
the righteous
blessed nation, whose *G. is*   *Ps 33:12;*
Lord   *144:15*
G. is our refuge and strength   *Ps 46:1;*
    62:8
G. is in midst of her, she   *Ps 46:5*
shall not be moved

G. is gone up with a shout;   *Ps 47:5;*
G. is King   *47:7*
G. is known in her palaces   *Ps 48:3*
for a refuge
for *G. is* judge himself   *Ps 50:6;*
    75:7
behold, *G is* my helper,   *Ps 54:4*
Lord is with them
turn back; this I know, for *G.*   *Ps 56:9*
is for me
I will wait, for *G. is* my   *Ps 59:9;*
defence   *59:17*
in *G. is* my salvation and   *Ps 62:7;*
glory   *Isa 12:2*
father of the fatherless *is G.*   *Ps 68:5*
in his habitation
truly *G. is* good to Israel,   *Ps 73:1*
even to such as are
G. is strength of my heart,   *Ps 73:26*
and portion for ever
G. is my King of old,   *Ps 74:12*
working salvation
G. is greatly to be feared in   *Ps 89:7*
the assembly
gracious is the Lord, our *G.*   *Ps 116:5*
is merciful
G. is the Lord that hath   *Ps 118:27*
shewed us light
for *G. is* in heaven, and thou   *Ec 5:2*
on earth
G. that *is* holy shall be   *Isa 5:16*
sanctified in righteousness
for *G. is* with us; surely *G.*   *Isa 8:10;*
is in thee   *45:14*
we have heard that *G. is*   *Zec 8:23*
with you
G. is able of these stones to   *M't 3:9;*
raise   *Lu 3:8*
G. is not God of the dead,   *M't 22:32*
but of the living
hath set to his seal that *G.*   *Joh 3:33*
is true
G. is a Spirit   *Joh 4:24*
G. is glorified in him   *Joh 13:31*
G. is no respecter of persons   *Ac 10:34*
for *G. is* my witness, whom I   *Ro 1:9*
serve
for *G. is* able to graff them   *Ro 11:23*
in again
for *G. is* able to make him   *Ro 14:4*
stand
G. is faithful, by whom ye   *1Co 1:9*
were called
G. is faithful who will not   *1Co 10:13*
suffer you
report that *G. is* in you of   *1Co 14:25*
a truth
G. is not author of   *1Co 14:33*
confusion, but of peace
as *G. is* true, our word was   *2Co 1:18*
not yea, nay
G. is able to make all grace   *2Co 9:8*
abound to you
but *G. is* one; *G. is* not   *Ga 3:20;*
mocked   *6:7*
G. who *is* rich in mercy   *Eph 2:4*
quickened us
G. is my record, how greatly   *Ph'p 1:8*
I long after
many walk, whose *g. is*   *Ph'p 3:19*
their belly
nor cloke of covetousness, *G.*   *1Th 2:5*
is witness
G. is not unrighteous to   *Heb 6:10*
forget your work
G. is not ashamed to be   *Heb 11:16*
called their God
for our *G. is* a consuming   *Heb 12:29*
fire
for with such sacrifices *G.*   *Heb 13:16*
is well pleased
G. is light   *1Jo 1:5*
G. is greater than our heart,   *1Jo 3:20*
knows all
for *G. is* love   *1Jo 4:8; 4:16*

GOD *OF HEAVEN*

earth hath the Lord *G.* of   *2Ch 36:23;*
heaven given me   *Ezr 1:2*
we are the servants of the *G.*   *Ezr 5:11*
of heaven
our fathers have provoked   *Ezr 5:12*
the *G. of heaven*
for burnt offerings of the *G.*   *Ezr 6:9*
of heaven
a scribe of the law of the *G.*   *Ezr 7:12*
of heaven
whatever is commanded by   *Ezr 7:23*
the *G. of heaven*

I fasted and prayed before the   *Ne 1:4*
G. of heaven
so I prayed to the *G.* of   *Ne 2:4*
heaven, and said
O give thanks to the *G. of*   *Ps 136:26*
heaven
they would desire mercies of   *Da 2:18*
G. of heaven
then Daniel blessed the *G.* of   *Da 2:19*
heaven
the *G. of heaven* shall set up   *Da 2:44*
a kingdom
I fear the Lord, the *G.* of   *Jon 1:9*
heaven
the remnant gave glory to *G.*   *Re 11:13*
of heaven
and they blasphemed the *G.*   *Re 16:11*
of heaven

GOD *OF HOSTS*

turn us again, O *G. of hosts*   *Ps 80:7;*
    80:19
return, we beseech thee, O   *Ps 80:14*
G. of hosts
saith Lord, whose name is   *Am 5:27*
the *G. of hosts*

GOD *OF ISRAEL*

they went up, and saw the   *Ex 24:10*
G. of Israel
the *G. of Israel* hath   *Nu 16:9*
separated you
to give glory to the *G.* of   *Jos 7:19;*
Israel   *1Sa 6:5*
the *G. of Israel* was their   *Jos 13:33*
inheritance
trespass ye committed against   *Jos 22:16*
G. of Israel
what have ye to do with the   *Jos 22:24*
G. of Israel
incline your heart to the *G.*   *Jos 24:23*
of Israel
G. of Israel dispossessed   *J'g 11:23*
Amorites
full reward be given thee of   *Ru 2:12*
G. of Israel
the *G. of Israel* grant thy   *1Sa 1:17*
petition
send away the ark of the *G.*   *1Sa 5:11*
of Israel
Lord *G. of Israel* no God like   *1Ki 8:23;*
thee   *2Ch 6:14*
some good thing toward the   *1Ki 14:13*
G. of Israel
Jabez called on the *G.* of   *1Ch 4:10*
Israel
the Lord of hosts is the *G.*   *1Ch 17:24*
of Israel
who would not seek the *G.*   *2Ch 15:13*
of Israel
have freely offered to the *G.*   *Ezr 7:15*
of Israel
trembled at the words of the   *Ezr 9:4*
G. of Israel
blessed be Lord *G. of Israel*   *Ps 41:13;*
from everlasting   *72:18; 106:48; Lu 1:68*
I the *G. of Israel* will not   *Isa 41:17*
forsake them
I which call thee by name,   *Isa 45:3*
am *G. of Israel*
they stay themselves on the   *Isa 48:2*
G. of Israel
the glory of the *G. of Israel*   *Eze 8:4*
was there
the multitude glorified the   *M't 15:31*
G. of Israel

AGAINST GOD

how do this wickedness, and   *Ge 39:9*
sin *against G.*
the people spake *against G.*   *Nu 21:5;*
    Ps 78:19
and they transgressed   *1Ch 5:25*
against G.
spake *against* the *G.* of   *2Ch 32:19*
Jerusalem
thou turnest thy spirit   *Job 15:13*
against G.
for he stretcheth out his   *Job 15:25*
hand *against G.*
he multiplieth his words   *Job 34:37*
against G.
which speak amiss *against G.*   *Da 3:29*
of Shadrach
speak marvellous things   *Da 11:36*
against G. of gods

AGAINST GOD

she hath rebelled *against* her | Ho 13:16
G.
lest ye be found to fight | Ac 5:39
against G.
he hath spoken blasphemous | Ac 6:11
words *against* G.
let us not fight *against* G. | Ac 23:9
the carnal mind is enmity | Ro 8:7
against G.
who art thou that repliest | Ro 9:20
against G.
opened his mouth in | Re 13:6
blasphemy *against* G.

ANY GOD

that sacrifice to *any* g. save | Ex 22:20
the Lord
nor is there *any* G. beside | 2Sa 7:22;
| 1Ch 17:20
that they might not worship | Da 3:28
any g. except
who shall ask a petition of | Da 6:7;
any g. or man | 6:12
neither shall he regard *any* | Da 11:37
g.

BEFORE GOD

the earth was corrupt *before* | Ge 6:11
G.
eat bread with Moses' father | Ex 18:12
before G.
they presented themselves | Jos 24:1
before G.
the people abode till even | J'g 21:2
before G.
David and all Israel played | 1Ch 13:8
before G.
there Uzza died *before* G. | 1Ch 13:10
they offered burnt sacrifices | 1Ch 16:1
before G.
Manasseh humbled himself | 2Ch 33:12
before G.
Josiah's heart was humbled | 2Ch 34:27
before G.
deliver *before* the G. of | Ezr 7:19
Jerusalem
yea, thou restrainest prayer | Job 15:4
before G.
when shall I appear *before* G. | Ps 42:2
may walk *before* G. in light | Ps 56:13
of living
he shall abide *before* G. for | Ps 61:7
ever
let the righteous rejoice *before* | Ps 68:3
G.
every one in Zion appeareth | Ps 84:7
before G.
give to him that is good | Ec 2:26
before G.
heart hasty to utter any thing | Ec 5:2
before G.
because he feareth not *before* | Ec 8:13
G.
gave thanks *before* his G. as | Da 6:10
aforetime
found him making | Da 6:11
supplication *before* G.
that men tremble *before* the | Da 6:26
G. of Daniel
they were both righteous | Lu 1:6
before G.
not one of them is forgotten | Lu 12:6
before G.
a prophet mighty in deed | Lu 24:19
and word *before* G.
who found favour *before* G. | Ac 7:46
thine arms are come for a | Ac 10:4
memorial *before* G.
we are all here present | Ac 10:33
before G. to hear
I lived in all good conscience | Ac 23:1
before G.
not hearers of law are just | Ro 2:13
before G.
the world may become guilty | Ro 3:19
before G.
hath whereof to glory, but not | Ro 4:2
before G.
hast thou faith? have it to | Ro 14:22
thyself *before* G.
we speak *before* G. in | 2Co 12:19
Christ
behold, *before* G. I lie not | Ga 1:20
he may establish your hearts | 1Th 3:13
before G.
that is good and acceptable | 2Th 5:4
before G.

I charge thee *before* G. | 2Th 5:21;
| 2Ti 4:1
pure religion and undefiled | Jas 1:27
before G.
not found thy works perfect | Re 3:2
before G.
a voice from the horns of the | Re 9:13
altar *before* G.
which accused them *before* G. | Re 12:10
day and night
Babylon came in | Re 16:19
remembrance *before* G.
I saw dead, small and great, | Re 20:12
stand *before* G.

ETERNAL GOD

the *eternal* G. is thy refuge | De 33:27

EVERLASTING GOD

Abraham called on name of | Ge 21:33
everlasting G.
the *everlasting* G. fainteth | Isa 40:28
not, nor is weary
according to commandment | Ro 16:26
of *everlasting* G.

HIGH GOD

was priest of the most *high* | Ge 14:18;
G. | Heb 7:1
blessed be Abraham of the | Ge 14:19
most *high* G.
blessed be the most *high* G. | Ge 14:20
which delivered
I have lift up my hand to | Ge 14:22
the most *high* G.
I will cry unto G. most *high*, | Ps 57:2
unto G.
God was their rock, the *high* | Ps 78:35
G. their Redeemer
they tempted and provoked | Ps 78:56
the most *high* G.
servants of most *high* G. | Da 3:26
come forth
shew the wonders the *high* G. | Da 4:2
hath wrought
high G. gave Nebuchadnezzar | Da 5:18
a kingdom
till he knew that the most | Da 5:21
high G. ruled
and bow myself before the | Mic 6:6
most *high* G.
thou Son of the most *high* | M'k 5:7;
G. | Lu 8:28
these men are servants of | Ac 16:17
most *high* G.

HOLY GOD

he is an *holy* G. he is a | Jos 24:19
jealous God
who is able to stand before | 1Sa 6:20
this *holy* G.
for the Lord our G. is *holy* | Ps 99:9
G. that is *holy* shall | Isa 5:16
be sanctified in righteousness

LIVING GOD

that heard the voice of the | De 5:26
living G.
hereby know the *living* G. is | Jos 3:10
among you
should defy the armies of | 1Sa 17:26;
living G. | 17:36
whom the king of Assyria | 2Ki 19:4;
hath sent to reproach | 19:16; Isa 37:4, 17
the *living* G.
my soul thirsteth for God, the | Ps 42:2
living G.
my heart and flesh crieth out | Ps 84:2
for *living* G.
he is *living* G. an everlasting | Jer 10:10
King
have perverted the words of | Jer 23:36
the *living* G.
he is the *living* G. and | Da 6:26
stedfast for ever
shall be said, Ye are sons of | Ho 1:10
the *living* G.
art Christ, Son of *living* G. | M't 16:16;
| Joh 6:69
I adjure thee by the *living* | M't 26:63
G. tell us
turn from these vanities to | Ac 14:15
the *living* G.
they shall be called children | Ro 9:26
of *living* G.

but with the Spirit of the | 2Co 3:3
living G.
for ye are the temple of the | 2Co 6:16
living G.
from idols to serve *living* and | 1Th 1:9
true G.
which is the church of the | 1Ti 3:15
living G.
because we trust in the | 1Ti 4:10;
living G. | 6:17
an evil heart in departing | Heb 3:12
from *living* G.
purge your conscience to | Heb 9:14
serve the *living* G.
it is fearful to fall into | Heb 10:31
hands of *living* G.
ye are come to Zion, the | Heb 12:22
city of *living* G.
angel having the seal of the | Re 7:2
living G.

MERCIFUL GOD

the Lord, the Lord G. | Ex 34:6
merciful, gracious
the Lord thy God is a | De 4:31
merciful G.
Lord your G. is *merciful* if | 2Ch 30:9
ye turn
thou art a gracious and | Ne 9:31
merciful G.
gracious is the Lord, our G. | Ps 116:5
is *merciful*
I knew that thou art a G. | Jon 4:2
merciful

MIGHTY GOD

bow abode by hands of | Ge 49:24
mighty G. of Jacob
Lord is among you, a *mighty* | De 7:21;
G. | 10:17
now therefore our God, the | Ne 9:32
mighty G.
behold, G. is *mighty,* and | Job 36:5
despiseth not any
the *mighty* G. the Lord hath | Ps 50:1
spoken
how he vowed to the *mighty* | Ps 132:2
G. of Jacob
till I find an habitation *mighty* | Ps 132:5
G. of Jacob
his name shall be called the | Isa 9:6
mighty G.
the remnant shall return to | Isa 10:21
the *mighty* G.
mighty G. the Lord of hosts | Jer 32:18
is his name
O *mighty* G. thou hast | Hab 1:12
stablished them

MY GOD

Jacob said, Then shall the | Ge 28:21
Lord be *my* G.
he is *my* G. *my* father's G. I | Ex 15:2
will exalt
thy people be my people, thy | Ru 1:16
God *my* G.
I cried to *my* G. he heard | 2Sa 22:7;
| Ps 18:6
and have not departed | 2Sa 22:22;
from *my* G. | Ps 18:21
by *my* G. I have leaped | 2Sa 22:30;
over a wall | Ps 18:29
for God, even *my* G. will | 1Ch 28:20
be with thee
what *my* G. saith, that will | 2Ch 18:13
I speak
think upon me, *my* G. for | Ne 5:19;
good | 13:31
remember me, *my* G. | Ne 13:14;
concerning this | 13:22
My G. *my* G. why hast thou | Ps 22:1;
forsaken me | M't 27:46
thou art *my* G. from my | Ps 22:10
mother's belly
I trusted in thee, I said, | Ps 31:14
Thou art *my* G.
O *my* G. be not far from | Ps 38:21;
me | 71:12
he shall cry, Thou art my | Ps 89:26
Father, *my* G.
I will sing praises to *my* | Ps 104:33;
G. | 146:2
thou art *my* G. and I will | Ps 118:28
praise thee
I will extol thee, *my* G. O | Ps 145:1
King, and bless

and take the name of *my* G. *Pr 30:9*
in vain
but will ye weary *my* G. also *Isa 7:13*
my judgment is passed over *Isa 40:17*
from *my* G.
he saith, Deliver me, for *Isa 44:17*
thou art *my* G.
my soul shall be joyful in *Isa 61:10*
my G.
my G. hath sent his angel, *Da 6:22*
hath shut lions'
they shall say, Thou art *my* *Ho 2:23*
G.
Israel shall cry to me, My *G.* *Ho 8:2*
we know the
my G. will cast them away, *Ho 9:17*
not hearken
I will wait, for *my* G. will *Mic 7:7*
hear me
and say, I ascend to *my* G. *Joh 20:17*
and your God
Thomas answered and said, *Joh 20:28*
My Lord and *my* G.
I thank *my* G. through Jesus *Ro 1:8;*
Christ   *1Co 1:4; 14:18; Ph'p 1:3*
lest when I come, *my* G. *2Co 12:21*
will humble
my G. shall supply all your *Ph'p 4:19*
need
I will write on him the name *Re 3:12*
of *my* G.

NO GOD

I, even I am he, there is *no* *De 32:39*
G. with me
there is *no* G. like thee *1Ki 8:23;*
           2Ch 6:14
it is because there is *no* G. *2Ki 1:16*
in Israel
now I know there is *no* G. in *2Ki 5:15*
all the earth
no G. of any nation able *2Ch 32:15*
to deliver
the fool hath said, There is *Ps 14:1;*
no G.   *53:1*
before me there was *no* G. *Isa 43:10*
formed
besides me there is *no* G. *Isa 44:6;*
     44:8; 45:5, 14, 21
but thou shalt be a man, *Eze 28:9*
and *no* G.
and thou shalt know *no* G. *Ho 13:4*
but me

O GOD

heal her now, O G. I *Nu 12:13*
beseech thee
strengthen me, only this *J'g 16:28*
once, O G.
hear me, O G. of my *Ps 4:1*
righteousness
redeem Israel, O G. out of *Ps 25:22*
all his troubles
deliver me from *Ps 51:14*
bloodguiltiness, O G.
thy vows are upon me, O G. *Ps 56:12*
I will render
nor hath the eye seen, O G. *Isa 64:4*
besides thee
I said, Lo, I come to do thy *Heb 10:7;*
will, O G.   *10:9*

OF GOD

hearkened not, for the *2Ch 10:15*
cause was *of* G.
Amaziah would not hear, *2Ch 25:20*
for it came *of* G.
my defence is *of* G. who *Ps 7:10*
saveth upright
did esteem him smitten *of* G. *Isa 53:4*
and afflicted
savourest not things *of* G. *M't 16:23;*
          M'k 8:33
born not of the will of man, *Joh 1:13*
but *of* G.
he which is *of* G. hath seen *Joh 6:46*
the Father
shall know of doctrine *Joh 7:17*
whether it be *of* G.
he that is *of* G. heareth: ye *Joh 8:47*
are not *of* G.
this man is not *of* G.; if he *Joh 9:16;*
were not *of* G.   *9:33*
loved the praise of men *Joh 12:43*
more than *of* G.

if it be *of* G. ye cannot *Ac 5:39*
overthrow it
whose praise is not of men, *Ro 2:29*
but *of* G.
but *of* G. that sheweth mercy *Ro 9:16*
no power but *of* G. powers *Ro 13:1*
ordained *of* G.
who *of* G. is made unto us *1Co 1:30*
wisdom
which ye have *of* G. ye are *1Co 6:19*
not your own
but all things are *of* G. *1Co 11:12;*
          2Co 5:18
but as *of* G. in the sight of *2Co 2:17*
G. speak we
we are not sufficient, our *2Co 3:5*
sufficiency is *of* G.
but to you of salvation, and *Ph'p 1:28*
that *of* G.
the righteousness which is *of* *Ph'p 3:9*
G. by faith
he that was called *of* G. as *Heb 5:4*
was Aaron
doeth not righteousness, is *1Jo 3:10*
not *of* G.
beloved, try the spirits *1Jo 4:1*
whether they are *of* G.
confesseth not that Christ is *1Jo 4:3*
come, is not *of* G.
we are *of* G.; we know we *1Jo 4:6;*
are *of* G.   *5:19*
follow good, he that doeth *3Jo 11*
good is *of* G.

OTHER GOD

thou shalt worship no *other* *Ex 34:14*
g.
because there is no *other* g. *Da 3:29*
can deliver
there is none *other* g. but one *1Co 8:4*

OUR GOD

let us go and sacrifice to *our* *Ex 5:8*
G.
because *our* G. is not *De 31:17*
amongst us
ascribe ye greatness unto *our* *De 32:3*
G.
we will serve the Lord, he is *Jos 24:18*
our G.
because we have forsaken *J'g 10:10*
our G.
neither is there any rock like *1Sa 2:2*
our G.
people, and for the cities *2Sa 10:12;*
of *our* G.   *1Ch 19:13*
who is a rock, save *our* G. *2Sa 22:32;*
           Ps 18:31
therefore, *our* G. we thank *1Ch 29:13*
thee
for great is *our* G. above all *2Ch 2:5*
gods
thou art *our* G. let not *2Ch 14:11*
man prevail
art not thou *our* G. who *2Ch 20:7*
didst drive out
now, O *our* G. what shall we *Ezr 9:10*
say after
hear, O *our* G.; *our* G. shall *Ne 4:4;*
fight for us   *4:20*
that this work was wrought *Ne 6:16*
of *our* G.
therefore *our* G. the great, *Ne 9:32*
mighty God
our G. turned the curse into *Ne 13:2*
a blessing
put a new song, even praise *Ps 40:3*
to *our* G.
this God is *our* G. for ever *Ps 48:14*
and ever
our G. shall come and not *Ps 50:3*
keep silence
and God even *our* own G. *Ps 67:6*
shall bless us
he that is *our* G. is the God *Ps 68:20*
of salvation
who is so great a God as *Ps 77:13*
our G.
he is *our* G.; *our* G. is in *Ps 95:7;*
heavens   *115:3*
gracious is the Lord, *our* G. *Ps 116:5*
is merciful
this is *our* G. we have waited *Isa 25:9*
for him
to *our* G. for he will *Isa 55:7*
abundantly pardon

and departing away from *Isa 59:13*
our G.
to proclaim the day of *Isa 61:2*
vengeance of *our* G.
our G. whom we serve is *Da 3:17*
able to deliver
he that remaineth shall be for *Zec 9:7*
our G.
sanctified by Spirit of *our* *1Co 6:11*
G.
for *our* G. is a consuming *Heb 12:29*
fire
made us to *our* G. kings and *Re 5:10*
priests
salvation to *our* G. who *Re 7:10*
sitteth on throne
blessing, and honour, and *Re 7:12*
power be to *our* G.

STRANGE GOD

there was no *strange* g. with *De 32:12*
them
stretched out our hands to a *Ps 44:20*
strange g.
no *strange* g. be in thee, nor *Ps 81:9*
worship *strange* g.
when there was no *strange* g. *Isa 43:12*
among them
thus shall he do with a *Da 11:39*
strange g.

THEIR GOD

I will be *their* G. *Ge 17:8;*
Ex 29:45; Jer 24:7; 31:33; 32:38;
Eze 11:20; 34:24; 37:23, 27; Zec 8:8;
         2Co 6:16; Re 21:3
they shall be holy to *their* G., *Le 21:6*
and bread of *their* G. they
do offer
that I might be *their* G. *Le 26:45;*
           Eze 14:11
thou art become *their* G. *2Sa 7:24;*
           1Ch 17:22
the eye of *their* G. was on the *Ezr 5:5*
elders
where is *their* G. *Ps 79:10;*
      115:2; Joe 2:17
should not a people seek to *Isa 8:19*
their G.
shall fret, and curse their *Isa 8:21*
king, and *their* G.
and forsook not the *Isa 58:2*
ordinance of *their* G.
they know not the judgment *Jer 5:4;*
of *their* G.   *5:5*
but the people that know *Da 11:32*
their G.
have gone a whoring from *Ho 4:12*
under *their* G.
not frame their doings to turn *Ho 5:4*
to *their* G.
my strength in the Lord of *Zec 12:5*
hosts *their* G.
he is not ashamed to be *Heb 11:16*
called *their* G.

THY GOD

thou shalt fear *thy* G. *Le 19:14;*
       25:17, 36, 43
he is *thy* praise, and he is *De 10:21*
thy G.
avouched this day the Lord to *De 26:17*
be *thy* G.
thy people my people, *thy* G. *Ru 1:16*
my God
let not *thy* G. deceive thee *2Ki 19:10;*
         Isa 37:10
peace to thee, for *thy* G. *1Ch 12:18*
helpeth thee
because *thy* G. loved Israel *2Ch 9:8*
made thee king
according to law of *thy* G. *Ezr 7:14*
in thy hand
after the wisdom of *thy* G. *Ezr 7:25*
laws of *thy* G.
this is *thy* G. that brought *Ne 9:18*
thee up
continually say to me, Where *Ps 42:3;*
is *thy* G.   *42:10*
God, *thy* G. hath anointed *Ps 45:7;*
thee   *Heb 1:9*
hear, O Israel, I am God, *Ps 50:7*
even *thy* G.
thy G. hath commanded thy *Ps 68:28*
strength
praise the Lord, praise *thy* *Ps 147:12*
G. O Zion

be not dismayed, for I am *thy G.*   Isa 41:10
they are full of the rebuke of *thy G.*   Isa 51:20
that saith to Zion, *Thy G.* reigneth   Isa 52:7
Lord shall be a light, and *thy G.* thy glory   Isa 60:19
so shall *thy G.* rejoice over thee   Isa 62:5
thy G. whom thou servest will deliver   Da 6:16
is *thy G.* whom thou servest continually able   Da 6:20
to chasten thyself before *thy G.*   Da 10:12
thou hast forgotten the law of *thy G.*   Ho 4:6
thou hast gone a whoring from *thy G.*   Ho 9:1
turn thou to *thy G.* and wait on *thy G.*   Ho 12:6
prepare to meet *thy G.* O Israel   Am 4:12
O sleeper, arise, call upon *thy G.*   Jon 1:6
and to walk humbly with *thy G.*   Mic 6:8

TO, UNTO GOD

do not interpretations belong *to G.*   Ge 40:8
they cried, and their cry came up *to G.*   Ex 2:23
for he is holy *unto* his *G.*   Le 21:7
sacrifice to devils not *to G.*   De 32:17; 1Co 10:20
there is none like *to* the *G.* of Jeshurun   De 33:26
shall be a Nazarite *unto G.*   J'g 13:5; 13:17; 16:7
shall meet three men going up *to G.*   1Sa 10:3
for every matter pertaining *to G.*   1Ch 26:32
can a man be profitable *to G.*   Job 22:2
it is meet to be said *unto G.* I have   Job 34:31
I have heard, power belongeth *to G.*   Ps 62:11
to G. the Lord belong issues from death   Ps 68:20
Ethiopia shall stretch her hands *unto G.*   Ps 68:31
it is good for me to draw near *to G.*   Ps 73:28
I cried *to G.* even *to G.* with my voice   Ps 77:1
and the spirit shall return *unto G.*   Ec 12:7
they take delight in approaching *to G.*   Isa 58:2
let us lift up our heart with hands *to G.*   La 3:41
render *unto G.* the things which are God's   M't 22:21; M'k 12:17; Lu 20:25
that he was come from God, went *to G.*   Joh 13:3
to hearken to you more than *unto G.*   Ac 4:19
thou hast not lied unto men, but *unto G.*   Ac 5:4
to turn them from power of Satan *unto G.*   Ac 26:18
turn *to G.* and do works meet for repentance   Ac 26:20
he liveth *unto G.*; but alive *unto G.*   Ro 6:10; 6:11
yield yourselves *unto G.* as alive from dead   Ro 6:13
that we should bring forth fruit *unto G.*   Ro 7:4
present your bodies living sacrifice *unto G.*   Ro 12:1
every one give account of himself *to G.*   Ro 14:12
speaketh not unto men but *unto G.*   1Co 14:2
shall have delivered up kingdom *to G.*   1Co 15:24
now *unto G.* our Father be glory   Ph'p 4:20
is able to save them that come *unto G.*   Heb 7:25
he that cometh *to G.* must believe that he is   Heb 11:6
but ye are come *to G.* the Judge of all   Heb 12:23

submit yourselves therefore *to G.*   Jas 4:7
Christ once suffered, might bring us *to G.*   1Pe 3:18
but live according *to G.* in the Spirit   1Pe 4:6
redeemed us *to G.* by thy blood   Re 5:9
her child was caught up *into G.* to his   Re 12:5
being firstfruits *unto G.* and the Lamb   Re 14:4

WITH GOD

Enoch walked *with G.* and was not   Ge 5:22; 5:24
Noah walked *with G.*   Ge 6:9
Jacob hath power *with G.*   Ge 32:28
Moses brought people to meet *with G.*   Ex 19:17
he hath wrought *with G.* this day   1Sa 14:45
although my house be not so *with G.*   2Sa 23:5
forbear from meddling *with G.*   2Ch 35:21
how should man be just *with G.*   Job 9:2
and I desire to reason *with*   Job 13:3
that one might plead for man *with G.*   Job 16:21
how can a man be justified *with G.*   Job 25:4
this portion of a wicked man *with G.*   Job 27:13
that he should delight himself *with G.*   Job 34:9
he should enter into judgment *with G.*   Job 34:23
with G. is terrible majesty   Job 37:22
whose spirit is not stedfast *with G.*   Ps 78:8
but Judah yet ruleth *with G.*   Ho 11:12
Jacob by strength had power *with G.*   Ho 12:3
with G. all things possible   M't 19:26; M'k 10:27; Lu 1:37; 18:27
for thou hast found favour *with G.*   Lu 1:30
Jesus increased in favour *with G.*   Lu 2:52
Word was *with G.* the Word was God   Joh 1:1
making himself equal *with G.*   Joh 5:18; Ph'p 2:6
there is no respect of persons *with G.*   Ro 2:11
justified by faith, we have peace *with G.*   Ro 5:1
is unrighteousness *with G.?* God forbid   Ro 9:14
we are labourers together *with G.*   1Co 3:9
wisdom of world is foolishness *with G.*   1Co 3:19
let every man therein abide *with G.*   1Co 7:24
righteous thing *with G.* to recompense   2Th 1:6
friendship of world is enmity *with G.*   Jas 4:4
take patiently, this is acceptable *with G.*   1Pe 2:20

YOUR GOD

your G. hath given you treasure in sacks   Ge 43:23
go ye, sacrifice to *your G.* in the land   Ex 8:25
Lord bringeth out of Egypt to be *your G.*   Le 11:45; 22:33; 25:38; Nu 15:41
I will be *your G.* and ye shall be my people   Le 26:12; Jer 7:23; 11:4; 30:22; Eze 36:28
be to you a memorial before *your G.*   Nu 10:10
do my commandments, be holy to *your G.*   Nu 15:40
stone be witness, lest ye deny *your G.*   Jos 24:27
ye have this day rejected *your G.*   1Sa 10:19
that *your G.* should deliver you   2Ch 32:14
much less shall *your G.* deliver you   2Ch 32:15

let us build, for we seek *your G.*   Ezr 4:2
your G. will come with vengeance   Isa 35:4
comfort ye my people, saith *your G.*   Isa 40:1
say to the cities of Judah, Behold *your G.*   Isa 40:9
iniquities separated between you and *your G.*   Isa 59:2
I am *your G.* saith the Lord God   Eze 34:31
truth it is, *your G.* is a God of gods   Da 2:47
ye are not my people, I will not be *your G.*   Ho 1:9
of whom ye say that he is *your G.*   Joh 8:54
I ascend to my God and *your G.*   Joh 20:17

GOD-APPOINTED

a *G.* Judge (B)   Ac 10:42

GODDESS

Solomon went after *g.* of Zidonians   1Ki 11:5
they have worshipped Ashtoreth, the *g.*   1Ki 11:33
temple of great *g.* Diana be despised   Ac 19:27
Ephesians are worshippers of the *g.* Diana   Ac 19:35
nor yet blasphemers of your *g.*   Ac 19:37

GODHEAD

nor think that the *g.* is like to gold   Ac 17:29
even his eternal power and *g.*   Ro 1:20
in him dwelleth the fulness of the *g.* bodily   Col 2:9

GODLESS

the *g.* (B)   1Sa 2:9
the *g.* (A)(R)   2Sa 23:6
a polluted and *g.* man (A)(B)(E)(R)   Job 13:16
the *g.* (A)(B)(E)(R)   Job 15:34; 36:13; Isa 33:14
the *g.* (B)   Job 16:11
the *g.* and polluted (A)(E)(R)   Job 17:8
the *g.* and defiled (A)(B)(E)(R)   Job 20:5
the *g.* and polluted (A)   Job 27:8
the *g.* (B)(E)(R)   Job 27:8; 34:30
the *g.* strut around (A)   Ps 12:8
the *g.* gathered together (S)   Ps 35:15
g. men deride me (R)   Ps 119:51; 119:69, 78, 85, 122
expectation of the *g.* (A)(R)   Pr 11:7
the *g.* man destroys (A)(E)(R)   Pr 11:9
the *g.* (B)(R)   Isa 9:17
a *g.* nation (B)   Isa 10:6
g. wickedness (N)   Ro 1:18
avoid impure *g.* fictions (A)(P)   1Ti 4:7
g. myths, fit only for (N)(R)   1Ti 4:7
g. mixture of contradictory notions (P)(R)   1Ti 6:20
stray in *g.* courses (N)   2Ti 2:16
renounce *g.* ways (N)   Tit 2:12
a *g.* world (B)(N)(R)   2Pe 2:5; 2:6; 3:7
filthy lives of the *g.* (P)   2Pe 2:6
filthy lives of *g.* (P)   2Pe 2:7
the *g.* desires (N)(P)   Jude 15; 18

GODLESSNESS

in *g.* of evil (P)   Ro 1:18
renounce *g.* (B)(P)   Tit 2:12

GODLINESS

through our own *g.* (E)(N)   Ac 3:12
that we may lead quiet life in all *g.*   1Ti 2:2
which becometh women professing *g.*   1Ti 2:10
great is mystery of *g.*: God in flesh   1Ti 3:16
and exercise thyself rather unto *g.*   1Ti 4:7

but *g.* is profitable unto all things   1Ti 4:8
to the doctrine which is according to *g.*   1Ti 6:3
corrupt men, supposing that gain is *g.*   1Ti 6:5
but *g.* with contentment is great gain   1Ti 6:6
follow after righteousness, *g.* faith, love   1Ti 6:11
having a form of *g.* but denying power   2Ti 3:5
acknowledging the truth which is after *g.*   Tit 1:1
all things that pertain to life and *g.*   2Pe 1:3
add to patience *g.* to *g.*   2Pe 1:6;
brotherly kindness   1:7
what manner of persons ought to be in all *g.*   2Pe 3:11

GODLY

Lord hath set apart him that is *g.*   Ps 4:3
help, Lord, for the *g.* man ceaseth   Ps 12:1
as for *g.* in the land (B)   Ps 16:3
love the Lord all ye *g.* (B)   Ps 31:23
for this shall every one that is *g.* pray   Ps 32:6
in presence of the *g.* (R)   Ps 52:9
praise of his *g.* ones (A)(B)   Ps 148:14
congregation of *g.* (B)   Ps 149:1; 149:5, 9
walks in *g.* wisdom (A)   Pr 28:26
that he might seek a *g.* seed   Mal 2:15
in *g.* sincerity had our conversation   2Co 1:12
we were made sorry after a *g.* manner   2Co 7:9; 7:11
for *g.* sorrow worketh repentance   2Co 7:10
I am jealous over you with *g.* jealousy   2Co 11:2
all that will live *g.* in Christ, suffer   2Ti 3:12
that ye should live *g.* in this world   Tit 2:12
let us serve God with reverence and *g.* fear   Heb 12:28
by *g.* lives of wives (A)   Jas 3:1
the Lord knoweth how to deliver the *g.*   2Pe 2:9
if thou bring forward after a *g.* sort   3Jo 6

GODS

shall be as *g.* knowing good and evil   Ge 3:5
yet wherefore hast thou stolen my *g.*   Ge 31:30
against all *g.* of Egypt I will execute   Ex 12:12
shalt not make with me *g.* of silver or gold   Ex 20:23
thou shalt not revile the *g.* nor curse ruler   Ex 22:28
thou shalt not bow down to their *g.*   Ex 23:24
shalt make no covenant with them nor their *g.*   Ex 23:32
bring him to the *g.* (B)   Ex 21:6
up, make us *g.* to go before us   Ex 32:1; 32:23; Ac 7:40
these be thy *g.* O Israel, which brought   Ex 32:4
Moses said, They have made them *g.* of gold   Ex 32:31
lest they go a whoring after their *g.*   Ex 34:15
goat-like *g.* (A)(E)   Le 17:7
called people to the sacrifices of their *g.*   Nu 25:2
upon the Egyptians' *g.* also   Nu 33:4;
the Lord executed judgment   Jer:4 12; 13; 46:25
the images of their *g.* shall ye burn   De 7:25
Lord your God is God of *g.*   De 10:17
Lord of lords
ye shall hew down the images of their *g.*   De 12:3
that thou enquire not after their *g.*   De 12:30
abomination to their *g.*   De 12:31
burnt sons and daughters in fire to their *g.*

entice thee to the *g.* of people round about   De 13:7
not to do as they have done to their *g.*   De 20:18
ye shall say, Where are their *g.*   De 32:37
the Lord God of *g.* knoweth   Jos 22:22
nor make mention of name of their *g.*   Jos 23:7
they chose new *g.* then was war   J'g 5:8
I said, Fear not the *g.* of the Amorites   J'g 6:10
go and cry to *g.* ye have chosen   J'g 10:14
the man Micah had an house of *g.*   J'g 17:5
ye have taken away my *g.* which I made   J'g 18:24
thy sister in law is gone back to her *g.*   Ru 1:15
these are *g.* that smote Egyptians   1Sa 4:8
lighten his hand from off you and your *g.*   1Sa 6:5
the Philistine cursed David by his *g.*   1Sa 17:43
I saw *g.* ascending out of the earth   1Sa 28:13
redeemest from Egypt and their *g.*   2Sa 7:23
will turn your heart after their *g.*   1Ki 11:2
Solomon burnt incense and sacrificed to their *g.*   1Ki 11:8
is too much to go up, behold thy *g.*   1Ki 12:28
call ye on the name of your *g.*   1Ki 18:24; 18:25
let *g.* do so to me and more also   1Ki 19:2; 20:10
their *g.* are *g.* of the hills, therefore   1Ki 20:23
every nation made *g.* of their own   2Ki 17:29
feared the Lord, and served their own *g.*   2Ki 17:33
hath any of the *g.*   2Ki 18:33;
delivered his land   19:12; 2Ch 32:13-14; Isa 36:18; 37:12
where are the *g.* of Hamath   2Ki 18:34; Isa 36:19
cast their *g.* into fire, they were no *g.*   2Ki 19:18
went whoring after *g.* of the land   1Ch 5:25
put Saul's armour in house of their *g.*   1Ch 10:10
they left their *g.* David burnt them   1Ch 14:12
golden calves Jeroboam made for *g.*   2Ch 13:8
same may be a priest to them that are no *g.*   2Ch 13:9
Amaziah brought *g.* of Seir to be his *g.*   2Ch 25:14
Ahaz sacrificed to the *g.* of Damascus   2Ch 28:23
the *g.* of the nations have not delivered   2Ch 32:17
Nebuchadnezzar put vessels in the house of his *g.*   Ezr 1:7
God standeth, he judgeth among the *g.*   Ps 82:1
I have said, Ye are *g.*   Ps 82:6; Joh 10:34
O give thanks unto the God of *g.*   Ps 136:2
before the *g.* will I sing praise unto thee   Ps 138:1
Babylon is fallen, and her *g.* broken   Isa 21:9
that we may know that ye are *g.*   Isa 41:23
that say to molten images, ye are our *g.*   Isa 42:17
hath a nation changed her *g.* are no *g.*   Jer 2:11
where are thy *g.* thou hast made? according to number of cities are thy *g.*   Jer 2:28; 11:13
children sworn by them that are no *g.*   Jer 5:7
the *g.* that have not made the heavens   Jer 10:11
cry to the *g.* to whom they offer incense   Jer 11:12
shall a man make *g.* and they are no *g.*   Jer 16:20

whoring after strange *g.* (S)   Jer 31:16
to cease him that burneth incense to his *g.*   Jer 48:35
no other can shew it, except the *g.*   Da 2:11
of a truth it is, that your God is a God of *g.*   Da 2:47
in whom is the spirit of the holy *g.*   Da 4:8
I know spirit of holy *g.* is in thee   Da 4:9; 4:18; 5:14
they praised the *g.* of gold and silver   Da 5:4; 5:23
and wisdom like the wisdom of the *g.*   Da 5:11
carry captives into Egypt *g.* with princes   Da 11:8
shall speak marvellous things against God of *g.*   Da 11:36
neither will we say more, Ye are our *g.*   Ho 14:3
out of the house of thy *g.* I will cut off   Na 1:14
if he called them *g.* to whom the word   Joh 10:35
the *g.* are come down to us like men   Ac 14:11
they be no *g.* which are made with hands   Ac 19:26
be that are called *g.* there be *g.* many   1Co 8:5
did service to them which by nature no *g.*   Ga 4:8

ALL GODS

I know the Lord is greater than *all g.*   Ex 18:11
to be feared above *all g.*   1Ch 16:25; Ps 96:4
all g. of the people are idols   1Ch 16:26; Ps 96:5
great is God above *all g.*   2Ch 2:5; Ps 135:5
the Lord is a great King above *all g.*   Ps 95:3
worship him, *all* ye *g.*;   Ps 97:7;
exalted above *all g.*   97:9
he will famish *all* the *g.* of the earth   Zep 2:11

AMONG THE GODS

among the g. who is like thee, O Lord   Ex 15:11
who *among the g.* could deliver their country   2Ki 18:35; 2Ch 32:14; Isa 36:20
among the g. there is none like thee   Ps 86:8

MOLTEN GODS

shalt make no *molten g.*   Ex 34:17; Le 19:4

OTHER GODS

shalt have no *other g.* before me   Ex 20:3; De 5:7
make no mention of names of *other g.*   Ex 23:13
ye shall not go after *other g.*   De 6:14; 11:28; 28:14; 1Ki 11:10; Jer 25:6; 35:15
they will turn thy son to serve *other g.*   De 7:4
if thou walk after *other g.* and serve them   De 8:19
let us go after *other g.* and serve them   De 13:2; 13:6, 13
hath gone and served *other g.*   De 17:3; 29:26; Jos 23:16; J'g 10:13; 1Sa 8:8; Jer 11:10
prophet that shall speak in name of *other g.*   De 18:20
drawn away, and worship *other g.* and serve them   De 30:17;
in that day they turned to *other g.*   De 31:18
then will they turn to *other g.* and provoke   De 31:20
forsook the Lord, and followed *other g.*   J'g 2:12
went a whoring after *other g.* bowed to   J'g 2:17
in following *other g.* to serve them, and to   J'g 2:19
driven me out, saying, Go serve *other g.*   1Sa 26:19

taken hold upon *other* g.   1Ki 9:9;
    2Ch 7:22

his wives turned his heart   1Ki 11:4
after *other* g.

for thou hast gone and made   1Ki 14:9
thee *other* g.

I will not offer sacrifice to   2Ki 5:17
other g.

Israel had sinned, and had   2Ki 17:7
feared *other* g.

not fear *other* g. nor bow   2Ki 17:35;
    17:37-38

have forsaken me, and   2Ki 22:17;
burnt incense to *other* g.   2Ch 34:25;
    Jer 1:16; 19:4

Ahaz burnt incense to   2Ch 28:25
other g.

nor walk after *other* g. to   Jer 7:6
your hurt

walk after *other* g. whom ye   Jer 7:9;
know not   13:10

have forsaken me, and   Jer 16:11
walked after *other* g.

hearkened not to burn no   Jer 44:5
incense to *other* g.

burning incense to *other* g.   Jer 44:8;
in land of Egypt   44:15

look to *other* g. and love   Ho 3:1
flagons of wine

STRANGE GODS

put away the *strange* g.   Ge 35:2;
    1Sa 7:3

they gave Jacob the *strange*   Ge 35:4;
g.   Jos 24:23

provoked him to jealousy   De 32:16
with *strange* g.

if ye forsake Lord, and serve   Jos 24:20
strange g.

they put away their *strange*   J'g 10:16
g.

Asa took away the altar of   2Ch 14:3
strange g.

Josiah took away the   2Ch 33:15
strange g. and idol

as ye served *strange* g. so   Jer 5:19
serve strangers

seemeth to be a setter forth   Ac 17:18
of *strange* g.

GOD'S

shall be G. house   Ge 28:22

I in G. stead who hath   Ge 30:2
withheld

this is G. host   Ge 32:2
G. anger was kindled   Nu 22:22
because

the judgment is G.   De 1:17
battle is not yours, but G.   2Ch 20:15
to walk in G. law   Ne 10:29
according to thy wish in G.   Job 33:6
stead

my righteousness is more   Job 35:2
than G.

I have yet to speak on G.   Job 36:2
behalf

by heaven: for it is G.   M't 5:34
throne

unto God the things that   M't 22:21;
are G.   M'k 12:17; Lu 20:25
many of G. people (N)   M't 27:52;
    Ac 26:10

to mislead G. chosen   M'k 13:22
(N)(P)

for the kingdom of G. sake   Lu 18:29
that is of God heareth G.   Joh 8:47
words

speaking G. message (P)   Joh 16:6
Revilest thou G. high priest   Ac 23:4
G. loved ones (B)(R)   Ro 1:7
thing to the charge of G.   Ro 8:33
elect

being ignorant of G.   Ro 10:3
righteousness

they are G. ministers,   Ro 13:6
attending

Ye are G. husbandry, G.   1Co 3:9
building

ye are Christ's; Christ is G.   1Co 3:23
in your spirit, which are G.   1Co 6:20
heralded G. gospel (B)   1Th 2:9
according to faith of G. elect   Tit 1:1
as being lords over G. heritage   1Pe 5:3

GOD-WARD

Be thou for the people to   Ex 18:19
G.

have we through Christ to   2Co 3:2
G.

your faith to G. is spread   1Th 1:8

GOEST

will keep thee in places thou   Ge 28:15

whither g. thou   Ge 32:17;
    J'g 19:17; Zec 2:2; Joh 13:36; 16:5

is it not in that thou g. with   Ex 33:16
us

no covenant with inhabitants   Ex 34:12
whither thou g.

thou g. before them by   Nu 14:14
day time

the land whither thou g.   De 7:1;
    11:10, 29

God cut off nations whither   De 12:29
thou g.

when thou g. to battle and   De 20:1;
seest   21:10

God bless thee whither thou   De 23:20;
g.   Jos 1:7

blessed shalt thou be when   De 28:6
thou g. out

cursed shalt thou be when   De 28:19
thou g. out

pestilence cleave to thee   De 28:21
whither thou g.

be plucked off the land   De 28:63
whither thou g.

and die in the mount whither   De 32:50
thou g.

the Lord is with thee whither   Jos 1:9
thou g.

that thou g. to take a wife of   J'g 14:3
Philistines

for whither thou g. I will go   Ru 1:16
wherefore g. thou also with   2Sa 15:19
us

on the day thou g. over the   1Ki 2:37;
brooks   2:42

thou g. not forth with our   Ps 44:9
armies

thou g. steps shall not be   Pr 4:12
straitened

when thou g. it shall lead thee   Pr 6:22
keep foot when thou g. to house   Ec 5:1
of God

nor wisdom in the grave   Ec 9:10
whither thou g.

I will give for a prey whither   Jer 45:5
thou g.

I will follow thee whither g.   M't 8:19;
    Lu 9:57

when thou g. with thine   Lu 12:58
adversary

sought to stone thee, g. thither   Joh 11:8
again

Lord, we know not whither   Joh 14:5
thou g.

GOETH

lo, he g. out unto the water   Ex 7:15
shall deliver it by that the sun   Ex 22:26
g. down

Aaron shall bear them when   Ex 28:29
he g. in

shall be on Aaron's heart   Ex 28:30
when he g.

his sound shall be heard when   Ex 28:35
he g. in

these ye may eat that g. on all   Le 11:21
four

he that g. into house shall be   Le 14:46
unclean

law of him whose seed g.   Le 15:32;
from him   22:4

none in the tabernacle when   Le 16:17
he g. in

who g. to holy things having   Le 22:3
uncleanness

field, when it g. out in jubile,   Le 27:21
be holy

this is the law, when a wife g.   Nu 5:29
aside

the Lord which g. before shall   De 1:30
fight

thy God is he that g. over   De 9:3
before you

as when man g. into wood with   De 19:5
neighbours

the Lord your God is he that g.   De 20:4
with you

when the host g. forth against   De 23:9
thy enemies

deliver the pledge when the   De 24:13
sun g. down

be as the sun when he g. forth   J'g 5:31
in might

as David who g. at thy   1Sa 22:14
bidding

as his part is that g. down to   1Sa 30:24
the battle

my master g. to house of   2Ki 5:18
Rimmon

be with king as he g. out   2Ki 11:8;
    2Ch 23:7

this work g. fast on and   Ezr 5:8
prospereth

g. down to grave come up no   Job 7:9
more

lo, he g. by me, and I see him   Job 9:11
not

when g. in company with   Job 34:8
workers of iniquity

hear the sound that g. out of   Job 37:2
his mouth

he g. on to meet the armed   Job 39:21
men

prayer that g. not out of   Ps 17:1
feigned lips

when he g. abroad, he telleth it   Ps 41:6
such a one as g. on in his   Ps 68:21
trespasses

thy fierce wrath g. over me   Ps 88:16
fire g. before him, and burneth   Ps 97:3
up enemies

man g. forth to his work   Ps 104:23
until evening

he that g. forth and weepeth,   Ps 126:6
bearing

his breath g. forth; he   Ps 146:4
returneth to earth

so he that g. in to his   Pr 6:29
neighbour's wife

g. after her, as an ox g. to the   Pr 7:22
slaughter

when it g. well with righteous,   Pr 11:10
city rejoices

pride g. before destruction, a   Pr 16:18
haughty spirit

that g. about as a talebearer   Pr 20:19
reveals secrets

as a thorn g. up into the hand   Pr 26:9
of a drunkard

where no wood is, there the   Pr 26:20
fire g. out

her candle g. not out by night   Pr 31:18
sun g. down and hasteth to his   Ec 1:5
place

spirit of man g. up, spirit of   Ec 3:21
beast g. down

because man g. to his long   Ec 12:5
home

that g. down sweetly, causing   Ca 7:9
the lips

from the time it g. forth, it   Isa 28:19
shall take

when one g. with a pipe to   Isa 30:29
come to mount

so shall my word be that g.   Isa 55:11
forth of mouth

whoso g. therein shall not   Isa 59:8
know peace

as a beast g. down into the   Isa 63:14
valley

every one that g. out shall be   Jer 5:6
torn

woe unto us, for the day g.   Jer 6:4
away

that g. out to Chaldeans shall   Jer 21:9;
live   38:2

but weep sore for him that g.   Jer 22:10
away

whirlwind of the Lord g.   Jer 30:23
forth with fury

we will do what g. out of our   Jer 44:17
mouth

every one that g. by it be   Jer 49:17;
astonished   50:13

they have blown, but none g.   Eze 7:14
to battle

their heart g. after their   Eze 33:31
covetousness

in the day that he g. into the   Eze 44:27
sanctuary

your goodness is as early dew, it   Ho 6:4
g. away

thy judgments are as light that   Ho 6:5
g. forth

this is the curse that g. forth   Zec 5:3
he said, This is an ephah that g.   Zec 5:6
forth

say Go, and he g.   M't 8:9; Lu 7:8
then g. he and taketh   M't 12:45;
    Lu 11:26

for joy thereof g. and selleth M't 13:44
all he hath
not that which g. into mouth M't 15:11
defileth
this kind g. not out but by M't 17:21
prayer
Son of man g. as it is M't 26:24;
written of him M'k 14:21; Lu 22:22
he g. before you into Galilee M't 28:7;
M'k 16:7
but canst not tell whither it g. Joh 3:8
hast a devil; who g. about to Joh 7:20
kill thee
he g. before them, the sheep Joh 10:4
follow him
she g. unto the grave to weep Joh 11:31
there
knoweth not whither he g. Joh 12:35;
1Jo 2:11
but brother g. to law with 1Co 6:6
brother
g. a warfare any time at own 1Co 9:7
charges
he beholdeth himself and g. his Jas 1:24
way
follow the Lamb whithersoever Re 14:4
he g.
and is of the seven, and g. Re 17:11
into perdition
and out of his mouth g. a Re 19:15
sharp sword

GOG

sons of Joel, G. his son, Shimei 1Ch 5:4
his son
son of man, set thy face Eze 38:2
against G.
say, Behold, I am against Eze 38:3;
thee, O G. 39:1
when I shall be sanctified in Eze 38:16
thee, O G.
G. shall come against the Eze 38:18
land of Israel
give to G. a place of graves Eze 39:11
in Israel
G. and Magog, to gather Re 20:8
together

GOIIM

the G. in Gilgal (S) Jos 12:23

GOING

sun g. down, a deep sleep fell Ge 15:12
on Abram
his hands steady, to g. down Ex 17:12
of sun
if thou meet thine enemy's ox Ex 23:4
g. astray
g. forth of border from south Nu 34:4
to Kadesh
sacrifice the passover at g. De 16:6
down of sun
he said, Rejoice, Zebulun, in De 33:18
thy g. out
and smote them in the g. down Jos 7:5
as they were in the g. down Jos 10:11
to Beth-horon
at g. down of the sun Jos 10:27
carcases taken down
I am g. the way of all the Jos 23:14
earth
I am now g. to the house of J'g 19:18
the Lord
up, let us be g. but none J'g 19:28
answered
meet thee three men g. up to 1Sa 10:3
God
in g. turned not from 2Sa 2:19
following Abner
hearest a sound of g. in trees 2Sa 5:24;
1Ch 14:15
as she was g. to fetch it, he 1Ki 17:11
called
went a proclamation at g. 1Ki 22:36
down of the sun
g. by the way, children 2Ki 2:23
mocked him
they smote Ahaziah at the g. 2Ki 9:27
up to Gur
at time of sun g. down, he 1Ch 18:34
died
from g. to and fro in the earth Job 1:7;
2:2
deliver him from g. down to Job 33:24
the pit
he will deliver his soul from Job 33:28
g. into the pit

his g. forth is from the end of Ps 19:6
heaven
mighty God calleth the earth, Ps 50:1;
from rising of sun to g. down 113:3;
Mal 1:11
the sun knoweth his g. down Ps 104:19
g. down to the chambers of Pr 7:27
death
but the prudent man looketh Pr 14:15
well to his g.
three go well, yea, four are Pr 30:29
comely in g.
the sun shall be darkened in Isa 13:10
his g. forth
in the g. up to Luhith; in the g. Jer 48:5
down of Horonaim
g. and weeping they shall seek Jer 50:4
the Lord
the g. up had eight steps Eze 40:31;
40:34
with every g. forth of the Eze 44:5
sanctuary
after his g. forth, one Eze 46:12
shut the gate
and laboured till g. down of Da 6:14
the sun
from the g. forth of the Da 9:25
commandment
his g. forth is prepared as the Ho 6:3
morning
rise, let us be g. behold, he is M't 26:46
at hand
what king g. to war with Lu 14:31
another
g. through midst of them, so Joh 8:59
passed by
these g. before, tarried at Ac 20:5
Troas
g. about to establish their Ro 10:3
righteousness
some men's sins g. before to 1Ti 5:24
judgment
is a disannulling of command Heb 7:18
g. before
g. after strange flesh are set Jude 7
forth an example

GOINGS

and Moses wrote their g. out Nu 33:2
the g. out of their borders Nu 34:5;
34:8-9, 12; Jos 15:4, 7, 11; 16:3, 8;
18:12, 14
his eyes are on man, he seeth Job 34:21
all his g.
hold up my g. in thy paths that Ps 17:5
footsteps
he set my feet on a rock, Ps 40:2
established my g.
they have seen thy g. even the Ps 68:24
g. of God
who have purposed to Ps 140:4
overthrow my g.
before Lord, and he pondereth Pr 5:21
all his g.
man's g. are of the Lord, how Pr 20:24
can a man
there is no judgment in their g. Isa 59:8
their g. out were according to Eze 42:11
fashion
shew them g. out thereof and Eze 43:11
comings in
whose g. forth have been from Mic 5:2
of old

GOLAN

G. in Bashan De 4:43; Jos 20:8;
1Ch 6:71
of Manasseth they gave G. in Jos 21:27

GOLD

whole land of Havilah, where Ge 2:11
there is g.
the g. of that land is good, Ge 2:12
there is bdellium
he put a chain of g. on Ge 41:42
Joseph's neck
borrow g. articles (B) Ex 3:22
jewelry of silver and g. (R) Ex 3:22
nor shall ye make you gods of Ex 20:23
g.
cast four rings of g. for the Ex 25:12;
ark 25:26; 26:29; 28:23, 26-27; 37:3, 13
staves of shittim wood, Ex 25:13;
overlay them with g. 25:28; 26:29, 37;
30:5; 37:4, 15, 28
make two cherubims of g. Ex 25:18;
37:7

thou shalt make fifty taches of Ex 26:6;
g. 36:13
their hooks shall be of g. Ex 26:32;
26:37; 36:38
ephod g. Ex 28:6
girdle g. Ex 28:8
to be set in ouches of g. Ex 28:11;
28:13; 39:6, 13, 16
breastplate g. Ex 28:15
chains of g. thou shalt make Ex 28:24;
28:33
bells of g. Ex 32:24
who hath any g. let him break
it off
oh, this people have made Ex 32:31
them gods of g.
they brought jewels of g. an Ex 35:22
offering of g.
he overlaid the boards with g. Ex 36:34
bars with g.
he overlaid their chapiters Ex 36:38
and fillets with g.
all the g. that was occupied in Ex 38:24
the work
they did beat the g. into thin Ex 39:3
plates
thou shalt set the altar of g. Ex 40:5
before the ark
one spoon of ten shekels of g. Nu 7:14;
7:20
at dedication of the altar Nu 7:84
twelve spoons of g.
all the g. of the spoons was 120 Nu 7:86
shekels
the captains' oblation, jewels Nu 31:50
of g. chains
Achan took a wedge of g. of Jos 7:21
50 shekels
Joshua took Achan and the Jos 7:24
wedge of g.
the earrings 1700 shekels of g. J'g 8:26
and put the jewels of g. in a 1Sa 6:8
coffer
they laid even and the mice 1Sa 6:11
of g. on the cart
Levites took the coffer with 1Sa 6:15
the jewels of g.
David took shields of g. 2Sa 8:7;
1Ch 18:7
house, altar, he overlaid with 1Ki 6:22
g.
he overlaid cherubims with g. 1Ki 6:28;
2Ch 3:10
Solomon made the altar and 1Ki 7:48
table of g.
lamps and tongs of g.; hinges 1Ki 7:49;
of g. 7:50
furnished Solomon with g. 1Ki 9:11;
and cedar trees 10:11; 2Ch 9:10
queen of Sheba came with g. 1Ki 10:2;
2Ch 9:9
the weight of g. come in one 1Ki 10:14;
year 2Ch 9:13
Solomon made 200 targets of 1Ki 10:16
beaten g.
he made three hundred 1Ki 10:17
shields of g.
he overlaid the throne with 1Ki 10:18
the best g.
Jeroboam made two calves 1Ki 12:28
of g.
Jehoshaphat made ships to 1Ki 22:48
go for g.
Hezekiah cut off g. from the 2Ki 18:16
doors
David gave of g. by weight 1Ch 28:14
for g.
and the g. was g. of Parvaim 2Ch 3:6
ten candlesticks of g.; basins 2Ch 4:7;
of g. 4:8
snuffers, censers, and spoons 2Ch 4:22
of pure g.
steps to the throne, with a 2Ch 9:18
footstool of g.
Shishak carried away the 2Ch 12:9
shields of g.
basins of g. copper precious as Ezr 8:27
g.
Tirshatha gave thousand Ne 7:70
drams of g.
chief of fathers gave g. Ne 7:71
people gave g. Ne 7:72
lay up g. as dust, the g. of Job 22:24
Ophir
when tried, I shall come Job 23:10
forth like g.
as for the earth, it hath the Job 28:6
dust of g.
wisdom cannot be gotten for Job 28:15
g. nor silver

it cannot be valued with the   *Job 28:16*
g. of Ophir
the g. and the crystal cannot   *Job 28:17*
equal it
if I made g. my hope, or said   *Job 31:24*
to fine g.
will he esteem thy riches? no   *Job 36:19*
not g.
every one gave Job an   *Job 42:11*
earring of g.
more to be desired are they   *Ps 19:10*
than g.
did stand the queen in g. of   *Ps 45:9*
Ophir
to him shall be given of the g.   *Ps 72:15*
of Sheba
as a jewel of g. in a swine's   *Pr 11:22*
snout
much better it is to get   *Pr 16:16*
wisdom than g.
there is g. and a multitude of   *Pr 20:15*
rubies
thy neck is comely with chains   *Ca 1:10*
of g.
his hands are as g. rings set   *Ca 5:14*
with beryl
ye shall defile ornament of   *Isa 30:22*
thy images of g.
the goldsmith spreadeth it   *Isa 40:19*
over with g.
for brass I will bring g. for   *Isa 60:17*
iron bring silver
thou deckest thee with   *Jer 4:30*
ornaments of g.
how is the g. become dim! fine   *La 4:1*
g. changed
merchants of Sheba occupied   *Eze 27:22*
with g.
art head of g.;   *Da 2:38;*
Nebuchadnezzar made image   *3:1*
of g.
and thou hast praised the gods   *Da 5:23*
of g.
they put a chain of g. about   *Da 5:29*
Daniel's neck
and behold a candlestick all of   *Zec 4:2*
g.
and I will try them as g. is   *Zec 13:9*
tried
they presented to him g. and   *M't 2:11*
myrrh
whoso shall swear by g. of   *M't 23:16*
the temple
for whether is greater, g. or   *M't 23:17*
the temple
not adorned with g. or pearls   *1Ti 2:9;*
  1Pe 3:3
the ark overlaid round about   *Heb 9:4*
with g.
if there come a man with a g.   *Jas 2:2*
ring
trial of faith more precious   *1Pe 1:7*
than g.
I counsel thee to buy of me g.   *Re 3:18*
tried
the elders had on their heads   *Re 4:4*
crowns of g.
the locusts had on their heads   *Re 9:7*
crowns of g.
woman was decked with g. and   *Re 17:4*
pearls
that great city that was   *Re 18:16;*
decked with g.   *25:24*

GOLD with SILVER

Abram was rich in *silver* and   *Ge 13:2;*
g.   *24:35*
steal out of my lord's house   *Ge 44:8*
silver or g.
jewels of *silver* and g.   *Ex 3:22;*
  11:2; 12:35
this is the offering, take *silver*   *Ex 25:3*
and g.
to work in g. *silver*, and brass   *Ex 31:4;*
  35:32
his house full of *silver* and g.   *Nu 22:18;*
  24:13
only g. and *silver* that may   *Nu 31:22*
abide the fire
not desire *silver* and g. on idols   *De 7:25*
when thy *silver* and g. is   *De 8:13*
multiplied
nor greatly multiply *silver* and   *De 17:17*
g.
ye have seen their idols, *silver*   *De 29:17*
and g.
silver and g. are consecrated   *Jos 6:19;*
to Lord   *6:24*

return to your tents with *silver*   *Jos 22:8*
and g.
silver and g. David dedicated   *2Sa 8:11;*
  1Ki 7:51
we will have no *silver* or g. of   *2Sa 21:4*
Saul
Asa brought into house of   *1Ki 15:15;*
Lord *silver* and g.   *2Ch 15:18*
Asa took all the *silver* and g.   *1Ki 15:18;*
  2Ch 16:2
I have sent a present of   *1Ki 15:19;*
silver and g.   *2Ch 16:3*
silver and g. is mine; deliver   *1Ki 20:3;*
silver and g.   *20:5*
carried thence *silver* and g.   *2Ki 7:8*
raiment
Jehoash took the *silver*   *2Ki 12:18;*
and g.   *2Ch 25:24*
Ahaz took *silver* and g. found   *2Ki 16:8*
in Lord's house
Hezekiah shewed them *silver*   *2Ki 20:13;*
and g.   *Isa 39:2*
Jehoiakim gave *silver* and g.   *2Ki 23:35*
exacted *silver* and g.
things of g. in g. of *silver* in   *2Ki 25:15;*
silver   *Jer 52:19*
of my own proper good, of g.   *1Ch 29:3*
and *silver*
the king made *silver* and g.   *2Ch 1:15*
plenteous
men of his place help with   *Ezr 1:4*
silver and g.
gave *silver* and g.; to carry   *Ezr 2:69;*
silver and g.   *7:15*
they weighed them the *silver*   *Ezr 8:25;*
and g.   *8:33*
beds were of g. and *silver* on a   *Es 1:6*
pavement
there is a vein for *silver*, a   *Job 28:1*
place for g.
covered with *silver* her   *Ps 68:13*
feathers with g.
he brought them out with   *Ps 105:37*
silver and g.
their idols are *silver* and g.   *Ps 115:4;*
  135:15
thy law is better than g. and   *Ps 119:72*
silver
not *silver* receive knowledge   *Pr 8:10*
rather than g.
fining pot for *silver*, furnace   *Pr 17:3;*
for g.   *27:21*
loving favour rather than *silver*   *Pr 22:1*
or g.
like apples of g. in pictures of   *Pr 25:11*
silver
I gathered me also *silver* and g.   *Ec 2:8*
make borders of g. with studs   *Ca 1:11*
of *silver*
he made the pillars of *silver*,   *Ca 3:10*
bottom of g.
the land also is full of *silver* and   *Isa 2:7*
g.
a man shall cast his idols of   *Isa 2:20;*
silver and g.   *31:7*
which shall not regard *silver*   *Isa 13:17*
or g.
they lavish g. out of the bag,   *Isa 46:6*
and weigh *silver*
to bring their *silver* and g. with   *Isa 60:9*
them
they deck it with *silver* and g.   *Jer 10:4*
cast away *silver* and g. *silver*   *Eze 7:19;*
and g. not able to deliver   *Zep 1:18*
thus wast thou decked with   *Eze 16:13*
g. and *silver*
then was *silver* and g. broken   *Da 2:35;*
to pieces   *2:45*
they praised the gods of *silver*   *Da 5:4;*
and g.   *5:23*
a god shall he honour with g.   *Da 11:38*
and *silver*
have power over treasures of   *Da 11:43*
g. and *silver*
did not know I multiplied her   *Ho 2:8*
silver and g.
of their *silver* and g. have they   *Ho 8:4*
made idols
because ye have taken my *silver*   *Joe 3:5*
and g.
take the spoil of *silver* and spoil   *Na 2:9*
of g.
behold, it is laid over with   *Hab 2:19*
silver and g.
the *silver* is mine, and the g. is   *Hag 2:8*
mine
take *silver* and g. and make   *Zec 6:11*
crowns

he shall purge them as g. and   *Mal 3:3*
silver
provide neither g. nor *silver*,   *M't 10:9*
nor brass
Peter said, Silver and g. have I   *Ac 3:6*
none
nor think Godhead is like to   *Ac 17:29*
silver and g.
I have coveted no man's *silver*   *Ac 20:33*
or g.
if any build on this   *1Co 3:12*
foundation g. *silver*
in a great house vessels of   *2Ti 2:20*
silver and g.
your g. and *silver* cankered,   *Jas 5:3*
rust of them
we were not redeemed with   *1Pe 1:18*
silver and g.
repented not of idols of *silver*   *Re 9:20*
and g.

PURE GOLD

overlay the ark with *pure* g.   *Ex 25:11;*
  25:24; 30:3; 37:2, 11, 26
thou shalt make a mercy seat   *Ex 25:17;*
of *pure* g.   *37:6*
dishes, spoons and covers of   *Ex 25:29;*
pure g.   *37:16, 23*
make a candlestick of *pure* g.   *Ex 25:31;*
  37:17; 1Ki 7:49
snuffdishes *pure* g.   *Ex 25:38;*
  1Ki 7:50; 2Ch 4:22
two chains of *pure* g. at ends   *Ex 28:14;*
  28:22; 39:15
thou shalt make a plate of   *Ex 28:36;*
pure g.   *39:30*
the oracle he overlaid with   *1Ki 6:20*
pure g.
vessels of Lebanon of *pure*   *1Ki 10:21;*
g.   *2Ch 9:20*
pure g. for fleshhooks,   *1Ch 28:17*
bowls, cups
overlaid the porch within with   *2Ch 3:4*
pure g.
he overlaid the throne with   *2Ch 9:17*
pure g.
wisdom not to be valued with   *Job 28:19*
pure g.
settest a crown of *pure* g. on   *Ps 21:3*
his head
city was *pure* g.   *Re 21:18*
street of *pure* g.   *Re 21:21*

TALENT, TALENTS
OF GOLD

of a *talent* of pure g. shall he   *Ex 25:39*
make it
of a *talent* of pure g. made he   *Ex 37:24*
it
weight of crown a *talent*   *2Sa 12:30;*
of g.   *1Ch 20:2*
Hiram sent Solomon 120   *1Ki 9:14*
talents of g.
they sent from Ophir 420   *1Ki 9:28*
talents of g.
she gave Solomon 120   *1Ki 10:10;*
talents of g.   *2Ch 9:9*
in one year came to   *1Ki 10:14*
Solomon 666 *talents* of g.
put the land to a *talent* of g.   *2Ki 23:33;*
  2Ch 36:3
David prepared 100,000   *1Ch 22:14*
talents of g.
prepared of my proper good   *1Ch 29:4*
3000 *talents* of g.
the chief of the fathers gave   *1Ch 29:7*
5000 *talents* of g.
took from Ophir 450 *talents*   *2Ch 8:18*
of g.
I weighed of g. vessels 100   *Ezr 8:26*
talents

VESSELS OF GOLD

Toi sent to David *vessels* of g.   *2Sa 8:10;*
  1Ch 18:10
Solomon's drinking *vessels*   *1Ki 10:21;*
were of g.   *2Ch 9:20*
every man brought present,   *1Ki 10:25;*
vessels of g.   *2Ch 9:24*
not made for house of Lord   *2Ki 12:13*
vessels of g.
Nebuchadnezzar cut in pieces   *2Ki 24:13*
vessels of g.
of rest of money made they   *2Ch 24:14*
vessels of g.

all the *vessels of g.* and silver Ezr 1:11 5400
all the *vessels of g.* Cyrus Ezr 5:14 delivered to one
I weighed of *vessels of g.* 100 Ezr 8:26 talents
they gave them drink in *vessels* Es 1:7 *of g.*
shall also carry into Egypt Da 11:8 *vessels of g.*
not only *vessels of g.* but of 2Ti 2:20 wood

GOLDEN

a *g.* crown to the border Ex 25:25 round about
a *g.* bell; two *g.* rings Ex 28:34; 30:4; 39:20
Aaron said, Break off the *g.* Ex 32:2 earrings
upon forefront he put the *g.* Le 8:9 plate
one *g.* spoon of ten shekels full Nu 7:26 of incense
had *g.* earrings, because J'g 8:24 Ishmaelites
the weight of *g.* earrings he J'g 8:26 requested
five *g.* emerods, five *g.* mice 1Sa 6:4; 6:17-18
Jehu departed not from the 2Ki 10:29 *g.* calves
for the *g.* basins he gave gold 1Ch 28:17
there are with you *g.* calves 2Ch 13:8
and also let the *g.* vessels be Ezr 6:5 restored
king shall hold out a *g.* sceptre Es 4:11; 5:2; 8:4
or the *g.* bowl be broken, or Ec 12:6 pitcher
man more precious than *g.* Isa 13:12 wedge of Ophir
how hath the oppressor, the *g.* Isa 14:4 city ceased
Babylon hath been *g.* cup in Jer 51:7 Lord's hand
fall down and worship the *g.* Da 3:5; image 3:12
Belshazzar commanded to bring Da 5:2 the *g.* vessels
they brought the *g.* vessels taken Da 5:3 out of temple
through the *g.* pipes, empty Zec 4:12 the *g.* oil
had the *g.* censer and ark Heb 9:4 where was *g.* pot
being turned, I saw seven *g.* Re 1:12 candlesticks
one girt about the paps with a Re 1:13 *g.* girdle
the mystery of the seven *g.* Re 1:20 candlesticks
who walketh in the midst of the Re 2:1 *g.* candlesticks
g. vials Re 5:8
having a *g.* censer Re 8:3; 15:7
on his head a *g.* crown Re 14:14
a *g.* cup full Re 17:4
had a *g.* reed to measure the Re 21:15 city and gates

GOLDSMITH

the *g.* spreadeth it over with Isa 40:19 gold
so the carpenter encouraged Isa 41:7 the *g.*
they hire a *g.* and he maketh it Isa 46:6 a god
the hands of the *g.* (S) Jer 10:9; 10:14; 51:17

GOLDSMITHS

son of Hanaiah of the *g.* Ne 3:8
repaired the *g.* and merchants Ne 3:32

GOLDSMITH'S

repaired Malchiah thy *g.* son Ne 3:31 into

GOLGOTHA

a place called *G.*, a place of M't 27:32; a skull M'k 15:22; Joh 19:17

GOLIATH

G. of Gath a champion went 1Sa 17:4; out 17:23

the sword of *G.* the Philistine 1Sa 21:9 is here
he gave him the sword of *G.* 1Sa 22:10 the Philistine
slew the brother of *G.* 2Sa 21:19; 1Ch 20:5

GOMER

sons of Japheth, *G.* Magog Ge 10:2; 1Ch 1:5
the sons of *G.* Ashkenaz, Ge 10:3; Riphath 1Ch 1:6
G. and all his bands, house of Eze 38:6 Togarmah
he took *G.* the daughter of Ho 1:3 Diblaim

GOMORRAH

before the Lord destroyed Ge 13:10 Sodom and *G.*
they took all the goods of Ge 14:11 Sodom and *G.*
because the cry of Sodom and Ge 18:20 *G.* is great
the Lord rained on *G.* fire Ge 19:24 from heaven
Abraham looked towards Ge 19:28 Sodom and *G.*
like the overthrow of Sodom De 29:23; and *G.* Isa 1:9; 13:19; Jer 23:14; 49:18; 50:40; Am 4:11; Ro 9:29; 2Pe 2:6; Jude 7
for their vine is of the fields De 32:32 of *G.*
give ear to the law, ye people Isa 1:10 of *G.*
children of Ammon shall be as Zep 2:9 *G.*

GOMORRHA

for the land of Sodom and *G.* M't 10:15 more tolerable for Sodom and M'k 6:11 *G.*
been made like unto *G.* Ro 9:29
turning the cities of Sodom and 2Pe 2:6 *G.*
Even as Sodom and *G.* and the Jude 7

GONE

now though thou wouldest Ge 31:30 needs be *g.*
take our daughter, and we Ge 34:17 will be *g.*
take food for your Ge 42:33 households, and be *g.*
take your flocks and herds, Ex 12:32 and be *g.*
when he seeth their power is De 32:36 *g.*
we people knew not Jonathan 1Sa 14:3 was *g.*
number now, and see who is 1Sa 14:17 *g.* from us
I have *g.* the way which Lord 1Sa 15:20 sent me
as soon as the lad was *g.* 1Sa 20:41 David arose
g. in to my father's concubine 2Sa 3:7
he is quite *g.*; Amnon said, 2Sa 3:24; Arise, be *g.* 13:15
that Shimei had *g.* from 1Ki 2:41 Jerusalem
when he was *g.* a lion met 1Ki 13:24 him by the way
as a man takes away dung 1Ki 14:10 till it be all *g.*
as soon as I am *g.* Spirit 1Ki 18:12 shall carry thee
as I was busy here and there, 1Ki 20:40 he was *g.*
the messenger that was *g.* to 1Ki 22:13 call Micaiah
but have *g.* from tent to tent 1Ch 17:5
when shall I rise, and the night Job 7:4 be *g.*
he hath destroyed me, and I Job 19:10 am *g.*
they are exalted for a while, Job 24:24 but are *g.*
they are dried up and *g.* away Job 28:4 from men
as for light of mine eyes, it Ps 38:10 also is *g.*
I had *g.* with multitude to Ps 42:4 house of God

but as for me, my feet were Ps 73:2 almost *g.*
is his mercy clean *g.* for ever Ps 77:8
the wind passeth over it, and Ps 103:16 it is *g.*
I am *g.* like the shadow that Ps 109:23 declineth
the good man is *g.* a long Pr 7:19 journey
when he is *g.* his way, then he Pr 20:14 boasteth
who had come and *g.* from Ec 8:10 place of holy
winter is past, the rain is over Ca 2:11 and *g.*
my beloved had withdrawn, and Ca 5:6 was *g.*
whither is thy beloved *g.* O thou Ca 6:1 fairest
therefore my people are *g.* into Isa 5:13 captivity
all joy darkened, mirth of the Isa 24:11 land *g.*
by the way he had not *g.* with Isa 41:3 his feet
what iniquity in me, that they Jer 2:5 are *g.*
canst thou say, I have not *g.* Jer 2:23 after Baalim
but this people are revolted Jer 5:23 and *g.*
beasts are *g.*; thou art *g.* Jer 9:10; backward 15:6
none that are *g.* into Egypt Jer 44:14 shall escape
all the remnant that are *g.* Jer 44:28 shall know
they have *g.* from mountain to Jer 50:6 hill
Judah is *g.*; Zion's children are La 1:3; *g.* 1:5
g. without strength; my virgins La 1:6; are *g.* 1:18
take Israel from heathen Eze 37:21 whither *g.*
the king said, The thing is *g.* Da 2:5; from me 2:8
for lo, they are *g.* because of Ho 9:6 destruction
when will new moon be *g.* that Am 8:5 we may
angels were *g.* from them into Lu 2:15 heaven
he made as if he would have Lu 24:28 *g.* further
for his disciples were *g.* to buy Joh 4:8 meat
behold, the world is *g.* after Joh 12:19 him
their masters saw hope of Ac 16:19 gains was *g.*
I have *g.* preaching the Ac 20:25 kingdom of God
who is *g.* into heaven on right 1Pe 3:22 hand
they have *g.* in the way of Cain Jude 11

GONE ABOUT

Saul is *g. about* and passed 1Sa 15:12 to Gilgal
when days of their feastings Job 1:5 were *g. about*
for the city is *g. about* borders Isa 15:8 of Moab
hath *g. about* to profane the Ac 24:6 temple

GONE ASIDE

if thou hast not *g. aside* to Nu 5:19 uncleanness
if hast *g. aside* to another Nu 5:20 unstead of husband
they are all *g. aside*, they are Ps 14:3 filthy
when they were *g. aside*, they Ac 26:31 talked

GONE ASTRAY

I have *g. astray* like a lost Ps 119:176 sheep
all we like sheep have *g. astray* Isa 53:6
have 100 sheep, one be *g.* M't 18:12 *astray*, he seeketh that *g. astray*
forsaken the right way, and 2Pe 2:15 are *g. astray*

GONE AWAY

but Abner was g. away in | 2Sa 3:22;
peace | 3:23
and the men of Israel were g. | 2Sa 23:9
away
even the waters are g. away | Job 28:4
from men
they are g. away backward | Isa 1:4
Levites which are g. away | Eze 44:10
from me
ye are g. away from mine | Mal 3:7
ordinances
but his disciples were g. away | Joh 6:22
alone

GONE BACK

behold, thy sister in law is g. | Ru 1:15
back
nor have I g. back from | Job 23:12
commandment
every one is g. back, none | Ps 53:3
doeth good
while he was not yet g. back he | Jer 40:5
said

GONE DOWN

Saul is passed, and g. down | 1Sa 15:12
to Gilgal
Adonijah is g. down, and slain | 1Ki 1:25
oxen
Ahab g. down to possess | 1Ki 21:18
Naboth's vineyard
by which the shadow had g. | 2Ki 20:11;
down in the dial of Ahaz | Isa 38:8
my beloved is g. down into his | Ca 6:2
garden
her sun is g. down while it was | Jer 15:9
yet day
his young men are g. down to | Jer 48:15
slaughter
all people g. down from his | Eze 31:12
shadow
the strong are g. down slain | Eze 32:21
by the sword
there is Elam; Tubal; Zidon | Eze 32:24;
g. down | 32:27
Jonah was g. down to sides of | Jon 1:5
ship

GONE FORTH

in third month when Israel was | Ex 19:1
g. forth
when servant of Elisha was g. | 2Ki 6:15
forth
God is g. forth before to | 1Ch 14:15
smite
my salvation is g. forth, and | Isa 51:5
my arms
he is g. forth to make thy land | Jer 4:7
desolate
my children are g. forth of | Jer 10:20
me, and are
is profaneness g. forth into all | Jer 23:15
the land
a whirlwind of the Lord is g. | Jer 23:19
forth in fury
brethren that are not g. forth | Jer 29:16
into captivity
day is come, the morning is g. | Eze 7:10
forth
these are people of the Lord | Eze 36:20
and are g. forth
g. forth to slay wise men of | Da 2:14
Babylon
when I am g. forth, prince of | Da 10:20
Grecia come
when he was g. forth one | M'k 10:17
came running

GONE OUT

as soon as I am g. out I will | Ex 9:29
spread hands
there is wrath g. out from the | Nu 16:46
Lord
certain men g. out, and | De 13:13
withdrawn
that which is g. out of thy | De 23:23
lips, shalt keep
is not the Lord g. out before | J'g 4:14
thee
hand of the Lord is g. out | Ru 1:13
against me
when the wine was g. out of | 1Sa 25:37
Nabal
Syrians had g. out by | 2Ki 5:2
companies

we be hungry, therefore they | 2Ki 7:12
are g. out
afore Isaiah was g. out into | 2Ki 20:4
the court
their line is g. out through all | Ps 19:4
earth
alter the thing that is g. out of | Ps 89:34
my lips
the word is g. out of my | Isa 45:23
mouth
pot, whose scum is not g. out | Eze 24:6
of it
when unclean spirit is g. out | M't 12:43;
| Lu 11:24
give us your oil, our lamps are | M't 25:8
g. out
that virtue had g. out of him | M'k 5:30;
| Lu 8:46
devil is g. out of daughter | M'k 7:29;
| M'k 7:30; Lu 11:14
when he was g. out, Jesus | Joh 13:31
said
they are all g. out of way, | Ro 3:12
unprofitable
many false prophets are g. out | 1Jo 4:1
into world

GONE OVER

they be g. over the brook of | 2Sa 17:20
water
mine iniquities are g. over my | Ps 38:4
head
all thy waves and billows are g. | Ps 42:7
over me
then the stream had g. over | Ps 124:4
our soul
the proud waters had g. over | Ps 124:5
our soul
they are g. over the passage, | Isa 10:29
and taken up
they are g. over the sea | Isa 16:8;
| Jer 48:32
shall not have g. over the | M't 10:23
cities of Israel

GONE UP

from the prey, my son, thou | Ge 49:9
art g. up
not come off bed on which g. | 2Ki 1:4;
up | 6:16
God is g. up with a shout, sing | Ps 47:5
praises
he is g. up to Bajith and to | Isa 15:2
Dibon
discovered to another than me, | Isa 57:8
art g. up
she is g. up on every high | Jer 3:6
mountain
and the cry of Jerusalem is g. | Jer 14:2
up
king of Babylon's army, | Jer 34:21
which are g. up
Moab is spoiled, and g. up | Jer 48:15
out of her cities
the glory of the God of Israel | Eze 9:3
was g. up
ye have not g. up into the gaps | Eze 13:5
for they are g. up to Assyria, a | Ho 8:9
wild ass
but when his brethren were g. | Joh 7:10
up
when he had g. up and saluted | Ac 18:22
church

GONE A WHORING

after whom they have g. a | Le 17:7
whoring
because thou hast g. a whoring | Eze 23:30
g. a whoring from under their | Ho 4:12
God
for thou hast g. a whoring from | Ho 9:1
thy God

GOOD

Hagar sat her down a g. way | Ge 21:16
off
I pray thee, send me g. speed | Ge 24:12
this day
as we have done to thee | Ge 26:29
nothing but g.
Rebekah said, What g. shall | Ge 27:46
my life do me
thou saidst, I will surely do | Ge 32:12
thee g.
g. ears; g. kine; g. years | Ge 41:5;
| 41:26, 35

thy servant our father is in g. | Ge 43:28
health
I will give you the g. of the | Ge 45:18
land of Egypt
for the g. of the land of Egypt | Ge 45:20
is yours
Joseph wept on his father's | Ge 46:29
neck a g. while
God meant it unto g. to bring | Ge 50:20
to pass
make it g. (R) | Le 24:21
Lord hath spoken g. | Nu 10:29
concerning Israel
they have spoken g. (S) | De 18:17
an abundance of g. things (B) | De 28:11
for g. will of him that dwelt | De 33:16
in bush
consume you, after he hath | Jos 24:20
done you g.
my sons, it is no g. report that | 1Sa 2:24
I hear
g. news (A) | 1Sa 4:10;
1Ki 1:42; 2Ki 7:9; Isa 41:27; Lu 1:19;
2:10; 8:1; Ac 13:32; 1Th 3:6
g. news (B) | 1Sa 4:10;
18:19, 31; 1Ki 1:42; 2Ki 7:9; 1Ch 10:9;
Isa 41:27; Lu 2:10; 8:1
g. news (R) | 1Sa 4:10;
1Ki 1:42; 2Ki 7:9; 1Ch 10:9; Lu 1:19;
2:10; 8:1; Ac 13:32; Ro 10:15; 1Th 3:6
I will teach you the g. and | 1Sa 12:23
right way
behold, if there be g. toward | 1Sa 20:12
David
for thou hast rewarded me g. | 1Sa 24:17
for evil
wherefore the Lord rewarded | 1Sa 24:19
thee g.
men were very g. to us, we | 1Sa 25:15
were not hurt
according to all the g. he | 1Sa 25:30
hath spoken
I know that thou art g. in my | 1Sa 29:9
sight
to carry g. news (R) | 1Sa 31:9
slain a g. man (B) | 2Sa 4:11
make g. four times over (B) | 2Sa 12:6
it had been g. for me to been | 2Sa 14:32
there
see thy matters are g. and | 2Sa 15:3
right
Lord will requite g. for his | 2Sa 16:12
cursing this day
the g. reports (B) | 2Sa 18:27
and to do what the king | 2Sa 19:18
thought g.
that thou teach them the g. | 1Ki 8:36
way
hath not failed one word of | 1Ki 8:56
his g. promise
and speak g. words to them | 1Ki 12:7;
| 2Ch 10:7
g. is the word of the Lord | 2Ki 20:19;
| Isa 39:8
words of prophets declare g. | 1Ch 12:13;
to king with one mouth | 2Ch 18:12
I have prepared of mine own | 1Ch 29:3
proper g.
the Lord shall be with thee g. | 2Ch 19:11
because he had done g. in | 2Ch 24:16
Israel
saying, The g. Lord pardon | 2Ch 30:18
every one
the g. hand of his God on him | Ezr 7:9;
| Ne 2:8
and by the g. hand of our God | Ezr 8:18
upon us
be strong, and eat the g. of the | Ezr 9:12
land
thou gavest them true laws, g. | Ne 9:13
statutes
thou gavest thy g. Spirit to | Ne 9:20
instruct them
houses filled with g. things | Ne 9:25
(A)(B)(E)(R)
who had spoken g. for the king | Es 7:9
shall we receive g. at the hand | Job 2:10
of God
hear it, and know thou it for | Job 5:27
thy g.
mine eye shall no more see g. | Job 7:7
my days flee away, they see no | Job 9:25
g.
is it g. that thou shouldest | Job 10:3
oppress
is it g. that he should search | Job 13:9
you out
or with speeches wherewith he | Job 15:3
can do no g.

lo, their g. is not in their hand *Job 21:16*

be at peace, thereby g. shall come to thee *Job 22:21*

and he doeth not g. to the window *Job 24:21*

their young ones are in g. liking *Job 39:4*

many say, Who will shew us any g. *Ps 4:6*

none doeth g. not one *Ps 14:1* *14:3; 53:1; 3; Ro 3:12*

g. and upright is the Lord *Ps 25:8*

and loveth many days, that he may see g. *Ps 34:12*

steps of a g. man are ordered by the Lord *Ps 37:23*

I was dumb, I held my peace, even from g. *Ps 39:2*

my heart is inditing a g. matter *Ps 45:1*

proclaimed the g. news (B) *Ps 68:11*

thou, Lord, art g. ready to forgive *Ps 86:5; 119:68*

thou openest hand, they are filled with g. *Ps 104:28*

that I may see the g. of thy chosen *Ps 106:5*

a g. man sheweth favour, and lendeth *Ps 112:5*

turn reproach, thy judgments are g. *Ps 119:39*

teach me g. judgment and knowledge *Ps 119:66*

because of house of Lord I will seek thy g. *Ps 122:9*

shalt see the g. of Jerusalem all thy life *Ps 128:5*

thou shalt understand every g. path *Pr 2:9*

that thou mayest walk in the way of g. men *Pr 2:20*

but a g. word maketh the heart glad *Pr 2:25*

withhold not g. from them to whom due *Pr 3:27*

the merciful man doth g. to his own soul *Pr 11:17*

beautiful woman who neglects g. taste (B) *Pr 11:22*

he that diligently seeketh g. procureth *Pr 11:27*

a g. wife (R) *Pr 12:4; 31:10*

a man satisfied with g. by fruit of his mouth *Pr 12:14*

a man shall eat g. by the fruit of his mouth *Pr 13:2*

but to the righteous g. shall be repaid *Pr 13:21*

the evil bow before the g. and the wicked *Pr 14:19*

mercy and truth be to them that devise g. *Pr 14:22*

and a word in due season, how g. is it *Pr 15:23*

and a g. report maketh the bones fat *Pr 15:30*

handleth a matter wisely, shall find g. *Pr 16:20*

he that hath a froward heart, findeth no g. *Pr 17:20*

a merry heart doeth g. like a medicine *Pr 17:22*

he that keepeth understanding shall find g. *Pr 19:8*

g. sense makes men restrain (A)(R) *Pr 19:11*

and with g. advice make war *Pr 20:18*

a g. name rather to be chosen than riches *Pr 22:1*

the upright shall have g. things *Pr 28:10*

make his soul enjoy g. *Ec 2:24; 3:13; 5:18*

I know that there is no g. in them *Ec 3:12*

whom do I labour, and bereave my soul of g. *Ec 4:8*

they have a g. reward for their labour *Ec 4:9*

what g. is there to the owners thereof *Ec 5:11*

his soul be not filled with g. and no burial *Ec 6:3*

yet hath he seen no g. all go to one place *Ec 6:6*

not a man just, that doeth g. and sinneth not *Ec 7:20*

there is one event to the g. and to the clean *Ec 9:2*

but one sinner destroyeth much g. *Ec 9:18*

or whether they both shall be alike g. *Ec 11:6*

if willing, ye shall eat the g. of the land *Isa 1:19*

that bringeth good tidings of g. of salvation *Isa 52:7*

where is the g. way, and walk therein *Jer 6:16*

we looked for peace, no g. came *Jer 8:15; 14:19*

he shall not see when g. cometh *Jer 17:6*

if it do evil, I will repent of the g. *Jer 18:10*

I stood before thee to speak g. for them *Jer 18:20*

g. figs; very g.; like g. figs, so will I *Jer 24:21; 24:3, 5*

I will perform my g. word toward you *Jer 29:10*

neither shall he behold the g. *Jer 29:32*

I will do I will bring all the g. I have promised *Jer 32:42*

which shall hear all the g. that I do them *Jer 33:9*

I took them away as I saw g. *Eze 16:50*

planted in a g. soil by great waters *Eze 17:8*

gather every g. piece, thigh, and shoulder *Eze 24:4*

I thought it g. to shew the signs *Da 4:2*

Lord answered the angel with g. words *Zec 1:13*

in these days I thought to do g. (S) *Zec 8:15*

receiveth it with g. will at your hand *Mal 2:13*

Joseph was a g. man (P) *M't 1:19*

announcing the g. news (B) (A)(B)(E)(R) *M't 4:23*

sends rain on the g. *M't 5:45*

know how to give g. gifts *M't 7:11; Lu 11:13*

every g. tree bringeth forth g. fruit *M't 7:17*

daughter, be of g. comfort *M't 9:22; Lu 8:48*

poor are hearing g. news (N) *M't 11:5*

it is lawful to do g. on the sabbath (S) *M't 12:12*

fell in g. ground *M't 13:8; 13:23; M'k 4:8, 20; Lu 8:8, 15*

g. seed; g. Master, what g. thing *M't 13:24; 19:16*

wicked from the g. (N)(P) *M't 13:49*

why calledst thou me g.? *M't 19:17*

none g. but one is thine eye evil because I am *M't 20:15*

well done, thou g. and faithful servant *M't 25:21*

been g. for that man had not been born *M't 26:24*

that g. man (P) *M't 27:19*

this g. man's blood (B) *M't 27:24*

believe the g. news (B)(P) *M'k 1:15*

spread the g. news (N) *M'k 5:20*

a g. and holy man (N) *M'k 6:20*

proclaim the g. news (N)(P) *M'k 16:15*

to the wisdom of g. men (P) *Lu 1:17*

g. news (N) *Lu 1:19; 2:10; 8:1; Ro 10:15; 1Th 3:6*

g. news (P) *Lu 1:19; 8:1; Ac 13:32*

peace on earth, g. will towards men *Lu 2:14*

announce the g. news (N) *Lu 4:18*

g. measure, pressed down, shaken together *Lu 6:38*

and Mary hath chosen that g. part *Lu 10:42*

eat, drink, have a g. time (P) *Lu 12:19*

it is your Father's g. pleasure to give you *Lu 12:32*

but thou hast kept the g. wine until now *Joh 2:10*

that have done g. to the resurrection *Joh 5:29*

I am the g. Shepherd, the g. Shepherd giveth *Joh 10:11*

men of g. reputation (B)(N)(P) *Ac 6:3*

men of g. report (E) *Ac 6:3*

men of g. repute (R) *Ac 6:3*

who went about doing g. and healing *Ac 10:38*

in that he did g. and gave us rain *Ac 14:17*

ye know how that a g. while ago *Ac 15:7*

to bring g. news (N)(P) *Ac 16:10*

to attest the g. news (A) *Ac 20:24*

honour to every man that worketh g. *Ro 2:10*

commandment is holy, and just, and g. *Ro 7:12*

who publish g. news (B)(N) *Ro 10:15*

bring glad tidings of g. things (E)(P) *Ro 10:15*

what is that g. and perfect will of God *Ro 12:2*

g., innocent, guileless (A) *Ro 16:19*

what g. is my fighting (B)(P) *1Co 15:32*

evil communications corrupt g. man *1Co 15:33*

affect you, but not g. (S) *Ga 4:17*

g., beneficial to spiritual progress (A) *Eph 4:29*

not g. children to resentment (N) *Eph 6:4*

we thought it g. to be left at Athens *1Th 3:1*

that ye have g. remembrance of us *1Th 3:6*

the g. message (B) *1Th 3:6*

rich in g. deeds, liberal, generous (R) *1Ti 6:18*

despisers of those that are g. *2Ti 3:3*

a bishop must be a lover of g. men *Tit 1:8*

that have tasted the g. word of God *Heb 6:5*

spirits of g. men (N)(P) *Heb 12:23*

every g. gift; sit in a g. place *Jas 1:17*

show by his g. life (E) *Jas 3:13*

be subject not only to the g. *1Pe 2:18*

and gentle he that will love life, and see g. days *1Pe 3:10*

Lot, who was a g. man (N) *2Pe 2:7*

who hath this world's g. and shutteth up *1Jo 3:17*

AS GOOD

sprang of one, and him as g. as dead *Heb 11:12*

FOR GOOD

to fear the Lord for our g. always *De 6:24*

which I command thee this day for thy g. *De 10:13*

the Lord will again rejoice over thee for g. *De 30:9*

hand of our God on all of them for g. *Ezr 8:22*

think upon me, O my God, for g. *Ne 5:19; 13:31*

hear it, and know thou it for thy g. *Job 5:27*

shew me a token for g. they may see *Ps 86:17*

be surety for thy servant for g. *Ps 119:122*

pray not for this people for their g. *Jer 14:11*

whom I sent out of this place for their g. *Jer 24:5*

for I will set mine eyes on them for g. *Jer 24:6*

may fear me for fear, for the g. of them *Jer 32:39*

Maroth waited carefully for g. *Mic 1:12*

we know all things work together for g. *Ro 8:28*

he is the minister of God to thee for g. *Ro 13:4*

let every one please his neighbour for g. *Ro 15:2*

IS GOOD

and the gold of that land is g. *Ge 2:12*

the thing which thou hast spoken is g. *De 1:14*

do that which is g. in the sight of the Lord *De 6:18*

coming in with me in the host is g. *1Sa 29:6*

and Shimei said, The saying is g. *1Ki 2:38*

the word that I have heard is g. *1Ki 2:42*

and speak that which *is g.*   *1Ki 22:13*
I have done that which *is g.*   *2Ki 20:3;*
    Isa 38:3
the Lord *is g.*   *1Ch 16:34;*
    2Ch 5:13;   7:3;   Ezr 3:11;   Ps 100:5;
    106:1;   107:1;   118:1,   29;   135:3;   136:1;
    145:9;   Jer 33:11;   La 3:25;   Na 1:7
Lord do that which *is g.* in   *1Ch 19:13*
his sight
know among ourselves what *is*   *Job 34:4*
g.
taste and see that the Lord *is*   *Ps 34:8*
g.
hear me, for thy   *Ps 69:16*
loving kindness *is g.*
truly God *is g.* to Israel, to   *Ps 73:1*
such as are
the Lord shall give that which   *Ps 85:12*
is g.
because thy mercy *is g.*   *Ps 109:21*
deliver me
thy Spirit *is g.* lead me into   *Ps 143:10*
the land
desire of the righteous *is* only   *Pr 11:23*
so *is g.* news from a far   *Pr 25:25*
country
she perceiveth her   *Pr 31:18*
merchandise *is g.*
a man that *is g.* in his sight,   *Ec 2:26*
may give to him that *is g.*
who knoweth what *is g.* for   *Ec 6:12*
man in life
wisdom *is g.* with an   *Ec 7:11*
inheritance
as *is* the *g.* so is the sinner   *Ec 9:2*
eat ye that which *is g.* let your   *Isa 55:2*
soul
this girdle which *is g.* for   *Jer 13:10*
nothing
because the shadow thereof *is*   *Ho 4:13*
g.
he hath shewed thee, O man,   *Mic 6:8*
what *is g.*
ye say, Every one that doeth   *Mal 2:17*
evil *is g.*
salt *is g.* but if the salt   *M'k 9:50;*
    Lu 14:34
bringeth forth that which *is g.*   *Lu 6:45*
none *is g.* save one, that is   *Lu 18:19*
God
was then that which *is g.* made   *Ro 7:13*
death
but how to perform that *is g.* I   *Ro 7:18*
find not
abhor evil, cleave to that   *Ro 12:9*
which *is g.*
I would have you wise to that   *Ro 16:19*
which *is g.*
that this *is g.* for the present   *1Co 7:26*
no communication but that *is*   *Eph 4:29*
g.
follow that which *is g.*   *1Th 5:15; 3Jo 11*
prove all things, hold fast that   *1Th 5:21*
which *is g.*
but we know that the law *is g.*   *1Ti 1:8*
this *is g.* and acceptable in sight   *1Ti 2:3*
of God
for every creature of God *is g.*   *1Ti 4:4*
for that *is g.* and acceptable   *1Ti 5:4*
before God
if ye be followers of that   *1Pe 3:13*
which *is g.*

IT IS GOOD

I will wait on thy name, for *it*   *Ps 52:9;*
is g.   *54:6*
it is g. for me to draw near to   *Ps 73:28*
God
it is a *g.* thing to give thanks   *Ps 92:1*
unto the Lord
it is g. for me that I have   *Ps 119:71*
been afflicted
it is g. to sing praises unto our   *Ps 147:1*
God
my son, eat thou honey,   *Pr 24:13*
because *it is g.*
it is g. and comely for one to   *Ec 5:18*
eat and drink
it is g. that thou shouldest take   *Ec 7:18*
hold
it is g. that a man should both   *La 3:26*
hope
it is g. that a man bear the yoke   *La 3:27*
in his youth
it is g. for nothing but to be   *M't 5:13*
cast out
it is g. for us to be here   *M't 17:4;*
    M'k 9:5; Lu 9:33

I consent unto the law, that *it*   *Ro 7:16*
is g.
it is g. neither to eat flesh nor   *Ro 14:21*
drink wine
it is g. for man not to touch   *1Co 7:1*
woman
I say, *it is g.* for a man so   *1Co 7:26*
to be
it is g. to be zealously affected   *Ga 4:18*

NOT GOOD

not g. that man should be   *Ge 2:18*
alone
the counsel is *not g.* at this   *2Sa 17:7*
time
setteth himself in a way that is   *Ps 36:4*
not g.
leadeth him into way that is   *Pr 16:29*
not g.
also to punish the just is *not g.*   *Pr 17:26*
is *not g.* to accept person of   *Pr 18:5*
wicked
that soul be without knowledge   *Pr 19:2*
is *not g.*
and a false balance is *not g.*   *Pr 20:23*
not g. to have respect of   *Pr 24:23;*
persons   *28:21*
it is *not g.* to eat much honey   *Pr 25:27*
which walketh in a way that is   *Isa 65:2*
not g.
did that which is *not g.*   *Eze 18:18*
among
I gave them statutes that   *Eze 20:25*
were *not g.*
remember your doings that   *Eze 36:31*
were *not g.*
if case be so, it is *not g.* to   *M't 19:10*
marry
Paul thought *not g.* to take   *Ac 15:38*
him with
your glorying is *not g.* know ye   *1Co 5:6*
not

SEEM, SEEMED, SEEMETH GOOD

as it *seemeth g.* to thee to do   *Jos 9:25;*
unto us   *J'g 10:15;   1Sa 14:36,   40;*
    Ezr 7:18;   Es 3:11;   Jer 26:14;   40:4
do to them what *seemeth g.*   *J'g 19:24*
unto you
do what *seemeth g.*   *1Sa 1:23;*
    3:18; 11:10; 24:4
Abner spake all *seemed g.* to   *2Sa 3:19*
Israel
the Lord do that *seemeth*   *2Sa 10:12;*
him *g.*   *15:26*
do to Chimham what shall   *2Sa 19:37;*
seem g.   *19:38*
take and offer up what   *2Sa 24:22*
seemeth g. unto him
if it *seem g.* to thee   *1Ki 21:2; Jer 40:4*
if it *seem g.* to you, let us   *1Ch 13:2*
send
if it *seem g.* to the king   *Ezr 5:17; Es 5:4*
as *seemed g.* to the potter to   *Jer 18:4*
make it
so it *seemed g.* in sight   *M't 11:26;*
    Lu 10:21
seemed g. to me, having perfect   *Lu 1:3*
understanding
seemed g. unto us, being   *Ac 15:25*
assembled
it *seemed g.* to the Holy   *Ac 15:28*
Ghost and to us

WAS GOOD

God saw that it *was g.*   *Ge 1:4;*
    1:10, 12, 18, 21, 25
God saw everything, it *was*   *Ge 1:31*
very *g.*
woman saw that the tree *was g.*   *Ge 3:6*
for food
the baker saw the   *Ge 40:16*
interpretation *was g.*
thing *was g.* in eyes of   *Ge 41:37*
Pharaoh
Issachar saw that rest *was g.*   *Ge 49:15*
and the land
Saul and people spared all   *1Sa 15:9*
that *was g.*
Asa did that which *was g.*   *2Ch 14:2*
and right
Hezekiah wrought that   *2Ch 31:20*
which *was g.*
the hand of my God which *was*   *Ne 2:18*
g.

till I might see what *was* that *g.*   *Ec 2:3*
for sons

GOOD HEED

take ye *g. heed*   *De 2:4; 4:15; Jos 23:11*
preacher gave *g. heed,* and   *Ec 12:9*
sought out

GOOD LAND

come to bring them to *g. land*   *Ex 3:8;*
    De 8:7
the land we searched is a *g.*   *Nu 14:7*
land
it is a *g. land* which the Lord   *De 1:25*
doth
none of that generation see   *De 1:35*
that *g. land*
let me go over, and see the *g.*   *De 3:25*
land
Lord sware I should not go   *De 4:21*
unto that *g. land*
ye shall go over and possess   *De 4:22*
that *g. land*
mayest go in and possess the *g.*   *De 6:18*
land
Lord thy God bringeth thee into   *De 8:7*
g. land
bless the Lord thy God for   *De 8:10*
g. land
giveth not *g. land* for thy   *De 9:6*
righteousness
lest ye perish from off *g. land*   *De 11:17*
Lord giveth
until ye perish from this *g.*   *Jos 23:13*
land
perish quickly from off the *g.*   *Jos 23:16*
land
we have seen *land,* and it is   *J'g 18:9*
very *g.*
shall root Israel out of *g.*   *1Ki 14:15*
land
mar every *g.* piece of *land*   *2Ki 3:19;*
    3:25
that ye may possess this *g.*   *1Ch 28:8*
land

GOOD with MAKE

the owner of pit shall *make* it   *Ex 21:34;*
g.   *22:14*
the owner shall not *make* it *g.*   *Ex 22:11;*
    22:13, 15
he that killeth a beast shall   *Le 24:18*
make it *g.*
hath spoken, shall he not   *Nu 23:19*
make it *g.*
make your ways and doings *g.*   *Jer 18:11*

GOOD MAN

king said, Ahimaaz is a *g.*   *2Sa 18:27*
man
steps of *g. man* ordered by the   *Ps 37:23*
Lord
a *g. man* sheweth favour and   *Ps 112:5*
lendeth
g. man is not at home, he is   *Pr 7:19*
gone
a *g. man* obtaineth favour of   *Pr 12:2*
the Lord
a *g. man* leaveth an   *Pr 13:22*
inheritance to
a *g. man* is satisfied from   *Pr 14:14;*
himself   *12:14*
g. man is perished out of the   *Mic 7:2*
earth
g. man out of good treasure   *M't 12:35;*
    Lu 6:45
they murmured against the *g.*   *M't 20:11*
man
if *g. man* of house had   *M't 24:43;*
known in what watch   *Lu 12:39*
Joseph was a *g. man,* and a   *Lu 23:50*
just
some said, He is a *g. man,*   *Joh 7:12*
other said, Nay
Barnabas was a *g. man* full of   *Ac 11:24*
Holy Ghost
a *g. man* some would even dare   *Ro 5:7*
to die

GOOD with THING

the *thing* that thou doest is   *Ex 18:17*
not *g.*
thou shalt rejoice in every *g.*   *De 26:11*
thing

there failed not aught of any   *Jos 21:45*
g. thing
this *thing* is not *g.* thou hast   *1Sa 26:16*
done
in him there is found some *g.*   *1Ki 14:13*
thing
Hazael took of every *g. thing*   *2Ki 8:9*
of Damascus
that seek Lord not want any *g.*   *Ps 34:10*
thing
because I follow the *thing* that   *Ps 38:20*
g. is
no *g. thing* will he withhold   *Ps 84:11*
from them
is a *g. thing* to give thanks   *Ps 92:1*
unto Lord
whoso findeth a wife, findeth   *Pr 18:22*
g. thing
I will perform *g. thing*   *Jer 33:14*
promised
Israel hath cast off the *thing*   *Ho 8:3*
that is *g.*
what *g. thing* shall I do to   *M't 19:16*
inherit life
can any *g. thing* come out of   *Joh 1:46*
Nazareth
that is in my flesh, dwelleth no   *Ro 7:18*
g. thing
good to be zealously affected   *Ga 4:18*
in a *g. thing*
working with his hands *thing*   *Eph 4:28*
which is *g.*
knowing that what *g. thing* any   *Eph 6:8*
man doeth
that *g. thing* committed unto   *2Ti 1:14*
thee, keep
by acknowledging every *g.*   *Ph'm 6*
thing in you
is a *g. thing* the heart be   *Heb 13:9*
established

GOOD *THINGS*

to give thee houses full of all *g.*   *De 6:11*
things
not one failed of all the *g.*   *Jos 23:14*
things
that as all *g. things* are come   *Jos 23:15*
upon you
in Judah there were *g. things*   *2Ch 12:12*
in Jehoshaphat there are *g.*   *2Ch 19:3*
things found
yet he filled their houses with   *Job 22:18*
g. things
who satisfieth thy mouth with   *Ps 103:5*
g. things
the upright shall have *g. things*   *Pr 28:10*
your sins have withholden *g.*   *Jer 5:25*
things
give *g. things* to them that ask   *M't 7:11*
him
how can ye being evil speak   *M't 12:34*
g. things
a good man bringeth forth *g.*   *M't 12:35*
things
hath filled hungry with *g.*   *Lu 1:53*
things
in lifetime receivedst thy *g.*   *Lu 16:25*
things
and bring glad tidings of *g.*   *Ro 10:15*
things
communicate unto him in all *g.*   *Ga 6:6*
things
aged women be teachers of *g.*   *Tit 2:3*
things
things are *g.* and profitable unto   *Tit 3:8*
men
Christ being an high priest of   *Heb 9:11*
g. things
law having shadow of *g.*   *Heb 10:1*
things to come

GOOD *TIDINGS*

thinking to have brought *g.*   *2Sa 4:10*
tidings
good man, and cometh with   *2Sa 18:27*
g. tidings
valiant man, and bringest *g.*   *1Ki 1:42*
tidings
this day is a day of *g. tidings*   *2Ki 7:9*
O Zion, that bringest *g. tidings*   *Isa 40:9*
will give Jerusalem one that   *Isa 41:27*
bringeth *g. tidings*
the feet of him that bringeth *g.*   *Isa 52:7*
tidings
he hath anointed me to preach   *Isa 61:1*
g. tidings
behold feet of him who   *Na 1:15*
bringeth *g. tidings*

I bring you *g. tidings* of great   *Lu 2:10*
joy
brought us *g. tidings* of your   *1Th 3:6*
faith

GOOD *UNDERSTANDING*

Abigail was a woman of *g.*   *1Sa 25:3*
understand.
g. understanding have all that   *Ps 111:10*
do his commandments
so shalt thou find favour and *g.*   *Pr 3:4*
understanding
g. understanding giveth favour   *Pr 13:15*

GOOD *WORK*

strengthen their hands for this   *Ne 2:18*
g. work
hath wrought a *g. work*   *M't 26:10;*
            M'k 14:6
for a *g. work* we stone thee   *Joh 10:33*
not
that ye may abound to every *g.*   *2Co 9:8*
work
that he which hath begun a *g.*   *Ph'p 1:6*
work
being fruitful in every *g. work*   *Col 1:10*
stablish you in every *g.* word   *2Th 2:17*
and *work*
office of a bishop, desireth a *g.*   *1Ti 3:1*
work
if she diligently followed every   *1Ti 5:10*
g. work
and prepared unto every *g.*   *2Ti 2:21*
work
and unto every *g. work*   *Tit 1:16*
reprobate
in mind to be ready to every *g.*   *Tit 3:1*
work
make you perfect in every *g.*   *Heb 13:21*
work

GOOD *WORKS*

his *works* to thee have been   *1Sa 19:4*
very *g.*
that they may see your *g.*   *M't 5:16*
works
many *g. works* have I shewed   *Joh 10:32*
you
Dorcas full of *g. works* and   *Ac 9:36*
almsdeeds
for rulers are not a terror to *g.*   *Ro 13:3*
works
created in Christ Jesus unto *g.*   *Eph 2:10*
works
that women be adorned with   *1Ti 2:10*
g. works
a widow well reported of for   *1Ti 5:10*
g. works
g. works of some are manifest   *1Ti 5:25*
beforehand
charge rich, that they be rich   *1Ti 6:18*
in *g. works*
thoroughly furnished to all *g.*   *2Ti 3:17*
works
shewing thyself a pattern in *g.*   *Tit 2:7*
works
a peculiar people, zealous of *g.*   *Tit 2:14*
works
they be careful to maintain *g.*   *Tit 3:8;*
works   *3:14*
to provoke unto love and *g.*   *Heb 10:24*
works
may be your *g. works* glorify   *1Pe 2:12*
God

GOOD-FOR-NOTHING

your maid a *g.* (B)   *1Sa 1:16*
g., ne'er-do-wells (B)   *2Ch 13:7*
g. servant (A)   *M't 25:30*

GOOD-LOOKING

intelligent and *g.* (B)   *1Sa 25:3*

GOOD-SIZED

four *g.* horns (B)   *Da 8:8*

GOODLIER

not in Israel a *g.* person than   *1Sa 9:2*
Saul

GOODLIEST

he will take your *g.* young men   *1Sa 8:16*
thy children, even the *g.* are   *1Ki 20:3*
mine

GOODLINESS

the *g.* thereof as the flower of   *Isa 40:6*
the field

GOODLY

g. things of master's (E)   *Ge 24:10*
Rebekah took *g.* raiment of   *Ge 27:15*
her son
Joseph was a *g.* person, and   *Ge 39:6*
well favoured
Naphtali a hind let loose,   *Ge 49:21*
giveth *g.* words
when she saw he was a *g.* child   *Ex 2:2*
they made *g.* bonnets of fine   *Ex 39:28*
linen
on first day boughs of the *g.*   *Le 23:40*
trees
how *g.* are thy tents, O Jacob   *Nu 24:5*
they burnt all their *g.* castles   *Nu 31:10*
with fire
let me see that *g.* mountain and   *De 3:25*
Lebanon
great and *g.* cities which thou   *De 6:10*
buildest not
lest when thou hast built *g.*   *De 8:12*
houses
I saw a *g.* Babylonish garment   *Jos 7:21*
Saul, a choice young man, and   *1Sa 9:2*
g.
David was ruddy and *g.* to   *1Sa 16:12*
look to
Benaiah slew an Egyptian, a   *2Sa 23:21*
g. man
Adonijah also was a very *g.*   *1Ki 1:6*
man
all manner of *g.* vessels (E)   *2Ch 32:27*
brought to Babylon the *g.*   *2Ch 36:10*
vessels
burnt palaces, and destroyed   *2Ch 36:19*
g. vessels
gavest *g.* wings to the   *Job 39:13*
peacocks
yea, I have a *g.* heritage   *Ps 16:6*
the boughs were like the *g.*   *Ps 80:10*
cedars
how shall I give thee a *g.*   *Jer 3:19*
heritage
green olive tree, fair and of   *Jer 11:16*
g. fruit
like a *g.* vessel (E)   *Jer 25:34*
was planted, that it might be a   *Eze 17:8*
g. vine
it shall bear fruit, and be a *g.*   *Eze 17:23*
cedar
they have made *g.* images   *Ho 10:1*
all *g.* vessels (E)   *Ho 13:15*
carried into your temples my *g.*   *Joe 3:5*
things
all *g.* furniture (E)   *Na 2:9*
hath made them as his *g.*   *Zec 10:3*
horse in battle
g. price that I was prized at   *Zec 11:13*
of them
a merchant man seeking *g.*   *M't 13:45*
pearls
how it was adorned with *g.*   *Lu 21:5*
stones
if there come a man in *g.*   *Jas 2:2*
apparel
all things dainty and *g.* are   *Re 18:14*
departed

GOODMAN

For the *g.* is not at home   *Pr 7:19*
against the *g.* of the house   *M't 20:11*
if *g.* of house had known   *M't 24:43;*
            Lu 12:39
say to *g.* of house   *M'k 14:14; Lu 22:11*

GOODNESS

Jethro rejoiced for all *g.* Lord   *Ex 18:9*
had done
I will make all my *g.* pass   *Ex 33:19*
before thee
the Lord God abundant in *g.*   *Ex 34:6*
and truth
that what *g.* the Lord shall do   *Nu 10:32*
to us
thou promisedst this *g.*   *2Sa 7:28;*
            1Ch 17:26
joyful for *g.* Lord had done   *1Ki 8:66;*
            2Ch 7:10
let thy saints rejoice in *g.*   *2Ch 6:41*
Hezekiah his *g.*   *2Ch 32:32*
Josiah and his *g.*   *2Ch 35:26*

and delighted themselves in thy *Ne 9:25*
g.
have not served thee in thy *Ne 9:35*
great g.
my g. extendeth not to thee *Ps 16:2*
for thou preventest him with *Ps 21:3*
blessings of g.
surely g. and mercy shall follow *Ps 23:6*
me
remember thou me, for thy g. *Ps 25:7*
sake
I had believed to see the g. of *Ps 27:13*
the Lord
O how great is thy g. thou *Ps 31:19*
hast laid up
the earth is full of the g. of the *Ps 33:5*
Lord
the g. of God endureth *Ps 52:1*
continually
we shall be satisfied with the g. *Ps 65:4*
of thy house
thou crownest the year with *Ps 65:11*
thy g.
thou hast prepared of thy g. *Ps 68:10*
for the poor
praise the Lord for his g. *Ps 107:8;*
107:15, 21, 31
filleth the hungry soul with g. *Ps 107:9*
my g. and my fortress, my *Ps 144:2*
high tower
they shall utter the memory of *Ps 145:7*
thy g.
most men will proclaim every *Pr 20:6*
one his g.
the great g. toward the house *Isa 63:7*
of Israel
I brought you to eat the g. *Jer 2:7*
thereof
they shall flow together to g. *Jer 31:12*
of the Lord
people shall be satisfied with *Jer 31:14*
my g.
they shall fear and tremble for *Jer 33:9*
all the g.
they shall fear the Lord and his *Ho 3:5*
g.
your g. is as a morning cloud *Ho 6:4*
and early dew
according to g. of his land they *Ho 10:1*
made images
for how great is his g. and his *Zec 9:17*
beauty
be all g. (N) *M't 5:48*
talking about g. (N) *Ac 24:25*
despisest riches of his g. not *Ro 2:4*
knowing g. of God leadeth
the g. and severity of God, *Ro 11:22*
toward the g. if thou continue
in his g.
I am persuaded that you are *Ro 15:14*
full of g.
g. and innocent (B)(N) *Ro 16:19*
the fruit of the Spirit is g. *Ga 5:22;*
Eph 5:9
fulfill all the good pleasures of *2Th 1:11*
his g.
your g. should (E)(R) *Ph'm 14*

GOODNESS'

remember thou me for thy g. *Ps 25:7*
sake

GOODS

Abram brought back all the g. *Ge 14:16*
recaptured all the loot (B) *Ge 14:16*
give me the persons, and take *Ge 14:21*
the g. to thyself
wilt thou destroy the g. (E) *Ge 18:23;*
18:24-25
the g. of his master were in *Ge 24:10*
his hand
all sorts of master's treasures *Ge 24:10*
(A)(B)
goodly things of his master's *Ge 24:10*
(E)
all sorts of choice gifts (R) *Ge 24:10*
Jacob carried away all his g. *Ge 31:18;*
46:6
all his gain (A) *Ge 31:18*
all moveable property (B) *Ge 31:18*
all his substance (E) *Ge 31:18*
my g. (A)(B) *Ge 31:37*
my g. (R) *Ge 31:37; 45:20; Ex 22:7*
regard not your g. (A) *Ge 45:20;*
Ex 22:7
not put hand to his *Ex 22:8;*
neighbor's g. *22:11*

the earth swallowed them and *Nu 16:32*
their g.
Israel took the spoil of Midian *Nu 31:9*
and their g.
the suburbs shall be for *Nu 35:3*
Levites' cattle and g.
Lord shall make thee *De 28:11*
plenteous in g.
make you have a surplus of *De 28:11*
prosperity (A)
an abundance of good things *De 28:11*
(B)
make thee plenteous in goods *De 28:11*
(E)
make you abound in *De 28:11*
prosperity (R)
the Lord will smite thy *2Ch 21:14*
wives, thy g.
let the men of his place help *Ezr 1:4*
him with g.
all about them strengthened *Ezr 1:6*
their hands with g.
that of king's g. expenses be *Ezr 6:8*
given to these men
to banishment or to *Ezr 7:26*
confiscation of g.
all our g. (B)(R) *Ezr 8:21;*
Pr 1:13; 6:31; Ob 13
they possessed houses full of *Ne 9:25*
all g.
houses filled with good things *Ne 9:25*
(A)(B)(E)(R)
and his hands shall restore *Job 20:10*
their g.
therefore shall no man look *Job 20:21*
for his g.
his g. shall flow away in the *Job 20:28*
day of his wrath
snatches away his g. (A) *Ps 35:10*
when g. increase, they are *Ec 5:11*
increased
which have gotten cattle and *Eze 38:12*
g.
art thou come to take away *Eze 38:13*
cattle and g.
plunder, spoil, g. (A)(R) *Da 11:24*
their g. shall become a booty *Zep 1:13*
enter strong man's house, *M't 12:29;*
and spoil g. *M'k 3:27*
rob his belongings (B) *M't 12:29*
steal his property (P) *M't 12:29*
he shall make him ruler over *M't 24:47*
all his g.
over all his possessions *M't 24:47*
(A)(R)
in charge of all his property *M't 24:47*
(B)(N)(P)
over all that he hath (E) *M't 24:47*
who called and delivered to *M't 25:14*
them his g.
entrusted them with his *M't 25:14*
property (A)(P)(R)
committed to them his *M't 25:14*
belongings (B)
put his capital in their hands *M't 25:14*
(N)
of him that taketh away thy g. *Lu 6:30*
ask not
your belongings (B) *Lu 6:30*
what belongs to you (P) *Lu 6:30*
keepeth his palace, his g. are *Lu 11:21*
in peace
his belongs (A)(B) *Lu 11:21*
his possessions are safe (N) *Lu 11:21*
his property is in peace (P) *Lu 11:21*
there will I bestow all my *Lu 12:18*
fruits and my g.
store my g. *Lu 12:18*
(A)(E)(N)(P)(R)
thou hast much g. laid up for *Lu 12:19*
many years
give me the portion of g. that *Lu 15:12*
falleth to me
share of property *Lu 15:12*
(A)(B)(N)(P)(R)
portion of substance (E) *Lu 15:12*
was accused to him that he *Lu 16:1*
wasted his g.
squandering his possessions *Lu 16:1*
(A)
wasting his belongings (B) *Lu 16:1*
squandering his property (N) *Lu 16:1*
the half of my g. I give to the *Lu 19:8*
poor
half of my belongings (B) *Lu 19:8*
half my possessions to the poor *Lu 19:8*
(N)(P)
sold their g. and parted them *Ac 2:45*
to all men

sold possessions and property *Ac 2:45*
(A)(B)
tho' I bestow all my g. to feed *1Co 13:3*
the poor
dole out all I have *1Co 13:3*
(A)(N)(R)
give all my belongings (B) *1Co 13:3*
dispose of all I possess (P) *1Co 13:3*
ye took joyfully the spoiling *Heb 10:34*
of your g.
plundering of your *Heb 10:34*
belongings (A)
plundering your property *Heb 10:34*
(B)(R)
seizure of your possessions *Heb 10:34*
(N)
I am rich, and increased with *Re 3:17*
g.
I have prospered and grown *Re 3:17*
wealthy (A)(B)
I have everything I want in *Re 3:17*
world (N)
I am rich, I have prospered *Re 3:17*
(P)(R)

GOPHER

Make thee an ark of g. wood *Ge 6:14*
ark of resinous wood (B) *Ge 6:14*

GORE

If an ox g. a man or a woman *Ex 21:28*
ox g. people in time past *Ex 21:29*
(E)(R)

GORED

Whether he have g. a son *Ex 21:31*
or have g. a daughter *Ex 21:31*

GORGE

about to g. himself (B) *Job 20:23*

GORGEOUS

arrayed him in a g. robe, and *Lu 23:11*
sent
put a bright robe upon him *Lu 23:11*
(B)

GORGEOUSLY

and rulers clothed most g. *Eze 23:12*
they which are g. apparelled *Lu 7:25*
wear fine apparel (A)(P) *Lu 7:25*
stylishly dressed (B) *Lu 7:25*
for grand clothes (N) *Lu 7:25*

GORING

ox g. people (B) *Ex 21:29*

GOSHEN

dwell in the land of G. and *Ge 45:10;*
thou *46:28-29, 34; 47:1, 4, 6, 27; 50:8*
sever in that day the land of G. *Ex 8:22*
Only in the land of G. where *Ex 9:26*
and all the country of G. even *Jos 10:41*
and all the land of G. and the *Jos 11:16*
and G. and Holon, and Giloh *Jos 15:51*

GOSPEL

preaching the g. of the *M't 4:23;*
kingdom *9:35; M'k 1:14*
have the g. preached to them *M't 11:5*
this g. of the kingdom shall *M't 24:14*
be
Wheresoever this g. shall be *M't 26:13*
beginning of the g. of Jesus *M'k 1:1*
Christ
repent ye, and believe the g. *M'k 1:15*
believe the good news (B)(P) *M'k 1:15*
the g. must first be published *M'k 13:10*
this g. shall be preached *M'k 14:9*
throughout
preach the g. to every *M'k 16:15*
creature
to preach the g. to the poor *Lu 4:18*
to the poor the g. is preached *Lu 7:22*
preaching the g. and healing *Lu 9:6*
in the temple, and preached the *Lu 20:1*
g.
preached the g. in many *Ac 8:25*
villages
And there they preached the g. *Ac 14:7*
And when they had preached *Ac 14:21*
the g.

should hear the word of the g. *Ac 15:7*
to preach the g. unto them *Ac 16:10*
testify the g. of the grace of *Ac 20:24*
God
separated unto the g. of God *Ro 1:1*
my spirit in the g. of his Son *Ro 1:9*
to preach the g. to you that are *Ro 1:15*
For I am not ashamed of the *Ro 1:16*
g.
by Jesus Christ according to *Ro 2:16*
my g.
them that preach the g. of *Ro 10:15*
peace
they have not all obeyed the *Ro 10:16*
g.
As concerning the g. they are *Ro 11:28*
ministering the g. of God *Ro 15:16*
have fully preached the g. of *Ro 15:19*
Christ
have I strived to preach the g. *Ro 15:20*
of the blessing of the g. of *Ro 15:29*
Christ
stablish you according to my *Ro 16:25*
g.
but I preach the g.: not with *1Co 1:17*
the folly of the g. (N)(P)(R) *1Co 1:21*
simplemindedness of the g. *1Co 1:21*
message (P)
the g. I proclaimed (N) *1Co 2:4*
have begotten you through *1Co 4:15*
the g.
we should hinder the g. of *1Co 9:12*
Christ
that they which preach the g. *1Co 9:14*
should live of the g. *1Co 9:14*
For though I preach the g. I *1Co 9:16*
have
is unto me, if I preach not the *1Co 9:16*
g.
a dispensation of the g. is *1Co 9:17*
that, when I preach the g. I *1Co 9:18*
may
I may make the g. of Christ *1Co 9:18*
of no
that I abuse not my power in *1Co 9:18*
the g.
the g. which I preached unto *1Co 15:1*
you
to preach Christ's g. and a *2Co 2:12*
door
But if our g. be hid, it is hid to *2Co 4:3*
them
lest the light of the glorious g. *2Co 4:4*
whose praise is in the g. *2Co 8:18*
subjection unto the g. of *2Co 9:13*
Christ
in preaching the g. of Christ *2Co 10:14*
To preach the g. in the *2Co 10:16*
regions
or another g. which ye have *2Co 11:4*
not
have preached to you the g. of *2Co 11:7*
God
grace of Christ unto another g. *Ga 1:6*
and would pervert the g. of *Ga 1:7*
Christ
preach any other g. unto you *Ga 1:8*
than
if any man preach any other g. *Ga 1:9*
that the g. which was preached *Ga 1:11*
communicated unto them that *Ga 2:2*
g.
the truth of the g. might *Ga 2:5*
continue
the g. of the uncircumcision was *Ga 2:7*
as the g. of the circumcision *Ga 2:7*
was
according to the truth of the g. *Ga 2:14*
before the g. unto Abraham *Ga 3:8*
I preached the g. unto you *Ga 4:13*
of truth the g. of your *Eph 1:13*
salvation
promise in Christ by the g. *Eph 3:6*
the preparation of the g. of *Eph 6:15*
peace
make known the mystery of *Eph 6:19*
the g.
For your fellowship in the g. *Ph'p 1:5*
and confirmation of the g. ye *Ph'p 1:7*
unto the furtherance of the g. *Ph'p 1:12*
I am set for the defence of *Ph'p 1:17*
the g.
be as it becometh the g. of *Ph'p 1:27*
Christ
together for the faith of the *Ph'p 1:27*
g.
he hath served with me in the *Ph'p 2:22*
g.

which laboured with me in the *Ph'p 4:3*
g.
that in the beginning of the g. *Ph'p 4:15*
in the word of the truth of the *Col 1:5*
g.
away from the hope of the g. *Col 1:23*
For our g. came not unto you *1Th 1:5*
to speak unto you the g. of *1Th 2:2*
God
to be put in trust with the g. *1Th 2:4*
not the g. of God only, but also *1Th 2:8*
we preached unto you the g. of *1Th 2:9*
God
heralded God's g. (B) *1Th 2:9*
fellowlabourer in the g. of *1Th 3:2*
Christ
and that obey not the g. of our *2Th 1:8*
he called you by our g. to the *2Th 2:14*
According to the glorious g. of *1Ti 1:11*
partaker of the afflictions of the *2Ti 1:8*
g.
immortality to light through *2Ti 1:10*
the g.
from the dead according to my *2Ti 2:8*
g.
unto me in the bonds of the g. *Ph'm 13*
For unto us was the g. *Heb 4:2*
preached
by them that have preached *1Pe 1:12*
the g.
by the g. is preached unto you *1Pe 1:25*
was the g. preached also to *1Pe 4:6*
them
them that obey not the g. of *1Pe 4:17*
God
the everlasting g. to preach *Re 14:6*

GOSPEL'S

his life for my sake and the g. *M'k 8:35*
or lands, for my sake, and *M'k 10:29*
the g.
And this I do for the g. sake *1Co 9:23*

GOSSIP

g. about those wounded *Ps 69:28*
(A)(B)
talk and g. of (A)(B)(R) *Eze 36:3*

GOSSIPERS

not g. (A) *1Ti 3:11*

GOSSIPING

every neighbor goes about g. *Jer 9:4*
(B)

GOSSIPS

gossips (B) *Ro 1:30*

GOT

which he had g. in the land *Ge 36:6*
her hand, and fled, and g. him *Ge 39:12*
out
with me, and fled, and g. him *Ge 39:15*
out
they g. not the land in *Ps 44:3*
possession
I g. me servants and maidens *Ec 2:7*
So I g. a girdle according to *Jer 13:2*
Take the girdle that thou hast *Jer 13:4*
g.

GOTTEN

I have g. a man from the Lord *Ge 4:1*
souls that they had g. in Haran *Ge 12:5*
our father's hath he g. all this *Ge 31:1*
glory
all his goods which he had g. *Ge 31:18*
of his getting, which he had g. *Ge 31:18*
their goods, which they had g. *Ge 46:6*
when I have g. me honour *Ex 14:18*
upon
thing which he hath deceitfully *Le 6:4*
g.
what every man hath g. of *Nu 31:50*
mine hand hath g. me this *De 8:17*
Moreover, if he be g. into a *2Sa 17:13*
city
It cannot be g. for gold *Job 28:15*
because mine hand hath g. *Job 31:25*
much
arm, hath g. him the victory *Ps 98:1*
Wealth g. by vanity shall be *Pr 13:11*
inheritance may be g. hastily *Pr 20:21*

and have g. more wisdom than *Ec 1:16*
the abundance they have g. *Isa 15:7*
riches that he hath g. are *Jer 48:36*
perished
thou hast g. thee riches *Eze 28:4*
and hast g. gold and silver *Eze 28:4*
which have g. cattle and *Eze 38:12*
goods
and hast g. thee renown, as at *Da 9:15*
after we were g. from them *Ac 21:1*
them that had g. the victory *Re 15:2*

GOURD

And the Lord God prepared a *Jon 4:6*
g.
Jonah was exceeding glad of *Jon 4:6*
the g.
it smote the g. that it withered *Joh 4:7*
thou well to be angry for the g. *Jon 4:9*
Thou hast had pity on the g. *Jon 4:10*

GOURDS

gathered thereof wild g. his *2Ki 4:39*
lap
figures of g. (R) *2Ch 4:3*

GOVERN

Dost thou now g. the kingdom *1Ki 21:7*
exercise kingship over Israel *1Ki 21:7*
(B)
to g. wisely (B) *2Ch 1:11*
to g. all the people (B) *2Ch 7:25*
Shall even he that hateth *Job 34:17*
right g.
and g. the nations upon earth *Ps 67:4*
guide nations on earth *Ps 67:4*
(A)(B)(R)
also g. my house (B) *Zec 13:7*

GOVERNED

g. by selfish ambition (N) *Ro 2:8*

GOVERNMENT

the g. shall be upon his shoulder *Isa 9:6*
Of the increase of his g. and *Isa 9:7*
peace
and I will commit thy g. into *Isa 22:21*
his
commit your authority to *Isa 22:21*
(A)(B)(R)
all g. and authority (B)(N) *Eph 1:21*
of uncleanness, and despise g. *2Pe 2:10*
revile dignitaries (A) *2Pe 2:10*
despise authority *2Pe 2:10*
(B)(N)(P)(R)
despise dominion (E) *2Pe 2:10*

GOVERNMENTS

helps, g., diversities of *1Co 12:28*
tongues
administrators (A)(R) *1Co 12:28*
administrating (B) *1Co 12:28*
power to guide them (N) *1Co 12:28*
organizers (P) *1Co 12:28*
g. and authorities (N) *Tit 3:1*

GOVERNOR

Joseph was the g. over the land *Ge 42:6*
he is g. over all the land *Ge 45:26*
Obadiah, which was g. of the *1Ki 18:3*
steward of his house (B) *1Ki 18:3*
was over the household *1Ki 18:3*
(E)(R)
Amon the g. of the city, and *1Ki 22:26*
gate of Joshua the g. of the *2Ki 23:8*
city
Ahikam the g. (S) *2Ki 25:22*
of Babylon had made *2Ki 25:23*
Gedaliah g.
unto the Lord to be the chief *1Ch 29:22*
g.
anointed him as ruler (B) *1Ch 29:22*
anointed him to be prince *1Ch 29:22*
(E)(R)
every g. in all Israel, the chief *2Ch 1:2*
back to Amon the g. of the *2Ch 18:25*
city
and Azrikam the g. of the *2Ch 28:7*
house
Maaseiah the g. of the city, *2Ch 34:8*
Rehum the g. (B) *Ezr 4:8; 4:17*
them Tatnai, g. on this side the *Ezr 5:3; 6:13*

that Tatnai, g. on this side the   *Ezr 5:6*
Sheshbazzar, whom he had   *Ezr 5:14*
made g.
Tatnai, g. beyond the river   *Ezr 6:6*
the g. of the Jews and the elders   *Ezr 6:7*
the throne of the g. on this side *Ne 3:7*
I was appointed to be their g.   *Ne 5:14*
I have not eaten the bread of   *Ne 5:14*
the g.
required not I the bread of the   *Ne 5:18*
g.
in the days of Nehemiah the   *Ne 12:26*
g.
the g. and rulers   *Es 8:9; 9:3*
he is the g. among the nations   *Ps 22:28*
ruler over the nations (A)(E)   *Ps 22:28*
rules over the nations (B)(R)   *Ps 22:28*
chief g. in the house of the   *Jer 20:1*
Lord
and their g. shall proceed   *Jer 30:21*
from
prince be one of themselves   *Jer 30:21*
(A)(B)(E)(R)
made g. over the cities of   *Jer 40:5*
Judah
has made Gedaliah g. in the   *Jer 40:7*
land
Babylon had made g. over the   *Jer 41:2*
land
of Babylon made g. in the   *Jer 41:18*
land
son of Shealtiel, g. of   *Hag 1:1;*
Judah   *1:14; 2:2, 21*
he shall be as a g. in Judah   *Zec 9:7*
he shall be as chieftain (A)(E)   *Zec 9:7*
he shall be as the clan-head (B)   *Zec 9:7*
it shall be like a clan in Judah   *Zec 9:7*
(R)
offer it now unto thy g.; will he   *Mal 1:8*
shall come a G. that shall rule   *M't 2:6*
leader shall arise (A)(B)(N)   *M't 2:6*
shall come a ruler (R)   *M't 2:6*
him to Pontius Pilate the g.   *M't 27:2*
And Jesus stood before the g.   *M't 27:11*
and the g. asked him, saying   *M't 27:11*
that the g. marvelled greatly   *M't 27:14*
the g. was wont to release   *M't 27:15*
unto
g. answered, and said unto   *M't 27:21*
them
And the g. said, Why, what   *M't 27:23*
evil
the soldiers of the g. took   *M't 27:27*
Jesus
when Cyrenius was g. of Syria   *Lu 2:2*
Pontius Pilate being g. of   *Lu 3:1*
Judaea
the power and authority of   *Lu 20:20*
the g.
And bear unto the g. of the   *Joh 2:8*
feast
carry to the table manager   *Joh 2:8*
(A)(B)
bear to the ruler of the feast   *Joh 2:8*
(E)
take it to the steward of the   *Joh 2:8*
feast (N)(R)
take to the master of   *Joh 2:8*
ceremonies (P)
the g. of the feast called the   *Joh 2:9*
and he made him g. over Egypt   *Ac 7:10*
bring him safe unto Felix the   *Ac 23:24*
g.
unto the most excellent g.   *Ac 23:26*
Felix
and delivered the epistle to   *Ac 23:33*
the g.
when the g. had read the   *Ac 23:34*
letter
who informed the g. against   *Ac 24:1*
Paul
after that the g. had beckoned   *Ac 24:10*
unto
the king rose up, and the g.   *Ac 26:30*
the g. under Aretas the king   *2Co 11:32*
kept
withersoever the g. listeth   *Jas 3:4*
the helmsman determines   *Jas 3:4*
(A)(B)(N)(P)
the steersman willeth (E)   *Jas 3:4*
the pilot directs (R)   *Jas 3:4*

GOVERNORS

My heart is toward the g. of   *J'g 5:9*
Israel
out of Machir came down g.   *J'g 5:14*
and of the g. of the country   *1Ki 10:15*
the g. of the sanctuary, and g.   *1Ch 24:5*
g. of the country brought gold   *2Ch 9:14*

and the g. of the people, and   *2Ch 23:20*
and to the g. on this side the   *Ezr 8:36*
river
given me to the g. beyond the   *Ne 2:7*
river
Then I came to the g. beyond   *Ne 2:9*
But the former g. that had   *Ne 5:15*
been
and to the g. that were over   *Es 3:12*
every
and chief of the g. over all the   *Da 2:48*
gather together the princes, the   *Da 3:2*
g.
Then the princes, the g. and   *Da 3:3*
And the princes, g. and   *Da 3:27*
captains
kingdom, the g. and the princes   *Da 6:7*
And the g. of Judah shall say   *Zec 12:5*
the chiefs of Judah   *Zec 12:5;*
(A)(B)(E)   *12:6*
the clans of Judah (R)   *Zec 12:5; 12:6*
day will I make the g. of   *Zec 12:6*
Judah
And ye shall be brought   *M't 10:18*
before a g.
But is under tutors and g. until   *Ga 4:2*
under guardians and   *Ga 4:2*
administrators (A)
under guardians and trustees   *Ga 4:2*
(B)(N)(P)(R)
under guardians and stewards   *Ga 4:2*
(E)
Or unto g. as unto them that   *1Pe 2:14*

GOVERNOR'S

And if this come to the g.   *M't 28:14*
ears
unto the G. headquarters   *Joh 18:28*
(N)

GOZAN

and in Habor by the river of   *2Ki 17:6;*
G.   *18:11*
my fathers have destroyed;   *2Ki 19:12;*
as G.   *Isa 37:12*
and Hora, and to the river G.   *1Ch 5:26*

GRABBER

no money g. (N)   *Tit 1:7*

GRABBERS

g. and swindlers (N)   *1Co 5:10; 6:10*

GRABBING

not fond of money g. (P)   *1Ti 3:3*

GRACE

cords of the g. (B)   *2Sa 22:6*
for a little space g. hath been   *Ezr 9:8*
shewed
Esther obtained g. in his sight   *Es 2:17*
felt more love for Esther (B)   *Es 2:17*
obtained favor and kindness   *Es 2:17*
(E)
g. is poured into lips, God hath   *Ps 45:2*
anointed
graciousness is poured upon   *Ps 45:2*
(A)(B)
the Lord is a sun, he will give   *Ps 84:11*
g. and glory
bestows mercy and honor (B)   *Ps 84:11*
bestows favor and honor (R)   *Ps 84:11*
terrors of the g. (B)   *Ps 116:3*
they shall be an ornament of g.   *Pr 1:9*
to head
so shall they be life and g. to   *Pr 3:22*
thy neck
but he giveth g. to the lowly   *Pr 3:34;*
  Jas 4:6
shall give to thine head an   *Pr 4:9*
ornament of g.
for the g. of his lips the king   *Pr 22:11*
be his friend
greed like the g. (B)   *Jon 2:5*
with shoutings, crying, G., g.   *Zec 4:7*
unto it
I will pour the Spirit of g.   *Zec 12:10*
and supplications
begotten of Father, full of g.   *Joh 1:14*
and truth
of his fulness we have all   *Joh 1:16*
received, g. for g.
but g. and truth came by Jesus   *Joh 1:17*
Christ
and great g. was on them all   *Ac 4:33*

which gave testimony to the   *Ac 14:3*
word of his g.
helped them which had   *Ac 18:27*
believed through g.
I commend you to the word   *Ac 20:32*
of his g.
by whom we received g. and   *Ro 1:5*
apostleship
undeserved gift of apostleship   *Ro 1:5*
(B)
g. and peace to you from God   *Ro 1:7;*
our Father   *1Co 1:3; 2Co 1:2; Ga 1:3;*
  Eph 1:2; Ph'p 1:2; Col 1:2; 1Th 1:1;
  2Th 1:2; Ph'm 3
being justified freely by his g.   *Ro 3:24*
through redemption
justified freely through his   *Ro 3:24*
mercy (B)
the reward is not reckoned of g.   *Ro 4:4*
but of debt
counted as a favor or a gift   *Ro 4:4*
(A)(P)(R)
not credited as a favor (B)(N)   *Ro 4:4*
it is of faith, that it might be   *Ro 4:16*
by g.
we have access into this g.   *Ro 5:2*
wherein we stand
much more they who receive   *Ro 5:17*
abundance of g.
where sin abounded g.   *Ro 5:20*
did much more abound
even so might g. reign through   *Ro 5:21*
righteousness
shall we continue in sin,   *Ro 6:1*
that g. may abound
under g.   *Ro 6:14*
shall we sin, because under g.   *Ro 6:15*
a remnant according to the   *Ro 11:5*
election of g.
agreement with his gracious   *Ro 11:5*
choice (B)
and if by g. then it is no more   *Ro 11:6*
of works
for I say, through the g. given   *Ro 12:3*
unto me
gifts differing according to the   *Ro 12:6*
g. given to us
because of the g. given to me   *Ro 15:15*
of God
Christian g. (A)   *1Co 1:7*
for if I by g. be a partaker,   *1Co 10:30*
why
his g. bestowed upon me was   *1Co 15:10*
not in vain
abundant g. might redound to   *2Co 4:15*
glory of God
so he would also finish in you   *2Co 8:6*
the same g. also
beneficent and gracious   *2Co 8:6*
contribution (A)
complete this gracious   *2Co 8:6*
arrangement (B)
work of generosity to   *2Co 8:6*
completion (N)(P)
complete this gracious work   *2Co 8:6*
(R)
see that ye abound in this g.   *2Co 8:7*
also
who was chosen to travel with   *2Co 8:19*
us with this g.
and God is able to make all g.   *2Co 9:8*
abound to you
he said, My g. is sufficient for   *2Co 12:9*
thee
removed from him who called   *Ga 1:6*
you to g.
when it pleased God, who   *Ga 1:15*
called me by his g.
when James perceived the g.   *Ga 2:9*
given to me
justified by the law, ye are   *Ga 5:4*
fallen from g.
to the praise of the glory of   *Eph 1:6*
his g.
forgiveness, according to the   *Eph 1:7*
riches of his g.
by g. ye are saved through   *Eph 2:5;*
faith   *2:8*
he might shew the exceeding   *Eph 2:7*
riches of his g.
to me the least of all saints is   *Eph 3:8*
this g. given
but unto every one of us is   *Eph 4:7*
given g.
that it may minister g. to the   *Eph 4:29*
hearers
g. be with all that love our   *Eph 6:24*
Lord Jesus
ye all are partakers of my g.   *Ph'p 1:7*

singing with *g.* in your hearts | Col 3:16
to the Lord
sung with a lovely feeling (B) | Col 3:16
sing thankfully in your hearts | Col 3:16
(N)
singing God's praises with | Col 3:16
joyful hearts (P)
sing with thankfulness in | Col 3:16
hearts (R)
let speech be alway with *g.* | Col 4:6
seasoned with salt
speech be gracious | Col 4:6
(A)(B)(N)(R)
Speak pleasantly to them (P) | Col 4:6
g. be with you | Col 4:18;
2Ti 4:22; Tit 3:15; Heb 13:25
hath given us good hope | 2Th 2:16
through *g.*
graciously given us eternal | 2Th 2:16
comfort (B)
g., mercy, and peace from God | 1Ti 1:2;
2Ti 1:2; Tit 1:4; 2Jo 3
g. of our Lord was exceeding | 1Ti 1:14
abundant
g. be with thee. Amen | 1Ti 6:21
who called us according to his | 2Ti 1:9
g.
be strong in the *g.* that is in | 2Ti 2:1
Christ Jesus
being justified by his *g.* we | Tit 3:7
should be heirs
let us come boldly to the | Heb 4:16
throne of *g.*
hath done despite to the | Heb 10:29
Spirit of *g.*
let us have *g.* to serve God | Heb 12:28
acceptably
Let us be grateful (B)(R) | Heb 12:28
Let us give thanks to God | Heb 12:28
(N)
it is good the heart be | Heb 13:9
established with *g.*
the *g.* of the fashion of it | Jas 1:11
perisheth
he giveth more *g.* giveth *g.* to | Jas 4:6
the humble
g. and peace be multiplied | 1Pe 1:2;
2Pe 1:2
who prophesied of the *g.* to | 1Pe 1:10
come to you
hope for the *g.* | 1Pe 1:13
as being heirs of *g.* | 1Pe 3:7
God resisteth the proud, giveth | 1Pe 5:5
g. to humble
the God of *g.* who hath called | 1Pe 5:10
us to glory
grow in *g.* and knowledge of | 2Pe 3:18
Jesus Christ
turning the *g.* of God into | Jude 4
lasciviousness
g. and peace from him which is | Re 1:4
and was

GRACE *OF GOD*

and the *g.* of God was upon | Lu 2:40
him
when he had seen *g.* of God, | Ac 11:23
was glad
persuaded them to continue in | Ac 13:43
the *g.* of God
had been recommended to *g.* | Ac 14:26;
of God | 15:40
to testify the gospel of the *g.* | Ac 20:24
of God
much more the *g.* of God hath | Ro 5:15
abounded
g. of God given you by Jesus | 1Co 1:4
Christ
according to *g.* of God which | 1Co 3:10
is given to me
by *g.* of God I am what I | 1Co 15:10
am, but the *g.* of God which
by the *g.* of God we had our | 2Co 1:12
conversation
that ye receive not the *g.* of | 2Co 6:1
God in vain
of the *g.* of God bestowed on | 2Co 8:1
the churches
for the exceeding *g.* of God in | 2Co 9:14
you
I do not frustrate the *g.* of | Ga 2:21
God
if have heard of dispensation | Eph 3:2
of *g.* of God
according to gift of *g.* of God | Eph 3:7
given me
since the day ye knew the *g.* of | Col 1:6
God

ye in him, according to *g.* of | 2Th 1:12
God
the *g.* of God that bringeth | Tit 2:11
salvation
that he by *g.* of God should | Heb 2:9
taste death
looking lest any man fail of | Heb 12:15
the *g.* of God
good stewards of the manifold | 1Pe 4:10
g. of God
testifying that this is the true | 1Pe 5:12
g. of God

GRACE *OF OUR LORD JESUS*

through *g.* of Lord Jesus we | Ac 15:11
shall be saved as
g. of our Lord Jesus Christ | Ro 16:20;
be with you 16:24; 1Co 16:23; Ph'p 4:23;
1Th 5:28; 2Th 3:18
for ye know the *g.* of our Lord | 2Co 8:9
Jesus Christ
g. of our Lord Jesus Christ, | 2Co 13:14
love of God, communion of
g. of our Lord Jesus Christ be | Ga 6:18
with spirit
g. of our Lord Jesus Christ be | Re 22:21
with you all

GRACEFUL

a *g.* doe (B)(R) | Pr 5:19

GRACEFULLY

behave ourselves *g.* (B) | Ro 13:13

GRACES

g. of healing (B) | 1Co 12:9
the choicest *g.* (B) | 1Co 12:31

GRACIOUS

and he said, God be *g.* to thee | Ge 43:29
my son
when he crieth, I will hear, | Ex 22:27
for I am *g.*
I will be *g.* to whom I will be | Ex 33:19
g.
the Lord, the Lord God, *g.,* | Ex 34:6;
2Ch 30:9; Ps 103:8; 116:5; 145:8;
Joe 2:13
the Lord make his face shine, | Nu 6:25
and be *g.*
who can tell whether God | 2Sa 12:22
will be *g.*
and the Lord was *g.* unto | 2Ki 13:23
them
a God ready to pardon, *g.,* | Ne 9:17;
merciful 9:31
then he is *g.* to him, and | Job 33:24
saith, Deliver
hath God forgotten to be *g.* | Ps 77:9
but thou, O Lord, art God, *g.* | Ps 86:15;
111:4; 112:4
merciful and *g.* (A)(E)(R) | Ps 86:15
a *g.* woman retaineth honour | Pr 11:16
the words of a wise man's | Ec 10:12
mouth are *g.*
the Lord will wait that he | Isa 30:18
may be *g.*
he will be very *g.* to thee; be | Isa 30:19;
g. to us 33:2
how *g.* when pangs come | Jer 22:23
upon thee
may be Lord will be *g.* to | Am 5:15
remnant
for I knew that thou art a *g.* | Jon 4:2
God
beseech God that he will be *g.* | Mal 1:9
to us
wondered at *g.* words which | Lu 4:22
proceeded
agreement with his *g.* choice | Ro 11:5
(B)
complete *g.* arrangement | 2Co 8:6
(B)(R)
speech be *g.* (A)(B)(N)(R) | Col 4:6
if ye have tasted that the Lord | 1Pe 2:3
is *g.*

GRACIOUSLY

children which God hath *g.* | Ge 33:5
me
because God hath dealt *g.* | Ge 33:11
with me
and grant me thy law *g.* | Ps 119:29

take away iniquity, receive us | Ho 14:2
g.
g. given us eternal comfort | 2Th 2:16
(B)

GRACIOUSNESS

g. is poured out (A)(B) | Ps 45:2

GRADUALLY

g. waters kept lowering (B) | Ge 8:5

GRAFF

God is able to *g.* them in | Ro 11:23
again

GRAFFED

wert *g.* in among them, and | Ro 11:17
broken off, that I might be *g.* | Ro 11:19
in
not still in unbelief, shall be | Ro 11:23
g. in
and wert *g.* contrary to nature | Ro 11:24
be *g.* into their own olive tree | Ro 11:24

GRAFT

shall be *g.* in again (S) | Ro 11:23

GRAFTED

were *g.* in (S) | Ro 11:17; 11:19, 23-24

GRAIN

grain (S) | Ge 27:28;
27:37; 41:5, 35, 49, 57; 42:1, 2, 3, 5, 19,
25, 26; 43:2; 44:2; 45:23; 47:14; Ex 22:6;
Le 2:14, 16; 23:14; Nu 18:27; De 7:13;
11:14; 12:17; 14:23; 16:9, 13; 18:4; 23:25;
25:4; 28:51; 33:28; Jos 5:11, 12; J'g 15:5;
Ru 2:2, 14; 3:7; 1Sa 17:17; 25:18;
2Sa 17:19, 28; 2Ki 4:42; 18:32; 19:26;
2Ch 31:5; 32:28; Ne 5:2, 3, 10, 11; 10:31
39; 13:5, 12; Job 5:26; 24:6, 24; Ps 4:7;
65:9, 13; 72:16; 78:24; Pr 11:26;
Isa 17:5; 21:10; 28:28; 36:17; 37:27;
La 2:12; Eze 36:29; Ho 2:8, 22; 7:14;
10:11; 14:7; Joe 1:10, 17; 2:19; Am 8:5;
9:9; Hag 1:11; Zec 9:17; M't 12:1;
M'k 2:23; 4:28; Lu 6:1; Joh 12:24;
Ac 7:12; 1Co 9:9; 1Ti 5:18
heads of full *g.* (B) | Ge 41:5
seven ears of *g.* (E)(R) | Ge 41:5
grain (A)(B)(E)(R) | Ge 41:57;
42:1-5, 19, 25-26; 43:2; 44:2; 45:23;
47:14; Ex 22:6; Le 2:14, 16; 23:14;
Nu 7:13; 18:12; 18:27; De 7:13; 11:14;
12:17; 14:23; 16:9, 13; 18:4; 23:25; 25:4;
28:51; 33:28; Jos 5:11; J'g 15:5; Ru 2:2,
14; 3:7; 1Sa 17:17; 25:18; 2Sa 17:19, 28;
2Ki 18:32; 2Ch 31:5; 32:28; Ne 5:2-3,
10-11; 10:39; 13:5, 12; Ps 4:7; 78:24;
Pr 11:26; Isa 17:5; 62:8; Eze 36:29;
Ho 2:8-9; 2:22; 7:14; 9:1; Joe 1:10;
2:19; Am 8:5; Hag 1:11; Zec 9:17;
Lu 5:1; 11:33; 12:18
yet shall not the least *g.* fall | Am 9:9
like to a *g.* of mustard seed, | M't 13:31
which
faith as a *g.* of mustard seed | M't 17:20;
Lu 17:6
It is like a *g.* of mustard seed | M'k 4:31;
Lu 13:19
body that shall be, but bare | 1Co 15:37
g.
of wheat, or of some other *g.* | 1Co 15:37

GRAINFIELD

into the *g.* (B) | De 23:25

GRAINFIELDS

through the *g.* (S) | M't 12:1

GRAINS

offerings of *g.* and vines (B) | Ex 22:29

GRANARIES

our *g.* filled (B)(R) | Ps 144:13;
Joe 1:17

GRANARY

store in his g.   *M't 3:12*
(B)(N)(P)(R)(S)

GRAND

for g. clothes (N)   *Lu 7:25*

GRANDCHILDREN

children or g.   *1Ti 5:4*
(A)(B)(E)(N)(P)(R)

GRANDEUR

g., exceeding greatness of   *2Co 4:7*
power (A)

GRANDMOTHER

which dwelt first in thy g. Lois   *2Ti 1:5*

GRANDMOTHER'S

avoid g. tales (A)   *1Ti 4:7*

GRANDSON

son nor g. (A)(E)   *Job 18:19*

GRANDSONS

thirty g. (B)(E)(R)(S)   *J'g 12:14*

GRANT

shall g. a redemption for the   *Le 25:24*
land
Lord g. you that ye may find   *Ru 1:9*
rest
God of Israel g. thee thy   *1Sa 1:17*
petition
G. me the place of this   *1Ch 21:22*
shalt g. it me for the full   *1Ch 21:22*
price
I will g. them some   *2Ch 12:7*
deliverance
according to the g. that they   *Ezr 3:7*
had
and g. him mercy in the sight   *Ne 1:11*
of
it please the king to g. my   *Es 5:8*
petition
and that God would g. me the   *Job 6:8*
thing
G. thee according to thine own   *Ps 20:4*
g. the king thy justice (B)(R)   *Ps 72:1*
O Lord, and g. us thy salvation   *Ps 85:7*
and g. me thy law graciously   *Ps 119:29*
G. not, O Lord, the desires of   *Ps 140:8*
G. that these my two sons   *M't 20:21*
may
G. unto us that we may sit,   *M'k 10:37*
one
That he would g. unto us, that   *Lu 1:74*
we
g. unto thy servants, that with   *Ac 4:29*
all
g. you to be likeminded one   *Ro 15:5*
toward
That he would g. you.   *Eph 3:16*
according to
Lord g. unto him that he may   *2Ti 1:18*
find
that overcometh will I g. to sit   *Re 3:21*

GRANTED

And God g. him that which   *1Ch 4:10*
he
and knowledge is g. unto thee   *2Ch 1:12*
and the king g. him all his   *Ezr 7:6*
request
And the king g. me, according   *Ne 2:8*
to
petition? and it shall be g. thee   *Es 5:6;*
   9:12
Esther? and it shall be g. thee   *Es 7:2*
the king g. the Jews which were   *Es 8:11*
in
let it be g. to the Jews which   *Es 9:13*
are in
Thou hast g. me life and   *Job 10:12*
favour
desire of the righteous shall   *Pr 10:24*
be g.
a murderer to be g. unto you   *Ac 3:14*
Gentiles g. repentance unto   *Ac 11:18*
life

g. signs and wonders to be   *Ac 14:3*
done
g. and accredited to us (A)(B)   *Ro 4:24*
to her was it g. that she should   *Re 19:8*

GRAPE

outflow of g. juice (A)   *Ex 22:29*
neither shalt thou gather every   *Le 19:10*
g.
drink the pure blood of the g.   *De 32:14*
He shall shake off his unripe   *Job 15:33*
g.
the vines with the tender g.   *Ca 2:13*
give
whether the tender g. appear   *Ca 7:12*
and the sour g. is ripening in   *Isa 18:5*
flower a ripening g.   *Isa 18:5*
(A)(B)(E)(R)
The fathers have eaten a sour   *Jer 31:29*
g.
every man that eateth the   *Jer 31:30*
sour g.

GRAPEGATHERER

turn back thine hand as a g.   *Jer 6:9*
into

GRAPEGATHERERS

If g. come to thee, would they   *Jer 49:9*
not
if the g. came to thee, would they   *Ob 5*

GRAPEGLEANINGS

as the g. of the vintage   *Mic 7:1*

GRAPES

thereof brought forth ripe g.   *Ge 40:10*
and I took the g. and pressed   *Ge 40:11*
them
and his clothes in the blood   *Ge 49:11*
of g.
neither gather the g. of thy vine   *Le 25:5*
nor gather the g. in it of thy   *Le 25:11*
vine
shall he drink any liquor of g.   *Nu 6:3*
nor eat moist g. or dried   *Nu 6:3*
was the time of the firstripe g.   *Nu 13:20*
a branch with one cluster of   *Nu 13:23*
g.
because of the cluster of g.   *Nu 13:24*
thou mayest eat g. thy fill at   *De 23:24*
thine
When thou gatherest the g. of   *De 24:21*
thy
shalt not gather the g.   *De 28:30*
thereof
nor gather the g. for the   *De 28:39*
worms
their g. are g. of gall, their   *De 32:32*
clusters
the gleaning of the g. of   *J'g 8:2*
Ephraim
and trode the g. and made   *J'g 9:27*
merry
also wine, g. and figs, and all   *Ne 13:15*
for our vines have tender g.   *Ca 2:15*
and thy breasts to clusters of g.   *Ca 7:7*
that it should bring forth g. and   *Isa 5:2*
it brought forth wild g.   *Isa 5:2*
looked that it should bring   *Isa 5:4*
forth g.
brought it forth wild g.   *Isa 5:4*
gleaning g. shall be left in it, as   *Isa 17:6*
the gleaning g. when the   *Isa 24:13*
vintage
there shall be no g. on the vine   *Jer 8:13*
as they that tread the g.   *Jer 25:30*
against
they not leave some gleaning g.   *Jer 49:9*
The fathers have eaten sour g.   *Eze 18:2*
Israel like g. in the wilderness   *Ho 9:10*
the treader of g. him that   *Am 9:13*
soweth
would they not leave some g.   *Ob 5*
Do men gather g. of thorns, or   *M't 7:16*
figs
of a bramble bush gather they   *Lu 6:44*
g.
the earth; for her g. are fully   *Re 14:18*
ripe

GRASP

g. God's secret (N)(P)   *Col 2:2*

GRASPING

an unscrupulous g. man (A)   *Pr 3:31*
g. self-indulgence (A)   *M't 23:25*
grasping (N)   *1Co 5:11*
the avaricious and g. (B)   *1Co 6:10*

GRASS

Let the earth bring forth g. the   *Ge 1:11*
earth brought forth g. and herb   *Ge 1:12*
ox licketh up the g. of the field   *Nu 22:4*
I will send g. in thy fields   *De 11:15*
nor any g. groweth therein   *De 29:23*
and as the showers upon the g.   *De 32:2*
g. springing out of the earth   *2Sa 23:4*
peradventure we may find g. to   *1Ki 18:5*
they were as the g. of the   *2Ki 19:26*
field
herb, as the g. on the house   *2Ki 19:26*
tops
offspring as the g. of the earth   *Job 5:25*
the wild ass bray when he hath   *Job 6:5*
g.
with thee; he eateth g. as an   *Job 40:15*
ox
shall soon be cut down like the   *Ps 37:2*
g.
upon the mown g.: as showers   *Ps 72:6*
that
of the city shall flourish like g.   *Ps 72:16*
in the morning they are like g.   *Ps 90:5*
When the wicked spring as the   *Ps 92:7*
g.
is smitten, and withered like g.   *Ps 102:4*
and I am withered like g.   *Ps 102:11*
As for man, his days are as g.   *Ps 103:15*
the g. to grow for the cattle   *Ps 104:14*
similitude of an ox that   *Ps 106:20*
eateth g.
as the g. upon the housetops   *Ps 129:6*
g. to grow upon the   *Ps 147:8*
mountains
his favour is as dew upon the   *Pr 19:12*
g.
the tender g. sheweth itself   *Pr 27:25*
the g. faileth, there is no green   *Isa 15:6*
shall be g. with reeds and   *Isa 35:7*
rushes
they were as the g. of the field   *Isa 37:27*
as the g. on the housetops,   *Isa 37:27*
and as
What shall I cry? All flesh is g.   *Isa 40:6*
The g. withereth, the flower   *Isa 40:7;*
fadeth   *40:8*
upon it: surely the people is g.   *Isa 40:7*
shall spring up as among the g.   *Isa 44:4*
man which shall be made as   *Isa 51:12*
g.
forsook it, because there was   *Jer 14:5*
no g.
did fail, because there was no   *Jer 14:6*
g.
as the heifer at g. and bellow   *Jer 50:11*
in the tender g. of the field   *Da 4:15*
the beasts in the g. of the earth   *Da 4:15*
brass, in the tender g. of the   *Da 4:23*
field
and they shall make thee to eat   *Da 4:25*
g.
they shall make thee to eat   *Da 4:32*
g. as
did eat g. as oxen, and his   *Da 4:33*
body
they fed him with g. like oxen   *Da 5:21*
make an end of eating the g. of   *Am 7:2*
as the showers upon the g. that   *Mic 5:7*
of rain, to every one g. in the   *Zec 10:1*
field
God so clothe the g. of the   *M't 6:30;*
field   *Lu 12:28*
to sit down on the g. and   *M't 14:19*
took
by companies upon the green   *M'k 6:39*
g.
there was much g. in the place   *Joh 6:10*
as the flower of the g. he shall   *Jas 1:10*
pass
it withereth the g. and the   *Jas 1:11*
flower
For all flesh is as g. and all   *1Pe 1:24*
glory of man as the flower of   *1Pe 1:24*
g.
The g. withereth, and the   *1Pe 1:24*
flower
and all green g. was burnt up   *Re 8:7*
should not hurt the g. of the   *Re 9:4*
earth

GRASSHOPPER

kind, and the g. after his kind *Le 11:22*
thou make him afraid as a g. *Job 39:20*
leap like a locust *Job 39:20*
(A)(B)(E)(R)
the g. shall be a burden, and *Ec 12:5*
desire

GRASSHOPPERS

we were in our own sight as *Nu 13:33*
g.
they came as g. for multitude *J'g 6:5*
lay along in the valley like g. *J'g 7:12*
the inhabitants thereof are as *Isa 40:22*
g.
because they are more than *Jer 46:23*
the g.
more numerous than locusts *Jer 46:23*
(A)(B)(E)(R)
young g. (B)(R) *Joe 3:15*
he formed g. in the beginning of *Am 7:1*
formed locusts (A)(B)(E)(R) *Am 7:1*
as the great g. which camp in *Na 3:17*

GRATE

shalt make for it a g. of *Ex 27:4*
network
with his brasen g. his staves *Ex 35:16*
he made for the altar a brasen *Ex 38:4*
g.
the four ends of the g. of brass *Ex 38:5*
and the brasen g. for it, and *Ex 38:30*
brasen altar, and his g. of *Ex 39:39*
brass

GRATEFUL

let us be g. (B)(R) *Heb 12:28*

GRAVE

Jacob set a pillar upon her g. *Ge 35:20*
that is the pillar of Rachel's g. *Ge 35:20*
go down into the g. unto my *Ge 37:35*
son
gray hairs with sorrow to *Ge 42:38;*
the g. *44:29*
our father with sorrow to the *Ge 44:31*
g.
Lo, I die: in my g. which I *Ge 50:5*
have
and g. on them the names of *Ex 28:9*
and g. upon it, like the *Ex 28:36*
engravings
a g. shall be unclean seven *Nu 19:16*
days
or one slain, or one dead, or *Nu 19:18*
a g.
grave (B) *De 34:6;*
2Sa 2:32; 4:12; 21:14; 1Ki 13:22;
2Ki 21:26; 23:17, 30
he bringeth down to the g., and *1Sa 2:6*
and wept at the g. of Abner *2Sa 3:32*
be buried by the g. of my *2Sa 19:37*
father
head go down to the g. in peace *1Ki 2:6*
head bring thou down to the g. *1Ki 2:9*
he laid his carcase in his own *1Ki 13:30*
g.
grave (A) *1Ki 13:31;*
2Ki 13:21; Ro 3:13
of Jeroboam shall come to *1Ki 14:13*
the g.
thou shalt be gathered into *2Ki 22:20*
thy g.
to g. with the cunning men that *2Ch 2:7*
also to g. any manner of *2Ch 2:14*
graving
be gathered to thy g. in *2Ch 34:28*
peace
are glad, when they can find *Job 3:22*
the g.
Thou shalt come to thy g. in a *Job 5:26*
full
goeth down to the g. shall come *Job 7:9*
carried from the womb to the *Job 10:19*
g.
wouldest hide me in the g. *Job 14:13*
g. is mine house: I have *Job 17:13*
made
in a moment go down to the *Job 21:13*
g.
he be brought to the g. and *Job 21:32*
shall
so doth the g. those which *Job 24:19*
have

stretch out his hand to the g. *Job 30:24*
soul draweth near unto the g. *Job 33:22*
in the g. who shall give thee *Ps 6:5*
brought up my soul from the g. *Ps 30:3*
let them be silent in the g. *Ps 31:17*
sheep they are laid in the g. *Ps 49:14*
beauty shall consume in the g. *Ps 49:14*
my soul from the power of the *Ps 49:15*
g.
my life draweth nigh unto the *Ps 88:3*
g.
like the slain that lie in the g. *Ps 88:5*
be declared in the g.? or thy *Ps 88:11*
his soul from the hand of the *Ps 89:48*
g.
life from the g. (B) *Ps 103:4*
terrors of the g. had hold (B) *Ps 116:3*
swallow them up alive as the g. *Pr 1:12*
go down to the g. (B) *Pr 30:3;30:9*
The g.; and the barren womb *Pr 30:16*
knowledge, nor wisdom, in the *Ec 9:10*
g.
death; jealousy is cruel as the *Ca 8:6*
g.
pomp is brought down to the *Isa 14:11*
g.
thou art cast out of thy g. like *Isa 14:19*
an
I shall go to the gates of the *Isa 38:10*
g.
the g. cannot praise thee, *Isa 38:18*
death
he made his g. with the wicked *Isa 53:9*
my mother might have been *Jer 20:17*
my g.
when he went down to the g. *Eze 31:15*
company is round about her *Eze 32:23*
g.
her multitude round about her *Eze 32:24*
g.
them from the power of the g. *Ho 13:14*
O g. I will be thy destruction *Ho 13:14*
make thy g.; for thou art *Na 1:14*
vile
he had lain in the g. four *Joh 11:17*
days
She goeth unto the g. to weep *Joh 11:31*
in himself cometh to the g. *Joh 11:38*
he called Lazarus out of his *Joh 12:17*
abandoned soul in the g. (B) *Ac 2:27*
sting? O g. where is thy *1Co 15:55*
victory
Likewise must the deacons be g. *1Ti 3:8*
Even so must their wives be g. *1Ti 3:11*
aged men be sober, g., temperate *Tit 2:2*
keys of death and g. (P) *Re 1:18*
death, and the g. followed (P) *Re 6:8*
death and the g. (P) *Re 21:13; 20:14*

GRAVECLOTHES

bound hand and foot with g. *Joh 11:44*

GRAVED

he g. cherubims, lions, and *1Ki 7:36*
palm
and g. cherubims on the walls *2Ch 3:7*
engraved cherubims (A) *2Ch 3:7*
which cherubim were carved *2Ch 3:7*
(B)(R)

GRAVEL

his mouth shall be filled with *Pr 20:17*
g.
offspring of thy bowels like *Isa 48:19*
the g.
descendents like the sand *Isa 48:19*
(A)(B)(E)(R)
broken my teeth with g. stones *La 3:16*

GRAVEN

was the writing of God g. on *Ex 32:16*
tables
engraved (B)(R) *Ex 32:16;*
39:6; Job 19:24
g. as signets are g. with the *Ex 39:6*
names of Israel
that they were g. with an *Job 19:24*
iron pen
it is g. upon the table of their *Jer 17:1*
heart
engraved on tablet of heart *Jer 17:1*
(A)(B)(R)
that the Godhead is like gold *Ac 17:29*
g. by art

GRAVEN *IMAGE*

thou shalt not make unto thee *Ex 20:4;*
any g. *image* *Le 26:1; De 5:8*
lest ye corrupt and make a g. *De 4:16;*
image *4:25*
cursed the man that maketh *De 27:15*
any g. *image*
make a carved or molten *De 27:15*
image (B)
the silver for my son to make a *J'g 17:3*
g. *image*
an engraved image (B) *J'g 17:3;*
17:4; 18:14, 17
gave them to the founder, who *J'g 17:4*
made a g. *image*
there is in these houses a g. *J'g 18:14*
image
the g. *image* *J'g 18:17*
Dan set up the g. image *J'g 18:30; 18:31*
Manasseh set g. *image* in *2Ki 21:7*
house of God
the workman melteth a g. *Isa 40:19*
image
he seeketh workman to *Isa 40:20*
prepare g. *image*
they that make a g. *image* are *Isa 44:9*
vanity
who hath molten a g. *image* *Isa 44:10*
not profitable
with the residue thereof he *Isa 44:17*
maketh his g. *image*
that set up the wood of their *Isa 45:20*
g. *image*
and my g. *image* hath *Isa 48:5*
commanded them
founder confounded by g. *Jer 10:14;*
image *51:17*
I will cut off the g. and molten *Na 1:14*
image
what profiteth the g. *image* *Hab 2:18*

GRAVEN *IMAGES*

ye shall burn their g. *images* *De 7:5;*
with fire *7:25*
ye shall hew down the g. *De 12:3*
images of their gods
feared the Lord and served g. *2Ki 17:41*
images
set up g. *images* before he *2Ch 33:19*
was humbled
when he had beaten the g. *2Ch 34:7*
images to powder
moved him to jealousy with g. *Ps 78:58*
images
confounded be all they that *Ps 97:7*
serve g. *images*
whose g. *images* did excel *Isa 10:10*
them of Jerusalem
Babylon is fallen, and all the g. *Isa 21:9*
images
shall defile the covering of thy *Isa 30:22*
g. *images*
neither will I give my praise to *Isa 42:8*
g. *images*
shall be greatly ashamed that *Isa 42:17*
trust in g. *images*
provoked me to anger with *Jer 8:19*
their g. *images*
it is the land of g. *images*, *Jer 50:38*
they are mad
I will do judgment on the g. *Jer 51:47;*
images *51:52*
they burnt incense to g. *images* *Ho 11:2*
all the g. *images* shall be *Mic 1:7*
beaten to pieces
thy g. *images* also will I cut *Mic 5:13*
off

GRAVES

Because there were no g. in *Ex 14:11*
Egypt
the powder thereof upon the *2Ki 23:6*
g. of
strowed it upon the g. of *2Ch 34:4*
them
extinct, the g. are ready for *Job 17:1*
me
Which remain among the g. *Isa 65:4*
of Jerusalem, out of their g. *Jer 8:1*
out of their sepulchres (B) *Jer 8:1*
out of their tombs (R) *Jer 8:1*
cast his dead body into the g. *Jer 26:23*
of
into the cemetery (B) *Jer 26:23*
burial place of common *Jer 26:23*
people (R)

company; his *g.* are about | Eze 32:22
him
Whose *g.* are set in the sides | Eze 32:23
of the
her *g.* are round about him | Eze 32:25;
| 32:26
I will open your *g.* and cause | Eze 37:12
you
you to come up out of your | Eze 37:12
g.
when I have opened your *g.*, | Eze 37:13
O my
and brought you up out of | Eze 37:13
your *g.*
give unto Gog a place there | Eze 39:11
of *g.*
for burial in Israel | Eze 39:11
(A)(B)(E)(R)
the *g.* were opened; and | M't 27:52
many
tombs were opened | M't 27:52;
(A)(B)(E)(R) | 27:53
And came out of the *g.* after | M't 27:53
his
for ye are as *g.* which appear | Lu 11:44
not
unseen tombs (B)(E) | Lu 11:44
that are in the *g.* shall hear his | Joh 5:28
who are in tombs (A)(E)(R) | Joh 5:28
those dead and buried (P) | Joh 5:28
their dead bodies to be put in | Re 11:9
g.
to be put in a tomb | Re 11:9
(A)(E)(R)
to be entombed (B) | Re 11:9
refuse them burial (N)(P) | Re 11:9

GRAVE'S

are scattered at the *g.* mouth | Ps 141:7

GRAVETH

and that *g.* an habitation for | Isa 22:16
hews him a sepulchre | Isa 22:16
(A)(B)(E)
hewn out a tomb (R) | Isa 22:16

GRAVING

fashioned it with a *g.* tool | Ex 32:4
also to grave any manner of | 2Ch 2:14
g.
engrave any type of engraving | 2Ch 2:14
(A)
carving all kinds of | 2Ch 2:14
engravings (B)(R)
I will engrave the *g.* thereof | Zec 3:9
carve upon it its inscription | Zec 3:9
(A)
engraving its inscription | Zec 3:9
(B)(R)

GRAVINGS

also upon the mouth of it | 1Ki 7:31
were *g.*
at its opening were carvings | 1Ki 7:31
(A)(R)
upon the mouth were | 1Ki 7:31
engravings (B)

GRAVITY

children in subjection with all | 1Ti 3:4
g.
under control with true dignity | 1Ti 3:4
(A)(B)
command respect of children | 1Ti 3:4
(P)
children submissive and | 1Ti 3:4
respectful (R)
uncorruptness, *g.*, sincerity | Tit 2:7

GRAY

down my *g.* hairs with sorrow | Ge 42:38;
| 44:29
g. hairs of thy servant our | Ge 44:31
father
also with the man of *g.* hairs | De 32:25
g. head (S) | 1Ki 2:6; 2:9; Isa 46:4
g. hairs are here and there upon | Ho 7:9

GRAYHEADED

I am old and *g.*; and, behold | 1Sa 12:2
the *g.* and very aged men, | Job 15:10
much
Now also when I am old and | Ps 71:18
g.

GREASE

Their heart is as fat as *g.* | Ps 119:70

GREAT

I will bless thee, make thy | Ge 12:2
name *g.*
Abraham my master is | Ge 24:35
become *g.*
with *g.* wrestlings have I | Ge 30:8
wrestled
how can I do this *g.* | Ge 39:9
wickedness and sin
to save your lives by a *g.* | Ge 45:7
deliverance
I know it, my son, he also | Ge 48:19
shall be *g.*
beside unwalled towns a *g.* | De 3:5
many
Lord your God is a *g.* God | De 10:17;
| 2Ch 2:5
your eyes have seen *g.* acts of | De 11:7
Lord
neither let me see this *g.* fire | De 18:16
any more
what meaneth the heat of this | De 29:24
g. anger
what wilt thou do unto thy *g.* | Jos 7:9
name
thou heardest cities were *g.* | Jos 14:12
and fenced
build there a *g.* altar by | Jos 22:10
Jordan to see to
for he did those *g.* signs in | Jos 24:17
our sight
divisions of Reuben *g.* thoughts | J'g 5:15
of heart
may perceive your | 1Sa 12:17
wickedness is *g.*
David went on, and grew *g.* | 2Sa 5:10
I have made thee a *g.* name | 2Sa 7:9
thou art *g.* O Lord God, none | 2Sa 7:22
is like thee
given *g.* occasion to enemies | 2Sa 12:14
to blaspheme
thy gentleness hath made me | 2Sa 22:36;
g. | Ps 18:35
shall hear of thy *g.* name | 1Ki 8:42;
| 1Ch 6:32
because the journey is too *g.* | 1Ki 19:7
for thee
passed to Shunem, where was | 2Ki 4:8
g. woman
g. is the wrath of the Lord | 2Ki 22:13
that is kindled
g. is the Lord | 1Ch 16:25;
| Ps 48:1; 96:4; 135:5; 145:3
by *g.* and terrible things (S) | 1Ch 17:21
into Lord's hand, very *g.* are | 1Ch 21:13
mercies
and in thine hand it is to | 1Ch 29:12
make *g.*
house I build is *g.* for *g.* is our | 2Ch 2:5
God
house I build shall be | 2Ch 2:9
wonderful *g.*
Jehoshaphat waxed *g.* | 2Ch 17:12
exceedingly
There cometh a *g.* multitude | 2Ch 20:2
our trespass is *g.*; *g.* wrath | 2Ch 28:13;
poured | 34:21
remember the Lord who is *g.* | Ne 4:14
and terrible
therefore our God, the *g.* the | Ne 9:32
mighty God
published thro' all his empire, | Es 1:20
for it is *g.*
shalt know that thy seed shall | Job 5:25
be *g.*
is not thy wickedness *g.* | Job 22:5
iniquities infinite
by *g.* force of my disease | Job 30:18
garment changed
yet he knoweth it not in *g.* | Job 35:15
extremity
a *g.* ransom; God is *g.* we | Job 36:18;
know him not | 36:26
or because the number of thy | Job 38:21
days is *g.*
wilt thou trust him, because | Job 39:11
strength is *g.*
great (S) | Ps 2:5;
Ec 5:13, 16; Jer 52:6; Eze 21:10;
| Mic 2:10
there were they in *g.* fear | Ps 14:5; 53:5
in keeping of them there is *g.* | Ps 19:11
reward
his glory is *g.* in thy salvation, | Ps 21:5
honour

O Lord, pardon mine iniquity, | Ps 25:11
for it is *g.*
O how *g.* is thy goodness thou | Ps 31:19
hast laid up
thou art *g.* and doest | Ps 86:10
wondrous things
how *g.* are thy works | Ps 92:5
O God, how *g.* is the sum of | Ps 139:17
them
this wisdom seemed *g.* unto me | Ec 9:13
houses even *g.* and fair without | Isa 5:9
inhabitant
sat in darkness, have seen *g.* | Isa 9:2;
light | M't 4:16
g. is the Holy One of Israel in | Isa 12:6
midst of thee
he shall send them a Saviour | Isa 19:20
a *g.* one
I will divide him a portion | Isa 53:12
with the *g.*
g. shall be the peace of thy | Isa 54:13
children
therefore they are become *g.* | Jer 5:27
and rich
thou art *g.* and thy name is *g.* | Jer 10:6
in might
and her womb to be always *g.* | Jer 20:17
with me
the *g.* the mighty God in his | Jer 32:18
name
g. in counsel, and mighty in | Jer 32:19
work
behold, I have sworn by my *g.* | Jer 44:26
name
they are new, *g.* is thy | La 3:23
faithfulness
thou hast increased and waxed | Eze 16:7
g.
a *g.* eagle with *g.* wings, | Eze 17:3;
longwinged *g.* | 17:7
I will even make the pile for | Eze 24:9
fire *g.*
to serve a *g.* service against | Eze 29:18
Tyrus
waters made him *g.* the deep | Eze 31:4
set
and I will sanctify my *g.* | Eze 36:23
name
how *g.* his signs, how mighty his | Da 4:3
wonders
I saw the ram pushing, and he | Da 8:4
became *g.*
get you down, for their | Joe 3:13
wickedness is *g.*
and from thence go to Hamath | Am 6:2
the *g.*
now shall he be *g.* unto ends of | Mic 5:4
the earth
how *g.* his goodness, how *g.* | Zec 9:17
his beauty
my name shall be *g.* among | Mal 1:11
Gentiles
rejoice and be exceeding glad, | M't 5:12;
for *g.* is your reward | Lu 6:23, 35
shall be called *g.* in the | M't 5:19
kingdom of heaven
if light be darkness, how *g.* | M't 6:23
is that darkness
one pearl of *g.* price; *g.* is | M't 13:46;
thy faith | 15:28
for he had *g.* possessions | M't 19:22;
| M'k 10:42
they that are *g.* exercise | M't 20:25
authority
whosoever will be *g.* among | M't 20:26;
you | M'k 10:43
Master, which is the *g.* | M't 22:36
commandment
this is the first and *g.* | M't 22:38
commandment
he shall be *g.* in sight of the | Lu 1:15
Lord
that is least among you, the | Lu 9:48
same shall be *g.*
the harvest truly is *g.* but the | Lu 10:2
labourers few
between us and you there is a | Lu 16:26
g. gulf
giving out that he was some *g.* | Ac 8:9
one
g. is Diana of the Ephesians | Ac 19:34;
| 19:34
g. is my boldness, *g.* is my | 2Co 7:4
glorying
that he hath a *g.* zeal for you | Col 4:13
and them
g. is mystery of godliness, | 1Ti 3:16
God manifest

in *g.* house not only vessels of   *2Ti 2:20* gold
the glorious appearing of the   *Tit 2:13* *g.* God
now consider how *g.* this man   *Heb 7:4* was
how *g.* a matter a little fire   *Jas 3:5* kindleth
the tribulation, the. (S)   *Re 7:14*
and I saw another sign in   *Re 15:11* heaven, *g.*
g. Babylon came in   *Re 16:19* remembrance before God
Babylon the *g.* the mother of   *Re 17:5;* harlots   *18:2*
gather together unto the   *Re 19:17* supper of the *g.* God

GREAT *EVIL*

then he hath done us this *g. evil 1Sa 6:9*
hearken to you to do all this   *Ne 13:27* *g. evil*
this also is vanity, and a *g. evil Ec 2:21*
wherefore Lord pronounced   *Jer 16:10* this *g. evil*
thus might we procure *g. evil Jer 26:19* against our souls
I have brought this *g. evil Jer 32:42* upon this people
why commit this *g. evil* against *Jer 44:7* your souls
confirmed, by bringing upon us *Da 9:12* a *g. evil*

GREAT *KING, KINGS*

thus saith the *g. king*   *2Ki 18:19;*   *18:28; Isa 36:4, 13*
which a *g. king* of Israel   *Ezr 5:11* builded
the Lord is a *g. King* over all *Ps 47:2* the earth
is mount Zion, the city of the *g. Ps 48:2 King*
the Lord is a *g. King* above all *Ps 95:3* gods
give thanks to him that   *Ps 136:17* smote *g. kings*
and there came a *g. king Ec 9:14* against it
g. kings shall serve   *Jer 25:14;* themselves   *27:7*
for I am a *g. King*, saith the *Mal 1:14* Lord
Jerusalem is the city of the *g. M't 5:35 King*

GREAT *MEN*

like name of *g. men* in earth   *2Sa 7:9;*   *1Ch 17:8*
Ahab's sons were with *g. men 2Ki 10:6* of city
Jehu slew all Ahab's *g. men 2Ki 10:11* and kinsfolks
Zabdiel overseer, son of one   *Ne 11:14* of *g. men*
g. men are not always wise, *Job 32:9* nor the aged
a gift bringeth him before *g. Pr 18:16 men*
and stand not in the place of *Pr 25:6 g. men*
I will get me unto *g. men* and *Jer 5:5* speak
all the houses of the *g. men Jer 52:13* burnt he
it is the sword of the *g. men Eze 21:14* slain
all her *g. men* were bound in *Na 3:10* chains
g. men hid themselves in dens *Re 6:15* and rocks
thy merchants were the *g. men Re 18:23* of the earth

GREAT *MULTITUDE,* MULTITUDES

Reuben, Gad had a *g.*   *Nu 32:1* multitude or cattle
hast thou seen all this *g. 1Ki 20:13* multitude
I will deliver this *g. 1Ki 20:28* multitude into thine hand
ye be a *g. multitude* ye have *2Ch 13:8* golden calves
there cometh a *g. multitude 2Ch 20:2* against thee

not dismayed by reason of   *2Ch 20:15* this *g. multitude*
carried a *g. multitude* captives *2Ch 28:5* to Damascus
did I fear a *g. multitude* or *Job 31:34* did contempt
all that *g. multitude* shall be *Isa 16:14* contemned
women that stood by, even a *Jer 44:15 g. multitude*
there shall be a very *g. Eze 47:9 multitude* of fish
king of south shall set forth a *Da 11:11 g. multitude*
g. multitudes followed him   *M't 4:25;* *8:1; 12:15; 19:2; 20:29; M'k 30:7;*   *Joh 6:2*
when Jesus saw *g. multitude M't 8:18;*   *14:14; M'k 9:14*
g. multitudes came, having   *M't 15:30* lame, blind, dumb
whence so much bread as to *M't 15:33* fill so *g.* a multitude
a *g. multitude* spread their   *M't 21:8* garments in way
with Judas a *g. multitude M't 26:47;* with swords   *M'k 14:43*
they inclosed a *g. multitude* of *Lu 5:6* fishes
a *g. multitude* came together to *Lu 5:15* hear and be healed
in these lay a *g. multitude* of *Joh 5:3* impotent folk
a *g. multitude* of Jews and   *Ac 14:1* Greeks believed
and of the devout Greeks a *g. Ac 17:4* multitude
a *g. multitude* which no man   *Re 7:9* could number
I heard as it were the voice of a *Re 19:6 g. multitude*

GREAT *NATION, NATIONS*

I will make of thee a *g. nation, Ge 12:2;* and will bless thee *18:18; 46:3; Ex 32:10*
I will make Ishmael a *g. Ge 17:20;* nation   *21:18*
surely this *g. nation* is a wise *De 4:6* people
he became there a *nation g. De 26:5* and mighty
hath driven out before you *Jos 23:9 g. nations*
who smote *g. nations,* and slew *Ps 135:10* kings
a *g. nation* shall be raised from *Jer 6:22* the sides
I will raise against Babylon *Jer 50:9* an assembly of *g. nations*
people shall come from north, *Jer 50:41* a *g. nation*
under his shadow dwelt all   *Eze 31:6 g. nations*

GREAT *PEOPLE*

the Emims dwelt therein, a   *De 2:10 people g.*
Zamzummims, a *people g.* many *De 2:21* and tall
a *people g.* and tall, children   *De 9:2* of Anakims
why but one lot, seeing   *Jos 17:14* thou a *g. people*
if thou be a *g. people;* art *Jos 17:15;* a *g. people*   *17:17*
a *g. people* that cannot be   *1Ki 3:8* numbered
who is able to judge this *g. 1Ki 3:9;* people   *2Ch 1:10*
given David a wise son over *1Ki 5:7* this *g. people*
the noise in mountains like as *Isa 13:4* of *g. people*
a *g. people* hath not been ever *Joe 2:2* the like

GREAT *POWER*

brought out of Egypt with   *Ex 32:11;* *g. power*   *2Ki 17:36; Ne 1:10*
let the *power* of my lord be *g. Nu 14:17*
thou art a great people and *Jos 17:17* hast *g. power*
will he plead against me with *Job 23:6 g. power*
great is our Lord and of *g. Ps 147:5 power*
made earth, man, and beast *Jer 27:5;* by my *g. power*   *32:17*

it shall wither even without *g. Eze 17:9 power*
the Lord is slow to anger, *g.* in *Na 1:3 power*
coming in the clouds with *g. M'k 13:26 power*
with *g. power* gave the apostles *Ac 4:33* witness
saying, This man is the *g. Ac 8:10 power* of God
thou hast taken to thee thy *g. Re 11:17 power*
angel come from heaven,   *Re 18:1* having *g. power*

GREAT *SEA*

ye shall have the *g. sea* for a *Nu 34:6* border
from the wilderness unto the *g. Jos 1:4 sea*
when the kings in the coasts of *Jos 9:1 g. sea* heard
the west border was to the *g. Jos 15:12 sea* and coast
inheritance of Judah, to the   *Jos 15:47 g. sea* and border
with all nations I have cut off *Jos 23:4* to the *g. sea*
as fish of the *g. sea* exceeding *Eze 47:10* many
border of land toward north *Eze 47:15* from the *g. sea*
the four winds strove upon the *Da 7:2 g. sea*

GREAT *SLAUGHTER*

slew them with a *g. slaughter Jos 10:10* at Gibeon
made an end of slaying them *Jos 10:20* with *g. slaughter*
Jephthah smote Ammon with *J'g 11:33 g. slaughter*
Samson smote the Philistines   *J'g 15:8* with *g. slaughter*
Philistines smote Israel with *1Sa 4:10;* *g. slaughter*   *4:17*
Lord had smitten the people *1Sa 6:19* with a *g. slaughter*
David slew Philistines with a *1Sa 19:8;* *g. slaughter*   *23:5*
a *g. slaughter* that day of   *2Sa 18:7* 20,000 men
king of Israel slew Assyria *1Ki 20:21*
Abijah slew Israel with a *g. 2Ch 13:17 slaughter*
king of Israel smote Ahaz   *2Ch 28:5* with a *g. slaughter*
in day of *g. slaughter* when *Isa 30:25* the towers fall
Lord hath a *g. slaughter* in *Isa 34:6* land of Idumea

GREAT *STONE, STONES*

a *g. stone* was upon the well's *Ge 29:2* mouth
set up *g. stones* and plaster *De 27:2* them
Lord cast down *g. stones Jos 10:11* from heaven
roll *g. stones* upon the mouth *Jos 10:18* of the cave
took a *g. stone,* and set it up *Jos 24:26* there
cart came where there was a *1Sa 6:14 g. stone*
and the Levites put them on the *1Sa 6:15 g. stone*
to *g. stone* of Abel, whereon *1Sa 6:18* they set ark
ye have transgressed, roll a *g. 1Sa 14:33 stone* unto me
when they were at *g. stone* in *2Sa 20:8* Gibeon
they brought *g. stones* to lay *1Ki 5:17* foundation
foundation was of *g. stones 1Ki 7:10;*   *7:11*
he made engines to shoot *g. 2Ch 26:15 stones*
three rows of *g. stones* and a *Ezr 6:4* row of timber
take *g. stones* and hide them in *Jer 43:9* clay
he rolled a *g. stone* to door *M't 27:60* of sepulchre

GREAT *THING, THINGS*

whether any such thing as this	De 4:32
g. thing is	
he is thy God that hath done	De 10:21
g. things	
stand and see this g. thing	1Sa 12:16
Lord will do	
consider how g. things he	1Sa 12:24
hath done for you	
thou shalt both do g. things	1Sa 26:25
and prevail	
for word's sake hast done g.	2Sa 7:21
things	
to do for you g. things and	2Sa 7:23
terrible	
if prophet bid thee do some g.	2Ki 5:13
things	
tell me all the g. things Elisha	2Ki 8:4
hath done	
is he a dog, that he should do	2Ki 8:13
this g. thing	
in making known these g.	1Ch 17:19
things	
to God who doeth g. things	Job 5:9;
	9:10; 37:5
who hast done g. things, who	Ps 71:19
is like thee	
they forgat God who had	Ps 106:21
done g. things	
the Lord hath done g. things	Ps 126:2;
for them	126:3
I will shew thee g. and mighty	Jer 33:3
things	
seekest thou g. things for	Jer 45:5
thyself	
a mouth speaking g. things	Da 7:8;
	7:20; Re 13:5
I have written the g. things of	Ho 8:12
my law	
because he hath done g. things	Joe 2:20
fear not, O land, the Lord will	Joe 2:21
do g. things	
when they heard what g. things	M'k 3:8
he did	
tell how g. things Lord hath	M'k 5:19;
done	Lu 8:39
he that is mighty hath done g.	Lu 1:49
things	
he published how g. things	Lu 8:39
Jesus had done	
shew how g. things he must	Ac 9:16
suffer	
is it a g. thing if we reap	1Co 9:11
carnal things	
no g. thing if his ministers	2Co 11:15
be transformed	
tongue a little member boasteth	Jas 3:5
g. things	

GREAT *WATERS*

in floods of g. waters shall not	Ps 32:6
come nigh	
thy way is in sea, thy path in	Ps 77:19
g. waters	
they that do business in g.	Ps 107:23
waters	
send from above, deliver me	Ps 144:7
out of g. waters	
and by g. waters the seed of	Isa 23:3
Sihor	
found Ishmael by g. waters of	Jer 41:12
Gibeon	
when her waves do roar like	Jer 51:55
g. waters	
noise of their wings like g.	Eze 1:24
waters	
he placed of the seed by g.	Eze 17:5
waters, set it	
it was planted in a good soil	Eze 17:8
by g. waters	
when g. waters shall cover	Eze 26:19
thee	
thy rowers brought thee into	Eze 27:26
g. waters	
he was fair, for his root was	Eze 31:7
by g. waters	
I restrained floods, the g.	Eze 31:15
waters were stayed	
I will destroy all beasts	Eze 32:13
beside g. waters	
didst walk through heap of g.	Hab 3:15
waters	

GREAT *WHILE*

hast spoken of thy servant's	2Sa 7:19;
house for a g. while	1Ch 17:17

rising up a g. while before day,	M'k 1:35
he went	
had g. while ago repented in	Lu 10:13
sackcloth	
after the barbarians looked a	Ac 28:6
g. while	

GREAT *WORK, WORKS*

Israel saw that g. work the	Ex 14:31
Lord did	
who had seen all the g. works of	J'g 2:7
the Lord	
my son is young, and the	1Ch 29:1
work is g.	
the work is g. and we are	Ne 4:19
separated	
I am doing a g. work, I cannot	Ne 6:3
come down	
the works of the Lord are g.	Ps 111:2;
	Re 15:3
I made g. works, I builded me	Ec 2:4
houses	

SMALL AND GREAT

smote men with blindness	Ge 19:11
small and g.	
but ye shall hear small as well	De 1:17
as g.	
not have divers weights, a g.	De 25:13
and small	
shalt not have divers	De 25:14
measures, a g. and small	
smote men small and g. with	1Sa 5:9
emerods	
my father will do nothing g.	1Sa 20:2
or small	
they slew not any either g. or	1Sa 30:2
small	
nothing lacking neither small	De 30:19
nor g.	
fight not with small nor g.	1Ki 22:31;
	2Ch 18:30
small and g. went to house	2Ki 33:2;
	2Ch 34:30
all people small and g. came	2Ki 25:26
to Egypt	
they cast lots as well the	1Ch 26:13
small as g.	
be put to death, whether	2Ch 15:13
small or g.	
to give to brethren by	2Ch 31:15
courses, g. and small	
gave into his hand vessels, g.	2Ch 36:18
and small	
Ahasuerus made a feast unto g.	Es 1:5
and small	
shall give to husbands honour	Es 1:20
g. and small	
small and g. are there, servant	Job 3:19
is free	
he saith to the small rain, and	Job 37:6
to g. rain	
are things creeping, small	Ps 104:25
and g.	
bless them that fear the Lord,	Ps 115:13
small and g.	
I had possessions of g. and	Ec 2:7
small cattle	
g. and small shall die in this	Jer 16:6
land	
making the ephah small, the	Am 8:5
shekel g.	
I continue witnessing to small	Ac 26:22
and g.	
reward to them that fear him,	Re 11:18
small and g.	
he caused small and g. to	Re 13:16
receive a mark	
praise our God, ye that fear	Re 19:5
him, small and g.	
that ye may eat flesh of all	Re 19:18
men, small and g.	
I saw the dead, small and g.	Re 20:12
stand before God	

SO GREAT

hast brought so g. a sin upon	Ex 32:21
them	
what nation so g. hath God so	De 4:7;
nigh	4:8
able to judge so g. people	1Ki 3:9;
	2Ch 1:10
who is so g. a God as our God	Ps 77:13
so g. is his mercy to them	Ps 103:11
that fear him	
not found so g. faith	M't 8:10; Lu 7:9

bread as to fill so g. a	M't 15:33
multitude	
who delivered us from so g. a	2Co 1:10
death	
how escape, if we neglect so g.	Heb 2:3
a salvation	
compassed with so g. a cloud	Heb 12:1
of witnesses	
ships so g. yet turned with an	Jas 3:4
helm	
so mighty an earthquake and	Re 16:18
so g.	
in one hour so g. riches come	Re 18:17
to nought	

VERY GREAT

Isaac grew till he became very	Ge 26:13
g.	
the man Moses was very g. in	Ex 11:3
the land	
Lord smote people with a	Nu 11:33
very g. plague	
and the cities are walled and	Nu 13:28
very g.	
I will promote thee unto very	Nu 22:17
g. honour	
the sin of the young men was	1Sa 2:17
very g.	
and there was a very g.	1Sa 4:10
slaughter	
very g. trembling; very g.	1Sa 14:15;
discomfiture	14:20
Nabal was a very g. man, he	1Sa 25:2
had 3000 sheep	
they laid a very g. heap on	2Sa 18:17
Absalom	
for Barzillai was a very g.	2Sa 19:32
man	
queen of Sheba came with a	1Ki 10:2
very g. train	
for very g. are his mercies	1Ch 21:13
they made a very g. burning	2Ch 16:14
for Asa	
Lord delivered a very g. host	2Ch 24:24
into their hand	
assembled a very g.	2Ch 30:13;
congregation	Ezr 10:1
Manasseh raised up the wall	2Ch 33:14
a very g. height	
and there was a very g.	Ne 8:17
gladness	
Job a very g. household,	Job 1:3
greatest in the east	
for they saw that his grief was	Job 2:13
very g.	
O Lord my God, thou art very	Ps 104:1
g.	
there shall be very g.	Eze 47:9
multitude of fish	
therefore the he goat waxed	Da 8:8
very g.	
king of south stirred up with	Da 11:25
very g. army	
for his camp is very g. he is	Joe 2:11
strong	
and there shall be a very g.	Zec 14:4
valley	
very g. multitude spread their	M't 21:8
garments	
the multitude very g. having	M'k 8:1
nothing	
stone was rolled away, for it	M'k 16:4
was very g.	

WAS GREAT

God saw the wickedness of	Ge 6:5
man was g.	
their substance was g. so that	Ge 13:6
they could	
to Gibeon, that was the g. high	1Ki 3:4
place	
there was g. indignation	2Ki 3:27
against Israel	
where the decree came was g.	Es 4:3
mourning	
Mordecai was g. in the king's	Es 9:4;
house	10:3
if I rejoiced because my	Job 31:25
wealth was g.	
I was g. and increased more	Ec 2:9
than all before	
she that was g. among the	La 1:1
nations	
the tree's height was g. and it	Da 4:10
grew	
it fell, and g. was the fall of it	M't 7:27;
	Lu 6:49

GREATER

God made g. light to rule day   Ge 1:16
my punishment is g. than I can   Ge 4:13 bear
there is none g. in this house   Ge 39:9 than I
only in the throne will I be g.   Ge 41:40 than thou
his younger brother shall be g.   Ge 48:19 than he
I know the Lord is g. than all   Ex 18:11 gods
make of thee g. nation   Nu 14:12; De 9:14
the people is g. and taller than   De 1:28 we
drive nations g. than thou   De 4:38; 7:1; 9:1; 11:23
because Gibeon was g. than Ai   Jos 10:2
had there been a much g.   1Sa 14:30 slaughter
the hatred was g. than the   2Sa 13:15 love
this evil is g. than the other   2Sa 13:16 thou didst me
make his throne g. than   1Ki 1:37; David   1:46
David waxed g. and g. Lord   1Ch 11:9 was with
the g. house he ceiled with   2Ch 3:5 fir tree
for this man Mordecai waxed g.   Es 9:4 and g.
I will answer, that God is g.   Job 33:12 than man
is g. than the punishment of   La 4:6 Sodom
thou shalt see g. abominations   Eze 8:6; 8:13, 15
shall set forth a multitude g.   Da 11:13 than former
or their border g. than your   Am 6:2 border
the glory of latter house g.   Hag 2:9 than former
not a g. than John the   M't 11:11; Baptist, least in kingdom   Lu 7:28 g. than he
in this place is one g. than the   M't 12:6 temple
behold, a g. than Jonas is   M't 12:41; here   Lu 11:32
behold, a g. than Solomon is   M't 12:42; here   Lu 11:31
receiving g. damnation   M't 23:14; M'k 12:40; Lu 20:47
for whether is g. the gold, or   M't 23:17 the temple
for whether is g. the gift or   M't 23:19 the altar
sown, it becometh g. than all   M'k 4:32 herbs
there is no other   M'k 12:31 commandment g. than these
I will pull down my barns,   Lu 12:18 and build g.
whether is g. he that sitteth or   Lu 22:27 that serveth g.
thou shalt see g. things   Joh 1:50; 5:20; 14:12
art thou g. than our father   Joh 4:12 Jacob
I have a g. witness than that   Joh 5:36 of John
art thou g. than our father   Joh 8:53 Abraham
my Father is g. than all   Joh 10:29; 14:28
the servant is not g. than his   Joh 13:16; lord   15:20
g. love hath no man than this   Joh 15:13 to lay down
he that delivered me to thee   Joh 19:11 hath the g. sin
to lay upon you no g. burden   Ac 15:28 than these
the g. part (S)   Ac 19:32; 27:12
for g. is he that prophesieth,   1Co 14:5 than he
of whom the g. part remain   1Co 15:6 unto this present
love grows ever g. (N)   2Th 1:3
because he could swear by no   Heb 6:13 g. he swore
for men verily swear by the g.   Heb 6:16 and an oath
by a g. and more perfect   Heb 9:11 tabernacle

esteeming the reproach of   Heb 11:26 Christ g. riches
knowing we shall receive g.   Jas 3:1 condemnation
whereas angels which are g. in   2Pe 2:11 power
God is g. than our heart, and   1Jo 3:20 knoweth
g. is he that is in you, than he   1Jo 4:4 in the world
witness of God is g.: this is the   1Jo 5:9 witness of God
I have no g. joy than to hear that   3Jo 4 children

GREATEST

least was over 100 g. over a   1Ch 12:14 thousand
hitherto the g. part had kept   1Ch 12:29 the ward of Saul
this man was the g. of all in the   Job 1:3 east
from least to g. given to   Jer 6:13; covetousness   8:10
all know me, from least to   Jer 31:34; the g.   Heb 8:11
all people from the least to the   Jer 42:1 g. came near
Jeremiah called the people   Jer 42:8 from least to the g.
they shall die, from the least   Jer 44:12 to the g.
put on sackcloth, from the g. to   Jon 3:5 the least
when grown, it is the g.   M't 13:32 among herbs
who is the g. in the kingdom   M't 18:1 of heaven
humble himself as this little   M't 18:4 child, same is g.
but he that is g. shall be your   M't 23:11 servant
disputed who should be g.   M'k 9:34; Lu 9:46
there was a strife who should   Lu 22:24 be g.
he that is g. let him be as   Lu 22:26 younger
all gave heed from the least to   Ac 8:10 the g.
but the g. of these is charity   1Co 13:13

GREATLY

I will g. multiply thy sorrow   Ge 3:16
Lot pressed upon them g. and   Ge 19:3 they turned in
the Lord hath blessed my   Ge 24:35 master g.
greatly (S)   Ge 31:30; Ps 38:2; Isa 23:5; 59:11; M't 17:15; M'k 14:33
then Jacob was g. afraid and   Ge 32:7 distressed
and the whole mount quaked   Ex 19:18 g.
anger of the Lord was   Nu 11:10 kindled g.
Moses told, and the people   Nu 14:39 mourned g.
Lord shall g. bless thee in the   De 15:4 land
nor shall he g. multiply silver   De 17:17 and gold
Lord against them, they were g.   J'g 2:15 distressed
Israel was g. impoverished by   J'g 6:6 Midian
Saul's anger was kindled g.   1Sa 11:6
Saul and all the men of Israel   1Sa 11:15 rejoiced g.
people g. feared the Lord and   1Sa 12:18 Samuel
he loved him g. became his   1Sa 16:21 armour-bearer
when heard Philistine they   1Sa 17:11 were g. afraid
Saul saw the Philistines his   1Sa 28:5 heart trembled g.
David was g. distressed, for   1Sa 30:6 the people spake
the men were g. ashamed   2Sa 10:5; 1Ch 19:5
David's anger was g. kindled   2Sa 12:5 against the man
David said, I have sinned g.   2Sa 24:10; 1Ch 21:8
Solomon's kingdom was   1Ki 2:12 established g.

Hiram heard Solomon's words,   1Ki 5:7 he rejoiced g.
now Obadiah feared the Lord   1Ki 18:3 g.
the house of their fathers   1Ch 4:38 increased g.
great is Lord, g. to be   1Ch 16:25; praised   Ps 48:1; 96:4; 145:3
their anger was g. kindled   2Ch 25:10 against Judah
Manasseh humbled himself   2Ch 33:12 g. before God
yet thy latter end should g.   Job 8:7 increase
in thy salvation how g. shall he   Ps 21:1 rejoice
my heart g. rejoiceth, I will   Ps 28:7 praise
I am bowed down g. go   Ps 38:6 mourning all day
so shall the king g. desire thy   Ps 45:11 beauty
shields of earth belong to God,   Ps 47:9 he is g. exalted
he is my defence, I shall not be   Ps 62:2 g. moved
thou g. enrichest it with the   Ps 65:9 river of God
my lip shall g. rejoice when I   Ps 71:23 sing unto thee
he was wroth, and g. abhorred   Ps 78:59 Israel
he increased his people g.   Ps 105:24; 107:38
I will g. praise the Lord with   Ps 109:30 my mouth
blessed that delighteth g. in   Ps 112:1 his commandments
I was g. afflicted, I said in   Ps 116:10 my haste
the proud have had me in g.   Ps 119:51 derision
father of righteous shall g.   Pr 23:24 rejoice
shall be g. ashamed that trust   Isa 42:17 in images
I will g. rejoice in the Lord   Isa 61:10
shall not that land be g. polluted   Jer 3:1
surely thou hast g. deceived   Jer 4:10 this people
g. confounded, have forsaken   Jer 9:19 the land
persecutors shall be g.   Jer 20:11 ashamed not prosper
and my sabbaths they g.   Eze 20:13 polluted
because that Edom hath g.   Eze 25:12 offended
then was king Belshazzar g.   Da 5:9 troubled
for thou art g. beloved   Da 9:23; 10:11, 19
I made thee small, thou art g.   Ob 2 despised
the great day of the Lord   Zep 1:14 hasteth g.
rejoice g. O daughter of Zion,   Zec 9:9 shout
insomuch that governor   M't 27:14 marvelled g.
Jairus besought him g. saying,   M'k 5:23 My daughter
he seeth them that wept and   M'k 5:38 wailed g.
when they beheld, they were   M'k 9:15 amazed g.
God of the living, ye   M'k 12:27 therefore do g. err
rejoiceth g. because of   Joh 3:29 bridegroom's voice
all the people ran to porch, g.   Ac 3:11 wondering
number of disciples multiplied   Ac 6:7 in Jerusalem g.
I g. desired Apollos to come   1Co 16:12 unto you
how g. I long after you all in   Ph'p 1:8 Jesus Christ
I rejoiced in the Lord g. that   Ph'p 4:10 at last your care
desiring g. to see us, as we to   1Th 3:6 see you
g. desiring to see thee, that I   2Ti 1:4 may be filled
for he hath g. withstood our   2Ti 4:15 words
ye g. rejoice tho' now ye are in   1Pe 1:6 heaviness

rejoiced g. that I found children walking 2Jo 4
I rejoiced g. when the brethren testified 3Jo 3

GREATNESS

in g. of thy excellency overthrow them Ex 15:7
by g. of thine arm they shall be as a stone Ex 15:16
pardon according to g. of thy mercies Nu 14:19
thou hast begun to shew thy servant thy g. De 3:24
the Lord hath shewed us his glory and g. De 5:24
which thou hast redeemed through thy g. De 9:26
not with children who have not seen his g. De 11:2
ascribe ye g. unto our God, he is the rock De 32:3
to thy own hurt hast done all this g. 1Ch 17:19
to make thee a name of g. and terribleness 1Ch 17:21
thine, O Lord, is the g. power and glory 1Ch 29:11
one half of g. of thy wisdom not shewed 2Ch 9:6
and the g. of the burdens laid upon him 2Ch 24:27
spare me according to g. of thy mercy Ne 13:22
the declaration of the g. of Mordecai Es 10:2
by g. of thy power enemies submit to Ps 66:3
thou shalt increase my g. and comfort me Ps 71:21
according to the g. of thy power, preserve Ps 79:11
his g. is unsearchable; I declare thy g. Ps 145:3; 145:6
praise him according to his excellent g. Ps 150:2
in the g. of his folly he shall go astray Pr 5:23
he calleth by name, by g. of his might Isa 40:26
thou art wearied in the g. of thy way Isa 57:10
travelling in the g. of his strength Isa 63:1
for g. of iniquity thy skirts discovered Jer 13:22
whom art thou like in thy g. Eze 31:2
thus was he fair in his g. in his branches Eze 31:7
thy g. is grown and reacheth to heaven Da 4:22
the g. of the kingdom shall be given to saints Da 7:27
exceeding g. of power (A)(E) 2Co 4:7
what is the exceeding g. of his power Eph 1:19

GREAVES

Goliath had g. of brass upon his legs 1Sa 17:6
bronze leggings on both legs (B) 1Sa 17:6

GRECIA

the rough goat is the king of G. Da 8:21
when I am gone king of G. shall come Da 10:20
he shall stir up all against the realm of G. Da 11:2

GRECIANS

the children of Judah have ye sold to the G. Joe 3:6
there arose a murmuring of the G. Ac 6:1
Paul spake boldly and disputed against the G. Ac 9:29
who spake to the G., preaching the Lord Jesus Ac 11:20

GREECE

the king of G. (S) Da 8:21
the prince of G. (S) Da 10:20
the realm of G. (S) Da 11:2

thy sons, O Zion, against thy sons, O G. Zec 9:13
Paul came to G. and there abode Ac 20:2

GREED

g. like the grave (B) Jon 2:5
a look for g. (N)(R) 1Th 2:5

GREEDILY

he coveteth g. all the day long Pr 21:26
thou hast g. gained of thy neighbours Eze 22:12
they ran g. after the error of Balaam Jude 11

GREEDINESS

trapped in g. (E) Pr 11:6
given over to work all uncleanness with g. Eph 4:19
greediness (A)(B)(N) Eph 5:3
conceal g. motives (A) 1Th 2:5

GREEDY

like as a lion that is g. of his prey Ps 17:12
so is every one that is g. of gain Pr 1:19
taken in iniquity, g. desire (A) Pr 11:6
be that is g. of gain troubleth his house Pr 15:27
the g. man stirs up (A)(B)(E)(R) Pr 28:25
they are g. dogs, can never have enough Isa 56:11
g., dishonest (N)(P) Lu 18:11
g. and sobbers (B)(R) 1Co 5:10; 6:10
greed, g. (A)(B)(R) 1Co 5:11
conceal g. motives (P) 1Th 2:5
not g. of filthy lucre, but patient 1Ti 3:3; 3:8
not g. of gain (B)(P)(R) Tit 1:7
not our for g. gain (B) 1Pe 5:2

GREEDYGRASPERS

greedygraspers (A) 1Co 5:10; 6:10

GREEK

the woman was a G. a Syrophenician M'k 7:26
superscription written in G. Lu 23:38; Joh 19:20
the father of Timotheus was a G. Ac 16:1; 16:3
chief captain said, Canst thou speak G. Ac 21:37
to Jew first, and also to G. Ro 1:16
to the G. as well Ro 2:9
no difference between Jew and G. Ro 10:12; (A)(B)(E)(N)(P)(R)
nor Titus who was with me, being a G. Ga 2:3
but in G. tongue hath his name Apollyon Re 9:11

GREEKS

the G. (B) Joh 7:35
certain G. came to worship at the feast Joh 12:20
spake unto the G. (S) Ac 11:20
a multitude of G. believed Ac 14:1; 17:4, 12
he persuaded the Jews and the G. Ac 18:4
then the G. took Sosthenes and beat him Ac 18:17
Jews and G. heard the word of Lord Ac 19:10
this was known to all the G. at Ephesus Ac 19:17
testifying to the Jews and G. repentance Ac 20:21
he brought the G. also into the temple Ac 21:28
I am a debtor both to G. and Barbarians Ro 1:14
and the G. seek after wisdom 1Co 1:22
we preach Christ crucified, to G. foolishness 1Co 1:23
Jews and G., Christ the power of God 1Co 1:24

GREEN

to beast I have given every g. herb Ge 1:30
as the g. herb have I given you all things Ge 9:3
Jacob took rods of g. poplar and hazel Ge 30:37
there remained not any g. thing in trees Ex 10:15
offer for thy firstfruits g. ears of corn Le 2:14
eat no g. ears, till ye have brought an offering Le 23:14
if they bind me with seven g. withs J'g 16:7
then they brought to her seven g. withs J'g 16:8
inhabitants were as g. herbs 2Ki 19:26; Isa 37:27
where were white, g. and blue hangings Es 1:6
he is g. before the sun, branch shooteth Job 8:16
and his branch shall not be g. Job 15:32
the wild ass searcheth after every g. thing Job 39:8
he maketh me lie down in g. pastures Ps 23:2
and they shall wither as the g. herb Ps 37:2
I have seen wicked spreading like a g. bay tree Ps 37:35
thou art fair, also our bed is g. Ca 1:16
the fig tree putteth forth her g. figs Ca 2:13
the grass faileth, there is no g. thing Isa 15:6
the Lord called thy name, a g. olive Jer 11:16
as tree spreadeth her roots, leaf shall be g. Jer 17:8
I am like a g. fir tree, from me Ho 14:8
sit down by companies on the g. grass M'k 6:39
horse sickly g. in color (P) Re 6:8
hail and fire, and all g. grass was burnt up Re 8:7
were commanded not to hurt any g. thing Re 9:4

GREEN TREE

nations served gods under every g. tree De 12:2
images under every g. tree 1Ki 14:23; 2Ki 17:10
Asa sacrificed under every g. tree 2Ki 16:4; 2Ch 28:4
I am like a g. olive tree in house of God Ps 52:8
inflaming yourselves under every g. tree Isa 57:5
when under every g. tree thou wanderest Jer 2:20
under every g. tree, there played the harlot Jer 3:6
hast scattered thy ways under every g. tree Jer 3:13
thy slain shall be under every g. tree Eze 6:13
know that I have dried up the g. tree Eze 17:24
it shall devour every g. tree and dry tree Eze 20:47
if they do these things in a g. tree Lu 23:31

GREEN TREES

whilst children remember groves by g. trees Jer 17:2

GREENISH

if the plague be g. in the garment Le 13:49
if plague be with hollow strakes g. or red Le 14:37
g. or reddish cavities (R) Le 14:37

GREENNESS

whilst it is yet in his g. and not cut Job 8:12

GREET

greet (S) 1Sa 10:4; 25:14; 2Sa 8:10; 2Ki 4:29; 10:13; M't

5:47; 10:12; Lu 10:4; Ac 25:13; Ro 16:5,
7, 9-10, 12-16, 21-22; 1Co 16:19;
2Co 13:13; Ph'p 4:21-22; Col 4:15;
2Ti 4:19; Tit 3:15; Ph'm 23; Heb 13:24;
               3Jo 14
go to Nabal and g. him in my   1Sa 25:5
name
g. Priscilla and Aquila helpers   Ro 16:3
in Christ Jesus
g. church; g. Mary who   Ro 16:5;
bestowed labour   16:6
g. Amplias; g. the household   Ro 16:8;
of Narcissus   16:11
all the brethren g. you   1Co 16:20;
             Ph'p 4:21
g. ye one another   1Co 16:20;
       2Co 13:12; 1Pe 5:14
Luke the physician and Demas   Col 4:14
g. you
g. the brethren with an holy   1Th 5:26
kiss
g. them that love us in the   Tit 3:15
faith
the children of thy elect sister g.   2Jo 13
thee
peace be to thee, g. the friends   3Jo 14
by name

GREETED

greeted (S)   J'g 18:15;
1Sa 17:22; 30:21; 2Ki 10:15; M'k 9:15;
Lu 1:40; Ac 18:22; 21:7, 19

GREETETH

greeteth (S)   Ro 16:23;
       Col 4:10, 12; 1Pe 5:13
Eubulus g. thee, Pudens, and   2Ti 4:21
Linus

GREETING

greeting (S)   Lu 1:29; 1:41, 44
send g. unto the brethren   Ac 15:23
which
excellent governor Felix   Ac 23:26
sendeth g.
which are scattered abroad, g.   Jas 1:1

GREETINGS

send g. (S)   Ezr 4:11
And g. in the markets, and to   M't 23:7
be
synagogues and g. in the   Lu 11:43
markets
love g. in the markets, and the   Lu 20:46

GREW

herb of the field before it g.   Ge 2:5
that which g. upon the ground   Ge 19:25
the child g. and was weaned   Ge 21:8
God was with the lad: and he   Ge 21:20
g.
And the boys g.: and Esau   Ge 25:27
was
g. until he became very great   Ge 26:13
had possession therein, and g.   Ge 47:27
the more they multiplied and g.   Ex 1:12
And the child g. and she   Ex 2:10
brought
grew (S)   De 8:4;
32:15; Jos 23:1; 2Sa 3:1; 1Ch
11:9; 2Ch 24:15; Es 9:4; Da 8:8-10;
            Ac 13:46
and his wife's sons g. up and   J'g 11:2
they
and the child g. and the Lord   J'g 13:24
child Samuel g. before the   1Sa 2:21
Lord
the child Samuel g. on, and   1Sa 2:26
was
And Samuel g. and the Lord   1Sa 3:19
was
And David went on and g.   2Sa 5:10
great
it g. up together with him, and   2Sa 12:3
g. and became a spreading   Eze 17:6
vine
wither in the furrows where   Eze 17:10
it g.
The tree g. and was strong   Da 4:11
tree that thou sawest, which g.   Da 4:20
thorns g. up, and choked it   M'k 4:7
bettered, but rather g. worse   M'k 5:26
And the child g. and waxed   Lu 1:80;
strong   2:40
it g. and waxed a great tree   Lu 13:19

people g. and multiplied in   Ac 7:17
Egypt
the word of God g. and   Ac 12:24
multiplied
So mightily g. the word of   Ac 19:20
God

GREY

beauty of old men is the g.   Pr 20:29
head

GREYHEADED

Now also when I am old and   Ps 71:18
g.

GREYHOUND

A g.; an he goat also; and a   Pr 30:31

GRIDDLE

baked on a g. (A)(B)(R)   Le 2:5;
          6:21; 7:9
baked in a g. (A)   1Ch 23:29

GRIEF

multiply g. and suffering in   Ge 3:16
pregnancy (A)
it is g. to me to have (B)   Ge 6:7
Which were a g. of mind unto   Ge 26:35
Isaac
brought great distress to (B)   Ge 26:35
made life bitter for Isaac (R)   Ge 26:35
with g. (A)   Ge 42:38;
Job 17:7; Isa 50:11; Lu 22:45; Joh 16:21;
         Ro 9:2; 2Co 7:10
complaint and g. have I   1Sa 1:16
spoken
great complaint and bitter   1Sa 1:16
provocation (A)
under stress of provocation,   1Sa 1:16
distress (B)
my complaint and provocation   1Sa 1:16
(E)
my great anxiety and vexation   1Sa 1:16
(R)
this shall be no g. unto thee   1Sa 25:31
be no staggering g. (A)(R)   1Sa 25:31
his own sore and his own g.   2Ch 6:29
his own affliction and sorrow   2Ch 6:29
(A)(R)
his own plagues and pain (B)   2Ch 6:29
his own plagues and sorrow   2Ch 6:29
(E)
saw that his g. was very great   Job 2:13
his suffering was very great   Job 2:13
(B)
my g. were thoroughly weighed   Job 6:2
my vexation was weighed   Job 6:2
(A)(B)(E)(R)
of my lips should assuage   Job 16:5
your g.
would soothe my suffering   Job 16:5
(B)
would assuage your pain (R)   Job 16:5
I speak, my g. is not assuaged   Job 16:6
my sorrow is not soothed (A)   Job 16:6
my sorrow is not lessened (B)   Job 16:6
my pain is not assuaged (R)   Job 16:6
dim by reason of g. (R)   Job 17:7;
          Jer 8:18; 2Co 7:10
eye is consumed because of g.   Ps 6:7
note trouble, g., vexation   Ps 10:17
(A)(B)
mine eye is consumed with g.   Ps 31:9
For my life is spent with g.   Ps 31:10
life spent with sorrow   Ps 31:10
(A)(B)(E)(R)
they talk to the g. of those   Ps 69:26
whom
the gossip about those   Ps 69:26
wounded (A)
gossip of pain of pierced ones   Ps 69:26
(B)
tell of the sorrow of these   Ps 69:26
wounded (E)
this I said in my g. (A)(R)   Ps 77:10
grief (B) Ps 90:10; 116:3; Pr 15:13; 17:21
A foolish son is a g. to his   Pr 17:25
father
For in much wisdom is much g.   Ec 1:18
in more wisdom is more   Ec 1:18
vexation (A)(B)(R)
days are sorrows, and his   Ec 2:23
travail g.
his work is vexation (A)(R)   Ec 2:23

his task vexations (B)   Ec 2:23
grief (B)   Ec 5:17;
11:10; Joh 16:20, 22; Ph'p 2:27; Re 21:4
g. and wrath (R)   Ec 5:17
shall be a heap in the day of g.   Isa 17:11
in day of desperate sorrow,   Isa 17:11
sickening (A)
sorrows, and acquainted with   Isa 53:3
g.
acquainted with grief and   Isa 53:3
sickness (A)
acquainted with sickness (B)   Isa 53:3
he hath put him to g.: when   Isa 53:10
thou
before me continually is g. and   Jer 6:7
Truly this is a g. and I must   Jer 10:19
bear
did not Lord feel g. (B)   Jer 20:1
Lord hath added g. to my   Jer 45:3
sorrow
though he cause g. yet will he   La 3:32
head, to deliver him from his g.   Jon 4:6
filled with g. (N)   M't 17:23
break with g. (N)   M't 26:38
overwhelmed with g. (A)   M'k 14:34
sleeping for g. (N)   Lu 22:45; Ro 9:2
plunged into g. (N)   Joh 16:20; 16:21
if any have caused g. he hath   2Co 2:5
do it with joy, and not with   Heb 13:17
g.
conscience toward God   1Pe 2:19
endure g.
endures pain of unjust   1Pe 2:19
suffering (A)
mete out g. and torment   Re 18:7
(N)(R)

GRIEFS

hath borne our g. and carried   Isa 53:4
our
borne our griefs-sickness,   Isa 53:4
weakness, and distress (A)
He has borne our sicknesses   Isa 53:4
(B)
many thorny g. (N)   1Ti 6:10

GRIEVANCE

help bear my g. (B)   Job 7:13
and cause me to behold g.   Hab 1:3
cause me to see perverseness,   Hab 1:3
trouble (A)
makest me look on   Hab 1:3
perverseness (B)(E)
see wrongs and look upon   Hab 1:3
trouble (R)
if one feels a g. (B)   Col 3:13

GRIEVANCES

those with g. (B)   1Sa 22:2

GRIEVE

thine eyes, and to g. thine   1Sa 2:33
heart
wear out your life (B)   1Sa 2:33
g. over Saul (B)(R)   1Sa 16:1
from evil, that it may not g.   1Ch 4:10
me
that it might not hurt me   1Ch 4:10
(A)(R)
so that no pain assails me   1Ch 4:10
(B)
be not to my sorrow (E)   1Ch 4:10
do not g. (B)(E)(R)   Ne 8:10
the body shall g. (A)   Job 14:22
wilderness, and g. him in the   Ps 78:40
desert
willingly nor g. the children of   La 3:33
shall mourn and g. (B)   Isa 3:26
shall weep and g. (A)   Joh 16:20
g. our many (P)   2Co 12:21
And g. not the holy Spirit of   Eph 4:30
God
you g. not   1Th 4:13
(A)(B)(N)(P)(R)

GRIEVED

and it g. him at his heart   Ge 6:6
and the men were g. and they   Ge 34:7
disgusted and angry beyond   Ge 34:7
words (B)
indignant and very angry (R)   Ge 34:7
be not g. nor angry with   Ge 45:5
yourselves
The archers have sorely g.   Ge 49:23
him

bitterly attacked and sorely worried him (A) — Ge 49:23
archers harassed, shot at him (B)(R) — Ge 49:23
And they were g. because of the — Ex 1:12
were vexed and alarmed (A) — Ex 1:12
became frightened because of Israel (B) — Ex 1:12
were in dread because of Israel (R) — Ex 1:12
Lord felt g. (B) — Ex 32:14; 2Sa 24:16
wearied and g. by them (A) — Le 20:23
thine heart shall not be g. when — De 15:10
heart shall not be grudging (A)(R) — De 15:10
heavy at heart (B) — De 15:10
soul was g. for the misery of Israel — J'g 10:16
Israelites felt g. (B) — J'g 21:6; 21:15
thou not? and why is thy heart g. — 1Sa 1:8
why are you grieving (A) — 1Sa 1:8
why so downhearted (B) — 1Sa 1:8
why is your heart sad (R) — 1Sa 1:8
I am deeply g. (B) — 1Sa 1:15
it g. Samuel; and he cried unto — 1Sa 15:11
I am g. I made Saul (B) — 1Sa 15:11
it g. God he had (B) — 1Sa 15:35
Jonathan know this, lest he be g. — 1Sa 20:3
it may distress him (B) — 1Sa 20:3
was g. for David, because his father — 1Sa 20:34
the soul of all the people was g. — 1Sa 30:6
people were in an ugly mood (B) — 1Sa 30:6
people were bitter in soul (R) — 1Sa 30:6
the king was g. for his son — 2Sa 19:2
it g. them exceedingly that there — Ne 2:10
distressed them exceedingly (A) — Ne 2:10
were much displeased (B)(R) — Ne 2:10
neither be g. (S) — Ne 8:10
the day is holy; neither be ye g. — Ne 8:11
And it g. me sore: therefore I cast — Ne 13:8
was the queen exceedingly g. — Es 4:4
queen was deeply shocked (B) — Es 4:4
queen was deeply distressed (R) — Es 4:4
with thee, wilt thou be g. — Job 4:2
will you be offended (A)(R) — Job 4:2
would it distress you (B) — Job 4:2
was not my soul g. for the poor — Job 30:25
Thus my heart was g. and I was — Ps 73:21
my heart was bitter (B) — Ps 73:21
my soul was embittered (R) — Ps 73:21
Forty years long was I g. with — Ps 95:10
I was disgusted with that generation (B) — Ps 95:10
I loathed that generation (R) — Ps 95:10
felt g. according to (B) — Ps 106:45
The wicked shall see it, and be g. — Ps 112:10
wicked shall see with vexation (B) — Ps 112:10
wicked sees it and is angry (R) — Ps 112:10
the transgressors, and was g. — Ps 119:158
am not I g. with those that rise up — Ps 139:21
thee as a woman forsaken and g. — Isa 54:6
hand; therefore thou wast not g. — Isa 57:10
you were not faint or heartsick (A) — Isa 57:10
you were not exhausted (B) — Isa 57:10
you were not faint (R) — Isa 57:10
g. his Holy Spirit (A)(B)(E) — Isa 63:10
have not g.; thou hast consumed — Jer 5:3
I Daniel was g. in my spirit — Da 7:15
my spirit was distressed (B) — Da 7:15
spirit within me was anxious (R) — Da 7:15
he shall be g. and return — Da 11:30
he shall burn with rage (B) — Da 11:30
turn back and be enraged (R) — Da 11:30
feels g. over punishment (B) — Joe 2:13
they are not g. for the affliction — Am 6:6
was g. at calamity (B) — Jon 4:2
g. for assembly (A) — Zep 3:18

deeply g. (A) — M't 17:23
g. for the hardness of their hearts — M'k 3:5
vexed at their callousness of heart (B) — M'k 3:5
anger, sorrow at obstinate stupidity (N) — M'k 3:5
at that saying, and went away g. — M'k 10:22
went away saddened (B) — M'k 10:22
went away sorrowful (E)(R) — M'k 10:22
went away with a heavy heart (N) — M'k 10:22
went away in deep distress (P) — M'k 10:22
Peter was g. because he said unto — Joh 21:17
Peter felt distressed (B) — Joh 21:17
Peter was deeply hurt (P) — Joh 21:17
g. that they taught the people — Ac 4:2
vexed and indignant (A) — Ac 4:2
chagrined because they taught (B) — Ac 4:2
sore troubled because they taught (E) — Ac 4:2
exasperated at their teaching (N) — Ac 4:2
thoroughly incensed that they should (P) — Ac 4:2
annoyed because they were teaching (R) — Ac 4:2
Paul, being g. turned and said — Ac 16:18
Paul, being sorely annoyed (A)(B) — Ac 16:18
Paul, being sore troubled (E) — Ac 16:18
Paul, could bear it no longer (N) — Ac 16:18
Paul, in a burst of irritation (P) — Ac 16:18
Paul was annoyed (R) — Ac 16:18
g. especially over (B) — Ac 20:38
if thy brother be g. with thy meat — Ro 14:15
if brother is pained, feelings hurt, or is injured by what you eat (A) — Ro 14:15
If brother is pained at your eating (B) — Ro 14:15
If brother is outraged by what you eat (N) — Ro 14:15
seriously upsets your brother (P) — Ro 14:15
brother being injured by what you eat (R) — Ro 14:15
g. and made sad (A)(B)(P) — 2Co 2:2
not that ye should be g. but — 2Co 2:4
he hath not g. me but in part — 2Co 2:5
g. and mourning (A) — 2Co 6:10
made you g. (A)(B)(P) — 2Co 7:8
made you g. (B)(R) — 2Co 7:9
I was g. with that generation — Heb 3:10
provoked with that generation (A)(R) — Heb 3:10
became sorely displeased with (B)(E)(P) — Heb 3:10
indignant with that generation (N) — Heb 3:10
with whom was he g. forty years — Heb 3:17

GRIEVES

it g. and makes (A) — Ge 6:7
g. me — Ps 77:10

GRIEVETH

for it g. me much for your sakes — Ru 1:13
it is exceeding bitter (A)(R) — Ru 1:13
harder for me than for you (B) — Ru 1:13
it g. him to bring it again to his — Pr 26:15
distresses, wearies him (A) — Pr 26:15
tires him to return to mouth (B) — Pr 26:15
wearieth to bring it to mouth (E) — Pr 26:15
wears him out to bring it to (R) — Pr 26:15

GRIEVING

why are you g. (A) — Isa 1:8
I am weary of g. (B) — Jer 15:6
nor any g. thorn of all that are — Eze 28:24

a hurting thorn to all (A)(E) — Eze 28:24
to pricking thorns and painful briers (B) — Eze 28:24
a brier to prick or a thorn to hurt (R) — Eze 28:24

GRIEVOUS

the famine was g. in the land — Ge 12:10
famine was severe in the land (B)(R) — Ge 12:10
famine was sore in the land (E) — Ge 12:10
and because their sin is very g. — Ge 18:20
the thing was very g. in Abraham's — Ge 21:11
proposal seemed very wrong (B) — Ge 21:11
thing was very displeasing to (R) — Ge 21:11
Let it not be g. in thy sight — Ge 21:12
Do not consider it objectionable (B) — Ge 21:12
Do not be displeased (R) — Ge 21:12
following: for it shall be very g. — Ge 41:31
it will be wholly severe (B) — Ge 41:31
is a g. mourning to the Egyptians — Ge 50:11
This is a deep-felt mourning (B) — Ge 50:11
there came a g. swarm of flies — Ex 8:24
there shall be a very g. murrain — Ex 9:3
a very severe plague (A)(R) — Ex 9:3
a dreadful plague (B) — Ex 9:3
will cause it to rain a very g. hail — Ex 9:18
fire mingled with the hail, very g. — Ex 9:24
coasts of Egypt: very g. were they — Ex 10:14
cursed me with a g. curse in the — 1Ki 2:8
cursed me violently (B) — 1Ki 2:8
Thy father made our yoke g. — 1Ki 12:4
made our yoke heavy (A)(R) — 1Ki 12:4
made our yoke unbearable (B) — 1Ki 12:4
thou the g. service of thy father — 1Ki 12:4
Thy father made our yoke g. now — 2Ch 10:4
the g. servitude of thy father — 2Ch 10:4
His ways are always g.: thy — Ps 10:5
be put to silence: which speak g. — Ps 31:18
which speak insolently against (A)(B)(E)(R) — Ps 31:18
wrath: but g. words stir up anger — Pr 15:1
harsh words stirs up anger (B)(R) — Pr 15:1
Correction is g. unto him that — Pr 15:10
there is severe discipline (A)(B)(R) — Pr 15:10
under the sun is g. unto me — Ec 2:17
seemed bad to me (B) — Ec 2:17
his life shall be g. unto him — Isa 15:4
his soul trembles within him (B)(E)(R) — Isa 15:4
A g. vision is declared unto me — Isa 21:2
a harsh vision is declared to me (B) — Isa 21:2
a stern vision is told me (R) — Isa 21:2
They are all g. revolters — Jer 6:28
for my hurt! my wound is g. — Jer 10:19
a great breach, with a very g. blow — Jer 14:17
with a very ugly wound (B) — Jer 14:17
with a very great wound (R) — Jer 14:17
They shall die of g. deaths — Jer 16:4
die of deadly diseases (A)(R) — Jer 16:4
shall die of the pestilence (E) — Jer 16:4
in fury, even a g. whirlwind — Jer 23:19
incurable, and thy wound is g. — Jer 30:12
thy wound is g.: all that hear — Na 3:19
heavy burdens and g. to be borne — M't 23:4
hard to bear (A)(R) — M't 23:4
with burdens g. to be borne, and ye — Lu 11:46
shall g. wolves enter in among you — Ac 20:29
ferocious wolves will get in (A) — Ac 20:29
savage wolves will make (B)(N)(P) — Ac 20:29
fierce wolves will come (R) — Ac 20:29
and g. complaints against Paul — Ac 25:7

GRIEVOUS (continued)

bringing many great accusations (A)	Ac 25:7
numerous and weighty charges (B)	Ac 25:7
to me indeed is not g. but for	Ph'p 3:1
is not irksome (A)(B)(E)(R)	Ph'p 3:1
is no trouble to me (N)	Ph'p 3:1
it doesn't bore me to repeat (P)	Ph'p 3:1
g. times shall come (E)	2Ti 3:1
seemeth to be joyous, but g.	Heb 12:11
not enjoyable, but painful (B)	Heb 12:11
at the time it seems painful (N)	Heb 12:11
it is in fact most unpleasant (P)	Heb 12:11
all discipline seems painful (R)	Heb 12:11
and his commandments are not g.	1Jo 5:3
these orders of his are not irksome, burdensome, oppressive, or grievous (A)	1Jo 5:3
His commands are not irksome (B)	1Jo 5:3
they are not burdensome (N)(P)(R)	1Jo 5:3
noisome and g. sore upon the men	Re 16:2
foul and painful ulcers came (A)	Re 16:2
loathsome and malignant ulcers (B)(P)	Re 16:2
foul and malignant sores appeared (N)	Re 16:2
foul and evil sores came upon men (R)	Re 16:2

GRIEVOUSLY

afterward did more g. afflict her	Isa 9:1
whirlwind: it shall fall g. upon	Jer 23:19
Jerusalem hath g. sinned	La 1:8
for I have g. rebelled: abroad	La 1:20
against me by trespassing g.	Eze 14:13
sick of the palsy, g. tormented	M't 8:6
daughter is g. vexed with a devil	M't 15:22

GRIEVOUSNESS

that write g. which they have	Isa 10:1
bent bow, and from the g. of war	Isa 21:15
before the hardship of battle (B)	Isa 21:15
from the press of battle (R)	Isa 21:15

GRIND

and he did g. in the prison house	J'g 16:21
Then let my wife g. unto another	Job 31:10
pieces, and g. the faces of the poor	Isa 3:15
nor g. it with horsemen (S)	Isa 28:28
Take the millstones, and g. meal	Isa 47:2
They took the young men to g.	La 5:13
shall fall, it will g. him to powder	M't 21:44; Lu 20:18

GRINDERS

the g. cease because they are few	Ec 12:3

GRINDING

when the sound of the g. is low	Ec 12:4
when sound of the mill becomes low (B)	Ec 12:4
g. his teeth (A)(B)	M't 8:12; 13:42, 50; 22:13; 24:51; 25:30
Two women shall be g. at the mill	M't 24:41
Two women shall be g. together	Lu 17:35
g. misery upon (N)	Ro 9:2

GRINDS

g. his teeth (B)(E)(N)(P)(R)	M'k 9:18

GRIPPED

fatal fear g. city (B)	1Sa 5:11

GRISLED

ringstraked, speckled, and g.	Ge 31:10; 31:12
streaked, speckled, and spotted (A)	Ge 31:10
striped, speckled, and mottled (B)(R)	Ge 31:10
fourth chariot g. and bay horses	Zec 6:3
fourth chariot dappled horses (A)(B)(R)	Zec 6:3; 6:6
the g. go forth toward the south	Zec 6:6

GROAN

Men g. from out of the city	Job 24:12
g. because of heart (B)(R)	Ps 38:8
in restlessness I g. (B)	Ps 55:2
I am disquieted and g. (A)	Ps 77:3
at end of life you g. (R)	Pr 5:11
the people g. and sigh (A)(B)(R)	Pr 29:2
all her land the wounded shall g.	Jer 51:52
he shall g. before him with	Eze 30:24
How do the beasts g.! the herds	Joe 1:18
we ourselves g. within ourselves	Ro 8:23
sigh within ourselves (B)	Ro 8:23; 2Co 5:2, 4
in this we g. earnestly desiring to	2Co 5:2
we that are in this tabernacle do g.	2Co 5:4

GROANED

g. in the spirit, and was troubled	Joh 11:33
deeply moved in spirit and sighed (A)(R)	Joh 11:33
deeply indignant in spirit (B)	Joh 11:33
he sighed heavily (N)	Joh 11:33

GROANETH

g. and travaileth in pain together	Ro 8:22
moaning together in pains of labor (A)	Ro 8:22
sighing and in throes of unison (B)	Ro 8:22

GROANING

And God heard their g.	Ex 2:24
And I have also heard the g. of	Ex 6:5
my stroke is heavier than my g.	Job 23:2
I am weary with my g.; all the	Ps 6:6
and my g. is not hid from thee	Ps 38:9
my sighing is not hid (A)(B)(R)	Ps 38:9
By reason of the voice of my g. my	Ps 102:5
the sound of my sighing (B)	Ps 102:5
To hear the g. of the prisoner	Ps 102:20
therefore again g. in himself	Joh 11:38
and I have heard their g. and	Ac 7:34
g. in travail (R)	Ro 8:22

GROANINGS

because of their g. by reason of	J'g 2:18
g. poured out (A)(B)(E)(R)	Job 3:24
the g. of a deadly wounded man	Eze 30:24
with g. which cannot be uttered	Ro 8:26
with unspeakable yearnings and g. (A)	Ro 8:26
sighs too deep for words (B)(R)	Ro 8:26
agonizing longings never find words (P)	Ro 8:26

GROANS

g. as if in pangs of (N)(P)	Ro 8:22
through g. the Spirit pleading (N)	Ro 8:26

GROPE

thou shalt g. at noonday, as	De 28:29
g. in the noonday as in the night	Job 5:14
They g. in the dark without light	Job 12:25
We g. for the wall like the blind	Isa 59:10
and we g. as if we had no eyes	Isa 59:10

GROPETH

as the blind g. in darkness	De 28:29

GROSS

earth, and g. darkness the people	Isa 60:2
dense darkness all people (A)	Isa 60:2
dark cloud in the nations (B)	Isa 60:2
thick darkness the peoples (R)	Isa 60:2
of death, and make it g.	Jer 13:16
darkness	
For this people's heart is waxed g.	M't 13:15
heart has grown dull (B)(R)	M't 13:15
the heart of this people is waxed g.	Ac 28:27

GROSSLY

g. offensive thoughts (A)	Jer 14:14

GROUND

and there was not a man to till the g.	Ge 2:5
Lord God formed man of the dust of g.	Ge 2:7
out of the g. the Lord formed every beast	Ge 2:19
he said, Cursed is the g. for thy sake	Ge 3:17
Abel a keeper of sheep, but Cain a tiller of g.	Ge 4:2
thy brother's blood crieth to me from the g.	Ge 4:10
because of the g. the Lord hath cursed	Ge 5:29
I will not again curse the g. any more	Ge 8:21
Abram bowed himself toward the g.	Ge 18:2
Lot bowed himself with his face toward g.	Ge 19:1
where thou standest is holy g.	Ex 3:5; Ac 7:33
g. whereon they are shall be full of flies	Ex 8:21
the g. clave asunder under them	Nu 16:31
blessed shall be the fruit of thy g.	De 28:4; 28:11
Jael fastened the nail into the g.	J'g 4:21
he will set them to ear his g. and reap	1Sa 8:12
his spear stuck in the g. at his bolster	1Sa 26:7
where was a piece of g. full of lentiles	2Sa 23:11
he stood in midst of g. and defended it	2Sa 23:12
but the water is naught, and g. barren	2Ki 2:19
now take him and cast him into the plat of g.	2Ki 9:26
where was a parcel of g. full of barley	1Ch 11:13
the king did cast them in the clay g.	2Ch 4:17
and to bring the firstfruits of our g.	Ne 10:35
and bring the tithes of our g. to the Levites	Ne 10:37
nor doth trouble spring out of the g.	Job 5:6
and though the stock thereof die in the g.	Job 14:8
the snare is laid for him in the g.	Job 18:10
to satisfy the desolate and waste g.	Job 38:27
he swallows the g. with fierceness and rage	Job 39:24
locusts devoured the fruit of their g.	Ps 105:35
he turneth the watersprings into dry g.	Ps 107:33
and he turneth dry g. into watersprings	Ps 107:35
fallow g. (S)	Pr 13:23
doth he open and break clods at his g.	Isa 28:24
Bread corn is g. (S)	Isa 28:28

and thou shalt speak out of the *Isa 29:4*
g.
seed that thou shalt sow the *Isa 30:23*
g. withal
oxen and young asses that ear *Isa 30:24*
the *g.* shall eat
and the parched *g.* shall *Isa 35:7*
become a pool
and thou hast laid thy body *Isa 51:23*
as the *g.*
break up your fallow *g.* *Jer 4:3;*
Ho 10:12
my fury shall be poured on the *Jer 7:20*
fruit of the *g.*
because the *g.* is chapt, there *Jer 14:4*
was no rain
her gates are sunk into the *g.* *La 2:2*
cover thy face, thou see not *Eze 12:6*
the *g.*
veiled from the *g.* up to the *Eze 41:16*
windows
an he goat came, and touched *Da 8:5*
not the *g.*
Daniel's face was towards the *Da 8:18;*
g. *10:9, 15*
make covenant with them for *Ho 2:18*
things of *g.*
and the *g.* shall give her *Zec 8:12*
increase
he shall not destroy the fruits *Mal 3:11*
of your *g.*
but other fell into good *g.* *M't 13:8;*
Lu 8:8
he that received seed into *M't 13:23;*
good *g.* *Lu 8:15*
as if a man should cast seed *M'k 4:26*
into the *g.*
the *g.* of a certain rich man *Lu 12:16*
brought forth
cut it down, why cumbereth it *Lu 13:7*
the *g.*
the first said, I have bought a *Lu 14:18*
piece of *g.*
they shall lay thee even with *Lu 19:44*
the *g.*
near the parcel of *g.* Jacob gave *Joh 4:5*
Joseph
except a corn of wheat fall *Joh 12:24*
into the *g.*
common *g.* between (B) *2Co 6:14*

ON, UPON THE GROUND

he spilled it *on the g.* lest he *Ge 38:9*
should give
Joseph's brethren fell before *Ge 44:14*
him *on the g.*
cast the rod *on the g.* he cast it *Ex 4:3*
on the g.
thunder, and the fire ran along *Ex 9:23*
upon the g.
Israel shall go *on dry g.* *Ex 14:16*
through the sea
as small as the hoar frost on *Ex 16:14*
the *g.*
pour the blood *upon the g.* as *De 15:23*
water
if a bird's nest chance to be *on* *De 22:6*
the *g.*
woman that would not set her *De 28:56*
foot *upon a g.*
and *upon all the g.* let there be *J'g 6:39*
dew
and there was dew *upon all the* *J'g 6:40*
g.
and there was honey *upon* *1Sa 14:25*
the *g.*
the people slew oxen and *1Sa 14:32*
calves *on the g.*
as long as the son of Jesse *1Sa 20:31*
liveth *on the g.*
for we are as water spilt on *2Sa 14:14*
the *g.*
shall light on him as dew *2Sa 17:12*
falleth *on the g.*
he said, Smite *upon the g.* he *2Ki 13:18*
smote
Job fell *upon the g.* and *Job 1:20*
worshipped
they sat down with him *upon* *Job 2:13*
the *g.* seven days
he poureth out my gall *upon* *Job 16:13*
the *g.*
she being desolate shall sit *on* *Isa 3:26*
the *g.*
O daughter of Babylon, sit *on* *Isa 47:1*
the *g.*
they shall be dung *upon the g.* *Jer 25:33*

I have made man and beast *Jer 27:5*
upon the g.
elders of daughter of Zion sit *La 2:10*
on the g.
young and old lie *on the g. in* *La 2:21*
the streets
she poured it not *upon the g.* *Eze 24:7*
to cover it
then all the princes shall sit *Eze 26:16*
upon the g.
the multitude to sit *on the g.* *M't 15:35;*
M'k 8:6
some fell *on* stony *g.* it had *M'k 4:5;*
not earth *4:16*
and other fell *on* good *g.* *M'k 4:8;*
4:20; Lu 8:8, 15
he fell *on the g.* and wallowed *M'k 9:20*
foaming
he went forward, and fell on *M'k 14:35*
g. and prayed
he wrote *on the g.* *Joh 8:6; 8:8*
he spat *on the g.* *Joh 9:6*

TO, UNTO THE GROUND

till thou return *unto the g.* for *Ge 3:19*
out of it
Jacob bowed himself *to the g.* *Ge 33:3*
seven times
Manoah and his wife fell *to* *J'g 13:20*
the *g.*
Benjamin destroyed *to the g.* *J'g 20:21*
22,000 men
destroyed *to the g.* of Israel *J'g 20:25*
18,000 men
Ruth bowed and fell *to the g.* *Ru 2:10*
let none of his words fall *to* *1Sa 3:19*
the *g.*
Dagon was fallen on his face *to* *1Sa 5:4*
the *g.*
shall not one hair of his head *1Sa 14:45*
fall *to the g.*
David arose and fell on his *1Sa 20:41*
face *to the g.*
Abigail bowed *to the g.* *1Sa 25:23*
before David
Saul stooped with his face *to* *1Sa 28:14*
the *g.*
wherefore should I smite thee *2Sa 2:22*
to the g.
he smote Moab, casting him *2Sa 8:2*
down *to the g.*
woman of Tekoah fell on her *2Sa 14:4*
face *to the g.*
Joab fell *to the g.*; Absalom *2Sa 14:22;*
bowed *to the g.* *14:33*
why didst not thou smite him *2Sa 18:11*
to the g.
Joab shed out Amasa's *2Sa 20:10*
bowels *to the g.*
Nathan bowed *to the g.* before *1Ki 1:23*
the king
sons of the prophets bowed *to* *2Ki 2:15*
the *g.*
woman of Shunam bowed *2Ki 4:37*
herself *to the g.*
Ornan bowed *to the g.* to *1Ch 21:21*
David
all Israel bowed with their *2Ch 7:3*
faces *to the g.*
Jehoshaphat bowed with his *2Ch 20:18*
face *to the g.*
worshipped Lord with their *Ne 8:6*
faces *to the g.*
the dwelling place of thy name *Ps 74:7*
to the g.
profaned his crown, by casting *Ps 89:39*
it *to the g.*
thou hast cast his throne down *Ps 89:44*
to the g.
he hath smitten my life down *Ps 143:3*
to the g.
he casteth the wicked down *to* *Ps 147:6*
the *g.*
how art thou cut down *to the* *Isa 14:12*
g.
Babylon's images he hath *Isa 21:9*
broken *to the g.*
lay low, bring *to the g.* even *Isa 25:12*
to the dust
the lofty city he layeth even *to* *Isa 26:5*
the *g.*
her gates languish, are black *to* *Jer 14:2*
the *g.*
hath brought strong holds of *La 2:2*
Judah *to the g.*
virgins of Jerusalem hang their *La 2:10*
heads *to the g.*

I will bring down the wall *to* *Eze 13:14*
the *g.*
thy mother was cast down *to* *Eze 19:12*
the *g.*
thy strong garrison shall go *Eze 26:11*
down *to the g.*
I will cast thee *to the g.* I will *Eze 28:17*
lay thee
he cast the ram down *to the g.* *Da 8:7*
and stamped
it cast down some of hosts and *Da 8:10*
stars to the *g.*
and cast down the truth *to the* *Da 8:12*
g.
the horns of the altar shall fall *Am 3:14*
to the g.
saith, Who shall bring me down *to Ob 3*
the *g.*
one of them shall not fall *to* *M't 10:29*
the *g.*
as drops of blood falling *to* *Lu 22:44*
the *g.*
they went backward, and fell *Joh 18:6*
to the g.
fell *to the g.* and heard a voice *Ac 22:7*

GROUNDED

in every place where *g.* staff *Isa 30:22*
shall pass
that ye being rooted and *g.* in *Eph 3:17*
love
if ye continue in the faith, *g.* *Col 1:23*
and settled

GROUNDLESS

g. arguments (A) *Eph 5:6*

GROUNDLESSLY

Christ died *g.* (A) *Ga 2:21*

GROUP

a *g.* of nations (B) *Ge 35:11*
meet a *g.* of prophets (B) *1Sa 10:5;*
19:20
one *g.* with (A)(B) *1Ch 24:5*
large *g.* of priests (B) *Ac 6:7*

GROUPS

full into sharply divided *g.* *1Co 11:18*
(N)(P)

GROVE

And Abraham planted a *g.* in *Ge 21:33*
planted a tamarisk tree *Ge 21:33*
(A)(B)(E((R)
Thou shalt not plant thee a *g.* *De 16:21*
Do not plant an Asherah *De 16:21*
(A)(B)(E)(R)
cut down the *g.* that is by it *J'g 6:25*
wood of the Asherah (A) *J'g 6:25*
cut down the shame images *J'g 6:25;*
(B) *6:28*
the wood of the *g.* which thou *J'g 6:26*
the *g.* was cut down that was *J'g 6:28*
he hath cut down the *g.* that *J'g 6:30*
was
she had made an idol in a *g.* *1Ki 15:13*
made an Asherah *1Ki 15:13;*
(A)(B)(E)(R) *16:33*
Ahab made a *g.* and Ahab *1Ki 16:33*
remained the *g.* also in *2Ki 13:6*
Samaria
remained the Asherah *2Ki 13:6;*
(A)(E)(R) *17:16; 21:3; 23:4, 6, 15*
shame images remain (B) *2Ki 13:6;*
17:16; 21:3; 23:4, 6, 15
even two calves, and made a *2Ki 17:16*
g.
and made a *g.* as did Ahab *2Ki 21:3*
king
set a graven image of the *g.* *2Ki 21:7*
that
for Baal. and for the *g.* and *2Ki 23:4*
he brought out the *g.* from the *2Ki 23:6*
women wove hangings for the *2Ki 23:7*
g.
to powder, and burned the *g.* *2Ki 23:15*
she had made an idol in a *g.* *2Ch 15:16*

GROVES

images, and cut down their *g.* *Ex 34:13*
cut down their Asherim *Ex 34:13*
(A)(E)(R)
sacred trees, totem pole gods *Ex 34:13*
(B)

images, and cut down their *g.*   *De 7:5*
and burn their *g.* with fire   *De 12:3*
burn their Asherim   *De 12:3*
(A)(E)(R)
burn their sacred trees (B)   *De 12:3*
and served Baalim and the *g.*   *J'g 3:7*
served the Baals and the   *J'g 3:7*
Ashtaroth (A)(B)
served Balaam and the Asheroth *J'g 3:7*
(E)(R)
because they have made their *1Ki 14:15*
g.
made their Asherim   *1Ki 14:15;*
(A)(B)(E)(R)   *14:23*
and *g.* on every high hill, and *1Ki 14:23*
prophets of the *g.* four   *1Ki 18:19*
hundred
prophets of Asherah   *1Ki 18:19*
(A)(B)(E)(R)
and *g.* in every high hill, and *2Ki 17:10*
the images, and cut down the *2Ki 18:4*
g.
cut down the Asherah   *2Ki 18:4*
(A)(E)(R)
cut off shame images (B)   *2Ki 18:4*
the images, and cut down the *2Ki 23:14*
g.
cut down the Asherim   *2Ki 23:14*
(A)(E)(R)
cut off the shame images (B) *2Ki 23:14*
the images, and cut down the *2Ch 14:3*
g.
hewed down the Asherim   *2Ch 14:3*
(A)(E)(R)
chopped down the Asherahs *2Ch 14:3*
(B)
took away the high places and *2Ch 17:6*
g.
took away the Asherim   *2Ch 17:6;*
(A)(E)(R)   *31:1; 34:3, 7*
remove the shame images   *2Ch 17:6;*
(B)   *19:3; 31:1; 33:3; 34:3, 7*
thou hast taken away the *g.* *2Ch 19:3*
put away the Asheroth   *2Ch 19:3;*
(A)(B)   *33:3*
destroyed the Asherahs (R) *2Ch 19:3;*
  33:3
fathers, and served *g.* and *2Ch 24:18*
idols
in pieces, and cut down the *g.* *2Ch 31:1*
and made *g.* and worshipped *2Ch 33:3*
all
and set up *g.* and graven *2Ch 33:19*
images
the *g.* and the carved images *2Ch 34:3;*
  34:4
altars and the *g.* and had *2Ch 34:7*
beaten
either, the *g.* or the images *Isa 17:8*
the images of the Ashteroth *Isa 17:8*
(B)
their altars and their *g.* by the *Jer 17:2*
the goddess Ashteroth (A) *Jer 17:2*
their Asherim (B)(E)(R)   *Jer 17:2*
the *g.* and images shall not *Jer 27:9*
stand
the shame images (B)   *Jer 27:9;*
  Mic 5:14
I will pluck up thy *g.* out of *Mic 5:14*

GROW

the Lord God to *g.* every tree   *Ge 2:9*
and let them *g.* into a   *Ge 48:16*
multitude
locks of the hair of his head a *Nu 6:5*
the hair of his head began to *J'g 16:22*
g.
grow (S)   *1Sa 3:2;*
Job 14:8;   Isa 29:22;   50:9;   51:6;
M't 24:12; Lu 12:33; 1Ti 5:11
such things as *g.* of   *2Ki 19:29*
themselves
why should damage *g.* to the *Ezr 4:22*
hurt
Can the rush *g.* up without *Job 8:11*
mire
out of the earth shall others *g.* *Job 8:19*
washest away the things   *Job 14:19*
which *g.*
Let thistles *g.* instead of *Job 31:40*
wheat
good liking, they *g.* up with *Job 39:4*
corn
shall *g.* like a cedar in   *Ps 92:12*
Lebanon
causeth the grass to *g.* for the *Ps 104:14*
who maketh grass to *g.* upon *Ps 147:8*

how the bones do *g.* in the   *Ec 11:5*
womb
Branch shall *g.* out of his roots *Isa 11:1*
shalt thou make thy plant to *Isa 17:11*
For he shall *g.* up before him *Isa 53:2*
they have taken root: they *g.* *Jer 12:2*
yea
Branch of righteousness to *g.* *Jer 33:15*
up
nor suffer their locks to *g.* *Eze 44:20*
long
this side and on that side, *Eze 47:12*
shall *g.*
he shall *g.* as the lily, and cast *Ho 14:5*
as the corn, and *g.* as the vine *Ho 14:7*
neither madest it *g.* which *Jon 4:10*
came
he shall *g.* up out of his place *Zec 6:12*
and *g.* up as calves of the stall *Mal 4:2*
the lilies of the field, how they *M't 6:28*
g.
both *g.* together until the   *M't 13:30*
harvest
no fruit *g.* on thee hence- *M't 21:19*
forward
the seed should spring and *g.* *M'k 4:27*
up
Consider the lilies how they *g.* *Lu 12:27*
of them whereunto this would *Ac 5:24*
may *g.* up into him in all   *Eph 4:15*
things
g. up feeling inferior and   *Col 3:21*
frustrated (P)
g. stubborn as in (B)(R)   *Heb 3:15*
the word, that ye may *g.*   *1Pe 2:2*
thereby
g. in grace, and in the   *2Pe 3:18*
knowledge

GROWETH

every tree which *g.* for you out *Ex 10:5*
of
freckled spot that *g.* in the   *Le 13:39*
skin
That which *g.* of its own   *Le 25:5*
accord
reap that which *g.* of itself in *Le 25:11*
it
beareth, nor any grass *g.*   *De 29:23*
therein
the day *g.* to an end, lodge   *J'g 19:9*
here
When the dust *g.* into   *Job 38:38*
hardness
groweth (S)   *Ps 6:7; Heb 8:13*
they are like grass which *g.* up *Ps 90:5*
morning it flourisheth, and *g.* up *Ps 90:6*
which withereth afore it *g.* up *Ps 129:6*
eat this year such as *g.* of   *Isa 37:30*
itself
when it is sown, it *g.* up, and *M'k 4:32*
g. unto an holy temple in the *Eph 2:21*
Lord
that your faith *g.* exceedingly *2Th 1:3*

GROWING

go on *g.* in me (P)   *Joh 15:4*
qualities *g.* (P)   *2Pe 1:8*

GROWL

g. like lion's whelps   *Jer 51:38*
(B)(E)(R)

GROWLING

g. like lion's whelps (A)   *Jer 51:38*

GROWN

house, till Shelah my son be *g.* *Ge 38:11*
she saw that Shelah was *g.* *Ge 38:14*
when Moses was *g.* that he *Ex 2:11*
went
smitten: for they were not *g.* *Ex 9:32*
up
there is black hair *g.* up *Le 13:37*
therein
grown (S)   *De 31:20;*
Jer 5:27-28; 49:24; Re 18:3
thou art waxen fat, thou art *De 32:15*
g. thick
tarry for them till they were *g.* *Ru 1:13*
until your beards be *g.* and *2Sa 10:5*
then

that were *g.* up with him, and *1Ki 12:8*
that were *g.* up with him   *1Ki 12:10*
spake
And when the child was *g.* it *2Ki 4:18*
fell
as corn blasted before it be *2Ki 19:26;*
g. up   *Isa 37:27*
at Jericho until your beards *1Ch 19:5*
be *g.*
our trespass is *g.* up unto the *Ezr 9:6*
as plants *g.* up in their youth *Ps 144:12*
it was all *g.* over with thorns *Pr 24:31*
are *g.* fat as the heifer at *Jer 50:11*
grass
are fashioned, and thine hair *Eze 16:7*
is *g.*
that are *g.* and become strong *Da 4:22*
for thy greatness is *g.*   *Da 4:22*
till his hairs were *g.* like eagles *Da 4:33*
when it is *g.* it is the greatest *M't 13:32*
the full *g.* (A)   *1Co 2:6*
unto a full *g.* man (E)   *Eph 4:13*

GROWS

what *g.* of itself (A)(E)(R)   *Le 25:5*
my compassion *g.* warm and *Ho 11:8*
tender (R)
love *g.* ever greater (N)   *2Th 1:3*

GROWTH

the voluntary *g.*   *Le 25:5*
the shooting up of the latter *g.* *Am 7:1*
and, lo, it was the latter *g.* after *Am 7:1*
g. of another's character (P) *Ro 14:19*
the real *g.* of the church (P) *1Co 14:12*

GRUDGE

bear any *g.* against the   *Le 19:18*
children
g. food to a brother (R)   *De 28:54;*
  28:56
and *g.* if they be not satisfied *Ps 59:15*
Herodias held a *g.*   *M'k 6:19*
(A)(B)(N)(R)
G. not one against another   *Jas 5:9*

GRUDGING

heart be *g.* (A)(R)   *De 15:10*
cruel and *g.* of food (A)   *De 28:54*
one to another without *g.*   *1Pe 4:9*

GRUDGINGLY

g. toward brother (B)   *De 28:54; 28:56*
not *g.* or of necessity   *2Co 9:7*

GRUMBLE

who hears you *g.* (B)   *Ex 16:7;*
  Nu 14:36
do not *g.* among yourselves *Joh 6:43*
do not *g.* (B)(N)(R)   *1Co 10:10*

GRUMBLED

whole congregation *g.* (B) *Ex 16:2*
you have *g.* (B)   *Nu 14:29*
they *g.* (A)(B)(N)(P)(R) *M't 20:11*
Jews *g.* about him (B)   *Joh 6:41*

GRUMBLING

Pharisees were *g.* (A)(B)   *Lu 5:30*
began *g.* (N)   *Lu 15:2*
without *g.* (A)(B)(P)(R)   *Ph'p 2:14*
stop *g.* (A)   *Joh 6:43*
his disciples were *g.* (B)   *Joh 6:61*

GUARANTEE

Spirit in our hearts as *g.*   *2Co 1:22*
(A)(P)(R)
g. of purchase (P)(R)   *Eph 1:14*
g. of a better agreement (P) *Heb 7:22*
guarantee of living in him (P) *1Jo 4:13*

GUARANTEED

Spirit is *g.* inheritance (A) *Eph 1:14*
g. with an oath (N)   *Heb 6:17*

GUARANTY

I will stand *g.* for him (A)   *Ge 43:9*
I went *g.* for him (B)   *Ge 44:32*

GUARD

Pharaoh's and captain of the g. — Ge 37:36
of Pharaoh, captain of the g. — Ge 39:1
the house of the captain of the g. — Ge 40:3
the g. charged Joseph with them — Ge 40:4
servant to the captain of the g. — Ge 41:12
the rear g. (S) — Nu 10:25; Jos 6:9, 13; Isa 52:12; 58:8
put them under g. (A)(N) — 2Sa 20:3
And David set him over his g. — 2Sa 23:23; 1Ch 11:25
the hands of the chief of the g. — 1Ki 14:27
that the g. bare them, and brought — 1Ki 14:28
them back into the g. chamber — 1Ki 14:28
that Jehu said to the g. and to the — 2Ki 10:25
the g. and the captains cast them — 2Ki 10:25
with the captains and the g. — 2Ki 11:4
third part at the gate behind the g. — 2Ki 11:6
And the g. stood, every man with — 2Ki 11:11
Athaliah heard the noise of the g. — 2Ki 11:13
the captains, and the g. and all — 2Ki 11:19
gate of the g. to the king's house — 2Ki 11:19
Nebuzar-adan, captain of the g. — 2Ki 25:8; Jer 39:11
that were with the captain of the g. — 2Ki 25:10
the captain of the g. carry away — 2Ki 25:11; Jer 39:9; 52:15; 30
the captain of the g. left of the poor — 2Ki 25:12; Jer 39:10
the captain of the g. took away — 2Ki 25:15
the captain of the g. took Seraiah — 2Ki 25:18; Jer 52:24
captain of the g. took these guard (S) — 2Ki 25:20; 1Ch 12:29; Jer 37:13; Ac 12:10
the chief of the g. that kept — 2Ch 12:10
the g. came and fetched them — 2Ch 12:11
them again into the g. chamber — 2Ch 12:11
the court of the g. (S) — Ne 3:25
in the night they may be a g. to us — Ne 4:22
men of the g. which followed me — Ne 4:23
the gate of the g. (S) — Ne 12:39
g. them from this generation (B)(R) — Ps 12:7
g. my life (B) — Ps 64:1
above all you g., watch your heart (B) — Pr 4:23
eyes of Lord g. over (A) — Pr 22:12
the captain of the g. sent, and — Jer 39:13
the captain of the g. had let him go — Jer 40:1
the captain of the g. took Jeremiah — Jer 40:2
captain of the g. gave him victuals — Jer 40:5
captain of the g. had committed — Jer 41:10
the captain of the g. had left with — Jer 43:6
the captain of the g. which served — Jer 52:12
the captain of the g. brake down — Jer 52:14
the captain of the g. left certain of — Jer 52:16
took the captain of the g. away — Jer 52:19
the captain of the g. took them — Jer 52:26
thee, and be thou a g. unto them — Eze 38:7
Arioch the captain of the king's g. — Da 2:14
g. against breakdown of your faith (N) — Joh 16:19
be on g. (A) — Ac 20:31; 1Co 16:13
prisoners to the captain of the g. — Ac 28:16

the whole imperial g. (A)(B)(E)(R) — Ph'p 1:13
be on g. and composed (B) — 1Th 5:6
g. the deposit (B) — 1Ti 6:20
be on g. (B) — 1Pe 5:8

GUARDIAN

anointed g. cherub (R) — Eze 28:14
the g. cherub (A)(R) — Eze 28:16

GUARDIANS

the g. of the children (S) — 2Ki 10:5
foster fathers and g. (A)(B)(R) — Isa 49:23
made you g. (A)(R) — Ac 20:28
under g. (A)(B)(E)(N)(P)(R) — Ga 4:2

GUARDS

by g. (S) — 1Ch 9:23; Ne 7:3
g. his life takes heed to (B) — Pr 16:17
guards (S) — M't 26:58; M'k 14:54, 65
witness before palace (P) — Ph'p 1:13

GUARD'S

in the captain of the g. house — Ge 41:10

GUDGODAH

unto G.; and from G. to Jotbath — De 10:7

GUEST

gone to be g. with a man that is — Lu 19:7

GUESTCHAMBER

The Master saith, Where is the g. — M'k 14:14
saith unto thee, Where is the g. — Lu 22:11

GUESTS

Adonijah and all the g. that were — 1Ki 1:41
the g. that were with Adonijah — 1Ki 1:49
her g. are in the depths of hell — Pr 9:18
a sacrifice, he hath bid his g. — Zep 1:7
the wedding was furnished with g. — M't 22:10
when the king came to see the g. — M't 22:11
g. and visitors on earth (B) — Heb 11:13

GUIDANCE

by their own g. (A)(E)(R) — Job 37:12
where no g. is (A)(E)(R) — Pr 11:14

GUIDE

canst thou g. Arcturus with his — Job 38:32
The meek will be g. in judgment — Ps 25:9
name's sake lead me, and g. me — Ps 31:3
I will g. thee with mine eye — Ps 32:8
he will be our g. even unto death — Ps 48:14
my g. and mine acquaintance — Ps 55:13
Thou shalt g. me with thy counsel — Ps 73:24
will g. his affairs with discretion — Ps 112:5
forsaketh the g. of her youth — Pr 2:17
having no g., overseer, or ruler — Pr 6:7
of the upright shall g. them — Pr 11:3
and g. thine heart in the way — Pr 23:19
springs of water shall he g. them — Isa 49:10
There is none to g. her among all — Isa 51:18
And the Lord shall g. thee — Isa 58:11
thou art the g. of my youth — Jer 3:4
put ye not confidence in a g. — Mic 7:5
g. our feet into the way of peace — Lu 1:79
he will g. you into all truth — Joh 16:13
was g. to them that took Jesus — Ac 1:16
except some man should g. me — Ac 8:31
art a g. of the blind, a light of — Ro 2:19
g. the house, give none occasion — 1Ti 5:14

GUIDED

thou hast g. them in thy strength — Ex 15:13
other, and g. them on every side — 2Ch 32:22
a father, and I have g. her from — Job 31:18
and g. them in the wilderness — Ps 78:52
g. them by the skilfulness of his — Ps 78:72
g. by the Spirit (N) — Ga 5:16
g. by the Spirit (P) — Ga 5:25

GUIDES

Woe unto you, ye blind g. which — M't 23:16
Ye blind g. which strain at a gnat — M't 23:24
countless g. in Christ (R) — 1Co 4:15
g. nations on earth (A)(B)(R) — Ps 67:4
power to g. them (N) — 1Co 12:28
faith is our g. (N) — 2Co 5:7
g. her steps to you (A)(P) — 1Th 3:11

GUIDING

Manasseh's head, g. his hands — Ge 48:14

GUILE

came with g. (B)(E) — Ge 27:35
to slay him with g.; thou shalt — Ex 21:14
in whose spirit there is no g. — Ps 32:2
and thy lips from speaking g. — Ps 34:13
deceit and g. depart not from her — Ps 55:11
subverted me with g. (R) — Ps 119:78
Israelite indeed, in whom is no g. — Joh 1:47
full of all g. and villainy (E) — Ac 13:10
being crafty, I caught you with g. — 2Co 12:16
nor of uncleanness, nor in g. — 1Th 2:3
laying aside all malice, and all g. — 1Pe 2:1
neither was g. found in his mouth — 1Pe 2:22
his lips that they speak no g. — 1Pe 3:10
in their mouth was found no g. — Re 14:5

GUILELESS

good, innocent, g. (A)(R) — Ro 16:19

GUILT

g. offering (R) — Le 5:6; 5:7, 15-16, 18-19; 6:5-6, 17; 7:1-2, 5, 7; 37; 14:12-14, 17, 21, 24-25, 28; 19:21-22; Nu 6:12; 18:9; 1Sa 6:3-4, 8, 17; 2Ki 12:16; Eze 40:39; 42:13; 44:29; 46:20
g. offering (A) — Le 5:7; 6:17; 1Sa 6:3-4, 8, 17; Eze 46:20
restitution for g. (E) — Nu 5:7
shalt put away the g. of — De 19:13; 21:9
money from g. offering (B) — 2Ki 12:16
bring g. (A)(B)(R) — 1Ch 21:3; Ezr 10:10
causes g. (E) — 1Ch 21:3; Ezr 9:13; 10:19
inner g. (B)(R) — 2Ch 19:10; 24:18; 28:13; Ezr 9:6-7, 13; 10:10, 19
our g. is great (B)(R) — 2Ch 28:13
multiplied his g. (B)(R) — 2Ch 33:23
g. has grown (S) — Ezr 9:6
in your g. (A)(B)(E)(R) — Ezr 9:15
no g. or violence (A) — Job 16:17
g. offering (B) — Eze 40:39; 42:13; 44:22; 46:30
until they acknowledge g. (A)(B)(E)(R) — Ho 5:15
he incurred g. through Baal (R) — Ho 13:1
I find no g. or crime (A)(R) — Lu 23:4

GUILTINESS

shouldest have brought g. upon us — Ge 26:10
for their g. (R) — 2Ch 24:18; Ezr 9:6

GUILTLESS

the Lord will not hold him g. — Ex 20:7
the g. slay not (B) — Ex 23:7
the man be g. from iniquity — Nu 5:31

be *g.* before the Lord, and   *Nu 32:22*
before
the Lord will not hold him *g.*   *De 5:11*
upon his head, and we will be *Jos 2:19*
g.
the Lord's anointed, and be *g.* *1Sa 26:9*
I and my kingdom are *g.*   *2Sa 3:28*
the king and his throne be *g.* *2Sa 14:9*
hold him not *g.*: for thou art *1Ki 2:9*
even deliver one not *g.* (B) *Job 22:30*
would not have condemned *M't 12:7*
the *g.*

GUILTY

verily *g.* concerning our   *Ge 42:21*
brother
judges pronounce *g.* (B)   *Ex 22:9*
and that will by no means clear *Ex 34:7*
the *g.*
should not be done, and are *g.* *Le 4:13*
should not be done, and is *g.* *Le 4:22*
ought not to be done, and be *g.* *Le 4:27*
he also shall be unclean, and *g.* *Le 5:2*
knoweth of it, then, he shall be *Le 5:3*
g.
then he shall be *g.* in one of *Le 5:4*
these
he shall be *g.* in one of these *Le 5:5*
things
he wist it not, yet is he *g.*   *Le 5:17*
he is certainly *g.* (E)(R)   *Le 5:19*
he hath sinned, and is *g.* that he *Le 6:4*
done to become *g.*   *Le 6:7*
(A)(B)(E)(R)
the Lord, and that person be *g.* *Nu 5:6*
and by no means of clearing *Nu 14:18*
the *g.*
he shall not be *g.* of blood   *Nu 35:27*
a murderer, which is *g.* of   *Nu 35:31*
death
the *g.* (A)   *De 25:1;*
            Job 9:29; Isa 5:23; Na 1:3
the *g.* (B)   *De 25:1;*
       Job 9:29; 10:7; Isa 5:23; Na 1:3
the *g.* (R)   *De 25:1;*
      2Ch 6:23; Job 10:7; Na 1:3
at this time, that ye should be *J'g 21:22*
g.
as one that is *g.* (A)(E)   *2Sa 14:13*
do not hold me *g.* (B)(R)   *2Sa 19:19*
be *g.* (A)(B)   *2Ch 19:10; 28:13*
not be *g.* (E)   *2Ch 19:10; Ezr 9:7*
we are *g.* before Lord (A)   *2Ch 28:13*
exceedingly *g.* (A) *Ezr 9:7; 9:13; 10:19*
wives; and being *g.* they   *Ezr 10:19*
offered
hands *g.* of violence (B)   *Job 16:17*
their *g.* doings (B)(R)   *Ps 68:21*
g. of blood (B)   *Pr 28:17*
curse thee, and thou be found *Pr 30:10*
g.
who aquit the *g.* (B)(R)   *Isa 5:23*
declare a person *g.* (B)   *Isa 29:21*
shown herself less *g.* (A)(R) *Jer 3:11*
we are not *g.* (A)(B)(E)(R) *Jer 50:7*
Thou art become *g.* in thy   *Eze 22:4*
blood
let not Judah be *g.* (B)(R)   *Ho 4:15*
not acquit the *g.* (E)   *Na 1:3*
hold themselves not *g.*: and   *Zec 11:5*
they
gift that is upon it, he is *g.*   *M't 23:18*
and said, He is *g.* of death   *M't 26:66*
condemned him to be *g.* of   *M'k 14:64*
death
In case I am *g.* (B)(N)   *Ac 25:11*
world may become *g.* before *Ro 3:19*
God
who acquits the *g.* (N)   *Ro 4:5*
g. of immorality (A)(P)(R)   *1Co 5:11*
shall be *g.* of the body and   *1Co 11:27*
blood
found *g.* (A)(E)   *Heb 10:2*
without making them foolish or *Jas 1:5*
g. (P)
offend in one point, he is *g.* of *Jas 2:10*
all
fear brings torture of feeling *1Jo 4:18*
g. (P)

GUISE

agents in *g.* (N)   *Lu 20:20*
assume *g.* of a servant (A)   *Ph'p 2:7*

GULF

and you there is a great *g.*   *Lu 16:26*
fixed

GULL

the sea *g.* (A)(B)(R)(S)   *Le 11:16*

GULLIES

g. for torrents of rain (B)   *Job 38:25*

GUNI

Jahzeel, and *G.*, and Jezer   *Ge 46:24*
of *G.* the family of the   *Nu 26:48*
Gunites
the son of *G.* chief of the   *1Ch 5:15*
house of
Jahziel, and *G.*; and Jezer   *1Ch 7:13*

GUNITES

of Guni, the family of the *G.* *Nu 26:48*

GUR

they did so at the going up to *2Ki 9:27*
G.

GUR-BAAL

the Arabians that dwelt in *G.* *2Ch 26:7*

GUSH

our eyelids *g.* out with waters *Jer 9:18*

GUSHED

till the blood *g.* out upon   *1Ki 18:28*
them
that the waters *g.* out, and the *Ps 78:20*
and the waters *g.* out: they   *Ps 105:41*
ran in
rock also, and the waters *g.*   *Isa 48:21*
out
midst, and all his bowels *g.* out *Ac 1:18*

GUTSTRINGS

seven fresh *g.* (A)   *J'g 16:7*

GUTTER

Whosoever getteth up to the *g.* *2Sa 5:8*

GUTTERS

pilled before the flocks in the *Ge 30:38*
g.
the eyes of the cattle in the *g.* *Ge 30:41*

H

HA

H., h.; and he smelleth the   *Job 39:25*

HAAHASHTARI

Hepher, and Temeni, and *H.* *1Ch 4:6*

HABAIAH

the children of *H.* the children *Ezr 2:61;*
of   *Ne 7:63*

HABAKKUK

The burden which *H.* the   *Hab 1:1*
prophet
A prayer of *H.* the prophet   *Hab 3:1*
upon

HABAZINIAH

Jeremiah, the son of *H.* and   *Jer 35:3*

HABERGEON

as it were the hole of an *h.*   *Ex 28:32*
robe, as the hole of an *h.*   *Ex 39:23*
the spear, the dart, nor the *h.* *Job 41:26*

HABERGEONS

helmets, and *h.*, and bows   *2Ch 26:14*
shields, and the bows, and the *Ne 4:16*
h.

HABITABLE

in the *h.* part of his earth   *Pr 8:31*

HABITATION

and I will prepare him an *h.* *Ex 15:2*
in thy strength unto thy holy *Ex 15:13*
h.
thy holy dwelling place (B)   *Ex 15:13*
thy holy abode (R)   *Ex 15:13*
without the camp shall his *h.* *Le 13:46*
be
his abode outside the camp   *Le 13:46*
(A)(B)
out of camp be his dwelling   *Le 13:46*
(E)
even unto his *h.* shall ye seek *De 12:5*
his dwelling (A)(B)   *De 12:5;*
  2Ch 29:6; Job 8:6; Ps 33:14; 69:25;
                      132:13
Look down from thy holy *h.*   *De 26:15*
I have commanded in my *h.*   *1Sa 2:29*
shalt see an enemy in my *h.*   *1Sa 2:32*
shew me both it, and his *h.*   *2Sa 15:25*
see both it and his house (A) *2Sa 15:25*
its shrine (B)   *2Sa 15:25*
have built an house of *h.* for *2Ch 6:2*
thee
a fitting abode (A)   *2Ch 6:2*
a residence (B)   *2Ch 6:2*
their faces from the *h.* of the *2Ch 29:6*
Lord
Israel, whose *h.* is in   *Ezr 7:15*
Jerusalem
whose dwelling is in Jerusalem *Ezr 7:15*
(A)
who dwells (B)(R)   *Ezr 7:15; 2Ch 6:2*
root: but suddenly I cursed his *Job 5:3*
h.
thou shalt visit thy *h.* and   *Job 5:24*
shalt
h. of thy righteousness   *Job 8:6*
prosperous
shall be scattered upon his *h.* *Job 18:15*
I have loved the *h.* of thy house *Ps 26:8*
From the place of his *h.* he   *Ps 33:14*
looketh
the widows, is God in his holy *Ps 68:5*
h.
Let their *h.* be desolate: and   *Ps 69:25*
Be thou my strong *h.*   *Ps 71:3*
whereunto
judgment, the *h.* of thy   *Ps 89:14*
throne
foundation of thy throne   *Ps 89:14*
(A)(B)(E)(R)
refuge, even the most High, thy *Ps 91:9*
h.
Most High your dwelling place *Ps 91:9*
(A)
Most High your shelter (B)   *Ps 91:9*
judgment are the *h.* of his   *Ps 97:2*
throne
fowls of the heaven have   *Ps 104:12*
their *h.*
that they might go to a city of *Ps 107:7*
h.
to the residence city they   *Ps 107:7*
sought (B)
that they may prepare a city *Ps 107:36*
for *h.*
h. for the mighty God of   *Ps 132:5*
Jacob
tabernacle for the mighty God *Ps 132:5*
(B)
he hath desired it for his *h.*   *Ps 132:13*
but he blesseth the *h.* of the just *Pr 3:33*
the home of the just (A)   *Pr 3:33*
the dwelling of the righteous *Pr 3:33*
(B)
the abode of the righteous (R) *Pr 3:33*
graveth an *h.* for himself in a *Isa 22:16*
rock
carves out a dwelling (A)   *Isa 22:16*
hewing out a home in rock   *Isa 22:16*
(B)
and the *h.* forsaken, and left *Isa 27:10*
a dwelling left deserted (B)   *Isa 27:10*
people shall dwell in a   *Isa 32:18*
peaceable *h.*
eyes shall see Jerusalem a   *Isa 33:20*
quiet *h.*

and it shall be an *h*. of dragons   *Isa 34:13*

a haunt for jackals (B)(R)   *Isa 34:13; 35:7*

in the *h*. of dragons, where each   *Isa 35:7*

behold from the *h*. of thy holiness   *Isa 63:15*

dwelling place of your holiness (A)   *Isa 63:15*

thy holy and glorious abode (B)   *Isa 63:15*

Thine *h*. is in the midst of deceit   *Jer 9:6*

and have made his *h*. desolate   *Jer 10:25*

utter his voice from his holy *h*.   *Jer 25:30*

shall mightily roar upon his *h*.   *Jer 25:30*

O *h*. of justice, and mountain of   *Jer 31:23*

an *h*. of shepherds causing their   *Jer 33:12*

dwelt in the *h*. of Chimham   *Jer 41:17*

against the *h*. of the strong   *Jer 49:19*

the *h*. of justice, even the Lord   *Jer 50:7*

I will bring Israel again to his *h*.   *Jer 50:19*

Jordan unto the *h*. of the strong   *Jer 50:44*

he shall make their *h*. desolate   *Jer 50:45*

Pathros, into the land of their *h*.   *Eze 29:14*

fowls of the heaven had their *h*.   *Da 4:21*

whose *h*. is high; that saith in his   *Ob 3*

whose dwelling is high (B)(R)   *Ob 3*

and moon stood still in their *h*.   *Hab 3:11*

is raised up out of his holy *h*.   *Zec 2:13*

Let his *h*. be desolate, and let no   *Ac 1:20*

Let his residence become deserted (A)   *Ac 1:20*

Let his dwelling be desolate (B)   *Ac 1:20*

Let his homestead fall desolate (N)   *Ac 1:20*

and the bounds of their *h*.   *Ac 17:26*

boundaries of their settlements (B)   *Ac 17:26*

limits of their territory (N)   *Ac 17:26*

for an *h*. of God through the Spirit   *Eph 2:22*

fixed abode of God in Spirit (A)   *Eph 2:22*

dwelling of God in the Spirit (B)(R)   *Eph 2:22*

spiritual dwelling of God (N)   *Eph 2:22*

in which God himself lives by Spirit (P)   *Eph 2:22*

but left their own *h*. he hath   *Jude 6*

abandoned proper dwelling place (A)(B)(R)   *Jude 6*

abandoned their proper home (N)   *Jude 6*

abandoned their proper sphere (P)   *Jude 6*

and is become the *h*. of devils   *Re 18:2*

dwelling place of demons (A)(N)(R)   *Re 18:2*

a resort of demons (B)   *Re 18:2*

a haunt of devils (P)   *Re 18:2*

HABITATIONS

according to their *h*. in the land of   *Ge 36:43*

of cruelty are in their *h*.   *Ge 49:5*

in all your *h*. shall ye eat   *Ex 12:20*

kindle no fire throughout your *h*.   *Ex 35:3*

Ye shall bring out of your *h*. two   *Le 23:17*

the land of your *h*. which I give   *Nu 15:2*

These were their *h*. and their   *1Ch 4:33*

the *h*. that were found there   *1Ch 4:41*

possessions and *h*. were, Beth-el   *1Ch 7:28*

are full of the *h*. of cruelty   *Ps 74:20*

their camp, round about their *h*.   *Ps 78:28*

forth the curtains of thine *h*.   *Isa 54:2*

and for the *h*. of the wilderness   *Jer 9:10*

or who shall enter into our *h*.   *Jer 21:13*

the peaceable *h*. are cut down   *Jer 25:37*

he shall make their *h*. desolate   *Jer 49:20*

swallowed up all the *h*. of Jacob   *La 2:2*

toward Diblath, in all their *h*.   *Eze 6:14*

---

h. of the shepherds shall mourn   *Am 1:2*

receive you into everlasting *h*.   *Lu 16:9*

HABITS

shocked by dissolute *h*. (N)   *2Pe 2:7*

HABITUALLY

h. putting to death (A)   *Ro 8:13*

HABOR

placed him in Halah and in *H*.   *2Ki 17:6*

put them in Halah and in *H*. by   *2Ki 18:11*

brought them unto Halah, and *H*.   *1Ch 5:26*

HACHALIAH

words of Nehemiah the son of *H*.   *Ne 1:1*

the Tirshatha, the son of *H*.   *Ne 10:1*

HACHILAH

in the hill of *H*. which is on   *1Sa 23:19*

David hide himself in the hill of *H*.   *1Sa 26:1*

Saul pitched in the hill of *H*.   *1Sa 26:3*

HACHMONI

of *H*. was with the king's sons   *1Ch 27:32*

HACHMONITE

Jashobeam, an *H*. the chief of   *1Ch 11:11*

HAD

servants that ruled over all he *h*.   *Ge 24:2*

he knew not ought he *h*. save bread he eat   *Ge 39:6*

And when she *h*. opened it, she saw   *Ex 2:6*

he that gathered much *h*. nothing   *Ex 16:18*

And if she *h*. at all an husband   *Nu 30:6*

the Lord *h*. a delight in thy fathers   *De 10:15*

Joshua saved Rahab and all that she *h*.   *Jos 6:25*

Joshua took Achan and all that he *h*.   *Jos 7:24*

repented that he *h*. made Saul king   *1Sa 15:35*

Now David *h*. said, Surely in vain have   *1Sa 25:21*

of them shall I be *h*. in honour   *2Sa 6:22*

that David *h*. smitten all the host of   *2Sa 8:9*

ewe lamb, which he *h*. bought   *2Sa 12:3*

because he did this thing, and *h*. no pity   *2Sa 12:6*

when the Philistines *h*. slain Saul   *2Sa 21:12*

names of mighty men whom David *h*.   *2Sa 23:8*

for he *h*. heard that they *h*. anointed   *1Ki 5:1*

until he *h*. finished all the house   *1Ki 6:22*

daughter, whom he *h*. taken to wife   *1Ki 7:8*

she said, *H*. Zimri peace who slew   *2Ki 9:31*

Lord blessed his house and all he *h*.   *1Ch 13:14*

as for me, I *h*. in my heart to build an   *1Ch 28:2*

the pattern of all that he *h*. by the Spirit   *1Ch 28:12*

all they that *h*. separated themselves   *Ne 10:28*

I was not in safety, neither *h*. I rest   *Job 3:26*

if men said not, Oh that we *h*. of his flesh   *Job 31:31*

Lord gave him twice as much as he *h*.   *Job 42:10*

after he *h*. gone in to Bath-sheba   *Ps 51 title*

I said, O that I *h*. wings like a dove   *Ps 55:6*

I *h*. rather be a doorkeeper in house of   *Ps 84:10*

to be *h*. in reverance of all them about him   *Ps 89:7*

proud have *h*. me greatly in derision   *Ps 119:51*

as were oppressed, they *h*. no comforter   *Ec 4:1*

for peace I *h*. great bitterness   *Isa 38:17*

we grope as if we *h*. no eyes, we stumble   *Isa 59:10*

in my favour have I *h*. mercy on thee   *Isa 60:10*

I beheld the heavens, and they *h*. no light   *Jer 4:23*

Asa the king *h*. made for fear of   *Jer 41:9*

for then *h*. we plenty of victuals, were well   *Jer 44:17*

which *h*. the charge of the men of   *Jer 52:25*

her pleasant things she *h*. in days of old   *La 1:7*

she came down wonderfully, *h*. no comforter   *La 1:9*

yet *h*. he no wages for the service   *Eze 29:18*

but I *h*. pity for mine holy name   *Eze 36:21*

by his strength Jacob *h*. power with God   *Ho 12:3*

he *h*. power over the angel and prevailed   *Ho 12:4*

against which thou hast *h*. indignation   *Zec 1:12*

yet *h*. he the residue of the Spirit   *Mal 2:15*

he sold all that he *h*. and bought it   *M't 13:46*

whose wife of seven, for they all *h*. her   *M't 22:28*

she of her want did cast in all she *h*.   *M'k 12:44*

if the goodman of the house *h*. known   *Lu 12:39*

for thou hast *h*. five husbands   *Joh 4:18*

was made whole of whatsoever disease he *h*.   *Joh 5:4*

Judas is the bag, and bare what was in it   *Joh 12:6*

if I *h*. not come, they *h*. not *h*. sin   *Joh 15:22*

glory I *h*. with thee before the world was   *Joh 17:5*

all that believed *h*. all things common   *Ac 2:44*

Cornelius *h*. made enquiry for Simon's   *Ac 10:17*

having shorn his head, for he *h*. a vow   *Ac 18:18*

that after examination *h*. I might write   *Ac 25:26*

seal he *h*. yet being uncircumcised   *Ro 4:11; 4:12*

what fruit *h*. ye in things whereof ashamed   *Ro 6:21*

that have wives be as tho' they *h*. none   *1Co 7:29*

but we *h*. the sentence of death in us   *2Co 1:9*

what manner of entering in *h*. to you   *1Th 1:9*

and blessed him that *h*. the promises   *Heb 7:6*

old commandment which ye *h*. from beginning   *1Jo 2:7*

that which we *h*. from the beginning   *2Jo 5*

HADAD

And Husham died, and *H*. the son   *Ge 36:35*

And *H*. died, and Samlah of   *Ge 36:36*

an adversary unto Solomon, *H*.   *1Ki 11:14*

That *H*. fled, he and certain   *1Ki 11:17*

H. being yet a little child   *1Ki 11:17*

H. found great favour in the sight   *1Ki 11:19*

when *H*. heard in Egypt that   *1Ki 11:21*

H. said to Pharaoh, Let me depart   *1Ki 11:21*

besides the mischief that *H*. did   *1Ki 11:25*

Mishma, and Dumah, Massa, *H*.   *1Ch 1:30*

H. the son of Bedad, which smote   *1Ch 1:46*

when *H*. was dead, Samlah of   *1Ch 1:47*

Baal-hanan was dead, H.   1Ch 1:50
reigned
H. died also. And the dukes   1Ch 1:51
of

HADADEZER

David smote also H. the son of   2Sa 8:3
came to succour H. king of   2Sa 8:5
Zobah
that were on the servants of H.   2Sa 8:7
Betah, and, Berothai, cities   2Sa 8:8
of H.
had smitten all the host of H.   2Sa 8:9
because he had fought   2Sa 8:10
against H.
for H. had wars with Toi   2Sa 8:10
and of the spoil of H. son of   2Sa 8:12
which fled from his lord H.   1Ki 11:23

HADADRIMMON

as the mourning of H. in the   Zec 12:11

HADAR

H., and Tema, Jetur, Naphish   Ge 25:15
and H. reigned in his stead   Ge 36:39

HADAREZER

And H. sent, and brought out   2Sa 10:16
the captain of the host of H.   2Sa 10:16
the kings that were servants   2Sa 10:19
to H.
David smote H. king of   1Ch 18:3
Zobah
came to help H. king of   1Ch 18:5
Zobah
that were on the servants of H.   1Ch 18:7
and from Chun, cities of H.   1Ch 18:8
had smitten all the host of H.   1Ch 18:9
because he had fought   1Ch 18:10
against H.
for H. had war with Tou   1Ch 18:10
the captain of the host of H.   1Ch 19:16
when the servants of H. saw   1Ch 19:19
that

HADASHAH

Zenan, and H. and   Jos 15:37
Migdal-gad

HADASSAH

he brought up H. that is, Esther   Es 2:7

HADATTAH

Hazor, H. and Kerioth   Jos 15:25

HADES

brought down to H.   M't 11:23
(A)(B)(E)(R)(S)
the gates of H.   M't 16:18
(A)(E)(N)(S)
brought down to H.   Lu 10:15
(A)(B)(E)(R)
in H., in torment   Lu 16:23
(A)(B)(E)(N)(R)(S)
leaving it in H.   Ac 2:27;
(A)(E)(N)(P)(R)(S)   2:31
not left my soul in h. (S)   Ac 2:31
keys of H. (A)(E)(N)(R)(S)   Re 1:18
death and H.   Re 6:8
(A)(B)(E)(N)(R)(S)
death and h. (S)   Re 20:13; 20:14

HADID

The children of Lod, H. and   Ezr 2:33
Ono
of Lod, H., and Ono, seven   Ne 7:37
H., Zeboim, Neballat   Ne 11:34

HADLAI

and Amasa the son of H.   2Ch 28:12
stood

HADORAM

And H., and Uzal, and Diklah   Ge 10:27
H. also, and Uzal, and Diklah   1Ch 1:21
He sent H. his son to king   1Ch 18:10
David
Then king Rehoboam sent   2Ch 10:18
H.

HADRACH

word of the Lord in the land of   Zec 9:1
H.

HADST

For it was little which thou h.   Ge 30:30
before I
with me, surely thou h. sent   Ge 31:42
me away
thought that thou h. utterly   J'g 15:2
hated
except thou h. hasted and   1Sa 25:34
come to
As God liveth, unless thou h.   2Sa 2:27
spoken
then h. thou smitten Syria till   2Ki 13:19
thou h.
be angry with us till thou h.   Eze 9:14
consumed
land which thou h. sworn to   Ne 9:15
give them
concerning which thou h.   Ne 9:23
promised
because thou h. a favour unto   Ps 44:3
them
O God, which h. cast us off   Ps 60:10
or ever thou h. formed the   Ps 90:2
earth
thou h. removed it far unto   Isa 26:15
all the
O that thou h. hearkened to   Isa 48:18
my
and thou h. a whore's forehead   Jer 3:3
For thou h. cast me into the   Jon 2:3
deep
Saying, If thou h. known,   Lu 19:42
even thou
unto Jesus, Lord, if thou h.   Joh 11:21
been here
unto him, Lord, if thou h.   Joh 11:32
been here
glory, as if thou h. not received   1Co 4:7
it
not, neither h. pleasure   Heb 10:8
therein

HAFT

the h. also went in after the   J'g 3:22
blade

HAG

the night h. (R)   Isa 34:14

HAGAB

The children of H. the   Ezr 2:46
children

HAGABA

the children of H. the children   Ne 7:48
of

HAGABAH

the children of H. the children   Ezr 2:45
of

HAGAR

an Egyptian, whose name was   Ge 16:1
H.
Sarai, Abram's wife, took H.   Ge 16:3
her
he went in unto H. and she   Ge 16:4
he said, H., Sarai's maid,   Ge 16:8
whence
H. bare Abram a son: and   Ge 16:15
called his son's name, which   Ge 16:15
H. bare
when H. bare Ishmael to   Ge 16:16
Abram
Sarah saw the son of H. the   Ge 21:9
and gave it unto H. putting it   Ge 21:14
and the angel of God called to   Ge 21:17
H.
unto her, What aileth thee, H.   Ge 21:17
Ishmael, Abraham's son,   Ge 25:12
whom H.

HAGARENES

Ishmaelites; of Moab, and the   Ps 83:6
H.

HAGARITES

they made war with the H.   1Ch 5:10
who
they made war with the H.   1Ch 5:19
with
and the H. were delivered into   1Ch 5:20

HAGERITE

over the flocks was Jaziz the   1Ch 27:31
H.

HAGGAI

the prophets, H. the prophet   Ezr 5:1
through the prophesying of H.   Ezr 6:14
the Lord by H. the prophet   Hag 1:1
unto
the Lord by H. the prophet,   Hag 1:3
saying
and the words of H. the   Hag 1:12
prophet, as
Then spake H. the Lord's   Hag 1:13
of the Lord by the prophet   Hag 2:1;
H.   2:10
Then said H., If one that is   Hag 2:13
unclean
Then answered H., and said,   Hag 2:14
So is
came unto H. in the four and   Hag 2:20

HAGGEDOLIM

the son of H. (S)   Ne 11:14

HAGGERI

Mibhar the son of H.   1Ch 11:38

HAGGI

Ziphion, and H., Shuni, and   Ge 46:16
of H. the family of the   Ne 26:15
Haggites

HAGGIAH

Shimea his son, H. his son   1Ch 6:30

HAGGITES

of Haggi, the family of the H.   Nu 26:15

HAGGITH

fourth, Adonijah the son of H.   2Sa 3:4;
   1Ch 3:2
Adonijah the son of H. exalted   1Ki 1:5
the son of H. doth reign, and   1Ki 1:11
the son of H. came to   1Ki 2:13
Bath-sheba

HAI

Beth-el on the west, and H. on   Ge 12:8
between Beth-el and H.   Ge 13:3

HAIL

to rain a very grievous h.   Ex 9:18;
   9:19, 22-26, 28-29, 33-34
remaineth unto you from the   Ex 10:5
h.
even all that the h. hath left   Ex 10:12
of the trees which the h. had   Ex 10:15
left
thou seen the treasures of the   Job 38:22
h.
thick clouds passed, h. stones   Ps 18:12
his voice; h. stones and coals   Ps 18:13
of
He destroyed their vines with   Ps 78:47
h.
He gave up their cattle, to   Ps 78:48
the h.
He gave them h. for rain, and   Ps 105:32
Fire, and h.; snow, and   Ps 148:8
vapours
as a tempest of h. and a   Isa 28:2
destroying
the h. shall sweep away the   Isa 28:17
refuge
When it shall h. coming down   Isa 32:19
on
with mildew and with h. in all   Hag 2:17
and said, H., master; and   M't 26:49
kissed
mocked him, saying, H.,   M't 27:29
King of the
Jesus met them, saying, All h.   M't 28:9

salute him, *H.*, King of the   *M'k 15:18*
Jews
H., thou that art highly   *Lu 1:28*
favoured
And said, *H.*, King of the   *Joh 19:3*
Jews
followed *h.* and fire mingled   *Re 8:7*
with
and an earthquake, and great   *Re 11:19*
h.
there fell upon men a great   *Re 16:21*
because of the plague of the   *Re 16:21*
h.

HAILSTONES

more which died with *h.* than   *Jos 10:11*
scattering, and tempest, and   *Isa 30:30*
h.
ye, O great *h.* shall fall; and   *Eze 13:11*
and great *h.* in my fury to   *Eze 13:13*
and great *h.*, fire and   *Eze 38:22*
brimstone

HAIR

scarlet, and the fine linen, and   *Ex 25:4;*
goats' *h.*   *35:6*
shalt make curtains of goats' *h.* *Ex 26:7*
to
and goats' *h.* and red skins of   *Ex 35:23*
rams
them up in wisdom spun   *Ex 35:26*
goats' *h.*
And he made curtains of   *Ex 36:14*
goats' *h.*
and when the *h.* in the plague is *Le 13:3*
and the *h.* thereof be not   *Le 13:4*
turned
it have turned the *h.* white   *Le 13:10*
and the *h.* thereof be turned   *Le 13:20*
white
the *h.* in the bright spot be   *Le 13:25*
turned
no white *h.* in the bright spot   *Le 13:26*
there be in it a yellow thin *h.*   *Le 13:30*
and that there is no black *h.*   *Le 13:31*
there be in it no yellow *h.*   *Le 13:32*
priest shall not seek for yellow *Le 13:36*
h.
and that there is black *h.*   *Le 13:37*
grown up
whose *h.* is fallen off his head,   *Le 13:40*
he
he that hath his *h.* fallen off   *Le 13:41*
from
shave off all his *h.* and wash   *Le 14:8*
he shall shave all his *h.* off his *Le 14:9*
head
eyebrows, even all his *h.* he   *Le 14:9*
shall
let the locks of the *h.* of his   *Nu 6:5*
head
shall take the *h.* of the head   *Nu 6:18*
of the Nazarite, after the *h.* of *Nu 6:19*
his
of goats' *h.*, and all things   *Nu 31:20*
made of
the *h.* of his head began to   *J'g 16:22*
grow
could sling stones at an *h.*   *J'g 20:16*
breadth
there shall not one *h.* of his   *1Sa 14:45*
head
put a pillow of goats' *h.* for   *1Sa 19:13;*
his bolster   *19:16*
there shall not one *h.* of thy   *2Sa 14:11*
son
because the *h.* was heavy on   *2Sa 14:26*
him
he weighed the *h.* of his head   *2Sa 14:26*
there shall not an *h.* of him   *1Ki 1:52*
fall
plucked off the *h.* of my head   *Ezr 9:3*
and plucked off their *h.* and   *Ne 13:25*
made
the *h.* of my flesh stood up   *Job 4:15*
thy *h.* is as a flock of goats   *Ca 4:1;*
  6:5
and the *h.* of thine head like   *Ca 7:5*
instead of well set *h.* baldness   *Isa 3:24*
head, and the *h.* of the feet   *Isa 7:20*
to them that plucked off the *h.* *Isa 50:6*
Cut off thine *h.* O Jerusalem   *Jer 7:29*
balances to weigh and divide   *Eze 5:1*
the *h.*
and thine *h.* is grown, whereas *Eze 16:7*
nor was an *h.* of their head   *Da 3:27*
singed

and the *h.* of his head like the   *Da 7:9*
pure
John had his raiment of   *M't 3:4*
camel's *h.*
canst not make one *h.* white   *M't 5:36*
or
John was clothed with camel's   *M'k 1:6*
h.
But there shall not an *h.* of   *Lu 21:18*
your
and wiped his feet with her *h.* *Joh 11:2;*
  12:3
an *h.* fall from the head   *Ac 27:34*
if a man have long *h.* it is a   *1Co 11:14*
But if a woman have long *h.*   *1Co 11:15*
it is
for her *h.* is given her for a   *1Co 11:15*
not with broided *h.* or gold, or   *1Ti 2:9*
of plaiting the *h.* and of   *1Pe 3:3*
wearing
black as sackcloth of *h.*   *Re 6:12*
And they had *h.* as the *h.* of   *Re 9:8*

HAIRS

bring down my gray *h.* with   *Ge 42:38;*
sorrow   *44:29*
the gray *h.* of thy servant   *Ge 44:31*
our father
no white *h.* therein, and if it   *Le 13:21*
be
suckling also with the man of   *De 32:25*
gray *h.*
they are more than the *h.* of   *Ps 40:12*
mine
cause are more than the *h.* of   *Ps 69:4*
mine
even to hoar *h.* will I carry you *Isa 46:4*
his *h.* were grown like eagles' *Da 4:33*
gray *h.* are here and there upon *Ho 7:9*
him
the very *h.* of your head are   *M't 10:30*
all
wipe them with the *h.* of her   *Lu 7:38*
head
wiped them with the *h.* of her   *Lu 7:44*
head
But even the very *h.* of your   *Lu 12:7*
head
His head and his *h.* were white *Re 1:14*

HAIRY

red, all over like an *h.*   *Ge 25:25*
garment
Esau my brother is a *h.* man   *Ge 27:11*
because his hands were *h.* as   *Ge 27:23*
his
answered him, He was an *h.*   *2Ki 1:8*
the *h.* scalp of such an one as   *Ps 68:21*
goeth

HAKKATAN

Johannan the son of *H.* and   *Ezr 8:12*
with

HAKKOZ

The seventh to *H.* the   *1Ch 24:10*
eighth to

HAKUPHA

the children of *H.* the children *Ezr 2:51;*
of   *Ne 7:53*

HALAH

and placed them in *H.* and in   *2Ki 17:6*
and put them in *H.* and in   *2Ki 18:11*
Habor
and brought them unto *H.*   *1Ch 5:26*

HALAK

mount *H.* that goeth up to   *Jos 11:17;*
Seir   *12:7*

HALE

lest he *h.* thee to the judge   *Lu 12:58*

HALF

Moses took *h.* the blood, *h.* he *Ex 24:6*
sprinkled
take thou of sweet cinnamon   *Ex 30:23*
h. so much
h. of it in the morning, and *h.*   *Le 6:20*
at night

of whom the flesh is *h.*   *Nu 12:12*
consumed
take it of their *h.* and give it   *Nu 31:29*
to Eleazar
h. of them over against mount *Jos 8:33*
Ebal
within as it were an *h.* acre of *1Sa 14:14*
land
Hanun shaved off one *h.* of   *2Sa 10:4*
their beards
nor if *h.* of us die, will they   *2Sa 18:3*
care for us
h. the people of Israel   *2Sa 19:40*
conducted David
give *h.* of the child to one, *h.*   *1Ki 3:25*
to other
and behold, the *h.* was not   *1Ki 10:7;*
told   *2Ch 9:6*
if thou wilt give me *h.* thine   *1Ki 13:8*
house, I will not
h. of the people followed   *1Ki 16:21*
Tibni, *h.* Omri
the ruler of the *h.* part of   *Ne 3:9;*
Jerusalem   *3:12*
h. part of Bethzur; *h.* of   *Ne 3:16;*
Keilah   *3:17-18*
children spake *h.* in the   *Ne 13:24*
speech of Ashdod
to the *h.* of the kingdom   *Es 5:3;*
  7:2; M'k 6:23
bloody men shall not live *h.*   *Ps 55:23*
their days
nor hath Samaria committed   *Eze 16:51*
h. thy sins
be for time, times, and an   *Da 12:7;*
h.   *Re 12:14*
I bought her for *h.* an homer of *Ho 3:2*
barley
h. of the city shall go into   *Zec 14:2*
captivity
h. of mount toward the   *Zec 14:4;*
south; *h.* toward sea   *14:8*
and departed, leaving him *h.*   *Lu 10:30*
dead
behold, the *h.* of my goods I   *Lu 19:8*
give to the poor
h. of possessions (N)(P)   *Lu 19:8*
was silence about space of *h.* an *Re 8:1*
hour
shall see dead bodies three   *Re 11:9;*
days and an *h.*   *11:11*

HALHUL

H., Beth-zur, and Gedor   *Jos 15:58*

HALI

their border was Helkath,   *Jos 19:25*
and *H.*

HALING

h. men and women committed *Ac 8:3*
dragged men and women   *Ac 8:3*
(A)(B)(E)(P)(R)
seizing men and women (N)   *Ac 8:3*

HALL

made a *h.* of pillars (A)(R)   *1Ki 7:6*
the *h.* of judgment (R)   *1Ki 7:7*
took Jesus into the common *h.* *M't 27:27*
led him away into the *h.*   *M'k 15:16*
a fire in the midst of the *h.*   *Lu 22:55*
led unto the *h.* of judgment   *Joh 18:28*
went not into the judgment *h.* *Joh 18:28*
Pilate entered the judgment   *Joh 18:33*
h.
went again into the judgment   *Joh 19:9*
h.
to be kept in Herod's   *Ac 23:35*
judgment *h.*

HALLELUJAH

Hallelujah (S)   *Re 19:1; 19:3-4, 6*

HALLMARK

as the *h.* of righteousness (N)   *Ro 4:11*

HALLOHESH

H., Pileha, Shobek   *Ne 10:24*

HALLOW

the children of Israel shall *h.* *Ex 28:38*
in (A)

dedicate (A)(B)(R) Ex 28:38; Le 22:2
to h. them, to minister unto me Ex 29:1
consecrate (A)(B) Ex 29:1; Le 25:10
and shalt h. it, and all the Ex 40:9
vessels
cleanse it, and h. it from the Le 16:19
those things which they h. unto Le 22:2
me
which the children of Israel h. Le 22:3
unto
I am the Lord which h. you Le 22:32
who consecrates and makes Le 22:32
you holy (A)
I will be revered (B) Le 22:32
And ye shall h. the fiftieth Le 25:10
year
and shall h. his head that same Nu 6:11
day
same day did the king h. the 1Ki 8:64
middle
consecrated middle of the 1Ki 8:64
court (A)(R)
set apart center of the court 1Ki 8:64
(B)
to purify and h. them (A) Job 1:5
but h. ye the sabbath day, as Jer 17:22
I
keep sabbath day holy Jer 17:22
(A)(B)(R)
but h. the sabbath day, to do Jer 17:24
no
to h. the sabbath day, and not Jer 17:27
to
h. my sabbaths; and they Eze 20:20
shall
and they shall h. my sabbaths Eze 44:24
my sabbaths holy (A)(R) Eze 44:24
maintain sacredness of Eze 44:24
sabbaths

HALLOWED

h. it (E)(R) Ge 2:3
blessed the sabbath day and h. Ex 20:11
it
consecrated (B) Ex 20:11; 29:21
and he shall be h. and his Ex 29:21
garments
I will be h. in them (A)(B) Le 10:3
she shall touch no h. thing, nor Le 12:4
contact nothing holy (B) Le 12:4
profaned the h. thing of the Le 19:8
Lord
profaned a holy thing (A) Le 19:8
dedicated (B) Le 19:8
I will be h. among the Le 22:32
children
I will be revered (B) Le 22:32
I h. unto me all the firstborn Nu 3:13
every man's h. things shall be Nu 5:10
his
the sacred gifts (B) Nu 5:10
every man's holy things (R) Nu 5:10
the fire yonder; for they are Nu 16:37
h.
they are now sacred (B) Nu 16:37
they are holy (E)(R) Nu 16:37
therefore they are h.: and Nu 16:38
they
all the h. things of the children Nu 18:8
of
the consecrated things (A)(R) Nu 18:8
the holy gifts (B) Nu 18:8
even the h. part thereof out Nu 18:29
of it
the sacred portion (B) Nu 18:29
I have brought away the h. De 26:13
things
the consecrated portion (B) De 26:13
the sacred portion (R) De 26:13
there is h. bread; if the young 1Sa 21:4
consecrated bread (B) 1Sa 21:4; 21:6
holy bread (E)(R) 1Sa 21:4; 21:6
the priest gave him h. bread 1Sa 21:6
I have h. this house, which 1Ki 9:3
thou
consecrated this house (B)(R) 1Ki 9:3
which I have h. for my name 1Ki 9:7
money of h. things (E) 2Ki 12:4
all the h. things that 2Ki 12:18
Jehoshaphat
took sacred treasures (B) 2Ki 12:18
dedicated things (R) 2Ki 12:18
and his own h. things, and all 2Ki 12:18
Moreover Solomon h. the 2Ch 7:7
middle
h. this house (E) 2Ch 7:15

of the Lord which he had h. 2Ch 36:14
in
he had consecrated (B) 2Ch 36:14
in heaven, H. be thy name M't 6:9;
  Lu 11:2
thy name be kept holy (B) M't 6:9
your name be honored (P) M't 6:9
you were consecrated, h. (A) 1Co 6:11
h. by God's Word (N) 1Ti 4:5

HALOHESH

repaired Shallum the son of H. Ne 3:12

HALT

How long h. ye between two 1Ki 18:21
I am ready to h., and my Ps 38:17
sorrow
to enter into life h. or maimed M't 18:8
better for thee to enter h. into M'k 9:45
life
the maimed, and the h. and Lu 14:21
of blind, h., withered, waiting Joh 5:3
for

HALTED

him, and he h. upon his thigh Ge 32:31
limping upon thigh Ge 32:31
(A)(B)(E)(R)
they h. in the prison gate (S) Ne 12:39
I will make her that h. a Mic 4:7
remnant
put lame for a remnant Mic 4:7
(B)(E)(R)

HALTETH

will I assemble her that h. and Mic 4:6
gather the lame (B)(E)(R) Mic 4:6
I will save her that h. and Zep 3:19
gather
the one who limps Zep 3:19
that which is lame (B)(E)(R) Zep 3:19

HALTING

my familiars watched for my Jer 20:10
h.
my fall (B)(E)(R) Jer 20:10

HAM

Noah begat Shem, H. and Ge 5:32
Noah begat three sons, Shem, Ge 6:10
H.
Noah, and Shem, and H. and Ge 7:13
were Shem, and H., and Ge 9:18
Japheth
And H. is the father of Caanan Ge 9:18
And H, the father of Caanan, Ge 9:22
saw
Shem, H., and Japheth: and Ge 10:1
the sons of H.; Cush, and Ge 10:6
Mizraim
These are the sons of H. after Ge 10:20
their
and the Zuzims in H. and the Ge 14:5
Noah, Shem, H. and Japheth 1Ch 1:4
The sons of H.: Cush, and 1Ch 1:8
for they of H. had dwelt there 1Ch 4:40
of
strength in the tabernacles of Ps 78:51
H.
Jacob sojourned in the land Ps 105:23
of H.
and wonders in the land of Ps 105:27
H.
Wondrous works in the land Ps 106:22
of H.

HAMAN

H. the son of Hammedatha Es 3:1;
3:2-8, 10-12, 15; 5:4-5, 8-12, 14; 6:4-7,
  10-14
of the money that H. had Es 4:7
promised
let the king and H. come this Es 5:4;
day 5:5, 8-12, 14; 6:4-7, 10-14
So the king and H. came to Es 7:1
and enemy is this wicked H. Es 7:6;
  7:7-10
give the house of H. the Jews' Es 8:1;
  8:2-5, 7; 9:10, 12, 24

HAMAN'S

they covered H. face Es 7:8
and let H. ten sons be hanged Es 9:13
and they hanged H. ten sons Es 9:14

HAMATH

unto Rehob, as men come to Nu 13:21
H.
your border unto, entrance Nu 34:8
of H.
Hermon unto the entering into Jos 13:5
H.
Baal-hermon, entering in of H. J'g 3:3
When Toi king of H. heard 2Sa 8:9
that
from the entering in of H. 1Ki 8:65;
unto the 2Ki 14:25
and H. which belonged to 2Ki 14:28
Judah
and from H. and from 2Ki 17:24
Sepharvaim
and the men of H. made 2Ki 17:30
Ashima
Where are the gods of H. 2Ki 18:34
and of
Where is the king of H. and 2Ki 19:13;
  Isa 37:13
at Riblah in the land of H. 2Ki 23:33
that he
slew them at Riblah, land 2Ki 25:21
of H.
Hadarezer king of Zobah 1Ch 18:3
unto H.
when Tou king of H. heard 1Ch 18:9
how
of H. unto the river of Egypt 2Ch 7:8
store cities, which he built in 2Ch 8:4
H.
is not H. as Arpad? is not Isa 10:9
from H. and from the islands Isa 11:11
Where are the gods of H. and Isa 36:19
H. where he gave judgment Jer 39:5
upon
H. is confounded, and Arpad Jer 49:23
to Riblah in the land of H. Jer 52:9
to death in Riblah in the land Jer 52:27
of H.
H., Berothah, Sibraim, which Eze 47:16
is
of Damascus and the border Eze 47:16
of H.
northward, and the border of Eze 47:17
H.
till a man come over against Eze 47:20
H.
of Hethlon, as one goeth to H. Eze 48:1
Damascus northward, Eze 48:1
coast of H.
from thence go ye to H. the Am 6:2
great
H. also shall border thereby Zec 9:2

HAMATHITE

the Zemarite, and the H. Ge 10:18;
  1Ch 1:16

HAMATH-ZOBAH

And Solomon went to H. and 2Ch 8:3

HAMMATH

and H., Rakkath, and Jos 19:35

HAMMEDATHA

the son of H. the Agagite Es 3:1
Haman the son of H. the Es 3:10
Agagite
by Haman the son of H. the Es 8:5
sons of Haman the son of H. Es 9:10
son of H. the Agagite, the Es 9:24
enemy

HAMMELECH

Jerahmeel the son of H. and Jer 36:26
Malchiah the son of H. that Jer 38:6
was

HAMMER

took an h. in her hand, and J'g 4:21
went
right hand to the workmen's h. J'g 5:26
and with the h. she smote J'g 5:26

neither *h.* nor axe nor any tool *1Ki 6:7*
of
like a heavy sledge *h.* (A)   *Pr 25:18*
he that smootheth with the *h.*   *Isa 41:7*
and like a *h.* that breaketh   *Jer 23:29*
the *h.* of the whole earth   *Jer 50:23*

HAMMERS

work, at once with axes and   *Ps 74:6*
h.
and fashioneth it with *h.* and   *Isa 44:12*
fasten it with nails and with *h.*   *Jer 10:4*

HAMMOLEKETH

And his sister *H.* bare Ishod   *1Ch 7:18*

HAMMON

Hebron and Rehob, and *H.*   *Jos 19:28*
and *H.* with her suburbs, and   *1Ch 6:76*

HAMMOTH-DOR

and *H.* with her suburbs   *Jos 21:32*

HAMONAH

the name of the city shall be   *Eze 39:16*
H.

HAMON-GOG

shall call it The valley of *H.*   *Eze 39:11*
have buried it in the valley of   *Eze 39:15*
H.

HAMOR

at the hand of the children of   *Ge 33:19*
H.
when Shechem the son of *H.*   *Ge 34:2*
Shechem spake unto his father   *Ge 34:4*
H.
H. the father of Shechem went   *Ge 34:6*
And *H.* communed with them   *Ge 34:8*
answered Shechem and *H.* his   *Ge 34:13*
And their words pleased *H.*   *Ge 34:18*
H. and Shechem his son came   *Ge 34:20*
And unto *H.* and unto   *Ge 34:24*
Shechem
they slew *H.* and Shechem his   *Ge 34:26*
son
Jacob bought of the sons of   *Jos 24:32*
H.
serve the men of *H.* the father   *J'g 9:28*
of

HAMOR'S

and Shechem *H.* son   *Ge 34:18*

HAMSTRING

h. their horses (B)(R)(S)   *Jos 11:6*

HAMSTRUNG

in anger they *h.* oxen (S)   *Ge 49:6*
h. their horses (A)(B)(R)(S)   *Jos 11:9;*
                                       2Sa 8:4
he *h.* their horses (S)   *1Ch 18:4*

HAMUEL

H. his son, Zacchur his son   *1Ch 4:26*

HAMUL

sons of Pharez, Hezron, and   *Ge 46:12;*
H.   *1Ch 2:5*
of *H.* the family of the   *Nu 26:21*
Hamulites

HAMULITES

of Hamul, the family of the   *Nu 26:21*
H.

HAMUTAL

his mother's name was *H.*   *2Ki 23:31;*
                                       Jer 52:1
H. the daughter of Jeremiah   *2Ki 24:18*

HANAMEEL

Behold, *H.* the son of Shallum   *Jer 32:7*
So *H.* mine uncle's son came   *Jer 32:8*

And I bought the field of *H.*   *Jer 32:9*
in the sight of *H.* mine uncle's   *Jer 32:12*

HANAN

And Abdon, and Zichri, and   *1Ch 8:23*
H.
Sheariah, and Obadiah, and   *1Ch 8:38*
H.
Obadiah, and *H.*: these were   *1Ch 9:44*
H. the son of Maachah, and   *1Ch 11:43*
of Shalmai, the children of   *Ezr 2:46*
H.
The children of *H.* the children   *Ne 7:49*
Azariah, Jozabad, *H.*, Pelaiah   *Ne 8:7*
Kelita, Pelaiah, *H.*   *Ne 10:10*
Pelatiah, *H.*, Anaiah   *Ne 10:22*
And Ahijah, *H.*, Anan   *Ne 10:26*
and next to them was *H.* the   *Ne 13:13*
son
into the chamber of the sons   *Jer 35:4*
of *H.*

HANANEEL

sanctified it unto the tower of   *Ne 3:1*
H.
the tower of *H.* and the tower   *Ne 12:39*
of
the tower of *H.* unto the gate   *Jer 31:38*
the tower of *H.* unto the   *Zec 14:10*
king's

HANANI

came to Jehu the son of *H.*   *1Ki 16:1*
of the prophet Jehu, the son   *1Ki 16:7*
of *H.*
Hananiah, *H.*, Eliathah,   *1Ch 25:4*
Giddalti
The eighteenth to *H.*, he, his   *1Ch 25:25*
sons
at that time *H.* the seer came   *2Ch 16:7*
to
Jehu the son of *H.* the seer   *2Ch 19:2*
went
in the book of Jehu the son   *2Ch 20:34*
of *H.*
of the sons of Immer; *H.* and   *Ezr 10:20*
That *H.* one of my brethren   *Ne 1:2*
I gave my brother *H.* and   *Ne 7:2*
and Judah, *H.* with the   *Ne 12:36*
musical

HANANIAH

Meshullam, and *H.* and   *1Ch 3:19*
the sons of *H.*; Pelatiah, and   *1Ch 3:21*
H., and Elam, and Antothijah   *1Ch 8:24*
Jerimoth, *H.*, Hanani   *1Ch 25:4*
The sixteenth to *H.*, he, his   *1Ch 25:23*
sons
H. one of the king's captains   *2Ch 26:11*
Jehohanan, *H.*, Zabbai   *Ezr 10:28*
repaired *H.* the son of one of   *Ne 3:8*
repaired *H.*, the son of   *Ne 3:30*
Shelemiah
and *H.* the ruler of the palace   *Ne 7:2*
Hoshea, *H.*, Hashub   *Ne 10:23*
of Jeremiah, *H.*   *Ne 12:12*
Zechariah, and *H.* with   *Ne 12:41*
trumpets
H. the son of Azur the prophet   *Jer 28:1*
Jeremiah said unto the prophet   *Jer 28:5*
H.
Then *H.* the prophet took the   *Jer 28:10*
H. spake in the presence of all   *Jer 28:11*
after that *H.* the prophet had   *Jer 28:12*
Go and tell *H.* saying, Thus   *Jer 28:13*
saith
Then said Jeremiah unto   *Jer 28:15*
H.
the prophet, Hear now, *H.*   *Jer 28:15*
So *H.* the prophet died the   *Jer 28:17*
same
and Zedekiah the son of *H.*   *Jer 36:12*
Shelemiah the son of *H.*; and   *Jer 37:13*
Daniel, *H.*, Mishael, and   *Da 1:6*
Azariah
and to *H.*, of Shadrach; and to   *Da 1:7*
over Daniel, *H.*, Mishael, and   *Da 1:11*
none like Daniel, *H..* Mishael   *Da 1:19*
and made the thing known to   *Da 2:17*
H.

HAND

into your *h.* are they delivered   *Ge 9:2*
he left all that he had in   *Ge 39:6*
Joseph's *h.*

but the man in whose *h.* the   *Ge 44:17*
cup is found
with a strong *h.* shall he drive   *Ex 6:1*
them out
by strength of *h.* Lord brought   *Ex 13:3*
out
Israel went out with an high *h.*   *Ex 14:8;*
                                       Nu 33:3
stretch out thine *h.* over the   *Ex 14:16*
sea
there shall not a *h.* touch it,   *Ex 19:13*
but he shall
h. for *h.* foot for foot   *Ex 21:24;*
                                       De 19:21
hesitate lending a *h.* (B)   *Ex 23:5*
two tables of the testimony in   *Ex 34:29*
Moses' *h.*
on this *h.* and that *h.* were   *Ex 38:15*
hangings
remain in the *h.* of him that   *Le 25:28*
bought it
doeth aught with high *h.*   *Nu 15:30*
(E)(R)
afterwards the *h.* of all the   *De 13:9*
people
thou shalt cut off her *h.* pity   *De 25:12*
her not
his blood on our head if any *h.*   *Jos 2:19*
on him
h. of the house of Joseph   *J'g 1:35*
prevailed
the Lord shall sell Sisera into   *J'g 4:9*
h. of a woman
now fall into the *h.* of the   *J'g 15:18*
uncircumcised
Israel smote all that came to   *J'g 20:48*
h. of Benjamin
of whose *h.* have I received   *1Sa 12:3*
any bribe
nor spear found in the *h.* of   *1Sa 13:22*
any of Israel
there was no sword in the *h.*   *1Sa 17:50*
of David
didst hide thyself when the   *1Sa 20:19*
business was in *h.*
because their *h.* also is with   *1Sa 22:17*
David
that I may see, and eat it at   *2Sa 13:5;*
her *h.*   *13:6*
is not the *h.* of Joab with   *2Sa 14:19*
thee in all this
And he took three darts in   *2Sa 18:14*
his *h.*
had on every *h.* six fingers   *2Sa 21:20;*
                                       1Ch 20:6
let me not fall into *h.* of men   *2Sa 24:14;*
                                       1Ch 21:13
kingdom established in *h.* of   *1Ki 2:46*
Solomon
and the king's *h.* was restored   *1Ki 13:6*
again
there ariseth a cloud like a   *1Ki 18:44*
man's *h.*
go up, for Lord shall deliver   *1Ki 22:6;*
it into king's *h.*   *22:12, 15; 2Ch 28:5*
lord on whose *h.* the king   *2Ki 7:2;*
leaned   *17:17*
man with his weapons in his   *2Ki 11:11*
h.
went out from under *h.* of   *2Ki 13:5*
Syrians
were on a man's left *h.* at the   *2Ki 23:8*
gate
hath Lord left you in *h.* of   *2Ch 12:5*
Shishak
according to good *h.* of his God   *Ezr 7:9*
on him
the *h.* of princes have been   *Ezr 9:2*
chief in trespass
upon himself put not forth   *Job 1:12*
thine *h.*
earth is given into the *h.* of   *Job 9:24*
the wicked
into whose *h.* God bringeth   *Job 12:6*
abundantly
in whose *h.* is the soul of   *Job 12:10*
every living thing
every *h.* of the wicked shall   *Job 20:22*
come on him
lo, their good is not in their   *Job 21:16*
h.
the mighty shall be taken   *Job 34:20*
away without *h.*
he sealeth up the *h.* of every   *Job 37:7*
man
thou hast not shut me into *h.* of   *Ps 31:8*
enemy
let not the *h.* of the wicked   *Ps 36:11*
remove me

deliver me out of *h.* of wicked   Ps 71:4;
82:4; 97:10
as eyes of servants look to the   Ps 123:2
h. of masters
as arrows are in the *h.* of a   Ps 127:4
mighty man
let a two-edged sword be in   Ps 149:6
their *h.*
when thou art come into *h.* of   Pr 6:3
thy friend
becometh poor that dealeth   Pr 10:4
with slack *h.* but *h.* of diligent
tho' *h.* join *h.* wicked not   Pr 11:21;
unpunished   16:5
the *h.* of the diligent shall bear   Pr 12:24
rule
why a price in *h.* of a fool to   Pr 17:16
get wisdom
as a thorn goeth up into the *h.*   Pr 26:9
of a drunkard
the *h.* mirrors (S)   Isa 3:23
the staff in their *h.* is my   Isa 10:5
indignation
shake the *h.* that they may go   Isa 13:2
into the gates
and this is the *h.* that is   Isa 14:26
stretched out
I will give over into the *h.* of a   Isa 19:4
cruel lord
Lord shall cast down to the   Isa 28:2
earth with the *h.*
given dearly beloved into *h.* of   Jer 12:7
enemies
vessel was marred in the *h.* of   Jer 18:4
the potter
as clay in potter's *h.* so are ye   Jer 18:6
in mine
with an outstretched *h.* I will   Jer 21:5
fight against you
the *h.* of Ahikam was with   Jer 26:24
Jeremiah, not to give him
into *h.* of people
shout against her round, she   Jer 50:15
hath given her *h.*
we have given the *h.* to the   La 5:6
Egyptians
princes are hanged up by their   La 5:12
h.
an *h.* was sent me, and lo, a   Eze 2:9
roll
and he put forth the form of   Eze 8:3;
an *h.*   10:8
nor did she strengthen the *h.*   Eze 16:49
of the needy
I say, Ye shall be taken with   Eze 21:24
the *h.*
be no god in *h.* of him that   Eze 28:9
slayeth thee
I will require my flock at   Eze 34:10
their *h.*
take the stick which is in the   Eze 37:19
h. of Ephraim
and in the man's *h.* a   Eze 40:5
measuring reed
there came forth the fingers of a   Da 5:5
man's *h.*
in whose *h.* thy breath is   Da 5:23
but he shall be broken without   Da 8:25
h.
an *h.* touched me, which set   Da 10:10
me
sell sons and daughters into *h.*   Joe 3:8
of Judah
because it is in the power of   Mic 2:1
their *h.*
shall see plummet in *h.* of   Zec 4:10
Zerubbabel
he touched her *h.*   M't 8:15
bind him *h.*   M't 22:13
a man who had a withered *h.*   M'k 3:1;
3:3; Lu 6:8
Son of man is betrayed into   M'k 14:41
h. of sinners
as many have taken in *h.* to set   Lu 1:1
forth
being delivered out of *h.* of our   Lu 1:74
enemies
h. of him that betrayeth me is   Lu 22:21
with me
but he escaped out of their *h.*   Joh 10:39
that was dead came forth,   Joh 11:44
bound *h.* and foot
Peter beckoning to them with   Ac 12:17
the *h.*
because I am not the *h.* I   1Co 12:15
am not body
eye cannot say to the *h.* I   1Co 12:21
have no need of thee

ordained by angels in the *h.* of   Ga 3:19
a mediator
take little book open in *h.* of   Re 10:8
the angel
woman, having a golden cup in   Re 17:4
her *h.*
hath avenged the blood of   Re 19:2
servants at her *h.*

HAND with *ENEMIES*

ark of the covenant may save   1Sa 4:3;
us out of the *h.* of our *enemies*   12:10;
2Sa 3:18
deliver you out of *h.* of   1Sa 12:11;
enemies   2Ki 17:39
king saved us out of the *h.* of   2Sa 19:9
our *enemies*
I will deliver them into *h.* of   2Ki 21:14;
enemies   2Ch 25:20; Ne 9:27
leftest thou them in *h.* of their   Ne 9:28
enemies
deliver me from the *h.* of mine   Ps 31:15
enemies
give this city into *h.* of   Jer 20:5;
enemies   21:7; 34:20-21; Eze 39:23
I will give Pharaoh into *h.* of   Jer 44:30
his *enemies*
redeem thee from the *h.* of   Mic 4:10
thy *enemies*
delivered out of the *h.* of our   Lu 1:74
enemies

HAND *OF GOD*

h. of God was heavy on them   1Sa 5:11
of Ashdod
h. of God was to give them   2Ch 30:12
one heart
according to the good *h.* of   Ezr 7:9;
God   Ne 2:8
by good *h.* of God upon us,   Ezr 8:18
they brought us
h. of God is upon all them for   Ezr 8:22
good that seek
the *h.* of God is upon us, and   Ezr 8:31
he delivered us
then I told them of the *h.* of   Ne 2:18
God on me
shall we receive good at the *h.*   Job 2:10
of God
have pity on me, *h.* of God   Job 19:21
hath touched me
I will teach you by the *h.* of   Job 27:11
God
this I saw that it was from the   Ec 2:24
h. of God
the wise and their works are in   Ec 9:1
the *h.* of God
shalt be a royal diadem in *h.*   Isa 62:3
of thy God
sat on right *h.* of God   M'k 16:19;
Ro 8:34; Col 3:1; Heb 10:12; 1Pe 3:22
being by the right *h.* of God   Ac 2:33
exalted
saw Jesus standing on the   Ac 7:55;
right *h.* of God   7:56
humble yourselves under the *h.*   1Pe 5:6
of God

HAND *OF THE LORD,*
LORD'S HAND

the *h.* of the Lord is upon thy   Ex 9:3
cattle
would to God we had died by   Ex 16:3
h. of the Lord
said to Moses, Is Lord's *h.*   Nu 11:23
waxed short
the *h.* of the Lord was against   De 2:15
them to destroy
all people know that *h.* of   Jos 4:24
Lord is mighty
ye have delivered Israel out   Jos 22:3
of *h.* of the Lord
the *h.* of the Lord was against   J'g 2:15
them for evil
the *h.* of the Lord is gone out   Ru 1:13
against me
h. of Lord was heavy on them   1Sa 5:6
of Ashdod
h. of Lord was against the city   1Sa 5:9
with destruction
the *h.* of the Lord was against   1Sa 7:13
the Philistines
then shall the *h.* of the Lord   1Sa 12:15
be against you
let us fall into *h.* of Lord   2Sa 24:14;
1Ch 21:13

the *h.* of the Lord was on   1Ki 18:46
Elijah
that the *h.* of Lord came upon   2Ki 3:15
Elisha
king granted according to *h.* of   Ezr 7:6
Lord on him
h. of Lord hath wrought this   Job 12:9;
Isa 40:20
in the *h.* of the Lord there is a   Ps 75:8
cup
king's heart is in the *h.* of the   Pr 21:1
Lord
because of the shaking of the   Isa 19:16
h. of Lord
in this mountain shall the *h.*   Isa 25:10
of the Lord rest
she hath received of the Lord's   Isa 40:2
h. double
hast drunk at *h.* of Lord the   Isa 51:17
cup of his fury
Lord's *h.* is not shortened, that   Isa 59:1
it cannot save
thou shalt be a crown of glory   Isa 62:3
in *h.* of Lord
h. of Lord shall be known   Isa 66:14
toward servants
then took I the cup at the   Jer 25:17
Lord's *h.*
Babylon hath been a golden   Jer 51:7
cup in Lord's *h.*
the *h.* of the Lord was there   Eze 1:3
upon him
the *h.* of the Lord was upon   Eze 3:14;
me   8:1; 37:1
the *h.* of the Lord was on me   Eze 33:22
in the evening
the self-same day the *h.* of   Eze 40:1
Lord was with him
and the *h.* of the Lord was   Lu 1:66
with him
the *h.* of the Lord was with   Ac 11:21
them
the *h.* of the Lord is upon   Ac 13:11
thee

AT, AT THE HAND

at the *h.* of every beast, at the *h.*   Ge 9:5
of man, at the *h.* of man's brother
the days of mourning for my   Ge 27:41
father are at *h.*
field Jacob bought at *h.* of   Ge 33:19
children of Hamor
saying, The year of release is   De 15:9
at *h.*
for the day of their calamity   De 32:35
is at *h.*
I have here at *h.* fourth part of   1Sa 9:8
a shekel
let Lord require it at *h.* of   1Sa 20:16
David's enemies
may avenge blood at the *h.* of   2Ki 9:7
Jezebel
Pethahiah was at the king's *h.*   Ne 11:24
in all
day of Lord is at *h.*   Isa 13:6;
Joe 1:15; Zep 1:7
am I a God at *h.* and not a   Jer 23:23
God afar off
the days are at *h.* and effect   Eze 12:23
of vision
but his blood will I require at   Eze 33:6
watchman's *h.*
and yield fruit, for they are at   Eze 36:8
h. to come
the day of the Lord cometh, it   Joe 2:1
is nigh at *h.*
kingdom of heaven is at *h.*   M't 3:2;
4:17; 10:7
my time is at *h.*   M't 26:18
the hour is at *h.*   M't 26:45
he is at *h.* that doth   M't 26:46;
betray me   M'k 14:42
kingdom of God is at *h.*   M'k 1:15;
Lu 21:31
that summer is now nigh at *h.*   Lu 21:30
and the Jews' passover was at   Joh 2:13;
11:55
now the Jews' feast of   Joh 7:2
tabernacles was at *h.*
for the sepulchre was nigh at   Joh 19:42
h.
the night is far spent, the day   Ro 13:12
is at *h.*
let moderation be known, the   Ph'p 4:5
Lord is at *h.*
as that the day of Christ is at   2Th 2:2
h.

the time of my departure is *at* 2Ti 4:6
h.
the end of all things is *at h.* be 1Pe 4:7
ye sober
for the time is *at h.* Re 1:3; 22:10

BY THE HAND

send *by h.* of him whom thou Ex 4:13
wilt send
sum of tabernacle counted Ex 38:21
by h. of Ithamar
Lord commanded *by h.* of Le 8:36;
Moses 10:11; 26:46; Nu 4:37, 45,
49; 9:23; 10:13; 15:23; 16:40; 27:23;
36:13; Jos 14:2; 20:2; 21:2, 8; 22:9;
J'g 3:4; 1Ki 8:53, 56; 2Ch 33:8; 35:6;
Ne 9:14; Ps 77:20
send him away *by the h.* of a Le 16:21
fit man
not die *by the h.* of the Jos 20:9
avenger of blood
Samson said to lad that held J'g 16:26
by the h.
make David fall *by the h.* of 1Sa 18:25
Philistines
I shall one day perish *by the* 1Sa 27:1
h. of Saul
by the h. of my servant David 2Sa 3:18
I will save
David sent to comfort him *by* 2Sa 10:2
h. of servants
David wrote a letter, sent it 2Sa 11:14
by h. of Uriah
he sent *by the h.* of Nathan 2Sa 12:25
the prophet
they fell *by the h.* of David 2Sa 21:22;
1Ch 20:8
Solomon sent *by the h.* of 1Ki 2:25
Benaiah
which he spake *by the h.* of 1Ki 14:18
his servant Ahijah
also *by the h.* of Jehu came 1Ki 16:7
word of the Lord
which he spake *by the h.* of 2Ki 14:25
Jonah
he saved them *by the h.* of 2Ki 14:27
Jeroboam
word which he spake *by h.* of 2Ch 10:15
Ahijah
not pour out wrath *by the h.* 2Ch 12:7
of Shishak
bring out vessels *by the h.* of Ezr 1:8
Mithredath
the vessels weighed *by the h.* Ezr 8:33
of Meremoth
that sendeth a message *by h.* of Pr 26:6
a fool
is any that taketh her *by the* Isa 51:18
h.
send yokes *by the h.* of the Jer 27:3
messengers
in the day I took them *by the* Jer 31:32;
h. Heb 8:9
my vengeance on Edom *by h.* Eze 25:14
of Israel
I will lay the land waste *by h.* Eze 30:12
of strangers
he went in and took her *by* M't 9:25;
the h. M'k 1:31; 5:41; Lu 8:54
he took the blind man *by h.* M'k 8:23
and led him
Jesus took him that was M'k 9:27
possessed *by the h.*
send to be a deliverer *by h.* of Ac 7:35
the angel
he saw no man, but they led him Ac 9:8
by the h.
he went seeking some to lead Ac 13:11
him *by the h.*
the salutation *by the h.* of me, Col 4:18
Paul

FROM THE HAND

deliver me *from h.* of my Ge 32:11
brother Esau
Lord redeemed you *from the h.* De 7:8
of Pharaoh
thou hast delivered us *from h.* J'g 8:22
of Midian
pleaded my reproach *from h.* 1Sa 25:39
of Nabal
he saveth the poor *from the h.* Job 5:15
of mighty
or redeem me *from the h.* of Job 6:23
the mighty
deliver his soul *from the h.* Ps 89:48
of the grave

saved them *from the h.* of Ps 106:10
him that hated them,
redeemed *from h.* of enemy
deliver me *from h.* of strange Ps 144:7
children
deliver thyself as a roe *from h.* Pr 6:5
of hunter
he hath delivered poor *from* Jer 20:13
h. of evil
from h. of him that was Jer 31:11
stronger than he

HIS HAND

lest he put forth *his h.* and Ge 3:22
take tree of life
his h. will be against every Ge 16:12
man, and every man's hand
while he lingered, men laid Ge 19:16
hold on *his h.*
all the goods of his master Ge 24:10
were in *his h.*
Jacob took of that which Ge 32:13
came to *his h.*
Lord made all that he did Ge 39:3
prosper in *his h.*
Pharaoh took the ring off *his* Ge 41:42
h. and put it
he put forth *his h.*, it became a Ex 4:4
rod in *his h.*
when he took it out, *his h.* was Ex 4:6
leprous as snow
Moses took the rod of God in Ex 4:20
his h.
Aaron stretched out *his h.* over Ex 8:6;
the waters 8:17
Moses stretched forth *his h.* Ex 10:22
toward heaven
when Moses held up *his h.*: let Ex 17:11
down *his h.*
but God delivered him into Ex 21:13
his h.
if found in *his h.*, he die Ex 21:16;
under *his h.* 21:20
if the theft be certainly found Ex 22:4
in *his h.* alive
to see whether he hath put *his* Ex 22:8;
h. to goods 22:11
on the nobles of Israel he laid Ex 24:11
not *his h.*
two tables of testimony were Ex 32:15;
in *his h.* 34:4
he shall put *his h.* on head of Le 1:4
burnt offering
priest shall have in *his h.* bitter Nu 5:18
water
besides that that *his h.* shall Nu 6:21
get
and had taken all his land out Nu 21:26
of *his h.*
his sword drawn in *his h.* Nu 22:23;
22:31; 1Ch 21:16
Phinehas took a javelin in *his* Nu 25:7
h. and went
his h. fetcheth a stroke with De 19:5
the axe
a man with his sword drawn Jos 5:13
in *his h.*
Joshua drew not *his h.* back Jos 8:26
till destroyed
shall not deliver the slayer up Jos 20:5
into *his h.*
put forth the end of the staff in J'g 6:21
his h.
into *his h.* hath God delievered J'g 7:14
Midian
known why *his h.* is not 1Sa 6:3
removed from you
that it is not *his h.* that smote 1Sa 6:9
us, but chance
but no man put *his h.* to his 1Sa 14:26
mouth
but Jonathan put *his h.* to his 1Sa 14:27
mouth
that he shall play with *his h.* 1Sa 16:16
thou be well
took an harp and played 1Sa 16:23;
with *his h.* 18:10
David took his staff and his 1Sa 17:40
sling in *his h.*
with the head of the 1Sa 17:57
Philistine in *his h.*
he put his life in *his h.* and 1Sa 19:5
slew the Philistine
and Jonathan strengthened 1Sa 23:16
his h. in God
Uzzah put *his h.* to ark 2Sa 6:6;
1Ch 13:10
and hath with *his h.* fulfilled it 1Ki 8:15

nor take the whole kingdom 1Ki 11:34
out of *his h.*
his h. which he put forth 1Ki 13:4
against him dried up
call on Lord and strike *his h.* 2Ki 5:11
over place
he gave him *his h.* took him 2Ki 10:15
up in chariot
ye shall compass the king 2Ki 11:8;
every man with his 11:11; 2Ch 23:7
weapons in *his h.*
the kingdom was confirmed in 2Ki 14:5
his h.
his h. might be with him to 2Ki 15:19
confirm kingdom
on which if a man lean will 2Ki 18:21
go into *his h.*
I beseech thee, save us out of 2Ki 19:19
his h.
made me understand by *his* 1Ch 28:19
h. on me
Uzziah had a censer in *his h.* 2Ch 26:19
he gave them all into *his h.* 2Ch 36:17
sent his servant with open letter Ne 6:5
in *his h.*
he would let loose *his h.* and Job 6:9
cut me off
the day of darkness is ready Job 15:23
at *his h.*
for he stretcheth out *his h.* Job 15:25
against God
his h. hath formed the Job 26:13
crooked serpent
he would fain flee out of his Job 27:22
h.
he putteth forth *his h.* upon Job 28:9
the rock
the Lord upholdeth him with Ps 37:24
his h.
the Lord will not leave him in Ps 37:33
his h.
they remembered not *his h.* Ps 78:42
nor the day
I will set *his h.* also in the sea, Ps 89:25
and right hand
in *his h.* are the deep places of Ps 95:4
the earth
sheep of *his h.* to-day if ye will Ps 95:7
hear his voice
therefore he lifted up *his h.* Ps 106:26
against them
wherewith the mower filleth Ps 129:7
not *his h.*
a slothful man hideth *his h.* Pr 19:24;
26:15
begets a son, and nothing is in Ec 5:14
his h.
nothing which he may carry Ec 5:15
away in *his h.*
my beloved put in *his h.* by hole Ca 5:4
of door
his anger not turned away, Isa 5:25;
but *his h.* is stretched out still 5:9, 12,
17, 21; 10:4; 14:27
he shall shake *his h.* against Isa 10:32
mount Zion
Lord shall set *his h.* again Isa 11:11
second time
and he shall shake *his h.* over Isa 11:15
the river
I will commit thy government Isa 22:21
into *his h.*
while it is yet in *his h.* he Isa 28:4
eateth it up
when the Lord shall stretch out Isa 31:3
his h.
therefore, O Lord, save us Isa 37:20
from *his h.*
who measured waters in Isa 40:12
hollow of *his h.*
another shall subscribe with Isa 44:5
his h. to Lord
in the shadow of *his h.* hath he Isa 49:2
hid me
the pleasure of Lord shall Isa 53:10
prosper in *his h.*
and keepeth *his h.* from doing Isa 56:2
any evil
till I have consumed them by Jer 27:8
his h.
yoke of my transgression La 1:14
bound by *his h.*
he hath not withdrawn *his h.* La 2:8
from destroying
he turneth *his h.* against me all La 3:3
the day
even every man with his Eze 8:11
censer in *his h.*

every man with his destroying   *Eze 9:1*
weapon into *his h.*
despiseth oath, when lo, he   *Eze 17:18*
had given *his h.*
I will cause the sword to fall   *Eze 30:22*
out of *his h.*
and I will put my sword in   *Eze 30:24*
his h.
for lambs according as *his h.*   *Eze 46:7*
shall attain unto
none can stay *his h.* or say,   *Da 4:35*
What doest thou
neither any that could deliver   *Da 8:4;*
out of *his h.*   *8:7*
he shall cause craft to prosper   *Da 8:25*
in *his h.*
but the multitude shall be   *Da 11:11*
given into *his h.*
but these shall escape out of   *Da 11:41*
his h. even Edom
he stretched out *his h.* with   *Ho 7:5*
scorners
the balances of deceit are in   *Ho 12:7*
his h.
he had horns coming out of   *Hab 3:4*
his h.
passeth her shall hiss and wag   *Zep 2:15*
his h.
every man with staff in *his h.*   *Zec 8:4*
for very age
his h. rise up against the   *Zec 14:13*
hand of his neighbour
whose fan is in *his h.*   *M't 3:12; Lu 3:17*
he that dippeth *his h.* with   *M't 26:23*
me in the dish
and *his h.* was restored whole   *M'k 3:5;*
          Lu 6:10
they beseech him to put *his h.*   *M'k 7:32*
upon him
no man having put *his h.* to the   *Lu 9:62*
plough
put a ring on *his h.* and shoes   *Lu 15:22*
on his feet
and hath given all things into   *Joh 3:35*
his h.
an officer struck him with the   *Joh 18:22*
palm of *his h.*
how God by *his h.* would   *Ac 7:25*
deliver them
a viper fastened on *his h.* hang   *Ac 28:3;*
on *his h.*   *28:4*
he that sat had a pair of   *Re 6:5*
balances in *his h.*
and he had in *his h.* a little   *Re 10:2*
book open
receive his mark in his   *Re 14:9*
forehead, or in *his h.*
having golden crown, and in   *Re 14:14*
his h. sharp sickle
an angel came with a great   *Re 20:1*
chain in *his h.*

LEFT HAND

if thou want take *left h.* I will   *Ge 13:9*
go to right
Hobah which is on *left h.* of   *Ge 14:15*
Damascus
that I may turn to the right *h.*   *Ge 24:49*
or to the *left*
Ephraim toward Israel's *left*   *Ge 48:13*
h. and Manasseh in his *left h.*
Israel laid his *left h.* upon   *Ge 48:14*
Manasseh's head
waters a wall on the right *h.*   *Ex 14:22*
and *left*
pour the oil into his own *left*   *Le 14:15;*
h.   *14:27*
not turn to the right *h.* nor   *Nu 20:17;*
to the *left*   *De 2:27; 5:32; 17:11, 20;*
          28:14
no way to turn either to right   *Nu 22:26*
h. or *left*
from right *h.* or to *left*, that   *Jos 1:7;*
thou mayest prosper   *23:6; 1Sa 6:12;*
          Pr 4:27
Ehud put forth *left h.* and took   *J'g 3:21*
dagger
the companies held lamps in   *J'g 7:20*
their *left h.*
Samson took hold of other   *J'g 16:29*
pillar with *left h.*
he turned not to *left h.* from   *2Sa 2:19*
following
none can turn to the right *h.*   *2Sa 14:19*
or to the *left*
all the mighty men were on   *2Sa 16:6*
right *h.* and *left*
host of heaven on *left h.*   *1Ki 22:19;*
          2Ch 18:18

Josiah turned not to the right   *2Ki 22:2*
h. or *left*
which were on a man's *left h.*   *2Ki 23:8*
at the gate
the sons of Merari stood on   *1Ch 6:44*
the *left h.*
they could use both right *h.*   *1Ch 12:2*
and *left* in hurling
he called name of that on *left*   *2Ch 3:17*
h. Boaz
he put five on the *left h.* to   *2Ch 4:6*
wash in them
five candlesticks on right, five   *2Ch 4:7*
on *left h.*
Ezra on pulpit, on his *left h.*   *Ne 8:4*
stood Pedaiah
on *left h.* he doth work, not   *Job 23:9*
behold him
and in her *left h.* riches and   *Pr 3:16*
honour
but a fool's heart is at his *left*   *Ec 10:2*
h.
left h. is under my head, right   *Ca 2:6*
embraces
his *left h.* under my head, right   *Ca 8:3*
embrace me
he shall eat on *left h.* and not   *Isa 9:20*
be satisfied
ears hear a word, then ye   *Isa 30:21*
turn to the *left h.*
thou shalt break forth on the   *Isa 54:3*
right *h.* and *left*
her daughters dwell at thy   *Eze 16:46*
left h.
go thee either on the right *h.*   *Eze 21:16*
or on the *left*
I will smite thy bow out of   *Eze 39:3*
thy *left h.*
when he held up his *left h.* to   *Da 12:7*
heaven
cannot discern between right   *Jon 4:11*
h. and *left*
shall devour all people on   *Zec 12:6*
right *h.* and *left*
let not *left h.* know what thy   *M't 6:3*
right doeth
one on right *h.* other on *left*   *M't 20:21;*
          M'k 10:37
to sit on right *h.* and   *M't 20:23;*
left not mine   *M'k 10:40*
he shall set sheep on his right   *M't 25:33*
h. goats on *left*
he shall say to them on *left h.*   *M't 25:41*
Depart from me
one crucified on right *h.*   *M't 27:38;*
other on *left*   *M'k 15:27; Lu 23:33*
we left Cyprus on the *left h.*   *Ac 21:3*
and sailed
armour of righteousness on   *2Co 6:7*
right *h.* and *left*

MIGHTY HAND

will not let you go, no not with   *Ex 3:19*
mighty h.
people thou broughtest forth   *Ex 32:11*
with *mighty h.*
hast begun to shew servant by   *De 3:24*
mighty h.
assayed to take him a nation   *De 4:34*
by a *mighty h.*
out of Egypt by a *mighty h.*   *De 5:15;*
  6:21, 7:8, 19; 9:26; 11:2; 26:8; 34:12
stranger that is come for thy   *2Ch 6:32*
mighty h.
with a *mighty h.* will I rule   *Eze 20:33*
and I will bring you out with   *Eze 20:34*
a *mighty h.*
brought you out of Egypt with   *Da 9:15*
mighty h.
humble yourselves under   *1Pe 5:6*
mighty h. of God

MINE, MY HAND

I have lifted up *mine h.* unto   *Ge 14:22*
the Lord
seven ewe-lambs shalt thou   *Ge 21:30*
take of *my h.*
it is in the power of *my h.* to   *Ge 31:29*
do you hurt
I bear loss, of *my h.* didst   *Ge 31:39*
thou require it
I pray thee, receive my   *Ge 33:10*
present at *my h.*
deliver him into *my h.* I will   *Ge 42:37*
bring him thee
I'll be surety, of *my h.* shalt   *Ge 43:9*
thou require him

I'll smite with the rod that is in   *Ex 7:17*
mine h.
my h. shall destroy them; rod   *Ex 15:9;*
in *mine h.*   *17:9*
I will cover thee with *my h.*   *Ex 33:22*
while I pass
I will take away *mine h.* and   *Ex 33:23*
thou shalt see
if thou wilt deliver this people   *Nu 21:2*
into *my h.*
I would there were a sword in   *Nu 22:29*
mine h.
might of *my h.* hath gotten me   *De 8:17*
this wealth
went up, having the two tables   *De 10:3*
in *mine h.*
that can deliver out of *my h.*   *De 32:39;*
          Isa 43:13
I lift up *my h.* to heaven and   *De 32:40*
say, I live for ever
and if *mine h.* take hold on   *De 32:41*
judgment
if thou wilt save Israel by *my*   *J'g 6:36;*
h.   *6:37*
mine own *h.* hath saved me   *J'g 7:2*
when Lord hath delivered Zeba   *J'g 8:7*
into *mine h.*
would to God this people were   *J'g 9:29*
under *my h.*
the Lord delivered them into   *J'g 12:3*
my h.
dedicated the silver to the Lord   *J'g 17:3*
from *my h.*
that ye have not found ought   *1Sa 12:5*
in *my h.*
Lord will deliver thee this   *1Sa 17:46*
day into *mine h.*
Saul said, Let not *mine h.* be   *1Sa 18:17*
upon him
there is no common bread   *1Sa 21:4*
under *mine h.*
God hath delivered him into   *1Sa 23:7*
mine h.
to stretch *mine h.* against   *1Sa 24:6*
Lord's anointed
see skirt in *mine h.* no   *1Sa 24:11*
transgression in *mine h.*
but *mine h.* shall not be   *1Sa 24:12*
upon thee
what have I done? what evil   *1Sa 26:18*
is in *mine h.*
Lord delivered thee into *my*   *1Sa 26:23;*
h. to-day   *24:10*
I have put my life in *my h.*   *1Sa 28:21*
and hearkened
my h. shall be with thee to   *2Sa 3:12*
bring Israel
deliver Philistines into *mine*   *2Sa 5:19;*
h.   *1Ch 14:10*
yet not put forth *mine h.*   *2Sa 18:12*
against Absalom
that *my h.* may be restored me   *1Ki 13:6*
again
he leaneth on *my h.* in house   *2Ki 5:18*
of Rimmon
have they delivered Samaria   *2Ki 18:34*
out of *my h.*
delivered their country out of   *2Ki 18:35*
my h. Lord deliver Jerusalem
out of *mine h.*
given inhabitants of land   *1Ch 22:18*
into *my h.*
shall God deliver you out of   *2Ch 32:15;*
my h.   *32:17*
wherefore do I put my life in   *Job 13:14*
mine h.
and my bow was renewed in   *Job 29:20*
my h.
rejoiced because *mine h.* had   *Job 31:25*
gotten much
or my mouth hath kissed *my*   *Job 31:27*
h.
neither shall *my h.* be heavy   *Job 33:7*
upon thee
and turned *my h.* against their   *Ps 81:14*
enemies
with whom *my h.* shall be   *Ps 89:21*
established
my soul is continually in *my*   *Ps 119:109*
h.
I have stretched out *my h.* none   *Pr 1:24*
regarded
I will turn *my h.* upon me and   *Isa 1:25*
purge dross
as *my h.* hath found the   *Isa 10:10*
kingdoms of idols
by the strength of *my h.* I   *Isa 10:13*
have done it

my *h*. hath found as a nest   *Isa 10:14*
the riches of people
have they delivered Samaria   *Isa 36:19*
out of *my h*.
that Lord should deliver   *Isa 36:20*
Jerusalem out of *my h*.
mine h. also hath laid   *Isa 48:13*
foundation of earth
is *my h*. shortened; this ye   *Isa 50:2;*
have of *my h*.   *50:11*
have covered thee in the   *Isa 51:16*
shadow of *mine h*.
all those hath *mine h*. made   *Isa 66:2;*
   Ac 7:50
I will stretch out *my h*.   *Jer 6:12;*
will cause them to know *mine*   *Jer 16:21*
h. and might
so are ye in *mine h*. O house of   *Jer 18:6*
Israel
take the wine cup of this fury   *Jer 25:15*
at *my h*.
so will I stretch out *my h*.   *Eze 6:15*
upon them
in the even I digged thro' the   *Eze 12:7*
wall with *my h*.
mine h. shall be upon   *Eze 13:9*
prophets that see vanity
I lifted up *mine h*. saying, I   *Eze 20:5;*
am the Lord your God   *6:23, 28, 42;*
   36:7; 44:12; 47:14
I withdrew *my h*. and   *Eze 20:22*
wrought for name's sake
I have smitten *mine h*. at thy   *Eze 22:13*
dishonest gain
one stick, and they shall be   *Eze 37:19*
one in *mine h*.
none shall deliver her out of   *Ho 2:10*
mine h.
I will turn *mine h*. against   *Am 1:8*
Ekron
tho' into hell, thence shall *mine*   *Am 9:2*
h. take them
behold, I will shake *mine h*. on   *Zec 2:9*
them
I will turn *mine h*. upon the   *Zec 13:7*
little ones
nor shall any pluck them out   *Joh 10:28*
of *my h*.
none is able to pluck them   *Joh 10:29*
out of my Father's *h*.
except I shall thrust *my h*.   *Joh 20:25*
into his side
salutation of Paul with   *1Co 16:21;*
mine own *h*.   *2Th 3:17*
I have written with *my h*.   *Ga 6:11;*
   Ph'm 19

OUR HAND

let not *our h*. be on him, he is   *Ge 37:27*
our brother
and we have brought it again   *Ge 43:21*
in *our h*.
lest adversaries should say,   *De 32:27*
Our h. is high
our god hath delivered Samson   *J'g 16:23*
into *our h*.
Lord hath delivered them   *1Sa 14:10;*
into *our h*.   *30:28*
prophesy not, that thou die   *Jer 11:21*
not by *our h*.
to boast in things made   *2Co 10:16*
ready to *our h*.

OUT OF,
OUT OF THE HAND

which I took out of the *h*. of   *Ge 48:22*
Amorite
Egyptian delivered us out of *h*.   *Ex 2:19*
of shepherds
to deliver them out of *h*. of   *Ex 3:8;*
Egyptians   *14:30*
take jealousy-offering out of   *Nu 5:25*
woman's *h*.
if thus, kill me. I pray thee,   *Nu 11:15*
out of *h*.
deliver him out of *h*. of the   *Nu 35:25*
revenger of blood
deliver them out of the *h*. of   *Jos 9:26*
Israel
judges which delivered them   *J'g 2:16*
out of the *h*.
I delivered you out of the *h*. of   *J'g 6:9*
Egyptians
deliver Israel out of the *h*. of   *J'g 13:5*
the Philistines

who shall deliver us out of *h*. of   *1Sa 4:8*
these gods
Lord will deliver me out of *h*. of   *1Sa 17:37*
of this Philistine
I delivered thee out of *h*. of   *2Sa 12:7;*
Saul   *22:1*
plucked the spear out of the   *2Sa 23:21*
Egyptian's *h*.
will rend kingdom out of *h*.   *1Ki 11:12;*
of Solomon   *11:31*
we take it not out of *h*. of the   *1Ki 22:3*
king of Syria
took again out of *h*. of   *2Ki 13:25*
Ben-hadad
out of *h*. of the king of   *2Ki 20:6;*
Assyria   *Isa 38:6*
deliver me out of the *h*. of the   *Ps 71:4*
wicked
rid them out of the *h*. of the   *Ps 82:4*
wicked
he delivereth them out of *h*. of   *Ps 97:10*
the wicked
I will deliver thee out of *h*. of   *Jer 15:21*
the wicked
him spoiled out of *h*. of the   *Jer 21:12;*
oppressor   *22:3*
not escape out of *h*. of   *Jer 32:4;*
Chaldeans   *38:18, 23*
none doth deliver us out of *their*   *La 5:8*
h.
out of their *h*. I will not   *Zec 11:6*
deliver them
to take him, but he escaped   *Joh 10:39*
out of their *h*.
deliver me out of the *h*. of   *Ac 12:11*
Herod
ascended before God out of   *Re 8:4;*
angel's *h*.   *10:10*

RIGHT HAND

put his *right h*. on Ephraim's   *Ge 48:14;*
head   *48:18*
thy *right h*. O Lord, is become   *Ex 15:6*
glorious
put blood on thumb of their   *Ex 29:20;*
right h.   *Le 8:23, 24; 14:14, 17, 25, 28*
from his *right h*. went a fiery   *De 33:2*
law
her *right h*. to the workman's   *J'g 5:26*
hammer
Joab took Amasa with *right h*.   *2Sa 20:9*
to kiss
Bath-sheba sat on Solomon's   *1Ki 2:19*
right h.
on *right h*. of the mount of   *2Ki 23:13*
corruption
he hideth himself on the *right*   *Job 23:9*
h.
upon my *right h*., rise the   *Job 30:12*
youth, they push
that thine own *right h*. can   *Job 40:14*
save thee
he is at my *right h*. I shall not   *Ps 16:8*
be moved
at thy *right h*. are pleasures   *Ps 16:11*
for ever more
savest by thy *right h*. them that   *Ps 17:7*
trust in thee
and thy *right h*. hath holden   *Ps 18:35*
me up
with the saving strength of his   *Ps 20:6*
right h.
thy *right h*. shall find out   *Ps 21:8*
those that hate thee
and their *right h*. is full of   *Ps 26:10*
bribes
but thy *right h*. and thy arm   *Ps 44:3*
saved them
thy *right h*. shall teach thee   *Ps 45:4*
terrible things
on thy *right h*. did stand queen   *Ps 45:9*
in gold of Ophir
thy *right h*. is full of   *Ps 48:10*
righteousness
save with thy *right h*. and hear   *Ps 60:5*
me
my soul followeth, thy *right h*.   *Ps 63:8*
upholdeth me
thou hast holden me by my   *Ps 73:23*
right h.
why withdrawest thou thy   *Ps 74:11*
right h.
I will remember the years of   *Ps 77:10*
the *right h*.
to mountain which his *right h*.   *Ps 78:54*
purchased
the vineyard which thy *right h*.   *Ps 80:15*
planted

let thy hand be upon the man   *Ps 80:17*
of thy *right h*.
strong is thy hand, high is thy   *Ps 89:13*
right h.
I will also set his *right h*. in   *Ps 89:25*
the rivers
thou hast set up the *right h*. of   *Ps 89:42*
his adversaries
ten thousand shall fall at thy   *Ps 91:7*
right h.
his *right h*. hath gotten him the   *Ps 98:1*
victory
save with thy *right h*. and   *Ps 108:6*
answer me
and let Satan stand at his   *Ps 109:6*
right h.
for he shall stand at the *right*   *Ps 109:31*
h. of the poor
sit thou at my *right h*. till I   *Ps 110:1;*
make enemies thy footstool   *Lu 20:42;*
   Ac 2:34; Heb 1:13
the Lord at thy *right h*. shall   *Ps 110:5*
strike thro' kings
the *right h*. of the Lord doeth   *Ps 118:15*
valiantly
right h. of the Lord is   *Ps 118:16*
exalted, doeth valiantly
the Lord is thy shade upon thy   *Ps 121:5*
right h.
if I forget, let my *right h*.   *Ps 137:5*
forget her cunning
and thy *right h*. shall save me   *Ps 138:7*
even there thy *right h*. shall   *Ps 139:10*
hold me
looked on my *right h*. none   *Ps 142:4*
would know me
their *right h*. is a *right h*.   *Ps 144:8*
of falsehood
length of days is in her   *Pr 3:16*
right h.
the ointment of his *right h*.   *Pr 27:16*
bewrayeth
a wise man's heart is at his   *Ec 10:2*
right h.
and his *right h*. doth embrace   *Ca 2:6*
me
and his *right h*. should embrace   *Ca 8:3*
me
I will uphold thee with *right*   *Isa 41:10*
h. of righteousness
I the Lord thy God will hold   *Isa 41:13*
thy *right h*.
nor say, Is there not a lie in   *Isa 44:20*
my *right h*.
to Cyrus whose *right h*. I have   *Isa 45:1*
holden
my *right h*. hath spanned the   *Isa 48:13*
heavens
the Lord hath sworn by his   *Isa 62:8*
right h.
that led them by the *right h*.   *Isa 63:12*
of Moses
tho' Coniah were the signet   *Jer 22:24*
on my *right h*.
hath drawn back his *right h*.   *La 2:3*
from enemy
he stood with his *right h*. as an   *La 2:4*
adversary
at *right h*. divination for   *Eze 21:22*
Jerusalem
cup of Lord's *right h*. shall be   *Hab 2:16*
turned to
Satan standing at his *right h*.   *Zec 3:1*
to resist him
if thy *right h*.offend thee, cut   *M't 5:30*
it off
let not thy left know what thy   *M't 6:3*
right h. doeth
Son of man sitting on the   *M'k 14:6;*
right h. of power   *Lu 22:69*
sat on *right h*. of God   *M'k 16:19;*
   Heb 1:3; 8:1; 10:12; 12:2; 1Pe 3:22
was a man whose *right h*. was   *Lu 6:6*
withered
he is on my *right h*. I shall not   *Ac 2:25*
be moved
being by the *right h*. of God   *Ac 2:33;*
exalted   *5:31*
he took him by the *right h*. and   *Ac 3:7*
lift him up
saw Jesus standing on *right h*.   *Ac 7:55;*
of God   *7:56*
who is even at the *right h*. of   *Ro 8:34*
God
set him at his *right h*. in   *Eph 1:20*
heavenly places
where Christ sitteth on the   *Col 3:1*
right h. of God

he had in his *right h.* seven   *Re 1:16;*
stars   *1:20; 2:1*
laid *right h.* upon me, saying,   *Re 1:17*
Fear not
I saw in his *right h.* a book   *Re 5:1;*
written within   *5:7*
to receive mark in their *right*   *Re 13:16*
h. or foreheads

STRETCH FORTH, STRETCH OUT HAND

Abraham *stretched forth* his *h.*   *Ge 22:10*
to slay
I will *stretch out* my *h.* on   *Ex 3:20;*
Egypt   *7:5; 9:15*
stretch out thy *h.* over the sea   *Ex 14:16;*
   26:7, 19
Moses *stretched out* his *h.*   *Ex 14:21;*
over the sea   *14:27*
who can *stretch forth h.*   *1Sa 26:9*
against Lord's anointed
how wast not afraid to *stretch*   *2Sa 1:14*
forth thy *h.*
will *stretch forth* thine *h.*   *Ps 138:7*
against enemies
she *stretcheth out* her *h.* to the   *Pr 31:20*
poor
I will *stretch out* my *h.* on   *Eze 14:9*
that prophet
then will I *stretch out* mine   *Eze 14:13*
h. upon the land
I will *stretch out* mine *h.*   *Eze 25:7*
upon the Ammonites
I will also *stretch out* mine *h.*   *Eze 25:13*
upon Edom
I will *stretch out* mine *h.* on   *Eze 25:16*
the Philistines
I will *stretch out* mine *h.*   *Eze 35:3*
against mount Seir
shall *stretch forth* his *h.* on the   *Da 11:42*
countries
stretch forth my *h.* upon   *Zep 1:4*
Judah
stretch forth my *h.* against   *Zep 2:13*
Assyria

THINE, THY HAND

to receive thy brother's blood   *Ge 4:11*
from *thy h.*
thy maid is in *thy h.* do to her   *Ge 16:6*
as it pleaseth
and he said, Lay not *thine h.*   *Ge 22:12*
upon the lad
put, I pray, *thy h.* under my   *Ge 24:2;*
thigh   *47:29*
thy h. shall be in the neck of   *Ge 49:8*
thy enemies
what is that in *thine h.?* he said,   *Ex 4:2*
A rod
thou shalt take this rod in   *Ex 4:17;*
thine h.   *7:15; 17:5*
stretch forth *thine h.* over the   *Ex 8:5;*
rivers *9:22; 10:12, 21; M't 12:13; M'k 3:5*
it shall be for a sign on *thine*   *Ex 13:9;*
h.   *De 6:8; M'k 13:16*
put not *thine h.* with wicked   *Ex 23:1*
to be witness
for I have delivered Og into   *Nu 21:34*
thy h.
Lord thy God hath blessed thee   *De 2:7;*
in works of *thy h. 14:29; 15:10; 23:20;*
   28:8, 12, 20
behold, I have given into *thy h.*   *De 2:24*
Sihon
I will deliver Og and his people   *De 3:2*
into *thy h.*
thy h. shall be first on him, to   *De 13:9*
put him to death
shall cleave nought of cursed   *De 13:17*
thing to *thine h.*
thou shalt bind up the money   *De 14:25*
in *thine h.*
nor shut *thine h.* from thy poor   *De 15:7*
brother
thou shalt open *thine h.* wide   *De 15:8*
to thy brother
thou mayest pluck the ears   *De 23:25*
with *thine h.*
there shall be no might in   *De 28:32*
thine h.
make thee plenteous in every   *De 30:9*
work of *thine h.*
he loved the people, all his   *De 33:3*
saints are in *thy h.*
I have given into *thine h.*   *Jos 6:2*
Jericho
for I will give Ai into *thine h.*   *Jos 8:18*

now behold, we are in *thine h.*   *Jos 9:25*
to do to us
slack not *thy h.* from thy   *Jos 10:6*
servants, save us
I have delivered kings of   *Jos 10:8*
Canaan into *thy h.*
I will deliver Sisera into *thine h.*   *J'g 4:7*
I will deliver the Midianites into   *J'g 7:7*
thine h.
are hands of Zeba and   *J'g 8:15*
Zalmunna in thine h.
hold thy peace, lay *thine h.* on   *J'g 18:19*
thy mouth
I will deliver Benjamin into   *J'g 20:28*
thine h.
Saul said to the priest,   *1Sa 14:19*
Withdraw *thy h.*
what is under *thine h.?* give me   *1Sa 21:3*
five loaves
I will deliver Philistines into   *1Sa 23:4;*
thine h.   *2Sa 5:19*
bring meat, that I may eat of   *2Sa 13:10*
thine h.
it is enough, stay *thine h.*   *2Sa 24:16;*
   1Ch 21:15
let *thine h.* I pray, be against   *2Sa 24:17;*
me   *1Ch 21:17*
hast fulfilled it with *thine h.*   *1Ki 8:24;*
   2Ch 6:15
she said, Bring me a morsel of   *1Ki 17:11*
bread in *thine h.*
I will deliver Syrians into   *1Ki 20:13;*
thine h.   *20:28*
because thou hast let go out   *1Ki 20:42*
of *thy h.* a man
and take my staff in *thine h.*   *2Ki 4:29*
the king said, Take a present in   *2Ki 8:8*
thine h.
Elisha said, Take this box of oil   *2Ki 9:1*
in *thine h.*
give me *thine h.* and he gave   *2Ki 10:15*
him his hand
and he said, Put *thine h.*   *2Ki 13:16*
upon the bow
and that *thine h.* might be   *1Ch 4:10*
with me
in *thine h.* power; and to   *1Ch 29:12*
make great
all this store for house   *1Ch 29:16*
cometh of *thine h.*
In *thine h.* is there not power   *2Ch 20:6*
and might
the law of thy God which is in   *Ezr 7:14*
thine h.
after wisdom of God, that is   *Ezr 7:25*
in *thine h.*
but put forth *thine h.* and   *Job 1:11;*
touch   *2:5*
only upon himself put not   *Job 1:12*
forth *thine h.*
behold, he is in *thine h.* but   *Job 2:6*
save his life
there is none that can deliver   *Job 10:7*
out of *thine h.*
if iniquity be in *thine h.* put   *Job 11:14*
it far away
withdraw *thine h.* far from   *Job 13:21*
me. let not thy dread
or what receiveth he of *thine*   *Job 35:7*
h.
arise, O Lord, O God, lift up   *Ps 10:12*
thine h.
beholdest spite to requite it   *Ps 10:14*
with *thy h.*
from men which are *thy h.* O   *Ps 17:14*
Lord
thine h. shall find out all thine   *Ps 21:8*
enemies
into *thine h.* I commit my spirit   *Ps 31:5*
my times are in *thy h.* deliver   *Ps 31:15*
me from enemies
for day and night *thy h.* was   *Ps 32:4*
heavy upon me
thy h. presseth me; by blow of   *Ps 38:2;*
thine h.   *39:10*
why withdrawest thou *thy h.?*   *Ps 74:11*
pluck it out
let *thy h.* be upon the man of   *Ps 80:17*
thy right h.
and they are cut off from *thy h.*   *Ps 88:5*
thou openest *thy h.* filled   *Ps 104:28;*
with good   *145:16*
that they may know that this   *Ps 109:27*
is *thy h.*
let *thy h.* help me; laid *thine*   *Ps 119:173;*
h. on me   *139:5*
even there shall *thy h.* lead me   *Ps 139:10*
send *thine h.* from above, rid   *Ps 144:7*
me, deliver me

when it is in power of *thine h.*   *Pr 3:27*
to do it
if thou hast stricken *thy h.* with   *Pr 6:1*
a stranger
if thought evil, lay *thy h.* upon   *Pr 30:32*
thy mouth
yea also from this withdraw   *Ec 7:18*
not *thine h.*
whatsoever *thy h.* findeth to do,   *Ec 9:10*
do it
in the evening withhold not   *Ec 11:6*
thine h.
and let this ruin be under *thy h.*   *Isa 3:6*
when *thy h.* is lifted up, they   *Isa 26:11*
will not see
I the Lord will hold *thine h.*   *Isa 42:6*
and keep thee
I have given my inheritance   *Isa 47:6*
into *thine h.*
I have taken out of *thy h.* cup   *Isa 51:22*
of trembling
thou hast found the life of   *Isa 57:10*
thine h.
art our Father, we are the   *Isa 61:8*
work of *thy h.*
turn back *thine h.* as a grape   *Jer 6:9*
gatherer
I sat alone because of *thy h.*   *Jer 15:17*
thou hast filled
if they refuse to take the cup   *Jer 25:28*
at *thine h.*
take in *thy h.* the roll,   *Jer 36:14*
wherein thou hast read
free from chains which were   *Jer 40:4*
his blood will I require at   *Eze 3:18;*
thine h.   *3:20; 33:8*
smite with *thine h.* and stamp   *Eze 6:11*
with thy foot
and fill *thine h.* with coals of   *Eze 10:2*
fire
therefore I will give her cup   *Eze 23:31*
into *thine h.*
when they took hold of thee by   *Eze 29:7*
thy h.
go in and they shall become   *Eze 37:17*
one in *thine h.*
to turn *thine h.* upon the   *Eze 38:12*
desolate places
the fowls hath he given into   *Da 2:38*
thine h.
our God will deliver us out of   *Da 3:17*
thine h.
thine h. shall be lifted up on   *Mic 5:9*
thine adversaries
I will cut off witchcrafts out   *Mic 12:1*
of *thine h.*
if *thy h.* or foot offend thee   *Mt 18:8;*
   M'k 9:43
reach *thy h.* and thrust it into   *Joh 20:27*
my side
to do whatever *thy h.* and   *Ac 4:28*
counsel determined
by stretching forth *thine h.* to   *Ac 4:30*
heal

YOUR HAND

into *your h.* are they delivered   *Ge 9:2*
and take double money in   *Ge 43:12*
your h.
with shoes on your feet, staff   *Ex 12:11*
in *your h.*
the inhabitants of the land   *Ex 23:31*
into *your h.*
ye shall rejoice in all ye put   *De 12:7*
your h. to
God will deliver it into *your h.*   *Jos 8:7*
the Lord hath delivered them   *Jos 10:19*
into *your h.*
I gave the Amorites into *your*   *Jos 24:8;*
h.   *24:11*
Moabites; Midianites into   *J'g 3:28;*
your h.   *7:15*
shall I not require his blood of   *2Sa 4:11*
your h.
they shall be delivered into   *2Ch 18:14*
your h.
God hath delivered them into   *2Ch 28:9*
your h.
who hath required this at *your*   *Isa 1:12*
h.
I am in *your h.* do with me as   *Jer 26:14*
seemeth good
Zedekiah said, Behold, he is in   *Jer 38:5*
your h.
ye have spoken and fulfilled   *Jer 44:25*
with *your h.*

and they shall be no more in   *Eze 13:21*
your h.
I will deliver my people out   *Eze 13:23*
of *your* h.
nor will I accept an offering   *Mal 1:10*
at *your* h.
should I accept this of *your*   *Mal 1:13*
h.
or receiveth it with good-will   *Mal 2:13*
at *your* h.

HANDBAG

the h. purses (A)(P)   *Isa 3:22*

HANDBAGS

and the h. (S)   *Isa 3:22*
provide purses and h. (A)   *Lu 12:33*

HAND-BREADTH

a border of an h. round about   *Ex 25:25;*
                            37:12
three-inch frame around (B)   *Ex 25:25*
made a four-inch border (B)   *Ex 37:12*
a molten sea a h. thick   *1Ki 7:26;*
                           2Ch 4:5
it was four inches thick (B)   *1Ki 7:26*
thou hast made my days as an   *Ps 39:5*
h.
a reed of six cubits long, and   *Eze 40:5*
an h.
the cubit is a cubit and an h.   *Eze 43:13*

HAND *BROAD*

within were hooks an   *Eze 40:43*
h. *broad* fastened
Hooks three inches long (B)   *Eze 40:43*

HANDED

weary and weak h. and will   *2Sa 17:2*
h. him to jailers (P)(R)   *M't 18:34*

HANDFUL

priest take an h. of flour   *Le 2:2;*
   5:12; 6:15; 9:17; Nu 5:26
an h. of meal in a barrel, oil   *1Ki 17:12*
in a cruse
there shall be an h. of corn in   *Ps 72:16*
the earth
better is h. with quietness, than   *Ec 4:6*
both hands
and as the h. after the   *Jer 9:22*
harvestman

HANDFULS

and the earth brought forth   *Ge 41:47*
by h.
take to you h. of ashes of the   *Ex 9:8*
furnace
let fall also some h. of purpose   *Ru 2:16*
for her
if dust of Samaria shall   *1Ki 20:10*
suffice for h.
will ye pollute me for h. of   *Eze 13:19*
barley

HANDICAPPED

h. never frustrated (P)   *2Co 4:8*

HANDKERCHIEF

face muffled in a h. (P)   *Joh 11:44*
also the h. (B)(P)   *Joh 20:7*

HANDKERCHIEFS

from his body were brought   *Ac 19:12*
to the sick h.

HANDLE

Jubal was father of such as h.   *Ge 4:21*
the harp
h. your nobles (B)   *De 1:12*
they that h. the pen of the   *J'g 5:14*
writer
men that could h. spear   *1Ch 12:8;*
                        2Ch 25:5
they have hands, but they h.   *Ps 115:7*
not
and they that h. the law knew   *Jer 2:8*
me not
and the Libyans that h. the   *Jer 46:9*
shield
mariners to handle wares (B)   *Eze 27:9*
all that h. the oar, and all the   *Eze 27:29*
pilots

h. me and see   *Lu 24:39*
taste not, h. not   *Col 2:21*
touch not; taste not; h. not   *Col 2:21*

HANDLED

to be furbished, that it may   *Eze 21:11*
be h.
and they sent him away   *M'k 12:4*
shamefully h.
our hands have h. of the word   *1Jo 1:1*
of life

HANDLES

upon the h. of the lock   *Ca 5:5*

HANDLETH

he that h. matter wisely shall   *Pr 16:20*
find good
cut off him that h. sickle in   *Jer 50:16*
time of harvest
nor shall he stand that h. the   *Am 2:15*
bow

HANDLING

great company, all of them h.   *Eze 38:4*
swords
not h. the word of God   *2Co 4:2*
deceitfully
h. of liberal collection   *2Co 8:20*
(B)(N)
h. a right word of truth   *2Ti 2:15*
(E)(R)

HANDMAID

Sarai had an h. whose name   *Ge 16:1*
was Hagar
Laban gave Zilpah to be   *Ge 29:24;*
Leah's h.   *35:26*
Laban gave Bilhah to be   *Ge 29:29;*
Rachel's h.   *30:4; 35:25*
that son of thy h. may be   *Ex 23:12*
refreshed
there is bread and wine for   *J'g 19:19*
me and thy h.
for that thou hast spoken   *Ru 2:13*
friendly to thy h.
and she answered, I am Ruth   *Ru 3:9*
thine h.
if wilt look on the affliction of   *1Sa 1:11*
thine h.
count not thine h. for a   *1Sa 1:16*
daughter of Belial
Hannah said, Let thy h. find   *1Sa 1:18*
grace in thy sight
let thy h. speak; remember   *1Sa 25:24;*
thy h.   *25:31*
let thy h. be a servant to   *1Sa 25:41*
wash feet of servants
thy h. had two sons, they two   *2Sa 14:6*
strove
she said to him, Hear the   *2Sa 20:17*
words of thy h.
didst not thou, my lord, swear   *1Ki 1:13*
to thy h.
thou swearest by the Lord thy   *1Ki 1:17*
God to thy h.
she took my son while thine h.   *1Ki 3:20*
slept
thy h. hath not any thing, save   *2Ki 4:2*
pot of oil
nay, thou man of God, do not   *2Ki 4:16*
lie to thine h.
turn to me, and save the son   *Ps 86:16*
of thy h.
I am thy servant, and the son   *Ps 116:16*
of thy h.
and an h. that is heir to her   *Pr 30:23*
mistress
ye caused every man his h. to   *Jer 34:16*
return
behold the h. of the Lord, be it   *Lu 1:38*
to me

HANDMAIDEN

he hath regarded the low estate   *Lu 1:48*
of his h.

HANDMAIDENS

Then the h. came near   *Ge 33:6*
like unto one of thine h.   *Ru 2:13*
on my servants and on my h.   *Ac 2:18*

HANDMAIDS

Jacob divided the children to   *Ge 33:1*
the two h.
he put the h. and their children   *Ge 33:2*
foremost
though I be not like to one of   *Ru 2:13*
thy h.
who uncovered himself in eyes   *2Sa 6:20*
of the h.
they caused the h. to return   *Jer 34:11*
for h.
on the h. will I pour my spirit   *Joe 2:29;*
                     Ac 2:18

HANDS

return and submit thyself   *Ge 16:9*
under her h.
the voice is Jacob's, the h. are   *Ge 27:22*
the h. of Esau
h. were made strong by h. of   *Ge 49:24*
mighty God
but Moses' h. were heavy,   *Ex 17:12*
took a stone
and thou shalt put all in the h.   *Ex 29:24*
of Aaron
put all on Aaron's h. and on   *Le 8:27*
his son's h.
put the offering of memorial in   *Nu 5:18*
her h.
and shall put them on the h. of   *Nu 6:19*
the Nazarite
serve gods, the work of men's   *De 4:28;*
h.   *27:15; 2Ki 19:18; 2Ch 32:19*
the tables of the covenant were   *Nu 9:15*
in my two h.
cast them out of my two h. and   *De 9:17*
brake them
the h. of witnesses shall be first   *De 17:7*
on him
to provoke him through the   *De 31:29*
work of your h.
he delivered them into h. of the   *J'g 2:14*
spoilers
into h. of Midianites; into h.   *J'g 6:13;*
of Philistines   *10:7*
are h. of Zeba and Zalmunna in   *J'g 8:6;*
thy hand   *8:15*
delivered them out of h. of   *J'g 8:34;*
enemies   *1Sa 14:48*
for God hath given Laish into   *J'g 18:10*
your h.
and her h. were upon the   *J'g 19:27*
threshold
nor deliver me into h. of my   *1Sa 30:15*
master
let your h. be strong   *2Sa 2:7;*
               Zec 8:9, 13
then the h. of all with thee   *2Sa 16:21*
shall be strong
delivered them into the h. of   *2Sa 24:9*
the Gibeonites
because they cannot be taken   *2Sa 23:6*
with h.
into the h. of the guard   *1Ki 14:27;*
                 2Ch 12:10
who poured water on the h. of   *2Ki 3:11*
Elijah
they found the skull and the   *2Ki 9:35*
palms of her h.
the men whom I brought into   *2Ki 10:24*
your h.
sons of Asaph under the h. of   *1Ch 25:2*
Asaph
under the h. of Jeduthun; h.   *1Ch 25:3;*
of their father   *25:6*
be strong, let not your h. be   *2Ch 15:7*
weak
weakened the h. of the people   *Ezr 4:4*
of Judah
thou hast strengthened the   *Job 4:3*
weak h.
God hath turned me into the   *Job 16:11*
h. of the wicked
who is he that will strike h.   *Job 17:3*
with me
that hath clean h. shall be   *Job 17:9*
stronger and stronger
who shall ascend? he that hath   *Ps 24:4*
clean h.
in whose h. is mischief; clap   *Ps 26:10;*
your h.   *47:1*
ye weigh the violence of your h.   *Ps 58:2*
in the earth
Ethiopia shall stretch out her   *Ps 68:31*
h. unto God
idols, the work of men's h.   *Ps 115:4;*
             135:15; Isa 37:19

they have *h.* but handle not, *Ps 115:7*
feet, but walk not
lift up your *h.* in the *Ps 134:2*
sanctuary, and bless Lord
keep me, O Lord, from the *h.* *Ps 140:4*
of the wicked
a little folding of the *h.* to *Pr 6:10;*
sleep *24:33*
Lord doth hate the *h.* that shed *Pr 6:17*
innocent blood
the recompence of man's *h.* *Pr 12:14*
be rendered him
the foolish plucketh it down her *Pr 14:1*
h.
a man striketh *h.* and becometh *Pr 17:18*
surety
be not thou one of them that *Pr 22:26*
strike *h.*
spider taketh hold with her *h.* *Pr 30:28*
is in palaces
and she worketh willingly with *Pr 31:13*
her *h.*
she layeth her *h.* to the spindle, *Pr 31:19*
her *h.* hold
yea, she reacheth forth her *h.* *Pr 31:20*
to the needy
give her of the fruit of her *h.* *Pr 31:31*
and let her works
than both *h.* full with travail *Ec 4:6*
and vexation
her *h.* are as bands; the *Ec 7:26;*
idleness of *h.* *10:18*
the work of the *h.* of a *Ca 7:1*
cunning workman
when ye spread forth your *h.* I *Isa 1:15*
will hide my eyes from you;
your *h.* are full of blood
they worship the work of their *Isa 2:8*
own *h.*
therefore shall all *h.* be faint, *Isa 13:7*
and heart melt
idols which your own *h.* *Isa 31:7*
have made to you
strengthen ye the weak *h.* and *Isa 35:3*
confirm knees
or shall thy work say, He hath *Isa 45:9*
no *h.*
h. are defiled with blood, *Isa 59:3*
fingers with iniquity
that spreadeth her *h.* saying, *Jer 4:31*
Woe is me
a tree, the work of the *h.* of *Jer 10:3*
the workman
and of the *h.* of the founder, *Jer 10:9*
blue and purple
cause them to fall by *h.* that *Jer 19:7*
seek their lives
will turn back weapons that *Jer 21:4*
are in your *h.*
they strengthen also the *h.* of *Jer 23:14;*
evil doers, that none *Eze 13:22*
provoke me not with the *Jer 25:6;*
works of your *h.* *25:7*
shall pass under *h.* of him *Jer 33:13*
that telleth them
he weakeneth *h.* of men of *Jer 38:4*
war, *h.* of people
upon all the *h.* shall be *Jer 48:37*
cuttings
Zion spreadeth her *h.* none to *La 1:17*
comfort
how esteemed as the work of *h.* *La 4:2*
of the potter
that was overthrown, and no *h.* *La 4:6*
stayed on her
h. of pitiful women have sodden *La 4:10*
their children
all *h.* shall be feeble *Eze 7:17; 21:7*
till a stone was cut out *Da 2:34;*
without *h.* *2:45*
that they may do evil with both *Mic 7:3*
h. earnestly
all shall clap the *h.* over thee *Na 3:19*
in all labour of your *h.* I *Hag 2:17*
smote you
the *h.* of Zerubbabel laid the *Zec 4:9*
foundation
to eat with unwashen *h.* *M't 15:20;*
M'k 7:2, 5
the Son of man shall be *M't 17:22;*
betrayed into the *h.* of men *26:45;*
M'k 9:31; Lu 9:44
having two *h.* to be cast into *M't 18:8;*
fire *M'k 9:43*
temple made with *h.* another *M'k 14:58*
without *h.*
ye stretched forth no *h.* *Lu 22:53*
against me

must be delivered into the *h.* of *Lu 24:7*
sinful men
by wicked *h.* have crucified and *Ac 2:23*
slain
by *h.* of the apostles were *Ac 5:12*
wonders wrought
dwelleth not in temples made *Ac 5:48;*
with *h.* *17:24*
that through laying on the *Ac 8:18*
apostles' *h.*
sent to elders by the *h.* of *Ac 11:30*
Barnabas and Saul
neither is worshipped with *Ac 17:25*
men's *h.*
that they be no gods which *Ac 19:26*
are made with *h.*
that these *h.* have ministered *Ac 20:34*
to my necessities
shall deliver him into the *h.* of *Ac 21:11*
the Gentiles
we have an house not made *2Co 5:1*
with *h.*
the circumcision in flesh *Eph 2:11*
made by *h.*
with the circumcision made *Col 2:11*
without *h.*
that ye study to work with *1Th 4:11*
your own *h.*
men pray every where lifting *1Ti 2:8*
up holy *h.*
by laying on of *h.* of the *1Ti 4:14;*
presbytery *Heb 6:2*
by a greater tabernacle not *Heb 9:11*
with *h.*
Christ not entered into holy *Heb 9:24*
place made with *h.*
fearful to fall into the *h.* of *Heb 10:31*
the living God
wherefore lift up the *h.* *Heb 12:12*
which hang down
cleanse your *h.* ye sinners, *Jas 4:8*
purify your

HIS HANDS

his h. were hairy; guiding *his* *Ge 27:23;*
h. *48:11*
and Aaron and Hur stayed up *Ex 17:12*
his h.
and Moses cast the tables out *Ex 32:19*
of *his h.*
his own h. shall bring the *Le 7:30*
offering
and hath not rinsed *his h.* in *Le 15:11*
water
his h. full of sweet incense *Le 16:12*
beaten small
Aaron shall lay both *his h.* on *Le 16:21*
head of live goat
and Balak smote *his h.* *Nu 24:10*
together
let *his h.* be sufficient for him *De 33:7*
bless, Lord, and accept the *De 33:11*
work of *his h.*
for Moses had laid *his h.* upon *De 34:9*
Joshua
done according to the *J'g 9:16*
deserving of *his h.*
both the palms of *his h.* were *1Sa 5:4*
cut off
Jonathan climbed up on *his* *1Sa 14:13*
h. and his feet
Jonathan went and *1Sa 23:16*
strengthened *his h.* in God
when Saul's son heard, *his h.* *2Sa 4:1*
were feeble
Solomon spread forth *his h.* *1Ki 8:22;*
toward heaven *38:54; 2Ch 6:12, 13, 29*
in provoking him with the *1Ki 16:7*
work of *his h.*
he went up and put *his h.* *2Ki 4:34*
upon *his h.*
hath spared Naaman in not *2Ki 5:20*
receiving at *his h.*
Elisha put *his h.* upon the *2Ki 13:16*
king's hands
who hath with *his h.* fulfilled *2Ch 6:4*
with one of *his h.* wrought in *Ne 4:17*
the work
thou hast blessed the work of *Job 1:10*
his h.
he woundeth, and *his h.* make *Job 5:18*
whole
and *his h.* shall restore their *Job 20:10*
goods
for they all are the works of *Job 34:19*
his h.
for he clappeth *his h.* *Job 34:37*
amongst us

the wicked is snared in the *Ps 9:16*
work of *his h.*
they regard not the operation *Ps 28:5*
of *his h.*
he guided them by the *Ps 78:72*
skilfulness of *his h.*
his h. were delivered from the *Ps 81:6*
pots
the sea is his, and *his h.* formed *Ps 95:5*
dry land
the works of *his h.* are verity *Ps 111:7*
and judgment
for *his h.* refuse to labour *Pr 21:25*
the fool foldeth *his h.* together *Ec 4:5*
his h. are as gold rings set with *Ca 5:14*
beryl
the reward of *his h.* shall be *Isa 3:11*
given him
nor consider the operation of *Isa 5:12*
his h.
he shall not look to altars, the *Isa 17:8*
work of *his h.*
Lord spread forth *his h.* as *Isa 25:11*
he that swimmeth spreadeth
his h.
that shaketh *his h.* from *Isa 33:15*
holding bribes
why see every man with *his h.* *Jer 30:6*
on his loins
king heard the report, *his h.* *Jer 50:43*
waxed feeble
the deep lifted up *his h.* on *Hab 3:10*
high
his h. shall also finish the house *Zec 4:9*
should put *his h.* on them *M't 19:13;*
M'k 10:16
he washed *his h.* before the *M't 27:24*
multitude
such mighty works are *M'k 6:2*
wrought by *his h.*
when he had put *his h.* on his *M'k 8:23;*
eyes *8:13*
shewed them *his h.* and feet *Lu 24:40;*
Joh 20:20
and he lifted up *his h.* and *Lu 24:50*
blessed them
the Father had given all things *Joh 13:3*
into *his h.*
except I see in *his h.* the *Joh 20:25*
print of the nails
putting *his h.* on him, said, *Ac 9:17*
Brother Saul
Herod stretched forth *his h.* to *Ac 12:1*
vex the church
and his chains fell off from *his* *Ac 12:7*
h.
was let down by a wall, and *2Co 11:33*
escaped *his h.*
working with *his h.* thing that *Eph 4:28*
is good

MINE, MY HANDS

in innocency of *my h.* have I *Ge 20:5*
done this
God hath seen the labour of *Ge 31:42*
my h.
I will spread abroad *my h.* *Ex 9:29;*
Ezr 9:5
I put my life in *my h.* and *J'g 12:3*
passed over
according to cleanness of *my* *2Sa 22:21;*
h. *18:20, 24*
he teacheth *my h.* to war *2Sa 22:35;*
Ps 18:34; 144:1
seeing there is no wrong in *1Ch 12:17*
mine h.
now, therefore, O God, *Ne 6:9*
strengthen *my h.*
and if I make *my h.* never so *Job 9:30*
clean
not for any injustice in *mine* *Job 16:17*
h.
and if any blot hath cleaved to *Job 31:7*
mine h.
O Lord, if there be iniquity in *Ps 7:3*
my h.
they pierced *my h.* and my feet *Ps 22:16*
I will wash *mine h.* in *Ps 26:6*
innocency, so will I compass
when I lift up *my h.* toward thy *Ps 28:2*
holy oracle
I will lift up *my h.* in thy *Ps 63:4*
name
in vain I have washed *my h.* in *Ps 73:13*
innocency
I have stretched out *my h.* unto *Ps 88:9*
thee
my h. will I lift to thy *Ps 119:48*
commandments

MINE, MY HANDS (continued)

lifting up of *my h.* as the Ps 141:2
evening sacrifice
I stretch forth *my h.* to thee, Ps 143:6
my soul
on all the works that *my h.* had Ec 2:11
wrought
I rose, and *my h.* dropped with Ca 5:5
myrrh
blessed be Assyria, the work Isa 19:25
of *my h.*
when he seeth the work of Isa 29:33
mine h. in thee
ask me concerning the work Isa 45:11
of *my h.*
even *my h.* have stretched out Isa 45:12
the heavens
I have graven thee on the Isa 49:16
palms of *my h.*
thy people also the work of Isa 60:21
my h.
I have spread out *my h.* all day Isa 65:2
to rebellious
I will also smite *mine h.* Eze 21:17
together
who is God to deliver you out Da 3:15
of *my h.*
an hand which set me on the Da 10:10
palms of *my h.*
behold *my h.* and my feet Lu 24:39;
Joh 20:27
not feet only, but also *my h.* Joh 13:9
and head
all day I have stretched forth Ro 10:21
my h.
the gift in thee by putting on of 2Ti 1:6
my h.

OUR HANDS

shall comfort us concerning Ge 5:29
toil of *our h.*
other money have we brought Ge 43:22
in *our h.*
God delivered into *our h.* Og De 3:3
king of Bashan
shall say, *Our h.* have not shed De 21:7
this blood
Lord hath delivered into *our h.* Jos 2:24
all the land
not received a meat offering J'g 13:23
at *our h.*
our God hath delivered into J'g 16:24
our h. our enemy
and he will give you into *our* 1Sa 17:47
h.
or stretched out *our h.* to a Ps 44:20
strange god
establish thou the work of *our* Ps 90:17
h. upon us
we have heard the fame, *our h.* Jer 6:24
wax feeble
let us lift up our heart with *our* La 3:41
h. to God
nor say to work of *our h.,* Ye Ho 14:3
are our gods
Lysias took him away out of Ac 24:7
our h.
and labour working with *our* 1Co 4:12
own *h.*
our h. have handled the word 1Jo 1:1
of life

RIGHT HANDS

gave *right h.* of fellowship Ga 2:9

THEIR HANDS

he delivered him out of *their* Ge 37:21;
h. 37:22
shall put *their h.* on head of Ex 29:10
the bullock
shall put *their h.* on the head Ex 29:15;
of the ram 29:19
thou shalt receive them of Ex 29:25;
their h. Le 8:28
Israel shall put *their h.* on the Nu 8:10
Levites
the Levites shall lay *their h.* on Nu 8:12
the bullock
they brought of fruit of land in De 1:25
their h.
the elders shall wash *their h.* De 21:6
over the heifer
too many to give Midianites J'g 7:2
into *their h.*
ye delivered me not out of J'g 12:2
their h.
and they cut off *their h.* and 2Sa 4:12
their feet

they clapped *their h.* said, 2Ki 11:12
God save king
that they might provoke me 2Ki 22:17;
to anger with all the works 2Ch 34:25
of *their h.*
strengthened *their h.* with Ezr 1:6
vessels of silver
work goeth fast on and Ezr 5:8
prospereth in *their h.*
to strengthen *their h.* in the Ezr 6:22
work of the house
they gave *their h.* that they Ezr 10:19
would put away
so they strengthened *their h.* Ne 2:18
for the work
their h. shall be weakened from Ne 6:9
the work
gavest them into *their h.* with Ne 9:24
their kings
their h. cannot perform their Job 5:12
enterprise
whereto might strength of Job 30:2
their h. profit me
give them after the work of Ps 28:4
their h.
the men of might have not Ps 76:5
found *their h.*
the angels shall bear thee up Ps 91:12
in *their h.*
lest righteous put forth *their* Ps 125:3
h. to iniquity
pride, together with the spoils Isa 25:11
of *their h.*
and the act of violence is in Isa 59:6
their h.
mine elect shall enjoy the Isa 65:22
work of *their h.*
worshipped the works of their Jer 1:16
own *h.*
according to the works of Jer 25:14;
their h. La 3:64
provoked to anger with works Jer 32:30
of *their h.*
the Lord hath delivered me La 1:14
into *their h.*
their h. and wings full of eyes Eze 10:12
round
committed adultery, blood is Eze 23:37;
in *their h.* 23:45
turn from the violence that is Jon 3:8
in *their h.*
so is every work of *their h.* Hag 2:14
unclean
with *their h.* they shall bear M't 4:6;
thee up Lu 4:11
they wash not *their h.* when M't 15:2
they eat bread
smote with palms of *their h.* M't 26:67;
M'k 14:65
Jews, except they wash *their h.* M'k 7:3
eat not
and did eat, rubbing them in Lu 6:1
their h.
and they smote him with *their* Joh 19:3
h.
they rejoiced in the works of Ac 7:41
their h.
granted signs and wonders to Ac 14:3
be done by *their h.*
with white robes, and palms in Re 7:9
their h.
yet repented not of the works Re 9:20
of *their h.*
nor had received his mark in Re 20:4
their h.

THINE, THY HANDS

in sanctuary which *thy h.* Ex 15:17
have established
the Lord shall bless thee in De 16:15;
all works of *thine h.* therefore 24:19
shalt surely rejoice
afterward shall *thine h.* be J'g 7:11
strengthened
thy h. were not bound, nor feet 2Sa 3:34
in fetters
is it good to despise the work Job 10:3
of *thine h.*
thine h. have made and Job 10:8
fashioned me together
thou wilt have desire to the Job 14:15
work of *thine h.*
and it is delivered by Job 22:30
pureness of *thine h.*
to have dominion over the works Ps 8:6
of *thy h.*
I will triumph in the works of Ps 92:4
thy h.

and the heavens are the work Ps 102:25
of *thy h.*
thy h. have made me and Ps 119:73
fashioned me
for thou shalt eat the labour Ps 128:2
of *thine h.*
forsake not the works of *thine* Ps 138:8
own *h.*
I meditate, I muse on the Ps 143:5
work of *thy h.*
why should God destroy the Ec 5:6
work of *thine h.*
thou shalt go forth, and *thine* Jer 2:37
h. on thy head
lift up *thy h.* for the life of thy La 2:19
children
prophesy and smite *thine h.* Eze 21:14
together
can *thine h.* be strong in the Eze 22:14
day that I deal
shalt no more worship the Mic 5:13
work of *thine h.*
and to Zion, Let not *thine h.* Zep 3:16
be slack
what are these wounds in Zec 13:6
thine h.
Father, into *thy h.* I commend Lu 23:46
my spirit
thou shalt stretch forth *thy h.* Joh 21:18
the heavens are the works of Heb 1:10
thine h.
thou didst set him over the Heb 2:7
works of *thy h.*

HANDSOME

a *h.* person (S) Ge 39:6
a *h.* young man (S) 1Sa 9:2
h. to look at (S) 1Sa 16:12
a *h.* appearance (B)(R) 1Sa 16:12
he was a *h.* man (S) 1Ki 1:6
made *h.* images (S) Ho 10:1

HANDSPIKES

the *h.* and spears (S) Eze 39:9

HANDSTAVES

and shall burn the *h.* and Eze 39:9
spears

HANDWEAPON

or if he smite him with a Nu 35:18
h.

HANDWRITING

blotting out the *h.* of Col 2:14
ordinances

HANDYWORK

firmament showeth his *h.* Ps 19:1

HANES

his ambassadors came to H. Isa 30:4

HANG

Pharaoh shall *h.* thee on a Ge 40:19
tree
h. them before the Lord Nu 25:4
against the sun
and if thou *h.* him on a tree, De 21:22
his body
and thy life shall *h.* in doubt De 28:66
before thee
and we will *h.* them up unto 2Sa 21:6
the Lord
to speak to the king to *h.* Es 6:4
Mordecai
then the king said, H. him Es 7:9
thereon
whereon there *h.* a thousand Ca 4:4
bucklers
they shall *h.* upon him all the Isa 22:24
glory
the virgins of Jerusalem *h.* La 2:10
their heads
will men take pin to *h.* vessel Eze 15:3
on these two *h.* all the law M't 22:40
and prophets
saw the venomous beast *h.* on Ac 28:4
his hand
lift up hands *h.* down and Heb 12:12
feeble knees

HANGED

but he *h.* the chief baker   Ge 40:22;
   41:13
for he that is *h.* is accursed of   De 21:23
God
and the king of Ai be *h.* on a   Jos 8:29
tree
the five kings *h.* he on five   Jos 10:26
trees
Rechab and Baanah *h.* over   2Sa 4:12
the pool
Ahithophel *h.* himself;   2Sa 17:23;
Absalom *h.*   18:10
the seven sons of Saul *h.* they   2Sa 21:9
in the hill
and being set up, let him be *h.*   Ezr 6:11
thereon
the two chamberlains were *h.*   Es 2:23
on a tree
they *h.* Haman; they *h.* his ten   Es 7:10;
sons   9:14
we *h.* our harps on the willows   Ps 137:2
princes are *h.* up by their hands   La 5:12
they *h.* the shield and helmet   Eze 27:10
in thee
they *h.* their shields upon thy   Eze 27:11
walls round about
it were better for him that a   M't 18:6;
millstone were *h.*   M'k 9:42; Lu 17:2
about his neck
Judas departed, and went and   M't 27:5
h. himself
one of the thieves who were *h.*   Lu 23:39
railed on him
whom ye slew and *h.* on a tree   Ac 5:30;
   10:39

HANGETH

and he *h.* the earth upon   Job 26:7
nothing
cursed is every one that *h.* on a   Ga 3:13
tree

HANGING

thou shalt make an *h.* for door   Ex 26:36
of tent
thou shalt make for the *h.* five   Ex 26:37
pillars
h. for court gate   Ex 27:16;
   38:18; 39:40; 40:8, 33
the *h.* for the door at the   Ex 35:15;
entering in of tabernacle   36:37;
   39:38; 40:5, 28
they were *h.* upon trees until   Jos 10:26
they were *h.* on trees till the   Jos 10:26
evening

HANGINGS

h. of an hundred cubits   Ex 27:9;
   27:11; 38:9, 11
there shall be *h.* of fifty   Ex 27:12;
cubits   38:12
the *h.* on either side of gate   Ex 27:14;
   27:15; 38:14, 15
the *h.* of court, his pillars   Ex 35:17;
and their sockets   38:9, 16, 18; 39:40;
   Nu 3:36; 4:26
where women wove *h.* for the   2Ki 23:7
grove
blue *h.* fastened with cords of   Es 1:6
linen and purple

HANIEL

sons of Ulla; Arah, and *H.*   1Ch 7:39

HANNAH

the name of the one was *H.*   1Sa 1:2;
   1:5, 8, 9, 13, 15, 19
about after *H.* had conceived   1Sa 1:20
But *H.* went not up; for she   1Sa 1:22
said
H. prayed, and said, My heart   1Sa 2:1
the Lord visited *H.*, so that   1Sa 2:21

HANNATHON

it on the north side to *H.*   Jos 19:14

HANNIEL

Manasseh, *H.* the son of   Nu 34:23
Ephod

HANOCH

Ephah, and Epher, and *H.* and   Ge 25:4
of Reuben: *H.* and Phallu, and   Ge 46:9
H. and Pallu, Hezron, and   Ex 6:14
Carmi
H. of whom cometh the family   Nu 26:5
H. and Pallu, Hezron, and   1Ch 5:3
Carmi

HANOCHITES

cometh the family of the *H.*   Nu 26:5

HANUN

H. his son reigned in his stead   2Sa 10:1
I will shew kindness unto *H.*   2Sa 10:2
of Ammon said unto *H.* their   2Sa 10:3
lord
Wherefore took David's   2Sa 10:4
said, I will shew kindness   1Ch 19:2
unto *H.*
of the children of Ammon to   1Ch 19:2
H.
said to *H.* Thinkest thou that   1Ch 19:3
H. took David's servants, and   1Ch 19:4
H. and the children of   1Ch 19:6
Ammon
The valley gate repaired *H.*   Ne 3:13
and *H.* the sixth son of Zalaph   Ne 3:30

HAP

her *h.* was to light on a part of   Ru 2:3
she happened to get into field   Ru 2:3
(A)(B)(R)

HAPHRAIM

And *H.*, and Shion, and   Jos 19:19

HAPLY

if *h.* the people had eaten   1Sa 14:30
freely
if *h.* he might find any thing   M'k 11:13
Lest *h.* after he hath laid the   Lu 14:29
lest *h.* ye be found even to fight   Ac 5:39
if *h.* they might feel after him   Ac 17:27
Lest *h.* if they of Macedonia   2Co 9:4
come

HAPPEN

there shall no punishment *h.*   1Sa 28:10
There shall no evil *h.* to the   Pr 12:21
just
shew us what shall *h.*: let   Isa 41:22
them
what things should *h.* unto   M'k 10:32
him

HAPPENED

she *h.* to get into field   Ru 2:3
(A)(B)(R)(S)
it was a chance that *h.* to us   1Sa 6:9
As I *h.* by chance upon mount   2Sa 1:6
there *h.* to be there a man of   2Sa 20:1
all that had *h.* unto him, and of   Es 4:7
therefore this evil is *h.* unto   Jer 44:23
you
of all these things which had   Lu 24:14
h.
at that which had *h.* unto him   Ac 3:10
blindness in part is *h.* to   Ro 11:25
Israel
all these things *h.* unto them   1Co 10:11
that the things which *h.* unto   Ph'p 1:12
me
as though some strange thing   1Pe 4:12
h.
But it is *h.* unto them   2Pe 2:22
according to

HAPPENETH

that one event *h.* to them all   Ec 2:14
As it *h.* to the fool   Ec 2:15
so it *h.* even to me   Ec 2:15
men, unto whom it *h.*:   Ec 8:14
according
wicked men, to whom it *h.*   Ec 8:14
time and chance *h.* to them all   Ec 9:11

HAPPIER

But she is *h.* if she so abide   1Co 7:40

HAPPINESS

to my *h.* (B)   Ge 30:13
speaks of *h.* (B)(N)   Ro 4:6

HAPPY

Leah said, *H.* am I, for the   Ge 30:13
to my happiness (B)   Ge 30:13
H. art thou, O Israel: who is   De 33:29
like
Blessing is your (B)   De 33:29
felt *h.* at heart (B)   Ru 3:7
Nabal was in a *h.* mood (B)   1Sa 25:36
ate, drank, and were *h.* (R)   1Ki 4:20
H. are thy men, *h.* are these   1Ki 10:8
fortunate are your men,   1Ki 10:8
fortunate (B)
let your heart be *h.* (A)   1Ki 21:7
H. are thy men, and *h.* are   2Ch 9:7
these
h. is the man whom God   Job 5:17
correcteth
Blessed (B)   Job 5:17;
127:5; 137:8, 9; 144:15; 146:5; Pr 3:13;
28:14; Joh 13:17; Jas 5:11; 1Pe 3:14;
   4:14
H. is the man that hath his   Ps 127:5
quiver
h. shalt thou be, and it shall   Ps 128:2
be
h. shall he be, that rewardeth   Ps 137:8
thee
H. shall he be, that taketh   Ps 137:9
H. is that people, that is in   Ps 144:15
such a
h. is that people, whose God   Ps 144:15
H. is he that hath the God   Ps 146:5
H. is the man that findeth   Pr 3:13
wisdom
h. is every one that retaineth   Pr 3:18
hath mercy on the poor, *h.* is   Pr 14:21
he
a *h.* heart makes face look   Pr 15:13
sunny (B)
trusteth in the Lord, *h.* is he   Pr 16:20
cheerful, *h.* heart   Pr 17:22
(A)(B)(E)(R)
H. is the man that feareth   Pr 28:14
alway
he that keepeth the law, *h.* is   Pr 29:18
he
are all they *h.* that deal very   Jer 12:1
And now we call the proud *h.*   Mal 3:15
h. are ye if you do them   Joh 13:17
I think myself *h.* king Agrippa   Ac 26:2
consider myself fortunate   Ac 26:2
(A)(B)(N)(P)(R)
H. is he that condemneth not   Ro 14:22
we count them *h.* which   Jas 5:11
endure
we call those blessed (A)   Jas 5:11
for righteousness' sake, *h.* are   1Pe 3:14
ye
you will be blessed (R)   1Pe 3:14; 4:14
for the name of Christ, *h.* are   1Pe 4:14
ye

HARA

Habor, and *H.*, and to the   1Ch 5:26
river

HARADAH

Shapher, and encamped in *H.*   Nu 33:24
And they removed from *H.*   Nu 33:25

HARAN

begat Abram, Nahor, and *H.*   Ge 11:26;
   11:27, 32
when he departed out of *H.*   Ge 12:4
souls that they had gotten in   Ge 12:5
H.
thou to Laban my brother to   Ge 27:43
H.
Beer-sheba, and went toward   Ge 28:10
H.
And they said, Of *H.* are we   Ge 29:4
as Gozan, and *H.* and   2Ki 19:12
Rezeph
Caleb's concubine, bare *H.*   1Ch 2:46
and Gazez: and *H.* begat   1Ch 2:46
Gazez
Shelomith, and Haziel, and *H.*   1Ch 23:9

H., and Rezeph, and the children   *Isa 37:12*

H., and Canneh, and Eden   *Eze 27:23*

HARANGUED

Herod *h.* them (N)   *Ac 12:21*

HARARITE

Shammah the son of Agee the *H.*   *2Sa 23:11*

Shammah the *H.*, Ahiam the son of   *2Sa 23:33*

Ahiam the son of Sharar the *H.*   *2Sa 23:33*

Jonathan the son of Shage the *H.*   *1Ch 11:34*

Ahiam the son of Sacar the *H.*   *1Ch 11:35*

HARASS

h. the midianites (R)   *Nu 25:17*

they *h.* you (R)   *Nu 25:18*

HARASSED

archers *h.* (B)(R)(S)   *Ge 49:23*

ill or *h.* by unclean spirits (N)   *Ac 5:16*

Saul *h.* the church (P)   *Ac 8:3*

I suffer *h.* (E)(N)   *2Ti 2:9*

HARBONA

Biztha, *H.*, Bigtha, and Abagtha   *Es 1:10*

HARBONAH

H., one of the chamberlains   *Es 7:9*

HARD

Is any thing too *h.* for the Lord   *Ge 18:14*

they pressed *h.* against the man (S)   *Ge 19:9*

travailed, and she had *h.* labour   *Ge 35:16*

when she was in *h.* labour   *Ge 35:17*

make life *h.* for them (B)   *Ex 1:11*

their lives bitter with *h.* bondage   *Ex 1:14*

the *h.* causes they brought unto   *Ex 18:26*

he take off *h.* by the backbone   *Le 3:9*

the cause that is too *h.* for you   *De 1:17*

It shall not seem *h.* unto thee   *De 15:18*

If there arise a matter too *h.*   *De 17:8*

us, and laid upon us *h.* bondage   *De 26:6*

and went *h.* unto the door of   *J'g 9:52*

and pursued *h.* after them unto   *J'g 20:45*

even they also followed *h.* after   *1Sa 14:22*

there was *h.* fighting (S)   *1Sa 14:52*

the Philistines followed *h.* upon   *1Sa 31:2*

and horsemen followed *h.* after   *2Sa 1:6*

the sons of Zeruiah be too *h.*   *2Sa 3:39*

and Amnon thought it *h.* for him   *2Sa 13:2*

to prove him with *h.* questions   *1Ki 10:1*

h. by the palace of Ahab king   *1Ki 21:1*

Thou hast asked a *h.* thing   *2Ki 2:10*

the Philistines followed *h.* after   *1Ch 10:2*

in the midst *h.* by their buttocks   *1Ch 19:4*

prove Solomon with *h.* questions   *2Ch 9:1*

h. as a piece of the nether   *Job 41:24*

hast shewed thy people *h.* things   *Ps 60:3*

My soul followeth *h.* after thee   *Ps 63:8*

Thy wrath lieth *h.* upon me   *Ps 88:7*

they utter and speak *h.* things   *Ps 94:4*

hard (S)   *Ps 118:13; Isa 27:1; La 3:52*

the way of transgressors is *h.*   *Pr 13:15*

the *h.* bondage wherein thou   *Isa 14:3*

and there is nothing too *h.* for thee   *Jer 32:17*

is there any thing too *h.* for me   *Jer 32:27*

and of an *h.* language, but to   *Eze 3:5*

and of an *h.* language, whose words   *Eze 3:6*

and shewing of *h.* sentences   *Da 5:12*

men rowed *h.* to bring it to the land   *Jon 1:13*

h. is the way (S)   *M't 7:14*

that thou art in *h.* man, reaping   *M't 25:24*

h. of speech (B)   *M'k 7:32*

how *h.* is it for them that trust   *M'k 10:24*

a *h.* man (N)(P)   *Lu 19:21*

This is an *h.* saying; who can   *Joh 6:60*

h. for thee to kick against the   *Ac 9:5*

house joined *h.* to the synagogue   *Ac 18:7*

it is *h.* for thee to kick against   *Ac 26:14*

h. pressed on every side (N)   *2Co 4:8*

things to say, and *h.* to be uttered   *Heb 5:11*

some things *h.* to be understood   *2Pe 3:16*

and of all their *h.* speeches which   *Jude 15*

HARDEN

but I will *h.* his heart, that he   *Ex 4:21*

I will *h.* Pharaoh's heart, and   *Ex 7:3*

I will *h.* Pharaoh's heart, that he   *Ex 14:4*

will *h.* the hearts of the Egyptians   *Ex 14:17*

thou shalt not *h.* thine heart   *De 15:7*

was of the Lord to *h.* their hearts   *Jos 11:20*

Wherefore then do ye *h.* your   *1Sa 6:6*

yea, I would *h.* myself in sorrow   *Job 6:10*

H. not your heart, as in the   *Ps 95:8*

H. not your hearts, as in the   *Heb 3:8*

voice, *h.* not your hearts, as in the   *Heb 3:15*

his voice, *h.* not your hearts   *Heb 4:7*

HARDENED

And he *h.* Pharaoh's heart, that   *Ex 7:13*

Pharaoh's heart is *h.* he refuseth   *Ex 7:14*

Pharaoh's heart was *h.* neither   *Ex 7:22*

he *h.* his heart, and hearkened not   *Ex 8:15*

and Pharaoh's heart was *h.* and this   *Ex 8:19*

And Pharaoh *h.* his heart at this   *Ex 8:32*

And the heart of Pharaoh was *h.*   *Ex 9:7*

the Lord *h.* the heart of Pharaoh   *Ex 9:12*

sinned yet more, and *h.* his heart   *Ex 9:34*

And the heart of Pharaoh was *h.*   *Ex 9:35*

I have *h.* his heart, and the heart   *Ex 10:1*

the Lord *h.* Pharaoh's heart   *Ex 10:20; 10:27; 11:10*

the Lord *h.* the heart of Pharaoh   *Ex 14:8*

the Lord thy *God h.* his spirit   *De 2:30*

and Pharaoh *h.* their hearts   *1Sa 6:6*

would not hear, but *h.* their necks   *2Ki 17:14*

and *h.* his heart from turning   *2Ch 36:13*

h. their necks, and hearkened not   *Ne 9:16*

but *h.* their necks, and in their   *Ne 9:17*

h. their neck, and would not hear   *Ne 9:29*

who hath *h.* himself against him   *Job 9:4*

She is *h.* against her young   *Job 39:16*

from thy ways, and *h.* our heart   *Isa 63:17*

but *h.* their neck: they did worse   *Jer 7:26*

they have *h.* their necks, that   *Jer 19:15*

up, and his mind *h.* in pride   *Da 5:20*

loaves: for their heart was *h.*   *M'k 6:52*

have ye your heart yet *h.*   *M'k 8:17*

blinded their eyes, and *h.* their   *Joh 12:40*

But when divers were *h.* and   *Ac 19:9*

h. through the deceitfulness of sin   *Heb 3:13*

HARDENETH

A wicked man *h.* his face: but   *Pr 21:29*

but he that *h.* his heart shall fall   *Pr 28:14*

being often reproved *h.* his neck   *Pr 29:1*

mercy, and whom he will he *h.*   *Ro 9:18*

HARDER

Israel bore *h.* and *h.* (R)   *J'g 4:24*

h. for me than for you (B)   *Ru 1:13*

A brother offended is *h.* to be won   *Pr 18:19*

made their faces *h.* than a rock   *Jer 5:3*

As an adamant *h.* than flint   *Eze 3:9*

HARD-FACED

a *h.* king (B)   *Da 8:23*

HARDHEARTED

Israel are impudent and *h.*   *Eze 3:7*

HARDLY

And when Sarai dealt *h.* with her   *Ge 16:6*

Pharaoh would *h.* let us go   *Ex 13:15*

through it, *h.* bestead and hungry   *Isa 8:21*

a rich man shall *h.* enter into   *M't 19:23*

How *h.* shall they that have riches   *M'k 10:23*

bruising him *h.* departeth from   *Lu 9:39*

How *h.* shall they that have riches   *Lu 18:24*

And, *h.* passing it, came unto a   *Ac 27:8*

HARDNESS

the dust groweth into *h.* and   *Job 38:38*

h. of heart (A)   *La 3:65*

because of the *h.* of your hearts   *M't 19:8*

grieved for the *h.* of their hearts   *M'k 3:5*

For the *h.* of your heart he wrote   *M'k 10:5*

their unbelief and *h.* of heart   *M'k 16:14*

thy *h.* and impenitent heart   *Ro 2:5*

therefore endure *h.* as a good   *2Ti 2:3*

HARDSHIP

let not *h.* (R)   *Ne 9:32*

before *h.* of battle (B)   *Isa 21:15*

in toil and *h.* (A)(B)(R)   *2Co 11:27*

found to suffer *h.* (N)   *1Th 3:4*

preferring to suffer *h.* (N)   *Heb 11:35*

HARDSHIPS

all the *h.* (A)(B)(R)   *Ex 18:8*

enter kingdom for *h.* (N)   *Ac 14:22*

HARE

the *h.* because he cheweth the cud   *Le 11:6*

the camel, and the *h.* and the   *De 14:7*

HAREM

the *h.* daughters (B)   *Ca 6:8*

HAREPH

H. the father of Beth-gader   *1Ch 2:51*

HARETH

and came into the forest of *H.*   *1Sa 22:5*

HARHAIAH

the son of *H.*, of the goldsmiths   *Ne 3:8*

HARHAS

the son of *H.*, keeper of the   *2Ki 22:14*

HARHUR

of Hakupha, the children of *H.*   *Ezr 2:51*

of Hakupha, the children of *H.*   *Ne 7:53*

HARIM

The third to *H.*, the fourth to   *1Ch 24:8*

The children of *H.*, three hundred   *Ezr 2:32*

The children of *H.*, a   *Ezr* 2:39
thousand and
the sons of *H.*; Maaseiah, and *Ezr* 10:21
of the sons of *H.*; Eliezer,   *Ezr* 10:31
Ishijah
Malchijah the son of *H.*, and   *Ne* 3:11
The children of *H.*, three   *Ne* 7:35
hundred
The children of *H.*, a thousand *Ne* 7:42
H., Meremoth, Obadiah   *Ne* 10:5
Malluch, *H.*, Baanah   *Ne* 10:27
Of *H.*, Adna; of Meraioth,   *Ne* 12:15
Helkai

HARIPH

The children of *H.*, and   *Ne* 7:24
hundred
H., Anathoth, Nebai   *Ne* 10:19

HARLOT

with our sister as with an *h.*   *Ge* 34:31
he thought her to be an *h.*   *Ge* 38:15
Where is the *h.* that was   *Ge* 38:21
openly
There was no *h.* in this place   *Ge* 38:21
there was no *h.* in this place   *Ge* 38:22
daughter in law hath played   *Ge* 38:24
the *h.*
harlotry (B) *Ge* 38:24; *Le* 20:5; *Jer* 3:9;
                        Eze 23:27; 43:7
harlotry (R)   *Ge* 38:24;
Jer 3:9; *Eze* 23:27; 43:7; *Ho* 1:2; 4:18;
                                       6:10
played the *h.* (S)   *Ge* 38:24;
Le 20:5; *Nu* 25:1; *Eze* 16:17; 20:30;
Ho 4:10, 12, 14, 18; 5:3
play the *h.* (A)   *Ex* 34:15;
34:16; 17:7; 20:5, 6; 15:39; 31:16;
J'g 2:17; 8:33; *1Ch* 5:25; *2Ch* 21:13;
    Ps 106:39; *Eze* 23:30; *Ho* 4:12; 9:1
play the *h.* (E)   *Ex* 34:15;
34:16; *Le* 17:7; 20:5, 6; *Nu* 15:39;
De 31:16; *J'g* 2:17; 8:27, 33; *1Ch* 5:25;
2Ch 21:13; *Ps* 73:27; 106:39; *Eze* 6:9;
             23:30; *Ho* 4:12; 9:1
play the *h.* (R)   *Ex* 34:15;
34:16; 17:7; 20:5; *De* 31:16; *J'g* 2:17;
8:27, 33; *1Ch* 5:25; *Ps* 106:39; *Eze* 23:30;
                                       Ho 9:1
play the *h.* (S)   *Ex* 34:15;
34:16; *Le* 20:5, 6; *Nu* 15:39; *De* 31:16;
              2Ch 21:13; *Ps* 73:27
played the *h.* (S)   *Le* 17:7;
J'g 2:17; 8:33; *1Ch* 5:25; *Ps* 106:39;
       Eze 23:30; *Ho* 4:12; 9:1
harlot (A)(E)(R)   *Le* 19:29; 21:7, 9;
De 22:21; 23:18; *Pr* 23:27; *Isa* 57:3;
       Eze 16:28; *Re* 17:1, 15, 16; 19:2
harlot (S)   *Le* 19:29; 21:7, 9; *De* 22:21;
23:17, 18; *J'g* 19:2; *Pr* 23:27; *Isa* 57:3;
      Eze 16:28, 30; *Re* 17:1, 15, 16; 19:2
playing the *h.* (S)   *Le* 20:5;
Nu 25:1; *Eze* 16:17; *Ho* 4:10, 13, 14; 5:3
play the *h.* (E)   *Le* 20:5;
                  Nu 25:1; *Eze* 16:17; 20:30
harlot (B)   *Le* 21:9;
De 22:21; 23:18; *Pr* 23:27; *Isa* 57:3;
      Eze 16:28; *Re* 17:1, 15, 16; 19:2
or profane, or an *h.* these   *Le* 21:14
shall
playing the *h.* (A)   *De* 22:21
play the *h.* (B)   *De* 31:16;
                       Eze 23:30; *Ho* 9:1
only Rahab the *h.* shall live   *Jos* 6:17
Joshua saved Rahab the *h.*   *Jos* 6:25
alive
playing the *h.* (S)   *J'g* 8:27
played the *h.* (E)   *J'g* 19:2
he was the son of an *h.*   *J'g* 11:1
saw there an *h.* and went   *J'g* 16:1
to play the *h.* (E)   *2Ch* 21:11
played *h.* in doings (E)(R)   *Ps* 106:39
by means of a *h.*   *Pr* 6:26
(A)(B)(E)(R)
a woman with the attire of an   *Pr* 7:10
h.
the faithful city become an *h.*   *Isa* 1:21
years shall Tyre sin as an *h.*   *Isa* 23:15
thou *h.* that hast been   *Isa* 23:16
forgotten
tyre will play *h.*   *Isa* 23:17
(A)(B)(E)(R)
tree thou wanderest, playing   *Jer* 2:20
the *h.*
played the *h.* with many lovers   *Jer* 3:1
the brow of the *h.* (B)   *Jer* 3:3
tree, and there hath played the   *Jer* 3:6
h.

but went and played the *h.*   *Jer* 3:8
and playedst the *h.* because   *Eze* 16:15
of thy
and playedst the *h.* thereupon   *Eze* 16:16
played the *h.* (B)   *Eze* 16:17; 23:3
yea, thou hast played the *h.*   *Eze* 16:28
multiply your *h.* (A)(B)(R)   *Eze* 16:29
bold, domineering *h.*   *Eze* 16:30
(A)(B)(E)(R)
hast not been as an *h.* in that   *Eze* 16:31
thou
play the *h.* (R)   *Eze* 16:34; 23:3
O *h.* hear the word of the   *Eze* 16:35
Lord
thee to cease from playing   *Eze* 16:41
the *h.*
And Aholah played the *h.*   *Eze* 23:5
when she
wherein she had played the   *Eze* 23:19
h. in
unto a woman that playeth   *Eze* 23:44
the *h.*
their mother hath played   *Ho* 2:5
the *h.*
thou shalt not play the *h.* and   *Ho* 3:3
play the *h.* (B)   *Ho* 4:10;
                             4:14; 5:3; 6:10
play the *h.* (E)   *Ho* 4:10;
                        4:13, 14, 18; 5:3
Though thou, Israel, play the   *Ho* 4:15
h.
have given a boy for an *h.*   *Joe* 3:3
Thy wife shall be an *h.* in the   *Am* 7:17
city
she gathered it of the hire of   *Mic* 1:7
an *h.*
shall return to the hire of an *h.*   *Mic* 1:7
of the wellfavoured *h.* the   *Na* 3:4
mistress
make them the members of an   *1Co* 6:15
h.
is joined to an *h.* is one body   *1Co* 6:16
links himself with a *h.* (N)   *1Co* 6:16
By faith the *h.* Rahab   *Heb* 11:31
perished not
was not Rahab the *h.* justified   *Jas* 2:25
by

HARLOTRIES

harlotries (S)   *Nu* 14:33;
2Ki 9:22; *2Ch* 21:13; *Eze* 16:20, 22, 25,
26, 34, 36; 23:3, 7, 8, 11, 14, 18, 19, 29,
                          35, 43; *Na* 3:4
h. and seductions, sorceries   *2Ki* 9:22
(B)(R)
lewd *h.* (B)   *Jer* 13:27
harlotries (B)(R)   *Eze* 16:15
harlotries(A)   *Eze* 16:20;
     16:24, 36; 23:7, 8, 11, 14, 18, 19
harlotries (R)   *Eze* 16:20;
              16:22, 36; 23:7; *Na* 3:4
harlotries (A)(R)   *Eze* 16:33; 23:8
harlotries (A)   *Eze* 23:7; 23:14, 18
through her *h.* (B)(R)   *Na* 3:4

HARLOTRY

harlotry (S)   *Ge* 38:34;
Le 19:29; 20:5; *Nu* 25:1; *Jer* 3:2, 9;
13:27; *Eze* 16:17, 33; 20:30; 23:8, 17, 27;
43:7, 9; *Ho* 1:2; 2:2, 4; 4:10, 11, 12, 13,
                14, 18; 5:3; 4:5; 5:3; 6:10
h. after Maloch (B)   *Le* 20:5
h. after them (B)   *Le* 20:6
led you into *h.* (B)   *Nu* 15:39
harlotry (A)   *2Ch* 21:13;
Jer 3:2; *Eze* 16:25, 26, 29, 35; *Ho* 1:2;
                2:2, 4; 4:12; 5:4
harlotry (B)   *2Ch* 21:13;
Eze 16:20, 22, 25; 23:8, 29, 35; *Ho* 1:2;
                2:2, 4; 4:12; 5:4
play the *h.* (E) *2Ch* 21:13; *Eze* 23:3, 43
vile *h.* (B)   *Jer* 3:2;
Eze 16:25, 26; 23:8, 11, 14, 18, 19, 29, 35,
         43; *Ho* 1:2; 2:2; 4:12; 5:4
harlotry (A)   *Jer* 13:27;
        Eze 23:27; 43:9; *Ho* 1:2; 4:11
harlotry (B)   *Ho* 1:2; 4:13
a spirit of *h.* (B)(R)   *Ho* 4:12
h. and idolatry (A)   *Ho* 6:10

HARLOTS

two women, that were *h.* unto *1Ki* 3:16
he that keepeth company with *Pr* 29:3
h.
gifts to all *h.* (A)(B)(E)(S) *Eze* 16:33

they sacrifice with *h.*:   *Ho* 4:14
therefore
aside with *h.* (B)(E)(R)(S)   *Ho* 4:14
and the *h.* go into the   *M't* 21:31
kingdom
and the *h.* believed him: and *M't* 21:32
ye
devoured thy living with *h.*   *Lu* 15:30
thou
mother of *h.* and abominations *Re* 17:5

HARLOT'S

came into an *h.* house, named *Jos* 2:1
Go into the *h.* house, and bring *Jos* 6:22
thou hast a *h.* forehead (S)   *Jer* 3:3
loved a *h.* hire (A)(B)(E)(R)   *Ho* 9:1

HARLOTS'

by troops in the *h.* houses   *Jer* 5:7

HARM

harm (S)   *Ge* 26:29;
31:29; *Jos* 24:20; *1Sa* 24:9; *2Sa* 18:32
2Ki 14:10; *2Ch* 25:19; *Es* 9:2; *Jer* 7:6;
                          25:6, 7; 38:4
and this pillar unto me, for *h. Ge* 31:52
h. or injury (A)(B)(E)(R)   *Ge* 42:4;
                                       42:38
no *h.* follows (E)(R)   *Ex* 21:23
for the *h.* that he hath done in *Le* 5:16
his enemy, neither sought his *Nu* 35:23
h.
when I *h.* Philistines (B)   *J'g* 15:3
I will no more do thee *h.*   *1Sa* 26:21
the son of Bichri do us more   *2Sa* 20:6
h.
Saviour from *h.* (B)   *2Sa* 22:3
there was no *h.* in the pot   *2Ki* 4:41
and do my prophets no *h.*   *1Ch* 16:22
they plan to *h.* me (A)(B)(R)   *Ne* 6:2
and do my prophets no *h.*   *Ps* 105:15
if he have done thee no *h.*   *Pr* 3:30
look well to him, and do him *Jer* 39:12
no *h.*
Do thyself no *h.*: for we are *Ac* 16:28
all
to have gained this *h.* and loss *Ac* 27:21
into the fire, and felt no *h.*   *Ac* 28:5
saw no *h.* come to him, they   *Ac* 28:6
shewed or spake any *h.* of   *Ac* 28:21
thee
love works no *h.* to (B)   *Ro* 13:10
who is he that will *h.* you   *1Pe* 3:13

HARMLESS

wise as serpents, and *h.* as   *M't* 10:16
doves
That ye may be blameless   *Ph'p* 2:15
and *h.*
who is holy, *h.* undefiled   *Heb* 7:26

HARMON

shall be cast forth into *H.*   *Am* 4:3
(A)(E)(R)

HARMONIOUS

be *h.* (B)   *1Pe* 3:8

HARMONIOUSLY

brothers live *h.* (B)   *Ps* 133:1
h. framed together (B)   *Eph* 2:21; 4:16

HARMONIZED

h. the body (P)   *1Co* 12:24

HARMONY

in perfect *h.* (A)   *1Co* 1:10
what *h.* can there be   *2Co* 6:15
(A)(B)(P)
keep in *h.* (A)   *Eph* 4:3

HARNEPHER

Suah, and *H.*, and Shual   *1Ch* 7:36

HARNESS

him that girdeth on his *h.*   *1Ki* 20:11
boast
between the joints of the *h.*   *1Ki* 22:34

raiment, *h.* and spices, horses   *2Ch 9:24*
between the joints of the *h.*   *2Ch 18:33*
H. the horses; and get up, ye   *Jer 46:4*

HARNESSED

the children of Israel went up   *Ex 13:18*
h.

HAROD

and pitched beside the well of   *J'g 7:1*
H.

HARODITE

Shammah the *H.*, Elika the   *2Sa 23:25*
H.

HAROEH

H. and half of the   *1Ch 2:52*
Manahethites

HARORITE

Shammoth the *H.* Helez the   *1Ch 11:27*

HAROSHETH

which dwelt in *H.* of the   *J'g 4:2*
Gentiles
from *H.* of the Gentiles unto   *J'g 4:13*
the host, unto *H.* of the   *J'g 4:16*
Gentiles

HARP

such as handle the *h.* and   *Ge 4:21*
organ
songs, with tabret, and with   *Ge 31:27*
h.
a pipe, and a *h.* before them   *1Sa 10:5*
a cunning player on an *h.*   *1Sa 16:16*
David took an *h.* and played   *1Sa 16:23*
who prophesied with a *h.* to   *1Ch 25:3*
give
They take the timbrel and *h.*   *Job 21:12*
My *h.* also is turned to   *Job 30:31*
mourning
Praise the Lord with *h.*: sing   *Ps 33:2*
unto
the *h.* of ten strings (A)(B)   *Ps 33:2*
upon the *h.* will I praise thee   *Ps 43:4*
open my dark saying upon the   *Ps 49:4*
h.
awake, psaltery and *h.*: I   *Ps 57:8*
myself
unto thee will I sing with the   *Ps 71:22*
h.
the pleasant *h.* with the psaltery   *Ps 81:2*
upon the *h.* with a solemn   *Ps 92:3*
sound
Sing unto the Lord with the *h.*   *Ps 98:5*
with the *h.*, and the voice of a   *Ps 98:5*
Awake, psaltery, and *h.*: I   *Ps 108:2*
myself
a ten-stringed *h.* (B)(R)   *Ps 144:9*
sing praise upon the *h.* unto   *Ps 147:7*
unto him with the timbrel and   *Ps 149:3*
h.
praise him with the psaltery   *Ps 150:3*
and *h.*
the *h.* and the viol, the tabret   *Isa 5:12*
my bowels shall sound like an   *Isa 16:11*
h.
Take an *h.* go about the city   *Isa 23:16*
endeth, the joy of the *h.*   *Isa 24:8*
ceaseth.
flute, *h.* sackbut   *Da 3:5, 7, 10, 15*
chant to the sound of the *h.*   *Am 6:5*
(S)
giving sound, whether pipe or   *1Co 14:7*
h.

HARPED

be known what is piped or *h.*   *1Co 14:7*

HARPERS

I heard the voice of *h.* harping   *Re 14:2*
And the voice of *h.* and   *Re 18:22*
musicians

HARPING

voice of harpers *h.* with their   *Re 14:2*

HARPS

even on *h.* and on psalteries   *2Sa 6:5*
h. also and psalteries for   *1Ki 10:12*
singers
and with *h.* and with   *1Ch 13:8*
psalteries
psalteries and *h.* and   *1Ch 15:16*
cymbals
with *h.* on the Sheminith   *1Ch 15:21*
a noise with psalteries and *h.*   *1Ch 15:28*
Jeiel with psalteries and with   *1Ch 16:5*
h.
who should prophesy with *h.*   *1Ch 25:1*
with cymbals, psalteries, and   *1Ch 25:6*
h. for
cymbals and psalteries and *h.*   *2Ch 5:12*
and *h.* and psalteries for   *2Ch 9:11*
singers
with psalteries and *h.* and   *2Ch 20:28*
with psalteries, and with *h.*   *2Ch 29:25*
cymbals, psalteries, and with   *Ne 12:27*
h.
We hanged our *h.* upon the   *Ps 137:2*
willows
it shall be with tabrets and *h.*   *Isa 30:32*
sound of thy *h.* shall no more   *Eze 6:13*
hear the melody of the *h.* (S)   *Am 5:23*
having every one of them *h.*   *Re 5:8*
of harpers harping with their *h.*   *Re 14:2*
sea of glass, having the *h.* of   *Re 15:2*
God

HARROW

will he *h.* the valleys after   *Job 39:10*
thee

HARROWS

saws, and under *h.* of iron   *2Sa 12:31*
and with *h.* of iron, and with   *1Ch 20:3*
axes

HARRYING

Saul was *h.* the church (N)   *Ac 8:3*

HARSH

forced them by *h.* treatment   *Ex 1:14*
(B)
h. words stirs anger (B)(R)   *Pr 15:1*
a *h.* vision is declared (B)   *Isa 21:2*
h. wicked speaking (A)   *Isa 58:9*
a *h.* man (B)   *Lu 19:21*

HARSHA

of Mehida, the children of *H.*   *Ezr 2:52*
of Mehida, the children of *H.*   *Ne 7:54*

HARSHLY

Egyptians dealt *h.* with us   *Nu 20:15*
(R)
treated *h.* (B)(R)   *De 26:6*

HARSHNESS

service with *h.* (A)   *Ex 1:14*
rule over him with *h.* (A)(R)   *Le 25:43;*
  25:46, 53

HART

the roebuck, and as of the *h.*   *De 12:15*
deer (B)   *De 12:15;*
  1Ki 4:23; Ps 42:1; Isa 35:6
as the roebuck and the *h.* is   *De 12:22*
eaten
The *h.* and the roebuck, and   *De 14:5*
as the roebuck, and as the *h.*   *De 15:22*
As the *h.* panteth after the   *Ps 42:1*
water
is like a roe or a young *h.*   *Ca 2:9*
or a young *h.* upon the   *Ca 2:17*
mountains
to a young *h.* upon the   *Ca 8:14*
mountains
shall the lame man leap as an   *Isa 35:6*
h.

HARTS

an hundred sheep, beside *h.*   *1Ki 4:23*
her princes are become like *h.*   *La 1:6*
like stags without pasture (B)   *La 1:6*

HARUM

families of Aharhel the son of   *1Ch 4:8*
H.

HARUMAPH

repaired Jedaiah the son of *H.*   *Ne 3:10*

HARUPHITE

Shemariah, and Shephatiah   *1Ch 12:5*
the *H.*

HARUZ

Meshullemeth, the daughter   *2Ki 21:19*
of *H.*

HARVEST

seedtime and *h.* and cold and   *Ge 8:22*
in the days of wheat *h.* and   *Ge 30:14*
found
there shall be neither be earing   *Ge 45:6*
nor *h.*
in the *h.* (S)   *Ge 47:24*
thy *h.* and presses (E)(R)   *Ex 22:29*
the feast of *h.* the first fruits   *Ex 23:16*
in earing time and in *h.* thou   *Ex 34:21*
shalt
the firstfruits of wheat *h.* and   *Ex 34:22*
when ye reap the *h.* of your   *Le 19:9*
land
thou gather the gleanings of thy   *Le 19:9*
h.
shall reap the *h.* thereof, then   *Le 23:10*
ye
a sheaf of the firstfruits of   *Le 23:10*
your *h.*
when ye reap the *h.* of your   *Le 23:22*
land
thou gather any gleaning of   *Le 23:22*
thy *h.*
groweth of its own accord of   *Le 25:5*
thy *h.*
till its *h.* comes in (B)   *Le 25:22*
When thou cuttest down thine   *De 24:19*
h.
all his banks all the time of *h.*   *Jos 3:15*
in the time of wheat *h.*   *J'g 15:1*
in the beginning of barley *h.*   *Ru 1:22*
until they have ended all my *h.*   *Ru 2:21*
end of barley *h.* and of wheat   *Ru 2:23*
h.
their wheat *h.* in the valley   *1Sa 6:13*
to reap his *h.* and to make his   *1Sa 8:12*
Is it not wheat *h.* to day   *1Sa 12:17*
were put to death in the days   *2Sa 21:9*
of *h.*
in the beginning of barley *h.*   *2Sa 21:9*
from the beginning of *h.* until   *2Sa 21:10*
came to David in the *h.* time   *2Sa 23:13*
Whose *h.* the hungry eateth up   *Job 5:5*
and gathereth her food in the *h.*   *Pr 6:8*
he that sleepeth in *h.* is a son   *Pr 10:5*
therefore shall he beg in *h.* and   *Pr 20:4*
the cold of snow in the time of   *Pr 25:13*
h.
as rain in *h.* so honour is not   *Pr 26:1*
according to the joy in *h.* and as   *Isa 9:3*
thy summer fruits and for thy   *Isa 16:9*
h.
the *h.* shall be a heap in the   *Isa 17:11*
day of
like a cloud of dew in the heat   *Isa 18:4*
of *h.*
For afore the *h.* when the bud   *Isa 18:5*
the *h.* of the river is her   *Isa 23:3*
revenue
they shall eat up thine *h.* and   *Jer 5:17*
thy
us the appointed weeks of the   *Jer 5:24*
h.
The *h.* is past, the summer is   *Jer 8:20*
the sickle in the time of *h.*   *Jer 50:16*
the time of her *h.* shall come   *Jer 51:33*
he hath set an *h.* for thee   *Ho 6:11*
the *h.* of the field is perished   *Joe 1:11*
the sickle, for the *h.* is ripe   *Joe 3:13*
were yet three months to the *h.*   *Am 4:7*
the *h.* truly is plenteous, but   *M't 9:37*
Lord of the *h.* that he will   *M't 9:38*
send
send forth labourers into his   *M't 9:38*
h.
both grow together until the   *M't 13:30*
h.
and in the time of *h.* I will   *M't 13:30*
say

HARVEST

the h. is the end of the world	M't 13:39
the sickle, because the h. is come	M'k 4:29
The h. truly is great, but the	Lu 10:2
ye therefore the Lord of the h.	Lu 10:2
send forth labourers into his h.	Lu 10:2
gather my h. (A)(P)	Lu 12:17
four months, and then cometh h.	Joh 4:35
for they are white already to h.	Joh 4:35
h. for eternal life (B)(P)	Joh 4:36
yields a rich h. (A)(B)(N)(P)	Joh 12:24
reap some h. among you (B)(R)	Ro 1:13
what h. did you reap (P)	Ro 6:21
might yield God a h. (B)	Ro 7:4
yield death a h. (B)	Ro 7:5
the h. of the spirit is (N)	Ga 5:22
h. ruin of his flesh (B)	Ga 6:8
the h. of righteousness (A)(B)(P)(R)	Jas 3:18
waits for precious h. (A)(P)	Jas 5:7
the h. of the earth is ripe	Re 14:15

HARVESTMAN

when the h. gathereth the corn	Isa 17:5
as the handful after the h.	Jer 9:22

HARVESTS

be ashamed of their h. (B)(R)	Jer 12:13

HASADIAH

and H., Jushab-hesed, five	1Ch 3:20

HASENUAH

son of Hodaviah, the son of H.	1Ch 9:7

HASHABIAH

the son of H., the son of Amaziah	1Ch 6:45
son of H., of the sons of Merari	1Ch 9:14
Jeshaiah, and Mattithiah	1Ch 25:3
The twelfth, to H., he, his sons	1Ch 25:19
Hebronites, H. and his brethren	1Ch 26:30
Of the Levites, H. the son of Amaziah	1Ch 27:17
his brethren, and H. and Jeiel	2Ch 35:9
H., and with him Jeshaiah of	Ezr 8:19
H. and ten of their brethren	Ezr 8:24
Next unto him repaired H.	Ne 3:17
Micha, Rehob, H.	Ne 10:11
the son of H., the son of Bunni	Ne 11:15
the son of Bani, the son of H.	Ne 11:22
Of Hilkiah, H.; of Jedaiah	Ne 12:21
chief of the Levites: H., Sherebiah	Ne 12:24

HASHABNAH

Rehum, H., Masseiah	Ne 10:25

HASHABNIAH

repaired Hattush the son of H.	Ne 3:10
Bani, H., Sherebiah, Hadijah	Ne 9:5

HASHBADANA

Hashum, and H., Zechariah	Ne 8:4

HASHEM

The sons of H. the Gizonite	1Ch 11:34

HASHMONAH

from Mithcah, and pitched in H.	Nu 33:29
And they departed from H.	Nu 33:30

HASHUB

and H. the son of Pahath-moab	Ne 3:11
him repaired Benjamin and H.	Ne 3:23
Hoshea, Hananiah, H.	Ne 10:23
Shemaiah the son of H., the son	Ne 11:15

HASHUBAH

H., and Ohel, and Berechiah	1Ch 3:20

HASHUM

The children of H., two hundred	Ezr 2:19
Of the sons of H.; Mattenai	Ezr 10:33
The children of H., three hundred	Ne 7:22
and Malchiah, and H., and	Ne 8:4
Hodijah, H., Bezai	Ne 10:18

HASHUPHA

the children of H., the children	Ne 7:46

HASRAH

the son of H. keeper of the	2Ch 34:22

HASSENAAH

fish gate did the sons of H. build	Ne 3:3

HASSHUB

Shemaiah the son of H., the son	1Ch 9:14

HAST

h. thou here any besides?	Ge 19:12
whatsoever thou h. in city	
Esau said, H. thou but one blessing, father	Ge 27:38
as a prince h. thou power with God and men	Ge 32:28
Esau said, Keep that thou h. to thyself	Ge 33:9
come thou, thy flock, and all that thou h.	Ge 45:10
send and gather all that thou h. in field	Ex 9:19
every firstling thou h. shall be the Lord's	Ex 13:12
silver, gold, and all thou h. is multiplied	De 8:13
what makest thou? what h. thou here	J'g 18:3
and for that thou h. spoken friendly	Ru 2:13
Why h. thou deceived me so, and sent	1Sa 19:17
peace be to thee and all that thou h.	1Sa 25:6
h. thou not here with thee Zadok	2Sa 15:35
Why h. thou done so? and he also was	1Ki 1:6
Elisha said, Tell me, what h. in house	2Ki 4:2
h. thou eyes of flesh, or seest as man	Job 10:4
Surely thou h. spoken in mine	Job 33:8
h. thou an arm like God? or canst thunder	Job 40:9
thou h. broken the teeth of the ungodly	Ps 3:7
And h. not shut me up into the hands	Ps 31:8
thou h. set my feet in a large room	Ps 31:8
say not, Go, when thou h. it by thee	Pr 3:28
what h. thou here? whom h. thou here	Isa 22:16
and h. made thee a high place in every	Eze 16:24
are all thy ways, h. thou not glorified	Da 5:23
thou h. established them for correction	Hab 1:12
people, and h. sinned against thy soul	Hab 2:10
sell all thou h.	M't 19:21; M'k 10:21; Lu 18:22
there thou h. that is thine	M't 25:25
from whence then h. thou living water	Joh 4:11
and he whom thou now h. is not thine husband	Joh 4:18
to whom go? thou h. words of eternal life	Joh 6:68
the people said, Thou h. a devil	Joh 7:20; 8:48, 52
if I wash thee not, thou h. no part with me	Joh 13:8
thou h. neither part nor lot in this matter	Ac 8:21
thou h. shewed these things to me	Ac 23:22
thou who h. the form of knowledge	Ro 2:20
h. thou faith? have it to thyself before God	Ro 14:22
what h. thou that thou didst not receive	1Co 4:7
a man may say, Thou h. faith and I works	Jas 2:18
thou h. patience, and for my name's sake	Re 2:3
but this thou h.; thou h a name to live	Re 2:6; 3:1, 4
thou h. a little strength; hold what thou h.	Re 2:8
thou h. a little strength; hold what thou h.	Re 2:8; 2:11

HASTE

H. thee, escape thither	Ge 19:22
h. ye, and go up to thy father	Ge 45:9
Pharaoh called for Moses and Aaron h.	Ex 10:16
ye shall eat it in h. with your loins girded	Ex 12:11
might send them out of land in h.	Ex 12:33; De 16:3
king's business requireth h.	1Sa 21:8
Make speed, h., stay not	1Sa 20:38
H. thee, and come	1Sa 23:27
make h. to depart (A)(R)	2Sa 15:14
the Syrians had cast away in their h.	2Ki 7:15
they went up in h. to Jerusalem	Ezr 4:23
h. thee to help me	Ps 22:19
I said in my h. I am cut off	Ps 31:22
I said in my h. All men are liars	Ps 116:11
ye shall not go out with h. nor by flight	Isa 52:12
Arioch brought Daniel before king in h.	Da 2:25
the king rose up in h. and spake, and said	Da 3:24
the king went in h. unto the den of lions	Da 6:19
she came in straightway with h. to king	M'k 6:25
Mary went into the hill-country with h.	Lu 1:39
the shepherds came with h. and found Mary	Lu 2:16

HASTED

give it to young man, and he h. to dress it	Ge 18:7
she said, Drink, my lord, and she h.	Ge 24:18
and the task masters h. them, saying	Ex 5:13
the people h. and passed over Jordan	Jos 4:10
and when the king of Ai saw it, they h.	Jos 8:14
the ambush h. and set the city on fire	Jos 8:19
the sun h. not to go down a whole day	Jos 10:13
liers in wait h. and rushed on Gibeah	J'g 20:37
David h.; Abigail h.	1Sa 17:48; 25:23; 25:42
except thou hadst h. and come to meet	1Sa 25:34
the witch at En-dor h. and killed the calf	1Sa 28:24
Shimei, who was of Bahurim, h.	2Sa 19:16
the prophet h. and took ashes away	1Ki 20:41
they h. and put garments under Jehu	2Ki 9:13
yea, himself h. also to go out	2Ch 26:20
Haman h. to his house mourning	Es 6:12
they h. to bring Haman unto the banquet	Es 6:14
or if my foot hath h. to deceit	Job 31:5
they were troubled and h. away	Ps 48:5; 104:7
Paul h. to be at Jerusalem at Pentecost	Ac 20:16

HASTEN

h. hither Micaiah the son of   *1Ki 22:9*
Imlah
and see that ye *h.* the matter   *2Ch 24:5*
sorrows multiplied *h.* after   *Ps 16:4*
another god
I would *h.* my escape from the   *Ps 55:8*
windy storm
or who else can *h.* hereunto   *Ec 2:25*
more than I
let him *h.* his work that we   *Isa 5:19*
may see it
I the Lord will *h.* it in his   *Isa 60:22*
time
I will *h.* my word to perform it   *Jer 1:12*

HASTENED

And Abraham *h.* into the tent   *Ge 18:6*
then the angels *h.* Lot, saying   *Ge 19:15*
those in ambush *h.*   *J'g 20:37*
Howbeit the Levites *h.* it not   *2Ch 24:5*
himself *h.* to go (S)   *2Ch 26:20;*
  Ac 20:16
The posts went out, being *h.*   *Es 3:15*
being *h.* and pressed on by the   *Es 8:14*
I have not *h.* from being a   *Jer 17:16*
pastor

HASTENETH

he that *h.* to be rich (S)   *Pr 28:22*
The captive exile *h.* that he   *Isa 51:14*
may

HASTETH

as the eagle that *h.* to the prey   *Job 9:26*
drinketh up a river, and *h.*   *Job 40:23*
as a bird *h.* to the snare   *Pr 7:23*
and he that *h.* with his feet   *Pr 19:2*
sinneth
He that *h.* to be rich hath an   *Pr 28:22*
evil
the sun goeth down, and *h.* to   *Ec 1:5*
his
to come, and his affliction *h.*   *Jer 48:16*
fast
fly as the eagle that *h.* to eat   *Hab 1:8*
is near, it is near, and *h.*   *Zep 1:14*
greatly

HASTILY

and they brought him *h.* out   *Ge 41:14*
without driving them out *h.*   *J'g 2:23*
he called *h.* unto the young   *J'g 9:54*
man
And the man came in *h.* and   *1Sa 4:14*
told
and did *h.* catch it: and they   *1Ki 20:33*
said
inheritance may be gotten *h.*   *Pr 20:21*
Go not forth *h.* to strive, lest   *Pr 25:8*
thou
that she rose up *h.* and went   *Joh 11:31*
out

HASTING

judgment, and *h.*   *Isa 16:5*
righteousness
h. unto the coming of the day   *2Pe 3:12*

HASTY

but he that is *h.* of spirit   *Pr 14:29*
exalteth
every one that is *h.* only to   *Pr 21:5*
want
Seest thou a man that is *h.* in   *Pr 29:20*
his
let not thine heart be *h.* to utter   *Ec 5:2*
Be not *h.* in thy spirit to be   *Ec 7:9*
Be not *h.* to go out of his sight   *Ec 8:3*
the *h.* fruit before the summer   *Isa 28:4*
Why is the decree so *h.* from   *Da 2:15*
that bitter and *h.* nation,   *Hab 1:6*
which

HASUPHA

the children of *H.* the children   *Ezr 2:43*

HATACH

called Esther for *H.* one of the   *Es 4:5*
So *H.* went forth to   *Es 4:6*
Mordecai unto
And *H.* came and told Esther   *Es 4:9*
Esther spake unto *H.* and gave   *Es 4:10*

HATCH

make her nest, and lay, and *h.*   *Isa 34:15*
They *h.* cockatrice' eggs, and   *Isa 59:5*

HATCHETH

partridge sitteth on eggs, and   *Jer 17:11*
h.

HATE

let seed possess gate of those   *Ge 24:60*
that *h.*
they said, Joseph will   *Ge 50:15*
peradventure *h.* us
thou shalt not *h.* thy brother   *Le 19:17*
in heart
they that *h.* you shall reign   *Le 26:17*
over you
let them that *h.* thee flee   *Nu 10:35*
before thee
repayeth them that *h.* him to   *De 7:10*
face
he will lay them upon them   *De 7:15;*
that *h.* thee   *30:7*
if any man *h.* his neighbour   *De 19:11*
and lie in wait
if take a wife, and go in unto   *De 22:13*
her and *h.* her
if the latter husband *h.* her and   *De 24:3*
write a bill
smite through the loins of   *De 33:11*
them that *h.* him
and love them that *h.* the Lord   *2Ch 19:2*
that *h.* thee shall be clothed   *Job 8:22*
with shame
thy hand shall find those that *h.*   *Ps 21:8*
thee
they that *h.* the righteous   *Ps 34:21*
shall be desolate
they which *h.* us spoil for   *Ps 44:10*
themselves
let them also that *h.* him flee   *Ps 68:1*
before him
they that *h.* thee have lifted up   *Ps 83:2*
the head
and I will plague them that *h.*   *Ps 89:23*
him
ye that love the Lord *h.* evil   *Ps 97:10*
he turned their heart to *h.* his   *Ps 105:25*
people
let them be turned back that   *Ps 129:5*
h. Zion
how long, fools, will ye *h.*   *Pr 1:22*
knowledge
these six doth the Lord *h.*: A   *Pr 6:16*
proud look
fear of the Lord is to *h.* evil;   *Pr 8:13*
pride do I *h.*
reprove not a scorner, lest he *h.*   *Pr 9:8*
thee
all the brethren of the poor do   *Pr 19:7*
h. him
lest he be weary of thee, and   *Pr 25:17*
so *h.* thee
the bloodthirsty *h.* the upright   *Pr 29:10*
a time to love and a time to *h.*   *Ec 3:8*
delivered unto will of them   *Eze 16:27*
that *h.* thee
the dream be to them that *h.*   *Da 4:19*
thee
they *h.* him that rebuketh in   *Am 5:10*
the gate
h. the evil, and love the good,   *Am 5:15*
establish judgment
who *h.* the good, and love evil,   *Mic 3:2*
who pluck
been said, Love thy   *M't 5:43*
neighbour, *h.* enemy
do good to them that *h.* you   *M't 5:44;*
  Lu 6:27
either he will *h.* the one   *M't 6:24;*
  Lu 16:13
and shall betray and shall *h.*   *M't 24:10*
one another
saved from the hand of all that   *Lu 1:71*
h. us
blessed are ye when men shall   *Lu 6:22*
h. you
and *h.* not his father, and   *Lu 14:26*
mother, and wife
the world cannot *h.* you, but   *Joh 7:7*
me it hateth
marvel not if the world *h.*   *Joh 15:18;*
you   *1Jo 3:13*
the ten horns, these shall *h.*   *Re 17:16*
the whore

I HATE

there is one man, *I h.* him   *1Ki 22:8;*
  2Ch 18:7
I h. the work of them that   *Ps 101:3*
turn aside
therefore I *h.* every false   *Ps 119:104;*
way   *119:128*
I h. vain thoughts; *I h.* and   *Ps 119:113*
abhor lying
do not *I h.* them, O Lord,   *Ps 139:21*
that hate thee
yea, *I h.* them with perfect   *Ps 139:22*
hatred
the evil way and froward mouth   *Pr 8:13*
do *I h.*
I h. robbery for burnt offering   *Isa 61:8*
do not this abominable thing   *Jer 44:4*
that *I h.*
I h. I despise your feast days   *Am 5:21*
I h. his palaces, therefore will I   *Am 6:8*
deliver city
for all these are things that *I*   *Zec 8:17*
h. saith Lord
but what *I h.* that do I   *Ro 7:15*
the deeds of the Nicolaitans *I*   *Re 2:6;*
h.   *2:15*

HATE ME

why come ye to me, seeing ye   *Ge 26:27*
h. me
visiting iniquity to the third   *Ex 20:5;*
and fourth generation of them   *De 5:9*
that *h. me*
and I will reward them that *h.*   *De 32:41*
me
do not ye *h. me?*; thou dost   *J'g 11:7;*
h. me   *14:16*
destroy them that *h. me*   *2Sa 22:41;*
  Ps 18:40
trouble which I suffer of them   *Ps 9:13*
that *h. me*
and they *h. me* with cruel   *Ps 25:19*
hatred
let them wink that *h. me*   *Ps 35:19*
without a cause
they that *h. me* wrongfully are   *Ps 38:19;*
many   *69:4*
all that *h. me* whisper together   *Ps 41:7*
against me
they cast iniquity upon me, in   *Ps 55:3*
wrath *h. me*
let me be delivered from them   *Ps 69:14*
that *h. me*
that they which *h. me* may see   *Ps 86:17*
I shall see my desire upon   *Ps 118:7*
them that *h. me*
all they that *h. me* love death   *Pr 8:36*

HATED

Esau *h.* Jacob, because of the   *Ge 27:41*
blessing
the Lord saw Leah was *h.*;   *Ge 29:31;*
that I was *h.*   *29:33*
his brethren *h.* Joseph yet the   *Ge 37:4;*
more   *37:5, 8*
the archers shot at him and *h.*   *Ge 49:23*
him
and said, Because the Lord *h.*   *De 1:27;*
us   *9:28*
h. him not in times past   *De 4:42;*
  19:4, 6; Jos 20:5
another *h.*   *De 21:15*
before the son of the *h.*   *De 21:16*
shall acknowledge the son of   *De 21:17*
h. for firstborn
I thought that thou hadst   *J'g 15:2*
utterly *h.* her
the lame and blind that are *h.*   *2Sa 5:8*
of David's
Amnon *h.* Tamar; Absalom   *2Sa 13:15;*
h. Amnon   *13:22*
delivered from my strong   *2Sa 22:18;*
enemy and from them   *Ps 18:17*
that *h.* me
the Jews had rule over them that   *Es 9:1*
h. them
did what they would unto those   *Es 9:5*
that *h.* them
at the destruction of him that   *Job 31:29*
h. me
I have *h.* the congregation of   *Ps 26:5*
evil doers
I have *h.* them that regard lying   *Ps 31:6*
vanities
thou hast put them to shame,   *Ps 44:7*
that *h.* us

neither was it he that *h.* me,   *Ps 55:12*
that did magnify
he saved them from him that   *Ps 106:10*
h. them
and they that *h.* them ruled   *Ps 106:41*
over them
they *h.* knowledge, and did not   *Pr 1:29*
choose
and say, How have I *h.*   *Pr 5:12*
instruction
and a man of wicked devices   *Pr 14:17*
is *h.*
the poor is *h.* even of his own   *Pr 14:20*
neighbour
I *h.* life; I *h..*labour   *Ec 2:17; 2:18*
whereas thou hast been   *Isa 60:15*
forsaken and *h.*
brethren that *h.* you said, Lord   *Isa 66:5*
be glorified
therefore have I *h.* mine   *Jer 12:8*
heritage
I will gather all them that   *Eze 16:37*
thou hast *h.*
sith thou hast not *h.* blood,   *Eze 35:6*
blood pursue
for there, I *h.* them for   *Ho 9:15*
wickedness of doings
I loved Jacob, and *h.* Esau   *Mal 1:3;*
                Ro 9:13
ye shall be *h.*   *M't 10:22;*
      M'k 13:13; Lu 21:17
ye shall be *h.* of all nations for   *M't 24:9*
my name
his citizens *h.* him, and sent a   *Lu 19:14*
message
ye know that it *h.* me before   *Joh 15:18*
it *h.* you
have both seen and *h.* both   *Joh 15:24*
me and my Father
written in their law, they *h.*   *Joh 15:25*
me without a cause
world hath *h.* them, because   *Joh 17:14*
not of world
no man ever yet *h.* his own   *Eph 5:29*
flesh
thou hast loved righteousness   *Heb 1:9*
and *h.* iniquity

HATEFUL

made themselves *h.* (A)   *1Ch 19:6*
until his iniquity be found to be   *Ps 36:2*
h.
we were *h.* and hating one   *Tit 3:3*
another
a cage of every unclean and *h.*   *Re 18:2*
bird

HATEFULLY

and they shall deal with thee   *Eze 23:29*
h.

HATERS

the *h.* of Lord should have   *Ps 81:15*
submitted
backbiters, *h.* of God,   *Ro 1:30*
despiteful
h. of good (A)(R)   *2Ti 3:3*

HATEST

lovest thine enemies, and *h.*   *2Sa 19:6*
thy friends
thou *h.* all workers of iniquity   *Ps 5:5*
thou lovest righteousness, and   *Ps 45:7*
h. wickedness
thou *h.* instruction, and   *Ps 50:17*
castest my words
deliver thee into hand whom   *Eze 23:28*
thou *h.*
thou *h.* the deeds of the   *Re 2:6*
Nicolaitans

HATETH

if see ass of him that *h.* thee   *Ex 23:5*
lying
Lord not be slack to him that   *De 7:10*
h. him
every abomination he *h.* have   *De 12:31*
they done
nor set up any image which   *De 16:22*
the Lord *h.*
gave my daughter unto this   *De 22:16*
man, he *h.* her
he teareth me in his wrath,   *Job 16:9*
who *h.* me

shall even he that *h.* right,   *Job 34:17*
govern
him that loveth violence, his   *Ps 11:5*
soul *h.*
soul long dwelt with him that   *Ps 120:6*
h. peace
and he that *h.* suretyship is   *Pr 11:15*
sure
but he that *h.* reproof is   *Pr 12:1*
brutish
righteous man *h.* lying   *Pr 13:5*
he that spareth his rod *h.* his   *Pr 13:24*
son
and he that *h.* reproof shall   *Pr 15:10*
die
but he that *h.* gifts shall live   *Pr 15:27*
he that *h.* dissembleth with his   *Pr 26:24*
lips
a lying tongue *h.* those that   *Pr 26:28*
are afflicted
he that *h.* covetousness   *Pr 28:16*
prolong days
is partner with a thief *h.* his   *Pr 29:24*
own soul
your apointed feasts my soul *h.*   *Isa 1:14*
Lord saith, that he *h.* putting   *Mal 2:16*
away
every one that doeth evil *h.*   *Joh 3:20*
the light
but me the world *h.* because I   *Joh 7:7*
testify of it
he that *h.* his life in this   *Joh 12:25*
world shall keep
are not of world, therefore   *Joh 15:19*
world *h.* you
he that *h.* me *h.* my Father   *Joh 15:23*
also
he that *h.* his brother is in   *1Jo 2:9;*
darkness   *2:11*
whosoever *h.* his brother is a   *1Jo 3:15*
murderer
if say, I love God, and *h.*   *1Jo 4:20*
brother, is a liar

HATH

and unto him *h.* he given all   *Ge 24:36*
that he *h.*
whatsoever uncleanness he *h.*   *Le 22:5*
no devoted thing of all he *h.*   *Le 27:28*
shall be sold
he *h.* the strength of an   *Nu 23:22;*
unicorn   *24:8*
why name done away because   *Nu 27:4*
he *h.* no son
his sons to inherit that which   *De 21:16*
he *h.*
the firstborn a double portion   *De 21:17*
of all he *h.*
bring out thence woman and   *Jos 6:22*
all she *h.*
he shall be burnt with fire, he   *Jos 7:15*
and all he *h.*
and he *h.* requited me evil   *1Sa 25:21*
for good
h. Lord as great delight in   *1Sa 15:22*
offerings
thine handmaid, *h.* not any   *2Ki 4:2*
thing in house
verily she *h.* no child, her   *2Ki 4:14*
husband is old
that *h.* come upon us, on our   *Ne 9:32*
kings, on
hedge about all he *h.*; touch   *Job 1:10;*
all he *h.*   *1:11*
behold, all that he *h.* is in thy   *Job 1:12*
power
all that a man *h.* will he give   *Job 2:4*
for his life
so the poor *h.* hope: *h.* rain a   *Job 5:16;*
father   *38:28*
God *h.* delivered me to the   *Job 16:11*
ungodly
a little that a righteous man *h.*   *Ps 37:16*
is better
let the extortioner catch all   *Ps 109:11*
that he *h.*
happy is the man *h.* his quiver   *Ps 127:5*
full of them
h. chosen Zion: he *h.* desired   *Ps 132:13*
it for his
happy he that *h.* God of Jacob   *Ps 146:5*
for his help
he that is despised and *h.* a   *Pr 12:9*
servant is
the sluggard desireth, and *h.*   *Pr 13:4*
nothing

is that maketh himself rich, yet   *Pr 13:7*
h. nothing
understanding is life unto him   *Pr 16:22*
who *h.* it
a precious stone in eyes of him   *Pr 17:8*
that *h.* it
and he that *h.* it shall abide   *Pr 19:23*
satisfied
who *h.* woe? who *h.* sorrow?   *Pr 23:29*
who *h.* wounds
who *h.* gathered the wind in his   *Pr 30:4*
fists
who *h.* bound the waters in a   *Pr 30:4*
garment
who *h.* established all the ends   *Pr 30:4*
yea, he *h.* neither child nor   *Ec 4:8*
brother
for he *h.* not another to help   *Ec 4:10*
him up
to pay it: for he *h.* no pleasure   *Ec 5:4*
in fools
for what *h.* the wise more than   *Ec 6:8*
the fool
neither *h.* he power in the day of   *Ec 8:8*
death
a little sister, and she *h.* no   *Ca 8:8*
breasts
and say, How *h.* the oppressor   *Isa 14:4*
ceased
he is faint, and his soul *h.*   *Isa 29:8*
appetite
he *h.* no hands; and *h.* no   *Isa 45:9;*
light   *50:10*
he *h.* no form nor comeliness,   *Isa 53:2*
when see him
he that *h.* no money, come ye,   *Isa 55:1*
buy and eat
prophet *h.* a dream, let him   *Jer 23:28*
tell, he that *h.* my word, let
and he *h.* settled on his lees   *Jer 48:11*
and *h.* not been emptied from   *Jer 48:11*
vessel to
neither *h.* he gone into   *Jer 48:11*
captivity
h. Israel no sons? he *h.* no   *Jer 49:1*
heir
for the Lord *h.* afflicted her for   *La 1:5*
the Lord *h.* delivered me into   *La 1:14*
cursed be deceiver which *h.* in   *Mal 1:14*
flock a male
h. not where to lay head   *M't 8:20;*
              Lu 9:58
that *h.* ears to hear, let him   *M't 11:15;*
hear *13:9, 43; M'k 4:9; Lu 8:8; 14:35;*
              Re 2:7
eating, nor drinking, they   *M't 11:18*
say he *h.* a devil
whosoever *h.* to him shall   *M't 13:12;*
be given; who *h.* not,   *25:29; M'k 4:25;*
from him shall be   *Lu 8:18; 19:26*
taken that he *h.*
selleth all that he *h.* and   *M't 13:44*
buyeth that field
whence *h.* this man these   *M't 13:56;*
things   *M'k 6:2*
my heavenly Father *h.* not   *M't 15:13*
planted
he *h.* Beelzebub, and casteth   *M'k 3:22*
out devils
because they said, He *h.* an   *M'k 3:30*
unclean spirit
and ye say, He *h.* a devil   *Lu 7:33;*
              Joh 10:20
No man, when he *h.* lighted a   *Lu 11:33*
candle
he will make him ruler over   *Lu 12:44*
all that he *h.*
that forsaketh not all that he   *Lu 14:33*
h. cannot be
whose superscription *h.* it?   *Lu 20:24*
they said
he that *h.* a purse, he that *h.*   *Lu 22:36*
no sword
a spirit *h.* not flesh and bones,   *Lu 24:39*
as ye see me
he that *h.* the bride, is the   *Joh 3:29*
bridegroom
believeth *h.* everlasting life   *Joh 3:26;*
          5:24; 6:47, 54
as the Father *h.* life in   *Joh 5:26*
himself, so *h.* given
h. one judgeth him, the word   *Joh 12:48*
I have
he that *h.* my commandments   *Joh 14:21*
and keepeth
the prince of this world *h.*   *Joh 14:30*
nothing in me
greater love *h.* no man than   *Joh 15:13*
this, that a

all things that the Father *h.*   *Joh 16:15*
are mine
delivered thee unto me, *h.* the   *Joh 19:11*
greater sin
Who also *h.* gone about to   *Ac 24:6*
profane the
what advantage then *h.* the Jew   *Ro 3:1*
if justified by works, he *h.*   *Ro 4:2*
whereof to glory
h. not the potter power over the   *Ro 9:21*
clay
wife *h.* not power of her own   *1Co 7:4*
body
but every man *h.* his proper   *1Co 7:7*
gift of God
every one of you *h. a* psalm,   *1Co 14:26*
h. a doctrine
what fellowship *h.*   *2Co 6:14*
righteousness with uprightness?
what communion *h.* light with
what concord *h.* Christ?   *2Co 6:15*
h. temple of God   *2Co 6:16*
it is accepted according to   *2Co 8:12*
that a man *h.*
for the desolate *h.* more   *Ga 4:27*
children than she
nor idolater *h.* any inheritance   *Eph 5:5*
in kingdom
if any thinketh be *h.* whereof   *Ph'p 3:4*
may trust
builder *h.* more honour than   *Heb 3:3*
the house
this man *h.* an unchangeable   *Heb 7:24*
priesthood
confidence, which *h.*   *Heb 10:35*
recompense of reward
though a man say he *h.* faith,   *Jas 2:14*
not works
who denieth Son, same *h.* not   *1Jo 2:23*
Father
every man that *h.* this hope in   *1Jo 3:3*
him purifieth
ye know that no murderer *h.*   *1Jo 3:15*
eternal life
whoso *h.* this world's good,   *1Jo 3:17*
and seeth brother
we have believed the love that   *1Jo 4:16*
God *h.* to us
there is no fear in love,   *1Jo 4:18*
because fear *h.* torment
he that believeth on Son of   *1Jo 5:10*
God, *h.* witness
he that *h.* the Son *h.* life, *h.*   *1Jo 5:12*
not Son *h.* not life
abideth not in doctrine of Christ   *2Jo 9*
h. not God, that abideth *h.*
both Father and Son
that *h.* key of David opens, no   *Re 3:7*
man shuts
wilderness where she *h.* a   *Re 12:6*
place prepared of God
he knoweth that he *h.* but a   *Re 12:12*
short time
beast which *h.* the seven heads   *Re 17:7*
and ten horns
and here is the mind which *h.*   *Re 17:9*
wisdom
on such the second death *h.* no   *Re 20:6*
power

HATHATH

and the sons of Othniel; *H.*   *1Ch 4:13*

HATING

men of truth, *h.* covetousness   *Ex 18:21*
envy, hateful, and *h.* one   *Tit 3:3*
another
h. even the garment spotted by   *Jude 23*

HATIPHA

of Neziah, the children of *H.*   *Ezr 2:54;*
   Ne 7:56

HATITA

the children of *H.* the children   *Ezr 2:42;*
   Ne 7:45

HATRED

But if he thrust him of *h.*   *Nu 35:20*
that the *h.* wherewith he   *2Sa 13:15*
hated her
and they hate me with cruel *h.*   *Ps 25:19*
me about also with words of   *Ps 109:3*
h.
for good, and *h.* for my love   *Ps 109:5*

I hate them with perfect *h.*   *Ps 139:22*
H. stirreth up strifes: but love   *Pr 10:12*
He that hideth *h.* with lying   *Pr 10:18*
lips
than a stalled ox and *h.*   *Pr 15:17*
therewith
Whose *h.* is covered by deceit,   *Pr 26:26*
his
no man knoweth either love or   *Ec 9:1*
h.
Also their love, and their *h.* and   *Ec 9:6*
to destroy it for the old *h.*   *Eze 25:15*
thou hast had a perpetual *h.*   *Eze 35:5*
which thou hast used out of   *Eze 35:11*
thy *h.*
thine iniquity, and the great *h.*   *Ho 9:7*
h. in the house of his God   *Ho 9:8*
h., variance, emulations, wrath   *Ga 5:20*

HATS

their hosen, and their *h.* and   *Da 3:21*

HATTIL

the children of *H.,* the   *Ezr 2:57*
children
of Shephatiah, the children of   *Ne 7:59*
H.

HATTUSH

H., and Igeal, and Bariah   *1Ch 3:22*
Daniel: of the sons of David;   *Ezr 8:2*
H.
And next unto him repaired *H.*   *Ne 3:10*
H., Shebaniah, Malluch   *Ne 10:4*
Amariah, Malluch, *H.*   *Ne 12:2*

HAUGHTILY

necks; neither shall ye go *h.*   *Mic 2:3*
does not display itself *h.* (A)   *1Co 13:4*

HAUGHTINESS

before *h.* comes disaster (A)   *Pr 18:12*
the *h.* of men shall be bowed   *Isa 2:11*
the *h.* of men shall be made   *Isa 2:17*
low
will lay low the *h.* of the   *Isa 13:11*
terrible
his *h.* and his pride, and his   *Isa 16:6*
and the *h.* of his heart   *Jer 48:29*

HAUGHTY

thine eyes are upon the *h.*   *2Sa 22:28*
my heart is not *h.* nor mine   *Ps 131:1*
eyes
h. eyes (B)(E)(R)   *Pr 6:17; 21:4*
and an *h.* spirit before a fall   *Pr 16:18*
destruction the heart of man   *Pr 18:12*
is *h.*
Proud and *h.* scorner is his   *Pr 21:24*
name
the *h.* looks of man (R)   *Isa 2:11*
against the *h.* and proud   *Isa 2:12*
(A)(B)
the daughters of Zion are *h.*   *Isa 3:16*
and the *h.* shall be humbled   *Isa 10:33*
h. people of the earth do   *Isa 24:4*
languish
And they were *h.* and   *Eze 16:50*
committed
shalt no more be *h.* because of   *Zep 3:11*
my
do not be *h.* (B)   *Ro 11:20*

HAUNT

his place where his *h.* is and   *1Sa 23:22*
and his men were wont to *h.*   *1Sa 30:31*
a *h.* for jackals (B)(R)   *Isa 34:13; 35:7*
terror to be on all that *h.* it   *Eze 26:17*
a *h.* of devils (P)   *Re 18:2*

HAURAN

which is by the coast of *H.*   *Eze 47:16*
ye shall measure from *H.*   *Eze 47:18*

HAVE

I said, I *h.* gotten a man from   *Ge 4:1*
the Lord
Lord said, They *h.* all one   *Ge 11:6*
language
for I *h.* borne him a son in his   *Ge 21:7*
old age

thou shouldest *h.* brought   *Ge 26:10*
guiltiness
h. ye another brother; *h.* ye a   *Ge 43:7*
father
and they have brought all that   *Ge 46:32*
they *h.*
thou shalt *h.* no other gods   *Ex 20:3;*
   De 5:7
Priest that maketh atonement   *Le 7:7*
shall *h.* it
meat offering the sons of   *Le 7:10*
Aaron shall *h.*
a just ephah and a just hin   *Le 19:36*
shall ye *h.*
priest's daughter *h.* no child   *Le 22:13;*
   Nu 27:8, 9
whence should I *h.* flesh to   *Nu 11:13*
give unto all
h. I now any power at all to   *Nu 22:38*
say any thing
covenant of peace he and his   *Nu 25:13*
seed shall *h.* it
the cities shall they *h.* to dwell   *Nu 35:3*
in
from them that *h.* many,   *Nu 35:8*
them that *h.* few
who hath heard voice of God,   *De 5:26*
as we *h.*
ye will save alive father and all   *Jos 2:13*
they *h.*
though they *h.* iron chariots   *Jos 17:18*
and be strong
what *h.* you to do with Lord   *Jos 22:24*
God of Israel
h. ye called us to take that we   *J'g 14:15*
h.
ye *h.* taken my gods, and   *J'g 18:24*
what *h.* I more
I am too old to *h.* an husband,   *Ru 1:12*
if I should *h.* an husband also
but we will *h.* a king over us   *1Sa 8:19*
there is not a present to bring;   *1Sa 9:7*
what *h.* we
time the sun be hot, ye shall   *1Sa 11:9*
h. help
go and utterly destroy all that   *1Sa 15:3*
they *h.*
what can he *h.* more but the   *1Sa 18:8*
kingdom
his works *h.* been to thee-ward   *1Sa 19:4*
certainly knoweth that I *h.*   *1Sa 20:3*
found grace
h. I need of madmen, that ye   *1Sa 21:15*
h. brought
Amnon said, *H.* out all men   *2Sa 13:9*
from me
they *h.* there with them their   *2Sa 15:36*
two sons
what *h.* I to do with you, ye   *2Sa 16:10*
sons of Zeruiah
I *h.* no son to keep my name   *2Sa 18:18*
in remembrance
what right *h.* I yet to cry any   *2Sa 19:28*
more to king
Barzillai said unto king,   *2Sa 19:34*
How long *h.* I to live
Israel said, We *h.* ten parts   *2Sa 19:43*
in the king
This is the noise that ye *h.*   *1Ki 1:45*
heard
h. thou respect unto prayer of   *1Ki 8:28*
thy servant
my servant may *h.* a light   *1Ki 11:36*
alway
saying, What portion *h.* we   *1Ki 12:16*
in David
I *h.* not a cake, but an   *1Ki 17:12*
handful of meal
my lord, O king, I am thine,   *1Ki 20:4*
and all I *h.*
that I may *h.* it for a garden   *1Ki 21:2*
of herbs
Israel scattered as sheep that   *1Ki 22:17*
h. no shepherd
h. her forth without   *2Ki 11:15;*
   2Ch 23:14
Isaiah said, This sign shalt   *2Ki 20:9*
thou *h.* of the Lord
nor shall any after thee *h.* the   *2Ch 1:12*
like
from henceforth thou shalt *h.*   *2Ch 16:9*
wars
what *h.* I to do with thee,   *2Ch 35:21*
king of Judah
he said, *H.* me away, for I   *2Ch 35:23*
am sore wounded
therefore *h.* we sent and   *Ezr 4:14*
certified the

other men *h.* our lands and   *Ne 5:5*
vineyards
let it look for light but *h.* none   *Job 3:9*
O that I might *h.* my request,   *Job 6:8*
that God would
then should I yet *h.* comfort,   *Job 6:10*
yea, I would
what profit should we *h.* if   *Job 21:15*
pray unto him
they mar my path, they *h.* no   *Job 30:13*
helper
what profit shall I *h.* if be   *Job 35:3*
cleansed from sin
the Lord shall *h.* them in   *Ps 2:4*
derision
h. workers of iniquity no   *Ps 14:4;*
knowledge   *53:4*
in pleasant places, I *h.* a goodly *Ps 16:6*
heritage
let them not say, ah, so would   *Ps 35:25*
we *h.* it
whom *h.* I in heaven but thee? *Ps 73:25*
none upon
I will sing to my God while I *Ps 104:33*
h. my being
a good understanding *h.* all   *Ps 111:10*
they that do
they *h.* mouths; eyes *h.* they, *Ps 115:5*
but see not
they *h.* ears; noses *h.* they   *Ps 115:6;*
   115:7; 135:16, 17
so shall I *h.* wherewith to   *Ps 119:42*
answer him
great peace *h.* they which   *Ps 119:165*
love thy law
sing praise unto my God while *Ps 146:2*
I *h.* being
this honour *h.* all his saints, *Ps 149:9*
praise Ye Lord
cast in thy lot, let us all *h.* one *Pr 1:14*
purse
sluggard shall beg in harvest,   *Pr 20:4*
and *h.* nothing
shall *h.* him become his son at *Pr 20:21*
the length
and I *h.* not the understanding *Pr 30:2*
of a man
nor *h.* I the knowledge of the *Pr 30:3*
Holy
they *h.* all one breath, so that *Ec 3:19*
a man
that wisdom giveth life to them *Ec 7:12*
that *h.* it
neither *h.* they any more a   *Ec 9:5*
reward
neither *h.* they any more portion *Ec 9:6*
for ever
we *h.* a little sister and she hath *Ca 8:8*
no breasts
thou, O Solomon, must *h.* a   *Ca 8:12*
thousand
gone, because they *h.* no   *Isa 5:13*
knowledge
and as I *h.* purposed, so shall *Isa 14:24*
it stand
pass over, there also shalt   *Isa 23:12*
thou *h.* no rest
h. a strong city, salvation will *Isa 26:1*
God appoint
ye shall *h.* a song as in the   *Isa 30:29*
night
bring blind that *h.* eyes, death *Isa 43:8*
that *h.* ears
and my servant whom I *h.*   *Isa 43:10*
chosen
h. not I the Lord? there is no *Isa 45:21*
God beside me
in the Lord *h.* I righteousness *Isa 45:24*
and strength
children which thou shalt *h.*   *Isa 49:20*
shall say
me these, seeing I *h.* lost my *Isa 49:21*
children
is my hand shortened? *h.* I no *Isa 50:2*
power to deliver
this *h.* of my hand, ye shall   *Isa 50:11*
lie down in sorrow
therefore what *h.* I here, saith *Isa 52:5*
the Lord
are greedy dogs, which never *Isa 56:11*
h. enough
for your shame you shall *h.*   *Isa 61:7*
double
which *h.* eyes and see not,   *Jer 5:21*
which *h.* ears
my people love to *h.* it so,   *Jer 5:31*
what will ye do in
sword of Lord devour, no   *Jer 12:12*
flesh shall *h.* peace

the sword, neither shall ye *h.* *Jer 14:13*
famine
neither shalt *h.* sons nor   *Jer 16:2*
daughter in this place
the Lord hath said, Ye shall *Jer 23:17;*
h. peace   *29:7*
the shepherds shall *h.* no   *Jer 25:35*
way to flee
the peace thereof shall ye *h.* *Jer 29:7*
peace
end of all nations whither I *h.* *Jer 30:11*
scattered
ye shall not plant vineyard, nor *Jer 35:7*
h. any
he shall *h.* none to sit upon   *Jer 36:30*
throne of David
he shall *h.* his life for a prey, *Jer 38:2*
and shall live
to the which they *h.* a desire *Jer 44:14*
to return
little ones *h.* caused a cry to be *Jer 48:4*
heard
they will destroy till they *h.*   *Jer 49:9*
enough
the nation which *h.* neither   *Jer 49:31*
gates nor bars
this I recall to my mind,   *La 3:21*
therefore I. I hope
neither will I *h.* pity   *Eze 5:11;*
   7:4; 8:18; 9:10
let not your eye spare, neither *Eze 9:5*
h. ye pity
h. I any pleasure that the   *Eze 18:23*
wicked die
for I *h.* spoken it, saith the   *Eze 23:34*
Lord God
when I *h.* executed judgments *Eze 28:26*
upon all
for I *h.* poured out my spirit *Eze 39:29*
upon the
for any wisdom that I *h.* more *Da 2:30*
than any
I see four men loose, and they *Da 3:25*
h. no hurt
shall *h.* a chain of gold about *Da 5:7;*
his neck   *5:16*
and the king should *h.* no   *Da 6:2*
damage
for now they shall say we *h.* no *Ho 10:3*
king
that eat thy bread *h.* laid a wound *Ob 7*
night be unto you, ye shall not *Mic 3:6*
h. vision
this shall they *h.* for their   *Zep 2:10*
pride
eat, but ye *h.* not enough; ye *Hag 1:6*
drink
I *h.* chosen thee, saith the   *Hag 2:23*
Lord of hosts
h. we not all one father? hath *Mal 2:10*
not God
we *h.* Abraham to our father *M't 3:9;*
   Lu 3:8
take thy coat, let him *h.* thy *M't 5:40*
cloak also
if love them who love you   *M't 5:46*
what reward *h.*
verily I say, They *h.* their   *M't 6:2;*
reward   *6:5, 16*
the foxes *h.* holes, birds *h.*   *M't 8:20;*
nests   *Lu 9:58*
what *h.* we do with thee,   *M't 8:29;*
Jesus, thou Son of God   *M'k 1:24;*
   Lu 4:34
and he shall *h.* more   *M't 13:12;*
abundance   *25:29*
which ye hear, and *h.* not   *M't 13:17*
heard them
it is not lawful for thee to *h.* *M't 14:4;*
her   *M'k 6:18*
whence should we *h.* so much *M't 15:33*
bread in wilderness
how many loaves *h.* ye   *M't 15:34;*
   M'k 6:38; 8:5
if *h.* faith as a grain of   *M't 17:20;*
mustard   *21:21*
what shall I do, that I may *h.* *M't 19:16*
eternal life
followed thee, what shall we *M't 19:27*
h. therefore
ye *h.* the poor always, but   *M't 26:11;*
me ye *h.* not always   *M'k 14:7;*
   Joh 12:8
what further need *h.* we of   *M't 26:65*
witnesses
h. nothing to do with that   *M't 27:19*
just man
let him deliver him now, if he *M't 27:43*
will *h.* him

whole *h.* no need of the   *M'k 2:17*
physician
as long as they *h.* bridegroom *M'k 2:19*
with them
if any man *h.* ears to hear   *M'k 4:23;*
   7:16; Re 13:9
why so fearful, how is it ye *h.* *M'k 4:40*
no faith
saying, It is because we *h.* no *M'k 8:16*
bread
h. salt in yourselves, *h.* peace *M'k 9:50*
one with another
thou shalt *h.* treasure in   *M'k 10:21;*
heaven   *Lu 18:22*
but shall believe, shall *h.*   *M'k 11:23*
whatsoever he saith
believe ye receive them, and *M'k 11:24*
ye shall *h.* them
who love you, what thank *h.* *Lu 6:32;*
ye   *6:33, 34*
from him be taken what he   *Lu 8:18*
seemeth to *h.*
which of you shall *h.* a friend, *Lu 11:5*
and shall go
but rather give alms of   *Lu 11:41*
such things as ye *h.*
and after that *h.* no more that *Lu 12:4*
they can do
which neither *h.* storehouse *Lu 12:24*
nor barn
sell that ye *h.* and give alms, *Lu 12:33*
provide bags
must go and see it, I pray *h.* *Lu 14:18;*
me excused   *14:19*
art ever with me, all that I *h.* *Lu 15:31*
is thine
we will not *h.* this man to   *Lu 19:14*
reign over us
Satan hath desired to *h.* you, *Lu 22:31*
that he may
what communications ye *h.* *Lu 24:17*
one to another
spirit hath not flesh and   *Lu 24:39*
bones, as ye see me *h.*
he said, *H.* ye here any meat *Lu 24:41;*
   Joh 21:5
mother of Jesus said, They *h.* *Joh 2:3*
no wine
woman, what *h.* I to do with *Joh 2:4*
thee
should not perish, but *h.*   *Joh 3:15;*
everlasting life   *3:16*
woman answered and said, I *Joh 4:17*
h. no husband
he hath given the Son to *h.*   *Joh 5:26*
life in himself
and ye *h.* not his word abiding *Joh 5:38*
in you
know ye *h.* not the love of   *Joh 5:42*
God in you
believeth on him may *h.*   *Joh 6:40*
everlasting life
except ye eat his flesh, ye *h.* *Joh 6:53*
no life in you
tempting, that they might *h.* to *Joh 8:6*
accuse him
he that followeth me, shall *h.* *Joh 8:12*
the light of life
h. one father, even God; I *h.* *Joh 8:41;*
not a devil   *8:49*
if ye were blind, ye should *h.* *Joh 9:41*
no sin
I am come that they might *h.* *Joh 10:10*
life and
other sheep I *h.* which are *Joh 10:16*
not of this fold
walk while ye *h.* light, lest *Joh 12:35;*
darkness   *12:36*
that in me ye might *h.* peace, *Joh 16:33*
in world ye shall *h.* tribulation,
I *h.* overcome world
but ye *h.* a custom that I   *Joh 18:39*
should release one
we *h.* a law; we *h.* no king but *Joh 19:7;*
Caesar   *19:15*
that believing ye might *h.*   *Joh 20:31*
life thro' Jesus
silver and gold *h.* I none, but *Ac 3:6*
such as I *h.*
he said, Lord, what wilt thou *h.* *Ac 9:6*
me to do
in him we live, move, and *h.* *Ac 17:28*
our being
certain also of your own poets *Ac 17:28*
h. said
know that by this craft we *h.* *Ac 19:25*
our wealth
we *h.* four men which *h.* a   *Ac 21:23*
vow

when the Gentiles, which *h.*   Ro 2:14
not the law
ye *h.* your fruit unto holiness,   Ro 6:22
the end life
now if any man *h.* not Spirit of   Ro 8:9
Christ
this time I will come, and Sarah   Ro 9:9
shall *h.* a son
and all members *h.* not the   Ro 12:4
same office
hast thou faith? *h.* to thyself   Ro 14:22
before God
I *h.* whereof I may glory   Ro 15:17
through Christ
but we *h.* the mind of Christ   1Co 2:16
are naked, and *h.* no certain   1Co 4:11
dwellingplace
though instructors, yet *h.* ye   1Co 4:15
not many fathers
that one should *h.* his father's   1Co 5:1
wife
Holy Ghost which is in you,   1Co 6:19
which ye *h.* of God
to avoid fornication, let every   1Co 7:2
man *h.* his own wife, woman
h. her own husband
yet such shall *h.* trouble in the   1Co 7:28
flesh
they that *h.* wives be as tho'   1Co 7:29
they had none
I would *h.* you without   1Co 7:32
carefulness
I think also that I *h.* the   1Co 7:40
Spirit of God
we know, that we all *h.*   1Co 8:1
knowledge
h. we not power to eat and   1Co 9:4;
drink   9:5, 6
if a man *h.* long hair, it is a   1Co 11:14
shame to him
if a woman *h.* long hair, it is   1Co 11:15
a glory to her
we *h.* no such custom, nor   1Co 11:16
the churches of God
what, *h.* ye not houses to eat   1Co 11:22
and drink in
eye not say to hand, I *h.* no   1Co 12:21
need of thee
h. all the gifts of healing? do   1Co 12:30
all interpret
h. not charity, I am become   1Co 13:1
sounding brass
though I *h.* all faith and *h.*   1Co 13:2;
not charity   13:3
by your rejoicing which I *h.*   1Co 15:31
Christ Jesus
for some *h.* not the   1Co 15:34
knowledge of God
such trust *h.* we thro' Christ to   2Co 3:4
God-ward
seeing we *h.* this ministry, we   2Co 4:1
faint not
a performance out of that   2Co 8:11
which ye *h.*
he may *h.* to give to him that   Eph 4:28
needeth
h. no fellowship with the   Eph 5:11
unfruitful works
I *h.* you in my heart; but I *h.*   Ph'p 1:7;
all   4:18
and love which ye *h.* to all the   Col 1:4
saints
ye knew what great conflict I *h.*   Col 2:1
for you
if any man *h.* a quarrel   Col 3:13
against any
knowing that ye also *h.* a   Col 4:1
Master in heaven
ye suffered, as they *h.* of the   1Th 2:14
Jews
pray for us, for all men *h.* not   2Th 3:2
faith
not because we *h.* not power,   2Th 3:9
but to make
who will *h.* all men to be saved   1Ti 2:4
the eyes of him with whom   Heb 4:13
we *h.* to do
seeing then that we *h.* a great   Heb 4:14
high priest
by reason of use *h.* their   Heb 5:14
senses exercised
which hope we *h.* as an   Heb 6:19
anchor of the soul
we *h.* such an High Priest set   Heb 8:1
on right hand
that this man *h.* somewhat also   Heb 8:3
to offer
that ye *h.* in heaven a better   Heb 10:34
substance

be content with such things as   Heb 13:5
ye *h.*
we *h.* an altar whereof they   Heb 13:10
h. no right to eat
here *h.* we no continuing   Heb 13:14
city, we seek one
but let patience *h.* her perfect   Jas 1:4
work
h. not faith of Christ with   Jas 2:1
respect of persons
and *h.* not works can faith   Jas 2:14
save him
even so faith, if it *h.* not   Jas 2:17
works, is dead
a man may say, thou hast   Jas 2:18
faith, and I *h.* works
if ye *h.* bitter envy and strife   Jas 3:14
in your hearts
ye lust and *h.* not, ye desire to   Jas 4:2
h. ye fight and war, yet ye
h. not because ye ask not
above all things *h.* fervent   1Pe 4:8
charity
we *h.* a more sure word of   2Pe 1:19
prophecy
an heart they *h.* exercised with   2Pe 2:14
covetousness
if we say, We *h.* no sin, deceive   1Jo 1:8
ourselves
we *h.* an Advocate with the   1Jo 2:1
Father, Jesus
but ye *h.* an unction from the   1Jo 2:20
Holy One
and this commandment *h.* we   1Jo 4:21
from him
that ye may know that ye *h.*   1Jo 5:13
eternal life
this is the confidence that we   1Jo 5:14
h. in him
know we *h.* the petitions we   1Jo 5:15
desired of him
I *h.* no greater joy than to hear   3Jo 4
that my
Diotrephes, who loveth to *h.* the   3Jo 9
pre-eminence
I *h.* the keys of hell and of   Re 1:18
death
yet I *h.* somewhat against thee   Re 2:4;
      2:14, 20
and ye shall *h.* tribulation ten   Re 2:10
days
to you, and to as many as *h.*   Re 2:24
not this doctrine
but what ye *h.* already, hold   Re 2:25
fast till I come
which *h.* not the seal of God in   Re 9:4
their foreheads
and *h.* the testimony of Jesus   Re 12:17
Christ
they *h.* no rest day nor night   Re 14:11
these *h.* one mind, and give   Re 17:13
their power
of brethren that *h.* the   Re 19:10
testimony of Jesus
liars shall *h.* their part in the   Re 21:8
lake that burns
that they may *h.* right to the   Re 22:14
tree of life

HAVEN

dwell at the *h.* of the sea   Ge 49:13
he shall be for an *h.* of ships   Ge 49:13
them unto their desired *h.*   Ps 107:30
the *h.* was not commodious   Ac 27:12
which is an *h.* at Crete   Ac 27:12

HAVENS

place called The fair *h.*   Ac 27:8

HAVILAH

compasseth whole land of *H.*   Ge 2:11
Seba, *H.*, and Sabtah   Ge 10:7; 1Ch 1:9
Ophir, and *H.*   Ge 10:29; 1Ch 1:23
dwelt from *H.* unto Shur   Ge 25:18
from *H.* until thou comest to   1Sa 15:7

HAVING

h. his uncleanness upon him   Le 7:20;
      22:3
h. her sickness; *h.* a wen or   Le 20:18;
scurvy   22:22
into a trance, but *h.* his eyes   Nu 24:4;
open   24:16
would ye stay for them from *h.*   Ru 1:13
husbands
h. a drawn sword in his hand   1Ch 21:16

h. Judah and Benjamin on   2Ch 11:12
his side
mourning, and *h.* his head   Es 6:12
covered
which *h.* no guide, overseer, or   Pr 6:7
ruler
and *h.* neither bars nor gates   Eze 38:11
pass ye away, *h.* thy   Mic 1:11
shamenaked
thy king cometh to thee, *h.*   Zec 9:9
salvation
he taught as one *h.* authority   M't 7:29
under authority, *h.* soldiers   M't 8:9;
      Lu 7:8
were as sheep *h.* no shepherd   M't 9:36;
      M'k 6:34
rather than *h.* two hands or   M't 18:8
two feet
rather than *h.* two eyes to be   M't 18:9;
cast   M'k 9:43
how camest, not *h.* a   M't 22:12
wedding garment
if a man die, *h.* no children   M't 22:24;
      Lu 20:28
and *h.* no issue, left his wife   M't 22:25
to his brother
woman *h.* an alabaster box   M't 26:7;
      M'k 14:3
and *h.* nothing to eat, Jesus   M'k 8:1
called
h. eyes, see ye not? *h.* ears,   M'k 8:18
hear ye not
a fig tree *h.* leaves; *h.* one   M'k 11:13;
son   12:6
woman *h.* an issue of blood   Lu 8:43
twelve years
what man of you *h.* an   Lu 15:4
hundred sheep
either what woman *h.* ten   Lu 15:8
pieces of silver
but which of you *h.* a servant   Lu 17:7
ploughing
how knows he letters, *h.* never   Joh 7:15
learned
then Simeon Peter *h.* a sword   Joh 18:10
drew it
h. land, sold it, and brought   Ac 4:37
the money
h. a good report of the Jews   Ac 22:12
who dwelt
h. more perfect knowledge of   Ac 24:22
that way
h. not the law, are a law to   Ro 2:14
themselves
h. then gifts differing according   Ro 12:6
to grace given
h. a great desire these many   Ro 15:23
years
h. a matter against another, go   1Co 6:1
to law
he that standeth stedfast *h.* no   1Co 7:37
necessity
we *h.* the same spirit of faith,   2Co 4:13
as written
as *h.* nothing, and yet   2Co 6:10
possessing all things
h. therefore these promises,   2Co 7:1
beloved, cleanse
ye always *h.* all sufficiency in   2Co 9:8
all things
h. in a readiness to revenge   2Co 10:6
all disobedience
but *h.* hope, when your faith   2Co 10:15
is increased
h. ho hope; not *h.* spot or   Eph 2:12;
wrinkle   5:27
h. your loins girt about with   Eph 6:14
truth
h. a desire to depart, and be   Ph'p 1:23
with Christ
h. this confidence; *h.* the   Ph'p 1:25;
same conflict   1:30
h. same love; not *h.* my own   Ph'p 2:2;
righteousness   3:9
h. made peace thro' the blood   Col 1:20
of his cross
h. nourishment ministered, and   Col 2:19
knit together
h. his children in subjection   1Ti 3:4
with all gravity
h. the promise of the life that   1Ti 4:8
now is
h. damnation, because they   1Ti 5:12
have cast off
and *h.* food and raiment, let us   1Ti 6:8
be content
h. this seal, the Lord knoweth   2Ti 2:19
his

h. a form of godliness, denying   2Ti 3:5
the power
they shall heap teachers, *h.*   2Ti 4:3
itching ears
h. faithful children, not   Tit 1:6
accused of riot
but *h.* seen them afar off   Heb 11:13
h. conversation honest among   1Pe 2:12
Gentiles
h. a good conscience, they   1Pe 3:16
may be ashamed
h. eyes full of adultery, that   2Pe 2:14
cannot cease
these be sensual, *h.* not the   Jude 19
Spirit
h. seven horns; *h.* every one   Re 5:6;
harps   5:8
I saw an angel, *h.* the seal of the   Re 7:2
living God
h. a golden censer; *h.*   Re 8:3;
breastplates   9:17
h. seven heads; *h.* great wrath   Re 12:3;
   12:12
h. the everlasting gospel to   Re 14:6
preach to them
h. the harps of God; *h.* a   Re 15:2;
golden cup   17:4
h. great power; *h.* the key of   Re 18:1;
the pit   20:1
the holy Jerusalem, *h.* the   Re 21:11
glory of God

HAVOC

make *h.* of such places (A)(E)   Ps 74:8
made *h.* of them (E)   Ac 9:21
faith he once made *h.* (E)   Ga 1:23

HAVOCK

Saul, he made *h.* of the church   Ac 8:3
shamefully treated, laid waste the   Ac 8:3
church with cruelty and violence
(A)
Saul laid waste the church   Ac 8:3
(E)(R)
Saul was harrying the church   Ac 8:3
(N)
Saul harassed the church   Ac 8:3
bitterly (P)

HAVOTH-JAIR

thereof, and called them *H.*   Nu 32:41
which are called *H.* unto this   J'g 10:4
day

HAWK

the fish *h.*, the black eagle (B)   Le 11:13
the owl, and the night *h.* and   Le 11:16;
   De 14:15
cuckow, and the *h.* after his   Le 11:16;
kind   De 14:15
Doth the *h.* fly by thy   Job 39:26
wisdom
the *h.* and porcupine (R)   Isa 34:11

HAY

The *h.* appeareth, and the   Pr 27:25
tender
for the *h.* is withered away, the   Isa 15:6
silver, precious stones, wood,   1Co 3:12
h.

HAZAEL

anoint *H.* to be king over Syria   1Ki 19:15
that escapeth the sword of   1Ki 19:17
H. shall
the king said unto *H.*, Take a   2Ki 8:8
So *H.* went to meet him, and   2Ki 8:9
took
And *H.* said, Why weepeth my   2Ki 8:12
And *H.*, said, But what, is thy   2Ki 8:13
and *H.* reigned in his stead   2Ki 8:15
of Ahab to war against *H.*   2Ki 8:28
king of
Ramah, when he fought   2Ki 8:29
against *H.*
and all Israel, because of *H.*   2Ki 9:14
king
when he fought with *H.* king   2Ki 9:15
and *H.* smote them in all the   2Ki 10:32
Then *H.* king of Syria went   2Ki 12:17
up
and *H.* set his face to go up to   2Ki 12:17
and sent it to *H.* king of   2Ki 12:18
Syria

into the hand of *H.* king of   2Ki 13:3
Syria
hand of Ben-hadad the son of   2Ki 13:3
H.
But *H.* king of Syria oppressed   2Ki 13:32
So *H.* king of Syria died   2Ki 13:24
hand of Ben-hadad, the son   2Ki 13:25
of *H.*
to war against *H.* king of   2Ch 22:5
Syria
Ramah, when he fought with   2Ch 22:6
H.
send a fire into the house of *H.*   Am 1:4

HAZAIAH

Col-hozeh, the son of *H.* the   Ne 11:5
son

HAZAR-ADDAR

and shall go on to *H.* and pass   Nu 34:4

HAZARDED

Men that have *h.* their lives   Ac 15:26

HAZAR-ENAN

goings out of it shall be at *H.*   Nu 34:9
east border from *H.* to   Nu 34:10
Shepham
border from the sea shall be   Eze 47:17
H.
as one goeth to Hamath *H.*   Eze 48:1

HAZAR-GADDAH

H. and Heshmon, and   Jos 15:27
Beth-palet

HAZAR-HATTICON

H. which is by the coast of   Eze 47:16

HAZARMAVETH

Sheleph, and *H.* and Jerah   Ge 10:26;
   1Ch 1:20

HAZAR-SHUAL

And *H.* and Beer-sheba, and   Jos 15:28
H. and Balah, and Azem   Jos 19:3
Beer-sheba, and Moladah, and   1Ch 4:28
H.
at *H.* and at Beer-sheba and   Ne 11:27

HAZAR-SUSAH

and Beth-marcaboth, and *H.*   Jos 19:5

HAZAR-SUSIM

at Beth-marcaboth, and *H.*   1Ch 4:31

HAZAZON-TAMAR

they be in *H.* which is Engedi   2Ch 20:2

HAZEL

and of the *h.* and chestnut   Ge 30:37
tree

HAZELELPONI

the name of their sister was *H.*   1Ch 4:3

HAZERIM

the Avims which dwelt in *H.*   De 2:23

HAZEROTH

from Kibroth-hattaavah unto   Nu 11:35
H.
and abode at *H.*   Nu 11:35
the people removed from *H.*   Nu 12:16
and encamped at *H.*   Nu 33:17
And they departed from *H.*   Nu 33:18
Laban, and *H.*, and Dizahab   De 1:1

HAZEZON-TAMAR

the Amorites, that dwelt in *H.*   Ge 14:7

HAZIEL

Shelomith, and *H.*, and Haran   1Ch 23:9

HAZO

Chesed, and *H.*, and Pildash   Ge 22:22

HAZOR

when Jabin king of *H.* had   Jos 11:1
heard
and took *H.*, and smote the   Jos 11:10
king
for *H.* beforetime was the   Jos 11:10
head
and he burnt *H.* with fire   Jos 11:11
Israel burned none of them,   Jos 11:13
save *H.*
Madon, one; the king of *H.*,   Jos 12:19
one
And Kedesh, and *H.* and   Jos 15:23
Ithnan
And *H.* Hadattah, and   Jos 15:25
Kerioth, and Hezron, which   Jos 15:25
is *H.*
And Adamah, and Ramah,   Jos 19:36
and *H.*
king of Caanan, that reigned in   J'g 4:2
H.
peace between Jabin the king   J'g 4:17
of *H.*
of Sisera, captain of the host   1Sa 12:9
of *H.*
and *H.*, and Megiddo, and   1Ki 9:15
Gezer
Kedesh, and *H.*, and Gilead   2Ki 15:29
H.., Ramah, Gittaim   Ne 11:33
and concerning the kingdoms   Jer 49:28
of *H.*
dwell deep. O ye inhabitants   Jer 49:30
of *H.*
H. shall be a dwelling for   Jer 49:33
dragons

HE

and *h.* shall rule over thee   Ge 3:16
not always strive with man, for   Ge 6:3
h. is flesh
h. with whom it is found shall   Ge 44:10
be my servant
younger brother shall be   Ge 48:19
greater than *h.*
art *h.* whom thy brethren shall   Ge 49:8
praise
h. shall be thy spokesman to   Ex 4:16
people, and *h.* shall be to
thee instead of a mouth
and hardened his heart, *h.* and   Ex 9:34
his servants
h. hath put in his heart that   Ex 35:34
he may teach both *h.* and
h. among the sons of Aaron   Le 7:33
that offereth
shall go out in jubilee, *h.* and   Le 25:54
his children
and cursed is *h.* that curseth   Nu 24:9
thee
came, *h.* and all his people to   De 3:1
it is *h.* that giveth power to get   De 8:18
wealth
cursed be *h.*   De 27:16; 27:17-26
h. that doth go with thee, *h.*   De 31:6;
will not fail   31:8
is not *h.* thy Father that hath   De 32:6
bought thee
I, even I am *h.* and there is   De 32:39;
no God with me   Isa 41:4; 43:10. 13;
   46:4; 48:12
Lord your God is *h.* that   Jos 23:3;
fought for you   23:10
what man is *h.* will begin to   J'g 10:18
fight
I am *h.* that came out of the   1Sa 4:16
army
there was not a goodlier person   1Sa 9:2
this is *h.* as his name is so is   1Sa 16:12
h.
who fell on two men better   1Ki 2:32
than *h.*
she and *h.* and her house did   1Ki 17:15
eat many days
art thou *h.* that troublest   1Ki 18:17
Israel
is not that *h.* whose places   2Ki 18:22;
   Isa 36:7
h. in first year of reign opened   2Ch 29:3
doors
if not, where, and who is *h.*   Job 9:24

who is *h.* that will plead with   *Job 13:19*
me
man dieth, and where is *h.*   *Job 14:10;*
  20:7; Isa 63:11
thou art *h.* that took me out of   *Ps 22:9*
the womb
h. it is shall tread down   *Ps 60:12*
enemies   *108:13*
h. that is our God is the God   *Ps 68:20*
of salvation
h. is God, it is *h.* that hath   *Ps 100:3*
made us
it is *h.* that giveth salvation   *Ps 144:10*
to kings
that trusteth in Lord happy is   *Pr 16:20;*
h.   *29:18*
h. that is higher than the highest   *Ec 5:8*
regardeth
I say that an untimely birth is   *Ec 6:3*
better than *h.*
it is *h.* sitteth on the circle of   *Isa 40:22*
the earth
I, even I, am *h.* that   *Isa 51:12;*
comforteth you   *52:6; Joh 18:5, 6,8;*
  Re 1:18; 2:23
have belied Lord, and said, It   *Jer 5:12*
is not *h.*
art not thou *h.*, O Lord our   *Jer 14:22*
god
the king is not *h.* that can do   *Jer 38:5*
any thing
and *h.* also shall be in   *Jer 48:26*
derision
art thou *h.* of whom I have   *Eze 38:17*
spoken
the man that is more   *Hab 1:13*
righteous than *h.*
where is *h.* that is born king of   *M't 2:2*
the Jews
this is *h.* that was spoken of by   *M't 3:3*
the prophet
art thou *h.* that should come   *M't 11:3;*
  Lu 7:19, 20
h. that is not with me is   *M't 12:30;*
against me, and *h.* that   *Lu 11:23*
gathereth not with me
what think ye of Christ?   *M't 22:42*
whose son is *h.*
h. is in the desert, he is in the   *M't 24:26*
secret chamber
the same is *h.* hold him fast   *M't 26:48;*
  M'k 14:44
and there is none other but   *M'k 12:32*
h.
h. to whom the Son will   *Lu 10:22*
reveal him
and *h.* from within shall   *Lu 11:7*
answer and say
who is *h.* that gave thee this   *Lu 20:2*
authority
h. that sitteth at meat, or *h.*   *Lu 22:27*
that serveth
they said, *H.* is not here, but   *Lu 24:6*
is risen
we trusted *h.* should have   *Lu 24:21*
redeemed Israel
this was *h.* of whom I spake   *Joh 1:15;*
  1:30
Jesus saith, I that speak to   *Joh 4:26*
thee, am *h.*
where is *h.?* is not this *h.* they   *Joh 7:11;*
seek to kill   *7:25*
if ye believe not that I am *h.*   *Joh 8:24*
ye shall die
then shall ye know that I am   *Joh 8:28*
h.
they said, Is not this *h.* that sat   *Joh 9:8*
and begged
some said, This is *h.*; others   *Joh 9:9*
said, *H.* is like him: but *h.* said,
I am *h.*
who is *h.* Lord; *h.* that talketh   *Joh 9:36;*
with thee   *9:37*
I tell you that ye may   *Joh 13:19*
believe that I am *h.*
they knew it was *h.* who sat for   *Ac 3:10*
alms
this is *h.* that was in the church   *Ac 7:38*
in wilderness
is not this *h.* that destroyed   *Ac 9:21*
them who called
Peter said, I am *h.* whom   *Ac 10:21*
ye seek
h. that was ordained of God   *Ac 10:42*
to be the judge
whom think ye that I am? I   *Ac 13:25*
am not *h.*
h. is not a Jew that is one   *Ro 2:28*
outwardly

but *h.* is a Jew that is one   *Ro 2:29*
inwardly
h. that in these things serveth   *Ro 14:18*
Christ
are we stronger than *h.*   *1Co 10:22*
of himself think this again   *2Co 10:7*
that as *h.* is Christ's even so
are we Christ's
faithful is *h.* that calleth you,   *1Th 5:24*
will do it
h. who letteth, will let till *h.* be   *2Th 2:7*
taken
what son is *h.* the father   *Heb 12:7*
chasteneth not
but *h.* for our profit, that we   *Heb 12:10*
might be partakers
when *h.* testified (S)   *1Pe 1:11*
as *h.* which hath called you is   *1Pe 1:15*
holy
if we walk in light, as *h.* is in   *1Jo 1:7*
the light
when he shall appear, we may   *1Jo 2:28*
have confidence
is righteous, even as *h.* is   *1Jo 3:7*
righteous
dwelleth in him, and *h.* in him   *1Jo 3:24;*
  4:15
greater is *h.* that is in you, than   *1Jo 4:4*
h. in world
because as *h.* is so are we in   *1Jo 4:17*
this world
h. that hath the Son, hath life;   *1Jo 5:12*
and *h.* that hath not the Son
follow not evil, *h.* that doeth   *3 Jo 11*
good is of God; *h.* that doeth
evil hath not seen God
holy is *h.* that hath part in first   *Re 20:6*
resurrection
h. that is unjust, *h.* that is   *Re 22:11*
filthy

HE-GOATS

the *h.* (E)(S)   *2Ch 11:15*

HEAD

it shall bruise thy *h.*, thou   *Ge 3:15*
bruise his heel
yet Pharaoh shall lift up thy   *Ge 40:13;*
h.   *40:19*
blessings shall be on the *h.* of   *Ge 49:26;*
Joseph, and on the top of   *De 33:16*
the *h.* of him
Aaron and his sons shall put   *Ex 29:10;*
their hands upon *h.* of bullock   *Le 4:4;*
  8:14
put hands on *h.* of the ram   *Ex 29:15;*
  29:19; Le 8:18, 22
shall put hand on the *h.* of   *Le 1:4*
burnt offering
lay his hand on the *h.* of   *Le 3:2*
his offering
lay his hand on the *h.* of   *Le 4:29;*
sin offering   *4:33*
he is leprous, his plague is in   *Le 13:44*
his *h.*
his clothes shall be rent, and   *Le 13:45*
his *h.* bare
they shall not make baldness   *Le 21:5*
on their *h.*
shall not uncover his *h.* nor   *Le 21:10*
rend his clothes
h. of other's house (R)(S)   *Nu 3:24;*
  3:30, 35; 25:14
the priest shall uncover the   *Nu 5:18*
woman's *h.*
there shall no razor come on the   *Nu 6:5*
Nazarite's *h.*
the consecration of his God is   *Nu 6:7*
on his *h.*
then he shall shave his *h.*   *Nu 6:9;*
  6:18; De 21:12
and he shall hallow his *h.* that   *Nu 6:11*
same day
h. of clans (B)(E)(R)   *Nu 25:15*
his blood be on his *h.* blood on   *Jos 2:19*
our *h.*
she smote of Sisera's *h.* when   *J'g 5:26*
she had
shalt bear a son, no razor shall   *J'g 13:5*
come on his *h.*
Goliath's *h.*; cut off Saul's *h.*   *1Sa 17:57;*
  31:9
head (S)   *1Sa 19:13;*
  19:16; 26:7, 11, 12, 16
the wickedness of Nabal on   *1Sa 25:39*
his own *h.*

I will make thee keeper of my   *1Sa 28:2*
h. for ever
a man came, and earth upon   *2Sa 1:2;*
his *h.*   *15:32*
thy blood be upon thy *h.*   *2Sa 1:16;*
  1Ki 2:37
Abner was wroth, and said,   *2Sa 3:8*
Am I a dog's *h.*
let it rest on *h.* of Joab, on his   *2Sa 3:29*
house
let me go over, and take off   *2Sa 16:9*
his *h.*
take thy master from thy *h.*   *2Ki 2:3;*
to-day   *2:5*
and he said unto his father,   *2Ki 4:19*
My *h.* my *h.*
if the *h.* of Elisha shall stand   *2Ki 6:31*
on him
son of a murderer sent to take   *2Ki 6:32*
away my *h.*
the virgin despised thee, the   *2Ki 19:21;*
daughter of Jerusalem hath   *Isa 37:22*
shaken her *h.* at thee
did lift up the *h.* of   *2Ki 25:27;*
Jehoiachin   *Jer 52:31*
by recompensing his way on   *2Ch 6:23*
his *h.*
our iniquities are increased   *Ezr 9:6*
over our *h.*
and turn their reproach on their   *Ne 4:4*
own *h.*
his device should return on his   *Es 9:25*
own *h.*
Job arose, shaved his *h.* and   *Job 1:20*
fell down
if righteous, yet will I not lift   *Job 10:15*
up my *h.*
and I could shake my *h.* at   *Job 16:4*
you
my glory and the lifter up of   *Ps 3:3*
mine *h.*
his mischief shall return on his   *Ps 7:16*
own *h.*
they shoot out the lip, they   *Ps 22:7*
shake the *h.*
thou anointest my *h.* with oil,   *Ps 23:5*
cup runneth
now shall my *h.* be lifted up   *Ps 27:6*
above enemies
mine iniquities are gone over   *Ps 38:4*
mine *h.*
a shaking of the *h.* among the   *Ps 44:14*
people
Ephraim is the strength of my   *Ps 60:7;*
h.   *108:8*
God shall wound the *h.* of his   *Ps 68:21*
enemies
they that hate thee have lift up   *Ps 83:2*
the *h.*
therefore shall he lift up the *h.*   *Ps 110:7*
as for the *h.* of those that   *Ps 140:9*
compass me
be an oil, which shall not   *Ps 141:5*
break my *h.*
blessings are on the *h.* of the   *Pr 10:6*
just
blessing on the *h.* of him   *Pr 11:26*
which selleth corn
shalt heap coals of fire on his   *Pr 25:22;*
h.   *Ro 12:20*
the wise man's eyes are in his   *Ec 2:14*
h.
his left hand is under my *h.*   *Ca 2:6; 8:3*
my *h.* is filled with dew, my   *Ca 5:2*
locks with drops
his *h.* as most fine gold; thy *h.*   *Ca 5:11;*
as Carmel   *7:5*
the whole *h.* is sick and the   *Isa 1:5*
heart faint
everlasting joy shall be on   *Isa 51:11*
their *h.*
is it to bow down his *h.* as a   *Isa 58:5*
bulrush
he put on an helmet of   *Isa 59:17*
salvation on his *h.*
go forth, and thine hands on   *Jer 2:37*
thy *h.*
O that my *h.* were waters, mine   *Jer 9:1*
eyes tears
fall grievously on the *h.* of   *Jer 23:19;*
wicked   *30:23*
to be *h.* over you (A)   *Jer 31:7*
her adversaries are the *h.* (S)   *La 1:5*
recompense their way on their   *Eze 9:10*
h.
every *h.* was made bald,   *Eze 29:18*
shoulder peeled
O king, thou art this *h.* of gold   *Da 2:38*

return your recompense on   *Joe 3:4;*
your *h.*   *3:7*
that pant after dust on the *h.* of   *Am 2:7*
the poor
and I will bring baldness on   *Am 8:10*
every *h.*
he said, Cut them in the *h.* all   *Am 9:1*
of them
so that no man did lift up his   *Zec 1:21*
h.
then set the crowns on the *h.*   *Zec 6:11*
of Joshua
neither shalt thou swear by   *M't 5:36*
thy *h.*
whose *h.* is this (N)   *M't 22:20*
and they smote him on the   *M't 27:30;*
h.   *M'k 15:19*
she said, The *h.* of John the   *M'k 6:24*
Baptist
my *h.* with oil thou didst not   *Lu 7:46*
anoint
not feet only, but also my   *Joh 13:9*
hands and *h.*
creature's watching with   *Ro 8:19*
outstretched *h.* and expectancy
(B)
his *h.* covered, dishonoureth   *1Co 11:4*
his *h.*
the woman ought to have   *1Co 11:10*
power on her *h.*
the *h.* to the feet, I have no   *1Co 12:21*
need of you
put all things under his feet,   *Eph 1:22;*
and gave him as *h.* to the   *4:15; Col 1:18*
church
not holding the *h.* from which   *Col 2:19*
the body
eyes flame of fire, and his *h.*   *Re 19:12*
many crowns

HEAD for ruler, governor

one rod shall be for the *h.* of   *Nu 17:3*
the house
he was *h.* over a people of a   *Nu 25:15*
chief house
Lord will make thee the *h.*   *De 28:13*
not the tail
he shall be the *h.* and thou   *De 28:44*
shalt be the tail
each one an *h.* of house of   *Jos 22:14*
their fathers
he shall be *h.* over all Gilead   *J'g 10:18;*
  11:8
shall I be your *h.?* the people   *J'g 11:9;*
made him *h.*   *11:11*
wast thou not made the *h.* of   *1Sa 15:17*
Israel
thou hast kept me to be *h.*   *2Sa 22:44;*
  Ps 18:43
and thou art exalted as *h.*   *1Ch 29:11*
above all
h. of Damascus is Rezin, *h.* of   *Isa 7:8;*
Samaria   *7:9*
Lord will cut off from Israel *h.*   *Isa 9:14*
and tail
the ancient and honourable, he   *Isa 9:15*
is the *h.*
nor work which *h.* or tail, or   *Isa 19:15*
rush, may do
thou art Gilead to me, *h.* of   *Jer 22:6*
Lebanon
they shall appoint themselves   *Ho 1:11*
one *h.*
woundest the *h.* out of house   *Hab 3:13*
of wicked
thou didst strike through the   *Hab 3:14*
h. of his villages
that the *h.* of every man is   *1Co 11:3*
Christ, the *h.* of the woman
is the man, the *h.* of Christ. is
the husband is the *h.* of the   *Eph 5:23*
wife, even as Christ is *h.* of
who is the *h.* of all   *Col 2:10*
principality and power

HEAD for top, chief

which are on the *h.* of fat   *Isa 28:1;*
valleys   *28:4*
they lie at the *h.* of all the   *Isa 51:20*
streets
built high places at *h.* of the   *Eze 16:25*
way
choose it at the *h.* of the way   *Eze 21:19*
to the city
king of Babylon stood at the   *Eze 21:21*
h. of two ways

HEAD with *HAIR, HAIRS*

the man whose *hair* is fallen   *Le 13:40*
off his *h.*
the leper shall shave all his *hair*   *Le 14:9*
off his *h.*
let the locks of the *hair* of his *h.*   *Nu 6:5*
grow
and shalt take the *hair* of *h.* of   *Nu 6:18*
his separation
the *hair* of his *h.* began to   *J'g 16:22*
grow again
not an *hair* of his *h.* shall fall   *1Sa 14:45*
to ground
weighed *hair* of his *h.* at 200   *2Sa 14:26*
shekels
I plucked off the *hair* of my *h.*   *Ezr 9:3*
and beard
they are more than *hairs* of   *Ps 40:12;*
my *h.*   *69:4*
and the *hair* of thine *h.* like   *Ca 7:5*
purple
nor was an *hair* of their *h.*   *Da 3:27*
singed
the *hair* of his *h.* like the pure   *Da 7:9*
wool
hairs of your *h.* are   *M't 10:30;*
numbered   *Lu 12:7*
did wipe them with *hairs* of   *Lu 7:38;*
her *h.*   *7:44*
there shall not an *hair* of your   *Lu 21:18*
h. perish
not an *hair* fall from the *h.* of   *Ac 27:34*
any
his *h.* and *hairs* were white   *Re 1:14*
like wool

HEAD *OF THE CORNER*

is become the *h.* of the   *M't 21:42;*
corner   *M'k 12:10; Lu 20:17; Ac 4:11;*
  1Pe 2:7

AXE HEAD

and the *axe h.* slippeth from   *De 19:5*
the helve
axe h. fell into the water and   *2Ki 6:5*
he cried

BED'S HEAD

Israel bowed himself on the   *Ge 47:31*
bed's h.

HOARY HEAD

thou shalt rise before the   *Le 19:32*
hoary h.

SPEAR'S HEAD

spear's h. weighed 600 shekels   *1Sa 17:7;*
  2Sa 21:16

HEADACHE

overcharged with *h.* (A)   *Lu 21:34*

HEADBANDS

and their *h.* (S)   *Isa 3:18*
Lord will take away the *h.* and   *Isa 3:20*
tablets
the *h.* (A)(B)   *Isa 3:20*
battling with a *h.* (N)   *M't 14:24*
who is *h.* for death (P)   *2Co 4:16*

HEADDRESSES

The *h.* and ornaments (R)(S)   *Isa 3:20*

HEADLONG

road leads *h.* into (B)   *Nu 22:32*
the counsel of the froward is   *Job 5:13*
carried *h.*
that they might cast him down   *Lu 4:29*
h.
falling *h.* he burst asunder in   *Ac 1:18*
midst

HEADQUARTERS

into his *h.* (N)   *Joh 18:33; 19:9*
to all at *h.* (N)   *Ph'p 1:13*

HEADS

h. of full grain (B)   *Ge 41:5; Le 2:14*
they bowed down their *h.*   *Ge 43:28;*
  Ex 4:31

uncover not your *h.* lest ye die   *Le 10:6*
h. of the houses (E)(R)   *Nu 31:26;*
  24:31; 26:32; 2Ch 26:12;
  Ezr 1:5; Ne 7:70
h. of your tribes   *De 1:15*
(B)(E)(R)(S)
and put dust upon their *h.*   *Jos 7:6;*
  Job 2:12
so that they lifted up their *h.*   *J'g 8:28*
no more
all the evil did God render   *J'g 9:57*
upon their *h.*
h. of grain (B)   *Ru 2:2*
should it not be with the *h.* of   *1Sa 29:4*
these
let us, I pray, put ropes on   *1Ki 20:31*
our *h.*
put ropes on their *h.* and   *1Ki 20:32*
came to the king
take ye the *h.* of your master's   *2Ki 10:6*
sons
they have brought the *h.* of   *2Ki 10:8*
the king's sons
h. of father's houses (R)   *1Ch 7:3; 24:4*
h. of the clans (B)(E)(R)   *1Ch 7:40*
the *h.* of the fathers (S)   *1Ch 9:9;*
  9:33; 15:12; 29:6; 2Ch 19:8; 23:2;
  Ezr 1:5; 4:2, 3; 8:29; 10:16; Ne 8:13;
  12:12, 23
h. of the fathers' houses (S)   *2Ch 1:2;*
  26:12; Ezr 2:68; 3:12; 8:1
h. of the father's houses (S)   *Ne 7:70;*
  7:71; 11:13
h. of the province (B)   *Ne 11:3*
h. of grain (B)(R)   *Job 24:24*
lift up your *h.,* O ye gates, and   *Ps 24:7;*
be lift   *24:9*
thou hast caused men to ride   *Ps 66:12*
over our *h.*
thou brakest *h.* of the dragons   *Ps 74:13*
in waters
thou brakest the *h.* of   *Ps 74:14*
leviathan in pieces
they looked on me, they   *Ps 109:25*
shaked their *h.*
on all their *h.* shall be baldness   *Isa 15:2*
to Zion songs, and everlasting   *Isa 35:10*
joy on *h.*
they were ashamed and covered   *Jer 14:3*
h.
plowmen were ashamed, they   *Jer 14:4*
covered *h.*
and baldness shall be on all   *Eze 7:18*
their *h.*
I will recompense their way   *Eze 11:21;*
on *h.*   *22:31*
they laid their swords under   *Eze 32:27*
their *h.*
shall have linen bonnets on   *Eze 44:18*
their *h.*
nor shall they shave, they   *Eze 44:20*
shall poll their *h.*
reviled, wagging their *h.*   *M't 27:39;*
  M'k 15:29
then look up, and lift up your   *Lu 21:28*
h.
he said, Your blood be upon   *Ac 18:6*
your own *h.*
h. up in one word (B)   *Ro 13:9*
hung over our *h.*   *Col 2:14*
and on their *h.* were as it were   *Re 9:7*
crowns
their tails were like to serpents,   *Re 9:19*
and had *h.*
I saw a beast having seven *h.*   *Re 13:1*
and on his *h.*
I saw one of his *h.* as it were   *Re 13:3*
wounded to death
seven *h.* are seven mountains,   *Re 17:9*
on which
cast dust on their *h.* and cried,   *Re 18:19*
Alas!

HEADS for governors

and made them *h.* over the   *Ex 18:25*
people
they were *h.* of thousands in   *Nu 1:16*
Israel
take all *h.* of people and hang   *Nu 25:4*
them
Reuben and Gad answered   *Jos 22:21*
the *h.*
Joshua called for their *h.* and   *Jos 23:2*
judges
the *h.* of Israel were two   *1Ch 12:32*
hundred
Solomon assembled all the *h.*   *2Ch 5:2*
to bring

certain of the *h.* of Ephraim 2Ch 28:12
stood up
shall wound the *h.* over many Ps 110:6
countries
hear, O *h.* of Jacob, and Mic 3:1;
princes of Israel 3:9
h. thereof judge for reward, Mic 3:11
and priests teach

HEADSTONE

is become the *h.* of the Ps 118:22
corner
bring forth the *h.* with Zec 4:7
shoutings

HEADSTRONG

h. as they are (B) 2Pe 2:10

HEADTIRE

find the *h.* (E) Eze 24:17

HEAD-TIRES

h. shall thou make (E) Ex 28:40;
29:9; 39:28
the *h.* (E) Isa 3:20
your *h.* shall come (E) Jer 13:18

HEADY

Traitors, *h.*, highminded 2Ti 3:4

HEAL

h. her now, O God, I beseech Nu 12:13
thee
I kill and make alive, I De 32:39
wound, I *h.*
I will *h.* thee, and add to thy 2Ki 20:5
days
what shall be sign that Lord 2Ki 20:8
will *h.* me
I will forgive their sin, and 2Ch 7:14
will *h.* land
O Lord, *h.* me, my bones are Ps 6:2
vexed
h. my soul, for I have sinned Ps 41:4
against thee
h. the breaches thereof, for it Ps 60:2
shaketh
a time to kill, and a time to *h.* Ec 3:3
shall smite and *h.* it, and he Isa 19:22
shall *h.* them
I have seen his ways, and Isa 57:18;
will *h.* him 57:19
return, and I will *h.* your Jer 3:22
backslidings
h. me, O Lord, and I shall be Jer 17:14
healed
I will *h.* thee of thy wounds, Jer 30:17
saith the Lord
bring restoration and health, I Jer 33:6
will *h.* them (B)
for thy breach is great, who La 2:13
can *h.* thee
yet could he not *h.* you, nor Ho 5:13
cure you
let us return, he hath torn, and Ho 6:1
will *h.* us
I will *h.* their backslidings Ho 14:4
he shall not *h.* that that is Zec 11:16
broken
Jesus saith, I will come and *h.* M't 8:7
him
to *h.* all manner of sickness M't 10:1;
M'k 3:15
h. the sick, cleanse lepers M't 10:8;
Lu 9:2; 10:9
Is it lawful to *h.* on M't 12:10;
sabbath day Lu 14:3
I should *h.* them M't 13:15;
Joh 12:40; Ac 28:27
whether he would *h.* on M'k 3:2;
sabbath Lu 6:7
sent me to *h.* the Lu 4:18
brokenhearted
ye will surely say, Physician, Lu 4:23
h. thyself
power of Lord was present to Lu 5:17
h. them
beseeching that he would come Lu 7:3
and *h.*
he would come down and *h.* Joh 4:47
his son
by stretching forth thine hand Ac 4:30
to *h.*
ability to *h.* (P) 1Co 12:9

HEALED

God *h.* Abimelech and his Ge 20:17
wife
he shall cause him to be Ex 21:19
thoroughly *h.*
the bile is *h.*; the scall is *h.* Le 13:18;
13:37
and if the plague of leprosy be Le 14:3;
h. 14:48
with itch, whereof thou canst De 28:27
not be *h.*
till they were *h.* (S) Jos 5:8
return an offering, then he shall 1Sa 6:3
be *h.*
take it to their *h.* (S) 1Ki 8:47;
2Ch 6:37
have *h.* the waters; waters 2Ki 2:21;
were *h.* 2:22
king Joram went to be *h.* in 2Ki 8:29
Jezreel
Joram was returned to be *h.* 2Ki 9:15;
2Ch 22:6
the Lord, hearkened and *h.* 2Ch 30:20
the people
I cried to thee, and thou hast *h.* Ps 30:2
me
he sent his word, and *h.* them Ps 107:20
lest they see, and convert, and Isa 6:10
be *h.*
was bruised, and with his Isa 53:5
stripes we are *h.*
they have *h.* the hurt slightly Jer 6:14;
8:11
my wound incurable, which Jer 15:18
refuseth to be *h.*
heal me, O Lord, and I shall Jer 17:14
be *h.*
howl for her, take balm, if so Jer 51:8
be she may be *h.*
we would have *h.* Babylon, but Jer 51:9
she is not *h.*
lo, it shall not be bound up Eze 30:21
to be *h.*
neither have ye *h.* that which Eze 34:4
was sick
nor *h.* the sick (A)(B)(R) Eze 34:4
brought forth into sea, the Eze 47:8;
waters shall be *h.* 47:9
and the marishes thereof Eze 47:11
shall not be *h.*
when I would have *h.* Israel Ho 7:1
then iniquity
but they knew not that I *h.* Ho 11:3
them
those that had the palsy, and M't 4:24
he *h.* them
speak, and my servant shall be M't 8:8;
h. Lu 7:7
multitudes followed him, he M't 12:15;
h. them 14:14
h. instantly (R) M't 15:28
that she may be *h.* and she M'k 5:23
shall live
had spent all nor could be *h.* of Lu 8:43
any
therefore come and be *h.* and Lu 13:14
not on sabbath
when he saw that he was *h.* Lu 17:15
turned back
and he touched his ear, and *h.* Lu 22:51
him
he that was *h.* wist not who it Joh 5:13
was
and beholding the man who Ac 4:14
was *h.*
and they were *h.* every one Ac 5:16
and perceiving that he had Ac 14:9
faith to be *h.*
Paul prayed, and *h.* the father Ac 28:8
of Publius
be out of the way, but let it Heb 12:13
rather be *h.*
pray one for another, that ye Jas 5:16
may be *h.*
by whose stripes ye were *h.* 1Pe 2:24
and his deadly wound was *h.* Re 13:3;
13:12

HEALER

shall swear, saying, I will not be Isa 3:7
an *h.*
I am not able to restore (B) Isa 3:7

HEALETH

for I am the Lord that *h.* thee Ex 15:26
bless the Lord who *h.* all thy Ps 103:3
diseases

he *h.* the broken in heart, and Ps 147:3
bindeth up
and he *h.* the stroke of their Isa 30:26
wound

HEALING

it will be *h.* to your body Pr 3:8
(B)(R)
h. to all their flesh (B)(R) Pr 4:2
tongue of wise brings *h.* Pr 10:18
(A)(R)
faithful envoy bring *h.* Pr 13:17
(A)(B)(R)
h. to the body (A) Pr 16:24
h. to the bones (B) Pr 16:24
h. shall spring Isa 58:8
forth(A)(B)(E)(R)
looked for a time of *h.* Jer 8:15
(A)(B)(E)(R)
us, and there is no *h.* for us Jer 14:19
and for the time of *h.* and Jer 14:19
behold
up: thou hast no *h.* medicines Jer 30:13
no *h.* device (A) Jer 30:13
lay upon it health and *h.* Jer 33:6
(A)(R)
no *h.* remedy (A)(B)(E)(R) Jer 46:11
their deaf for *h.* Eze 47:12
(A)(B)(E)(R)
There is no *h.* of thy bruise Na 3:19
arise with *h.* in his wings Mal 4:2
h. all manner of sickness and M't 4:23
all
h. every sickness and every M't 9:35
disease
h. many sicknesses (A) Lu 7:21
the gospel, and *h.* every where Lu 9:6
healed them that had need of Lu 9:11
I do *h.* today (B) Lu 13:32
this miracle of *h.* was shewed Ac 4:22
and *h.* all that were oppressed Ac 10:38
gifts of *h.* by the same Spirit 1Co 12:9
extraordinary powers of *h.* 1Co 12:9
(A)(B)
Have all the gifts of *h.*? do 1Co 12:30
were for the *h.* of the nations Re 22:2

HEALINGS

perform *h.* (A) Lu 13:32
miracles, then gift of *h.* helps 1Co 12:28

HEALS

tongue of wise *h.* (B) Pr 10:18

HEALTH

servant our father is in good Ge 43:28
h.
Art thou in *h.* my brother 2Sa 20:9
Is all well with you 2Sa 20:9
(A)(B)(E)(R)
who is the *h.* of my Ps 42:11
countenance
the help of my countenance Ps 42:11
(A)(E)
my face-healer (B) Ps 42:11
my help and my God (R) Ps 42:11
who is the *h.* of my Ps 43:5
countenance
the help of my countenance Ps 43:5
(A)(E)
my face-saver (B) Ps 43:5
my help and my God (R) Ps 43:5
thy saving *h.* among all nations Ps 67:2
It shall be *h.* to thy navel, and Pr 3:8
it will be healing to your body Pr 3:8
(B)(R)
find them, and *h.* to all their Pr 4:22
flesh
healing and health to all their Pr 4:22
flesh (A)
healing to all their flesh Pr 4:22
(B)(R)
but the tongue of the wise is *h.* Pr 12:18
tongue of wise brings healing Pr 12:18
(A)(R)
tongue of the wise heals (B) Pr 12:18
but a faithful ambassador is *h.* Pr 13:17
faithful envoy brings healing Pr 13:17
(A)(B)(R)
life and *h.* of body (A)(B) Pr 14:30
the soul, and *h.* to the bones Pr 16:24
healing to the body (A) Pr 16:24
healing to the bones (B) Pr 16:24
and thine *h.* shall spring forth Isa 58:8

healing shall spring forth *Isa 58:8*
(A)(B)(E)(R)
and for a time of *h.* and *Jer 8:15*
behold
looked for a time of healing *Jer 8:15*
(A)(B)(E)(R)
the *h.* of the daugher of my *Jer 8:22*
For I will restore *h.* unto thee *Jer 30:17*
I will bring it *h.* and cure, and *Jer 33:6*
lay upon it *h.* and healing *Jer 33:6*
(A)(B)(R)
gave him perfect. (B)(P)(R) *Ac 3:16*
some meat: for this is for your *Ac 27:34*
h.
thou mayest prosper and be in *h.* *3Jo 2*

HEALTHY

h. and vigorous men (B)(S) *J'g 3:29*
heart be *h.* (B) *Ps 119:80*
if thine eye be *h.* (S) *M't 6:22*

HEAP

they took stones, and made *Ge 31:46*
an *h.*
they did eat there upon the *h.* *Ge 31:46*
This *h.* is a witness between *Ge 31:48*
me
Behold this *h.* and behold *Ge 31:51*
This *h.* be witness, and this *Ge 31:52*
pillar
I will not pass over this *h.* to *Ge 31:52*
thee
thou shalt not pass over this *h.* *Ge 31:52*
the floods stood upright as an *Ex 15:8*
h.
and it shall be an *h.* for ever *De 13:16*
I will *h.* mischiefs upon them *De 32:23*
and they shall stand upon an *Jos 3:13*
h.
rose up upon an *h.* very far *Jos 3:16*
from
over him a great *h.* of stones *Jos 7:26*
Ai, and made it an *h.* for ever *Jos 8:28*
raise thereon a great *h.* of *Jos 8:29*
stones
down at the end of the *h.* of *Ru 3:7*
corn
very great *h.* of stones upon *2Sa 18:17*
him
roots are wrapped about the *Job 8:17*
h.
I could *h.* up words against you *Job 16:4*
Though he *h.* up silver as the *Job 27:16*
dust
hypocrites in heart *h.* up *Job 36:13*
wrath
waters of the sea together as an *Ps 33:7*
h.
made the waters to stand as *Ps 78:13*
an *h.*
shalt *h.* coals of fire upon his *Pr 25:22*
head
gather and to *h.* up, that he *Ec 2:26*
may
thy belly is like a *h.* of wheat *Ca 7:2*
city, and it shall be a ruinous *Isa 17:1*
h.
the harvest shall be a *h.* in *Isa 17:11*
the day
thou hast made of a city an *h.* *Isa 25:2*
shall be builded on her own *Jer 30:18*
h.
it shall be a desolate *h.* and her *Jer 49:2*
H. on wood, kindle the fire *Eze 24:10*
make Samaria as an *h.* of the *Mic 1:6*
field
for they shall *h.* dust, and *Hab 1:10*
take it
through the *h.* of great waters *Hab 3:15*
came to an *h.* of twenty *Hag 2:16*
measures
body go to the rubbish *h.* (P) *M't 5:29;*
     5:30; 23:33; M'k 9:43, 45, 47
shalt *h.* coals of fire on his *Ro 12:20*
head
they *h.* to themselves teachers *2Ti 4:3*

HEAPED

and *h.* up silver as the dust, and *Zec 9:3*
Ye have *h.* treasures together *Jas 5:3*

HEAPETH

he *h.* up riches, and knoweth *Ps 39:6*
not
and *h.* unto him all people *Hab 2:5*

HEAPING

h. up phrases (A) *M't 6:7*

HEAPS

gathered them together upon *h.* *Ex 8:14*
the jawbone of an ass, *h.* *J'g 15:16*
upon *h.*
Lay ye them in two *h.* at the *2Ki 10:8*
waste fenced cities into *2Ki 19:25*
ruinous *h.*
turn to rubbish *h.* *2Ki 19:25*
(B)(E)(R)
their God, and laid them by *2Ch 31:6*
h.
to lay the foundation of the *h.* *2Ch 31:7*
the princes came and saw the *2Ch 31:8*
h.
and the Levites concerning *2Ch 31:9*
the *h.*
stones out of the *h.* of the *Ne 4:2*
rubbish
which are ready to become *h.* *Job 15:28*
they have laid Jerusalem on *h.* *Ps 79:1*
defenced cities into ruinous *h.* *Isa 37:26*
I will make Jerusalem and *Jer 9:11*
Jerusalem shall become *h.* *Jer 26:18*
up waymarks, make thee high *Jer 31:21*
h.
cast her up as *h.* and destroy *Jer 50:26*
her
And Babylon shall become *h.* *Jer 51:37*
their altars are as *h.* in the *Ho 12:11*
furrows
Jerusalem shall become *h.* and *Mic 3:12*

HEAR

so that all that *h.* will laugh *Ge 21:6*
with me
h. us, my lord, thou art a *Ge 23:6*
mighty prince
that the people may *h.* when I *Ex 19:9*
speak
but the noise of them that *Ex 32:18*
sing do I *h.*
h. I pray you, ye sons of Levi *Nu 16:8*
rise up, Balak, and *h.* hearken *Nu 23:18*
unto me
and her father *h.* her vow and *Nu 30:4*
her bond
h. the causes between your *De 1:16*
brethren
and I will make them *h.* my *De 4:10*
words
h. Israel the statutes and *De 5:1;*
judgments   *6:3; 9:1; 20:3; Isa 48:1;*
     M'k 12:29
and *h.* all that the Lord our *De 5:27*
God doth say
h. all these words which I *De 12:28*
command thee
if thou shalt *h.* say in one of *De 13:12*
thy cities
bring it, that we may *h.* it *De 30:12;*
and do it   *30:13*
that they may *h.* and fear *De 31:12;*
Lord   *30:13; Jer 6:10*
h. the words of the Lord your *Jos 3:9*
God
when ye *h.* the sound of the *Jos 6:5;*
trumpet, the people shall shout *Ne 4:20;*
     Da 3:5, 15
h. O ye kings, give ear, O ye *J'g 5:3*
princes
why abodest, to *h.* the *J'g 5:16*
bleatings of the flocks
put forth thy riddle, that we *J'g 14:13*
may *h.* it
for I *h.* of your evil dealings *1Sa 2:23*
by all
nay, my sons, it is no good *1Sa 2:24*
report that I *h.*
and the lowing of the oxen *1Sa 15:14*
which I *h.*
how can I go? if Saul *h.* it, he *1Sa 16:2*
will kill me
h. the words of thy *1Sa 25:24;*
handmaid   *2Sa 20:17*
let my lord the king *h.* words *1Sa 26:19*
of his servant
there is no man deputed of the *2Sa 15:3*
king to *h.* thee
as soon as ye *h.* the sound of *2Sa 15:10*
the trumpet
that what thing soever thou *2Sa 15:35*
shalt *h.*
ye shall send to me every *2Sa 15:36*
thing that ye *h.*

and let us *h.* likewise what *2Sa 17:5*
Hushai saith
a wise woman cried out of *2Sa 20:16*
the city, *H. h.*
soon as they *h.* shall be *2Sa 22:45;*
obedient   *Ps 18:44*
to *h.* the wisdom of Solomon *1Ki 4:34;*
  10:8, 24; 2Ch 9:7, 23; M't 12:42;
     Lu 11:31
then *h.* thou in heaven and *1Ki 8:30;*
forgive   *8:32, 34, 36, 39, 43, 45, 49;*
     2Ch 6:21
they called on Baal, saying, *1Ki 18:26*
O Baal, *h.* us
made the host to *h.* a noise of *2Ki 7:6*
chariots
h. the word of the great king *2Ki 18:28;*
     Isa 36:13
h. the words of Sennacherib *2Ki 19:16;*
     Isa 37:17
when thou shalt *h.* a sound of *1Ch 14:15*
going
that thou mayest *h.* the prayer *Ne 1:6*
of servant
h. O our God for we are *Ne 4:4*
despised, turn reproach
and all that could *h.* with *Ne 8:2*
understanding
h. it, and know thou it for thy *Job 5:27*
good
h. diligently my speech with *Job 13:17;*
ears   *21:2*
with God *h.* his cry *Job 27:9*
h. my words *Job 34:2*
h. I beseech thee, and I will *Job 42:4*
speak
h. my prayer, O God *Ps 4:1;*
  39:12; 54:2; 84:8; 102:1; 143:1
the Lord *h.* thee in the day of *Ps 20:1*
trouble
save, Lord, let the king *h.* us *Ps 20:9*
when we call
h. O Lord, when I cry with my *Ps 27:7*
voice
h. O Lord, and have mercy *Ps 30:10*
upon me
h. this, all ye people, give ear, *Ps 49:1*
all inhabitants
h. O my people, and I will *Ps 50:7;*
speak   *81:8*
make me to *h.* joy and *Ps 51:8*
gladness, that the bones
swords in lips, for who, say *Ps 59:7*
they, doth *h.*
h. my cry, O God, attend to my *Ps 61:1*
prayer
come, and *h.* all ye that fear *Ps 66:16*
God
h. groaning of the prisoner, *Ps 102:20*
to loose those
when they *h.* the words of thy *Ps 138:4*
mouth
cause me to *h.* thy *Ps 143:8*
lovingkindness in morning
my son, *h.* the instruction of thy *Pr 1:8*
father
h. ye children, the instruction of *Pr 4:1*
a father
h. O my son, and receive my *Pr 4:10;*
sayings   *19:20*
h. for I will speak of excellent *Pr 8:6*
things
h. instruction, and be wise, *Pr 8:33*
refuse it not
cease to *h.* instruction that *Pr 19:27*
causeth to err
bow thine ear, *h.* the words of *Pr 22:17*
the wise
h. thou, my son, be wise, and *Pr 23:19*
guide thy heart
and be more ready to *h.* than to *Ec 5:1*
give
it is better to *h.* the rebuke of *Ec 7:5*
the wise
let us *h.* the conclusion of the *Ec 12:13*
matter
hearken to thy voice, cause me *Ca 8:13*
to *h.* it
h. O heavens, and give ear, O *Isa 1:2*
earth
h. ye indeed, but understand *Isa 6:9;*
not   *M'k 4:12*
and when he bloweth a *Isa 18:3*
trumpet, *h.* ye
h. ye that are afar off what I *Isa 33:13*
have done
let the earth *h.* and all that is *Isa 34:1*
therein

h. ye deaf; who will *h.* for   *Isa 42:18;*
time to come   *42:23*
or let them *h.* and say, It is   *Isa 43:9*
truth
all ye, assemble yourselves   *Isa 48:14*
and *h.*
h. ye this, I have not spoken   *Isa 48:16*
in secret
h. and your soul shall live   *Isa 55:3;*
  Joh 5:25
shall I *h.* the sound of the   *Jer 4:21*
trumpet
therefore *h.* ye nations; *h.* O   *Jer 6:18;*
earth   *6:19*
h. ye the words of this   *Jer 11:2;*
covenant   *11:6*
forefathers who refused to *h.*   *Jer 11:10;*
  13:10
h. ye, give ear, for the Lord   *Jer 13:15*
hath spoken
then I will cause thee to *h.* my   *Jer 18:2*
words
and had caused my people to   *Jer 23:22*
h. my words
if the princes *h.* that I have   *Jer 38:25*
talked
therefore *h.* the counsel of   *Jer 49:20;*
the Lord   *50:45*
h. I pray you, all people, and   *La 1:18*
behold
h. what I say; *h.* at my mouth   *Eze 2:8;*
  3:17; 33:7
he that heareth, let him *h.* he   *Eze 3:27*
that forbears
by your lying to my people,   *Eze 13:19*
that *h.* our lies
h. what is the word that   *Eze 33:30*
cometh forth
they *h.* thy words, but will   *Eze 33:31;*
not do them   *33:32*
O God, *h.* the prayer of thy   *Da 9:17*
servant
O Lord, *h.* O Lord, forgive,   *Da 9:19*
hearken, and do
h. ye this, O priests, and   *Ho 5:1*
hearken, give ear
h. this, ye old men, and give   *Joe 1:2*
ear, all inhabitants
h. this word Lord hath spoken   *Am 3:1;*
  4:1; 5:1; 8:4
h. all ye people, hearken, O   *Mic 1:2*
earth
I said, *H.* I pray you, O heads   *Mic 3:1;*
of Jacob   *3:9*
h. ye, O mountains   *Mic 6:2*
h. ye the rod and him   *Mic 6:9*
all that *h.* the bruit of thee   *Na 3:19*
shall clap
lest they should *h.* the law and   *Zec 7:12*
words
shew John the things which ye   *M't 11:4*
h. and
lame walk, and deaf *h.*   *M't 11:5;*
  M'k 7:37; Lu 7:22
to *h.* those things that ye *h.*   *M't 13:17;*
  Lu 10:24
he said to the multitude, *H.*   *M't 15:10*
and understand
this is my beloved Son *h.* him   *M't 17:5;*
  M'k 9:7
he neglect to *h.* them, to *h.*   *M't 18:17*
the church
are such as *h.* the word   *M'k 4:18;*
  4:20; Lu 8:12, 13
take heed what ye *h.* you that   *M'k 4:24*
h. more given
pressed on him to *h.* the word of   *Lu 5:1*
God
multitudes came together to *h.*   *Lu 5:15*
and be healed
which came to *h.* him, and to   *Lu 6:17*
be healed
I say to you which *h.*, Love   *Lu 6:27*
your enemies
take heed therefore how ye *h.*   *Lu 8:18*
whoever hath
are these which *h.* the word   *Lu 8:21;*
and do it   *11:28*
but who is this of whom I *h.*   *Lu 9:9*
such things
then drew near publicans and   *Lu 15:1*
sinners to *h.* him
he said, How is it that I *h.* this   *Lu 16:2*
of thee?
they have Moses and prophets,   *Lu 16:29*
let them *h.* them
Lord said, *H.* what the unjust   *Lu 18:6*
judge saith

the people were very attentive   *Lu 19:48*
to *h.* him
came to him in the temple for   *Lu 21:38*
to *h.* him
as I *h.* I judge; who can *h.* it   *Joh 5:32;*
  6:60
doth our law judge a man   *Joh 7:51*
before it *h.* him
wherefore would ye *h.* it again   *Joh 9:27*
the sheep *h.* his voice, and he   *Joh 10:3*
calleth by name
if any man *h.* my words, and   *Joh 12:47*
believe not
and the word which ye *h.* is   *Joh 14:24*
not mine
how *h.* we every man in our   *Ac 2:8*
own tongue
hath shed forth this, which ye   *Ac 2:33*
now see and *h.*
to send for thee, and to *h.*   *Ac 10:22*
words of thee
to *h.* all things that are   *Ac 10:33*
commanded thee
and desired to *h.* the word of   *Ac 13:7*
God
the whole city came together   *Ac 13:44*
to *h.* the word
Gentiles by my mouth should   *Ac 15:7*
h. the word
either to tell or to *h.* some new   *Ac 17:21*
thing
ye *h.* Paul hath turned away   *Ac 19:26*
much people
h. ye my defence which I make   *Ac 22:1*
now to you
that thou wouldest *h.* us of thy   *Ac 24:4*
clemency
Agrippa said, I would *h.* the   *Ac 25:22*
man myself
but we desire to *h.* what thou   *Ac 28:22*
thinkest
I *h.* there be divisions among   *1Co 11:18*
you
or else be absent, I may *h.* of   *Ph'p 1:27*
your affairs
we *h.* that some walk   *2Th 3:11*
disorderly
shalt save thyself and them   *1Ti 4:16*
that *h.* thee
and that all the Gentiles might   *2Ti 4:17*
h.
let every one be swift to *h.*   *Jas 1:19*
slow to speak
we know that he *h.* us, what   *1Joh 5:15*
we ask
than to *h.* my children walk in   *3Jo 4*
truth
blessed that *h.* words of this   *Re 1:3*
prophecy
which neither can see, nor *h.*   *Re 9:20*
nor walk

HEAR ME

how then shall Pharaoh *h. me*   *Ex 6:12*
h. me, O Lord *h. me*, that   *1Ki 18:37*
this people
h. me, my brethren, and my   *1Ch 28:2*
people
h. me, thou Jeroboam, and all   *2Ch 13:4*
Israel
h. me, Asa; *h. me*, O Judah   *2Ch 15:2;*
  20:20
h. me, ye Levites, sanctify   *2Ch 29:5*
now yourselves
I will shew thee, *h. me*, I will   *Job 15:17*
declare
O that one would *h. me*, my   *Job 31:35*
desire is
h. me when I call, O God of my   *Ps 4:1*
righteousness
consider, and *h. me.*, O Lord   *Ps 13:3*
my God
I called upon thee, for thou   *Ps 17:6*
wilt *h. me*
for I said, *H. me.*, lest they   *Ps 38:16*
should rejoice
attend unto me, and *h. me*, I   *Ps 55:2*
mourn
save with thy right hand, and   *Ps 60:5*
h. me
O God, in the multitude of thy   *Ps 69:13*
mercy *h. me*
for I am in trouble, *h. me*   *Ps 69:17;*
speedily   *143:7*
I will wait for God, my God   *Mic 7:7*
will *h. me*
wherefore I beseech thee to *h.*   *Ac 26:3*
me

but also all that *h. me*, were   *Ac 26:29*
such as I am
yet for all that will they not   *1Co 14:21*
h. me

HEAR *NOT*, *NOT* HEAR

so thou wilt *not h.* but   *De 30:17*
worship other gods
the Lord will *not h.* you in   *1Sa 8:18*
that day
I cry unto thee, and thou dost   *Job 30:20*
not h. me
surely God will *not h.* vanity,   *Job 35:13*
nor regard it
if I regard iniquity, Lord will   *Ps 66:18*
not h. me
he that planted the ear, shall he   *Ps 94:9*
not h.
when pray I will *not h.*   *Isa 1:15;*
  Jer 7:16; 11:14; 14:12; Eze 8:18;
  Am 5:23
children that will *not h.* the   *Isa 30:9*
law of the Lord
neither his ear heavy that it   *Isa 59:1*
cannot h.
he will *not h.*; when I spake   *Isa 59:2;*
ye did not *h.*   *65:12*
when I spake, they did *not h.*   *Jer 66:4;*
  Zec 1:4
have ears and *h. not*   *Jer 5:21;*
  Eze 12:2; M'k 8:18
but if ye will *not h.*   *Jer 13:17;*
  22:5; Mal 2:2
that they might *not h.*   *Jer 17:23; 19:15;*
  Zec 7:11
I spake, but thou saidst, I will   *Jer 22:21*
not h.
praised gods of silver, which   *Da 5:23;*
see *not*, nor *h.* nor know   *Re 9:20*
shall cry to Lord, but he will   *Mic 3:4*
not h. them
how long shall I cry, and thou   *Hab 1:2*
will *not h.*
not receive you, *nor h.* your   *M't 10:14*
words
if he will *not h.* thee, then   *M't 18:16*
take one or two
if they *h. not* Moses and the   *Lu 16:31*
prophets
even because ye *cannot h.* my   *Joh 8:43*
word
ye therefore *h.* them *not*,   *Joh 8:47*
because not of God
he answered, I told you, and   *Joh 9:27*
ye did *not h.*
are robbers, but the sheep did   *Joh 10:8*
not h. them
every soul which will *not h.*   *Ac 3:23*
be destroyed
yet for all that will they *not*   *1Co 14:21*
h. me
ye under the law, do ye *not h.*   *Ga 4:21*
the law

HEAR *NOW*, *NOW* HEAR

and he said, *H.* now my   *Nu 12:6;*
words   *20:10*
then Saul said, *H.* now, ye   *1Sa 22:7*
Benjamites
h. now, thou son of Ahitub,   *1Sa 22:12*
he answered
h. now my reasoning, and   *Job 13:6*
hearken
h. me now, therefore O ye   *Pr 5:7*
children
and he said, *H.* ye now, O   *Isa 7:13*
house of David
yet now *h.* O Jacob my servant,   *Isa 44:1*
and Israel
h. now, thou that art given to   *Isa 47:8*
pleasures
therefore, *h.* now this, thou   *Isa 51:21*
afflicted
therefore, *h.* now this, O   *Jer 5:21*
foolish people
h. now Hananiah; *h.* now   *Jer 28:15;*
  3:8
h. now, I pray thee, O my Lord   *Jer 37:20*
the king
h. ye *now* what the Lord saith,   *Mic 6:1*
arise
shed forth this which ye *now*   *Ac 2:33*
see and *h.*
which ye saw in me, and now   *Ph'p 1:30*
h. to be in

HEAR *THE WORD* OF THE LORD

h. the word of the Lord　1Ki 22:19;
　　　2Ch 18:18; Jer 29:20; 42:15; Am 7:16
then Elisha said, *H.* ye the　2Ki 7:1;
word of the Lord　　　Jer 17:20; 21:11
h. word of Lord　2Ki 20:16; Isa 39:3
h. word of the Lord, ye rulers of Isa 1:10
Sodom
h. the word of the Lord, ye　Isa 28:14
scornful men
h. word of Lord, ye that　　Isa 66:5
tremble at his word
h. word of Lord, O house of　Jer 2:4;
Jacob　　　　　　　　　　　　　　　10:1
h. the word of the Lord, all ye　Jer 7:2
of Judah
yet *h.* the word of the Lord, O　Jer 9:20
ye women
h. word of Lord, O kings of　Jer 19:3;
Judah　　　　　　　　　　　　　　　22:2
O earth, earth, *h.* the word of Jer 22:29
the Lord
h. the word of the Lord, O ye　Jer 31:10
nations
yet *h.* word of Lord, O　　Jer 34:4
Zedekiah, king of Judah
h. the word of the Lord, all　Jer 44:24;
Judah　　　　　　　　　　　　　44:26
ye mountains of Israel, *h.* the　Eze 6:3;
word of the Lord　　　　　　　36:1, 4
say to prophets, *H.* ye the　Eze 13:2
word of the Lord
wherefore, O harlot, *h.* the　Eze 16:35
word of the Lord
forest of the south, *h.* the　Eze 20:47
word of the Lord
say to Ammonites, *h.* the　Eze 25:3
word of the Lord
ye shepherds, *h.* the word of Eze 34:7;
the Lord　　　　　　　　　　　34:9
O ye dry bones, *h.* the word of Eze 37:4
the Lord
h. word of the Lord, children of　Ho 4:1
Israel
h. thou *the word of the Lord*　Am 7:16

SHALL HEAR

the people *shall h.* and be　Ex 15:14;
afraid　De 13:11; 17:13; 19:20; 21:21
Moses, said, Then the　　　Nu 14:13
Egyptians *shall h.* it
ye *shall h.* small as well as　De 1:17
great
who *shall h.* report of thee,　De 2:25
and shall tremble
which *shall h.* all these statutes De 4:6
and say
the inhabitants of the land　Jos 7:9
shall h. of it
and thou *shalt h.* what they say J'g 7:11
Israel *shall h.* that thou art　2Sa 16:21
abhorred
for they *shall h.* of thy great　1Ki 8:42
name
and he *shall h.* a rumour　　2Ki 19:7;
　　　　　　　　　　　　　　Isa 37:7
shalt make prayer to him, he Job 22:27
shall h.
the humble *shall h.* thereof, and Ps 34:2
be glad
I will pray and cry, and he　Ps 55:17
shall h. my voice
God *shall h.* and afflict them, Ps 55:19
even he that
mine ears *shall h.* desire of the Ps 92:11
wicked
they *shall h.* my words, for　Ps 141:6
they are sweet
in that day *shall* the deaf *h.*　Isa 29:18
the words
when he *shall h.* it he will　Isa 30:19
answer thee
thine ears *shall h.* a word　Isa 30:21
behind thee
which *shall h.* all the good that Jer 33:9
I do
and the heaven *shall h.* the　Ho 2:21
earth
the earth *shall h.* the corn　Ho 2:22
and the wine
by hearing, ye *shall h.*　　　M't 13:14;
　　　　　　　　　　　　　Ac 28:26
if he *shall h.* thee thou hast　M't 18:15
gained thy

ye *shall h.* of wars　　　M't 24:6;
　　　　　　　M'k 13:7; Lu 21:9
the dead *shall h.* voice of the　Joh 5:25
Son of God
whatsoever he *shall h.* that　Joh 16:13
shall he speak
him *shall ye h.* in all things　Ac 3:22;
　　　　　　　　　　　　　　7:37
to-morrow, said he, thou *shalt* Ac 25:22
h. him
how *shall* they *h.* without a　Ro 10:14
preacher

WILL HEAR

speak with us, we *will h.*　　Ex 20:19;
　　　　　　　　　　　　　De 5:27
if they cry, I *will* surely *h.*　Ex 22:23;
their cry　　　　　　　　　　　22:27
I *will h.* what the Lord will　Nu 9:8
command
king *will h.* to deliver his　2Sa 14:16
handmaid
it may be thy God *will h.* the 2Ki 19:4
words
they *will* I *h.* from heaven　2Ch 7:14;
　　　　　　　　　　　　　　Ps 20:6
then thou *wilt h.* and help　2Ch 20:9;
　　　　　　　　　　　　　Ps 38:15
the Lord *will h.* thou *wilt h.*　Ps 4:3;
me　　　　　　　　　　　　　17:6
I *will h.* what God the Lord　Ps 85:8
will speak
he also *will h.* their cry, and Ps 145:19
save them
wise man *will h.* and increase　Pr 1:5
learning
the Lord *will h.* them, and not Isa 41:17
forsake
while they are yet speaking, I Isa 65:24
will h.
it may be the house of Judah　Jer 36:3
will h.
whether they *will h.* or forbear Eze 2:5;
　　　　　　　　　　　　2:7; 3:11
I *will h.* the heavens, they the Ho 2:21
earth
I will wait for God, my God　Mic 7:7
will h. me
I am their God and *will h.*　Zec 10:6;
them　　　　　　　　　　　　13:9
we *will h.* thee again of this　Ac 17:32
matter
for they *will h.* that thou art　Ac 21:22
come
I *will h.* thee, when thy　　Ac 23:35
accusers are come
salvation is sent to the　　Ac 28:28
Gentiles, they *will h.*

WOULD NOT HEAR

when he besought us, we　　Ge 42:21
would not h.
do not sin against the child,　Ge 42:22
ye *would not h.*
behold, hitherto, thou *wouldest* Ex 7:16
not h.
Israel *would not h.*　　　　De 1:43;
　　　　　　　　　3:26; 2Ki 17:14
Amaziah *would not h.*　　　2Ki 14:11;
　　　　　　　　　　　　　25:26
Israel *would not h.*　　　　2Ki 18:12;
　　　　　　　　　Ne 9:29; Zec 7:13
this is the refreshing, yet they Isa 28:12
would not h.
might be for praise, they　　Jer 13:11;
would not h.　　　　　　　　29:19
he *would not h.*; I *would not* Jer 36:25;
h.　　　　　　　　　　　　7:13

HEARD

because the Lord hath *h.* thy　Ge 16:11
affliction
neither yet *h.* I of it, but to-day Ge 21:26
because the Lord hath *h.* that Ge 29:33
I was hated
Joseph wept aloud, and the　Ge 45:2
Egyptians *h.*
God *h.* their groaning, and　Ex 2:24
remembered
for he hath *h.* your murmurings Ex 16:9
neither let it be *h.* out of thy　Ex 23:13
mouth
his sound shall be *h.* when he Ex 28:35
goeth in and
when the people *h.* these evil　Ex 33:4
tidings

let all that *h.* him lay their　Le 24:14
hands
the people complained, the　Nu 11:1
Lord *h.* it
Miriam spake against Moses,　Nu 12:2
the Lord *h.* it
they have *h.* thou art among　Nu 14:14
this people
the nations which have *h.*　Nu 14:15
the fame of thee
held his peace at her the day　Nu 30:7;
he *h.* it　　　　　　　　　　30:14
they *h.* that they were their　Jos 9:16
neighbours
Samuel cried, and the Lord *h.*　1Sa 7:9
him
will Saul come, as thy　　　1Sa 23:11
servant hath *h.*
hast not *h.* that Adonijah doth 1Ki 1:11
reign
nor was any tool of iron *h.* in　1Ki 6:7
the house
half not told me, thy wisdom 1Ki 10:7;
and prosperity excedeth fame　2Ch 9:6
which I *h.*
hast thou not *h.* long ago　2Ki 19:25;
　　　　　　　　　　　　　Isa 37:26
make one sound to be *h.* in　2Ch 5:13
praising
he was entreated and *h.* his　2Ch 33:13
supplications
people shouted, the noise was Ezr 3:13
h. afar
the joy of Jerusalem *h.* even　Ne 12:43
afar off
hast thou *h.* the secret of God Job 15:8
I cry out of wrong, but I am　Job 19:7
not *h.*
but how little a portion is *h.* Job 26:14
of him
when the ear *h.* me, then it　Job 29:11
blessed me
the Lord hath *h.* my supplication Ps 6:9
thou hast *h.* the desire of the　Ps 10:17
humble
save me, for thou hast *h.* me　Ps 22:21
from the horns
but when he cried he *h.*　　Ps 22:24;
　　　　　　　　　34:6; 40:1; 120:1
I sought the Lord, and he *h.* me, Ps 34:4
and delivered
but I as a deaf man *h.* not, I　Ps 38:13
was dumb
thou, O God hast *h.* my vows,　Ps 61:5
thou hast given
verily God hath *h.* me, he hath Ps 66:19
attended
cause judgment to be *h.* from　Ps 76:8
heaven
therefore the Lord *h.* this and Ps 78:21
was wroth
when God *h.* this, was wroth, Ps 78:59
and abhorred
where I *h.* a language that I　Ps 81:5
understood not
Zion *h.* and was glad, and Judah Ps 97:8
rejoiced
he regarded their affliction,　Ps 106:44
when he *h.*
for thou hast *h.* me, and art　Ps 118:21
my salvation
lo, we *h.* of it at Ephratah, we Ps 132:6
found it
he shall cry himself, but not　Pr 21:13
be *h.*
cause it to be *h.* unto Laish,　Isa 10:30
O Anathoth
have ye not *h.*? hath it not　Isa 40:21
been told you
hast thou not *h.* everlasting　Isa 40:28
God fainteth not
thou hast *h.* see all this, will　Isa 48:6
not ye declare
which they had not *h.* shall　Isa 52:15
they consider
violence shall no more be *h.*　Isa 60:18
in thy land
men have not *h.* what he hath Isa 64:4
prepared
the voice of weeping shall be　Isa 65:19
nor more *h.*
who hath *h.* such a thing,　Isa 66:8
who hath seen
to the isles afar off, that have Isa 66:19
not *h.* my fame
because thou hast *h.* sound of Jer 4:19
trumpet
she casteth out wickedness,　Jer 6:7
spoil is *h.* in her

I spake unto you, rising early,   *Jer 7:13* but ye *h.* not

I hearkened and *h.* but they   *Jer 8:6* spake not aright

ask the heathen, who hath *h.*   *Jer 18:13* such things

let cry be *h.* from houses   *Jer 18:22* when shalt bring

an howling of the flock shall   *Jer 25:36* be *h.*

for he hath prophesied as ye   *Jer 26:11* have *h.*

h. every one should let his   *Jer 34:10* manservant go

I have spoken, but they have   *Jer 35:17* not *h.*

the nations have *h.* of thy   *Jer 46:12* shame

and the cry is *h.* among the   *Jer 50:46* nations

a rumour that shall be *h.* in   *Jer 51:46* the land

they have *h.* that I sigh, there   *La 1:21* is none

thou hast *h.* their reproach, O   *La 3:61* Lord

the nations *h.* of him, he was   *Eze 19:4* taken

the sound of thy harps shall   *Eze 26:13* be no more *h.*

he *h.* the sound of the   *Eze 33:5* trumpet, and took

and I *h.* but I understood not   *Da 12:8*

chastise them, as their   *Ho 7:12* congregation hath *h.*

I cried unto the Lord, and he *h.*   *Jon 2:2* me

in fury, such as they have not   *Mic 5:15* *h.*

when I *h.* my belly trembled   *Hab 3:16*

and the Lord hearkened and *h.*   *Mal 3:16*

ye have *h.* it said   *M't 5:21; 5:27, 33, 38, 43*

they shall be *h.* for their much   *M't 6:7* speaking

ye hear, and have not *h.* them   *M't 13:17; Lu 10:24*

were offended after they *h.*   *M't 15:12* this saying

when the king *h.* thereof, he   *M't 22:7* was wroth

ye have *h.* his blasphemy   *M't 26:65; M'k 14:64*

but when they have *h.* Satan   *M'k 4:15* cometh

and when they *h.* it they   *M'k 14:11* were glad

fear not, thy prayer is *h.*   *Lu 1:13; Ac 10:31*

what ye have spoken, shall be   *Lu 12:3* *h.* in the light

when they *h.* it, they said,   *Lu 20:16* God forbid

what he hath *h.* that he   *Joh 3:32* testifieth

every man that hath *h.* of the   *Joh 6:45* Father

wrote on the ground, as tho' he   *Joh 8:6* *h.* them not

since the world began was it   *Joh 9:32* not *h.*

Father, I thank thee that   *Joh 11:41* thou hast *h.* me

ask them which *h.* me, what I   *Joh 18:21* have said

when Simon Peter *h.* that it was   *Joh 21:7* the Lord

wait for the promise ye have *h.*   *Ac 1:4* of me

when they *h.* this, they were   *Ac 2:37* pricked in heart

many of them which *h.* the word   *Ac 4:4* believed

fear came on all them that *h.*   *Ac 5:5* these things

when the Gentiles *h.* this they   *Ac 13:48* were glad

the same *h.* Paul speak, who   *Ac 14:9* beholding

a woman which worshipped   *Ac 16:14* God, *h.* us

sang praises to God, and the   *Ac 16:25* prisoners *h.* them

when they *h.* this, they were   *Ac 19:5* baptized

shall witness of what thou hast   *Ac 22:15* seen and *h.*

h. him concerning the faith in   *Ac 24:24* Christ

in him of whom they have not   *Ro 10:14* *h.*

but I say, have they not *h.*?   *Ro 10:18* yes, verily

they that have not *h.* shall   *Ro 15:21* understand

eye hath not seen, nor ear *h.*   *1Co 2:9* neither

for ye have *h.* of my   *Ga 1:13* conversation

after that ye *h.* the word of   *Eph 1:13* truth

after I *h.* of your faith in the   *Eph 1:15* Lord Jesus

if so be ye have *h.* him and   *Eph 4:21* been taught

that ye had *h.* that he had   *Ph'p 2:26* been sick

those things ye have *h.* and seen   *Ph'p 4:9* in me, do

since we *h.* of your faith in   *Col 1:4* Christ

since day ye *h.* of it and knew   *Col 1:6* the grace of God

since day we *h.* it, do not cease   *Col 1:9* to pray for you

things thou hast *h.* of me,   *2Ti 2:2* commit to

was confirmed to us by them   *Heb 2:3* that *h.* him

for some when they had *h.*   *Heb 3:16* did provoke

not being mixed with faith in   *Heb 4:2* them that *h.*

offered up prayers, and was   *Heb 5:7* *h.* in that he feared

ye have *h.* of the patience of   *Jas 5:11* Job

ye *h.* that antichrist shall come   *1Jo 2:18; 4:3*

have *h.* from the beginning   *1Jo 2:24; 3:11; 2Jo 6*

remember therefore how thou   *Re 3:3* hast *h.*

and all that are in them *h.* I,   *Re 5:13* saying

I *h.* the number of them which   *Re 7:4* were sealed

and I *h.* the number of the   *Re 9:16* horsemen

and I *h.* the angel of the waters   *Re 16:5* say

the voice of trumpeters shall   *Re 18:22* be *h.* no more

the voice of bride shall be *h.*   *Re 18:23* no more in thee

I saw these things, and *h.* them,   *Re 22:8* when I *h.*

HEARD *VOICE*

they *h.* voice of the Lord   *Ge 3:8* walking in garden

I *h.* thy voice, and was afraid,   *Ge 3:10* because naked

God *h.* the voice of the lad,   *Ge 21:17* the angel called

God hath *h.* my voice, and   *Ge 30:6* given me a son

when he *h.* that I lifted up my   *Ge 39:15* voice

then he *h.* the voice of one   *Nu 7:89* speaking

we cried, he *h.* our voice, and   *Nu 20:16* sent an angel

the Lord *h.* the voice of your   *De 1:34* words

saw no similitude, only he *h.* a   *De 4:12* voice

hear voice of God as thou   *De 4:33; 5:26* hast *h.* and live

ye *h.* the voice out of the midst   *De 5:23* of darkness

we have *h.* his voice out of the   *De 5:24* midst of the fire

and the Lord *h.* the voice of   *De 5:28* your words

we cried, the Lord *h.* our voice,   *De 26:7* and looked

let not thy voice be *h.* among   *J'g 18:25* us

her lips moved, her voice was   *1Sa 1:13* not *h.*

the Lord *h.* the voice of Elijah   *1Ki 17:22*

their voice was *h.* prayer   *2Ch 30:27* came up

there was silence, I *h.* a voice   *Job 4:16*

I have *h.* the voice of thy   *Job 33:8* words, saying

he will not stay them when his   *Job 37:4* voice is *h.*

I cried to the Lord with my   *Ps 3:4* voice, he *h.* me

the Lord hath *h.* the voice of my   *Ps 6:8* weeping

I called, he *h.* my voice out of   *Ps 18:6* his temple

there is no speech where their   *Ps 19:3* voice is not *h.*

because he hath *h.* the voice of   *Ps 28:6* my supplication

and make the voice of his   *Ps 66:8* praise to be *h.*

I love the Lord, because he   *Ps 116:1* hath *h.* my voice

the voice of the turtle is *h.* in   *Ca 2:12* our land

also I *h.* the voice of the Lord,   *Isa 6:8* saying

their voice shall be *h.* even   *Isa 15:4* unto Jahaz

Lord shall cause his glorious   *Isa 30:30* voice to be *h.*

nor cause his voice to be *h.* in   *Isa 42:2* the street

not fast, to make your voice   *Isa 58:4* be *h.* on high

voice of weeping shall no   *Isa 65:19* more be *h.* in her

a voice was *h.* upon the high   *Jer 3:21* places

I have *h.* a voice as of a   *Jer 4:31* woman in travail

for a voice of wailing is *h.* out   *Jer 9:19* of Zion

we have *h.* a voice of   *Jer 30:5* trembling, of fear

a voice was *h.* in Ramah   *Jer 31:15; M't 2:18*

thou hast *h.* my voice, hide not   *La 3:56* thine ear

and I *h.* a voice of one that   *Eze 1:28* spake

I *h.* behind me a voice of   *Eze 3:12* great rushing

that his voice should no more   *Eze 19:9* be *h.*

and shall cause their voice to   *Eze 27:30* be *h.* against thee

I *h.* a man's voice between the   *Da 8:16* banks

yet *h.* I the voice of his words,   *Da 10:9* when I

voice of thy messengers no   *Na 2:13* more be *h.*

ye have neither *h.* his voice at   *Joh 5:37* any time

h. a voice, saying, Saul, Saul   *Ac 9:4; 22:7; 26:14*

I *h.* a voice saying to me,   *Ac 11:7* Arise, slay and eat

they *h.* not the voice of him   *Ac 22:9* that spake

which voice they that *h.*   *Heb 12:19* entreated

the voice which came from   *2Pe 1:18* heaven we *h.*

I *h.* a great voice   *Re 1:10; 16:1; 19:1; 21:3*

the first voice I *h.* was as it were   *Re 4:1* of a trumpet

I beheld, and *h.* the voice of   *Re 5:11* many angels

I *h.* a voice in the midst of the   *Re 6:6* four beasts

I *h.* a voice of the fourth beast   *Re 6:7* say, Come and see

I *h.* a voice from the four   *Re 9:13* horns of the altar

I *h.* a voice from heaven   *Re 10:4; 10:8; 14:2, 13; 18:4*

and I *h.* a loud voice, saying   *Re 12:10* in heaven

I *h.* the voice of harpers   *Re 14:2* harping with harps

I *h.* as it were the voice of a   *Re 19:6* great multitude

HEARD with WORD, WORDS

and when he *h.* the words of   *Ge 24:30* Rebekah

when Abraham's servant *h.*   *Ge 24:52* their words

and when Esau *h.* the words   *Ge 27:34* of his father

Jacob *h.* the *words* of Laban's *Ge 31:1*
sons, saying
when his master *h.* the *words* *Ge 39:19*
of his wife
he hath said, which *h. words* *Nu 24:4;*
of God *24:16*
when heads of Israel *h. words* *Jos 22:30*
of Reuben
for it hath *h.* all the *words* of *Jos 24:27*
the Lord
when Zebul *h.* the *words* of *J'g 9:30*
Gaal
Samuel *h.* all the *words* of the *1Sa 8:21*
people
Saul and Israel *h.* Goliath's *1Sa 17:11*
words
according to the same *words,* *1Sa 17:23*
and David *h.* them
when the *words* were *h.* which *1Sa 17:31*
David spake
the *word* that I have *h.* is good *1Ki 2:42*
when Hiram *h.* Solomon's *1Ki 5:7*
words he rejoiced
when Ahab *h.* those *words,* *1Ki 21:27*
rent his clothes
when the king *h. words* of the *2Ki 6:30*
woman
be not afraid of *words* thou *2Ki 19:6;*
hast *h.* *19:6*
when the king had *h.* the *2Ki 22:11;*
words of book of law, he *22:18;*
 2Ch 34:19
Asa *h.* these *words,* he took *2Ch 15:8*
courage
h. these *words,* I sat down and *Neh 1:4*
wept
and I was angry when I *h.* *Neh 5:6*
these *words*
the people wept, when they *h.* *Neh 8:9*
words of the law
I have *h.* the voice of thy *Job 33:8*
words, saying
the poor man's *words* are not *Ec 9:16*
h.
the *words* of wise men are *h.* in *Ec 9:17*
quiet
will reprove the *words* which *Isa 37:4*
God hath *h.*
hath perceived, marked, and *Jer 23:18*
h. his *word*
therefore because ye have not *Jer 25:8*
h. my *words*
against this city all the *words* *Jer 26:12*
ye have *h.*
when the king and all the *Jer 26:21*
princes *h.* his *words*
declared unto them all the *Jer 36:13*
words he had *h.*
they were not afraid that *h.* *Jer 36:24*
these *words*
Pashur *h.* the *words* Jeremiah *Jer 38:1*
had spoken
when Darius *h.* these *words* *Da 6:14*
was displeased
thy *words* were *h.* I am come *Da 10:12*
for thy *words*
when they *h.* these *words* *M't 22:22*
they marvelled
as soon as Jesus *h.* the *word* *M'k 5:36*
spoken
Mary sat at Jesus' feet, and *h.* *Lu 10:39*
his *word*
Holy Ghost fell on them who *Ac 10:44*
h. word
caught up, and *h.* *2Co 12:4*
unspeakable *words*
after that ye *h.* the *word* of *Eph 1:13*
truth
whereof ye *h.* in the *word* of *Col 1:5*
the gospel
received the *word* which ye *h.* *1Th 2:13*
of us
hold fast form of sound *words* *2Ti 1:13*
which hast *h.* of me
they that *h.* entreated that *Heb 12:19*
the *word*
the *word* ye have *h.* from the *1Jo 2:17*
beginning

I HAVE HEARD

and as for Ishmael I have *h.* *Ge 17:20*
thee
I have *h.* say of thee thou *Ge 41:15;*
canst interpret dreams *Da 5:14, 16*
I have *h.* that there is corn in *Ge 42:2*
Egypt
I have *h.* their cry; I have *h.* *Ex 3:7;*
groaning *6:5*

I have *h.* the murmuring *Ex 16:12;*
 Nu 14:27
I have *h.* the voice of your *De 5:28*
words
now I have *h.* that thou hast *1Sa 25:7*
shearers
the word that I have *h.* is *1Ki 2:42*
good
I have *h.* thy prayer *1Ki 9:3;*
 2Ki 20:5; 2Ch 7:12; Isa 38:5
that which thou hast prayed *2Ki 19:20*
I have *h.*
I also have *h.* thee, saith *2Ki 22:19;*
Lord *2Ch 34:27*
I have *h.* many such things, *Job 16:2*
miserable comforters
I have *h.* the check of my *Job 20:3*
reproach
I have *h.* of thee by the *Job 42:5*
hearing of the ear
for I have *h.* the slander of *Ps 31:13*
many
twice I have *h.* this, power *Ps 62:11*
belongeth to God
that which I have *h.* of Lord *Isa 21:10*
of hosts
I have *h.* from the Lord a *Isa 28:22*
consumption
in an acceptable time have I *Isa 49:8;*
h. *2Co 6:2*
I have *h.* what the prophets *Jer 23:25*
said
I have *h.* Ephraim bemoaning *Jer 31:18*
himself thus
I have *h.* you, behold, I will *Jer 42:4*
pray unto the Lord
I have *h.* a rumour from the *Jer 49:14*
Lord
know I have *h.* all thy *Eze 35:12*
blasphemies
I have *h.* him and observed *Ho 14:8*
him
O Lord I have *h.* thy speech, *Hab 3:2*
and was afraid
I have *h.* the reproach of Moab *Zep 2:8*
I speak those things I have *h.* *Joh 8:26*
of him
told you the truth, which I *Joh 8:40*
have *h.* of God
all things that I have *h.* of *Joh 15:15*
my Father
I have *h.* their groaning, and *Ac 7:34*
am come
Lord I have *h.* by many of this *Ac 9:13*
man, how

WE HAVE HEARD

we have *h.* how the Lord dried *Jos 2:10*
Red sea
soon as we had *h.* these things *Jos 2:11*
hearts melt
we have *h.* the fame of him, *Jos 9:9*
and all he did
there is none like thee *2Sa 7:22;*
according to all we have *h.* *1Ch 17:20*
with our ears
we have *h.* kings of Israel are *1Ki 20:31*
merciful
we have *h.* the fame thereof *Job 28:22;*
 Jer 6:24
we have *h.* with our ears, our *Ps 44:1*
fathers told
as we have *h.* so have we seen *Ps 48:8*
in city of Lord
dark sayings which we have *h.* *Ps 78:3*
and known
we have *h.* of pride of Moab *Isa 16:6;*
 Jer 48:29
we have *h.* songs, glory to the *Isa 24:16*
righteous
we have *h.* a voice of *Jer 30:5*
trembling, of fear
confounded, because we have *Jer 51:51*
h. reproach
we have *h.* a rumour from the *Ob 1*
Lord
for we have *h.* that God is *Zec 8:23*
with you
we have *h.* him say, I will *M'k 14:58*
destroy
whatever we have *h.* done in *Lu 4:23*
Capernaum
we ourselves have *h.* of his *Lu 22:71*
own mouth
we believe, we have *h.* him *Joh 4:42*
ourselves
we have *h.* out of the law *Joh 12:34*
that Christ abideth

we cannot but speak things we *Ac 4:20*
have *h.*
we have *h.* him speak *Ac 6:11*
blasphemous words
we have *h.* him say, this Jesus *Ac 6:14*
shall destroy
we have *h.* that certain have *Ac 15:24*
troubled you
we have not *h.* whether there *Ac 19:2*
be any Holy Ghost
to give heed to things which *Heb 2:1*
we have *h.*
that which we have *h.* and seen *1Jo 1:1;*
 1:3
this is the message which we *1Jo 1:5*
have *h.* of him

HEARDEST

and thou *h.* his words out of *De 4:36*
the fire
for thou *h.* in that day how *Jos 14:12*
Anakims
when thou *h.* what I spake *2Ki 22:19;*
against this place *2Ch 34:27*
and thou *h.* their cry by the *Ne 9:9*
Red sea
they cried, thou *h.* them from *Ne 9:27;*
heaven *9:28*
thou *h.* the voice of my *Ps 31:22*
supplications
I have declared my ways, and *Ps 119:26*
thou *h.* me
before the day when thou *h.* *Isa 48:7*
them not
yea, thou *h.* not, yea, thou *Isa 48:8*
knewest not
out of belly of hell I cried, thou *Jon 2:2*
h.

HEARER

if any be a *h.* of the word, and *Jas 1:23*
not a doer
he being not a forgetful *h.* but *Jas 1:25*
doer of work

HEARERS

not the *h.* of the law are *Ro 2:13*
justified
that it may minister grace *Eph 4:29*
unto the *h.*
but to the subverting of the *h.* *2Ti 2:14*
be doers of the word, and not *Jas 1:22*
h. only

HEAREST

Boaz to Ruth, *h.* thou not, my *Ru 2:8*
daughter
wherefore *h.* thou men's *1Sa 24:9*
words
when *h.* sound in the *2Sa 5:24*
mulberry trees
when thou *h.,* forgive *1Ki 8:30;*
 2Ch 6:21
I cry in the day-time, but thou *Ps 22:2*
h. not
thou that *h.* prayer, unto thee *Ps 65:2*
all flesh come
said unto him, H. thou what *M't 21:16*
these say
h. thou not how many things *M't 27:13*
they witness
wind bloweth, and thou *h.* the *Joh 3:8*
sound
and I knew that thou *h.* me *Joh 11:42*
always

HEARETH

for that he *h.* your *Ex 16:7;*
 16:8
if father disallow her in day *Nu 30:5*
that he *h.*
when he *h.* the words of this *De 29:19*
curse
speak, Lord, for thy servant *h.* *1Sa 3:9;*
 3:10
do a thing at which ears of *1Sa 3:11;*
every one *h.* shall tingle *2Ki 21:12;*
 Jer 19:3
whosoever *h.* it will say, *2Sa 17:9*
There is a slaughter
and he *h.* the cry of the *Job 34:28*
afflicted
the righteous cry, and the *Ps 34:17*
Lord *h.*

thus I was as a man that *h.*   Ps 38:14
not
Lord *h.* poor, and despiseth   Ps 69:33
not his prisoners
blessed is the man that *h.* me,   Pr 8:34
watching
a wise son *h.* his father's   Pr 13:1
instruction
ransom his riches, but poor *h.*   Pr 13:8
not rebuke
but he *h.* the prayer of the   Pr 15:29
righteous
the ear that *h.* the reproof of   Pr 15:31;
life   15:32
he that answereth a matter   Pr 18:13
before he *h.* it
but the man that *h.* speaketh   Pr 21:28
constantly
lest he that *h.* it put thee to   Pr 25:10
shame
he *h.* cursing, and bewrayeth   Pr 29:24
it not
yea, there is none that *h.* your   Isa 41:26
words
opening the ears, but he *h.*   Isa 42:20
not
thou shalt say, he that *h.* let   Eze 3:27
him hear
whosoever *h.* the sound of the   Eze 33:4
trumpet
whoso *h.* these sayings   M't 7:24;
  7:26; Lu 6:47, 49
when any one *h.* the word of   M't 13:19
the kingdom
the same is he that *h.* the   M't 13:20;
word   13:22-23
he that *h.* you *h.* me, and that   Lu 10:16
despiseth
who standeth and *h.* him   Joh 3:29
rejoiceth greatly
he that *h.* my word, and   Joh 5:24
believeth on him
he that is of God *h.* God's   Joh 8:47
words
God *h.* not sinners, but if any   Joh 9:31
man doeth his will, him he *h.*
every one that is of the truth,   Joh 18:37
h. my voice
think of me above that he *h.*   2Co 12:6
of me
are of the world, and the world   1Jo 4:5
h. them
we are of God, he that knoweth   1Jo 4:6
God *h.* us
if we ask according to his will,   1Jo 5:14
he *h.* us
and let him that *h.* say, Come   Re 22:17
for I testify to every man   Re 22:18
that *h.* the words

HEARING

in *h.* of people (B)(R)   Ge 23:13; 23:16
hearing (S)   Ge 23:10;
23:13, 16; Ex 24:7; 1Ch 28:8; Ne 13:1;
  Lu 7:1; 20:45
this law before all Israel in   De 31:11
their *h.*
hearing (S)   J'g 7:3;
9:3; 1Sa 11:4; 2Sa 3:19; 2Ki 18:26; 23:2;
2Ch 34:30; Isa 36:6, 10, 13, 15, 20, 21
speak in thy *h.* (S)   1Sa 25:24
in our *h.*, the king charged   2Sa 18:12
thee
there was neither voice, nor *h.*   2Ki 4:31
Surely thou hast spoken in   Job 33:8
mine *h.*
heard of thee by the *h.* of the   Job 42:5
ear
The *h.* ear, and the seeing eye   Pr 20:12
turneth away his ear from *h.*   Pr 28:9
the law
seeing, nor the ear filled with *h.*   Ec 1:8
reprove after the *h.* of his ears   Isa 11:3
I was bowed down at the *h.*   Isa 21:3
of it
stoppeth his ears from *h.* of   Isa 33:15
blood
to the others he said in mine *h.*   Eze 9:5
it was cried unto them in my   Eze 10:13
h.
but of *h.* the words of the   Am 8:11
Lord
seeing see not; and *h.* they   M't 13:13
hear not
By *h.* ye shall hear, and shall   M't 13:14
not
and their ears are dull of *h.*   M't 13:15
and *h.* they may hear, and not   M'k 4:12

and many *h.* him were   M'k 6:2
astonished
both *h.* them, and asking them   Lu 2:46
and *h.* they might not   Lu 8:10
understand
h. the multitude pass by, he   Lu 18:36
asked
Ananias *h.* these words fell   Ac 5:5
down
Philip spake, *h.* and seeing the   Ac 8:6
h. a voice, but seeing no man   Ac 9:7
many of the Corinthians *h.*   Ac 18:8
believed
petitioning judicial *h.* (A)   Ac 25:15
reserved unto the *h.* of   Ac 25:21
Augustus
and was entered into the   Ac 25:23
place of *h.*
H. ye shall hear, and shall not   Ac 28:26
and their ears are dull of *h.*   Ac 28:27
So then faith cometh by *h.*   Ro 10:17
and *h.* by the word of God   Ro 10:17
body were an eye, where   1Co 12:17
were the *h.*
whole were *h.*, where the   1Co 12:17
smelling
of the law, or by the *h.* of   Ga 3:2;
faith   3:5
H. of thy love and faith, which   Ph'm 5
thou
to be uttered, seeing ye are   Heb 5:11
dull of *h.*
them, in seeing and *h.* vexed his   2Pe 2:8

HEARKEN

ye wives of Lamech, *h.* to my   Ge 4:23
speech
my lord, *h.* to me   Ge 23:15
h. to Israel your father   Ge 49:2
behold, how shall Pharaoh *h.*   Ex 6:30
to me
rise up, *h.* unto me, thou son   Nu 23:18
of Zippor
h. O Israel, to the statutes I   De 4:1
teach you
if ye *h.* to these judgments, and   De 7:12
keep them
if ye will *h.* diligently to my   De 11:13
commands
if thou carefully *h.* to voice of   De 15:5;
Lord   Jer 17:24
a prophet like to me, to him ye   De 18:15
shall *h.*
take heed, and *h.* O. Israel,   De 27:9
this day thou art
if thou *h.* to commandments   De 28:13;
  Ne 11:38
as to Moses, so will we *h.* unto   Jos 1:17
thee
he cried, *h.* to me, ye men of   J'g 9:7
Shechem
and to *h.* than the fat of   1Sa 15:22
rams
for who will *h.* to you in this   1Sa 30:24
matter
have thou respect to *h.* to cry   1Ki 8:28
and prayer
mayest *h.* to the prayer   1Ki 8:29;
  8:52; 2Ch 6:19, 20
h. to the supplications   1Ki 8:30;
  2Ch 6:21
he said, *H.* O people, every   1Ki 22:28
one of you
and he said, *H.* all ye people   2Ch 18:27
h. ye, all Judah, and ye   2Ch 20:15
inhabitants of Jerusalem
shall we *h.* then to you to do   Ne 13:27
all this
and *h.* to the pleadings of my   Job 13:6
lips
h. to me; *h.* to all my words   Job 32:10;
  33:1
h. unto me, ye men of   Job 34:10
understanding
let a wise man *h.*; *h.* to this,   Job 34:34;
O Job   37:14
h. I will teach you; *h.* O   Ps 34:11;
daughter   45:10
O Israel, if thou wilt *h.* unto   Ps 81:8
me
h. to me, therefore, O children   Pr 7:24;
  8:32
if a ruler *h.* to lies, servants   Pr 29:12
are wicked
hear my voice, *h.* and hear   Isa 28:23
my speech
and the ears of them that hear   Isa 32:3
shall *h.*

come near, ye nations, *h.* ye   Isa 34:1;
people   49:1
who will *h.* and hear for the   Isa 42:23
time to come
h. to me, O house of Jacob   Isa 46:3;
  48:12; Ho 5:1
h. to me, stout-hearted, are   Isa 46:12
far from righteousness
h. to me, ye that follow after   Isa 51:1
righteousness
h. unto me, my people, give   Isa 51:4
ear, O my nation
h. to me, ye that know   Isa 51:7
righteousness
h. diligently unto me, eat that   Isa 55:2
which is good
saying, *H.* to the sound of the   Jer 6:17
trumpet
if so be they will *h.* and turn   Jer 26:3
from evil
to *h.* to the prophets whom I   Jer 26:5
sent unto you
ye shall pray to me, and I will   Jer 29:12
h. unto you
will ye not receive instruction   Jer 35:13
to *h.* to words
but they refused to *h.* stopped   Zec 7:11
their ears
O Lord, *h.* and do; defer not,   Da 9:19
O my God
h. O earth, and all that therein   Mic 1:2
he said, *H.* to me, every one   M'k 7:14
of you
ye men of Judah, *h.* to my   Ac 2:14
words
to *h.* unto you more than unto   Ac 4:19
God
he said, Men, brethren, and   Ac 7:2
fathers, *h.*
as Peter knocked, a damsel   Ac 12:13
came to *h.*
saying, Men and brethren, *h.*   Ac 15:13
to me
h. my beloved brethren, hath   Jas 2:5
not God

HEARKEN *NOT*, *NOT* HEARKEN

if ye will *not h.* to be   Ge 34:17
circumcised
Pharaoh shall *not h.* to you   Ex 7:4;
  7:22; 11:9
but if ye will *not h.* to me   Le 26:14;
  26:18, 21, 27
thou shalt *not h.* to that   De 13:3
dreamer
not h. unto him, nor shall thine   De 13:8
eye pity him
the man that will *not h.* to the   De 17:12
priest
that whosoever will *not h.* to   De 18:19
my words
when chastened, he will *not h.*   De 21:18
to them
Lord would *not h.* to Balaam   De 23:5;
  Jos 24:10
and will *not h.* to thy words in   Jos 1:18
all
yet they would *not h.* to their   J'g 2:17
judges
the king of Edom would *not h.*   J'g 11:17
thereto
the men of Gibeah would *not*   J'g 19:25
h. to him
the children of Benjamin   J'g 20:13
would *not h.*
elders said, *H. not* to him,   1Ki 20:8
nor consent
did *not h.* but did after their   2Ki 17:40
manner
h. not to Hezekiah   2Ki 18:31; Isa 36:16
king Rehoboam would *not h.*   2Ch 10:16
to them
and the Lord spake, but they   2Ch 33:10
would *not h.*
if *not h.* hold thy peace, I   Job 33:33
shall teach thee
who will *not h.* to the voice of   Ps 58:5
charmers
but my people would *not h.* to   Ps 81:11
my voice
their ear is uncircumcised, they   Jer 6:10
cannot h.
but they said, We will *not h.*   Jer 6:17;
  44:16
thou shalt speak, they will *not*   Jer 7:27
h. unto thee

tho' they cry to me, I will *not* *Jer 11:11*
h. to them
after evil heart, that they may *Jer 16:12*
not h. to me
if ye will *not h.* to me *Jer 17:27;*
    26:4; Eze 20:39
h. not to prophets *Jer 23:16;*
    27:9, 14, 16, 17; 29:8
if I give counsel, wilt thou *Jer 38:15*
not h. to me
not h. to thee, for they will *not* *Eze 3:7*
h. to me
they rebelled, and would *not* *Eze 20:8*
h. unto me
because they did *not h.* to him *Ho 9:17;*
    Zec 1:4

HEARKENED

Abraham *h.* to Ephron, and *Ge 23:16*
weighed
God *h.* to Leah; God *h.* to *Ge 30:17;*
Rachel   *30:22*
to Hamor *h.* all that went out *Ge 34:24*
of the gate
that Joseph *h.* not to her, to *Ge 39:10*
lie by her
but they *h.* not to Moses *Ex 6:9; 16:20*
the children of Israel have not *Ex 6:12*
h. to me
Pharaoh *h.* not to them *Ex 7:13;*
    8:15, 19; 9:12
Lord *h.* to me at that time *De 9:19;*
    10:10
these nations *h.* to observers *De 18:14*
of times
Israel *h.* to Joshua as to *De 34:9;*
Moses   *Jos 1:17*
king of Ammonites *h.* not to *J'g 11:28*
Jephthah
the woman of Endor *h.* to *1Sa 28:21*
Saul's words
king *h.* not to people *1Ki 12:15;*
    12:16; 2Ch 10:15
they. therefore to the word *1Ki 12:24*
of the Lord
Ben-hadad *h.* to king Asa *1Ki 15:20;*
    2Ch 16:4
and he *h.* unto their voice, *1Ki 20:25*
and did
and the Lord *h.* to Jehoahaz *2Ki 13:4*
the king of Assyria *h.* to Asa *2Ki 16:9*
Hezekiah *h.* to the *2Ki 20:13*
messengers from Babylon
Judah *h.* not to the law, *2Ki 21:9*
Manasseh seduced
our fathers *h.* not to the *2Ki 22:13*
words of the book
then Joash *h.* to the princes *2Ch 24:17*
of Judah
Amaziah *h.* not to the *2Ch 25:16*
prophet's counsel
Lord *h.* to Hezekiah, and *2Ch 30:20*
healed the people
Josiah *h.* not to *2Ch 35:22*
Pharaoh-necho
our fathers *h.* not to thy *Ne 9:16;*
commandments   *9:29, 34; Jer 34:14*
now when Mordecai *h.* not to *Es 3:4*
them
O that my people had *h.* to me *Ps 81:13*
and he *h.* diligently with much *Isa 21:7*
heed
that thou hadst *h.* to my *Isa 48:18*
commandments
they have not *h.* to my word *Jer 6:19;*
7:24, 26; 25:3, 4, 7; 26:5; 29:19; 32:33;
34:17; 35:14, 15, 16; 36:31; 44:5
Irijah, *h.* not to Jeremiah, so *Jer 37:14*
he took him
had I sent, they would have *h.* to *Eze 3:6*
thee
neither have we *h.* to thy *Da 9:6*
servants
the Lord *h.* and heard it *Mal 3:16;*
    Jer 8:6
Paul said, Sirs, ye should *Ac 27:21*
have *h.* to me.

HEARKENEDST

because thou *h.* not to voice *De 28:45*
of the Lord

HEARKENETH

but whoso *h.* to me shall dwell *Pr 1:33*
safely
but he that *h.* to counsel is *Pr 12:15*
wise

HEARKENING

ye angels *h.* to the voice of *Ps 103:20*
his word

HEART

h. yearned for brother *Ge 43:30;*
(A)(E)(R)(S)   *1Ki 3:26*
Jacob's *h.* fainted, for he *Ge 45:26*
believed them not
the *h.* and liver (B) *Ex 12:9*
for ye know the *h.* of a *Ex 23:9*
stranger
they shall be on Aaron's *h.* *Ex 28:30*
when he goeth in
whoso is of a willing *h.* let him *Ex 35:5*
bring it
them hath he filled with *Ex 35:35*
wisdom of *h.*
shall consume eyes, cause *Le 26:16*
sorrow of *h.*
make soul pine away *Le 26:16*
(A)(E)(R)
saps the life (B) *Le 26:16*
wherefore discourage ye the *h.* *Nu 32:7*
of Israel
they discouraged the *h.* of the *Nu 32:9*
children of Israel
O that there were such an *h.* in *De 5:29*
them
h. and entire being (A) *De 10:12;*
    26:16; 30:2, 10
h. and entire being (A) *De 11:13;*
    11:18; 13:3
Lord shall smite with *De 28:28*
astonishment of *h.*
thou servedst not the Lord *De 28:47*
with gladness of *h.*
the Lord shall give thee there *De 28:65*
a trembling *h.*
Lord give sorrow of *h.* *De 28:65*
(B)(E)(R)
the Lord hath not given you a *De 29:4*
h. to perceive
they made the *h.* of the people *Jos 14:8*
melt
disheartened the people (B) *Jos 14:8*
for divisions were great *J'g 5:15*
thoughts of *h.*
great deliberations (B) *J'g 5:15*
for divisions there were great *J'g 5:16*
searchings of *h.*
his *h.* grieved (B) *J'g 16:16*
the priest's *h.* was glad, he *J'g 18:20*
took the ephod
felt happy at *h.* (B) *Ru 3:7*
now Hannah, she spake in her *1Sa 1:13*
h.
it was so that God gave him *1Sa 10:9*
another *h.*
but the Lord looketh on the *h.* *1Sa 16:7*
let no man's *h.* fail because *1Sa 17:32*
of him
David's *h.* smote him, because *1Sa 24:5*
he cut off
shall be no grief, nor offence *1Sa 25:31*
of *h.* to my lord
and Nabal's *h.* was merry *1Sa 25:36*
within him
she despised him in *h.* *2Sa 6:16;*
    1Ch 15:29
when Ammon's *h.* is merry *2Sa 13:28*
with wine
the *h.* of David (B) *2Sa 13:39*
that the king's *h.* was toward *2Sa 14:1*
Absalom
Joab thrust darts through the *2Sa 18:14*
h. of Absalom
he bowed the *h.* of all the *2Sa 19:14*
men of Judah
foreigners lost *h.* (R) *2Sa 22:46*
give thy servant an *1Ki 3:9*
understanding *h.*
an understanding mind *1Ki 3:9*
(A)(R)
an observant mind (B) *1Ki 3:9*
I have given thee an *1Ki 3:12*
understanding *h.*
a discerning mind (A)(R) *1Ki 3:12*
wise and perceptive mind (B) *1Ki 3:12*
her *h.* did yearn for son (S) *1Ki 3:26*
God gave Solomon wisdom *1Ki 4:29*
and largeness of *h.*
it was in the *h.* of David *1Ki 8:17;*
    2Ch 6:7
mind and *h.* (A)(R) *1Ki 8:48;*
    1Ch 22:19
people went to tents glad of *1Ki 8:66;*
h.   *2Ch 7:10*

communed of all was in her *1Ki 10:2;*
h.   *2Ch 9:1*
perfect, as was the *h.* of David *1Ki 11:4*
his father
then shall the *h.* of this *1Ki 12:27*
people turn
let your *h.* be happy (A) *1Ki 21:7*
the *h.* of king of Assyria was *2Ki 6:11*
troubled
that cometh into any man's *h.* *2Ki 12:4;*
    2Ch 29:31
they were not of double *h.* *1Ch 12:33*
let the *h.* of them rejoice *1Ch 16:10;*
    Ps 105:3
in the *h.* of God (A)(B)(R) *1Ch 28:8*
I know thou triest the *h.* *1Ch 29:17;*
    29:18; Jer 11:20
joyful and glad of *h.* (E)(R) *2Ch 7:10*
and all that came into *2Ch 7:11;*
Solomon's *h.*   *29:18*
turned the *h.* of the king of *Ezr 6:22*
Assyria
put such a thing as this in the *Ezr 7:27*
king's *h.*
this is nothing else but sorrow *Ne 2:2*
of *h.*
sadness of *h.* (R) *Ne 2:2*
when the *h.* of the king was *Es 1:10*
merry
Haman went forth that day with *Es 5:9*
a glad *h.*
he is wise in *h.* and mighty in *Job 9:4*
strength
he taketh away the *h.* of the *Job 9:24*
chief of people
the *h.* prepareth deceit (S) *Job 15:35*
my *h.* pines, faints *Job 19:27*
(A)(E)(R)(S)
I caused the widow's *h.* to sing *Job 29:13*
for joy
my *h.* is troubled *Job 30:27*
(A)(E)(R)(S)
but the hypocrites in *h.* heap *Job 36:13*
up wrath
he respecteth not any that *Job 37:24*
are wise of *h.*
who hath given *Job 38:36*
understanding to the *h.*
their *h.* is destruction *Ps 5:9*
(A)(B)(R)
and with a double *h.* do they *Ps 12:2*
speak
my *h.* instructs me *Ps 16:7*
(A)(E)(R)(S)
the statutes of Lord are right, *Ps 19:8*
rejoicing the *h.*
h. melted within me *Ps 22:14*
(A)(B)(E)(R)
try my *h.* (S) *Ps 26:2*
the lord is nigh them that are *Ps 34:18*
of a broken *h.*
not *h.* away in my heart *Ps 40:10*
(B)(E)(R)
for he knoweth the secrets of *Ps 44:21*
the *h.*
thine arrows are sharp in the *h.* *Ps 45:5*
of enemies
in *h.* ye work wickedness *Ps 58:2;*
the *h.* is deep   *Ps 64:6*
at *h.* they curse (B) *Ps 62:4*
they have more than *h.* could *Ps 73:7*
wish
I was pricked in my *h.* *Ps 73:21*
(A)(E)(R)(S)
a froward *h.* shall depart from *Ps 101:4*
me
perverse nature shall be absent *Ps 101:4*
(B)
an high look, and a proud *h.* *Ps 101:5*
will not I suffer
wine, that maketh glad the *h.* *Ps 104:15*
of man; bread, which
strengtheneth man's *h.*
my *h.* breaketh (A) *Ps 119:20*
h. be healthy (B) *Ps 119:80*
pleasant to your *h.* (A) *Pr 2:10; 29:17*
pleasant to your *h.* (R) *Pr 2:10;*
    19:18; 29:17; M't 22:37
an *h.* that deviseth wicked *Pr 6:18*
imaginations
behold, there met him a woman *Pr 7:10*
subtle of *h.*
a crafty mind (B) *Pr 7:10*
and ye fools, be ye of an *Pr 8:5*
understanding *h.*
make your mind understand (B) *Pr 8:5*
fools pay attention (R) *Pr 8:5*
let not your *h.* spare (B) *Pr 9:18*

the wise in *h.* will receive commandments — Pr 10:8
the *h.* of the wicked is little worth — Pr 10:20
they of a froward *h.* are abomination to Lord — Pr 11:20
the fool shall be servant to the wise of *h.* — Pr 11:29
he that is of perverse *h.* shall be despised — Pr 12:8
twisted thoughts shall be despised (B) — Pr 12:8
deceit is in the *h.* of them who imagine evil — Pr 12:20
heaviness in the *h.* of man maketh it stoop — Pr 12:25
hope deferred maketh the *h.* sick — Pr 13:12
the *h.* knoweth his own bitterness — Pr 14:10
even in laughter the *h.* is sorrowful — Pr 14:13
backslider in *h.* be filled with his own ways — Pr 14:14
a sound *h.* is the life of flesh, but envy — Pr 14:30
relaxed mind makes physical health (B) — Pr 14:30
wisdom resteth in *h.* of him that hath understanding — Pr 14:33
but the *h.* of the foolish doeth not so — Pr 15:7
merry *h.* maketh cheerful countenance; but by sorrow of *h.* the spirit is broken — Pr 15:13
a happy *h.* makes face look sunny (B) — Pr 15:13
h. of him that hath understanding — Pr 15:14
he that is of a merry *h.* hath a continual feast — Pr 15:15
without *h.* and sense (A) — Pr 15:21
the *h.* of the righteous studieth to answer — Pr 15:28
mind of righteous ponders (A)(B)(R) — Pr 15:28
the light of the eyes rejoiceth the *h.* — Pr 15:30
the preparations of *h.* in man from the Lord — Pr 16:1
every one proud in *h.* is an abomination to Lord — Pr 16:5
a man's *h.* deviseth his way, but Lord directs — Pr 16:9
the *h.* of the wise teacheth his mouth — Pr 16:23
a price in hand, seeing he hath no *h.* to it — Pr 17:16
he that hath a froward *h.* findeth no good — Pr 17:20
crooked mind finds no good (A)(B)(R) — Pr 17:20
a merry *h.* doeth good like a medicine — Pr 17:22
cheerful, happy *h.* (A)(B)(E)(R) — Pr 17:22
before destruction the *h.* of man is haughty — Pr 18:12
the *h.* of the prudent getteth knowledge — Pr 18:15
discerning mind gets knowle _ ᵉ (ᴬ)(B)(R) — Pr 18:15
there are many devices in a man's *h.* — Pr 19:21
Many plans in man's mind (A)(B)(R) — Pr 19:21
counsel in the *h.* of man is like deep water — Pr 20:5
planning in man's mind is deep (B)(R) — Pr 20:5
the king's *h.* is in the hand of the Lord — Pr 21:1
an high look, and a proud *h.* is sin — Pr 21:4
that loveth pureness of *h.* the king his friend — Pr 22:11
foolishness is bound in the *h.* of a child — Pr 22:15
my *h.* will rejoice (A)(B)(E)(S) — Pr 23:16
doth not he that pondereth the *h.* consider it — Pr 24:12
and the *h.* of kings is unsearchable — Pr 25:3
mind of kings is unsearchable (B)(R) — Pr 25:3
so is he that singeth songs to an heavy *h.* — Pr 25:20

a wicked *h.* is like a potsherd covered with — Pr 26:23
ointment and perfume rejoice the *h.* — Pr 27:9
so the *h.* of man answereth to man — Pr 27:19
he that is of a proud *h.* stirreth up strife — Pr 28:25
the *h.* of her husband doth safely trust her — Pr 31:11
by sadness of countenance the *h.* is better — Ec 7:3
h. of wise is in house of mourning, but *h.* of fools is in house of mirth — Ec 7:4
oppression makes mad, a gift destroyeth the *h.* — Ec 7:7
my *h.* seeketh (B) — Ec 7:28
wise man's *h.* discerneth both time and judgment — Ec 8:5
the *h.* of men is fully set in them to do evil — Ec 8:11
also the *h.* of the sons of men is full of evil — Ec 9:3
eat thy bread, and drink thy wine with merry *h.* — Ec 9:7
a wise man's *h.* is at right hand, fool's *h.* at left — Ec 10:2
h. grew desirous of him (B)(R)(S) — Ca 5:4
make their *h.* fat — Isa 6:10; M't 13:15; Ac 28:27
be not afraid or timid of *h.* (B)(E)(R) — Isa 7:4
that say in the pride and stoutness of *h.* — Isa 9:9
will punish the fruit of the stout *h.* of king — Isa 10:12
all hands faint, every man's *h.* shall melt — Isa 13:7
h. sounds like a harp (A)(E)(S) — Isa 16:11
h. of Egypt shall melt — Isa 19:1
ye shall have gladness of *h.* as when one — Isa 30:29
the *h.* of the rash shall understand knowledge — Isa 32:4
say to them that are of fearful *h.* Be strong — Isa 35:4
it burned him, yet he laid it not to *h.* — Isa 42:25
a deceived *h.* hath turned him aside — Isa 44:20
and no man layeth it to *h.* — Isa 57:1; Jer 12:11
and to revive the *h.* of the contrite ones — Isa 57:15
uttering from the *h.* words of falsehood — Isa 59:13
thy *h.* and mercy (S) — Isa 63:15
My servants shall sing for joy of *h.* cry for sorrow of *h.* — Isa 65:14
follow the *h.* (R) — Jer 3:17; 13:10; 18:12; Eze 37:24
the *h.* of the king and princes shall perish — Jer 4:9
but this people hath a rebellious *h.* — Jer 5:23
the house of Israel are uncircumcised in *h.* — Jer 9:26
O Lord, that triest the reins and the *h.* — Jer 11:20
the *h.* and the mind (S) — Jer 11:20; 20:12
far from their *h.* (A)(E)(R)(S) — Jer 12:2
the *h.* is deceitful above all things — Jer 17:9
I the Lord search the *h.* I try the reins — Jer 17:10
I try the *h.* (A)(E)(R) — Jer 17:10
O Lord, that seest the reins and *h.* — Jer 20:12
how long shall this be in the *h.* of prophets — Jer 23:26
and I will give them a *h.* to know me — Jer 24:7
h. yearneth for him (E)(R) — Jer 31:20
my whole *h.*, whole being (A) — Jer 32:41
be as the *h.* of a woman in her pangs — Jer 48:41; 49:22
my *h.* is troubled (S) — La 1:20; 2:11; Jer 31:20
arrows enter my *h.* (A)(R)(S) — La 3:13
give them sorrow of *h.* thy curse to them — La 3:65
I am broken with their whorish *h.* — Eze 6:9
I will take the stony *h.* out of their flesh — Eze 11:19

with lies ye made *h.* of the righteous sad — Eze 13:22
and make you a new *h.* and a new spirit — Eze 18:31
every *h.* shall melt, all hands shall be feeble — Eze 21:7
rejoiced in *h.* with all thy despite against Israel — Eze 25:6
have taken vengeance with a despiteful *h.* — Eze 25:15
shall weep for thee with bitterness of *h.* — Eze 27:31
and I will give you a *h.* of flesh — Eze 36:26
strangers uncircumcised in *h.* — Eze 44:7; 44:9; Ac 7:51
let a beast's *h.* be given unto him — Da 4:16
let a beast's nature and understanding be given him (A) — Da 4:16
an animal mind be given him (B)(R) — Da 4:16
and a man's *h.* was given to it — Da 7:4
mind of a man was given to it (B)(R) — Da 7:4
whoredom and wine take away the *h.* — Ho 4:11
Ephraim is like a silly dove without *h.* — Ho 7:11
my *h.* desired (B) — Mic 7:1
the *h.* melteth, and the knees smite — Na 2:10
this the city that said in her *h.* I am — Zep 2:15
lay it to *h.* to give glory, I will send a curse, because ye do not lay it to *h.* — Mal 2:2
shall turn the *h.* of fathers, and *h.* of children — Mal 4:6
at *h.* they are voracious wolves (B) — M't 7:15
come to me, I am meek and lowly in *h.* — M't 11:29
out of the abundance of the *h.* — M't 12:34; Lu 6:45
out of the treasure of the *h.* — M't 12:35; Lu 6:45
Son of man be in *h.* of the earth — M't 12:40
come forth from the *h.* and defile the man — M't 15:18
out of the *h.* proceed evil thoughts — M't 15:19; M'k 7:21
had a heavy *h.* (N) — M't 19:22
h. nearly breaking (P) — M't 26:38; M'k 14:34
went away with heavy *h.* (N) — M'k 10:22
my *h.* goes out to (P) — M'k 15:32
he upbraided them with hardness of *h.* — M'k 16:14
Mary kept and pondered them in her *h.* — Lu 2:19
pierce own *h.* (N) — Lu 2:35
but his mother kept these sayings in her *h.* — Lu 2:51
in the *h.* of the people (A)(R) — Lu 7:1
his *h.* went out to her (N)(P) — Lu 7:13
which in a good *h.* having heard the word — Lu 8:15
his *h.* sank (N) — Lu 18:23
in *h.* of people (B)(E)(N)(R) — Lu 20:45
O fools, slow of *h.* to believe the prophets — Lu 24:25
out of his *h.* shall flow (R)(S) — Joh 7:38
the devil having put into the *h.* of Judas — Joh 13:2
did eat their meat with singleness of *h.* — Ac 2:46
heard that, they were cut to the *h.* — Ac 5:33; 7:54
with purpose of *h.* they would cleave to Lord — Ac 11:23
after thy impenitent *h.* treasurest up — Ro 2:5
circumcision is that of the *h.* in the Spirit — Ro 2:29
ye have obeyed from the *h.* that doctrine — Ro 6:17
in my inmost *h.* (B) — Ro 7:22
with my *h.* I serve God (B) — Ro 7:25
with the *h.* man believeth to righteousness — Ro 10:10
neither have entered into the *h.* of man — 1Co 2:9
hath so decreed in his *h.* that he will keep — 1Co 7:37

out of much anguish of *h.* I   *2Co 2:4*
wrote you

not in stone, but written in   *2Co 3:3*
fleshly tables of *h.*

which glory in appearance,   *2Co 5:12*
and not in *h.*

his *h.* goes out to you   *2Co 7:15*
(A)(N)(R)

the same earnest care into the   *2Co 8:16*
h. of Titus

doing the will of God from the   *Eph 6:6*
h.

give *h.* to heavenly things (P)   *Col 3:2*

tenderness of *h.*   *Col 3:12*
(B)(E)(N)(P)(R)

so they may not lose *h.* (B)   *Col 3:21*

but in singleness of *h.* fearing   *Col 3:22*
God

taken from you in presence,   *1Th 2:17*
not in *h.*

my very *h.* (A)(B)(E)(R)(S)   *Ph'm 12*

refresh my *h.* (A)(E)(P)(R)   *Ph'm 20*

is a discerner of the intents of   *Heb 4:12*
the *h.*

let us draw near with a true   *Heb 10:22*
h. in assurance

it is good that the *h.* be   *Heb 13:9*
established with grace

let it be the hidden man of the   *1Pe 3:4*
h.

Lot vexed his *h.* (N)   *2Pe 2:8*

an *h.* exercised with covetous   *2Pe 2:14*
practices

his *h.* of compassion   *1Jo 3:17*
(A)(N)(P)(R)

for she saith in her *h.* I sit a   *Re 18:7*
queen

HEART with *ALL*

to serve him with *all* your *h.*   *De 11:13;*
  Jos 22:5; 1Sa 12:20, 24

love the Lord, with *all* your *h.*   *De 13:3;*
30:6;   *M't 22:37;*   *M'k 12:30,*   *33;*
  Lu 10:27

thou shalt keep and do them   *De 26:16*
with *all* thy *h.*

return to the *Lord* with *all*   *De 30:2;*
thine *h.*   *30:10; Joe 2:12*

that Samson told her *all* his   *J'g 16:17;*
h.   *16:18*

walk before me with *all* their   *1Ki 2:4;*
h.   *8:23*

return to thee with *all* their *h.*   *1Ki 8:48;*
  2Ki 23:25; 2Ch 6:38

David, who followed me with   *1Ki 14:8*
all his *h.*

Jehu took no heed to walk   *2Ki 10:31*
with *all* his *h.*

to walk before the Lord with   *2Ki 23:3;*
all their *h.* and all their soul   *2Ch 34:31*

seek God of fathers with *all*   *2Ch 15:12*
their *h.*

for they had sworn with *all*   *2Ch 15:15*
their *h.*

Jehoshaphat sought the Lord   *2Ch 22:9*
with *all* his *h.*

he did it with *all* his *h.* and   *2Ch 31:21*
prospered

I will praise thee, O Lord with   *Ps 86:12*
all my *h.*

trust in the Lord with *all* thy *h.*   *Pr 3:5*
lean not

when ye search for me with   *Jer 29:13*
all your *h.*

with the joy of *all* their *h.* to   *Eze 36:5*
cast it out

be glad with *all* the *h.* O   *Zep 3:14*
Jerusalem

if thou believest with *all* thy *h.*   *Ac 8:37*
mayest

HIS HEART

every imagination of his *h.* was   *Ge 6:5*
only evil

it repented the Lord and grieved   *Ge 6:6*
him at his *h.*

Lord said in his *h.*; Abraham   *Ge 8:21;*
in his *h.*   *17:17*

Esau said in his *h.* the days of   *Ge 27:41*
mourning

when seeth thee, he will be glad   *Ex 4:14*
in his *h.*

neither did he set his *h.* to this   *Ex 7:23*
also

every man that giveth willingly   *Ex 25:2*
with his *h.*

in the breastplate of   *Ex 28:29*
judgment upon his *h.*

he hath put in *his h.* that   *Ex 35:34*
he may teach

the Lord hath made *his h.*   *De 2:30*
obstinate

multiply wives, that *his h.*   *De 17:17*
turn not away

his h. be not lifted up above   *De 17:20*
his brethren

lest the avenger pursue, while   *De 19:6*
his h. is hot

lest his brethren's heart faint as   *De 20:8*
well as *his h.*

for he is poor, and setteth *his*   *De 24:15*
h. upon it

that he bless himself in *his h.*   *De 29:19*
saying

his h. was merry, he went to lie   *Ru 3:7*
down

his h. trembled for the ark of   *1Sa 4:13*
God

David laid up these words in   *1Sa 21:12*
his h.

it came to pass that *his h.*   *1Sa 21:37*
died within him

David said in *his h.*; *his h.*   *1Sa 27:1;*
trembled   *28:5*

thy servant hath found in *his*   *2Sa 7:27;*
h. to pray   *1Ch 17:25*

let not my lord take the   *2Ch 13:33*
thing to *his h.*

which God had put in *his h.*   *1Ki 10:24;*
  2Ch 9:23

and his wives turned away *his*   *1Ki 11:3;*
h.   *11:4, 9*

Jeroboam said in *his h.* the   *1Ki 12:26*
kingdom return

the arrow went out at *his h.*   *2Ki 9:24*
and sunk

because he prepared not *his*   *2Ch 12:14*
h. to

his h. was lifted up in the   *2Ch 17:6*
ways of the Lord

his h. was lifted up to his   *2Ch 26:16*
destruction

that prepareth *his h.* to seek   *2Ch 30:19*
God, Lord God

for *his h.* was lifted up,   *2Ch 32:25*
therefore was wrath

he humbled himself for the   *2Ch 32:26*
pride of *his h.*

that he might know all that   *2Ch 32:31*
was in *his h.*

Ezra prepared *his h.* to seek   *Ezr 7:10*
law of Lord

and foundest *his h.* faithful   *Ne 9:8*
before thee

Haman thought in *his h.* to   *Es 6:6*
whom the king

where is he that durst presume   *Es 7:5*
in *his h.* to do

if he set *his h.* upon man, if   *Job 34:14*
he gather

his h. is as firm as a stone,   *Job 41:24*
yea as hard

he hath said in *his h.*   *Ps 10:6;*
  11:13; 14:1; 53:1

that speaketh truth in *his h.*   *Ps 15:2*
shall dwell

the thoughts of *his h.* to all   *Ps 33:11*
generations

law of his God is in *his h.*   *Ps 37:31*
none of his steps

his h. gathereth iniquity to   *Ps 41:6*
itself

words were smooth, but war   *Ps 55:21*
was in *his h.*

he fed them according to   *Ps 78:72*
integrity of *his h.*

his h. is fixed, trusting in the   *Ps 112:7*
Lord

his h. is established, he shall   *Ps 112:8*
not be afraid

frowardness is in *his h.*   *Pr 6:14*
deviseth mischief

but that *his h.* may discover   *Pr 18:2*
itself

and *his h.* fretteth against the   *Pr 19:3*
Lord

as he thinketh in *his h.* so is he;   *Pr 23:7*
eat and drink, saith he, but
his h. is not with thee

but he hardeneth *his h.*   *Pr 28:14*
shall fall

yea *his h.* taketh not rest in the   *Ec 2:23*
night

God answereth him in the joy   *Ec 5:20*
of *his h.*

in the day of the gladness of   *Ca 3:11*
his h.

his h. was moved, and the heart   *Isa 7:2*
of his people

he meaneth not so, neither   *Isa 10:7*
doth *his h.* think so, but it is
in *his h.* to destroy

his h. will work iniquity, to   *Isa 32:6*
practise hypocrisy

none considereth in *his h.*   *Isa 44:19*
neither is there

he went on frowardly in the   *Isa 57:17*
way of *his h.*

but in *h.* he layeth *his* wait   *Jer 9:8*

he have performed the   *Jer 23:20*
thoughts of *his h.*

that engaged *his h.* to   *Jer 30:21*
approach unto me

until he have performed the   *Jer 30:24*
intents of *his h.*

we have heard the   *Jer 48:29*
haughtiness of *his h.*

that setteth up his idols in *his*   *Eze 14:4;*
h.   *14:7*

his h. lifted up in his height   *Eze 31:10;*
  Da 5:20

Daniel purposed in *his h.* that   *Da 1:8*
he would

let *his h.* be changed from   *Da 4:16;*
man's   *5:21*

the king set *his h.* on Daniel to   *Da 6:14*
deliver him

and he shall magnify himself   *Da 8:25*
in *his h.*

his h. shall be lifted up, shall   *Da 11:12*
cast down

his h. shall be against the   *Da 11:28*
holy covenant

that saith in *his h.*; Who shall   *Ob 3*
bring me down

hath committed adultery with   *M't 5:28*
her in *his h.*

and catcheth away that was   *M't 13:19*
sown in *his h.*

if evil servant shall say in   *M't 24:48;*
his h.   *Lu 12:45*

because it entereth not into   *M'k 7:19*
his h.

and shall not doubt in *his h.*   *M'k 11:23*
but believe

good man out of good treasure   *Lu 6:45*
of *his h.*, an evil man out of
evil treasure of *his h.*

it came into *his h.* to visit his   *Ac 7:23*
brethren

he that standeth stedfast in   *1Co 7:37*
his h.

thus are the secrets of *his h.*   *1Co 14:25*
made manifest

as he purposeth in *his h.* so let   *2Co 9:7*
him give

MINE, MY HEART

in the integrity of *my h.* have I   *Ge 20:5*
done this

done speaking in *mine h.*   *Ge 24:45*
Rebekah came

tho' I walk in the imagination   *De 29:19*
of *my h.*

I brought him word as it was   *Jos 14:7*
in *mine h.*

my h. is toward the governors of   *J'g 5:9*
Israel

she said, *My h.* rejoiceth in the   *1Sa 2:1*
Lord

shall do according to that   *1Sa 2:35*
which is in *mine h.*

mine h. be there perpetually   *1Ki 9:3;*
  2Ch 7:16

went not *mine h.* with thee   *2Ki 5:26*

is thine heart right, as *my h.*   *2Ki 10:15*
is with thy

hast done according to all   *2Ki 10:30*
that was in *mine h.*

if to help, *mine h.* shall be   *1Ch 12:17*
knit unto

I have in *mine h.* to build an   *1Ch 28:2*
house of rest

it is in *mine h.* to make a   *2Ch 29:10*
covenant

what God had put in *my h.* to   *Ne 2:12*
do

the thoughts of *my h.* are   *Job 17:11*
broken off

God maketh *my h.* soft and   *Job 23:16*
the Almighty

my *h.* shall not reproach me   *Job 27:6*
so long as I live
and *mine h.* walked after mine   *Job 31:7*
eyes
if *mine h.* have been deceived   *Job 31:9*
by a woman
and *my h.* hath been secretly   *Job 31:27*
enticed
my words shall be of the   *Job 33:3*
uprightness of *my h.*
at this also *my h.* trembleth,   *Job 37:1*
and is moved
thou hast put gladness in *my h.*   *Ps 4:7*
more than
how long take counsel, sorrow   *Ps 13:2*
in *my h.* daily
but I trusted, *my h.* shall   *Ps 13:5*
rejoice in thy salvation
my h. is glad; thou hast proved *Ps 16:9;*
mine h.   *17:3*
let the meditation of *my h.* be   *Ps 19:14*
acceptable
mine h. is like wax; try my   *Ps 22:14*
reins and *mine h.*   *26:2*
the troubles of *my h.* are   *Ps 25:17*
enlarged, O bring
my h. shall not fear though war *Ps 27:3*
should rise
my h. said to thee, Thy face,   *Ps 27:8*
Lord, will I seek
my h. trusted in him, *my h.*   *Ps 28:7*
greatly rejoiceth
the transgression of the wicked *Ps 36:1*
saith in *my h.*
by reason of the disquietness of *Ps 38:8*
my h.
my h. panteth, my strength   *Ps 38:10;*
faileth   *Isa 21:4*
my h. was hot within me, while *Ps 39:3*
musing
yea, thy law is within *my h.*   *Ps 40:8*
I have not hid thy   *Ps 40:10*
righteousness within *my h.*
not able to look up, therefore *Ps 40:12*
my h. faileth me
my h. is inditing a good matter, *Ps 45:1*
I speak
the meditation of *my h.* be of   *Ps 49:3*
understanding
my h. is sore pained within me, *Ps 55:4*
terrors of death
my h. is fixed, O God, *my h.* is *Ps 57:7;*
fixed   *108:1*
I will cry, when *my h.* is   *Ps 61:2*
overwhelmed
if I regard iniquity in *my h.*   *Ps 66:18*
Lord will not hear
reproach hath broken *my h.* I *Ps 69:20*
am full
verily I have cleansed *my h.* in *Ps 73:13*
vain
my h. was grieved, I was   *Ps 73:21*
pricked in my reins
my h. faileth, but God is the   *Ps 73:26*
strength of *my h.*
my h. and flesh crieth out for   *Ps 84:2*
the living God
unite *my h.* to fear thy name   *Ps 86:11*
my h. is smitten and withered *Ps 102:4*
like grass
and *my h.* is wounded within   *Ps 109:22*
me
thy word have I hid in *my h.* *Ps 119:11*
not to sin
I will run, when thou shalt   *Ps 119:32*
enlarge *my h.*
incline *my h.* to thy   *Ps 119:36*
testimonies, not covetousness
let *my h.* be sound in thy   *Ps 119:80*
statutes
thy testimonies are the   *Ps 119:111*
rejoicing of *my h.*
I have inclined *mine h.* to   *Ps 119:112*
perform thy statutes
Lord, *my h.* is not haughty,   *Ps 131:1*
nor eyes lofty
search me, and know *my h.*   *Ps 139:23*
try me
incline not *my h.* to any evil   *Ps 141:4*
thing
my h. within me is desolate   *Ps 143:4*
how hath *my h.* despised   *Pr 5:12*
reproof
who can say, I have made *my*   *Pr 20:9*
h. clean
if thine heart be wise, *my h.*   *Pr 23:15*
shall rejoice
I gave *my h.* to seek and   *Ec 1:13*
search out

my *h.* had great experience of *Ec 1:16*
wisdom
I gave *my h.* to know wisdom   *Ec 1:17*
and madness
I said in *mine h.* I will   *Ec 2:1;*
   2:15; 3:17, 18
I sought in *mine h.* to give   *Ec 2:3*
myself to wine
I withheld not *my h.* from any *Ec 2:10*
joy
to cause *my h.* to despair of all *Ec 2:20*
the labour
I applied *mine h.* to know and *Ec 7:25;*
search   *8:9, 16*
for all this I considered in *my h. Ec 9:1*
thou hast ravished *my h.* my   *Ca 4:9*
sister
I sleep, but *my h.* waketh, it is *Ca 5:2*
the voice
my h. shall cry out for Moab   *Isa 15:5*
for the day of vengeance is in *Isa 63:4*
mine h.
I will give you pastors   *Jer 3:15*
according to *mine h.*
I am pained at *my h. my h.*   *Jer 4:19*
maketh a noise
I commanded not, neither   *Jer 7:31*
came it into *my h.*
when I comfort myself, *my h. Jer 8:18*
is faint in me
hast seen me, and tried *mine h. Jer 12:3*
toward thee
thy word the joy and   *Jer 15:16*
rejoicing of *mine h.*
his word was in *mine h.* as a   *Jer 20:9*
burning fire
mine h. is broken; *my h.* shall *Jer 23:9;*
mourn   *48:31*
therefore *mine h.* shall sound *Jer 48:36*
for Moab
behold, *mine h.* is turned   *La 1:20*
within me
my sighs are many, and *my h. La 1:22*
is faint
mine eye affecteth *mine h.*   *La 3:51*
because of all
but I kept the matter in *my h. Da 7:28*
mine h. is turned within me,   *Ho 11:8*
my repentings
therefore did *my h.* rejoice,   *Ac 2:26*
tongue glad
what mean ye to weep, and   *Ac 21:13*
break *mine h.*
I have continual sorrow in my *Ro 9:2*
h.
because I have you in *my h.*   *Ph'p 1:7*
inasmuch

ONE HEART

hand of God was to give   *2Ch 30:12*
them *one h.*
I will give them *one h.*   *Jer 32:39;*
   Eze 11:19
multitude that believed were of *Ac 4:32*
one h.

OWN HEART

that ye seek not after your   *Nu 15:39*
own h.
sought man after his *own h.*   *1Sa 13:14;*
   Ac 13:22
according to thine *own h.*   *2Sa 7:21;*
hast thou done these things   *1Ch 17:19*
know every man plague of his *1Ki 8:38*
own h.
which he had devised of his   *1Ki 12:33*
own h.
thou feignest them out of   *Ne 6:8*
thine *own h.*
commune with your *own h.* on   *Ps 4:4*
your bed
grant thee according to thine   *Ps 20:4*
own h.
their sword shall enter into   *Ps 37:15*
their *own h.*
I commune with my *own h.* and *Ps 77:6*
my spirit
he that trusteth in his *own h.* *Pr 28:26*
is a fool
I communed with mine *own h. Ec 1:16*
saying
thy *own h.* knows thou hast   *Ec 7:22*
cursed others
after imagination of their *own Jer 9:14;*
h.   *23:17*

they speak a vision of their   *Jer 23:16*
own h.
prophesy the deceit of their   *Jer 23:26;*
own h.   *Eze 13:17*
may take house of Israel in   *Eze 14:5*
their *own h.*
but deceiveth his *own h.* this *Jas 1:26*
man's

OUR HEART

our brethren have discouraged *De 1:28*
our h.
for *our h.* shall rejoice in him *Ps 33:21*
our h. is not turned back,   *Ps 44:18*
neither our
let us lift up *our h.* with our   *La 3:41*
hands
the joy of *our h.* is ceased; *our La 5:15;*
h. is faint   *5:17*
did not *our h.* burn within us, *Lu 24:32*
while he
our mouth is open, *our h.* is   *2Co 6:11*
enlarged
if *our h.* condemn us, God is   *1Jo 3:20*
greater
if *our h.* condemn us not, we   *1Jo 3:21*
have confidence

PERFECT HEART

let your *h.* be *perfect* with   *1Ki 8:61*
the Lord
his *h.* was not *perfect* with the *1Ki 11:4;*
Lord   *15:3*
nevertheless Asa's *h.* was   *1Ki 15:14;*
perfect with the Lord all his *2Ch 15:17*
days
remember how I have walked *2Ki 20:3;*
before thee with a *perfect h.* *Isa 38:3*
came with *perfect h.* to make *1Ch 12:38*
David king
Solomon, my son, serve God *1Ch 28:9*
with a *perfect h.*
because with *perfect h.* they *1Ch 29:9*
offered willingly
and give unto Solomon my   *1Ch 29:19*
son a *perfect h.*
in behalf of them whose *h.* is *2Ch 16:9*
perfect
thus shall ye do in fear of   *2Ch 19:9*
Lord with *perfect h.*
Amaziah did right, but not   *2Ch 25:2*
with a *perfect h.*
I will walk in my house with   *Ps 101:2*
perfect h.

PURE HEART

who shall ascend? that hath a *Ps 24:4*
pure h.
blessed are *pure* in *h.* they shall *M't 5:8*
see God
end of commandment is charity *1Ti 1:5*
out of *pure h.*
that call on the Lord out of a   *2Ti 2:22*
pure h.
love one another with a *pure h. 1Pe 1:22*
fervently

THEIR HEART

their h. failed them, they were *Ge 42:28*
afraid
the kings of Amorites heard   *Jos 5:1*
their h. melted
thou hast turned *their h.* back *1Ki 18:37*
again
and prepare *their h.* unto   *1Ch 29:18*
thee
shall they not utter words out *Job 8:10*
of *their h.*
thou hast hid *their h.* from   *Job 17:4*
understanding
Lord, thou wilt prepare *their   *Ps 10:17*
h.*
a generation that set not *their h. Ps 78:8*
aright
they tempted God in *their h.*   *Ps 78:18*
by asking meat
their h. was not right with   *Ps 78:37*
him, nor were
it is a people that do err in   *Ps 95:10*
their h.
he turned *their h.* to hate his *Ps 105:25*
people
therefore he brought down   *Ps 107:12*
their h.
their h. is as fat as grease, I *Ps 119:70*
delight in thy law

which imagine mischiefs in | Ps 140:2
their h. with labour
for their h. studieth destruction | Pr 24:2
also he hath set the world in | Ec 3:11
their h.
madness is in their h. while they | Ec 9:3
live
understand with their h. | Isa 6:10;
| M't 13:15; Ac 28:27
their h. is far from me | Isa 29:13;
| M't 15:8; M'k 7:6
neither say they in their h., | Jer 5:24
Let us fear the Lord
which walk in the | Jer 13:10
imagination of their h.
the prophets prophesy the | Jer 14:14
deceit of their h.
sin of Judah is graven on the | Jer 17:1
table of their h.
their h. cried to the Lord O | La 2:18
wall of Zion
these have set up their idols in | Eze 14:3
their h.
for their h. went after their | Eze 20:16
idols
that their h. may faint, ruins | Eze 21:15
be multiplied
but their h. goeth after their | Eze 33:31
covetousness
they set their h. on their | Ho 4:8
iniquity
they have made ready their h. | Ho 7:6
like an oven
they have not cried unto me | Ho 7:14
with their h.
their h. is divided | Ho 10:2
their h. was exalted | Ho 13:6
I will rend the caul of their h. | Ho 13:8
and devour
I will punish the men that say | Zep 1:12
in their h.
their h. shall rejoice in the | Zec 10:7
Lord
the governors of Judah shall | Zec 12:5
say in their h.
for their h. was hardened | M'k 6:52;
| Ro 1:21
Jesus perceiving the thought of | Lu 9:47
their h.
hardened their h. that they | Joh 12:40
should not see nor understand
their h.
were pricked in their h. and said | Ac 2:37
to Peter
when Moses is read, veil is on | 2Co 3:15
their h.
because of the blindness of | Eph 4:18
their h.

THINE, THY HEART

thou didst this in the integrity | Ge 20:6
of thy h.
I will send all my plagues upon | Ex 9:14
thine h.
thou shalt not hate thy | Le 19:17
brother in thine h.
lest they depart from thy h. all | De 4:9
thy life
shalt find, if thou seek him | De 4:29
with all thy h.
know and consider it in thine | De 4:39;
h. | 8:5
thou shalt love the Lord with all | De 6:5
thine h.
if say in thine h. these nations | De 7:17;
are more than I | 8:17; 18:21; Jer 13:22
led thee, to know what was in | De 8:2
thine h.
then thine h. be lifted up, and | De 8:14
thou forget Lord
speak not thou in thine h. after | De 9:4
that the Lord
not for uprightness of thine h. | De 9:5
dost thou go to
to serve the Lord thy God with | De 10:12
all thy h.
there be not a thought in thy | De 15:9
wicked h.
thine h. shall not be grieved | De 15:10
when thou givest
for the fear of thine h. | De 28:67
wherewith shalt fear
circumcise thine h. and the | De 30:6
heart of thy seed
but the word is very nigh to | De 30:14
thee in thy h.
if thine h. turn, so that thou | De 30:17
wilt not hear
when thine h. is not with me | J'g 16:15

and let thine h. be merry | J'g 19:6;
| 19:9; 1Ki 21:7
the damsel's father said, | J'g 19:8
Comfort thine h.
why weepest thou? why is thy | 1Sa 1:8
h. grieved
the man of thine shall be to | 1Sa 2:33
grieve thine h.
I will tell thee all that is in | 1Sa 9:19
thine h.
do all that is in thine h. | 1Sa 14:7;
| 2Sa 7:3
behold, I am with thee, | 1Sa 14:7
according to thy h.
I know thy pride and | 1Sa 17:28
naughtiness of thy h.
reign over all that thine h. | 2Sa 3:21
desireth
knowest wickedness thine h. | 1Ki 2:44
is privy
in thine h. to build | 1Ki 8:18;
| 2Ch 1:11; 6:8
is thine h. right as my heart | 2Ki 10:15
is with thy h.
thine h. hath lifted thee up | 2Ki 14:10;
| 2Ch 25:19
because thine h. was tender | 2Ki 22:19;
| 2Ch 34:27
hast prepared thine h. to seek | 2Ch 19:3
God
and that thou shouldest set | Job 7:17
thine h. upon him
and these things hast thou | Job 10:13
hid in thine h.
if thou prepare thine h. and | Job 11:13
stretch out
why doth thine h. carry thee | Job 15:12
away
receive, and lay up his words | Job 22:22
in thine h.
and he shall strengthen thine | Ps 27:14
h.
and he shall give thee the | Ps 37:4
desires of thine h.
and apply thine h. to | Pr 2:2
understanding
when wisdom entereth into | Pr 2:10
thine h.
my son, let thine h. keep my | Pr 3:1
commandments
write them upon the table of | Pr 3:3;
thine h. | 7:3
he said, Let thine h. retain my | Pr 4:4;
words | 4:21
keep thy h. with all diligence, | Pr 4:23
for out of it
bind them continually upon | Pr 6:21
thine h.
lust not after her beauty in | Pr 6:25
thine h.
let not thine h. decline to her | Pr 7:25
ways
my son. if thine h. be wise, my | Pr 23:15
heart rejoice
let not thine h. envy sinners, | Pr 23:17
but be in fear
hear, my son, and guide thine | Pr 23:19
h. in the way
my son, give me thine h. let | Pr 23:26
thy eyes observe
and thine h. shall utter | Pr 23:33
perverse things
let not thine h. be glad when | Pr 24:17
he stumbleth
not thine h. be hasty to utter | Ec 5:2
any thing
let thy h. cheer thee; walk in | Ec 11:9
ways of thy h.
therefore remove sorrow | Ec 11:10
from thy h.
thou hast said in thine h. I | Isa 14:13
will ascend
thine h. shall meditate terror, | Isa 33:18
where is
thou didst not lay these things | Isa 47:7;
to thy h. | 57:11
that sayest in thine h. I am, | Isa 47:8;
and none else | 47:10
then shalt thou say in thine h. | Isa 49:21
Who hath
O Jerusalem wash thine h. | Jer 4:14
from wickedness
it is bitter, because it reacheth | Jer 4:18
unto thine h.
thine h. are not but for thy | Jer 22:17
covetousness
set thine h. toward the | Jer 31:21
highway, turn

the pride of thine h. deceived | Jer 49:16;
thee | Ob 3
pour out thine h. like water | La 2:19
before Lord
receive in thine h. hear with | Eze 3:10
thine ears
how weak is thine h. saith | Eze 16:30
the Lord God
can thine h. endure in days I | Eze 22:14
deal with thee
because thine h. is lifted up | Eze 28:2;
for thy riches | 28:5
thou hast set thine h. as the | Eze 28:6
heart of God
thine h. was lifted up because | Eze 28:17
of thy beauty
set thine h. upon all that I | Eze 40:4
shall shew thee
mightest know the thoughts of | Da 2:30
thy h.
and then hast not humbled | Da 5:22
thine h.
thou didst set thine h. to | Da 10:12
understand
why hath Satan filled thine h. | Ac 5:3
to lie
why hast thou conceived this in | Ac 5:4
thine h.
for thy h. is not right in the | Ac 8:21
sight of God
thought of thine h. may be | Ac 8:22
forgiven thee
say not in thine h.; Who shall | Ro 10:6
ascend
and shalt believe in thine h. | Ro 10:9
that God raised

UPRIGHT IN HEART

Levites were more upright in | 2Ch 29:34
h.
which saveth the upright in h. | Ps 7:10
that they may shoot at the | Ps 11:2
upright in h.
shout for joy, ye that are | Ps 32:11
upright in h.
continue thy righteousness to | Ps 36:10
upright in h.
and all the upright in h. shall | Ps 64:10
glory
and all the upright in h. shall | Ps 94:15
follow it
gladness is sown for the | Ps 97:11
upright in h.

UPRIGHTNESS OF HEART

he walketh in uprightness of h. | 1Ki 3:6;
| 9:4
I will praise thee with | Ps 119:7
uprightness of h.

WHOLE HEART

praise thee with my whole h. | Ps 9:1;
| 111:1; 138:1
blessed that seek him with | Ps 119:2
the whole h.
with my whole h. have I | Ps 119:10
sought thee
yea, I shall observe it with | Ps 119:34
my whole h.
I entreated thy favour with | Ps 119:58
my whole h.
I will keep thy precepts with | Ps 119:69
my whole h.
I cried with my whole h. | Ps 119:145
Hear me, O Lord
the whole head is sick, the | Isa 1:5
whole h. is faint
not turned with whole h. but | Jer 3:10
feignedly
they shall return unto me with | Jer 24:7
their whole h.
I will plant them in land with | Jer 32:41
my whole h.

WHOSE HEART

whose h. stirred him up | Ex 35:21;
| 35:29; 36:2
all the women whose h. | Ex 35:26
stirred them up
whose h. turneth away this | De 29:18
day from Lord
whose h. is as the heart of a | 2Sa 17:10
lion
whose h. thou knowest | 1Ki 8:39;
| 2Ch 6:30

in behalf of them *whose h.* is 2Ch 16:9
perfect
in *whose h.* are the ways of Ps 84:5
them
the woman *whose h.* is snares Ec 7:26
and nets
hearken ye people, in *whose h.* Isa 51:7
is my law
whose h. departeth from the Jer 17:5
Lord
whose h. walketh after Eze 11:21
detestable things
whose h. the Lord opened, she Ac 16:14
attended

YOUR HEART

circumcise foreskin of *your* De 10:16;
h.
take heed that *your h.* be not De 11:16
deceived
ye shall lay up these my De 11:18
words in *your h.*
surely they will turn away 1Ki 11:2
your h.
set *your h.* and soul to seek 1Ch 22:19
the Lord
meek shall eat, *your h.* shall Ps 22:26
live for ever
he shall strengthen *your h.* ye Ps 31:24
that hope
ye people, pour out *your h.* Ps 62:8
before him
if riches increase, set not *your* Ps 62:10
h. upon them
and *your h.* shall live that seek Ps 69:32
God
when ye see this *your h.* shall Isa 66:14
rejoice
and lest *your h.* faint, and ye Jer 51:46
fear
and rend *your h.* and not your Joe 2:13
garments
let none of you imagine evil in Zec 7:10
your h.
there will *your h.* be also M't 6:21;
Lu 12:34
have ye *your h.* yet hardened M'k 8:17
for the hardness of *your h.* he M'k 10:5
wrote
let not *your h.* be troubled Joh 14:1;
because I said this, sorrow Joh 16:6
hath filled *your h.*
I will see you, and *your h.* Joh 16:22
shall rejoice
in singleness of *your h.* as unto Eph 6:5
Christ

HEARTACHE

winketh causeth *h.* (B) Pr 10:10

HEARTBREAK

now comes the hour of *h.* Joh 12:27
(P)

HEARTED

they came, as many as were Ex 35:22
willing *h.*
the stout-*h.* are spoiled, they Ps 76:5
slept
new wine mourns, all the Isa 24:7
merry-*h.* do sigh
he hath sent me to bind up the Isa 61:1
broken-*h.*
all the house of Israel are Eze 3:7
hard-*h.*

FAINT-HEARTED

what man is there that is De 20:8
faint-*h.*

TENDER-HEARTED

Rehoboam was young and 2Ch 13:7
tender-*h.*
and be kind one to another, Eph 4:32
tender-*h.*

WISE-HEARTED

thou shalt speak unto all that Ex 28:3
are wise-*h.*
and in the hearts of all that are Ex 31:6
wise-*h.*
and every *wise-h.* among you Ex 35:10
shall come

all the women that were Ex 35:25
wise-h. did spin
then wrought every *wise-h.* Ex 36:1;
man 36:2, 8

HEARTEN

h., fortify one another (N) 1Th 5:11

HEARTH

knead it, and make cakes upon Ge 18:6
the *h.*
or *h.* for pots (A) Le 11:35
and my bones are burnt as an Ps 102:3
h.
not a sherd to take fire from Isa 30:14
the *h.*
a fire on the *h.* burning before Jer 36:22
him
cast the roll into fire that was Jer 36:23
on the *h.*
make government of Judah like Zec 12:6
h. of fire

HEARTILY

what ye do, do it *h.* as to the Col 3:23
Lord, not to

HEARTLESS

h. and loveless (A)(R) Ro 1:31

HEARTS

wherefore the *h.* of the people Jos 7:5
melted
band of men, whose *h.* God 1Sa 10:26
had touched
so Absalom stole the *h.* of 2Sa 15:6
Israel
the *h.* of the men of Israel are 2Sa 15:13
after Absalom
thou only knowest the *h.* 1Ki 8:39;
2Ch 6:30
minds and *h.* (B)(R) 1Ch 22:19;
2Ch 6:38
for the Lord searcheth all *h.* 1Ch 28:9
the righteous God trieth the *h.* Ps 7:9;
Pr 17:3
how much more then the *h.* of Pr 15:11
men
but the Lord pondereth the *h.* Pr 21:2
give wine to those that be of Pr 31:6
heavy *h.*
follow their *h.* (B)(R) Jer 9:14
mighty men's *h.* of Moab like Jer 48:41
a woman
their adulterous *h.* (B)(R) Eze 6:9
I will also vex the *h.* of many Eze 32:9
people
both these kings' *h.* shall be Da 11:27
to do mischief
turn the *h.* of the fathers to the Lu 1:17
children
that the thoughts of *h.* may be Lu 2:35
revealed
signs in the sun, men's *h.* Lu 21:26
failing them
which knowest the *h.* of all Ac 1:24;
men 15:8
he that searcheth the *h.* knoweth Ro 8:27
the
by fair speeches deceive the *h.* Ro 16:18
of the simple
make manifest the counsels of 1Co 4:5
the *h.*
open wide your own *h.* (B) 2Co 6:12
h. of the saints Ph'm 7
(A)(B)(E)(P)(R)
I am he that searcheth the Re 2:23
reins and *h.*

OUR HEARTS

as soon as we heard, *our h.* Jos 2:11
did melt
that he may incline *our h.* to 1Ki 8:58
him
filling *our h.* with food and Ac 14:17
gladness
the love of God is shed abroad Ro 5:5
in *our h.*
given the earnest of the Spirit 2Co 1:22
in *our h.*
ye are our epistle written in 2Co 3:2
our h.
God hath shined in *our h.* to 2Co 4:6
give the light

that you are in *our h.* to die 2Co 7:3
and live the light
that you are in *our h.* to die 2Co 7:3
and live with you
but pleasing God, who trieth 1Th 2:4
our h.
our h. sprinkled from an evil Heb 10:22
conscience
and shall assure *our h.* before 1Jo 3:19
him

THEIR HEARTS

I will send a faintness into Le 26:36
their h.
if then *their* uncircumcised *h.* Le 26:41
be humbled
their h. inclined to follow J'g 9:3
Abimelech
when *their h.* were merry, J'g 16:25
they said
as they were making *their h.* J'g 19:22
merry
walk before thee with all *their* 2Ch 6:14
h.
such as set *their h.* to seek 2Ch 11:16
the Lord God
the people had not prepared 2Ch 20:33
their h. to God
it may be my sons have cursed Job 1:5
God in *their h.*
speak peace, but mischief is in Ps 28:3
their h.
he fashioneth *their h.* alike, he Ps 33:15
considers
let them not say in *their h.*, Ps 35:25
Ah, so would we
they said in *their h.*; Let us Ps 74:8
destroy them
I gave them up to *their* own *h.* Ps 81:12
lust
and to them that are upright Ps 125:4
in *their h.*
hath shut *their h.* they cannot Isa 44:18
understand
and write my law in *their h.* Jer 31:33;
Heb 8:10
but I will put my fear in Jer 32:40
their h. not to depart
that prophesy out of *their* own Eze 13:2
h.
and they consider not in *their h.* Ho 7:2
yea, they made *their h.* as an Zec 7:12
adamant
sitting there, and reasoning in M'k 2:6
their h.
being grieved for the hardness M'k 3:5
of *their h.*
taketh away word sown in M'k 4:15;
their h. Lu 8:12
scattered proud in Lu 1:51
imaginations of *their h.*
all that heard laid them up in Lu 1:66
their h.
all men mused in *their h.* of Lu 3:15
John, whether Christ
in *their h.* turned back again to Ac 7:39
Egypt
through the lust of *their h.* to Ro 1:24
dishonour
shew the work of the law Ro 2:15
written in *their h.*
that *their h.* might be Col 2:2
comforted, being knit
said, They do always err in Heb 3:10
their h.
God hath put in *their h.* to Re 17:17
fulfil his will

YOUR HEARTS

comfort ye *your h.* after that Ge 18:5
pass on
O Israel, let not *your h.* faint, De 20:3
fear not
set *your h.* to all the words De 32:46
which I testify
and ye know in all *your h.* Jos 23:14
and souls
incline *your h.* to the Lord Jos 24:23
God of Israel
wherefore then do ye harden 1Sa 6:6
your h.
if ye return to the Lord with all 1Sa 7:3
your h. and prepare *your h.*
ye dissembled in *your h.* when Jer 42:20
ye sent
let none of you imagine evil in Zec 8:17
your h.

Jesus said, Wherefore think ye   *M't 9:4*
evil in *your* h.
if ye from *your* h. forgive not   *M't 18:35*
every one
because of the hardness of   *M't 19:8*
your h. suffered you
why reason ye these things in   *M'k 2:8*
your h.
Jesus said, What reason ye in   *Lu 5:22*
your h.
ye justify yourselves, God   *Lu 16:15*
knoweth *your* h.
settle it in *your* h. not to   *Lu 21:14*
meditate before
lest at any time *your* h. be   *Lu 21:34*
overcharged
and why do thoughts arise in   *Lu 24:38*
your h.
God sent the Spirit of his Son   *Ga 4:6*
into *your* h.
that Christ may dwell in *your*   *Eph 3:17*
h. by faith
making melody in *your* h. to   *Eph 5:19;*
the Lord   *Col 3:16*
I sent that he might comfort   *Eph 6:22*
your h.
keep *your* h. and minds   *Ph'p 4:7*
through Christ
let the peace of God rule in   *Col 3:15*
your h.
might know your estate and   *Col 4:8*
comfort *your* h.
he may establish *your* h.   *1Th 3:13*
unblameable
comfort *your* h. and stablish   *2Th 2:17*
you
the Lord direct *your* h. into the   *2Th 3:5*
love of God
if ye have strife in *your* h.   *Jas 3:14*
glory not
and purify *your* h. ye   *Jas 4:8*
double-minded
have been wanton, ye have   *Jas 5:5*
nourished *your* h.
be ye also patient, stablish *your*   *Jas 5:8*
h. the coming
sanctify the Lord God in *your*   *1Pe 3:15*
h.
till day dawn, and day star   *2Pe 1:19*
arise in *your* h.

HEART'S

your h. desire (R)   *1Sa 23:20*
wicked boasteth of h. desire   *Ps 10:3*
hast given him his h. desire   *Ps 21:2*
my h. desire and prayer to   *Ro 10:1*
God

HEARTS'

them up to their own h. lust   *Ps 81:12*

HEARTSICK

not faint our h. (A)   *Isa 57:10*

HEARTY

so the sweetness of a friend by   *Pr 27:9*
h. counsel

HEAT

cold, h., summer, winter, shall   *Ge 8:22*
not cease
sat in the tent door in the h. of   *Ge 18:1*
the day
what meaneth the h. of this   *De 29:24*
great anger
they shall be devoured with   *De 32:24*
burning h.
slew the Ammonites till h. of   *1Sa 11:11*
the day
and they came about the h. of   *2Sa 4:5*
the day
but he gat no h.   *1Ki 1:1*
my lord may get h.   *1Ki 1:2*
drought and h. consume the   *Job 24:19*
snow waters
my skin black, my bones are   *Job 30:30*
burnt with h.
there is nothing hid from the h.   *Ps 19:6*
thereof
if two lie together, then they   *Ec 4:11*
have h.
a shadow in the daytime from   *Isa 4:6;*
h.   *25:4*
I will take my rest, like a clear   *Isa 18:4*
h. on herbs, and like a cloud
of dew in the h. of harvest

---

as the h. in a dry place, even   *Isa 25:5*
the h.
neither shall the h. nor sun   *Isa 49:10*
smite them
and shall not see when h.   *Jer 17:8*
cometh
dead body shall be cast out in   *Jer 36:30*
the day to h.
in their h. I will make their   *Jer 51:39*
feasts
and I went in the h. of my   *Eze 3:14*
spirit
h. furnace more than wont to   *Da 3:19*
be
have borne the burden and h.   *M't 20:12*
of the day
when south wind blow, there   *Lu 12:55*
will be h.
there came a viper out of the h.   *Ac 28:3*
the sun no sooner risen with a   *Jas 1:11*
burning h.
the elements shall melt with   *2Pe 3:10*
fervent h.

HEATED

the furnace more than wont to   *Da 3:19*
be h.
are adulterers, as an oven h. by   *Ho 7:4*
the baker

HEATH

he shall be like the h. in the   *Jer 17:6*
desert
flee, and be like the h. in the   *Jer 48:6*
wilderness

HEATHEN

bondmen shall be of the h.   *Le 25:44*
round you
nations (B)(E)(R)   *Le 25:44;*
26:45; 2Sa 22:44; 2Ki 16:3; 17:8, 11;
2Ch 20:6; 33:2, 9; Ezr 6:21; Ne 5:9;
6:16
whom I brought forth in sight   *Le 26:45*
of the h.
kept me to be head of h.   *2Sa 22:44;*
Ps 18:43
walked according to   *2Ki 16:3*
abominations of the h.   *17:15; 21:2;*
2Ch 28:3; 36:14
Israel walked in the statutes   *2Ki 17:8*
of the h.
as did the h. whom the Lord   *2Ki 17:11*
carried away
save us, and deliver us from   *1Ch 16:35*
the h.
the world (B)   *1Ch 16:35*
the nations (E)   *1Ch 16:35*
thou rulest over all kingdoms   *2Ch 20:6*
of h.
but did like to the   *2Ch 33:2*
abominations of the h.
Manasseh made Judah to do   *2Ch 33:9*
worse than the h.
as had separated from   *Ezr 6:21*
filthiness of the h.
we redeemed the Jews who were   *Ne 5:8*
sold to h.
the Gentiles (B)   *Ne 5:8*
because of the reproach of the   *Ne 5:9*
h. our enemies
all the h. that were about us   *Ne 6:16*
saw these things
why do the h. rage   *Ps 2:1; Ac 4:25*
the nations (A)(B)(E)(R)   *Ps 2:1;*
2:8; 9:5, 15, 19; 10:16; 33:10; 44:2; 46:6;
47:8; 59:5, 8; 78:55; 79:1; 94:10; 98:2;
102:15; 105:44; 106:41; 111:6; 135:15;
149:7; Isa 16:8; Jer 49:14; La 1:10;
Eze 7:24; 11:12; 20:9, 32, 41; 22:4, 16;
23:30; 25:7, 8; 30:3; 31:11, 17; 34:28, 29;
36:3, 4, 6, 20, 23; 39:21; Joe 2:17; 3:11,
12
I shall give thee the h. for thy   *Ps 2:8*
inheritance
thou hast rebuked the h. thou   *Ps 9:5*
hast destroyed
the h. are sunk in the pit that   *Ps 9:15*
they made
arise, let the h. be judged in thy   *Ps 9:19*
sight
the h. are perished out of his   *Ps 10:16*
land
the Lord brings the counsel of   *Ps 33:10*
h. to nought
we heard how thou didst drive   *Ps 44:2*
out the h.

---

the h. raged, the kingdoms were   *Ps 46:6*
moved
God reigneth over the h. God   *Ps 47:8*
sitteth on
thou, therefore, awake to visit   *Ps 59:5*
all the h.
thou shalt have all the h. in   *Ps 59:8*
derision
he cast out the h. also before   *Ps 78:55;*
them   *80:8*
the h. are come into thine   *Ps 79:1*
inheritance
pour out thy wrath upon the h.   *Ps 79:6;*
Jer 10:25
the Gentile nations (A)   *Ps 79:6;*
79:10; Jer 49:14
wherefore should the h. say,   *Ps 79:10;*
Where is their God? let him   *115:2*
be known among the h.
he that chastiseth the h. shall   *Ps 94:10*
not he correct?
he hath openly shewed in the   *Ps 98:2*
sight of the h.
the h. shall fear the name of   *Ps 102:15*
the Lord
and gave them the lands of   *Ps 105:44*
the h.
and he gave them into the   *Ps 106:41*
hand of the h.
he may give them the heritage   *Ps 111:6*
of the h.
the idols of the h. are silver   *Ps 135:15*
and gold
to execute vengeance upon the   *Ps 149:7*
the lords of the h. have broken   *Isa 16:8*
down
learn not way of the h. be not   *Jer 10:2*
dismayed at signs of heaven,
for the h. dismayed at them
an ambassador is sent to the   *Jer 49:14*
h. saying
seen that the h. entered into   *La 1:10*
her sanctuary
I will bring the worst of the h.   *Eze 7:24*
but have done after the   *Eze 11:12*
manners of h.
should not be polluted before   *Eze 20:9;*
the h.   *14:22*
that ye say, We will be as   *Eze 20:32*
the h.
I will be sanctified before   *Eze 20:41;*
the h.   *28:25*
I have made thee a reproach   *Eze 22:4*
to the h.
take thine inheritance in   *Eze 22:16*
sight of the h.
thou hast gone a whoring   *Eze 23:30*
after the h.
I will deliver thee for a spoil   *Eze 25:7*
to the h.
behold, the house of Judah is   *Eze 25:8*
like to all the h.
day is near, it shall be time of   *Eze 30:3*
the h.
into the hand of the mighty   *Eze 31:11*
one of the h.
that dwelt under his shadow   *Eze 31:17*
in midst of the h.
they shall no more be a prey   *Eze 34:28*
to the h.
neither bear the shame of the   *Eze 34:29*
h. any more
might be a possession to the   *Eze 36:3*
residue of the h.
which became a derision to   *Eze 36:4*
the residue of the h.
because ye have borne the   *Eze 36:6*
shame of the h.
when they entered unto the   *Eze 36:20*
h. whither
h. know I am Lord   *Eze 36:23;*
36:36; 37:28; 38:16; 39:7
and all the h. shall see my   *Eze 39:21*
judgment
that the h. should rule over   *Joe 2:17*
them
and come, all ye h. and gather   *Joe 3:11*
yourselves
let the h. be wakened, and   *Joe 3:12*
come up to valley of Jehoshaphat,
there will I sit to judge all the h.
they may possess remnant of   *Am 9:12*
all the h.
the nations (A)(B)(E)(R)   *Am 9:12;*
Ob 15, 16; Mic 5:15; Hab 3:12;
Zep 2:11; Hag 2:22; Zec 1:15; 9:10;
14:14, 18

the day of the Lord is near on all *Ob 15*
the *h.*
so shall all the *h.* drink   *Ob 16*
continually
I will execute fury upon the *h. Mic 5:15*
thou didst thresh the *h.* in   *Hab 3:12*
anger
all the isles of the *h.* shall   *Zep 2:11*
worship him
I will destroy the strength of *Hag 2:22*
the *h.*
I am sore displeased with the *Zec 1:15*
h.
he shall speak peace to the *h. Zec 9:10*
the wealth of all the *h.* shall *Zec 14:14*
be gathered
the plague wherewith Lord   *Zec 14:18*
will smite the *h.*
do not even the *h.* so (S)   *M't 5:47*
use not vain repetitions as the   *M't 6:7;*
h. do
the Gentiles (A)(E)   *M't 6:7;*
                     2Co 11:26; Ga 2:9; 3:8
pagans (B)(P)   *M't 6:7*
let him be to thee as an *h.*   *M't 18:17*
man and publican
a pagan (A)(B)(N)(P)   *M't 18:17*
Gentile (R)   *M't 18:17*
in perils by the *h.* in perils in *2Co 11:26*
the sea
the Gentiles (B)(R)   *2Co 11:26;*
                                 Ga 2:9; 3:8
from foreigners (N)   *2Co 11:26*
from pagans (P)   *2Co 11:26*
that we should go unto the *h.*   *Ga 2:9*
the Gentiles (P)   *Ga 2:9; 3:8*
that God would justify the *h.*   *Ga 3:8*
through faith

AMONG THE HEATHEN

I will scatter you *among the h. Le 26:33*
       Jer 9:16; Eze 20:23; 22:15
the nations (A)(B)(E)(R)   *Le 26:33;*
26:38; De 4:27; 2Sa 22:50; 1Ch 16:24;
                              Ne 5:17; 6:6
and ye shall perish *among the Le 26:38*
h. and the land
ye shall be left few in number   *De 4:27*
among h.
I will give thanks to thee, O *2Sa 22:50:*
Lord, *among h.* and sing   *Ps 18:49*
praises to thy name
declare his glory *among h.*   *1Ch 16:24;*
                                   Ps 96:3
that came to us from *among   Ne 5:17*
the *h.*
it is reported *among the h.*   *Ne 6:6*
Gashmu saith it
thou hast scattered us *among   Ps 44:11*
the *h.*
the nations (A)(B)(E)(R)   *Ps 44:11;*
44:14; 46:10; 96:10; 106:35, 47; 110:6;
126:2; Jer 18:13; 49:15; La 1:3; 4:15, 20;
Eze 11:16; 12:16; 16:14; 36:19, 21, 24,
30; 39:21, 28; Joe 2:19; Ob 1, 2;
          Hab 1:5; Zec 8:13; Mal 1:11, 14
thou makest us a byword   *Ps 44:14*
among the h.
I am God, I will be exalted   *Ps 46:10*
among the h.
let him be known *among the   Ps 79:10*
h.* in sight
the Gentile nations (A)   *Ps 79:10*
say *among the h.* that the   *Ps 96:10*
Lord reigneth
but they were mingled *among Ps 106:35*
the *h.*
save us, O Lord, and gather   *Ps 106:47*
us from *among h.*
he shall judge *among the h.* he *Ps 110:6*
shall fill
said *among the h.* Lord hath   *Ps 126:2*
done great things
ask *among the h.* who heard   *Jer 18:13*
such things
I will make thee small *among   Jer 49:15*
the *h.*
she dwelleth *among the h.* she   *La 1:3*
findeth
said *among the h.* They shall   *La 4:15*
no more sojourn
under his shadow we shall live   *La 4:20*
among the h.
tho' I have cast them far off   *Eze 11:16*
among the h.
may declare their   *Eze 12:16*
abominations *among the h.*

thy renown went forth   *Eze 16:14*
among the h.
and I did scatter them *among   Eze 36:19*
the *h.*
which Israel profaned *among Eze 36:21;*
the *h.*   *22:23*
I will take you from *among   Eze 36:24;*
the *h.*   *37:21*
no more reproach of famine   *Eze 36:30*
among the h.
and I will set my glory   *Eze 39:21*
among the h.
caused them to be led into   *Eze 39:2*
captivity *among h.*
no more make you a reproach   *Joe 2:19*
among the h.
an ambassador is sent *among the Ob 1*
h.
behold, I have made thee small   *Ob 2*
among the h.
behold, ye *among the h.*   *Hab 1:5*
regard, wonder
that as ye were a curse *among Zec 8:13*
the *h.*
my name shall be great   *Mal 1:11*
among the h.
and my name is dreadful   *Mal 1:14*
among the h.
that I might preach him   *Ga 1:16*
among the h.
among the Gentiles   *Ga 1:16*
(A)(B)(E)(N)(R)
to the non-Jewish world (P)   *Ga 1:16*

HEAVE

the shoulder of the *h.* offering *Ex 29:27*
for it is an *h.* offering: and it *Ex 29:28*
be an *h.* offering from the   *Ex 29:28*
children
their *h.* offering unto the Lord *Ex 29:28*
an *h.* offering unto the Lord   *Le 7:14*
an *h.* offering of the sacrifices *Le 7:32*
and the *h.* shoulder have I   *Le 7:34*
taken of
the wave breast and *h.*   *Le 10:14*
shoulder
The *h.* shoulder and the wave   *Le 10:15*
the wave breast and *h.*   *Nu 6:20*
shoulder
shall offer up an *h.* offering   *Nu 15:19*
unto the
of your dough for an *h.*   *Nu 15:20*
offering
h. offering of the   *Nu 15:20*
threshingfloor
threshingfloor, so shall ye *h.* *Nu 15:20*
it
the Lord an *h.* offering in your *Nu 15:21*
the charge of mine *h.* offerings *Nu 18:8*
the *h.* offering of their gift, *Nu 18:11*
with all
the *h.* offerings of the holy   *Nu 18:19*
things
which they offer as an *h.*   *Nu 18:24*
offering
ye shall offer up an *h.* offering *Nu 18:26*
your *h.* offering shall be   *Nu 18:27*
reckoned
offer an *h.* offering unto the   *Nu 18:28*
Lord
the Lord's *h.* offering to   *Nu 18:28*
Aaron
offer every *h.* offering of the *Nu 18:29*
Lord
for an *h.* offering of the Lord *Nu 31:29*
which was the Lord's *h.*   *Nu 31:41*
offering
h. offerings of your hand, and *De 12:6*
your
and the *h.* offering of your   *De 12:11*
hand
or *h.* offering of thine hand   *De 12:17*

HEAVED

is waved, and which is *h.* up   *Ex 29:27*
When ye have *h.* the best   *Nu 18:30*
thereof
when ye have *h.* from it the   *Nu 18:32*
best of

HEAVEN

in the beginning God created *h. Ge 1:1*
and earth
and God called the firmament *h. Ge 1:8*
let there be lights in the   *Ge 1:14;*
firmament of *h.*   *1:15*
fowl that may fly in the open   *Ge 1:20*
firmament of *h.*

and the windows of *h.* were   *Ge 7:11*
opened
and the windows of *h.* were   *Ge 8:2*
stopped
most high God, possessor of   *Ge 14:19;*
h. and earth   *14:22*
Lord rained fire from the   *Ge 19:24*
Lord out of *h.*
the angel of God called to   *Ge 21:17*
Hagar out of *h.*
the angel called to Abraham   *Ge 22:11;*
out of *h.*   *22:15*
God give thee of the dew of   *Ge 27:28;*
h.   *27:39*
and he said, This is the gate   *Ge 28:17*
of *h.*
shall bless thee with   *Ge 49:25*
blessings of *h.* above
six days Lord made *h.* and   *Ex 20:11;*
earth   *31:17*
as it were the body of *h.* in his *Ex 24:10*
clearness
I will make your *h.* as iron,   *Le 26:19*
earth brass
the mountain burned to the   *De 4:11*
midst of *h.*
I call *h.* and earth to witness *De 4:26;*
                          30:19; 31:28
ask from the one side of *h.* to *De 4:32*
the other
out of *h.* he made thee hear his *De 4:36*
voice
behold, the *h.* and *h.* of   *De 10:14;*
heavens   *Ps 115:16*
and drinketh water of the   *De 11:11*
rain of *h.*
he shut up *h.*   *De 11:17;*
         1Ki 8:35; 2Ch 6:26; 7:13
be multiplied as the days of *h. De 11:21*
on the earth
open the *h.* to give thee rain   *De 28:12*
in his season
the *h.* that is over thy head   *De 28:23*
shall be brass
scatter thee to the utmost part *De 30:4;*
of *h.*   *Ne 1:9*
for the precious things of *h.*   *De 33:13*
for the dew
God of Jeshurun rideth upon   *De 33:26*
the *h.* in thy help
out of *h.* shall he thunder on   *1Sa 2:10*
them
he was taken up between *h.*   *2Sa 18:9*
and earth
till water dropped on them   *2Sa 21:10*
out of *h.*
the foundations of *h.* moved   *2Sa 22:8*
and shook
the *h.* and *h.* of heavens   *1Ki 8:27;*
cannot contain thee   *6:18*
when *h.* is shut up, and there   *1Ki 8:35*
is not rain
mean while the *h.* was black   *1Ki 18:45*
with clouds
thou hast made *h.* and earth   *2Ki 19:15;*
                  2Ch 2:12; Ne 9:6
angel stood between *h.* and   *1Ch 21:16*
earth
it is as high as *h.* what canst *Job 11:8*
thou do
the *h.* shall reveal his   *Job 20:27*
iniquity, earth rise up
is not God in height of *h.*?   *Job 22:12*
behold height
and he walketh in the circuit   *Job 22:14*
of *h.*
the pillars of *h.* tremble at   *Job 26:11*
his reproof
the hoary frost of *h.* who   *Job 38:29*
hath gendered it
knowest thou the ordinances   *Job 38:33*
of *h.*
or who can stay the bottles   *Job 38:37*
of *h.*
his going forth is from the end   *Ps 19:6*
of *h.*
he will hear him from his holy   *Ps 20:6*
h.
let *h.* and earth praise him,   *Ps 69:34*
the seas
and though he opened the   *Ps 78:23*
doors of *h.*
and had given them of the   *Ps 78:24*
corn of *h.*
his throne to endure as the   *Ps 89:29*
days of *h.*
for as the *h.* is high above   *Ps 103:11*
the earth

he satisfied them with the   Ps 105:40
bread of *h.*
the Lord made *h.* and earth   Ps 115:15;
121:2; 124:8; 134:3; 146:6; Isa 37:16;
Jer 32:17; Ac 4:24; 14:15; Re 14:7
who covereth *h.* with clouds,   Ps 147:8
who prepares
his glory is above the earth   Ps 148:13
and *h.*
the *h.* for height, the earth for   Pr 25:3
depth
they come from far, from the   Isa 13:5
end of *h.*
who hath meted out *h.* with a   Isa 40:12
span
h. my throne, earth my   Isa 66:1;
footstool   Ac 7:49
to make cakes to the queen of   Jer 7:18
h.
and be not dismayed at the   Jer 10:2
signs of *h.*
do not I fill *h.* and earth?   Jer 23:24
saith Lord
if *h.* above can be measured   Jer 31:37
if I have not appointed   Jer 33:25
ordinances of *h.*
burn incense to queen of *h.*   Jer 44:17;
44:18, 19, 25
four winds from the four   Jer 49:36
quarters of *h.*
hath stretched out the *h.* by   Jer 51:15
his understanding
the *h.* and earth shall sing for   Jer 51:48
Babylon
our enemies swifter than the   La 4:19
eagles of *h.*
the Spirit lifted me between   Eze 8:3
earth and *h.*
I will cover the *h.* and make   Eze 32:7
the stars dark
the lights of *h.* will I make   Eze 32:8
dark over thee
be wet with dew of *h.*   Da 4:15;
23:25, 33; 5:21
doeth according to his will in   Da 4:35
the army of *h.*
now I extol and honour the   Da 4:37
King of *h.*
hast lifted up thyself against   Da 5:23
the Lord of *h.*
the four winds of *h.* strove upon   Da 7:2
the sea
one like Son of man, came   Da 7:13
with clouds of *h.*
four horns toward the four   Da 8:8
winds of *h.*
his kingdom divided toward   Da 11:4
four winds of *h.*
he that buildeth his stories in   Am 9:6
the *h.*
the *h.* over you is stayed from   Hag 1:10
dew
I have spread you as the four   Zec 2:6
winds of *h.*
lifted the ephah between the   Zec 5:9
earth and *h.*
if I will not open the windows   Mal 3:10
of *h.*
till *h.* and earth pass, one jot   M't 5:18
not pass
nor swear by *h.* it is God's   M't 5:34;
throne   La 5:12
I thank thee, Father, Lord of   M't 11:25;
h.   Lu 10:21
he that shall swear by *h.*   M't 23:22
sweareth by God
appear sign of the Son of   M't 24:30;
man coming in clouds of *h.*   M'k 14:62
gather elect from one end of   M't 24:31
h. to the other
h., earth pass away   M't 24:35;
M'k 13:31; Lu 21:33
no, not the angels of *h.* but   M't 24:36
my Father only
gather his elect from utmost   M'k 13:27
part of *h.*
and Jesus praying, the *h.* was   Lu 3:21
opened
when the *h.* was shut up three   Lu 4:25
years
father, I have sinned against   Lu 15:18;
h.   15:21
it is easier for *h.* and earth   M'k 16:17
to pass
for the powers of *h.* shall be   M'k 21:26
shaken
hereafter see *h.* open, and   Joh 1:51
angels

whom the *h.* must receive until   Ac 3:21
the times
I saw *h.* opened, and a vessel   Ac 10:11;
Re 19:11
seeing that he is Lord of *h.*   Ac 17:24
and earth
he prayed again, and the *h.*   Jas 5:18
gave rain
a hint of the glories of *h.* (P)   1Pe 1:8
cometh down out of *h.* from   Re 3:12
my God
h. departed as a scroll when it   Re 6:14
is rolled
an angel flying through the   Re 8:13;
midst of *h.*   14:6
who created *h.* and the things   Re 10:6
therein
these have power to shut *h.*   Re 11:6
that it rain not
came a great voice out of the   Re 16:17
temple of *h.*
there fell on men a great hail   Re 16:21
out of *h.*
rejoice over her, thou *h.*   Re 18:20
to all the fowls that fly in the   Re 19:17
midst of *h.*
and fire came down from God   Re 20:9
out of *h.*
earth and *h.* fled away, and   Re 20:11
there was no place
I saw a new *h.* and earth, the   Re 21:1
first *h.* passed
holy Jerusalem descending out   Re 21:10
of *h.* from God

HEAVEN with *STARS*

God set *stars* in the firmament   Ge 1:17
of *h.*
multiply seed as *stars* of *h.*   Ge 22:17;
26:4; Ex 32:13; 1Ch 27:23; Ne 9:23
you are this day as *stars* of *h.*   De 1:10;
10:22
whereas ye were as *stars* of *h.*   De 28:62
for multitude
the *stars* of *h.* shall not *give*   Isa 13:10
light
I will cover *h.* and make *stars*   Eze 32:7
dark
multiplied merchants as *stars*   Na 3:16
of *h.*
the *stars* shall fall from *h.*   M't 24:29;
M'k 13:25
and the *stars* of *h.* fell on the   Re 6:13
earth
his tail drew the third part of   Re 12:4
stars of *h.*

FROM HEAVEN

and the rain *from h.* was   Ge 8:2
restrained
I will rain bread *from h.* for   Ex 16:4
you
I have talked with you *from*   Ex 20:22;
h.   Ne 9:13
look down *from h.*   De 26:15;
Isa 63:15; La 3:50
as dust *from h.* shall it come   De 28:24
down on thee
Lord cast great stones *from*   Jos 10:11
h. on them
they fought *from h.* the stars   J'g 5:20
fought
Lord thundered *from h.* and   2Sa 22:14
uttered
then let fire come down *from*   2Ki 1:10
h.
and there came down fire   2Ki 1:14
from h.
he answered him *from h.* by   1Ch 21:26
fire
hear thou *from h.* 2Ch 6:21; 6:23, 27, 30
the fire came down *from h.*   2Ch 7:1
and consumed
then will I hear *from h.* and   2Ch 7:14
will forgive
gavest them bread *from h.* for   Ne 9:15
hunger
they cried, thou heardest them   Ne 9:27;
from h.   9:28
the fire of God is fallen *from*   Job 1:16
h.
the Lord looked down *from h.*   Ps 14:2;
53:2
the Lord looketh *from h.* and   Ps 33:13
beholdeth
shall send *from h.* and save me   Ps 57:3
from reproach
didst cause judgment to be   Ps 76:8
heard *from h.*

O God, look down *from h.*   Ps 80:14
and behold
righteousness shall look down   Ps 85:11
from h.
from h. did the Lord behold   Ps 102:19
the earth
how art thou fallen *from h.* O   Isa 14:12
Lucifer
as snow falleth *from h.* and   Isa 55:10
returneth not
Lord cast down *from h.* beauty   La 2:1
of Israel
behold, a watcher came down   Da 4:13
from h.
the king saw an holy one   Da 4:23
coming down *from h.*
fell a voice *from h.* saying   Da 4:31;
M't 3:17; Lu 3:22; Joh 12:28
he would shew them a sign   M't 16:1
from h.
the baptism of John; *from*   M't 21:25;
h. or of men   M'k 11:30; Lu 20:4
the angel descended *from h.*   M't 28:2;
Re 10:1; 18:1; 20:1
seeking of him a sign *from h.*   M'k 8:11;
Lu 11:16
we command fire to come   Lu 9:54
down *from h.*
I behold Satan as lightning   Lu 10:18
fall *from h.*
it rained fire and brimstone   Lu 17:29
from h. on Sodom
and great signs shall there be   Lu 21:11
from h.
appeared an angel *from h.*   Lu 22:43
strengthening him
I saw the Spirit descending   Joh 1:32
from h.
but he that came down *from*   Joh 3:13;
h.   6:33
receive nothing, except it be   Joh 3:27
given him *from h.*
he that cometh *from h.* is   Joh 3:31
above all
he gave them bread *from h.* to   Joh 6:31
eat
Moses gave you not that bread   Joh 6:32
from h.
I came *from h.* not to do   Joh 6:38;
mine own will   6:42
bread which came down *from*   Joh 6:41;
h.   6:50, 51, 58
suddenly there came a sound   Ac 2:2
from h.
a light *from h.* shined about   Ac 9:3;
him   22:6; 26:13
as it had been a great sheet let   Ac 11:5
down *from h.*
but the voice answered me   Ac 11:9
again *from h.*
in that he did good, and gave   Ac 14:17
us rain *from h.*
the wrath of God is revealed   Ro 1:18
from h.
the second man is the Lord   1Co 15:47
from h.
clothed on with our house that   2Co 5:2
is *from h.*
an angel *from h.* preach any   Ga 1:8
other gospel
and to wait for his Son *from*   1Th 1:10
h.
the Lord himself shall descend   1Th 4:16
from h.
the Lord Jesus shall be   2Th 1:7
revealed *from h.*
if turn from him that   Heb 12:25
speaketh *from h.*
you with Holy Ghost sent   1Pe 1:12
down *from h.*
and there fell a great star *from*   Re 8:10
h.
and I saw a star fall *from h.* to   Re 9:1
the earth
I heard a voice *from h.*   Re 10:4;
10:8; 11:12; 14:2, 13; 18:4
that he maketh fire come   Re 13:13
down *from h.*

HOST, HOSTS OF HEAVEN

seest the *hosts of h.* shouldest   De 4:19
worship them
hath gone and worshipped the   De 17:3
host of h.
I saw the Lord and the *host*   1Ki 22:19;
of *h.* standing by him   2Ch 18:18
Israel worshipped the *host of*   2Ki 17:16
h.

Manasseh worshipped *host of* 2Ki 21:3;
h.   2Ch 33:3
he built altars for the *host of* 2Ki 21:5;
h.   2Ch 33:5
Josiah brought out vessels 2Ki 23:4
made for *host of h.*
put down them that burnt 2Ki 23:5
incense to *host of h.*
made *h.* of heavens with their Ne 9:6
host, and *host of h.* worshippeth
all the *host of h.* shall be Isa 34:4
dissolved
they shall spread them before Jer 8:2
the *host of h.*
they burnt incense to all the Jer 19:13
host of h.
as the *host of h.* cannot be Jer 33:29
numbered
it waxed great, even to the *host* Da 8:10
of *h.*
I will cut off them that worship Zep 1:5
host of h.
gave them up to worship the Ac 7:42
host of h.

IN HEAVEN

nor likeness of any thing *in h.* Ex 20:4;
   De 5:8
what god *in h.* can do like thy De 3:24
works
that the Lord he is *God in h.* De 4:39
above and earth
it is not *in h.* that thou De 30:12
shouldest say, Who
for Lord your God he is God Jos 2:11
in h. above
is no God like thee *in h.* 1Ki 8:23;
   2Ch 6:14
hear thou *in h.* 1Ki 8:30;
   8:32, 34, 36, 39, 43 ,45, 49
if the Lord make windows in 2Ki 7:2;
h.   7:19
all that is *in h.* and earth is 1Ch 29:11
thine
Lord God, art not thou God 2Ch 20:6
in h.
also now behold, my witness Job 16:19
is *in h.*
the Lord's throne is *in h.* his Ps 11:4
eyes behold
whom have I *in h.* but thee, Ps 73:25
none on earth
the voice of thy thunder was Ps 77:18
in the h.
he caused an east wind to Ps 78:26
blow *in h.*
who *in h.* can be compared to Ps 89:6
the Lord
shall be established as a Ps 89:37
faithful witness *in h.*
humbleth himself to behold Ps 113:6
things *in h.*
for ever, Lord, thy word is Ps 119:89
settled *in h.*
that did he *in h.* and earth, Ps 135:6
the seas
for God is *in h.* and thou upon Ec 5:2
earth
for my sword shall be bathed Isa 34:5
in h. behold
yea, the stork *in h.* knoweth her Jer 8:7
times
there is a God *in h.* that Da 2:28
revealeth secrets
worketh signs and wonders Da 6:27
in h. and earth
he that buildeth his stories *in* Am 9:6
the *h.*
rejoice, for great is your M't 5:12
reward *in h.*
and glorify your Father who is M't 5:16
in h.
the children of your Father M't 5:45
who is *in h.*
be perfect, as your Father *in* M't 5:48
h. is perfect
pray ye, Our Father which art M't 6:9;
in h.   Lu 11:2
will be done on earth, as it is M't 6:10;
in h.   Lu 11:2
but lay up for yourselves M't 6:20
treasures *in h.*
shall your Father *in h.* give M't 7:11
good things
that doth the will of my M't 7:21;
Father *in h.*   12:50
him will I confess before my M't 10:32
Father *in h.*

him will I deny before M't 10:33
my Father *in h.*
but my Father which is *in h.* M't 16:17
revealed it
shall be bound *in h.* be M't 16:19;
loosed *in h.*   18:18
these little ones, *in h.* angels M't 18:10
do always behold face of
my Father *in h.*
shall be done for them of my M't 18:19
Father *in h.*
thou shalt have treasure in M't 19:21;
h.   Lu 18:22
are as the angels of God *in h.* M't 22:30;
   M'k 12:25
for one is your Father M't 23:9
who is *in h.*
shall appear the sign of the M't 24:30
Son of man *in h.*
all power is given to me *in h.* M't 28:18
and in earth
now will your Father *in h.* M'k 11:26
forgive you
the powers that are *in h.* M'k 13:25
shall be shaken
no, not the angels which are M'k 13:32
in h. nor the Son
for behold, your reward is Lu 6:23
great *in h.*
because your names are Lu 10:20
written *in h.*
joy shall be *in h.* over one Lu 15:7
sinner that repenteth
peace *in h.* and glory in the Lu 19:38
highest
even the Son of man who is *in* Joh 3:13
h.
I will shew wonders *in h.* Ac 2:19
above and signs
and called gods, whether *in h.* 1Co 8:5
or in earth
he might gather in one, things Eph 1:10
in h.
of whom the whole family *in* Eph 3:15
h. is named
knowing that your master is Eph 6:9;
in h.   Col 4:1
every knee should bow, of Ph'p 2:10
things *in h.*
our conversation is *in h.* from Ph'p 3:20
whence we look
for the hope which is laid up Col 1:5
for you *in h.*
by him were all things created Col 1:16
that are *in h.*
by him to reconcile all things Col 1:20
in h. and earth
that ye have *in h.* a better Heb 10:34
substance
the firstborn which are Heb 12:23
written *in h.*
to an inheritance reserved *in h.* 1Pe 1:4
for you
there are three that bear record 1Jo 5:7
in h.
and behold, a door was opened Re 4:1
in h.
a throne was set *in h.* and one sat Re 4:2
on the throne
no man *in h.* or earth was able Re 5:3
to open book
every creature *in h.* saying, Re 5:13
Blessing, honour
was silence *in h.;* great voices Re 8:1;
in h.   11,15
the temple of God was opened Re 11:19
in h.
there appeared a great wonder Re 12:1;
in h.   12:3
there was war *in h.* Michael Re 12:7
and his angels
nor was their place found any Re 12:8
more *in h.*
I heard a loud voice saying Re 12:10;
in h.   19:1
to blaspheme them that dwell Re 13:6
in h.
angel came out of the temple Re 14:17
which is *in h.*
I saw another sign *in h.* great Re 15:1
and marvellous
the tabernacle of testimony *in* Re 15:5
h. was opened
the armies that were *in h.* Re 19:14
followed him

INTO HEAVEN

the Lord would take up Elijah 2Ki 2:1
into h.

Elijah went up by a 2Ki 2:11
whirlwind *into h.*
if I ascend *into h.* thou art Ps 139:8
there
who hath ascended *into h.* Pr 30:4;
   Ro 10:6
thou hast said, I will Isa 14:13
ascend *into h.*
the Lord was received up M'k 16:19
into h.
as the angels were gone away Lu 2:15
into h.
he was parted from them, Lu 24:51
carried up *into h.*
gazing up *into h.* taken from Ac 1:11
you *into h.* Jesus shall come
as ye have seen him go *into h.*
Stephen looked up stedfastly Ac 7:55
into h. and saw
the vessel was received up Ac 10:16;
into h.   11:10
but *into h.* itself, to appear Heb 9:24
for us
who is gone *into h.* on right 1Pe 3:22
hand of God

TO, UNTO HEAVEN

a tower whose top may reach Ge 11:4
unto h.
a ladder, and the top of it Ge 28:12
reached *to h.*
the cities great and walled up De 1:28;
to h.   9:1
and lest thou lift up thine eyes De 4:19
unto h.
who shall go up for us *to h.* De 30:12
and bring it to us
for I lift up my hand *to h.* De 32:40
and say, I live
the smoke of the city ascended Jos 8:20
up *to h.*
the flame of the city ascended J'g 20:40
up *to h.*
and the cry of the city went 1Sa 5:12
up *to h.*
with his hands spread up *to h.* 1Ki 8:54
in a rage that reacheth up 2Ch 28:9
unto h.
their prayer came up even 2Ch 30:27
unto h.
the prophet Isaiah prayed 2Ch 32:20
and cried *to h.*
they mount up *to h.* they go Ps 107:26
down
for her judgment reacheth *unto* Jer 51:9
h.
the tree whose height reached Da 4:11;
to h.   4:20
when he held up his left hand Da 12:7
unto h.
though they climb up *to h.* Am 9:2
thence will I
Capernaum, which art M't 11:23
exalted *to h.*
and looking up *to h.* M't 14:19;
   M'k 6:41; Lu 9:16
looking up *to h.* he sighed, M'k 7:34
and saith
not lift up so much as his eyes Lu 18:13
unto h.
and no man hath ascended up Joh 3:13
to h.
Jesus lift up his eyes *to h.* and Joh 17:1
said, Father
such an one caught up *to* 2Co 12:2
third *h.*
the angel lifted up his hand *to* De 10:5
h.
and they ascended up *to h.* in De 11:12
a cloud
for her sins have reached *unto* De 18:5
h.

TOWARD HEAVEN

look now *toward h.* and tell Ge 15:5
the stars
let Moses sprinkle it *toward* the Ex 9:8
h.
and Moses sprinkled it up Ex 9:10
toward h.
stretch forth thine hand Ex 9:22;
toward h.   10:21
Moses stretched forth his rod Ex 9:23
toward h.
Moses stretched forth his hand Ex 10:22
toward h.
when the flame went up J'g 13:20
toward h.

Solomon spread forth his *1Ki 8:22;*
hands *toward* h. *2Ch 6:13*
sprinkled dust on their heads *Job 2:12*
toward h.
they fly away as an eagle *Pr 23:5*
toward h.
while they looked stedfastly *Ac 1:10*
toward h.

UNDER HEAVEN

let the waters *under* h. be *Ge 1:9*
gathered
a flood to destroy all flesh *Ge 6:17*
from *under* h.
the high hills *under* the whole *Ge 7:19*
h. were covered
put out the remembrance of *Ex 17:14;*
Amalek from *under* h. *De 25:19*
the fear of thee on nations *De 2:25*
under h.
God hath divided to all *De 4:19*
nations *under* h.
shalt destroy their name from *De 7:24;*
under h. *9:14*
Lord shall blot out his name *De 29:90*
from *under* h.
blot out name of Israel from *2Ki 14:27*
under h.
for God seeth *under* the *Job 28:24*
whole h.
he directeth it *under* the whole *Job 37:3*
h.
whatsoever is *under* the *Job 41:11*
whole h. is mine
to search out all things done *Ec 1:13*
under h.
what was that good they should *Ec 2:3*
do *under* h.
a time to every purpose *under* *Ec 3:1*
the h.
that lighteneth out of one part *Lu 17:24*
under h.
devout men of every nation *Ac 2:5*
under h.
none other name *under* h. *Ac 4:12*
given among men
gospel preached to every *Col 1:23*
creature *under* h.

HEAVENLY

your h. Father will forgive you *M't 6:14*
yet your h. Father feedeth *M't 6:26*
them
your h. Father knoweth that ye *M't 6:32*
have need
every plant my h. Father *M't 15:13*
hath not planted
so shall my h. Father do also *M't 18:35*
to you
h. hosts be shaken (B) *M'k 13:25*
a multitude of the h. host *Lu 2:13*
praising God
your h. Father shall give the *Lu 11:13*
Spirit to them
how believe, if I tell you of h. *Joh 3:12*
things
I was not disobedient to the *Ac 26:19*
h. vision
as is the h. such are they *1Co 15:48*
that are h.
we shall also bear the image *1Co 15:49*
of the h.
with spiritual blessings in h. *Eph 1:3*
places in Christ
set him at his right hand in h. *Eph 1:20;*
places *2:6*
that now unto the powers in *Eph 3:10*
h. places
Lord will preserve me to his h. *2Ti 4:18*
kingdom
brethren, partakers of the h. *Heb 3:1*
calling
once enlightened, and have *Heb 6:4*
tasted of the h. gift
who serve to example and *Heb 8:5*
shadow of h. things
but h. things with better *Heb 9:23*
sacrifices than these
an h. country; the h. *Heb 11:16;*
Jerusalem *11:12, 22*
inexpressible h. joy (B) *1Pe 1:8*

HEAVENS

thus the h. and the earth were *Ge 2:1*
finished
generations of h. and earth in *Ge 2:4*
the day Lord made h. and earth

give ear, O h. I will speak *De 32:1;*
Isa 1:2
also his h. shall drop down *De 33:28*
dew
the earth trembled, the h. *J'g 5:4*
dropped
he bowed the h. and came *2Sa 22:10;*
Ps 18:9
the heaven of h. cannot *1Ki 8:27*
contain thee
the Lord made the h. *1Ch 16:26;*
Ne 9:6; Ps 96:5; 102:25; 136:5
let the h. be glad, let the *1Ch 16:31*
earth rejoice
then hear from the h. *2Ch 6:25;*
6:33, 35, 39
our trespass is grown up to the *Ezr 9:6*
h.
which alone spreadeth out the *Job 9:8*
h.
man riseth not till the h. be *Job 14:12*
no more
yea, the h. are not clean in *Job 15:15*
his sight
though his excellency mount *Job 20:6*
up to the h.
by his Spirit he hath *Job 26:13*
garnished the h.
look to the h. and see, and *Job 35:5*
behold the clouds
thou hast set thy glory above *Ps 8:1;*
the h. *113:4*
when I consider thy h. the work *Ps 8:3*
of thy fingers
the h. declare the glory of God, *Ps 19:1*
and firmament
by the word of the Lord were *Ps 33:6*
the h. made
shall call to the h. from above, *Ps 50:4*
and to earth
the h. shall declare his *Ps 50:6*
righteousness: God is judge
be thou exalted, O God, above *Ps 57:5;*
h. *57:11, 108:5*
for thy mercy is great unto the *Ps 57:10;*
h. *108:4*
extol him that rideth upon the *Ps 68:4;*
68:33
the h. also dropped at the *Ps 68:8*
presence of God
they set their mouth against the *Ps 73:9*
h.
the h. shall praise thy wonders, *Ps 89:5*
O Lord
the h. are thine, the earth also *Ps 89:11*
is thine
let the h. rejoice, earth be *Ps 96:11;*
glad *Re 12:12*
h. declare his righteousness, *Ps 97:6*
people see his glory
who stretchest out the h. *Ps 104:2;*
Isa 40:22
for thy mercy is great above *Ps 108:4*
the h.
the heavens, even the h. are *Ps 115:16*
the Lord's
bow thy h. O Lord, and come *Ps 144:5*
down, touch
praise ye the Lord from the h. *Ps 148:1*
praise him ye h. of h. and *Ps 148:4*
waters above the h.
by understanding he established *Pr 3:19*
the h.
when he prepared the h. I *Pr 8:27*
was there
will shake the h. and earth *Isa 13:13;*
Hag 2:6, 21
the h. shall be rolled together *Isa 34:4*
as a scroll
thus saith he that created the h. *Isa 42:5;*
45:18
sing, O ye h. for the Lord *Isa 44:23*
hath done it
Lord, that stretcheth forth h. *Isa 44:24;*
45:12; 51:13; Jer 10:12; Zec 12:1
drop down ye h. from above, *Isa 45:8*
let the skies pour
my right hand hath spanned *Isa 48:13*
the h.
sing, O h. and be joyful, O *Isa 49:13*
earth
I clothe h. with blackness, I *Isa 50:3*
make sackcloth
lift up eyes to h. and look, the *Isa 51:6*
h. shall vanish away like smoke
that I may plant the h. and *Isa 51:16*
lay foundations

for as the h. are higher than *Isa 55:9*
the earth
that thou wouldest rend the h. *Isa 64:1*
and come down
behold, I create new h. and a *Isa 65:17*
new earth
for as the new h. which I will *Isa 66:22*
make
be astonished, O ye h. and be *Jer 2:12*
afraid
I beheld the h. and they had *Jer 4:23*
no light
all the birds of the h. were *Jer 4:25;*
fled *9:10*
for this shall the earth mourn, *Jer 4:28*
h. above black
the gods that have not made *Jer 10:11*
the h. and the earth shall
perish, and from under these h.
or can the h. give showers? *Jer 14:22*
art not thou he
destroy them from under the h. *La 3:66*
that the h. were opened *Eze 1:1;*
M't 3:16
shalt have known that the h. *Da 4:26*
do rule
I will hear the h. they shall *Ho 2:21*
hear the earth
the h. shall tremble, sun and *Joe 2:10*
moon be dark
and the h. and the earth shall *Joe 3:16*
shake
God came, his glory covered *Hab 3:3*
the h.
the h. over you withhold dew *Hag 1:10*
(S)
these are the four spirits of the *Zec 6:5*
h.
and the h. shall give their dew *Zec 8:12*
the powers of the h. shall be *M't 24:29*
shaken
and coming up, he saw the h. *M'k 1:10*
opened
for David is not ascended into *Ac 2:34*
the h.
behold, I see the h. opened, and *Ac 7:56*
Son of man
the h. are the work of thine *Heb 1:10*
hands
we have an high priest that *Heb 4:14*
is passed into h.
an high priest made higher *Heb 7:26*
than the h.
by the word of God the h. were *2Pe 3:5*
of old
but the h. which are now, are *2Pe 3:7*
kept in store
the h. shall pass away with a *2Pe 3:10*
great noise
wherein the h. being on fire *2Pe 3:12*
shall be dissolved

IN THE HEAVENS

he that sitteth *in the* h. shall *Ps 2:4*
laugh
the Lord also thundered *in the* *Ps 18:13*
h.
thy mercy, O Lord, is *in the* h. *Ps 36:5*
thy faithfulness
thy faithfulness shalt thou *Ps 89:2*
establish *in the* h.
the Lord hath prepared his *Ps 103:19*
throne *in the* h.
God is *in the* h. he hath done *Ps 115:3*
what pleased
I lift my eyes, O thou that *Ps 123:1*
dwellest *in the* h.
the light is darkened *in the* h. *Isa 5:30*
thereof
a multitude of waters *in the* *Jer 10:13;*
h. *51:16*
let us lift up our hearts to God *La 3:41*
in the h.
I will shew wonders *in the* h. *Joe 2:30*
a treasure *in the* h. which *Lu 12:33*
faileth not
house not made with hands, *2Co 5:1*
eternal *in the* h.
of the throne of the Majesty *in* *Heb 8:1*
the h.
necessary that the patterns of *Heb 9:23*
things *in the* h.

HEAVEN'S

eunuchs for kingdom of h. *M't 19:12*
sake

HEAVIER

hand of Israel pressed *h*. (B)   *J'g 4:24*
now it would be *h*. than the   *Job 6:3*
sand
my stroke is *h*. than my   *Job 23:2*
groaning
a fool's wrath is *h*. than them   *Pr 27:3*
both

HEAVILY

wheels, that they drave them *h*.   *Ex 14:25*
battle went *h*. against Saul (S)   *1Sa 31:3*
his *h*. embossed shield (S)   *Job 15:26*
I bowed down *h*. as one that   *Ps 35:14*
hast thou very *h*. laid thy yoke   *Isa 47:6*
he sighted *h*. (N)   *Joh 11:33*

HEAVINESS

sacrifice I arose up from my *h*.   *Ezr 9:5*
I will leave off my *h*. and   *Job 9:27*
comfort
and I am full of *h*.: and I   *Ps 69:20*
looked
My soul melteth for *h*.:   *Ps 119:28*
strengthen
foolish son is the *h*. of his   *Pr 10:1*
mother
H. in the heart of man maketh   *Pr 12:25*
it
but the end of that mirth is *h*.   *Pr 14:13*
and there shall be *h*. and   *Isa 29:2*
sorrow
of praise for the spirit of *h*.   *Isa 61:3*
great *h*. and continual sorrow   *Ro 9:2*
would not come again to you   *2Co 2:1*
in *h*.
and was full of *h*., because   *Ph'p 2:26*
to mourning, and your joy to *h*.   *Jas 4:9*
ye are in *h*. through manifold   *1Pe 1:6*

HEAVY

Moses' hands were *h*.; and   *Ex 17:12*
they
for this thing is too *h*. for thee   *Ex 18:18*
alone, because it is too *h*. for   *Nu 11:14*
me
h. at heart (B)   *De 15:10*
for he was an old man, and *h*.   *1Sa 4:18*
But the hand of the Lord was   *1Sa 5:6*
h.
his hand is *h*. upon us (S)   *1Sa 5:7*
the hand of God was very *h*.   *1Sa 5:11*
because the hair was *h*. on   *2Sa 14:26*
him
his *h*. yoke which he put upon   *1Ki 12:4*
us
made our yoke *h*. (A)(R)   *1Ki 12:4*
Thy father made our yoke *h*.   *1Ki 12:10*
father did lade you with a *h*.   *1Ki 12:11*
yoke
My father made your yoke *h*.   *1Ki 12:14*
I am sent to thee with *h*.   *1Ki 14:6*
tidings
went to his house *h*. and   *1Ki 20:43*
displeased
Ahab came into his house *h*.   *1Ki 21:4*
his *h*. yoke that he put upon   *2Ch 10:4*
us
Thy father made our yoke *h*.   *2Ch 10:10*
my father put a *h*. yoke upon   *2Ch 10:11*
you
My father made your yoke   *2Ch 10:14*
h., but
bondage was *h*. upon this   *Ne 5:18*
people
neither shall my hand be *h*.   *Job 33:7*
upon
a *h*. metal mirror (S)   *Job 37:18*
night thy hand was *h*. upon me   *Ps 32:4*
over mine head: as an *h*.   *Ps 38:4*
burden
burden they are too *h*. for me   *Ps 38:4*
laid *h*. burden on hips (B)   *Ps 66:11*
Thy wrath lieth *h*. upon me (S)   *Ps 88:7*
our cattle *h*. with young (R)   *Ps 144:14*
like a *h*. sledge hammer (A)   *Pr 25:18*
that singeth songs to an *h*.   *Pr 25:20*
heart
stone is *h*. and the sand weighty   *Pr 27:3*
unto those that be of *h*. hearts   *Pr 31:6*
it is a *h*. travail (S)   *Ec 4:8*
make their ears *h*. and shut   *Isa 6:10*
their
transgression thereof shall be   *Isa 24:20*
h.

and the burden thereof is *h*.   *Isa 30:27*
your carriages were *h*. loaden   *Isa 46:1*
to undo the *h*. burdens, and   *Isa 58:6*
neither his ear *h*. that it cannot   *Isa 59:1*
get out: he hath made my chain   *La 3:7*
h.
the crop is *h*. (N)   *M't 9:37*
all ye that labour and are *h*.   *M't 11:28*
laden
had a *h*. heart (N)   *M't 19:22*
For they bind *h*. burdens and   *M't 23:4*
began to be sorrowful and   *M't 26:37*
very *h*.
asleep again: for their eyes   *M't 26:43*
were *h*.
went away with *h*. heart (N)   *M'k 10:22*
be sore amazed, and to be   *M'k 14:33*
very *h*.
asleep again, for their eyes   *M'k 14:40*
were *h*.
were with him were *h*. with   *Lu 9:32*
sleep

HEBER

and the sons of Beriah; *H*.   *Ge 46:17*
the sons of Beriah: of *H*. the   *Nu 26:45*
Now *H*. the Kenite, which was   *J'g 4:11*
of
the tent of Jael the wife of *H*.   *J'g 4:17*
and the house of *H*. of Kenite   *J'g 4:17*
Jael the wife of *H*. the Kenite   *J'g 5:24*
and *H*. the father of Socho   *1Ch 4:18*
Jachan, and Zia and *H*.,   *1Ch 5:13*
seven
And the sons of Beriah; *H*.   *1Ch 7:31*
And *H*. begat Japhlet, and   *1Ch 7:32*
Shomer
Meshullam, and Hezeki, and   *1Ch 8:17*
H.
And Ishpan, and *H*. and Eliel   *1Ch 8:22*
Phalec, which was the son of   *Lu 3:35*
H.

HEBERITES

of Heber, the family of the   *Nu 26:45*
H.: of

HEBER'S

Then Jael *H*. wife took a nail of   *J'g 4:21*

HEBREW

escaped, and told Abram the   *Ge 14:13*
H.
he hath brought in a *H*. unto   *Ge 39:14*
The *H*. servant, which thou   *Ge 39:17*
hast
with us a young man, an *H*.   *Ge 41:12*
Egypt spake to the *H*.   *Ex 1:15*
midwives
of a midwife to the *H*. women   *Ex 1:16*
Because the *H*. women are not   *Ex 1:19*
to thee a nurse of the *H*. women   *Ex 2:7*
spied an Egyptian smiting a *H*.   *Ex 2:11*
If thou buy an *H*. servant, six   *Ex 21:2*
years
an *H*. man or an *H*. woman   *De 15:12*
being an *H*. or an Hebrewess,   *Jer 34:9*
go
every man his brother an *H*.   *Jer 34:14*
And he said unto them, I am a   *Jon 1:9*
H.
of Greek, and Latin, and *H*.   *Lu 23:38*
called in the *H*. tongue   *Joh 5:2*
Bethesda
Pavement, but in the *H*.,   *Joh 19:13*
Gabbatha
which is called in the *H*.   *Joh 19:17*
Golgotha
written in *H*., and Greek, and   *Joh 19:20*
Latin
spake unto them in the *H*.   *Ac 21:40*
tongue
that he spake in the *H*. tongue   *Ac 22:2*
saying in the *H*., tongue, Saul,   *Ac 26:14*
Saul
of Benjamin, an *H*. of the   *Ph'p 3:5*
Hebrews
name in the *H*. tongue is   *Re 9:11*
Abaddon
in the *H*. tongue Armageddon   *Re 16:16*

HEBREWESS

being an Hebrew or an *H*., go   *Jer 34:9*
free

HEBREWS

away out of the land of the   *Ge 40:15*
H.
might not eat bread with the   *Ge 43:32*
H.
two men of the *H*. strove   *Ex 2:13*
together
God of the *H*. hath met with us   *Ex 3:18;*
    5:3
The Lord God of the *H*. hath   *Ex 7:16*
sent
saith the Lord God of the *H*.   *Ex 9:1;*
    9:13
Thus saith the Lord God of the   *Ex 10:3*
H.
great shout in the camp of the   *1Sa 4:6*
H.
that ye be not servants unto the   *1Sa 4:9*
H.
all the land, saying, Let the *H*.   *1Sa 13:3*
hear
some of the *H*. went over   *1Sa 13:7*
Jordan
the *H*. make them swords or   *1Sa 13:19*
spears
the *H*. come forth out of the   *1Sa 14:11*
holes
H. that were with the   *1Sa 14:21*
Philistines
What do these *H*. here? And   *1Sa 29:3*
of the Grecians against the *H*.   *Ac 6:1*
Are they *H*.? so am I. Are   *2Co 11:22*
they
of Benjamin, an Hebrew of   *Ph'p 3:5*
the *H*.

HEBREWS'

This is one of the *H*. children   *Ex 2:6*

HEBRON

Sarah died in Kirjath-arba,   *Ge 23:2;*
the same is *H*. *35:27; Jos 14:15; 20:7;*
    J'g 1:10
Jacob sent Joseph out of the   *Ge 37:14*
vale of *H*.
Amram, Izhar, and *H*.   *Ex 6:18;*
    Nu 3:19; 2Ch 6:2, 18; 23:12
H. was built seven years   *Nu 13:22*
before Zoan
as he did to *H*. so he did to   *Jos 10:39*
Debir
Joshua gave to Caleb *H*.   *Jos 14:13;*
    14:14; J'g 1:20
a present to them which were   *1Sa 30:31*
in *H*.
whither shall I go up? he said,   *2Sa 2:1*
unto *H*.
the time David was king in   *2Sa 2:11;*
H. was seven years *5:5; 1Ki 2:11;*
    1Ch 29:27
Joab and his men came to *H*.   *2Sa 2:32*
at break of day
to David were sons born in *H*.   *2Sa 3:2;*
    5:1; 1Ch 3:1, 4
they buried Abner in *H*. and   *2Sa 3:32*
the king wept
they buried the head of   *2Sa 4:12*
Ish-bosheth in *H*.
the elders of Israel came to *H*.   *2Sa 5:3;*
and David made a league   *1Ch 11:3*
with them in *H*.
took more wives after he was   *2Sa 5:13*
come from *H*.
which I have vowed to the   *2Sa 15:7*
Lord in *H*.
then ye shall say, Absalom   *2Sa 15:10*
reigneth in *H*.
cities of Judah, *H*. a city of   *2Sa 6:57*
refuge
all these came with a perfect   *2Sa 12:38*
heart to *H*.
the father of *H*.   *1Ch 2:42*
the sons of *H*.   *1Ch 2:43;*
    15:9; 23:19; 24:23
Rehoboam built Zorah, *H*.   *2Ch 11:10*
in Judah

HEBRONITES

and the family of the *H*. and   *Nu 3:27*
the family of the *H*., the   *Nu 26:58*
and the Izharites. the *H*.   *1Ch 26:23*
And of the *H*. Hashabiah   *1Ch 26:30*
and his
Among the *H*. was Jerijah   *1Ch 26:31*
the chief
even among the *H*.,   *1Ch 26:31*
according to

HEDGE

not thou made an *h.* about him	Job 1:10
slothful man is as an *h.* of thorns	Pr 15:19
whoso breaketh an *h.*, a serpent	Ec 10:8
I will take away the *h.* thereof	Isa 5:5
the *h.* for the house of Israel	Eze 13:5
them, that should make up the *h.*	Eze 22:30
I will *h.* up thy way with thorns	Ho 2:6
upright is sharper than a thorn *h.*	Mic 7:4
and set an *h.* about it, and digged	M'k 12:1

HEDGED

is hid, and whom God hath *h.* in	Job 3:23
He hath *h.* me about, that I cannot	La 3:7
a vineyard, and *h.* it round	M't 21:33
h. in, troubled, oppressed, cramped (A)(B)(R)	2Co 4:8

HEDGEHOG

the pelican and *h.* (A)(R)	Zep 2:14

HEDGEROWS

roads and *h.* (P)	Lu 14:21

HEDGES

that dwelt among plants and *h.*	1Ch 4:23
thou then broken down her *h.*	Ps 80:12
Thou hast broken down all his *h.*	Ps 89:40
and run to and fro by the *h.*	Jer 49:3
which camp in the *h.* in the cold	Na 3:17
Go out into the highways and *h.*	Lu 14:23

HEED

Take *h.* that thou speak not to	Ge 31:24
Take thou *h.* that thou speak not	Ge 31:29
Get thee from me, take *h.* to thyself	Ex 10:28
Take *h.* to yourselves, that ye go not	Ex 19:12
take *h.* to (E)(R)	Ex 23:13
Take *h.* to thyself, lest thou make	Ex 34:12
Must I not take *h.* to speak that	Nu 23:12
take ye good *h.* unto yourselves	De 2:4
Only take *h.* to thyself, and keep thy	De 4:9
Take ye therefore good *h.* unto	De 4:15
Take *h.* unto yourselves, lest ye	De 4:23
Take *h.* to yourselves, that your	De 11:16
Take *h.* to thyself that thou offer not	De 12:13
Take *h.* to thyself that thou forsake	De 12:19
Take *h.* to thyself that thou be not	De 12:30
Take *h.* in the plague of leprosy	De 24:8
Take *h.* and hearken, O Israel	De 27:9
But take diligent *h.* to do the	Jos 22:5
Take good *h.* therefore unto your	Jos 23:11
take *h.* to thyself until the morning	1Sa 19:2
Amasa took no *h.* to the sword that	2Sa 20:10
thy children take *h.* to their way	1Ki 2:4; 8:25
Jehu took no *h.* to walk in the law	2Ki 10:31
prosper if thou takest *h.* to fulfil	1Ch 22:13
Take *h.* now; for the Lord hath	1Ch 28:10
thy children take *h.* to their way	2Ch 6:16
Take *h.* what ye do: for ye judge	2Ch 19:6
take *h.* and do it: for there is no	2Ch 19:7

so that they will take *h.* to do all	2Ch 33:8
Take *h.* now that ye fail not to do	Ezr 4:22
Take *h.* regard not iniquity: for	Job 36:21
I said, I will take *h.* to my ways	Ps 39:1
by taking *h.* thereto according to	Ps 119:9
wicked doer giveth *h.* to false lips	Pr 17:4
Also take no *h.* unto all words	Ec 7:21
he gave good *h.* and sought out	Ec 12:9
Take *h.* and be quiet; fear him	Isa 7:4
hearkened diligently with much *h.*	Isa 21:7
Take ye *h.* every one of his	Jer 9:4
Take *h.* to yourselves, and bear no	Jer 17:21
us not give *h.* to any of his words	Jer 18:18
Give *h.* to me, O Lord, and hearken	Jer 18:19
have left off to take *h.* to the Lord	Ho 4:10
Therefore take *h.* to your spirit, and	Mal 2:15
therefore take *h.* to your spirit, that	Mal 2:16
Take *h.* that ye do not your alms	M't 6:1
Take *h.* and beware of the leaven	M't 16:6
Take *h.* that ye despise not one of	M't 18:10
Take *h.* that no man deceive you	M't 24:4
Take *h.* what ye hear: with what	M'k 4:24
Take *h.* beware of the leaven of	M'k 8:15
Take *h.* lest any man deceive	M'k 13:5
take *h.* to yourselves: for they shall	M'k 13:9
take ye *h.*: behold, I have foretold	M'k 13:23
Take ye *h.*, watch and pray: for ye	M'k 13:33
Take *h.* therefore how ye hear	Lu 8:18
Take *h.* therefore that the light	Lu 11:35
Take *h.*, beware of covetousness	Lu 12:15
Take *h.* to yourselves: If thy	Lu 17:3
Take *h.* that ye be not deceived	Lu 21:8
take *h.* to yourselves, lest at any	Lu 21:34
he gave *h.* unto them, expecting	Ac 3:5
take *h.* to yourselves what ye	Ac 5:35
accord gave *h.* unto those things	Ac 8:6
To whom they all gave *h.* from	Ac 8:10
Take *h.* therefore unto yourselves	Ac 20:28
Take *h.* what thou doest: for this	Ac 22:26
take *h.* lest he also spare not thee	Ro 11:21
every man take *h.* how he buildeth	1Co 3:10
But take *h.* lest by any means this	1Co 8:9
thinketh he standeth take *h.* lest he	1Co 10:12
take *h.* that ye be not consumed one	Ga 5:15
Take *h.* to the ministry which thou	Col 4:17
give *h.* to fables and endless	1Ti 1:4
giving *h.* to seducing spirits	1Ti 4:1
Take *h.* unto thyself, and unto	1Ti 4:16
Not giving *h.* to Jewish fables	Tit 1:14
the more earnest *h.* to the things	Heb 2:1
Take *h.* brethren, lest there be in	Heb 3:12
ye do well that ye take *h.* as unto	2Pe 1:19

HEEL

head, and thou shalt bruise his *h.*	Ge 3:15
his hand took hold on Esau's *h.*	Ge 25:26
The gin shall take him by the *h.*	Job 18:9
hath lifted up his *h.* against me	Ps 41:9
He took his brother by the *h.* in the	Ho 12:3
hath lifted up his *h.* against me	Joh 13:18

HEELS

adder that biteth the horse *h.*	Ge 49:17
thou settest a print upon the *h.* of	Job 13:27
iniquity of my *h.* shall compass	Ps 49:5
discovered and thy *h.* made bare	Jer 13:22

HEGAI

the palace, to the custody of *H.*	Es 2:8
custody of *H.* keeper of the women	Es 2:8
H. the king's chamberlain, the	Es 2:15

HEGE

unto the custody of *H.* the king's	Es 2:3

HEIFER

Take me an *h.* of three years old	Ge 15:9
bring thee a red *h.* without spot	Nu 19:2
one shall burn the *h.* in his sight	Nu 19:5
the midst of the burning of the *h.*	Nu 19:6
shall gather up the ashes of the *h.*	Nu 19:9
gathereth the ashes of the *h.* shall	Nu 19:10
ashes of the burnt *h.* of purification	Nu 19:17
elders of that city shall take an *h.*	De 21:3
down the *h.* unto a rough valley	De 21:4
shall wash their hands over the *h.*	De 21:6
If ye had not plowed with my *h.* ye	J'g 14:18
Take an *h.* with thee, and say, I am	1Sa 16:2
unto Zoar, an *h.* of three years old	Isa 15:5
Egypt is like a very fair *h.* but	Jer 46:20
voice as an *h.* of three years old	Jer 48:34
ye are grown fat as he *h.* at grass	Jer 50:11
slideth back as a backsliding *h.*	Ho 4:16
Ephraim is as an *h.* that is taught	Ho 10:11
the ashes of an *h.* sprinkling	Heb 9:13

HEIFERS

h. of Bashan (B)	Am 4:1

HEIFER'S

shall strike off the *h.* neck there	De 21:4

HEIGHT

and the *h.* of it thirty cubits	Ge 6:15
a cubit and a half the *h.* thereof	Ex 25:10; 25:2
the *h.* thereof shall be three cubits	Ex 27:1
and the *h.* five cubits of fine twined	Ex 27:18
two cubits shall be the *h.* thereof	Ex 30:2
and a cubit and a half the *h.* of	Ex 37:1
a cubit and a half the *h.* thereof	Ex 37:10
and two cubits was the *h.* of it; the	Ex 37:25
and three cubits the *h.* thereof	Ex 38:1
the *h.* in the breadth was five cubits	Ex 38:18
in the *h.* of Dor (S)	Jos 12:23
or on the *h.* of his stature	1Sa 16:7
whose *h.* was six cubits and a span	1Sa 17:4
and the *h.* thereof thirty cubits	1Ki 6:2
and twenty cubits in the *h.* thereof	1Ki 6:20
The *h.* of the one cherub was ten	1Ki 6:26
The *h.* thereof thirty cubits, upon	1Ki 7:2
the *h.* of the one chapiter was five	1Ki 7:16

the h. of the other chapter was five — 1Ki 7:16
all about, his h. was five cubits: and — 1Ki 7:23
thereof, and three cubits the h. of it — 1Ki 7:27
the h. of a wheel was a cubit — 1Ki 7:32
come up to the h. of the mountains — 2Ki 19:23
h. of the one pillar was eighteen — 2Ki 25:17
the h. of the chapiter three cubits — 2Ki 25:17
the h. was an hundred and twenty — 2Ch 3:4
and ten cubits the h. thereof — 2Ch 4:1
and five cubits the h. thereof — 2Ch 4:2
and raised it up a very great h. — 2Ch 33:14
the h. thereof threescore cubits — Ezr 6:3
Is not God in the h. of heaven — Job 22:12
behold the h. of the stars, how high — Job 22:12
down from the h. of his sanctuary — Ps 102:19
The heaven for h. and the earth — Pr 25:3
in the depth; or in the h. above — Isa 7:11
come up to the h. of the mountains — Isa 37:24
will enter into the h. of his border — Isa 37:24
come and sing in the h. of Zion, and — Jer 31:12
rock, that holdest the h. of the hill — Jer 49:16
should fortify the h. of her strength — Jer 51:53
the h. of one pillar was eighteen — Jer 52:21
and the h. of one chapiter was five — Jer 52:22
In the mountain of the h. of Israel — Eze 17:23
and she appeared in her h. with the — Eze 19:11
in the mountain of the h. of Israel — Eze 20:40
his h. was exalted above all — Eze 31:5
thou hast lifted up thyself in h. — Eze 31:10
and his heart is lifted up in his h. — Eze 31:10
exalt themselves for their h. — Eze 31:14
their trees stand up in their h. — Eze 31:14
and fill the valleys with thy h. — Eze 32:5
one reed; and the h. one reed — Eze 40:5
I saw also the h. of the house — Eze 41:8
whose h. was threescore cubits — Da 3:1
earth, and the h. thereof was great — Da 4:10
the h. thereof reached unto heaven — Da 4:11
whose h. reached unto heaven — Da 4:20
Amorite before them, whose h. — Am 2:9
was like the h. of the cedars — Am 2:9
Nor h. nor depth, nor any other — Ro 8:39
and length, and depth, and h. — Eph 3:18
breadth and the h. of it are equal — Re 21:16

HEIGHTENED

my strength is h. (B)(R) — 1Sa 2:1

HEIGHTS

h. of the hills (E) — Ps 95:4
the heavens: praise him in the h. — Ps 148:1
ascend above the h. of the clouds — Isa 14:14

HEINOUS

For this is an h. crime; yea, it is an — Job 31:11

HEIR

the h. of mine house is (S) — Ge 15:2
one born in my house is mine h. — Ge 15:3
This shall not be thine h.; but he — Ge 15:4
thine own bowels shall be thine h. — Ge 15:4

of this bondwoman shall not be h. — Ge 21:10
and we will destroy the h. also — 2Sa 14:7
handmaid that is h. to her mistress — Pr 30:23
Hath Israel no sons? hath he no h. — Jer 49:1
then shall Israel be h. unto them — Jer 49:2
Yet will I bring an h. unto thee — Mic 1:15
This is the h.; come, let us kill him — M't 21:38; Lu 20:14
he should be the h. of the world — Ro 4:13
That the h. as long as he is a child — Ga 4:1
then an h. of God through Christ — Ga 4:7
shall not be h. with the son of — Ga 4:30
whom appointed h. of all things — Heb 1:2
and became h. of the righteousness — Heb 11:7

HEIRS

unto them that were his h. saith — Jer 49:2
h. of the prophets (B)(N) — Ac 3:25
if they which are of the law be h. — Ro 4:14
And if children, then h.; of God — Ro 8:17
and h. according to the promise — Ga 3:29
equal h. (P) — Eph 5:6
by his grace, we should be made h. — Tit 3:7
them who shall be h. of salvation — Heb 1:14
to shew unto the h. of promise — Heb 6:17
h. with him of the same promise — Heb 11:9
rich in faith, and h. of the kingdom — Jas 2:5
h. together of the grace of life — 1Pe 3:7

HELAH

had two wives, H. and Naarah — 1Ch 4:5
the sons of H. were, Zereth, and — 1Ch 4:7

HELAM

the river: and they came to H. — 2Sa 10:16
passed over Jordan, and came to H. — 2Sa 10:17

HELBAH

nor of H. nor of Aphik, nor of — J'g 1:31

HELBON

in the wine of H. and white wool — Eze 27:18

HELD

wondering at her h. his peace — Ge 24:21
and Jacob h. his peace until they — Ge 34:5
and he h. up his father's hand, to — Ge 48:17
when Moses h. up his hand, that — Ex 17:11
h. up his hands (S) — Ex 17:12
the loops h. one curtain to another — Ex 36:12
glorified. And Aaron h. his peace — Le 10:3
and h. his peace at her in the day — Nu 30:7
heard it, and h. his peace at her. — Nu 30:11
he h. his peace at her in the day he — Nu 30:14
h. the lamps in their left hands — J'g 7:20
unto the lad that h. him by the hand — J'g 16:26
And when she h. it, he measured — Ru 3:15
no presents. But he h. his peace — 1Sa 10:27
behold, he h. a feast in his house — 1Sa 25:36
Israel: for Joab h. back the people — 2Sa 18:16

at that time Solomon h. a feast — 1Ki 8:65
king was h. up in chariot (S) — 1Ki 22:35; 2Ch 18:34
But the people h. their peace — 2Ki 18:36
received and h. three thousand — 2Ch 4:5
half of them h. both the spears — Ne 4:16
with the other hand h. a weapon — Ne 4:17
half of them h. the spears from — Ne 4:21
I h. a great assembly for them (S) — Ne 5:7
Then h. they their peace, and — Ne 5:8
king h. out to Esther the golden — Es 5:2
I had h. my tongue, although — Es 7:4
the king h. out the golden sceptre — Es 8:4
My foot hath h. his steps, his — Job 23:11
The nobles h. their peace and — Job 29:10
held (S) — Ps 18:35; Pr 5:22; Isa 45:1; Ac 2:24; Ro 14:4
whose mouth must be h. in with — Ps 32:9
I h. my peace, even from good — Ps 39:2
thy mercy, O Lord, h. me up — Ps 94:18
I h. him, and would not let him go — Isa 3:4
the king is h. in the galleries — Isa 7:5
they h. their peace, and answered — Isa 36:21
have not I h. my peace, even of old — Isa 57:11
took them captives h. them fast — Jer 50:33
when he h. up his right hand — Da 12:7
and h. a council against him, — M't 12:14
h. him to be a prophet (R) — M't 14:5
But Jesus h. his peace. And — M't 26:63
they came and h. him by the feet — M't 28:9
or to kill? But they h. their peace — M'k 3:4
But they h. their peace: for by — M'k 9:34
But he h. his peace, and answered — M'k 14:61
the chief priests h. a consultation — M'k 15:1
And they h. their peace. And he — Lu 14:4
at his answer, and h. their peace — Lu 20:26
the men that h. Jesus mocked him — Lu 22:63
man which was healed h. Peter — Ac 3:11
they h. their peace, and glorified — Ac 11:18
and part h. with the Jews, and part — Ac 14:4
and after they had h. their peace — Ac 15:13
being dead wherein we were h. — Ro 7:6
for the testimony which they h. — Re 6:9

HELDAI

H. the Netophathite, of Othniel — 1Ch 27:15
of them of the captivity, even of H. — Zec 6:10

HELEB

H. the son of Baanah, a — 2Sa 23:29

HELED

H. the son of Baanah the — 1Ch 11:30

HELEK

of H. the family of the Helekites — Nu 26:30
and for the children of H. and — Jos 17:2

HELEKITES

of Helek, the family of the H. — Nu 26:30

HELEM

And the sons of his brother H. — 1Ch 7:35
And the crowns shall be to H. — Zec 6:14

HELEPH

And their coast was from H. — Jos 19:33

HELEZ

H. the Paltite, Ira the son of	2Sa 23:26
Azariah begat *H.* and *H.* begat	1Ch 2:39
the Harorite, *H.* the Pelonite	1Ch 11:27
seventh month was *H.* the Pelonite	1Ch 27:16

HELI

Joseph, which was the son of *H.*	Lu 3:23

HELKAI

Of Harim, Adna; of Meraioth, *H.*	Ne 12:15

HELKATH

their border was *H.*, and Hali	Jos 19:25
H. with her suburbs, and Rehob	Jos 21:31

HELKATH-HAZZURIM

that place was called *H.*, which is	2Sa 2:16

HELL

shall burn unto the lowest *h.*	De 32:22
unto the lowest Sheol (A)(E)(R)	De 32:22
in the depths of the underworld (B)	De 32:22
The sorrows of *h.* compassed me	2Sa 22:6
the cords of Sheol were around (A)(E)(R)	2Sa 22:6
cords of the grave closed me (B)	2Sa 22:6
deeper than *h.*; what canst thou	Job 11:8
deeper than Sheol (A)(B)(E)(R)	Job 11:8
H. is naked before him, and	Job 26:6
Sheol naked before God (A)(B)(E)(R)	Job 26:6
The wicked shall be turned into *h.*	Ps 9:17
wicked turned into Sheol (A)(B)(E)(R)	Ps 9:17
thou wilt not leave my soul in *h.*	Ps 16:10
The sorrows of *h.* compassed me	Ps 18:5
let them go down quick into *h.*	Ps 55:15
go down alive into Sheol (A)(B)(E)(R)	Ps 55:15
my soul from the lowest *h.*	Ps 86:13
the pains of *h.* gat hold upon me	Ps 116:3
terrors of Sheol had hold (A)(E)(R)	Ps 116:3
terrors of the grave (B)	Ps 116:3
if I make my bed in *h.* behold	Ps 139:8
if I make my bed in Sheol (A)(E)(R)	Ps 139:8
if I make the underworld my couch (B)	Ps 139:8
death; her steps take hold on *h.*	Pr 5:5
her steps take hold of Sheol (A)(E)(R)	Pr 5:5
Her house is the way to *h.* going	Pr 7:27
house the way to Sheol (A)(B)(E)(R)	Pr 7:27
her guests are in the depths of *h.*	Pr 9:18
in the depths of Sheol (A)(B)(E)(R)	Pr 9:18; 15:24
H. and destruction are before	Pr 15:11
Sheol before the Lord (A)(B)(E)(R)	Pr 15:11
he may depart from *h.* beneath	Pr 15:24
and shalt deliver his soul from *h.*	Pr 23:14
deliver his life from Sheol (A)(B)(E)(R)	Pr 23:14
H. and destruction are never full	Pr 27:20
Sheol never satisfied (A)(B)(E)(R)	Pr 27:20
Therefore *h.* hath enlarged herself	Isa 5:14
Sheol has enlarged herself (A)(B)(E)(R)	Isa 5:14

H. from beneath is moved for thee	Isa 14:9
Sheol is stirred up (A)(B)(E)(R)	Isa 14:9
thou shalt be brought down to	Isa 14:15
brought down to Sheol (A)(B)(E)(R)	Isa 14:15
and with *h.* are we at agreement	Isa 28:15
agreement with Sheol (A)(B)(E)(R)	Isa 28:15; 28:18
agreement with *h.* shall not stand	Isa 28:18
didst debase thyself even unto *h.*	Isa 57:9
debased to Sheol (A)(B)(E)(R)	Isa 57:9
I cast him down to *h.* with them	Eze 31:16
cast down to Sheol (A)(B)(E)(R)	Eze 31:16
They also went down into *h.*	Eze 31:17
shall go down to Sheol (A)(E)(R)	Eze 31:17
into the realm of the dead (B)	Eze 31:17
speak to him out of the midst of *h.*	Eze 32:21
out of the midst of Sheol	Eze 32:21
gone down to *h.* with their weapons	Eze 32:27
are gone down to Sheol (A)(B)(E)(R)	Eze 32:27
Though they dig into *h.* thence	Am 9:2
dig into Sheol (A)(B)(E)(R)	Am 9:2
out of the belly of *h.* cried I	Jon 2:2
out of the belly of Sheol (A)(B)(E)(R)	Jon 2:2
who enlargeth his desire as *h.*	Hab 2:5
appetite large like Sheol (A)(E)(R)	Hab 2:5
greed like the grave (B)	Hab 2:5
fool, shall be in danger of *h.* fire	M't 5:22
unable to escape Gehenna of fire (A)	M't 5:22
heading straight for fire of destruction (P)	M't 5:22
body should be cast into *h.*	M't 5:29; 5:30
body go to the rubbish heap (B)	M't 5:29; 5:30
to destroy both soul and body in *h.*	M't 10:28
into the fires of destruction (P)	M't 10:28
shalt be brought down to *h.*	M't 11:23
brought down to Hades (A)(B)(E)(R)	M't 11:23
brought down to the depths (N)	M't 11:23
hurtling down among the dead (P)	M't 11:23
and the gates of *h.* shall not prevail	M't 16:18
the gates of Hades (A)(E)	M't 16:18
the forces of death (N)(P)(R)	M't 16:18
two eyes to be cast into *h.* fire	M't 18:9
thrown into the hell (Gehenna) of fire (A)	M't 18:9
thrown onto everlasting fire (P)	M't 18:9
more the child of *h.* than yourselves	M't 23:15
twice as ripe for destruction (P)	M't 23:15
can ye escape the damnation of *h.*	M't 23:33
the sentence of perdition (B)	M't 23:33
condemned to the rubbish heap (P)	M't 23:33
than having two hands to go into *h.*	M'k 9:43
thrown in Gehenna into the fire that cannot be put out (B)	M'k 9:43
go to the rubbish heap (P)	M'k 9:43; 9:45, 47
having two feet to be cast into *h.*	M'k 9:45
having two eyes to be cast into *h.* fire	M'k 9:47
heaven, shalt be thrust down to *h.*	Lu 10:15
brought down to Hades (A)(B)(E)(R)	Lu 10:15
brought down to the depths (N)	Lu 10:15

hurtling down among the dead (P)	Lu 10:15
killed hath power to cast into *h.*	Lu 12:5
cast into Gehenna (B)	Lu 12:5
throw you into destruction (P)	Lu 12:5
in *h.* he lift up his eyes, being	Lu 16:23
in Hades, being in torment (A)(B)(E)(N)(R)	Lu 16:23
thou wilt not leave my soul in *h.*	Ac 2:27
leaving it in Hades (A)(E)(N)(P)(R)	Ac 2:27; 2:31
abandoned my soul in the grave (B)	Ac 2:27
that his soul was not left in *h.*	Ac 2:31
to *h.* with you and money (P)	Ac 8:20
nature; and it is set on fire of *h.*	Jas 3:6
kindled by Gehenna (B)	Jas 3:6
sinned, but cast them down to *h.*	2Pe 2:4
to black dungeons of Tartarus (B)	2Pe 2:4
to pity of nether gloom (R)	2Pe 2:4
have the keys of *h.* and of death	Re 1:18
keys of Death and Hades (A)(E)(N)(R)	Re 1:18
keys of death and the grave (P)	Re 1:18
Death, and *H.* followed with him	Re 6:8
Death and Hades (A)(B)(E)(N)(R)	Re 6:8
death, and the grave followed	Re 6:8
death and *h.* delivered up the dead	Re 20:13
Death and Hades (A)(B)(E)(N)(R)	Re 20:13
death and the grave (P)	Re 20:13; 20:14
death and *h.* were cast into the lake	Re 20:14

HELM

turned about with a very small *h.*	Jas 3:4

HELMET

had an *h.* of brass upon his head	1Sa 17:5
put an *h.* of brass upon his head	1Sa 17:38
an *h.* of salvation upon his head	Isa 59:17
Ephraim is my *h.* (R)	Ps 60:7
buckler and shield and *h.* round	Eze 23:24
hanged the shield and *h.* in thee	Eze 27:10
all of them with shield and *h.*	Eze 38:5
And take the *h.* of salvation	Eph 6:17
and for an *h.* the hope of salvation	1Th 5:8

HELMETS

spears, and *h.* and habergeons	2Ch 26:14
stand forth with your *h.*; furbish	Jer 46:4

HELMSMAN

the *h.* (A)(B)(N)(P)	Jas 3:4
every *h.* (B)	Re 18:17

HELON

Of Zebulun; Eliab the son of *H.*	Nu 1:9
Eliab the son of *H.* shall be captain	Nu 2:7
Eliab the son of *H.* prince of	Nu 7:24
the offering of Eliab the son of *H.*	Nu 7:29
of Zebulun was Eliab the son of *H.*	Nu 10:16

HELP

will make him an *h.* meet for him	Ge 2:18
was not found an *h.* meet for him	Ge 2:20
of thy father, who shall *h.* thee	Ge 49:25
of my father, said he, was mine *h.*	Ex 18:4
and wouldest forbear to *h.* him	Ex 23:5

thou shalt surely *h*. with him   *Ex 23:5*
shalt surely *h*. him to lift them   *De 22:4* up
let them rise up and *h*. you   *De 32:38*
an *h*. to him from his enemies   *De 33:7*
rideth upon the heaven in thy   *De 33:26* *h*.
Lord, the shield of thy *h*. and   *De 33:29* who
men of valour, and *h*. them   *Jos 1:14*
Come up unto me, and *h*. me   *Jos 10:4*
us quickly, and save us, and   *Jos 10:6* *h*. us
of Gezer came up to *h*.   *Jos 10:33* Lachish
came not to the *h*. of the Lord   *J'g 5:23*
h. of the Lord against the mighty   *J'g 5:23*
the sun be hot, ye shall have *h*.   *1Sa 11:9*
for me, then thou shalt *h*. me   *2Sa 10:11*
thee, then I will come and *h*.   *2Sa 10:11* thee
Syrians feared to *h*. the   *2Sa 10:19* children of
did obeisance, and said, H. O   *2Sa 14:4* king
him, saying, *H*. my lord, O   *2Ki 6:26* king
not *h*. thee, whence shall I *h*.   *2Ki 6:27* thee
come peaceably unto me to   *1Ch 12:17* *h*. me
day there came to David to   *1Ch 12:22* *h*. him
Syrians of Damascus came to   *1Ch 18:5* *h*.
for me, then thou shalt *h*.   *1Ch 19:12* me: but
strong for thee, then I will *h*.   *1Ch 19:12* thee
Syrians *h*. the children of   *1Ch 19:19* Ammon
princes of Israel to *h*.   *1Ch 22:17* Solomon
Lord, it is nothing with thee   *2Ch 14:11* to *h*.
no power: *h*. us, O Lord our   *2Ch 14:11* God
Shouldest thou *h*. the ungodly   *2Ch 19:2*
together, to ask *h*. of the   *2Ch 20:4* Lord: even
then thou wilt hear and *h*.   *2Ch 20:9*
God hath power to *h*. and to   *2Ch 25:8* cast
to *h*. the king against the   *2Ch 26:13* enemy
unto the kings of Assyria to *h*.   *2Ch 28:16* him
the gods of the kings of Syria   *2Ch 28:23* to *h*.
I sacrifice to them, that they   *2Ch 28:23* may *h*. me
brethren the Levites did *h*.   *2Ch 29:34* them
the city: and they did *h*. him   *2Ch 32:3*
with us is the Lord our God   *2Ch 32:8* to *h*. us
of his place *h*. him with silver   *Ezr 1:4*
of soldiers and horsemen to *h*.   *Ezr 8:22* us
Is not my *h*. in me? and is   *Job 6:13* wisdom
neither will he *h*. the evil   *Job 8:20* doers
and him that had none to *h*.   *Job 29:12* him
when I saw my *h*. in the gate   *Job 31:21*
soul, There is no *h*. for him in   *Ps 3:2* God
H., Lord; for the godly man   *Ps 12:1*
Send thee *h*. from the sanctuary   *Ps 20:2*
trouble is near; there is none   *Ps 22:11* to *h*.
O my strength, haste thee to *h*.   *Ps 22:19* me
thou hast been my *h*.; leave me   *Ps 27:9* not
Lord: he is our *h*. and our   *Ps 33:20* shield
buckler, and stand up for mine   *Ps 35:2* *h*.
And the Lord shalt *h*. them   *Ps 37:40*
Make haste to *h*. me, O   *Ps 38:22* Lord my
me: O Lord, make haste to *h*.   *Ps 40:13* me
thou art my *h*. and my   *Ps 40:17* deliverer
for the *h*. of his countenance   *Ps 42:5*
the *h*. of my countenance   *Ps 42:11*

the *h*. of my countenance   *Ps 42:11;*
(A)(E)(R)   *42:5*
Arise for our *h*. and redeem us   *Ps 44:26*
a very present *h*. in trouble.   *Ps 46:1*
God shall *h*. her, and that right   *Ps 46:5*
fault: awake to *h*. me, and   *Ps 59:4* behold
Give us *h*. from trouble: for   *Ps 60:11* vain
trouble: for vain is the *h*. of   *Ps 60:11* man
Because thou hast been my *h*.   *Ps 63:7*
me; make haste to *h*. me, O   *Ps 70:1* Lord
thou art my *h*. and my deliverer   *Ps 70:5*
O my God, and make haste   *Ps 71:12* for my *h*.
H. us, O God of our salvation   *Ps 79:9*
h. and comfort me   *Ps 86:17* (A)(B)(E)(R)(S)
I have laid *h*. upon one that is   *Ps 89:19*
Unless the Lord had been my   *Ps 94:17* *h*.
fell down, and there was   *Ps 107:12* none to *h*.
Give us *h*. from trouble: for   *Ps 108:12* vain
trouble: for vain is the *h*. of   *Ps 108:12* man
H. me, O Lord my God: O   *Ps 109:26* save me
is their *h*. and their shield   *Ps 115:9; 115:10-11*
my part with them that *h*. me   *Ps 118:7*
persecute me wrongfully: *h*.   *Ps 119:86* thou
Let thine hand *h*. me; for I   *Ps 119:173* have
thee; and let thy judgments   *Ps 119:175* *h*. me
hills, from which cometh my *h*.   *Ps 121:1*
My *h*. cometh from the Lord,   *Ps 121:2* which
Our *h*. is in the name of the   *Ps 124:8* Lord
son of man, in whom there is   *Ps 146:3* no *h*.
hath the God of Jacob for his   *Ps 146:5* *h*.
he hath not another to *h*. him up   *Ec 4:10*
to whom will ye flee for *h*.   *Isa 10:3*
whither we flee for *h*. to be   *Isa 20:6* delivered
be an *h*. nor profit, but a   *Isa 30:5* shame
For the Egyptians shall *h*. in   *Isa 30:7* vain
them that go down to Egypt   *Isa 31:1* for *h*.
the *h*. of them that work   *Isa 31:2* iniquity
I will *h*. thee; yea, I will   *Isa 41:10* uphold
unto thee, Fear not; I will *h*.   *Isa 41:13* thee
I will *h*. thee, saith the Lord   *Isa 41:14*
from the womb, which will *h*.   *Isa 44:2* thee
the Lord God will *h*. me;   *Isa 50:7* therefore
Behold, the Lord God will *h*.   *Isa 50:9* me
I looked, and there was none   *Ec 63:5* to *h*.
which is come forth to *h*. you   *Jer 37:7*
the enemy, and none did *h*. her   *La 1:7*
eyes as yet failed for our vain   *La 4:17* *h*.
all that are about him to *h*.   *Eze 12:14* him
mighty army and company to   *Eze 17:17* *h*. (S)
midst of hell with them that   *Eze 32:21* *h*. him
of the chief princes, came to   *Da 10:13* *h*. me
they shall be holpen with a   *Da 11:34* little *h*.
receive a little *h*. (A)   *Da 11:34*
to his end, and none shall *h*.   *Da 11:45* him
thyself; but in me is thine *h*.   *Ho 13:9*
worshipped him, saying,   *M't 15:25* Lord *h*. me
have compassion on us, and   *M'k 9:22* *h*. us
I believe; *h*. thou mine   *M'k 9:24* unbelief

to *h*. him (A)(E)(P)(R)   *Lu 1:54*
that they should come and *h*.   *Lu 5:7* them
bid her therefore that she *h*.   *Lu 10:40* me
over into Macedonia, and *h*. us   *Ac 16:9*
Crying out, Men of Israel, *h*.:   *Ac 21:28* This
Having therefore obtained *h*.   *Ac 26:22* of
h. your spiritual life (P)   *2Co 12:19*
h. those women which laboured   *Ph'p 4:3*
able to *h*. those in test   *Heb 2:18* (N)(P)(R)
find grace to *h*. in time of   *Heb 4:16* need

HELPED

Moses stood up and *h*. them   *Ex 2:17*
Hitherto hath the Lord *h*. us   *1Sa 7:12*
and they following Adonijah *h*.   *1Ki 1:7* him
the thirty and two kings that   *1Ki 20:16* *h*. him
And they were *h*. against   *1Ch 5:20* them, and
Saul to battle: but they *h*.   *1Ch 12:19* them not
And they *h*. David against   *1Ch 12:21* the band
when God *h*. the Levites that   *1Ch 15:26* bare
cried out, and the Lord *h*.   *2Ch 18:31* him; and
every one *h*. to destroy   *2Ch 20:23* another
God *h*. him against the   *2Ch 26:7* Philistines
marvelously *h*. till he was   *2Ch 26:15* strong
king of Assyria: but he *h*.   *2Ch 28:21* him not
they *h*. the people (S)   *Ezr 8:36*
and Shabbethai the Levite   *Ezr 10:15* *h*. them
officers of the king, *h*. the Jews   *Es 9:3*
thou *h*. him that is without   *Job 26:2* power
heart trusted in him, and I am   *Ps 28:7* *h*.
h. children of Lot (A)(E)(S)   *Ps 83:8*
I was brought low, and he *h*.   *Ps 116:6* me
I might fall: but the Lord *h*.   *Ps 118:13* me
Judah who is *h*.   *Isa 31:3* (A)(B)(E)(R)
They *h*. every one his   *Isa 41:6* neighbour
in a day of salvation have I *h*.   *Isa 49:8* thee
shall be *h*. a little (E)   *Da 11:34*
and they *h*. forward the   *Zec 1:15* affliction
h. them much which had   *Ac 18:27* believed
I have *h*. thee (S)   *2Co 6:2*
the earth *h*. the woman, and   *Re 12:16*

HELPER

nor any left, nor any *h*. for   *2Ki 14:26* Israel
my calamity, they have no *h*.   *Job 30:13*
thou art the *h*. of the   *Ps 10:14* fatherless
upon me: Lord, be thou my *h*.   *Ps 30:10*
Behold, God is mine *h*.: the   *Ps 54:4* Lord is
poor also, and him that hath   *Ps 72:12* no *h*.
and Zidon every *h*. that   *Jer 47:4* remaineth
John as their *h*. (S)   *Ac 13:5*
has been a *h*. of many (S)   *Ro 16:2*
Salute Urbane, our *h*. in Christ   *Ro 16:9*
Lord is my *h*. and I will not   *Heb 13:6* fear

HELPERS

the mighty men, *h*. of the war   *1Ch 12:1*
unto thee, and peace be to   *1Ch 12:18* thine *h*.
the proud *h*. do stoop under   *Job 9:13* him
when all her *h*. shall be   *Eze 30:8* destroyed
Put and Lubim were thy *h*.   *Na 3:9*

and Aquila my *h.* in Christ Ro 16:3
Jesus
your faith, but are *h.* of your 2Co 1:24
joy

HELPETH

thine helpers: for thy God *h.* 1Ch 12:18
thee
both he that *h.* shall fall, and Isa 31:3
he
the Spirit also *h.* our Ro 8:26
infirmities
and to every one that *h.* with 1Co 16:16
us

HELPFUL

not everything is *h.* (B)(R) 1Co 10:23

HELPING

were the prophets of God *h.* Ezr 5:2
them
why art thou so far from *h.* me Ps 22:1
Ye also *h.* together by prayer 2Co 1:11
for us

HELPLESS

render *h.* (B) J'g 16:6; 16:19
Lord takes care of *h.* (B) Ps 116:6

HELPS

they used *h.* undergirding the Ac 27:17
ship
gifts of healings, *h.,* 1Co 12:28
governments

HELVE

and the head slippeth from the De 19:5
h.

HEM

upon the *h.* of it thou shall Ex 28:33
make
scarlet, round about the *h.* Ex 28:33
thereof
upon the *h.* of the robe round Ex 28:34
upon the *h.* of the robe, round Ex 39:25
round about the *h.* of the robe Ex 39:26
touched the *h.* of his garment M't 9:20
only touch the *h.* of his M't 14:36
garment

HEMAM

of Lotan were Hori and H. Ge 36:22

HEMAN

than Ethan the Ezrahite, and 1Ki 4:31
H.
of Zerah; Zimri, and Ethan, 1Ch 2:6
and H.
H. a singer, the son of Joel, 1Ch 6:33
the son
So the Levites appointed H. 1Ch 15:17
the son
the singers, H., Asaph, and 1Ch 15:19
Ethan
And with them H. and 1Ch 16:41
Jeduthun
H. and Jeduthun with 1Ch 16:42
trumpets
of the sons of Asaph, and of 1Ch 25:1
H. and
Of H.: the son of H.; Bukkiah 1Ch 25:4
H. the king's seer in the 1Ch 25:5
words of
And God gave to H. fourteen 1Ch 25:5
sons
order to Asaph, Jeduthun, and 1Ch 25:6
H.
of Asaph, of H. of Jeduthun 2Ch 5:12
the sons of H.; Jehiel, and 2Ch 29:14
Shimei
and Asaph, and H., and 2Ch 35:15
Jeduthun
Maschil of H. the Ezrahite Ps 88 title

HEMATH

the Kenites that came of H. the 1Ch 2:55
even unto the entering of H. 1Ch 13:5
the entering in of H. unto the Am 6:14

HEMDAN

H. and Eshban, and Ithran Ge 36:26

HEMLOCK

as *h.* in the furrows of the field Ho 10:4
the fruit of righteousness into Am 6:12
h.

HEMMED

hard-pressed, never *h.* in (N) 2Co 4:8

HEMMING

surrounding, *h.* in (P) Lu 19:43

HEMORRHAGE

had a *h.* (B)(N)(P)(R) M't 9:20
healed of her *h.* (P)(R) M'k 5:29
her *h.* was over (B)(N)(P) Lu 8:44

HEMORRHOIDS

with *h.* (B) 1Sa 5:6; 5:9, 12; 6:4, 5

HEMS

they made upon the *h.* of the Ex 39:24
robe

HEN

and to H. the son of Zec 6:14
Zephaniah
even as a *h.* gathereth her M't 23:37
chickens
as a *h.* doth gather her brood Lu 13:34
under

HENA

gods of Sepharvaim, H. and 2Ki 18:34
Ivah
city of Sepharvaim, of H. 2Ki 19:13
and Ivah
city of Sepharvaim, H. and Isa 37:13
Ivah

HENADAD

the sons of H. with their sons Ezr 3:9
and
Bavai the son of H. the ruler Ne 3:18
of the
him repaired Binnui the son of Ne 3:24
H.
Binnui of the sons of H., Ne 10:9
Kadmiel

HENCE

They are departed *h.;* for I Ge 37:17
heard
ye shall not go forth *h.* except Ge 42:15
your
ye shall carry up my bones Ge 50:25
from *h.*
afterwards he will let you go *h.* Ex 11:1
surely thrust you out *h.* Ex 11:1
altogether
carry up my bones away *h.* Ex 13:19
with you
and go up *h.* thou and the Ex 33:1
people
go not with me, carry us not Ex 33:15
up *h.*
Arise, get thee down quickly De 9:12
from *h.*
you *h.* out of the midst of Jos 4:3
Jordan
Depart not *h.* I pray thee, until J'g 6:18
I
neither go from *h.* but abide Ru 2:8
here
Get thee *h.* and turn thee 1Ki 17:3
eastward
strength, before I go *h.* and be Ps 39:13
no more
thou shalt say unto it, Get Isa 30:22
thee *h.*
Take from *h.* thirty men with Jer 38:10
thee
Get you *h.* walk to and fro Zec 6:7
through
Get thee *h.* Satan: for it is M't 4:10
written
Remove *h.* to yonder place M't 17:20
of God, cast thyself down from *h.* Lu 4:9

Get thee out, and depart *h.:* Lu 13:31
for
would pass from *h.* to you Lu 16:26
cannot
Take these things *h.;* make Joh 2:16
not my
Depart *h.* and go into Judæa, Joh 7:3
that
even so I do. Arise, let us go Joh 14:31
h.
but now is my kingdom not Joh 18:36
from *h.*
Sir, if thou have borne him *h.* Joh 20:15
tell me
Holy Ghost not many days *h.* Ac 1:5
send thee far *h.* unto the Ac 22:21
Gentiles
come they not *h.* even of your Jas 4:1
lusts

HENCEFORTH

it shall not *h.* yield unto thee Ge 4:12
her
Israel *h.* come nigh the Nu 18:22
tabernacle
Ye shall *h.* return no more De 17:16
that
shall *h.* commit no more any De 19:20
such
will not *h.* drive out any from J'g 2:21
before
for thy servant will *h.* offer 2Ki 5:17
neither
from *h.* thou shalt have wars 2Ch 16:9
his people from *h.* even for Ps 125:2
ever
in the Lord from *h.* and for Ps 131:3
ever
with justice from *h.* even for Isa 9:7
ever
for *h.* there shall no more Isa 52:1
come into
saith the Lord, from *h.* and Isa 59:21
for ever
shalt no more *h.* bereave Eze 36:12
them of men
over them in mount Zion from Mic 4:7
h.
Ye shall not see me *h.* till ye M't 23:39
I will not drink *h.* of this M't 26:29
fruit of
from *h.* all generations shall Lu 1:48
call me
not: from *h.* thou shalt catch Lu 5:10
men
h. there shall be five in one Lu 12:52
house
from *h.* ye know him, and Joh 14:7
have seen
H. I call you not servants; Joh 15:15
for the
speak *h.* to no man in this Ac 4:17
name
from *h.* I will go unto the Ac 18:6
Gentiles
that *h.* we should not serve sin Ro 6:6
should not *h.* live unto 2Co 5:15
themselves
h. know we no man after 2Co 5:16
yet now *h.* know we him no 2Co 5:16
more
From *h.* let no man trouble me Ga 6:17
That we *h.* be no more Eph 4:14
children
ye *h.* walk not as other Eph 4:17
Gentiles
H. there is laid up for me a 2Ti 4:8
crown
From *h.* expecting till his Heb 10:13
enemies
dead which die in the Lord Re 14:13
from *h.*

HENCEFORWARD

and *h.* among your Nu 15:23
generations
no fruit grow on thee *h.* for M't 21:19
ever

HENNA

h. flowers in the vineyard (S) Ca 1:14
h. with with spikenards (S) Ca 4:13
my *h.* and nard (R) Ca 4:13

HENNAS

lodge among the *h.* (B) Ca 7:11

HENOCH

H., Methuselah, Lamech, Noah   1Ch 1:3
Epher, and H., and Abido   1Ch 1:33

HEPHER

of H. the family of the   Nu 26:32
Hepherites
Zelophehad the son of H. had   Nu 26:33
no
the son of H. the son of Gilead   Nu 27:1
Tappuah, one; the king of H.   Jos 12:17
one
for the chilren of H. and for   Jos 17:2
But Zelophehad, the son of H.   Jos 17:3
Sochoh, and all the land of H.   1Ki 4:10
Naarah bare him Ahuzam, and   1Ch 4:6
H.
H. the Mecherathite, Ahijah   1Ch 11:36

HEPHERITES

of Hepher, the family of the   Nu 26:32
H.

HEPHZI-BAH

And his mother's name was   2Ki 21:1
H.
but thou shalt be called H. and   Isa 62:4

HER

brought h. to the man   Ge 2:22
gave h. husband with h.   Ge 3:62
between thy seed and h. seed   Ge 3:15
earth opened h. mouth   Ge 4:11
no rest for sole of h. feet   Ge 8:9
entreated him well for h. sake   Ge 12:16
obtain children by h.   Ge 16:2; 16:3-13
call h. name Sarah   Ge 17:15; 17:16
with h. pitcher   Ge 24:15;
    24:16, 17, 18, 20, 45, 46
he became h. son   Ex 2:10
wife and children be h.   Ex 21:4;
masters   21:6, 8, 9, 10, 11, 22
separation from h. infirmity   Le 12:2;
12:4-8; 15:19, 20, 21, 23, 24, 25, 26, 28,
                 29, 30
Heal h. now   Nu 12:12; 12:13-14
he hateth h.   De 22:16; 22:14-19
stone h. with stones   De 22:21
all that are in h. house   Jos 6:17; 6:22-23
h. suburbs   Jos 21:13; 21:14-39
she was left and h. two sons   Ru 1:5
Ruth clave to h.   Ru 1:14; 1:18, 22
show the princes h. beauty   Es 1:11
give h. royal estate to another   Es 1:19
made h. queen   Es 2:17
soul make h. boast in the   Ps 34:2
Lord
h. clothing is of wrought gold   Ps 45:13
God is in the midst of h.   Ps 46:5
God is known in h. palaces   Ps 48:3
earth yield h. increase   Ps 67:4
time of h. favor is come   Ps 102:13
seekest h. as silver, as hid   Pr 2:4
treasures
forsaketh the guide of h. youth   Pr 2:17
h. house inclineth unto death   Pr 2:18
Length of days in h. right   Pr 3:16;
hand   3:17-19
h. mouth smoother than oil   Pr 5:3; 7:5
h. end is as bitter as wormwood   Pr 5:3
h. feet go down to death   Pr 5:5
Remove thy way far from h.   Pr 5:8
h. price far above rubies   Pr 31:10
h. husband doth safely trust in   Pr 31:11
h.
h. warfare is accomplished   Isa 40:2
h. treacherous sister Judah saw   Jer 3:7
it
that conceived in h. is of   M't 1:20
Rachel weeping for h. children   M't 2:18
looketh on woman to lust   M't 5:28
after h.
she brought forth h. firstborn   Lu 2:7
son
Jesus saith unto h.   Joh 4:7;
    4:10, 13, 16, 17, 21
bound by the law to h. husband   Ro 7:2
every woman have h. own   1Co 7:2
husband
let h. not depart from   1Co 7:10
husband
prophesieth with h. head   1Co 11:5
uncovered
let h. be covered   1Co 11:6

power on h. head because of   1Co 11:10
angels
wife reverence h. husband   Eph 5:33
patience have h. perfect work   Jas 1:4
gave h. space to repent   Re 2:21
moon under h. feet, upon h.   Re 12:1
head
devour h. child as soon as born   Re 12:4
h. child caught up to God   Re 12:5
Come out of h. my people   Re 18:4
to h. it was granted that she   Re 19:8
prepared as a bride adorned   Re 21:2
for h.
h. light was like unto a stone   Re 21:11
yielded h. fruit every month   Re 22:2

HERALD

Then an h. cried aloud, To you   Da 3:4
it is
h. from the housetops (B)   M't 10:27
a h. of the kingdom (B)   Ac 20:25
h. the message (B)   2Ti 4:2

HERALDED

your long h. Christ (P)   Ac 3:20
the baptism John h. (B)   Ac 10:37
h. God's gospel (B)   1Th 2:9
h. among Gentiles (B)   1Ti 3:16

HERB

the h. yielding seed, and the   Ge 1:11
fruit
h. yielding seed after his kind   Ge 1:12
I have given you every h.   Ge 1:29
bearing
have given every green h. for   Ge 1:30
meat
every h. of the field before it   Ge 2:5
grew
and thou shalt eat the h. of the   Ge 3:18
field
even as the green h. have I given   Ge 9:3
every h. of the field, throughout   Ex 9:22
the hail smote every h. of the   Ex 9:25
field
and eat every h. of the land,   Ex 10:12
even all
and they did eat every h. of   Ex 10:15
the land
the small rain upon the tender   De 32:2
h.
and as the green h. as the   2Ki 19:26
grass on
it withereth before any other   Job 8:12
h.
the bud of the tender h. to   Job 38:27
spring
grass, and wither as the green   Ps 37:2
h.
and h. for the service of man   Ps 104:14
of the field, and as the green   Isa 37:27
h. as
your bones shall flourish like   Isa 66:14
an h.

HERBS

the trees, or in the h. of the   Ex 10:15
field
and with bitter h. they shall eat   Ex 12:8
with unleavened bread and   Nu 9:11
bitter h.
it with thy foot, as a garden of   De 11:10
h.
I may have it for a garden of   1Ki 21:2
h.
went out into the field to   2Ki 4:39
gather h.
did eat up all the h. in their   Ps 105:35
land
Better is a dinner of h. where   Pr 15:17
love
h. of the mountains are   Pr 27:25
gathered
like a clear heat upon h. and   Isa 18:4
like
thy dew is as the dew of h.   Isa 26:19
and the
and hills, and dry up all their   Isa 42:15
h.
and the h. of every field wither   Jer 12:4
grown, it is the greatest   M't 13:32
among h.
up, and becometh greater   M'k 4:32
than all h
mint and rue and all manner   Lu 11:42
of h.

another, who is weak, eateth h.   Ro 14:2
and bringeth forth h. meet for   Heb 6:7
them

HERD

And Abraham ran unto the h.   Ge 18:7
even of the h. and of the   Le 1:2
flock
offering be a burnt sacrifice of   Le 1:3
the h.
peace offering, if he offer it of   Le 3:1
the h.
concerning the tithe of the h.   Le 27:32
or of
the Lord, of the h. or of the   Nu 15:3
flock
shalt kill of thy h. and of thy   De 12:21
flock
that come of thy h. and of   De 15:19
thy flock
of the flock and the h. in the   De 16:2
place
came after the h. out of the   1Sa 11:5
field
of his own flock and of his   2Sa 12:4
own h.
the young of the flock and of   Jer 31:12
the h.
man nor beast, h. nor flock,   Jon 3:7
taste
and there shall be no h. in the   Hab 3:17
stalls
them an h. of many swine   M't 8:30
feeding
us to go away into the h. of   M't 8:31
swine
they went into the h. of swine   M't 8:32
the whole h. of swine ran   M't 8:32
violently
mountains a great h. of swine   M'k 5:11
feeding
the h. ran violently down a   M'k 5:13
steep place
an h. of many swine feeding on   Lu 8:32
the h. ran violently down a   Lu 8:33
steep place

HERDMAN

but I was an h. and a gatherer   Am 7:14

HERDMEN

between the h. of Abram's   Ge 13:7
cattle
cattle and the h. of Lot's cattle   Ge 13:7
between my h. and thy h.; for   Ge 13:8
we be
And the h. of Gerar did strive   Ge 26:20
of Gerar did strive with   Ge 26:20
Isaac's h.
the chiefest of the h. that   1Sa 21:7
belonged to
who was among the h. of   Am 1:1
Tekoa

HERDS

with Abram, had flocks, and h.   Ge 13:5
hath given him flocks, and h.   Ge 24:35
and possession of h. and great   Ge 26:14
store
the flocks, and h. and the   Ge 32:7
camels
and the flocks and h.   Ge 33:13
with young are
and thy h. and all that thou   Ge 45:10
hast
and their h., and all that they   Ge 46:32;
have   47:1
for the cattle of the h. and for   Ge 47:17
my lord also hath our h. of   Ge 47:18
cattle
their flocks, and their h. they   Ge 50:8
left
flocks and with our h. will we   Ex 10:9
go
your flocks and your h. be   Ex 10:24
stayed
take your flocks and your h.   Ex 12:32
as ye
flocks, and h. even very much   Ex 12:38
cattle
flocks nor h. feed before that   Ex 34:3
mount
Shall the flocks and the h. be   Nu 11:22
slain
when thy h. and thy flocks   De 8:13
multiply
firstlings of your h. and of your   De 12:6

firstlings of thy *h.* or of thy   *De 12:17*
flock
the firstlings of thy *h.* and of   *De 14:23*
thy
herds (B)(R)   *De 28:4; 28:51; 2Sa 17:29*
David took all the flocks and   *1Sa 30:20*
the *h.*
had exceeding many flocks   *2Sa 12:2*
and *h.*
And over the *h.* that fed in   *1Ch 27:29*
Sharon
over the *h.* that were in the   *1Ch 27:29*
valleys
and possessions of flocks   *2Ch 32:29*
and *h.* in
firstlings of our *h.* and of our   *Ne 10:36*
flocks
thy flocks, and look well to   *Pr 27:23*
thy *h.*
a place for the *h.* to lie down   *Isa 65:10*
their flocks and their *h.* their   *Jer 3:24*
sons
shall eat up thy flocks and   *Jer 5:17*
thine *h.*
and with their *h.* to seek the   *Ho 5:6*
Lord
the *h.* of cattle are perplexed   *Joe 1:18*

HERE

here (S)   *Ge 15:16;*
37:17; 42:15; 45:5, 8, 13; 50:25; Ex 11:1;
13:19; 33:1, 15; De 9:12; J'g 16:2; 18:3;
19:12; Ru 2:8, 14; 1Sa 13:9; 14:18, 34,
36, 38; 15:32; 16:11, 28; 23:9; 30:9;
2Sa 1:10; 5:6; 14:32; 20:16; 1Ki 17:3;
2Ki 8:7; 1Ch 11:5; Ps 73:10; Isa 57:3;
Eze 40:4; Da 7:28; M't 8:29; 14:18;
  17:17, 20
the men said, Hast thou *h.*   *Ge 19:12*
any besides
arise, take thy two daughters   *Ge 19:15*
which are *h.*
now therefore swear unto me   *Ge 21:23*
h. by God
h. I am   *Ge 22:1;*
7:11; 27:1, 18; 31:11; 37:13; 46:2;
Ex 3:4; 1Sa 3:4, 5, 6, 8, 16; 2Sa 1:7;
  15:26; Isa 6:8
abide ye *h.* with the ass, I and   *Ge 22:5*
lad will go yonder
behold, I stand *h.* by the well   *Ge 24:13*
of water
set it *h.* before my brethren   *Ge 31:37*
that they may
and *h.* also have I done   *Ge 40:15*
nothing to put me
leave one of your brethren *h.*   *Ge 42:33*
with me
lo, *h.* is seed for you, ye shall   *Ge 47:23*
sow the land
tarry ye *h.* for us, till we come   *Ex 24:14*
to you
saying, Lo, we be *h.* and will   *Nu 14:40*
go up
lodge *h.* this night, I will   *Nu 22:8;*
bring you word   *22:19*
build *h.* seven altars, prepare   *Nu 23:1;*
h. oxen   *23:29*
shall your brethren go to war,   *Nu 32:6*
and you sit *h.*
we will build sheepfolds *h.*   *Nu 32:16*
for our cattle
even us, who are all of us *h.*   *De 5:3*
alive this day
after all the things we do *h.*   *De 12:8*
this day
with him that standeth *h.* that   *De 29:15*
is not *h.*
that I may cast lots for you   *Jos 18:6;*
h.   *18:8*
is there any man *h.*? thou   *J'g 4:20*
shalt say, No
and what hast thou *h.*; lodge *h.* *J'g 18:3;*
  19:9
behold, *h.* is my daughter, a   *J'g 19:24*
maiden
give *h.* your advice and counsel *J'g 20:7*
but abide *h.* fast by my maidens *Ru 2:8*
unto whom he said, Turn   *Ru 4:1;*
aside, sit down *h.*   *4:2*
I am the woman that stood by   *1Sa 1:26*
thee *h.*
they went up the hill and said, *1Sa 9:11*
Is the seer *h.*
behold, *h.* I am   *1Sa 12:3;*
  22:12; Isa 58:9
slay them *h.* and eat, and sin   *1Sa 14:34*
not against Lord
Samuel said to Jesse, Are *h.*   *1Sa 16:11*
all thy children

is there not *h.* under thine   *1Sa 21:8*
hand a spear
it is *h.* wrapped in a cloth, none *1Sa 21:9*
save that *h.*
behold, we be afraid *h.* in   *1Sa 23:3*
Judah; how much
the princes said, What do   *1Sa 29:3*
these Hebrews *h.*
tarry *h.* to day; turn aside *h.* *2Sa 11:12;*
  18:30
be thou *h.* present; *h.* be oxen *2Sa 20:4;*
  24:22
and he said, Nay, but I will   *1Ki 2:30*
die *h.*
tell thy lord, behold, Elijah is *1Ki 18:8;*
  11:14
he said, What doest thou *h.*   *1Ki 19:9;*
Elijah   *19:13*
as thy servant was busy *h.*   *1Ki 20:40*
and there
is there not *h.* a prophet of   *1Ki 22:7;*
Lord   *2Ki 3:11*
Elijah said, Tarry *h.* I pray   *2Ki 2:2;*
thee   *2:6*
h. is Elisha   *2Ki 3:11*
why sit we *h.* until we die   *2Ki 7:3*
the lepers said, If we sit still *h.* *2Ki 7:4*
we die also
look there be *h.* none of the *2Ki 10:23*
servants of Lord
with joy thy people present   *1Ch 29:17*
h. to offer
there not *h.* a prophet of the *2Ch 18:6*
Lord
h. shall thy proud waves be   *Job 38:11*
stayed
that lightnings may say unto *Job 38:35*
thee, *H.* we are
this is my rest, *h.* will I dwell *Ps 132:14*
behold, *h.* cometh a chariot of *Isa 21:9*
men
what hast thou *h.*? whom   *Isa 22:16*
hast thou *h.*
h. a little, and there a little   *Isa 28:10;*
  28:13
now therefore, what have I *h.* *Isa 52:5*
the house of Israel committeth *Eze 8:6;*
h.   *8:17*
gray hairs are *h.* and there   *Ho 7:9*
upon him
a great than Jonas is *h.*   *M't 12:41;*
  Lu 11:32
a greater than Solomon is *h.*   *M't 12:42;*
  Lu 11:31
give me *h.* John Baptist's head *M't 14:8*
in a charger
we have *h.* but five loaves,   *M't 14:17*
and two fishes
there be some standing *h.*   *M't 16:28;*
  Lu 9:27
Lord, it is good for us to be *h.* *M't 17:4*
let us make *h.*
shall not be left *h.* one stone   *M't 24:2*
upon another
if any say to you, Lo, *h.* is   *M't 24:23;*
Christ   *M'k 13:21*
sit ye *h.* while I go and pray   *M't 26:36;*
  M'k 14:32
tarry ye *h.* and watch with   *M't 26:38*
me
he is not *h.* he is risen   *M't 28:6;*
  M'k 16:6; Lu 24:6
and are not his sisters *h.* with *M'k 6:3*
us
Master, see what stones and   *M'k 13:1*
buildings are *h.*
what heard done, do *h.* in thy *Lu 4:23*
country
for we are *h.* in a desert place *Lu 9:12*
neither shall they say, Lo *h.*   *M't 17:21*
or lo there
say to you, See *h.* or see   *Lu 17:23*
there, go not after them
behold, *h.* is thy pound which *Lu 19:20*
I have kept
h. are two swords, he said, It *Lu 22:38*
is enough
he said unto them, Have ye   *Lu 24:41*
h. any meat
there is a lad *h.* which hath five *Joh 6:9*
loaves
Lord, if thou hadst been *h.*   *Joh 11:21*
my brother
h. is water   *Ac 8:36*
behold, I am *h.* Lord   *Ac 9:10*
and *h.* he hath authority from *Ac 9:14*
the priests
are we all *h.* present before   *Ac 10:33*
God, to hear

do thyself no harm, for we are *Ac 16:28*
all *h.*
who ought to have been *h.*   *Ac 24:19*
before thee
and all men which are *h.*   *Ac 25:24*
present with us
make known unto you all   *Col 4:9*
things done *h.*
and *h.* men that die receive   *Heb 7:8*
tithes
for *h.* have we no continuing *Heb 13:14*
city, seek one
sit *h.* in a good place, or sit *h.* *Jas 2:3*
under
pass time of your sojourning, *1Pe 1:17*
h. in fear
h. is the patience of the   *Re 13:10;*
saints   *14:12*
h. is wisdom; let him that   *Re 13:18*
hath understanding
h. are they that kept the   *Re 14:12*
commandments
and *h.* is the mind which hath *Re 17:9*
wisdom

HEREAFTER

shew the things that are to   *Isa 41:23*
come *h.*
h. also, if ye will not hearken *Eze 20:39*
unto me
what should come to pass *h.*   *Da 2:29;*
  2:45
h. shall ye see the Son of   *M't 26:64*
man sitting
no man eat fruit of thee *h.*   *M'k 11:14*
for ever
h. shall Son of man sit on   *Lu 22:69*
right hand
I say, *H.* ye shall see heaven *Joh 1:51*
opened
thou knowest not now, thou   *Joh 13:7*
shalt know *h.*
h. I will not talk much with *Joh 14:30*
you
pattern to them which *h.*   *1Ti 1:16*
believe on him
write the things which shall be *Re 1:19*
h.
I will shew thee things which   *Re 4:1*
must be *h.*
and behold, there come two   *Re 9:12*
woes more *h.*

HEREBY

H. ye shall be proved: By the *Ge 42:15*
life
H. shall I know that ye   *Ge 42:33*
are true men
And Moses said, *H.* ye shall   *Nu 16:28*
know
And Joshua said, *H.* ye shall   *Jos 3:10*
know
yet am I not *h.* justified: but *1Co 4:4*
And *h.* we do know that we do *1Jo 2:3*
h. know we that we are in him *1Jo 2:5*
H. perceive we the love of   *1Jo 3:16*
God
And *h.* we know that we are of *1Jo 3:19*
h. we know that he abideth in *1Jo 3:24*
H. know ye the Spirit of God *1Jo 4:2*
H. know we the spirit of truth *1Jo 4:6*
H. know we that we dwell in *1Jo 4:13*

HEREIN

Only *h.* will the men consent   *Ge 34:22*
unto
H. thou hast done foolishly   *2Ch 16:9*
And *h.* is that saying true,   *Joh 4:37*
One
Why *h.* is a marvellous thing *Joh 9:30*
H. is my Father glorified, that *Joh 15:8*
And *h.* do I exercise myself, *Ac 24:16*
to
And *h.* I give my advice: for *2Co 8:10*
H. is love, not that we loved *1Jo 4:10*
God
H. is our love made perfect   *1Jo 4:17*

HEREOF

the fame *h.* went abroad into *M't 9:26*
And by reason *h.* he ought, as *Heb 5:3*

HERES

Amorites would dwell in   *J'g 1:35*
mount *H.*

HERESH

Bakbakkar, *H.* and Galal, and *1Ch 9:15*

HERESIES

there must be also *h.* among you *1Co 11:19*
have to be factions or parties among (A) *1Co 11:19*
there have to be dissensions among (B)(N) *1Co 11:19*
there must be factions among (E)(R) *1Co 11:19*
there must be cliques among you (P) *1Co 11:19*
wrath, strife, seditions, *h.,* envyings *Ga 5:20*
divisions, party spirit (A) *Ga 5:20*
dissensions, a factional spirit (B)(N) *Ga 5:20*
factions, divisons (E) *Ga 5:20*
factions, party spirit (P) *Ga 5:20*
dissensions, party spirit (R) *Ga 5:20*
shall bring in damnable *h.* even *2Pe 2:1*

HERESY

ringleader of the Nazarene *h.* (B) *Ac 24:5*
after the way which they call *h.* *Ac 24:14*
as far as this *h.* is (B) *Ac 28:22*

HERETICAL

a *h.* sectarian (A) *Tit 3:10*

HERETICK

A man that is an *h.* after the first *Tit 3:10*
factious, a heretical sectarian (A) *Tit 3:10*
a factious person (B)(E)(R) *Tit 3:10*
still argumentative (P) *Tit 3:10*

HERETOFORE

not eloquent, neither *h.* nor since *Ex 4:10*
people straw to make brick, as *h.* *Ex 5:7*
the bricks, which they did make *h.* *Ex 5:8*
both yesterday and to day, as *h.* *Ex 5:14*
for ye have not passed this way *h.* *Jos 3:4*
a people which thou knewest not *h.* *Ru 2:11*
hath not been such a thing *h.* *1Sa 4:7*
write to them which *h.* have sinned *2Co 13:2*

HEREUNTO

who else can hasten *h.* more than *Ec 2:25*
For even *h.* were ye called *1Pe 2:21*

HEREWITH

and yet thou wast not satisfied *h.* *Eze 16:29*
prove me now *h.* saith the Lord of *Mal 3:10*

HERITAGE

I will give land to you for an *h.* *Ex 6:8*
give it to you as a legacy (B) *Ex 6:8*
give it to you as a possession (R) *Ex 6:8*
the *h.* appointed by God for him *Job 20:29*
the legacy allotted him of God (B) *Job 20:29*
the *h.* of oppressors they shall receive *Job 27:13*
I have a goodly *h.* *Ps 16:6*
a good inheritance is mine (B) *Ps 16:6*
given me *h.* of those that fear thy name *Ps 61:5*
they afflict thine *h.* *Ps 94:5*
may give them the *h.* of the heathen *Ps 111:6*
Thy testimonies have I taken as an *h.* *Ps 119:111*
children are an *h.* of the Lord *Ps 127:3*

children are a legacy from the Lord (B) *Ps 127:3*
gave their land for an *h.* *Ps 135:12; 136:21, 22*
this is *h.* of servants of Lord *Isa 54:17*
feed thee with the *h.* of Jacob *Isa 58:14*
made mine *h.* an abomination *Jer 2:7*
My inheritance an abomination (B) *Jer 2:7*
how shall I give thee a goodly *h.* *Jer 3:19*
left mine *h.,* mine *h.* is as lion *Jer 12:7; 12:8*
Mine *h.* is as a speckled bird *Jer 12:9*
will bring again every man to his *h.* *Jer 12:15*
each to his inheritance (B) *Jer 12:15*
shalt discontinue from thine *h.* *Jer 17:4*
I give abandon your *h.* (B)(R) *Jer 17:4*
destroyers of mine *h.* because grown *Jer 50:11*
give not thine *h.* to reproach *Joe 2:17*
will plead with them for my *h.* Israel *Joe 3:2*
they oppress a man and his *h.* *Mic 2:2*
feed flock of thine *h.* with thy rod *Mic 7:14*
flock of your inheritance (A)(B)(R) *Mic 7:14*
passeth by transgression of his *h.* *Mic 7:18*
remnant of his inheritance (B)(R) *Mic 7:18*
laid Esau's *h.* waste *Mal 1:3*
neither as being lords over God's *h.* *1Pe 5:3*
domineering over those in your charge (A) *1Pe 5:3*
lording it over your charges (B)(R) *1Pe 5:3*
lording it over the charge allotted (E) *1Pe 5:3*

HERITAGES

to cause to inherit desolate *h.* *Isa 49:8*
re-inherit the desolate possessions (B) *Isa 49:8*

HERMAS

Phlegon, *H.,* Patrobas *Ro 16:14*

HERMES

H. and the brethren which are *Ro 16:14*

HERMOGENES

of whom are Phygellus and *H.* *2Ti 1:15*

HERMON

river Arnon unto mount *H.* *De 3:8*
which *H.* the Sidonians call Sirion *De 3:9*
from Aroer to mount Sion, which is *H.* *De 4:48*
H. in land of Mizpeh *Jos 11:3; 11:17; 12:1, 5; 13:5, 11; 1Ch 5:23*
Tabor and *H.* shall rejoice in *Ps 89:12*
As the dew of *H.,* and as the dew *Ps 133:3*
from top of Shenir and *H.* *Ca 4:8*

HERMONITES

remember thee from land of *H.* *Ps 42:6*

HERO

mighty *h.* (B) *J'g 6:12; 1Ch 26:6*
brave *h.* (B) *J'g 11:1*

HEROD

in days of *H.* the king *M't 2:1; 2:3, 7, 12, 13, 15, 16, 19, 22; Lu 1:5*
H. the tetrarch heard of fame of Jesus *M't 14:1; M'k 6:14, 16; Lu 3:1, 19; 9:7*
H. had laid hold on John *M't 14:3; M'k 6:17*
H. made a supper *M't 14:6; M'k 6:18-22*
John said to *H.* *M'k 6:18; Lu 9:9*
For *H.* feared John, knowing *M'k 6:20*
the leaven of *H.* *M'k 8:15*
H. said, John have I beheaded *Lu 9:9*

depart thence: for *H.* will kill thee *Lu 13:31*
he sent him to *H.* *Lu 23:7; 23:8, 11, 12, 15*
H. and Pontius Pilate against Jesus *Ac 4:27*
H. vexed certain of the church *Ac 12:1; 12:11, 19*
H. was highly displeased with them *Ac 12:20*
upon a set day *H.* arrayed in *Ac 12:21*
brought up with *H.* the tetrarch *Ac 13:1*

HERODIANS

sent disciples with *H.* *M't 22:16; M'k 12:13*
took counsel with *H.* *M'k 3:6*

HERODIAS

daughter of *H.* danced *M't 14:6; M'k 6:22*
H. had a quarrel against John *M'k 6:19*
being reproved by him for *H.* *Lu 3:19*

HERODIAS'

put him in prison for *H.* sake *M't 14:3; M'k 6:17*

HERODION

Salute *H.* my kinsman *Ro 16:11*

HEROD'S

when *H.* birthday was kept *M't 14:8*
the wife of Chuza *H.* steward *Lu 8:3*
he belonged to *H.* jurisdiction *Lu 23:7*
him to be kept in *H.* judgment hall *Ac 23:35*

HEROES

powerful *h.* (B) *1Ch 7:2; 7:5; 7:11*

HERON

h. after his kind *Le 11:19; De 14:18*

HERS

if firstborn be *h.* *De 21:15*
with five damsels of *h.* *1Sa 25:42*
restore all that was *h.* *2Ki 8:6*
though they were not *h.* *Job 39:16*

HERSELF

Sarah laughed within *h.* *Ge 18:12*
she *h.* said, He is my brother *Ge 20:5*
took a veil and covered *h.* *Ge 24:65*
with a veil, and wrapped *h.* *Ge 38:14*
came down to wash *h.* at river *Ex 2:5*
number to *h.* seven days *Le 15:28*
if profane *h.* by playing whore *Le 21:9*
she thrust *h.* unto the wall *Nu 22:25*
bind *h.* by a bond *Nu 30:3*
she returned answer to *h.* *J'g 5:29*
bowed *h.* to the ground *Ru 2:10; 1Sa 4:19; 25:23, 41; 2Ki 4:37*
saw a woman washing *h.* *2Sa 11:2*
she shall feign *h.* to be *1Ki 14:5*
she lifted *h.* on high *Job 39:18*
the swallow a nest for *h.* *Ps 84:3*
maketh *h.* coverings of tapestry *Pr 31:22*
hell hath enlarged *h.* *Isa 5:14*
find for *h.* a place of rest *Isa 34:14*
bride adorneth *h.* with jewels *Isa 61:10*
backsliding Israel justified *h.* *Jer 3:11*
Zion, that bewaileth *h.* *Jer 4:31*
turneth *h.* to flee *Jer 49:24*
maketh idols to defile *h.* *Eze 22:3; 23:7*
She hath wearied *h.* with lies *Eze 24:12*
she decked *h.* with earrings *Ho 2:13*
Tyrus did build *h.* a stronghold *Zec 9:3*
she said within *h.,* If I may *M't 9:21*
earth bringeth forth fruit of *h.* *M'k 4:28*
hid *h.* five months, saying *Lu 1:24*
could in no wise lift up *h.* *Lu 13:11*
she turned *h.* back *Joh 20:14; 20:16*
Through faith Sarah *h.* received *Heb 11:11*
Jezebel calleth *h.* a prophetess *Re 2:20*
How much she glorified *h.* *Re 18:7*
his wife hath made *h.* ready *Re 19:7*

HESED

The son of *H.* in Aruboth   *1Ki 4:10*

HESHBON

in *H.* and its villages   *Nu 21:25;*
  Jos 13:17
H. the city of Sihon   *Nu 21:26;*
21:27; De 2:24, 26, 30; 3:6; 29:7;
Jos 9:10; 12:5; 13:10, 21, 27; J'g 11:19
Amorites dwelt in *H.* Nu 21:34; De 1:4;
  3:2; 4:46; Jos 12:2
the children of Reuben built *Nu 32:37*
H.
H. and her suburbs *Jos 21:39; 1Ch 6:81*
while Israel dwelt in *h.*   *J'g 11:26*
eyes like the fishpools of *H.*   *Ca 7:4*
H. shall cry   *Isa 15:4; 16:9; Jer 48:34*
the fields of *H.* languish   *Isa 16:8*
in *H.* they have devised evil   *Jer 48:2*
Howl, O *H.*, for Ai is spoiled   *Jer 49:3*

HESHMON

Hazar-Gaddah, and *H.*   *Jos 15:27*

HESITATION

accompany them without *h.*   *Ac 10:20*
(R)
without *h.*, misgivings, or   *Ac 11:12*
discrimination (A)(B)(R)
without slightest *h.* (P)   *Heb 10:23*

HESITATE

h. lending a hand (B)   *Ex 23:5*

HETH

begat Sidon, and *H.*   *Ge 10:15; 1Ch 1:13*
the sons of *H.*   *Ge 23:3; 23:16, 20; 25:10*
the children of *H.*   *Ge 23:5;*
  23:7, 10, 18; 49:32
the daughters of *H.*   *Ge 27:46*

HETHLON

the way of *H.*   *Eze 47:15; 48:1*

HEW

H. two tables of stone *Ex 34:1; De 10:1*
h. down the graven images   *De 12:3*
with his neighbor to *h.* wood   *De 19:5*
h. me cedar trees   *1Ki 5:6; 5:18*
set masons to *h.* wrought   *1Ch 22:2*
stones
thousand to *h.* in the   *2Ch 2:2*
mountains
H. down trees and cast them   *Jer 6:6*
H. down the tree, cut off   *Da 4:14; 4:23*

HEWED

he *h.* two tables of stone   *Ex 34:4;*
  De 10:3
oxen and *h.* them in pieces   *1Sa 11:7*
Samuel *h.* Agag in pieces   *1Sa 15:33*
h. stones for temple   *1Ki 5:17;*
  6:36; 7:9, 11, 12
to buy timber and *h.* stones   *2Ki 12:12*
h. down the Asherim   *2Ch 14:3*
(A)(E)(R)
thou hast *h.* thee out a   *Isa 22:16*
sepulchre
h. them out cisterns, broken   *Jer 2:13*
have I *h.* them by the prophets   *Ho 6:5*

HEWER

the *h.* of wood unto the   *De 29:11*
drawer
no *h.* is come up (E)(R)   *Isa 14:8*

HEWERS

let them be *h.* of wood   *Jos 9:21;*
  9:23, 27
thousand *h.* in the mountains   *1Ki 5:15*
masons, and *h.* of stone   *2Ki 12:12*
h. and workers of stone   *1Ch 22:15*
the *h.* that cut timbers   *2Ch 2:10*
thousand to be *h.* in   *2Ch 2:18*
mountains
her with axes, as *h.* of wood   *Jer 46:22*

HEWETH

axe boast against him that *h.*   *Isa 10:15*
as he that *h.* him out a   *Isa 22:16*
sepulchre
He *h.* him down cedars, and   *Isa 44:14*
taketh

HEWING

h. out home in the rock (B)   *Isa 22:16*

HEWN

shalt not build it with *h.* stone *Ex 20:25*
timber and *h.* stone to repair   *2Ki 22:6*
to buy *h.* stone and timber   *2Ch 34:11*
she hath *h.* out her seven pillars   *Pr 9:1*
we will build with *h.* stones   *Isa 9:10*
high ones of stature be *h.*   *Isa 10:33*
down
h. out a tomb (R)   *Isa 22:16*
Lebanon is ashamed and *h.*   *Isa 33:9*
down
unto rock from whence ye are *Isa 51:1*
h.
four tables of *h.* stone   *Eze 40:42*
have built houses of *h.* stone   *Am 5:11*
h. down, cast into fire   *M't 3:10;*
  7:19; Lu 3:9
had *h.* of rock   *M't 37:60;*
  M'k 15:46; Lu 23:53

HEWS

h. him a sepulchre   *Isa 22:16*
(A)(B)(E)

HEZEKI

Meshullam, and *H.*   *1Ch 8:17*

HEZEKIAH

H. his son reigned   *2Ki 16:20;*
18:1-21:3; 2Ch 28:27-33:3; Isa 36:1-39:8
in fourteenth year of *H.* did   *2Ki 18:13*
Assyria come
H. gave him all the silver   *2Ki 18:15;*
  18:16
altars *H.* hath taken away   *2Ki 18:22;*
  Isa 36:1
let not *H.* deceive you   *2Ki 18:29;*
  18:31-32; 2Ch 32:15; Isa 36:14
when *H.* heard it he rent   *2Ki 19:1;*
  Isa 37:1
H. prayed   *2Ki 19:15;*
  2Ch 30:18; Isa 37:15
Isaiah sent to *H.*   *2Ki 19:20;*
  Isa 37:9-14; 39:5
H. sick to death   *2Ki 20:1;*
  2Ch 32:24; Isa 38:1
H. wept sore   *2Ki 20:3; 2Ch 32:26;*
  Isa 38:3
sent letters and a present to   *2Ki 20:12;*
H.   *Isa 39:1*
H. shewed them his riches   *2Ki 20:13;*
  Isa 39:2
H. sent to all Israel and   *2Ch 30:1*
Judah
Lord hearkened to *H.* and   *2Ch 30:20*
healed
H. appointed the courses   *2Ch 31:2*
Lord saved *H.* from   *2Ch 32:22*
Sennacherib
H. had exceeding much   *2Ch 32:27*
riches
H. also stopped the upper   *2Ch 32:30*
watercourse
H. prospered in all his works *2Ch 32:30*
children of Ater of *H.*   *Ezr 2:16;*
  Neh 7:21
proverbs the men of *H.* copied   *Pr 25:1*
out
because of Manasseh the son   *Jer 15:4*
of *H.*
prophecied in days of *H.*   *Jer 26:18*
Uzziah, Jotham, Ahaz, and *H.*   *Ho 1:1;*
  Isa 1:1; Mic 1:1

HEZION

son of *H.*, king of Syria   *1Ki 15:18*

HEZIR

seventeenth to *H.*   *1Ch 24:15*
Magpiash, Meshullam, *H.*   *Ne 10:20*

HEZRAI

H. the Carmelite   *2Sa 23:35*

HEZRO

H. the Carmelite   *1Ch 11:37*

HEZRON

sons of Reuben, *H.*   *Ge 46:9;*
  Ex 6:14; 1Ch 5:3
sons of Pharez were *H.*   *Ge 46:12;*
Hamul   *Ru 4:18; 1Ch 2:5; 4:1*
Of *H.* the family of   *Nu 26:6;*
Hezronites   *26:21*
passed along to *H.*   *Jos 15:3; 15:25*
Pharez begat *H. H.* begat Ram *Ru 4:19*
sons also of *H.* that were born *1Ch 2:9*
Caleb the son of *H.* begat   *1Ch 2:18*
children
H. went in to the daughter of *1Ch 2:21*
Machi
after that *H.* was dead   *1Ch 2:24*
sons of Jerahmeel, firstborn   *1Ch 2:25*
of *H.*

HEZRONITES

Of Hezron, the family of *H.*   *Nu 26:6;*
  26:21

HEZRON'S

Abiah *H.* wife bare him   *1Ch 2:24*
Ashur

HID

Adam and wife *h.* themselves   *Ge 3:8*
afraid because naked, I *h.*   *Ge 3:10*
myself
from thy face shall I be *h.*   *Ge 4:14*
Jacob *h.* them under the oak   *Ge 35:4*
she *h.* Moses three months   *Ex 2:2*
Moses slew Egyptian, *h.* him in *Ex 2:12*
sand
Moses *h.* his face, he was afraid *Ex 3:6*
they shall suck treasures *h.* in *De 33:19*
sand
Rahab *h.* the spies with flax *Jos 2:4; 2:6*
she *h.* messengers we sent *De 6:17; 6:25*
they are *h.* in the earth   *De 7:21; 7:22*
five kings *h.* in cave *De 10:16; 10:17, 27*
Jotham was left for he *h.*   *J'g 9:5*
himself
Samuel told Eli and *h.* nothing *1Sa 3:18*
Saul *h.* himself among the   *1Sa 10:22*
stuff
David *h.* himself in the field *1Sa 20:24*
he is *h.* now in some pit   *2Sa 17:9*
no matter *h.* from the king *2Sa 18:13;*
  1Ki 10:3; 2Ch 9:2
Obadiah *h.* the prophets   *1Ki 18:4;*
  18:13
the Lord hath *h.* it from me   *2Ki 4:27*
I said, Give thy son, she hath *2Ki 6:29*
h.
lepers went and *h.* it   *2Ki 7:8*
they *h.* him and his nurse   *2Ki 11:2;*
  11:3; 2Ch 22:11, 12
Ornan and four sons *h.*   *1Ch 21:20*
themselves
Ahaziah was *h.* in Samaria   *2Ch 22:9*
nor *h.* sorrow from mine eyes   *Job 3:10*
dig for it more than for *h.*   *Job 3:21*
treasures
light given to a man whose   *Job 3:23*
way is *h.*
snow *h.*   *Job 6:16*
things hast thou *h.* in thine   *Job 10:13;*
heart   *28:11*
thou hast *h.* their heart from   *Job 17:4*
seeing it is *h.* from eyes of all *Job 28:21*
living
young men saw and *h.*   *Job 29:8*
themselves
the waters are *h.*   *Job 38:30*
net they *h.* is their own feet *Ps 9:15*
taken
belly thou fillest with *h.*   *Ps 17:14*
treasure
nothing is *h.* from the heat   *Ps 19:6*
thereof
neither hath he *h.* his face   *Ps 22:24*
from him
without cause they *h.* for me   *Ps 35:7*
their net
not *h.* away in my house   *Ps 40:10*
(B)(E)(R)

let his net that he hath *h.* catch *Ps 35:8*
then I would have *h.* myself *Ps 55:12*
from him
Thy word have I *h.* in mine *Ps 119:11*
heart
proud have *h.* a snare for me *Ps 140:5*
search for her as for *h.* treasure *Pr 2:4*
under falsehood we *h.* *Isa 28:15*
ourselves
why say, My way is *h.* from *Isa 40:27*
Lord
they are *h.* in prison houses *Isa 42:22*
in his quiver hath he *h.* me *Isa 49:2*
I *h.* not my face from shame *Isa 50:6*
we *h.* as it were our faces from *Isa 53:3*
him
in little wrath I *h.* my face from *Isa 54:8*
I *h.* me and was wroth *Isa 57:17*
your sins have *h.* his face from *Isa 59:2*
you
thou hast *h.* thy face from *Isa 64:7*
because they are *h.* from mine *Isa 65:16*
eyes
I went and *h.* it by Euphrates *Jer 13:5*
took girdle from place I *h.* it *Jer 13:7*
nor their iniquity *h.* from mine *Jer 16:17*
eyes
they have *h.* snares for my *Jer 18:22*
feet
I have *h.* my face from this *Jer 33:5*
city
to take them, but Lord *h.* *Jer 36:25*
them
will set throne on stones I *Jer 43:10*
have *h.*
have *h.* eyes from my *Eze 22:26*
sabbaths
h. I my face from them *Eze 39:23;*
39:24
sin of Ephraim bound up, sin *Ho 13:12*
is *h.*
relenting *h.* from (A)(B) *Ho 13:14*
compassion is *h.* from (R) *Ho 13:14*
nothing *h.* that shall not be *M't 10:26;*
known *M'k 4:22; Lu 8:17; 12:2*
h. things from wise *M'k 11:25; Lu 10:21*
h. in three measures of meal *M't 13:33;*
Lu 13:21
he went and *h.* his lord's *M't 25:18*
money
I went and *h.* thy talent in *M't 25:25*
earth
Elizabeth *h.* herself five months *Lu 1:24*
nothing *h.* but shall be *Lu 8:17*
disclosed (A)(E)(R)
this saying was *h.* from them *Lu 9:45;*
18:34
now they are *h.* from thine *Lu 19:42*
eyes
Jesus *h.* himself, and went out *Joh 8:59*
from beginning hath been *h.* in *Eph 3:9*
God
mystery hath been *h.* from *Col 1:26*
ages
in whom are *h.* all treasures of *Col 2:3*
your life is *h.* with Christ in *Col 3:3*
God
by faith Moses was *h.* three *Heb 11:23*
months
bondman, freeman *h.* *Re 6:15*
themselves

BE HID

from thy face shall I *be h.* *Ge 4:14*
thing *be h.* from assembly *Le 4:13;*
5:3, 4
it *be h.* from eyes of her *Nu 5:13*
husband
shall *be h.* from scourge of *Job 5:21*
tongue
darkness *be h.* in his secret *Job 20:26*
places
understanding of prudent *Isa 29:14*
men *be h.*
repentance shall *be h.* from *Ho 13:14*
my eyes
though they *be h.* from my *Am 9:3*
sight
thou shalt *be h.* *Na 3:11; Zep 2:3*
if our gospel *be h.*, it is hid to *2Co 4:3*

CANNOT BE HID

city set on an hill *cannot be h.* *M't 5:14*
but he could *not be h.* *M'k 7:24*
that are otherwise *cannot be* *1Ti 5:25*
h.

NOT HID

told from fathers, and *not h.* *Job 15:18*
it
mine iniquity have I *not h.* *Ps 32:5*
my groaning is *not h.* from thee *Ps 38:9*
I have *not h.* thy righteousness *Ps 40:10*
within
my sins are *not h.* from thee *Ps 69:5*
substance was *not h.* when I *Ps 139:15*
was made
ways, iniquities *not h.* from *Jer 16:17*
my eyes
Israel is *not h.* from me *Ho 5:3*
woman saw she was *not h.* *Lu 8:47*
came

HIDDAI

H. of the brooks of Gaash *2Sa 23:30*

HIDDEKEL

name of third river is *H.* *Ge 2:14;*
Da 10:4

HIDDEN

if it be *h.* from him, he shall be *Le 5:2*
it is not *h.* from thee, nor is it *De 30:11*
afar
as an *h.* untimely birth *Job 3:16*
number of years *h.* to the *Job 15:20*
oppressor
seeing times are not *h.* from *Job 24:1*
thee
in *h.* part make me know *Ps 51:6*
wisdom
they consulted against thy *h.* *Ps 83:3*
ones
when wicked rise, a man is *h.* *Pr 28:12*
I will give thee *h.* riches *Isa 45:3*
have shewed new things, *h.* *Isa 48:6*
things
how are his *h.* things sought up *Ob 6*
none of these things are *h.* *Ac 26:26*
from me
even *h.* wisdom, which God *1Co 2:7*
ordained
bring to light *h.* things of *1Co 4:5*
darkness
renounced *h.* things of *2Co 4:2*
dishonesty
let it be *h.* man of the heart *1Pe 3:4*
I will give to eat the *h.* manna *Re 2:17*

HIDE

shall I *h.* from Abraham what *Ge 18:17*
I do
will not *h.* it from my lord, *Ge 47:18*
how
when she could no longer *h.* him *Ex 2:3*
his *h.* and flesh be burnt *Le 8:17*
ways *h.* their eyes from the *Le 20:4*
man
go astray, *h.* from them *De 22:1; 22:3-4*
h. yourselves there three days *Jos 2:16*
tell, *h.* it not from me *Jos 7:19*
to *h.* wheat from the *J'g 6:11*
Midianites
h. it not from me *1Sa 3:17; 2Sa 14:18*
h. thyself *1Sa 19:2; 20:19; 1Ki 17:3*
why should father *h.* this from *1Sa 20:2*
me
h. myself *1Sa 20:5; Job 13:20*
thou wouldest *h.* me in the *Job 14:13*
grave
though he *h.* it under his *Job 20:12*
tongue
from his purpose, *h.* pride *Job 33:17*
from man
h. them in the dust together *Job 40:13*
h. me under shadow of thy *Ps 17:8*
wings
in time of trouble he shall *h.* *Ps 27:5*
me
didst *h.* thy face, I was troubled *Ps 30:7*
h. them in secret of thy *Ps 31:20*
presence
h. not thyself from my *Ps 55:1*
supplication
h. me from secret counsel of *Ps 64:2*
wicked
not *h.* them from their children *Ps 78:4*
how long wilt thou *h.* thyself *Ps 89:46*
h. not thy commandments *Ps 119:19*
from me
deliver me, I flee to thee to *h.* *Ps 143:9*
me

h. my commandments with thee *Pr 2:1*
I will *h.* my eyes from you, I *Isa 1:15*
will not
h. thee in the dust, for fear of *Isa 2:10*
Lord
they *h.* not their sin *Isa 3:9*
h. the outcasts; bewray not *Isa 16:3*
him that
h. thyself for a little moment *Isa 26:20*
h. not thyself from thine own *Isa 58:7*
flesh
h. it there in hole of the rock *Jer 13:4;*
13:6
go, *h.* thee, thou and *Jer 36:19*
Jeremiah
ask thee a thing, *h.* nothing *Jer 38:14*
from me
h. it not from us *Jer 38:25*
h. them in the clay *Jer 43:9*
is no secret they can *h.* from *Eze 28:3*
thee
cedars in garden of God could *Eze 31:8*
not *h.*
neither will I *h.* my face from *Eze 39:29*
them
shall *h.* a multitude of sins *Jas 5:20*
h. us from face of him that *Re 6:16*
sitteth

HIDE HIMSELF

doth not David *h. himself* *1Sa 23:19;*
26:1
can any *h. himself* in secret *Jer 23:24*
places
not be able to *h. himself* *Jer 49:10*
Jesus did *h. himself* from *Joh 12:36*
them

HIDE THEMSELVES

till they that *h. themselves* be *De 7:20*
people did *h. themselves* in *1Sa 13:6*
caves
Syrians gone to *h. themselves* *2Ki 7:12*
poor of the earth *h.* *Job 24:4*
themselves
workers of iniquity *h.* *Job 34:22*
themselves
they *h. themselves*, they mark *Ps 56:6*
my
when wicked rise, men *h.* *Pr 28:28*
themselves
so they fled to *h. themselves* *Da 10:7*
tho' they *h. themselves* in top *Am 9:3*

HIDEST

wherefore *h.* thou thy face *Job 13:24;*
Ps 44:24; 88:14
why *h.* thyself in times of *Ps 10:1*
trouble
Thou *h.* thy face, they are *Ps 104:29*
troubled
thou art a God that *h.* thyself *Isa 45:15*

HIDETH

find lurking places where he *1Sa 23:23*
h.
He *h.* himself on the right hand *Job 23:9*
when he *h.* his face who can *Job 34:29*
find
who is he that *h.* counsel *Job 42:3*
without
he *h.* his face, he will never *Ps 10:11*
see
darkness *h.* not from thee *Ps 139:12*
he that *h.* hatred with lying *Pr 10:18*
lips
slothful *h.* hand in bosom *Pr 19:24;*
26:15
prudent man *h.* himself *Pr 22:3; 27:12*
Whosoever *h.* her, *h.* the wind *Pr 27:16*
that *h.* eyes shall have many a *Pr 28:27*
curse
that *h.* his face from Jacob *Isa 8:17*
which when a man hath *M't 13:44*
found he *h.*

HIDING

finds all his *h.* *1Sa 23:23*
by *h.* mine iniquity in my *Job 31:33*
bosom
wait in *h.* places (A) *Job 38:40*
made darkness his *h.* place (E) *Ps 18:11*
thou art my *h.* place *Ps 32:7; 119:114*
h. place of thunder (B) *Ps 81:7*
a sheltered *h.* place (A)(B) *Isa 16:4*

waters shall overflow *h.* place Isa 28:17
man shall be as an *h.* place Isa 32:2
from
a *h.* place (A)(B)(E) Isa 32:2
there was the *h.* of his power Hab 3:4

HIEL

H. Beth-elite built Jericho 1Ki 16:34

HIERAPOLIS

are in Laodicea, and them in Col 4:13
H.

HIGGAION

work of his own hands, *H.* Ps 9:16

HIGH

lo, it is yet *h.* day Ge 29:7
went out with *h.* hand Ex 14:8; Nu 33:3
stretch forth wings on *h.* Ex 25:20; 37:9
quails as it were two cubits *h.* Nu 11:31
doeth aught with *h.* hand Nu 15:30
(E)(R)
they were in *h.* spirits (B) J'g 16:25
house, which is *h.* 1Ki 9:8; 2Ch 7:21
man of great stature, five 1Ch 11:23
cubits *h.*
gallows be made fifty cubits *h.* Es 5:14;
7:9
it is as *h.* as heaven Job 11:8
he judgeth those that are *h.* Job 21:22
behold the stars, how *h.* they Job 22:12
are
the *h.* arm shall be broken Job 38:15
he beholdeth all *h.* things Job 41:34
thou shalt bring down *h.* looks Ps 18:27
give ear, both low and *h.* Ps 49:2
men of *h.* degree are a lie Ps 62:9;
1Ch 17:17
Thy righteousness is very *h.* Ps 71:19
built his sanctuary like *h.* Ps 78:69
palaces
him that hath a *h.* look Ps 101:5;
Pr 21:4
exercise myself in things too *h.* Ps 131:1
for
though Lord be *h.* yet hath he Ps 138:6
respect
such knowledge is *h.* I cannot Ps 139:6
attain
let *h.* praises of God be in Ps 149:6
mouth
praise him upon *h.* sounding Ps 150:5
cymbals
as an *h.* wall in his own Pr 18:11
conceit
wisdom is too *h.* for a fool Pr 24:7
day of Lord on all cedars that Isa 2:13
are *h.*
Lord sitting on a throne *h.* and Isa 6:1
lifted
punish the glory of his *h.* Isa 10:12
looks
h. ones of stature be hewn Isa 10:33
down
my servant shall be very *h.* Isa 52:13
saith the *h.* and lofty One Isa 57:15
a glorious *h.* throne from Jer 17:12
beginning
though make thy nest *h.* as Jer 49:16
the eagle
her *h.* gates shall be burnt Jer 51:58
with fire
their rings were very *h.* Eze 1:18
have brought down the *h.* Eze 17:24
tree
exalt the low, abase him that Eze 21:26
is *h.*
h. to be brought low (A) Eze 21:26
the Assyrian was of *h.* stature Eze 31:3
two horns were *h.*, one was Da 8:3
higher
whose habitation is *h.* Ob 3
whose dwelling is *h.* (B)(R) Ob 3
that sabbath was an *h.* day Joh 19:31
with an *h.* arm brought them Ac 13:17
out
mind not *h.* things, but Ro 12:16
condescend
it is *h.* time we awake out of Ro 13:11
sleep
casting down every *h.* thing 2Co 10:5
that
worthy of *h.* calling (P) Eph 4:1
for the prize of the *h.* calling Ph'p 3:14
holy Jerusalem had a *h.* wall Re 21:12

HIGH *ABOVE*

make thee *h. above* all De 26:19
nations
God will set the *h. above* all De 28:1
Lord, art *h. above* all the earth Ps 97:9
He is *h. above* all the people Ps 99:2
heaven is *h. above* the earth Ps 103:11
Lord is *h. above* all nations Ps 113:4

HIGH *HILL*

on every *h. hill* 1Ki 14:23; 2Ki 17:10
an *h. hill* as the hill of Bashan Ps 68:15
upon every *h. hill* Isa 30:25;
Eze 6:13; 34:6
they saw every *h. hill*, and all Eze 20:28
and upon every *h. hill* Eze 34:14

HIGH *HILLS*

all the *h. hills* under heaven Ge 7:19
Why leap ye, ye *h. hills* Ps 68:16
h. hills are a refuge for wild Ps 104:18
goats
by green trees upon the *h. hills* Jer 17:2

HIGH *MOUNTAIN*

banner upon the *h. mountain* Isa 13:2
upon every *h. mountain*, and Isa 30:25
upon
get up into the *h. mountain* Isa 40:9
Upon a lofty and *h. mountain* Isa 57:7
upon every *h. mountain* and Jer 3:6
under
plant it upon an *h. mountain* Eze 17:22
set me upon a very *h.* Eze 40:2
mountain
into an exceeding *h.* M't 4:8; Lu 4:5
mountain
into an *h. mountain* M't 17:1; M'k 9:2
spirit into a great and *h.* Re 21:10
mountain

HIGH *MOUNTAINS*

upon the *h. mountains*, and De 12:2
upon
upon all the *h. mountains* and Isa 2:14
upon

HIGH *PLACE*

h. place of sacrifice Nu 23:3;
1Sa 9:12, 13, 14, 19, 25; 10:5, 13;
1Ki 3:4; 11:7; 2Ki 23:15; 1Ch 16:39;
21:29; 2Ch 1:3, 13; Isa 16:12; Eze 16:24,
25, 31; 20:29

HIGH *PLACES*

h. places for sacrifice Le 26:30;
Nu 21:28; 22:41; 33:52; De 32:13; 33:29;
J'g 5:18; 1Sa 13:6; 2Sa 1:19, 25; 22:34;
1Ki 3:2, 3; 12:31, 32; 13:2, 32, 33; 14:23;
15:14; 22:43; 2Ki 12:3; 14:4; 15:4, 35;
16:4; 17:9, 11, 29, 32; 18:4, 22; 21:3;
23:5, 8, 9, 13, 19, 20; 2Ch 11:15; 14:3,
5; 15:17; 17:6; 20:33; 21:11; 28:4, 25;
31:1; 32:12; 33:3, 17, 19; 34:3;
Ps 78:58; Pr 8:2; 9:14; Isa 15:2; 36:7;
Jer 3:2, 21; 4:11; 7:29, 31; 12:12; 14:6;
17:3; 19:5; 26:18; 32:35; 48:35; Eze 6:3,
6; 16:16, 39; 36:2; 43:7; Ho 10:8;
Mic 1:5
maketh peace in his *h. places* Job 25:2
setteth me upon my *h. places* Ps 18:33
I will open rivers in *h. places* Isa 41:18
pastures in all *h. places* Isa 49:9
ride upon *h. places* of the Isa 58:14
earth
tread upon *h. places* Am 4:13; Mic 1:3
h. places of Isaac be desolate Am 7:9
as the *h. places* of the forest Mic 3:12
walk upon mine *h. places* Hab 3:19
spiritual wickedness in *h.* Eph 6:12
places

HIGH *PRIEST*

he that is *h. priest* among you Le 21:10
unto the death of the *h.* Nu 35:25;
priest 35:28; Jos 20:6
the *h. priest* came up 2Ki 12:10
Hilkiah, *h. priest* 2Ki 22:4;
22:8; 23:4; 2Ch 34:9
Eliashib the *h. priest* Ne 3:1;
3:20; 13:28

Josedech the *h. priest* Hag 1:1;
1:12, 14; 2:2, 4; Zec 6:11
Joshua the *h. priest* Zec 3:1; 3:8
palace of *h. priest* M't 26:3;
26:58; M'k 14:54; Joh 18:15
servant of *h. priest* M't 26:51;
M'k 14:47; Lu 22:50; Joh 18:10, 26
Caiaphas the *h. priest* M't 26:57;
26:62, 63; M'k 14:53, 60, 61; Lu 3:2;
Joh 11:49, 51; 18:24
the *h. priest* rent clothes M't 26:65;
M'k 14:63
Abiathar the *h. priest* M'k 2:26
one of maids of the *h. priest* M'k 14:66
Annas the *h. priest* Ac 4:6;
5:17, 21, 24, 27
Ananias the *h. priest* Ac 23:2;
23:4-5; 24:1
Christ the *h. priest* Heb 2:17;
3:1; 4:14-15; 5:5, 10; 6:20; 7:26-28; 8:1;
9:11; 10:21

HIGH *TOWER*

my *h. tower* 2Sa 22:3; Ps 18:2; 144:2
upon every *h. tower* Isa 2:15
against the *h. towers* Zep 1:16

HIGH *WALL*

cities fenced with *h. walls* De 3:5
thy *h. walls* come down De 28:52
swelling out in a *h. wall* Isa 30:13
had a *h. wall* Re 21:12

MOST HIGH

priest of the *most H.* God Ge 14:18
Abram of the *most H.* God Ge 14:19
blessed be the *most H.* God Ge 14:20
unto the Lord, the *most H.* Ge 14:22
God
knew knowledge of the *most* Nu 24:16
H.
when the *most H.* divided the De 32:8
nations
when the *most H.* uttered his 2Sa 22:14
voice
sing praise to Lord *most H.* Ps 7:17;
9:2; 92:1
through mercy of the *most H.* Ps 21:7
the tabernacle of the *most H.* Ps 46:4
Lord *most H.* is terrible, a Ps 47:2
great
pay thy vows to the *most H.* Ps 50:14
that fight against me, O thou Ps 56:2
most H.
I will cry unto God *most H.* Ps 57:2
is there knowledge in the *most* Ps 73:11
H.
years of right hand of the Ps 77:10
most H.
by provoking the *most H.* Ps 78:17;
78:56
all of you are children of the Ps 82:6
most H.
Thou art *most H.* over all the Ps 83:18
earth
dwelleth in secret place of *most* Ps 91:1
H.
made the *most H.* thy Ps 91:9
habitation
Thou art *most H.* for evermore Ps 92:8
contemned the counsel of the Ps 107:11
most H.
I will be like the *most H.* Isa 14:14
turn aside before face of the La 3:35
most H.
out of mouth of *most H.* La 3:38
proceedeth
the *most H.* ruleth in kingdom Da 4:17;
4:25
this is decree of the *most H.* Da 4:24
I blessed the *most H.* and Da 5:34
praised
saints of *most H.* shall take Da 7:18
kingdom
judgment given to saints of Da 7:22
most H.
speak great words against Da 7:25
most H.
people of saints of the *most H.* Da 7:27
they return, but not to the Ho 7:16
most H.
they called them to the *most* M'k 11:7
H.
Jesus, son of the *most H.* God M'k 5:7;
Lu 8:28
the *most H.* dwelleth not in Ac 7:48
temples

servants of the *most H.* God   *Ac 16:17*
priest of the *most h.* God   *Heb 7:1*

ON HIGH

cherubims stretch wings *on h.*   *Ex 25:20;*
      37:9
lace of blue, to fasten it *on h.*   *Ex 39:31*
set thee *on h.* above all   *De 28:1;*
nations   *Job 5:11; Ps 69:29; 91:14;*
      107:41; Eze 31:4
hast lifted me up *on h.*   *2Sa 22:49*
man who was raised up *on h.*   *2Sa 23:1*
   said
set Naboth *on h.* among   *1Ki 21:9;*
people   *21:12*
lifted up eyes *on h.* *2Ki 19:22; Isa 37:23*
his kingdom was lifted up *on* *1Ch 14:2*
   h.
stood to praise God *on h.*   *2Ch 29:30*
my record is *on h.*   *Job 16:19*
inheritance of Almighty from *Job 31:2*
   on h.
she lifteth up herself *on h.*   *Job 39:18*
eagle mount up, make nest   *Job 39:27*
   on h.
for their sakes return *on h.*   *Ps 7:7*
Thou hast ascended *on h.*   *Ps 68:18;*
      Eph 4:8
lift up your horn *on h.*   *Ps 75:5*
Lord *on h.* is mightier than the *Ps 93:4*
   noise
God who dwelleth *on h.*   *Ps 113:5;*
      Isa 33:5
hewn him out a sepulchre *on* *Isa 22:16*
   h.
windows from *on h.* are open *Isa 24:18*
punish host of high ones *on* *Isa 24:21*
   h.
bringeth down them that dwell *Isa 26:5*
   on h.
till Spirit be poured from *on* *Isa 32:15*
   h.
lift up your eyes *on h.*   *Isa 40:26*
to make voice be heard *on h.* *Isa 58:4*
Lord shall roar from *on h.*   *Jer 25:30*
may set his nest *on h.*   *Hab 2:9*
the deep lifted up hands *on h.* *Hab 3:10*
dayspring from *on h.* visited *Lu 1:78*
till be endued with power   *Lu 24:49*
   from *on h.*
on right hand of the Majesty *Heb 1:3*
   on h.

HIGHER

his king shall be *h.* than Agag *Nu 24:7*
Saul was *h.* than any of the   *1Sa 9:2*
   people
Jotham built *h.* gate of the   *2Ki 15:35*
   house
on the *h.* places, I set the   *Ne 4:13*
   people
clouds, which are *h.* than thou *Job 35:5*
lead me to rock that is *h.* than I *Ps 61:2*
I will make him *h.* than kings *Ps 89:27*
as heavens are *h.* than earth, *Isa 55:9*
so my ways *h.* than your ways
then read Baruch in the *h.*   *Jer 36:10*
   court
six men came from way of *h.*   *Eze 9:2*
   gate
the galleries were *h.* than these *Eze 42:5*
this shall be *h.* place of the   *Eze 43:13*
   altar
one horn *h.* that the other, *h.*   *Da 8:3*
   came
he shall say, Friend, go up *h.* *Lu 14:10*
be subject to the *h.* powers   *Ro 13:1*
an high priest made *h.* than *Heb 7:26*
   heavens

HIGHEST

Lord thundered, the *H.* gave   *Ps 18:13*
   voice
the *H.* himself shall establish *Ps 87:5*
   her
nor the *h.* part of the dust of *Pr 8:26*
   world
she crieth upon *h.* places of city *Pr 9:3*
he that is higher than the *h.*   *Ec 5:8*
to the *h.* branch of the cedar *Eze 17:3;*
      17:22
from the lowest chamber to   *Eze 41:7*
   the *h.*
Hosanna in the *h.* *M't 21:9; M'k 11:10*
shall be called the Son of the   *Lu 1:32*
   H.

---

power of the *H.* shall   *Lu 1:35*
   overshadow thee
be called the prophet of the *H.* *Lu 1:76*
glory to God in the *h.* *Lu 2:14; 19:38*
shall be children of the *H.*   *Lu 6:35*
when bidden sit not down in *h.* *Lu 14:8*
   room
love *h.* seats in the synagogues *Lu 20:46*

HIGHLY

angel said, Thou art *h.* favoured *Lu 1:28*
which is *h.* esteemed among   *Lu 16:15*
   men
exalted and *h.* thought of (A) *Lu 16:15*
Herod was *h.* displeased with *Ac 12:20*
   Tyre
not think of himself more *h.*   *Ro 12:3*
   than
God also hath *h.* exalted him *Ph'p 2:9*
esteem them very *h.* in love   *1Th 5:13*

HIGHMINDED

be not *h.* but fear   *Ro 11:20; 1Ti 6:17*
traitors, heady, *h.*   *2Ti 3:4*

HIGHNESS

by reason of his *h.* I could   *Job 31:23*
   not
them that rejoice in my *h.*   *Isa 13:3*

HIGH-SOUNDING

h. nonsense (P)   *2Pe 2:18*

HIGHWAY

on east side of the *h.* that   *J'g 21:19*
   goeth
went along the *h.* lowing as   *1Sa 6:12*
   they
in blood in midst of the *h.*   *2Sa 20:12;*
      20:13
in *h.* of fuller's field   *2Ki 18:17;*
      Isa 7:3; 36:2
h. of the upright is to depart *Pr 16:17*
   from
an *h.* for the remnant   *Isa 11:16*
be a *h.* out of Egypt   *Isa 19:23*
an *h.* shall be there, and a way *Isa 35:8*
in the desert a *h.* for our God *Isa 40:3*
cast up the *h.;* gather out the *Isa 62:10*
set thine heart toward the *h.* *Jer 31:21*
Bartimaeus sat by the *h.* side *M'k 10:46*
   begging

HIGHWAYS

the *h.* were unoccupied, and the *J'g 5:6*
in the *h.* as one goeth up   *J'g 20:31;*
      20:32, 45
The *h.* is waste, the wayfaring *Isa 33:8*
   man
a way, and my *h.* shall be   *Isa 49:11*
   exalted
shall say in all *h.,* Alas! alas! *Am 5:16*
Go ye into the *h.*   *M't 22:9;*
      22:10; Lu 14:23

HILARIOUS

drank and got *h.* (B)   *Ge 43:34*

HILEN

H. with her suburbs   *1Ch 6:58*

HILKIAH

Eliakim the son of *H.*   *2Ki 18:18;*
      18:26, 37; Isa 22:20, 22
H. the priest   *2Ki 22:4;*
22:8, 10, 12, 14; 23:4, 24; 2Ch 34:9, 14,
      18
Shallum begat *H.;* and *H.*   *1Ch 6:13*
   begat
the son of Amaziah, the son   *1Ch 6:45*
   of *H.*
Azariah the son of *H. 1Ch 9:11; Ezr 7:1*
H. the second   *1Ch 26:11*
H. answered and said to   *2Ch 34:15*
   Shaphan
the king commanded *H.*   *2Ch 34:20*
H. went to Huldah the   *2Ch 34:22*
   prophetess
H. and Zechariah   *2Ch 35:8*
Urijah, and *H.*   *Ne 8:4; 12:7, 21*

Seraiah the son of *H.*   *Ne 11:11*
Jeremiah the son of *H.*   *Jer 1:1*
Gemariah the son of *H.*   *Jer 29:3*

HILKIAH'S

H. son, which was over the   *Isa 36:3*
   house

HILL

I will stand on top of the *h.*   *Ex 17:9*
   with
Hur went up to top of the *h.* *Ex 17:10*
builded an altar under the *h.*   *Ex 24:4*
Canaanites dwelled in that *h.* *Nu 14:45;*
      14:44
were ready to go into the *h.*   *De 1:41;*
      1:43
circumcised Israel at *h.* of   *Jos 5:3*
   foreskins
they said, The *h.* is not   *Jos 17:16*
   enough for us
Joshua buried on *h.* of   *Jos 24:30;*
   Gaash   *J'g 2:9*
Eleazar was buried in *h.* that *Jos 24:33*
   pertained
the *h.* country (S)   *J'g 2:9;*
   3:27; 1Sa 9:4; 1Ch 6:67; 2Ch 13:4; 15:8
Midianites were by *h.* of Moreh *J'g 7:1*
ark into house of Abinadab in *1Sa 7:1*
   the *h.*
Saul and servants went up the *1Sa 9:11*
   h.
after that thou shalt come to *1Sa 10:5;*
   H.   *10:10*
David hid in *h.* of Hachilah *1Sa 23:19;*
      26:1
Abigail came down by covert *1Sa 25:20*
   of *h.*
they were come to *h.* of   *2Sa 2:24*
   Ammah
much people came by *h.*   *2Sa 13:34*
   behind him
hanged them in *h.* before the *2Sa 21:9*
   Lord
Solomon built in *h.* for   *1Ki 11:7*
   Chemosh
Omri bought the *h.* Samaria *1Ki 16:24*
she came to man of God to   *2Ki 4:27*
   the *h.*
who shall ascend into *h.* of the *Ps 24:3*
   Lord
I will remember thee from *h.*   *Ps 42:6*
   Mizar
h. of God is as the *h.* of   *Ps 68:15*
   Bashan
the *h.* God desireth to dwell in *Ps 68:16*
get me to the *h.* of frankincense *Ca 4:6*
hath vineyard in very fruitful *h.* *Isa 5:1*
shake hand against *h.* of   *Isa 10:32*
   Jerusalem
left as an ensign on an *h.*   *Isa 30:17*
Lord shall fight for the *h.*   *Isa 31:4*
every mountain and *h.* be   *Isa 40:4*
   made low
shall hunt them from every *h.* *Jer 16:16*
measuring line upon the *h.*   *Jer 31:39*
   Gareb
that holdest the height of the *Jer 49:16*
   h.
have gone from mountain to *h. Jer 50:6*
make places about my *h.* of *Eze 34:26*
   blessing
city set on an *h.* cannot be hid *M't 5:14*
every *h.* shall be brought low *Lu 3:5*
led him to the brow of the *h.* *Lu 4:29*
when they came down from the *Lu 9:37*
   h.
Paul stood in midst of Mar's *Ac 17:22*
   h.

HILL *COUNTRY*

inhabitants of *h. country* will I *Jos 13:6*
   drive
gave sons of Aaron, Arba in *Jos 21:11*
   h. country
Mary went in the *h. country*   *Lu 1:39*
   with
noised throughout *h. country* *Lu 1:65*
   of Judea

HILL *TOP*

I will stand on *top* of the *h.*   *Ex 17:9*
Moses, Hur, Aaron went to *Ex 17:10*
   top of *h.*
presumed to go to the *h. top* *Nu 14:44*

Samson carried them to *top* of J'g 16:3
h.
David stood on *top* of h.   1Sa 26:13
Abner stood on *top* of h.   2Sa 2:25
David was a little past *top* of 2Sa 16:1
h.
Elijah sat on *top* of h.   2Ki 1:9

HIGH HILL

groves on every *high* h.   1Ki 14:23;
                    2Ki 17:10
is a *high* h. as the hill of   Ps 68:15
Bashan
on every *high* h. rivers of   Isa 30:25
waters
on every *high* h. wanderest   Jer 2:20;
                     2:23
slain men on every *high* h.   Eze 6:13
they saw every *high* h. and   Eze 20:28
trees
My sheep wandered on every Eze 34:6
high h.

HOLY HILL

have set my king on my *holy* h. Ps 2:6
Lord heard me out of his *holy* h. Ps 3:4
who shall dwell in thy *holy* h.   Ps 15:1
bring me into thy *holy* h.   Ps 43:3
worship at his *holy* h.   Ps 99:9

HILLEL

Abdon, son of *H.*   J'g 12:13; 12:15

HILLS

utmost bound of the   Ge 49:26
everlasting h.
from the h. I behold him   Nu 23:9
spring out of valleys and h.   De 8:7
out of whose h. mayest dig   De 8:9
brass
it is a land of h. and valleys   De 11:11
scorching bases of the h. (B)   De 32:22
precious things of the lasting De 33:15
h.
Joshua smote all country of Jos 10:40;
h.   11:16
gods are gods of the h.   1Ki 20:23;
                       20:28
saw all Israel scattered on 1Ki 22:17
the h.
burnt incense on h.   2Ki 16:4; 2Ch 28:4
wast thou made before the h. Job 15:7
foundations of the h. moved   Ps 18:7
cattle on a thousand h. are   Ps 50:10
mine
the little h. rejoice on every   Ps 65:12
the little h. by righteousness   Ps 72:3
h. covered with shadow of it   Ps 80:10
the strength of h. is his also   Ps 95:4
heights of the h. (E)   Ps 95:4
the h. melted like wax at   Ps 97:5
presence
let the h. be joyful together   Ps 98:8
springs, which run among the Ps 104:10
h.
He watereth h. from his   Ps 104:13
chambers
he toucheth h. and they   Ps 104:32
smoke
the little h. skipped like lambs Ps 114:4;
                     114:6
lift up mine eyes to the h.   Ps 121:1
whence
mountains and all h. praise   Ps 148:9
the Lord
before the h. I was brought forth Pr 8:25
he cometh skipping upon the h. Ca 2:8
shall be exalted above h.   Isa 2:2;
                     Mic 4:1
day of Lord be upon all the h. Isa 2:14
the h. did tremble, their   Isa 5:25
carcases
on all h. that shall be digged Isa 7:25
who hath weighed h. in a   Isa 40:12
balance
shalt make the h. as chaff   Isa 41:15
will make waste mountains   Isa 42:15
and h.
mountains depart, h. be   Isa 54:10
removed
the h. shall break forth into   Isa 55:12
singing
have blasphemed me upon the Isa 65:7
h.
in vain is salvation hoped from Jer 3:23
h.

I beheld the h. moved lightly   Jer 4:24
seen thy abominations on the Jer 13:27
h.
thus saith Lord to the h.   Eze 6:3;
                     36:4, 6
his slain men in thy h. and   Eze 35:8
valleys
they burn incense on h. under Ho 4:13
oaks
shall say to the h., Fall on us Ho 10:8
the h. shall flow with milk   Joe 3:18
drop wine, and all h. shall melt Am 9:13
arise, let the h. hear thy voice Mic 6:1
the h. melt, the earth is burned Na 1:5
the perpetual h. did bow   Hab 3:6
a great crashing upon the h.   Zep 1:10
begin to say to the h., Cover Lu 23:30
us

HILL'S

Shimei went along h. side   2Sa 16:13
cursing

HIGH HILLS

all *high* h. that were under   Ge 7:19
heaven
Why leap ye, ye *high* h.   Ps 68:16
high h. are refuge for wild   Ps 104:18
goats
by green trees upon the *high* h. Jer 17:2

HILT

the h. went in after the blade J'g 3:22
(S)

HIM

me he restored, and h. he   Ge 41:13
hanged
whoso hath sinned, h. I will   Ex 32:33
blot out
Caleb, h. will I bring into the Nu 14:24
land
h. whom he hath chosen   Nu 16:5
h. shalt thou serve, to h.   De 10:20
cleave
Lord hath chosen h. and sons De 18:5
for ever
see h. whom Lord hath   1Sa 10:24
chosen
h. that dieth in city   1Ki 14:11;
                     16:4; 21:24
h. that pisseth against wall   1Ki 21:21;
                     2Ki 9:8
hid h. even h. and his nurse 2Ki 11:2
h. that followed her, kill with 2Ki 11:15
sword
h. shall ye fear, h. shall ye   2Ki 17:36
worship
h. did outlandish woman   Ne 13:26
cause to sin
h. they have hanged on gallows Es 8:7
h. that is deceived trust in   Job 15:31
vanity
delivered h. that had none to Job 29:12
help h.
who teacheth like h.   Job 36:22
canst thunder with a voice like Job 40:9
h.
Job pray for you, for h. will I Job 42:8
accept
Lord hath set apart h. that is   Ps 4:3
godly
h. shall he teach in the way   Ps 25:12
He is thy Lord, worship h.   Ps 45:11
h. who hath no helper   Ps 72:12
h. will I cut off, h. with high Ps 101:5
look
h. that soweth discord among Pr 6:19
brethren
h. shall the people curse   Pr 24:24
h. that is in reputation   Ec 10:1
cut of h. that offereth an   Mal 2:12
offering
h. only shalt thou serve   M't 4:10;
                     Lu 4:8
and ministered unto h. (S)   M't 8:15
confess me before men, h.   M't 10:32;
                     Lu 12:8
h. will I deny before my   M't 10:33
Father
receiveth h. that sent me   M't 10:40;
                     M'k 9:37
my Son, hear ye h.   M't 17:5;
                  Ac 3:22; 7:37
tell h. between thee and h.   M't 18:15
alone

nor let h. in field return   M't 24:18;
                     M'k 13:16
h. they compelled to beat his M't 27:32
cross
let h. that readeth   M'k 13:14
understand
let h. on housetop not go   M'k 13:15
down
whom he sent, h. ye believe   Joh 5:38
not
come in own name, h. ye shall Joh 5:43
receive
h. hath God the Father sealed Joh 6:27
h. that cometh to me, I will in Joh 6:37
doeth his will, h. he heareth   Joh 9:31
serve me, h. will my Father   Joh 12:26
honour
h. hath God exalted   Ac 5:31; Ph'p 2:9
h. God raised up the third day Ac 10:40
whom ye worship, h. declare I Ac 17:23
to you
h. that is weak in the faith   Ro 14:1
receive
let not h. that eateth, despise Ro 14:3
h. that
any defile temple, h. shall God 1Co 3:17
let h. that thinketh he   1Co 10:12
standeth take
made h. to be sin for us   2Co 5:21
let h. that is taught in word   Ga 6:6
give
let h. that stole steal no more Eph 4:28
h. whose coming is after   2Th 2:9
working
might destroy h. that had   Heb 2:14
power of
sprang of one and h. as good Heb 11:12
as dead

ABOUT HIM

servants standing *about* h.   1Sa 22:6
king said to footmen stood 1Sa 22:17
about h.
not build for wars *about* h.   1Ki 5:3
compassed *about* h. to fight 2Ch 18:31
hast made an hedge *about* h.   Job 1:10
let all *about* h. bring presents Ps 76:11
had in reference of all *about* h. Ps 89:7
all ye that are *about* h.   Jer 48:17
bemoan him
Moab be a dismaying to all   Jer 48:39
about h.
it shall devour all round   Jer 50:32
about h.
his adversaries round *about* h. La 1:17
scatter all that are *about* h.   Eze 12:14
his graves are round *about*   Eze 32:22;
h.   23
when Jesus saw multitudes   M't 8:18
about h.
multitude sat *about* h. and   M'k 3:32
said
came the Jews round *about* h. Joh 10:24
four beasts each had six wings Re 4:8
about h.

AFTER HIM

with him and his seed *after* h. Ge 17:19
command his household *after* Ge 18:19
h.
shall be a statute for his seed Ex 28:43
after h.
holy garments be his son's   Ex 29:29
after h.
cut off all that go whoring *after* Le 20:5
h.
if ye turn away from *after* h.   Nu 32:15
pursue *after* h.   Jos 20:5; J'g 1:6; 3:28
Abiezer was gathered *after* h.   J'g 6:34
his armourbearer *after* h.   1Sa 14:13
I went out *after* h. and smote 1Sa 17:35
him
David saw that Saul came   1Sa 26:3
after h.
horsemen followed hard *after* 2Sa 1:6
h.
all the people *after* h.   2Sa 15:17; 23:10
on throne *after* h.   1Ki 1:20; 1:27; 15:4
set up his son *after* h. and   1Ki 15:4
establish
will run *after* h. and take   2Ki 5:20
somewhat
Jehu followed *after* h., and   2Ki 9:27
said, Smite
sent *after* h. to Lachish   2Ki 14:19;
                     2Ch 25:27
after h. was none like him   2Ki 18:5;
                     23:25

Zebadiah his son *after h.* 1Ch 27:7
Azariah the priest went *after* 2Ch 26:17 h.
After h. repaired Ne 3:16; 3:17, 18, 20, 21, 22, 23, 24, 25, 27, 29, 30, 31
they that came *after h.* shall Job 18:20
what pleasure in his house Job 21:21 *after h.*
every man shall draw *after h.* Job 21:33
maketh a path to shine *after* Job 41:32 h.
his glory not descend *after h.* Ps 49:17
his children are blessed *after h.* Pr 20:7
see what shall be *after h.* Ec 3:22; 6:12; 10:14
man should find nothing *after* Ec 7:14 h.
go ye *after h.* and smite Eze 9:5
sent a message *after h.* saying Lu 19:14
the world is gone *after h.* Joh 12:19
drew away much people *after* Ac 5:37 h.
give it to him, and seed *after h.* Ac 7:5
seek Lord, if haply might feel Ac 17:27 *after h.*
believe on him which come Ac 19:4 *after h.*

AGAINST HIM

every man's hand *against h.* Ge 16:12
saw he prevailed not *against* Ge 32:25 h.
they conspired *against h.* Ge 37:18; 1Ki 15:27; 16:9; 2Ki 14:19; 15:10, 25; 21:23
hear murmurings which ye Ex 16:8; murmur *against h.* Nu 14:36; 16:11
stood for an adversary Nu 22:22 *against h.*
if any man rise up *against h.* De 19:11; 19:16
smite through loins that rise De 33:11 *against h.*
stood a man over *against h.* Jos 5:13
a young lion roared *against h.* J'g 14:5
the Philistines shouted *against* J'g 15:14 h.
Lord said, Go up *against h.* J'g 20:23
front of battle was *against h.* 2Sa 10:9
hand he put forth *against h.* 1Ki 13:4 dried up
sons of Belial bear witness 1Ki 21:10 *against h.*
Josiah went up *against h.* 2Ki 23:29
Lord sent *against h.* bands of 2Ki 24:2 Chaldees
to rail and speak *against h.* 2Ch 32:17
shalt not prevail *against h.* Es 6:13
thou movedst me *against h.* Job 2:3
if children have sinned *against* Job 8:4 h.
hardened himself *against h.* and Job 9:4
prevailest for ever *against h.* Job 14:20
why dost thou strive *against* Job 33:13 h.
what doest thou *against h.* Job 35:6
they sinned yet more *against* Ps 78:17 h.
cruel messenger be sent Pr 17:11 *against h.*
if one prevail *against h.* Ec 4:12
shall axe boast *against h.* that Isa 10:15 heweth? or the saw *against* h.
shepherds are called *against h.* Isa 31:4
all that are incensed *against* Isa 45:24 h.
Spirit of Lord lift up Isa 59:19 standard *against h.*
we shall prevail *against h.* Jer 20:10
since I spake *against h.* I Jer 31:20 remember
against h. that bendeth, let Jer 51:3 archer
prophesy *against h.* Eze 29:2; 38:2
I will call for sword *against* Eze 38:21 h.
I will plead *against h.* with Eze 38:22 pestilence
because we have sinned Da 9:11 *against h.*
he that cometh *against h.* Da 11:16 shall do
they prepare war *against h.* Mic 3:5
because I have sinned *against* Mic 7:9 h.
take up a parable *against h.* Hab 2:6
held counsel *against h.* M't 12:14; M'k 3:6

to meet him that cometh Lu 14:31 *against h.*
wherefore they cried *against h.* Ac 22:24
to say what they had *against* Ac 23:30 h.
high priest desired favor Ac 25:3 *against h.*
Jews desiring judgment Ac 25:15 *against h.*
durst not bring *against h.* a Jude 9 railing
ungodly sinners have spoken Jude 15 *against h.*
make war *against h.* that sat Re 19:19 on horse

AT HIM

archers shot *at h.* and hated Ge 49:23 him
Saul cast a javelin *at h.* to 1Sa 20:33 smite him
Shimei threw stones *at h.* 2Sa 16:13
men clap their hands *at h.* Job 27:23
in safety from him that puffeth Ps 12:5 *at h.*
Lord shall laugh *at h.* for he Ps 37:13 seeth
righteous also shall see and Ps 52:6 laugh *at h.*
suddenly do they shoot *at h.* Ps 64:4
kings shall shut their mouths Isa 52:15 *at h.*
king of south push *at h.* Da 11:40
mountains quake *at h.* and hills Na 1:5 melt
they were offended *at h.* M'k 6:3
at h. they cast stones, M'k 12:4 wounded him
they marvelled *at h.* M'k 12:17
he marvelled *at h.* and turned Lu 7:9 about
they could not come *at h.* for Lu 8:19
Jews then murmured *at h.* Joh 6:41
then took they up stones to Joh 8:59 cast *at h.*

BEFORE HIM

there was set meat *before h.* Ge 24:33 to eat
Jacob sent messengers *before* Ge 32:3 h. to
went the present over *before* Ge 32:21 h.
they cried *before h.*, Bow the Ge 41:43 knee
they sat *before h.* according Ge 43:33 to youth
they fell *before h.* on the Ge 44:14 ground
Lord passed by *before h.* Ex 34:6
have wept *before h.* saying Nu 11:20
ascend up every man straight Jos 6:5 *before h.*
do service of Lord *before h.* Jos 22:27
fled *before h.* J'g 9:40; 2Sa 10:13; 1Ch 19:14
wept *before h.* J'g 14:16; 14:17
the Lord's anointed in *before* 1Sa 16:6 h.
stood *before h.* 1Sa 16:21; 1Ki 3:16; 2Ki 4:12
one bearing shield went *before* 1Sa 17:7 h.
eat and drink *before h.* 2Sa 11:13
they set bread *before h.* 2Sa 12:20
fifty men to run *before h.* 2Sa 15:1; 1Ki 1:5
was upright *before h.* 2Sa 22:24; Ps 18:23
did worse than all *before h.* 1Ki 16:25; 16:30, 33
set two men, sons of Belial 1Ki 21:10 *before h.*
bowed to ground *before h.* 2Ki 2:15
sons of prophets sitting *before* 2Ki 4:38 h.
sent a man from *before h.* 2Ki 6:32
stood not *before h.* how shall 2Ki 10:4 we
not as kings that were *before* 2Ki 17:2; h. 18:5
Amorites did, which were 2Ki 21:11 *before h.*
like Josiah there was no king 2Ki 23:25 *before h.*
did eat bread *before h.* 2Ki 25:29; Jer 52:33
bring offering, and come 1Ch 16:29 *before h.*

fear *before h.* 1Ch 16:30; Ps 96:9; Ec 3:14; 8:12
not any *before h.* like 1Ch 29:25 Solomon for
to burn *before h.* sweet 2Ch 2:4; incense 2:6
the kingdom was quiet *before* 2Ch 14:5 h.
Lord chose you to stand 2Ch 29:11 *before h.*
that wine was *before h.* Ne 2:1
to make request *before h.* for Es 4:8 her
proclaim *before h.* Es 6:9; 6:11
shalt surely fall *before h.* Es 6:13
I will maintain my ways Job 13:15 *before h.*
an hypocrite shall not come Job 13:16 *before h.*
as there are innumerable Job 21:33 *before h.*
would order my cause *before* Job 23:4 h.
hell is naked *before h.* Job 26:6
judgment is *before h.* Job 35:14
sorrow turned into joy *before* Job 41:22 h.
my cry came *before h.* even to Ps 18:6 his
at brightness that was *before* Ps 18:12 h.
all that go to dust shall bow Ps 22:29 *before h.*
God come, a fire shall devour Ps 50:3 *before h.*
pour out your heart *before h.* Ps 62:8
let them that hate him flee Ps 68:1 *before h.*
sing and rejoice *before h.* Ps 68:4
dwell in wilderness shall bow Ps 72:9 *before h.*
kings all *before h.*, nations Ps 72:11 serve him
righteousness shall go *before* Ps 85:13 h.
honour and majesty are *before* Ps 96:6 h.
fear *before h.* all the earth Ps 96:9
a fire goeth *before h.* and Ps 97:3 burneth
had not Moses stood *before* Ps 106:23 h.
I showed *before h.* my Ps 142:2 trouble
rejoicing always *before h.* Pr 8:30
wisdom is *before h.* that hath Pr 17:24
his work *before h.* Isa 40:10; 62:11
all nations *before h.* are as Isa 40:17 nothing
gave nations *before h.*, and Isa 41:2 made
holden to subdue nations Isa 45:1 *before h.*
present supplications *before h.* Jer 42:9
wilt thou say *before h.* that Eze 28:9 slayeth
groan *before h.* with Eze 30:24 groanings
10,000 times 10,000 stood Da 7:10 *before h.*
no beasts might stand *before h.* Da 8:4; 8:7
none shall stand *before h.* Da 11:16; 11:22
shall come *before h.* with Mic 6:6 offerings
let all earth keep silence Hab 2:20 *before h.*
before h. went pestilence and Hab 3:5
book of remembrance written Mal 3:16 *before h.*
before h. shall be gathered all M't 25:32 nations
bowed the knee *before h.* and M't 27:29 mocked
fell down *before h.* and M'k 3:11; cried 5:33
shall go *before h.* in spirit of Lu 1:17 Elias
in holiness *before h.* all days of Lu 1:75 life
sought means to lay him *before* Lu 5:18
I have nothing to set *before h.* Lu 11:6
I said, that I am sent *before h.* Joh 3:28
they presented Paul *before h.* Ac 23:33
before h. whom he believed Ro 4:17
holy, without blame *before h.* Eph 1:4 in love
for joy set *before h.* endured Heb 12:2

not be ashamed *before h.* at   *1Jo 2:28*
coming
assure our hearts *before h.*   *1Jo 3:19*
all power of first beast *before*   *Re 13:12*
h.
false prophet wrought   *Re 19:20*
miracles *before h.*

BEHIND HIM

Sarah heard in tent door   *Ge 18:10*
behind h.
the spear came out *behind h.*   *2Sa 2:23*
sound of master's feet *behind* *2Ki 6:32*
h.
repent, leave blessing *behind*   *Joe 2:14*
h.
behind h. were red horses,   *Zec 1:8*
speckled
woman diseased came *behind* *M't 9:20;*
h. and touched hem   *Lu 8:44*
brother die, leave wife   *M'k 12:19*
behind h.
stood at feet *behind h.* weeping *Lu 7:38*

BESIDE HIM

God, there is none *beside h.*   *De 4:35*
his servants passed on *beside* *2Sa 15:18*
h.
beside h. stood Mattithiah and *Ne 8:4*
Shema

BETWEEN HIM

law Lord made *between h.*   *Le 26:46*
and Israel
discern *between h.* that   *Mal 3:18*
serveth God

BEYOND HIM

shot an arrow *beyond h.*   *1Sa 20:36*

BY HIM

Sihon would not let us pass *by* *De 2:30*
h.
beloved of Lord shall dwell   *De 33:12*
safely *by h.*
by h. Israel sent a present   *J'g 3:15*
all that stood *by h.* went out   *J'g 3:19*
from him
by h. actions are weighed   *1Sa 2:3*
be sure evil is determined *by* *1Sa 20:7*
h.
host of heaven standing *by h. 1Ki 22:19*
enquire of the Lord *by h. 2Ki 3:11; 8:8*
by h. Lord had given deliverance *2Ki 5:1*
three hundred slain *by h.*   *1Ch 11:11*
at one time
the queen also sitting *by h.*   *Ne 2:6*
Tobiah the Ammonite was *by h. Ne 4:3*
every one that sweareth *by h. Ps 63:11*
slaughter of them slain *by h. Isa 27:7*
by h. daily sacrifice was taken *Da 8:11*
away
sware *by h.* that liveth for   *Da 12:7;*
                       Re 10:6
rocks are thrown down *by h.*   *Na 1:6*
sweareth *by h.*   *M't 23:21; 23:22*
Herod being reproved *by h.*   *Lu 3:19*
shut up
Herod heard all that was done *Lu 9:7*
by h.
glorious things done *by h.*   *Lu 13:17;*
                       Ac 2:22
all things were made *by h.*   *Joh 1:3;*
                       1:10
faith which is *by h.*   *Ac 3:16; 4:10*
by h. all that believe are   *Ac 13:39*
justified
night following Lord stood *by Ac 23:11*
h.
in every thing enriched *bv h.*   *1Co 1:5*
by whom are all things, we *by 1Co 8:6*
h.
heard him and been taught   *Eph 4:21*
by h.
by h. all things created in   *Col 1:16*
heaven
before all things, *by h.* all   *Col 1:17*
things
by h. to reconcile all things *by Col 1:20*
h. giving
giving thanks to God the   *Col 3:17*
Father *by h.*
taken captive *by h.* at his will *2Ti 2:26*
save them that come to God   *Heb 7:25*
by h.

by *h.* let us offer sacrifice of *Heb 13:15*
praise
who *by h.* do believe in God   *1Pe 1:21*
are sent *by h.* for punishment *1Pe 2:14*

CONCERNING HIM

made an oath *concerning h.*   *J'g 21:5*
word Lord hath spoken   *2Ki 19:21;*
concerning h.   *Isa 37:22*
king commanded *concerning h. Es 3:2*
made proclamation *concerning Da 5:29*
h.
murmuring *concerning h. Joh 7:12; 7:32*
Jews did not believe   *Joh 9:18*
concerning h.
David speaketh *concerning h.*   *Ac 2:25*
inquire something *concerning Ac 23:15*
h.
concerning h. that hath done   *1Co 5:3*
this

FOR HIM

make him an help meet *for h. Ge 2:18;*
                       2:20
Joseph's father wept *for h.*   *Ge 37:35*
I will be surety *for h.*   *Ge 43:9*
blood shed *for h.*   *Ex 22:2; 22:3*
atonement *for h.*   *Le 1:4;*
   4:26, 31; 5:13; 14:18, 19, 20, 31; 15:15;
           19:22; Nu 5:8; 6:11, 15:28
priest ask counsel *for h.*   *Nu 27:21*
take no satisfaction *for h.*   *Nu 35:32*
lie in wait *for h.*   *De 19:11; 1Sa 15:2*
let his hands be sufficient *for h. De 33:7*
he that will plead *for h.*   *J'g 6:31*
if man sin, who shall entreat *1Sa 2:25*
for h.
Saul sent *for h.*   *1Sa 17:31*
he inquired of the Lord *for 1Sa 22:10;*
h.   *22:15*
he sought no more again *for 1Sa 27:4*
h.
servants shall till land *for h.*   *2Sa 9:10*
ask *for h.* the kingdom, even *1Ki 2:22*
for h.
saddled *for h.* the ass   *1Ki 13:23*
Israel shall mourn *for h.* and *1Ki 14:13*
bury him
made very great burning *for 2Ch 16:14;*
h.   *21:19*
banquet I have prepared *for h. Es 5:4*
Haman saw he moved not *for h. Es 5:9*
servants said nothing done *for Es 6:3*
hang on gallows he prepared *for Es 6:4*
h.
will you talk deceitfully *for h. Job 13:7*
I weep *for h.* that was in   *Job 30:25*
trouble
there is no help *for h.* in God   *Ps 3:2*
rest in Lord, wait patiently *for Ps 37:7*
h.
nor give to God a ransom *for Ps 49:7*
h.
prayer also be made *for h.*   *Ps 72:15*
continually
for h. that wanteth   *Pr 9:4;*
understanding   *9:16*
he shall gather it *for h.* that will *Pr 28:8*
my bowels were moved *for h.*   *Ca 5:4*
wait upon Lord and look *for Isa 8:17*
h.
we have waited *for h.*   *Isa 25:9*
that lay a snare *for h.* that   *Isa 29:21*
reproveth
blessed are they that wait *for Isa 30:18*
h.
Lord come, his arm shall rule *Isa 40:10*
for h.
prepared *for h.* that waiteth   *Isa 64:4*
for h.
they shall not lament *for h.*   *Jer 22:18*
my bowels are troubled *for h. Jer 31:20*
Lord is good to them that wait *La 3:25*
for h.
covered the deep *for h.,*   *Eze 31:15*
mourn *for h.,* the trees of field
fainted *for h.*
so shalt thou do *for h.* that is *Eze 45:20*
simple
nor shall she be *for h.*   *Da 11:17*
fall in snare where no gin is *for Am 3:5*
h.
not sought Lord nor inquired   *Zep 1:6*
for h.
mourn *for h.* be in bitterness *Zec 12:10*
for h.
was not lawful *for h.* to eat   *M't 12:4*
better *for h.* that millstone   *M't 18:6;*

hanged about neck   *M'k 9:42; Lu 17:2*
when looketh not *for h.*   *M't 24:50;*
                       Lu 12:46
great things Jesus had done   *M'k 5:20*
for *h.*
brought in child to do *for h.*   *Lu 2:27*
after the
they were all waiting *for h.*   *Lu 8:40*
they went to make ready *for h. Lu 9:52*
prayer was made unto God *for Ac 12:5*
h.
I look *for h.* with the   *1Co 16:11*
brethren
all things created by him and   *Col 1:16*
for h.
to them that look *for h.* shall *Heb 9:28*
he

FROM HIM

God went up *from h.*   *Ge 35:13*
it be hid *from h.* when he   *Le 5:3*
knoweth it
all by him went out *from h.*   *J'g 3:19;*
                       2Sa 13:9
locks, his strength went   *J'g 16:19*
from h.
Samuel hid nothing *from h.*   *1Sa 3:18*
retire *from h.*   *1Sa 11:15*
whether any thing come *from 1Ki 20:33*
h.
all his army scattered *from h. 2Ki 25:5*
wrath of the Lord turned   *2Ch 12:12*
from h.
turn *from h.* that he may rest *Job 14:6*
nor hath he hid his face *from Ps 22:24*
h.
the poor *from h.* that spoileth *Ps 35:10*
him
I would have hid myself *from Ps 55:12*
h.
God, *from h.* cometh my   *Ps 62:1*
salvation
righteousness of the righteous *Isa 5:23*
from h.
we hid as it were our faces   *Isa 53:3*
from h.
go *from h.* and become another *Jer 3:1*
man's
part of the hand was sent *from Da 5:24*
h.
take *from h.* burdens of wheat *Am 5:11*
he arose, and laid his robe   *Jon 3:6*
from h.
from h. that would borrow of *M't 5:42*
thee
from h. be taken   *M't 13:12;*
     25:29; M'k 4:25; Lu 8:18; 19:26
prayed the hour might pass   *M'k 14:35*
from h.
taketh *from h.* all his armour *Lu 11:22*
I am *from h.* he hath sent me *Joh 7:29*
will flee *from h.* for they know *Joh 10:5*
not
so soon removed *from h.* that   *Ga 1:6*
called
if we turn away *from h.* that *Heb 12:25*
speaketh
shutteth bowels of compassion *1Jo 3:17*
from h.
this commandment have we   *1Jo 4:21*
from h.
peace *from h.* which is, which   *Re 1:4*
was

IN HIM

all nations of earth be blessed *Ge 18:18*
in h.
beware of him, for my name   *Ex 23:21*
is *in h.*
men of Shechem put   *J'g 9:26*
confidence *in h.*
there was not strength *in h.*   *1Sa 28:20*
I have found no fault *in h.*   *1Sa 29:3;*
                       Joh 19:4, 6
in h. will I trust   *2Sa 22:3; Ps 91:12*
buckler to all that trust *in h. 2Sa 22:31;*
                       Isa 36:6
if wickedness be *in h.* he shall *1Ki 1:52*
die
saw the wisdom of God was   *1Ki 3:28*
in h.
because *in h.* was found   *1Ki 14:13*
some good
there was no breath left *in h. 1Ki 17:17*
because they put trust *in h.*   *1Ch 5:20*
Though he slay me, yet will I *Job 13:15*
trust *in h.*

judgment is before him, trust   *Job 35:14*
in *h.*
blessed are they that put trust   *Ps 2:12;*
in *h.;*   *34:8*
buckler to all that trust in *h.*   *Ps 18:30*
my heart trusteth *in h.*   *Ps 28:7*
heart shall rejoice *in h.*   *Ps 33:21;*
                66:6; 149:2
none that trust *in h.* shall be   *Ps 34:22*
desolate
trust *in h.*   *Ps 37:5; 62:8*
he will deliver because they   *Ps 37:40*
trust *in h.*
righteous shall be glad and   *Ps 64:10*
trust *in h.*
men shall be blessed *in h.*   *Ps 72:17*
is no unrighteousness *in h.*   *Ps 92:15;*
                Joh 7:18
perceivest not *in h.* lips of   *Pr 14:7*
knowledge
is shield to them that put trust   *Pr 30:5*
in h.
that come after shall not   *Ec 4:16*
rejoice *in h.*
nations shall bless themselves in   *Jer 4:2*
h.
Pharaoh and all that trust in   *Jer 46:25*
h.
therefore his taste remained   *Jer 48:11*
in h.
my portion, therefore will I   *La 3:24*
hope *in h.*
delivered his servants who   *Da 3:28*
trusted *in h.*
nor any error or fault found in   *Da 6:4*
h.
there is none understanding *in h.*   *Ob 7*
he knoweth them that trust *in h.*   *Na 1:7*
his soul is not upright *in h.*   *Hab 2:4*
they were offended *in h.*   *M't 13:57*
mighty works shew themselves   *M't 14:2*
in h.
have found no cause of death   *Lu 23:22*
in h.
in h. was life, life was light of   *Joh 1:4*
men
whosoever believeth *in h.*   *Joh 3:15;*
                Ac 10:43
be *in h.* well of water   *Joh 4:14*
springing up
dwelleth in me, I *in h.*   *Joh 6:56;*
              10:38; 15:5
neither did brethren believe in   *Joh 7:5*
h.
because there is no truth *in h.*   *Joh 8:44*
works of God-made manifest *in*   *Joh 9:3*
h.
because there is no light *in h.*   *Joh 11:10*
God is glorified *in h.*   *Joh 13:31; 13:32*
in h. we live, move, have our   *Ac 17:28*
being
how shall they believe *in h.* of   *Ro 10:14*
whom
in h. shall the Gentiles trust   *Ro 15:12*
save spirit of man which is *in*   *1Co 2:11*
h.
are all things, we *in h.*   *1Co 8:6;*
              1Jo 5:20
but *in h.* was yea   *2Co 1:19; 1:20*
be made righteousness of God   *2Co 5:21*
in h.
for we are weak *in h.* but live   *2Co 13:4*
with him
he has chosen us *in h.* from the   *Eph 1:4*
gather together all things *in h.*   *Eph 1:10*
may win Christ, and be found   *Ph'p 3:9*
in h.
in h. should all fulness dwell   *Col 1:19*
as received Christ, so walk ye   *Col 2:6*
in h.
rooted and built up *in h.*   *Col 2:7*
in h. dwelleth fulness of   *Col 2:9*
Godhead
ye are complete *in h.* who is   *Col 2:10*
head
again, I will put my trust *in*   *Heb 2:13*
h.
My soul shall have no   *Heb 10:38*
pleasure *in h.*
is a liar, and truth is not *in h.*   *1Jo 2:4*
whoso keepeth word *in h.* is   *1Jo 2:5*
love perfected, hereby we know
we are *in h.*
that saith he abideth *in h.*   *1Jo 2:6*
ought to
which things are true *in h.* and   *1Jo 2:8*
in you
none occasion of stumbling *in*   *1Jo 2:10*
h.

love of the Father is not *in h.*   *1Jo 2:15;*
               3:17
as taught you, ye shall abide   *1Jo 2:27;*
in h.   *2:28*
every man that hath this hope   *1Jo 3:3*
in h.
take away our sin, *in h.* is no   *1Jo 3:5*
sin
Whosoever abideth *in h.*   *1Jo 3:6*
sinneth not
seed remaineth *in h.* and   *1Jo 3:9*
cannot sin
no murderer hath eternal life   *1Jo 3:15*
in h.
dwelleth *in h.,* he *in h.*   *1Jo 3:24;*
            4:13, 15, 16
this is the confidence we have   *1Jo 5:14*
in h.

INTO HIM

let child's soul come *into h.*   *1Ki 17:21*
again
soul of child came *into h.*   *1Ki 17:22*
again
many devils were entered *into*   *Lu 8:30*
h.
after the sop, Satan entered   *Joh 13:27*
into h.
may grow up *into h.* in all   *Eph 4:15*
things

OF HIM

Lord was entreated *of h.*   *Ge 25:21;*
            2Ch 33:13, 19
beware *of h.* and obey his   *Ex 23:21*
voice
wot not what is become *of h.*   *Ex 32:1;*
               32:23
toucheth flesh *of h.* that hath   *Le 15:7;*
issue   *15:33*
take thou no usury *of h.* nor   *Le 25:36*
increase
by the blood *of h.* that shed it   *Nu 35:33*
I will require it *of h.*   *De 18:19*
shalt not be afraid *of h.*   *De 18:22;*
             2Ki 1:15
let no man's heart fail   *1Sa 17:32*
because *of h.*
I will run and take somewhat   *2Ki 5:20*
of h.
his life shall be for the life *of*   *2Ki 10:24*
h.
of h. came the chief ruler, but   *1Ch 5:2*
they were the ruin *of h.* and   *2Ch 28:23*
Israel
to seek *of h.* a right way for us   *Ezr 8:21*
eye *of h.* hath seen me shall see   *Job 7:8*
despised in thought *of h.* at   *Job 12:5*
ease
is place *of h.* that knoweth   *Job 18:21*
not God
when I consider, I am afraid   *Job 23:15*
of h.
fret not thyself because *of h.*   *Ps 37:7*
his mouth craveth it *of h.*   *Pr 16:26*
begetteth wise child have joy   *Pr 23:24*
of h.
more hope of a fool than *of*   *Pr 26:12;*
h.   *29:20*
take pledge *of h.* for strange   *Pr 27:13*
woman
shall the work say *of h.* that   *Isa 29:16*
made it
feet *of h.* bring good tidings   *Isa 52:7;*
              Na 1:15
I will make mention *of h.*   *Jer 20:9*
be not afraid *of h.* saith the   *Jer 42:11*
Lord
the punishment *of h.* that   *Eze 14:10*
seeketh
king of Babylon take an oath   *Eze 17:13*
of h.
no pleasure in death *of h.*   *Eze 18:32*
that dieth
nations also heard *of h.* he   *Eze 19:4*
was taken
in hand *of h.* that slayeth thee   *Eze 28:9*
take hold of skirt *of h.* that is   *Zec 8:23*
a Jew
encamp because *of h.* that   *Zec 9:8*
returneth
as written *of h.*   *M't 26:24;*
            M'k 9:13; 14:21
I suffered in a dream,   *M't 27:19*
because *of h.*
that they should tell no man   *M'k 8:30*
of h.
of h. Son of man ashamed   *M'k 8:38;*
              Lu 9:26

of h. that taketh goods, ask not   *Lu 6:30*
again
much given *of h.* much be   *Lu 12:48*
required
say *of h.* whom the Father   *Joh 10:36*
sanctified
justifier *of h.* that believeth in   *Ro 3:26*
Jesus
not of works but *of h.* that   *Ro 9:11*
calleth
it is not *of h.* that willeth, but   *Ro 9:16*
of God
of h. and through him are all   *Ro 11:36*
things
of h. are ye in Christ, who of   *1Co 1:30*
God
shew forth praises *of h.* who   *1Pe 2:9*
called
ye may be found *of h.* in   *2Pe 3:14*
peace
is the message we have heard *of*   *1Jo 1:5*
h.
anointing which ye received *of*   *1Jo 2:27*
h.
that doeth righteousness is   *1Jo 2:29*
born *of h.*
all kindreds shall wail because   *Re 1:7*
of h.

ON HIM

lay hold *on h.*   *1Ki 13:4*
if head of Elisha stand *on h.*   *2Ki 6:31*
today
on h. they laid the cross   *Lu 23:26*
Spirit descending it abode   *Joh 1:32;*
on h.   *1:33*
he that believeth *on h.*   *Joh 3:18;*
       5:24; 6:40; Ro 9:33; 1Pe 2:6
shall look *on h.* whom they   *Joh 19:37*
pierced
Saul set his eyes *on h.* and said   *Ac 13:9*
not only believe *on h.* but to   *Ph'p 1:29*
suffer
God had mercy *on h.,* not *on*   *Ph'p 2:27*
h. only
took not *on h.* the nature of   *Heb 2:16*
angels
he that sat *on h.*   *Re 6:2; 6:5, 8; 19:11*

OVER HIM

thou shalt rule *over h.*   *Ge 4:7*
confess *over h.* all the   *Le 16:21*
iniquities
not rule *over h.* with rigour   *Le 25:43;*
              25:53
all people wept again *over h.*   *2Sa 3:34*
they mourned *over h.* saying,   *1Ki 13:30*
Alas
burnt king's house *over h.*   *1Ki 16:18*
with fire
set a wicked man *over h.,* let   *Ps 109:6*
Satan
nations spread their net *over*   *Eze 19:8*
h.
let seven times pass *over h.*   *Da 4:16;*
              4:23
devout men lamented *over h.*   *Ac 8:2*
death hath no more dominion   *Ro 6:9*
over h.
is any sick? let them pray *over*   *Jas 5:14*
h.

THROUGH HIM

all men *through h.* might   *Joh 1:7*
believe
the world *through h.* might be   *Joh 3:17*
saved
shall be saved from wrath   *Ro 5:9*
through h.
more than conquerors   *Ro 8:37*
through h.
of him, *through h.* and to him   *Ro 11:36*
are all
through h. we have access to   *Eph 2:18*
Father
sent Son that we might live   *1Jo 4:9*
through h.

TO HIM

to Seth, *to h.* also there was   *Ge 4:26*
born a son
at set time God had spoken *to*   *Ge 21:2*
h.
shalt be *to h.* instead of God   *Ex 4:16*
not be *to h.* as an usurer,   *Ex 22:25*
neither

to *h*. will I give the land   De 1:36
to do *to h.* as he hath done to   J'g 15:10
us
Lord hath done *to h.* as he   1Sa 28:17
spake
sworn to David, even so do *to*   2Sa 3:9
h.
wherefore wilt thou go *to h.*   2Ki 4:23
today
even *to h.* and his sons by   2Ch 13:5
covenant
to h. that is afflicted, pity   Job 6:14
should be
to h. that rideth on the   Ps 68:33
heavens
to h. shall be given gold of   Ps 72:15
Sheba
to h. that made great lights   Ps 136:7
to h. that smote great kings   Ps 136:17
all things come alike *to h.*   Ec 9:2
that sacrificeth, *to h.* that
sacrificeth not
people turneth not *to h.* that   Isa 9:13
smiteth
turn *to h.* from whom Israel   Isa 31:6
revolted
counted *to h.* less than   Isa 40:17
nothing
even *to h.* shall men come,   Isa 45:24
and all
to h. whom man despiseth   Isa 49:7
peace *to h.* that is afar off,   Isa 57:19
and *to h.*
will look *to h.* that is poor and   Isa 66:2
contrite
to h. that knocketh, it shall be   M't 7:8
opened
to h. that smiteth thee on one   Lu 6:29
cheek
whosoever hath, *to h.* shall be   Lu 8:18
given
to h. that blasphemeth Holy   Lu 12:10
Ghost
to h. the porter openeth, sheep   Joh 10:3
hear
to h. they agreed, and called   Ac 5:40
apostles
to h. they had regard because   Ac 8:11
to h. gave all the prophets   Ac 10:43
witness
now *to h.* that worketh, is the   Ro 4:4
reward
to h. that worketh not, but   Ro 4:5
believeth
even *to h.* who is raised from   Ro 7:4
the dead
to h. are all things, to whom   Ro 11:36
be glory
to h. that esteemeth, *to h.* is   Ro 14:14
unclean
now *to h.* that is of power to   Ro 16:25
establish
I be *to h.* who speaketh a   2Co 14:11
barbarian
it was accounted *to h.* for   Ga 3:6
righteousness
I will be *to h.* a Father, he to   Heb 1:5
me a son
to h. that was able to save   Heb 5:7
from death
to h. that knoweth to do good,   Jas 4:17
to h.
to h. that overcometh,   Re 2:7;
     2:17; 3:21
to h. will I give power over   Re 2:26
nations

TOWARD HIM

it was not *toward h.* as before   Ge 31:2
their anger was abated *toward*   J'g 8:3
h.
them whose heart is perfect   2Ch 16:9
toward h.
stretch out thine hands   Job 11:13
toward h.
lift up thy hands *toward h.*   La 2:19
whose branches turned *toward*   Eze 17:6
h.
confirm your love *toward h.*   2Co 2:8

UNDER HIM

took a stone and put it *under*   Ex 17:12
h.
mule that was *under h.* went   2Sa 18:9
away
proud helpers do stoop *under*   Job 9:13
h.

spread sackcloth and ashes   Isa 58:5
under h.
roots thereof were *under h.*   Eze 17:6
all things put *under h.*   1Co 15:27;
     15:28; Heb 2:8

UNTO HIM

altar to Lord, who appeared   Ge 12:7
unto h.
shall a child be born *unto h.*   Ge 17:17
that is
unto h. hath he given all he   Ge 24:36
hath
unto h. shall gathering of   Ge 49:10
people be
shall be statute for ever *unto*   Ex 28:43;
h.   30:21
raise up a prophet *unto h.*   De 18:15
so it fell out *unto h.*, the   2Ki 7:20
people trode
the king, so shall ye say *unto*   2Ch 34:26
h.
if thou sinnest, what doest   Job 35:6
thou *unto h.*
what likeness will ye compare   Isa 40:18
unto h.
God of living, for all live *unto*   Lu 20:38
h.
I go *unto h.* that sent me   Joh 7:33; 16:5
unto h. be glory in the church   Eph 3:21
was imputed *unto h.* for   Jas 2:23
righteousness
unto h. that loved us, and   Re 1:5
washed us
will give *unto h.* that is athirst   Re 21:6

UPON HIM

give whatsoever is laid *upon*   Ex 21:30
h.
eateth, having his uncleanness   Le 7:20
upon h.
if her flowers be *upon h.* he is   Le 15:24
unclean
shalt rebuke, not suffer sin   Le 19:17
upon h.
he cursed father, his blood be   Le 20:9
upon h.
anointing oil of his God is   Le 21:12
upon h.
took of Spirit that was *upon*   Nu 11:25
h.
his iniquity shall be *upon h.*   Nu 15:31
Spirit of Lord came *upon h.*   Nu 24:2;
J'g 3:10; 14:6, 19; 15:14; 1Sa 10:10;
     19:23
seeing him not, cast it *upon*   Nu 35:23
h. that
thine hand shall be first *upon*   De 13:9;
h.   17:7
all curses written in book lie   De 29:20
upon h.
be on our head, if any hand be   Jos 2:19
upon h.
hand of Philistines be *upon*   1Sa 18:17
h.
will come *upon h.* while he is   2Sa 17:2
weary
an oath be laid *upon h.*   1Ki 8:31;
     2Ch 6:22
she shut the door *upon h.* and   2Ki 4:21
went out
people trode *upon h.* in gate   2Ki 7:17;
     7:20
therefore there was wrath   2Ch 32:25
upon h.
hand of Lord his God *upon h.*   Ezr 7:6;
     7:9
thou shouldest set heart *upon*   Job 7:17
h.
in prosperity destroyer come   Job 15:21
upon h.
hand of wicked shall come   Job 20:22
upon h.
shall rain it *upon h.* while   Job 20:23
eating
sword cometh; terrors *upon*   Job 20:25
h.
hear, when trouble cometh   Job 27:9
upon h.
I will call *upon h.* as long as I   Ps 116:2
live
Lord nigh to all that call   Ps 145:18
upon h. in
I will pour water *upon h.* that   Isa 44:3
is thirsty
chastisement of our peace was   Isa 53:5
upon h.

call *upon h.* while he is near   Isa 55:6
he will have mercy *upon h.*   Isa 55:7
I will surely have mercy *upon*   Jer 31:20
h.
my net will I spread *upon h.*   Eze 12:13
righteousness of righteous be   Eze 18:20
upon h.; wickedness of
wicked be *upon h.*
gray hairs are here, there *upon*   Ho 7:9
h.
he shall leave his blood *upon h.*   Ho 12:14
h.
I will put my Spirit *upon h.*   M't 12:18
they spit *upon h.* and smote   M't 27:30
him
shut him up, and set a seal   Re 20:3
upon h.

WITH HIM

master saw that the Lord was   Ge 39:3
with h.
have given *with h.* Aholiab   Ex 31:6
     38:23
with h. will I speak mouth to   Nu 12:8;
mouth   Jer 32:4
Lord his God is *with h.* and   Nu 23:21
the shout
with h. with us, *with h.* not   De 29:15
here today
there was no strange god *with*   De 32:12
h.
Lord was *with h.*   1Sa 3:19;
18:12, 14; 2Sa 5:10; 2Ki 18:7; 1Ch 9:20;
     11:9; 2Ch 1:1; 15:9; Ac 7:9; 10:38
the Lord is *with h.*   1Sa 16:18
folly is *with h.*   1Sa 25:25
his will I be, *with h.* will I   2Sa 16:18
abide
all Israel *with h.*   1Ki 8:65; 2Ch 7:8
the word of Lord is *with h.*   2Ki 3:12
that his hand might be *with*   2Ki 15:19
h.
Lord with you, while ye be   2Ch 15:2
with h.
with h. fourscore priests of   2Ch 26:17
the Lord
there be more with us than   2Ch 32:7
with h.
with h. is an arm of flesh,   2Ch 32:8
with us the
Lord his God be *with h.*   2Ch 36:23;
     Ezr 1:3
with h. 150 males   Ezr 8:3; 8:4-12
with h. is wisdom and   Job 12:13;
strength   12:16
his candle shall be put out   Job 18:6
with h.
acquaint thyself *with h.* and   Job 22:21
be at peace
My mercy shall be *with h.*   Ps 89:24
I will be *with h.* in trouble   Ps 91:15
with h. is plenteous   Ps 130:7
redemption
was I as one brought up *with h.*   Pr 8:30
that shall abide *with h.* of his   Ec 8:15
labour
say to righteous, shall be well   Isa 3:10
with h.
unto wicked, it shall be ill *with*   Isa 3:11
h.
His reward is *with h.*   Isa 40:10; 62:11
with h. that is of contrite   Isa 57:15
spirit
then it was well *with h.*   Jer 22:15; 22:16
mighty one, he shall deal   Eze 31:11
with h.
My covenant was *with h.* of   Mal 2:5
life
agree while in the way *with h.*   M't 5:25
ordained twelve to be *with h.*   M'k 3:14
prayed he might be *with h.*   M'k 5:18;
     Lu 8:38
hand of Lord was *with h.*   Lu 1:66
This man was also *with h.*   Lu 22:56
do miracles, except God be   Joh 3:2
with h.
we will come make our   Joh 14:23
abode *with h.*
that feareth him is accepted   Ac 10:35
with h.
multitude crying, Away *with*   Joh 21:36
h.
buried *with h.* by baptism   Ro 6:4;
     Col 2:12
live *with h.*   Ro 6:8;
     2Co 13:4; 1Th 5:10; 2Ti 2:11
shall he not *with h.* give us all   Ro 8:32
things

sleep in Jesus, will God bring *1Th 4:14*
with h.
we shall reign *with* h.   *2Ti 2:12;*
               Re 20:6
heirs *with* h. of same promise *Heb 11:9*
when we were *with* h. in holy *2Pe 1:18*
mount
I will sup *with* h. and he with *Re 3:20*
me
with h. 144,000 having Father's *Re 14:1*
name
they *with* h. are called chosen *Re 17:14*

WITHIN HIM

his soul *within* h. shall   *Job 14:22*
mourn
his meat is gall of asps   *Job 20:14*
within h.
layeth up deceit *within* h.   *Pr 26:24*
put his holy spirit *within* h.   *Isa 63:11*
formeth the spirit of man   *Zec 12:1*
within h.

WITHOUT HIM

without h. was not any thing   *Joh 1:3*
made

HIMSELF

they set on for him by h. and *Ge 43:32*
for them
if came by h. he shall go out by *Ex 21:3*
h.
himself (R)   *Ex 30:12;*
32:2; Ps 24:4; 25:13; 89:48; Pr 6:30;
18:7; 22:5; Ec 2:24; Isa 44:20
himself (R)   *Ex 30:12;*
Job 14:22; Ps 25:13; 49:18; Pr 18:7;
               Isa 53:10
sin offering for h.   *Le 9:8; 16:6, 11*
shall number to h. seven days *Le 15:13*
for his
make an atonement for h.   *Le 16:11;*
              16:17, 24
separated you to bring you   *Nu 16:9*
near to h.
men of war took spoil, every *Nu 31:53*
man for h.
chosen thee to be a people to h. *De 7:6;*
    14:2; 28:9; 29:13; 2Sa 7:23
he provided first part for h.   *De 33:21*
let the Lord h. require it   *Jos 22:23*
he h. turned again from the   *J'g 3:19*
quarries
David encouraged h. in the   *1Sa 30:6*
Lord
taken and reared up for h. a *2Sa 18:18*
pillar
Elijah h. requested for h. he   *1Ki 19:4*
might die
God h. is with us for our   *2Ch 13:12*
captain
thrust him out, h. hasted to *2Ch 26:20*
go out
h. separated from the   *Ezr 10:8*
congregation
only on h. put not forth hand *Job 1:12*
wise may be profitable to h.   *Job 22:2*
will he delight h. in the   *Job 27:10*
Almighty
because he justified h. rather *Job 32:2*
than God
he should delight h. with God *Job 34:9*
when raiseth h. the mighty   *Job 41:25*
are afraid
set apart him that is godly for h. *Ps 4:3*
the poor committeth h. unto *Ps 10:14*
thee
let his net he hath hid catch h. *Ps 35:8*
setteth h. in a way that is not *Ps 36:4*
good
for God is judge h.   *Ps 50:6*
the highest h. shall establish her *Ps 87:5*
on h. shall his crown flourish *Ps 132:18*
Lord hath chosen Jacob to h. *Ps 135:4*
own iniquities shall take wicked *Pr 5:22*
h.
he that watereth shall be   *Pr 11:25*
watered h.
maketh h. rich, that maketh h. *Pr 13:7*
poor
good man shall be justified   *Pr 14:14*
from h.
Lord hath made all things for   *Pr 16:4*
h.
he that laboureth, laboureth *Pr 16:26*
for h.

shall cry h. but shall not be   *Pr 21:13*
heard
foreseeth evil, and hideth h.   *Pr 22:3;*
              27:12
child left to h. bringeth to   *Pr 29:15*
shame
my beloved hath withdrawn h.   *Ca 5:6*
the Lord h. shall give you a   *Isa 7:14*
sign
hath spoken, and h. hath   *Isa 38:15*
done it
another call h. by the name of *Isa 44:5*
Jacob
departeth from evil, maketh *Isa 59:15*
h. a prey
to make h. an everlasting   *Isa 63:12*
name
the way of man is not in h.   *Jer 10:23*
mad man maketh h. a   *Jer 29:26*
prophet
Lord hath sworn by h.   *Jer 51:14;*
             Am 6:8
that day shall prince prepare *Eze 45:22*
for h.
Messiah shall be cut off not for *Da 9:26*
h.
he hath withdrawn h. from   *Ho 5:6*
them
Israel bringeth forth fruit to h. *Ho 10:1*
nor shall the mighty deliver h. *Am 2:14*
is swift of foot shall not   *Am 2:15*
deliver h.
Father h. shall reward   *M't 6:4*
thee openly
h. took our infirmities, bare *M't 8:17*
sickness
hath not root in h. dureth a *M't 13:21*
while
went up into a mountain by *M't 14:23*
h. (S)
h. he cannot save *M't 27:42; M'k 15:31*
they said, He is beside h.   *M'k 3:21*
let him deny h., take cross   *M'k 8:34;*
             Lu 9:23
to love his neighbor as h. is *M'k 12:33*
more than
sent them whither he h. would *Lu 10:1*
come
seven spirits more wicked   *Lu 11:26*
than h.
knew his lord's will, prepared *Lu 12:47*
not h.
when he came to h. he said, *Lu 15:17*
How
nobleman went to receive for *Lu 19:12*
h. a
that he h. is Christ, a king   *Lu 23:2*
who also h. waited for   *Lu 23:51*
kingdom of God
he expounded things   *Lu 24:27*
concerning h.
Jesus h. stood in the midst of *Lu 24:36*
them
Jesus h. baptized not, but   *Joh 4:2*
disciples
God was his Father, making   *Joh 5:18*
h. equal
the Son can do nothing of h. *Joh 5:19*
Father hath life in h. so the *Joh 5:26*
Son hath
he h. knew what he would do   *Joh 6:6*
Jesus knew in h. that his   *Joh 6:61*
disciples
he h. seeketh to be known   *Joh 7:4*
openly
speaketh of h. seeketh his own *Joh 7:18*
glory
he shall speak for h.   *Joh 9:21*
this spake he not of h. but   *Joh 11:51*
being high
God shall glorify him in h.   *Joh 13:32*
he shall speak of h., but   *Joh 16:13*
whatsoever
the Father h. loveth you,   *Joh 16:27*
because
whoso maketh h. king   *Joh 19:12*
speaketh
Jesus shewed h. again to   *Joh 21:1;*
disciples   *21:14*
of rest durst no man join h. to *Ac 5:13*
them
rose up boasting h. to be   *Ac 5:36*
somebody
giving out that h. was some   *Ac 8:9*
great one
whom speaketh the prophet   *Ac 8:34*
his? of h.

while Peter doubted in h.   *Ac 10:17*
what this
when Peter was come to h.   *Ac 12:11*
he said
He left not h. without witness *Ac 14:17*
while he answered for h.   *Ac 25:8;*
             26:1, 24
Paul was suffered to dwell by *Ac 28:16*
h.
the Spirit. h. (S)   *Ro 8:16; 8:26*
not think of h. more highly   *Ro 12:3*
than he
none liveth to h., nor dieth to *Ro 14:7*
h.
even Christ pleased not h.   *Ro 15:3*
yet h. is judged of no man   *1Co 2:15*
he h. shall be saved, yet so as *1Co 3:15*
by fire
let a man examine h. so let *1Co 11:28*
him eat
then shall Son h. be subject *1Co 15:28*
to him
who hath reconciled us to h. *2Co 5:18;*
             5:19
if any man trust h. let him of *2Co 10:7*
h. think
ye suffer if a man exalt h.   *2Co 11:20*
who gave h. for our sins, that *Ga 1:4*
loved me and gave h. for me *Ga 2:20*
if a man think h. to be   *Ga 6:3*
something
then shall he have rejoicing in *Ga 6:4*
h. alone
to make in h. of twain one   *Eph 2:15*
new man
Jesus h. being the chief corner *Eph 2:20*
stone
hath given h. for us   *Eph 5:2; 5:25*
might present it to h.   *Eph 5:27*
glorious church
love his wife, even as h. *Eph 5:33; 5:28*
by him to reconcile all things *Col 1:20*
to h.
sitteth, shewing h. that he is *2Th 2:4*
God
who gave h. a ransom for all *1Ti 2:6*
who gave h. for us, to purify to *Tit 2:14*
h.
he sinneth, being condemned *Tit 3:11*
of h.
when he had by h. purged our *Heb 1:3*
sins
he also h. likewise took part *Heb 2:14*
of same
in that he h. hath suffered, *Heb 2:18*
being
for that he h. also is   *Heb 5:2*
compassed with
so also for h. to offer for sins *Heb 5:3*
no man taketh this honour to *Heb 5:4*
h.
Christ glorified not h. to be *Heb 5:5*
made
He sware by h.   *Heb 6:13*
when he offered up h.   *Heb 7:27*
to put away sin by sacrifice of *Heb 9:26*
h.
committed h. to him that   *1Pe 2:23*
judgeth
ought h. to walk, even as he   *1Jo 2:6*
walked
hath this hope, purifieth h. as he *1Jo 3:3*
he that believeth hath witness *1Jo 5:10*
in h.
nor doth he h. receive the   *3Jo 10*
brethren
had name that no man knew *Re 19:12*
but h.
God h. shall be with them, and *Re 21:3*
be

HIN

with a fourth part of an h. of *Ex 29:40*
oil
with 2½ pints of oil (B)   *Ex 29:40*
take also of oil olive an h.   *Ex 30:24*
six quarts of olive oil (B)   *Ex 30:24*
a just ephah and h. shall ye *Le 19:36*
have
an honest gallon (B)   *Le 19:36*
a fourth part of an h.   *Le 23:13;*
            Nu 15:4; 28:14
three pints of oil (B)   *Le 23:13*
fourth part of a h. of wine   *Nu 15:5*
three pints of wine (B)   *Nu 15:5*
third part of an h. of oil   *Nu 15:6*
two quarts of oil (B)   *Nu 15:6*
half an h. of oil   *Nu 15:9*
three quarts of oil (B)   *Nu 15:9*

shalt drink sixth part of an *h.*   Eze 4:11
of water
two pints of water (B)   Eze 4:11
an *h.* of oil for an ephah   Eze 45:24;
  46:5, 7, 11
1½ gallons of oil to a   Eze 45:24
bushel (B)
third part of an *h.* of oil to   Eze 46:14
temper
half a gallon of oil (B)   Eze 46:14

HIND

Naphtali is a *h.* let loose   Ge 49:21
Naphtali is a deer (B)   Ge 49:21;
  2Sa 22:34
Let her be as the loving *h.*   Pr 5:19
the *h.* also calved in the field   Jer 14:5

HINDER (verb)

h. me not, seeing the Lord   Ge 24:56
hath
let nothing *h.* thee from   Nu 22:16
coming
to come and fight, and *h.*   Ne 4:8
building
he taketh away, who can *h.*   Job 9:12
him
if he cut off who can *h.* him   Job 11:10
who will *h.* it (S)   Isa 43:13
what doth *h.* me to be baptized   Ac 8:36
we should *h.* the gospel   1Co 9:12
did *h.* you that ye should not   Ga 5:7
obey
hindereth will continue to *h.*   2Th 2:7
(S)

HINDER (adjective)

the *h.* end of the spear smote   2Sa 2:23
him
all *h.* parts were inward   1Ki 7:25;
  2Ch 4:4
smote enemies in the *h.* parts   Ps 78:66
his *h.* part toward the utmost   Joe 2:20
sea
half of them toward the *h.* sea   Zec 14:8
he was in the *h.* part of the   M'k 4:38
ship
but the *h.* part was broken   Ac 27:41

HINDERED

these men, that they be not *h.*   Ezr 6:8
the waters were *h.* (S)   Pr 4:12
them that were entering in ye   Lu 11:52
h.
been much *h.* from coming to   Ro 15:22
you
once and again; but Satan *h.*   1Th 2:18
us
of life; that your prayers be not   1Pe 3:7
h.

HINDERETH

he that rules is persecuted,   Isa 14:6
none *h.*
h. will continue to hinder (S)   2Th 2:7

HINDERING

if eating is *h.* progress (A)   1Co 8:13

HINDERMOST

put Rachel and Joseph *h.*   Ge 33:2
the *h.* of the nations shall be   Jer 50:12

HINDMOST

shall go *h.* with their standards   Nu 2:31
smote the *h.* of thee, even all   De 25:18
enemies, and smote the *h.* of   Jos 10:19
them

HINDRANCE

Satan, you are a *h.* to me (R)   M't 16:23

HINDS

mark when the *h.* do calve   Job 39:1
the Lord maketh the *h.* to calve   Ps 29:9
h. of the field that ye stir not   Ca 2:7;
up   3:5

HINDS'

maketh my feet like *h.* feet   2Sa 22:34;
  Ps 18:33
he will make my feet like *h.*   Hab 3:19
feet

HINGES

the *h.* of gold, both for the   1Ki 7:50
As the door turneth upon its   Pr 26:14
h.

HINNOM

the valley of the son of H.   Jos 15:8;
  18:16; 2Ch 28:3; 33:6; Jer 7:31, 32; 19:2,
  6; 32:35
the valley of H.   Jos 15:8;
  18:16; Ne 11:30
the valley of the children of   2Ki 23:10
H.

HINT

a *h.* of the glories of heaven (P)   1Pe 1:8

HIP

he smote them *h.* and thigh   J'g 15:8
with a

HIPS

fastened on his *h.* (A)   2Sa 20:8
laid heavy burden on *h.* (B)   Ps 66:11
daughters carried on the *h.*   Isa 60:4
(B)

HIRAH

Adullamite whose name was   Ge 38:1;
H.   38:12

HIRAM

H. king of Tyre sent   2Sa 5:11;
messenger to David   1Ch 14:1
H. king of Tyre sent servants   1Ki 5:1;
  5:8
H. was ever a lover of David   1Ki 5:1
Solomon sent to H. saying   1Ki 5:2
H. heard the words of Solomon   1Ki 5:7
H. gave Solomon cedar trees   1Ki 5:10
Solomon gave H.   1Ki 5:11; 9:11
was peace between H. and   1Ki 5:12
Solomon
sent and fetched H. out of   1Ki 7:13
Tyre
H. make lavers, shovels   1Ki 7:40;
  7:45; 9:11
H. came from Tyre to see the   1Ki 9:12
cities
H. sent to the king sixscore   1Ki 9:14
H. sent in navy his servants   1Ki 9:27;
  10:11, 22

HIRAM'S

Solomon's builders and H.   1Ki 5:18
builders

HIRE

God hath given me my *h.*   Ge 30:18
such shall be my *h.*   Ge 30:32;
  30:33; 31:8
if an hired thing, it came for   Ex 22:15
his *h.*
shalt bring the *h.* of a whore   De 23:18
into
At his day thou shalt give him   De 24:15
his *h.*
to thee will I give *h.* to thy   1Ki 5:6
servants
to *h.* them chariots and   1Ch 19:6
horsemen
lurking in *h.* places (A)   Ps 17:12
clear me of *h.*, unconscious   Ps 19:12
faults (A)(E)(R)
is not *h.* from me (S)   Ps 38:9
keeps the matter *h.*   Pr 11:13
(A)(B)(R)
better than love that is *h.*   Pr 27:5
(A)(E)(R)
Tyre shall turn to her *h.*   Isa 23:17
her *h.* shall be holiness to the   Isa 23:18
Lord

the balance, and *h.* a goldsmith   Isa 46:6
uncovered his *h.* places   Jer 49:10
(A)(R)
an harlot, in that thou   Eze 16:31
scornest *h.*
thou also shall give no *h.* any   Eze 16:41
more
she gathered it of the *h.* of an   Mic 1:7
harlot
priests thereof teach for *h.*   Mic 3:11
no *h.* for man, nor any *h.* for   Zec 8:10
beast
h. since foundation of world   M't 13:35
(A)(B)(E)(P)(R)
h. labourers in his vineyard   M't 20:1;
  20:8
nothing *h.* but shall be   Lu 8:17
disclosed (B)(N)(P)
the labourer is worthy of his   Lu 10:7
h.
wisdom of God once *h.*   1Co 2:7
(A)(N)(R)
renounced *h.* ways of shame   2Co 4:2
(E)(N)
great truth *h.* here (N)   Eph 5:32
make known the *h.* purpose   Eph 6:19
(N)
the *h.* principle of lawlessness   2Th 2:7
(B)
the *h.* truth of faith (B)(N)   1Ti 3:9
h. truth of godliness (A)(B)   1Ti 3:16
laborer worthy of his *h.*   1Ti 5:18
(A)(E)(P)
h. of labourers who have reaped   Jas 5:4
loved *h.* of wrongdoing   2Pe 2:15
(E)(R)
h. reefs in your feasts (A)(E)   Jude 12
h. meaning of seven stars   Re 1:20
(A)(N)(P)
h. purpose of God (N)   Re 10:7

HIRED

I have *h.* thee with my son's   Ge 30:16
mandrakes
an *h.* servant shall not eat   Ex 12:45
thereof
be an *h.* thing, it came for his   Ex 22:15
hire
wages of him that is *h.* shall   Le 99:13
not abide
h. servant shall not eat of holy   Le 22:10
thing
thy *h.* servant and for the   Le 25:6
stranger
as an *h.* servant and as a   Le 25:40
sojourner
to the time of an *h.* servant   Le 25:50;
  25:53
worth a double *h.* servant to   De 15:18
thee
h. against thee Balaam   De 23:4
not oppress an *h.* servant that   De 24:14
is poor
Abimelech *h.* vain persons   J'g 9:4
Micah hath *h.* me, I am his   J'g 18:4
priest
have *h.* themselves out for   1Sa 2:5
bread
Ammon sent and *h.* the   2Sa 10:6
Syrians
Israel hath *h.* against us the   2Ki 7:6
kings
So they *h.* thirty two thousand   1Ch 19:7
h. masons and carpenters to   2Ch 24:12
repair
He *h.* an hundred thousand   2Ch 25:6
mighty
h. counsellors against them   Ezr 4:5
Tobiah and Sanballat had *h.*   Ne 6:12;
him   6:13
but *h.* Balaam against them,   Ne 13:2
that he
Lord shave with a razor that is   Isa 7:20
h.
her *h.* men are in the midst of   Jer 46:21
her
Ephraim hath *h.* lovers   Ho 8:9; 8:10
because no man hath *h.* us   M't 20:7;
  20:9
the ship with the *h.* servants   M'k 1:20
h. himself out to (P)   Lu 15:15
many *h.* servants of my   Lu 15:17
father's
make me as one of thy *h.*   Lu 15:19
servants
two whole years in his own *h.*   Ac 28:30
house

HIRELING

his days as the days of an *h.*   *Job 7:1*
like those of a hired man (B)   *Job 7:1;*
  14:6; Isa 16:14; Joh 10:12
as an *h.* looketh for reward of   *Job 7:2*
work
like a laborer who longs for   *Job 7:2*
wages (B)
shall accomplish, as an *h.,* his   *Job 14:6*
day
in three years as years of an   *Isa 16:14;*
h.   *21:16*
that oppress the *h.* in his wages *Mal 3:5*
the wage earner (B)   *Mal 3:5*
is an *h.* and not the shepherd *Joh 10:12*
the *h.* fleeth, because he is an *Joh 10:13*
h.

HIRES

all the *h.* thereof shall be   *Mic 1:7*
burned

HIREST

gifts to lovers and *h.* them   *Eze 16:33*
bribing them to come to you *Eze 16:33*
(B)(E)(R)

HIS

Onan knew the seed should not *Ge 38:9*
be *h.*
the dead beast shall be *h.*   *Ex 21:34*
which another challengeth to   *Ex 22:9*
be *h.*
add the fifth part and it shall *Le 27:15*
be *h.*
a man's hallowed things shall *Nu 5:10*
be *h.*
to morrow Lord will shew who *Nu 16:5*
is *h.*
let my last end be like *h.*   *Nu 23:10*
the right of the firstborn is *h.* *De 21:17*
h. will I be, with him will I *2Sa 16:18*
abide
for it was *h.* from the Lord *1Ki 2:15*
captain of *h.* conspired *2Ki 15:25*
against him
is one law of *h.* to be put to *Es 4:11*
death
the deceived and the deceiver *Job 12:16*
are *h.*
in *h.* tabernacle, because *Job 18:15*
none of it *h.*
sing unto the Lord, all saints of *Ps 30:4*
h.
the strength of the hills is *h.* *Ps 95:4*
also
ye ministers of *h.* that do *h.* *Ps 103:21*
pleasure
my beloved is mine, and I am *Ca 2:16*
h.
on every one passeth by, *h.* it *Eze 16:15*
was
it shall be *h.* to the year of *Eze 46:17*
liberty
blessed be God, wisdom, might *Da 2:20*
are *h.*
cut off those of *h.* that did *Ob 14*
escape, deliver up those of
h. that remain
increaseth that which is not *h.* *Hab 2:6*
My doctrine is not mine, but *Joh 7:16*
h.
baptized, he and all *h.*   *Ac 16:33*
straightway
if any man have not the Spirit *Ro 8:9*
of Christ, he is none of *h.*
Lord knoweth them that are *h.* *2Ti 2:19*
ceased from works, as God *Heb 4:10*
did from *h.*

HISS

at this house every one shall *h.* *1Ki 9:8*
every one passing by shall *1Ki 9:8*
whistle (B)
men shall *h.* him out of his *Job 27:23*
place
he will *h.* to them from end of *Isa 5:26*
earth
whistles for them from ends of *Isa 5:26*
(B)(R)
Lord shall *h.* for the fly in *Isa 7:18*
Egypt
whistle for the fly in Egypt *Isa 7:18*
(A)(B)(R)
passeth by shall *h.*   *Jer 19:8;*
  49:17; 50:13

---

they *h.* at the daughter of   *La 2:15*
Jerusalem
thy enemies *h.* and gnash teeth *La 2:16*
the merchants shall *h.* at thee *Eze 27:36*
every one that passeth by her *Zep 2:15*
shall *h.*
I will *h.* for them and gather *Zec 10:8*
them
I will whistle for them (B) *Zec 10:8*
I will signal for them (R) *Zec 10:8*

HISSING

delivered them to *h.*   *2Ch 29:8*
to make their land a   *Jer 18:16*
perpetual *h.*
will make this city desolate *Jer 19:8*
and an *h.*
I will make them an *h.*   *Jer 25:9;*
  25:18; 29:18
Babylon be an *h.* without *Jer 51:37*
inhabitant
make inhabitants thereof an *Mic 6:16*
h.
the inhabitants to scorn (B) *Mic 6:16*

HISTORY

h. of Jacob's family (R)   *Ge 37:2*
all human *h.* shall be   *Eph 1:10*
consummated in Christ (P)

HIT

hit (B)   *Nu 22:23;*
  1Sa 17:49; 19:10; 2Ch 18:33
the archers *h.* Saul   *1Sa 31:3; 1Ch 10:3*

HITHER

they shall come *h.* again   *Ge 15:16*
except your youngest brother *Ge 42:15*
come *h.*
be not angry that ye sold me   *Ge 45:5;*
h.   *45:8*
haste and bring down thy   *Ge 45:13*
father *h.*
draw not nigh *h.* put off thy   *Ex 3:5*
shoes
there came men in *h.* tonight *Jos 2:2*
come *h.* and hear the word of *Jos 3:9*
bring the description *h.* to me *Jos 18:6*
Samson is come *h.*   *J'g 16:2*
who brought thee *h.*   *J'g 18:3*
we will not turn aside *h.* into *J'g 19:12*
city
At mealtime come thou *h.* *Ru 2:14*
Bring *h.* a burnt offering to me *1Sa 13:9*
Bring *h.* the ark of God *1Sa 14:18*
Bring me *h.* every man his ox *1Sa 14:34*
Let us draw near *h.* unto *1Sa 14:36*
God
bring *h.* Agag the king of *1Sa 15:32*
Amalekites
Why camest thou down *h.* *1Sa 17:28*
Abiathar, bring *h.* the ephod   *1Sa 23:9;*
  30:7
I have brought *h.* unto my *2Sa 1:10*
lord
Hasten *h.* Micaiah the son of *1Ki 22:9*
Imlah
Jordan divided *h.* and thither   *2Ki 2:8;*
  2:14
shall not bring in captives *h.* *2Ch 28:13*
king of Assur, which brought *Ezr 4:2*
us up *h.*
therefore his people return *h.* *Ps 73:10*
take a psalm, bring *h.* the *Ps 81:2*
timbrel
whoso is simple, turn in *h.* *Pr 9:4; 9:16*
it be said unto thee, Come up *Pr 25:7*
h.
draw near *h.* ye sons of *Isa 57:3*
sorceress
bring them *h.* to me   *M't 14:18;*
  17:17; Lu 9:41
friend, how camest thou in *h. M't 22:12*
bring in *h.* the poor and *Lu 14:21*
maimed
bring *h.* the fatted calf and kill *Lu 15:23*
bring *h.* and slay them before *Lu 19:27*
me
colt tied, loose him, bring him *Lu 19:30*
h.
Rabbi, when camest thou *h.* *Joh 6:25*
reach *h.* finger, reach *h.* hand *Joh 20:27*
came *h.* for that intent, that he *Ac 9:21*
call *h.* Simon, whose surname *Ac 10:32*
is Peter

---

have brought *h.* these men, *Ac 19:37*
which are
Come up *h.,* and I will shew *Re 4:1;*
thee   *11:12; 17:1; 21:9*

HITHERTO

h. thou wouldst not hear *Ex 7:16*
the Lord hath blessed me *h.* *Jos 17:14*
h. thou hast mocked me *J'g 16:13*
out of my grief have I spoken *1Sa 1:16*
h.
h. hath the Lord helped us *1Sa 7:12*
thou hast brought me *h.*   *2Sa 7:18;*
  1Ch 17:16
I have been thy father's *2Sa 15:34*
servant *h.*
who *h.* waited in the king's *1Ch 9:18*
gate
h. the greatest part kept the *1Ch 12:29*
ward
H. shalt thou come, but no *Job 38:11*
further
h. have I declared thy *Ps 71:17*
wondrous works
a people terrible *h.*   *Isa 18:2; 18:7*
H. is the end of the matter *Da 7:28*
my Father worketh *h.* and I *Joh 5:17*
work
H. have asked nothing in my *Joh 16:24*
name
purposed to come, but was let *Ro 1:13*
h.
h. ye were not able to bear it *1Co 3:2*

HITTITE

Ephron the *H.*   *Ge 23:10;*
  49:29, 30; 50:13
Ephron the son of Zohar the *Ge 25:9*
H.
Judith the daughter of Beeri *Ge 26:34*
the *H.*
daughter of Elon the *H. Ge 26:34; 36:2*
drive out the *H.*   *Ex 23:28; 33:2; 34:11*
the *H.* and Amorite gathered *Jos 9:1;*
  11:3
David said to Ahimelech the *1Sa 26:6*
H.
Uriah the *H.*   *2Sa 11:3;*
  11:6, 17, 21, 24; 12:9, 10; 1Ch 11:41
thou hast killed Uriah the *H.* *2Sa 12:9*
with
taken the wife of Uriah the *2Sa 12:10*
H.
Uriah the *H.:* thirty seven in *2Sa 23:39*
all
only in the matter of Uriah *1Ki 15:5*
the *H.*
thy mother an *H.*   *Eze 16:3; 16:45*

HITTITES

the land of the *H.*   *Ge 15:20;*
Ex 3:8, 17; 13:5; Jos 1:4; J'g 1:26;
  Ne 9:8
unto the Amorites and the *H. Ge 23:23*
the *H.* and the Jebusites *Nu 13:29*
destroy the *H.*   *De 7:1;*
  20:17; Jos 3:10; 12:8
the Canaanites and the *H. Jos 24:11*
dwelt among the Canaanites, *H. J'g 3:5*
that were left of the *H.*   *1Ki 9:20;*
  2Ch 8:7
so for all the kings of the *H.* *1Ki 10:29;*
  2Ch 1:17
Edomites, Zidonians, and *1Ki 11:1*
hired against us the kings of *2Ki 7:6*
the *H.*
even to the Canaanites, the *H.* *Ezr 9:1*

HIVITE

And the *H.,* and the Arkite *Ge 10:17;*
  1Ch 1:15
Shechem the son of Hamor the *Ge 34:2*
H.
Anah the daughter of Zibeon *Ge 36:2*
the *H.*
which shall drive out the *H.* *Ex 23:28*
Perizzite, the *H. Ex 33:2; 34:11; Jos 9:1*
to the *H.* under Hermon in the *Jos 11:3*

HIVITES

the *H.,* the Jebusites   *Ex 3:8;*
3:17; 13:5; De 7:1; 20:17; 1Ki 9:20;
  2Ch 8:7
the Canaanites, the *H.,* and *Ex 23:23*
the

H., and the Perizzites | *Jos 3:10; 12:8*
men of Israel said unto the *H.* | *Jos 9:7*
save the *H.*, the inhabitants | *Jos 11:19*
the Girgashites, the *H.* | *Jos 24:11*
H. that dwelt in mount Lebanon | *J'g 3:3*
to all the cities of the *H.* | *2Sa 24:7*

HIZKIAH

the son of *H.*, in the days of | *Zep 1:1*

HIZKIJAH

Ater, *H.*, Azzur, Hodijah, Bani | *Ne 10:17*

HO

unto whom he said, *H.*, such a one | *Ru 4:1*
H., every one that thirsteth | *Isa 55:1*
H., *h.*, come forth, and flee | *Zec 2:6*

HOAR

small as the *h.* on ground | *Ex 16:14*
let not his *h.* head go down | *1Ki 2:6; 2:9*
even the *h.* hairs will I carry | *Isa 46:4*

HOARFROST

he scattereth the *h.* like ashes | *Ps 147:16*

HOARY

shalt rise up *h.* head | *Le 19:32*
the *h.* frost of heaven | *Job 38:29*
one would think the deep to be *h.* | *Job 41:32*
The *h.* head is a crown of glory | *Pr 16:31*

HOBAB

Moses said unto *H.*, the son | *Nu 10:29*
the children of *H.* | *J'g 4:11*

HOBAH

pursued them to *H.* | *Ge 14:15*

HOCK

shalt *h.* their horses (A)(E) | *Jos 11:6*

HOCKED

h. their horses (E) | *Jos 11:9; 2Sa 8:4*

HOCUS-POCUS

no *h.*, no clever tricks (P) | *2Co 4:2*

HOD

Bezer, and *H.*, and Shamma | *1Ch 7:37*

HODAIAH

sons of Elioenai were *H.*, and | *1Ch 3:24*

HODAVIAH

Jeremiah, and *H.* | *1Ch 5:24*
the son of *H.*, the son of | *1Ch 9:7*
the children of *H.*, seventy four | *Ezr 2:40*

HODESH

begat of *H.* his wife | *1Ch 8:9*

HODEVAH

the children of *H.* seventy four | *Ne 7:43*

HODIAH

the sons of his wife, *H.* | *1Ch 4:19*

HODIJAH

Shabbethai, *H.*, Maaseiah | *Ne 8:7*
Sherebiah, *H.*, Shebaniah | *Ne 9:5; 10:10*
H., Bani, Beninu, *H.*, Hashum | *Ne 10:18; 10:13*

HOE

tilled with a *h.* (B) | *Isa 7:25*

HOED

which used to be *h.* (R)(S) | *Isa 7:25*

HOGLAH

were Mahlah, Noah, *H.* | *Nu 26:33; 27:1; 36:11; Jos 17:3*

HOHAM

sent unto *H.* king of Hebron | *Jos 10:3*

HOISTED

we *h.* the sail (S) | *Ac 27:17*
h. up the mainsail to the wind | *Ac 27:40*

HOLD

laid *h.* upon his hand | *Ge 19:16*
lift up the lad, *h.* him in hand | *Ge 21:18*
that they may *h.* a feast to me | *Ex 5:1; 10:9*
refuse to let them go, wilt *h.* them | *Ex 9:2*
Lord will not *h.* him guiltless | *Ex 20:7; De 5:11*
they entered into a *h.* of the god | *J'g 9:46*
they put them in the *h.*, set *h.* on fire | *J'g 9:49*
bring the veil, and *h.* it | *Ru 3:15*
David in the *h.* | *1Sa 22:4; 24:22; 2Sa 5:17; 23:14*
abide not in the *h.* depart | *1Sa 22:5*
how should I *h.* up my face to Joab | *2Sa 2:22*
Uzzah took *h.* of ark | *2Sa 6:6; 1Ch 13:9*
now therefore *h.* him not guiltless | *1Ki 2:9*
came of Judah to the *h.* to David | *1Ch 12:16*
no power to *h.* his kingdom (S) | *2Ch 22:9*
king shall *h.* out the golden sceptre | *Es 4:11*
do you still *h.* fast (A)(B)(E)(R) | *Job 2:9*
teach me, I will *h.* my tongue | *Job 6:24*
thou wilt not *h.* me innocent | *Job 9:28*
if I *h.* my tongue, I shall give up ghost | *Job 13:19*
righteous shall *h.* on his way | *Job 17:9*
I *h.* in derision (A) | *Job 30:1*
spear, dart, habergeon cannot *h.* | *Job 41:26*
h. up my goings in the paths | *Ps 17:5*
horror hath taken *h.* upon me | *Ps 119:53*
h. me up, and I shall be safe | *Ps 119:117*
thy right hand shall *h.* me | *Ps 139:10*
h. fast my words (A)(B)(R) | *Pr 4:4*
her hands *h.* the distaff | *Pr 31:19*
they all *h.* swords, being expert in war | *Ca 3:8*
I the Lord will *h.* thy right hand | *Isa 41:13*
I will *h.* thine hand, and keep thee | *Isa 42:6*
hewed broken cisterns, can *h.* no water | *Jer 2:13*
astonishment hath taken *h.* on me | *Jer 8:21*
they shall *h.* the bow and lance | *Jer 50:42*
anguish took *h.* of him, pangs | *Jer 50:43*
make it strong to the *h.* | *Eze 30:21*
might have *h.*, had not *h.* in sword | *Eze 41:6*
then shall he say, *H.* thy tongue | *Am 6:10*
slay them, *h.* themselves not guilty | *Zec 11:5*
else he will *h.* to the one | *M't 6:24; Lu 16:13*
gates of hell not *h.* out (B) | *M't 16:18*
for all *h.* John as a prophet | *M't 21:26*
other things have received to *h.* | *M'k 7:4*
h. the tradition of men, as washing | *M'k 7:8*
put them in *h.* unto next day | *Ac 4:3*
who *h.* the truth in unrighteousness | *Ro 1:18*
receive him, *h.* such in reputation | *Ph'p 2:29*
h. lovingly in highest regard (B)(P) | *1Th 5:13*
h. traditions ye have been taught | *2Th 2:15*

if we *h.* beginning of confidence | *Heb 3:14*
them that *h.* the doctrine of Balaam | *Re 2:14*
them that *h.* doctrine of Nicolaitans | *Re 2:15*
become the *h.* of every foul spirit | *Re 18:2*

HOLD *FAST*

he shall *h. fast*, but shall not endure | *Job 8:15*
my righteousness I *h. fast* | *Job 27:6*
they *h. fast* deceit, refuse to return | *Jer 8:5*
prove all things, *h. fast* that is good | *1Th 5:21*
h. fast the form of sound words | *2Ti 1:13*
if we *h. fast* the confidence and | *Heb 3:6*
let us *h. fast* our profession | *Heb 4:14; 10:23*
h. fast till I come | *Re 2:25*
h. fast and repent | *Re 3:3*
h. fast that which thou hast | *Re 3:11*

HOLD *PEACE*

h. your *peace* | *Ex 14:14; 2Ki 2:3, 5; Ne 8:11; Job 13:5, 13*
h. his *peace* | *Nu 30:4; 30:14; 1Co 14:30*
h. thy *peace* | *J'g 18:19; 2Sa 13:20; Job 33:31, 33; Isa 64:12; Zep 1:7; M'k 1:25*
h. our *peace* | *2Ki 7:9*
h. their *peace* | *Job 11:3; Isa 62:6; M't 20:31; M'k 10:48; Lu 18:39; 19:40; Ac 12:17*
h. not thy *peace* | *Ps 83:1; 109:1*
not *h.* my *peace* | *Isa 62:1; Jer 4:19; Ac 18:9*

HOLDEN

not *h.* such a passover | *2Ki 23:22; 23:23*
if they be *h.* in cords of affliction | *Job 36:8*
held in cords of affliction (A) | *Job 36:8*
caught in cords of affliction (B)(R) | *Job 36:8*
taken in the cords of affliction (E) | *Job 36:8*
thy right hand hath *h.* me up | *Ps 18:35*
right hand has held me up (A) | *Ps 18:35*
right hand sustains me (B) | *Ps 18:35*
right hand supported me (R) | *Ps 18:35*
by thee have I been *h.* up from the | *Ps 71:6*
took me from mother's womb (A)(B)(R) | *Ps 71:6*
hast *h.* me up by my right hand | *Ps 73:23*
dost hold my right hand (A)(B)(R) | *Ps 73:23*
shall be *h.* with cords of sins | *Pr 5:22*
held with the cords of sins (A)(B) | *Pr 5:22*
caught in the cords of sin (R) | *Pr 5:22*
I have long *h.* my peace and | *Isa 42:14*
long time held my peace (A) | *Isa 42:14*
I was silent, restraining myself (B)(E) | *Isa 42:14*
long time I have held my peace (R) | *Isa 42:14*
whose right hand have I *h.* to subdue | *Isa 45:1*
right hand I have held (A) | *Isa 45:1*
right hand I hold fast (B) | *Isa 45:1*
right hand I have grasped (R) | *Isa 45:1*
eyes were *h.* they should not know him | *Lu 24:16*
their eyes were held (A)(N) | *Lu 24:16*
eyes were kept from recognizing (B)(R) | *Lu 24:16*
something prevented recognizing (P) | *Lu 24:16*
it was not possible he should be *h.* of | *Ac 2:24*
not possible to be controlled or retained by it (A) | *Ac 2:24*
could not be held in its grip (B) | *Ac 2:24*
not be that death keep him in grip (P) | *Ac 2:24*
not allow pains of death to touch (P) | *Ac 2:24*
not possible to be held by it (R) | *Ac 2:24*

he should be *h.* up, for God is　*Ro 14:4*
able to
he shall stand and be upheld　*Ro 14:4*
(A)(R)
Lord enable him to stand　*Ro 14:4*
(B)(E)(N)

HOLDEST

if thou *h.* thy peace this time　*Es 4:14*
if you keep still (B)　*Es 4:14*
if you keep silence at such a　*Es 4:14*
time (R)
wherefore *h.* me for an　*Job 13:24*
enemy
alienate me as your enemy　*Job 13:14*
(A)
consider me thy enemy (B)　*Job 13:24*
count me as an enemy (R)　*Job 13:24*
Thou *h.* my eyes waking, I am　*Ps 77:4*
troubled
thou that *h.* the height of the　*Jer 49:16*
hill
h. thy tongue when the　*Hab 1:13*
wicked
dost keep silent (A)(B)　*Hab 1:13*
thou *h.* my name, hast not　*Re 2:13*
denied
holding my name (A)(B)(N)　*Re 2:13*
hold fast to My name (P)(R)　*Re 2:13*

HOLDETH

still he *h.* his integrity　*Job 2:3*
He *h.* back the face of his　*Job 26:9*
throne
He withdraws His throne (A)　*Job 26:9*
He encloseth the face of His　*Job 26:9*
throne (E)
bless God who *h.* our soul in life *Ps 66:9*
keeps us among the living　*Ps 66:9*
(A)(R)
man of understanding *h.* his　*Pr 11:12*
peace
man of understanding keeps　*Pr 11:12*
quiet (A)
man of understanding will hold *Pr 11:12*
peace (B)
man of understanding remains　*Pr 11:12*
silent (R)
fool when he *h.* peace is　*Pr 17:28*
counted wise
fool when he is silent is wise　*Pr 17:28*
(B)(R)
none *h.* with me but Michael　*Da 10:21*
none is joining force with me　*Da 10:21*
but (B)
none contends by my side but　*Da 10:21*
(R)
cut off him that *h.* the sceptre *Am 1:5;*
　　　　　　　　　　　　　1:8
cut off the holder of the sceptre *Am 1:5*
(B)
that *h.* seven stars in right hand *Re 2:1*
who holds seven stars　*Re 2:1*
(A)(B)(N)(P)(R)

HOLDING

shaketh hands from *h.* of　*Isa 33:15*
bribes
free from taking bribes (A)　*Isa 33:15*
shakes his hands, refusing　*Isa 33:15*
bribes (B)(R)
shaketh his hands from　*Isa 33:15*
taking bribes (E)
I am weary with *h.* in, I will　*Jer 6:11*
pour fury
I am weary of restraining it　*Jer 6:11*
(A)
eat not, *h.* tradition of the　*M'k 7:3*
elders
adhering to traditions of elders *M'k 7:3*
(A)
observe the tradition of elders　*M'k 7:3*
(B)
obedience to established　*M'k 7:3*
tradition (N)
following a traditional rule　*M'k 7:3*
(P)
observing tradition of the　*M'k 7:3*
elders (R)
not *h.* misdeeds against (N)　*2Co 5:19*
h. forth the word of life　*Ph'p 2:16*
so attached to the word of　*Ph'p 2:16*
life (A)
hold in hands the very word　*Ph'p 2:16*
of life (P)
not *h.* the head, from which　*Col 2:19*
the body

h. faith and a good conscience *1Ti 1:19*
Keeping fast hold on faith　*1Ti 1:19*
(A)
possessed of faith (B)　*1Ti 1:19*
armed with faith (N)(P)　*1Ti 1:19*
h. mystery of faith in pure　*1Ti 3:9*
conscience
possess the mystic secret of　*1Ti 3:9*
faith (A)
keeping hold on hidden truth　*1Ti 3:9*
(B)
with a firm hold on deep truths *1Ti 3:9*
(N)
hold the mystery of the faith　*1Ti 3:9*
(P)(R)
h. fast faithful word, as been　*Tit 1:9*
taught
hold fast to sure and　*Tit 1:9*
trustworthy word (A)
hold to the trustworthy message *Tit 1:9*
(B)
adhere to the true doctrine (P)　*Tit 1:9*
hold firm to the true word (R)　*Tit 1:9*
four angels *h.* the four winds of *Re 7:1*
earth
restraining the four winds (B)　*Re 7:1*

HOLDS

whether in tents, or strong *h.*　*Nu 13:19;*
　　　　　　　　　　　　　J'g 6:2
abode in wilderness in　*1Sa 23:14;*
strong *h.*　　　　　　　　*23:19, 29*
their strong *h.* wilt thou set on *2Ki 8:12*
fire
he fortified the strong *h.*　*2Ch 11:11;*
　　　　　　　　　　　　　Na 3:14
hast brought his strong *h.* to　*Ps 89:40*
ruin
every one who *h.* her fast　*Pr 3:18*
(A)(B)(R)
to destroy the strong *h.*　*Isa 23:11;*
　Jer 48:18, 41; La 2:5; Mic 5:11
they have remained in their *h.* *Isa 51:30*
they brought them into strong　*Eze 19:9*
h.
devises against the strong *h.*　*Da 11:24;*
　　　　　　　　　　　　　11:39
All thy strong *h.* shall be like　*Na 3:12*
fig
to the pulling down of strong　*2Co 10:4*
h.

HOLE

shall be an *h.* in the top of it　*Ex 28:32;*
　　　　　　　　　　　　　39:23
Jehoiada bored a *h.* in the lid *2Ki 12:9*
of it
fallen into the *h.* he made　*Ps 7:15*
(A)(B)(R)
put his hand by the *h.* of the　*Ca 5:4*
door
shall play on the *h.* of an asp　*Isa 11:8*
h. of pit whence ye are digged　*Isa 51:1*
hide it in a *h.* of the rock　*Jer 13:4*
behold a *h.* in the wall　*Eze 8:7*

HOLES

Hebrews came forth out of　*1Sa 14:11*
the *h.*
shall go into *h.* of the rocks　*Isa 2:19;*
　　　　　　　　　　　　　7:19
the *h.* in the rocks (S)　*Isa 2:19*
they are all of them snared in　*Isa 42:22*
h.
hunt them out of the *h.* of the *Jer 16:16*
rocks
they shall not move out of　*Mic 7:17*
their *h.*
the lion filled his *h.* with prey *Nah 2:12*
wages to put it in a bag with *h.* *Hag 1:6*
eyes shall consume in their *h.* *Zec 14:12*
foxes have *h.*　*M't 8:20; Lu 9:58*

HOLE'S

nest in sides of the *h.* mouth　*Jer 48:28*

HOLIER

come not near, for I am *h.*　*Isa 65:5*
than thou
Keep yourself, do not come　*Isa 65:5*
near (A)
Keep your distance, come not　*Isa 65:5*
near (B)
Stand by thyself, come not　*Isa 65:5*
near (R)

HOLIES

the holy of *h.* (A)　*1Ki 6:5;*
6:15, 19, 20, 21, 22, 31; 7:49; 8:6, 8;
　　　　　　　　　　　　　2Ch 5:9
the Holy of *H.* (B)　*2Ch 5:7*
into the Holy of *H.* (B)　*Heb 6:19*
Holy of *H.* (A)(P)(R)　*Heb 9:3;*
　　　　　　　　　　　　　9:8; 10:19

HOLIEST

tabernacle which is called the　*Heb 9:3*
H. of all
Holy of Holies (A)(P)(R)　*Heb 9:3;*
　　　　　　　　　　　　　9:8; 10:19
the Most Holy Place (N)　*Heb 9:3*
way into the *h.* was not yet　*Heb 9:8*
made
the holy place (E)　*Heb 9:8; 10:19*
to enter into *h.* by the blood　*Heb 10:19*
of Jesus
the sanctuary (N)(R)　*Heb 10:19; 10:19*

HOLILY

how *h.* and justly and　*1Th 2:10*
unblameably
how unworldly, upright,　*1Th 2:10*
blameless (A)
how pure, fair, irreproachable *1Th 2:10*
(B)
how devout, just, blameless　*1Th 2:10*
(N)
how honest, straightforward,　*1Th 2:10*
above criticism (P)
how holy, righteous,　*1Th 2:10*
blameless (R)

HOLINESS

who is like thee, glorious in *h.* *Ex 15:11*
h. to the Lord　*Ex 28:36;*
　39:30; Zec 14:20-21
worship in beauty of *h.*　*1Ch 16:29;*
　　　　　　　　Ps 29:2; 96:9
praise in the beauty of *h.*　*1Ch 20:21*
sanctified themselves in *h.*　*1Ch 31:18*
in the matter of holy things　*1Ch 31:18*
(B)
keeping themselves holy (R)　*1Ch 31:18*
at remembrance of his *h.*　*Ps 30:4; 97:12*
remembrance of his holy name *Ps 30:4*
(A)
praise his sacred memory (B)　*Ps 30:4*
give thanks to his holy　*Ps 30:4*
memorial name (E)
give thanks to his holy name　*Ps 30:4*
(R)
God sitteth upon throne of his *Ps 47:8*
h.
sits upon his holy thorne　*Ps 47:8*
(A)(B)(E)(R)
praised in the mountain of his *Ps 48:1*
h.
in his holy mountain　*Ps 48:1*
(A)(B)(E)(R)
God hath spoken in his *h.*　*Ps 60:6;*
　　　　　　　　　　　　　108:7
once have I sworn by my *h.* I *Ps 89:35*
will
h. becometh thine house　*Ps 93:5*
people be willing in beauties　*Ps 110:3*
of *h.*
her hire shall be *h.* to the　*Isa 23:18*
Lord
shall be dedicated to the Lord *Isa 23:18*
(A)(R)
be set apart to the Lord (B)　*Isa 23:18*
shall be called the way of *h.*　*Isa 35:8*
called the Holy Way　*Isa 35:8*
(A)(B)(R)
drink in the courts of thy *h.*　*Isa 62:9*
the courts of my sanctuary　*Isa 62:9*
(B)(E)(R)
behold from the habitation of　*Isa 63:15*
thy *h.*
Thy holy and glorious abode　*Isa 63:15*
(B)(R)
people of thy *h.* have　*Isa 63:18*
possessed it
Your holy people possessed　*Isa 63:18*
(A)(B)(E)(R)
Israel was *h.* to the Lord　*Jer 2:3*
Israel was holy to the Lord　*Jer 2:3*
(B)(R)
because of words of his *h.*　*Jer 23:9*
Because of his holy words　*Jer 23:9*
(A)(B)(E)(R)

Lord bless thee, O mountain *Jer 31:23* of *h.*
O holy mountain (A)(B) *Jer 31:23*
O holy hill (R) *Jer 31:23*
manifest my *h.* (A)(R) *Eze 20:41*
Lord hath sworn by his *h.* *Am 4:2*
but upon mount Zion shall be *h.* *Ob 17*
it shall be holy (A)(E)(R) *Ob 17*
it shall be a sanctuary (B) *Ob 17*
Judah hath profaned *h.* of the *Mal 2:11* Lord
profaned the- holy sanctuary *Mal 2:11* (A)(R)
profaned the Lord's sanctuary *Mal 2:11* (B)
might serve him in *h.* *Lu 1:75*
as though by our *h.* made man *Ac 3:12* well
through our own piety *Ac 3:12* (A)(B)(P)(R)
through our own godliness *Ac 3:12* (E)(N)
among all made *h.* (B) *Ac 20:32*
power, according to Spirit of *h.* *Ro 1:4*
yield members servants of *Ro 6:19* righteousness to *h.*
righteousness to sanctification *Ro 6:19* (A)(E)(R)
of righteousness to holy living *Ro 6:19* (B)
making for a holy life (N) *Ro 6:19*
purpose of becoming really *Ro 6:19* good (P)
have your fruit unto *h.* and the *Ro 6:22* end
unto sanctification (E)(R) *Ro 6:22*
reap fruit of being made *Ro 6:22* righteous (P)
consecrated and made *h.* *Ro 15:16* (A)(B)(N)
those consecrated, made *h.* *1Co 1:2* (A)(B)(P)
made our *h.* (B) *1Co 1:30*
perfecting *h.* in fear of God *2Co 7:1*
bring consecration to *2Co 7:1* completeness (A)
complete our dedication (B) *2Co 7:1*
complete our consecration (N) *2Co 7:1*
consecrating to him completely *2Co 7:1* (P)
new man created in *Eph 4:24* righteousness and *h.*
stablish hearts unblameable in *1Th 3:13* *h.*
spotlessly holy before God *1Th 3:13* (B)
holy and faultless (N) *1Th 3:13*
holy and blameless in heart *1Th 3:13* (P)
not called to uncleanness, but *1Th 4:7* to *h.*
but to consecration, thorough *1Th 4:7* purity (A)
but to a holy life (B) *1Th 4:7*
but in sanctification (E) *1Th 4:7*
but to the most thorough *1Th 4:7* purity (P)
if they continue in faith and *h.* *1Ti 2:15*
continues in faith, love, *1Ti 2:15* consecration (B)
continue in sanctification with *1Ti 2:15* (E)
be in behaviour as becometh *h.* *Tit 2:3*
those engaged in sacred services *Tit 2:3* (A)
might be partakers of his *h.* *Heb 12:10*
follow peace with all men, *Heb 12:14* and *h.*
lives of *h.* and godliness (R) *2Pe 3:11*

HOLLOW

touched the *h.* of his thigh *Ge 32:25; 32:32*
make the altar *h.* with *Ex 27:8; 38:7*
if plague be in walls with *h.* *Le 14:37* strakes
God clave an *h.* place in the *J'g 15:19* jaw
measured waters in *h.* of his *Isa 40:12* hand
the pillar, it was *h.* *Jer 52:21*

HOLON

Goshen, and *H.*, and Gilah *Jos 15:51*
H. with her suburbs *Jos 21:15*
upon *H.* and upon Jahazah *Jer 48:21*

HOLPEN

they have *h.* children of Lot *Ps 83:8*
helped the children of Lot *Ps 83:8* (A)(E)
a strong support to children of *Ps 83:8* Lot (B)
the strong arm of children of *Ps 83:8* Lot (R)
because thou, Lord, hast *h.* me *Ps 86:17*
help and comfort me *Ps 86:17* (A)(B)(E)(R)
he that is *h.* shall fall down *Isa 31:3*
Judah who is helped shall fall *Isa 31:3* (A)
he who is helped stumbles *Isa 31:3* (B)(E)(R)
they shall be *h.* with little help *Da 11:34*
they shall receive a little help *Da 11:34* (A)
they shall receive aid (B)(R) *Da 11:34*
they shall be helped a little *Da 11:34* (E)
hath *h.* his servant Israel in *Lu 1:54*
to help him, to espouse his *Lu 1:54* cause (A)
he sustained Israel (B) *Lu 154*
he has given help to Israel *Lu 1:54* (E)(P)(R)
ranged himself on the side of *Lu 1:54* Israel (N)

HOLY

place thou standest is *h.* ground *Ex 3:5*
a *h.* assembly (A) *Ex 12:16; Le 23:21*
to-morrow is the rest of the *h.* *Ex 16:23* sabbath
shall be to me a *h.* nation *Ex 19:6; 1Pe 2:9*
remember the sabbath day to *Ex 20:8* keep it *h.*
Israel shall hallow in all their *Ex 28:38* *h.* gifts
and put the *h.* crown upon the *Ex 29:6* mitre
because they are *h.*; because *Ex 29:33; 29:34* it is *h.*
make it an oil of *h.* ointment *Ex 30:25* compound
it is *h.* and it shall be *h.* unto *Ex 30:32* you
perfume tempered together, *Ex 30:35* pure and *h.*
keep sabbath, for it is *h.* unto *Ex 31:14; 31:15* you
and he put upon Aaron the *h.* *Le 8:9* crown
put difference between *h.* and *Le 10:10* unholy
contact nothing *h.* (B) *Le 12:4*
he shall put on the *h.* linen coat *Le 16:4*
make atonement for the *h.* *Le 16:33* sanctuary
for I the Lord your God am *h.* *Le 19:2; 21:8*
profaned a *h.* thing (A) *Le 19:8*
be ye *h.* for he is *h.* unto his *Le 20:7; 21:7* God
a man sanctify his house to be *Le 27:14* *h.* to the Lord
the tithe of the land is *h.* unto *Le 27:30* the Lord
every man's *h.* things (R) *Nu 5:10*
and the priest shall take *h.* *Nu 5:17* water
may remember, and be *h.* to *Nu 15:40* your God
all the congregation are *h.* *Nu 16:3*
Lord will shew who are his, *Nu 16:5* and who is *h.*
they are *h.* (E)(R) *Nu 16:37*
thou shalt not redeem them, *Nu 18:17* they are *h.*
sent Phinehas with the *h.* *Nu 31:6* instruments
which was anointed with *h.* *Nu 35:25* oil
thou art an *h.* people *De 7:6; 14:2, 21; 26:19*
Only thy *h.* things *De 12:26*
shall thy camp be *h.* *De 23:14*
Look down from *h.* *De 26:15* habitation
establish thee an *h.* people *De 28:9*
thousands of *h.* ones (E) *De 33:2*
Grim be with thy *h.* one *De 33:8*
place thou standest is *h.* *Jos 5:15*
are *h.* unto Jehovah (E) *Jos 6:19*
for he is an *h.* God *Jos 24:19*

for there is none *h.* as the Lord *1Sa 2:2*
guard feet of *h.* ones (A)(E) *1Sa 2:9*
the *h.* bread (E)(R) *1Sa 21:4 21:6*
and the vessels of the young *1Sa 21:5* men are *h.*
the *h.* of holies (A) *1Ki 6:5; 6:15, 19-22, 31; 7:49; 8:6, 8; 2Ch 5:7*
the most *h.* place (R) *1Ki 6:16*
the *h.* place (B) *1Ki 6:31*
brought up the ark, *1Ki 8:4;*
tabernacle, and all *h.* vessels *2Ch 5:5*
I perceive this is an *h.* man of *2Ki 4:9* God
money of thing, (R) *2Ki 12:4*
bring the *h.* vessels into *1Ch 22:19* house of God
all I have prepared for *h.* *1Ch 29:3* house
in the matter of *h.* things *1Ch 31:18* (B)
keeping themselves *h.* (R) *1Ch 31:18*
the *H.* of Holies (B) *2Ch 5:7*
they shall go in, for they are *2Ch 23:6* *h.*
keeping themselves *h.* (R) *2Ch 31:18*
Levites which were *h.* to the *2Ch 35:3*
Lord put the *h.* ark into house
the other *h.* offerings sod *2Ch 35:13* they in pots
ye are *h.* to the Lord., vessels *Ezr 8:28* are *h.* also
h. seed mingled themselves with *Ezr 9:2* people
madest known unto them thy *Ne 9:14* *h.* sabbath
which of the *h.* ones *Job 5:1* (A)(B)(E)(R)
puts trust in his *h.* ones *Job 15:15* (A)(B)(E)(R)
he will hear him from his *h.* *Ps 20:6* heaven
thou art *h.* O thou that *Ps 22:3* inhabitest praises
when I lift my hands towards *Ps 28:2* thy *h.* oracle
remembrance of his *h.* name *Ps 30:4* (A)(E)(R)
sits upon his *h.* throne *Ps 47:8* (A)(B)(E)(R)
in his *h.* mountain *Ps 48:1* (A)(B)(E)(R)
gather all the *h.* ones (B) *Ps 50:5*
in midst of the *h.* place (A)(R) *Ps 74:4*
preserve my soul, for I am *h.* O *Ps 86:2* God, save
assembly of *h.* ones *Ps 89:5* (A)(B)(R)
his *h.* arm hath gotten him the *Ps 98:1* victory
worship at his footstool, for he *Ps 99:5* is *h.*
exalt the Lord, and worship at *Ps 99:9* his *h.* hill
for he remembered his *h.* *Ps 105:42* promise
the *h.* one (A)(B)(R) *Ps 106:16; Da 8:13*
the Lord is *h.* in all his works *Ps 145:17*
knowledge of the *h.* is *Pr 9:10* understanding
to man, who devoureth that *Pr 20:25* which is *h.*
nor have I the knowledge of the *Pr 30:3* *h.*
remaineth in Jerusalem shall be *Isa 4:3* called *h.*
h. in righteousness (A)(B)(R) *Isa 5:16*
one cried, *H.*, *h.*, *h.*, is the Lord *Isa 6:3* of hosts
the *h.* seed shall be the *Isa 6:13* substance thereof
regard him as *h.* (A)(B)(R) *Isa 8:13*
worship in the *h.* mountains *Isa 27:13* at Jerusalem
a song, as when a *h.* *Isa 30:29* solemnity is kept
called the *H.* way (A)(B)(R) *Isa 35:8*
the Lord hath made bare his *Isa 52:10* *h.* arm
call sabbath *h.* of the Lord *Isa 58:13*
h. people possessed *Isa 63:18* (A)(B)(E)(R)
thy *h.* cities are a wilderness *Isa 64:10*
our *h.* and beautiful house is *Isa 64:11* burnt up
thy *h.* and glorious abode *Isa 65:15*
Israel was *h.* to the Lord *Jer 2:3* (B)(R)

the *h.* flesh is passed from thee	*Jer 11:15*
keep sabbath day *h.* (A)(B)(R)	*Jer 17:22*
because of his *h.* words (A)(B)(E)(R)	*Jer 23:9*
O *h.* mountains (A)(B)	*Jer 31:23*
O *h.* hill (R)	*Jer 31:23*
put no difference between *h.* and profane	*Eze 22:26*
I will increase them as the *h.* flock	*Ez 36:38*
they be *h.* chambers where priests eat	*Eze 42:13*
there lay their garments, for they are *h.*	*Eze 42:14*
and lay them in the *h.* chambers	*Eze 44:19*
teach difference between *h.* and profane	*Eze 44:23*
my sabbaths *h.* (A)(R)	*Eze 44:24*
shall offer an *h.* portion of the land	*Eze 45:1;* 45:4
against the oblation of *h.* portion	*Eze 45:6;* 45:7; 48:18
into the *h.* chambers of the priests	*Eze 46:19*
for the priests shall be this *h.* oblation	*Eze 48:10*
not sell firstfruits, for it is *h.* unto the Lord	*Eze 48:14*
offer the *h.* oblation foursquare	*Eze 48:20;* 48:21
Daniel came in before me, in	*Da 4:8;*
whom is spirit of *h.* gods	*4:9, 18; 5:11*
his heart shall be against the *h.* covenant	*Da 11:28*
against *h.* covenant, intelligence with them	*Da 11:30*
that forsake *h.* covenant	
with faithful *H.* One (A)(B)(E)(R)	*Ho 11:12*
it shall be *h.* (A)(E)(R)	*Ob 17*
if one hear *h.* flesh, and with his skirt touch bread or wine shall it be *h.*	*Hag 2:12*
Lord shall inherit Judah in the *h.* land	*Zec 2:12*
Lord is raised up out of his *h.* habitation	*Zec 2:13*
all the *h.* ones (A)(B)(E)(R)	*Zec 14:5*
thy name be kept *h.* (B)	*M't 6:9*
give not that which is *h.* unto the dogs	*M't 7:6*
shall come and all the *h.* angels with him	*M't 25:31*
bodies of *h.* men (P)	*M't 27:52*
knowing that he was a just man and *h.*	*M'k 6:20*
cometh in glory with *h.* angels	*M'k 8:38;* *Lu 9:26*
by mouth of *h.* prophets	*Lu 1:70;* *Ac 3:21*
and to remember his *h.* covenant	*Lu 1:72*
every male shall be called *h.* to the Lord	*Lu 2:23*
h. Father keep those thou hast given me	*Joh 17:11*
against thy *h.* child Jesus, whom thou	*Ac 4:27*
wonders be done by name of thy *h.* child	*Ac 4:30*
the place where thou standest is *h.* ground	*Ac 7:33*
was warned from God by an *h.* angel	*Ac 10:22*
many faithful *h.* ones (A)	*Ac 26:10*
which he had promised in *h.* scriptures	*Ro 1:2*
righteousness to *h.* living (B)	*Ro 6:19*
the commandment is *h.*, just, and good	*Ro 7:12*
if the firstfruit be *h.* if the root be *h.*	*Ro 11:16*
that ye present your bodies a *h.* sacrifice to God	*Ro 12:1*
salute with *h.* kiss	*Ro 16:16; 1Co 16:20;* *2Co 13:12; 1Th 5:26; 1Pe 5:14*
made righteous and *h.* (P)	*1Co 1:30*
the temple of God is *h.* which temple	*1Co 3:17*
you were made *h.* (B)	*1Co 6:11*
but now are they *h.* that she may be *h.*	*1Co 7:14;* 7:34
we should be *h.* and without blame	*Eph 1:4;* 5:27
to present you *h.* and unblameable	*Col 1:22*

put on, as elect of God, *h.* and beloved	*Col 3:12*
how *h.*, righteous, blameless (R)	*1Th 2:10*
H. and blameless (B)(N)(P)	*1Th 3:13*
your growing *h.* (B)(N)(P)	*1Th 4:3*
make you *h.* (B)(N)(P)	*1Th 5:23*
this epistle be read to all *h.* brethren	*1Th 5:27*
lifting up *h.* hands without wrath	*1Ti 2:8*
who hath called us with an *h.* calling	*2Ti 1:9*
hast known *h.* scriptures able to make	*2Ti 3:15*
a bishop must be sober, *h.* temperate	*Tit 1:8*
those being made *h.* (A)	*Heb 2:11*
h. brethren partakers of heavenly calling	*Heb 3:1*
into the *H.* of Holies (B)	*Heb 6:19*
such an high priest became us, who is *h.*	*Heb 7:26*
H. of Holies (A)(P)(R)	*Heb 9:3;* 9:8; 10:19
the most *H.* Place (N)	*Heb 9:3*
the *h.* place (E)	*Heb 9:8; 10:19*
those made *h.* (A)(B)	*Heb 10:10*
perfected those made *h.* (A)(P)	*Heb 10:14*
blood which made *h.* (B)(P)	*Heb 10:29*
so be ye *h.* in all conversation	*1Pe 1:15;* 1:16
h. priesthood to offer spiritual sacrifices	*1Pe 2:5*
the *h.* women also who trusted in God	*1Pe 3:5*
when we were with him in *h.* mount	*2Pe 1:18*
but *h.* men spake as moved by Holy Ghost	*2Pe 1:21*
than to turn from the *h.* commandment	*2Pe 2:21*
words spoken before by the *h.* prophets	*2Pe 3:2*
what persons to be in all *h.* conversation	*2Pe 3:11*
with myriads of *h.* ones (B)(E)(P)	*Jude 14*
with his *h.* myriads (R)	*Jude 14*
write these things, saith he that is *h.*	*Re 3:7*
saying, *H.*, *h.*, *h.*, Lord God Almighty	*Re 4:8*
cried, saying, How long, O Lord, *h.* and true	*Re 6:10*
be tormented in presence of the *h.* angels	*Re 14:10*
who shall not fear thee? for thou art *h.*	*Re 15:4*
rejoice over her, ye *h.* apostles and prophets	*Re 18:20*
h. is he that hath part in the first resurrection	*Re 20:6*
and he shewed me the *h.* Jerusalem	*Re 21:10*
Lord God of the *h.* prophets sent his angel	*Re 22:6*
and he that is *h.* let him be *h.* still	*Re 22:11*

HOLY DAY

the seventh shall be an *h.* day	*Ex 35:2*
this *day* is *h.* unto the Lord	*Ne 8:9;* 8:10, 11
not buy it of them on sabbath or *h.* day	*Ne 10:31*
with a multitude that kept *h.* day	*Ps 42:4*
from doing thy pleasure on my *h.* day	*Isa 58:13*
let no man judge you in respect of an *h.* day	*Col 2:16*

HOLY GHOST

was found with child of the *H.* Ghost	*M't 1:18*
what is conceived in her is of the *H.* Ghost	*M't 1:20*
baptize you with *H.* Ghost and fire	*M't 3:11; M'k 1:8; Lu 3:16; Joh 1:33;* *Ac 1:5*
blasphemy against *H.* Ghost not be forgiven unto men	*M'k 3:29;* *Lu 12:10*
whosoever speaketh against the *H.* Ghost	*M't 12:32*

baptize in name of Father, Son, and *H.* Ghost	*M't 28:19*
David said by the *H.* Ghost	*M'k 12:36;* *Ac 1:16*
it is not ye that speak, but *H.* Ghost	*M'k 13:11*
John shall be filled with *H.* Ghost	*Lu 1:15*
the *H.* Ghost shall come upon thee	*Lu 1:35*
and Elisabeth was filled with the *H.* Ghost	*Lu 1:41*
his father Zacharias was filled with *H.* Ghost	*Lu 1:67*
Simeon, and *H.* Ghost was upon him	*Lu 2:25*
it was revealed unto him by the *H.* Ghost	*Lu 2:26*
the *H.* Ghost descended in a bodily shape	*Lu 3:22*
Jesus being full of the *H.* Ghost returned	*Lu 4:1*
H. Ghost shall teach you in same hour	*Lu 12:12*
for the *H.* Ghost was not yet given	*Joh 7:39*
but the Comforter, who is the *H.* Ghost	*Joh 14:26*
he saith, Receive ye the *H.* Ghost	*Joh 20:22;* *Ac 2:38*
after that he through *H.* Ghost had given	*Ac 1:2*
after that the *H.* Ghost is come upon you	*Ac 1:8*
they were all filled with the *H.* Ghost	*Ac 2:4;* 4:31
having received the promise of the *H.* Ghost	*Ac 2:33*
Peter, filled with *H.* Ghost said unto them	*Ac 4:8*
Satan filled thy heart to lie to *H.* Ghost	*Ac 5:3*
we are his witnesses, so is also *H.* Ghost	*Ac 5:32*
look out men full of *H.* Ghost and wisdom	*Ac 6:3*
chose Stephen, a man full of the *H.* Ghost	*Ac 6:5*
stiffnecked, ye always resist the *H.* Ghost	*Ac 7:51*
being full of *H.* Ghost looked up to heaven	*Ac 7:55*
prayed that they might receive the *H.* Ghost	*Ac 8:15*
hands on them, they received the *H.* Ghost	*Ac 8:17*
when Simon saw that the *H.* Ghost was given	*Ac 8:18*
on whom I lay hands, he may receive *H.* Ghost	*Ac 8:19*
thou mightest be filled with the *H.* Ghost	*Ac 9:17*
walking in the comfort of the *H.* Ghost	*Ac 9:31*
how God anointed Jesus with *H.* Ghost	*Ac 10:38*
H. Ghost fell on all which heard the word	*Ac 10:44*
on Gentiles was poured the gift of *H.* Ghost	*Ac 10:45*
which have received *H.* Ghost as well as we	*Ac 10:47*
H. Ghost fell on them as on us at beginning	*Ac 11:15*
but ye shall be baptized with the *H.* Ghost	*Ac 11:16*
Barnabas, full of the *H.* Ghost and faith	*Ac 11:24*
H. Ghost said, Separate Barnabas and Saul	*Ac 13:2*
being sent forth by the *H.* Ghost departed	*Ac 13:4*
Paul, filled with *H.* Ghost set his eyes on him	*Ac 13:9*
the disciples were filled with the *H.* Ghost	*Ac 13:52*
giving them *H.* Ghost as he did unto us	*Ac 15:8*
it seemed good to the *H.* Ghost and to us	*Ac 15:28*
were forbidden of the *H.* Ghost to preach in Asia	*Ac 16:6*
have ye received the *H.* Ghost	*Ac 19:2*
we have not heard whether there be any *H.* Ghost	
laid hands on them, the *H.* Ghost came on them	*Ac 19:6*
the *H.* Ghost witnesseth in every city	*Ac 20:23*

over which *H. Ghost* made   *Ac 20:28*
you overseers
thus saith the *H. Ghost*, So   *Ac 21:11*
shall the Jews
well spake *H. Ghost* by   *Ac 28:25*
Esaias the prophet
love of God shed in hearts by   *Ro 5:5*
H. Ghost
conscience bearing me witness   *Ro 9:1*
in *H. Ghost*
the kingdom of God is joy in   *Ro 14:17*
the *H. Ghost*
abound in hope through   *Ro 15:13*
power of the *H. Ghost*
acceptable, being sanctified   *Ro 15:16*
by the *H. Ghost*
but in words which the *H.*   *1Co 2:13*
Ghost teacheth
your body is the temple of the   *1Co 6:19*
H. Ghost
say that Jesus is Lord, but by   *1Co 12:3*
the *H. Ghost*
by kindness, by the *H. Ghost*   *2Co 6:6*
by love
the communion of the *H.*   *2Co 13:14*
Ghost be with you
for our gospel came in the *H.*   *1Th 1:5*
Ghost
received the word with joy of   *1Th 1:6*
the *H. Ghost*
that good thing keep by the *H.*   *2Ti 1:14*
Ghost
he saved us by the renewing of   *Tit 3:5*
the *H. Ghost*
bearing witness with gifts of   *Heb 2:4*
the *H. Ghost*
as *H. Ghost* saith, To-day if   *Heb 3:7*
ye will hear
and were made partakers of   *Heb 6:4*
the *H. Ghost*
the *H. Ghost* this signifying,   *Heb 9:8*
that the way
whereof the *H. Ghost* is a   *Heb 10:15*
witness to us
with the *H. Ghost* sent down   *1Pe 1:12*
from heaven
spake as they were moved by   *2Pe 1:21*
the *H. Ghost*
the Father, the Word, and the   *1Jo 5:7*
H. Ghost
but ye, beloved, praying in *H.*   *Jude 20*
Ghost

HOLY *MOUNTAIN*

his foundation is in the *h.*   *Ps 87:1*
mountain
nor destroy in my *h.*   *Isa 11:9;*
mountain   *65:25*
even them will I bring to my *h.*   *Isa 56:7*
mountain
and he shall inherit my *h.*   *Isa 57:13*
mountain
ye are they that forget my *h.*   *Isa 65:11*
mountain
on mules and swift beasts to   *Isa 66:20*
my *h. mountain*
in my *h. mountain* they shall   *Eze 20:40*
serve me
thou wast upon the *h.*   *Eze 28:14*
mountain of God
let thy anger be turned from   *Da 9:16*
thy *h. mountain*
presenting supplication for the   *Da 9:20*
h. mountain
plant tabernacles in glorious   *Da 11:45*
h. mountain
sound an alarm in my *h.*   *Joe 2:1*
mountain
the Lord, dwelling in Zion   *Joe 3:17*
my *h. mountain*
for as ye have drunk on my *h.*   *Ob 16*
mountain
no more haughty, because of   *Zep 3:11*
h. mountain
mountain of Lord called *h.*   *Zec 8:3*
mountain

HOLY *NAME*

seed to Molech, to profane *h.*   *Le 20:3*
name
and that they profane not my   *Le 22:2*
h. name
neither shall ye profane my *h.*   *Le 22:32*
name
glory ye in his *h. name*   *1Ch 16:10;*
   Ps 105:3
we give thanks to thy *h.*   *1Ch 16:35;*
name   *Ps 106:47*

to build thee an house for   *1Ch 29:16*
thy *h. name*
because we trusted in his *h.*   *Ps 33:21*
name
praise thy terrible *name*, for it   *Ps 99:3*
is *h.*
bless the Lord, bless his *h.*   *Ps 103:1;*
name   *145:21*
h. and reverend is his *name*   *Ps 111:9;*
   Lu 1:49
saith the lofty One, whose   *Isa 57:15*
name is *h.*
pollute you my *h. name* no   *Eze 20:39*
more
profaned my *h. name* when   *Eze 36:20*
they said
but I had pity for mine *h.*   *Eze 36:21*
name
not for your sakes, but my *h.*   *Eze 36:22*
name's sake
make my *h. name* known in   *Eze 39:7*
Israel not let them pollute my *h.*
name any more
and I will be jealous for my   *Eze 39:25*
h. name
my *h. name* shall Israel no   *Eze 43:7*
more defile
defiled my *h. name* by their   *Eze 43:8*
abominations
go in to same maid, to profane   *Am 2:7*
my *h. name*

HOLY *OIL*

it shall be an *h.* annointing   *Ex 30:25;*
oil   *30:31*
and be made the *h.* anointing   *Ex 37:29*
oil
the high priest was anointed   *Nu 35:25*
with *h. oil*
with my *h. oil* have I anointed   *Ps 89:20*
him

HOLY *ONE*

Thummim and Urim be with   *De 33:8*
thy *h. One*
not concealed the words of the   *Job 6:10*
h. One
not leave soul in hell, nor   *Ps 16:10;*
suffer *h. One* to see corruption   *Ac 2:7;*
   13:35
thou spakest in vision to thy   *Ps 89:19*
h. One
his *h. One* shall be for a flame   *Isa 10:17*
they shall sanctify the *h. One*   *Isa 29:23*
of Jacob
to whom shall I be equal?   *Isa 40:25*
saith *h. One*
I am the Lord your *h. One,*   *Isa 43:15*
the Creator
thus saith the Redeemer of   *Isa 49:7*
Israel his *h. One*
an *h. One* came down from   *Da 4:13;*
heaven   *4:23*
for I am the *h. One* in the   *Ho 11:9*
midst of thee
art thou not from everlasting   *Hab 1:12*
my *h. One*
the *h. One* came from mount   *Hab 3:3*
Paran
unclean spirit said, I know   *M'k 1:24;*
thee who thou art, the *h.*   *Lu 4:31*
One of God
but ye denied the *h. One* and   *Ac 3:14*
the Just
ye have an unction from the *h.*   *1Jo 2:20*
One

HOLY *ONE OF ISRAEL*

thou hast lifted thy eyes   *2Ki 19:22;*
against the *h. One of Israel*   *Isa 37:23*
to thee will I sing, O thou *h.*   *Ps 71:22*
One of Israel
yea, they limited the *h. One* of   *Ps 78:41*
Israel
and the *h. One of Israel* is our   *Ps 89:18*
king
they have provoked the *h. One*   *Isa 1:4*
of Israel
let counsel of *h. One of Israel*   *Isa 5:19*
draw nigh
despised the word of the *h.*   *Isa 5:24*
one of Israel
shall stay on the Lord, *h. One*   *Isa 10:20*
of Israel
great is *h. One of Israel* in   *Isa 12:6*
midst of thee

his eyes shall have respect to *h.*   *Isa 17:7*
One of Israel
the poor shall rejoice in *h.*   *Isa 29:19*
One of Israel
cause *h. One of Israel* to   *Isa 30:11*
cease from us
thus saith the *h. One* of   *Isa 30:12;*
Israel   *30:15*
they look not unto *h. One of*   *Isa 31:1*
Israel
saith thy Redeemer, *h. One of*   *Isa 41:14*
Israel
and thou shalt glory in *h. One*   *Isa 41:16*
of Israel
and the *h. One of Israel* hath   *Isa 41:20*
created it
I am Lord the *h. One of Israel*   *Isa 43:3*
thus saith your Redeemer, *h.*   *Isa 43:14*
One of Israel
Lord the *h. One of Israel*   *Isa 45:11*
Lord of hosts is his name, *h.*   *Isa 47:4*
One of Israel
saith thy Redeemer, *h. One*   *Isa 48:17;*
of Israel   *54:5*
the Redeemer of Israel, and   *Isa 49:7*
his *h. One*
nations run unto thee, for *h.*   *Isa 55:5*
One of Israel
bring their gold to *h. One of*   *Isa 60:9*
Israel
shall call thee, the Zion of *h.*   *Isa 60:14*
One of Israel
Babylon proud against *h. One*   *Jer 50:29*
of Israel
land filled with sin against *h.*   *Jer 51:5*
One of Israel
that I am the Lord, *h. One* in   *Eze 39:7*
Israel

HOLY *ONES*

the demand by the word of the   *Da 4:17*
h. ones

HOLY *PEOPLE*

art an *h. people* to the Lord   *De 7:6;*
   14:2, 21
thou mayest be an *h. people*   *De 26:19*
to the Lord
Lord establish thee an *h.*   *De 28:9*
people to himself
they shall call them, the *h.*   *Isa 62:12*
people
prosper, and destroy the *h.*   *Da 8:24*
people
to scatter the power of the *h.*   *Da 12:7*
people

HOLY *PLACE*

when he goeth in unto the *h.*   *Ex 28:29;*
place   *28:35*
come near to minister in the   *Ex 28:43;*
h. place   *29:30*
thou shalt seethe his flesh in   *Ex 29:31*
the *h. place*
may make sweet incense for   *Ex 31:11*
the *h. place*
to do service in the *h. place*   *Ex 35:19;*
   39:1, 41
the gold in all the work of the   *Ex 38:24*
h. place
with unleavened bread it shall   *Le 6:16;*
be eaten in the *h. place*   *6:26; 7:6; 10:13;*
   24:9
thou shalt wash that in the *h.*   *Le 6:27*
place
brought to reconcile withal in   *Le 6:30*
the *h. place*
have ye not eaten sin offering   *Le 10:7*
in the *h. place*
blood was not brought in   *Le 10:18*
within the *h. place*
shall slay the burnt offering in   *Le 14:13*
the *h. place*
that he come not at all times   *Le 16:2*
into the *h. place*
thus shall Aaron come into the   *Le 16:3*
h. place
he shall make an atonement for   *Le 16:16*
the *h. place*
goeth to make atonement in   *Le 16:17;*
the *h. place*   *16:27*
hath made an end of   *Le 16:20*
reconciling the *h. place*
he put on when he went into   *Le 16:23*
the *h. place*

HOLY *PLACE* (continued)

shall wash his flesh with water *Le 16:24*
in the *h. place*
the *place* whereon thou *Jos 5:15*
standest is *h.*
the staves were seen out in the *1Ki 8:8*
h. place
priests come out of the *h.* *1Ki 8:10; place* *2Ch 5:11*
keep the charge of the *h.* *1Ch 23:32*
place
carry filthiness out of the *h.* *2Ch 29:5*
place
nor offered burnt offerings in *2Ch 29:7*
the *h. place*
prayer came up to his *h.* *2Ch 30:27*
dwelling *place*
stand in the *h. place* *2Ch 35:5*
according to divisions
and to give us a nail in his *h.* *Ezr 9:8*
place
and who shall stand in his *h.* *Ps 24:3*
place
streams whereof make glad *h.* *Ps 46:4*
place
among them as in Sinai, in the *Ps 68:17*
h. place
who had gone from the *place* *Ec 8:10*
of the *h.*
I dwell in the high and *h.* *Isa 57:15*
place
he said to me, This is most *h.* *Eze 41:4*
place
the *place* is *h.*; not go out of *Eze 42:13; h. place* *42:14*
it shall be an *h. place* for the *Eze 45:4*
sanctuary
ye see abomination stand in *M't 24:15*
h. place
blasphemous words against *Ac 6:13*
this *h. place*
this man hath polluted this *h. Ac 21:28*
place
Christ entered in once into *h. Heb 9:12*
place
high priest entered every year *Heb 9:25*
into *h. place*

HOLY *PLACES*

because the *places* are *h.* *2Ch 8:11*
whereunto
thou art terrible out of thy *h.* *Ps 68:35*
places
and their *h. places* shall be *Eze 7:24*
defiled
and drop thy word toward the *Eze 21:2*
h. places
Christ is not entered into *h. Heb 9:24*
places made

HOLY *SPIRIT*

and take not thy *h. spirit* *Ps 51:11*
from me
they rebelled and vexed his *h. Isa 63:10*
spirit
where is he that put his *h. Isa 63:11*
spirit within him
your heavenly Father gave *H. Lu 11:13*
Spirit
sealed with that *h. Spirit* of *Eph 1:13*
promise
grieve not the *h. Spirit* of *Eph 4:30*
God, whereby
hath given unto us his *h. Spirit 1Th 4:8*

HOLY *TEMPLE*

I will worship toward thy *h.* *Ps 5:7; temple* *138:2*
Lord is in his *h. temple*, his *Ps 11:4*
eyes behold
be satisfied with the goodness *Ps 65:4*
of thy *h. temple*
thy *h. temple* have they defiled, *Ps 79:1*
they laid
I will look again toward thy *h. Jon 2:4*
temple
prayer came in unto thee, to thy *Jon 2:7*
h. temple
Lord from his *h. temple* be *Mic 1:2*
witness
but the Lord is in his *h. Hab 2:20*
temple
groweth to an *h. temple* in the *Eph 2:21*
Lord

HOLY *THING*

no stranger shall eat of *h.* *Le 22:10*
thing
if a man eat of the *h. thing* *Le 22:14*
unwittingly
thy estimation as an *h. thing* to *Le 27:23*
Lord
they shall not touch any *h.* *Nu 4:15*
thing
oblation be to them a *thing Eze 48:12*
most *h.*
therefore that *h. thing* born of *Lu 1:35*
thee

HOLY *THINGS*

Aaron may bear the iniquity *Ex 28:38*
of *h. things*
sin thro' ignorance in *h. things Le 5:15*
of Lord
separate themselves from *h. Le 22:2*
things of Israel
whosoever he be that goeth *Le 22:3*
unto *h. things*
not eat of *h. things* till he be *Le 22:4; 22:6, 12*
clean
be clean, and shall afterward *Le 22:7*
eat of *h. things*
shall not profane *h. things* of *Le 22:15*
Israel
to bear iniquity, when they eat *Le 22:16*
h. things
not go in to see, when *h. things Nu 4:20*
are covered
every offering of *h. things* shall *Nu 5:9; 18:19*
be his
neither shall ye pollute the *h. Nu 18:32*
things
h. things take and go to the *De 12:26*
place
their office was in purifying *1Ch 23:28*
h. things
they brought in the tithe of *h. 2Ch 31:6*
things
we made ordinances for *h. Ne 10:33*
things
they sanctified *h. things* to the *Ne 12:47*
Levites
there will I require your *h. Eze 20:40*
things
thou hast despised mine *h. Eze 22:8*
things
her priests have profaned my *Eze 22:26*
h. things
have not kept charge of my *h. Eze 44:8*
things
shall not come near to any of *Eze 44:13*
my *h. things*
they who minister about *h. 1Co 9:13*
things

MOST *HOLY*

between holy place and *most Ex 26:33*
h.
on ark of the testimony in *Ex 26:34*
most h. place
and it shall be an altar *most Ex 29:37; h.* *40:10*
it is most *h.*; that they may *Ex 30:10; 30:29*
be most *h.*
the perfume shall be to you *Ex 30:36*
most *h.*
remnant of meat offering shall *Le 2:3;*
be Aaron's, it is most *h. 2:3; 6:17; 10:12*
the sin offering is most *h. Le 6:25; 6:29; 10:17*
the trespass offering is most *h. Le 7:1; 10:17*
eat bread of God, both of *Le 21:22; 7:6; 14:13*
most *h.* and holy
the cakes of fine flour are *most Le 24:9*
h. to him
every devoted thing is most *h. Le 27:28*
to Lord
this shall be service about *most Nu 4:4*
h. things
thus do, when they approach *Nu 4:19*
most *h. things*
offering they render to me *Nu 18:9*
shall be most *h.*
in the most *h.* place shalt *Nu 18:10*
thou eat it
he built them for the *most 1Ki 6:16*
place
Solomon made vessels for the *1Ki 7:50*
most *h.* place

HOME (continued right column)

brought the ark unto *most h. 1Ki 8:6;
place* *2Ch 5:7*
Aaron and sons for work of *1Ch 6:49*
most *h.*
Aaron separated to sanctify *1Ch 23:13*
most *h.* things
Solomon made the *most h. 2Ch 3:8*
house
in *most h.* house he made two *2Ch 3:10*
cherubims
inner doors thereof for the *2Ch 4:22*
most *h.* place
Kore to distribute the *most 2Ch 31:14*
h. things
not eat of the *most h.* things *Ezr 2:63;
Ne 7:65*
the whole limit shall be *most Eze 43:12*
h.
shall not come near in the *Eze 44:13*
most *h.* place
in it shall be the sanctuary *Eze 45:3*
and most *h.* place
this oblation shall be a thing *Eze 48:12*
most *h.*
seventy weeks to anoint the *Da 9:24*
most *h.*
building yourselves on your *Jude 20*
most *h.* faith

SHALL BE HOLY

and ye *shall be h.* men unto *Ex 22:31*
me
whatsoever toucheth the altar *Ex 29:37*
shall be h.
whatsoever toucheth them *Ex 30:29; shall be h.* *Le 6:18*
it is holy, and it *shall be h. Ex 30:32; 30:37*
unto you
anoint the tabernacle, and it *Ex 40:9*
shall be h.
shall touch the flesh thereof *Le 6:27*
shall be h.
ye *shall be h.* for I am holy *Le 11:44; 11:45; 19:2; 20:26*
fruit thereof *shall be h.* to *Le 19:24*
praise the Lord
the priests *shall be h.* unto their *Le 21:6*
God
shall be h. to the Lord for the *Le 23:20*
priest
it is the jubilee, it *shall be h. Le 25:12*
unto you
that any man giveth to Lord *Le 27:9*
shall be h.
then the exchange thereof *Le 27:10; shall be h.* *27:33*
in the jubilee it *shall be h.* to *Le 27:21*
the Lord
the tenth *shall be h.* unto the *Le 27:32*
Lord
Nazarite *shall be h.* unto the *Nu 6:5*
Lord
man whom Lord doth choose *Nu 16:7*
he *shall be h.*
every male shall eat it, it *shall Nu 18:10*
be *h.* unto thee
therefore *shall* thy camp be *h. De 23:14*
the gate towards the east shall *Jer 31:40*
be *h.*
holy portion *shall be h.* with *Eze 45:1*
borders
I dwell in Zion, then *shall Joe 3:17*
Jerusalem be *h.*

HOLYDAY

with a multitude that kept *h. Ps 42:4*
in respect of an *h.*, or of *Col 2:16*

HOMAGE

paid *h.* to (A) *J'g 8:27*
fell on knees and paid *h.* (B) *1Ki 1:31*
fell upon knees, did *h.* (B) *1Ki 1:16*

HOMAM

sons of Lotan; Hori and *H. 1Ch 1:39*

HOME

my father's *h.* (B) *Ge 20:13*
in her parental *h.* (B) *Ge 38:11*
laid up garment till her lord *Ge 39:16*
came *h.*
bring these men *h.* slay and *Ge 43:16*
make ready

man and beast not brought *h.*   *Ex 9:19*
shall die
one lamb for each *h.* (B)   *Ex 12:3*
thou shalt bring her *h.* to thy   *De 21:12*
house
but he shall be free at *h.* one   *De 24:5*
year
bring all father's household *h.*   *Jos 2:18*
to thee
if ye bring me *h.* again to fight   *J'g 11:9*
get on your way, that thou   *J'g 19:9*
mayest go *h.*
the Lord hath brought me *h.*   *Ru 1:21*
empty
and they went unto their own   *1Sa 2:20*
h.
and bring their calves *h.* from   *1Sa 6:7*
them
and the men shut up their   *1Sa 6:10*
calves at *h.*
Saul also went *h.* to Gibeah   *1Sa 10:26;*
                        24:22
let him go no more *h.* to his   *1Sa 18:2*
father's house
then David sent *h.* to Tamar   *2Sa 13:7*
the king doth not fetch *h.* his   *2Sa 14:13*
banished
Ahithophel gat him *h.* to his   *2Sa 17:23*
house
a month in Lebanon, two   *1Ki 5:14*
months at *h.*
come *h.* with me and refresh   *1Ki 13:7;*
thyself   *13:15*
and tarry at *h.*   *2Ki 14:10; 2Ch 25:19*
bring the ark of God *h.* to   *1Ch 13:12*
me
so David brought not the ark   *1Ch 13:13*
h. to himself
Amaziah separated army of   *2Ch 25:10*
Ephraim to go *h.* returned *h.*
Haman came *h.* called his   *Es 5:10*
friends
believe that he will bring *h.*   *Job 39:12*
thy seed
she that tarried at *h.* divided   *Ps 68:12*
spoil
the *h.* of the just (A)   *Pr 3:33*
the good man is not at *h.* he is   *Pr 7:19*
gone
and he will come *h.* at the day   *Pr 7:20*
appointed
because man goeth to his long   *Ec 12:5*
h.
that Gedaliah should carry   *Jer 39:14*
him *h.*
abroad the sword, at *h.* there is   *La 1:20*
as death
he is a proud man, neither   *Hab 2:5*
keepeth at *h.*
when ye brought it *h.* I did   *Hag 1:9*
blow upon it
my servant lieth at *h.* sick of   *M't 8:6*
the palsy
enter into the *h.* (B)   *M't 10:12; 12:25*
make their *h.* there (A)   *M't 12:45*
courtyard of high priest's *h.*   *M't 26:58*
(A)(B)(E)(P)(R)
go *h.* to thy friends and tell   *M'k 5:19*
them
let first bid them farewell   *Lu 9:61*
which are at *h.*
when he cometh *h.* he calleth   *Lu 15:6*
his friends
that disciple took her to his   *Joh 19:27*
own *h.*
the disciples went away to   *Joh 20:10*
their own *h.*
we took ship, and they   *Ac 21:6*
returned *h.* again
finds a *h.* with you (B)(P)   *Ro 8:9*
sin which is at *h.* in me   *Ro 7:17*
(A)(B)(P)
if any man hunger let him   *1Co 11:34*
eat at *h.*
let them ask their husbands   *1Co 14:35*
at *h.*
that whilst we are at *h.* in the   *2Co 5:6*
body
let them learn to shew piety at   *1Ti 5:4*
h.
to be discreet, chaste, keepers at   *Tit 2:5*
h.

HOMEBORN

one law shall be to him that is   *Ex 12:49*
h.
thy sister whether *born* at *h.* or   *Le 18:9*
abroad

---

is Israel a servant? is he a   *Jer 2:14*
h. slave

HOMER

an *h.* of barley seed shall be   *Le 27:16*
valued
ten bushels of barley (B)   *Le 27:16*
seed of an *h.* shall yield an   *Isa 5:10*
ephah
ten bushels of seed (B)   *Isa 5:10*
the measure shall be after the   *Eze 45:11*
h.
ten-bushel (B)   *Eze 45:11; 5:13, 14*
sixth part of an ephah of an   *Eze 45:13*
h. of wheat
tenth part of a bath, for ten   *Eze 45:14*
baths are an *h.*
I bought her for an *h.* and half   *Ho 3:2*
an *h.*
fifteen bushels of barley (B)   *Ho 3:2*

HOMERS

gathered least gathered ten *h.*   *Nu 11:32*

HOMES

the immigrant *h.* (B)   *Eze 47:23*

HOMESTEAD

let his *h.* fall desolate (N)   *Ac 1:20*

HOMOSEXUALITY

who participate in *h.*   *1Co 6:9*
(A)(B)(N)

HOMOSEXUALS

nor *h.* (R)   *1Co 6:9*

HONEST

done with *h.* heart (B)   *Ge 20:5; 20:6*
we are *h.* (B)   *Ge 42:11;*
           42:31, 33; 2Co 6:8; Heb 10:22
we are *h.* (B)   *Ge 42:11;*
              42:19, 31, 33, 34
we are *h.* (A)   *Ge 42:33; 42:34*
h. scales, *h.* bushel, *h.* weights,   *Le 19:36*
h. gallon (B)
you have been *h.* (R)   *1Sa 29:6*
no one *h.* among men (B)   *Mic 7:2*
rain on *h.* and dishonest (P)   *M't 5:45*
you are *h.* (N)(P)   *M't 22:16;*
                   M'k 12:14
look like *h.* men (N)   *M't 23:28*
they, which in an *h.* and good   *Lu 8:15*
heart
just, noble, virtuous, worthy   *Lu 8:15*
heart (A)
in a good, well-disposed heart   *Lu 8:15*
(B)
pretended to be *h.*   *Lu 20:20*
(A)(B)(N)(P)
look out among you seven men   *Ac 6:3*
of *h.* report
men of good, attested character,   *Ac 6:3*
repute (A)
men of good reputation   *Ac 6:3*
(B)(N)(P)
men of good report (E)   *Ac 6:3*
men of good repute (R)   *Ac 6:3*
provide things *h.* in sight of   *Ro 12:17*
all men
determine on noblest ways in   *Ro 12:17*
dealing (B)
Take thought for things   *Ro 12:17*
honorable (E)(N)
public behaviour above   *Ro 12:17*
criticism (P)
what is noble in sight of all   *Ro 12:17*
(R)
truthful and *h.* (A)   *2Co 6:8*
provide *h.* things in sight of   *2Co 8:21*
Lord and men
we intend to do the fair thing   *2Co 8:21*
(B)
take thought for things   *2Co 8:21*
honorable (E)
our aims are entirely   *2Co 8:21*
honorable (N)(R)

---

to be absolutely aboveboard   *2Co 8:21*
(P)
but that ye should do that   *2Co 13:7*
which is *h.*
continue doing what is right   *2Co 13:7*
(A)(N)(R)
that you may behave well (B)   *2Co 13:7*
may do that which is   *2Co 13:7*
honorable (E)
are true, whatsoever things are   *Ph'p 4:8*
h.
how *h.*, above criticism (P)   *1Th 2:10*
h. and trustworthy (N)(P)   *Tit 2:10*
your conversation *h.* among the   *1Pe 2:12*
Conduct yourselves properly   *1Pe 2:12*
(A)
Conduct yourselves honorably   *1Pe 2:12*
(B)
having your behaviour seemly   *1Pe 2:12*
(E)
behaviour such as pagans   *1Pe 2:12*
recognize good (N)
conduct always good and right   *1Pe 2:12*
(P)
Maintain good conduct (R)   *1Pe 2:12*

HONESTLY

who walks *h.* (B)   *Mic 2:7*
teach way of God *h.* (B)(N)   *M't 22:16*
Let us walk *h.* as in the day   *Ro 13:13*
conduct ourselves honorably   *Ro 13:13*
(A)
behave ourselves gracefully   *Ro 13:13*
(B)
Let us walk becomingly   *Ro 13:13*
(E)(R)
Let us behave decently (N)   *Ro 13:13*
fling away things men do in   *Ro 13:13*
dark (P)
That ye may walk *h.* toward   *1Th 4:12*
them
be correct and honorable (A)   *1Ti 4:12*
behaviour be honorable (B)   *1Ti 4:12*
walk becomingly toward them   *1Th 4:12*
without (E)
be dependent on nobody (R)   *1Th 4:12*
in all things willing to live *h.*   *Heb 13:18*
we want to behave nobly   *Heb 13:18*
(B)
desiring to live honorably   *Heb 13:18*
(E)
one desire to always do right   *Heb 13:18*
(N)
desiring to act honorably   *Heb 13:18*
(R)

HONESTY

my *h.* shall answer for me (S)   *Ge 30:33*
h. cannot enter (B)   *Isa 59:14*
quiet life in all godliness and   *1Ti 2:2*
h.
pass a quiet, undisturbed life, a   *1Ti 2:2*
peaceable one in all godliness,
reverence (A)
lead a quiet and undisturbed   *1Ti 2:2*
life (B)
in all godliness and gravity (E)   *1Ti 2:2*
life in high standards of   *1Ti 2:2*
morality (N)
life godly and respectable (R)   *1Ti 2:2*

HONEY

a little balm, and a little *h.*   *Ge 43:11*
spices
a land flowing with milk and *h.*   *Ex 3:8;*
3:17; 13:5; 33:3; Jer 11:5; 32:22;
                      Eze 20:6, 15
of it was like wafers made   *Ex 16:31*
with *h.*
burn no leaven, nor any *h.* in   *Le 2:11*
any
land that floweth with milk   *Le 20:24;*
and *h.*   *Nu 13:27; 14:8; 16:13-14;*
De 6:3; 11:9; 26:9, 15; 27:3; 31:20;
                         Jos 5:6
a land of oil olive, and *h.*   *De 8:8*
made him to suck *h.* out of   *De 32:13*
the rock
was a swarm of bees and *h.*   *J'g 14:8*
in the
had taken the *h.* out of the   *J'g 14:9*
carcase

What is sweeter than *h.*? and *J'g 14:18*
and there was *h.* upon the *1Sa 14:25*
ground
the *h.* dropped; but no man *1Sa 14:26*
put his
because I tasted a little of *1Sa 14:29*
this *h.*
I did but taste a little *h.* with *1Sa 14:43*
And *h.* and butter, and *2Sa 17:29*
sheep, and
and cracknels, and a cruse of *1Ki 14:8*
h.
a land of oil olive and of *h.* *2Ki 18:32*
that ye
wine, and oil, and *h.* and of *2Ch 31:5*
all the
floods, the brooks of *h.* and *Job 20:17*
butter
gold: sweeter also than *h.* and *Ps 19:10*
and with *h.* out of the rock *Ps 81:16*
should I
yea, sweeter than *h.* to my *Ps 119:103*
mouth
son, eat thou *h.* because it is *Pr 24:13*
good
Hast thou found *h.*? eat so *Pr 25:16*
much as
It is not good to eat much *h.* *Pr 25:27*
h. and milk are under thy *Ca 4:11*
tongue
eaten my honeycomb with my *h.* *Ca 5:1*
Butter and *h.* shall he eat, *Isa 7:15*
that he
for butter and *h.* shall every *Isa 7:22*
one eat
and of barley, and of oil, and *Jer 41:8*
of *h.*
in my mouth as *h.* for *Eze 3:3*
sweetness
didst eat fine flour, and *h.* *Eze 16:13*
and oil
gave thee, fine flour and oil, *Eze 16:19*
and *h.*
Pannag, and *h.* and oil, and *Eze 27:17*
balm
his meat was locusts and wild *M't 3:4*
h.
and he did eat locusts and wild *M'k 1:6*
h.
it shall be in thy mouth sweet *Re 10:9*
as *h.*
it was in my mouth sweet as *Re 10:10*
h.

HONEYCOMB

and dipped it in an *h.* and *1Sa 14:27*
put
also than honey and the *h.* *Ps 19:10*
a strange woman drop as an *h.* *Pr 5:3*
Pleasant words are as an *h.* *Pr 16:24*
the *h.* which is sweet to thy *Pr 24:13*
taste
The full soul loatheth an *h.*; *Pr 27:7*
but to
lips, O my spouse, drop as the *Ca 4:11*
h.
have eaten my *h.* with my honey *Ca 5:1*
a broiled fish, and of an *h.* *Lu 24:42*

HONOR

acted in good faith and *h.* (R) *J'g 9:19*
bestows favor and *h.* (B)(R) *Ps 84:11*
thou shalt have *h.* (S) *Lu 14:10*
no obligation of *h.* (P) *Ro 1:31*
through *h.* and shame (B) *2Co 6:8*
in highest *h.* (P) *1Th 5:13*

HONORABLY

conduct ourselves *h.* (A) *Ro 13:3;*
1Pe 2:12
desiring to live *h.* (E)(R) *Heb 13:5*
conduct yourselves *h.* (B) *1Pe 2:12*

HONORED

your name be *h.* (P) *M't 6:9*

HONOUR

mine *h.* be not thou united: for *Ge 49:6*
and I will get me *h.* upon *Ex 14:17*
Pharaoh
I have gotten me *h.* upon *Ex 14:18*
Pharaoh

H. thy father and thy mother *Ex 20:12*
nor *h.* the person of the *Le 19:15*
mighty
and *h.* the face of the old *Le 19:32*
man, and
promote thee unto very great *Nu 22:17*
h.
able indeed to promote thee *Nu 22:37*
to *h.*
to promote thee unto great *Nu 24:11*
h.: but
Lord hath kept thee back *Nu 24:11*
from *h.*
put some of thine *h.* upon *Nu 27:20*
him
h. thy father and thy mother, *De 5:16*
as
in praise, and in name, and in *De 26:19*
h.
thou takest shall not be for *J'g 4:9*
thine *h.*
by me they *h.* God and man *J'g 9:9*
come to pass we may do thee *J'g 13:17*
they
them that *h.* me I will *h.* and *1Sa 2:30*
sinned: yet *h.* me now, I pray *1Sa 15:30*
thee
of, of them shall I be had in *h.* *2Sa 6:22*
thou that David doth *h.* thy *2Sa 10:3*
father
hast not asked, both riches, *1Ki 3:13*
and *h.*
Glory and *h.* are in his *1Ch 16:27*
presence
to thee, for the *h.* of thy *1Ch 17:18*
servant
thou that David doth *h.* thy *1Ch 19:3*
father
Both riches and *h.* come of *1Ch 29:12*
thee
old age, full of days, riches, *1Ch 29:28*
and *h.*
hast not asked riches, wealth, *2Ch 1:11*
or *h.*
give thee riches, and wealth, *2Ch 1:12*
and *h.*
he had riches and *h.* in *2Ch 17:5*
abundance
had riches and *h.* in *2Ch 18:1*
abundance, and
neither shall it be for thine *2Ch 26:18*
h. from
exceeding much riches and *h.* *2Ch 32:27*
inhabitants of Jerusalem did *2Ch 32:33*
him *h.*
and the *h.* of his excellent *Es 1:4*
majesty
shall give to their husbands *h.*, *Es 1:20*
both
What *h.* and dignity hath been *Es 6:3*
done
whom the king delighteth to *h.* *Es 6:6*
would the king delight to do *h.* *Es 6:6*
more
whom the king delighteth to *h.* *Es 6:7;*
6:9
whom the king delighteth to *h.* *Es 6:9*
light, and gladness, and joy, *Es 8:16;*
and *h.* *6:11*
sons come to *h.* and he *Job 14:21*
knoweth
earth, and lay mine *h.* in the *Ps 7:5*
dust
crowned him with glory and *h.* *Ps 8:5*
h. and majesty hast thou laid *Ps 21:5*
upon
the place where thine *h.* *Ps 26:8*
dwelleth
man being in *h.* abideth not: *Ps 49:12*
he is
that is in *h.* and understandeth *Ps 49:20*
not
Sing forth the *h.* of his name *Ps 66:2*
praise and with thy *h.* all the *Ps 71:8*
day
I will deliver him, and *h.* him *Ps 91:15*
H. and majesty are before him *Ps 96:6*
art clothed with *h.* and *Ps 104:1*
majesty
his horn shall be exalted with *Ps 112:9*
h.
the glorious *h.* of thy majesty *Ps 145:5*
written: this *h.* have all his *Ps 149:9*
saints
H. the Lord with thy substance *Pr 3:9*

and in her left hand riches and *Pr 3:16*
h.
she shall bring thee to *h.* when *Pr 4:8*
Lest thou give thine *h.* unto *Pr 5:9*
others
Riches and *h.* are with me; yea *Pr 8:18*
A gracious woman retaineth *Pr 11:16*
h.
multitude of people is the *Pr 14:28*
king's *h.*
wisdom; and before *h.* is *Pr 15:33*
humility
haughty, and before *h.* is *Pr 18:12*
humility
It is an *h.* for a man to cease *Pr 20:3*
from
findeth life, righteousness, and *Pr 21:21*
h.
the Lord are riches, and *h.* and *Pr 22:4*
life
but the *h.* of kings is to search *Pr 25:2*
out
harvest, so *h.* is not seemly for *Pr 26:1*
a fool
so is he that giveth *h.* to a fool *Pr 26:8*
h. shall uphold the humble in *Pr 29:23*
spirit
Strength and *h.* are her *Pr 31:25*
clothing
riches, wealth, and *h.* so that he *Ec 6:2*
is in reputation for wisdom *Ec 10:1*
and *h.*
with their lips do *h.* me, but *Isa 29:13*
have
The beast of the field shall *h.* *Isa 43:20*
me
and shalt *h.* him, not doing *Isa 58:13*
thine
a praise and an *h.* before all *Jer 33:9*
me gifts and rewards and great *Da 2:6*
h.
of my power, and for the *h.* of *Da 4:30*
mine *h.* and brightness *Da 4:36*
returned
extol and *h.* the King of *Da 4:37*
heaven, all
and majesty, and glory, and *h.* *Da 5:18*
not give the *h.* of the kingdom *Da 11:21*
shall be *h.* the God of forces *Da 11:38*
his fathers knew not shall he *Da 11:38*
h.
I be a father, where is mine *h.* *Mal 1:6*
A prophet is not without *h.* *M't 13:57*
save in
H. thy father and thy mother: *M't 15:4*
and he
h. not his father or his mother, *M't 15:6*
he
H. thy father and thy mother *M't 19:19*
A prophet is not without *h.* *M'k 6:4*
but in
H. thy father and thy mother *M'k 7:10*
not; *H.* thy father and mother *M'k 10:19*
h. thy father and thy mother *Lu 18:20*
hath no *h.* in his own country *Joh 4:44*
that all men should *h.* the Son *Joh 5:23*
the Son, even as they *h.* the *Joh 5:23*
Father
I receive not *h.* from men *Joh 5:41*
which receive *h.* one of *Joh 5:44*
another
the *h.* that cometh from God *Joh 5:44*
only
but I *h.* my Father, and ye do *Joh 8:49*
Jesus answered, If I *h.* myself *Joh 8:54*
If I myself, my *h.* is nothing *Joh 8:54*
serve me, him will my Father *Joh 12:26*
h.
Jesus gained in *h.* (N) *Ac 19:17*
for glory and *h.* and immortality *Ro 2:7*
But glory, *h.* and peace, to *Ro 2:10*
every
to make one vessel unto *h.* and *Ro 9:21*
love; in *h.* preferring one *Ro 12:10*
another
fear to whom fear; *h.* to whom *Ro 13:7*
h.
these we bestow more *1Co 12:23*
abundant *h.*
given more abundant *h.* to *1Co 12:24*
that
h. and dishonour, by evil *2Co 6:8*
report
H. thy father and mother; *Eph 6:2*
which
not in any *h.* to the satisfying *Col 2:23*
his vessel in sanctification and *1Th 4:4*
be *h.* and glory for ever and *1Ti 1:17*
ever

HONOUR (continued)

H. widows that are widows indeed   *1Ti 5:3*
be counted worthy of double h.   *1Ti 5:17*
their own masters worthy of all h.   *1Ti 6:1*
whom be h. and power everlasting   *1Ti 6:16*
some to h. and some to dishonour   *2Ti 2:20*
be a vessel unto h. sanctified   *2Ti 2:21*
crownedst him with glory and h.   *Heb 2:7*
death, crowned with glory and h.   *Heb 2:9*
builded the house hath more h.   *Heb 3:3*
no man taketh this h. unto himself   *Heb 5:4*
might be found unto praise and h.   *1Pe 1:7*
H. all men. Love the brotherhood.   *1Pe 2:17*
Fear God. H. the king   *1Pe 2:17*
giving h. unto the wife, as unto   *1Pe 3:7*
from God the Father h. and glory   *2Pe 1:17*
beasts give glory and h. and thanks   *Re 4:9*
to receive glory and h. and power   *Re 4:11*
and h. and glory, and blessing   *Re 5:12*
Blessing, and h. and glory, and   *Re 5:13*
h. and power, and might, be unto   *Re 7:12*
Salvation, and glory, and h.   *Re 19:1*
and rejoice, and give h. to him   *Re 19:7*
do bring their glory and h. into it   *Re 21:24*
bring the glory and h. of the nations   *Re 21:26*

HONOURABLE

was more h. than all the house of   *Ge 34:19*
more, and more h. than they   *Nu 22:15*
man of God, and he is an h. man   *1Sa 9:6*
bidding, and is h. in thine house   *1Sa 22:14*
Was he not most h. of three   *2Sa 23:19*
He was more h. than the thirty   *2Sa 23:23*
man with his master, and h.   *2Ki 5:1*
was more h. than his brethren   *1Ch 4:9*
three, he was more h. than the two   *1Ch 11:21*
he was h. among the thirty, but   *1Ch 11:25*
and the h. man dwelt in it   *Job 22:8*
were among thy h. women: upon   *Ps 45:9*
His work is h. and glorious   *Ps 111:3*
of fifty, and the h. man, and   *Isa 3:3*
ancient, and base against the h.   *Isa 3:5*
and their h. men are famished, and   *Isa 5:13*
ancient and h. he is the head   *Isa 9:15*
traffickers are the h. of the earth   *Isa 23:8*
contempt all the h. of the earth   *Isa 23:9*
magnify the law, and make it h.   *Isa 42:21*
thou hast been h. and I have loved   *Isa 43:4*
delight, the holy of the Lord, h.; and   *Isa 58:13*
and they cast lots for her h. men   *Na 3:10*
of Arimathæa, an h. counsellor   *M'k 15:43*
more h. man than thou be bidden   *Lu 14:8*
up the devout and h. women   *Ac 13:50*
of h. women which were Greeks   *Ac 17:12*
thought for things h. (E)(N)   *Ro 12:17*
for things h. (E)(N)(R)   *2Co 8:21*
ye are h. but we are despised   *1Co 4:10*
body, which we think to be less h.   *1Co 12:23*
do that which is h. (E)   *2Co 13:7*
be correct and h. (A)(B)   *1Th 4:12*
Marriage is h. in all, and the bed   *Heb 13:4*

HONOURED

and I will be h. upon Pharaoh   *Ex 14:4*
that regardeth reproof shall be h.   *Pr 13:18*

---

waiteth on his master shall be h.   *Pr 27:18*
hast thou h. me with thy sacrifices   *Isa 43:23*
all that h. her despise her, because   *La 1:8*
the faces of elders were not h.   *La 5:12*
and h. him that liveth for ever   *Da 4:34*
also h. us with many honours   *Ac 28:10*
one member, be h. all the members   *1Co 12:26*

HONOUREST

and h. thy sons above me, to make   *1Sa 2:29*

HONOURETH

but he h. them that fear the Lord   *Ps 15:4*
better than he that h. himself   *Pr 12:9*
that h. him hath mercy on the poor   *Pr 14:31*
A son, h. his father, and a servant   *Mal 1:6*
mouth, and h. me with their lips   *M't 15:8*
This people h. me with their lips   *M'k 7:6*
that h. not the Son h. not the Father   *Joh 5:23*
it is my Father that h. me; of   *Joh 8:54*

HONOURS

also honoured us with many h.   *Ac 28:10*

HOODS

linen, and the h. and the veils   *Isa 3:23*

HOOF

shall not an h. be left behind   *Ex 10:26*
Whatsoever parteth the h. and   *Le 11:3*
cud, or of them that divide the h.   *Le 11:4*
the swine, though he divide the h.   *Le 11:7*
every beast which divideth the h.   *Le 11:26*
And every beast that parteth the h.   *De 14:6*
of them that divide the cloven h.   *De 14:7*
chew the cud, but divide not the h.   *De 14:7*
swine, because it divideth the h.   *De 14:8*

HOOFS

or bullock that hath horns and h.   *Ps 69:31*
horses' h. shall be counted like   *Isa 5:28*
the noise of the stamping of the h.   *Jer 47:3*
the h. of his horses shall he tread   *Eze 26:11*
nor the h. of beasts trouble them   *Eze 32:13*
iron, and I will make thy h. brass   *Mic 4:13*

HOOK

I will put my h. in thy nose   *2Ki 19:28*
draw out leviathan with an h.   *Job 41:1*
thou put an h. into his nose   *Job 41:2*
with a h. or spike (A)(E)(R)   *Job 41:2*
will I put my h. in thy nose   *Isa 37:29*
take up with the h. (A)(B)(R)   *Hab 1:15*
go thou to the sea, and cast an h.   *M't 17:27*

HOOKS

their h. shall be of gold, upon   *Ex 26:32*
gold, and their h. shall be of gold   *Ex 26:37*
h. of the pillars and their fillets   *Ex 27:10; 27:11*
their h. shall be of silver, and   *Ex 27:17*
his h. (A)(R)   *Ex 35:11*
with gold: their h. were of gold   *Ex 36:36*
the five pillars of it with their h.   *Ex 36:38*
the h. of the pillars and   *Ex 38:10; 38:11, 12, 17*

---

their h. of silver, and the overlaying   *Ex 38:19*
shekels he made h. for the pillars   *Ex 38:28*
his h. (R)   *Ex 39:33; 2Ch 33:11*
took Mannaseh with h. (A)(B)(R)   *2Ch 33:11*
cut off the sprigs with pruning h.   *Isa 18:5*
But I will put h. in thy jaws   *Eze 29:4*
thee back, and put h. into thy jaws   *Eze 38:4*
And within were h. an hand broad   *Eze 40:43*
that he will take you away with h.   *Am 4:2*

HOOPOE

the h. (S)   *Le 11:19; De 14:18*

HOPE

If I should say, I have h. if I   *Ru 1:12*
yet now there is h. in Israel   *Ezr 10:2*
thy fear, thy confidence, thy h.   *Job 4:6*
So the poor hath h. and iniquity   *Job 5:16*
is my strength, that I should h.   *Job 6:11*
shuttle, and are spent without h.   *Job 7:6*
and the hypocrite's h. shall perish   *Job 8:13*
Whose h. shall be cut off; and   *Job 8:14*
be secure, because there is h.   *Job 11:18*
their h. shall be as the giving up   *Job 11:20*
hope (E)   *Job 13:15*
hope (R)   *Job 13:15; Isa 51:5; M't 12:21; Joh 5:45; Ro 15:12, 24; 1Co 16:7; 2Co 1:10; , 13; 5:11; 13:6; Ph'p 2:19; 2Ti 4:10; 6:17; 2Jo 12; 2Jo 14*
there is h. of a tree, if it be cut down   *Job 14:7*
and thou destroyest the h. of man   *Job 14:19*
And where is now my h.   *Job 17:15*
as for my h. who shall see it   *Job 17:15*
mine h. hath he removed like a tree   *Job 19:10*
For what is the h. of the hypocrite   *Job 27:8*
If I have made gold my h. or have   *Job 31:24*
Behold, the h. of him is in vain   *Job 41:9*
my flesh also shall rest in h.   *Ps 16:9*
didst make me h. when I was   *Ps 22:9*
heart, all ye that h. in the Lord   *Ps 31:24*
upon them that h. in his mercy   *Ps 33:18*
upon us, according as we h. in thee   *Ps 33:22*
in thee, O Lord, do I h.: thou   *Ps 38:15*
what wait I for? my h. is in thee   *Ps 39:7*
disquieted in me? h. thou in God   *Ps 42:5*
within me? h. thou in God   *Ps 42:11*
disquieted within me? h. in God   *Ps 43:5*
h. in thy name (E)   *Ps 52:9*
For thou art my h. O Lord God   *Ps 71:5*
But I will h. continually, and   *Ps 71:14*
they might set their h. in God   *Ps 78:7*
which thou hast caused me to h.   *Ps 119:49*
salvation: but I h. in thy word   *Ps 119:81*
and my shield: I h. in thy word   *Ps 119:114*
let me not be ashamed of my h.   *Ps 119:116*
doth wait, and in his word do I h.   *Ps 130:5*
Let Israel h. in the Lord: for   *Ps 130:7*
Let Israel h. in the Lord from   *Ps 131:3*
my spirit is losing h. (B)   *Ps 143:4*
whose h. is in the Lord his God   *Ps 146:5*
him, in those that h. in his mercy   *Ps 147:11*
The h. of the righteous shall be   *Pr 10:28*
the h. of unjust men perisheth   *Pr 11:7*
H. deferred maketh the heart sick   *Pr 13:12*
the righteous hath h. in his death   *Pr 14:32*

Chasten thy son while there is *Pr 19:18*
h.
is more h. of a fool than of *Pr 26:12;*
him *Pr 29:20*
joined to all the living there is h. *Ec 9:4*
into the pit cannot h. for thy *Isa 38:18*
truth
saidst thou not, There is no h. *Isa 57:10*
but thou saidst, There is no h. *Jer 2:25*
O the h. of Israel, the saviour *Jer 14:8*
Lord, and whose h. the Lord is *Jer 17:7*
O Lord, the h. of Israel, all *Jer 17:13*
thou art my h. in the day of *Jer 17:17*
evil
And they said, There is no h. *Jer 18:12*
And there is h. in thine end *Jer 31:17*
the Lord, the h. of their fathers *Jer 50:7*
strength and my h. is perished *La 3:18*
to my mind, therefore have I *La 3:21*
soul; therefore will I h. in him *La 3:24*
good that a man should both h. *La 3:26*
the dust; if so be there may be *La 3:29*
h.
and they have made others to *Eze 13:6*
h.
had waited, and her h. was *Eze 19:5*
lost
bones are dried, and our h. is *Eze 37:11*
lost
the valley of Achor for a door *Ho 2:15*
of h.
Lord will be the h. of his *Joe 3:16*
people
the strong hold, ye prisoners *Zec 9:12*
of h.
nations h. in him (B) *M't 12:21*
Gentiles h. (E) *M't 12:21; Ro 15:12*
hope (N) *M't 12:21; Joh 5:45;*
Ro 15:12, 24; 1Co 16:7; 2Co 1:10;
5:11; 13:6; Ph'p 2:10; 4:10; 6:17;
Ph'm 22; 2Jo 12; 3Jo 14
hope (P) *M't 12:21;*
Ro 15:12, 24; 1Co 16:7; Ph'p 2:19;
Ph'm 22; 2Jo 12; 3Jo 14
to them of whom ye h. to *Lu 6:34*
receive
also my flesh shall rest in h. *Ac 2:26*
that the h. of their gains was *Ac 16:19*
gone
the h. and resurrection of the *Ac 23:6*
dead
And have h. toward God *Ac 24:15*
am judged for the h. of the *Ac 26:6*
promise
God day and night, h. to come *Ac 26:7*
all h. that we should be saved *Ac 27:20*
was
that for the h. of Israel I am *Ac 28:20*
bound
Who against h. believed in h. *Ro 4:18*
and rejoice in h. of the glory of *Ro 5:2*
God
experience; and experience, h. *Ro 5:4*
And h. maketh not ashamed *Ro 5:5*
who hath subjected the same *Ro 8:20*
in h.
for we are saved by h. *Ro 8:24*
but h. that is seen is not h. *Ro 8:24*
man seeth, why doth he yet h. *Ro 8:24*
But if we h. for that we see not *Ro 8:25*
Rejoicing in h.; patient in *Ro 12:12*
of the scriptures might have h. *Ro 15:4*
in him Gentiles h. (A)(B) *Ro 15:12*
the God of h. fill you with all *Ro 15:13*
joy and
that ye may abound in h. *Ro 15:13*
hope (A) *Ro 15:24; 1Co 16:7;*
2Co 1:13; 5:11; 13:6; Ph'p 2:19; 2Jo 12;
3Jo 14
hope (B) *Ro 15:24;*
1Co 16:7; 2Co 1:10; 13:6; Ph'p 2:19;
1Ti 4:10; 6:17; Ph'm 22; 2Jo 12; 3Jo 14
hope (E) *Ro 15:24; 1Co 16:7; 2Co 1:13;*
5:11; 13:6; Ph'p 2:19; Ph'm 22; 2Jo 12;
3Jo 14
he that ploweth should plow *1Co 9:10*
in h.
and that he that thresheth in *1Co 9:10*
h.
should be partaker of his h. *1Co 9:10*
And now abideth faith, h. *1Co 13:13*
charity
If in this life only we have h. *1Co 15:19*
And our h. of you is stedfast, *2Co 1:7*
set out h. in (A)(E) *2Co 1:10; 1Ti 6:17*
Seeing them that we have *2Co 3:12*
such h.
but having h. when your *2Co 10:15*
faith is

wait for the h. of righteousness *Ga 5:5*
know what is the h. of his *Eph 1:18*
calling
having no h. and without God *Eph 2:12*
are called in one h. of your *Eph 4:4*
calling
my earnest expectation and *Ph'p 1:20*
my h.
I passionately h. (N) *Ph'p 1:20*
Him therefore I h. to send *Ph'p 2:23*
the h. which is laid up for you *Col 1:5*
away from the h. of the gospel *Col 1:23*
Christ in you, the h. of glory *Col 1:27*
patience of h. in our Lord *1Th 1:3*
Jesus
For what is our h. or joy, or *1Th 2:19*
crown
even as others which have no *1Th 4:13*
h.
for an helmet, the h. of *1Th 5:8*
salvation
and good h. through grace *2Th 2:16*
Lord Jesus Christ, which is our *1Ti 1:1*
h.
our h. in God (E) *1Ti 4:10*
fixed her h. in God *1Ti 5:5*
(A)(B)(E)(N)(P)(R)
In h. of eternal life, which God *Tit 1:2*
Looking for that blessed h. and *Tit 2:13*
according to the h. of eternal *Tit 3:7*
life
confidence and rejoicing of the *Heb 3:6*
h.
full assurance of h. unto the *Heb 6:11*
end
lay hold upon the h. set before *Heb 6:18*
us
which h. we have as an *Heb 6:19*
anchor of
the bringing in of a better h. *Heb 7:19*
begotten us again unto a lively *1Pe 1:3*
h.
and h. to the end for the grace *1Pe 1:13*
that
your faith and h. might be in *1Pe 1:21*
God
a reason of the h. that is in *1Pe 3:15*
you
every man that hath this h. in *1Jo 3:3*
him

HOPED

the enemies of the Jews h. to *Es 9:1*
have
confounded because they had *Job 6:20*
for I have h. in thy *Ps 119:43*
judgments
because I have h. in thy word *Ps 119:74*
and cried: I h. in thy word *Ps 119:147*
Lord, I have h. for thy *Ps 119:166*
salvation
Truly in vain is salvation h. for *Jer 3:23*
from
he h. to have seen some *Lu 23:8*
miracle
we had h. that it was he (S) *Lu 24:21*
He h. also that the money *Ac 24:26*
should
And this they did, not as we h. *2Co 8:5*
is the substance of things h. *Heb 11:1*
women h. in God *1Pe 3:5*
(A)(B)(E)(R)

HOPES

h. confidently in you (A) *Isa 26:3*
set h. in him (A) *M't 12:21*

HOPE'S

For which h. sake, king *Ac 26:7*
Agrippa, I

HOPETH

believeth all things, h. all *1Co 13:7*
things

HOPHNI

two sons of Eli, H. and *1Sa 1:3*
Phinehas
thy two sons, on H. and *1Sa 2:34*
Phinehas
H. and Phinehas, were there *1Sa 4:4*
with
two sons of Eli, H. and *1Sa 4:11*
Phinehas
H. and Phinehas are dead *1Sa 4:17*

HOPING

I keep h. (B) *Job 13:15*
and lend, h. for nothing again *Lu 6:35*
thee, h. to come unto thee *1Ti 3:14*
shortly

HOPPED

h. about the altar (B) *1Ki 18:26*

HOPPER

the h. stripper (B)(R) *Joe 2:25*

HOR

Kadesh, and came unto *Nu 20:22*
mount H.
unto Moses and Aaron in *Nu 20:23*
mount H.
and bring them up unto *Nu 20:25*
mount H.
and they went up into mount *Nu 20:27*
H.
And they journeyed from *Nu 21:4*
mount H.
Kadesh, and pitched in *Nu 33:37*
mount H.
the priest went up into mount *Nu 33:38*
H.
years old when he died in *Nu 33:39*
mount H.
And they departed from *Nu 33:41*
mount H.
ye shall point out tor you *Nu 34:7*
mount H.
From mount H. ye shall point *Nu 34:8*
out
thy brother died in mount H. *De 32:50*

HORAM

Then H. king of Gezer came *Jos 10:33*

HORDE

this h. will now lick (R) *Nu 22:4*

HORDES

head of enemy's h. (A) *Hab 3:14*

HOREB

the mountain of God, even to H. *Ex 3:1*
thee there upon the rock in H. *Ex 17:6*
their ornaments by the mount *Ex 33:6*
H.
are eleven days' journey from *De 1:2*
H.
Lord our God spake unto us in *De 1:6*
H.
And when we departed from *De 1:19*
H. we
before the Lord thy God in H. *De 4:10*
Lord spake unto you in H. out *De 4:15*
God made a covenant with us in *De 5:2*
H.
Also in H. ye provoked the *De 9:8*
Lord to
desiredst of the Lord thy God *De 18:16*
in H.
which he made with them in *De 29:1*
H.
stone, which Moses put there at *1Ki 8:9*
H.
nights unto H. the mount of *1Ki 19:8*
God
which Moses put therein at H. *2Ch 5:10*
made a calf in H. and *Ps 106:19*
worshipped
which I commanded unto him *Mal 4:4*
in H.

HOREM

And Iron, and Migdal-el, H. *Jos 19:38*

HOR-HAGIDGAD

Bene-jaakan, and encamped *Nu 33:32*
at H.
they went from H. and *Nu 33:33*
pitched

HORI

of Lotan were H. and Hemam *Ge 36:22*
are the dukes that came of H. *Ge 36:30*

of Simeon, Shaphat, the son of   *Nu 13:5*
H.
the sons of Lotan; *H.* and   *1Ch 1:39*
Homam

HORIMS

The *H.* also dwelt in Seir   *De 2:12*
when he destroyed the *H.* from   *De 2:22*

HORITE

These are the sons of Seir the   *Ge 36:20*
H.

HORITES

And the *H.* in their mount Seir   *Ge 14:6*
these are the dukes of the *H.*   *Ge 36:21*
are the dukes that came of   *Ge 36:29*
the *H.*

HORMAH

discomfited them, even unto   *Nu 14:45*
H.
he called the name of the place   *Nu 21:3*
H.
destroyed you in Seir, even   *De 1:44*
unto *H.*
The king of *H.* one; the king   *Jos 12:14*
And Eltolad, and Chesil, and   *Jos 15:30*
H.
And Eltolad, and Bethul, and   *Jos 19:4*
H.
the name of the city was called   *J'g 1:17*
H.
And to them which were in   *1Sa 30:30*
H.
And at Bethuel, and at *H.*   *1Ch 4:30*

HORN

ox were wont to push with his   *Ex 21:29*
h.
ox was wont to gore in time   *Ex 21:29*
past (A)(E)(R)
ox repeatedly goring people   *Ex 21:29*
(B)
a long blast with the ram's *h.*   *Jos 6:5*
mine *h.* is exalted in the Lord   *1Sa 2:1*
my strength is heightened   *1Sa 2:1*
(B)(R)
and exalt the *h.* of his   *1Sa 2:10*
anointed
he enhances the might of his   *1Sa 2:10*
anointed (B)
he will give strength to his   *1Sa 2:10*
king (E)(R)
fill thine *h.* with oil, and go, I   *1Sa 16:1*
will
Then Samuel took the *h.* of   *1Sa 16:13*
oil, and
shield, and the *h.* of my   *2Sa 22:3*
salvation
Zadok the priest took an *h.* of   *1Ki 1:39*
oil
the words of God, to lift up   *1Ch 25:5*
the *h.*
promise of God to exalt him   *1Ch 25:5*
(A)(R)
God exalted his power (B)   *1Ch 25:5*
skin, and defiled my *h.* in the   *Job 16:15*
dust
buckler, and the *h.* of my   *Ps 18:2*
salvation
to the wicked, Lift not up the   *Ps 75:4*
h.
Lift not up your *h.* on high;   *Ps 75:5*
speak
thy favour our *h.* shall be   *Ps 89:17*
exalted
in my name shall his *h.* be   *Ps 89:24*
exalted
But my *h.* shalt thou exalt like   *Ps 92:10*
thou exalt like the *h.* of an   *Ps 92:10*
unicorn
his *h.* shalt be exalted with   *Ps 112:9*
honour
will I make the *h.* of David   *Ps 132:17*
to bud
also exalteth the *h.* of his   *Ps 148:14*
people
The *h.* of Moab is cut off, and   *Jer 48:25*
his fierce anger all the *h.* of   *La 2:3*
Israel
set up the *h.* of thine   *La 2:17*
adversaries
the *h.* of the house of Israel   *Eze 29:21*
to bud

horn (S)   *Da 3:5; 3:7, 10, 15; Ho 5:8*
up among them another little *h.*   *Da 7:8*
in this *h.* were eyes like the eyes   *Da 7:8*
great words which the *h.* spake   *Da 7:11*
even of that *h.* that had eyes   *Da 7:20*
same *h.* made war with the   *Da 7:21*
saints
the goat had a notable *h.*   *Da 8:5*
strong, the great *h.* was broken   *Da 8:8*
one of them came forth a little   *Da 8:9*
h.
great *h.* that is between his eye   *Da 8:21*
I will make thine *h.* iron, and   *Mic 4:12*
the Gentiles, which lifted up   *Zec 1:21*
their *h.*
hath raised up an *h.* of   *Lu 1:69*
salvation

HORNED

the *h.* owl (S)   *Le 11:17*

HORNET

God will send the *h.* among   *De 7:20*
them
I sent the *h.* before you,   *Jos 24:12*
which drave

HORNETS

And I will send *h.* before thee   *Ex 23:28*

HORNS

ram caught in a thicket by his   *Ge 22:13*
h.
And thou shalt make the *h.* of   *Ex 27:2*
his *h.* shall be of the same; and   *Ex 27:2*
and put it upon the *h.* of the   *Ex 29:12*
altar
the *h.* thereof shall be of the   *Ex 30:2*
same
round about, and the *h.* thereof   *Ex 30:3*
an atonement upon the *h.* of it   *Ex 30:10*
once
the *h.* thereof were of the   *Ex 37:25*
same
round about, and the *h.* of it   *Ex 37:26*
he made the *h.* thereof on the   *Ex 38:2*
four
it; the *h.* thereof were of the   *Ex 38:2*
same
blood upon the *h.* of the altar of   *Le 4:7*
blood upon the *h.* of the altar   *Le 4:18*
which
upon the *h.* of the altar of   *Le 4:25;*
  4:30, 34
and put it upon the *h.* of the   *Le 8:15;*
altar   *16:18*
the *h.* of a wild ox (R)   *Nu 23:22*
his *h.* are like the *h.* of   *De 33:17*
unicorns
ark seven trumpets of rams' *h.*   *Jos 6:4*
bear seven trumpets of rams' *h.*   *Jos 6:6*
seven trumpets of rams' *h.*   *Jos 6:8*
seven trumpets of rams' *h.*   *Jos 6:13*
before
caught hold on the *h.* of the   *1Ki 1:50;*
altar   *1:51; 2:28*
And Zedekiah made him   *1Ki 22:11;*
h. of iron   *2Ch 18:10*
me from the *h.* of the unicorns   *Ps 22:21*
or bullock that hath *h.* and   *Ps 69:31*
hoofs
the *h.* of the wicked also will I   *Ps 75:10*
cut
h. of the righteous shall be   *Ps 75:10*
exalted
even unto the *h.* of the altar   *Ps 118:27*
and upon the *h.* of your altars   *Jer 17:1*
for a present *h.* of ivory and   *Eze 27:15*
ebony
pushed all the diseased with   *Eze 34:21*
your *h.*
altar and upward shall be   *Eze 43:15*
four *h.*
thereof, and on the four *h.* of   *Eze 43:20*
it
were before it; and it had ten *h.*   *Da 7:7*
I considered the *h.* and behold   *Da 7:8*
three of the first *h.* plucked up   *Da 7:8*
the ten *h.* that were in his head   *Da 7:20*
And the ten *h.* out of this   *Da 7:24*
kingdom
the river a ram which had two   *Da 8:3*
h.
and the two *h.* were high; but   *Da 8:3*
one

came to the ram that had two *h.*   *Da 8:6*
smote the ram, and brake his   *Da 8:7*
two *h.*
four good sized *h.* (B)(R)   *Da 8:8*
sawest having two *h.* are the   *Da 8:20*
kings
the *h.* of the altar shall be cut   *Am 3:14*
Have we not taken to us *h.* by   *Am 6:13*
our
he had *h.* coming out of his   *Hab 3:4*
hand
eyes, and saw, and behold   *Zec 1:18*
four *h.*
h. which have scattered Judah   *Zec 1:19;*
  1:21
to cast out the *h.* of the   *Zec 1:21*
Gentiles
having seven *h.* and seven eyes   *Re 5:6*
from the four *h.* of the golden   *Re 9:13*
altar
sea, having seven heads and ten *h.*   *Re 12:3*
ten *h.*   *Re 13:1*
and upon his *h.* ten crowns   *Re 13:1*
he had two *h.* like a lamb,   *Re 13:11*
and he
having seven heads, and ten *h.*   *Re 17:3*
hath the seven heads and ten *h.*   *Re 17:7*
the ten *h.* which thou sawest   *Re 17:12;*
  17:16

HORONAIM

in the way of *H.* they shall   *Isa 15:5*
raise
A voice of crying shall be from   *Jer 48:3*
H.
for in the going down of *H.*   *Jer 48:5*
the
voice, from Zoar even unto   *Jer 48:34*
H.

HORONITE

When Sanballat the *H.* and   *Ne 2:10*
But when Sanballat the *H.* and   *Ne 2:19*
was son in law to Sanballat   *Ne 13:28*
the *H.*

HORRIBLE

brimstone, and an *h.* tempest   *Ps 11:6*
brought me up also out of an *h.*   *Ps 40:2*
pit
A wonderful and *h.* thing is   *Jer 5:30*
Israel hath done a very *h.*   *Jer 18:13*
thing
prophets of Jerusalem an *h.*   *Jer 23:14*
thing
I have seen an *h.* thing in the   *Ho 6:10*
house

HORRIBLY

heavens, at this, and be *h.*   *Jer 2:12*
afraid
their kings shall be *h.* afraid   *Eze 32:10*

HORRIFIED

greatly *h.* (P)   *M't 18:31*

HORROR

an *h.* of great darkness fell   *Ge 15:12*
become an object of *h.*   *De 28:27*
(B)(R)
an object of *h.* (B)(R)   *2Ch 29:8*
filled with *h.* (B)(R)   *Job 18:20*
and *h.* hath overwhelmed me   *Ps 55:5*
thing of *h.* to them (R)   *Ps 88:8*
H. hath taken hold upon me   *Ps 119:53*
h. terrifies me (A)(B)(R)   *Isa 21:4*
make them a *h.*   *Jer 25:9*
horror (S)   *Jer 25:9;*
25:11, 18; 29:18; 42:18; 44:12, 22; 51:37,
41; Eze 5:15; 23:33
a *h.* to all about him (S)   *Jer 48:39*
a *h.* (A)(B)(E)(R)   *Jer 49:17*
a *h.* and a kissing (B)(R)   *Jer 51:37*
an *h.* to the nations (B)(R)   *Eze 7:18*
h. shall cover them; and   *Eze 7:18*
shame
cup of *h.* (B)(R)   *Eze 23:33*
h. and dismay came (N)(P)   *M'k 14:33*
in *h.* and dismay (N)   *M'k 14:34*
performed shameful *h.* (P)   *Ro 1:27*

HORSE

the path, that biteth the *h.*   *Ge 49:17*
heels
the *h.* and his rider hath he   *Ex 15:1*
thrown
For the *h.* of Pharaoh went in   *Ex 15:19*
the *h.* and his rider hath he   *Ex 15:21*
thrown
and an *h.* for an hundred and   *1Ki 10:29*
fifty
king of Syria escaped on an   *1Ki 20:20*
h. with
h. for *h.* and chariot for   *1Ki 20:25*
chariot
and an *h.* for an hundred and   *2Ch 1:17*
fifty
come to the entering of the   *2Ch 23:15*
h. gate
From above the *h.* gate   *Ne 3:28*
repaired
the *h.* that the king rideth upon   *Es 6:8*
this apparel and *h.* be delivered   *Es 6:9*
and take the apparel and the *h.*   *Es 6:10*
took Haman the apparel and   *Es 6:11*
the *h.*
she scorneth the *h.* and his   *Job 39:18*
rider
Hast thou given the *h.*   *Job 39:19*
strength
Be ye not as the *h.* or as the   *Ps 32:9*
mule
An *h.* is a vain thing for safety   *Ps 33:17*
both the chariot and *h.* are cast   *Ps 76:6*
not in the strength of the *h.*   *Ps 147:10*
The *h.* is prepared against the   *Pr 21:31*
day
A whip for the *h.* a bridle for   *Pr 26:3*
bringeth forth the chariot and   *Isa 43:17*
h.
the deep, as an *h.* in the   *Isa 63:13*
wilderness
as the *h.* rusheth into the battle   *Jer 8:6*
unto the corner of the *h.* gate   *Jer 31:40*
toward
break in pieces the *h.* and his   *Jer 51:21*
rider
he that rideth the *h.* deliver   *Am 2:15*
himself
behold a man riding upon a red   *Zec 1:8*
h.
and the *h.* from Jerusalem   *Zec 9:10*
them as his goodly *h.* in the   *Zec 10:3*
battle
smite every *h.* with   *Zec 12:4*
astonishment
smite every *h.* of the people   *Zec 12:4*
And so shall be the plague of   *Zec 14:15*
the *h.*
I saw, and behold a white *h.*   *Re 6:2*
went out another *h.* that was red   *Re 6:4*
I beheld, and lo a black *h.;*   *Re 6:5*
and he
And I looked, and behold a pale   *Re 6:8*
h.
winepress, even unto the *h.*   *Re 14:20*
bridles
opened, and behold a white *h.*   *Re 19:11*
war against him that sat on   *Re 19:19*
the *h.*
sword of him that sat upon   *Re 19:21*
the *h.*

HORSEBACK

there went one on *h.* to meet   *2Ki 9:18*
Then he sent out a second on   *2Ki 9:19*
h.
on *h.* through the street of the   *Es 6:9*
on *h.* through the street of the   *Es 6:11*
city
and sent letters by posts on *h.*   *Es 8:10*

HORSEHOOFS

Then were the *h.* broken by   *J'g 5:22*

HORSELEACH

the *h.* hath two daughters   *Pr 30:15*

HORSEMAN

Joram said, Take an *h.* and   *2Ki 9:17*
send
The *h.* lifteth up both the bright   *Na 3:3*

HORSEMEN

up with him both chariots and   *Ge 50:9*
h.

chariots of Pharaoh, and his *h.*   *Ex 14:9*
his chariots, and upon his *h.*   *Ex 14:17;*
    14:18
horses, his chariots, and his *h.*   *Ex 14:23*
their chariots, and upon their   *Ex 14:26*
h.
covered the chariots, and the   *Ex 14:28*
h.
in with his chariots and with   *Ex 15:19*
his *h.*
with chariots and *h.* unto the   *Jos 24:6*
Red
for his chariots, and to be his   *1Sa 8:11*
h.
chariots, and six thousand *h.*   *1Sa 13:5*
h. followed hard after him   *2Sa 1:6*
chariots, and seven hundred *h.*   *2Sa 8:4*
the Syrians, and forty   *2Sa 10:18*
thousand *h.*
he prepared him chariots and   *1Ki 1:5*
h.
chariots, and twelve thousand   *1Ki 4:26*
h.
for his chariots, and cities for   *1Ki 9:19*
his *h.*
rulers of his chariots, and his   *1Ki 9:22*
h.
gathered together chariots   *1Ki 10:26*
and *h.*
chariots, and twelve   *1Ki 10:26*
thousand *h.*
escaped on an horse with the   *1Ki 20:20*
h.
chariot of Israel, and the *h.*   *2Ki 2:12*
thereof
he leave of the people but   *2Ki 13:7*
fifty *h.*
chariot of Israel, and the *h.*   *2Ki 13:14*
thereof
on Egypt for chariots and for   *2Ki 18:24*
chariots, and seven thousand   *1Ch 18:4*
silver to hire them chariots   *1Ch 19:6*
and *h.*
Solomon gathered chariots   *2Ch 1:14*
and *h.*
chariots, and twelve thousand   *2Ch 1:14*
h.
cities, and the cities of the *h.*   *2Ch 8:6*
and captains of his chariots   *2Ch 8:9*
and *h.*
chariots, and twelve thousand   *2Ch 9:25*
h.
and threescore thousand *h.*   *2Ch 12:3*
with very many chariots and *h.*   *2Ch 16:8*
a band of soldiers and *h.* to   *Ezr 8:22*
help us
had sent captains of the army   *Ne 2:9*
and *h.*
he saw a chariot with a couple   *Isa 21:7*
of *h.*
chariot of men, with a couple   *Isa 21:9*
of *h.*
quiver with chariots of men   *Isa 22:6*
and *h.*
the *h.* shall set themselves in   *Isa 22:7*
array
his cart, nor bruise it with his   *Isa 28:28*
h.
in *h.* because they are very   *Isa 31:1*
strong
on Egypt for chariots, and for   *Isa 36:9*
h.
for the noise of the *h.* and   *Jer 4:29*
bowmen
get up, ye *h.* and stand forth   *Jer 46:4*
young men *h.* riding upon   *Eze 23:6*
horses
h. riding upon horses, all of   *Eze 23:12*
them
with chariots, and with *h.* and   *Eze 26:7*
shall shake at the noise of   *Eze 26:10*
the *h.*
in thy fairs with horses and   *Eze 27:14*
h. and
and all thine army, horses and   *Eze 38:4*
h.
with chariots, and with *h.* and   *Da 11:40*
nor by battle, by horses, nor by   *Ho 1:7*
h.
and as *h.* so shall they run   *Joe 2:4*
their *h.* shall spread themselves   *Hab 1:8*
and their *h.* shall come from   *Hab 1:8*
far
and *h.* threescore ten, and   *Ac 23:23*
they left the *h.* to go with him   *Ac 23:32*
the number of the army of the   *Re 9:16*
h.

HORSES

them bread in exchange for *h.*   *Ge 47:17*
field, upon the *h.* upon the asses   *Ex 9:3*
all the *h.* and chariots of   *Ex 14:9*
Pharaoh
even all Pharaoh's *h.* his   *Ex 14:23*
chariots
unto their *h.* and to their   *De 11:4*
chariots
he shall not multiply *h.* to   *De 17:16*
himself
the end that he should multiply   *De 17:16*
h.
and seest *h.* and chariots   *De 20:1*
with *h.* and chariots very many   *Jos 11:4*
thou shalt hough their *h.* and   *Jos 11:6*
burn
he houghed their *h.* and burnt   *Jos 11:9*
David houghed all the chariot   *2Sa 8:4*
h.
prepared him chariots and *h.*   *2Sa 15:1*
had forty thousand stalls of *h.*   *1Ki 4:26*
Barley also and straw for the   *1Ki 4:28*
h. and
armour, and spices, *h.* and   *1Ki 10:25*
mules
had *h.* brought out of Egypt   *1Ki 10:28*
grass to save the *h.* and mules   *1Ki 18:5*
alive
with him, and *h.* and chariots   *1Ki 20:1*
and smote the *h.* and   *1Ki 20:21*
chariots, and
people as thy people, my *h.* as   *1Ki 22:4*
thy *h.*
a chariot of fire, and *h.* of fire   *2Ki 2:11*
as thy people, and my *h.* as thy   *2Ki 3:7*
Naaman came with his *h.* and   *2Ki 5:9*
sent he thither *h.* and chariots   *2Ki 6:14*
the city both with *h.* and   *2Ki 6:15*
chariots
was full of *h.* and chariots of   *2Ki 6:17*
fire
noise of chariots, and a noise   *2Ki 7:6*
of *h.*
left their tents, and their *h.* and   *2Ki 7:7*
but *h.* tied, and asses tied, and   *2Ki 7:10*
five of the *h.* that remain   *2Ki 7:13*
They took therefore two   *2Ki 7:14*
chariot *h.*
sprinkled on the wall, and on   *2Ki 9:33*
the *h.*
there are with you chariots   *2Ki 10:2*
and *h.*
way by the which the *h.*   *2Ki 11:16*
came into
And they brought him on *h.*   *2Ki 14:20*
I will deliver thee two   *2Ki 18:23*
thousand *h.*
he took away the *h.* that the   *2Ki 23:11*
kings
also houghed all the chariot   *1Ch 18:4*
h., but
had *h.* brought out of Egypt   *2Ch 1:16*
so brought they out *h.* for all   *2Ch 1:17*
the
harness, and spices, *h.* and   *2Ch 9:24*
mules
had four thousand stalls for   *2Ch 9:25*
h. and
unto Solomon *h.* out of Egypt   *2Ch 9:28*
h. and
And they brought him upon   *2Ch 25:28*
h. and
Their *h.* were seven hundred   *Ezr 2:66*
thirty
Their *h.* seven hundred thirty   *Ne 7:68*
trust in chariots, and some in *h.*   *Ps 20:7*
I have seen servants upon *h.*   *Ec 10:7*
to a company of *h.* in Pharaoh's   *Ca 1:9*
their land is also full of *h.*   *Isa 2:7*
neither
said, No; for we will flee   *Isa 30:16*
upon *h.*
stay on *h.* and trust in chariots   *Isa 31:1*
and their *h.* flesh, and not   *Isa 31:3*
spirit
I will give thee two thousand   *Isa 36:8*
h.
the Lord out of all nations   *Isa 66:20*
upon *h.*
his *h.* are swifter than eagles   *Jer 4:13*
They were as fed *h.* in the   *Jer 5:8*
morning
they ride upon *h.* set in array   *Jer 6:23*
The snorting of his *h.* was   *Jer 8:16*
heard

how canst thou contend with *Jer 12:5*
h.
riding in chariots and on *h.* *Jer 17:25;*
22:4
Harness the *h.;* and get up, ye *Jer 46:4*
Come up, ye *h.;* and rage, ye *Jer 46:9*
stamping of hoofs of his *Jer 47:3*
strong *h.*
A sword is upon their *h.* and *Jer 50:37*
they shall ride upon *h.* every *Jer 50:42*
one
cause the *h.* to come up as the *Jer 51:27*
rough
that they might give him *h.* *Eze 17:15*
men, horsemen riding upon *h.* *Eze 23:6*
horsemen riding upon *h.* all *Eze 23:12*
whose issue is like the issue *Eze 23:20*
of *h.*
renowned, all of them riding *Eze 23:23*
upon *h.*
with *h.* and with chariots, and *Eze 26:7*
By reason of the abundance *Eze 26:10*
of his *h.*
the hoofs of his *h.* shall he *Eze 26:11*
tread
with *h.* and horsemen and *Eze 27:14*
mules
all thine army, *h.* and *Eze 38:4*
horsemen
all of them riding upon *h.* a *Eze 38:15*
great
at my table with *h.* and *Eze 39:20*
chariots
by battle, by *h.* nor by *Ho 1:7*
horsemen
save us; we will not ride upon *Ho 14:3*
h.
of them is as the appearance of *Joe 2:4*
h.
and have taken away your *h.* *Am 4:10*
Shall *h.* run upon the rock *Am 6:12*
that I will cut off thy *h.* out of *Mic 5:10*
of the wheels and of the *Na 3:2*
pransing *h.*
Their *h.* are also swifter than *Hab 1:8*
that thou didst ride upon thine *Hab 3:8*
h.
walk through the sea with *Hab 3:15*
thine *h.*
the *h.* and their riders shall *Hag 2:22*
come
and behind him were there red *Zec 1:8*
h.
In the first chariot *Zec 6:2*
were red *h.*
and in the second chariot black *Zec 6:2*
h.
And in the third chariot white *Zec 6:3*
h.
fourth chariot grisled and bay *Zec 6:3*
h.
The black *h.* which are therein *Zec 6:6*
go
riders on *h.* shall be *Zec 10:5*
confounded
there be upon the bells of the *Zec 14:20*
h.
of the locusts were like unto *h.* *Re 9:7*
the chariots of many *h.* running *Re 9:9*
And thus I saw the *h.* in the *Re 9:17*
vision
heads of the *h.* were as the *Re 9:17*
heads
and *h.* and chariots, and *Re 18:13*
slaves
heaven followed him upon *Re 19:14*
white *h.*
of mighty men, and the flesh *Re 19:18*
of *h.*

HORSES'

their *h.* hoofs shall be counted *Isa 5:28*
we put bits in the *h.* mouths *Jas 3:3*

HOSAH

and the coast turneth to H. *Jos 19:29*
of Jeduthun and H. to be *1Ch 16:38*
porters
Also H. of the children of *1Ch 26:10*
Merari
and brethren of H. were *1Ch 26:11*
thirteen
To Shuppim and H. the lot *1Ch 26:16*
came

HOSANNA

H. to the son of David: *M't 21:9*
Blessed
name of the Lord; H. in the *M't 21:9*
highest
and saying, H. to the son of *M't 21:15*
David
H.; Blessed is he that cometh *M'k 11:9*
in
name of the Lord; H. in the *M'k 11:10*
highest
H: Blessed is the King of *Joh 12:13*
Israel

HOSEA

of the Lord that came unto H. *Ho 1:1*
of the word of the Lord by H. *Ho 1:2*
Lord said to H., Go, take unto *Ho 1:2*
thee

HOSEN

were bound in their coats, *Da 3:21*
their *h.*

HOSHAIAH

And after them went H. and *Ne 12:32*
half
and Jezaniah the son of H. *Jer 42:1*
Then spake Azariah the son of *Jer 43:2*
H.

HOSHAMA

Jecamiah, H. and Nedabiah *1Ch 3:18*

HOSHEA

people, he, and H. the son of *De 32:44*
Nun
And H. the son of Elah made *2Ki 15:30*
began H. the son of Elah to *2Ki 17:1*
reign
and H. became his servant *2Ki 17:3*
of Assyria found conspiracy *2Ki 17:4*
in H.
in the ninth year of H. the *2Ki 17:6*
king of
in the third year of H. son of *2Ki 18:1*
Elah
which was the seventh year of *2Ki 18:9*
H.
that is the ninth year of H. *2Ki 18:10*
king of
of Ephraim, H. the son of *1Ch 27:20*
Azaziah
H., Hananiah, Hashub *Ne 10:23*

HOSPITABLY

entertained *h.* (N)(R) *Ac 28:7*

HOSPITALITY

entertained with hearty *h.* (A) *Ac 28:7*
necessity of saints; given to *h.* *Ro 12:13*
given to *h.* apt to teach *1Ti 3:2*
have practiced *h.* *1Ti 5:10*
(A)(B)(E)(N)(R)
But a lover of *h.* a lover of good *Tit 1:8*
Use *h.* one to another without *1Pe 4:9*

HOST

the earth was finished, and all *h.* *Ge 2:1*
of them
Phichol the chief captain of *Ge 21:22;*
his *h.* *21:32*
Jacob saw them, he said, This *Ge 32:2*
is God's *h.*
I will be honoured on all his *h.* *Ex 14:4;*
14:17
Lord looked to *h.* of *Ex 14:24*
Egyptians thro' pillar of
fire and troubled the *h.* of Egypt
the waters covered all the *h.* *Ex 14:28*
of Pharaoh
in morning the dew lay round *Ex 16:13*
about the *h.*
his *h.* and those that were *Nu 2:4;*
numbered of them *2:6, 8, 11, 13, 15, 19,*
21, 23
all that entered him into the *h.* *Nu 4:3*
to do the work
over the *h.* of Judah *Nu 10:14;*
10:15, 16, 18, 19
Moses was wroth with the *Nu 31:14*
officers of *h.*
the officers of the *h.* came *Nu 31:48*
near to Moses
men of war were wasted from *De 2:14*
the *h.*
destroy them from among *h.* *De 2:15*
till consumed
when the *h.* goeth forth against *De 23:9*
enemies
pass thro' the *h.* and command *Jos 1:11*
the people
after three days officers went *Jos 3:2*
thro' the *h.*
as captain of the *h.* of Lord *Jos 5:14*
am I come
came again to Joshua to the *h.* *Jos 18:9*
at Shiloh
the captain of whose *h.* was *J'g 4:2*
Sisera
all the *h.* of Sisera fell on the *J'g 4:16*
sword
the *h.* of Midian was beneath in *J'g 7:8*
the valley
God said, Arise, get thee down *J'g 7:9;*
unto the *h.* *7:10*
a cake of bread tumbled into *J'g 7:13*
the *h.* of Midian
and all the *h.* ran, and cried, *J'g 7:21*
and fled
Gideon went up and smote the *J'g 8:11*
h.: the *h.* secure
Gideon pursued and *J'g 8:12*
discomfited all the *h.*
Saul came into the *h.* in the *1Sa 11:11*
morning
there was trembling in the *h.* *1Sa 14:15*
in the field
the noise of the *h.* went on *1Sa 14:19*
and increased
captain of Saul's *h.* was *1Sa 14:50*
Abner son of Ner
David came as the *h.* was *1Sa 17:20*
going forth to fight
when Saul saw the *h.* of the *1Sa 28:5*
Philistines
Lord shall deliver the *h.* of *1Sa 28:19*
Israel to Philistines
thy going and coming in with *1Sa 29:6*
me in *h.* is good
Lord shall smite the *h.* of the *2Sa 5:24*
Philistines
when Toi king of Hamath *2Sa 8:9;*
heard David had smitten *1Ch 18:9*
all *h.* of Hadadezer
Syrians fled, David smote *2Sa 10:18;*
Shobach, captain of their *h.* *1Ch 18:18*
Absalom made Amasa *2Sa 17:25*
captain of the *h.*
if thou be not captain of *h.* in *2Sa 19:13*
room of Joab
Joab was over all the *h.* *2Sa 20:23;*
1Ch 18:15
these three brake thro' the *h.* *2Sa 23:16;*
1Ch 11:18
Abner son of Ner captain of *1Ki 2:32*
h. of Israel and Amasa
the king put Benaiah over the *1Ki 2:35;*
4:4
Israel made Omri captain of *1Ki 16:16*
the king
Benhadad gathered all his *h.* *1Ki 20:1*
together
And all the *h.* of heaven *1Ki 22:19*
standing
turn thy hand and carry me *1Ki 22:34*
out of the *h.*
there was no water for the *h.* *2Ki 3:9*
and cattle
wouldest be spoken for to the *2Ki 4:13*
captain of the *h.*
therefore sent he horses and *2Ki 6:14*
great *h.* to Dothan
Benhadad gathered his *h.* and *2Ki 6:24*
went up
come and let us fall unto the *h.* *2Ki 7:4*
of the Syrians
Lord made the *h.* to hear the *2Ki 7:6*
noise of a great *h.*
behold the captains of the *h.* *2Ki 9:5*
were sitting
Sennacherib sent a great *h.* *2Ki 18:17*
against Jerusalem
came and his *h.* against *2Ki 25:1*
Jerusalem
the principal scribe of the *h.* *2Ki 25:19;*
Jer 52:25
their fathers over the *h.* of the *1Ch 9:19*
Lord

HOST (cont.)

till it was a great *h*. like the · *1Ch 12:22*
h. of God

was the chief of all the · *1Ch 27:3*
captains of the *h*.

against them Zerah came with · *2Ch 14:9*
an *h*.

not relied, therefore the *h*. of · *2Ch 16:7*
Syria escaped

were not the Ethiopians and · *2Ch 16:8*
Lubims a huge *h*.

turn thy hand and carry me · *2Ch 18:33*
out of the *h*.

the Lord delivered a great *h*. · *2Ch 24:24*
into their hand

Uzziah had an *h*. of fighting · *2Ch 26:11*
men for war

Oded went out before the *h*. · *2Ch 28:9*
and said, Behold

though an *h*. should encamp · *Ps 27:3*
against me

all *h*. of them made by breath · *Ps 33:6*
of thy mouth

no king is saved by the · *Ps 33:16*
multitude of an *h*.

a great *h*. (A)(B)(E)(R) · *Ps 68:11*

but overthrew Pharaoh and · *Ps 136:15*
h. in Red sea

Lord of hosts mustereth the *h*. · *Isa 13:4*
of battle

Lord shall punish the *h*. of · *Isa 24:21*
the high ones

that bringeth out their *h*. by · *Isa 40:26*
number

and all their *h*. have I · *Isa 45:12*
commanded

spare not, destroy ye utterly all · *Jer 51:3*
her *h*.

the voice of speech, as the · *Eze 1:24*
noise of an *h*.

bring up a *h*. (A)(R) · *Eze 23:46*

and it cast down some of the · *Da 8:10*
h.

he magnified himself to the · *Da 8:11*
prince of the *h*.

an *h*. was given him against · *Da 8:12*
the daily sacrifice

to give the *h*. to be trodden · *Da 8:13*
under foot

the captivity of this *h*. shall · *Ob 20*
possess that

multitude of the heavenly *h*. · *Lu 2:13*
praising God

two pence, gave them to the · *Lu 10:35*

a vast *h*. (B) · *Joh 6:5*

Gaius mine *h*. and of the · *Ro 16:23*
church

HOSTILE

h. to God (A)(B)(R) · *Ro 8:7*

abolished the *h*. dividing wall · *Eph 2:14*
(A)

HOSTILITY

show *h*. (B) · *Ps 103:9*

cherished animosity, *h*. (A) · *Ac 12:20*

h. which preaching (P) · *Ga 5:11*

broken down middle wall of · *Eph 2:14*
h. (R)

removed *h*. of law (P) · *Eph 2:15*

bringing *h*. to an end (R) · *Eph 2:16*

HOSTS

the *h*. of the Lord went out · *Ex 12:41*
from

standard, throughout their *h*. · *Nu 1:52;*
2:32; 10:25

and went up, they and all their · *Jos 10:5*
h.

went out, they and all their *h*. · *Jos 11:4*
with

in Karkor, and their *h*. with · *J'g 8:10*
them

that were left of all the *h*. of · *J'g 8:10*

the Lord of *h*. *1Sa 1:3; 4:4; 15:3; 17:45;*
2Sa 6:2, 18; 7:8, 26, 27; 1Ki 18:15;
2Ki 3:14; 19:31; 1Ch 11:9; 17:7, 24;
Ps 24:10; 46:7; 48:8; 84:1, 3, 12; Isa 1:9,
24; 2:12; 3:1; 5:7, 9, 16, 24; 6:3, 5;
8:13, 18; 9:7, 13, 19; 10:16; 10:26, 33;
13:4, 13; 14:22, 23, 24, 27; 17:3; 18:7;
19:4, 12, 16-20, 25; 21:10; 22:14; 23:9;
24:23; 25:6; 28:5, 29; 29:6; 31:4-5; 37:16,
32; 39:5; 44:6; 45:13; 47:4; 48:2; 51:15;
54:5; Jer 6:6, 9; 7:3, 21; 8:3; 9:7, 15,
17; 10:16; 11:17, 20, 22; 16:9; 19:3, 11,
15; 20:12; 23:15, 16, 36; 25:8, 27, 28,
29, 32; 26:18; 27:4, 18, 19, 21; 28:2, 14;
29:4, 8, 17, 21, 25; 30:8; 31:23, 35;
32:14, 15, 18; 33:11, 12; 35:13, 17-19;
39:16; 42:15, 18; 43:10; 44:2, 7, 11, 25;
46:18, 25; 48:1, 15; 49:7, 26, 35; 50:18,
33-34; 51:5, 14, 19, 33, 57, 58; Mic 4:4;
Na 2:13; 3:5; Hab 2:13; Zep 2:9, 10;
Hag 1:2, 5, 7, 9, 14; 2:4, 6-9, 11, 23;
Zec 1:3, 4, 6, 12, 14, 16-17; 2:8-9, 11;
3:7, 9-10; 4:6, 9; 5:4; 6:12, 15; 7:3,
4, 9, 12-13; 8:1-4, 6-7, 9, 11, 14, 18-23;
9:15; 10:3; 12:5; 13:2, 7; 14:16-17, 21;
Mal 1:4, 6, 8-11, 13-14; 2:2, 4, 7-8, 12,
16; 3:1, 5, 7, 10-12, 14, 17; 4:1, 3

the Lord God of *h*. · *2Sa 5:10;*
1Ki 19:10, 14; Ps 59:5; 69:6; 80:4, 7, 19;
84:8; 89:8; Isa 3:15; 10:23, 24; 22:5, 12,
14, 15; 28:22; Jer 2:19; 5:14; 15:16;
46:10; 49:5; 50:25, 31; Ho 12:5;
Am 5:15; 9:5

bands of *h*. for war (E) · *1Ch 7:4*

God of *h*. · *Ps 80:14;*
Jer 38:17; Am 3:13; 4:13; 5:14, 16, 27;
6:8, 14

heavenly *h*. be shaken (B) · *M'k 13:25*

Lord of *h*. (A)(B)(N)(R) · *Ro 9:29;*
Jas 5:4

innumerable *h*. of angels · *Heb 12:22*
(E)

HOT

when the sun waxed *h*. it · *Ex 16:21*
melted

And my wrath shall wax *h*. · *Ex 22:24*

that my wrath may wax *h*. · *Ex 32:10*

why doth thy wrath wax *h*. · *Ex 32:11*

and Moses' anger waxed *h*. · *Ex 32:19*
and he

not the anger of my lord wax · *Ex 32:22*
h.

grew *h*. with anger (B) · *Ex 39:19*

skin whereof there is a *h*. · *Le 13:24*
burning

of the anger and *h*. displeasure · *De 9:19*

the slayer, while his heart is *h*. · *De 19:6*

This our bread, we took *h*. for · *Jos 9:12*

the anger of the Lord was *h*. · *J'g 2:14;*
2:20

anger of the Lord was *h*. against · *J'g 3:8*

Let not thine anger be *h*. · *J'g 6:39*
against

anger of the Lord was *h*. · *J'g 10:7*
against

by that time the sun be *h*. ye · *1Sa 11:9*
shall

to put *h*. bread in the day · *1Sa 21:6*
when it

be opened until the sun be *h*. · *Ne 7:3*

when it is *h*. they are · *Job 6:17*
consumed

chasten me in thy *h*. displeasure *Ps 6:1;*
38:1

My heart was *h*. within me, · *Ps 39:3*
while

their flocks to *h*. thunderbolts · *Ps 78:48*

Can one go upon *h*. coals, and · *Pr 6:28*
his

that the brass of it may be *h*. · *Eze 24:11*

and the furnace exceeding *h*. · *Da 3:22*

They are all *h*. as an oven, and · *Ho 7:7*

comfort with *h*. air (B) · *Zec 10:2*

conscience seared with a *h*. · *1Ti 4:2*
iron

not *h*. tempered (B)(P) · *Tit 1:7*

that thou art neither cold nor · *Re 3:15*

I would thou wert cold or *h*. · *Re 3:15*

lukewarm, and neither cold nor · *Re 3:16*
h.

HOTHAM

Japhlet, and Shomer, and H. · *1Ch 7:32*

HOTHAN

Shama and Jehiel the sons of · *1Ch 11:44*
H.

HOTHIR

Mallothi, H. and Mahazioth · *1Ch 25:4*

The one and twentieth to H. · *1Ch 25:28*

HOTLY

thou hast so *h*. pursued after · *Ge 31:36*

poor are *h*. pursued (E) · *Ps 10:2*

HOTTEST

in the forefront of the *h*. · *1Sa 11:15*
battle

front line of heaviest fighting · *2Sa 11:15*
(A)(B)

forefront of hardest fighting · *2Sa 11:15*
(R)

HOUGH

shalt *h*. their horses, and burn · *Jos 11:6*

shalt hock their horses · *Jos 11:6*
(A)(E)

hamstring their horses (B)(R) · *Jos 11:6*

HOUGHED

he *h*. their horses, and burnt · *Jos 11:9*

he hamstrung their horses · *Jos 11:9*
(A)(B)(R)

he hocked their horses (E) · *Jos 11:9*

David *h*. all the chariot horses · *2Sa 8:4*

he hamstrung all their horses · *2Sa 8:4*
(A)(B)(R)

hocked all their chariot horses · *2Sa 8:4*
(E)

David also *h*. all the chariot · *1Ch 18:4*
horses

HOUR

the same *h*. be cast into the · *De 3:6*
midst

be cast the same *h*. into the · *De 3:15*
midst

was astonied for one *h*. and his · *De 4:19*

stood aghast for a time (B) · *De 4:19*

was stricken dumb for a while · *De 4:19*
(E)

was dismayed for a long time · *De 4:19*
(R)

woman was made whole from · *M't 9:22*
that *h*.

her daughter made whole · *M't 15:28*
from that very *h*.

from that moment · *M't 15:28*
(A)(B)(N)(P)

daughter was healed instantly · *M't 15:28*
(R)

the child was cured from that · *M't 17:18*
very *h*.

the boy was cured instantly · *M't 17:18*
(A)(R)

from that exact moment · *M't 17:18*
(B)(N)(P)

he went out about the third *h*. · *M't 20:3*

about nine o'clock · *M't 20:3*
(A)(B)(P)

going out about three hours · *M't 20:3*
later (N)

about the sixth, and ninth *h*. · *M't 20:5*

about twelve and at three · *M't 20:5*
(A)(B)(N)(P)

the eleventh *h*. · *M't 20:6*

saying, These last have · *M't 20:12*
wrought but one *h*.

that *h*. knoweth no man · *Mt 24:36;*
24:42; M'k 13:32

such an *h*. as ye think not · *M't 24:44;*
24:50; Lu 12:40, 46

for ye know neither the day · *M't 25:13*
nor the *h*.

could ye not watch one *h*. · *M't 26:40;*
M'k 14:37

the *h*. is at hand, the Son of · *M't 26:45*
man is betrayed

from the sixth *h*. was · *M't 27:45*

darkness over the · *M'k 15:33; Lu 23:44*
land to the ninth *h*.

twelve o'clock until three · *M't 27:45*
(A)(B)(N)(P)

about the ninth *h*. Jesus · *M't 27:46;*
cried · *M'k 15:34*

about three o'clock · *M't 27:46*
(A)(B)(N)(P)

whatsoever shall be given · *M'k 13:11*
you in that *h*.

that if possible the *h*. might · *M'k 14:35*
pass from him

it was the third *h*. and they · *M'k 15:25*
crucified him

it was nine o'clock · *M'k 15:25*
(A)(B)(N)(P)

in that *h*. Jesus rejoiced in · *Lu 10:21*
spirit and said

had known what *h*. the thief · *Lu 12:39*
would come

and when the *h.* was come, he *Lu 22:14*
sat down
but this is your *h.* and the *Lu 22:53*
power of darkness
about the space of one *h.* *Lu 22:59*
after another affirmed
abode that day, for it was *Joh 1:39*
about tenth *h.*
about four o'clock *Joh 1:39*
(A)(B)(N)(P)
Jesus saith, Woman, mine *h.* is *Joh 2:4*
not yet come
Jesus sat, it was about the *Joh 4:6;*
sixth *h.* *19:14*
it was about noon (A)(B)(N) *Joh 4:6*
it was about midday (P) *Joh 4:6*
woman, believe me, the *h.* *Joh 4:21;*
cometh *4:23*
then inquired he the *h.* when *Joh 4:52*
he began to amend, yesterday
at seventh *h.* the fever left him
the *h.* is coming, and now is *Joh 5:25;*
5:28; 16:32
about one o'clock *Joh 5:52*
(A)(B)(N)(P)
because his *h.* was not yet *Joh 7:30;*
come *8:20*
the *h.* is come, Son should *Joh 12:23;*
be glorified *17:1*
my soul is troubled, Father, *Joh 12:27*
save me from this *h.* for this
cause came I to this *h.*
now comes the *h.* of *Joh 12:27*
heartbreak (P)
when Jesus knew that his *h.* *Joh 13:1*
was come
woman hath sorrow, because *Joh 16:21*
her *h.* is come
from that *h.* that disciple *Joh 19:27*
took her home
not drunken, seeing it is third *Ac 2:15*
h. of day
it is only nine o'clock *Ac 2:15*
(A)(B)(N)(P)
at the *h.* of prayer being the *Ac 3:1*
ninth *h.*
for the three o'clock hour *Ac 3:1*
A)(B)(N)(P)
he saw about the ninth *h.* an *Ac 10:3*
angel coming
about three o'clock *Ac 10:3*
(A)(B)(N)(P)
Peter went up to pray about *Ac 10:9*
the sixth *h.*
about noontime *Ac 10:9*
(A)(B)(N)(P)
four days ago I was fasting *Ac 10:30*
until this *h.*
make ready at the third *h.* of *Ac 23:23*
the night
at nine tonight *Ac 23:23*
(A)(B)(N)(P)
to this present *h.* both hunger *1Co 4:11*
and thirst
some with conscience of the *1Co 8:7*
idol unto this *h.*
and why stand we in *1Co 15:30*
jeopardy every *h.*
to whom we gave place, no not *Ga 2:5*
for an *h.*
not know what *h.* I will come *Re 3:3*
upon thee
I will keep thee from the *h.* of *Re 3:10*
temptation
there was silence about the *Re 8:1*
space of half an *h.*
which were prepared for an *h.* *Re 9:15*
and a day
fear God, for the *h.* of his *Re 14:7*
judgment is come
but receive power as kings *Re 17:12*
one *h.* with beast
for in one *h.* is thy judgment *Re 18:10*
come
in one *h.* so great riches is *Re 18:17*
come to nought
that great city in one *h.* is she *Re 18:19*
made desolate

SAME HOUR

the *same h.* be cast into the *Da 3:6;*
furnace *3:15*
the *same h.* was the thing *Da 4:33*
fulfilled on Nebuchadnezzar
in the *same h.* came forth *Da 5:5*
fingers, and wrote
his servant was healed the *M't 8:13*
same h.

it shall be given you the *M't 10:19;*
same *h.* *Lu 12:12*
in the *same h.* said Jesus to *M't 26:55*
the multitude
that *same h.* cured many of *Lu 7:21*
their plagues
scribes *same h.* sought to lay *Lu 20:19*
hands on him
rose up *same h.* returned to *Lu 24:33*
Jerusalem
father knew that it was at the *Joh 4:53*
same h.
and he came out the *same h.* *Ac 16:18*
he took them *same h.* of the *Ac 16:33*
night and washed
and the *same h.* I looked up *Ac 22:13*
upon him
the *same h.* was there a great *Re 11:13*
earthquake

HOURS

are there not twelve *h.* in the *Joh 11:9*
day
wife came in about space of *Ac 5:7*
three *h.* after
all cried about two *h.*, Great *Ac 19:34*
is Diana of Ephesians

HOUSE

men of Sodom compassed the *Ge 19:4*
h. round
Lord led me to the *h.* of my *Ge 24:27*
master's brethren
I have prepared the *h.* and *Ge 24:31*
room for camels
go to the *h.* of Bethuel, thy *Ge 28:2*
mother's father
the family of Bethuel (B) *Ge 28:2*
blessed Egyptian's *h.* for *Ge 39:5*
Joseph's sake
blessed the Egyptian's *Ge 39:5*
household (B)
the Egyptians and the *h.* of *Ge 45:2*
Pharaoh heard
Pharaoh's household heard *Ge 45:2*
(A)(B)(R)
frogs shall come into the *h.* of *Ex 8:3*
thy servants
a lamb according to the *h.* of *Ex 12:3*
their fathers
one lamb for each home (B) *Ex 12:3*
a lamb for each household *Ex 12:3*
(E)(R)
was not an *h.* where there was *Ex 12:30*
not one dead
thou shalt not carry of the *Ex 12:46*
flesh out of the *h.*
remember day ye came out *Ex 13:3;*
from Egypt, out of the *13:14; De 5:6;*
h. of bondage *6:12*
shalt not covet neighbour's *h.* *Ex 20:17;*
De 5:21
neighbor's household (B) *Ex 20:17*
priest shall command they *Le 14:36*
empty the *h.*
priest shall go out of the *h.* *Le 14:38*
and shut up
he shall break down the *h.* *Le 14:45*
and mortar of *h.*
he that goeth into the *h.* shall *Le 14:46*
be unclean
he shall take to cleanse the *h.* *Le 14:49*
two birds
h. sold in walled city, not go *Le 25:30*
out in jubilee
and it she vowed in her *Nu 30:10*
husband's *h.*
redeemed you out of the *h.* of *De 7:8*
bondmen
brought you out of the *h.* of *De 8:14;*
bondage *13:5, 10; Jos 24:17; J'g 6:8;*
Jer 34:13; Mic 6:4
the *h.* of him that hath his *De 25:10*
shoe loosed
for her *h.* was upon the town *Jos 2:15*
wall
neither shewed kindness to *h.* *J'g 8:35*
of Jerubbaal
all the *h.* of Millo made *J'g 9:6*
Abimelech king
let fire come from *h.* of Millo, *J'g 9:20*
and devour
Ammon fought against the *h.* *J'g 10:9*
of Ephraim
that I may feel pillars *J'g 16:26*
whereon *h.* standeth
the *h.* was full of men; *h.* fell *J'g 16:27;*
on the lords *16:30*

Micah had an *h.* of gods, made *J'g 17:5*
an ephod
and they came unto the *h.* of *J'g 18:13*
Micah
there is no man that receiveth *J'g 19:18*
me to *h.*
the sons of Belial beset the *h.* *J'g 19:22;*
round *20:5*
therefore I have sworn unto *h.* *1Sa 3:14*
of Eli
they brought the ark into the *h.* *1Sa 5:2*
of Dagon
and brought the ark into the *h.* *1Sa 7:1*
of Abinadab
tell me, I pray thee, where the *1Sa 9:18*
seer's *h.* is
return to his father's *h.* (B) *1Sa 18:2*
Nabal was churlish, and of *1Sa 25:3*
the *h.* of Caleb
Lord will certainly make my *1Sa 25:28*
lord a sure *h.*
long war between *h.* of Saul and *2Sa 3:1*
h. of David
do shew kindness to the *h.* of *2Sa 3:8*
Saul thy father
let there not fail from the *h.* *2Sa 3:29*
of Joab one
came to *h.* of Ishbosheth, who *2Sa 4:5*
lay on bed at
the lame and blind shall not *2Sa 5:8*
come into the *h.*
Lord blessed *h.* of *2Sa 6:11;*
Obed-edom, David *6:12; 1Ch 13:14*
brought ark from his *h.*
I have not dwelt in any *h.* *2Sa 7:6;*
1Ch 17:5
Lord telleth thee, he will *2Sa 7:11*
make thee an *h.*
to bless the *h.* of thy servant *2Sa 7:29;*
1Ch 17:27
is there any that is left of the *h.* *2Sa 9:1*
of Saul
and I gave thee thy master's *h.* *2Sa 12:8*
and wives
go now to thy brother *2Sa 13:7*
Amnon's *h.* and dress
see both it and his *h.* (A) *2Sa 15:25*
came a man of the family of *2Sa 16:5*
the *h.* of Saul
who made me an *h.* as he *1Ki 2:24*
promised
which he spake concerning the *1Ki 2:27*
h. of Eli
and the whole *h.* he overlaid *1Ki 6:22*
with gold
he burnt incense, so Solomon *1Ki 9:25*
finished the *h.*
they came to Pharaoh, who *1Ki 11:18*
gave him an *h.*
Jeroboam made an *h.* of his *1Ki 12:31*
high places
I will bring an evil on the *h.* *1Ki 14:10;*
of Jeroboam *14:14*
Baasha smote all the *h.* of *1Ki 15:29*
Jeroboam
Zimri slew all the *h.* of *1Ki 16:11*
Baasha, he left none
she, and he, and her *h.* did *1Ki 17:15*
eat many days
I will make thy *h.* like the *h.* *1Ki 21:22*
of Jeroboam
to cry to the king for her *h.* *2Ki 8:3*
and land
as did the *h.* of Ahab *2Ki 8:18;*
8:27; 2Ch 21:6; 22:4
for the whole *h.* of Ahab shall *2Ki 9:8*
perish
look out the best, fight for *2Ki 10:3*
your master's *h.*
h. of Baal was full from one *2Ki 10:21*
end to another
they made the *h.* of Baal a *2Ki 10:27*
draught *h.*
for all that was laid out for *2Ki 12:12*
h. to repair it
Hezekiah shewed *h.* of *2Ki 20:13;*
precious things, all *h.* *Isa 39:2*
of armour
h. of which I said, My name *2Ki 23:27*
shall be there
every great man's *h.* he burnt *2Ki 25:9*
with fire
sons of Salma; Ataroth the *h.* *1Ch 2:54*
of Joab
and to his sons, the *h.* of *1Ch 26:15*
Asuppim
glory of Lord filled the *h.* *2Ch 7:1;*
Eze 43:4-5
chosen this place to myself *2Ch 7:12*
for *h.* of sacrifice

so the *h.* of Ahaziah had no power to keep *2Ch 22:9*
but against the *h.* wherewith I have war *2Ch 35:21*
that we went to the *h.* of the great God *Ezr 5:8*
let the *h.* be builded, the place where offered *Ezr 6:3*
and for the *h.* which I shall enter into *Ne 2:8*
gather all the virgins to the *h.* of Es 2:3 women
king did give the *h.* of Haman to Esther *Es 8:1; 8:7*
drinking wine in eldest brother's *h.* *Job 1:13; 1:18*
wind came and smote corners of *h.* *Job 1:19*
hath taken away a *h.* which he builded not *Job 20:19*
for ye say, Where is the *h.* of the prince *Job 21:28*
and to the *h.* appointed for all living *Job 30:23*
thou shouldest know paths to *h.* thereof *Job 38:20*
whose *h.* I have made the wilderness *Job 39:6*
my rock be for a *h.* of defence to save me *Ps 31:2*
yea, the sparrow hath found an *h.* *Ps 84:3*
as for the stork, fir trees are her *h.* *Ps 101:17*
her *h.* inclineth to death, paths to dead *Pr 2:18*
the young man went the way to her *h.* *Pr 7:8*
loud and stubborn, her feet abide not in her *h.* *Pr 7:11*
her *h.* is the way to hell, going to death *Pr 7:27*
wisdom hath builded her *h.,* hath hewn pillars *Pr 9:1*
but the *h.* of the righteous shall stand *Pr 12:7*
the *h.* of the wicked shall be overthrown *Pr 14:11*
the Lord will destroy the *h.* of the proud *Pr 15:25*
than an *h.* full of sacrifices with strife *Pr 17:1*
h. and riches are the inheritance of fathers *Pr 19:14*
righteous wisely considereth the *h.* of wicked *Pr 21:12*
thro' wisdom is an *h.* built and established *Pr 24:3*
withdraw thy foot from thy neighbour's *h.* *Pr 25:17*
nor go into brother's *h.* in day of calamity *Pr 27:10*
to go to *h.* of mourning, than *h.* of feasting *Ec 7:2*
thro' idleness of hands the *h.* droppeth thro' *Ec 10:18*
when the keepers of the *h.* shall tremble *Ec 12:3*
beams of our *h.* are cedar, and rafters *Ca 1:17*
brought me to the banqueting *h.* his banner *Ca 2:4*
till I had brought him into my mother's *h.* *Ca 3:4*
I would bring thee into my mother's *h.* *Ca 8:2*
woe to them that join *h.* to *h.,* field to field *Isa 5:8*
and the *h.* was filled with smoke *Isa 6:4*
that opened not the *h.* of his prisoners *Isa 14:17*
so that there is no *h.* *Isa 23:1*
every *h.* shut *Isa 23:10; 23:24*
he will arise against the *h.* of evildoers *Isa 31:2*
and I will glorify the *h.* of my glory *Isa 60:7*
our holy and beautiful *h.* is burned up *Isa 64:11*
enter not into the *h.* of mourning *Jer 16:5*
thou shalt not go into *h.* of feasting with them *Jer 16:8*
touching the *h.* of the king of Judah *Jer 21:11; 22:1*
go to the *h.* of the Rechabites and speak *Jer 35:2*
not to return to *h.* of Jonathan *Jer 37:20; 38:26*

they are a rebellious *h.* *Eze 2:5; 3:9, 26-27; 12:3*
be not thou rebellious like that rebellious *h.* *Eze 2:8*
he said to them, Defile the *h.* go ye forth *Eze 9:7*
thou dwellest in the midst of a rebellious *h.* *Eze 12:2*
in your days, O rebellious *h.* will I say *Eze 12:25*
say now to the rebellious *h.,* Know ye not *Eze 17:12*
and utter a parable to the rebellious *h.* *Eze 24:3*
if ashamed, shew them the form of *h.* *Eze 43:11*
this is the law of *h.* on the top of mountain *Eze 43:12*
so shall ye reconcile the *h.* *Eze 45:20*
which he carried to the *h.* of his god *Da 1:2*
avenge blood of Jezreel on the *h.* of Jehu *Ho 1:4*
I will send a fire into the *h.* of Hazael *Am 1:4*
that holdeth the sceptre from the *h.* of Eden *Am 1:5*
I will smite the winter *h.* with summer *h.* *Am 3:15*
went into *h.* and leaned his hand on wall *Am 5:19*
he will smite the great *h.* and the little *h.* *Am 6:11*
I will rise against *h.* of Jeroboam with sword *Am 7:9*
drop not thy word against the *h.* of Isaac *Am 7:16*
the *h.* of Esau shall be for stubble *Ob 18*
mountain of the *h.* be as high places *Mic 3:12*
let us go up to the *h.* of the God of Jacob *Mic 4:2*
all the works of the *h.* of Ahab are kept *Mic 6:16*
out of the *h.* of thy gods will I cut off *Na 1:14*
enter into the *h.* of the thief, into the *h.* of him that sweareth *Zec 5:4*
the family of the *h.* of Nathan apart *Zec 12:12*
and beat upon that *h.* *M't 7:25; 7:27; Lu 6:48*
and when ye come into an *h.* salute it *M't 10:12*
enter into the home (B) *M't 10:12; 12:25*
if *h.* be worthy, let your peace come *M't 10:13; Lu 10:5*
every *h.* divided against itself *M't 12:25; M'k 3:25*
how enter into a strong man's *h.* *M't 12:29; M'k 3:27*
murmured against the good man of the *h.* *M't 20:11*
your *h.* is left to you desolate *M't 23:38; Lu 13:25*
if good man of *h.* had known watch thief would come *M't 24:43; Lu 12:39*
a *h.* divided against itself, that *h.* cannot *M'k 3:25*
household divided *M'k 3:25*
that hath left *h.* or brethren for my sake *M'k 10:29*
the good man of the *h.* *M'k 14:14; Lu 22:11*
in that *h.* remain, go not from *h.* to *h.* *Lu 10:7*
named Martha, received him into her *h.* *Lu 10:38*
guards his own *h.* (P) *Lu 11:21*
doth not light candle and sweep *h.* and seek *Lu 15:8*
h. was filled with the odour of the ointment *Joh 12:3*
a sound from heaven filled all the *h.* *Ac 2:2*
breaking bread from *h.* to *h.* did eat their *Ac 2:46*
in every *h.* ceased not to teach *Ac 5:42*
Simon a tanner, whose *h.* is by the sea side *Ac 10:6*
and we entered into the man's *h.* *Ac 11:12*
he came to the *h.* of Mary, mother of John *Ac 12:12*
but the Jews assaulted the *h.* of Jason *Ac 17:5*
whose *h.* joined hard to the synagogue *Ac 18:7*

they fled out of that *h.* naked and wounded *Ac 19:16*
I taught you publicly, and from *h.* to *h.* *Ac 20:20*
entered into the *h.* of Philip the evangelist *Ac 21:8*
greet the church in their *h.* *Ro 16:5; 1Co 16:19*
by them which are of the *h.* of Chloe *1Co 1:11*
ye know the *h.* of Stephanas the firstfruits *1Co 16:15*
if earthly *h.* be dissolved, we have an *h.* *2Co 5:1*
desiring to be clothed upon with *h.* from heaven *2Co 5:2*
wandering about from *h.* to *h.* and tattlers *1Ti 5:13*
that the younger women guide the *h.* *1Ti 5:14*
Lord gave mercy to *h.* of Onesiphorus *2Ti 1:16*
in a great *h.* there are vessels of gold and *2Ti 2:20*
he who built the *h.* more honour than *h.* *Heb 3:3*
for every *h.* is built by some man, he that built *Heb 3:4*
whose *h.* 're we, if we hold fast the confidence *Heb 3:6*
we are his household (B) *Heb 3:6*
receive him not into your *h.* nor bid him *2Jo 10*

HOUSE *OF GOD*

this is none other but the *h.* of God *Ge 28:17*
this stone which I set shall be God's *h.* *Ge 28:22*
from being drawers of water for *h.* of God *Jos 9:23*
all the time *h. of God* was in Shiloh *J'g 18:31*
Israel arose and went up to the *h. of God* *J'g 20:18*
all the people came unto the *h. of God* *J'g 20:26; 21:2*
highway of which one goeth up to *h. of God* *J'g 20:31*
Azariah ruler of *h. of God* *1Ch 9:11; Ne 11:11*
governors of *h. of God* were sons of Eleazar *1Ch 24:5*
glory of the Lord filled the *h.* of God *2Ch 5:14*
he was with them hid in *h.* of God six years *2Ch 22:12*
and they set the *h. of God* in his state *2Ch 24:13*
Manasseh set a carved image in the *h. of God* *2Ch 33:7*
they burnt the *h. of God* and brake the wall *2Ch 36:19*
we went to the *h.* of the great God *Ezr 5:8*
let the *h. of God* be builded in his place *Ezr 5:15; 6:7*
what more shall be needful for the *h. of God* *Ezr 7:20*
let it be done for the *h.* of the God of heaven *Ezr 7:23*
let us meet in *h. of God* in the temple *Ne 6:10*
then I said, Why is the *h. of God* forsaken *Ne 13:11*
I went with them to the *h. of God* *Ps 42:4; 55:14*
I am like a green olive tree in the *h. of God* *Ps 52:8*
I had rather be doorkeeper in *h. of God* *Ps 84:10*
keep thy foot when thou goest to *h. of God* *Ec 5:1*
come, let us go up to the *h. of God* *Isa 2:3; Mic 4:2*
the prophet is hated in the *h. of God* *Ho 9:8*
drink offering withholden from *h. of God* *Joe 1:13*
joy and gladness cut off from the *h. of God* *Joe 1:16*
when they had sent to *h. of God* men to pray *Zec 7:2*
entered into the *h. of God,* and did eat *M't 12:4; M'k 2:26; Lu 6:4*
how to behave thyself in the *h. of God* *1Ti 3:15*
having an high priest over the *h. of God* *Heb 10:21*

judgment must begin at the *h.*   *1Pe 4:17*
of God

HOUSE *OF JACOB*

all the souls of *h. of Jacob*   *Ge 46:27*
were seventy
thus shalt thou say to the *h. of*   *Ex 19:3*
Jacob
h. of Jacob from people of   *Ps 114:1*
strange language
O *h. of Jacob,* let us walk in   *Isa 2:5*
light of Lord
thou hast forsaken thy people,   *Isa 2:6*
the *h. of Jacob*
Lord that hideth his face from   *Isa 8:17*
h. of Jacob
such as are escaped of the   *Isa 10:20*
h. of Jacob
and they shall cleave to the *h.*   *Isa 14:1*
of Jacob
thus saith the Lord   *Isa 29:22*
concerning *h. of Jacob*
hearken unto me, O *h. of*   *Isa 46:3*
Jacob and Israel
hear ye this, O *h. of Jacob,*   *Isa 48:1*
which are called
spare not, shew the *h. of Jacob* *Isa 58:1*
their sins
hear the word of the Lord, O *h.*   *Jer 2:4*
of Jacob
declare this in the *h. of Jacob,*   *Jer 5:20*
publish it
I lifted up my hand to the   *Eze 20:5*
h. of Jacob
hear ye, and testify in the *h.*   *Am 3:13*
of Jacob
I will not utterly destroy the   *Am 9:8*
h. of Jacob
the *h. of Jacob* shall possess   *Ob 17*
possessions
h. of Jacob shall be a fire   *Ob 18*
O thou that art named the *h.*   *Mic 2:7*
of Jacob
hear this, I pray, ye heads of   *Mic 3:9*
the *h. of Jacob*
he shall reign over the *h. of*   *Lu 1:33*
Jacob

HOUSE *OF JOSEPH*

he brought the men into   *Ge 43:17*
Joseph's *h.*
the *h. of Joseph* shall abide in *Jos 18:5*
their coast
the *h. of Joseph* went up   *J'g 1:22*
against Bethel
the *h. of Joseph* sent to descry *J'g 1:23*
Bethel
yet the hand of the *h. of*   *J'g 1:35*
Joseph prevailed
am come first of all the *h. of* *2Sa 19:20*
Joseph
ruler over the charge of *h. of* *1Ki 11:28*
Joseph
lest he break out like fire in *h.*   *Am 5:6*
of Joseph
and the *h. of Joseph* shall be a   *Ob 18*
flame
and I will save the *h. of*   *Zec 10:6*
Joseph

HOUSE *OF ISRAEL*

let *h. of Israel* bewail the   *Le 10:6*
burning
what man of the *h. of Israel*   *Le 17:3;*
that killeth an ox   *17:8, 10; 22:18*
all the *h. of Israel* mourned   *Nu 20:29*
for Aaron
the *h. of Israel* lamented after *1Sa 7:2*
the Lord
they mourned for the *h. of*   *2Sa 1:12*
Israel
all the *h. of Israel* played   *2Sa 6:5*
before the Lord
David and the *h. of Israel*   *2Sa 6:15*
brought up the ark
I gave thee the *h. of Israel*   *2Sa 12:8*
and Judah
to-day shall *h. of Israel*   *2Sa 16:3*
restore the kingdom
kings of *h. of Israel* are   *1Ki 20:31*
merciful kings
remembered his truth toward *h.* *Ps 98:3*
of Israel
he will bless us, he will bless   *Ps 115:12*
the *h. of Israel*
bless ye the Lord, O *h. of*   *Ps 135:19*
Israel bless Lord

the vineyard of the Lord is the   *Isa 5:7*
h. of Israel
the *h. of Israel* shall possess   *Isa 14:2*
them in the land
the remnant of the *h. of Israel,* *Isa 46:3*
hearken to me
the great goodness toward the   *Isa 63:7*
h. of Israel
hear, all the families of the *h. of* *Jer 2:4*
Israel
as a thief, so is the *h. of Israel* *Jer 2:26*
ashamed
the house of Judah shall walk   *Jer 3:18*
with *h. of Israel*
you dealt treacherously, O *h.*   *Jer 3:20;*
of Israel   *5:11*
all the *h. of Israel* are   *Jer 9:26*
uncircumcised in heart
the *h. of Israel* have broken   *Jer 11:10*
my covenant
pronounced evil for evil, of   *Jer 11:17*
the *h. of Israel*
caused to cleave to me the   *Jer 13:11*
whole *h. of Israel*
the Lord liveth, who led the *h.* *Jer 23:8*
of Israel
I will sow the *h. of Israel*   *Jer 31:27*
with seed of man
I will make new covenant   *Jer 31:31;*
with *h. of Israel*   *31:33*
perform that I promised to   *Jer 33:14*
the *h. of Israel*
as the *h. of Israel* was   *Jer 48:13*
ashamed of Beth-el
eat roll, speak to *h. of Israel*   *Eze 3:1;*
   17:2; 20:27, 30; 24:21; 33:10; 36:22
go, get thee unto the *h. of*   *Eze 3:4*
Israel, and speak
but thou art sent to the *h. of*   *Eze 3:5*
Israel
h. of Israel will not hearken to *Eze 3:7*
me, *h. of Israel* are
I made thee a watchman to   *Eze 3:17;*
h. of Israel   *33:7*
this shall be a sign to the *h. of*   *Eze 4:3*
Israel
and lay the iniquity of the *h. of* *Eze 4:4*
Israel upon it
thou shalt bear the iniquity of   *Eze 4:5*
the *h. of Israel*
a fire shall come forth into the   *Eze 5:4*
h. of Israel
the evil abominations of the   *Eze 6:11;*
h. of Israel   *8:6*
all the idols of the *h. of Israel* *Eze 8:10*
are pourtrayed
seventy men of the ancients   *Eze 8:11;*
of *h. of Israel*   *8:12*
iniquity of *h. of Israel*   *Eze 9:9*
exceeding great
thus have ye said, O *h. of*   *Eze 11:5*
Israel, for I know
and all the *h. of Israel* wholly *Eze 11:15*
are they
hath not the *h. of Israel* said   *Eze 12:9;*
   12:27; 18:29
nor any more divination   *Eze 12:24*
within the *h. of Israel*
nor made up the hedge for the *Eze 13:5*
h. of Israel
written in the writing of the *h.* *Eze 13:9*
of Israel
every one of *h. of Israel* that *Eze 14:4;*
setteth up idols   *14:7*
that the *h. of Israel* may go   *Eze 14:11*
no more astray
nor lift his eyes to the idols   *Eze 18:6;*
of *h. of Israel*   *18:15*
hear, O *h. of Israel* is not   *Eze 18:25*
my way equal
therefore I will judge you, O   *Eze 18:30*
h. of Israel
for why will ye die, O *h. of*   *Eze 18:31;*
Israel   *33:11*
but the *h. of Israel* rebelled   *Eze 20:13*
against me
h. of Israel go serve idols,   *Eze 20:39*
if ye will not hearken
there shall all the *h. of Israel* *Eze 20:40*
serve me
according to your corrupt   *Eze 20:44*
doings, O *h. of Israel*
the *h. of Israel* is to me   *Eze 22:18*
become dross
no more a pricking briar to   *Eze 28:24*
h. of Israel
when I shall have gathered *h.* *Eze 28:25*
of Israel
have been a staff of a reed to   *Eze 29:6*
h. of Israel

be no more the confidence of   *Eze 29:16*
h. of Israel
I will cause horn of *h. of*   *Eze 29:21*
Israel to bud
that they, even *h. of Israel*   *Eze 34:30*
are my people
and I will multiply all the *h.*   *Eze 36:10*
of Israel
when *h. of Israel* dwelt in   *Eze 36:17*
their own land
my holy name which *h. of*   *Eze 36:21*
Israel profaned
I do not this for your sakes,   *Eze 36:22*
O *h. of Israel*
be ashamed for your ways, O *Eze 36:32*
h. of Israel
I will for this be inquired of   *Eze 36:37*
by *h. of Israel*
these bones are the whole *h.*   *Eze 37:11*
of Israel
write on it, for *h. of Israel*   *Eze 37:16*
his companions
seven months shall *h. of*   *Eze 39:12*
Israel be burying
h. of Israel shall know that I *Eze 39:22*
am the Lord
h. of Israel went into   *Eze 39:23*
captivity
I will have mercy on whole *h.* *Eze 39:25*
of Israel
I have poured out my Spirit   *Eze 39:29*
on *h. of Israel*
declare all that thou seest to   *Eze 40:4*
h. of Israel
son of man, shew the house   *Eze 43:10*
to *h. of Israel*
say to the rebellious, even to   *Eze 44:6*
h. of Israel
caused *h. of Israel* to fall into *Eze 44:12*
iniquity
shall take maidens of the   *Eze 44:22*
seed of *h. of Israel*
possession shall be for whole *Eze 45:6*
h. of Israel
the rest of the land shall they *Eze 45:8*
give to *h. of Israel*
to make reconciliation for *h.* *Eze 45:17*
of Israel
cause to cease the kingdom of   *Ho 1:4*
h. of Israel
I will no more have mercy on *h.*   *Ho 1:6*
of Israel
and hearken, ye *h. of Israel,*   *Ho 5:1*
and give ear
have seen an horrible thing in *Ho 6:10*
h. of Israel
h. of Israel compasseth me   *Ho 11:12*
with deceit
the city shall leave ten to the *h.* *Am 5:3*
saith the Lord to *h. of Israel,*   *Am 5:4*
Seek ye me
have ye offered sacrifices 40   *Am 5:25*
years, *h. of Israel*
chief of nations, to whom *h. of* *Am 6:1*
Israel came
I will raise against you a   *Am 6:14*
nation, *h. of Israel*
hath conspired against thee   *Am 7:10*
in *h. of Israel*
I will sift *h. of Israel* among all *Am 9:9*
nations
for the sins of *h. of Israel* is all *Mic 1:5*
this
hear, ye princes of *h. of Israel* *Mic 3:1;*
   3:9
that as ye were a curse, *h. of* *Zec 8:13*
Israel
go to lost sheep of *h. of Israel* *M't 10:6;*
   15:24
let all *h. of Israel* know   *Ac 2:36*
assuredly
h. of Israel, have ye offered to *Ac 7:42*
me beasts
make a new covenant with *h.* *Heb 8:8;*
of Israel   *8:10*

HOUSE *OF JUDAH*

men of Judah anointed David *2Sa 2:4;*
king over *h. of Judah*   *2:7, 11; 1Ch 28:4*
I gave thee the *h. of Judah*   *2Sa 12:8*
and of Israel
he assembled all the *h. of*   *1Ki 12:21*
Judah
speak to all the *h. of Judah*   *1Ki 12:23*
and Benjamin
remnant that is escaped of   *2Ki 19:30;*
h. of Judah shall take root   *Isa 37:31*

Zebadiah the ruler of the *h.* 2Ch 19:11
of Judah
the rulers were behind the *h. of* Ne 4:16
Judah
he shall be a father to the *h.* Isa 22:21
of Judah
h. of Judah shall walk with Jer 3:18
house of Israel
the *h. of Judah* hath dealt Jer 5:11
treacherously
the *h. of Judah* hath broken Jer 11:10
my covenant
for evil of the *h. of Judah* Jer 11:17
that they have done
I will pluck *h. of Judah* from Jer 12:14
among them
I caused to cleave to me the Jer 13:11
h. of Judah
I will sow the *h. of Judah* Jer 31:27
with seed of man
I will make a new covenant Jer 31:31
with *h. of Judah*
perform that good I promised Jer 33:14
to *h. of Judah*
it may be *h. of Judah* will hear Jer 36:3
all the evil
bear the iniquity of *h. of Judah* Eze 4:6
forty days
is it a light thing to the *h. of* Eze 8:17
Judah
the iniquity of the *h. of Judah* Eze 9:9
is great
Ammonites said, Aha, against Eze 25:3
the *h. of Judah*
the *h. of Judah* is like to all Eze 25:8
the heathen
Edom hath dealt against the Jer 25:12
h. of Judah
but I will have mercy upon the Ho 1:7
h. of Judah
I will be to the *h. of Judah* as Ho 5:12
rottenness
I will be as a young lion to the Ho 5:14
h. of Judah
coast shall be for remnant of *h.* Zep 2:7
of Judah
as ye were a curse, O *h. of* Zec 8:13
Judah
I have thought to do well to Zec 8:15
the *h. of Judah*
the fast shall be to *h. of Judah* Zec 8:19
joy and gladness
for the Lord hath visited the Zec 10:3
h. of Judah
I will strengthen the *h. of* Zec 10:6
Judah
I will open mine eyes unto the Zec 12:4
h. of Judah
I will make new covenant with Heb 8:8
h. of Judah

HOUSE *OF LEVI*

and there went a man of the *h.* Ex 2:1
of Levi
rod of Aaron for *h. of Levi* Nu 17:8
was budded
bless the Lord, O *h. of Levi* Ps 135:20
the family of the *h. of Levi* Zec 12:13
apart

HOUSE with *FATHER,*
FATHERS

Lord said, Get thee from thy Ge 12:1
father's h.
thy father's household (B) Ge 12:1;
    46:31
when God caused to wander Ge 20:13
from *father's h.*
my father's home (B) Ge 20:13
God, which took me from my Ge 24:7
father's h.
thou shalt go to my *father's h.* Ge 24:38
and take a wife
shalt take a wife for my son Ge 24:40
of my *father's h.*
is there any portion for us in Ge 31:14
our *father's h.*
remain a widow at *father's h.* Ge 38:11
Tamar dwelt in *father's h.*
in her parental home (B) Ge 38:11
God hath made me forget my Ge 41:51
father's h.
my brethren and *father's h.* Ge 46:31
are come to me
Joseph dwelt in Egypt, he and Ge 50:22
his *father's h.*

his father's household (A) Ge 50:22
Joseph and his father's family Ge 50:22
(B)
a lamb, according to *h.* of their Ex 12:3
fathers
a lamb for his parental family Ex 12:3
(A)(B)
if she is returned to her Le 22:13
father's h.
take sum of Israel by *h.* of Nu 1:2;
their *fathers* 1:18, 20, 22, 24
by their father's houses (A) Nu 1:2
according to families and clans Nu 1:2
(B)
tribe, every one head of the Nu 1:4;
h. of his *fathers* 1:44; Jos 22:14
leader of his clan (B) Nu 1:4
that were numbered by the *h.* Nu 1:45
of their *fathers*
every man pitch with ensign of Nu 2:2
their *father's h.*
their father's houses (A) Nu 2:2
standard of clans' ensigns (B) Nu 2:2
number of children of Levi Nu 3:15;
after the *h.* of their *fathers* 3:20; 4:46
their father's houses (A) Nu 3:15
their clans and families (B) Nu 3:15
Gershon, Merari after *h.* of Nu 4:38;
their *fathers* 4:42
according to *h.* of their Nu 17:2;
fathers twelve rods 17:3
a rod for each clan (B) Nu 17:2
thou and *father's h.* bear Nu 18:1
iniquity of sanctuary
woman vow a vow, being in Nu 30:3;
her *father's h.* 30:16
Reuben, Gad, according to Nu 34:14
the *h.* of their *father*
their father's houses (A) Nu 34:14
according to respective clans Nu 34:14
(B)
to play the whore in her De 22:21
father's h.
ye will shew kindness to my Jos 2:12
father's h.
and I am the least in my J'g 6:15
father's h.
and ye are risen up against my J'g 9:18
father's h.
thou shalt not inherit in our J'g 11:2
father's h.
inheritance in father's estate J'g 11:2
(B)
lest we burn thee and thy J'g 14:15
father's h. with fire
all the *h.* of his *father* came J'g 16:31
and buried him
kinsmen of all the tribal J'g 16:31
family (A)
brothers and relatives came J'g 16:31
buried (B)
his concubine went to his J'g 19:2
father's h.
and she brought him into her J'g 19:3
father's h.
did I plainly appear to *h.* 1Sa 2:27
of thy *father*
I said the *h.* of thy *fathers* 1Sa 2:30
should walk before me
family of your fathers walk (B) 1Sa 2:30
is it not on thee, and on all 1Sa 9:20
thy *father's h.*
king will make his *father's h.* 1Sa 17:25
free in Israel
his father's family (B) 1Sa 17:25
let him go no more home to 1Sa 18:2
his *father's h.*
return to his father's home 1Sa 18:2
(B)
the king sent to call all his 1Sa 22:11
father's h.
his whole family (B) 1Sa 22:11; 22:16
thou and all thy *father's h.* 1Sa 22:16
shall die
wilt not destroy my name out 1Sa 24:21
of *father's h.*
my father's family (B) 1Sa 24:21
let it rest on Joab and all his 2Sa 3:29
father's h.
the iniquity be on me, and on 2Sa 14:9
my *father's h.*
all of my *father's h.* were but 2Sa 19:28
dead men
let thy hand, I pray thee, be 2Sa 24:17;
against my *father's h.* 1Ch 21:17
take innocent blood from me 1Ki 2:31
and *father's h.*
thou and *father's h.* have 1Ki 18:18
troubled Israel

Hemath *father* of the *h.* of 1Ch 2:55
Rechab
the *h.* of their *fathers* 1Ch 4:38
increased greatly
Guni, chief of house their 1Ch 5:15;
father's h. 5:24; 7:2, 7, 9, 40
with them after the *h.* of 1Ch 7:4
fathers were bands
chief in the *h.* of their *fathers* 1Ch 9:9;
    9:13; 12:30
of Zadok, his *father's h.* 1Ch 12:28
twenty-two captains
God chose me before the *h.* of 1Ch 28:4
my *father*
slain thy brethren of thy 2Ch 21:13
father's h.
could not shew their *father's* Ezr 2:59;
h. Ne 1:1
chief of the *h.* of their *father* Ezr 10:16
examined
both I and my *father's h.* have Ne 1:6
sinned
thou and thy *father's h.* shall Es 4:14
be destroyed
forget thy people and thy Ps 45:10
father's h.
take hold of his brother of *h.* of Isa 3:6
his *father*
bring on thy *father's h.* days Isa 7:17
that have not come
shall be for glorious throne to Isa 22:23
his *father's h.*
hang on him all the glory of Isa 22:24
his *father's h.*
the *h.* of thy *father* dealt Jer 12:6
treacherously
I pray thee, send him to my Lu 16:27
father's h.
make not my *Father's h.* an Joh 2:16
house of
in my *Father's h.* are many Joh 14:2
mansions
Moses was nourished in his Ac 7:20
father's h.

HOUSE with *LORD*

firstfruits bring into the *h.* of Ex 23:19;
the Lord 34:26; Ne 10:35
not bring price of a dog into De 23:18
h. of Lord
put into the treasury of *h.* of Jos 6:24
Lord
I am now going to the *h.* of J'g 19:18
Lord
when she went up to the *h.* of 1Sa 1:7
Lord
Hannah brought him unto *h.* 1Sa 1:24;
of Lord 2Ki 12:4, 9, 13; 22:4; 2Ch 34:14
then David came into *h.* of 2Sa 12:20
the Lord
made an end of building the *h.* 1Ki 3:1
of Lord
foundation of *h.* of the Lord 1Ki 6:37;
laid 2Ch 8:16; Ezr 3:11; Zec 8:9
work he made for *h.* of Lord 1Ki 7:40;
    7:45, 51; 2Ch 4:16; 5:1; 24:14
the cloud filled *h.* of Lord 1Ki 8:10;
    8:11; 2Ch 5:13; 7:2; Eze 44:4
so Israel dedicated the *h.* of 1Ki 8:63
the Lord
he went up unto *h.* of Lord 1Ki 10:5;
    2Ch 9:4
hid in the *h.* of Lord six years 2Ki 11:3
he took an oath of them in the 2Ki 11:4
h. of the Lord
let her not be slain in *h.* of 2Ki 11:15;
Lord 2Ch 23:14
appointed officers over *h.* of 2Ki 11:18;
Lord 2Ch 23:18
they brought from the 2Ki 11:19;
h. of the Lord 23:6
found in *h.* of the Lord 2Ki 12:10;
    14:14; 16:8; 18:15
had the oversight of the *h.* of 2Ki 12:11
the Lord
trespass money was not 2Ki 12:16
brought into *h.* of Lord
the king's entry, turned he 2Ki 16:18
from *h.* of Lord
third day shalt go up unto *h.* 2Ki 20:5
of Lord
heal me, that I shall go to 2Ki 20:8;
h. of Lord Isa 38:22
read words of covenant 2Ki 23:2
found in *h.* of Lord 23:24; 2Ch 34:17, 30
houses of Sodomites that were 2Ki 23:7
by *h.* of the Lord
the horses at entering in the 2Ki 23:11
h. of the Lord

and he burnt the *h.* of the   2Ki 25:9;
Lord   Jer 52:13
service of song in the *h.* of the 1Ch 6:31
Lord
then David said, This is the *h.* 1Ch 22:1
of the Lord
now, my son, build the *h.* of 1Ch 22:11
the Lord thy God
have prepared for the *h.* of 1Ch 22:14
the Lord
to set forward the work of the 1Ch 23:4
h. of the Lord
porters, to minister in the *h.* 1Ch 26:12
of the Lord
so the *h.* of the Lord was   2Ch 8:16
perfected
for he was cut off from the   2Ch 26:21;
of Lord   Joe 1:9
ye Levites, sanctify the *h.* of 2Ch 29:5
the Lord
they came to cleanse the *h.* 2Ch 29:15
of the Lord
Manasseh took the idol out 2Ch 33:15
of *h.* of Lord
I found the book of the law 2Ch 34:15
in *h.* of Lord
the priests polluted the *h.* of 2Ch 36:14
the Lord
to beautify *h.* of the Lord in   Ezr 7:27
Jerusalem
I will dwell in the *h.* of the   Ps 23:6
Lord for ever
that I may dwell in the *h.* of   Ps 27:4
Lord all my life
those that he planted in the *h.* Ps 92:13
of the Lord
I will pay my vows in courts Ps 116:19
of Lord's *h.*
we have blessed you out of Ps 118:26
the *h.* of Lord
when they said, Let us go into Ps 122:1
h. of the Lord
because of the *h.* of Lord I   Ps 122:9
will seek thy good
ye that stand in the *h.* of the Ps 134:1;
Lord   135:2
mountain of Lord's *h.* be   Isa 2:2;
established in top of   Mic 4:1
Hezekiah went up unto the *h.* Isa 37:14
of the Lord
sacrifices of praise to the *h.* Jer 17:26
of the Lord
Pashur was governor in the *h.* Jer 20:1
of the Lord
the high gate, which was by *h.* Jer 20:2
of the Lord
which come to worship in the Jer 26:2
Lord's *h.*
speaking these words in *h.* of Jer 26:7
Lord
Hananiah spake to me in *h.* of Jer 28:1
Lord
the people that stood in *h.*   Jer 28:5
of the Lord
ye should be officers in *h.* of Jer 29:26
Lord
bring the Rechabites into *h.* of Jer 35:2
Lord
I am shut up, I cannot go into Jer 36:5
h. of Lord
read in Lord's *h.* upon the   Jer 36:6
fasting day
the third entry that is in *h.* of Jer 38:14
Lord
to bring them to the *h.* of   Jer 41:5
Lord
come into the sanctuaries of Jer 51:51
Lord's *h.*
they have made a noise in *h.*   La 2:7
of Lord
time that Lord's *h.* should be Hag 1:2
built

HIS HOUSE

Lord plagued Pharaoh and   Ge 12:17
his h.
all the men of *his h.* were   Ge 17:27
circumcised
he made him overseer over *his* Ge 39:4;
h.   39:5
hath made me lord of all   Ge 45:8;
his h.   Ac 7:10
and make an atonement for   Le 16:6;
his h.   16:11
and when a man shall sanctify Le 27:14
his h.
if he that sanctified it will   Le 27:15
redeem *his h.*

if Balak would give me *his h.* Nu 22:18;
full of silver and   24:13
let him go and return to *his h.* De 20:5;
                  20:6-8
then let him send her out of *his* De 24:1
h.
thou shalt not go into *his h.*   De 24:10
to fetch his pledge
which thing became a snare to J'g 8:27
his h.
if dealt well with Jerubbaal   J'g 9:16;
and *his h.*   9:19
which I have spoken   1Sa 3:12
concerning *his h.*
I told, that I will judge *his h.* 1Sa 3:13
for ever
his return was to Ramah, for 1Sa 7:17
there was *his h.*
Israel buried Samuel in *his h.* 1Sa 25:1
at Ramah
the people departed every one 2Sa 6:19
which chose me before thy   2Sa 6:21
father and *his h.*
it came to pass, when the king 2Sa 7:1
sat in *his h.*
hast spoken concerning *his h.* 2Sa 7:25;
              1Ch 17:23
but Uriah went not down to   2Sa 11:9;
his h.   11:10, 13
David fetched her to *his h.*   2Sa 11:27
became his wife
why last to bring the king   2Sa 19:11
back to *his h.*
it is for Saul and *his* bloody *h.* 2Sa 21:1
because he slew
have no silver nor gold of   2Sa 21:4
Saul, nor of *his h.*
on *his h.* there shall be peace 1Ki 2:33
from Lord
Solomon was building, and   1Ki 7:1
finished all *his h.*
return every man to *his h.*   1Ki 12:24;
     22:17; 1Ch 16:43; 2Ch 11:4; 18:16
did eat bread in *his h.* and   1Ki 13:19
drank water
came the sword against   1Ki 16:7
Baasha and *his h.*
king of Israel went to *his h.* 1Ki 20:43;
heavy   21:4
Elisha sat in *his h.* and elders 2Ki 6:32
with him
nothing in *his h.* Hezekiah   2Ki 20:13
shewed not
because it went evil with *his* 1Ch 7:23
h.
Saul, his sons, and all *his h.* 1Ch 10:6
died together
the ark remained in *his h.*   1Ch 13:14
three months
had done good toward God 2Ch 24:16
and *his h.*
let *his h.* be made a dunghill Ezr 6:11
for this
every one repaired over against Ne 3:28
his h.
so God shake out every man   Ne 5:13
from *his h.*
and every one to be over against Ne 7:3
his h.
hast not thou made an hedge Job 1:10
about *his h.*
he shall return no more to   Job 7:10
h.
he shall lean on *his h.* it shall Job 8:15
not stand
the increase of *his h.* shall   Job 20:28
depart
for what pleasure hath he in Job 21:21
his h. after him
he buildeth *his h.* as a moth, Job 27:18
as a booth
when the glory of *his h.* is   Ps 49:16
increased
he made him Lord of *his h.*   Ps 105:21
and ruler
wealth and riches shall be in Ps 112:3
his h.
give the substance of *his h.*   Pr 6:31;
                Ca 8:7
evil shall not depart from *his* Pr 17:13
h.
I will even punish that man   Jer 23:34
and *his h.*
so they oppress a man and *his* Mic 2:2
h.
covereth an evil covetousness Hab 2:9
to *his h.*
it shall remain in the midst of Zec 5:4
his h.

then he will spoil *his h.*   M't 12:29;
               M'k 3:27
to take any thing out of *his* M't 24:17;
h.   M'k 13:15
not have suffered *his h.* to be M't 24:43
broken up
besought that he would come Lu 8:41
into *his h.*
this man went down to *his h.* Lu 18:14
justified
and himself believed and *his* Joh 4:53
whole *h.*
one that feared God, with all Ac 10:2
his h.
was warned to send for thee Ac 10:22
into *his h.*
shewed how he had seen an Ac 11:13
angel in *his h.*
they spake to him and to all Ac 16:32
in *his h.*
jailer brought them into *his* Ac 16:34;
h., believing God with *his h.*   18:8
salute the church which is in Col 4:15
his h.
Moses was faithful in all *his* Heb 3:2;
h.   3:5
Noah prepared an ark for the Heb 11:7
saving of *his h.*

KING'S HOUSE

David walked on roof of the   2Sa 11:2
king's h.
and Uriah departed out of   2Sa 11:18
the *king's h.*
what thou shalt hear out of 2Sa 15:35
the *king's h.*
when Solomon had finished the 1Ki 9:1
king's h.
took away treasure of *king's* 1Ki 14:26;
h.   15:18; 2Ki 16:8; 2Ch 12:9; 25:24
Zimri burnt the *king's h.*   1Ki 16:18
over him with fire
they told it to the *king's h.*   2Ki 7:11
within
he burnt the *king's h.*   2Ki 25:9;
             Jer 39:8; 52:13
a third part shall be at the   2Ch 23:5
king's h.
Jotham his son was over the 2Ch 26:21
king's h.
took away a portion out of 2Ch 28:21
the *h.* of the *king*
let expences be given out of the Ezr 6:4
king's h.
gave her seven maidens out   Es 2:9
of *king's h.*
think not thou shalt escape in Es 4:13
the *king's h.*
for Mordecai was great in the Es 9:4
king's h.
and give ye ear, O *h.* of the *king* Ho 5:1

IN THE HOUSE

she took raiment of Esau that Ge 27:15
were in the *h.*
they spoiled even all that was Ge 34:29
in the *h.*
the blessing of the Lord was on Ge 39:5
all in the *h.*
my master wotteth not what is Ge 39:8
with me in the *h.*
the fame thereof was heard in Ge 45:16
Pharaoh's *h.*
in one *h.* shall the passover Ex 12:46
be eaten
I put the plague of leprosy in Le 14:34;
a *h.*   14:35
if plague come again and   Le 14:43
break out in the *h.*
behold, if the plague be   Le 14:44
spread in the *h.*
he that lieth, that eateth in the Le 14:47
h. shall wash
behold, the plague hath not Le 14:48
spread in the *h.*
whoso with thee in the *h.* his Jos 2:19
blood on us
Rahab live, all that are with Jos 6:17
her in the *h.*
and they were in the *h.* of J'g 17:4;
Micah   17:12
may find rest, each in *h.* of her Ru 1:9
husband
until now, that she tarried a   Ru 2:7
little in the *h.*
the woman had a fat calf in 1Sa 28:24
the *h.*

sent to publish it *in the h.* of   *1Sa 31:9*
their idols
they put his armour *in the h.*   *1Sa 31:10*
of Ashtaroth
I and this woman dwell   *1Ki 3:17*
in one *h.*, was delivered of
child *in the h.*
there was not any tool of iron   *1Ki 6:7*
heard *in the h.*
is found some good *in the*   *1Ki 14:13*
h. of Jeroboam
drinking himself drunk *in the*   *1Ki 16:9*
h. of Arza
what hast thou *in the h.?*   *2Ki 4:2*
handmaid hath not any thing
in the h.
he returned, and walked *in the*   *2Ki 4:35*
h. to and fro
leaneth on my hand, bow *in h.*   *2Ki 5:18*
of Rimmon
he took them, and bestowed   *2Ki 5:24*
them *in the h.*
worshipping *in h.* of Nisroch   *2Ki 19:37;*
  Isa 37:38
Manasseh set a graven image   *2Ki 21:7*
in the h.
slew young men *in the h.* of   *2Ch 36:17*
sanctuary
and had put them *in the h.* of   *Ezr 1:7*
his gods
search was made *in the h.* of   *Ezr 6:1*
the rolls where
will he force the queen also *in*   *Es 7:8*
the h.
behold. the gallows standeth *in*   *Es 7:9*
h. of Haman
been my songs *in the h.* of   *Ps 119:54*
my pilgrimage
curse of Lord is *in the h.* of   *Pr 3:33*
wicked
thy labours be *in the h.* of a   *Pr 5:10*
stranger
she is loud, her feet abide not   *Pr 7:11*
in her h.
in the h. of the righteous is   *Pr 15:6*
much treasure
heart of wise *in h.* of mourning;   *Ec 7:4*
heart of fools *in h.* of mirth
maketh idol that it may   *Isa 44:13*
remain *in the h.*
set their abominations *in the*   *Jer 7:30;*
h.   *32:34*
ye made a covenant before   *Jer 34:15*
me *in the h.*
put him *in the h.* of Jonathan   *Jer 37:15*
the scribe
if there remain ten men *in one*   *Am 6:9*
h.
in the h. of Aphrah roll   *Mic 1:10*
thyself in dust
treasures of wickedness *in the*   *Mic 6:10*
h. of wicked
I was wounded *in the h.* of my   *Zec 13:6*
friends
giveth light unto all that are *in*   *M't 5:15*
the h.
and it was noised that he was   *M'k 2:1*
in the h.
being *in the h.* he asked them   *M'k 9:33*
What was it
in the h. his disciples asked   *M'k 10:10*
of the matter
being in Bethany, *in the h.* of   *M'k 14:3*
Simon the leper
nor abode *in* any *h.* but in the   *Lu 8:27*
tombs
the servant abideth not *in the*   *Joh 8:35*
h.
Martha met him, Mary sat   *Joh 11:20*
still *in the h.*
inquire *in the h.* of Judas for   *Ac 9:11*
one Saul
Peter is lodged *in the h.* of   *Ac 10:32*
Simon a tanner

MINE, MY HOUSE

the steward of *my h.* is this   *Ge 15:2*
Eliezer
one born *in my h.* is mine heir   *Ge 15:3*
and I shall be destroyed, I   *Ge 34:30*
and *my h.*
thou shalt be over *my h.* and   *Ge 41:40*
according to
Moses not so, who is faithful   *Nu 12:7*
in all *mine h.*
the hallowed things out of   *De 26:13*
mine h.
for me and *my h.* we will   *Jos 24:15*
serve Lord

cometh forth of the doors of   *J'g 11:31*
my h.
seeking this man come into   *J'g 19:23*
my h.
not cut off thy kindness from   *1Sa 20:15*
my h.
shall this fellow come into   *1Sa 21:15*
my h.
what is *my h.* that thou hast   *2Sa 7:18;*
brought me hitherto   *1Ch 17:16*
shall I then go into *mine h.*   *2Sa 11:11*
to eat and drink
tho' *my h.* be not so with God,   *2Sa 23:5*
yet he hath
give it me, because it is near   *1Ki 21:2*
to *my h.*
all things in *mine h.*   *2Ki 20:15; Isa 39:4*
I will settle him in *mine h.*   *1Ch 17:14*
for ever
if I wait, the grave is *mine h.*   *Job 17:13*
I have made
I will walk in *my h.* with a   *Ps 101:2*
perfect heart
I will not come into the   *Ps 132:3*
tabernacle of *my h.*
at the window of *my h.* I looked   *Pr 7:6*
through
in *my h.* is neither bread nor   *Isa 3:7*
clothing
unto them will I give in *mine*   *Isa 56:5*
h. a name
joyful in *my h.* of prayer,   *Isa 56:7;*
mine h. be   *M't 21:13; M'k 11:17;*
called an house of prayer   *Lu 19:46*
what hath my beloved to do   *Jer 11:15*
in *mine h.*
I have forsaken *mine h.* I left   *Jer 12:7*
mine heritage
in *my h.* have I found their   *Jer 23:11*
wickedness
as I sat in *mine h.* and elders   *Eze 8:1*
before me
thus have they done in midst   *Eze 23:39*
of *mine h.*
in my sanctuary to pollute it,   *Eze 44:7*
even *my h.*
I Nebuchadnezzar was at rest in   *Da 4:4*
mine h.
I will drive them out of *mine*   *Ho 9:15*
h.
why? because of *mine h.* that is   *Hag 1:9*
waste
then thou shalt also judge *my*   *Zec 3:7*
h. and keep
I will encamp about *mine h.* for   *Zec 9:8*
the army
that there may be meat in   *Mal 3:10*
mine h.
I will return into *my h.*   *M't 12:44;*
  Lu 11:24
let me bid them farewell at *my*   *Lu 9:61*
h.
compel them, that *my h.* may   *Lu 14:23*
be filled
at the ninth hour I prayed in   *Ac 10:30*
my h.
saying, Come into *my h.* and   *Ac 16:15*
abide there

OWN HOUSE

armed his servants born in his   *Ge 14:14*
own h.
when shall I provide for mine   *Ge 30:30*
own h. also
thou shalt bring it unto thine   *De 22:2*
own h.
shall return and come unto his   *Jos 20:6*
own h.
Jerubbaal went and dwelt in   *J'g 8:29*
his *own h.*
slain a righteous person in his   *2Sa 4:11*
own h.
raise evil against thee out of   *2Sa 12:11*
thy *own h.*
let him turn to his *own h.* so   *2Sa 14:24*
Absalom returned to his *own h.*
king is come again in peace   *2Sa 19:30*
to his *own h.*
Joab buried in his *own h.* in   *1Ki 2:34*
wilderness
he had made an end of building   *1Ki 3:1*
his *own h.*
Solomon was building his *own*   *1Ki 7:1*
h. thirteen years
Solomon raised a levy to build   *1Ki 9:15*
his *own h.*
see to thine *own h.*, David   *1Ki 12:16;*
  2Ch 10:16

arise therefore, get thee into   *1Ki 14:12*
thine *own h.*
Manasseh was buried in   *2Ki 21:18;*
garden of *own h.*   *2Ch 33:20*
slew king in his *own h.*   *2Ki 21:23;*
  2Ch 33:24
came in heart to make in his   *2Ch 7:11*
own h.
Solomon built house of Lord   *2Ch 8:1*
and his *own h.*
every man should bear rule in   *Es 1:22*
his *own h.*
he that troubleth his *own h.*   *Pr 11:29*
shall
that is greedy of gain   *Pr 15:27*
troubleth his *own h.*
lie in glory, every one in his   *Isa 14:18*
own h.
a man's enemies are the men   *Mic 7:6*
of his *own h.*
and ye run every man unto his   *Hag 1:9*
own h.
a prophet is not without   *M't 13:57;*
honour, save in his *own h.*   *M'k 6:4*
he departed to his *own h.* Lu 1:23; 5:25
Mary returned to her *own h.*   *Lu 1:56*
Levi made him a great feast in   *Lu 5:29*
his *own h.*
return to thy *own h.*   *Lu 8:39*
and shew how great things
and every man went unto his   *Joh 7:53*
own h.
Paul dwelt two years in his   *Ac 28:30*
own h.
a bishop, one that ruleth well   *1Ti 3:4*
his *own h.*
for if a man know not how to   *1Ti 3:5*
rule his *own h.*
and especially for those of his   *1Ti 5:8*
own h.
but Christ as a son over his   *Heb 3:6*
own h.

THIS HOUSE

there is none greater in *this h.*   *Ge 39:9*
than I
think on me, and bring me   *Ge 40:14*
out of *this h.*
concerning *this h.* thou art   *1Ki 6:12*
building
how much less *this h.* that I   *1Ki 8:27*
have builded
eyes be opened toward *this h.*   *1Ki 8:29;*
  2Ch 6:20
before thine altar in *this h.*   *1Ki 8:31;*
  2Ch 6:22
make supplication to thee in   *1Ki 8:33;*
this h.   *8:42; 2Ch 6:24, 32*
spread forth his hands   *1Ki 8:38*
towards *this h.*
I have hallowed *this h.*   *1Ki 9:3;*
  2Ch 7:16, 20
at *this h.* every one shall hiss   *1Ki 9:8;*
  2Ch 7:21
this h. I have chosen   *2Ki 21:7;*
  2Ch 33:7
when evil cometh we stand   *2Ch 20:9*
before *this h.* name is in *this h.*
the foundation of *this h.* was   *Ezr 3:12*
laid before
Nebuchadnezzar who   *Ezr 5:12*
destroyed *this h.*
this h. was finished on third   *Ezr 6:15*
day of Adar
and come and stand before me   *Jer 7:10*
in *this h.*
is *this h.* become a den of   *Jer 7:11*
robbers in your eyes
therefore will I do to *this h.* as   *Jer 7:14*
to Shiloh
then shall there enter in by the   *Jer 22:4*
gates of *this h.*
that *this h.* shall become a   *Jer 22:5*
desolation
then will I make *this h.* like   *Jer 26:6*
Shiloh
saying, *This h.* shall be like   *Jer 26:9*
Shiloh
the Lord sent me to prophesy   *Jer 26:12*
against *this h.*
to dwell in houses, and *this h.*   *Hag 1:4*
lie waste
who is left that saw *this h.* in   *Hag 2:3*
her first glory
I will fill *this h.* with glory,   *Hag 2:7*
saith the Lord
the glory of *this* latter *h.*   *Hag 2:9*
greater than former

Zerubbaal laid the foundation   *Zec 4:9*
this h.
ye enter, first say, Peace be to   *Lu 10:5*
this h.
Jesus said, This day is salvation   *Lu 19:9*
come to *this h.*

THINE, THY HOUSE

come thou and all *thy h.* into   *Ge 7:1*
the ark
thus have I been twenty years   *Ge 31:41*
in *thy h.*
frogs shall go up and come into   *Ex 8:3*
thine h.
every one that is clean in *thy*   *Nu 18:11;*
h.   *18:13*
talk when thou sittest in *thine*   *De 6:7;*
h.   *11:19*
shalt write them on the posts of   *De 6:9;*
thy h.   *11:20*
nor shalt bring an abomination   *De 7:26*
into *thine h.*
because he loveth thee and   *De 15:16*
thine h.
then thou shalt bring her   *De 21:12*
home to *thine h.*
shall remain in *thine h.* and   *De 21:13*
bewail her father
that thou bring not blood upon   *De 22:8*
thine h.
shalt not have in *thine h.*   *De 25:14*
divers measures
good thing God given to thee   *De 26:11*
and *thine h.*
bring men which are entered   *Jos 2:3*
into *thine h.*
whosoever shall go out of the   *Jos 2:19*
doors of *thy h.*
we will burn *thine h.* on thee   *J'g 12:1*
with fire
bring forth the man that came   *J'g 19:22*
into *thine h.*
make woman that is come into   *Ru 4:11*
thine h.
let *thy h.* be like the house of   *Ru 4:12*
Pharez
that *thy h.* should walk before   *1Sa 2:30*
me
there shall not be an old man   *1Sa 2:31*
in *thine h.*
the increase of *thine h.* shall   *1Sa 2:33*
die in flower of age
every one in *thine h.* shall   *1Sa 2:36*
crouch to him
as David, who is honourable   *1Sa 22:14*
in *thine h.*
peace be to *thine h.* and to all   *1Sa 25:6*
thou hast
David said to her, Go up in   *1Sa 25:35*
peace to *thine h.*
thine h. shall be established   *2Sa 7:16*
for ever
go down to *thy h.* and wash   *2Sa 11:8*
thy feet
why then didst not thou go   *2Sa 11:10*
down to *thine h.*
the sword shall never depart   *2Sa 12:10*
from *thine h.*
the king said, Go to *thine h.*   *2Sa 14:8;*
                         1Ki 1:53
if thou wilt give me half *thine*   *1Ki 13:8*
h.
bring him back with thee   *1Ki 13:18*
into *thine h.*
make *thy h.* like the h. of   *1Ki 16:3;*
Jeroboam   *21:22*
my servants, they shall search   *1Ki 20:6*
thine h.
set *thine h.* in order   *2Ki 20:1; Isa 38:1*
what have they seen in *thine*   *2Ki 20:15;*
h.   *Isa 39:4*
all in *thine h.* shall be   *2Ki 20:17;*
carried   *Isa 39:6*
I will come to *thy h.* in   *Ps 5:7*
multitude of thy mercy
I have loved the habitation of   *Ps 26:8*
thy h.
they shall be satisfied with   *Ps 36:8*
fatness of *thy h.*
I will take no bullock out of   *Ps 50:9*
thy h.
we shall be satisfied with   *Ps 65:4*
goodness of *thy h.*
I will go into *thy h.* with burnt   *Ps 66:13*
offerings
zeal of *thine h.* hath eaten me   *Ps 69:9;*
up   *Joh 2:17*
holiness becometh *thine h.* O   *Ps 93:5*
Lord, for ever

wife as a fruitful vine by sides   *Ps 128:3*
of *thine h.*
bring the poor that are cast   *Isa 58:7*
out to *thy h.*
go forth, thou shalt live, and   *Jer 38:17*
thine h.
Spirit said, Shut thyself within   *Eze 3:24*
thine h.
may cause the blessing to rest   *Eze 44:30*
in *thine h.*
thou hast consulted shame to   *Hab 2:10*
thy h.
arise, go to *thy h.*   *M't 9:6;*
            M'k 2:11; Lu 5:24
I will keep the passover at   *M't 26:18*
thy h.
I entered *thy h.* thou gavest me   *Lu 7:44*
no water
come down, for to-day I must   *Lu 19:5*
abide at *thy h.*
thou and all *thy h.* shall be   *Ac 11:14;*
saved   *16:31*
to the church in *thy h.* grace to   *Ph'm 2*
you

HOUSEBREAKING

find it by *h.* (A)   *Jer 2:34*

HOUSEHOLD

thy father's *h.* (B)   *Ge 12:1; 46:31*
his children and his *h.* after   *Ge 18:19*
him
a great *h.* (B)(E)   *Ge 26:14*
hast thou found of all *thy h.*   *Ge 31:37*
stuff
my *h.* goods (A)(B)   *Ge 31:37*
Jacob said unto his *h.* and to   *Ge 35:2*
all
blessed Egyptian's *h.* (B)   *Ge 39:5*
Pharaoh's *h.* heard   *Ge 45:2*
(A)(B)(R)
lest thou, and *thy h.* and all   *Ge 45:11*
that
and all his father's *h.* with   *Ge 47:12*
bread
his father's *h.* (A)   *Ge 50:22*
man and his *h.* came with Jacob   *Ex 1:1*
one lamb for each *h.* (E)(R)   *Ex 12:3*
if the *h.* be too little for the   *Ex 12:4*
lamb
for himself, and for his *h.* and   *Le 16:17*
neighbor's *h.* (A)   *Le 20:17*
upon Pharaoh, and upon all   *De 6:22*
his *h.*
thou shalt rejoice, thou, and   *De 14:26*
thy h.
Lord shall choose, thou and   *De 15:20*
thy h.
all *thy* father's *h.* home unto   *Jos 2:18*
thee
harlot alive, and her father's *h.*   *Jos 6:25*
the *h.* which the Lord shall   *Jos 7:14*
take
And he brought his *h.* man   *Jos 7:18*
by man
because he feared his father's   *J'g 6:27*
h.
lose thy life, with the lives of   *J'g 18:25*
thy h.
our master, and against all   *1Sa 25:17*
his *h.*
and his men, every man with   *1Sa 27:3*
his *h.*
bring up, every man with his *h.*   *2Sa 2:3*
blessed Obed-edom, and all   *2Sa 6:11*
his *h.*
Then David returned to bless   *2Sa 6:20*
his *h.*
went forth, and all his *h.*   *2Sa 15:16*
after him
asses be for the king's *h.* to   *2Sa 16:2*
ride on
put his *h.* in order, and   *2Sa 17:23*
hanged
ferry boat to carry over the   *2Sa 19:18*
king's *h.*
have brought the king, and   *2Sa 19:41*
his *h.*
Ahishar was over the *h.*: and   *1Ki 4:6*
victuals for the king and his *h.*   *1Ki 4:7*
my desire, in giving food for   *1Ki 5:9*
my *h.*
measures of wheat for food to   *1Ki 5:11*
his *h.*
and Genubath was in   *1Ki 11:20*
Pharaoh's *h.*
we may go and tell the king's *h.*   *2Ki 7:9*

go thou and thine *h.* and   *2Ki 8:1*
sojourn
she went with her *h.* and   *2Ki 8:2*
sojourned
Hilkiah, which was over the   *2Ki 18:18;*
h.   *18:37*
sent Eliakim, which was over   *2Ki 19:2*
the *h.*
one principal *h.* being taken   *1Ch 24:6*
for
I cast forth all the *h.* stuff of   *Ne 13:8*
Tobiah
she asses, and a very great *h.*   *Job 1:3*
for the food of thy *h.* and for   *Pr 27:27*
giveth meat to her *h.* and a   *Pr 31:15*
portion
not afraid of the snow for   *Pr 31:21*
her *h.*
for all her *h.* are clothed with   *Pr 31:21*
scarlet
looketh well to the ways of   *Pr 31:27*
her *h.*
son of Hilkiah, that was over   *Isa 36:22*
the *h.*
sent Eliakim, who was over   *Isa 37:2*
the *h.*
more shall they call them of   *M't 10:25*
his *h.*
man's foes shall be they of   *M't 10:36*
his own *h.*
his lord hath made ruler over   *M't 24:45*
his *h.*
the *h.* divided (B)   *M'k 3:25*
carry any *h.* equipment (A)   *M'k 11:16*
his lord shall make ruler over   *Lu 12:42*
his *h.*
he called two of his *h.* servants   *Ac 10:7*
when she was baptized, and   *Ac 16:15*
her *h.*
them which are of   *Ro 16:10*
Aristobulus' *h.*
them that be of the *h.* of   *Ro 16:11*
Narcissus
baptized also the *h.* of   *1Co 1:16*
Stephanas
unto them who are of the *h.* of   *Ga 6:10*
faith
with the saints, and of the *h.*   *Eph 2:19*
of God
chiefly they that are of   *Ph'p 4:22*
Caesar's *h.*
and the *h.* of Onesiphorus   *2Ti 4:19*
we are his *h.* (B)   *Heb 3:6*

HOUSEHOLDER

servants of the *h.* came and   *M't 13:27*
said
is like unto a man that is an   *M't 13:52;*
h.   *20:1*
murmured against the *h.*   *M't 20:11*
was a certain *h.* which   *M't 21:33*
planted a
if the *h.* had known (S)   *M't 24:43*

HOUSEHOLDS

food for the famine of your *h.*   *Ge 42:33*
take your father and your *h.*   *Ge 45:18*
your food, and for them of   *Ge 47:24*
your *h.*
eat it in every place, ye and   *Nu 18:31*
your *h.*
swallowed them up, and their   *De 11:6*
h.
put your hand unto, ye and   *De 12:7*
your *h.*
Lord shall take shall come by   *Jos 7:14*
h.

HOUSES

go, carry corn for the famine   *Ge 42:19*
of your *h.*
midwives feared God, he made   *Ex 1:21*
them *h.*
these by the heads of their   *Ex 6:14*
fathers' *h.*
to destroy the frogs from thee   *Ex 8:9;*
and thy *h.*   *8:11*
and the frogs died out of the   *Ex 8:13*
h. and the fields
I will send swarms of flies into   *Ex 8:21;*
thy *h.*   *8:24*
he made his servants and cattle   *Ex 9:20*
flee into the *h.*
locusts fill thy *h.* and *h.* of all   *Ex 10:6*
servants, and *h.* of all Egyptians
strike it on the upper door   *Ex 12:7*
posts of the *h.*

blood be for a token upon *h*. *Ex 12:13*
where you are
ye shall put away leaven out *Ex 12:15*
of your *h*.
there shall be no leaven found *Ex 12:19*
in your *h*.
not suffer the destroyer to *Ex 12:23*
come in to your *h*.
passed over and delivered our *Ex 12:27*
h. in Egypt
h. of villages be counted as *Le 25:31*
the fields
h. of cities of their possession *Le 25:32;*
    25:33
by their father's *h*. (A) *Nu 1:2*
their father's *h*. (A) *Nu 2:2; 3:15; 34:14*
sum of Gershon thro' *h*. their *Nu 4:22*
fathers
the earth swallowed them up *Nu 16:32*
and their *h*.
for each prince, according to *Nu 17:6*
their fathers' *h*.
we will not return unto our *h*. *Nu 32:18*
till Israel
to give thee *h*. full of all good *De 6:11*
things
when hast built goodly *h*. and *De 8:12*
dwelt therein
dwellest in their cities and *h*. *De 19:1;*
    Ne 9:25
we took hot provision out of *Jos 9:12*
our *h*.
do ye know that there is in *J'g 18:14*
these *h*.
men that were in *h*. near to *J'g 18:22*
Micah's
he cried against *h*. of high *1Ki 13:32*
places
they shall search the *h*. of thy *1Ki 20:6*
servants
put them in *h*. of the high *2Ki 17:29*
places
which sacrificed in the *h*. of *2Ki 17:32*
the high places
he brake down the *h*. of the *2Ki 23:7*
Sodomites
the *h*. of the high places *2Ki 23:19*
Josiah took away
he burnt all the *h*. of *2Ki 25:9;*
Jerusalem *Jer 52:13*
the fathers' *h*. (S) *1Ch 8:10;*
    8:28; 9:9; 23:9; 24:6, 31
David made *h*. in the city of *1Ch 15:1*
David
built *h*. for himself (S) *1Ch 15:1*
David gave to Solomon the *1Ch 28:11*
pattern of the *h*.
to overlay the walls of the *h*. *1Ch 29:4*
withal
to buy timber to floor the *h*. *2Ch 34:11*
and prepare yourselves by *h*. *2Ch 35:4*
of your fathers
fight for your wives and your *Ne 4:14*
h.
some said, We have mortgaged *Ne 5:3*
our lands and *h*.
restore to them their vineyards *Ne 5:11*
and *h*.
but the people are few, and *h*. *Ne 7:4*
not builded
we cast lots after the *h*. of our *Ne 10:34*
fathers
his sons went and feasted in *Job 1:4*
their *h*.
with princes, who filled their *Job 3:15*
h. with silver
much less in them that dwell *Job 4:19*
in *h*. of clay
he dwelleth in *h*. which no *Job 15:28*
man inhabiteth
their *h*. are safe from fear, nor *Job 21:9*
is rod of God
yet he filled their *h*. with *Job 22:18*
good things
in dark they dig through *h*. *Job 24:16*
which they
that their *h*. shall continue for *Ps 49:11*
ever
let us take the *h*. of God in *Ps 83:12*
possession
we shall fill our *h*. with spoil *Pr 1:13*
yet make they their *h*. in the *Pr 30:26*
rocks
I builded me *h*. I planted me *Ec 2:4*
vineyards
the spoil of the poor is in your *Isa 3:14*
h.
of a truth, many *h*. shall be *Isa 5:9;*
desolate *6:11*

for a rock of offence to both *Isa 8:14*
the *h*. of Israel
their *h*. be spoiled, their wives *Isa 13:16*
ravished
their *h*. shall be full of doleful *Isa 13:21*
creatures
the wild beasts shall cry in *Isa 13:22*
their desolate *h*.
on the tops of their *h*. every *Isa 15:3*
one shall howl
ye have numbered *h*. of *Isa 22:10*
Jerusalem, and *h*. have ye
yea, upon all the *h*. of joy in *Isa 32:13*
the joyous city
they shall build *h*. and inhabit *Isa 65:21*
them
and assembled by troops in the *Jer 5:7*
harlot's *h*.
as cage is full of birds, their *h*. *Jer 5:27*
full of deceit
and their *h*. shall be turned *Jer 6:12*
unto others
let a cry be heard from their *Jer 18:22*
h.
h. of Jerusalem and *h*. of the *Jer 19:13*
kings of Judah be defiled
build ye *h*. and dwell in them *Jer 29:5;*
    29:28
h. and fields be possessed in *Jer 32:15*
this land
h. on whose roofs they *Jer 32:29*
offered incense to Baal
concerning *h*. of this city, and *Jer 33:4*
h. of kings
they burnt the *h*. of the people *Jer 39:8*
with fire
I will kindle a fire in *h*. of *Jer 43:12*
gods of Egypt
our *h*. turned to aliens, we are *La 5:2*
orphans
the heathen shall possess their *Eze 7:24*
h.
which say, It is not near, let us *Eze 11:3*
build *h*.
they shall burn thine *h*. with *Eze 16:41;*
fire *23:47*
and they shall destroy thy *Eze 26:12*
pleasant *h*.
they shall build *h*. and plant *Eze 28:26*
vineyards
talking against thee in the *Eze 33:30*
doors of the *h*.
the holy portion shall be a *Eze 45:4*
place for their *h*.
and your *h*. shall be made a *Da 2:5*
dunghill
and their *h*. shall be made a *Da 3:29*
dunghill
I will place them in their *h*. *Ho 11:11*
saith Lord
they shall climb up upon the *h*.; *Joe 2:9*
shall enter
h. of ivory perish, great *h*. *Am 3:15*
have an end
the *h*. of Achzib shall be a lie *Mic 1:14*
to kings
and they covet *h*. and take *Mic 2:2*
them away
the women ye cast out from *Mic 2:9*
their pleasant *h*.
fill their master's *h*. with *Zep 1:9*
violence
their *h*. become a desolation, *Zep 1:13*
they shall build *h*. but not
in the *h*. of Ashkelon shall they *Zep 2:7*
lie down
is time for you to dwell in *Hag 1:4*
your ceiled *h*.
h. shall be rifled, and the *Zec 14:2*
women ravished
they that wear soft clothing *M't 11:8*
are in kings' *h*.
every one that hath forsaken *M't 19:29*
h. or wife
devour widows' *h*. *M't 23:14;*
    M'k 12:40; Lu 20:47
if send them away fasting to *M'k 8:3*
their own *h*.
that they may receive me into *Lu 16:4*
their *h*.
as many as were possessors of *Ac 4:34*
h. sold
have ye not *h*. to eat and *1Co 11:22*
drink in
deacons ruling their own *h*. *1Ti 3:12*
well
of this sort are they which *2Ti 3:6*
creep into *h*.
who subvert whole *h*. teaching *Tit 1:11*
things

HOUSETOP

better to dwell in a corner of *Pr 21:9;*
the *h*. *25:24*
Let him which is on the *h*. *M't 24:17;*
not *M'k 13:15*
they went upon the *h*. and let *Lu 5:19*
him
he which shall be upon the *h*. *Lu 17:31*
Peter went up upon the *h*. to *Ac 10:9*
pray

HOUSETOPS

them be as the grass upon the *Ps 129:6*
h.
thou art wholly gone up to the *Isa 22:1*
h.
as the grass on the *h*. and as *Isa 37:27*
corn
upon all the *h*. of Moab, and *Jer 48:38*
in the
the host of heaven upon the *h*. *Zep 1:5*
the ear, that preach ye upon *M't 10:27*
the *h*.
herald from the *h*. (B) *M't 10:27*
shall be proclaimed upon the *h*. *Lu 12:3*

HOW

and *h*. saidst thou, She is my *Ge 26:9*
sister
h. is it thou hast found it so *Ge 27:20*
quickly
Jacob said, *H*. dreadful is this *Ge 28:17*
place
h. then can I do this great *Ge 39:9*
wickedness
what shall we speak? *h*. shall *Ge 44:16*
we clear ourselves
h. shall I go to my father, lad *Ge 44:34*
not with me
h. is it that ye are come so *Ex 2:18*
soon to-day
h. then shall Pharaoh hear me *Ex 6:12*
of uncircumcized
and *h*. shall Pharaoh hearken *Ex 6:30*
unto me
H. long shall this man be a *Ex 10:7*
snare
may know *h*. that the Lord *Ex 11:7*
doth put
Moses told *h*. the Lord *Ex 18:8*
delivered them
ye have seen *h*. I bare you *Ex 19:4;*
    De 1:31
h. we are to encamp in the *Nu 10:31*
wilderness
h. shall I curse whom God *Nu 23:8*
not cursed? *h*. shall I defy
h. goodly are thy tents, O *Nu 24:5*
Jacob, and
h. can I myself bear your *De 1:12*
cumbrance
if thou shalt say, *H*. can I *De 7:17*
dispossess them
h. the earth opened her mouth *De 11:6*
and swallowed
h. did these nations serve *De 12:30*
their gods
h. he met thee by the way and *De 25:18*
smote thee
ye know *h*. we have dwelt in *De 29:16*
Egypt. and *h*. we came through
h. should one chase a *De 32:30*
thousand, and two put
h. shall we make a league with *Jos 9:7*
you
h. shall we order the child, *h*. *J'g 13:12*
do to him
she said, *H*. canst thou say, I *J'g 16:15*
they said, Tell us, *h*. was this *J'g 20:3*
wickedness
h. do for wives for them that *J'g 21:7;*
remain *21:16*
till thou know *h*. the matter *Ru 3:18*
will fall
said, *H*. shall this man save *1Sa 10:27*
us
see *h*. mine eyes have been *1Sa 14:29*
enlightened
h. can I go? if Saul hear he *1Sa 16:2*
will kill me
h. went the matter, I pray *2Sa 1:4*
thee, tell me
h. knowest thou that Saul and *2Sa 1:5*
Jonathan be dead
h. are the mighty fallen *2Sa 1:19;*
    1:25, 27

H. shall the ark of the Lord come *2Sa 6:9*

h. Joab did, h. the people did, and h. the war *2Sa 11:7*

h. then will he vex himself, if we tell him *2Sa 12:18*

I know not h. to go out or come in *1Ki 3:7*

h. do you advise, that I may answer people *1Ki 12:6*

h. Jeroboam warred, and h. he reigned *1Ki 14:19*

h. I hid an hundred men of Lord's prophets *1Ki 18:13*

and see h. the man seeketh mischief *1Ki 20:7*

h. he seeketh a quarrel against me *2Ki 5:7*

h. shall I help (S) *2Ki 6:27*

two kings stood not, h. then shall we stand *2Ki 10:4*

taught them h. they should fear the Lord *2Ki 17:28*

h. then wilt thou turn away *2Ki 18:24; Isa 36:9*

heard long ago, h. I have done it *2Ki 19:25; Isa 37:26*

h. I have walked before thee *2Ki 20:3; Isa 38:3*

behold, I say, h. they reward us *2Ch 20:11*

his prayer, and h. God was entreated of him *2Ch 33:19*

see h. Jerusalem lieth waste, gates burnt *Ne 2:17*

Mordecai walked, to know h. Esther did *Es 2:11*

h. can I endure to see evil that shall come *Es 8:6*

but h. should a man be just with God *Job 9:2*

and thou sayest, H. doth God know *Job 22:13*

h. hast helped him without power? h. savest arm that *Job 26:2*

but h. little a portion is heard of him *Job 26:14*

h. say ye to my soul, flee as a bird *Ps 11:1*

h. thou didst drive out heathen, h. afflict *Ps 44:2*

say to God, h. terrible art thou in thy works *Ps 66:3*

h. doth God know *Ps 73:11*

h. amiable are thy tabernacles, O Lord *Ps 84:1*

h. short my time *Ps 89:47*

O Lord, h. manifold are thy works *Ps 104:24*

O h. love I thy law, it is my meditation *Ps 119:97*

h. sweet are thy words unto my taste *Ps 119:103*

consider h. I love thy precepts, quicken me *Ps 119:159*

h. he sware unto the Lord and vowed *Ps 132:2*

h. precious are thy thoughts unto me *Pr 139:17*

a word in due season, h. good is it *Pr 15:23*

there is a generation, O h. lofty their eyes *Pr 30:13*

he knoweth not h. to go to the city *Ec 10:15*

knowest not h. the bones grow in the womb *Ec 11:5*

h. fair is thy love, my sister, spouse *Ca 4:10; 7:6*

I have put off my coat, h. shall I put it on *Ca 5:3*

h. beautiful are thy feet with shoes, O daughter *Ca 7:1*

h. art thou fallen from heaven, O Lucifer *Isa 14:12*

shall say in that day, and h. shall we escape *Isa 20:6*

for h. should my name be polluted *Isa 48:11*

I should know h. to speak a word in season *Isa 50:4*

h. beautiful are the feet of him *Isa 52:7; Ro 10:15*

h. canst thou say, I am not polluted *Jer 2:23*

I said, H. shall I put thee among the children *Jer 3:19*

h. shall I pardon? h. do ye say *Jer 5:7; 8:8; 48:14*

h. are we spoiled? to ask h. thou doest *Jer 9:19; 15:5*

h. long wilt thou cut thyself *Jer 47:5*

h. can it be quiet, seeing the Lord hath given *Jer 47:7*

h. is the hammer of the whole earth cut *Jer 50:23*

h. doth the city sit solitary as a widow *La 1:1*

h. are they esteemed as earthen *La 4:2*

h. weak is thy heart, saith the Lord *Eze 16:30*

if we pine away in sins, h. should we live *Eze 33:10*

h. shall I give thee up? h. make thee as Admah and *Ho 11:8*

h. do the beasts groan herds of cattle *Joe 1:18*

if thieves came to thee, h. art thou cut off *Ob 5*

h. is she become desolate place for beasts *Zep 2:15*

h. do you see it now? is it not as nothing *Hag 2:3*

h. great is his goodness and his beauty *Zec 9:17*

h. have we robbed thee (S) *Mal 3:8*

if light be darkness, h. great is that darkness *M't 6:23*

h. wilt thou say to thy brother, Let me pull *M't 7:4*

if ye know h. to give good gifts *M't 7:11; Lu 11:13*

take no thought h. or what ye shall speak *M't 10:19*

h. they might destroy him *M't 12:14; M'k 3:6; 11:18*

h. shall his kingdom stand *M't 12:26; Lu 11:18*

h. can ye, being evil, speak good things *M't 12:34*

h. is it that ye do not understand that I spake *M't 16:11*

h. think ye? if a man have an hundred sheep *M't 18:12*

h. soon is the fig tree withered away *M't 21:20*

h. camest thou in hither not having a garment *M't 22:12*

if call him Lord h. is he his son *M't 22:45; Lu 20:44*

h. can ye escape damnation of hell *M't 23:33*

h. then shall the scriptures be fulfilled *M't 26:54*

h. is it that he eateth with sinners *M'k 2:16*

h. he went into the house of God *M'k 2:26; Lu 6:4*

seed should grow up, he knoweth not h. *M'k 4:27*

he said, H. is it that ye have no faith *M'k 4:40*

h. hardly they that have riches enter *M'k 10:23*

sought h. they might take him by craft *M'k 14:1*

sought h. he might betray him *M'k 14:11; Lu 22:4*

h. shall this be, seeing I know not a man *Lu 1:34*

h. is it that ye sought me? wist ye not *Lu 2:49*

take heed h. ye hear; h. readest thou *Lu 8:18; 10:26*

h. am I straitened till it be accomplished *Lu 12:50*

h. is it that ye do not discern this time *Lu 12:56*

he said, H. is it that I hear this of thee *Lu 16:2*

remember h. he spake unto you in Galilee *Lu 24:6*

h. he was known of them in breaking bread *Lu 24:35*

h. can a man be born, when he is old *Joh 3:4*

h. can these things be; h. can ye believe *Joh 3:9; 5:44*

if not his writing, h. believe my words *Joh 5:47*

h. can this man give us his flesh to eat *Joh 6:52*

saying, H. knoweth this man letters *Joh 7:15*

h. were thy eyes opened; h. opened eyes *Joh 9:10; 9:26*

h. loved him; h. can we know the way *Joh 11:36; 14:5*

h. is it thou wilt manifest thyself to us *Joh 14:22*

finding nothing h. they might punish them *Ac 4:21*

h. is it ye agreed together to tempt *Ac 5:9*

h. God by his hand would deliver them *Ac 7:25*

h. can I, except some man guide me *Ac 8:31*

told, h. he had seen the Lord in the way *Ac 9:27*

h. God anointed Jesus of Nazareth with Holy Ghost *Ac 10:38*

shewed h. he had seen an angel in house *Ac 11:13*

h. he had opened the door of faith *Ac 14:27*

let us go again, and see h. they do *Ac 15:36*

knoweth not h. that the city *Ac 19:35*

h. kept back nothing that was profitable *Ac 20:20*

h. labouring, ye ought to support weak *Ac 20:35*

for then h. shall God judge the world *Ro 3:6*

h. we that are dead to sin live longer therein *Ro 6:2*

h. to perform what is good, I find not *Ro 7:18*

h. shall he not with him freely give all *Ro 8:32*

h. shall they call? h. shall believe? h. hear *Ro 10:14*

h. he maketh intercession to God against Israel *Ro 11:2*

h. unsearchable his judgments, and ways *Ro 11:33*

take heed, h. he buildeth thereupon *1Co 3:10*

unmarried careth h. he may please the Lord *1Co 7:32*

that is married careth h. he may please wife *1Co 7:33*

she careth h. she may please her husband *1Co 7:34*

h. shall it be known what is piped or harped *1Co 14:7*

h. shall it be known what is spoken *1Co 14:9*

h. say some that there is no resurrection *1Co 15:12*

some will say, H. are dead raised up *1Co 15:35*

h. with fear and trembling received him *2Co 7:15*

h. that in a great trial of affliction their joy *2Co 8:2*

know ye not h. that Jesus Christ is in you *2Co 13:5*

h. turn ye again to the weak elements *Ga 4:9*

see h. large letter I have written *Ga 6:11*

but that ye also may know h. I do *Eph 6:21*

so soon as I shall see h. it will go with me *Ph'p 2:23*

I know h. to be abased, and know h. to abound *Ph'p 4:12*

ye may know h. ye ought to answer *Col 4:6*

and h. ye turned to God from idols to *1Th 1:9*

h. holily we behaved ourselves among you *1Th 2:10*

h. we exhorted you; h. ye ought to walk *1Th 2:11; 4:1*

know h. to possess his vessel in honour *1Th 4:4*

for you know h. ye ought to follow us *2Th 3:7*

if a man know not h. to rule own house, h. shall he take care of the church *1Ti 3:5*

mayest know h. thou oughtest to behave *1Ti 3:15*

h. shall escape if neglect so great salvation *Heb 2:3*

consider h. great this man was, to whom *Heb 7:4*

ye see h. that by works a man is justified *Jas 2:24*

h. great a matter a little fire kindleth *Jas 3:5*

the Lord knoweth h. to deliver the godly *2Pe 2:9*

h. dwelleth the love of God in *1Jo 3:17* him

h. can he love God whom he *1Jo 4:20* hath not seen

h. that the Lord having saved *Jude 5* the people

h. canst not bear them who are *Re 2:2* evil

remember *h.* thou hast received *Re 3:3* and heard

HOW *LONG*

h. long wilt refuse to humble *Ex 10:3* thyself

h. long shall this man be a *Ex 10:7* snare unto us

h. long refuse to keep my *Ex 16:28* commandments

h. long will people provoke *Nu 14:11* me? *h. long* will it be ere

h. long shall I bear with evil *Nu 14:27* congregation

h. long are ye slack to go to *Jos 18:3* possess land

Eli said, *H. long* wilt thou be *1Sa 1:14* drunken

h. long wilt thou mourn for *1Sa 16:1* Saul, seeing I have

Barzillai said, *H. long* have I *2Sa 19:34* to live

h. long halt ye between two *1Ki 18:21* opinions

king said, For *h. long* shall thy *Ne 2:6* journey be

h. long wilt thou not depart *Job 7:19* from me

h. long wilt thou speak? *h. long Job 8:2* shall words of mouth be like wind

h. long will it be ere you make *Job 18:2* end of words

h. long will ye vex my soul *Job 19:2* and break me

h. long will ye turn glory into *Ps 4:2* shame? *h. long* ye love vanity

my soul is vexed; but thou, O *Ps 6:3* Lord, *h. long*

h. long wilt thou forget me, O *Ps 13:1* Lord for ever

h. long shall I take counsel in *Ps 13:2* my soul? *h. long* enemy be

Lord *h. long* wilt thou look *Ps 35:17* on? rescue my soul

h. long will ye imagine mischief *Ps 62:3* against man

nor is there any among us that *Ps 74:9* knoweth *h. long*

O God, *h. long* shall the *Ps 74:10* adversary reproach

h. long wilt thou be angry for *Ps 79:5;* ever *80:4*

h. long wilt judge unjustly and *Ps 82:2* accept persons

h. long Lord, wilt thou hide *Ps 89:46* thyself? for ever

return, O Lord, *h. long?* let it *Ps 90:13* repent thee

h. long wicked, *h. long* wicked *Ps 94:3* triumph

h. long shall they utter hard *Ps 94:4* things

h. long simple ones, will love *Pr 1:22* simplicity

h. long wilt thou sleep, O *Pr 6:9* sluggard? when arise

then said I, Lord, *h. long?* he *Isa 6:11* answered

h. long shall vain thoughts *Jer 4:14* lodge in thee

h. long shall I see standard, *Jer 4:21* and hear trumpet

h. long shall land mourn and *Jer 12:4* herbs wither

h. long shall this be in the *Jer 23:26* heart of prophets

baldness on Gaza, *h. long* wilt *Jer 47:5* cut thyself

sword of the Lord, *h. long* ere *Jer 47:6* thou be quiet

h. long shall be vision of daily *Da 8:13* sacrifice

h. long shall it be to end of *Da 12:6* these wonders

h. long will it be ere they attain *Ho 8:5* innocency

h. long shall I cry, and thou *Hab 1:2* wilt not hear

woe to him increaseth what *Hab 2:6* not his, *h. long*

---

h. long wilt thou not have *Zec 1:12* mercy on Jerusalem

h. long shall I be with you, *M't 17:17;* *h. long* suffer you *M'k 9:19; Lu 9:41*

h. long is it ago since this *M'k 9:21* came to him

h. long dost thou make us to *Joh 10:24* doubt

h. long, O Lord holy and *Re 6:10* true, dost thou not

HOW *MANY*

h. many are mine iniquities *Job 13:23* and sins

h. many are the days of thy *Ps 119:84* servants

h. many loaves have ye *M't 15:34;* *M'k 6:38; 8:5*

h. many baskets ye took up *M't 16:9;* *M'k 8:19-20*

h. many things they witness *M'k 15:4* against thee

h. many hired servants of my *Lu 15:17* father's have

in *h. many* things he *2Ti 1:18* ministered to me

HOW *MANY TIMES*

h. many times I adjure thee, *1Ki 22:16;* tell nothing but *2Ch 18:15*

HOW *MUCH*

h. much rather when he saith, *2Ki 5:13* Wash

and salt without prescribing *h. Ezr 7:22* much

h. much better is it to get *Pr 16:16* wisdom than gold

h. much better is thy love than *Ca 4:10* wine

h. much better is a man *M't 12:12* better than a sheep

h. much owest thou to my lord *Lu 16:5;* *16:7*

h. much every man hath *Lu 19:15* gained by trading

h. much evil he hath done thy *Ac 9:13* saints at Jerusalem

by *h. much* he is Mediator of *Heb 8:6* better covenant

of *h. much* sorer *Heb 10:29* punishment, suppose ye

h. much she hath glorified *Re 18:7* herself

HOW *MUCH LESS*

heaven cannot contain thee, *1Ki 8:27;* *h. much less* this house *2Ch 6:18*

h. much less shall your God *2Ch 32:15* deliver

h. much less in them dwell in *Job 4:19* houses of clay

h. much less shall I answer *Job 9:14* him, choose words

h. much less is man that is *Job 25:6* worm and son of man

h. much less to him that *Job 34:19* accepteth not persons

h. much less shall it be meet *Eze 15:5* for work

HOW *MUCH MORE*

and *h. much more* after my *De 31:27* death

h. much more if people had *1Sa 14:30* eaten freely

h. much more then if we come *1Sa 23:3* to Keilah

h. much more when wicked *2Sa 4:11* men have slain

h. much more now may this *2Sa 16:11* Benjamite do it

h. much more abominable *Job 15:16* and filthy is man

h. much more than the hearts *Pr 15:11* of men

h. much more do his friends *Pr 19:7* go far from him

h. much more when with a *Pr 21:27* wicked mind

h. much more when send *Eze 14:21* sore judgments

h. much more heavenly *M't 7:11;*

Father give good things to *Lu 11:13* them

h. much more shall call them *M't 10:25* of his household

h. much more are ye better *Lu 12:24* than the fowls

h. much more will clothe you, *Lu 12:28* O ye of little faith

h. much more their fulness *Ro 11:12*

h. much more these which be *Ro 11:24* natural branches

h. much more things that *1Co 6:3* pertain to life

a brother to me, *h. much Ph'm 16* more* to thee

HOW *OFT, OFTEN*

h. oft is candle of wicked *Job 21:17* put out? *h. oft* cometh destruction upon them

h. oft did they provoke him in *Ps 78:40* wilderness

h. oft shall my brother sin *M't 18:21* against me

h. often would I have *M't 23:37;* gathered children as a hen *Lu 13:34*

HOWBEIT

h. Sisera fled on his feet to tent *J'g 4:17* of Jael

h. the king of Ammonites *J'g 11:28* hearkened not

h. the hair of his head began *J'g 16:22* to grow again

h. the name of the city was *J'g 18:29* Laish at first

h. we may not give them *J'g 21:18* wives of our daughters

h. there is a kinsman nearer *Ru 3:12* than I

h. yet protest solemnly unto *1Sa 8:9* them

h. Asahel refused to turn aside *2Sa 2:23*

h. because by this deed hast *2Sa 12:14* given occasion

h. he would not hearken unto *2Sa 13:14* her voice

h. he would not go, but *2Sa 13:25* blessed him

h. he attained not first three *2Sa 23:19;* *1Ch 11:21*

h. the kingdom is turned *1Ki 2:15* about

h. I believed not the words *1Ki 10:7;* *2Ch 9:6*

h. I will not rend all the *1Ki 11:13;* kingdom *11:34*

I have lacked nothing, *h.* let *1Ki 11:22* me go in any wise

h. slingers went about it and *2Ki 3:25* smote it

h. Lord shewed me, that he *2Ki 8:10* shall surely die

h. from sins of Jeroboam *2Ki 10:29* Jehu turned not

h. there were not made for *2Ki 12:13* house bowls

h. high places were not taken *2Ki 14:4;* away *15:35; 2Ch 20:33*

h. every nation made gods of *2Ki 17:29* their own

h. they did not hearken, but *2Ki 17:40* did after their

h. there was no reckoning *2Ki 22:7* made with them

h. the Lord God of Israel *1Ch 28:4* chose me

h. the king of Israel stayed *2Ch 18:34* himself up

h. the Levites hastened it not *2Ch 24:5*

h. he entered not into temple *2Ch 27:2* of the Lord

h. in business of *2Ch 32:31* ambassadors, God left him

h. thou art just in all brought *Ne 9:33* on us

h. our God turned curse into a *Ne 13:2* blessing

h. he will not stretch out his *Job 30:24* hand

h. he meaneth not so, nor *Isa 10:7* thinketh so

h. I sent to you all my *Jer 44:4* servants, prophets

h. this kind goeth not out but *M't 17:21* by prayer

h. Jesus suffered him not, but *M'k 5:19* saith to him

h. in vain do they worship me, *M'k 7:7*
teaching
h. there came boats from *Joh 6:23*
Tiberias
h. no man spake openly of *Joh 7:13*
him for fear
h. we know this man whence *Joh 7:27*
he is
if he sleep, do well, *h.* Jesus *Joh 11:13*
spake of his
h. when he the Spirit of truth *Joh 16:13*
is come
h. many who heard the word *Ac 4:4*
believed
h. the Most High dwelleth not *Ac 7:48*
in temples
h. he rose up and came into *Ac 14:20*
the city
h. certain men clave to him *Ac 17:34*
and believed
h. we must be cast upon a *Ac 27:26*
certain island
h. they looked when he should *Ac 28:6*
have swollen
h. we speak wisdom among the *1Co 2:6*
perfect
h. there is not in every man *1Co 8:7*
that knowledge
h. in the Spirit he speaketh *1Co 14:2*
mysteries
h. in malice be children, in *1Co 14:20*
understanding, men
h. that was not first which is *1Co 15:46*
spiritual
h. wherein soever any is *2Co 11:21*
bold, I am also
h. when ye knew not God ye *Ga 4:8*
did service
h. for this cause I obtained *1Ti 1:16*
mercy
h. not all that came out of *Heb 3:16*
Egypt by Moses

HOWL

they *h.* (B) *Job 30:7*
h. ye for the day of Lord is at *Isa 13:6*
hand
h. O gate; Moab shall *h.* *Isa 14:31;*
15:2-3; 16:7
h. ye ships of Tarshish, for it *Isa 23:1*
is laid waste
pass over to Tarshish; *h.* ye *Isa 23:6*
inhabitants of isle
make them to *h.; h.* for *Isa 52:5;*
vexation 65:14
lament and *h.* *Jer 4:8; 48:20*
h. ye shepherds *Jer 25:34*
and all the inhabitants of the *Jer 47:2*
land shall *h.*
I will *h.* for Moab; they shall *Jer 48:31;*
h. 48:39
h. O Heshbon; *h.* for Babylon *Jer 49:3;*
51:8
cry and *h.* son of man, for it *Eze 21:12*
shall be
prophesy and say, *H.* ye, woe *Eze 30:2*
h. ye drinkers; *h.* ye *Joe 1:5;*
vinedressers 1:11
lament and *h.* ye ministers of *Joe 1:13*
the altar
therefore I will wail and *h.* will *Mic 1:8*
go stripped
h. ye inhabitants of Maktesh *Zep 1:11*
h. fir tree, *h.* O ye oaks of *Zec 11:2*
Bashan
go to, now, ye rich men, weep *Jas 5:1*
and *h.*

HOWLED

when they *h.* upon their beds *Ho 7:14*

HOWLING

and in the waste *h.* *De 32:10*
wilderness; he
h. creatures (B)(R) *Isa 13:21*
Moab: the *h.* thereof unto *Isa 15:8*
Eglaim
and the *h.* thereof unto *Isa 15:8*
Beer-elim
an *h.* of the principal of the *Jer 25:36*
flock
and an *h.* from the second *Zep 1:10*
voice of the *h.* of the *Zec 11:3*
shepherds

HOWLINGS

songs of the temple shall be *h.* *Am 8:3*

HOWSOEVER

h. let all thy wants lie upon *J'g 19:20*
me
h. let me, I pray thee, also *2Sa 18:22*
But *h.* said he, Let me run *2Sa 18:23*
be cut off *h.* I punished them *Zep 3:7*

HUBBUB

because of *h.* (N) *Ac 21:34*

HUBS

spokes and *h.* were cast *1Ki 7:33*
(A)(B)(R)(S)

HUGE

and the Lubims a *h.* host, with *2Ch 16:8*

HUKKOK

and goeth out from thence to *Jos 19:34*
H.

HUKOK

And *H.* with her suburbs, and *1Ch 6:75*

HUL

Uz, and *H.,* and Gether, and *Ge 10:23*
Mash
and Aram, Uz, and *H.,* and *1Ch 1:17*
Gether

HULDAH

went unto *H.* the *2Ki 22:14;*
prophetess the *2Ch 34:22*

HUMAN

no *h.* power renders one mighty *1Sa 2:9*
(B)
how can a *h.* being be just *Job 25:4*
(B)(E)
no. *h.* being endure *M't 24:22*
(A)(P)(R)
claim righteousness in *h.* eyes *Lu 16:15*
(B)
you judge by *h.* standards *Joh 8:15*
(B)(P)
h. beings of nature like yours *Ac 14:15*
(A)(B)(N)(P)
anguish on every *h.* being (R) *Ro 2:9*
no *h.* being shall (B)(N)(R) *Ro 3:20*
h. ancestor (B)(N)(P) *Ro 4:1*
your *h.* weakness (B)(N) *Ro 6:19*
my *h.* nature under sin's *Ro 7:25*
control (B)
in *h.* lineage (B) *Ro 9:5*
as far as *h.* descent goes (P) *Ro 9:5*
no *h.* may boast (N)(R) *1Co 1:29*
words of *h.* philosophy (A) *1Co 2:1*
tablets of *h.* hearts *2Co 3:3*
(A)(B)(N)(R)
all *h.* history shall be *Eph 1:10*
consummated in Christ (P)
bearing *h.* likeness, revealed in *Ph'p 2:7*
h. shape (N)

HUMANITY

all *h.* be boastless (B) *1Co 1:29*

HUMANLY

our forefather *h.* speaking (A) *Ro 4:1*

HUMBLE

long wilt thou refuse to *h.* *Ex 10:3*
thyself
will you decline submission to *Ex 10:3*
me (B)
h. yourselves (B) *Le 16:29;*
20:25; 23:27; Nu 29:7
to *h.* thee, and to prove thee *De 8:2*
that he might *h.* thee, and that *De 8:16*
he
and *h.* ye them, and do with *J'g 19:24*
them
debase them (A) *J'g 19:24*
ravish them (B)(R) *J'g 19:24*

If my people shall *h.* *2Ch 7:14*
themselves
thou didst *h.* thyself before *2Ch 34:27*
God
might *h.* ourselves (A) *Ezr 8:21*
and he shall save the *h.* *Job 22:29*
he forgetteth not the cry of the *Ps 9:12*
forgetteth not cry of the poor *Ps 9:12*
does not forget cry of afflicted *Ps 9:12*
(R)
up thine hand: forget not the *Ps 10:12*
h.
forget not the afflicted (B)(R) *Ps 10:12*
forget not the poor (E) *Ps 10:12*
hast heard the desire of the *h.* *Ps 10:17*
heard longing of the afflicted *Ps 10:17*
(B)
heard the desire of the meek *Ps 10:17*
(E)(R)
guide *h.* in right (B)(R) *Ps 25:9*
the *h.* shall hear thereof, and be *Ps 34:2*
meek shall hear and be glad *Ps 34:2*
(E)
afflicted hear and be glad (R) *Ps 34:2*
God shall *h.* them (A)(B)(R) *Ps 55:19*
The *h.* shall see this, and be *Ps 69:32*
glad
meek have seen it and are glad *Ps 69:32*
(E)
oppressed see it and be glad *Ps 69:32*
(R)
go, *h.* thyself, and make sure thy *Pr 6:3*
importune your neighbor (R) *Pr 6:3*
Better it is to be of an *h.* spirit *Pr 16:19*
better be of lowly spirit *Pr 16:19*
(E)(R)
but honour shall uphold the *h.* *Pr 29:23*
lowly in spirit obtains honor *Pr 29:23*
(B)(E)(R)
that is of a contrite and *h.* *Isa 57:15*
spirit
to revive the spirit of the *h.* *Isa 57:15*
to *h.* himself (A)(R) *Isa 58:5*
the queen, *H.* yourselves, sit *Jer 13:18*
down
take a lowly seat (B)(R) *Jer 13:18*
h. women (B)(R) *Eze 22:10; 22:11*
h. thyself before God *Da 10:12*
(A)(B)(E)(N)
Whosoever therefore shall *h.* *M't 18:4*
and he that shall *h.* himself *M't 23:12*
shall
h. been lifted high (N)(P) *Lu 1:52*
think in a *h.* way (B) *Ro 12:3*
give yourselves to *h.* talks *Ro 12:16*
(A)
adjust to *h.* situations (B) *Ro 12:16*
go about with *h.* folk (N) *Ro 12:16*
h. enough when face to face *2Co 10:1*
(P)(R)
my God will *h.* me among *2Co 12:21*
you
God shall humiliate me (N) *2Co 12:21*
God make me ashamed of *2Co 12:21*
you (P)
h. in mind (P) *Col 3:12*
but giveth grace unto the *h.* *Jas 4:6*
gives grace to the lowly (A) *Jas 4:6*
grants grace to humble-minded *Jas 4:6*
(B)
the grace he gives is stronger *Jas 4:6*
(N)
h. yourselves in sight of Lord *Jas 4:10*
take a lowly position before (B) *Jas 4:10*
have to feel very small before *Jas 4:10*
(P)
proud, and giveth grace to the *1Pe 5:5*
h.
H. yourselves therefore under *1Pe 5:6*

HUMBLED

h. her (E)(R) *Ge 34:2*
their uncircumcised hearts be *Le 26:41*
h.
And he *h.* thee, and suffered *De 8:3*
thee
her, because thou hast *h.* her *De 21:14*
he hath *h.* his neighbour's *De 22:24*
wife
because he hath *h.* her, he *De 22:29*
may not
and thou hast *h.* thyself *2Ki 22:19*
before
Israel and the king *h.* *2Ch 12:6*
themselves
Lord saw that they *h.* *2Ch 12:7*
themselves

saying, They have h.   2Ch 12:7
themselves
And when he h. himself, the   2Ch 12:12
wrath
and of Zebulun h.   2Ch 30:11
themselves, and
Hezekiah h. himself for the   2Ch 32:26
pride
and h. himself greatly before   2Ch 33:12
graven images, before he   2Ch 33:19
was h.
And h. not himself before   2Ch 33:23
the Lord
Manasseh his father had h.   2Ch 33:23
himself
h. not himself before   2Ch 36:12
Jeremiah
he has h. me (B)(R)   Job 30:11
I h. my soul with fasting; and   Ps 35:13
I h. myself (A)(R)   Ps 69:10
The lofty looks of man shall be   Isa 2:11
h.
and the mighty man shall be h.   Isa 5:15
the eyes of the lofty shall be h.   Isa 5:15
down, and the haughty shall   Isa 10:33
be h.
They are not h. even unto this   Jer 44:10
remembrance, and is h. in me   La 3:20
thee. have they h. her that   Eze 22:10
was set
humble women (B)(R)   Eze 22:10;
  22:11
another in thee hath h. his   Eze 22:11
sister
Belshazzar, hast not h. thine   Da 5:22
heart
shall be h.   M't 23:12
(A)(B)(E)(N)(P)(R)
he h. himself, and became   Ph'p 2:8
obedient

HUMBLEDST

and h. thyself before me, and   2Ch 34:27

HUMBLE-MINDED

grants grace to h. (B)   Jas 4:6
kindly and h. (N)   1Pe 3:8

HUMBLE-MINDEDNESS

humble-mindedness (B)   Col 3:12

HUMBLENESS

kindness, h. of mind,   Col 3:12
meekness
a lowly opinion of yourselves   Col 3:12
(A)
humble-mindedness (B)   Col 3:12
lowliness (E)(R)   Col 3:12
humble in mind (P)   Col 3:12

HUMBLETH

how Ahab h. himself before   1Ki 21:29
me
because he h. himself before   1Ki 21:29
me
He croucheth, and h. himself   Ps 10:10
Who h. himself to behold the   Ps 113:6
and the great man h. himself   Isa 2:9
that h. himself shall be   Lu 14:11;
exalted   18:14

HUMBLING

sin in h. myself (B)(E)(R)   2Co 11:7

HUMBLY

I h. beseech thee that I may   2Sa 16:4
find grace
I do obeisance (A)(E)(R)   2Sa 16:4
I prostrate myself before you   2Sa 16:4
(B)
to love mercy, to walk h. with   Mic 6:8
God

HUMILIATE

God h. me (N)   2Co 12:21

HUMILIATED

greatly h. (B)   2Sa 10:5; 1Ch 19:5
I have been h. (B)   Ps 69:7
will be h. (B)   Isa 19:9
h. and has no redress (N)   Ac 8:33
our h. body (B)   Ph'p 3:2
insulted, h. poor (A)   Jas 2:6

HUMILIATION

Egypt be your h. (R)   Isa 30:3
h., impropriety (A)   Lu 14:9
in his h. his judgment was   Ac 8:33
taken away
body of h. (A)   Ph'p 3:2

HUMILITY

and before honour is h.   Pr 15:33; 18:12
by h. are riches, and honour,   Pr 22:4
and life
serving the Lord with all h. of   Ac 20:19
mind
let no man beguile you in a   Col 2:18
voluntary h.
have a shew of wisdom in   Col 2:23
will-worship and h.
be subject one to another,   1Pe 5:5
clothed with h.

HUMPS

the h. of camels (S)   Isa 30:6

HUNDRED

Shem was an h. years old and   Ge 11:10
begat
shall a child be born to him   Ge 17:17;
that is a h. years old   21:5; Ro 4:19
Jacob bought for an h. pieces   Ge 33:19;
  Jos 24:32
hangings h. cubits long   Ex 27:9;
  27:11; 38:9, 11
the length of the court shall   Ex 27:18
be an h. cubits
an h. sockets were cast of the   Ex 38:27
h. talents
five shall chase a h. and a h.   Le 26:8
put to flight
shall amerce him in h. shekels   De 22:19
of silver
so Gideon and the h. men with   J'g 7:19
him came
we will take ten of an h. an h.   J'g 20:10
of a 1000
Israel destroyed of Benjamin   J'g 20:35
25.000 and an h.
but an h. foreskins   1Sa 18:25; 2Sa 3:14
an h. clusters of raisins   1Sa 25:18;
  2Sa 16:1
reserved for an h. chariots   2Sa 8:4;
  1Ch 18:4
Solomon's provision for one   1Ki 4:23
day h. sheep
length of the house of the   1Ki 7:2
forest an h. cubits
Obadiah took an h. prophets   1Ki 18:4;
and hid them   18:13
what should I set this before   2Ki 4:43
an h. men
put land to tribute of h.   2Ki 23:33;
talents   2Ch 36:3
one of the least was over an   1Ch 12:14
h.
children of Simeon seven   1Ch 12:25
thousand and one h.
Lord make his people an h.   1Ch 21:3
times so many
Solomon made an h.   2Ch 3:16
pomegranates
and he made an h. basins of   2Ch 4:8
gold
he hired also men for an h.   2Ch 25:6
talents of silver
what shall we do for the h.   2Ch 25:9
talents I have given
Ammon gave Jotham an h.   2Ch 27:5
talents of silver
the congregation brought an   2Ch 29:32
h. rams
they gave one h. priests'   Ezr 2:69
garments
offered at the dedication an h.   Ezr 6:17
bullocks
h. talents of silver, h measures   Ezr 7:22
of wheat, h. baths of oil
vessels an h. talents of gold,   Ezr 8:26
an h. talents
restore to them the h. part of   Ne 5:11
the money
more than an h. stripes into a   Pr 17:10
fool
if a man beget an h. children   Ec 6:3
and live years
tho' sinner do evil h. times,   Ec 8:12
days be prolonged

child die an h. years old, but   Isa 65:20
sinner being an h. years old be
he measured an h. cubits   Eze 40:19
eastward
he measured from gate to   Eze 40:23;
gate an h. cubits   40:27
the court an h. cubits long,   Eze 40:47
an h. cubits broad
so he measured the house an   Eze 41:13
h. cubits long
of the separate place toward   Eze 41:14
east, an h. cubits
the galleries on one side and   Eze 41:15
other, an h. cubits
and lo, before the temple were   Eze 42:8
an h. cubits
city by a 1000, shall leave an h.   Am 5:3
that which went forth by an
h. shall leave ten
half h. weight of flour (N)   M't 13:33
if a man have an h. sheep   M't 18:12;
  Lu 15:4
went and found one who   M't 18:28
owed him an h. pence
and he said, An h. measures of   Lu 16:6
oil
how much owest thou? an h.   Lu 16:7
measure of wheat
mixture of myrrh and aloes   Joh 19:39
an h. weight

ONE HUNDRED AND FIVE

Seth lived one h. and five years,   Ge 5:6
begat Enos

ONE HUNDRED AND TEN

Joseph lived one h. and ten   Ge 50:22;
years   50:26
Joshua died an h. ten years   Jos 24:29;
old   J'g 2:8
with Johanan an h. and ten   Ezr 8:12
males

ONE HUNDRED AND TWELVE

of the sons of Uzziel an h.   1Ch 15:10
and twelve
the children of Jorah, an h.   Ezr 2:18
and twelve
the children of Hariph, an h.   Ne 7:24
and twelve

ONE HUNDRED AND NINETEEN

Nahor lived after begat Terah   Ge 11:25
h. and nineteen

ONE HUNDRED AND TWENTY

yet his days shall be h. and   Ge 6:3
twenty years
gold of spoons h. and twenty   Nu 7:86
shekels
I am an h. and twenty years   De 31:2
old this day
Moses an h. and twenty years   De 34:7
old when he died
gave king an h. and twenty   1Ki 10:10;
talents of gold, spices   2Ch 9:9
Uriel and brethren an h. and   1Ch 15:5
twenty
height of porch an h. and   2Ch 3:4
twenty cubits
with them an h. and twenty   2Ch 5:12
priests, sounding
to set over kingdom an h. and   Da 6:1
twenty princes
number of names were about   Ac 1:15
an h. and twenty

ONE HUNDRED TWENTY-TWO

men of Michmash, h.   Ezr 2:27;
twenty-two   Ne 7:31

ONE HUNDRED TWENTY-THREE

Aaron h. twenty-three years   Nu 33:39
when he died
children of Beth-lehem an h.   Ezr 2:21;
twenty and three   Ne 7:32

ONE HUNDRED
TWENTY-SEVEN

Sarah was an *h. twenty-seven*   *Ge 23:1*
years, and died
Ahasuerus reigned over *h.* and   *Es 1:1;*
twenty-seven provinces   *8:9; 9:30*

ONE HUNDRED
TWENTY-EIGHT

men of Anathoth *h.*   *Ezr 2:23;*
twenty-eight   *Ne 7:27*
children of Asaph an *h.*   *Eze 2:41*
twenty-eight
their brethren an *h.* and *Ne 11:14*
twenty-eight

ONE HUNDRED
THIRTY

Adam lived *h. thirty* years, and   *Ge 5:3*
begat son
years of my pilgrimage are an   *Ge 47:9*
h. and *thirty*
weight thereof was a *h. thirty*   *Nu 7:13;*
shekels   *7:19, 25*
each charger weighing an *h.*   *Nu 7:85*
thirty shekels
Joel and brethren an *h.* and   *1Ch 15:7*
thirty
Jehoiada was an *h. thirty*   *2Ch 24:15*
years old

ONE HUNDRED
THIRTY-THREE

years of life of Kohath an *h.*   *Ex 6:18*
thirty-three

ONE HUNDRED
THIRTY-SEVEN

life of Ishmael an *h.* and   *Ge 25:17*
thirty-seven years
the years of Levi were *h.* and   *Ex 6:16*
thirty-seven
the years of Amram were an *h.*   *Ex 6:20*
thirty-seven

ONE HUNDRED
THIRTY-EIGHT

the children of Shobai of Ater   *Ne 7:45*
h. thirty-eight

ONE HUNDRED
THIRTY-NINE

children of Shobai in all an *h.*   *Ezr 2:42*
thirty-nine

ONE HUNDRED
FORTY

after this lived Job an *h.*   *Job 42:16*
forty years

ONE HUNDRED
FORTY-FOUR

measured the wall an *h.*   *Re 21:17*
forty-four cubits

ONE HUNDRED
FORTY-SEVEN

whole age of Jacob an *h.*   *Ge 47:28*
forty-seven

ONE HUNDRED
FORTY-EIGHT

singers, the children of Asaph   *Ne 7:44*
h. forty-eight

ONE HUNDRED
FIFTY

waters prevailed an *h. fifty*   *Ge 7:24;*
days   *8:3*
an horse for an *h. fifty*   *1Ki 10:29;*
shekels   *2Ch 1:17*
Ulam's sons and sons' sons an   *1Ch 8:40*
h. fifty

were reckoned of males, an *h.*   *Ezr 8:3*
and *fifty*
there were at my table an *h.*   *Ne 5:17*
fifty Jews

ONE HUNDRED
FIFTY-THREE

drew the net full of fishes an   *Joh 21:11*
h. fifty-three

ONE HUNDRED
FIFTY-SIX

the children of Magbish, an *h.*   *Ezr 2:30*
fifty-six

ONE HUNDRED
SIXTY

Shelomith, and with him *h.*   *Ezr 8:10*
sixty males

ONE HUNDRED
SIXTY-TWO

Jared lived *h. sixty-two* years,   *Ge 5:18*
begat Enoch

ONE HUNDRED
SEVENTY-TWO

the porters and brethren *h.*   *Ne 11:19*
seventy-two

ONE HUNDRED
SEVENTY-FIVE

Abraham's life was an *h.*   *Ge 25:7*
seventy-five

ONE HUNDRED
EIGHTY

the days of Isaac an *h.* and   *Ge 35:28*
eighty years
Ahasuerus feast for an *h.* and   *Es 1:4*
eighty days

ONE HUNDRED
EIGHTY-TWO

Lamech lived *h. eighty-two*   *Ge 5:28*
and begat Noah

ONE HUNDRED
EIGHTY-SEVEN

Methuselah lived *h.*   *Ge 5:25*
eighty-seven begat Lamech

ONE HUNDRED
EIGHTY-EIGHT

the men of Beth-lehem an *h.*   *Ne 7:26*
eighty-eight

HUNDRED THOUSAND

all numbered in Judah were an   *Nu 2:9*
h. thousand
numbered in the camp of   *Nu 2:16*
Reuben an *h. thousand*
slew of the Syrians *h.*   *1Ki 20:29*
thousand footmen
an *h. thousand* lambs, an *h.*   *2Ki 3:4*
thousand rams
took from Hagarites an *h.*   *1Ch 5:21*
thousand men
of Israel a thousand thousand   *1Ch 21:5*
an *h. thousand*
for house of Lord *h.*   *1Ch 22:14*
thousand talents of gold
and gave an *h. thousand*   *1Ch 29:7*
talents of iron
hired *h. thousand* men of   *2Ch 25:6*
valour

HUNDRED EIGHT
THOUSAND, AN HUNDRED

numbered of Ephraim, *108,100*   *Nu 2:24*

HUNDRED TWENTY
THOUSAND

there fell of the Midianites   *J'g 8:10*
120,000
sacrifice of an *120,000*   *1Ki 8:63;*
                            2Ch 7:5
of Reuben, Gad, and   *1Ch 12:37*
Manasseh, *120,000*
Pekah slew in Judah in one   *2Ch 28:6*
day *120,000*
in Nineveh were about   *Jon 4:11*
120,000 persons

HUNDRED FORTY-FOUR
THOUSAND

were sealed *144,000* of all the   *Re 7:4*
tribes of Israel
with him *144,000*, having his   *Re 14:1*
Father's name
no man could learn that song   *Re 14:3*
but the *144,000*

HUNDRED FIFTY
THOUSAND

Israel an *h. fifty thousand*   *2Ch 2:17*

HUNDRED EIGHTY
THOUSAND

with Benjamin *180,000*   *1Ki 12:21;*
                          2Ch 11:1
with Jehozabad were   *2Ch 17:18*
180,000, for war

HUNDRED EIGHTY-FIVE
THOUSAND

angel smote of the   *2Ki 19:35;*
Assyrians, *185,000*   *Isa 37:36*

TWO HUNDRED

Serug lived after begat Nahor   *Ge 11:23*
two h. years
two h. she goats, and *two h.*   *Ge 32:14*
ewes for Esau
Achan saw *two h.* shekels of   *Jos 7:21*
silver
his mother took *two h.* shekels   *J'g 17:4*
of silver
David slew of the Philistines   *1Sa 18:27*
two h. men
two h. abode by the stuff   *1Sa 25:13*
                               30:10, 21
Abigail took *two h.* loaves,   *1Sa 25:18*
two h. cakes of figs
Absalom weighed hair *two h.*   *2Sa 14:26*
shekels
with Absalom went *two h.*   *2Sa 15:1*
men out of Jerusalem
Ziba brought David *two h.*   *2Sa 16:1*
loaves of bread
the pomegranates were *two h.*   *1Ki 7:20*
in rows
Solomon made *two h.*   *1Ki 10:16;*
targets   *2Ch 9:15*
for burnt offerings *two h.*   *2Ch 29:32*
lambs
were among them *two h.*   *Ezr 2:65*
singing men
and offered at the dedication   *Ezr 6:17*
two h. rams
those that keep the fruit   *Ca 8:12*
thereof *two h.*
ye shall offer one lamb out of   *Eze 45:15*
two h.
two h. pennyworth is not   *Joh 6:7*
sufficient
make ready *two h.* soldiers to   *Ac 23:23*
go, and spearmen *two h.*

TWO HUNDRED FIVE

the days of Terah were *two*   *Ge 11:32*
h. five years

TWO HUNDRED SEVEN

Reu lived *two h. seven* years   *Ge 11:21*
and begat

TWO HUNDRED NINE

Peleg lived *two h. nine* years   *Ge 11:19*
and begat

TWO HUNDRED *TWELVE*

porters in the gates were *two* 1Ch 9:22
h. twelve

TWO HUNDRED *EIGHTEEN*

with Obadiah *two h. eighteen* Ezr 8:9
males

TWO HUNDRED *TWENTY*

for service of Levites *two h.* Ezr 8:20
twenty Nethinim

TWO HUNDRED *TWENTY-THREE*

men of Beth-el and Ai *two h.* Ezr 2:28
twenty-three

TWO HUNDRED *THIRTY-TWO*

of princes of provinces *two* 1Ki 20:15
h. thirty-two

TWO HUNDRED *FORTY-TWO*

chief of the fathers *two h.* Ne 11:13
forty-two

TWO HUNDRED *FORTY-FIVE*

their mules *two h.* and Ezr 2:66
forty-five
had *two h. forty-five* singing Ne 7:67
men and women
their mules *two h.* and Ne 7:68
forty-five

TWO HUNDRED *FIFTY*

cinnamon *two h.* and *fifty,* of Ex 30:23
calamus *two h.* and *fifty* shekels
two h. and *fifty* princes of the Nu 16:2
assembly
and bring ye before Lord *two* Nu 16:17
h. and *fifty* censers
a fire consumed the *two h.* Nu 16:35
and *fifty* men
two h. and *fifty* that bare rule 2Ch 8:10
suburbs toward north *two h.* Eze 48:17
fifty

TWO HUNDRED *SEVENTY-SIX*

in all the ship *two h.* Ac 27:37
seventy-six souls

TWO HUNDRED *EIGHTY-FOUR*

Levites in the holy city *two h.* Ne 11:18
eighty-four

TWO HUNDRED *EIGHTY-EIGHT*

all cunning in songs *two h.* 1Ch 25:7
eighty-eight

TWO HUNDRED *FIFTY-THOUSAND*

took away of sheep *two h.* 1Ch 5:21
fifty thousand

THREE HUNDRED

Enoch walked with God *three* Ge 5:22
h. years
the length of the ark shall be Ge 6:15
three h. cubits
he gave Benjamin *three h.* Ge 45:22
pieces of silver
the number that lapped were J'g 7:6
three h. men
and he retained those *three h.* J'g 7:8
men
the *three h.* men that were with J'g 8:4
him were faint
Israel by the coast of Arnon J'g 11:26
three h. years

Samson went and caught *three* J'g 15:4
h. foxes
whose spear weighed *three h.* 2Sa 21:16
shekels
Abishai lifted up his spear 2Sa 23:18;
against *three h.* 1Ch 11:11, 20
he made *three h.* shields of 1Ki 10:17
beaten gold
Solomon had *three h.* 1Ki 11:3
concubines
appointed to Hezekiah *three* 2Ki 18:14
h. talents
three h. shekels of gold went 2Ch 9:16
to one shield
Zera came against Asa with 2Ch 14:9
three h. chariots
gave to priests for 2Ch 35:8
passover offering *three h.* oxen
with Shechaniah *three h.* males Ezr 8:5
the Jews slew *three h.* men at Es 9:15
Shushan
this ointment sold for *three h.* Joh 12:5
pence

THREE HUNDRED *EIGHTEEN*

Abram went with *three h.* Ge 14:14
eighteen servants

THREE HUNDRED *TWENTY*

the children of Harim *three h.* Ezr 2:32;
and *twenty* Ne 7:35

THREE HUNDRED *TWENTY-THREE*

the children of Bezai *three h.* Ezr 2:17;
twenty-three Ne 7:23

THREE HUNDRED *TWENTY-EIGHT*

children of Hashum *three h.* Ne 7:22
twenty-eight

THREE HUNDRED *FORTY-FIVE*

children of Jericho *three h.* Ezr 2:34;
forty-five Ne 7:36

THREE HUNDRED *FIFTY*

Noah lived after flood *three h.* Ge 9:28
fifty years

THREE HUNDRED *SIXTY*

so that of Israel *three h.* 2Sa 2:31
sixty men died

THREE HUNDRED *SIXTY-FIVE*

Enoch's days were *three h.* Ge 5:23
sixty-five years

THREE HUNDRED *SEVENTY-TWO*

children of Shephatiah *three h.* Ezr 2:4;
seventy-two Ne 7:9

THREE HUNDRED *NINETY*

according to number of days, Eze 4:5;
three h. ninety 4:9

THREE HUNDRED *THOUSAND*

of them that went out to war Nu 31:36
300,000
Israel were *300,000* 1Sa 11:8; 2Ch 14:8
with Adnah mighty men 2Ch 17:14
300,000
found Judah and Benjamin to 2Ch 25:5
be *300,000*

THREE HUNDRED *SEVEN THOUSAND FIVE* HUNDRED

Uzziah had an army of 2Ch 26:13
307,500

THREE HUNDRED *AND THIRTY SEVEN THOUSAND FIVE* HUNDRED

the half that pertained unto Nu 31:43
the congregation was *337,500*
sheep

FOUR HUNDRED

afflict them *four h.* years Ge 15:13;
Ac 7:6
land is worth *four h.* shekels Ge 23:15;
of silver 23:16
Esau cometh to thee with *four* Ge 32:6;
h. men 33:1
found *four h.* virgins of J'g 21:12
Jabesh-gilead
were with David, *four h.* 1Sa 22:2;
25:13; 30:10
save *four h.* young men on 1Sa 30:17
camels that fled
four h. pomegranates for 1Ki 7:42
networks
and the prophets of the 1Ki 18:19
groves *four h.*
Ahab gathered prophets 1Ki 22:6;
about *four h.* and said 2Ch 18:5
brake down wall of 2Ki 14:13;
Jerusalem *four h.* cubits 2Ch 25:23
offered at dedication of house, Ezr 6:17
four h. lambs
to whom about *four h.* joined Ac 5:36
themselves

FOUR HUNDRED *AND THREE*

Arphaxad lived *four h. three* Ge 11:13
years, and begat
Salah lived after he begat Ge 11:15
Eber *four h. three* years

FOUR HUNDRED *AND TEN*

silver basins of a second sort Ezr 1:10
four h. ten

FOUR HUNDRED *AND TWENTY*

fetched from thence gold, 1Ki 9:28
four h. twenty talents

FOUR HUNDRED *THIRTY*

Eber lived *four h. thirty* years Ge 11:17
and begat sons
sojourning in Egypt *four h.* Ex 12:40;
thirty years 12:41
the law which was *four h.* Ga 3:17
thirty years after cannot

FOUR HUNDRED *THIRTY-FIVE*

their camels were *four h.* Ezr 2:67;
thirty-five Ne 7:69

FOUR HUNDRED *AND FIFTY*

gather the prophets of Baal 1Ki 18:19;
four h. fifty 18:22
gave judges about *four h. fifty* Ac 13:20
years

FOUR HUNDRED *FIFTY-FOUR*

the children of Adin *four h.* Ezr 2:15
fifty-four

FOUR HUNDRED *SIXTY-EIGHT*

all the sons of Perez were Ne 11:6
four h. sixty eight men

FOUR HUNDRED EIGHTY

in *four h. eighty* years Solomon   *1Ki 6:1*
began to build

FOUR HUNDRED THOUSAND

Israel besides Benjamin   *J'g 20:2;*
400,000   *20:17*
set the battle in array with   *2Ch 13:3*
400,000 men

FOUR HUNDRED SEVENTY THOUSAND

Judah was 470,000 that drew   *1Ch 21:5*
the sword

FIVE HUNDRED

Noah was *five h.* years old and   *Ge 5:32*
begat Shem
Shem lived after *five h.* years   *Ge 11:11*
and begat
take of pure myrrh *five h.*   *Ex 30:23*
shekels
of cassia *five h.* shekels after   *Ex 30:24*
shekel of sanctuary
levy one soul of *five h.* for the   *Nu 31:28*
Lord
for passover offerings *five h.*   *2Ch 35:9*
oxen
Jews slew at Shushan *five h.*   *Es 9:6;*
men   *9:12*
five h. yoke of oxen, *five h.*   *Job 1:3*
she asses
he measured *five h.* reeds   *Eze 42:16;*
  42:17-20
for the sanctuary *five h.* in   *Eze 45:2*
length, *five h.* in breadth
the one owed *five h.* pence,   *Lu 7:41*
the other fifty
was seen of above *five h.*   *1Co 15:6*
brethren at once

FIVE HUNDRED AND THIRTY

gave *five h. and thirty* priests'   *Ne 7:70*
garments

FIVE HUNDRED AND FIFTY

five h. and fifty bare rule over   *1Ki 9:23*
people

FIVE HUNDRED THOUSAND

the men of Judah were   *2Sa 24:9*
500,000 men
there were slain of Israel   *2Ch 13:17*
500,000 men

SIX HUNDRED

Noah *six h.* years old when   *Ge 7:6;*
flood came   *7:11*
Pharaoh took *six h.* chariots   *Ex 14:7*
to pursue Israel
Shamgar slew with an ox goad   *J'g 3:31*
six h.
Danites sent out of Eshtaol   *J'g 18:11;*
six h.   *18:16-17*
six h. Benjamites fled to rock   *J'g 20:47*
Rimmon
Saul numbered the people   *1Sa 13:15;*
six h.   *14:2*
Goliath's spear head weighed   *1Sa 17:7*
six h. shekels
David and his men about   *1Sa 23:13;*
six h.   *27:2; 30:9*
all the Gittites were *six h.*   *2Sa 15:18*
men
Solomon made targets, *six*   *1Ki 10:16;*
h. shekels of gold   *2Ch 9:15*
a chariot went for *six h.*   *1Ki 10:29;*
shekels   *2Ch 1:17*
David gave Ornan *six h.*   *1Ch 21:25*
shekels
overlaid house with gold to *six*   *2Ch 3:8*
h. talents
the consecrated things were   *2Ch 29:33*
six h. oxen

SIX HUNDRED TWENTY-ONE

child of Ramah *six h.*   *Ezr 2:26;*
twenty-one   *Ne 7:30*

SIX HUNDRED TWENTY-THREE

the children of Bebai, *six h.*   *Ezr 2:11*
twenty-three

SIX HUNDRED TWENTY-EIGHT

the children of Bebai, *six h.*   *Ne 7:16*
twenty-eight

SIX HUNDRED FORTY-TWO

the children of Bani, *six h.*   *Ezr 2:10*
forty-two
the children of Nekoda, *six h.*   *Ne 7:62*
forty-two

SIX HUNDRED FORTY-EIGHT

the children of Binnui, *six h.*   *Ne 7:15*
forty-eight

SIX HUNDRED AND FIFTY

weighed to their hand *six h.*   *Ezr 8:26*
fifty talents

SIX HUNDRED FIFTY-TWO

the children of Nekoda, *six h.*   *Ezr 2:60*
fifty-two
the children of Arah, *six h.* and   *Ne 7:10*
fifty-two

SIX HUNDRED SIXTY-SIX

gold to Solomon in year *six*   *1Ki 10:14*
h. sixty-six talents
children of Adonikam, *six h.*   *Ezr 2:13*
sixty-six
and his number is *six h.* and   *Re 13:18*
sixty-six

SIX HUNDRED SIXTY-SEVEN

children of Adonikam, *six h.*   *Ne 7:18*
sixty-seven

SIX HUNDRED SEVENTY-FIVE

Lord's tribute of sheep was   *Nu 31:37*
six h. seventy-five

SIX HUNDRED NINETY

Jeuel and brethren were *six h.*   *1Ch 9:6*
ninety

SIX HUNDRED THOUSAND

Israel journeyed about   *Ex 12:37*
600,000 on foot
a bekah for every man for   *Ex 38:26*
600,000 men
all that were numbered were   *Nu 1:46*
600,000
Moses said, The people are   *Nu 11:21*
600,000 footmen

SIX HUNDRED SEVENTY-FIVE THOUSAND

the rest of the prey was   *Nu 31:32*
675,000 sheep

SEVEN HUNDRED

of Gibeah were *seven h.*   *J'g 20:15;*
chosen men   *20:16*
David took from him *seven h.*   *2Sa 8:4*
horsemen
David slew men of *seven h.*   *2Sa 10:18*
chariots of Syrians
Solomon had *seven h.* wives,   *1Ki 11:3*
princesses
the king of Moab took *seven*   *2Ki 3:26*
h. men
they offered to the Lord   *2Ch 15:11*
seven h. oxen

SEVEN HUNDRED TWENTY-ONE

children of Lod, Hadid, Ono   *Ne 7:37*
seven h. twenty-one

SEVEN HUNDRED TWENTY-FIVE

children of Lod, Hadid, Ono,   *Ezr 2:33*
seven h. twenty-five

SEVEN HUNDRED THIRTY-SIX

their horses were *seven h.*   *Ezr 2:66;*
thirty-six   *Ne 7:68*

SEVEN HUNDRED FORTY-THREE

the children of Kirjath-arim   *Ezr 2:25*
seven h. forty-three

SEVEN HUNDRED FORTY-FIVE

took away captive of the Jews   *Jer 52:30*
seven h. forty-five

SEVEN HUNDRED SIXTY

the children of Zaccai *seven*   *Ezr 2:9;*
h. sixty   *Ne 7:14*

SEVEN HUNDRED SEVENTY-FIVE

the children of Arah, *seven h.*   *Ezr 2:5*
seventy-five

SEVEN HUNDRED SEVENTY-SEVEN

all the days of Lamech were   *Ge 5:31*
seven h. seventy-seven years

SEVEN HUNDRED EIGHTY-TWO

Methusaleh lived *seven h.*   *Ge 5:26*
eighty-two years, begat Lamech

EIGHT HUNDRED

Adam after he begat Seth lived   *Ge 5:4*
eight h. years
Jared after he begat Enoch lived   *Ge 5:19*
eight h. years
he lifted up his spear against   *2Sa 23:8*
eight h.

EIGHT HUNDRED SEVEN

Seth lived after he begat Enos   *Ge 5:7*
eight h. seven

EIGHT HUNDRED FIFTEEN

Enos after he begat Cainan   *Ge 5:10*
eight h. fifteen years

EIGHT HUNDRED TWENTY-TWO

their brethren that did work   *Ne 11:12*
were *eight h. twenty-two*

EIGHT HUNDRED THIRTY

Mahalaleel after he begat   Ge 5:16
Jared *eight h. thirty* years

EIGHT HUNDRED THIRTY-TWO

Nebuchadnezzar carried   Jer 52:29
captive *eight h. thirty-two*

EIGHT HUNDRED FORTY

Cainan after he begat   Ge 5:13
Mahalaleel *eight h. forty*

EIGHT HUNDRED FORTY-FIVE

the children of Zattu were   Ne 7:13
eight h. forty-five

EIGHT HUNDRED NINETY-FIVE

all the days of Mahalaleel were   Ge 5:1
eight h. ninety-five years

NINE HUNDRED

Jabin had *nine h.* chariots of   J'g 4:3;
iron   4:13

NINE HUNDRED FIVE

all the days of Enos were *nine*   Ge 5:11
h. five years

NINE HUNDRED TEN

all the days of Cainan *nine h.*   Ge 5:14
ten years

NINE HUNDRED TWELVE

all the days of Seth were *nine*   Ge 5:8
h. twelve years

NINE HUNDRED TWENTY-EIGHT

and after him Gabbai, Sallai,   Ne 11:8
nine h. twenty-eight

NINE HUNDRED THIRTY

all days that Adam lived were   Ge 5:5
nine h. thirty years

NINE HUNDRED FORTY-FIVE

the children of Zattu *nine h.*   Ezr 2:8
forty-five

NINE HUNDRED FIFTY

all the days of Noah were *nine*   Ge 9:29
h. fifty years

NINE HUNDRED FIFTY-SIX

brethren according to   1Ch 9:9
generations *nine h. fifty-six*

NINE HUNDRED SIXTY-TWO

all the days of Jared were *nine*   Ge 5:20
h. sixty-two years

NINE HUNDRED SIXTY-NINE

the days of Methuselah were   Ge 5:27
nine h. sixty-nine years

NINE HUNDRED SEVENTY-THREE

the children of Jedaiah *nine*   Ezr 2:36;
h. seventy-three   Ne 7:39

HUNDREDFOLD

in the same year an *h.*   Ge 26:12
many soever they be, an *h.*   2Sa 24:3
some an *h.*   M't 13:8; 13:23
shall receive an *h.*, and shall   M't 19:29
he shall receive an *h.* now in   M'k 10:30
sprang up, bare fruit an *h.*   Lu 8:8

HUNDREDS

be rulers of *h.* and tens   Ex 18:21;
    18:25; De 1:15
Moses was wroth with   Nu 31:14
captains over *h.*
Moses took the gold of the   Nu 31:54
captains of *h.*
will son of Jesse make you   1Sa 22:7
captains of *h.*
the lords of the Philistines   1Sa 29:2
passed on by *h.*
David set captains of *h.* over   2Sa 18:1
them
the king stood, all the people   2Sa 18:4
came out by *h.*
Jehoiada sent and set the   2Ki 11:4
rulers over *h.*
to captains over *h.* did the   2Ki 11:10;
priest give spears and shields   2Ch 23:9
David consulted with the   1Ch 13:1
captains of *h.*
which the captains over *h.*   1Ch 26:26
had dedicated
David assembled the captains   1Ch 28:1
over the *h.*
then the captains of *h.* offered   1Ch 29:6
willingly
Jehoiada took captains of *h.*   2Ch 23:1
into covenant
Amaziah made them captains   2Ch 25:5
over *h.*
they sat down in ranks by *h.*   M'k 6:40
and fifties

HUNDREDTH

In the six *h.* year of Noah's life   Ge 7:2
in the six *h.* and first year   Ge 8:13
also an *h.* part of the money   Ne 5:11

HUNG

hung (S)   De 21:23; Ps 137:2;
    La 5:12; Eze 27:10-11; M'k 9:42

HUNGER

to kill this whole assembly with   Ex 16:3
h.
kill all of us by starving (B)   Ex 16:3
he suffered thee to *h.* and fed   De 8:3
with manna
thou shalt serve thine enemies   De 28:48
in *h.*
they shall be burnt with *h.*   De 32:24
and devoured
wasted by famine shall be   De 32:24
devoured (B)
thou gavest bread from   Ne 9:15
heaven for their *h.*
the young lions do lack and   Ps 34:10
suffer *h.*
and an idle soul shall suffer *h.*   Pr 19:15
they shall not *h.* nor thirst, nor   Isa 49:10
sun smite
he is like to die for *h.* where he   Jer 38:9
he will starve on the spot (B)   Jer 38:9
die because of the famine (E)   Jer 38:9
we shall see no war, nor have   Jer 42:14
h. of bread
that faint for *h.* in the top of   La 2:19
every street
are better than they that be slain   La 4:9
with *h.*
they shall be no more   Eze 34:29
consumed with *h.*
subjected to famine (B)(E)   Eze 34:29
blessed are they that *h.*   M't 5:6; Lu 6:21
woe to you who are full, for ye   Lu 6:25
shall *h.*
have bread enough, and I   Lu 15:17
perish with *h.*
here I am starving (B)(N)   Lu 15:17

he that cometh to me shall   Joh 6:35
never *h.*
therefore if thine enemy *h.*   Ro 12:20
feed him
we both *h.* and thirst, and are   1Co 4:11
naked
and if any man *h.* let him eat   1Co 11:34
at home
I have been in *h.* and thirst,   2Co 11:27
in fastings
and power was given them to kill   Re 6:8
with *h.*
kill with famine   Re 6:8
(A)(B)(E)(N)(P)(R)
they shall *h.* no more, neither   Re 7:16
thirst

HUNGER-BITTEN

his strength shall be *h.*   Job 18:12
destruction

HUNGERED

he was afterwards an *h.*   M't 4:2; Lu 4:2
hungry (A)(B)(R)   M't 4:2;
    12:1, 3; 21:18; 25:35, 37, 42; Lu 6:3
he was famished (N)   M't 4:2
his disciples were an *h.* and   M't 12:1
began to pluck ears
hungry (N)   M't 12:1;
    12:3; 21:18; 25:35, 37, 42; Lu 6:3
what David did when he was   M't 12:3;
an *h.*   M'k 2:25
now as he returned into the   M't 21:18
city he *h.*
for I was an *h.* and ye gave   M't 25:35;
me meat   25:42
Lord when saw we thee an   M't 25:37;
h. and fed thee   25:44
what David did when himself   Lu 6:3
was an *h.*

HUNGRY

and they that were *h.* ceased   1Sa 2:5
the people is *h.*, weary, and   2Sa 17:29
thirsty
they know that we be *h.*   2Ki 7:12
therefore
whose harvest the *h.* eateth up   Job 5:5
and taketh it
thou hast withholden bread   Job 22:7
from the *h.*
they take away the sheaf   Job 24:10
from the *h.*
if I were *h.* I would not tell   Ps 50:12
thee
h. and thirsty, their soul   Ps 107:5
fainted in them
for he filleth the *h.* soul with   Ps 107:9
goodness
and there he maketh the *h.* to   Ps 107:36
dwell
hope is in Lord who giveth   Ps 146:7
food to the *h.*
if he steal to satisfy his soul   Pr 6:30
when he is *h.*
if thine enemy be *h.* give him   Pr 25:21
bread to eat
to the *h.* soul every bitter thing   Pr 27:7
is sweet
and *h.* when they shall be   Isa 8:21
h. they shall fret
he shall snatch on the right   Isa 9:20
hand, and be *h.*
it shall even be as when a *h.*   Isa 29:8
man dreameth
to make empty the soul of the   Isa 32:6
h.
yea, he is *h.* and his strength   Isa 44:12
faileth
is it not to deal thy bread to   Isa 58:7
the *h.*
and if thou draw out thy soul   Isa 58:10
to the *h.*
my servants shall eat, but ye   Isa 65:13
shall be *h.*
hath given his bread to the *h.*   Eze 18:7;
    18:16
he was *h.* (S)   M't 4:2;
    12:3; 21:18; M'k 2:25; Lu 4:2; 6:3
his disciples were *h.* (S)   M't 12:1
I was *h.* (S)   M't 25:35; 25:37, 42, 44
when were come from   M'k 11:12
Bethany he was *h.*
he hath filled the *h.* with good   Lu 1:53
things
Peter became very *h.* would   Ac 10:10
have eaten

HUNGRY (cont.)

one is h. and another is drunken	1Co 11:21
I know how to be full and to be h.	Ph'p 4:12

HUNT

went to the field to h. for venison	Ge 27:5
h. a partridge in the mountains	1Sa 26:20
Wilt thou h. the prey for the lion	Job 38:39
evil shall h. the violent man	Ps 140:11
adulteress will h. for the precious	Pr 6:26
shall h. them from every mountain	Jer 16:16
They h. our steps, that we cannot	La 4:18
head of every stature to h. souls	Eze 13:18
Will ye h. the souls of my people	Eze 13:18
wherewith ye there the souls to	Eze 13:20
even the souls that ye h. to make	Eze 13:20
they h. every man his brother	Mic 7:2

HUNTED

hide the h. (B)	Isa 16:3
be no more in your hand to be h.	Eze 13:21

HUNTER

was a mighty h. before the Lord	Ge 10:9
Even as Nimrod the mighty h.	Ge 10:9
Esau was a cunning h. a man	Ge 25:27
as a roe from the hand of the h.	Pr 6:5

HUNTERS

and after will I send for many h.	Jer 16:16

HUNTEST

thee; yet thou h. my soul to take it	1Sa 24:11
Thou h. me as a fierce lion	Job 10:16

HUNTETH

which h. and catcheth any beast	Le 17:13

HUNTING

his brother came in from his h.	Ge 27:30
roasteth not that, he took in h.	Pr 12:27

HUPHAM

H., the family of the Huphamites	Nu 26:39

HUPHAMITES

of Hupham, the family of the H.	Nu 26:39

HUPPAH

thirteenth to H., the fourteenth	1Ch 24:13

HUPPIM

Rosh, Muppim, and H. and Ard	Ge 46:21
Shuppim also, and H., the children	1Ch 7:12
Machir took to wife the sister of H.	1Ch 7:15

HUR

Moses, Aaron, H. went up to top of hill	Ex 17:10
and Aaron and H. stayed up his hands	Ex 17:12
behold, Aaron and H. are with you	Ex 24:14
Lord hath called Bezaleel son of H. of the tribe of Judah	Ex 31:2; 35:30; 38:22
they slew Evi, Rekem, Zur, H. and Reba	Nu 31:8; Jos 13:21
the son of H. in mount Ephraim	1Ki 4:8
Caleb took Ephratah, which bare H.	1Ch 2:19
H. begat Uri; sons of Judah, H., Shobal	1Ch 2:20; 4:1
these were the sons of Caleb the son of H.	1Ch 2:50
these are the sons of H. Ephratah, Ashur	1Ch 4:4
Rephaiah son of H. repaired next to them	Ne 3:9

HURAI

H. of the brooks of Gaash, Abiel	1Ch 11:32

HURAM

Shephuphan, and H.	1Ch 8:5
Solomon sent to H. the king of Tyre	2Ch 2:3; 2:11-13
H. made pots and finished	2Ch 4:11; 4:16
cities which H. had restored	2Ch 8:2
H. sent by the hands of servants of H.	2Ch 8:18 2Ch 9:10; 9:21

HURI

Abihail the son of H. the son of	1Ch 5:14

HURL

or h. at him by laying of wait	Nu 35:20

HURLED

insults fools have h. (B)	Ps 74:22
h. abuse at him (N)	M't 27:39; M'k 15:29
h. abuse at him (P)	M'k 15:32
h. him into the abyss (A)(B)(E)(N)(P)(R)	Re 20:3

HURLETH

as a storm h. him out of his place	Job 27:21

HURLING

in h. stones and shooting arrows	1Ch 12:2

HURT

and a young man to my h.	Ge 4:23
That thou wilt do us no h. as we	Ge 26:29
but God suffered him not to h. me	Ge 31:7
the power of my hand to do you h.	Ge 31:29
strive, and h. a woman with child	Ex 21:22
if one man's ox h. another's, that he	Ex 21:35
and it die, or be h. or driven away	Ex 22:10
ought of his neighbour, and it be h.	Ex 22:14
neither have I h. one of them	Nu 16:15
then he will turn and do you h.	Jos 24:20
there is peace to thee, and no h.	1Sa 20:21
Behold, David seeketh thy h.	1Sa 24:9
which were with us, we h. them not	1Sa 25:7
good unto us, and we were not h.	1Sa 25:15
rise against thee to do thee h.	2Sa 18:32
shouldest thou meddle to thy h.	2Ki 14:10
shouldest thou meddle to thine h.	2Ch 25:19
grow to the h. of the kings	Ezr 4:22
hand on such as sought their h.	Es 9:2
Thy wickedness may h. a man	Job 35:8
He that sweareth to his own h.	Ps 15:4
to confusion that devise my h.	Ps 35:4
together that rejoice at mine h.	Ps 35:26
that seek my h. speak mischievous	Ps 38:12
who desire my h. (B)(E)(R)	Ps 40:14
against me do they devise my h.	Ps 41:7
put to confusion, that desire my h.	Ps 70:2
and dishonour that seek my h.	Ps 71:13
unto shame, that seek my h.	Ps 71:24
Whose feet they h. with fetters	Ps 105:18
for the owners thereof to their h.	Ec 5:13
ruleth over another to his own h.	Ec 8:9
Whoso removeth stones shall be h.	Ec 10:9
They shall not h. nor destroy in all	Isa 11:9
lest any h. it, I will keep it night	Isa 27:3
the h. of my people (A)(E)(R)	Isa 30:26
They shall not h. nor destroy in all	Isa 65:25
healed also the h. of the daughter	Jer 6:14
walk after other gods to your h.	Jer 7:6
healed the h. of the daughter	Jer 8:11
the h. of the daughter of my people	Jer 8:21
the daughter of my people am I h.	Jer 8:21
Woe is me for my h.! my wound is	Jer 10:19
kingdoms of the earth for their h.	Jer 24:9
hands; and I will do you no h.	Jer 25:6
works of your hands to your own h.	Jer 25:7
the welfare of this people, but the h.	Jer 38:4
a thorn to h. (R)	Eze 28:24
of the fire, and they have no h.	Da 3:25
mouths, that they have not h. me	Da 6:22
thee, O king, have I done no h.	Da 6:22
no manner of h. was found upon	Da 6:23
sad and h. (A)	M'k 14:19
deadly thing, it shall not h. them	M'k 16:18
he came out of him, and h. him not	Lu 4:35
nothing shall by any means h. you	Lu 10:19
no man shall set on thee to h. thee	Ac 18:10
will be with h. and much damage	Ac 27:10
shall not be h. of the second death	Re 2:11
see thou h. not the oil and the wine	Re 6:6
it was given to h. the earth and	Re 7:2
H. not the earth, neither the sea	Re 7:3
should not h. the grass of the earth	Re 9:4
power was to h. men five months	Re 9:10
had heads, and with them they do h.	Re 9:19
any man will h. them, fire proceedeth	Re 11:5
if any man will h. them, he must in	Re 11:5

HURTFUL

rebellious city, and h. unto kings	Ezr 4:15
his servant from the h. sword	Ps 144:10
a h. disease (B)	Ec 6:2
and into many foolish and h. lusts	1Ti 6:9

HURTING

slain a man for h. me (S)	Ge 4:23
hath kept me back from h. thee	1Sa 25:34
a h. thorn to all (A)(E)	Eze 28:24

HURTLING

h. down among the dead (P)	M't 11:23

HURTS

it never *h.* anybody (A)(P)   *Ro* 13:10

HUSBAND

surely a bloody *h.* art thou to me   *Ex* 4:25; 4:26
a blood bridegroom to me (B)(E)(R)   *Ex* 4:25
as the woman's *h.* will lay upon him   *Ex* 21:22
that is betrothed to a *h.*   *Le* 19:20; *De* 22:23
his sister who hath had no *h.*   *Le* 21:3; *Eze* 44:25
h. among his people (R)   *Le* 21:4
if she had at all an *h.* when she vowed   *Nu* 30:6
lying with a woman married to a *h.*   *De* 22:22
and if the latter *h.* hate her or die   *De* 24:3
her former *h.* may not take her again   *De* 24:4
perform the duty of a *h.* brother to her   *De* 25:5
her eye be evil toward *h.* of her bosom   *De* 28:56
h. of the woman slain, answered   *J'g* 20:4
Elimelech, Naomi's *h.* died, she was left   *Ru* 1:3
I am too old to have an *h.* if I should have a *h.*   *Ru* 1:12
my *h.* is not at home (S)   *Pr* 7:19
the *h.* with the wife shall be taken   *Jer* 6:11
although I was a *h.* to them   *Jer* 31:32
girded with sackcloth for *h.* of her youth   *Joe* 1:8
Jacob begat Joseph the *h.* of Mary   *M't* 1:16
she had lived with a *h.* seven years   *Lu* 2:36
I have no *h.* Thou hast well said, I have no *h.*   *Joh* 4:17
if *h.* be dead, she is loosed from her *h.*   *Ro* 7:2; 7:3
let *h.* render to wife due benevolence, likewise wife to *h.*   *1Co* 7:3
also the *h.* hath not power of his own body   *1Co* 7:4
and let not the *h.* put away his wife   *1Co* 7:11
woman who hath a *h.* that believeth not   *1Co* 7:13
unbelieving *h.* is sanctified by wife, unbelieving wife sanctified by *h.*   *1Co* 7:14
for I have espoused you to one *h.*   *2Co* 11:2
more children than she who hath a *h.*   *Ga* 4:27
h. is head of wife, as Christ of church   *Eph* 5:23
bishop blameless, *h.* one wife   *1Ti* 3:2; *Tit* 1:6

HER HUSBAND

Eve did eat of the fruit, and gave to *her h.*   *Ge* 3:6
Sarai Abram's wife gave Hagar to *her h.* Abram   *Ge* 16:3
not take a woman put away from *her h.*   *Le* 21:7
if it be hid from the eyes of *her h.*   *Nu* 5:13
if she have done trespass against *her h.*   *Nu* 5:27
when one goeth aside to another instead of *her h.*   *Nu* 5:29
and *her h.* heard it, and held his peace   *Nu* 30:7; 30:11, 14
if *her h.* disallow her on the day he heard it   *Nu* 30:8
and if she vowed in *her h.* house or bound   *Nu* 30:10
if *her h.* hath utterly made them void on day   *Nu* 30:12
her h. may establish it, or may make it void   *Nu* 30:13
thou shalt go in unto her, and be *her h.*   *De* 21:13
the wife draweth near to deliver *her h.*   *De* 25:11
then the woman came and told *her h.*   *J'g* 13:6

but Manoah *her h.* was not with her   *J'g* 13:9
the woman made haste, and shewed *her h.*   *J'g* 13:10
her h. arose and went after her, to speak   *J'g* 19:3
Naomi left of her two sons and *her h.*   *Ru* 1:5
find rest each of you in the house of *her h.*   *Ru* 1:9
Naomi had kinsman of *her h.* a man of wealth   *Ru* 2:1
then said Elkanah *her h.* to her   *1Sa* 1:8; 1:23
she said unto *her h.*, I will not go up till child   *1Sa* 1:22
when she came up with *her h.* to offer sacrifice   *1Sa* 2:19
she heard that her father and *her h.* were dead   *1Sa* 4:19
because of *her h.*; she told not *her h.*   *1Sa* 4:21; 25:19
Ish-bosheth sent and took her from *her h.*   *2Sa* 3:15
her h. went with her along weeping behind her   *2Sa* 3:16
when the wife of Uriah heard *her h.* was dead, she mourned for *her h.*   *2Sa* 11:26
she said to her *h.* Behold, now I perceive   *2Ki* 4:9
verily she hath no child, and *her h.* is old   *2Ki* 4:14
she called unto *her h.* and said, Send me one   *2Ki* 4:22
a virtuous wife is a crown to *her h.*   *Pr* 12:4
the heart of *her h.* doth safely trust in her   *Pr* 31:11
her h. is known in the gates among the elders   *Pr* 31:23
her h. also riseth up, and he praiseth her   *Pr* 31:28
surely as a wife departeth from *her h.*   *Jer* 3:20
who taketh strangers instead of *her h.*   *Eze* 16:32
that loatheth *her h.* and her children, thou art   *Eze* 16:45
she is not my wife, neither am I *her h.*   *Ho* 2:2
now Joseph *her h.* being a just man   *M't* 1:19
if a woman shall put away *her h.*   *M'k* 10:12
whoso marrieth her put away from *her h.*   *Lu* 16:18
buried her by *her h.*   *Ac* 5:10
is bound by law to *her h.* so long as he liveth   *Ro* 7:2
if *her h.* be dead, she is free from that law   *Ro* 7:3
and let every woman have *her* own *h.*   *1Co* 7:2
let not the wife depart from *her h.*   *1Co* 7:10
remain unmarried or be reconciled to *her h.*   *1Co* 7:11
is married, careth how she may please *her h.*   *1Co* 7:34
is bound by law as long as *her h.* liveth   *1Co* 7:39
and the wife see that she reverence *her h.*   *Eph* 5:33
prepared as a bride adorned for *her h.*   *Re* 21:2

MY HUSBAND

now therefore *my h.* will love me   *Ge* 29:32
now this time will *my h.* be joined to me   *Ge* 29:34
is it small matter that thou hast taken *my h.*   *Ge* 30:15
because I have given my maiden to *my h.*   *Ge* 30:18
Leah said, Now will *my h.* dwell with me   *Ge* 30:20
am a widow, *my h.* is dead   *2Sa* 14:5; *2Ki* 4:1
shall not leave to *my h.* a name on the earth   *2Sa* 14:7
shall say, I will go and return to *my* first *h.*   *Ho* 2:7

THY HUSBAND

thy desire shall be to *thy h.* he shall rule   *Ge* 3:16
with another instead of *thy h.*   *Nu* 5:19; 5:20
they said to Samson's wife, Entice *thy h.*   *J'g* 14:15
done to thy mother since death of *thy h.*   *Ru* 2:11
and say to her, Is it well with *thy h.*   *2Ki* 4:26
thy Maker is *thy h.* the Lord is his name   *Isa* 54:5
go call *thy h.*, he is not *thy h.*   *Joh* 4:16; 4:18
the feet of them that have buried *thy h.*   *Ac* 5:9
knowest whether thou shalt save *thy h.*   *1Co* 7:16

HUSBANDMAN

Noah began to be an *h.* and he planted a vineyard (A)   *Ge* 9:20
Noah began his farming with planting a vineyard (B)   *Ge* 9:20
Noah was the first tiller of the soil (R)   *Ge* 9:20
I break in pieces the *h.* and his yoke   *Jer* 51:23
I will shatter the farmer (B)(R)   *Jer* 51:23
they shall call the *h.* to mourning   *Am* 5:16
call the plowman to mourning (B)   *Am* 5:16
call the farmers to mourning (R)   *Am* 5:16
I am no prophet, I am an *h.*   *Zec* 13:5
man who cultivates the ground (B)   *Zec* 13:5
I am a tiller of the ground (E)(R)   *Zec* 13:5
true vine, and my Father is the *h.*   *Joh* 15:1
my Father is the Vinedresser (A)(P)(R)   *Joh* 15:1
my Father is the Tiller (B)   *Joh* 15:1
my Father is the Gardener (N)   *Joh* 15:1
The *h.* that laboureth must be first   *2Ti* 2:6
the hard-working farmer (A)(R)   *2Ti* 2:6
man who works on the land (P)   *2Ti* 2:6
the *h.* waiteth for the precious fruit   *Jas* 5:7
the farmer waits (A)(B)(N)(P)(R)   *Jas* 5:7

HUSBANDMEN

the land to be vine dressers and *h.*   *2Ki* 25:12
vinedressers and soil tillers (A)   *2Ki* 25:12
vinedressers and farmers (B)   *2Ki* 25:12
vinedressers and plowmen (R)   *2Ki* 25:12
h. also, and vine dressers in   *2Ch* 26:10
farmers and vinedressers (A)(R)   *2Ch* 26:10
plowmen and vinedressers (B)   *2Ch* 26:10
h. and they that go with flocks   *Jer* 31:24
farmers (B)   *Jer* 31:24; *Joe* 1:11
land for vinedressers and for *h.*   *Jer* 52:16
Be ye ashamed, O ye *h.*; howl   *Joe* 1:11
tillers of the soil (R)   *Joe* 1:11
left it out to *h.*, and went into a far   *M't* 21:33
tenants (A)(R)   *M't* 21:33; 21:34, 38, 40-41; *M'k* 12:2, 9
tillers (B)   *M't* 21:33; 21:34, 40; *M'k* 12:2
vine-growers (N)   *M't* 21:33; *M'k* 12:2
farm workers (P)   *M't* 21:33; 21:34, 38-41; *M'k* 12:2
he sent his servants to the *h.*   *M't* 21:34
tenants (N)   *M't* 21:34; 21:38, 40-41; *M'k* 12:2, 9
the *h.* took his servants, and beat   *M't* 21:35
when the *h.* saw the son, they said   *M't* 21:38

what will he do unto those *h.*   *M't 21:40*

let out his vineyard unto other *h.*   *M't 21:41*

let it out to *h.* and went into a far   *M'k 12:1*

he sent to the *h.* a servant, that he   *M'k 12:2*

receive from the *h.* of the fruit of   *M'k 12:2*

those *h.* said among themselves   *M'k 12:7*

will come and destroy the *h.*   *M'k 12:9*

a vineyard and let it forth to *h.*   *Lu 20:9*

sent a servant to the *h.,* that   *Lu 20:10*

the *h.* beat him, and sent him away   *Lu 20:10*

when the *h.* saw him, they reasoned   *Lu 20:14*

shall come and destroy these *h.*   *Lu 20:16*

HUSBANDRY

and in Carmel: for he loved *h.*   *2Ch 26:10*

he loved farming (A)   *2Ch 26:10*

he loved the soil (B)(R)   *2Ch 26:10*

with God: ye are God's *h.* ye are   *1Co 3:9*

God's garden, vineyard, field under cultivation (A)   *1Co 3:9*

God's farmland (B)   *1Co 3:9*

God's garden (N)   *1Co 3:9*

a field under God's cultivation (P)(R)   *1Co 3:9*

HUSBANDS

womb, that they may be your *h.*   *Ru 1:11*

ye stay for them from having *h.*   *Ru 1:13*

they shall despise their *h.* in their   *Es 1:17*

wives shall give to their *h.* honour   *Es 1:20*

and give your daughters to *h.*   *Jer 29:6*

without our *h.* (S)   *Jer 44:19*

loathed their *h.* and their children   *Eze 16:45*

For thou hast had five *h.,* and   *Joh 4:18*

let them ask their *h.* at home: for it   *1Co 14:35*

submit yourselves unto your own *h.*   *Eph 5:22; Col 3:18*

be to their own *h.* in every thing   *Eph 5:24*

H., love your wives, even as Christ   *Eph 5:25*

H. love your wives, and be not bitter   *Col 3:19*

deacons be the *h.* of one wife, ruling   *1Ti 3:12*

love their *h.* to love their children   *Tit 2:4*

obedient to their own *h.* that   *Tit 2:5*

wives, in subjection to your own *h.*   *1Pe 3:1*

in subjection unto their own *h.*   *1Pe 3:5*

Likewise, ye *h.* dwell with them   *1Pe 3:7*

HUSBAND'S

vowed in her *h.* house, or bound   *Nu 30:10*

her *h.* brother shall go in unto her   *De 25:5*

perform the duty of an *h.* brother   *De 25:5*

My *h.* brother refuseth to raise up   *De 25:7*

perform the duty of my *h.* brother   *De 25:7*

kinsman of her *h.* a mighty man   *Ru 2:1*

HUSHAH

Gedor, and Ezer the father of *H.*   *1Ch 4:4*

HUSHAI

H. the Archite came to meet him   *2Sa 15:32*

So *H.* David's friend came into the   *2Sa 15:37*

when *H.* the Archite, David's friend   *2Sa 16:16*

that *H.* said unto Absalom, God   *2Sa 16:16*

Absalom said to *H.,* Is this thy   *2Sa 16:17*

H. said unto Absalom, Nay   *2Sa 16:18*

Call now *H.* the Archite also   *2Sa 17:5*

when *H.* was come to Absalom   *2Sa 17:6*

And *H.* said unto Absalom, The counsel   *2Sa 17:7*

For, said *H.,* thou knowest thy   *2Sa 17:8*

The counsel of *H.* the Archite is   *2Sa 17:14*

Then said *H.* unto Zadok and to   *2Sa 17:15*

Baanah the son of *H.* was in Asher   *1Ki 4:16*

and *H.* the Archite was the king's   *1Ch 27:33*

HUSHAM

and *H.* of the land of Temani   *Ge 36:34*

And *H.* died, and Hadad the son of   *Ge 36:35*

H. of the land of the Temanites   *1Ch 1:45*

when *H.* was dead, Hadad the son   *1Ch 1:46*

HUSHATHITE

then Sibbechai the *H.* slew Saph   *2Sa 21:18*

the Anethothite, Mebunnai the *H.*   *2Sa 23:27*

Sibbecai the *H.,* Ilai the Ahohite   *1Ch 11:29*

time Sibbechai the *H.* slew Sippai   *1Ch 20:4*

eighth month was Sibbecai the *H.*   *1Ch 27:11*

HUSHIM

And the sons of Dan; *H.*   *Ge 46:23*

the children of Ir, and *H.* the sons   *1Ch 7:12*

H. and Baara were his wives   *1Ch 8:8*

And of *H.* he begat Abitub   *1Ch 8:11*

HUSK

from the kernels even to the *h.*   *Nu 6:4*

seeds and skins (B)(R)   *Nu 6:4*

ears of corn in the *h.* thereof   *2Ki 4:42*

HUSKS

filled his belly with the *h.* that   *Lu 15:16*

with the carob pods (A)   *Lu 15:16*

with bean pods (B)   *Lu 15:16*

the food the pigs were eating (P)   *Lu 15:16*

the pods that the swine ate (R)   *Lu 15:16*

HUZ

H. his firstborn, and Buz his   *Ge 22:21*

HUZZAB

And *H.* shall be led away captive   *Na 2:7*

HYENAS

H. cry in its towers (R)   *Isa 13:22*

to bear *h.* (P)   *Ac 5:41*

HYMENAEUS

Of whom is *H.* and Alexander   *1Ti 1:20*

Of whom is *H.* and Philetus   *2Ti 2:17*

HYMN

they had sung an *h.* they went out   *M't 26:30; M'k 14:26*

HYMNS

in psalms and *h.* and spiritual   *Eph 5:19; Col 3:16*

HYPOCRISIES

and all guile, and *h.* and envies   *1Pe 2:1*

HYPOCRISY

work iniquity, to practise *h.*   *Isa 32:6*

practicing profane ungodliness (A)   *Isa 32:6*

practice profaneness (E)   *Isa 32:6*

to practice ungodliness (R)   *Isa 32:6*

in sheer *h.* (A)   *Isa 33:10*

within ye are full of *h.* and   *M't 23:28*

full of pretense (A)(P)   *M't 23:28*

knowing their *h.* said unto them   *M'k 12:15*

saw how crafty their question was (N)   *M'k 12:15*

leaven of the Pharisees, which is *h.*   *Lu 12:1*

love be without *h.* (E)(S)   *Ro 12:9*

carried way with *h.* (A)(B)   *Ga 2:13*

Speaking lies in *h.;* having their   *1Ti 4:2*

by hypocritical liars (B)   *1Ti 4:2*

through specious falsehoods of (N)   *1Ti 4:2*

men who are lying hypocrites (P)   *1Ti 4:2*

the pretensions of liars (R)   *1Ti 4:2*

without partiality and without *h.*   *Jas 3:17*

impartial and unfeigned (A)   *Jas 3:17*

impartial and unpretentious (B)   *Jas 3:17*

straightforward and sincere (N)   *Jas 3:17*

without uncertainty and insincerity (R)   *Jas 3:17*

HYPOCRITE

for an *h.* shall not come before   *Job 13:16*

a polluted and godless man (A)   *Job 13:16*

stir up himself against the *h.*   *Job 17:8*

the godless and polluted (A)   *Job 17:8*

the wicked (B)   *Job 17:8*

the godless (E)(R)   *Job 17:8*

the joy of the *h.* but for a moment   *Job 20:5*

the godless and defiled (A)   *Job 20:5*

joys of godless but for moment (B)(E)(R)   *Job 20:5*

For what is the hope of the *h.*   *Job 27:8*

the godless and polluted (A)   *Job 27:8*

the godless (B)(E)(R)   *Job 27:8; 34:30*

That the *h.* reign not lest   *Job 34:30*

An *h.* with his mouth destroyeth (A)(E)(R)   *Pr 11:9*

profane man destroys his (B)   *Pr 11:9*

for every one is a *h.* and an   *Isa 9:17*

profane (A)(E)   *Isa 9:17*

the godless (B)(R)   *Isa 9:17*

Thou *h.* first cast out the beam   *M't 7:5; Lu 6:42*

Thou *h.* doth not each one of you   *Lu 13:15*

rest of Jews played *h.* (B)   *Ga 2:13*

HYPOCRITES

the congregation of *h.* shall   *Job 15:34*

the godless (A)(B)(E)(R)   *Job 15:34; 36:13; Isa 33:14*

But the *h.* in heart heap up wrath   *Job 36:13*

hath surprised the *h.*   *Isa 33:14*

as the *h.* do in the synagogues   *M't 6:2*

thou shalt not be as the *h.* are   *M't 6:5*

when ye fast. be not as the *h.*   *M't 6:16*

Ye *h.* well did Esaias prophesy of   *M't 15:7*

O ye *h.,* ye can discern the face   *M't 16:3*

and said, Why tempt ye me, ye *h.*   *M't 22:18*

scribes and Pharisees, *h.!* for   *M't 23:13; 23:14-15; 23:23, 25, 27; Lu 11:44*

ye scribes and Pharisees, *h.!*   *M't 23:29*

because appoint him his portion with the *h.*   *M't 24:51*

Esaias prophesied of you *h.* as it is   *M'k 7:6*

Ye *h.,* ye can discern the face of   *Lu 12:56*

who are lying *h.* (P)   *1Ti 4:2*

HYPOCRITE'S

and the *h.* hope shall perish   *Job 8:13*

HYPOCRITICAL

With *h.* mockers in feasts, they   *Ps 35:16*
profane mockers (A)(B)(E)   *Ps 35:16*
the impiously mocked (R)   *Ps 35:16*
will send him against an *h.* nation   *Isa 10:6*
a godless nation (B)   *Isa 10:6*
a profane nation (E)(R)   *Isa 10:6*

HYSSOP

ye shall take a bunch of *h.* and dip   *Ex 12:22*
cedar wood, and scarlet, and *h.*   *Le 14:4; 14:49*
wood, and the scarlet, and the *h.*   *Le 14:6*
the cedar wood, and the *h.* and the   *Le 14:51; 14:52; Nu 19:6*
a clean person shall take *h.*   *Nu 19:18*
the *h.* that springeth out of the   *1Ki 4:33*
Purge me with *h.* and I shall be   *Ps 51:7*
with vinegar, and put it upon *h.*   *Joh 19:29*
water, and scarlet wool, and *h.* and   *Heb 9:19*

I

I

I, even *I*, do bring a flood on earth   *Ge 6:17*
I, behold *I*, establish my covenant   *Ge 9:9*
I shall be destroyed, *I* and my house   *Ge 34:30*
shall *I*, thy mother, and brethren bow   *Ge 37:10*
child is not, and *I*, whither shall *I* go   *Ge 37:30*
none greater in this house than *I*   *Ge 39:9*
who am *I*, that *I* should go to Pharaoh   *Ex 3:11*
Lord is righteous, *I* and my people   *Ex 9:27*
I, behold *I*, will harden the hearts   *Ex 14:17*
I thy father in law Jethro am come to   *Ex 18:6*
I, behold *I*, have given with him Aholiab   *Ex 31:6*
I, even *I*, will chastise you for sins   *Le 26:28*
I, behold *I*, have taken the   *Nu 3:12; Le 18:6*
nations more than *I*, how can *I*   *De 7:17*
I, even *I*, am he, there is no God   *De 32:39*
forty years old was *I* when Moses sent me   *Jos 14:7*
I, even *I*, will sing to the Lord God   *J'g 5:3*
till *I* Deborah arose, *I* arose a mother   *J'g 5:7*
when *I* blow, *I* and all that are with   *J'g 7:18*
may bewail my virginity, *I* and my   *J'g 11:37*
I and my people were at strife with   *J'g 12:2*
I came to Gibeah, *I* and my concubine   *J'g 20:4*
thou art more righteous than *I*   *1Sa 24:17*
I and my kingdom are guiltless   *2Sa 3:28*
I, whither shall *I* cause my shame   *2Sa 13:13*
I and Solomon be counted offenders   *1Ki 1:21*
I, even *I*, only remain a prophet   *1Ki 18:22; 19:10, 14; Ro 11:3*
who am *I*, what my people   *1Ch 29:14; 2Ch 2:6*
what *I* and fathers have done to people   *2Ch 32:13*
I, even *I* Artaxerxes, make a decree   *Ezr 7:21*
so did *I*, because of fear of God   *Ne 5:15*
I also and my maidens will fast   *Es 4:16*
I only am escaped   *Job 1:15; 1:16-17, 19*
own mouth condemneth thee, not *I*   *Job 15:6*

whether thou refuse or choose, not *I*   *Job 34:33*
lead me to rock that is higher than *I*   *Ps 61:2*
persecutors, they are stronger than *I*   *Ps 142:6*
who can hasten hereunto more than *I*   *Ec 2:25*
I am rose of Sharon, lily of valley   *Ca 2:1*
I am my beloved's   *Ca 6:3; 7:10*
I am a wall, and my breasts like   *Ca 8:10*
I and children given me   *Isa 8:18; Heb 2:13*
I the Lord, the first, and with the last; *I* am he   *Isa 41:4; 43:11, 25*
I am with thee, *I* am thy God   *Isa 41:10; 43:5*
I am the first, *I* am the last   *Isa 44:6; 48:12; Re 1:11, 17; 2:8; 22:13*
who as *I* shall call, shall declare   *Isa 44:7*
I, even my hands stretched out heaven   *Isa 45:12*
even to old age *I* am he, *I* have made   *Isa 46:4*
I am God, there is none else, *I* am   *Isa 46:9*
I, even *I* have spoken, I have called   *Isa 48:15*
from time that it was, there am *I*   *Isa 48:16*
yet shall *I* be glorious in eyes of Lord   *Isa 49:5*
I, even *I* am he that comforteth you   *Isa 51:12*
I am he that doth speak; behold it is *I*   *Isa 52:6*
stand by thyself, for *I* am holier than *I*   *Isa 65:5*
I am deceived, thou art stronger than *I*   *Jer 20:7*
I, even *I*, will utterly forget you   *Jer 23:39*
I, even *I*, am against thee   *Eze 5:8*
I, even *I*, will bring a sword upon   *Eze 6:3*
I, even *I*, will search sheep   *Eze 34:11*
I, even *I*, will judge between fat   *Eze 34:20*
I am their inheritance, *I* am their   *Eze 44:28*
when *I*, even *I* Daniel had seen   *Da 8:15*
I, even *I*, will tear, I will take   *Ho 5:14*
I am with you, saith the Lord   *Hag 1:13*
for *I* was but little pleased, they   *Zec 1:15*
should *I* accept of your hands   *Mal 1:13*
after me is mightier than *I*   *M't 3:11; M'k 1:7*
It is *I*, be not afraid   *M't 14:27; M'k 6:50; Joh 6:20*
whom do men say that *I* the son of   *M't 16:13*
two or three, there am *I* in midst of   *M't 18:20*
many come, saying *I* am Christ   *M't 24:5; Lu 21:8*
every one began to say, Lord, is it *I*   *M't 26:22*
all shall be offended, yet will not *I*   *M'k 14:29*
father and *I* sought thee sorrowing   *Lu 2:48*
if *I* by Beelzebub cast out devils, by   *Lu 11:19*
if *I* with finger of God cast out   *Lu 11:20*
I am among you as he that serveth   *Lu 22:27*
it is *I* myself, handle me and see   *Lu 24:39*
confessed, *I* am not Christ   *Joh 1:20; 3:28*
I knew him not; but he that sent me   *Joh 1:33*
I that speak unto thee am he   *Joh 4:26*
I am not alone, but *I* and the Father   *Joh 8:16*
I am from above, *I* am not of world   *Joh 8:23*
I am he, *I* do nothing of myself   *Joh 8:28*
Jesus said, Before Abraham was *I* am   *Joh 8:58*

I and my Father are one   *Joh 10:30*
Father in me, *I* in him   *Joh 10:38; 15:5; 17:21*
I, if *I* be lifted up, will draw all   *Joh 12:32*
if *I* then your Lord and Master have   *Joh 13:14*
I in my Father, and ye in me   *Joh 14:20*
I go to my Father, my Father greater   *Joh 14:28*
Abide in me, and *I* in you   *Joh 15:4*
I in them, and thou in me   *Joh 17:23*
I have known them, and these have   *Joh 17:25*
love may be in them, and *I* in them   *Joh 17:26*
Pilate answered, Am *I* a Jew   *Joh 18:35*
what was *I*, that *I* could withstand   *Ac 11:17*
I obtained freedom; *I* was free born   *Ac 22:28*
no more *I*, but sin   *Ro 7:17; 7:20*
I am of Paul, *I* of Apollos, *I* of Cephas, and *I* of Christ   *1Co 1:12; 3:4*
I, brethren, when *I* came to you   *1Co 2:1*
I, brethren, could not speak to you as   *1Co 3:1*
I would that all men were as *I* myself   *1Co 7:7*
It is good to abide even as *I*   *1Co 7:8*
I command, yet not *I*, but the Lord   *1Co 7:10*
or *I* only and Barnabas, have we not   *1Co 9:6*
I so run, so fight *I*, not as one that   *1Co 9:26*
be followers of me, as *I* am of Christ   *1Co 11:1*
by grace *I* am what *I* am, yet not *I*   *1Co 15:10*
whether it were *I* or they, so we   *1Co 15:11*
he worketh work of Christ, even as *I*   *1Co 16:10*
are they Hebrews? so am *I* Israelites? so am I. Seed of Abraham? so am *I*   *2Co 11:22*
Are they ministers of Christ? *I* am   *2Co 11:23*
five time received *I* forty stripes save   *2Co 11:24*
I was beaten with rods, once was *I* stoned, thrice *I* suffered shipwreck, *I* have been in the deep   *2Co 11:25*
I am not weak? *I* burn not   *2Co 11:29*
If *I* must needs glory, *I* will glory   *2Co 11:30*
I knew a man in Christ above fourteen years, *I* cannot tell, *I* knew such a man, of such an one will *I* glory   *2Co 12:2*
I through law am dead to law, that *I*   *Ga 2:19*
I live, yet not *I*, but Christ liveth   *Ga 2:20*
be as *I* am, for *I* am as ye are   *Ga 4:12*
I, brethren, if *I* yet preach circumcision   *Ga 5:11*
that *I* should glory save in cross, world crucified to me, *I* unto world   *Ga 6:14*
I also, after *I* heard of your faith   *Eph 1:15*
I therefore, prisoner of the Lord   *Eph 4:1*
be ye holy, for *I* am holy   *1Pe 4:16*
I am Alpha and Omega, beginning and   *Re 1:8*
as many as *I* love, *I* rebuke   *Re 3:19*
I also overcame, and am set down   *Re 3:21*
I John saw the holy city   *Re 21:2*
I John saw these things, *I* fell   *Re 22:8*
I am thy fellow-servant, and   *Re 22:9*
I Jesus have sent my angel to testify these things, *I* am root   *Re 22:16*

IBEX

the ibex (A)(R)   *De 14:5*

IBHAR

I. also, and Elishua   *2Sa 5:15; 1Ch 3:6*
And *I*, Elishua, and Elpalet   *1Ch 14:5*

IBLEAM

I. and her towns, and the — *Jos 17:11*
nor the inhabitants of *I*. and — *J'g 1:27*
her
going up to Gur, which is by — *2Ki 9:27*
I.

IBNEIAH

And *I*. the son of Jeroham, and — *1Ch 9:8*

IBNIJAH

the son of Reuel, the son of *I*. — *1Ch 9:8*

IBRI

Shoham, Zaccur, and *I*. — *1Ch 24:27*

IBZAN

after him, *I* of Beth-lehem — *J'g 12:8*
Then died *I*., and was buried — *J'g 12:10*
in

ICE

are blackish by reason of the — *Job 6:16*
i.
i, is given (A)(B)(E)(R) — *Job 38:10*
Out of whose womb came — *Job 38:29*
the *i*.
He casteth forth his *i*. like — *Ps 147:17*
morsels

I-CHABOD

she named the child *I*., saying — *1Sa 4:21*

I-CHABOD'S

the son of Ahitub, *I*. brother — *1Sa 14:3*

ICONIUM

against them, and came unto — *Ac 13:51*
I.
And it came to pass in *I*., that — *Ac 14:1*
certain Jews from Antioch — *Ac 14:19*
and *I*.
to Lystra, and to *I*., and — *Ac 14:21*
Antioch
brethren that were at Lystra — *Ac 16:2*
and *I*.
unto me at Antioch, at *I*., at — *2Ti 3:11*
Lystra

IDALAH

and Shimron, and *I*., and — *Jos 19:15*

IDBASH

Jezreel, and Ishma, and *I*. — *1Ch 4:3*

IDDO

Ahinadab the son of *I*. had — *1Ki 4:14*
Joah his son, *I*. his son, Zerah — *1Ch 6:21*
his
I. the son of Zechariah; of — *1Ch 27:21*
and in the visions of *I*. the — *2Ch 9:29*
seer
and of *I*. the seer concerning — *2Ch 12:15*
written in the story of the — *2Ch 13:22*
prophet *I*.
and Zechariah the son of *I*. — *Ezr 5:1;*
                    6:14
with commandment unto *I*. — *Ezr 8:17*
what they should say unto *I*. — *Ezr 8:17*
I., Ginnetho, Abijah — *Ne 12:4*
of *I*., Zechariah: of Ginnethon — *Ne 12:16*
the son of Berechiah, the son of — *Zec 1:1*
I.
the son of *I*. the prophet, — *Zec 1:7*
saying

IDENTIFY

did not *i*. him (B) — *Ge 27:23*

IDIOT

he is a conceited *i*. (P) — *1Ti 6:4*

IDLE

for they be *i*.: therefore they cry — *Ex 5:8*
they are lazy (B) — *Ex 5:8; 5:17*
But he said, Ye are *i*., ye are *i*. — *Ex 5:17*

---

and an *i*. soul shall suffer — *Pr 19:15*
hunger
That every *i*. word that men — *M't 12:36*
shall
every useless word (B) — *M't 12:36*
thoughtless word (N) — *M't 12:36*
every careless word (P)(R) — *M't 12:36*
and saw others standing *i*. in — *M't 20:3*
standing without employment — *M't 20:3*
(B)
standing about with nothing — *M't 20:3*
to do (P)
found others standing *i*. and — *M't 20:6*
saith
Why stand ye here all the day — *M't 20:6*
i.
words seemed to them as *i*. — *Lu 24:11*
tales
reports seemed nonsense to — *Lu 24:11*
them (B)(N)
struck them as sheer — *Lu 24:11*
imagination (P)
admonish the *i*. (R) — *1Th 5:14*
And withal they learn to be *i*. — *1Ti 5:13*
not only *i*. but tattlers also and — *1Ti 5:13*
learn to be idlers (A)(R) — *1Ti 5:13*
become worse than lazy (P) — *1Ti 5:13*

IDLENESS

and eateth not the bread of *i*. — *Pr 31:27*
and through *i*. of the hands — *Ec 10:18*
through *i*. the house leaks (A) — *Ec 10:18*
and abundance of *i*. was in — *Eze 16:49*
her

IDLERS

learn to be *i*. (A)(R) — *1Ti 5:13*

IDOL

she had made an *i*. in a — *1Ki 15:13*
grove
she had her image (A) — *1Ki 15:13*
made a destestable image to — *1Ki 15:13*
Asherah (B)
made image for an Asherah — *1Ki 15:13*
(E)(R)
Asa destroyed her *i*. and — *1Ki 15:13*
burnt it
an *i*. (S) — *1Ki 16:33*
  2Ki 13:6; 17:16; 21:3, 7; 1Ki 6-7, 15
because she had made an *i*. — *2Ch 15:16*
in a
grove: and Asa cut down her — *2Ch 15:16*
i.
image, the *i*. which he had — *2Ch 33:7*
made
the *i*. out of the house of the — *2Ch 13:15*
Lord
Mine *i*. hath done them, and — *Isa 48:5*
incense, as if he blessed an *i*. — *Isa 66:3*
man Coniah a despised broken — *Jer 22:28*
i.
the *i*. of resentment (B) — *Eze 8:3*
Woe to the *i*. shepherd that — *Zec 11:17*
leaveth
and offered a sacrifice unto the — *Ac 7:41*
i.
we know that an *i*. is nothing — *1Co 8:4*
with conscience of the *i*. unto — *1Co 8:7*
this
eat it as a thing offered unto — *1Co 8:7*
an *i*.
say I then? that the *i*. is any — *1Co 10:19*
thing

IDOLATER

a fornicator, or covetous, or — *1Co 5:11*
an *i*.
nor covetous man, who is an *i*. — *Eph 5:5*

IDOLATERS

or extortioners, or with *i*. — *1Co 5:10*
neither fornicators, nor *i*., nor — *1Co 6:9*
Neither be *i*. as were some of — *1Co 10:7*
i. and all liars, shall have their — *Re 21:8*
and murderers, and *i*. and — *Re 22:15*

IDOLATRIES

banquetings, and abominable *i*. — *1Pe 4:3*

IDOLATROUS

he put down the *i*. priests, — *2Ki 23:5*
whom
without *i*. pillar (A)(B)(E)(R) — *Ho 3:4*

IDOLATRY

stubbornness is as iniquity — *1Sa 15:23*
and *i*.
put away *i*. (R) — *Eze 43:9*
he saw the city wholly given — *Ac 17:16*
to *i*.
my dearly beloved, flee from — *1Co 10:14*
i.
i., witchcraft, hatred, variance — *Ga 5:20*
and covetousness, which is *i*. — *Col 3:5*

IDOLS

idols (S) — *Ex 34:13;*
  De 7:5; 12:3; J'g 3:7; 1Ki 14:15, 23;
  2Ki 17:10; 18:4, 19; 23:14; 2Ch 14:3;
  17:6; 19:3; 31:1; 33:3, 19; 34:3-4, 7;
  Isa 17:8; 27:9; Jer 17:2; Ho 4:12;
                        Mic 5:14
Turn ye not unto *i*. nor make — *Le 19:4*
Ye shall make you no *i*. nor — *Le 26:1*
graven
upon the carcases of your *i*. — *Le 26:30*
breakage of your *i*. — *Le 26:30*
(B)(E)(R)
destroy all their stone *i*. (S) — *Nu 33:52*
and their *i*. wood and stone, — *De 29:17*
silver
their *i*. (A)(R) — *De 32:21; 1Ki 16:13, 26*
i., mere nothings (B) — *1Sa 12:21*
publish it in the house of their — *1Sa 31:9*
i.
abandoned their *i*. (B)(R) — *2Sa 5:21*
and removed all the *i*. that — *1Ki 15:12*
his
their vain *i*. (B) — *1Ki 16:13;*
                      16:26; Ps 31:6
did very abominably in — *1Ki 21:26*
following *i*.
For they served *i*. whereof the — *2Ki 17:12*
made Judah also to sin with — *2Ki 21:11*
his *i*.
served the *i*. that his father — *2Ki 21:21*
served
and the images, and the *i*. — *2Ki 23:24*
and all
to carry tidings unto their *i*. — *1Ch 10:9*
all the gods of the people are — *1Ch 16:26*
i.
put away the abominable *i*. — *2Ch 15:8*
out
and served groves and *i*. and — *2Ch 24:18*
cut down all the *i*. throughout — *2Ch 34:7*
all
vain *i*. (A) — *Ps 31:6*
the gods of the nations are *i*. — *Ps 96:5*
that boast themselves of *i*.: — *Ps 97:7*
worship
And they served their *i*. — *Ps 106:36*
sacrificed unto the *i*. of — *Ps 106:38*
Canaan
Their *i*. are silver and gold — *Ps 115:4*
The *i*. of the heathen are — *Ps 135:15*
silver and
Their land also is full of *i*: they — *Isa 2:8*
and the *i*. he shall utterly — *Isa 2:18*
abolish
day a man shall cast his *i*. of — *Isa 2:20*
silver
and his *i*. of gold, which they — *Isa 2:20*
made
hath found the kingdoms of — *Isa 10:10*
the *i*.
have done unto Samaria and — *Isa 10:11*
her *i*.
so do to Jerusalem and her *i*. — *Isa 10:11*
the *i*. of Egypt shall be moved — *Isa 19:1*
and they shall seek to the *i*. — *Isa 19:3*
and to
man shall cast away his *i*. of — *Isa 31:7*
silver
and his *i*. of gold, which your — *Isa 31:7*
own
together that are makers of *i*. — *Isa 45:16*
their *i*. were upon the beasts — *Isa 46:1*
Enflaming yourselves with *i*. — *Isa 57:5*
under
foreign *i*. (A)(B)(R) — *Jer 8:19*
her *i*. are confounded, her — *Jer 50:2*
images
and they are mad upon their — *Jer 50:38*
i.
your slain men before your *i*. — *Eze 6:4*
children of Israel before their *i*. — *Eze 6:5*
your *i*. may be broken and — *Eze 6:6*
cease
which go a whoring after their — *Eze 6:9*
i.

shall be among their *i*. round about   *Eze 6:13*

offer sweet savour to all their *i*.   *Eze 6:13*

and all the *i*. of the house of Israel   *Eze 8:10*

man, these men have set up their *i*.   *Eze 14:3*

that setteth up his *i*. in his heart   *Eze 14:4*

according to the multitude of his *i*.   *Eze 14:4*

estranged from me through their *i*.   *Eze 14:5*

turn yourselves from your *i*.   *Eze 14:6*

setteth up his *i*. in his heart   *Eze 14:7*

with all the *i*. of thy abominations   *Eze 16:36*

eyes to the *i*. of the house of Israel   *Eze 18:6; 18:15*

hath lifted up his eyes to the *i*.   *Eze 18:12*

not yourselves with the *i*. of Egypt   *Eze 20:7*

did they forsake the *i*. of Egypt   *Eze 20:8*

for their heart went after their *i*.   *Eze 20:16*

nor defile yourselves with their *i*.   *Eze 20:18*

eyes were after their fathers' *i*.   *Eze 20:24*

pollute yourselves with all your *i*.   *Eze 20:31*

Go ye, serve ye every one his *i*. and   *Eze 20:39*

with your gifts, and with your *i*.   *Eze 20:39*

maketh *i*. against herself to defile   *Eze 22:3*

defiled thyself in thine *i*. which   *Eze 22:4*

with all their *i*. she defiled herself   *Eze 23:7*

thou art polluted with their *i*.   *Eze 23:30*

with their *i*. have they committed   *Eze 23:37*

had slain their children to their *i*.   *Eze 23:39*

you, and ye bear the sins of your *i*.   *Eze 23:49*

I will also destroy the *i*. and I will   *Eze 30:13*

lift up your eyes toward your *i*.   *Eze 33:25*

shed upon the land, and for their *i*.   *Eze 36:18*

from all your *i*. will I cleanse you   *Eze 36:25*

themselves any more with their *i*.   *Eze 37:23*

astray away from me after their *i*.   *Eze 44:10*

unto them before their *i*., and   *Eze 44:12*

senseless wood *i*. (A)(B)(R)   *Ho 4:12*

Ephraim is joined to *i*. let him   *Ho 4:17*

their gold have they made them *i*.   *Ho 8:4*

and *i*. according to their own   *Ho 13:2*

have I to do any more with *i*.   *Ho 14:8*

all the *i*. thereof will I lay desolate   *Mic 1:7*

trusteth therein, to make dumb *i*.   *Hab 2:18*

For the *i*. have spoken vanity   *Zec 10:2*

cut off the names of the *i*. out of   *Zec 13:2*

they abstain from pollutions of *i*.   *Ac 15:20*

abstain from meats offered to *i*.   *Ac 15:29*

from things offered to *i*., and   *Ac 21:25*

thou that abhorrest *i*. dost thou   *Ro 2:22*

as touching things offered to *i*.   *1Co 8:1*

that are offered in sacrifice unto *i*.   *1Co 8:4*

those things which are offered to *i*.   *1Co 8:10*

which is offered in sacrifice to *i*. is   *1Co 10:19*

offered in sacrifice unto *i*. eat not   *1Co 10:28*

carried away unto these dumb *i*.   *1Co 12:2*

hath the temple of God with *i*.   *2Co 6:16*

ye turned to God from *i*. to serve   *1Th 1:9*

children, keep yourselves from *i*.   *1Jo 5:21*

eat things sacrificed unto *i*. and   *Re 2:14*

and to eat things sacrificed unto *i*.   *Re 2:20*

i. of gold, and silver, and brass   *Re 9:20*

IDOL'S

sit at meat in the *i*. temple   *1Co 8:10*

IDUMAEA

from Jerusalem, and from I.   *M'k 3:8*

IDUMEA

it shall come down upon I. and   *Isa 34:5*

great slaughter in the land of I.   *Isa 34:6*

O mount Seir, and all I. even all   *Eze 35:15*

of the heathen, and against all I.   *Eze 36:5*

IF

I. thou doest well, shalt thou not   *Ge 4:7*

i. thou doest not well, sin lieth at   *Ge 4:7*

I. Cain should be avenged   *Ge 4:24*

i. they will not believe thee, neither   *Ex 4:8*

i. they will not believe also these   *Ex 4:9*

and *i*. thou refuse to let him go   *Ex 4:23*

and *i*. thou refuse to let them go   *Ex 8:2*

Else, *i*. thou wilt not let my people   *Ex 8:21*

For *i*. thou refuse to let them go   *Ex 9:2*

Else, *i*. thou refuse to let my people   *Ex 10:4*

And *i*. the household be too little for   *Ex 12:4*

i. thou wilt not redeem it, then thou   *Ex 13:13*

I. thou wilt diligently hearken to   *Ex 15:26*

I. ye walk in my statutes, and keep   *Le 26:3*

But *i*. ye will not hearken unto me   *Le 26:14*

And *i*. ye shall despise my statutes   *Le 26:15*

And *i*. ye will not yet for all this   *Le 26:18*

And *i*. ye walk contrary unto me   *Le 26:21*

And *i*. ye will not be reformed by   *Le 26:23*

And *i*. ye will not for all this   *Le 26:27*

I. they shall confess their iniquity   *Le 26:40*

i. then their uncircumcised hearts   *Le 26:41*

But *i*. from thence thou shalt seek   *De 4:29*

i. thou seek him with all thy heart   *De 4:29*

i. thou turn to the Lord thy God   *De 4:30*

i. we hear the voice of the Lord   *De 5:25*

i. we observe to do all these   *De 6:25*

i. ye hearken to these judgments   *De 7:12*

I. thou shalt say in thine heart   *De 7:17*

i. thou do at all forget the Lord   *De 8:19*

i. ye shall hearken diligently unto   *De 11:13*

For *i*. ye shall diligently keep all   *De 11:22*

i. ye obey the commandments of   *De 11:27*

i. ye will not obey the   *De 11:28*

I. the place which the Lord thy   *De 12:21*

I. there arise among you a prophet   *De 13:1*

i. thou shalt hearken diligently   *De 28:1*

i. thou shalt hearken unto the   *De 28:2*

i. thou shalt keep commandments   *De 28:9*

i. that thou hearken unto the   *De 28:13*

i. thou wilt not hearken unto the   *De 28:15*

I. thou wilt not observe to do all   *De 28:58*

And *i*. it seem evil unto you to serve   *Jos 24:15*

I. ye forsake the Lord, and serve   *Jos 24:20*

I. ye will fear the Lord, and serve   *1Sa 12:14*

But *i*. ye will not obey the voice of   *1Sa 12:15*

But *i*. ye shall still do wickedly, ye   *1Sa 12:25*

I. he commit iniquity, I will chasten   *2Sa 7:14*

i. there be any iniquity in me   *2Sa 14:32*

I. thy children take heed to their   *1Ki 2:4*

i. thou wilt walk in my ways   *1Ki 3:14; 6:12*

i. they sin against thee   *1Ki 8:46; 2Ch 6:36*

i. thou seek him, he will be found   *1Ch 28:9*

but *i*. you forsake him, he will   *1Ch 28:9*

I. they return to thee with all their heart   *2Ch 6:38*

I. my people, which are called by my name   *2Ch 7:14*

i. thou wilt walk before me, as   *2Ch 7:17*

But *i*. ye turn away, and forsake my   *2Ch 7:19*

i. ye seek him, he will be found of you   *2Ch 15:2*

but *i*. ye forsake him, he will forsake you   *2Ch 15:2*

i. ye turn again unto the Lord: *i*. ye return   *2Ch 30:9*

I. ye transgress, I will scatter you   *Ne 1:8*

But *i*. ye turn unto me, and keep my   *Ne 1:8*

I. I regard iniquity in my heart, the Lord   *Ps 66:18*

I. his children forsake my law,   *Ps 89:30*

and *i*. they break my statutes

I. ye be willing and obedient, ye shall   *Isa 1:19*

But *i*. ye refuse and rebel, ye shall   *Isa 1:20*

I. thou wilt return, O Israel   *Jer 4:1; 7:5; 17:24; 26:3*

But *i*. they will not obey, I will   *Jer 12:17; 17:27; 26:4*

Yet *i*. thou warn the wicked   *Eze 3:19; 3:21; 33:8-9*

i. we follow on to know the Lord   *Ho 6:3*

but *i*. the salt have lost his savour   *M't 5:13*

i. ye forgive men. *i*. ye forgive not   *M't 6:14; 6:15; 18:35; M'k 11:25-26; Lu 17:3-4*

I. ye have faith as a grain of mustard seed   *M't 17:20; 21:21; Lu 17:6*

i. two of you shall agree on earth   *M't 18:19*

I. thou canst believe, all things are possible   *M'k 9:23*

I. ye continue in my word, then   *Joh 8:31*

I. a man abide not in me, he is cast   *Joh 15:6*

I. ye abide in me, and my words abide   *Joh 15:7*

For *i*. ye live after the flesh, ye shall die   *Ro 8:13*

but *i*. ye though the Spirit do mortify   *Ro 8:13*

i. the fall of them be the riches of the   *Ro 11:12*

i. the casting away of them be   *Ro 11:16*

I. God spared not the natural branches   *Ro 11:21*

i. thou continue in his goodness   *Ro 11:22*

i. any man defile the temple of God   *1Co 3:17*

saved, *i*. ye keep in memory what I   *1Co 15:2*

I. ye continue in the faith, rooted   *Col 1:23*

now we live, *i*. we stand fast in the Lord   *1Th 3:8*

i. they continue in the faith   *1Ti 2:15*

i. we deny him, he also will deny us; *i*. we believe not   *2Ti 2:12; 2:13*

i. we neglect so great salvation   *Heb 2:3*

i. we hold fast the confidence   *Heb 3:6*

i. we hold the beginning of our confidence   *Heb 3:14*

I. they shall fall away, to renew them   *Heb 6:6*

For *i*. we sin wilfully after that we   *Heb 10:26*

but *i*. any man draw back, my soul   *Heb 10:38*

i. we turn away from him that — *Heb 12:25*

Brethren, *i.* any of you do err from truth — *Jas 5:19*

i. God spared not the angels that sinned — *2Pe 2:4*

i. after they have escaped the pollutions — *2Pe 2:20*

i. we walk in the light, as he is in the — *1Jo 1:7*

i. any man sin, we have an advocate — *1Jo 2:1*

IGAL

Issachar, *I.* the son of Joseph — *Nu 13:7*

I. the son of Nathan of Zobah — *2Sa 23:36*

IGDALIAH

of *I.*, a man of God, which was — *Jer 35:4*

IGEAL

Hattush, and *I.*, and Bariah — *1Ch 3:22*

IGNITES

it *i.* the thickets — *Isa 9:18*

IGNOBLE

one for noble, one for *i.* (A)(B) — *Ro 9:21*

some menial and *i.* (A)(B(R) — *2Ti 2:20*

IGNOMINY

being filled with *i.* (E) — *Job 10:15*

contempt, and with *i.* reproach — *Pr 18:3*

with inner baseness comes outer shame (A) — *Pr 18:3*

with disdain brings reproach (B) — *Pr 18:3*

with dishonor comes disgrace (R) — *Pr 18:3*

strife and *i.* shall cease (E) — *Pr 22:10*

IGNORAMUS

a pompous *i.* (N) — *1Ti 6:4*

IGNORANCE

If a soul shall sin through *i.* — *Le 4:2*

sin unwittingly (A)(E)(R) — *Le 4:2; 4:22, 27*

sins ignorantly (B) — *Le 4:2; 4:13, 22, 27; Nu 15:25*

of Israel sin through *i.* — *Le 4:13*

sins unintentionally (A) — *Le 4:13*

whole congregation of Israel err (E) — *Le 4:13*

sin unwittingly (R) — *Le 4:13*

done somewhat through *i.* — *Le 4:22*

common people sin through *i.* — *Le 4:27*

a trespass, and sin through *i.* — *Le 5:15*

his *i.* wherein he erred and wist it — *Le 5:18*

if ought be committed by *i.* — *Nu 15:24*

shall be forgiven; for it is *i.* — *Nu 15:25*

it was an error (A)(E)(R) — *Nu 15:25*

before the Lord, for their *i.* — *Nu 15:25*

seeing all the people were in *i.* — *Nu 15:26*

if any soul sin through *i.* then he — *Nu 15:27*

he sinneth by *i.* before the Lord — *Nu 15:28*

for him that sinneth through *i.* — *Nu 15:29*

brethren, I wot that through *i.* ye did — *Ac 3:17*

behaved ignorantly (B) — *Ac 3:17*

you worship in *i.* (E)(P) — *Ac 17:23*

the times of this *i.* God winked at — *Ac 17:30*

God through the *i.* that is in them — *Eph 4:18*

to the former lusts in your *i.* — *1Pe 1:14*

to silence the *i.* of foolish men — *1Pe 2:15*

foolishness of thoughtless people (B) — *1Pe 2:15*

IGNORANT

he was *i.* of it (B) — *Le 5:17*

So foolish was I, and *i.*: I was — *Ps 73:22*

---

they are all *i.* they are all — *Isa 56:10*

though Abraham be *i.* of us — *Isa 63:16*

Abraham does not know us (A)(B)(E)(R) — *Isa 63:16*

they were unlearned and *i.* men — *Ac 4:13*

unlearned and untrained in schools (A) — *Ac 4:13*

without schooling or skill (B) — *Ac 4:13*

were untrained laymen (N) — *Ac 4:13*

uneducated and untrained men (P) — *Ac 4:13*

uneducated, and common men (R) — *Ac 4:13*

Now I would not have you *i.* — *Ro 1:13*

I want you to know (A)(N)(P)(R) — *Ro 1:13*

do not want you to be unaware (B) — *Ro 1:13*

For they being *i.* of God's — *Ro 10:3*

that ye should be *i.* of this mystery — *Ro 11:25*

I would not that ye should be *i.* — *1Co 10:1*

brethren, I would not have you *i.* — *1Co 12:1*

if any man be *i.* let him be *i.* — *1Co 14:38*

if anyone disregards it, he is disregarded (A)(B) — *1Co 14:38*

if anyone does not recognize this, he should not be recognized (N)(R) — *1Co 14:38*

would not, brethren, have you *i.* — *2Co 1:8*

of us: for we are not *i.* of his devices — *2Co 2:11*

But I would not have you to be *i.* — *1Th 4:13*

i. speculations (N) — *2Ti 2:23*

Who can have compassion on the *i.* — *Heb 5:2*

For this they willingly are *i.* of one thing — *2Pe 3:5*

beloved, be not *i.* of this — *2Pe 3:8*

i. and steadfast wrest (E)(N)(R) — *2Pe 3:16*

IGNORANTLY

sins *i.* (B) — *Le 4:2; 4:13, 22, 27; Nu 15:25*

eat *i.* of (B) — *Le 22:14*

for the soul that sinneth *i.* when — *Nu 15:28*

Whoso killeth neighbour *i.* — *De 19:4*

kills his neighbor unintentionally (A) — *De 19:4*

killing is unintentional (B) — *De 19:4*

killeth his neighbor unawares (E) — *De 19:4*

i. considered him stricken (A) — *Isa 53:4*

behaved *i.* (B) — *Ac 3:17*

Whom therefore ye *i.* worship him — *Ac 17:23*

already worshiping as unknown (A) — *Ac 17:23*

you revere without knowing it (B) — *Ac 17:23*

you worship in ignorance (E)(P) — *Ac 17:23*

you worship, but you do not know (N) — *Ac 17:23*

you worship as unknown (R) — *Ac 17:23*

mercy, because I did it *i.* in unbelief — *1Ti 1:13*

IGNORES

the discerning *i.* an insult (A)(B)(R) — *Pr 12:16*

IIM

And they departed from *I.* — *Nu 33:45*

Baalah, and *I.*, and Azem — *Jos 15:29*

IJE-ABARIM

and pitched at *I.* in the — *Nu 21:11*

and pitched in *I.* in the border — *Nu 33:44*

IJON

and smote *I.*, and Dan, and — *1Ki 15:20; 2Ch 16:4*

took *I.* and Abel-beth-maachah — *2Ki 15:29*

IKKESH

Ira the son of *I.* the Tekoite — *2Sa 23:26; 1Ch 11:28*

sixth month was Ira the son of *I.* — *1Ch 27:9*

ILAI

the Hushathite, *I.* the Ahohite — *1Ch 11:29*

ILL

them out of the river, *i.* favoured — *Ge 41:3*

ugly and lean (B) — *Ge 41:3*

gaunt and thin (R) — *Ge 41:3*

the *i.* favoured and leanfleshed kine — *Ge 41:4*

up after them, poor and very *i.* — *Ge 41:19*

the lean and the *i.* favoured kine — *Ge 41:20*

they were still *i.* favoured, as at — *Ge 41:21*

the seven thin and *i.* favoured kine — *Ge 41:27*

dealt so *i.* with me, as to tell — *Ge 43:6*

did me such a wrong (A) — *Ge 43:6*

treat me so shabbily (B) — *Ge 43:6*

dealt *i.* with (A)(R) — *Nu 11:11*

Egyptians dealt *i.* with us (E) — *Nu 20:15*

blind, or have any *i.* blemish — *De 15:21*

became *i.* of the illness (A) — *1Ki 13:14*

leaving him *i.* (A) — *2Ch 24:25*

it shall go *i.* with him that is left — *Job 20:26*

so that it went *i.* with Moses — *Ps 106:32*

your *i.* repute has no end (A)(B)(E)(R) — *Pr 25:10*

it shall be *i.* with him for the — *Isa 3:11*

if it seem *i.* unto thee to come — *Jer 40:4*

if it seem bad to you to come (A) — *Jer 40:4*

seem wrong to you to come (B)(R) — *Jer 40:4*

and his *i.* savour shall come up — *Joe 2:20*

they have behaved themselves *i.* — *Mic 3:4*

made their deeds evil (A)(B)(E)(R) — *Mic 3:4*

all who were *i.* (N) — *M't 14:35*

i. or harassed by unclean spirits (N) — *Ac 5:16*

Love worketh no *i.* to his — *Ro 13:10*

it never hurts anybody (A)(P) — *Ro 13:10*

Love works no harm to his neighbor (B) — *Ro 13:10*

Love cannot wrong a neighbor (N)(R) — *Ro 13:10*

ILLEGITIMATE

not *i.* children (A)(P) — *Joh 8:41*

ILLEGITIMATELY

born *i.* (B) — *Joh 8:41*

ILLICIT

i. relations (B) — *Nu 25:1*

ILL-INFORMED

the *i.* (P)(R) — *2Pe 3:16*

ILLNESS

became ill of this *i.* (A)(B) — *1Ki 13:14*

recover of this *i.* (A) — *2Ki 1:2*

recover from this *i.* (B) — *2Ki 8:8*

this *i.* grew severe (B) — *2Ch 16:12*

i. because of wicked ways (B) — *Ps 107:17*

frequent spells of *i.* (P) — *1Ti 5:23*

ILLNESSES

took our *i.* (N) — *M't 8:17*

their *i.* were removed (B) — *Ac 19:12*

your frequent *i.* (A)(B) — *1Ti 5:23*

ILL-TREAT

if you *i.* (B)(R) — *Ge 31:50*

i. them (S) — *Ac 7:6*

ILL-TREATED

i. and killed them (B)	*M't 22:6*
they *i.* our fathers (S)	*Ac 7:19*
ill-treated (E)(P)(R)	*Heb 11:37*
those *i.* (A)(E)(R)	*Heb 13:3*

ILL-TREATMENT

ill-treatment (E)	*Heb 11:25*
suffering *i.* (A)(B)(N)	*Jas 5:10*

ILLUMINATE

lightnings *i.* world (A)(B)	*Ps 97:4*

ILLUMINATED

in which, after ye were *i.* ye	*Heb 10:32*
were first spiritually enlightened (A)	*Heb 10:32*
after enjoying the light (B)	*Heb 10:32*
after ye were enlightened (E)(N)(R)	*Heb 10:32*
when you had received the light (P)	*Heb 10:32*

ILLUMINATION

inner *i.* of spirit (P)	*Eph 1:18*

ILLUMINED

granting you *i.* eyes (B)(N)	*Eph 1:18*
once for all *i.* (B)	*Heb 6:4*

ILLUSION

blinded in world of *i.* (P)	*Eph 4:17*

ILLUSIONS

see no more *i.* (B)	*Eze 13:23*

ILLUSTRATIONS

told you in *i.* (B)	*Joh 16:25*

ILLYRICUM

and round about unto *I.,* I have	*Ro 15:19*

IMAGE

said, Let us make man in our *i.*	*Ge 1:26*
God created man in his own *i.*	*Ge 1:27*
in the *i.* of God created he him	*Ge 1:27*
in his own likeness, after his *i.*	*Ge 5:3*
for in the *i.* of God made he man	*Ge 9:6*
not make unto thee any graven *i.*	*Ex 20:4*
make you no idols nor graven *i.*	*Le 26:1*
neither rear you up a standing *i.*	*Le 26:1*
neither shall ye set up any *i.* of	*Le 26:1*
and make you a graven *i.*	*De 4:16*
a form was before my eyes (A)(B)(E)(R)	*De 4:16*
and make you a graven *i.* or	*De 4:23*
and make a graven *i.* or the	*De 4:25*
shalt not make thee any graven *i.*	*De 5:8*
they have made them a molten *i.*	*De 9:12*
shalt thou set thee up any *i.*	*De 16:22*
maketh any graven or molten *i.*	*De 27:15*
for my son, to make a graven *i.*	*J'g 17:3*
and a molten *i.:* now therefore	*J'g 17:3*
thereof a graven *i.* and a molten *i.*	*J'g 17:4*
and a graven *i.* and a molten *i.*	*J'g 18:14*
and took the graven *i.* and the	*J'g 18:17*
teraphim, and the molten *i.*	*J'g 18:17; 18:18*
and fetched the carved *i.* the ephod	*J'g 18:18*
the teraphim, and the graven *i.*	*J'g 18:25*
children of Dan set up the graven *i.*	*J'g 18:30*
them up Micah's graven *i.* which	*J'g 18:31*
Michal took an *i.* and laid it in	*1Sa 19:13*
behold, there was an *i.* in the bed	*1Sa 19:16*
she had her *i.*	*1Ki 15:13*
(A)(B)(E)(R)	
he put away the *i.* of Baal that	*2Ki 3:2*
they brake down the *i.* of Baal, and	*2Ki 10:27*
he set a graven *i.* of the grove	*2Ki 21:7*
that he made two cherubims of *i.* work	*2Ch 3:10*
two cherubim of sculptured work (B)	*2Ch 3:10*
And he set a carved *i.* the idol	*2Ch 33:7*
an *i.* was before mine eyes	*Job 4:16*
thou shalt despise their *i.*	*Ps 73:20*
despise their outward show (A)	*Ps 73:20*
despise their imaginings (B)	*Ps 73:20*
despise their phantoms (R)	*Ps 73:20*
Horeb, and worshipped the molten *i.*	*Ps 106:19*
the *i.* of a calf (A)(B)(R)	*Ps 106:20*
The workman melteth a graven *i.*	*Isa 40:19*
workman to prepare a graven *i.*	*Isa 40:20*
They that make a graven *i.* are	*Isa 44:9*
formed a god, or molten a graven *i.*	*Isa 44:10*
he maketh it a graven *i.* and falleth	*Isa 44:15*
he maketh a god, even his graven *i.*	*Isa 44:17*
set up the wood of their graven *i.*	*Isa 45:20*
hath done them, and my graven *i.*	*Isa 48:5*
and my molten *i.* hath commanded	*Isa 48:5*
is confounded by the graven *i.*	*Jer 10:14*
for his molten *i.* is falsehood	*Jer 10:14; 51:17*
is confounded by the graven *i.*	*Jer 51:17*
was the seat of the *i.* of jealousy	*Eze 8:3*
the idol of resentment (B)	*Eze 8:3*
altar this *i.* of jealousy in the entry	*Eze 8:5*
king, sawest, and behold a great *i.*	*Da 2:31*
This great *i.* whose brightness was	*Da 2:31*
which smote the *i.* upon his feet	*Da 2:34*
and the stone that smote the *i.*	*Da 2:35*
the king made an *i.* of gold	*Da 3:1*
to the dedication of the *i.* which	*Da 3:2*
unto the dedication of the *i.* that	*Da 3:3*
set up; and they stood before the *i.*	*Da 3:3*
fall down and worship the golden *i.*	*Da 3:5; 3:10*
down and worshipped the golden *i.*	*Da 3:7*
nor worship the golden *i.* which	*Da 3:12; 3:14, 18*
fall down and worship the *i.* which	*Da 3:15*
and without an *i.* and without an	*Ho 3:4*
without an idolatrous pillar (A)(B)(E)(R)	*Ho 3:4*
cut off the graven *i.* and the molten	*Na 1:14*
What profiteth the graven *i.* that	*Hab 2:18*
the molten *i.* and a teacher of lies	*Hab 2:18*
Whose is this *i.* and superscription	*M't 22:20; M'k 12:16*
whose likeness and title (A)(B)(R)	*M't 22:20*
whose head is this (N)	*M't 22:20*
whose face is this (P)	*M't 22:20*
i. and inscription (B)(N)(P)(R)	*M'k 12:16; Lu 20:24*
Whose *i.* and superscription hath	*Lu 20:24*
i. which fell down from Jupiter	*Ac 19:35*
into an *i.* made like to corruptible	*Ro 1:23*
conformed to the *i.* of his Son	*Ro 8:29*
the likeness of his Son (B)(N)(P)	*Ro 8:29*
not bowed the knee to the *i.* of Baal	*Ro 11:4*
as he is the *i.* and glory of God	*1Co 11:7*
as we have borne the *i.* of the earthy	*1Co 15:49*
the likeness of (B)	*1Co 15:49; 2Co 3:18; 4:4; Col 3:10*
also bear the *i.* of the heavenly	*1Co 15:49*
changed into the same *i.* from glory	*2Co 3:18*
gospel of Christ, who is the *i.* of God	*2Co 4:4*
Who is the *i.* of the invisible God	*Col 1:15*
after the *i.* of him that created him	*Col 3:10*
and the express *i.* of his person	*Heb 1:3*
the true expression of his being (B)	*Heb 1:3*
the stamp of God's very being (N)	*Heb 1:3*
flawless expression of nature of God (P)	*Heb 1:3*
the very stamp of his nature (R)	*Heb 1:3*
not the very image of the things	*Heb 10:1*
instead of fully expressing those (A)	*Heb 10:1*
without expressing them in reality (B)	*Heb 10:1*
did not actually reproduce them (P)	*Heb 10:1*
instead of true form of these realities (R)	*Heb 10:1*
they should make an *i.* to the beast	*Re 13:14*
erect a statue (B)(P)	*Re 13:14; 13:15; 14:9, 11; 15:2; 16:2; 19:20; 20:4*
to give life unto the *i.* of the beast	*Re 13:15*
statue of the beast (A)	*Re 13:15; 14:9; 15:2; 19:20; 20:4*
i. of the beast should both speak	*Re 13:15*
not worship the *i.* of the beast	*Re 13:15*
man worship the beast and his *i.*	*Re 14:9*
who worship the beast and his *i.*	*Re 14:11*
victory over the beast, and over his *i.*	*Re 15:2*
upon them which worshipped his *i.*	*Re 16:2*
and them that worshipped his *i.*	*Re 19:20*
worshipped the beast, neither his *i.*	*Re 20:4*

IMAGERY

man in the chambers of *i.*	*Eze 8:12*

IMAGES

Rachel had stolen the *i.*	*Ge 31:19*
stole household gods (A)(B)(R)	*Ge 31:19*
stole teraphim that were her (E)	*Ge 31:19*
Rachel had taken the *i.* and	*Ge 31:34*
he searched, but found not the *i.*	*Ge 31:35*
and quite break down their *i.*	*Ex 23:24*
break their worship pillars (B)(E)(R)	*Ex 23:24*
break their *i.* and cut down their	*Ex 34:13*
cut down your *i.* and cast your	*Le 26:30*
breakage of your idols (B)(E)(R)	*Le 26:30*
destroy all their molten *i.* and	*Nu 33:52*
and break down their *i.* and cut	*De 7:5*
and burn their graven *i.* with fire	*De 7:5*
The graven *i.* of their gods shall ye	*De 7:25*
ye shall hew down the graven *i.* of	*De 12:3*
cut down shame *i.* (B)	*J'g 6:25; 6:28*
ye shall make *i.* of your emerods	*1Sa 6:5*
and *i.* of your mice that mar	*1Sa 6:5*
of gold and the *i.* of their emerods	*1Sa 6:11*
And there they left their *i.* and	*2Sa 5:21*
abandoned their idols (B)(R)	*2Sa 5:21*
shame-*i.* remained (B)	*1Ki 13:6; 17:16; 21:3; 23:4, 6, 15*
made thee other gods, and molten	*1Ki 14:9*

molten *i.* to irritate me (B)   *1Ki 14:9*
built them high places, and *i.*   *1Ki 14:23*
high places, pillars, Asherim   *1Ki 14:23*
(A)(B)(E)(R)
forth the *i.* out of the house   *2Ki 10:26*
of Baal
pillars as obelisks (A)   *2Ki 10:26*
out the pillar of Baal   *2Ki 10:26*
(B)(E)(R)
and his *i.* brake they in   *2Ki 11:18*
pieces
they set them up *i.* and   *2Ki 17:10*
groves
made them molten *i.*, even   *2Ki 17:16*
two calves
and served their graven *i.*   *2Ki 17:41*
both
brake the *i.* and cut down the   *2Ki 18:4*
And he brake in pieces the *i.*   *2Ki 23:14*
wizards, and the *i.* and the   *2Ki 23:24*
idols
the teraphim, household   *2Ki 23:24*
gods (A)
teraphim and disgusting idols   *2Ki 23:24*
(B)(E)(R)
brake down the *i.*, and cut   *2Ch 14:3*
the pillars or obelisks, and the   *2Ch 14:3*
Asherim (A)
shattered pillars, Asherahs   *2Ch 14:3*
(B)(E)(R)
away, the high places and the   *2Ch 14:5*
i.
his altars and his *i.* in pieces   *2Ch 23:17*
and made also molten *i.* for   *2Ch 28:2*
Baalim
Judah, and brake the *i.* in   *2Ch 31:1*
pieces
and set up groves and graven   *2Ch 33:19*
i.
sacrificed unto all the carved   *2Ch 33:22*
i.
and the groves, and the   *2Ch 34:3*
carved *i.*
the groves, and the molten   *2Ch 34:3;*
i.   *34:4*
and the *i.* that were on high   *2Ch 34:4*
above
beaten the graven *i.* into   *2Ch 34:7*
powder
him to jealousy with their   *Ps 78:58*
graven *i.*
be all they that serve graven *i.*   *Ps 97:7*
and whose graven *i.* did excel   *Isa 10:10*
made, either the groves, or the *i.*   *Isa 17:8*
Asherim (sacred poles),   *Isa 17:8*
sun-images (A)(E)
images of Ashteroth,   *Isa 17:8*
sun-images (B)
the Asherim or the altars of   *Isa 17:8*
incense (R)
and all the graven *i.* of her   *Isa 21:9*
gods
the groves and *i.* shall not   *Isa 27:9*
stand
the Asherim and sun-images   *Isa 27:9*
(A)(E)
shame images and sun pillars   *Isa 27:9*
(B)
the Asherim or incense altars   *Isa 27:9*
(R)
covering of thy graven *i.* of   *Isa 30:22*
silver
ornament of thy molten *i.* of   *Isa 41:22*
gold
their molten *i.* are wind and   *Isa 41:29*
confusion
neither my praise to graven *i.*   *Isa 42:8*
ashamed, that trust in graven   *Isa 42:17*
i.
that say to the molten *i.*, Ye   *Isa 42:17*
are our
me to anger with their graven   *Jer 8:19*
i.
He shall break also the *i.* of   *Jer 43:13*
images and obelisks of   *Jer 43:13*
Heliopolis (A)
the obelisks of Bethshemesh   *Jer 43:13*
(B)
the pillars of Bethshemesh   *Jer 43:13*
(E)
confounded, her *i.* are broken   *Jer 50:2*
in
for it is the land of graven *i.*   *Jer 50:38*
upon the graven *i.* of Babylon   *Jer 51:47*
do judgment upon her graven   *Jer 51:52*
i.
your *i.* shall be broken: and I   *Eze 6:4*
will
your sun-pillars shall be broken   *Eze 6:4*
(A)

your incense altars shall be   *Eze 6:4*
broken (B)(R)
your sun-images shall be   *Eze 6:4*
broken (E)
and your *i.* may be cut down   *Eze 6:6*
sun images may be hewn down   *Eze 6:6*
(A)(B)(E)
your incense altars cut down   *Eze 6:6*
(R)
made the *i.* of their   *Eze 7:20*
abominations
and madest to thyself *i.* of   *Eze 16:17*
men, and
he consulted with *i.*, he   *Eze 21:21*
looked in
consults the teraphim   *Eze 21:21*
(A)(B)(E)(R)
the *i.* of the Chaldeans   *Eze 23:14*
pourtrayed
pictures of the Chaldeans   *Eze 23:14*
(A)
figures like those of the   *Eze 23:14*
Chaldeans (B)
cause their *i.* to cease out of   *Eze 30:13*
Noph
his land they have made   *Ho 10:1*
goodly *i.*
goodly pillars or obelisks (A)   *Ho 10:1*
he made his sacred pillars (B)   *Ho 10:1*
made goodly pillars (E)   *Ho 10:1*
he improved his pillars (R)   *Ho 10:1*
their altars, he shall spoil their   *Ho 10:2*
i.
destroy their idolatrous pillars   *Ho 10:2*
(A)
their sacred stones he will   *Ho 10:2*
destroy (B)
he will destroy their pillars   *Ho 10:2*
(E)(R)
and burned incense to graven   *Ho 11:2*
i.
and have made them molten *i.*   *Ho 13:2*
of their
Moloch and Chiun your *i.* the   *Am 5:26*
all the graven *i.* thereof shall   *Mic 1:7*
be
Thy graven *i.* also will I cut   *Mic 5:13*
off
and thy standing *i.* out of the   *Mic 5:13*
midst

IMAGE'S

this *i.* head was of fine gold   *Da 2:32*

IMAGINATION

every *i.* of the thoughts of his   *Ge 6:5*
intention of all human thinking   *Ge 6:5*
produced nothing but evil (B)
the *i.* of man's heart is evil   *Ge 8:21*
from
he is evil-minded from his   *Ge 8:21*
youth (B)
I walk in the *i.* of mine heart   *De 29:19*
congratulates himself in his   *De 29:19*
heart (B)
bless himself in his heart   *De 29:19*
(E)(R)
for I know their *i.* which they   *De 31:21*
go
the thoughts they are forming   *De 31:21*
(B)
their purposes they are   *De 31:21*
already forming (R)
keep this for ever in the *i.* of   *1Ch 29:18*
the thoughts of the people's   *1Ch 29:18*
hearts (B)(R)
after the *i.* of their evil heart   *Jer 3:17*
and in the *i.* of their evil heart   *Jer 7:24*
the *i.* of their own heart, and   *Jer 9:14*
after
one in the *i.* of their evil heart   *Jer 11:8*
walk in the *i.* of their heart   *Jer 13:10*
one after the *i.* of his evil   *Jer 16:12*
heart
every one do the *i.* of his evil   *Jer 18:12*
heart
after the *i.* of his own heart   *Jer 23:17*
walks after stubbornness of   *Jer 23:17*
mind (A)(B)(E)
stubbornly follows his own   *Jer 23:17*
heart (R)
proud in the *i.* of their hearts   *Lu 1:51*
struck with sheer *i.* (P)   *Lu 24:11*
contrived by human art or *i.*   *Ac 17:29*
(P)(R)
followed impulse and *i.* of evil   *Eph 2:3*
nature (P)

IMAGINATIONS

all the *i.* of the thoughts: if   *1Ch 28:9*
thou
all wanderings of the thoughts   *1Ch 28:9*
(A)
every development of   *1Ch 28:9*
thoughts (B)
understands every plan and   *1Ch 28:9*
thought (R)
An heart that deviseth wicked *i.*   *Pr 6:18*
manufactures wicked thoughts   *Pr 6:18*
and plans (A)
deviseth wicked schemes (B)   *Pr 6:18*
deviseth wicked purposes (E)   *Pr 6:18*
devises wicked plans (R)   *Pr 6:18*
and all their *i.* against me   *La 3:60*
all their devices   *La 3:60;*
(A)(B)(E)(R)   *3:61*
Lord, and all their *i.* against   *La 3:61*
me
became vain in their *i.* and   *Ro 1:21*
their
with vain imaginings (A)   *Ro 1:21*
indulged in useless   *Ro 1:21*
speculations (B)
became vain in reasonings (E)   *Ro 1:21*
misguided minds plunged into   *Ro 1:21*
darkness (N)
became fatuous in   *Ro 1:21*
argumentations (P)
became futile in thinking (R)   *Ro 1:21*
Casting down *i.* and every   *2Co 10:5*
high
refute arguments, theories,   *2Co 10:5*
reasonings (A)
tear down calculations (B)   *2Co 10:5*
we demolish sophistries (N)   *2Co 10:5*
bring down every deceptive   *2Co 10:5*
fantasy (P)
every proud obstacle to   *2Co 10:5*
knowledge (R)

IMAGINE

Do ye *i.* to reprove words   *Job 6:26*
the devices which ye   *Job 21:27*
wrongfully *i.*
devices with which you   *Job 21:27*
would (A)(E)
schemes to do me wrong   *Job 21:27*
(B)(R)
and the people *i.* a vain thing   *Ps 2:1*
devise an empty scheme (A)(B)   *Ps 2:1*
meditate a vain thing (E)   *Ps 2:1*
peoples plot in vain (R)   *Ps 2:1*
and *i.* deceits all the day long   *Ps 38:12*
meditate treachery and deceit   *Ps 38:12*
(A)
think up treacheries all day   *Ps 38:12*
(B)
meditate deceits all day (E)   *Ps 38:12*
meditate treachery all day (R)   *Ps 38:12*
i. the worst for me (R)   *Ps 41:7*
will ye *i.* mischief against a   *Ps 62:3*
man
Which *i.* mischiefs in their   *Ps 140:2*
heart
devise mischiefs in heart   *Ps 140:2*
(A)(E)
hearts devise evil plots (B)   *Ps 140:2*
plan evil things in hearts (R)   *Ps 140:2*
in the heart of them that *i.* evil   *Pr 12:20*
who devise evil (A)(E)(R)   *Pr 12:20*
who plan evil (B)   *Pr 12:20*
yet do they *i.* mischief against   *Ho 7:15*
devise evil against me (A)(R)   *Ho 7:15*
they think only evil (B)   *Ho 7:15*
devise mischief against me (E)   *Ho 7:15*
What do ye *i.* against the Lord   *Na 1:9*
attempt to plot aganst (A)(R)   *Na 1:9*
your plotting is against (B)   *Na 1:9*
devise against Jehovah (E)   *Na 1:9*
you *i.* evil against his brother   *Zec 7:10*
think evil in his heart (B)   *Zec 7:10*
devise evil against brother   *Zec 7:10*
(E)(R)
none of you *i.* evil in your   *Zec 8:17*
hearts
rage, and the people *i.* vain   *Ac 4:25*
things
people devise vain things (B)   *Ac 4:25*
lay their plots in vain (N)   *Ac 4:25*

IMAGINED

them, which they have *i.* to do   *Ge 11:6*
nothing they plan to do (B)   *Ge 11:6*
nothing they purpose to do   *Ge 11:6*
(E)

nothing they propose to do   *Ge 11:6*
(R)
in the devices that they have *i.*   *Ps 10:2*
the schemes they have devised   *Ps 10:2*
(A)(B)(R)
the devises they have conceived   *Ps 10:2*
(E)
they *i.* a mischievous device   *Ps 21:11*
they conceived a mischievous   *Ps 21:11*
plot (A)
they have devised a plot (B)   *Ps 21:11*
they conceived a devise (E)   *Ps 21:11*
they devise mischief (R)   *Ps 21:11*

IMAGINETH

that *i.* evil against the Lord   *Na 1:11*
who plots evil against the Lord   *Na 1:11*
(A)
a plotter of evil against the   *Na 1:11*
Lord (B)
that deviseth evil against   *Na 1:11*
Jehovah (E)
who plotted evil against the   *Na 1:11*
Lord (R)

IMAGININGS

despise their *i.* (B)   *Ps 73:20*
with vain *i.* (A)   *Ro 1:21*
inflated by unspiritual *i.* (P)   *Col 2:18*

IMITATE

i. their faith (P)(R)   *Heb 13:7*

IMITATION

have no *i.* love (P)   *Ro 12:9*

IMLA

the same is Micaiah the son   *2Ch 18:7*
of *I.*
quickly Micaiah the son of *I.*   *2Ch 18:8*

IMLAH

one man, Micaiah the son of   *1Ki 22:8*
I.
hither Micaiah the son of *I.*   *1Ki 22:9*

IMMANUEL

a son, and shall call his name   *Isa 7:14*
I.
fill the breadth of the land, O *I.*   *Isa 8:8*

IMMATURE

i. and faithhearted (B)   *2Ch 13:7*
teacher of *i.* (B)(N)   *Ro 2:20*
is obviously *i.* (P)   *Heb 5:13*

IMMEDIATELY

immediately (S)   *1Sa 9:13;*
28:20;   M't 13:20-21;   Ac 5:10;   9:20;
16:33;   22:29;   23:30;   Jas 1:24
And they *i.* left the ship, and   *M't 4:22*
And *i.* his leprosy was cleansed   *M't 8:3*
And *i.* Jesus stretched forth   *M't 14:31*
his
i. their eyes received sight   *M't 20:34*
i. after the tribulation of   *M't 24:29*
those
the man. And *i.* the cock   *M't 26:74*
crew
i. the spirit driveth him into   *M'k 1:12*
i. his fame spread abroad   *M'k 1:28*
i. the fever left her, and she   *M'k 1:31*
i. the leprosy departed from   *M'k 1:42*
him
i. when Jesus perceived in his   *M'k 2:8*
And *i.* he arose, took up the   *M'k 2:12*
bed
and *i.* it sprang up, because it   *M'k 4:5*
Satan cometh *i.* and taketh   *M'k 4:15*
away
word, *i.* receive it with   *M'k 4:16*
gladness
word's sake, *i.* they are   *M'k 4:17*
offended
i. he putteth in the sickle   *M'k 4:29*
i. there met him out of the   *M'k 5:2*
tombs
Jesus, *i.* knowing in himself   *M'k 5:30*
that
i. the king sent an executioner   *M'k 6:27*

i. he talked with them, and   *M'k 6:50*
saith
And *i.* he received his sight   *M'k 10:52*
And *i.* while he yet spake   *M'k 14:43*
And his mouth was opened *i.*   *Lu 1:64*
i. she arose and ministered   *Lu 4:39*
unto
i. the leprosy departed from   *Lu 5:13*
him
And *i.* he rose up before them   *Lu 5:25*
beat vehemently, and *i.* it fell   *Lu 6:49*
and *i.* her issue of blood   *Lu 8:44*
stanched
him, and how she was healed *i.*   *Lu 8:47*
they may open unto him *i.*   *Lu 12:36*
and *i.* she was made straight   *Lu 13:13*
And *i.* he received his sight   *Lu 18:43*
kingdom of God should *i.*   *Lu 19:11*
appear
peace, the stones would *i.* cry   *Lu 19:40*
out
And *i.* while he yet spake, the   *Lu 22:60*
i. the man was made whole   *Joh 5:9*
i. the ship was at the land   *Joh 6:21*
received the sop went *i.* out   *Joh 13:30*
again: and *i.* the cock crew   *Joh 18:27*
and *i.* came out blood and   *Joh 19:34*
water (S)
forth, and entered into a ship   *Joh 21:3*
i.
and *i.* his feet and ancle bones   *Ac 3:7*
i. there fell from his eyes as it   *Ac 9:18*
make thy bed. And he arose *i.*   *Ac 9:34*
I. therefore I sent to thee; and   *Ac 10:33*
i. there were three men   *Ac 11:11*
already
and *i.* the angel departed (S)   *Ac 12:10*
And *i.* the angel of the Lord   *Ac 12:23*
smote
And *i.* there fell on him a mist   *Ac 13:11*
i. we endeavoured to go into   *Ac 16:10*
and *i.* all the doors were   *Ac 16:26*
opened
the brethren *i.* sent away Paul   *Ac 17:10*
i. the brethren sent away Paul   *Ac 17:14*
Who *i.* took soldiers and   *Ac 21:32*
i. I conferred not with flesh   *Ga 1:16*
And *i.* I was in the spirit: and   *Re 4:2*

IMMENSE

i. wealth of every kind   *Eze 27:18*
(A)(B)(R)

IMMER

son of Meshillemith, the son   *1Ch 9:12;*
of *I.*   *Ne 11:13*
to Bilgah, the sixteenth to *I.*   *1Ch 24:14*
The children of *I.* a thousand   *Ezr 2:37*
fifty
Tel-harsa, Cherub, Addan,   *Ezr 2:59*
and *I.*
of the sons of *I.*; Hanani   *Ezr 10:20*
them repaired Zadok the son   *Ne 3:29*
of *I.*
The children of *I.*, a thousand   *Ne 7:40*
fifty
Tel-haresha, Cherub, Addon,   *Ne 7:61*
and *I.*
Now Pashur the son of *I.* the   *Jer 20:1*
priest

IMMIGRANT

came here an an *i.* (B)   *Ge 19:9*
you are an *i.* (B)   *Ge 21:23*
a stranger and an *i.* (B)   *Ge 23:4*
violate rights of *i.* (B)   *De 24:17*
the *i.* homes (B)   *Eze 47:23*

IMMIGRANTS

immigrants (B)   *Ge 36:7;*
De 10:19; 24:14; Ps 46:9; Eze 47:22
Lord protects the *i.* (B)   *Ps 145:20*
i. who reside (B)   *Eze 47:22*
strangers and *i.* (B)   *Eph 2:19*

IMMORAL

like the *i.* pack in Israel (B)   *2Sa 13:13*
were *i.* in practices (B)   *Ps 106:39*
don't mix with the *i.* (P)   *1Co 5:11*
no *i.* or unclean person (P)(R)   *Eph 5:5*
for *i.* persons (A)(P)   *1Ti 1:10*
i. and worldly minded (N)   *Heb 12:16*
i. or irreligious (R)   *Heb 12:16*
the *i.* and adulterers (R)   *Heb 13:4*

by *i.* behavior (B)   *2Pe 2:7*
appeal to *i.* passions (B)   *2Pe 2:18*

IMMORALITY

all sexual *i.* (P)   *Ac 15:20*
immorality (B)   *Ro 1:29*
not in *i.* and debauchery   *Ro 13:13*
(A)(S)
sexual *i.* (A)(B)(N)(P)(R)   *1Co 5:1*
immorality (P)(R)   *2Co 12:21*
i., sexual vice (A)(P)(R)   *Eph 5:2*
sexual *i.* (P)   *Eph 5:3*
clean from sexual *i.* (P)(R)   *1Th 4:3*
pervert grace into *i.* (A)(P)   *Jude 4*
abandoned to sexual *i.* (B)(P)   *Jude 7;*
   Jude 8
her *i.* (A)(P)(R)   *Re 2:21*
wine of *i.* (B)   *Re 17:2*

IMMORALLY

acted *i.* (R)   *Jude 7*

IMMORTAL

raised *i.* (N)(R)   *1Co 15:42; 15:53*
Now unto the King eternal, *i.*   *1Ti 1:17*
i., unsullied, unfading (B)   *1Pe 1:4*

IMMORTALITY

glory and honour and *i.*, eternal   *Ro 2:7*
not in *i.* (A)   *Ro 13:13*
perishable cannot possess *i.*   *1Co 15:50*
(N)
and this mortal must put on   *1Co 15:53*
i.
this mortal shall have put on   *1Co 15:54*
i.
Who only hath *i.* dwelling   *1Ti 6:16*
in the
hath brought life and *i.* to   *2Ti 1:10*
light

IMMUTABILITY

the *i.* of his counsel,   *Heb 6:17*
confirmed it
unchangeableness of purpose   *Heb 6:17*
(A)(B)
how unchanging was his   *Heb 6:17*
purpose (N)
his plan was unchangeable   *Heb 6:17*
(P)
unchangeable character of   *Heb 6:17*
purpose (R)

IMMUTABLE

That by two *i.* things, in   *Heb 6:18*
which it
by two unchangeable things   *Heb 6:18*
(A)(R)
by two unalterable facts (B)   *Heb 6:18*
Here are two irrevocable facts   *Heb 6:18*
(N)

IMNA

Zophah, and *I.* and Shelesh   *1Ch 7:35*

IMNAH

sons of Asher; *I.* and Ishuah   *1Ch 7:30*
And Kore the son of *I.* the   *2Ch 31:14*
Levite

IMPACT

i. of teaching (P)   *Ro 6:17*

IMPAIR

i. the revenue of kings (S)   *Ezr 4:13*

IMPALED

let him be *i.* thereon (S)   *Ezr 6:11*

IMPART

let him *i.* to him that hath none   *Lu 3:11*
let him share with him   *Lu 3:11*
(A)(B)(N)(P)(R)
i. unto you some spiritual gift   *Ro 1:11*
bestow upon you some spiritual   *Ro 1:11*
(B)
bring to you some spiritual gift   *Ro 1:11*
(N)(P)

IMPARTED

hath he *i.* to her　　　　　　*Job 39:17*
understanding
were willing to have *i.* unto　　*1Th 2:8*
you

IMPARTIAL

you must be *i.* (B)　　　　　　*De 16:19*
i. and unfeigned (A)(B)　　　　*Jas 3:17*

IMPARTIALITY

act with strict *i.* (N)(P)　　　　*1Ti 5:21*
judges each *i.* (A)(B)(N)(R)　　*1Pe 1:17*

IMPATIENT

he became *i.* (R)　　　　　　　*Nu 21:4*
you are *i.* (R)　　　　　　　　*Job 4:5*
why not be *i.* (B)(R)　　　　　*Job 21:4*

IMPEDED

deficient and *i.* speech (A)　　*Ex 6:12;*
　　　　　　　　　　　　　　6:30

IMPEDIMENT

deaf, and had an *i.* in his　　　*M'k 7:32*
speech
had difficulty in speaking (A)　*M'k 7:32*
hard of speech (B)　　　　　　*M'k 7:32*
unable to speak intelligibly　　*M'k 7:32*
(P)

IMPENITENT

But, after thy hardness and *i.*　*Ro 2:5*
heart

IMPERIAL

the whole *i.* guard (A)(B)　　*Ph'p 1:13*

IMPERIOUS

the work of an *i.* whorish　　*Eze 16:30*
woman
work of a bold, domineering　*Eze 16:30*
harlot (A)
doings of a brazenfaced　　　*Eze 16:30*
harlot (B)
work of an impudent harlot　*Eze 16:30*
(E)
the deeds of a brazen harlot　*Eze 16:30*
(R)

IMPERISHABLE

an *i.* crown (B)(R)　　　　　　*1Co 9:25*
raised *i.* (A)　*1Co 15:42; 15:50, 53-54*
imperishable (R)　　　　　　　*1Co 15:42*
raised *i.* (A)(B)(R)　　　　　　*1Co 15:52*
i., undefiled, unfading (B)　　*1Pe 1:4*
i. qualities of the spirit (B)(R)　*1Pe 3:4*

IMPIETY

i. and wickedness (B)　　　　*Ro 1:18*

IMPIOUS

the *i.* scoff at thee (R)　　　　*Ps 74:22*
the *i.* and sinful (B)(E)(N)　　*1Pe 4:18;*
　　　　　　　　　　　　　　Jude 4
the *i.* (R)　　　　　　　　　　*Jude 15*
the *i.* passions (B)(R)　　　　*Jude 18*

IMPLACABLE

without natural affection, *i.*　*Ro 1:31*
conscienceless, faithless,　　*Ro 1:31*
heartless, and loveless (A)
without conscience, fidelity　*Ro 1:31*
(B)(N)
foolish, faithless, heartless (R)　*Ro 1:31*

IMPLANTED

i. and rooted (A)(B)(E)(R)　　*Jas 1:21*

IMPLEAD

deputies: let them *i.* one　　*Ac 19:38*
another
let them bring charges against　*Ac 19:38*
(A)(B)(R)
let them accuse one another　*Ac 19:38*
(E)

let the parties bring their　　　*Ac 19:38*
charges and counter-charges
(N)
let them bring legal action　　*Ac 19:38*
(P)

IMPLEMENT

carry an *i.* (B)　　　　　　　*M'k 11:16*

IMPLEMENTED

personally *i.* promises (P)　　*Ro 15:8*

IMPLEMENTS

i. of violence (B)　　　　　　*Ge 49:5*
i. of foolish shepherd　　　　*Zec 11:15*
(A)(R)
i. of righteousness (B)(N)　　*Ro 6:13*

IMPLORE

I solemnly *i.* (A)　*M'k 5:7; Ac 19:13*
began to *i.* him (S)　　　　　*M'k 5:17*

IMPLORED

the devil *i.* him (S)　　　　　*M'k 5:18*
i. that no further (B)　　　　*Heb 12:19*

IMPORTANT

who makes you *i.* (N)　　　　*1Co 4:7*

IMPORTUNE

i. your neighbor (R)(S)　　　*Pr 6:3*

IMPORTUNITY

yet because of his *i.* he will rise　*Lu 11:8*
because of his shameless　　　*Lu 11:8*
persistence and insistence (A)
on account of his brazen　　　*Lu 11:8*
insistence (B)
very shamelessness of the　　*Lu 11:8*
request (N)
yet if he persists (P)　　　　　*Lu 11:8*

IMPOSE

it shall not be lawful to *i.* toll　*Ezr 7:24*
shall not have to pay taxes　　*Ezr 7:24*
(B)
i. a fine (B)(R)　　　　　　　*Pr 17:26*
i. on her torture (B)(R)　　　*Pr 18:7*

IMPOSED

i. himself upon (N)　　　　　*Lu 15:15*
i. on them until the time of　*Heb 9:10*

IMPOSSIBLE

will a pure heart be *i.* (B)　　*Ho 8:5*
and nothing shall be *i.* unto　*M't 17:20*
you
With men this is *i.*; but with　*M't 19:26*
God
With men it is *i.* but not　　*M'k 10:27*
with God
with God nothing shall be *i.*　*Lu 1:37*
is *i.* but that offences will come　*Lu 17:1*
things which are *i.* with men　*Lu 18:27*
are
For it is *i.* for those who were　*Heb 6:4*
once
in which it was *i.* for God to　*Heb 6:18*
lie
without faith it is *i.* to please　*Heb 11:6*
him

IMPOSTER

you *i.* and charlatan (N)　　*Ac 13:10*

IMPOSTERS

i. shall go from bad　　　　　*2Ti 3:13*
(A)(B)(E)(R)

IMPOTENT

lay a great multitude of *i.* folk　*Joh 5:3*
The *i.* man answered him, Sir, I　*Joh 5:7*
the good deed done to the *i.*　*Ac 4:9*
man
certain man at Lystra, *i.* in his　*Ac 14:8*
feet
i. and useless (E)(N)　　　　*Heb 7:18*

IMPOVERISH

called us to *i.* us (S)　　　　*J'g 14:5*
they shall *i.* thy fenced cities　*Jer 5:17*

IMPOVERISHED

And Israel was greatly *i.*　　*J'g 6:6*
because
is so *i.* that he hath no　　　*Isa 40:20*
oblation
Whereas, Edom saith, We are *i.*　*Mal 1:4*

IMPRISONED

know that I *i.* and beat in　　*Ac 22:19*
every

IMPRESS

i. fellowmen with　　　　　　*Lu 16:15*
righteousness (N)
love not anxious to *i.* (P)　　*1Co 13:4*

IMPRISONED

i. by sin (A)(B)(P)　　　　　*Ga 3:22*

IMPRISONMENT

or to confiscation of goods,　*Ezr 7:26*
or to *i.*
yea, moreover of bonds and　*Heb 11:36*
i.

IMPRISONMENTS

In stripes, in *i.*, in tumults, in　*2Co 6:5*

IMPROPER

offered *i.* fire (R)　　　　*Nu 3:4; 26:61*
i. conduct (R)　　　　　　　*Ro 1:28*

IMPROVE

the hour he began to *i.* (S)　*Joh 4:52*

IMPROVEMENT

we pray for your *i.* (R)　　　*2Co 13:9*

IMPUDENCE

i. and ugly heart (B)　　　　*1Sa 17:28*

IMPUDENT

kissed him, and with an *i.* face　*Pr 7:13*
i. children and stiff hearted　*Eze 2:4*
i. and hard of heart　　　　*Eze 2:4*
(A)(B)(R)
all the house of Israel are *i.*　*Eze 3:7*
work of an *i.* harlot (E)　　*Eze 16:30*

IMPULSE

not act on own *i.* (B)　　　　*Nu 16:28*
followed *i.* and imaginations of　*Eph 2:3*
evil nature (P)
where *i.* of helmsman (A)(E)　*Jas 3:4*

IMPULSES

obeying *i.* of flesh (A)　　　*Eph 2:3*
all sorts of *i.* (B)(R)　　　　*2Ti 3:6*

IMPURE

every thing *i.* (A)　　　　　*M't 23:27*
i. motives (B)　　　　　　　*Eph 4:19*
i. godless fictions (A)　　　*1Ti 4:7*
wine of her *i.* passion (R)　　*Re 14:8*
the impure (P)　　　　　　　*Re 22:15*

IMPURITIES

all *i.* burned up (B)　　　　*Eze 24:13*
cleansed from all *i.* (B)　　*Eze 36:25*
full of offences, *i.*, lewdness　*Re 17:4*
(B)(R)

IMPURITY

days of her *i.* (E)　　　　　*Le 12:2*
her *i.* be upon him (S)　　　*Le 15:24*
the days of her *i.* (E)(R)　　*Le 15:25*
sick of her *i.* (S)　　　　　　*Le 15:33*
water of his *i.* (A)(E)(R)　　*Nu 19:9;*
　　　　　　　　　　　19:21; 31:23

unclean from her *i.*   *Eze 22:16*
(B)(E)(R)
impurity (B)   *M't 23:27;*
Ro 1:24;   6:19;   2Co 12:21;   Ga 5:19;
Eph 4:19;   5:3;   Col 3:5
all sexual *i.* (A)   *Ac 15:20*
gave them up to sexual *i.*   *Ro 1:24*
(A)(R)
to *i.* (A)(N)   *Ro 6:19;*
2Co 12:21;   Ga 5:19;   Eph 4:19;   5:3;
Col 3:5
not sorry for *i.* (P)   *2Co 12:21*
impurity (N)(P)   *Ga 5:19;   1Th 4:7*
any form of *i.* (P)   *Eph 4:19;   1Th 4:7*
i., every evil (P)   *Jas 1:21*
gave themselves to *i.* (A)   *Jude 7*
earth's foul *i.* (P)   *Re 17:4*
practice *i.* (A)   *Re 22:15*

IMPUTE

king *i.* any thing unto his   *1Sa 22:15*
servant
let not king accuse servant   *1Sa 22:15*
(B)
Let not my Lord *i.* iniquity   *2Sa 19:19*
unto
do not hold me guilty   *2Sa 19:19*
(B)(R)
to whom the Lord will not *i.* sin   *Ro 4:8*
take no account or reckon (A)   *Ro 4:8*
Lord will take no account (B)   *Ro 4:8*
Lord will not reckon   *Ro 4:8*
sin (E)(P)(N)
Lord does not count against   *Ro 4:8*
(N)

IMPUTED

it be *i.* unto him that offereth it   *Le 7:18*
neither be credited to him   *Le 7:18*
(A)(R)
it will be no credit to him (B)   *Le 7:18*
blood shall be *i.* unto that man   *Le 17:4*
he
shall be counted guilty (B)   *Le 17:4*
might be *i.* unto them also   *Ro 4:11*
righteousness might be   *Ro 4:11*
accredited (B)
righteousness reckoned to   *Ro 4:11*
them (E)(R)
righteousness is counted to   *Ro 4:11*
them (N)
therefore it was *i.* to him for   *Ro 4:22*
faith was credited to him (A)   *Ro 4:22;*
4:23
it was accredited to him (B)   *Ro 4:22;*
4:23
it was reckoned to him   *Ro 4:22;*
(E)(P)(R)   *4:23*
faith was counted to him (N)   *Ro 4:22;*
4:23
sake alone, that it was *i.* to   *Ro 4:23*
him
to whom it shall be *i.* if we   *Ro 4:24*
believe
granted and accredited to us   *Ro 4:24*
(A)(B)
shall be reckoned (E)(P)(R)   *Ro 4:24*
shall be counted in the same   *Ro 4:24*
way (N)
sin is not *i.* when there is no   *Ro 5:13*
law
sin is not charged to men's   *Ro 5:13*
account (A)
sin is not charged up (B)   *Ro 5:13*
no reckoning is kept of sin   *Ro 5:13*
(N)
sin is not counted where no   *Ro 5:13*
law (R)
and it was *i.* unto him for   *Jas 2:23*

IMPUTETH

whom the Lord *i.* not iniquity   *Ps 32:2*
the Lord does not charge   *Ps 32:2*
iniquity (B)
unto whom God *i.* righteousness   *Ro 4:6*
whom God credits righteousness   *Ro 4:6*
(A)
whom God attributes   *Ro 4:6*
righteousness (B)
God reckoneth righteousness   *Ro 4:6*
without (P)
whom God counts as just (N)   *Ro 4:6*
whom God accounts righteous   *Ro 4:6*
(P)
to whom God reckons   *Ro 4:6*
righteousness (R)

IMPUTING

offend, *i.* this his power unto   *Hab 1:11*
his God
not *i.* their trespasses unto   *2Co 5:19*
them
not counting up and holding   *2Co 5:19*
against (A)
not counting up their sins   *2Co 5:19*
against (B)(R)
not reckoning unto them their   *2Co 5:19*
(E)
no longer holding misdeeds   *2Co 5:19*
against (P)

IMRAH

and Shual, and Beri, and *I.*   *1Ch 7:36*

IMRI

the son of *I.* the son of Bani   *1Ch 9:4*
them builded Zaccur the son of   *Ne 3:2*
I.

IN

I. the beginning God created   *Ge 1:1*
heaven
whose seed is *i.* itself   *Ge 1:11*
because that *i.* it he had rested   *Ge 2:3*
tree *i.* the midst of the garden   *Ge 3:3*
i. the day ye eat thereof   *Ge 3:5; 2:17*
I. the day that God created man   *Ge 5:1*
before me *i.* this generation   *Ge 7:1*
i. the image of God made he   *Ge 9:6*
man
after their families, *i.* their   *Ge 10:5;*
nations   *10:20, 32*
if ye walk *i.* my statutes   *Le 26:3*
rain *i.* due season   *Le 26:4*
sow your seed *i.* vain   *Le 26:16; 26:20*
i. counsel, *i.* the way, *i.*   *Ps 1:1*
the seat
delight is *i.* the law of the Lord   *Ps 1:2*
dwelleth *i.* secret place of most   *Ps 90:1*
High
i. the day of   *Isa 1:1;*
          Jer 1:2; Ho 1:1; Am 1:1
arise with healing *i.* his wings   *Mal 4:2*
appeared unto him *i.* a dream   *M't 1:20;*
          2:12
come *i.* my name, saying, I am   *M't 24:5*
Christ
I. the beginning was the Word   *Joh 1:1;*
          1:2
I. him was life, and the life was   *Joh 1:4*
light
Son of man which is *i.* heaven   *Joh 3:13*
whosoever believeth *i.* him   *Joh 3:15;*
          3:16, 18
shall be *i.* him a well of water   *Joh 4:14*
dwelleth *i.* me, and I *i.* him   *Joh 6:56*
ye believe *i.* God, believe also   *Joh 14:1*
i. me
I. my father's house are many   *Joh 14:2*
mansions
I am *i.* the Father, the   *Joh 14:10;*
Father *i.* me   *14:11*
whatsoever ye ask, *i.* my   *Joh 14:13;*
name   *14:14; 16:23-26*
dwelleth with you, shall be *i.*   *Joh 14:17*
you
Comforter the father will   *Joh 14:26*
send *i.* my name
Every branch *i.* me. Abide   *Joh 15:2;*
i. me   *15:4-6*
If ye abide *i.* me, and my   *Joh 15:7*
words abide *i.* you
abide *i.* my love, abide *i.* his   *Joh 15:10*
love
i. the name of Jesus Christ   *Ac 2:38;*
          3:16, 16; 9:29
promised by prophets *i.* the holy   *Ro 1:2*
scriptures
by continuance *i.* well doing   *Ro 2:7*
seek for
rejoice *i.* hope of the glory of   *Ro 5:2*
God
glory *i.* tribulations also   *Ro 5:3*
love of God shed abroad *i.* our   *Ro 5:5*
hearts
we should walk *i.* newness of   *Ro 6:4*
life
righteousness fulfilled *i.* us who   *Ro 8:4*
walk not
they that are *i.* the flesh cannot   *Ro 8:8*
please
ye are not *i.* the flesh, but *i.* the   *Ro 8:9*
Spirit

Christ be *i.* you, Spirit   *Ro 8:10;*
dwelleth *i.* you   *8:9*
if any man be *i.* Christ, he is   *2Co 5:17*
a new
the faithful *i.* Christ Jesus   *Eph 1:1*
I. whom we have redemption   *Eph 1:7*
I. whom ye also trusted   *Eph 1:13*
created *i.* righteousness and   *Eph 4:24*
true holiness
the dead *i.* Christ shall rise   *1Th 4:16*
first
But let him ask *i.* faith, nothing   *Jas 1:6*
But if we walk *i.* the light, as he   *1Jo 1:7*
his seed remaineth *i.* him   *1Jo 3:9*
hath part *i.* the first   *Re 20:6*
resurrection
may enter *i.* through the gates   *Re 22:14*
the things written *i.* this book   *Re 22:19*

INACTIVE

my mind is *i.* (P)   *1Co 14:14*
faith is *i.,* ineffective (A)   *Jas 2:20*

INARTICULATE

through our *i.* groans the Spirit   *Ro 8:26*
pleads (N)

INASMUCH

of death, *i.* as he hated him not   *De 19:6*
I. as thou followedst not young   *Ru 3:10*
I. as ye have done it unto one   *M't 25:40*
I. as ye did it not to one of   *M't 25:45*
i. as I am the apostle of the   *Ro 11:13*
i. as both in my bonds, and in   *Ph'p 1:7*
i. as he who hath builded the   *Heb 3:3*
And *i.* as not without an oath   *Heb 7:20*
i. as ye are partakers of   *1Pe 4:13*
Christ's

INAUGURATED

law was *i.* in (P)   *Ga 3:19*
i. and ratified   *Heb 9:18*
(A)(B)(N)(R)

INCALCULABLE

the *i.* riches of Christ (A)(P)   *Eph 3:8*

INCENSE

for anointing oil, and for sweet   *Ex 25:6*
i.
make an altar to burn *i.* upon   *Ex 30:1;*
30:7-8, 27; 31:8; 35:15; 37:25; 40:5;
Le 4:7; 1Sa 2:28; 1Ki 13:1; 1Ch 6:49;
          28:18; 2Ch 26:16, 18-19; 29:11
sweet *i.*   *Ex 30:7;*
31:11; 35:8; 35:15, 28; 39:38; 40:27
          Le 16:12; Nu 4:16; 2Ch 2:4; 13:11
perpetual *i.*   *Ex 30:8*
strange *i.*   *Ex 30:9*
an *i.,* a perfume (E)(R)   *Ex 30:35*
pure *i.*   *Ex 37:29*
golden spoon full of *i.*   *Nu 7:14;*
7:20, 26, 32, 38, 44, 50, 56, 62, 68, 74,
          80, 86
put *i.* in them before the Lord   *Nu 16:7*
man his censer, and put *i.*   *Nu 16:17*
them
fire in them, and laid *i.*   *Nu 16:18*
thereon
hundred and fifty men that   *Nu 16:35*
offered *i.*
near to offer *i.* before the   *Nu 16:40*
Lord
from off the altar, and put on   *Nu 16:46*
i.
put on *i.* and made an   *Nu 16:47*
atonement
they shall put *i.* before thee   *De 33:10*
burnt *i.*   *1Ki 3:3;*
9:25; 11:8; 12:33; 22:43; 2Ki 12:3; 14:4;
15:4, 35; 16:4; 17:11; 18:4; 22:17; 23:5,
8; 2Ch 25:14; 28:3-4, 25; 29:7; Jer 44:21,
          23
stood by the altar to burn *i.*   *1Ki 13:1*
high places that burn *i.* upon   *1Ki 13:2*
thee
all the altars for *i.* took they   *2Ch 30:14*
away
one altar, and burn *i.* upon it   *2Ch 32:12*
and have burned *i.* unto   *2Ch 34:25*
other gods
of fatlings, with the *i.* of rams   *Ps 66:15*
prayer be set forth before thee   *Ps 141:2*
as *i.*

i. is an abomination unto me   *Isa 1:13*
offering, nor wearied thee   *Isa 43:23*
with *i.*
they shall bring gold and *i.*   *Isa 60:6*
burneth *i.* upon altars of brick *Isa 65:3*
burned *i.* upon the mountains *Isa 65:7*
he that burneth *i.* as if he   *Isa 66:3*
blessed
burned *i.* to other gods   *Jer 1:16;*
  11:12; 18:15; 19:4; 44:5, 8, 15; 48:35
cometh to me *i.* from Sheba   *Jer 6:20*
burned *i.* to Baal   *Jer 7:9;*
  11:13, 17; 32:29
burned *i.* to all the host of *Jer 19:13*
heaven
burn *i.* for you (E)   *Jer 34:5*
burn *i.* to the queen of   *Jer 44:17;*
heaven   *44:18-19, 25*
your *i.* altars broken (B)(R) *Eze 6:4*
your *i.* altars cut down (B) *Eze 6:6*
and a thick cloud of *i.* went *Eze 8:11*
up
set mine oil and mine *i.*   *Eze 16:18*
before
thou hast set mine *i.* and   *Eze 23:41*
mine oil
offering and *i.* be offered   *Da 2:46*
(A)(R)
wherein she burned *i.* to them *Ho 2:13*
burn *i.* upon the hills, under *Ho 4:13*
oaks
and burned *i.* to graven images *Ho 11:2*
and burn *i.* unto their drag *Hab 1:16*
in every place *i.* shall be   *Mal 1:11*
offered
his lot was to burn *i.* when he *Lu 1:9*
went
praying without at the time of *Lu 1:10*
i.
on the right side of the altar of *Lu 1:11*
i.
golden bowls full of *i.*   *Re 5:8*
(A)(B)(E)(N)(P)(R)(S)
there was given unto him much *Re 8:3*
i.
the smoke of the *i.,* which came *Re 8:4*
i. and perfume   *Re 18:13*
(A)(B)(E)(N)

INCENSED

all they that were *i.* against *Isa 41:11*
thee
and all that are *i.* against him *Isa 45:24*
shall
thoroughly *i.* (P)   *Ac 4:2*

INCENTIVE

opponent *i.* for slandering (B) *1Ti 5:14*

INCEST

it is *i.* (B)   *Le 18:17; 20:14*

INCH

three *i.* frame around (B) *Ex 25:25*
made a four *i.* border (B) *Ex 37:12*

INCHES

it was four *i.* thick (B) *1Ki 7:26*
hooks three *i.* long (B) *Eze 40:43*

INCITED

he *i.* David to number (S) *2Sa 24:1*
but hast *i.* me (S)   *Eze 16:43*

INCLINE

and *i.* your heart unto the *Jos 24:23*
Lord
give your hearts to the Lord *Jos 24:23*
(B)
That he may *i.* our hearts *1Ki 8:58*
unto him
i. thine ear unto me, and hear *Ps 17:6*
my
and consider, and *i.* thine ear *Ps 45:10*
I will *i.* mine ear to a parable *Ps 49:4*
escape: *i.* thine ear unto me *Ps 71:2*
i. your ears to the words of my *Ps 78:1*
listen to the words of my mouth *Ps 78:1*
(B)
thee; *i.* thine ear unto my cry *Ps 88:2*
i. thine ear unto me: in the *Ps 102:2*
day

i. my heart unto thy   *Ps 119:36*
testimonies
i. not my heart to any evil *Ps 141:4*
thing
thou *i.* thine ear into wisdom *Pr 2:2*
i. thine ear unto my sayings *Pr 4:20*
i. toward her ways (A)(B) *Pr 7:25*
I. thine ear, O Lord, and hear *Isa 37:17*
I. your ear, and come unto me *Isa 55:3*
O my God, *i.* thine ear, and *Da 9:18*
hear

INCLINED

and their hearts *i.* to follow *J'g 9:3*
and he *i.* unto me, and heard *Ps 40:1*
my
bent over to me and heard my *Ps 40:1*
cry (B)
Because he hath *i.* his ear unto *Ps 116:2*
me
I have *i.* mine heart to   *Ps 119:112*
perform
I have set my heart on   *Ps 119:112*
practicing (B)
nor *i.* mine ear to them that *Pr 5:13*
i. ear to instructors (B)(R) *Pr 5:13*
hearkened not, nor *i.* their ear *Jer 7:24*
not unto me, nor *i.* their ear *Jer 7:26*
they obeyed, not, nor *i.* their *Jer 11:8*
ear
obeyed not, neither *i.* their *Jer 17:23*
ear
hearkened, nor *i.* your ear to *Jer 25:4*
hear
not unto me, neither *i.* their *Jer 34:14*
ear
ye have not *i.* your ear, nor *Jer 35:15*
nor *i.* their ear to turn from *Jer 44:5*
their

INCLINETH

her house *i.* unto death, and her *Pr 2:18*
her house sinks down to death *Pr 2:18*
(A)(B)(R)

INCLOSE

we will *i.* her with boards of *Ca 8:9*
cedar

INCLOSED

onyx stones *i.* in ouches of gold *Ex 39:6*
they were *i.* in ouches of gold *Ex 39:13*
in
Thus they *i.* the Benjamites *J'g 20:43*
They are *i.* in their own fat *Ps 17:10*
assembly of the wicked have *i.* *Ps 22:16*
me
A garden *i.* is my sister, my *Ca 4:12*
He hath *i.* my ways with hewn *La 3:9*
they *i.* a great multitude of *Lu 5:6*
fishes

INCLOSINGS

shall be set in gold in their *i.* *Ex 28:20*
in ouches of gold in their *i.* *Ex 39:13*

INCLUSION

their full *i.* (R)   *Ro 11:12*

INCOME

the *i.* of the wicked (A)(B)(R) *Pr 15:6*
than a large *i.* (B)   *Pr 16:8*

INCONSISTENCY

no shadow of *i.*   *Jas 1:17*
(A)(B)(E)(N)(P)(R)

INCONSISTENT

you are *i.* (N)   *Jas 2:4*

INCONTINENCY

Satan tempt you not for your *i.* *1Co 7:5*
lack of restraint of sexual (A) *1Co 7:5*
lack of self-control (B) *1Co 7:5*
for lack of self-control (E)(N) *1Co 7:5*

INCONTINENT

false accusers, *i.,* fierce, *2Ti 3:3*
despisers

uncontrolled (A)(B)   *2Ti 3:3*
without self-control (E) *2Ti 3:3*
intemperate (N)   *2Ti 3:3*
passionate and unprincipled *2Ti 3:3*
(P)

INCORRECT

mind utter things *i.* (A) *Pr 23:33*

INCORRIGIBLENESS

which brings *i.* (B)   *Eph 5:18*

INCORRUPTIBLE

corruptible crown; but we an *1Co 9:25*
i.
crown of eternal blessedness *1Co 9:25*
(A)
an imperishable crown   *1Co 9:25*
(B)(R)
a wreath that never fades (N) *1Co 9:25*
an eternal crown (P)   *1Co 9:25*
and the dead shall be raised *1Co 15:52*
i.
raised imperishable   *1Co 15:52*
(A)(B)(R)
rise immortal (N)   *1Co 15:52*
raised beyond reach of   *1Co 15:52*
corruption (P)
i. love (A)(E)   *Eph 6:24*
To an inheritance *i.* and *1Pe 1:4*
undefiled
which is beyond reach of *1Pe 1:4*
change and decay, unsullied,
and unfading (A)(P)
immortal, unsullied, and *1Pe 1:4*
unfading (B)
that nothing can destroy, spoil, *1Pe 1:4*
wither (N)
imperishable, undefiled, *1Pe 1:4*
unfading (R)
corruptible seed, but of *i.* *1Pe 1:23*
one that is immortal (A)(N) *1Pe 1:23*
from an imperishable sperm *1Pe 1:23*
(B)(R)
i., unboding spirit (A)(E)(N) *1Pe 3:4*

INCORRUPTION

in corruption; it is raised in *1Co 15:42*
i.
raised imperishable (A) *1Co 15:42;*
  15:50, 53-54
raised immortal (B)   *1Co 15:42*
imperishable (N)(R) *1Co 15:42; 15:53*
neither doth corruption *1Co 15:50*
inherit *i.*
imperishable (B) *1Co 15:50; 15:53-54*
must put on *i.* and this *1Co 15:53*
mortal
corruptible shall have put on *1Co 15:54*
i.

INCREASE

to pass in the *i.* that ye shall *Ge 47:24*
give
gather the *i.* (E)   *Ex 23:10*
may yield unto you the *i.* *Le 19:25*
thereof
shall all the *i.* thereof be meat *Le 25:7*
ye shall eat the *i.* thereof out of *Le 25:12*
thou shalt *i.* the price thereof *Le 25:16*
shall not sow, nor gather in *Le 25:20*
Take thou no usury of him, or *Le 25:36*
i.
nor lend him thy victuals for *i.* *Le 25:37*
the land shall yield her *i.* and *Le 26:4*
your land shall not yield her *i.* *Le 26:20*
as the *i.* of the threshing floor *Nu 18:30*
and as the *i.* of the winepress *Nu 18:30*
an *i.* of sinful men, to augment *Nu 32:14*
that ye may *i.* mightily, as the *De 6:3*
the *i.* of thy kine, and the *De 7:13*
flocks
once, lest the beasts of the field *De 7:22*
i.
truly tithe all the *i.* of thy seed *De 14:22*
bring forth all the tithe of *De 14:28*
thine *i.*
God shall bless thee in all *De 16:15*
thine *i.*
tithing all the tithes of thine *i.* *De 26:12*
thy cattle, the *i.* of thy kine *De 28:4*
the *i.* of thy kine, and the *De 28:18*
flocks of

or the *i.* of thy kine, or flocks   *De 28:51*
of thy
he might eat the *i.* of the   *De 32:13*
fields
consume the earth with her *i.*   *De 32:22*
and destroyed the *i.* of the earth   *J'g 6:4*
I. thine army, and come out   *J'g 9:29*
all the *i.* of thine house shall   *1Sa 2:33*
die
Lord had said he would *i.*   *1Ch 27:23*
Israel
over the *i.* of the vineyards   *1Ch 27:27*
for the
and of all the *i.* of the field   *2Ch 31:5*
Storehouses also for the *i.* of   *2Ch 32:28*
corn
wives, to *i.* the trespass of   *Ezr 10:10*
Israel
yieldeth much *i.* unto the kings   *Ne 9:37*
thy latter end should greatly *i.*   *Job 8:7*
The *i.* of his house shall   *Job 20:28*
depart
and would root out all mine   *Job 31:12*
i.
not *i.* thy wealth by their price   *Ps 44:12*
if riches, *i.* set not your heart   *Ps 62:10*
upon
Then shall the earth yield her *i.*   *Ps 67:6*
Thou shalt *i.* my greatness   *Ps 71:21*
in the world: they *i.* in riches   *Ps 73:12*
also their *i.* unto the   *Ps 78:46*
caterpiller
and our land shall yield her *i.*   *Ps 85:12*
which may yield fruits of *i.*   *Ps 107:37*
The Lord shall *i.* you more   *Ps 115:14*
man will hear, and will *i.*   *Pr 1:5*
learning
with the firstfruits of all thine *i.*   *Pr 3:9*
man, and he will *i.* in learning   *Pr 9:9*
that gathereth by labour shall   *Pr 13:11*
i.
much *i.* is by the strength of   *Pr 14:4*
the ox
the *i.* of his lips shall he be   *Pr 18:20*
filled
oppresseth the poor to *i.* his   *Pr 22:16*
riches
when they perish, the   *Pr 28:28*
righteous *i.*
he that loveth abundance with   *Ec 5:10*
i.
When goods *i.* they are   *Ec 5:11*
increased
there be many things that *i.*   *Ec 6:11*
vanity
Of the *i.* of his government and   *Isa 9:7*
The meek also shall *i.* their   *Isa 29:19*
joy
and bread of the *i.* of the   *Isa 30:23*
earth
and didst *i.* thy perfumes, and   *Isa 57:9*
and the first fruits of his *i.*: all   *Jer 2:3*
that
and they shall be fruitful and *i.*   *Jer 23:3*
I will *i.* the famine upon you   *Eze 5:16*
usury, neither hath taken any   *Eze 18:8*
i.
upon usury, and hath taken *i.*   *Eze 18:13*
that hath not received usury   *Eze 18:17*
nor *i.*
thou hast taken usury and *i.*   *Eze 22:12*
and the earth shall yield her   *Eze 34:27*
i.
and they shalt *i.* and bring   *Eze 36:11*
fruit
I will call for the corn, and   *Eze 36:29*
will *i.* it
of the tree, and the *i.* of the   *Eze 36:30*
field
I will *i.* them with men like a   *Eze 36:37*
flock
and the *i.* thereof shall be for   *Eze 48:18*
food
acknowledge and *i.* with glory   *Da 11:39*
whoredom, and shall not *i.*   *Ho 4:10*
and the ground shall give her   *Zec 8:12*
i.
shall *i.* as they have increased   *Zec 10:8*
said unto the Lord, *I.* our faith   *Lu 17:5*
He must *i.*, I must decrease   *Joh 3:30*
i. the trespass (A)(R)   *Ro 5:20*
Apollos watered; but God gave   *1Co 3:6*
the *i.*
watereth; but God that giveth   *1Co 3:7*
the *i.*
i. the fruits of your   *2Co 9:10*
righteousness
i. of the body unto the   *Eph 4:16*
edifying

increaseth with the *i.* of God   *Col 2:19*
the Lord make you to *i.* and   *1Th 3:12*
abound
i., overflow with love (A)   *1Th 3:12*
that ye *i.* more and more   *1Th 4:10*
they will *i.* unto more   *2Ti 2:16*
ungodliness

INCREASED

and the waters *i.* and bare up   *Ge 7:17*
and were *i.* greatly upon the   *Ge 7:18*
earth
and it is now *i.* unto a   *Ge 30:30*
multitude
And the man *i.* exceedingly   *Ge 30:43*
were fruitful, and *i.* abundantly   *Ex 1:7*
thou be *i.* and inherit the land   *Ex 23:30*
of the Philistines went on   *1Sa 14:19*
and *i.*
for the people *i.* continually   *2Sa 15:12*
with
And the battle *i.* that day   *1Ki 22:35*
house of their fathers *i.*   *1Ch 4:38*
greatly
they *i.* from Bashan unto   *1Ch 5:23*
And the battle *i.* that day: *2Ch 18:34*
howbeit
for our iniquities are *i.* over our   *Ezr 9:6*
and his substance is *i.* in the   *Job 1:10*
land
Lord, how are they *i.* that   *Ps 3:1*
trouble
that their corn and their wine *i.*   *Ps 4:7*
when the glory of his house is   *Ps 49:16*
i.
And he *i.* his people greatly   *Ps 105:24*
and the years of thy life shall   *Pr 9:11*
be *i.*
so I was great, and *i.* more than   *Ec 2:9*
increase, they are *i.* that eat   *Ec 5:11*
them
the nation, and not *i.* the joy   *Isa 9:3*
Thou hast *i.* the nation, O   *Isa 26:15*
Lord
thou hast *i.* the nation: thou   *Isa 26:15*
art
and blessed him, and *i.* him   *Isa 51:2*
ye be multiplied and *i.* in the   *Jer 3:16*
land
and their backslidings are *i.*   *Jer 5:6*
Their widows are *i.* to me   *Jer 15:8*
above
that ye may be *i.* there, and   *Jer 29:6*
not
iniquity; because thy sins   *Jer 30:14*
were *i.*
because thy sins were *i.* I   *Jer 30:15*
have
hath *i.* in the daughter of Judah   *La 2:5*
and thou hast *i.* and waxen   *Eze 16:7*
great
and hast *i.* thy whoredoms,   *Eze 16:26*
And that she *i.* her   *Eze 23:14*
whoredoms
thy traffick hast thou *i.* thy   *Eze 28:5*
riches
so *i.* from the lowest chamber   *Eze 41:7*
and fro, and knowledge shall   *Da 12:4*
be *i.*
As they were *i.* so they sinned   *Ho 4:7*
of his fruit he hath *i.* the altars   *Ho 10:1*
fig trees and your olive trees *i.*   *Ho 4:9*
they shall increase as they   *Zec 10:8*
have *i.*
yield fruit that sprang up and   *M'k 4:8*
i.
Jesus *i.* in wisdom and stature   *Lu 2:52*
And the word of God *i.*; and the   *Ac 6:7*
Saul *i.* the more in strength   *Ac 9:22*
the faith, and *i.* in number   *Ac 16:5*
daily
having hope, when your   *2Co 10:15*
faith is *i.*
I am rich, and *i.* with goods   *Re 3:17*

INCREASEST

and *i.* thine indignation upon   *Job 10:17*
me

INCREASETH

For it *i.* Thou huntest me as   *Job 10:16*
a
He *i.* the nations, and   *Job 12:23*
destroyeth
rise up against thee *i.*   *Ps 74:23*
continually

is that scattereth, and yet *i.*   *Pr 11:24*
sweetness of the lips *i.*   *Pr 16:21*
learning
i. the transgressors among   *Pr 23:28*
men
yea, a man of knowledge *i.*   *Pr 24:5*
strength
that by usury and unjust gain *i.*   *Pr 28:8*
are multiplied, transgression *i.*   *Pr 29:16*
he that *i.* knowledge, *i.* sorrow   *Ec 1:18*
that have no might he *i.*   *Isa 40:29*
strength
he daily *i.* lies and desolation   *Ho 12:1*
to him that *i.* that which is not   *Hab 2:6*
his
together, *i.* with the increase   *Col 2:19*
of God

INCREASING

and *i.* in the knowledge of   *Col 1:10*
God
i., overflowing love (P)   *1Th 3:12*

INCREASINGLY

possess these qualities *i.* (B)   *2Pe 1:8*

INCREDIBLE

it be thought a thing *i.* with   *Ac 26:8*
you

INCREDULITY

reproached for *i.* and   *M'k 16:14*
dullness (N)

INCURABLE

his bowels with an *i.* disease   *2Ch 21:18*
wound is *i.* without   *Job 34:6*
transgression
my wound *i.*, which refuseth   *Jer 15:18*
to be
Thy bruise is *i.*, and thy   *Jer 30:12*
wound is
thy sorrow is *i.* for the   *Jer 30:15*
multitude
For her wound is *i.*: for it is   *Mic 1:9*
come

INCURRED

he *i.* guilt through Baal (R)   *Ho 13:1*

INDEBTED

forgive every one that is *i.* to   *Lu 11:4*
us

INDECENCY

out of heart proceeds *i.* (N)   *M'k 7:22*
works of flesh manifest, *i.*   *Ga 5:19*
(A)(N)
i. of any kind (B)(N)   *Eph 5:3; Col 3:5*

INDECENTLY

behave *i.* (N)   *Ro 1:27*

INDECOROUS

something *i.* about (P)   *1Co 14:35*

INDEED

thy wife shall bear thee a son   *Ge 17:19*
i.
And yet *i.* she is my sister;   *Ge 20:12*
she is
to him, Shalt thou *i.* reign over   *Ge 37:8*
us
or shalt thou *i.* have dominion   *Ge 37:8*
over us
thy brethren *i.* come to bow   *Ge 37:10*
down
For *i.* I was stolen away out   *Ge 40:15*
of the
And said, O sir, we came *i.*   *Ge 43:20*
down at
drinketh, and whereby *i.* he   *Ge 44:5*
divineth
if ye will obey my voice *i.* and   *Ex 19:5*
keep
But if thou shalt *i.* obey his   *Ex 23:22*
voice, and
ye should *i.* have eaten it in   *Le 10:18*
the holy

Hath the Lord *i.* spoken only by | *Nu 12:2*
If thou wilt *i.* deliver this people | *Nu 21:2*
am I not able *i.* to promote thee to | *Nu 22:37*
for *i.* the hand of the Lord was | *De 2:15*
of the hated, which is *i.* the firstborn | *De 21:16*
I. I have sinned against the Lord | *Jos 7:20*
if thou wilt *i.* look on the affliction of | *1Sa 1:11*
I said *i.* that thy house, and the house | *1Sa 2:30*
I am *i.* a widow woman, and mine | *2Sa 14:5*
shall bring me again *i.* to Jerusalem | *2Sa 15:8*
But will God *i.* dwell on the earth | *1Ki 8:27*
Thou hast *i.* smitten Edom, and thine | *2Ki 14:10*
Oh that thou wouldest bless me *i.* and | *1Ch 4:10*
It is that have sinned and done evil *i.* | *1Ch 21:17*
And be it *i.* that I have erred | *Job 19:4*
If *i.* ye will magnify yourselves | *Job 19:5*
Do ye *i.* speak righteousness, O | *Ps 58:1*
people, Hear ye *i.* but understand not | *Isa 6:9*
and see ye *i.* but perceive not | *Isa 6:9*
For if ye do this thing *i.* then shall | *Jer 22:4*
I *i.* baptize you with water unto | *M't 3:11*
Which *i.* is the least of all seeds | *M't 13:32*
them, Ye shall drink *i.* of my cup | *M't 20:23*
which *i.* appear beautiful outward | *M't 23:27*
the spirit *i.* is willing, but the flesh | *M't 26:41*
I *i.* have baptized you with water | *M'k 1:8*
That Elias is *i.* come, and they | *M'k 9:13*
Ye shall *i.* drink of the cup that | *M'k 10:39*
John, that he was a prophet *i.* | *M'k 11:32*
The Son of man *i.* goeth, as it is | *M'k 14:21*
I *i.* baptize you with water; but | *Lu 3:16*
for they *i.* killed them, and ye build | *Lu 11:48*
And we *i.* justly; for we receive the | *Lu 23:41*
Saying, The Lord is risen *i.* | *Lu 24:34*
Behold an Israelite *i.* in whom is | *Joh 1:47*
this is *i.* the Christ, the Saviour of | *Joh 4:42*
For my flesh is meat *i.* | *Joh 6:55*
and my blood is drink *i.* | *Joh 6:55*
know *i.* that this is the very Christ | *Joh 7:26*
word, then are ye my disciples *i.* | *Joh 8:31*
make you free, ye shall be free *i.* | *Joh 8:36*
for that *i.* a noble miracle hath | *Ac 4:16*
John *i.* baptized with water; but ye | *Ac 11:16*
that were with me saw *i.* the light | *Ac 22:9*
to be dead *i.* unto sin, but alive | *Ro 6:11*
the law of God, neither *i.* can be | *Ro 8:7*
All things *i.* are pure; but it is evil | *Ro 14:20*
For a man *i.* ought not to cover his | *1Co 11:7*
For *i.* he accepted the exhortation | *2Co 8:17*
in my folly: and *i.* bear with me | *2Co 11:1*
Some *i.* preach Christ even of envy | *Ph'p 1:15*
For *i.* he was sick nigh unto death | *Ph'p 2:27*
to me *i.* is not grievous, but for you | *Ph'p 3:1*
Which things have *i.* a shew of | *Col 2:23*
And *i.* ye do it toward all the | *1Th 4:10*
Honour widows that are widows *i.* | *1Ti 5:3*

Now she that is a widow *i.* and relieve them that are widows *i.* | *1Ti 5:5* / *1Ti 5:16*
disallowed *i.* of men, but chosen of | *1Pe 2:4*

INDESCRIBABLE

i., free gift (A)(P) | *2Co 9:15*

INDIA

from *I.* even unto Ethiopia | *Es 1:1*
which are from *I.* unto Ethiopia | *Es 8:9*

INDICTMENT

has an *i.* against all nations (R) | *Jer 25:31*

INDIGNANT

i. and angry (R) | *Ge 34:7*
descending in *i.* anger (A) | *Isa 30:30*
i. at two brothers (A)(B)(N)(P)(R) | *M't 20:24*
they were *i.* (A)(P)(R) | *M't 21:15*
they were *i.* (A)(N)(P)(R) | *M't 26:8*
he was *i.* (A)(B)(N)(P)(R) | *M'k 10:14*
began to be *i.* (A)(B)(N)(P) | *M'k 10:41*
i. because Jews (A)(B)(N)(R) | *Lu 13:14*
vexed and *i.* (A) | *Ac 4:2*
i. with that (N) | *Heb 3:10*

INDIGNANTLY

asked him *i.* (N) | *M't 21:15*
disciples said *i.* (B) | *M't 26:8*
kept muttering *i.* (P) | *Lu 5:30*

INDIGNATION

indignation (A) | *Ex 15:7;*
32:11; Ps 38:1; 85:3; 88:7; 102:10; Re 11:18
indignation (B) | *Ex 22:24;*
32:10; Nu 25:11; 1Sa 28:18; 2Ch 19:2; 28:11; 32:25; Ezr 7:24; 8:22; Job 21:20; 36:13; Ps 2:5; 21:9; 78:31, 38, 49; 95:11; Isa 10:6; Eze 7:12, 14; 22:31; 38:19; Ho 5:10; Zep 1:18; Zec 7:12; Ro 1:18; 2:8; 4:15; 5:9; 9:22; Eph 2:3; 5:6; 1Th 2:16; 5:9; Heb 3:11; Re 6:16; 14:10, 19; 15:1; 16:1; 19:15
the awful *i.* of Lord (B) | *De 9:19*
anger and *i.* (B) | *De 29:23*
and in wrath, and in great *i.* | *De 29:28*
there was great *i.* against Israel | *2Ki 3:27*
was wroth, and took great *i.* | *Ne 4:1*
he was angry, in a great rage (A) | *Ne 4:1*
he was furious and insulted (B) | *Ne 4:1*
he was angry and greatly enraged (R) | *Ne 4:1*
he was full of *i.* against Mordecai | *Es 5:9*
he was filled with wrath (A)(E)(R) | *Es 5:9*
Haman's temper grew against Mordecai (B) | *Es 5:9*
i. slay the simple (A)(B)(R) | *Job 5:2*
and increasest thine *i.* upon me | *Job 10:17*
increase thine anger toward me (B) | *Job 10:17*
increase thy vexation toward me (R) | *Job 10:17*
Pour out thine *i.* upon them | *Ps 69:24*
anger, wrath, and *i.*, and trouble | *Ps 78:49*
Because of thine *i.* and thy wrath | *Ps 102:10*
day of his *i.* (A)(B) | *Ps 110:5*
the staff in their hand is mine *i.* | *Isa 10:5*
the *i.* shall cease, and mine anger | *Isa 10:25*
the weapons of his *i.* to destroy | *Isa 13:5*
moment, until the *i.* be overpast | *Isa 26:20*
his lips are full of *i.* and his tongue | *Isa 30:27*

His lips are filled with fury (B) | *Isa 30:27*
with the *i.* of his anger, and descending in indignant anger (A) | *Isa 30:30* / *Isa 30:30*
descending in furious anger (B)(R) | *Isa 30:30*
i. of the Lord is upon all nations | *Isa 34:2*
and his *i.* toward his enemies | *Isa 66:14*
shall not be able to abide his *i.* | *Jer 10:10*
hand: for thou hast filled me with *i.* | *Jer 15:17*
brought forth the weapons of his *i.* | *Jer 50:25*
hath despised in the *i.* of his anger | *La 2:6*
I will pour out mine *i.* upon thee | *Eze 21:31*
nor rained upon in the day of *i.* | *Eze 22:24*
I poured out mine *i.* upon | *Eze 22:31*
shall be in the last end of the *i.* | *Da 8:19*
have *i.* against the holy covenant | *Da 11:30*
burn with rage against holy | *Da 11:30*
enraged and take action (R) | *Da 11:30*
prosper till the *i.* be accomplished | *Da 11:36*
I will bear the *i.* of the Lord | *Mic 7:9*
does not maintain *i.* (B) | *Mic 7:18*
Who can stand before his *i.* | *Na 1:6*
didst march through the land in *i.* | *Hab 3:12*
to pour upon them mine *i.* even all | *Zep 3:8*
hast had *i.* these threescore | *Zec 1:12*
whom the Lord hath *i.* for ever | *Mal 1:4*
were moved with *i.* against the two | *M't 20:24*
indignant at two brothers (A)(B)(N)(P)(R) | *M't 20:24*
moved to *i.* (E) | *M't 21:15; 10:41*
they had *i.* saying, To what purpose | *M't 26:8*
they were indignant (A)(N)(P)(R) | *M't 26:8*
disciples said indignantly (B) | *M't 26:8*
in warm *i.* (N) | *M'k 1:41*
moved with *i.* (E) | *M'k 10:14*
some that had *i.* within themselves | *M'k 14:4*
of the synagogue answered with *i.* | *Lu 13:14*
indignant because Jesus healed (A)(B)(N)(R) | *Lu 13:14*
in his annoyance at Jesus (P) | *Lu 13:14*
i. on this people (A) | *Lu 21:23*
Sadducees, and were filled with *i.* | *Ac 5:17*
were insufferably jealous (B) | *Ac 5:17*
were filled with jealousy (E)(R) | *Ac 5:17*
goaded into action by jealousy (B) | *Ac 5:17*
in a fury of jealousy (P) | *Ac 5:17*
unrighteousness, and wrath | *Ro 2:8*
yea, what *i.* yea, what fear | *2Co 7:11*
of judgment and fiery *i.* | *Heb 10:27*
mixture into the cup of his *i.* | *Re 14:10*

INDIGNITY

to suffer *i.* (N) | *Ac 5:41*

INDISTINCT

an *i.* sound (B)(R) | *1Co 14:8*

INDISTINCTLY

we see *i.* in a mirror (B) | *1Co 13:12*

INDITING

My heart is *i.* a good matter: I | *Ps 45:1*
heart overflows with goodly theme (A)(B)(R) | *Ps 45:1*
overfloweth with a goodly matter (E) | *Ps 45:1*

INDOLENCE

through *i.* the house leaks (R) | *Ec 10:18*

INDUCED

entreated, *i.* us (A)   *Ac 16:15*

INDUCING

i. people to rebellion (B)   *Lu 23:14*

INDULGE

i. in lust of (A)(B)   *2Pe 2:10*

INDULGED

i. all foulness (P)   *2Pe 2:10*
i. in unnatural vice (A)(R)   *Jude 7*

INDULGING

i. in unbridled lusts (B)   *1Pe 4:3*

INDUSTRIOUS

young man that he was *i.,* he   *1Ki 11:28*

INDUSTRY

business, *i.* (N)   *Ac 19:25*

INEDIBLE

fruit *i.* for you (A)   *Le 19:23*

INEFFABLE

heard *i.* sayings (B)   *2Co 12:4*

INEFFECTIVE

this is also *i.* (B)   *Ec 8:10*
faith is inactive, *i.* (A)   *Jas 2:20*

INEFFECTUAL

rendered death *i.* (B)   *2Ti 1:10*

INEVITABLE

i. disintegration lust produces   *2Pe 1:4*
(P)

INEXCUSABLE

Therefore thou art *i.* O man   *Ro 2:1*
no excuse, defense, or   *Ro 2:1*
justification (A)
you can offer no excuse (B)   *Ro 2:1*
Thou art without excuse (E)   *Ro 2:1*
You therefore have no defense   *Ro 2:1*
(N)
Therefore you have no excuse   *Ro 2:1*
(R)

INEXHAUSTIBLE

i., boundless (A)   *Ps 147:5*

INEXPERIENCED

young and *i.* (B)(R)   *1Ch 22:5; 29:1*
irresolute and *i.* (A)   *2Ch 13:7*
not *i.* (B)   *Heb 5:13*

INEXPRESSIBLE

i., free gift (A)(R)   *2Co 9:15*
i. glorious joy (A)(B)   *1Pe 1:8*

INFALLIBLE

by many *i.* proofs, being seen of   *Ac 1:3*
them
by many convincing proofs   *Ac 1:3*
(B)(E)(R)
gave ample proof that he was   *Ac 1:3*
alive (N)
showed himself alive in many   *Ac 1:3*
convincing ways (P)

INFAMOUS

making one *i.* (A)   *Ge 34:30*
worthless, *i.* men (B)   *Job 30:8*
shall mock thee, which art *i.*   *Eze 22:5*
ban your name as *i.* (N)   *Lu 6:22*

INFAMY

shame, and thine *i.* turn not   *Pr 25:10*
away

your ill repute has no end   *Pr 25:10*
(A)(B)(R)
talkers, and are an *i.* of the   *Eze 36:3*
people
became talk and gossip of   *Eze 36:3*
people (A)(B)(R)
the evil report of the people   *Eze 36:3*
(E)
the proceeds of *i.* (P)   *Ac 1:18*

INFANCY

from *i.* (B)   *2Ti 3:15*

INFANT

slay both man and woman, *i.*   *1Sa 15:3*
be no more thence an *i.* of   *Isa 65:20*
days
a mere *i.* (A)(B)(N)   *Heb 5:13*

INFANTS

been; as *i.* which never saw   *Job 3:16*
light
their *i.* shall be dashed in   *Ho 13:16*
pieces
they brought unto him also *i.*   *Lu 18:15*
as to mere *i.* in Christ (A)(N)   *1Co 3:1*
although *i.* in wickedness   *1Co 14:20*
(B)
like newborn *i.* (N)   *1Pe 2:2*

INFATUATED

i. with a loose woman   *Pr 5:19*
(A)(B)(R)
be *i.* with them (B)   *Ga 4:17*

INFECTED

having *i.* sores (B)   *Le 22:22*

INFERIOR

I am not *i.* to you; yea, who   *Job 12:3*
I know also: I am not *i.* unto   *Job 13:2*
you
arise another kingdom *i.* to   *Da 2:39*
thee
you were *i.* to other churches   *2Co 12:13*
grow up feeling *i.* and   *Col 3:21*
frustrated (P)

INFIDEL

hath he that believeth with an   *2Co 6:15*
i.
believer with unbeliever   *2Co 6:15*
(A)(B)(E)(N)(P)(R)
the faith, and is worse than an   *1Ti 5:8*
i.
worse than an unbeliever   *1Ti 5:8*
(A)(B)(E)(N)(R)
than a man who makes no   *1Ti 5:8*
profession (P)

INFINITE

great? and thine iniquities *i.*   *Job 22:5*
no end to iniquities   *Job 22:5*
(A)(B)(E)(R)
power: his understanding is *i.*   *Ps 147:5*
understanding inexhaustible,   *Ps 147:5*
boundless (A)
understanding is unlimited   *Ps 147:5*
(B)
understanding is beyond   *Ps 147:5*
measure (R)
her strength, and it was *i.*   *Na 3:9*
Egypt her strength without limit   *Na 3:9*
(A)(R)
Egypt her strength unlimited   *Na 3:9*
(B)

INFIRMITIES

Himself took our *i.* and bare   *M't 8:17*
our
weaknesses (B)   *M't 8:17*
illnesses (N)   *M't 8:17*
and to be healed by him of   *Lu 5:15*
their *i.*
diseases (B)(P)   *Lu 5:15; 7:21*
ailments (N)   *Lu 5:15*
cured many of their *i.* and   *Lu 7:21*
plagues
sicknesses (A)(E)   *Lu 7:21*
diseases, plagues (N)(R)   *Lu 7:21*

been healed of evil spirits and *i.*   *Lu 8:2*
the Spirit also helpeth our *i.*   *Ro 8:26*
weakness (A)(B)(N)(R)   *Ro 8:26*
out present limitations (P)   *Ro 8:26*
to bear the *i.* of the weak, and   *Ro 15:1*
not
frailties (A)   *Ro 15:1*
weaknesses (B)   *Ro 15:1*
tender scruples of weaker men   *Ro 15:1*
(N)
doubts and qualms of others   *Ro 15:1*
(P)
the failings of the weak (R)   *Ro 15:1*
of the things which concern   *2Co 11:30*
my *i.*
weakness (B)(E)(N)(P)(R)   *2Co 11:30*
I will not glory, but in mine *i.*   *2Co 12:5*
weakness (N)   *2Co 12:10*
weaknesses (E)(N)(P)(R)   *2Co 12:5;
12:10*
will I rather glory in my *i.* that   *Ro 12:9*
Therefore I take pleasure in *i.*   *Ro 12:10*
stomach's sake and thine often   *1Ti 5:23*
i.
your frequent illnesses (A)(B)   *1Ti 5:23*
your frequent ailments   *1Ti 5:23*
(N)
frequent spells of illness (P)   *1Ti 5:23*
touched with the feeling of   *Heb 4:15*
our *i.*
weaknesses (B)(N)(P)(R)   *Heb 4:15*

INFIRMITY

days of the separation for her *i.*   *Le 12:2*
during her monthly discomfort   *Le 12:2*
(A)
time of her menstruation   *Le 12:2*
(B)(R)
the days of her impurity (E)   *Le 12:2*
And I said, This is my *i.*: but   *Ps 77:10*
this is my grief (A)(R)   *Ps 77:10*
this grieves me (B)   *Ps 77:10*
spirit of a man will sustain his   *Pr 18:14*
i.
sustain him in bodily pain,   *Pr 18:14*
trouble (A)
man's spirit will endure   *Pr 18:14*
sickness (B)(R)
a woman which had a spirit   *Lu 13:11*
of *i.*
a weakening spirit (B)   *Lu 13:11; 13:12*
thou art loosed from thine *i.*   *Lu 13:12*
had an *i.* thirty and eight years   *Joh 5:5*
men because of the *i.* of your   *Ro 6:19*
flesh
your natural limitations   *Ro 6:19*
(A)(R)
your human weakness (B)(N)   *Ro 6:19*
the Spirit helps our *i.* (S)   *Ro 8:26*
Ye know how through *i.* of the   *Ga 4:13*
flesh
on account of bodily ailment   *Ga 4:13*
(A)(R)
bodily illness (N)(P)   *Ga 4:13*
himself also is compassed with   *Heb 5:2*
i.
moral weakness and physical   *Heb 5:2*
infirmity (A)
liable to weakness (B)   *Heb 5:2*
he too is beset by weakness   *Heb 5:2*
(N)(R)
he himself is prone to human   *Heb 5:2*
weakness (P)
men high priests which have   *Heb 7:28*
i.

INFLAME

until night, till wine *i.* them   *Isa 5:11*

INFLAMMATION

clean: for it is an *i.* of the   *Le 13:28*
burning
it is the scar of the burn   *Le 13:28*
(A)(B)(E)(R)
and with a fever, and with an   *De 28:22*
i.
charged with *i.* (B)   *Ps 38:7*

INFLATED

may not be *i.* with pride (N)   *1Co 4:6*
grown *i.* with pride (B)   *1Co 4:18*
love does not cherish *i.* ideas   *1Co 13:4*
(P)
is *i.* by his worldly mind   *Col 2:18*
(B)(P)

INFLICT

i. this people (B)	*2Ki 6:18*
i. his wrath (A)(B)(R)	*Ro 3:5*
i. God's punishment (P)	*Ro 13:4*

INFLICTED

i. judgments (B)	*Nu 33:4*
he *i.* heavy losses (B)	*1Sa 23:5*
this punishment, which was *i.*	*2Co 2:6*
of many	
this censure of many (A)(B)	*2Co 2:6*
punishment by the majority	*2Co 2:6*
(R)	
suffering hurt for the hurt *i.*	*2Pe 2:13*
(N)	

INFLUENCE

grew irresistibly in power and	*Ac 19:20*
i. (P)	

INFLUENCED

i. from the east (B)	*Isa 2:6*

INFLUENCES

bind the sweet *i.* of Pleiades	*Job 38:31*
bind the chains of Pleiades	*Job 38:31*
(A)(R)	
bind the bonds of Pleiades	*Job 38:31*
(B)	
bind the cluster of Pleiades	*Job 38:31*
(E)	
woe to world for *i.* to do	*M't 18:7*
wrong (A)(B)	

INFLUENTIAL

the *i.* women (N)(P)	*Ac 17:4*

INFOLDING

a fire *i.* itself, and a brightness	*Eze 1:4*

INFORM

i. you what this is (B)	*Nu 24:14*
according to all that they *i.*	*De 17:10*
thee	
inform (S)	*2Sa 15:28;*
	Ezr 4:16; 5:10; 7:24
i. a wise man (B)	*Pr 6:23*

INFORMATION

i. in spiritual matters (P)	*1Co 12:1*

INFORMED

i. the king (S)	*Ezr 4:14; Es 2:22*
And he *i.* me, and talked with	*Da 9:22*
me	
are *i.* of thee, that thou	*Ac 21:21*
teachest	
they were *i.* concerning thee	*Ac 21:24*
who *i.* the governor against	*Ac 24:1*
Paul	
of the Jews *i.* him against Paul	*Ac 25:2*
and the elders of the Jews *i.*	*Ac 25:15*
me	

INGATHERING

and the feast of *i.* which is in	*Ex 23:16*
the feast of *i.* at the year's end	*Ex 34:22*
full number of *i.* (A)(P)(R)	*Ro 11:25*

INGENUITY

springs from human *i.* (B)	*Eph 4:14*

INGOTS

make it into *i.* (B)	*2Ki 12:10*

INGRATIATING

i. words of flattery (B)	*Ro 16:18*

INHABIT

the land which ye shall *i.*	*Nu 35:34*
wherein	
the wicked shall not *i.* the	*Pr 10:30*
earth	
the villages that Kedar doth *i.*	*Isa 42:11*

shall build houses, and *i.*	*Isa 65:21*
them	
shall not build and another *i.*	*Isa 65:22*
but shall *i.* the parched places	*Jer 17:6*
in	
Thou daughter that dost *i.*	*Jer 48:18*
Dibon	
they that *i.* those wastes of	*Eze 33:24*
the land	
build the waste cities, and *i.*	*Am 9:14*
them	
also build houses, but not *i.*	*Zep 1:13*
them	
nobody to *i.* them (B)	*Zep 3:10*

INHABITANT

flood breaketh out from the *i.*	*Job 28:4*
even great and fair, without *i.*	*Isa 5:9*
fair without occupants (B)	*Isa 5:9*
Until the cities be wasted	*Isa 6:11*
without *i.*	
ruins without residents (B)	*Isa 6:11;*
	9:9; 12:6; 33:24
and the *i.* of Samaria that say	*Isa 9:9*
in	
Cry out and shout, thou *i.* of	*Isa 12:6*
Zion	
And the *i.* of this isle shall say	*Isa 20:6*
in	
are upon thee, O *i.* of the	*Isa 24:17*
earth	
And the *i.* shall not say, I am	*Isa 33:24*
sick	
his cities are burned without *i.*	*Jer 2:15*
shall be laid waste, without an *i.*	*Jer 4:7*
of Judah desolate, without an *i.*	*Jer 9:11*
out of the land, O *i.* of the	*Jer 10:17*
fortress	
I am against thee, O *i.* of the	*Jer 21:13*
valley	
O *i.* of Lebanon, that makest	*Jer 22:23*
thy	
city shall be desolate without	*Jer 26:9*
an *i.*	
without man, and without *i.*	*Jer 33:10*
of Judah a desolation without	*Jer 34:22*
an *i.*	
and a curse, without an *i.* as	*Jer 44:22*
waste and desolate without	*Jer 46:19*
an *i.*	
O *i.* of Aroer, stand by the	*Jer 48:19*
way, and	
O inhabitress of Aroer (B)	*Jer 48:19*
thee, O *i.* of Moab, saith the	*Jer 48:43*
Lord	
Babylon a desolation without	*Jer 51:29*
an *i.*	
Babylon, shall the *i.* of Zion	*Jer 51:35*
say	
and an hissing, without an *i.*	*Jer 51:37*
cut off the *i.* from the plain of	*Am 1:5*
Aven	
I will cut off the *i.* from	*Am 1:8*
Ashdod	
Pass ye away, thou *i.* of	*Mic 1:11*
Saphir	
dwellers (B)	*Mic 1:11; 1:12-13, 15*
the *i.* of Zaanan came not	*Mic 1:11*
forth in	
the *i.* of Maroth waited	*Mic 1:12*
carefully for	
O thou *i.* of Lachish, bind the	*Mic 1:13*
heir unto thee, O *i.* of	*Mic 1:15*
Mareshah	
thee, that there shall be no *i.*	*Zep 2:5*
is no man, that there is none *i.*	*Zep 3:6*
nobody to inhabit them (B)	*Zep 3:6*

INHABITANTS

he overthrew all the *i.* of the	*Ge 19:25*
cities	
shall take hold of the *i.* of	*Ex 15:14*
Palestina	
all the *i.* of Canaan shall melt	*Ex 15:15*
away	
dwellers of Canaan (B)	*Ex 15:15*
the land itself vomiteth out	*Le 18:25*
her *i.*	
shall proclaim liberty to all	*Le 25:10*
the *i.* thereof	
is a land that eateth up the *i.*	*Nu 13:32*
thereof	
have withdrawn the *i.* of their	*De 13:13*
city	
thou shalt surely smite the *i.*	*De 13:15*
of that city	
even the *i.* of the country do	*Jos 2:24*
faint	

all *i.* (B)	*Jos 10:28; 10:32, 35, 37, 39*
that made peace, save the *i.*	*Jos 11:19*
of Gibeon	
could not drive out the *i.*	*Jos 17:12;*
	J'g 1:19, 27
make no league with the *i.*	*J'g 2:2*
of this land	
the *i.* of the villages ceased till	*J'g 5:7*
arose	
curse ye bitterly the *i.* thereof	*J'g 5:23*
be head over all the *i.* of	*J'g 10:18;*
Gilead	*11:8*
were none of the *i.* of	*J'g 21:9*
Jabesh-gilead there	
go and smite the *i.* of Jabesh-	*J'g 21:10*
gilead	
saying, Buy it before the *i.* and	*Ru 4:4*
elders	
Elijah who was of the *i.* of	*1Ki 17:1*
Gilead	
their *i.* were of small power	*2Ki 19:26*
first *i.* that dwelt in their	*1Ch 9:2*
possessions	
stood against the *i.* of	*2Ch 20:23*
mount Seir	
are formed from under the *i.*	*Job 26:5*
thereof	
all the *i.* of world stand in	*Ps 33:8*
awe of him	
he looketh on all the *i.* of the	*Ps 33:14*
earth	
hear this, give ear, all ye *i.* of	*Ps 49:1*
the world	
the earth and all the *i.* thereof	*Ps 75:3*
are dissolved	
put down the *i.* like a valiant	*Isa 10:13*
man	
all ye *i.* of the world, see ye,	*Isa 18:3*
when he	
be still, ye *i.* of the isle, thou	*Isa 23:2;*
whom	*23:6*
and scattereth abroad the *i.*	*Isa 24:1*
thereof	
the earth is defiled under the	*Isa 24:5*
i. thereof	
therefore the *i.* of the earth are	*Isa 24:6*
burned	
the *i.* of the world will learn	*Isa 26:9*
righteousness	
nor have the *i.* of the world	*Isa 26:18*
fallen	
behold man no more with the	*Isa 38:11*
i. of the world	
the *i.* thereof are as	*Isa 40:22*
grasshoppers	
isles and *i.* sing to the Lord a	*Isa 42:10*
new song	
let the *i.* of the rock sing, let	*Isa 42:11*
them shout	
land too narrow by reason of	*Isa 49:19*
the *i.*	
I will fill the *i.* with	*Jer 13:13*
drunkenness	
thus will I do to the *i.* thereof	*Jer 19:12*
I will smite the *i.* of this city,	*Jer 21:6*
man and beast	
as Sodom, and the *i.* thereof	*Jer 23:14*
as Gomorrah	
for a sword upon the *i.*	*Jer 25:29;*
thereof	*50:35*
ye shall bring innocent blood	*Jer 26:15*
on the *i.*	
turn back, dwell deep, O *i.* of	*Jer 49:8;*
Dedan	*49:30*
the Lord will disquiet the *i.* of	*Jer 50:34*
Babylon	
and my blood upon the *i.* of	*Jer 51:35*
Chaldea	
i. of the world would not have	*La 4:12*
believed	
i. of Egypt shall know I am	*Eze 29:6*
the Lord	
i. of the earth are reputed as	*Da 4:35*
nothing	
the *i.* thereof have spoken lies	*Mic 6:12*
that I should make the *i.*	*Mic 6:16*
thereof an hissing	
there shall come the *i.* of	*Zec 8:20*
many cities	
the *i.* of one city shall go to	*Zec 8:21*
another	
the *i.* of the earth have been	*Re 17:2*
made drunk	

INHABITANTS *OF THE LAND*

to make me to stink among	*Ge 34:30*
the *i. of land*	
I will deliver the *i. of land*	*Ex 23:31*
into your hand	

lest thou make a covenant *Ex 34:12;*
with *i. of land* *34:15*
dwell in cities because of the *Nu 32:17*
i. of land
shall drive out the *i. of land Nu 33:52;*
 33:55; 2Ch 20:7
all the *i. of the land* faint *Jos 2:9*
because of you
all the *i. of land* shall hear of it *Jos 7:9*
and environ
to destroy all the *i. of the land Jos 9:24*
from before you
these nations were of old the *1Sa 27:8*
i. of land
he hath given *i. of land* into *1Ch 22:18*
my hand
an evil shall break forth on all *Jer 1:14*
the *i. of land*
behold, I will fling out the *i. Jer 10:18*
of land at once
men shall cry, and all the *i. of Jer 47:2*
land shall howl
Lord hath a controversy with *Ho 4:1*
the *i. of land*
let all the *i. of the land* tremble *Joe 2:1*
for the day
for I will no more pity the *i. Zec 11:6*
of the land

INHABITED

eat manna, till they came to a *Ex 16:35*
land *i.*
goat bear their iniquities to a *Le 16:22*
land not *i.*
it shall never be *i.* nor dwelt *Isa 13:20*
in
thou shalt be *i.*; formed it to *Isa 44:26;*
be *i.* *45:18*
and make the desolate cities to *Isa 54:3*
be *i.*
lest I make thee a land not *i. Jer 6:8*
shall inhabit in a salt land and *Jer 17:6*
not *i.*
I will make thee cities which *Jer 22:6*
are not *i.*
afterward it shall be *i.* as in *Jer 46:26*
the days of old
it shall not be *i.* no more *i. Jer 50:13;*
for ever *50:39*
the cities that are *i.* shall be *Eze 12:20*
laid waste
when I shall set thee, that *Eze 26:20*
thou be not *i.*
nor shall it be *i.* forty years *Eze 29:11*
the cities shall be *i.* and the *Eze 36:10*
wastes builded
upon the desolate places that *Eze 38:12*
are now *i.*
i. forever (A)(B) *Joe 3:20*
Jerusalem be *i.* as towns *Zec 2:4*
without walls
from Gaza, and Ashkelon shall *Zec 9:5*
not be *i.*
Jerusalem shall be *i.* again in *Zec 12:6*
her place
it shall be lifted up, and *i.* in *Zec 14:10*
her place
no destruction, but Jerusalem *Zec 14:11*
shall be safely *i.*

INHABITERS

woe, woe, woe, to *i.* of the *Re 8:13*
earth
woe to the *i.* of the earth and *Re 12:12*
of the sea

INHABITEST

O. thou that *i.* the praises of *Ps 22:3*
Israel

INHABITETH

he dwelleth in houses which *Job 15:28*
no man *i.*
thus saith the lofty One that *Isa 57:15*
i. eternity

INHABITING

be meat to the people *i.* the *Ps 74:14*
wilderness

INHABITRESS

i. of Aroer (B) *Jer 48:19*

INHABITS

no man passes through or *i.* (B) *Jer 2:6*

INHERIT

whereby shall I know that I *Ge 15:8*
shall *i.* it
assured it will be mine (B) *Ge 15:8*
know that I shall possess it *Ge 15:8*
(R)
and they shall *i.* it for ever *Ex 32:13*
they shall possess it for ever *Ex 32:13*
(B)
I have given it to the Levites *Nu 18:24*
to *i.*
according to the names of *Nu 26:55*
tribes they shall *i.*
we will not *i.* on yonder side *Nu 32:19*
Jordan
fallen heir to our possession *Nu 32:19*
(B)
for he shall cause Israel to *i.* it *De 1:38*
which the Lord God giveth *De 12:10*
you to *i.*
he maketh his sons to *i.* what *De 21:16*
he hath
shalt not *i.* in our father's *J'g 11:2*
house
to make them *i.* the throne of *1Sa 2:8*
glory
and his seed shall *i.* the earth *Ps 25:13*
that wait on the Lord shall *i. Ps 37:9*
the earth
the meek shall *i.* the earth *Ps 37:11;*
 M't 5:5
such as be blessed of him shall *Ps 37:22*
i. the earth
the seed also of his servants *Ps 69:36*
shall *i.* it
O God, for thou shalt *i.* all *Ps 82:8*
nations
the wise shall *i.* glory, but *Pr 3:35*
shame
cause those who love me to *i. Pr 8:21*
substance
troubleth his own house, shall *Pr 11:29*
i. wind
the simple *i.* folly, but the *Pr 14:18*
prudent
to cause to *i.* the desolate *Isa 49:8*
heritages
and thy seed shall *i.* the *Isa 54:3*
Gentiles
mine elect shall *i.* it, and my *Isa 65:9*
servants
I have caused my people *Jer 12:14*
Israel to *i.*
why then doth their king *i., Jer 49:1*
Gad
ye shall *i.* it one as well as *Eze 47:14*
another
the Lord shall *i.* Judah his *Zec 2:12*
portion
and shall *i.* everlasting life *M't 19:29*
come *i.* the kingdom *M't 25:34*
prepared for you
i. eternal life *M'k 10:17;*
 Lu 10:25; 18:18
i. new kinds of mischief (N) *Ro 1:30*
unrighteous not *i.* the kingdom *1Co 6:9*
of God
neither shall extortioners *i.* *1Co 6:1;*
 Ga 5:21
flesh and blood cannot *i.* *1Co 15:50*
kingdom of
perishable *i.* imperishable *1Co 15:50*
(A)(B)(R)
who through faith *i.* the *Heb 6:12*
promises
called, that ye should *i.* a *1Pe 3:9*
blessing
he that overcometh shall *i.* all *Re 21:7*
things

INHERIT LAND

to give thee this *land* to *i.* it *Ge 15:7*
thou mayest *i. land* wherein a *Ge 28:4*
stranger
I have said, Ye shall *i.* their *Le 20:24*
land
this is the *land* ye shall *i.* by *Nu 34:13*
lot
possess, that thou mayest *i.* his *De 2:31*
land
i. the *land* the Lord giveth *De 16:20;*
thee *19:3*
the righteous shall *i.* the *land Ps 37:29*
and he shall exalt thee to *i.* the *Ps 37:34*
land
they shall *i.* the *land* for ever *Isa 60:21*
whereby ye shall *i.* the *land Eze 47:13*

INHERITANCE

is there any portion or *i.* for *Ge 31:14*
us
after name of their brethren in *Ge 48:6*
their *i.*
plant them in mountain of *Ex 15:17*
thine *i.*
for ever take them as an *i.* for *Le 25:46*
ever
or given us *i.* of fields or *Nu 16:14*
vineyards
have no *i.* for I am thy part *Nu 18:20*
and thine *i.*
shall cause his *i.* to pass to his *Nu 27:8*
daughters
i. to brethren *Nu 27:9*
i. to father's brethren *Nu 27:10*
our *i.* is fallen on this side *Nu 32:19;*
 32:32; 34:15
take one prince, to divide the *Nu 34:18*
land by *i.*
and shall be put to the *i.* of *Nu 36:3;*
the tribe *36:4*
nor *i.* remove from one tribe *Nu 36:9*
to another
a people of *i.* as ye are this day *De 4:20*
destroy not thine *i.*; they are *De 9:26;*
thy *i.* *9:29*
Jacob is the lot of his *i. De 32:9*
sacrifices of Lord their *i.* *Jos 13:14;*
 18:7
the Lord God of Israel was *Jos 13:33*
their *i.*
by lot was their *i.* *Jos 14:2; Ps 78:55*
Hebron therefore became the *Jos 14:14*
i. of Caleb
daughters of Manasseh had *i. Jos 17:6*
among sons
every man to his *i.* *Jos 24:28;*
 J'g 2:6; 21:24
must be an *i.* for them that *J'g 21:17*
escaped
cannot redeem *i.* lest mar mine *Ru 4:6*
own *i.*
anointed thee captain over his *1Sa 10:1*
i.
from abiding in the *i.* of the *1Sa 26:19*
Lord
nor *i.* in son of Jesse *2Sa 20:1;*
 1Ki 12:16
that ye may bless the *i.* of the *2Sa 21:3*
Lord
they be thy people and thy *i.* *1Ki 8:51;*
 8:53
give the *i.* of my fathers to *1Ki 21:3;*
thee *21:4*
will forsake the remnant of *2Ki 21:14*
mine *i.*
land of Canaan, the lot of *1Ch 16:18*
your *i.*
in all cities, every one in his *i. Ne 11:20*
what *i.* of the Almighty from *Job 31:2*
on high
the Lord is the portion of mine *Ps 16:5*
i.
a good *i.* is mine (B) *Ps 16:6*
bless thine *i.*; chosen for his *i. Ps 28:9;*
 33:12
and their *i.* shall be for ever *Ps 37:18*
he shall choose our *i.* for us *Ps 47:4*
whereby thou didst confirm *Ps 68:9*
thine *i.*
the rod of thine *i.* thou hast *Ps 74:2*
redeemed
and was wroth with his *i.* *Ps 78:62*
he brought him to feed Israel *Ps 87:71*
his *i.*
O God, the heathen are come *Ps 79:1*
into thine *i.*
not cast off, neither will he *Ps 94:14*
forsake his *i.*
the land of Canaan, the lot *Ps 105:11*
of your *i.*
that I may glory with thine *i. Ps 106:5*
insomuch, that he abhorred *Ps 106:40*
his own *i.*
good man leaveth *i.* to *Pr 13:22*
children
have part of *i.* among the *Pr 17:2*
brethren
house and riches are the *i.* of *Pr 19:14*
fathers
an *i.* may be gotten hastily at *Pr 20:21*
beginning
wisdom is good with an *i.* *Ec 7:11*
blessed be Israel mine *i.* *Isa 19:25*
I have polluted mine *i.* and *Isa 47:6*
given them

thy servants' sake, the tribes *Isa 63:17*
of thine *i.*
my *i.* an abomination (B) *Jer 2:7*
Israel is the rod of his *i.* *Jer 10:16;*
51:19
each in his *i.* (B) *Jer 12:15*
right of *i.* is thine, redemption *Jer 32:8*
is thine
our *i.* is turned to strangers, our *La 5:2*
houses
shall possess thee, thou shalt *Eze 36:12*
be their *i.*
shall be unto them for an *i.* I *Eze 44:28*
am their *i.*
i. thereof shall be his sons' *Eze 46:16;*
46:17
not take of people's *i.* by *Eze 46:18*
oppression
they shall have *i.* with you *Eze 47:22;*
among zhins *47:23*
flock of your *i.* (A)(B)(R) *Mic 7:14*
remnant of his *i.* (B)(R) *Mic 7:18*
kill him, and let us seize on *M't 21:38*
his *i.*
and the *i.* shall be ours *M'k 12:7;*
Lu 20:14
speak, that he divide the *i.* *Lu 12:13*
with me
to give you an *i.* among all *Ac 20:32*
sanctified
and *i.* among them sanctified *Ac 26:18*
by faith, in me
if the *i.* be of the law, it is no *Ga 3:18*
more
in whom also we have *Eph 1:11*
obtained an *i.*
which is earnest of our *i.* till *Eph 1:14*
redemption
the riches of the glory of his *i.* *Eph 1:18*
in the saints
hath an *i.* in the kingdom of *Eph 5:5*
Christ and God
to be partakers of the *i.* of the *Col 1:12*
saints
and ye shall receive the *Col 3:24*
reward of the *i.*
as he hath by *i.* obtained a *Heb 1:4*
name
might receive the promise of *Heb 9:15*
eternal *i.*
begotten us to an *i.* *1Pe 1:4*
incorruptible

FOR INHERITANCE

pardon our sin, and take us *for* *Ex 34:9*
thine *i.*
all the tenth in Israel *for* an *Nu 18:21;*
i. *18:26*
the land shall be divided *for* *Nu 26:53;*
i. *33:54; 34:2; 36:2; De 4:21, 38; 15:4;*
19:10; Jos 13:6-7, 32; 14:1; 19:49, 51;
Eze 45:1; 47:22; 48:29
the Lord doth give thee *for* *De 20:16;*
i. 21:23; 24:4; 25:19; 26:1; Jos 11:23;
13:6; 14:13; 1Ki 8:36; 2Ch 6:27; Jer 3:18
leave it *for* an *i.* for children *1Ch 28:8;*
Ezr 9:12
I shall give thee the heathen *for* *Ps 2:8*
thy *i.*
the land is given us *for* an *i.* *Eze 33:24*
it shall be to them *for* an *i.* *Eze 44:28*
this land shall fall unto you *Eze 47:14*
for an *i.*
which he should after receive *Heb 11:8*
for an *i.*

NO, NONE INHERITANCE

thou shalt have *no i.* *Nu 18:20;*
18:23-24; 26:62; De 10:9; 14:27, 29;
18:1-2; Jos 13:14, 33; 14:3
we have *no i.* in the son of *2Ch 10:16*
Jesse
and he gave him *none i.* in it *Ac 7:5*

INHERITANCES

these are the *i.* Joshua *Jos 19:51*
divided by lot

INHERITED

we will not return till Israel *Nu 32:18*
have *i.*
children of Israel *i.* land of *Jos 14:1*
Canaan
they *i.* the labour of the *Ps 105:44*
people

surely our fathers have *i.* lies *Jer 16:19*
Abraham was one, and he *i.* *Eze 33:24*
land
when he would have *i.* the *Heb 12:17*
blessing

INHERITETH

according to his inheriting *Nu 35:8*
which he *i.*

INHERITOR

out of Judah an *i.* of my *Isa 65:9*
mountains

INIQUITIES

confess over the goat all the *i.* *Le 16:21*
pine
in *i.* of their fathers shall they *Le 26:39*
pine
bear your *i.* (E) *Nu 14:33*
our *i.* are increased over our *Ezr 9:6*
head
our *i.* have we, our kings, been *Ezr 9:7*
delivered
punished us less than our *i.* *Ezr 9:13*
deserve
Israel confessed the *i.* of their *Ne 9:2*
fathers
how many are mine *i.* and *Job 13:23*
sins
makest me to possess *i.* of *Job 13:26*
my youth
thy wickedness great, and *Job 22:5*
thine *i.* infinite
mine *i.* are gone over my head *Ps 38:4*
mine *i.* have taken hold on me *Ps 40:12*
hide face from my sins, blot *Ps 51:9*
out all *i.*
they search out *i.; i.* prevail *Ps 64:6;*
against *65:3*
remember not against us *Ps 79:8*
former *i.*
set our *i.* before thee, our secret *Ps 90:8*
sins
bless the Lord, who forgiveth *Ps 103:3*
all thine *i.*
nor rewarded us according to *Ps 103:10*
our *i.*
if Lord shouldest mark *i.* who *Ps 130:3*
stand
he shall redeem Israel from all *Ps 130:8*
his *i.*
his own *i.* shall take wicked *Pr 5:22*
himself
thou hast wearied me with *Isa 43:24*
thine *i.*
but he was bruised for our *i.* *Isa 53:5*
and as for our *i.* we know *Isa 59:12*
them
our *i.* like wind have taken us *Isa 64:6*
away
thou hast consumed us because *Isa 64:7*
of our *i.*
turned back to *i.* of their *Jer 11:10*
forefathers
O Lord, though our *i.* testify *Jer 14:7*
against us
for *i.* of her priests that shed *La 4:13*
blood
by multitude of thine *i.* *Eze 28:18*
defiled
break off thine *i.* by shewing *Da 4:27*
mercy
we might turn from our *i.* *Da 9:13*
for our sins, and for the *i.* of *Da 9:16*
our fathers
he will turn, he will subdue *Mic 7:19*
our *i.*
to bless in turning every one *Ac 3:26*
from his *i.*
blessed are they whose *i.* are *Ro 4:7*
forgiven
merciful to their *i.* *Heb 8:12*
(E)(P)(R)
for God hath remembered her *Re 18:5*
i.

THEIR INIQUITIES

the goat shall bear on him all *Le 16:22*
their i.
fools because of *their i.* are *Ps 107:17*
afflicted
justify many, for he shall bear *Isa 53:11*
their i.
and I will pardon all *their i.* *Jer 33:8*
whereby
our fathers sinned, we have *La 5:7*
borne *their i.*

but *their i.* shall be on their *Eze 32:27*
bones
that they may be ashamed of *Eze 43:10*
their i.
their i. will I remember no *Heb 8:12;*
more *10:17*

YOUR INIQUITIES

forty years shall ye bear *your* *Nu 14:34*
i.
for *your i.* have you sold *Isa 50:1*
yourselves
your i. separated between you *Isa 59:2*
and God
your i. I will recompense *Isa 65:7*
your i. have turned away these *Jer 5:25*
things
ye shall pine away for *your i.* *Eze 24:23*
and shall loathe yourselves *Eze 36:31*
for *your i.*
I shall have cleansed you *Eze 36:33*
from all *your i.*
therefore I will punish you for *Am 3:2*
all *your i.*

INIQUITOUS

decree *i.* decrees (R) *Isa 10:1*

INIQUITY

i. of the Amorites is not yet *Ge 15:16*
full
lest thou be consumed in *i.* of *Ge 19:15*
the city
God hath found out the *i.* of *Ge 44:16*
thy servants
visiting *i.* of fathers upon the *Ex 20:5;*
children *34:7; Nu 14:18; De 5:9*
sins of fathers (B) *Ex 20:5*
forgiving *i.* and transgression *Ex 34:7;*
Nu 14:18
go amongst us, and pardon our *Ex 34:9*
i.
therefore I do visit the *i.* *Le 18:25*
thereof
offering bringing *i.* to *Nu 5:15*
remembrance
be innocent of any sin (B) *Nu 5:15;*
14:19; 23:21; Jos 22:17
then shall the man be guiltless *Nu 5:31*
from *i.*
pardon, I pray thee, the *i.* *Nu 14:19*
of people
he hath not beheld *i.* in *Nu 23:21*
Jacob, nor seen
nor rise up against a man for *De 19:15*
any *i.*
he is a God of truth and *De 32:4*
without *i.* just
is the *i.* of Peor too little *Jos 22:17*
for us
judge for the *i.* which he *1Sa 3:13*
knoweth
the *i.* of Eli's house shall not *1Sa 3:14*
be purged
and stubbornness is as *i.* and *1Sa 15:23*
idolatry
is as wickedness (B) *1Sa 15:23*
if there be in me *i.* slay me *1Sa 20:8*
thyself
upon me let this *i.* be *1Sa 25:24;*
2Sa 14:9
if there be *i.* in me, let him *2Sa 14:32*
kill me
let not my Lord impute *i.* to *2Sa 19:19*
me
take away *i.* of servant *2Sa 24:10;*
1Ch 21:8
for there is no *i.* with Lord *2Ch 19:7*
our God
they that plow *i.* reap the same *Job 4:8*
poor hath hope, and *i.* stoppeth *Job 5:16*
her mouth
return, I pray you, let it not *Job 6:29*
be *i.* return
is there *i.* in my tongue? *Job 6:30*
cannot my taste
God exacteth less than thine *i.* *Job 11:6*
deserveth
if *i.* be in thy hand, put it far *Job 11:14*
away
for thy mouth uttereth thine *i.* *Job 15:5*
filthy is man which drinketh *Job 15:16*
i. like water
shalt put away *i.* far from thy *Job 22:23*
tabernacles
it is an *i.* to be punished by *Job 31:11;*
judges *31:28*

I am innocent, nor is there *i.* *Job 33:9*
in me
if I have done *i.* I will do no *Job 34:32*
more
he commandeth that they *Job 36:10*
return from *i.*
take heed, regard not *i.* for *Job 36:21*
this hast chosen
or who can say, Thou hast *Job 36:23*
wrought *i.*
O Lord, if there be *i.* in my *Ps 7:3*
hands
he travaileth with *i.* and *Ps 7:14*
conceived
blessed to whom Lord imputeth *Ps 32:2*
not *i.*
and thou forgavest the *i.* of my *Ps 32:5*
sin
the words of his mouth are *i.* *Ps 36:3*
and deceit
when thou dost correct man *Ps 39:11*
for *i.*
his heart gathereth *i.* to itself *Ps 41:6*
when *i.* of my heels shall *Ps 49:5*
compass me
I was shapen in *i.* and in sin *Ps 51:5*
mother
are corrupt, and have done *Ps 53:1*
abominable *i.*
cast *i.* upon me, and in wrath *Ps 55:3*
hate me
shall they escape by *i.*? cast *Ps 56:7*
down
if I regard *i.* in heart, *Ps 66:18*
Lord not hear me
thou hast forgiven the *i.* of thy *Ps 85:2*
people
throne of *i.* have fellowship *Ps 94:20*
with thee
and all *i.* shall stop her *Ps 107:42*
mouth
let the *i.* of his fathers be *Ps 109:14*
remembered
they also do no *i.* they walk in *Ps 119:3*
his ways
let not any *i.* have dominion *Ps 119:133*
over me
lest they put forth their hands *Ps 125:3*
to *i.*
by mercy and truth *i.* is purged *Pr 16:6*
the mouth of the wicked *Pr 19:28*
devoureth *i.*
he that soweth *i.* shall reap *Pr 22:8*
vanity
place of righteousness *i.* was *Ec 3:16*
there
people laden with *i.* seed of evil *Isa 1:4*
doers
it is *i.* even the solemn meeting *Isa 1:13*
woe to them that draw *i.* with *Isa 5:18*
cords
thine *i.* is taken away, and sin *Isa 6:7*
purged
prepare for the *i.* of their *Isa 14:21*
fathers
this *i.* shall not be purged *Isa 22:14*
from you
by this shall the *i.* of Jacob be *Isa 27:9*
purged
and all that watch for *i.* are *Isa 29:20*
cut off
this *i.* shall be to you as a *Isa 30:13*
breach
cry unto her, her *i.* is pardoned *Isa 40:2*
Lord hath laid on him the *i.* of *Isa 53:6*
us all
for *i.* of his covetousness was *Isa 57:17*
I wroth
for your fingers are defiled *Isa 59:3*
with *i.*
bring forth *i.*; their works are *Isa 59:4*;
works of *i.* *59:6*
their thoughts are thoughts of *Isa 59:7*
i. wasting
be not wroth, nor remember *i.* *Isa 64:9*
for ever
what *i.* have fathers found in *Jer 2:5*
me
thine *i.* is marked before me *Jer 2:22*
only acknowledge thine *i.* that *Jer 3:13*
thou
for greatness of thine *i.* are *Jer 13:22*
thy skirts
we acknowledge the *i.* of our *Jer 14:20*
fathers
what is our *i.*: *i.* hid from *Jer 16:10*;
mine eyes *16:17*
for multitude of thine *i.* *Jer 30:14*;
  30:15; Ho 9:7

recompensest *i.* of fathers *Jer 32:18*
into the bosom
the *i.* of Israel be sought for, *Jer 50:20*
and none
flee out of Babylon, be not cut *Jer 51:6*
off in her *i.*
they have not discovered thine *La 2:14*
i.
for the punishment of the *i.* of *La 4:6*
my people
punishment of *i.* is *La 4:22*
accomplished, will visit thine *i.*
lay *i.* of the house of Israel *Eze 4:4*
upon it
nor strengthen himself in *i.* of *Eze 7:13*
his life
the *i.* of the house of Israel is *Eze 9:9*
great
this was the *i.* of thy sister *Eze 16:49*
Sodom
that hath withdrawn his hand *Eze 18:8*
from *i.*
he shall not die for the *i.* of *Eze 18:17*
his father
repent, so *i.* shall not be your *Eze 18:30*
ruin
he will call to remembrance *Eze 21:23*;
your *i.* *21:24*
when *i.* shall have an end *Eze 21:25*;
  21:29; 35:5
wast perfect, till *i.* was *Eze 28:15*
found in thee
defiled thy sanctuaries by *i.* *Eze 28:18*
of thy traffic
caused house of Israel to fall *Eze 44:12*
into *i.*
to make reconciliation for *i.* *Da 9:24*
the *i.* of Ephraim was *Ho 7:1*
discovered
against children of *i.*; ye *Ho 10:9*;
reaped *i.* *10:13*
find no *i.* in me; is there *i.* in *Ho 12:8*;
Gilead *12:11*
i. of Ephraim is bound up, *Ho 13:12*
his sin hid
return, for thou hast fallen by *Ho 14:1*
thine *i.*
take away all *i.* and receive us *Ho 14:2*
graciously
woe to them that devise *i.* on *Mic 2:1*
their beds
they build up Jerusalem with *Mic 3:10*
i.
who is a God like to thee, *Mic 7:18*
that pardoneth *i.*
why dost thou shew me *i.* and *Hab 1:3*
cause me
of purer eyes, and thou canst *Hab 1:13*
not look on *i.*
woe to him that establisheth *Hab 2:12*
a city by *i.*
the just Lord, he will not do *i.* *Zep 3:5*
the remnant of Israel shall not *Zep 3:13*
do *i.*
I have caused thine *i.* to pass *Zec 3:4*
from thee
I will remove the *i.* of that land *Zec 3:9*
in one day
i. was not found in his lips, *Mal 2:6*
and did turn many away from *i.*
they shall gather them which *M't 13:41*
do *i.*
within ye are full of *M't 23:28*
hypocrisy and *i.*
because *i.* abound, love wax *M't 24:12*
cold
purchased a field with the *Ac 1:18*
reward of *i.*
for I perceive thou art in the *Ac 8:23*
bond of *i.*
your members servants to *i.* *Ro 6:19*
unto *i.*
rejoiceth not in *i.* but in the *1Co 13:6*
truth
mystery of *i.* doth already work *2Th 2:7*
that nameth Christ, depart *2Ti 2:19*
from *i.*
that he might redeem us from *Tit 2:14*
all *i.*
thou hast hated *i.* therefore *Heb 1:9*
God
the tongue is a fire, a world *Jas 3:6*
of *i.*

HIS INIQUITY

his i. shall be upon him *Nu 15:31*
that man perished not alone *Jos 22:20*
in *his i.*
the heavens shall reveal *his i.* *Job 20:27*

God layeth up *his* i. for his *Job 21:19*
children
until *his i.* be found to be *Ps 36:2*
hateful
die for *his i.* *Jer 31:30*;
  Eze 3:18-19; 7:16; 18:26
the stumblingblock of *his i.* *Eze 14:7*;
  14:14
even he shall die in *his i.* *Eze 18:18*;
  33:8-9
he is taken away in *his i.* but *Eze 33:6*
his blood
Balaam was rebuked for *his i.* *2Pe 2:16*

MINE INIQUITY

what is *mine i.* and what is my *1Sa 20:1*
sin
I kept myself from *mine i.* *2Sa 22:24*;
  Ps 18:23
why dost thou not take away *Job 7:21*
mine i.
that thou inquirest after *mine* *Job 10:6*
i.
thou wilt not acquit me from *Job 10:14*
mine i.
sealed in a bag, thou sewest *Job 14:17*
up *mine i.*
if I covered, by hiding *mine* *Job 31:33*
i. in my bosom
pardon *mine i.* for it is great *Ps 25:11*
my strength faileth because of *Ps 31:10*
mine i.
and *mine i.* have I not hid, I *Ps 32:5*
said
I will declare *mine i.* I will be *Ps 38:18*
sorry for
wash me thoroughly from *mine* *Ps 51:2*
i. cleanse

THEIR INIQUITY

left of you, shall pine away in *Le 26:39*
their i.
if they confess *their i.* and the *Le 26:40*
iniquity of fathers
accept of the punishment of *Le 26:41*;
their i. *26:43*
and cover not *their i.* let not *Ne 4:5*
their sin be
add iniquity unto *their i.* and *Ps 69:27*
let them
he forgave *their i.*, I will visit *Ps 78:38*;
their i. *89:32*
he shall bring upon them *their* *Ps 94:23*
i.
they were brought low for *Ps 106:43*
their i.
I will punish the wicked for *Isa 13:11*
their i.
to punish inhabitants of earth *Isa 26:21*
for *their i.*
the people shall be forgiven *Isa 33:24*
their i.
he will now remember *their i.* *Jer 14:10*
and first, he will recompense *Jer 16:18*
their i.
forgive not *their i.* nor blot *Jer 18:23*
out sin
I will punish that nation for *Jer 25:12*
their i.
all know me, for I will forgive *Jer 31:34*
their i.
I will cleanse them from all *Jer 33:8*
their i.
that I may forgive *their i.* and *Jer 36:3*
sin
I will punish his servants for *Jer 36:31*
their i.
I have laid on thee years of *Eze 4:5*
their i.
may consume away for *their i.* *Eze 4:17*
the stumblingblock of *their i.* *Eze 7:19*;
  14:3
shall bear the punishment of *Eze 14:10*
their i.
which bringeth *their i.* to *Eze 29:16*
remembrance
Israel went into captivity for *Eze 39:23*
their i.
and they set their heart on *their* *Ho 4:8*
i.
shall Israel and Ephraim fall in *Ho 5:5*
their i.
he will remember *their i.* he will *Ho 9:9*
visit sins

WORK INIQUITY

to practise works with men *Ps 141:4*
that *work i.*

against the help of them that *work i.* — *Isa 31:2*

his heart will *work i.* to practise hypocrisy — *Isa 32:6*

Gilead is a city of them that *work i.* — *Ho 6:8*

depart from me, ye that *work i.* — *M't 7:23*

WORKERS OF INIQUITY

strange punishment to *workers of i.* — *Job 31:3*

goeth in company with *workers of i.* — *Job 34:8*

where *workers of i.* may hide themselves — *Job 34:22*

foolish not stand, thou hatest all *workers of i.* — *Ps 5:5*

depart from me all ye *workers of i.* — *Ps 6:8; Lu 13:27*

have all the *workers of i.* no knowledge — *Ps 14:4; 53:4*

draw me not away with the *workers of i.* — *Ps 28:3*

there are *workers of i.* fallen, they are cast down — *Ps 36:12*

nor be thou envious against *workers of i.* — *Ps 37:1*

deliver me from *workers of i.* and save me — *Ps 59:2*

from the insurrection of the *workers of i.* — *Ps 64:2*

when all the *workers of i.* do flourish — *Ps 92:7*

all the *workers of i.* shall be scattered — *Ps 92:9*

all the *workers of i.* boast themselves — *Ps 94:4*

or who will stand up for me against the *workers of i.* — *Ps 94:16*

lead them forth with the *workers of i.* — *Ps 125:5*

keep me from the gins of the *workers of i.* — *Ps 141:9*

destruction shall be to *workers of i.* — *Pr 10:29; 21:15*

INITIATED

He *i.*, dedicated (A) — *Heb 10:20*

INJUNCTION

in spite of the *i.* (B) — *Es 4:16*

containing *i.* and conditions (B) — *Jer 32:11*

INJUNCTIONS

keep all his *i.* (B) — *Ex 15:26*

soul abhors my *i.* (B) — *Le 26:15*

i. and statutes he gave (B) — *Ps 99:7*

walking in agreement with all *i.* (B) — *Lu 1:6*

INJURED

if brother is *i.* (A) — *Ro 14:15*

as ye are: ye have not *i.* me at all — *Ga 4:12*

ye did me no wrong (A)(B)(E)(N)(R) — *Ga 4:12*

INJURING

if possiblity of *i.* my brother (P) — *1Co 8:13*

INJURIOUS

and a persecutor, and *i.*: but I (B) — *1Ti 1:13*

persecutor and an oppressor (B) — *1Ti 1:13*

persecution and outrage (N) — *1Ti 1:13*

persecuted and insulted (P)(R) — *1Ti 1:13*

INJURY

recover from this *i.* (E)(R) — *2Ki 1:2*

will be with *i.* and much damage (S) — *Ac 27:10*

INJUSTICE

do no *i.* (A)(R) — *Le 19:15; 19:35*

no *i.* with God (A)(B) — *2Ch 19:7*

Not for any *i.* in mine hands — *Job 16:17*

---

no guilt or violence in my hands (A) — *Job 16:17*

hands guilty of no violence (B) — *Job 16:17*

no violence in my hands (E)(R) — *Job 16:17*

destroyed because of *i.* (A)(E)(R) — *Pr 8:23*

tongue muttered *i.* (B) — *Isa 59:3*

city full of *i.* (B)(R) — *Eze 9:9*

every kind of *i.* (N) — *Ro 1:29*

our *i.* (P)(R) — *Ro 3:5*

is there *i.* on God's part (A)(B)(N)(R) — *Ro 9:14*

INK

and I wrote them with *i.* in — *Jer 36:18*

written not with *i.* but with the — *2Co 3:3*

would not write with paper and *i.* — *2Jo 12*

I will not with *i.* and pen write unto — *3Jo 13*

INKHORN

with a writer's *i.* by his side — *Eze 9:2; 9:3*

linen, which had the *i.* by his side — *Eze 9:11*

INLET

notice an *i.* (B) — *Ac 27:39*

INMOST

my *i.* self (B) — *Ps 94:19*

far from their *i.* selves (B) — *Jer 12:2*

arrows enter *i.* parts (B) — *La 3:13*

in my *i.* self (A)(N)(R) — *Ro 7:22*

in my *i.* heart — *Ro 7:22*

INN

to give his ass provender in the *i.* — *Ge 42:27*

when we came to the *i.* that we — *Ge 43:21*

came to pass by the way in the *i.* — *Ex 4:24*

was no room for them in the *i.* — *Lu 2:7*

and brought him to an *i.* and took — *Lu 10:34*

INNER

the *i.* room (B) — *1Ki 6:5*

the *i.* sanctuary (R) — *1Ki 6:5; 6:31; 7:49; 8:6, 8*

the *i.* sanctuary (S) — *1Ki 6:5; 6:16, 19-23, 31; 7:49; 8:6, 8; 2Ch 3:16; 4:20; 5:7, 9*

an *i.* sanctuary (B)(R) — *1Ki 6:16*

the *i.* room (A) — *1Ki 6:19*

the cherubims within the *i.* house — *1Ki 6:27; 7:50; Eze 41:17; 42:15*

the *i.* court — *1Ki 6:36; 7:12; Es 4:11; 5:1; Eze 8:3, 16; 10:3; 40:19, 23, 27-28, 32, 44; 42:3; 43:5; 44:17, 21, 27; 45:19; 46:1*

the *i.* chamber — *1Ki 20:30; 22:25; 2Ki 9:2; 2Ch 18:24*

the *i.* parlours — *1Ch 28:11*

the *i.* doors — *2Ch 4:22*

the *i.* part of the house — *2Ch 29:16*

wisdom in *i.* self (B) — *Job 38:36*

our *i.* selves (A) — *Ps 33:20*

desire truth in *i.* being (A)(B)(R) — *Ps 51:6*

my *i.* being (A) — *Ps 71:23*

your *i.* self (A) — *Pr 3:22*

my *i.* being sounds like a harp (A) — *Isa 16:11*

I try the *i.* self (B) — *Jer 17:10*

entered into *i.* chamber (A) — *Eze 21:14*

the *i.* gate — *Eze 40:15; 40:44*

the *i.* temple — *Eze 41:15*

my *i.* self trembled (A) — *Hab 3:16*

enter your *i.* room (B)(E) — *M't 6:6*

i. rooms, chambers — *M't 24:26*

(E)(N)(P)(R)

the *i.* prison — *Ac 16:24*

i. illumination of spirit (P) — *Eph 1:18*

his Spirit in the *i.* man — *Eph 3:16*

reveal *i.* motives (P) — *1Co 4:5*

our *i.* self being renewed (A)(B) — *2Co 4:16*

our *i.* nature being renewed (R) — *2Co 4:16*

INNERMOST

the *i.* part (B)(R) — *1Ki 6:19*

down into *i.* parts of belly — *1Ki 18:8; 26:22*

searching *i.* parts (A)(B)(E)(R) — *Pr 20:27; 20:30*

strokes reach *i.* parts (A)(B)(E)(R) — *Pr 20:30*

from his *i.* being (A)(B) — *Joh 7:38*

from his *i.* heart (P) — *Joh 7:38*

the *i.* shrine (P) — *Heb 6:19*

INNERPARTS

its *i.* (A)(R) — *Ex 12:9*

INNOCENCE

i. of my hands (R) — *Ge 20:5*

wash hands in *i.* (A)(B)(R) — *Ps 26:6*

wash hands in *i.* (B)(R) — *Ps 73:13*

INNOCENCY

and *i.* of my hands have I done — *Ge 20:5*

an honest heart and clean hands (B) — *Ge 20:5*

innocence of my hands (R) — *Ge 20:5*

I will wash mine hands in *i.*: so will — *Ps 26:6*

wash my hands in innocence (A)(B)(R) — *Ps 26:6*

in vain, and washed my hands in *i.* — *Ps 73:13*

washed my hands in innocence (B)(R) — *Ps 73:13*

as before him *i.* was found in me — *Da 6:22*

I was found innocent (A)(B) — *Da 6:22*

I was found blameless (R) — *Da 6:22*

long will it be ere they attain to *i.* — *Ho 8:5*

until they attain to purity (A) — *Ho 8:5*

How long pure heart impossible (B) — *Ho 8:5*

till they are pure in Israel (R) — *Ho 8:5*

INNOCENT

an *i.* nation (B)(R) — *Ge 20:40*

the *i.* and righteous slay thou not — *Ex 23:7*

submits cause of *i.* (B) — *De 16:19*

That *i.* blood be not shed in thy — *De 19:10*

the guilt of *i.* blood from Israel — *De 19:13*

and lay not *i.* blood unto thy people — *De 21:8*

put away the guilt of *i.* blood from — *De 21:9*

may acquit the *i.* (B)(R) — *De 25:1*

taketh reward to slay an *i.* person — *De 27:25*

then wilt thou sin against *i.* blood — *1Sa 19:5*

mayest take away the *i.* blood — *1Ki 2:31*

Manasseh shed *i.* blood very much — *2Ki 21:16*

also for the *i.* blood that he shed — *2Ki 24:4*

he filled Jerusalem with *i.* blood — *2Ki 24:4*

thee, who ever perished, being *i.* — *Job 4:7*

i. cut off (B)(R) — *Job 4:7; 34:5*

though I am *i.* (A)(B)(R) — *Job 9:20*

he will laugh at the trial of the *i.* — *Job 9:23*

know that thou wilt not hold me *i.* — *Job 9:28*

the *i.* shall stir up himself against — *Job 17:8*

and the *i.* laugh them to scorn — *Job 22:19*

He shall deliver the island of the *i.* — *Job 22:30*

on, and the *i.* shall divide the silver — *Job 27:17*

without transgression, I am *i.* — *Job 33:9*

places doth he murder the *i.* — *Ps 10:8*

nor taketh reward against the *i.* — *Ps 15:5*

i. from the great transgression — *Ps 19:13*

shoot at the *i.* (B) — *Ps 64:4*

and condemn the *i.* blood — *Ps 94:21*

And shed *i.* blood, even the blood — *Ps 106:38*

let us lurk privily for the *i.* without — *Pr 1:11*

and hands that shed *i.* blood Pr 6:17
toucheth her shall not be *i.* Pr 6:29
haste to be rich shall not be *i.* Pr 28:20
condemned the *i.* (N)(P) Isa 5:6
thrust aside the *i.* (A) Isa 29:21
they make haste to shed *i.* Isa 59:7
blood
Yet thou sayest, Because I am Jer 2:35
i.
and shed not *i.* blood in this Jer 7:6
place
neither shed *i.* blood in this Jer 22:3
place
and for to shed *i.* blood and Jer 22:17
for
ye shall surely bring *i.* blood Jer 26:15
upon
I was found *i.* (A)(B) Da 6:22
they have shed *i.* blood in Joe 3:19
their land
and lay not upon us *i.* blood Jon 1:14
in that I have betrayed the *i.* M't 27:4
blood
that *i.* man (B)(N) M't 27:19
I am *i.* of the blood of this M't 27:24
just
the hearts of the *i.* (S) Ro 16:18
good, *i.*, guileless (A)(B) Ro 16:19
as *i.* of evil as babes (N)(P) 1Co 14:20
present you *i.* (N) Col 1:22

INNOCENTS

blood of the souls of the poor Jer 2:34
i.
filled this place with the blood Jer 19:4
of *i.*

INNUMERABLE

as there are *i.* before him Job 21:33
For *i.* evils have compassed Ps 40:12
me
how *i.* are thy works (B) Ps 104:24
wherein are things creeping *i.* Ps 104:25
the grasshoppers, and are *i.* Jer 46:23
an *i.* multitude of people Lu 12:1
sand which is by the sea Heb 11:12
shore *i.*
and to an *i.* company of Heb 12:22
angels

INORDINATE

was more corrupt in her *i.* Eze 23:11
love
uncleanness, *i.* affection, evil Col 3:5

INQUIRE

judges *i.* diligently (A) De 19:18
i. of (B)(R) J'g 18:5; 20:18; 1Sa 14:37

INQUIRY

make careful *i.* (B) De 19:18
shall make diligent *i.* (S) De 19:18;
 Es 2:23
investigate and make *i.* (B) De 40:8
look on *i.* (A) 2Sa 16:12
he seeth *i.* (A)(E)(R) Job 11:11
bring forth *i.* (A)(E) Job 15:35;
 Ps 10:7
taken in *i.*, greedy desire Pr 11:6
(A)(E)(S)
cords of *i.* (A) Isa 5:18
who devise *i.* (A)(B)(E)(R) Eze 11:2
have ploughed *i.* (R) Ho 10:13
all who do *i.* (A)(E) M't 13:41
after an exhaustive *i.* (P) Ac 15:7

INQUISITION

the judges shall make diligent De 19:18
i.
judges shall inquire diligently De 19:18
(A)
make careful inquiry (B) De 19:18
when *i.* was made of the matter Es 2:23
(A)
matter was investigated Es 2:23
(A)(B)(R)
When he maketh *i.* for blood, Ps 9:12
he

INQUISITORS

delivered him to the *i.* (S) M't 18:34

INSANE

pretended to be *i.* (A) 1Sa 21:13
which were *i.* (P) M't 4:24

INSATIABLE

i. for wealth (A) 1Ti 3:3

INSCRIPTION

carving its *i.* (A)(B)(R) Zec 3:9
whose *i.* (N)(P)(R) M't 22:20
image and *i.* (B)(N)(P)(R) M'k 12:16
the *i.* was (A)(B)(N)(R) M'k 15:26
image and *i.* Lu 20:24
(A)(B)(N)(P)(R)
i. was written (A)(B)(N)(R) Lu 23:38
altar with this *i.* To The Ac 17:23
Unknown
with this *i.* (N)(P) 2Ti 2:19

INSCRUTABLE

how *i.* his judgments (B) Ro 11:33

INSECT

every winged *i.* (S) Le 11:21

INSECTS

among winged *i.* (A)(B)(R) Le 11:21
all flying winged *i.* (S) Le 11:23

INSIDE

covered them on the *i.* with 1Ki 6:15
wood
inside (S) 1Ki 6:15; 6:21; Joh 20:26
on the *i.* of the chariot (S) 1Ki 22:35
on the *i.* of the tabernacle 2Sa 6:17;
(S) 1Ch 16:1
my *i.* boils (B) Job 30:27
the gate *i.* (S) Eze 40:9
round about *i.* (S) Eze 40:16
the *i.* of the house (S) Am 6:10
i. are devouring wolves (A) M't 7:15

INSIGHT

i. and understanding (B) 1Ch 22:12
I, wisdom, dwell with *i.* (B) Pr 8:12
a man of *i.* (B) Pr 12:23;
 Pr 13:16; 14:8, 15, 18
cause many to gain *i.* (B) Da 11:33
greatest wisdom and *i.* Eph 1:8
(B)(N)(R)

INSIGNIFICANT

poor and *i.* (B) 1Sa 18:23

INSINCERITY

carried away by *i.* (R) Ga 2:13
without uncertainty and *i.* (R) Jas 3:17

INSINUATE

i. themselves in private homes 2Ti 3:6
(N)

INSIPID

can the *i.* be eaten (B) Job 6:6

INSISTED

i. disciples aboard (P) M't 14:22
he *i.* and repeated (N) M'k 14:31
i. on our going (N)(P) Ac 16:15

INSISTENCE

his brazen *i.* (A)(B) Lu 11:8

INSISTENT

with *i.* good behavior (B) Ro 2:7

INSOLENCE

in their *i.* they (B) Ge 49:6
your *i.* has come (B) 2Ki 19:28
full of *i.* (A) Ro 1:30

INSOLENT

i. men (R) Ps 54:3
speak with *i.* neck (B)(R) Ps 75:5

i. men have risen (R) Ps 86:14
rebuke the *i.* (R) Ps 119:21
the *i.* men (R) Jer 43:2
insolent Ro 1:30
(B)(E)(N)(P)(R)(S)
living in shameless, *i.* 1Pe 4:3
wantonness (A)

INSOLENTLY

struck cheek *i.* (A)(B)(R) Job 16:10
speak *i.* against Ps 31:18
(A)(B)(E)(R)
who deals *i.* with me (R) Ps 55:12

INSOMUCH

i. that he abhorred his own Ps 106:40
i. that he regardeth not the Mal 2:13
offering
i. that the ship was covered M't 8:24
with
i. that the blind and dumb M't 12:22
both
i. that they were astonished M't 13:54
I. that the multitude M't 15:31
wondered
i. that, if it were possible, M't 24:24
they shall
i. that the governor marvelled M't 27:14
i. that they questioned among M'k 1:27
i. that Jesus could no more M'k 1:45
openly
i. that there was no room to M'k 2:2
receive
i. that they were all amazed M'k 2:12
i. that they pressed upon him M'k 3:10
for to
dead; *i.* that many said, He is M'k 9:26
dead
i. that they trode one upon Lu 12:1
another
i. as that field is called in Ac 1:19
their
I., that they brought forth the Ac 5:15
sick
i. that we despaired even of life 2Co 1:8
I. that we desired Titus, that as 2Co 8:6
i. that Barnabas also was Ga 2:13
carried

INSPECTION

in the day of *i.* (A) 1Pe 2:12

INSPIRATION

the *i.* of the Almighty giveth Job 32:8
them
the breath of the Almighty Job 32:8
(A)(B)(E)(R)
scripture is given by *i.* of God 2Ti 3:16
All scripture is inspired 2Ti 3:16
(B)(E)(P)(R)

INSPIRED

man who is *i.* (A) Ho 5:7
i. to predict (N) Ac 11:28
a prophet or *i.* (B)(N) 1Co 14:37
doctrines *i.* by devils (N) 1Ti 4:1
all scriptures *i.* 2Ti 3:16
(B)(E)(N)(P)(R)

INSPIRES

work of Lord *i.* awe (R) Ex 34:10

INSTABILITY

and by their lies and *i.* (S) Jer 23:32
will reveal *i.* (P) Jas 1:8

INSTALLATION

seven days to *i.* (B) Ex 29:35

INSTALLED

you are *i.* today (B) Ex 32:29
i. in priestly office (B) Nu 3:3

INSPIRING

angel very awe *i.* (B) J'g 13:6
awe *i.* terror (B) De 26:8
awe *i.* deeds (B) Ps 45:4;
 65:5; 66:3; 68:35; 99:3; 106:22; 145:6
awe *i.* God (B) Ps 47:2
awesome, reverence *i.* (A) Ps 99:3

INSTANT

yea, it shall be at an *i.* suddenly	*Isa 29:5*
breaking cometh suddenly at an *i.*	*Isa 30:13*
At what *i.* I shall speak concerning	*Jer 18:7; 18:9*
she coming in that *i.* gave thanks	*Lu 2:38*
And they were *i.* with loud voices	*Lu 23:23*
continuing *i.* in prayer	*Ro 12:12*
be *i.* in season, out of season	*2Ti 4:2*

INSTANTLY

they besought him *i.* saying	*Lu 7:4*
i. serving God day and night	*Ac 26:7*

INSTEAD

and closed up the flesh *i.* thereof	*Ge 2:21*
me another seed *i.* of Abel	*Ge 4:25*
let thy servant abide *i.* of the lad a	*Ge 44:33*
even he shall be to thee *i.* of a mouth	*Ex 4:16*
and thou shalt be to him *i.* of God	*Ex 4:16*
of Egypt to gather stubble *i.* of straw	*Ex 5:12*
of Israel *i.* of all the firstborn	*Nu 3:12*
i. of all the firstborn among	*Nu 3:41*
i. of all the firstlings among the	*Nu 3:41*
the Levites *i.* of all the firstborn	*Nu 3:45*
of the Levites *i.* of their cattle	*Nu 3:45*
with another *i.* of thy husband	*Nu 5:19*
aside to another *i.* of thy husband	*Nu 5:20*
aside to another *i.* of her husband	*Nu 5:29*
i. of such as open every womb	*Nu 8:16*
even *i.* of the firstborn of all	*Nu 8:16*
thou mayest be to us *i.* of eyes	*Nu 10:31*
she? take her, I pray thee, *i.* of her	*J'g 15:2*
captain of the host *i.* of Joab	*2Sa 17:25*
made thy servant king *i.* of David	*1Ki 3:7*
him king *i.* of his father Amaziah	*2Ki 14:21*
of Samaria *i.* of the children of	*2Ki 17:24*
as king *i.* of David his father, and	*1Ch 29:23*
i. of which king Rehoboam made	*2Ch 12:10*
the king be queen *i.* of Vashti	*Es 2:4*
and made her queen *i.* of Vashti	*Es 2:17*
i. of wheat, and cockle *i.* of barley	*Job 31:40*
I. of thy fathers shall be thy	*Ps 45:16*
i. of sweet smell there shall be	*Isa 3:24*
stink; and *i.* of a girdle a rent	*Isa 3:24*
and *i.* of well set hair baldness	*Isa 3:24*
and *i.* of a stomacher a girding of	*Isa 3:24*
sackcloth; and burning *i.* of beauty	*Isa 3:24*
I. of the thorn shall come up the fir	*Isa 55:13*
i. of the brier shall come up	*Isa 55:13*
which reigned *i.* of Josiah his father	*Jer 22:11*
son of Josiah reigned *i.* of Coniah	*Jer 37:1*
taketh strangers *i.* of her husband	*Eze 16:32*

INSTIGATED

i. and instructed men (A)(B)(R)	*Ac 6:11*

INSTINCTIVE

cut nerve of *i.* actions (P)	*Ro 8:13*

INSTINCTS

live on level of *i.* (P)	*Ro 8:12*
obeyed promptings of *i.* (N)	*Eph 2:3*

INSTITUTE

i. elders in every town (N)	*Tit 1:5*

INSTITUTED

i. in Mount Sinai (B)	*Nu 28:6*
are *i.* by him (N)(R)	*Ro 13:1*

INSTITUTION

an everlasting *i.* (B)	*Ex 23:21*
resisting a divine *i.* (N)	*Ro 13:2*
to every human *i.* (A)(B)(N)(R)	*1Pe 2:13*

INSTITUTIONS

i. and usages (A)	*Ac 6:14*

INSTRUCT

his voice, that he might *i.* thee	*De 4:36*
correct, discipline and admonish (A)	*De 4:36*
in order to discipline you (B)(R)	*De 4:36*
also thy good spirit to *i.* them	*Ne 9:20*
with the Almighty *i.* him	*Job 40:2*
find fault with Almighty contend with (A)	*Job 40:2*
Will faultfinder contend with (B)(R)	*Job 40:2*
he that cavilleth contend with (E)	*Job 40:2*
my reins also *i.* me in the night	*Ps 16:7*
my emotions admonish me (B)	*Ps 16:7*
I will *i.* thee and teach thee in the	*Ps 32:8*
your discipline and *i.* (A)(B)	*Ps 94:12*
mother's house, who would *i.* me	*Ca 8:2*
his God doth *i.* him to discretion	*Isa 28:26*
among the people shall *i.* many	*Da 11:33*
cause many to gain insight (B)	*Da 11:33*
shall make many understand (R)	*Da 11:33*
of the Lord, that he may *i.* him	*1Co 2:16*

INSTRUCTED

he *i.* him, he kept him as the	*De 32:10*
kept him as the pupil of his eye (A)	*De 32:10*
tended them with care (B)	*De 32:10*
cared for him (E)(R)	*De 32:10*
Jehoiada the priest *i.* him	*2Ki 12:2*
he *i.* about the song, because he	*1Ch 15:22*
brethren that were *i.* in the songs	*1Ch 25:7*
Solomon was *i.* for the building	*2Ch 3:3*
Behold, thou hast *i.* many, and	*Job 4:3*
be *i.* ye judges of the earth	*Ps 2:10*
be warned, O rulers of earth (B)(R)	*Ps 2:10*
mine ear to them that *i.* me	*Pr 5:13*
inclined ear to my instructors (B)(R)	*Pr 5:13*
when the wise is *i.* he receiveth	*Pr 21:11*
and *i.* me that I should not walk	*Isa 8:11*
and who *i.* him and taught him	*Isa 40:14*
Be thou *i.* O Jerusalem, lest my	*Jer 6:8*
and after that I was *i.* I smote	*Jer 31:19*
is *i.* unto the kingdom of heaven	*M't 13:52*
who is versed in the kingdom (B)	*M't 13:52*
who has been made a disciple (E)(P)	*M't 13:52*
has become a learner in kingdom (N)	*M't 13:52*
has been trained in the kingdom (R)	*M't 13:52*
being before *i.* of her mother	*M't 14:8*
prompted by her mother (A)(N)(P)(R)	*M't 14:8*
put forward by her mother (E)	*M't 14:8*
things, wherein thou hast been *i.*	*Lu 1:4*
instigated and *i.* men (A)(B)(R)	*Ac 6:11*
man was *i.* in the way of the Lord	*Ac 18:25*
excellent, being *i.* out of the law	*Ro 2:18*
all things I am *i.* both to be full	*Ph'p 4:12*

INSTRUCTING

In meekness *i.* those that oppose	*2Ti 2:25*
correct his opponents with courtesy (A)	*2Ti 2:25*
discipline those in opposition (B)	*2Ti 2:25*
correcting them that oppose (E)	*2Ti 2:25*
when discipline is needed for (N)	*2Ti 2:25*
correct those that oppose his message (P)	*2Ti 2:25*
correcting his oponents (R)	*2Ti 2:25*

INSTRUCTION

i. from his mouth (B)(R)	*Job 22:22*
ears of men, and sealeth their *i.*	*Job 33:16*
affirms warnings directed to them (B)	*Job 33:16*
terrifies them with warnings (R)	*Job 33:16*
Seeing thou hatest *i.* and castest	*Ps 50:17*
you hate correction (B)	*Ps 50:17*
you hate discipline (R)	*Ps 50:17*
To know wisdom and *i.*; to	*Pr 1:2*
To receive the *i.* of wisdom	*Pr 1:3*
but fools despise wisdom and *i.*	*Pr 1:7*
My son, hear the *i.* of thy father	*Pr 1:8*
Hear, ye children, the *i.* of a father	*Pr 4:1*
Take fast hold of *i.*; let her not go	*Pr 4:13*
How have I hated *i.* and my heart	*Pr 5:12*
I hated discipline (B)(R)	*Pr 5:12*
He shall die without *i.*; and in	*Pr 5:23*
dies for lack of discipline (B)(R)	*Pr 5:23*
reproofs of *i.* are the way of life	*Pr 6:23*
reproofs of discipline way of life (A)(B)(R)	*Pr 6:23*
Receive my *i.* and not silver	*Pr 8:10*
Hear *i.* and be wise, and refuse it	*Pr 8:33*
Give *i.* to a wise man, and he will be	*Pr 9:9*
Inform a wise man he will be wiser (B)	*Pr 9:9*
in the way of life that keepeth *i.*	*Pr 10:17*
Whoso loveth *i.* loveth knowledge	*Pr 12:1*
Whoever loves discipline loves (B)(R)	*Pr 12:1*
Whoso loveth correction loveth (E)	*Pr 12:1*
A wise son heareth his father's *i.*	*Pr 13:1*
wise son accepts father's correction (B)	*Pr 13:1*
shall be to him that refuseth *i.*	*Pr 13:18*
A fool despiseth his father's *i.*	*Pr 15:5*
refuseth *i.* despiseth his own soul	*Pr 15:32*
who ignores correction despises (B)(R)	*Pr 15:32*
fear of the Lord is the *i.* of	*Pr 15:33*
hath it: but the *i.* of fools is folly	*Pr 16:22*
folly is the chastisement of fools (B)(R)	*Pr 16:22*
correction of fools is their folly (E)	*Pr 16:22*
Hear counsel, and receive *i.* that	*Pr 19:20*
to hear the *i.* that causeth to err	*Pr 19:27*
Apply thine heart unto *i.* and	*Pr 23:12*
wisdom, and *i.* and understanding	*Pr 23:23*
I looked upon it, and received *i.*	*Pr 24:32*
i. of idols (A)(B)(E)(R)	*Jer 10:8*
they might not hear, nor receive *i.*	*Jer 17:23*

have not hearkened to receive *Jer 32:33* *i.*

Will ye not receive *i.* to *Jer 35:13* hearken to

Will you not receive *Jer 35:13* correction (B)

an *i.* and an astonishment *Eze 5:15* unto

a warning and a horror *Eze 5:15* (A)/(B)/(R)

wilt fear me, thou wilt receive *Zep 3:7* *i.*

bring them up in *i.* (B)(N) *Eph 6:4*

correction, for *i.* in *2Ti 3:16* righteousness

profitab'e for teaching *2Ti 3:16* (B)(E)(N)(P)(R)

i. sound, fit, wise (A) *Tit 2:8*

INSTRUCTIONS

walk in my *i.* (B) *Ex 16:4; Ps 78:1*
refuse to keep my *i.* (B) *Ex 16:28*
all the legal *i.* (B) *Ex 24:3*
Lord gave *i.* that (N) *1Co 9:14*
wholesome *i.* (B) *2Ti 4:3*

INSTRUCTOR

an *i.* of every artificer in brass *Ge 4:22*
an *i.* of lies (B) *Hab 2:18*
An *i.* of the foolish, a teacher *Ro 2:20* of

INSTRUCTORS

ye have ten thousand *i.* in *1Co 4:15* Christ

10,000 teachers in Christ *1Co 4:15* (A)(P)

a myriad of tutors in Christ *1Co 4:15* (B)

10,000 tutors in Christ *1Co 4:15* (E)(N)

countless guides in Christ (R) *1Co 4:15*

INSTRUMENT

if he smite him with an *i.* of *Nu 35:16* iron

the psaltery and an *i.* of ten *Ps 33:2* strings

the harp of ten strings *Ps 33:2* (A)(B)(R)

Upon an *i.* of ten strings, and *Ps 92:3* upon

upon a psaltery and an *i.* of *Ps 144:9* ten strings

a ten-stringed harp (B)(R) *Ps 144:9*
are not threshed with a *Isa 28:27* threshing *i.*

with a threshing sledge *Isa 28:27;* (B)(R) *41:15*

make thee a new sharp *Isa 41:15* threshing *i.*

bringeth forth an *i.* for his *Isa 54:16* work

produces weapon for its *Isa 54:16* purpose (A)(E)(R)

produce a tool for his work *Isa 54:16* (B)

voice, and can play well on *Eze 33:32* an *i.*

chosen *i.* (B)(N)(P)(R) *Ac 9:15*

INSTRUMENTS

i. of cruelty are in their *Ge 49:5*
weapons of violence *Ge 49:5* (A)(E)(R)

implements of violence (B) *Ge 49:5*
the pattern of all the *i.* thereof *Ex 25:9*
furniture (A)(B)(E)(R) *Ex 25:9*
i. of the tabernacle (E) *Ex 27:19;* *39:40; Nu 3:36*

keep all the *i.* of the tabernacle *Nu 3:8*
the furnishings (B)(R) *Nu 3:8*
shall take all the *i.* of ministry *Nu 4:12*
ministering utensils (A)(B) *Nu 4:12*
the vessels of the ministry (E) *Nu 4:12*
the vessels of the service (N) *Nu 4:12*
cords, and all the *i.* of their *Nu 4:26* service

with all their *i.* and with all *Nu 4:32* their

ye shall reckon the *i.* of the *Nu 4:32* charge

sanctified it, and all the *i.* *Nu 7:1* thereof

with the holy *i.* and the *Nu 31:6* trumpets

his *i.* of war, and *i.* of his *1Sa 8:12* chariots

weapons and chariot equipment *1Sa 8:12* (B)

with joy, and with *i.* of musick *1Sa 18:6*
on all manner of *i.* made of fir *2Sa 6:5* wood

burnt sacrifice, and threshing *2Sa 24:22* *i.*

and other *i.* of the oxen for *2Sa 24:22* wood

their flesh with the *i.* of the *1Ki 19:21* oxen

and all the *i.* of the sanctuary *1Ch 9:29*
with all *i.* of war, fifty *1Ch 12:33* thousand

with all manner of *i.* of war *1Ch 12:37* for the

to be the singers with *i.* of *1Ch 15:16* musick

sound, and with musical *i.* *1Ch 16:42* of God

and the threshing *i.* for *1Ch 21:23* wood, and

Lord with the *i.* which I made *1Ch 23:5*
for all *i.* of all manner of *1Ch 28:14* service

silver also for all *i.* of silver *1Ch 28:14*
for all *i.* of every kind of *1Ch 28:14* service

and all their *i.* did Huram his *2Ch 4:16*
and all the *i.* put he among the *2Ch 5:1*
and cymbals and *i.* of musick *2Ch 5:13* Lord

also with *i.* of musick of the *2Ch 7:6* Lord

the singers with *i.* of musick *2Ch 23:13*
Levites stood with the *i.* of *2Ch 29:26* David

with the *i.* ordained by *2Ch 29:27* David king

singing with loud *i.* unto the *2Ch 30:21* Lord

all that could skill of *i.* of *2Ch 34:12* musick

with the musical *i.* of David *Ne 12:36*
prepared for him the *i.* of death *Ps 7:13*
deadly weapons (A)(R) *Ps 7:13*
weapons of death (B) *Ps 7:13*
the players on *i.* followed after *Ps 68:25*
as the players on *i.* shall be *Ps 87:7* there

him with stringed *i.* and *Ps 150:4* organs

as musical *i.* and that of all sorts *Ec 2:8*
The *i.* also of the churl are evil *Isa 32:7*
sing my songs to the stringed *Isa 38:20* *i.*

i. wherewith they slew the *Eze 40:42* burnt

neither were *i.* of musick *Da 6:18* brought

Gilead with threshing *i.* of iron *Am 1:3*
with iron sledges (A) *Am 1:3*
with iron threshing sleds (B) *Am 1:3*
with threshing sledges of iron *Am 1:3* (R)

invent to themselves *i.* of *Am 6:5* musick

chief singer on my stringed *i.* *Hab 3:19*
yet the *i.* of a foolish *Zec 11:15* shepherd

implements of a foolish *Zec 11:15* shepherd (A)(R)

equipment of a foolish *Zec 11:15* shepherd (B)

as *i.* of unrighteousness unto *Ro 6:13* sin

Implements (A)(B)(N) *Ro 6:13*
weapons (P) *Ro 6:13*
as *i.* of righteousness unto God *Ro 6:13*

INSUBORDINATE

being profligate or *i.* (R) *Tit 1:6*
many *i.* men (R) *Tit 1:10*

INSUFFERABLY

were *i.* jealous (B) *Ac 5:17*

INSULT

insults of those who *i.* me (R) *Ps 69:9*
my enemies *i.* me (B) *Ps 102:8*

a prudent man ignores *i.* *Pr 12:16* (A)(B)(R)

from *i.* and spitting (B) *Isa 50:6*
outlaw and *i.* you (N) *Lu 6:22*
you *i.* us (B) *Lu 11:45*
to insult (A)(P) *Ac 14:5*
i. for *i.* (A)(P) *1Pe 3:9*

INSULTED

mocked and *i.* (A)(R) *2Ki 19:22; 19:23*
he was furious and *i.* (B) *Ne 4:1*
jeered and *i.* him *Lu 18:32* (A)(B)(P)(R)

persecuted and *i.* (P)(R) *1Ti 1:13*
i. the Spirit of grace (P) *Heb 10:29*
i., humiliated poor (A)(N)(P) *Jas 2:6*

INSULTING

are *i.* us (N)(P) *Lu 11:45*
i. Holy Spirit (A) *Heb 10:29*
do not bring *i.* criticisms (P) *2Pe 2:11*
condemn with *i.* words (N) *Jude 9*

INSULTS

my eye dwells on their *i.* (A) *Job 17:2*
i. of those who insult me (R) *Ps 69:9*
i. fools have hurled (B) *Ps 74:22*
oppress poor *i.* his Maker *Pr 14:31;* (B)(R) *17:5*

in *i.* (A)(P) *2Co 12:10; Heb 10:33*
abuse, *i.*, slander (A) *1Ti 6:4*
i., continual wrangling *1Ti 6:5*
do not employ *i.* in (N) *2Pe 2:11*

INSURRECTION

time hath made *i.* against *Ezr 4:19* kings

rise up against kings (B)(R) *Ezr 4:19*
the *i.* of the workers of iniquity *Ps 64:2*
conspiracy of ungodly men *Ps 64:2* (A)(B)

from secret counsel of *Ps 64:2* evil-doers (E)

from secret plots of wicked (R) *Ps 64:2*
bound with them that had *M'k 15:7* made *i.*

had committed murder in the *M'k 15:7* *i.*

confined with insurrectionists *M'k 15:7* (B)

in custody with the rebels *M'k 15:7* (N)

with some other rioters (P) *M'k 15:7*
for certain *i.* (E)(R) *Lu 23:19*
for *i.* and murder (E)(N)(R) *Lu 23:19*
the Jews made *i.* with one *Ac 18:12* accord

made an attack on Paul *Ac 18:12* (A)(R)

Jews rose unanimously *Ac 18:12* against Paul (B)

with one accord rose against *Ac 18:12* Paul'(E)

Jews set upon Paul in a body *Ac 18:12* (N)

Jews banded together to *Ac 18:12* attack Paul (P)

a mover of *i.* (E) *Ac 24:5*

INSURRECTIONISTS

confined with *i.* (B) *M'k 15:7*

INSURRECTIONS

i., do not be alarmed (A)(N) *Lu 21:9*

INTEGRITY

the *i.* of my heart and *Ge 20:5* innocency

done from honest heart (B) *Ge 20:5;* *20:6*

didst this in the *i.* of thy heart *Ge 20:6*
thy father walked, in *i.* of heart *1Ki 9:4*
a heart of *i.* (B) *1Ch 29:19*
heart full of *i.* (B) *2Ch 16:9*
and still he holdeth fast his *i.* *Job 2:3*
him, Dost thou still retain thine *Job 2:9* *i.*

till I die, I will not remove *Job 27:5* mine *i.*

that God may know mine *i.* *Job 31:6*
according to mine *i.* that is in *Ps 7:8* me

waketh in *i.* (B) *Ps 15:2*
Let *i.* and uprightness preserve *Ps 25:21*

Lord; for I have walked in mine i. *Ps 26:1*
as for me, I will walk in mine i. *Ps 26:11*
me, thou upholdest me in mine i. *Ps 41:12*
according to the i. of his heart *Ps 78:72*
walking in i. (B)(R) *Pr 2:7; 10:9*
The i. of the upright shall guide *Pr 11:3*
is the poor that walketh in his i. *Pr 19:1*
The just man walketh in his i. *Pr 20:7*
who walks in i. (R) *Pr 28:18*
speaks with i. (B) *Am 5:10*

INTELLECT
my i. lies fallow (N) *1Co 14:14*

INTELLECTUALISM
spoils faith through i. (P) *Col 2:8*

INTELLIGENCE
put ability and i. (R) *Ex 36:1; 36:2*
and have i. with them that forsake *Da 11:30*
make common cause with them (A)(B) *Da 11:30*
have regard to them that forsake (E) *Da 11:30*
give heed to those who forsake (R) *Da 11:30*

INTELLIGENT
i. and prudent man (B) *Ge 41:33*
i. and good-looking (B) *1Sa 25:3*
is deemed i. (B)(R) *Pr 17:28*
from the clever and i. (P) *M't 11:25*
an i. and sensible man (A)(B)(N)(P)(R) *Ac 13:7*

INTEMPERANCE
intemperance (B) *M't 23:25*

INTEMPERATE
intemperate (N) *2Ti 3:3*

INTEND
and did not i. to go up against *Jos 22:33*
ye i. to add more to our sins and to *2Ch 28:13*
i. my hurt (A) *Ps 35:4*
and i. to bring this man's blood *Ac 5:28*
what ye i. to do as touching these *Ac 5:35*

INTENDED
For they i. evil against thee; they *Ps 21:11*

INTENDEST
i. thou to kill me, as thou killedst *Ex 2:14*

INTENDING
which of you, i. to build a tower *Lu 14:28*
i. after Easter to bring him forth *Ac 12:4*
Assos, there i. to take in Paul *Ac 20:13*

INTENSE
have i. and unfailing love (A)(B)(R) *1Pe 4:8*

INTENSIFY
word of Lord i. (B) *Ac 19:20*

INTENT
kill a person without i. (S) *Jos 20:9*
i. that the Lord might bring evil *2Sa 17:14*
to the i. that he might destroy *2Ki 10:19*
to the i. that he might let none go *2Ch 16:1*

brings with evil i. (B)(R) *Pr 21:27*
the i. that I might shew them unto *Eze 40:4*
to the i. that the living may know *Da 4:17*
not there, to the i. ye may believe *Joh 11:15*
for what i. he spake this unto *Joh 13:28*
and came hither for that i. *Ac 9:21*
for what i. ye have sent for me *Ac 10:29*
to the i. we should not lust after *1Co 10:6*
To the i. that now unto the *Eph 3:10*

INTENTION
i. of all human thinking (B) *Ge 6:5*
brings with evil i. (A) *Pr 21:27*
have performed the i. of his heart *Jer 30:24*
of the thoughts and i. of the heart *Heb 4:12*

INTERCEDE
who will i. for him (B) *1Sa 2:25*
do not i. for me (B)(R) *Jer 7:16*
let them i. with (R) *Jer 27:18*
i. and intervene (A)(B)(P) *Heb 7:25*

INTERCEDES
Spirit i. with sighs (B)(R) *Ro 8:26*

INTERCEDING
all entreaty, i. (A)(N) *Eph 6:18*

INTERCESSION
and made i. for the transgressors *Isa 53:12*
for them, neither make i. to me *Jer 7:16*
do not intercede for me (B)(R) *Jer 7:16*
let them now make i. to the Lord *Jer 27:18*
let them plead with the Lord (B) *Jer 27:18*
let them intercede with the Lord (R) *Jer 27:18*
Gemariah had made i. to the king *Jer 36:25*
tried to persuade the king (A) *Jer 36:25*
cautioned the king (B) *Jer 36:25*
urged the king (R) *Jer 36:25*
the Spirit itself maketh i. for us *Ro 8:26*
Spirit himself goes to meet our *Ro 8:26*
supplication, pleads in our behalf with unspeakable yearnings and groanings too deep for (A)
Spirit himself intercedes on our behalf with sighs too deep for words (B)(R) *Ro 8:26*
through our inarticulate groans the Spirit himself is pleading for us (N) *Ro 8:26*
Spirit within us is actually praying in agonizing longings which never find words (P) *Ro 8:26*
maketh i. for the saints according *Ro 8:27*
of God, who also maketh i. for us *Ro 8:34*
he maketh i. to God against Israel *Ro 11:2*
how he pleads with God against Israel (A) *Ro 11:2*
complains to God against Israel (B)(N)(R) *Ro 11:2*
pleadeth with God against Israel (E) *Ro 11:2*
pleaded with God on Israel's behalf (P) *Ro 11:2*
he ever liveth to make i. for them *Heb 7:25*
to make petition to God and intercede with him and intervene for them (A) *Heb 7:25*
he does forever intercede for them (B) *Heb 7:25*
always living to plead on their behalf (N) *Heb 7:25*
always living to intercede on behalf (P) *Heb 7:25*

INTERCESSIONS
prayers, i. and giving of thanks *1Ti 2:1*

INTERCESSOR
wondered that there was no i. *Isa 59:16*
there was none to interpose (B) *Isa 59:16*
no one to intervene (R) *Isa 59:16*

INTERCOURSE
normal sexual i. (P) *1Co 7:5*

INTEREST
interest (A)(E) *Ex 22:25; Le 25:36, 37; De 23:19-20; Ne 5:10; Ps 15:5; Pr 28:8; Eze 18:8, 17; 22:12; M't 25:27; Lu 19:23*
interest (B) *Ex 22:25; Le 25:36-37; De 23:19-20; Ne 5:7, Ps 15:5; Pr 28:8; Eze 18:7; M't 25:27; Lu 19:23*
interest (R) *Ex 22:25; Le 25:36-37; De 23:19-20; Ne 5:7, 10; Ps 15:5; Pr 28:8; Eze 18:8, 13; M't 25:27; Lu 19:23*
interest (S) *Le 25:36; 25:37; De 23:19-20; Ne 5:7; Ps 15:5; Pr 28:8; Isa 24:2; Jer 15:10; Eze 18:8, 13, 17; 22:12; Lu 19:23*
my deep i. in temple (B) *1Ch 29:3*
receive i. (N)(P) *M't 25:27; Lu 19:23*
take real i. in people (P) *Ro 12:16*
common i. between (P) *2Co 6:14*
keen i. on my behalf (P) *2Co 7:7*
keen in i. (A)(P) *2Co 8:17*

INTERESTED
so deeply i. in you (B) *2Co 8:17*

INTERESTS
you of divided i. (A)(B) *Jas 4:8*

INTERLACING
i. her tracks (B) *Jer 2:23*

INTERMARRYING
i. with people (A)(B)(R) *Ezr 9:14*

INTERMEDDLE
a stranger doth not i. with his joy *Pr 14:10*
no stranger shares its joy (A)(R) *Pr 14:10*
can intermingle with its joy (B) *Pr 14:10*

INTERMEDDLETH
seeketh and i. with all wisdom *Pr 18:1*
seeks own desire and pretext to break out against all wise, sound wisdom (A)(B) *Pr 18:1*
seeketh own desire and rageth against all sound wisdom (E) *Pr 18:1*
seeks pretexts to break out against all sound wisdom (R) *Pr 18:1*

INTERMEDIARY
an i. person (A)(N)(P)(R) *Ga 3:19; 3:20*
one i. between (P) *1Ti 2:5*

INTERMINABLE
i. genealogies (B) *1Ti 1:4*
i. myths (N) *1Ti 1:4*

INTERMINGLE
can i. with joy (B) *Pr 14:10*

INTERMISSION
and ceaseth not, without any i. *La 3:49*

INTERPOSE
there is none to i. (B) *Isa 59:16*
intercede and i. (A)(B)(P) *Heb 7:25*

INTERPOSED

i. by an oath (E)(R)　　　　　Heb 6:17

INTERPRET

there was none that could *i.*　　Ge 41:8
them
according to his dream he did　Ge 41:12
i.
and there is none that can *i.* it　Ge 41:15
canst understand a dream to　Ge 41:15
i. it
i. appearance of sky　　　　M't 16:3
(A)(P)(R)
all speak with tongues? do　1Co 12:30
all *i.*
speaketh with tongues, except　1Co 14:5
he *i.*
tongue pray that he may *i.*　1Co 14:13
and that by course; and let　1Co 14:27
one *i.*

INTERPRETATION

according to the *i.* of his　　Ge 40:5
dream
own dream with personal　　Ge 40:5
significance (B)
each dream with its own　　Ge 40:5
meaning (R)
This is the *i.* of it: The three　Ge 40:12
baker saw that the *i.* was　Ge 40:16
good
This is the *i.* thereof: The　Ge 40:18
three
according to the *i.* of his　Ge 41:11
dream
of the dream, and the *i.* thereof　J'g 7:15
understand a proverb, and the *i.* Pr 1:6
who knoweth *i.* of a thing　Ec 8:1
the dream, and we will shew the　Da 2:4
i.
we will show its meaning (B)　Da 2:4;
　　　　　　　　　　　4:19; 7:16
me the dream, with the *i.*　Da 2:5;
thereof　　　　　　　　　　　2:6
shew the dream and the *i.*　Da 2:6
thereof
dream, and we will shew the *i.*　Da 2:7
of it
that ye can shew me the *i.*　Da 2:9
thereof
that he would shew the king　Da 2:16
the *i.*
I will shew unto the king the *i.*　Da 2:24
make known unto the king the　Da 2:25
i.
I have seen, and the *i.* thereof　Da 2:26
make known the *i.* to the king　Da 2:30
and we will tell the *i.* thereof　Da 2:36
before
is certain, and the *i.* thereof　Da 2:45
sure
known unto me the *i.* of the　Da 4:6
dream
make known unto me the *i.*　Da 4:7
thereof
that I have seen, and the *i.*　Da 4:9
thereof
declare the *i.* thereof,　Da 4:18
forasmuch
able to make known unto me　Da 4:18
the *i.*
dream, or the *i.* thereof,　Da 4:19
trouble
and the *i.* thereof to thine　Da 4:19
enemies
This is the *i.* O King, and this　Da 4:24
is
writing, and shew me the *i.*　Da 5:7
thereof
known to the king the *i.* thereof　Da 5:8
be called, and he will shew the　Da 5:12
i.
make known unto me the *i.*　Da 5:15
thereof
could not shew the *i.* of the　Da 5:15
thing
known to me the *i.* thereof,　Da 5:16
thou
and make known to him the *i.*　Da 5:17
This is the *i.* of the thing:　Da 5:26
Mene
made me know the *i.* of the　Da 7:16
things
Cephas, which is by *i.*, A　Joh 1:42
stone
translated is Peter - meaning　Joh 1:42
Stone (A)(B)

Cephas (Peter, meaning a　Joh 1:42
rock) (P)
Cephas (which means Peter)　Joh 1:42
(R)
pool of Siloam, which is by *i.*　Joh 9:7
Sent
Siloam which means Sent　Joh 9:7
(A)(N)(R)
Siloam - translated Sent (B)　Joh 9:7
Siloam means "one who has　Joh 9:7
been sent" (P)
which by *i.* is called Dorcas　Ac 9:36
Tabitha, which (in Greek)　Ac 9:36
means Dorcas or (in English)
Gazelle (A)
Tabitha, that is, translated　Ac 9:36
Dorcas (B)
Tabitha, meaning gazelle (P)　Ac 9:36
Tabitha, which means Dorcas　Ac 9:36
or Gazelle (R)
sorcerer (for so is his name by　Ac 13:8
i.)
Elymas the wise man, for this　Ac 13:8
is the translation of his name (A)
Elymas, the magician, such is　Ac 13:8
his name translated (B)(P)(R)
Elymas the sorcerer, so his　Ac 13:8
name may be translated (N)
to another the *i.* of tongues　1Co 12:10
tongue, hath a revelation,　1Co 14:26
hath an *i.*
being by *i.* King of　　　　Heb 7:2
righteousness
name when translated, king of　Heb 7:2
righteousness (A)
the name explains, king of　Heb 7:2
righteousness (B)
Melchizedek means king of　Heb 7:2
righteousness (P)
by translation king of　　Heb 7:2
righteousness (R)
the scripture is of any private　2Pe 1:20
i.
no prophetic scripture can be　2Pe 1:20
explained by one's unaided
mental powers (B)
no one can interpret any　　2Pe 1:20
prophecy of Scripture by
himself (N)

INTERPRETATIONS

Do not *i.* belong to God? tell　Ge 40:8
me
that thou canst make *i.* and　Da 5:16
can make *i.* (A)(E)(R)　　Da 5:16
give explanations and solve　Da 5:16
problems (B)

INTERPRETED

baker: as Joseph had *i.* to　Ge 40:22
them
him, and he *i.* to us our　Ge 41:12
dreams
to pass, as he *i.* to us, so it　Ge 41:13
was
and *i.* in the Syrian tongue　Ezr 4:7
which being *i.* is, God with us　M't 1:23
Emmanuel, means God with us　M't 1:23
(A)(N)(R)
Immanuel, which means　　M't 1:23
God-with-us (B)(P)
cumi; which is, being *i.*　M'k 5:41
Damsel
Talitha cumi, which translated　M'k 5:41
is, Little girl, I say to you,
arise (A)(R)
Talitha Koum, which is　　M'k 5:41
translated, Maiden, I tell you,
rise (B)
Talitha cum, which means,　M'k 5:41
Get up, my child (N)
is, being *i.*, The place of a　M'k 15:22
skull
Golgotha (in Latin,　　　　M'k 15:22
Calvary), meaning the place
of a skull (A)(N)(R)
Golgotha, which means skull　M'k 15:22
(B)(P)
which is being *i.* My God, my　M'k 15:34
God
Eloi, Eloi, lama sabachthani,　M'k 15:34
which means My God, my God,
why have you forsaken me
(A)(B)(N)(P)(R)
i. scriptures (E)(R)　　　　Lu 24:27
which is to say, being *i.*　Joh 1:38
Master

Rabbi, translated is Teacher　Joh 1:38
(A)(B)(N)(R)
which is, being *i.* the Christ　Joh 1:41
being *i.* The son of consolation　Ac 4:36
Barnabas, translated Son of　Ac 4:36
Consolation (B)
Barnabas, means Son of　Ac 4:36
Exhortation (N)
Barnabas, meaning son of　Ac 4:36
comfort (P)
Barnabas, means Son of　Ac 4:36
encouragement (R)

INTERPRETER

a dream, and there is no *i.* of it　Ge 40:8
for he spake unto them by an　Ge 42:23
i.
an *i.* one among a thousand　Job 33:23
an angel, a mediator, one of　Job 33:23
the (R)
if there be no *i.* let him keep　1Co 14:28

INTERPRETERS

without *i.* (R)　　　　　　Ge 35:11;
　　　　　　　　　Nu 35:15; Jos 20:9
related to the *i.* (B)　　　　Ge 41:24

INTERPRETING

understanding, *i.* of dreams　Da 5:12
explaining and *i.* (A)　　Lu 24:27

INTERSECTIONS

the noisy *i.* (A)(B)　　　　Pr 1:21

INTERVENE

no one to *i.* (R)　　　　Isa 59:16

INTERVIEWED

king *i.* them (B)　　　　Da 1:19

INTERWEAVING

with *i.* and knotting of hair　1Pe 3:3
(A)

INTESTINAL

i. disease (A)　　　　2Ch 21:15; 21:18

INTESTINES

his *i.* poured out (B)　　　2Sa 20:10
disease of the *i.* (S)　　　2Ch 21:15;
　　　　　　　　　　　　21:18-19
his *i.* poured out (A)(B)(P)　Ac 1:18

INTIMATE

my *i.* friends avoid me　　Job 19:19
(B)(R)
i. counsel is with (B)　　　Pr 3:32
not get *i.* with (B)　　　1Co 5:11

INTIMIDATED

unsettled or *i.* (B)　　　Joh 14:27

INTO

breathed *i.* his nostrils the　・Ge 2:7
breath of
parted, and became *i.* four　Ge 2:10
heads
and put him *i.* the garden of　Ge 2:15
Eden
and thou shalt come *i.* the ark　Ge 6:18
sort shalt thou bring *i.* the ark　Ge 6:19
thou and all thy house *i.* the ark　Ge 7:1
i. the south　　　　　　　Ge 13:1
i. thy hand　　　　　　　Ge 14:20;
　　　　　　　De 2:30; 3:2; Jos 8:1
i. thy bosom　　　　Ge 16:5; 2Sa 12:8
i. the tent　　　　　　　Ge 18:6;
　　　　　　　Ex 18:7 ;40:32, 35; J'g 4:18
i. the house　　Ge 19:10; 39:11; 43:26
i. the prison　　　　Ge 39:20; 40:3
i. the wilderness　　　　Ex 4:27;
18:5; 19:1; Le 16:10, 21, 23; Nu 14:25;
De 1:40; 2:1; 1Sa 26:3; Eze 20:10, 35;
　　　　　　　　　　　　M't 4:1
i. the sea　　　Ex 15:1; 15:4, 19, 21
i. the mount　　　　　　Ex 19:12;
24:12-13, 15, 18; De 5:5; 9:9; 10:1, 3
i. the house of the Lord　　Ex 23:19;

De 23:18; 2Sa 12:20; 1Ki 14:28; 15:15;
2Ki 11:4; 12:4, 9, 13, 16; 19:1, 14; 20:8;
                           22:4
i. the ark   *Ex* 25:16; 40:20; 1Sa 6:19
i. the tabernacle   *Ex* 29:30;
  30:20; 33:8-9; 40:21; Le 6:30; 9:23; 10:9;
                           Nu 7:89; 17:8
i. the camp   *Ex* 33:11;
Le 14:8; 16:26, 28; De 23:11; Jos 6:11,
         14; 1Sa 4:3, 5-7
i. the holy place   *Le* 16:2; 16:3, 23
i. the land   *Le* 19:23;
23:10; 25:2; Nu 15:18; De 2:29; 6:10;
7:1; 9:28; 18:9; 30:5; 31:20-21; Jos 2:18
all that enter *i.* the host, to do   *Nu* 4:3
i. the congregation   *De* 23:1; 23:2-3, 8
removed *i.* all kingdoms   *De* 28:25;
                  Jer 15:4; 24:9; 34:17
go *i.* captivity   *De* 28:41;
Isa 46:2; Jer 20:6; 22:22; 29:16; 30:16;
46:19; 48:7; 49:3; La 1:3, 5, 18; 4:22;
                           Am 7:17
i. covenant with the Lord   *De* 29:12
i. the hand of Israel   *Jos* 10:30;
  10:32; 11:8; J'g 11:21; 1Sa 14:12, 37
turned *i.* another man   *1Sa* 10:6
i. the city of David   *2Sa* 6:12; 6:16
i. the temple of the Lord   *2Ch* 27:2
wicked shall be turned *i.* hell   *Ps* 9:17
go down quick *i.* hell   *Ps* 55:15
go *i.* lower parts of the earth   *Ps* 63:9
if I ascend *i.* heaven   *Ps* 139:8; Pr 30:4
beat swords *i.* plowshares   *Isa* 2:4
to deliver us *i.* the hand of the   *Jer* 43:3
shall remove and go *i.*   *Eze* 12:11
  captivity
in no case enter *i.* the   *M't* 5:20;
  kingdom   18:3
cast them *i.* furnace of fire   *M't* 13:42;
                           13:50
enter *i.* life   *M't* 18:8; 18:9; M'k 9:43
cast *i.* hell fire   *M't* 18:9; 25:41, 46
harlots enter *i.* kingdom of   *M't* 21:31
  God
cannot enter *i.* kingdom of God *Joh* 3:5
enter *i.* rest   *Heb* 3:11;
            3:18; 4:1, 3, 5, 10-11
in through the gates *i.* the city *Re* 24:14

INTOLERABLE

i. anguish (A)   *M't* 24:8; M'k 13:8

INTOXICANTS

men mixing *i.* (B)   *Isa* 5:22

INTOXICATED

long wilt thou be *i.* (S)   *1Sa* 1:14

INTRACTABLE

an *i.* evil (N)   *Jas* 3:8

INTREAT

i. for me to Ephron the son of   *Ge* 23:8
ask Ephron for me (A)   *Ge* 23:8
request for me of Ephron (B)   *Ge* 23:8
I. the Lord, that he may take   *Ex* 8:8
pray to the Lord (B)   *Ex* 8:8
when shall I *i.* for thee, and for *Ex* 8:9
  thy
I shall plead for you (B)   *Ex* 8:9
not go very far away: *i.* for   *Ex* 8:28
  me
i. the Lord that the swarms of *Ex* 8:29
  flies
I. the Lord (for it is enough)   *Ex* 9:28
  that
once, and *i.* the Lord your   *Ex* 10:17
  God
Ruth said, *I.* me not to   *Ru* 1:16
  leave thee
do not urge me to desert you   *Ru* 1:16
  (A)(B)
the Lord, who shall *i.* for him *1Sa* 2:25
who will intercede for him   *1Sa* 2:25
  (B)
I. now the face of the Lord   *1Ki* 13:6
  thy
who will intercede for him   *1Ki* 13:6
  (A)
plead with the Lord (B)   *1Ki* 13:6
the people shall *i.* thy favour *Ps* 45:12
shall seek your favor with   *Ps* 45:12
  gifts (B)
will sue your favor with gifts *Ps* 45:12
  (R)

will *i.* the favour of the prince *Pr* 19:6
Being defamed, we *i.*: we are *1Co* 4:13
we (try to) answer softly,   *1Co* 4:13
  bring comfort (A)
we bring comfort (B)   *1Co* 4:13
we humbly make our appeal   *1Co* 4:13
  (N)
men curse us, but we return a *1Co* 4:13
  blessing (P)
when slandered, we try to   *1Co* 4:13
  conciliate (R)
I i. thee also, true yokefellow *Ph'p* 4:3
I exhort you too, genuine   *Ph'p* 4:3
  yokefellow (A)
I beg of you also, genuine   *Ph'p* 4:3
  yokefellow (B)
I beseech thee also, true   *Ph'p* 4:3
  yokefellow (E)
I beg, and you too, my   *Ph'p* 4:3
  loyal comrade (N)(P)
an elder, but *i.* him as a father *1Ti* 5:1
address him as a father (B)   *1Ti* 5:1
exhort him as a father (E)(R) *1Ti* 5:1
appeal to him as your father   *1Ti* 5:1
  (N)(P)

INTREATED

Isaac *i.* the Lord for his wife *Ge* 25:21
prayed to the Lord   *Ge* 25:21;
  (A)(B)(R)
and the Lord was *i.* of him   *Ge* 25:21
out from Pharaoh, and *i.* the *Ex* 8:30
  Lord   10:18
Then Manoah *i.* the Lord, and *J'g* 13:8
  said
petitioned the Lord (B)   *J'g* 13:8
after that God was *i.* for the *2Sa* 21:14
  land
his people prayed for the   *2Sa* 21:14
  land (A)
answered the prayers of the *2Sa* 21:14;
  land (B)   24:25; 1Ch 5:20
God heeded supplications of *2Sa* 21:14
  the land (R)
So the Lord was *i.* for the   *2Sa* 24:25
  land, and
in the battle, and he was *i.* of *1Ch* 5:20
  them
and he was *i.* of him, and   *2Ch* 33:13
  heard
also, and how God was *i.* of *2Ch* 33:19
  him
God for this: and he was *i.* of *Ezr* 8:23
  us
listened to their entreaty   *Ezr* 8:23
  (A)(R)
he heard us (B)   *Ezr* 8:23
answer: I *i.* him with my   *Job* 19:16
  mouth
I beseech him with words   *Job* 19:16
  (A)(R)
I i. for the children's sake of *Job* 9:17
I i. thy favour with my whole *Ps* 119:58
Wholeheartedly I sought thy *Ps* 119:58
  favor (A)
Lord, and he shall be *i.* of   *Isa* 19:22
  them
listen to their entreaties (A)   *Isa* 19:22
He will heed their petitions   *Isa* 19:22
  (B)
He will heed their   *Isa* 19:22
  supplications (R)
came his father out, and *i.*   *Lu* 15:28
  him
began to plead with him   *Lu* 15:28
  (A)(N)
came out to invite him (B)   *Lu* 15:28
came outside and called him *Lu* 15:28
  (P)
i. that the word should not   *Heb* 12:19
  be
beg that nothing more be   *Heb* 12:19
  said (A)
implored that no further   *Heb* 12:19
  message (B)
begged to hear no more (N)   *Heb* 12:19
prayed that it might stop   *Heb* 12:19
  speaking (P)
and easy to be *i.* full of mercy *Jas* 3:17
willing to yield to reason (A)   *Jas* 3:17
congenial (B)   *Jas* 3:17
open to reason (N)(R)   *Jas* 3:17
approachable (P)   *Jas* 3:17

INTREATIES

The poor useth *i.*; but the rich *Pr* 18:23

INTREATY

Praying us with much *i.* that *2Co* 8:4
we

INTRICATELY

i. wrought in the lowest part *Ps* 139:15
(S)

INTRIGUES

acquire royalty by devious *i.* *Da* 11:21
(B)
the devil's *i.* (B)   *Eph* 6:11

INTRUDING

i. into those things which he *Col* 2:18
hath

INVADE

thou wouldest not let Israel *2Ch* 20:10
i.
he will *i.* them with his troops *Hab* 3:16

INVADED

for the Philistines have *i.* the *1Sa* 23:27
  land
went up, and *i.* the Geshurites *1Sa* 27:8
the Amalekites had *i.* the   *1Sa* 30:1
  south
bands of the Moabites *i.* the *2Ki* 13:20
  land
Philistines also had *i.* the   *2Ch* 28:18
  cities

INVALID

made them *i.* (B)   *Ge* 30:13
many are *i.* (A)   *1Co* 11:30

INVALIDATED

it cannot be *i.* (N)   *Ga* 3:17

INVALIDS

no *i.* among them (B)   *Ps* 105:37

INVASION

We made an *i.* upon the   *1Sa* 30:14
south of

INVENT

i. to themselves instruments of *Am* 6:5
i. new kinds of mischief (N)   *Ro* 1:30

INVENTED

engines, *i.* by cunning men   *2Ch* 26:15
constructed or *i.* (A)(B)   *Ac* 17:29
i. stories (B)   *1Ti* 1:4

INVENTEST

thou *i.* them (S)   *Ne* 6:8

INVENTING

i. them of own mind (A)(R)   *Ne* 6:8

INVENTION

neither work nor *i.* (B)   *Ec* 9:10

INVENTIONS

thou tookest vengeance of their *Ps* 99:8
  i.
avenging evil-doings and   *Ps* 99:8
  practices (A)
make them pay for their evil   *Ps* 99:8
  practices (B)
tookest vengeance of their   *Ps* 99:8
  doings (E)
an avenger of their   *Ps* 99:8
  wrong-doings (R)
provoked him to anger with   *Ps* 106:29
  their *i.*
make Lord angry with   *Ps* 106:29
  practices (A)(B)
provoked the Lord with   *Ps* 106:29
  doings (E)(R)
went a whoring with their   *Ps* 106:39
  own *i.*

were immoral in their *Ps 106:39*
practices (B)
played harlot in their doings *Ps 106:39*
(E)(R)
and find out knowledge of witty *Pr 8:12*
i.
find out knowledge and *Pr 8:12*
discretion (A)(E)(R)
find out knowledge through *Pr 8:12*
deliberating (B)
devised *i.* and schemes (A) *Jer 11:19*
but they have sought out many *Ec 7:29*
i.
sought out many devices for *Ec 7:29*
evil (A)(B)(R)
minds teemed with diabolical *i.* *Ro 1:30*
(P)

INVENTORS

machines devised by *i.* *2Ch 26:15*
(A)(B)
i. of evil things, disobedient to *Ro 1:30*
invent new kinds of mischief *Ro 1:30*
(N)
minds teemed with diabolical *Ro 1:30*
inventions (P)

INVESTIGATE

i. and make inquiry (B) *De 40:8*
did not dare *i.* (B) *Ac 7:32*
i. more particularly (B) *Ac 23:20*

INVESTIGATED

matter was *i.* (A)(B)(R) *Es 2:23*

INVESTIGATOR

investigator (A)(B) *1Co 1:20*

INVISIBLE

he became *i.* (B) *Lu 24:31*
For the *i.* things of him from *Ro 1:20*
Who is the image of the *i.* *Col 1:15*
God
and that are in earth, visible *Col 1:16*
and *i.*
things seen and unseen *Col 1:16*
(A)(P)
unto the King eternal, *1Ti 1:17*
immortal, *i.*
endured, as seeing him who *Heb 11:27*
is *i.*

INVITE

came out to *i.* him (B) *Lu 15:28*

INVITED

since I said, I have *i.* the *1Sa 9:24*
people
and Absalom *i.* all the king's *2Sa 13:23*
sons
invited (S) *2Sa 15:11;*
1Ki 1:9-10, 19. 25-26
am I *i.* unto her also with the *Es 5:12*
king

INVOKE

and to *i.* and praise (S) *1Ch 16:4*

INWARD

the *i.* parts (S) *Ex 12:9; Ps 139:13*
is in the side of the ephod *i.* *Ex 28:26*
was on the side of the ephod *i.* *Ex 39:19*
it is fret *i.* whether it be *Le 13:55*
bare
round about from Millo and *i.* *2Sa 5:9*
the *i.* parts (S) *2Sa 20:10; Ps 109:18*
and all their hinder parts *1Ki 7:25;*
were *i.* *2Ch 4:4*
their feet, and their faces *2Ch 3:13*
were *i.*
All my *i.* friends abhorred me *Job 19:19*
my familiar friends abhor me *Job 19:19*
(A)(E)
my intimate friends avoid me *Job 19:19*
(B)(R)
hath put wisdom in the *i.* *Job 38:36*
parts
wisdom in the inner self (B) *Job 38:36*
their *i.* part is very wickedness *Ps 5:9*
their heart is destruction - a *Ps 5:9*
destructive chasm, a yawning gulf
(A)

their heart is a destructive *Ps 5:9*
chasm (B)
their heart is destruction (R) *Ps 5:9*
Their *i.* thought is, that their *Ps 49:11*
thou desirest truth in the *i.* *Ps 51:6*
parts
desire truth in the inner being *Ps 51:6*
(A)
desirest truth in the inner self *Ps 51:6*
(B)
desirest truth in the inward *Ps 51:6*
being (R)
i. thought of every one of them *Ps 64:6*
seeped into *i.* life (A)(E) *Ps 109:18*
did form my *i.* parts *Ps 139:3*
(A)(E)(R)
Lord be your *i.* parts (B) *Pr 3:26*
all the *i.* parts of the belly *Pr 20:27*
searching all innermost parts *Pr 20:27*
(A)(E)(R)
do stripes the *i.* parts of the *Pr 20:30*
belly
strokes reach innermost parts *Pr 20:30*
(A)(B)(E)(R)
and mine *i.* parts for *Isa 16:11*
Kir-haresh
my inner being sounds like a *Isa 16:11*
harp (A)
my feelings are moved for *Isa 16:11*
Moab (B)
my heart soundeth for Moab *Isa 16:11*
(E)
my soul moans like a lyre for *Isa 16:11*
Moab (R)
I will put my law in their *i.* *Jer 31:33*
parts
put my law within them *Jer 31:33*
(A)(R)
their *i.* parts to shake (S) *Eze 29:7*
and the porch of the gate was *Eze 40:9*
i.
and windows were round *Eze 40:16*
about *i.*
Then went he *i.* and measured *Eze 41:3*
a walk of ten cubits breadth *i.* *Eze 42:4*
your *i.* part is full of ravening *Lu 11:39*
the law of God after the *i.* man *Ro 7:22*
in my inmost self (A)(N)(R) *Ro 7:22*
in my inmost heart (B) *Ro 7:22*
conscious mind wholeheartedly *Ro 7:22*
endorses (P)
disclose *i.* motives (N) *1Co 4:5*
the *i.* man is renewed day by *2Co 4:16*
day
our inner self is being *2Co 4:16*
renewed (A)(B)
we are inwardly renewed (N) *2Co 4:16*
our inner nature is being *2Co 4:16*
renewed (R)
his *i.* affection is more *2Co 7:15*
abundant

INWARDLY

their mouth, but they curse *i.* *Ps 62:4*
but at heart they curse (B) *Ps 62:4*
but *i.* they are ravening wolves *M't 7:15*
inside they are devouring *M't 7:15*
wolves (A)
at heart they are voracious *M't 7:15*
wolves (B)
underneath they are savage *M't 7:15*
wolves (N)
but are really greedy wolves *M't 7:15*
(P)
he is a Jew, which is one *i.* *Ro 2:29*
we are *i.* renewed (N) *2Co 4:16*

INWARDS

its *i.* thereof (E) *Ex 12:9*
all the fat that covereth the *i.* *Ex 29:13*
in pieces, and wash the *i.* of *Ex 29:17*
him
and the fat that covereth the *Ex 29:22*
his *i.* and his legs shall he wash *Le 1:9*
in
he shall wash the *i.* and the legs *Le 1:13*
the fat that covereth the *i.* *Le 3:3;*
3:9, 14; 4:8; 7:3
and all the fat that is upon the *i. Le 3:3;*
3:9, 14; 4:8; 8:25
and with his legs, and his *i.* and *Le 4:11*
his
took all the fat that was upon *Le 8:16*
the *i.*
And he washed the *i.* and the *Le 8:21;*
legs *9:14*
and that which covereth the *i.* *Le 9:19*

IOTA

not one *i.* (B)(R) *M't 5:18; Lu 16:17*

IPHEDEIAH

And *I.* and Penuel, the sons *1Ch 8:25*
of

IR

and Huppim, the children of *1Ch 7:12*
I.

IRA

I. also the Jairite was a chief *2Sa 20:26*
I. the son of Ikkesh the *2Sa 23:26;*
Tekoite *1Ch 11:28; 27:9*
I. an Ithrite, Gareb an Ithrite *2Sa 23:38;*
1Ch 11:40

IRAD

And unto Enoch was born *I.* *Ge 4:18*
I. begat Mehujael: and *Ge 4:18*
Mehujael

IRAM

Duke Magdiel, duke *I.*, these *Ge 36:43*
be
Duke Magdiel, duke *I.* These *1Ch 1:54*
are

IRI

and *I.*, five; heads of the house *1Ch 7:7*

IRIJAH

whose name was *I.*, the son of *Jer 37:13*
I. took Jeremiah, and brought *Jer 37:14*
him

IRKSOME

is not *i.* (A)(B)(E)(R)(S) *Ph'p 3:1*
orders not *i.* (A)(B) *1Jo 5:3*

IR-NAHASH

and Tehinnah, the father of *I.* *1Ch 4:12*

IRON

of every artificer in brass and *i.* *Ge 4:22*
I will make your heaven as *i.* *Le 26:19*
the silver, the brass, the *i.*, the *Nu 31:22*
tin
smite him with an instrument *Nu 35:16*
of *i.*
his bedstead was a bedstead of *De 3:11*
i.
you forth out of the *i.* furnace, *De 4:20*
even
a land whose stones are *i.* and *De 8:9*
thou shalt not lift up any *i.* *De 27:5*
tool
earth that is under thee shall *De 28:23*
be *i.*
shall put a yoke of *i.* upon thy *De 28:48*
neck
Thy shoes shall be *i.* and *De 33:25*
brass
gold, and vessels of brass and *Jos 6:19*
i.
and the vessels of brass and of *Jos 6:24*
i.
which no man hath lift up any *i. Jos 8:31*
i.
of the valley have chariots *Jos 17:16*
of *i.*
though they have *i.* chariots *Jos 17:18*
And *I.* and Migdal-el, Horem *Jos 19:38*
gold, and with brass, and with *Jos 22:8*
i.
because they had chariots of *i.* *J'g 1:19*
he had nine hundred chariots *J'g 4:3*
of *i.*
even nine hundred chariots of *J'g 4:3*
i.
weighed six hundred shekels of *1Sa 17:7*
i.
saws, and under harrows of *i.* *2Sa 12:31*
and under axes of *i.* and *2Sa 12:31*
made

be fenced with *i*. and the staff   *2Sa 23:7*
of a
any tool of *i*. heard in the   *1Ki 6:7*
house
from the midst of the furnace   *1Ki 8:51*
of *i*.
Chenaanah made him horns   *1Ki 22:11*
of *i*.
it in thither; and the *i*. did   *2Ki 6:6*
swim
with harrows of *i*. and with   *1Ch 20:3*
axes
David prepared *i*. in   *1Ch 22:3*
abundance
and of brass and *i*. without   *1Ch 22:14*
weight
the brass, and the *i*. there is   *1Ch 22:16*
no
of brass, the *i*. for things of *i*.   *1Ch 29:2*
one hundred thousand talents   *1Ch 29:7*
of *i*.
in brass, and in *i*. and in   *2Ch 2:7*
purple
in silver, in brass, in *i*., in   *2Ch 2:14*
stone
had made him horns of *i*.   *2Ch 18:10*
also such as wrought *i*. and   *2Ch 24:12*
brass
they were graven with an *i*.   *Job 19:24*
pen
He shall flee from the *i*.   *Job 20:24*
weapon
I. is taken out of the earth   *Job 28:2*
brass; his bones are like bars   *Job 40:18*
of *i*.
He esteemeth *i*. as straw, and   *Job 41:27*
brass
shalt break them with a rod of *i*.   *Ps 2:9*
hurt with fetters: he was laid   *Ps 105:18*
in *i*.
being bound in affliction and   *Ps 107:10*
i.
and cut the bars of *i*. in   *Ps 107:16*
sunder
and their nobles with fetters   *Ps 149:8*
of *i*.
I. sharpeneth *i*.; so a man   *Pr 27:17*
If the *i*. be blunt, and he do   *Ec 10:10*
not
the thickets of the forest with   *Isa 10:34*
i.
and cut in sunder the bars of *i*.   *Isa 45:2*
thy neck is as an *i*. sinew, and   *Isa 48:4*
gold, and for *i*. I will bring   *Isa 60:17*
silver
for wood brass, and for   *Isa 60:17*
stones *i*.
and an *i*. pillar, and brasen   *Jer 1:18*
walls
they are brass and *i*.; they are   *Jer 6:28*
all
land of Egypt, from the *i*.   *Jer 11:4*
furnace
Shall *i*. break the northern *i*.   *Jer 15:12*
of Judah is written with a pen   *Jer 17:1*
of *i*.
shalt make for them yokes of   *Jer 28:13*
i.
have put a yoke of *i*. upon the   *Jer 28:14*
neck
take thou unto thee an *i*. pan   *Eze 4:3*
and set it for a wall of *i*.   *Eze 4:3*
between
are brass, and tin, and *i*. and   *Eze 22:18*
lead
silver, and brass, and *i*. and   *Eze 22:20*
lead
with silver, *i*., tin, and lead   *Eze 27:12*
bright *i*. cassia, and calamus,   *Eze 27:19*
were
His legs of *i*. his feet part of *i*.   *Da 2:33*
image upon his feet that were   *Da 2:34*
of *i*.
Then was the *i*., the clay, the   *Da 2:35*
brass
kingdom shall be strong as *i*.   *Da 2:40*
i. breaketh in pieces and   *Da 2:40*
subdueth
and as *i*. that breaketh all   *Da 2:40*
these
part of potters' clay, and part   *Da 2:41*
of *i*.
be in it of the strength of the *i*.   *Da 2:41*
sawest the *i*. mixed with miry   *Da 2:41;*
clay   *2:43*
the toes of the feet were part   *Da 2:42*
of *i*.
even as *i*. is not mixed with   *Da 2:43*
clay

it brake in pieces the *i*. the   *Da 2:45*
brass
even with a band of *i*. and   *Da 4:15;*
brass   *4:23*
of gold, and of silver, of brass,   *Da 5:4*
of *i*.
gods of silver, and gold, of   *Da 5:23*
brass, *i*.
it had great *i*. teeth; it devoured   *Da 7:7*
whose teeth were of *i*. and his   *Da 7:19*
nails
with threshing instruments of *i*.   *Am 1:3*
for I will make thine horn *i*.   *Mic 4:13*
they came unto the *i*. gate   *Ac 12:10*
that
conscience seared with a hot *i*.   *1Ti 4:2*
he shall rule them with a rod   *Re 2:27;*
of *i*.   *19:15*
as it were breastplates of *i*.   *Re 9:9*
to rule all nations with a rod of   *Re 12:5*
i.
and of brass, and *i*., and   *Re 18:12*
marble

IRONS

thou fill his skin with barbed *i*.   *Job 41:7*
hurt with *i*. (B)   *Ps 105:18*

IRPEEL

Rekem, and *I*., and Taralah   *Jos 18:27*

IRREPROACHABLE

i. we behaved ourselves (B)   *1Th 2:10*
stainless, *i*. (A)(B)(N)   *1Ti 6:14*

IRRELIGION

renounce *i*. (R)   *Tit 2:12*

IRRELIGIOUS

i., empty discussions (B)   *1Ti 6:20*
immoral or *i*. (R)   *Heb 12:16*

IRRESISTIBLY

grew *i*. in power and influence   *Ac 19:20*
(P)

IRRESOLUTE

i. and inexperienced (A)   *2Ch 13:7*

IRREVERENT

avoid *i*. legends (A)   *1Ti 4:7*

IRREVOCABLE

there are two *i*. facts (N)   *Heb 6:18*

IRRITABLE

love is not *i*. (B)(R)   *1Co 13:5*

IRRITATE

molten images to *i*. me (B)   *1Ki 14:9*
do not *i*. your children (B)   *Col 3:21*

IRRITATED

because you *i*. me (B)   *1Ki 21:22*
provoked, *i*., embittered God   *Heb 3:15*
(A)

IRRITATION

i. came to such pass (B)   *Ac 15:39*
in a burst of *i*. (P)   *Ac 16:18*

IR-SHEMESH

was Zorah, and Eshtaol, and   *Jos 19:41*
I.

IRU

Caleb the son of Jephunneh;   *1Ch 4:15*
I.

IS

that they are double to that   *Job 11:6*
which *is*
who son *is*, and who Father *is*   *Lu 10:22*
an Israelite indeed, in whom   *Joh 1:47*
is no guile

born of flesh *is* flesh, of Spirit   *Joh 3:6*
is spirit
but the Son of man which *is*   *Joh 3:13*
in heaven
he that hath the bride *is* the   *Joh 3:29*
bridegroom
but the hour cometh, and now   *Joh 4:23*
is
no man knoweth whence he *is*   *Joh 7:27*
that *is* of God   *Joh 8:47*
we know not from whence he   *Joh 9:29;*
is   *9:30*
is of the truth   *Joh 18:37*
made the sea, and all that in   *Ac 4:24*
them *is*
what new doctrine whereof   *Ac 17:19*
thou speakest *is*
understanding what the will   *Eph 5:17*
of Lord *is*
above all that *is* called God, *is*   *2Th 2:4*
worshipped, shewing himself he
is God
having promise of life that now   *1Ti 4:8*
is
must believe he *is*, and is a   *Heb 11:6*
rewarder
for we shall see him as he *is*   *1Jo 3:2*
as he *is* pure   *1Jo 3:3*
sin *is* transgression of law   *1Jo 3:4*
which *is*, was, and *is* to come   *Re 1:4;*
  1:8; 4:8
behold the beast that was, *is*   *Re 17:8*
not, yet *is*
one *is* and the other *is* not yet   *Re 17:10*
come

IS IT

this city near, *is it* not a little   *Ge 19:20*
one
wherefore *is it* thou askest   *Ge 39:29*
after my name
that *is it* that I spake to you,   *Ge 42:14*
ve are spies
this *is it* that their fathers   *Ge 49:28*
spake to them
how *is it* that you are come so   *Ex 2:18*
soon
why *is it* that ye have left the   *Ex 2:20*
man
Moses said, Why *is it* that thou   *Ex 5:22*
hast sent
neither *is it* the voice of them   *Ex 32:18*
that cry
is it not in that thou goest   *Ex 33:16*
with us
is it not in Rabbath of Ammon   *De 3:11*
nor *is it* far off; nor *is it*   *De 30:11;*
beyond the sea   *30:13*
to take that we have, *is it* not   *J'g 14:15*
so
is it not on thee, and on   *1Sa 9:20*
father's house
is it not because the Lord hath   *1Sa 10:1*
anointed
is it not wheat harvest to-day?   *1Sa 12:17*
I will call
is it not because no God in   *2Ki 1:3;*
Israel   *1:6, 16*
is it well with thee, *is it* well   *2Ki 4:26*
with husband
and let him say, Is *it* peace   *2Ki 9:17;*
  9:18-19, 22
is it not good, if peace be in   *2Ki 20:19*
my days
is it not I that commanded   *1Ch 21:17*
the people
is it good   *Job 10:3*
saying, Where *is it*   *Job 13:9; 15:23*
is it any pleasure to the   *Job 22:3*
Almighty that
a word in due season, how   *Pr 15:23*
good *is it*
is it a small thing for you to   *Isa 7:13*
weary men
is it not yet a very little while,   *Isa 20:17*
and Lebanon
is it not he whose high places   *Isa 36:7*
and altars
is it such a fast that I have   *Isa 58:5*
chosen
is it not to deal thy bread to   *Isa 58:7*
the hungry
neither also *is it* in them to do   *Jer 10:5*
good
is it nothing to you, all ye that   *La 1:12*
pass by
is it true, O Shadrach,   *Da 3:14*
Meshach

is it not even thus, O children *Am 2:11*
of Israel
transgression of Jacob, *is it* not *Mic 1:5*
Samaria
is it not for you to know *Mic 3:1*
judgment
is it not of the Lord of hosts *Hab 2:13*
that people
is it not in your eyes as *Hag 2:3*
nothing
what *is it* *Zec 5:6;*
M't 26:62; M'k 14:60; Ac 10:4; 21:22;
2Co 12:13; Eph 4:9
is it not evil; what profit *is it* *Mal 1:8;*
3:14
is it lawful to heal on *M't 12:10;*
Lu 14:3
how *is it* ye do not *M't 16:11;*
understand *M'k 8:21*
is it lawful to put away his *M't 19:3;*
wife *M'k 10:2*
is it not lawful for me to do *M't 20:15*
what I will
is it lawful to give tribute to *M't 22:17;*
Caesar, or not *M'k 12:14; Lu 20:22*
began to say, Lord *is it* I *M't 26:22;*
26:25; M'k 14:19
what *is it* which these *M't 26:62;*
witness *M'k 14:60*
whether *is it* easier to say, Thy *M'k 2:9*
sins
how *is it* that he eateth with *M'k 2:16*
publicans
is it lawful to do good on *M'k 3:4;*
sabbath *Lu 6:9*
he said, How *is it* that you *M'k 4:40*
have no faith
how long *is it* ago since this *M'k 9:21*
came to him
hard *is it* for them that trust *M'k 10:24*
in riches
to them, *is it* not written *M'k 11:17;*
Joh 10:34
he said to them, How *is it* ye *Lu 2:49*
sought me
how *is it* that ye do not *Lu 12:56*
discern this time
how *is it* that I hear this of *Lu 16:2*
thee
prophesy, who *is it* that smote *Lu 22:64*
thee
how *is it* thou being a Jew *Joh 4:9*
askest of me
how *is it* that thou wilt *Joh 14:22*
manifest thyself
how *is it* that ye have agreed *Ac 5:9*
together
is it lawful for you to scourge *Ac 22:25*
a Roman
is it so, that there is not a wise *1Co 6:5*
man
is it a great matter if we reap *1Co 9:11*
your carnal
is it not the communion of *1Co 10:16*
blood of Christ
is it therefore not of the *1Co 12:15;*
body *12:16*
how *is it* every one of you *1Co 14:26*
hath a psalm
what glory *is it* if when ye be *1Pe 2:20*
buffeted
even now already *is it* in the *1Jo 4:3*
world

IS *NOT*

the child *is not;* and one is *Ge 37:30;*
not *37:32; 42:13*
and Jacob said, Joseph *is not,* *Ge 42:36*
Simeon *is not*
is not this it in which my lord *Ge 44:5*
drinketh
is not Aaron the Levite thy *Ex 4:14*
brother
is not this the word that we *Ex 14:12*
did tell thee
my servant Moses *is not* so, *Nu 12:7*
who is
is not of seed of Aaron, come *Nu 16:40*
near to offer
God *is not* a man that he *Nu 23:19*
should lie
the land *is not* as the land of *De 11:10*
Egypt
also with him that *is not* here *De 29:15*
this day
because our God *is not* *De 31:17*
amongst us
is not he thy Father that *De 32:6*
bought thee

for their rock *is not* as our *De 32:31*
rock
is not this laid up in store *De 32:34*
with me
is not the Lord gone out before *J'g 4:14*
thee
a city that *is not* of children *J'g 19:12*
of Israel
he *is not* a man that he *1Sa 15:29*
should repent
he cried, *Is not* the arrow *1Sa 20:37*
beyond thee
is not this David king of the *1Sa 21:11;*
land *29:3, 5*
is not this Bath-sheba wife of *2Sa 11:3*
Uriah
is not the band of Joab with *2Sa 14:19*
thee in this
and Joab said, The matter *is* *2Sa 20:21*
not so
is not this blood of the men *2Sa 23:17*
that went
stranger that *is not* of Israel *1Ki 8:41;*
2Ch 6:32
this *is not* the way, nor this *2Ki 6:19*
the city
is not the sound of his *2Ki 6:32*
master's feet behind
is not the Lord your God *1Ch 22:18*
with you
for the Lord *is not* with Israel *2Ch 25:7*
which *is not* according to the *Es 4:16*
law
is not this thy fear, thy *Job 4:6*
confidence
is not my help in me; he is *Job 6:13;*
not man as *9:32*
lo, their good *is not* in their *Job 21:16*
hand
is not thy wickedness great *Job 22:5*
and infinite
is not God in the height of *Job 22:12*
heaven
behold, I go forward but he *is* *Job 23:8*
not there
rich man openeth his eyes, *Job 27:19*
and he *is not*
for the good man *is not* at *Pr 7:19*
home, he is
wilt thou set thy eyes on that *Pr 23:5*
which *is not*
eat, saith he, but his heart *is* *Pr 23:7*
not with thee
I saw the race *is not* to the *Ec 9:11*
swift
is not Calno, *is not* Hamath, *is* *Isa 10:9*
not Samar
and behold, before the *Isa 17:14*
morning he *is not*
spend money for that which *is* *Isa 55:2*
not bread
and the word *is not* in the *Jer 5:13*
prophets
is not Lord in Zion, *is not* her *Jer 8:19*
King in her
portion of Jacob *is not* like *Jer 10:16;*
them *51:19*
I know that way of man *is* *Jer 10:23*
not in himself
is not my word like as a fire *Jer 23:29*
the king *is not* he that can do *Jer 38:5*
any thing
and Esau *is not;* but she is *Jer 49:10;*
not healed *51:9*
ye say way of Lord *is not* *Eze 18:25;*
equal, *is not* my way equal *18:29; 33:17,*
20
gods, whose dwelling *is not* *Da 2:11*
with flesh
as for me, this secret *is not* *Da 2:30*
revealed to me
is not this great Babylon, that *Da 4:30*
I have built
she *is not* my wife, nor I her *Ho 2:2*
husband
arise, depart, for this *is not* *Mic 2:10*
your rest
they say, *Is not* the Lord *Mic 3:11*
among us
his soul which is lifted up *is* *Hab 2:4*
not upright
is not this a brand plucked out *Zec 3:2*
of the fire
is not this the carpenter's son, *M't 13:55*
is not his
on my left, *is not* mine to *M't 20:23;*
give *M'k 10:40*
God *is not* the God of the *M't 22:32;*
dead, but *M'k 12:27; Lu 20:38*

come to pass, but end *is not* *M't 24:6;*
yet *Lu 21:9*
he *is not* here for he is risen *M't 28:6;*
Lu 24:6
the disciple *is not* above his *Lu 6:40*
master
is not he that sitteth at meat *Lu 22:27*
greater
he that believeth *is not* *Joh 3:18*
condemned
my witness *is not* true; this *Joh 5:31;*
man *is not* *9:16*
Jesus said, This sickness *is not* *Joh 11:4*
unto death
word which you hear *is not* *Joh 14:24;*
mine *7:16*
my kingdom *is not* of this *Joh 18:36*
world
he *is not* a Jew that is one *Ro 2:28*
outwardly
whose praise *is not* of men but *Ro 2:29*
of God
is not he also of Gentiles, yes, *Ro 3:29*
of Gentiles
but hope that is seen *is not* *Ro 8:24*
hope
kingdom of God *is not* meat *Ro 14:17*
and drink
for whatsoever *is not* of faith *Ro 14:23*
is sin
the kingdom of God *is not* in *1Co 4:20*
word
now the body *is not* for *1Co 6:13*
fornication
a brother or sister *is not* *1Co 7:15*
under bondage
for the man *is not* of the *1Co 11:8*
woman, but the
this *is not* to eat the Lord's *1Co 11:20*
supper
the body *is not* one member, *1Co 12:14*
but many
charity envieth not, *is not* *1Co 13:4*
puffed up
all flesh *is not* the same flesh, *1Co 15:39*
but there is
that your labour *is not* in *1Co 15:58*
vain in the Lord
which *is not* another, but some *Ga 1:7*
trouble you
the gospel preached by me *is* *Ga 1:11*
not after man
law *is not* of faith; *is not* *Ga 3:12;*
mediator of one *3:20*
be not deceived, God *is not* *Ga 6:7*
mocked
to write the same to me *is not* *Ph'p 3:1*
grievous
for God *is not* unrighteous to *Heb 6:10*
forget
the Lord *is not* slack *2Pe 3:9*
concerning his
truth *is not* in us *1Jo 1:8; 2:4*
word *is not* in *1Jo 1:10*
the love of the Father *is not* in *1Jo 2:15*
him
is not of the Father, but is of *1Jo 2:16*
the world
doth not righteousness, *is not* *1Jo 3:10;*
of God *4:3, 6*
if brother sin a sin which *is* *1Jo 5:16*
not unto death
beast thou sawest, was, and *is* *Re 17:8;*
not *17:11*

IS *THERE*

is there yet any portion or *Ge 31:14*
inheritance
what God *is there* in heaven or *De 3:24*
earth
what nation *is there* so great, *De 4:7;*
who hath God *8:8*
who *is there* of all flesh that *De 5:26*
hath heard
what man *is there* that hath *De 20:5;*
built *20:7-8*
nor *is there* any *De 32:28*
understanding in them
is there any man; *is there* *J'g 4:20;*
never a *14:3*
who *is there* among all the *J'g 21:5;*
tribes of Israel *21:8*
neither *is there* any rock like *1Sa 2:2*
our God
and David said, *Is there* not *1Sa 17:29*
a cause
nor *is there* any God besides *2Sa 7:22;*
thee *Isa 44:8*

is there any that is left of   2Sa 9:1;
Saul's house   9:3
is there not here a prophet of   1Ki 22:7;
the Lord besides   2Ki 3:11; 2Ch 18:6
in thy hand *is there* not power 2Ch 20:6
and might
who *is there* among you his   2Ch 36:23;
people   Ezr 1:3
who *is there* being as I am   Ne 6:11
would go
is there iniquity in my tongue Job 6:30;
  33:9
is there any secret thing with Job 15:11
thee
what profit *is there* in my blood Ps 30:9
when I go
is there a price in the hand of Pr 17:16
a fool
is there any thing whereof it   Ec 1:10
may be said
what good *is there* to the   Ec 5:11
owners thereof
nor *is there* any end of their   Isa 2:7
treasures, nor *is there* any end
nor *is there* knowledge to say, Isa 44:19
I have burnt
nor say, Is *there* not a lie in Isa 44:20
my right hand
is there no balm in Gilead, *is*   Jer 8:22
there no physician
I am Lord, *is there* any thing Jer 32:27
too hard for me
asked him, Is *there* any word Jer 37:17
from the Lord
is there iniquity in Gilead,   Ho 12:11
surely vanity
is there yet any with thee. he   Am 6:10
shall say, No
what man *is there* of you,   M't 7:9
whom if his son
nor *is there* salvation in any   Ac 4:12
other, for no
what profit *is there* of   Ro 3:1
circumcision
is there unrighteousness with Ro 9:14
God

IT IS

it is in the power of my hand Ge 31:29
to do hurt
and Joseph answered, *It is* not Ge 41:16
in me
go up and see the land what   Nu 13:18
it is
he *it is* that doth go before   De 31:8
thee
it is the Lord, let him do what 1Sa 3:18
seems
so *it is*   2Sa 13:35; Job 5:27; Lu 12:54
it is for Saul and for his   2Sa 21:1
bloody house
is thine heart right as my   2Ki 10:15
heart? *it is*
he *it is* that executeth the   1Ch 6:10
priest's office
even I *it is* that have sinned, 1Ch 21:17
and done evil
and there *it is* unto this day   2Ch 5:9
how hast thou declared the   Job 26:3
thing as *it is*
to know the measure of my   Ps 39:4
days what *it is*
it is even the time of Jacob's Jer 30:7
trouble
it is of Lord's mercies not   La 3:22
consumed
till he come whose right *it is* Eze 21:27
will be done on earth, as *it is* M't 6:10
in heaven
of good cheer, *it is* I, be not   M't 14:27;
afraid   Joh 6:20
it is because we have no   M't 16:7;
bread   M'k 8:16
he *it is* who coming after me   Joh 1:27
is preferred
not because *it is* of Moses, but Joh 7:22
the fathers
he *it is* to whom I shall give   Joh 13:26
a sop
hath commandments, he *it is* Joh 14:21
that loveth
then said they, *It is* his angel Ac 12:15
try every man's work, of what 1Co 3:13
sort *it is*
that if a man have long hair 1Co 11:14
it is a shame
if a woman have long hair *it* 1Co 11:15
is a glory to her

it is to God, or if we be sober 2Co 5:13
it is for
but as then, even so *it is* now Ga 4:29
is come to you, as *it is* in all   Col 1:6
the world
be glorified, even as *it is* with 2Th 3:1
you

IT IS NOT

it is not good   Ge 2:18;
Pr 18:5; 25:27; 28:21; Ho 8:6; M't 19:10
that *it is not* towards me as   Ge 31:5
before
it is not in me, God shall give Ge 41:16
Moses said, *It is not* meet so to Ex 8:26
do
for *it is not* a vain thing for   De 32:47
you
know *it is not* his hand that   1Sa 6:9
smote
Jonathan said, God forbid, *it* 1Sa 20:2
is not so
been in building, yet *it is not* Ezr 5:16
finished
I would speak, but *it is not* so Job 9:35
with me
it is not in me, sea saith, It is Job 28:14
not with
but now because *it is not* so, Job 35:15
he hath visited
it is not for kings, O Lemuel, to Pr 31:4
drink
it is not he; *it is not* in man to Jer 5:12;
direct   10:23
which say, *It is not* near, let   Eze 11:3
us build
it is not ye that speak, but   M't 10:20
Spirit
to you it is given, but to   M't 13:11
them *it is not* given
it is not law, to have her   M't 14:4;
  27:6; M'k 6:18
it is not meet to take   M't 15:26;
children's   M'k 7:27
even so *it is not* the will of   M't 18:14
your Father
it is not for you to know the   Ac 1:7
times
it is not reason that we should Ac 6:2
leave word
for *it is not* fit that he should Ac 22:22
live
it is not the manner of the   Ac 25:16
Romans
so then *it is not* of him that   Ro 9:16
willeth
it is not expedient for me to   2Co 12:1
glory

THERE IS

there is a plague in the house Le 14:35
there is nothing at all besides Nu 11:6
manna
I am he, and *there is* no god De 32:39
with me
there is both straw and   J'g 19:19
provender
there is a feast of the Lord in J'g 21:19
Shiloh
there is no restraint to the   1Sa 14:6
Lord
may know that *there is* a   1Sa 17:46
God in Israel
there is but a step between me 1Sa 20:3
and death
then came thou, for *there is* 1Sa 20:21
peace to thee
there is neither adversary nor 1Ki 5:4
evil
there is no God like thee in   1Ki 8:23;
heaven   2Ch 6:14
there is no man that sinneth   1Ki 8:46;
not   2Ch 6:36
there is Ahijah the prophet   1Ki 14:2
who told
there is yet one man, Micaiah 1Ki 22:8
son of Imlah
he shall know *there is* a prophet 2Ki 5:8
in Israel
yet *there is* hope in Israel   Ezr 10:2;
  Job 11:18
there is a certain people   Es 3:8
scattered
that ye may know *there is*   Job 19:29
judgment
then thou shalt say, There is   Job 22:29
lifting up

there is a spirit in man, the   Job 32:8
inspiration
the fool hath said, There is no Ps 14:1;
God   53:1
in keeping them *there is* great Ps 19:11
reward
there is no want to them that   Ps 34:9
fear him
there is a river whose streams Ps 46:4
make glad
verily *there is* a reward for the Ps 58:11
righteous
there is little Benjamin with   Ps 68:27
their ruler
put not trust in man, in whom Ps 146:3
there is no help
there is that scattereth, yet   Pr 11:24
increaseth
there is that maketh himself   Pr 13:7
rich, yet hath
but among the righteous there   Pr 14:9
is favour
there is a way that seemeth   Pr 14:12;
right to man   16:25
in all labour *there is* profit;   Pr 14:23;
there is an end   23:18
there is a generation that   Pr 30:11;
curseth   30:12-14
to every thing *there is* a season, Ec 3:1
and a time
there is a just man, *there is* a   Ec 7:15
wicked man
where the word of a king is,   Ec 8:4
there is power
there is that neither day nor   Ec 8:16
night seeth sleep
there is one event; for to him   Ec 9:2;
there is hope   9:4
and besides me *there is* no   Isa 43:11
Saviour
and beside me *there is* no God Isa 44:6;
  44:8; 45:5
there is no throne, O daughter Isa 47:1
of the Chaldeans
there is no peace to wicked   Isa 48:22;
  57:21; Jer 6:14
because *there is* no water,   Isa 50:2;
there is no beauty   53:2
saidst not, There is no hope Isa 57:10;
  Jer 2:25; 18:12
there is hope in thy end; he   Jer 31:17;
said, There is   37:17
there is a conspiracy of her   Eze 22:25
prophets
there is Elam; *there is*   Eze 32:24;
Edom, her kings   32:29
were scattered, because *there* Eze 34:5
is no shepherd
there is a God that revealeth Da 2:28
secrets
there is a man in thy kingdom Da 5:11
in whom is
because *there is* no truth nor   Ho 4:1
mercy
there is no healing of thy   Na 3:19
bruise, thy wound
Sadducees say *there is* no   M't 22:23;
resurrection   M'k 12:18; 1Co 15:12
there is none good but one,   M'k 10:18
that is God
and yet *there is* room; *there* Lu 14:22;
is joy in   15:10
because *there is* no truth in   Joh 8:44
him
stumbleth, because *there is*   Joh 11:10
no light in him
there is among you envying   1Co 3:3
and strife
reported *there is* fornication   1Co 5:1
among you
to us *there is* but one God, the 1Co 8:6
Father
there is a natural body, *there* 1Co 15:44
is a spiritual body
temperance, against such *there* Ga 5:23
is no law
and *there is* no respect of   Col 3:25
persons
there is no fear in love, but   1Jo 4:18
perfect love
there is a sin unto death, I do 1Jo 5:16
not say
and *there is* a sin not unto   1Jo 5:17
death

THERE IS NOT

there is not ought left in sight Ge 47:18
of my lord

slain king's sons, *there is not*   2Sa 13:30
one left
there is not among us that   1Ki 5:6
can skill to hew
not because *there is not* a God   2Ki 1:3;
      1:6
to birth, and *there is not*   2Ki 19:3
strength to bring forth
upon earth *there is not* his   Job 41:33
like
there is one alone, *there is not*   Ec 4:8
second
there is not one barren among   Ca 6:6
them
there is not a greater prophet   Lu 7:28
than John
there is not a wise man   1Co 6:5
amongst you
there is not in every man that   1Co 8:7
knowledge

ISAAC

thou shalt call his name *I.*   Ge 17:19;
      21:3
but my covenant will I   Ge 17:21
establish with *I.*
shall not be heir with my son,   Ge 21:10
even *I.*
hearken to Sarah, for in *I.*   Ge 21:12;
shall thy seed be called   Ro 9:7;
      Heb 11:18
take thine only son *I.*   Ge 22:2
Abraham bound *I.*   Ge 22:9
take a wife for *I.*; appointed   Ge 24:4;
for *I.*   24:14
I. went out to meditate in the   Ge 24:63
field
I. was comforted after his   Ge 24:67
mother's death
Abraham gave all that he had   Ge 25:5
unto *I.*
his sons *I.* and Ishmael buried   Ge 25:9
Abraham
God blessed *I.*   Ge 25:11
I. forty years old when he   Ge 25:20
took Rebekah
and *I.* entreated the Lord for   Ge 25:21
his wife
I. was sixty years old when   Ge 25:26
she bare Esau
I. loved Esau   Ge 25:28
I. went to Abimelech king of   Ge 26:1
Philistines
I. was sporting with Rebekah   Ge 26:8
his wife
I. sowed and received an   Ge 26:12
hundredfold
I. servants digged in valley   Ge 26:19
and found well
which was grief of mind to *I.*   Ge 26:35
and Rebekah
as *I.* had made an end of   Ge 27:30
blessing Jacob
I. called Jacob, blessed him,   Ge 28:1
and charged
I. sent Jacob away, he went to   Ge 28:5
Padan-aram
except the fear of *I.* had been   Ge 31:42
with me
Jacob came to *I.*; *I.* gave up   Ge 35:27;
the ghost   35:29
offered sacrifices to the God of   Ge 46:1
his father *I.*
God, before whom my father   Ge 48:15
I. did walk
let the name of my father *I.*   Ge 48:16
be on them
there they buried *I.*; he sware   Ge 49:31;
to *I.*   50:24
God remembered his covenant   Ex 2:24;
with Abraham with *I.*   Le 26:42
the God of *I.*   Ge 32:9;
  Ex 3:6;   3:15-16;   4:5;   1Ki 18:36;
  1Ch 29:18;   2Ch 30:6;   M't 22:32;
  M'k 12:26; Lu 20:37; Ac 3:13;   7:32
I multiplied his seed and gave   Jos 24:3
him *I.*
I gave unto *I.* Jacob and Esau,   Jos 24:4
and to Esau
his oath unto *I.*   1Ch 16:16; Ps 105:9
his seed to be rulers over the   Jer 33:26
seed of *I.*
and the high places of *I.* shall   Am 7:9
be desolate
drop not thy word against the   Am 7:16
house of *I.*
Abraham begat *I.* and *I.* begat   M't 1:2;
Jacob   Lu 3:34; Ac 7:8

many shall sit down with *I.* in   M't 8:11
the kingdom
when ye shall see *I.* in   Lu 13:28
kingdom of God
Rebekah had conceived by our   Ro 9:10
father *I.*
we, brethren, as *I.* was, are of   Ga 4:28
the promise
dwelling in tabernacles with   Heb 11:9
I. and Jacob
by faith Abraham offered   Heb 11:17;
up *I.*   Jas 2:21
by faith *I.* blessed Jacob,   Heb 11:20
Esau, about things

ISAAC'S

I. servants digged in the valley   Ge 26:19
Gerar did strive with *I.*   Ge 26:20
herdmen
there *I.* servants digged a well   Ge 26:25
I. servants came and told him   Ge 26:32

ISAIAH

to *I.* the prophet the son of   2Ki 19:2
Amoz
of king Hezekiah came to *I.*   2Ki 19:5
And *I.* said unto them, Thus   2Ki 19:6
shall
Then *I.* the son of Amoz sent   2Ki 19:20
to
I. the son of Amoz came to   2Ki 20:1
him
I. was gone out into the   2Ki 20:4
middle
And *I.* said, Take a lump of   2Ki 20:7
figs
Hezekiah said unto *I.*, What   2Ki 20:8
shall
I. said, This sign shalt thou   2Ki 20:9
have of
I. the prophet cried unto the   2Ki 20:11
Lord
I. the prophet unto King   2Ki 20:14
Hezekiah
I. said unto Hezekiah, Hear   2Ki 20:16
said Hezekiah unto *I.*, Good   2Ki 20:19
is the
did *I.* the prophet, the son of   2Ch 26:22
Amoz
I. the son of Amoz, prayed   2Ch 32:20
in the vision of *I.* the   2Ch 32:32
prophet
The vision of *I.* the son of Amoz   Isa 1:1
word that *I.* the son of Amoz   Isa 2:1
saw
Then said the Lord unto *I.*, Go   Isa 7:3
which *I.* the son of Amoz did   Isa 13:1
see
the same time spake the Lord   Isa 20:2
by *I.*
my servant *I.* hath walked   Isa 20:3
naked
unto *I.* the prophet the son of   Isa 37:2
Amoz
of king Hezekiah came to *I.*   Isa 37:5
I. said unto them, Thus shall   Isa 37:6
ye say
Then *I.* the son of Amoz sent   Isa 37:21
unto
I. the prophet the son of Amoz   Isa 38:1
came the word of the Lord to   Isa 38:4
I.
I. had said, Let them take a   Isa 38:21
lump
I. the prophet unto king   Isa 39:3
Hezekiah
Then said *I.* to Hezekiah, Hear   Isa 39:5
Then said Hezekiah to *I.* Good   Isa 39:8

ISCAH

of Milcah, and the father of *I.*   Ge 11:29

ISCARIOT

Judas *I.* who also betrayed   M't 10:4;
him   M'k 3:19
one of the twelve, called   M't 26:14
Judas *I.*
And Judas *I.* one of the   M'k 14:10
twelve
Judas *I.* which also was the   Lu 6:16
traitor
Satan into Judas surnamed *I.*   Lu 22:3
spake of Judas *I.* the son of   Joh 6:71
Simon
one of his disciples, Judas *I.*   Joh 12:4

now put it into the heart of   Joh 13:3
Judas *I.*
the sop, he gave it to Judas *I.*   Joh 13:26
Judas saith unto him, not *I.*,   Joh 14:22
Lord

ISHBAH

and *I.* the father of Eshtemoa   1Ch 4:17

ISHBAK

and Midian, and *I.* and Shuah   Ge 25:2;
      1Ch 1:32

ISHBI-BENOB

And *I.* which was of the sons   2Sa 21:16
of

ISH-BOSHETH

took *I.* the son of Saul, and   2Sa 2:8
I. Saul's son was forty years   2Sa 2:10
old
the servants of *I.* the son of   2Sa 2:12
Saul
pertained to *I.* the son of Saul   2Sa 2:15
I. said to Abner, Wherefore   2Sa 3:7
hast
very wroth for the words of *I.*   2Sa 3:8
David sent messengers to *I.*   2Sa 3:14
Saul's
I. sent, and took her from her   2Sa 3:15
I.
heat of the day to the house of   2Sa 4:5
I.
brought the head of *I.* unto   2Sa 4:8
David
Behold the head of *I.* the son of   2Sa 4:8
they took the head of *I.*, and   2Sa 4:12
buried

ISHI

of Appaim; *I.* And the sons   1Ch 2:31
of *I.*
the sons of *I.* were, Zoheth,   1Ch 4:20
and
and Uzziel, the sons of *I.*   1Ch 4:42
of their fathers, even Epher,   1Ch 5:24
and *I.*
Lord, that thou shalt call me *I.*   Ho 2:16

ISHIAH

and Obadiah, and Joel, *I.* five   1Ch 7:3

ISHIJAH

the sons of Harim; Eliezer, *I.*   Ezr 10:31

ISHMA

Jezreel, and *I.* and Idbash: and   1Ch 4:3

ISHMAEL

thou shalt call his name *I.*   Ge 16:11;
      16:15
Abram was 86 years old when   Ge 16:16
Hagar bare *I.*
said to God, O that *I.* might   Ge 17:18
live before thee
as for *I.* I have heard thee, I   Ge 17:20
have blessed him
I. was 13 years old when he   Ge 17:25
was circumcised
his sons Isaac and *I.* buried   Ge 25:9
Abraham
the generations of *I.*   Ge 25:12;
      25:13, 16; 1Ch 1:29, 31
these are the years of the life   Ge 25:17
of *I.*
then went Esau unto *I.* and   Ge 28:9
took Mahalath
I. came to Gedaliah   2Ki 25:23; Jer 40:8
I. came and ten men with him   2Ki 25:25;
      Jer 41:1
the sons of Abraham, Isaac   1Ch 1:28
and *I.*
Bocheru and *I.* were sons of   1Ch 8:38;
Azel   9:44
Zebadiah son of *I.* the ruler   2Ch 19:11
Jehoiada took *I.* into   2Ch 23:1
covenant with him
I. Elasah, had taken strange   Ezr 10:22
wives
king of the Ammonites hath   Jer 40:14
sent *I.*
I will slay *I.*   Jer 40:15

ISHMAEL

not do this thing, for thou *Jer 40:16*
speakest falsely of *I.*
I. smote Gedaliah *Jer 41:2*
I. went forth to meet them, *Jer 41:6*
weeping
then *I.* carried away captive *Jer 41:10*
residue of people
then Johanan went to fight *Jer 41:12*
with *I.*
but *I.* escaped from Johanan *Jer 41:15*
with eight men

ISHMAELITE

the camels also was Obil the *1Ch 27:30*
I.

ISHMAELITES

earrings, because they were *I.* *J'g 8:24*
tabernacles of Edom, and the *I* *Ps 83:6*

ISHMAEL'S

And Bashemath *I.* daughter, *Ge 36:3*
sister

ISHMAIAH

Zebulun, *I.* the son of *1Ch 27:19*
Obadiah

ISHMEELITE

of Amasa was Jether the *I.* *1Ch 2:17*

ISHMEELITES

I. came from Gilead, with *Ge 37:25*
their
Come, and let us sell him to *Ge 37:27*
the *I.*
sold Joseph to the *I.* for *Ge 37:28*
twenty
bought him of the hands of the *Ge 39:1*
I.

ISHMERAI

I. also, and Jezliah, and *1Ch 8:18*
Jobab

ISHOD

his sister Hammoleketh bare *1Ch 7:18*
I.

ISHPAN

And *I.* and Heber, and Eliel *1Ch 8:22*

ISH-TOB

and of *I.* twelve thousand men *2Sa 10:6*
of Zoba, and of Rehob, and *I.* *2Sa 10:8*

ISHUAH

and *I.* and Isui, and Beriah *Ge 46:17*

ISHUAI

and Isuah, and *I.* and Beriah *1Ch 7:30*

ISHUI

Saul were Jonathan, and *I.* *1Sa 14:49*

ISLAND

shall deliver the *i.* of the *Job 22:30*
innocent
even deliver one who is not *Job 22:30*
innocent (A)(E)
even deliver one not guiltless *Job 22:30*
(B)
He delivers the innocent man *Job 22:30*
(R)
meet with the wild beasts of *Isa 34:14*
the *i.*
wild beasts of the desert *Isa 34:14*
(A)(B)(E)
a certain *i.* which is called *Ac 27:16*
Clauda
we must be cast upon a *Ac 27:26*
certain *i.*
knew that the *i.* was called *Ac 28:1*
Melita

the chief man of the *i.* whose *Ac 28:7*
name
which had diseases in the *i.* *Ac 28:9*
came
every mountain and *i.* were *Re 6:14*
moved
And every *i.* fled away, and *Re 16:20*

ISLANDERS

i., seeing make (N) *Ac 28:4*

ISLANDS

Hamath, and from the *i.* of *Isa 11:11*
the sea
countries bordering the *Isa 11:11*
Mediterranean (A)
the coastlands of the sea (R) *Isa 11:11*
the wild beasts of the *i.* shall *Isa 13:22*
cry in
will cry in the deserted *Isa 13:22*
castles (A)
shall howl within the castles *Isa 13:22*
(B)(E)
Hyenas will cry in its towers *Isa 13:22*
(R)
Keep silence before me, O *i.* *Isa 41:1*
and declare his praise in the *i.* *Isa 42:12*
I will make the rivers *i.* and I *Isa 42:15*
will
to the *i.* he will repay *Isa 59:18*
recompence
beasts of the *i.* shall dwell *Jer 50:39*
there
wild beasts of the desert *Jer 50:39*
(A)(B)(E)

ISLE

inhabitants of this *i.* shall say *Isa 20:6*
inhabitants of the coastland *Isa 20:6*
(A)(B)(E)(R)
Be still, ye inhabitants of the *i.* *Isa 23:2*
inhabitants of the coast *Isa 23:2;*
(A)(E)(R)						*23:6*
inhabitants of the coastlands *Isa 23:2;*
(B)						*23:6*
howl, ye inhabitants of the *i.* *Isa 23:6*
gone through the *i.* unto *Ac 13:6*
Paphos
which had wintered in the *i.* *Ac 28:11*
was in the *i.* that is called *Re 1:9*
Patmos

ISLES

were the *i.* of the Gentiles *Ge 10:5*
divided
the coastland peoples spread *Ge 10:5*
(A)(R)
the coastlands of the Gentiles *Ge 10:5*
(B)
the land, and upon the *i.* of the *Es 10:1*
sea
the coastlands of the sea *Es 10:1*
(A)(R)
the islands of the sea (B) *Es 10:1*
and of the *i.* shall bring *Ps 72:10*
presents
kings of the coasts (A) *Ps 72:10*
the multitude of *i.* be glad *Ps 97:1*
thereof
let the many islands be glad *Ps 97:1*
(B)
let the many coastlands be glad *Ps 97:1*
(R)
God of Israel in the *i.* of the *Isa 24:15*
sea
in the islands of the sea (B) *Isa 24:15*
the coastlands of the sea (R) *Isa 24:15*
taketh up the *i.* as a very little *Isa 40:15*
thing
islands (B) *Isa 40:15;*
*41:5;	42:4,	10;	49:1;	51:5;	66:19;*
Jer 31:10; Eze 27:15; Zep 2:11
The *i.* saw it, and feared; the *Isa 41:5*
ends
coastlands (A)(B)(R) *Isa 41:5;*
Eze 26:15
and the *i.* shall wait for his law *Isa 42:4*
Islands and coastal regions *Isa 42:4;*
(A) *42:10; 66:19*
the coastlands shall wait for *Isa 42:4*
his law (R)
the *i.* and the inhabitants *Isa 42:10*
thereof
Listen, O *i.* unto me; and *Isa 49:1*
hearken

the *i.* shall wait upon me, and *Isa 51:5*
islands (A) *Isa 51:5*
the coastlands wait for me (R) *Isa 51:5*
Surely the *i.* shall wait for me *Isa 60:9*
to Tubal, and Javan, to the *i.* *Isa 66:19*
afar off
pass over the *i.* of Chittim, and *Jer 2:10*
see
the coasts of Cyprus (A)(R) *Jer 2:10*
the *i.* which are beyond the *Jer 25:22*
sea
islands and coastlands across *Jer 25:22*
sea (A)
the coastland across the sea *Jer 25:22*
(B)(R)
declare it in the *i.* afar off, *Jer 31:10*
and say
the *i.* shake at the sound of *Eze 26:15*
thy fall
the *i.* tremble in the day of *Eze 26:18*
thy fall
the *i.* that are in the sea shall *Eze 26:18*
be
merchant of the people for *Eze 27:3*
many *i.*
people of many coasts (B) *Eze 27:3*
brought out of the *i.* of *Eze 27:6*
Chittim
the coasts of Cyprus (A)(R) *Eze 27:6*
the pines of Cyprus (B) *Eze 27:6*
the isles of Kittim (E) *Eze 27:6*
and purple from the *i.* of *Eze 27:7*
Elishah
the coasts of Elishah (A)(R) *Eze 27:7*
the coastlands of Elishah (B) *Eze 27:7*
many *i.* were the *Eze 27:15*
merchandise of
All the inhabitants of the *i.* *Eze 27:35*
shall be
dwellers of the coastlands *Eze 27:35*
(B)(R)
them that dwell carelessly in *Eze 39:6*
the *i.*
dwell securely in the *Eze 39:6*
coastlands (A)(B)(R)
shall he turn his face unto the *Da 11:18*
i.
attention to the coastlands *Da 11:18*
(B)(R)
place, even all the *i.* of the *Zep 2:11*
heathen
coastlands of the nations (A) *Zep 2:11*
the isles of the nations (E) *Zep 2:11*
the lands of the nations (R) *Zep 2:11*

ISMACHIAH

and Jozabad, and Eliel, and *2Ch 31:13*
I.

ISMAIAH

And *I.* the Gibeonite, a *1Ch 12:4*
mighty

ISOLATED

be *i.* (B) *Le 13:46*
render her *i.* (B) *Re 17:16*

ISPAH

And Michael, and *I.*, and *1Ch 8:16*
Joha

ISRAEL

thy name shall be no more *Ge 32:28*
Jacob but *I.*
but *I.* shall be thy name *Ge 35:10;*
1Ki 18:31
I. dwelt in the land of Egypt, *Ge 47:27*
in Goshen
and *I.* bowed himself upon *Ge 47:31*
the bed's head
in thee shall *I.* bless, saying, *Ge 48:20*
God make thee
from thence is the shepherd, *Ge 49:24*
the stone of *I.*
I. is my son *Ex 4:22*
that I should obey his voice to *Ex 5:2*
let *I.* go
that we have let *I.* go from *Ex 14:5*
serving us
let us flee from *I.* for Lord *Ex 14:25*
fighteth for them
the Lord saved *I.* that day *Ex 14:30*
from Egyptians
I. prevailed *Ex 17:11*
remember Abraham, Isaac, *Ex 32:13*
and *I.* thy

her son and a man of *I*. strove *Le 24:10*
together
Lord hath spoken good *Nu 10:29*
concerning *I*.
return, O Lord, to the many *Nu 10:36*
thousands of *I*.
thus saith thy brother *I*. Let us *Nu 20:14*
pass
I. vowed a vow unto the Lord, *Nu 21:2*
and said
then *I*. sang this song, *Nu 21:17*
Spring up, O well
defy *I*. *Nu 23:7*
shall be said of *I*. What hath *Nu 23:23*
God wrought
a sceptre rise out of *I*. *Nu 24:17*
Edom a possession, and *I*. *Nu 24:18*
shall do valiantly
Phinehas went after the man *Nu 25:8*
of *I*. and thrust
that his name be not put out of *De 25:6*
I.
shall each *I*. thy law, Jacob *De 33:10*
thy
I. then shall dwell in safety *De 33:28*
alone, fountain
when *I*. turned their backs *Jos 7:8*
before enemies
I. hath sinned *Jos 7:11*
so Joshua took the mountain *Jos 7:16*
of *I*.
I. he shall know *Jos 22:22*
I. served the Lord all the days *Jos 24:31*
of Joshua
it came to pass when *I*. was *J'g 1:28*
strong
that through them I may *J'g 2:22;*
prove *I*. *3:1, 4*
my heart is toward the *J'g 5:9*
governors of *I*.
I. was greatly impoverished by *J'g 6:6*
Midianites
save *I*. *J'g 6:14; 6:15, 36-37; 7:2*
so that *I*. was sore distressed *J'g 10:9*
his soul was grieved for the *J'g 10:16*
misery of *I*.
because *I*. took away my land *J'g 11:13*
even to Jabbok
the Lord smote Benjamin *J'g 20:35*
before *I*.
I. was smitten *1Sa 4:2*
I. is fled *1Sa 4:10; 4:17*
on whom is the desire of *I*.? *1Sa 9:20*
Is it not on thee
heard that *I*. also was had in *1Sa 13:4*
abomination
also the strength of *I*. will not *1Sa 15:29*
lie
in the name of the God of *1Sa 17:45*
the armies of *I*.
the beauty of *I*. is slain on *2Sa 1:19*
high places
what one nation is like thy *2Sa 7:23*
people *I*.
the ark, and *I*. and Judah *2Sa 11:11*
abide in tents
like the immoral pack in *I*. *2Sa 13:13*
(B)
for *I*. had fled every man to *2Sa 19:8*
his tent
Judah and *I*. were many as *1Ki 4:20*
the sand
Judah and *I*. dwelt safely *1Ki 4:25;*
Jer 23:6
I shall be a proverb among all *1Ki 9:7*
people
he abhorred *I*.: so *I*. *1Ki 11:25;*
rebelled *12:19*
Lord shall smite *I*. as a reed *1Ki 14:15*
is shaken
Ahab said, Art thou he that *1Ki 18:17*
troubleth *I*.
the Lord began to cut *I*. *2Ki 10:32*
short
Judah was put to the worse *2Ki 14:12*
before *I*.
not that he would blot out *2Ki 14:27*
he named *I*.
carried *I*. away into Assyria *2Ki 17:6;*
17:23; 23:27
the children of Jacob, whom *2Ki 17:34*
he named *I*.
the word of the Lord *1Ch 11:10*
concerning *I*.
all they of *I*. were a thousand *1Ch 21:5*
thousand
The God of *I*. *1Ch 29:18;*
1Ki 18:36; 2Ch 6:16; 30:6; Jer 31:1
because thy God loved *I*. to *2Ch 9:8*
establish

whether they were of *I*. *Ezr 2:59;*
Ne 7:61
his mercy endureth for ever *Ezr 3:11*
towards *I*.
strange wives to increase the *Ezr 10:10*
trespass of *I*.
Jacob shall rejoice *I*. shall be *Ps 14:7;*
glad *53:6*
glorify him, and fear him, all *Ps 22:23*
ye seed of *I*.
redeem *I*. O God, out of all *Ps 25:22*
his troubles
bless ye the Lord from the *Ps 68:26*
fountain of *I*.
when God heard this, he *Ps 78:59*
abhorred *I*.
would not hearken, *I*. would *Ps 81:11*
none of me
O that my people *I*. had *Ps 81:13*
walked in my ways
name of *I*. be no more in *Ps 83:4*
remembrance
Judah was his sanctuary, *I*. his *Ps 114:2*
dominion
he that keepeth *I*. shall neither *Ps 121:4*
slumber
but peace shall be upon *I*. *Ps 125:5;*
128:6
let *I*. hope in the Lord *Ps 130:7; 131:3*
he gathereth together the *Ps 147:2*
outcasts of *I*.
let *I*. rejoice in him that made *Ps 149:2*
him
but *I*. doth not know nor *Isa 1:3*
consider
blessed be *I*. mine *Isa 19:25*
inheritance
I. shall blossom and bud, and *Isa 27:6*
fill the world
but thou *I*. art my servant, *Isa 41:8*
seed of Abraham
who gave *I*. to robbers? did *Isa 42:24*
not the Lord
and I have given *I*. to *Isa 43:28*
reproaches
shall surname himself by the *Isa 44:5*
name of *I*.
for *I*. mine elect's sake, I have *Isa 45:4*
called thee
I. shall be saved in Lord with *Isa 45:17*
everlasting salvation
in the Lord shall the seed of *I*. *Isa 45:25*
be justified
which are called by the name *Isa 48:1*
of *I*.
though *I*. be not gathered, *I*. *Isa 49:5*
shall be glorious
be my servant to restore the *Isa 49:6*
preserved of *I*.
the Lord which gathereth the *Isa 56:8*
outcasts of *I*.
and though *I*. acknowledge us *Isa 63:16*
not
I. was holiness to the Lord and *Jer 2:3*
firstfruits
is *I*. a servant? the salvation *Jer 2:14;*
of *I*. *3:23*
I. is the rod of his *Jer 10:16;*
inheritance *51:19*
O Lord, hope of *I*. Saviour in *Jer 14:8;*
thee *17:13*
for was not *I*. a derision unto *Jer 48:27*
thee
hath *I*. no sons? hath he no *Jer 49:1*
heir
I. shall be heir to them that *Jer 49:2*
were his heirs
I. is a scattered sheep, lions *Jer 50:17*
have driven
I will bring *I*. again to his *Jer 50:19*
habitation
iniquity of *I*. be sought for *Jer 50:20*
and shall be none
I. hath not been forsaken of *Jer 51:5*
his God
and *I*. is the rod of his *Jer 51:19*
inheritance
the Lord hath swallowed up *I*. *La 2:5*
I will judge you in the border *Eze 11:10*
of *I*.
ah Lord God, wilt thou make *Eze 11:13*
a full end of *I*.
eyes to the idols of the house *Eze 18:15*
of *I*.
shall know that I the Lord do *Eze 37:28*
sanctify *I*.
are gone from me, when *I*. *Eze 44:10*
went astray
though thou *I*. play harlot, let *Ho 4:15*
not Judah

I. slideth back as a *Ho 4:16*
backsliding heifer
I. is not hid from me, *I*. is *Ho 5:3;*
defiled *6:10*
I shall fall; *I*. shall cry to me, *Ho 5:5;*
my God *8:2*
I. hath cast off the thing that is *Ho 8:3*
good
I. is swallowed up *Ho 8:8*
I. hath forgotten his Maker, *Ho 8:14*
and buildeth
I. shall know it *Ho 9:7*
I found *I*. like grapes in the *Ho 9:10*
wilderness
I. is an empty vine *Ho 10:1*
I. shall be ashamed of his own *Ho 10:6*
counsel
the sin of *I*. be destroyed *Ho 10:8*
when *I*. was a child, then I *Ho 11:1*
loved him
how shall I deliver thee, *I*. *Ho 11:8*
I. served and kept sheep for a *Ho 12:12*
wife
will plead with them for my *Joe 3:2*
heritage *I*.
I. shall surely be led captive *Am 7:11;*
7:17
shall come to Adullam the *Mic 1:15*
glory of *I*.
they shall smite the judge of *I*. *Mic 5:1*
with a rod
he hath holpen his servant *I*. in *Lu 1:54*
mercy
art thou a master of *I*. and *Joh 3:10*
knowest not
that for the hope of *I*. I am *Ac 28:20*
bound
for they are not all *I*. which are *Ro 9:6*
of *I*.
Esaias crieth concerning *I*. tho' *Ro 9:27*
number of *I*.
I. which followed the law of *Ro 9:31*
righteousness
but I say, Did not *I*. know? *Ro 10:19*
Moses saith
I. hath not obtained what he *Ro 11:7*
seeketh for
behold, *I*. after the flesh *1Co 10:18*
peace and mercy on them, and *Ga 6:16*
on *I*.
of the stock of *I*. of tribe of *Ph'p 3:5*
Benjamin

AGAINST ISRAEL

Arad fought *against I*.; Sihon *Nu 21:1;*
against I. *21:23*
is there any divination *Nu 23:23*
against I.
anger of Lord was kindled *Nu 25:3;*
against I. *32:13; J'g 2:14, 20; 3:8; 10:7;*
2Sa 24:1; 2Ki 13:3; 1Ch 27:24;
2Ch 28:13; Ps 78:21
the kings of Canaan *against I*. *Jos 8:14;*
11:5
Balak king of Moab warred *Jos 24:9*
against I.
Eglon *against I*.; Midian *J'g 3:12;*
against I. *6:2*
children of Ammon made war *J'g 11:4;*
against I. *11:5, 20*
Balak, did he ever strive *J'g 11:25*
against I.
Philistines in array *against I*. *1Sa 4:2;*
7:7, 10; 31:1; 1Ch 10:1
Ben-hadad *against I*. *1Ki 20:26;*
2Ki 6:8
then Moab rebelled *against I*. *2Ki 1:1*
there was great indignation *2Ki 3:27*
against I.
yet the Lord testified *against* *2Ki 17:13*
I.
and Satan stood up *against I*. *1Ch 21:1*
Rehoboam went out *against I*. *2Ch 11:1*
write the words I have spoken *Jer 36:2*
against I.
thou sayest, Prophesy not *Am 7:16*
against I.
he maketh intercession *against* *Ro 11:2*
I.

ALL ISRAEL

Moses chose able men out of *Ex 18:25*
all *I*.
all *I*. round about fled at cry *Nu 16:34*
of them
all *I*. shall hear and fear *De 13:11;*
21:21
all *I*. stoned Achan with stones *Jos 7:25*

all *I.* went a whoring after the *J'g 8:27* ephod

Eli heard all that his sons did *1Sa 2:22* to all *I.*

all *I.* knew that Samuel was a *1Sa 3:20* prophet

word of Samuel came to all *I.* *1Sa 4:1* Now Israel went

that I may lay it for a *1Sa 11:2* reproach on all *I.*

but all *I.* and Judah loved *1Sa 18:16* David

all *I.* had lamented *1Sa 23:3* Samuel, and buried

to bring about all *I.* unto thee *2Sa 3:12*

all *I.* understood it was not of *2Sa 3:37* king David

but I will do this thing before *2Sa 12:12* all *I.*

in all *I.* none so much praised *2Sa 14:25* as Absalom

all *I.* shall hear that thou art *2Sa 16:21* abhorred

all *I.* know thy father is a *2Sa 17:10* mighty man

and all *I.* fled every one to *2Sa 18:17* his tent

seeing the speech of all *I.* is *2Sa 19:11* come to me

the eyes of all *I.* are upon thee *1Ki 1:20*

thou knowest that all *I.* set *1Ki 2:15* their faces on me

all *I.* heard of the judgment of *1Ki 3:28* Solomon

the king and all *I.* offered *1Ki 8:62* sacrifice before Lord

all *I.* stoned Adoram with *1Ki 12:18* stones that he died

all *I.* shall mourn for him, *1Ki 14:13* and bury him

gather to me all *I.* unto *1Ki 18:19* mount Carmel

I saw all *I.* scattered *1Ki 22:17;* *2Ch 18:16*

David and all *I.* went to *1Ch 11:4* Jerusalem

David and all *I.* played before *1Ch 13:8* God with might

all *I.* brought up the ark of *1Ch 15:28* the covenant

wheresoever I have walked *1Ch 17:6* with all *I.*

all *I.* and the princes obeyed *1Ch 29:23* Solomon

all *I.* forsook the law of the *2Ch 12:1* Lord

Abijah said, Hear me, *2Ch 13:4* Jeroboam, and all *I.*

God smote Jeroboam and all *2Ch 13:15* *I.*

to make an atonement for *2Ch 29:24;* all *I.* *Ezr 6:17*

all *I.* went out and brake the *2Ch 31:1* images

all *I.* dwelt in their cities *Ezr 2:70;* *Ne 7:73*

he made all *I.* swear to do this *Ezr 10:5* thing

all *I.* gave the portions of the *Ne 12:47* singers

confusion of faces belongeth to *Da 9:7* us, to all *I.*

yea, all *I.* have transgressed *Da 9:11* thy law

remember ye the law of Moses *Mal 4:4* for all *I.*

for they are not all *I.* which are *Ro 9:6* of Israel

so all *I.* shall be saved, as it is *Ro 11:26* written

CAMP OF ISRAEL

angel which went before the *Ex 14:19* camp of *I.*

a cloud between Egyptians *Ex 14:20* and the camp of *I.*

lest ye make the camp of *I.* a *Jos 6:18* curse

they left them without the *Jos 6:23* camp of *I.*

out of the camp of *I.* am *I* *2Sa 1:3* escaped

when they came to the camp *2Ki 3:24* of *I.*

FOR ISRAEL

all that God had done for *I.* *Ex 18:1;* *18:8; Jos 24:31; J'g 2:7, 10; 1Ki 8:66*

for the Lord fought for *I.* *Jos 10:14;* *10:42*

the Midianites left no *J'g 6:4* sustenance for *I.*

Samuel cried unto the Lord for *1Sa 7:9* *I.*

that David made it an *1Sa 30:25* ordinance for *I.*

not any helper for *I.* *2Ki 14:26*

to make an atonement for *I.* *1Ch 6:49;* as Moses commanded *22:1; Ne 10:33*

this was statute for *I.*, law of *Ps 81:4* God of Jacob

place salvation in Zion for *I.* *Isa 46:13* my glory

the burden of the word of the *Zec 12:1* Lord for *I.*

my prayer to God for *I.* is, they *Ro 10:1* be saved

FROM ISRAEL

shalt be cut off from *I.* *Ex 12:15;* *Nu 19:13*

that wrath may be turned *Nu 25:4* away from *I.*

put evil from *I.* *De 17:12;* *22:22; J'g 20:13*

there is one tribe cut off from *J'g 21:6* *I.*

the glory is departed from *I.* *1Sa 4:21;* *4:22*

the cities taken from *I.* were *1Sa 7:14* restored

that taketh away the *1Sa 17:26* reproach from *I.*

and the plague was stayed *2Sa 24:25* from *I.*

separated from *I.* the mixed *Ne 13:3* multitude

Lord will cut off from *I.* head *Isa 9:14* and tail

for from *I.* was it also, the *Ho 8:6* workman made it

IN ISRAEL

he had wrought folly in *I.* *Ge 34:7;* *De 22:21; Jos 7:15; J'g 20:6, 10*

divide them in Jacob, scatter *Ge 49:7* them in *I.*

strangers sojourn in *I.* *Le 20:2;* *22:18; Eze 14:7*

able to go forth to war in *I.* *Nu 1:3;* *1:45; 26:2*

these were heads of thousands *Nu 1:16;* in *I.* *10:4*

I hallowed to me all the *Nu 3:13* firstborn in *I.*

every thing devoted in *I.* shall *Nu 18:14* be thine

given all the tenth in *I.* for an *Nu 18:21* inheritance

nor hath he seen perverseness *Nu 23:21* in *I.*

abomination is wrought in *I.* *De 17:4;* *22:21*

to raise up to his brother a *De 25:7* name in *I.*

his name be called in *I.* the *De 25:10* house of him that

arose not a prophet since in *I.* *De 34:10* like Moses

Rahab dwelleth in *I.* because *Jos 6:25* hid spies

they ceased in *I.* till that *J'g 5:7*

Deborah arose, a mother in *I.* *J'g 5:8*

was there a spear seen among *40,000 in *I.*

custom in *I.* to lament *J'g 11:39* Jephthah's daughter

was no king in *I.* *J'g 17:6;* *18:1; 19:1; 21:25*

or that thou be priest to a *J'g 18:19* family in *I.*

come to pass in *I.* one tribe *J'g 21:3* lacking in *I.*

manner in former times in *I.* *Ru 4:7* concerning redeeming, a testimony in *I.*

that his name may be famous *Ru 4:14* in *I.*

behold, I will do a thing in *I.* *1Sa 3:11*

beforetime in *I.* when a man *1Sa 9:9* went to inquire

Lord hath wrought salvation *1Sa 11:13;* in *I.* *14:45*

will make his father's house *1Sa 17:25* free in *I.*

the earth may know that *1Sa 17:46* there is a God in *I.*

or what is my father's family *1Sa 18:18* in *I.*

David said to Abner, Who is *1Sa 26:15* like to thee in *I.*

there is a great man fallen in *2Sa 3:38* *I.*

thou broughtest in *I.* *2Sa 5:2; 1Ch 11:2*

no such thing ought to be *2Sa 13:12* done in *I.*

thou shalt be as one of the *2Sa 13:13* fools in *I.*

shall any be put to death this *2Sa 19:22* day in *I.*

I am faithful and peaceable *2Sa 20:19* in *I.* thou seekest to destroy a mother in *I.*

nor for us shalt thou kill any *2Sa 21:4* man in *I.*

I will cut off him that is shut *1Ki 14:10;* up and left in *I.* *21:21; 2Ki 9:8*

let it be known, that thou art *1Ki 18:36* God in *I.*

yet I have left me seven *1Ki 19:18* thousand in *I.*

because there is not a God in *2Ki 1:3;* *I.* *1:6, 16*

he shall know that there is a *2Ki 5:8* prophet in *I.*

there is no God in all the *2Ki 5:15* earth but in *I.*

prophet in *I.* telleth the king of *2Ki 6:12* Israel

for there was joy in *I.* *2Ch 12:40*

not fail thee a man to be ruler *2Ch 7:18* in *I.*

buried him, because he had *2Ch 24:16* done good in *I.*

inquire for them that are left *2Ch 34:21* in *I.*

Josiah made all present in *I.* *2Ch 34:33* to serve the Lord

was no passover like to that *2Ch 35:18* kept in *I.*

singing men made them an *2Ch 35:25* ordinance in *I.*

yet there is hope in *I.* *Ezr 10:2* concerning this

known in Judah, his name is *Ps 76:1* great in *I.*

testimony in Jacob, and he *Ps 78:5* appointed law in *I.*

are for signs and for wonders *Isa 8:18* in *I.*

the Lord hath glorified *Isa 44:23* himself in *I.*

they have committed villainy *Jer 29:23* in *I.*

which hast set signs and *Jer 32:20* wonders in *I.*

no more use it as a proverb *Eze 12:23;* in *I.* *18:3*

shall know that I am the holy *Eze 39:7* One in *I.*

will give to Gog a place of *Eze 39:11* graves in *I.*

ye shall give them no *Eze 44:28* possession in *I.*

every dedicated thing in *I.* *Eze 44:29* shall be theirs

in the land shall be his *Eze 45:8* possession in *I.*

shall give this oblation for *Eze 45:16* the prince in *I.*

Ephraim spake, he exalted *Ho 13:1* himself in *I.*

come out of thee, that is to be *Mic 5:2* ruler in *I.*

an abomination is committed *Mal 2:11* in *I.*

so great faith, no not in *I.* *M't 8:10;* *Lu 7:9*

marvelled, saying, It was *M't 9:33* never so seen in *I.*

LAND OF ISRAEL

no smith found in all the *1Sa 13:19* land of *I.*

brought a little maid out of *2Ki 5:2* land of *I.*

bands of Syria came no more *2Ki 6:23* into land of *I.*

send to brethren left in land *1Ch 13:2* of *I.*

gather together strangers in *1Ch 22:2;* the land of *I.* *2Ch 2:17; 30:25*

cut down idols through the *2Ch 34:7* land of *I.*

thus saith the Lord to the land *Eze 7:2* of *I.*

and I will give you the *land*   *Eze 11:17*
of *I.*
thus saith the Lord of the   *Eze 12:19*
land of *I.*
nor shall they enter into *land Eze 13:9;*
of *I.*   *20:38*
bring you into the *land* of *I. Eze 20:42;*
   37:12
and prophesy against the *land Eze 21:2*
of *I.*
thou saidst, Aha, against the   *Eze 25:3*
land of *I.*
rejoicedst with despite against *Eze 25:6*
the *land* of *I.*
Judah and *land* of *I.* were thy *Eze 27:17*
merchants
when Gog shall come against   *Eze 38:18*
the *land* of *I.*
shall be a great shaking in   *Eze 38:19*
the *land* of *I.*
in visions he brought me into   *Eze 40:2*
land of *I.*
go into the *land* of *I.* for they *M't 2:20*
are dead
took the child and came into   *M't 2:21*
the *land* of *I.*

MADE ISRAEL SIN

Jeroboam *made I.* to *sin*   *1Ki 14:16;*
   15:26, 30, 34; 16:19, 26; 22:52
Jeroboam *made I.* to *sin* (S) *1Ki 14:16;*
10:29, 31; 13:2, 6, 11; 14:24; 15:9, 18,
   24, 28; 23:15
Baasha *made* my people *I.* to *1Ki 16:2;*
sin   *16:13*
Ahab provoked the Lord,   *1Ki 21:22*
and *made I.* to *sin*

MEN OF ISRAEL

Joshua called for all the *men*   *Jos 10:24*
of *I.*
men of *I.* gathered against the *J'g 20:11*
city
men of *I.* went out;   *J'g 20:20;*
encouraged themselves   *20:22*
the *men* of *I.* gave place to *J'g 20:36*
the Benjamites
the *men* of *I.* were distressed *1Sa 14:24*
that day
the *men* of *I.* fled from the   *1Sa 31:1*
Philistines
Abner was beaten and the   *2Sa 2:17*
men of *I.*
hearts of the *men* of *I.* are   *2Sa 15:13*
after Absalom
whom the *men* of *I.* choose,   *2Sa 16:18*
his will I be
words of Judah fiercer than   *2Sa 19:43*
of the *men* of *I.*
and the *men* of *I.* were gone *2Sa 23:9*
away
smote down the chosen *men*   *Ps 78:31*
of *I.*
fear not, ye *men* of *I.* I will *Isa 41:14*
help you
ye *men* of *I.* hear these words *Ac 2:22*
ye *men* of *I.* why marvel ye at *Ac 3:12*
this
ye *men* of *I.* take heed to   *Ac 5:35*
yourselves
Paul said, Ye *men* of *I.* give   *Ac 13:16*
audience
Jews in Asia crying out, Men *Ac 21:28*
of *I.* help

O ISRAEL

they said, These be thy gods, O. *Ex 32:4*
I.
how goodly are thy   *Nu 24:5*
tabernacles, O *I.*
hearken, O. *I.*   *De 4:1;*
   27:9; Isa 48:12
hear; O *I.*   *De 5:1; 6:3-4;*
9:1; 20:3; Ps 50:7; 81:8; Isa 44:1;
   M'k 12:29
happy art thou, O *I.* who is *De 33:29*
like to thee
an accursed thing in the midst *Jos 7:13*
of thee, O *I.*
he said, Every man to his   *2Sa 20:1;*
tents, O *I.*   *1Ki 12:16; 2Ch 10:16*
behold thy gods, O *I.* which *1Ki 12:28*
brought
O *I.* trust thou in the Lord,   *Ps 115:9*
their help
why speakest thou, O *I.* my   *Isa 40:27*
way is hid

O *I.* fear not   *Isa 43:1; Jer 30:10; 46:27*
but thou hast been weary of   *Isa 43:22*
me, O *I.*
these, O *I.* for thou art   *Isa 44:21;*
servant, O *I.* thou shalt not   *49:3*
be forgotten
if thou wilt return, O *I.*   *Jer 4:1;*
   Ho 14:1
O *I.* thy prophets are like the *Eze 13:4*
foxes
rejoice not, O *I.* for joy, as   *Ho 9:1*
other people
O *I.* thou hast sinned from   *Ho 10:9*
the days of Gibeah
O *I.* thou hast destroyed thyself *Ho 13:9*
but in me help
prepare to meet thy God, O *I. Am 4:12*
shout, O. *I.* be glad and   *Zep 3:14*
rejoice with heart

OVER ISRAEL

Abimelech reigned three years *J'g 9:22*
over *I.*
the Philistines had dominion *J'g 14:4*
over *I.*
Samuel made his sons judges *1Sa 8:1*
over *I.*
when Saul had reigned two   *1Sa 13:1*
years over *I.*
Lord hath rejected thee from *1Sa 15:26*
being king over *I.*
Ish-bosheth Saul's son reigned *2Sa 2:10*
over *I.*
David over *I.*   *2Sa 3:10;*
   5:2-3; 12, 17; 6:21; 1Ch 11:3
the Lord of hosts is the God *2Sa 7:26*
over *I.*
Solomon over *I.*; Jeroboam *1Ki 1:34;*
   13:37
the Lord shall raise up a king *1Ki 14:14*
over *I.*
Nadab over *I.*   *1Ki 15:25*
Elah over *I.*   *1Ki 16:8*
Omri over *I.*   *1Ki 16:16*
Ahab; Ahaziah reigned over *1Ki 16:29;*
   22:51
Jeroram over *I.*   *2Ki 3:1;*
   9:3, 6, 12; 10:36
Jehoahaz; Jehoash; Zachariah *2Ki 13:1;*
over *I.*   *13:10; 15:8*
Menahem; Pekahiah;   *2Ki 15:17;*
Hoshea over *I.*   *15:23; 17:1*
Chenaniah for outward   *1Ch 26:29*
business over *I.*
times that went over *I.* are *1Ch 29:30*
written
strength to God, his excellency *Ps 68:34*
is over *I.*
I the preacher was king over *I. Ec 1:12*

PRINCES OF ISRAEL

princes of *I.* being twelve men *Nu 1:44*
princes of *I.*, heads of   *Nu 7:2;*
tribes offered at setting up   *7:84*
David commanded *princes* *1Ch 22:17*
of *I.* to help
David assembled the *princes 1Ch 23:2;*
of *I.*   *28:1*
the *princes* of *I.* humbled   *2Ch 12:6*
themselves
Jehoram slew divers of the   *2Ch 21:4*
princes of *I.*
take up lamentation for the   *Eze 19:1*
princes of *I.*
a sword shall be upon all the *Eze 21:12*
princes of *I.*
the *princes* of *I.* were on thee *Eze 22:6*
to shed blood
Lord saith, Let it suffice you, *Eze 45:9*
O *princes* of *I.*

TO, UNTO ISRAEL

God spake *unto I.* in the   *Ge 46:2*
visions of night
hear and hearken *unto I.* your *Ge 49:2*
father
goodness which the Lord hath *Ex 18:9*
done *to I.*
Joshua gave it for   *Jos 11:23;*
inheritance *to I.*   *21:43*
Lord hath given rest *unto I.*   *Jos 23:1*
from all enemies
the goodness he had shewed   *J'g 8:35*
unto I.
remember what Amalek did *to 1Sa 15:2*
I.

Abner spake all that seemed   *2Sa 3:19*
good *to I.*
Rezon was an adversary *to I. 1Ki 11:25*
confirmed for a law, and *to 1Ch 16:17;*
I. for everlasting covenant   *Ps 105:10*
why will he be a cause of   *1Ch 21:3*
trespass *to I.*
I will give quietness *to I.* in his *1Ch 22:9*
days
this is an ordinance for ever   *2Ch 2:4*
to I.
Ezra the priest, scribe of   *Ezr 7:11*
statutes *to I.*
law, which Lord commanded   *Ne 8:1*
to I.
truly God is good *to I.* even   *Ps 73:1*
to such
even an heritage *unto I.*   *Ps 135:12;*
   136:22
the Lord sheweth his   *Ps 147:19*
judgments *to I.*
as it was *to I.* in the day that *Isa 11:16*
he came
have I been a wilderness *unto I. Jer 2:31*
I am a father *to I.* Ephraim is *Jer 31:9*
my firstborn
I will be as the dew *to I.* he   *Ho 14:5*
shall grow
I am full of power to declare *Mic 3:8*
to I. his sin
the burden of the word of the *Mal 1:1*
Lord *to I.*
till the day of his shewing *unto Lu 1:80*
I.
that he should be made   *Joh 1:31*
manifest *to I.*
wilt thou restore the kingdom *to Ac 1:6*
I.
him hath God exalted to give *Ac 5:31*
repentance *to I.*
God hath raised *unto I.* a   *Ac 13:23*
Saviour Jesus
to I. he saith, All day long   *Ro 10:21*
stretched out
that blindness in part is   *Ro 11:25*
happened *to I.*

TRIBES OF ISRAEL

Dan shall judge as one of   *Ge 49:16*
tribes of *I.*
all these are the twelve *tribes Ge 49:28*
of *I.*
twelve pillars according to   *Ex 24:4*
twelve *tribes* of *I.*
thousand through all *tribes* of *Nu 31:4*
I. to war
if married to any of the other *Nu 36:3*
tribes of *I.*
every one of *tribes* of *I.* shall *Nu 36:9*
keep to his own
separate him to evil out of   *De 29:21*
tribes of *I.*
when the *tribes* of *I.* were   *De 33:5*
gathered together
take twelve men out of the   *Jos 3:12*
tribes of *I.*
stones according to number of *Jos 4:5;*
tribes of *I.*   *4:8*
so Joshua brought *I.* by their *Jos 7:16*
tribes
the land which Joshua gave to *Jos 12:7*
the *tribes* of *I.*
which heads of fathers of   *Jos 19:51*
tribes of *I.* divided
princes through *tribes* of *I.* *Jos 22:14*
sent to Reuben
Joshua gathered all *tribes* of *I. Jos 24:1*
to Shechem
inheritance of Dan not among *J'g 18:1*
tribes of *I.*
the chief of *tribes* of *I.*   *J'g 20:2*
presented before God
take ten men of an hundred *J'g 20:10*
out of all *tribes* of *I.*
who among the *tribes* of *I.*   *J'g 21:5;*
came not up   *21:8*
Lord hath made a breach in *J'g 21:15*
the *tribes* of *I.*
did I choose him out of all   *1Sa 2:28*
tribes of *I.*
I am of the smallest of the   *1Sa 9:21*
tribes of *I.*
Samuel caused all the *tribes 1Sa 10:20*
of *I.* to come
wast thou not made head of *1Sa 15:17*
the *tribes* of *I.*
then came all the *tribes* of *I.*   *2Sa 5:1*
to David

spake I a word with any of the   *2Sa 7:7*
tribes of I.
thy servant is one of the *tribes*   *2Sa 15:2*
of I.
Absalom sent spies through   *2Sa 15:10*
all the *tribes of I.*
people were at strife thro' the   *2Sa 19:9*
tribes of I.
go through all *tribes of I.* and   *2Sa 24:2*
number
chose no city of all *tribes of*   *1Ki 8:16;*
I. to build an house in   *2Ch 6:5*
chosen Jerusalem out of all   *1Ki 11:32;*
tribes of I. 14:21; 2Ki 21:7; 2Ch 12:13;
                                 33:7
after them out of all the   *2Ch 11:16*
tribes of I.
offered twelve goats according   *Ezr 6:17*
to *tribes of I.*
made *tribes of I.* to dwell in   *Ps 78:55*
their tents
I will take *tribes of I.* put   *Eze 37:19*
with Judah
according to the twelve   *Eze 47:13;*
tribes of I.   *21:22*
serve the city out of all the   *Eze 48:19*
tribes of I.
gates be after the names of   *Eze 48:31*
the *tribes of I.*
among *tribes of I.* have I made   *Ho 5:9*
known
the eyes of all *tribes of I.* be   *Zec 9:1*
toward Lord
judging the twelve *tribes of I.*   *M't 19:28;*
                            Lu 22:30
gates with names of twelve   *Re 21:12*
tribes of I.

WITH ISRAEL

Amalek fought *with I.* in   *Ex 17:8*
Rephidim
I have made a covenant *with*   *Ex 34:27*
thee and *I.*
Levites shall have no   *De 18:1*
inheritance *with I.*
Gad executed his judgments   *De 33:21*
with I.
the kings of Canaan fought   *Jos 9:2*
with I.
the inhabitants of Gibeon made *Jos 10:1*
peace *with I.*
the Philistines gathered   *1Sa 13:5*
themselves to fight *with I.*

ISRAEL with *PEOPLE*

much *people of I.* died by   *Nu 21:6*
serpents
be merciful, O Lord, to thy   *De 21:8*
people I.
look down and bless thy   *De 26:15*
people I.
that they should bless the   *Jos 8:33*
people of I.
drave Amorites before his   *J'g 11:23*
people I.
fat with the offerings of *I.* my *1Sa 2:29*
people
shall anoint Saul captain over *1Sa 9:16*
my *people I.*
hath made his *people I.*   *1Sa 27:12*
utterly to abhor him
by David I will save my *people* *2Sa 3:18*
I.
to feed my *people I.*   *2Sa 5:2;*
                 7:7; 1Ch 11:2
exalted his kingdom for his   *2Sa 5:12*
people I. sake
appoint place for my *people*   *2Sa 7:10;*
I.   *1Ch 17:9*
thou hast confirmed to thyself *2Sa 7:24*
thy *people I.*
I will not forsake my *people I.* *1Ki 6:13*
when thy *people I.* be smitten *1Ki 8:33;*
                        2Ch 6:24
what prayer shall be made by *1Ki 8:38*
thy *people I.*
all people may fear thee, as do *1Ki 8:43*
thy *people I.*
the Lord hath given rest to his *1Ki 8:56*
people I.
was lifted up, because of his   *1Ch 14:2*
people I.
be ruler over my *people I.*   *1Ch 17:7;*
                        2Ch 6:5
what one nation in earth is   *1Ch 17:21*
like thy *people I.*
thy *people I.* didst thou   *1Ch 17:22*
make thine own

goodness of Lord shewed *I.*   *2Ch 7:10*
his *people*
they blessed the Lord and his   *2Ch 31:8*
people I.
serve now the Lord your God *2Ch 35:3*
and his *people I.*
all they of *people* of *I.* minded *Ezr 7:13*
to go
people of *I.* have not separated *Ezr 9:1*
themselves
gave for an heritage to *I.* his   *Ps 135:12*
people
tho' thy *people I.* be as sand, *Isa 10:22*
a remnant
for the wickedness of my   *Jer 7:12*
people I.
which I caused my *people I.* to *Jer 12:14*
inherit
they have caused my *people I.* *Jer 23:13*
to err
I will bring again the captivity *Jer 30:3;*
of my *people I.* and Judah   *Am 9:14*
lay vengeance on Edom by   *Eze 25:14*
my *people I.*
ye shall yield your fruit to my *Eze 36:8*
people I.
I will cause my *people I.* to   *Eze 36:12*
walk upon you
when my *people I.* dwelleth   *Eze 38:14*
safely
thou shalt come up against   *Eze 38:16*
my *people I.*
was confessing the sin of my   *Da 9:20*
people I.
Lord said, Go, prophesy unto   *Am 7:15*
my *people I.*
the end is come upon my   *Am 8:2*
people I.
a Governor, that shall rule my *M't 2:6*
people I.
and the glory of thy *people I.*   *Lu 2:32*
people of *I.* were gathered   *Ac 4:27*
against Jesus
God of this *people I.* chose   *Ac 13:17*
our fathers
John preached repentance to   *Ac 13:24*
all *people* of *I.*

ISRAELITE

the name of the *I.* that was   *Nu 25:14*
slain, Zimri
Amasa was the son of Ithra,   *2Sa 17:25*
an *I.*
behold an *I.* indeed, in whom *Joh 1:47*
is no guile
I also am an *I.* of the seed of   *Ro 11:1*
Abraham

ISRAELITES

was not one of the cattle of the *Ex 9:7*
I. dead
all that are *I.* born shall dwell *Le 23:42*
in booths
all the *I.* passed over on dry   *Jos 3:17*
ground
only divide it by lot to the *I.*   *Jos 13:6*
for inheritance
the Benjamites destroyed of   *J'g 20:21*
the *I.*
so the priest's servant did to   *1Sa 2:14*
all *I.*
I. went to the Philistines to   *1Sa 13:20*
sharpen his axe
the Hebrews turned to be   *1Sa 14:21*
with the *I.*
all the *I.* lamented Samuel and *1Sa 25:1*
buried him
the *I.* pitched by a fountain in *1Sa 29:1*
Jezreel
the *I.* were troubled at Abner's *2Sa 4:1*
death
the *I.* rose and smote the   *2Ki 3:24*
Moabites
they are as all the multitude   *2Ki 7:13*
of the *I.*
the first inhabitants were the *I.* *1Ch 9:2*
who are *I.* to whom pertaineth *Ro 9:4*
adoption
are they Hebrews? are they   *2Co 11:22*
I.? so am I

ISRAELITISH

the son of an *I.* woman strove *Le 24:10*
in camp
I. woman's son blasphemed   *Le 24:11*
the name of Lord

his right hand toward *I.*   *Ge 48:13*
to Egyptians for *I.* sake   *Ex 18:8*
Reuben, *I.* eldest son   *Nu 1:20*
children of *I.* half   *Nu 31:30;* 31:42, 47
blood unto thy people of *I.*   *De 21:8*
charge
for his people *I.* sake   *2Sa 5:12*
one of the king of *I.* servants   *2Ki 3:11*

ISSACHAR

and Leah called his name *I.*   *Ge 30:18*
Leah's son, *I.*   *Ge 35:23*
sons of *I.*   *Ge 46:13; 1Ch 7:1*
I. is a strong ass, couching   *Ge 49:14*
down between
Israel's son's, *I.*, Zebulun   *Ex 1:3;*
                        1Ch 2:1
the princes of *I.* Nethaneel   *Nu 1:8;*
                   2:5; 7:18
I. and Joseph shall stand to   *De 27:12*
bless
rejoice, Zebulun and *I.* in thy *De 33:18*
tents
they met together in *I.* on the *Jos 17:10*
east
Manasseh had in *I.* and   *Jos 17:11*
Asher, Beth-shean
princes of *I.* with Deborah,   *J'g 5:15*
even *I.*
Tola, a man of *I.* arose to   *J'g 10:1*
defend Israel
Jehoshaphat was an officer in *1Ki 4:17*
I.
Baasha son of Ahijah of the *1Ki 15:27*
house of *I.*
that were nigh to *I.* brought *1Ch 12:40*
bread
I. the seventh son of   *1Ch 26:5*
Obed-edom
captain of *I.* Omri the son of *1Ch 27:18*
Michael
many of *I.* had not cleansed *2Ch 30:18*
themselves
by the border of Simeon, *I.* a *Eze 48:25*
portion
by the border of *I.* Zebulun a *Eze 48:26*
portion
one gate of *I.* one gate of   *Eze 48:33*
Zebulun

TRIBE OF ISSACHAR

that were numbered of the   *Nu 1:29*
tribe of I.
that pitch next Judah shall be   *Nu 2:5*
the *tribe of I.*
over the *tribe of I.* was   *Nu 10:15*
Nethaneel
of the *tribe of I.* to spy the   *Nu 13:7*
land
prince of the *tribe of I.*   *Nu 34:26*
Paltiel
the inheritance of the *tribe of Jos 19:23*
I.
Gershon had by lot out of   *Jos 20:6;*
families of the   *21:28; 1Ch 6:62, 72*
tribe of I.
of the *tribe of I.* were seated   *Re 7:7*
12,000

ISSHIAH

sons of Rehabiah, the first   *1Ch 24:21*
was *I.*
The brother of Michah was   *1Ch 24:25*
I.

ISSUE

And thy *i.* which thou begettest *Ge 48:6*
cleansed from the *i.* of her   *Le 12:7*
blood
When any man hath a running *Le 15:2;*
i.   *15:3-4, 6-9, 11-13, 15*
And if a woman have an *i.*   *Le 15:19;*
             15:25-26, 28, 30
is the law of him that hath an *Le 15:32*
i.
of him that hath an *i.* of the *Le 15:33*
man
is a leper, or hath a running *i.* *Le 22:4*
leper, and every one that hath *Nu 5:2*
an *i.*
house of Joab one that hath   *2Sa 3:29*
an *i.*

of thy sons that shall *i.* from   *2Ki 20:18*
thee
house, the offspring and the   *Isa 22:24*
i. all
thy sons that shall *i.* from thee   *Isa 39:7*
and whose *i.* is like the *i.* of   *Eze 23:20*
horses
waters *i.* out toward the east   *Eze 47:8*
with an *i.* of blood twelve   *M't 9:20;*
years   *M'k 5:25; Lu 8:43*
having no *i.* left his wife   *M't 22:25*
unto his
and immediately her *i.* of blood *Lu 8:44*

ISSUED

the other *i.* out of the city   *Jos 8:22*
against
as if it had *i.* out of the womb *Job 38:8*
waters *i.* out from under the   *Eze 47:1*
waters they *i.* out of the   *Eze 47:12*
sanctuary
A fiery stream *i.* and came   *Da 7:10*
forth
out of their mouths *i.* fire and   *Re 9:17*
which *i.* out of their mouths.   *Re 9:18*

ISSUES

the Lord belong the *i.* from   *Ps 68:20*
death
for out of it are the *i.* of life   *Pr 4:23*

ISUAH

Imnah, and *I.* and Ishuai, and *1Ch 7:30*

ISUI

Jimnah, and Ishuah, and *I.*   *Ge 46:17*

IT

keep heart, for out of *it* are   *Pr 4:23*
issues of life
in *it* shall be a tenth, and *it*   *Isa 6:13*
shall return
thus saith the Lord, *It* shall not *Isa 7:7*
stand
to *it* shall the Gentiles seek,   *Isa 11:10*
and his rest
a word, saying, This is the   *Isa 30:21*
way, walk in *it*
art thou not *it* that hath cut   *Isa 51:9*
Rahab
art thou not *it* which hath   *Isa 51:10*
dried the sea

ITALIAN

of the band called the *I.* band   *Ac 10:1*

ITALY

in Pontus, lately come from *I.*   *Ac 18:2*
that we should sail into *I.*   *Ac 27:1*
ship of Alexandria sailing into *Ac 27:6*
I.
the saints. They of *I.* salute *Heb 13:24*
you

ITCH

and with the scab, and with   *De 28:27*
the *i.*
i. to get hands on (P)   *Eph 5:3*

ITCHING

teachers, having *i.* ears   *2Ti 4:3*

ITEMS

personal *i.* of (B)   *Ne 13:8*

ITHAI

I. the son of Ribai of   *1Ch 11:31*
Gibeah, that

ITHAMAR

Nadab and Abihu, Eleazar,   *Ex 6:23;*
and *I.*   *Nu 26:60; 1Ch 6:3; 24:1*
Abihu, Eleazar and *I.* Aaron's *Ex 28:1*
sons
by the hand of *I.* son to   *Ex 38:21*
Aaron the

---

unto Eleazar and unto *I.,* his   *Le 10:6*
sons
Aaron, unto Eleazar and unto *Le 10:12*
I.
he was angry with Eleazar and *Le 10:16*
I.
firstborn, and Abihu, Eleazar, *Nu 3:2*
and *I.*
I. ministered in the priest's   *Nu 3:4*
office
shall be under the hand of *I.*   *Nu 4:28*
under the hand of *I.* the son of *Nu 4:33;*
  7:8
Eleazar and *I.* executed the   *1Ch 24:2*
priest's
and Ahimelech of the sons of *1Ch 24:3*
I.
of Eleazar, and of the sons of *1Ch 24:4;*
I.   *24:5*
and eight among the sons of   *1Ch 24:4*
I.
for Eleazar, and one taken for *1Ch 24:6*
I.
Gershom: of the sons of *I.;*   *Ezr 8:2*
Daniel

ITHIEL

son of Maaseiah, the son of *I.* *Ne 11:7*
man spake unto *I.* even unto *I.* *Pr 30:1*

ITHMAH

of Elnaam, and *I.* the   *1Ch 11:46*
Moabite

ITHNAN

And Kedesh, and Hazor, and *Jos 15:23*
I.

ITHRA

whose name was *I.* an   *2Sa 17:25*
Israelite

ITHRAN

Hemdan, and Eshban, and *I.*   *Ge 36:26*
Amram, and Eshban, and *I.*   *1Ch 1:41*
and Shilshah, and *I.* and   *1Ch 7:37*
Beera

ITHREAM

sixth, *I.* by Eglah David's wife *2Sa 3:5*
the sixth, *I.* by Eglah his wife *1Ch 3:3*

ITHRITE

Ira an *I.,* Gareb an *I.*   *2Sa 23:38*
Ira the *I.,* Gareb the *I.*   *1Ch 11:40*

ITHRITES

families of Kirjath-jearim; the *1Ch 2:53*
I.

ITINERANT

i. Jewish exorcists (P)(R)   *Ac 19:13*

ITINERARY

this is the *i.* of (B)   *Nu 33:1*

ITS

That which groweth of *i.* own *Le 25:5*
accord

ITSELF

whose seed is in *i.* upon the   *Ge 1:11*
earth
yielding fruit, whose seed was *Ge 1:12*
in *i.*
fat of the beast that dieth of *i.* *Le 7:24*
soul that eateth that which   *Le 17:15*
dieth of *i.*
land *i.* vomiteth out her   *Le 18:25*
inhabitants
That which dieth of *i.* or torn *Le 22:8*
neither reap that which   *Le 25:11*
groweth of *i.*
not eat of any thing that died *De 14:21*
of *i.*
undersetters were of the very *1Ki 7:34*
base *i.*

A land of darkness, as   *Job 10:22*
darkness *i.*
his heart gathereth iniquity to *i.* *Ps 41:6*
Sinai *i.* was moved at the   *Ps 68:8*
presence
but that his heart may discover *Pr 18:2*
i.
in the cup, when it moveth   *Pr 23:31*
i. aright
of his right hand, which   *Pr 27:16*
bewrayeth *i.*
and the tender grass sheweth *i.* *Pr 27:25*
Shall the axe boast *i.* against *Isa 10:15*
him that
shall the saw magnify *i.*   *Isa 10:15*
against him
rod should shake *i.* against   *Isa 10:15*
them that
as if the staff should lift up *i.* *Isa 10:15*
as if it
eat this year such as groweth *Isa 37:30*
of *i.;* and
and let your soul delight *i.* in *Isa 55:2*
fatness
neither shall thy moon   *Isa 60:20*
withdraw *i.*
there shall dwell in Judah *i.*   *Jer 31:24*
and in
a great cloud, and a fire   *Eze 1:4*
infolding *i.*
not eaten of that which dieth *Eze 4:14*
of *i.*
be base, that it might not lift *Eze 17:14*
i. up
neither shall it exalt *i.* any   *Eze 29:15*
more above
eat of any thing that is dead *Eze 44:31*
of *i.*
a bear, and it raised up *i.* on one *Da 7:5*
side
take thought for the things of *M't 6:34*
i.
Every kingdom divided   *M't 12:25*
against *i.*
city or house divided against *M't 12:25*
i.
if a kingdom be divided   *M'k 3:24*
against *i.*
if a house be divided against *M'k 3:25*
i.
Every kingdom divided   *Lu 11:17*
against *i.* is
the branch cannot bear fruit of *Joh 15:4*
i.
wrapped together in a place by *Joh 20:7*
i.
even the world *i.* could not   *Joh 21:25*
contain
Spirit *i.* beareth witness with *Ro 8:16*
our
creature *i.* also shall be   *Ro 8:21*
delivered
the Spirit *i.* maketh   *Ro 8:26*
intercession for
there is nothing unclean of *i.* *Ro 14:14*
Doth not even nature *i.*   *1Co 11:14*
teach you
charity vaunteth not *i.* is not *1Co 13:4*
puffed
Doth not behave *i.* unseemly *1Co 13:5*
every high thing that exalteth *2Co 10:5*
i.
of the body unto the edifying *Eph 4:16*
of *i.*
into heaven *i.,* now to appear *Heb 9:24*
in the
of all men, and of the truth *i.*   *3Jo 12*

ITTAH-KAZIN

the east to Gittah-hepher, to *Jos 19:13*
I.

ITTAI

said the king to *I.* the Gittite *2Sa 15:19*
I. answered the king, and   *2Sa 15:21*
said
David said to *I.,* Go and pass *2Sa 15:22*
over
and *I.* the Gittite passed over *2Sa 15:22*
a third part, under the hand   *2Sa 18:2*
of *I.*
commanded Joab and   *2Sa 18:5*
Abishai and *I.*
charged thee and Abishai   *2Sa 18:12*
and *I.*
I. the son of Ribai out of   *2Sa 23:29*
Gibeah

ITURAEA

his brother Philip tetrarch of *I*.   *Lu 3:1*

IVAH

of Sepharvaim, Hena, and *I*.   *2Ki 18:34; 19:13*
city of Sepharvaim, Hena,   *Isa 37:13*
and *I*.

IVORY

the king made a great throne   *1Ki 10:18*
of *i*.
silver, *i*., and apes, and   *1Ki 10:22;*
peacocks   *2Ch 9:21*
and the *i*. house which he   *1Ki 22:39*
made
the king made a great throne   *2Ch 9:17*
of *i*.
and cassia, out of the *i*. palaces   *Ps 45:8*
his belly is as bright *i*. overlaid   *Ca 5:14*
Thy neck is as a tower of *i*.,   *Ca 7:4*
thine
have made thy benches of *i*.   *Eze 27:6*
for a present horns of *i*. and   *Eze 27:15*
ebony
houses of *i*. shall perish, and   *Am 3:15*
That lie upon beds of *i*. and   *Am 6:4*
stretch
wood, and all manner vessels   *Re 18:12*
of *i*.

IZEHAR

families; Amram, and *I*.,   *Nu 3:19*
Hebron

IZEHARITES

and the family of the *I*. and   *Nu 3:27*

IZHAR

sons of Kohath; Amram, and   *Ex 6:18;*
I.   *1Ch 6:2*
the sons of *I*.; Korah, and   *Ex 6:21*
Nepheg
the son of *I*. the son of Kohath   *Nu 16:1;*
   1Ch 6:38
of Kohath were, Amram, and   *1Ch 6:18*
I.
of Kohath; Amram, *I*.,   *1Ch 23:12*
Hebron
sons of *I*., Shelomith the   *1Ch 23:18*
chief

IZHARITES

Of the *I*.; Shelomoth: of the   *1Ch 24:22*
sons
Of the Amramites, and the *I*.   *1Ch 26:23*
Of the *I*., Chenaniah and his   *1Ch 26:29*
sons

IZRAHIAH

And the sons of Uzzi; *I*.: and   *1Ch 7:3*
sons of *I*.; Michael, and   *1Ch 7:3*
Obadiah

IZRAHITE

fifth month was Shamhuth the   *1Ch 27:8*
I.

IZRI

fourth to *I*., he, his sons, and   *1Ch 25:11*
his

J

JAAKAN

Beeroth of the children of *J*. to   *De 10:6*

JAAKOBAH

Elioenai, and *J*. and   *1Ch 4:36*
Jeshohaiah

JAALA

The children of *J*., the children   *Ne 7:58*

JAALAH

The children of *J*., the children   *Ezr 2:56*
of

JAALAM

Aholibamah bare Jeush, and *J*.   *Ge 36:5*
to Esau Jeush and *J*., and   *Ge 36:14*
Korah
duke Jeush, duke *J*., duke   *Ge 36:18*
Korah
and Jeush, and *J*. and Korah   *1Ch 1:35*

JAANAI

and *J*. and Shaphat in Bashan   *1Ch 5:12*

JAARE-OREGIM

where Elhanan the son of *J*.   *2Sa 21:19*

JAASAU

Mattaniah, Mattenai, and *J*.   *Ezr 10:37*

JAASIEL

of Benjamin, *J*. the son of   *1Ch 27:21*
Abner

JAAZANIAH

and *J*. the son of a   *2Ki 25:23*
Maachathite
Then I took *J*. the son of   *Jer 35:3*
Jeremiah
them stood *J*. the son of   *Eze 8:11*
Shaphan
whom I saw *J*. the son of Azur   *Eze 11:1*

JAAZER

And Moses sent to spy out *J*.   *Nu 21:32*
And Atroth, Shophan, and *J*.   *Nu 32:35*

JAAZIAH

and Mushi: the sons of *J*.;   *1Ch 24:26*
Beno
The sons of Merari by *J*.;   *1Ch 24:27*
Beno, and

JAAZIEL

degree, Zechariah, Ben, and   *1Ch 15:18*
J.

JABAL

Adah bare *J*.: he was the   *Ge 4:20*
father

JABBOK

and passed over the ford *J*.   *Ge 32:22*
his land from Arnon unto *J*.   *Nu 21:24*
nor unto any place of the river   *De 2:37*
the border even unto the river   *De 3:16*
J.
half Gilead, even unto the   *Jos 12:2*
river *J*.
from Arnon even unto *J*. and   *J'g 11:13*
Amorites, from Arnon even   *J'g 11:22*
unto *J*.

JABESH

the men of *J*. said unto   *1Sa 11:1*
Nahash
And the elders of *J*. said unto   *1Sa 11:3*
him
him the tidings of the men of   *1Sa 11:5*
J.
and shewed it to the men of *J*.   *1Sa 11:9*
the men of *J*. said, To   *1Sa 11:10*
morrow we
and came to *J*. and burnt   *1Sa 31:12*
them
and buried them under a tree   *1Sa 31:13*
at *J*.
the son of *J*. conspired   *2Ki 15:10*
against him
the son of *J*. began to reign   *2Ki 15:13*
and smote Shallum the son   *2Ki 15:14*
of *J*.
and brought them to *J*., and   *1Ch 10:12*
buried
their bones under the oak in   *1Ch 10:12*
J.

JABESH-GILEAD

none to the camp from *J*. to   *J'g 21:8*
none of the inhabitants of *J*.   *J'g 21:9*
and smite the inhabitants of   *J'g 21:10*
J.
among the inhabitants of *J*.   *J'g 21:12*
saved alive of the women of *J*.   *J'g 21:14*
up, and encamped against *J*.   *1Sa 11:1*
shall ye say unto the men of *J*.   *1Sa 11:9*
inhabitants of *J*. heard of   *1Sa 31:11*
that
men of *J*. were they that buried   *2Sa 2:4*
messengers unto the men of *J*.   *2Sa 2:5*
his son from the men of *J*.   *2Sa 21:12*
J. heard all that the   *1Ch 10:11*
Philistines

JABEZ

of the scribes which dwelt at   *1Ch 2:55*
J.
J. was more honourable than   *1Ch 4:9*
his
and his mother called his name   *1Ch 4:9*
J.
And *J*. called on the God of   *1Ch 4:10*
Israel

JABIN

when *J*. king of Hazor had   *Jos 11:1*
heard
into the hand of *J*. king of   *J'g 4:2*
Canaan
was peace between *J*. the king   *J'g 4:17*
of
God subdued on that day *J*. the   *J'g 4:23*
prevailed against *J*. the king of   *J'g 4:24*
until they had destroyed *J*. king   *J'g 4:24*
of
as to *J*. at the brook of Kison   *Ps 83:9*

JABIN'S

Sisera, the captain of *J*. army   *J'g 4:7*

JABNEEL

mount Baalah, and went unto   *Jos 15:11*
Adami, Nekeb, and *J*. unto   *Jos 19:33*
Lakum

JABNEH

wall of Gath, and the wall of   *2Ch 26:6*
J.

JACHAN

Jorai, and *J*. and Zia, and   *1Ch 5:13*
Heber

JACHIN

Jamin, and Ohad, and *J*. and   *Ge 46:10;*
   Ex 6:15
of *J*. the family of the   *Nu 26:12*
Jachinites
and called the name thereof *J*.   *1Ki 7:21*
Jedaiah, and Jehoiarib, and *J*.   *1Ch 9:10*
The one and twentieth to *J*.   *1Ch 24:17*
name of that on the right   *2Ch 3:17*
hand *J*.
Jedaiah the son of Joiarib, *J*.   *Ne 11:10*

JACHINITES

of Jachin, the family of the *J*.   *Nu 26:12*

JACINTH

the third row a *j*. (S)   *Ex 28:19; 39:12*
breastplates of fire and of *j*.   *Re 9:17*
the eleventh, a *j*.; the twelfth   *Re 21:20*

JACKALS

brother of *j*. (A)(B)(E)(R)   *Job 30:29*
jackals (S)   *Job 30:29;*
Ps 44:19; Isa 13:22; 34:13; 35:7; 43:20;
Jer 9:11; 10:22; 14:6; 49:33; 51:37;
   Mic 1:8; Mal 1:3
place of *j*. (A)(E)(R)   *Ps 44:19*
jackals (A)(E)(R)   *Isa 13:22;*
34:13; 35:7; 43:20; Jer 9:11; 10:22; 14:6;
   49:33; 51:37; Mic 1:8; Mal 1:3
they pant like *j*.   *Jer 14:6*
(A)(B)(E)(R)(S)
j. draw out the breast   *La 4:3*
(A)(B)(E)(R)

JACKAL'S

before the *j.* well (S)   Ne 2:13

JACKET

wrapped his work *j.* about   Joh 21:7
him (B)(N)

JACOB

he was called *J.*	Ge 25:26
J. was a plain man	Ge 25:27
J. sod pottage	Ge 25:29
the voice is *J.*; *J.* was scarce	Ge 27:22;
gone out	27:30
Esau said, Is not he rightly	Ge 27:36
named *J.*	
Esau hated *J.*; if *J.* take a	Ge 27:41;
wife of Heth	27:46
Isaac sent away *J.*; *J.* obeyed	Ge 28:5;
his father	28:7
J. awakened out of sleep; *J.*	Ge 28:16;
vowed a vow	28:20
J. saw Rachel the daughter of	Ge 29:10
Laban	
and *J.* served seven years for	Ge 29:20
Rachel	
and *J.* did so, and fulfilled her	Ge 29:28
week	
J. gave Esau pottage	Ge 29:34
J. came out of the field in the	Ge 30:16
evening	
and *J.* took him rods of green	Ge 30:37
poplar	
J. hath taken all that was our	Ge 31:1
father's	
J. stole away unawares to	Ge 31:20
Laban the Syrian	
J. sware by the fear of his	Ge 31:53
father Isaac	
J. sent messengers before him	Ge 32:3
to Esau	
J. saith thus; then *J.* was	Ge 32:4;
greatly afraid	32:7
J. was left alone, and there	Ge 32:24
wrestled a man	
thy name shall be no more *J.*	Ge 32:28;
but Israel	35:10
J. called the name of the	Ge 32:30
place Peniel	
J. looked, and behold, Esau	Ge 33:1
came	
J. journeyed to Succoth; to	Ge 33:17;
Shalem	33:18
J. held his peace until they	Ge 34:5
were come	
sons of *J.*	Ge 34:7;
13:25; 35:26; 49:1-2; 1Ki 18:31	
J. came to Luz; *J.* called the	Ge 35:6;
place Beth-el	35:15
these are the generations of *J.*	Ge 37:2
J. rent his clothes, put	Ge 37:34
sackcloth on his loins	
J. and all his seed came into	Ge 46:6
Egypt	
all the souls that came with *J.*	Ge 46:26
were sixty-six	
J. blessed Pharaoh; the	Ge 47:10;
whole age of *J.*	47:28
by hands of the mighty God	Ge 49:24;
of *J.*	Ex 3:6, 15-16; 4:5; 2Sa 23:1;
	Ps 20:1
remembered his covenant with	Ex 2:24;
J.	Le 26:42
come, curse me *J.* and defy	Nu 23:7
Israel	
who can count dust of *J.* and	Nu 23:10
number of Israel	
there is no enchantment	Nu 23:23
against *J.*, it shall be said	
of *J.* and Israel	
there shall come a Star out of	Nu 24:17
J. and Sceptre	
out of *J.* come he that shall	Nu 24:19
have dominion	
J. is the lot of his inheritance	De 32:9
they shall teach *J.* thy	De 33:10
judgments and Israel	
fountain of *J.* shall be on land	De 33:28
of corn, wine	
O ye seed of Israel his	1Ch 16:13;
servant, ye children of *J.* his	Ps 105:6
chosen	
J. shall rejoice, Israel shall be	Ps 14:7;
glad	53:6
the name of the God of *J.*	Ps 20:1
defend thee	

all ye seed of *J.* glorify him	Ps 22:23
and fear him	
my king, O God: command	Ps 44:4
deliverances for *J.*	
the God of *J.*	Ps 46:7;
46:11; 75:9; 76:6; 81:1, 4; 84:8; 94:7;	
114:7; 132:2, 5; 146:5	
the excellency of *J.* whom he	Ps 47:4;
loved	Na 2:2
a fire was kindled against *J.*	Ps 78:21
anger against Israel	
he brought him to feed *J.* his	Ps 78:71
people	
for they have devoured *J.* and	Ps 79:7
laid waste	
thou hast brought back the	Ps 85:1
captivity of *J.*	
gates of Zion more than all the	Ps 87:2
dwellings of *J.*	
and *J.* sojourned in the land	Ps 105:23
of Ham	
the Lord hath chosen *J.* unto	Ps 135:4
himself	
the God of *J.*	Isa 2:3;
41:21; Mic 4:2; M't 22:32; M'k 12:26;	
Lu 20:37; Ac 3:13; 7:32, 46	
the remnant of *J.* shall return	Isa 10:21
to God	
for the Lord will have mercy	Isa 14:1
on *J.*	
in that day the glory of *J.* shall	Isa 17:4
be made thin	
shall cause them that come of	Isa 27:6
J. to take root	
by this shall the iniquity of *J.*	Isa 27:9
be purged	
they shall sanctify the Holy	Isa 29:23
One of *J.*	
J. whom I have chosen, the	Isa 41:8
seed of Abraham	
fear not, thou worm *J.* and	Isa 41:14
ye men of Israel	
who gave *J.* for a spoil? did	Isa 42:24
not the Lord	
therefore I have given *J.* to	Isa 43:28
the curse	
another shall call himself by	Isa 44:5
the name of *J.*	
for the Lord hath redeemed	Isa 44:23;
J.	Jer 31:11
for *J.* my servant's sake, I	Isa 45:4
called thee	
the Lord hath redeemed his	Isa 48:20
servant *J.*	
that formed me to bring *J.*	Isa 49:5
again to him	
be my servant to raise up the	Isa 49:6
tribes of *J.*	
thy Redeemer, the mighty	Isa 49:26;
One of *J.*	60:16
I will feed thee with the	Isa 58:14
heritage of *J.*	
I will bring forth a seed out of	Isa 65:9
J. and Judah	
the portion of *J.* not like	Jer 10:16;
them	51:19
for they have eaten up *J.* and	Jer 10:25
devoured him	
therefore fear thou not, O my	Jer 30:10
servant *J.*	
saith the Lord, Sing with	Jer 31:7
gladness for *J.*	
then will I cast away the seed	Jer 33:26
of *J.*	
J. shall return to be in rest	Jer 46:27
and ease	
Lord hath commanded	La 1:17
concerning *J.*	
he burned against *J.* like a	La 2:3
flaming fire	
Judah shall plow, *J.* shall	Ho 10:11
break his clods	
I will punish *J.*; *J.* fled into	Ho 12:2;
Syria	12:12
I abhor the excellency of *J.* and	Am 6:8
by whom shall *J.* arise, for he	Am 7:2;
is small	7:5
the Lord hath sworn by the	Am 8:7
excellency of *J.*	
for the transgression of *J.* is all	Mic 1:5
this	
and I said, Hear, I pray you, O	Mic 3:1
heads of *J.*	
remnant of *J.* shall be among	Mic 5:7
the Gentiles	
therefore, ye sons of *J.* are not	Mal 3:6
consumed	
Isaac begat *J.*; Matthan begat	M't 1:2;
J.	1:15

shall sit down with Abraham,	M't 8:11
Isaac, and *J.*	
when ye see *J.* in the kingdom	Lu 13:28
of God	
Joseph called his father *J.* to	Ac 7:14
him	
J. have I loved, but Esau have	Ro 9:13
I hated	
and shall turn away	Ro 11:26
ungodliness from *J.*	
Abraham dwelling in	Heb 11:9
tabernacles with *J.*	
by faith Isaac blessed *J.*; *J.*	Heb 11:20;
blessed sons	11:21

IN JACOB

I will divide them *in J.* and	Ge 49:7
scatter then	
he hath not beheld iniquity *in*	Nu 23:21
J.	
let them know that God ruleth	Ps 59:13
in J.	
for he established a testimony	Ps 78:5
in J. and a law	
thou executest judgment and	Ps 99:4
righteousness *in J.*	
to them that turn from	Isa 59:20
transgression *in J.*	

O JACOB

how goodly are thy tents, *O J.*	Nu 24:5
the generation that seek thy	Ps 24:6
face, *O J.*	
why sayest thou, *O J.* my way	Isa 40:27
is hid	
saith the Lord that created thee,	Isa 43:1
O J.	
but thou hast not called upon	Isa 43:22
me *O J.*	
yet hear, *O J.*	Isa 44:1
fear not, *O J.* my servant	Isa 44:2;
	Jer 46:27-28
remember these, *O J.* for thou	Isa 44:21
art my servant	
hearken unto me, *O J.*	Isa 48:12
I will surely assemble, *O J.* all	Mic 2:12
of thee	

TO, UNTO JACOB

speak not *to J.* either good or	Ge 31:24;
bad	31:29
God appeared *unto J.* and	Ge 35:9
blessed him	
the land which he sware to	Ge 50:24;
give *to J.*	Ex 6:8; 33:1; Nu 32:11;
De 6:10; 29:13; 30:20; 34:4; Eze 37:25	
and hath confirmed the	1Ch 16:17;
same *to J.* for a law	Ps 105:10
he shewed his word *unto J.*	Ps 147:19
his statutes	
the Lord sent a word *unto J.* it	Isa 9:8
lighted on	
to declare *unto J.* his	Mic 3:8
transgression and	
wilt perform truth *to J.* and	Mic 7:20
mercy to Abraham	

JACOB'S

voice is *J.* voice, but the	Ge 27:22
hands	
Rebekah, *J.* and Esau's mother	Ge 28:5
And *J.* anger was kindled	Ge 30:2
against	
were Laban's, and the	Ge 30:42
stronger *J.*	
And Laban went into *J.* tent	Ge 31:33
shall say, They be thy servant	Ge 32:18
hollow of *J.* thigh was out of	Ge 32:25
joint	
he touched the hollow of *J.*	Ge 32:32
thigh	
in Israel in lying with *J.*	Ge 34:7
daughter	
he had delight in *J.* daughter	Ge 34:19
Reuben, *J.* first born, and	Ge 35:23
Simeon	
J. heart fainted, for he	Ge 45:26
believed	
and his sons: Reuben, *J.*	Ge 46:8
firstborn	
sons of Rachel *J.* wife;	Ge 46:19
Joseph, and	

JACOB'S

of his loins, besides J. son's   Ge 46:26
wives
it is even the time of J. trouble   Jer 30:7
again the captivity of J. tents   Jer 30:18
Was not Esau J. brother? saith   Mal 1:2
Now J. well was there. Jesus   Joh 4:6

JADA

of Onam were, Shammai, and   1Ch 2:28
J.
And the sons of J. the brother   1Ch 2:32
of

JADAU

Zabad, Zebina, J., and Joel   Ezr 10:43

JADDUA

Meshezabeel, Zadok, J.   Ne 10:21
Jonathan, and Jonathan begat   Ne 12:11
J.
Joiada, and Johanan, and J.   Ne 12:22

JADON

and J. the Meronothite, the men   Ne 3:7

JAEL

away on his feet to the tent of   J'g 4:17
J.
And J. went out to meet Sisera   J'g 4:18
J. Heber's wife took a nail of   J'g 4:21
J. came out to meet him, and   J'g 4:22
said
in the days of J. the highways   J'g 5:6
were
Blessed above women shall J.   J'g 5:24

JAGUR

were Kabzeel, and Eder, and   Jos 15:21
J.

JAH

upon the heavens by his name   Ps 68:4
J.

JAHATH

Reaiah the son of Shobal begat   1Ch 4:2
J.
and J. begat Ahumai, and   1Ch 4:2
Lahad
Libni his son, J. his son,   1Ch 6:20
Zimmah
The son of J., the son of   1Ch 6:43
Gershom
sons of Shimei were, J., Zina   1Ch 23:10
And J. was the chief, and   1Ch 23:11
Zirah
of the sons of Shelomoth; J.   1Ch 24:22
the overseers of them were J.   2Ch 34:12

JAHAZ

he came to J. and fought   Nu 21:23
against
he and all his people, to fight   De 2:32
at J.
pitched in J. and fought   J'g 11:20
against
voice shall be heard even unto   Isa 15:4
J.
even unto J. have I uttered   Jer 48:34

JAHAZA

J. and Kedemoth, and   Jos 13:18
Mephaath

JAHAZAH

suburbs, and J. with her   Jos 21:36
suburbs
and upon J., and upon   Jer 48:21
Mephaath

JAHAZIAH

and J. the son of Tikvah were   Ezr 10:15

JAHAZIEL

Jeremiah, and J., and   1Ch 12:4
Johanan

Benaiah also and J. the   1Ch 16:6
priests
J. the third, and Jekameam   1Ch 23:19
J. the third, Jekameam the   1Ch 24:23
fourth
Then upon J. the son of   2Ch 20:14
Zechariah
the son of J., and with him   Ezr 8:5
three

JAHDAI

sons of J.; Regem, and   1Ch 2:47
Jotham

JAHDIEL

and J., mighty men of valour   1Ch 5:24

JAHDO

the son of J., the son of Buz   1Ch 5:14

JAHLEEL

Zebulun; Sered, and Elon,   Ge 46:14
and J.
of J., the family of the   Nu 26:26
Jahleelites

JAHLEELITES

of Jahleel, the family of the J.   Nu 26:26

JAHMAI

and Jeriel, and J., and Jibsam   1Ch 7:2

JAHZAH

suburbs, and J. with her   1Ch 6:78
suburbs

JAHZEEL

sons of Naphtali; J., and   Ge 46:24
Guni
J., the family of the   Nu 26:48
Jahzeelites

JAHZEELITES

of Jahzeel, the family of the   Nu 26:48
J.

JAHZERAH

Adiel, the son of J. the son of   1Ch 9:12

JAHZIEL

sons of Naphtali; J., and   1Ch 7:13
Guni

JAILERS

handed him to j. (P)(R)   M't 18:34

JAILOR

charging the j. to keep them   Ac 16:23

JAIR

J. the son of Manasseh went   Nu 32:41
J. the son of Manasseh took all   De 3:14
towns of J., which are in   Jos 13:30
Bashan
And after him arose J., a   J'g 10:3
Gileadite
J. died, and was buried in   J'g 10:5
Camon
to him pertained the towns of   1Ki 4:13
Segub begat J., who had three   1Ch 2:22
and Aram, with the towns of   1Ch 2:23
J.
Elhanan the son of J. slew   1Ch 20:5
Lahmi
name was Mordecai, the son of   Es 2:5
J.

JAIRITE

Ira also the J. was a chief   2Sa 20:26
ruler

JAIRUS

of the synagogue, J. by name   M'k 5:22
there came a man named J.   Lu 8:41

JAKAN

Ezer; Bilhan, and Zavan, and   1Ch 1:42
J.

JAKEH

The words of Agur the son of   Pr 30:1
J.

JAKIM

And J., and Zichri, and Zabdi   1Ch 8:19
to Eliashib, the twelfth to J.   1Ch 24:12

JALON

and Mered, and Epher, and J.   1Ch 4:17

JAMBRES

Jannes and J. withstood Moses   2Ti 3:8

JAMES

saw two brethren J. and John   M't 4:21;
    M'k 1:19
J. the son of Zebedee   M't 10:2;
    M'k 3:17
J. the son of Alpheus   M't 10:3;
    M'k 3:18; Ac 1:13
and his brethren J. and   M't 13:55;
Joses   M'k 6:3
Jesus taketh Peter, J. and   M't 17:1;
John   M'k 5:37; 9:2; 14:33; Lu 8:51
Mary Magdalene and Mary   M'k 15:40;
mother of J.   16:1; Lu 24:10
began to be much displeased   M'k 10:41
with J.
Peter, J. and John asked him   M'k 13:3
privately
J. was astonished at draught of   Lu 5:10
fishes
where abode both Peter, J. and   Ac 1:13
John
Herod killed J. brother of John   Ac 12:2
with sword
Peter said, Shew these things   Ac 12:17
to J.
J. answered, saying, Hearken   Ac 15:13
unto me
Paul went in with us unto J.   Ac 21:18
and elders
after that was seen of J. then   1Co 15:7
of apostles
I saw none, save J. the Lord's   Ga 1:19
brother
when J. perceived the grace   Ga 2:9
given to me
certain came from J. did eat   Ga 2:12
with Gentiles
J. a servant of God   Jas 1:1
Jude the brother of J.   Jude 1

JAMIN

Jemuel, and J. and Ohad, and   Ge 46:10;
    Ex 6:15
of J. the family of the   Nu 26:12
Jaminites
of Jerahmeel were, Maaz, and   1Ch 2:27
J.
of Simeon were, Nemuel, and   1Ch 4:24
J.
Sherebiah, J., Akkub,   Ne 8:7
Shabbethai

JAMINITES

of Jamin, the family of the J.   Nu 26:12

JAMLECH

Meshobab, and J., and Joshah   1Ch 4:34

JANGLING

turned aside unto vain j.; have   1Ti 1:6
wandered away into vain   1Ti 1:6
arguments, discussions, and
purposeless talk (A)
turned off into empty talk (B)   1Ti 1:6
turned aside unto vain talking   1Ti 1:6
(E)
gone astray into a wilderness of   1Ti 1:6
words (N)
lost themselves in endless words   1Ti 1:6
(P)
wandered away into vain   1Ti 1:6
discussion (R)

JANNA

Melchi, which was the son of *J.*   *Lu 3:24*

JANNES

J. and Jambres withstood Moses   *2Ti 3:8*

JANOAH

J. and Kedesh, and Hazor   *2Ki 15:29*

JANOHAH

and passed by it on the east to *J.*   *Jos 16:6*

it went down from *J.* to Ataroth   *Jos 16:7*

JANUM

And *J.* and Beth-tappuah   *Jos 15:53*

JAPHETH

Noah begat Shem, Ham, and *J.*   *Ge 5:32*

three sons, Shem, Ham, and *J.*   *Ge 6:10*

Noah, and Shem, and Ham, and *J.*   *Ge 7:13*

ark, were Shem, and Ham, and *J.*   *Ge 9:18*

And Shem and *J.* took a garment   *Ge 9:23*

shall enlarge *J.* and he shall dwell   *Ge 9:27*

sons of Noah, Shem, Ham, and *J.*   *Ge 10:1*

The sons of *J.*; Gomer, and Magog   *Ge 10:2; 1Ch 1:5*

of Eber, brother of *J.* the elder   *Ge 10:21*

Noah, Shem, Ham, and *J.*   *1Ch 1:4*

JAPHIA

and unto *J.* king of Lachish   *Jos 10:3*

out to Daberath, and goeth up to *J.*   *Jos 19:12*

and Elishua, and Nepheg, and *J.*   *2Sa 5:15*

And Nogah, and Nepheg, and *J.*   *1Ch 3:7; 14:6*

JAPHLET

Heber begat *J.* and Shomer   *1Ch 7:32*

And the sons of *J.*; Pasach   *1Ch 7:33*

These are the children of *J.*   *1Ch 7:33*

JAPHLETI

down westward to the coast of *J.*   *Jos 16:3*

JAPHO

Rakkon, with the border before *J.*   *Jos 19:46*

JAR

water *j.* (A)(R)   *Ge 24:15; 24:16-18, 20, 43, 45-46*

in a clay *j.* (B)   *Nu 5:17*

every *j.* filled with (B)(R)   *Jer 13:12*

potter's earthen *i.* (B)   *Jer 19:1*

a *j.* of vinegar (N)   *Joh 19:29*

an earthenware *j.* (P)   *2Co 4:7*

JARAH

And Ahaz begat *J.*; and *J.* begat   *1Ch 9:42*

JAREB

the Assyrian, and sent to king *J.*   *Ho 5:13*

Assyria for a present to king *J.*   *Ho 10:6*

JARED

sixty and five years, and begat   *Ge 5:15*

Mahalaleel lived after he begat   *Ge 5:16*

J. lived an hundred sixty and two   *Ge 5:18*

And *J.* lived after he begat Enoch   *Ge 5:19*

the days of *J.* were nine hundred   *Ge 5:20*

Enoch, which was the son of *J.*   *Lu 3:37*

JARESIAH

J. and Eliah, and Zichri, the sons   *1Ch 8:27*

JARHA

an Egyptian, whose name was *J.*   *1Ch 2:34*

Sheshan gave his daughter to *J.*   *1Ch 2:35*

JARIB

and Jamin, *J.* Zerah, and Shaul   *1Ch 4:24*

for Elnathan, and for *J.* and   *Ezr 8:16*

and Eliezer, and *J.* and Gedaliah   *Ezr 10:18*

JARMUTH

unto Piram king of *J.* and unto   *Jos 10:3*

king of *J.* the king of Lachish   *Jos 10:3; 10:5*

The king of *J.*, one; the king of   *Jos 12:11*

J. and Adullam, Socoh, and Azekah   *Jos 15:35*

J. with her suburbs,   *Jos 21:29*

and at Zareah, and at *J.*   *Ne 11:29*

JAROAH

the son of Huri, the son of *J.*   *1Ch 5:14*

JARS

go to the water *j.* (B)   *Ru 2:9*

dash *j.* in pieces (B)(R)(S)   *Jer 48:12*

as clay *j.* are broken (B)   *Re 2:27*

JASHEN

the Shaalbonite, of the sons of *J.*   *2Sa 23:32*

JASHER

not this written in the book of *J.*   *Jos 10:13*

it is written in the book of *J.*   *2Sa 1:18*

JASHOBEAM

J., an Hachmonite, the chief of the   *1Ch 11:11*

and Joezer, and *J.*, the Korhites   *1Ch 12:6*

month was *J.*, the son of Zabdiel   *1Ch 27:2*

JASHUB

J. the family of the Jashubites   *Nu 26:24*

Puah, *J.*, and Shimron, four   *1Ch 7:1*

and Adaiah, *J.* and Sheal, and   *Ezr 10:29*

JASHUBI-LEHEM

had the dominion in Moab, and *J.*   *1Ch 4:22*

JASHUBITES

Of Jashub, the family of the *J.*   *Nu 26:24*

JASIEL

and Obed, and *J.* the Mesobaite   *1Ch 11:47*

JASON

and assaulted the house of *J.*   *Ac 17:5*

they drew *J.* and certain brethren   *Ac 17:6*

Whom *J.* hath received: and these   *Ac 17:7*

when they had taken security of *J.*   *Ac 17:9*

Lucius, and *J.* and Sosipater, my   *Ro 16:21*

JASPER

a beryl, and an onyx, and a *j.*   *Ex 28:20*

row, a beryl, an onyx, and a *j.*   *Ex 39:13*

the onyx, and the *j.* the sapphire   *Eze 28:13*

to look upon like a *j.* and a sardine   *Re 4:3*

even like a *j.* stone, clear as crystal   *Re 21:11*

building of the wall of it was of *j.*   *Re 21:18*

The first foundation was *j.* the   *Re 21:19*

JATHNIEL

Zebadiah the third, *J.* the fourth   *1Ch 26:2*

JATTIR

in the mountains, Shamir, and *J.*   *Jos 15:48*

J. with her suburbs, and Eshtemoa   *Jos 21:14*

and to them which were in *J.*   *1Sa 30:27*

Libnah with her suburbs, and *J.*   *1Ch 6:57*

JAVAN

and *J.* and Tubal, and Meshech   *Ge 10:2*

And the sons of *J.*; Elishah   *Ge 10:4; 1Ch 1:7*

and *J.*, and Tubal, and Meshech   *1Ch 1:5*

that draw the bow, to Tubal, and *J.*   *Isa 66:19*

J., Tubal, and Meshech, they were   *Eze 27:13*

Dan also and *J.* going to and fro   *Eze 27:19*

JAVELIN

and took a *j.* in his hand   *Nu 25:7*

bronze *j.* across (A)(B)(E)(R)   *1Sa 17:6*

and there was a *j.* in Saul's hand   *1Sa 18:10*

And Saul cast the *j.*; for he said, I   *1Sa 18:11*

in his house with his *j.* in his hand   *1Sa 19:9*

David even to the wall with the *j.*   *1Sa 19:10*

and he smote the *j.* into the wall   *1Sa 19:10*

Saul cast a *j.* at him to smite him   *1Sa 20:33*

the dart, not the *j.* (S)   *Job 41:26*

JAW

with the *j.* of an ass have I slain a   *J'g 15:16*

clave an holy place that in the *j.*   *J'g 15:19*

or bore his *j.* through with a thorn   *Job 41:2*

their *j.* teeth as knives, to devour   *Pr 30:14*

JAWBONE

he found a new *j.* of an ass   *J'g 15:15*

With the *j.* of an ass, heaps upon   *J'g 15:16*

he cast away the *j.* out of his hand   *J'g 15:17*

JAWS

I brake the *j.* of the wicked   *Job 29:17*

and my tongue cleaveth to my *j.*   *Ps 22:15*

be a bridle in the *j.* of the people   *Isa 30:28*

I will put hooks in thy *j.* and I will   *Eze 29:4*

thee back, and put hooks into thy *j.*   *Eze 38:4*

that take off the yoke on their *j.*   *Ho 11:4*

JAZER

and when they saw the land of *J.*   *Nu 32:1*

Ataroth, and Dibon, and J.   *Nu 32:3*
their coast was J., and all the   *Jos 13:25*
cities
her suburbs, J. with her   *Jos 21:39;*
suburbs   *1Ch 6:81*
of the river of Gad, and   *2Sa 24:5*
toward J.
them men of valour at J. of   *1Ch 26:31*
Gilead
they are come even unto J.   *Isa 16:8*
I will bewail with the weeping   *Isa 16:9*
of J.
weep for thee with the   *Jer 48:32*
weeping of J.
they reach even to the sea of   *Jer 48:32*
J.

JAZIZ

over the flocks was J. the   *1Ch 27:31*
Hagerite

JEALOUS

for I the Lord thy God am a j.   *Ex 20:5;*
God   *34:14; De 4:24; 5:9; 6:15; Jos 24:19*
and he be j. of his wife   *Nu 5:14*
I have been j. for the Lord   *1Ki 19:10;*
of hosts   *19:14*
do not be j. of an unscrupulous   *Pr 3:31*
grasping man (A)
and will be j. for my holy   *Eze 39:25*
name
then will the Lord be j. for his   *Joe 2:18*
land
God is j. and the Lord   *Na 1:2*
revengeth
I am j. for Jerusalem; was   *Zec 1:14;*
j. for Zion   *8:1*
were insufferably j. (B)   *Ac 5:17*
make my kinfolk j. (P)(R)   *Ro 11:14*
j. and quarreling   *1Co 3:3*
(B)(E)(N)(P)(R)
for I am j. over you with   *2Co 11:2*
godly jealousy
j. and quarrelsome spirit (N)   *Ph'p 1:15*

JEALOUSIES

this is the law of j. when wife   *Nu 5:29*
goeth aside

JEALOUSY

the spirit of j. come upon him   *Nu 5:14*
for it is an offering of j. and   *Nu 5:15;*
of memorial   *5:18*
then priest shall take j. offering   *Nu 5:25*
from woman
that I consumed not Israel in   *Nu 25:11*
my j.
his j. shall smoke against that   *De 29:20*
man
they provoked him to j.   *De 32:16;*
  1Ki 14:22
have moved me to j. I will   *De 32:21*
move them to j.
they moved him to j. with   *Ps 78:58*
images
how long, Lord, shall thy j.   *Ps 79:5*
burn like fire
for j. is the rage of man, he will   *Pr 6:34*
not spare
j. long since vanished (B)   *Ec 9:6*
j. is cruel as the grave   *Ca 8:6*
he shall stir up j. like a man   *Isa 42:13*
of war
where was the seat of the   *Eze 8:3*
image of j.
behold at gate of altar this   *Eze 8:5*
image of j. in entry
and I will give thee blood in   *Eze 16:38*
fury and j.
my j. shall depart from thee   *Eze 16:42*
and will be quiet
I will set my j. against thee,   *Eze 23:25*
they shall deal
in the fire of j. have I spoken   *Eze 36:5;*
  36:6; 38:19
whose land devoured by fire   *Zep 1:18;*
of his j.   *3:8*
I am jealous for Zion with   *Zec 1:14;*
great j.   *8:2*
were filled with j.   *Ac 5:17*
(E)(N)(P)(R)
Moses saith, Will provoke you   *Ro 10:19*
to j.
salvation to Gentiles, to   *Ro 11:11*
provoke them to j.

arouse to j. (B)(E)(S)   *Ro 11:14*
do you provoke the Lord to j.   *1Co 10:22*
for I am jealous over you   *2Co 11:2*
with godly j.
variance, j., wrath (S)   *Ga 5:20*
preaching out of j. (P)   *Ph'p 1:15*

JEARIM

passed along unto the side of   *Jos 15:10*
mount J.

JEATERAI

his son, Zerah his son, J. his   *1Ch 6:21*
son

JEBERECHIAH

priest, and Zechariah the son of   *Isa 8:2*
J.

JEBUS

departed, came over   *J'g 19:10*
against J.
And when they were by J. the   *J'g 19:11*
day
went to Jerusalem, which is J.   *1Ch 11:4*
the inhabitants of J. said to   *1Ch 11:5*
David

JEBUSI

to the side of J. on the south   *Jos 18:16*
Eleph, and J. which is   *Jos 18:28*
Jerusalem

JEBUSITE

the J. and the Amorite, and   *Ge 10:16*
the Perizzite, the Hivite, and   *Ex 33:2;*
the J.   *34:11*
Hivite, and the J., heard thereof   *Jos 9:1*
and the J. in the mountains   *Jos 11:3*
unto the south side of the J.   *Jos 15:8*
threshingplace of Araunah   *2Sa 24:16*
the J.
threshingfloor of Araunah   *2Sa 24:18*
the J.
The J. also, and the Amorite   *1Ch 1:14*
threshingfloor of Ornan the   *1Ch 21:15;*
J.   *21:18, 28; 2Ch 3:1*
in Judah, and Ekron as a J.   *Zec 9:7*

JEBUSITES

and the Girgashites, and the   *Ge 15:21*
J.
and the Hivites, and the J.   *Ex 3:8;*
  3:17; 13:5
Canaanites, the Hivites, and   *Ex 23:23*
the J.
the J. and the Amorites, dwell   *Nu 13:29*
in
and the Hivites, and the J. seven   *De 7:1*
Perizzites, the Hivites, and   *De 20:17;*
the J.   *Jos 12:8; J'g 3:5*
and the Amorites, and the J.   *Jos 3:10*
J. the inhabitants of   *Jos 15:63*
Jerusalem
J. dwell with the children of   *Jos 15:63*
Judah
Girgashites, the Hivites, and   *Jos 24:11*
the J.
out the J. that inhabited   *J'g 1:21*
Jerusalem
the J. dwell with the children   *J'g 1:21*
of
let us turn in into this city of   *J'g 19:11*
the J.
men went to Jerusalem unto   *2Sa 5:6*
the J.
and smiteth the J. and the lame   *2Sa 5:8*
Hittites, Perizzites, Hivites,   *1Ki 9:20*
and J.
where the J. were, the   *1Ch 11:4*
inhabitants
Whosoever smiteth the J. first   *1Ch 11:6*
shall
and the Hivites, and the J.,   *2Ch 8:7*
which
the Hittites, the Perizzites, the   *Ezr 9:1*
J.
and the J. and the Girgashites   *Ne 9:8*

JECAMIAH

and Shenazar, J., Hoshama   *1Ch 3:18*

JECHOLIAH

And his mother's name was J.   *2Ki 15:2*

JECHONIAS

Josias begat J. and his   *M't 1:11*
brethren
to Babylon, J. begat Salathiel   *M't 1:12*

JECOLIAH

His mother's name also was   *2Ch 26:3*
J. of

JECONIAH

J. his son, Zedekiah his son   *1Ch 3:16*
the sons of J.; Assir, Salathiel   *1Ch 3:17*
which had been carried away   *Es 2:6*
with J.
had carried away captive J. the   *Jer 24:1*
son
when he carried away captive   *Jer 27:20*
J.
I will bring again to this place   *Jer 28:4*
J.
(After that J. the king, and the   *Jer 29:2*

JEDAIAH

the son of Allon, the son of J.   *1Ch 4:37*
of the priests; J., and   *1Ch 9:10*
Jehoiarib
forth to Jehoiarib, the second   *1Ch 24:7*
to J.
the children of J., of the house   *Ezr 2:36*
of
repaired J. the son of   *Ne 3:10*
Harumaph
the children of J., of the house   *Ne 7:39*
Of the priests; J. the son of   *Ne 11:10*
Joiarib
Shemaiah, and Joiarib, J.   *Ne 12:6*
Sallu, Amok, Hilkiah, J.   *Ne 12:7*
of Joiarib, Mattenai; of J.,   *Ne 12:19*
Uzzi
Hashabiah; of J., Nethaneel   *Ne 12:21*
of Heldai, of Tobijah, and of   *Zec 6:10*
J.
Helem, and to Tobijah, and to   *Zec 6:14*
J.

JEDIAEL

Bela, and Becher, and J., three   *1Ch 7:6*
The sons also of J., Bilhan   *1Ch 7:10*
All these the sons of J., by the   *1Ch 7:11*
J. the son of Shimri, and   *1Ch 11:45*
Joha his
and Jozabad, and J., and   *1Ch 12:20*
Michael
the firstborn, J. the second   *1Ch 26:2*

JEDIDAH

his mother's name was J. the   *2Ki 22:1*

JEDIDIAH

called his name J. because of   *2Sa 12:25*

JEDUTHUN

son of Galal, the son of J. and   *1Ch 9:16*
Obed-edom also the son of   *1Ch 16:38*
J. and
And with them Heman and   *1Ch 16:41;*
J. and   *16:42*
And the sons of J. were   *1Ch 16:42*
porters
of Asaph, and of Heman, and   *1Ch 25:1;*
of J.   *2Ch 5:12*
Of J.: the sons of J.;   *1Ch 25:3*
Gedaliah, and
under the hands of their   *1Ch 25:3*
father J.
order to Asaph, J., and   *1Ch 25:6*
Heman
and of the sons of J.;   *2Ch 29:14*
Shemaiah
and Heman, and J. the   *2Ch 35:15*
king's seer
the son of Galal, the son J.   *Ne 11:17*
to the chief Musician, even   *Ps 39 title;*
to J.   *Ps 62; 77 title*

JEER

began to j. at him (P)   *Lu 14:29*

JEERED

j. at him (R)	2Ki 2:23
then j. at him (N)(P)	M't 27:29
spoke abusively, j. him (A)	M't 27:39
j. and insulted (A)(P)	Lu 18:32
rulers j. at him (N)	Lu 23:35

JEERING

sneering and j. (B)	Isa 57:4
j. at him (P)	M't 27:41

JEERS

had to face j. (N)	Heb 11:36

JEEZER

of J., the family of the Jeezerites	Nu 26:30

JEEZERITES

of Jeezer, the family of the J.	Nu 26:30

JEGAR-SAHADUTHA

And Laban called it J.: but Jacob	Ge 31:47

JEHALELEEL

the sons of J.: Ziph, and Ziphah	1Ch 4:16

JEHALELEL

and Azariah the son of J.	2Ch 29:12

JEHDEIAH

of the sons of Shubael; J.	1Ch 24:20
the asses was J. the Meronothite	1Ch 27:30

JEHEZEKEL

to Pethahiah, the twentieth to J.	1Ch 24:16

JEHIAH

J. were doorkeepers for the ark	1Ch 15:24

JEHIEL

dwelt the father of Gibeon, J.	1Ch 9:35
Shama and J. the sons of Hothan	1Ch 11:44
Shemiramoth, and J. and Unni	1Ch 15:18; 15:20
and Shemiramoth, and J. and	1Ch 16:5
the chief was J. and Zetham	1Ch 23:8
J. the son of Hachmoni was with the	1Ch 27:32
by the hand of J. the Gershonite	1Ch 29:8
Azariah, and J. and Zechariah	2Ch 21:2
sons of Heman; J. and Shimei	2Ch 29:14
And J. and Azaziah, and Nahath	2Ch 31:13
and Zechariah and J. rulers of	2Ch 35:8
Obadiah the son of J. and with him	Ezr 8:9
Shechaniah the son of J. one of the	Ezr 10:2
and Elijah, and Shemaiah, and J.	Ezr 10:21
Zechariah, and J., and Abdi	Ezr 10:26

JEHIELI

Laadan the Gershonite, were J.	1Ch 26:21
The sons of J.; Zetham, and Joel	1Ch 26:22

JEHIZKIAH

J. the son of Shallum, and Amasa	2Ch 28:12

JEHOADAH

Ahaz begat J.; and J. begat	1Ch 8:36

JEHOADDAN

And his mother's name was J.	2Ki 14:2; 2Ch 25:1

JEHOAHAZ

J. his son reigned in his stead	2Ki 10:35
J. the son of Jehu began to reign	2Ki 13:1
J. besought the Lord, and the Lord	2Ki 13:4
leave of the people to J. but fifty	2Ki 13:7
the rest of the acts of J., and all	2Ki 13:8
J. slept with his fathers; and	2Ki 13:9
began Jehoash the son of J. to reign	2Ki 13:10
oppressed Israel all the days of J.	2Ki 13:22
Jehoash the son of J. took again	2Ki 13:25
he had taken out of the hand of J.	2Ki 13:25
the second year of Joash son of J.	2Ki 14:1
Jehoash, the son of J. son of Jehu	2Ki 14:8
after the death of Jehoash son of J.	2Ki 14:17
the land took J. the son of Josiah	2Ki 23:30
J. was twenty and three years old	2Ki 23:31; 2Ch 36:2
to Jehoiakim, and took J. away	2Ki 23:34
save J. the youngest of his sons	2Ch 21:17
and sent to Joash, the son of J.	2Ch 25:17
the son of Joash, the son of J., at	2Ch 25:23
after the death of Joash son of J.	2Ch 25:25
the land took J. the son of Josiah	2Ch 36:1
Necho took J. his brother	2Ch 36:4

JEHOASH

Seven years old was J. when he	2Ki 11:21
year of Jehu J. began to reign	2Ki 12:1
J. did that which was right in	2Ki 12:2
J. said to the priests, All the money	2Ki 12:4
three and twentieth year of king J.	2Ki 12:6
Then king J. called for Jehoiada the	2Ki 12:7
And J. king of Judah took all the	2Ki 12:18
began J. the son of Jehoahaz to	2Ki 13:10
J. the son of Jehoahaz took again	2Ki 13:25
Amaziah sent messengers to J.	2Ki 14:8
J. the king of Israel sent to Amaziah	2Ki 14:9
Therefore J. king of Israel went up	2Ki 14:11
And J. king of Israel took Amaziah	2Ki 14:13
the son of J. the son of Ahaziah	2Ki 14:13
rest of the acts of J. which he did	2Ki 14:15
J. slept with his fathers and	2Ki 14:16
the death of J. son of Jehoahaz	2Ki 14:17

JEHOHANAN

J. the sixth, Elioenai the seventh	1Ch 26:3
And next to him was J. the captain	2Ch 17:15
Jeroham, and Ishmael the son of J.	2Ch 23:1
Of the sons also of Bebai; J.	Ezr 10:28
Ezra, Meshullam; of J.	Ne 12:13
Amariah, J.	
Uzzi, and J., and Malchijah	Ne 12:42

JEHOIACHIN

J. his son reigned in his stead	2Ki 24:6; 2Ch 36:8
J. was eighteen years old when he	2Ki 24:8
J. the king of Judah went out to	2Ki 24:12
he carried away J. to Babylon, and	2Ki 24:15
thirtieth year of the captivity of J.	2Ki 25:27; Jer 52:31
lift up the head of J. king of Judah	2Ki 25:27
J. was eight years old when he	2Ch 36:9
lifted up the head of J. king of	Jer 52:31

JEHOIACHIN'S

fifth year of king J. captivity	Eze 1:2

JEHOIADA

Benaiah the son of J.	2Sa 8:18; 20:23; 23:20, 22; 1Ki 1:8, 26, 32, 36, 38, 44; 2:25; 29, 34-35, 46; 4:4; 1Ch 11:22; 24; 18:17; 27:5, 34
J. the priest sent and fetched	2Ki 11:4
J. the priest sent and commanded	2Ki 11:9; 11:15; 12:7, 9; 2Ch 23:8
J. made a covenant	2Ki 11:17; 2Ch 23:16
J. the priest instructed him	2Ki 12:2
J. was leader of the Aaronites	1Ch 12:27
the wife of J.	2Ch 22:11
J. strengthened himself	2Ch 23:1
J. and his sons anointed him	2Ch 23:11
J. apointed the offices of	2Ch 23:18
J. took for him two wives	2Ch 24:2
J. waxed old	2Ch 24:15; 24:17
gate repaired J. the son of Paseah	Ne 3:6
made thee priest instead of J.	Jer 29:26

JEHOIAKIM

turned his name to J.	2Ki 23:34; 2Ch 36:4
J. gave the silver and gold	2Ki 23:35
J. was twenty and five years old	2Ki 23:36
J. became his servant three years	2Ki 24:1
rest of the acts of J.	2Ki 24:5; 2Ch 36:8
J. slept with his fathers	2Ki 24:6
firstborn Johanan, the second J.	1Ch 3:15
the sons of J.: Jeconiah his son	1Ch 3:16
It came to pass in the days of J.	Jer 1:3
thus saith the Lord concerning J.	Jer 22:18
Coniah the son of J.	Jer 22:24; 24:1; 37:1
fourth year of J. the son of Josiah	Jer 25:1
In beginning of the reign of J.	Jer 26:1; 27:1
J. the king	Jer 26:21; 26: 22-23
captive Jeconiah the son of J.	Jer 27:20; 28:4
in the days of J. the son of Josiah	Jer 35:1
in the fourth year of J.	Jer 36:1; 45:1; 46:2
in the fifth year of J.	Jer 36:9
J. king of Judah	Jer 36:28; 36:29-32; Da 1:2
In the third year of J.	Da 1:1

JEHOIARIB

Jedaiah, and J. and Jachin	1Ch 9:10
Now the first lot came forth to J.	1Ch 24:7

JEHONADAB

he lighted on J. the son of Rechab	2Ki 10:15
thy heart? And J. answered, It is	2Ki 10:15
went, and J. the son of Rechab	2Ki 10:23

JEHONATHAN

castles, was J. the son of Uzziah	1Ch 27:25

and Shemiramoth, and *J.*, and 2Ch 17:8
Shammua: of Shemaiah, *J.* Ne 12:18

JEHORAM

J. his son reigned in his stead 1Ki 22:50;
    2Ch 21:1; 21:3-5, 9, 16
And *J.* reigned in his stead 2Ki 1:17
J. the son of Ahab began to 2Ki 3:1
reign
King *J.* went out of Samaria 2Ki 3:6
J. the son of Jehoshaphat 2Ki 8:16
Ahaziah son of *J.* king of 2Ki 8:25;
Judah 2Ch 22:1
smote *J.* between his arms 2Ki 9:24
with them Elishama and *J.*, 2Ch 17:8
priests
J. son of Ahab king of Israel 2Ch 22:5
went out with *J.* son of Ahab 2Ch 22:7
daughter of king *J.*, the wife 2Ch 22:11
of

JEHOSHABEATH

But *J.* the daughter of the 2Ch 22:11
king
J., the daughter of king 2Ch 22:11
Jehoram

JEHOSHAPHAT

J. the son of Ahilud was 2Sa 8:16;
recorder 20:24; 1Ki 4:3; 1Ch 18:15
J. son of Paruah was in 1Ki 4:17
Issachar
J. the son of Asa reigned 1Ki 15:24;
    2Ch 17:1
J. came down to Ahab king of 1Ki 22:2
Israel
Ahab and *J.* sat each on his 1Ki 22:10;
throne 2Ch 18:9
J. went up to 1Ki 22:29;
Ramoth-gilead 2Ch 18:28
J. cried out 1Ki 22:32
let my servants go, but *J.* 1Ki 22:49
would not
J. slept with his fathers 1Ki 22:50
were it not that I regard 2Ki 3:14
presence of *J.*
look out there Jehu the son of 2Ki 9:2
J. and go in
J. blew with the trumpet 1Ch 15:24
before ark
Lord was with *J.* because he 2Ch 17:3
walked
so that they made no war 2Ch 17:10
against *J.*
J. waxed great exceedingly 2Ch 17:12
and built castles
J. had riches and honour in 2Ch 18:1
abundance
J. feared and set himself to 2Ch 20:3
seek the Lord
they returned and *J.* in the 2Ch 20:27
forefront of them
after this did *J.* join with 2Ch 20:35
Ahaziah king of Israel
then Eliezer prophesied 2Ch 20:37
against *J.* because
thou hast not walked in the 2Ch 21:12
ways of *J.*
because, said they, he is the 2Ch 22:9
son of *J.*
bring them down to the valley Joe 3:2
of *J.*
let the heathen come up to the Joe 3:12
valley of *J.*

JEHOSHEBA

J. the daughter of king Joram 2Ki 11:2

JEHOSHUA

called Oshea the son of Nun Nu 13:16
J.

JEHOSHUAH

Non his son, *J.* his son 1Ch 7:27

JEHOVAH

name *J.* was I not known to Ex 6:3
them
thou, whose name alone is *J.* Ps 83:18
J. is my strength and my song Isa 12:2
the Lord *J.* is everlasting Isa 26:4
strength

JEHOVAH-JIREH

called the name of that place Ge 22:14
J.

JEHOVAH-NISSI

altar, and called the name of Ex 17:15
it *J.*

JEHOVAH-SHALOM

unto the Lord, and called it *J.* J'g 6:24

JEHOZABAD

J. the son of Shomer, his 2Ki 12:21
servants
J. the second, Joah the third 1Ch 26:4
next him was *J.*, and with 2Ch 17:18
him an
J. the son of Shimrith a 2Ch 24:26
Moabitess

JEHOZADAK

Seraiah, and Seraiah begat *J.* 1Ch 6:14
J. went into captivity, when 1Ch 6:15

JEHU

word came to *J.* son of 1Ki 16:1;
Hanani 16:7, 12
J. son of Nimshi shalt thou 1Ki 19:16
anoint king
shall *J.* slay; that escapeth 1Ki 19:17
the sword of *J.*
look out there *J.*; *J.* is king 2Ki 9:2;
    9:13
J. son of Nimshi conspired 2Ki 9:14
against Joram
a watchman spied company of 2Ki 9:17
J. as he came
the driving is like the driving 2Ki 9:20
of *J.* son of
J. drew a bow with his full 2Ki 9:24
strength, smote
J. slew all that remained of 2Ki 10:11
house of Ahab
Ahab served Baal, *J.* shall 2Ki 10:18
serve Baal much
J. departed not from the sins 2Ki 10:29
of Jeroboam
J. took no heed to walk in 2Ki 10:31
the law of God
this was the word which he 2Ki 15:12
spake to *J.*
Obed begat *J.* and *J.* begat 1Ch 2:38
Azariah
J. son of Josibiah; *J.* son of 1Ch 4:35;
Azmaveth 12:3
J. went out to meet 2Ch 19:2
Jehoshaphat
written in the book of *J.* son 2Ch 20:34
of Hanani
J. was executing judgment on 2Ch 22:8
Ahab
I will avenge the blood of Ho 1:4
Jezreel on *J.*

JEHUBBAH

of Shamer; Ahi, and Rohgah, 1Ch 7:34
J.

JEHUCAL

king sent *J.* the son of Jer 37:3
Shelemiah

JEHUD

And *J.*, and Bene-berak, and Jos 19:45

JEHUDI

Therefore all the princes sent *J.* Jer 36:14
So the king sent *J.* to fetch Jer 36:21
the roll
J. read it in the ears of the Jer 36:21
king
J. had read three or four Jer 36:23
leaves, he

JEHUDIJAH

And his wife *J.* bare Jered the 1Ch 4:18

JEHUSH

J. the second, and Eliphelet 1Ch 8:39

JEIEL

were the chief, *J.*, and Zechariah 1Ch 5:7
Obed-edom, and *J.*, the 1Ch 15:18
porters
Obed-edom, and *J.*, and 1Ch 15:21
Azaziah
and next to him Zechariah, *J.* 1Ch 16:5
J. with psalteries and with 1Ch 16:5
harps
of Benaiah, the son of *J.*, the 2Ch 20:14
son of
account by the hand of *J.* 2Ch 26:11
the scribe
sons of Elizaphan; Shimri, 2Ch 29:3
and *J.*
Hashabiah and *J.* and 2Ch 35:9
Jozabad
names are these, Eliphelet, *J.* Ezr 8:13
the sons of Nebo; *J.*, Ezr 10:43
Mattithiah

JEKABZEEL

at *J.*, and in the villages Ne 11:25
thereof

JEKAMEAM

the third, and *J.* the fourth 1Ch 23:19
Jahaziel the third, *J.*, the 1Ch 24:23
fourth

JEKAMIAH

Shallum begat *J.*, and *J.* begat 1Ch 2:41

JEKUTHIEL

and *J.* the father of Zanoah 1Ch 4:18

JEMIMA

he called the name of the Job 42:14
first, *J.*

JEMUEL

sons of Simeon; *J.*, and Jamin Ge 46:10;
    Ex 6:15

JEOPARDED

a people that *j.* their lives unto J'g 5:18

JEOPARDIZED

j. his life (A)(B) J'g 9:17

JEOPARDY

the men that went in *j.* of 2Sa 23:17
their lives
that have put their lives in *j.* 1Ch 11:19
for with the *j.* of their lives 1Ch 11:19
they brought
master Saul to the *j.* of our 1Ch 12:19
heads
filled with water, and were in *j.* Lu 8:23
And why stand we in *j.* every 1Co 15:30
hour

JEPHTHAE

Barak, and of Samson, and Heb 11:32
of *J.*

JEPHTHAH

J. the Gileadite was a mighty J'g 11:1
man of valour, Gilead begat *J.*
J. fled from his brethren, and J'g 11:3
dwelt in Tob
J. uttered all his words before J'g 11:11
the Lord
the king hearkened not to J'g 11:28
words of *J.*
the Spirit came on *J.*; *J.* J'g 11:29;
vowed a vow 11:30
went yearly to lament the J'g 11:40
daughter of *J.*
J. judged Israel six years, then J'g 12:7
died *J.*
the Lord sent *J.* and 1Sa 12:11
delivered you
for the time would fail me to Heb 11:32
tell of *J.*

JEPHUNNEH

Caleb the son of *J.*   *Nu 13:6;*
14:6, 30, 38; 26:65; 32:12; 34:19;
De 1:36; Jos 14:6; 13-14; 15:13; 21:12;
                  1Ch 4:15: 6:56
sons of Jether; *J.* and Pispah   *1Ch 7:38*

JERAH

and Hazarmaveth, and *J.*   *Ge 10:26;*
                   1Ch 1:20

JERAHMEEL

J. and Ram and Chelubai   *1Ch 2:9;*
           2:25-27, 33, 42
Kish; the son of Kish was *J.*   *1Ch 24:29*
J. the son of Hammelech   *Jer 36:26*

JERAHMEELITES

and against the south of the   *1Sa 27:10*
J.
which were in the cities of   *1Sa 30:29*
the *J.*

JERED

Kenan, Mahalaleel, *J.*   *1Ch 1:2*
wife Jehudijah bare *J.* the   *1Ch 4:18*
father of

JEREMAI

Zabad, Eliphelet, *J.,*   *Ezr 10:33*
Manasseh

JEREMIAH

his mother's name was   *2Ki 23:31;*
Hamutal daughter of *J.*   *24:18; Jer 52:1*
J. a mighty man   *1Ch 5:24; 12:4, 10, 13*
and *J.* lamented for Josiah   *2Ch 35:25*
Zedekiah humbled not   *2Ch 36:12*
himself before *J.*
to fulfil word of the Lord by *2Ch 36:21;*
J. till land   *36:22; Ezr 1:1*
Azariah, *J.* sealed the covenant *Ne 10:2*
Seraiah, *J.* went up with   *Ne 12:1*
Zerubbabel
in days of Joiakim, of *J.*   *Ne 12:12*
Hananiah was priest
J. and Shemaiah went after   *Ne 12:34*
them
the words of *J.* the son of   *Jer 1:1*
Hilkiah
the word that came to *J.*   *Jer 7:1;*
         11:1; 14:1; 18:1
come, let us devise devices   *Jer 18:18*
against *J.*
Pashur smote *J.* and put him *Jer 20:2*
in the stocks
then said the Lord, What seest *Jer 24:3*
thou, *J.*
all the people were gathered   *Jer 26:9*
against *J.*
the hand of Ahikam was with *Jer 26:24*
J. not to put
why hast thou not reproved   *Jer 29:27*
J. of Anathoth
J. was shut up in the court of *Jer 32:2*
the prison
J. spake all these words to   *Jer 34:6*
Zedekiah
then I took Jaazaniah the son *Jer 35:3*
of *J.*
the princes said, Go hide thee, *Jer 36:19*
thou and *J.*
Lord hid Baruch the scribe   *Jer 36:26*
and *J.* the prophet
J. came in and went out   *Jer 37:4*
among the people
so Irijah took *J.* and brought *Jer 37:14*
him to princes
wherefore the princes were   *Jer 37:15*
wroth with *J.*
when *J.* was entered into the *Jer 37:16*
dungeon
to commit *J.* into the court of *Jer 37:21*
the prison
then they cast *J.* into the   *Jer 38:6*
dungeon
drew up *J.* with cords out of *Jer 38:13*
the dungeon
Zedekiah the king sware   *Jer 38:16*
secretly to *J.*
Nebuchadrezzar gave charge *Jer 39:11*
concerning *J.*

then went *J.* to Gedaliah son *Jer 40:6*
of Ahikam
so *J.* wrote in a book all the *Jer 51:60*
evil on Babylon
thus far are the words of *J.*   *Jer 51:64*
fulfilled that was spoken by   *M't 2:17;*
J.   *27:9*
others say thou art *J.* or one *M't 16:14*
of prophets

JEREMIAH'S

yoke from off the prophet *J.*   *Jer 28:10*
neck

JEREMIAS

others, *J.,* or one of the   *M't 16:14*
prophets

JEREMOTH

And Ahio, Shashak, and *J.*   *1Ch 8:14*
Mahli, and Eder, and *J.,*   *1Ch 23:23*
three
The fifteenth to *J.,* he, his   *1Ch 25:22*
sons, and
and Jehiel, and Abdi, and *J.* *Ezr 10:26*
Mattaniah, and *J.,* and   *Ezr 10:27*
Zabad, and

JEREMY

that which was spoken by *J.*   *M't 2:17;*
                       27:9

JERIAH

Of the sons of Hebron; *J.*   *1Ch 23:19*
the first
J. the first, Amariah the   *1Ch 24:23*
second

JERIBAI

Eliel the Mahavite, and *J.*   *1Ch 11:46*

JERICHO

go view *J.; J.* was straitly shut *Jos 2:1;*
up   *2:6*
the people passed over right   *Jos 3:16*
against *J.*
Lord said, See, I have given into *Jos 6:2*
thine hand *J.*
cursed be the man that   *Jos 6:26*
buildeth the city *J.*
Joshua sent men from *J.* to   *Jos 7:2*
view Ai
ye came to *J.* and the men of *Jos 24:11*
J. fought
king said, Tarry at *J.* till your *2Sa 10:5;*
beards be grown   *1Ch 19:5*
in his days did Hiel build *J.*   *1Ki 16:34*
for the Lord hath sent me to *J.* *2Ki 2:4*
Chaldees pursued and   *2Ki 25:5;*
overtook him in   *Jer 39:5; 52:8*
the plains of *J.*
they brought the captives to *2Ch 28:15*
J.
a certain man went down to *J.* *Lu 10:30*
and fell
by faith the walls of *J.* fell   *Heb 11:30*
down

JERIEL

Uzzi, and Rephaiah, and *J.*   *1Ch 7:2*

JERIJAH

the Hebronites was *J.* the   *1Ch 26:31*
chief

JERIMOTH

Uzzi, and Uzziel, and *J.,* and *1Ch 7:7*
Iri
and Elioenai and Omri, and *J.* *1Ch 7:8*
Eluzai, and *J.,* and Bealiah   *1Ch 12:5*
of Mushi; Mahli, and Eder,   *1Ch 24:30*
and *J.*
Mattaniah, Uzziel, Shebuel,   *1Ch 25:4*
and *J.*
of Naphtali, *J.* the son of   *1Ch 27:19*
Azriel
him Mahalath the daughter   *2Ch 11:18*
of *J.*
and Nahath, and Asahel,   *2Ch 31:13*
and *J.*

JERIOTH

of Azubah his wife, and of *J.*   *1Ch 2:18*

JEROBOAM

J. was a mighty man of   *1Ki 11:28*
valour
Solomon sought to kill *J.* and *1Ki 11:40*
J. fled
J. dwelt in Egypt; *J.* was   *1Ki 12:2;*
come again   *12:20*
J. built Shechem, and dwelt *1Ki 12:25*
therein
J. ordained a feast in the   *1Ki 12:32*
eighth month
J. stood by the altar to burn *1Ki 13:1*
incense
after this *J.* returned not   *1Ki 13:33*
from his evil way
this thing became sin to the   *1Ki 13:34*
house of *J.*
at that time Abijah the son of *1Ki 14:1*
J. fell sick
Ahijah, said, Come in, thou *1Ki 14:6*
wife of *J.*
behold, I will bring evil upon *1Ki 14:10*
the house of *J.*
him that dieth of *J.* shall the *1Ki 14:11*
dogs eat
for he only of *J.* shall come *1Ki 14:13*
to the grave
because of the sins of *J.*   *1Ki 14:16;*
                      15:30
there was war between   *1Ki 14:30*
Rehoboam and *J.*
Baasha left not to *J.* any that *1Ki 15:29*
breathed
Baasha did evil, walked in   *1Ki 15:34;*
way of *J.*   *2Ki 10:31; 13:6; 14:24; 17:22*
J. son of Joash sat on his   *2Ki 13:13*
throne
the Lord saved Israel by the *2Ki 14:27*
hand of *J.*
J. drave Israel from   *2Ki 17:21*
following the Lord
reckoned by genealogies in   *1Ch 5:17*
days of *J.*
J. had cast off the Levites   *2Ch 11:14*
from
golden calf which *J.* made for *2Ch 13:8*
your gods
God smote *J.* and all Israel *2Ch 13:15*
before Abijah
neither did *J.* recover   *2Ki 13:20*
strength again in days
prophesied in the days of *J.*   *Ho 1:1;*
                      Am 1:1
rise against house of *J.* with the *Am 7:9*
sword
thus Amos saith, *J.* shall die *Am 7:11*
by the sword

JEROBOAM with *NEBAT*

J. son of *Nebat* lifted up his *1Ki 11:26*
hand
Ahijah the Shilonite to *J.*   *1Ki 12:15;*
the son of *Nebat*   *2Ch 10:15*
I will make thy house like the *1Ki 16:3;*
house of *J.* the son of *Nebat*   *21:22;*
                      2Ki 9:9
for he walked in all the way *1Ki 16:26;*
of *J.* the son of   *16:31; 22:52; 2Ki 3:3*
Nebat
Jehu departed not from sins *2Ki 10:29;*
of *J.* son of *Nebat*   *13:2, 11; 14:24;*
               15:9; 18:24, 28

JEROBOAM'S

J. wife did so, and arose   *1Ki 14:4*
J. wife arose, and departed *1Ki 14:17*

JEROHAM

name was Elkanah, son of *J.*   *1Sa 1:1*
J. his son, Elkanah his son   *1Ch 6:27*
son of Elkanah, the son of *J.* *1Ch 6:34*
and Zichri, the sons of *J.*   *1Ch 8:27*
Ibneiah the son of *J.*   *1Ch 9:8*
Adaiah the son of *J. 1Ch 9:12; Ne 11:12*
the sons of *J.* of Gedor   *1Ch 12:7*
Azareel the son of *J.*   *1Ch 27:22*
Azariah the son of *J.*   *2Ch 23:1*

JERUBBAAL

on that day he called him *J.*   *J'g 6:32*
saying

then J. (who is Gideon) rose up *J'g* 7:1
early
and J. went and dwelt in his   *J'g* 8:29
own house
nor shewed they kindness to   *J'g* 8:35
the house of J.
either that all sons of J. reign,   *J'g* 9:2
or one reign
Abimelech slew his brethren the   *J'g* 9:5
sons of J.
if ye dealt well with J.; if   *J'g* 9:16;
sincerely with J.   9:19
who is Abimelech? is not he the *J'g* 9:28
son of J.
the Lord sent J. and   1Sa 12:11
delivered you

JERUBBESHETH

who smote Abimelech the   2Sa 11:21
son of J.

JERUEL

brook, before the wilderness 2Ch 20:16
of J.

JERUSALEM

Jebusi, which is J.   *Jos* 18:28; *J'g* 19:10
David brought Goliath's   1Sa 17:54
head to J.
king David and his men went   2Sa 5:6
to J.
David brought the shields of   2Sa 8:7
gold to J.
so David and all people   2Sa 12:31
returned to J.
if Lord shall bring me again   2Sa 15:8
to J. then
they carried the ark of God   2Sa 15:29
again to J.
the day that my lord went   2Sa 19:19
out of J.
came to J. at end of nine   2Sa 24:8
months
when angel stretched out   2Sa 24:16;
hand on J. to destroy it   1Ch 21:15
made an end of building the   1Ki 3:1
wall of J.
she came to J. with a very   1Ki 10:2
great train
to set up his son after him and 1Ki 15:4
to establish J.
that Lord shall deliver J.   2Ki 18:35;
out of mine hand   *Isa* 36:20
out of J. go forth a remnant 2Ki 19:31;
                    Isa 37:32
I will bring such evil upon J.   2Ki 21:12
I will wipe J. as a man   2Ki 21:13
wipeth a dish
shed innocent blood till he   2Ki 21:16;
had filled J.   24:4
I will cast off J. which I have 2Ki 23:27
chosen
he carried away all J. and the 2Ki 24:14
princes
Nebuzar-adan burnt all the   2Ki 25:9
houses of J.
But I have chosen J. that my   2Ch 6:6
name
my wrath shall not be poured 2Ch 12:7
on J.
they came to J. with   2Ch 20:28
psalteries, harps
wrath was upon J.   2Ch 24:18;
               29:8; 32:25
Ahaz made altars in every   2Ch 28:24
corner of J.
they spake against the God   2Ch 32:19
of J.
Josiah began to purge J. from 2Ch 34:3
high places
thou art sent to inquire   Ezr 7:14
concerning J.
those deliver thou before the   Ezr 7:19
God of J.
so I came to J.   Ne 2:11; 7:6; 13:7
merchants lodged without J.   Ne 13:20
once or
do good to Zion, build thou   Ps 51:8
walls of J.
the heathens have laid J. on   Ps 79:1
heaps
their blood have they shed   Ps 79:3
round about J.
J. is builded as city compact   Ps 122:3
together
pray for the peace of J. they   Ps 122:6
shall prosper

as the mountains are round   Ps 125:2
about J.
thou shalt see the good of J.   Ps 128:5
all thy life
if I prefer not J. above my   Ps 137:6
chief joy
remember children of Edom in Ps 137:7
the day of J.
the Lord doth build up J. he   Ps 147:2
gathereth
thou art comely, O my love, as   Ca 6:4
the vision he saw concerning J. Isa 1:1;
                        2:1
J. is ruined   Isa 3:8
the Lord shall have purged the Isa 4:4
blood of J.
so will I do to J.   Isa 10:11
Lord hath performed his   Isa 10:12
whole work on J.
and ye have numbered the   Isa 22:10
houses of J.
so will the Lord of hosts   Isa 31:5
defend J.
thine eyes see J. a quiet   Isa 33:20
habitation
speak ye comfortably to J. and Isa 40:2
cry to her
give to J. one that bringeth   Isa 41:27
good tidings
that saith to J. Thou shalt be   Isa 44:26
inhabited
sing together, ye waste places Isa 52:9
of J. for Lord hath redeemed J.
give him no rest till he make J. Isa 62:7
a praise
Zion is a wilderness, J. a   Isa 64:10
desolation
for behold, I create J. a   Isa 65:18
rejoicing
rejoice ye with J. and be glad Isa 66:10
with her
go, and cry in the ears of J.   Jer 2:2
saying
they shall call J. the throne of Jer 3:17
the Lord
run ye to and fro through the   Jer 5:1
streets of J.
gather you to flee out of the   Jer 6:1
midst of J.
why then is this people of J.   Jer 8:5
slidden back
I will make J. heaps, and a den Jer 9:11
of dragons
proclaim these words in the   Jer 11:6
streets of J.
I will mar the great pride of   Jer 13:9
Judah and J.
Judah mourneth, the cry of J. Jer 14:2
is gone up
they shall come from the places Jer 17:26
about J.
I will make void the counsel of Jer 19:7
J.
the houses of J. shall be   Jer 19:13
defiled as Tophet
have seen in prophets of J. an Jer 23:14
horrible thing
J. shall become heaps   Jer 26:18;
                 Mic 3:12
in the places about J. shall   Jer 33:13
flocks pass
in those days J. shall dwell   Jer 33:16
safely, this is
let us go to J. for fear of the Jer 35:11
Chaldeans
till day that J. was taken   Jer 38:28
the Chaldeans brake down the Jer 39:8
wall of J.
ye have seen the evil I have   Jer 44:2
brought on J.
mine anger was kindled in the Jer 44:6
streets of J.
let J. come into your mind,   Jer 51:50
remember Lord
J. hath grievously sinned   La 1:8
J. is as a menstruous woman   La 1:17
among them
this is J.; go through the midst Eze 5:5;
of J.   9:4
son of man cause J. to know   Eze 16:2
her abominations
the king of Babylon is come   Eze 17:12
to J.
that the sword may come to   Eze 21:20
Judah in J.
at his right hand the   Eze 21:22
divination for J.

I will gather you into the   Eze 22:19
midst of J.
one that had escaped out of Eze 33:21
J. came to me
as the flock of J. in her   Eze 36:38
solemn feasts
his windows being open   Da 6:10
toward J.
not been done, as hath been   Da 9:12
done upon J.
from going forth of the   Da 9:25
commandment to build J.
when I bring again the captivity Joe 3:1
of J.
then shall J. be holy; J. shall Joe 3:17;
dwell   3:20
foreigners entered and cast lots Ob 11
upon J.
are they not J.   Mic 1:5
build up Zion with blood, J.   Mic 3:10
with iniquity
I will search J. with candles   Zep 1:12
and punish
how long wilt thou not have a Zec 1:12
mercy on J.
jealous for J.   Zec 1:14
Lord shall yet comfort Zion   Zec 1:17;
and choose J.   2:12
these are the horns which have Zec 1:19
scattered J.
whither goest thou? I go to   Zec 2:2
measure J.
J. shall be inhabited as towns Zec 2:4
without walls
so again have I thought to do Zec 2:15
well to J.
behold, I will make J. a cup of Zec 12:2
trembling
that day I will make J. a   Zec 12:3
burdensome stone
but J. shall be safely   Zec 14:11
inhabited
the offering of J. shall be   Mal 3:4
pleasant
then went out to him J.   M't 3:5;
                 M'k 1:5
neither swear by J.   M't 5:35
Jesus began to shew how he   M't 16:21
must go to J.
come into J.   M't 21:10
his parents brought him to J.   Lu 2:22
they turned back again to J.   Lu 2:45
seeking him
a great multitude out of J.   Lu 6:17
came to hear
his face was as though he   Lu 9:53
would go to J.
it cannot be that a prophet   Lu 13:33
perish out of J.
spake a parable, because he   Lu 19:11
was nigh to J.
when ye shall see J.   Lu 21:20
compassed with armies
J. shall be trodden down of   Lu 21:24
the Gentiles
tarry ye in J. till endued with Lu 24:49
power
and they returned to J. with   Lu 24:52
great joy
when heard that Jesus was   Joh 12:12
coming to J.
ye have filled J. with your   Ac 5:28
doctrine
that he might bring them bound Ac 9:2
unto J.
I go bound in the spirit to J.   Ac 20:22
tidings came that all J. was in Ac 21:31
an uproar
make haste, get thee quickly   Ac 22:18
out of J.
I asked him whether he would Ac 25:20
go to J.
that my service for J. may be Ro 15:31
accepted
will send to bring your   1Co 16:3
liberality unto J.
Agar answereth to J. which   Ga 4:25
now is
but J. which is above is free,   Ga 4:26
mother of us all
the new J.   Re 3:12
the holy J.   Re 21:2; 21:10

AGAINST JERUSALEM

Judah hath fought *against* J.   J'g 1:8
and taken it
Shishak came *against* J.   1Ki 14:25;
               2Ch 12:9

Sennacherib *against J.*   2Ki 18:17;
  2Ch 32:2
the king of Babylon came   2Ki 24:10;
against J. 25:1; *Jer* 34:1, 7; 39:1; 52:4;
  Eze 24:2
Rehum, Shimshai, wrote   *Ezr* 4:8
against J.
they conspired to come and   *Ne* 4:8
fight *against J.*
publish *against J.*   *Jer* 4:16
cast a mount *against J.*   *Jer* 6:6
because that Tyrus hath said   *Eze* 26:2
against J.
destroy nations that come   *Zec* 12:9;
against J.   14:12

AT JERUSALEM

the Jebusites dwelt with   *Jos* 15:63
Judah *at J.*
David came to his house *at J.*   2Sa 20:3
go up to sacrifice in house   *1Ki* 12:27;
of Lord *at J.*   2Ch 9:25; Isa 27:13
these chief fathers dwelt *at J.* 1Ch 9:34;
  9:38
Solomon began to build house 2Ch 3:1;
of Lord *at J.*   *Ezr* 1:2; 5:2
willingly offered themselves to   *Ne* 11:2
dwell *at J.*
but in all this time was not I *at*   *Ne* 13:6
J.
because of thy temple *at J.*   *Ps* 68:29
bring presents
blessed be the Lord who   *Ps* 135:21
dwelleth *at J.*
the people shall dwell in Zion   *Isa* 30:19
at J.
let us go into Jerusalem so   *Jer* 35:11
we dwell *at J.*
and Judah also shall fight *at*   *Zec* 14:14
J.
decease which he should   *Lu* 9:31
accomplish *at J.*
Herod himself was also *at J.* at   *Lu* 23:7
that time
preached among all nations,   *Lu* 24:47
beginning *at J.*
nor yet shall ye *at J.* worship   *Joh* 4:21
the Father
having seen all things that he   *Joh* 4:45
did *at J.*
it was known to all the   *Ac* 1:19
dwellers *at J.*
a great persecution against the   *Ac* 8:1
church *at J.*
what evil he hath done to thy   *Ac* 9:13
saints *at J.*
they that dwell *at J.* have   *Ac* 13:27
fulfilled them
he hasted to be *at J.* the day   *Ac* 20:16
of Pentecost
so shall the Jews *at J.* bind   *Ac* 21:11
the man
but also to die *at J.* for the   *Ac* 21:13
name of Jesus
but shewed first to them of   *Ac* 26:20
Damascus *at J.*
contribution for the poor   *Ro* 15:26
saints *at J.*

FROM JERUSALEM

told that Shimei had gone   *1Ki* 2:41
from J.
Hazael went away *from J.*   2Ki 12:18
carried into captivity *from J.* 2Ki 24:15;
to Babylon   *Es* 2:6; *Jer* 24:1; 27:20;
  29:1; 52:29
the word of the Lord *from J.*   *Isa* 2:3;
  Mic 4:2
the Lord doth take away *from*   *Isa* 3:1
J. the stay
the Lord utter his voice *from*   *Joe* 3:16
J.
I will cut off the horse *from J.*   *Zec* 9:10
that living waters shall go out   *Zec* 14:8
from J.
multitudes followed him *from*   *M't* 4:25
J.
a certain man went down   *Lu* 10:30
from J.
which was *from J.* about sixty   *Lu* 24:13
furlongs
that they should not depart   *Ac* 1:4
from J.
the way that goeth down *from J.* *Ac* 8:26
to Gaza
there came prophets *from J.*   *Ac* 11:27
to Antioch

---

from J. to Illyricum I have   *Ro* 15:19
preached

IN JERUSALEM

Jebusites dwell with Benjamin   *J'g* 1:21
in J.
I will feed thee with me *in J.*   2Sa 19:33
build thee an house *in J.* and   *1Ki* 2:36
dwell
may have a light alway   *1Ki* 11:36;
before me *in J.*   15:4
ye shall worship before this   2Ki 18:22
altar *in J.*
the Lord said, In *J.* will I put   2Ki 21:4
my name
now Huldah dwelt *in J.* in   2Ki 22:14
the college
these dwelt *in J.*   1Ch 8:28; 8:32; 9:3
that they may dwell *in J.* for 1Ch 23:25
ever
the king made silver *in J.* as   2Ch 9:27
stones
they took away the altars   2Ch 30:14
that were *in J.*
there was great joy *in J.* not 2Ch 30:26
the like *in J.*
the house of the Lord which is   *Ezr* 1:3
in J.
God of Israel, whose   *Ezr* 7:15
habitation is *in J.*
and to give us a wall in Judah   *Ezr* 9:9
and *in J.*
ye have no right nor memorial   *Ne* 2:20
in J.
I said, Let every one lodge *in J. Ne* 4:22
cast lots, to bring one of ten to   *Ne* 11:1
dwell *in J.*
to declare in Zion and his   *Ps* 102:21
praises *in J.*
that have been before me *in J. Ec* 1:16;
  2:7, 9
that remaineth *in J.* be called   *Isa* 4:3
holy
when the Lord of hosts shall *Isa* 24:23
reign *in J.*
hear, ye scornful men that rule *Isa* 28:14
in J.
whose fire is in Zion, his   *Isa* 31:9
furnace *in J.*
I will rejoice *in J.* and joy in *Isa* 65:19
my people
and ye shall be comforted *in*   *Isa* 66:13
J.
publish *in J.* and say, Blow the   *Jer* 4:5
trumpet
for that which Manasseh did *in Jer* 15:4
J.
I will break the staff of bread   *Eze* 4:16
in J.
in mount Zion and *in J.* shall   *Joe* 2:32
be deliverance
Jerusalem be inhabited in her   *Zec* 12:6
place, even *in J.*
every pot *in J.* shall be   *Zec* 14:21
holiness to Lord
an abomination is committed   *Mal* 2:11
in J.
a man *in J.* whose name was   *Lu* 2:25
Simeon
spake to all that looked for   *Lu* 2:38
redemption *in J.*
the child Jesus tarried behind   *Lu* 2:43
in J.
were sinners above all that   *Lu* 13:4
dwelt *in J.*
one said, Art thou only a   *Lu* 24:18
stranger *in J.*
in J. is the place where to   *Joh* 4:20
worship
shall be witnesses to me *in J.*   *Ac* 1:8;
  10:39
number of disciples multiplied   *Ac* 6:7
in J.
for as thou hast testified of   *Ac* 23:11
me *in J.*
which thing I also did *in J.*   *Ac* 26:10
many saints

INHABITANTS OF
JERUSALEM

ye *inhabitants of J.* be not   2Ch 20:15
afraid
thus the Lord saved the   2Ch 32:22
inhabitants of J.
inhabitants of J. did him   2Ch 32:33
honour

---

inhabitants of J. did   2Ch 34:32
according to covenant
O *inhabitants of J.* judge   *Isa* 5:3
betwixt me and vineyard
for a gin and snare to the   *Isa* 8:14
inhabitants of J.
he shall be a father to the   *Isa* 22:21
inhabitants of J.
inhabitants of J. shall remain *Jer* 17:25
for ever
go and tell Judah and the   *Jer* 35:13
inhabitants of J.
to whom *inhabitants of J.*   *Eze* 11:15
have said
so will I give the *inhabitants*   *Eze* 15:6
of J. for fuel
the *inhabitants of J.* shall be my *Zec* 12:5
strength
the glory of the *inhabitants*   *Zec* 12:7
of J. do not magnify
the Lord shall defend the   *Zec* 12:8
inhabitants of J.
pour upon *inhabitants of J.*   *Zec* 12:10
the spirit of grace
a fountain opened to the   *Zec* 13:1
inhabitants of J.

O JERUSALEM

pay my vows in midst of   *Ps* 116:19
thee, *O J.*
our feet stand within thy   *Ps* 122:2
gates, *O J.*
if I forget, *O J.*; praise Lord, *Ps* 137:5;
O J.   147:12
O J. that bringest good tidings, *Isa* 40:9
lift up
stand up, *O J.*   *Isa* 51:17
put on thy beautiful garments, *Isa* 52:1
O J.
arise, and sit down, *O J.*   *Isa* 52:2
O J. wash thy heart from   *Jer* 4:14
wickedness
be thou instructed, *O J.* lest I   *Jer* 6:8
depart from thee
cut off thine hair, *O J.* and cast *Jer* 7:29
it away
woe to thee, *O J.* wilt not be   *Jer* 13:27
made clean
for who shall have pity upon   *Jer* 15:5
thee, *O J.*
O J. that killest prophets   *M't* 23:37;
and stonest them sent to thee   *Lu* 13:34

UP TO JERUSALEM

that I should go *up* with the   2Sa 19:34
king *to J.*
it is too much for you to go   *1Ki* 12:28
up to J.
Hazar set his face to go *up*   2Ki 12:17
to J.
Rezin and Pekah came *up to*   2Ki 16:5
J. to war
and let him go *up to J.*   *Ezr* 1:3; 7:13
we go *up to J.* Son of man   *M't* 20:18;
shall be betrayed   *M'k* 10:33; Lu 18:31
they were in the way going   *M'k* 10:32
up to J.
he went before, ascending *up*   *Lu* 19:28
and when Peter was come *up*   *Ac* 11:2
to J.
they should go *up to J.* to the   *Ac* 15:2
apostles
who said, That he should not   *Ac* 21:4;
go *up to J.*   21:12
wilt thou go *up to J.* and there *Ac* 25:9
be judged
neither went I *up to J.* to them   *Ga* 1:17
I went *up to J.* to see Peter   *Ga* 1:18
and abode with him
I went *up to J.* with Barnabas,   *Ga* 2:1
took Titus

JERUSALEM'S

for *J.* sake which I have   *1Ki* 11:13
chosen
David's sake, and for *J.* sake *1Ki* 11:32
and for *J.* sake I will not rest, *Isa* 62:1
until

JERUSHA

And his mother's name was   2Ki 15:33
J. the

JERUSHAH

His mother's name also was *J.* 2Ch 27:1

JESAIAH

of Hananiah; Pelatiah, and J.   *1Ch 3:21*
the son of Ithiel, the son of J.   *Ne 11:7*

JESHAIAH

and Zeri, and J., and Hashabiah   *1Ch 25:3*
The eighth to J., he, his sons   *1Ch 25:15*
Rehabiah his son, and J. his   *1Ch 26:25*
son
of Elam; J. the son of Athaliah   *Ezr 8:7*
with him J. of the sons of   *Ezr 8:19*
Merari

JESHANAH

and J. with the towns   *2Ch 13:19*
thereof, and

JESHARELAH

The seventh to J., he, his   *1Ch 25:14*
sons

JESHEBEAB

to Huppah, the fourteenth to   *1Ch 24:13*
J.

JESHER

sons are these; J., and Shobab   *1Ch 2:18*

JESHIMON

Pisgah, which looketh toward   *Nu 21:20*
J.
of Peor, that looketh toward   *Nu 23:28*
J.
which is on the south of J.   *1Sa 23:19*
in the plain on the south of J.   *1Sa 23:24*
of Hachilah, which is before   *1Sa 26:1;*
J.   *26:3*

JESHISHAI

the son of J., the son of Jahdo   *1Ch 5:14*

JESHOHAIAH

Elioenai, and Jaakobah, and   *1Ch 4:36*
J.

JESHUA

were Eden, and Miniamin,   *2Ch 31:15*
and J.
J., Nehemiah, Seraiah, Reelaiah   *Ezr 2:2*
of the children of J. and Joab,   *Ezr 2:6*
two
of Jedaiah, of the house of J.,   *Ezr 2:36*
nine
the children of J. and   *Ezr 2:40*
Kadmiel, of
stood up J. the son of Jozadak   *Ezr 3:2*
and J. the son of Jozadak, and   *Ezr 3:8*
Then stood J. with his sons and   *Ezr 3:9*
But Zerubbabel, and J. and the   *Ezr 4:3*
rest
and J. the son of Jozadak   *Ezr 5:2*
them was Jozabad the son of   *Ezr 8:33*
J.
the sons of J. the son of   *Ezr 10:18*
Jozadak
to him repaired Ezer the son   *Ne 3:19*
of J.
with Zerubbabel, J., Nehemiah   *Ne 7:7*
of the children of J. and Joab   *Ne 7:11*
of Jedaiah, of the house of J.   *Ne 7:39*
the children of J., of Kadmiel   *Ne 7:43*
Also J., and Bani, and   *Ne 8:7*
Sherebiah
since the days of J. the son of   *Ne 8:17*
Nun
stairs, of the Levites, J., and   *Ne 9:4*
Bani
Then the Levites, J., and   *Ne 9:5*
Kadmiel
both J. the son of Azaniah,   *Ne 10:9*
Binnui
And J., and at Moladah   *Ne 11:26*
the son of Shealtiel, and J.   *Ne 12:1*
of their brethren in the days of   *Ne 12:7*
J.
the Levites: J., Binnui, Kadmiel   *Ne 12:8*
And J. begat Joiakim,   *Ne 12:10*
Joiakim also

and J. the son of Kadmiel   *Ne 12:24*
the days of Joiakim the son   *Ne 12:26*
of J.

JESHUAH

The ninth to J., the tenth to   *1Ch 24:11*

JESHURUN

But J. waxed fat, and kicked   *De 32:15*
he was king in J., when the   *De 33:5*
heads
is none like unto the God of   *De 33:26*
J.

JESIAH

Elkanah, and J., and Azareel   *1Ch 12:6*
Micah the first, and J. the   *1Ch 23:20*
second

JESIMIEL

and Adiel, and J., and Benaiah   *1Ch 4:36*

JESSE

Obed the father of J.   *Ru 4:17; M't 1:5*
Obed begat J. and J. begat   *Ru 4:22;*
David   *M't 1:6*
I will send thee to J.   *1Sa 16:1*
sanctified J. and sons and   *1Sa 16:9*
called them
I have seen a son of J. that is   *1Sa 16:18*
cunning
Saul sent messengers unto J.   *1Sa 16:19*
David said, I am the son of   *1Sa 17:58*
thy servant J.
I know thou hast chosen the   *1Sa 20:30*
son of J.
as long as the son of J. liveth   *1Sa 20:31*
will the son of J. give you   *1Sa 22:7*
fields
my son made league with the   *1Sa 22:8*
son of J.
Doeg said, I saw the son of J.   *1Sa 22:9*
coming to Nob
who is David? who is the son   *1Sa 25:10*
of J.
neither have we inheritance   *2Sa 20:1;*
in the son of J.   *1Ki 12:16; 2Ch 10:16*
turned kingdom to David the   *1Ch 10:14*
son of J.
on thy side are we, thou son   *1Ch 12:18*
of J. peace
shall come a rod out of the   *Isa 11:1*
stem of J.
there shall be a root of J.   *Isa 11:10;*
  Ro 15:12
I have found David the son of   *Ac 13:22*
J.

JESTED

as one who j. (B)   *Ge 19:14*

JESTING

to be j. (R)   *Ge 19:14*
nor foolish talking, nor j.,   *Eph 5:4*
which
no course, stupid or flippant   *Eph 5:4*
talk (N)
conversation should not be   *Eph 5:4*
nastiness, silliness, or flippancy
(P)
no filthiness, nor silly talk (R)   *Eph 5:4*

JESUI

of J., the family of the   *Nu 26:44*
Jesuites

JESUITES

of Jesui, the family of the J.   *Nu 26:44*

JESURUN

thou, J., whom I have chosen   *Isa 44:2*

JESUS

call his name J. for he shall   *M't 1:21;*
save people from sins   *1:25; Lu 1:31;*
  2:21
J. was led up of the Spirit into   *M't 4:1*
wilderness

from that time J. began to   *M't 4:17*
preach and say
J. put forth his hand and   *M't 8:3*
touched him
when J. heard it, he marvelled,   *M't 8:10*
and said
what have we to do with   *M't 8:29;*
thee, J. thou Son of God   *M'k 1:24; 5:7;*
  Lu 8:28
the whole city came out to   *M't 8:34*
meet J.
J. seeing their faith   *M't 9:2*
as J. sat at meat   *M't 9:10*
J. turned him about; J.   *M't 9:22;*
departed thence   *9:27*
J. knew their thoughts, and   *M't 12:25*
said to them
these things spake J. to the   *M't 13:34*
multitude
at that time Herod heard of   *M't 14:1*
the fame of J.
Peter walked on the water to   *M't 14:29*
go to J.
saw no man save J. only   *M't 17:8;*
  M'k 9:8
J. rebuked the devil and he   *M't 17:18*
departed
when come into the house, J.   *M't 17:25*
prevented him
J. called a little child to him,   *M't 18:2*
and set him
two blind men heard that J.   *M't 20:30*
passed by
J. had compassion on them,   *M't 20:34*
touched their eyes
this is J. the prophet of   *M't 21:11*
Nazareth of Galilee
but J. perceived their   *M't 22:18*
wickedness and said
they might take J. by subtilty   *M't 26:4*
and kill him
the disciples did as J. had   *M't 26:19*
appointed them
J. took bread and blessed it   *M't 26:26;*
  M'k 14:22
thou also wast with J.   *M't 26:69;*
  26:71; M'k 14:67
and Peter remembered the   *M't 26:75*
words of J.
written, This is J. the king of   *M't 27:37*
the Jews
J. cried with a loud voice   *M't 27:46;*
  M'k 15:37
J. met them; J. came and   *M't 28:9;*
spake to them   *28:18*
J. could no more enter into   *M'k 1:45*
the city
J. withdrew himself with his   *M'k 3:7*
disciples
J. gave them leave; J.   *M'k 5:13;*
suffered him not   *5:19*
J. knowing that virtue had   *M'k 5:30*
gone out of him
Elias and Moses were talking   *M'k 9:4*
with J.
then J. beholding him, loved   *M'k 10:21*
him
when J. saw that he   *M'k 12:34*
answered discreetly
they bound J. and carried him   *M'k 15:1*
away
let him down in the midst   *Lu 5:19*
before J.
they communed what they   *Lu 6:11*
might do to J.
Zaccheus sought to see J. who   *Lu 19:3*
he was
that he might bear the cross   *Lu 23:26*
after J.
J. himself drew near and went   *Lu 24:15*
with them
they said, Is not this J. son of   *Joh 6:42*
Joseph
a man, that is called J. made   *Joh 9:11*
clay, anointed
J. spake of his death; J.   *Joh 11:13;*
wept   *11:35*
Sir, we would see J.   *Joh 12:21*
when J. knew that his hour   *Joh 13:1*
was come
leaning on J.   *Joh 13:23*
whom seek ye? they said,   *Joh 18:7*
J. of Nazareth
one of the officers that stood   *Joh 18:22*
by struck J.
then came J. forth, wearing   *Joh 19:5*
crown of thorns
now there stood by the cross   *Joh 19:25*
of J. his mother

J. knowing that all things *Joh 19:28* were accomplished
took the body of J.; there *Joh 19:40;* laid they J. *19:42*
and she knew not that it was *Joh 20:14;* J. *21:4*
of all that J. began to do and *Ac 1:1* teach
this same J. which is taken up *Ac 1:11* from you
Judas, who was guide to them *Ac 1:16* who took J.
this J. hath God raised up *Ac 2:32; 3:26; 5:30*
God of Abraham hath glorified *Ac 3:13* his Son J.
preaching thro' J. resurrection *Ac 4:2* from the dead
they took knowledge that they *Ac 4:13* had been with J.
they commanded not to teach *Ac 4:18* in the name of J.
for of a truth against thy holy *Ac 4:27* child J.
signs done by the name of thy *Ac 4:30* holy child J.
they should not speak in the *Ac 5:40* name of J.
this J. shall destroy this place *Ac 6:14* and change
he saw J. standing on the right *Ac 7:55* hand of God
then Philip preached unto him *Ac 8:35* J.
I am J. whom thou persecutest *Ac 9:5; 22:8; 26:15*
even J. that appeared to thee in *Ac 9:17* the way
had preached at Damascus in *Ac 9:27* the name of J.
how God anointed J. with the *Ac 10:38* Holy Ghost
God hath raised to Israel a *Ac 13:23* Saviour J.
saying, that there is another *Ac 17:7* king, one J.
because he preached J. and *Ac 17:18* the resurrection
we adjure you by J. whom *Ac 19:13* Paul preacheth
J. I know, and Paul I know, *Ac 19:15* but who are ye
had questions of one J. who *Ac 25:19* was dead
persuading concerning J. law *Ac 28:23* and prophets
the justifier of him that *Ro 3:26* believes in J.
the Spirit of him that raised up *Ro 8:11* J. from dead
no man speaking by Spirit *1Co 12:3* calleth J.
that the life of J. might be *2Co 4:10* made manifest
that he who raised J. shall *2Co 4:14* raise up also by J.
for if he that cometh, preach *2Co 11:4* another J.
been taught by him as the *Eph 4:21* truth is in J.
at the name of J. every knee *Ph'p 2:10* should bow
even J. who delivered us from *1Th 1:10* wrath
so them that sleep in J. will *1Th 4:14* God bring
we see J. who was made lower *Heb 2:9* than angels
we have a great high priest, *Heb 4:14;* J. son of God *6:20*
by so much was J. made *Heb 7:22* surety of better testament
to enter into the holiest by *Heb 10:19* the blood of J.
looking unto J. the author of *Heb 12:2* our faith
to J. the Mediator of the new *Heb 12:24* covenant
wherefore J. suffered *Heb 13:12* without the gate
whoso shall confess J. is Son *1Jo 4:15* of God
that believeth that J. is the Son *1Jo 5:5* of God
here are they that keep the *Re 14:12* faith of J.
woman drunken with blood of *Re 17:6* martyrs of J.

that were beheaded for the *Re 20:4* witness of J.
I J. have sent mine angel to *Re 22:16* testify to you

JESUS for Joshua

brought in with J. into *Ac 7:45* possession of Gentiles
for if J. had given them rest *Heb 4:8* then would not

JESUS with LORD

all the time the Lord J. went in *Ac 1:21* and out
God made that same J. both *Ac 2:36* Lord and Christ
Stephen saying, Lord J. receive *Ac 7:59* my spirit
were baptized in the name of *Ac 8:16* the Lord J.
he spake boldly in the name of *Ac 9:29* the Lord J.
spake to Grecians, preaching *Ac 11:20* the Lord J.
believe on the Lord J. Christ *Ac 16:31* and be saved
all in Asia heard the word of *Ac 19:10* the Lord J.
and the name of the Lord J. *Ac 19:17* was magnified
and to remember the words of *Ac 20:35* the Lord J.
Lord J. same night he was *1Co 11:23* betrayed
that no man can say that J. is *1Co 12:3* the Lord
as ye are ours in the day of *2Co 1:14* the Lord J.
always bearing about the *2Co 4:10* dying of Lord J.
I bear in my body the marks *Ga 6:17* of Lord J.
who both killed Lord J. and *1Th 2:15* prophets
we beseech and exhort you by *1Th 4:1* the Lord J.
what commandments we gave *1Th 4:2* you by Lord J.
when the Lord J. shall be *2Th 1:7* revealed
brought again from dead *Heb 13:20* our Lord J.
through the knowledge of J. *2Pe 1:2* our Lord
I come quickly, even so, come *Re 22:20* Lord J.

JESUS SAID

Peter called to mind the *M'k 14:72* word J. said
the disciples believed the word *Joh 2:22* J. said
it was at the same hour in *Joh 4:53* which J. said
when J. had thus said, he *Joh 13:21* was troubled
yet J. said not to him, He *Joh 21:23* shall not die

JESUS'

and cast them down at J. feet *M't 15:30* who also himself was J. *M't 27:57* disciple
saw it, he fell down at J. knees *Lu 5:8* fell down at J. feet, and *Lu 8:41* besought
Mary, which also sat at J. feet *Lu 10:39* they came not for J. sake only *Joh 12:9* Now there was leaning on J. *Joh 13:23* bosom
He then lying on J. breast *Joh 13:25* saith
ourselves your servants for J. *2Co 4:5* sake
delivered unto death for J. *2Co 4:11* sake

JETHER

he said unto J. his firstborn, *J'g 8:20* Up
Ner, and unto Amasa, the son *1Ki 2:5* of J.
and Amasa, the son of J. *1Ki 2:32* captain of

and the father of Amasa was *1Ch 2:17* J. the
of Shammai; J., and Jonathan *1Ch 2:32* and J. died without children *1Ch 2:32* sons of Ezra were, J., and *1Ch 4:17* Mered
sons of J.; Jephunneh, and *1Ch 7:38* Pispah

JETHETH

Timnah, duke Alvah, duke J. *Ge 36:40* Timnah, duke Aliah, duke J. *1Ch 1:51*

JETHLAH

Shaalabbin, and Ajalon, and *Jos 19:42* J.

JETHRO

Now Moses kept the flock of J. *Ex 3:1* Moses went and returned to J. *Ex 4:18* And J. said to Moses, Go in *Ex 4:18* peace
When J., the priest of Midian *Ex 18:1* Then J., Moses' father in law, *Ex 18:2;* took *18:12*
J., Moses' father in law, came *Ex 18:5* with
father in law J. am come unto *Ex 18:6* thee
J. rejoiced for all the goodness *Ex 18:9* J. said, Blessed be the Lord, *Ex 18:10* who

JETUR

Hadar, and Tema, J., Naphish *Ge 25:15* J., Naphish, and Kedemah. *1Ch 1:31* These
Hagarites, with J., and *1Ch 5:19* Nephish

JEUEL

the sons of Zerah; J., and their *1Ch 9:6*

JEUSH

Aholibamah bare J., and *Ge 36:5* Jaalam
she bare to Esau J., and *Ge 36:14* Jaalam
duke J., duke Jaalam, duke *Ge 36:18* Korah
Reuel, and J., and Jaalam *1Ch 1:35* J., and Benjamin, and Ehud *1Ch 7:10* Jahath, Zina, and J., and *1Ch 23:10* Beriah
J. and Beriah had not many *1Ch 23:11* sons
J., and Shamariah, and *2Ch 11:19* Zaham

JEUZ

And J., and Shachia, and *1Ch 8:10* Mirma

JEW

the palace there was a certain J. *Es 2:5* he had told them that he was a *Es 3:4* J.
Mordecai the J. sitting at the *Es 5:13* king's
do even so to Mordecai the J., *Es 6:10* that
the queen and to Mordecai the *Es 8:7* J.
of Abihail, and Mordecai the *Es 9:29* J.
Mordecai the J., and Esther the *Es 9:31* Mordecai the J. was next unto *Es 10:3* king
them, to wit, of a J. his *Jer 34:9* brother
hold of the skirt of him that is *Zec 8:23* a J.
being a J., askest drink of me *Joh 4:9* Pilate answered, Am I a J. *Joh 18:35* man that is a J. to keep *Ac 10:28* company
a J., whose name was Bar-jesus *Ac 13:6* found a certain J. named *Ac 18:2* Aquila
certain J. named Apollos, *Ac 18:24* born at

Sceva, a *J.*, and chief of the   *Ac 19:14*
priests
when they knew that he was a   *Ac 19:34*
J.
a man which am a *J.* of   *Ac 21:39*
Tarsus
man which am a *J.* born in   *Ac 22:3*
Tarsus
the *J.* first, and also to the   *Ro 1:16*
Greek
the *J.* first, and also to the   *Ro 2:9*
Gentile
the *J.* first, and also to the   *Ro 2:10*
Gentile
Behold, thou art called a *J.* and *Ro 2:17*
is not a *J.*which is one   *Ro 2:28*
outwardly
he is a *J.*, which is one   *Ro 2:29*
inwardly
What advantage then hath the *J. Ro 3:1*
between the *J.* and the Greek *Ro 10:12*
And to the Jews I became as *1Co 9:20*
a *J.*
If thou, being a *J.* livest after *Ga 2:14*
There is neither *J.* nor Greek *Ga 3:28*
Where there is neither Greek *Col 3:11*
nor *J.*

JEWEL

As a *j.* of gold in a swine's   *Pr 11:22*
snout
ring of gold in a swine's   *Pr 11:22*
(A)(B)(E)(R)
lips of knowledge are a   *Pr 20:15*
precious *j.*
a vase of preciousness (A)   *Pr 20:15*
one *j.* of necklace (A)(R)   *Ca 4:9*
I put a *j.* on thy forehead   *Eze 16:12*
put a ring on your nostril   *Eze 16:12*
(A)(B)(E)(R)

JEWELED

cheeks with *j.* spangles (B)   *Ca 1:10*
limbs like *j.* chains (A)   *Ca 7:1*
thighs are a jeweled chain (B)   *Ca 7:1*

JEWELRY

j. of silver (R)   *Ge 24:53*
j. of silver and gold (R)   *Ex 3:22*
all sorts of gold *j.* (B)   *Ex 35:22*
was worked *j.* entirely (B)   *Nu 31:51*
precious stones and *j.* (B)   *Da 11:38*

JEWELS

servant brought forth *j.* of   *Ge 24:53*
silver
articles of silver (B)   *Ge 24:53*
jewelry of silver (R)   *Ge 24:53*
and *j.* of gold and raiment   *Ge 24:53;*
                                        Ex 12:35
sojourneth in her house, *j.* of *Ex 3:22*
silver
borrow gold articles (B)   *Ex 3:22*
jewelry of silver and gold (R)   *Ex 3:22*
and *j.* of gold, and raiment: *Ex 3:22*
and ye
neighbour, *j.* of silver, and *j.* of *Ex 11:2*
gold
of the Egyptians *j.* of silver *Ex 12:35*
rings, and tablets, all *j.* of *Ex 35:22*
gold
all sorts of gold jewelry (B)   *Ex 35:22*
all sorts of gold objects (R)   *Ex 35:22*
of *j.* of gold, chains, and   *Nu 31:50*
bracelets
gold of them, even all   *Nu 31:51*
wrought *j.*
all wrought articles (A)(R)   *Nu 31:51*
which was worked jewelry   *Nu 31:51*
entirely (B)
put the *j.* of gold, which ye   *1Sa 6:8*
return
the figures of gold (A)(R)   *1Sa 6:8*
gold articles for atonement (B) *1Sa 6:8*
with it, wherein the *j.* of gold *1Sa 6:15*
were
precious *j.*, which they   *2Ch 20:25*
stripped off
found precious things   *2Ch 20:25*
(A)(R)
found precious articles (B)   *2Ch 20:25*
and for all manner of   *2Ch 32:27*
pleasant *j.*
all kinds of costly vessels   *2Ch 32:27*
(A)(R)

---

all sorts of precious articles *2Ch 32:27*
(B)
all manner of goodly vessels *2Ch 32:27*
(E)
it shall not be for *j.* of fine *Job 28:17*
gold
more precious than *j.* (B)(R) *Ps 31:10*
wisdom more valuable than *j.* *Pr 3:15*
(B)(R)
cheeks are comely with rows of *Ca 1:10*
j.
strings of *j.* (A)(E)(R)   *Ca 1:10*
cheeks with jeweled spangles *Ca 1:10*
(B)
joints of thy thighs are like *j.* *Ca 7:1*
The rings, and nose *j.*   *Isa 3:21*
bride adorneth herself with *Isa 61:10*
her *j.*
Thou hast also taken thy fair *Eze 16:17*
j. of
shall take thy fair *j.* and   *Eze 16:39*
leave thee
clothes and take away thy *Eze 23:26*
fair *j.*
with her earrings and her *j.* *Ho 2:13*
that day when I make up my *Mal 3:17*
j.
I prepare my special   *Mal 3:17*
possession (B)(R)
my own possession (E)   *Mal 3:17*

JEWESS

certain woman, which was a *J. Ac 16:1*
his wife Drusilla, which was a *Ac 24:24*
J.

JEWISH

in the *J.* language (N)   *Ac 21:40*
Not giving heed to *J.* fables *Tit 1:14*

JEWRY

king my father brought out of *Da 5:13*
J.
people, teaching throughout all *Lu 23:5*
J.
he would not walk in *J.*,   *Joh 7:1*
because

JEWS

Syria, and drave the *J.* from *2Ki 16:6*
Elath
the *J.* and the Chaldees that *2Ki 25:25*
were
the *J.* which came up from *Ezr 4:12*
thee
in haste to Jerusalem unto the *Ezr 4:23*
J.
son of Iddo, prophesied unto *Ezr 5:1*
the *J.*
God was upon the elders of the *Ezr 5:5*
J.
alone; let the governors of the *Ezr 6:7*
J.
and the elders of the *J.* built *Ezr 6:7*
this
shall do to the elders of these *J. Ezr 6:8*
the elders of the *J.* builded *Ezr 6:14*
concerning the *J.* that had *Ne 1:2*
escaped
neither had I as yet told it to *Ne 2:16*
the *J.*
indignation, and mocked the *Ne 4:1*
J.
and said, What do these feeble *Ne 4:2*
J.
the *J.* which dwelt by them *Ne 4:12*
came
wives against their brethren the *Ne 5:1*
J.
have redeemed our brethren *Ne 5:8*
the *J.*
were at my table, *J.* and rulers *Ne 5:17*
that thou and the *J.* think to *Ne 6:6*
rebel
In those days also saw I *J. Ne 13:23*
that
Haman sought to destroy all the *Es 3:6*
J.
kill, and to cause to perish, all *Es 3:13*
J.
was great mourning among the *J. Es 4:3*
to the king's treasuries for the *J. Es 4:7*
king's house, more than all the *Es 4:13*
J.
and deliverance arise to the *J. Es 4:14*

---

gather together all the *J.* that *Es 4:16*
are
Mordecai be of the seed of the *Es 6:13*
J
that he had devised against the *Es 8:3*
J.
which he wrote to destroy the *J. Es 8:5*
he laid his hand upon the *J. Es 8:7*
Write ye also for the *J.*, as it *Es 8:8*
liketh
Mordecai commanded unto the *Es 8:9*
J.
the *J.* according to their writing *Es 8:9*
Wherein the king granted the *J. Es 8:11*
J. should be ready against that *Es 8:13*
day
The *J.* had light, and gladness *Es 8:16*
the *J.* had joy and gladness, a *Es 8:17*
feast
the people of the land became *Es 8:17*
J.
the fear of the *J.* fell upon them *Es 9:1*
J. hoped to have power over *Es 9:1*
there
the *J.* had rule over them that *Es 9:1*
J. gathered themselves together *Es 9:2*
officers of the king, helped the *J. Es 9:3*
the *J.* smote all their enemies *Es 9:5*
with
Shushan the palace the *J.* slew *Es 9:6*
the enemy of the *J.* slew they *Es 9:10*
The *J.* have slain and destroyed *Es 9:12*
king, let it be granted to the *J. Es 9:13*
For the *J.* that were in Shushan *Es 9:15*
J. that were in the king's *Es 9:16*
provinces
J. that were in Shushan *Es 9:18*
assembled
Therefore the *J.* of the villages *Es 9:19*
sent letters unto all the *J.* that *Es 9:20*
the *J.* rested from their enemies *Es 9:22*
the *J.* undertook to do as they *Es 9:23*
had
Agagite, the enemy of all the *J. Es 9:24*
devised against the *J.* to destroy *Es 9:24*
which he devised against the *J. Es 9:25*
J. ordained, and took upon *Es 9:27*
them
should not fail from among the *Es 9:28*
J.
he sent the letters unto all the *Es 9:30*
J.
Ahasuerus, great among the *J. Es 10:3*
J. that sat in the court of the *Jer 32:12*
prison
afraid of the *J.* that are fallen *Jer 38:19*
to
when all the *J.* that were in *Jer 40:11*
Moab
all the *J.* returned out of all *Jer 40:12*
places
all the *J.* which are gathered *Jer 40:15*
unto
Ishmael also slew all the *J. Jer 41:3*
that
concerning all the *J.* which *Jer 44:1*
dwell
the seventh year three *Jer 52:28*
thousand *J.*
carried away captive of the *J. Jer 52:30*
came near, and accused the *J. Da 3:8*
certain *J.* whom thou hast set *Da 3:12*
is he that is born King of the *J. M't 2:2*
saying, Art thou the King of *M't 27:11;*
the *J.   M'k 15:2; Lu 23:3*
him, saying, Hail, King of *M't 27:29*
the *J.*
This Is Jesus The King Of *M't 27:37*
The *J.*
is commonly reported among *M't 28:15*
the *J.*
For the Pharisees, and all the *M'k 7:3*
J.
release unto you the King of *M'k 15:9*
the *J.*
whom ye call the King of *M'k 15:12*
J.
to salute him, Hail, King of *M'k 15:18*
the *J.*
written over, The King Of *M'k 15:26*
The *J.*
sent unto him the elders of the *Lu 7:3*
J.
If thou be the king of the *J. Lu 23:37*
save
This Is The King Of The *J. Lu 23:38*
was of Arimathaea, a city of *Lu 23:51*
the *J.*

when the *J.* sent priests and   *Joh 1:19*
Levites
manner of the purifying of the   *Joh 2:6*
J.
Then answered the *J.* and said   *Joh 2:18*
unto
Then said the *J.,* Forty and six   *Joh 2:20*
named Nicodemus, a ruler of   *Joh 3:1*
the *J.*
of John's disciples and the *J.*   *Joh 3:25*
the *J.* have no dealings with the   *Joh 4:9*
worship: for salvation is of   *Joh 4:22*
the *J.*
this there was a feast of the *J.*   *Joh 5:1*
J. therefore said unto him that   *Joh 5:10*
was
and told the *J.* that it was   *Joh 5:15*
Jesus
therefore did the *J.* persecute   *Joh 5:16*
Jesus
the *J.* sought the more to kill   *Joh 5:18*
him
passover, a feast of the *J.,* was   *Joh 6:4*
nigh
The *J.* then murmured at him   *Joh 6:41*
The *J.* therefore strove among   *Joh 6:52*
because the *J.* sought to kill him   *Joh 7:1*
Then the *J.* sought him at the   *Joh 7:11*
feast
openly of him for fear of the   *Joh 7:13*
J.
And the *J.* marvelled, saying,   *Joh 7:15*
How
said the *J.* among themselves   *Joh 7:35*
said the *J.* Will he kill himself   *Joh 8:22*
Jesus to those *J.* which believed   *Joh 8:31*
Then answered the *J.* and said   *Joh 8:48*
Then said the *J.* unto him,   *Joh 8:52*
Now we
Then said the *J.* unto him,   *Joh 8:57*
Thou
the *J.* did not believe   *Joh 9:18*
concerning
parents, because they feared   *Joh 9:22*
the *J.*
for the *J.* had agreed already,   *Joh 9:22*
that
was a division, again among   *Joh 10:19*
the *J.*
Then came the *J.* round   *Joh 10:24*
about him
Then the *J.* took up stones   *Joh 10:31*
again
The *J.* answered him, saying,   *Joh 10:33*
For
the *J.* of late sought to stone   *Joh 11:8*
thee
many of the *J.* came to   *Joh 11:19*
Martha
The *J.* then which were with   *Joh 11:31*
her
weeping, and the *J.* also   *Joh 11:33*
weeping
Then said the *J.,* Behold   *Joh 11:36*
how he
many of the *J.* which came to   *Joh 11:45*
Mary
no more openly among the *J.*   *Joh 11:54*
people of the *J.* therefore   *Joh 12:9*
knew
of him many of the *J.* went   *Joh 12:11*
away
as I said unto the *J.,* Whither   *Joh 13:33*
I go
and officers of the *J.* took   *Joh 18:12*
Jesus
he, which gave counsel to the   *Joh 18:14*
J.
whither the *J.* always resort   *Joh 18:20*
The *J.* therefore said unto   *Joh 18:31*
him, It
him, Art thou the King of   *Joh 18:33*
the *J.*
I should not be delivered to   *Joh 18:36*
the *J.*
he went out again unto the *J.*   *Joh 18:38*
release unto you the King of   *Joh 18:39*
the *J.*
And said, Hail, King of the *J.*   *Joh 19:3*
J. answered him, We have a   *Joh 19:7*
law
but the *J.* cried out, saying,   *Joh 19:12*
If thou
he saith unto the *J.,* Behold   *Joh 19:14*
your
Of Nazareth The King Of   *Joh 19:19*
The *J.*
This title then read many of   *Joh 19:20*
the *J.*

Then said the chief priests of   *Joh 19:21*
the *J.*
Write not, The King of the *J.*   *Joh 19:21*
but
that he said, I am King of   *Joh 19:21*
the *J.*
The *J.* therefore, besought   *Joh 19:31*
Pilate
but secretly for fear of the *J.*   *Joh 19:38*
as the manner of the *J.* is to   *Joh 19:40*
bury
were assembled for fear of   *Joh 20:19*
the *J.*
were dwelling at Jerusalem *J.*   *Ac 2:5*
of Rome, *J.* and proselytes   *Ac 2:10*
the *J.* which dwelt at   *Ac 9:22*
Damascus
the *J.* took counsel to kill him   *Ac 9:23*
among all the nation of the *J.*   *Ac 10:22*
he did both in the land of the   *Ac 10:39*
J.
word to none but unto the *J.*   *Ac 11:19*
only
because he saw it pleased the *J.*   *Ac 12:3*
expectation of the people of   *Ac 12:11*
the *J.*
of God in the synagogues of   *Ac 13:5*
the *J.*
J. were gone out of the   *Ac 13:42*
synagogue
many of the *J.* and religious   *Ac 13:43*
when the *J.* saw the multitudes   *Ac 13:45*
the *J.* stirred up the devout   *Ac 13:50*
into the synagogue of the *J.*   *Ac 14:1*
great multitude both of the *J.*   *Ac 14:1*
the unbelieving *J.* stirred up   *Ac 14:2*
and part held with the *J.* and   *Ac 14:4*
part
and also of the *J.* with their   *Ac 14:5*
rulers
thither certain *J.* from   *Ac 14:13*
Antioch
circumcised him because of the   *Ac 16:3*
J.
being *J.,* do exceedingly   *Ac 16:20*
trouble
where was a synagogue of the   *Ac 17:1*
J.
But the *J.* which believed not   *Ac 17:5*
went into the synagogue of   *Ac 17:10*
the *J.*
But when the *J.* of   *Ac 17:13*
Thessalonica
he in the synagogue of the *J.*   *Ac 17:17*
all *J.* to depart from Rome   *Ac 18:2*
persuaded the *J.* and the Greeks   *Ac 18:4*
testified to the *J.* that Jesus was   *Ac 18:5*
the *J.* made insurrection with   *Ac 18:12*
one
Gallio said unto the *J.,* If it   *Ac 18:14*
were
O ye *J.* reason would that I   *Ac 18:14*
should
and reasoned with the *J.*   *Ac 18:19*
For he mightily convinced the   *Ac 18:28*
J.
Lord Jesus, both *J.* and   *Ac 19:10*
Greeks
Then certain of the vagabond   *Ac 19:13*
J.
And this was known to all the   *Ac 19:17*
J.
the *J.* putting him forward   *Ac 19:33*
And when the *J.* laid wait for   *Ac 20:3*
him
me by the lying in wait of the   *Ac 20:19*
J.
Testifying both to the *J.,* and   *Ac 20:21*
also
So shall the *J.* at Jerusalem   *Ac 21:11*
bind
how many thousands of *J.*   *Ac 21:20*
there are
thou teachest all the *J.* which   *Ac 21:21*
are
the *J.* which were of Asia,   *Ac 21:27*
when
a good report of all the *J.*   *Ac 22:12*
which
wherefore he was accused of   *Ac 22:30*
the *J.*
certain of the *J.* banded   *Ac 23:12*
together
The *J.* have agreed to desire   *Ac 23:20*
thee
This man was taken of the *J.*   *Ac 23:27*
that the *J.* laid wait for the   *Ac 23:30*
man

mover of sedition among all   *Ac 24:5*
the *J.*
the *J.* also assented, saying that   *Ac 24:9*
certain *J.* from Asia found me   *Ac 24:18*
willing to shew the *J.* a   *Ac 24:27*
pleasure
the chief of the *J.* informed   *Ac 25:2*
him
the *J.* which came down from   *Ac 25:7*
Neither against the law of the   *Ac 25:8*
J.
willing to do the *J.* a pleasure   *Ac 25:9*
to the *J.* have I done no   *Ac 25:10*
wrong, as
the elders of the *J.* informed   *Ac 25:15*
me
the multitude of the *J.* have   *Ac 25:24*
dealt
whereof I am accused of the *J.*   *Ac 26:2*
questions which are among the   *Ac 26:3*
J.
at Jerusalem, know all the *J.*   *Ac 26:4*
Agrippa, I am accused of the *J.*   *Ac 26:7*
the *J.* caught me in the temple   *Ac 26:21*
days Paul called the chief of   *Ac 28:17*
the *J.*
But when the *J.* spake against   *Ac 28:19*
it
said these words, the *J.*   *Ac 28:29*
departed
before proved both *J.* and   *Ro 3:9*
Gentiles
Is he the God of the *J.* only   *Ro 3:29*
called, not of the *J.* only, but   *Ro 9:24*
also
For the *J.* require a sign, and   *1Co 1:22*
unto the *J.* a stumbling block   *1Co 1:23*
are called, both *J.* and Greeks   *1Co 1:24*
And unto the *J.* I became as a   *1Co 9:20*
Jew
that I might gain the *J.* to   *1Co 9:20*
them
none offence, neither to the   *1Co 10:32*
J. nor
whether we be *J.* or Gentiles   *1Co 12:13*
Of the *J.* five times received   *2Co 11:24*
I forty
the other *J.* dissembled   *Ga 2:13*
likewise
of Gentiles, and not as do the   *Ga 2:14*
the Gentiles to live as do the *J.*   *Ga 2:14*
not
We who are *J.* by nature, and   *Ga 2:15*
even as they have of the *J.*   *1Th 2:14*
which say they are *J.,* and are   *Re 2:9;*
not   *3:9*

JEWS'

talk not with us in the *J.*   *2Ki 18:26*
language
a loud voice in the *J.*   *2Ki 18:28;*
language   *Isa 36:13*
with a loud voice in the *J.*   *2Ch 32:18*
speech
not speak in the *J.* language   *Ne 13:24*
the Agagite, the *J.* enemy   *Es 3:10*
the house of Haman the *J.*   *Es 8:1*
enemy
speak not to us in the *J.*   *Isa 36:11*
language
the *J.* passover was at hand   *Joh 2:13*
the *J.* feast of tabernacles was   *Joh 7:2*
at
the *J.* passover was nigh at   *Joh 11:55*
hand
because of the *J.* preparation   *Joh 19:42*
day
in time past in the *J.* religion   *Ga 1:13*
profited in the *J.* religion above   *Ga 1:14*

JEZANIAH

and *J.* the son of a   *Jer 40:8*
Maachathite
Kareah. and *J.* the son of   *Jer 42:1*
Hoshaiah

JEZEBEL

he took to wife *J.* the   *1Ki 16:31*
daughter of
when *J.* cut off the prophets of   *1Ki 18:4*
what I did when *J.* slew the   *1Ki 18:13*
prophets
And Ahab told *J.* all that   *1Ki 19:1*
Elijah had
J. sent a messenger unto   *1Ki 19:2*
Elijah

J. his wife came to him, and said   *1Ki 21:5*
J. his wife said unto him, Dost thou   *1Ki 21:7*
did as *J.* had sent unto them   *1Ki 21:11*
sent to *J.*, saying, Naboth is stoned   *1Ki 21:14*
J. heard that Naboth was stoned   *1Ki 21:15*
that *J.* said to Ahab, Arise, take   *1Ki 21:15*
And of *J.* also spake the Lord   *1Ki 21:23*
The dogs shall eat *J.* by the wall of   *1Ki 21:23*
Lord, whom *J.* his wife stirred up   *1Ki 21:25*
of the Lord, at the hand of *J.*   *2Ki 9:7*
the dogs shall eat *J.* in the portion   *2Ki 9:10*
as the whoredoms of thy mother *J.*   *2Ki 9:22*
was come to Jezreel, *J.* heard of it   *2Ki 9:30*
Jezreel shall dogs eat the flesh of *J.*   *2Ki 9:36*
the carcase of *J.* shall be as dung   *2Ki 9:37*
so that they shall not say, This is *J.*   *2Ki 9:37*
thou sufferest that woman *J.*   *Re 2:20*

JEZEBEL'S

four hundred which eat at *J.* table   *1Ki 18:19*

JEZER

and Guni, and *J.*, and Shillem   *Ge 46:24*
Of *J.*, the family of the Jezerites   *Nu 26:49*
and Guni, and *J.*, and Shallum   *1Ch 7:13*

JEZERITES

of Jezer, the family of the *J.*   *Nu 26:49*

JEZIAH

Ramiah, and *J.*, and Malchiah   *Ezr 10:25*

JEZIEL

and *J.*, and Pelet, the sons of   *1Ch 12:3*

JEZLIAH

J., and Jobab, the sons of Elpaal   *1Ch 8:18*

JEZOAR

of Helah were, Zereth, and *J.*   *1Ch 4:7*

JEZRAHIAH

sang loud, with *J.* their overseer   *Ne 12:42*

JEZREEL

Amalek pitched in the valley of *J.*   *J'g 6:33*
David also took Ahinoam of *J.*   *1Sa 25:43*
Israel pitched by a fountain which is in *J.*   *1Sa 29:1*
Abner made Ish-bosheth king over *J.*   *2Sa 2:9*
and Ahab rode and went to *J.*   *1Ki 18:45*
Elijah ran before Ahab to entrance of *J.*   *1Ki 18:46*
Naboth had a vineyard which was in *J.*   *1Ki 21:1*
dogs eat Jezebel by wall of *J.*   *1Ki 21:23; 2Ki 9:10, 36*
Joram went back to *J.*   *2Ki 8:29; 2Ch 22:6*
so Jehu rode in a chariot, and went to *J.*   *2Ki 9:16*
come to me to *J.* by to-morrow this time   *2Ki 10:6*
they sent the heads of the king's sons to *J.*   *2Ki 10:7*
these were of the father of Etam, *J.*   *1Ch 4:3*

call his name *J.* for I will avenge blood of *J.* on house of   *Ho 1:4*
I will break the bow of Israel in valley of *J.*   *Ho 1:5*
one head, for great shall be the day of *J.*   *Ho 1:11*
the corn, wine, and oil shall hear *J.*   *Ho 2:22*

JEZREELITE

that Naboth the *J.* had a vineyard   *1Ki 21:1*
Naboth the *J.* had spoken to him   *1Ki 21:4*
Because I spake unto Naboth the *J.*   *1Ki 21:6*
thee the vineyard of Naboth the *J.*   *1Ki 21:7*
of the vineyard of Naboth the *J.*   *1Ki 21:15*
to the vineyard of Naboth the *J.*   *1Ki 21:16*
him in the portion of Naboth the *J.*   *2Ki 9:21*
of the field of Naboth the *J.*   *2Ki 9:25*

JEZREELITESS

his two wives, Ahinoam the *J.*   *1Sa 27:3*
taken captives, Ahinoam the *J.*   *1Sa 30:5*
two wives also, Ahinoam the *J.*   *2Sa 2:2*
was Amnon, of Ahinoam the *J.*   *2Sa 3:2; 1Ch 3:1*

JIBSAM

and Jahmai, and *J.*, and Shemuel   *1Ch 7:2*

JIDLAPH

and Pildash, and *J.*, and Bethuel   *Ge 22:22*

JIMNA

of *J.*, the family of the Jimnites   *Nu 26:44*

JIMNAH

sons of Asher; *J.* and Ishuah   *Ge 46:17*

JIMNITES

of Jimna, the family of the *J.*   *Nu 26:44*

JIPHTAH

And *J.*, and Ashnah, and Nezib   *Jos 15:43*

JIPHTHAH-EL

thereof are in the valley of *J.*   *Jos 19:14*
to the valley of *J.* toward the north   *Jos 19:27*

JOAB

three sons of Zeruiah, *J.*, Abishai   *2Sa 2:18*
how should I hold up my face to *J.* thy brother   *2Sa 2:22*
J. also and Abishai pursued after Abner   *2Sa 2:24*
let the blood of Abner rest on the head of *J.*   *2Sa 3:29*
so *J.* and Abishai his brother slew Abner   *2Sa 3:30*
J. the son of Zeruiah was over the host   *2Sa 8:16; 20:23; 1Ch 11:6; 18:15; 27:34*
David demanded of Uriah how *J.* did   *2Sa 11:7*
Israel and Judah abide in tents, and my lord *J.*   *2Sa 11:11*
in the morning David wrote a letter to *J.*   *2Sa 11:14*
J. fought against Rabbah of Ammon   *2Sa 12:26*
so *J.* put the words in the widow's mouth   *2Sa 14:3*
is not the hand of *J.* with thee in all this   *2Sa 14:19*
Absalom sent for *J.*   *2Sa 14:29*
J. killed Amasa   *2Sa 20:9*
woman said, Art thou *J.*   *2Sa 20:17*

the king's word prevailed against *J.* and captains   *2Sa 24:4; 1Ch 21:4*
Adonijah confered with *J.* son of Zeruiah   *1Ki 1:7*
moreover thou knowest what *J.* did to me   *1Ki 2:5*
J. fled to tabernacle of Lord and caught horns   *1Ki 2:28*
six months *J.* remain, every male in Edom   *1Ki 11:16*
Seraiah begat *J.*   *1Ch 4:14*
J. led the army   *1Ch 20:1*
for the king's word was abominable to *J.*   *1Ch 21:6*
all that Abner and *J.* had dedicated   *1Ch 26:28*
of children of Jeshua and *J.*   *Ezr 2:6; Ne 7:11*
of the sons of *J.* Obadiah went with Ezra   *Ezr 8:9*

JOAB'S

J. field is near mine, and he hath   *2Sa 14:30*
Nahash, sister to Zeruiah *J.* mother   *2Sa 17:25*
the son of Zeruiah, *J.* brother   *2Sa 18:2*
young men that bare *J.* armour   *2Sa 18:15*
there went out after him *J.* men   *2Sa 20:7*
J. garment that he had put on was   *2Sa 20:8*
to the sword that was in *J.* hand   *2Sa 20:10*
one of *J.* men stood by him   *2Sa 20:11*

JOAH

J. the son of Asaph the recorder   *2Ki 18:18; 18:37; Isa 36:22*
Shebna, and *J.* unto Rab-shakeh   *2Ki 18:26*
J. his son, Iddo his son, Zerah his   *1Ch 6:21*
J. the third, and Sacar the fourth   *1Ch 26:4*
Gershonites; *J.* the son of Zimmah   *2Ch 29:12*
and Eden the son of *J.*   *2Ch 29:12*
J. the son of Joahaz the recorder   *2Ch 34:8*
and *J.*, Asaph's son, the recorder   *Isa 36:3*
Shebna and *J.* into Rab-shakeh   *Isa 36:11*

JOAHAZ

Joah the son of *J.* the recorder   *2Ch 34:8*

JOANNA

Which was the son of *J.*, which   *Lu 3:27*
and *J.* the wife of Chuza Herod's   *Lu 8:3*
It was Mary Magdalene, and *J.*   *Lu 24:10*

JOASH

that pertaineth to *J.* the Abi-ezrite   *J'g 6:11*
save the sword of Gideon the son of *J.*   *J'g 7:14*
carry him back to Amon and *J.* the king's son   *1Ki 22:26; 2Ch 18:25*
Jehosheba stole *J.*   *2Ki 11:2; 2Ch 22:11*
J. the son of Jehoahaz reigned in his stead   *2Ki 13:9*
J. the king of Israel wept over Elisha   *2Ki 13:14*
J. beat Ben-hadad three times, and recovered   *2Ki 13:25*
by the hand of Jeroboam the son of *J.*   *2Ki 14:27*
the sons of Becher, Zemira and *J.*   *1Ch 7:8*
J. the son of Shemaiah the Gibeathite   *1Ch 12:3*
and over the cellars of oil was *J.*   *1Ch 27:28*
thus *J.* remembered not the kindness   *2Ch 24:22*
so they executed judgment against *J.*   *2Ch 24:24*

JOATHAM

And Ozias begat J.; and J.   *M't 1:9*
begat

JOB

the sons of Issachar J. and   *Ge 46:13*
Shimron
a man in the land of Uz whose   *Job 1:1*
name was J.
hast thou considered my   *Job 1:8;*
servant J.   *2:3*
Satan said, Doth J. fear God   *Job 1:9*
for nought
in all this J. sinned not with   *Job 1:22;*
his lips   *2:16*
Satan went and smote J. with   *Job 2:7*
sore boils
so these three men ceased to   *Job 32:1*
answer J.
against J. was Elihu's wrath   *Job 32:2*
kindled
because they found no answer   *Job 32:3*
and condemned J.
there was none of you that   *Job 32:12*
convinced J.
mark well, O J. hearken unto   *Job 33:31*
me
what man is like J. who   *Job 34:7*
drinketh scorning
J. hath spoken without   *Job 34:35*
knowledge
my desire is that J. may be   *Job 34:36*
tried to the end
therefore doth J. open his   *Job 35:16*
mouth in vain
ye have not spoken as my   *Job 42:7;*
servant J. hath   *42:8*
take seven bullocks and go to   *Job 42:8*
my servant J.
did as Lord commanded, the   *Job 42:9*
Lord also accepted J.
the Lord gave J. twice as   *Job 42:10*
much as he had
so the Lord blessed the latter   *Job 42:12*
end of J.
no women found so fair as   *Job 42:15*
the daughters of J.
after this lived J. 140 years   *Job 42:16*
and saw his sons
so J. died, being old and full   *Job 42:17*
of days
tho' Noah, Daniel and J.   *Eze 14:14;*
were in it   *14:20*
ye have heard of the patience   *Jas 5:11*
of J.

JOB'S

when J. three friends heard of   *Job 2:11*
all

JOBAB

And Ophir, and Havilah, and   *Ge 10:29;*
J.   *1Ch 1:23*
and J. the son of Zerah of   *Ge 36:33;*
Bozrah   *1Ch 1:44*
And J. died, and Husham of   *Ge 36:34*
he sent to J. king of Madon   *Jos 11:1*
And when J. was dead,   *1Ch 1:45*
Husham
he begat of Hodesh his wife, J.   *1Ch 8:9*
Ishmerai also, and Jezliah   *1Ch 8:18*
and J.

JOCHEBED

Amram took him J. his father's   *Ex 6:20*
the name of Amram's wife   *Nu 26:59*
was J.

JOCKEYING

teaching j. men (P)   *Eph 4:14*

JOED

the son of J., the son of   *Ne 11:7*
Pedaiah

JOEL

the name of his firstborn was J.   *1Sa 8:2*
J., and Jehu the son of   *1Ch 4:35*
Josibiah
The sons of J.; Shemaiah his   *1Ch 5:4*
son
the son of J., who dwelt in   *1Ch 5:8*
Aroer

J. the chief, and Shapham the   *1Ch 5:12*
next
Heman a singer, the son of J.   *1Ch 6:33*
Elkanah, the son of J., the   *1Ch 6:36*
son of
and Obadiah, and J., Ishiah,   *1Ch 7:3*
five
J. the brother of Nathan,   *1Ch 11:38*
Mibhar
the sons of Gershom; J. the   *1Ch 15:7*
chief
Levites, for Uriel, Asaiah,   *1Ch 15:11*
and J.
appointed Heman the son of   *1Ch 15:17*
J.
Jehiel, and Zatham, and J.,   *1Ch 23:8*
three
Zetham, and J. his brother,   *1Ch 26:22*
which
Manasseh, J. the son of   *1Ch 27:20*
Pedaiah
Amasai, and J. the son of   *2Ch 29:12*
Azariah
Zabad, Zebina, Jadau, and J.   *Ezr 10:43*
And J. the son of Zichri was   *Ne 11:9*
their
word of the Lord that came to   *Joe 1:1*
J.
was spoken by the prophet J.   *Ac 2:16*

JOELAH

J., and Zebadiah, the sons of   *1Ch 12:7*

JOEZER

and Jesiah, and Azareel, and   *1Ch 12:6*
J.

JOGBEHAH

Shophan, and Jaazer, and J.   *Nu 32:35*
tents on the east of Nobah and   *J'g 8:11*
J.

JOGLI

of Dan, Bukki the son of J.   *Nu 34:22*

JOHA

And Michael, and Ispah, and   *1Ch 8:16*
J.
son of Shimri, and J. his   *1Ch 11:45*
brother

JOHANAN

J. came to Gedaliah   *2Ki 25:23;*
   Jer 40:8, 13
the sons of Josiah, the   *1Ch 3:15*
firstborn J.
Ezra went into the chamber of   *Ezr 10:6*
J.
but when J. heard of all the   *Jer 41:11*
evil
so J. obeyed not the voice of   *Jer 43:4*
the Lord

JOHN, the apostle

James and J. the sons of   *M't 4:21;*
Zebedee   *10:2; M'k 1:19; 3:17*
Jesus sent Peter and J. to   *Lu 22:8*
prepare
Peter and J. went up into the   *Ac 3:1*
temple
and as the lame man held Peter   *Ac 3:11*
and J.
when they saw the boldness of   *Ac 4:13*
Peter and J.
the apostles sent to Samaria   *Ac 8:14*
Peter and J.
Herod killed James the brother   *Ac 12:2*
of J.
signified it by his angel to his   *Re 1:1*
servant J.
J. to the seven churches which   *Re 1:4*
are in Asia
I J. who also am your brother   *Re 1:9*
and companion
I J. saw the holy city new   *Re 21:2*
Jerusalem coming

JOHN, a priest

J. and Alexander gathered   *Ac 4:6*
together

JOHN, son of Zacharias

J. had raiment of camel's hair   *M't 3:4;*
   M'k 1:6
Jesus came to be baptized, but   *M't 3:14*
J. forbad him
then J. was cast into prison   *M't 4:12;*
   M'k 1:14
then came to him the   *M't 9:14;*
disciples of J. *M'k 2:18; Lu 5:33; 7:18;*
   11:1; Joh 3:25
J. had heard the works of   *M't 11:2;*
Christ   *Lu 7:19*
go and shew J. these things   *M't 11:4;*
   Lu 7:22
Jesus began to say concerning   *M't 11:7;*
J.   *Lu 7:24*
the law prophesied till J.   *M't 11:13;*
   Lu 16:16
Herod beheaded J.   *M't 14:10;*
   M'k 6:16; Lu 9:9
all hold J. a prophet   *M't 21:26;*
   M'k 11:32; Lu 20:6
J. came in the way of   *M't 21:32*
righteousness
Herod feared J. knowing he   *M'k 6:20*
was just man
bear a son, thou shalt call his   *Lu 1:13;*
name J.   *1:60*
all men mused in their hearts   *Lu 3:15*
of J.
it was said, that J. was risen   *Lu 9:7*
from the dead
a man sent from God, whose   *Joh 1:6*
name was J.
and this is the record of J.   *Joh 1:19;*
   1:32
next day J. seeth Jesus coming   *Joh 1:29*
unto him
J. also was baptizing in Enon   *Joh 3:23*
near to Salim
for J. was not yet cast into   *Joh 3:24*
prison
that Jesus made more disciples   *Joh 4:1*
than J.
ye sent to J. and he bare   *Joh 5:33*
witness to the truth
but I have greater witness   *Joh 5:36*
than that of J.
J. did not miracle; but all   *Joh 10:41*
that J. spake
for J. truly baptized with water   *Ac 1:5;*
   11:16
when J. had first preached   *Ac 13:24*
before his coming
and as J. fulfilled his   *Ac 13:25*
course, he said whom

JOHN MARK

Peter came to house of J.   *Ac 12:12*
surnamed *Mark*
took with them J. whose   *Ac 12:25*
surname was *Mark*
and they had also J. to their   *Ac 13:5*
minister
J. departing from them,   *Ac 13:13*
returned to Jerusalem
Barnabas determined to take   *Ac 15:37*
with him J. *Mark*

JOHN'S

took up J. body   *M'k 6:29*
(A)(B)(N)(P)(R)
between some of J. disciples   *Joh 3:25*
And they said, Unto J. baptism *Ac 19:3*

JOIADA

Eliashib, and Eliashib begat   *Ne 12:10*
J.
J. begat Jonathan, and   *Ne 12:11*
Jonathan
Levites in the days of   *Ne 12:22*
Eliashib, J.
one of the sons of J., the son   *Ne 13:28*
of

JOIAKIM

Jeshua begat J., J. also begat   *Ne 12:10*
in the days of J. were priests   *Ne 12:12*
in the days of J. the son of   *Ne 12:26*
Jeshua

JOIARIB

for J. and for Elnathan, men   *Ezr 8:16*
the son of Adaiah, the son of   *Ne 11:5*
J.

the priests: Jedaiah the son of *Ne 11:10* J.
Shemaiah, and J., Jedaiah *Ne 12:6*
of J., Mattenai; of Jedaiah, *Ne 12:19* Uzzi

JOIN

they *j.* also unto our enemies *Ex 1:10*
side with our enemies (B) *Ex 1:10*
king of Judah *j.* himself with *2Ch 20:35*
made an alliance with *2Ch 20:35;*
(B) *Da 11:6*
and *j.* in afinity with the *Ezr 9:14*
people of
intermarry with the people *Ezr 9:14*
(A)
by intermarrying with (B)(R) *Ezr 9:14*
Though hand *j.* in hand, the *Pr 11:21* wicked
though hand *j.* in hand, he shall *Pr 16:5* not
unto them that *j.* house to house *Isa 5:8*
him, and *j.* his enemies *Isa 9:11* together
that *j.* themselves to the Lord *Isa 56:6*
let us *j.* ourselves to the Lord *Jer 50:5* in a
j. them one to another into *Eze 37:17* one
they shall *j.* themselves *Da 11:6* together
durst no man *j.* himself to *Ac 5:13* them
near, and *j.* thyself to this *Ac 8:29* chariot

JOINED

these were *j.* together in the *Ge 14:3* vale
met in the Siddim (B) *Ge 14:3*
they *j.* battle with them in the *Ge 14:8* vale
will my husband be *j.* unto me *Ge 29:34*
will be a companion to me *Ge 29:34* (A)
will grow attached to me (B) *Ge 29:34*
j. one to another (E) *Ex 26:17*
shoulderpieces thereof *j.* at the *Ex 28:7* two
and so it shall be *j.* together *Ex 28:7*
that they may be *j.* unto thee *Nu 18:2*
they shall be *j.* unto thee, and *Nu 18:4* keep
Israel *j.* himself unto Baal-peor *Nu 25:3*
men that were *j.* unto *Nu 25:5* Baal-peor
they *j.* battle, Israel was *1Sa 4:2* smitten
drew up to battle (A)(B)(R) *1Sa 4:2*
of the wheels were *j.* to the *1Ki 7:32* base
the seventh day the battle *1Ki 20:29* was *j.*
and *j.* affinity with Ahab *2Ch 18:1*
was allied with Ahab (A) *2Ch 18:1*
made a marriage alliance with *2Ch 18:1* (B)(R)
j. himself with him to make *2Ch 20:36* ships
thou hast *j.* thyself with *2Ch 20:37* Ahaziah
thereof, and *j.* the foundations *Ezr 4:12*
repaired the foundations *Ezr 4:12* (A)(E)(R)
digging its foundations (B) *Ezr 4:12*
all the wall was *j.* together unto *Ne 4:6*
j. with brothers (A)(B)(R) *Ne 10:29*
the people *j.* in the covenant *2Ki 23:3* (S)
such as *j.* themselves unto them *Es 9:27*
not be *j.* unto the days of the *Job 3:6* year
counted in the number of *Job 3:6* month (B)(E)(R)
They are *j.* one to another *Job 41:17*
flakes of his flesh are *j.* *Job 41:23* together
Assur also is *j.* with them: they *Ps 83:8*
j. themselves also unto *Ps 106:28* Baal-peor
to him that is *j.* to all the living *Ec 9:4*
every one that is *j.* unto them *Isa 13:15*
strangers shall be *j.* with them *Isa 14:1*
shalt not be *j.* with them in *Isa 14:20* burial
that hath *j.* himself to the Lord *Isa 56:3*
wings were *j.* one to another *Eze 1:9*

two wings of every one were *j.* *Eze 1:11*
there were courts *j.* of forty *Eze 46:22* cubits
Ephraim is *j.* to idols: let him *Ho 4:17*
Ephraim is wedded to his idols *Ho 4:17* (B)
nations shall be *j.* to the Lord *Zec 2:11*
therefore God hath *j.* together *M't 19:6;* *M'k 10:9*
and *j.* himself to a citizen of *Lu 15:15*
forced (glued) himself upon *Lu 15:15* (A)
imposed himself upon a *Lu 15:15* citizen (B)
attached himself to one of *Lu 15:15* (N)
hired himself out to a citizen *Lu 15:15* (P)
about four hundred *j.* *Ac 5:36* themselves
a number of men allied *Ac 5:36* themselves (A)
men adhered to him (B) *Ac 5:36*
had a following of four hundred *Ac 5:36* men (P)
Go up and contact that chariot *Ac 8:29* (B)
Approach this chariot (P) *Ac 8:29*
assayed to *j.* himself to the *Ac 9:26* disciples
made efforts to associate with *Ac 9:26* (B)
j. Paul (N)(R) *Ac 17:4*
i. him (A)(N)(P)(R)(S) *Ac 17:34*
house *j.* hard to the synagogue *Ac 18:7*
that ye be perfectly *j.* together *1Co 1:10*
be in perfect harmony, full *1Co 1:10* agreement (A)
be agreeable mutually in mind, *1Co 1:10* attitude (B)
be perfected together in same *1Co 1:10* mind (E)
be united in the same mind *1Co 1:10* (R)
not that he which is *j.* to an *1Co 6:16* harlot
who unites with a prostitute *1Co 6:16* (B)
who links himself with a harlot *1Co 6:16* (N)
he that is *j.* unto the Lord is *1Co 6:17* one
who is united to the Lord *1Co 6:17* (A)(R)
who unites with the Lord (B) *1Co 6:17*
who links himself to Christ (N) *1Co 6:17*
i. together (A)(R) *Eph 2:21*
the whole body fitly *j.* *Eph 4:16* together
united by every contributing *Eph 4:16* ligament (B)
fitly framed and knit together *Eph 4:16* (E)
Bonded and knit together *Eph 4:16* (P)
knit together (P) *Eph 4:16*
shall be *j.* unto his wife, and *Eph 5:31*

JOINING

j. to the wing of the other *2Ch 3:12* cherub

JOININGS

their *j.* (A) *Ex 27:10;* *36:38; 38:10-12, 17, 19, 28*
doors of the gates, and for the *1Ch 22:3* *j.*

JOINT

of Jacob's thigh was out of *j.* *Ge 32:25*
Jacob's thigh was dislocated *Ge 32:25*
hollow of Jacob's thigh was *Ge 32:25* strained (E)
and all my bones are out of *j.* *Ps 22:14*
broken tooth, and a foot out *Pr 25:19* of *j.*
j. inheritors (B) *Eph 3:6*
by that which every *j.* *Eph 4:16* supplieth

JOINT-HEIRS

heirs of God, and *j.* with *Ro 8:17* Christ

fellow heirs with Christ *Ro 8:17* (A)(R)
God's heirs jointly with Christ *Ro 8:17* (B)
God's heirs and Christ's *Ro 8:17* fellow-heirs (N)
all that Christ claims as his *Ro 8:17* will belong to all of us as well (P)

JOINTS

between the *j.* of the harness *1Ki 22:34*
between scale armor and *1Ki 22:34* breastplate (B)(R)
between the *j.* of the harness *2Ch 18:33*
lower armor of the *2Ch 18:33* breastplate (A)
between the layers of *2Ch 18:33* breastplate and body armor (B)
between scale armor and *2Ch 18:33* breastplate (R)
the *j.* of thy thighs are like *Ca 7:1* jewels
that the *j.* of his loins were *Da 5:6* loosed
all the body by *j.* and bands *Col 2:19* having
by ligaments and sinews (B) *Col 2:19*
spirit, and of the *j.* and *Heb 4:12* marrow

JOKDEAM

And Jezreel, and J., and *Jos 15:56* Zanoah

JOKE

made a *j.* of it (A) *Ac 2:13*

JOKIM

J., and the men of Chozeba *1Ch 4:22*

JOKING

as if he were *j.* (A) *Ge 19:14*
I am *j.* (A)(B) *Pr 26:19*

JOKMEAM

and J. with her suburbs, and *1Ch 6:68*

JOKNEAM

the king of J. of Carmel, one *Jos 12:22*
to the river that is before J. *Jos 19:11*
J. with her suburbs, and *Jos 21:34* Kartah
unto the place that is beyond *1Ki 4:12* J.

JOKSHAN

she bare him Zimran, and J. *Ge 25:2;* *1Ch 1:32*
And J. begat Sheba, and *Ge 25:3* Dedan
the sons of J.; Sheba, and *1Ch 1:32* Dedan

JOKTAN

and his brother's name was J. *Ge 10:25;* *1Ch 1:19*
J. begat Almodad, and *Ge 10:26;* Sheleph *1Ch 1:20*
Jobab; all these were the sons *Ge 10:29* of J.
Joab. All these were the sons *1Ch 1:23* of J.

JOKTHEEL

and Dilean, and Mizpeh, and *Jos 15:38* J.
and called the name of it J. *2Ki 14:7* unto

JONA

Thou art Simon the son of J. *Joh 1:42*

JONADAB

had a friend, whose name was *2Sa 13:3* J.

and *J.* was a very subtle man   2Sa 13:3
J. said unto him, Lay thee   2Sa 13:5
down
and *J.*, the son of Shimeah   2Sa 13:32
David's
And *J.* said unto the king,   2Sa 13:35
Behold
for *J.* the son of Rechab our   Jer 35:6
father
have we obeyed the voice of *J.*   Jer 35:8
that *J.* our father commanded   Jer 35:10
us
the words of *J.* the son of   Jer 35:14
Rechab
the sons of *J.* the son of   Jer 35:16
Rechab
obeyed the commandment of   Jer 35:18
J.
J. the son of Rechab shall not   Jer 35:19

JONAH

by the hand of his servant *J.*   2Ki 14:25
the word of the Lord came   Jon 1:1
unto *J.*
J. rose up to flee unto Tarshish   Jon 1:3
J. was gone down into the sides   Jon 1:5
of
cast lots, and the lot fell upon   Jon 1:7
J.
took up *J.*, and cast him forth   Jon 1:15
into
a great fish to swallow up *J.*   Jon 1:17
J. was in the belly of the fish   Jon 1:17
three
J. prayed unto the Lord his   Jon 2:1
God
it vomited out *J.* upon the dry   Jon 2:10
land
word of the Lord came unto *J.*   Jon 3:1
So *J.* arose, and went unto   Jon 3:3
Nineveh
J. began to enter into the city a   Jon 3:4
But it displeased *J.* exceedingly   Jon 4:1
J. went out of the city, and sat   Jon 4:5
on
and made it to come up over *J.*   Jon 4:6
J. was exceeding glad of the   Jon 4:6
gourd
the sun beat upon the head of   Jon 4:8
J.
God said unto *J.*, Doest thou   Jon 4:9
well

JONAN

Joseph, which was the son of *J.*   Lu 3:30

JONAS

it, but the sign of the prophet   M't 12:39
J.
For as *J.* was three days and   M't 12:40
three
repented at the preaching of   M't 12:41;
J.   Lu 11:32
behold, a greater than *J.* is   M't 12:41;
here   Lu 11:32
it, but the sign of the prophet   M't 16:4
J.
it, but the sign of the *J.* the   Lu 11:29
prophet
J. was a sign unto the   Lu 11:30
Ninevites
Simon, son of *J.*, lovest   Joh 21:15;
thou   21:16-17

JONATHAN

J. and his sons were priests to   J'g 18:30
Dan
a thousand men were with *J.*   1Sa 13:2
in Gibeah
but with Saul and *J.* were   1Sa 13:22
swords found
the people knew not that *J.*   1Sa 14:3
was gone
J. climbed up upon his hands   1Sa 14:13
and his feet
J. heard not when his father   1Sa 14:27
charged the people
though it be in *J.* my son, he   1Sa 14:39
shall surely die
I and *J.* my son will be on   1Sa 14:40
the other side
J. was taken; thou shalt   1Sa 14:42;
surely die, *J.*   14:44
so the people rescued *J.* that   1Sa 14:45
he died not

the soul of *J.* was knit with   1Sa 18:1
the soul of David
but *J.* Saul's son delighted   1Sa 19:2
much in David
J. spake good of David to   1Sa 19:4
Saul his father
let not *J.* know this lest he be   1Sa 20:3
grieved
the Lord do so, and much   1Sa 20:13
more to *J.*
J. made a covenant with the   1Sa 20:16
house of David
then Saul's anger was kindled   1Sa 20:30
against *J.*
J. knew it was determined to   1Sa 20:33
slay David
J. cried after the lad; *J.* and   1Sa 20:37;
David knew   20:39
J. arose and went to David   1Sa 23:16
into the wood
the Philistines slew *J.*   1Sa 31:2;
  1Ch 10:2
Saul and *J.* his son are dead   2Sa 1:4
also
the bow of *J.* turned not back,   2Sa 1:22
sword of Saul
Saul and *J.* were lovely in   2Sa 1:23
their lives
I am distressed for thee, my   2Sa 1:26
brother *J.*
J. had a son that was lame of   2Sa 4:4;
his feet   9:3
J. the son of Abiathar   2Sa 15:27;
  15:36; 1Ki 1:42-43
now *J.* and Ahimaaz stayed   2Sa 17:17
by En-rogel
the king spared Mephibosheth   2Sa 21:7
the son of *J.*
David took the bones of Saul   2Sa 21:12
and *J.*
J. the son of Shimea slew   2Sa 21:21;
him   1Ch 20:7
of the sons of Jashen, *J.* a   2Sa 23:32
valiant man
the sons of Jada, Jether, and   1Ch 2:32
J.
the sons of Hashem, *J.*   1Ch 11:34
Ahiham, and Eliphal
also *J.* David's uncle was a   1Ch 27:32
counsellor
Ebed the son of *J.* went up with   Ezr 8:6
Ezra
only *J.* and Jehaziah were   Ezr 10:15
employed
Joiada begat *J.*; of Melicu, *J.*   Ne 12:11;
  12:14
Zechariah the son of *J.* with a   Ne 12:35
trumpet
put Jeremiah in prison in the   Jer 37:15
house of *J.*
not to return to the house of   Jer 37:20;
J.   38:26
Johanan and *J.* came to   Jer 40:8
Gedaliah to Mizpeh

JONATHAN'S

J. lad gathered up the arrows   1Sa 20:38
shew him kindness for *J.* sake   2Sa 9:1
to return to *J.* house, to die   Jer 38:26
there

JONATH-ELEM-RECHOKIM

the chief Musician upon *J.*   Ps 56 title

JOPPA

it to thee in floats by sea to *J.*   2Ch 2:16
trees from Lebanon to the sea   Ezr 3:7
of *J.*
of the Lord, and went down to   Jon 1:3
J.
there was at *J.* a certain   Ac 9:36
disciple
as Lydda was nigh to *J.*, and   Ac 9:38
it was known throughout all *J.*   Ac 9:42
he tarried many days in *J.* with   Ac 9:43
now send men to *J.*, and call   Ac 10:5
for one
unto them, he sent them to *J.*   Ac 10:8
and certain brethren from *J.*   Ac 10:23
Send therefore to *J.*, and call   Ac 10:32
I was in the city of *J.* praying   Ac 11:5
Send men to *J.*, and call for   Ac 11:13
Simon

JORAH

The children of *J.*, an hundred   Ezr 2:18

JORAI

Sheba, and *J.*, and Jachan   1Ch 5:13

JORAM

Toi sent *J.* his son to king   2Sa 8:10
David
J. of Ahab; *J.* son of   2Ki 8:16
Jehoshaphat
Syrians wounded *J.*; *J.* went   2Ki 8:28;
to Jezreel   8:29
Jehu son of Jehoshaphat   2Ki 9:14
conspired against *J.*
drew a bow and smote *J.*   2Ki 9:24
between his arms
Jehosheba the daughter of *J.*   2Ki 11:2
took Joash
of the Levites, *J.* over   1Ch 26:25
treasures
destruction of Ahaziah by   2Ch 22:7
coming to *J.*
Josaphat begat *J.* and *J.*   M't 1:8
begat Ozias

JORDAN

Lot chose him all the plain of   Ge 13:11
the border shall go down to   Nu 34:12;
J.   Jos 13:27; 18:12
when ye are come to *J.* stand   Jos 3:8
still in *J.*
the ark passeth over before   Jos 3:11
you into *J.*
J. overfloweth all his banks in   Jos 3:15
harvest
take twelve stones out of the   Jos 4:3
midst of *J.*
commanded the priests, Come   Jos 4:17
ye up out of *J.*
the Lord your God dried the   Jos 4:23
waters of *J.*
Lord hath made *J.* a border   Jos 22:25
between us
they took the fords of *J.*   J'g 3:28;
  7:24; 12:5
then they slew him at the   J'g 12:6
passages of *J.*
the king returned and came   2Sa 19:15
to *J.*
Shimei came down to meet me   1Ki 2:8
at *J.*
in plain of *J.* did the king   1Ki 7:46;
cast them in clay ground   2Ch 4:17
Elijah by the brook Cherith   1Ki 17:3;
before *J.*   17:5
tarry here, Lord hath sent me   2Ki 2:6
to *J.*
they two stood by *J.*; Elisha   2Ki 2:7;
stood by *J.*   2:9
saying, Go and wash in *J.*   2Ki 5:10
seven times
Naaman dipped himself seven   2Ki 5:14
times in *J.*
let us go, we pray thee, to *J.*   2Ki 6:2
and take a beam
and they went after the   2Ki 7:15
Syrians to *J.*
he trusteth that he can draw   Job 40:23
up *J.*
I will remember thee from the   Ps 42:6
land of *J.*
the sea fled, *J.* was driven   Ps 114:3;
back   114:5
how wilt thou do in the swelling   Jer 12:5
of *J.*
jungle of the *J.* (B)(R)   Jer 12:5;
  49:19; 50:44
like a lion from the swelling   Jer 49:19;
of *J.*   50:44
for the pride of *J.* is   Zec 11:3
spoiled
were baptized of him in *J.*   M't 3:6;
  M'k 1:5, 9
then cometh Jesus from   M't 3:13
Galilee to *J.* to be baptized

BEYOND JORDAN

the floor of Atad which is   Ge 50:10
beyond *J.*
called Abel-mizraim, which is   Ge 50:11
beyond *J.*
see the good land that is   De 3:25
beyond *J.*
did to the kings of Amorites   Jos 9:10
beyond *J.*
inheritance Moses gave them   Jos 13:8;
beyond *J.*   18:7

Gilead abode *beyond J.* Dan in   *J'g 5:17*
ships
land of Zebulun and Naphtali   *Isa 9:1;*
beyond J. in Galilee of nations *M't 4:15*
these things done in   *Joh 1:28*
Bethabara *beyond J.*
he that was with thee *beyond Joh 3:26*
J. baptizeth

ON OTHER SIDE JORDAN

Gerizim, Ebal, are they not   *De 11:30*
on other side J.
been content and dwelt *on*   *Jos 7:7*
other side J.
Reuben, Gad, and half the   *Jos 12:1;*
tribe *on the other side J.* 13:27; 14:3;
                   17:5; 22:4
on other side J. Bezer,   *Jos 20:8*
Ramoth, cities of refuge
Amorites who dwelt *on the*   *Jos 24:8*
other side J.
brought heads of Oreb, Zeeb   *J'g 7:25*
on other side J.
Israel *on other side J.*   *J'g 10:8*
oppressed by the Amorites
they *on other side J.* forsook *1Sa 31:7*
their cities
to children of Merari cities *on 1Ch 6:78*
other side J.
on the other side J. were   *1Ch 12:37*
120,000 men

ON THIS SIDE JORDAN

our inheritance is fallen *on*   *Nu 32:19;*
this side J. eastward   32:32; 34:15;
               Jos 1:14-15; 22:7
give three cities *on this side Nu 35:14;*
J.   *De 4:41*
on this side J. Moses began to   *De 1:5*
declare this law
we took the land *on this side J. De 3:8*
from Arnon
kings *on this side J.* gathered   *Jos 9:1*
against Joshua
of Hebronites 1700 officers   *1Ch 26:30*
this side J.

OVER JORDAN

with my staff I passed *over*   *Ge 32:10*
this *J.*
give us this land, bring us not *Nu 32:5*
over J.
if ye will go all of you armed *Nu 32:21*
over J.
we will pass *over J.* armed   *Ge 32:32*
before the Lord
when passed *over J.* into   *Nu 33:51;*
land of Canaan *35:10; De 12:10; 27:4,*
                         12
thou shalt not go *over J.*   *De 3:27;*
                4:21; 31:2
I must die in this land, I must *De 4:22*
not go *over J.*
thou art to pass *over J.* this day *De 9:1;*
                      11:31
go *over* this *J.* thou and all this *Jos 1:2*
people
within three days ye shall pass *Jos 1:11*
over J.
the people were passed clean *Jos 3:17;*
over J.   4:1
Israel came *over* this *J.* on dry *Jos 4:22*
land
brought this people *over J.* to   *Jos 7:7*
deliver us
ye went *over J.* and came   *Jos 24:11*
unto Jericho
Ammon passed *over J.* to fight *J'g 10:9*
some of the Hebrews went   *1Sa 13:7*
over J.
Abner and his men passed   *2Sa 2:29*
over J.
David and the people passed *2Sa 17:22*
over J.
Absalom and all Israel   *2Sa 17:24*
passed *over J.*
Judah came to conduct the   *2Sa 19:15;*
king *over J.*   19:31
these are they that passed *1Ch 12:15*
over J.
David passed *over J.* against *1Ch 19:17*
the Syrians

JORIM

Eliezer, which was the son of *J. Lu 3:29*

JORKOAM

begat Raham, the father of *J. 1Ch 2:44*

JOSABAD

Johanan, and *J.* the   *1Ch 12:4*
Gederathite

JOSAPHAT

Asa begat *J.;* and *J.* begat   *M't 1:8*
Joram

JOSE

Which was the son of *J.,* which *Lu 3:29*

JOSEDECH

to Joshua the son of *J.,* the   *Hag 1:1;*
high   1:12; 2:2
spirit of Joshua the son of *J.,* *Hag 1:14*
the
Joshua, son of *J.,* the high   *Hag 2:4*
priest
the head of Joshua the son of *Zec 6:11*
J.

JOSEPH

she called his name *J.* and   *Ge 30:24*
said
Jacob put Rachel and *J.*   *Ge 33:2*
hindermost
sons of Jacob twelve, the   *Ge 35:24;*
sons of Rachel, *J.*   *46:19; 1Ch 2:2*
and Benjamin
J. brought to his father their *Ge 37:2*
evil report
Israel loved *J.*   *Ge 37:3*
J. dreamed a dream   *Ge 37:5*
his brethren sold *J.*   *Ge 37:8*
J. is rent in pieces   *Ge 37:33*
but the Lord was with *J. Ge 39:2; 39:21*
his master's wife cast her eyes *Ge 39:7*
upon *J.*
the chief butler told his dream *Ge 40:9*
to *J.*
yet did not the chief butler *Ge 40:23*
remember *J.*
they brought *J.* out of the   *Ge 41:14*
dungeon
J. 30 years old when he stood *Ge 41:46*
before Pharaoh
J. gathered corn as the sand *Ge 41:49*
of the sea
go to *J.; J.* knew his brethren *Ge 41:55;*
                     42:8
J. is not; the man did as *J. Ge 42:36;*
bade   43:17
J. made haste, for his bowels *Ge 43:30*
did yearn
I am *J.;* say, Thus saith thy *Ge 45:3;*
son *J.*   9
they told him, saying, *J.* is   *Ge 45:26;*
yet alive   45:28
J. shall put his hand upon   *Ge 46:4*
thine eyes
J. went up to meet Israel his *Ge 46:29*
father
J. nourished his father and   *Ge 47:12*
his brethren
money failed, all the Egyptians *Ge 47:15*
Israel must die, and he called *Ge 47:29*
his son *J.*
one told Jacob, Thy son *J.*   *Ge 48:2*
cometh to thee
J. brought them from between *Ge 48:12*
his knees
Jacob blessed *J.* and said,   *Ge 48:15*
God bless the lads
J. is a fruitful bough, even a *Ge 49:22*
bough by a well
blessing shall be on head of *Ge 49:26*
J. and on him
and *J.* went up to bury his   *Ge 50:7*
father
J. will peradventure hate us *Ge 50:15*
and requite
and they sent a messenger to *Ge 50:16*
J. saying
J. wept when they spake unto *Ge 50:17*
him
J. took an oath of the   *Ge 50:25*
children of Israel
new king which knew not *J.*   *Ex 1:8;*
                   Ac 7:18

Moses took the bones of *J.*   *Ex 13:19*
with him
sons of *J.* Manasseh,   *Nu 26:28;*
Ephraim   26:37
these on Gerizim to bless,   *De 27:12*
Judah, *J.*
of *J.* he said, Blessed of the *De 33:13*
Lord be his land
let the blessing come upon the *De 33:16*
head of *J.*
hast redeemed the sons of   *Ps 77:15*
Jacob and *J.*
moreover he refused the   *Ps 78:67*
tabernacle of *J.*
give ear, thou that leadest *J.*   *Ps 80:1*
like a flock
this he ordained in *J.* for a   *Ps 81:5*
testimony
even *J.* who was sold for a   *Ps 105:17*
servant
write for *J.* the stick of   *Eze 37:16;*
Ephraim   37:19
tribes of Israel, *J.* shall have *Eze 47:13*
two portions
one gate of *J.* one gate of   *Eze 48:32*
Benjamin
Lord will be gracious to the   *Am 5:15*
remnant of *J.*
but they are not grieved for the *Am 6:6*
affliction of *J.*
near the ground that Jacob   *Joh 4:5*
gave to *J.*
the patriarchs sold *J.* into   *Ac 7:9*
Egypt
at the second time *J.* was made *Ac 7:13*
known
then *J.* called his father Jacob *Ac 7:14*
to him
by faith Jacob blessed the   *Heb 11:21*
sons of *J.*
J. made mention of Israel's *Heb 11:22*
departing

JOSEPH with *TRIBE*
and *CHILDREN*

of the *children* of *J.* of   *Nu 1:10;*
Ephraim   1:32
of the *tribe* of *J.* namely of   *Nu 13:11*
Manasseh
the princes of the *children* of *Nu 34:23*
J. Hanniel
the *tribe* of the sons of *J.* hath *Nu 36:5*
said well
the *children* of *J.* two tribes   *Jos 14:4;*
                     16:4
the lot of *children* of *J.* fell   *Jos 16:1*
from Jordan
the *children* of *J.* spake to   *Jos 17:14;*
Joshua   17:16
in these dwelt the *children* of *1Ch 7:29*
J.
of the *tribe* of *J.* were sealed   *Re 7:8*
12,000

JOSEPH, husband of Mary

Jacob begat *J.* the husband of *M't 1:16*
Mary
when as his mother Mary was *M't 1:18*
espoused to *J.*
J. her husband being a just   *M't 1:19*
man was minded
J. did as angel of Lord had   *M't 1:24*
bidden him
the angel of the Lord   *M't 2:13;*
appeared to *J.*   2:19
his name was *J.* of the house of *Lu 1:27*
David
J. also went up from Galilee to *Lu 2:4*
be taxed
the shepherds found Mary, *J.*   *Lu 2:16*
and the babe
and *J.* and his mother knew   *Lu 2:43*
not of it
being as was supposed, the son *Lu 3:23*
of *J.*

JOSEPH,
the name of divers men

of the tribe of Issachar, Igal   *Nu 13:7*
son of *J.*
of the sons of Asaph, Zaccur, *1Ch 25:2;*
J.   25:9
Shallum, *J.* had taken strange *Ezr 10:42*
wives

of Shebaniah, J. was a priest　Ne 12:14
Jesus' disciple, J. of　M't 27:57;
Arimathea　27:59; M'k 15:43, 45;
　Lu 23:50; Joh 19:38
who was the son of J.　Lu 3:24; 26:30
they appointed two, J. called　Ac 1:23
Barsabas

JOSEPH'S

they took J. coat and killed a　Ge 37:31
kid
the Egyptian's house for J.　Ge 39:5
sake
he left all that he had in J.　Ge 39:6
hand
J. master took him, and put　Ge 39:20
him
prison committed to J. hand　Ge 39:22
all the
his hand, and put it upon J.　Ge 41:42
hand
called J. name　Ge 41:45
Zaphnath-paaneah
J. ten brethren went down to　Ge 42:3
buy
Benjamin, J. brother, Jacob　Ge 42:4
sent
J. brethren came, and bowed　Ge 42:6
down
man brought the men into J.　Ge 43:17;
house　43:24
they were brought into J.　Ge 43:18
house
near to the steward of J.　Ge 43:19
house
and his brethren came to J.　Ge 44:14
house
house, saying, J. brethren are　Ge 45:16
come
Israel beheld J. sons, and said,　Ge 48:8
Who
J. brethren saw that their　Ge 50:15
father
were brought up upon J.　Ge 50:23
knees
ruler; but the birthright was J.　1Ch 5:2
And they said, Is not this J.　Lu 4:22
son
J. kindred was made known　Ac 7:13
unto

JOSES

James, and J., and Simon　M't 13:55
Mary the mother of James　M't 27:56
and J.
the brother of James, and J.　M'k 6:3
mother of James the less and　M'k 15:40
of J.
Mary the mother of J.　M'k 15:47
beheld where
J., who was surnamed　Ac 4:36
Barnabas

JOSHAH

and J. the son of Amaziah　1Ch 4:34

JOSHAPHAT

Maachah, and J. the　1Ch 11:43
Mithnite

JOSHAVIAH

Jeribai, and J. the sons of　1Ch 11:46
Elnaam

JOSHBEKASHAH

J., Mallothi, Hothir, and　1Ch 25:4
The seventeenth to J., he, his　1Ch 25:24
sons

JOSHUA

J. discomfited Amalek with the　Ex 17:13
sword
write this, and rehearse it in　Ex 17:14
the ears of J.
and Moses rose up and his　Ex 24:13
minister J.
when J. heard the noise of the　Ex 32:17
people
J. departed not out of the　Ex 33:11
tabernacle
save Caleb and J.　Nu 14:30;
　14:38; 26:65; 32:12

take thee J.; he set J. before　Nu 27:18;
Eleazar　27:22
Eleazar and J. shall divide the　Nu 34:17
land
but J. shall go in thither　De 1:38; 31:3
charge J. and encourage him　De 3:28;
　31:23
J. was full of the spirit of　De 34:9
wisdom
then J. commanded the officers　Jos 1:10
J. sent two men to spy secretly　Jos 2:1
the land
Lord said to J.　Jos 3:7;
　5:9; 6:2; 7:10; 8:18; 10:8
the children of Israel did as J.　Jos 4:8
commanded
on that day the Lord　Jos 4:14
magnified J. in sight
their children, them J.　Jos 5:7
circumcised
J. fell on his face to the earth　Jos 5:14
and did worship
and J. did so; so the Lord was　Jos 5:15;
with J.　6:27
J. rent his clothes; pursued　Jos 7:6;
after J.　8:16
then J. built an altar to the　Jos 8:30
Lord
which J. read not before all　Jos 8:35
the congregation
then spake J. and said, Sun,　Jos 10:12
stand still
and their land did J. take at　Jos 10:42
one time
J. did unto them as the Lord　Jos 11:9
bade him
now J. was old and stricken　Jos 13:1;
in years　23:1
so J. blessed Caleb and gave　Jos 14:13
him Hebron
J. cast lots for them before　Jos 18:10
the Lord
Israel gave an inheritance to　Jos 19:49
J.
J. blessed the Reubenites and　Jos 22:6
Gadites
J. gathered the tribes of　Jos 24:1
Israel to Shechem
so J. made a covenant with　Jos 24:25
the people
J. the servant of the Lord　Jos 24:29;
died　J'g 2:8
Israel served the Lord all the　Jos 24:31;
days of J. and of the　J'g 2:7
elders that overlived J.
the cart came into the field of　1Sa 6:14
J.
which he spake by J. the son　1Ki 16:34
of Nun
in the entering in of the gate　2Ki 23:8
of J.
J. son of Josedech　Hag 1:1;
　1:2, 14; 2:2, 4
and he shewed me J. the　Zec 3:1
high priest
now J. was clothed with filthy　Zec 3:3
garments
behold, the stone that I have　Zec 3:9
laid before J.
make crowns, set them upon　Zec 6:11
the head of J.

JOSIAH

house of David, J. by name　1Ki 13:2
made J. king　2Ki 21:24;
　21:26; 22:1, 3; 2Ch 33:25; 34:1
J. took away, J. put away　2Ki 23:16;
　23:24
rest of the acts of J.　2Ki 23:28;
　2Ch 35:26
Amon his son, J. his son　1Ch 3:14
the sons of J. were　1Ch 3:15
J. kept the passover　2Ch 35:1; 35:18-19
J. had prepared the temple　2Ch 35:20
archers shot at king J.　2Ch 35:23
Jerusalem mourned for J.　2Ch 35:24;
　35:25
days of J. son of Amon　Jer 1:2;
　3:6; 36:2
Jehoiakim the son of J.　Jer 1:3;
　22:18; 25:1; 26:1; 27:1; 35:1; 36:1, 9;
　45:1; 46:2
Zedekiah the son of J.　Jer 1:3; 37:1
Shallum the son of J.　Jer 22:11
days of J. the son of Amon,　Zep 1:1
king of
house of J. the son of　Zec 6:10
Zephaniah

JOSIAS

Amon begat J. and J. begat　M't 1:10;
　1:11

JOSIBIAH

Jehu the son of J.　1Ch 4:35

JOSIPHIAH

the son of J.　Ezr 8:10

JOSTLE

j. one against another (S)　Na 2:4

JOT

one j. or tittle shall in no wise　M't 5:18

JOTBAH

daughter of Haruz of J.　2Ki 21:19

JOTBATH

from Gudgodah to J.　De 10:7

JOTBATHAH

and pitched at J.　Nu 33:33
removed from J. and　Nu 33:34
encamped

JOTHAM

J. youngest son of Jerubbaal　J'g 9:5
escaped
on them came the curse of J.　J'g 9:57
son of Jerubbaal
J. judged the people　2Ki 15:5;
　2Ch 26:21
the sons of Jahdai, Regem　1Ch 2:47
and J.
Amaziah his son, Azariah his　1Ch 3:12
son, J. his son
were reckoned by genealogies　1Ch 5:17
in the days of J.

JOURNEY

the Lord had made his j.　Ge 24:21
prosperous
his trip successful (A)(B)　Ge 24:21
made my j. successful (B)　Ge 24:46
Jacob went on his j. and came　Ge 29:1
to the east
went briskly and cheerfully on　Ge 29:1
his way (A)
Jacob then traveled on (B)　Ge 29:1
Laban pursued after him　Ge 31:23
seven days' j.
pursued after Jacob (A)　Ge 31:23
pursuit of him seven days　Ge 31:23
(B)(R)
let us take our j.　Ge 33:12
travel on together (B)　Ge 33:12
Israel took his j.　Ge 40:1
they took their j. from　Ex 13:20
Succoth
they trekked on from Succoth　Ex 13:20
(B)
they moved on from Succoth　Ex 13:20
(R)
Israelites took their j. from　Ex 16:1
Elim
Israelites set out from Elim　Ex 16:1
(B)(R)
be in a j. yet shall keep the　Nu 9:10
passover
is on a long trip (B)　Nu 9:10
is not in a j. and forbeareth to　Nu 9:13
keep passover
and not traveling (B)　Nu 9:13
they first took their j.　Nu 10:13
according to the
they broke camp (B)　Nu 10:13
they set out for the first time　Nu 10:13
(R)
there are eleven days' j. from　De 1:2
Horeb
arise, take thy j. before the　De 10:11
people
take victuals with you for your　Jos 9:11
j.
become old, by reason of the　Jos 9:13
very long j.
the j. thou takest is not for thy　J'g 4:9
honour

and the Lord sent thee on a *j.* *1Sa 15:18*
sent you on a mission *1Sa 15:18*
(A)(R)
sent you out under orders *1Sa 15:18*
(B)
camest thou not from thy *j.* *2Sa 11:10*
or he is in a *j.* *1Ki 18:27*
he is on a trip (B) *1Ki 18:27*
the *j.* is great *1Ki 19:7*
fetched a compass of seven *2Ki 3:9*
days *j.*
roundabout march for seven *2Ki 3:9*
days (B)
made a circuitous march seven *2Ki 3:9*
days (B)
for how long shall thy *j.* be *Ne 2:6*
how long will you be gone *Ne 2:6*
(B)(R)
the good man is gone a long *j.* *Pr 7:19*
nor scrip for your *j.* nor two *M't 10:10*
coats
no pack for the road (N) *M't 10:10*
take nothing for their *j.* *M'k 6:8; Lu 9:3*
nothing for the trip (B) *M'k 6:8*
take nothing for the road (P) *M'k 6:8*
a friend of mine in his *j.* is *Lu 11:6*
come to me
come to me from a trip (B) *Lu 11:6*
I must *j.* today (P) *Lu 13:33*
the younger took his *j.* into a *Lu 15:13*
far country
traveled to a distant country *Lu 15:13*
(B)
left home for a distant *Lu 15:13*
country (N)
went off to a foreign land (P) *Lu 15:13*
Jesus wearied with his *j.* sat *Joh 4:6*
thus
wearied by his travel (B) *Joh 4:6*
might have a prosperous *j.* to *Ro 1:10*
come
be prospered and come to you *Ro 1:10*
(A)
be sped on my way to visit you *Ro 1:10*
(B)
be prospered by the will of *Ro 1:10*
God to come to you (E)
succeed at long last in coming *Ro 1:10*
to (N)(R)
at long last, to come to Rome *Ro 1:10*
(P)
for I trust to see you in my *j.* *Ro 15:24*
that ye may bring me on my *j.* *1Co 16:6*
may escort me wherever I go *1Co 16:6*
(B)
help me on my way (N) *1Co 16:6*
bring Zenas and Apollos on *Tit 3:13*
their *j.*
whom if thou bring forward on *3Jo 6*
their *j.*

DAY'S JOURNEY

the quails fall a *day's j.* on *Nu 11:31*
this side
himself went a *day's j.* into *1Ki 19:4*
wilderness
began to enter city a *day's j.* *Jon 3:4*
and cried
one day's travel (B) *Jon 3:4*
went a *day's j.* among their *Lu 2:44*
acquaintance
traveled a day (B) *Lu 2:44*
is from Jerusalem a sabbath *Ac 1:12*
day's j.

JOURNEYED

that as they *j.* they found a *Ge 11:2*
plain
in moving in the East (B) *Ge 11:2*
as men migrated in the east *Ge 11:2*
(R)
Abram *j.* going on toward the *Ge 12:9;*
south *20:1*
Abram traveled on (B) *Ge 12:9*
Lot *j.* east *Ge 13:11*
he traveled east (A) *Ge 13:11*
Lot moved eastward (B) *Ge 13:11*
Jacob *j.* to Succoth *Ge 33:17*
Israel *j.* toward Bethel, and the *Ge 35:5*
terror
They broke camp (B) *Ge 35:5*
j. from Bethel *Ge 35:16*
They moved on from Bethel *Ge 35:16*
(B)
j. to the tower of Edar *Ge 35:21*
cloud not taken up, they *j.* *Ex 40:37;*
not *Nu 9:21*

they would not move on until *Ex 40:37*
(B)
they did not go onward till *Ex 40:37*
(R)
after that the children of *Nu 9:17;*
Israel *j.* *9:18*
Israel would break camp (B) *Nu 9:17;*
9:19
after that Israel set out (R) *Nu 9:17;*
9:19-20
kept the charge of the Lord, *Nu 9:19*
and *j.* not
at the commandment of the *Nu 9:20;*
Lord they *j.* *9:23*
they would decamp (B) *Nu 9:20*
j. not till Miriam was brought *Nu 12:15*
in again
people did not leave (B) *Nu 12:15*
people did not set out on (R) *Nu 12:15*
came to the house of Micah as *J'g 17:8*
he *j.*
in his travels he came (B) *J'g 17:8*
as Saul *j.* he came near to *Ac 9:3*
Damascus
as he traveled he came (B) *Ac 9:3*
still on road Damascus (N) *Ac 9:3*
the men which *j.* with him *Ac 9:7;*
stood *26:13*
who had taken the road with *Ac 9:7*
him (B)
men travelling with him *Ac 9:7*
(N)(R)

JOURNEYING

make trumpets for *j.* of the *Nu 10:2*
camps
for breaking camp (B)(R) *Nu 10:2*
we are *j.* to the place of *Nu 10:29*
which Lord said
we are on our way to the *Nu 10:29*
place (B)
we are setting out (R) *Nu 10:29*
and as he went *j.* towards *Lu 13:22*
Jerusalem
Making his way to Jerusalem *Lu 13:22*
(B)
he went on his way (P)(R) *Lu 13:22*

JOURNEYS

Abram went on his *j.* from the *Ge 13:3*
South
he journeyed on (A) *Ge 13:3*
he traveled by stages (B) *Ge 13:3*
j. according to the *Ex 17:1*
commandment
moved on from the wilderness *Ex 17:1*
(A)(R)
traveled by stages from (B) *Ex 17:1*
taken up, they went on in *j.* *Ex 40:36;*
Nu 10:12
move ahead on their trek (B) *Ex 40:36*
the cloud was on tabernacle *Ex 40:38*
thro all their *j.*
during all their travels (B) *Ex 40:38*
they shall blow an alarm for *Nu 10:6*
their *j.*
start to break camp (B) *Nu 10:6*
shall set out (R) *Nu 10:6*
these are the *j.* of Israel with *Nu 33:1;*
armies *33:2*
this is the itinerary of (B) *Nu 33:1*
these are the stages of (R) *Nu 33:1*

JOY

came out to meet king Saul *1Sa 18:6*
with *j.*
for there was *j.* in Israel *1Ch 12:40*
singers, by lifting up the *1Ch 15:16*
voice with *j.*
went to bring the ark of the *1Ch 15:25*
covenant with *j.*
now have I seen with *j.* the *1Ch 29:17*
people offer
to go again to Jerusalem *2Ch 20:27*
with *j.*
not discern noise of the shout *Ezr 3:13*
of *j.*
dedication of the house of *Ezr 6:16*
God with *j.*
and kept the feast seven days *Ezr 6:22*
with *j.*
the *j.* of the Lord is your *Ne 8:10*
strength
the *j.* of Jerusalem was heard *Ne 12:43*
afar off
the Jews had light, *j.* and *Es 8:16*
honour

turned from sorrow to *j.*, make *Es 9:22*
them days of feasting and *j.*
behold, this is the *j.* of his way *Job 8:19*
the *j.* of the hypocrite is but *Job 20:5*
for a moment
I caused the widow's heart to *Job 29:13*
sing for *j.*
and he will see his face with *Job 33:26*
j.
and sorrow is turned into *j.* *Job 41:22*
before him
in thy presence is fulness of *j.* *Ps 16:11*
offer in his tabernacles *Ps 27:6*
sacrifices of *j.*
but *j.* cometh in the morning *Ps 30:5*
I went with the voice of *j.* and *Ps 42:4*
praise
then will I go to God my *Ps 43:4*
exceeding *j.*
the *j.* of the whole earth is *Ps 48:2*
mount Zion
restore to me the *j.* of thy *Ps 51:12*
salvation
let the nations be glad and sing *Ps 67:4*
for *j.*
he brought forth his people *Ps 105:43*
with *j.*
they that sow in tears shall *Ps 126:5*
reap in *j.*
if I prefer not Jerusalem above *Ps 137:6*
my chief *j.*
but to the counsellors of peace *Pr 12:20*
is *j.*
a stranger not intermeddle *Pr 14:10*
with his *j.*
folly is *j.* to him destitute of *Pr 15:21*
wisdom
a man hath *j.* by the answer of *Pr 15:23*
his mouth
and the father of a fool hath *Pr 17:21*
no *j.*
it is *j.* to the just to do *Pr 21:15*
judgment
who begetteth a wise child *Pr 23:24*
shall have *j.*
I withheld not my heart from *j.* *Ec 2:10*
God giveth him wisdom, *Ec 2:26*
knowledge, and *j.*
God answered him in the *j.* of *Ec 5:20*
his heart
go thy way, eat thy bread with *j.* *Ec 9:7*
not increased the *j.* according to *Isa 9:3*
the *j.*
Lord shall have no *j.* in their *Isa 9:17*
young men
with *j.* shall ye draw water out *Isa 12:3*
of wells
j. is taken out of the plentiful *Isa 16:10*
field
j. of the harp ceaseth; *j.* is *Isa 24:8;*
darkened *24:11*
the meek shall increase their *Isa 29:19*
j. in Lord
on all houses of *j.*; a *j.* of *Isa 32:13;*
wild asses *32:14*
and rejoice even with *j.* and *Isa 35:2*
singing
with everlasting *j.* on their *Isa 35:10;*
heads *51:11*
break forth into *j.*; go out *Isa 52:9;*
with *j.* *55:12*
I will make thee a *j.* of many *Isa 60:15*
generations
to give them the oil of *j.* for *Isa 61:3*
mourning
everlasting *j.* shall be unto *Isa 61:7*
them
my servants shall sing for *j.* *Isa 65:14*
of heart
for behold, I create her *Isa 65:18*
people a *j.*
I will rejoice and *j.* in my *Isa 65:19*
people
but he shall appear to your *j.* *Isa 66:5*
rejoice for *j.* with her, all ye *Isa 66:10*
that mourn
the word was to me the *j.* of *Jer 15:16*
my heart
I will turn their mourning *Jer 31:13*
into *j.*
it shall be to me a name of *j.* a *Jer 33:9*
praise
again there shall be heard the *Jer 33:11*
voice of *j.*
since thou spakest, thou *Jer 48:27*
skippedst for *j.*
j. is taken from the plentiful *Jer 48:33*
field

the city of praise, the city of   Jer 49:25
my j.
the city, the j. of the whole   La 2:15
earth
the j. of our heart is ceased,   La 5:15
our dance
take from them the j. of their   Eze 24:25
glory
appointed, with the j. of all   Eze 36:5
their heart
rejoice not, O Israel, for j. as   Ho 9:1
other people
because j. is withered away   Joe 1:12
from men
I will j. in the God of my   Hab 3:18
salvation
he will j. over thee with   Zep 3:17
singing
he will rejoice over thee with   Zep 3:17
j.
anon with j. receiveth it   M't 13:20;
    Lu 8:13
for j. thereof goeth and   M't 13:44
selleth all he hath
enter thou into the j. of thy   M't 25:21;
Lord   25:23
the babe leaped in my womb   Lu 1:44
for j.
rejoice ye in that day, and leap   Lu 6:23
for j.
the seventy returned again   Lu 10:17
with j.
j. shall be in heaven over one   Lu 15:7
sinner that
there is j. in the presence of   Lu 15:10
the angels
while they yet believed not for   Lu 24:41
j.
this my j. therefore is fulfilled   Joh 3:29
spoken that my j. might   Joh 15:11
remain in you, and your
j. might be full
your sorrow shall be turned   Joh 16:20
into j.
for j. that a man is born into   Joh 16:21
the world
and your j. no man taketh   Joh 16:22
from you
ye shall receive, that your j.   Joh 16:24
may be full
might have my j. fulfilled in   Joh 17:13
themselves
make me full of j. with thy   Ac 2:28
countenance
disciples filled with j. and the   Ac 13:52
Holy Ghost
that I might finish my course   Ac 20:24
with j.
but we also j. in God thro' our   Ro 5:11
Lord Jesus
kingdom of God is j. in the   Ro 14:17
Holy Ghost
God fill you with all j. in   Ro 15:13
believing
may come to you with j. by   Ro 15:32
the will of God
but we are helpers of your j.   2Co 1:24
that my j. is the j. of you all   2Co 2:3
the more joyed we for the j.   2Co 7:13
of Titus
the abundance of their j.   2Co 8:2
abounded to riches
the fruit of the Spirit is love, j.   Ga 5:22
in prayer, making request with   Ph'p 1:4
j.
abide for your furtherance   Ph'p 1:25
and j. of faith
fulfil ye my j.   Ph'p 2:2
yea, I j. and rejoice with you   Ph'p 2:17
all
for the same cause also do ye   Ph'p 2:18
j. and rejoice
my j. and crown   Ph'p 4:1
received the word with j. of   1Th 1:6
Holy Ghost
what is our hope or j., ye   1Th 2:19;
are our j.   2:20
for the j. wherewith we j.   1Th 3:9
before God
that I may be filled with j.   2Ti 1:4
let me have j. of thee in the   Ph'm 20
Lord
who for the j. that was set   Heb 12:2
before him
they may do it with j. and   Heb 13:17
not with grief
count it j. when ye fall into   Jas 1:2
temptation

and your j. be turned into   Jas 4:9
heaviness
ye rejoice with j. unspeakable   1Pe 1:8
ye may be glad also with   1Pe 4:13
exceeding j.
that your j. may be full   1Jo 1:4;
    2Jo 12
I have no greater j. than to hear   3Jo 4
that my
to present you faultless with   Jude 24
exceeding j.

GREAT JOY

the people rejoiced with great   1Ki 1:40
j.
David the king rejoiced with   1Ch 29:9
great j.
so there was great j. in   2Ch 30:26
Jerusalem
God had made them rejoice   Ne 12:43
with great j.
saw the star, they rejoiced   M't 2:10
with great j.
went from sepulchre with fear   M't 28:8
and great j.
I bring you good tidings of   Lu 2:10
great j.
they returned to Jerusalem   Lu 24:52
with great j.
and there was great j. in that   Ac 8:8
city
they caused great j. to all the   Ac 15:3
brethren
for we have great j. in thy love   Ph'm 7

SHOUT, SHOUTED FOR JOY

and many shouted aloud for j.   Ezr 3:12
and all the sons of God   Job 38:7
shouted for j.
let them ever shout for j.   Ps 5:11; 35:27
shout for j. all ye that are   Ps 32:11
upright in heart
the valleys shout for j. they   Ps 65:13
also sing
and let thy saints shout for j.   Ps 132:9;
    132:16

JOYED

the more j. we for the joy of   2Co 7:13
Titus

JOYFUL

they went to their tents j. and   1Ki 8:66
glad
for the Lord hath made them   Ezr 6:22
j.
then Haman went forth that day   Es 5:9
j.
let no j. voice come therein   Job 3:7
let them that love thy name be   Ps 5:11
j. in thee
and my soul shall be j. in the   Ps 35:9
Lord
my mouth shall praise thee with   Ps 63:5
j. lips
make a j. noise to God, all ye   Ps 66:1
lands
make a j. noise to the God of   Ps 81:1
Jacob
blessed is the people that   Ps 89:15
know the j. sound
make a j. noise to the rock of   Ps 95:1
our salvation
a j. noise to him with psalms   Ps 95:2;
    98:4; 100:1
make a j. noise before the Lord   Ps 98:6
the king
let the hills be j. together before   Ps 98:8
the Lord
the barren to be a j. mother of   Ps 113:9
children
let the children of Zion be j. in   Ps 149:2
their king
let the saints be j. in glory; let   Ps 149:5
them sing
in the day of prosperity be   Ec 7:14
j. but in
sing, O heavens, and be j. O   Isa 49:13
earth
I will make them j. in my   Isa 56:7
house of prayer
my soul shall be j. in my God   Isa 61:10
I am exceeding j. in all our   2Co 7:4
tribulation

JOYFULLY

live j. with the wife whom thou   Ec 9:9
lovest
Zaccheus came down and   Lu 19:6
received him j.
ye took j. the spoiling of   Heb 10:34
your goods

JOYFULNESS

because servedst not the Lord   De 28:47
with j.
strengthened to longsuffering   Col 1:11
with j.

JOYING

absent, yet am I with you in the   Col 2:5
spirit, j.

JOYOUS

thou art full of stirs, a j. city   Isa 22:2
is this your j. city, whose   Isa 23:7
antiquity is
on all the houses of joy in the   Isa 32:13
j. city
no chastening seemeth to be   Heb 12:11
j.

JOZABAD

J., and Jediael, and Michael   1Ch 12:20
J. and Elihu, and Zilthai,   1Ch 12:20
captains
and Jerimoth, and J., and   2Ch 31:13
Eliel
Jeiel and J., chief of the   2Ch 35:9
Levites
with them was J. the son of   Ezr 8:33
Jeshua
Ishmael, Nethaneel, J., and   Ezr 10:22
Elasah
Also of the Levites; J., and   Ezr 10:23
Shimei
Azariah, J., Hanan, Pelaiah   Ne 8:7
Shabbethai and J., of the chief   Ne 11:16

JOZACHAR

For J. the son of Shimeath   2Ki 12:21

JOZADAK

stood up Jeshua the son of J.   Ezr 3:2
and Jeshua the son of J., and   Ezr 3:8
and Jeshua the son of J., and   Ezr 5:2
began
of the sons of Jeshua the son   Ezr 10:18
of J.,
the son of Jeshua, the son of   Ne 12:26
J.,

JUBAL

And his brother's name was J.   Ge 4:21

JUBILANT

j. and above reproach (N)   Jude 24

JUBILE

the trumpet of the j. to sound   Le 25:9
on
it shall be a j. unto you; and   Le 25:10
ye
A j. shall that fiftieth year be   Le 25:11
For it is the j.; it shall be holy   Le 25:12
unto
In the year of this j. ye shall   Le 25:13
return
after the j. thou shalt buy of   Le 25:15
thy
hath bought it until the year   Le 25:28
of j.
in the j. it shall go out, and he   Le 25:28
shall
it shall not go out in the j.   Le 25:30
and they shall go out in the j.   Le 25:31
shall go out in the year of j.   Le 25:33
shall serve thee unto the year   Le 25:40
of j.
was sold to him unto the year   Le 25:50
of j.
but few years unto the year of   Le 25:52
j.

then he shall go out in the year of *j.*   Le 25:54

sanctify his field from the year of *j.*   Le 27:17

if he sanctify his field after the *j.*   Le 27:18

remain, even unto the year of the *j.*   Le 27:18

field, when it goeth out in the *j.*   Le 27:21

even unto the year of the *j.*   Le 27:23

year of *j.* the field shall return   Le 27:24

when the *j.* of the children of Israel   Nu 36:4

JUCAL

and *J.* the son of Shelemiah   Jer 38:1

JUDA

thou Bethlehem, in the land of *J.*   M't 2:6

the least among the princes of *J.*   M't 2:6

of James, and Joses, and of *J.*   M'k 6:3

with haste, into a city of *J.*   Lu 1:39

of Joseph, which was the son of *J.*   Lu 3:26

of Simeon, which was the son of *J.*   Lu 3:30

Phares, which was the son of *J.*   Lu 3:33

that our Lord sprang out of *J.*   Heb 7:14

behold, the Lion of the tribe of *J.*   Re 5:5

Of the tribe of *J.* were sealed   Re 7:5

JUDAEA

Jesus was born in Bethlehem of *J.*   M't 2:1

said unto him, In Bethlehem of *J.*   M't 2:5

heard that Archelaus did reign in *J.*   M't 2:22

preaching in the wilderness of *J.*   M't 3:1

out to him Jerusalem, and all *J.*   M't 3:5

and from Jerusalem, and from *J.*   M't 4:25

the coasts of *J.* beyond Jordan   M't 19:1

be in *J.* flee into the mountains   M't 24:16

out unto him all the land of *J.*   M'k 1:5

Galilee followed him, and from *J.*   M'k 3:7

and cometh into the coasts of *J.*   M'k 10:1

that be in *J.* flee to the mountains   M'k 13:14

the days of Herod, the king of *J.*   Lu 1:5

all the hill country of *J.*   Lu 1:65

out of the city of Nazareth, into *J.*   Lu 2:4

Pontius Pilate being governor of *J.*   Lu 3:1

out of every town of Galilee, and *J.*   Lu 5:17

multitude of people out of all *J.*   Lu 6:17

him went forth throughout all *J.*   Lu 7:17

are in *J.* flee to the mountains   Lu 21:21

his disciples into the land of *J.*   Joh 3:22

He left *J.*, and departed again   Joh 4:3

that Jesus was come out of *J.*, into Galilee   Joh 4:47

he was come out of *J.*   Joh 4:54

he would not walk in *J.* (S)   Joh 7:1

Depart hence, and go into *J.*   Joh 7:3

disciples, Let us go into *J.* again   Joh 11:7

and in all *J.*, and in Samaria   Ac 1:8

dwellers in Mesopotamia, and in *J.*   Ac 2:9

Ye men of *J.*, and all ye that dwell   Ac 2:14

the regions of *J.* and Samaria   Ac 8:1

rest throughout all *J.* and Galilee   Ac 9:31

was published throughout all *J.*   Ac 10:37

and brethren that were in *J.* heard   Ac 11:1

unto the brethren which dwelt in *J.*   Ac 11:29

he went down from *J.* to Caesarea   Ac 12:19

men which came down from *J.*   Ac 15:1

there came down from *J.* a certain   Ac 21:10

and throughout all the coasts of *J.*   Ac 26:20

neither received letters out of *J.*   Ac 28:21

from them that do not believe in *J.*   Ro 15:31

be brought on my way toward *J.*   2Co 1:16

by face unto the churches of *J.*   Ga 1:22

which in *J.* are in Christ Jesus   1Th 2:14

JUDAH

therefore she called his name *J.*   Ge 29:35

the sons of Leah, *J.*, Issachar, Zebulun   Ge 35:23

J. thought Tamar to be an harlot   Ge 38:15

J. acknowledged the signet and bracelets   Ge 38:26

sons of *J.*   Ge 46:12; Nu 26:19; 1Ch 2:3; 4:1

Jacob sent *J.* before him to Joseph   Ge 46:28

J. thou art he whom thy brethren shall praise   Ge 49:8

J. is a lion's whelp, he couched as a lion   Ge 49:9

sceptre shall not depart *J.* till Shiloh come   Ge 49:10

the sons of Israel, Levi, *J.*   Ex 1:2; 1Ch 2:1

J., Nashan son of Amminadab was prince   Nu 1:7

the camp of *J.* shall pitch on the east side   Nu 2:3

all that were numbered in the camp of *J.*   Nu 2:9

Simeon, Levi, *J.* shall stand to bless   De 27:12

this is the blessing of *J.* the voice of *J.*   De 33:7

Joshua brought the family of *J.*   Jos 7:17

J. shall abide in their coast on the south   Jos 18:5

the Lord said, *J.* shall go up first   J'g 1:2

the Lord was with *J.*; fight against *J.*   J'g 1:19; 10:9

like Pharez, whom Tamar bare to *J.*   Ru 4:12

search him thro' all thousands of *J.*   1Sa 23:23

which against *J.* do shew kindness   2Sa 3:8

David reigned over *J.* seven years, six months   2Sa 5:5

the ark, Israel, and *J.* abide in tents   2Sa 11:11

J. came to Gilgal to meet the king   2Sa 19:15

David said, Go number Israel and *J.*   2Sa 24:1

Joab slew Amasa captain of host of *J.*   1Ki 2:32

J. and Israel were many as the sand by sea   1Ki 4:20

J. and Israel dwelt safely under Solomon   1Ki 4:25

came man of God out of *J.*   1Ki 13:1; 2Ki 23:17

J. did evil in the sight of the Lord   1Ki 14:22

Abijam reigned over *J.*; Asa over *J.*   1Ki 15:1; 15:9

Baasha went up against *J.*   1Ki 15:17; 2Ch 16:1

Jehoshaphat began to reign over *J.*   1Ki 22:41

yet the Lord would not destroy *J.*   2Ki 8:19

Edom revolted from *J.*   2Ki 8:20; 8:22; 2Ch 21:8, 10

Ahaziah began to reign over *J.*   2Ki 9:29

to fall, thou and *J.* with thee   2Ki 14:10; 2Ch 25:19

J. was put to the worse   2Ki 14:12; 2Ch 25:22

Azariah restored Elath to *J.*   2Ki 14:22; 2Ch 26:2

the Lord began to send against *J.* Rezin   2Ki 15:37

yet the Lord testified against Israel and *J.*   2Ki 17:13

J. kept not the commandments of the Lord   2Ki 17:19

Manasseh made *J.* to sin   2Ki 21:11; 21:16; 2Ch 33:9

behold, I am bringing such evil upon *J.*   2Ki 21:12

his anger kindled against *J.*   2Ki 23:26; 2Ch 25:10

I will remove *J.* also out of my sight   2Ki 23:27

the Lord sent bands of Chaldees against *J.*   2Ki 24:2

at the command of the Lord came this on *J.*   2Ki 24:3

so *J.* was carried away   2Ki 25:21; 1Ch 6:15

J. prevailed above his brethren   1Ch 5:2

Aaron then gave the cities of *J.*   1Ch 6:57

of *J.* Elihu one of David's brethren was captain   1Ch 27:18

for he hath chosen *J.* to be the ruler   1Ch 28:4

so they were before *J.* and behind   2Ch 13:13

the children of Israel fled before *J.*   2Ch 13:16

Asa commanded *J.* to seek the Lord   2Ch 14:4

Jehoshaphat took the groves out of *J.*   2Ch 17:6

Jehoram compelled *J.* to commit fornication   2Ch 21:11

hast made *J.* and Jerusalem go a whoring   2Ch 21:13

wrath came upon *J.*   2Ch 24:18; 28:9; 29:8; 32:25

the Lord brought *J.* low, made *J.* naked   2Ch 28:19

seven lambs for a sin offering for *J.*   2Ch 29:21

all the congregation of *J.* rejoiced   2Ch 30:25

Manasseh commanded *J.* to serve the Lord   2Ch 33:16

in 12th year Josiah began to purge *J.*   2Ch 34:3; 34:5

sons of *J.* to set forward the workmen   Ezr 3:9

thou art sent to inquire concerning *J.*   Ezr 7:14

J. and Eliezer had taken strange wives   Ezr 10:22

that thou wouldst send me to *J.*   Ne 2:5

that they may convey me till I come into *J.*   Ne 2:7

the nobles of *J.* sent letters to Tobiah   Ne 6:17

J. son of Senuah was second over city   Ne 11:9

for *J.* rejoiced for the priests that waited   Ne 12:44

Gilead is mine, *J.* is my lawgiver   Ps 60:7; 108:8

J. was his sanctuary, Israel his dominion   Ps 114:2

vision which he saw concerning *J.*   Isa 1:1; 2:1

Lord doth take from *J.* stay and staff of bread   Isa 3:1

J. is fallen; let us go up against *J.*   Isa 3:8; 3:6

from day that Ephraim departed from *J.*   Isa 7:17

shall pass through *J.* shall overflow, go over   Isa 8:8

and they together shall be against *J.*   Isa 9:21

he shall gather together the dispersed of *J.*   Isa 11:12

the adversaries of *J.* shall be cut off; Ephraim shall not envy *J.* and *J.* not vex Ephraim   Isa 11:13

he discovered the covering of *J.*   Isa 22:8

and are come forth out of the waters of *J.*   Isa 48:1

and out of *J.* an inheritor of my mountains   Isa 65:9

as number of cities are thy gods, O *J.*   Jer 2:28

her sister *J.* saw it, and feared not   Jer 3:7; 3:8

Egypt, and *J.* and Edom are uncircumcised   Jer 9:26

after this manner will I mar the pride of *J.*   Jer 13:9

J. shall be carried away captive all of it   Jer 13:19

J. mourneth   Jer 14:2

hast thou utterly rejected *J.* and loathed Zion   Jer 14:19

the sin of J. is written with a   Jer 17:1
pen of iron
I will void the counsel of J.   Jer 19:7
and Jerusalem
J. shall be saved   Jer 23:6
they should do this to cause J.   Jer 32:35
to sin
I will cause the captivity of J.   Jer 33:7
to return
the words that I have spoken   Jer 36:2
against J.
hear the word of the Lord, ye   Jer 42:15
remnant of J.
not named in mouth of any   Jer 44:26
man of J.
the sins of J. shall not be   Jer 50:20
found
J. hath not been forsaken of   Jer 51:5
his God
J. was carried away captive   Jer 52:27;
                               La 1:3
that the sword may come to   Eze 21:20
J. in Jerusalem
J. and Israel were thy   Eze 27:17
merchants
write upon it for J. and for   Eze 37:16
Israel
by the border of Reuben, a   Eze 48:7
portion for J.
one gate of Reuben, one gate   Eze 48:31
of J. one of Levi
tho' Israel play harlot, yet let   Ho 4:15
not J. offend
J. shall fall; when J. saw his   Ho 5:5;
wound   5:13
O J. what shall I do unto thee?   Ho 6:4
for your good
J. shall plow, Jacob shall   Ho 10:11
break his clods
but J. ruleth yet with God,   Ho 11:12
and is faithful
the Lord hath also a   Ho 12:2
controversy with J.
but J. shall dwell for ever, and   Joe 3:20
Jerusalem
for three transgressions of J.   Am 2:4
and for four
but I will send a fire on J. it   Am 2:5
shall devour
her wound is incurable, it is   Mic 1:9
come to J.
though thou be little among the   Mic 5:2
thousands of J.
I will stretch out mine hand   Zep 1:4
upon J.
the horns which have   Zec 1:19;
scattered J.   1:21
Lord shall inherit J. his   Zec 2:12
portion in holy land
when I have bent J. for me,   Zec 9:13
filled the bow
the Lord shall save the tents   Zec 12:7
of J. first
J. also shall fight at   Zec 14:14
Jerusalem
J. hath dealt treacherously; J.   Mal 2:11
hath profaned the holiness of
then shall the offering of J. be   Mal 3:4
pleasant
Jacob begat J.; J. begat   M't 1:2;
Phares   1:3
Phares, which was the son of J.   Lu 3:33
for it is evident that our Lord   Heb 7:14
sprang of J.

ALL JUDAH

but all Israel and all J. loved   1Sa 18:16
David
David reigned 33 years over all   2Sa 5:5
J.
all J. rejoiced at the oath   2Ch 15:15
all J. stood before the Lord   2Ch 20:13
with their wives
all J. did honour Hezekiah   2Ch 32:33
at his death
all J. and Jerusalem   2Ch 35:24
mourned for Josiah
then all J. brought the tithe of   Ne 13:12
the corn
I will give all J. to the king of   Jer 20:4
Babylon
I will set my face to cut off all   Jer 44:11
J.

IN JUDAH

behold, we be afraid here in J.   1Sa 23:3
like unto the feast that is in   1Ki 12:32
J.

Lord it came to pass in   2Ki 24:20;
Jerusalem and J.   Jer 52:3
cunning men that are with me   2Ch 2:7
in J.
and also in J. things went   2Ch 12:12
well
they taught in J. and had   2Ch 17:9
book of law of Lord
Pekah slew in J. 120,000 in   2Ch 28:6
one day
in J. hand of God was to   2Ch 30:12
give one heart
inquire for them that are left   2Ch 34:21
in J.
prophesied to the Jews that   Ezr 5:1
were in J.
but hath extended mercy to give   Ezr 9:9
us a wall in J.
to preach, saying, There is a king   Ne 6:7
in J.
I saw in J. some treading   Ne 13:15
wine presses
in J. is God known, his name is   Ps 76:1
great
declare ye in J. publish in   Jer 4:5;
Jerusalem   5:20
none shall prosper, ruling any   Jer 22:30
more in J.
he shall be as a governor in J.   Zec 9:7
every pot in J. be holiness to   Zec 14:21
the Lord

LAND OF JUDAH

Lord shewed him all the land   De 34:2
of J.
thus went to return into the   Ru 1:7
land of J.
depart, get thee into the land   1Sa 22:5
of J.
people that remained in land   2Ki 25:22
of J.
Jehoshaphat set garrisons in   2Ch 17:2
land of J.
the land of J. shall be a terror   Isa 19:17
to Egypt
this song shall be sung in the   Isa 26:1
land of J.
use this speech in the land of   Jer 31:23
J.
the poor, who had nothing in   Jer 39:10
the land of J.
they have committed in the   Jer 44:9
land of J.
that they should return into   Jer 44:14
the land of J.
flee, thou seer, into the land   Am 7:12
of J.
lift up their horn over the land   Zec 1:21
of J.
thou, Bethlehem, in the land of   M't 2:6
J.

MEN OF JUDAH

men of J. said, Why are ye   J'g 15:10
come against us
the men of J. anointed David   2Sa 2:4
king
he bowed the heart of all the   2Sa 19:14
men of J.
the words of the men of J.   2Sa 19:43
were fiercer
but the men of J. clave to   2Sa 20:2
their king
assemble the men of J. within   2Sa 20:4
three days
the men of J. were five   2Sa 24:9
hundred thousand
then the men of J. gave a   2Ch 13:15
shout
all the men of J. gathered   Ezr 10:9
together
the men of J. are his pleasant   Isa 5:7
plant
circumcise your hearts, ye men   Jer 4:4
of J.
a conspiracy is found among   Jer 11:9
the men of J.
bring upon the men of J. all   Jer 36:31
the evil
hide them in the sight of the   Jer 43:9
men of J.
all the men of J. shall be   Jer 44:27
consumed
but confusion belongeth to the   Da 9:7
men of J.

TRIBE OF JUDAH

Bezaleel of the tribe of J.   Ex 31:2;
                          35:30; 38:22
that were numbered of the   Nu 1:27
tribe of J.
Nahshon, the prince of the   Nu 7:12
tribe of J.
of the tribe of J. Caleb to spy   Nu 13:6;
                             34:19
Achan of tribe of J. took of   Jos 7:1
accursed thing
and the tribe of J. was taken   Jos 7:16;
                             7:18
this was the lot of the tribe of   Jos 15:1
J.   15:20
Levites out of the tribe of J.   Jos 21:4;
                      21:9; 2Ch 6:65
the tribe of J. only followed   1Ki 12:20
David
none left but the tribe of J.   2Ki 17:18
only
but he chose the tribe of J.   Ps 78:68
mount Sion
the Lion of the tribe of J. hath   Re 5:5
prevailed
of the tribe of J. were sealed   Re 7:5
12,000

JUDAH'S

Er, J. firstborn was wicked   Ge 38:7
daughter of Shuah J. wife   Ge 38:12
died
which was in the king of J.   Jer 32:2
house
left in the king of J. house   Jer 38:22

JUDAISM

a former convert to J. (N)(P)   Ac 6:5
previous career in J. (B)(R)   Ga 1:13;
                               1:14

JUDAS

his brethren Joses, Simon,   M't 13:55
and J.
J. one of the twelve came,   M't 26:47;
and   M'k 14:43; Lu 22:47; Joh 18:3, 5
then J. repented himself and   M't 27:3
brought 30 pieces
some thought because J.   Joh 13:29
had the bag
J. saith unto him, not   Joh 14:22
Iscariot, How is it
David spake before concerning   Ac 1:16
J.
from which J. by transgression,   Ac 1:25
fell
after this man rose up J. of   Ac 5:37
Galilee
inquire in the house of J. for   Ac 9:11
one Saul
they sent J. surnamed   Joh 15:22;
Barsabas   15:27
J. and Silas exhorted the   Ac 15:32
brethren

JUDAS ISCARIOT

J. Iscariot, who betrayed him   M't 10:4;
             M'k 3:19; Lu 6:16; Joh 6:71; 13:2
J. Iscariot went to chief   M't 26:14;
priests   M'k 14:10
then entered Satan into J.   Lu 22:3
Iscariot
he gave the sop to J. Iscariot   Joh 13:26

JUDE

J. the servant of Jesus Christ   Jude 1

JUDEA

we went into the province of J.   Ezr 5:8

JUDGE

this fellow came, and will   Ge 19:9
needs be j.
made thee a j. over us   Ex 2:14;
                           Ac 7:27, 35
come to the j. that shall be in   De 17:9
those days
the man that will not hearken   De 17:12
to the j.
that the j. shall cause him to   De 25:2
lie down
then the Lord was with the j.   J'g 2:18

the *j.* was dead, they corrupted   *J'g 2:19*
themselves
if a man sin, the *j.* shall judge   *1Sa 2:25*
him
Absalom said, O that I were   *2Sa 15:4*
made *j.*
an iniquity to be punished by   *2Sa 31:28*
the *j.*
doth take away from Jerusalem   *Isa 3:2*
the *j.*
I will cut off the *j.* from the   *Am 2:3*
midst thereof
prince asketh, and the *j.* asketh   *Am 7:3*
for a reward
adversary deliver thee to *j.*   *M't 5:25;*
the *j.* deliver to officer   *Lu 12:58*
man, who made me a *j.* over   *Lu 12:14*
you
saying, There was in a city, a *j.*   *Lu 18:2*
feared not God
the Lord said, Hear what the   *Lu 18:6*
unjust *j.* saith
for I will be no *j.* of such   *Ac 18:15*
matters
hast been of many years a *j.*   *Ac 24:10*
of this nation
ye are come to God the *J.* of   *Heb 12:23*
all
thou art not a doer of the law,   *Jas 4:11*
but a *j.*

JUDGE, God and Christ

the Lord *j.* between me and   *Ge 16:5;*
thee   *1Sa 24:12, 15*
shall not *j.* of all the earth do   *Ge 18:25*
right
God of their father, *j.* betwixt   *Ge 31:53*
us
they said, The Lord look on you   *Ex 5:21*
and *j.*
for the Lord shall *j.* his   *De 32:36;*
people   *Ps 50:4; 135:14; Heb 10:30*
the Lord be *J.* this day   *J'g 11:27*
between us
Lord shall *j.* the ends of the   *1Sa 2:10;*
earth   *24:12, 15*
hear, and *j.* thy servants   *1Ki 8:32;*
  2Ch 6:23
cometh to *j.* the earth   *1Ch 16:33;*
  Ps 96:13; 98:9
O our God, wilt thou not *j.*   *2Ch 20:12*
them
would make supplication to   *Job 9:15;*
my *j.*   *23:7*
can he *j.* through the dark   *Job 22:13*
cloud
The Lord shall *j.* the people   *Ps 7:8;*
righteously   *9:8; 50:4; 96:10*
j. the fatherless and the   *Ps 10:18;*
oppressed   *68:5*
J. me, O Lord   *Ps 26:1;*
  35:24; 43:1; 54:1; La 3:59
for God is the *J.* himself   *Ps 50:6;*
  75:7; 2Ti 4:8
arise, O God, *j.* the earth: thou   *Ps 82:8*
shalt inherit
he shall *j.* the world with   *Ps 96:13;*
righteousness   *98:9; Ac 17:31*
he shall *j.* among the heathen   *Ps 110:6*
God shall *j.* the righteous and   *Ec 3:17*
wicked
and he shall *j.* among the   *Isa 2:4*
nations
the Lord standeth to *j.* the   *Isa 3:13*
people
he shall not *j.* after the sight of   *Isa 11:3*
his eyes
and mine arm shall *j.* the   *Isa 51:5*
people
and will *j.* thee according to thy   *Eze 7:3*
ways
behold I *j.* between cattle   *Eze 34:17*
and cattle
the *J.* was seated (A)   *Da 7:10*
there will I sit to *j.* the   *Joe 3:12*
heathen
he shall *j.* among many people   *Mic 4:3*
they shall smite the *J.* of Israel   *Mic 5:1*
as I hear, I *j.*; my judgment is   *Joh 5:30*
just
I *j.* no man; and yet if I *j.*   *Joh 8:15;*
  8:16
I have many things to say and   *Joh 8:26*
to *j.* of you
I *j.* him not, I came not to *j.*   *Joh 12:47*
the world
God to be the *J.* of the quick   *Ac 10:42;*
  2Ti 4:1; 1Pe 4:5

when God shall *j.* the secrets   *Ro 2:16*
of men
for then how shall God *j.* the   *Ro 3:6*
world
the Lord will *j.* his people   *Heb 10:30*
to God the *J.* of all   *Heb 12:23*
adulterers God will *j.*   *Heb 13:4*
the *j.* standeth before the door   *Jas 5:9*
dost thou not *j.* and avenge our   *Re 6:10*
blood
in righteousness he doth *j.*   *Re 19:11*
and make war

JUDGE, man, other things

that they may *j.* betwixt us   *Ge 31:37*
both
Dan shall *j.* his people as one   *Ge 49:16*
of the tribes
that Moses sat to *j.* the people   *Ex 18:13*
administer justice (B)   *Ex 18:13;*
  18:16, 22
they come, I *j.* between one   *Ex 18:16*
and another
but every small matter they   *Ex 18:22*
shall *j.*
in righteousness shalt thou *j.*   *Le 19:15;*
thy neighbour   *De 1:16; 16:18*
the congregation *j.* between   *Nu 35:24*
the slayer
the assembly shall decide (B)   *Nu 35:24*
come, that the judges may *j.*   *De 25:1*
them
if a man sin, the judge shall *j.*   *1Sa 2:25*
him
thou art old, make us a king to   *1Sa 8:5;*
j. us   *8:20*
give understanding heart to *j.*   *1Ki 3:9;*
who is able to *j.* this   *2Ch 1:10*
great people
a porch for the throne where   *1Ki 7:7*
he might *j.*
a porch of judgment (B)   *1Ki 7:7*
where he was to proclaim   *1Ki 7:7*
judgment (R)
that thou mayest *j.* my people   *2Ch 1:11*
so as to govern wisely my   *2Ch 1:11*
people (B)
that you may rule my people   *2Ch 1:11*
(R)
for ye *j.* not for man, but for   *2Ch 19:6*
the Lord
you are not judging for men   *2Ch 19:6*
(B)
set judges which may *j.* all the   *Ezr 7:25*
people
to govern all the people (B)   *Ezr 7:25*
j. world in righteousness   *Ps 9:8*
  (A)(B)(E)(R)
do ye *j.* uprightly, O ye sons of   *Ps 58:1*
men
he shall *j.* thy people   *Ps 72:2*
with righteousness
he shall *j.* the poor of the   *Ps 72:4;*
people   *Pr 31:9*
how long will ye *j.* unjustly, and   *Ps 82:2*
accept
j. the fatherless, plead for the   *Isa 1:17*
widow
defend the fatherless (A)(R)   *Isa 1:17*
protect the orphan (B)   *Isa 1:17*
they *j.* not the fatherless   *Isa 1:23;*
  Jer 5:28
protect the orphan (B)   *Isa 1:23*
defend the fatherless (R)   *Isa 1:23*
j. I pray you betwixt me and my   *Isa 5:3*
vineyard
arbitrate between me and my   *Isa 5:3*
vineyard (B)
let us *j.* together (B)   *Isa 43:26*
j. with truth (B)   *Eze 8:16*
wilt thou *j.* them, son of man   *Eze 20:4;*
  22:2
and they shall *j.* thee   *Eze 23:24;*
  23:45; 24:14
son of man, wilt *j.* Aholah   *Eze 23:36*
and Aholibah
they shall *j.* it according to   *Eze 44:24*
my judgments
and *j.* their sins (S)   *Ho 8:13;*
  9:9; Am 3:14
and will *j.* them (S)   *Joe 3:2*
saviours come to *j.* the mount of   *Ob 21*
Esau
the heads thereof *j.* for   *Mic 3:11*
reward
deal out judgment for a bribe   *Mic 3:11*
(B)(R)
then thou shalt also *j.* my house   *Zec 3:7*

shall rule my house (A)(R)   *Zec 3:7*
also govern my house (B)   *Zec 3:7*
j. not that ye be not judged   *M't 7:1*
do not pass judgment (B)(N)   *M't 7:1*
Don't criticize people (P)   *M't 7:1*
for with what judgment ye *j.*   *M't 7:2;*
  Lu 6:37
the way you *j.* will be judged   *M't 7:2*
(A)(B)(N)
j. not, not be judged   *Lu 6:37*
(A)(B)(E)(N)(P)(R)
yea, and why *j.* ye not what is   *Lu 12:57*
right
personally decide what is   *Lu 12:57*
right (B)(P)
to *j.*-pass sentence   *Joh 3:17*
(A)(E)(N)(P)
to act as *j.* (B)(P)   *Joh 5:27*
j. not according to the   *Joh 7:24*
appearance, *j.* righteous judgment
j. fairly and righteously   *Joh 7:24*
(A)(B)(P)
doth our law *j.* any man   *Joh 7:51*
before it hear
Does our law convict a man   *Joh 7:51*
(A)
Our law does not condemn   *Joh 7:51*
without (B)(P)
pass judgment on a man   *Joh 7:51*
unless (N)
ye *j.* after flesh; same shall *j.*   *Joh 8:15;*
him   *12:48*
take and *j.* him according to   *Joh 18:31*
your law
sentence him according to   *Joh 18:31*
(A)(B)
try him by your own law (N)   *Joh 18:31*
j. ye; *j.* yourselves unworthy   *Ac 4:19;*
  13:46
for sittest thou to *j.* me after   *Ac 23:3*
the law
uncircumcision if it fulfil the   *Ro 2:27*
law, *j.* thee
i. him that eateth   *Ro 14:3*
criticize and pass judgment on   *Ro 14:3*
(A)(P)
censure the eater (B)   *Ro 14:3; 14:13*
must not hold in contempt (N)   *Ro 14:3*
pass judgment on (R)   *Ro 14:3*
why *j.* thy brother   *Ro 14:10*
let us not *j.* one another, but   *Ro 14:13*
j. this rather
criticize, blame, pass   *Ro 14:13*
judgment on (A)
cease judging one another (N)   *Ro 14:13*
stop turning critical eyes on   *Ro 14:13*
one (P)
let us no more pass judgment   *Ro 14:13*
on (R)
no reason to *j.* himself   *Ro 14:22*
(A)(R)
I *j.* not myself; *j.* not, before   *1Co 4:3;*
time   *4:5*
what have I to do to *j.* them   *1Co 5:12*
that are without, do ye not *j.*
them that are within
God will *j.* those outside   *1Co 5:13*
(B)(N)(P)(R)
do ye not know the saints shall   *1Co 6:2*
j. the world
know ye not that we shall *j.*   *1Co 6:3*
angels
set them to *j.* who are least   *1Co 6:4*
esteemed in church
shall be able to *j.* between his   *1Co 6:5*
brethren
competent enough to decide   *1Co 6:5*
between (A)
capable of deciding between   *1Co 6:5*
brothers (B)
able to decide between   *1Co 6:5*
brethren (E)
able to give a decision in a   *1Co 6:5*
cause (N)
one man with enough sense to   *1Co 6:5*
decide (P)
wise enough to decide between   *1Co 6:5*
(R)
i. ye what I say   *1Co 10:15*
I appeal to your reason,   *1Co 10:15*
discernment (A)
I appeal to your intelligence   *1Co 10:15*
(B)
Form your own judgment   *1Co 10:15*
(N)
think over what I am saying   *1Co 10:15*
(P)
j. in yourselves   *1Co 11:13*

for if we would *j.* ourselves, *1Co 11:31*
we should
if we searchingly examined *1Co 11:31*
ourselves-detecting our
shortcomings and recognizing
our own condition (A)
If we scrutinized ourselves *1Co 11:31*
(B)
if we discerned ourselves *1Co 11:31*
(E)
if we examined ourselves *1Co 11:31*
(N)(P)
let the prophets speak, and *1Co 14:29*
the other *j.*
rest pay attention, weigh, *1Co 14:29*
discern (A)(B)
let the others discern (E) *1Co 14:29*
rest exercise their judgment *1Co 14:29*
(N)
others think over what has *1Co 14:29*
been said (P)
let the others weigh what is *1Co 14:29*
said (R)
because we thus *j.* that if one *2Co 5:14*
died
of the opinion and conviction *2Co 5:14*
that (A)
brings us to this conclusion *2Co 5:14*
(B)
we have reached the *2Co 5:14*
conclusion that (N)
we look at it like this (P) *2Co 5:14*
we are convinced that one has *2Co 5:14*
died (A)
let no man therefore *j.* you in *Col 2:16*
meat
let no man sit in judgment on *Col 2:16*
you (A)
Allow no one to be your judge *Col 2:16*
(B)
Allow no one to take you to *Col 2:16*
task (N)
don't let anyone worry you by *Col 2:16*
criticising (P)
let no one pass judgment on *Col 2:16*
you (R)
but if thou *j.* the law, thou art *Jas 4:11*
not
to *j.* your neighbor *Jas 4:12*
(N)(P)(R)
committed it to righteous *j.* *1Pe 2:23*
(B)

I WILL JUDGE

I told that *I will j.* his house *1Sa 3:13*
for ever
execute justice over his house *1Sa 3:13*
(B)
I am about to punish his *1Sa 3:13*
house (R)
when shall receive, *I will j.* *Ps 75:2*
uprightly
I will render fair judgments *Ps 75:2*
(B)
I will j. according to thy *Eze 7:3;*
ways *8:27; 33:20*
I will j. you in the border of *Eze 11:10;*
Israel *11:11*
I will execute judgments (B) *Eze 11:10*
I will j. thee as women that *Eze 16:38*
break wedlock
therefore *I will j.* you, O *Eze 18:30*
house of Israel
I will j. thee in the place *Eze 21:30*
where thou wast
I, even *I, will j.* between fat *Eze 34:20;*
cattle *34:22*

WILL I JUDGE

the nation they shall serve *Ge 15:14;*
will I j. *Ac 7:7*
bring judgment on that nation *Ge 15:14*
(A)(R)
I will punish the nation (B) *Ge 15:14*
out of thine own mouth *will I* *Lu 19:22*
j. thee
convict you from your own *Lu 19:22*
(B)
your own words condemn you *Lu 19:22*
(P)
condemn you out of own *Lu 19:22*
mouth (R)

JUDGED

God hath *j.* me and heard my *Ge 30:6*
voice

God has done me justice (B) *Ge 30:6*
j. the people, small matter *Ex 18:26*
they *j.*
Othniel *j.* *J'g 3:10*
Deborah *j.* Israel *J'g 4:4*
Tola *j.* *J'g 10:2*
Jair *j.* *J'g 10:3*
Jephthah *j.* *J'g 12:7*
Ibzan *j.* *J'g 12:8*
Elon *j.* *J'g 12:11*
Abdon *j.* Israel *J'g 12:14*
Samson *j.* Israel twenty years *J'g 15:20;*
16:31
Eli *j.* *1Sa 4:18*
Samuel *j.* Israel *1Sa 7:6; 7:15-17*
heard the judgment the king *1Ki 3:28*
had *j.*
heard decision, king had *1Ki 3:28*
rendered (B)(R)
from the days of the judges *2Ki 23:22*
that *j.*
let the heathen be *j.* in thy sight *Ps 9:19*
not condemn him when he is *j.* *Ps 37:33*
when he shall be *j.* let him be *Ps 109:7*
condemned
when his case is tried (B) *Ps 109:7*
when he is tried (R) *Ps 109:7*
he *j.* the cause of the poor *Jer 22:16*
and needy
as women that shed blood *Eze 16:38*
are *j.*
thou also who hast *j.* thy *Eze 16:52*
sisters, bear shame
and the wounded shall be *j.* *Eze 28:23*
in her
make myself known, when I *Eze 35:11*
have *j.* thee
according to their doings I *j.* *Eze 36:19*
them
and against our judges that *j.* *Da 9:12*
us
our rulers who directed us (B) *Da 9:12*
our rulers who ruled us (R) *Da 9:12*
j. her for (S) *Ho 2:13*
that ye be not *j.* *M't 7:1*
shall be *j.* *M't 7:2; Lu 6:37*
the way you judge will be *j.* *M't 7:2*
(B)(N)
judge not, not be *j.* *Lu 6:37*
(A)(B)(E)(N)(P)(R)
he said to him, Thou hast *Lu 7:43*
rightly *j.*
j. worthy of a place (N) *Lu 20:35*
the prince of this world is *j.* *Joh 16:11*
if ye have *j.* me to be faithful *Ac 16:15*
If you consider me faithful *Ac 16:15*
(B)
If you are satisfied I am a *Ac 16:15*
true (P)
we would have *j.* according to *Ac 24:6*
our law
sentenced by our law (A)(B) *Ac 24:6*
then we arrested him (N) *Ac 24:6*
when we overcame him (P) *Ac 24:6*
we seized him (R) *Ac 24:6*
there be *j.* of these things *Ac 25:9;*
before ,me *25:20*
there be put to trial (A) *Ac 25:9*
there be tried before me (B) *Ac 25:9*
stand trial on these charges *Ac 25:9*
(N)
stand you trial over these *Ac 25:9*
matters (P)
to be tried on these charges *Ac 25:9*
(R)
Paul said, I stand, where I *Ac 25:10*
ought to be *j.*
where I ought to be tried *Ac 25:10*
(A)(B)(N)(R)
and am *j.* for the hope of the *Ac 26:6*
promise
I am standing trial for hope *Ac 26:6*
(B)(P)(R)
shall be *j.* by the law *Ro 2:12; Jas 2:12*
thou mightest overcome when *Ro 3:4*
thou art *j.*
might triumph when tried (B) *Ro 3:4*
prevail when comest to *Ro 3:4*
judgment (E)(P)
win verdict when on trial (N) *Ro 3:4*
why yet am I also *j.* as a sinner *Ro 3:7*
condemned as a sinner *Ro 3:7*
(B)(N)(R)
j. not himself (E) *Ro 14:22*
are spiritually *j.* (E)(N) *1Co 2:14*
yet he himself is *j.* of no man *1Co 2:15*
he is properly valued by none *1Co 2:15*
(B)

is not himself a subject of *1Co 2:15*
judgment (N)
a small thing that I should be *1Co 4:3*
j. of you
I should be put on trial by you *1Co 4:3*
(A)
I am called to account by you *1Co 4:3*
(N)
I have *j.* already, as though *1Co 5:3*
I were present
passed judgment, as actually *1Co 5:3*
present (A)
as if present, passed sentence *1Co 5:3*
on (B)
my judgment upon the man is *1Co 5:3*
given (N)
already pronounced judgment *1Co 5:3*
in name (P)(R)
and if the world shall be *j.* by *1Co 6:2*
you
for why is my liberty *j.* of *1Co 10:29*
another man's
why should another man's *1Co 10:29*
scruples apply to me, my
liberty action be (A)
why should my freedom be *1Co 10:29*
arraigned before other person's
conscience (B)
my freedom to be called to *1Co 10:29*
question by (N)
my freedom to eat be at the *1Co 10:29*
mercy of (P)
my liberty be determined by *1Co 10:29*
another man's scruples (R)
if we would judge we should *1Co 11:31*
not be *j.*
when we are *j.* we are *1Co 11:32*
chastened of the Lord
judgments from Lord serve *1Co 11:32*
(B)
fall under Lord's judgment *1Co 11:32*
(N)
he is convinced of all, he is *j.* *1Co 14:24*
of all
he is told of his sin, *1Co 14:24*
reproved, convicted, and
convinced by all (A)
he would be convicted by all *1Co 14:24*
(B)(R)
searches his conscience, *1Co 14:24*
brings conviction, and secrets
of heart are laid bare (N)
convicted and challenged by *1Co 14:24*
your united speaking the truth
(P)
be *j.* and condemned *2Th 2:12*
(A)(E)(R)(S)
j. me faithful (A)(R) *1Ti 1:12*
because she *j.* him faithful *Heb 11:11*
who had
she considered (God) *Heb 11:11*
reliable, trustworthy, and
true to his word (A)
she regarded the Promiser *Heb 11:11*
trustworthy (B)
she counted him faithful *Heb 11:11*
who promised (E)
she believed that the one *Heb 11:11*
who had given promise
was utterly trustworthy (P)
considered him faithful who *Heb 11:11*
promised (R)
j. with greater strictness *Jas 3:1*
(N)(R)
j. with much higher standard *Jas 3:1*
(P)
may not be *j.* (A)(E)(R)(S) *Jas 5:9*
they might be *j.* according to *1Pe 4:6*
men
time of the dead, that they *Re 11:18*
should be *j.*
art righteous because thou hast *Re 16:5*
j. thus
art just in his decisions *Re 16:5*
(A)(B)
God who has *j.* her (B) *Re 18:8*
righteous, for he hath *j.* the *Re 19:2*
great whore
the dead were *j.* out of those *Re 20:12*
things
were *j.* every man according *Re 20:13*
to his works

JUDGES

master shall bring him unto the *Ex 21:6*
j.
shall bring him to the gods (B) *Ex 21:6*
shall bring him unto God *Ex 21:6*
(E)(R)

he shall pay as the *j.* determine | Ex 21:22
house shall be brought unto the *j.* | Ex 22:8
parties shall come before the *j.* | Ex 22:9
whom the *j.* shall condemn, he | Ex 22:9
Moses said unto the *j.* of Israel | Nu 25:5
And I charged your *j.* at that time | De 1:16
j. and officers shalt thou make | De 16:18
before the priests and *j.* which | De 19:17
j. shall make diligent inquisition | De 19:18
elders and thy *j.* shall come forth | De 21:2
that the *j.* may judge them | De 25:1
our enemies themselves being *j.* | De 32:31
our foes themselves concluding (B) | De 32:31
their *j.* stood on this side the ark | Jos 8:33
for their *j.* and for their officers | Jos 23:2; 24:1
Nevertheless the Lord raised up *j.* | J'g 2:16
would not hearken unto their *j.* | J'g 2:17
when the Lord raised them up *j.* | J'g 2:18
pass in the days when the *j.* ruled | Ru 1:1
that he made his sons *j.* over Israel | 1Sa 8:1
Abiah: they were *j.* in Beer-sheba | 1Sa 8:2
since the time that I commanded *j.* | 2Sa 7:11
the days of the *j.* that judged Israel | 2Ki 23:22
I a word to any of the *j.* of Israel | 1Ch 17:6
since the time that I commanded *j.* | 1Ch 17:10
six thousand were officers and *j.* | 1Ch 23:4
over Israel, for officers and *j.* | 1Ch 26:29
to the *j.* and to every governor | 2Ch 1:2
he set *j.* in the land throughout all | 2Ch 19:5
said to the *j.*, Take heed what ye do | 2Ch 19:6
thine hand, set magistrates and *j.* | Ezr 7:25
of every city, and the *j.* thereof | Ezr 10:14
covereth the faces of the *j.* thereof | Job 9:24
spoiled, and maketh the *j.* fools | Job 12:17
iniquity to be punished by the *j.* | Job 31:11
be instructed, ye *j.* of the earth | Ps 2:10
O rulers of the earth (A)(B)(R) | Ps 2:10
in midst of *j.* he gives (B) | Ps 82:1
their *j.* are overthrown in places | Ps 141:6
princes, and all *j.* of the earth | Ps 148:11
nobles, even all the *j.* of the earth | Pr 8:16
he who *j.* the wicked (B) | Pr 17:15
I will restore thy *j.* as at the first | Isa 1:26
maketh the *j.* of the earth as vanity | Isa 40:23
makes dignitaries look like nothing (B) | Isa 40:23
makes rulers of earth as nothing (R) | Isa 40:23
they shall stand as *j.* (S) | Eze 44:24
governors, and the captains, the *j.* | Da 3:2; 3:3
against our *j.* that judged us | Da 9:12
our rulers who directed us (B)(R) | Da 9:12
oven, and have devoured their *j.* | Ho 7:7
consume their rulers (B)(R) | Ho 7:7
thy *j.* of whom thou saidst, Give me | Ho 13:10
all your princes besides (B)(R) | Ho 13:10
her *j.* are evening wolves; they | Zep 3:3
therefore they shall be your *j.* | M't 12:27; Lu 11:19
And after that he gave unto them *j.* | Ac 13:20
sitting on *j.* seat (A) | Ac 18:12

And are become *j.* of evil thoughts | Jas 2:4
disparages and *j.* the law (N) | Jas 4:11
one who *j.* fairly (A)(N)(P)(R) | 1Pe 2:23
God who *j.* her (A)(P)(R) | Re 18:8
authority to act as *j.* (A)(B)(P) | Re 20:4

JUDGEST

and be clear when thou *j.* | Ps 51:4
faultless in your judgment (A)(R) | Ps 51:4
pure in thy judging (B) | Ps 51:4
O Lord of hosts, that *j.* righteously | Jer 11:20
O man, whosoever thou art that *j.* | Ro 2:1
who judges and condemns another (A) | Ro 2:1
by passing sentence on another (B) | Ro 2:1
who sit in judgment (N) | Ro 2:1
feel inclined to set yourself up as a judge of those who sin (P) | Ro 2:1
when you judge another (R) | Ro 2:1
for wherein thou *j.* another thou | Ro 2:1
thou that *j.* doest the same things | Ro 2:1
that *j.* them which do such things | Ro 2:3
when you judge and condemn those who (A)(R) | Ro 2:3
who condemn those practicing such evils (B) | Ro 2:3
who pass judgment on the guilty while (N) | Ro 2:3
who readily judge the sins of others (P) | Ro 2:3
Who art thou that *j.* another man's | Ro 14:4
pass judgment on and censure another's (A) | Ro 14:4
to censure Another's servant (B) | Ro 14:4
pass judgment on someone else's (N)(R) | Ro 14:4
criticise the servant of somebody else (P) | Ro 14:4
who art thou that *j.* another | Jas 4:12
pass judgment on your neighbor (A) | Jas 4:12
to be judging your neighbor (B) | Jas 4:12
who are you to judge your neighbor (N)(R) | Jas 4:12
silly to imagine you are neighbor's judge (P) | Jas 4:12

JUDGETH

seeing he *j.* those that are high | Job 21:22
by them *j.* he the people; he giveth | Job 36:31
God *j.* the righteous, and God | Ps 7:11
God is a righteous judge (A)(B)(E)(R) | Ps 7:11
he is a God that *j.* in the earth | Ps 58:11
God who judges the earth (A)(R) | Ps 58:11
God who is judging the earth (B) | Ps 58:11
the mighty; he *j.* among the gods | Ps 82:1
he gives judgment among the gods (A) | Ps 82:1
in midst of judges he gives judgment (B) | Ps 82:1
in midst of the gods he holds judgment (R) | Ps 82:1
The king that faithfully *j.* the poor | Pr 29:14
the Father *j.* no man, but hath | Joh 5:22
does not even sentence any man (B) | Joh 5:22
Father does not judge any one (N)(R) | Joh 5:22
The Father is no man's judge (P) | Joh 5:22
there is one that seeketh and *j.* | Joh 8:50
not my words, hath one that *j.* him | Joh 12:48
But he that is spiritual *j.* all things | 1Co 2:15
but he that *j.* me is the Lord | 1Co 4:4
But them that are without God *j.* | 1Co 5:13

God alone sits in judgment on those (A) | 1Co 5:13
God will judge (B)(N)(P) | 1Co 5:13
God judges those outside (R) | 1Co 5:13
evil, brother, and *j.* his brother | Jas 4:11
evil of the law, and judgeth the law | Jas 4:11
maligning, criticizing, judging Law (A) | Jas 4:11
maligns and criticizes the Law (B) | Jas 4:11
disparages and judges the law (N) | Jas 4:11
become a critic of the Law (P) | Jas 4:11
j. according to every man's work | 1Pe 1:17
himself to him that *j.* righteously | 1Pe 2:23
committed it to the righteous judge (B) | 1Pe 2:23
one who judges fairly, justly (A)(N)(P)(R) | 1Pe 2:23
strong is the Lord God who *j.* her | Re 18:8
Lord God who judges her (A)(P)(R) | Re 18:8
Lord God, who has judged her (B) | Re 18:8
God who has pronounced her doom (N) | Re 18:8

JUDGING

house, *j.* the people of the land | 2Ki 15:5; 2Ch 26:21
thou satest in the throne *j.* right | Ps 9:4
establish his throne for *j.* (B) | Ps 9:7
seats are placed for *j.* (B) | Ps 122:5
of David, *j.*, and seeking judgment | Isa 16:5
j. the twelve tribes of Israel | M't 19:28
thrones *j.* the twelve tribes of Israel | Lu 22:30

JUDGMENT

against the gods I will execute *j.* | Ex 12:12
to decline after many, to wrest *j.* | Ex 23:2; 23:6
toward majority to thwart justice (B) | Ex 23:2
after multitude to wrest justice (E) | Ex 23:2
according to this *j.* be it done to him | Ex 21:31
thou shalt make the breastplate of *j.* | Ex 28:15
make the judicial breastplate (B) | Ex 28:15
Aaron bear names in breastplate of *j.* | Ex 28:29; 28:36
to Israel a statute of *j.* | Nu 27:11; 35:29
a statute and ordinance (A)(E)(R) | Nu 27:11
statute for determining legal right (B) | Nu 27:11
after the *j.* of Urim before the Lord | Nu 27:21
the decision of the Urim (B) | Nu 27:21
not afraid of man, for the *j.* is God's | De 1:17
no partiality in decisions (B) | De 1:17
he doth execute the *j.* of the fatherless | De 10:18
executes justice for the fatherless (A) | De 10:18
secures justice for orphan and widow (B)(E)(R) | De 10:18
they shall judge the people with just *j.* | De 16:18
administer proper justice (B) | De 16:18
not wrest *j.* | De 16:19
not distort justice (B) | De 16:19
not wrest justice (E) | De 16:19
not pervert justice (R) | De 16:19
they shall shew thee the sentence of *j.* | De 17:9
will tell you of their decision (A)(B)(R) | De 17:9
according to the *j.* | De 17:11
thou shalt not pervert the *j.* of the stranger | De 24:17
not wrest the justice due to sojourner, or fatherless (A)(E)(R) | De 24:17
Do not violate rights of the immigrant or of the orphan (B) | De 24:17

be a controversy, and they come unto *j*.   *De 25:1*

take case to court for judicial decision (B)   *De 25:1*

cursed be he that perverteth *j*. of stranger (B)   *De 27:19*

perverts the justice due an alien (A)(B)   *De 27:19*

wresteth justice due a sojourner (E)(R)   *De 27:19*

for all his ways are *j*.; a God of truth   *De 32:4*

all his ways are justice (A)(E)(R)   *De 32:4*

all his ways of just (B)   *De 32:4*

if my hand take hold on *j*. I will render   *De 32:11*

stand before the congregation for *j*.   *Jos 20:6*

tried before the congregation (A)   *Jos 20:6*

appear before assembly for trial (B)   *Jos 20:6*

Israel came up to Deborah for *j*.   *J'g 4:5*

his sons took bribes and perverted (A)   *1Sa 8:3*

accepted presents; they twisted justice (B)   *1Sa 8:3*

David of sound *j*. (B)   *1Sa 16:18*

David executed *j*.   *2Sa 8:15; 1Ch 18:14*

executed justice and righteousness (A)(E)   *2Sa 8:15*

executing justice and maintaining right (B)   *2Sa 8:15*

administered justice and equity (R)   *2Sa 8:15*

when any man came to the king for *j*.   *2Sa 15:2; 15:6*

hast asked understanding to discern (R)   *1Ki 3:11*

recognize what is just and right (A)   *1Ki 3:11*

understanding to recognize justice (B)(E)   *1Ki 3:11*

understanding to discern what is right (R)   *1Ki 3:11*

all Israel heard of the *j*. the king judged   *1Ki 3:28*

heard about the decision (B)   *1Ki 3:28*

the porch of *j*.   *1Ki 7:7*

so shall thy *j*. be   *1Ki 20:40*

took the king and gave *j*. upon him   *2Ki 25:6*

pronounced sentence upon him (A)(R)   *2Ki 25:6*

chief of fathers for *j*. of the Lord   *2Ch 19:8*

when evil cometh on us as the sword, *j*.   *2Ch 20:9*

when Jehu was executing *j*. on Ahab   *2Ch 22:8*

so they executed *j*. against Joash   *2Ch 24:24*

let *j*. be executed speedily on him   *Ezr 7:26*

towards all that knew law and *j*.   *Es 1:13*

who knew law and justice (B)   *Es 1:13*

doth God pervert *j*. or pervert justice   *Job 8:3*

justice (A)(B)(E)   *Job 8:3; 9:19; 32:9, 12*

if I speak of *j*.   *Job 9:19*

but there is no *j*.   *Job 19:7*

that ye may know there is a *j*.   *Job 19:29*

neither do the aged understand *j*.   *Job 32:9*

understand what is right (N)   *Job 32:9*

let us choose to us *j*. know what is good   *Job 34:4*

choose that which is right (A)(B)(E)(R)   *Job 34:4*

neither will the Almighty pervert *j*.   *Job 34:12*

yet *j*. is before him, trust in him   *Job 35:14*

thou hast fulfilled the *j*. of the wicked, *j*. and justice   *Job 36:17*

awake for me to the *j*. thou hast commanded   *Ps 7:6*

justice and vindication (A)   *Ps 7:6*

he hath prepared his throne for *j*.   *Ps 9:7*

established his throne for judging (B)   *Ps 9:7*

shall minister *j*. to the people in righteousness   *Ps 9:8*

judge world in righteousness (A)(B)(E)   *Ps 9:8*

judges world with righteousness (R)   *Ps 9:8*

the Lord is known by the *j*. he executeth   *Ps 9:16*

he loveth righteousness and *j*.   *Ps 33:5; 37:28*

justice (A)(B)(R)(S)   *Ps 33:5; 37:30; 72:2; 89:14; 94:15; 99:4; 101:1; 106:3; Pr 1:3; 2:8; 8:20; 17:23; 19:28; 28:5; 29:4; 29:26; Ec 5:8; Isa 1:17, 27; 5:7; 10:2; 28:6; 30:18; 32:16; 33:5; 40:14; 42:3-4; 56:1; 59:8-9, 15; 61:8; Jer 7:5; Am 5:15, 24; 6:12; Mic 3:1, 9; Hab 1:4; Mal 2:17*

he shall bring forth thy *j*. as the noonday   *Ps 37:6*

and his tongue talketh of *j*.   *Ps 37:30*

and he shall judge thy poor with *j*.   *Ps 72:2*

thou didst cause *j*. to be heard from heaven   *Ps 76:8*

caused, sentence to be heard (A)(E)   *Ps 76:8*

God arose to *j*. to save meek of earth   *Ps 76:9*

justice and *j*. are the habitation   *Ps 89:14; 97:2*

but *j*. shall return to righteousness   *Ps 94:15*

the king's strength also loveth *j*.   *Ps 99:4*

I will sing of mercy and *j*. to thee, O Lord   *Ps 101:1*

Lord executeth *j*. for the oppressed   *Ps 103:6; 146:7*

executes righteousness, justice (A)(B)(R)   *Ps 103:6*

blessed are they that keep *j*.   *Ps 106:3*

then Phinehas stood up and executed *j*.   *Ps 106:30*

the works of his hands are verity and *j*.   *Ps 111:7*

are truth and justice (A)(E)   *Ps 111:7*

are faithful and right (B)   *Ps 111:7*

are faithful and just (R)   *Ps 111:7*

maintain cause in *j*. (E)   *Ps 112:5*

teach me good *j*. and knowledge   *Ps 119:66*

Teach me good taste (B)   *Ps 119:66*

I have done *j*. and justice leave me not   *Ps 119:121*

done justice, righteousness (A)(B)(E)   *Ps 119:121*

done what is just and right (R)   *Ps 119:121*

O Lord, quicken me according to thy *j*.   *Ps 119:149*

according to your righteous decree (A)   *Ps 119:149*

according to thy ordinances (B)(E)   *Ps 119:149*

in thy justice preserve my life (R)   *Ps 119:149*

for there are set thrones of *j*.   *Ps 122:5*

seats are placed for judging (B)   *Ps 122:5*

to execute upon them the *j*. written   *Ps 149:9*

to receive the instruction of wisdom and *j*.   *Pr 1:3*

he keepeth the paths of *j*. and preserveth   *Pr 2:8*

then shalt thou understand *j*. and equity   *Pr 2:9*

I lead in the midst of the paths of *j*.   *Pr 8:20*

there is that is destroyed for want of *j*.   *Pr 13:23*

destroyed because of injustice (A)(E)(R)   *Pr 13:23*

swept away for lack of justice (B)   *Pr 13:23*

lack good *j*. (B)   *Pr 17:18*

taketh a gift to pervert the ways of *j*.   *Pr 17:23*

an ungodly witness scorneth *j*.   *Pr 19:28*

a king that sitteth in the throne of *j*.   *Pr 20:8*

evil men understand not *j*. but they that seek   *Pr 28:5*

the king by *j*. establisheth the land   *Pr 29:4*

every man's *j*. cometh from the Lord   *Pr 29:26*

nor pervert the *j*. of any of the afflicted   *Pr 31:5*

pervert the justice due (A)(E)   *Pr 31:5*

pervert the rights of the afflicted (B)(R)   *Pr 31:5*

I saw under the sun the place of *j*.   *Ec 3:16*

the place of justice (A)(R)   *Ec 3:16*

the place of righteousness (E)   *Ec 3:16*

seest violent perverting of *j*. and   *Ec 5:8*

justice

and a wise man discerneth both time and *j*.   *Ec 8:5*

because to every purpose there is time and *j*.   *Ec 8:6*

seek *j*.; it was full of *j*.   *Isa 1:17; 1:21*

Zion shall be redeemed with *j*.   *Isa 1:27*

we shall receive greater *j*. (S)   *Isa 3:1*

shall have purged Jerusalem by the spirit of *j*.   *Isa 4:4*

and looked for *j*.   *Isa 5:7*

and to establish it with *j*. and with justice   *Isa 9:7*

with justice and righteousness (A)(B)(E)(R)   *Isa 9:7*

to turn aside the needy from *j*.   *Isa 10:2*

execute *j*.   *Isa 16:3; Jer 21:12; 22:3; Eze 18:8; 45:9; Zec 7:9; 8:12*

execute justice (A)(E)(R)   *Isa 16:3*

arbitrate justly (B)   *Isa 16:3*

seeking *j*.   *Isa 16:5*

for a spirit of *j*.   *Isa 28:6*

I will lay *j*. to the line   *Isa 28:17*

will have mercy, for the Lord is a God of *j*.   *Isa 30:18*

then *j*. shall dwell in the wilderness   *Isa 32:16*

Lord hath filled Zion with *j*. and righteousness   *Isa 33:5*

and upon the people of my curse to *j*.   *Isa 34:5*

and who taught him in the path of *j*.   *Isa 40:14*

let us come near together to *j*.   *Isa 41:1*

he shall bring forth *j*. to the Gentiles   *Isa 42:1*

he shall bring forth *j*. unto truth   *Isa 42:3*

he shall not fail, till he have set *j*. in the earth   *Isa 42:4*

he was taken from prison and from *j*.   *Isa 53:8*

keep ye *j*. and do justice   *Isa 56:1; Ho 12:6*

and there is no *j*. in their goings   *Isa 59:8*

therefore is *j*. far from us, neither doth justice   *Isa 59:9*

we look for *j*. but there is none   *Isa 59:11*

j. is turned away backward; and justice   *Isa 59:14*

it displeased him that there was no *j*.   *Isa 59:15*

I the Lord love *j*. I hate robbery   *Isa 61:8*

Lord will execute *j*. (A)(B)(E)(R)   *Isa 66:16*

speak in *j*. against (A)(B)(E)(R)   *Jer 4:12*

if there be any that executeth *j*.   *Jer 5:1*

they know not the *j*. of their God   *Jer 5:4; 8:7*

they have known the *j*. of their God   *Jer 5:5*

if ye thoroughly execute *j*. between a man   *Jer 7:5*

in the time of their *j*. (S)   *Jer 8:12; 10:15; 11:23; 23:12; 46:21; 48:44; 50:27; 51:18; Ho 9:7; Mic 7:4*

which exercise *j*. and righteousness in earth   *Jer 9:24*

justice and righteousness (B)(E)(R)   *Jer 9:24*

correct me, but with *j*. not in anger   *Jer 10:24*

correct me, but justly (B)   *Jer 10:24*

correct me, but in just measure (E)(R)   *Jer 10:24*

execute *j*. in the morning, and deliver him   *Jer 21:12*

execute justice (A)(E)(R)   *Jer 21:12; 23:5*

practice *j*. (B)   *Jer 21:12*

branch shall execute *j*. in the earth   *Jer 23:5; 33:15*

execute *j*. and righteousness (B)   *Jer 23:5*

enter into *j*. (A)(E)   *Jer 25:31*

to Riblah, where he gave *j.*　*Jer 39:5;*
upon him　*52:9*
passed sentence upon him　*Jer 39:5*
(A)(B)(R)
and *j.* is come upon the plain *Jer 48:21*
country
thus far is the *j.* of Moab　*Jer 48:47*
they whose *j.* was not to　*Jer 49:12*
drink of the cup
forsake her, for her *j.* reacheth *Jer 51:9*
unto heaven
city full of wresting of *j.* (E)　*Eze 9:9*
enter into *j.* (A)(E)(R)　*Eze 17:20;*
　38:22
enter into *j.* (S)　*Eze 17:20;*
　20:35-36; 38:22
for they had executed *j.* on　*Eze 23:10*
her
I will set *j.* before them, they *Eze 23:24*
shall judge
king of heaven, all whose ways *Da 4:37*
are *j.*
his ways are just (A)(R)　*Da 4:37*
his dealings are just (B)　*Da 4:37*
his ways are justice (E)　*Da 4:37*
j. was set　*Da 7:10*
the Judge was seated (A)　*Da 7:10*
j. was given to the saints of the *Da 7:22*
most High
the court took its seat (B)　*Da 7:22*
but the *j.* shall sit　*Da 7:26*
give ye ear, for *j.* is toward you *Ho 5:1*
who does justice (A)(B)(R)　*Ho 5:1*
that doeth justly (B)　*Ho 5:1*
thus *j.* springeth up as hemlock *Ho 10:4*
in the field
enter into *j.* with　*Joe 3:2*
(A)(B)(E)(R)
ye who turn *j.* into wormwood　*Am 5:7*
turn justice into bitterness　*Am 5:7*
(A)(B)(E)(R)
love the good, and establish *j.* *Am 5:15*
in the gate
but let *j.* run down as waters　*Am 5:24*
and righteousness
for ye have turned *j.* into gall *Am 6:12*
is it not to know *j.*　*Mic 3:1*
I am full of *j.*　*Mic 3:8*
that abhor *j.*　*Mic 3:9*
deal out *j.* for a bribe (B)(R) *Mic 3:11*
and execute *j.* for me　*Mic 7:9*
law is slacked, *j.* doth never go *Hab 1:4*
forth
their *j.* shall proceed of　*Hab 1:7*
themselves
O Lord, thou hast ordained　*Hab 1:12*
them for *j.*
all ye which have wrought his *j.* *Zep 2:3*
every morning doth he bring *j.* *Zep 3:5*
to light
yet ye say, Where is the God *Mal 2:17*
of *j.*
shall be in danger of the *j.*　*M't 5:21;*
　5:22
escape punishment imposed　*M't 5:21*
by the court (A)
is liable before the court (B)　*M't 5:21*
must stand his trial (P)　*M't 5:21*
with what *j.* ye judge, ye shall *M't 7:2*
be judged
judge, criticize, and condemn　*M't 7:2*
(A)
the way you judge will be　*M't 7:2*
judged (B)(N)
he shall shew *j.* to the　*M't 12:18*
Gentiles
justice to the Gentiles　*M't 12:18*
(B)(R)
till he send forth *j.* unto　*M't 12:20*
victory
brings justice　*M't 12:20*
(A)(B)(N)(R)
greater *j.* (B)　*M't 23:14*
and have omitted *j.*, mercy, *M't 23:23*
and faith
right, justice, mercy, fidelity *M't 23:23*
(A)(B)
justice, mercy, and faith　*M't 23:23*
(E)(N)(P)(R)
escape *j.* of hell (E)　*M't 23:33*
and pass over *j.* and the love *Lu 11:42*
of God
neglect justice and love　*Lu 11:42*
(A)(B)(E)(N)(P)(R)
this is the *j.* (A)(E)(P)(R)　*Joh 3:19*
but hath committed all *j.* to　*Joh 5:22*
the Son
does not come into *j.*　*Joh 5:24*
(A)(E)(N)(P)(R)(S)

hath given him authority to　*Joh 5:27*
execute *j.* also
resurrection of *j.* (E)(P)(R)　*Joh 5:29*
not to appearance, but judge　*Joh 7:24*
righteous *j.*
judge fairly and righteously　*Joh 7:24*
(A)(B)
judge by the reality (P)　*Joh 7:24*
for *j.* I am come into this　*Joh 9:39*
world
now is the *j.* of this world,　*Joh 12:31*
now shall
Now is this world's sentence *Joh 12:31*
(B)
he will reprove the world of *j.* *Joh 16:8;*
　16:11
in his humiliation his *j.* was　*Ac 8:33*
taken away
he was deprived of his trial (B) *Ac 8:33*
humiliated and has no redress *Ac 8:33*
(N)
humiliation justice was denied *Ac 8:33*
him (R)
it is my *j.* that　*Ac 15:19*
(B)(E)(N)(R)(S)
giving *j.* (E)(R)　*Ac 21:25*
as he reasoned of *j.* Felix　*Ac 24:25*
trembled
the Jews desiring to have *j.*　*Ac 25:15*
against him
petitioning judicial hearing　*Ac 25:15*
and condemnation of him (A)
request for sentence against　*Ac 25:15*
him (B)(E)(R)
demanding his condemnation *Ac 25:15*
(N)
demanded his conviction (P) *Ac 25:15*
who knowing the *j.* of God,　*Ro 1:32*
that they which
fully aware of God's righteous *Ro 1:32*
decree (A)
knowing God's ordinance　*Ro 1:32*
(B)(E)
know the just decree of God　*Ro 1:32*
(N)(R)
well aware of God's　*Ro 1:32*
pronouncement (P)
who sat in *j.* (N)　*Ro 2:1*
are sure that the *j.* of God is *Ro 2:2*
according to truth
God's sentence rests in all　*Ro 2:2*
fairness (B)
thinkest that thou shalt escape *Ro 2:3*
the *j.* of God
escape God's sentence (B)　*Ro 2:3*
revelation of the righteous *j.* of *Ro 2:5*
God
for the *j.* was by one to　*Ro 5:16*
condemnation
sentence of one brought　*Ro 5:16*
condemnation (A)(R)
j. came on all men to　*Ro 5:18*
condemnation
receive *j.* (E)(R)(S)　*Ro 13:2*
pass *j.* on scruples (A)　*Ro 14:1*
pass *j.* on another's　*Ro 14:4*
(A)(N)(R)
pass *j.* on (R)　*Ro 14:13*
but be joined together in the　*1Co 1:10*
same *j.*
that I should be judged of　*1Co 4:3*
man's *j.*
passed *j.* on (A)(N)(P)(R)　*1Co 5:3*
seek *j.* in pagan court (B)(P) *1Co 6:1*
drinks verdict of *j.* (A)(S)　*1Co 11:29*
drink *j.* (E)(N)(P)(R)(S)　*1Co 11:29*
fall under Lord's *j.* (N)　*1Co 11:32*
to bring *j.*　*1Co 11:34*
(A)(B)(E)(N)(P)
let no man sit in *j.* (A)　*Col 2:16*
token of the righteous *j.* of　*2Th 1:5*
God
God's fair verdict (B)　*2Th 1:5*
may receive *j.* (B)(N)　*2Th 2:12*
j. contrived by the devil (N)　*1Ti 3:6*
some sins are open, going　*1Ti 5:24*
before to *j.*
and of eternal *j.*　*Heb 6:2*
eternal punishment (B)　*Heb 6:2*
after this the *j.*　*Heb 9:27*
but a certain fearful looking *Heb 10:27*
for of *j.*
dreadful anticipation of　*Heb 10:27*
(B)
passed *j.* and sentence on　*Heb 11:7*
(A)(B)
he shall have *j.* without mercy *Jas 2:13*
that shewed no mercy, and
mercy rejoiceth against *j.*

received heavier *j.* (E)　*Jas 3:1*
so you may incur no *j.*　*Jas 3:12*
(B)(E)(N)
pass *j.* on neighbor (A)　*Jas 4:12*
come under *j.* (B)(N)　*Jas 5:9*
that *j.* must begin at the house *1Pe 4:17*
of God
whose *j.* lingereth not　*2Pe 2:3*
of old the sentence for them　*2Pe 2:3*
(A)(B)
j. decreed (N)　*2Pe 2:3*
of old their condemnation has *2Pe 2:3*
not been (R)
reserved to *j.*　*2Pe 2:4*
do not pronounce railing *j.* (R) *2Pe 2:11*
to *j.* of the great day　*Jude 6*
warning of fire of *j.* (P)　*Jude 7*
to execute *j.*　*Jude 15*
fear God, for the hour of his *j.* *Re 14:7*
is come
will shew thee the *j.* of the　*Re 17:1*
great whore
doom of the great whore　*Re 17:1*
(A)(B)
alas, alas, for in one hour is　*Re 18:10*
thy *j.* come
they sat on them, and *j.* was *Re 20:4*
given to them
authority to act as judges and *Re 20:4*
pass sentence was entrusted (A)(B)
appointed judges seated upon *Re 20:4*
them (P)

DO JUDGMENT

to *do* justice and *j.*　*Ge 18:19;*
　1Ki 10:9; Pr 21:3; Jer 22:15
doing what is right and fair　*Ge 18:19*
(B)
wisdom of God was in him to *1Ki 3:28*
do j.
to administer justice　*1Ki 3:28*
(B)(E)(R)
set over them to *do* justice and *2Ch 9:8*
j.
to administer equity and　*2Ch 9:8*
justice (B)
to do justice and righteousness *2Ch 9:8*
(E)(R)
because they refuse to *do j.*　*Pr 21:7*
refuse to do justice (A)(E)　*Pr 21:7*
refuse to act with fairness (B) *Pr 21:7*
refuse to do what is just (R)　*Pr 21:7*
it is joy to the just to *do j.* but *Pr 21:15*
destruction
when justice is done it is a joy *Pr 21:15*
(A)(R)
doing justice is joy to　*Pr 21:15*
righteous (B)(E)
I will *do j.* on the graven　*Jer 51:47*
images
I will *do j.* on her graven　*Jer 51:52*
images

IN JUDGMENT

do no unrighteousness *in j.*　*Le 19:15;*
　19:34
no unfairness in a court　*Le 19:15*
decision (B)
stand before the congregation *Nu 35:12*
in j.
stood trial before the　*Nu 35:12*
assembly (B)
ye shall not respect persons *in De 1:17*
j.
if there arise a matter too hard *De 17:8*
for thee *in j.*
too difficult for you to decide *De 17:8*
(B)
case requiring decision too　*De 17:8*
difficult (R)
ye that sit *in j.* and walk by the *J'g 5:10*
way
for the Lord, who is with you *2Ch 19:6*
in j.
and we should come together *Job 9:32*
in j.
come together in court for　*Job 9:32*
trial (A)(B)
he is excellent in power and *Job 37:23*
in j.
he will disregard no right　*Job 37:23*
(A)
will not pervert justice (B)　*Job 37:23*
the ungodly shall not stand *in j.* *Ps 1:5*
the meek will he guide *in j.* and *Ps 25:9*
teach

guide humble in what is right *Ps 25:9* (B)(R)
meek he will guide in justice *Ps 25:9* (E)
his mouth transgresseth not in *Pr 16:10* *j.*
not good to overthrow the *Pr 18:5* righteous *in j.*
deprive righteous of justice *Pr 18:5* (A)(B)(R)
not good to have respect of *Pr 24:23* persons *in j.*
but the Lord of hosts shall be *Isa 5:16* exalted *in j.*
shall be exalted in justice *Isa 5:16* (A)(B)(E)(R)
him that sitteth *in j.* *Isa 28:6*
him who executes justice (B) *Isa 28:6*
they stumble *in j.* *Isa 28:7*
behold princes shall rule *in j.* *Isa 32:1*
princes shall rule in justice *Isa 32:1* (A)(B)(E)(R)
every tongue that shall rise *Isa 54:17* against thee *in j.*
the Lord liveth in righteousness *Jer 4:2* and *in j.*
in justice and in righteousness *Jer 4:2* (B)(E)(R)
in controversy they stand *in* *Eze 44:24* *j.*
I will betroth thee to me *in j.* *Ho 2:19*
in righteousness and justice *Ho 2:19* (A)(B)(E)(R)
Ephraim is oppressed and *Ho 5:11* broken *in j.*
he crushes justice to earth (B) *Ho 5:11*
and I will come near to you *in* *Mal 3:5* *j.*
the men of Nineveh shall rise *M't 12:41* *in j.*
queen of south shall rise *in* *M't 12:42;* *j.* *Lu 11:31-32*
I pray, that your love may *Ph'p 1:9* abound *in j.*

INTO JUDGMENT

and bringest me *into j.* with *Job 14:3* thee
will he reprove, will he enter *Job 22:4* with thee *into j.*
that he should enter *into j.* *Job 34:23* with God
enter not *into j.* with thy *Ps 143:2* servant
for these God will bring thee *Ec 11:9* *into j.*
God will call you to account *Ec 11:9* (B)
God shall bring every work *Ec 12:14* *into j.*
Lord will enter *into j.* with *Isa 3:14* ancients

MY JUDGMENT

who hath taken away *my j.* *Job 27:2;* 34:5
taken away my right, denied *Job 27:2* me justice (A)
taken away my right *Job 27:2* (B)(E)(R)
my j. was as a robe and a *Job 29:14* diadem
my justice was like a robe *Job 29:14* (A)(E)(R)
my fairness dressed me as a *Job 29:14* robe (B)
wilt thou also disannul *my j.* *Job 40:8*
discredit my justice (B) *Job 40:8*
put me in the wrong (R) *Job 40:8*
stir up thyself, and awake to *Ps 35:23* *my j.*
awake to the justice due me *Ps 35:23* (A)(E)
awake for my right (R) *Ps 35:23*
my j. is passed over from my *Isa 40:27* God
my right is passed over (A) *Isa 40:27*
your rights are overlooked *Isa 40:27* (B)
justice due me is passed away *Isa 40:27* (E)
my right is disregarded by *Isa 40:27* God (R)
yet surely *my j.* is with the *Isa 49:4* Lord
my right is with the Lord *Isa 49:4* (A)(B)(R)

justice due me is with Jehovah *Isa 49:4* (E)
I will make *my j.* to rest for a *Isa 51:4* light of people
my justice for a light to *Isa 51:4* (A)(B)(E)(R)
all the heathen shall see *my j.* *Eze 39:21*
and *my j.* is just *Joh 5:30*
my j. is true *Joh 8:16*
yet I give *my j.* *1Co 7:25*
I give my opinion and advice *1Co 7:25* (A)(B)(P)(R)
happier in *my j.* *1Co 7:40*

JUDGMENT HALL

they led Jesus to *hall* of *j.* *Joh 18:28*
themselves went not into *j. hall* *Joh 18:28*
into the praetorium *Joh 18:28* (A)(B)(E)(R)
into the Governor's *Joh 18:28* headquarters (N)
into the palace (P) *Joh 18:28*
then Pilate entered into the *Joh 18:33* *j. hall* again
entered the palace again *Joh 18:33* (B)(P)
again into the praetorium *Joh 18:33* (E)(R)
into his headquarters (N) *Joh 18:33*
went into the *j. hall* and saith *Joh 19:9* to Jesus
Again he entered the palace *Joh 19:9* (B)(P)
entered the praetorium again *Joh 19:9* (E)(R)
back into his headquarters *Joh 19:9* (N)
to be kept in Herod's *j. hall* *Ac 23:35*
in Herod's palace—the *Ac 23:35* praetorium (A)
kept in Herod's palace *Ac 23:35* (E)(N)(P)
guarded in Herod's *Ac 23:35* praetorium (R)

JUDGMENT SEAT

he was set down on *j.* seat *M't 27:19;* *Joh 19:13*
seated on the tribunal (B) *M't 27:19*
sitting in court (N) *M't 27:19*
sitting on the Bench (P) *M't 27:19*
the Jews brought him to the *Ac 18:12* *j.* seat
sitting on the judge's seat (A) *Ac 18:12*
led him before the court *Ac 18:12* (B)(N)(P)
brought him before the *Ac 18:12* tribunal (R)
and he drave them from the *Ac 18:16* *j.* seat
drove him from the court *Ac 18:16* (B)(N)(P)
drove him from the tribunal *Ac 18:16* (R)
the Greeks beat Sosthenes *Ac 18:17* before the *j.* seat
in front of the court gave a *Ac 18:17* beating (A)
beating in full view of the *Ac 18:17* bench (N)
beat him in front of the *Ac 18:17* courthouse (P)
beat him in front of the *Ac 18:17* tribunal (R)
I stand at Caesar's *j.* seat *Ac 25:10*
I take my stand at Caesar's *Ac 25:10* tribunal (B)(N)
I am standing in Caesar's *Ac 25:10* court (P)
I am standing before Caesar's *Ac 25:10* tribunal (R)
I sat on *j.* seat *Ac 25:17*
stand before *j.* seat of Christ *Ro 14:10;* *2Co 5:10*
placed at God's tribunal *Ro 14:10* (B)(N)
rich men draw you before the *Jas 2:6* *j.* seats
drag you into law courts *Jas 2:6* (A)(B)(N)(R)
drag you into litigation (P) *Jas 2:6*

JUDGMENTS

I will redeem you with great *j.* *Ex 6:6;* 7:4
these are the *j.* thou shalt set *Ex 21:1* before them

these are the ordinances *Ex 21:1* (A)(E)(R)
these are the legal orders (B) *Ex 21:1*
and Moses told the people all *Ex 24:3* the *j.*
all the ordinances (A)(E)(R) *Ex 24:3*
all the legal instructions (B) *Ex 24:3*
on their gods the Lord *Nu 33:4* executed (B)
shall judge according to these *Nu 35:24* *j.*
according to these regulations *Nu 35:24* (B)
according to these ordinances *Nu 35:24* (E)(R)
these are the *j.* which the *Nu 36:13* Lord commanded
these are the commands and *Nu 36:13* ordinances (A)(E)(R)
these are the commands and *Nu 36:13* regulations (B)
j. are upright and just (A) *De 4:8*
if ye hearken to these *j.* and *De 7:12* keep them
hearken to these precepts (A) *De 7:12*
show obedience to these *De 7:12* ordinances (B)
And his statutes and his *j.* *De 30:16*
they shall teach Jacob thy *j.* *De 33:10* and law
he executed the *j.* of the Lord *De 33:21* with Israel
his *j.* were before me *2Sa 22:23;* *Ps 18:22*
remember *j.* of his mouth *1Ch 6:12;* *Ps 105:5*
his *j.* are in all the earth *1Ch 16:14;* *Ps 105:7*
but sinned against thy *j.* *Ne 9:29*
thy *j.* are far above out of sight *Ps 10:5*
the *j.* of the Lord are true and *Ps 19:9* righteous
thy *j.* are a great deep; O *Ps 36:6* Lord thou preservest
let Judah be glad because of *Ps 48:11* thy *j.*
because of thy just decisions *Ps 48:11* (B)
give the king thy *j.* O God, and *Ps 72:1* righteousness
grant unto the king thy justice *Ps 72:1* (B)(R)
Judah rejoiced, because of thy *Ps 97:8* *j.* O Lord
because of thy justice (B) *Ps 97:8*
when I have learned thy *Ps 119:7* righteous *j.*
with my lips I declared all *Ps 119:13* the *j.* of thy mouth
ordinances (A)(B)(E)(R) *Ps 119:13* 119:20, 30, 39, 43, 62, 102, 106, 108, 147:20
for the longing that it hath *Ps 119:20* unto thy *j.*
thy *j.* have I laid before me *Ps 119:30*
turn away my reproach, for *Ps 119:39* thy *j.* are good
I hoped in thy *j.* *Ps 119:43*
I remembered thy *j.* *Ps 119:52*
give thanks, because of thy *Ps 119:62;* righteous *j.* 119:164
I know, O Lord, that thy *j.* *Ps 119:75* are right
I have not departed from *Ps 119:102*
I have sworn that I will *Ps 119:106* keep thy righteous *j.*
teach me thy *j.* *Ps 119:108*
I am afraid of thy *j.* *Ps 119:120*
righteous art thou, and *Ps 119:137* upright are thy *j.*
O Lord, quicken me *Ps 119:156* according to thy *j.*
according to thy justice (R) *Ps 119:156*
every one of thy righteous *j.* *Ps 119:160* endureth
let my soul live, and let thy *j.* *Ps 119:175* help me
his *j.* they have not *Ps 147:20* known them
j. are prepared for scorners, *Pr 19:29* stripes
in the way of thy *j.* we waited *Isa 26:8* for thee
for when thy *j.* are in the *Isa 26:9* earth, inhabitants
ask of me righteous *j.* *Isa 58:2* (A)(E)(R)

yet let me talk with thee of thy *Jer 12:1*
j.
plead and reason the case with *Jer 12:1*
you (A)(E)(R)
argue with thee about justice *Jer 12:1*
(B)
nor done according to the j. of *Eze 5:7*
the nations
ordinances of the nations *Eze 5:7*
(A)(B)(E)(R)
execute j. in the midst of thee *Eze 5:8;*
5:10, 15; 11:9
execute j. on thee in sight of *Eze 16:41*
women
they shall judge thee *Eze 23:24*
according to their j.
and I will execute j. on Moab *Eze 25:11*
executed j. on all those that *Eze 28:26*
despise them
I will execute j. in No *Eze 30:14*
thus will I execute j. in Egypt *Eze 30:19*
I will destroy, I will feed *Eze 34:16*
them with j.
we sinned by departing from *Da 9:5*
thy j.
swerved from commands, *Da 9:5*
ordinances (A)(B)(E)(R)
thy j. are as the light that *Ho 6:5*
goeth forth
the Lord hath taken away thy *Zep 3:15*
j.
dismissed the sentence against *Zep 3:15*
you (B)
how unsearchable are his j. *Ro 11:33*
and ways
if ye have j. of things of this *1Co 6:4*
life
j. from the Lord serve (B) *1Co 11:32*
for thy j. are made manifest *Re 15:4*
true and righteous are thy j. *Re 16:7;*
19:2

MY JUDGMENTS

ye shall do *my* j. I am the Lord *Le 18:4*
practice my regulations (B) *Le 18:4*
Mine ordinances ye shall do *Le 18:4*
(E)(R)
ye shall therefore keep *my* j. *Le 18:5;*
25:18
if your soul abhor *my* j. so *Le 26:15*
that ye do not
soul abhors my injunctions *Le 26:15*
(B)
abhor my ordinances (E)(R) *Le 26:15*
because, even because they *Le 26:43*
despised *my* j.
despised my ordinances *Le 26:43*
(B)(E)(R)
if ye be constant to do *my* j. *1Ch 28:7*
if his children walk not in *my* *Ps 89:30*
j.
I will utter *my* j. against them *Jer 1:16*
she changed *my* j. into *Eze 5:6*
wickedness
rebelled against my ordinances *Eze 5:6;*
(B)(E)(R) *5:7*
neither have kept *my* j. nor *Eze 5:7*
done
when I send *my* four sore j. *Eze 14:21*
on Jerusalem
and ye shall keep *my* j. and *Eze 36:27*
do them
observe my ordinances *Eze 36:27*
(B)(E)(R)
they shall judge it according *Eze 44:24*
to *my* j.
according to my laws (B) *Eze 44:24*
according to my ordinances *Eze 44:24*
(E)

STATUTES AND JUDGMENTS

keep my *statutes and* my j. *Le 18:5;*
18:26; 20:22; De 7:11; 11:1; 26:16-17;
30:16; 1Ki 2:3; 8:58; 9:4; 11:33
keep my law and my *Le 18:5*
ordinances (B)
keep my statutes and *Le 18:5*
ordinances (E)(R)
ye shall observe all my *Le 19:37;*
statutes and j. De 11:32; 12:1; 2Ch 7:17
observe my laws and *Le 19:37*
ordinances (B)
observe my statutes and *Le 19:37*
ordinances (E)(R)
these are the *statutes and* j. *Le 26:46;*
Lord made *De 4:45*
these are statutes and *Le 26:46*
ordinances (B)(E)(R)

hearken to *statutes and* j. *De 4:1;*
which I teach *5:1*
laws and ordinances *De 4:1;*
(A)(B)(E)(R) *4:5, 14; 5:31; 6:20; 8:11*
I taught you *statutes and* j. *De 4:5*
hath *statutes and* j. so righteous *De 4:8*
commanded to teach *statutes De 4:14;*
and j. *6:1; Ezr 7:10*
I will speak the *statutes and* j. *De 5:31*
thou shalt teach
thy son asketh thee, What mean *De 6:20*
the *statutes and* j.
forget Lord in not keeping his *De 8:11;*
statutes and j. *Ne 1:7*
walk in my *statutes and* *1Ki 6:12*
execute my j.
if thou takest heed to fulfil *1Ch 22:13*
statutes and j.
what cause shall come *2Ch 19:10*
between *statutes and* j.
and thou gavest them right *Ne 9:13*
statutes and j.
entered into a curse, to do all *Ne 10:29*
his *statutes and* j.
he sheweth his *statutes and* j. *Ps 147:19*
to Israel
for they refused my j. *and* my *Eze 5:6*
statutes
for ye have not walked in *Eze 11:12;*
my *statutes,* nor executed my j. *20:13,*
16, 21
walked in my *statutes and* j. *Eze 18:9;*
18:17; 20:19; 37:24
give them my *statutes, and* *Eze 20:11*
shewed my j.
not in *statutes* of fathers, nor *Eze 20:18*
observe their j.
gave them *statutes* not good, *Eze 20:25*
and j. whereby
remember ye law of Moses *Mal 4:4*
with *statutes and* j.

JUDICIAL

make the j. breastplate (B) *Ex 28:15*
take case to court for j. *De 25:1*
decision
petitioning j. hearing and *Ac 25:15*
condemnation of him (A)
for the j. action (N) *Ro 5:16*

JUDITH

Esau, when he took to wife J. *Ge 26:34*

JUG

the water j. (B)(R) *1Sa 26:11;*
26:12; 1Ki 14:3
oil in a j. (B) *1Sa 17:12; 17:14; 19:6*

JUICE

outflow of grape j. (A) *Ex 22:29*
wine of the j. of my *Ca 8:2*
pomegranate

JULIA

Salute Philologus, and J., *Ro 16:15*
Nereus

JULIUS

unto one named J., a centurion *Ac 27:1*
And J. courteously entreated *Ac 27:3*
Paul

JUMPING

horses, and of the j. chariots *Na 3:2*

JUNIA

Salute Andronicus and J., my *Ro 16:7*

JUNGLE

wander in a j. (B) *Job 12:24*
j. of the Jordan (B)(R) *Jer 12:5;*
49:19; 50:44

JUNIPER

Elijah came and sat under a *1Ki 19:4;*
j. tree *19:5*
under a broom bush (B)(R) *1Ki 19:4*
as he lay and slept under a j. *1Ki 19:5*
tree

bushes, and j. roots for their *Job 30:4*
meat
roots of the broom *Job 30:4*
(A)(B)(E)(R)
arrows of the mighty with *Ps 120:4*
coals of j.
the broom tree (A)(B)(R) *Ps 120:4*

JUPITER

And they called Barnabas, J. *Ac 14:12*
called Barnabas Zeus *Ac 14:12;*
(A)(B)(R) *14:13*
Then the priest of J. which *Ac 14:13*
was
image which fell down from J. *Ac 19:35*

JURISDICTION

that he belonged unto Herod's *Lu 23:7*
j.

JURIST

bring Zenas the j. (B) *Tit 3:13*

JUSHAB-HESED

and Berechiah, and Hasadiah, *1Ch 3:20*
J.

JUST

Noah was a j. man, and *Ge 16:9*
perfect, and
Noah was an upright man (B) *Ge 6:9*
Noah was a righteous man *Ge 6:9*
(E)(R)
a right and j. nation (A) *Ge 20:4;*
38:26; Job 15:14
thwarts j. man's testimony (B) *Ex 23:8*
j. balances, j. weights, a j. *Le 19:36;*
ephah, a j. hin *De 25:15; Eze 45:10*
honest scales, honest bushel, *Le 19:36*
honest (B)
judgments are upright and j. (A) *De 4:8*
they shall judge people with j. *De 16:18*
judgments
judge with righteous judgment *De 16:18*
(A)(E)(R)
administer proper justice (B) *De 16:18*
that is altogether j. shalt thou *De 16:20*
follow
Strive for justice (B)(R) *De 16:20*
a God without iniquity, j. and *De 32:4*
right is he
all his ways are j. (B) *De 32:4*
commands and j. decrees (S) *De 33:21*
slain a j. man (A) *2Sa 4:11*
rulers decree what is j. (R) *2Sa 8:15*
he that ruleth over men must *2Sa 23:3*
be j.
recognize what is j. and right *1Ki 3:11*
you are j. and innocent (A) *1Ki 10:9*
thou art j. in all that is brought *Ne 9:33*
on us
shall mortal man be more j. *Job 4:17*
than God
Can man be pure before his *Job 4:17*
Maker (A)(B)
Can mortal man be righteous *Job 4:17*
before God (R)
but how should man be j. with *Job 9:2*
God
man be right before God *Job 9:2*
(A)(B)
the j. upright man is laughed *Job 12:4*
to scorn
how can a human being be j. *Job 25:4*
(B)(E)
he may prepare it, but the j. *Job 27:17*
shall put it on
behold, in this thou art not j. *Job 33:12*
in this claim you are not fair *Job 33:12*
(B)
in this you are not right (R) *Job 33:12*
let wickedness end, but establish *Ps 7:9*
the j.
establish the upright, righteous *Ps 7:9*
(A)(B)(E)(R)
the wicked plotteth against the *Ps 37:12*
j.
because of thy j. decisions (B) *Ps 48:11*
works are faithful and j. (R) *Ps 111:7*
done what is j. and right *Ps 119:121*
(R)
but he blesseth the habitation *Pr 3:33*
of the j.

the righteous (A)(B)(E)(R) Pr 3:33;
4:18; 9:9; 10:6-7, 20, 31; 11:9; 12:13, 21;
13:22; 17:15, 26; 21:15; 24:16; 29:27;
Ec 7:15, 20; 8:14; Eze 18:5; Am 5:12;
Hab 2:4
the path of the *j.* is as the Pr 4:18
shining light
teach a *j.* man, and he will Pr 9:9
increase in learning
blessings are upon the head of Pr 10:6
the *j.*
the memory of the *j.* is blessed Pr 10:7
the tongue of the *j.* is as Pr 10:20
choice silver
the mouth of the *j.* bringeth Pr 10:31
forth wisdom
but a *j.* weight is his delight Pr 11:1
an accurate weight is his Pr 11:1
delight (B)
but through knowledge shall Pr 11:9
the *i.* be delivered
but the *j.* shall come out of Pr 12:13
trouble
there shall no evil happen to Pr 12:21
the *j.*
the wealth of the sinner is laid Pr 13:22
up for the *j.*
a *j.* weight and balance are the Pr 16:11
Lord's
scales of justice are the Lord's Pr 16:11
(B)
he that condemneth the *j.* is Pr 17:15
abomination
also to punish the *j.* is not Pr 17:26
good
he that is first in his own Pr 18:17
cause seemeth *j.*
states his case seems right Pr 18:17
(A)(B)(R)
the *j.* man walketh in his Pr 20:7
integrity
refuse to do what is *j.* (R) Pr 21:7
it is a joy to the *j.* to do Pr 21:15
judgment
a *j.* man falleth seven times Pr 24:16
and riseth again
hate the upright, but the *j.* Pr 29:10
seek his soul
an unjust man is an Pr 29:27
abomination to the *i.*
there is a *j.* man that perisheth Ec 7:15
in his
not a *j.* man upon earth that Ec 7:20
sinneth not
there by *j.* men to whom it Ec 8:14
happeneth
way of *j.* is uprightness, thou Isa 26:7
most upright dost weigh path of *i.*
turn aside the *j.* for a thing of Isa 29:21
nought
thrust aside the innocent, Isa 29:21
righteous (A)
turn aside person who is in Isa 29:21
right (B)(R)
I the Lord, a *j.* God, and a Isa 45:21
Saviour
righteous and rescuing God Isa 45:21
(B)
a righteous God and a Savior Isa 45:21
(R)
correct me, but in *j.* measure Jer 10:24
(E)(R)
that have shed the blood of the La 4:13
j. in her
but if a man be *j.* and do that Eze 18:5
is right
he is *i.* he shall surely live, saith Eze 18:9
the Lord God
The Lord is not *j.* (R) Eze 18:25; 25:29
his ways are *i.* (A)(B)(R) Da 4:27
ways of Lord right, *j.* shall Ho 14:9
walk in them
they afflict the *j.* they take a Am 5:12
bribe
but the *j.* shall live by faith Hab 2:4;
Ro 1:17; Ga 3:11; Heb 10:38
the *i.* Lord is in the midst Zep 3:5
thereof
Lord uncompromisingly Zep 3:5
righteous (A)(B)(E)(R)
he is *j.* and having salvation, Zec 9:9
lowly
righteous and victorious (B) Zec 9:9
triumphant and victorious (R) Zec 9:9
Joseph her husband, being a *j.* M't 1:19
man
Joseph was fairminded (B) M't 1:19
Joseph, being a righteous man M't 1:19
(E)

Being a man of principle (N) M't 1:19
Joseph was a good man (P) M't 1:19
and sendeth rain on the *j.* and M't 5:45
on unjust
rain on the good M't 5:45
(A)(B)(E)(N)
rain upon the honest and M't 5:45
dishonest (P)
and sever the wicked from M't 13:49
among the *j.*
wicked from the righteous M't 13:49
(A)(B)(E)(R)
wicked from the good M't 13:49
(N)(P)
have nothing to do with that M't 27:19
j. man
that innocent man (B)(N) M't 27:19
that righteous man (E)(R) M't 27:19
that good man (P) M't 27:19
I am innocent of the blood M't 27:24
of this *j.* person
this righteous man's blood M't 27:24
(A)(E)
this good man's blood (B) M't 27:24
knowing that he was a *j.* man M'k 6:20
and holy
a righteous and a holy man M'k 6:20
(A)(E)(R)
a straight and holy man (B) M'k 6:20
a good and holy man (N) M'k 6:20
the disobedient to the wisdom Lu 1:17
of the *j.*
to the wisdom of the upright Lu 1:17
(A)
to the wisdom of the righteous Lu 1:17
(B)
to the ways of the righteous Lu 1:17
(N)
to the wisdom of good men Lu 1:17
(P)
Simeon was *j.* and devout, Lu 2:25
waiting for
was righteous and devout Lu 2:25
(A)(E)(R)
an upright and devout man Lu 2:25
(B)(N)(P)
acknowledges God is *j.* (B) Lu 7:29
be recompensed at the Lu 14:14
resurrection of the *j.*
more than over ninety and nine Lu 15:7
j. persons
ninety-nine righteous Lu 15:7
(A)(B)(E)(N)(P)(R)
declare yourselves *j.* and Lu 16:15
upright (A)
spies which should feign Lu 20:20
themselves *j.*
pretended to be honest Lu 20:20
(A)(B)(P)
feigned themselves to be Lu 20:20
righteous (E)
in the guise of honest men Lu 20:20
(N)
pretended to be sincere (R) Lu 20:20
Joseph of Arimathea was a Lu 23:50
good man and *j.*
a good man and righteous Lu 23:50
(A)(E)(R)
a good and upright man Lu 23:50
(B)(N)
as I hear I judge, and my Joh 5:30
judgment is *j.*
my judgment is right, fair Joh 5:30
(A)(B)
my judgment is righteous (E) Joh 5:30
my judgment is true (P) Joh 5:30
Cornelius the centurion, a *j.* Ac 10:22
man
shall be resurrection both of *j.* Ac 24:15
and unjust
for not the hearers of the law Ro 2:13
are *j.*
not hearers are righteous Ro 2:13
(A)(B)(R)
not by hearing men will be Ro 2:13
justified (N)
not familiarity with law Ro 2:13
justifies (P)
whose damnation is *j.* Ro 3:8
he might be *j.* Ro 3:26
and the commandment holy, *j.* Ro 7:12
and good
finally, whatsoever things are Ph'p 4:8
i., pure
give servants that which is *j.* Col 4:1
and equal
a bishop must be *j.* holy, Tit 1:8
temperate

upright and fair-minded Tit 1:8
(A)(P)
fair, of holy life (B) Tit 1:8
upright, holy, self-controlled Tit 1:8
(R)
received a *j.* recompence of Heb 2:2
reward
and to the spirits of *j.* men Heb 12:23
made perfect
spirits of righteous men Heb 12:23
(A)(B)
spirits of good men (N)(P) Heb 12:23
ye have condemned and killed Jas 5:6
the *i.*
murdered the righteous (A) Jas 5:6
murdered the upright (B) Jas 5:6
killed the righteous one (E)(R) Jas 5:6
condemned the innocent and Jas 5:6
murdered him (N)(P)
Christ suffered, the *j.* for the 1Pe 3:18
unjust
delivered *j.* Lot, vexed with 2Pe 2:7
conversation
delivered righteous Lot 2Pe 2:7
(A)(E)(P)(R)
rescued upright Lot (B) 2Pe 2:7
Lot, who was a good man (N) 2Pe 2:7
if we confess, he is *j.* to forgive 1Jo 1:9
us our sins
j. and true are thy ways, thou Re 15:3
King

JUST ONE

ye denied the Holy One and Ac 3:14
the *J.* One
Holy and Righteous One Ac 3:14
(B)(E)(N)(P)(R)
shewed before of the coming of Ac 7:52
the *J.* One
coming of Righteous One Ac 7:52
(A)(B)(E)(N)(P)(R)
shouldest know his will, and Ac 22:14
see that *J.* One
the Righteous One Ac 22:14
(A)(E)(N)(P)

MOST JUST

wilt thou condemn him that Job 34:17
is *most j.*
condemn the Righteous and Job 34:17
Mighty (B)(E)(R)

JUSTICE

keep way of Lord to do *j.* and Ge 18:19
judgment
doing what is right and fair Ge 18:19
(B)
righteousness and *j.* (S) Ge 18:19;
Ps 89:14; Pr 1:3; 21:3
he executeth the *j.* of Lord Ge 33:21
and judgments
did the righteous will of Lord Ge 33:21
(B)
executed righteousness of Ge 33:21
Jehovah (E)
executed commands and just Ge 33:21
decrees (R)
God has done me *j.* (B) Ge 50:6
majority to thwart *j.* (B)(E) Ex 23:2
j. due me (S) Ex 23:6;
De 27:19; Isa 40:27; 49:4
secure *j.* for widow (B) De 10:12
executes *j.* for fatherless De 10:18
(A)(B)(E)(R)(S)
administer proper *j.* (B) De 16:18
not distort *j.* (B)(E)(R) De 16:19
strive for *j.* (B)(R) De 16:20
wrest *i.* of sojourner De 24:17
(A)(E)(R)
j. due an alien De 27:19
(A)(B)(E)(R)
execute *j.* over his house (B) 1Sa 3:13
accepted presents; twisted *j.* 1Sa 8:3
(A)(B)(R)(S)
do me *j.* (B) 1Sa 24:15
David executed *j.* 2Sa 8:15; 1Ch 18:14
rulers decree righteously (B) 2Sa 8:15
rulers decree what is just (R) 2Sa 8:15
executed *j.* and righteousness 2Sa 8:15
(A)(B)(E)(S)
j. and righteousness (S) 2Sa 8:15;
1Ch 18:14; 2Ch 9:8; Ps 119:121; Ec 5:8;
Jer 22:15; 23:5; Eze 45:9
O that I were made judge, I 2Sa 15:4
would do it
to recognize *j.* (B)(E)(S) 1Ki 3:11

to administer *j.* 1Ki 3:28
(B)(E)(R)(S)
to execute *j.* and righteousness 1Ki 10:9
(S)
to do *j.* and righteousness 2Ch 9:8
(B)(E)(R)
no perversion of *j.* with God 2Ch 19:7
(B)(E)(R)
who knew law and *j.* (B) Es 1:13
or doth the Almighty pervert *j.* Job 8:3
doth God pervert *j.* Job 8:3;
(A)(B)(E) 9:19; 32:9, 12
pervert *j.* (S) Job 8:3;
34:12; Pr 17:23; 31:5
do men *j.* (B) Job 16:21
there is no *j.* (S) Job 19:7
denied me *j.* (A) Job 27:2
my *J.* was like a robe Job 29:14
(A)(E)(R)(S)
neither do the aged Job 32:9
understand *j.*
yet *j.* is before him (S) Job 35:14
judgment and *j.* take hold on Job 36:17
thee
is excellent in plenty of *j.* will Job 37:23
not afflict
will not pervert *j.* (B) Job 37:23
discredit my *j.* (B) Job 40:8
j. and vindication (A) Ps 7:6
meek he will guide in *j.* (E)(S) Ps 25:9
administer *j.* (A)(E) Ps 31:9
justice (A)(B)(E)(R) Ps 33:5;
37:30; 72:2; 89:14; 94:15; 99:4; 101:1;
106:3; Pr 1:3; 2:8; 8:20; 17:23; 19:28;
28:5; 29:4, 26; Ec 5:8; Isa 1:17, 27; 5:7;
10:2; 28:6; 30:18; 32:16; 33:5; 40:14;
42:3-4; 56:1; 59:8-9, 15; 61:8; Jer 7:5;
Am 5:15, 24; 6:12; Mic 3:1, 9; Hab 1:4;
Mal 2:17
loveth *j.* (S) Ps 33:5; 37:28; 99:4
awake to *j.* due me (A)(E) Ps 35:23
thy *j.* as the noonday (S) Ps 37:6
his tongue talketh of *j.* (S) Ps 37:30
grant the king thy *j.* (B)(R) Ps 72:1
judge the poor in *j.* (S) Ps 72:2
do *j.* to the afflicted and needy Ps 82:3
j. and judgment are habitation Ps 89:14
of thy throne
righteousness and *j.* are Ps 97:2
habitation (S)
justice (B)(S) Ps 98:9;
Pr 1:3; 2:9; Isa 11:4; Mic 3:9
executeth *j.* and righteousness Ps 99:4;
(S) 146:7
sing of mercy and *j.* (S) Ps 101:1
executes *j.* (A)(B)(R) Ps 103:6
they that observe *j.* (S) Ps 106:3
works are truth and *j.* Ps 111:7
(A)(E)(S)
conducts affairs with *j.* Ps 112:5
(A)(R)
I have done judgment and *j.* Ps 119:121
leave me not
done *j.. righteousness Ps 119:121
(A)(B)(E)
in thy *j.* preserve my life Ps 119:149
(R)
according to thy *j.* (R) Ps 119:156
to receive the instruction of *j.* Pr 1:3
and equity
justice (A) Pr 1:3; 2:9; Isa 11:4
justice (S) Pr 2:8;
2:9; 8:20; 13:23; 19:28; 21:7, 15; 28:5;
29:4; Ec 3:16; Isa 1:21, 27; 5:7, 16; 10:2;
33:5; 40:14; 51:4; 56:1; 59:8-9, 15;
Jer 4:2; 9:24; 10:24; 34:16; Ho 2:19;
12:6; Am 5:7, 15, 24; 6:12; Mic 3:1, 9;
Zep 3:5; Mal 2:17; M't 12:20
by me kings reign, and princes Pr 8:15
decree *j.*
swept away for lack of *j.* (B) Pr 13:23
scales of *j.* are the Lord's (B) Pr 16:11
deprive righteous in *j.* Pr 18:5
(A)(B)(E)
refuse to do *j.* (A)(E) Pr 21:7
when *j.* is done (A)(R) Pr 21:15
doing *j.* is joy (B)(E) Pr 21:15
pervert the *j.* due (A)(E) Pr 31:5
the place of *j.* (A)(R) Ec 3:16
if thou seest the perverting of *j.* Ec 5:8
violent taking away *j.* Ec 5:8
(A)(B)(E)(S)
seek *j.* (S) Isa 1:12; 16:5
by the spirit of *j.* Isa 4:4; 28:6
shall be exalted in *j.* Isa 5:16
(A)(B)(E)(S)
to establish his throne with *j.* Isa 9:7
and judgment

with *j.* and righteousness Isa 9:7
(A)(B)(E)(R)(S)
execute *j.* (A)(E)(R) Isa 16:3
him who executes *j.* (B) Isa 26:6
J. will I lay to the line (S) Isa 28:17
he is a God of *j.* (S) Isa 30:18
princes rule in *j.* Isa 32:1
(A)(B)(E)(R)(S)
princes shall rule in *j.* (S) Isa 32:1
j. due me is passed away (E) Isa 40:27
bring forth *j.* to the Gentiles Isa 42:1;
(S) M't 12:18
bring forth *j.* unto truth (S) Isa 42:3
till he set *j.* in the earth (S) Isa 42:4
j. due me is with Jehovah (E) Isa 49:4
my *j.* for a light Isa 51:4
(A)(B)(E)(R)
keep ye judgment, and do *j.* Isa 56:1
for my salvation
they ask of me the ordinances Isa 58:2
of *j.*
ask of me righteous ordinances Isa 58:2
(B)
ask of me righteous judgments Isa 58:2
(E)(R)
none calleth for *j.* Isa 59:4
nor doth *j.* overtake us Isa 59:9
we look for *j.* (S) Isa 59:11
j. standeth afar off, truth is Isa 59:14
fallen in the street
j. cannot enter (A)(S) Isa 59:14
j. your ruler (B) Isa 60:17
I love *j.* (S) Isa 61:8
in *j.* and righteousness Jer 4:2
(B)(E)(R)
execute *j.* (S) Jer 5:1;
7:5; 21:12; 22:3; 33:15; Eze 18:8
execute *j.* (B)(E)(R) Jer 9:24
execute *j.* (A)(E)(R) Jer 21:12; 23:5
shall execute judgment and *j.* in Jer 23:5
the earth
execute judgment and Jer 23:5
righteousness (B)
Lord bless thee, O habitation Jer 31:23
of *j.*
habitation of righteousness Jer 31:23
(B)(E)(R)
sinned against the Lord, the Jer 50:7
habitation of *j.*
habitation of righteousness Jer 50:7
(B)(E)
the Lord, their true habitation Jer 50:7
(R)
O princes, execute judgment Eze 45:9
and *j.*
to refuse a man *j.* (B) La 3:36
his ways are *j.* (E) Da 4:27
in righteousness and *j.* Ho 2:19
(A)(B)(E)(R)
who does *j.* (A)(B)(R) Ho 5:1
turn *j.* into bitterness Ho 5:7
(A)(B)(E)(R)
he crushes *j.* to earth (B) Ho 5:11
but to do *j.* (B)(R) Mic 6:8
j. to the Gentiles (B)(R) M't 12:18
brings *j.* (B)(N)(R) M't 12:20
right, *j.,* mercy (A)(B) M't 23:23
j., mercy, faith M't 23:23
(E)(N)(P)(R)(S)
acknowledged *j.* of God (A) Lu 7:29
neglect *j.* and love Lu 11:42
(A)(B)(E)(N)(P)(R)
do *j.* in short order (B)(P) Lu 18:8
humiliation *j.* was denied him Ac 8:33
(R)
argued about *j.* (R) Ac 24:25
j. will not allow him to live Ac 28:4
(B)(E)(N)(P)(R)
j. brought to light (N) Ro 3:21
j. is mine (N) Heb 10:30

JUSTIFICATION

Christ was raised again for our Ro 4:25
j.
but the free gift is of many Ro 5:16
offences to *j.*
the free gift came on all men Ro 5:18
to *j.* of life
to acquittal, right standing Ro 5:18
with God, and life for all men (A)
for all men a justified life (B) Ro 5:18
acquittal and life for all men Ro 5:18
(N)(R)
all men freely acquitted before Ro 5:18
God (P)
aim at *j.* by law (B) Ga 5:4

JUSTIFIED

should a man full of talk be *j.* Job 11:2
man full of talk be free from Job 11:2
guilt (A)
must a glib talker be right (B) Job 11:2
man full of talk be vindicated Job 11:2
(R)
behold now, I know that I Job 13:18
shall be *j.*
I shall be vindicated (B)(R) Job 13:18
I know that I am righteous Job 13:18
(E)
how then can man be *j.* with Job 25:4
God or be clean
how can a human being be Job 25:4
just (B)(E)
how can man be righteous Job 25:4
(R)
because he *j.* himself rather Job 32:2
than God
that thou mayest be *j.* (S) Job 40:8
thou mightest be *j.* when thou Ps 51:4
speakest
in thy sight shall no man Ps 143:2
living be
no man living is righteous Ps 143:2
(B)(E)(R)
they may be *j.* Isa 43:9
produce witnesses to justify Isa 43:9
them (B)(R)
thou mayest be *j.* Isa 43:20
j. thy sisters in all Eze 16:51;
abominations 16:52
in the Lord shall all the seed Eze 45:25
of Israel be *j.*
the backsliding Israel hath *j.* Jer 3:11
herself
shown herself less guilty Jer 3:11
(A)(R)
shown herself more righteous Jer 3:11
(B)(E)
wisdom is *j.* of her children M't 11:19;
Lu 7:35
wisdom is vindicated by M't 11:19
efforts (B)
wisdom is proved right by M't 11:19
results (N)
wisdom stands or falls by her M't 11:19
own action (P)
for by thy words thou shalt M't 12:37
be *j.*
by your words you will be M't 12:37
acquitted (B)
your words that will acquit M't 12:37
you (P)
all the people and publicans *j.* Lu 7:29
God
acknowledged the justice of Lu 7:29
God (A)
acknowledged God as just (B) Lu 7:29
this man went down *j.* rather Lu 18:14
than the other
went home made righteous Lu 18:14
(B)
went home acquitted of his Lu 18:14
sins (N)
all that believe are *j.* from all Ac 13:39
things which could not be *j.* by
every believer is absolved Ac 13:39
(A)(B)(P)
everyone who has faith is Ac 13:39
acquitted of everything (N)
is freed from everything (R) Ac 13:39
but the doers of the law shall Ro 2:13
be *j.*
doers of law be pronounced Ro 2:13
righteous (B)
by hearing men will be *j.* (N) Ro 2:13
obedience to law justifies (P) Ro 2:13
that thou mightest be *j.* in thy Ro 3:4
sayings
thou mightest be vindicated Ro 3:4
there shall no flesh be *j.* in his Ro 3:20
sight
be made righteous in God's Ro 3:20
sight (B)
being *j.* freely by his grace Ro 3:24;
Tit 3:7
a man is *j.* by faith Ro 3:28;
5:1; Ga 2:16; 3:24
if Abraham were *j.* by works, he Ro 4:2
hath
being *j.* by faith we have peace Ro 5:1
with God
we are made righteous through Ro 5:1;
faith (B) 5:9; 8:30; 1Co 6:11; Ga 2:16

being now *j.* by his blood, we *Ro 5:9*
shall be saved
for all men a *j.* life (B) *Ro 5:18*
and whom he *j.* them he also *Ro 8:30*
glorified
I know nothing, yet am I not *1Co 4:4*
hereby *j.*
ye are *j.* in the name of the *1Co 6:11*
Lord Jesus
a man is not *j.* by the works *Ga 2:16;*
of law *3:11*
whosoever of you is *j.* by law, *Ga 5:4*
ye are fallen
aim at justification by law (B) *Ga 5:4*
God manifest in the flesh, *j.* in *1Ti 3:16*
the Spirit
vindicated by the Spirit *1Ti 3:16*
(B)(N)(R)
was not Abraham our father *j.* *Jas 2:21*
by works
made righteous due to works *Jas 2:21*
(B)
ye see how that by works a *Jas 2:24*
man is *j.*
pronounced righteous due *Jas 2:24;*
(B) *2:25*
was not Rahab the harlot *j.* by *Jas 2:25*
works

JUSTIFIER

the *j.* of him who believeth in *Ro 3:26*
Jesus

JUSTIFIES

that *j.* the wicked (A)(R) *Pr 17:15*
not familiarity with law *j.* (P) *Ro 2:13*
j. the circumcised (B) *Ro 3:30*
j. Gentiles through faith (B) *Ga 3:8*

JUSTIFIETH

he that *j.* the wicked, is *Pr 17:15*
abomination
that justifies the wicked *Pr 17:15*
(A)(R)
He who judges the wicked (B) *Pr 17:15*
he is near that *j.* who will *Isa 50:8*
contend with me
Who declares me in the right *Isa 50:8*
(A)
who vindicates me is near *Isa 50:8*
(B)(R)
but believeth on him that *j.* the *Ro 4:5*
ungodly
who makes the ungodly *Ro 4:5*
righteous (B)
who acquits the guilty (N) *Ro 4:5*
to the charge of God's elect? it *Ro 8:33*
is God that *j.*
God is the Acquitter (B) *Ro 8:33*
God who pronounces the *Ro 8:33*
acquittal (N)

JUSTIFY

for I will not *j.* the wicked *Ex 23:7*
then they shall *j.* the righteous *De 25:1*
justifying the innocent (A) *De 25:1*
may acquit the innocent (B) *De 25:1*
acquitting the innocent (R) *De 25:1*
if I *j.* myself, my own mouth *Job 9:20*
shall condemn
Though I am innocent *Job 9:20*
(A)(B)(R)
Though I be righteous, mine *Job 9:20*
own (E)
God forbid that I should *j.* *Job 27:5*
you
I should acknowledge you to *Job 27:5*
be right (B)(R)
answer me, speak, for I *Job 33:32*
desire to *j.* thee
which *j.* the wicked for reward *Isa 5:23*
who acquit the guilty for a *Isa 5:23*
bribe (B)(R)
produce witnesses to *j.* them *Isa 43:9*
(B)(R)
by knowledge shall my *Isa 53:11*
righteous servant *j.* many
Righteous Servant make many *Isa 53:11*
righteous (B)(R)
he, willing to *j.* himself, said *Lu 10:29*
to Jesus
acquit himself of reproach *Lu 10:29*
(A)
wishing to absolve himself *Lu 10:29*
(B)

wanted to vindicate himself *Lu 10:29*
(N)
ye are they which *j.* yourselves *Lu 16:15*
before men
declare yourselves just and *Lu 16:15*
upright (A)
claim righteousness in human *Lu 16:15*
eyes (B)
impress fellowmen with *Lu 16:15*
righteousness (N)
advertise your goodness *Lu 16:15*
before men (P)
one God shall *j.* circumcision *Ro 3:30*
by faith
justifies the circumcised (B) *Ro 3:30*
foreseeing that God would *j.* the *Ga 3:8*
heathen
justifies the Gentiles through *Ga 3:8*
faith (B)

JUSTIFYING

j. the innocent (A) *De 25:1*
and *j.* the righteous *1Ki 8:32; 2Ch 6:23*
acquitting the righteous (B) *1Ki 8:32*
vindicating the righteous (R) *1Ki 8:32*

JUSTLE

the chariots shall *j.* one against *Na 2:4*
another

JUSTLY

arbitrate *j.* (B) *Isa 16:3*
correct me, but *j.* (B) *Jer 10:24*
that doeth *j.* (E) *Ho 5:1*
what doth the Lord require, *Mic 6:8*
but to do *j.*
but to do justice (B)(R) *Mic 6:8*
we indeed *j.* for we receive the *Lu 23:41*
reward
how holily and *j.* we behaved *1Th 2:10*
unworldly, upright, blameless *1Th 2:10*
(A)
pure, fair, and irreproachable *1Th 2:10*
(B)
holily, righteously, *1Th 2:10*
unblamably (E)
devout, just, blameless (N) *1Th 2:10*
honest, straightforward, *1Th 2:10*
above criticism (P)
holy, righteous, blameless (R) *1Th 2:10*

JUSTUS

Barsabas, who was surnamed *Ac 1:23*
J.
J., one that worshipped God *Ac 18:7*
And Jesus, which is called *J.* *Col 4:11*

JUTTAH

Maon, Carmel, and Ziph, and *Jos 15:55*
J.
and *J.* with her suburbs, and *Jos 21:16*

K

KABZEEL

coast of Edom southward *Jos 15:21*
were *K.*
the son of a valiant man, of *2Sa 23:20;*
K. *1Ch 11:22*

KADESH

came to En-mishpat, which is *Ge 14:7*
K.
behold, it is between *K.* and *Ge 16:14*
Bered
dwelled between *K.* and Shur *Ge 20:1*
the wilderness of Paran, to *K.* *Nu 13:26*
the people abode in *K.*; and *Nu 20:1*
Miriam
Moses sent messengers from *Nu 20:14*
K.
behold, we are in *K.*, a city in *Nu 20:16*
congregation, journeyed from *Nu 20:22*
K.
that is the water of Meribah *Nu 27:14*
in *K.*
the wilderness of Zin, which *Nu 33:36*
is *K.*

they removed from *K.*, and *Nu 33:37*
pitched
abode in *K.* many days, *De 1:46*
according
unto the Red sea, and came to *J'g 11:16*
K.
consent: and Israel abode in *J'g 11:17*
K.
Lord shaketh the wilderness of *Ps 29:8*
K.
even to the waters of strife in *Eze 47:19*
K.
unto the waters of strife in *Eze 48:28*
K.

KADESH-BARNEA

sent them from *K.* to see the *Nu 32:8*
land
shall be from the south to *K.* *Nu 34:4*
by the way of mount Seir unto *De 1:2*
K.
commanded us; and we came *De 1:19*
to *K.*
space in which we came from *De 2:14*
K.
when the Lord sent you from *De 9:23*
K.
Joshua smote them from *K.* *Jos 10:41*
even
God concerning me and thee *Jos 14:6*
in *K.*
servant of the Lord sent me *Jos 14:7*
from *K.*
up on the south side unto *K.* *Jos 15:3*

KADMIEL

the children of Jeshua and *K.* *Ezr 2:40;*
Ne 7:43
K. and his sons, the sons of *Ezr 3:9*
Judah
the Levites, Jeshua, and Bani, *Ne 9:4*
K.
the Levites, Jeshua, and *K.*, *Ne 9:5*
Bani
Binnui of the sons of Henadad, *Ne 10:9*
K.
Binnui, *K.*, Sherebiah, Judah *Ne 12:8*
and Jeshua the son of *K.*, *Ne 12:24*
with their

KADMONITES

and the Kennizzites, and the *Ge 15:19*
K.

KALLAI

Of Sallai, *K.*; of Amok, Eber *Ne 12:20*

KANAH

westward into the river *K.* *Jos 16:8*
coast descended unto the river *Jos 17:9*
K.
and *K.*, even unto great *Jos 19:28*
Zidon

KAREAH

and Jonathan the sons of *K.* *Jer 40:8*
Johanan the son of *K.* and all *Jer 40:13;*
41:13; 43:2
the son of *K.* spake to *Jer 40:15*
Gedaliah in
said unto Johanan the son of *Jer 40:16*
K.
when Johanan the son of *K.* *Jer 41:11*
went unto Johanan the son of *Jer 41:14*
K.
took Johanan the son of *K.*, *Jer 41:16*
and all
and Johanan the son of *K.* *Jer 42:1*
called he Johanan the son of *K.* *Jer 42:8*
So Johanan the son of *K.*, and *Jer 43:4*
all
But Johanan the son of *K.*, *Jer 43:5*
and all

KARKAA

and fetched a compass to *K.* *Jos 15:3*

KARKOR

Zebah and Zalmunna were in *J'g 8:10*
K.

KARNAIM

the Rephaims in Ashteroth K.   *Ge 14:5*

KARTAH

suburbs, and K. with her   *Jos 21:34*
suburbs

KARTAN

K. with her suburbs; three   *Jos 21:32*
cities

KATTATH

And K., and Nahallal, and   *Jos 19:15*

KEDAR

of Ishmael, Nebajoth; and K   *Ge 25:13*
of Ishmael, Nebaioth; then K.   *1Ch 1:29*
that I dwell in the tents of K.   *Ps 120:5*
of Jerusalem, the tents of K.   *Ca 1:5*
and all the glory of K. shall   *Isa 21:16*
fail
mighty men of the children of   *Isa 21:17*
K.
the villages that K. doth   *Isa 42:11*
inhabit
the flocks of K. shall be   *Isa 60:7*
gathered
and send unto K., and consider   *Jer 2:10*
Concerning K., and   *Jer 49:28*
concerning the
go up to K., and spoil the   *Jer 49:28*
men of
Arabia, and all the princes of   *Eze 27:21*
K.

KEDEMAH

Tema, Jetur, Naphish, and K.   *Ge 25:15*
Jetur, Naphish, K. These are   *1Ch 1:31*

KEDEMOTH

out of the wilderness of K.   *De 2:26*
unto
Jahaza, and K., and   *Jos 13:18*
Mephaath
K. with her suburbs, and   *Jos 21:37*
Mephaath
K. also with her suburbs, and   *1Ch 6:79*

KEDESH

The king of K., one; the king   *Jos 12:22*
And K., and Hazor, and   *Jos 15:23*
Ithnan
And K., and Edrei, and   *Jos 19:37*
En-hazor
And they appointed K. in   *Jos 20:7*
Galilee
K. in Galilee with her   *Jos 21:32*
suburbs
arose, and went with Barak to   *J'g 4:9*
K.
Zebulun and Naphtali to K.   *J'g 4:10*
plain of Zaanaim, which is by   *J'g 4:11*
K.
and K. and Hazor, and   *2Ki 15:29*
Gilead, and
K. with her suburbs,   *1Ch 6:72*
Daberath
K. in Galilee with her   *1Ch 6:76*
suburbs, and

KEDESH-NAPHTALI

the son of Abinoam out of K.   *J'g 4:6*

KEEN

telling you how k. others are   *2Co 8:8*
(N)
k. in enthusiasm (A)(P)   *2Co 8:17*

KEENNESS

set aside k. of the sagacious   *1Co 1:19*
(B)

KEEP

put him in garden of Eden   *Ge 2:15*
to k. it
and they shall k. the way of   *Ge 18:19*
the Lord

and behold I am with thee to   *Ge 28:15;*
k. thee   *28:20*
I will again feed and k. thy   *Ge 30:31*
flock
my brother, k. that thou hast   *Ge 33:9*
to thyself
and let them k. food in the   *Ge 41:35*
cities
whom the Egyptians k. in   *Ex 6:5*
bondage
shall k. it till the fourteenth   *Ex 12:6*
day of month
ye shall k. it a feast to the   *Ex 12:14;*
Lord through   *23:15; 34:18; Le 23:41*
that ye shall k. this service   *Ex 12:25;*
   13:5
and the congregation of Israel   *Ex 12:47*
shall k. it
thou shalt k. this ordinance in   *Ex 13:10*
his season
remember the sabbath day to   *Ex 20:8;*
k. it holy   *31:13-14, 16; De 5:12, 15*
if a man deliver money or   *Ex 22:7;*
stuff to k.   *22:10*
k. thee far from a false matter   *Ex 23:7*
three times shalt thou k. a   *Ex 23:14*
feast to me
I send an angel to k. thee in   *Ex 23:20*
the way
and lie in that delivered him to   *Le 6:2;*
k.   *6:4*
ye shall k. my ordinances, I   *Le 18:4;*
am the Lord   *18:30; 22:9; Le 11:20*
shall k. my sabbaths   *Le 19:3;*
   19:30; 26:2; Isa 56:4
k. away from holy things (R)   *Le 22:2*
shall k. a feast seven days   *Le 23:39;*
   2Ch 30:13
ye shall k. my judgments and   *Le 25:18*
do them
the Lord bless thee and k. thee   *Nu 6:24*
in the fourteenth day at even ye   *Nu 9:3*
shall k. it
day of second month at even   *Nu 9:11*
they shall k. it
thou and thy sons shall k. your   *Nu 18:7*
priests' office
ye shall k. a feast to the Lord   *Nu 29:12*
seven days
shall k. himself to the   *Nu 36:7;*
inheritance of tribe   *36:9*
k. therefore and do them   *De 4:6; 5:1*
k. it holy (R)   *De 5:12*
he might k. us alive (B)   *De 6:24*
because the Lord loved you,   *De 7:8*
would k. the oath
if ye k. them, the Lord shall k.   *De 7:12*
the covenant
thou shalt k. the feast of   *De 16:10*
weeks to the Lord
shalt k. a solemn feast to the   *De 16:15*
Lord thy God
may learn to k. all the words   *De 17:19*
of this law
then k. thee from every wicked   *De 23:9*
thing
that which is gone out of thy   *De 23:23*
lips thou shalt k.
k. therefore the words of this   *De 29:9*
covenant
k. yourselves from the   *Jos 6:18*
accursed thing
and set men by the cave for   *Jos 10:18*
to k. them
to k. all that is written in the   *Jos 23:6*
law of Moses
whether they will k. the way of   *J'g 2:22*
Lord
thou shalt k. fast by my young   *Ru 2:21*
men
he will k. the feet of his saints   *1Sa 2:9*
Eleazar his son, to k. the ark of   *1Sa 7:1*
the Lord
king left ten women which   *2Sa 15:16;*
were concubines to k. house   *16:21; 20:3*
I have no son to k. my name   *2Sa 18:18*
in remembrance
k. with thy servant David   *1Ki 8:25;*
   2Ch 6:16
brought a man to me and   *1Ki 20:39*
said. K. this
that thou wouldest k. me   *1Ch 4:10*
from evil
fifty thousand, which could   *1Ch 12:33;*
k. rank   *12:38*
that thou mayest k. the law   *1Ch 22:12*
of the Lord
k. this for ever in the   *1Ch 29:18*
imagination of heart

had no power to k. still the   *2Ch 22:9*
kingdom
ye purpose to k. under the   *2Ch 28:10*
children of Judah
for they could not k. it at that   *2Ch 30:3*
time
assembly took counsel to k.   *2Ch 30:23*
other seven days
watch and k. them till ye weigh   *Ezr 8:29*
them
to k. the dedication with   *Ne 12:27*
gladness
that the Levites should k. the   *Ne 13:22*
gates
nor k. they the king's laws   *Es 3:8*
if you k. still (B)(R)   *Es 4:14*
that they would k. those two   *Es 9:27*
days at Purim
O that thou wouldest k. me   *Job 14:13*
secret till
though he k. it still within his   *Job 20:13*
mouth
does not k. wicked alive (R)   *Job 36:6*
thou shalt k. them, O Lord   *Ps 12:7;*
   31:20
k. and protect me (A)   *Ps 16:1*
k. me as the apple of the eye,   *Ps 17:8*
hide me
k. back also from   *Ps 19:13*
presumptuous sins
O k. my soul, and deliver me,   *Ps 25:20*
I trust
k. thy tongue from evil, and   *Ps 34:13*
thy lips
and k. his way; I will k. my   *Ps 37:34;*
mouth   *39:1*
k. my life (B)   *Ps 86:2*
my mercy will I k. for him for   *Ps 89:28*
ever
his angels charge, to k. thee in   *Ps 91:11*
all thy ways
nor chide, nor will he k. his   *Ps 103:9*
anger for ever
they might observe and k. his   *Ps 105:45*
laws
blessed are they that k.   *Ps 106:3*
judgment
he maketh the barren woman   *Ps 113:9*
to k. house
blessed are they that k. his   *Ps 119:2*
testimonies
thou hast commanded us to k.   *Ps 119:4*
thy precepts
that I may live and k. thy   *Ps 119:17;*
word   *119:101*
teach me, and I shall k. it to   *Ps 119:33*
the end
give understanding, I shall   *Ps 119:34;*
k. thy law   *119:44*
O Lord, I have said, that I   *Ps 119:57*
would k. thy words
I am a companion of them   *Ps 119:63*
that k. thy precepts
I will k. thy precepts with my   *Ps 119:69;*
heart   *119:134*
I will k. the testimony of thy   *Ps 119:88*
mouth
I understand, because I k.   *Ps 119:100*
thy precepts
I will k. thy righteous   *Ps 119:106*
judgments
wonderful, therefore doth   *Ps 119:129*
my soul k. them
down my eyes, because they   *Ps 119:136*
k. not thy law
save me, and I shall k. thy   *Ps 119:146*
testimonies
k. from all evil   *Ps 121:7*
(A)(B)(E)(R)
k. your going out (A)(E)(R)   *Ps 121:8*
except the Lord k. the city the   *Ps 127:1*
watchman
k. me from the hands of the   *Ps 140:4*
wicked
O Lord, k. the door of my lips   *Ps 141:3*
k. me from the snares they   *Ps 141:9*
have laid for me
understanding shall k. thee   *Pr 2:11*
thou mayest k. the paths of the   *Pr 2:20*
righteous
my son, k. sound wisdom and   *Pr 3:21*
discretion
Lord shall k. thy foot from   *Pr 3:26*
being taken
love wisdom, and she shall k.   *Pr 4:6*
thee
she shall k. you (R)   *Pr 4:6*
k. instruction, let her not go,   *Pr 4:13*
for she is thy life

k. my sayings in the midst of   *Pr 4:21*
thy heart
k. thy heart with all diligence,   *Pr 4:23*
for out of it
and that thy lips may *k.*   *Pr 5:2*
knowledge
when thou sleepest it shall *k.*   *Pr 6:22*
thee
to *k.* thee from the evil woman *Pr 6:24*
my son, *k.* my words, and lay up *Pr 7:1*
my commandments
they may *k.* thee from the   *Pr 7:5*
strange woman
k. alive a young cow   *Pr 7:21*
(A)(B)(E)(R)
for blessed are they that *k.* my *Pr 8:32*
ways
he that doth *k.* his soul shall be *Pr 22:5*
far from them
it is pleasant if thou *k.* them *Pr 22:18*
within thee
such as *k.* the law contend with *Pr 28:4*
them
there is a time to *k.* and to cast *Ec 3:6*
away
k. thy foot when thou goest to *Ec 5:1*
the house
that *k.* the fruit thereof, two *Ca 8:12*
hundred
thou wilt *k.* him in perfect *Isa 26:3*
peace
I the Lord do *k.* it, I will *k.* it *Isa 27:3*
night and day
I the Lord have called thee, I *Isa 42:6*
will *k.* thee
k. not back; *k.* ye judgment *Isa 43:6;*
                   56:1
will he *k.* his anger to the end *Jer 3:5*
and I will not *k.* anger forever *Jer 3:12*
and *k.* him as a shepherd *Jer 31:10*
doth his flock
did not *k.* terms of covenant *Jer 34:18*
(A)(B)(R)
I will *k.* nothing back from *Jer 42:4*
you
k. my judgments and do *Eze 20:19;*
them   *36:27*
that they may *k.* the whole *Eze 43:11*
form thereof
k. mercy and judgment, wait *Ho 12:6*
on God
k. the doors of thy mouth *Mic 7:5*
from her that
k. thy feasts; *k.* the munition *Na 1:15;*
                     2:1
dost *k.* silent (A)(B) *Hab 1:13*
then thou shalt also *k.* my *Zec 3:7*
courts
man suffered me to *k.* cattle *Zec 13:5*
from my youth
and to *k.* the feast of *Zec 14:16;*
tabernacles   *14:18-19*
for the priests' lips should *k.* *Mal 2:7*
knowledge
worker earns his *k.* (N)(P) *M't 10:10*
that ye may *k.* your own *M'k 7:9*
tradition
he shall give his angels charge *Lu 4:10*
to *k.* thee
they who having heard the *Lu 8:15*
word *k.* it
blessed are they that hear the *Lu 11:28*
word and *k.* it
thy enemies shall *k.* thee in on *Lu 19:43*
every side
if *k.* my saying shall never see *Joh 8:51;*
death   *8:52*
but I know him, and *k.* his *Joh 8:55*
saying
he that hateth his life in this *Joh 12:25*
world shall *k.* it
if a man love me he will *k.* *Joh 14:23*
my words
if kept my saying, they will *k.* *Joh 15:20*
yours also
k. thro' thy name; *k.* from *Joh 17:11;*
evil   *17:15*
and to *k.* back part of the price *Ac 5:3*
of land
for a man that is a Jew to *k.* *Ac 10:28*
company
and delivered him to soldiers *Ac 12:4*
to *k.* him
to command them to *k.* the law *Ac 15:5*
of Moses
ye must be circumcised, and *Ac 15:24*
k. the law
from which if ye *k.* *Ac 15:29*
yourselves, ye do well

they delivered them the decrees *Ac 16:4*
for to *k.*
charging the jailer to *k.* *Ac 16:23*
them safely
I must by all means *k.* this *Ac 18:21*
feast in Jerusalem
k. themselves from things *Ac 21:25*
offered to idols
he commanded a centurion to *Ac 24:23*
k. Paul
circumcision profiteth, if thou *Ro 2:25*
k. the law
if uncircumcision *k.* the *Ro 2:26*
righteousness of law
let us *k.* the feast; not *k.* *1Co 5:8;*
company   *5:11*
decreed that he will *k.* his *1Co 7:37*
virgin, doeth well
I *k.* under my body and bring *1Co 9:27*
it into subjection
that ye *k.* the ordinances, as I *1Co 11:2*
delivered to them
if ye *k.* in memory what I *1Co 15:2*
preached to you
kept myself, and so will I *k.* *2Co 11:9*
myself
neither do circumcised *k.* the *Ga 6:13*
law
endeavouring to *k.* the unity of *Eph 4:3*
the Spirit
the peace of God shall *k.* your *Ph'p 4:7*
hearts
k. yourselves from lewdness *1Th 4:3*
(B)
k. you sound in spirit (N) *1Th 5:23*
who shall establish and *k.* you *2Th 3:3*
from evil
nor partaker of sins, *k.* thyself *1Ti 5:22*
pure
k. that which is committed to *1Ti 6:20*
thy trust
able to *k.* that I committed to *2Ti 1:12*
him
good thing committed to thee *2Ti 1:14*
k. by Holy Ghost
k. me safe until (N)(P) *2Ti 4:18*
and to *k.* himself unspotted *Jas 1:27*
from world
for whosoever shall *k.* the *Jas 2:10*
whole law
k. clear of desires of lower *1Pe 2:11*
nature (P)
children, *k.* yourselves from *1Jo 5:21*
idols
k. yourselves in the love of *Jude 21*
God, looking
to him that is able to *k.* you *Jude 24*
from falling
blessed are they that hear and *k.* *Re 1:3*
those
I will *k.* thee from the hour of *Re 3:10*
temptation
of them who *k.* the sayings of *Re 22:9*
this book

KEEP *ALIVE*

bring into the ark to *k.* them *Ge 6:19;*
alive   *6:26*
to *k.* seed *alive* on the face of *Ge 7:3*
all the earth
women, children *k.* alive for *Nu 31:18*
yourselves
he measured with one full line *2Sa 8:2*
to *k.* alive
and none can *k.* alive his own *Ps 22:29*
soul
to deliver and *k.* them *alive* in *Ps 33:19*
famine
the Lord will preserve him and *Ps 41:2*
k. him *alive*

KEEP *CHARGE*

and *k.* the *charge* of the Lord *Le 8:35;*
                    1Ki 2:3
Levites *k.* *charge* of the *Nu 1:53;*
tabernacle of testimony *18:4; 31:30;*
                  1Ch 23:32
they shall *k.* his *charge* *Nu 3:7;*
         8:26; 18:3; De 11:1
they shall *k.* the *charge* of the *Nu 3:8*
children of Israel
k. *charge* of the sanctuary *Nu 3:32;*
           18:5; 1Ch 23:32
to minister to me, and *k.* my *Eze 44:16*
charge
if thou wilt *k.* my *charge* then *Zec 3:7*
shalt judge

KEEP *COMMANDMENTS*

how long refuse ye to *k.* my *Ex 16:28*
commandments
shewing mercy to them that *k.* *Ex 20:6;*
my commandments *De 5:10; 7:9; Da 9:4*
therefore shall ye *k.* my *Le 22:31;*
commandments and do them *De 4:40;*
                 6:17; 7:11
if ye *k.* my commandments *Le 26:3;*
   De 11:22; 19:9; 28:9; 30:10; 1Ki 3:14
that ye may *k.* the *De 4:2*
commandments of the Lord
O that they would fear me and *De 5:29*
k. my commandments
know whether thou wouldest *k.* *De 8:2*
his commandments
thou shalt *k.* the *De 8:6;*
commandments *11:1, 8; 13:4, 18*
doth Lord require him to *k.* *De 10:13;*
commandments *27:1; 30:16*
thou hast avouched the Lord *De 26:17*
to *k.* his commandments
Lord avouched thee, that thou *De 26:18*
shouldest *k.* commandments
because thou hearkened not *De 28:45*
to *k.* his commandments
take heed to *k.* *Jos 22:5*
commandments to cleave to him
keep the charge of the Lord to *1Ki 2:3*
k. his commandments
k. my commandments *1Ki 6:12;*
          2Ki 17:13; Pr 4:4; 7:2
that he may incline our hearts *1Ki 8:58*
to *k.* his commandments
let your heart be perfect to *k.* *1Ki 8:61*
his commandments
if ye will not *k.* my *1Ki 9:6*
commandments I will cut off
if thou wilt *k.* my *1Ki 11:38;*
commandments *Ne 1:9; Joh 15:10*
made a covenant to *k.* *2Ki 23:3;*
commandments *2Ch 34:31*
k. and seek for all the *1Ch 28:8*
commandments of the Lord
give to Solomon a perfect *1Ch 29:19*
heart to *k.* thy commandments
not forget the works of God, *Ps 78:7*
but *k.* his commandments
I made haste and delayed not *Ps 119:60*
to *k.* thy commandments
depart ye evil doers, for I *Ps 119:115*
will *k.* commandments of God
forget not my law, let thy heart *Pr 3:1*
k. my commandments
my son, *k.* thy father's *Pr 6:20*
commandments forsake
not the law
I counsel thee to *k.* the king's *Ec 8:2*
commandments
fear God and *k.* his *Ec 12:13*
commandments this is the
whole duty
if thou wilt enter into life, *k.* *M't 19:17*
the commandments
if ye love me, *k.* my *Joh 14:15*
commandments
that thou *k.* this *commandment 1Ti 6:14*
without spot
we know that we know him if *1Jo 2:3*
we *k.* his commandments
what we ask we receive, *1Jo 3:22*
because we *k.* commandments
when we love God and *k.* his *1Jo 5:2*
commandments
this is the love of God, that we *1Jo 5:3*
k. his commandments
make war with her seed which *Re 12:17*
k. commandments
here are they which *k.* the *Re 14:12*
commandments of God

KEEP *PASSOVER*

when stranger will *k.* passover *Ex 12:48*
let males be circumcised, then
let him *k.* *passover*
let children of Israel *k.* *Nu 9:2;*
passover *9:4; De 16:1; 2Ki 23:21*
could not *k.* the *passover* *Nu 9:6*
he shall *k.* the *passover* *Nu 9:10*
all the ordinances of *passover Nu 9:12*
they shall *k.* it
and forbeareth to *k.* the *Nu 9:13*
passover that soul cut off
if a stranger will *k.* the *Nu 9:14*
passover to the Lord
come to *k.* the *passover* to *2Ch 30:1*
the God of Israel

KEEP PASSOVER

taken counsel, to *k. passover* 2Ch 30:2
in the second month
all the service was prepared 2Ch 35:16
to *k. passover*
nor did all the kings of 2Ch 35:18
Israel *k.* such a *passover*
say to him, I will *k. passover* M't 26:18
at thy house

KEEP SILENCE

who said, *K. silence*, and all J'g 3:19
went out
k. not *silence* Ps 35:22;
50:3; 83:1
a time to *k. silence* and a time Ec 3:7
to speak
k. silence before me, O islands, Isa 41:1
and let people
k. not *silence;* behold, I will Isa 62:6;
not *k. silence* 65:6
the elders of daughter of Zion La 2:10
k. silence
the prudent shall *k. silence* in Am 5:13
that time
Lord in his temple, let the Hab 2:20
earth *k. silence* in the
let him *k. silence* in the 1Co 14:28
church
let your women *k. silence* in 1Co 14:34
the churches

KEEP STATUTES

if thou wilt *k.* all his *statutes* Ex 15:26;
De 30:10; 1Ki 9:4; 11:38
you shall *k.* my *statutes* and Le 18:5;
judgments 18:26; 19:19; 20:8, 22;
Eze 44:24
thou shalt *k.* therefore his De 4:40;
statutes 26:16
that thou mightest fear Lord to De 6:2
k. his *statutes*
thou hast avouched the Lord De 26:17
to *k.* his *statutes*
thou hearkenedst not to *k.* his De 28:45
statutes
not walked in my ways to *k.* 1Ki 11:33
my *statutes*
that my ways were directed to Ps 119:5
k. thy *statutes*
I will *k.* thy *statutes* Ps 119:8;
119:145
if wicked will turn and *k.* my Eze 18:21
statutes

KEEPER

Abel was a *k.* of sheep, my Ge 4:2;
brother's *k.* 4:9
Lord gave Joseph favour in Ge 39:21
sight of the *k.*
the *k.* of the prison Ge 39:22
committed to Joseph
the *k.* of the prison looked Ge 39:23
not to any thing
David let the sheep with the 1Sa 17:20
k.
David left his carriage in the 1Sa 17:22
hand of the *k.*
I will make the *k.* of mine 1Sa 28:2
head for ever
k. of the wardrobe 2Ki 22:14;
2Ch 34:22
Asaph the *k.* of the king's forest Ne 2:8
after him Shemaiah *k.* of the Ne 3:29
east gate
custody of Hege *k.* of women Es 2:3;
2:8, 15
you watcher and *k.* of man (A) Job 7:20
and as a booth that the *k.* Job 27:18
maketh
Lord is thy *k.* the Lord is thy Ps 121:5
shade
they made me the *k.* of the Ca 1:6
vineyards
Maaseiah the son of Shallum Jer 35:4
k. of the door
and the *k.* of the prison Ac 16:27
awaking
the *k.* of the prison told this Ac 16:36
saying to Paul

KEEPERS

a third part shall be *k.* of the 2Ki 11:5
watch
k. of the gates of the 1Ch 9:19
tabernacle

when the *k.* of the house Ec 12:3
tremble
the *k.* took away my veil from Ca 5:7
me
Solomon let out the vineyard Ca 8:11
to *k.*
as *k.* of the field are they Jer 4:17
against her
k. of the flocks (B) Jer 25:35
k. of charge of house Eze 40:45;
40:46; 44:8, 14
for fear of him the *k.* did M't 28:4
shake
the *k.* standing before the Ac 5:23
doors
k. kept the prison; Herod Ac 12:6;
examined the *k.* 18:19
to be discreet, chaste, *k.* at Tit 2:5
home, good

KEEPEST

who *k.* covenant and mercy 1Ki 8:23;
with thy servants 2Ch 6:14; Ne 9:32
thou walkest orderly and *k.* Ac 21:24
the law

KEEPETH

and he died not, but *k.* his bed Ex 21:18
faithful God which *k.* covenant De 7:9;
Ne 1:5
and behold he *k.* the sheep 1Sa 16:11
he *k.* back his soul from the Job 33:18
pit
he *k.* all his bones, none is Ps 34:20
broken
he that *k.* thee will not Ps 121:3;
slumber 121:4
Lord God, which *k.* truth for Ps 146:6
ever
he *k.* the paths of judgment Pr 2:8
he is in the way of life that *k.* Pr 10:17
instruction
he that *k.* his mouth *k.* his life Pr 13:3;
21:23
righteousness *k.* him upright in Pr 13:6
the way
that *k.* his way preserveth his Pr 16:17;
soul 19:16
he that *k.* understanding shall Pr 19:8
find good
that *k.* thy soul, doth not he Pr 24:12
know
whoso *k.* the fig tree shall eat Pr 27:18
fruit
whoso *k.* the law is a wise son Pr 28:7
that *k.* company with harlots, Pr 29:3
spendeth
but a wise man *k.* it in till Pr 29:11
afterwards
but he that *k.* the law, happy Pr 29:18
is he
k. the commandments shall feel Ec 8:5
no evil
that nation which *k.* truth may Isa 26:2
enter in
that *k.* the sabbath from Isa 56:2;
polluting it, and *k.* his hand 56:6
cursed be he that *k.* back his Jer 48:10
sword
he sitteth alone and *k.* silence La 3:28
he is a proud man, neither *k.* Hab 2:5
at home
when a strong man armed *k.* Lu 11:21
his palace
and yet none of you *k.* the law Joh 7:19
is not of God, because he *k.* Joh 9:16
not the sabbath
that hath my commandments Joh 14:21
and *k.* them
he that loveth me not, *k.* not Joh 14:24
my sayings
that saith, I know him, and *k.* 1Jo 2:4
not
whoso *k.* his word, in him is 1Jo 2:5;
love 3:24
he that is begotten of God *k.* 1Jo 5:18
himself
he that overcometh and *k.* my Re 2:26
works
blessed is he that *k.* his Re 16:15
garments, lest he
blessed is he that *k.* the sayings Re 22:7
of this book

KEEPING

K. mercy for thousands, Ex 34:7
forgiving

k. the charge of the sanctuary Nu 3:28;
3:38
God, in not *k.* his De 8:11
commandments
we were with them *k.* the 1Sa 25:16
sheep
were porters *k.* the ward at Ne 12:25
in *k.* of them there is great Ps 19:11
reward
by *k.* of his covenant it might Eze 17:14
stand
k. the covenant and mercy to Da 9:4
them
k. watch over their flock by Lu 2:8
night
k. of the commandments of 1Co 7:19
God
k. body pure (P) 1Th 4:4
safe *k.* of Jesus Christ (N) Jude 1
commit the *k.* of their souls to 1Pe 4:19
him

KEEPS

man of understanding *k.* quiet Ps 11:12
(A)
k. us among the living (A)(R) Ps 66:9

KEHELATHAH

from Rissah, and pitched in Nu 33:22
K.
they went from K., and Nu 33:23
pitched in

KEILAH

K. and Achzib, and Jos 15:44
Mareshah
the Philistines fight against 1Sa 23:1;
K. 1:2-13
the father of K. the Garmite 1Ch 4:19
the ruler of the half part of K. Ne 3:17;
3:18

KELAIAH

Jozabad, and Shimei, and K. Ezr 10:23

KELITA

and Kelaiah, (the same is Ezr 10:23
K.)
Maaseiah, K., Azariah, Jozabad Ne 8:7
Hodijah, K., Pelaiah, Hanan Ne 10:10

KEMUEL

and K. the father of Aram Ge 22:21
Ephraim, K. the son of Nu 34:24
Shiphtan
Levites, Hashabiah the son 1Ch 27:17
of K.

KENAN

K., Mahalaleel, Jered 1Ch 1:2

KENATH

And Nobah went and took K. Nu 32:42
with K. and the towns thereof 1Ch 2:23

KENAZ

Omar, Zepho, and Gatam, Ge 36:11
and K.
duke Omar, duke Zepho, Ge 36:15
duke K.
Duke K. duke Teman, duke Ge 36:42;
1Ch 1:53
Othniel the son of K., the Jos 15:17
brother
And Othniel the son of K, J'g 1:13
Caleb's
even Othniel the son of K. J'g 3:9
Caleb's
And Othniel the son of K. died J'g 3:11
Zephi, and Gatam, K., and 1Ch 1:36
Timna
And the sons of K.: Othniel 1Ch 4:13
and the sons of Elah, even K. 1Ch 4:15

KENEZITE

the son of Jephunneh the K. Nu 32:12;
Jos 14:6; 14:14

KENITE

the K. shall be wasted, until Nu 24:22
children of the K., Moses' J'g 1:16
father

Now Heber the *K.*, which was   *J'g 4:11*
of
of Jael the wife of Heber the   *J'g 4:17*
K.
and the house of Heber the *K.*   *J'g 4:17*
Jael the wife of Heber the *K.*   *J'g 5:24*

KENITES

The *K.*, and the Kenizzites   *Ge 15:19*
he looked on the *K.*, and took   *Nu 24:21*
up
had severed himself from the   *J'g 4:11*
K.
Saul said unto the *K.*, Go,   *1Sa 15:6*
depart
So the *K.* departed from   *1Sa 15:6*
among
and against the south of the   *1Sa 27:10*
K.
which were in the cities of   *1Sa 30:29*
the *K.*
These are the *K.* that came of   *1Ch 2:55*

KENIZZITES

The Kenites, and the *K.*   *Ge 15:19*

KEPT

Abraham *k.* my charge and my   *Ge 26:5*
laws
Rachel came with sheep, for   *Ge 29:9*
she *k.* them
neither hath he *k.* back any   *Ge 39:9*
thing from me
send one, and ye shall be *k.* in   *Ge 42:16*
prison
now Moses *k.* the flock of Jethro   *Ex 3:1*
lay up for you, to be *k.* till the   *Ex 16:23*
morning
pot of manna to be *k.* for   *Ex 16:32;*
generations   *16:33-34*
if the owner hath not *k.* him   *Ex 21:29;*
in   *21:36*
and it be *k.* close, and she be   *Nu 5:13*
defiled
they *k.* the passover; why are   *Nu 9:5;*
we *k.* back   *9:7*
then Israel *k.* the charge of   *Nu 9:19;*
the Lord   *9:23*
bring Aaron's rod to be *k.* for   *Nu 17:10*
a token
water of separation *k.* for the   *Nu 19:9*
congregation
Lord hath *k.* thee back from   *Nu 24:11*
honour
which *k.* the charge of the   *Nu 31:47*
tabernacle
he *k.* them as the apple of his   *De 32:10*
eye
they observed thy word, *k.* thy   *De 33:9*
covenant
Israel *k.* the passover in Gilgal   *Jos 5:10*
the Lord hath *k.* me alive   *Jos 14:10*
these 45 years
you have *k.* all that Moses   *Jos 22:2*
commanded
have *k.* the charge of   *Jos 22:3*
commandment of Lord
so she *k.* fast by the maidens   *Ru 2:23*
of Boaz
to this time it hath been *k.* for   *1Sa 9:24*
thee
hast not *k.* the   *1Sa 13:13;*
commandment of Lord   *13:14*
David said, Thy servant *k.* his   *1Sa 17:34*
father's sheep
have *k.* themselves at least   *1Sa 21:4*
from women
David said, Surely in vain   *1Sa 25:21*
have I *k.* all that
blessed be thou who hast *k.*   *1Sa 25:33*
me this day
the Lord God hath *k.* me   *1Sa 25:34;*
from evil   *25:39*
why hast thou not *k.* thy lord   *1Sa 26:15*
the king
because ye have not *k.* your   *1Sa 26:16*
master, the Lord's
the young man that *k.* the   *2Sa 13:34*
watch
I have *k.* the ways of the   *2Sa 22:2;*
Lord   *Ps 18:21*
I have *k.* myself from   *2Sa 22:24;*
iniquity   *Ps 18:23*
thou hast *k.* me to be head of   *2Sa 22:44*
the heathen

why hast thou not *k.* the oath   *1Ki 2:43*
of Lord
thou hast *k.* for him this great   *1Ki 3:6*
kindness
hast *k.* with David my father   *1Ki 8:24;*
that thou promisedst him   *2Ch 6:15*
Solomon *k.* not that the Lord   *1Ki 11:10*
commanded
and thou hast not *k.* my   *1Ki 11:11*
covenant and statutes
because David *k.* my   *1Ki 11:34;*
commandments   *14:8*
man of God from Judah not   *1Ki 13:21*
k. commandments
Judah *k.* not the   *1Ki 17:19*
commandments
Hezekiah *k.* the   *1Ki 18:6*
commandments of the Lord
the word of the Lord Saul *k.*   *1Ch 10:13*
not
while David *k.* himself close   *1Ch 12:1*
because of Saul
Solomon *k.* the feast seven   *2Ch 7:8*
days
for they *k.* the dedication of the   *2Ch 7:9*
altar seven days
k. feast of unleavened bread   *2Ch 30:21;*
  Ezr 6:22
and they *k.* other seven days   *2Ch 30:23*
with gladness
because our fathers have not   *2Ch 34:21*
k. the word
Josiah and Israel *k.* the   *2Ch 35:1;*
passover   *35:17, 19*
there was no passover like to   *2Ch 35:18*
that *k.* in Israel
they *k.* also the feast of   *Ezr 3:4*
tabernacles
k. the dedication of this house   *Ezr 6:16*
with joy
the children of the captivity *k.*   *Ezr 6:19*
the passover
we have not *k.* the   *Ne 1:7*
commandments
and they *k.* the feast seven days   *Ne 8:18*
nor our priests nor our fathers   *Ne 9:34*
k. thy law
that these days of Purim should   *Es 9:28*
be *k.*
his ways have I *k.* and not   *Job 23:11*
declined
and *k.* close from the fowls   *Job 28:21*
of the air
I have *k.* me from paths of the   *Ps 17:4*
destroyer
hast *k.* me alive   *Ps 30:3*
that *k.* holy day   *Ps 42:4*
they *k.* not the covenant of   *Ps 78:10*
God
they tempted God, and *k.* not   *Ps 78:56*
his testimonies
they *k.* his testimonies and the   *Ps 99:7*
ordinance
for I have *k.* thy testimonies   *Ps 119:22;*
  119:167
I have *k.* thy law   *Ps 119:55;*
  119:56
now have I *k.* thy word; *k.*   *Ps 119:67;*
not thy word   *119:158*
k. thy precepts   *Ps 119:168*
what my eyes desired I *k.* not   *Ec 2:10*
from them
riches *k.* for the owners thereof   *Ec 5:13*
to their hurt
but my own vineyard have I not   *Ca 1:6*
k.
a song as when a holy   *Isa 30:29*
solemnity is *k.*
I have *k.* you (R)   *Isa 49:8*
not *k.* my laws; *k.* his   *Jer 16:11;*
precepts   *35:18*
k. all his precepts (E)(R)   *Jer 35:18*
nor have *k.* my judgments   *Eze 5:7;*
  5:20-21
hath *k.* my judgments; *k.* my   *Eze 18:9;*
statutes   *18:19*
ye have not *k.* the charge of   *Eze 44:8*
my holy things
that *k.* the charge of my   *Eze 44:15;*
sanctuary   *48:11*
whom he would, he *k.* alive, he   *Da 5:19*
set up
but I *k.* the matter in my heart   *Da 7:28*
Israel served for a wife, and *k.*   *Ho 12:12*
k. sheep
and Edom *k.* his wrath for   *Am 1:11*
ever
Judah hath not *k.* his   *Am 2:1*
commandments

for the statutes of Omri are *k.*   *Mic 6:16*
which have *k.* his judgment (S)   *Zep 2:3*
according as ye have not *k.* my   *M't 2:9;*
ways   *3:7*
what profit that we have *k.* his   *M't 3:14*
ordinance
and they that *k.* the swine fled,   *M't 8:33*
and told
will utter things which have   *M't 13:35*
been *k.* secret
but when Herod's birthday   *M't 14:6*
was *k.*
these have I *k.* from my   *M't 19:20;*
youth   *Lu 18:21*
nor was any thing *k.* secret,   *M'k 4:22*
but that it
and they *k.* that saying   *M'k 9:10;*
  Lu 9:36
Mary *k.* these things in her   *Lu 2:19;*
heart   *2:51*
and he was *k.* bound with   *Lu 8:29*
chains, in letters
thy pound, which I have *k.* in   *Lu 19:20*
a napkin
but thou hast *k.* the good wine   *Joh 2:10*
till now
against day of my burying   *Joh 12:7*
hath she *k.* this
as I have *k.* my father's   *Joh 15:10*
commandments
if *k.* my saying, they will   *Joh 15:20*
keep yours
thine they were, and have *k.*   *Joh 17:6*
thy word
k. in thy name, those thou   *Joh 17:12*
gavest me I have *k.*
and spake to her that *k.* the   *Joh 18:16*
door
then saith the damsel that *k.*   *Joh 18:17*
the door to Peter
sold, and *k.* back part of the   *Ac 5:2*
price
who received the law, and have   *Ac 7:53*
not *k.* it
Æneas had *k.* his bed eight   *Ac 9:33*
years, was sick
Peter was *k.* in prison   *Ac 12:5*
k. the prison   *Ac 12:6*
I *k.* back nothing profitable to   *Ac 20:20*
you
and *k.* the raiment of them   *Ac 22:20*
that slew him
and he commanded him to   *Ac 23:35;*
be *k.*   *25:21*
Festus answered that Paul   *Ac 25:4*
should be *k.*
the centurion *k.* them from   *Ac 27:43*
their purpose
Paul dwelt with a soldier that   *Ac 28:16*
k. him
mystery *k.* secret since the   *Ro 16:25*
world began
I *k.* myself from being   *2Co 11:9*
burdensome
the governor *k.* the city with   *2Co 11:32*
a garrison
before faith came, we were *k.*   *Ga 3:23*
under law
k. spotless, sound (P)(R)   *1Th 5:23*
have finished my course, I *k.*   *2Ti 4:7*
the faith
through faith Moses *k.* the   *Heb 11:28*
passover
the hire that is *k.* back by   *Jas 5:4*
fraud, crieth
who are *k.* by the power of   *1Pe 1:5*
God thro' faith
which by the same word are *k.*   *2Pe 3:7*
in store
k. for Jesus Christ   *Jude 1*
(A)(B)(E)(P)(R)
the angels which *k.* not their   *Jude 6*
first estate
hast *k.* my word, and not denied   *Re 3:8*
my name
because thou hast *k.* the word   *Re 3:10*
of my patience
k. safe and fed (A)   *Re 12:14*

KEPT *SILENCE*

men gave ear, and *k.* silence   *Job 29:21*
at my counsel
did I fear a great multitude,   *Job 31:34*
that I *k.* silence
when I *k.* silence, my bones   *Ps 32:3*
waxed old
these things hast thou done,   *Ps 50:21*
and I *k.* silence

then all the multitude *k.*   Ac 15:12
silence
that he spake Hebrew, they *k.*   Ac 22:2
the more *silence*

KERCHIEFS

make *k.* upon the head of   Eze 13:18
every
Your *k.* also will I tear, and   Eze 13:21
deliver

KEREN-HAPPUCH

and the name of the third, *K.*   Job 42:14

KERIOTH

Hadattah, and *K.,* and   Jos 15:25
Hezron
And upon *K.,* and upon   Jer 48:24
Bozrah
K. is taken, and the strong   Jer 48:41
holds

KERNEL

the main *k.* of Ammon (A)   Da 11:41
yet shall not the least *k.* fall   Am 9:9
(S)

KERNELS

from the *k.* even to the husk   Nu 6:4

KEROS

The children of *K.,* the   Ezr 2:44;
children   Ne 7:47

KESIL

made *K.* Kimah, the Pleiades   Job 9:9
(B)

KETTLE

he struck it into the pan,   1Sa 2:14
or *k.,* or

KETURAH

took a wife, and her name was   Ge 25:1
K.
All these were the children of   Ge 25:4
K.
Now the sons of *K.,*   1Ch 1:32
Abraham's
All these are the sons of *K.*   1Ch 1:33

KEY

they took a *k.* and opened   J'g 3:25
them
the *k.* of the house of David   Isa 22:22
will I
taken away the *k.* of   Lu 11:52
knowledge
true, he that hath the *k.* of   Re 3:7
David
given the *k.* of the bottomless   Re 9:1
pit
having the *k.* of the bottomless   Re 20:1
pit

KEYS

the *k.* of the kingdom of   M't 16:19
heaven
have the *k.* of hell and of death   Re 1:18

KEZIA

and the name of the second,   Job 42:14
K.

KEZIZ

Beth-hoglah, and the valley of   Jos 18:21
K.

KIBROTH-HATTAAVAH

called the name of that place   Nu 11:34
K.
journeyed from *K.* unto   Nu 11:35
Hazeroth
desert of Sinai, and pitched   Nu 33:16
at *K.*
And they departed from *K.*   Nu 33:17
and at *K.,* ye provoked the   De 9:22
Lord to

KIBZAIM

And *K.* with her suburbs, and   Jos 21:22

KICK

Wherefore *k.* ye at my   1Sa 2:29
sacrifice
for thee to *k.* against the pricks   Ac 9:5;
   26:14

KICKED

Jeshurun waxed fat, and *k.*   De 32:15

KID

killed a *k.* of the goats, and   Ge 37:31
dipped
will send thee a *k.* from the   Ge 38:17
flock
Judah sent the *k.* by the hand   Ge 38:20
I sent this *k.,* and thou hast   Ge 38:23
not
seethe a *k.* in his mother's   Ex 23:19;
milk   34:26; De 14:21
a *k.* of the goats, a male without   Le 4:23
his offering, a *k.* of the   Le 4:28
goats
a *k.* of the goats, for a sin   Le 5:6;
offering   9:3; Nu 7:16; 27:22, 28,
   34, 40, 46, 52, 58, 64, 70, 76, 81
shall sacrifice one *k.* of the   Le 23:19
goats
for one ram, or for a lamb, or   Nu 15:11
a *k.*
one *k.* of the goats for a sin   Nu 15:24;
   28:15; 29:5, 11, 16, 19, 25
one *k.* of the goats to make   Nu 28:30
an
went in, and made ready a *k.*   J'g 6:19
have made ready a *k.* for thee   J'g 13:15
took a *k.* with a meat offering   J'g 13:19
him as he would have rent a *k.*   J'g 14:6
visited his wife with a *k.*   J'g 15:1
and a bottle of wine, and a *k.*   1Sa 16:20
leopard shall lie down with the   Isa 11:6
k.
offer a *k.* of the goats   Eze 43:22
without
a *k.* of the goats daily for a   Eze 45:23
sin
thou never gavest me a *k.* that   Lu 15:29
I

KIDNAPERS

law made for *k.* (S)   1Ti 1:10

KIDNEYS

the two *k.,* and the fat that is   Ex 29:13;
   29:22; Le 3:4, 10, 15; 4:9; 7:4
caul above the liver, with the *k.*   Le 3:4;
   3:10, 15; 4:9
that is above the liver, with the   Le 7:4
k.
above the liver, and the two *k.*   Le 8:16;
   8:25
the fat, and the *k.,* and the caul   Le 9:10
the *k.,* and the caul above the   Le 9:19
liver
goats, with the fat of *k.* of   De 32:14
wheat
he slashes open my *k.* (R)   Job 16:13
he cleaveth my *k.* asunder   Job 16:13
(S)
goats, with the fat of the *k.* of   Isa 34:6
rams

KIDRON

himself passed over the   2Sa 15:23
brook *K.*
and passest over the brook *K.*   1Ki 2:37
idol, and burnt it by the brook   1Ki 15:13
K.
Jerusalem in the fields of *K.*   2Ki 23:4
Jerusalem, unto the brook *K.*   2Ki 23:6
and burned it at the brook *K.*   2Ki 23:6
dust of them into the brook   2Ki 23:12
K.
it, and burnt it at the brook   2Ch 15:16
K.
it out abroad into the brook   2Ch 29:16
K.
and cast them into the brook   2Ch 30:14
K.
all the fields unto the brook   Jer 31:40
of *K.*

KIDS

thence two good *k.* of the goats   Ge 27:9
put the skins of the *k.* of the   Ge 27:16
goats
two *k.* of the goats for a sin   Le 16:5
the *k.* of the goats for sin   Nu 7:87
offering
Beth-el, one carrying three   1Sa 10:3
k.
of the flock, lambs and *k.,* all   2Ch 35:7
feed thy *k.* beside the shepherds   Ca 1:8

KILL

will *k.* me (A)(B)   Ge 4:14
any finding him should *k.* him   Ge 4:15
they will *k.* me, but they will   Ge 12:12
save
will *k.* me (B)(R)   Ge 20:11
place should *k.* me for   Ge 26:7
Rebekah
I will *k.* my brother   Ge 27:41
(A)(B)(R)
himself, purposing to *k.* thee   Ge 27:42
conspired to *k.* him   Ge 37:18;
(A)(B)(R)   37:20
and said, Let us not *k.* him   Ge 37:21
k. an animal (A)   Ge 43:16
it be a son then ye shall *k.* him   Ex 1:16
intendest thou to *k.* me, as   Ex 2:14
thou
took steps to *k.* Moses (B)(R)   Ex 2:15
to *k.* your first born (B)   Ex 4:23
met him, and sought to *k.* him   Ex 4:24
a sword to *k.* us (B)(R)   Ex 5:21
Israel shall *k.* it in the evening   Ex 12:6
your families, and *k.* the   Ex 12:21
passover
to *k.* this whole assembly with   Ex 16:3
to *k.* us and our children and   Ex 17:3
Thou shalt not *k.*   Ex 20:13
ox, or a sheep, and *k.* it or sell   Ex 22:1
it
and I will *k.* you with the   Ex 22:24
sword
thou shalt *k.* the bullock   Ex 29:11
before
Then shalt thou *k.* the ram   Ex 29:20
k. them in the mountains (B)   Ex 32:12
shall *k.* the bullock before the   Le 1:5
Lord
he shall *k.* it on the side of the   Le 1:11
altar
k. it at the door of the   Le 3:2
tabernacle
k. it before the tabernacle of   Le 3:8;
the   3:13
and *k.* the bullock before the   Le 4:4
Lord
and *k.* it in the place where   Le 4:24
they
k. the burnt offering before the   Le 4:24
Lord
k. at the place (A)(E)(R)   Le 4:29
where they *k.* the burnt   Le 4:33;
offering   7:2
shall they *k.* the trespass offering   Le 7:2
where he shall *k.* the sin   Le 14:13
he shall *k.* the lamb   Le 14:13
(A)(B)(E)(R)
he shall *k.* the burnt offering   Le 14:19
k. the lamb of the trespass   Le 14:25
offering
he shall *k.* the one of the birds   Le 14:50
in
k. the bullock of the sin   Le 16:11
offering
he *k.* the goat of the sin   Le 16:15
offering
seed unto Molech, and *k.* him   Le 20:4
not
k. the animal (B)(R)   Le 20:15
thou shalt *k.* the woman, and   Le 20:16
ye shall not *k.* it and her   Le 22:28
young
thus with me, *k.* me, I pray   Nu 11:15
thee
thou shalt *k.* all this people as   Nu 14:15
one
to *k.* us in the wilderness,   Nu 16:13
except
hand, for now would I *k.* thee   Nu 22:29
k. every male among the little   Nu 31:17
ones
k. every woman that hath   Nu 31:17
known
revenger of blood *k.* the   Nu 35:27
slayer

should k. his neighbour   De 4:42
unawares
Thou shalt not k.   De 5:17
k. and eat flesh in all thy   De 12:15
gates
shalt k. of thy herd and of thy   De 12:21
thou shalt surely k. him; thine   De 13:9
I k. and I make alive; I   De 32:39
wound
kill (R)   Jos 9:18;
20:5;   2Sa 11:21;   1Ki 15:29;   25:25;
2Ch 25:13
I would not k. you (B)   J'g 8:19
stand up and k. them (B)   J'g 8:20
if the Lord were pleased to k.   J'g 13:23
us
but surely we will not k. thee   J'g 15:13
when it is day, we shall k. him   J'g 16:2
to smite of the people, and k.   J'g 20:31
began to k. (B)   J'g 20:31;
20:39; 1Sa 20:39
smite and k. of the men of   J'g 20:39
Israel
k. us and our people (B)   1Sa 5:10; 5:11
if Saul hear it, he will k. me   1Sa 16:2
fight with me, and to k. me   1Sa 17:9
prevail against him, and k.   1Sa 17:9
him
that they should k. David   1Sa 19:1
Saul my father seeketh to k.   1Sa 19:2
thee
k. him in the morning   1Sa 19:11
(A)(B)(R)
that I may k. him (R)   1Sa 19:15
Let me go; why should I k.   1Sa 19:17
thee
k. me yourself (A)   1Sa 20:8
determined to k. David   1Sa 20:33
(A)(B)
k. the priests (R)   1Sa 22:17
some bade me k. thee: but   1Sa 24:10
mine
God, that thou wilt neither k.   1Sa 30:15
me
stand and k. me (B)   2Sa 1:9
Amnon; then k. him, fear not   2Sa 13:28
that we may k. him, for the   2Sa 14:7
life of
any iniquity in me, let him k.   2Sa 14:32
me
shalt thou k. any man in Israel   2Sa 21:4
not k. his servant   1Ki 1:51
do not k. him (B)   1Ki 3:26; 3:27
sought therefore to k.   1Ki 11:40
Jeroboam
they shall k. me, and go   1Ki 12:27
again to
to k. my son (B)   1Ki 17:18
to k. him (B)(R)   1Ki 18:9
he will k. me (A)(B)(R)   1Ki 18:12;
18:14
he will k. (B)   1Ki 19:17
a lion will k. you (B)(R)   1Ki 20:36
Am I God, to k. and make   2Ki 5:7
alive
and if they k. us we shall but   2Ki 7:4
die
young men you will k. (B)   2Ki 8:12
enter and k. them (B)   2Ki 10:25
followeth her k. with the   2Ki 11:15
sword
So k. the passover, and   2Ch 35:6
sanctify
they are coming to k. you   Ne 6:10
(A)(B)(R)
to k. and to cause to perish, all   Es 3:13
k. and exterminate (B)   Es 8:11
watched the house to k. him   Ps 59 title
then k. the widow (B)   Ps 94:6
A time to k. and a time to heal   Ec 3:3
I will k. thy root with famine   Isa 14:30
to year; let them k. sacrifices   Isa 29:1
the wool, ye k. them that are   Eze 34:3
fed
all its princes I will k. (B)   Ho 2:3
young child to k. him (P)   M't 2:13
of old time, Thou shalt not k.   M't 5:21
shall k. shall be in danger of   M't 5:21
fear not them which k. the   M't 10:28
body
but are not able to k. the soul   M't 10:28
they shall k. him, and the   M't 17:23
third day
you shall not k.   M't 19:18
(A)(B)(E)(R)
let us k. him, and let us seize   M't 21:38
on his
k. those murderers   M't 22:7
(A)(N)(P)

some of them ye shall k. and   M't 23:34
crucify
up to be afflicted, and shall k.   M't 24:9
you
take Jesus by subtilty, and k.   M't 26:4
him
or to do evil? to save life, or to   M'k 3:4
k.
hands of men, and they shall   M'k 9:31
k. him
Do not k., Do not steal, Do   M'k 10:19
not
spit upon him, and shall k.   M'k 10:34
him
let us k. him, and the   M'k 12:7
inheritance
they will k.   Lu 11:49
(B)(E)(N)(P)(R)
not afraid of them that k. the   Lu 12:4
body
depart hence: for Herod will   Lu 13:31
k. thee
hither the fatted calf, and k. it   Lu 15:23
Do not commit adultery, Do   Lu 18:20
not k.
is the heir: come, let us k.   Lu 20:14
him
sought how they might k. him   Lu 22:2
sought to k. him (A)   Joh 5:16
the Jews sought the more to k.   Joh 5:18
him
because the Jews sought to k.   Joh 7:1
him
the law? Why go ye about to   Joh 7:19
k. me
devil: who goeth about to k.   Joh 7:20
thee
Is not this he, whom they seek   Joh 7:25
to k.
said the Jews, Will he k.   Joh 8:22
himself
ye seek to k. me, because my   Joh 8:37
word
now ye seek to k. me, a man   Joh 8:40
that
not, but for to steal, and to   Joh 10:10
k., and
they wanted to k. them   Ac 5:33
(A)(B)(N)(P)(R)
Wilt thou k. me, as thou didst   Ac 7:28
the Jews took counsel to k. him   Ac 9:23
the gates day and night to k.   Ac 9:24
him
seeking to k. him (E)(R)   Ac 9:29
to him, Rise, Peter; k., and   Ac 10:13
eat
k. and eat   Ac 11:7
(A)(B)(E)(N)(P)(R)
And as they went about to k.   Ac 21:31
him
he come near, are ready to k.   Ac 23:15
him
laying wait in the way to k.   Ac 25:3
him
temple, and went about to k.   Ac 26:21
me
counsel was to k. the   Ac 27:42
prisoners
Thou shalt not k., Thou shalt   Ro 13:9
not
k. the evil desire (A)   Col 3:5
adultery, said also, Do not k.   Jas 2:11
yet if thou k., thou art become   Jas 2:11
ye k., and desire to have, and   Jas 4:2
I will k. her children with   Re 2:23
death
that they should k. one another   Re 6:4
to k. with sword, and with   Re 6:8
hunger
given that they should not k.   Re 9:5
them
k. one third of men   Re 9:15
(B)(E)(N)(P)(R)
shall overcome them, and k.   Re 11:7
them

KILLED

k. a kid of the goats, and   Ge 37:31
dipped
him in, but that he hath k. a   Ex 21:29
man
the bullock shall be k. before   Le 4:15
place where the burnt offering   Le 6:25
is k.
sin offering be k. before the   Le 6:25
Lord
And he k. it; and Moses   Le 8:19
sprinkled
k. them (A)   Le 10:2

one of the birds be k. in an   Le 14:5
earthen
in the blood of the bird that   Le 14:6
was k.
Ye have k. the people of the   Nu 16:41
Lord
whosoever hath k. any person   Nu 31:19
killed (A)   Jos 7:5;
20:5; 2Sa 11:21; 1Ki 15:29; Isa 37:38
k. with the sword (A)(R)   Jos 13:22
then were k. (B)   J'g 20:32; 2Ch 25:16
women are k. (B)   J'g 21:16
skirt of thy robe, and k. thee   1Sa 24:11
not
that I have k. for my   1Sa 25:11
shearers
hasted, and k. it, and took   1Sa 28:24
flour
hast k. Uriah the Hittite with   2Sa 11:21
smote the Philistine, and k.   2Sa 21:17
him
Baasha k. him (B)(R)   1Ki 15:28
Jeroboam; and because he k.   1Ki 16:7
him
in and smote him, and k. him   1Ki 16:10
Hast thou k., and also taken   1Ki 21:19
k. him, and reigned in his   2Ki 15:25
room
k. some of them (B)   2Ki 17:26
his sons k. him (A)   2Ki 19:37
k. Shophach the captain of   1Ch 19:18
the host
Ahab k. sheep and oxen for   2Ch 18:2
him
servants that had k. the king   2Ch 25:3
his
So they k. the bullocks, and   2Ch 29:22
when they had k. the rams,   2Ch 29:22
they
they k. also the lambs, and   2Ch 29:22
And the priests k. them, and   2Ch 29:24
k. the passover on the   2Ch 30:15;
fourteenth   35:1
they k. the passover, and the   2Ch 35:11
k. the passover for all the   Ezr 6:20
children
for thy sake are we k. all the   Ps 44:22
day
She hath k. her beasts; she hath   Pr 9:2
anger; thou hast k., and not   La 2:21
pitied
be k. and be raised again the   M't 16:21
third
beat one,, and k. another,   M't 21:35
and stoned
my fatlings are k., and all   M't 22:4
things
of them which k. the   M't 23:31
prophets
him, and would have k. him   M'k 6:19
and be k. and after three days   M'k 8:31
rise
after that he is k. he shall rise   M'k 9:31
and him they k. and many   M'k 12:5
others
they took him, and k. him,   M'k 12:8
and cast
when they k. the passover   M'k 14:12
prophets, and your fathers k.   Lu 11:47
them
for they indeed k. them, and   Lu 11:48
ye build
after he hath k. hath power to   Lu 12:5
cast
and k. them (S)   Lu 13:4; 1Jo 3:12
thy father hath k. the fatted   Lu 15:27
calf
thou hast k. for him the fatted   Lu 15:30
calf
out of the vineyard, and k.   Lu 20:15
him
when the passover must be k.   Lu 22:7
And k. the Prince of life, whom   Ac 3:15
God
he k. James the brother of   Ac 12:2
John
sword, and would have k.   Ac 16:27
himself
eat nor drink till they had k.   Ac 23:12
Paul
eat nor drink till they have k.   Ac 23:21
him
and should have been k. of   Ac 23:27
them
For thy sake we are k. all the   Ro 8:36
day
Lord, they have k. thy prophets   Ro 11:3
k. by poisonous serpents (A)   1Co 10:9
we live; as chastened, and not   2Co 6:9
k.

KILLED (continued)

Who both k. the Lord Jesus *1Th 2:15*
have condemned and k. the just *Jas 5:6*
should be k. as they were *Re 6:11*
three was the third part of men *Re 9:18*
k.
which were not k. by these *Re 9:20*
plagues
them, he must in this manner *Re 11:5*
be k.
sword must be k. with the *Re 13:10*
sword
the image of the beast should *Re 13:15*
be k.

KILLEDST

kill me, as thou k. the Egyptian *Ex 2:14*
me into thine hand, thou k. *1Sa 24:18*
me not

KILLEST

Jerusalem, that k. the *M't 23:37;*
prophets *Lu 13:34*

KILLETH

of Israel, that k. an ox, or lamb *Le 17:3*
camp, or that k. it out of the *Le 17:3*
camp
he that k. any man shall surely *Le 24:17*
that k. a beast shall make it *Le 24:18*
good
he that k. a beast, he shall *Le 24:21*
restore
he that k. a man, he shall be *Le 24:21*
put to
which k. any person at *Nu 35:11*
unawares
one that k. any person *Nu 35:15*
unawares
Whoso k. any person, the *Nu 35:30*
murderer
Whoso k. his neighbour *De 19:4*
ignorantly
slayer that k. any person *Jos 20:3*
unawares
whosoever k. any, at *Jos 20:9*
unawares
The Lord k., and maketh alive *1Sa 2:6*
who k. him, the king will *1Sa 17:25*
enrich
to the man that k. this *1Sa 17:26*
Philistine
it be done to the man that k. *1Sa 17:27*
him
For wrath k. the foolish man *Job 5:2*
the light k. the poor and *Job 24:14*
needy
The desire of the slothful k. *Pr 21:25*
him
He that k. an ox is as if he *Isa 66:3*
slew
whosoever k. you will think *Joh 16:2*
that he
letter k., but the spirit giveth *2Co 3:6*
life
he that k. with the sword *Re 13:10*
must be

KILLING

him in the k. of his brethren *J'g 9:24*
returned from k. of Goliath (A) *1Sa 17:57*
from k. the Philistine (A) *1Sa 18:6*
they are k. them (A)(R) *2Ki 17:26*
charge of the k. of the *2Ch 30:17*
passovers
slaying oxen, and k. sheep, *Isa 22:13*
eating
By swearing, and lying, and k. *Ho 4:2*
others; beating some, and k. *M'k 12:5*
some

KILLS

k. him with design (B)(R) *Ex 21:14*

KIMAH

made Kesil K., the Pleiades *Job 9:9*
(B)

KIN

any that is near of k. to him *Le 18:6*
for he uncovereth his near k. *Le 20:19*
for his k. that is near unto him *Le 21:2*

if any of his k. come to *Le 25:25*
redeem it
any that is nigh of k. unto him *Le 25:49*
man is near of k. unto us, one *Ru 2:20*
of our
Because the king is near of k. *2Sa 19:42*
to us
country, and among his own k. *M'k 6:4*
her k. (B) *Lu 1:58*

KINAH

K. and Dimonah, and *Jos 15:22*
Adadah

KIND

tree yielding fruit after his k. *Ge 1:11;*
1:12
every winged fowl after his k. *Ge 1:21;*
6:20; 7:14; Le 11:14-16, 19; De 14:13-15
the living creature after his k. *Ge 1:24;*
1:25; 6:20; 7:14; Le 11:22, 29; 19:19
two of every k. (B) *Ge 6:19; 6:20; 7:14*
after his k. (A) *Ge 7:14*
the stork, and the heron after *De 14:18*
her k.
instruments of every k. of *1Ch 28:14*
service
If thou be k. to this people *2Ch 10:7*
merchants and sellers of all k. *Ne 13:20*
of ware
trees in them of all k. of fruits *Ec 2:5*
of the multitude of all k. of *Eze 27:12*
riches
the sea, and gathered of *M't 13:47*
every k.
this k. goeth not out but by *M't 17:21*
prayer
how k. he has been (P) *M'k 5:19*
This k. can come forth by *M'k 9:29*
nothing
he is k. unto the unthankful *Lu 6:35*
Charity suffereth long, and is *1Co 13:4*
k.
but there is one k. of flesh of *1Co 15:39*
men
And be ye k. one to another *Eph 4:32*
a k. of first fruits of his *Jas 1:18*
creatures
For every k. of beasts, and of *Jas 3:7*

KINDLE

shall k. no fire throughout your *Ex 35:3*
is a contentious man to k. *Pr 26:21*
strife
k. in the thickets of the forest *Isa 9:18*
it ignites the thickets (B) *Isa 9:18*
k. a burning like the burning *Isa 10:16*
of
a stream of brimstone, doth *Isa 30:33*
k. it
breath of the Lord setting it *Isa 30:33*
on fire (B)
shall the flame k. upon thee *Isa 43:2*
you shall not be burned (B) *Isa 43:2*
all ye that k. a fire, that *Isa 50:11*
compass
wood, and the fathers k. the *Jer 7:18*
fire
then will I k. a fire in the *Jer 17:27*
gates
I will k. a fire in the forest *Jer 21:14*
thereof
and to k. meat offerings, and *Jer 33:18*
to do
burn offerings, oblations *Jer 33:18*
(A)(B)(E)(R)
k. a fire in the houses of the *Jer 43:12*
gods
k. a fire in the wall of *Jer 49:27*
Damascus
and I will k. a fire in his *Jer 50:32*
cities
God; Behold, I will k. a fire *Eze 20:47*
in thee
k. the fire, consume the flesh *Eze 24:10*
k. a fire in the wall of Rabbah *Am 1:14*
they shall k. in them, and devour *Ob 18*
neither do ye k. fire on mine *Mal 1:10*
altar

KINDLED

And Jacob's anger was k. *Ge 30:2*
against

to me; that his wrath was k. *Ge 39:19*
grew hot with anger (B) *Ge 39:19*
of the Lord was k. against *Ex 4:14*
Moses
he that k. the fire shall surely *Ex 22:6*
burning which the Lord hath k. *Le 10:6*
heard it; and his anger was k. *Nu 11:1*
anger of the Lord was k. *Nu 11:10*
greatly
wrath of the Lord was k. *Nu 11:33*
against
Lord's anger flared up (B) *Nu 11:33*
and the anger of the Lord was *Nu 12:9*
k.
And God's anger was k. *Nu 22:22*
because he
Balaam's anger was k., and he *Nu 22:27*
Balak's anger was k. against *Nu 24:10*
anger of the Lord was k. *Nu 25:3;*
against *De 29:27; Jos 7:1; 2Sa 6:7;*
24:1; 2Ki 13:3; 2Ch 25:15
Lord's anger was k. the same *Nu 32:10*
time
Lord's anger was k. against *Nu 32:13*
Israel
anger of the Lord thy God be *De 6:15*
k.
the anger of the Lord be k. *De 7:4*
against
Lord's wrath be k. against *De 11:17*
you
my anger shall be k. against *De 31:17*
them
For a fire is k. in mine anger *De 32:22*
shall the anger of the Lord *Jos 23:16*
be k.
the son of Ebed, his anger was *J'g 9:30*
k.
And his anger was k., and he *J'g 14:19*
went
and his anger was k. greatly *1Sa 11:6*
Eliab's anger was k. against *1Sa 17:28*
David
Saul's anger was k. against *1Sa 20:30*
And David's anger was greatly *2Sa 12:5*
k.
devoured: coals were k. by it *2Sa 22:9;*
Ps 18:8
before him were coals of fire *2Sa 22:13*
k.
wrath of the Lord that is k. *2Ki 22:13*
against
my wrath shall be k. against *2Ki 22:17*
this
his anger was k. against *2Ki 23:26*
Judah
And the anger of the Lord *1Ch 13:10*
was k.
wherefore their anger was *2Ch 25:10*
greatly k.
hath also k. his wrath against *Job 19:11*
me
Then was k. the wrath of *Job 32:2*
Elihu
against Job was his wrath k. *Job 32:2*
his three friends was his wrath *Job 32:3*
k.
three men, then his wrath was *Job 32:5*
k.
My wrath is k. against thee *Job 42:7*
when his wrath is k. but a little *Ps 2:12*
so a fire was k. against Jacob *Ps 78:21*
a fire was k. in their *Ps 106:18*
company
was the wrath of the Lord k. *Ps 106:40*
their wrath was k. against us *Ps 124:3*
is the anger of the Lord k. *Isa 5:25*
against
and in the sparks that ye have *Isa 50:11*
k.
tumult hath k. fire upon it *Jer 11:16*
a fire is k. in mine anger, *Jer 15:14*
which
ye have k. a fire in mine anger *Jer 17:4*
was k. in the cities of Judah *Jer 44:6*
hath k. a fire in Zion, and it *La 4:11*
hath
see that I the Lord have k. *Eze 20:48*
mine anger is k. against them *Ho 8:5*
me, my repentings are k. *Ho 11:8*
together
was k. against the shepherds *Zec 10:3*
what will I, if it be already k. *Lu 12:49*
they had k. a fire in the midst *Lu 22:55*
of
for they k. a fire, and received *Ac 28:2*
us
k. by Gehenna (B) *Jas 3:6*

KINDLETH

His breath k. coals, and a flame	Job 41:21
yea, he k. it; and baketh bread	Isa 44:15
how great a matter a little fire k.	Jas 3:5

KINDLY

if ye will deal k. and truly with	Ge 24:49
treat my master k. (B)	Ge 24:49
and spake k. unto the damsel	Ge 34:3
and deal k. and truly with me	Ge 47:29
and spake k. unto them	Ge 50:21
will deal k. and truly with thee	Jos 2:14
k. and faithfully (B)(R)	Jos 2:14
speak k. unto her (A)(E)(R)	J'g 19:3
Lord deal k. with you, as ye have	Ru 1:8
spoken k. to me (B)(E)(R)	Ru 2:13
shalt deal k. with thy servant	1Sa 20:8
speak k. unto thy servants (S)	2Sa 19:7
he spake k. to him, and set his	2Ki 25:28; Jer 52:32
Be k. affectioned one to another	Ro 12:10
k. and humble minded (N)	1Pe 3:8

KINDNESS

shown wonderful k. (B)(R)	Ge 19:19
is thy k. which thou shalt shew	Ge 20:13
to the k. that I have done unto thee	Ge 21:23
shew k. unto my master Abraham	Ge 24:12
hast shewed k. unto my master	Ge 24:14
least of all k. (B)	Ge 32:10
be well with thee, and shew k.	Ge 40:14
Lord, since I have shewed you k.	Jos 2:12
shew k. unto my father's house	Jos 2:12
shewed they k. to the house of	J'g 8:35
not left off his k. to the living	Ru 2:20
shewed more k. in the latter end	Ru 3:10
ye shewed k. to all the children of	1Sa 15:6
I live shew me the k. of the Lord	1Sa 20:14
not cut off thy k. from my	1Sa 20:15
have shewed this k. unto your lord	2Sa 2:5
the Lord shew k. and truth unto	2Sa 2:6
will requite you this k. because	2Sa 2:6
Judah do shew k. this day unto	2Sa 3:8
shew him k. for Jonathan's sake	2Sa 9:1
may shew the k. of God unto him	2Sa 9:3
shew thee k. for Jonathan thy	2Sa 9:7
will shew k. unto Hanun the son of	2Sa 10:2; 1Ch 19:2
as his father shewed k. unto me	2Sa 10:2
Hushai, Is this thy k. to thy friend	2Sa 16:17
shew k. unto the sons of Barzillai	1Ki 2:7
hast kept for him this great k.	1Ki 3:6
because his father shewed k. to me	1Ch 19:2
king remembered not the k. which	2Ch 24:22
slow to anger, and of great k.	Ne 9:17
him, and she obtained k. of him	Es 2:9
obtained favor and k. (E)	Es 2:17
hath shewed me his marvellous k.	Ps 31:21
For his merciful k. is great toward	Ps 117:2
thy merciful k. be for my comfort	Ps 119:76
smite me; it shall be a k.	Ps 141:5
The desire of a man is his k.	Pr 19:22
and in her tongue is the law of k.	Pr 31:26
with everlasing k. will I have	Isa 54:8
my k. shall not depart from thee	Isa 54:10
remember thee, the k. of thy youth	Jer 2:2
k. and compassion (B)	Jer 16:5
find k. and compassion (E)	Da 1:9

slow to anger, and of great k.	Joe 2:13; Jon 4:2
show k. and mercy (R)	Zec 7:9
people shewed us no little k.	Ac 28:2
by k. by the Holy Ghost, by love	2Co 6:6
in his k. toward us through Christ	Eph 2:7
k., humbleness of mind, meekness	Col 3:12
after that the k. and love of God	Tit 3:4
your k. may be (N)	Ph'm 14
to godliness brotherly k.; and	2Pe 1:7
and to brotherly k. charity	2Pe 1:7
k. before the congregation (N)	3Jo 6

KINDRED

of thy country, and from thy k.	Ge 12:1
go unto my country, and to my	Ge 24:4
from the land of my k., and which	Ge 24:7
my father's house, and to my k.	Ge 24:38
take a wife for my son of my k.	Ge 24:40
oath, when thou comest to my k.	Ge 24:41
land of thy fathers, and to thy k.	Ge 31:3
return unto the land of thy k.	Ge 31:13
unto thy country, and to thy k.	Ge 32:9
straitly of our state, and of our k.	Ge 43:7
to mine own land, and to my k.	Nu 10:30
and they brought out all her k.	Jos 6:23
who was of the k. of Elimelech	Ru 2:3
And now is not Boaz of our k.	Ru 3:2
of Benjamin, the k. of Saul	1Ch 12:29
not shewed her people nor her k.	Es 2:10
Esther had not yet shewed her k.	Es 2:20
to see the destruction of my k.	Es 8:6
the Buzite, of the k. of Ram	Job 32:2
thy brethren, the men of thy k.	Eze 11:15
thy k. that is called by this name	Lu 1:61
were of the k. of the high priest	Ac 4:6
of thy country, and from thy k.	Ac 7:3
Joseph's k. was made known unto	Ac 7:13
all his k. threescore and fifteen	Ac 7:14
same dealt subtilly with our k.	Ac 7:19
blood out of every k., and tongue	Re 5:9
every nation, and k., and tongue	Re 14:6

KINDREDS

unto the Lord, ye k. of the people	1Ch 16:28
all the k. of the nations shall	Ps 22:27
O ye k. of the people, give unto	Ps 96:7
all the k. of the earth be blessed	Ac 3:25
all k. of the earth shall wail	Re 1:7
of all nations, and k., and people	Re 7:9
and k. and tongues and nations	Re 11:9
power was given him over all k.	Re 13:7

KINDS

upon the earth, after their k.	Ge 8:19
two k. (A)(B)(E)(R)	De 22:9; J'g 5:30
odours and divers k. of spices	2Ch 16:14
various k. (A)(B)(R)	2Ch 16:14
the k. of (S)	Ne 13:16; Re 18:12
I will appoint over them four k.	Jer 15:3
fish shall be according to their k.	Eze 47:10
dulcimer, and all k. of musick	Da 3:5
all k. of musick, all the people	Da 3:7
and all k. of musick, shall fall down	Da 3:10
all k. of musick, ye fall down	Da 3:15
another divers k. of tongues	1Co 12:10
so many k. of voices in the world	1Co 14:10
all k. of trials (P)	Jas 1:2

KINE

forty k. and ten bulls, twenty she	Ge 32:15
cows (A)(B)(R)	Ge 32:15; 41:2-3, 26-27; 1Sa 6:7, 10, 14
river seven well favoured k.	Ge 41:2
seven other k. came up after them	Ge 41:3; 41:19
the other k. upon the brink of	Ge 41:3
ill favoured and leanfleshed k.	Ge 41:4
the seven well favoured and fat k.	Ge 41:4
came up out of the river seven	Ge 41:18
the lean and ill favoured k.	Ge 41:20
did eat	
did eat up the first seven fat	Ge 41:20
The seven good k. are seven years	Ge 41:26
the seven thin and ill favoured k.	Ge 41:27
increase of thy k. and the flocks	De 7:13; 28:4, 18
cattle (A)	De 28:4; 28:51
herds (B)(R)	De 28:4; 28:51; 2Sa 17:29
increase of thy k., or flocks of	De 28:51
Butter of k., and milk of sheep	De 32:14
new cart, and take two milch k.	1Sa 6:7
no yoke, and tie the k. to the cart	1Sa 6:7
and took two milch k. and tied	1Sa 6:10
the k. took the straight way to	1Sa 6:12
and offered the k. a burnt offering	1Sa 6:14
sheep, and cheese of k., for David	2Sa 17:29
Hear this word, ye k. of Bashan	Am 4:1
cows of Bashan (A)(R)	Am 4:1
heifers of Bashan (B)	Am 4:1

KING

Melchizedek k. of Salem	Ge 14:18; Heb 7:1
before there reigned any k.	Ge 36:31; 1Ch 1:43
over Israel	
there arose up a new k. over Egypt	Ex 1:8
the shout of a k. is among them	Nu 23:21
and his k. shall be higher than Agag	Nu 24:7
shalt say, I will set a k. over me	De 17:14
thou shalt in any wise set him k. over thee	De 17:15
Lord shall bring thee and thy k. to a nation	De 28:36
and he was k. in Jeshurun when the heads	De 33:5
each resembled the children of a k.	J'g 8:18
the trees went to anoint a k. over them	J'g 9:8
in those days no k. in Israel	J'g 17:6; 18:1; 19:1; 21:25
Lord shall give strength to his k.	1Sa 2:10
go make us a k. to judge us like the nations	1Sa 8:5
give us a k.	1Sa 8:6
shew the manner of the k.	1Sa 8:9; 8:11
ye shall cry out on that day because of your k.	1Sa 8:18
we will have a k.	1Sa 8:19
that our k. may judge us, and go before us	1Sa 8:20
and make them a k.	1Sa 8:22
ye said unto him, Nay, but set a k. over us	1Sa 10:19
the people shouted, and said, God save the k.	1Sa 10:24; 2Sa 16:16; 2Ki 11:12; 2Ch 23:11
behold, I have made a k. over you	1Sa 12:1
and now behold, the k. walketh before you	1Sa 12:2
ye said unto me, Nay, but a k. reign over us, when Lord God was your k.	1Sa 12:12
behold the k. whom ye have chosen	1Sa 12:13

that your wickedness is great *1Sa 12:17*
in asking a *k*.

have added to our sins this *1Sa 12:19*
evil, to ask us a *k*.

ye shall be consumed, both *1Sa 12:25*
you and your *k*.

the Lord sent me to anoint *1Sa 15:1*
thee to be *k*.

he hath rejected thee from *1Sa 15:23;*
being *k*.   *15:26*

I have provided me a *k*. *1Sa 16:1*
among his sons

let not the *k*. sin against his *1Sa 19:4*
servant David

I should not fail to sit with *1Sa 20:5*
the *k*. at meat

let not the *k*. impute any *1Sa 22:15*
thing to his servant

I know that thou shalt surely *1Sa 24:20*
be *k*.

Nabal held a feast like the *1Sa 25:36*
feast of a *k*.

against the enemies of my lord *1Sa 29:8*
the *k*.

he made Ish-bosheth *k*. over *2Sa 2:9*
Gilead

what the *k*. did, pleased all the *2Sa 3:36*
people

that it was not of the *k*. to *2Sa 3:37*
slay Abner

the Lord had established him *2Sa 5:12*
k. over Israel

there followed him a mess of *2Sa 11:8*
meat from *k*.

thus saith Lord, I anointed *2Sa 12:7*
thee *k*. over Israel

therefore I pray thee, speak *2Sa 13:13*
to the *k*.

and the *k*. and his throne be *2Sa 14:9*
guiltless

as an angel of God so is my *2Sa 14:17;*
Lord the *k*.   *19:27*

that had a controversy, came *2Sa 15:2*
to the *k*.

there is none deputed of the *k*. *2Sa 15:3*
to hear thee

abide with the *k*. for thou art *2Sa 15:19*
a stranger

in what place my lord the *k*. *2Sa 15:21*
shall be

why should this dead dog *2Sa 16:9*
curse the *k*.

people shall flee, I will smite *2Sa 17:2*
the *k*. only

there is no matter hid from *2Sa 18:13*
the *k*.

the *k*. saved us out of the *2Sa 19:9*
hand of our enemies

the speech of all Israel is *2Sa 19:11*
come to the *k*.

that the *k*. should take it to *2Sa 19:19*
his heart

I know that I am this day *k*. *2Sa 19:22*
over Israel

what right have I to cry any *2Sa 19:28*
more to the *k*.

because the *k*. is near of kin *2Sa 19:42*
to us

and said, We have ten parts *2Sa 19:43*
in the *k*.

he is the tower of salvation *2Sa 22:51*
for his *k*.

these did Araunah as a *k*. *2Sa 24:23*
give to the *k*.

then Adonijah said, I will be *k*. *1Ki 1:5*

for Solomon shall be *k*. in my *1Ki 1:35*
stead

well, I will speak for thee to *1Ki 2:18*
the *k*.

as the *k*. hath said, so will thy *1Ki 2:38*
servant do

hast made thy servant *k*. *1Ki 3:7*
instead of David

thus the women spake before *1Ki 3:22*
the *k*.

Israel heard the judgment the *1Ki 3:28*
k. judged

the *k*. and all Israel offered *1Ki 8:62*
sacrifice

there was not any thing hid *1Ki 10:3*
from the *k*.

Jeroboam lifted up his hand *1Ki 11:26*
against the *k*.

thou shalt reign and shalt be *1Ki 11:37*
k. over Israel

Ahijah, who told me I should *1Ki 14:2*
be *k*.

the Lord shall raise him up a *1Ki 14:14*
k. over Israel

in the fifth year of *k*. *1Ki 14:25*
Rehoboam

Zimri conspired and hath *1Ki 16:16*
slain the *k*.

thou didst blaspheme God *1Ki 21:10*
and the *k*.

prophets declare good to the *1Ki 22:13;*
k.   *2Ch 18:12*

there was then no *k*. in *1Ki 22:47*
Edom, a deputy was *k*.

O man of God, *k*. said, Come *2Ki 1:11*
down

wouldest thou be spoken for *2Ki 4:13*
to the *k*.

then a lord on whose hand the *2Ki 7:2*
k. leaned

she went to cry to the *k*. for her *2Ki 8:3*
house

the Lord hath shewed that *2Ki 8:13*
thou shalt be *k*.

Edom revolted, made a *k*. *2Ki 8:20*
over themselves

sent, saying, We will not make *2Ki 10:5*
any *k*.

and be with the *k*. as he goeth *2Ki 11:8*
out and cometh

made covenant between Lord *2Ki 11:17*
and *k*. between *k*. also and people

had slain the *k*. his father *2Ki 14:5;*
                   2Ch 25:3

brought the *k*. word *2Ki 22:9;*
    22:20; 2Ch 34:16, 28

Shaphan read it before the *2Ki 22:10;*
k.   *2Ch 34:18*

they took the *k*. and brought *2Ki 25:6;*
him   *Jer 52:9*

they dwelt with the *k*. for his *1Ch 4:23*
work

Shemaiah wrote them before *1Ch 24:6*
the *k*.

bowed and worshipped the *1Ch 29:20*
Lord and the *k*.

he hath made thee *k*. over *2Ch 2:11;*
them   *9:8*

so the *k*. hearkened not to *2Ch 10:15*
the people

for he thought to make him *2Ch 11:22*
k.

they stoned him at the *2Ch 24:21*
command of the *k*.

be it known to the *k*. that *Ezr 4:12;*
            4:13; 5:8

and pray for the life of *k*. and *Ezr 6:10*
sons

who will not do the law of the *Ezr 7:26*
k.

to require of the *k*. a band of *Ezr 8:22*
soldiers

what do ye? will ye rebel *Ne 2:19*
against the *k*.

mayest be their *k*. according to *Ne 6:6*
these words

to preach, saying, There is a *k*. *Ne 6:7*
in Judah

there no *k*. like him, God *Ne 13:26*
made him *k*. over all Israel

so will I go in unto the *k*. if I *Es 4:16*
perish

whom the *k*. delighteth to *Es 6:6;*
honour   *6:7*

for Mordecai, who had spoken *Es 7:9*
good for the *k*.

shall prevail, as a *k*. ready to *Job 15:24*
the battle

it shall bring him to the *k*. of *Job 18:14*
terrors

I sat chief, and dwelt as a *k*. *Job 29:25*
in the army

is it fit to say to the *k*., Thou *Job 34:18*
art wicked

he is a *k*. over all the *Job 41:34*
children of pride

I set my *k*. upon my holy hill of *Ps 2:6*
Zion

hearken to my cry, my *k*. and *Ps 5:2;*
my God   *84:3*

the Lord is *k*. for ever and *Ps 10:16;*
ever   *29:10*

great deliverance giveth he to *Ps 18:50*
his *k*.

let the *k*. hear us when we call *Ps 20:9*

the *k*. shall joy in thy strength, *Ps 21:1*
O Lord

for the *k*. trusteth in the Lord *Ps 21:7*
and not be moved

and the *k*. of glory shall come *Ps 24:7;*
in   *24:9*

who is *k*. of glory? the Lord *Ps 24:8*
strong and mighty

the Lord of hosts he is the *k*. *Ps 24:10*
of glory

no *k*. saved by the multitude *Ps 33:16*
of an host

art my *k*. O God, command *Ps 44:4*
deliverances

of the things I have made *Ps 45:1*
touching the *k*.

so shall the *k*. greatly desire *Ps 45:11*
thy beauty

she shall be brought to the *k*. *Ps 45:14*
in raiment

sing praises to our *k*.; God is *Ps 47:6;*
the *k*.   *47:7*

but the *k*. shall rejoice in God, *Ps 63:11*
every one

they have seen the goings of *Ps 68:24*
my God, my *k*.

give the *k*. thy judgments, O *Ps 72:1*
God

God is my *k*. of old, working *Ps 74:12*
salvation

the holy One of Israel is our *k*. *Ps 89:18*

make a joyful noise before the *Ps 98:6*
Lord the *k*.

the *k*. sent and loosed him, *Ps 105:20*
let him go free

let the children of Zion be *Ps 149:2*
joyful in their *k*.

mercy and truth preserve the *Pr 20:28*
k.

for grace of his lips, the *k*. *Pr 22:11*
shall be his friend

my son, fear thou the Lord *Pr 24:21*
and the *k*.

take away the wicked from *Pr 25:5*
before the *k*.

the locusts have no *k*. yet go *Pr 30:27*
they forth

and a *k*. against whom there is *Pr 30:31*
no rising up

what can the man do that *Ec 2:12*
cometh after *k*.

the *k*. himself is served by the *Ec 5:9*
field

where the word of a *k*. is, there *Ec 8:4*
is power

woe to thee, O land, when thy *Ec 10:16*
k. is a child

blessed when thy *k*. is the son *Ec 10:17*
of nobles

curse not the *k*. no, not in thy *Ec 10:20*
thought

the *k*. brought me into his *Ca 1:4*
chamber

while the *k*. sitteth at his table, *Ca 1:12*
my spikenard

behold *k*. Solomon with the *Ca 3:11*
crown

the *k*. is held in the galleries *Ca 7:5*

mine eyes have seen the *k*. the *Isa 6:5*
Lord of hosts

let us set a *k*. in the midst of it, *Isa 7:6*
son of Tabeal

curse their *k*. and their God, *Isa 8:21*
and look up

and a fierce *k*. shall rule over *Isa 19:4*
them

according to the days of one *Isa 23:15*
k.

for Tophet, yea, for the *k*. it *Isa 30:33*
is prepared

behold, a *k*. shall reign in *Isa 32:1*
righteousness

thine eyes shall see the *k*. in *Isa 33:17*
his beauty

the Lord is our *k*. he will save *Isa 33:22*
us

bring your reasons, saith the *Isa 41:21*
k. of Jacob

I am the Creator of Israel *Isa 43:15*
your *k*.

and thou wentest to the *k*. with *Isa 57:9*
ointment

that the heart of the *k*. shall *Jer 4:9*
perish

is not the Lord in Zion? is not *Jer 8:19*
her *k*. in her

the Lord is the true God, an *Jer 10:10*
everlasting *k*.

say to the *k*. and queen, *Jer 13:18*
Humble yourselves

a *k*. shall reign and prosper *Jer 23:5*
and execute

thus saith the Lord, of the *k* *Jer 29:16*
that sitteth

for the *k.* is not he that can do   *Jer 38:5*
any thing
declare what hast said to the   *Jer 38:25*
k. the *k.* to thee
as I live, saith the *k.* whose   *Jer 46:18;*
name is the Lord of hosts   *48:15; 51:57*
why doth their *k.* inherit Gad   *Jer 49:1*
and dwell in
I will destroy from thence the   *Jer 49:38*
k. and the princes
the Lord hath despised the *k.*   *La 2:6*
and priest
the *k.* shall mourn, and the   *Eze 7:27*
prince
hath taken the *k.* and princes   *Eze 17:12*
thereof
hath taken of the *k.* seed and   *Eze 17:13*
made a covenant
where the *k.* dwelleth that   *Eze 17:16*
made him a
I will bring a *k.* of kings from   *Eze 26:7*
the north
and one *k.* shall be *k.* to   *Eze 37:22;*
them all   *37:24*
there is no *k.* asked such things   *Da 2:10*
at any
there is none that can shew it   *Da 2:11*
before the *k.*
bring me in before the *k.* and I   *Da 2:24*
will shew the *k.*
they brought these men before   *Da 3:13*
the *k.*
decree which is come upon my   *Da 4:24*
lord the *k.*
I praise, extol, and honour the   *Da 4:37*
k. of heaven
the *k.* saw the part of the hand   *Da 5:5*
that wrote
the princes assembled together   *Da 6:6*
to the *k.*
a *k.* of fierce countenance shall   *Da 8:23*
stand up
and a mighty *k.* shall stand up   *Da 11:3*
to rule
the *k.* shall do according to   *Da 11:36*
his will
Israel shall abide many days   *Ho 3:4*
without a *k.*
Israel shall seek the Lord, and   *Ho 3:5*
David their *k.*
then Ephraim sent to *k.*   *Ho 5:13;*
Jareb   *10:6*
they make the *k.* glad with   *Ho 7:3*
their wickedness
in the day of our *k.* princes   *Ho 7:5*
made him sick
we have no *k.* what then   *Ho 10:3*
should a *k.* do
her *k.* is cut off, as the foam   *Ho 10:7*
upon the water
but the Assyrian shall be his   *Ho 11:5*
k. because
I will be thy *k.* give me a *k.*   *Ho 13:10*
and princes
I gave thee a *k.* in mine   *Ho 13:11*
anger and took him
and their *k.* shall go into   *Am 1:15*
captivity
and their *k.* shall pass before   *Mic 2:13*
them
why dost thou cry? is there no   *Mic 4:9*
k. in thee
and the *k.* shall perish from   *Zec 9:5*
Gaza
behold thy *k.* cometh to thee   *Zec 9:9;*
  M't 21:5
will deliver every one into the   *Zec 11:6*
hand of his *k.*
the Lord shall be *k.* over all   *Zec 14:9*
the earth
every one even go up to   *Zec 14:16;*
worship the *k.*   *14:17*
kingdom likened to a certain   *M't 18:23;*
k.   *22:2*
when the *k.* came in to see   *M't 22:11*
the guests
she came with haste to the *k.*   *M'k 6:25*
and asked
what *k.* goeth to war against   *Lu 14:31*
another *k.*
blessed be the *k.* that cometh   *Lu 19:38*
in name of Lord
saying, that he himself is   *Lu 23:2*
Christ, a *K.*
to make him a *k.;* thy *k.*   *Joh 6:15;*
cometh   *12:15*
Pilate said to him, Art thou a   *Joh 18:37*
k. then
whosoever maketh himself a   *Joh 19:12*
k. speaketh

Pilate saith to the Jews,   *Joh 19:14*
Behold your *k.*
shall I crucify your *k.?* have   *Joh 19:15*
no, *k.* but Cæsar
till another *k.* arose, who knew   *Ac 7:18*
not Joseph
afterward they desired a *k.*   *Ac 13:21*
and God gave
saying, That there is another *k.*   *Ac 17:7*
one Jesus
for the *k.* knoweth of these   *Ac 26:26*
things
death is *k.* **(B)**   *Ro 5:17*
now to the *k.* eternal,   *1Ti 1:17*
immortal
who is the *k.* of kings, and   *1Ti 6:15*
Lord of lords
Moses not fearing the wrath   *Heb 11:27*
of the *k.*
whether to the *k.* as supreme,   *1Pe 2:13*
or governors
honour all men, fear God   *1Pe 2:17*
honour the *k.*
they had a *k.* over them, the   *Re 9:11*
angel
just are thy ways, thou *K.* of   *Re 15:3*
saints
he is Lord of lords, *K.* of   *Re 17:14;*
kings   *19:16*

KING *OF ASSYRIA*

Pul the *k. of Assyria* came   *2Ki 15:19*
against land
Menahem exacted money to   *2Ki 15:20*
give *k. of Assyria*
turned he from house of   *2Ki 16:18*
Lord to *k. of Assyria*
in ninth year of Hoshea *k. of*   *2Ki 17:6*
Assyria took Samaria
k. of Assyria did carry   *2Ki 18:11*
away Israel to Assyria
speak, thus saith great king   *2Ki 18:19*
the *k. of Assyria*
delivered his land out of   *2Ki 18:33*
hand of *k. of Assyria*
saith Lord concerning *k. of*   *2Ki 19:32;*
Assyria   *Isa 37:33*
turned the heart of *k. of*   *Ezr 6:22*
Assyria to them
Lord shall bring upon thee the   *Isa 7:17*
k. of Assyria
shall shave by *k. of Assyria* the   *Isa 7:20*
head and hair
first the *k. of Assyria* hath   *Jer 50:17*
devoured him
I will punish Babylon as I   *Jer 50:18*
punished *k. of Assyria*
thy shepherds slumber, O *k. of*   *Na 3:18*
Assyria

KING *OF EGYPT*

midwives did not as *k. of*   *Ex 1:17*
Egypt commanded
I am sure the *k. of Egypt* will   *Ex 3:19*
not let you go
the Lord gave them a charge to   *Ex 6:13*
the *k. of Egypt*
the *k. of Egypt* came not again   *2Ki 24:7*
any more that pertained *k. of*
Egypt
k. of Egypt came up against   *2Ch 12:2*
Jerusalem
the *k. of Egypt* put him down   *2Ch 36:3*
at Jerusalem
the *k. of Egypt* made Eliakim   *2Ch 36:4*
his brother king
so is the *k. of Egypt* to all that   *Isa 36:6*
trust in him

KING *OF ISRAEL*

after whom is the *k. of Israel*   *1Sa 24:14*
come out
for the *k. of Israel* is come   *1Sa 26:20*
out to seek a flea
how glorious was the *k.* of   *2Sa 6:20*
Israel to-day
let us, I pray thee, go out to   *1Ki 20:31*
k. of Israel
fight not, save only with the   *1Ki 22:31*
k. of Israel
they said, Surely it is *k.* of   *1Ki 22:32;*
Israel   *2Ch 18:31*
shew me which of us is for *k.*   *2Ki 6:11*
of Israel
save me out of the hand of *k.*   *2Ki 16:7*
of Israel
fight ye not, save only with   *2Ch 18:30*
k. of Israel

captains perceived that it   *2Ch 18:32*
was not *k. of Israel*
son of David *k. of Israel* did   *2Ch 35:3;*
build   *Ezr 5:11*
did not Solomon *k. of Israel*   *Ne 13:26*
sin by these
thus saith the Lord, the *k. of*   *Isa 44:6*
Israel
in a morning shall the *k. of*   *Ho 10:15*
Israel be cut off
the *k. of Israel* is in the midst   *Zep 3:15*
of thee
if he be *k. of Israel* let him   *M't 27:42;*
descend   *M'k 15:32*
thou art *k. of Israel*   *Joh 1:49*
blessed is *k. of Israel*   *Joh 12:13*

KING *OF JUDAH*

Jehoshaphat being then *k. of*   *2Ki 8:16*
Judah
but to *k. of Judah* which sent   *2Ki 22:18*
you to inquire
and as for *k. of Judah* who   *2Ch 34:26*
sent you
what have I to do with thee,   *2Ch 35:21*
thou *k. of Judah*
hear the word of the Lord O   *Jer 34:4*
k. of Judah
thus shall ye say to *k. of Judah*   *Jer 37:7*
who sent you

KING *OF MOAB*

Balak *k. of Moab* brought me   *Nu 23:7*
from Aram
the *k. of Moab* warred against   *Jos 24:9*
Israel
Israel served Eglon the *k. of*   *J'g 3:14*
Moab eighteen years
Israel in like manner sent to   *J'g 11:17*
k. of Moab
art thou any thing better than   *J'g 11:25*
Balak *k. of Moab*
sold them into the hand of *k.*   *1Sa 12:9*
of Moab
David brought father and   *1Sa 22:4*
mother to *k. of Moab*
and Mesha *k. of Moab* was a   *2Ki 3:4*
sheepmaster
the *k. of Moab* rebelled   *2Ki 3:5;*
against Israel   *3:7*
when the *k. of Moab* saw the   *2Ki 3:26*
battle was too sore
send bonds and yokes to the *k.*   *Jer 27:3*
of Moab

KING *OF PERSIA*

as Cyrus, *k. of Persia* hath   *Ezr 4:3*
commanded us
even till the reign of Darius *k.*   *Ezr 4:5*
of Persia
Bishlam wrote unto Artaxerxes   *Ezr 4:7;*
k. of Persia   *6:14*
extended mercy to us in sight of   *Ezr 9:9*
the *k. of Persia*

KING *OF SYRIA*

Ben-hadad *k. of Syria*   *1Ki 20:20*
escaped on a horse
the *k. of Syria* will come up   *1Ki 20:22*
against thee
Naaman captain of host of *k.*   *2Ki 5:1*
of Syria
k. of Syria was sick; *k. of*   *2Ki 6:7;*
Syria hath sent me to thee   *6:9*
because the *k. of Syria*   *2Ki 13:4*
oppressed them
for the *k. of Syria* had   *2Ki 13:7*
destroyed them
save me out of the hand of the   *2Ki 16:7*
k. of Syria
because thou hast relied on *k.*   *2Ch 16:7*
of Syria

KING *OF TYRE*

k. of Tyre sent messengers to   *2Sa 5:11;*
David   *1Ch 14:1*
the *k. of Tyre* sent servants to   *1Ki 5:1*
Solomon
Hiram the *k. of Tyre* had   *1Ki 9:11*
furnished Solomon
Solomon sent to Huram the *k.*   *2Ch 2:3*
of Tyre
Huram the *k. of Tyre*   *2Ch 2:11*
answered in writing

O KING

Abner said, O k. I cannot tell   *1Sa 17:55*
now, therefore, O k. come down   *1Sa 23:20*
my lord, O k.   *1Sa 26:17; 2Sa 14:9, 22; 16:4; 19:26; 1Ki 1:13, 20, 24; 20:4; 2Ki 6:12, 26; 8:5*
woman of Tekoah said, Help, O k.   *2Sa 14:4*
if thou say, I will be thy servant, O k.   *2Sa 15:34*
O k. let not the army of Israel go   *2Ch 25:7*
I will extol thee, my God, O k.   *Ps 145:1*
who would not fear thee, O k. of nations   *Jer 10:7*
O k. live for ever   *Da 2:4; 3:9; 5:10; 6:21*
as for thee, O k.; thou, O k.   *Da 2:29;*
sawest an image   *2:31*
thou, O k. art a king of kings, for God hath   *Da 2:37*
thou, O k. hast made a decree, that every man   *Da 3:10*
he will deliver us out of thy hand, O k.   *Da 3:17*
be it known to thee, O k.   *Da 3:18*
true, O k.   *Da 3:24*
it is thou, O k.; O k. let my counsel be   *Da 4:22; 4:27*
saying, O k. Nebuchadnezar to thee it is spoken   *Da 4:31*
O thou k. the most high God gave thy father   *Da 5:18*
shall ask a petition save of thee, O k.   *Da 6:7*
now, O k. establish the decree, and sign it   *Da 6:8*
regardeth not thee, O k.   *Da 6:13*
know, O k.   *Da 6:15*
also before thee, O k. have I done no hurt   *Da 6:22*
at mid-day, O k. I saw in the way a light   *Ac 26:13*
whereupon, O k. I was not disobedient   *Ac 26:19*

KINGDOM

and ye shall be to me a k. of priests   *Ex 19:6*
the k. of Sihon and the k. of Og   *Nu 32:33; De 3:13; Jos 13:12, 21, 27, 30*
took the k. of Og in Bashan sixty cities   *De 3:4*
of the matter of k. he told him not   *1Sa 10:16*
then Samuel told the manner of the k.   *1Sa 10:25*
renew the k. there; Saul took k.   *1Sa 11:14; 14:47*
Lord hath rent the k. of Israel   *1Sa 15:28; 28:17*
and what can he have more but the k.   *1Sa 18:8*
to translate the k. from house of Saul   *2Sa 3:10*
Israel shall restore me k. of my father   *2Sa 16:3*
hath delivered the k. into hand of Absalom   *2Sa 16:8*
thou knowest that the k. was mine   *1Ki 2:15*
ask for him the k. for he is my elder brother   *1Ki 2:22*
not the like made in any k.   *1Ki 10:20; 2Ch 9:19*
I will surely rend the k. from thee   *1Ki 11:11; 31:35*
tear the k. away (S)   *1Ki 11:11*
I will not rend away all the k.   *1Ki 11:13; 11:34*
to bring k. again to Rehoboam   *1Ki 12:21; 2Ch 11:1*
now shall k. return again to house of David   *1Ki 12:26*
I rent the k. away from the house of David   *1Ki 14:8*
no k. where my lord hath not sent to seek   *1Ki 18:10*
dost thou now govern the k. of Israel   *1Ki 21:7*
as soon as the k. was confirmed   *2Ki 14:5*
with him, to confirm the k. in his hand   *2Ki 15:19*
in all this k. (B)   *2Ki 20:13*

and turned the k. to David   *1Ch 10:14; 12:23*
from one k. to another people   *1Ch 16:20; Ps 105:13*
thine is the k. O Lord   *1Ch 29:11; Ps 22:28; M't 6:13*
think to withstand the k. of the Lord   *2Ch 13:8*
the k. was quiet before him   *2Ch 14:5*
the k. gave he to Jehoram the firstborn   *2Ch 21:3*
Jehoram was risen up to the k. of his father   *2Ch 21:4*
Ahaziah had no power to keep still the k.   *2Ch 22:9*
for a sin offering for the k. and Judah   *2Ch 29:21*
for no god of any nation or k. was able   *2Ch 32:15*
for they have not served thee in their k.   *Ne 9:35*
seven princes which sat first in the k.   *Es 1:14*
thou art come to the k. for such a time   *Es 4:14*
it shall be given to the half of the k.   *Es 5:3; 5:6; 7:2*
they shall fight, k. against k.   *Isa 19:2; M't 24:7; M'k 13:8; Lu 21:10*
they shall call the nobles thereof to the k.   *Isa 34:12*
the k. that will not serve thee   *Isa 60:12; Jer 27:8*
I speak concerning a k. to destroy it   *Jer 18:7*
concerning a k. to build and to plant it   *Jer 18:9*
he hath polluted the k. and the princes   *La 2:2*
and thou didst prosper into a k.   *Eze 16:13*
that the k. might be base, and not lift itself   *Eze 17:14*
and they shall be there a base k.   *Eze 29:14*
the God of heaven hath given thee a k.   *Da 2:37*
in their days shall God of heaven set up a k.   *Da 2:44*
the most High ruleth in the k. of men   *Da 4:17; 25:32*
O king, the k. is departed from thee   *Da 4:31*
no fault against Daniel concerning the k.   *Da 6:4*
the saints shall take the k. and possess the k.   *Da 7:18*
the time came that the saints possessed the k.   *Da 7:22*
the most High, whose k. is an everlasting k.   *Da 7:27*
they shall not give the honour of the k.   *Da 11:21*
and will cause to cease the k. of Israel   *Ho 1:4*
the eyes of the Lord are upon the sinful k.   *Am 9:8*
and the k. shall be the Lord's   *Ob 21*
k. shall come to the daughter of Jerusalem   *Mic 4:8*
the gospel of the k.   *M't 4:23; 9:35; 24:14*
the children of the k. shall be cast out   *M't 8:12*
every k. divided against itself is brought   *M't 12:25; M'k 3:24; Lu 11:17*
the good seed are the children of the k.   *M't 13:38*
shall shine as the sun in the k. of their father   *M't 13:43*
inherit the k. prepared for you from the   *M't 25:34*
till I drink it new in my Father's k.   *M't 26:29*
blessed be the k. of our father David   *M'k 11:10*
Father's good pleasure to give you k.   *Lu 12:32*
a nobleman went to receive for himself a k.   *Lu 19:12*
he was returned, having received the k.   *Lu 19:15*
I appoint unto you a k. as my Father   *Lu 22:29*
wilt thou restore again the k. to Israel   *Ac 1:6*
when he shall have delivered up the k.   *1Co 15:24*
hath translated us into the k. of his Son   *Col 1:13*

wherefore we receiving a k. that cannot   *Heb 12:28*
heirs of the k. which he hath promised   *Jas 2:5*
an entrance ministered into everlasting k.   *2Pe 1:11*
a k. of priests (S)   *Re 1:6; 5:10*
companion in the k. and patience of Jesus   *Re 1:9*
the k. of this world (S)   *Re 11:15*
ten kings, which have received no k. as yet   *Re 17:12*
to agree, and give their k. to the beast   *Re 17:17*

KINGDOM *OF GOD*

but seek ye first the k. of God   *M't 6:33; Lu 12:31*
k. of God is come unto   *M't 12:28; Lu 10:9, 11; 11:20*
through eye of needle, rich man enter k. of God   *M't 19:24; M'k 10:23; Lu 18:24*
the harlots go into the k. of God before you   *M't 21:31*
the k. of God shall be taken from you   *M't 21:43*
preaching k. of God   *M'k 1:14; Ac 8:12; 20:25; 28:31*
the k. of God is at hand, repent and believe   *M'k 1:15*
to know the mystery of k. of God   *M'k 4:11; Lu 8:10*
and he said, So is the k. of God as if a man cast   *M'k 4:26*
whereunto shall liken k. of God   *M'k 4:30; Lu 13:18, 20*
till they have seen k. of God come with power   *M'k 9:1*
better to enter into the k. of God with one eye   *M'k 9:47*
children, for of such is k. of God   *M'k 10:14; 18:16*
whoso shall not receive k. of God   *M'k 10:15; Lu 18:17*
riches to enter into k. of God   *M'k 10:24; 10:25; Lu 18:25*
he said, Thou art not far from the k. of God   *M'k 12:34*
till that day I drink it new in the k. of God   *M'k 14:25*
which waited for the k. of God   *M'k 15:43; Lu 23:51*
I must preach the k. of God to other cities   *Lu 4:43*
blessed be ye poor, for yours is the k. of God   *Lu 6:20*
that is least in the k. of God is greater than he   *Lu 7:28*
preaching and shewing glad tidings of k. of God   *Lu 8:1*
and he sent them to preach the k. of God   *Lu 9:2; 9:60*
received them, and spake to them of k. of God   *Lu 9:11*
shall not taste of death, till they see k. of God   *Lu 9:27*
and looking back, is fit for the k. of God   *Lu 9:62*
ye shall see all the prophets in the k. of God   *Lu 13:28*
and they shall sit down in the k. of God   *Lu 13:29*
blessed is he that shall eat bread in the k. of God   *Lu 14:15*
since that time the k. of God is preached   *Lu 16:16*
was demanded when k. of God should come   *Lu 17:20*
the k. of God cometh not with observation   *Lu 17:20*
for behold, the k. of God is within you   *Lu 17:21*
left wife or children for the k. of God's sake   *Lu 18:29*
they thought that k. of God should appear   *Lu 19:11*
know ye that the k. of God is nigh at hand   *Lu 21:31*
nor eat till it be fulfilled in the k. of God   *Lu 22:16*
I will not drink until the k. of God shall come   *Lu 22:18*
except man be born again, cannot see k. of God   *Joh 3:3*
born of water, he cannot enter into the k. of God   *Joh 3:5*

things pertaining to *k.* of God   *Ac 1:3;*
   8:12; 19:8
thro' much tribulation enter   *Ac 14:22*
into *k. of God*
to whom he expounded, and   *Ac 28:23*
testified *k. of God*
for the *k. of God* is not meat   *Ro 14:17*
and drink
the *k. of God* is not in word,   *1Co 4:20*
but in power
the unrighteous shall not   *1Co 6:9*
inherit the *k. of God*
inherit the *k. of God*   *Ga 5:21; Eph 5:5*
flesh and blood cannot   *1Co 15:50*
inherit the *k. of God*
my fellow workers unto the *k.*   *Col 4:11*
of God
may be counted worthy of the   *2Th 1:5*
k. of God
now is come the *k.* of our   *Re 12:10*
God

KINGDOM *OF HEAVEN*

repent, for *k. of heaven* is at   *M't 3:2;*
hand   *4:17; 10:7*
blessed are poor in spirit,   *M't 5:3;*
theirs is *k. of heaven*   *5:10*
shall be called least in *k. of*   *M't 5:19*
heaven great in *k. of heaven*
shall in no case enter into *k.*   *M't 5:20;*
of heaven   *18:3*
not that saith, Lord, shall   *M't 7:21*
enter *k. of heaven*
shall sit down with Abraham *M't 8:11*
in *k. of heaven*
he that is least in *k. of heaven M't 11:11*
is greater than he
k. of heaven suffereth   *M't 11:12*
violence
to know the mysteries of the   *M't 13:11*
k. of heaven
the *k. of heaven* is like   *M't 13:24;*
31, 33, 44-45, 47, 52; 18:23; 20:1; 22:2;
   25:1, 14
I will give to thee the keys of *M't 16:19*
k. of heaven
who is the greatest in the *k.*   *M't 18:1;*
of heaven   *18:4*
for ye shut up the *k.* of   *M't 23:13*
heaven against men

HIS KINGDOM

and the beginning of *his k.*   *Ge 10:10*
was Babel
and *his k.* shall be exalted   *Nu 24:7*
he sitteth on the throne of *his De 17:18*
k.
that he may prolong his days   *De 7:20*
in *his k.*
perceived that he had exalted *2Sa 5:12*
his k.
strengthened with him in *his 1Ch 11:10*
k.
for *his k.* was lifted up on   *1Ch 14:2*
high for Israel
Solomon was strengthened in   *2Ch 1:1*
his k.
determined to build a house *2Ch 2:1;*
for *his k.*   *2:12*
brought him again to   *2Ch 33:13*
Jerusalem into *his k.*
and *his k.* ruleth over all   *Ps 103:19*
and the glorious majesty of   *Ps 145:12*
his k.
whereas he that is born in *his Ec 4:14*
k.
upon *his k.* to order and   *Isa 9:7*
establish it
the high God, *his k.* is an   *Da 4:3*
everlasting kingdom
his k. from generation to   *Da 4:34;*
generation   *6:26; 7:14*
his k. shall be broken and   *Da 11:4*
plucked up
the king of the south shall   *Da 11:9*
come into *his k.*
how shall *his k.* stand   *M't 12:26;*
   Lu 11:18
they shall gather out of *his k. M't 13:41*
all things
they see the Son of man   *M't 16:28*
coming in *his k.*
and of *his k.* there shall be no *Lu 1:33*
end
who hath called you to *his k. 1Th 2:12*
and glory

who shall judge at his   *2Ti 4:1*
appearing and *his k.*
and *his k.* was full of darkness *Re 16:10*

MY KINGDOM

hast brought on me and *my k. Ge 20:9*
a great sin
I and *my k.* are guiltless   *2Sa 3:28*
before the Lord
I will settle him in *my k.* for *1Ch 17:14*
ever
and for the glory of *my k.* in   *Da 4:36*
my k.
in every dominion of *my k*   *Da 6:26*
men tremble
I will give it, to the half of   *M'k 6:23*
my k.
may eat and drink at my table *Lu 22:30*
in *my k.*
my k. is not of this world, if *Joh 18:36*
my k. were, but now *my k.* is not

THY KINGDOM

but now *thy k.* shall not   *1Sa 13:14*
continue
sceptre of *thy k.* a right   *Ps 45:6;*
sceptre   *Heb 1:8*
they shall speak of the glory   *Ps 145:11*
of *thy k.*
thy k. is an everlasting   *Ps 145:13*
kingdom thy
thy k. shall be sure to thee,   *Da 4:26*
after that
there is a man in *thy k.;*   *Da 5:11;*
God numbered *thy k.*   *5:26*
thy k. is divided to the Medes *Da 5:28*
and Persians
thy k. come, thy will be done *M't 6:10;*
   Lu 11:2
and the other on the left in   *M't 20:21*
thy k.
remember me when thou   *Lu 23:42*
comest to *thy k.*

KINGDOMS

so shall the Lord do all the *k. De 3:21*
whither
be removed into all the *k.* of   *De 28:25*
the earth
Hazor was the head of all   *Jos 11:10*
those *k.*
I delivered you out of hand   *1Sa 10:18*
of all *k.*
Solomon reigned over all *k.*   *1Ki 4:21*
the God of all the *k.* of   *2Ki 19:15*
earth
that all the *k.* may know   *2Ki 19:19;*
   Isa 37:20
times that went over all the   *1Ch 29:30*
k.
they may know the service of *2Ch 12:8*
the *k.*
the fear of the Lord fell on   *2Ch 17:10;*
the *k.*   *20:29*
thou rulest over all the *k.* of *2Ch 20:6*
the heathen
all *k.* hath the Lord given   *2Ch 36:23;*
me   *Ezr 1:2*
thou gavest them *k.* and   *Ne 9:22*
nations
the heathen raged, the *k.* were *Ps 46:6*
moved
sing unto God, ye *k.* of the   *Ps 68:32*
earth
thy wrath on the *k.* that have *Ps 79:6*
not called
the *k.* are gathered to serve   *Ps 102:22*
the Lord
who smote all the *k.* of   *Ps 135:11*
Canaan
as my hand hath found the *k. Isa 10:10*
of idols
the noise of the *k.* of nations *Isa 13:4*
gathered
Babylon the glory of *k.* as   *Isa 13:19;*
Sodom   *47:5*
is this the man that did shake *Isa 14:16*
k.
he shook the *k.*; God of all   *Isa 23:11;*
k.   *37:16*
and over the *k.* I have set thee *Jer 1:10*
and in all their *k.* none like   *Jer 10:7*
thee
to be removed into all *k.*   *Jer 15:4;*
   24:9; 34:17
all the *k.* of the world shall   *Jer 25:26*
drink

the prophets prophesied   *Jer 28:8*
against great *k.*
I will make them a terror to   *Jer 29:18*
all *k.*
all the *k.* fought against   *Jer 34:1*
Jerusalem
concerning Kedar and the *k. Jer 49:28*
of Hazor
and with thee will I destroy *k. Jer 51:20*
call together against her the   *Jer 51:27*
k. of Ararat
it shall be the basest of the *k. Eze 29:15*
nor shall they be divided into *Eze 37:22*
two *k.*
and it shall consume all these   *Da 2:44*
k.
which shall be diverse from all *Da 7:23*
k.
four *k.* shall stand up out of   *Da 8:22*
the nation
go to Gath; be they better than *Am 6:2*
these *k.*
and I will shew the *k.* thy shame *Na 3:5*
that I may assemble the *k.* to   *Zep 3:8*
pour on
overthrow throne of *k.* and   *Hag 2:22*
destroy strength of *k.* of the
shewed him all the *k.* of world *M't 4:8;*
   Lu 4:5
who through faith subdued   *Heb 11:33*
k. wrought
k. of this world become *k.* of *Re 11:15*
the Lord

KINGLY

he was deposed from his *k.*   *Da 5:20*
throne

KINGS

k. shall come out of thee   *Ge 17:6;*
   17:16; 35:11
these are the *k.* that reigned *Ge 36:31*
in Edom
and they sew the *k.* of Midian *Nu 31:8*
and Lord hath done to these   *De 3:21*
two *k.*
he shall deliver their *k.* into thy *De 7:24*
hand
five *k.* of Amorites gathered   *Jos 10:5*
together
these five *k.* fled; bring out   *Jos 10:16;*
those five *k.*   *10:22*
come near, put your feet on   *Jos 10:24*
necks of these *k.*
so Joshua smote all their *k.*   *Jos 10:40;*
   11:17
all these *k.* thirty and one   *Jos 12:24*
seventy *k.* having their thumbs *J'g 1:7*
cut off
hear, O ye *k.*; the *k.* came and *J'g 5:3;*
fought   *5:19*
the time when *k.* go forth to   *2Sa 11:1*
battle
not be any among the *k.* like   *1Ki 3:13;*
thee   *10:23; 2Ch 1:12; 9:22*
Solomon over all the *k.* on   *1Ki 4:24*
this side the river
Ben-hadad and thirty-two *k.*   *1Ki 20:1*
with him
hath called these three *k.*   *2Ki 3:10*
together
this is blood, the *k.* are surely *2Ki 3:23*
slain
hath hired against us the *k.* of *2Ki 7:6*
the Hittites
behold, two *k.* stood not   *2Ki 10:4*
before him
he reproved *k.* for them   *1Ch 16:21;*
   Ps 105:14
all *k.* sought the presence of   *2Ch 9:23*
Solomon
but not in the sepulchres of   *2Ch 21:20;*
the *k.*   *24:25*
in field of the burial which   *2Ch 26:23*
belonged to *k.*
shalt endamage the revenue of *Ezr 4:13*
the *k.*
this city hath been hurtful to   *Ezr 4:15*
k. and provinces
this city hath made   *Ezr 4:19*
insurrection against *k.*
there have been mighty *k.* over *Ezr 4:20*
Jerusalem
God destroy *k.* that shall alter *Ezr 6:12*
this house
Artaxerxes king of *k.* to Ezra *Ezr 7:12*
the priest
our *k.* and priests have been   *Ezr 9:7;*
delivered   *Ne 9:24*

trouble seem little to us and   Ne 9:32
our k.
nor have our k. or princes kept   Ne 9:34
thy law
had I been at rest with k. and   Job 3:14
counsellors
he looseth the bond of k. and   Job 12:18
girdeth
but with k. are they on the   Job 36:7
throne
k. of the earth set themselves   Ps 2:2;
                           Ac 4:26
be wise, therefore, O ye k. be   Ps 2:10
instructed
lo, the k. were assembled, they   Ps 48:4
passed by
k. of armies did flee apace,   Ps 68:12
she that tarried
when the Almighty scattered   Ps 68:14
k. in it
shall k. bring presents to thee   Ps 68:29
yea, all k. shall fall down   Ps 72:11
before him
he is terrible to the k. of the   Ps 76:12
earth
make him higher than the k.   Ps 89:27
of the earth
the k. of the earth shall fear   Ps 102:15
thy glory
he shall strike thro' k. in the   Ps 110:5
day of wrath
I will speak of thy   Ps 119:46
testimonies before k.
smote great nations, and slew   Ps 135:10
mighty k.
to him which smote great k.   Ps 136:17;
                               136:18
all k. of the earth shall praise   Ps 138:4;
thee   148:11
it is he that giveth salvation   Ps 144:10
to k.
to bind their k. with chains,   Ps 149:8
their nobles
by me k., princes decree justice   Pr 8:15
an abommation for k. to   Pr 16:12
commit wickedness
righteous lips are the delight   Pr 16:13
of k.
the diligent in business shall   Pr 22:29
stand before k.
it is the honour of k. to search   Pr 25:2
a matter
and the heart of k. is   Pr 25:3
unsearchable
nor thy ways to that which   Pr 31:3
destroyeth k.
it is not for k. O Lemuel, to   Pr 31:4
drink wine
gold and the peculiar treasure of   Ec 2:8
k.
the land shall be forsaken of   Isa 7:16
both her k.
are not my princes altogether   Isa 10:8
k.
it hath raised all the k. of the   Isa 14:9
nations
all the k. of the nations lie in   Isa 14:18
glory
how say ye, I am the son of   Isa 19:11
ancient k.
Lord shall punish the k. of the   Isa 24:21
earth on earth
who raised up and made him   Isa 41:2
ruler over k.
I will loose the loins of k. to   Isa 45:1
open gates
k. shall see and arise, princes   Isa 49:7
shall worship
k. shall be thy nursing fathers   Isa 49:23
and queens
the k. shall shut their mouths   Isa 52:15
at him
and k. to the brightness of thy   Isa 60:3
rising
and their k. shall minister to   Isa 60:10
thee
thy gates open, that their k.   Isa 60:11
may be brought
thou shalt also suck the   Isa 60:16
breast of k.
and all k. shall see thy glory   Isa 62:2
they, their k. and princes   Jer 2:26
ashamed
even k. that sit upon David's   Jer 13:13
throne
shall enter into the gates of   Jer 17:25
this city, k.
k. sitting upon the throne of   Jer 22:4
David

I made Judah and k. drink of   Jer 25:18
the cup
k. of Tyrus; all the k. of   Jer 25:22;
Arabia   25:24
the k. of Zimri; all the k. of   Jer 25:25;
the north   25:26
to provoke me to anger, they,   Jer 32:32
their k.
and with the burnings of   Jer 34:5
former k. before thee
as we, our k. and princes to   Jer 44:17
burn incense
your k. and princes burnt   Jer 44:21
incense in Judah
I will punish their k. and   Jer 46:25
their gods
for their k. shall go into   Jer 49:3
captivity, and priests
man k. shall be raised up   Jer 50:41
from the earth
Lord raised up the spirit of k.   Jer 51:11
of the Medes
k. of the earth would not have   La 4:12
believed
their k. shall be sore afraid   Eze 27:35;
                               32:10
I will lay thee before k. to   Eze 28:17
behold thee
there is Edom, her k. and all   Eze 32:29
her princes
their k. shall no more defile   Eze 43:7
my holy name
he removeth k. and setteth up   Da 2:21
in the days of these k. shall   Da 2:44
God set up a kingdom
of a truth it is, that your God   Da 2:47
is a Lord of k.
the four great beasts are four   Da 7:17
k. shall arise
the ten horns are ten k. shall   Da 7:24
subdue three k.
which spake in thy name to our   Da 9:6
k. our princes
to our k. and princes belongs   Da 9:8
confusion of face
I remained there with the k.   Da 10:13
of Persia
stand up three k.   Da 11:2
are hot as an oven, all their k.   Ho 7:7
are fallen
they have set up k. but not by   Ho 8:4
me
they shall scoff at k. and   Hab 1:10
princes
shall be brought before   M't 10:18;
governors and k.   M'k 13:9; Lu 21:12
of whom do the k. of the   M't 17:25
earth take custom
prophets and k. have desired   Lu 10:24
to see
k. of Gentiles exercise   Lu 22:25
lordship over them
a chosen vessel to bear my   Ac 9:15
name before k.
ye have reigned as k. without   1Co 4:8
us
that prayers be made for k. and   1Ti 2:2
for all
King of k. Lord of lords   1Ti 6:15;
                     Re 17:14; 19:16
Abraham returned from   Heb 7:1
slaughter of the k.
Jesus Christ the prince of the   Re 1:5
k. of the earth
hath made us k. and priests   Re 1:6;
unto God   5:10
the k. of the earth hid   Re 6:15
themselves in the dens
thou must prophesy again   Re 10:11
before k.
the way of the k. of east   Re 16:12
might be prepared
spirits which go forth to the   Re 16:14
k. of the earth
with whom k. of earth   Re 17:2
committed fornication
there are seven k. five are   Re 17:10
fallen, and one is
are ten k. which receive   Re 17:12
power as k. with beasts
that great city which reigneth   Re 17:18
over k. of earth
k. of the earth have committed   Re 18:3
fornication
k. of earth who shall bewail   Re 18:9
her and lament
that ye may eat the flesh of k.   Re 19:18
and captains

k. of the earth gathered to   Re 19:19
make war against
the k. of the earth do bring   Re 21:24
their glory

KINGS *OF THE AMORITES*

two k. of Amorites   De 4:47;
             31:4; Jos 2:10; 9:10; 24:12
came to pass, when all k. of   Jos 5:1
Amorites heard
therefore five k. of Amorites   Jos 10:5;
gathered together   10:6

KINGS *OF ISRAEL*

written in book of   1Ki 14:19;
chronicles of k. of Israel   15:31; 16:5;
14, 20, 27; 22:39; 2Ki 1:18; 10:34; 13:8,
   12; 14:15, 28; 15:11, 15, 21, 26, 31
Ahab provoked Lord more   1Ki 16:33
than all k. of Israel
we heard that k. of Israel   1Ki 20:31
are merciful kings
Jehoram walked in way of k.   2Ki 8:18
of Israel
Joash was buried with the k.   2Ki 13:13;
of Israel   14:16
Jeroboam slept with his   2Ki 14:29
fathers k. of Israel
Ahaz walked in the way of the   2Ki 16:3
k. of Israel
Hoshea did evil, but not as   2Ki 17:2
the k. of Israel
Israel walked in the statutes   2Ki 17:8
of the k. of Israel
Josiah took away houses the   2Ki 23:19
k. of Israel made
not such a passover in the   2Ki 23:22
days of the k. of Israel
written in book of k. of Israel   1Ch 9:1;
and   2Ch 16:11; 25:26; 27:7; 28:26;
                   32:32; 33:18
Jehu who is mentioned in   2Ch 20:34;
book of k. of Israel   35:27; 36:8
Ahaz was not brought into   2Ch 28:27
sepulchres of k. of Israel
houses of Achzib shall be a lie   Mic 1:14
to k. of Israel

KINGS *OF JUDAH*

Ziklag pertained to the k. of   1Sa 27:6
Judah
book of the chronicles of k.   1Ki 14:29;
of Judah 15:7, 23; 22:45; 2Ki 8:23; 15:6,
   36; 16:19; 20:20; 21:17, 25; 23:28; 24:5
hallowed things the k. of   2Ki 12:18
Judah
book of chronicles of k. of   2Ki 12:19;
Judah 14:18; 2Ch 25:26; 28:26; 32:32;
                   35:27; 36:8
there was none like him of all   2Ki 18:5
the k. of Judah
Josiah put down priests k. of   2Ki 23:5
Judah ordained
took horses the k. of Judah had   2Ki 23:11
given to the sun
beat down altars which k. of   2Ki 23:12
Judah had made
not such a passover in all   2Ki 23:22
days of k. of Judah
to floor houses k. of Judah   2Ch 34:11
destroyed
the vision of Isaiah in days of   Isa 1:1
the k. of Judah
I have made an iron pillar   Jer 1:18
against k. of Judah
they shall bring out bones of the   Jer 8:1
k. of Judah
stand in gate, whereby k. of   Jer 17:19
Judah come in
hear the word of the Lord,   Jer 17:20;
ye k. of Judah   19:3
burnt incense to gods k. of   Jer 19:4
Judah have not known
the houses of the k. of Judah   Jer 19:13
shall be defiled
treasures of k. of Judah will I   Jer 20:5
give to enemies
concerning houses of k. of   Jer 33:4
Judah thrown down
have ye forgotten wickedness   Jer 44:9
of k. of Judah
the word of the Lord that came   Ho 1:1;
in the days of k. of Judah   Mic 1:1

KING'S

k. dale   Ge 14:17; 2Sa 18:18
k. prisoners   Ge 39:20

k. highway _Nu 20:17; 21:22_
k. son in law _1Sa 18:22;_
_18:23, 26-27; 22:14_
k. table _1Sa 20:29; 2Sa 9:13_
k. business _1Sa 21:8; Da 8:27_
k. hand _1Sa 23:20;_
_1Ki 13:6; 22:12; 2Ch 18:5; Ne 11:24_
k. spear _1Sa 26:16; 26:22_
k. sons _2Sa 9:11;_
_13:23, 27-36; 1Ki 1:9, 25; 2Ki 10:6-8;_
_11:2; 1Ch 27:32; 2Ch 22:11_
k. house _2Sa 11:2;_
_11:8-9; 15:35; 1Ki 9:1, 10; 10:12; 14:26-_
_27; 15:18; 16:18; 2Ki 7:11; 11:5-16, 19-_
_20; 12:18; 14:14; 15:25; 16:8; 18:15;_
_24:13; 25:9; 2Ch 7:11; 12:9-10; 16:2;_
_21:17; 23:5, 15, 20; 25:24; 26:21;_
Ezr 6:4; Es 2:8-9, 13; 4:13; 5:1; 6:4;
9:4; Jer 22:6; 26:10; 36:12; 38:7-8;
_39:8; 52:13_
k. wrath _2Sa 11:20; Es 7:10; Pr 19:12_
k. servants _2Sa 11:24;_
_15:15; 1Ki 1:9, 47; Es 2:2; 4:11; 6:2, 5_
k. crown _2Sa 12:30_
k. son _2Sa 13:4;_
_18:12, 20; 1Ki 22:26; 2Ki 11:4, 12; 15:5;_
_2Ch 18:25; 23:3, 11; 28:7; Ps 72:1_
k. daughters _2Sa 13:18;_
Ps 45:9; Jer 41:10; 43:6
k. heart _2Sa 14:1_
k. face _2Sa 14:24, 28, 32; Es 1:14_
k. weight _2Sa 14:26_
k. household _2Sa 16:2; 19:18; 2Ki 7:9_
k. servant _2Sa 18:29;_
_2Ki 22:12; 2Ch 34:20_
k. cost _2Sa 19:42_
k. word _2Sa 24:4; 1Ch 21:4, 6;_
_Da 3:28_
k. presence _1Ki 1:28; 2Ki 25:19_
k. mule _1Ki 1:44_
k. mother _1Ki 2:19_
k. friend _1Ki 4:5_
k. merchants _1Ki 10:28; 2Ch 1:16_
k. seed _1Ki 11:14; Eze 17:13; Da 1:3_
k. daughter _2Ki 9:34; Ps 45:13; Da 11:6_
k. scribe _2Ki 12:10;_
_2Ch 24:11; Es 3:12; 8:9_
k. hands _2Ki 13:16_
k. burnt sacrifice _2Ki 16:15_
k. entry _2Ki 16:18_
k. commandment _2Ki 18:36;_
_2Ch 24:8; 35:10; Ne 11:23; Es 1:12; 2:8;_
_3:3, 5; 4:3; 8:14, 17; 9:1; Pr 21:1; Ec 8:2;_
Isa 36:21; Da 3:22; Heb 11:23
k. wives _2Ki 24:15_
k. garden _2Ki 25:4;_
Ne 3:15; Jer 39:4; 52:7
k. gate _1Ch 9:18;_
_Es 2:19, 21; 3:2-3; 4:2, 6; 5:9, 13; 6:10,_
_12_
k. treasures _1Ch 27:25; Es 3:9; 4:7_
k. counsellor _1Ch 27:33; Da 3:27_
k. companion _1Ch 27:33_
k. army _1Ch 27:34_
k. work _1Ch 29:6_
k. palace _2Ch 9:11;_
Ezr 4:14; Es 1:5; Ps 45:15; Da 1:4; 5:5
k. ships _2Ch 9:21_
k. matters _2Ch 19:11; Da 2:10, 23_
k. office _2Ch 24:11_
k. counsel _2Ch 25:16_
k. captains; captain _2Ch 26:11; Da 2:15_
k. seer _2Ch 29:25; 35:15_
k. portion _2Ch 31:3_
k. substance _2Ch 35:7_
k. dishonour _Ezr 4:14_
k. treasure house _Ezr 5:17_
k. good _Ezr 6:8_
k. treasure _Ezr 7:20_
k. heart _Ezr 7:27; Pr 21:1_
k. mighty princes _Ezr 7:28; Es 1:18; 6:9_
k. commissions _Ezr 8:36_
k. lieutenants _Ezr 8:36; Es 3:12_
k. cupbearer _Ne 1:11_
k. forest _Ne 2:8_
k. letters _Ne 2:9_
k. pool _Ne 2:14_
k. words _Ne 2:18_
k. high house _Ne 3:25_
k. tribute _Ne 5:4_
k. manner toward all _Es 1:13_
k. decree _Es 1:20; Da 6:12_
k. provinces _Es 1:22;_
_3:13; 4:11; 8:5; 9:12, 16_
k. chamberlain _Es 2:3;_
_2:14-15, 21; 4:5; Ac 12:20_
k. laws _Es 3:8_
k. profit _Es 3:8_
k. ring _Es 3:12; 8:8, 10_
k. chamberlains _Es 6:2; 6:14_

k. damage _Es 7:4_
k. mouth _Es 7:8; Da 4:31_
k. name _Es 8:8_
k. enemies _Ps 45:5_
k. life _Ps 61:6_
k. strength _Ps 99:4_
k. honour _Pr 14:28_
k. favour _Pr 14:35_
k. countenance _Pr 16:15; Da 5:6_
k. person _Jer 52:25_
k. meat _Da 1:5; 1:8, 13_
k. guard _Da 2:14_
k. wise men _Da 5:8_
k. mowings _Am 7:1_
k. chapel _Am 7:13_
k. court _Am 7:13_
k. children _Zep 1:8_
k. winepresses _Zec 14:10_
k. country _Ac 12:20_

KINGS'

k. daughters were among thy _Ps 45:9_
her hands, and is in k. palaces _Pr 30:28_
both these k. hearts shall be _Da 11:27_
to do
wear soft clothing are in k. _M't 11:8_
houses
and live delicately, are in k. _Lu 7:25_
courts

KINGSHIP

exercise k. over Israel (B) _1Ki 21:7_

KINSFOLK

My k. have failed, and my _Job 19:14_
familiar
kinsfolk (E)(R) _Lu 1:58_
they sought him among their k. _Lu 2:44_

KINSFOLKS

neither of his k. nor of his _1Ki 16:11_
his great men, and his k. and _2Ki 10:11_
and brethren, and k. and _Lu 21:16_
friends

KINSMAN

the man have no k. to _Nu 5:8_
recompence
give his inheritance unto his _Nu 27:11_
k.
Naomi had a k. of her _Ru 2:1_
husband's
handmaid; for thou art a near _Ru 3:9_
k.
it is true that I am thy near k. _Ru 3:12_
howbeit there is a k. nearer _Ru 3:12_
than I.
perform unto thee the part of a _Ru 3:13_
k.
will not do the part of a k. to _Ru 3:13_
thee
will I do the part of a k. to _Ru 3:13_
thee
the k. of whom Boaz spake _Ru 4:1_
came
he said unto the k. Naomi, that _Ru 4:3_
is
the k. said, I cannot redeem it _Ru 4:6_
the k. said unto Boaz, Buy it for _Ru 4:8_
not left thee this day without a _Ru 4:14_
k.
k. of (R) _2Ki 10:13; 1Ch 12:2_
being his k. whose ear Peter _Joh 18:26_
cut
Salute Herodion my k. Greet _Ro 16:11_
them

KINSMAN'S

let him do the k. part: but if _Ru 3:13_

KINSMEN

we are k. (B)(R) _Ge 13:8_
k. of tribal family (A) _J'g 16:31_
of kin unto us, one of our next _Ru 2:20_
k.
neither of his k. (S) _1Ki 16:11_
sore; and my k. stand afar off _Ps 38:11_
neither thy k. nor thy rich _Lu 14:12_
together his k. and near _Ac 10:24_
friends
my k. according to the flesh _Ro 9:3_
Andronicus and Junia, my k. _Ro 16:7_
and Jason, and Sosipater, my _Ro 16:21_
k.

KINSWOMAN

sister: she is my father's near _Le 18:12_
k.
for she is thy mother's near k. _Le 18:13_
and call understanding thy k. _Pr 7:4_
thy k. (E)(N)(R) _Lu 1:36_

KINSWOMEN

for they are her near k.: it is _Le 18:17_

KIR

the people of it captive to K. _2Ki 16:9_
K. of Moab is laid waste _Isa 15:1_
and K. uncovered the shield _Isa 22:6_
shall go into captivity unto K. _Am 1:5_
Caphtor, and the Syrians from _Am 9:7_
K.

KIR-HARASETH

in K. left they the stones _2Ki 3:25_
thereof

KIR-HARESETH

foundations of K. shall ye _Isa 16:7_
mourn

KIR-HARESH

and mine inward parts for K. _Isa 16:11_

KIR-HERES

shall mourn for the men of K. _Jer 48:31_
sound like pipes for the men _Jer 48:36_
of K.

KIRIATHAIN

and the Emims in Shaveh K. _Ge 14:5_
K. is confounded and taken _Jer 48:1_
upon K. and upon _Jer 48:23_
Beth-gamul
Baal-meon, and K. _Eze 25:9_

KIRIOTH

it shall devour the palaces of K. _Am 2:2_

KIRJATH

Jerusalem, Gibeath, and K. _Jos 18:28_

KIRJATHAIM

Heshbon, and Elealeh, and K. _Nu 32:37_
And K., and Sibmah, and _Jos 13:19_
suburbs, and K. with her _1Ch 6:76_
suburbs

KIRJATH-ARBA

And Sarah died in K.; the _Ge 23:2_
same
the name of Hebron before _Jos 14:15_
was K.
and K., which is Hebron, and _Jos 15:54_
Zior
and K., which is Hebron, in _Jos 20:7_
name of Hebron before was K. _J'g 1:10_
the children of Judah dwelt at _Ne 11:25_
K.

KIRJATH-ARIM

The children of K., Chephirah _Ezr 2:25_

KIRJATH-BAAL

K., which is Kirjath-jearim _Jos 15:60_
the goings out thereof were at _Jos 18:14_
K.

KIRJATH-HUZOTH

Balak, and then came unto K. _Nu 22:39_

KIRJATH-JEARIM

Chephirah, and Beeroth, and _Jos 9:17_
K.
was drawn to Baalah, which is _Jos 15:9_
K.
Kirjath-baal, which is K., and _Jos 15:60_
K., a city of the children of _Jos 18:14_
Judah

quarter was from the end of   *Jos 18:15*
K.
they went up, and pitched in   *J'g 18:12*
K.
this day; behold, it is behind   *J'g 18:12*
K.
sent, to the inhabitants of   *1Sa 6:21*
K.
the men of K. came, and   *1Sa 7:1*
fetched
to pass, while the ark abode in   *1Sa 7:2*
K.
Ephratah; Shobal the father   *1Ch 2:50*
of K.
Shobal the father of K. had   *1Ch 2:52*
sons
the families of K.; the Ithrites   *1Ch 2:53*
to bring the ark of God from   *1Ch 13:5*
K.
all Israel, to Baalah, that is,   *1Ch 13:6*
to K.
had David brought up from   *2Ch 1:4*
The men of K., Chephirah, and   *Ne 7:29*
Urijah the son of Shemaiah   *Jer 26:20*
of K.

KIRJATH-SANNAH

Dannah, and K., which is   *Jos 15:49*
Debir

KIRJATH-SEPHER

the name of Debir before was   *Jos 15:15;*
K.   *J'g 1:11*
He that smiteth K., and   *Jos 15:16;*
taketh it   *J'g 1:12*

KISH

of Benjamin, whose name was   *1Sa 9:1*
K.
asses of K. Saul's father were   *1Sa 9:3*
lost
K. said to Saul his son, Take   *1Sa 9:3*
now
that is come unto the son of   *1Sa 10:11*
K.
and Saul the son of K. was   *1Sa 10:21*
taken
K. was the father of Saul;   *1Sa 14:51*
and Ner
in the sepulchre of K. his   *2Sa 21:14*
father
son Abdon, and Zur, and K.   *1Ch 8:30;*
                       9:36
Ner begat K., and K. begat   *1Ch 8:33;*
Saul   *9:39*
because of Saul the son of K.   *1Ch 12:1*
the sons of Mahli; Eleazar,   *1Ch 23:21*
and K.
brethren the sons of K. took   *1Ch 23:22*
them
Concerning K.; the son of K.   *1Ch 24:29*
Saul the son of K., and   *1Ch 26:28*
Abner
sons of Merari, K. the son of   *2Ch 29:12*
Abdi
Shimei, the son of K., a   *Es 2:5*
Benjamite

KISHI

Ethan the son of K., the son   *1Ch 6:44*

KISHION

And Rabbith, and K., and   *Jos 19:20*
Abez

KISHON

of Issachar, K. with her   *Jos 21:28*
suburbs
draw unto thee to the river K.   *J'g 4:7*
of the Gentiles unto the river   *J'g 4:13*
of K.
The river of K. swept them   *J'g 5:21*
away
that ancient river, the river   *J'g 5:21*
K.
brought them down to the   *1Ki 18:40*
brook K.

KISON

as to Jabin, at the brook of K.   *Ps 83:9*

KISS

near now, and k. me, my son   *Ge 27:26*
to k. my sons and my   *Ge 31:28*
daughters
beard with the right hand to   *2Sa 20:9*
k. him
thee, k. my father and my   *1Ki 19:20*
mother
K. the Son, lest he be angry   *Ps 2:12*
shall k. his lips that giveth a   *Pr 24:26*
right
Let him k. me with the kisses of   *Ca 1:2*
his
find thee without, I would k.   *Ca 8:1*
thee
the men that sacrifice k. the   *Ho 13:2*
calves
Whomsoever I shall k. that   *M't 26:48;*
same   *M'k 14:44*
Thou gavest me no k.: but this   *Lu 7:45*
in hath not ceased to k. my feet   *Lu 7:45*
drew near unto Jesus to k.   *Lu 22:47*
him
thou the Son of man with a k.   *Lu 22:48*
Salute one another with an   *Ro 16:16*
holy k.
ye one another with an holy   *1Co 16:20*
k.
Greet one another with an   *2Co 13:12*
holy k.
all the brethren with an holy   *1Th 5:26*
k.
ye one another with a k. of   *1Pe 5:14*
charity

KISSED

And he came near, and k. him   *Ge 27:27*
Jacob k. Rachel, and lifted up   *Ge 29:11*
his
him, and embraced him, and   *Ge 29:13*
k. him
and k. his sons and his   *Ge 31:55*
daughters
and fell on his neck, and k.   *Ge 33:4;*
him   *Lu 15:20*
Moreover he k. all his brethren   *Ge 45:15*
he k. them, and embraced   *Ge 48:10*
them
and wept upon him, and k. him   *Ge 50:1*
in the mount of God, and k.   *Ex 4:27*
him
law, and did obeisance, and k.   *Ex 18:7*
him
Then she k. them; and they   *Ru 1:9*
lifted up
and Orpah k. her mother in   *Ru 1:14*
law
poured it upon his head, and   *1Sa 10:1*
k. him
they k. one another, and   *1Sa 20:41*
wept one
the king: and the king k.   *2Sa 14:33*
Absalom
his hand, and took him, and   *2Sa 15:5*
k. him
the king k. Barzillai, and   *2Sa 19:39*
blessed
every mouth which hath not   *1Ki 19:18*
or my mouth hath k. my   *Job 31:27*
hand
righteousness and peace have   *Ps 85:10*
k.
So she caught him, and k. him   *Pr 7:13*
said, Hail, master; and k.   *M't 26:49*
him
saith, Master, master; and k.   *M'k 14:45*
him
and k. his feet, and anointed   *Lu 7:38*
them
and fell on Paul's neck, and k.   *Ac 20:37*
him

KISSES

the k. of an enemy are deceitful   *Pr 27:6*
kiss me with the k. of his mouth   *Ca 1:2*

KITE

vulture, and the k. after his   *Le 11:14*
kind
the k. and the vulture after   *De 14:13*
his kind

KITES

the k. (A)(E)(R)(S)   *Isa 34:15*

KITHLISH

Cabbon, and Lahmam, and   *Jos 15:40*
K.

KITRON

drive out the inhabitants of K.   *J'g 1:30*

KITS

the k. of the young men (B)   *1Sa 21:5*

KITTIM

and Tarshish, K., and   *Ge 10:4;*
Dodanim   *1Ch 1:7*

KNAPSACK

no k. (P)   *M't 10:10*

KNEAD

of fine meal, k. it, and make   *Ge 18:6*
cakes
and the women k. their dough   *Jer 7:18*

KNEADED

took flour, and k. it, and did   *1Sa 28:24*
bake
she took flour, and k. it and   *2Sa 13:8*
made
raising after he hath k. the   *Ho 7:4*
dough

KNEADING

thy k. trough   *De 28:5*
(A)(B)(E)(R)(S)

KNEADINGTROUGHS

into thine ovens, and into thy k.   *Ex 8:3*
k. being bound up in their   *Ex 12:34*
clothes

KNEE

they cried before him, Bow   *Ge 41:43*
the k.
That unto me every k. shall   *Isa 45:23*
bow
they bowed the k. before   *M't 27:29*
him, and
have not bowed the k. to the   *Ro 11:4*
image
the Lord, every k. shall bow   *Ro 14:11*
to me
name of Jesus every k.   *Ph'p 2:10*
should bow

KNEEL

he made his camels to k.   *Ge 24:11*
down
let us k. before the Lord our   *Ps 95:6*
maker

KNEELED

k. down upon his knees   *2Ch 6:13*
before
he k. upon his knees three   *Da 6:10*
times
came one running, and k. to   *M'k 10:17*
him
cast, and k. down, and prayed   *Lu 22:41*
he k. down, and cried with a   *Ac 7:60*
forth, and k. down, and prayed   *Ac 9:40*
he k. down, and prayed with   *Ac 20:36*
we k. down on the shore, and   *Ac 21:5*

KNEELING

from k. on his knees with his   *1Ki 8:54*
a certain man, k. down to   *M't 17:14*
him
beseeching him, and k. down   *M'k 1:40*
to him

KNEES

she shall bear upon my k. that   *Ge 30:3*
them out from between his k.   *Ge 48:12*
were brought up upon   *Ge 50:23*
Joseph's k.
The Lord shall smite thee in   *De 28:35*
the k.

boweth down upon his *k.* to drink   *J'g 7:5*

down upon their *k.* to drink water   *J'g 7:6*

made him sleep upon her *k.*   *J'g 16:19*

fell upon *k.*, did homage (B)   *1Ki 1:16*

kneeling on his *k.* with his hands   *1Ki 8:54*

and put his face between his *k.*   *1Ki 18:42*

k. which have not bowed unto Baal   *1Ki 19:18*

and fell on his *k.* before Elijah   *2Ki 1:13*

he sat on her *k.* till noon, and then   *2Ki 4:20*

kneeled down upon his *k.* before all   *2Ch 6:13*

I fell upon my *k.*, and spread out   *Ezr 9:5*

Why did the *k.* prevent me? or why   *Job 3:12*

hast strengthened the feeble *k.*   *Job 4:4*

My *k.* are weak through fasting   *Ps 109:24*

hands, and confirm the feeble *k.*   *Isa 35:3*

sides, and be dandled upon her *k.*   *Isa 66:12*

and all *k.* shall be weak as water   *Eze 7:17; 21:7*

waters; the waters were to the *k.*   *Eze 47:4*

and his *k.* smote one against   *Da 5:6*

kneeled upon his *k.*, three times a   *Da 6:10*

which set me upon my *k.* and   *Da 10:10*

and the *k.* smite together, and   *Na 2:10*

bowing their *k.* worshipped him   *M'k 15:19*

he fell down at Jesus' *k.*, saying   *Lu 5:8*

I bow my *k.* unto the Father of our   *Eph 3:14*

hang down, and the feeble *k.*   *Heb 12:12*

KNELT

man *k.* to him (B)   *Es 3:2; 3:5*

KNEW

Adam and Eve *k.* that they were naked   *Ge 3:7*

Adam *k.* Eve his wife   *Ge 4:1; 4:17, 25; 38:26*

Noah *k.* what his younger son Ge 9:24 had done

Jacob *k.* it, and said, It is my son's coat   *Ge 37:33*

Onan *k.* the seed should not be his   *Ge 38:9*

Joseph saw and *k.* his brethren   *Ge 42:7; 42:8*

knew (S)   *Ex 16:15; 34:29; Le 5:17-18; Jos 2:4; 8:14; J'g 16:20; M'k 9:6; 14:40; Lu 2:49; Joh 5:13; Ac 12:9; 23:5*

and *k.* the knowledge of the most High   *Nu 24:16*

been rebellious from the day I *k.* you   *De 9:24*

a prophet whom the Lord *k.* face to face   *De 34:10*

such as before *k.* nothing thereof   *J'g 3:2*

Jephthah's daughter *k.* no man   *J'g 11:39*

Manoah *k.* that he was an angel of God   *J'g 13:21*

they *k.* the voice of the young man   *J'g 18:3*

they *k.* her and abused her all night   *J'g 19:25*

Elkanah *k.* Hannah his wife   *1Sa 1:19*

all Israel *k.* Samuel was a prophet   *1Sa 3:20*

Saul *k.* that the Lord was with David   *1Sa 18:28*

for if I *k.* then would I not tell thee   *1Sa 20:9*

Jonathan *k.* that it was determined by Saul   *1Sa 20:33*

only David and Jonathan *k.* the matter   *1Sa 20:39*

for the servant *k.* nothing of all this   *1Sa 22:15*

slay the priests, because they *k.* when he fled   *1Sa 22:17*

David said to Abiathar, I *k.* it that day   *1Sa 22:22*

David *k.* that Saul secretly practised against   *1Sa 23:9*

Saul *k.* David's voice, and said, Is this thy   *1Sa 26:17*

where he *k.* that valiant men were   *2Sa 11:16*

the king *k.* her not   *1Ki 1:4*

Obadiah *k.* Elijah, and fell on his face   *1Ki 18:7*

then Manasseh *k.* the Lord was God   *2Ch 33:13*

manner to all that *k.* law and judgment   *Es 1:13*

O that I *k.* where I might find him   *Job 23:3*

because I *k.* that thou art obstinate   *Isa 48:4*

lest thou shouldest say, Behold I *k.* them   *Isa 48:7*

I *k.* that thou wouldest deal very treacherously   *Isa 48:8*

before I formed thee, I *k.* thee   *Jer 1:5*

then I *k.* this was the word of the Lord   *Jer 32:8*

he had slain Gedaliah, and no man *k.* it   *Jer 41:4*

men which their wives had *k.* burnt incense   *Jer 44:15*

I *k.* that they were the cherubims   *Eze 10:20*

and he *k.* their desolate palaces, laid waste   *Eze 19:7*

till he *k.* that the most High ruled   *Da 5:21*

when Daniel *k.* the writing was signed   *Da 6:10*

I *k.* that thou art a gracious God   *Jon 4:2*

k. that it was the word of the Lord   *Zec 11:11*

Joseph *k.* her not, till she   *M't 1:25*

I will profess I never *k.* you   *M't 7:23*

when Jesus *k.* he withdrew himself   *M't 12:15*

Jesus *k.* their thoughts   *M't 12:25; Lu 6:8*

I *k.* thee, that thou art an hard man   *M't 25:24*

he *k.* that for envy they had delivered   *M't 27:18*

not to speak because they *k.* him   *M'k 1:34*

out of the ship, straightway they *k.* him   *M'k 6:54*

k. he had spoken parable against them   *M'k 12:12*

devils, for they *k.* that he was Christ   *Lu 4:41*

that servant which *k.* his lord's will   *Lu 12:47*

nor *k.* they the things that were spoken   *Lu 18:34*

their eyes were opened, and they *k.* him   *Lu 24:31*

but the servants *k.* whence it was   *Joh 2:9*

not commit himself, because he *k.* all men   *Joh 2:24*

any testify, for he *k.* what was in man   *Joh 2:25*

the father *k.* it was at the same hour   *Joh 4:53*

Jesus *k.* he had been long in that case   *Joh 5:6*

for he himself *k.* what he would do   *Joh 6:6*

Jesus *k.* that his disciples murmured   *Joh 6:61*

Jesus *k.* from the beginning who believed not   *Joh 6:64*

I *k.* that thou hearest me always   *Joh 11:42*

that if any man *k.* where he were, to shew it   *Joh 11:57*

when Jesus *k.* that his hour was come   *Joh 13:1*

for he *k.* who should betray him   *Joh 13:11*

no man at the table *k.* for what intent   *Joh 13:28*

Jesus *k.* that they were desirous to ask   *Joh 16:19*

Judas which betrayed him *k.* the place   *Joh 18:2*

k. that it was he that sat for alms   *Ac 3:10*

which when the brethren *k.* they brought   *Ac 9:30*

when Rhoda *k.* Peter's voice she opened   *Ac 12:14*

they *k.* all that his father was a Greek   *Ac 16:3*

but when they *k.* that he was a Jew   *Ac 19:34*

afraid after he *k.* that he was a Roman   *Ac 22:29*

which *k.* me from the beginning a Pharisee   *Ac 26:5*

then they *k.* the island was called Melita   *Ac 28:1*

because that when they *k.* God   *Ro 1:21*

which none of the princes of this world *k.*   *1Co 2:8*

he made him to be sin, who *k.* no sin   *2Co 5:21*

I *k.* a man in Christ above fourteen years ago   *2Co 12:2; 12:3*

in you since ye *k.* the grace of God in truth   *Col 1:6*

I would you *k.* what great conflict I have   *Col 2:1*

put in remembrance, tho' ye once *k.* this   *Jude 5*

he had a name written that no man *k.*   *Re 19:12*

KNEW *NOT*

Lord is in this place, and I *k.* it *not*   *Ge 28:16*

Jacob *k. not* that Rachel had stolen them   *Ge 31:32*

Judah *k. not* she was his daughter in law   *Ge 38:16*

he *k. not* aught he had   *Ge 39:6*

but they *k. not* him   *Ge 42:8*

there arose a new king which *k. not* Joseph   *Ex 1:8*

I *k. not* that thou stoodest in the way   *Nu 22:34*

with manna which thy fathers *k. not*   *De 8:16*

served gods which thy fathers *k. not*   *De 29:26; 32:17*

a generation which *k. not* the Lord   *J'g 2:10*

Manoah *k. not* that he was an angel   *J'g 13:16*

his father *k. not* that it was of the Lord   *J'g 14:4*

Benjamin *k. not* that evil was near   *J'g 20:34*

now the sons of Eli *k. not* the Lord   *1Sa 2:12*

the people *k. not* that Jonathan was gone   *1Sa 14:3*

the lad *k. not* any thing, only Jonathan   *1Sa 20:39*

sent after Abner, but David *k. not* it *not*   *2Sa 3:26*

k. ye *not* they would shoot from the wall   *2Sa 11:20*

they went in simplicity, and *k. not* any thing   *2Sa 15:11*

I saw a tumult, but I *k. not* what it was   *2Sa 18:29*

a people which I *k. not* shall serve me   *2Sa 22:44*

gathered gourds for they *k.* them *not*   *2Ki 4:39*

the rulers *k. not* whither I went   *Ne 2:16*

Job's friends *k.* him *not*, and wept   *Job 2:12*

the cause which I *k. not* I searched out   *Job 29:16*

things which I *k. not* too wonderful for me   *Job 42:3*

they laid to my charge things I *k. not*   *Ps 35:11*

abjects gathered against me, and I *k.* it *not*   *Ps 35:15*

if thou sayest, Behold, we *k.* it *not*   *Pr 24:12*

I will bring the blind by a way they *k. not*   *Isa 42:16*

it hath set him on fire, yet he *k. not*   *Isa 42:25*

and nations that *k. not* thee, shall run to thee   *Isa 55:5*

and they that handle the law *k. not* me   *Jer 2:8*

I *k. not* that they had devised devices   *Jer 11:19*

went to serve other gods whom they *k. not*   *Jer 44:3*

honour a god whom his fathers *k. not*   *Da 11:38*

they have made princes and I *k.* it *not*   *Ho 8:4*

but they *k. not* that I healed them   *Ho 11:3*

among nations whom they *k. not*   *Zec 7:14*

Elias is come, and they *k. him not*   *M't 17:12*

k. not till the flood came and took them   *M't 24:39*

Joseph and his mother *k. not* of it   *Lu 2:43*

that *k. not* and did commit things worthy   *Lu 12:48*

the world *k. him not; I k. him not*   *Joh 1:10; 1:31, 33*

when the governor *k. not* whence it was   *Joh 2:9*

for as yet they *k. not* the scriptures that he   *Joh 20:9*

and *k. not* that it was Jesus   *Joh 20:14; 21:4*

for they, because they *k. him not*   *Ac 13:27*

the more part *k. not* wherefore they came   *Ac 19:32*

when it was day, they *k. not* the land   *Ac 27:39*

the world by wisdom *k. not* God, it pleased   *1Co 1:21*

howbeit, then when ye *k. not* God, ye did   *Ga 4:8*

world knoweth us not, because *k. him not*   *1Jo 3:1*

KNEWEST

he fed thee with manna, which *thou k. not*   *De 8:3*

art come to a people which *thou k. not*   *Ru 2:11*

thou *k.* that they dealt proudly against   *Ne 9:10*

then thou *k.* my path in the way   *Ps 142:3*

thou heardest not, yea, thou *k. not*   *Isa 48:8*

not humbled thy heart, thou *k.* all this   *Da 5:22*

thou *k.* I reaped where   *M't 25:26; Lu 19:22*

thou *k.* not the time of thy visitation   *Lu 19:44*

if thou *k.* the gift of God, and who it is   *Joh 4:10*

KNIFE

Abraham took the *k.* in his hand   *Ge 22:6; 22:10*

took a flint *k.* (A)(B)   *Ex 4:29*

took a *k.* and laid hold on his concubine   *J'g 19:29*

and put a *k.* to thy throat, if given to   *Pr 23:2*

son of man, take thee a sharp *k.*   *Eze 5:1*

take a third part, and smite about it with a *k.*   *Eze 5:2*

KNIT

Israel were *k.* together as one man   *J'g 20:11*

were united as one man (A)(B)(R)   *J'g 20:11*

the soul of Jonathan was *k.* to David   *1Sa 18:1*

soul was in unison with David (B)   *1Sa 18:1*

if come, my heart shall be *k.* to you   *1Ch 12:17*

my heart being united with yours (B)   *1Ch 12:17*

his thighs are *k.* (S)   *Job 40:17*

k. together (S)   *La 1:14*

I saw a sheet *k.* at the four corners   *Ac 10:11*

firmly *k.* together (A)(E)(N)(P)(R)   *Eph 4:16*

their hearts being *k.* together in love   *Col 2:2*

welded together in love (B)   *Col 2:2*

in the unity of love (N)   *Col 2:2*

body *k.* together increaseth with increase of God   *Col 2:19*

held together by ligaments and sinews (B)   *Col 2:19*

KNIVES

make thee sharp *k.* and circumcise   *Jos 5:2*

---

make *k.* of flint (A)(B)(E)(R)   *Jos 5:2*

Joshua made them sharp *k.* and circumcised   *Jos 5:3*

they cut themselves with *k.* and lancets   *1Ki 18:28*

nine and twenty *k.* Cyrus brought   *Ezr 1:9*

their jaw teeth as *k.* to devour the poor   *Pr 30:14*

KNOB

his *k.* and flower (S)   *Ex 25:33*

their *k.* and their branches (S)   *Ex 25:35; 25:36; 37:21*

KNOBS

his *k.* and flowers (S)   *Ex 25:21; 25:34; 37:17, 20; 37:22*

house within carved with *k.* (S)   *1Ki 6:18*

there were *k.* compassing it (S)   *1Ki 7:24*

KNOCK

k., and it shall be opened unto   *M't 7:7; Lu 11:9*

stand without, and to *k.* at the door   *Lu 13:25*

Behold, I stand at the door, and *k.*   *Re 3:20*

KNOCKED

And as Peter *k.* at the door of   *Ac 12:13*

KNOCKETH

is the voice of my beloved that *k.*   *Ca 5:2*

to him that *k.* it shall be opened   *M't 7:8; Lu 11:10*

that when he cometh and *k.* they   *Lu 12:36*

KNOCKING

made great game of *k.* him about (P)   *Lu 22:63*

But Peter continued *k.:* and when   *Ac 12:16*

KNOP

a *k.* and a flower in one branch   *Ex 25:33*

a branch, with a *k.* and a flower   *Ex 25:33*

k. under two branches of in one branch, a *k.* and a flower   *Ex 25:35*

in another branch, a *k.* and a flower   *Ex 37:19*

k. under two branches of the   *Ex 37:21*

KNOPS

his *k.,* and his flowers, shall be   *Ex 25:31*

with their *k.* and their flowers   *Ex 25:34*

k. and their branches shall be   *Ex 25:36*

his *k.,* and his flowers, were of   *Ex 37:17*

almonds, his *k.,* and his flowers   *Ex 37:20*

k. and their branches were of   *Ex 37:22*

carved with *k.* and open flowers   *1Ki 6:18*

about there were *k.* compassing it   *1Ki 7:24*

the *k.* were cast in two rows   *1Ki 7:24*

KNOTS

solve riddles, unravel *k.* (B)   *Da 5:12*

KNOTTING

with *k.* of hair (A)   *1Pe 3:3*

KNOTTY

solve *k.* problems (A)   *Da 5:12*

KNOW

God doth *k.* your eyes shall be opened   *Ge 3:5*

man is become as one of us, to *k.* good and evil   *Ge 3:22*

---

said to Abram, *K.* thy seed shall be a stranger   *Ge 15:13*

I will go down and see, and if not, I will *k.*   *Ge 18:21*

if thou restore her not, *k.* thou shalt die   *Ge 20:7*

know (S)   *Ge 21:26; 44:15; Ex 32:1, 23; Nu 22:6; Jos 2:5; Ac 3:17; 7:40; Ro 11:2; Ph'p 1:22*

I make them *k.* the statutes of God   *Ex 18:16*

hast not let me *k.* whom thou wilt send   *Ex 33:12*

they shall *k.* the land ye have despised   *Nu 14:31*

k. this day and consider it   *De 4:39; 11:2*

to prove thee and *k.* what was in thy heart   *De 8:2*

nor did thy father *k.* he might make thee *k.*   *De 8:3*

proveth you, to *k.* whether ye love the Lord   *De 13:3*

then ye shall let your children *k.*   *Jos 4:22*

the Lord knoweth, and Israel he shall *k.*   *Jos 22:22*

we *k.* the Lord is (A)(B)(E)(R)   *Jos 22:31*

to *k.* whether they would hearken to   *J'g 3:4*

city of my people doth *k.* thou art   *Ru 3:11*

she rose up before one could *k.* another   *Ru 3:14*

sit still, my daughter, till thou *k.* how matter   *Ru 3:18*

k. your wickedness (A)(B)(E)(R)   *1Sa 12:17*

and all this assembly shall *k.* the Lord   *1Sa 17:47*

he saith, Let not Jonathan *k.* this, lest he grieved   *1Sa 20:3*

let no man *k.* any thing of the business   *1Sa 21:2*

k. and see that there is no evil in me   *1Sa 24:11*

therefore *k.* and consider what thou   *1Sa 25:11*

Achish said to David, *K.* assuredly that   *1Sa 28:1*

surely thou shalt *k.* what thy servant can do   *1Sa 28:2*

to *k.* thy going out, to *k.* all thou doest   *2Sa 3:25*

done these things to make thy servant *k.* them   *2Sa 7:21*

to *k.* all things that are in the earth   *2Sa 14:20*

thy servant doth *k.* that I have sinned   *2Sa 19:20*

k. every man the plague   *1Ki 8:38; 2Ch 6:29*

he shall *k.* that there is a prophet in Israel   *2Ki 5:8*

they *k.* that we be hungry, therefore   *2Ki 7:12*

k. now that there shall fall nothing of word   *2Ki 10:10*

Issachar, to *k.* what Israel ought to do   *1Ch 12:32*

my son, *k.* thou the God of thy father   *1Ch 28:9*

ought ye not to *k.* that the Lord gave   *2Ch 13:5*

k. that this city is a rebellious city   *Ezr 4:15*

all such as *k.* the laws of thy God and teach   *Ezr 7:25*

Mordecai walked to *k.* how Esther did   *Es 2:11*

to *k.* what it was, and why it was   *Es 4:5*

people *k.* whosoever shall come to the king   *Es 4:11*

thou shalt *k.* thy tabernacle in peace   *Job 5:24*

thou shalt *k.* that thy seed shall be great   *Job 5:25*

hear it, and *k.* thou it for thy good   *Job 5:27*

nor shall his place *k.* him any more   *Job 7:10*

we are but of yesterday, and *k.* nothing   *Job 8:9*

k. therefore that God exacteth less than thine   *Job 11:6*

it is deeper than hell, what canst thou *k.*   *Job 11:8*

make me to *k.* my transgression and sin   *Job 13:23*
k. now that God hath overthrown me   *Job 19:6*
God rewardeth him, and he shall *k.* it   *Job 21:19*
and thou sayest, How doth God *k.*   *Job 22:13*
do they that *k.* him not see his days   *Job 24:1*
if one *k.* them, they are in terrors of shadow   *Job 24:17*
let us *k.* among ourselves what is good   *Job 34:4*
dost thou *k.* when God disposed them   *Job 37:15*
dost thou *k.* the balancings of the clouds   *Job 37:16*
and caused the dayspring to *k.* his place   *Job 38:12*
that thou shouldest *k.* the paths to the house   *Job 38:20*
but *k.* the Lord hath set apart the godly   *Ps 4:3*
they that *k.* thy name put their trust in thee   *Ps 9:10*
continue thy lovingkindness to them *k.* thee   *Ps 36:10*
Lord, make me to *k.* mine end, and measure   *Ps 39:4*
be still, and *k.* that I am God   *Ps 46:10*
in hidden part thou shalt make me to *k.*   *Ps 51:6*
and let them *k.* that God ruleth in Jacob   *Ps 59:13*
how doth God *k.*   *Ps 73:11*
I thought to *k.* this   *Ps 73:16*
I will mention Babylon to them that *k.* me   *Ps 87:4*
blessed are they that *k.* the joyful sound   *Ps 89:15*
the place thereof shall *k.* it no more   *Ps 103:16*
k. my heart, try me, and *k.* my thoughts   *Ps 139:23*
there was no man that would *k.* me   *Ps 142:4*
cause me *k.* the way wherein I should walk   *Ps 143:8*
to *k.* wisdom and instruction, to perceive   *Pr 1:2*
hear, and attend to *k.* understanding   *Pr 4:1*
the lips of righteous *k.* what is acceptable   *Pr 10:32*
be thou diligent to *k.* the state of thy flocks   *Pr 27:23*
and I gave my heart to *k.* wisdom   *Ec 1:17*
I applied my heart to *k.*   *Ec 7:25*
wisdom and folly
when I applied my heart to *k.*   *Ec 8:16*
wisdom and see
tho' a wise man think to *k.* it yet not able   *Ec 8:17*
the living *k.* they shall die, but the dead   *Ec 9:5*
but *k.* that God will bring thee to judgment   *Ec 11:9*
for before the child shall *k.* to refuse evil   *Isa 7:16*
and all the people shall *k.* even Ephraim   *Isa 9:9*
the Egyptians shall *k.* the Lord in that day   *Isa 19:21*
that they may see and *k.* and consider   *Isa 41:20*
that we may *k.* the latter end of them   *Isa 41:22*
all flesh shall *k.* that I am thy Saviour   *Isa 49:26*
should *k.* how to speak in season to weary   *Isa 50:4*
therefore my people shall *k.* my name   *Isa 52:6*
they seek me, and delight to *k.* my ways   *Isa 58:2*
thou shalt *k.* that I the Lord am thy Saviour   *Isa 60:16*
k. and see that it is an evil thing to forsake   *Jer 2:19*
see thy way in valley, *k.* what thou hast done   *Jer 2:23*
k. O congregation, what is among them   *Jer 6:18*
thro' deceit they refuse to *k.* me, saith Lord   *Jer 9:6*
k. that for thy sake I have suffered rebuke   *Jer 15:15*

I will cause them to *k.*, they shall *k.* that my name is Lord   *Jer 16:21*
the heart is deceitful, who can *k.* it   *Jer 17:9*
was not this to *k.* me? saith the Lord   *Jer 22:16*
I will give them an heart to *k.* me   *Jer 24:7*
k. the Lord for they shall all *k.* me   *Jer 31:34; Heb 8:11*
go, hide thee, let no man *k.* where ye be   *Jer 36:19*
he said, Let no man *k.* of these words   *Jer 38:24*
slay Ishmael and no man shall *k.* it   *Jer 40:15*
Judah shall *k.* whose words shall stand   *Jer 44:28*
k. that there hath been a prophet   *Eze 2:5; 33:33*
shall *k.* I the Lord hath spoken in my zeal   *Eze 5:13*
Jerusalem to *k.* her abomination   *Eze 16:2; 20:4*
and they shall *k.* my vengeance, saith Lord   *Eze 25:14*
all that *k.* thee shall be astonished at thee   *Eze 28:19*
thus shall they *k.* that I am with them   *Eze 34:30*
and the heathen shall *k.*   *Eze 37:28; 39:23*
givest knowledge to them who *k.* understanding   *Da 2:21*
till thou *k.* that the most High ruleth   *Da 4:25; 4:32*
and made me *k.* the interpretation   *Da 7:16*
I would *k.* the truth of the fourth beast   *Da 7:19*
I will make thee *k.* what shall be   *Da 8:19*
k. therefore and understand, that from   *Da 9:25*
people that *k.* their God shall be strong   *Da 11:32*
thou shalt *k.* the Lord; shall *k.* it   *Ho 2:20; 9:7*
and thou shalt *k.* no God but me   *Ho 13:4*
who is prudent, and he shall *k.* them   *Ho 14:9*
is it not for you to *k.* judgment   *Mic 3:1*
thou shalt *k.* that the Lord sent me   *Zec 2:11; 4:9*
and ye shall *k.* that I have sent this   *Mal 2:4*
let not thy left hand *k.* what thy right doeth   *M't 6:3*
if ye *k.* how to give good gifts   *M't 7:11; Lu 11:13*
see no man *k.* it   *M't 9:30; M'k 5:43; 7:24; 9:30*
it is given to you to *k.*   *M't 13:11; M'k 4:11; Lu 8:10*
k. desolation is near   *M't 24:33; M'k 13:29; Lu 21:20*
but *k.* this, if the goodman   *M't 24:43; Lu 12:39*
we *k.* that this is indeed the Christ   *Joh 4:42*
if any do his will, he shall *k.* of the doctrine   *Joh 7:17*
do the rulers *k.* indeed; *k.* what he doeth   *Joh 7:26; 7:51*
the sheep follow him, for they *k.* his voice   *Joh 10:4*
I *k.* my sheep; thou shalt *k.* hereafter   *Joh 10:14; 13:7*
by this shall all men *k.* ye are my disciples   *Joh 13:35*
ask them, behold, they *k.* what I said   *Joh 18:21*
it is not for you to *k.* the times or seasons   *Ac 1:7*
let all the house of Israel *k.* assuredly that God   *Ac 2:36*
shouldest *k.* his will and see that Just One   *Ac 22:14*
they *k.* I imprisoned them that believed on thee   *Ac 22:19*
my manner of life from my youth *k.* all Jews   *Ac 26:4*
I speak to them that *k.* the law   *Ro 7:1*
but I say, Did not Israel *k.* first Moses   *Ro 10:19*
neither can he *k.* them, because they are   *1Co 2:14*

he knoweth nothing as he ought to *k.*   *1Co 8:2*
but I would have you *k.* that the head is Christ   *1Co 11:3*
and to *k.* the love of Christ, which passeth   *Eph 3:19*
for this cause I sent to *k.* your faith   *1Th 3:5*
every one should *k.* how to possess his vessel in   *1Th 4:4*
to *k.* them who labour among you, and are   *1Th 5:12*
of them which believe and *k.* the truth   *1Ti 4:3*
this *k.* also that in the last days perilous   *2Ti 3:1*
they profess that they *k.* God, but in works   *Tit 1:16*
but wilt thou *k.* O vain man   *Jas 2:20*
let him *k.* he which converteth a sinner   *Jas 5:20*
but what they *k.* naturally, as brute beasts   *Jude 10*
all the churches shall *k.* that I am he who   *Re 2:23*
I will make them to *k.* that I have loved thee   *Re 3:9*

KNOW *NOT*, *NOT* KNOW

Lord said, Where is Abel? he said, I *k. not*   *Ge 4:9*
I am old, I *k. not* the day of my death   *Ge 27:2*
I *k. not* the Lord, nor will I let Israel go   *Ex 5:2*
we *k. not* with what we must serve the Lord   *Ex 10:26*
or if thou *k.* him *not*, then bring it   *De 22:2*
now Samuel did *not* yet *k.* the Lord   *1Sa 3:7*
take my bread, give to men whom I *k. not*   *1Sa 25:11*
I *k. not* how to go out or come in   *1Ki 3:7*
the Spirit shall carry thee whither I *k. not*   *1Ki 18:12*
they *k. not* the manner of God of land   *2Ki 17:26*
and teach ye them that *k.* them *not*   *Ezr 7:25*
they shall *not k.* nor see, till we come   *Ne 4:11*
though perfect, yet would I *not k.* my soul   *Job 9:21*
what knowest thou that we *k. not*   *Job 15:9*
and do ye *not k.* their tokens   *Job 21:29*
they *k. not* the ways thereof, nor abide in   *Job 24:13*
they dig in the dark, they *k. not* the light   *Job 24:16*
for I *k. not* to give flattering titles   *Job 32:22*
God is great, and we *k.* him *not*   *Job 36:26*
for I *k. not* the numbers thereof   *Ps 71:15*
they *k. not*, neither will they understand   *Ps 82:5*
he that teacheth man, shall *not* he *k.*   *Ps 94:10*
I will *not k.* a wicked person   *Ps 101:4*
they *k. not* at what they stumble   *Pr 4:19*
ways are moveable, that thou canst *not k.* them   *Pr 5:6*
doth *not* he *k.* it, and shall *not* he render   *Pr 24:12*
lest thou *k. not* what to do in the end   *Pr 25:8*
but the wicked regardeth *not* to *k.* it   *Pr 29:7*
yea, there are four things which I *k. not*   *Pr 30:18*
but the dead *k. not* any thing   *Ec 9:5*
if thou *k. not*, fairest among women   *Ca 1:8*
but Israel doth *not k.* nor consider   *Isa 1:3*
shall ye *not k.* it; I *k. not* any   *Isa 43:19; 44:8*
thou shalt *not k.* from whence it ariseth   *Isa 47:11*
even hidden things, and thou didst *not k.*   *Isa 48:6*
way of peace they *k. not*, shall *not k.* peace   *Isa 59:8*

for they *k. not* the way of the   *Jer 5:4*
Lord
will ye walk after other gods,   *Jer 7:9*
whom ye *k. not*
but my people *k. not* the   ,   *Jer 8:7*
judgments of the Lord
and they *k. not* me, saith the   *Jer 9:3*
Lord
thy fury on the heathen that   *Jer 10:25*
k. thee not
go about into a land that   *Jer 14:18;*
they *k. not*   *22:28*
dwelleth safely, shalt thou   *Eze 38:14*
not *k.* it
she did *not k.* that I gave her   *Ho 2:8*
corn, wine
for they *k. not* to do right,   *Am 3:10*
saith the Lord
they *k. not* the thoughts of the   *Mic 4:12*
Lord
verily I say unto you, I *k.*   *M't 25:12*
you not
Peter said, I *k. not* what thou   *M't 26:70*
sayest
swear, saying, I *k. not* the   *M't 26:72;*
man   *26:74; M'k 14:68, 71*
Jesus said, Ye *k. not* what ye   *M'k 10:38*
ask
ye err, because ye *k. not* the   *M'k 12:24*
scriptures
how shall this be, seeing I *k.*   *Lu 1:34*
not a man
he shall say, I *k. not* whence   *Lu 13:25;*
you are   *13:27*
denied him, saying, Woman, I   *Lu 22:57*
k. him *not*
Peter said, Man, I *k. not* what   *Lu 22:60*
thou sayest
forgive them, they *k. not* what   *Lu 23:34*
they do
eyes holden, that they should   *Lu 24:16*
not k. him
standeth one among you   *Joh 1:26*
whom ye *k. not*
if I should say, I *k.* him *not,* I   *Joh 8:55*
should lie
the blind man said, I *k. not*   *Joh 9:12;*
                          9:25
or who hath opened his eyes,   *Joh 9:21*
we *k. not*
for this fellow, we *k. not* from   *Joh 9:29*
whence he is
for they *k. not* the voice of   *Joh 10:5*
strangers
Lord, we *k. not* whither thou   *Joh 14:5*
goest
because they *k. not* him that   *Joh 15:21*
sent me
we *k. not; k. not* where they   *Joh 20:2;*
have laid him   *20:13*
and when he could *not k.* the   *Ac 21:34*
certainty
for we *k. not* what we should   *Ro 8:26*
pray for
I *k. not* whether I baptized   *1Co 1:16*
any other
I determined *not* to *k.* any   *1Co 2:2*
thing among you
if I *k. not* the meaning of the   *1Co 14:11*
voice
as the Gentiles which *k. not*   *1Th 4:5*
God
vengeance on them that *k. not*   *2Th 1:8*
God
if a man *k. not* how to rule his   *1Ti 3:5*
house
these speak evil of things they   *Jude 10*
k. not.
thou shalt *not k.* what hour I   *Re 3:3*
will come

KNOW YE NOT, YE KNOW NOT

k. ye not that there is a prince   *2Sa 3:38*
fallen
k. ye not what I and my   *2Ch 32:13*
fathers have
have not asked, do *ye not k.*   *Job 21:29*
their tokens
k. ye not what these things   *Eze 17:12*
mean
Jesus said, Ye *k. not* what ye   *M't 20:22*
ask
ye k. not what hour your   *M't 24:42*
Lord doth come
he said to them, *K. ye not*   *M'k 4:13*
this parable
ye err, because *ye k. not* the   *M'k 12:24*
scriptures

watch, for *ye k. not* when   *M'k 13:33;*
the time is   *13:35*
ye k. not what manner of spirit   *Lu 9:55*
ye be of
standeth one among you,   *Joh 1:26*
whom ye *k. not*
ye worship *ye k. not* what;   *Joh 4:22*
meat ye *k. not*
he that sent me is true, whom   *Joh 7:28*
ye k. not
ye neither *k.* me nor my   *Joh 8:19*
Father
that *ye k. not* from whence he   *Joh 9:30*
is, and yet
k. ye not that so many as were   *Ro 6:3*
baptized
k. ye not that to whom ye yield   *Ro 6:16*
servants
k. ye not, brethren, for I speak   *Ro 7:1*
to them that
k. ye not ye are temple of   *1Co 3:16;*
God   *6:15, 19*
k. ye not that a little leaven   *1Co 5:6*
leaveneth the lump
do *ye not k.* the saints shall   *1Co 6:2*
judge the world
k. ye not that we shall judge   *1Co 6:3*
angels
k. ye not, the unrighteous shall   *1Co 6:9*
not inherit
k. ye not, that he which is   *1Co 6:16*
joined to an harlot
do *ye not k.* that they which   *1Co 9:13*
minister
k. ye not, that they which run   *1Co 9:24*
in a race, run all
k. ye not yourselves, that   *2Co 13:5*
Jesus is in you
k. ye not that the friendship of   *Jas 4:4*
the world
ye k. not what shall be on the   *Jas 4:14*
morrow
not written, because *ye k. not*   *1Jo 2:21*
the truth

KNOW THAT I AM THE LORD

ye shall *k. that I am the Lord*   *Ex 6:7;*
16:12; 1Ki 20:28; Eze 6:7, 13; 7:4, 9;
11:10, 12; 12:20; 13:9, 14, 21, 23; 14:8;
15:7; 20:38, 42, 44; 23:49; 24:24; 25:5;
35:9; 36:11; 37:6, 13; Joe 3:17
and the Egyptians shall *k. that*   *Ex 7:5;*
I am the Lord   *14:4, 18*
thou shalt *k. that I am the*   *Ex 7:17;*
Lord   1Ki 20:13; Isa 49:23; Eze 16:62;
22:16; 25:7; 35:4, 12
to end that thou mayest *k. that*   *Ex 8:22*
I am the Lord
that ye may *k. that I am the*   *Ex 10:2;*
Lord   31:13; Eze 20:20
they shall *k. that I am the*   *Ex 29:46;*
Lord   Eze 6:10,   14; 7:27;   12:15-16;
16, 21; 30:8, 19, 25-26; 32:15; 33:29;
34:27; 35:15; 36:38; 38:23; 39:6, 28
that ye might *k. that I am the*   *De 29:6*
Lord
I will give them an heart to *k.*   *Jer 24:7*
I am the Lord
my sabbaths that they might   *Eze 20:12;*
k. I am the Lord   *20:26*
and the heathen shall *k. I*   *Eze 36:23;*
am the Lord   *39:7*
the house of Israel shall *k.*   *Eze 39:22*
that I am the Lord

I KNOW

now *I k.* that thou art a fair   *Ge 12:11*
woman
whereby shall *I k.* that I shall   *Ge 15:8*
inherit it
I k. that he will command his   *Ge 18:19*
children
I k. thou didst this in integrity   *Ge 20:6*
of thy heart
for now *I k.* that thou fearest   *Ge 22:12*
God
thereby shall *I k.* that thou   *Ge 24:14*
hast shewed
his father said, *I k.* it, my   *Ge 48:19*
son, *I k.* it
the Lord said, *I k.* their sorrows   *Ex 3:7*
Aaron thy brother, *I k.* he can   *Ex 4:14*
speak well
I k. that ye will not yet fear the   *Ex 9:30*
Lord God

I k. the Lord is greater than   *Ex 18:11*
all gods
yet thou hast said, *I k.* thee   *Ex 33:12;*
by name   *33:17*
I k. their imagination even   *De 31:21*
now
for *I k.* thy rebellion and thy   *De 31:27*
stiff neck
I k. that after my death ye   *De 31:29*
will utterly corrupt
I k. the Lord hath given you the   *Jos 2:9*
land
then shall *I k.* that thou wilt   *J'g 6:37*
save
now *k. I* that the Lord will do   *J'g 17:13*
me good
I k. thy pride and the   *1Sa 17:28*
naughtiness of heart
do not *I k.* thou hast chosen   *1Sa 20:30*
son of Jesse
till *I k.* what God will do for   *1Sa 22:3*
me
I k. well that thou shalt   *1Sa 24:20*
surely be king
I k. that thou art good in my   *1Sa 29:9*
sight, as angel
yea *I k.* it, hold you your   *2Ki 2:3;*
peace   *2:5*
I k. that there is no God in   *2Ki 5:15*
earth, but in Israel
I k. the evil that thou wilt do   *2Ki 8:12*
to Israel
I k. thy abode and going out   *2Ki 19:27;*
                    Isa 37:28
I k. that thou triest the heart   *1Ch 29:17*
I k. that God hath   *2Ch 25:16*
determined
I k. it is so of a truth, but how   *Job 9:2*
should
I k. thou wilt not hold me   *Job 9:28*
innocent
things hast hid, *I k.* that this   *Job 10:13*
is with thee
what ye know, the same do *I*   *Job 13:2*
k. also
behold, *I k.* that I shall be   *Job 13:18*
justified
I k. that my Redeemer liveth   *Job 19:25*
and shall
I k. thoughts and devices ye   *Job 21:27*
imagine
for *I k.* that thou wilt bring   *Job 30:23*
me to death
I k. that thou canst do every   *Job 42:2*
thing
I k. that the Lord saveth his   *Ps 20:6*
anointed
by this *I k.* that thou favourest   *Ps 41:11*
me
I k. all the fowls of the   *Ps 50:11*
mountains
this *I k.* for God is for me   *Ps 56:9*
I k. that thy judgments are   *Ps 119:75*
right
I k. the Lord is great and   *Ps 135:5*
above all gods
I k. the Lord will maintain   *Ps 140:12*
the cause
I k. that there is no good in   *Ec 3:12*
them
I k. that whatsoever God   *Ec 3:14*
doeth, it shall be
I k. it shall be well with them   *Ec 8:12*
that fear God
nor shall *I k.* the loss of   *Isa 47:8*
children
and *I k.* that I shall not be   *Isa 50:7*
ashamed
I k. their works and their   *Isa 66:18*
thoughts
I k. the way of man is not in   *Jer 10:23*
himself
hath given me knowledge,   *Jer 11:18*
I k.
for *I k.* the thoughts that I   *Jer 29:11*
think
I k. and am a witness, saith   *Jer 29:23*
the Lord
I k. his wrath, saith the Lord,   *Jer 48:30*
it shall
I k. things that come into your   *Eze 11:5*
mind
tell me the dream, and *I* shall   *Da 2:9*
k.
I k. Ephraim, and Israel is not   *Ho 5:3*
hid
I did *k.* thee in the wilderness   *Ho 13:5*
I k. your manifold   *Am 5:12*
transgressions

I k. that for my sake this   *Jon 1:12*
tempest is
fear not ye, *I k.* that ye seek   *M't 28:5*
Jesus
I k. thee who thou art   *M'k 1:24;*
       Lu 4:34
whereby shall *I k.* this, for I   *Lu 1:18*
am old
I k. that Messias cometh,   *Joh 4:25*
called Christ
but I k. you; *I k.* whence I   *Joh 5:42;*
came   *8:14*
I k. that ye are Abraham's   *Joh 8:37*
seed
but *I k.* him; one thing *I k.*   *Joh 8:55*
       9:25
as Father knoweth me, so I   *Joh 10:15*
k. the Father
and *I k.* my sheep, and they   *Joh 10:27*
follow me
I k. that what thou wilt ask   *Joh 11:22*
of God
Martha said, *I k.* that he   *Joh 11:24*
shall rise again
I k. his commandment is life   *Joh 12:50*
everlasting
I speak not of all, *I k.* whom   *Joh 13:18*
I have chosen
now *I k.* of a surety that the   *Ac 12:11*
Lord sent
Jesus *I k.* and Paul *I k.* but   *Ac 19:15*
who are ye
I k. that ye shall see my face   *Ac 20:25*
no more
I k. this, that after my   *Ac 20:29*
departing, wolves
I will *k.* the uttermost of your   *Ac 24:22*
matter
because *I k.* thee to be expert   *Ac 26:3*
in customs
king Agrippa, *I k.* that thou   *Ac 26:27*
believest
I k. that in me dwelleth no   *Ro 7:18*
good thing
I k. nothing by myself, yet am   *1Co 4:4*
I not
now *I k.* in part, then shall I   *1Co 13:12*
k. as I am
I k. the forwardness of your   *2Co 9:2*
mind
I k. this shall turn to my   *Ph'p 1:19*
salvation
I k. that I shall abide with   *Ph'p 1:25*
you all
be of good comfort, when *I*   *Ph'p 2:19*
k. your estate
I k. how to be abased, *I k.*   *Ph'p 4:12*
how to abound
for *I k.* whom I have believed   *2Ti 1:12*
he that saith, *I k.* him and   *1Jo 2:4*
keepeth
I k. thy works   *Re 2:2;*
       2:9, 13, 19; 3:1, 8, 15
I k. the blasphemy of them, who   *Re 2:9*
say

MAY, MAYEST, MIGHT KNOW

mayest k. there is none like   *Ex 8:10;*
God   *9:14*
that thou *mayest k.* that earth   *Ex 9:29*
is Lord's
ye *may k.* the Lord doth put a   *Ex 11:7*
difference
that *I may k.* what to do to   *Ex 33:5*
thee
shew me thy way, that I *may*   *Ex 33:13*
k. thee
that your generations *may k.*   *Le 23:43*
that
that *I may k.* what Lord   *Nu 22:19*
will say
that thou *mightest k.* that   *De 4:35*
Lord is God
may k. way by which ye should   *Jos 3:4*
go
they *may k.* that as I was with   *Jos 3:7*
Moses
all people *might k.* the hand of   *Jos 4:24*
Lord
that Israel *might k.* to teach   *J'g 3:2*
them war
may k. whether our way be   *J'g 18:5*
prosperous
if not, then tell me, that I *may*   *Ru 4:4*
k.
all earth *may k.* there is a   *1Sa 17:46;*
God   *1Ki 8:43, 60; 2Ki 19:19*

that *I may k.* number of   *2Sa 24:2*
people
this people *may k.* thou art   *1Ki 18:37*
God
all people *may k.* thy name,   *2Ch 6:33*
may k. this house is called by
his servants, that they *may k.*   *2Ch 12:8*
my service
that ye *may k.* there is a   *Job 19:29*
judgment
be weighed, that God *may k.*   *Job 31:6*
my integrity
that all men *may k.* his work   *Job 37:7*
nations *may k.* themselves to be   *Ps 9:20*
but men
measure of days, that *may k.*   *Ps 39:4*
how frail I am
that the generation to come   *Ps 78:6*
might *k.* them
that men *may k.* that thou art   *Ps 83:18*
the most High
that they *may k.* that this is   *Ps 109:27*
thy hand
that *I may k.* thy   *Ps 119:125*
testimonies
let counsel draw nigh that we   *Isa 5:19*
may k. it
that he *may k.* to refuse the   *Isa 7:15*
evil
that all *may k.* that thou art   *Isa 37:20*
the Lord
that we *may k.* ye are gods,   *Isa 41:23*
yea, do good
who hath declared, that we   *Isa 41:26*
may k. and before
ye *may k.* and believe me,   *Isa 43:10*
and understand
that thou *mayest k.* that I am   *Isa 45:3*
the God of Israel
that they *may k.* from the   *Isa 45:6*
rising of the sun
that thou *mayest k.* and try   *Jer 6:27*
their way
that ye *may k.* that my words   *Jer 44:29*
shall stand
all flesh *may k.* I have drawn   *Eze 21:5*
my sword
against the land, that   *Eze 38:16*
heathen *may k.* me
mightest k. the thoughts of thy   *Da 2:30*
heart
to the intent that the living   *Da 4:17*
may k.
come, let us cast lots, that we   *Jon 1:7*
may k.
ye *may k.* the righteousness of   *Mic 6:5*
the Lord
ye *may k.* Son of man hath   *M't 9:6;*
power to forgive   *M'k 2:10; Lu 5:24*
ye *may k.* and believe the   *Joh 10:38*
Father is in me
that the world *may k.* love   *Joh 14:31;*
Father   *17:23*
that they *might k.* thee the   *Joh 17:3*
only true God
that ye *may k.* that I find no   *Joh 19:4*
fault in him
may we *k.* what this new   *Ac 17:19*
doctrine is
all *may k.* that those things   *Ac 21:24*
are nothing
we *might k.* things given us of   *1Co 2:12*
God
that ye *might k.* the love I have   *2Co 2:4*
to you
that I *might k.* proof of you,   *2Co 2:9*
whether ye be
that ye *may k.* the hope of his   *Eph 1:18*
calling
whom I sent, that ye *might k.*   *Eph 6:22*
our affairs
that *I may k.* him, and power   *Ph'p 3:10*
of his
ye *may k.* how to answer every   *Col 4:6*
man
whom I sent, that he *might k.*   *Col 4:8*
your estate
thou *may k.* how thou   *1Ti 3:15*
oughtest to behave
that ye *may k.* ye have eternal   *1Jo 5:13*
life
given us, that we *may k.* him   *1Jo 5:20*
that is true

WE KNOW, KNOW WE

know ye Laban? they said, We   *Ge 29:5*
k. him
if thou say, How shall we *k.*   *De 18:21*
the word

then shall *we k.* it is not his   *1Sa 6:9*
hand
we have no might, nor *k.* we   *2Ch 20:12*
what to do
behold, God is great, and we   *Job 36:26*
k. him not
as for our iniquities, *we k.*   *Isa 59:12*
them
then shall *we k.* if we follow   *Ho 6:3*
on to know
Israel shall cry to me, My God,   *Ho 8:2*
we k. thee
we k. thou art true, and   *M't 22:16;*
       M'k 12:14; Lu 20:21
we k. thou art a teacher come   *Joh 3:2*
from God
verily I say to thee, We speak   *Joh 3:11*
that *we do k.*
we k. what we worship; for   *Joh 4:22*
salvation is of
Jesus, whose father and   *Joh 6:42*
mother *we k.*
howbeit, *we k.* whence this   *Joh 7:27*
man is
now *we k.* that thou hast a   *Joh 8:52*
devil
we k. that this is our son who   *Joh 9:20*
was blind
said to him, *We k.* that this   *Joh 9:24*
man is a sinner
we k. that God spake to   *Joh 9:29*
Moses, as for this
now *we k.* that God heareth   *Joh 9:31*
not sinners
Thomas saith; Lord *we k.* not   *Joh 14:5*
whither thou goest, and how
can *we k.* the way
and *we k.* that his testimony   *Joh 21:24*
is true
we would *k.* what these things   *Ac 17:20*
mean
we k. it is every where spoken   *Ac 28:22*
against
we k. that what things the law   *Ro 3:19*
saith
we k. that the law is spiritual,   *Ro 7:14*
but I am
we k. the whole creation   *Ro 8:22*
groaneth and travaileth
we k. that all things work   *Ro 8:28*
together for good
we k. that we all have   *1Co 8:1*
knowledge
we k. that an idol is nothing in   *1Co 8:4*
world
for *we k.* in part, and prophesy   *1Co 13:9*
in part
for *we k.* that if our earthly   *2Co 5:1*
house
k. we no man after flesh, *k.*   *2Co 5:16*
we him no more
but *we k.* that the law is good   *1Ti 1:8*
for *we k.* him that hath said,   *Heb 10:30*
Vengeance
hereby *we k.* that *we k.* him, if   *1Jo 2:3*
we keep
hereby *k.* we that we are in him   *1Jo 2:5*
whereby *we k.* that it is the   *1Jo 2:18*
last time
but *we k.* that when he shall   *1Jo 3:2*
appear
we k. that we have passed   *1Jo 3:14*
from death to life
hereby *we k.* that we are of   *1Jo 3:19*
the truth
hereby *we k.* that he abideth   *1Jo 3:24*
in us
hereby *k.* we the spirit of truth   *1Jo 4:6*
and error
hereby *k.* we that we dwell in   *1Jo 4:13*
him
by this *we k.* we love the   *1Jo 5:2*
children of God
if we *k.* that he heareth us, we   *1Jo 5:15*
k. we have the petitions we
we k. whosoever is born of   *1Jo 5:18*
God, sinneth not
we k. that we are of God, and   *1Jo 5:19*
world lieth
we k. the Son of God is come,   *1Jo 5:20*
that *we may k.* him that is true

YE KNOW, KNOW YE

he said, *K.* ye Laban the son of   *Ge 29:5*
Nahor
ye k. that with all my power I   *Ge 31:6*
served your
ye k. that my wife bare me   *Ge 44:27*
two sons

at even *ye* shall *k.* the Lord brought   *Ex 16:6*

ye k. the heart of a stranger, seeing ye were   *Ex 23:9*

ye shall *k.* my breach of promise   *Nu 14:34*

ye shall *k.* that the Lord hath sent me   *Nu 16:28*

ye shall *k.* the living God is among you   *Jos 3:10*

and *ye k.* in all your hearts and souls   *Jos 23:14*

ye k. there is in these houses an ephod   *J'g 18:14*

k. ye that Ramoth in Gilead is ours   *1Ki 22:3*

ye k. the man and his communication   *2Ki 9:11*

what *ye k.* the same do I know   *Job 13:2*

k. ye that the Lord he is God   *Ps 100:3*

hearken, *ye* that *k.* righteousness   *Isa 51:7*

k. ye for certain, if ye put me to death   *Jer 26:15*

all *ye* that *k.* his name, say, How is   *Jer 48:17*

ye shall *k.* that I have not done   *Eze 14:23*

ye shall *k.* I the Lord have spoken   *Eze 17:21; 37:14*

ye shall *k.* that I am in midst of Israel   *Joe 2:27*

ye shall *k.* the Lord hath sent me   *Zec 2:9; 6:15*

ye shall *k.* them by their fruits   *M't 7:16; 7:20*

ye k. princes of the Gentiles   *M't 20:25; M'k 10:42*

ye k. summer nigh   *M't 24:32; M'k 13:28; Lu 21:30*

watch, for *ye k.* neither day nor hour   *M't 25:13*

he said to them, *K. ye* not this parable   *M'k 4:13*

k. ye that the kingdom of God is nigh   *Lu 21:31*

ye both *k.* me, and know whence I am   *Joh 7:28*

ye shall *k.* I am he; *ye* shall *k.* the truth   *Joh 8:28; 8:32*

k. ye nothing   *Joh 11:49*

k. ye what I have done   *Joh 13:12*

if *ye k.* these things, happy are ye if do them   *Joh 13:17*

whither I go *ye k.* and the way *ye k.*   *Joh 14:4*

from henceforth *ye k.* him, and have seen   *Joh 14:7; 14:17*

ye shall *k.* I am in my Father, and you in me   *Joh 14:20*

ye k. that it hated me before it hated you   *Joh 15:18*

man approved, as *ye* yourselves also *k.*   *Ac 2:22*

ye k. how that it is unlawful for a Jew   *Ac 10:28*

brethren, *ye k.* how that a good while ago   *Ac 15:7*

ye k. that by this craft we have our wealth   *Ac 19:25*

ye k. from the first day that I came   *Ac 20:18*

ye k. that ye were Gentiles, carried   *1Co 12:2*

ye k. your labour is not in vain in the Lord   *1Co 15:58*

brethren, *ye k.* the house of Stephanas   *1Co 16:15*

ye k. the grace of our Lord Jesus Christ   *2Co 8:9*

I trust *ye* shall *k.* we are not reprobates   *2Co 13:6*

k. ye that they which are of faith   *Ga 3:7*

ye k. how through infirmities I preached   *Ga 4:13*

for this *ye k.* that no whoremonger   *Eph 5:5*

ye k. the proof of him, that as a son   *Ph'p 2:22*

as *ye k.* what manner of men we were   *1Th 1:5*

and were shamefully entreated, as *ye k.*   *1Th 2:2*

nor used we flattering words, as *ye k.*   *1Th 2:5*

ye k. how we exhorted and comforted   *1Th 2:11*

even as it came to pass, and *ye k.*   *1Th 3:4*

ye k. what commandments we gave by Lord   *1Th 4:2*

and now *ye k.* what withholdeth   *2Th 2:6*

ye k. when he would have inherited   *Heb 12:17*

k. ye that our brother Timothy is set at   *Heb 13:23*

ye k. that ye were not redeemed with   *1Pe 1:18*

put you in remembrance, tho' *ye k.* them   *2Pe 1:12*

seeing *ye k.* these things before, beware   *2Pe 3:17*

ye k. all things; because *ye k.* it   *1Jo 2:20; 2:21*

if *ye k.* he is righteous, *ye k.* that every one   *1Jo 2:29*

ye k. he was manifested to take away our sins   *1Jo 3:5*

ye k. no murderer hath eternal life in him   *1Jo 3:15*

hereby *k. ye* the Spirit of God, every spirit   *1Jo 4:2*

and *ye k.* that our record is true   *3Jo 12*

KNOWEST

thou *k.* my service that I have done   *Ge 30:26*

thou *k.* how I have served thee   *Ge 30:29*

if thou *k.* any man of activity among   *Ge 47:6*

k. thou not that Egypt is destroyed   *Ex 10:7*

thou *k.* the travail that hath mischief   *Nu 20:14*

for thou *k.* how we are to encamp   *Nu 10:31*

thou *k.* the travel that hath befallen   *Nu 20:14*

diseases of Egypt, which thou *k.*   *De 7:15*

children of the Anakims, whom thou *k.*   *De 9:2*

a nation thou *k.* not, shall eat up   *De 28:33*

thou *k.* the thing that the Lord said   *Jos 14:6*

k. thou not Phlistines are rulers   *J'g 15:11*

woman said, Thou *k.* what Saul hath done   *1Sa 28:9*

how *k.* thou that Saul and Jonathan be dead   *2Sa 1:5*

k. thou not that it will be bitterness in end   *2Sa 2:26*

thou *k.* Abner, son of Ner, that he came   *2Sa 3:25*

Lord, *k.* thy servant   *2Sa 7:20; 1Ch 17:18*

for, said Hushai, thou *k.* thy father   *2Sa 17:8*

my lord the king, thou *k.* it not   *1Ki 1:18*

thou *k.* also what Joab did to me   *1Ki 2:5*

thou *k.* what thou oughtest to do to him   *1Ki 2:9*

thou *k.* that the kingdom was mine   *1Ki 2:15*

k. all wickedness thou didst to David   *1Ki 2:44*

whose heart thou *k.* thou only *k.*   *1Ki 8:39; 2Ch 6:30*

k. thou Lord will take thy master   *2Ki 2:3; 2:5*

thou *k.* that thy servant did fear the Lord   *2Ki 4:1*

thou *k.* that I am not wicked   *Job 10:7*

what *k.* thou that we know not   *Job 15:9*

k. thou not this of old, since man was   *Job 20:4*

therefore speak what thou *k.*   *Job 34:33*

who hath laid measures of earth, if thou *k.*   *Job 38:5*

breadth of the earth, declare, if thou *k.* it all   *Job 38:18*

k. thou it, because thou wast then born   *Job 38:21*

k. thou the ordinances of heaven   *Job 38:33*

k. thou when the wild goats bring forth   *Job 39:1; 39:2*

not refrained, O Lord thou *k.*   *Ps 40:9; Jer 15:15*

O God, thou *k.* my foolishness   *Ps 69:5*

thou *k.* my downsitting and uprising   *Ps 139:2*

lo, O Lord, thou *k.* it altogether   *Ps 139:4*

thou *k.* not what a day may bring forth   *Pr 27:1*

thou *k.* not what evil shall be   *Ec 11:2*

k. not what is the way of the Spirit, even so thou *k.* not   *Ec 11:5*

for thou *k.* not whether shall prosper   *Ec 11:6*

thou shalt call a nation that thou *k.* not   *Isa 55:5*

a nation whose language thou *k.* not   *Jer 5:15*

but thou, O Lord, *k.* me, thou hast seen me   *Jer 12:3*

into a land which thou *k.* not   *Jer 15:14; 17:4*

nor have I desired the woeful day, thou *k.*   *Jer 17:16*

thou *k.* all their counsel to slay me   *Jer 18:23*

I will shew these things which thou *k.* not   *Jer 33:3*

and I answered, O Lord God, thou *k.*   *Eze 37:3*

said, *K.* thou wherefore I come to thee   *Da 10:20*

angel said, *K.* thou not what these be   *Zec 4:5; 4:13*

k. thou that the Pharisees were offended   *M't 15:12*

thou *k.* commandments   *M'k 10:19; Lu 18:20*

shall thrice deny that thou *k.* me   *Lu 22:34*

Nathanael said, Whence *k.* thou me   *Joh 1:48*

art thou a master, and *k.* not these things   *Joh 3:10*

Jesus said, What I do, thou *k.* not now   *Joh 13:7*

we are sure thou *k.* all things   *Joh 16:30; 21:17*

k. thou not I have power to crucify   *Joh 19:10*

yea, Lord, thou *k.* that I love thee   *Joh 21:15; 21:16*

thou which *k.* the hearts of all men   *Ac 1:24*

I have done no wrong, as thou very well *k.*   *Ac 25:10*

k. his will, and approvest the things   *Ro 2:18*

what *k.* thou, O wife, *k.* thou, O man   *1Co 7:16*

thou *k.* that all they in Asia be turned   *2Ti 1:15*

how he ministered to me, thou *k.* very well   *2Ti 1:18*

and *k.* not that thou art wretched, blind   *Re 3:17*

and I said unto him, Sir, thou *k.*   *Re 7:14*

KNOWETH

my lord *k.* the children are tender   *Ge 33:13*

when he *k.* of it, he shall be guilty   *Le 5:3; 5:4*

he *k.* thy walking thro' this wilderness   *De 2:7*

no man *k.* of Moses' sepulchre to this day   *De 34:6*

Lord God of gods, he *k.* and Israel   *Jos 22:22*

Eli's house for the iniquity which he *k.*   *1Sa 3:13*

thy father certainly *k.* that I found grace   *1Sa 20:3*

and that also Saul my father *k.*   *1Sa 23:17*

thy servant *k.* that I found grace   *2Sa 14:22*

all Israel *k.* thy father is a mighty man   *2Sa 17:10*

he *k.* vain men, he seeth wickedness   *Job 11:11*

he *k.* the day of darkness is ready at hand   *Job 15:23*

but he *k.* the way that I take   *Job 23:10*

there is a path which no fowl *k.*   *Job 28:7*

God understandeth and *k.* the place thereof   *Job 28:23*

he *k.* their works and overturneth   *Job 34:25*

the Lord *k.* the way of the righteous   *Ps 1:6*

the Lord *k.* the days of the upright   *Ps 37:18*

for he *k.* the secrets of the heart   *Ps 44:21*

nor is there any among us that *k.* how long   *Ps 74:9*

Lord *k.* the thoughts of man are vanity   *Ps 94:11*

k. our frame, remembereth we are dust   *Ps 103:14*

moon for seasons, sun *k.* his going down   *Ps 104:19*

but the proud he *k.* afar off   *Ps 138:6*

works, and that my soul *k.* right well   *Ps 139:14*

foolish woman is simple and *k.* nothing   *Pr 9:13*

heart *k.* his own bitterness, and stranger   *Pr 14:10*

poor, that *k.* to walk before the living   *Ec 6:8*

thine own heart *k.* hast cursed others   *Ec 7:22*

no man *k.* either love or hatred by all that   *Ec 9:1*

ox *k.* his owner, the ass his master's crib   *Isa 1:3*

stork *k.* her appointed times, and turtle   *Jer 8:7*

glory, that he understandeth and *k.* me   *Jer 9:24*

he *k.* what is in the darkness, and light   *Da 2:22*

Lord is good, he *k.* them that trust in him   *Na 1:7*

he faileth not, but unjust *k.* no shame   *Zep 3:5*

your Father *k.* what things ye need   *M't 6:8*

k. ye have need of all these things   *M't 6:32; Lu 12:30*

no man *k.* Son but the Father, nor any *k.* Father   *Lu 10:22*

of that day *k.* no man   *M't 24:36; M'k 13:32*

ye justify, but God *k.* your hearts   *Lu 16:15*

saying, How *k.* this man letters   *Joh 7:15*

when Christ cometh. no man *k.* whence he is   *Joh 7:27*

as the Father *k.* me; nor *k.* him   *Joh 10:15; 14:17*

he saw it, and he *k.* that he saith true   *Joh 19:35*

God which *k.* the hearts bare witness   *Ac 15:8*

for the king *k.* of these things before whom   *Ac 26:26*

he *k.* what is the mind of the Spirit   *Ro 8:27*

what man *k.* things of man, even so things of God *k.* no man   *1Co 2:11*

if any man think he *k.* any thing, he *k.* nothing   *1Co 8:2*

because I love you not? God *k.*   *2Co 11:11*

God *k.* I lie not; I cannot tell, God *k.*   *2Co 11:31; 12:2-3*

the Lord *k.* them that are his   *2Ti 2:19*

to him that *k.* to do good, and doeth not   *Jas 4:17*

the Lord *k.* how to deliver the godly   *2Pe 2:9*

and *k.* all things; that that *k.* God   *1Jo 3:20; 4:6*

he that loveth is born of God, and *k.* God   *1Jo 4:7*

a new name written, which no man *k.*   *Re 2:17*

because he *k.* that he hath but a short time   *Re 12:12*

KNOWETH *NOT,* *WHO* KNOWETH

doth reign, and David our Lord *k.* it *not*   *1Ki 1:11*

who k. whether thou art come to kingdom   *Es 4:14*

yea, *who k. not* such things as these   *Job 12:3*

who k. not in all these, that the hand of Lord   *Job 12:9*

his sons come to honour, he *k.* it *not*   *Job 14:21*

this is the place of him that *k. not* God   *Job 18:21*

man *k. not* the price thereof, nor is it found   *Job 28:13*

---

he hath visited in anger, yet he *k.* it *not*   *Job 35:15*

riches, and *k. not* who shall gather them   *Ps 39:6*

who k. the power of thine anger   *Ps 90:11*

a brutish man *k. not,* nor a fool understand this   *Ps 92:6*

and *k. not* that it is for his life   *Pr 7:23*

but he *k. not* that the dead are there   *Pr 9:18*

and *who k.* the ruin of them both   *Pr 24:22*

who k. whether he be wise or a fool   *Ec 2:19*

who k. the spirit of man that goeth upward   *Ec 3:21*

for *who k.* what is good for man in life   *Ec 6:12*

who k. the interpretation of a   *Ec 8:1*

for he *k. not* that which shall be   *Ec 8:7*

for man also *k. not* his time, as the fishes   *Ec 9:12*

because he *k. not* how to go to the city   *Ec 10:15*

and they say, Who seeth us, *who k.* us   *Isa 29:15*

gray hairs here and there, yet he *k. not*   *Ho 7:9*

who k. if he will return and repent   *Joe 2:14*

and seed should grow up, he *k. not* how   *M'k 4:27*

but this people, *who k. not* the law   *Joh 7:49*

walketh in darkness, *k. not* whither he goeth   *Joh 12:35*

the servant *k. not* what his lord doeth   *Joh 15:15*

what man that *k. not* that Ephesians   *Ac 19:35*

walketh in darkness *k. not* whither go   *1Jo 2:11*

therefore the world *k.* us *not,* it knew him not   *1Jo 3:1*

he that loveth not, *k. not* God, for God is love   *1Jo 4:8*

KNOWING

ye shall be as gods, *k.* good and evil   *Ge 3:5*

slew them, my father David not *k.*   *1Ki 2:32*

to David a wise son, *k.* prudence   *2Ch 2:12*

Jesus *k.* their thoughts   *M't 9:4; Lu 11:17*

ye err, not *k.* the scriptures nor power of God   *M't 22:29*

Jesus immediately *k.* in himself virtue   *M'k 5:30*

but the woman *k.* what was done in her   *M'k 5:33*

feared John, *k.* that he was a just man   *M'k 6:20*

but he *k.* their hypocrisy, said to them   *M'k 12:15*

they laughed, *k.* that she was dead   *Lu 8:53*

and one for Elias, not *k.* what he said   *Lu 9:33*

Jesus *k.* the Father had given all things   *Joh 13:3*

Jesus *k.* all things that should come upon him   *Joh 18:4*

Jesus *k.* that all things were accomplished   *Joh 19:28*

none durst ask him, *k.* that it was the Lord   *Joh 21:12*

k. that God had sworn with an oath   *Ac 2:30*

his wife also *k.* (S)   *Ac 5:2*

his wife not *k.* what was done came in   *Ac 5:7*

he taught, *k.* only the baptism of John   *Ac 18:25*

not *k.* the things that shall befall me there   *Ac 20:22*

who k. the judgment of God that they   *Ro 1:32*

not *k.* that the goodness of God leadeth thee   *Ro 2:4*

k. that tribulation worketh patience   *Ro 5:3*

k. this, that our old man is crucified with him   *Ro 6:6*

k. Christ being raised from dead, dieth no more   *Ro 6:9*

---

k. the time, now it is high time to awake   *Ro 13:11*

k. that as ye are partakers of sufferings   *2Co 1:7*

k. that he which raised the Lord Jesus   *2Co 4:14*

k. that whilst we are at home in the body   *2Co 5:6*

k. the terror of the Lord, we persuade men   *2Co 5:11*

k. that a man is not justified by the law   *Ga 2:16*

k. that whatsoever good any man doeth   *Eph 6:8*

k. that your master is in heaven   *Eph 6:9; Col 4:1*

k. that I am set for defence of gospel   *Ph'p 1:17*

k. that of the Lord ye shall receive reward   *Col 3:24*

k. beloved, your election of God   *1Th 1:4*

k. this, that the law is made for lawless   *1Ti 1:9*

is proud, *k.* nothing, but doting about questions   *1Ti 6:4*

questions, *k.* that they do gender strifes   *2Ti 2:23*

k. of whom thou hast learned them   *2Ti 3:14*

k. that he that is such, is subverted   *Tit 3:11*

k. that thou wilt do more than I say   *Ph'm 21*

k. ye have in heaven a better substance   *Heb 10:34*

he went out, not *k.* whither he went   *Heb 11:8*

k. this, that the trying of your faith   *Jas 1:3*

k. we shall receive greater condemnation   *Jas 3:1*

blessing, *k.* that ye are thereunto called   *1Pe 3:9*

k. the same afflictions are accomplished in   *1Pe 5:9*

k. that shortly I must put off this tabernacle   *2Pe 1:14*

k. this, that no prophecy of scripture is of   *2Pe 1:20*

k. that there shall come scoffers in last days   *2Pe 3:3*

KNOWLEDGE

and the tree of *k.* of good and evil   *Ge 2:9; 2:17*

tree of knowing good and evil (B)   *Ge 2:9*

I have filled Bezaleel in *k.*   *Ex 31:3; 35:31*

in skill, intelligence, understanding (B)   *Ex 31:3*

or if his sin come to his *k.*   *Le 4:23; 4:28*

and knew the *k.* of the most High   *Nu 24:16*

that thou shouldest take *k.* of me   *Ru 2:10*

blessed be he that did take *k.* of thee   *Ru 2:19*

for the Lord is a God of *k.*   *1Sa 2:3*

see, take *k.* of all the lurking places   *1Sa 23:23*

shipment that had *k.* of sea   *1Ki 9:27; 2Ch 8:18*

give me *k.* that I may go out but hast asked *k.; k.* is granted thee   *2Ch 1:10; 2Ch 1:11; 1:12*

every one having *k.* separated   *Ne 10:28*

should a wise man utter vain *k.*   *Job 15:2*

for we desire not the *k.* of thy ways   *Job 21:14*

shall any teach God *k.* seeing he judgeth   *Job 21:22*

and my lips shall utter *k.* clearly   *Job 33:3*

give ear unto me, ye that have *k.*   *Job 34:2*

I will fetch my *k.* from afar, and will ascribe   *Job 36:3*

he that is perfect in *k.* is with thee   *Job 36:4; 37:16*

and night unto night sheweth *k.*   *Ps 19:2*

and is there *k.* in the most High   *Ps 73:11*

he that teacheth man *k.* shall not he know   *Ps 94:10*

teach me good judgment and *k.*   *Ps 119:66*

such *k.* is too wonderful for *Ps 139:6* me

what is man that thou takest *k.* *Ps 144:3* of him

to give the young man *k.* and *Pr 1:4* discretion

the fear of the Lord is the *Pr 1:7* beginning of *k.*

fools hate *k.* *Pr 1:22*

for that they hated *k.* and did *Pr 1:29* not choose

if thou criest after *k.* *Pr 2:3*

out of his mouth cometh *k.* and *Pr 2:6* understanding

and when *k.* is pleasant to thy *Pr 2:10* soul

by his *k.* the depths are *Pr 3:20* broken up

and that thy lips may keep *k.* *Pr 5:2*

they are right to them that *Pr 8:9* find *k.*

k. rather than gold; and find *Pr 8:10; 8:12* out *k.*

and the *k.* of the Holy is *Pr 9:10* understanding

wise men lay up *k.* but the *Pr 10:14* foolish

but through *k.* shall the just be *Pr 11:9* delivered

whoso loveth instruction loveth *Pr 12:1* *k.*

a prudent man concealeth *k.* *Pr 12:23* but fools

every prudent man dealeth *Pr 13:16* with *k.*

k. is easy to him that *Pr 14:6* understandeth

thou perceivest not in him the *Pr 14:7* lips of *k.*

but the prudent are crowned *Pr 14:18* with *k.*

the tongue of the wise useth *k.* *Pr 15:2* aright

the lips of the wise disperse *k.* *Pr 15:7*

the heart that hath *Pr 15:14* understanding seeketh *k.*

he that hath *k.* spareth his *Pr 17:27* words

heart of the prudent getteth *k.* *Pr 18:15* and the ear of the wise seeketh *k.*

reprove, and he will *Pr 19:25* understand *k.*

cease, my son, to err from the *Pr 19:27* words of *k.*

the lips of *k.* are a precious *Pr 20:15* jewel

when the wise is instructed, he *Pr 21:11* receiveth *k.*

the eyes of the Lord preserve *Pr 22:12* *k.*

and apply thine heart unto my *Pr 22:17* *k.*

written excellent things in *Pr 22:20* counsels and *k.*

and apply thine ears to the *Pr 23:12* words of *k.*

by *k.* shall the chambers be *Pr 24:4* filled with riches

yea, a man of *k.* increaseth *Pr 24:5* strength

so shall the *k.* of wisdom be to *Pr 24:14* thy soul

by a man of *k.* the state shall *Pr 28:2* be prolonged

nor learned wisdom, nor have *Pr 30:3* the *k.* of Holy

yea, my heart had experience *Ec 1:16* of *k.*

he that increaseth *k.* increaseth *Ec 1:18* sorrow

for there is a man whose labour *Ec 2:21* is in *k.*

God giveth to a man wisdom, *k.* *Ec 2:26* and joy

but the excellency of *k.* is that *Ec 7:12* wisdom giveth

nor *k.* in the grave, whither *Ec 9:10* thou goest

the preacher still taught the *Ec 12:9* people *k.*

for before the child shall have *Isa 8:4* *k.* to cry

the spirit of *k.* and of the fear *Isa 11:2* of the Lord

whom shall he teach *k.*? them *Isa 28:9* that are weaned

the heart of the rash shall *Isa 32:4* understand *k.*

wisdom and *k.* shall be *Isa 33:6* stability of thy times

who taught him *k.*; nor is *Isa 40:14; 44:19* there *k.*

and maketh their *k.* foolish *Isa 44:25*

thy wisdom and thy *k.* hath *Isa 47:10* perverted thee

by his *k.* my righteous servant *Isa 53:11* justify many

pastors, which shall feed you *Jer 3:15* with *k.*

every man is brutish in his *k.* *Jer 10:14; 51:17*

the Lord hath given me *k.* of *Jer 11:18* it

children well favoured and *Da 1:4* cunning in *k.*

God gave them *k.*; he giveth *Da 1:17; 2:21* *k.* to them

excellent spirit and *k.* were *Da 5:12* found in Daniel

many run to and fro, and *k.* *Da 12:4* shall be increased

my people are destroyed for *Ho 4:6* lack of *k.* because thou hast rejected *k.*

the earth filled with the *k.* of *Hab 2:14* the Lord

for the priest's lips should keep *Mal 2:7* *k.*

the men of that place had *k.* *M't 14:35* of him

to give *k.* of salvation by *Lu 1:77* remission of sins

ye have taken away the key of *Lu 11:52* *k.*

they marvelled and took *k.* of *Ac 4:13* them

having more perfect *k.* of that *Ac 24:22* way

did not like to retain God in *Ro 1:28* their *k.*

which hast the form of *k.* and *Ro 2:20* of truth

no flesh justified, for by law is *Ro 3:20* the *k.* of sin

they have a zeal, but not *Ro 10:2* according to *k.*

that ye also are filled with all *Ro 15:14* *k.* able to

are enriched in all utterance *1Co 1:5* and all *k.*

we know that we all have *k.* K. *1Co 8:1* puffeth up

howbeit there is not in every *1Co 8:7* man that *k.*

if any man see thee which *1Co 8:10* hast *k.* sit at meat

through the *k.* shall thy weak *1Co 8:11* brother perish

to another the word of *k.* by *1Co 12:8* the same Spirit

though understand all *1Co 13:2* mysteries and all *k.*

whether there be *k.* it shall *1Co 13:8* vanish away

except I speak to you by *1Co 14:6* revelation or *k.*

maketh manifest the savour *2Co 2:14* of his *k.*

to give the light of the *k.* of the *2Co 4:6* glory of God

by pureness, by *k.* by *2Co 6:6* longsuffering, by kindness

as ye abound in faith, *2Co 8:7* utterance, and *k.*

though I be rude in speech, *2Co 11:6* yet not in *k.*

may give you wisdom in the *Eph 1:17* *k.* of him

when ye read, ye may *Eph 3:4* understand my *k.*

the love of Christ which *Eph 3:19* passeth *k.*

till we come in the unity of *Eph 4:13* the *k.* of the Son

that your love may abound *Ph'p 1:9* more in *k.*

I count all things but loss for *Ph'p 3:8* the *k.* of Christ

that ye might be filled with the *Col 1:9* *k.* of his will

in whom are hid the treasures *Col 2:3* of wisdom and *k.*

put on the new man which is *Col 3:10* renewed in *k.*

all men to come to the *k.* of the *1Ti 2:4* truth

falsely called *k.* *1Ti 6:20* (A)(B)(E)(N)(P)(R)

never able to come to the *k.* of *2Ti 3:7* the truth

if we sin after we have *Heb 10:26* received the *k.*

who is a wise man, and *Jas 3:13* endued with *k.*

husbands dwell with them *1Pe 3:7* according to *k.*

thro' the *k.* of him that hath *2Pe 1:3* called us

add to virtue *k.* and to *k.* *2Pe 1:5* temperance

nor unfruitful in the *k.* of our *2Pe 1:8* Lord Jesus Christ

grow in grace and in the *k.* of *2Pe 3:18* our Lord Jesus

KNOWLEDGE *OF GOD*

then shalt thou find the *k.* of *Pr 2:5* God

there is no truth, nor *k. of God* *Ho 4:1* in the land

desired the *k. of God* more than *Ho 6:6* burnt offerings

the riches both of wisdom, *Ro 11:33* and *k. of God*

for some have not the *k.* of *1Co 15:34* God

high thing exalteth itself *2Co 10:5* against *k. of God*

and increasing in the *k.* of *Col 1:10* God

peace be multiplied, thro' the *2Pe 1:2* *k. of God*

KNOWLEDGE *OF THE LORD*

that taught the good *k.* of *2Ch 30:22* the Lord

the earth shall be full of the *k.* *Isa 11:9* of the Lord

escaped pollutions thro' the *k.* *2Pe 2:20* of the Lord

NO KNOWLEDGE

your children which in that day *De 1:39* had *no k.*

have the workers of iniquity *Ps 14:4; 53:4* *no k.*

gone into captivity because *Isa 5:13* they have *no k.*

they have *no k.* that set up *Isa 45:20* their images

we afflicted our soul, and thou *Isa 58:3* takest *no k.*

but to do good, they have *no k.* *Jer 4:22*

WITHOUT KNOWLEDGE

committed *without k.* of the *Nu 15:24* congregation

Job hath spoken *without k.* *Job 34:35* and wisdom

he multiplieth words *without* *Job 35:16* *k.*

shall perish by sword, and *Job 36:12* die *without k.*

darkeneth counsel by words *Job 38:2; 42:3* *without k.*

it is not good that the soul be *Pr 19:2* *without k.*

KNOWN

was a virgin, nor had any *Ge 24:16* man *k.* her

Moses said, Surely this thing is *Ex 2:14* *k.*

if it be *k.* that the ox hath *Ex 21:36* used to push

for wherein shall it be *k.* here *Ex 33:16* that I and

when the sin they have sinned *Le 4:14* is *k.*

is a witness whether he hath *Le 5:1* seen or *k.* of it

kill every woman that hath *k.* *Nu 31:17* man

take wise men, and *k.* among *De 1:13; 1:15* tribes

k. as Rephaim (A)(R) *De 2:11*

and it be not *k.* who hath slain *De 21:1* him

and which had *k.* the works *Jos 24:31* of the Lord

and it shall be *k.* to you why *1Sa 6:3* his hand

let it be *k.* that thou art God *1Ki 18:36* in Israel

be it *k.* to the king *Ezr 4:12; 4:13; 5:8*

when enemies heard that it was *Ne 4:15*
k. to us
the thing was *k.* to Mordecai *Es 2:22*
who told it
the Lord is *k.* by the judgment *Ps 9:16*
which
thou hast *k.* my soul in *Ps 31:7*
adversities
God is *k.* in her palaces for a *Ps 48:3*
refuge
that thy way may be *k.* on *Ps 67:2*
earth, thy health
thou hast *k.* my reproach *Ps 69:19*
and my shame
in Judah is God *k.*: his name is *Ps 76:1*
great in Israel
thy way in the sea, thy *Ps 77:19*
footsteps are not *k.*
sayings of old, which we have *Ps 78:3*
heard and *k.*
let him be *k.* among the *Ps 79:10*
heathen in our sight
shall thy wonders be *k.* in the *Ps 88:12*
dark
set him on high, because he *Ps 91:14*
hath *k.* my name
those that have *k.* thy *Ps 119:79*
testimonies
I have *k.* of old thou hast *Ps 119:152*
founded them for ever
O Lord, thou hast searched *Ps 139:1*
me, and *k.* me
but he that perverteth his ways *Pr 10:9*
shall be *k.*
a fool's wrath is presently *k.* *Pr 12:16*
but a prudent
a child is *k.* by his doings *Pr 20:11*
whether his work
her husband is *k.* in the gates, *Pr 31:23*
when he sitteth
a fool's voice is *k.* by multitude *Ec 5:3*
of words
and it is *k.* that it is man, nor *Ec 6:10*
may contend
excellent things, this is *k.* in all *Isa 12:5*
the earth
and the Lord shall be *k.* to *Isa 19:21*
Egypt
their seed shall be *k.* among *Isa 61:9*
the Gentiles
hand of the Lord shall be *k.* *Isa 66:14*
to his servants
for they have *k.* the way of the *Jer 5:5*
Lord
then shall prophet be *k.* the *Jer 28:9*
Lord sent him
saith the Lord God, Be it *k.* *Eze 36:32;*
to you *Ac 4:10, 13:38; 28:28*
I will be *k.* in the eyes of *Eze 38:23*
many nations
but if not, be it *k.* to thee, O *Da 3:18*
king
after thou shalt have *k.* the *Da 4:26*
heavens rule
you only have I *k.* of all *Am 3:2*
families of earth
a day which shall be *k.* to the *Zec 14:7*
Lord
but if ye had *k.* what this *M't 12:7*
meant
the tree is *k.* by his fruit *M't 12:33;*
Lu 6:44
if the good man of house *M't 24:43;*
had *k.* *Lu 12:39*
if he were a prophet, he would *Lu 7:39*
have *k.*
saying, If thou hadst *k.* in this *Lu 19:42*
thy day
how he was *k.* of them in *Lu 24:35*
breaking of bread
he himself seeketh to be *k.* *Joh 7:4*
openly
nor know me nor my Father, *Joh 8:19;*
if ye had *k.* me ye should *14:7*
have *k.* my Father also
I know my sheep, and am *k.* *Joh 10:14*
of mine
now they have *k*; and have *k.* *Joh 17:7;*
surely *17:8*
I have *k.* thee, these have *k.* *Joh 17:25*
that thou sent me
that disciple which was *k.* to *Joh 18:15;*
high priest *18:16*
and it was *k.* to all dwellers at *Ac 1:19*
Jerusalem
be this *k.* unto you, and *Ac 2:14*
hearken to my words
but their laying await was *k.* of *Ac 9:24*
Saul

it was *k.* throughout all Joppa *Ac 9:42*
many believed
k. unto God are all his works *Ac 15:18*
from beginning
this was *k.* to all the Jews and *Ac 19:17*
Greeks
he would have *k.* the *Ac 22:30;*
certainty *23:28*
because that which may be *k.* *Ro 1:19*
of God
who hath *k.* the mind of *Ro 11:34;*
Lord *1Co 2:16*
for had they *k.* it; same is *k.* *1Co 2:8;*
of him *8:3*
then shall I know, even as I *1Co 13:12*
also am *k.*
how shall it be *k.* what is *1Co 14:7*
piped or harped
how shall it be *k.* what is *1Co 14:9*
spoken
are our epistle *k.* and read of *2Co 3:2*
all men
though we have *k.* Christ *2Co 5:16*
after the flesh
as unknown and yet well *k.* as *2Co 6:9*
dying and
make *k.* to you (S) *2Co 8:1;*
Ga 1:11
after ye have *k.* God or are *k.* *Ga 4:9*
of God
might be *k.* by church the *Eph 3:10*
wisdom of God
let your moderation be *k.* to *Ph'p 4:5*
all men
thou hast fully *k.* my doctrine *2Ti 3:10*
from a child thou hast *k.* the *2Ti 3:15*
holy scriptures
that by me the preaching *2Ti 4:17*
might be fully *k.*
I write, because ye have *k.* *1Jo 2:13;*
him *2:14*
we have *k.* and believed the *1Jo 4:16*
love God hath
and all them that have *k.* the *2Jo 1:1*
truth

MADE, MADEST KNOWN

while Joseph *made* himself *k.* to *Ge 45:1*
brethren
and *madest k.* to them thy holy *Ne 9:14*
sabbath
the Lord hath *made k.* his *Ps 98:2*
salvation
he *made k.* his ways to Moses, *Ps 103:7*
his acts
that which is in the midst of *Pr 14:33*
fools is *made k.*
I have *made k.* to thee this *Pr 22:19*
day, even to thee
and *made* myself *k.* to them *Eze 20:5;*
20:9
then Arioch *made* the thing *k.* *Da 2:15*
to Daniel
Daniel *made* the thing *k.* to *Da 2:17*
Hananiah
hast *made k.* to me, *made k.* *Da 2:23*
to us the king's matter
the great God hath *made k.* to *Da 2:45*
the king
have I *made k.* that which shall *Ho 5:9*
surely be
which the Lord hath *made k.* *Lu 2:15*
to us
had seen it, they *made k.* *Lu 2:17*
abroad the saying
all that I heard, I have *made* *Joh 15:15*
k. to you
thou hast *made k.* to me the *Ac 2:28*
ways of life
at second time Joseph was *Ac 7:13*
made k. Joseph's kindred
made k. to Pharaoh
m. k. to all nations for *Ro 16:26*
obedience of
having *made k.* to us the *Eph 1:9*
mystery of his will
how by revelation he *made k.* *Eph 3:3*
to me the mystery
let your requests be *made k.* to *Ph'p 4:6*
God
when we *made k.* the coming *2Pe 1:16*
of our Lord

MAKE, MAKING KNOWN

I will *make* myself *k.* to him in *Nu 12:6*
a vision
thou mayest *make k.* to me *1Sa 28:15*
what I shall do

make k. his deeds among *1Ch 16:8;*
people *Ps 105:1*
in *making k.* all these great *1Ch 17:19*
things
that they should *make* them *k.* *Ps 78:5*
with my mouth will I *make k.* *Ps 89:1*
thy faithfulness
that he might *make k.* his *Ps 106:8*
mighty power
to *make k.* to sons of men his *Ps 145:12*
mighty acts
I will *make k.* my words to you *Pr 1:23*
the father to children shall *Isa 38:19*
make k. thy truth
to *make* thy name *k.* to thy *Isa 64:2*
adversaries
I will *make* myself *k.* among *Eze 35:11*
them
so will I *make* my holy name *k.* *Eze 39:7*
in Israel
found a man that will *make k.* *Da 2:25*
to the king
art thou able to *make k.* to me *Da 2:26*
the dream
but the Lord *maketh k.* to the *Da 2:28;*
king *2:29*
shall *make k.* the *Da 2:30;*
interpretation *5:15-17*
O Lord, in the midst of the *Hab 3:2*
years *make k.*
God willing to *make k.* his power *Ro 9:22*
k.
that he might *make k.* the *Ro 9:23*
riches of his glory
to *make k.* the mystery of the *Eph 6:19*
gospel
Tychicus shall *make k.* to you *Eph 6:21*
all things
to whom God will *make k.* *Col 1:27*
what is the riches
they shall *make k.* to you all *Col 4:9*
things done here

NOT KNOWN

I have two daughters which *Ge 19:8;*
have not *k.* man *Nu 31:18, 35; J'g 21:12*
it could not be *k.* they had *Ge 41:21*
eaten them
and the plenty shall not be *k.* *Ge 41:31*
in the land
by my name JEHOVAH was I *Ex 6:3*
not *k.*
with children which have not *De 11:2;*
k. *31:13*
to go after gods which ye *De 11:28;*
have not *k.* *13:6, 13*
neither thou nor thy fathers *De 28:36;*
have *k.* *28:64*
as many as had not *k.* the wars *J'g 3:1*
of Canaan
brake the withs, so his strength *J'g 16:9*
was not *k.*
but make not thyself *k.* to the *Ru 3:3*
man
let it not be *k.* that a woman *Ru 3:14*
came in
spread corn, and the thing *2Sa 17:19*
was not *k.*
be not *k.* to be the wife of *1Ki 14:2*
Jeroboam
people whom I have not *k.* *Ps 18:43*
shall serve me
way is in the sea, and thy *Pr 77:19*
footsteps are not *k.*
pour wrath on heathen that *Ps 79:6*
have not *k.* thee
and they have not *k.* my ways *Ps 95:10;*
Heb 3:10
thy judgments, they have not *Ps 147:20*
k. them
he hath not seen the sun, nor *k.* *Ec 6:5*
any thing
have ye not *k.*? hast thou not *Isa 40:21;*
k. *40:28*
lead them in paths that they *Isa 42:16*
have not *k.*
they have not *k.* nor *Isa 44:18*
understood, he hath shut
I surnamed thee, tho' thou *Isa 45:4;*
hast not *k.* me *45:5*
my people is foolish, they have *Jer 4:22*
not *k.* me
into countries which thou hast *Eze 32:9*
not *k.*
if ye will not make *k.* the *Da 2:5;*
dream *2:9*
they did not make *k.* to me *Da 4:7;*
interpretation *5:8*

and they have *not* k. the Lord   Ho 5:4
their place is *not* k. where they   Na 3:17
are
fear not, for there is nothing   M't 10:26;
hid that shall *not* be k.   Lu 8:17; 12:2
they should *not* make him k.   M't 12:16;
   M'k 3:12
a stranger, and hast *not* k.   Lu 24:18
these things
yet ye have *not* k. him, but I   Joh 8:55
know him
so long time, and yet hast   Joh 14:9
thou *not* k. me, Philip
because they have *not* k. the   Joh 16:3
Father nor me
O righteous Father the   Joh 17:25
world hath *not* k. thee
the way of peace have they *not*   Ro 3:17
k.
I had *not* k. sin but by the law,   Ro 7:7
I had *not* k. lust
which in other ages was *not*   Eph 3:5
made k.
been better *not* k. way of   2Pe 2:21
righteousness
the sinner hath not seen *not* k.   1Jo 3:6
him
which have *not* k. the depths of   Re 2:24
Satan

KOA

Shoa, and K., and all the   Eze 23:23

KOHATH

the sons of Levi, Gershon, K.   Ge 46:11;
and Merari   Ex 6:16; Nu 3:17
the sons of K.   Ex 6:18;
Nu 3:19, 27, 29-30; 16:1; 1Ch 6:2, 22, 61
the years of the life of K. were   Ex 6:18
133 years
take the sum of the sons of K.   Nu 4:2
of Levi
this be the service of the sons   Nu 4:4;
of K.   4:15; 7:9
of the sons of K. Uriel the   1Ch 15:5
chief

KOHATHITES

cut ye not off the family of the   Nu 4:18
K.
Moses and Aaron numbered   Nu 4:34;
the sons of K.   4:37
the K. set forward bearing   Nu 10:21
the sanctuary
the lot came out for K.   Jos 21:4;
   1Ch 6:54
the sons of K. sanctified   2Ch 29:12
themselves
the sons of the K. to set the   2Ch 34:12
work forward

KOLAIAH

the son of K.   Ne 11:7; Jer 29:21

KORAH

Aholibamah bare K.; duke K.   Ge 36:5;
   36:16
sons of Izhar, K., Nepheg   Ex 6:21;
   Nu 16:1
take censers, K. and all his   Nu 16:6
company
K. gathered all the   Nu 16:19
congregation against them
get you up from about the   Nu 16:24
tabernacle of K.
that he be not as K. and as   Nu 16:40
his company
Dathan who strove in the   Nu 26:9
company of K.
notwithstanding the children   Nu 26:11
of K. died not
our father was not in the   Nu 27:3
company of K.
the sons of Esau, Joalam and   1Ch 1:35
K.
son of Hebron, K.; K. of   1Ch 2:43;
Amminadab   6:22
son of K. and his brethren   1Ch 9:19
over the work
they perished in the gain-   Jude 11
saying of K.

KORAHITE

the firstborn of Shallum the K.   1Ch 9:31

KORAHITES

the K. were over the work   1Ch 9:19

KORATHITES

the family of the K.   Nu 26:58

KORE

Shallum the son of K.   1Ch 9:19
Meshelemiah the son of K.   1Ch 26:1
porters among the sons of K.   1Ch 26:19
K. the son of Imnah the   2Ch 31:14
Levite

KORHITES

the families of the K.   Ex 6:24
Jashobeam, the K.   1Ch 12:6
K. was Meshelemiah the son   1Ch 26:1
of
of the children of the K.   2Ch 20:19

KOUM

Talitha K., translated (B)   M'k 5:41

KOZ

the children of K.   Ezr 2:61; Ne 7:63
the son of K.   Ne 3:4; 3:21

KUE

K.; the king's merchants   1Ki 10:28
received them from K. (S)

KUSHAIAH

Ethan the son of K.   1Ch 15:17

L

LAADAH

L. the father of Mareshah   1Ch 4:21

LAADAN

L. his son   1Ch 7:26
Of the Gershonites were L.   1Ch 23:7;
   26:21
The sons of L.   1Ch 23:8; 26:21
the chief of the fathers of L.   1Ch 23:9

LABAN

Rebekah had a brother, his   Ge 24:29
name was L.
flee thou to L. my brother, to   Ge 27:43
Haran
take thee a wife of the   Ge 28:2
daughters of L.
know ye L.; L. gave to Rachel,   Ge 29:5;
Bilhah   29:29
Jacob beheld the countenance   Ge 31:2
of L.
for I have seen all that L.   Ge 31:12
doth to thee
Jacob stole away unawares to   Ge 31:20
L. the Syrian
God came to L. in a dream by   Ge 31:24
night
L. searched all the tent, but   Ge 31:34
found them not
Jacob chode with L.; L.   Ge 31:36;
kissed his sons   31:55
I have sojourned with L. and   Ge 32:4
stayed until now
words Moses spake between   De 1:1
Paran and L.

LABAN'S

Jacob fed the rest of L. flocks   Ge 30:36
put them not unto L. cattle   Ge 30:40
feebler were L., and the   Ge 30:42
stronger
heard the words of L. sons   Ge 31:1

LABOR

forced l. (A)   De 16:10; 17:13;
J'g 1:28;   1Ki 4:6; 12:18; 2Ch 10:18;
   Pr 12:24

force, conscripted l. (S)   1Ki 5:13;
   5:14; 9:15
conscripted the l. corps   1Ki 9:15
(B)(R)
conscript l. (A)   2Ki 4:6;
   9:21; 12:18; 2Ch 8:8
the painful l. (A)   Ec 3:10; 4:4, 6
woman in l. (B)   Jer 4:31
as a woman in l. (B)   Jer 6:24;
   13:21; 22:23; 49:24; 50:43; Mic 4:10
like a woman in l. (A)(R)   Jer 30:6;
   Mic 4:9
woman in l. (R)   Joh 16:2
in l. and travail (E)   2Co 11:27
l. pains of a woman (A)   1Th 5:3

LABORERS

battalion of conscript l. (B)   1Ki 5:13;
   5:14

LABORIOUS

l. work (R)   Le 23:9

LABOUR

God hath seen the l. of my   Ge 31:42
hands
Rachel travailed and had   Ge 35:16;
hard l.   35:17
Rachel felt the birth pangs   Ge 35:16
(B)
that they may l. therein   Ex 5:9
six days l.   Ex 20:9; De 5:13
the Lord heard, and looked on   De 26:7
our l.
make not all the people to l.   Jos 7:3
for which he did not l.   Jos 24:13
be a guard to us, and l. on the   Ne 4:22
day
shake out every man from his   Ne 5:13
l.
why l. I in vain   Job 9:29
why should I weary myself in   Job 9:29
vain (B)
or wilt thou leave thy l. to   Job 39:11
him
he l. is in vain without fear   Job 39:16
he gave their l. to the locust   Ps 78:46
yet is their strength l. and   Ps 90:10
sorrow, soon cut
man goeth to his l. till the   Ps 104:23
evening
they inherited the l. of the   Ps 105:44
people
he brought down their heart   Ps 107:12
with l.
let the stranger spoil his l.   Ps 109:11
except Lord build they l. in   Ps 127:1
vain
eat the l. of thy hands   Ps 128:2
eat the product of your hands   Ps 128:2
(B)
oxen may be strong to l.   Ps 144:14
when our oxen are well   Ps 144:14
loaded (A)
our oxen well burdened (B)   Ps 144:14
our oxen well laden (E)   Ps 144:14
our cattle be heavy with   Ps 144:14
young (R)
the l. of the righteous tendeth   Pr 10:16
to life
he that gathereth by l. shall   Pr 13:11
increase
in all l. there is profit, but the   Pr 14:23
talk of lips
the slothful, his hands refuse   Pr 21:25
to l.
his hands refuse to work (B)   Pr 21:25
l. not to be rich   Pr 23:4
Weary not yourself to be rich   Pr 23:4
(A)(E)
Do not toil to get wealth   Pr 23:4
(B)(R)
what profit hath a man of all his   Ec 1:3
l.
all things are full of l. man   Ec 1:8
cannot utter it
rejoiced in all my l. my portion   Ec 2:10
of all my l.
yea, I hated all my l. which I   Ec 2:18
had taken
yet shall he have rule over all   Ec 2:19
my l.
to cause my heart to despair of   Ec 2:20
the l. I took
for there is a man whose l. is in   Ec 2:21
wisdom
what hath man of all his l.   Ec 2:22
under the sun

make his soul enjoy good in *l.*   Ec 2:24; 3:13; 5:18
yet there is no end of all his *l.*   Ec 4:8
for whom do I *l.*   Ec 4:8
working and denying myself (B)   Ec 4:8
I toiling, depriving myself (R)   Ec 4:8
because they have a good   Ec 4:9
reward for their *l.*
nothing of his *l.* which he may   Ec 5:15
carry away
to rejoice in his *l.* this is the   Ec 5:19
gift of God
all the *l.* of man is for his   Ec 6:7
mouth, and yet
for that shall abide with him of   Ec 8:15
his *l.*
though a man *l.* to seek it out   Ec 8:17
however much a man may toil   Ec 8:17
(A)(R)
that is thy portion in thy *l.*   Ec 9:9
under the sun
the *l.* of the foolish wearieth   Ec 10:15
every one
l. not to comfort me   Isa 22:4
the *l.* of Egypt shall come   Isa 45:14
over to thee
why spend your *l.* for that   Isa 55:2
which satisfieth not
they shall not *l.* in vain   Isa 65:23
shame devoured the *l.* of our   Jer 3:24
fathers
wherefore came I out of the   Jer 20:18
womb to see *l.*
the people shall *l.* in vain   Jer 51:58
we *l.* and have no rest   La 5:5
weary and are allowed no rest   La 5:5
(A)
we toil without rest (B)   La 5:5
weary, and have no rest (E)(R)   La 5:5
they shall take away all thy *l.*   Eze 23:29
I have given him the land of   Eze 29:20
Egypt for his *l.*
l. to bring forth, O Zion   Mic 4:10
the people should *l.* in the fire   Hab 2:13
though the *l.* of the olive   Hab 3:17
should fail
a drought on all the *l.* of the   Hag 1:11
hands
come unto me all ye that *l.*   M't 11:28
to reap wherein ye bestowed   Joh 4:38
no *l.*
l. not for the meat that   Joh 6:37
perisheth
greet Mary, who bestowed   Ro 16:6
much *l.* on us
who *l.* in the Lord   Ro 16:12
every man shall receive   1Co 3:8
according to his *l.*
l. working with our own   1Co 4:12;
hands   Eph 4:28
you know that your *l.* is not   1Co 15:58
in vain
we *l.* to be accepted of him   2Co 5:9
I am afraid of you, lest I   Ga 4:11
bestowed *l.* in vain
if I live in the flesh, this is   Ph'p 1:22
fruit of my *l.*
Epaphroditus, my companion   Ph'p 2:25
in *l.* brother
I also *l.* striving according to   Col 1:29
remembering your *l.* of love,   1Th 1:3
and patience
for ye remember, brethren, our   1Th 2:9
l. and travail
tempter have tempted you, and   1Th 3:5
our *l.* be in vain
to know them which *l.* among   1Th 5:12
you
but wrought with *l.* and travail   2Th 3:8
night
we both *l.* and suffer reproach   1Ti 4:10
they that *l.* in word and   1Ti 5:17
doctrine
l. therefore to enter into that   Heb 4:11
rest
not unrighteous to forget   Heb 6:10
your *l.* of love
I know, thy works, and *l.* and   Re 2:2
patience

LABOURED

So we *l.* in the work: and half   Ne 4:21
of
which he *l.* for shall he   Job 20:18
restore
on the labour that I had *l.* to   Ec 2:11
do
all my labour wherein I have *l.*   Ec 2:19

to a man that hath not *l.*   Ec 2:21
therein
wherein he hath *l.* under the   Ec 2:22
sun
hath he that hath *l.* for the   Ec 5:16
wind
thou hast *l.* from thy youth   Isa 47:12
with whom thou hast *l.* even   Isa 47:15
Then I said, I have *l.* in vain, I   Isa 49:4
have
thy wine, for the which thou   Isa 62:8
hast *l.*
he *l.* till the going down of the   Da 6:14
sun
for the which thou hast not *l.*   Jon 4:10
other men *l.* and ye are   Jon 4:38
entered
Persis, which *l.* much in the   Re 16:12
Lord
I *l.* more abundantly than   1Co 15:10
they all
not run in vain, neither *l.* in   Ph'p 2:16
vain
which *l.* with me in the gospel   Ph'p 4:3
and for my name's sake hast *l.*   Re 2:3

LABOURER

for the *l.* is worthy of his hire   Lu 10:7
And, The *l.* is worthy of his   1Ti 5:18
reward

LABOURERS

is plenteous, but the *l.* are few   M't 9:37
will send forth *l.* into his   M't 9:38
harvest
morning to hire *l.* into his   M't 20:1
vineyard
agreed with the *l.* for a penny   M't 20:2
a day
Call the *l.* and give them their   M't 20:8
hire
truly is great, but the *l.* are few   Lu 10:2
that he would send forth *l.* into   Lu 10:2
For we are *l.* together with   1Co 3:9
God
the hire of the *l.* who have   Jas 5:4
reaped

LABOURETH

He that *l.*, for himself; for   Pr 16:26
l. for himself; for his mouth   Pr 16:26
he that worketh wherein he *l.*   Ec 3:9
one that helpeth with us, and   1Co 16:16
l.
husbandman that *l.* must be   2Ti 2:6
first

LABOURING

The sleep of a *l.* man is sweet   Ec 5:12
so *l.* ye ought to support the   Ac 20:35
weak
l. fervently for you in prayers   Col 4:12
for *l.* night and day, because   1Th 2:9
we

LABOURS

of harvest, the firstfruits of   Ex 23:16
thy *l.*
gathered in thy *l.* out of the   Ex 23:16
field
The fruit of thy land, and all   De 28:33
thy *l.*
l. be in the house of a stranger   Pr 5:10
pleasure, and exact all your *l.*   Isa 58:3
of this city, and all the *l.*   Jer 20:5
thereof
my *l.* they shall find none   Ho 12:8
iniquity
hail in all the *l.* of your hands   Hag 2:17
and ye are entered into their *l.*   Joh 4:38
in imprisonments, in tumults,   2Co 6:5
in *l.*
measure, that is, of other   2Co 10:15
men's *l.*
in *l.* more abundant, in   2Co 11:23
stripes
that they may rest from their   Re 14:13
l.

LACE

rings of the ephod with a *l.* of   Ex 28:28;
blue   39:21
And thou shalt put it on a   Ex 28:37
blue *l.*

And they tied unto it a *l.* of   Ex 39:31
blue, to

LACERATE

turn and *l.* you (S)   M't 7:6

LACHISH

the Lord delivered L. to   Jos 10:32
Israel
the king of L. one; Judah   Jos 12:11;
had L.   15:39
Amaziah fled to L.   2Ki 14:19;
  2Ch 25:27
Hezekiah sent to king of   2Ki 18:14
Assyria to L.
the king of Assyria sent   2Ki 18:17;
Rab-shakeh from L. with   Isa 36:2
Rehoboam built L. and   2Ch 11:9
Azekah
the king of Babylon fought   Jer 34:7
against L.
O inhabitant of L. bind   Mic 1:13
the chariot

LACK

there shall *l.* five of the fifty   Ge 18:28
destroy all the city for *l.* of   Ge 18:28
five
he that gathered little had no   Ex 16:18
l.
thou shalt not *l.* any thing in it   De 8:9
lack (S)   De 28:48;
28:57; Ps 34:9-10; Isa 34:16; Jer 33:17-
18; 35:19; La 4:9; Eze 4:17; Am 4:6
old lion perisheth for *l.* of   Job 4:11
prey
God, they wander for *l.* of   Job 38:41
meat
The young lions do *l.* and   Ps 34:10
suffer
who lack sense (B)(R)   Pr 15:21
giveth unto the poor shall not   Pr 28:27
l.
and let thy head *l.* no ointment   Ec 9:8
are destroyed for *l.* of   Ho 4:6
knowledge
from my youth up: what *l.* I   M't 19:20
yet
reproached for *l.* of faith   M'k 16:14
(P)
contributed of her *l.* (A)   Lu 21:4
l. out of self-control   1Co 7:5
(A)(B)(E)(R)
that had gathered little had   2Co 8:15
no *l.*
to supply your *l.* of service   Ph'p 2:30
toward
that ye may have *l.* of   1Th 4:12
nothing
If any of you *l.* wisdom, let him   Jas 1:5

LACKED

with thee; thou hast *l.* nothing   De 2:7
l. of David's servants nineteen   2Sa 2:30
the morning light there *l.* not   2Sa 17:22
one
man in his month: they *l.*   1Ki 4:27
nothing
But what hast thou *l.* with   1Ki 11:22
me
wilderness, so that they *l.*   Ne 9:21
nothing
away, because it *l.* moisture   Lu 8:6
scrip, and shoes, *l.* ye any   Lu 22:35
thing
was there any among them that   Ac 4:34
l.
honour to that part which *l.*   1Co 12:24
also careful, but ye *l.*   Ph'p 4:10
opportunity

LACKEST

said unto him, One thing   M'k 10:21
thou *l.*
unto him, Yet *l.* thou one   Lu 18:22
thing

LACKETH

and there *l.* not one man of   Nu 31:49
us
lacketh (S)   De 15:8;
Pr 9:4; 1019; 28:16; Ec 6:2
on the sword, or that *l.* bread   2Sa 3:29
with a woman *l.* understanding   Pr 6:32
honoureth himself, and *l.* bread   Pr 12:9
that *l.* these things is blind   2Pe 1:9

LACKING

to be *l.* from thy meat offering　*Le 2:13*
thing superfluous or *l.* in his　*Le 22:23*
parts
be to day one tribe *l.* in Israel　*J'g 21:3*
And there was nothing *l.* to　*1Sa 30:19*
them
lacking (S)　*Ec 1:15; Jas 1:4*
neither shall they be *l.* saith the　*Jer 23:4*
that which was *l.* on your　*1Co 16:17*
part they
that which was *l.* to me the　*2Co 11:9*
brethren
that which is *l.* in your faith　*1Th 3:10*

LAD

let it not be grievous because　*Ge 21:12*
of the *l.*
death of the *l.* (A)　*Ge 21:16*
and God heard the voice of　*Ge 21:17*
the *l.*
arise, lift up the *l.*; she gave　*Ge 21:18;*
the *l.* drink　　　　　　　　　*21:19*
God was with the *l.* and he　*Ge 21:20*
grew and dwelt
I and the *l.* will go yonder and　*Ge 22:5*
worship
he said, Lay not thine hand　*Ge 22:12*
upon the *l.*
the *l.* was with the sons of　*Ge 37:2*
Bilhah
the *l.* is not (B)(R)　*Ge 37:30; 42:22*
do not sin against the *l.* (B)　*Ge 42:22*
send the *l.* with me, and we　*Ge 43:8*
will arise and go
we said, The *l.* cannot leave　*Ge 44:22*
his father
my father, and the *l.* be not　*Ge 44:31;*
with us　　　　　　　　　　　*44:34*
thy servant became surety for　*Ge 44:32*
the *l.*
abide instead of the *l.* let the　*Ge 44:33*
l. go up
Samson said to the *l.* that　*J'g 16:26*
held him
the *l.* to Eli (B)　*1Sa 1:25; 3:8*
the *l.* girded (B)　*1Sa 2:18*
and behold I will send a *l.*　*1Sa 20:21*
saying, Go
Jonathan said to the *l.*, Run,　*1Sa 20:36*
as the *l.* ran
Jonathan cried after the *l.*,　*1Sa 20:37;*
Make speed　　　　　　　　　　*20:38*
but the *l.* knew not any thing,　*1Sa 20:39*
only David
Jonathan gave his artillery to　*1Sa 20:40*
his *l.*
a *l.* saw them and told　*2Sa 17:18*
Absalom
a mere *l.* (A)(B)　*1Ki 3:7*
the *l.* will fare (B)　*1Ki 14:3*
there is a *l.* here hath five　*Joh 6:9*
barley loaves

LADDER

Jacob dreamed, and behold a　*Ge 28:12*
l. set up

LADE

l. your beasts, and go, get you　*Ge 45:17*
did *l.* you with a heavy yoke　*1Ki 12:11*
l. men with burdens grievous　*Lu 11:46*

LADED

they *l.* their asses with the　*Ge 42:26*
corn
and *l.* every man his ass, and　*Ge 44:13*
bare burdens, with those that *l. Ne 4:17*
l. us with such things as were　*Ac 28:10*

LADEN

ten asses *l.* with the good　*Ge 45:23*
things
ten she asses *l.* with corn and　*Ge 45:23*
And Jesse took an ass *l.* with　*1Sa 16:20*
bread
our oxen well *l.* (E)　*Ps 144:14*
fountains *l.* with water (A)　*Pr 8:24*
l. with blood (E)　*Pr 28:17*
people *l.* with iniquity, a seed of *Isa 1:4*
carriages were heavily *l.* (S)　*Isa 46:1*
all ye that labour and are　*M't 11:28*
heavy *l.*
captive silly women *l.* with sins　*2Ti 3:6*

LADETH

that *l.* himself with thick clay　*Hab 2:6*

LADIES

Her wise *l.* answered her　*J'g 5:29*
l. of Persia and Media say this　*Es 1:18*
day

LADING

bringing in sheaves, and *l.*　*Ne 13:15*
asses
not only of the *l.* and ship　*Ac 27:10*

LADS

me from all evil, bless the *l.*　*Ge 48:16*
some *l.* came (E)　*2Ki 2:23*

LAD'S

his life is bound up in the *l.*　*Ge 44:30*
life

LADY

be called, The *l.* of kingdoms　*Isa 47:5*
thou saidst, I shall be a *l.* for　*Isa 47:7*
ever
unto the elect *l.* and her children　*2Jo 1*
I beseech thee, *l.*, not as though　*2Jo 5*

LAEL

shall be Eliasaph the son of *L. Nu 3:24*

LAG

never *l.* in zeal (A)　*Ro 12:11*
not to become *l.* (N)　*Heb 6:12*

LAHAD

Jahath begat Ahumai, and *L.*　*1Ch 4:2*

LAHAI-ROI

came from the way of the　*Ge 24:62*
well *L.*
and Isaac dwelt by the well *L. Ge 25:11*

LAHMAM

And Cabbon, and *L.* and　*Jos 15:40*
Kithlish

LAHMI

the son of Jair slew *L.* the　*1Ch 20:5*

LAID

l. it upon both their shoulders　*Ge 9:23*
l. each piece one against　*Ge 15:10*
another
l. hold upon his hand　*Ge 19:16*
l. it upon Isaac, *l.* wood in　*Ge 22:6*
order
l. him on the altar　*Ge 22:9*
l. rods before their eyes　*Ge 30:41*
l. by her veil　*Ge 38:19*
l. up his garment by her, until　*Ge 39:16*
l. up the food in the cities　*Ge 41:48*
l. it upon Ephraim's head　*Ge 48:14;*
　　　　　　　　　　　　　　　48:17
l. it in the flags by the river　*Ex 2:3*
l. up till the morning　*Ex 16:24; 16:34*
l. before their faces all these　*Ex 19:7*
l. on him a sum of money　*Ex 21:30*
l. not his hand upon elders　*Ex 24:11*
l. their hands upon bullock　*Le 8:14;*
　　　　　　　　　　　　　　8:18, 22
l. incense thereon　*Nu 16:18*
l. up the rods before the Lord　*Nu 17:7*
　　　　　　　　　　　　　　Nu 21:30;
Ps 79:7; Isa 15:1; 23:1, 14; 64:11;
Jer 4:7; 27:17; Eze 6:6; 12:20; 19:7; 26:2
　　　　　　29:12; Am 7:9; Na 3:7
　　　　　　　　　　　　　　Nu 27:23;
l. hands upon
De 34:9; 2Ki 11:16; 2Ch 23:15; 29:23;
M't 18:28; 19:15; 26:50; M'k 6:5; 14:51;
Lu 4:40; 13:13; Ac 4:3; 5:18; 6:6; 8:17;
　　　　　　　13:3; 19:6; 21:27; 28:8
l. upon us hard bondage　*De 26:6*
l. down　　　　　　　　　*Jos 2:8;*
4:8; Ru 3:7; 1Sa 3:2-3; 2Sa 13:8

l. them out before Lord　*Jos 7:23;*
　　　　　　　　　　　　　　1Sa 10:25
l. great stones in the cave's　*Jos 10:27*
mouth
l. wait　　　　　　　*J'g 9:34; 9:43; 16:2;*
1Sa 15:2-5; Job 31:9; La 4:19; Ac 23:30
l. it upon shoulder　*J'g 9:48*
l. hold on　*J'g 19:29;*
　　1Sa 15:27; M't 14:3; 26:57; M'k 6:17
l. it in her bosom　*Ru 4:16; 1Ki 3:20*
l. foundation　*1Ki 6:37;*
16:34; Ezr 3:6, 10-12; 5:16; 6:3;
Isa 44:28; Hag 2:18; Zec 4:9; 8:9;
　　　　　　　　Lu 14:29; Heb 1:10
l. siege　*1Ki 15:27; 2Ch 32:9; Mic 5:1*
l. him down　*1Ki 17:19;*
　　　　　　19:6; 21:4; 2Ki 4:21
l. it upon the boil　*2Ki 20:7*
l. up in store　*2Ki 20:17*
greatness of the burdens *l.*　*2Ch 24:27*
upon him
l. the beams　*Ne 3:3; 3:6*
l. a burden upon (S)　*Ne 5:15*
l. not their hand　*Es 9:10; 9:15-16*
l. a tribute　*Es 10:1*
l. horn in dust (B)(E)(R)　*Job 16:15*
l. up for his treasures (S)　*Job 20:26*
l. hand upon mouth　*Job 29:9*
l. on him the whole world　*Job 34:13*
(A)(R)
l. corner stone　*Job 38:6*
l. me down and slept　*Ps 3:5*
l. to my charge things I knew　*Ps 35:11*
not
l. in the grave　*Ps 49:14*
l. in the balance　*Ps 62:9*
l. Jerusalem in heaps　*Ps 79:1*
l. snare for me　*Ps 119:110;*
　　　　　141:9; 142:3; Jer 50:24
l. it upon my mouth　*Isa 6:7*
l. waste (E)　*Isa 24:3;*
Jer 4:20; 25:36; 48:1, 15, 20; 49:3
l. foundations of the earth　*Isa 48:13;*
　　　　51:13; Job 38:4; Ps 102:25; 104:5
l. waste (A)　*Jer 4:20;*
　　　　　　　　48:1; 49:3; Zec 11:2
l. waste (B)　*Jer 4:20;*
　　　　25:36; 48:1, 20; 49:3
l. land desolate　*Jer 33:29; 35:12*
it is *l.* waste (R)　*Jer 48:1; 48:20; 49:3*
no hands are *l.* upon her (S)　*La 4:6*
foundations *l.* bare (B)(R)　*Eze 13:14*
l. axe to root of trees　*M't 3:10; Lu 3:9*
l. sick of a fever　*M't 8:14*
l. it in his own new tomb　*M't 27:60*
l. sick in the streets　*M'k 6:56*
l. them up in their hearts　*Lu 1:66*
l. him in a manger　*Lu 2:7*
l. at his gate full of sores　*Lu 16:20*
no man *l.* hands on him　*Joh 7:30;*
　　　　　　　　　　　　　7:44; 8:20
Where have ye *l.* him　*Joh 11:34; 11:41*
l. aside his garments　*Joh 13:4*
There *l.* they Jesus　*Joh 19:42;*
　　　　　　　　　　　20:2, 13, 15
l. daily at the gate of the temple　*Ac 3:2*
l. them down at apostles' feet　*Ac 4:35;*
　　　　　　　　　　　　　4:37; 5:2
l. them on beds and couches　*Ac 5:15*
l. down their clothes at the feet　*Ac 7:58*
l. many stripes upon them　*Ac 16:23*
l. many and grievous　*Ac 25:7*
complaints
l. crimes against him　*Ac 25:16; 25:27*
l. down their own necks　*Ro 16:4*
I have *l.* the foundation　*1Co 3:10; 3:11*
limit God *l.* down (N)(R)　*2Co 10:13*
hope which is *l.* up for you in　*Col 1:5*
l. up for me a crown of　*2Ti 4:8*
l. down his life for us　*1Jo 3:16*
l. his right hand upon me　*Re 1:17*
l. hold on the dragon, that old　*Re 20:2*

LAIDST

thou *l.* affliction upon our　*Ps 66:11*
loins

LAIN

If no man have *l.* with thee　*Nu 5:19*
some man have *l.* with thee　*Nu 5:20*
woman that hath *l.* by man　*J'g 21:11*
I have *l.* still and been quiet　*Job 3:13*
thou hast been *l.* with (S)　*Jer 3:2*
had *l.* in the grave four days　*Joh 11:17*
already
where the body of Jesus had　*Joh 20:12*
l.

LAISH

men departed, and came to L. *J'g 18:7*
went to spy out the country of *J'g 18:14*
L.
which he had, and came unto *J'g 18:27*
L.
the name of the city was L. *J'g 18:29*
David's wife, to Phalti the *1Sa 25:44*
son of L.
even from Phaltiel the son of *2Sa 3:15*
L.
cause it to be heard unto L. *Isa 10:30*

LAKE

into the *l.* and drowned (P) *M't 8:32*
hear, stood by the *l.* of *Lu 5:1*
Gennesareth
saw two ships standing by the *l. Lu 5:2*
over unto the other side of the *Lu 8:22*
l.
down a storm of wind on the *l. Lu 8:23*
down a steep place into the *l. Lu 8:33*
both were cast alive into a *l. Re 19:20*
of fire
them was cast into the *l.* of *Re 20:10*
fire
and hell were cast into the *l. Re 20:14*
of fire
of life was cast into the *l.* of *Re 20:15*
fire
their part in the *l.* which *Re 21:8*
burneth

LAKUM

Nekeb, and Jabneel, unto L. *Jos 19:33*

LAMA

saying, Eli, Eli, *l. M't 27:46*
sabachthani
saying, Eloi, Eloi, *l. M'k 15:34*
sabachthani

LAMB

but where is the *l.* for a *Ge 22:7*
burnt offering
my son, God will provide *Ge 22:8*
himself a *l.*
they shall take to them every *Ex 12:3;*
man a *l.* *12:21*
your *l.* shall be without *Ex 12:5*
blemish, a male
an ass shalt thou redeem with *Ex 13:13;*
a *l.* *34:20*
one *l.* offer in the morning, *Ex 29:39;*
and the other *l.* offer at evening *29:41;*
Nu 28:4
with a *l.* a tenth deal of flour *Ex 39:40;*
mingled *Nu 28:21, 29; 29:4, 10, 15*
if he offer a *l. Le 3:7;*
4:32; 5:6; 22:23; 23:12
he shall take away the fat, as *Le 4:35*
the fat of a *l.*
if he be not able to bring a *l. Le 5:7;*
12:8
take a *l.* of the first year *Le 9:3;*
without blemish *14:10; Nu 6:12; 7:15, 21*
the priest shall take the *l.* and *Le 14:12*
offer him
slay the *l.; l.* of *Le 14:13;*
trespass-offering *14:24*
that killeth an ox, or a *l.* or *Le 17:3*
goat in the camp
shall offer a *l.* without blemish *Le 23:12*
offer one he *l.,* ewe *l.* for a *Nu 6:14*
sin offering
shalt prepare with the sacrifice *Nu 15:5*
for one *l.*
thus done for one *l. Nu 15:11;*
28:7, 13-14; Eze 46:15
Samuel offered a sucking *l.* to *1Sa 7:9*
the Lord
there came a lion and bear *1Sa 17:34*
and took a *l.*
took the poor man's *l.* and *2Sa 12:4*
dressed it
and he shall restore the *l. 2Sa 12:6*
fourfold
the wolf also shall dwell with *Isa 11:6*
the *l.*
send ye the *l.* to the ruler of *Isa 16:1*
the land
was brought as *l.* to the *Isa 53:7;*
slaughter *Jer 11:19*
the wolf and the *l.* shall feed *Isa 65:25*
together

that sacrificeth a *l.* as if he cut *Isa 66:3*
off dog's neck
one *l.* out of flock for a *Eze 45:15*
peace offering
a *l.* of the first year thou *Eze 46:13*
shalt prepare
Lord will feed them as *l.* in a *Ho 4:16*
large place
behold *l.* of God that takes *Joh 1:29;*
away sin *1:36*
like a *l.* dumb before the *Ac 8:32*
shearer
as of a *l.* without blemish and *1Pe 1:19*
spot
in the midst of the elders stood *Re 5:6*
a *l.* slain
the four beasts fell down before *Re 5:8*
the *l.*
saying, Worthy is the *l.* that *Re 5:12*
was slain
honour, glory, and power, be *Re 5:13*
to the *l.* for ever
I saw when the *l.* opened one of *Re 6:1*
the seals
and hide us from the wrath of *Re 6:16*
the *l.* that sits
a great multitude stood before *l. Re 7:9*
clothed
saying, Salvation to our God *Re 7:10*
and to the *l.*
and made them white in the *Re 7:14*
blood of the *l.*
for the *l.* shall feed and lead *Re 7:17*
them to fountains
they overcame him by the *Re 12:11*
blood of the *l.*
the *l.* slain from the foundation *Re 13:8*
of the world
he had two horns like a *l.* and *Re 13:11*
spake as dragon
I looked, and lo, a *l.* stood on *Re 14:1*
the mount Sion
these are they that follow the *l. Re 14:4*
whithersoever
tormented in the presence of *Re 14:10*
angels and the *l.*
they sing the song of Moses *Re 15:3*
and song of the *l.*
war with the *l.* and the *l.* shall *Re 17:14*
overcome
for the marriage of the *l.* is *Re 19:7*
come, and his wife
that are called to the marriage *Re 19:9*
supper of the *l.*
the names of the twelve *Re 21:14*
apostles of the *l.*
God Almighty and the *l.* are *Re 21:22*
the temple of it
God did lighten it, and the *l. Re 21:23*
is light thereof
proceeding out of throne of *Re 22:1;*
God and of *l.* *22:3*

LAMBS

and Jacob did separate the *l. Ge 30:40*
rams twelve, *l.* of the first year *Nu 7:87*
twelve
sixty *l. Nu 7:88*
fourteen *l. Nu 29:13;*
29:15, 17, 20, 23, 26, 29, 32
drink offerings for the *Nu 29:18*
bullocks, *l.* and rams
milk of sheep, with fat of *l. De 32:14*
and rams
but Saul spared the best of the *1Sa 15:9*
l.
Moab rendered to Israel *2Ki 3:4*
100,000 *l.*
they offered to the Lord a *1Ch 29:21*
thousand *l.*
priests killed *l.* and sprinkled *1Ch 29:22*
blood
the number of burnt *2Ch 29:32*
offerings two hundred *l.*
Josiah gave to the people *l. 2Ch 35:7*
and kids
that thou mayest buy speedily *Ezr 7:17*
l.
the wicked shall be as the fat *Ps 37:20*
of *l.*
mountains skipped, little hills *Ps 114:4*
skipped like *l.*
ye little hills that skipped like *Ps 114:6*
l. are for thy clothing, and *Pr 27:26*
goats
I delight not in the blood of *l. Isa 1:11*
or goats

then shall the *l.* feed after their *Isa 5:17*
manner
the sword of the Lord filled *Isa 34:6*
with blood of *l.*
he shall gather the *l.* with his *Isa 40:11*
arm, carry
I will bring them like *l.* to *Jer 51:40*
slaughter
Arabia occupied with thee in *Eze 27:21*
l.
ye shall drink the blood of *l. Eze 39:18*
and rams
in the sabbath six *l. Eze 46:4*
meat offering for the *l.* as *Eze 46:5;*
able to give *46:7*
in new moons six *l. Eze 46:6*
and eat the *l.* out of the flock, *Am 6:4*
and calves
I send you forth as *l.* among *Lu 10:3*
wolves
Jesus saith to Peter, Feed my *Joh 21:15*
l.

FIVE LAMBS

five l. of the first year *Nu 7:17;*
7:23, 29, 35, 41, 47

SEVEN LAMBS

Abraham set *seven* ewe *l.* by *Ge 21:28*
themselves
what mean these *seven* ewe *l. Ge 21:29*
set by themselves
these *seven* ewe *l.* thou shalt *Ge 21:30*
take of my hand
ye shall offer with the bread *Le 23:18*
seven l.
ye shall offer *seven l.* of the *Nu 28:11;*
first year without spot *19, 27; 29:2, 8, 36*
a tenth deal throughout *Nu 28:21;*
seven l. *28:29; 29:4, 10*
they brought *seven l.* for a *2Ch 29:21*
sin offering

TWO LAMBS

two l. of the first year offer *Ex 29:38;*
Nu 28:3
on the eighth day he shall take *Le 14:10*
two l.
then ye shall sacrifice *two l.* of *Le 23:19*
the first year
on the sabbath *two l.* of the *Nu 28:9*
first year

LAMB'S

shew thee the bride, the L. wife *Re 21:9*
are written in the L. book of *Re 21:27*
life

LAME

a blind man, or a *l.* or he that *Le 21:18*
hath
as if it be *l.* or blind, or have *De 15:21*
any ill
had a son that was *l.* of his feet *2Sa 4:4*
to flee, that he fell, and became *2Sa 4:4*
l.
take away the blind and the *l. 2Sa 5:6*
Jebusites, and the *l.* and the *2Sa 5:8*
blind
the *l.* shall not come into the *2Sa 5:8*
house
yet a son, which is *l.* on his feet *2Sa 9:3*
table; and was *l.* on both his *2Sa 9:13*
feet
the king; because thy servant *2Sa 19:26*
is *l.*
the blind, and feet was I to *Job 29:15*
the *l.*
The legs of the *l.* are not equal *Pr 26:7*
spoil divided; the *l.* take the *Isa 33:23*
prey
shall the *l.* man leap as an hart *Isa 35:6*
and with them the blind and *Jer 31:8*
the *l.*
gather the *l.* (B)(E)(R) *Mic 4:6*
her that was *l.* (S) *Mic 4:6; Zep 3:19*
put *l.* for a remnant *Mic 4:7*
(B)(E)(R)
that which is *l.* (B)(E)(R) *Zep 3:19*
offer the *l.* and sick, is it not *Mal 1:8*
evil
was torn, and the *l.* and the *Mal 1:13*
sick
l. walk, the lepers are cleansed *M't 11:5;*
Lu 7:22

with them those that were *l.*   *M't 15:30*
blind
the *l.* to walk, and the blind   *M't 15:31*
to see
enter into life *l.* (S)   *M't 18:8; M'k 9:45*
the *l.* came to him in the   *M't 21:14*
temple
poor, the maimed, the *l.,* the   *Lu 14:13*
blind
the maimed and the *l.* (S)   *Lu 14:21;*
                                        Joh 5:3
man *l.* from his mother's womb   *Ac 3:2*
the *l.* man which was healed   *Ac 3:11*
held
and that were *l.,* were healed   *Ac 8:7*
which is *l.* be turned out of   *Heb 12:13*
the way

LAMECH

and Methusael begat *L.*   *Ge 4:18;*
                                    4:19, 23-24
and seven years, and begat *L.*   *Ge 5:25;*
                                    5:26, 28, 30-31
Henoch, Methuselah, *L.*   *1Ch 1:3*
Noe, which was the son of *L.*   *Lu 3:36*

LAMENT

came to *l.* and weep (B)   *Ge 23:2*
to *l.* the daughter of Jephthah   *J'g 11:40*
And her gates shall *l.* and   *Isa 3:26*
mourn
shall mourn and grieve (B)   *Isa 3:26*
cast angle into the brooks shall   *Isa 19:8*
l.
fishermen shall *l.*   *Isa 19:8*
(A)(B)(E)(R)
They shall *l.* for the teats, for   *Isa 32:12*
beat upon their breasts   *Isa 32:12*
(A)(E)(R)
beat your breasts in mourning   *Isa 32:12*
(B)
you with sackcloth, *l.* and howl   *Jer 4:8*
neither go to *l.* nor bemoan   *Jer 16:5*
them
neither shall men *l.* for them   *Jer 16:6*
They shall not *l.* for him,   *Jer 22:18*
saying
they will *l.* thee, saying, Ah   *Jer 34:5*
lord
l. and run to and fro by the   *Jer 49:3*
hedges
the rampart and the wall to *l.*   *La 2:8*
wall and rampart to languish   *La 2:8*
(B)
for thee, and *l.* over thee,   *Eze 27:32*
saying
wherewith they shall *l.* her   *Eze 32:16*
daughters of the nations shall   *Eze 32:16*
l. her
shall *l.* for her, even for   *Eze 32:16*
Egypt
l. like a virgin girded with   *Joe 1:8*
Wail like a virgin (B)   *Joe 1:8*
Gird yourselves and *l.,* ye   *Joe 1:13*
priests
Gird yourselves and mourn   *Joe 1:13*
(B)
l. and wail (S)   *Mic 1:8*
and *l.* with a doleful   *Mic 2:4*
lamentation
That ye shall weep and *l.,* but   *Joh 16:20*
you shall weep and grieve   *Joh 16:20*
(A)
you will be weeping and   *Joh 16:20*
mourning (B)
beat breasts, mourn, *l.* (A)(N)   *Re 1:7*
shall bewail her, and *l.* for her   *Re 18:9*
weep and beat the breast for   *Re 18:9*
her (B)
weep and wail over her   *Re 18:9*
(E)(R)

LAMENTABLE

cried with a *l.* voice unto   *Da 6:20*
Daniel
cried out in a voice of anguish   *Da 6:20*
(A)
cried in tone of anguish and   *Da 6:20*
anxiety (B)
cried out in tone of anguish   *Da 6:20*
(R)

LAMENTATION

with a great and very sore *l.*   *Ge 50:10*
with this *l.* over Saul and over   *2Sa 1:17*

and their widows made no *l.*   *Ps 78:64*
widows made no mourning   *Ps 78:64*
(B)
treasure and *l.* (B)   *Pr 15:16*
as for an only son most bitter   *Jer 6:26*
l.
and take up a *l.* on high places   *Jer 7:29*
habitations of the wilderness a   *Jer 9:10*
l.
a dirge for pastures of the   *Jer 9:10*
desert (B)
and every one her neighbour *l.*   *Jer 9:20*
in Ramah, *l.* and bitter   *Jer 31:15*
weeping
There shall be *l.* generally   *Jer 48:38*
upon
every one is wailing (B)   *Jer 48:38*
daughter of Judah mourning   *La 2:5*
and *l.*
multiplied moaning and   *La 2:5*
mourning (B)
up for a *l.* for the princes of   *Eze 19:1*
Israel
take up a dirge (B)   *Eze 19:1;*
                            19:14; 28:12; 32:2; Am 8:10
This is a *l.* and shall be for a   *Eze 19:14*
l.
they shall take up a *l.* for   *Eze 26:17;*
thee, and   *27:32*
son of man, take up a *l.* for   *Eze 27:2*
Tyrus
take up a *l.* upon the king of   *Eze 28:12*
Tyrus
up a *l.* for Pharaoh king of   *Eze 32:2*
Egypt
l. wherewith they shall   *Eze 32:16*
lament her
you, even as *l.,* O house, of   *Am 5:1*
Israel
against you as a complaint (B)   *Am 5:1*
such as are skilful of *l.* to   *Am 5:16*
wailing
and all your songs into *l.*   *Am 8:10*
and lament with a doleful *l.*   *Mic 2:4*
a voice heard, *l.* and weeping   *M't 2:18*
burial, and made great *l.* over   *Ac 8:2*
him

LAMENTATIONS

women spake of Josiah in   *2Ch 35:25*
their *l.*
behold, they are written in   *2Ch 35:25*
the *l.*
fastings and their *l.* (S)   *Es 9:31*
there was written therein *l.*   *Eze 2:10*

LAMENTED

the people *l.* because the Lord   *1Sa 6:19*
had
house of Israel *l.* after the Lord   *1Sa 7:2*
and *l.* him, and buried him in   *1Sa 25:1*
Israel had *l.* him, and buried   *1Sa 28:3*
him
And David *l.* with this   *2Sa 1:17*
lamentation
the king *l.* over Abner, and   *2Sa 3:33*
said
And Jeremiah *l.* for Josiah: *2Ch 35:25*
and all
they shall not be *l.;* neither   *Jer 16:4*
shall
they shall not be *l.* neither   *Jer 25:33*
gathered
unto you, and ye have not *l.*   *M't 11:17*
which also bewailed and *l.*   *Lu 23:27*
him

LAMENTING

l. and moaning (A)(R)   *Na 2:7*

LAMP

burning *l.* that passed   *Ge 15:17*
between
smoking fire pot and flaming   *Ge 15:17*
torch (A)(E)
a smoking oven and burning   *Ge 15:17*
torch (B)
smoking fire pot and flaming   *Ge 15:17*
torch (R)
to cause the *l.* to burn always   *Ex 27:20*
l. of God went out in the   *1Sa 3:3*
temple the
For thou art my *l.,* O Lord   *2Sa 22:29*
his God give him a *l.* in   *1Ki 15:4*
Jerusalem

as a *l.* despised in the thought   *Job 12:5*
of
l. shall be dark in his   *Job 18:6*
tent (S)
the *l.* of the wicked be put   *Job 2:17;*
out   *Pr 13:9; 24:20*
his *l.* shone over my head   *Job 29:2*
(A)(E)
his *l.* shined upon my head   *Job 29:3*
(S)
thou wilt light my *l.* (S)   *Ps 18:28*
Thy word is a *l.* unto my   *Ps 119:105*
feet
ordained a *l.* for mine   *Ps 132:17*
anointed
For the commandment is a *l.*   *Pr 6:23*
(S)
l. shall be put out in   *Pr 20:20*
obscure
spirit of man is the *l.* of the   *Pr 20:27*
Lord (S)
her *l.* goeth not out by night   *Pr 31:18*
(S)
quenched like a *l.* wick   *Isa 43:17*
(S)
the salvation thereof as a *l.*   *Isa 62:1*
that
the light of the *l.* (S)   *Jer 25:10*
neither do men light a *l.* (S)   *M't 5:15;*
   M'k 4:21; Lu 8:16; 11:33
the *l.* of the body is the eyes   *M't 6:22;*
(S)   *Lu 11:34*
bright shining of a *l.* (S)   *Lu 11:36*
woman doth light a *l.* (S)   *Lu 15:8*
heaven, burning as it were a *l.*   *Re 8:10*
burning like a torch   *Re 8:10*
(A)(B)(E)(N)(P)(R)
light of a *l.* no longer be (S)   *Re 18:23*
the lamb is the *l.* thereof (S)   *Re 21:23*
they need no *l.* (S)   *Re 22:5*

LAMPS

they shall light the *l.* thereof   *Ex 25:37*
when he dresseth the *l.* he shall   *Ex 30:7*
when Aaron lighteth the *l.* at   *Ex 30:8*
even
and his *l.,* with the oil for the   *Ex 35:14*
light
candlestick, with the *l.* thereof   *Ex 39:37*
even with the *l.* to be set in   *Ex 39:37*
order
candlestick, and light the *l.*   *Ex 40:4*
thereof
he lighted the *l.* before the   *Ex 40:25*
Lord
to cause the *l.* to burn   *Le 24:2*
continually
the *l.* upon the pure candlestick   *Le 24:4*
the light, and his *l.* and his   *Nu 4:9*
tongs
unto him, When thou lightest   *Nu 8:2*
the *l.*
lighted the *l.* thereof over   *Nu 8:3*
against
and *l.* within the pitchers   *J'g 7:16*
torches inside (A)(B)(E)(R)   *J'g 7:16;*
   7:20
and held the *l.* in their left   *J'g 7:20*
hands
and the *l.* and the tongs of   *1Ki 7:49*
gold
and for their *l.* of gold, by   *1Ch 28:15*
weight
candlestick, and for the *l.*   *1Ch 28:15*
thereof
and also for the *l.* thereof   *1Ch 28:15*
the candlesticks with their *l.*   *2Ch 4:20*
that
flowers, and the *l.* and the   *2Ch 4:21*
tongs
of gold with the *l.* thereof, to   *2Ch 13:11*
burn
put out the *l.* and have not   *2Ch 29:7*
burned
Out of his mouth go burning   *Job 41:19*
l.
go burning torches   *Job 41:19*
(A)(B)(E)(R)
fire, and like the appearance   *Eze 1:13*
of *l.*
like torches moving to and fro   *Eze 1:13*
(A)(B)(E)(R)
lightning, and his eyes as lamps   *Da 10:6*
of fire
eyes like flaming torches   *Da 10:6*
(A)(B)(E)(R)
I will search Jerusalem with *l.*   *Zep 1:12*
(S)
ten virgins, which took their *l.*   *M't 25:1*

foolish took their *l.* and took *M't 25:3*
no oil
took oil in their vessels with *M't 25:4*
their *l.*
virgins arose, and trimmed *M't 25:7*
their *l.*
of your oil; for our *l.* are gone *M't 25:8*
out
and your *l.* burning (S) *Lu 12:35*

SEVEN LAMPS

thou shalt make the *seven l.* *Ex 25:37*
thereof
he made his *seven l.* of pure *Ex 37:23*
gold
the *seven l.* shall give light over *Nu 8:2*
against
and behold a candlestick and *Zec 4:2*
seven l.
there were *seven l.* of fire *Re 4:5*
burning before

LAMPSTAND

make a *l.* (S) *Ex 25:31;*
25:32-35
set the *l.* over against (S) *Ex 26:35;*
40:4, 24; Le 24:4
the *l.* and his vessels with *Ex 30:27;*
31:8; 35:14; 39:27; Nu 3:21; 4:9
he made the *l.* (S) *Ex 37:17;*
37:18-20; Nu 8:4
give light over against the *l.* *Nu 8:2;*
(S) *8:3*
a stool and a *l.* (S) *2Ki 4:10*
the *l.* of gold (S) *2Ch 13:11; Zec 4:2*
wrote over against the *l.* (S) *Da 5:5*
upon the right side of the *l.* *Zec 4:11*
(S)
but on a *l.* (S) *M't 5:15;*
M'k 4:21; Lu 8:16; 11:33
wherein was the *l.* (S) *Heb 9:2*
I saw seven golden *l.* (S) *Re 1:12;*
1:13, 20; 2:1, 5
two olive trees and two *l.* (S) *Re 11:4*

LAMPSTANDS

the *l.* of pure gold (S) *1Ki 7:49;*
1Ch 28:15; 2Ch 4:7, 20
the caldrons and *l.* (S) *Jer 52:19*

LANCE

they that hold the *l.* are cruel, *Jer 50:42*
will not
hold the bow and spear *Jer 50:42*
(B)(E)(R)

LANCES

cut themselves with swords *1Ki 18:28*
and *l.* (S)

LANCETS

cut themselves with *l.* till *1Ki 18:28*
blood

LAND

and the gold of that *l.* is good *Ge 2:12*
out of that *l.* went forth *Ge 10:11*
Ashur
get thee into a *l.* I will shew *Ge 12:1;*
thee *Ac 7:3*
and the *l.* was not able to bear *Ge 13:6*
is not the whole *l.* before thee, *Ge 13:9*
separate
country (B) *Ge 13:9; 17:8*
I will give thee and seed the *l.* *Ge 17:8;*
28:13; 35:12
behold, my *l.* is before thee, *Ge 20:15*
dwell where
of the Canaanite, in whose *l.* *Ge 24:37*
I dwell
Isaac sowed in that *l.* and *Ge 26:12*
received in year
that the *l.* perish not *Ge 41:36*
bought the *l.* so the *l.* became *Ge 47:20*
Pharaoh's
only the *l.* of the priests *Ge 47:22*
bought he not
the *l.* was corrupted by the flies *Ex 8:24*
so that the *l.* was darkened, *Ex 10:15*
and they eat
that thy days may be long *Ex 20:12*
upon the *l.*

goat bear iniquities into *l.* not *Le 16:22*
inhabited
desolate region, in the desert *Le 16:22*
(B)
and the *l.* is defiled, therefore *Le 18:25;*
18:27
that the *l.* spue not you out *Le 18:28;*
also *20:22*
then shall the *l.* keep a *Le 25:2;*
sabbath *26:34*
the *l.* shall not be sold, for the *Le 25:23*
l. is mine
the *l.* shall yield her increase *Le 26:4;*
25:19
the *l.* of your enemies shall eat *Le 26:38*
you up
and I will remember the *l.* *Le 26:42*
the *l.* also shall be left of *Le 26:43*
them, and enjoy
see the *l.* what it is, and the *Nu 13:18*
people
the *l.* is a *l.* that eateth up the *Nu 13:32*
inhabitants
surely they shall not see the *l.* *Nu 14:23*
I sware to
my servant Caleb will I bring *Nu 14:24*
to the *l.*
when ye be come into the *l.* of *Nu 15:2;*
your habitation *15:18; De 17:14; 18:9;*
26:1
delivered into thy hand his *l.* *Nu 21:34*
De 3:2
the country the Lord smote is *Nu 32:4*
a *l.* for cattle
for blood defileth the *l.* and the *Nu 35:33*
l. cannot
to him will I give the *l.* he hath *De 1:36*
that was accounted a *l.* of *De 2:20;*
giants *3:13*
a *l.* of wheat, and barley, and *De 8:8*
vines
l. wherein eat bread, *l.* whose *De 8:9*
stones are iron
was not able to bring them *De 9:28*
into the *l.*
to Jotbath, a *l.* of rivers of *De 10:7*
waters
a *l.* which the Lord thy God *De 11:12*
careth for
the whole *l.* thereof is *De 29:23*
brimstone and salt
cast them into another *l.* as at *De 29:28*
this day
found him in a desert *l.* and *De 32:10*
wilderness
he will be merciful to his *l.* *De 32:43*
and people
he said, Blessed of the Lord *De 33:13*
be his *l.*
and the Lord shewed him all *De 34:1*
the *l.*
sent two men, saying, Go view *Jos 2:1*
the *l.*
the Lord hath given you the *l.* *Jos 2:9;*
21:43
Joshua took all that *l.*, the *Jos 11:16;*
hills *11:23*
and the *l.* had rest from war *Jos 14:15*
given you a *l.* for which ye *Jos 24:13*
did not labour
the *l.* had rest forty years *J'g 3:11; 5:31*
and the *l.* had rest fourscore *J'g 3:30*
years
thou art come to fight against *J'g 11:12*
me in my *l.*
when ye go ye shall come to a *J'g 18:10*
large *l.*
till the day of the captivity of *J'g 18:30*
the *l.*
its own *l.* (A)(R) *1Sa 6:9*
my father hath troubled the *l.* *1Sa 14:29*
is not this David the king of *1Sa 21:11*
the *l.*
Abner sent, saying, Whose is *2Sa 3:12*
the *l.*
I will restore thee all the *l.* of *2Sa 9:7*
Saul
God was entreated for the *l.* *2Sa 21:14;*
24:25
and he called them the *l.* of *1Ki 9:13*
Cabul
appointed him victuals and *1Ki 11:18*
gave him *l.*
went to cry to the king for her *2Ki 8:3*
l.
since the day that she left the *l.* *2Ki 8:6*
even till now
the manner of the God of the *2Ki 17:26;*
l. *17:27*

take you to *l.* of corn and *2 Ki 18:32;*
wine *Isa 36:17*
any god delivered his *l.* *2Ki 8:33;*
Isa 36:18
2Ch 33:8
move any more out of the *l.* *2Ki 21:8;*
23:8
the king of Egypt came no *2Ki 24:7*
more out of his *l.*
left of the poor of the *l.* *2Ki 25:12;*
Jer 52:16
and the *l.* was wide, and quiet *1Ch 4:40*
men of Gath, who were born *1Ch 7:21*
in that *l.*
I will pluck them up out of *2Ch 7:20*
my *l.*
make walls, while the *l.* is yet *2Ch 14:7*
before us
when he had purged the *l.* and *2Ch 34:8*
the house
that ye may eat the good of *l.* *Ezr 9:12;*
Isa 1:19
work of wall, nor bought we *Ne 5:16*
any *l.*
for the *l.* behold we are *Ne 9:36*
servants in it
if my *l.* cry against me, or *Job 31:38*
furrows
whether for correction, or his *Job 37:13*
l. or mercy
and the barren *l.* his dwellings *Job 39:6*
the heathen are perished out *Ps 10:16*
of his *l.*
remember thee from the *l.* of *Ps 42:6*
Jordan
for they got not the *l.* in *Ps 44:3*
possession
and root thee out of the *l.* of *Ps 52:5*
the living
to take deep root, and it filled *Ps 80:9*
the *l.*
mine eyes shall be on the *Ps 101:6*
faithful of the *l.*
I will destroy all the wicked of *Ps 101:8*
the *l.*
he called for a famine on the *Ps 105:16*
l.
the *l.* brought forth frogs in *Ps 105:30*
abundance
yea, they despised the *Ps 106:24*
pleasant *l.*
and the *l.* was polluted with *Ps 106:38*
blood
he turneth the fruitful *l.* into *Ps 107:34*
barrenness
my soul thirsts after thee as a *Ps 143:6*
thirsty *l.*
lead me into the *l.* of *Ps 143:10*
uprightness
that tilleth his *l.* shall be *Pr 12:11;*
satisfied *28:19*
for the transgression of a *l.* *Pr 28:2*
many princes
woe to thee, O *l.* when thy *Ec 10:16*
king is a child
blessed art thou, O *l.* when thy *Ec 10:17*
king is son
if one look unto the *l.* behold *Isa 5:30*
sorrow
the *l.* that thou abhorrest shall *Isa 7:16*
be forsaken
because all *l.* shall become *Isa 7:24*
briers and thorns
l. of Zebulun, *l.* of Naphtali *Isa 9:1;*
M't 4:15
through the wrath of the Lord *Isa 9:19*
is *l.* darkened
they come to destroy the whole *Isa 13:5*
l.
I will break the Assyrian in *Isa 14:25*
my *l.*
woe to the *l.* shadowing with *Isa 18:1*
wings
whose *l.* the rivers have *Isa 18:2;*
spoiled *18:7*
shall be a blessing in the *Isa 19:24*
midst of the *l.*
cometh from the desert, from *Isa 21:1*
a terrible *l.*
from the *l.* of Chittim it is *Isa 23:1*
revealed
the *l.* shall be utterly emptied *Isa 24:3*
and spoiled
joy is darkened, the mirth of *Isa 24:11*
l. is gone
into the *l.* of trouble and *Isa 30:6*
anguish
as shadow of a great rock in a *Isa 32:2*
weary *l.*
on the *l.* of my people shall *Isa 32:13*
come thorns

and behold the *l.* that is very   *Isa 33:17* far off
l. thereof shall become burning   *Isa 34:9* pitch
and the thirsty *l.* springs of   *Isa 35:7* water
and lo, these from the *l.* of   *Isa 49:12* Sinim
the *l.* of thy destruction be   *Isa 49:19* too narrow
he was cut off out of the *l.* of   *Isa 53:8* the living
an iron pillar against the   *Jer 1:18* whole *l.*
wentest after me, in *l.* that not   *Jer 2:2* sown
led us through *l.* of deserts, *l.*   *Jer 2:6* of drought
when he entered, ye defiled my   *Jer 2:7;* *l.*   *3:9*
the young lions made his *l.*   *Jer 2:15* waste
how shall I give thee a   *Jer 3:19* pleasant *l.*
the whole *l.* is spoiled,   *Jer 4:20* suddenly are
strangers in a *l.* that is not   *Jer 5:19* yours
lest I make thee a *l.* not   *Jer 6:8* inhabited
the whole *l.* trembled at the   *Jer 8:16* sound
for what the *l.* perisheth and is   *Jer 9:12* burnt
because we have forsaken the   *Jer 9:19* *l.*
let us cut him off from *l.* of   *Jer 11:19* the living
how long shall *l.* mourn, herbs   *Jer 12:4* wither
from one end of the *l.* even to   *Jer 12:12* the other
I will bring again every man   *Jer 12:15* to his *l.*
brought Israel from *l.* of the   *Jer 16:15;* north   *31:16*
because they have defiled my   *Jer 16:18* *l.* they filled
inhabit wilderness in a salt *l.* not   *Jer 17:6* inhabited
to *l.* whereunto they desire to   *Jer 22:27* return
is profaneness gone forth into   *Jer 23:15* the *l.*
I will bring on that *l.* all my   *Jer 25:13* words
till the very time of his *l.* come   *Jer 27:7*
behold, all the *l.* is before thee   *Jer 40:4*
thy shame, and thy cry hath   *Jer 46:12* filled the *l.*
I will punish king of Babylon   *Jer 50:18* and his *l.*
for it is *l.* of graven images,   *Jer 50:38* they are mad
a dry *l.* a *l.* wherein no man   *Jer 51:43* dwelleth
her whole *l.* shall be   *Jer 51:47* confounded
for the *l.* is full of bloody   *Eze 7:23* crimes
they have filled the *l.* with   *Eze 8:17* violence
and the *l.* is full of blood, and   *Eze 9:9* the city
when the *l.* sinneth against me   *Eze 14:13*
bring a sword on *l.;* a   *Eze 14:17;* pestilence into *l.*   *14:19*
he took also of seed of *l.* and   *Eze 17:5* planted
he hath taken the might of   *Eze 17:13* the *l.*
both shall come forth out of   *Eze 21:19* one *l.*
thou art *l.* not cleansed nor   *Eze 22:24* rained on
should stand in the gap   *Eze 22:30* before me for the *l.*
then will I leave thee upon *l.* I   *Eze 32:4* will cast
when I bring the sword upon   *Eze 33:2* a *l.*
if when he seeth the sword   *Eze 33:3* come upon the *l.*
the *l.* is given us for   *Eze 33:24* inheritance
have appointed my *l.* into   *Eze 36:5* their possession
thou *l.* devourest up men   *Eze 36:13*
thou shalt be like cloud to   *Eze 38:9;* cover *l.*   *39:16*

I will go up to the *l.* of   *Eze 38:11* unwalled villages
and I will bring thee against   *Eze 38:16* my *l.*
that they may cleanse the *l.*   *Eze 39:12*
remain upon the face of the   *Eze 39:14* *l.* (S)
thus shall they cleanse the *l.*   *Eze 39:16*
and this shall be the border   *Eze 47:15* of the *l.*
he shall stand in the glorious   *Da 11:16;*   *11:4*
therefore shall *l.* mourn and   *Ho 4:3* languish
for a nation is come up upon   *Joe 1:6* my *l.* strong
the *l.* is as the garden of Eden   *Joe 2:3* before them
then will the Lord be jealous   *Joe 2:18* for his *l.*
fear not, O *l.* be glad; and   *Joe 2:21;* parted my *l.*   *3:2*
she is forsaken upon her *l.*   *Am 5:2* there is none
the *l.* is not able to bear all his   *Am 7:10* words
even to make the poor of the *l.*   *Am 8:4* to fail
shall not the *l.* tremble for this   *Am 8:8*
Lord God of hosts is he that   *Am 9:5* toucheth the *l.*
I consume all things from off   *Zep 1:2* the *l.*
whole *l.* shall be devoured by   *Zep 1:18* fire of jealousy
I will get them praise and   *Zep 3:19* fame in every *l.*
ho, ho, flee from the *l.* of the   *Zec 2:6* north
I will remove the iniquity of   *Zec 3:9* that *l.* in one
of a crown lifted up, as an   *Zec 9:16* ensign upon his *l.*
the *l.* shall mourn, every   *Zec 12:12* family apart
and the unclean spirit to pass   *Zec 13:2* out of the *l.*
in all the *l.* two parts therein   *Zec 13:8* shall be cut off
all the *l.* shall be turned as a   *Zec 14:10* plain
for ye shall be a delightsome   *Mal 3:12* *l.*
fame hereof went abroad into   *M't 9:26* all that *l.*
more tolerable for the *l.* of   *M't 10:15;* Sodom   *11:24*
ye compass sea and *l.* to   *M't 23:15* make one proselyte
was darkness over all the *l.*   *M't 27:45;*   *M'k 15:33*
ship was in the sea, and he   *M'k 6:47* alone on the *l.*
neither fit for the *l.* nor   *Lu 14:35* dunghill
there arose a great famine in   *Lu 15:14* that *l.*
immediately the ship was at   *Joh 6:21* the *l.*
Peter drew net to *l.* full of   *Joh 21:11* great fishes
having *l.* sold it, and brought   *Ac 4:37* money
tell me whether ye sold the *l.* for   *Ac 5:8* so much
when it was day, they knew   *Ac 27:39* not the *l.*
cast themselves into the sea,   *Ac 27:43* and get to *l.*
that they escaped all safe to *l.*   *Ac 27:44*
l. produced its crops (A)(N)   *Jas 5:18*

DRY LAND

let *dry l.* appear; called *dry l.*   *Ge 1:9;* earth   *1:10*
of all that was in the *dry l.*   *Ge 7:22* died
take and pour water on *dry l.*   *Ex 4:9* and become blood on *dry l.*
and the Lord made the sea   *Ex 14:21* *dry l.*
Israel walked on *dry l.*   *Ex 14:29;*   *15:19; Ne 9:11*
priests' feet were lifted up on   *Jos 4:18* *dry l.*
Israel came over this Jordan   *Jos 4:22* on *dry l.*
my flesh longeth for thee in a   *Ps 63:1* *dry l.*

he turned the sea into *dry l.*   *Ps 66:6*
but the rebellious dwell in a *dry*   *Ps 68:6* *l.*
sea is his, and his hands   *Ps 95:5* formed *dry l.*
I will make *dry l.* springs of   *Isa 41:18* water
hindermost of nations shall   *Jer 50:12* be a *dry l.*
her cities are a *dry l.* and   *Jer 51:43* wilderness
I set her as a *dry l.* and slay   *Ho 2:3* her
I fear God, who made sea and   *Jon 1:9* *dry l.*
the fish vomited out Jonah on   *Jon 2:10* the *dry l.*
and I will shake the sea and   *Hag 2:6* *dry l.*
they passed the Red sea as   *Heb 11:29* by *dry l.*

IN THE LAND

the Canaanite dwelt then *in the*   *Ge 13:7* *l.*
and we shall be fruitful *in the*   *Ge 26:22* *l.*
the plenty shall not be known   *Ge 41:31* *in the l.*
I shall know, ye shall traffick   *Ge 42:34* *in the l.*
for to sojourn *in the l.* are we   *Ge 47:4* come
go ye, sacrifice to your God *in*   *Ex 8:25* *the l.*
to-morrow the Lord shall do this   *Ex 9:5* thing *in the l.*
he will say, They are entangled   *Ex 14:3* *in the l.*
I will give peace *in the l.*   *Le 26:6* any ye
that ye may do them *in the l.*   *De 4:14* whither ye go
that it may go well with thee   *De 5:16* *in the l.*
that you may prolong days *in*   *De 11:9;* *the l.*   *11:21; 25:15*
God hath given thee rest *in*   *De 25:19*
he shall bless thee *in the l.*   *De 28:8;*   *28:11; 30:16*
fear the Lord as long as ye   *De 31:13* live *in the l.*
there was no magistrate *in the*   *J'g 18:7* *l.*
and if he be *in the l.* I will   *1Sa 23:23* search
O that I were made judge *in*   *2Sa 15:4* *the l.*
if there be famine *in the l.*   *1Ki 8:37;*   *2Ch 6:28*
fear thee so long as they live   *2Ch 6:31* *in the l.*
and Jehoshaphat set judges *in*   *2Ch 19:5* *the l.*
inquire of wonder that was   *2Ch 32:31* done *in the l.*
nor is it found *in the l.* of the   *Job 28:13* living
goodness of the Lord *in the l.*   *Ps 27:13* of living
they devise deceitful matter *in*   *Ps 35:20* *the l.*
they burnt the synagogues of   *Ps 74:8* God *in the l.*
walk before Lord *in the l.* of   *Ps 116:9* living
thou art my portion *in the l.*   *Ps 142:5* of living
for honey shall every one eat   *Isa 7:22* *in the l.*
in the l. of uprightness he will   *Isa 26:10* deal unjustly
I shall not see the Lord *in*   *Isa 38:11* *the l.* of living
shall all of them *in the l.*   *Eze 20:40* serve me
I shall set glory *in the l.* of   *Eze 26:20* the living
caused terror *in the l.* of the   *Eze 32:23;* living   *24:32*
I will make them one nation   *Eze 37:22* *in the l.*
in the l. shall be his possession   *Eze 45:8* in Israel
because there is no truth *in the*   *Ho 4:1* *l.*
I will raise up a Shepherd *in*   *Zec 11:16* *the l.*

there shall be great distress *in* Lu 21:23
the *l.*
by faith he sojourned *in the l.* Heb 11:9

OUR LAND

buy us and *our l.* for bread, Ge 47:19
and we and *our l.*
and *our l.* shall yield her Ps 85:12
increase
the voice of the turtle is heard Ca 2:12
in *our l.*
the Assyrian shall come into Mic 5:5
our l.
he shall deliver us when he Mic 5:6
cometh into *our l.*

OWN LAND

Jethro went into his *own l.* Ex 18:27;
Nu 10:30
a true report I heard in my 1Ki 10:6;
own l. 2Ch 9:5
Israel carried out of their 2Ki 17:23
own l.
take you to a land like your 2Ki 18:32;
own l. Isa 36:17
and he shall return to his *own* 2Ki 19:7
l.
he returned with shame to 2Ch 32:21
his *own l.*
and flee every one to his *own* Isa 13:14
l.
choose Israel, and set them in Isa 14:1
their *own l.*
and fall by the sword in his Isa 37:7
own l.
they shall dwell in their *own l.* Jer 23:8;
27:11
return to Egypt, into their Jer 37:7;
own l. 42:12
they shall flee every one of his Jer 50:16
own l.
I will bring them into their Eze 34:13;
own l. 36:24; 37:14, 21; 39:28
when Israel dwelt in their Eze 36:17
own l.
Israel led captive out of their Am 7:11
own l.

THEIR LAND, LANDS

wherefore the priests sold not Ge 47:22
their l.
but I said, Ye shall inherit Le 20:24
their l.
Aaron had no inheritance in Nu 18:20
their l.
for I will not give you of *their* De 2:5;
l. 2:9
bring thee, and give thee *their* De 4:38;
l. J'g 6:9
we took *their l.* and gave it De 29:8;
Jos 10:42
and the Lord rooted them out De 29:28
of *their l.*
return and pray to thee 1Ki 8:48
toward *their l.*
forgive their sin and heal 2Ch 7:14
their l.
he gave them flaming fire in Ps 105:32
their l.
and gave *their l.* for an Ps 135:12;
heritage 136:21
their l. is full of silver and Isa 2:7
horses
their l. also is full of idols, they Isa 2:8
worship
their l. shall be soaked with Isa 34:7
blood
behold, I will pluck them out Jer 12:14
of *their l.*
I will bring them again into Jer 16:15
their l.
not forsaken, tho' *their l.* was Jer 51:5
filled with sin
and they shall be safe in *their* Eze 34:27
l.
when they dwelt safely in Eze 39:26
their l. and
and I will plant them on *their* Am 9:15
l.

THIS LAND

the Lord said, Unto thy seed I Ge 12:7;
will give *this l.* 15:18; 24:7; 48:4;
Ex 32:13
I will bring thee again into Ge 28:15
this l.

get thee out from *this l.* and Ge 31:13
return to land
and God will bring you out of Ge 50:24
this l.
why hath the Lord brought us Nu 14:3
unto *this l.*
then he will bring us into *this* Nu 14:8
l. and give it
let *this l.* be given to thy Nu 32:5
servants
this l. shall be your Nu 32:22
possession of the Lord
this l. shall fall to you Nu 34:2;
34:13; Jos 13:2
but I must die in *this l.* and not De 4:22
go over
and he hath given us *this l.* De 26:9;
Jos 1:13
wherefore hath the Lord De 29:24;
done this to *this l.* 29:27; 1Ki 9:8;
2Ch 7:21
no league with the inhabitants J'g 2:2
of *this l.*
Lord said, Go up against 2Ki 18:25;
this l. Isa 36:10
they shall come again into 2Ch 30:9
this l.
say, The sword shall not be in Jer 14:15
this l.
their fathers that begat them in Jer 16:3
this l.
both great and small shall die Jer 16:6
in *this l.*
therefore I will cast you out of Jer 16:13
this l.
and he shall see *this l.* no Jer 22:12
more
and I will bring them again to Jer 24:6
this l.
and I will bring them against Jer 25:9
this l.
and *this* whole *l.* shall be a Jer 25:11
desolation
a man who prophesied Jer 26:20
against *this l.*
houses shall be possessed Jer 32:15
again in *this l.*
and I will plant them in *this l.* Jer 32:41
assuredly
the king of Babylon shall Jer 36:29
destroy *this l.*
shall not come against you, Jer 37:19
nor *this l.*
if ye abide in *this l.* I will Jer 42:10
build you
if ye say, We will not dwell in Jer 42:13
this l.
I will pluck up even *this* whole Jer 45:4
l.
to us is *this l.* given in Eze 11:15
possession
this l. shall fall unto you for Eze 47:14
inheritance
this is the *l.* which ye shall Eze 48:29
divide
he removed him into *this l.* Ac 7:4
wherein

THY LAND

six years thou shalt sow *thy l.* Ex 23:10
nothing shall cast their young Ex 23:26
in *thy l.*
they shall not dwell in *thy l.* Ex 23:33
lest they
nor shall any man desire *thy l.* Ex 34:24
Israel said, Let me pass Nu 21:22;
through *thy l.* De 2:27; J'g 11:17, 19
he will bless the fruit of *thy l.* De 7:13
bury him, that *thy l.* be not De 21:23
defiled
to give the rain to *thy l.* in his De 28:12
season
cursed shall be the fruit of De 28:18;
thy l. 28:42
and to do great things for *thy* 2Sa 7:23
l.
shall famine come to thee 2Sa 24:13
thy l.
thou hast been favourable to Ps 85:1
thy l.
his wings shall fill the breadth Isa 8:8
of *thy l.*
because thou hast destroyed Isa 14:20
thy l.
pass through *thy l.* as a river, Isa 23:10
O Tarshish
violence shall no more be Isa 60:18
heard in *thy l.*

nor shall *thy l.* be termed Isa 62:4
desolate; *thy l.* shall be married
and I will set darkness upon Eze 32:8
thy l.
and *thy l.* shall be divided by Am 7:17
line
I will cut off the cities of *thy l.* Mic 5:11
gates of *thy l.* shall be set wide Na 3:13
open

YOUR LAND

I have bought you and *your l.* Ge 47:23
this day
when ye reap the harvest of Le 19:9;
your l. 23:22
children, which they begat in Le 25:45
your l.
ye shall eat, and dwell in *your* Le 26:5
l. safely
nor shall the sword go through Le 26:6
your l.
for *your l.* shall not yield her Le 26:20
increase
if you go to war in *your l.* then Nu 10:9
blow
get into *your l.* Nu 22:19
this shall be *your l.* Nu 34:12
give you the rain of *your l.* in De 11:14
season
he will lighten his hand from 1Sa 6:5
off *your l.*
and have served strange gods Jer 5:19
in *your l.*
prophesy, to remove you far Jer 27:10
from *your l.*
therefore is *your l.* a Jer 44:22
desolation and astonishment

LANDED

when we had *l.* at Caesarea Ac 18:22
and sailed into Syria, and *l.* at Ac 21:3
Tyre

LANDING

l. at Syracuse we tarried three Ac 28:12
days

LANDMARK

thou shalt not remove thy De 19:14;
neighbour's *l.* Pr 22:28; 23:10
cursed that removeth De 27:17
neighbour's *l.*

LANDMARKS

some remove the *l.*, and Job 24:2
take away

LANDS

all these *l.* (A)(E)(R) Ge 26:3
and the dearth was in all *l.* Ge 41:54;
41:57
not ought left but our bodies Ge 47:18
and *l.*
wherefore they sold not their Ge 47:22
l.
restore those *l.* again J'g 11:13
peaceably
gods of the *l.* (B) 2Ki 18:35
heard what the kings of 2Ki 19:11;
Assyria have done to all *l.* Isa 37:11
the fame of David went into 1Ch 14:17
all *l.*
glory through all *l.* 1Ch 22:5
(A)(B)(R)
priests after the manner of 2Ch 13:9
other *l.*
fear fell on all the *l.* round 2Ch 17:10
about
kingdoms of all *l.* (B) 2Ch 20:29
as the gods of other *l.* have 2Ch 32:17
not delivered
neighboring. (B) Ezr 3:3
have not separated from people Ezr 9:1
of *l.*
have mingled with people of Ezr 9:2;
those *l.* 9:11
some said, We have mortgaged Ne 5:3;
our *l.* 5:4
other men have our *l.* and Ne 5:5
vineyards
restore I pray you, this day Ne 5:11
their *l.*
had separated from people of Ne 10:28
the *l.*

call their *l.* after their own   *Ps 49:11*
names
make a joyful noise all ye *l.*   *Ps 66:1;*
     100:1
and gave them the *l.* of the   *Ps 105:44*
heathen
lifted his hand, to scatter   *Ps 106:27*
them in the *l.*
gathered them out of the *l.*   *Ps 107:3*
from east
brought up Israel from *l.*   *Jer 16:15*
whither
all *l.* (B)(E)   *Jer 23:3; Eze 22:4*
have given all these *l.* to   *Jer 27:6*
Nebuchadnezzar
into a land which is glory of   *Eze 20:6;*
all *l.*   *20:15*
gathered them out of their   *Eze 39:27*
enemies' *l.*
hath forsaken houses, *l.*   *M't 19:29;*
     M'k 10:29
shall receive an hundred   *M'k 10:30*
fold, *l.*
as many as were possessors of *l.*   *Ac 4:34*
sold

LANES

go out quickly into *l.* of the   *Lu 14:21*
city
great streets and small streets   *Lu 14:21*
(A)
streets and alleys of the city   *Lu 14:21*
(B)(N)
roads and hedgerows (P)   *Lu 14:21*

LANGUAGE

after his *l.* (A)(B)(R)   *Ge 10:5*
whole earth was of one *l.* and   *Ge 11:1*
speech
people is one, and they have all   *Ge 11:6*
one *l.*
go down, and there counfound   *Ge 11:7;*
their *l.*   *11:9*
confuse their speech (B)   *Ge 11:7*
whose *l.* thou shalt (A)   *De 28:49*
speak in the Syrian *l.*   *2Ki 18:26;*
     Isa 36:11
Speak to servants in (A)   *2Ki 18:26*
Rab-shakeh cried in the   *2Ki 18:28;*
Jews' *l.*   *Isa 36:13*
in the Jewish *l.*   *2Ch 32:18*
(A)(B)(E)(R)
written in Syrian *l.* (A)(B)   *Ezr 4:7*
children could not speak in   *Ne 13:24*
Jews' *l.* but according to *l.* of
the *l.* of Ashdod (R)   *Ne 13:24*
to every people after their *l.*   *Es 1:22;*
     3:12; 8:9
every people in own tongue (B)   *Es 1:22*
no *l.* where their voice is not   *Ps 19:3*
heard
no speech, nor spoken word   *Ps 19:3*
(A)
no speech, nor words their   *Ps 19:3*
voice (B)(R)
where I heard a *l.* that I   *Ps 81:5*
understood not
speech of one whom I know   *Ps 81:5*
not (A)
speech of those I knew not (B)   *Ps 81:5*
a voice I had not known (R)   *Ps 81:5*
house of Jacob from a people   *Ps 114:1*
of strange *l.*
a people of alien speech (B)   *Ps 114:1*
their *l.* and doings (B)   *Isa 3:8*
five cities speak the *l.* of   *Isa 19:18*
Canaan
another *l.* will he speak (B)   *Isa 28:11*
a nation, whose *l.* thou   *Jer 5:15*
knowest not
not sent to a people of hard *l.*   *Eze 3:5;*
     3:6
I decree, every *l.* that speaketh   *Da 3:29*
amiss
I will turn to the people a pure   *Zep 3:9*
l.
understand my *l.* (N)   *Joh 8:43*
in their own *l.* (R)   *Ac 1:19*
every man heard them speak in   *Ac 2:6*
his own *l.*
speak in his own dialect (A)   *Ac 2:6*
our own native *l.* (P)   *Ac 2:11*
in the Hebrew *l.* (B)(N)   *Ac 21:40;*
     26:14
in their own *l.* (N)   *Ac 22:2*
my *l.* and my message (A)(R)   *1Co 2:4*
human and angelic *l.* (B)   *1Co 13:1*

a *l.* of ecstasy (N)   *1Co 14:2;*
     14:4, 13, 19, 27
10,000 words in a strange *l.*   *1Co 14:18;*
(A)   *14:19*
no foul *l.* (A)(B)(N)(P)   *Eph 4:29;*
     Col 3:3
every tribe and *l.* (A)(N)   *Re 5:9; 14:6*

LANGUAGES

after their *l.* (A)(B)(R)   *Ge 10:30;*
     10:31
to you, O people, nations, and *l.*   *Da 3:4*
nations, races of every tongue   *Da 3:4*
(B)
all *l.* fell down and worshipped   *Da 3:7*
the image
Nebuchadnezzar to all *l.*   *Da 4:1*
all *l.* trembled and feared   *Da 5:19*
before him
Darius to all *l.*   *Da 6:25*
all people, nations, and *l.*   *Da 7:14*
should serve him
ten men out of all *l.* shall take   *Zec 8:23*
hold
speak in new *l.* (A)   *M'k 16:15*
appeared different *l.* (P)   *Ac 2:3*
speaking in other *l.* (A)(B)   *Ac 2:4;*
     10:40
our own *l.* (B)   *Ac 2:11*
many *l.* in the world (B)(R)   *1Co 14:10*
men of strange *l.* (A)(B)   *1Co 14:21*
and *l.* (A)(N)(P)   *Re 7:9;*
     10:11; 11:9; 13:7; 17:15

LANGUISH

for the fields of Heshbon *l.* and   *Isa 16:8*
vine
and they that spread nets on   *Isa 19:8*
waters shall *l.*
top of the water will pine away   *Isa 19:8*
(B)
the haughty people of the   *Isa 24:4*
earth do *l.*
gates of Judah *l.* and are black   *Jer 14:2*
to ground
l. any more (R)   *Jer 31:12*
wall and rampart to *l.* (B)   *La 2:8*
every one that dwelleth therein   *Ho 4:3*
shall *l.*

LANGUISHED

rampart and wall to lament, *l.*   *La 2:8*
together

LANGUISHETH

hath many children *l.* (S)   *1Sa 2:5*
the world *l.* and fadeth away   *Isa 24:4*
the vine *l.*   *Isa 24:7*
the earth mourneth and *l.*   *Isa 33:9*
she that hath born seven *l.*   *Jer 15:9*
given up ghost
the oil *l.*   *Joe 1:10*
the fig tree *l.*   *Joe 1:12*
Bashan *l.* and Carmel, the   *Na 1:4*
flower *l.*

LANGUISHING

l. spirit (B)(R)   *De 28:6*
I am *l.* (R)   *Ps 6:2*
Lord will strengthen him on the   *Ps 41:3*
bed of *l.*

LANTERNS

Judas cometh with *l.* and   *Joh 18:3*
torches

LAODICEA

what great conflict I have for   *Col 2:1*
them at L.
he hath a zeal for them that   *Col 4:13*
are in L.
salute brethren which are in L.   *Col 4:15*
and Nymphas
that ye likewise read the   *Col 4:16*
epistle from L.

LAODICEANS

that it be read in the church   *Col 4:16*
of the L.
to the angel of the church of   *Re 3:14*
the L.

LAP

and gathered wild gourds, his   *2Ki 4:39*
l. full
I shook my *l.* and said, So God   *Ne 5:13*
shake
the lot is cast into the *l.* but   *Pr 16:33*
disposing

LAPIDOTH

the wife of L., she judged Israel   *J'g 4:4*

LAPPED

the number that *l.* were three   *J'g 7:6*
hundred
the Lord said, By them that *l.* I   *J'g 7:7*
will save you

LAPPETH

every one that *l.* of the water as   *J'g 7:5*
a dog

LAPSES

justification out of many *l.* (B)   *Ro 5:16*

LAPWING

heron and the *l.*   *Le 11:19; De 14:18*

LARGE

the land, behold it is *l.*   *Ge 34:21*
enough for them
to bring them into a good and *l.*   *Ex 3:8*
land
when ye go, ye shall come   *J'g 18:10*
into a *l.* land
he brought me into *l.* place   *2Sa 22:20;*
     Ps 18:19
I said to people, The work is   *Ne 4:19*
great and *l.*
the city was *l.* and great, but the   *Ne 7:4*
people few
have not served thee in the *l.*   *Ne 9:35*
and fat land
thou hast set my feet in a *l.*   *Ps 31:8*
room
Lord answered me, and set me   *Ps 118:5*
in a *l.* place
he will toss thee into a *l.*   *Isa 22:18*
country
in that day shall thy cattle   *Isa 30:23*
feed in *l.* pastures
Tophet is ordained, he made   *Isa 30:33*
it deep and *l.*
that saith, I will build *l.*   *Jer 22:14*
chambers
drink of thy sister's cup deep   *Eze 23:32*
and *l.*
Lord will feed them as a lamb   *Ho 4:16*
in a *l.* place
they gave *l.* money to the   *M't 28:12*
soldiers
will shew a *l.* upper room   *M'k 14:15;*
     Lu 22:12
ye see how *l.* a letter I have   *Ga 6:11*
written
the length is as *l.* as the   *Re 21:16*
breadth

LARGENESS

God gave Solomon *l.* of heart   *1Ki 4:29*

LASCIVIOUS

l. life of wicked (E)   *2Pe 2:7*

LASCIVIOUSNESS

out of the heart of men   *M'k 7:22*
proceed *l.*
unrestrained (indecent)   *M'k 7:22*
conduct (A)
lewdness (B)   *M'k 7:22*
indecency (N)   *M'k 7:22*
sensuality (P)   *M'k 7:22*
licentiousness (R)   *M'k 7:22*
and have not repented of the   *2Co 12:21*
l.
sensuality (A)(B)(N)   *2Co 12:21*
lustfulness (P)   *2Co 12:21*
licentiousness (R)   *2Co 12:21*
the works of the flesh are   *Ga 5:19*
manifest, *l.*

indecency (A)(N) Ga 5:19
lewdness (B) Ga 5:19
sensuality (P) Ga 5:19
licentiousness (R) Ga 5:19
who have given themselves Eph 4:19
over to l.
abandoned to unbridled Eph 4:19
sensuality (A)(B)
abandoned themselves to vice Eph 4:19
(N)
surrendered themselves to Eph 4:19
sensuality (P)
given themselves to Eph 4:19
licentiousness (R)
when we walked in l. lusts, 1Pe 4:3
excess
living in shameless, insolent 1Pe 4:3
wantonness (A)
indulging in unbridled lusts 1Pe 4:3
(B)
walked in l. (E) 1Pe 4:3
lived in licence and debauchery 1Pe 4:3
(N)
meant sensuality, lust (P) 1Pe 4:3
living in licentiousness, 1Pe 4:3
passions (P)
turning the grace of our God Jude 4
into l.
pervert grace of God into Jude 4
(lawlessness, wantonness, and)
immorality (A)
pervert the grace of God into Jude 4
unbridled lust (B)
pervert the free favour of God Jude 4
into licentiousness (N)
abuse his grace as an Jude 4
opportunity of immorality (P)
pervert the grace of God into Jude 4
licentiousness (R)

LASEA

whereunto was the city of L. Ac 27:8

LASHA

Admah, and Zeboim, even Ge 10:19
unto L.

LASHARON

the king of L., one Jos 12:18

LAST

l. night (S) Ge 19:34; 31:29; 31:42
their children l. of all (S) Ge 33:2
but Gad shall overcome at the Ge 49:19
l.
they shall go l. (S) Nu 2:31
and let my l. end be like his Nu 23:10
why are ye l. to bring the 2Sa 19:11;
king 19:12
now these be the l. words of 2Sa 23:1
David
for by the l. words of David 1Ch 23:27
now the acts of David the 1Ch 29:29
king, first and l.
the acts of Solomon first and 2Ch 9:29
l.
of Rehoboam first and l.; of 2Ch 12:15;
Asa, first and l. 16:11
the acts of Jehoshaphat first 2Ch 20:34
and l.
the acts of Amaziah first and 2Ch 25:26
l.
of Uzziah first and l.; of 2Ch 26:22;
Ahaz first and l. 28:26
Josiah's deeds first and l. are 2Ch 35:27
written
and of the l. sons of Ezr 8:13
Adonikam
from the first day to the l. he Ne 8:18
read
and thou mourn at the l. when Pr 5:11
at the l. it biteth like a Pr 23:32
serpent, and stingeth
I the Lord, the first, and with Isa 41:4;
the l. 44:6; 48:12; Re 1:11, 17; 2:8; 22:13
they said, He shall not see our Jer 12:4
l. end
at l. Nebuchadnezzar hath Jer 50:17
broken his bones
she remembereth not her l. end La 1:9
at the l. Daniel came in before Da 4:8
me
but one was higher, and the Da 8:3
higher came up l.
make thee know what shall be Da 8:19
in the l. end

I will slay the l. of them with Am 9:1
sword
l. state of that man is worse M't 12:45;
Lu 11:26
many that are first shall be l. M't 19:30;
and the l. first 20:16; M'k 10:31;
Lu 13:30
beginning from the l. to the M't 20:8
first
these l. have wrought but one M't 20:12
hour
I will give to this l. even as M't 20:14
unto thee
l. of all he sent his son, M't 21:37;
saying M'k 12:6
l. of all the woman died also M't 22:27;
M'k 12:22; Lu 20:32
at the l. came two false M't 26:60
witnesses
the l. error shall be worse M't 27:64
than the first
if desire to be first, the same M'k 9:35
shall be l.
till thou hast paid the l. mite Lu 12:59
work for food that does not l. Joh 6:27
(P)
beginning at the eldest, even to Joh 8:9
the l.
God hath set forth us the 1Co 4:9
apostles l.
and l. of all he was seen of 1Co 15:8
me also
l. enemy is death; the l. 1Co 15:26;
Adam 15:45
all be changed in a moment, 1Co 15:52
at the l. trump
at l. your care of me Ph'p 4:10
flourished again
the l. works to be more than Re 2:19
the first
seven angels, having the seven Re 15:1
l. plagues
seven vials full of the seven l. Re 21:9
plagues

LAST DAY, DAYS

which shall befall you in the l. Ge 49:1
days
come to pass in l. days Isa 2:2;
Mic 4:1; Ac 2:17
should raise it up at the l. day Joh 6:39;
6:40, 44, 54
in the l. day, the great day of Joh 7:37
the feast
I know that he shall rise Joh 11:24
again at the l. day
the same shall judge him in Joh 12:48
the l. day
in l. days perilous times shall 2Ti 3:1
come
hath spoken in these l. days by Heb 1:2
his Son
ye have heaped treasure for the Jas 5:3
l. days
there shall come in the l. days 2Pe 3:3
scoffers

LAST TIME, TIMES

ready to be revealed in the l. 1Pe 1:5
time
but was manifest in these l. 1Pe 1:20
times for you
little children, it is the l. time, 1Jo 2:18
whereby we know it is the
l. time
told there should be mockers in Jude 18
the l. time

LASTED

and she wept while the feast l. J'g 14:17

LASTING

for the precious things of the De 33:15
l. hills
abundance of everlasting hills De 33:15
(A)(B)(E)(R)

LATCH

put his hand by the l. (S) Ca 5:4

LATCHET

nor the l. of their shoes be Isa 5:27
broken
his sandal-strap does not break Isa 5:27
(B)

not a sandal-thong broken (R) Isa 5:27
the l. of whose shoes M'k 1:7
Lu 3:16; Joh 1:27
sandals I am not worthy to M'k 1:7
unloose (A)(R)
sandal straps not fit to untie M'k 1:7
(B)
not fit to unfasten his shoes M'k 1:7
(N)
not good enough to undo his M'k 1:7
shoes (P)

LATE

it is in vain for you to sit up l. Ps 127:2
of l. my people is risen up as Mic 2:8
an enemy
the time is l. (S) M't 14:15
the Jews of l. sought to stone Joh 11:8
thee

LATELY

found Aquila a Jew l. come Ac 18:2
from Italy

LATIN

written in Hebrew and L. Lu 23:38;
Joh 19:20

LATRINE

made it a l. unto this day (S) 2Ki 10:27

LATTER

they will believe the voice of l. Ex 4:8
sign
they will give you first rain, De 11:14
and l. rain
and if her l. husband hate her De 24:3
or die
my Redeemer shall stand at l. Job 19:25
day
they opened their mouth, as Job 29:23
for l. rain
his favour is as a cloud of l. Pr 16:15
rain
that thou mayest be wise in Pr 19:20
the l. end
and there hath been no l. rain Jer 3:3
both the former and l. rain in Jer 5:24
his season
remembered not her l. end (S) La 1:9
in the l. years thou shalt come Eze 38:8
in the l. time of their kingdom Da 8:23
but it shall not be as the Da 11:29
former or the l.
he shall come as l. and former Ho 6:3
rain
and the l. rain in the first Joe 2:23
month
in the beginning of the l. Am 7:1
growth
glory of the l. house shall be Hag 2:9
greater
ask ye rain in the time of the Zec 10:1
l. rain
that in the l. times some shall 1Ti 4:1
depart

LATTICE

Sisera's mother cried though J'g 5:28
the l.
Ahaziah fell down through the 2Ki 1:2
l.
shewing himself through the l. Ca 2:9

LAUD

praise the Lord and l. him, all Ro 15:11
ye people
let all people praise him Ro 15:11
(A)(E)(N)(P)(R)
greatly sing his praises (B) Ro 15:11

LAUGH

wherefore did Sarah l. saying Ge 18:13
and he said, Nay, but thou Ge 18:15
didst l.
God hath made me to l. all will Ge 21:6
l. with me
at destruction and famine Job 5:22
thou shalt l.
he will l. at the trial of the Job 9:23
innocent
and the innocent l. them to Job 22:19
scorn

he that sitteth in the heavens shall *l.*	*Ps 2:4*	and he set the *l.*	*Ex 40:30*	people wept when they heard the words of *l.*	*Ne 8:9*

he that sitteth in the heavens shall *l.* *Ps 2:4*

all they that see me *l.* me to scorn *Ps 22:7*

the Lord shall *l.* at him, for he seeth *Ps 37:13*

the righteous also shall *l.* at him *Ps 52:6*

but thou, O Lord, shalt *l.* at them *Ps 59:8*

and our enemies *l.* among themselves *Ps 80:6*

I also will *l.* at your calamity *Pr 1:26*

whether he rage or *l.* there is no rest *Pr 29:9*

a time to weep, and a time to *l.* *Ec 3:4*

l. at every fortress (B)(R) *Hab 1:10*

blessed are ye that weep, ye shall *l.* *Lu 6:21*

woe unto you that *l.* now, ye shall weep *Lu 6:25*

onlookers will *l.* at him (N) *Lu 14:29*

LAUGHED

Abraham *l.*; Sarah *l.* in herself *Ge 17:17; 18:12*

then Sarah denied, saying, I *l.* not *Ge 18:15*

lest we be *l.* at (R) *Ge 38:23*

daughter of Zion hath *l.* *2Ki 19:21; Isa 37:22*

they *l.* them to scorn, and mocked *2Ch 30:10*

they *l.* us to scorn, and despised us *Ne 2:19*

the just and upright man is *l.* to scorn *Job 12:4*

if I *l.* on them, they believed not *Job 29:24*

thou shalt be *l.* to scorn, and had *Eze 23:32*

they *l.* to scorn *M't 9:24; M'k 5:40; Lu 8:53*

others *l.* mockingly (P) *Ac 2:13*

some of them *l.* outright (P) *Ac 17:32*

LAUGHETH

he *l.* at the shaking of a spear *Job 41:29*

LAUGHING

till he fill thy mouth with *l.* and thy lips *Job 8:21*

I am a *l.* stock (A)(B)(E)(R) *Job 1:4*

I became a *l.* stock (B) *Ps 69:11*

became a *l.* stock (B) *Ps 109:25; Jer 30:8*

LAUGHS

he *l.* at terror (B)(R) *Job 39:22*

LAUGHTER

then was our mouth filled with *l.* *Ps 126:2*

even in *l.* the heart is sorrowful *Pr 14:13*

I said of *l.*, It is mad, and of mirth *Ec 2:2*

sorrow is better than *l.*; so is *l.* of the fool *Ec 7:3; 7:6*

let your *l.* be turned to mourning *Jas 4:9*

LAUNCH

he said to Simon, L. out into the deep *Lu 5:4*

LAUNCHED

let us go over, and they *l.* forth *Lu 8:22*

that after we had *l.* *Ac 21:1; 27:2, 4*

LAVER

thou shalt also make a *l.* of brass *Ex 30:18*

wash basin (B) *Ex 30:18; 38:8; 40:7, 11*

the *l.* and his foot *Ex 30:28 31:9; 35:16; 39:39*

washbowl (B) *Ex 30:28*

he made the *l.* of brass, and the foot brass *Ex 38:8*

thou shall set the *l.* *Ex 40:7*

and thou shalt anoint the *l.* and his foot *Ex 40:11*

he anointed both the *l.* and his foot *Le 8:11*

the basin and its base (B) *Le 8:11*

under the *l.* were undersetters molten *1Ki 7:30*

every *l.* was forty baths, and every *l.* was *1Ki 7:38*

and king Ahaz removed the *l.* *2Ki 16:17*

LAVERS

then made he ten *l.* of brass *1Ki 7:38*

and Hiram made the *l.* and *1Ki 7:40*

and the ten *l.* on the bases *1Ki 7:43; 2Ch 4:6, 14*

LAVISH

they *l.* gold out of the bag, and weigh *Isa 46:6*

in a wealth of *l.* generosity (A)(B) *2Co 8:2*

l. upon us every (A)(N)(R) *Eph 1:8*

LAVISHED

l. their lusts (B) *Eze 23:8*

LAVISHLY

l. open-handed (N) *2Co 8:2*

LAW

Joseph made it a *l.* over the land *Ge 47:26*

established it as a regulation (B) *Ge 47:26*

Joseph made it a statute (E)(R) *Ge 47:26*

one *l.* to homeborn and to the stranger *Ex 12:49; Le 24:22; Nu 15:16, 29*

I will give thee a *l.* and commandment *Ex 24:12*

according to the sentence of the *l.* *De 17:11*

not depart from the verdict (B)(R) *De 17:11*

from his right hand went a fiery *l.* for them *De 33:2*

flames of fire at right hand (B)(R) *De 33:2*

Moses commanded us a *l.* even the inheritance *De 33:4*

mayest observe to do according to all the *l.* *Jos 1:7*

wrote on the stones a copy of the *l.* of Moses *Jos 8:32*

afterward he read all the words of the *l.* *Jos 8:34*

take heed to the *l.* *Jos 22:5; 2Ki 17:13, 37; 21:8*

taking *l.* in own hands (B) *1Sa 25:26; 25:33*

nor do after the *l.* and commandment *2Ki 17:34*

that he might perform the words of the *l.* *2Ki 23:24*

according to all the *l.* of Moses *2Ki 23:25*

hath confirmed to Jacob for a *l.* *1Ch 16:17*

defined for Jacob a statute (B)(E)(R) *1Ch 16:17*

that thou mayest keep the *l.* of God *1Ch 22:12*

commanded Judah to do the *l.* between *l.* and commandment, statutes *2Ch 14:4; 2Ch 19:10*

stood in their place according to *l.* of Moses *2Ch 30:16*

Hezekiah did in every work, and in the *l.* *2Ch 31:21*

take heed to do according to the whole *l.* *2Ch 33:8*

when Josiah heard the words of the *l.* *2Ch 34:19*

he was a ready scribe in the *l.* *Ezr 7:6; 12:21*

to inquire according to the *l.* of thy God *Ezr 7:14*

will not do the *l.* of God and *l.* of the king *Ezr 7:26*

and let it be done according to the *l.* *Ezr 10:3*

Ezra the priest brought the *l.* before *Ne 8:2*

Levites caused the people to understand the *l.* *Ne 8:7*

were gathered together to understand the *l.* *Ne 8:13*

had separated themselves to *l.* of God *Ne 10:28*

entered into an oath to walk in God's *l.* *Ne 10:29*

to gather into them the portions of the *l.* *Ne 12:44*

when they had heard the *l.* they separated *Ne 13:3*

the drinking was according to the *l.* *Es 1:8*

according to the rule (B) *Es 1:8*

what do to the queen Vashti according to the *l.* *Es 1:15*

be handled legally (B) *Es 1:15*

there is one *l.* of his to put him to death *Es 4:11*

there is one penalty, execution (B) *Es 4:11*

I will go in, which is not according to the *l.* *Es 4:16*

in spite of the injunction (B) *Es 4:16*

receive the *l.* from his mouth, lay up *Job 22:22*

instruction from his mouth (B)(R) *Job 22:22*

in his *l.* he meditates day and night *Ps 1:2*

the *l.* of his God is in his heart *Ps 37:31*

for he appointed a *l.* in Israel, which he *Ps 78:5*

and they refused to walk in his *l.* *Ps 78:10*

this was a *l.* of the God of Jacob *Ps 81:4*

ordinance of God of Jacob (A)(B)(E)(R) *Ps 81:4*

which frameth mischief by a *l.* *Ps 94:20*

and confirmed the same to Jacob for a *l.* *Ps 105:10*

confirmed to Jacob by a decree (B) *Ps 105:10*

confirmed to Jacob by a statute (E)(R) *Ps 105:10*

the *l.* of thy mouth is better than gold *Pr 119:72*

forsake not the *l.* of thy mother *Pr 1:8; 6:20*

teaching of thy mother (A)(B)(R) *Pr 1:8*

commandment is a lamp, and the *l.* is light *Pr 6:23*

the teaching a light (B)(R) *Pr 6:23*

the *l.* of the wise is a fountain of life *Pr 13:14*

teaching of the wise is a (A)(B)(R) *Pr 13:14*

they that forsake *l.* praise wicked, but such as keep *l.* contend *Pr 28:4*

whoso keepeth the *l.* is a wise son *Pr 28:7*

he that turns away his ear from hearing the *l.* *Pr 28:9*

but he that keepeth the *l.* happy is he *Pr 29:18*

lest they drink and forget the *l.* *Pr 31:5*

forget what is decreed (B)(R) *Pr 31:5*

and in her tongue is the *l.* of kindness *Pr 31:26*

teaching is on her tongue (B) *Pr 31:26*

and give ear to the *l.* of our God *Isa 1:10*

to the teaching of our God (B)(R) *Isa 1:10*

out of Zion shall go forth the *l.* *Isa 2:3; Mic 4:2*

Zion shall instruction go forth (B) *Isa 2:3*

seal the *l.*; to the *l.* and the testimony *Isa 8:16; 8:20*

and the isles shall wait for his *l.* *Isa 42:4*

the Lord will magnify the *l.* and make it *Isa 42:21*

neither were they obedient to his *l.* *Isa 42:24*

for a *l.* shall proceed from me *Isa 51:4*

they that handle the *l.* knew me not *Jer 2:8*

the *l.* of their God (S) *Jer 5:4; 5:5; 8:7*

the *l.* shall not perish from the priest *Jer 18:18*

evidence was sealed according to *l.* and custom *Jer 32:11*

containing terms of conditions (A)(R) *Jer 32:11*

containing injunction and conditions (B) *Jer 32:11*

ye have not obeyed, nor walked in his *l*. *Jer 44:23*

the *l*. is no more, prophets find no vision *La 2:9*

the *l*. shall perish from the priests *Eze 7:26*

there is but one *l*. (E) *Da 2:9*

except concerning the *l*. of his God *Da 6:5*

in connection with service to his god (B) *Da 6:5*

true according to the *l*. of the Medes *Da 6:12; 6:15*

thou hast forgotten the *l*. of thy God *Ho 4:6*

therefore the *l*. is slacked, and judgment *Hab 1:4*

her priests have done violence to the *l*. *Zep 3:4*

ask now the priests concerning the *l*. *Hag 2:11*

lest they should hear the *l*. and words *Zec 7:12*

the *l*. of truth was in his mouth *Mal 2:6*

and they should seek the *l*. at his mouth *Mal 2:7*

ye have caused many to stumble at the *l*. *Mal 2:8*

not kept my ways, but have been partial in the *l*. *Mal 2:9*

remember the *l*. of Moses my servant *Mal 4:4*

think not I am come to destroy the *l*. *M't 5:17*

one tittle shall in no wise pass from the *l*. *M't 5:18*

and if any man will sue thee at the *l*. *M't 5:40*

the *l*. prophesied till John *M't 11:13; Lu 16:16*

have ye not read in the *l*. how that on *M't 12:5*

which is the great commandment in *l*. *M't 22:36*

on these two commandments hang all the *l*. *M't 22:40*

have omitted the weightier matters of the *l*. *M't 23:23*

to do for him after the custom of the *l*. *Lu 2:27*

there were doctors of the *l*. sitting by *Lu 5:17*

than for one tittle of the *l*. to fail *Lu 16:17*

for the *l*. was given by Moses, but grace *Joh 1:17*

him of whom Moses in the *l*. did write *Joh 1:45*

did not Moses give you the *l*. and yet none of you keepeth the *l*. *Joh 7:19*

that the *l*. of Moses should not be broken *Joh 7:23*

people who knoweth not the *l*. are cursed *Joh 7:49*

doth our *l*. judge any man before it hear him *Joh 7:51*

now Moses in the *l*. commanded us *Joh 8:5*

is it not written in your *l*. ye are gods *Joh 10:34*

we have heard out of the *l*. that Christ *Joh 12:34*

might be fulfilled what is written in their *l*. *Joh 15:25*

and judge him according to your *l*. *Joh 18:31*

we have a *l*. and by our *l*. he ought to die *Joh 19:7*

then stood up Gamaliel, a doctor of the *l*. *Ac 5:34*

to speak blasphemous words against the *l*. *Ac 6:13*

who have received the *l*. by angels *Ac 7:53*

after reading of the *l*. and prophets *Ac 13:15*

ye could not be justified by the *l*. of Moses *Ac 13:39*

to command them to keep the *l*. of Moses *Ac 15:5*

ye must be circumcised and keep the *l*. *Ac 15:24*

men to worship God contrary to the *l*. *Ac 18:13*

but if it be a question of your *l*. look ye to it *Ac 18:15*

the *l*. is open; zealous of the *l*. *Ac 19:38; 21:20*

but that thou thyself keepest the *l*. *Ac 21:24*

this is the man that teacheth against the *l*. *Ac 21:28*

taught according to the manner of the *l*. *Ac 22:3*

Ananias a devout man according to the *l*. *Ac 22:12*

sittest to judge me after *l*. and commandest me to be smitten contrary to *l*. *Ac 23:3*

and would have judged according to our *l*. *Ac 24:6*

nor against the *l*. of the Jews, nor temple *Ac 25:8*

persuading them out of the *l*. and prophets *Ac 28:23*

sinned in the *l*. shall be judged by the *l*. *Ro 2:12*

lost without *l*. (B) *Ro 2:12*

not the hearers of the *l*. are just before God *Ro 2:13*

Gentiles which have not the *l*. do by nature things contained in the *l*. these having not the *l*. are a *l*. unto themselves *Ro 2:14*

which shew the work of the *l*. written in *Ro 2:15*

thou art called a Jew, and restest in the *l*. *Ro 2:17*

knowest, being instructed out of the *l*. *Ro 2:18*

which hast the form of the truth in the *l*. *Ro 2:20*

makest thy boast of the *l*. through breaking the *l*. *Ro 2:23*

circumcision verily profitteth if thou keep the *l*. but if thou be a breaker of the *l*. *Ro 2:25*

therefore if keep the righteousness of the *l*. *Ro 2:26*

uncircumcision, if it fulfil the *l*. judge thee who dost transgress the *l*. *Ro 2:27*

we know what things soever the *l*. saith *Ro 3:19*

by the deeds of *l*. no flesh be *Ro 3:20;*

justified, for by the *l*. is *3:28; Ga 2:16*

the righteousness of God is witnessed the *l*. *Ro 3:21*

by what *l*. excluded? by the *l*. of faith *Ro 3:27*

do we make void the *l*.? we establish the *l*. *Ro 3:31*

for the promise was not through the *l*. *Ro 4:13*

for if they which are of the *l*. be heirs *Ro 4:14*

the *l*. worketh wrath, for where no *l*. is *Ro 4:15*

be sure, not to that only which is of the *l*. *Ro 4:16*

for until the *l*. sin was in the world, but sin is not imputed where there is no *l*. *Ro 5:13*

the *l*. entered, that the offence might abound *Ro 5:20*

l. intruded to multiply law-breaking (N) *Ro 5:20*

I speak to them which know the *l*. *Ro 7:1*

l. the *l*. hath dominion over

l. lords it over a person (B) *Ro 7:1*

woman is bound by *l*. to *Ro 7:2;*

husband, if he be dead, she is loosed from *l*. *7:3*

ye also are become dead to the *l*. by Christ *Ro 7:4*

the motions of sins which were by the *l*. *Ro 7:5*

but now we are delivered from the *l*. *Ro 7:6*

is the *l*. sin? I had not known sin but by *l*. nor lust, except *l*. *Ro 7:7*

for without the *l*. sin was dead *Ro 7:8*

the *l*. is holy, and commandment holy, just *Ro 7:12*

the *l*. is spiritual *Ro 7:14*

the *l*. is good *Ro 8:16; 1Ti 1:8*

I find a *l*.; I delight in the *l*. of God *Ro 7:21; 7:22*

I see another *l*. warring against the *l*. of my mind, bringing me into captivity to *l*. of sin *Ro 7:23*

with mind I serve *l*. of God, flesh, *l*. of sin *Ro 7:25*

the *l*. of life made me free from the *l*. of sin *Ro 8:2*

for what the *l*. could not do, in that weak *Ro 8:3*

the righteousness of the *l*. might be fulfilled *Ro 8:4*

the carnal mind is not subject to the *l*. of God *Ro 8:7*

to whom pertaineth the giving of the *l*. *Ro 9:4*

Israel followed after the *l*. of righteousness *Ro 9:31*

because they sought it by the works of the *l*. *Ro 9:32*

Christ is the end of the *l*. for righteousness *Ro 10:4*

describes the righteousness which is of the *l*. *Ro 10:5*

he that loveth another, hath fulfilled the *l*. *Ro 13:8*

therefore love is the fulfilling of the *l*. *Ro 13:10*

dare any of you go to *l*. before the unjust *1Co 6:1*

seek judgment before a pagan court (B)(P) *1Co 6:1*

take it to pagan law-courts (N) *1Co 6:1*

but brother goeth to *l*. with brother *1Co 6:6*

because ye go to *l*. one with another *1Co 6:7*

wife is bound by the *l*. as long as her husband *1Co 7:39*

or saith not the *l*. the same also *1Co 9:8*

to be under obedience, as also saith the *l*. *1Co 14:34*

of death is sin, and strength of sin is the *l*. *1Co 15:56*

man is not justified by the works of the *l*. *Ga 2:16*

I thro' the *l*. am dead to the *l*. that I might live *Ga 2:19*

for if righteousness come by the *l*. then *Ga 2:21*

received ye the Spirit by the works of the *l*. *Ga 3:2*

miracles, doeth he it by the works of the *l*. *Ga 3:5*

as many as are of the works of *l*. *Ga 3:10*

that no man is justified by the *l*. is evident *Ga 3:11*

and the *l*. is not of faith, but the man *Ga 3:12*

Christ hath redeemed us from the curse of *l*. *Ga 3:13*

the covenant in Christ, the *l*. cannot disannul *Ga 3:17*

if the inheritance be of the *l*. not of promise *Ga 3:18*

wherefore then serveth the *l*.? it was added *Ga 3:19*

is the *l*. then against the promises? if a *l*. *Ga 3:21*

given righteousness been by *l*.

the *l*. was our schoolmaster to bring us to Christ *Ga 3:24*

tell me, do ye not hear the *l*. *Ga 4:21*

that he is a debtor to do the whole *l*. *Ga 5:3*

for whosoever of you are justified by the *l*. *Ga 5:4*

all the *l*. is fulfilled in one word, even in this *Ga 5:14*

temperance, against such there is no *l*. *Ga 5:23*

bear ye, and so fulfil the *l*. of Christ *Ga 6:2*

nor themselves keep the *l*. but desire to have *Ga 6:13*

having abolished in his flesh the *l*. *Eph 2:15*

as touching the *l*. a Pharisee *Ph'p 3:5*

touching the righteousness in the *l*. blameless *Ph'p 3:6*

not having mine own righteousness, of the *l*. *Ph'p 3:9*

desiring to be teachers of the *l*. *1Ti 1:7*

the *l*. is not made for a righteous man *1Ti 1:9*

but avoid contentions about the *l*. *Tit 3:9*

to take tithes of people according to the *l*. *Heb 7:5*

for under it the people received the *l*. *Heb 7:11*

there is made of necessity a change of the *l*. *Heb 7:12*

not after the *l*. of a carnal commandment *Heb 7:16*

for the *l*. made nothing perfect, but bringing *Heb 7:19*

l. maketh men high priests,   *Heb 7:28*
but the word of the oath
which was since the *l.*
there are priests offer gifts   *Heb 8:4*
according to the *l.*
when Moses had spoken   *Heb 9:19*
according to the *l.*
all things are by the *l.* purged   *Heb 9:22*
with blood
the *l.* having a shadow of   *Heb 10:1*
good things
he that despised Moses' *l.*   *Heb 10:28*
died without mercy
whoso looketh into perfect *l.*   *Jas 1:25*
of liberty
if ye fulfil the royal *l.* ye do well   *Jas 2:8*
and are convinced of the *l.* as   *Jas 2:9*
transgressors
for whosoever shall keep the   *Jas 2:10*
whole *l.*
if thou kill, thou art a   *Jas 2:11*
transgressor of the *l.*
they that shall be judged by   *Jas 2:12*
the *l.* of liberty
that speaketh evil of the *l.* and   *Jas 4:11*
judgeth the *l.*
transgresseth also *l.* for   *1Jo 3:4*
sin is transgression of *l.*
lawbreaking (B)
doeth lawlessness; sin is   *1Jo 3:4*
lawlessness (E)(R)

LAW OF THE LORD

that *the Lord's l.* may be in thy   *Ex 13:9*
mouth
Jehu took no heed to walk in   *2Ki 10:31*
l. of the Lord
Rehoboam forsook *l. of the*   *2Ch 12:1*
Lord and Israel
that they might be encouraged   *2Ch 31:4*
in the *l. of the Lord*
Josiah's goodness according   *2Ch 35:26*
to *l. of the Lord*
prepared his heart to seek the   *Ezr 7:10*
l. of the Lord
delight is in the *l. of the Lord*   *Ps 1:2*
the *l. of the Lord* is perfect,   *Ps 19:7*
converting the soul
blessed are they who walk in   *Ps 119:1*
the *l. of the Lord*
because they have cast away   *Isa 5:24*
the *l. of the Lord*
children that will not hear the   *Isa 30:9*
l. of the Lord
how do ye say, The *l. of the*   *Jer 8:8*
Lord is with us
because they have despised the   *Am 2:4*
l. of the Lord
had performed according to   *Lu 2:39*
the *l. of the Lord*

MY LAW

whether they will walk in *my l.*   *Ex 16:4*
or no
my instructions (B)   *Ex 16:4; Ps 78:1*
so that thy children walk in   *2Ch 6:16*
my l.
give ear, O my people, to *my l.*   *Ps 78:1*
my teaching (A)   *Ps 78:1*
if his children forsake *my l.*   *Ps 89:30*
and walk
my son, forget not *my l.* but   *Pr 3:1*
keep
my teaching (A)(B)(R)   *Pr 3:1; 4:2*
forsake not *my l.;* keep *my l.* as   *Pr 4:2;*
the apple   *7:2*
the people in whose heart is   *Isa 51:7*
my l.
my instruction (B)   *Isa 51:7*
they have not hearkened unto   *Jer 6:19*
my l.
my words, my teaching   *Jer 6:19;*
(B)   *16:11; 26:4*
because they have forsaken *my*   *Jer 9:13*
l.
have forsaken me, and have   *Jer 16:11*
not kept *my l.*
if ye will not hearken to walk   *Jer 26:4*
in *my l.*
I will put *my l.* in their   *Jer 31:33*
inward parts
nor have they feared nor   *Jer 44:10*
walked in *my l.*
her priests have violated *my*   *Eze 22:26*
l.
because they trespassed against   *Ho 8:1*
my l.

have written to him the great   *Ho 8:12*
things of *my l.*

THIS LAW

this shall be the *l.* of leper in   *Le 14:2*
cleansing
the priest shall execute on her   *Nu 5:30*
this l.
this is the ordinance of the *l.*   *Nu 19:2;*
  31:21
began Moses to declare *this l.*   *De 1:5*
saying
all *this l.* which I set before you   *De 4:8*
this day
he shall write him a copy of   *De 17:18*
this l. in a book
he may learn to keep all the   *De 17:19*
words of *this l.*
shall write on them the words   *De 27:3;*
of *this l.*   *27:8*
cursed that confirmeth not the   *De 27:26*
words of *this l.*
if thou wilt not observe the   *De 28:58*
words of *this l.*
that we may do all the words   *De 29:29;*
of *this l.*   *31:12*
Moses wrote *this l.;* thou shalt   *De 31:9;*
read *this l.*   *31:11*
of writing the words of *this l.*   *De 31:24*
in a book
your children to do the words   *De 32:46*
of *this l.*

THIS IS THE LAW

this is the l. of the burnt   *Le 6:9;*
offering   *7:37*
this is the l. of meat offering;   *Le 6:14;*
of sin offering   *6:25*
this is the l. of the trespass   *Le 7:1*
offering, it is holy
this is the l. of the beasts and   *Le 11:46*
of the fowl
this is the l. of her that hath   *Le 12:7*
born male and female
this is the l. of plague of   *Le 13:59;*
leprosy   *14:32, 57*
this is the l. for all manner of   *Le 14:54*
plague of scall
this is the l. of him that hath   *Le 15:32*
an issue
this is the l. of jealousies,   *Nu 5:29*
when a wife
this is the l. of the Nazarite,   *Nu 6:13*
when days
this is the l. when a man   *Nu 19:14*
dieth in a tent
this is the l. which Moses set   *De 4:44*
before Israel
this is the l. of the house, on   *Eze 43:12*
top of mountain
do to them, for *this is the l.*   *M't 7:12*
and prophets

THY LAW

they shall teach Israel *thy l.*   *De 33:10*
they cast *thy l.* behind their   *Ne 9:26*
backs
thou mightest bring them again   *Ne 9:29*
to *thy l.*
nor our kings, nor our princes   *Ne 9:34*
kept *thy l.*
yea, *thy l.* is within my heart   *Ps 40:8*
chastenest, and teachest him   *Ps 94:12*
out of *thy l.*
behold wondrous things out   *Ps 119:18*
of *thy l.*
way of lying, and grant me   *Ps 119:29*
thy l. graciously
give understanding, and I   *Ps 119:34*
shall keep *thy l.*
so shall I keep *thy l.*   *Ps 119:44*
continually for ever
yet have I not declined from   *Ps 119:51*
thy l.
because of the wicked that   *Ps 119:53*
forsake *thy l.*
I remembered thy name, and   *Ps 119:55*
kept *thy l.*
have robbed me, but I have   *Ps 119:61*
not forgotten *thy l.*
their heart is fat, but I   *Ps 119:70*
delight in *thy l.*
I may live, for *thy l.* is my   *Ps 119:77;*
delight   *119:92, 174*
proud digged pits; which are   *Ps 119:85*
not after *thy l.*
O how I love *thy l.;* do I not   *Ps 119:97;*
forget *thy l.*   *119:109*

but *thy l.* do I love; made   *Ps 119:113;*
void *thy l.*   *119:126*
waters run down, because   *Ps 119:136*
they keep not *thy l.*
thy l. is truth; are far from   *Ps 119:142;*
thy l.   *119:150*
great peace have they who   *Ps 119:165*
love *thy l.*
they obeyed not, nor walked   *Jer 32:23*
in *thy l.*
all Israel have transgressed *thy*   *Da 9:11*
l.

UNDER THE LAW

it saith to them that are *under*   *Ro 3:19*
the *l.*
ye are not *under the l.* but   *Ro 6:14*
under grace
shall we sin because we are not   *Ro 6:15*
under the l.
to them that are *under the l.*   *1Co 9:20*
as *under the l.* that I might
gain them that are *under the l.*   *1Co 9:21*
not without law to God, but
under l. to Christ
we were kept *under the l.;*   *Ga 3:23;*
made *under the l.*   *4:4*
sent his Son to redeem them   *Ga 4:5*
that were *under the l.*
tell me, ye that desire to be   *Ga 4:21*
under the l.
if ye be led by Spirit, are not   *Ga 5:18*
under the l.

WITHOUT LAW

a long season, Israel hath   *2Ch 15:3*
been *without l.*
as many as sinned *without l.*   *Ro 2:12*
perish *without l.*
the righteousness of God   *Ro 3:21*
without l. is manifested
for *without l.* sin was read; I   *Ro 7:8;*
was alive *without l.* once   *7:9*
that are *without l.* as   *1Co 9:21*
without l. being not *without*
l. to God

WRITTEN IN THE LAW

as written in the *l.* of Moses   *1Ki 2:3;*
2Ch 23:18; 25:4; 31:3; Ezr 3:2; Ne 10:34,
36; Da 9:13; Lu 2:23
do according to all *written*   *1Ch 16:40;*
in the l.   *2Ch 35:26*
and they found *written in the*   *Ne 8:14*
l. that Israel
and the oath that is *written*   *Da 9:11*
in the l. of Moses
what is *written in the l.* how   *Lu 10:26*
readest thou
all must be fulfilled, which   *Lu 24:44*
were *written in the l.*
believing all things that are   *Ac 24:14*
written in the l.
it is *written in the l.*   *1Co 9:9;*
  14:21

LAWBREAKER

became a *l.* (N)   *Jas 2:11*

LAW-BREAKING

law intruded to multiply *l.* (N)   *Ro 5:20*
loose living and *l.* (P)   *Tit 1:6*
practices *l.;* sin is *l.* (B)   *1Jo 3:4*

LAWFUL

shall not be *l.* to impose toil   *Ezr 7:24*
on them
shall the *l.* captive be   *Isa 49:24*
delivered
do that which is *l.*   *Eze 18:5;*
  21:27; 33:14, 19
the son hath done that   *Eze 18:19;*
which is *l.*   *33:16*
do what is not *l.*   *M't 12:2;*
  M'k 2:24; Lu 6:2
was not *l.* for him to eat   *M't 12:4;*
  M'k 2:26; Lu 6:4
they asked him, Is it *l.* to   *M't 12:10;*
heal on the   *12:12; M'k 3:4; Lu 6:9;*
sabbath days   *14:3*
it is not *l.* for thee to have   *M't 14:4;*
her   *M'k 6:18*
is it *l.* for man to put away   *M't 19:3;*
wife   *M'k 10:2*
tell us, Is it *l.* to give tribute   *M't 22:17;*
to Caesar or not   *M'k 12:14; Lu 20:22*

it is not *l.* to put them in the   *M't 27:6*
treasury
it is not *l.* for thee to carry thy   *Joh 5:10*
bed
it is not *l.* for us to put any   *Joh 18:31*
man to death
teach customs which are not *l.*   *Ac 16:21*
to receive
it shall be determined in a *l.*   *Ac 19:39*
assembly
is it *l.* for you to scourge a   *Ac 22:25*
Roman
all things are *l.* to me, *l.* for   *1Co 6:12;*
me   *10:23*
which is not *l.* for a man to   *2Co 12:4*
utter

LAWFULLY

the law is good, if a man use it   *1Ti 1:8*
l.
yet is not crowned, except he   *2Ti 2:5*
strive *l.*

LAWGIVER

nor a *l.* from between his feet   *Ge 49:10*
nor leader's staff from   *Ge 49:10*
between (A)(B)
nor ruler's staff from between   *Ge 49:10*
(E)(R)
digged the well by direction   *Nu 21:18*
of the *l.*
hollowed with scepter and   *Nu 21:18*
staves (A)(B)(E)
in a portion of the *l.* was he   *De 33:21*
seated
the leader's portion (A)   *De 33:21*
that was the commander's   *De 33:21*
portion (B)(R)
Gilead is mine, Judah is my *l.*   *Ps 60:7;*
108:8
the Lord is our *l.* and our   *Isa 33:22*
king
there is one *l.* who is able to   *Jas 4:12*
save

LAWLESS

by *l.* hands (B)(E)(R)   *Ac 2:23*
the *l.* one (A)(B)(E)(P)(R)   *1Th 2:8*
the law is for the *l.* and   *1Ti 1:9*
disobedient
living in *l.* idolatry (R)   *1Pe 4:3*
the ungodless and *l.*   *2Pe 2:7;*
(A)(B)(N)(R)   *3:17*

LAWLESSNESS

gather those practicing *l.* (B)   *M't 13:41*
l., moral anarchy (N)   *Ro 6:19*
the hidden principle of *l.* (B)   *2Th 2:7*
death *l.*; sin is *l.* (E)(R)   *1Jo 3:4*
pervert grace into *l.* (A)(N)(R)   *Jude 4*

LAW-REMINDING

their *l.* tassels (B)   *M't 23:5*

LAWS

Abraham kept my statutes and   *Ge 26:5*
my *l.*
how long refuse ye to keep my   *Ex 16:28*
l.
my instructions (B)   *Ex 16:28*
I do make them know the *l.* of   *Ex 18:16*
God
rules and *l.* (B)   *Ex 18:16*
thou shalt teach them   *Ex 18:20*
ordinances and *l.*
observe my *l.* and ordinances   *Le 19:37*
(B)
these are the *l.* which the Lord   *Le 26:46*
made
l. and ordinances   *De 4:1;*
(A)(B)(E)(R)   *4:5, 14; 5:31; 6:20; 8:11*
hear all these *l.* (B)   *De 4:6*
my *l.* (B)   *2Ch 9:19*
all such as know the *l.* of thy   *Ezr 7:25*
God
camest down, thou gavest them   *Ne 9:13*
true *l.*
and commandedst them   *Ne 9:14*
statutes and *l.*
to be written among the *l.* of   *Es 1:19*
the Persians
certain people, their *l.* are   *Es 3:8*
diverse from all people, neither
keep they the king's *l.*

know the *l.* of heaven (B)   *Job 38:33*
that they might keep his *l.*   *Ps 105:45*
because they have transgressed   *Isa 24:5*
the *l.*
shew them all the *l.* thereof   *Eze 43:11*
hear all the *l.*; they shall keep   *Eze 44:5;*
my *l.*   *44:24*
and think to change times and   *Da 7:25*
l.
nor have we obeyed to walk in   *Da 9:10*
his *l.*
those in defiance of its *l.* (P)   *M't 13:41*
I will put my *l.* into their   *Heb 8:10*
mind
I will put my *l.* into their   *Heb 10:16*
hearts

LAWYER

a *l.* by the name of (P)   *Ac 24:1*
one that was a *l.* asked him   *M't 22:35;*
Lu 10:25
bring Zenas the *l.* and Apollos   *Tit 3:13*
Zenas the jurist (B)   *Tit 3:13*

LAWYERS

the *l.* rejected the counsel of   *Lu 7:30*
God
then answered one of the *l.*   *Lu 11:45*
and said
woe unto you, *l.*   *Lu 11:46;*
Jesus spake to *l.*   *11:52; 14:3*

LAY

the tale of bricks ye shall *l.* upon   *Ex 5:8*
them
the dew *l.* round about the   *Ex 16:13;*
host   *16:14*
as woman's husband will *l.*   *Ex 21:22*
upon him
neither shalt thou *l.* upon him   *Ex 22:25*
usury
and *l.* the wood in order on the   *Le 1:7*
fire
the priests shall *l.* the parts in   *Le 1:8;*
order   *1:12*
thou shalt *l.* the frankincense   *Le 2:15*
thereon
and *l.* the burnt offering in   *Le 6:12*
order upon it
alas, my Lord, *l.* not the sin   *Nu 12:11*
upon us
but will *l.* them on them that   *De 7:15*
hate thee
shall *l.* the fear of you upon   *De 11:25*
all the land
l. not innocent blood to thy   *De 21:8*
people Israel
l. thee an ambush for the city   *Jos 8:2*
behind it
Samson *l.* till midnight, and   *J'g 16:3*
arose
and behold, a woman *l.* at his   *Ru 3:8*
feet
and Samuel *l.* till the morning   *1Sa 3:15*
and *l.* it for a reproach on all   *1Sa 11:2*
Israel
Saul *l.* in the trench, people   *1Sa 26:5;*
about him   *26:7*
Ish-bosheth, who *l.* on a bed at   *2Sa 4:5*
noon
ewe lamb eat of his meat, and   *2Sa 12:3*
l. in his bosom
David *l.* all night on the   *2Sa 12:16;*
earth   *13:31*
she *l.* on it (S)   *1Ki 3:19*
l. my bones beside his bones   *1Ki 13:31*
l. it on wood and put no fire   *1Ki 18:23*
under
and as he *l.* and slept under a   *1Ki 19:5*
juniper tree
Ahab fasted and *l.* in   *1Ki 21:27*
sackcloth
he went up and *l.* upon the   *2Ki 4:34*
child
l. ye them in two heaps at the   *2Ki 10:8*
gate
long as she *l.* desolate, she   *2Ch 36:21*
kept sabbath
many *l.* in sackcloth and ashes   *Es 4:3*
the dew *l.* all night upon my   *Job 29:19*
branch
he will not *l.* on man more   *Job 34:23*
than right
let him *l.* mine honour in the   *Ps 7:5*
dust
they that seek my life, *l.*   *Ps 38:12*
snares for me

found a nest, where she may *l.*   *Ps 84:3*
her young
l. up my commandments (S)   *Pr 2:1*
and the living will *l.* it to heart   *Ec 7:2*
woe to them that *l.* field to field   *Isa 5:8*
to *l.* the land desolate *Isa 13:9; Eze 33:28*
I will *l.* low the haughtiness   *Isa 13:11*
of the terrible
key of house of David *l.* on   *Isa 22:22*
his shoulder
and the fortress shall he *l.* low   *Isa 25:12*
behold, I will *l.* in Zion a   *Isa 28:16*
tried stone
judgment will I *l.* to the line,   *Isa 28:17*
and righteousness
that *l.* a snare for him that   *Isa 29:21*
reproveth
the staff which the Lord shall   *Isa 30:32*
l. on him
there shall the great owl *l.*   *Isa 34:15*
and hatch
a lump of figs, and *l.* it for a   *Isa 38:21*
plaister
so thou didst not *l.* these   *Isa 47:7*
things to thy heart
I will *l.* thy stones with fair   *Isa 54:11*
colours
I will *l.* stumblingblock   *Jer 6:21;*
Eze 3:20
take thee a tile, and *l.* it before   *Eze 4:1*
thee
l. siege against it   *Eze 4:2; 4:3*
l. the iniquity of the house of   *Eze 4:4*
Israel upon it
l. bands on thee   *Eze 4:8*
I will *l.* my vengeance on   *Eze 25:14;*
Edom   *25:17*
I will *l.* thee before kings to   *Eze 28:17*
behold thee
I will *l.* thy flesh on the   *Eze 32:5*
mountains, and fill
and I will *l.* no famine upon   *Eze 36:29*
you
the land shall be tilled,   *Eze 36:34*
whereas it *l.* desolate
I will *l.* sinews upon you and   *Eze 37:6*
bring flesh
there *l.* the most holy things *Eze 42:13;*
42:14; 44:19
O Lord, *l.* not on us innocent   *Jon 1:14*
blood
the idols thereof will I *l.*   *Mic 1:7*
desolate
though it *l.* wait (B)   *Hab 2:3*
if ye will not *l.* it to heart, I   *Mal 2:2*
will send a curse, because ye
do not *l.* it to heart
hath not where to *l.* his head   *M't 8:20;*
Lu 9:58
bind, and *l.* them on men's   *M't 23:4*
shoulders
come, see the place where the   *M't 28:6*
Lord *l.*
the bed wherein the sick of the   *M'k 2:4*
palsy *l.*
and shall *l.* thee even with the   *Lu 19:44*
ground
in these *l.* impotent folk, blind,   *Joh 5:3*
halt
it was a cave, and a stone *l.*   *Joh 11:38*
upon it
Lord, *l.* not this sin to their   *Ac 7:60*
charge
to *l.* on you no greater burden   *Ac 15:28*
than these
and no small tempest *l.* on us,   *Ac 27:20*
all hope
l. any thing to the charge of   *Ro 8:33*
God's elect
behold, I *l.* in Zion a   *Ro 9:33*
stumblingblock
let every one *l.* by him in store   *1Co 16:2*
let us *l.* aside every weight,   *Heb 12:1*
and the sin
wherefore *l.* apart all filthiness   *Jas 1:21*
I *l.* in Zion a chief cornerstone   *1Pe 2:6*

LAY *DOWN*

before they *l. down* men of   *Ge 19:4*
Sodom compassed
and Lot perceived not when   *Ge 19:33;*
she *l. down*   *19:35*
Jacob *l. down* in that place   *Ge 28:11*
to sleep
couched, he *l. down* as a lion,   *Nu 24:9*
as a young
he *l. down* at her feet, he   *J'g 5:27*
bowed, he fell

uncover his feet, and *l.* thee *down*	*Ru 3:4*
lie down, and Samuel went	*1Sa 3:5;*
and *l. down*	*3:9*
Saul *l. down* naked, all that day and night	*1Sa 19:24*
Jonadab said, L. thee *down* on thy bed	*2Sa 13:5*
so Amnon *l. down* and made himself sick	*2Sa 13:6*
l. down now, put me in surety with thee	*Job 17:3*
I will *l.* me *down* in peace and sleep	*Ps 4:8*
young lions *l.* them *down* in their dens	*Ps 104:22*
thy mother *l. down* among lions	*Eze 19:2*
they *l.* themselves *down* on clothes	*Am 2:8*
and I *l. down* my life for my sheep	*Joh 10:15;* *10:17*
I *l.* it *down* of myself, I have power to *l.* it *down*	*Joh 10:18*
I will *l. down* my life for thy sake	*Joh 13:37;* *13:38*
that a man *l. down* his life for his friends	*Joh 15:13*
we ought to *l. down* our lives for the brethren	*1Jo 3:16*

LAY *HAND*

he said, L. not thy *hand* on the lad	*Ge 22:12*
shed no blood, *l.* no *hand* upon Joseph	*Ge 37:22*
that I may *l.* my *hand* upon Egypt	*Ex 7:4*
l. his *hand* on the head of his offering	*Le 3:2;* *3:8*
l. his *hand* on the head of the goat	*Le 3:13;* *4:24*
he shall *l.* his *hand* on the bullock's head	*Le 4:4;* *4:15*
he shall *l.* his *hand* on the sin offering	*Le 4:29;* *4:33*
the Lord said, L. thy *hand* on Joshua	*Nu 27:18*
l. thy *hand* upon thy mouth, and go	*J'g 18:19*
and sought to *l. hand* on the king	*Es 2:21*
to *l. hand* on such as sought their hurt	*Es 9:2*
any daysman to *l.* his *hand* on us both	*Job 9:33*
mark me, and *l.* your *hand* upon your mouth	*Job 21:5*
shall I answer I will *l.* my *hand* on my mouth	*Job 40:4*
l. thy *hand* upon him, remember the battle	*Job 41:8*
if thou thought evil, *l. hand* on mouth	*Pr 30:32*
they shall *l.* their *hand* on Edom	*Isa 11:14*
they shall *l.* their *hand* on their mouth	*Mic 7:16*
come, and *l.* thy *hand* on her	*M't 9:18*

LAY *HANDS*

Aaron shall *l.* both his *hands* on the goat	*Le 16:21*
all that heard him *l.* their *hands* on head	*Le 24:14*
the Levites *l.* their *hands* on the bullocks	*Nu 8:12*
if ye do so again, I will *l. hands* on you	*Ne 13:21*
he thought scorn to *l. hands* on Mordecai alone	*Es 3:6*
they sought to *l. hands* on him	*M't 21:46;* *Lu 20:19*
come and *l.* thy *hands* on her	*M'k 5:23*
l. hands on the sick, and they shall recover	*M'k 16:18*
they shall *l. hands* on you, and persecute	*Lu 21:12*
on whomsoever I *l. hands* he may receive	*Ac 8:19*
l. hands suddenly on no man, nor be	*1Ti 5:22*

LAY *HOLD*

then shall his father *l. hold* on him	*De 21:19*
and *l. hold* on her, and lie with her	*De 22:28*

l. thee *hold* on one of the young men	*2Sa 2:21*
put forth his hand, saying, L.	*1Ki 13:4*
hold on him a tree of life to them that *l. hold* on her	*Pr 3:18*
and I sought to *l. hold* on folly, till I might	*Ec 2:3*
they shall roar, and *l. hold* on the prey	*Isa 5:29*
they shall *l. hold* on bow and spear	*Jer 6:23*
every one shall *l. hold* on his neighbour	*Zec 14:13*
will he not *l. hold* on it, and lift it out	*M't 12:11*
his friends went out to *l. hold* on him	*M'k 3:21*
they sought to *l. hold* on him, but feared	*M'k 12:12*
l. hold on eternal life, whereunto	*1Ti 6:12;* *6:19*
to *l. hold* on the hope set before us	*Heb 6:18*

LAY *UP*

l. up corn under the hand of Pharaoh	*Ge 41:35*
l. up manna for you till the morning	*Ex 16:23*
l. up a pot of manna to be kept for generations	*Ex 16:38*
shall *l.* them *up* in the tabernacle	*Nu 17:4*
l. them *up* without the camp in a clean place	*Nu 19:9*
l. up these my words in your heart	*De 11:18*
and shall *l.* it *up* within thy gates	*De 14:28*
and *l. up* his words in thy heart	*Job 22:22*
then shalt *l. up* gold as dust and stones	*Job 22:24*
l. up my commandments with thee	*Pr 7:1*
wise men *l. up* knowledge, but the foolish	*Pr 10:14*
l. not *up* for you treasures on earth	*M't 6:19*
l. up for yourselves treasures in heaven	*M't 6:20*
children not to *l. up* for the parents	*2Co 12:14*

LAY *WAIT*

delivered us from such as *l.* in wait	*Ezr 8:31*
that *l. wait* for my soul take counsel	*Ps 71:10*
let us *l. wait* for blood, let us lurk	*Pr 1:11*
and they *l. wait* for their own blood, and lurk	*Pr 1:18*
l. not *wait* against the righteous	*Pr 24:15*
they *l. wait* as he that setteth snares	*Jer 5:26*

LAY *WASTE*

that shouldest be to *l. waste*	*2Ki 19:25;* *Isa 37:26*
I will *l.* it *waste*, it shall not be pruned	*Isa 5:6*
I will *l.* thy cities *waste*, thou shalt	*Eze 35:4*

LAY, with a woman

the firstborn *l.* with her father	*Ge 19:33;* *19:34-35*
and Jacob *l.* with Leah that night	*Ge 30:16*
Shechem *l.* with Dinah and defiled her	*Ge 34:2*
Reuben went and *l.* with Bilhah	*Ge 35:22*
man that *l.* with woman, both shall die	*De 22:22*
the man only that *l.* with her shall die	*De 22:25*
the man that *l.* with her give fifty shekels	*De 22:29*
Eli heard they *l.* with the women	*1Sa 2:22*
she came, and he *l.* with her	*2Sa 11:4;* *12:24*

Amnon forced Tamar and *l.* with her	*2Sa 13:14*
for in her youth they *l.* with her	*Eze 23:8*

LAYEDST

takest up that thou *l.* not down	*Lu 19:21*

LAYERS

l. of fat on loins (A)(B)(E)(R)	*Job 15:27*

LAYEST

thou *l.* the burden of this people on me	*Nu 11:11*
wherefore *l.* thou a snare for my life	*1Sa 28:9*

LAYETH

God *l.* up his iniquity for his children	*Job 21:19*
soul crieth out, yet God *l.* not folly to them	*Job 24:12*
the sword of him that *l.* at him cannot hold	*Job 41:26*
he *l.* up the depth in storehouses	*Ps 33:7*
he *l.* the beams of his chambers in waters	*Ps 104:3*
he *l.* up wisdom for the righteous	*Pr 2:7*
deals with knowledge, but a fool *l.* open folly	*Pr 13:16*
dissembleth, and *l.* up deceit with him	*Pr 26:24*
she *l.* her hands to the spindle, her hands	*Pr 31:19*
the lofty city he *l.* low to the ground	*Isa 26:5*
blessed is the man that *l.* hold on it	*Isa 56:2*
righteous perisheth, and no man *l.* it to heart	*Isa 57:1*
in heart he *l.* wait; *l.* it to heart	*Jer 9:8;* *12:11*
Lord *l.* the foundation of the earth	*Zec 12:1*
so is he that *l.* up treasure for himself	*Lu 12:21*
found, he *l.* it on his shoulders rejoicing	*Lu 15:5*

LAYING

or hurl at him by *l.* wait, that he die	*Nu 35:20*
have cast on him any thing without *l.* wait	*Nu 35:22*
they commune of *l.* snares privily	*Ps 64:5*
l. Babylon waste (R)	*Jer 51:55*
l. bare from (A)(B)(E)(R)	*Hab 3:13*
for *l.* aside the commandment of God	*M'k 7:8*
l. wait for him, and seeking to catch	*Lu 11:54*
that through *l.* on the apostles' hands	*Ac 8:18*
but their *l.* wait was known of Saul	*Ac 9:24*
l. before them the facts (N)	*Ac 11:4*
Paul's kinsmen heard of their *l.* in wait	*Ac 23:16*
send for him, *l.* wait in the way to kill him	*Ac 25:3*
with *l.* on of the hands of the presbytery	*1Ti 4:14*
l. up in store a good foundation for time to	*1Ti 6:19*
not *l.* again the foundation of repentance	*Heb 6:1*
of doctrine of baptisms, and of *l.* on of hands	*Heb 6:2*
l. aside all malice, guile, and hypocrisies	*1Pe 2:1*

LAYMEN

untrained *l.* (N)	*Ac 4:13*

LAZARUS

there was a certain beggar named L.	*Lu 16:20*
he seeth L. in Abraham's bosom	*Lu 16:23*
send L.	*Lu 16:24*

and likewise *L.* received evil things, but now | *Lu 16:25*
Mary whose brother *L.* was sick | *Joh 11:2*
Jesus loved *L.*; our friend *L.* sleepeth | *Joh 11:5; 11:11*
L. is dead; he cried, *L.* come forth | *Joh 11:14; 11:43*
L. was one of them that sat at the table | *Joh 12:2*
much people came that they might see *L.* | *Joh 12:9*
when he called *L.* out of grave and raised him | *Joh 12:17*

LAZINESS

l. makes one sleep heavy (B) | *Pr 19:15*

LAZY

for they are *l.* (B) | *Ex 5:8; 5:17*
by field of the *l.* man (A)(B) | *Pr 24:30*
the *l.* man on his bed (B)(E)(R) | *Pr 26:14*
l., idle, servant (A) | *M't 25:26*
despicable and *l.* slave (B)(N)(P) | *M't 25:26*
become worse than *l.* (P) | *1Ti 5:13*

LEAD

I will *l.* on softly, according as the | *Ge 33:14*
of a cloud, to *l.* them the way | *Ex 13:21*
sank as *l.* in the mighty waters | *Ex 15:10*
l. the people unto the place of | *Ex 32:34*
which may *l.* them out, and | *Nu 27:17*
brass, the iron, the tin, and the *l.* | *Nu 31:22; Eze 22:18*
whither the Lord shall *l.* you | *De 4:27*
of the armies to *l.* the people | *De 20:9*
whither the Lord shall *l.* thee | *De 28:37*
the Lord alone did *l.* him, and | *De 32:12*
and *l.* thy captivity captive | *J'g 5:12*
that they may *l.* them away | *1Sa 30:22*
were to *l.* with lyres (A)(R)(S) | *1Ch 15:21*
before them that *l.* them captive | *2Ch 30:9*
by day, to *l.* them in the way | *Ne 9:19*
graven with an iron pen and *l.* | *Job 19:24*
L. me, O Lord, in thy righteousness | *Ps 5:8*
L. me in thy truth, and teach me | *Ps 25:5*
l. me in a plain path, because | *Ps 27:11*
name's sake *l.* me, and guide me | *Ps 31:3*
let them *l.* me; let them bring me | *Ps 43:3*
city? who will *l.* me into Edom | *Ps 60:9; 108:10*
l. me to the rock that is higher | *Ps 61:2*
Lord shall *l.* them forth with | *Ps 125:5*
Even there shall thy hand *l.* me | *Ps 139:10*
and *l.* me in the way everlasting | *Ps 139:24*
l. me into the land of uprightness | *Ps 143:10*
When thou goest, it shall *l.* thee | *Pr 6:22*
I *l.* in the way of righteousness | *Pr 8:20*
I would *l.* thee, and bring thee | *Ca 8:2*
they which *l.* thee cause thee to err | *Isa 3:12*
and a little child shall *l.* them | *Isa 11:6*
of Assyria *l.* away the Egyptians | *Isa 20:4*
shall gently *l.* those that are | *Isa 40:11*
l. them in paths that they have not | *Isa 42:16*
hath mercy on them shall *l.* them | *Isa 49:10*
I will *l.* him also, and restore | *Isa 57:18*
so didst thou *l.* thy people, to make | *Isa 63:14*
the *l.* is consumed of the fire | *Jer 6:29*
with supplications will I *l.* them | *Jer 31:9*
he shall *l.* Zedekiah to Babylon | *Jer 32:5*
silver, and brass, and iron, and *l.* | *Eze 22:20*
silver, iron, tin, and *l.* they | *Eze 27:12*
maids shall *l.* her as with the voice | *Na 2:7*
there was lifted up a talent of *l.* | *Zec 5:7*
the weight of *l.* upon the mouth | *Zec 5:8*

And *l.* us not into temptation | *M't 6:13; Lu 11:4*
if the blind *l.* the blind, both shall | *M't 15:14*
when they shall *l.* you, and deliver | *M'k 13:11*
take him and *l.* him away safely | *M'k 14:44*
them, Can the blind *l.* the blind | *Lu 6:39*
stall, and *l.* him away to watering | *Lu 13:15*
l. a life of daily luxury (P) | *Lu 16:19*
seeking some to *l.* him by the hand | *Ac 13:11*
we not power to *l.* about a sister | *1Co 9:5*
may *l.* a quiet and peaceable life | *1Ti 2:2*
l. captive silly women laden with | *2Ti 3:6*
settle nothing, *l.* nowhere (P) | *Tit 3:9*
to *l.* them out of the land of Egypt | *Heb 8:9*
that would *l.* you astray (E)(P) | *1Jo 2:26*
shall *l.* them into living fountains | *Re 7:17*

LEADER

clan *l.* (B) | *Nu 3:24; 3:30, 35; 25:14*
leader (S) | *Nu 3:32; 4:46; 2Sa 23:13; 1Ki 8:1; 9:23; 1Ch 9:34; 15:16; Ne 12:24, 46*
was the *l.* of the Aaronites | *1Ch 12:27*
and hundreds, and with every *l.* | *1Ch 13:1*
Jezrahiah as *l.* (A)(R) | *Ne 12:42*
a *l.* and commander to the people | *Isa 55:4*
the *l.* of the nations (B) | *Jer 31:7*
l. shall arise (A)(B)(N) | *M't 2:6*
who would be *l.* (N)(P) | *3Jo 9*

LEADERS

the tribal *l.* (B) | *Nu 31:26*
which were *l.* of Sihon (S) | *Jos 13:21*
who are *l.* in Moab (B) | *Jos 4:22*
leaders (B) | *1Ch 7:3; 24:4; Ezr 5:10*
the clan *l.* (B) | *1Ch 9:34; 24:31; 26:32; 2Ch 26:12*
the *l.* and captains in the camp of | *2Ch 32:21*
l. of the people (A) | *Job 12:24*
the *l.* of this people cause them | *Isa 9:16*
alone: they be blind *l.* of the blind | *M't 15:14*

LEADER'S

nor *l.* staff from (A)(B) | *Ge 49:10*
the *l.* portion (A) | *De 33:21*

LEADERSHIP

attain to *l.* (B) | *Pr 1:5*
where there is no *l.* (B) | *Pr 11:14*

LEADEST

thou that *l.* Joseph like a flock | *Ps 80:1*

LEADETH

turned unto the way that *l.* to Ophrah | *1Sa 13:17*
He *l.* counsellors away spoiled | *Job 12:17*
He *l.* princes away spoiled | *Job 12:19*
he *l.* me beside the still waters | *Ps 23:2*
l. me in paths of righteousness | *Ps 23:3*
l. into the way that is not good | *Pr 16:29*
which *l.* thee by the way that thou | *Isa 48:17*
is the way, that *l.* to destruction | *M't 7:13*
narrow is the way, which *l.* unto life | *M't 7:14*
l. them up into an high mountain | *M'k 9:2*
sheep by name, and *l.* them out | *Joh 10:4*
the iron gate that *l.* unto the city | *Ac 12:10*
of God *l.* thee to repentance | *Ro 2:4*
He that *l.* into captivity shall go | *Re 13:10*

LEADING

harps for *l.* off (B)(E) | *1Ch 15:21*
l. men (B)(R) | *Ezr 7:28*
l. men (N)(P)(R) | *Ac 13:50*
the *l.* woman (A)(R) | *Ac 17:4*
teaching and *l.* astray (A) | *Re 2:20*

LEADS

road *l.* headlong into (B) | *Nu 22:32*
wicked *l.* them astray (A)(B)(R) | *Pr 12:26*
who *l.* a loose life (N) | *1Co 5:11*

LEAF

lo, in her mouth was an olive *l.* | *Ge 8:11*
the sound of a shaken *l.* shall chase | *Le 26:36*
thou break a *l.* driven to and fro | *Job 13:25*
his *l.* also shall not wither: and | *Ps 1:3*
flourish like a green *l.* (B)(E)(R) | *Pr 11:28*
shall be as an oak whose *l.* fadeth | *Isa 1:30*
whose *l.* withers (A)(R) | *Isa 1:30*
as the *l.* falleth off from the vine | *Isa 34:4*
rags, and we all do fade as a *l.* | *Isa 64:6*
on the fig tree, and the *l.* shall fade | *Jer 8:13*
cometh, but her *l.* shall be green | *Jer 17:8*
whose *l.* shall not fade, neither shall | *Eze 47:12*
and the *l.* thereof for medicine | *Eze 47:12*

LEAGUE

therefore make ye a *l.* with us | *Jos 9:6*
make a covenant with us (A)(E)(R) | *Jos 9:6*
make a treaty with us (B) | *Jos 9:6; 9:15*
how shall we make a *l.* with you | *Jos 9:7*
therefore now make ye a *l.* with us | *Jos 9:11*
them, and made a *l.* with them | *Jos 9:15*
after they had made a *l.* with them | *Jos 9:16*
make no *l.* with the inhabitants of | *J'g 2:2*
make no covenant with (A)(B)(E)(R) | *J'g 2:2*
made a *l.* with the son of Jesse | *1Sa 22:8*
made a covenant with (B) | *1Sa 22:8*
Make thy *l.* with me, and | *2Sa 3:12*
Well; I will make a *l.* with thee | *2Sa 3:13*
that they may make a *l.* with thee | *2Sa 3:21*
king David made a *l.* with them | *2Sa 5:3*
made a covenant with (A)(E)(R) | *2Sa 5:3*
made a compact with (B) | *2Sa 5:3*
and they two made a *l.* together | *1Ki 5:12*
agreed to a treaty (A)(B)(R) | *1Ki 5:12*
There is a *l.* | *1Ki 15:19; 2Ch 16:3*
between me and thee | *1Ki 15:19; 2Ch 16:3*
a treaty between (B) | *1Ki 15:19; 2Ch 16:3*
break thy *l.* with Baasha king | *2Ch 16:3*
thou shalt be in *l.* with the stones | *Job 5:23*
Syria is in *l.* with Ephraim (R) | *Isa 7:2*
and the men of the land that is in *l.* | *Eze 30:5*
after the *l.* made with him he shall | *Da 11:23*
time that an alliance was made (A)(R) | *Da 11:23*
when a treaty has been made (B) | *Da 11:23*

LEAH

the name of the elder daughter was *L.* | *Ge 29:16*
L. was tender eyed, but Rachel was beautiful | *Ge 29:17*
in the morning, behold it was *L.* | *Ge 29:25*
when the Lord saw that *L.* was hated | *Ge 29:31*
L. conceived and bare a son | *Ge 29:32; 30:19*

Jacob came out of the field, *L.* *Ge 30:16;*
met him
Jacob called Rachel and *L.* to *Ge 31:4*
his flock
Jacob put *L.* and her children *Ge 33:2*
after
Dinah the daughter of *L.* *Ge 34:1*
went out to see
the sons of *L.* Reuben, *Ge 35:23;*
Simeon *46:15*
they buried Abraham, there I *Ge 49:31*
buried *L.*
the Lord make this woman like *Ru 4:11*
L.

LEAH'S

Zilpah *L.* maid before Jacob *Ge 30:10;*
a son *30:12*
into Jacob's tent, and into *L.* *Ge 31:33*
tent
went he out of *L.* tent and *Ge 31:33*
entered
the sons of Zilpah, *L.* *Ge 35:26*
handmaid

LEAKS

through idleness the house *l.* *Ec 10:18*
(A)(B)(R)

LEAN

ugly and *l.* (B) *Ge 41:3*
l. and the ill favoured kine *Ge 41:20*
did eat
l. toward the majority (B) *Ex 23:2*
the land is, whether it be fat *Nu 13:20*
or *l.*
standeth, that I may *l.* upon *J'g 16:26*
them
the king's son, *l.* from day to *2Sa 13:4*
day
on which if a man *l.* it will *2Ki 18:21*
go into
He shall *l.* upon his house, but *Job 8:15*
l. not unto thine *Pr 3:5*
understanding
shall no more *l.,* but shall *l.* *Isa 10:20*
(S)
fatness of his flesh shall wax *l.* *Isa 17:4*
whereon if a man *l.* it will go *Isa 36:6*
fat cattle and between the *l.* *Eze 34:20*
cattle
yet will they *l.* upon the Lord *Mic 3:11*

LEANED

behold Saul *l.* upon his spear *2Sa 1:6*
a Lord on whose hand the king *2Ki 7:2*
l.
the lord on whose hand he *l.* *2Ki 7:17*
to have
and when they *l.* upon thee, *Eze 29:7*
thou
house, and *l.* his hand on the *Am 5:19*
wall
also *l.* on his breast at supper *Joh 21:20*

LEANETH

or that *l.* on a staff, or that *2Sa 3:29*
falleth
and he *l.* on my hand, and I *2Ki 5:18*
bow

LEANFLESHED

the river, ill favoured, and *l.* *Ge 41:3*
ill favoured and *l.* kine did eat *Ge 41:4*
poor and very ill favoured *Ge 41:19*
and *l.*

LEANING

wilderness *l.* upon her beloved *Ca 8:5*
there was *l.* on Jesus' bosom *Joh 13:23*
one
worshipped, *l.* upon the top *Heb 11:21*
of his staff

LEANNESS

and my *l.* rising up in me *Job 16:8*
beareth
request but sent *l.* into their *Ps 106:15*
soul
hosts, send among his fat *Isa 10:16*
ones *l.*
I said, My *l.* my *l.,* woe unto *Isa 24:16*
me

LEANNOTH

Musician upon Mahalath *L.* *Ps 88 title*

LEANS

l. on you (A) *Isa 26:3*

LEAP

the rams, which *l.* upon the *Ge 31:12*
cattle
feet, to *l.* withal upon the earth *Le 11:21*
whelp: he shall *l.* from *De 33:22*
Bashan
l. like a locust *Job 39:20*
(A)(B)(E)(R)
lamps, and sparks of fire *l.* *Job 41:19*
out
Why *l.* ye, ye high hills *Ps 68:16*
look with grudging envy (A) *Ps 68:16*
gaze with envious hostility *Ps 68:16*
(B)
look ye askance (E) *Ps 68:16*
look ye with envy (R) *Ps 68:16*
Then shall the lame man *l.* as *Isa 35:6*
the tops of mountains shall *Joe 2:5*
they *l.*
all those that *l.* on the threshold *Zep 1:9*
ye in that day, and *l.* for joy *Lu 6:23*

LEAPED

the rams which *l.* upon the *Ge 31:10*
cattle
by my God have I *l.* over a *2Sa 22:30;*
wall *Ps 18:29*
vault over a wall (B) *2Sa 22:30*
they *l.* upon the altar which *1Ki 18:26*
(A)(R)
limped about the altar *1Ki 18:26*
hopped about the altar (B) *1Ki 18:26*
of Mary, the babe *l.* in her *Lu 1:41*
womb
the babe *l.* in my womb for joy *Lu 1:44*
on thy feet. And he *l.* and *Ac 14:10*
walked
sprang up and walked *Ac 14:10*
(B)(N)(P)(R)
the evil spirit was *l.* on them *Ac 19:16*

LEAPING

David *l.* and dancing before *2Sa 6:16*
the
he cometh *l.* upon the *Ca 2:8*
mountains
And he *l.* up stood, and walked *Ac 3:8*
walking and *l.,* and praising *Ac 3:8*
God

LEARN

to *l.* whether the Lord had *Ge 24:21*
(S)
that they may *l.* to fear me all *De 4:10*
that ye may *l.* them, and keep *De 5:1*
mayest *l.* to fear the Lord thy *De 14:23*
God
he may *l.* to fear the Lord his *De 17:19*
God
not *l.* to do after the *De 18:9*
abominations
that they may *l.* and fear the *De 31:12*
Lord
and *l.* to fear the Lord your *De 31:13*
God
to *l.* what it was (S) *Es 4:5*
that I might *l.* thy statutes *Ps 119:71*
that I may *l.* thy *Ps 119:73*
commandments
Lest thou *l.* his ways, and get *Pr 22:25*
L. to do well; seek judgment *Isa 1:17*
neither shall they *l.* war any *Isa 2:4*
more
of the world will *l.* *Isa 26:9*
righteousness
yet will he not *l.* righteousness *Isa 26:10*
that murmured shall *l.* *Isa 29:24*
doctrine
Lord, *L.* not the way of the *Jer 10:2*
heathen
diligently *l.* the ways of my *Jer 12:16*
people
neither shall they *l.* war any *Mic 4:3*
more
go ye and *l.* what that *M't 9:13*
meaneth
my yoke upon you, and *l.* of *M't 11:29*
me

Now *l.* a parable of the fig *M't 24:32;*
tree *M'k 13:28*
l. its lesson (A)(B)(N)(R) *M't 24:32*
might *l.* in us not to think of *1Co 4:6*
men
one by one, that all may *l.* *1Co 14:31*
and all
And if they will *l.* any thing, *1Co 14:35*
let
This only would I *l.* of you *Ga 3:2*
l. to master own body (N)(P) *1Th 4:4*
they may *l.* not to blaspheme *1Ti 1:20*
Let the woman *l.* in silence *1Ti 2:11*
them *l.* first to shew piety at *1Ti 5:4*
home
withal they *l.* to be idle, *1Ti 5:13*
wandering
also *l.* to maintain good works *Tit 3:14*
no man could *l.* that song but *Re 14:3*

LEARNED

I have *l.* by experience that *Ge 30:27*
I have *l.* by divination (B) *Ge 30:27*
Mordecai *l.* all that was done *Es 4:1*
(S)
the heathen, and *l.* their *Ps 106:35*
works
have *l.* thy righteous *Ps 119:7*
judgments
I neither *l.* wisdom nor have *Pr 30:3*
men deliver to one that is *l.* *Isa 29:11*
delivered to him that is not *l.* *Isa 29:12*
thee: and he saith, I am not *l.* *Isa 29:12*
given me the tongue of the *l.* *Isa 50:4*
mine ear to hear as the *l.* *Isa 50:4*
lion and it *l.* to catch the *Eze 19:3;*
prey *19:6*
from wise, *l.,* and intelligent *M't 11:25*
(B)(N)
heard, and hath *l.* of the *Joh 6:45*
Father
this man letters, having never *Joh 7:15*
l.
Moses was *l.* in all the wisdom *Ac 7:22*
to the doctrine which ye have *Ro 16:17*
l.
destroy wisdom of *l.* (B) *1Co 1:19;*
1:27
But ye have not so *l.* Christ *Eph 4:20*
things, which ye have both *l.* *Ph'p 4:9*
for I have *l.* in whatsoever *Ph'p 4:11*
state I
As ye also *l.* of Epaphras our *Col 1:7*
dear
in the things which thou hast *2Ti 3:14*
l. and
knowing of whom thou hast *l.* *2Ti 3:14*
them
yet *l.* he obedience by the *Heb 5:8*
things

LEARNER

become a *l.* (N) *M't 13:52*

LEARNING

will hear, and will increase *l.* *Pr 1:5*
just man, and he will increase in *Pr 9:9*
l.
sweetness of the lips *Pr 16:21*
increaseth *l.*
his mouth, and addeth *l.* to his *Pr 16:23*
lips
a man of *l.* (B) *Isa 18:24*
whom they might teach the *l.* *Da 1:4*
them knowledge and skill in all *Da 1:17*
l.
much *l.* doth make thee mad *Ac 26:24*
aforetime were written for our *Ro 15:4*
l.
Ever *l.* and never able to come *2Ti 3:7*

LEASE

he will *l.* his vineyard to *M't 21:41*
others (S)

LEASED

leased (S) *Ca 8:11;*
M't 21:33; M'k 12:1; Lu 20:9

LEASING

ye love vanity, and seek after *l.* *Ps 4:2*
seek after lies (A)(R) *Ps 4:2*
pursue falsehood (B) *Ps 4:2*
seek after falsehood (E) *Ps 4:2*
shalt destroy them that speak *l.* *Ps 5:6*
who speak lies (A)(B)(E)(R) *Ps 5:6*

LEAST

not worthy of the *l.* or the Ge 32:10
mercies
that gathered *l.* gathered ten Nu 11:32
homers
I am the *l.* in my father's house J'g 6:15
my family, the *l.* of all 1Sa 9:21
families
one captain of *l.* of master's 2Ki 18:24
servants
l. of flock shall draw them Jer 49:20;
50:45
not the *l.* grain fall upon the Am 9:9
earth
art not the *l.* among the princes M't 2:6
of Judah
break one of these *l.* M't 5:19
commandments, be called *l.* in
John Baptist, he that is *l.* in M't 11:11;
the kingdom of heaven Lu 7:28
which indeed is the *l.* of all M't 13:32
seeds
as ye have done it to the *l.* M't 25:40;
of these 25:45
he that is *l.* among you, the Lu 9:48
same shall
if ye be not able to do that Lu 12:26
which is *l.*
he that is faithful in the *l.* Lu 16:10
unjust in *l.*
heed, from the *l.* to the greatest Ac 8:10
set them to judge who are *l.* 1Co 6:4
esteemed
for I am the *l.* of the apostles, 1Co 15:9
not meet
who am I less than the *l.* of all Eph 3:8
saints
me, from the *l.* to the greatest Heb 8:11

AT LEAST, AT THE LEAST

damsel abide with us, *at the l.* Ge 24:55
ten days
at the l. such as before knew J'g 3:2
nothing
if kept themselves *at l.* from 1Sa 21:4
women
hadst known *at l.* in this thy Lu 19:42
day
that *at the l.* the shadow of Ac 5:15
Peter passing

LEATHER

an hairy man, girt with a girdle 2Ki 1:8
of *l.*
wore a *l.* girdle M't 3:4
(A)(B)(N)(P)(R)
l. belt (S) M't 3:4; M'k 1:6

LEATHERN

John had a *l.* girdle about his M't 3:4
loins
wore a leather girdle M't 3:4
(A)(B)(N)(P)(R)

LEAVE

man *l.* father and mother, and Ge 2:24;
cleave to wife M't 19:5; M'k 10:7;
Eph 5:31
let me *l.* with thee some of the Ge 33:15
folk
l. one of your brethren here Ge 42:33
with me
the lad cannot *l.* his father, if Ge 44:22
he *l.* him
let no man *l.* manna till the Ex 16:19
morning
what they *l.* the beasts of the Ex 23:11
field shall eat
not *l.* any of the peace offering Le 7:15;
22:30
shall put off garments and *l.* Le 16:23
them there
thou shalt *l.* them for the Le 19:10;
poor 23:22
l. none of the passover till Nu 9:12
morning
and he said, *L.* us not, I pray Nu 10:31
thee
for the Lord refuseth to give Nu 22:13
me *l.* to
will yet again *l.* them in the Nu 32:15
wilderness
shall not *l.* thee either corn, De 28:51
wine, or oil

the remnant of children which De 28:54
he shall *l.*
and *l.* them in the lodging place Jos 4:3
the olive said, Should I *l.* my J'g 9:9
fatness
vine said, Should I *l.* my wine, J'g 9:13
which cheereth
Ruth said, Entreat me not to *l.* Ru 1:16
thee
lest my father *l.* caring for the 1Sa 9:5
asses
Saul said, Let us not *l.* a man 1Sa 14:36
of them
David earnestly asked *l.* of 1Sa 20:6;
me 20:28
if I *l.* of all that pertain to 1Sa 25:22
him
shall not *l.* to my husband a 2Sa 14:7
name
let him not *l.* us nor forsake 1Ki 8:57
us
they shall eat and shall *l.* 2Ki 4:43
thereof
nor did he *l.* of the people but 2Ki 13:7
fifty horsemen
may possess this good land, 1Ch 28:8
and *l.* it
grace from Lord to *l.* us a Ezr 9:8
remnant to escape
l. it for an inheritance to your Ezr 9:12
children for ever
I pray you let us *l.* off this Ezr 5:10
usury
why should the work cease Ezr 6:3
whilst I *l.* it.
that we would *l.* the seventh Ezr 10:31
year
after certain days obtained I *l.* Ezr 13:6
of the king
or wilt thou *l.* thy labour to Job 39:11
him
thou wilt not *l.* my soul in Ps 16:10;
hell Ac 2:27
they *l.* their substance to their Ps 17:14
babes
thou hast been my help, *l.* me Ps 27:9;
not 119:121
they die and *l.* their wealth to Ps 49:10
others
O God, my trust, *l.* not my Ps 141:8
soul destitute
who *l.* the paths of uprightness Pr 2:13
l. off contention, before it be Pr 17:14
meddled with
because I should *l.* it to the Ec 2:18
man after me
yet shall he *l.* it for his portion Ec 2:21
if ruler rise up against thee, *l.* Ec 10:4
not thy place
and where will ye *l.* your glory Isa 10:3
and ye shall *l.* your name for Isa 65:15
a curse
I might *l.* my people, and go Jer 9:2
from them
O Lord, we are called by thy Jer 14:9
name, *l.* us not
riches, he shall *l.* them in Jer 17:11
midst of his days
will a man *l.* the snow of Jer 18:14
Lebanon
child and suckling, to *l.* you Jer 44:7
none to remain
l. the cities and dwell in the Jer 48:28
rock
would they not *l.* some Jer 49:9
gleaning grapes
l. thy fatherless children, I Jer 49:11
will preserve them
and *l.* thee naked and bare Eze 16:39;
23:29
will turn thee, and *l.* but a Eze 39:2
sixth part of thee
l. the stump of his root Da 4:15;
4:23, 26
therefore shall he *l.* his blood Ho 12:14
upon him
will return, and *l.* a blessing Joe 2:14
behind him
shall *l.* an hundred, shall *l.* ten Am 5:3
to Israel
ye, who *l.* off righteousness in Am 5:7
the earth
grape gatherers, would they not *l.* Ob 5
grapes
that it shall *l.* them neither Mal 4:1
root nor branch
l. there thy gift before the M't 5:24
altar
doth he not *l.* the ninety and M't 18:12;
nine Lu 15:4

to have done, and not to *l.* M't 23:23
other undone
and forthwith Jesus gave M'k 5:13
them *l.*
and *l.* his wife, and *l.* no M'k 12:19
children
they shall not *l.* in thee one Lu 19:44
stone
my peace I *l.* with you, peace Joh 14:27
I give
l. the world and go to the Joh 16:28
Father
ye shall *l.* me alone, yet I am Joh 16:32
not alone
Pilate gave him *l.* to take Joh 19:38
away body
it is not reason we should *l.* the Ac 6:2
word
Paul took his *l.* of the Ac 18:18
brethren
when we had taken our *l.* one Ac 21:6
of another
to dwell with her, let her not 1Co 7:13
l. him
taking my *l.* I went to 2Co 2:13
Macedonia
I will never *l.* thee nor Heb 13:5
forsake thee
the court *l.* out, and measure it Re 11:2
not

I WILL, WILL I LEAVE

if I say, *I will l.* off my Job 9:27
heaviness
I will l. my complaint on Job 10:1
myself, I will speak
yet *I will l. a* remnant; but I Eze 6:8;
will *l.* a few 12:16
and *I will l.* you there and Eze 22:20
melt you
I will l. thee thrown into the Eze 29:5
wilderness
then *I will l.* thee upon the Eze 32:4
lane and cast
I will l. in midst of thee a Zep 3:12
poor people

I WILL NOT LEAVE

I will not l. thee until I have Ge 28:15
done that
as the Lord liveth, *I will not l.* 2Ki 2:2;
thee 4:30
he said, As they soul liveth, I 2Ki 2:4;
will *not l.* thee 2:6
Lord *I will not l.* him in his Ps 37:33
hand, nor condemn
I will not l. thee together Jer 30:11;
unpunished 46:28
I will not l. you comfortless, I Joh 14:19
will come

LEAVED

to open before him the two *l.* Isa 45:1
gates

LEAVEN

ye shall put away *l.* seven Ex 12:15;
days 12:19
neither shall be *l.* seen in all Ex 13:7
thy quarters
not offer the blood of my Ex 34:25
sacrifice with *l.*
no meat offering shall be made Le 2:11
with *l.*
it shall not be baken with *l.* I Le 6:17
have given
take and eat the meat offering Le 10:12
without *l.*
be of fine flour, they shall be Le 23:17
baken with *l.*
offer a sacrifice of thanksgiving Am 4:5
with *l.*
kingdom of heaven is like *l.* M't 13:33;
Lu 13:21
beware of the *l.* of Pharisees, M't 16:6;
and of Sadducees 16:11; M'k 8:15;
Lu 12:1
bade them not beware of the M't 16:12
l. of bread
little *l.* leaveneth the whole 1Co 5:6;
lump Ga 5:9
purge out therefore the old *l.* 1Co 5:7
that ye may be
let us keep the feast, not with 1Co 5:8
old *l.* or of malice

LEAVENED

for whosoever eateth *l.* bread   *Ex 12:15; 12:19*
ye shall eat nothing *l.* in all   *Ex 12:20*
your habitations
people took their dough   *Ex 12:34;*
before it was *l.*   *12:39*
there shall no *l.* bread be eaten   *Ex 13:3; 13:7*
after he hath kneaded the   *Ho 7:4*
dough till it be *l.*
till the whole was *l.*   *M't 13:33; Lu 13:21*

LEAVENETH

a little leaven *l.* the whole   *1Co 5:6;*
lump   *Ga 5:9*

LEAVES

they sewed fig *l.* together, and   *Ge 3:7*
the two *l.* of the one door   *1Ki 6:34*
were
the two *l.* of the other door   *1Ki 6:34*
were
oak shedding withering *l.* (B)   *Isa 1:30*
is in them, when they cast   *Isa 6:13*
their *l.*
Jehudi had read three or four   *Jer 36:23*
l.
wither in all the *l.* of her   *Eze 17:9*
spring
had two *l.* apiece, two turning   *Eze 41:24*
l.
two *l.* for the one door   *Eze 41:24*
and two *l.* for the other door   *Eze 41:24*
The *l.* thereof were fair, and   *Da 4:12*
off his branches, shake off his   *Da 4:14*
l.
Whose *l.* were fair, and the   *Da 4:21*
fruit
found nothing thereon, but *l.*   *M't 21:19*
only
yet tender, and putteth forth   *M't 24:32*
l.
seeing a fig tree afar off   *M'k 11:13*
having *l.*
came to it, he found nothing   *M'k 11:13*
but *l.*
yet tender, and putteth forth   *M'k 13:28*
l.
love *l.* no choice (N)   *2Co 5:14*
l. of the trees were for the   *Re 22:2*
healing

LEAVETH

Which *l.* her eggs in the earth   *Job 39:14*
A good man *l.* an inheritance   *Pr 13:22*
to his
like a sweeping rain which *l.* no   *Pr 28:3*
food
the idol shepherd that *l.* the   *Zec 11:17*
flock
Then the devil *l.* him, and   *M't 4:11*
coming, and *l.* the sheep, and   *Joh 10:12*
fleeth

LEAVING

l. Nazareth, he came and   *M't 4:13*
dwelt
and departed *l.* him half dead   *Lu 10:30*
l. the natural use of the woman   *Ro 1:27*
l. the principles of the doctrine   *Heb 6:1*
of
suffered for us, *l.* us an   *1Pe 2:21*
example

LEAVINGS

a cab of dove's *l.* (S)   *2Ki 6:25*

LEBANA

The children of *L.,* the children   *Ne 7:48*

LEBANAH

The children of *L.,* the   *Ezr 2:45*
children

LEBANESE

of *L.* lumber (B)   *1Ki 7:2*

LEBANON

let me see that goodly   *De 3:25*
mountain and *L.*

the Hivites that dwelt in mount   *J'g 3:3*
L.
he sent ten thousand a month   *1Ki 5:14*
to *L.*
the house of the forest of *L.*   *1Ki 7:2; 10:17, 21*
the thistle in *L.* sent to cedar   *2Ki 14:9;*
in *L.*   *2Ch 25:18*
I am come up to the sides of   *2Ki 19:23;*
L.   *Isa 37:24*
thy servants can skill to cut   *2Ch 2:8*
timber in *L.*
L. and Sirion like a young   *Ps 29:6*
unicorn
the fruit thereof shall shake   *Ps 72:16*
like *L.*
he shall grow like a cedar in   *Ps 92:12*
L.
Solomon made a chariot of the   *Ca 3:9*
wood of *L.*
come with me from *L.* my   *Ca 4:8*
spouse, from *L.*
smell of thy garments is like   *Ca 4:11*
the smell of *L.*
a well of living waters, and   *Ca 4:15*
streams from *L.*
his countenance is as *L.*   *Ca 5:15*
excellent as cedars
thy nose is as tower of *L.*   *Ca 7:4*
toward Damascus
L. shall fall   *Isa 10:34*
L. shall be turned into a   *Isa 29:17*
fruitful field
L. is ashamed   *Isa 33:9*
the glory of *L.* shall be given   *Isa 35:2*
unto it
L. is not sufficient to burn for   *Isa 40:16*
burnt offering
the glory of *L.* shall come to   *Isa 60:13*
thee
will a man leave the snow of   *Jer 18:14*
L.
thou art Gilead, and the head   *Jer 22:6*
of *L.* to me
go up to *L.* and cry, Lift up   *Jer 22:20*
thy voice in Bashan
a great eagle, longwinged,   *Eze 17:3*
came to *L.*
and I caused *L.* to mourn for   *Eze 31:15*
him
he shall cast forth his roots as   *Ho 14:5*
L.
his smell as *L.*; the scent as   *Ho 14:6;*
the wine of *L.*   *14:7*
Bashan and the flower of *L.*   *Na 1:4*
languisheth
the violence of *L.* shall cover   *Hab 2:17*
thee
I will bring them into the   *Zec 10:10*
land of *L.*
open thy doors, O *L.* that fire   *Zec 11:1*
may devour

LEBAOTH

And *L.* and Shilhim, and Ain   *Jos 15:32*

LEBBAEUS

James the son of Alphæus,   *M't 10:3*
and *L.*

LEBONAH

Shechem, and on the south of   *J'g 21:19*
L.

LECAH

Er the father of *L.* and   *1Ch 4:21*
Laadah

LED

I being in the way, the Lord *l.*   *Ge 24:27*
me
blessed Lord, who *l.* me in   *Ge 24:48*
right way
Moses *l.* the flock to back side   *Ex 3:1*
of desert
God *l.* them not thro' the land   *Ex 13:17*
of Philistines
but God *l.* them about thro'   *Ex 13:18*
the wilderness
thou in mercy hast *l.* forth the   *Ex 15:13*
people
the way which the Lord *l.* thee   *De 8:2*
forty years
who *l.* thee through that great   *De 8:15*
wilderness

I have *l.* you forty years in the   *De 29:5*
wilderness
he *l.* him about, he instructed   *De 32:10*
him
I *l.* him through all the land of   *Jos 24:3*
Canaan
enemies, which *l.* them away   *1Ki 8:48*
captive
but Elisha *l.* them to Samaria   *2Ki 6:19*
Joab *l.* forth the power of the   *1Ch 20:1*
army
l. Judah astray (S)   *2Ch 21:11*
and Amaziah *l.* forth his   *2Ch 25:11*
people
in the day he *l.* them with a   *Ps 78:14*
cloud
he *l.* them on safely, so that   *Ps 78:53*
they feared not
so he *l.* them thro' the depths   *Ps 106:9;*
as thro' a wilderness   *136:16; Isa 63:13*
he *l.* them forth by the right   *Ps 107:7*
way
I have *l.* thee in right paths   *Pr 4:11*
they that are *l.* of them are   *Isa 9:16*
destroyed
they thirsted not when they *l.*   *Isa 48:21*
them thro'
for ye shall be *l.* forth with   *Isa 55:12*
peace
that *l.* them by the right hand   *Isa 63:12*
of Moses
where is the Lord that *l.* us   *Jer 2:6*
thro' wilderness
hath forsaken God, when he *l.*   *Jer 2:17*
thee by the way
shall die in the place whither   *Jer 22:12*
they have *l.* him
the Lord liveth which *l.* the   *Jer 23:8*
house of Israel
he hath *l.* me into darkness, not   *La 3:2*
light
and *l.* them with him to   *Eze 17:12*
Babylon
who caused them to be *l.*   *Eze 39:28*
into captivity
l. me about to the outer gate   *Eze 47:2*
eastward
also I *l.* you 40 years thro' the   *Am 2:10*
wilderness
Israel shall surely be *l.* captive   *Am 7:11*
out of land
and Huzzah shall be *l.* away   *Na 2:7*
captive
then was Jesus *l.* of the Spirit   *M't 4:1; Lu 4:1*
they *l.* him to Caiaphas the   *M't 26:57;*
high priest   *M'k 14:53; Lu 22:54; Joh 18:13*
they *l.* him to Pontius Pilate   *M't 27:2;*
the governor   *27:30; M'k 15:16, 20; Lu 22:54; Joh 18:13*
he took the blind man and *l.*   *M'k 8:23*
him out
they *l.* Jesus to the brow of the   *Lu 4:29*
hill
they shall be *l.* away captive   *Lu 21:24*
into all nations
and *l.* him into their council,   *Lu 22:66*
saying
the whole multitude *l.* him to   *Lu 23:1*
Pilate
two other malefactors were *l.*   *Lu 23:32*
with him
he *l.* them out as far as   *Lu 24:50*
Bethany
they *l.* Jesus unto the hall of   *Joh 18:28*
judgment
he was *l.* as a sheep to the   *Ac 8:32*
slaughter
they *l.* Saul by the hand to   *Ac 9:8; 22:11*
Damascus
as Paul was to be *l.* into the   *Ac 21:37*
castle
as many as are *l.* by Spirit of   *Ro 8:14*
God
carried away to idols, even as   *1Co 12:2*
ye were *l.*
but if ye be *l.* by the Spirit, ye   *Ga 5:18*
are
silly women, *l.* away with divers   *2Ti 3:6*
lusts
beware, lest being *l.* away   *2Pe 3:17*
with error of wicked

LEDDEST

wast he that *l.* out Israel   *2Sa 5:2; 1Ch 11:2*

l. them in the day by a cloudy   *Ne 9:12*
pillar
thou *l.* thy people like a flock   *Ps 77:20*
l. into the wilderness four   *Ac 21:38*
thousand

LEDGE

even to the lowest *l.* (S)   *Eze 43:14*
highest *l.* of temple (P)   *M't 4:5; 4:9*

LEDGER

red *l.* of regulations (B)   *Eph 2:14*

LEDGES

the borders were between   *1Ki 7:28*
the *l.*
borders between the frames   *1Ki 7:28;*
(B)   *7:35-36*
the borders that were between   *1Ki 7:29*
the *l.*
the *l.* and borders thereof   *1Ki 7:35*
were of the same
on the plates of the *l.* he   *1Ki 7:36*
graved cherubims

LEEKS

and the *l.* and the onions, and   *Nu 11:5*

LEES

things, a feast of wines on the   *Isa 25:6*
of wines on the *l.* well refined   *Isa 25:6*
hath settled on his *l.* and hath   *Jer 48:11*
not
the men that are settled on   *Zep 1:12*
their *l.*

LEFT

he had *l.* communing with   *Ge 18:33*
Abraham
who hath not *l.* destitute my   *Ge 24:27*
master
his name Judah, and *l.*   *Ge 29:35;*
bearing   *30:9*
then the other company which   *Ge 32:8*
is *l.*
he *l.* all that he had in Joseph's   *Ge 39:6*
hand
he *l.* his garment in her hand   *Ge 39:12;*
  39:13, 15, 18
Joseph gathered corn till *l.*   *Ge 41:49*
numbering
at the eldest, and *l.* at the   *Ge 44:12*
youngest
not enough *l.* but our bodies   *Ge 47:18*
and lands
their little ones *l.* they in   *Ge 50:8*
Goshen
why is it that ye have *l.* the   *Ex 2:20*
man
l. his servants and his cattle in   *Ex 9:21*
field
what is *l.* (A)   *Ex 10:5;*
  Isa 44:17; Eze 48:21; Da 7:1, 19
what is *l.* (B)   *Ex 10:5;*
  Isa 21:17; Eze 9:8
eat every herb, all that the   *Ex 10:12;*
hail *l.*   *10:13*
there shall not an hoof be *l.*   *Ex 16:26*
behind
but some of them *l.* of it till   *Ex 16:20*
morning
nor sacrifice of passover be *l.*   *Ex 34:25*
till morning
that which is *l.* of the meat   *Le 2:10*
offering
and to Ithamar, his sons that   *Le 10:12*
were *l.*
they that are *l.* of you shall   *Le 26:39*
pine away
the land also shall be *l.* of   *Le 26:43*
them and enjoy
there was not *l.* a man of   *Nu 26:65;*
them   *Jos 8:17; J'g 4:16; Ho 9:12*
we utterly destroyed, we *l.*   *De 2:34*
none to remain   *Jos 10:33, 37, 39-40;*
  11:8, 11, 14
ye shall be *l.* few in number   *De 4:27;*
among the heathen   *28:62; Isa 24:6;*
  Jer 42:2
till they that are *l.* be destroyed   *De 7:20*
he hath nothing *l.* him in the   *De 28:55*
siege
power gone, and there is none   *De 32:36*
shut up or *l.*

l. them without the camp of   *Jos 6:23*
Israel
they *l.* the city open, and   *Jos 8:17*
pursued Israel
he *l.* nothing undone of all   *Jos 11:15*
commanded
there was none of the   *Jos 11:22*
Anakims *l.* in the land
ye have not *l.* your brethren to   *Jos 22:3*
this day
of nations which Joshua *l.*   *J'g 2:21*
when he died
therefore the Lord *l.* those   *J'g 2:23;*
nations   *3:1*
l. no sustenance for Israel,   *J'g 6:4*
neither sheep
yet Jotham the youngest son   *J'g 9:5*
was *l.*
and she was *l.* and her two sons   *Ru 1:3;*
  1:5
was minded to go, then she *l.*   *Ru 1:18*
speaking to her
how thou hast *l.* thy father and   *Ru 2:11*
mother
Ruth did eat and was sufficed,   *Ru 2:14*
and *l.*
Lord not *l.* thee this day   *Ru 4:14*
without kinsman
every one that is *l.* in thy   *1Sa 2:36*
house
only the stump of Dagon was *l.*   *1Sa 5:4*
to him
that which is *l.* set it before   *1Sa 9:24*
thee and eat
thy father hath *l.* the care of   *1Sa 10:2*
the asses
so that two of them were not   *1Sa 11:11*
l. together
David rose up and *l.* the   *1Sa 17:20*
sheep with a keeper
David *l.* his carriage in the   *1Sa 17:22*
hand of a keeper
not been *l.* any that pisseth   *1Sa 25:34*
against wall
David *l.* neither man nor   *1Sa 27:9*
woman alive
and there they *l.* their images   *2Sa 5:21*
is there yet any *l.* of the house   *2Sa 9:1*
of Saul
the king's sons, there is not   *2Sa 13:30*
one of them *l.*
so they shall quench my coal   *2Sa 14:7*
which is *l.*
the king *l.* ten concubines   *2Sa 15:16;*
  16:21
there shall not be *l.* so much   *2Sa 17:12*
as one
there was *l.* not one (S)   *2Sa 17:22*
their children that were *l.*   *1Ki 9:21;*
  2Ch 8:8
cut off him that is shut up   *1Ki 14:10;*
and *l.*   *2Ki 9:8*
he *l.* not Jeroboam any that   *1Ki 15:29*
breathed
he *l.* Baasha not one that   *1Ki 16:11*
pisseth against
sickness that there was no   *1Ki 17:17*
breath *l.* in him
and *l.* his servant there; I   *1Ki 19:3;*
only am *l.*   *9:10*
yet I have *l.* me 7000; he *l.*   *1Ki 19:18;*
oxen and   *19:20*
have some *l.* (S)   *2Ki 4:43*
and they did eat and *l.* thereof   *2Ki 4:44*
they arose and *l.* tents; all that   *2Ki 7:7;*
are *l.*   *7:13*
since the day she *l.* the land   *2Ki 8:6*
even until now
Jehu slew all, till he *l.* him   *2Ki 10:11*
none remaining
so that there was not a man   *2Ki 10:21*
l. that came not
for there was not any *l.* nor   *2Ki 14:26*
any helper
they *l.* the commandments of   *2Ki 17:16*
the Lord
this prayer for remnant that   *2Ki 19:4;*
are *l.*   *Isa 37:4*
nothing shall be *l.* saith the   *2Ki 20:17*
Lord
l. of poor of the land   *2Ki 25:12;*
  Jer 39:10; 52:16
send to our brethren that are   *1Ch 13:2*
l.
for the Levites *l.* their   *2Ch 11:14*
suburbs
I have also *l.* you in the hand   *2Ch 12:5*
of Shishak
so that there was never a son   *2Ch 21:17*
l. him

and they *l.* the house of the   *2Ch 24:18*
Lord God
for they *l.* Joash in great   *2Ch 24:25*
diseases
we had enough to eat, and   *2Ch 31:10*
have *l.* plenty
God *l.* him to try him, that   *2Ch 32:31*
he might know
go, inquire for them that are   *2Ch 34:21*
l. in Israel
I asked concerning the Jews   *Ne 1:2*
which had *l.*
the remnant that are *l.* are in   *Ne 1:3*
great affliction
the wall that there was no   *Ne 6:1*
breach *l.* therein
there shall none of his meat   *Job 20:21*
be *l.*
it shall go ill with him that is   *Job 20:26*
l. in his tabernacle
there was not one of them *l.*   *Ps 106:11*
a child *l.* to himself bringeth   *Pr 29:15*
to shame
Zion is *l.* as a cottage in a   *Isa 1:8*
vineyard
except Lord had *l.* us a   *Isa 1:9;*
remnant   *Ro 9:29*
he that is *l.* in Zion shall be   *Isa 4:3*
called holy
butter and honey shall every   *Isa 7:22*
one eat that is *l.*
as one gathereth eggs that are   *Isa 10:14*
l.
a highway for the remnant   *Isa 11:16*
that shall be *l.*
yet gleaning grapes shall be *l.*   *Isa 17:6*
in it
in the city is *l.* desolation,   *Isa 24:12*
and the gate
till ye be *l.* as a beacon on a   *Isa 30:17*
mountain
nothing shall be *l.* saith the   *Isa 39:6*
Lord
I *l.* my heritage; *l.* of the   *Jer 12:7;*
sword   *31:2*
how is the city of praise not *l.*   *Jer 49:25*
the city of joy
destroy her, let nothing of her   *Jer 50:26*
be *l.*
behold, therein shall be *l.* a   *Eze 14:22*
remnant
nor *l.* her whoredoms brought   *Eze 23:8*
from Egypt
strangers have cut him off   *Eze 31:12*
and have *l.* him
the kingdom shall not be *l.* to   *Da 2:44*
other people
what the palmerworm *l.* the   *Joe 1:4*
locust hath *l.*
who is *l.* that saw this house in   *Hag 2:3*
her glory
the third part shall be *l.*   *Zec 13:8*
therein
l. their nets; they *l.* their ships   *M't 4:20;*
  4:22
he touched her, and fever *l.*   *M't 8:15;*
her   *M'k 1:31*
took up of the meat that was   *M't 15:37;*
l.   *M'k 8:8*
he *l.* his wife to his brother   *M't 22:25;*
  M'k 12:20
your house is *l.* unto you   *M't 23:38*
desolate
there shall not be *l.* one stone   *M't 24:2;*
upon another   *M'k 13:2; Lu 21:6*
one taken, other *l.*   *M't 24:40;*
  24:41; Lu 17:34-36
Jesus *l.* them, and prayed the   *M't 26:44*
third time
we have *l.* all and followed   *M'k 10:28*
thee
no man that hath *l.* house   *M'k 10:29;*
  Lu 18:28-29
and the seven had her, and *l.*   *M'k 12:22*
no seed
he *l.* all, rose up, and   *Lu 5:28*
followed him
that my sister hath *l.* me to   *Lu 10:40*
serve alone
the woman then *l.* her   *Joh 4:28*
waterpot
at the seventh hour the fever *l.*   *Joh 4:52*
him
of Christ, that his soul was not   *Ac 2:31*
l. in hell
he *l.* not himself without   *Ac 14:17*
witness
when saw captain, they *l.*   *Ac 21:32*
beating of Paul

and Felix *l.* Paul bound   *Joh 24:27;*
   25:14
we thought good to be *l.* at   *1Th 3:1*
Athens alone
the cloak that I *l.* at Troas   *2Ti 4:13*
bring
Trophimus have I *l.* sick at   *2Ti 3:20*
Miletum
for this cause I *l.* thee at Crete   *Tit 1:5*
he *l.* nothing that is not put   *Heb 2:8*
under
let us fear, lest a promise being   *Heb 4:1*
l. of entering
the angels which *l.* their own   *Jude 6*
habitation
because thou hast *l.* thy first   *Re 2:4*
love

LEFT *CORNER*

guard stood to the *l. corner*   *2Ki 11:11*
about king

LEFTHANDED

raised Ehud a Benjamite, a   *J'g 3:15*
man *l.*
were seven hundred chosen   *J'g 20:16*
men *l.*

LEFT *OFF*

and they *l. off* to build the city   *Ge 11:8*
l. off talking with him, and   *Ge 17:22*
God went up
who hath not *l. off* his kindness   *Ru 2:20*
Baasha *l. off* building   *1Ki 15:21;*
   2Ch 16:5
answered no more, they *l. off*   *Job 32:15*
speaking
he hath *l. off* to be wise and to   *Ps 36:3*
do good
so they *l. off* speaking with   *Jer 38:27*
him
since we *l. off* to burn incense   *Jer 44:18*
to the queen
because they have *l. off* to take   *Ho 4:10*
heed

LEFT *PILLAR*

he set up the *l. pillar* and   *1Ki 7:21*
called it Boaz

LEFT *SIDE*

five bases on the *l. side* of the   *1Ki 7:39*
house
five candlsticks on the *l. side*   *1Ki 7:49*
before
with his weapon from right   *2Ch 23:10*
to *l. side*
they had the face of an ox on   *Eze 1:10*
the *l. side*
lie also on thy *l. side* and lay   *Eze 4:4*
the iniquity
other olive tree upon *l. side*   *Zec 4:3;*
thereof   *4:11*

LEFTEST

therefore *l.* thou them in the   *Ne 9:28*
hand

LEG

make bare the *l.* uncover the   *Isa 47:2*

LEGACY

give it to you as a *l.* (B)   *Ex 6:8*
the *l.* allotted him (B)   *Job 20:29*
children are a *l.* from (B)   *Ps 127:3*
pledge- deposit of our *l.* (B)   *Eph 1:14*

LEGAL

these are *l.* orders (B)   *Ex 21:1*
all the *l.* instructions (B)   *Ex 24:3*
statute for determining *l.* right   *Nu 27:11*
(B)
l. usages by Moses (B)   *Ac 6:14*
let them bring *l.* action (P)   *Ac 19:38*
cancelled *l.* demands (R)   *Col 2:14*

LEGALLY

be handled *l.* (B)   *Es 1:8*

LEGENDS

l. and endless genealogies (A)   *1Ti 1:4*
avoid irreverent *l.*, (A)   *1Ti 4:7*

LEGGINGS

bronze *l.* (B)   *1Sa 17:6*

LEGION

My name is *L.*: for we are   *M'k 5:9*
many
with the devil, and had the *l.*   *M'k 5:15*
What is thy name? And he   *Lu 8:30*
said, *L.*

LEGIONS

me more than twelve *l.* of   *M't 26:53*
angels

LEGITIMATE

every *l.* officer is (P)   *Ro 13:4*

LEGS

his head with his *l.* and with   *Ex 12:9*
wash the inwards of him, and   *Ex 29:17*
his *l.*
inwards and his *l.* shall he wash   *Le 1:9*
he shall wash the inwards and   *Le 1:13*
the *l.*
flesh, with his head, and with   *Le 4:11*
his *l.*
he washed the inwards and the   *Le 8:21*
l.
he did wash the inwards and   *Le 9:14*
the *l.*
which have *l.* above their feet   *Le 11:21*
thee in the knees, and in the *l.*   *De 28:35*
had greaves of brass upon his   *1Sa 17:6*
l.
not pleasure in the *l.* of a   *Ps 147:10*
man
The *l.* of the lame are not equal   *Pr 26:7*
His *l.* are as pillars of marble,   *Ca 5:15*
set
the ornaments of the *l.* and the   *Isa 3:20*
His *l.* of iron, his feet part of   *Da 2:33*
iron
out of the mouth of the lion   *Am 3:12*
two *l.*
that their *l.* might be broken   *Joh 19:31*
and brake the *l.* of the first,   *Joh 19:32*
and of
dead already, they brake not   *Joh 19:33*
his *l.*

LEHABIM

Ludim, and Anamim, and *L.*   *Ge 10:13*
begat Ludim, and Anamim,   *1Ch 1:11*
and *L.*

LEHI

and spread themselves in *L.*   *J'g 15:9*
And when he came unto *L.*   *J'g 15:14*
which is in *L.* unto this day   *J'g 15:19*

LEISURE

they had no *l.* so much as to   *M'k 6:31*
eat
could not conveniently eat   *M'k 6:31*
(B)

LEMUEL

words of king *L.*, the prophecy   *Pr 31:1*
O *L.* it is not for kings to drink   *Pr 31:4*

LEND

thou *l.* money to any of my   *Ex 22:25*
people
l. him thy victuals for increase   *Le 25:37*
thou shalt *l.* unto many nations   *De 15:6*
shalt surely *l.* him sufficient for   *De 15:8*
his
Thou shalt not *l.* upon usury   *De 23:19;*
   23:20
When thou dost *l.* thy brother   *De 24:10*
any
the man to whom thou dost *l.*   *De 24:11*
shall
thou shalt *l.* unto many   *De 28:12*
nations
l. to thee, and thou shalt not   *De 28:44*
l. to
if ye *l.* to them of whom ye   *Lu 6:34*
hope to
sinners also *l.* to sinners, to   *Lu 6:34*
receive

and *l.* hoping for nothing again   *Lu 6:35*
him, Friend, *l.* me three loaves   *Lu 11:5*

LENDER

the borrower is servant to the *l.*   *Pr 22:7*
as with the *l.*, so with the   *Isa 24:2*
borrower

LENDETH

Every creditor that *l.* ought   *De 15:2*
unto
He is ever merciful, and *l.*   *Ps 37:26*
good man sheweth favour, and   *Ps 112:5*
l.
pity upon the poor *l.* unto the   *Pr 19:17*
Lord

LENDING

hesitate *l.* a hand (B)   *Ex 23:5*

LENGTH

arise, walk thro' the land in   *Ge 13:17*
the *l.* of it
he is thy life, and the *l.* of   *De 30:20*
thy days
and in *l.* of days,   *Job 12:12*
understanding
even *l.* of days for ever and   *Ps 21:4*
ever
for *l.* of days shall they add to   *Pr 3:2*
thee
l. of days is in her right hand,   *Pr 21:16*
riches
and to see what is the *l.* thereof   *Zec 2:2*
the *l.* of the roll is twenty cubits   *Zec 5:2*
be able to comprehend *l.* of   *Eph 3:18*
love of Christ
and the *l.* as large as the   *Re 21:16*
breadth

AT LENGTH

shall have him become his son   *Pr 29:21*
at *l.*
if now *at l.* I may have a   *Ro 1:10*
journey

LENGTHEN

did walk then will I *l.* thy days   *1Ki 3:14*
l. thy cords, and strengthen thy   *Isa 54:2*

LENGTHENED

that thy days may be *l.* in the   *De 25:15*
land

LENGTHENING

if it may be a *l.* of thy   *Da 4:27*
tranquillity

LENT

l. unto them such things as   *Ex 12:36*
they
of any thing that is *l.* upon   *De 23:19*
usury
also I have *l.* him to the Lord   *1Sa 1:28*
he liveth he shall be *l.* to the   *1Sa 1:28*
Lord
the loan which is *l.* to the   *1Sa 2:20*
Lord
I have neither *l.* on usury, nor   *Jer 15:10*
nor men have *l.* to me on   *Jer 15:10*
usury

LENTIL

red *l.* stew (A)   *Ge 25:30; 25:34*

LENTILES

gave Esau bread and pottage   *Ge 25:34*
of *l.*
parched corn, and beans, and   *2Sa 17:28*
was a piece of ground full of   *2Sa 23:11*
l.
and beans, and *l.* and millet   *Eze 4:9*

LEOPARD

the *l.* shall lie down with the   *Isa 11:6*
kid
a *l.* shall watch over their cities   *Jer 5:6*

change his skin, or the *l.* his   *Jer 13:23*
spots
I beheld, and lo another, like a   *Da 7:6*
l.
as a *l.* by the way will I   *Ho 13:7*
observe
which I saw was like unto a *l.*   *Re 13:2*

LEOPARDS

from the mountains of the *l.*   *Ca 4:8*
horses also are swifter than   *Hab 1:8*
the *l.*

LEPER

And the *l.* in whom the plague   *Le 13:45*
is
this shall be the law of the *l.* in   *Le 14:2*
plague of leprosy be healed in   *Le 14:3*
the *l.*
soever of the seed of Aaron is a   *Le 22:4*
l.
they put out of the camp every   *Nu 5:2*
l.
that hath an issue, or that is a   *2Sa 3:29*
l.
man in valour, but he was a *l.*   *2Ki 5:1*
over the place, and recover   *2Ki 5:11*
the *l.*
he went out from his presence   *2Ki 5:27*
a *l.*
was a *l.* unto the day of his   *2Ki 15:5*
death
Uzziah the king was a *l.*   *2Ch 26:21*
unto the
dwelt in a several house,   *2Ch 26:21*
being a *l.*
the kings: for they said, He   *2Ch 26:23*
is a *l.*
there came a *l.* and worshipped   *M't 8:2*
in the house of Simon the *l.*   *M't 26:6*
there came a *l.* to him,   *M'k 1:40*
beseeching
in the house of Simon the *l.*   *M'k 14:3*
as he

LEPERS

l. came to the uttermost part of   *2Ki 7:8*
sick, cleanse the *l.* raise the   *M't 10:8*
dead
the *l.* are cleansed, and the   *M't 11:5*
deaf
And many *l.* were in Israel in   *Lu 4:27*
the *l.* are cleansed, the deaf   *Lu 7:22*
hear
there met him ten men that   *Lu 17:12*
were *l.*

LEPROSY

and it be in the skin like the   *Le 13:2*
plague of *l.*
it is a plague of *l.*   *Le 13:3;*
   13:8, 11, 15, 25, 27, 30, 42, 49
when the plague of *l.* is in a   *Le 13:9*
man, then he shall
if a *l.* break out; if the *l.*   *Le 13:12;*
covered his flesh   *13:13*
as the *l.* appeareth in the skin   *Le 13:43*
of the flesh
the garment that the plague of   *Le 13:47*
l. is in
this is the law of the plague   *Le 13:59;*
of *l.*   *14:54-55, 57*
if the plague of *l.* be healed in   *Le 14:3*
the leper
shall sprinkle him that is to be   *Le 14:7*
cleansed from *l.*
the law of him in whom is the   *Le 14:32*
plague of *l.*
take heed in the plague of *l.* to   *De 24:8*
observe
for he would recover him of   *2Ki 5:3;*
his *l.*   *5:7*
that thou mayest recover him   *2Ki 5:6*
of his *l.*
cure the *l.* (S)   *2Ki 5:11*
the *l.* of Naaman shall cleave   *De 5:27*
unto thee
the *l.* rose up in his forehead   *2Ch 26:19*
his *l.* was cleansed   *M't 8:3;*
   M'k 1:42; Lu 5:13
behold, a man full of *l.*   *Lu 5:12*
besought him

LEPROUS

behold, his hand was *l.* as snow   *Ex 4:6*
He is a *l.* man, he is unclean   *Le 13:44*

a *l.* spot (S)   *Le 13:55*
Miriam became *l.* white as   *Nu 12:10*
snow
Miriam, and, behold, she was   *Nu 12:10*
l.
were four *l.* men at the entering   *2Ki 7:3*
in
behold, he was *l.* in his   *2Ch 26:20*
forehead

LESHEM

Dan went up to fight against   *Jos 19:47*
L.
dwelt therein, and called *L.*   *Jos 19:47*
Dan

LESS

looked *l.* favorably (A)   *Ge 31:2*
and gathered some more,   *Ex 16:17*
some *l.*
the poor shall not give *l.* than   *Ex 30:15*
half a shekel
go beyond the word of the   *Nu 22:18*
Lord to do *l.*
to few thou shalt give *l.*   *Nu 26:54;*
inheritance   *33:54*
thy servant knew nothing *l.*   *1Sa 22:15*
or more
Abigail told him nothing *l.* or   *1Sa 25:36*
more
punished us *l.* than our   *Ezr 9:13*
iniquities deserve
God exacteth *l.* than iniquity   *Job 11:6*
deserveth
much *l.* do lying lips a prince   *Pr 17:7*
much *l.* for a servant to rule   *Pr 19:10*
over princes
all nations are counted *l.* than   *Isa 40:17*
nothing
when it is sown is *l.* than all   *M'k 4:31*
seeds
Mary the mother of James   *M'k 15:40*
the *l.*
those members we think *l.*   *1Co 12:23*
honourable
the more I love, the *l.* I am   *2Co 12:15*
loved
who am I *l.* than the least of all   *Eph 3:8*
saints
and that I may be the *l.*   *Ph'p 2:28*
sorrowful
the *l.* is blessed of better   *Heb 7:7*
without contradiction

LESSER

and the *l.* light to rule the   *Ge 1:16*
night
and for the treading of *l.* cattle   *Isa 7:25*
and from the *l.* settle even to   *Eze 43:14*

LESSON

learn its *l.* (A)(B)(N)(R)   *M't 24:32*

LESSONS

beginnings of God's *l.* (B)   *Heb 5:12*

LEST

neither shall ye touch it *l.* ye   *Ge 3:3*
die
l. he put forth his hand, and   *Ge 3:22*
take
l. any finding him should kill   *Ge 4:15*
him
l. we be scattered abroad upon   *Ge 11:4*
l. thou shouldest say, I have   *Ge 14:23*
made
l. thou be consumed in the   *Ge 19:15*
mountain, *l.* thou be consumed   *Ge 19:17*
l. some evil take me, and I die   *Ge 19:19*
did not *l.* (R)   *Ge 20:6;*
De 8:3; Job 31:30; M't 3:15; 24:43;
   Ac 19:30
l. said he, the men of the place   *Ge 26:7*
Because I said, *L.* I die for her   *Ge 26:9*
him, *l.* he will come and smite   *Ge 32:11*
me
l. that he should give seed to   *Ge 38:9*
his
L. peradventure he die also,   *Ge 38:11*
as his
her take it to her, *l.* we be   *De 38:23*
shamed
L. peradventure mischief befall   *Ge 42:4*
l. peradventure I see the evil   *Ge 44:34*
that

l. thou, and thy household,   *Ge 45:11*
and all
l. they multiply, and it come to   *Ex 1:10*
pass
l. he fall upon us with pestilence   *Ex 5:3*
L. peradventure the people   *Ex 13:17*
repent
l. they break through unto the   *Ex 19:21*
Lord
l. the Lord break forth upon   *Ex 19:22*
them
Lord, *l.* he break forth upon   *Ex 19:24*
them
let not God speak with us, *l.*   *Ex 20:19*
we die
l. the land become desolate   *Ex 23:29*
l. they make thee sin against   *Ex 23:33*
me
l. I consume thee in the way   *Ex 33:3*
l. thou make a covenant with   *Ex 34:12;*
   34:15
l. it be for a snare in the midst   *Ex 34:12*
of
neither rend your clothes; *l.* ye   *Le 10:6*
l. wrath come upon all the   *Le 10:6*
people
of the congregation, *l.* ye die   *Le 10:7;*
   10:9
l. the land fall to whoredom   *Le 19:29*
l. they bear sin for it, and die   *Le 22:9*
not touch any holy thing, *l.*   *Nu 4:15*
they die
the holy things are covered, *l.*   *Nu 4:20*
they die
l. ye be consumed in all their   *Nu 16:26*
sins
L. the earth swallow us up also   *Nu 16:34*
congregation, *l.* they bear sin,   *Nu 18:22*
and die
of the children of Israel, *l.* ye   *Nu 18:32*
die
l. thou forget the things which   *De 4:9*
l. they depart from thy heart all   *De 4:9*
L. ye corrupt yourselves, and   *De 4:16*
make
And *l.* thou lift up thine eyes   *De 4:19*
unto
l. ye forget the covenant of the   *De 4:23*
Lord
Then beware *l.* thou forget the   *De 6:12*
Lord
l. the anger of the Lord thy   *De 6:15*
God be
l. the beasts of the field   *De 7:22*
increase
unto thee, *l.* thou be snared   *De 7:25*
therein
l. thou be a cursed thing like it   *De 7:26*
L. when thou hast eaten and   *De 8:12*
art
L. the land whence thou   *De 9:28*
broughtest
l. ye perish quickly from off   *De 11:17*
the good
L. the avenger of the blood   *De 19:6*
pursue
l. he die in the battle   *De 20:5; 20:6-7*
l. his brethren's heart faint as   *De 20:8*
well
l. the fruit of thy seed which   *De 22:9*
thou
l. he cry against thee unto the   *De 24:15*
Lord
l. if he should exceed, and beat   *De 25:3*
L. there should be among you   *De 29:18*
man
l. there should be among you   *De 29:18*
a root
l. their adversaries should   *De 32:27*
behave
and *l.* they should say, Our   *De 32:27*
hand is
l. the pursuers meet you   *Jos 2:16*
l. ye make yourselves accursed   *Jos 6:18*
let them live, *l.* wrath be upon   *Jos 9:20*
us
unto you, *l.* ye deny your God   *Jos 24:27*
l. Israel vaunt themselves   *J'g 7:2*
against
l. we burn thee and thy   *J'g 14:15*
father's
l. angry fellows run upon thee   *J'g 18:25*
l. I mar mine own inheritance   *Ru 4:6*
l. my father leave caring for the   *1Sa 9:5*
L. the Hebrews make them   *1Sa 13:19*
swords
l. I destroy you with them: for   *1Sa 15:6*
ye
know this, *l.* he be grieved   *1Sa 20:3*

L. they should tell on us, saying	1Sa 27:11
l. in the battle he be an adversary	1Sa 29:4
l. these uncircumcised come	1Sa 31:4
l. the daughters of the Philistines rejoice,	2Sa 1:20
l. the daughters of the	2Sa 1:20
l. I take the city, and it be called	2Sa 12:28
go, *l*. we be chargeable unto thee	2Sa 13:25
any more, *l*. they destroy my son	2Sa 14:11
depart, *l*. he overtake us suddenly	2Sa 15:14
l. the king be swallowed up, and all	2Sa 17:16
l. he get him fenced cities, and	2Sa 20:6
l. peradventure the spirit of	2Ki 2:16
l. these uncircumcised come	1Ch 10:4
L. ye should say, We have found	Job 32:13
reign not, *l*. the people be ensnared	Job 34:30
beware *l*. he take thee away with	Job 36:18
l. I deal with you after your folly	Job 42:8
Kiss the Son, *l*. he be angry	Ps 2:12
L. he tear my soul like a lion	Ps 7:2
eyes, *l*. I sleep the sleep of death	Ps 13:3
L. mine enemy say, I have prevailed	Ps 13:4
l. if thou be silent to me, I become	Ps 28:1
l. they come near unto thee	Ps 32:9
l. otherwise they should rejoice	Ps 38:16
l. I tear you in pieces, and there be	Ps 50:22
Slay them not, *l*. my people forget	Ps 59:11
his wrath, *l*. he should destroy them	Ps 106:23
l. the righteous put forth	Ps 125:3
device; *l*. they exalt themselves	Ps 140:8
l. I be like unto them that go down	Ps 143:7
L. thou shouldest ponder the	Pr 5:6
L. thou give thine honour unto	Pr 5:9
L. strangers be filled with thy	Pr 5:10
not a scorner, *l*. he hate thee	Pr 9:8
not sleep, *l*. thou come to poverty	Pr 20:13
L. thou learn his ways, and get a	Pr 22:25
L. the Lord see it, and it displease	Pr 24:18
l. thou know not what to do in	Pr 25:8
L. he that heareth it put thee to	Pr 25:10
l. thou be filled therewith, and	Pr 25:16
l. he be weary of thee, and so hate	Pr 25:17
folly, *l*. thou also be like unto him	Pr 26:4
l. he be wise in his own conceit	Pr 26:5
l. he reprove thee, and thou be	Pr 30:6
L. I be full, and deny thee and	Pr 30:9
l. he curse thee, and thou be found	Pr 30:10
L. they drink, and forget the law	Pr 31:5
l. thou hear thy servant curse	Ec 7:21
l. they see with their eyes, and	Isa 6:10
l. any hurt it, I will keep it night	Isa 27:3
l. your bands be made strong	Isa 28:22
Beware *l*. Hezekiah persuade you	Isa 36:18
l. thou shouldest say, Mine idol	Isa 48:5
l. thou shouldest say, Behold, I	Isa 48:7
l. I confound thee before them	Jer 1:17
l. my fury come forth like fire	Jer 4:4
l. my soul depart from thee	Jer 6:8
l. I make thee desolate, a land not	Jer 6:8
anger, *l*. thou bring me to nothing	Jer 10:24
l. my fury go out like fire, and burn	Jer 21:12
Jonathan the scribe, *l*. I die there	Jer 37:20
l. they deliver me into their hand	Jer 38:19
And *l*. your heart faint, and ye fear	Jer 51:46

L. I strip her naked, and set her as	Ho 2:3
l. he break out like fire in the house	Am 5:6
l. they should hear the law	Zec 7:12
l. I come and smite the earth with	Mal 4:6
l. at any time thou dash thy foot	M't 4:6; Lu 4:11
l. at any time the adversary deliver	M't 5:25
l. they trample them under their	M't 7:6
l. at any time they should see with	M't 13:15
l. while ye gather up the tares, ye	M't 13:29
fasting, *l*. they faint in the way	M't 15:32
l. we should offend them, go	M't 17:27
l. there be not enough for us	M't 25:9
l. there be an uproar among	M't 26:5
l. his disciples come by night	M't 27:64
l. they should throng him	M'k 3:9
l. time they should be converted	M'k 4:12
Take heed *l*. any man deceive you	M'k 13:5
L. coming suddenly he find you	M'k 13:36
l. there be an uproar of the people	M'k 14:2
l. ye enter into temptation	M'k 14:38; Lu 22:46
l. they should believe and be	Lu 8:12
him; *l*. he hale thee to the judge	Lu 12:58
l. a more honourable man than	Lu 14:8
l. they also bid thee again, and a	Lu 14:12
L. haply, after he hath	Lu 14:29
l. they also come into this	Lu 16:28
l. by her continual coming she	Lu 18:5
l. at any time your hearts be	Lu 21:34
l. his deeds should be reproved	Joh 3:20
l. a worse thing come unto thee	Joh 5:14
l. darkness come upon you	Joh 12:35
l. they should be put out of	Joh 12:42
hall, *l*. they should be defiled	Joh 18:28
l. they should have been stoned	Ac 5:26
l. haply ye be found even to fight	Ac 5:39
therefore, *l*. that come upon you	Ac 13:40
fearing *l*. Paul should have been	Ac 23:10
fearing *l*. they should fall into	Ac 27:17
fearing *l*. we should have fallen	Ac 27:29
l. any of them should swim out	Ac 27:42
l. they should see with their eyes	Ac 28:27
take heed *l*. he also spare not thee	Ro 11:21
l. ye should be wise in your	Ro 11:25
l. I should build upon another	Ro 15:20
L. any should say that I had	1Co 1:15
l. the cross of Christ should be	1Co 1:17
heed *l*. by any means this liberty	1Co 8:9
l. I make by brother to offend	1Co 8:13
l. we should hinder the gospel	1Co 9:12
l. that by any means, when I have	1Co 9:27
he standeth take heed *l*. he	1Co 10:12
l., when I came, I should have	2Co 2:3
l. perhaps such a one should be	2Co 2:7
L. Satan should get an	2Co 2:11
l. the light of the glorious	2Co 4:4
l. our boasting of you should	2Co 9:3
L. haply if they of Macedonia	2Co 9:4
l. by any means, as the serpent	2Co 11:3
l. any man should think of me	2Co 12:6
l. I should be, above measure	2Co 12:7
For fear *l*., when I come, I shall	2Co 12:20
l. there be debates, envyings	2Co 12:20
l., when I come again, my God	2Co 12:21
l. being present I should use	2Co 13:10
l. by any means I should run	Ga 2:2
l. I have bestowed upon you labour	Ga 4:11
thyself, *l*. thou also be tempted	Ga 6:1
only *l*. they should suffer	Ga 6:12
l. any man should boast	Eph 2:9

l. I should have sorrow upon	Ph'p 2:27
l. any man should beguile	Col 2:4
Beware *l*. any man spoil you	Col 2:8
l. they be discouraged	Col 3:21
l. by some means the tempter have	1Th 3:5
l. being lifted up with pride	1Ti 3:6
l. he fall into reproach and the	1Ti 3:7
l. at any time we should let them	Heb 2:1
l. there be in any of you an evil	Heb 3:12
l. any of you be hardened	Heb 3:13
fear, *l*. a promise being left us of	Heb 4:1
l. any man fall after the same	Heb 4:11
l. he that destroyed the	Heb 11:28
l. ye be wearied and faint in	Heb 12:3
l. that which is lame be	Heb 12:13
l. any man fail of the grace of God	Heb 12:15
l. any root of bitterness springing	Heb 12:15
L. there be any fornicator, or	Heb 12:16
l. ye be condemned: behold	Jas 5:9
l. ye fall into condemnation	Jas 5:12
beware *l*. ye also, being led	2Pe 3:17
l. he walk naked, and they see	Re 16:15

LET

And God said, *L*. there be light	Ge 1:3
L. there be a firmament in the midst	Ge 1:6
L. the waters, the heaven be gathered	Ge 1:9
L. the earth bring forth grass	Ge 1:11
L. there be lights in the firmament of	Ge 1:14
l. them be for signs, and for seasons	Ge 1:14
l. them be for lights in the firmament	Ge 1:15
L. the waters bring forth abundantly	Ge 1:20
seas, and *l*. fowl multiply in the earth	Ge 1:22
L. the earth bring forth the living	Ge 1:24
L. us make man in our image, after	Ge 1:26
l. them have dominion over the fish	Ge 1:26
to *l*. us make brick, and burn them	Ge 11:3
Go to, *l*. us build us a city and a tower	Ge 11:4
and *l*. us make us a name, lest we be	Ge 11:4
Go, to *l*. us go down, and there	Ge 11:7
L. there be no strife, I pray thee	Ge 13:8
Mamre; *l*. them take their portion	Ge 14:24
L. a little water, I pray you, be fetched	Ge 18:4
Oh *l*. not the Lord be angry, and I	Ge 18:30; 18:32
l. me, I pray you, bring them out unto	Ge 19:8
a little one: oh, *l*. me escape thither	Ge 19:20
l. us make our father drink wine	Ge 19:32
l. us make him drink wine this night	Ge 19:34
L. it not be grievous in thy sight	Ge 21:12
L. me not see the death of the child	Ge 21:16
And *l*. it come to pass, that the damsel	Ge 24:14
L. down thy pitcher, I pray	Ge 24:14
l. the same be she that thou hast	Ge 24:14
L. me, I pray thee, drink a little	Ge 24:17
she hasted, and *l*. down her pitcher	Ge 24:18
l. the same be the woman whom the	Ge 24:44
unto her, *L*. me drink, I pray thee	Ge 24:45
haste, and *l*. down her pitcher and	Ge 24:46
and *l*. her be thy master's son's wife	Ge 24:51
L. the damsel abide with us a few	Ge 24:55

l. thy seed possess the gate of Ge 24:60
those
L. there be now an oath Ge 26:28
betwixt us
and *l.* us make a covenant Ge 26:28
with thee
L. people serve thee, and Ge 27:29
nations bow
l. thy mother's sons bow Ge 27:29
down to thee
L. my father arise, and eat of Ge 27:31
his son's
whom I have served thee, and Ge 30:26
l. me go
thou findest thy gods, *l.* him Ge 31:32
not live
L. it not displease my lord Ge 31:35
that I
l. us make a covenant, I and Ge 31:44
thou
l. it be for a witness between Ge 31:44
me and
L. me go, for the day Ge 32:26
breaketh
I will not *l.* thee go, except Ge 32:26
thou
L. us take our journey, and *l.* Ge 33:12
us go
L. my lord, I pray thee, pass Ge 33:14
over
L. me now leave with thee Ge 33:15
some of
l. me find grace in the sight of Ge 33:15
my
L. me find grace in your eyes Ge 34:11
therefore *l.* them dwell in the Ge 34:21
land
l. us take their daughters to Ge 34:21
us for
and *l.* us give them our Ge 34:21
daughters
only *l.* us consent unto them, Ge 34:23
and they
And *l.* us arise, and go up to Ge 35:3
Bethel
heard them say, **L.** us go to Ge 37:17
Dothan
l. us slay him, and cast him Ge 37:20
into some
hands; and said, **L.** us not kill Ge 37:21
him
and *l.* us sell him to the Ge 37:27
Ishmeelites
and *l.* not our hand be upon Ge 37:27
him; for
I pray thee, *l.* me come in Ge 38:16
unto thee
L. her take it to her lest we be Ge 38:23
Bring her forth, and *l.* her be Ge 38:24
burnt
therefore *l.* Pharaoh look out Ge 41:33
a man
L. Pharaoh do this, and *l.* him Ge 41:34
appoint
l. them gather all the food of Ge 41:35
those
and *l.* them keep food in the Ge 41:35
cities
l. him fetch your brother, and Ge 42:16
ye shall
l. one of your brethren be Ge 42:19
bound in
then *l.* me bear the blame Ge 43:9
forever
both *l.* him die, and we also Ge 44:9
will be
Now also *l.* it be according Ge 44:10
unto your
lord, *l.* thy servant, I pray Ge 44:18
thee, speak
l. not thine anger burn Ge 44:18
against thy
l. thy servant abide instead of Ge 44:33
the lad
and *l.* the lad go up with his Ge 44:33
brethren
Now *l.* me die, since I have Ge 46:30
seen thy
l. thy servants dwell in the land Ge 47:4
of
in the land of Goshen *l.* them Ge 47:6
dwell
l. us find grace in the sight of Ge 47:25
my
l. my name be named on Ge 48:16
them, and the
l. them grow into a multitude Ge 48:16
in the
Naphtali is a hind *l.* loose: he Ge 49:21
giveth

Now therefore *l.* me go up, I Ge 50:5
pray thee
l. us deal wisely with them; lest Ex 1:10
they
now *l.* us go, we beseech thee Ex 3:18
king of Egypt will not *l.* you go Ex 3:19
and after that he will *l.* you go Ex 3:20
L. me go, I pray thee, and Ex 4:18
return unto
that he shall not *l.* the people Ex 4:21
go
L. my son go, that he may Ex 4:23
serve
and if thou refuse to *l.* him go Ex 4:23
So he *l.* him go: then she said Ex 4:26
L. my people go, that they may Ex 5:1;
  7:16; 8:1, 20; 9:1, 13; 10:3
obey his voice to *l.* Israel go Ex 5:2
Lord, neither will I *l.* Israel go Ex 5:2
l. us go, we pray thee, three days' Ex 5:3
l. the people from their works Ex 5:4
l. them go and gather straw for Ex 5:7
L. us go and sacrifice to our Ex 5:8
God
L. there more work be laid upon Ex 5:9
and *l.* them not regard vain Ex 5:9
words
L. us go and do sacrifice to the Ex 5:17
Lord
with a strong hand shall he *l.* Ex 6:1
them go
he *l.* the children of Israel go Ex 6:11
out
he refuseth to *l.* the people go Ex 7:14
And if thou refuse to *l.* them go Ex 8:2
I will *l.* the people go, that they Ex 8:8
may
if thou wilt not *l.* my people go Ex 8:21
said, I will *l.* you go, that ye Ex 8:28
may
l. not Pharaoh deal deceitfully Ex 8:29
neither would he *l.* the people Ex 8:32
go
For if thou refuse to *l.* them go Ex 9:2
and he did not *l.* the people go Ex 9:7
l. Moses sprinkle it toward the Ex 9:8
heaven
that thou wilt not *l.* them go Ex 9:17
I will *l.* you go, and ye shall Ex 9:28
stay as
he *l.* the children of Israel go Ex 9:35
if thou refuse to *l.* my people Ex 10:4
go
l. the men go, that they may Ex 10:7
serve
them, **L.** the Lord be so with Ex 10:10
you
I will *l.* you go, and your little Ex 10:10
ones
not *l.* the children of Israel go Ex 10:20
only *l.* your flocks and your Ex 10:24
herds be
l. your little ones also go with Ex 10:24
you
and he would not *l.* them go Ex 10:27
afterwards he will *l.* you go Ex 11:1
hence
when he shall *l.* you go, he Ex 11:1
shall
l. every man borrow of his Ex 11:2
neighbour
would not *l.* the children of Ex 11:10
Israel go
l. him and his neighbour Ex 12:4
next
shall *l.* nothing of it remain Ex 12:10
until the
Lord, *l.* all his males be Ex 12:48
circumcised
then *l.* him come near and Ex 12:48
keep it
Pharaoh would hardly *l.* us go Ex 13:15
when Pharaoh had *l.* the Ex 13:17
people go
have *l.* Israel go from serving Ex 14:5
us
L. us alone, that we may serve Ex 14:12
L. us flee from the face of Ex 14:25
Israel
L. no man leave of it till the Ex 16:19
morning
l. no man go out of his place Ex 16:29
on the
when he *l.* down his hand, Ex 17:11
Amalek
l. them judge the people at all Ex 18:22
seasons
Moses *l.* his father in law Ex 18:27
depart

morrow, and *l.* them wash Ex 19:10
their clothes
And *l.* the priests Ex 19:22
also, sanctify
but *l.* not the priests and Ex 19:24
people break
l. not God speak with us, lest Ex 20:19
we die
then shall he *l.* her be redeemed Ex 21:8
l. him go free for his eye's Ex 21:26
sake
l. him go free for his tooth's Ex 21:27
sake
pieces, then *l.* him bring it for Ex 22:13
witness
thou shalt *l.* it rest and lie still Ex 23:11
neither *l.* it be heard out of Ex 23:13
thy mouth
matters to do, *l.* him come Ex 24:14
unto them
And *l.* them make me a Ex 25:8
sanctuary
Now therefore *l.* me alone, Ex 32:10
that
L. not the anger of my lord Ex 32:22
wax hot
hath any gold, *l.* them break it Ex 32:24
off
the Lord's side? *l.* him come Ex 32:26
unto me
l. me know whom thou wilt Ex 33:12
send
neither *l.* any man be seen Ex 34:3
throughout
neither *l.* the flocks nor herds Ex 34:3
feed
Lord, *l.* my Lord, I pray thee, Ex 34:9
go among
l. him bring it, an offering of Ex 35:5
the Lord
L. neither man nor woman Ex 36:6
make any
l. him offer a male without Le 1:3
blemish
then *l.* him bring for his sin, Le 4:3
which he
but *l.* your brethren, the whole Le 10:6
house
shall *l.* the living bird loose into Le 14:7
l. go the living bird out of the Le 14:53
city
to *l.* him go for a scapegoat Le 16:10
into the
l. go the goat in the wilderness Le 16:22
l. go the goat for the Le 16:26
scapegoat
thou shalt not *l.* any of thy Le 18:21
seed pass
not *l.* thy cattle gender with a Le 19:19
diverse
l. him not approach to offer Le 21:17
the bread
l. all that heard him lay their Le 24:14
hands
and *l.* all the congregation Le 24:14
stone him
Then *l.* him count the years of Le 25:27
the sale
l. the trespass he recompensed Nu 5:8
unto
shall *l.* the locks of his head Nu 6:5
grow
them, and *l.* them shave all their Nu 8:7
flesh
and *l.* them wash their clothes Nu 8:7
Then *l.* them take a young Nu 8:8
bullock
L. the children of Israel also Nu 9:2
keep the
and *l.* thine enemies be Nu 10:35
scattered
l. them that hate thee flee Nu 10:35
before thee
and *l.* me not see my Nu 11:15
wretchedness
l. them fall by the camp, as it Nu 11:31
were
L. her not be as one dead, of Nu 12:12
whom
l. her be shut out from the Nu 12:14
camp seven
after that *l.* her be received in Nu 12:14
again
L. us go up at once, and Nu 13:30
possess it
L. us make a captain, and Nu 14:4
and *l.* us return into Egypt Nu 14:4
l. the power of my Lord be Nu 14:17
great

l. them make them broad plates for a   *Nu 16:38*

L. us pass, I pray thee, through thy   *Nu 20:17*

L. me pass through thy land: we will   *Nu 21:22*

l. the city of Sihon be built   *Nu 21:27*

L. nothing, I pray thee, hinder thee   *Nu 22:16*

L. me die the death of the righteous   *Nu 23:10*

and *l.* my last end be like his   *Nu 23:10*

L. the Lord, set a man over   *Nu 27:16*

l. them go against the Midianites, and   *Nu 31:3*

l. this land be given unto thy   *Nu 32:5*

those which ye *l.* remain of them shall   *Nu 33:55*

L. them marry to whom they think   *Nu 36:6*

L. me pass through thy land: I will   *De 2:27*

Heshbon would not *l.* us pass by him   *De 2:30*

I pray thee, *l.* me go over, and see the   *De 3:25*

Lord said unto me, *L.* it suffice thee   *De 3:26*

L. me alone, that I may destroy   *De 9:14*

L. us go after other gods, which thou   *De 13:2*

hast not known, and *l.* us serve them   *De 13:2*

L. us go and serve other gods   *De 13:6; 13:13*

shalt *l.* him go free from thee   *De 15:12*

shalt not *l.* him go away empty   *De 15:13*

L. me not hear again the voice of the   *De 18:16*

neither *l.* me see his great fire any   *De 18:16*

l. not your hearts faint, fear not, and   *De 20:3*

l. him go and return to his house   *De 20:5*

l. him also go and return unto his   *De 20:6*

l. him go and return unto his   *De 20:7; 20:8*

shalt *l.* her go whither she will   *De 21:14*

shalt in any wise *l.* the dam go   *De 22:7*

l. him write her a bill of divorcement   *De 24:1*

l. his brother's wife go up to the gate   *De 25:7*

l. them rise up and help you, and be   *De 32:38*

L. Reuben live, and not die   *De 33:6*

and *l.* not his men be few   *De 33:6*

l. his hands be sufficient for him   *De 33:7*

L. thy Thummim and thy Urim be   *De 33:8*

l. the blessing come upon the head of   *De 33:16*

L. Asher be blessed with children   *De 33:24*

l. him be acceptable to his brethren   *De 33:24*

and *l.* him dip his foot in oil   *De 33:24*

Then she *l.* them down by a cord   *Jos 2:15*

which thou didst *l.* us down by   *Jos 2:18*

ye shall *l.* your children know, saying   *Jos 4:22*

l. seven priests bear seven trumpets   *Jos 6:6*

l. him that is armed pass on before the   *Jos 6:7*

unto him, *L.* not all the people go up   *Jos 7:3*

but *l.* about two or three thousand   *Jos 7:3*

they *l.* none of them remain or escape   *Jos 8:22*

a league with them, to *l.* them live   *Jos 9:15*

we will even *l.* them live, lest wrath   *Jos 9:20*

said unto them, *L.* them live   *Jos 9:21*

but *l.* them be hewers of wood   *Jos 9:21*

were therein; he *l.* none remain   *Jos 10:28; 10:30*

thereon, *l.* the Lord himself require it   *Jos 22:23*

L. us now prepare to build us an   *Jos 22:26*

So Joshua *l.* the people depart   *Jos 24:28*

they *l.* go the man and all his family   *J'g 1:25*

when Joshua had *l.* the people go   *J'g 2:6*

So *l.* all thine enemies perish, O Lord   *J'g 5:31*

l. them that love him be as the sun   *J'g 5:31*

l. him be put to death whilst it is yet   *J'g 6:31*

he be a god, *l.* him plead for himself   *J'g 6:31*

L. Baal plead against him   *J'g 6:32*

L. not thine anger be hot against   *J'g 6:39*

l. me prove, I pray thee, but this once   *J'g 6:39*

l. it now be dry only upon the fleece   *J'g 6:39*

upon all the ground *l.* there be dew   *J'g 6:39*

l. him return and depart early   *J'g 7:3*

l. all the other people go every man   *J'g 7:7*

if not *l.* fire come out of the bramble   *J'g 9:15*

l. him also rejoice in you   *J'g 9:19*

if not, *l.* fire come out from Abimelech   *J'g 9:20*

and *l.* fire come out from the men of   *J'g 9:20*

l. them deliver you in the time of your   *J'g 10:14*

L. me, I pray thee, pass through thy   *J'g 11:17*

L. us pass, we pray thee, through thy   *J'g 11:19*

father, *L.* this thing be done for me   *J'g 11:37*

l. me alone two months, that I   *J'g 11:37*

L. me go over; that the men of Gilead   *J'g 12:5*

l. the man of God which thou didst   *J'g 13:8*

said, Now *l.* thy words come to pass   *J'g 13:12*

I said unto the woman *l.* her beware   *J'g 13:13*

neither *l.* her drink wine or strong   *J'g 13:14*

that I commanded her *l.* her observe   *J'g 13:14*

thee, *l.* us detain thee, until we shall   *J'g 13:15*

l. them go into the standing corn   *J'g 15:5*

said, *L.* me die with the Philistines   *J'g 16:30*

L. not thy voice be heard among us   *J'g 18:25*

all night and *l.* thine heart be merry   *J'g 19:6*

and *l.* us turn in into this city of the   *J'g 19:11*

l. us draw near to one of these places   *J'g 19:13*

l. all thy wants lie upon me; only   *J'g 19:20*

day began to spring, they *l.* her go   *J'g 19:25*

said unto her, Up, and *l.* us be going   *J'g 19:28*

L. us flee, and draw them from the   *J'g 20:32*

l. me now go to the field, and glean   *Ru 2:2*

l. me glean and gather after the   *Ru 2:7*

L. thine eyes be on the field that they   *Ru 2:9*

L. me find favour in thy sight   *Ru 2:13*

L. her glean even among the sheaves   *Ru 2:15*

l. fall also some of the handfuls   *Ru 2:16*

l. him do the kinsman's part: but if he   *Ru 3:13*

L. it not be known that a woman came   *Ru 3:14*

And *l.* thy house be like the house of   *Ru 4:12*

L. thine handmaid find grace in thy   *1Sa 1:18*

l. not arrogancy come out of your   *1Sa 2:3*

L. them not fail to burn the fat   *1Sa 2:16*

l. him do what seemeth him good   *1Sa 3:18*

did *l.* none of his words fall to   *1Sa 3:19*

L. us fetch the ark of the covenant   *1Sa 4:3*

L. the ark of the God be carried   *1Sa 5:8*

and *l.* it go again to his own place   *1Sa 5:11*

did they not *l.* the people go   *1Sa 6:6*

with him, Come, and *l.* us return   *1Sa 9:5*

now *l.* us go thither; peradventure he   *1Sa 9:6*

Come, and *l.* us go to the seer: for he   *1Sa 9:9*

his servant, Well said; come, *l.* us go   *1Sa 9:10*

to-morrow I will *l.* thee go   *1Sa 9:19*

And *l.* it be, when these signs are   *1Sa 10:7*

Come, and *l.* us go to Gilgal   *1Sa 11:14*

land, saying, *L.* the Hebrews hear   *1Sa 13:3*

and *l.* us go over to the Philistines   *1Sa 14:1*

and *l.* us go over unto the garrison of   *1Sa 14:6*

L. us go down after the Philistines   *1Sa 14:36*

and *l.* us not leave a man of them   *1Sa 14:36*

L. our lord now command thy   *1Sa 16:16*

L. David, I pray thee, stand before   *1Sa 16:22*

you, and *l.* him come down to me   *1Sa 17:8*

L. no man's heart fail because of him   *1Sa 17:32*

l. him go no more home to his   *1Sa 18:2*

said, *L.* not mine hand be upon him   *1Sa 18:17*

l. the hand of the Philistines be upon   *1Sa 18:17*

L. not the king sin against his servant   *1Sa 19:4*

so Michal *l.* David down through   *1Sa 19:12*

L. me go; why should I kill thee   *1Sa 19:17*

L. not Jonathan know this, lest he be   *1Sa 20:3*

l. me go, that I may hide myself   *1Sa 20:5*

Come, and *l.* us go out into the field   *1Sa 20:11*

L. the Lord even require it at   *1Sa 20:16*

l. me go, I pray thee; for our   *1Sa 20:29*

l. me get away, I pray thee   *1Sa 20:29*

L. no man know any thing of   *1Sa 21:2*

l. his spittle fall down upon his   *1Sa 21:13*

L. my father and my mother, I pray   *1Sa 22:3*

l. not the king impute any thing unto   *1Sa 22:15*

l. them (A)   *1Sa 24:7; Job 31:30*

will he *l.* him go well away   *1Sa 24:19*

l. the young men find favour in thine   *1Sa 25:8*

my lord, upon me *l.* this iniquity be   *1Sa 25:24*

l. thine handmaid, I pray thee, speak   *1Sa 25:24*

L. not my lord, I pray thee, regard   *1Sa 25:25*

now *l.* thine enemies, be as Nabal   *1Sa 25:26*

l. it even be given unto the young   *1Sa 25:27*

l. thine handmaid be a servant to   *1Sa 25:41*

therefore *l.* me smite him, I pray thee   *1Sa 26:8*

and the cruse of water, and *l.* us go   *1Sa 26:11*

l. my lord the king hear the words of   *1Sa 26:19*

against me, *l.* him accept an offering   *1Sa 26:19*

l. not my blood fall to the earth before   *1Sa 26:20*

l. one of the young men come over   *1Sa 26:22*

so *l.* my life be much set by in the   *1Sa 26:24*

l. him deliver me out of all tribulation   *1Sa 26:24*

l. them give me a place in some town   *1Sa 27:5*

l. me set a morsel of bread before   *1Sa 28:22*
l. him not go down with us to   *1Sa 29:4*
of Gilboa, *l.* there be no dew   *2Sa 1:21*
neither *l.* there be rain upon you, nor   *2Sa 1:21*
now *l.* your hands be strengthened   *2Sa 2:7*
L. the young men now arise, and play   *2Sa 2:14*
And Joab said, *L.* them arise   *2Sa 2:14*
L. it rest on the head of Joab, and on   *2Sa 3:29*
l. there not fail from the house   *2Sa 3:29*
l. it be, when thou hearest the sound   *2Sa 5:24*
And *l.* thy name be magnified for ever   *2Sa 7:26*
l. the house of David be established   *2Sa 7:26*
now *l.* it please thee to bless the house   *2Sa 7:29*
l. the house of thy servant be blessed   *2Sa 7:29*
and *l.* us play the men for our people   *2Sa 10:12*
to-morrow I will *l.* thee depart   *2Sa 11:12*
Joab, *L.* not this thing displease thee   *2Sa 11:25*
l. my sister Tamar come, and give me   *2Sa 13:5*
l. Tamar my sister come, and make   *2Sa 13:6*
l. the king, I beseech thee, and his   *2Sa 13:24*
Nay, my son, *l.* us not all now go   *2Sa 13:25*
l. my brother Amnon go with us   *2Sa 13:26*
l. Amnon and all the king's sons go   *2Sa 13:27*
L. not my lord suppose that they have   *2Sa 13:32*
l. not my lord the king take the thing   *2Sa 13:33*
l. the king remember the Lord thy   *2Sa 14:11*
L. thine handmaid, I pray thee, speak   *2Sa 14:12*
said, *L.* my lord the king now speak   *2Sa 14:18*
said, *L.* him turn to his own house   *2Sa 14:24*
and *l.* him not see my face   *2Sa 14:24*
therefore *l.* me see the king's face   *2Sa 14:32*
be any inquity in me, *l.* him kill me   *2Sa 14:32*
pray thee, *l.* me go and pay my vow   *2Sa 15:7*
at Jerusalem, Arise, and *l.* us flee   *2Sa 15:14*
l. him do to me as seemeth good unto   *2Sa 15:26*
l. me go over, I pray thee, and take   *2Sa 16:9*
so *l.* him curse, because the Lord hath   *2Sa 16:10*
l. him alone, and *l.* him curse; for   *2Sa 16:11*
L. me now choose out twelve thousand   *2Sa 17:1*
and *l.* us hear likewise what he saith   *2Sa 17:5*
L. me now run, and bear the king   *2Sa 18:19*
l. me, I pray thee, also run after Cushi   *2Sa 18:22*
But howsoever, said he, *l.* me run   *2Sa 18:23*
L. not my lord impute iniquity unto   *2Sa 19:19*
l. him take all, forasmuch as my lord   *2Sa 19:30*
L. thy servant, I pray thee, turn back   *2Sa 19:37*
l. him go over with my lord the king   *2Sa 19:37*
that is for David, *l.* him go after Joab   *2Sa 20:11*
L. seven men of his sons be delivered   *2Sa 21:6*
l. neither (B)   *2Sa 21:10; Ac 14:16*
l. us fall now into the hand of us   *2Sa 24:14*
l. me not fall into the hand of man   *2Sa 24:14*

l. thine hand, I pray thee, be against   *2Sa 24:17*
L. my lord the king take and offer up   *2Sa 24:22*
L. there be sought for my lord the   *1Ki 1:2*
and *l.* her stand before the king   *1Ki 1:2*
before the king, and *l.* her cherish   *1Ki 1:2*
and *l.* her lie in thy bosom, that my   *1Ki 1:12*
l. me, I pray thee, give thee counsel   *1Ki 1:12*
L. my lord king David live for ever   *1Ki 1:31*
l. Zadok the priest and anoint him   *1Ki 1:34*
L. king Solomon swear unto me to   *1Ki 1:51*
l. not his hoar head go down to   *1Ki 2:6*
l. them be of those that eat at   *1Ki 2:7*
L. Abishag the Shunammite be given   *1Ki 2:17*
L. it be neither mine nor thine   *1Ki 3:26*
l. thy word, I pray thee, be verified   *1Ki 8:26*
l. him not leave us, nor forsake us   *1Ki 8:57*
And *l.* these my words be nigh unto   *1Ki 8:59*
L. your heart therefore be perfect   *1Ki 8:61*
L. me depart that I may go to   *1Ki 11:21*
howbeit *l.* me go in any wise   *1Ki 11:22*
l. this child's soul come into him   *1Ki 17:21*
L. them give us two bullocks   *1Ki 18:23*
l. them choose one bullock for   *1Ki 18:23*
that answereth by fire, *l.* him be God   *1Ki 18:24*
l. it be known this day that thou art   *1Ki 18:36*
of Baal; *l.* not one of them escape   *1Ki 18:40*
So *l.* the gods do to me, and more   *1Ki 19:2*
L. me, I pray thee, kiss my father and   *1Ki 19:20*
L. not him that girdeth on his harness   *1Ki 20:11*
l. us fight against them in the plain   *1Ki 20:23*
l. us, I pray thee, put sackcloth on   *1Ki 20:31*
saith, I pray thee, *l.* me live   *1Ki 20:32*
hast *l.* go out of thy hand a man   *1Ki 20:42*
bread, and *l.* thine heart be merry   *1Ki 21:7*
said, *L.* not the king say so   *1Ki 22:8*
l. thy word, I pray thee, be like the   *1Ki 22:13*
l. them return every man to his   *1Ki 22:17*
L. my servants go with thy   *1Ki 22:49*
l. fire come down from heaven   *2Ki 1:10; 1:12*
l. my life, and the life be precious in   *2Ki 1:13*
l. my life now be precious in thy sight   *2Ki 1:14*
l. a double portion of thy spirit be   *2Ki 2:9*
l. them go, we pray thee, and seek   *2Ki 2:16*
L. us make a little chamber, I pray   *2Ki 4:10*
l. us set for him there a bed, and a   *2Ki 4:10*
man of God said, *L.* her alone   *2Ki 4:27*
l. him come now to me, and he shall   *2Ki 5:8*
and he *l.* the men go, and they   *2Ki 5:24*
L. us go, we pray thee, unto   *2Ki 6:2*
l. us make us a place there, where we   *2Ki 6:2*
l. us fall unto the host of the Syrians   *2Ki 7:4*
L. some take, I pray thee, five of the   *2Ki 7:13*
consumed:) and *l.* us send and see   *2Ki 7:13*
l. none go forth nor escape out of the   *2Ki 9:15*
meet them, and *l.* him say, Is it peace   *2Ki 9:17*
all his priests; *l.* none be wanting   *2Ki 10:19*

and slay them; *l.* none come forth   *2Ki 10:25*
within the ranges, *l.* him be slain   *2Ki 11:8*
L. her not be slain in the house of the   *2Ki 11:15*
L. the priests take it to them, every   *2Ki 12:5*
l. them repair the breaches of   *2Ki 12:5*
when the man was *l.* down   *2Ki 13:21*
l. us look one another in the face   *2Ki 14:8*
and *l.* them go and dwell there   *2Ki 17:27*
l. him teach them the manner of   *2Ki 17:27*
the king, *L.* not Hezekiah deceive you   *2Ki 18:29*
Neither *l.* Hezekiah make you trust in   *2Ki 18:30*
L. not thy God in whom thou trustest   *2Ki 19:10*
but *l.* the shadow return backward   *2Ki 20:10*
l. them deliver it into the hand of   *2Ki 22:5*
l. them give it to the doers of   *2Ki 22:5*
L. him alone: *l.* no man move his   *2Ki 23:18*
So they *l.* his bones alone, with the   *2Ki 23:18*
l. us send abroad unto our   *1Ch 13:2*
l. us bring again the ark of our God to   *1Ch 13:3*
l. the heart of them rejoice that seek   *1Ch 16:10*
L. the heavens be glad, and *l.*   *1Ch 16:31*
and *l.* men, say among the nations, the   *1Ch 16:31*
L. the sea roar, and the fulness   *1Ch 16:32*
l. the fields rejoice, and all that is   *1Ch 16:32*
l. the thing that thou, be established   *1Ch 17:23*
L. it even be established, that thy   *1Ch 17:24*
l. the house of David be established   *1Ch 17:24*
l. it please thee to bless the house of   *1Ch 17:27*
and *l.* us behave ourselves valiantly   *1Ch 19:13*
and *l.* the Lord do that which is good   *1Ch 19:13*
l. me fall now into the hand of the   *1Ch 21:13*
but *l.* me not fall into the hand of man   *1Ch 21:13*
l. thine hand, O Lord my God, be on me   *1Ch 21:17*
l. my lord the king do that which is   *1Ch 21:23*
l. thy promise unto David my father   *2Ch 1:9*
of, *l.* him send unto his servants   *2Ch 2:15*
God of Israel, *l.* thy word be verified   *2Ch 6:17*
l. I beseech thee, thine eyes be open   *2Ch 6:40*
l. thine ears be attent unto the prayer   *2Ch 6:40*
l. thy priests, O Lord God, be clothed   *2Ch 6:41*
and *l.* thy saints rejoice in goodness   *2Ch 6:41*
unto Judah, *L.* us build these cities   *2Ch 14:7*
God; *l.* not man prevail against thee   *2Ch 14:11*
l. not your hands be weak   *2Ch 15:7*
that he might *l.* none go out   *2Ch 16:1*
of Ramah, and *l.* his work cease   *2Ch 16:5*
said, *L.* not the king say so   *2Ch 18:7*
l. thy word therefore, I pray thee, be like   *2Ch 18:12*
l. them return therefore every man   *2Ch 18:16*
now *l.* the fear of the Lord be upon   *2Ch 19:7*
thou wouldest not *l.* Israel invade   *2Ch 20:10*
But *l.* none come into the house of the   *2Ch 23:6*
her, *l.* him be slain with the sword   *2Ch 23:14*
l. not the army of Israel go with thee   *2Ch 25:7*

l. us see one another in the   2Ch 25:17
face

therefore *l.* not Hezekiah   2Ch 32:15
deceive you

his God be with him, and *l.*   2Ch 36:23
him go up

l. him go up to Jerusalem,   Ezr 1:3
which is in

l. the men of his place help him   Ezr 1:4

L. us build with you: for we   Ezr 4:2
seek

l. the house of God be builded   Ezr 5:15
in his

l. there be search made in the   Ezr 5:17
king's

l. the king send his pleasure to   Ezr 5:17
us

L. the house be builded, the   Ezr 6:3
place

l. the foundations thereof be   Ezr 6:3
strongly

l. the expences be given out of   Ezr 6:4

l. the golden and silver   Ezr 6:5
vessels be restored

L. the work of this house of   Ezr 6:7
God alone

l. the governor of the Jews   Ezr 6:7
build

l. it be given them day by day   Ezr 6:9
without

l. timber be pulled down from   Ezr 6:11
his

set up, *l.* him be hanged   Ezr 6:11
thereon

and *l.* his house be made a   Ezr 6:11
dunghill for

a decree; *l.* it be done with   Ezr 6:12
speed

l. it be diligently done for the   Ezr 7:23
house of

l. judgment be executed   Ezr 7:26
speedily

l. us make a covenant with our   Ezr 10:3
God

and *l.* it be done according to   Ezr 10:3
the law

L. now our rulers of all   Ezr 10:14
the stand

l. all them which have   Ezr 10:14
taken, and

L. thine ear now be attentive   Ne 1:6

l. now thine ear be attentive to   Ne 1:11
the king, *L.* the king live for
ever

l. letters be given me to the   Ne 2:7

l. us build up the wall of   Ne 2:17
Jerusalem

And they said, *L.* us rise up   Ne 2:18
and build

l. not their sin be blotted out   Ne 4:5
from

L. every one with his servant   Ne 4:22
lodge

I pray you, *l.* us leave off this   Ne 5:10
usury

Come, *l.* us meet together in   Ne 6:2
some one

and *l.* us take counsel together   Ne 6:7

L. us meet together in the   Ne 6:10
house of

and *l.* us shut the doors of the   Ne 6:10
temple

L. not the gates of Jerusalem   Ne 7:3
be

l. them shut the doors, and bar   Ne 7:3
them

l. not all the trouble seem little   Ne 9:32
before

l. there go a royal   Es 1:19
commandment

l. it be written among the laws   Es 1:19
of the

l. the king give her royal estate   Es 1:19

L. there be fair young virgins   Es 2:2
sought

And *l.* the king appoint officers   Es 2:3
in all

l. their things for purification be   Es 2:3
given

l. the maiden which pleaseth be   Es 2:4
queen

l. it be written that they may be   Es 3:9

l. the king and Haman come this   Es 5:4
day

l. the king and Haman come to   Es 5:8
the queen did *l.* no man come   Es 5:12
in with

L. a gallows be made of fifty   Es 5:14
cubits

And the king said, *L.* him come   Es 6:5
in

L. the royal apparel be brought   Es 6:8

l. this apparel and horse be   Es 6:9
delivered

l. nothing fail of all that thou   Es 6:10
hast

l. my life be given me at my   Es 7:3

l. it be written to reverse the   Es 8:5
letters

l. it be granted to the Jews   Es 9:13
which

l. Haman's ten sons be hanged   Es 9:13
upon

L. the day perish wherein I was   Job 3:3
born

l. that day be darkness   Job 3:4

l. not God regard it from above   Job 3:4

neither *l.* the light shine upon it   Job 3:4

L. darkness and the shadow of   Job 3:5
death

stain it; *l.* a cloud dwell upon it   Job 3:5

L. the blackness of the day   Job 3:5
terrify it

that night, *l.* darkness seize   Job 3:6
upon it

l. it not be joined unto the days   Job 3:6
of the

l. it not come into the number   Job 3:6
of the

Lo, *l.* that night be solitary   Job 3:7

l. no joyful voice come therein   Job 3:7

L. them curse it that curse the   Job 3:8
day

L. the stars of the twilight   Job 3:9
thereof be

l. it look for light, but have   Job 3:9
none

neither *l.* it see the dawning of   Job 3:9

he would *l.* loose his hand, and   Job 6:9
cut me

l. him not spare; for I have   Job 6:10
not

l. it not be iniquity; yea,   Job 6:29
return again

not live alway: me alone; for   Job 7:16

nor *l.* me alone till I swallow   Job 7:19
down

L. him take his rod away from   Job 9:34
me

and *l.* not his fear terrify me   Job 9:34

and *l.* me alone, that I may   Job 10:20
take

and *l.* not wickedness dwell   Job 11:14
in thy

Hold your peace, *l.* me alone,   Job 13:13
that I

speak, and *l.* come on me   Job 13:13
what will

and *l.* not thy dread make me   Job 13:21
afraid

or *l.* me speak, and answer   Job 13:22
thou me

L. not him that is deceived   Job 15:31
trust in

my blood, and *l.* my cry have   Job 16:18
no place

and *l.* this be your   Job 21:2
consolations

I hold fast, and will not *l.* it   Job 27:6
go

L. my enemy be as the wicked,   Job 27:7
and he

have also *l.* loose the bridle   Job 30:11
before me

L. me be weighed in an even   Job 31:6
balance

Then *l.* me sow, and *l.* another   Job 31:8
eat

Yea, *l.* my offspring be rooted   Job 31:8
out

Then *l.* my wife grind unto   Job 31:10
another

and *l.* others bow down upon   Job 31:10
her

l. mine arm fall from my   Job 31:22
shoulder

L. thistles grow instead of   Job 31:40
wheat, and

L. me not, I pray you, accept   Job 32:21
any

neither *l.* me give flattering   Job 32:21
titles unto

L. us choose to us judgment   Job 34:4

l. us know among ourselves   Job 34:4
what is

L. men of understanding tell   Job 34:34
me

and *l.* a wise man hearken   Job 34:34
unto me

reproveth God, *l.* him answer   Job 40:2
it

L. us break their bands   Ps 2:3
asunder, and

l. them fall by their own   Ps 5:10
counsels

l. all those that put their   Ps 5:11
trust rejoice

l. them ever shout for joy   Ps 5:11

l. them that love thy name be   Ps 5:11
joyful

L. all mine enemies be ashamed   Ps 6:10

l. them return and be ashamed   Ps 6:10

L. the enemy persecute my soul   Ps 7:5

l. him tread down my life upon   Ps 7:5

l. the wickedness of the wicked   Ps 7:9
come

Arise, O Lord; *l.* not man   Ps 9:19
prevail

l. the heathen be judged in thy   Ps 9:19
sight

l. them be taken in the devices   Ps 10:2
that

L. my sentence come forth   Ps 17:2
from thy

l. thine eyes behold the things   Ps 17:2
that are

l. the God of my salvation be   Ps 18:46
exalted

l. them not have dominion   Ps 19:13
over me

L. the words of my mouth be   Ps 19:14
acceptable

l. the king hear us when we   Ps 20:9
call

l. him deliver him, seeing he   Ps 22:8
delighted

trust in thee: *l.* me not be   Ps 25:2
ashamed

l. not mine enemies triumph   Ps 25:2
over me

l. none that wait on thee be   Ps 25:3
ashamed

l. them be ashamed which   Ps 25:3
transgress

l. me not be ashamed; for I   Ps 25:20
put my

L. integrity and uprightness   Ps 25:21
preserve

put my trust; *l.* me never be   Ps 31:1
ashamed

L. me not be ashamed, O Lord;   Ps 31:17
for I

upon thee: *l.* the wicked be   Ps 31:17
ashamed

and *l.* them be silent in the   Ps 31:17
grave

L. the lying lips be put to   Ps 31:18
silence

L. all the earth fear the Lord   Ps 33:8

l. all the inhabitants stand in   Ps 33:8
awe

L. thy mercy, O Lord, be upon   Ps 33:22
us

me, and *l.* us exalt his name   Ps 34:3
together

L. them be confounded and put   Ps 35:4
to

l. them be turned back and   Ps 35:4
brought

L. them be as chaff before the   Ps 35:5
wind

l. the angel of the Lord chase   Ps 35:5
them

L. their way be dark and   Ps 35:6
slippery

l. the angel of the Lord   Ps 35:6
persecute

L. destruction come upon him   Ps 35:8

l. his net that he hath hid catch   Ps 35:8

into that very destruction *l.* him   Ps 35:8
fall

L. not them mine enemies   Ps 35:19
rejoice

neither *l.* them wink with the   Ps 35:19
eye that

and *l.* them not rejoice over   Ps 35:24
me

L. them not say in their   Ps 35:25
hearts, Ah, so

l. them not say, We have   Ps 35:25
swallowed

L. them be ashamed and   Ps 35:26
brought to

l. them be clothed with shame   Ps 35:26

L. them shout for joy, and be   Ps 35:27
glad

cause: yea, *l.* them say   Ps 35:27
continually

L. the Lord be magnified, which hath   Ps 35:27
L. not the foot of pride come against   Ps 36:11
l. not the hand of the wicked remove   Ps 36:11
l. thy lovingkindness and truth preserve me   Ps 40:11
L. them be ashamed and confounded   Ps 40:14
l. them be driven backward and put to   Ps 40:14
L. them be desolate for a reward of   Ps 40:15
L. all those that seek thee rejoice   Ps 40:16
l. such as love thy salvation say   Ps 40:16
light and thy truth: *l.* them lead me   Ps 43:3
l. them bring me unto thy holy hill   Ps 43:3
L. mount Zion rejoice   Ps 48:11
l. the daughters of Judah be glad   Ps 48:11
L. death seize upon them   Ps 55:15
and *l.* them go down quick into hell   Ps 55:15
l. thy glory be above all the earth   Ps 57:5; 57:11
L. them melt away as waters which   Ps 58:7
his arrows, *l.* them be as cut in pieces   Ps 58:7
l. every one of them pass away   Ps 58:8
God shall *l.* me see my desire upon   Ps 59:10
l. them even be taken in their pride   Ps 59:12
l. them know that God ruleth in Jacob   Ps 59:13
And at evening *l.* them return   Ps 59:14
l. them make a noise like a dog, and   Ps 59:14
L. them wander up and down   Ps 59:15
l. not the rebellious exalt themselves   Ps 66:7
L. the people praise thee, O God   Ps 67:3; 67:5
l. all the people praise thee   Ps 67:3; 67:5
O *l.* the nations be glad and sing for   Ps 67:4
L. God arise, *l.* his enemies be   Ps 68:1
l. them also that hate him flee before   Ps 68:1
so *l.* the wicked perish at the presence   Ps 68:2
But *l.* the righteous be glad   Ps 68:3
l. them rejoice before God   Ps 68:3
yea, *l.* them exceedingly rejoice   Ps 68:3
L. not them that wait on be ashamed   Ps 69:6
l. not those that seek be confounded   Ps 69:6
out of the mire, and *l.* me not sink   Ps 69:14
l. me be delivered from them that hate   Ps 69:14
L. not the waterflood overflow me   Ps 69:15
neither *l.* the deep swallow me up   Ps 69:15
l. not the pit shut her mouth upon me   Ps 69:15
L. their table become a snare before   Ps 69:22
for their welfare, *l.* it become a trap   Ps 69:22
L. their eyes be darkened, that they   Ps 69:23
l. thy wrathful anger take hold of   Ps 69:24
L. their habitation be desolate   Ps 69:25
and *l.* none dwell in their tents   Ps 69:25
and *l.* them not come into thy   Ps 69:27
L. them be blotted out of the book of   Ps 69:28
l. thy salvation, O God, set me up on   Ps 69:29
L. the heaven and earth praise him   Ps 69:34
L. them be ashamed and confounded   Ps 70:2
l. them be turned backward, and put   Ps 70:2
L. them be turned back for a reward   Ps 70:3
L. all those that seek thee rejoice and   Ps 70:4

and *l.* such as love thy salvation say   Ps 70:4
say continually, *L.* God be magnified   Ps 70:4
trust: *l.* me never be put to confusion   Ps 71:1
L. my mouth be filled with thy praise   Ps 71:8
L. them be confounded and consumed   Ps 71:13
l. them be covered with reproach and   Ps 71:13
l. the whole earth be filled with his   Ps 72:19
hearts, *L.* us destroy them together   Ps 74:8
O *l.* not the oppressed return ashamed   Ps 74:21
l. the poor and needy praise thy name   Ps 74:21
l. all that be round about him bring   Ps 76:11
he *l.* it fall in the midst of their camp   Ps 78:28
l. thy tender mercies speedily prevent   Ps 79:8
l. him be known among the heathen in   Ps 79:10
L. the sighing of the prisoner come   Ps 79:11
L. thy hand be upon the man of thy   Ps 80:17
l. us cut them off from being a nation   Ps 83:4
L. us take to ourselves the houses of   Ps 83:12
L. them be confounded and troubled   Ps 83:17
l. them be put to shame, and perish   Ps 83:17
l. them not turn again to folly   Ps 85:8
L. my prayer come before thee   Ps 88:2
l. it repent thee concerning thy   Ps 90:13
L. thy work appear unto thy servants   Ps 90:16
l. the beauty of the Lord our God be   Ps 90:17
O come, *l.* us sing unto the Lord   Ps 95:1
l. us make a joyful noise to the rock   Ps 95:1
L. us come before his presence with   Ps 95:2
O come, *l.* us worship and bow down   Ps 95:6
l. us kneel before the Lord our maker   Ps 95:6
L. the heavens rejoice, and *l.* the earth   Ps 96:11
l. the sea roar, and the fulness thereof   Ps 96:11; 98:7
L. the field be joyful, and all that is   Ps 96:12
l. the earth rejoice; *l.* the multitude   Ps 97:1
L. the floods clap their hands   Ps 98:8
l. the hills be joyful together   Ps 98:8
Lord reigneth; *l.* the people tremble   Ps 99:1
cherubims; *l.* the earth be moved   Ps 99:1
L. them praise thy great and terrible   Ps 99:3
O Lord, and *l.* my cry come unto thee   Ps 102:1
L. the sinners be consumed out of the   Ps 104:35
and *l.* the wicked be no more. Bless   Ps 104:35
l. the heart of them rejoice that seek   Ps 105:3
ruler of the people, and *l.* him go free   Ps 105:20
and *l.* all the people say, Amen   Ps 106:48
L. the redeemed of the Lord say so   Ps 107:2
And *l.* them sacrifice the sacrifices of   Ps 107:22
L. them exalt him also in the   Ps 107:32
and *l.* Satan stand at his right hand   Ps 109:6
be judged, *l.* him be condemned   Ps 109:7
and *l.* his prayer become sin   Ps 109:7
L. his days be few; and *l.* another   Ps 109:8
L. his children be fatherless   Ps 109:9
L. his children be continually   Ps 109:10

l. them seek their bread also out of   Ps 109:10
L. the extortioner catch all that he   Ps 109:11
and *l.* the strangers spoil his labour   Ps 109:11
L. there be none to extend mercy unto   Ps 109:12
neither *l.* there be any to favour his   Ps 109:12
L. his posterity be cut off; and in the   Ps 109:13
following *l.* their name be blotted out   Ps 109:13
L. the iniquity of his fathers be   Ps 109:14
and *l.* not the sin of his mother be   Ps 109:14
L. them be before the Lord   Ps 109:15
loved cursing, so *l.* it come unto him   Ps 109:17
not in blessing, so *l.* it be far from him   Ps 109:17
so *l.* it come into his bowels like water   Ps 109:18
L. it be unto him as the garment   Ps 109:19
L. this be the reward of mine   Ps 109:20
L. them curse, but bless thou: when   Ps 109:28
they arise, *l.* them be ashamed   Ps 109:28
but *l.* thy servant rejoice   Ps 109:28
L. mine adversaries be clothed with   Ps 109:29
l. them cover themselves with their   Ps 109:29
L. Israel now say, that his mercy   Ps 118:2
L. the house of Aaron now say, that   Ps 118:3
L. them now that fear the Lord say   Ps 118:4
O *l.* me not wander from thy   Ps 119:10
L. thy mercies come also unto me, O   Ps 119:41
L. I pray thee, thy merciful kindness   Ps 119:76
L. thy tender mercies come unto me   Ps 119:77
L. the proud be ashamed; for they   Ps 119:78
L. those that fear thee turn unto me   Ps 119:79
L. my heart be sound in thy statutes   Ps 119:80
and *l.* me not be ashamed of my hope   Ps 119:116
good: *l.* not the proud oppress me   Ps 119:122
l. not any iniquity have dominion over   Ps 119:133
L. my cry come near before thee, O   Ps 119:169
L. my supplication come before thee   Ps 119:170
L. thine hand help me; for I have   Ps 119:173
L. my soul live, and it shall praise   Ps 119:175
thee; and *l.* thy judgments help me   Ps 119:175
L. us go into the house of the Lord   Ps 122:1
L. them all be confounded and turned   Ps 129:5
L. them be as the grass upon   Ps 129:6
l. thine ears be attentive to the voice   Ps 130:2
L. Israel hope in the Lord: for with   Ps 130:7
L. Israel hope in the Lord from   Ps 131:3
L. thy priests be clothed with   Ps 132:9
and *l.* thy saints shout for joy   Ps 132:9
l. my right hand forget her cunning   Ps 137:5
l. my tongue cleave to the roof of my   Ps 137:6
l. the mischief of their own lips cover   Ps 140:9
L. burning coals fall upon them   Ps 140:10
l. them be cast into the fire; into deep   Ps 140:10
L. not an evil speaker be established   Ps 140:11
L. my prayer be set forth before thee   Ps 141:2

and *l.* me not eat of their   *Ps 141:4*
dainties
L. the righteous smite me; it   *Ps 141:5*
shall be
l. him reprove me; it shall be   *Ps 141:5*
L. the wicked fall into their   *Ps 141:10*
own nets
l. all flesh bless his holy name   *Ps 145:21*
for ever
L. them praise the name of   *Ps 148:5;*
the Lord   *148:13*
L. Israel rejoice in him that   *Ps 149:2*
made
l. the children of Zion be   *Ps 149:2*
joyful in their
L. them praise his name in the   *Ps 149:3*
dance
l. them sing praises unto him   *Ps 149:3*
with the
L. the saints be joyful in glory   *Ps 149:5*
l. them sing aloud upon their   *Ps 149:5*
beds
L. the high praises of God be   *Ps 149:6*
in their
L. everything that hath breath   *Ps 150:6*
praise
Come with us, *l.* us lay wait   *Pr 1:11*
for blood
l. us lurk privily for the   *Pr 1:11*
innocent
L. us swallow them up alive as   *Pr 1:12*
among us; *l.* us all have one   *Pr 1:14*
purse
l. thine heart keep my   *Pr 3:1*
commandments
L. not mercy and truth forsake   *Pr 3:3*
thee
l. not them depart from thine   *Pr 3:21*
eyes
me, *L.* thine heart retain my   *Pr 4:4*
words
l. her not go: keep her; for she   *Pr 4:13*
is
L. them not depart from thine   *Pr 4:21*
eyes
L. thine eyes look right on, and   *Pr 4:25*
L. thine eyelids look straight   *Pr 4:25*
before
and *l.* all thy ways be   *Pr 4:26*
established
L. thy fountains be dispersed   *Pr 5:16*
abroad
L. them be only thine own, and   *Pr 5:17*
not
L. thy fountain be blessed: and   *Pr 5:18*
L. her be as the loving hind and   *Pr 5:19*
l. her breasts satisfy thee at all   *Pr 5:19*
times
neither *l.* her take thee with her   *Pr 6:25*
l. us take our fill of love until   *Pr 7:18*
l. us solace ourselves with loves   *Pr 7:18*
L. not thine heart decline to her   *Pr 7:25*
ways
is simple, *l.* him turn in hither   *Pr 9:4;*
                         9:16
L. a bear robbed of her   *Pr 17:12*
whelps meet a
l. not thy soul spare for his   *Pr 19:18*
crying
L. not thine heart envy   *Pr 23:17*
sinners: but
and *l.* thine eyes observe my   *Pr 23:26*
ways
l. not thine heart be glad when   *Pr 24:17*
he
L. another man praise thee,   *Pr 27:2*
and not
flee to the pit; *l.* no man stay   *Pr 28:17*
him
L. him drink, and forget his   *Pr 31:7*
poverty
l. her own works praise her in   *Pr 31:31*
l. not thine heart be hasty to   *Ec 5:2*
utter any
earth: therefore *l.* thy words be   *Ec 5:2*
few
L. thy garments be always white   *Ec 9:8*
and *l.* thy head lack no ointment   *Ec 9:8*
l. him remember the days of   *Ec 11:8*
darkness
l. thy heart cheer thee in the   *Ec 11:9*
days of
L. us hear the conclusion of   *Ec 12:13*
the whole
L. him kiss me with the kisses   *Ca 1:2*
of his
l. me see thy countenance, *l.*   *Ca 2:14*
me hear
held him, and would not *l.* him   *Ca 3:4*
go

L. my beloved come into his   *Ca 4:16*
garden
beloved, *l.* us go forth into the   *Ca 7:11*
field
l. us lodge in the villages   *Ca 7:11*
L. us get up early to the   *Ca 7:12*
vineyards
l. us see if the vine flourish,   *Ca 7:12*
whether
l. out the vineyards unto   *Ca 8:11*
keepers
Come now, and *l.* us reason   *Isa 1:18*
together
l. us go up to the mountain of   *Isa 2:3*
l. us walk in the light of the   *Isa 2:5*
Lord
and *l.* this ruin be under thy   *Isa 3:6*
hand
only *l.* us be called by thy   *Isa 4:1*
name, to
L. him make speed and hasten   *Isa 5:19*
his
l. the counsel of the   *Isa 5:19*
Holy draw nigh
L. us go up against Judah, and   *Isa 7:6*
vex it
l. us make a breach therein for   *Isa 7:6*
us
hosts himself; and *l.* him be   *Isa 8:13*
your fear
and *l.* him be your dread   *Isa 8:13*
L. mine outcasts dwell with   *Isa 16:4*
thee
wise men? and *l.* them tell   *Isa 19:12*
thee now
l. them know what the Lord   *Isa 19:12*
of hosts
l. him declare what he seeth   *Isa 21:6*
l. us eat and drink; for   *Isa 22:13*
to-morrow we
L. favour be shewed to the   *Isa 26:10*
wicked, yet
Or *l.* him take hold of my   *Isa 27:5*
strength
ye year to year; *l.* them kill   *Isa 29:1*
sacrifices
l. the earth hear, and all that is   *Isa 34:1*
king, *L.* not Hezekiah deceive   *Isa 36:14*
you
Neither *l.* Hezekiah make you   *Isa 36:15*
trust in
L. not thy God, in   *Isa 37:10*
whom, deceive thee
had said, *L.* them take a lump   *Isa 38:21*
of figs
l. the people renew their   *Isa 41:1*
strength
l. them come near; then *l.*   *Isa 41:1*
them speak
l. us come near together to   *Isa 41:1*
judgment
L. them bring them forth, and   *Isa 41:22*
shew us
l. them shew the former   *Isa 41:22*
things, what
L. the wilderness and the   *Isa 42:11*
cities thereof
l. the inhabitants of the rock   *Isa 42:11*
sing
l. them shout from the top of   *Isa 42:11*
L. them give glory unto the   *Isa 42:12*
Lord
L. all the nations be gathered   *Isa 43:9*
together
and *l.* the people be assembled   *Isa 43:9*
l. them bring forth their   *Isa 43:9*
witnesses
or *l.* them hear, and say, It is   *Isa 43:9*
truth
I will work, and who shall *l.*   *Isa 43:13*
it
in remembrance: *l.* us plead   *Isa 43:26*
together
shall come, *l.* them shew unto   *Isa 44:7*
them
l. them all be gathered   *Isa 44:11*
together
l. them stand up; yet they   *Isa 44:11*
shall fear
l. the skies pour down   *Isa 45:8*
righteousness
l. the earth open, and *l.* them   *Isa 45:8*
bring
l. righteousness spring up   *Isa 45:8*
together
L. the potsherd strive with the   *Isa 45:9*
he shall *l.* go my captives, not   *Isa 45:13*
l. them take counsel together   *Isa 45:21*
L. now the astrologers,   *Isa 47:13*
stand up

contend with me? *l.* us stand   *Isa 50:8*
together
adversary? *l.* him come near to   *Isa 50:8*
me
l. him trust in the name of the   *Isa 50:10*
Lord
l. them stretch forth the   *Isa 54:2*
curtains of
l. your soul delight itself in   *Isa 55:2*
fatness
L. the wicked forsake his way   *Isa 55:7*
l. him return unto the Lord   *Isa 55:7*
Neither *l.* the son of   *Isa 56:3*
neither *l.* the eunuch say,   *Isa 56:3*
Behold, I
criest, *l.* thy companies deliver   *Isa 57:13*
thee
to *l.* the oppressed go free, and   *Isa 58:6*
L. the Lord be glorified: but   *Isa 66:5*
he shall
l. them arise, if they can save   *Jer 2:28*
thee in
and *l.* us go into the defenced   *Jer 4:5*
cities
L. us now fear the Lord our   *Jer 5:24*
God, that
her; arise, and *l.* us go up at   *Jer 6:4*
noon
Arise, and *l.* us go by night   *Jer 6:5*
and *l.* us destroy her palaces   *Jer 6:5*
l. us enter into the defenced   *Jer 8:14*
cities
and *l.* us be silent there: for   *Jer 8:14*
the Lord
And *l.* them make haste, and   *Jer 9:18*
take up
and *l.* your ear receive the   *Jer 9:20*
word of his
L. not the wise man glory in   *Jer 9:23*
his
neither *l.* the mighty man glory   *Jer 9:23*
in his
l. not the rich man glory in his   *Jer 9:23*
riches
But *l.* him that glorieth glory   *Jer 9:24*
in this
L. us destroy the tree with the   *Jer 11:19*
fruit
l. us cut him off from the land   *Jer 11:19*
of the
l. me see thy vengeance on   *Jer 11:20*
them
l. me talk with thee of thy   *Jer 12:1*
judgments
L. mine eyes run down with   *Jer 14:17*
tears
night and day, and *l.* them not   *Jer 14:17*
cease
out of my sight, and *l.* them go   *Jer 15:1*
forth
l. them return unto thee; but   *Jer 15:19*
the word of the Lord? *l.* it   *Jer 17:15*
come now
L. them be confounded that   *Jer 17:18*
persecute
but *l.* not me be confounded   *Jer 17:18*
l. them be dismayed   *Jer 17:18*
but *l.* not me be dismayed   *Jer 17:18*
l. us devise devices against   *Jer 18:18*
Jeremiah
and *l.* us smite him with the   *Jer 18:18*
tongue
l. us not give heed to any of   *Jer 18:18*
his words
l. their wives be bereaved of   *Jer 18:21*
their
and *l.* their men be put to   *Jer 18:21*
death
l. their young men be slain by   *Jer 18:21*
L. a cry be heard from their   *Jer 18:22*
houses
but *l.* them be overthrown   *Jer 18:23*
before thee
l. me see thy vengeance on   *Jer 20:12*
them
l. not the day wherein my   *Jer 20:14*
mother bare
And *l.* that man be as the   *Jer 20:16*
cities which
l. him hear the cry in the   *Jer 20:16*
morning
that hath a dream, *l.* him tell   *Jer 23:28*
a dream
world *l.* him speak my word   *Jer 23:28*
faithfully
those will I *l.* remain still in   *Jer 27:11*
their
L. not your prophets and your   *Jer 29:8*
intercession to the

l. them now make — Jer 27:18
l. us go up to Zion unto the — Jer 31:6
Lord our
man should *l.* his — Jer 34:9
manservant go free
one should *l.* his — Jer 34:10
manservant go free
then they obeyed, and *l.* them — Jer 34:10
go
whom they had *l.* go free, to — Jer 34:11
return
l. ye go every man his brother — Jer 34:14
thou shalt *l.* him go free from — Jer 34:14
thee
and *l.* us go to Jerusalem for — Jer 35:11
fear of
and *l.* no man know where ye — Jer 36:19
be
l. my supplication be — Jer 37:20
accepted
thee, *l.* this man be put to — Jer 38:4
death
they *l.* down Jeremiah with — Jer 38:6
cords
and *l.* them down by cords — Jer 38:11
into the
L. no man know of these — Jer 38:24
words, and
captain of the guard had *l.* him — Jer 40:1
go
victuals and a reward, and *l.* — Jer 40:5
him go
Mizpah secretly, saying, L. — Jer 40:15
me go
L. our supplication be — Jer 42:2
accepted
L. not the swift flee away, nor — Jer 46:6
and *l.* the mighty men come — Jer 46:9
forth
l. us go again to our own — Jer 46:16
people
l. us cut it off from being a — Jer 48:2
nation
alive; and *l.* thy widows trust — Jer 49:11
in me
and *l.* us join ourselves to the — Jer 50:5
Lord
her utterly: *l.* nothing of her — Jer 50:26
be left
l. them go down to the — Jer 50:27
slaughter
about; *l.* none therefore — Jer 50:29
escape
them fast; they refused to *l.* — Jer 50:33
them go
bendeth *l.* the archer bend his — Jer 51:3
bow
l. us go every one into his own — Jer 51:9
l. us declare in Zion the work — Jer 51:10
of the
l. Jerusalem come into your — Jer 51:50
mind
L. all their wickedness come — La 1:22
before
l. tears run down like a river — La 2:18
day
l. not the apple of thine eye — La 2:18
cease
L. us search and try our ways — La 3:40
L. us lift up our heart with our — La 3:41
hands
stood, they *l.* down their wings — Eze 1:24
stood, and had *l.* down their — Eze 1:25
wings
God; He that heareth, *l.* him — Eze 3:27
hear
and he that forbeareth, *l.* him — Eze 3:27
forbear
l. not the buyer rejoice, nor — Eze 7:12
the seller
l. not your eye spare, neither — Eze 9:5
have ye
l. us build houses: this city is — Eze 11:3
will *l.* the souls go, even the — Eze 13:20
souls
and *l.* the sword be doubled — Eze 21:14
the third
l. them seethe the bones of it — Eze 24:5
therein
piece by piece; *l.* no lot fall — Eze 24:6
upon it
spice it well, *l.* the bones be — Eze 24:10
burned
I will not *l.* them pollute my — Eze 39:7
holy
Now *l.* them put away their — Eze 43:9
whoredom
and *l.* them measure the — Eze 43:10
pattern

Israel, *l.* it suffice you of all — Eze 44:6
your
l. them give us pulse to eat, — Da 1:12
and water
l. our countenance's be looked — Da 1:13
upon
L. the king tell his servants the — Da 2:7
dream
l. the beasts get away from — Da 4:14
under it
l. it be wet with the dew of — Da 4:15;
heaven — 4:23
l. his portion be with the — Da 4:15
beasts in the
L. his heart be changed from — Da 4:16
man's
l. a beast's heart be given unto — Da 4:16
him
and *l.* seven times pass over — Da 4:16
him
l. not the dream, or — Da 4:19
l. his portion be with the — Da 4:23
beasts of the
l. my counsel be acceptable — Da 4:27
unto thee
ever: *l.* not thy thoughts — Da 5:10
trouble thee
nor *l.* thy countenance be — Da 5:10
changed
now *l.* Daniel be called, and he — Da 5:12
will
L. thy gifts be to thyself, and — Da 5:17
give thy
l. thine anger and thy fury be — Da 9:16
turned
said, L. my lord speak; for — Da 10:19
thou hast
l. her therefore put away her — Ho 2:2
Yet *l.* no man strive, nor reprove — Ho 4:4
the harlot, yet *l.* not Judah — Ho 4:15
offend
is joined to idols: *l.* him alone — Ho 4:17
and *l.* us return unto the Lord — Ho 6:1
L. the men that sacrifice kiss — Ho 13:2
l. your children tell their — Joe 1:3
children, and
l. all the inhabitants of — Joe 2:1
l. the bridegroom go forth of — Joe 2:16
his
L. the priests weep, *l.* them — Joe 2:17
say
men, *l.* all the men of war draw — Joe 3:9
near
l. them come up — Joe 3:9
spears: *l.* the weak say, I am — Joe 3:10
strong
L. the heathen be wakened, — Joe 3:12
and come
their masters, Bring, and *l.* us — Am 4:1
drink
But *l.* judgment run down as — Am 5:24
waters
and *l.* us rise up against her in — Ob 1
battle
Come, and *l.* us cast lots, that — Jon 1:7
we may
l. us not perish for this man's — Jon 1:14
life, and
L. neither man nor beast, — Jon 3:7
herd
l. them not feed, nor drink — Jon 3:7
water
But *l.* man and beast be — Jon 3:8
covered with
l. them turn every one from his — Jon 3:8
l. the Lord God be witness — Mic 1:2
against
and *l.* us go up to the mountain — Mic 4:2
of the
L. her be defiled, and *l.* our — Mic 4:11
eye look
and *l.* the hills hear thy voice — Mic 6:1
l. them feed in Bashan and — Mic 7:14
Gilead, as
also, and *l.* thy foreskin be — Hab 2:16
uncovered
l. all the earth keep silence — Hab 2:20
before
to Zion, L. not thine hands be — Zep 3:16
slack
l. them set a fair mitre upon — Zec 3:5
his head
l. none of you imagine evil — Zec 7:10
against his
L. your hands be strong, ye that — Zec 8:9
hear
fear not, but *l.* your hands — Zec 8:13
be strong

l. none of you imagine evil in — Zec 8:17
your
L. us go speedily to pray — Zec 8:21
before the
not feed you: that that dieth, — Zec 11:9
l. it die
that that is to be cut off, *l.* it — Zec 11:9
be cut off
and *l.* the rest eat every one — Zec 11:9
the flesh
l. none deal treacherously — Mal 2:15
against the
his wife, *l.* him give her a — M't 5:31
writing of
l. your communication be, — M't 5:37
Yea
thy coat, *l.* him have thy cloke — M't 5:40
also
L. me pull out the mote out of — M't 7:4
thine
me; and *l.* the dead bury their — M't 8:22;
dead — Lu 9:60
be worthy, *l.* your peace — M't 10:13
come upon it
worthy, *l.* your peace return — M't 10:13
to you
He that hath ears to hear, *l.* — M't 11:15;
him hear — M'k 4:9; Lu 8:8; 14:35
Who hath ears to hear, *l.* him — M't 13:9;
hear — 13:43
L. both grow together until — M't 13:30
father or mother, *l.* him die — M't 15:4
the death
L. them alone: they be — M't 15:14
blind
l. him deny himself, and take — M't 16:24;
up his — M'k 8:34; Lu 9:23
l. us make here three — M't 17:4;
tabernacles — Lu 9:33
l. him be unto thee as an — M't 18:17
heathen
together, *l.* not man put — M't 19:6
asunder
able to receive it, *l.* him — M't 19:12
receive it
you, *l.* him be your minister — M't 20:26
among you, *l.* him be your — M't 20:27
servant
L. no fruit grow on thee — M't 21:19
henceforward
l. it out to husbandmen and — M't 21:33
went
This is the heir; come, *l.* us — M't 21:38;
kill him — M'k 12:7; Lu 20:14
will *l.* out his vineyard unto — M't 21:41
other
whoso readeth, *l.* him — M't 24:15
understand
l. them which be in Judaea — M't 24:16;
flee into the — M'k 13:14; Lu 21:21
L. him which is on the — M't 24:17;
housetop not — M'k 13:15
Neither *l.* him which is in the — M't 24:18
field
be possible, *l.* this cup pass — M't 26:39
from me
l. us be going: behold, he is — M't 26:46
at hand
all say unto him, L. him be — M't 27:22
crucified
the more, saying, L. him be — M't 27:23
crucified
l. him now come down from — M't 27:42
the cross
l. him deliver him now, if he — M't 27:43
will
The rest said, L. be — M't 27:49
l. us see whether Elias will — M't 27:49;
come — M'k 15:36
L. us alone: what have we — M'k 1:24
to do
L. us go into the next towns, — M'k 1:38
that I
l. down the bed wherein the — M'k 2:4
sick
man have ears to hear, *l.* him — M'k 4:23;
hear — 7:16
L. us pass over unto the other — M'k 4:35
side
father or mother, *l.* him die — M'k 7:10
the death
her, L. the children first be — M'k 7:27
filled
and *l.* us make three — M'k 9:5
tabernacles
together, *l.* not man put — M'k 10:9
asunder

commanded: and they *l.* them *M'k 11:6* go

l. it out to husbandmen, and *M'k 12:1* went

not, *l.* him that readeth *M'k 13:14* understand

And *l.* him that is in the field *M'k 13:16* not turn

And Jesus said, *L.* her alone: *M'k 14:6* why

Rise up, *l.* us go; lo, he that *M'k 14:42* betrayeth

L. Christ, the King of Israel *M'k 15:32* descend

to drink, saying, *L.* alone *M'k 15:36*

L. us now go even unto *Lu 2:15* Bethlehem

l. him impart to him that hath *Lu 3:11* none

he that hath meat, *l.* him do *Lu 3:11* likewise

Saying, *L.* us alone; what have *Lu 4:34*

l. your nets down for a draught *Lu 5:4*

at thy word I will *l.* down the *Lu 5:5* net

and *l.* him down through the *Lu 5:19* tiling

l. me pull out the mote that is *Lu 6:42* in

L. us go over unto the other *Lu 8:22* side of

L. these sayings sink down into *Lu 9:44* your

l. me first go bid them farewell *Lu 9:61*

L. your loins be girded about *Lu 12:35*

Lord *l.* it alone this year also, *Lu 13:8* till I

him, and healed him, and *l.* *Lu 14:4* him go

kill it; and *l.* us eat, and be *Lu 15:23* merry

and the prophets; *l.* them hear *Lu 16:29* them

l. him not come down to take *Lu 17:31* it away

field, *l.* him likewise not *Lu 17:31* return back

L. little children come unto me *Lu 18:16* (S)

and *l.* it forth to husbandmen *Lu 20:9*

l. them which are in the midst *Lu 21:21* depart

l. not them in the countries *Lu 21:21* enter

among you, *l.* him be as the *Lu 22:26* younger

l. him take it, and likewise his *Lu 22:36* script

l. him sell his garment, and *Lu 22:36* buy one

ye will not answer me, nor *l.* *Lu 22:68* me go

therefore chastise him, and *l.* *Lu 23:22* him go

l. him save himself, if he be *Lu 23:35* Christ, the

thirst, *l.* him come unto me *Joh 7:37* and drink

you, *l.* him first cast a stone at *Joh 8:7* her

disciples, *L.* us go into Judaea *Joh 11:7* again

nevertheless *l.* us go unto him *Joh 11:15*

*L.*us also go, that we may die *Joh 11:16* with

them, Loose him, and *l.* him *Joh 11:44* go

If we *l.* him thus alone, all *Joh 11:48* men will

said Jesus, *L.* her alone: *Joh 12:7* against

any man serve me, *l.* him *Joh 12:26* follow me

L. not your heart be troubled *Joh 14:1; 14:27*

neither *l.* it be afraid *Joh 14:27*

even so I do. Arise, *l.* us go *Joh 14:31* hence

ye seek me, *l.* these go their *Joh 18:8* way

If thou *l.* this man go, thou *Joh 19:12* art not

L. us not rend it, but cast *Joh 19:24* lots for it

L. his habitation be desolate *Ac 1:20* and *l.* no man dwell therein *Ac 1:20* and his bishoprick *l.* another *Ac 1:20* take

l. me freely speak unto you of *Ac 2:29*

l. all the house of Israel know *Ac 2:36*

he was determined to *l.* him go *Ac 3:13*

l. us straitly threaten them, *Ac 4:17* that they

threatened them, they *l.* them *Ac 4:21* go

And being *l.* go, they went to *Ac 4:23* their own

these men, and *l.* them alone *Ac 5:38*

in the name of Jesus, and *l.* *Ac 5:40* them go

l. him down by the wall in a *Ac 9:25* corners, and *l.* down to the *Ac 10:11* earth

sheet, *l.* down from heaven by *Ac 11:5* four

they were *l.* go in peace from *Ac 15:33*

L. us go again and visit our *Ac 15:36* brethren

serjeants, saying, *L.* those *Ac 16:35* men go

magistrates have sent to *l.* you *Ac 16:36* go

l. them come themselves and *Ac 16:37* fetch us

and of the other, they *l.* them *Ac 17:9* go

deputies: *l.* them implead one *Ac 19:38* another

to him, *l.* us not fight against *Ac 23:9* God

then *l.* the young man depart *Ac 23:22*

Or else *l.* these same here say, *Ac 24:20* if they

keep Paul, and to *l.* him have *Ac 24:23* liberty

L. them therefore, go down *Ac 25:5* with me

up into the wind, we *l.* her *Ac 27:15* drive

had *l.* down the boat into the *Ac 27:30* sea

ropes of the boat, and *l.* her *Ac 27:32* fall off

examined me, would have *l.* *Ac 28:18* me go

unto you, (but was *l.* hitherto) *Ro 1:13*

yea, *l.* God be true, but every *Ro 3:4* man a

L. us do evil, that good may *Ro 3:8* come

L. not sin therefore reign in *Ro 6:12* your

L. their table be made a snare, *Ro 11:9* and a

L. their eyes be darkened, *Ro 11:10* that they

l. us prophesy according to the *Ro 12:6* ministry, *l.* us wait on our *Ro 12:7* ministering

giveth, *l.* him do it with *Ro 12:8* simplicity

L. love be without *Ro 12:9* dissimulation

L. every soul be subject unto *Ro 13:1*

l. us therefore cast off the *Ro 13:12* works of

and *l.* us put on the armour *Ro 13:12* of light

L. us walk honestly, as in the *Ro 13:13* day

L. not him that eateth despise *Ro 14:3* him

L. not him which eateth not *Ro 14:3* judge him

L. every man be fully *Ro 14:5* persuaded in

L. us not therefore judge one *Ro 14:13* another

L. not then your good be *Ro 14:16* evil spoken

L. us therefore follow after *Ro 14:19* the things

L. every one please his *Ro 15:2* neighbour

that glorieth, *l.* him glory in *1Co 1:31* the Lord

l. every man take heed how he *1Co 3:10* buildeth

L. no man deceive himself. If *1Co 3:18* any

l. him become a fool, that he *1Co 3:18* may be

Therefore *l.* no man glory in *1Co 3:21* men

L. a man so account of us, as *1Co 4:1*

Therefore *l.* us keep the feast *1Co 5:8*

l. every man have his own *1Co 7:2* wife, and

l. every woman have her own *1Co 7:2* husband

L. the husband render unto the *1Co 7:3* wife

if they cannot contain, *l.* them *1Co 7:9* marry

L. not the wife depart from *1Co 7:10* her

she depart, *l.* her remain *1Co 7:11* unmarried

l. not the husband put away his *1Co 7:11* wife

with him, *l.* him not put her *1Co 7:12* away

to dwell with her, *l.* her not *1Co 7:13* leave him

the unbelieving depart, *l.* him *1Co 7:15* depart

hath called every one, so *l.* *1Co 7:17* him walk

l. him not become *1Co 7:18* uncircumcised

l. him not be circumcised *1Co 7:18*

L. every man abide in the *1Co 7:20* same calling

l. every man, wherein he *1Co 7:24* is

need so require, *l.* him do *1Co 7:36* what he will

will he sinneth not: *l.* them *1Co 7:36* marry

Neither *l.* us commit *1Co 10:8* fornication, as

Neither *l.* us tempt Christ, as *1Co 10:9* some of

l. him that standeth take *1Co 10:12* heed

L. no man seek his own, but *1Co 10:24* every

be not covered, *l.* her also be *1Co 11:6* shorn

be shorn or shaven, *l.* her be *1Co 11:6* covered

But *l.* a man examine himself *1Co 11:28* so *l.* him eat of that bread, *1Co 11:28* and drink

any man hunger, *l.* him eat *1Co 11:34* at home

l. him that speaketh in *1Co 14:13*

L. all things be done unto *1Co 14:26* edifying

l. it be by two, or at most by *1Co 14:27* three

that by course; and *l.* one *1Co 14:27* interpret

l. him keep silence in the *1Co 14:28* church

l. him speak to himself, and *1Co 14:28* to God

L. the prophets speak two or *1Co 14:29* three

two or three, and *l.* the other *1Co 14:29* judge

sitteth by, *l.* the first hold his *1Co 14:30* peace

L. your women keep silence *1Co 14:34* in the

l. them ask their husbands at *1Co 14:35* home

l. him acknowledge that the *1Co 14:37* things

man be ignorant, *l.* him be *1Co 14:38* ignorant

L. all things be done decently *1Co 14:40* and in

l. us eat and drink; for *1Co 15:32* to morrow we

l. every one of you lay by *1Co 16:2* him in store

L. no man therefore despise *1Co 16:11* him: but

L. all your things be done *1Co 16:14* with charity

l. him be Anathema *1Co 16:22* Maran-atha

l. us cleanse ourselves from all *2Co 7:1*

purposeth in his heart, so *l.* him *2Co 9:7* give

l. him of himself think this *2Co 10:7* again, that

L. such an one think this, *2Co 10:11* that, such

that glorieth, *l.* him glory in *2Co 10:17* the Lord

say again, *L.* no man think *2Co 11:16* me a fool

basket was I *l.* down by the *2Co 11:33* wall

unto you, *l.* him be accursed *Ga 1:8*

have received, *l.* him be *Ga 1:9* accursed

the Spirit, *l.* us also walk in the   *Ga 5:25*
Spirit
L. us not be desirous of vain   *Ga 5:26*
glory
But *l.* every man prove his own   *Ga 6:4*
work
L. him that is   *Ga 6:6*
taught communicate
l. us not be weary in well doing   *Ga 6:9*
l. us do good unto all men,   *Ga 6:10*
especially
henceforth *l.* no man trouble   *Ga 6:17*
me
l. not the sun go down upon   *Eph 4:26*
your
L. him that stole steal no   *Eph 4:28*
more: but
but rather *l.* him labour,   *Eph 4:28*
working with
L. no corrupt communication   *Eph 4:29*
proceed
L. all bitterness be put   *Eph 4:31*
away
l. it not be once named among   *Eph 5:3*
you, as
L. no man deceive you with   *Eph 5:6*
vain
l. the wives be to their own   *Eph 5:24*
husbands
l. every one of you in   *Eph 5:33*
particular so love
l. your conversation be as it   *Ph'p 1:27*
becometh
L. nothing be done through   *Ph'p 2:3*
strife or
mind *l.* each esteem other   *Ph'p 2:3*
better than
L. this mind be in you, which   *Ph'p 2:5*
was also
L. us therefore be thus   *Ph'p 3:15*
minded
attained, *l.* us walk by the   *Ph'p 3:16*
same rule
l. us mind the same things   *Ph'p 3:16*
L. your moderation be known   *Ph'p 4:5*
unto all
l. your requests be made   *Ph'p 4:6*
known unto
L. no man therefore judge you   *Col 2:16*
L. no man beguile you of your   *Col 2:18*
reward
l. the peace of God rule in   *Col 3:15*
your hearts
L. the word of Christ dwell in   *Col 3:16*
you
L. your speech be alway with   *Col 4:6*
grace
Therefore *l.* us not sleep, as do   *1Th 5:6*
others
but *l.* us watch and be sober   *1Th 5:6*
But *l.* us, who are of the day,   *1Th 5:8*
be sober
L. no man deceive you by any   *2Th 2:3*
means
only he who now letteth will *l.*   *2Th 2:7*
L. the woman learn in silence   *1Ti 2:11*
with all
and *l.* these also first be   *1Ti 3:10*
proved; then
then *l.* them use the office of a   *1Ti 3:10*
deacon
L. the deacons be the   *1Ti 3:12*
husbands of
L. no man despise thy youth;   *1Ti 4:12*
but be
l. them learn first to show piety   *1Ti 5:4*
at
L. not a widow be taken into   *1Ti 5:9*
have widows, *l.* them relieve   *1Ti 5:16*
them
and *l.* not the church be   *1Ti 5:16*
charged; that
L. the elders that rule well be   *1Ti 5:17*
counted
L. as many servants as are   *1Ti 6:1*
masters, *l.* them not despise   *1Ti 6:2*
them
raiment *l.* us be therewith   *1Ti 6:8*
content
L. every one that   *2Ti 2:19*
nameth
authority. *L.* no man despise   *Tit 2:15*
thee
l. ours also learn to maintain   *Tit 3:14*
good
l. me have joy of thee in the   *Ph'm 20*
Lord
l. all the angels of God   *Heb 1:6*
worship him

at any time we should *l.* them   *Heb 2:1*
slip
L. us therefore fear, lest, a   *Heb 4:1*
promise
L. us labour therefore to   *Heb 4:11*
enter into
of God, *l.* us hold fast our   *Heb 4:14*
profession
L. us therefore come   *Heb 4:16*
boldly unto the
of Christ, *l.* us go on unto   *Heb 6:1*
perfection
L. us draw near with a true   *Heb 10:22*
heart in
L. us hold fast the   *Heb 10:23*
profession of our
l. us consider one another to   *Heb 10:24*
provoke
l. us lay aside every weight   *Heb 12:1*
l. us run with patience the   *Heb 12:1*
race that is
of the way; but *l.* it rather   *Heb 12:13*
be healed
l. us have grace, whereby we   *Heb 12:28*
may
L. brotherly love continue   *Heb 13:1*
L. your conversation be   *Heb 13:5*
without
L. us go forth therefore unto   *Heb 13:13*
him
l. us offer the sacrifice of   *Heb 13:15*
praise to God
But *l.* patience have her perfect   *Jas 1:4*
work
you lack wisdom, *l.* him ask of   *Jas 1:5*
God
But *l.* him ask in faith, nothing   *Jas 1:6*
For *l.* not that man think that   *Jas 1:7*
he shall
L. the brother of low degree   *Jas 1:9*
rejoice
L. no man say when he is   *Jas 1:13*
tempted, I
l. every man be swift to hear,   *Jas 1:19*
slow to
l. him shew out of a good   *Jas 3:13*
conversation
l. your laughter be turned to   *Jas 4:9*
mourning
l. your yea be yea; and your   *Jas 5:12*
nay, nay
any among you afflicted? *l.*   *Jas 5:13*
him pray
Is any merry? *l.* him sing   *Jas 5:13*
psalms
l. him call for the elders of the   *Jas 5:14*
church
l. them pray over him,   *Jas 5:14*
anointing him
l. him know, that he which   *Jas 5:20*
converteth
l. it not be that outward   *1Pe 3:3*
adorning
But *l.* it be the hidden man of   *1Pe 3:4*
l. him refrain his tongue from   *1Pe 3:10*
evil
L. him eschew evil, and do   *1Pe 3:11*
good
l. him seek peace, and ensue it   *1Pe 3:11*
l. him speak as the oracles of   *1Pe 4:11*
God
l. him do it as of the ability   *1Pe 4:11*
which
l. none of you suffer as a   *1Pe 4:15*
murderer
as a Christian, *l.* him not be   *1Pe 4:16*
ashamed
but *l.* him glorify God on this   *1Pe 4:16*
behalf
l. them that suffer according   *1Pe 4:19*
to the
L. that therefore abide in you   *1Jo 2:24*
Little children, *l.* no man   *1Jo 3:7*
deceive you
little children, *l.* us not love in   *1Jo 3:18*
word
l. us love one another; for love   *1Jo 4:7*
is of
l. him hear what the Spirit   *Re 2:7;*
   2:11, 17, 29; 3:6, 13, 22
If any man have an ear, *l.*   *Re 13:9*
him hear
L. him that hath   *Re 13:18*
understanding count
L. us be glad and rejoice, and   *Re 19:7*
that is unjust, *l.* him be unjust   *Re 22:11*
still
he which is filthy, *l.* him be   *Re 22:11*
filthy still

is righteous, *l.* him be   *Re 22:11*
righteous still
and he that is holy, *l.* him be   *Re 22:11*
holy still
And *l.* him that heareth say,   *Re 22:17*
Come
And *l.* him that is athirst   *Re 22:17*
come
l. him take the water of life   *Re 22:17*
freely

LETTER

David wrote a *l.* to Joab and   *2Sa 11:14*
sent
wrote a message to Joab (N)   *2Sa 11:14*
And he wrote in the *l.* saying,   *2Sa 11:15*
Set
and I will send a *l.* unto the   *2Ki 5:5*
king of
And he brought the *l.* to the   *2Ki 5:6*
king of
Now when this *l.* is come unto   *2Ki 5:6*
thee
the king of Israel had read the   *2Ki 5:7*
l.
as soon as this *l.* cometh to   *2Ki 10:2*
you
Then he wrote a *l.* the second   *2Ki 10:6*
time
to pass, when the *l.* came to   *2Ki 10:7*
them
And Hezekiah received the *l.*   *2Ki 19:14*
of the
writing of the *l.* was written in   *Ezr 4:7*
and Shimshai the scribe wrote   *Ezr 4:8*
a *l.*
the copy of the *l.* that they   *Ezr 4:11*
sent unto
The *l.* which ye sent unto us   *Ezr 4:18*
hath
the copy of king Artaxerxes' *l.*   *Ezr 4:23*
was
returned answer by *l.*   *Ezr 5:5*
concerning
The copy of the *l.* that Tatnai   *Ezr 5:6*
They sent a *l.* unto him,   *Ezr 5:7*
wherein
is the copy of the *l.* that the   *Ezr 7:11*
king
And a *l.* unto Asaph the keeper   *Ne 2:8*
time with an open *l.* in his hand   *Ne 6:5*
Therefore for all the words of   *Es 9:26*
this *l.*
to confirm this second *l.* of   *Es 9:29*
Purim
make the second document (B)   *Es 9:29*
Hezekiah received the *l.* from   *Isa 37:14*
words of the *l.* that Jeremiah   *Jer 29:1*
the priest read this *l.* in the   *Jer 29:29*
ears of
not one smallest *l.* (A)(N)   *M't 5:18*
he wrote a *l.* after this manner   *Ac 23:25*
when the governor had read   *Ac 23:34*
the *l.*
who by the *l.* and circumcision   *Ro 2:27*
heart, in the spirit, and not in   *Ro 2:29*
the *l.*
and not in the oldness of the *l.*   *Ro 7:6*
not under old code of written   *Ro 7:6*
regulations, but of the Spirit in
newness (A)
not in old relationship of
literalness (B)
serve God in new way in   *Ro 7:6*
contrast to the old way, the way
of a written code (N)(R)
letter (A)(N)(R)   *Ro 16:22;*
   1Co 5:9; 2Co 3:2-3; 7:8; 1Th 5:27;
   2Th 2:15; 3:14, 17; 2Pe 3:1
letter (B)   *Ro 16:22;*
   1Co 5:9; 2Co 7:8; 2Th 2:15; 2Pe 3:1
letter (P)   *1Co 5:9;*
   2Co 3:2; 7:8; Col 4:16; 1Th 5:27;
   2Th 3:17; 2Pe 3:1
not of the *l.* but of the spirit   *2Co 3:6*
the *l.* killeth, but the spirit   *2Co 3:6*
giveth
though I make you sorry with   *2Co 7:8*
an *l.*
Ye see how large a *l.* I have   *Ga 6:11*
nor by word, nor by *l.* as from   *2Th 2:2*
us
I have written a *l.* unto you   *Heb 13:22*
in few

LETTERS

So she wrote *l.* in Ahab's   *1Ki 21:8*
name

and sent the *l.* unto the elders *1Ki 21:8*
And she wrote in the *l.* saying *1Ki 21:9*
as it was written in the *l.* *1Ki 21:11*
which she
And Jehu wrote *l.* and sent to *2Ki 10:1*
sent *l.* and a present unto *2Ki 20:12*
Hezekiah
and wrote *l.* also to Ephraim *2Ch 30:1*
the posts went with the *l.* *2Ch 30:6*
from the
He wrote also *l.* to rail on *2Ch 32:17*
the Lord
let *l.* be given me to the *Ne 2:7*
governors
river, and gave them the king's *Ne 2:9*
l.
Judah sent many *l.* unto *Ne 6:17*
Tobiah
the *l.* of Tobiah came unto *Ne 6:17*
them
And Tobiah sent *l.* to put me *Ne 6:19*
in fear
For he sent *l.* into all the king's *Es 1:22*
the *l.* were sent by posts into all *Es 3:13*
let it be written to reverse the *l.* *Es 8:5*
and sent *l.* by posts on *Es 8:10*
horseback
sent *l.* unto all the Jews that *Es 9:20*
were
he commanded by *l.* that his *Es 9:25*
wicked
And he sent the *l.* unto all the *Es 9:30*
Jews
sent *l.* and a present to *Isa 39:1*
Hezekiah
thou hast sent *l.* in thy name *Jer 29:25*
unto
written over him in *l.* of *Lu 23:38*
Greek
How knoweth this man *l.* *Joh 7:15*
having
And desired of him *l.* to *Ac 9:2*
Damascus
And they wrote *l.* by them *Ac 15:23*
after this
I received *l.* unto the brethren *Ac 22:5*
We neither received *l.* out of *Ac 28:21*
Judaea
whomsoever approve by *1Co 16:3*
your *l.*
you, or *l.* of commendation *2Co 3:1*
from you
letters (A)(B)(N)(R) *2Co 3:1; 2Pe 3:16*
seem as if I would terrify you *2Co 10:9*
by *l.*
For his *l.,* say they, are *2Co 10:10*
weighty
in word by *l.* when we are *2Co 10:11*
absent

LETTEST

l. such words go out of thy *Job 15:13*
mouth
with a cord which thou *l.* *Job 41:1*
down
now *l.* thou thy servant depart *Lu 2:29*

LETTETH

he that *l.* him go, his life *2Ki 10:24*
shall be for
strife is as when one *l.* out *Pr 17:14*
water
only he who now *l.* will let, *2Th 2:7*
until

LETTING

in not *l.* the people go to *Ex 8:29*
sacrifice

LETUSHIM

of Dedan were Asshurim, and *Ge 25:3*
L.

LEUMMIM

Asshurim, and Letushim, and *Ge 25:3*
L.

LEVEL

live on *l.* of instincts (P) *Ro 8:12*

LEVI

therefore was his name called *Ge 29:34*
L.
the sons of *L.* *Ge 46:11;*
                  Ex 6:16; Nu 3:17
Simeon, *L.* are brethren, *Ge 49:5*
instruments of cruelty
the years of the life of *L.* were *Ex 6:16*
137 years
talk too much upon you, *Nu 16:7*
sons of *L.*
Amram's wife Jochebed, *Nu 26:59*
daughter of *L.*
L. hath no part with his *De 10:9*
brethren
the priests the sons of *L.* shall *De 21:5*
come near
of *L.* he said, Let thy *De 33:8*
Thummim and Urim
made priests which were not *1Ki 12:31*
of *L.*
but *L.* and Benjamin counted *1Ch 21:6*
he not
I found there none of the sons *Ezr 8:15*
of *L.*
bless the Lord, O house of *L.* *Ps 135:20*
the sons of Zadok among the *Eze 40:46*
sons of *L.*
one gate of Judah, one gate *Eze 48:31*
of *L.*
the family of the house of *L.* *Zec 12:13*
apart
that my covenant might be *Mal 2:4*
with *L.*
ye have corrupted the covenant *Mal 2:8*
of *L.*
and he shall purify the sons of *Mal 3:3*
L.
he saw *L.* the son of *M'k 2:14*
Alphaeus sitting
Matthat, which was the son of *Lu 3:24;*
L.   *3:29*
he saw a publican named *L.* *Lu 5:27*
sitting at
L. made him a great feast in *Lu 5:29*
his own house
L. who received tithes, payed *Heb 7:9*
tithes in Abraham

LEVIATHAN

canst thou draw out *l.* with an *Job 41:1*
hook
thou breakest the heads of *l.* *Ps 74:14*
in pieces
there is that *l.* thou hast *Ps 104:26*
made to play
shall punish *l.* even *l.* that *Isa 27:1*
crooked serpent

LEVITE

is not Aaron the *L.* thy brother *Ex 4:14*
rejoice ye before the Lord *De 12:12;*
your God, and the *L.* *12:18; 16:11, 14;*
                           26:11, 13
and the *L.* shall come and eat *De 14:29;*
                                    26:12
if a *L.* come from any of thy *De 18:6*
gates
a young man a *L.;* so the *L.* *J'g 17:7;*
went in   *17:9-10*
the *L.* was content to dwell *J'g 17:11*
with the man
Micah consecrated the *L.;* a *J'g 17:12;*
L. to my priest   *17:13*
they knew the voice of the *J'g 18:3*
young man the *L.*
there was a certain *L.* *J'g 19:1*
sojourning on mount
the *L.* said, I came into *J'g 20:4*
Gibeah of Benjamin
on Jahaziel the *L.* came the *2Ch 20:14*
Spirit
Cononiah the *L.* over the *2Ch 31:12*
dedicated things
Kore the *L.* over the freewill *2Ch 31:14*
offerings
Shabbethai, the *L.* helped *Ezr 10:15*
them
likewise a *L.* came and looked *Lu 10:32*
on
Barnabas a *L.* having land, sold *Ac 4:36*
it

LEVITES

these heads of the fathers of *Ex 6:25*
the *L.*
it was counted for the service *Ex 38:21*
of the *L.*
cities of *L.* may *L.* redeem at *Le 25:32*
any time
the cities of the *L.* are their *Le 25:33*
possession
but the *L.* were not numbered *Nu 1:47;*
                                    2:33
shalt appoint the *L.* over the *Nu 1:50*
tabernacle
the *L.* shall take it down; the *Nu 1:51;*
L. shall pitch   *1:53*
and thou shalt give the *L.* unto *Nu 3:9*
Aaron
I have taken the *L.* the *L.* shall *Nu 3:12*
be mine
all that were numbered of the *Nu 3:39;*
L.   *4:46*
and thou shalt take the *L.* for *Nu 3:41;*
me   *3:45; 8:14*
thou shalt give wagons unto the *Nu 7:5*
L.
take the *L.* from Israel and *Nu 8:6*
cleanse them
bring the *L.* before the *Nu 8:9;*
tabernacle   *8:10*
Aaron shall offer the *L.* before *Nu 8:11*
the Lord
then after that shall the *L.* go *Nu 8:15;*
in   *8:22*
this is it that belongeth unto *Nu 8:24*
the *L.*
this shalt thou do to *L.* *Nu 8:26*
touching their
I have taken the *L.* to do *Nu 18:6;*
service   *18:23*
tithes I have given to *L.* to *Nu 18:24*
inherit
that they give to the *L.* cities *Nu 34:2;*
round   *35:8*
minister, as his brethren the *L.* *De 18:7*
do
to *L.* he gave none inheritance *Jos 14:3*
Israel gave these cities to the *Jos 21:3;*
L.   *21:8*
all the cities of the *L.* were *Jos 21:41*
forty-eight
L. took down the ark of the *1Sa 6:15*
Lord
Zadok and the *L.* were with *2Sa 15:24*
him
children of the *L.* bare the *1Ch 15:15*
ark
when God helped the *L.* that *1Ch 15:26*
bare the ark
one of the *L.* wrote them *1Ch 24:6*
before the king
the *L.* which were singers *2Ch 5:12;*
stood   *7:6*
the *L.* left their suburbs and *2Ch 11:14*
possession
have ye not cast out the sons *2Ch 13:9*
of Aaron and *L.*
also the *L.* shall be officers *2Ch 19:11*
before you
L. shall compass the king *2Ch 23:6;*
round about   *23:7*
howbeit, the *L.* hastened it *2Ch 24:5*
not
hear me, ye *L.* sanctify now *2Ch 29:5*
yourselves
Hezekiah spake comfortably *2Ch 30:22*
to the *L.*
of the *L.* there were scribes *2Ch 34:13*
and officers
Josiah said to the *L.* which *2Ch 35:3*
taught Israel
the chief of the *L.* gave to the *2Ch 35:9*
L. 500 oxen
therefore the *L.* prepared for *2Ch 35:14;*
themselves   *35:15*
they set the *L.* in their courses *Ezr 6:18*
after him repaired the *L.* *Ne 3:17*
Rehum
L. caused the people to *Ne 8:7*
understand the law
the *L.* stilled the people, *Ne 8:11*
saying, Hold your peace
the overseer of the *L.* was *Ne 11:22*
Uzzi
at the dedication they sought *Ne 12:27*
the *L.*
portions of *L.* had not been *Ne 13:10*
given them, for *L.* were fled

they have defiled the | Ne 13:29
priesthood of the *L.*
I will multiply the *L.* that | Jer 33:22
minister
the *L.* that are gone shall bear | Eze 44:10
iniquity
went not astray when the *L.* | Eze 48:11
went astray

PRIESTS AND LEVITES

thou shalt come to *priests and* | De 17:9
L. and judge
to do all that the *priests and L.* | De 24:8
shall teach
when ye see the *priests and L.* | Jos 3:3
bearing the ark
priests and L. brought up the | 1Ki 8:4
ark of the Lord
priests and L. shall be porters | 2Ch 23:4
of the doors
priests and L. were more | 2Ch 29:34
upright in heart than
priests and L. were ashamed, | 2Ch 30:15
and sanctified
L. and the *priests* praised the | 2Ch 30:21
Lord day by day
then the *priests and L.* | 2Ch 30:27
blessed the people
Hezekiah questioned with the | 2Ch 31:9
priests and L.
his princes gave willingly to | 2Ch 35:8
the *priests and L.*
so *priests and L.* dwelt in their | Ezr 2:70
cities
for the *priests and L.* were | Ezr 6:20
purified together
there went up of the *priests and* | Ezr 7:7
L. and singers
the *priests and L.* have not | Ezr 9:1
separated themselves
Ezra arose and made the | Ezr 10:5
priests and L. to swear
our princes, *L.* and *priests* seal | Ne 9:38
to it
we cast lots among *priests* | Ne 10:34
and L. the people
the *priests and L.* purified | Ne 12:30
themselves and the wall
Judah rejoiced for the *priests* | Ne 12:44
and L. that waited
I will take of them for *priests* | Isa 66:21
and L.
priests and L. not want a man | Jer 33:18
to offer
and with the *L.* the *priests* my | Jer 33:21
ministers
but the *priests and L.* that | Eze 44:15
kept the charge
when the Jews sent *priests and* | Joh 1:19
L. to ask him

LEVITICAL

if perfection were by the *L.* | Heb 7:11
priesthood

LEVY

And *l.* a tribute unto the Lord | Nu 31:28
king Solomon raised a *l.* out | 1Ki 5:13
of all
battalion of conscript | 1Ki 5:13;
laborers (B) | 5:14
and the *l.* was thirty thousand | 1Ki 5:13
men
and Adoniram was over the *l.* | 1Ki 5:14
the *l.* which king Solomon | 1Ki 9:15
raised
conscripted the labor corps | 1Ki 9:15
(B)
forced labor Solomon levied | 1Ki 9:15
(R)
upon those did Solomon *l.* a | 1Ki 9:21
tribute
upon those did Solomon lay | 1Ki 9:21
tribute (B)
according to number of their | 2Ch 26:11
l. (B)

LEWD

committed *l.* and wanton deed | J'g 20:6
(B)
your *l.* harlotries (B)(R) | Jer 13:27
their *l.* heart (E) | Eze 6:9
which are ashamed of thy *l.* | Eze 16:27
way

and unto Aholibah, the *l.* | Eze 23:44
women
certain *l.* fellows of the baser | Ac 17:5
sort
brother is *l.* (B) | 1Co 5:11
the *l.* and adulterous (A)(B) | Re 21:8

LEWDLY

hath *l.* defiled his daughter in | Eze 22:11
law

LEWDNESS

committed *l.* and folly in Israel | J'g 20:6
all *l.* committed (B) | J'g 20:10
she hath wrought *l.* with | Jer 11:15
many
she has committed wicked | Jer 11:15
acts (B)
she has done vile deeds (R) | Jer 11:15
neighings, the *l.* of thy | Jer 13:27
whoredom
your lewd harlotries (B)(R) | Jer 13:27
broken with *l.* (A) | Eze 6:9
shalt not commit this *l.* | Eze 16:43
above all
Thou hast borne thy *l.* and | Eze 16:58
thine
in the midst of thee they | Eze 22:9
commit *l.*
to remembrance the *l.* of thy | Eze 23:21
youth
Thus will I make thy *l.* to | Eze 23:27
cease
both thy *l.* and thy | Eze 23:29
whoredoms
therefore bear thou also thy | Eze 23:35
l. and
Thus will I cause *l.* to cease | Eze 23:48
out of
be taught not to do after | Eze 23:48
your *l.*
shall recompense your *l.* | Eze 23:49
upon you
In thy filthiness is *l.*: because | Eze 24:13
And now will I discover her *l.* | Ho 2:10
by consent: for they commit *l.* | Ho 6:9
out of heart proceeds *l.* (B) | M'k 7:22
a matter of wrong or wicked | Ac 18:14
misdemeanor or villainy | Ac 18:14
(A)(E)
crookedness, wicked | Ac 18:14
unscrupulousness (B)
crime or grave misdemeanor | Ac 18:14
(N)
crime or wrongdoing (P) | Ac 18:14
wrongdoing or vicious crime | Ac 18:14
(R)
work of flesh manifest, *l.* (B) | Ga 5:1
keep yourselves from *l.* (B) | 1Th 4:3
filth of her *l.* and vice (A) | Re 17:4
offences, impurities, *l.* (B) | Re 17:4
poisoned earth with *l.* (A)(B) | Re 19:2
practicing *l.* (B) | Re 21:27

LIABLE

is *l.* before the court (B) | M't 5:21
is *l.* to moral weakness and | Heb 5:2
physical infirmity (A)(B)

LIAR

not so now, who will make | Job 24:25
me a *l.*
l. giveth ear to a naughty | Pr 17:4
tongue
a poor man is better than a *l.* | Pr 19:22
thee, and thou be found a *l.* | Pr 30:6
thou be altogether unto me as | Jer 15:18
a *l.*
for he is a *l.*, and the father of | Joh 8:44
it
him not, I shall be a *l.* like | Joh 8:55
unto you
let God be true, but every man | Ro 3:4
a *l.*
have not sinned, we make him | 1Jo 1:10
a *l.*
not his commandments, is a *l.* | 1Jo 2:4
Who is a *l.* but he that denieth | 1Jo 2:22
that
and hateth his brother, he is a | 1Jo 4:20
l.
not God hath made him a *l.* | 1Jo 5:10

LIARS

shall be found *l.* unto thee | De 33:29
I said in my haste, All men | Ps 116:11
are *l.*
frustrateth the tokens of the *l.* | Isa 44:25
A sword is upon the *l.*; and | Jer 50:36
for *l.* for perjured persons, and | 1Ti 1:10
by hypocritical *l.* (B)(R) | 1Ti 4:2
said, The Cretians are alway | Tit 1:12
l.
are not, and hast found them *l.* | Re 2:2
sorcerers, and idolaters, and all | Re 21:8
l.

LIBERAL

The *l.* soul shall be made fat | Pr 11:25
the charitable soul will (B) | Pr 11:25
person shall be no more called | Isa 32:5
l.
no more be called noble | Isa 32:5;
(A)(B)(E)(R) | 32:8
But the *l.* deviseth *l.* things | Isa 32:8
and by *l.* things shall he stand | Isa 32:8
for your *l.* distribution unto | 2Co 9:13
them
liberality (A)(B)(E) | 2Co 9:13
your liberal contribution (N) | 2Co 9:13
generosity of your | 2Co 9:13
contribution (R)
rich in good deeds, *l.* (R) | 1Ti 6:18

LIBERALITY

let him do it with *l.* (S) | Ro 12:8
to bring your *l.* unto | 1Co 16:3
Jerusalem
gift of charity | 1Co 16:3
(A)(B)(N)(P)(R)
your bounty to Jerusalem (E) | 1Co 16:3
abounded unto the riches of | 2Co 8:2
their *l.*
in a wealth of lavish generosity | 2Co 8:2
(A)(B)
lavishly open-handed (N) | 2Co 8:2
generous-hearted *l.* | 2Co 9:13
(A)(B)(E)

LIBERALLY

furnish him *l.* out of thy flock | De 15:14
ask of God, that giveth to all | Jas 1:5
men *l.*
without reserve, without | Jas 1:5
faultfinding (B)
God is a generous giver who | Jas 1:5
neither refuses nor reproaches
anyone (N)
who gives generously to all men | Jas 1:5
without making them feel
foolish and guilty (P)
who gives generously without | Jas 1:5
reproaching (R)

LIBERATE

did *l.* Jehoiachin (S) | 2Ki 25:27

LIBERATING

l. from pangs of death | Ac 2:24
(A)(E)(N)(R)

LIBERATION

your *l.* is near (N) | Lu 21:28
through act of *l.* (N) | Ro 3:24
marked for final *l.* (N) | Eph 4:30

LIBERTINES

is called the synagogue of the *L.* | Ac 6:9

LIBERTY

proclaim *l.* throughout all the | Le 25:10
land
And I will walk at *l.*; for I | Ps 119:45
seek thy
I walk with freedom (B) | Ps 119:45
to proclaim *l.* to the captives | Isa 61:1
to proclaim *l.* unto them | Jer 34:8
in proclaiming *l.* every man to | Jer 34:15
his

he had set at *l.* at their *Jer 34:16*
pleasure
in proclaiming *l.*, every one to *Jer 34:17*
his
behold, I proclaim a *l.* for *Jer 34:17*
you, saith
then it shall be his to the *Eze 46:17*
year of *l.*
until the year of release (B) *Eze 46:17*
to set at *l.* them that are *La 4:18*
bruised
to send forth delivered those *La 4:18*
who are oppressed,
downtrodden, bruised, crushed
and broken down with
calamity (A)
to set free the downtrodden (B) *La 4:18*
to let the broken victims go *La 4:18*
free (N)
to keep Paul, and to let him *Ac 24:23*
have *l.*
This man might have been set *Ac 26:32*
at *l.*
gave him *l.* to go unto his *Ac 27:3*
friends
glorious *l.* of the children of *Ro 8:21*
God
she is at *l.* to be married to *1Co 7:39*
whom
any means this *l.* of yours *1Co 8:9*
become
for why is my *l.* judged of *1Co 10:29*
another
the Spirit of the Lord is, there *2Co 3:17*
is *l.*
to spy out our *l.* which we have *Ga 2:4*
in
the *l.* wherewith Christ hath *Ga 5:1*
made
freedom Christ made free *Ga 5:1*
(A)(B)(E)(P)(R)
Christ set us free, to be free *Ga 5:1*
men (N)
For ye have been called unto *Ga 5:13*
l.
only use not *l.* for an occasion *Ga 5:13*
to
our brother Timothy is set *Heb 13:23*
at *l.*
looketh into the perfect law of *Jas 1:25*
l.
that shall be judged by the law *Jas 2:12*
of *l.*
and not using your *l.* for a *1Pe 2:16*
cloke of
While they promise them *l.* *2Pe 2:19*
they

LIBNAH

Rimmon-parez, and pitched *Nu 33:20*
in *L.*
they removed from *L.* and *Nu 33:21*
pitched
unto *L.* and fought against *L.* *Jos 10:29*
And Joshua passed from *L.* *Jos 10:31*
and all
to all that he had done to *L.* *Jos 10:32*
as he had done also to *L.* and *Jos 10:39*
The king of *L.* one; the king *Jos 12:15*
of
L. and Ether, and Ashan *Jos 15:42*
slayer: and *L.* with her *Jos 21:13*
suburbs
Then *L.* revolted at the same *2Ki 8:22*
time
king of Assyria warring *2Ki 19:8;*
against *L.* *Isa 37:8*
the daughter of Jeremiah of *2Ki 23:31;*
L. *24:18; Jer 52:1*
of refuge, and *L.* with her *1Ch 6:57*
suburbs
did *L.* revolt from under his *2Ch 21:10*
hand

LIBNI

sons of Gershom; *L.* and *Ex 6:17*
Shimi
Gershon by their families; *L.* *Nu 3:18*
sons of Gershom; *L.* and *1Ch 6:17*
Shimei
Of Gershom; *L.* his son, *1Ch 6:20*
Jahath his
L. his son, Shimei his son, *1Ch 6:29*
Uzza his

LIBNITES

Gershon was the family of the *Nu 3:21*
L.

the family of the *L.*, the *Nu 26:58*
family of

LIBYA

Ethiopia, and *L.* and Lydia *Eze 30:5*
Ethiopia, and *L.* with *Eze 38:5*
them
and in the parts of *L.* about *Ac 2:10*
Cyrene

LIBYANS

the Ethiopians and the *L.* *Jer 46:9*
that
the *L.* and the Ethiopians *Da 11:43*
shall be

LICE

may become *l.* throughout all *Ex 8:16*
it became *l.* in man, and in *Ex 8:17*
beast
all the dust of the land became *Ex 8:17*
l.
enchantments to bring forth *l.* *Ex 8:18*
so there were *l.* upon man, and *Ex 8:18*
of flies, and *l.* in all their *Ps 105:31*
coasts

LICENCE

when he had given him *l.* Paul *Ac 21:40*
and have *l.* to answer for *Ac 25:16*
himself
lived in *l.* and debauchery (N) *1Pe 4:3*

LICENTIOUS

l. and wicked (B) *Le 19:29*

LICENTIOUSNESS

out of heart proceeds *l.* (R) *M'k 7:22*
debauchery and *l.* (R) *Ro 13:13*
not repented of *l.* (R) *2Co 12:21*
work of flesh manifest *l.* (R) *Ga 5:19*
given themselves to *l.* (R) *Eph 4:19*
the *l.* (A)(B)(E)(N) *1Ti 1:9*
living in *l.*, passions (R) *1Pe 4:3*
by *l.* of wicked (R) *2Pe 2:7*

LICK

Now shall this company *l.* up *Nu 22:4*
all
of Naboth shall dogs *l.* thy *1Ki 21:19*
blood
and his enemies shall *l.* the dust *Ps 72:9*
and *l.* up the dust of thy feet *Isa 49:23*
They shall *l.* the dust like a *Mic 7:17*
serpent

LICKED

l. up the water that was in *1Ki 18:38*
where dogs *l.* the blood of *1Ki 21:19*
Naboth
and the dogs *l.* up his blood *1Ki 22:38*
the dogs came and *l.* his sores *Lu 16:21*

LICKETH

as the ox *l.* up the grass of the *Nu 22:4*

LID

and bored a hole in the *l.* of it *2Ki 12:9*

LIE

drink wine, and we will *l.* *Ge 19:32*
with him
and go thou in, and *l.* with *Ge 19:34*
him
therefore he shall *l.* with thee *Ge 30:15*
to-night
she said, Come *l.* with me *Ge 39:7;*
 39:12; 2Sa 13:11
he came in unto me to *l.* with *Ge 39:14*
me
I will *l.* with my fathers, not *Ge 47:30*
in Egypt
if a man *l.* with a maid not *Ex 22:16*
betrothed
thou shalt let the ground *l.* *Ex 23:11*
still
if a soul *l.* to his neighbour in *Le 6:2*
that

woman with whom man shall *Le 15:18*
l. with seed
if any man *l.* with her at all, *Le 15:24*
he is unclean
not *l.* carnally with thy *Le 18:20*
neighbour's wife
shalt not *l.* with mankind; *Le 18:22;*
nor *l.* with beast *18:23*
ye shall not steal, nor *l.* one to *Le 19:11*
another
and if a man *l.* with his *Le 20:12*
daughter in law
if *l.* with mankind; if *l.* with *Le 20:13;*
a beast *20:15*
if a man *l.* with a woman *Le 20:18*
having her sickness
if a man *l.* with his uncle's *Le 20:20*
wife, he hath
if a man *l.* with her, and it be *Nu 5:13*
hid from
God is not a man, that he *Nu 23:19*
should *l.*
and a man find her, and *l.* *De 22:23*
with her
if the man force her, and *l.* *De 22:25*
with her
if find a damsel, not *De 22:28*
betrothed, and *l.* with her
betroth a wife, and another *l.* *De 28:30*
with her
all the curses in this book *De 29:20*
shall *l.* on him
and they went to *l.* in ambush *Jos 8:9;*
 8:12
let all thy wants *l.* on me, only *J'g 19:20*
lodge
thou shalt mark the place where *Ru 3:4*
he shall *l.*
strength of Israel will not *l.* *1Sa 15:29*
nor repent
shall I then go to *l.* with my *2Sa 11:11*
wife
and let her *l.* in thy bosom, that *1Ki 1:2*
king
my lord, do not *l.* to thy *2Ki 4:16*
handmaid
look on me, for it is evident to *Job 6:28*
you if I *l.*
should I *l.* against my right, *Job 34:6*
my wound is
I will *l.* me down in peace (S) *Ps 4:8*
I *l.* among them that are set on *Ps 57:4*
fire
and men of high degree are a *l.* *Ps 62:9*
ye *l.* among pots (S) *Ps 68:13*
like the slain that *l.* in the grave *Ps 88:5*
once sworn that I will not *l.* to *Ps 89:35*
David
the proud have forged a *l.* *Ps 119:69*
against me
a faithful witness will not *l.* but *Pr 14:5*
a false
if two *l.* together they have *Ec 4:11*
heat
he shall *l.* all night betwixt my *Ca 1:13*
breasts
wild beasts of the desert shall *Isa 13:21*
l. there
all the kings of the nations *l.* *Isa 14:18*
in glory
is there not a *l.* in my right *Isa 44:20*
hand
thy sons *l.* at the head of all *Isa 51:20*
the streets
they are my people, children *Isa 63:8*
that will not *l.*
they *l.* wait *Jer 5:26*
prophesy a *l.* *Jer 27:10; 27:14-16*
thou makest this people to *Jer 28:15*
trust in a *l.*
and he caused you to trust in *Jer 29:31*
a *l.*
the young and old *l.* on the *La 2:21*
ground
l. thou also upon thy left side *Eze 4:4*
and lay
l. again on thy right side *Eze 4:6*
shalt *l.* 390 days *Eze 4:9*
whilst they divine a *l.* to thee *Eze 21:29*
shalt *l.* in the midst of the *Eze 31:18*
uncircumcised
they *l.* uncircumcised, slain *Eze 32:21;*
by sword *32:30*
and they shall not *l.* with the *Eze 32:27*
mighty
l. with the slain; *l.* with *Eze 32:28;*
uncircumcised *32:29*
there shall they *l.* in a good *Eze 34:14*
fold

come, *l.* all night in sackcloth   *Joe 1:13*
that *l.* on beds of ivory, and   *Am 6:4*
stretch
houses of Achzib shall be a *l.*   *Mic 1:14*
to kings
if a man walking in falsehood   *Mic 2:11*
do *l.*
at the end it shall speak and   *Hab 2:3*
not *l.*
for the diviners have seen a *l.*   *Zec 10:2*
and told
when Jesus saw him *l.* he saith   *Joh 5:6*
to him
when he speaketh a *l.* he   *Joh 8:44*
speaketh
Simon Peter seeth the linen   *Joh 20:6*
clothes *l.*
why hath Satan filled thy heart   *Ac 5:3*
to *l.*
who changed the truth of God   *Ro 1:25*
into a *l.*
hath more abounded thro' my *l.*   *Ro 3:7*
to his glory
I say truth in Christ I *l.* not   *Ro 9:1;*
         1Ti 2:7
Father of our Lord knoweth   *2Co 11:31*
I *l.* not
which I wrote to you, behold I   *Ga 1:20*
l. not
l. not one to another seeing ye   *Col 3:9*
have put off
delusion, that they should   *2Th 2:11*
believe a *l.*
God that cannot *l.* promised   *Tit 1:2;*
         Heb 6:18
glory not, *l.* not against the   *Jas 3:14*
truth
if we say, we have fellowship   *1Jo 1:6*
with him, and walk in darkness,
we *l.*
ye know that no *l.* is of the   *1Jo 2:21*
truth
anointing teach you of all   *1Jo 2:27*
things, and is no *l.*
which say they are Jews, but do   *Re 3:9*
l.
dead bodies shall *l.* in the   *Re 11:8*
street of
neither whatsoever maketh a   *Re 21:27*
l.
without are whosoever loveth   *Re 22:15*
and maketh a *l.*

LIE *DOWN*

before a beast, to *l. down*   *Le 18:23;*
thereto   *20:16*
ye shall *l. down* and none shall   *Le 26:6*
make you afraid
Israel shall not *l. down* till he   *Nu 23:24*
eat prey
judge cause him to *l. down* and   *De 25:2*
beaten
Boaz went to *l. down* at the end   *Ru 3:7*
of heap
tarry this night, *l. down* until   *Ru 3:13*
the morning
Eli said, I called not, *l. down*   *1Sa 3:5;*
again   *3:6, 9*
at even he went to *l. down* on   *2Sa 11:13*
his bed
when I *l. down* I say, when   *Job 7:4*
shall I arise
thou shalt *l. down* and none   *Job 11:19*
make thee afraid
which shall *l. down* with him   *Job 20:11*
in the dust
they shall *l. down* alike in the   *Job 21:26*
dust
the rich man shall *l. down* but   *Job 27:19*
not be gathered
he maketh me *l. down* in green   *Ps 23:2*
pastures
thou shalt *l. down* and thy sleep   *Pr 3:24*
be sweet
the leopard shall *l. down* with   *Isa 11:6*
the kid
their young ones shall *l. down*   *Isa 11:7*
together
and the needy shall *l. down* in   *Isa 14:30*
safety
they shall be for flocks which   *Isa 17:2*
shall *l. down*
there shall the calf feed and *l.*   *Isa 27:10*
down
the army and the power shall   *Isa 43:17*
l. down together
this ye have, ye shall *l. down*   *Isa 50:11*
in sorrow

shall be a place for the herds   *Isa 63:10*
to *l. down* in
we *l. down* in our shame and   *Jer 3:25*
confusion
shepherds causing their flocks   *Jer 33:12*
to *l. down*
and I will cause them to *l.*   *Eze 34:15*
down
I will make them to *l. down*   *Ho 2:18*
safely
they shall *l. down* in the   *Zep 2:7*
evening
flocks shall *l. down;* for   *Zep 2:14;*
beasts to *l. down* in   *2:15*
the remnant of Israel shall   *Zep 3:13*
feed and *l. down*

LIE *IN WAIT*

if a man *l.* not *in wait*, but   *Ex 21:13*
God deliver
if a man hate his neighbour,   *De 19:11*
and *l. in wait*
ye shall *l. in wait* against the   *Jos 8:4*
city
up by night, and *l. in wait* in the *J'g 9:32*
field
saying, Go and *l. in wait* in the *J'g 21:20*
vineyards
hast stirred up my servant to   *1Sa 22:8;*
l. in wait   *22:13*
and abide in the covert to *l.*   *Job 38:40*
in wait
for lo, they *l. in wait* for my   *Ps 59:3*
soul
the words of the wicked are to   *Pr 12:6*
l. in wait
heart like an oven, whiles they   *Ho 7:6*
l. in wait
they all *l. in wait* for blood,   *Mic 7:2*
they hunt
there *l. in wait* for him more   *Ac 23:21*
than forty men
whereby they *l. in wait* to   *Eph 4:14*
deceive me

LIE *WASTE*

the highways *l. waste;* it shall   *Isa 33:8;*
l. waste   *34:10*
to dwell in houses, and this   *Hag 1:4*
house *l. waste*

LIED

drink water. But he *l.* unto   *1Ki 13:18*
him
l. unto him with their tongues   *Ps 78:36*
or feared, that thou hast *l.*   *Isa 57:11*
thou hast not *l.* unto men, but   *Ac 5:4*
unto

LIEN

lightly have *l.* with thy wife   *Ge 26:10*
Though ye have *l.* among the   *Ps 68:13*
pots
where thou hast not been *l.* with *Jer 3:2*

LIERS

l. in wait on the west of the   *Jos 8:13*
city
were *l.* in ambush against him   *Jos 8:14*
of Shechem set *l.* in wait for   *J'g 9:25*
him in
l. in wait abiding in the   *J'g 16:12*
chamber
set *l.* in wait round about   *J'g 20:29*
Gibeah
the *l.* in wait of Israel came   *J'g 20:33*
forth
they trusted unto the *l.* in wait   *J'g 20:36*
which
the *l.* in wait hasted, and   *J'g 20:37*
rushed
the *l.* in wait drew themselves   *J'g 20:37*
along
the men of Israel and the *l.* in   *J'g 20:38*
wait

LIES

trusting in *l.* (B)   *Ex 5:9*
hast mocked me, and told me   *J'g 16:10;*
l.   *16:13*
thy *l.* make men hold their   *Job 11:3*
peace
But ye are forgers of *l.* ye are   *Job 13:4*

walked with *l.* (B)   *Job 31:5*
seek after *l.* (A)(R)   *Ps 4:2*
gives birth to *l.* (A)(R)   *Ps 7:14*
they utter *l.* (R)   *Ps 12:2; 144:8, 11*
proud, nor such as turn aside   *Ps 40:4*
to *l.*
soon as they be born, speaking   *Ps 58:3*
l.
they delight in *l.:* they bless   *Ps 62:4*
with
mouth of them that speak *l.*   *Ps 63:11*
shall be
telleth *l.* shall not tarry in my   *Ps 101:7*
sight
A false witness that speaketh *l.*   *Pr 6:19*
lie: but a false witness will   *Pr 14:5*
utter *l.*
but a deceitful witness   *Pr 14:25*
speaketh *l.*
he that speaketh *l.* shall not   *Pr 19:5*
escape
and he that speaketh *l.* shall   *Pr 19:9*
perish
If a ruler hearken to *l.*, all his   *Pr 29:12*
far from me vanity and *l.*   *Pr 30:8*
the prophet that teacheth *l.* he   *Isa 9:15*
wrath: but his *l.* shall not be   *Isa 16:6*
so
we have made *l.* our refuge   *Isa 28:15*
shall sweep away the refuge   *Isa 28:17*
of *l.*
your lips have spoken *l.* your   *Isa 59:3*
lips have spoken *l.* (R)   *Isa 59:3*
they trust in vanity, and speak   *Isa 59:4*
l.
their tongue like their bow for *l.*   *Jer 9:3*
taught their tongue to speak *l.*   *Jer 9:5*
prophets prophesy *l.* in my   *Jer 14:14*
name
Surely our fathers have   *Jer 16:19*
inherited *l.*
to whom thou hast prophesied   *Jer 20:6*
l.
commit adultery, and walk in   *Jer 23:14*
l.
said, that prophesy *l.* in my   *Jer 23:25*
name
of the prophets that prophesy *l.*   *Jer 23:26*
cause my people to err by   *Jer 23:32*
their *l.*
be so; his *l.* shall not so   *Jer 48:30*
effect it
ye have spoken vanity, and   *Eze 13:8*
seen *l.*
that see vanity, and that   *Eze 13:9*
divine *l.*
to my people that hear your   *Eze 13:19*
l.
with *l.* ye have made the   *Eze 13:22*
heart of
vanity, and divining *l.* unto   *Eze 22:28*
them
She hath wearied herself with   *Eze 24:12*
l.
they shall speak *l.* at one table   *Da 11:27*
and the princes with their *l.*   *Ho 7:3*
they have spoken *l.* against me   *Ho 7:13*
ye have eaten the fruit of *l.*   *Ho 10:13*
compasseth me about with *l.*   *Ho 11:12*
daily increaseth *l.* and   *Ho 12:1*
desolation
and their *l.* caused them to err   *Am 2:4*
inhabitants thereof have   *Mic 6:12*
spoken *l.*
city! it is all full of *l.* and   *Na 3:1*
robbery
molten image, and a teacher   *Hab 2:18*
of *l.*
shall not do iniquity, nor   *Zep 3:13*
speak *l.*
speakest *l.* in the name of the   *Zec 13:3*
Lord
Speaking *l.* in hypocrisy; having *1Ti 4:2*

LIEST

land whereon thou *l.* to thee   *Ge 28:13*
will
when thou *l.* down, and when   *De 6:7;*
thou   *11:19*
l. thou thus upon thy face   *Jos 7:10*
When thou *l.* down, thou shalt   *Pr 3:24*
not

LIETH

doest not well, sin *l.* at the door   *Ge 4:7*
blessings of the deep that *l.*   *Ge 49:25*
under

Whosoever *l.* with a beast shall   *Ex 22:19*
was lost, and *l.* concerning it   *Le 6:3*
he that *l.* in the house shall wash   *Le 14:47*
whereon he *l.* that hath the issue   *Le 15:4*
every thing that she *l.* upon in   *Le 15:20*
her
bed whereon he *l.* shall be unclean   *Le 15:24*
Every bed whereon she *l.* all   *Le 15:26*
him that *l.* with her that is unclean   *Le 15:33*
whosoever *l.* carnally with a woman   *Le 19:20*
man that *l.* with his father's wife   *Le 20:11*
mankind, as he *l.* with a woman   *Le 20:13*
her sabbaths, as long as it *l.* desolate   *Le 26:34*
As long as it *l.* desolate it shall rest   *Le 26:35*
while she *l.* desolate without them   *Le 26:43*
and *l.* upon the border of Moab   *Nu 21:15*
be he that *l.* with his father's wife   *De 27:20*
that *l.* with any manner of beast   *De 27:21*
Curse be he that *l.* with his sister   *De 27:22*
he that *l.* with his mother in law   *De 27:23*
mountain that *l.* before the valley of   *Jos 15:8*
Michmethah, that *l.* before Shechem   *Jos 17:7*
the hill that *l.* on the south side of the   *Jos 18:13*
the hill that *l.* before Beth-horon   *Jos 18:14*
the mountain that *l.* before the valley   *Jos 18:16*
Judah, which *l.* in the south of Arad   *J'g 1:16*
and see wherein his great *l.*   *J'g 16:5*
thee, wherein thy great strength *l.*   *J'g 16:6*
told me wherein thy great strength *l.*   *J'g 16:15*
in the valley that *l.* by Beth-rehob   *J'g 18:28*
when he *l.* down, that thou shalt   *Ru 3:4*
that *l.* before Giah by the way of   *2Sa 2:24*
city that *l.* in the midst of the river of   *2Sa 24:5*
of my fathers' sepulchres, *l.* waste   *Ne 2:3*
Jerusalem *l.* waste, and the gates   *Ne 2:17*
tower which *l.* out from the king's   *Ne 3:25*
the east, and the tower that *l.* out   *Ne 3:26*
against the great tower that *l.* out   *Ne 3:27*
So man *l.* down, and riseth not   *Job 14:12*
He *l.* under the shady trees, in the   *Job 40:21*
l. in wait secretly as a lion in   *Ps 10:9*
he *l.* in wait to catch the poor   *Ps 10:9*
now that he *l.* he shall rise up no   *Ps 41:8*
Thy wrath *l.* hard upon me, and   *Ps 88:7*
and *l.* in wait at every corner   *Pr 7:12*
She also *l.* in wait as for a prey   *Pr 23:28*
thou shalt be as he that *l.* down in   *Pr 23:34*
as he that *l.* upon the top of a mast   *Pr 23:34*
in heart he *l.* in wait (S)   *Jer 9:8*
gate, which *l.* toward the north   *Eze 9:2*
great dragon that *l.* in the midst   *Eze 29:3*
from her that *l.* in thy bosom   *Mic 7:5*
my servant *l.* at home sick of   *M't 8:6*
daughter *l.* at the point of death   *M'k 5:23*
unto the region that *l.* round about   *Ac 14:6*
l. toward the south-west and north   *Ac 27:12*

as much as *l.* in you, live peaceably   *Ro 12:18*
the whole world *l.* in wickedness   *1Jo 5:19*
And the city *l.* foursquare   *Re 21:16*

LIEUTENANTS

commissions unto the king's *l.*   *Ezr 8:36*
had commanded unto the king's *l.*   *Es 3:12*
unto the Jews, and to the *l.* and   *Es 8:9*
rulers of the provinces, and the *l.*   *Es 9:3*

LIFE

the moving creature that hath *l.*   *Ge 1:20*
and to every thing wherein there is *l.*   *Ge 1:30*
God breathed into his nostrils the breath of *l.*   *Ge 2:7*
the tree of *l.* in the midst of the garden   *Ge 2:9; 3:22*
cherubims to keep the way of the tree of *l.*   *Ge 3:24*
to destroy all wherein is the breath of *l.*   *Ge 6:17; 7:22*
flesh with the *l.* shall ye not eat   *Ge 9:4; Le 17:14*
of every man will I require the *l.* of man   *Ge 9:5*
my *l.* (A)   *Ge 12:13; 19:20; 1Sa 24:11; 26:21; Job 10:1; 27:2; 30:16; Ps 6:4; 7:2, 5, 23:3; 30:3; 31:7; 34:2; 35:4, 7; 40:14; 42:6; 54:34; 55:18; 56:6, 13; 57:4; 59:3; 63:9; 69:1; 70:2; 86:2, 14; 88:3; 109:20; 116:8; 119:25, 28, 109; 120:6; 141:8; 142:4, 7; 143:11; Isa 38:17; Jer 12:7; 18:20*
my *l.* (B)   *Ge 12:13; 19:20; 1Sa 24:11; 26:21; Job 9:21; Ps 26:9; 54:4; 86:4, 14; 109:20; 119:109; 141:8; 143:11; Jer 18:20*
my *l.* (R)   *Ge 12:13; 19:20; 1Sa 24:11; 26:21; 2Sa 4:9; Job 9:21; 10:1; Ps 6:3; 7:5; 25:20; 26:9; 35:4, 7, 17; 40:14; 54:3-4; 56:6; 59:9; 70:2; 86:2, 14; 109:20; 119:109; 143:3; Isa 38:17; Jer 18:20*
I will return according to the time of *l.*   *Ge 18:10; 18:14*
these were the years of the *l.* of Sarah   *Ge 23:1*
years of Abraham's *l.*   *Ge 25:7*
Ishmael's *l.*   *Ge 25:17*
by the *l.* of Pharaoh, ye shall not go   *Ge 42:15; 42:16*
God did send me before to preserve *l.*   *Ge 45:5*
not attained to the years of *l.* of my fathers   *Ge 47:9*
the years of the *l.* of Levi were   *Ex 6:16*
years of *l.* of Kohath; *l.* of Amram   *Ex 6:18; 6:20*
his *l.* (B)   *Ex 12:13; Pr 16:17; 29:10; Isa 53:11; Jer 51:6; Eze 18:27; 33:5; M't 16:26*
shalt give *l.* for *l.*   *Ex 21:23; De 19:21*
for the *l.* of the flesh is in the blood   *Le 17:11*
besides the other in her *l.* time   *Le 18:18*
l. pine away (A)(B)(E)(R)   *Le 26:16*
your *l.* (A)   *De 4:9; 6:5; 1Sa 25:29; Ps 121:7; Pr 24:14; Isa 58:10; Hab 2:10*
your *l.* (B)   *De 4:9; 1Sa 25:29; Ps 121:7; Pr 24:14; Isa 58:10; Hab 2:10*
blood is the *l.* not eat *l.* with flesh   *De 12:23*
our *l.* (A)   *De 13:6; Ps 123:4; 1Sa 18:1; Pr 6:32; 19:8, 16; 20:2; 29:24; M't 16:26*
for the tree of the field is man's *l.*   *De 20:19*
for he taketh a man's *l.* to pledge   *De 24:6*
I have set before thee *l.*   *De 30:15; 30:19; Jer 21:8*
it is not a vain thing, because it is your *l.*   *De 32:47*
the men answered, Our *l.* for yours   *Jos 2:14*
wear out your *l.* (B)   *1Sa 2:33*
shall be bound up in the bundle of *l.*   *1Sa 25:29*
life (A)   *1Sa 25:29; Job 12:10; 24:12; Ps 34:22; 49:8; 72:14; 74:19; 94:21; 107:5; Pr 25:13; Jer 4:10; 20:13; 31:12, 14; La 2:12; Jon 2:5*

life (B)   *1Sa 25:29; Job 12:10; Ps 34:22; 49:8; 72:14; 94:21; Pr 22:23; Jer 4:10; 20:13; 31:12; La 2:12*
your *l.* (R)   *1Sa 25:29; Ps 121:7; Jer 38:17; Eze 3:19; Hab 2:10*
for the *l.* of his brother whom he slew   *2Sa 14:7*
whether in death or *l.* there will I be   *2Sa 15:21*
not asked for thyself long *l.*   *1Ki 3:11*
nor asked *l.* of thine enemies   *2Ch 1:11*
life (B)   *1Ki 17:21; Job 12:10; Ps 49:8; 74:19; 94:21; Jer 20:13; Jon 2:5*
time of *l.* thou shalt embrace a son   *2Ki 4:16; 4:17*
left the camp as it was, and fled for their *l.*   *2Ki 7:7*
they may pray for the *l.* of the king   *Ezr 6:10*
granted the Jews to stand for their *l.*   *Es 8:11*
why is *l.* given to the bitter in soul   *Job 3:20*
thou hast granted me *l.* and favour   *Job 10:12*
my *l.* is ruined (B)   *Job 17:1*
he riseth up, and no man is sure of *l.*   *Job 24:22*
life (A)   *Job 27:8; 33:28; Ps 11:5; 109:13; Pr 16:17; 23:14; 29:10; Ec 6:3; Isa 53:12; Jer 51:6; Eze 18:27; 33:5; M't 16:26*
his *l.* (R)   *Job 27:8; 31:30; 33:20; Pr 16:17; 23:14; 29:10; Jer 51:6; Eze 18:27; 33:5; M't 16:26*
or the owners thereof to lose their *l.*   *Job 31:39*
the breath of the Almighty hath given me *l.*   *Job 33:4*
he preserveth not the *l.* of the wicked   *Job 36:6*
and their *l.* is among the unclean   *Job 36:14*
thou wilt shew me the path of *l.*   *Ps 16:11*
he asked *l.* of thee, thou gavest him   *Ps 21:4*
my dear *l.* (A)(R)   *Ps 22:20*
in his favour is *l.* weeping may endure   *Ps 30:5*
what man is he that desireth *l.*   *Ps 34:12*
my *l.* (A)(R)   *Ps 35:17*
for with thee is the fountain of *l.*   *Ps 36:9*
manner of *l.* (S)   *Ps 37:14; Ga 1:13; Eph 2:3; 4:22; Heb 13:5, 7; Jas 3:13; 1Pe 1:15, 18; 3:16; 2Pe 2:7*
thou wilt prolong the king's *l.*   *Ps 61:6*
thy lovingkindness is better than *l.*   *Ps 63:3*
bring down their *l.* blood (A)(B)(E)(R)   *Ps 63:6*
bless God, who holdeth our soul in *l.*   *Ps 66:9*
l. of your poor (A)(E)(R)   *Ps 74:19*
l. of the afflicted ones (B)   *Ps 74:19*
but gave their *l.* over to the pestilence   *Ps 78:50*
give us *l.*   *Ps 80:18*
with long *l.* will I satisfy him   *Ps 91:16*
give me *l.* (A)(B)(R)   *Ps 119:37*
life (A)(R)(S)   *Ps 119:40; 119:50, 93; Joh 5:21; Ro 4:17; 8:11*
give *l.* to me (A)(R)   *Ps 119:88*
granted me *l.* (B)(R)   *Ps 119:93*
give me *l.* (A)(R)   *Ps 119:156*
the blessing, even *l.* for evermore   *Ps 133:3*
save my *l.* (A)(B)(R)   *Ps 143:11*
which taketh away the *l.* of the owners   *Pr 1:19*
nor take they hold of the paths of *l.*   *Pr 2:19*
long *l.* and peace shall they add to thee   *Pr 3:2*
she is a tree of *l.* to them that lay hold on her   *Pr 3:18*
so shall they be *l.* to thy soul   *Pr 3:22*
for they are *l.* to those that find them   *Pr 4:22*
keep thy heart, for out of it are the issues of *l.*   *Pr 4:23*
lest thou shouldest ponder the path of *l.*   *Pr 5:6*
reproofs of instruction are the way of *l.*   *Pr 6:23*

adulteress will hunt for the   Pr 6:26
precious *l.*
whoso findeth me findeth *l.* and   Pr 8:35
shall obtain
the mouth of the righteous is a   Pr 10:11
well of *l.*
is in the way of *l.* that keepeth   Pr 10:17
instruction
the fruit of the righteous is a   Pr 11:30
tree of *l.*
righteous regardeth the *l.* of   Pr 12:10
his beast
in the way of righteousness is   Pr 12:28
l. and no death
the ransom of a man's *l.* are his   Pr 13:8
riches
when desire cometh, it is a   Pr 13:12
tree of *l.*
the law of the wise is a   Pr 13:14
fountain of *l.*
the fear of the Lord is a   Pr 14:27
fountain of *l.*
a sound heart is the *l.* of the   Pr 14:30
flesh, but envy
l. and health of the body (A)   Pr 14:30
a wholesome tongue is a tree of   Pr 15:4
l.
the way of *l.* is above to the   Pr 15:24
wise
heareth reproof of *l.* abideth   Pr 15:31
among the wise
in the light of the king's   Pr 16:15
countenance is *l.*
understanding is a wellspring   Pr 16:22
of *l.* to him
death and *l.* are in the power   Pr 18:21
of the tongue
loves his own *l.* (B)   Pr 19:8;
   20:2; M't 16:26
keep his own *l.* (R)   Pr 19:16;
   20:2; 29:24; M't 16:26
he that followeth mercy,   Pr 21:21
findeth *l.*
by humility are riches, honour   Pr 22:4
and *l.*
she will do him good all the   Pr 31:12
days of her *l.*
good they should do all the days   Ec 2:3
of their *l.*
therefore I hated *l;* wisdom   Ec 2:17;
giveth *l.*   7:12
in all these things is the *l.* of   Isa 38:16
my spirit
we will sing songs all the days   Isa 38:20
of our *l.*
thou hast found the *l.* of thy   Isa 57:10
hand
and death shall be chosen rather   Jer 8:3
than *l.*
hands of them that seek their   Jer 21:7;
l.   34:20-21
   Jer 41:8
set before you the way of *l.*   Jer 21:8
and of death
I will cause Elam to be   Jer 49:37
dismayed before their enemies,
before them that seek their *l.*
lift up thy hands for the *l.* of   La 2:19
thy children
should not return by   Eze 13:22
promising him *l.*
if the wicked walk in the   Eze 33:15
statutes of *l.*
let us not perish for this man's   Jon 1:14
l.
my covenant was with him of *l.*   Mal 2:5
are dead which sought the   M't 2:20
child's *l.*
take no thought for your *l.*   M't 6:25;
   Lu 12:22
to enter into *l.* halt or   M't 18:8;
maimed   M'k 9:43
better to enter into *l.* with   M't 18:9;
one eye   M'k 9:45
if wilt enter into *l.* keep the   M't 19:17
commandments
is it lawful to save *l.* or to kill   M'k 3:4;
   Lu 6:9
in holiness all the days of our *l.*   Lu 1:75
for a man's *l.* consisteth not   Lu 12:15
in abundance
your *l.* be required (R)   Lu 12:20
the *l.* more than meat, the   Lu 12:23
body than raiment
lead a *l.* of daily luxury (P)   Lu 16:19
in him was *l.* and the *l.* was   Joh 1:4
light of men
that believeth not the Son,   Joh 3:36
shall see *l.*

as Father hath *l.* in himself, so   Joh 5:26
hath he given to Son to
have *l.* in himself
have done good, to the   Joh 5:29
resurrection of *l.*
will not come to me that   Joh 5:40;
might have *l.*   10:10
giveth *l.* unto world   Joh 6:33;
   6:35
I am bread of *l.*   Joh 6:35; 6:48
which I will give for the *l.* of   Joh 6:51
the world
and drink his blood, ye have   Joh 6:53
no *l.* in you
the words that I speak to you,   Joh 6:63
they are *l.*
not in darkness, but shall have   Joh 8:12
the light of *l.*
I am the resurrection and the   Joh 11:25;
l.   14:6
believing ye might have *l.*   Joh 20:31
through his name
hast made known to me the   Ac 2:28
ways of *l.*
and killed the Prince of *l.*   Ac 3:15
whom God raised
seeing he giveth to all *l.* and   Ac 17:25
breath
the manner of *l.* from my   Ac 26:4
youth, Jews know
there shall be no loss of any   Ac 27:22
man's *l.*
shall reign in *l.* by one, Jesus   Ro 5:17
Christ
came on all men to   Ro 5:18
justification of *l.*
even so we should walk in   Ro 6:4
newness of *l.*
the law of the Spirit of *l.* in   Ro 8:2
Christ Jesus
to be spiritually minded is *l.* and   Ro 8:6
peace
the Spirit is *l.* because of   Ro 8:10
righteousness
restore to *l.* (A)   Ro 8:11
give *l.* to mortal bodies   Ro 8:11
(E)(N)(R)
I am persuaded that neither   Ro 8:38
death nor *l.*
danger to *l.* and limb (P)   Ro 8:38
the receiving them be, but *l.*   Ro 11:15
from the dead
he brought to *l.*   1Co 2:13
(B)(E)(N)(R)
the world, or *l.* or death, all   1Co 3:22
are yours
who leads a loose *l.* (N)   1Co 5:11
even things without *l.* giving   1Co 14:7
sound
does not come to *l.*   1Co 15:36
(A)(B)(N)(R)
insomuch that we despaired   2Co 1:8
even of *l.*
to the other the savour of *l.*   2Co 2:16
unto *l.*
the letter killeth, but the spirit   2Co 3:6
giveth *l.*
that the *l.* of Jesus might be   2Co 4:10
manifested
death worketh in us, but *l.* in   2Co 4:12
you
that mortality might be   2Co 5:4
swallowed up of *l.*
former manner of *l.*   Ga 1:13
(A)(E)(N)(R)
the *l.* which I now live in the   Ga 2:20
flesh
a law given which could have   Ga 3:21
given *l.*
being alienated from the *l.* of   Eph 4:18
God
whether it be by *l.* or by   Ph'p 1:20
death
holding forth word of *l.* that   Ph'p 2:16
I may rejoice
and your *l.* is hid with Christ in   Col 3:3
God
when Christ who is our *l.* shall   Col 3:4
appear
we may lead a peaceable *l.* in   1Ti 2:2
all godliness
having the promise of the *l.*   1Ti 4:8
that now is
according to the promise of *l.*   2Ti 1:1
in Christ
and hath brought *l.* to light by   2Ti 1:10
the gospel
thou hast fully known my   2Ti 3:10
manner of *l.*
the breath of *l.* (A)   Heb 4:12

l. and spirit (N)   Heb 4:12
neither beginning of days, nor   Heb 7:3
end of *l.*
who is made after the power   Heb 7:16
of an endless *l.*
considering the issue of their   Heb 13:7
l. (E)
he shall receive the crown of *l.*   Jas 1:12
whole *l.* a blazing hell (P)   Jas 3:6
show by good *l.* (E)   Jas 3:13
for what is your *l.?*it is even a   Jas 4:14
vapour
vain manner of *l.* (E)   1Pe 1:18
as being heirs together of the   1Pe 3:7
grace of *l.*
for he that will love *l.* and see   1Pe 3:10
good days
l. being your good Christian   1Pe 3:16
behavior (P)
came to *l.* again in spirit (P)   1Pe 3:18
for the time past of our *l.* may   1Pe 4:3
suffice us
hath given us all things   2Pe 1:3
pertaining to *l.*
lascivious *l.* of wicked (E)   2Pe 2:7
our hands have handled the   1Jo 1:1
word of *l.*
for the *l.* was manifested, and   1Jo 1:2
we have seen it
the pride of *l.* is not of the   1Jo 2:16
Father but of world
he that hath the Son hath *l.*   1Jo 5:12
and he that hath not the Son
of God hath not *l.*
he shall give him *l.* for them   1Jo 5:16
that sin not
to him will I give to eat of the   Re 2:7
tree of *l.*
be faithful, and I will give thee   Re 2:10
a crown of *l.*
third part of the creatures that   Re 8:9
had *l.* died
the Spirit of *l.* from God   Re 11:11
entered into them
he had power to give *l.* to the   Re 13:15
beast
I will give to thirsty of the water   Re 21:6
of *l.* freely
he shewed me a pure river of   Re 22:1
water of *l.*
the tree of *l.* bare twelve   Re 22:2
manner of fruits
that they may have right to   Re 22:14
the tree of *l.*
let him take the water of *l.*   Re 22:17
freely

HIS LIFE

seeing *his l.* is bound up in   Ge 44:30
the lad's life
he shall give for the ransom   Ex 21:30
of *his l.*
shall read therein all the days   De 17:19
of *his l.*
they feared him all the days of   Jos 4:14
his l.
for my father adventured *his l.*   J'g 9:17
far
more than they which he slew   J'g 16:30
he did put *his l.* in his hand,   1Sa 19:5
and slew
saw that Saul was come out   1Sa 23:15
to seek *his l.*
if not spoken this word   1Ki 2:23
against *his l.*
when he saw that, he arose   1Ki 19:3
and went for *his l.*
then shall thy life be for *his*   1Ki 20:39;
l.   20:42
his l. shall be for the life of   2Ki 10:24
him
would go into the temple to   Ne 6:11
save *his l.*
Haman stood to make request   Es 7:7
for *his l.*
all that a man hath will he give   Job 2:4
for *his l.*
behold, he is in thy hand, but   Job 2:6
save *his l.*
and *his l.* from perishing by   Job 33:18
the sword
his l. abhorreth bread; *his l.*   Job 33:20;
to destroyers   33:22
he will deliver, and *his l.*   Job 33:28
shall see the light
and knoweth not that it is for   Pr 7:23
his l.

he that keepeth his mouth,   *Pr 13:3*
keepeth *his l.*
for a man to rejoice and do   *Ec 3:12*
good in *his l.*
there is a wicked man that   *Ec 7:15*
prolongeth *his l.*
shall abide of his labours all   *Ec 8:15*
the days of *his l.*
Moab, *his l.* shall be grievous   *Isa 15:4*
to him
his l. shall be to him for a   *Jer 21:9;*
prey   *38:2*
into the hand of them that   *Jer 44:30*
seek *his l.*
nor speakest to warn, to save   *Eze 3:18*
his l.
nor strengthen himself in   *Eze 7:13*
iniquity of *his l.*
shall tremble, every man for   *Eze 32:10*
his l.
he that findeth *his l.* shall   *M't 10:39;*
lose it; he that loseth *his l.*   *16:25;*
shall find it   *M'k 8:35; Lu 9:24; 17:33;*
                 Joh 12:25
to give *his l.* a ransom for   *M't 20:28;*
many   *M'k 10:45*
yea, and hate not *his* own *l.*   *Lu 14:26*
also
good Shepherd giveth *his l.*   *Joh 10:11*
for sheep
that a man lay down *his l.*   *Joh 15:13*
for his friends
for *his l.* is taken from the   *Ac 8:33*
earth
trouble not yourselves, *his l.* is   *Ac 20:10*
in him
much more we shall be saved   *Ro 5:10*
by *his l.*
not regarding *his l.* to supply   *Ph'p 2:30*
your lack
love of God because he laid   *1Jo 3:16*
down *his l.*

MY LIFE

mercy thou hast shewed in   *Ge 19:19*
saving *my l.*
I am weary of *my l.* what   *Ge 27:46*
good shall *my l.* do
my l. is preserved; fed me all   *Ge 32:30;*
my l.   *48:15*
I put *my l.* in my hands, and   *J'g 12:3*
passed over
what is *my l.* or my father's   *1Sa 18:18*
family
what is my sin, that he seeketh   *1Sa 20:1*
my l.
he that seeketh *my l.* seeketh   *1Sa 22:23*
thy life
so that *my l.* be much set by   *1Sa 26:24*
in the eyes
wherefore layest thou a snare   *1Sa 28:9*
for *my l.*
I put *my l.* in my hand, and   *1Sa 28:21*
hearkened to
because *my l.* is yet whole in me   *2Sa 1:9*
behold, my son of my bowels   *2Sa 16:11*
seeketh *my l.*
have wrought falsehood   *2Sa 18:13*
against *my l.*
it is enough, now, take away   *1Ki 19:4*
my l.
they seek *my l.* to take it   *1Ki 19:10;*
away   *19:14; Ro 11:3*
let *my l.* be precious in thy   *2Ki 1:13;*
sight   *1:14*
let *my l.* be given me at my   *Es 7:3*
petition
my end that I should prolong   *Job 6:11*
my l.
O remember that *my l.* is but   *Job 7:7*
wind
my soul chooseth death rather   *Job 7:15*
than *my l.*
tho' I were perfect, yet I   *Job 9:21*
would despise *my l.*
my soul is weary of *my l.* I will   *Job 10:1*
leave
wherefore do I put *my l.* in   *Job 13:14*
my l. from me
let him tread down *my l.* on the   *Ps 7:5*
earth
mercy shall follow me all the   *Ps 23:6*
days of *my l.*
gather not *my l.* with bloody   *Ps 26:9*
men
the Lord is the strength of *my l.*   *Ps 27:1*
dwell in the house of the Lord   *Ps 27:4*
all days of *my l.*

my l. is spent with grief and   *Ps 31:10*
sighing
they devised to take away *my*   *Ps 31:13*
l.
that seek after *my l.* lay snares   *Ps 38:12*
for me
and my prayer to the God of   *Ps 42:8*
my l.
preserve *my l.* from fear of the   *Ps 64:1*
enemy
and *my l.* draweth nigh to the   *Ps 88:3*
grave
he hath smitten *my l.* to the   *Ps 143:3*
ground
I have cut off like a weaver   *Isa 38:12*
my l.
they cut off *my l.* in the   *La 3:53*
dungeon
O Lord, thou hast redeemed   *La 3:58*
my l.
hast brought up *my l.* from   *Jon 2:6*
corruption
O Lord, take, I beseech thee,   *Jon 4:3*
my l. from me
and I lay down *my l.* for the   *Joh 10:15*
sheep
my Father loveth me,   *Joh 10:17*
because I lay down *my l.*
Lord, I will lay down *my l.*   *Joh 13:37*
for thy sake
nor count I *my l.* dear to   *Ac 20:24*
myself

THIS LIFE

men which have their portion   *Ps 17:14*
in *this l.*
knoweth what is good for a   *Ec 6:12*
man in *this l.*
that is thy portion in *this l.*   *Ec 9:9*
and in labour
are choked with the cares of   *Lu 8:14*
this l.
hearts overcharged with the   *Lu 21:34*
cares of *this l.*
go, speak all the words of *this*   *Ac 5:20*
l.
much more things that pertain   *1Co 6:3*
to *this l.*
have judgment of things   *1Co 6:4*
pertaining to *this l.*
if in *this l.* only we have   *1Co 15:19*
hope in Christ
entangleth himself with affairs   *2Ti 2:4*
of *this l.*
eternal life, and *this l.* is in his   *1Jo 5:11*
Son

THY LIFE

escape for *thy l.* look not   *Ge 19:17*
behind thee
the men are dead which sought   *Ex 4:19*
thy l.
thy l. hang in doubt before   *De 28:66*
thee; thou shalt have no
assurance of *thy l.*
they run on thee, and thou   *J'g 18:25*
lose *thy l.*
he shall be to thee a restorer of   *Ru 4:15*
thy l.
if thou save not *thy l.*   *1Sa 19:11*
to-night
he that seeketh my life seeketh   *1Sa 22:23*
thy l.
as *thy l.* was much set by this   *1Sa 26:24*
day, so my life
the head of thine enemy that   *2Sa 4:8*
sought *thy l.*
thy servants which this day   *2Sa 19:5*
saved *thy l.*
come that thou mayest save   *1Ki 1:12*
thy l.
if I make not *thy l.* as the life   *1Ki 19:2*
of one of them
go out, peradventure he   *1Ki 20:31*
will save *thy l.*
if he be missing *thy l.* be for   *1Ki 20:39;*
his life   *20:42*
who redeemeth *thy l.* from   *Ps 103:4*
destruction
and the years of *thy l.* shall be   *Pr 4:10;*
many   *9:11*
let her not go, keep her, for she   *Pr 4:13*
is *thy l.*
and the years of *thy l.* shall be   *Pr 9:11*
increased
therefore will I give people for   *Isa 43:4*
thy l.
thy lovers, they will seek *thy l.*   *Jer 4:30*

of the men that seek *thy l.*   *Jer 11:21;*
             22:25; 38:16
thy l. shall be for a prey to   *Jer 39:18;*
thee   *45:5*
thou in *thy l.* receivedst good   *Lu 16:25*
things
wilt thou lay down *thy l.* for   *Joh 13:38*
my sake

TO LIFE

whose son he had restored *to l.*   *2Ki 8:1;*
             8:5
the labour of the righteous   *Pr 10:16*
tendeth *to l.*
as righteousness tendeth *to l.*   *Pr 11:19*
so that pursueth
the fear of the Lord tendeth   *2Ki 19:23*
to l.
narrow is the way that leadeth   *M't 7:14*
to l.
but is passed from death *to l.*   *Joh 5:24;*
             1Jo 3:14
God to Gentiles granted   *Ac 11:18*
repentance *to l.*
the commandment ordained *to*   *Ro 7:10*
l.
women received their dead   *Heb 11:35*
raised *to l.*

LIFE-GIVING

a *l.* spirit (S)   *1Co 15:45*

LIFETIME

Absalom in his *l.* had taken   *2Sa 18:18*
thou in thy *l.* receivedst good   *Lu 16:25*
all *l.* subject to bondage   *Heb 2:15*

LIFT

the ark was *l.* up above the   *Ge 7:17*
earth
l. up the lad, and hold him in   *Ge 21:18*
thine hand
they *l.* up Joseph out of the   *Ge 37:28*
pit
Pharaoh shall *l.* up thine   *Ge 40:13;*
head   *40:19*
l. up the rod and smote waters   *Ex 7:20;*
             14:16
if thou *l.* up a tool on it thou   *Ex 20:25*
hast polluted
Lord *l.* up his countenance   *Nu 6:26*
upon thee
l. it high (S)   *Nu 15:20*
wherefore then *l.* ye up   *Nu 16:3*
yourselves
and *l.* himself as a young   *Nu 23:24*
lion
shalt help him to *l.* them up   *De 22:4*
again
not *l.* up an iron tool on them   *De 27:5;*
            Jos 8:31
the soles of the priests' feet   *Jos 4:18*
were *l.* up
he *l.* up His spear against 800   *2Sa 23:8*
he *l.* up his spear against 300   *2Sa 23:18;*
            1Ch 11:11
he *l.* up his face to the   *2Ki 9:32*
window
l. up thy prayer for the   *2Ki 19:4;*
remnant   *Isa 37:4*
l. up the head of Jehoiachin   *2Ki 25:27*
king of Judah
all these were to *l.* up the   *1Ch 25:5*
horn
I blush to *l.* up my face to thee,   *Ezr 9:6*
my God
if righteous, yet will I not *l.*   *Job 10:15*
up my head
then shalt thou *l.* up thy face   *Job 11:15;*
             22:26
l. up the light of thy   *Ps 4:6*
countenance on us
arise, O Lord, in thine anger, *l.*   *Ps 7:6*
up thyself
up heads, ye gates, be *l.* ye   *Ps 24:7;*
doors   *24:9*
to thee, O Lord, I *l.* my soul   *Ps 25:1;*
           86:4; 143:8
hear my voice when I *l.* up my   *Ps 28:2*
hands
feed them also, and *l.* them up   *Ps 28:9*
forever
hath *l.* up his heel against me   *Ps 41:9;*
            Joh 13:18
l. up thy feet to the perpetual   *Ps 74:3*
desolations

LIFT (continued)

and to the wicked, *l.* not up the Ps 75:4; 75:5
the floods have *l.* up their waves Ps 93:3
l. up thyself, thou judge of the Ps 94:2
earth
therefore shall he *l.* up the Ps 110:7
head
if they fall, the one will *l.* up Ec 4:10
his fellow
nation not *l.* up sword against Isa 2:4;
nation Mic 4:3
he will *l.* up an ensign to the Isa 5:26
nations
as if staff should *l.* up itself as Isa 10:15
if no wood
smite, and shall *l.* up his staff Isa 10:24
against thee
so shall *l.* it up after the Isa 10:26
manner of Egypt
l. ye up a banner upon the Isa 13:2
high mountain
now will I rise, now will I *l.* Isa 33:10
up myself
the Lord shall *l.* up a standard Isa 59:19
against him
l. up a standard for the Isa 62:10
people
nor *l.* up cry nor prayer for Jer 7:16;
them 11:14
they shall *l.* up a shout Jer 51:14
against thee
let us *l.* up our heart with our La 3:41
hands
Spirit *l.* me up between the Eze 8:3;
earth
that it might not *l.* itself up, Eze 17:14
but stand
and shall *l.* up the buckler Eze 26:8
against thee
no man did *l.* up his head, Zec 1:21
which *l.* up horn over land
will he not *l.* it out on the M't 12:11
sabbath
took her by the hand, and *l.* M'k 1:31
her up
and could in no wise *l.* up Lu 13:11
herself
l. up your heads, your Lu 21:28
redemption draweth
humble yourselves, and he Jas 4:10
shall *l.* up

LIFT *HAND, HANDS*

I have *l.* up mine *hand* to the Ge 14:22
Lord
without thee shall no man *l.* Ge 41:44
up his *hand*
I *l.* up my *hand* and say I live De 32:40
for ever
l. thine *hand*, forget not the Ps 10:12
humble
when I *l.* up my *hands* toward Ps 28:2
thine oracle
I will *l.* up my *hands* in thy Ps 63:4
name
my *hands* will I *l.* up to thy Ps 119:48
commandments
l. up your *hands* in the Ps 134:2
sanctuary and bless
I will *l.* up mine *hand* to the Isa 49:22
Gentiles
l. up thy *hands* towards him La 2:19
for the life
wherefore *l.* up the *hands* Heb 12:12
that hang down

LIFT *VOICE*

and Hagar *l.* up her *voice* and Ge 21:16
wept
canst thou *l.* up thy *voice* to Job 38:34
the clouds
l. up thy *voice*, O daughter of Isa 10:30
Gallim
they shall *l.* up their *voice*, Isa 24:14
shall sing
l. up thy *voice* with strength, Isa 40:9
lift it up
he shall not cry nor *l.* up his Isa 42:2
voice
let the wilderness and cities *l.* Isa 42:11
up their *voice*
thy watchmen shall *l.* up the Isa 52:8
voice
cry, spare not, *l.* up thy *voice* Isa 58:1
like a trumpet
cry, and *l.* up thy *voice* in Jer 22:20
Bashan
to *l.* up the *voice* with Eze 21:22
shouting

LIFTED

Lot *l.* up his eyes and beheld Ge 13:10
Jordan
Abraham *l.* up his eyes and Ge 18:2;
looked 22:13
Esau *l.* up voice Ge 27:38
and Jacob *l.* up his voice and Ge 29:11
wept
Jacob *l.* up his eyes saw in a Ge 31:10;
dream 33:1
as I *l.* up my voice Ge 39:18
Pharaoh *l.* up the head of the Ge 40:20
butler
and have *l.* up (S) Ex 29:27
Aaron *l.* up his hand towards Le 9:22
the people
the congregation *l.* up their Nu 14:1
voice
When ye have *l.* up (S) Nu 18:30
Moses *l.* up his hand and Nu 20:11
smote the rock
then thy heart be *l.* up and De 8:14
thou forget
that his heart be not *l.* above De 17:20
his brethren
the people *l.* up their voice and J'g 2:4;
wept 21:2; 1Sa 11:4
so they *l.* up their heads no J'g 8:28
more
Jotham *l.* up his voice and cried, J'g 9:7
Hearken to me
Orpah and Ruth *l.* up voice Ru 1:9;
and wept 1:14
and Saul *l.* up his voice and 1Sa 24:16
wept
David and people *l.* up voice 1Sa 30:4;
  2Sa 3:32
king's sons came and *l.* up 2Sa 13:36
their voice
Sheba hath *l.* up his hand 2Sa 20:21
against king
thou also hast *l.* up on high 2Sa 22:49
Jeroboam *l.* up hand against 1Ki 11:26;
king 11:27
and thine heart hath *l.* thee 2Ki 14:10
up
his kingdom was *l.* up on high 1Ch 14:2
as trumpeters and singers *l.* 2Ch 5:13
up voice
his heart was *l.* up in the ways 2Ch 17:6
of the Lord
heart was *l.* up to 2Ch 26:16;
destruction 32:25
they *l.* up their voice and wept Job 2:12
if I have *l.* up my hand Job 31:21
against fatherless
or *l.* up myself when evil Job 31:29
found him
who hath not *l.* up his soul Ps 24:4
unto vanity
now shall my head be *l.* up Ps 27:6
above
extol thee, for thou hast *l.* me Ps 30:1;
up 102:10
as he *l.* up axes upon the thick Ps 74:5
trees
they that hate thee have *l.* up Ps 83:2
the head
the floods have *l.* up their Ps 93:3
voice, O Lord
therefore he *l.* up his hand Ps 106:26
against them
lofty eyes, and their eyelids Pr 30:13
are *l.* up
day of the Lord on every one Isa 2:12
that is *l.* up
on cedars that are *l.* Isa 2:13
mountains *l.* up Isa 2:14
the Lord sitting on a throne Isa 6:1
high and *l.* up
when thy hand is *l.* up they Isa 26:11
will not see
against whom hast thou *l.* up Isa 37:23
thine eyes
your skirts are *l.* (B)(R) Jer 13:22
her judgment is *l.* up to the Jer 51:9
skies
creatures were *l.* up from the Eze 1:19
earth
the wheels were *l.* up Eze 1:20;
  1:21; 10:17
the Spirit *l.* me up (S) Eze 3:12
so the Spirit *l.* me up and took Eze 3:14
me away
cherubims *l.* up their wings Eze 10:16;
  10:19; 11:22
and *l.* up my hand to the seed Eze 20:5;
of Jacob 20:6
yet *l.* up mine hand in the Eze 20:15;

wilderness 20:23
when I brought into land for Eze 20:28;
which I *l.* up mine hand 20:42; 47:14
because thine heart is *l.* up Eze 28:2
  28:5, 17; 31:30
thus saith the Lord, I have *l.* Eze 36:7
up mine hand
have I *l.* up my hand against Eze 44:12
them
when his heart was *l.* up and Da 5:20
hardened
but hast *l.* up thyself against Da 5:23
the Lord
the first beast was *l.* up from the Da 7:4
earth
then I *l.* up mine eyes and saw Da 8:3;
  10:5
thine hand shall be *l.* up on Mic 5:9
adversaries
his soul which is *l.* up is not Hab 2:4
upright
the deep *l.* up his hands on Hab 3:10
high
behold, there was *l.* up a talent Zec 5:7
of lead
and they *l.* up the ephah Zec 5:9
between the earth
shall be as the stones of a Zec 9:16
crown, *l.* up
the land shall be *l.* up and Zec 14:10
inhabited
but Jesus *l.* him up, and he M'k 9:27
arose
l. up the lowly (B)(N)(P) Lu 1:52
he *l.* up his eyes on his Lu 6:20
disciples
a certain woman *l.* up her Lu 11:27
voice and said
ten lepers *l.* up their voices Lu 17:13
and said
and he *l.* up his hands and Lu 24:50
blessed them
as Moses *l.* up serpent in Joh 3:14
wilderness, even so must Son
of man be *l.* up
when ye have *l.* up the Son of Joh 8:28
man
I, if I be *l.* up, will draw all Joh 12:32
men to me
sayest thou, Son of man must Joh 12:34
be *l.* up
Peter *l.* up his voice and said to Ac 2:14
them
l. high my right hand (A)(B) Ac 2:33
l. up their voice to God with Ac 4:24
one accord
l. up their voices in the speech Ac 14:11
of Lycaonia
and then *l.* up their voices and Ac 22:22
said. Away
lest being *l.* up with pride he 1Ti 3:6
fall
the angel *l.* up his hand to Re 10:5
heaven

LIFTER

my glory, and the *l.* up of mine Ps 3:3
head

LIFTEST

thou *l.* me up to the wind, Job 30:22
thou causest
that *l.* me up from the gates of Ps 9:13
death
l. above those that rise up Ps 18:48
against me
and *l.* up thy voice for Pr 2:3
understanding

LIFTETH

the Lord bringeth low, and *l.* 1Sa 2:7;
up 2:8
thine heart *l.* thee up to 2Ch 28:19
boast
what time the ostrich *l.* up Job 39:18
herself
wind which *l.* up the waves Ps 107:25
thereof
he *l.* the needy out of the Ps 113:7
dunghill
the Lord *l.* up the meek, he Ps 147:6
casteth wicked
see ye when he *l.* up an ensign Isa 18:3
on mount
that *l.* himself up in his Jer 51:3
brigandine
the horseman *l.* up the bright Na 3:3
sword

LIFTING

Abishai chief, for *l.* up his   *1Ch 11:20*
spear
sounding, by *l.* up the voice   *1Ch 15:16*
with joy
answered, Amen, with *l.* up their   *Ne 8:6*
hands
then thou shalt say, There is   *Job 22:29*
l. up
l. up of my hands as the   *Ps 141:2*
evening sacrifice
hast done foolishly in *l.* up   *Pr 30:32*
thyself
they shall mount up like the *l.*   *Isa 9:18*
up of smoke
at *l.* up of thyself nations are   *Isa 33:3*
scattered
men pray every where, *l.* up   *1Ti 2:8*
holy hands

LIGAMENT

united by every *l.* (B)   *Eph 4:16*
by *l.* and sinews (B)   *Col 2:19*

LIGHT

God said, Let there be *l.* and   *Ge 1:3*
there was *l.*
God saw the *l.*; God called the   *Ge 1:4;*
l. day   *1:5*
the greater *l.* the lesser *l.* to   *Ge 1:16*
rule the night
a *l.* made to the ark (E)   *Ge 6:16*
as soon as the morning was *l.*   *Ge 44:3*
the men
Israel had *l.* in their dwellings   *Ex 10:23*
but the pillar gave *l.* by night   *Ex 14:20*
to these
this is the offering, oil for the   *Ex 25:6;*
l.   *27:20; 35:8, 14, 28; 39:37; Le 24:2*
priest pertaineth the oil of the   *Nu 4:16*
l.
our soul loatheth this *l.* bread   *Nu 21:5*
cursed that setteth *l.* by his   *De 27:16*
father
Abimelech hired vain and *l.*   *J'g 9:4*
persons
fell at door of the house till it   *J'g 19:26*
was *l.*
and spoil them till the   *1Sa 14:36*
morning *l.*
and as soon as ye have *l.*   *1Sa 29:10*
depart
Asahel was *l.* of foot as a wild   *2Sa 2:18*
roe
and we will *l.* on him as the   *2Sa 17:12*
dew
that thou quench not the *l.* of   *2Sa 21:17*
Israel
he shall be as the *l.* of the   *2Sa 23:4*
morning
l. was against *l.* in three ranks   *1Ki 7:4;*
    7:5
that David my servant may   *1Ki 11:36*
have a *l.*
made *l.* of us (B)   *Ne 2:19*
nor pillar of fire by night to   *Ne 9:19*
shew them *l.*
the Jews had *l.* joy and gladness   *Es 8:16*
neither let the *l.* shine upon it   *Job 3:4*
let it look for *l.* but have none   *Job 3:9*
I had been as infants which   *Job 3:16*
never saw *l.*
wherefore is *l.* given to him   *Job 3:20;*
in misery   *3:23*
without order, where the *l.* is   *Job 10:22*
as darkness
bringeth out to *l.* the shadow   *Job 12:22*
of death
they grope in the dark   *Job 12:25*
without *l.*
the *l.* of the wicked shall be   *Job 18:5*
put out
the *l.* shall be dark in his   *Job 18:6*
tabernacle
and the *l.* shall shine on thy   *Job 22:28*
ways
they are of those that rebel   *Job 24:13*
against the *l.*
the murderer rising with the   *Job 24:14*
l. killeth
marked in the daytime, they   *Job 24:16*
know not the *l.*
and upon whom doth not his   *Job 25:3*
l. arise
the thing that is hid bringeth   *Job 28:11*
he to *l.*
will deliver, and his life shall   *Job 33:28*
see the *l.*

to be enlightened with the *l.*   *Job 33:30*
of the living
behold he spreadeth his *l.*   *Job 36:30*
upon it
with clouds he covereth *l.*   *Job 36:32*
and commandeth
and caused the *l.* of his cloud   *Job 37:15*
to shine
men see not the bright *l.* in   *Job 37:21*
the clouds
from the wicked their *l.* is   *Job 38:15*
withholden
where is the way where *l.*   *Job 38:19*
dwelleth
by what way is the *l.* parted?   *Job 38:24*
which scattereth
by his neesings a *l.* doth   *Job 41:18*
shine, and his eyes
lift up the *l.* of thy countenance   *Ps 4:6*
on us
The Lord is my *l.* and my   *Ps 27:1*
salvation
he shall bring forth thy   *Ps 37:6*
righteousness as *l.*
l. of mine eyes is gone, it is   *Ps 38:10*
gone from me
he shall go, they shall never   *Ps 49:19*
see *l.*
thou hast prepared the *l.* and   *Ps 74:16*
the sun
and all the night with a *l.* of   *Pr 78:14*
fire
l. is sown for the righteous,   *Ps 97:11*
and gladness
who coverest thyself with *l.* as   *Ps 104:2*
with garment
God is the Lord, who hath   *Ps 118:27*
shewed us *l.*
thy word is a lamp, and a *l.*   *Ps 119:105*
to my path
the entrance of thy words   *Ps 119:130*
giveth *l.*
even the night shall be *l.*   *Ps 139:11*
about me
darkness and *l.* are both alike   *Ps 139:12*
to thee
praise him, sun, and all ye   *Ps 148:3*
stars of *l.*
the path of the just is as the   *Pr 4:18*
shining *l.*
for the commandment is a   *Pr 6:23*
lamp, the law is *l.*
l. of righteous rejoiceth, but   *Pr 13:9*
lamp of wicked
the *l.* of the eyes rejoiceth the   *Pr 15:30*
heart
truly the *l.* is sweet and   *Ec 11:7*
pleasant
while the sun or the *l.* be not   *Ec 12:2*
darkened
put darkness for *l.* and *l.* for   *Isa 5:20*
darkness
and the *l.* is darkened in the   *Isa 5:30*
heavens thereof
it is because there is no *l.* in   *Isa 8:20*
them
have seen a great *l.* on them   *Isa 9:2*
hath *l.* shined
the *l.* of Israel shall be for a   *Isa 10:17*
fire
sun darkened, moon not   *Isa 13:10;*
cause her *l.* to shine   *M't 24:29;*
    M'k 13:24
l. of the moon shall be as the   *Isa 30:26*
l. of sun, *l.* of sun as *l.* of seven
my judgment to rest for a *l.* to   *Isa 51:4*
people
we wait for *l.* but behold   *Isa 59:9*
obscurity
look for the *l.* (R)   *Isa 59:9*
the Lord shall be to thee an   *Isa 60:19*
everlasting *l.*
I beheld the heavens, and they   *Jer 4:23*
had no *l.*
I will take from them the *l.* of   *Jer 25:10*
the candle
Lord giveth sun for *l.* by day;   *Jer 31:35*
ordinances of moon and stars
for *l.* by night
and the *l.* dwelleth with him   *Da 2:22*
l. and understanding found in   *Da 5:11;*
Daniel   *5:14*
thy judgments as *l.* that goeth   *Ho 6:5*
forth
when morning is *l.* they   *Mic 2:1*
practice it
the Lord will bring me forth to   *Mic 7:9*
the *l.*
and his brightness was as the *l.*   *Hab 3:4*
at the *l.* of thine arrows they   *Hab 3:11*
went

her prophets are *l.* and   *Zep 3:4*
every morning bring judgment   *Zep 3:5*
to *l.*
in that day the *l.* shall be not   *Zec 14:6*
clear
at evening time it shall be *l.*   *Zec 14:7*
to them that sat in death, *l.* is   *M't 4:16*
sprung up
ye are the *l.* of the world   *M't 5:14*
it giveth *l.*   *M't 5:15*
nor do men *l.* a candle   *M't 5:15;*
    Lu 8:16; 15:8
let your *l.* so shine before   *M't 5:16*
men, that they see
l. of body is the eye, if eye   *M't 6:22;*
single, thy whole body be   *Lu 11:34, 36*
full of *l.*
my yoke is easy, my burden   *M't 11:30*
is *l.*
and his raiment was white as   *M't 17:2*
the *l.*
but made *l.* of it, and went   *M't 22:5*
their ways
it should come to *l.* (S)   *M'k 4:22; 8:17*
a *l.* to lighten the Gentiles, and   *Lu 2:32*
the glory
they which enter in may see   *Lu 8:16;*
the *l.*   *11:33*
of this world are wiser than the   *Lu 16:8*
children of *l.*
in him was life, and life was   *Joh 1:4*
the *l.* of men
the same came to bear witness   *Joh 1:7;*
of that *l.*   *1:8*
that was the true *l.* which   *Joh 1:9*
lighteth every man
condemnation that *l.* is come   *Joh 3:19*
into the world
every one that doeth evil   *Joh 3:20*
hateth the *l.*
but he that doeth truth   *Joh 3:21*
cometh to the *l.*
he was a burning and a   *Joh 5:35*
shining *l.* and ye rejoice
in his *l.*
Jesus saying, I am the *l.* of   *Joh 8:12;*
the world, he that followeth   *9:5*
me shall have the *l.* of life
he stumbleth not, because he   *Joh 11:9*
seeth the *l.*
he stumbleth, because there   *Joh 11:10*
is no *l.* in him
yet a little while is the *l.* with   *Joh 12:35*
you
while ye have the *l.* believe in   *Joh 12:36*
the *l.* that ye
I am come a *l.* into the   *Joh 12:46*
world, that whosoever
there shined about him a *l.* from   *Ac 9:3*
heaven
a *l.* shined in the prison, and   *Ac 12:7*
he smote
I have set thee to be a *l.* to   *Ac 13:47*
the Gentiles
then he called for a *l.* and   *Ac 16:29*
sprang in
there shone a great *l.* round   *Ac 22:6*
about me
they that were with me saw   *Ac 22:9*
indeed the *l.*
when I could not see for the   *Ac 22:11*
glory of that *l.*
at midday, O king, I saw in   *Ac 26:13*
the way a *l.*
should shew *l.* to the people   *Ac 26:23*
and Gentiles
a *l.* of them which are in   *Ro 2:19*
darkness
and let us put on the armour   *Ro 13:12*
of *l.*
who will bring to *l.* hidden   *1Co 4:5*
things
lest the *l.* of the gospel should   *2Co 4:4*
shine
who commanded *l.* to shine   *2Co 4:6*
out of darkness
our *l.* affliction worketh for us   *2Co 4:17*
Satan is transformed into an   *2Co 11:14*
angel of *l.*
but now are ye *l.* walk as   *Eph 5:8*
children of *l.*
live like children of *l.* (B)(P)   *Eph 5:8*
manifest by *l.* whatsoever   *Eph 5:13*
doth make manifest is *l.*
meet for inheritance of the   *Col 1:12*
saints in *l.*
ye are all children of the *l.* and   *1Th 5:5*
day
dwelling in *l.* no man can   *1Ti 6:16*
approach

who brought life and 2Ti 1:10
immortality to *l.*
had received *l.* (B)(P) Heb 10:32
who called you into his 1Pe 2:9
marvellous *l.*
take heed, as to a *l.* shining in 2Pe 1:19
dark place
God is *l.* and in him is no 1Jo 1:5
darkness
nor shall sun *l.* on them Re 7:16
the *l.* of a candle shall shine Re 18:23
no more
her *l.* was like a stone most Re 21:11
precious
glory lighten it, and the Re 21:23
Lamb is the *l.* thereof
glory of God did *l.* it (S) Re 21:23
they need not *l.* of the sun, the Re 22:5
Lord giveth *l.*

LIGHT *THING*

seemeth it a *l. thing* to be 1Sa 18:23
had been a *l. thing* for him 1Ki 16:31
is but a *l. thing* in the sight of 2Ki 20:10
the Lord
it is a *l. thing* for the shadow 2Ki 20:10
to go down
It is a *l. thing* that thou Isa 49:6
Is it a *l. thing* to the Eze 8:17

GIVE LIGHT

and let them be to *give l.* on Ge 1:15
the earth
and God set the stars to *give l.* Ge 1:17
on the earth
in a pillar of fire to *give them* Ex 13:21
l.
the lamps may *give l.* over Ex 25:37;
against it Nu 8:2
he promised to *give him* a *l.* 2Ki 8:19;
2Ch 21:7
to *give* them *l.* in the way they Ne 9:12
should go
and fire to *give l.* in the night Ps 105:39
the stars of heaven shall not Isa 13:10
give their *l.*
I will *give* thee for a *l.* to the Isa 42:6;
Gentiles 49:6
nor shall the moon *give l.* to Isa 60:19;
thee Eze 32:7
it *give l.* to all in the house M't 5:15;
Lu 11:36
to *give* the *l.* of the knowledge 2Co 4:6
of God
awake, and Christ shall *give* Eph 5:14
thee *l.*

IN THE LIGHT

that I may walk *in the l.* of Ps 56:13
the living
come, let us walk *in the l.* of the Isa 2:5
Lord
walk *in the l.* of your fire, and Isa 50:11
in the sparks
while ye have the light, Joh 12:36
believe *in the l.*
but if we walk *in the l.* as he is 1Jo 1:7
in the l.
he that saith he is *in the l.* and 1Jo 2:9
hateth his brother
that loveth his brother, 1Jo 2:10
abideth *in the l.*
nations that are saved shall Re 21:24
walk *in the l.*

THY LIGHT

and in *thy l.* shall we see light Ps 36:9
O send out *thy l.* and thy truth, Ps 43:3
let them lead
then shall *thy l.* break forth as Isa 58:8
morning
then shall *thy l.* rise in Isa 58:10
obscurity
Arise, shine, for *thy l.* is come Isa 60:1
the Gentiles shall come to *thy* Isa 60:3
l. and kings
the sun shall be no more *thy* Isa 60:19
l. by day
for the Lord shall be *thy* Isa 60:20
everlasting *l.*

LIGHT-BRINGER

l., day star (A) Isa 14:12

LIGHTED

she *l.* off her camel Ge 24:64
he *l.* on a certain place Ge 28:11
he *l.* the lamps Ex 40:25; Nu 8:3
l. off ass Jos 15:18; J'g 1:14; 1Sa 25:23
l. down off chariot J'g 4:15; 2Ki 5:21
l. the torches (S) J'g 15:5
l. on Jehonadab the son of 2Ki 10:15
it hath *l.* on Israel Isa 9:8
l. a candle Lu 8:16; 11:33

LIGHTEN

he will *l.* his hand from off you 1Sa 6:5
and the Lord will *l.* my 2Sa 22:29
darkness
that our God may *l.* our eyes Ezr 9:8
l. mine eyes, lest I sleep the Ps 13:3
sleep
lightnings *l.* the world (R) Ps 97:4
ship into the sea, to *l.* it of Jon 1:5
them
A light to *l.* the Gentiles, and Lu 2:32
the glory of God did *l.* it, and Re 21:23

LIGHTENED

looked unto him, and were *l.* Ps 34:5
the lightnings *l.* the world: the Ps 77:18
his lightnings *l.* the world (S) Ps 97:4
the next day they *l.* the ship Ac 27:18
they *l.* the ship, and cast out Ac 27:38
the earth was *l.* with his glory Re 18:1

LIGHTENETH

the Lord *l.* both their eyes Pr 29:13
that *l.* out of the one part Lu 17:24
under

LIGHTER

which he put upon us *l.* 1Ki 12:4
father did put upon us *l.* 1Ki 12:9
heavy, but make thou it *l.* 1Ki 12:10
unto us
make thou it somewhat *l.* for 2Ch 10:10
us
they are altogether *l.* than Ps 62:9
vanity

LIGHTEST

unto him, When thou *l.* the Nu 8:2
lamps

LIGHTETH

when Aaron *l.* the lamps at Ex 30:8
even
and *l.* upon his neighbour, that De 19:5
which *l.* every man that cometh Joh 1:9

LIGHT-FINGERED

not be *l.* (P) Tit 2:10

LIGHTHEADED

l. and foolhardy (B) J'g 9:4

LIGHTING

shall shew the *l.* down of his Isa 30:30
arm
like a dove, and *l.* upon him M't 3:16

LIGHTLY

might *l.* have lien with thy Ge 26:10
wife
and *l.* esteemed the Rock of De 32:15
his
despise me shall be *l.* esteemed 1Sa 2:30
I am a poor man, and *l.* 1Sa 18:23
esteemed
he *l.* afflicted the land of Isa 9:1
Zebulun
trembled, and all the hills Jer 4:24
moved *l.*
that can *l.* speak evil of me M'k 9:39
think *l.* of his wealth (A) Ro 2:4

LIGHTNESS

through the *l.* of her whoredom Jer 3:9
err by their lies, and by their *l.* Jer 23:32
was thus minded, did I use *l.* 2Co 1:17

LIGHTNING

them; *l.* and discomfited 2Sa 22:15
them
a way for the *l.* of the Job 28:26
thunder
his *l.* unto the ends of the Job 37:3
earth
or a way for the *l.* of thunder Job 38:25
Cast forth *l.* and scatter Ps 144:6
and out of the fire went forth Eze 1:13
l.
as the appearance of a flash of Eze 1:14
l.
his face as the appearance of *l.* Da 10:6
his arrow shall go forth as the Zec 9:14
l.
For as the *l.* cometh out of M't 24:27
the east
His countenance was like *l.* M't 28:3
I beheld Satan as *l.* fall from Lu 10:18
heaven
For as the *l.* that lighteneth Lu 17:24
out of

LIGHTNINGS

that there were thunders and *l.* Ex 19:16
saw the thunderings, and the Ex 20:18
l.
Canst thou send *l.* that they Job 38:35
may
and he shot out *l.* and Ps 18:14
discomfited
the *l.* lightened the world: the Ps 77:18
earth
His *l.* enlightened the world Ps 97:4
he maketh *l.* for the rain; he Ps 135:7
he maketh *l.* with rain, and Jer 10:13;
bringeth 51:16
torches, they shall run like the *l.* Na 2:4
out of the throne proceeded *l.* Re 4:5
were voices, and thunderings, Re 8:5
and *l.*
and there were *l.* and voices Re 11:19
were voices, and thunders, Re 16:18
and *l.*

LIGHTS

Let there be *l.* in the firmament Ge 1:14
let them be for *l.* in the Ge 1:15
firmament
God made two great *l.;* the Ge 1:16
greater
he made windows of narrow *l.* 1Ki 6:4
To him that made great *l.:* for Ps 136:7
his
bright *l.* of heaven will I make Eze 32:8
about, and your *l.* burning Lu 12:35
there were many *l.* in the upper Ac 20:8
whom ye shine as *l.* in the Ph'p 2:15
world
cometh down from the Father Jas 1:17
of *l.*

LIGN

as the trees of *l.* aloes which Nu 24:6
the Lord

LIGURE

And the third row a *l.* an Ex 28:19
agate
the third row, a *l.* an agate Ex 39:12

LIKE

Sodom was *l.* the land of Ge 13:10
Egypt
who is *l.* unto thee Ex 15:11;
De 33:29; 1Ki 8:23; 2Ch 6:14; Ps 35:10;
71:19
manna was *l.* coriander seed, Ex 16:31
white
the glory of the Lord was *l.* Ex 24:17
devouring fire
nor shall ye make any Ex 30:32
ointment *l.* it
whosoever compoundeth any Ex 30:33;
l. it 30:38
of each shall there be a *l.* Ex 30:34
weight
hew two tables *l.* to the first Ex 34:1;
34:4; De 10:1, 3
and let my last end be *l.* his Nu 23:10
or any thing that hath been De 4:32
heard *l.*
lest thou be a cursed thing *l.* it De 7:26

set king over me l. all nations *De 17:14;*
1Sa 8:5, 20
they shall have l. portions to *De 18:8*
eat
prophet of thy brethren l. *De 18:15;*
me *Ac 3:22; 7:37*
I will raise a prophet from *De 18:18*
brethren l. to thee
l. the overthrow of Sodom *De 29:23*
and Gomorrah
there arose not a prophet l. to *De 34:10*
Moses
no day l. that before or after *Jos 10:14*
it
his countenance l. an angel of *J'g 13:6*
God
he brake them from his arms *J'g 16:12*
l. a thread
I shall become weak and l. *J'g 16:17*
any other man
tho' I be not l. to one of thy *Ru 2:13*
handmaidens
Lord make the woman l. Rachel *Ru 4:11*
and l. Leah
let thy house be l. the house of *Ru 4:12*
Pharez
nor is there any rock l. our God *1Sa 2:2*
be strong, quit yourselves l. *1Sa 4:9;*
men *1Co 16:13*
the staff of his spear was l. a *1Sa 17:7*
weaver's beam
Nabal held a feast l. the feast *1Sa 25:36*
of a king
a valiant man, and who is l. *1Sa 26:15*
to thee in Israel
l. to the name of the great men *2Sa 7:9*
one nation in earth is l. thy *2Sa 7:23*
people Israel
he maketh my feet l. hinds' *2Sa 22:34*
feet
none l. thee before not arise *1Ki 3:12;*
l. thee *3:13*
there was not the l. made in *1Ki 10:20*
any kingdom
Jeroboam ordained a feast l. *1Ki 12:32*
that in Judah
l. the house of Jeroboam *1Ki 16:3;*
16:7; 21:22; 2Ki 9:9
there ariseth a little cloud l. a *1Ki 18:44*
man's hand
number thee an army l. the *1Ki 20:25*
army thou lost
pitched before them l. two *1Ki 20:27*
little flocks of kids
word l. word of one of those *1Ki 22:13;*
2Ch 18:12
but not l. his father and l. his *2Ki 3:2*
mother
his flesh came again l. flesh of *2Ki 5:14*
a little child
and l. the house of Baasha son *2Ki 9:9*
of Ahijah
had made them l. dust by *2Ki 13:7*
threshing
yet not l. David his father *2Ki 14:3;*
16:2; 2Ch 28:1
the Lord charged they should *2Ki 17:15*
not do l. them
take you to a land l. your own *2Ki 18:32;*
Isa 36:17
l. to him was there no king *2Ki 23:25;*
Ne 13:26
a great host l. the host of *1Ch 12:22*
God
would increase Israel l. the *1Ch 27:23*
stars of heaven
over a people, l. the dust of the *2Ch 1:9*
earth
no burning for him l. *2Ch 21:19*
burning of fathers
be not ye l. your fathers and *2Ch 30:7*
your brethren
l. to the abominations of the *2Ch 33:2*
heathen
there was no passover l. to *2Ch 35:18*
that in Israel
to grave l. as a shock of corn *Job 5:26*
cometh in
hast thou not curdled me l. *Job 10:10*
cheese
though man be born l. a wild *Job 11:12*
ass's colt
he maketh them to stagger l. *Job 12:25*
a drunken man
your remembrances are l. to *Job 13:12*
ashes
he cometh forth l. a flower *Job 14:2*
and is cut down
filthy is man, who drinketh *Job 15:16*
iniquity l. water

he runneth upon me l. a giant *Job 16:14*
he shall perish for ever l. his *Job 20:7*
own dung
they send their little ones l. a *Job 21:11*
flock
what man is l. Job, who *Job 34:7*
drinketh scorning
God exalteth by power, who *Job 36:22*
teacheth l. him
gird up now thy loins l. a *Job 38:3;*
man *40:7*
hast thou an arm l. God, or *Job 40:9*
canst thunder
on earth there is not his l. *Job 41:33*
who is made
ye have not spoken right l. my *Job 42:8*
servant Job
he shall be l. a tree planted by *Ps 1:3*
the rivers
ungodly are not so, but are l. the *Ps 1:4*
chaff
lest he tear my soul l. a lion, *Ps 7:2*
rending it
l. as a lion that is greedy of *Ps 17:12*
his prey
I am poured out l. water, my *Ps 22:14*
heart l. wax
I become l. them that go down *Ps 28:1*
to the pit
I am forgotten, I am l. a *Ps 31:12*
broken vessel
thy righteousness is l. the great *Ps 36:6*
mountains
they shall be soon cut down l. *Ps 37:2*
grass
and spreading himself l. a *Ps 37:35*
green bay tree
thou makest his beauty to *Ps 39:11*
consume l. moth
thou hast given us l. sheep for *Ps 44:11*
meat
man is l. the beasts that *Ps 49:12;*
perish *49:20*
thy tongue is l. a sharp razor *Ps 52:2*
working
but I am l. a green olive tree in *Ps 52:8*
the house of God
O that I had wings l. a dove, I *Ps 55:6*
would fly
l. the poison of a serpent, l. the *Ps 58:4*
deaf adder
they make a noise l. a dog *Ps 59:6;*
59:14
who whet their tongue l. a *Ps 64:3*
sword
he shall come down l. rain on *Ps 72:6*
the grass
nor are they plagued l. other *Ps 73:5*
men
thou leddest thy people l. a *Ps 77:20;*
flock *78:52*
they dealt unfaithfully l. their *Ps 78:57*
fathers
their blood have shed l. water *Ps 79:3*
round Jerusalem
the boughs thereof l. the *Ps 80:10*
goodly cedars
but shall die l. men, and fall l. *Ps 82:7*
one of princes
O my God, make them l. a *Ps 83:13*
wheel
a strong Lord l. to thee *Ps 89:8;*
113:5; Mic 7:18
righteous shall flourish l. *Ps 92:12*
palm tree, he shall grow l. a
cedar in Lebanon
my heart is smitten, withered *Ps 102:4;*
l. grass *102:11*
I am l. a pelican, l. an owl of *Ps 102:6*
the desert
all of them shall wax old l. a *Ps 102:26*
garment
l. as a father pitieth his *Ps 103:13*
children, so Lord
who stretchest out the heavens *Ps 104:2*
l. a curtain
they ran in the dry places l. a *Ps 105:41*
river
they reel and stagger l. a *Ps 107:27*
drunken man
l. water, l. oil let it come into *Ps 109:18*
his bones
they that make them are l. to *Ps 115:8;*
them *135:18*
captivity of Zion, we were l. *Ps 126:1*
them dream
lest I be l. them that go down *Ps 143:7*
to the pit
man is l. to vanity, his days as *Ps 144:4*
a shadow

he giveth snow l. wool, hoar *Ps 147:16*
frost l. ashes
their contentions l. the bars of *Pr 18:19*
a castle
counsel in the heart of man is l. *Pr 20:5*
deep water
it biteth l. a serpent, stingeth l. *Pr 23:32*
an adder
in an unfaithful man is l. a *Pr 25:19*
broken tooth
l. a city broken down, and *Pr 25:28*
without walls
answer not a fool, lest thou be *Pr 26:4*
l. to him
my beloved is l. a roe or young *Ca 2:9*
hart
turn, my beloved, and be thou *Ca 2:17;*
l. a roe *8:14*
who is this that cometh l. pillars *Ca 3:6*
of smoke
thy teeth are l. a flock of sheep *Ca 4:2*
even shorn
thy lips l. scarlet, temples l. a *Ca 4:3*
pomegranate
thy neck is l. the tower of David *Ca 4:4*
for armoury
thy two breasts are l. two *Ca 4:5;*
young roes *7:3*
his lips l. lilies dropping sweet *Ca 5:13*
myrrh
my soul made me l. chariots of *Ca 6:12*
Ammin-adib
the joints of thy thighs are l. *Ca 7:1*
jewels
thy navel is l. a goblet, thy belly *Ca 7:2*
is l. wheat
eyes; head, hair; stature l. a *Ca 7:4;*
palm tree *7:7*
and the smell of thy nose l. *Ca 7:8*
apples
should have been l. Gomorrah *Isa 1:9;*
Ro 9:29
tho your sins be red l. crimson, *Isa 1:18*
shall be as wool
put down the inhabitants l. a *Isa 10:13*
valiant man
and the lion shall eat straw l. *Isa 11:7*
the ox
shall be an highway, l. as it *Isa 11:16*
was to Israel
they shall say, Art thou *Isa 14:10*
become l. to us
I will ascend, I will be l. the *Isa 14:14*
most High
thou art cast out l. an *Isa 14:19*
abominable branch
my bowels shall sound l. an *Isa 16:11*
harp for Moab
in that day shall Egypt be l. *Isa 19:16*
unto women
l. as my servant Isaiah hath *Isa 20:3*
walked naked
will toss thee l. a ball into a *Isa 22:18*
large country
l. a woman with child that *Isa 26:17*
draweth near
breath of the Lord l. a stream *Isa 30:33*
of brimstone
Sharon is l. a wilderness, *Isa 33:9*
Bashan and Carmel
I have cut off l. a weaver my *Isa 38:12*
life
l. a crane or swallow so did I *Isa 38:14*
chatter
now will I cry l. a travailing *Isa 42:14*
woman
to whom will ye compare me *Isa 46:5*
that we may be l.
the wicked are l. the troubled *Isa 57:20*
sea
spare not, lift up thy voice l. a *Isa 58:1*
trumpet
be l. a watered garden, *Isa 58:11*
and l. a spring
we grope for the wall l. the *Isa 59:10*
blind
we roar all l. bears, and *Isa 59:11*
mourn sore l. doves
when the enemy shall come in *Isa 59:19*
l. a flood
l. him that treadeth in the *Isa 63:2*
winevat
our iniquities l. wind have *Isa 64:6*
taken us away
I will extend peace to her l. a *Isa 66:12*
river
lest my fury come forth l. fire *Jer 4:4;*
21:12
l. as ye have forsaken me, and *Jer 5:19*
served gods

the portion of Jacob is not *l.*   *Jer 10:16*
them
I was *l.* a lamb brought to   *Jer 11:19*
the slaughter
for he shall be *l.* the heath in   *Jer 17:6*
the desert
is not my word *l.* fire, and *l.*   *Jer 23:29*
a hammer
then will I make this house   *Jer 26:6;*
l. Shiloh   *26:9*
saying, Zion shall be plowed   *Jer 26:18*
l. a field
make thee *l.* Zedekiah and *l.*   *Jer 29:22*
Ahab
were added besides to them   *Jer 36:32*
many *l.* words
he is *l.* to die with hunger   *Jer 38:9*
where he is
Egypt is *l.* a very fair heifer   *Jer 46:20*
flee, be *l.* the heath in the   *Jer 48:6*
wilderness
be *l.* dove   *Jer 48:28*
shall come *l.* a lion   *Jer 49:19; 50:44*
who is *l.* me, who will appoint   *Jer 49:19*
the portion of Jacob is not *l.*   *Jer 51:19*
them
whereto I will not do any   *Eze 5:9*
more the *l.*
l. as I have done, so shall it   *Eze 12:11*
be done them
and doth the *l.* to any of   *Eze 18:10*
these things
the house of Judah is *l.* to   *Eze 25:8*
all the heathen
whom art thou *l.* in thy   *Eze 31:2;*
greatness   *31:18*
not any tree was *l.* to him in   *Eze 31:8*
his beauty
in the seventh month shall   *Eze 45:25*
he do the *l.*
the form of the fourth is *l.*   *Da 3:25*
the Son of God
his heart was made *l.* the   *Da 5:21*
beasts, *l.* oxen
one *l.* the Son of man came   *Da 7:13*
with clouds
and there shall be *l.* people, *l.*   *Ho 4:9*
priest
the princes *l.* them that remove   *Ho 5:10*
the bound
but they *l.* men have   *Ho 6:7*
transgressed the covenant
I am *l.* a green fir tree, from   *Ho 14:8*
me is fruit
there hath not been ever the *l.*   *Joe 2:2*
nor shall be
lest he break out *l.* fire in   *Am 5:6*
Joseph
and invent instruments of   *Am 6:5*
music *l.* David
l. as the Lord of hosts thought   *Zec 1:6*
to do
make the governors of Judah   *Zec 12:6*
l. a hearth
Spirit descending *l.* a dove   *M't 3:16;*
and lighting on him *M'k 1:10; Lu 3:22;*
  Joh 1:32
be not ye therefore *l.* unto them *M't 6:8*
was not arrayed *l.* one of   *M't 6:29;*
these   *Lu 12:27*
l. children sitting in the   *M't 11:16;*
market   *Lu 7:32*
it was restored whole *l.* as   *M't 12:13*
the other
kingdom of heaven is *l.* to a   *M't 13:31;*
grain of mustard seed   *M'k 4:31;*
  Lu 13:19
kingdom of heaven is *l.* to   *M't 13:33;*
leaven   *Lu 13:21*
l. to a treasure   *M't 13:44*
l. to a merchant   *M't 13:45*
l. to a net   *M't 13:47*
l. an householder   *M't 13:52; 20:1*
the kingdom of heaven is *l.* to   *M't 22:2*
a certain king
and the second is *l.* to it   *M't 22:39;*
  M'k 12:31
for ye are *l.* to whited   *M't 23:27*
sepulchres
his countenance was *l.*   *M't 28:3*
lightning and raiment
I will shew you to whom he is   *Lu 6:47*
l.
to what are they *l.*; are *l.*   *Lu 7:31;*
children   *7:32*
he said, To what is the   *Lu 13:18*
kingdom of God *l.*
answered, Never man spake *l.*   *Joh 7:46*
this man

I shall be a liar *l.* unto you,   *Joh 8:55*
but I know
some, This is he, others said, He *Joh 9:9*
is *l.* him
l. a lamb dumb before his   *Ac 8:32*
shearer
forasmuch as God gave them   *Ac 11:17*
the *l.* gift
we are also men of *l.*   *Ac 14:15*
passions with you
not to think the Godhead is *l.*   *Ac 17:29*
gold or silver
with the workmen of *l.*   *Ac 19:25*
occupation
an image made *l.* to   *Ro 1:23*
corruptible man
did not *l.* to retain God   *Ro 1:28*
l. as Christ was raised up from   *Ro 6:4*
the dead
behaving *l.* the unconverted   *1Co 3:3*
(B)
fashioned *l.* unto his glorious   *Ph'p 3:21*
body
suffered *l.* things of your   *1Th 2:14*
countrymen
it behoved him to be made *l.*   *Heb 2:17*
his brethren
was in all points tempted *l.* as   *Heb 4:15*
we are
but made *l.* to the Son of God,   *Heb 7:3*
abides a priest
that wavereth is *l.* a wave of the   *Jas 1:6*
sea
he is *l.* a man beholding his   *Jas 1:23*
natural face
Elias was a man subject to *l.*   *Jas 5:17*
passions
l. figure whereunto baptism   *1Pe 3:21*
save us
I have obtained *l.* precious faith *2Pe 1:1*
with us
he shall appear, we shall be *l.*   *1Jo 3:2*
him
one *l.* the Son of man, clothed   *Re 1:13;*
  14:14
worshipped, saying, Who is *l.* to *Re 13:4*
the beast
he had two horns *l.* a lamb,   *Re 13:11*
and he spake as
I saw three unclean spirits *l.*   *Re 16:13*
frogs come
saying, What city is *l.* to this   *Re 18:18*
great city

LIKE *MANNER*

did in *l. manner* with their   *Ex 7:11*
enchantments
in *l. manner* thou shalt deal   *Ex 23:11*
with thy vineyard
in *l. manner* shalt thou do with   *De 22:3*
his ass
in *l. manner* they sent to king   *J'g 11:17*
of Moab
he prophesied before Samuel *1Sa 19:24*
in *l. manner*
Sanballat sent in *l. manner* the   *Ne 6:5*
fifth time
that dwell there shall die in *l.*   *Isa 51:6*
manner
ye, in *l. manner* when ye see   *M'k 13:29*
these things
in *l. manner* did their fathers   *Lu 6:23*
to prophets
third took her, in *l. manner*   *Lu 20:31*
the seventh also
shall so come in *l. manner* as   *Ac 1:11*
ye have seen
in *l. manner* that women adorn *1Ti 2:9*
themselves
in *l. manner* giving themselves   *Jude 7*
to fornication

NONE *LIKE*

none *l.* the Lord our God   *Ex 8:10;*
  9:14; De 33:26; 2Sa 7:22; 1Ch 17:20
none *l.* the hail; none *l.* cry of *Ex 9:24;*
Egypt   *11:6*
none *l.* Saul among all the   *1Sa 10:24*
people
David said, There is none *l.*   *1Sa 21:9*
that, give it me
there was *none l.* Solomon;   *1Ki 3:12;*
none *l.* Ahab   *21:25*
so that after there was *none*   *2Ki 18:5*
l. Hezekiah
that there is none *l.* him in the   *Job 1:8;*
earth   *2:3*
among the gods *none l.* to thee   *Ps 86:8;*
  Jer 10:6-7

for I am God, and there is   *Isa 46:9*
none l. me
alas, that day is great, so that   *Jer 30:7*
none l. it
among all was found *none l.*   *Da 1:19*
Daniel

SUCH LIKE

considereth, and doeth not   *Eze 18:14*
such l.
many other *such l.* things ye   *M'k 7:8;*
do   *7:13*
envyings, drunkenness, and   *Ga 5:21*
such l.

LIKED

did to him as they *l.* (A)(B)   *M't 17:12*

LIKELY

he is *l.* to die (S)   *Jer 38:9*

LIKEMINDED

to be *l.* one toward another   *Ro 15:5*
Fulfil ye my joy, that ye be *l.*   *Ph'p 2:2*
For I have no man *l.* who   *Ph'p 2:20*
will
be ye all *l.* (E)   *1Pe 3:8*

LIKEN

To whom then will ye *l.* God   *Isa 40:18*
To whom then will ye *l.* me   *Isa 40:25*
To whom will ye *l.* me, and   *Isa 46:5*
make
what thing shall I *l.* to thee, O   *La 2:13*
I will *l.* him unto a wise man   *M't 7:24*
whereunto shall I *l.* this   *M't 11:16*
generation
shall we *l.* the kingdom of   *M'k 4:30*
God
then shall I *l.* the men of this   *Lu 7:31*
shall I *l.* the kingdom of God   *Lu 13:20*

LIKENED

mighty can be *l.* unto the Lord   *Ps 89:6*
have *l.* the daughter of Zion to a   *Jer 6:2*
shall be *l.* unto a foolish man   *M't 7:26*
of heaven is *l.* unto a man   *M't 13:24*
which
of heaven *l.* unto a certain   *M't 18:23*
king
of heaven be *l.* unto ten   *M't 25:1*
virgins

LIKENESS

man in our image, after our *l.*   *Ge 1:26*
man, in the *l.* of God made he   *Ge 5:1*
him
begat a son in his own *l.* after   *Ge 5:3*
his
or any *l.* of any thing that is in   *Ex 20:4*
figure, the *l.* of male or female   *De 4:16*
The *l.* of any beast that is on   *De 4:17*
the *l.* of any winged fowl, that   *De 4:17*
flieth
The *l.* of any thing that   *De 4:18*
creepeth on
the *l.* of any fish that is in the   *De 4:18*
image, or the *l.* of any thing   *De 4:23*
graven image or the *l.* of any   *De 4:25*
thing
any *l.* of any thing that is in   *De 5:8*
heaven
satisfied, when I awake, with   *Ps 17:15*
thy *l.*
the *l.* of an ox (E)   *Ps 106:20*
what *l.* will ye compare unto   *Isa 40:18*
him
came the *l.* of four living   *Eze 1:5*
creatures
they had the *l.* of a man   *Eze 1:5*
As for the *l.* of their faces,   *Eze 1:10*
they four
As for the *l.* of the living   *Eze 1:13*
creatures
a beryl; and they four had one   *Eze 1:16*
l.
the *l.* of the firmament upon   *Eze 1:22*
their heads was the *l.* of a   *Eze 1:26*
throne
and upon the *l.* of the throne   *Eze 1:26*
was the
l. as the appearance of a man   *Eze 1:26*
above
of the *l.* of the glory of the   *Eze 1:28*
Lord

and lo a *l.* as the appearance of | Eze 8:2
fire
the appearance of the *l.* of a | Eze 10:1
throne
appearances, they four had | Eze 10:10
one *l.*
and the *l.* of the hands of a | Eze 10:21
man
the *l.* of their faces was the | Eze 10:22
same
l. of sons of men (A)(E)(R) | Da 10:16
whose *l.* and title | M't 22:20
(A)(B)(R)
come down to us in the *l.* of | Ac 14:11
men
together in the *l.* of his death | Ro 6:5
be also in the *l.* of his | Ro 6:5
resurrection
his own Son in the *l.* of sinful | Ro 8:3
flesh
the *l.* of his Son (B)(N)(P) | Ro 8:29
the *l.* of (B) | 1Co 15:49;
  | 2Co 3:18; 4:4; Col 3:10
and was made in the *l.* of men | Ph'p 2:7
l. of Melchizedek (A)(E)(R) | Heb 7:15
made in God's *l.* | Jas 3:9
(A)(B)(E)(N)(P)(R)

LIKES

wind blows where it *l.* (P) | Joh 3:8

LIKETH

thy gates, where it *l.* him best | De 23:16
ye also for the Jews, as it *l.* you | Es 8:8
for this *l.* you, O ye children of | Am 4:5

LIKEWISE

l. shalt thou do with thine | Ex 22:30
oxen
serve their gods, even so will I | De 12:30
do *l.*
to thy maidservant thou shalt | De 15:17
do *l.*
to thy brother's lost goods | De 22:3
shalt thou do *l.*
he said to them, Look on me, | J'g 7:17
and do *l.*
sent messengers, and they | 1Sa 19:21
prophesied *l.*
fell *l.* on his sword, and died | 1Sa 31:5
with him
and let us hear *l.* what he saith | 2Sa 17:5
and *l.* did he for all his | 1Ki 11:8
strange wives
l. fled before Abishai his | 1Ch 19:15
brother
to praise every morning and | 1Ch 23:30
l. at even
I *l.* might exact of them money | Ne 5:10
I also and my maidens will fast | Es 4:16
l.
l. the fool and brutish person | Ps 49:10
perish
God shall *l.* destroy thee for | Ps 52:5
ever
knowest thou thyself *l.* hast | Ec 7:22
cursed others
and doeth *l.* (S) | Eze 18:14
l. in the feast of seven days | Eze 42:25
(S)
though they be quiet and *l.* | Na 1:12
many, yet
l. shall also Son of man | M't 17:12
suffer of them
so *l.* shall my heavenly | M't 18:35
Father do to you
he went about the sixth hour, | M't 20:5
and did *l.*
they *l.* received every man a | M't 20:10
penny
I in *l.* will tell by what | M't 21:24
authority
he came to the second and | M't 21:30
said *l.*
other servants, and they did | M't 21:36
unto them *l.*
l. the second and third died | M't 22:26;
  | M'k 12:21
so *l.* when ye see these | M't 24:33;
things | Lu 21:31
l. he that had received two | M't 25:17
talents
l. also said all his disciples | M't 26:35;
  | M'k 14:31
l. the chief priests mocked | M't 27:41;
  | M'k 15:31
and she gave thanks *l.* to the | Lu 2:38
Lord

let him do *l.* | Lu 3:11
do ye also to them *l.* | Lu 6:31
go and do *l.* | Lu 10:37
ye shall *l.* perish | Lu 13:3; 13:5
l. who forsaketh not all that | Lu 14:33
he hath
l. joy shall be in heaven over | Lu 15:7;
one | 15:10
l. Lazarus received evil things, | Lu 16:25
but now
so *l.* when ye shall have done | Lu 17:10
all things
l. also the cup after supper, | Lu 22:20
saying
what he doeth, these also | Joh 5:19
doeth the Son *l.*
prophets have *l.* foretold of | Ac 3:24
these days
l. the men leaving the natural | Ro 1:27
use
l. reckon yourselves to be | Ro 6:11
dead to sin
l. the Spirit helpeth our | Ro 8:26
infirmities
and *l.* also the wife to the | 1Co 7:3
husband
other Jews dissembled *l.* with | Ga 2:13
him
l. the good works of some are | 1Ti 5:25
manifest
young men *l.* exhort to be | Tit 2:6
sober minded
he also himself *l.* took part of | Heb 2:14
the same
arm yourselves *l.* with the same | 1Pe 4:1
mind
l. these filthy dreamers defile the | Jude 8
flesh
the day shone not, the night *l.* | Re 8:12

LIKHI

Anian, and Shechem, and L. | 1Ch 7:19

LIKING

Their young ones are in good | Job 39:4
l.
should he see your faces worse | Da 1:10
l.

LILIES

brim of a cup, with flowers of | 1Ki 7:26;
l. | 2Ch 4:5
I am his: he feedeth among the | Ca 2:16
l.
are twins, which feed among the | Ca 4:5
l.
his lips like *l.* dropping sweet | Ca 5:13
l. dropping liquid myrrh | Ca 5:13
(A)(B)(E)(R)
in the gardens, and to gather *l.* | Ca 6:2
is mine: he feedeth among the *l.* | Ca 6:3
an heap of wheat set about with | Ca 7:2
l.
Consider the *l.* of the field | M't 6:28
Consider the *l.* how they grow | Lu 12:27

LILY

pillars were of *l.* work in the | 1Ki 7:19
porch
the top of the pillars, was *l.* | 1Ki 7:22
work
like the flower of the *l.* (S) | 2Ch 4:5
of Sharon, and the *l.* of the | Ca 2:1
valleys
As the *l.* among thorns, so is my | Ca 2:2
he shall grow as the *l.* and cast | Ho 14:5

LIMB

danger to life and *l.* (P) | Ro 8:38

LIME

shall be as the burnings of *l.* | Isa 33:12
bones of the king of Edom into | Am 2:1
l.

LIMIT

dost thou *l.* wisdom (S) | Job 15:6
the whole *l.* thereof round | Eze 43:12
about
strength without *l.* (A)(R) | Na 3:9
l. God laid down (N)(R) | 2Co 10:13

LIMITATIONS

your natural *l.* (A)(R) | Ro 6:19
helps our *l.* (P) | Ro 8:26

LIMITED

and *l.* the Holy One of Israel | Ps 78:41

LIMITETH

he *l.* a certain day, saying to | Heb 4:7
David

LIMITLESS

l. deceit of wickedness (B) | 2Th 2:10

LIMITS

the *l.* of the Almighty (B)(R) | Job 11:7
everything has its *l.* (A)(B) | Ps 119:96

LIMPED

he *l.* upon his thigh (S) | Ge 32:31
l. about the altar (A)(R) | 1Ki 18:26

LIMPING

l. upon his thigh | Ge 32:31
(A)(B)(E)(R)
my stumbling *l.* (A)(B)(R) | Ps 35:15

LIMPS

the one who *l.* (B) | Zep 3:19

LINE

this is Jacob's *l.* (A) | Ge 37:2
shalt bind this *l.* of scarlet | Jos 2:18
thread
bound the scarlet *l.* in the | Jos 2:21
window
and measured them with a *l.* | 2Sa 8:2
and with one full *l.* to keep | 2Sa 8:2
alive
a *l.* of twelve cubits did | 1Ki 7:15
compass
a *l.* of thirty cubits did | 1Ki 7:23
compass
over Jerusalem the *l.* of | 2Ki 21:13
Samaria
a *l.* of thirty cubits did | 2Ch 4:2
compass it
who hath stretched the *l.* upon | Job 38:5
it
Their *l.* is gone out through all | Ps 19:4
divided them an inheritance | Ps 78:55
by *l.*
l. upon *l.*, *l.* upon *l.*; here a | Isa 28:10;
  | 28:13
Judgment also will I lay to | Isa 28:17
the *l.*
out upon it the *l.* of confusion | Isa 34:11
hand hath divided it unto | Isa 34:17
them by *l.*
he marketh it out with a *l.*; he | Isa 44:13
the measuring *l.* shall yet go | Jer 31:39
forth
he hath stretched out a *l.*, he | La 2:8
hath
with a *l.* of flax in his hand | Eze 40:3
man that had the *l.* in his | Eze 47:3
hand
thy land shall be divided by *l.* | Am 7:17
cast a *l.* by lot (A)(B)(E)(R) | Mic 2:5
a *l.* shall be stretched forth | Zec 1:16
upon
with a measuring *l.* in his hand | Zec 2:1
not to boast in another | 2Co 10:16
man's *l.*

LINEAGE

was of the house and *l.* of David | Lu 2:4
without *l.* (N) | Heb 7:3

LINEAGES

declared their *l.* (S) | Nu 1:18

LINED

the greater house he *l.* (S) | 2Ch 3:5

LINEN

vestures of fine *l.* | Ge 41:42
purple, scarlet, and fine *l.* | Ex 25:4;
  | 28:5; 35:6, 23, 25, 35; 38:23; 39:3

curtains of fine twined *l.*   Ex 26:1;
   26:31, 36; 27:9, 16, 18; 28:6, 8, 15; 36:8,
   35, 37; 38:9, 16, 18; 39:2, 5, 8, 24
coat of fine *l.*   Ex 28:39
mitre of fine *l.*   Ex 28:39; Le 16:4
breeches of fine *l.*   Ex 28:42;
   39:28; Le 6:10; 16:4; Eze 44:18
coats of fine *l.*   Ex 39:27; Le 16:4
bonnets of fine *l.*   Ex 39:28; Eze 44:18
girdle of fine *l.*   Ex 39:29;
   Le 16:4; Jer 13:1
priest put on *l.* garment   Le 6:10; 13:47
l. or woolen   Le 13:48;
   13:52, 59; 19:19; De 22:11
l. garments   Le 16:23;
   16:32; Es 8:13; Eze 44:17
l. ephod   1Sa 2:18;
   22:18; 2Sa 6:14; 1Ch 15:27
l. yarn of Egypt   1Ki 10:28;
   2Ch 1:16; Pr 7:16
house of them that wrought   1Ch 4:21
   in fine *l.*
robe of fine *l.*   1Ch 15:27
fine *l.* and crimson   2Ch 2:14;
   3:14
arrayed in white *l.*   2Ch 5:12
cords of fine *l.*   Es 1:6
clothing in fine *l.*   Ps 31:22
   (A)(B)(E)(R)
she maketh fine *l.*   Pr 31:24
The glasses, and fine *l.*   Isa 3:23
the *l.* wrappers (S)   Isa 3:23
clothed with fine *l.*   Eze 9:2;
   9:11; 10:2, 6-7; Da 10:5; 12:6-7
I girded thee with fine *l.*   Eze 16:10
raiment of fine *l.*   Eze 16:13
Fine *l.* with broidered work   M't 27:7;
   27:16
wrapped it in a *l.* cloth   M't 27:59;
   M'k 15:46; Lu 23:53; Joh 19:40
l. cloth cast about his body   M'k 14:51;
   14:52
was clothed in purple and fine   Lu 16:19
   l.
the *l.* clothes laid by   Lu 24:12;
   themselves   Joh 20:5-7
clothed in pure and white *l.*   De 15:6;
   19:14
pearls, and fine *l.* and purple   Re 18:12
city, that was clothed in fine *l.*   Re 18:16
that she should be arrayed in   Re 19:8
   fine *l.*
the fine *l.* is the righteousness of   Re 19:8
   saints

LINES

even with two *l.* measured   2Sa 8:2
   he to
The *l.* are fallen unto me in   Ps 16:6
   pleasant

LINGER

l., dwell awhile (A)   Ge 27:44

LINGERED

And while he *l.* the men laid   Ge 19:16
   hold
For except we had *l.* surely   Ge 43:10
   now

LINGERETH

judgment now of a long time *l.*   2Pe 2:3
   not

LINKS

l. himself with a harlot (N)   1Co 6:16
l. himself to Christ (N)   1Co 6:17

LINTEL

strike the *l.* and the two side   Ex 12:22
   posts
when he seeth the blood upon   Ex 12:23
   the *l.*
the *l.* and side posts were a   1Ki 6:31
   fifth
he said, Smite the *l.* of the door   Am 9:1

LINTELS

shall lodge in the upper *l.* of it   Zep 2:14

LINUS

and L., and Claudia, and all   2Ti 4:21

LION

Judah couched as a *l.* who shall   Ge 49:9
   rouse
Israel lay down as a *l.* as a   Nu 24:9
   great *l.*
Gad dwelleth as a *l.* and   De 33:20
   teareth
lurks as a *l.* (B)   De 33:20
carcase of *l.* bees and honey in   J'g 14:8
   carcase of *l.*
the men said, What is stronger   J'g 14:18
   than a *l.*
there came a *l.* and took a   1Sa 17:34
   lamb
whose heart is as the heart of   2Sa 17:10
   a *l.*
slew *l.* in midst of pit   2Sa 23:20;
   1Ch 11:22
a *l.* met him by way and slew   1Ki 13:24
   him, the *l.* stood by carcase
men saw the *l.* standing by   1Ki 13:25;
   the carcase   13:28
the Lord hath delivered him   1Ki 13:26
   to the *l.*
as soon as thou art departed,   1Ki 20:36
   a *l.* shall slay thee; a *l.* found
the roaring of the *l.* voice of   Job 4:10
   fierce *l.*
thou huntest me as a fierce *l.*   Job 10:16
nor the fierce *l.* passed by it   Job 28:8
wilt thou hunt the prey for   Job 38:39
   the *l.*
lest he tear my soul like a *l.*   Ps 7:2
   rending
he lieth in wait secretly as a *l.*   Ps 10:9
like a *l.* that is greedy of his   Ps 17:12
   prey
they gaped on me as a roaring   Ps 22:13
   l.
thou shalt tread on the *l.* and   Ps 91:13
   adder
the king's wrath is as the   Pr 19:12
   roaring of a *l.*
the fear of a king is as the   Pr 20:2
   roaring of a *l.*
the slothful saith, There is a *l.*   Pr 22:13
   in the way
there is a *l.* in the way, a *l.* in   Pr 26:13
   the street
but the righteous are bold as a   Pr 28:1
   l.
a *l.* which is strongest among   Pr 30:30
   beasts
a living dog is better than a   Ec 9:4
   dead *l.*
their roaring shall be like a *l.*   Isa 5:29
   shall roar
the *l.* shall eat straw like the   Isa 11:7;
   ox   65:25
he cried, A *l.* my Lord, I   Isa 21:8
   stand on watch
no *l.* shall be there, nor   Isa 35:9
   ravenous beast
as a *l.* so will he break all my   Isa 38:13
   bones
hath devoured your prophets   Jer 2:30
   like a *l.*
the *l.* is come up from his   Jer 4:7
   thicket
a *l.* out of the forest shall slay   Jer 5:6
   them
my heritage is to me as a *l.* in   Jer 12:8
   the forest
he hath forsaken his covert as   Jer 25:38
   the *l.*
he shall come up like a *l.*   Jer 49:19;
   50:44
he was to me as a *l.* in secret   La 3:10
   places
the face of a *l.* on the right   Eze 1:10
   side
and the third was the face of   Eze 10:14
   a *l.*
a conspiracy of prophets like   Eze 22:25
   a roaring *l.*
the first was like a *l.* and had   Da 7:4
   wings
for I will be to Ephraim as a *l.*   Ho 5:14
he shall roar like a *l.* when he   Ho 11:10
   shall roar
I will be to them as a *l.;* I will   Ho 13:7;
   devour as a *l.*   13:8
teeth of a *l.* cheek teeth of a   Joe 1:6
   great *l.*
will a *l.* roar when he hath no   Am 3:4
   prey
the *l.* hath roared, who will   Am 3:8
   not fear

as shepherd taketh out of the   Am 3:12
   mouth of the *l.*
the remnant of Jacob shall be   Mic 5:8
   as a *l.*
l. did tear in pieces enough for   Na 2:12
   his whelps
I was delivered out of mouth   2Ti 4:17
   of the *l.*
devil as a roaring *l.* walketh   1Pe 5:8
   about
and the first beast was like a *l.*   Re 4:7
the *l.* of the tribe of Judah hath   Re 5:5
   prevailed
cried with a loud voice, as   Re 10:3
   when a *l.* roareth
and his mouth as the mouth of   Re 13:2
   a *l.*

OLD LION

as an *old l.* who shall rouse   Ge 49:9
   him up
the *old l.* perisheth for lack of   Job 4:11
   prey
from whence come the young   Isa 30:6
   and *old l.*
where the lion, even the *old l.*   Na 2:11
   walked

YOUNG LION

and shall lift up himself as a   Nu 23:24
   young l.
behold, a *young l.* roared   J'g 14:5
   against him
as it were a *young l.* lurking in   Ps 17:12
   secret
the *young l.* shalt thou trample   Ps 91:13
   under feet
the calf and *young l.* lie down   Isa 11:6
   together
like as the *young l.* roaring on   Isa 31:4
   his prey
it became a *young l.* and   Eze 19:3;
   learned to catch   19:6
then she took another, and   Eze 19:5
   made him a *young l.*
thou art like a *young l.* of the   Eze 32:2
   nations
face of a *young l.* was   Eze 41:19
   towards the palm tree
I will be as a *young l.* to the   Ho 5:14
   house of Judah
will a *young l.* cry out of his   Am 3:4
   den, if taken
as a *young l.* among the flocks   Mic 5:8
   of sheep

LIONESS

and say, What is thy mother?   Eze 19:2
   a *l.*

LIONESSES

the lion strangled for his *l.* and   Na 2:12
   filled

LIONLIKE

slew two *l.* men of Moab   2Sa 23:20;
   1Ch 11:22

LIONS

Saul and Jonathan stronger   2Sa 1:23
   than *l.*
on the borders were *l.* beneath   1Ki 7:29
   the *l.*
he graved cherubims, *l.* and   1Ki 7:36
   palm trees
two *l.* stood beside the stays   1Ki 10:19;
   2Ch 9:18
twelve *l.* stood on the one   1Ki 10:20;
   side   2Ch 9:19
the Lord sent *l.* among them   2Ki 17:25
therefore he hath sent *l.*   2Ki 17:26
   among them
whose faces were like faces of   1Ch 12:8
   l.
Lord, rescue my darling from   Ps 35:17
   the *l.*
my soul is among *l.* I lie even   Ps 57:4
   among them
l. upon him that escapeth of   Isa 15:9
   Moab
the *l.* have driven Israel away   Jer 50:17
they shall roar together like *l.*   Jer 51:38

a lioness, she lay down among   *Eze 19:2*
l.

he went up and down among   *Eze 19:6*
the *l.*

and the *l.* had the mastery of   *Da 6:24*
them

who delivered Daniel from   *Da 6:27*
power of the *l.*

where is the dwelling of the *l.*   *Na 2:11*

her princes within are roaring   *Zep 3:3*
l.

through faith stopped   *Heb 11:33*
mouths of *l.*

their teeth were as the teeth of *l.*   *Re 9:8*

heads of the horses were as the   *Re 9:17*
heads of *l.*

YOUNG LIONS

the teeth of the *young l.* are   *Job 4:10*
broken

wilt thou fill the appetite of   *Job 38:39*
the *young l.*

young l. do lack and suffer   *Ps 34:10*
hunger

break out the great teeth of the   *Ps 58:6*
young l.

the *young l.* roar after their   *Ps 104:21*
prey

they shall roar like *young l.*   *Isa 5:29*
and lay hold

young l. roared upon him and   *Jer 2:15*
yelled

she nourished her whelps   *Eze 19:2*
among *young l.*

with all the *young l.* shall say   *Eze 38:13*
to thee

where is the feeding place of   *Na 2:11*
young l.

and the sword shall devour   *Na 2:13*
thy *young l.*

there is a voice of roaring of   *Zec 11:3*
young l.

LION'S

Judah is a *l.* whelp: from the   *Ge 49:9*
prey

of Dan he said, Dan is *l.*   *De 33:22*
whelp

the stout *l.* whelps are   *Job 4:11*
scattered

The *l.* whelps have not   *Job 28:8*
trodden it

Save me from the *l.* mouth   *Ps 22:21*

old lion, walked, and the *l.*   *Na 2:11*
whelp

LIONS'

and Hermon, from the *l.* dens   *Ca 4:8*

lions; they shall yell as *l.*   *Jer 51:38*
whelps

angel, and hath shut the *l.*   *Da 6:22*
mouths

LIP

put a covering upon his upper   *Le 13:45*
l.

give *l.* service (B)   *2Ki 18:20*

they shoot out the *l.* they shake   *Ps 22:7*

The *l.* of truth shall be   *Pr 12:19*
established

LIPS

who am of uncircumcised *l.*   *Ex 6:12;*
      6:30

or uttered ought out of her *l.*   *Nu 30:6;*
      30:8, 12

spake in her heart, only her *l.*   *1Sa 1:13*
moved

with flattering *l.* do they speak   *Ps 12:2*

the Lord shall cut off all   *Ps 12:3*
flattering *l.*

our *l.* are our own, who is lord   *Ps 12:4*
over us

prayer that goeth not out of   *Ps 17:1*
feigned *l.*

let the lying *l.* be put to silence   *Ps 31:18*

swords are in their *l.* who doth   *Ps 59:7*
hear

for the words of their *l.* let   *Ps 59:12*
them be taken

my mouth shall praise thee   *Ps 63:5*
with joyful *l.*

deliver my soul, O Lord, from   *Ps 120:2*
lying *l.*

adders' poison is under their *l.*   *Ps 140:3*

let the mischief of their own *l.*   *Ps 140:9*
cover them

and perverse *l.* put far from thee   *Pr 4:24*

l. of strange woman drop as an   *Pr 5:3*
honeycomb

with flattering of her *l.* she   *Pr 7:21*
forced him

in the *l.* of him that hath   *Pr 10:13*
understanding

he that hideth hatred with   *Pr 10:18*
lying *l.* is a fool

the *l.* of the righteous feed   *Pr 10:21*
many, but fools

the *l.* of righteous know   *Pr 10:32*
what is acceptable

lying *l.* are an abomination   *Pr 12:22*
to the Lord

but the *l.* of the wise shall   *Pr 14:3*
preserve them

when perceivest not in him   *Pr 14:7*
l. of knowledge

the talk of the *l.* tendeth   *Pr 14:23*
only to penury

the *l.* of the wise disperse   *Pr 15:7*
knowledge

a divine sentence is in the *l.*   *Pr 16:10*
of the king

righteous *l.* are the delight of   *Pr 16:13*
kings

the sweetness of the *l.*   *Pr 16:21*
increaseth learning

a wicked doer giveth heed to   *Pr 17:4*
false *l.*

much less do lying *l.* become   *Pr 17:7*
a prince

a fool's *l.* enter into contention   *Pr 18:6*

the *l.* of knowledge are a   *Pr 20:15*
precious jewel

that opens wide his *l.* (B)(E)   *Pr 20:19*

and their *l.* talk of mischief   *Pr 24:2*

burning *l.* are like a potsherd   *Pr 26:23*
covered

the *l.* of a fool will swallow   *Ec 10:12*
himself

causing the *l.* of those asleep to   *Ca 7:9*
speak

I am undone, man of unclean *l.*   *Isa 6:5*
I dwell in midst of people of
unclean *l.*

for with stammering *l.* will he   *Isa 28:11*
speak

this people with their *l.* do   *Isa 29:13*
honour me

I create the fruit of the *l.*   *Isa 57:19*
peace to him

your *l.* have spoken lies, your   *Isa 59:3*
tongue

the *l.* of those that rose against   *La 3:62*
me

ye shall not cover your *l.* nor   *Eze 24:22*
eat

ye are taken up in the *l.* of   *Eze 36:3*
talkers

so will we render the calves   *Ho 14:2*
of our *l.*

they shall cover their *l.* no   *Mic 3:7*
answer of God

the priest's *l.* should keep   *Mal 2:7*
knowledge

honoureth me with their *l.*   *M't 15:8;*
      M'k 7:6

the poison of asps is under   *Ro 3:13*
their *l.*

with other *l.* will I speak to   *1Co 14:21*
this

the fruit of our *l.* giving   *Heb 13:15*
thanks

HIS LIPS

pronouncing with *his l.* to do   *Le 5:4*
evil

in all this did not Job sin   *Job 2:10*
with *his l.*

O that God would open *his*   *Job 11:5*
l. against thee

not gone back from   *Job 23:12*
commandment of *his l.*

not withholden the request of   *Ps 21:2*
his l.

so that he spake unadvisedly   *Ps 106:33*
with *his l.*

he that refraineth *his l.* is wise   *Pr 10:19*

wicked is snared by   *Pr 12:13*
transgression of *his l.*

openeth wide *his l.* shall have   *Pr 13:3*
destruction

the heart of the wise addeth   *Pr 16:23*
learning to *his l.*

and in *his l.* there is as a   *Pr 16:27*
burning fire

moving *his l.* he bringeth evil   *Pr 16:30*
to pass

shutteth *his l.* is a man of   *Pr 17:28*
understanding

and *his l.* are the snare of his   *Pr 18:7*
soul

with the increase of *his l.* shall   *Pr 18:20*
he be filled

he that is perverse in *his l.* and   *Pr 19:1*
is a fool

with him that flattereth with   *Pr 20:19*
his l.

for grace of *his l.* the king   *Pr 22:11*
will be his friend

shall kiss *his l.* that gives a   *Pr 24:26*
right answer

he that hateth dissembleth   *Pr 26:24*
with *his l.*

his l. like lilies dropping myrrh   *Ca 5:13*

with breath of *his l.* slay   *Isa 11:4*
wicked

his l. are full of indignation   *Isa 30:27*

and iniquity was not found in   *Mal 2:6*
his l.

and *his l.* that they speak no   *1Pe 3:10*
guile

MY LIPS

hear now to the pleading of   *Job 13:6*
my l.

moving of *my l.* should   *Job 16:5*
assuage your grief

my l. shall not speak   *Job 27:4*
wickedness

I will speak, I will open *my l.*   *Job 32:20*
and answer

and *my l.* shall utter   *Job 33:3*
knowledge clearly

nor take up their names into   *Ps 16:4*
my l.

I have not refrained *my l.* O   *Ps 40:9*
Lord

open thou *my l.; my l.* shall   *Ps 51:15;*
praise thee   *63:3*

I will pay vows, which *my l.*   *Ps 66:14*
have uttered

my l. shall greatly rejoice   *Ps 71:23*
when I sing

nor alter the thing gone out of   *Ps 89:34*
my l.

with *my l.* have I declared   *Ps 119:13*
thy judgments

my l. shall utter thy praise,   *Ps 119:171*
when hast taught

O Lord, keep the door of *my l.*   *Ps 141:3*

the opening of my *l.* shall be   *Pr 8:6*
right things

wickedness is an abomination to   *Pr 8:7*
my l.

that which came out of *my l.*   *Jer 17:16*
was right

one like the sons of men   *Da 10:16*
touched *my l.*

I heard, *my l.* quivered at the   *Hab 3:16*
voice

THY LIPS

that which is gone out of *thy*   *De 23:23*
l. perform

I will put my bridle in *thy l.*   *2Ki 19:28;*
      Isa 37:29

till he fill *thy l.* with rejoicing   *Job 8:21*

yea, *thy* own *l.* testify against   *Job 15:6*
thee

by the word of *thy l.* I have   *Ps 17:4*
kept me from

keep *thy l.* from speaking guile   *Ps 34:13*

grace is poured into *thy l.*   *Job 45:2*
therefore God blessed

and that *thy l.* may keep   *Pr 5:2*
knowledge

they shall withal be fitted in   *Pr 22:18*
thy l.

rejoice when *thy l.* speak right   *Pr 23:16*
things

deceive not with *thy l.* say not,   *Pr 24:28*
I will do so

let another praise thee, and not   *Pr 27:2*
thy own *l.*

thy l. are like a thread of scarlet   *Ca 4:3*

thy l. O my spouse, drop as the   *Ca 4:11*
honeycomb

and sad, lo, this hath touched   *Isa 6:7*
thy l.

cover not *thy l.* and eat not   *Eze 24:17*
bread

LIQUIDATING

l. devil's activities (P)　　　　*1Jo 3:8*

LIQUOR

nor shall he drink any *l.* of　　*Nu 6:3*
grapes
drink no grape juice　　　　　*Nu 6:3*
(A)(B)(E)(R)
a round goblet, which wanteth　*Ca 7:2*
not *l.*
mingled wine is never missing　*Ca 7:2*
(B)(E)
never lacks mixed wine (R)　　*Ca 7:2*

LIQUORS

nor delay to offer the first of　*Ex 22:29*
thy *l.*
outflow of your grape juice　　*Ex 22:29*
(A)
offerings of grains and vines　*Ex 22:29*
(B)
offer the overflow of presses　*Ex 22:29*
(E)(R)

LISTED

done to him whatsoever *l.*　　*M't 17:12;*
　　　　　　　　　　　　　M'k 9:13
did to him as they liked　　　*M't 17:12*
(A)(P)
done to him as they pleased　*M't 17:12*
(B)(R)
did unto him whatsoever　　　*M't 17:12*
they would (E)
worked their will upon him　*M't 17:12*
(N)

LISTEN

l. to the demands (B)　　　　*J'g 20:13*
not *l.* to father's (B)　　　　*1Sa 2:25*
l. to Lord's message (B)　　　*1Sa 15:1*
l. to her words (B)　　　　　*2Sa 13:14*
did not *l.* to Lord (B)　　　*1Ki 20:36*
if you *l.* to me (B)　　　　　*2Ki 10:6*
would not *l.* (S)　　　　　　*Ne 9:30*
l. to my pleadings (B)　　　　*Job 13:6*
l. to words of my mouth (B)　*Ps 78:1*
l. O isles, unto me, and　　　*Isa 49:1*
hearken from far
ye that fear God, *l.* (S)　　　*Ac 13:16*

LISTENED

l. to their plan (B)　　　　　*1Ki 20:25*
l. to him (A)(N)(P)(R)(S)　　*Ac 15:12;*
　　　　　　　　　　　　　22:22

LISTENING

to the *l.* people (B)　　　　　*Lu 7:1*

LISTETH

the wind bloweth where it *l.*　*Joh 3:8*
wind blows where it will　　　*Joh 3:8*
(A)(E)(N)(R)
wind blows where it pleases　*Joh 3:8*
(B)
wind blows where it likes (P)　*Joh 3:8*
the ships, withersoever the　　*Jas 3:4*
governor *l.*
wherever impulse of helmsman　*Jas 3:4*
determines (A)
wherever helmsman's whim　　*Jas 3:4*
determines (B)
wherever impulse of steersman　*Jas 3:4*
willeth (E)
whatever course helmsman　　*Jas 3:4*
chooses (N)
the course chosen by the　　　*Jas 3:4*
helmsman (P)
wherever the will of the pilot　*Jas 3:4*
directs (R)

LITERALNESS

not in old relationship of *l.* (B)　*Ro 7:6*

LITIGATION

drag you into *l.* (P)　　　　　*Jas 2:6*

LITTERS

shall bring your brethren　　　*Isa 66:20*
chariots and *l.*

LITTLE

let a *l.* water, I pray you, be　*Ge 18:4*
fetched
let me drink a *l.* water of thy　*Ge 24:17*
pitcher
it was but *l.* thou hadst before　*Ge 30:30*
I came
there was but a *l.* way to　　*Ge 35:16;*
Ephrath　　　　　　　　　　*48:7*
buy us a *l.* food　　　　　　*Ge 43:2; 44:25*
l. balm, *l.* honey　　　　　　*Ge 43:11*
if the household be too *l.* for　*Ex 12:4*
the lamb
he that gathered *l.* had no　*Ex 16:18;*
lack　　　　　　　　　　　*2Co 8:15*
by *l.* and *l.* I will drive them　*Ex 23:30;*
out　　　　　　　　　　　　*De 7:22*
carry much out, and gather　*De 28:38*
but *l.* in
coast of Dan went out too *l.*　*Jos 19:47*
for them
is the iniquity of Peor too *l.*　*Jos 22:17*
for us
give me *l.* water to drink　　*J'g 4:19;*
　　　　　　　　　　　　　1Ki 17:10
that she tarried a *l.* in the house　*Ru 2:7*
his mother made him a *l.* coat　*1Sa 2:19*
because I tasted a *l.* of this　*1Sa 14:29;*
honey　　　　　　　　　　　*14:43*
when thou wast *l.* in thine　*1Sa 15:17*
own sight
had nothing, save one *l.* ewe　*2Sa 12:3*
lamb
if that had been too *l.* I would　*2Sa 12:8*
have given such
thy servant will go a *l.* way　*2Sa 19:36*
over Jordan
because the brasen altar was　*1Ki 8:64*
too *l.*
my *l.* finger thicker than　　*1Ki 12:10;*
　　　　　　　　　　　　　2Ch 10:10
and a *l.* oil in a cruse; make　*1Ki 17:12;*
a *l.* cake　　　　　　　　　*17:13*
there ariseth a *l.* cloud like a　*1Ki 18:44*
man's hand
Israel pitched like two *l.*　　*1Ki 20:27*
flocks of kids
had brought away captive a *l.*　*2Ki 5:2*
maid
Ahab served Baal a *l.* but　*2Ki 10:18*
Jehu much
for a *l.* space, give us a *l.*　*Ezr 9:8*
reviving
let not all the trouble seem *l.*　*Ne 9:32*
and my ear received a *l.*　　*Job 4:12*
thereof
cease then, that I may take　*Job 10:20*
comfort a *l.*
but how *l.* a portion is heard　*Job 26:14*
of him
suffer me a *l.* and I will shew　*Job 36:2*
thee
when his wrath is kindled but a　*Ps 2:12*
l.
made him a *l.* lower than the　*Ps 8:5;*
angels　　　　　　　　　　　*Heb 2:7*
a *l.* that a righteous man　　*Ps 37:16*
hath is better
the *l.* hills rejoice on every　*Ps 65:12*
side
there is *l.* Benjamin, with their　*Ps 68:27*
ruler
and the *l.* hills by righteousness　*Ps 72:3*
and the *l.* hills skipped like　*Ps 114:4;*
lambs　　　　　　　　　　　*114:6*
a *l.* sleep, *l.* slumber, a *l.*　*Pr 6:10;*
folding　　　　　　　　　　*24:33*
the heart of the wicked is *l.*　*Pr 10:20*
worth
better is a *l.* with the fear of　*Pr 15:16*
the Lord
better is a *l.* with righteousness,　*Pr 16:8*
than great
four things that are *l.* on the　*Pr 30:24*
earth
is sweet, whether he eat *l.* or　*Ec 5:12*
much
there was a *l.* city, and few　*Ec 9:14*
men in it
so a *l.* folly him that is in　*Ec 10:1*
reputation
take us the foxes, the *l.* foxes　*Ca 2:15*
was but a *l.* that I passed from　*Ca 3:4*
them
we have a *l.* sister, and she hath　*Ca 8:8*
no breasts
hide thyself for a *l.* moment　*Isa 26:20*
till indignation

line upon line, here a *l.* and　*Isa 28:10;*
there a *l.*　　　　　　　　　*28:13*
he taketh up the isles as a　*Isa 40:15*
very *l.* thing
in a *l.* wrath I hid my face from　*Isa 54:8*
thee
I will be to them a *l.*　　　*Eze 11:16*
sanctuary
but as if that were a very *l.*　*Eze 16:47*
thing
and sent out her *l.* rivers to　*Eze 31:4*
the trees
there came up another *l.* horn　*Da 7:8;*
　　　　　　　　　　　　　8:9
they shall be holpen with a *l.*　*Da 11:34*
help
they shall sorrow a *l.* for the　*Ho 8:10*
burden
he will smite the *l.* house with　*Am 6:11*
clefts
though *l.* among the thousands　*Mic 5:2*
of Judah
ye have sown much, and bring　*Hag 1:6*
in *l.*
ye looked for much, and, lo, it　*Hag 1:9*
came to *l.*
for I was but a *l.* displeased　*Zec 1:15*
clothe you, O ye of *l.* faith　*M't 6:30;*
　　　　　　　　　　8:26; 16:8; Lu 12:28
O thou of *l.* faith, why didst　*M't 14:31*
thou doubt
they said, Seven, and a few *l.*　*M't 15:34*
fishes
he went a *l.* further　　　　*M't 26:39;*
　　　　　　　　　　M'k 1:19; 14:35
my *l.* daughter lieth at point　*M'k 5:23*
of death
L. girl, I say unto you (S)　　*M'k 5:41*
to whom *l.* is forgiven, the　*Lu 7:47*
same loveth *l.*
fear not, *l.* flock; he was *l.* of　*Lu 12:32;*
stature　　　　　　　　　　*19:3*
thou hast been faithful in a　*Lu 19:17*
very *l.*
that every one of them may　*Joh 6:7*
take a *l.*
to put the apostles forth a *l.*　*Ac 5:34*
space
young man alive, and were　*Ac 20:12*
not a *l.* comforted
the barbarians shewed us no *l.*　*Ac 28:2*
kindness
a *l.* leaven leaveneth the lump　*1Co 5:6;*
　　　　　　　　　　　　　Ga 5:9
could bear with me a *l.* in my　*2Co 11:1*
folly
receive me, that I may boast　*2Co 11:16*
myself a *l.*
bodily exercise profiteth *l.* but　*1Ti 4:8*
godliness
use a *l.* wine for thy stomach's　*1Ti 5:23*
sake
who was made a *l.* lower than　*Heb 2:9*
the angels
tongue is a *l.* member, a *l.* fire　*Jas 3:5*
kindleth
life, a vapour that appeareth　*Jas 4:14*
for a *l.* time
thou hast a *l.* strength, and hast　*Re 3:8*
kept
rest a *l.* season; be loosed a *l.*　*Re 6:11;*
season　　　　　　　　　　*20:3*

LITTLE *ONE, ONES*

Lot said, It is a *l.* one, is it　*Ge 19:20*
not a *l.* one
all their *l.* ones took they　*Ge 34:29*
captive
we may live, both we, and　*Ge 43:8*
thou, and our *l.* ones
we have a *l.* one, and his　*Ge 44:20*
brother is dead
take wagons out of Egypt　*Ge 45:19*
for your *l.* ones
carried their *l.* ones; food for　*Ge 46:5;*
your *l.* ones　　　　　　　　*17:24*
only their *l.* ones left they in　*Ge 50:8*
Goshen
fear not, I will nourish you　*Ge 50:21*
and your *l.* ones
I will let you go and your *l.*　*Ex 10:10;*
ones　　　　　　　　　　　*10:24*
but your *l.* ones, them will I　*Nu 14:31*
bring
took women of Midian　　　*Nu 31:9*
captives and *l.* ones
therefore kill every male　*Nu 31:17*
among the *l.* ones
we will build cities for our *l.*　*Nu 32:16*
ones

our *l.* ones shall dwell in the   *Nu 32:17;*
fenced cities   *32:26*
we destroyed men, women, and   *De 2:34*
l. ones
but the women and *l.* ones   *De 20:14*
take to thyself
Joshua read before the women   *Jos 8:35*
and *l.* ones
so they put the *l.* ones before   *J'g 18:21*
them
Ittai passed over and all the   *2Sa 15:22*
l. ones
Judah stood before Lord and   *2Ch 20:13*
l. ones
and to the genealogy of all   *2Ch 31:18*
their *l.* ones
to seek a right way for our *l.*   *Ezr 8:21*
ones
to cause to perish *l.* ones and   *Es 8:11*
women
they send forth their *l.* ones   *Job 21:11*
like a flock
that dasheth thy *l.* ones against   *Ps 137:9*
the stones
a *l.* one shall become a   *Isa 60:22*
thousand
their nobles sent their *l.* ones   *Jer 14:3*
to the pit
her *l.* ones have caused a cry   *Jer 48:4*
to be heard
and I will turn my hand on   *Zec 13:7*
the *l.* ones
give to drink to one of these   *M't 10:42*
l. ones
who should offend one of   *M't 18:6;*
these *l.* ones   *M'k 9:42*
take heed that ye despise not   *M't 18:10*
one of these *l.* ones
that one of these *l.* ones   *M't 18:14*
should perish
than that he offend one of   *Lu 17:2*
these *l.* ones

LITTLE *WHILE*

they are exalted for a *l.* while   *Job 24:24*
but are gone
yet a *l.* while and the wicked   *Ps 37:10*
shall not be
yet a *l.* while and the   *Isa 10:25*
indignation shall cease
is it not yet a very *l.* while,   *Isa 29:17*
and Lebanon
thy people have possessed it   *Isa 63:18*
but a *l.* while
yet a *l.* while and her harvest   *Jer 51:33*
shall come
yet a *l.* while and I will avenge   *Ho 1:4*
the blood
a *l.* while and I will shake the   *Hag 2:6*
heavens
and after a *l.* while another   *Lu 22:58*
saw him
yet a *l.* while and I am with   *Joh 7:33;*
you   *13:33*
yet a *l.* while is the light with   *Joh 12:35*
you, walk
a *l.* while, and the world seeth   *Joh 14:19*
me no more
again a *l.* while, and ye shall   *Joh 16:16;*
see me; a *l.* while and ye   *16:17, 19*
shall not see me
a *l.* while; we cannot tell   *Joh 16:18*
what he saith
for yet a *l.* while, and he   *Heb 10:37*
that shall come

LITTLE-FAITHS

you *l.* (P)   *M't 6:30;*
   8:26; 14:31; Lu 12:28

LIVE

lest he take of tree of life, and   *Ge 3:22*
l. for ever
and my soul shall *l.* because   *Ge 12:13*
of thee
l. on borders of kinsman   *Ge 16:12*
(A)(B)
l. in my presence (B)   *Ge 17:1*
O that Ishmael might *l.*   *Ge 17:18*
before thee
O let me escape, and my soul   *Ge 19:20*
shall *l.*
he shall pray for thee, and   *Ge 20:7*
thou shalt *l.*
by sword shalt thou *l.* and   *Ge 27:40*
serve thy brethren
and findest thy goods, let him   *Ge 31:32*
not *l.*

Joseph said, This do, and *l.* for   *Ge 42:18*
I fear God
I am Joseph, doth my father   *Ge 45:3*
yet *l.*
if it be a daughter, then she   *Ex 1:16*
shall *l.*
for there shall no man see me   *Ex 33:20*
and *l.*
there be *l.* raw flesh (S)   *Le 13:10; 13:24*
he shall *l.* alone (A)   *Le 13:46*
which if a man do, he shall *l.*   *Le 18:5;*
in them   *Ne 9:29; Eze 20:11, 13, 21*
l. in (B)   *Le 23:42; 2Ki 4:13; 17:27*
when he looketh upon serpent,   *Nu 21:8*
shall *l.*
alas, who shall *l.* when God   *Nu 24:23*
doeth this
may fear me all the days they   *De 4:10*
shall *l.*
did ever people hear, as thou   *De 4:33*
hast, and *l.*
but by every word of the Lord   *De 8:3*
doth man *l.*
all the days that ye *l.* on the   *De 12:1*
earth
he shall flee to one of these   *De 19:5*
cities and *l.*
learn to fear Lord as long as   *De 31:13;*
ye *l.*   *1Ki 8:40*
let Reuben *l.* and not die, men   *De 33:6*
not be few
only Rahab harlot shall *l.* and   *Jos 6:17*
her house
perhaps you *l.* among us   *Jos 9:7*
(A)(B)
Joshua made a league with   *Jos 9:15*
them to let them *l.*
we will let them *l.* lest wrath   *Jos 9:20;*
be on us   *9:21*
to *l.* awhile (B)   *Ru 1:1;*
   Jer 42:22; 44:12
not only while I *l.* shew me   *1Sa 20:14*
kindness
l. thou and thy children of the   *2Ki 4:7*
rest
if they save us alive, we shall *l.*   *2Ki 7:4*
walk in thy ways so long as   *2Ch 6:31*
they *l.*
if a man die, shall he *l.*   *Job 14:14*
again? all days
wherefore do the wicked *l.*   *Job 21:7*
become old
praise Lord, your heart shall *l.*   *Ps 22:26*
for ever
he should still *l.* and not see   *Ps 49:9*
corruption
will I bless thee while I *l.*: lift   *Ps 63:4*
up hands
live (B)   *Ps 65:8;*
84:10; 107:36; Pr 21:19; Isa 11:6; 13:21;
16:4; 40:22; 49:20; Jer 40:5, 10;
Ho 12:9; 14:7; Mic 4:10; 7·14; Zec 9:6
God makes the lonely to *l.* (B)   *Ps 68:6*
your hearts shall *l.* that seek   *Ps 69:32*
God
he shall *l.*; I shall not die, but   *Ps 72:15;*
l.   *118:17*
give me understanding, and I   *Ps 119:144*
shall *l.*
let my soul *l.* and it shall   *Ps 119:175*
praise thee
while I *l.* will I prise the Lord   *Ps 146:2*
keep my commandments, and *l.*   *Pr 4:4;*
   7:2
forsake foolish and *l.*   *Pr 9:6*
but he that hateth gifts shall *l.*   *Pr 15:27*
if a man *l.* many years   *Ec 6:3; 6:6; 11:8*
madness is in their heart while   *Ec 9:3*
they *l.*
l. joyfully with the wife whom   *Ec 9:9*
thou lovest
a seraphim, having a *l.* coal in   *Isa 6:6*
hand
thy dead men shall *l.* together   *Isa 26:19*
by these things men *l.* make   *Isa 38:16*
me to *l.*
come to me, hear, and your soul   *Isa 55:3*
shall *l.*
to Chaldeans shall *l.*   *Jer 21:9;*
   27:12, 17; 38.2. 17
obey, I pray thee, and thy   *Jer 38:20*
soul shall *l.*
under his shadow we shall *l.*   *La 4:20*
he shall surely *l.*   *Eze 3:21;*
   18:9, 17; 33:13, 15·16
I said, When thou wast in thy   *Eze 16:6*
blood, *l.*
kept my statutes shall *l.*   *Eze 18:19;*
   18:21-22; 20:11, 25

shall he *l.*; turn yourselves   *Eze 18:24;*
and *l.*   *18:32; 33:11*
if our sins be on us, how   *Eze 33:10*
should we then *l.*
do that which is lawful and   *Eze 33:19*
right, he shall *l.*
he said, Son of man, can these   *Eze 37:3*
bones *l.*
cause breath to enter you,   *Eze 37:5;*
and ye shall *l.*   *37:6, 14*
every thing which liveth and   *Eze 47:9*
moveth shall *l.* everything shall *l.*
l. in agreement with (B)   *Da 9:10*
he will revive us, we shall *l.* in   *Ho 6:2*
his sight
saith Lord, Seek me, and ye   *Am 5:4;*
shall *l.*   *5:6*
it is better for me to die than   *Jon 4:3;*
to *l.*   *4:8*
l. alone in the forest (B)   *Mic 7:14*
just shall *l.* by his faith   *Hab 2:4;*
   Ro 1:17
they shall *l.* with their children   *Zec 10:9*
lay hand on her, and she shall   *M't 9:18;*
l.   *M'k 5:23*
enter and *l.* there (B)   *M't 12:45*
they which *l.* delicately are in   *Lu 7:25*
courts
he said to him, This do, and   *Lu 10:28*
thou shalt *l.*
he is not God of dead, for all   *Lu 20:38*
l. unto him
dead hear voice of the Son of   *Joh 5:25*
God, and *l.*
as I *l.* by Father, so he that   *Joh 6:57*
eateth me, even he shall *l.* by me
believeth, tho' he were dead,   *Joh 11:25*
yet shall he *l.*
l. in darkness (A)   *Joh 12:46*
because I *l.*, ye shall *l.* also   *Joh 14:19*
for in him we *l.* and move   *Ac 17:28*
for it is not fit that he should   *Ac 22:22*
l.
l. by himself (A)(B)(P)   *Ac 28:16*
that are dead to sin, *l.* any   *Ro 6:2*
longer therein
we believe that we shall also *l.*   *Ro 6:8*
with him
make mortal bodies *l.* (B)   *Ro 8:11*
we are debtors, not to *l.* after   *Ro 8:12*
the flesh
l. on level of instincts (P)   *Ro 8:12*
if *l.* after the flesh, ye shall die,   *Ro 8:13*
if thro' Spirit mortify deeds of
body, ye shall *l.*
doeth these things shall *l.* by   *Ro 10:5;*
them   *Ga 3:12*
if possible, *l.* peaceably with   *Ro 12:18*
all men
whether we *l.* we *l.* to the   *Ro 14:8*
Lord: whether we *l.* or die
consents to *l.* with him   *1Co 7:12*
(A)(N)(P)(R)
they *l.* of the things of the   *1Co 9:13*
temple
they who preach gospel   *1Co 9:14*
should *l.* of gospel
for we which *l.* are delivered   *2Co 4:11*
to death
as dying, and behold, we *l.* as   *2Co 6:9*
chastened
ye are in our hearts to die, and   *2Co 7:3*
l. with you
we shall *l.* with him by the   *2Co 13:4*
power of God
brethren, be of one mind, *l.*   *2Co 13:11*
in peace
why compellest the Gentiles to   *Ga 2:14*
l. as Jews
dead to the law, that I might   *Ga 2:19*
l. unto God
I *l.* yet not I, the life I now *l.*   *Ga 2:20*
in flesh, I *l.* by faith of
the just shall *l.* by faith   *Ga 3:11;*
   Heb 10:38
if we *l.* in Spirit, let us walk in   *Ga 5:25*
Spirit
l. up to your calling (N)   *Eph 4:1*
no longer *l.* like Gentiles (R)   *Eph 4:17;*
M'k 7:5; Ph'p 3:17-18; Col 2:6; 1Th 4:1;
   2Th 3:11
l. with sense of responsibility   *Eph 5:15*
(P)
for me to *l.* is Christ, and to   *Ph'p 1:21*
die is gain
if I *l.* in the flesh, this is the   *Ph'p 1:22*
fruit of my labour
how to *l.* simply, relish plenty   *Ph'p 4:12*
(B)

l. worthy of the Lord (B)   *Col 1:10*
l. lives in union with him   *Col 2:6*
  (B)(N)
l. lives worthy of God   *1Th 2:12*
  (N)(P)
for now we *l.* if ye stand fast in *1Th 3:8*
  Lord
died, that we should *l.*   . *1Th 5:10*
  together with him
if dead, we shall also *l.* with *2Ti 2:11*
  him
all that will *l.* godly shall suffer *2Ti 3:12*
  persecution
teaching us that we should *l.*   *Tit 2:12*
  soberly
be in subjection to Father of *Heb 12:9*
  spirits and *l.*
in all things willing to *l.*   *Heb 13:18*
  honestly
if the Lord will we shall *l.* and *Jas 4:15*
  do this
that we should *l.* to   *1Pe 2:24*
  righteousness
that he should no longer *l.* in *1Pe 4:2*
  the flesh
but *l.* according to God in the *1Pe.4:6*
  Spirit
an ensample to those that *l.*   *2Pe 2:6*
  ungodly
those that escaped from them *2Pe 2:18*
  who *l.* in error
sent his Son, that we might *l.* *1Jo 4:9*
  thro' him
God does actually *l.* in us (P) *1Jo 4:12*
you who *l.* in heaven (P)   *Re 12:12*
beast which had the wound   *Re 13:14*
  and did *l.*
he will *l.* among them (A)(P) *Re 21:3*

AS I LIVE

as truly *as I l.* earth shall be *Nu 14:21;*
  filled   *14:28*
so long *as I l.*   *Job 27:6;*
   Ps 104:33; 116:2
as I l. saith the Lord   *Isa 49:18;*
Jer 22:24; Eze 5:11; 14:16, 18, 20; 16:48;
17:16, 19; 18:3; 20:3, 33; 33:11, 27; 34:8;
      35:6, 11; Zep 2:9; Ro 14:11
as I l. saith the king, surely as *Jer 46:18*
  Tabor

MAY, MIGHT, MAYEST LIVE

that we *may l.* and not die   *Ge 42:2;*
   43:8; 47:19
relieve him that he *may l.* with *Le 25:35*
  thee
take no usury, that thy   *Le 25:36*
  brother *may l.*
but thus do to them that they *Nu 4:19*
  may l.
do to them, ye *may l.*   *De 4:1;*
   5:33; 8:1; 30:6, 16
that fleeing to one of these   *De 4:42*
  cities he *might l.*
what is just follow, that thou *De 16:20*
  may l.
choose life, that thou and thy *De 30:19*
  seed *may l.*
gracious to me, that the child *2Sa 12:22*
  may l.
to a land of bread, that you *2Ki 18:32*
  may l.
hold out the sceptre, that he *Es 4:11*
  may l.
deal bountifully, that I *may l.* *Ps 119:17*
let thy mercies come to me, *Ps 119:77*
  that I *may l.*
uphold me according to thy *Ps 119:116*
  word, that I *may l.*
dwell in tents, that ye *may l.* *Jer 35:7*
  many days
breathe on these slain, that *Eze 37:9*
  they *may l.*
seek good, and not evil, that *Am 5:14*
  ye *may l.*
and thou *mayest l.* long on the *Eph 6:3*
  earth

NOT LIVE

that touch the mountain shall *Ex 19:13*
  not l.
thou shalt *not* suffer a witch *Ex 22:18*
  to *l.*
man doth *not l.* by bread only, *De 8:3;*
but by word of Lord   *M't 4:4; Lu 4:4*
for I was sure that he could *2Sa 1:10*
  not l.

whosoever is wanting he   *2Ki 10:19*
  shall *not l.*
set house in order, thou shalt *2Ki 20:1;*
  not l.   *Isa 38:1*
I loathe it, I would *not l.*   *Job 7:16*
  always
wicked shall *not l.* half their *Ps 55:23*
  days
they are dead, they shall *not l.* *Isa 26:14*
to save the souls that should *Eze 13:19*
  not l.
shall he then live? he shall *Eze 18:13*
  not l.
shall say to him, Thou shalt *Zec 13:3*
  not l.
cast out children, that they   *Ac 7:19*
  might *not l.*
crying, that he ought *not* to *l.* *Ac 25:24*
  any longer
yet vengeance suffereth *not* to *Ac 28:4*
  l.
they should *not l.* to   *2Co 5:15*
  themselves, but

LIVED

l. as a stranger (B)   *Ge 21:34*
from Isaac his son, while he   *Ge 25:6*
  yet *l.*
Jacob *l.* in the land of Egypt *Ge 47:28*
  seventeen years
you *l.* in Egypt (B)   *Le 18:3;*
   Nu 31:10; Jer 39:14
but Joshua and Caleb *l.* still *Nu 14:38*
when he beheld the serpent of *Nu 21:9*
  brass he *l.*
that heard the voice of God   *De 5:26*
  and *l.*
l. beyond the river (A)(B)(E) *Jos 24:2*
if Absalom had *l.* and we had *2Sa 19:6*
  died
old men that stood before   *1Ki 12:6;*
  Solomon while he yet *l.*   *2Ch 10:6*
Amaziah *l.* after death of   *2Ki 14:17;*
  Jehoash fifteen years   *2Ch 25:25*
while he *l.* he blessed his soul *Ps 49:18*
breath came into them, and   *Eze 37:10*
  they *l.*
had *l.* with a husband seven *Lu 2:36*
  years
l. in luxury (A)(B)(N)(P)(R) *Lu 7:25*
l. among us (P)   *Joh 1:14*
l. as strangers in Egypt (B) *Ac 13:17*
Jews who *l.* there (B)(P)(R) *Ac 22:12*
I have *l.* in all good conscience *Ac 23:1*
  before God
after sect of our religion I *l.* a *Ac 26:5*
  Pharisee
Paul *l.* there two years   *Ac 28:30*
  (A)(R)
once *l.* (A)(E)(R)   *Eph 2:3*
walked sometime, when ye *l.* in *Col 3:7*
  them
he *l.* around in (B)   *Heb 11:7*
ye have *l.* in pleasure on the *Jas 5:5*
  earth
l. in licence and debauchery *1Pe 4:3*
  (N)
how much she hath *l.*   *Re 18:7;*
  deliciously   *18:9*
they *l.* with Christ; rest *l.* not *Re 20:4;*
  again   *20:5*

LIVELY

because the Hebrew women are *Ex 1:19*
  l.
l. themselves (B)   *Nu 23:9*
my enemies are *l.* and are   *Ps 38:19*
  strong
who received *l.* oracles to give *Ac 7:38*
  to us
hath begotten us again to a *l.* *1Pe 1:3*
  hope
as *l.* stones, are built a spiritual *1Pe 2:5*
  house

LIVER

the heart and *l.* (B)   *Ex 12:9*
caul above the *l.*   *Ex 29:13;*
29:22; Le 3:4, 10, 15; 4:9; 7:4; 8:16, 25;
      9:10, 19
till a dart strike through his *l.* *Pr 7:23*
my *l.* is poured upon the earth *La 2:11*
he consulted, he looked in   *Eze 21:21*
  the *l.*

LIVES

your blood of your *l.* will I   *Ge 9:5*
  require

to save your *l.* by a great   *Ge 45:7*
  deliverance
thou hast saved our *l.* let us *Ge 47:25*
  find grace
made their *l.* bitter with   *Ex 1:14*
  bondage
own *l.* (R)   *Nu 16:38;*
1Sa 25:29; Ps 72:18; 97:10; Pr 14:25;
   Eze 14:14, 20; 22:25, 27; Lu 21:19
and deliver our *l.* from death *Jos 2:13*
therefore we were sore afraid *Jos 9:24*
  of our *l.*
were a people that jeoparded *J'g 5:18*
  their *l.*
lose thy life with *l.* of thy   *J'g 18:25*
  household
Saul and Jonathan lovely in *2Sa 1:23*
  their *l.*
who saved *l.* of thy sons, wives *2Sa 19:5*
went in jeopardy of their *l.* *2Sa 23:17;*
   1Ch 11:19
defend their *l.* (S)   *Es 8:11*
Jews gathered and stood for *Es 9:16*
  their *l.*
devout and dedicated *l.* (N) *Job 3:11*
our *l.* are bowed down (A) *Ps 44:25*
they lurk privily for their own *l.* *Pr 1:18*
fall by them which seek their *Jer 19:7;*
  l.   *46:26*
they that seek their *l.* shall *Jer 19:9*
  straiten them
save your *l.* be like heath in *Jer 48:6*
  wilderness
we gat our bread with peril of *La 5:9*
  our *l.*
their *l.* were prolonged for a *Da 7:12*
  season
Son of man is not come to   *Lu 9:56*
  destroy men's *l.*
l. continually in me (A)(P) *Joh 14:10*
he *l.* with you (A)   *Joh 14:17*
men that have hazarded their *Ac 15:26*
  l. for our
this voyage will be with   *Ac 27:10*
  damage of our *l.*
in which God himself *l.* (P) *Eph 2:22*
live *l.* in union with him   *Col 2:6*
  (B)(N)
live *l.* worthy of God (N)(P) *1Th 2:12*
holy in every department of *1Pe 1:15*
  your *l.* (P)
by godly *l.* of wives (A)   *1Pe 3:1*
to lay down our *l.* for the *1Jo 3:16*
  brethren
love God *l.* in him (P)   *1Jo 3:17*
they loved not their *l.* to the *Re 12:11*
  death

LIVEST

forsake not the Levite as long *De 12:19*
  as thou *l.*
if thou being a Jew *l.* after the *Ga 2:14*
  manner
hast a name that thou *l.* and art *Re 3:1*
  dead

LIVETH

every thing *l.* shall be meat for *Ge 9:3*
  you
God doth talk with man, and *De 5:24*
  he *l.*
have lent him to the Lord as *1Sa 1:28*
  long as he *l.*
as long as son of Jesse *l.* on *1Sa 20:31*
  ground
thus shall say to him that *l.* in *1Sa 25:6*
  prosperity
as God *l.* unless thou hadst *2Sa 2:27*
  spoken
as my lord the king *l.* surely *2Sa 15:21*
the Lord *l.* blessed be my *2Sa 22:47;*
  rock   *Ps 18:46*
one saith, This is my son that *1Ki 3:23*
and Elijah said, See thy son *l.* *1Ki 17:23*
for I know that my   *Job 19:25*
  Redeemer *l.*
as God *l.* who hath taken away *Job 27:2*
  my judgment
what man that *l.* and shall not *Ps 89:48*
  see death
thou shalt swear, the Lord *l.* in *Jer 4:2*
  truth
they say, The Lord *l.* they swear *Jer 5:2*
  falsely
to swear by my name, Lord *l.* *Jer 12:16*
  as they
no more be said, The Lord *l.* *Jer 16:14;*
   16:15; 23:7-8

in the land of Egypt, saying, *Jer 44:26*
The Lord *l.*
every thing that *l.* and moveth *Eze 47:9*
shall live
nor go ye up, nor swear, the *Ho 4:15*
Lord *l.*
that swear, thy God, O Dan, *l. Am 8:14*
and the manner of Beer-sheba.
Jesus said, Go thy way, thy *Joh 4:50;*
son *l.* *4:51, 53*
whosoever *l.* and believeth in *Joh 11:26*
me never die
but in that he *l.* he *l.* to God *Ro 6:10*
law hath dominion over man as *Ro 7:1;*
long as he *l.* *7:2*
so if while her husband *l.* she be' *Ro 7:3*
married
for none of us *l.* or dieth to *Ro 14:7*
himself
wife is bound as long as her *1Co 7:39*
husband *l.*
yet he *l.* by the power of God *2Co 13:4*
I live, yet not I, but Christ *l.* in *Ga 2:20*
me
that *l.* in pleasure is dead while *1Ti 5:6*
she *l.*
of whom it is witnessed that he *Heb 7:8*
l.
he ever *l.* to make *Heb 7:25*
intercession for them
testament is of no strength *Heb 9:1*
while testator *l.*
I am he that *l.* and was dead *Re 1:18*

AS THE LORD LIVETH

as the Lord *l.* if ye saved them *J'g 8:19*
alive
I will do the part of kinsman, *Ru 3:13*
as the Lord *l.*
for *as the Lord l.* tho' it be in *1Sa 14:39*
Jonathan
as the Lord *l.* *1Sa 14:45;*
19:6; 20:21; 25:26; 26:10, 16; 28:10; 29:6
2Sa 4:9; 12:5; 14:11; 1Ki 1:29
as the Lord *l.* there is but a *1Sa 20:3*
step between me
as the Lord God of Israel *l.* *1Sa 25:34*
who kept me
as the Lord *l.* and as my lord *2Sa 15:21*
the king liveth
as the Lord *l.* *1Ki 2:24;*
2Ki 5:20; 2Ch 18:13; Jer 38:16
as the Lord God of Israel *l.* *1Ki 17:1;*
18:15
as the Lord thy God *l. 1Ki 17:12; 18:10*
as Lord *l.* and thy soul liveth *2Ki 2:2;*
4:6; 4:30
as Lord of hosts *l.* before *2Ki 3:14;*
whom I stand *5:16*

AS THY SOUL LIVETH

as thy soul *l.* I am woman who *1Sa 1:26*
stood praying
Abner said, *As thy soul l.* O *1Sa 17:55*
king, I cannot tell
as thy soul *l.* there is but one *1Sa 20:3*
step between me and death
as thy soul *l.* seeing Lord *1Sa 25:26*
hath withholden thee
as thy soul *l.* I will not do *2Sa 11:11*
this thing
as thy soul *l.* none can turn to *2Sa 14:19*
right or left hand
as thy soul *l.* I will not leave *2Ki 2:2*
thee, so they went

LIVING

have dominion over every *l.* *Ge 1:28*
thing
man became a *l.* soul; Eve, *Ge 2:7;*
mother of all *l.* *3:20*
and of every *l.* thing of all *Ge 6:19*
flesh, two
and every *l.* substance I will *Ge 7:4*
destroy
and every *l.* substance was *Ge 7:23*
destroyed
God remembered Noah and *Ge 8:1*
every *l.* thing
I will not smite any more every *Ge 8:21*
thing *l.*
among whom I am *l.* (B) *Ge 24:3*
of any *l.* thing which is in the *Le 11:10*
water
as for the *l.* bird he shall take *Le 14:6;*
14:6, 7, 53

not make abominable by any *l. Le 20:25*
thing
he stood between the dead *Nu 16:48*
and the *l.*
your *l.* (A)(R) *J'g 17:10*
l. temporarily in (A)(B) *J'g 19:1*
hath not left off his kindness to *Ru 2:20*
the *l.*
they were shut up *l.* in *2Sa 20:3*
widowhood
the *l.* is my son, the dead thy *1Ki 3:22;*
3:23
divide the *l.* children in two, *1Ki 3:25*
and give half to one
whose the *l.* child was, give *1Ki 3:26*
her the *l.* child
then the king said, Give her *1Ki 3:27*
the *l.* child
old prophet *l.* (B) *1Ki 13:11*
in whose hand is soul of *Job 12:10*
every *l.* thing
nor is it found in the land of *Job 28:13*
the *l.*
seeing it is hid from the eyes *Job 28:21*
of all *l.*
and to the house appointed *Job 30:23*
for all *l.*
to be enlightened with light *Job 33:30*
of *l.*
to see goodness of Lord in *Ps 27:13*
land of *l.*
and root thee out of the land of *Ps 52:5*
the *l.*
that I may walk in the light of *Ps 56:13*
the *l.*
shall take them away both *l. Ps 58:9*
and in wrath
let them be blotted out of *Ps 69:28*
book of *l.*
walk before the Lord in the *Ps 116:9*
land of the *l.*
thou art my portion in the *Ps 142:5*
land of the *l.*
in thy sight shall no man *l.* be *Ps 143:2*
justified
thou satisfiest the desire of *Ps 145:16*
every *l.* thing
dead, more than the *l.* which *Ec 4:2*
are alive
I considered all the *l.* under the *Ec 4:15*
sun
poor, that knoweth to walk *Ec 6:8*
before the *l.*
end of all men, and the *l.* will *Ec 7:2*
lay it to heart
that is joined to all the *l.* a *l. Ec 9:4*
dog is better
for the *l.* know that they shall *Ec 9:5*
die, but dead
a well of *l.* water, streams from *Ca 4:15*
Lebanon
that is written among *l.* in *Isa 4:3*
Jerusalem
l. among (B) *Isa 6:5; Jer 29:32*
seek to their God for the *l.* to *Isa 8:19*
the dead
not see the Lord in the land *Isa 38:11*
of the *l.*
the *l.* the *l.* he shall praise *Isa 38:19*
thee, as I do
he was cut off out of the land *Isa 53:8*
of the *l.*
forsaken fountain of *l.* waters *Jer 2:13;*
17:13
let us cut him off from the *Jer 11:19*
land of the *l.*
wherefore doth a *l.* man *La 3:39*
complain
I shall set glory in the land of *Eze 26:20*
the *l.*
all slain, which caused *Eze 32:23;*
terror in land of *l.* *32:24-27, 32*
any wisdom that I have more *Da 2:30*
than any *l.*
to the intent that the *l.* may *Da 4:17*
know
l. waters shall go out from *Zec 14:8*
Jerusalem
deserves his *l.* (A) *M't 10:10*
God is not the God of the *M't 22:32;*
dead, but of the *l.* *M'k 12:27; Lu 20:38*
no *l.* thing survive (N) *M't 24:22*
she cast in all she had, even *M'k 12:44*
all her *l.*
woman had spent all her *l.* on *Lu 8:43*
physicians
and he divided unto them his *Lu 15:12*
l.
there wasted his substance *Lu 15:13;*
with riotous *l.* *15:30*

enjoyed luxurious *l.* (B) *Lu 16:19*
why seek ye the *l.* among the *Lu 24:5*
dead
he would have given thee *l. Joh 4:10*
water
from whence hast thou that *l. Joh 4:11*
water
I am the *l.* bread which came *Joh 6:51*
down from
as the *l.* Father hath sent me, *Joh 6:57*
and I live
out of his belly flow rivers of *Joh 7:38*
l. water
received the *l.* Word *Ac 7:38*
(B)(N)(P)(S)
the *l.* and the dead *Ac 10:42;*
(A)(B)(E)(N)(P)(R)(S) *1Pe 4:5*
l. as aliens in Egypt (N) *Ac 13:17*
l. by same sort of faith (P) *Ro 4:12*
ye present your bodies a *l. Ro 12:1*
sacrifice
he might be Lord both of dead *Ro 14:9*
and *l.*
enjoys *l.* with him (B) *1Co 7:12*
first man Adam was made a *1Co 15:45*
l. soul
in *l.* men and women (P) *2Co 3:3*
give up *l.* like pagans (N) *Eph 4:17*
old way of *l.* (P) *Eph 4:22*
l. in love (N)(P) *Eph 5:2*
l. like children of light (B)(P) *Eph 5:8*
l. in the world, are ye subject *Col 2:20*
to ordinances
loose *l.* and lawbreaking (P) *Tit 1:6*
l. in malice, envy, and hating *Tit 3:3*
one another
boldness to enter by a new *Heb 10:20*
and *l.* way
by his noble *l.* show (A) *Jas 3:13*
unto a *l.* hope (S) *1Pe 1:3*
manner of *l.* (A)(E) *1Pe 1:15*
futile way of *l.* (P)(R) *1Pe 1:18*
to whom coming as to a *l. 1Pe 2:4*
stone, chosen
l. in shameless, insolent *1Pe 4:3*
wantonness (A)
l. in licentiousness, passions *1Pe 4:3*
(R)
in all holy *l.* (S) *2Pe 3:11*
guarantee of *l.* with him (P) *1Jo 4:13*
l. creatures (S) *Re 4:6;*
4:7-9; 5:6, 8, 11, 14; 6:1, 3, 5-7; 7:11;
14:3; 15:7; 19:4
the Lamb shall lead them to *l. Re 7:17*
fountains
and every *l.* soul died in the sea *Re 16:3*

LIZARD

kinds of great *l.* (A)(E)(R) *Le 11:29*
the *l.* snail, and mole unclean *Le 11:30*
to you

LO

l. Sarah thy wife shall have a *Ge 18:10*
son
l. it is yet high day, water ye *Ge 29:7*
the sheep
l. I die; *l.* I come in a cloud *Ge 50:5;*
Ex 19:9
l. we be here, and will go up *Nu 14:40*
to place
l. the Lord hath kept thee *Nu 24:11*
from honour
I did but taste honey, and *l.* I *1Sa 14:43*
must die
I have sinned and done *2Sa 24:17*
wickedly
if I speak of strength, *l.* he is *Job 9:19*
strong
he passed away, and *l.* he was *Ps 37:36*
not
l. I come *Ps 40:7*
l. the man that made not God *Ps 52:7*
his strength
l. they that are far from thee *Ps 73:27*
shall perish
l. thine enemies, for *l.* thine *Ps 92:9*
enemies perish
we heard it at Ephratah *Ps 132:6*
l. this only have I found, that *Ec 7:29*
God made
l. the winter is past, the rain is *Ca 2:11*
over
l. this is our God, we have *Isa 25:9*
waited for him
the earth, and *l.* it was without *Jer 4:23*
form

I beheld, and *l.* there was no *Jer 4:25*
man, birds fled
l. certainly in vain made he it *Jer 8:8*
for *l.* I begin to bring evil on *Jer 25:29*
the city
when *l.* he had given him his *Eze 17:18*
hand
for *l.* it cometh; *l.* it will *Eze 30:9;*
come *33:33*
for *l.* they are gone, because of *Ho 9:6*
destruction
that *l.* the days shall come upon *Am 4:2*
you
ye looked for much, and *l.* it *Hag 1:9*
came to little
and *l.* the heavens were *M't 3:16*
opened
l. here is Christ, or there, *M't 24:23*
believe it not
l. I have told you; *l.* I am *M't 28:7;*
with you *28:20*
Satan bound, *l.* these eighteen *Lu 13:16*
years
l. nothing worthy of death is *Lu 23:15*
done to him
unworthy, *l.* we turn to the *Ac 13:46*
Gentiles
l. I come to do thy will, O *Heb 10:7;*
God *10:9*

LOAD

l. your beasts (S) *Ge 45:17; Lu 11:46*

LOADED

they *l.* their asses (S) *Ge 42:26;*
44:13; 45:23
when our oxen are well *l.* *Ps 144:14*
(A)
return *l.* with loot (B) *Da 11:28*

LOADEN

on the cattle your carriages *Isa 46:1*
were heavy *l.*

LOADETH

Lord, who daily *l.* us with *Ps 68:19*
benefits

LOADING

and *l.* asses (S) *Ne 13:15*

LOAF

one *l.* of bread, one cake of *Ex 29:23*
oiled bread
David dealt to every one a *l.* *1Ch 16:3*
of bread
neither had they more than *M'k 8:14*
one *l.*
the whole *l.* is holy (P) *Ro 11:16*

LO-AMMI

call his name L. for ye are not *Ho 1:9*
my people

LOAN

for the *l.* which is lent to the *1Sa 2:20*
Lord

LOATHE

Egyptians shall *l.* to drink of *Ex 7:18*
my soul *l.* you (B) *Le 26:30*
detest and *l.* it (B) *De 7:26*
I *l.* it; I would not live alway *Job 7:16*
makes him *l.* food (A)(R) *Job 33:20*
does not *l.* evil (B) *Ps 36:4*
l. the covenant (A) *Ps 89:39*
I *l.* that generation (R) *Ps 95:10*
shall *l.* themselves for the evils *Eze 6:9*
l. yourselves in your own *Eze 20:43*
sight for *Eze 36:31*
you *l.* idolatry (P) *Ro 2:22*

LOATHED

he *l.* Israel (B) *1Ki 11:25*
hath thy soul *l.* Zion? why *Jer 14:19*
which *l.* their husbands and *Eze 16:45*
my soul *l.* them, and their soul *Zec 11:8*
they *l.* me (A)(B)(E) *Zec 11:8*

LOATHETH

our soul *l.* this light bread *Nu 21:5*
The full soul *l.* an honeycomb *Pr 27:7*
l. her husband and her *Eze 16:45*
children

LOATHING

l. her ways (A) *Ps 78:59*
an object of *l.* (B) *Ps 88:8*
open field, to the *l.* of thy *Eze 16:5*
person
l. evil (N) *Ro 12:9*
l. clothing polluted (B)(N) *Jude 23*

LOATHSOME

repulsive, *l.* (B) *Le 7:18*
it is *l.* (A) *Le 19:7*
nostrils, and it shall be *l.* to *Nu 11:20*
you
as *l.* meat (B)(E)(R)(S) *Job 6:7*
my skin is broken, become *l.* *Job 7:5*
l. and foul (B) *Job 15:16*
wound *l.* and corrupt (A)(E) *Ps 38:5*
loins filled with *l.* disease *Ps 38:7*
detestable and *l.* (A) *Pr 8:7*
a wicked man is *l.* and cometh *Pr 13:5*
to
l. impurities (B) *Eze 5:11*
made *l.* images (B) *Eze 7:20*
l., abominable impurities (B) *Eze 11:18*
l., destestable things (A) *Eze 20:30;*
Ho 9:10
detestable and *l.* (A) *Tit 1:16*
dungeon of *l.* spirit (A) *Re 18:2*
l., malignant ulcers (B)(P) *Re 21:3*

LOAVES

take ten *l.* and run to the *1Sa 17:17*
camp
Abigail made haste and took *1Sa 25:18*
200 *l.*
take with thee ten *l.* and *1Ki 14:3*
cracknels
a man brought the man of *2Ki 4:42*
God twenty *l.*
they say, We have here but *M't 14:17*
five *l.*
and he took the five *l.* *M't 14:19;*
M'k 6:38; Lu 9:13
said, How many *l.* have ye *M't 15:34;*
M'k 6:38; 8:5
he took the seven *l.* and the *M't 15:36;*
fishes *M'k 8:6*
nor remember the five *l.* of the *M't 16:9*
5000
nor the seven *l.* of the 4000 *M't 16:10*
they that did eat of the *l.* *M'k 6:44*
were 5000
they considered not the *M'k 6:52*
miracle of the *l.*
say to him, Friend, lend me *Lu 11:5*
three *l.*
a lad here who hath five barley *Joh 6:9*
l.
Jesus took the *l.* and *Joh 6:11*
distributed to the disciples
with the fragments of the five *Joh 6:13*
barley *l.*
because ye did eat of the *l.* *Joh 6:26*
and were filled

WAVE LOAVES

shall bring two *wave l.* of two *Le 23:17*
tenth deals

LOCK

dropping myrrh on the handles *Ca 5:5*
of the *l.*
handles of the bolt (A)(E)(R) *Ca 5:5*
handles of the bar (B) *Ca 5:5*
and he took me by a *l.* of my *Eze 8:3*
head

LOCKED

Ehud shut the doors and *l.* *J'g 3:23*
them
behold, the doors of the *J'g 3:24*
parlour were *l.*

LOCKS

let the *l.* of the hair of his head *Nu 6:5*
grow
if thou weavest the seven *l.* of *J'g 16:13*
my head
she caused him to shave off *J'g 16:19*
the seven *l.*
set up doors, and *l.* thereof *Ne 3:3;*
3:6, 13-15
l. up the stars (B) *Job 9:7*
thou hast doves' eyes within thy *Ca 4:1*
l.

like a piece of pomegranate *Ca 4:3*
within thy *l.*
my *l.* are filled with the drops *Ca 5:2*
of the night
his *l.* are bushy, and black as a *Ca 5:11*
raven
a pomegranate are thy temples *Ca 6:7*
within thy *l.*
uncover thy *l.* make bare the *Isa 47:2*
leg
nor suffer their *l.* to grow *Eze 44:20*
long

LOCUST

there remained not one *l.* in *Ex 10:19*
all Egypt
l. after his kind, and bald *l.* ye *Le 11:22*
may eat
all thy trees shall the *l.* *De 28:42*
consume
if there be in the land *l.* *1Ki 8:37;*
2Ch 6:28
leap like a *l.* (A)(B)(E)(R) *Job 39:20*
he gave also their labour to *Ps 78:46*
the *l.*
I am tossed up and down as *Ps 109:23*
the *l.*
hath he *l.* eaten, and that which *Joe 1:4*
l. left
hopping *l.* eaten (A)(B)(R) *Joe 1:4*
I will restore the years that the *Joe 2:25*
l. hath eaten
the crawling *l.* (A) *Joe 2:25*

LOCUSTS

behold, to-morrow I will bring *Ex 10:4*
l.
stretch out thy hand over *Ex 10:12*
Egypt for the *l.*
in the morning the east wind *Ex 10:13*
brought the *l.*
no such *l.*; the west wind *Ex 10:14;*
took away the *l.* *10:19*
for the *l.* shall consume it *De 28:38*
if I command the *l.* to devour *2Ch 7:13*
he spake, and *l.* came, and *Ps 105:34*
caterpillars
the *l.* have no king, ye go by *Pr 30:27*
bands
as the running to and fro of *l.* *Isa 33:4*
shall be run
more numerous than *l.* *Jer 46:23*
(A)(B)(E)(R)
licking *l.* (A)(B)(R) *Joe 3:15*
the *l.* are eating (B)(R) *Am 4:9*
make thyself many as the *l.* *Na 3:15*
thy crowned are as the *l.* and *Na 3:17*
thy captains
his meat was *l.* and wild honey *M't 3:4;*
M'k 1:6
there came out of the smoke *l.* *Re 9:3*
on the earth
shapes of *l.* were like to horses *Re 9:7*
for battle

LOD

Shamed, who built Ono and *1Ch 8:12*
L.
The children of L. *Ezr 2:33; Ne 7:37*
L. and Ono, the valley of *Ne 11:35*
craftsmen

LO-DEBAR

son of Ammiel in L. *2Sa 9:4; 9:5; 17:27*

LODGE

is there room in the house for *Ge 24:23*
us to *l.* in
we have provender enough, *Ge 24:25*
and room to *l.* in
he said to him, L. here this *Nu 22:8*
night
spend the night here (B) *Nu 22:8;*
Jos 4:3
in the place where ye shall *l.* *Jos 4:3*
this night
l. here, that thy heart may be *J'g 19:9*
merry
please stay all night (B) *J'g 19:9*
tarry all night (R) *J'g 19:9*
to *l.* in Gibeah or in Ramah *J'g 19:13;*
19:15; 20:4
spend the night (A)(B)(R) *J'g 19:13*
the old man said, Only *l.* not *J'g 19:20*
in the street
do not stay in the street (B) *J'g 19:20*

do not spend the night in the   *J'g 19:20*
square (R)
where thou lodgest I will *l.*   *Ru 1:16*
thy father will not *l.* with the   *2Sa 17:8*
people
not going to stop with the   *2Sa 17:8*
people (B)
will not spend night with   *2Sa 17:8*
people (R)
l. not this night in the plains   *2Sa 17:16*
of the wilderness
spend the night at the desert   *2Sa 17:16*
fords (B)
the stranger did not *l.* in the   *2Sa 31:32*
street
let every one *l.* within   *Ne 4:22*
Jerusalem
I said, Why *l.* ye about the   *Ne 13:21*
wall
they cause the naked to *l.*   *Job 24:7*
without clothing
pass the night naked   *Job 24:7*
(A)(B)(E)(R)
I *l.* near Mesech (B)   *Ps 120:5*
come, my beloved, let us *l.* in   *Ca 7:11*
the villages
in the forest in Arabia shall   *Isa 21:13*
ye *l.*
and *l.* in monuments, and eat   *Isa 65:4*
swine's flesh
how long shall vain thoughts *l.*   *Jer 4:14*
in thee
the beasts shall *l.* in the upper   *Zep 2:14*
lintels
so that birds of air come   *M't 13:32;*
and *l.* in the branches thereof   *M'k 4:32*
come and find shelter (A)   *M't 13:32*
come and roost in its   *M't 13:32*
branches (B)(N)
come and nest in its branches   *M't 13:32*
(P)
make nests in its branches   *M't 13:32*
(R)
brought Mnason with whom   *Ac 21:16*
we should *l.*
we were to be entertained (B)   *Ac 21:16*
allowed to *l.* alone (N)(R)   *Ac 28:16*
with whom we were going to   *Ac 21:16*
stay (P)

LODGED

Jacob *l.* there that same night   *Ge 31:13*
and himself *l.* that night in   *Ge 32:21*
the company
the spies came into an harlot's   *Jos 2:1*
house, and *l.*
they encamped (B)   *Jos 2:1*
and lay there (E)   *Jos 2:1*
to Jordan, he and all Israel, and   *Jos 3:1*
l. there
they encamped (B)   *Jos 3:1*
carried them over to the place   *Jos 4:8*
where they *l.*
bringing them to the camp (B)   *Jos 4:8;*
  6:11
they came into the camp, and   *Jos 6:11*
l. in the camp
but Joshua *l.* that night among   *Jos 8:9*
the people
spent the night with the troops   *Jos 8:9*
(B)(R)
came to house of Micah, they   *J'g 18:2*
l. there
so they did eat and drink, and   *J'g 19:4*
l. there
spent the nights there (B)   *J'g 19:4; 19:7*
urged him, therefore he *l.* there   *J'g 19:7*
again
came into a cave, and *l.* there   *1Ki 19:9*
they *l.* round about the house   *1Ch 9:27*
of God
the merchants *l.* without   *Ne 13:20*
Jerusalem
righteousness *l.* in it, but now   *Isa 1:21*
murderers
he went to Bethany and *l.*   *M't 21:17*
there
asked whether Simon were *l.*   *Ac 10:18*
there
then called he them in, and *l.*   *Ac 10:23*
them
Publius *l.* us three days   *Ac 28:7*
courteously
if they have *l.* strangers, if she   *1Ti 5:10*
washed
practiced hospitality   *1Ti 5:10*
(A)(B)(E)(N)(R)

LODGER

l. in her house (B)   *Ex 3:22*

LODGERS

l. and tenants (B)   *Le 25:23*

LODGES

l. in shadow of almighty (B)   *Ps 91:1*
sin that *l.* in me (N)   *Ro 7:17; 7:18*

LODGEST

Ruth said, Where thou *l.* I will   *Ru 1:16*
lodge

LODGETH

he *l.* with one Simon a tanner   *Ac 10:6*

LODGING

twelve stones, and leave them in   *Jos 4:3*
the *l.*
place them in the camp (B)   *Jos 4:3*
no man took them to his   *J'g 19:15*
house to *l.*
they have taken up their *l.* at   *Isa 10:29*
Geba
make Geba their camping   *Isa 10:29*
place (A)
stay overnight in Geba (B)   *Isa 10:29*
that I had in the wilderness a *l.*   *Jer 9:2*
place
birds have their *l.* places (A)   *M't 8:20*
there came many to him unto   *Ac 28:23*
his *l.*
but withal prepare me also a *l.*   *Ph'm 22*
love of God *l.* in him (B)   *1Jo 3:17*

LODGINGS

I will enter into the *l.* of his   *2Ki 19:23*
borders

LOFT

he took him and carried him   *1Ki 17:19*
into a *l.*
Eutychus fell down from the   *Ac 20:9*
third *l.*

LOFTILY

oppression: they speak *l.*   *Ps 73:8*

LOFTINESS

the *l.* of man shall be bowed   *Isa 2:17*
down
haughtiness of man (B)   *Isa 2:17*
we heard the pride of Moab,   *Jer 48:29*
his *l.*

LOFTY

heart is not haughty, nor mine   *Ps 131:1*
eyes *l.*
nor my eyes disdainful (B)   *Ps 131:1*
my eyes are not raised too   *Ps 131:1*
high (R)
my *l.* stronghold (B)   *Ps 144:2*
a generation, O how *l.* are their   *Pr 30:13*
eyes
eyes lifted and eyelids raised   *Pr 30:13*
(B)
the *l.* looks of man shall be   *Isa 2:11;*
humbled   *5:15*
the proud looks of man   *Isa 2:11*
(A)(B)
the haughty looks of man (R)   *Isa 2:11*
the day of the Lord be on   *Isa 2:12*
every one that is *l.*
against all haughty and proud   *Isa 2:12*
(A)(B)
the *l.* city he layeth low to the   *Isa 26:5*
ground
on a *l.* mountain hast thou set   *Isa 57:7*
thy bed
thus saith the high and *l.*   *Isa 57:15*
One, that inhabiteth
a *l.* mountain height   *Eze 17:22*
(B)(E)(R)
l. words of eloquence (A)(R)   *1Co 2:1*

LOG

mingled with oil, and one *l.*   *Le 14:10;*
of oil   *14:12, 15, 21, 24*

LOGICIAN

logician (B)   *1Co 1:20*

LOINS

and kings shall come out of   *Ge 35:11*
thy *l.*
and Jacob put sackcloth upon   *Ge 37:34*
his *l.*
the souls which came out of   *Ge 46:26;*
his *l.*   *Ex 1:5*
ye shall eat it, with your *l.*   *Ex 12:11*
girded
your waist belted (B)   *Ex 12:11*
breeches reach from the *l.*   *Ex 28:42*
unto the thighs
from waist to thigh (A)(B)   *Ex 28:42*
on them at the *l.* (A)(B)(E)(R)   *Le 3:4*
smite through the *l.* of them   *De 33:11*
that rise
a girdle with a sword fastened   *2Sa 20:8*
on his *l.*
fastened around his hips (A)   *2Sa 20:8*
fastened on his waist (B)   *2Sa 20:8*
put the blood in the girdle   *1Ki 2:5*
around his *l.*
son shall come forth of thy *l.*   *1Ki 8:19*
thicker than my father's *l.*   *1Ki 12:10;*
  2Ch 10:10
Elijah girded up his *l.* and   *1Ki 18:46*
ran before Ahab
let us, I pray, put sackcloth   *1Ki 20:31*
on our *l.*
so they girded sackcloth on   *1Ki 20:32*
their *l.* and ropes
hairy man, and girt with girdle   *2Ki 1:8;*
of leather about *l.*   *M't 3:4; M'k 1:6*
gird up thy *l.*   *2Ki 4:29*
  9:1; Job 38:3; 40:7; Jer 1:17
he girdeth the *l.* of kings with   *Job 12:18*
a girdle
layers of fat on *l.*   *Job 15:27*
(A)(B)(E)(R)
if his *l.* have not blessed me   *Job 31:20*
lo, now his strength is in his   *Job 40:16*
l.
my *l.* are filled with a   *Ps 38:7*
loathsome disease
thou laidst affliction upon our   *Ps 66:11*
l.
laid heavy burden on our hips   *Ps 66:11*
(B)
and make their *l.* continually   *Ps 69:23*
to shake
she girdeth her *l.* with strength   *Pr 31:17*
neither shall the girdle of their   *Isa 5:27*
l. be loosed
righteousness shall be the   *Isa 11:5*
girdle of his *l.*
girdle of his waist   *Isa 11:5*
(A)(B)(E)(R)
loose the sackcloth from off   *Isa 20:2*
thy *l.* put off
therefore are my *l.* filled with   *Isa 21:3*
pain
make bare, gird sackcloth   *Isa 32:11*
upon your *l.*
I will loose the *l.* of kings to   *Isa 45:1*
open before
get a linen girdle and put it   *Jer 13:1*
upon thy *l.*
as the girdle cleaveth to the *l.*   *Jer 13:11*
of a man
see every man with his hands   *Jer 30:6*
on his *l.*
and upon the *l.* shall be   *Jer 48:37*
sackcloth
from the appearance of his *l.*   *Eze 1:27*
upward
from his *l.* downward, fire;   *Eze 8:2*
from his *l.* upward
sigh with the breaking of thy   *Eze 21:6*
l. and bitterness
girded with girdles upon   *Eze 23:15*
their *l.*
thou madest all their *l.* to be   *Eze 29:7*
at a stand
they shall have linen breeches   *Eze 44:18*
their *l.*
he measured, the waters were   *Eze 47:4*
to the *l.*
so the joints of his *l.* were   *Da 5:6*
loosed
whose *l.* were girded with fine   *Da 10:5*
gold of Uphaz
I will bring sackcloth on your *l.*   *Am 8:10*
make thy *l.* strong; pain is in   *Na 2:1;*
all *l.*   *2:10*

let your *l.* be girded about,   *Lu 12:35*
and lights
that of his *l.* he would raise up   *Ac 2:30*
Christ
having our *l.* girt about with   *Eph 6:14*
truth
belt of truth tightened about   *Eph 6:14*
waist (B)
buckle on the belt of truth   *Eph 6:14*
(N)
with truth as your belt (P)   *Eph 6:14*
tho' they came out of the *l.* of   *Heb 7:5*
Abraham
for he was yet in the *l.* of his   *Heb 7:10*
Father
wherefore gird up the *l.*   *1Pe 1:13*
of your mind
bracing up your minds   *1Pe 1:13*
(A)(B)(P)
men stripped for action,   *1Pe 1:13*
perfectly controlled (N)
gird up your minds, be sober   *1Pe 1:13*
(R)

LOIS

which dwelt in thy grandmother   *2Ti 1:5*
L.

LONELY

l. self (B)   *Ps 22:20*
God makes the *l.* to live (B)   *Ps 68:6*
how *l.* sits the city (R)(S)   *La 1:1*
went to a *l.* spot (B)(N)(R)   *M'k 1:35*

LONG

God who fed me all my life *l.*   *Ge 48:15*
to this day
when the trumpet soundeth *l.*   *Ex 19:13;*
                                19:19
that thy days may be *l.* on the   *Ex 20:12*
land
when the cloud tarried *l.* on   *Nu 9:19*
tabernacle
ye dwelt *l.* enough in this   *De 1:6;*
mount   *2:3*
and shalt have remained *l.*   *De 4:25*
in the land
and if the way be too *l.* for   *De 14:24*
thee
and overtake him, because the   *De 19:6*
way is *l.*
make great plagues and of *l.*   *De 28:59*
continuance
when they make a *l.* blast with   *Jos 6:5*
the horn
are old, by reason of the very   *Jos 9:13*
l. journey
ye dwelt in the wilderness a *l.*   *Jos 24:7*
season
there was *l.* war between house   *2Sa 3:1*
of Saul
and hast not asked *l.* life   *1Ki 3:11;*
                          2Ch 1:11
for a *l.* season Israel was   *2Ch 15:3*
without God
which *l.* for death, but cometh   *Job 3:21*
not
God grant me thing that I *l.* for   *Job 6:8*
with *l.* life will I satisfy him   *Ps 91:16*
forty years *l.* was I grieved   *Ps 95:10*
with this generation
my soul *l.* dwelt with him that   *Ps 120:6*
hateth peace
the plowers made *l.* their   *Ps 129:3*
furrows
to dwell, as those that have   *Ps 143:3*
been *l.* dead
and *l.* life shall they add to thee   *Pr 3:2*
the good man is gone a *l.*   *Pr 7:19*
journey
they that tarry *l.* at the wine,   *Pr 23:30*
that go
by *l.* forbearing is a prince   *Pr 25:15*
persuaded
because man goeth to his *l.*   *Ec 12:5*
home
my elect shall *l.* enjoy work of   *Isa 65:22*
their hands
this captivity is *l.* build ye   *Jer 29:28*
houses
shall women eat their children   *La 2:20*
of span *l.*
a great eagle *l.* winged, full of   *Eze 17:3*
feathers
his branches became *l.*   *Eze 31:5*
because of waters
nor shave, nor suffer their   *Eze 44:20*
locks to grow *l.*

but the time appointed was *l.*   *Da 10:1*
not stay *l.* in the place of   *Ho 13:13*
breaking forth
repented *l.* ago in sackcloth   *M't 11:21*
and ashes
devour widows' houses, for   *M't 23:14;*
pretence make *l.* prayers   *M'k 12:40;*
                          Lu 20:47
professing that you pray *l.*   *M't 23:14*
(B)
who go in *l.* clothing   *M'k 12:38;*
                          Lu 20:46
sitting clothed in a *l.* white   *M'k 16:5*
garment
avenge, though he bear *l.* with   *Lu 18:7*
them
for he was desirous to see him   *Lu 23:8*
of a *l.* season
your *l.* heralded Christ (P)   *Ac 3:20*
as Paul was *l.* preaching, he   *Ac 20:9*
sunk with
not *l.* after there arose a   *Ac 27:14*
tempest Euroclydon
after *l.* abstinence Paul stood   *Ac 27:21*
in midst of
I *l.* to see you, that I may   *Ro 1:11*
impart
if a man have *l.* hair, it is a   *1Co 11:14*
shame
if a woman have *l.* hair, it is   *1Co 11:15*
a glory to her
by their prayer which I *l.*   *2Co 9:14*
after
that thou mayest live *l.* on the   *Eph 6:3*
earth
how greatly I *l.* after you all   *Ph'p 1:8*
if I tarry *l.* that thou mayest   *1Ti 3:15*
know
the husbandman hath *l.*   *Jas 5:7*
patience for it

LONG TIME

when he had been there a *l.*   *Ge 26:8*
time
and we have dwelt in Egypt a   *Nu 20:15*
l. time
when thou shalt besiege a city   *De 20:19*
a *l. time*
Joshua made war a *l. time*   *Jos 11:18*
with kings
a *l. time* after that Joshua   *Jos 23:1*
waxed old
while the ark abode the *time*   *1Sa 7:2*
was *l.*
as a woman that had *l. time*   *2Sa 14:2*
mourned
for they had not done it of a   *2Ch 30:5*
l. time
I have *l. time* holden my   *Isa 42:14*
peace, been still
forget us, and forsake us so *l.*   *La 5:20*
time
after *l. time* the lord of   *M't 25:19;*
those servants cometh   *Lu 20:9*
a certain man which had devils   *Lu 8:27*
l. time
a man went into a far country   *Lu 20:9*
for a *l. time.*
knew that he had been a *l. time*   *Joh 5:6*
in that case
have I been so *l. time* with   *Joh 14:9*
you, and yet
because of *l. time* he had   *Ac 8:11*
bewitched them
l. time abode they with the   *Ac 14:3;*
disciples   *14:28*
whose judgment of *l. time*   *2Pe 2:3*
lingereth not

LONG WHILE

he talked a *l. while* till break   *Ac 20:11*
of day

AS LONG AS

as *l. as* she is put apart for   *Le 18:19*
uncleanness
enjoy sabbaths, as *l. as* it   *Le 26:34;*
lieth desolate   *26:35*
as *l. as* the cloud abode, they   *Nu 9:18*
rested
forsake not the Levite as *l. as*   *De 12:19*
thou livest
fear the Lord as *l. as* you live   *De 31:13*
in the land
lent to the Lord, as *l. as* he   *1Sa 1:28*
liveth
as *l. as* son of Jesse liveth on   *1Sa 20:31*
the ground

any thing as *l. as* we were   *1Sa 25:15*
conversant
as *l. as* he sought the Lord he   *2Ch 26:5*
prospered
as *l. as* she lay desolate she   *2Ch 36:21*
kept sabbath
fear thee as *l. as* sun and moon   *Ps 72:5*
endure
his name shall be continued as   *Ps 72:17*
l. as the sun
I will sing to the Lord as *l. as*   *Ps 104:33*
I live
I will call upon him as *l. as* I   *Ps 116:2*
live
as *l. as* they, and as broad as   *Eze 42:11*
they
as *l. as* bridegroom is with   *M't 9:15;*
them   *M'k 2:19*
as *l. as* I am in the world, I am   *Joh 9:5*
the light
dominion over a man as *l. as* he   *Ro 7:1*
liveth
wife is bound as *l. as* her   *1Co 7:39*
husband liveth
the heir, as *l. as* he is a child,   *Ga 4:1*
differeth not
whose daughters ye are as *l. as*   *1Pe 3:6*
ye do well
as *l. as* I am in this tabernacle   *2Pe 1:13*

SO LONG

why is his chariot *so l.* in   *J'g 5:28*
coming
what found in thy servant, so   *1Sa 29:8*
l. as I have
so *l.* as the whoredoms of thy   *2Ki 9:22*
mother
they may fear thee *so l.* as   *2Ch 6:31*
they live
so *l.* as I see Mordecai sitting   *Es 5:13*
at the gate
shall not reproach me *so l.* as   *Job 27:6*
I live
peace *so l.* as the moon   *Ps 72:7*
endureth
and marvelled that he tarried   *Lu 1:21*
so l.
bound to her husband *so l.* as   *Ro 7:2*
he liveth
to-day, after *so l.* a time, as it   *Heb 4:7*
is said

LONGED

David *l.* to go forth unto   *2Sa 13:39*
Absalom
David *l.* and said, O that   *2Sa 23:15;*
one   *1Ch 11:17*
behold, I have *l.* after thy   *Ps 119:40*
precepts
for I *l.* for thy   *Ps 119:131*
commandments
I have *l.* for thy salvation, O   *Ps 119:174*
Lord
l. to see (A)(B)   *Lu 10:24*
for he *l.* after you all; and *l.*   *Ph'p 2:26;*
for   *4:1*

LONGEDST

thou sore *l.* after thy father's   *Ge 31:30*
house

LONGER

when she could no *l.* hide him   *Ex 2:3*
I will let you go, and ye shall   *Ex 9:28*
stay no *l.*
could not any *l.* stand before   *J'g 2:14*
enemies
my mouth no *l.* silent (A)   *1Sa 2:1*
he tarried *l.* than the set time   *2Sa 20:5*
should I wait for the Lord any   *2Ki 6:33*
l.
the measure thereof is *l.* than   *Job 11:9*
the earth
so that the Lord could no *l.*   *Jer 44:22*
bear
no *l.* be admonished (S)   *Ec 4:13;*
                          La 4:16
for thou mayest be no *l.*   *Lu 16:2*
steward
Paul could bear it no *l.* (N)   *Ac 16:18*
when they desired him to   *Ac 18:20*
tarry *l.*
Paul discoursed *l.* (E)   *Ac 20:9*
Paul's address became *l.* and *l.*   *Ac 20:9*
(P)
crying, that he ought not to   *Ac 25:24*
live any *l.*

that are dead to sin, live any *l.*   Ro 6:2
therein
no *l.* under lower nature (N)   Ro 8:4
we are no *l.* under a   Ga 3:25
schoolmaster
when we could no *l.* forbear   1Th 3:1;
                                               3:5
drink no *l.* water, but use a   1Ti 5:23
little wine
that he no *l.* live the rest of his   1Pe 4:2
time
that there should be time no *l.*   Re 10:6

LONGETH

my son Shechem *l.* for your   Ge 34:8
daughter
because thy soul *l.* to eat flesh   De 12:20
my flesh *l.* for thee in a dry   Ps 63:1
land
my soul *l.* for the courts of the   Ps 84:2
Lord

LONG-HAIRED

l. heads of the enemy (S)   De 32:42

LONGING

thine eyes shall fail with *l.* for   De 28:32
them
for he satisfieth the *l.* soul   Ps 107:9
my soul breaketh for the *l.*   Ps 119:20
that it hath
l. to stuff himself (P)   Lu 15:16
waits with eager *l.* (R)   Ro 8:19
you are *l.* for us   2Co 7:7
(B)(E)(N)(R)
l. to see thee (E)(N)(P)(R)   2Ti 1:4

LONGINGS

praying in agonizing *l.* (P)   Ro 8:26

LONGS

l. for the shade (A)(R)   Job 7:2
as the heart *l.* for flowing   Ps 38:10
streams (R)
l. earnestly for God's sons (A)   Ro 8:19

LONGSUFFERING

Lord God merciful and   Ex 34:6;
gracious, *l.*   Nu 14:18; Ps 86:15;
                                          2Pe 3:9
O Lord take me not away in   Jer 15:15
thy *l.*
or despisest thou riches of his   Ro 2:4
l.
endured with much *l.* vessels   Ro 9:22
of wrath
by knowledge, by *l.* by kindness   2Co 6:6
fruit of the Spirit is love, *l.*   Ga 5:22
with *l.*, forbearing one another   Eph 4:2
strengthened to all *l.* with   Col 1:11
joyfulness
put on, as elect of God,   Col 3:12
meekness, *l.*
that in me Christ might shew   1Ti 1:16
all *l.*
thou hast fully known my   2Ti 3:10
faith, *l.*
rebuke, exhort with all *l.* and   2Ti 4:2
doctrine
when *l.* of God waited in days   1Pe 3:20
the *l.* of our Lord is salvation   2Pe 3:15

LONGWINGED

eagle with great wings, *l.*   Eze 17:3

LOOK

l. from the place where thou   Ge 13:14
art
l. towards heaven, and tell the   Ge 15:5
stars
escape for thy life, *l.* not   Ge 19:17
behind thee
wherefore *l.* ye so sadly to-day   Ge 40:7
now let Pharaoh *l.* out a man   Ge 41:33
discreet
Jacob said Why *l.* ye one upon   Ge 42:1
another
l. to it; for evil is before you   Ex 10:10
and their faces shall *l.* one to   Ex 25:20
another
l. that thou make them after   Ex 25:40
their pattern
then the priest shall *l.* if the   Le 13:39
spots

if the priest shall *l.* and   Le 13:53;
behold   13:56
then the priest shall *l.* if the   Le 14:3;
plague   14:39, 44
l. no to the stubbornness of   De 9:27
this people
thine eyes shall *l.* and fail   De 28:32
with longing
David was ruddy, and goodly   1Sa 16:12
to *l.* to
l. how brethren fare, and   1Sa 17:18
take pledge
go up now, *l.* toward the sea   1Ki 18:43
I would not *l.* toward thee,   2Ki 3:14
nor see
l. when messenger cometh,   2Ki 6:32
shut the door
l. out there, Jehu, and go in,   2Ki 9:2
make him rise
l. even out best and meetest of   2Ki 10:3
master's sons
l. there be none of the   2Ki 10:23
servants of the Lord
come, let us *l.* one another in   2Ki 14:8
the face
the God of our fathers *l.*   1Ch 12:17
thereon
let us *l.* one another in the   2Ch 25:17
face (S)
l. upon with contempt (S)   Es 1:17
let it *l.* for light, but have none   Job 3:9
How long wilt thou not *l.*   Job 7:19
away (S)
therefore shall no man *l.* for   Job 20:21
his goods
l. to heavens and see, and   Job 35:5
behold the clouds
I will direct my prayer to thee,   Ps 5:3
and *l.* up
iniquities so that I am not   Ps 40:12
able to *l.* up
l. with grudging envy   Ps 68:16
(A)(E)(R)
that hath a high *l.* I will not   Ps 101:5
suffer
l. to thee (R)   Ps 104:27; 123:2; 145:15
as the eyes of servants *l.* to   Ps 123:2
their masters
l. to the Lord (A)(E)   Ps 123:2
let thine eyes *l.* right on,   Pr 4:25
and eyelids
Lord hateth a proud *l.*   Pr 6:17
a high *l.* and proud heart   Pr 21:4
to know thy flocks, and *l.* well   Pr 27:23
to thy herds
that *l.* out at the windows be   Ec 12:3
darkened
l. from top of Amana, Shenir,   Ca 4:8
Hermon
if one *l.* unto the land, behold   Isa 5:30
darkness
I will wait on the Lord, I will   Isa 8:17
l. for him
shall curse their king and God,   Isa 8:21
and *l.* upward
they shall *l.* unto earth, and   Isa 8:22
behold trouble
at that day shall a man *l.* to   Isa 17:7
his Maker
he shall not *l.* to the altars,   Isa 17:8
work of his hands
l. away from me, I will weep   Isa 22:4
bitterly
thou didst *l.* in that day to the   Isa 22:8
armour
they *l.* not to the Holy One of   Isa 31:1
Israel
hear, ye deaf, *l.* ye blind, that   Isa 42:18
ye may see
l. unto me, and be saved, all   Isa 45:22
ends of earth
l. to the rock whence ye are   Isa 51:1
hewn
l. to Abraham your father, and   Isa 51:2
to Sarah
they all *l.* to their own way   Isa 56:11
for gain
l. for the light (R)   Isa 59:9
we *l.* for judgment, but there is   Isa 59:11
none
but to this man will I *l.* that is   Isa 66:2
poor
and while ye *l.* for light, he   Jer 13:16
turn it
take and *l.* well to him, do   Jer 39:12
him no harm
come with me, and I will *l.*   Jer 40:4
well to thee
their mighty ones are fled, and   Jer 46:5
l. not back

the fathers shall not *l.* back to   Jer 47:3
their children
all of them princes to *l.* us to   Eze 23:15
Babylon
iniquity to remembrance   Eze 29:16
when they *l.*
whose *l.* was more stout than   Da 7:20
his
who *l.* to other gods, and love   Ho 3:1
wine
I will *l.* again towards thy holy   Jon 2:4
temple
therefore will I *l.* to the Lord,   Mic 7:7
will wait
stand, stand, but none shall *l.*   Na 2:8
back
make their *l.* unsightly (B)   M't 6:16
or do we *l.* for another   M'k 11:3;
                                  Lu 7:19-20
put hands on eyes, and made   M'k 8:25
him *l.* up
when these things begin, then   Lu 21:28
l. up
search and *l.* for out of   Joh 7:52
Galilee no prophet
l. ye out seven men of honest   Ac 6:3
report
if it be a question of words, *l.*   Ac 18:15
ye to it
I *l.* for him with the brethren   1Co 16:11
Israel could not stedfastly *l.*   2Co 3:13
to the end
while we *l.* at things which   2Co 4:18
are seen
from whence we *l.* for the   Ph'p 3:20
Saviour
to them that *l.* for him shall   Heb 9:28
he appear
which the angels desire to *l.*   1Pe 1:12
into
nevertheless we *l.* for new   2Pe 3:13
heavens
seeing ye *l.* for such things, be   2Pe 3:14
diligent that
l. to yourselves, that we lose not   2Jo 8
and no man was able to *l.*   Re 5:3
thereon
found worthy to read the book,   Re 5:4
nor *l.* thereon

LOOK *DOWN*

l. down from thy holy   De 26:15
habitation
l. down, behold, and visit this   Ps 80:14
vine
righteousness shall *l. down*   Ps 85:11
from heaven
l. down from heaven, and   Isa 63:15
behold from
till Lord *l. down*, and behold   La 3:50
from heaven

LOOK *ON, UPON*

bow shall be in cloud, and I   Ge 9:16
will *l. upon* it
I know thou art a fair woman   Ge 12:11
to *l. upon*
Rebekah was very fair to *l.*   Ge 24:16;
upon   26:7
Moses was afraid to *l. upon*   Ex 3:6
God
the Lord *l. upon* you, and   Ex 5:21
judge, because
and Moses did *l. upon* all the   Ex 39:43
work
priest shall *l.* on the plague   Le 13:3;
       13:21, 25-26, 31-32, 34, 43, 50
the priest shall *l. upon* it, and   Le 14:48
                                 13:5-6, 27, 36
the priest shall *l. upon* it, and   Le 14:48
behold
for a fringe, that ye may *l.*   Nu 15:39
upon it
Gideon said, L. on me, and   J'g 7:17
do likewise
if thou wilt indeed *l.* on the   1Sa 1:11
affliction
l. not *on* his countenance or   1Sa 16:7
stature
shouldest *l. upon* such a dead   2Sa 9:8
dog as I am
the woman was very beautiful   2Sa 11:2
to *l. upon*
it may be the Lord will *l.* on   2Sa 16:12
my affliction
he said, Lord, *l. upon* it, and   2Ch 24:22
require it
Vashti the queen was fair to *l.*   Es 1:11
on

now, therefore, be content, *l.*   *Job 6:28*
upon me
l. on every one that is proud,   *Job 40:12*
and bring low
my bones stare and *l. upon* me   *Ps 22:17*
l. upon mine affliction and my   *Ps 25:18*
pain, forgive
Lord, how long wilt thou *l.*   *Ps 35:17*
on? rescue
and *l. upon* the face of thine   *Ps 84:9*
Anointed
l. thou *upon* me, and be   *Ps 119:132*
merciful to me
let thine eyes *l.* right *on,* and   *Pr 4:25*
eyelids
l. not thou *upon* the wine   *Pr 23:31*
when it is red
l. not *upon* me because I am   *Ca 1:6*
black
return, return, that we may *l.*   *Ca 6:13*
upon thee
that see thee, shall narrowly *l.*   *Isa 14:16*
upon thee
l. upon Zion; *l. upon* the   *Isa 33:20;*
earth beneath   *51:6*
go forth and *l. upon* the   *Isa 66:24*
carcases of the men
be defiled, and let our eye *l.*   *Mic 4:11*
upon Zion
that *l. upon* thee, shall flee from   *Na 3:7*
thee
of purer eyes than to *l. upon*   *Hab 1:13*
iniquity
that thou mayest *l. upon* their   *Hab 2:15*
nakedness
shall *l. upon* me whom they   *Zec 12:10*
pierced
master, I beseech thee, *l. upon*   *Lu 9:38*
my son
lift up your eyes and *l. upon*   *Joh 4:35*
the fields
they shall *l. upon* him whom   *Joh 19:37*
they pierced
Peter and John said, *L. on* us   *Ac 3:4;*
  3:12
l. upon things after outward   *2Co 10:7*
appearance
l. not every man *on* his own   *Ph'p 2:4*
things
he that sat was to *l. upon* like a   *Re 4:3*
jasper

LOOKED

l. sad and depressed (A)   *Ge 4:5*
God *l.* on the earth, and it was   *Ge 6:12*
corrupt
the men rose up, and *l.*   *Ge 18:16*
toward Sodom
his wife *l.* back; *l.* out at a   *Ge 19:26;*
window   *26:8*
the Lord hath *l.* upon my   *Ge 29:32*
affliction
l. less favourably (A)   *Ge 31:2*
keeper of the prison *l.* not to   *Ge 39:23*
any thing
Joseph *l.* on them, behold they   *Ge 40:6*
were sad
Moses went and *l.* on their   *Ex 2:11*
burdens
he *l.* this way and that way,   *Ex 2:12*
and saw no man
and God *l.* upon the children of   *Ex 2:25*
Israel
Lord had *l.* on their affliction   *Ex 4:31;*
  De 26:7
the Lord *l.* on the host of the   *Ex 14:24*
Egyptians
that they *l.* toward the   *Ex 16:10*
wilderness
the people *l.* after Moses till he   *Ex 33:8*
was gone
Aaron *l.* on Miriam, she was   *Nu 12:10*
leprous
that they *l.* towards the   *Nu 16:42*
tabernacle
he *l.* on Amalek, he took up   *Nu 24:20*
his parable
l. on the Kenites, and took up   *Nu 24:21*
his parable
when the men of Ai *l.* behind   *Jos 8:20*
them
the mother of Sisera *l.* out at a   *J'g 5:28*
window
the Lord *l.* upon him, and said,   *J'g 6:14*
Go in might
and Manoah and his wife *l.*   *J'g 13:19;*
on   *13:20*
the Benjamites *l.* behind   *J'g 20:40*
them, and behold

because they had *l.* into the   *1Sa 6:19*
ark
I have *l.* on my people,   *1Sa 9:16*
because cry came to
the watchmen of Saul *l.* and   *1Sa 14:16*
behold
when they were come, he *l.* on   *1Sa 16:6*
Eliab
the Philistine *l.* about, and   *1Sa 17:42*
saw David
Saul *l.* behind him, David   *1Sa 24:8;*
stood   *2Sa 1:7*
Abner *l.* behind him and said   *2Sa 2:20*
Michal *l.* through a window,   *2Sa 6:16*
and saw David
they *l.* but there was none to   *2Sa 22:42*
save
when I had *l.* at it (S)   *1Ki 3:21*
Elijah's servant went up and   *2Ki 18:43*
l.
Elisha turned back and *l.* on   *2Ki 2:24*
them
the people *l.* and behold he   *2Ki 6:30*
had sackcloth
Jezebel painted, and *l.* out at a   *2Ki 9:30*
window
l. one another in the face at   *2Ki 14:11*
Beth-shemesh
when Judah *l.* back, the   *2Ch 13:14*
battle
they *l.* one another in the   *2Ch 25:21*
face (S)
l. on him, and behold he was   *2Ch 26:20*
leprous
favour in the sight of all who *l.*   *Es 2:15*
on her
the troops of Tema *l.* Sheba   *Job 6:19*
waited
the Lord *l.* to see if any did   *Ps 14:2*
understand
they *l.* to him, and were   *Ps 34:5*
lightened
God *l.* down on the children of   *Ps 53:2*
men
he hath *l.* down from his   *Ps 102:19*
sanctuary
when they *l.* they shaked   *Ps 109:25*
their heads
because the sun hath *l.* on me   *Ca 1:6*
he *l.* that it should bring forth   *Isa 5:2*
grapes
he *l.* for judgment, but behold   *Isa 5:7*
oppression
but ye have not *l.* to the   *Isa 22:11*
maker thereof
didst terrible things which we   *Isa 63:3*
l. not for
we *l.* for peace, no good came   *Jer 8:15;*
  14:19
certainly this is the day that we   *La 2:16*
l. for
whither the head *l.* they   *Eze 10:11*
followed
he consulted with images, he   *Eze 21:21*
l. in the liver
let our countenances be *l.* on   *Da 1:13*
before thee
not have *l.* on the day of thy   *Ob 12*
brother
thou shouldest not have *l.* on   *Ob 13*
their affliction
ye *l.* for much, and lo it came   *Hag 1:9*
to little
when he *l.* round about   *M'k 3:5;*
  5:32; 10:23
he *l.* up to heaven, and   *M'k 6:41*
blessed and brake
he *l.* and said, I see men as   *M'k 8:24*
trees walking
when they *l.* they saw the   *M'k 16:4*
stone rolled
l. on me, to take away my   *Lu 1:25*
reproach
spake to all that *l.* for   *Lu 2:38*
redemption in Jerusalem
likewise a Levite came and *l.*   *Lu 10:32*
on him
the Lord turned, and *l.* upon   *Lu 22:61*
Peter
then the disciples *l.* one on   *Joh 13:22*
another
l. in bewilderment (N)   *Joh 13:22*
while they *l.* stedfastly toward   *Ac 1:10*
heaven
after they had *l.* a great while   *Ac 28:6*
and saw no
for he *l.* for a city which   *Heb 11:10*
hath foundation
that which we have *l.* upon,   *1Jo 1:1*
declare we

LOOKED, *EYES*

Jacob lifted up his *eyes* and *l.*   *Ge 33:1*
Esau came
they lifted up their *eyes* and *l.*   *Ge 37:25*
and behold
then I lifted up mine *eyes l.* and   *Da 10:5*
behold
Zechariah lifted his *eyes* and   *Zec 2:1;*
l.   *5:9; 6:1*

I LOOKED

have *I* also here *l.* after him   *Ge 16:13*
that seeth
I l. and behold ye had sinned   *De 9:16*
when *I l.* for good, then evil   *Job 30:26*
came
and *I I.* for some to take pity   *Ps 69:20*
I l. on my right hand, and   *Ps 142:4*
beheld
at the window, *I l.* through my   *Pr 7:6*
casement
I l. upon it, and received   *Pr 24:32*
instruction
I l. on all the works that my   *Ec 2:11*
hands
I l. it should bring forth grapes,   *Isa 5:4*
it brought
and *I l.* and there was none to   *Isa 63:5*
help
I l. and behold   *Eze 1:4;*
  2:9; 8:7; 10:1, 9; 44:4
then *I* Daniel *l.* and behold   *Da 12:5*
there stood
I have *l.* and behold a   *Zec 4:2*
candlestick
and the same hour *I I.* up   *Ac 22:13*
upon him
I l. and behold   *Re 4:1;*
  6:8; 14:1, 14; 15:5

LOOKEST

thou *l.* narrowly to all my   *Job 13:27*
paths
why *l.* on them that deal   *Hab 1:13*
treacherously

LOOKETH

if leprosy cover wheresoever   *Le 13:12*
priest *l.*
when he *l.* on the serpent, he   *Nu 21:8*
shall live
Pisgah, which *l.* toward   *Nu 21:20;*
Jeshimon   *23:28*
man *l.* on the outward   *1Sa 16:7*
appearance
as an hireling *l.* for the reward   *Job 7:2*
of work
for he *l.* to the ends of the   *Job 28:24*
earth
he *l.* on men, and if any say,   *Job 33:27*
I have sinned
the Lord *l.* from heaven, he   *Ps 33:13*
beholdeth
he *l.* on all the inhabitants of   *Ps 33:14*
the world
he *l.* on the earth, and it   *Ps 104:32*
trembleth
the prudent *l.* well to his   *Pr 14:15*
goings
she *l.* well to the ways of her   *Pr 31:27*
household
behold, he *l.* forth at the   *Ca 2:9*
window
who is she that *l.* forth as the   *Ca 6:10*
morning
as the tower which *l.* toward   *Ca 7:4*
Damascus
when he that *l.* upon it seeth it   *Isa 28:4*
the door that *l.* toward the   *Eze 8:3*
north
the gate which *l.* eastward   *Eze 11:1;*
  40:6, 22; 43:1; 44:1; 46:1, 12; 47:2
gate of the court that *l.*   *Eze 40:20*
toward the north
whosoever *l.* on a woman to   *M't 5:28*
lust after
lord come when *l.* not for   *M't 24:50;*
him   *Lu 12:46*
whoso *l.* into the perfect law   *Jas 1:25*
of liberty

LOOKING

better *l.* (B)   *J'g 15:2*
was fine *l.* (A)   *1Sa 16:7*

three oxen *l.* toward the north   *1Ki 7:25*
which were *l.* on (S)   *2Ki 2:15*
Michal *l.* out at a window,   *1Ch 15:29*
saw David
three oxen *l.* toward the south   *2Ch 4:4*
keep on *l.* all night (S)   *Ps 59:15*
mine eyes fail with *l.* upward   *Isa 38:14*
l. up to heaven, he blessed   *M't 14:19;*
                      Lu 9:16
worse *l.* than the children (S)   *Da 1:10*
better *l.* (A)   *Da 1:15*
and *l.* up to heaven, he sighed   *M'k 7:34*
there were also women *l.* on   *M'k 15:40*
afar off
l. round about upon them all,   *Lu 6:10*
he said
and *l.* back, is fit for the   *Lu 9:62*
kingdom of God
men's hearts failing them for   *Lu 21:26*
l. after
John *l.* on Jesus saith, Behold   *Joh 1:36*
the Lamb
l. in, saw linen clothes lying,   *Joh 20:5*
yet went not in
l. stedfastly on him, saw his   *Ac 6:15*
face as it
are they ready, *l.* for a   *Ac 23:21*
promise from thee
l. for that blessed hope and   *Tit 2:13*
appearing
but a certain fearful *l.* for of   *Heb 10:27*
judgment
l. unto Jesus the author and   *Heb 12:2*
finisher of faith
l. diligently, lest any fail of   *Heb 12:15*
the grace of God
l. for the coming of the day of   *2Pe 3:12*
God
l. for the mercy of our Lord   *Jude 21*
Jesus Christ

LOOKING *GLASS*

spread out the sky as a   *Job 37:18*
molten *l. glass*

LOOKING *GLASSES*

made laver and foot of *l.*   *Ex 38:8*
glasses of women

LOOKS

admired their *l.* (B)   *Ge 6:2*
pay no attention to his *l.* (B)   *1Sa 16:7*
thou changest his *l.* (B)   *Job 14:20*
wilt bring down high *l.*   *Ps 18:27*
lofty *l.* of man shall be   *Isa 2:11*
humbled
the glory of his high *l.*   *Isa 10:12*
nor be dismayed at their high   *Eze 2:6;*
l.   *3:9*
our *l.* (B)   *Da 1:13*

LOOPS

thou shalt make *l.* of   *Ex 26:4;*
blue   *26:5, 10*
l. shalt thou make; put taches   *Ex 26:5;*
in the *l.*   *26:11*
made *l.* of blue, fifty *l.* made   *Ex 36:11;*
he   *36:12, 17*

LOOSE

Naphtali is a hind let *l.:* he   *Ge 49:21*
giveth
box *l.* the people from their   *Ex 5:4*
work (S)
people were broken *l.* (E)(R)   *Ex 32:25*
the living bird *l.* into the open   *Le 14:7*
field
and *l.* his shoe from off his   *De 25:9*
foot
L. thy shoe from off thy foot   *Jos 5:15*
that he would let *l.* his hand   *Job 6:9*
also let *l.* the bridle before   *Job 30:11*
me
Pleiades, or *l.* the bands of   *Job 38:31*
Orion
l. those that are appointed to   *Ps 102:20*
death
l. women (A)   *Pr 2:16;*
   5:20; 6:24; 7:5; 22:14; 23:27, 33
l. women (B)   *Pr 2:16;*
         5:3; 20; 7:5; 22:14
l. women (R)   *Pr 2:16; 5:3, 20*
infatuated with a *l.* woman   *Pr 5:20*
(A)(B)(R)

l. woman (A)   *Pr 7:5*
l. the sackcloth from off thy   *Isa 20:2*
loins
I will *l.* the loins of kings, to   *Isa 45:1*
open
l. thyself from the bands of thy   *Isa 52:2*
neck
to *l.* the bands of wickedness   *Isa 58:6*
I *l.* thee this day from the   *Jer 40:4*
chains
Lo, I see four men *l.,* walking   *Da 3:25*
whatsoever thou shalt *l.* on   *M't 16:19*
earth
whatsoever ye shall *l.* on   *M't 18:18*
earth shall
l. them, and bring them unto   *M't 21:2*
me
not worthy to *l.* (S)   *M'k 1:7;*
          Lu 3:16; Joh 1:27
man sat; *l.* him, and bring   *M'k 11:2*
him
two ways met; and they *l.* him   *M'k 11:4*
on the sabbath *l.* his ox or his   *Lu 13:15*
ass
sat: *l.* him, and bring him   *Lu 19:30*
thither
any man ask you, Why do ye   *Lu 19:31*
l. him
said unto them, Why *l.* ye the   *Lu 19:33*
colt
unto them, *L.* him, and let   *Joh 11:44*
him go
of his feet I am not worthy to   *Ac 13:25*
l.
him of Paul, that he might *l.*   *Ac 24:26*
him
who leads a *l.* life (N)   *1Co 5:11*
l. living and lawbreaking (P)   *Tit 1:6*
and to *l.* the seven seals thereof   *Re 5:2;*
                     5:5
L. the four angels which are   *Re 9:14*
bound

LOOSED

the breastplate be not *l.* from   *Ex 28:28*
the breastplate might not be *l.*   *Ex 39:21*
from
house of him that hath his   *De 25:10*
shoe *l.*
his bands *l.* from off his hands   *J'g 15:14*
Because he hath *l.* my cord   *Job 30:11*
l. any bowstring (A)(B)   *Job 30:11*
hath *l.* the bands of the wild   *Job 39:5*
ass
The king sent and *l.* him;   *Ps 105:20*
even
handmaid: thou hast *l.* my   *Ps 116:16*
bonds
Or ever the silver cord be *l.* or   *Ec 12:6*
shall the girdle of their loins   *Isa 5:27*
be *l.*
Thy tacklings are *l;* they   *Isa 33:23*
could
exile hasteneth that he may   *Isa 51:14*
be *l.*
that the joints of his loins were   *Da 5:6*
l.
loose on earth shall be *l.* in   *M't 16:19;*
heaven   *18:18*
with compassion, and *l.* him   *M't 18:27*
and the string of his tongue   *M'k 7:35*
was *l.*
and his tongue *l.* and he spake   *Lu 1:64*
thou art *l.* from thine   *Lu 13:12*
infirmity
l. from this bond on the   *Lu 13:16*
sabbath
up, having *l.* the pains of death   *Ac 2:24*
and his company *l.* from   *Ac 13:13*
Paphos
and every one's bands were *l.*   *Ac 16:26*
Jews, he *l.* him from his bands   *Ac 22:30*
me, and not have *l.* from   *Ac 27:21*
Crete
l. the rudder bands, and   *Ac 27:40*
hoisted up
is *l.* from the law of her   *Ro 7:2*
husband
unto a wife? seek not to be *l.*   *1Co 7:27*
Art thou *l.* from a wife? seek   *1Co 7:27*
not
l. and freed from sins (A)(E)   *Re 1:5*
And the four angels were *l.*   *Re 9:15*
that he must be *l.* a little season   *Re 20:3*
Satan shall be *l.* out of his   *Re 20:7*
prison

LOOSETH

He *l.* the bond of kings, and   *Job 12:18*
hungry, The Lord *l.* the   *Ps 146:7*
prisoners

LOOSING

unto them, What do ye, *l.* the   *M'k 11:5*
colt
And as they were *l.* the colt   *Lu 19:33*
Therefore *l.* from Troas, we   *Ac 16:11*
came
l. thence, they sailed close by   *Ac 27:13*

LOOT

recaptured all the *l.* (B)   *Ge 14:16*
loot (B)   *Ge 49:27*
threw themselves on the *l.*   *1Sa 14:32*
(B)
have their *l.* taken (B)   *Ps 76:5*
return loaded with *l.* (B)   *Da 11:28*

LOOTED

looted (B)   *Ge 34:29; Isa 13:16; 24:3*

LOP

shall *l.* the bough with terror   *Isa 10:33*

LORD

is any thing too hard for the   *Ge 18:14*
L.
the *L.* before whom I   *Ge 24:40*
walk will send
we saw certainly the *L.* was   *Ge 26:28*
with thee
I come again, then shall the   *Ge 28:21*
L. be my God
and the *L.* was with Joseph   *Ge 39:2;*
               39:21, 23
who is the *L.* that I should obey   *Ex 5:2*
him
and the *L.* did so, and there   *Ex 8:24*
came flies
the *L.* be so with you, as I will   *Ex 10:10*
let you go
because of that which the *l.*   *Ex 13:8*
did to me
it shall be unto thee holy   *Ex 30:37*
for *L.* whose name is   *Ex 34:14*
Aaron shall cast one lot for   *Le 16:8;*
the *L.*   *25:4; 27:2*
thou, *L.* art among this   *Nu 14:14*
people, that thou, *L.* art
therefore the *L.* will not be   *Nu 14:43*
with you
to you they are given as a gift   *Nu 18:6*
for the *L.*
that I may know what the *L.*   *Nu 22:19*
will say
all that the *L.* speaketh that   *Nu 23:26*
must I do
the *L.* hath kept thee back   *Nu 24:11*
from honour
we have brought an oblation   *Nu 31:50*
for the *L.*
they have followed the *L.*   *Nu 32:12;*
               De 1:36
so shall the *L.* do to all   *De 3:21*
kingdoms
know that the *L.* he is God   *De 4:35;*
         4:39; 1Ki 18:39
I stood between the *L.* and you   *De 5:5*
at that time
behold the heaven of heavens   *De 10:14*
is the *L.*
L. of lords, a great God a   *De 10:17*
ye have seen all the *L.* did in   *De 29:2*
Egypt
yet the *L.* hath not given you   *De 29:4*
an heart to
wherefore hath the *L.* done   *De 29:24;*
thus to this land   *1Ki 9:8; 2Ch 7:21*
L. shall do to them as he did to   *De 31:4*
Sihon
do ye thus requite the *L.* O   *De 32:6*
foolish
to flight, except the *L.* had   *De 32:30*
shut them up
happy art thou, O people   *De 33:29*
saved by the *L.*
swear unto me by the *L.*   *Jos 2:12;*
                 1Sa 24:21
even the *L.* of all the earth   *Jos 3:11;*
passeth over   *3:13*
thus shall the *L.* do to all   *Jos 10:25*
your enemies

if so be the *L.* will be with me, then   *Jos 14:12*

L. was with Judah, and he drave   *J'g 1:19*

and the *L.* was with the house of Joseph   *J'g 1:22*

arose a generation which knew not the *L.*   *J'g 2:10*

is not the *L.* gone out before thee   *J'g 4:14*

if the *L.* be with us, why is this befallen us   *J'g 6:13*

cometh to meet me shall surely be the *L.*   *J'g 11:31*

now know I that the *L.* will do me good   *J'g 17:13*

L. do so to me and more   *Ru 1:17; 1Sa 20:13*

the *L.* be with you   *Ru 2:4; 2Ch 20:17; 2Th 3:16*

there is none holy as the *L.* for   *1Sa 2:2*

it is the *L.:* let him do what seems   *1Sa 3:18; Joh 21:7*

Samuel grew, *L.* was with him   *1Sa 3:19; 18:12, 14; 2Ki 18:7; 1Ch 9:20*

this great thing which the *L.* will do   *1Sa 12:16*

the *L.* be with thee   *1Sa 17:37; 20:13; 1Ch 22:11, 16*

the *L.* be between thee and me   *1Sa 20:23; 20:42*

L. art become their God   *2Sa 7:24; 1Ch 17:22*

L. do what seemeth him good   *2Sa 10:12; 1Ch 19:13*

if the *L.* be God, follow him, if Baal   *1Ki 18:21*

if the *L.* do not help, whence shall I   *2Ki 6:27*

what shall I wait for the *L.* any longer   *2Ki 6:33*

come with me and see my zeal for the *L.*   *2Ki 10:16*

am I now come without the *L.*   *2Ki 18:25; Isa 36:10*

for great is the *L.*   *1Ch 16:25; Ps 48:1; 145:3*

and now, *L.* thou art God and hast promised   *1Ch 17:26*

not take that which is thine for the *L.*   *1Ch 21:24*

ye judge not for man, but for the *L.*   *2Ch 19:6*

and the *L.* shall be with good   *2Ch 19:11*

Manasseh knew that the *L.* was God   *2Ch 33:13*

even that thou art *L.* alone   *Ne 9:6; Isa 37:20*

know the *L.* hath set apart the godly   *Ps 4:3*

blessed is the nation whose God is the *L.*   *Ps 33:12*

my bones say, *L.* who is like unto thee   *Ps 35:10*

for he is thy *L.* worship thou him   *Ps 45:11*

if I regard iniquity, the *L.* will not hear me   *Ps 66:18*

which is the *L.* (S)   *Ps 68:4*

whose name alone is *L.* (S)   *Ps 83:18*

for thou *L.* art good, ready to forgive   *Ps 86:5*

thou *L.* art most high for ever   *Ps 92:8; 97:9*

know ye that the *L.* he is God, he made us   *Ps 100:3*

do thou for me, O God the *L.*   *Ps 109:21; 140:7*

they may know that thou *L.* hast done it   *Ps 109:27*

gracious is the *L.* and righteous   *Ps 116:5*

God is the *L.*   *Ps 118:27*

if it had not been the *L.* who was on   *Ps 124:1; 124:2*

if *L.* shouldest mark iniquity, who stand   *Ps 130:3*

till I find out a place for the *L.*   *Ps 132:5*

lest *L.* see it, and it displease him   *Pr 24:18*

lest I deny thee, and say, Who is the *L.*   *Pr 30:9*

shall stay upon the *L.* the Holy One   *Isa 10:20*

the *L.* is my strength (S)   *Isa 12:2*

and the *L.* shall be known to Egypt   *Isa 19:21*

L. will be to us a place of broad rivers   *Isa 33:21*

did not the *L.*, he against whom we sinned   *Isa 42:24*

sing, O heavens, for the *L.* hath done it   *Isa 44:23*

the *L.* will go before you, your rereward   *Isa 52:12*

where is the *L.* that brought us   *Jer 2:6; 2:8*

is not the *L.* in Zion   *Jer 8:19*

they shall know that my name is the *L.*   *Jer 16:21*

if so be that the *L.* will deal with us   *Jer 21:2*

called, the *L.* our Righteousness   *Jer 23:6; 33:16*

saying, Know the *L.*   *Jer 31:24; Heb 8:11*

even the *L.* the hope of their fathers   *Jer 50:7*

remember the *L.* afar off, let Jerusalem   *Jer 51:50*

for the *L.* will not cast off for ever   *La 3:31*

till the *L.* look down from heaven   *La 3:50*

possess it, whereas the *L.* was there   *Eze 35:10*

truth it is, your God is a *L.* of kings   *Da 2:47*

betroth thee, thou shalt know the *L.*   *Ho 2:20*

and they have not known the *L.*   *Ho 5:4*

shall walk after the *L.* he shall roar   *Ho 11:10*

his reproach shall his *L.* return to him   *Ho 12:14*

fear not, for *L.* will do great things   *Joe 2:21*

be evil in city, and *L.* hath not done   *Am 3:6*

and so the *L.* shall be with you   *Am 5:14*

and the *L.* on the head of them   *Mic 2:13*

lean on *L.* and say, Is not *L.* among   *Mic 3:11*

L. shall reign over them in mount Zion   *Mic 4:7*

and what doth the *L.* require of thee   *Mic 6:8*

that swear by the *L.* and by Malcham   *Zep 1:5*

when eyes of man shall be toward *L.*   *Zec 9:1*

the *L.* shall be seen over them   *Zec 9:14*

then shall *L.* go forth and fight   *Zec 14:3*

that day shall there be one *L.* his name one   *Zec 14:9*

not every one that saith, *L. L.*   *M't 7:21*

shall enter into kingdom   *22:22, 44; Lu 13:25*

L. if thou wilt, thou canst make   *M't 8:2; Lu 5:12*

L. save us   *M't 8:25; 9:28*

they said, Yea *L.*   *M't 13:51*

L. save me; saying, *L.* help me   *M't 14:30; 15:25*

she said, Truth *L.*   *M't 15:27*

L. hath need of   *M't 21:3; M'k 11:3; Lu 19:31, 34*

how then doth David call him *L.*   *M't 22:43; 22:45; M'k 12:37; Lu 20:44*

ye know not what hour your *L.* will come   *M't 24:42*

whom his *L.* shall find so doing   *M't 24:46; Lu 12:43*

the *L.* of that servant shall come   *M't 24:50; Lu 12:46*

L. L. open to   *M't 25:11*

enter thou into the joy of thy *L.*   *M't 25:21*

L. when saw we thee an hungered   *M't 25:37; 25:44*

L. is it I? place where the *L.* lay   *M't 26:22; 28:6*

Son of man is *L.* of sabbath   *M'k 2:28; Lu 6:5*

how great things the *L.* hath done for thee   *M'k 5:19*

L. I believe, help thou   *M'k 9:24; Joh 9:38; 11:27*

L. that I may receive my sight   *M'k 10:51; M't 20:33*

preached, the *L.* working with them   *M'k 16:20*

to make ready a people for the *L.*   *Lu 1:17*

thus *L.* dealt with me, to take my reproach   *Lu 1:25*

born a Saviour, which is Christ the *L.*   *Lu 2:11*

why call ye me *L. L.*, and do not what I say   *Lu 6:46*

a man said to him, *L.* I will follow thee   *Lu 9:57; 9:61*

L. teach us to pray, as John taught his disciples   *Lu 11:1*

L. let it alone this year, till I dig about it   *Lu 13:8*

that servant shewed his *L.*   *Lu 14:21*

apostles said unto the *L.*, Increase our faith   *Lu 17:5*

where *L.*; *L.* remember me when thou   *Lu 17:37; 23:42*

saying, The *L.* is risen indeed, and appeared   *Lu 24:34*

L. to whom shall we go, thou hast life   *Joh 6:68*

no man *L.*; who is the *L.* that I might   *Joh 8:11; 9:36*

they said to him, *L.* come and see   *Joh 11:34*

ye call me Master and *L.* and say well   *Joh 13:13*

L. who is it   *Joh 13:25*

they have taken the *L.* out of the sepulchre   *Joh 20:2*

we have seen the *L.*   *Joh 20:25*

none durst ask him, knowing it was the *L.*   *Joh 21:12*

Peter saith, *L.* what shall this man do   *Joh 21:21*

whom ye crucified both *L.* and Christ   *Ac 2:36*

L. thou art God; now *L.* behold threatenings   *Ac 4:24; 4:29*

and he said, Who art thou *L.*   *Ac 9:5; 26:15*

and said, What is it, *L.*   *Ac 10:4; 10:14*

not so *L.*   *Ac 11:8*

peace by Jesus Christ, he is *L.* of all   *Ac 10:36*

and I said, What shall I do, *L.*   *Ac 22:10*

because a short work will the *L.* make   *Ro 9:28*

for the same *L.* over all is rich unto all   *Ro 10:12*

that he might be *L.* of the dead and living   *Ro 14:9*

not have crucified the *L.* of glory   *1Co 2:8*

even as the *L.* gave to every man   *1Co 3:5*

but he that judgeth me is the *L.*   *1Co 4:4*

I will come to you, if the *L.* will   *1Co 4:19; Jas 4:15*

but for the *L.*; yet not I, but the *L.*   *1Co 6:13; 7:10*

differences of administrations, but the same *L.*   *1Co 12:5*

second man is the *L.* from heaven   *1Co 15:47*

and to be present with the *L.*   *2Co 5:8*

I speak it not after the *L.* but as it were   *2Co 11:17*

one *L.*; even as the *L.* the church   *Eph 4:5; 5:29*

tongue confess that Jesus Christ is *L.*   *Ph'p 2:11*

moderation be known, the *L.* is at hand   *Ph'p 4:5*

so shall we ever be with the *L.*   *1Th 4:17*

that the day of the *L.* is (S)   *2Th 2:2*

the King of kings, and *L.* of lords   *1Ti 6:15*

with them that call on the *L.*   *2Ti 2:22*

out of them all the *L.* delivered me   *2Ti 3:11*

which the *L.* shall give me at that day   *2Ti 4:8*

notwithstanding the *L.* stood with me   *2Ti 4:17*

which at first began to be spoken by the *L.*   *Heb 2:3*

saying, Know the *L.* for all shall know   *Heb 8:11*

and the *L.* shall raise the sick   *Jas 5:15*

one day is with the *L.* as a thousand   *2Pe 3:8*

Michael said, The *L.* rebuke thee   *Jude 9*

where also our *L.* was crucified   *Re 11:8*

are become the kingdoms of   *Re 11:15*
our *L*. and his Christ
overcome, for he is *L*. of   *Re 17:14;*
lords   *19:16*

LORD, as applied to man

after I am old, my *l*. being old *Ge 18:12*
also
nay, my *l*. hear me; my *l*.   *Ge 23:11;*
hearken to me   *23:15*
drink, my *l*. and she hasted   *Ge 24:18*
and let down
be *l*. over thy brethren, let thy *Ge 27:29*
mother's
Isaac answered, I have made   *Ge 27:37*
him thy *l*.
Rachel said, Let it not   *Ge 31:35*
displease my *l*.
saying, Thus shall ye speak to   *Ge 32:4*
my *l*. Esau
I have sent to tell my *l*. that I   *Ge 32:5*
may find grace
shall say, It is a present sent   *Ge 32:18*
to my *l*. Esau
laid up his garment, until his   *Ge 39:16*
l. come home
had offended their *l*. the king   *Ge 40:1*
of Egypt
nay, my *l*. but to buy food are   *Ge 42:10*
we come
the man who is the *l*. of the   *Ge 42:30;*
land   *42:33*
is not this it, in which my *l*.   *Ge 44:5*
drinketh
we came up, we told him the   *Ge 44:24*
words of my *l*.
and he hath made me *l*. of all   *Ge 45:8*
his house
God hath made me *l*. of all   *Ge 45:9*
Egypt, come down
we will not hide it from my *l*.   *Ge 47:18*
nothing left in sight of my *l*.
let not the anger of my *l*. wax   *Ex 32:22*
hot
l. it over him with severity   *Le 25:43*
(B)
not severely *l*. it over him (B)   *Le 25:53*
and said, My *l*. Moses forbid   *Nu 11:28*
them
my *l*. I beseech thee, lay not   *Nu 12:11*
sin on us
servants do as my *l*.   *Nu 32:25;*
commandeth   *32:27*
the Lord commanded my *l*. to   *Nu 36:2*
give land
their *l*. was fallen down dead   *J'g 3:25*
on earth
turn in, my *l*. turn in to me   *J'g 4:18*
the woman fell down where   *J'g 19:26*
her *l*. was
and her *l*. rose up in the   *J'g 19:27*
morning and opened
let me find favour in thy sight,   *Ru 2:13*
my *l*.
my *l*. I am of a sorrowful   *1Sa 1:15*
spirit
O my *l*. as thy soul liveth, my   *1Sa 1:26*
l. I am woman
and he answered, Here I am,   *1Sa 22:12*
my *l*.
and cried after Saul, saying,   *1Sa 24:8*
My *l*. the king
on me, my *l*. on me let this   *1Sa 25:24*
iniquity be
let not my *l*. regard this man   *1Sa 25:25*
of Belial
they that seek evil to my *l*. be   *1Sa 25:26*
as Nabal
it be given to young men that   *1Sa 25:27*
follow my *l*.
when the Lord shall have   *1Sa 25:31*
dealt with my *l*.
why hast thou not kept thy *l*.   *1Sa 26:15*
the king
David said, It is my voice,   *1Sa 26:17*
my *l*. O king
why doth my *l*. this pursue   *1Sa 26:18*
after his servant
that may not fight against   *1Sa 29:8*
enemies of my *l*.
and brought them hither to   *2Sa 1:10*
my *l*.
I will gather all Israel to my *l*. *2Sa 3:21*
the king
according to all that my *l*. hath *2Sa 9:11*
commanded
Uriah slept with all the   *2Sa 11:9*
servants of his *l*.

let not my *l*. suppose they   *2Sa 13:32*
have slain
let thine handmaid speak to   *2Sa 14:12*
my *l*.
as an angel of God, so is my *l*. *2Sa 14:17*
the king
none can turn from aught my   *2Sa 14:19*
l. hath spoken
my *l*. is wise according to   *2Sa 14:20*
wisdom of an angel
why should this dead dog   *2Sa 16:9*
curse my *l*. king
and Cushi said, Tidings, my *l*. *2Sa 18:31*
the king
let not my *l*. impute iniquity   *2Sa 19:19*
to me, the day my *l*. the king
I am come the first to go   *2Sa 19:20*
down to meet my *l*.
forasmuch as my *l*. is come   *2Sa 19:30*
again in peace
that the eyes of my *l*. the king *2Sa 24:3*
may see it, but why doth my *l*.
let my *l*. take and offer up   *2Sa 24:22*
what seemeth good
that my *l*. the king may get heat *1Ki 1:2*
is this thing done by my *l*. the *1Ki 1:27*
king
the Lord God of my *l*. the   *1Ki 1:36*
king say so too
as the Lord hath been with my *1Ki 1:37*
l. the king
as my *l*. the king hath said, so *1Ki 2:38*
will I do
O my *l*. I and this woman   *1Ki 3:17*
dwell in one house
O my *l*. give her the living   *1Ki 3:26*
child, not slay it
who fled from his *l*.   *1Ki 11:23*
Hadadezer king of
Obadiah said, Art thou that   *1Ki 18:7*
my *l*. Elijah
was it not told my *l*. what I   *1Ki 18:13*
did, when Jezebel
go tell thy *l*. Behold Elijah is *1Ki 18:14*
here, he slay
my *l*. I am thine, and all that I *1Ki 20:4*
have
tell my *l*. all thou didst send   *1Ki 20:9*
for, I will do
the situation is pleasant as   *2Ki 2:19*
my *l*. seeth
nay, my *l*. do not lie to thine   *2Ki 4:16*
handmaid
did I desire a son of my *l*.? did *2Ki 4:28*
I not say
would God my *l*. were with the *2Ki 5:3*
prophet
one went in and told his *l*.   *2Ki 5:4*
saying
and one of his servants said,   *2Ki 6:12*
None, my *l*.
a woman cried, saying, Help   *2Ki 6:26*
my *l*. O king
then a *l*. on whose hand the   *2Ki 7:2;*
king leaned   *7:17*
my *l*. O king, this is the   *2Ki 8:5*
woman, and her son
and Hazael said, Why weepeth *2Ki 8:12*
my *l*.
Jehu came forth to the   *2Ki 9:11*
servants of his *l*.
now, I pray thee, give   *2Ki 18:23*
pledges to my *l*.
with the cunning men of my *l*. *2Ch 2:14*
David
according to the counsel of my *Ezr 10:3*
l.
our lips are our own, who is *l*. *Ps 12:4*
over us
saying, Ah *l*. or ah his glory   *Jer 22:18;*
                                34:5
therefore hear now, I pray   *Jer 37:20*
thee, my *l*.
my *l*. the king, these men have *Jer 38:9*
done evil
said to Daniel, I fear my *l*. the *Da 1:10*
king
there is no king nor *l*. that   *Da 2:10*
asked such things
my *l*. the dream be to them   *Da 4:19*
that hate thee
decree which is come upon my *Da 4:24*
l. the king
nor is the servant above his *l*. *M't 10:24*
it is enough that the servant   *M't 10:25*
be as his *l*.
I. have patience with me, and *M't 18:26*
I will pay
they came, and told their *l*.   *M't 18:31*
all that was done

l. it over them   *M't 20:25*
(A)(B)(E)(N)(P)(R)
my *l*. delayeth his coming   *M't 24:48;*
                              Lu 12:45
and ye like men that wait for *Lu 12:36*
their *l*.
my *l*. taketh away from me the *Lu 16:3*
stewardship
How much owest thou to   *Lu 16:5*
my *l*.
servant knoweth not what *l*.   *Joh 15:15*
I said, the servant is not   *Joh 15:20*
greater than his *l*.
I have no certain thing to   *Ac 25:26*
write to my *l*.
l. it over your faith (B)(R)   *2Co 1:24*
differs not from a servant,   *Ga 4:1*
though *l*. of all
Sarah obeyed Abraham, calling *1Pe 3:6*
him *l*.

LORD GOD

he said, Blessed be the *L*. God *Ge 9:26*
of Shem
Abram said, *L*. God what wilt *Ge 15:2*
thou give me
L. God, whereby shall I know *Ge 15:8*
I shall inherit
blessed be the *L*. God of my   *Ge 24:27*
master Abraham
I am the *L*. God of Abraham *Ge 28:13*
thy father
the *L*. God of Israel   *Ex 32:27;*
Jos 9:18-19; 10:40, 42; 13:14, 33; 14:14
Lord, the *L*. God merciful and *Ex 34:6*
gracious
Joshua said, Alas, O *L*. God, *Jos 7:7*
wherefore
the *L*. God of gods, the *L*.   *Jos 22:22*
God of gods
what have ye to do with *L*.   *Jos 22:24*
God of Israel
the *L*. God of Israel   *Jos 24:2;*
J'g 4:6; 5:3, 5; 11:21, 23; 21:3; Ru 2:12;
1Sa 2:30; 14:41; 20:12; 23:10; 25:32, 34;
                  1Ki 1:30; 1Ch 23:25; 24:19
Gideon said, Alas, O *L*. God *J'g 6:22*
O *L*. God, remember me only *J'g 16:28*
this once
who is able to stand before this *1Sa 6:20*
holy *L*. God
the *L*. God of hosts was with *2Sa 5:10*
him
who am I, O *L*. God, and   *2Sa 7:18*
what is my house
is this the manner of man, O *2Sa 7:19*
L. God
for thou, *L*. God, knowest thy *2Sa 7:20*
servant
wherefore thou art great, O *L*. *2Sa 7:22*
God, none like
the *L*. God of my lord the   *1Ki 1:36*
king say so
king said, Blessed be the *L*.   *1Ki 1:48;*
God of Israel   *8:15; 1Ch 16:36; 29:10*
found some good thing   *1Ki 14:13*
toward the *L*. God
Elijah said, As the *L*. God of *1Ki 17:1*
Israel liveth
may know thou art *L*. God   *1Ki 18:37;*
                             2Ki 19:19
said, Where is *L*. God of   *2Ki 2:14*
Elijah
state of a man of high   *1Ch 17:17*
degree, O *L*. God
fight ye not against *L*. God   *2Ch 13:12*
of fathers
they left the house of *L*. God *2Ch 24:18*
of fathers
nor shall it be for thy   *2Ch 26:18*
honour from *L*. God
his servants spake more   *2Ch 32:16*
against *L*. God
thou art the *L*. God, didst   *Ne 9:7*
choose Abram
hast redeemed me, O *L*. God of *Ps 31:5*
truth
blessed be *L*. God from   *Ps 41:13;*
everlasting to everlasting *72:18; 106:48;*
                              Lu 1:68
that the *L*. God might dwell *Ps 68:18*
among them
thou art my hope, O *L*. God   *Ps 71:5*
thou art my trust
for *L*. God is a sun and shield, *Ps 84:11*
will give grace
I will hear what the *L*. God will *Ps 85:8*
speak

LORD *GOD*

for I have heard from the *L. Isa 28:22*
God of hosts
for the *L. God* will help me, *Isa 50:7;*
therefore *50:9*
for *L. God* shall slay thee, *Isa 65:15*
and call servants
not named, saying, The *L. Jer 44:26*
God liveth
as I live, saith the *L. God Eze 5:11;*
14:16
know I am the *L. God Eze 13:9;*
23:49; 24:24
and thus it was, saith the *L. Eze 16:19*
God
woe, woe unto thee, saith the *Eze 16:23*
L. God
according to his ways, saith *Eze 18:30*
the *L.* God
be brought to pass, saith the *Eze 21:7*
the *L.* God
it shall be no more, saith *Eze 21:13*
the *L.* God
and hast forgotten me, saith *Eze 22:12*
L. God
because they wrought for me, *Eze 29:20*
saith *L.* God
and I am your God, saith the *Eze 34:31*
L. God
know that I am the Lord *Eze 36:23*
saith *L.* God
not for your sakes do I this, *Eze 36:32*
saith *L.* God
and I answered, O *L. God, Eze 37:3*
thou knowest
for I have spoken it, saith the *Eze 39:5;*
L. God *23:34; 26:14; 28:10*
it is come, and it is done, *Eze 39:8*
saith the *L.* God
I will accept you saith the *L. Eze 43:27*
God
I set my face unto the *L. God, Da 9:3*
to seek
even *L. God* of hosts in his *Ho 12:5*
memorial
a remnant of Philistines shall *Am 1:8*
perish, saith *L.* God
L. God will do nothing, but he *Am 3:7*
revealeth
the *L. God* hath spoken, who *Am 3:8*
can but prophesy
for this liketh you, saith the *L. Am 4:5*
God
L. God of hosts is he that *Am 9:5*
toucheth the land
let the *L. God* be witness *Mic 1:2*
against you
the *L. God* is my strength, he *Hab 3:19*
will make
sanctify the *L. God* in your *1Pe 3:15*
hearts
holy, holy, *L. God* Almighty *Re 4:8;*
11:17; 16:7
marvellous are thy works, *L. Re 15:3*
God Almighty
for strong is the *L. God* who *Re 18:8*
judgeth her
for the *L. God* omnipotent *Re 19:6*
reigneth
the *L. God* and the Lamb are *Re 21:22*
the temple
for the *L. God* giveth them *Re 22:5*
light

LORD *HIS GOD*

Moses besought the *L. his God Ex 32:11*
the commandments of the *L. Le 4:22*
his God
the *L. his God* is with him *Nu 23:21*
that he may learn to fear the *De 17:19*
L. his God
he shall minister in name of *De 18:7*
the *L. his* God
David encouraged himself *1Sa 30:6*
in *L. his* God
an house unto the name of *L. 1Ki 5:3*
his God
heart was not perfect with *L. 1Ki 11:4;*
his God *15:3*
the *L. his God* give him lamp *1Ki 15:4*
in Jerusalem
not right in the sight of the *L. 2Ki 16:2*
his God
the *L. his God* was with him, *2Ch 1:1*
and magnified
good and right in the eyes of *2Ch 14:2*
the *L. his* God
Asa cried unto the *L. his 2Ch 14:11*
God, and said
when they saw that *L. his 2Ch 15:9*
God was with him

Uzziah transgressed against *2Ch 26:16*
the *L. his* God
Jotham prepared his ways *2Ch 27:6*
before *L. his* God
L. his God delivered Ahaz *2Ch 28:5*
into hands of Syria
Hezekiah wrought right *2Ch 31:20*
before *L. his* God
Manasseh in affliction *2Ch 33:12*
besought *L. his* God
Josiah sent to repair the *2Ch 34:8*
house of *L. his* God
Jehoiakim did evil in sight of *2Ch 36:5;*
L. his God *36:12*
L. his God be with him, and *2Ch 36:23*
let him go up
according to hand of the *L. his Ezr 7:6*
God upon him
happy he whose hope is in the *Ps 146:5*
L. his God
then Jonah prayed to the *L. his Jon 2:1*
God
feed in majesty of the name of *Mic 5:4*
L. his God

LORD *IS*

surely the *L. is* in this place *Ge 28:16*
the *L. is* righteous, I wicked *Ex 9:27;*
2Ch 12:6
the *L. is* my strength and song, *Ex 15:2*
he is my God
the *L. is* a man of war, the *L. is Ex 15:3*
his name
I know that *L. is* greater than *Ex 18:11*
all gods
the *L. is* with us, fear them not *Nu 14:9*
the *L. is* longsuffering, of *Nu 14:18;*
great *Na 1:3*
go not up, for the *L. is* not *Nu 14:42*
among you
are holy every one, the *L. is Nu 16:3*
among them
the *L. is* his inheritance, *De 10:9*
according
the *L. is* their inheritance, as *De 18:2*
he said
shall be a witness, that *L. is Jos 22:34*
God
and said, The *L. is* with thee *J'g 6:12;*
Lu 1:28
for the *L. is* a God of *1Sa 2:3*
knowledge
the *L. is* with David *1Sa 16:18; 2Sa 7:3*
seeing the *L. is* departed *1Sa 28:16*
from thee
he said, The *L. is* my rock *2Sa 22:2;*
Ps 18:2
people may know that the *L. 1Ki 8:60*
is God
Syrians said, The *L. is* the *1Ki 20:28*
God of hills
but as for us, the *L. is* our *2Ch 13:10*
God
the *L. is* with you while ye be *2Ch 15:2*
with him
L. is known by judgment which *Ps 9:16*
the *L. is* king for ever and ever *Ps 10:16*
the *L. is* in his holy temple, his *Ps 11:4*
eyes behold
counsel of poor, because the *L. Ps 14:6*
is his refuge
The *L. is* the portion of mine *Ps 16:5*
inheritance
The *L. is* my shepherd, I shall *Ps 23:1*
not want
the *L. is* my light, and my *Ps 27:1*
salvation, the *L. is* the strength
of my life of whom be afraid
the *L. is* my strength and *Ps 28:7;*
shield *118:14*
L. is their strength, and he is *Ps 28:8*
saving strength
O taste and see that the *L. is Ps 34:8*
good, blessed is
for the *L.* most high *is* terrible, *Ps 47:2*
a great king
the *L. is* our defence and Holy *Ps 89:18*
One our king
to shew that *L. is* upright he is *Ps 92:15*
my rock
the *L. is* clothed with strength *Ps 93:1*
but the *L. is* my defence and *Ps 94:22*
my rock
the *L. is* a great God *Ps 95:3;*
96:4; 99:2; 135:5
the *L. is* good *Ps 100:5;*
34:8; 135:3; 145:9; Jer 33:11; La 3:25;
Na 1:7

L. is merciful and gracious *Ps 103:8;*
111:4; 145:8
the *L. is* high; the *L. is* on my *Ps 113:4;*
side *118:6*
the *L. is* thy keeper, the *L. is Ps 121:5*
thy shade
so the *L. is* round about his *Ps 125:2*
people
L. is right *Ps 129:4;*
145:17; La 1:18; Da 9:14
the *L. is* nigh to all them that *Ps 145:18*
call on him
the *L. is* far from the wicked *Pr 15:29*
the *L. is* the maker of them all *Pr 22:2*
for the *L. is* a God of *Isa 30:18*
judgment
the *L. is* exalted; *L. is* our *Isa 33:5;*
judge our *33:22*
L. is well pleased for his *Isa 42:21*
righteousness
the *L. is* the true God, the *Jer 10:10*
living God
whose hope the *L. is;* the *L. is Jer 17:7;*
with me *20:11*
the *L. is* my portion, saith my *La 3:24*
soul
the name of the city, the *L. is Eze 48:35*
there
maketh the stars, the *L. is* his *Am 5:8;*
name *9:6*
but the *L. is* in his holy *Hab 2:20*
temple
the just *L. is* in the midst *Zep 3:5;*
thereof *3:15*
they shall fight because *L. is Zec 10:5*
with them
and they shall say, The *L. is Zec 13:9*
my God
the *L. is* risen indeed, and *Lu 24:34*
appeared
now the *L. is* that Spirit, and *2Co 3:17*
moderation be known, the *L. is Ph'p 4:5*
at hand
the *L. is* the avenger of all such *1Th 4:6*
but the *L. is* faithful, who shall *2Th 3:3*
keep
the *L. is* my helper, I will not *Heb 13:6*
fear
L. is very pitiful, and of tender *Jas 5:11*
mercy
if ye have tasted that the *L. is 1Pe 2:3*
gracious
the *L. is* not slack concerning *2Pe 3:9*
his promise

LORD *MY GOD*

not go beyond the word of *L. Nu 22:18*
my God
even as the *L. my God De 4:5*
commanded me
not hear again the voice of *De 18:16*
the *L. my* God
have hearkened to the voice *De 26:14*
of *L. my* God
but I wholly followed the *L. Jos 14:8*
my God
I offer burnt offerings to the *2Sa 24:24*
L. my God
O *L. my* God *1Ki 3:7;*
8:28; 17:20-21; 1Ch 21:17; 2Ch 6:19;
Ps 7:1, 3; 13:3; 30:2, 12; 35:24; 38:15;
40:5; 86:12; 109:26; Jon 2:5; Hab 1:12
the *L. my God* hath given me *1Ki 5:4*
rest on every side
to build an house unto name *1Ki 5:5;*
of *L. my* God *1Ch 22:7; 2Ch 2:4*
as the hand of the *L. my God Ezr 7:28*
was upon me
and I spread out my hands to *Ezr 9:5*
the *L. my* God
the *L. my God* will enlighten *Ps 18:28*
my darkness
turn thou me, for thou art *L. Jer 31:18*
my God
I prayed unto the *L. my God, Da 9:4*
and said
while I was present, my *Da 9:20*
supplication before *L. my* God
thus saith the *L. my God, Feed Zec 11:4*
the flock
the *L. my God* shall come, and *Zec 14:5*
all saints

LORD *OF HOSTS*

O *L.* of hosts *1Sa 1:11;*
Ps 59:5; 84:1, 3, 12; 2Sa 7:27; Jer 11:20;
20:12

called by the name of the *L. of*   2Sa 6:2
hosts
saying, The *L. of hosts* is God 2Sa 7:26
over Israel
Elijah said, As *L. of hosts*   1Ki 18:15;
liveth   2Ki 3:14
the zeal of the *L. of hosts*   2Ki 9:31;
shall do this   Isa 9:7; 37:32
greater, for the *L. of hosts*   1Ch 11:9
was with him
the *L. of hosts* God of Israel 1Ch 17:24
the *L. of hosts* he is the King Ps 24:10
of glory
the *L. of hosts* is with us   Ps 46:7;
                           46:11
in city *L. of hosts*   Ps 48:8
therefore saith the Lord, the   Isa 1:24
L. of hosts
the day of the *L. of hosts* shall Isa 2:12
be on the proud
and one said, Holy, holy, holy Isa 6:3
is the *L. of hosts*
mine eyes have seen the King, Isa 6:5
the *L. of hosts*
sanctify the *L. of hosts*   Isa 8:13
himself, let him be
for the *L. of hosts* hath   Isa 14:27;
purposed it   23:9
five cities shall swear to the Isa 19:18
L. of hosts
L. of hosts is his name   Isa 47:4;
48:2; 51:15; 54:5; Jer 10:16; 31:35;
          32:18; 50:34; 51:19
king, whose name is the *L.* Jer 46:18;
of hosts   48:15
L. of hosts saith, I will punish Jer 46:25
the multitude
is it not of the *L. of hosts*   Hab 2:13
that the people
work for I am with you, saith Hag 2:4
L. of hosts
like as the *L. of hosts* thought Zec 1:6
to do to us
shall know that the *L. of hosts* Zec 2:9;
sent me   2:11; 4:9
came a great wrath from the Zec 7:12
L. of hosts
they cried, I would not hear, Zec 7:13
saith the *L. of hosts*
let us go to pray, and to seek Zec 8:21
the *L. of hosts*
many people shall come to Zec 8:22
seek the *L. of hosts*
go up to worship the King, Zec 14:16;
L. of hosts   14:17
every pot shall be holiness Zec 14:21
unto the *L. of hosts*
for I am a great King, saith Mal 1:14
L. of hosts

LORD *OUR GOD*

sacrifice to *L. our God*   Ex 3:18;
         5:3; 8:27; 10:25
there is none like to *L. our*   Ex 8:10;
God   Ps 113:5
thereof must we take to serve Ex 10:26
the *L. our God*
the *L. our God* spake unto us in De 1:6
Horeb
through wilderness, as *L. our* De 1:19;
God commanded   1:41; 6:20
which *L. our God* doth give De 1:20;
unto us   1:25; 2:29
L. our God delivered him   De 2:33;
before us   2:36; 3:3
nor unto whatsoever *L. our*   De 2:37
God forbade us
so nigh to them as *L. our God* De 4:7
is in all things
L. our God made a covenant   De 5:2
us in Horeb
the *L. our God* hath shewed us De 5:24
his glory
if we hear the voice of *L. our* De 5:25
God any more
go and hear all that the *L. our* De 5:27
God shall say
O Israel, *L. our God* is one   De 6:4;
Lord   M'k 12:29
to fear *L. our God;* to do   De 6:24;
before *L. our God*   6:25
that standeth this day before De 29:15
the *L. our God*
the secret things belong to the De 29:29
L. our God
cast lots for you before the   Jos 18:6
L. our God
an altar, beside the altar of   Jos 22:19;
L. our God   22:29

L. our God, he it is that   Jos 24:17
brought us up out of
the people said, The *L. our* Jos 24:24
God will we serve
whomsoever *L. our God* shall J'g 11:24
drive out
cease not to cry to the *L. our* 1Sa 7:8
God for us
L. our God be with us, as with 1Ki 8:57
fathers
let these my words be nigh   1Ki 8:59
L. our God
but if ye say, We trust in *L.* 2Ki 18:22
our God
O *L. our God,* save thou   2Ki 19:19
us out of his hand
and that it be of *L. our God* 1Ch 13:2
let us send
the *L. our God* made a   1Ch 15:13
breach on us, for that
he. is. *L. our God* his   1Ch 16:14;
judgments   Ps 105:7
O *L. our God*   1Ch 29:16;
2Ch 14:11; Ps 99:8; 106:47; Isa 26:13;
       37:20; Jer 14:22; Da 9:15
we keep the charge of the   2Ch 13:11
L. our God
because we have sought the 2Ch 14:7
L. our God
there is no iniquity with the 2Ch 19:7
L. our God
but with us is the *L. our God* 2Ch 32:8
to help us
L. our God shall deliver us 2Ch 32:11
out of the hand
grace hath been shewed from Ezr 9:8
the *L. our God*
will remember the name of   Ps 20:7
the *L. our God*
let the beauty of the *L. our God* Ps 90:17
be on us
yea, the *L. our God* shall cut Ps 94:23
them off
exalt ye the *L. our God* and   Ps 99:5;
worship at his   99:9
for the *L. our God* is holy; for Ps 99:9;
he is the *L. our God*   105:7
because of the house of the *L.* Ps 122:9
our God
so our eyes wait on the *L. our* Ps 123:2
God
we come to thee, for thou art Jer 3:22
the *L. our God*
in the *L. our God* is the   Jer 3:23
salvation of Israel
sinned against the *L. our God,* Jer 3:25
and have not obeyed voice of
L. our God
wherefore doth the *L. our God* Jer 5:19
these things
let us now fear the *L. our God* Jer 5:24
that giveth rain
for the *L. our God* hath put us Jer 8:14
to silence
sin we have committed against Jer 16:10
the *L. our God*
hath spoken to us in the name Jer 26:16
of *L. our God*
arise, and let us go up to Zion, Jer 31:6
to the *L. our God*
saying, Pray now to *L. our*   Jer 37:3;
God for us   42:20
we will obey the voice of the Jer 42:6
L. our God
the *L. our God* hath not sent Jer 43:2
thee to say, Go not
to declare the vengeance of Jer 50:28
the *L. our God*
let us declare in Zion the work Jer 51:10
of *L. our God*
to the *L. our God* belong   Da 9:9
mercies, tho' we
nor have we obeyed the voice Da 9:10
of the *L. our God*
for the *L. our God* is righteous Da 9:14
in all his works
we will walk in the name of the Mic 4:5
L. our God
they shall be afraid of the *L.* Mic 7:17
our God
as many as the *L. our God*   Ac 2:39
shall call
glory, honour, and power to   Re 19:1
the *L. our God*

LORD *SAID*

the *L. said* in his heart, I will Ge 8:21
not curse
he hearkened not as the *L.*   Ex 7:13;
said 7:22; 8:15, 19; De 9:3; J'g 2:15; 6:27

this is that which the *L. said,* Ex 16:23
Tomorrow
Moses told them all the words Ex 24:3
the *L. said*
all that the *L. said* we will do   Ex 24:7;
                       Nu 32:31
journeying to place of which Nu 10:29
L. said
as the *L. said* to him by the   Nu 16:40
hand of Moses
the *L. had said,* They shall Nu 26:65
surely die
as the *L. hath said*   De 31:3;
      Jos 14:12; Joe 2:32
according to all the *L. said*   Jos 11:23
to Moses
thou knowest the thing that   Jos 14:6
the *L. said*
what is the thing that *L. said* to 1Sa 3:17
thee
tell thee what the *L. said* to   1Sa 15:16
me this night
behold, the day of which the   1Sa 24:4
L. said to thee
the *L. said* to him, Curse   2Sa 16:10
David
L. said he would dwell   1Ki 8:12;
                      2Ch 6:1
nations, concerning which *L.* 1Ki 11:2
said to Israel
L. said not that he would   2Ki 14:27
blot out
whereof the *L. had said,* Ye 2Ki 17:12
shall not do
of which *L. said* in Jerusalem 2Ki 21:4;
         21:7; 2Ch 33:4
Solomon had made in temple 2Ki 24:13
as the *L. said*
L. hath said unto me, thou art Ps 2:7
my Son
L. said unto my Lord   Ps 110:1;
M't 22:44; M'k 12:36; Lu 20:42; Ac 2:34
then said the *L.*   Isa 7:3; 8:3;
Eze 44:2; Ho 3:1; Jon 4:10; Lu 20:13
for so *L. said* unto me, I will Isa 18:4
take my rest
thus hath *L. said* unto me   Isa 21:16;
             Jer 4:27; 6:6
wherefore *L. said,* Forasmuch Isa 29:13
as this people
cause my fury rest, I the *L.* Eze 21:17
have said
his *L. said* unto him, Well   M't 25:21;
done   25:23
to him said the *L.* in a vision, Ac 9:10
Ananias
I remembered the word of *L.* Ac 11:16
how he *said*

LORD with *SEEK*

if from thence thou shalt *seek* De 4:29
the *L.*
heart rejoice, that *seek L.*   1Ch 16:10;
                       Ps 105:3
seek the *L.* and his strength 1Ch 16:11;
                       Ps 105:4
set your heart to *seek* the *L.* 1Ch 22:19;
                    2Ch 11:16
prepared not his heart to   2Ch 12:14
seek the *L.*
and commanded Judah to   2Ch 14:4
seek the *L.* God
they entered into a covenant 2Ch 15:12
to *seek* the *L.*
that whosoever would not   2Ch 15:13
seek the *L.* God
Jehoshaphat set himself to   2Ch 20:3
seek the *L.*
out of the cities of Judah they 2Ch 20:4
came to *seek L.*
were come to *seek* the *L.* God Ezr 6:21
of Israel
they shall praise the *L.* that Ps 22:26
seek him
they that *seek* the *L.* shall not Ps 34:10
want any good
they that *seek L.* understand all Pr 28:5
things
neither do they *seek L.*   Isa 9:13;
            31:1; Ho 7:10
hearken to me, ye that *seek* the Isa 51:1
L. look to
seek ye the *L.* while he may be Isa 55:6
found
they shall go and *seek* the *L.* Jer 50:4
their God
shall return and *seek* the *L.* Ho 3:5
their God
they shall go with their herds Ho 5:6
to *seek* the *L.*

for it is time to *seek* the *L.*   Ho 10:12
till he come
seek ye the *L.* and ye shall live,   Am 5:6
lest he break
seek ye the *L.* all ye meek of the Zep 2:3
earth
saying, Let us go to *seek* the *L.* Zec 8:21
of hosts
many people shall come to   Zec 8:22
seek the *L.*
the *L.* whom ye *seek* shall   Mal 3:1
suddenly come
that the residue of men might   Ac 15:17
seek the *L.*
that they should *seek* the *L.* if Ac 17:27
haply might

LORD with *SENT*

the *L. sent* him forth from the   Ge 3:23
garden
we will destroy, the *L. sent* us Ge 19:13
to destroy it
told all the words of *L.* who had Ex 4:28
sent him
the *L.* God of the Hebrews *sent* Ex 7:16
me to thee
and *L. sent* thunder and hail on Ex 9:23
Egypt
ye shall know that the *L.* hath Nu 16:28
sent him
if die common death, then *L.* Nu 16:29
hath not *sent*
and when we cried, the *L.*   Nu 20:16
sent an angel
the *L. sent* fiery serpents   Nu 21:6
among the people
when *L. sent* you from   De 9:23
Kadesh-barnea
in all wonders which the *L.* De 34:11
sent him to do
that the *L. sent* a prophet unto J'g 6:8
Israel
then the *L. sent* Moses and   1Sa 12:8
Aaron
and the *L. sent* Jerubbaal;   1Sa 12:11;
the *L. sent* thunder   12:18
the *L. sent* me to anoint thee 1Sa 15:1
king over Israel
the *L. sent* thee on a journey, 1Sa 15:18
and said
I have gone the way which   1Sa 15:20
the *L. sent* me
go thy way, the *L.* hath *sent* 1Sa 20:22
thee away
the *L. sent* Nathan to David, 2Sa 12:1
and he came
L. sent pestilence on Israel   2Sa 24:15;
                  1Ch 21:14
tarry, for the *L.* hath *sent* me 2Ki 2:2
to Beth-el
L. hath *sent* me to Jericho; 2Ki 2:4;
sent me to Jordan   2:6
therefore the *L. sent* lions   2Ki 17:25
among them
the *L. sent* against him bands 2Ki 24:2
of the Chaldees
the *L. sent* an angel, who cut 2Ch 32:21
off
the *L. sent* a word into Jacob, Isa 9:8
and it lighted
whither the *L. sent* him to   Jer 19:14
prophesy
and the *L.* hath *sent* to you all Jer 25:4
his servants
nations to drink to whom the   Jer 25:17
L. had *sent* me
L. sent me to prophesy   Jer 26:12;
against this house   26:15
be known that the *L.* hath   Jer 28:9
truly *sent* him
hear Hananiah, the *L.* hath   Jer 28:15
not *sent* thee
Lord saith, and the *L.* hath   Eze 13:6
not *sent* them
the *L. sent* out a great wind   Jon 1:4
into the sea
obeyed, as the *L.* their God   Hag 1:12
had *sent* him
whom the *L.* hath *sent* to walk Zec 1:10
to and fro
know *L.* of hosts hath *sent* me Zec 2:9;
           2:11; 4:9; 6:15
lest hear the words which the   Zec 7:12
L. hath *sent*
Saul, the *L.* Jesus hath *sent* me, Ac 9:17
that thou
now know I that the *L.* hath   Ac 12:11
sent his angel

LORD *SPAKE*

called the name of *L.* that   Ge 16:13
spake to her
this is it that the *L. spake,*   Le 10:3
saying, I will
in the day the *L. spake* with   Nu 3:1;
Moses   9:1
as the *L. spake* unto Moses, so Nu 5:4
did Israel
that is the well whereof *L.*   Nu 21:16
spake to Moses
L. spake to you out of the   De 4:12
midst of fire
ye saw no similitude in the day De 4:15
the *L. spake*
these words the *L. spake* to   De 5:22
your assembly
written all the words which the De 9:10
L. spake
the ten commandments which   De 10:4
the *L. spake*
since the *L. spake* this word   Jos 14:10
to Moses
this mountain whereof *L.*   Jos 14:12
spake in that day
Samuel did that which the *L.* 1Sa 16:4
spake
L. may continue his word   1Ki 2:4
which he *spake*
fulfil the word of the *L.* which 1Ki 2:27
he *spake*
as the *L. spake* to David my   1Ki 5:5
father, saying
L. hath performed word he   1Ki 8:20;
spake   2Ki 10:10
perform his saying the *L.*   1Ki 12:15;
spake   2Ch 10:15
according to the word of the 1Ki 13:26;
L. which he *spake*   14:18;
16:12, 36; 17:16; 22:38; 2Ki 10:10; 24:2
according to saying of *L.*   1Ki 15:29;
spake by Ahijah   2Ki 10:17
and of Jezebel also *spake* the 1Ki 21:23
L. saying
this is the word of *L.* which he 2Ki 9:36
spake
the word of the *L.* which he 2Ki 15:12
spake to Jehu
the *L. spake* by his servants   2Ki 21:10
the prophets
L. spake unto Gad, David's   1Ch 21:9
seer, saying
L. spake to Manasseh and   2Ch 33:10
his people
moreover, the *L. spake* again Isa 7:10
to Ahaz
the *L. spake* also unto me   Isa 8:5
again, saying
for the *L. spake* thus to me   Isa 8:11
with a strong hand
at the same time *spake* the *L.* Isa 20:2
by Isaiah
these are the words that the *L.* Jer 30:4
spake
the word that the *L. spake*   Jer 50:1
against Babylon
for the *L.* hath done that   Jer 51:12
which he *spake*
the *L. spake* unto the fish, it Jon 2:10
vomited
then *spake* the *L.* to Paul in Ac 18:9
the night

LORD with *SPOKEN*

Abram departed as *L.* had   Ge 12:4;
spoken 21:1; 24:51; Ex 9:12, 35; De 6:19
Moses spake the words the *L.* Ex 4:30
had *spoken*
and said, All that the *L.* hath Ex 19:8
spoken will we do
gave in commandment all the Ex 34:32
L. had *spoken*
teach the statutes the *L.* hath Le 10:11
spoken
for *L.* had spoken to Moses,   Nu 1:48;
saying   15:22
the *L.* hath *spoken* good   Nu 10:29
concerning Israel
hath the *L.* indeed *spoken* only Nu 12:2
by Moses
Balak said to him, What   Nu 23:17
hath the *L. spoken*
word which *L.* hath not   De 18:21;
spoken   18:22
failed not ought which *L.* had Jos 21:45
spoken
L. have done the good he   1Sa 25:30
hath *spoken*

now then do it, for the *L.* hath 2Sa 3:18
spoken
it may continue, for thou, O   2Sa 7:29
L. hath *spoken* it
this is the sign which *L.* hath 1Ki 13:3
spoken
L. hath *spoken* it   1Ki 14:11;
Isa 21:17; 22:25; 24:3; 25:8; Joe 3:8;
                 Ob 18
after the *L.* had *spoken* these Job 42:7
words to Job
the *L.* hath *spoken*, and called Ps 50:1
the earth
for thus hath the *L. spoken* to Isa 31:4
me, like as
L. will do this thing that he   Isa 38:7
hath *spoken*
to whom the mouth of the *L.* Jer 9:12
hath *spoken*
give ear, be not proud, for the Jer 13:15
L. hath *spoken*
and ye shall say, what hath   Jer 23:35;
L. spoken   23:37
as the *L.* hath *spoken* against Jer 27:13
the nation
shall be destroyed, as the *L.* Jer 48:8
hath *spoken*
I the *L.* have *spoken* it   Eze 5:13;
5:15, 17; 17:21, 24; 21:32; 22:14; 24:14;
     26:14; 30:12; 34:24; 36:36; 37:14
thus saith the Lord, when the Eze 22:28
L. hath not *spoken*
for I have *spoken* it, saith *L.* Eze 26:5;
               28:10; 39:5
hear this word that the *L.* hath Am 3:1
spoken
the *L.* God hath *spoken*, who   Am 3:8
can but prophesy
the mouth of the *L.* of hosts   Mic 4:4
hath *spoken* it
fulfilled which was *spoken* of M't 1:22;
the *L.*   2:15
so then after the *L.* had   M'k 16:19
spoken to them
had seen the *L.* and that he   Ac 9:27
had *spoken*
at the first began to be *spoken* Heb 2:3
by the *L.*

LORD *THEIR GOD*

serve *L. their* God   Ex 10:7;
        2Ch 34:33; Jer 30:9
they shall know that I am the Ex 29:46;
L. their God Eze 28:26; 34:30; 39:22, 28
break covenant I am *L. their* Le 26:44;
God   Zec 10:6
forgat *L. their* God   J'g 3:7;
     8:34; 1Sa 12:9; Jer 3:21
because they forsook *L. their* 1Ki 9:9;
God   Jer 22:9
Israel had sinned against the   2Ki 17:7
L. their God
that were not right against the 2Ki 17:9
L. their God
fathers, that did not believe   2Ki 17:14
in the *L. their* God
they left all the   2Ki 17:16
commandments of the
L. their God
Judah kept not   2Ki 17:19
commandments of the
L. their God
obeyed not voice of the *L.*   2Ki 18:12;
their God   Jer 7:28
were consecrated to the *L.*   2Ch 31:6
their God
did sacrifice unto the *L. their* 2Ch 33:17
God only
words of *L. their* God which Jer 43:1
L. their God had sent him
they shall go and seek the *L.* Jer 50:4;
their God   Ho 3:5
and I will save them by the *L.* Ho 1:7
their God
and they do not return to the Ho 7:10
L. their God
people obeyed the voice of   Hag 1:12
the *L. their* God
the *L. their* God shall save   Zec 9:16
them in that day
and many shall he turn to the Lu 1:16
L. their God

LORD *THY GOD*

I am the *L. thy* God   Ex 20:2;
Ps 81:10; Isa 51:15; Ho 12:9; 13:4
for I the *L. thy* God am a   Ex 20:5;
jealous God   De 5:9

the *L. thy God* hath been with | De 2:7
thee
the *L. thy God* is a consuming | De 4:24
fire, a jealous God
for the *L. thy God* is a | De 4:31
merciful God
know therefore that the *L. thy* | De 7:9
God, he is God
for the *L. thy God* is among | De 7:21;
you | 23:14
as a man his son, so the *L.* | De 8:5
thy God chasteneth thee
thou shalt not do so to the *L.* | De 12:31
thy God
for the *L. thy God* is with thee | De 20:1
who brought
and thou shalt say before the | De 26:5;
L. thy God | 26:13
mayest fear this fearful name, | De 28:58
L. thy God
be strong, for the *L. thy God* is | Jos 1:9
with thee
only the *L. thy God* be with | Jos 1:17
thee as with Moses
therefore the *L. thy God* will | 2Sa 14:17
be with thee
Araunah said, The *L. thy* | 2Sa 24:23
God accept thee
entreat now the face of the *L.* | 1Ki 13:6
thy God
as the *L. thy God* liveth I | 1Ki 17:12;
have not a cake | 18:10
I am the *L. thy God* the holy | Isa 43:3
One of Israel
shall run to thee, because of | Isa 55:5
the *L. thy God*
pray for us to the *L. thy God* | Jer 42:2
even for this
that the *L. thy God* may shew | Jer 42:3
us the way wherein
which said to me, Where is | Mic 7:10
the *L. thy God*
the *L. thy God* in midst of | Zep 3:17
thee is mighty
thou shalt not tempt the *L.* | M't 4:7;
thy God | Lu 4:12

LORD *YOUR GOD*

ye shall be holy, for I *L. your* | Le 19:2
God am holy
L. your God hath multiplied | De 1:10
you as stars
the *L. your God* he shall fight | De 1:30;
for you | 3:22
ye shall not tempt the *L. your* | De 6:16
God as in Massah
the *L. your God* is God of | De 10:17
gods Lord of lords
the *L. your God* is he that | De 20:4
goeth with you
the *L. your God* is God in | Jos 2:11
heaven above
the *L. your God* is he that | Jos 23:3;
hath fought for you | 23:10
when the *L. your God* was | 1Sa 12:12
your king
but the *L. your God* ye shall | 2Ki 17:39
fear
is not the *L. your God* with | 1Ch 22:18
you
believe in the *L. your God* | 2Ch 20:20
so shall ye
ye dissembled, when ye sent | Jer 42:20
me to *L. your God*
so shall ye know that I am the | Joe 3:17
L. your God
a prophet shall the *L. your* | Ac 3:22;
God raise | 7:37

AGAINST THE LORD

I have sinned *against the L.* | Ex 10:16;
your God | Jos 7:20; 2Sa 12:13
that he heareth your | Ex 16:7;
murmurings *against the L.* | 16:8
have trespassed *against the L.* | Le 5:19;
| Nu 5:6; 31:16
if a soul commit trespass *against* | Le 6:2
the *L.*
only rebel not *against the L.* | Nu 14:9;
| Jos 22:19
are gathered together *against* | Nu 16:11;
the *L.* | 27:3; Ps 2:2; Ac 4:26
we have sinned, for we have | Nu 21:7
spoken *against the L.*
company of Korah, when they | Nu 26:9
strove *against the L.*
ye have sinned *against the L.* | Nu 32:23;
| Jer 40:3; 44:23

I have sinned *against the L.* | De 1:4;
| 1Sa 7:6; Jer 8:14
ye have been rebellious *against* | De 9:7;
the *L.* | 9:24; 31:27
that ye might rebel this day | Jos 22:16
against the L.
it will be, seeing ye rebel this | Jos 22:18
day *against the L.*
or if in transgression *against* | Jos 22:22
the *L.* save us not
God forbid we should rebel | Jos 22:29
against the L.
have not committed this | Jos 22:31
trespass *against the L.*
if a man sin *against the L.* who | 1Sa 2:25
shall entreat
sin *against the L.* in ceasing | 1Sa 12:23
to pray for you
behold, the people sin *against* | 1Sa 14:33
the *L.* in that
slay them here and eat, and | 1Sa 14:34
sin not *against the L.*
Israel had sinned *against the L.* | 2Ki 17:7
their God
did secretly things not right | 2Ki 17:9
against the L. God
transgression he committed | 1Ch 10:13
against the L.
because they had transgressed | 2Ch 12:2
against the L.
warn them that they trespass | 2Ch 19:10
not *against the L.*
whereas we have offended | 2Ch 28:13
already *against the L.*
Ahaz transgressed sore | 2Ch 28:19
against the L.
in distress did he trespass yet | 2Ch 28:22
more *against the L.*
rulers take counsel *against the* | Ps 2:2
L. and Anointed
and his heart fretteth *against* | Pr 19:3
the *L.*
there is no wisdom nor | Pr 21:30
counsel *against the L.*
because their doings are *against* | Isa 3:8
the *L.*
will work iniquity to utter error | Isa 32:6
against the L.
in transgressing and lying | Isa 59:13
against the L.
hast taught rebellion *against* | Jer 28:16;
the *L.* | 29:32
for he magnified himself | Jer 48:26;
against the L | 48:42
because they have sinned | Jer 50:7
against the L.
against Babylon he hath | Jer 50:14;
sinned *against the L.* | 50:29
because thou hast striven | Jer 50:24;
against the L. | Zep 1:17
but hast lifted up thyself | Da 5:23
against the L.
they have dealt treacherously | Ho 5:7
against the L.
what do ye imagine *against the* | Na 1:9
L. he will make
there is one that imagineth | Na 1:11
evil *against the L.*

ANGER OF THE LORD

anger of the L. was kindled | Ex 4:14
against Moses
anger of the L. was kindled | Nu 11:10;
against Israel | 25:3; Jos 7:1; J'g 2:14, 20;
| 3:8; 10:7; 2Sa 24:1; 2Ki 13:3; Isa 5:25
anger of the L. kindled against | Nu 12:9
Aaron and Miriam
that the fierce *anger of the L.* | Nu 25:4
may be turned away
to augment yet the *anger of* | Nu 32:14
the *L.* toward Israel
lest the *anger of the L.* be | De 6:15
kindled against thee
so will *anger of the L.* be | De 7:4;
kindled against you | Jos 23:16
then the *anger of the L.* shall | De 29:20
smoke against that man
anger of the L. was kindled | De 29:27
against this land
anger of the L. kindled | 2Sa 6:7;
against Uzzah | 1Ch 13:10
thro' *anger of the L.* it | 2Ki 24:20;
came to pass | Jer 52:3
anger of the L. kindled | 2Ch 25:15
against Amaziah
fierce *anger of the L.* is not | Jer 4:8
turned back from us
ashamed because of the fierce | Jer 12:13
anger of the L.

anger of the L. shall not | Jer 23:20;
return till | 30:24
deliver every man his soul | Jer 51:45
from *anger of the L.*
the *anger of the L.* hath | La 4:16
divided them
before the fierce *anger of the* | Zep 2:2
L. come upon you
be hid in day of the *anger of* | Zep 2:3
the *L.*

BEFORE THE LORD

Nimrod was a mighty hunter | Ge 10:9
before the L.
well watered, *before the L.* | Ge 13:10
destroyed Sodom
men of Sodom were sinners | Ge 13:13
before the L. exceedingly
but Abraham stood yet *before* | Ge 18:22
the *L.* and said
that I may eat and bless thee | Ge 27:7
before the L.
say to congregation, Come near | Ex 16:9
before the L.
lay it up *before the L.* to be | Ex 16:33;
kept | 1Sa 10:25
three times in year all males | Ex 23:17;
appear *before the L.* | 34:24; De 16:16;
| 1Sa 1:22
Aaron shall order the lamps | Ex 27:21;
before the L. | 40:25
Aaron shall bear their names | Ex 28:12
before the L.
for a memorial *before the L.* | Ex 28:29;
| 30:16; Nu 31:54
sprinkle seven times *before the* | Le 4:6;
L. | 4:17; 14:16, 27
there came a fire out from | Le 9:24
before the L.
went out fire, and they died | Le 10:2;
before the L. | Nu 3:4
bring her near, set her *before* | Nu 5:16;
the *L.* | 5:18, 30
shall be remembered *before* | Nu 10:9
the *L.* your God
it is a covenant of salt for | Nu 18:19
ever *before the L.*
hang them up *before the L.* | Nu 25:4
against the sun
Moses brought their cause | Nu 27:5
before the L.
I fell down *before the L.* | De 9:18
forty days
thou must eat them *before the* | De 12:18
L. thy God
his brethren which stand there | De 18:7
before the L.
controversy is, shall stand | De 19:17
before the L.
cursed be man *before the L.* | Jos 6:26
that buildeth
uttered his words *before the* | J'g 11:11
L. in Mizpeh
before the L. is your way | J'g 18:6
wherein ye go
all the people sat there *before* | J'g 20:26;
the *L.* | 2Sa 7:18
sin of the men was very great | 1Sa 2:17
before the L.
here I am, witness against me | 1Sa 12:3
before the L.
that I may reason with you | 1Sa 12:7
before the L.
was there that day detained | 1Sa 21:7
before the L.
if they be men, cursed be | 1Sa 26:19
they *before the L.*
it was *before the L.* which | 2Sa 6:21
chose me
they hanged them in the hill | 2Sa 21:9
before the L.
Hezekiah spread it *before* | 2Ki 19:14;
the *L.* | Isa 37:14
and the land is subdued | 1Ch 22:18
before the L.
did eat and drink *before the* | 1Ch 29:22
Lord with gladness
before the L. for he cometh to | Ps 96:13;
judge | 98:9
let them be *before the L.* | Ps 109:15
continually
walk *before the L.* in land of | Ps 116:9
living
hell and destruction are *before* | Pr 15:11
the *L.*
shall be for them that dwell | Isa 23:18
before the L.
present their supplications | Jer 36:7
before the L.

shall sit in it to eat bread   *Eze 44:3*
before the L.
made we not our prayer *before*   *Da 9:13*
the L.
wherewith shall I come *before*   *Mic 6:6*
the L. *and bow*
be silent, O all flesh, *before*   *Zec 2:13*
the L. *for he*
their men to pray *before the* L. *Zec 7:2;*
     8:21-22
we have walked mournfully   *Mal 3:14*
before the L.
charging them *before the* L.   *2Ti 2:14*
that they strive
bring no railing accusation   *2Pe 2:11*
before the L.

FROM THE LORD

I have gotten a man *from the*   *Ge 4:1;*
L.: fire *from the* L.   *19:24*
Laban said, The thing   *Ge 24:50*
proceedeth *from the* L.
there went forth a wind *from*   *Nu 11:31*
the L.
came out a fire *from the* L.   *Nu 16:35*
and consumed
there is wrath gone out *from*   *Nu 16:46*
the L. *the plague*
evil spirit *from the* L.   *1Sa 16:14;*
troubled him   *19:9*
deep sleep *from the* L. *was*   *1Sa 26:12*
fallen on them
it was his *from the* L.; *shall be 1Ki 2:15;*
peace *from the* L.   *2:33*
he shall receive the blessing   *Ps 24:5*
from the L.
reward of mine adversaries   *Ps 109:20*
from the L.
my help cometh *from the* L.   *Ps 121:2*
who made heaven
the answer of the tongue is   *Pr 16:1*
from the L.
and a prudent wife is *from the Pr 19:14*
L.
every man's judgment cometh   *Pr 29:26*
from the L.
seek to hide their counsel   *Isa 29:15*
from the L.
why sayest thou, My way is   *Isa 40:27*
hid *from the* L.
word that came to Jeremiah   *Jer 7:1;*
from the L.   *11:1; 18:1; 21:1; 26:1;*
27:1; 30:1; 32:1; 34:1, 8, 12; 35:1; 36:1;
     40:1
cursed whose heart departeth   *Jer 17:5*
from the L.
king asked, Is there any word   *Jer 37:17*
from the L.
I have heard a rumour *from*   *Jer 49:14*
the L. *an*
her prophets find no vision *from La 2:9*
the L.
my strength and hope is   *La 3:18*
perished *from the* L.
Jerusalem said, Get ye far   *Eze 11:15*
from the L.
hear what is the word that   *Eze 33:30*
cometh *from the* L.
committed whoredom,   *Ho 1:2*
departing *from the* L.
we have heard a rumour *from*   *Ob 1*
the L. *arise*
evil came down *from the* L. *to Mic 1:12*
the gate
remnant of Jacob shall be as a   *Mic 5:7*
dew *from the* L.
them that are turned back *from Zep 1:6*
the L.
tumult *from the* L. *shall be*   *Zec 14:13*
among them
things which were told her   *Lu 1:45*
from the L.
in the body we are absent *from 2Co 5:6*
the L.

I AM THE LORD

I am the L. that brought thee   *Ge 15:7*
out of Ur
I am the L.   *Ex 6:2;*
6:6, 8, 29; 12:12; Le 18:5-6, 21; Nu 3:13;
     Isa 43:11, 15
I am the L. thy God who   *Ex 20:2*
brought thee out of Egypt
I am the L. which hallow   *Le 22:32*
you, that brought
I am the L. that is my name;   *Isa 42:8;*
shall say, I am the L.   *44:5*

---

glory, that he knoweth that *I*   *Jer 9:24*
am the L.
behold, *I am the* L. *the God*   *Jer 32:27*
of all flesh
for *I am the* L. *I change not*   *Mal 3:6*

I AM THE LORD YOUR GOD

ye shall know that *I am the* L.   *Ex 6:7;*
your God   *16:12*
I am the L. *your God*   *Le 11:44;*
18:30; 19:3; 20:7; 23:22; J'g 6:10;
     Eze 20:5, 7, 19-20; Joe 2:27

I THE LORD

for *I the* L. *your God am holy*   *Le 19:2;*
     20:26; 21:8
for *I the* L. *do sanctify him*   *Le 21:15;*
     21:23; 22:9, 16
I the L. *have said it, I will*   *Nu 14:35;*
do it   *Eze 21:17*
I the L. *do keep it, I will water Isa 27:3*
it every
I the L. *the first, and with the Isa 41:4*
last I am he
when the needy seek, *I the* L. *Isa 41:17*
will hear them
I. *the* L. *have called thee in*   *Isa 42:6*
righteousness
that *I the* L. *which call thee by Isa 45:3*
thy name
I the L. *do all these things*   *Isa 45:7*
I the L. *created it*   *Isa 45:8*
I the L. *speak righteousness, I Isa 45:19*
declare things
have not *I the* L. *and there is Isa 45:21*
no God else
shalt know that *I the* L. *am*   *Isa 60:16*
thy Saviour
I the L. *will hasten it in his*   *Isa 60:22*
time
for *I the* L. *love judgment, I*   *Isa 61:8*
hate robbery
I the L. *search the heart, and*   *Jer 17:10*
try reins
I the L. *have spoken it*   *Eze 5:13;*
5:15, 17; 17:21; 21:32; 22:14; 24:14;
     26:14; 30:12
I the L. *will answer him that Eze 14:4;*
cometh   *14:7*
I the L. *have deceived that*   *Eze 14:9*
prophet
I the L. *have brought down,*   *Eze 17:24*
I the L. *have done it*
all shall see that *I the* L. *have Eze 20:48*
kindled it
that *I the* L. *have drawn forth Eze 21:5*
my sword
I the L. *will be their God*   *Eze 34:24*
David their prince
know that *I the* L. *their God Eze 34:30*
am with them
that *I the* L. *do build, I the*   *Eze 36:36*
L. *will do it*
know that *I the* L. *have*   *Eze 37:14*
performed it
shall know that *I the* L. *do*   *Eze 37:28*
sanctify Israel

IN THE LORD

he believed *in the* L. *and he*   *Ge 15:6*
counted it
Reuben, Gad, ye have no   *Jos 22:25;*
part *in the* L.   *22:27*
my heart rejoiceth *in the* L. *is 1Sa 2:1*
exalted *in the* L.
offer sacrifice, and put your trust *Ps 4:5*
in the L.
in the L. *put I my trust*   *Ps 11:1;*
     26:1; 31:6; 73:28
all ye that hope *in the* L.;   *Ps 31:24;*
be glad *in the* L.   *32:11*
my soul shall make her boast *in Ps 34:2*
the L.
my soul shall be joyful *in the* L. *Ps 35:9*
delight also thyself *in the* L.   *Ps 37:4;*
     Isa 58:14
rest *in the* L.; *in the* L. *will I Ps 37:7;*
praise his word   *56:10*
the righteous shall be glad *in Ps 64:10;*
     104:34
trust *in the* L., *with all thine Pr 3:5*
heart
putteth his trust *in the* L. *shall Pr 29:25*
be safe
in the L. *Jehovah is*   *Isa 26:4*
everlasting strength

---

the meek shall increase their   *Isa 29:19*
joy *in the* L.
but Israel shall be saved *in*   *Isa 45:17*
the L.
in the L. *have I righteousness Isa 45:24*
and strength
in the L. *shall all the seed of Isa 45:25*
Israel be justified
in the L. *is the salvation of*   *Jer 3:23*
Israel
she trusted not *in the* L. *drew Zep 3:2*
not near
Jerusalem shall be my strength *Zec 12:5*
in the L.
it was known, and many   *Ac 9:42*
believed *in the* L.
they abode, speaking boldly *in Ac 14:3*
the L.
ye receive her *in the* L.;   *Ro 16:2;*
great Amplias *in the* L.   *16:8*
salute Persis, who laboured   *Ro 16:12*
much *in the* L.
salute Rufus, chosen *in the*   *Ro 16:13*
L. *and his mother*
I Tertius who wrote this   *Ro 16:22*
salute you *in the* L.
glorieth, let him glory *in the*   *1Co 1:31;*
L.   *2Co 10:17*
and faithful *in the* L.; *called 1Co 4:17;*
in the L.   *7:22*
be married to whom she will, *1Co 7:39*
only *in the* L.
am I not an apostle, are not   *1Co 9:1*
ye may work *in the* L.
the seal of my apostleship are *1Co 9:2*
ye *in the* L.
nor the woman without the   *1Co 11:11*
man *in the* L.
that your labour is not in   *1Co 15:58*
vain *in the* L.
groweth to an holy temple *in Eph 2:21*
the L.
and testify *in the* L.; *now*   *Eph 4:17;*
are ye *in the* L.   *5:8*
children obey your parents *in Eph 6:1*
the L. *for this*
finally, my brethren, be strong *Eph 6:10*
in the L.
Tychicus a faithful minister   *Eph 6:21*
in the L.
brethren *in the* L. *waxing*   *Ph'p 1:14*
confident
I trust *in the* L. *I shall come Ph'p 2:24*
to you shortly
receive him therefore *in the*   *Ph'p 2:29*
L. *with gladness*
my brethren, stand fast *in the Ph'p 4:1;*
L.   *1Th 3:8*
that they be of the same mind *Ph'p 4:2*
in the L.
but I rejoiced *in the* L.   *Ph'p 4:10*
greatly, that at last
submit to your own husbands *Col 3:18*
in the L.
Tychicus who is a   *Col 4:7*
fellow-servant *in the* L.
ministry which thou hast   *Col 4:17*
received *in the* L.
know them which are over   *1Th 5:12*
you *in the* L.
we have confidence *in the* L.   *2Th 3:4*
touching
to thee, both in the flesh and   *Ph'm 16*
in the L.
joy of thee *in the* L. *refresh*   *Ph'm 20*
my bowels *in the* L.
blessed are the dead which die *Re 14:13*
in the L.

MOUTH OF THE LORD

word that proceedeth out of   *De 8:3*
mouth of the L.
and asked not counsel at the   *Jos 9:14*
mouth of the L.
thou hast disobeyed the   *1Ki 13:21*
mouth of the L.
for the *mouth of the* L. *hath Isa 1:20;*
spoken it *40:5; 58:14; Jer 9:12; Mic 4:4*
by a new name, which the   *Isa 62:2*
mouth of the L. *shall name*
and they speak not out of   *Jer 23:16*
mouth of the L.

MY LORD

Lot said unto him, Oh, not so, *Ge 19:18*
my L.
Moses said, O *my* L. I am not *Ex 4:10*
eloquent

O *my L.* send by hand of whom   *Ex 4:13*
thou wilt send
now let the power of *my L.*   *Nu 14:17*
be great
he said, What saith *my L.* to   *Jos 5:14*
his servant
O *my L.* if the Lord be with   *J'g 6:13*
us, why is this
O *my L.* wherewith shall I save   *J'g 6:15*
Israel
O *my L.* let the man of God   *J'g 13:8*
come again to us
thou hast said to the Lord,   *Ps 16:2*
Thou art *my L.*
stir up thyself, my God,   *Ps 35:23;*
my L.   *Joh 20:28*
the Lord said to *my L.*   *Ps 110:1;*
M't 22:44; M'k 12:36; Lu 20:42; Ac 2:34
my L. I stand on the   *Isa 21:8*
watchtower
but Zion saith, *My L.* hath   *Isa 49:14*
forgotten me
O *my L.* by the vision my   *Da 10:16*
sorrows
can the servant of *my L.* talk   *Da 10:17*
with this *my L.*
and I said, Let *my L.* speak,   *Da 10:19*
for thou hast
O *my L.* what shall be end of   *Da 12:8*
these things
said I, O *my L.* what are   *Zec 1:9;*
these   *6:4; 4:5; 4:13*
no, *my L.*   *Zec 1:19*
that the mother of *my L.*   *Lu 1:43*
should come
because they have taken   *Joh 20:13*
away *my L.*
the knowledge of Christ Jesus   *Ph'p 3:8*
my L.

NAME OF THE LORD

Abraham called on the *name*   *Ge 12:8*
of the L.
she called the *name of the L.*   *Ge 16:13*
that spake to her
Isaac called on *name of the*   *Ge 26:25*
L. and pitched there
shalt not take *name of the L.*   *Ex 20:7;*
in vain   *De 5:11*
I will proclaim *name of the L.*   *Ex 33:19*
before thee
and the Lord proclaimed   *Ex 34:5*
name of the L.
woman's son blasphemed the   *Le 24:11;*
name of the L.   *24:16*
to stand to minister in *name of*   *De 18:5;*
the L.   *18:7*
when a prophet speaketh in   *De 18:22*
the *name of the L.*
them hath God chosen to bless   *De 21:5*
in *name of the L.*
see that thou art called by the   *De 28:10*
name of the L.
because I will publish *name of*   *De 32:3*
the L. ascribe
thy servants are come because   *Jos 9:9*
of *name of the L.*
I come to thee in *name of the*   *1Sa 17:45*
L. of hosts
we have sworn both of us in   *1Sa 20:42*
name of the L.
whose name is called by the   *2Sa 6:2*
name of the L.
blessed the people in the   *2Sa 6:18;*
name of the L.   *1Ch 16:2*
no house built to the *name of*   *1Ki 3:2;*
the L.   *5:3, 5; 8:17, 20; 1Ch 22:7, 19;*
   2Ch 2:1, 4; 6:10
queen of Sheba heard   *1Ki 10:1*
concerning *name of the L.*
Elijah built an altar in the   *1Ki 18:32*
name of the L.
that which is true in *name*   *1Ki 22:16;*
of the L.   *2Ch 18:15*
and Elisha cursed them in   *2Ki 2:24*
name of the L.
which he spake in *name of*   *1Ch 21:19;*
the L.   *2Ch 33:18*
blessed be the *name of the L.*   *Job 1:21;*
   Ps 113:2
I will sing praises to *name*   *Ps 7:17*
of the L. most high
but we will remember *name*   *Ps 20:7*
of the L. our God
so the heathen shall fear the   *Ps 102:15*
name of the L.
to declare *name of the L.*   *Ps 102:21*
in Zion, and his praise

praise the *name of the L.*   *Ps 113:1;*
   135:1; 148:5, 13; Joe 2:26
then called I on *name of the*   *Ps 116:4*
L. O Lord, deliver
but the *name of the L.* will I   *Ps 118:10;*
destroy them   *118:11-12*
blessed be he that cometh in   *Ps 118:26*
the *name of the L.*
our help in the *name of the L.*   *Ps 124:8*
who made heaven
they which go by say, We   *Ps 129:8*
bless you in *name of the L.*
the *name of the L.* is a strong   *Pr 18:10*
tower, the righteous
to the place of the *name of*   *Isa 18:7*
the L. of hosts
glorify the *name of the L.* in   *Isa 24:15*
the isles of sea
the *name of the L.* cometh   *Isa 30:27*
from far, burning with
which swear by *name of the*   *Isa 48:1*
L. and make mention
let him trust in *name of the*   *Isa 50:10*
L. and stay on God
and to love the *name of the*   *Isa 56:6*
L. to be his servants
so shall they fear the *name of*   *Isa 59:19*
the L. from west
to bring their silver and gold   *Isa 60:9*
to *name of the L.*
all nations gathered to *name of*   *Jer 3:17*
the L.
saying, Prophesy not in the   *Jer 11:21*
name of the L.
why hast thou prophesied in   *Jer 26:9*
the *name of the L.*
he hath spoken to us in the   *Jer 26:16;*
name of the L.   *44:16*
Urijah that prophesied in the   *Jer 26:20*
name of the L.
we may not make mention of   *Am 6:10*
name of the L.
we will walk in *name of the L.*   *Mic 4:5*
for ever and ever
ye shall feed in the majesty of   *Mic 5:4*
the *name of the L.*
and they shall trust in *name*   *Zep 3:12*
of the L.
thou speakest lies in the *name*   *Zec 13:3*
of the L.
blessed is he that cometh in   *M't 21:9;*
the *name of the L.*   *23:39; M'k 11-9-10;*
   Lu 13:35; 19:38; Joh 12:13
and he spake boldly in *name of*   *Ac 9:29*
the *L.* Jesus
commanded them to be   *Ac 10:48*
baptized in *name of the L.*
to call over them the *name*   *Ac 19:13*
of the L. Jesus, saying
and the *name of the L.* Jesus   *Ac 19:17*
was magnified
for I am ready to die for the   *Ac 21:13*
name of the L. Jesus
wash away thy sins, calling on   *Ac 22:16*
the *name of the L.*
that the *name of the L.*   *2Th 1:12*
Jesus may be glorified
we command you in the *name*   *2Th 3:6*
of the L. Jesus Christ
prophets, who have spoken in   *Jas 5:10*
name of the L.
anointing him with oil in the   *Jas 5:14*
name of the L.

O LORD

I have waited for thy   *Ge 49:18*
salvation, O *L.*
who is like to thee, O *L.*   *Ex 15:11*
among gods
return, O *L.* unto Israel   *Nu 10:36;*
   Ps 6:4
which thou, O *L.* hast given   *De 26:10*
me
O *L.* what shall I say, Israel   *Jos 7:8*
turneth
so let all thy enemies perish, O   *J'g 5:31*
L.
O *L.* turn counsel of   *2Sa 15:31*
Ahithophel
thou art my lamp, O *L.* and   *2Sa 22:29*
Lord will
be it far from me, O *L.* that I   *2Sa 23:17*
should
O *L.* there is none like thee   *1Ch 17:20*
thine, O *L.* is the greatness,   *1Ch 29:11*
thine, O *L.*
help us, O *L.* our God O. *L.*   *2Ch 14:11*
thou art

arise, O *L.* save me; lead me,   *Ps 3:7;*
   5:8
O *L.*   *Ps 6:2*
O *L.* heal me   *Ps 6:2*
but thou, O *L.* how long   *Ps 6:3*
arise, O *L.*   *Ps 7:6; 9:19; 10:12; 17:13*
judge me, O *L.* according to my   *Ps 7:8;*
righteousness   *26:1*
O *L.* our Lord   *Ps 8:1; 8:9*
I will praise thee, O *L.*   *Ps 9:1*
have mercy upon me, O *L.*   *Ps 9:13;*
consider my trouble   *31:9; 86:3; 123:3*
I will love thee, O *L.* my   *Ps 18:1;*
strength   *19:14*
be not thou far from me, O   *Ps 22:19;*
L.   *35:22*
hear, O *L.*   *Ps 27:7;*
30:10; 39:12; 69:16; 86:6; 102:1; 119:145;
   140:6
I trusted in thee, O. *L.* I said   *Ps 31:14*
among the gods none like to   *Ps 86:8*
thee, O *L.*
teach me thy way, O *L.* I   *Ps 86:11;*
walk   *25:4; 27:11*
not unto us, O *L.* not unto us,   *Ps 115:1*
but to thy name
thou art near, O *L.* thy   *Ps 119:151*
commandments truth
hear my prayer, O *L.*   *Ps 143:1;*
   143:7; Isa 37:17; Da 9:19
O *L.* thou art my God, I will   *Isa 25:1*
exalt thee
thou, O *L.* art our Father   *Isa 63:16;*
our Redeemer   *64:8*
O *L.* thou art great; so be it,   *Jer 10:6;*
O *L.*   *11:5*
but thou, O *L.* knowest   *Jer 12:3*
me, thou hast seen
yet thou, O *L.* art in the midst   *Jer 14:9*
of us
O *L.* the hope of Israel, all   *Jer 17:13*
that forsake
heal me, O *L.* and I shall be   *Jer 17:14*
healed, save me
see, O *L.* and consider I am   *La 1:11;*
vile   *2:20*
thou, O *L.* remainest for ever,   *La 5:19*
thy throne
turn us unto thee, O *L.* we shall   *La 5:21*
be turned
we beseech thee, O *L.* we   *Jon 1:14*
beseech thee
O *L.* thou hast ordained   *Hab 1:12*
them for judgment
O *L.* revive thy work in midst   *Hab 3:2*
of the years
O *L.* thou Son of David   *M't 15:22;*
   20:30-31
depart, for I am a sinful man, O   *Lu 5:8*
L.
thou art worthy, O *L.* to   *Re 4:11*
receive glory
saying, How long, O *L.* holy   *Re 6:10*
and true
who shall not fear thee, O *L.*   *Re 15:4*
and glorify
O *L.* which art, and wast, and   *Re 16:5*
shalt be

OF THE LORD

for it was *of the L.* to harden   *Jos 11:20*
hearts
because I have asked him *of*   *1Sa 1:20*
the L.
he rehearsed them in the ears   *1Sa 8:21*
of the L.
Saul said, Blessed be ye *of*   *1Sa 23:21;*
the L.   *2Sa 2:5*
his name Jedidiah because *of*   *2Sa 12:25*
the L.
according to the saying *of*   *1Ki 15:29*
the L.
he said, Behold this evil is *of*   *2Ki 6:33*
the L.
meet the man of God and   *2Ki 8:8*
enquire *of the L.* by him
according to the saying *of*   *2Ki 10:17*
the L. to Elijah
one man, by whom we may   *2Ch 18:7*
enquire *of the L.*
go, enquire *of the L.* for me,   *2Ch 34:21*
and for Israel
I will say *of the L.* He is my   *Ps 91:2*
refuge
but the disposing thereof is *of*   *Pr 16:33*
the L.
man's going are *of the L.;*   *Pr 20:24;*
safety is *of the L.*   *21:31*

worship because *of the L.* that is faithful   *Isa 49:7*

O arm *of the L.* awake as in ancient days   *Isa 51:9*

enquire, I pray thee, *of the L.* for us   *Jer 21:2*

pay that I vowed, salvation is *of* the L.   *Jon 2:9*

ceased, saying, The will *of the L.* be done   *Ac 21:14*

I have received *of the L.* that which   *1Co 11:23*

and a door was opened to me *of the L.*   *2Co 2:12*

the same shall he receive *of the* L.   *Eph 6:8*

knowing that *of the L.* ye receive reward   *Col 3:24*

grant that he may find mercy *of the L.*   *2Ti 1:18*

that he shall receive any thing *of the L.*   *Jas 1:7*

and ye have seen the end *of the* L.   *Jas 5:11*

longsuffering *of the L.* is salvation   *2Pe 3:15*

PROPHET, PROPHETS OF THE LORD

Samuel established to be a *prophet of the L.*   *1Sa 3:20*

when Jezebel cut off the *prophet of the L.*   *1Ki 18:4*

Jezebel slew the *prophets of the L.*; I only remain a   *1Ki 18:13; 18:22*

is there not here a *prophet of the L.* to inquire of him   *1Ki 22:7; 2Ki 3:11; 2Ch 18:6*

a *prophet of the L.* was there, whose name was Oded   *2Ch 28:9*

SAITH THE LORD

thus *saith the L.*   *Ex 4:22; 5:1; 7:17; 1Sa 2:27; 2Sa 12:11; 24:12*

what *the L. saith*, that will I speak   *Nu 24:13*

thus *saith the L.* God of Israel   *Jos 7:13; 24:2; J'g 6:8; 2Sa 12:7*

but now *the L. saith*, Be it far from me   *1Sa 2:30*

thus *saith the L.* of hosts   *1Sa 15:2; 2Sa 7:8; 1Ch 17:7; Jer 6:9; 7:3, 21*

what *the L. saith*, that will I speak   *1Ki 22:14*

iniquity shall not be purged, *saith the L.*   *Jer 5:14; 35:17; 49:5; 50:31*

now will I rise, *saith the L.*, now will I   *Isa 33:10; Ps 12:5*

now *saith the L.* that formed me from the womb   *Isa 49:5*

be removed *saith the L.* that hath mercy on thee   *Isa 54:10*

for I am with thee, *saith the L.*   *Jer 1:8; 1:19; 30:11*

and that my fear is not in thee, *saith the L.*   *Jer 2:19*

played the harlot, yet return upon me, *saith the L.*   *Jer 3:1*

if thou wilt return, *saith the L.* return unto me   *Jer 4:1*

fear ye not me *saith the L.*; I have seen it, *saith the L.*   *Jer 5:22; 7:11*

from evil to evil, they know not me, *saith the L.*   *Jer 9:3*

was not this to know me? *saith the L.*   *Jer 22:16*

am I a God at hand, *saith the* Jer 23:23 L.

can any hide, that I shall not see him, *saith the L.*   *Jer 23:24*

what burden? I will even forsake you, *saith the L.*   *Jer 23:33*

for I have not seen him, *saith the L.*   *Jer 27:15*

they prophesy, I have not sent them, *saith the L.*   *Jer 29:9*

L. saith and the Lord hath not sent them   *Eze 13:6; 13:7*

I am against you *saith the L.*;   *Eze 13:8;*
thus it was, *saith the L.*   *16:19*

even the rod, it shall be no more, *saith the L.*   *Eze 21:13*

ye my flock are men, and I am your God *saith the L.*   *Eze 34:31*

behold, it is come, and it is done, *saith the L.* God   *Eze 39:8*

and I will accept you, *saith the L.* God   *Eze 43:27*

is it not even thus, O Israel *saith the L.*   *Am 2:11*

this liketh you *saith the L.*; shall not be *saith the L.*   *Am 4:5; 7:3*

are called by my name, *saith the L.* that doeth this   *Am 9:12*

hear ye now what *the L. saith*, Arise thou   *Mic 6:1*

behold, I am against thee, *saith the L.*   *Na 2:13; 3:5*

therefore wait ye upon me, *saith the L.*   *Zep 3:8*

why? *saith the L.* of hosts; I am with you, *saith the L.*   *Hag 1:9; 1:13*

for I, *saith the L.* will be to her a wall of fire   *Zec 2:5*

not by might nor power, but by my Spirit, *saith the L.*   *Zec 4:6*

I have loved you, *saith the L.* yet ye say   *Mal 1:2*

should I accept this of your hand, *saith the L.*   *Mal 1:13*

for I am a great king, *saith the L.* of hosts   *Mal 1:14*

that oppress, and fear not me, *saith the L.* of hosts   *Mal 3:5*

and prove me now herewith, *saith the L.* of hosts   *Mal 3:10*

and they shall be mine, *saith the L.* of hosts   *Mal 3:17*

in the day that I shall do this, *saith the L.* of hosts   *Mal 4:3*

saith the L. who doeth all these things   *Ac 15:17*

vengeance is mine, I will repay *saith the L.*   *Ro 12:19*

they will not hear me for all this, *saith the L.*   *1Co 14:21*

come out and be ye separate, *saith the L.*   *2Co 6:17*

and I regarded them not, *saith the L.*   *Heb 8:9*

who hath said, I will recompense, *saith the L.*   *Heb 10:30*

I am the Beginning and Ending, *saith the L.*   *Re 1:8*

SERVANT, SERVANTS OF THE LORD

Moses the *servant of the L.* died there in Moab   *De 34:5*

after the death of Moses, the *servant of the L.*   *Jos 1:1*

which Moses the *servant of the L.* commanded   *Jos 1:13; 8:31, 33; 11:12; 22:2, 5; 2Ki 18:12*

which Moses the *servant of the L.* gave you   *Jos 1:15; 12:6; 13:8; 18:7; 22:4*

them did Moses the *servant of the L.* smite   *Jos 12:6*

when Moses the *servant of the L.* sent me from Kadesh   *Jos 14:7*

Joshua son of Nun the *servant of the L.* died   *Jos 24:29; J'g 2:8*

avenge the blood of all the *servants of the L.*   *2Ki 9:7*

see there be here none of the *servants of the L.*   *2Ki 10:23*

tabernacle Moses the *servant of the L.* made   *2Ch 1:3*

according to commandment of Moses the *servant of the L.*   *2Ch 21:6*

praise, O ye *servants of the L.*   *Ps 113:1; 135:1*

behold, bless ye the Lord, O all ye *servants of the L.*   *Ps 134:1*

this is the heritage of the *servants of the L.*   *Isa 54:17*

and the *servants of the L.* must not strive   *2Ti 2:24*

SERVE THE LORD

men go, that they may *serve the* L. their God   *Ex 10:7*

said, Go *serve the L.* your God   *Ex 10:8; 11:24; 12:31*

serve the L. our God, we know not with what we must *serve the* L.   *Ex 10:26*

ye shall *serve the L.* your God, ye shall bless   *Ex 23:25*

to *serve the L.* thy God with all thy heart   *De 10:12*

therefore fear and *serve the* L.   *Jos 24:14*

if it seem evil unto you to *serve the L.* choose you   *Jos 24:15*

therefore will we *serve the L.* he is our God   *Jos 24:18; 21:24*

Joshua said, Ye cannot *serve the L.* for he is holy   *Jos 24:19*

that ye have chosen you the L. to *serve* him   *Jos 24:22*

but *serve the L.* with all your heart   *1Sa 12:20*

will bring me again, then I will *serve the* L.   *2Sa 15:8*

but yield, and *serve the L.* your God   *2Ch 30:8; 35:3*

and commanded Judah to *serve the* L.   *2Ch 33:16; 34:33*

serve the L. with fear, and rejoice with   *Ps 2:11*

serve the L. with gladness   *Ps 100:2*

and the kingdoms gathered to *serve the* L.   *Ps 102:22*

receive reward, for ye *serve the* L. Christ   *Col 3:24*

SIGHT OF THE LORD

Er was wicked in *sight of the* L. and he slew him   *Ge 38:7*

should have been accepted in *sight of the* L.   *Le 10:19*

do that which is good in *sight of the* L.   *De 6:18; 12:28*

do what is right in *sight of the* L.   *De 12:25; 2Ki 12:2; 14:3; 15:3, 24; 18:3; 22:2; 2Ch 20:32; 24:2; 25:2; 26:4; 27:2; 29:2; 34:2*

wickedness done in the *sight of the* L.   *1Sa 12:17; 1Ki 21:25; 2Ki 21:6*

this is but a light thing in *sight of the* L.   *2Ki 3:18*

did not what was right in *sight of the* L.   *2Ki 16:2; 2Ch 28:1*

precious in *sight of the* L. is death of his saints   *Ps 116:15*

ye say, He that doeth evil, is good in *sight of the* L.   *Mal 2:17*

for he shall be great in the *sight of the* L.   *Lu 1:15*

not only in the *sight of the* L. but of men   *2Co 8:21*

humble yourselves in the *sight of the* L.   *Jas 4:10*

SPIRIT OF THE LORD

Spirit of the L. came on Othniel, and he judged   *J'g 3:10*

Spirit of the L. came on Gideon, on Jephtha   *J'g 6:34; 11:29*

Spirit of the L. began to move Samson   *J'g 13:25; 14:6, 19; 15:14*

Spirit of the L. will come on Saul   *1Sa 10:6*

Spirit of the L. came on David   *1Sa 16:13*

but the *Spirit of the L.* departed from Saul   *1Sa 16:14*

Spirit of the L. spake by me, his word was   *2Sa 23:2*

Spirit of the L. shall carry thee   *1Ki 18:12*

which way went *Spirit of the L.* from me to speak   *1Ki 22:24; 2Ch 18:23*

lest the *Spirit of the L.* hath taken him up   *2Ki 2:16*

on Jahaziel came *Spirit of the L.* in midst   *2Ch 20:14*

Spirit of the L. shall rest upon him   *Isa 11:2*

Spirit of the L. bloweth upon it; hath directed *Spirit of the L.*   *Isa 40:7; 40:13*

the *Spirit of the L.* shall lift up a standard   *Isa 59:19*

Spirit of the L. is upon me   *Isa 61:1; Lu 4:18*

Spirit of the L. caused him to rest   *Isa 63:14*

Spirit of the L. fell upon me; carried in *Spirit of the L.*   *Eze 11:5; 37:1*

O house of Jacob is the *Spirit of the L.* straitened   *Mic 2:7*

but truly I am full of power by the *Spirit of the L.*   *Mic 3:8*

how is it ye have agreed to tempt *Spirit of the L.*   *Ac 5:9*

the *Spirit of the L.* caught   *Ac 8:39*
away Philip
where the *Spirit of the L.* is,   *2Co 3:17*
there is liberty
from glory to glory, even as   *2Co 3:18*
by the *Spirit of the L.*

TEMPLE OF THE LORD

Eli sat on a seat by a post of   *1Sa 1:9*
the *temple of the L.*
and ere the lamp of God went   *1Sa 3:3*
out in the *temple of the L.*
she came to the people into   *2Ki 11:13*
temple of the L.
Hezekiah cut gold off from   *2Ki 18:16*
doors of *temple of the L.*
bring out of the *temple of*   *2Ki 23:4*
the L. vessels made for Baal
all vessels Solomon had   *2Ki 24:13*
made in the *temple of the L.*
Uzziah went in *temple of*   *2Ch 26:16*
L. to
Jotham entered not into the   *2Ch 27:2*
temple of the L.
took away uncleanness   *2Ch 29:16*
found in *temple of the L.*
foundation of the *temple of*   *Ezr 3:6*
the L. was not yet laid
laid foundation of *temple*   *Ezr 3:10;*
of the L.   *Hag 2:18*
temple of the L., the temple   *Jer 7:4*
of the L. are these
basket of figs were set before   *Jer 24:1*
the *temple of the L.*
at door of *temple of the L.*   *Eze 8:16*
were 25 men with backs toward
temple of the L.
consider before a stone was   *Hag 2:15*
laid in *temple of the L.*
and he shall build the   *Zec 6:12;*
temple of the L.   *6:13, 15*
crown shall be for a memorial   *Zec 6:14*
in *temple of the L.*
when Zacharias went into the   *Lu 1:9*
temple of the L.

TO, UNTO THE LORD

I have lift up mine hands *to*   *Ge 14:22*
the L. most high
I have taken on me to speak   *Ge 18:27;*
to the L.   *18:31*
let us go, and do sacrifice *to*   *Ex 5:17;*
the L.   *8:8, 29*
we must hold a feast *to the L.*   *Ex 10:9;*
  12:14; Nu 29:12
sing *to the L.*   *Ex 15:1;*
15:21; J'g 5:3; 1Ch 16:23; Ps 13:6; 30:4;
68:32; 95:1; 96:1-2; 98:1, 5; 104:33;
147:7; 149:1; Isa 12:5; 42:10; Jer 20:13
for to-day is a sabbath *to the*   *Ex 16:25;*
L.   *35:2; Le 25:2*
he that sacrificeth save *unto*   *Ex 22:20*
the L. only
it is most holy *unto the L.*   *Ex 30:10;*
31:15; Le 23:20; 27:21, 30, 32; Nu 6:8;
  Ezr 8:28
said, Pray *to the L.*   *Nu 21:7;*
  Jer 29:7; Ac 8:24
these things ye shall do *to the*   *Nu 29:39*
L. in feasts
thou shalt not do so *to the L.*   *De 12:31*
thy God
I have opened my mouth *to*   *J'g 11:35;*
the L.   *11:36*
I had wholly dedicated the   *J'g 17:3*
silver *to the L.*
that came not up *to the L.* to   *J'g 21:8*
Mizpeh
Hannah prayed *to the L.* and   *1Sa 1:10*
wept sore
displeased Samuel, and he   *1Sa 8:6*
prayed *to the L.*
there is no restraint *to the L.*   *1Sa 14:6*
to save by many
will hang them up *to the L.* in   *2Sa 21:6*
Gibeah
Abiathar from being priest *to*   *1Ki 2:27*
the L.
Elisha shut door, prayed *to*   *2Ki 4:33;*
the L.   *6:18*
Hezekiah clave *to the L.* and   *2Ki 18:6*
kept his command
Hezekiah turned face to wall,   *2Ki 20:2;*
prayed *to the L.*   *2Ch 32:24; Isa 37:15;*
  38:2

this passover holden *to the L.*   *2Ki 23:23*
in Jerusalem
not drink it, but poured it   *1Ch 11:18*
out *to the L.*
give thanks *to the L.* call on   *1Ch 16:8;*
his name   *16:41; Ps 92:1*
they burn *to the L.* morning   *2Ch 13:11*
and evening
to bring *to the L.* the   *2Ch 24:9*
collection that Moses
but yield yourselves *to the L.*   *2Ch 30:8*
and serve him
salvation belongeth *to the L.* thy   *Ps 3:8*
blessing
they cried *unto the L.* but he   *Ps 18:41*
answered not
and *to the L.* I made   *Ps 30:8;*
supplication   *142:1*
who can be compared *to the*   *Ps 89:6*
L. be likened *to the L.*
what shall I render *to the L.*   *Ps 116:12*
for benefits
I said *to the L.,* Thou art my   *Ps 140:6*
God, hear voice
abomination *to the L.*   *Pr 3:32;*
11:1, 20; 12:22; 15:8-9, 26; 16:5; 17:15;
  20:10, 23
commit thy works *to the L.*   *Pr 16:3*
lendeth *to the L.*   *Pr 19:17*
shall vow a vow *to the L.* and   *Isa 19:21*
perform it
they shall return even *to the*   *Isa 19:22*
L. he shall heal
shall be holiness *to the L.*   *Isa 23:18;*
  Jer 2:3; Zec 14:20
it shall be *to the L.* for a   *Isa 55:13*
name, for a sign
that hath joined himself *to the*   *Isa 56:3;*
L.   *56:6*
wilt thou call this an   *Isa 58:5*
acceptable day *to the L.*
Jeremiah prayed *to the L.*   *Jer 32:16*
they have left off to take heed   *Ho 4:10*
to the L.
Jonah prayed *to the L.* and said   *Jon 4:2*
consecrate gain *unto the L.*   *Mic 4:13*
and substance *unto the L.*
therefore I will look *to the L.* I   *Mic 7:7*
will wait for
one day, which shall be known   *Zec 14:7*
to the L.
but shalt perform *to the L.*   *M't 5:33*
thine oaths
brought him to present him *to*   *Lu 2:22*
the L.
every male shall be called holy   *Lu 2:23*
to the L.
believers were the more added   *Ac 5:14*
to the L.
exhorted that they would   *Ac 11:23*
cleave *to the L.*
as they ministered *unto the L.*   *Ac 13:2*
and fasted
had prayed, they commended   *Lu 14:23*
them *to the L.*
if ye have judged me faithful   *Ac 16:15*
to the L.
regardeth it *to the L.* eateth *to*   *Ro 14:6*
the L.
whether we live, we live *to the*   *Ro 14:8*
L. we die *to the L.*
but first gave their own selves   *2Co 8:5*
to the L.
proving what is acceptable *to*   *Eph 5:10*
the L.
submit yourselves as *to the*   *Eph 5:22;*
L.   *6:7; Col 3:23*

VOICE OF THE LORD

and obey *voice of the L.*   *De 30:8;*
  Jer 26:13; 38:20
obeyed not the *voice of the*   *Jos 5:6;*
L.   *1Sa 28:18; 1Ki 20:36; Jer 3:25;*
7:28; 42:13, 21; 43:4, 7; 44:23; Da 9:10
wherefore didst thou not   *1Sa 15:19*
obey *voice of the L.*
Saul said, Yea, I have obeyed   *1Sa 15:20*
the *voice of the L.*
and sacrifices, as in obeying   *1Sa 15:22*
the *voice of the L.*
the *voice of the L.* is upon the   *Ps 29:3*
waters
the *voice of the L.* is   *Ps 29:4;*
powerful   *29:5*
the *voice of the L.* divideth the   *Ps 29:7*
flames of fire
the *voice of the L.* shaketh the   *Ps 29:8*
wilderness of Kadesh

the *voice of the L.* maketh the   *Ps 29:9*
hinds to calve
they hearkened not to the   *Ps 106:25*
voice of the L.
I heard the *voice of the L.*   *Isa 6:8*
saying
thro' *voice of the L.* shall   *Isa 30:31*
Assyrians be beaten
a *voice of the L.* that rendereth   *Isa 66:6*
recompence
we will obey *voice of the L.*   *Jer 42:6*
that it may be well with us when
we obey *voice of the L.*
remnant of the people obeyed   *Hag 1:12*
voice of the L.
if ye will diligently obey the   *Zec 6:15*
voice of the L.
the *voice of the L.* came to   *Ac 7:31*
Moses, saying

WAY OF THE LORD

command his household to   *Ge 18:19*
keep *way of the L.*
whether they will keep the *way*   *J'g 2:22*
of the L.
Amon walked not in the *way*   *2Ki 21:22*
of the L.
blessed are they who walk in   *Ps 119:1*
way of the L.
the *way of the L.* is strength   *Pr 10:29*
to the upright
prepare *way of the L.*   *Isa 40:3;*
  M't 3:3; M'k 1:3; Lu 3:4
are foolish, they know not *way*   *Jer 5:4*
of the L.
great men, for they have known   *Jer 5:5*
way of the L.
the *way of the L.* is not   *Eze 18:25;*
equal   *18:29; 33:17, 20*
one crying, Make straight *way*   *Joh 1:23*
of the L.
Apollos was instructed in *way*   *Ac 18:25*
of the L.

WAYS OF THE LORD

for I have kept the *ways of*   *2Sa 22:22;*
the L.   *Ps 18:21*
Jehoshaphat was lifted up in   *2Ch 17:6*
ways of the L.
yea, they shall sing in the *ways*   *Ps 138:5*
of the L.
the *ways of the L.* are right,   *Ho 14:9*
and the just
cease to pervert the right *ways*   *Ac 13:10*
of the L.

WORD OF THE LORD

he that feared the *word of the*   *Ex 9:20*
L. amongst
and he that regarded not the   *Ex 9:21*
word of the L. left
according to the *word of the*   *Nu 3:16;*
L. 3:51; 4:45; 36:5; De 34:5; Jos 8:27;
19:50; 22:9; 1Ki 12:24; 13:26; 14:18;
16:12, 34; 17:5, 16; 22:38; 2Ki 1:17
  4:44; 7:16; 9:26; 14:25
because he hath despised the   *Nu 15:31*
word of the L.
I cannot go beyond the *word*   *Nu 22:18*
of the L. my God
at that time to shew you the   *De 5:5*
word of the L.
the *word of the L.* was   *1Sa 3:1*
precious in those days
nor was *word of the L.* yet   *1Sa 3:7*
revealed to Samuel
because thou hast rejected   *1Sa 15:23;*
the *word of the L.*   *15:26*
the *word of the L.* is tried   *2Sa 22:31;*
  Ps 18:30
might fulfil *word of the L.*   *1Ki 2:27;*
  2Ch 36:21
they hearkened therefore to   *1Ki 12:24;*
the *word of the L.*   *2Ch 11:4; Jer 37:2*
came a man of God by *word*   *1Ki 13:1*
of the L. to Bethel
he cried against the altar in   *1Ki 13:2*
the *word of the L.*
the sign the man of God had   *1Ki 13:5*
given by *word of the L.*
so it was charged me by   *1Ki 13:9*
word of the L. saying
angel spake by *word of the*   *1Ki 13:18*
L. saying, Bring him back

the man who was disobedient   1Ki 13:26
unto the word of the L.
for the saying he cried by the   1Ki 13:32
word of the L.
they buried him according to   1Ki 14:18
the word of the L.
and that word of the L.   1Ki 17:24
in my mouth is truth
prophet in word of the L.   1Ki 20:35
Smite me, I pray
enquire, I pray thee, at   1Ki 22:5;
word of the L.   2Ch 18:4
Jehoshaphat said, Word of the   2Ki 3:12
L. is with him
this is word of the L.   2Ki 9:36;
  15:12
fall to the earth nothing of   2Ki 10:10
the word of the L.
this was the word of the L.   2Ki 15:12
Hezekiah said, Good is   2Ki 20:19;
the word of the L.   Isa 39:8
according to the word of the   2Ki 23:16;
L. 24:2; 1Ch 11:3   10;   12:23;   15:15;
  Jer 13:2; Jon 3:3
committed even against word   1Ch 10:13
of the L.
to do commandment of   2Ch 30:12
king by word of the L.
our fathers have not kept the   2Ch 34:21
word of the L.
that word of the L. might be   2Ch 36:22;
accomplished   Ezr 1:1
for the word of the L. is right,   Ps 33:4
and his works
by word of the L. were   Ps 33:6
heavens made, and all host
till his word came, the word   Ps 105:19
of the L. tried him
and the word of the L. from   Isa 2:3;
Jerusalem   Mic 4:2
the word of the L. was to   Isa 28:13
them precept on precept
O generation, see ye the word   Jer 2:31
of the L.
the word of the L. is to   Jer 6:10;
them a reproach   20:8
lo, they have rejected the word   Jer 8:9
of the L. and what
behold, they say to me, Where   Jer 17:15
is the word of the L.
to this day the word of the L.   Jer 25:3
hath come unto me
if the word of the L. be   Jer 27:18
with them, let them make
then I knew that this was the   Jer 32:8
word of the L.
the word of the L. that came   Ho 1:2
to Hosea son of
they shall wander to seek the   Am 8:12
word of the L.
the word of the L. is   Zep 2:5
against you, O Canaan
this is word of the L. to   Zec 4:6
Zerubbabel, saying
the burden of the word of the   Zec 9:1;
L. in the land of Hadrach   12:1; Mal 1:1
poor of the flock knew that it   Zec 11:11
was word of the L.
Peter remembered word of   Lu 22:61;
the L.   Ac 11:16
they had testified, and had   Ac 8:25;
preached the word of the L.   13:49;
  15:35-36; 16:32
and glorified the word of the   Ac 13:48
L.
heard the word of the L. Jesus   Ac 19:10
for from you sounded out the   1Th 1:8
word of the L.
for this we say to you by the   1Th 4:15
word of the L.
that the word of the L. may   2Th 3:1
have free course
but the word of L. endureth   1Pe 1:25
for ever

WORDS OF THE LORD

Moses told people, all words   Ex 24:3;
of the L.   Nu 11:24
and Moses wrote all the   Ex 24:4
words of the L. and rose up
this stone heard all the words   Jos 24:27
of the L.
Samuel told the people words   1Sa 8:10
of the L.
hearken thou to the voice of   1Sa 15:1
the words of the L.
came by words of the L.   2Ch 29:15
to cleanse the house

words of the L. are pure words,   Ps 12:6
as silver
Baruch wrote all words of the   Jer 36:4
L. from mouth of
read in the roll thou hast   Jer 36:6;
written words of the L.   36:8
had heard out of the book all   Jer 36:11
the words of the L.
but a famine of hearing the   Am 8:11
words of the L.

WORK OF THE LORD

all the people shall see the   Ex 34:10
work of the L.
they regard not the work of   Isa 5:12
the L. nor consider
cursed that doeth the work   Jer 48:10
of the L. deceitfully
this is the work of the L.;   Jer 50:25;
declare the work of the L.   51:10
always abounding in the   1Co 15:58
work of the L.
for he worketh the work of   1Co 16:10
the L. as I also do

WORKS OF THE LORD

which had known all the   Jos 24:31
works of the L.
which had seen all the great   J'g 2:7
works of the L.
because they regard not the   Ps 28:5
works of the L.
come, behold the works of   Ps 46:8
the L. what desolations
I will remember the works of   Ps 77:11
the L. and thy wonders
these see the works of the L.   Ps 107:24
and his wonders
the works of the L. are great;   Ps 111:2;
declare works of the L.   118:17

WRATH OF THE LORD

ere it was chewed wrath of   Nu 11:33
the L. was kindled
for great is the wrath of   2Ki 22:13;
the L.   2Ch 34:21
the wrath of the L. turned   2Ch 12:12
from him, that
wrath of the L. was   2Ch 29:8
upon Judah and Jerusalem
so that the wrath of the L.   2Ch 32:26
came not upon them
until wrath of the L. arose   2Ch 36:16
against his people
therefore was wrath of the L.   Ps 106:40
kindled
thro' the wrath of the L. is the   Isa 9:19
land darkened
the earth shall remove in the   Isa 13:13
wrath of the L.
because the wrath of the L.   Jer 50:13
not be inhabited
gold not be able to deliver   Eze 7:19;
them in day of wrath of the   Zep 1:18
L.

LORDLY

brought forth butter in a l. dish   J'g 5:25
a l. price (S)   Zec 11:13

LORDS

he said, Behold now, my l. turn   Ge 19:2
the l. of the high places of   Nu 21:28
Arnon
God is God of gods, and Lord   De 10:17
of l.
five l. of the Philistines; the   Jos 13:3
five l. of the Philistines, and all   J'g 3:3
l. of the Philistines came up   J'g 16:5
l. of the Philistines brought   J'g 16:8
up to
called for the l. of the   J'g 16:18
Philistines
l. of the Philistines came up   J'g 16:18
unto
the l. of the Philistines   J'g 16:23
gathered
l. of the Philistines were there   J'g 16:27
the house fell upon the l. and   J'g 16:30
upon
gathered all the l. of the   1Sa 5:8
Philistines

together all the l. of the   1Sa 5:11
Philistines
number of the l. of the   1Sa 6:4
Philistines
was on you all, and on your l.   1Sa 6:4
l. of the Philistines went after   1Sa 6:12
them
five l. of the Philistines had   1Sa 6:16
seen it
Philistines belonging to the   1Sa 6:18
five l.
l. of the Philistines went up   1Sa 7:7
against
the l. of the Philistines passed   1Sa 29:2
nevertheless the l. favour thee   1Sa 29:6
displease not the l. of the   1Sa 29:7
Philistines
for the l. of the Philistines   1Ch 12:19
upon
his l. and all Israel there   Ezr 8:25
present
O give thanks to the Lord of l.   Ps 136:3
l. of the heathen have broken   Isa 16:8
down
other l. beside thee have had   Isa 26:13
say my people, We are l.   Jer 2:31
l. of the flock (R)   Jer 25:34; 25:35
and rulers, great l. and   Eze 23:23
renowned
and my l. sought unto me; and   Da 4:36
a great feast to a thousand of   Da 5:1
his l.
in him, and his l. were   Da 5:9
astonied
of the words of the king and   Da 5:10
his l.
thou and thy l. thy wives, and   Da 5:23
and with the signet of his l.   Da 6:17
birthday made a supper to his   M'k 6:21
l.
there be gods many, and l.   1Co 8:5
many
the King of kings, and Lord of   1Ti 6:15
l.
as being l. over God's heritage   1Pe 5:3
is Lord of l. and King of   Re 17:14
kings
King Of Kings, And Lord Of   Re 19:16
L.

LORD'S

him in the ward of his l. house   Ge 40:7
we steal out of thy l. house   Ge 44:8
silver
and we also will be my l.   Ge 44:9
bondmen
behold, we are my l. servants,   Ge 44:16
both
speak a word in my l. ears,   Ge 44:18
and let
know how that the earth is the   Ex 9:29
L.
it in haste: it is the L.   Ex 12:11
passover
is the sacrifice of the L.   Ex 12:27
passover
the L. law may be in thy mouth   Ex 13:9
hast; the male shall be the L.   Ex 13:12
Who is on the L. side? let him   Ex 32:26
they brought the L. offering to   Ex 35:21
and brass brought the L.   Ex 35:24
offering
sweet savour: all the fat is the   Le 3:16
L.
goat upon which the L. lot fell   Le 16:9
month at even is the L.   Le 23:5
passover
which should be the L.   Le 27:26
firstling
it be ox, or sheep: it is the L.   Le 27:26
Is the L. hand waxed short   Nu 11:23
all the L. people were   Nu 11:29
prophets
the L. heave offering to   Nu 18:28
Aaron
the L. tribute of the sheep was   Nu 31:37
the L. tribute was three score   Nu 31:38;
  31:39
the L. tribute was thirty and   Nu 31:40
two
which was the L. heave   Nu 31:41
offering
L. anger was kindled the   Nu 32:10
same
the L. anger was kindled   Nu 32:13
against
of heavens it the L. thy God   De 10:14

L. wrath be kindled against *De 11:17*
you
because it is called the L. *De 15:2*
release
For the L. portion is his people *De 32:9*
Moses the L. servant gave you *Jos 1:15*
captain of the L. host said *Jos 5:15*
unto
wherein the L. tabernacle *Jos 22:19*
Ammon, shall surely be the L. *J'g 11:31*
the pillars of the earth are the *1Sa 2:8*
L.
make the L. people to *1Sa 2:24*
transgress
son of Eli, the L. priest in *1Sa 14:3*
Shiloh
the L. anointed is before him *1Sa 16:6*
for the battle is the L. and he *1Sa 17:47*
will
for me, and fight the L. *1Sa 18:17*
battles
that Saul had slain the L. *1Sa 22:21*
priests
unto my master, the L. *1Sa 24:6*
anointed
lord; for he is the L. anointed *1Sa 24:10*
his hand against the L. *1Sa 26:9*
anointed
hand against the L. anointed *1Sa 26:11*
your master, the L. anointed *1Sa 26:16*
hand to destroy the L. *2Sa 1:14*
anointed
I have slain the L. anointed *2Sa 1:16*
because he cursed the L. *2Sa 19:21*
anointed
take thou thy l. servants, and *2Sa 20:6*
L. oath that was between them *2Sa 21:7*
an hundred men of the L. *1Ki 18:13*
prophets
that they should be the L. *2Ki 11:17*
people
The arrow of the L. *2Ki 13:17*
deliverance
are they not all my l. servants *1Ch 21:3*
glory had filled the L. house *2Ch 7:2*
that they should be the L. *2Ch 23:16*
people
the L. throne is in heaven; his *Ps 11:4*
For the kingdom is the L.; and *Ps 22:28*
earth is the L. and the fulness *Ps 24:1*
the L. name is to be praised *Ps 113:3*
even the heavens, are the L. *Ps 115:16*
in the courts of the L. house *Ps 116:19*
This is the L. doing; it is *Ps 118:23*
How shall we sing the L. song *Ps 137:4*
weight and balance are the L. *Pr 16:11*
that the mountain of the L. *Isa 2:2*
house
shall be the shame of thy l. *Isa 22:18*
house
is the day of the L. vengeance *Isa 34:8*
received of the L. hand double *Isa 40:2*
and blind as the L. servant *Isa 42:19*
One shall say, I am the L.; and *Isa 44:5*
the L. hand is not shortened *Isa 59:1*
for they are not the L. *Jer 5:10*
Stand in the gate of the L. *Jer 7:2*
house
L. flock is carried away *Jer 13:17*
captive
stood in the court of the L. *Jer 19:14*
house
took I the cup at the L. hand *Jer 25:17*
Stand in the court of the L. *Jer 26:2*
house
come to worship in the L. *Jer 26:2*
house
of the new gate of the L. *Jer 26:10*
house
the vessels of the L. house *Jer 27:16*
shall
all the vessels of the L. house *Jer 28:3*
again the vessels of the L. *Jer 28:6*
house
ears of the people in the L. *Jer 36:6*
house
words of the Lord in the L. *Jer 36:8*
house
of the new gate of the L. *Jer 36:10*
house
is the time of the L. vengeance *Jer 51:6*
been a golden cup in the L. *Jer 51:7*
hand
the sanctuaries of the L. *Jer 51:51*
house
day of the L. anger none *La 2:22*
escaped

of the L. mercies that we are *La 3:22*
not
door of the gate of the L. *Eze 8:14*
house
inner court of the L. house *Eze 8:16*
of the brightness of the L. *Eze 10:4*
of the east gate of the L. *Eze 10:19*
house
unto the east gate of the L. *Eze 11:1*
house
that is desolate, for the L. sake *Da 9:17*
shall not dwell in the L. land *Ho 9:3*
priests, the L. ministers, mourn *Joe 1:9*
and the kingdom shall be the L. *Ob 21*
O mountains, the L. *Mic 6:2*
controversy
The L. voice crieth unto the *Mic 6:9*
city
the cup of the L. right hand *Hab 2:16*
shall
pass in the day of the L. *Zep 1:8*
sacrifice
them in the day of the L. *Zep 1:18*
wrath
before the day of the L. anger *Zep 2:2*
be hid in the day of the L. *Zep 2:3*
anger
that the L. house should be *Hag 1:2*
built
spake Haggai the L. *Hag 1:13*
messenger
in the L. message unto the *Hag 1:13*
people
the foundation of the L. *Hag 2:18*
temple
pots in the L. house shall be *Zec 14:20*
this is the L. doing, and it is *M't 21:42*
in the earth, and hid his l. *M't 25:18*
money
This was the L. doing, and it *M'k 12:11*
before he had seen the L. *Lu 2:26*
Christ
that servant, which knew his *Lu 12:47*
will
he called every one of his l. *Lu 16:5*
debtors
live therefore, or die, we are *Ro 14:8*
the L.
being a servant, is the L. *1Co 7:22*
freeman
cannot be partakers of the *1Co 10:21*
L. table
the earth is the L. and the *1Co 10:26*
fulness
earth is the L. and the *1Co 10:28*
fulness
this is not to eat the L. *1Co 11:20*
supper
do shew the L. death till he *1Co 11:26*
come
himself, not discerning the *1Co 11:29*
L. body
none, save James, the L. *Ga 1:19*
brother
ordinance of man for the L. *1Pe 2:13*
sake
I was in the Spirit on the L. *Re 1:10*
day

LORDSHIP

Gentiles exercise l. over *M'k 10:42;*
them *Lu 22:45*
death hold l. over (B) *Ro 6:9*
l. over your faith (N) *2Co 1:24*
all government, authority, *Eph 1:21*
power, and l. (B)

LORDSHIPS

thrones or l. rulers or *Col 1:16*
authorities (B)

LO-RUHAMAH

said unto him, Call her name L. *Ho 1:6*
Now when she had weaned L. *Ho 1:8*

LOSE

and thou l. thy life, with the *J'g 18:25*
lives
alive, that we l. not all the *1Ki 18:5*
beasts
the owners thereof to l. their *Job 31:39*
life
vomit up, and l. thy sweet *Pr 23:8*
words
A time to get, and a time to l. a *Ec 3:6*

better to l. one of members *M't 5:29;*
(A)(B)(N)(P)(R) 5:30
He that findeth his life shall *M't 10:39*
l. it
he shall in no wise l. his *M't 10:42*
reward
will save his life shall l. it *M't 16:25*
will l. his life for my sake *M't 16:25*
shall find
whole world, and l. his own *M't 16:26*
soul
many will l. their faith *M't 24:10*
(N)(P)
even if everyone l. faith in *M't 26:33*
you, I never will (P)
will save his life shall l. it *M'k 8:35*
shall l. his life for my sake *M'k 8:35*
whole world, and l. his own *M'k 8:36*
soul
unto you, he shall not l. his *M'k 9:41*
reward
will save his life shall l. it *Lu 9:24*
will l. his life for my sake *Lu 9:24*
gain the whole world, and l. *Lu 9:25*
himself
hundred sheep, if he l. one of *Lu 15:4*
them
if she l. one piece, doth not *Lu 15:8*
light a
shall seek to save his life shall *Lu 17:33*
l. it
shall l. his life shall preserve it *Lu 17:33*
He that loveth his life shall l. *Joh 12:25*
nothing
He that loveth his life shall l. *Joh 12:25*
it
so they may not l. heart (B) *Col 3:21*
l. not those things which we have *2Jo 8*

LOSES

who never l. faith in me (P) *M't 11:6*

LOSETH

l. his life for my sake shall *M't 10:39*
find it

LOSS

not unto thee; I bare the l. of *Ge 31:39*
it
he shall pay for the l. of his *Ex 21:19*
time
shall I know the l. of children *Isa 47:8*
in one day, the l. of children *Isa 47:9*
to have gained this harm and *Ac 27:21*
l.
be no l. of any man's life *Ac 27:22*
among
shall be burned, he shall *1Co 3:15*
suffer l.
me, those I counted l. for *Ph'p 3:7*
Christ
I count all things but l. for *Ph'p 3:8*
I have suffered the l. of all *Ph'p 3:8*

LOST

or for any manner of l. thing *Ex 22:9*
Or have found that which was l. *Le 6:3*
keep, or the l. thing which he *Le 6:4*
found
days that were before shall be *Nu 6:12*
l.
Hesbon is l. even to (B) *Nu 21:30*
with all l. thing of thy brother's *De 22:3*
which he hath l. and thou hast *De 22:3*
the asses of Kish Saul's father *1Sa 9:3*
were l.
as for thine asses that were l. *1Sa 9:20*
three
foreigners l. heart (R) *2Sa 22:46*
like the army that thou hast l. *1Ki 20:25*
l. their manly vigor (B)(R) *Job 30:2*
I have gone astray like a l. *Ps 119:176*
sheep
have, after thou hast l. the *Isa 49:20*
other
seeing I have l. my children *Isa 49:21*
My people hath been l. sheep *Jer 50:6*
she had waited, and her hope *Eze 19:5*
was l.
have ye sought that which was *Eze 34:4*
l.
I will seek that which was l. *Eze 34:16*
bones are dried, and our *Eze 37:11*
hope is l.

but if the salt have *l.* his savour	M't 5:13
Lord, save, we are *l.* (B)	M't 8:25
the *l.* sheep of the house of Israel	M't 10:6; 15:24
is come to save that which was	M't 18:11
little ones should be *l.* (B)(N)(P)	M't 18:14
if the salt have *l.* his saltness	M'k 9:50
but if the salt have *l.* his savour	Lu 14:34
and go after that which is *l.*	Lu 15:4
I have found my sheep which was *l.*	Lu 15:6
I have found the piece which I had *l.*	Lu 15:9
alive again; he was *l.* and is found	Lu 15:24
alive again; and was *l.* and is found	Lu 15:32
to seek and to save that which was *l.*	Lu 19:10
not a hair of head he *l.* (B)(N)	Lu 21:18
should not be *l.* (P)	Joh 3:16
that remain, that nothing be *l.*	Joh 6:12
and none of them is *l.* but the	Joh 17:12
which thou gavest me have I *l.* none	Joh 18:9
l. without law (B)	Ro 2:12
fallen asleep are *l.* (B)(N)	1Co 15:18
be hid, it is hid to them that are *l.*	2Co 4:3
plain proof they are *l.* (P)	Ph'p 1:28
l. the power of reason (N)	2Ti 3:8
shrink back and are *l.* (P)	Heb 10:3
what was lovely to look at is *l.* (N)	Jas 1:11
not willing any be *l.* (N)	2Pe 3:9

LOT

one *l.* for Lord other for scapegoat	Le 16:8; 16:9-10
land shall be divided by *l.*	Nu 26:55; Eze 48:29
he shall divide the land by *l.* for an inheritance	Nu 33:54; 36:2; Jos 13:6; Eze 47:22
this is the land ye shall inherit by *l.*	Nu 34:13
Jacob is the *l.*of his inheritance	De 32:9
this was the *l.* of the tribe of Judah	Jos 15:1
the *l.* of Joseph	Jos 16:1
was a *l.* for Manasseh	Jos 17:1
why hast thou given me but one *l.*	Jos 17:14
thou shalt not have one *l.* only, but mountain	Jos 17:17
the *l.* of the tribe of Benjamin came up	Jos 18:11
and the second *l.* came forth to Simeon	Jos 19:1
the third *l.* came for the children of Zebulun	Jos 19:10
the fourth *l.* came out to Issachar	Jos 19:17
fifth *l.* to Asher	Jos 19:24
sixth *l.* to Naphtali	Jos 19:32
the seventh *l.* came for the tribe of Dan	Jos 19:40
l. for families of Kohathites	Jos 21:4; 1Ch 6:54
Gershon had by *l.*	Jos 21:6
gave by *l.* to the Levites	Jos 21:8
come up with me into my *l.* to fight, likewise go with thee into thy *l.*	J'g 1:3
we will go up by *l.* against it, and take ten men	J'g 20:9
Saul said to God, Give a perfect *l.*	1Sa 14:41
to sons of Merari were given by *l.*	1Ch 6:63
to thee will I give the land of Canaan, the *l.* of your inheritance	1Ch 16:18; Ps 105:11
to thee they were divided by *l.*	1Ch 24:5
now the first *l.* came forth to Jehoiarib	2Ch 24:7
now the first *l.* came forth for Asaph	1Ch 25:9
they cast Pur, that is *l.* before Haman	Es 3:7
portion of cup, thou maintainest my *l.*	Ps 16:5

shall not rest on the *l.* of the righteous	Ps 125:3
cast in thy *l.* among us, let us all have	Pr 1:14
l. is cast into lap, disposing of the Lord	Pr 16:33
the *l.* causeth contentions to cease	Pr 18:18
this is the *l.* of them that rob	Isa 17:14
and he hath cast the *l.* for	Isa 34:17
the smooth stones of the stream are thy *l.*	Isa 57:6
this is thy *l.* from me, saith the Lord	Jer 13:25
bring it out, let no *l.* fall upon	Eze 24:6
shalt stand in thy *l.* at end of the days	Da 12:13
shalt have none that shall cast a cord by *l.*	Mic 2:5
cast a line by *l.* (A)(B)(E)(R)	Mic 2:5
his *l.* was to burn incense when he went	Lu 1:9
the *l.* fell on Matthias, was numbered	Ac 1:26
thou hast no *l.* or part in this matter	Ac 8:21
he divided their land to them by *l.*	Ac 13:19
threw in *l.* with Paul (P)	Ac 17:4

LOT a person

Haran begat *L.*	Ge 11:27
Terah took *L.*	Ge 11:31
Abram departed, *L.* went with him	Ge 12:4; 13:1
L. had flocks	Ge 13:5
was a strife between herdmen of Abram and *L.*	Ge 13:7
then *L.* chose him all the plain of Jordan	Ge 13:11
they took *L.* prisoner	Ge 14:12
L. sat in the gate of Sodom; *L.* seeing them	Ge 19:1
pulled *L.* into house	Ge 19:10
angels hastened *L.*	Ge 19:15
God sent *L.* out of the midst of the overthrow	Ge 19:29
both the daughters of *L.* were with child	Ge 19:36
I have given Ar to the children of *L.*	De 2:9; 2:19
they have holpen the children of *L.*	Ps 83:8
likewise as it was in the days of *L.*	Lu 17:28
delivered just *L.* vexed with filthy conversation	2Pe 2:7

LOTAN

L. and Shobal, and Zibeon	Ge 36:20
the children of *L.* were Hori	Ge 36:22
that came of the Horites; duke *L.*	Ge 36:29
L. and Shobal, and Zibeon	1Ch 1:38
the sons of *L.*: Hori, and Homan	1Ch 1:39

LOTAN'S

Hemam; and *L.* sister was Timna	Ge 36:22
Homam: and Timna was *L.* sister	1Ch 1:39

LOTS

shall cast *l.* upon the two goats	Le 16:8
cast *l.* for you here before the Lord	Jos 18:6
here cast *l.* for you before the Lord	Jos 18:8
Joshua cast *l.* for them in Shiloh	Jos 18:10
Cast *l.* between me and Jonathan my	1Sa 14:42
cast *l.* over against their brethren	1Ch 24:31
they cast *l.* ward against ward, as	1Ch 25:8
they cast *l.* as well the small	1Ch 26:13
son, a wise counsellor, they cast *l.*	1Ch 26:14
we cast the *l.* among the priests, the	Ne 10:34
the rest of the people also cast *l.* to	Ne 11:1

them, and cast *l.* upon my vesture	Ps 22:18
they have cast *l.* for my people	Joe 3:3
gates, and cast *l.* upon Jerusalem	Ob 11
Come, and let us cast *l.* that we	Jon 1:7
So they cast *l.* and the lot fell	Jon 1:7
they cast *l.* for her honourable men	Na 3:10
parted his garments, casting *l.*	M't 27:35
upon my vesture did they cast *l.*	M't 27:35
garments, casting *l.* upon them	M'k 15:24
they parted his raiment, and cast *l.*	Lu 23:34
Let us not rend it, but cast *l.* for it	Joh 19:24
and for my vesture they did cast *l.*	Joh 19:24
they gave forth their *l.*; and the lot	Ac 1:26

LOT'S

and the herdman of *L.* cattle	Ge 13:7
Remember *L.* wife	Lu 17:32

LOUD

singing with *l.* instruments to	2Ch 30:21
the people shouted with a *l.*	Ezr 3:13
the singers sang *l.* with Jezrahiah	Ne 12:42
and Mordecai cried with a *l.* cry	Es 4:1
sing to him, play skilfully with a *l.* noise	Ps 33:3
make a *l.* noise and rejoice and sing praise	Ps 98:4
praise him on *l.* cymbals	Ps 150:5
she is *l.* and stubborn, her feet abide not	Pr 7:11
another angel cried with a *l.* cry to him	Re 14:18

LOUD VOICE

he came to me, I cried with a *l.* voice	Ge 39:14
the voice of the trumpet exceeding *l.*	Ex 19:16
the Levites shall speak with a *l.* voice	De 27:14
all the country wept with a *l.* voice	2Sa 15:23
he blessed congregation with a *l.* voice	1Ki 8:55
they sware to the Lord with a *l.* voice	2Ch 15:14
to praise Lord with a *l.* voice	2Ch 20:19; Lu 19:37
many wept with a *l.* voice, many shouted	Ezr 3:12
the congregation answered with a *l.* voice	Ezr 10:12
he blesseth his friend with a *l.* voice	Pr 27:14
and though they cry with a *l.* voice	Eze 8:18
he cried with a *l.* voice, saying, Cause them	Eze 9:1
she spake out with a *l.* voice, and said, Blessed art thou	Lu 1:42
unclean spirit cried with a *l.* voice	Lu 8:28; Ac 8:7
turned back and with a *l.* voice glorified God	Lu 17:15
said with a *l.* voice; Stand upright on feet	Ac 14:10
Festus said with a *l.* voice, Paul, thou art beside	Ac 26:24
a strong angel proclaiming with a *l.* voice	Re 5:2
many angels saying with a *l.* voice, Worthy is	Re 5:12
angel saying with a *l.* voice	Re 8:13; 14:7, 9, 15
Woe, woe	
and I heard a *l.* voice saying in heaven	Re 12:10

LOUD VOICES

and they were instant with *l.* voices	Lu 23:23

LOUDER

the voice of the trumpet waxed *l.* and *l.*	Ex 19:19

LOUNGERS

l. in the market (A)(B)(P) *Ac 17:5*

LOVE

a few days for the *l.* he had to *Ge 29:20*
least of all stedfast *l.* (R) *Ge 32:10;*
 1Ch 6:42
thou shalt *l.* thy neighbour as *Le 19:18;*
thyself *19:34; M't 19:19; 22:39;*
 M'k 12:31
thou shalt *l.* the Lord thy God *De 6:5;*
with all thy heart *10:12; 11:1, 13, 22;*
 19:9; 30:6
he is God, the faithful God, *De 7:9;*
which keepeth covenant with *Da 9:4*
them that *l.* him
he will *l.* thee, bless thee, and *De 7:13*
multiply thee
Lord had a delight in thy *De 10:15*
fathers to *l.* them
l. therefore the stranger, for *De 10:19*
ye were strangers
to know whether ye *l.* the Lord *De 13:3*
your God
in that I command thee to *l.* *De 30:16*
Lord thy God
that thou mayest *l.* the Lord *De 30:20*
and obey his voice
take heed to *l.* the Lord your *Jos 22:5;*
God *23:11*
let them that *l.* him be as the *J'g 5:31*
sun
and all the king's servants *l.* *1Sa 18:22*
thee
wonderful, passing the *l.* of *2Sa 1:26*
women
the hatred was greater than *2Sa 13:15*
the *l.* he had
hate those who *l.* you *2Sa 19:6*
(A)(B)(E)(R)
shouldest thou *l.* them that *2Ch 19:2*
hate Lord
God keepeth mercy for them *Ne 1:5*
that *l.* him
felt more *l.* for Esther (B) *Es 2:17*
O ye sons, how long will ye *l.* *Ps 4:2*
vanity
let them that *l.* thy name be *Ps 5:11*
joyful in thee
I will *l.* thee, O Lord, my *Ps 18:1*
strength
O *l.* the Lord, all ye saints, *Ps 31:23*
Lord preserves
let such as *l.* thy salvation say *Ps 40:16;*
 70:4
they that *l.* his name shall dwell *Ps 69:36*
there
ye that *l.* the Lord hate evil, *Ps 97:10*
he preserveth
abundance of stedfast *l.* (R) *Ps 106:7;*
 106:45
let your stedfast *l.* come (R) *Ps 119:41*
usest to do to those that *l.* *Ps 119:132*
thy name
great peace have they who *l.* *Ps 119:165*
thy law
they shall prosper that *l.* thee *Ps 122:6*
the Lord preserveth them that *Ps 145:20*
l. him
how long, ye simple, will ye *l.* *Pr 1:22*
simplicity
l. wisdom, and she shall keep *Pr 4:6*
thee
be thou ravished always with *Pr 5:19*
her *l.*
let us take our fill of *l.* till the *Pr 7:18*
morning
all they that hate me, *l.* death *Pr 8:36*
rebuke a wise man, and he will *l.* *Pr 9:8*
thee
hatred stirreth up strifes, but *l.* *Pr 10:12*
covereth sins
better is a dinner of herbs *Pr 15:17*
where *l.* is, than
kings *l.* him that speaketh *Pr 16:13*
right
he that covereth a transgression *Pr 17:9*
seeketh *l.*
they that *l.* it shall eat the fruit *Pr 18:2*
open rebuke is better than *Pr 27:5*
secret *l.*
better than *l.* that is hidden *Pr 27:5*
(A)(B)(E)(R)
a time to *l.* and a time to hate *Ec 3:8*
no man knoweth either *l.* or *Ec 9:1*
hatred
also their *l.* and hatred is now *Ec 9:6*
perished

therefore do the virgins *l.* thee *Ca 1:3*
love more than wine, the *Ca 1:4*
upright *l.* thee
and his banner over me was *l.* *Ca 2:4*
comfort me with apples, for I *Ca 2:5;*
am sick of *l.* *5:8*
the midst thereof being paved *Ca 3:10*
with *l.*
how pleasant art thou, O *l.* for *Ca 7:6*
delights
l. is strong as death, jealousy is *Ca 8:6*
cruel as grave
many waters cannot quench *l.* if *Ca 8:7*
a man would give all his substance
for *l.* it would be contemned
to serve and *l.* the name of the *Isa 56:6*
Lord
the Lord *l.* judgment, I hate *Isa 61:8*
be glad with Jerusalem all ye *Isa 66:10*
that *l.* her
I remember thee, the *l.* of thy *Jer 2:2*
espousals
why trimmest thou thy way to *Jer 2:33*
seek *l.*
and my people *l.* to have it so *Jer 5:3*
I have loved thee with an *Jer 31:3*
everlasting *l.*
behold, thy time was the time *Eze 16:8*
of *l.*
the age of courting (B) *Eze 16:8*
she was more corrupt in her *Eze 23:11*
inordinate *l.*
more corrupt in foolish *Eze 23:11*
fondness (A)
more corruptly in her lusting *Eze 23:11*
(B)
more corrupt in her doting *Eze 23:11*
(E)(R)
the Babylonians came to her *Eze 23:17*
into bed of *l.*
came into her bed of amours *Eze 23:17*
(B)
with their mouth they shew *Eze 33:31*
much *l.*
brought Daniel into tender *l.* *Da 1:9*
with prince
find favor, compassion, loving *Da 1:9*
kindness (A)
granted favor and sympathy *Da 1:9*
(B)
find kindness and compassion *Da 1:9*
(E)
find favor and compassion (R) *Da 1:9*
according to the *l.* of Lord *Ho 3:1*
toward Israel
l. a woman beloved, *l.* flagons *Ho 3:1*
of wine
her rulers with shame, do *l.* *Ho 4:18*
give ye
l. shame more than glory (S) *Ho 4:18*
drive them out, I will *l.* them *Ho 9:15*
no more
I drew them with bands of *l.* *Ho 11:4*
and cords
I will *l.* them freely, for mine *Ho 11:4*
anger turned
so ye *l.* to do (S) *Am 4:5*
hate the evil, and *l.* the good, *Am 5:15*
establish
who hate the good, and *l.* the *Mic 3:2*
evil
but to *l.* mercy, and to walk *Mic 6:8*
humbly
l. no false oath; *l.* the truth *Zec 8:17;*
 8:19
it hath been said, L. thy *Zec 5:43*
neighbour
but I say, L. your enemies *M't 5:44;*
 Lu 6:27, 35
if ye *l.* them which *l.* you *M't 5:46;*
 Lu 6:32
they *l.* to pray standing in the *M't 6:5*
synagogues
hate the one, and *l.* the other *M't 6:24;*
 Lu 16:13
thou shalt *l.* the Lord thy *M't 22:37;*
God with all thy heart *M'k 12:30;*
 Lu 10:27
and *l.* the uppermost rooms at *M't 23:6*
feasts
the *l.* of many shall wax cold *M't 24:12*
scribes who *l.* to go in long *M'k 12:38*
clothing
which of them will *l.* him most *Lu 7:42*
ye *l.* greetings in the markets *Lu 11:43;*
 20:46
if ye have *l.* one to another *Joh 13:35*
I will *l.* him, and manifest *Joh 14:21*
myself

if a man *l.* me, my Father will *Joh 14:23*
l. him
commandment that ye *l.* one *Joh 15:12;*
another *15:17*
greater *l.* hath no man than *Joh 15:13*
this, that he lay
if were of world, the world *Joh 15:19*
would *l.* his own
the *l.* wherewith thou hast *Joh 17:26*
loved me
all things work for good to *Ro 8:28*
them *l.* God
who shall separate us from *l.* *Ro 8:35*
of Christ
let *l.* be without dissimulation *Ro 12:9*
be kindly affectioned with *Ro 12:10*
brotherly *l.*
owe nothing to any, but to *l.* *Ro 13:8*
one another
in this saying, Thou shalt *l.* thy *Ro 13:9;*
neighbour as thyself *Ga 5:14; Jas 2:8*
l. worketh no ill, therefore *l.* *Ro 13:10*
is fulfilling
walkest thou not in *l.* (S) *Ro 14:15*
I beseech you, for the *l.* of the *Ro 15:30*
Spirit
God hath prepared for them *1Co 2:9*
that *l.* him
goodwill, benevolence edifies *1Co 8:1*
(A)
l. builds up *1Co 8:1*
(B)(E)(N)(P)(R)
knowledge puffeth up, but *l.* *1Co 8:1*
edifieth (S)
if any man *l.* God, the same is *1Co 8:3*
known of him
love (A)(B)(E)(N)(P)(R) *1Co 13:1;*
 13:2, 4, 8, 13; 14:1; 16:14; Col 3:13;
 1Th 3:6; 2Th 1:3; 1Ti 1:5; 2:15; 4:12;
 2Ti 2:22; 3:10; Tit 2:2; 1Pe 4:8; 5:14;
 Re 2:19
and have not *l.* (S) *1Co 13:1; 13:2-3*
l. suffereth long, is envieth *1Co 13:4*
not, *l.* vaunteth not itself (S)
L. never faileth (S) *1Co 13:8*
now abideth faith, hope, *l.* *1Co 13:13*
the greatest of these is *l.* (S)
follow after *l.* (S) *1Co 14:1*
let all things (S) *1Co 16:14*
that you may know the *l.* I *2Co 2:4*
have to you
that ye would confirm your *l.* *2Co 2:8*
toward him
for the *l.* of Christ *2Co 5:14*
constraineth us
by the Holy Ghost, by *l.* *2Co 6:6*
unfeigned
and to prove the sincerity of *2Co 8:8*
your *l.*
shew to the churches the *2Co 8:24*
proof of your *l.*
and of the God of *l.* shall be *2Co 13:11*
with you
but faith which worketh by *l.* *Ga 5:6*
but brethren, by *l.* serve one *Ga 5:13*
another
but the fruit of the Spirit is *l.* *Ga 5:22*
joy, peace
he planned in his purpose of *l.* *Eph 1:5*
(P)
after I heard of your *l.* to all *Eph 1:15*
the saints
to know the *l.* of Christ, *Eph 3:19*
passeth knowledge
husband *l.* your wives, as *Eph 5:25;*
Christ loved the *5:28, 33; Col 3:19*
and *l.* with faith, from God *Eph 6:23*
the Father
grace be with all them that *l.* *Eph 6:24*
our Lord Jesus
deepest Christian *l.* (P) *Ph'p 1:8*
this I pray that your *l.* may *Ph'p 1:9*
abound
but the other of *l.* doth *Ph'p 1:17*
preach Christ
if there be therefore any *Ph'p 2:1*
comfort of *l.*
that ye be like-minded, having *Ph'p 2:2*
the same *l.*
and of the *l.* which ye have to *Col 1:4*
all the saints
who declared to us your *l.* in *Col 1:8*
the Spirit
above all, put on *l.* (S) *Col 3:14*
remembering your labour of *l.* *1Th 1:3*
tidings of your faith and *l.* (S) *1Th 3:6*
touching brotherly *l.* ye need *1Th 4:9*
not that I write

ye are taught of God to *l*. 1Th 4:9
one another
putting on breast-plate of faith 1Th 5:8
and *l*.
mutual *l*. increasing 2Th 1:3
(B)(N)(P)(R)(S)
they received not the *l*. of the 2Th 2:10
truth
the end of commandment is *l*. 1Ti 1:5
(S)
exceeding abundant with faith 1Ti 1:14
and *l*.
if they continue in faith and *l*. 1Ti 2:15
(S)
example in *l*. (S) 1Ti 4:12
the *l*. of money is the root of 1Ti 6:10
all evil
follow after righteousness, *l*., 1Ti 6:11
patience
not given the spirit of fear, but 2Ti 1:7
of *l*.
follow righteousness, faith, *l*. 2Ti 2:22
(S)
no *l*. for the good (B)(E) 2Ti 3:3
known my doctrine, *l*. (S) 2Ti 3:10
but to all them that *l*. his 2Ti 4:8
appearing
example in *l*. (S) 1Ti 4:12
sound in faith, *l*. (S) Tit 2:2
teach young women to *l*. their Tit 2:4
husbands
greet them that *l*. us in the Tit 3:15
faith
to forget your work and Heb 6:10
labour of *l*.
to provoke unto *l*. and to Heb 10:24
good works
let brotherly *l*. continue, Heb 13:1
entertain strangers
Lord promised to them that *l*. Jas 1:12;
him 2:5
l. of world is enmity to God Jas 4:4
(N)
whom having not seen ye *l*. in 1Pe 1:8
whom
see ye *l*. one another with a 1Pe 1:22
pure heart
to unfeigned *l*. of the brethren 1Pe 1:22
honour all men, *l*. the 1Pe 2:17
brotherhood
l. as brethren; he that will *l*. 1Pe 3:8;
life 3:10
have intense unfailing *l*. 1Pe 4:8
(A)(B)(R)
keep your *l*. at full strength 1Pe 4:8
(N)
have real deep *l*. (P) 1Pe 4:8
above all have fervent *l*. (S) 1Pe 4:8
great with a kiss of *l*. (S) 1Pe 5:14
Christian *l*. (A)(B)(E)(N)(R) 2Pe 1:7
to brotherly kindness *l*. (S) 2Pe 1:7
l. not the world, if any man 1Jo 2:15
the world
the *l*. of the Father is not in 1Jo 2:15
him
behold what manner of *l*. the 1Jo 3:1
Father hath
message ye heard from the 1Jo 3:11;
beginning that we should 4:7, 11; 2Jo 5
l. one another
from death to life, because we 1Jo 3:14
l. the brethren
l. of God lodging in him (B) 1Jo 3:17
l. one another, as he gave 1Jo 3:23
commandment
let us *l*. one another, for *l*. is 1Jo 4:7
of God
God is *l*.; herein is *l*. not that 1Jo 4:8;
we loved God 4:10
if we *l*. one another, God 1Jo 4:12
dwelleth in us
known the *l*. that God hath to 1Jo 4:16
us, God is *l*.
herein is our *l*. made perfect, 1Jo 4:17
to have boldness
there is no fear in *l*.; perfect *l*. 1Jo 4:18
casteth out fear
we *l*. him because he first loved us 1Jo 4:19
how can he *l*. God whom he 1Jo 4:20
hath not seen
he who loveth God, *l*. his 1Jo 4:21
brother also
we *l*. the children of God when 1Jo 5:2
we *l*. God
this is *l*. that we walk after his 2Jo 6
commandment

l. and friendship (A)(E)(P)(R) 3Jo 6
borne witness of thy *l*. (S) 3Jo 6
mercy to you, peace and *l*. be Jude 2
multiplied
l. feasts (A)(B)(E)(N)(R) Jude 12
your *l*. feasts (S) Jude 12
because thou hast left thy first *l*. Re 2:4
I know thy works and *l*. (S) Re 2:19

LOVE ME

now therefore my husband Ge 29:32
will *l*. me
shewing mercy to them *l*. me Ex 20:6;
De 5:10
I love them that *l*. me, and Pr 8:17
those that seek
cause those that *l*. me to inherit Pr 8:21
substance
if God were your Father you Joh 8:42
would *l*. me
therefore doth my Father *l*. Joh 10:17
me, because
if ye *l*. me, keep my Joh 14:15
commandments
if a man *l*. me, he will keep Joh 14:23
my words

LOVE *NOT*

l. not sleep, lest thou come to Pr 20:13
poverty
if any man *l*. not the Lord 1Co 16:22
Jesus Christ
because I *l*. you *not*? God 2Co 11:11
knoweth
l. not the world 1Jo 2:15
let us *not l*. in word 1Jo 3:18

LOVE *OF GOD*

ye pass over judgment and the Lu 11:42
l. of God
I know that ye have not *l*. of Joh 5:42
God in you
because *l*. of God is shed abroad Ro 5:5
in our hearts
shall be able to separate us Ro 8:39
from the *l*. of God
the *l*. of God be with you all, 2Co 13:14
Amen
direct your hearts into the *l*. of 2Th 3:5
God
after the kindness and *l*. of God Tit 3:4
appeared
in him verily is the *l*. of God 1Jo 2:5
perfected
hereby perceive we *l*. of God 1Jo 3:16
because he laid
how dwelleth the *l*. of God in 1Jo 3:17
him
in this was manifested the *l*. of 1Jo 4:9
God towards us
this is *l*. of God that we keep 1Jo 5:3
his commandments
keep yourselves in the *l*. of Jude 21
God, looking for

HIS LOVE

Lord did not set *his l*. upon you De 7:7
because he hath set *his l*. upon Ps 91:14
me
in *his l*. and in his pity he Isa 63:9
redeemed them
he will rest in *his l*. he will joy Zep 3:17
over
I kept commandments, and Joh 15:10
abide in *his l*.
but God commended *his l*. Ro 5:8
toward us
if love one another *his l*. is 1Jo 4:12
perfected

I LOVE

make me savoury meat, such Ge 27:4
as I *l*.
if servant shall say, I *l*. my Ex 21:5
master
how canst thou say, I *l*. thee J'g 16:15
I *l*. Tamar my brother 2Sa 13:4
Absalom's sister
I *l*. the Lord, because he hath Ps 116:1
heard
O how I *l*. thy law; thy law I Ps 119:97;
l. 119:113, 163
therefore I *l*. thy testimonies Ps 119:119

therefore I *l*. thy Ps 119:127
commandments above gold
consider how I *l*. thy Ps 119:159
precepts, quicken me
thy testimonies I *l*. Ps 119:167
exceedingly
I *l*. them that love me and Pr 8:17
those that
world may know that I *l*. the Joh 14:31
Father
Lord, thou knowest that I *l*. Joh 21:15;
thee 21:16-17
though the more I *l*. you, the 2Co 12:15
less I be
if a man say, I *l*. God, and 1Jo 4:20
hateth
whom I *l*. in the truth 2Jo 1;
3Jo 1
as many as I *l*. rebuke and Re 3:19
chasten

IN LOVE

Solomon clave unto these *in l*. 1Ki 11:2
hast *in l*. to my soul delivered Isa 38:17
it from pit
shall I come to you with a rod 1Co 4:21
or *in l*.
as ye abound *in* your *l*. to us, 2Co 8:7
see that
we should be without blame Eph 1:4
before him *in l*.
that ye being rooted, and Eph 3:17
grounded *in l*.
in meekness, forbearing one Eph 4:2
another *in l*.
but speaking the truth *in l*. Eph 4:15
may grow up to
maketh increase to the Eph 4:16
edifying of itself *in l*.
walk *in l*. as Christ hath loved Eph 5:2
us and given
hearts be comforted, being knit Col 2:2
together *in l*.
the Lord make you to 1Th 3:12
increase *in l*.
esteem them highly *in l*. for 1Th 5:13
work's sake
in faith and *l*. which is in 2Ti 1:13
Christ Jesus
he that dwelleth *in l*. dwelleth 1Jo 4:16
in God
no fear *in l*. that feareth not 1Jo 4:18
made perfect *in l*.
Jesus the Son of the Father *in* 2Jo 3
truth and *l*.

MY LOVE

for *my l*. they are my Ps 109:4
adversaries
they have rewarded me hatred Ps 109:5
for *my l*.
I have compared thee, O *my l*. Ca 1:9
to horses
behold, thou art fair, *my l*. Ca 1:15;
4:1
as lily, so is *my l*. among the Ca 2:2
daughters
nor awake *my l*. till he please Ca 2:7;
3:5; 8:4
rise up *my l*. Ca 2:10;
2:13; 5:2
open to me, *my l*. my dove Ca 4:7
art all fair, *my l*. there is no
spot in thee
thou art beautiful, O *my l*. as Ca 6:4
Tirzah
continue ye in *my l*. Joh 15:9
abide in *my l*. Joh 15:10
my l. be with you all, in 1Co 16:24
Christ Jesus

THY LOVE

thy l. was wonderful, passing 2Sa 1:26
the love of women
for *thy l*. is better than wine Ca 1:2;
4:10
we will remember *thy l*. more Ca 1:4
than wine
how fair is *thy l*. my sister, my Ca 4:10
spouse
hearing of *thy l*. and faith Ph'm 5
towards Jesus
we have great joy and Ph'm 7
consolation in *thy l*.
because thou hast left *thy* first *l*. Re 2:4

LOVED

Isaac took Rebekah to wife, *Ge 24:67*
and *l.* her
Isaac *l.* Esau, but Rebekah *l.* *Ge 25:28*
Jacob
his mother made such as his *Ge 27:14*
father *l.*
Jacob *l.* Rachel more than *Ge 29:18;*
Leah   *29:30*
Shechem *l.* Dinah, and spake *Ge 34:3*
kindly to her
Israel *l.* Joseph more than all *Ge 37:3;*
his children   *37:4*
and because he *l.* thy fathers *De 4:37*
but because the Lord *l.* you *De 7:8;*
                                    23:5; 33:3
Samson *l.* a woman in the *J'g 16:4*
valley of Sorek
Elkanah *l.* Hannah *1Sa 1:5*
Saul *l.* David *1Sa 16:21*
Jonathan *l.* David as his own *1Sa 18:1;*
soul   *18:3; 20:17*
Israel and Judah *l.* David, *1Sa 18:16*
because he went
and Michal, Saul's daughter, *1Sa 18:20*
l. David
Lord *l.* Solomon, and he sent *2Sa 12:24*
Nathan
Amnon, the son of David, *l.* *2Sa 13:1*
Tamar
hatred greater than love *2Sa 13:15*
wherewith he *l.* her
Solomon *l.* the Lord walking *1Ki 3:3*
in statutes
because the Lord *l.* Israel *1Ki 10:9;*
                                    2Ch 9:8
king Solomon *l.* many strange *1Ki 11:1*
women
the Lord *l.* his people *2Ch 2:11;*
                                    Isa 48:14
Rehoboam *l.* Maacah above *2Ch 11:21*
all his wives
Uzziah had husbandmen, he *2Ch 26:10*
l. husbandry
the king *l.* Esther above all the *Es 2:17*
women
they whom I *l.* are turned *Job 19:19*
against me
the excellency of Jacob whom *Ps 47:4*
he *l.*
but chose the mount Zion *Ps 78:68*
which he *l.*
as he *l.* cursing, so let it come *Ps 109:17*
to him
all the host of heaven whom *Jer 8:2*
they have *l.*
thus have they *l.* to wander, *Jer 14:10*
they have not
I will gather all them that *Eze 16:37*
thou hast *l.*
thou hast *l.* a reward on every *Ho 9:1*
cornfloor
their abominations were *Ho 9:10*
according as they *l.*
when Israel was a child, then I *Ho 11:1*
l. him
yet ye say, wherein hast thou *l.* *Mal 1:2*
us
Judah profaned holiness *Mal 2:11*
of Lord which he *l.*
then Jesus beholding him, *l.* *M'k 10:21*
him
many sins are forgiven, for she *Lu 7:47*
l. much
God so *l.* the world *Joh 3:16*
l. darkness *Joh 3:19*
Jesus *l.* Martha and her sister, *Joh 11:5*
and Lazarus
then said the Jews, Behold *Joh 11:36*
how he *l.* him
for they *l.* praise of men more *Joh 12:43*
than praise
having *l.* his own, he *l.* them to *Joh 13:1*
the end
disciple whom Jesus *l.* *Joh 13:23;*
                    19:26; 20:2; 21:7, 20
he that loveth me shall be *l.* *Joh 14:21*
of my Father
if ye *l.* me, ye would rejoice, *Joh 14:28*
because I go to my
as the Father *l.* me, so have I *Joh 15:9*
l. you
Father himself loveth you, *Joh 16:27*
because ye *l.* me
and hast *l.* them, as thou hast *Joh 17:23*
l. me
love wherewith thou hast *l.* *Joh 17:26*
me, may be in them

more than conquerors thro' *Ro 8:37*
him that *l.* us
the more I love you, the less *2Co 12:15*
I be *l.*
who *l.* me, and gave himself *Ga 2:20*
for me
for his great love wherewith he *Eph 2:4*
l. us
l. children (B) *Eph 5:1*
as Christ also *l.* us *Eph 5:2*
Christ *l.* the church *Eph 5:25*
God our Father, which hath *l.* *2Th 2:16*
Demas having *l.* this present *2Ti 4:10*
world
hast *l.* righteousness, and *Heb 1:9*
hated iniquity
Balaam *l.* the wages of *2Pe 2:15*
unrighteousness
not that we *l.* God, but that he *1Jo 4:10*
l. us
because he first *l.* us *1Jo 4:19*
to him that *l.* us and washed us *Re 1:5*
from sins
they *l.* not their lives to the *Re 12:11*
death

I HAVE LOVED

I have *l.* the habitation of thy *Ps 26:8*
house
delight in thy commands *Ps 119:47;*
which I have *l.*   *119:48*
I have *l.* thee, therefore will I *Isa 43:4*
give men
I have *l.* strangers, and after *Jer 2:25*
them will I go
I have *l.* thee with an *Jer 31:3*
everlasting love
I have *l.* you, yet ye say, *Mal 1:2*
Wherein hast thou
as I have *l.* you, that ye also *Joh 13:34;*
love   *15:12*
as the Father loved me, so I *Joh 15:9*
have *l.* you
as it is written, Jacob I have *l.* *Ro 9:13*
but Esau
I will make them know that I *Re 3:9*
have *l.* thee

LOVEDST

thou *l.* their bed where thou *Isa 57:8*
sawest it
thou *l.* me before foundation *Joh 17:24*
of world

LOVELESS

heartless and *l.* (A)(R) *Ro 1:21*
faithless, heartless, *l.* (A) *Ro 1:31*

LOVELY

beautiful and *l.* (R) *Ge 29:17*
Saul and Jonathan were *l.* in *2Sa 1:23*
their lives
he is altogether *l.* O daughters *Ca 5:16*
of Jerusalem
thou art to them as a very *l.* *Eze 33:32*
song
one a *l.* vase, another a pipe *Ro 9:21*
for sewage (P)
whatsoever things are *l.* think *Ph'p 4:8*
on these
that the *l.* sight is destroyed *Jas 1:11*
(N)(P)

LOVER

for Hiram was ever a *l.* of *1Ki 5:1*
David
l. and friend hast thou put far *Ps 88:18*
from me
no *l.* of money (A)(E)(N)(R) *1Ti 3:3*
a *l.* of hospitality, a *l.* of good *Tit 1:8*
men, sober
being world's *l.* means (P) *Jas 4:4*

LOVERS

my *l.* and friends stand aloof *Ps 38:11*
from my
thou hast played the harlot with *Jer 3:1*
many *l.*
thy *l.* will despise thee, they *Jer 4:30*
will seek thy life
go up and cry, for all thy *l.* *Jer 22:20*
are destroyed

thy *l.* shall go into captivity, *Jer 22:22*
shalt be ashamed
all thy *l.* have forgotten thee, *Jer 30:14*
they seek
among all her *l.* hath none to *La 1:2*
comfort her
I called for my *l.* but they *La 1:19*
deceived me
thou givest thy gifts to all thy *Eze 16:33*
l.
thy nakedness discovered *Eze 16:36*
with thy *l.* and idols
I will gather thy *l.* *Eze 16:37*
doted on her *l.* *Eze 23:5*
I have delivered her into the *Eze 23:9*
hand of her *l.*
behold, I will raise up thy *l.* *Eze 23:22*
against thee
I will go after my *l.* *Ho 2:5*
shall follow her *l.* *Ho 2:7*
I will discover her lewdness in *Ho 2:10*
the sight of *l.*
these rewards that my *l.* have *Ho 2:12*
given me
and she went after her *l.* and *Ho 2:13*
forgat me
are gone up to Assyria, *Ho 8:9*
Ephraim hath hired *l.*
for men shall be *l.* of their own *2Ti 3:2*
selves
heady, *l.* of pleasures more than *2Ti 3:4*
l. of God

LOVES

come, let us solace ourselves *Pr 7:18*
with *l.*
there will I give thee my *l.* *Ca 7:12*
l. bribes (A)(B)(E)(R) *Isa 1:23*

LOVE'S

for *l.* sake I rather beseech thee *Ph'm 9*

LOVEST

take thine only son Isaac *Ge 22:2*
whom thou *l.*
thou dost but hate me, and *l.* *J'g 14:16*
me not
in that thou *l.* thine enemies, *2Sa 19:6*
and hatest
thou *l.* righteousness, therefore *Ps 45:7*
God thy
thou *l.* evil more than good, *Ps 52:3*
and lying
thou *l.* all devouring words, O *Ps 52:4*
thou deceitful
live joyfully with the wife whom *Ec 9:9*
thou *l.*
behold, he whom thou *l.* is *Joh 11:3*
sick
Simon, son of Jonas, *l.* thou *Joh 21:15;*
me   *21:16-17*

LOVETH

make meat for thy father, such *Ge 27:9*
as he *l.*
a child, a little one, and his *Ge 44:20*
father *l.* him
Lord *l.* the stranger in giving *De 10:18*
him food
I will not go away because he *De 15:16*
l. thee
for thy daughter in law who *l.* *Ru 4:15*
thee
and him that *l.* violence his soul *Ps 11:5*
hateth
for the righteous Lord *l.* *Ps 11:7;*
righteousness   *33:5*
what man is he that *l.* many *Ps 34:12*
days
for the Lord *l.* judgment *Ps 37:28; 99:4*
the Lord *l.* gates of Zion more *Ps 87:2*
than dwellings
word is very pure, therefore *Ps 119:140*
thy servant *l.*
Lord openeth the eyes, Lord *l.* *Ps 146:8*
the righteous
for whom the Lord *l.* he *Pr 3:12*
correcteth
whoso *l.* instruction, *l.* *Pr 12:1*
knowledge
but he that *l.* him, chasteneth *Pr 13:24*
him betimes
he *l.* him that followeth after *Pr 15:9*
righteousness
a scorner *l.* not one that *Pr 15:12*
reproveth him

a friend *l.* at all times, and a brother is born *Pr 17:17*
l. transgression that *l.* strife, he that exalteth *Pr 17:19*
he that getteth widom *l.* his own soul *Pr 19:8*
he that *l.* pleasure, he that *l.* wine and oil *Pr 21:17*
he that *l.* pureness of heart, the king his *Pr 22:11*
whoso *l.* wisdom rejoiceth his father *Pr 29:3*
he that *l.* silver, he that *l.* abundance *Ec 5:10*
tell me, O thou whom my soul *l.* *Ca 1:7*
by night on my bed I sought him whom soul *l.* *Ca 3:1*
I will arise and seek him whom my soul *l.* *Ca 3:2*
to whom I said, Saw ye him whom my soul *l.* *Ca 3:3*
I found him whom my soul *l.* I held him *Ca 3:4*
every one *l.* gifts and follows after rewards *Isa 1:23*
Ephraim as heifer *l.* to tread out corn *Ho 10:11*
he is a merchant, he *l.* to oppress *Ho 12:7*
that *l.* father or mother, he that *l.* son *M't 10:37*
he *l.* our nation *Lu 7:5*
the same *l.* little *Lu 7:47*
the Father *l.* the Son, hath given *Joh 3:35; 5:20*
he that *l.* his life shall lose it *Joh 12:25*
he it is that *l.* me, and he that *l.* me shall be loved *Joh 14:21*
he that *l.* me not, keepeth not my sayings *Joh 14:24*
the Father himself *l.* you, because loved me *Joh 16:27*
he that *l.* another hath fulfilled the law *Ro 13:8*
or of necessity, for God *l.* a cheerful giver *2Co 9:7*
he that *l.* his wife, *l.* himself *Eph 5:28*
for whom the Lord *l.* he chasteneth *Heb 12:6*
he that *l.* his brother, abideth in light *1Jo 2:10*
he that *l.* not his brother, is not of God *1Jo 3:10*
l. not his brother, abideth in death *1Jo 3:14; 4:8, 20*
every one that *l.* is born of God, and knows God *1Jo 4:7*
that he who *l.* God, *l.* his brother also *1Jo 4:21*
that *l.* him that begat, *l.* him that is begotten *1Jo 5:1*
Diotrephes *l.* to have the pre-eminence *3Jo 9*
unto him that *l.* us (S) *Re 1:5*
and whosoever *l.* and maketh a lie *Re 22:15*

LOVING

l. kindness, steadfastness (B) *Ge 24:27*
least of *l.* kindness (E) *Ge 32:10*
the acts of *l.* kindness (B)(E) *2Ch 6:42*
shown me his *l.* kindness (B) *Ps 31:21*
tokens of *l.* kindness (A)(B)(E) *Ps 106:7; 106:45*
may thy *l.* kindness come (B)(E) *Ps 119:41*
let her be as the *l.* hind and pleasant roe *Pr 5:19*
and *l.* favour rather than silver *Pr 22:1*
sleeping, lying down, *l.* to slumber *Isa 56:10*

LOVINGKINDNESS

Shew thy marvelous *l.* *Ps 17:7*
For thy *l.* is before mine eyes *Ps 26:3*
How excellent is thy *l.* *Ps 36:7*
continue thy *l.* unto them that *Ps 36:10*
I have not concealed thy *l.* *Ps 40:10*
let thy *l.* and truth continually *Ps 40:11*
the Lord will command his *l.* *Ps 42:8*
We have thought of thy *l.* *Ps 48:9*
according to thy *l.* *Ps 51:1; 119:149, 159*
thy *l.* is better than life *Ps 63:3*
for thy *l.* is good *Ps 69:16*
rich in *l.* (B)(E) *Ps 86:5*
abundant in *l.* (A)(B)(E) *Ps 86:15*
Shall thy *l.* be declared in the grave *Ps 88:11*
my *l.* will I not utterly take *Ps 89:33*
To shew forth thy *l.* in the morning *Ps 92:2*
crowneth thee with *l.* and tender *Ps 103:4*
shall understand the *l.* of Lord *Ps 107:43*
Quicken me after thy *l.* *Ps 119:88*
for thy *l.* and for thy truth *Ps 138:2*
me to hear thy *l.* in the morning *Ps 143:8*
I am the Lord which exercise *l.* *Jer 9:24*
saith the Lord, even *l.* and mercies *Jer 16:5*
with *l.* have I drawn thee *Jer 31:3*
Thou shewest *l.* unto thousands *Jer 32:18*
and in *l.*, and mercies *Ho 2:19*

LOVINGKINDNESSES

thy tender mercies and thy *l.* *Ps 25:6*
where are thy former *l.* *Ps 89:49*
I will mention the *l.* of Lord *Isa 63:7*
according to multitude of his *l.* *Isa 63:7*

LOVINGLY

hold *l.* in highest regard (B) *1Th 5:13*

LOW

l. and worthless (A) *De 25:3*
and thou shalt come down very *l.* *De 28:43*
the Lord bringeth *l.* and lifteth *1Sa 2:7*
as sycamore trees in the *l.* plains *2Ch 9:27*
Uzziah had much cattle in the *l.* country *2Ch 26:10*
Philistines invaded cities of the *l.* country *2Ch 28:18*
to set up on high those that be *l.* *Job 5:11*
look on every one proud, and bring him *l.* *Job 40:12*
both high and *l.* rich and poor together *Ps 49:2*
surely men of *l.* degree are vanity *Ps 62:9*
who remembered us in our *l.* estate *Ps 136:23*
a man's pride shall bring him *l.* *Pr 29:23*
and the rich sit in *l.* place *Ec 10:6*
when the sound of the grinding is *l.* *Ec 12:4*
I will lay *l.* the haughtiness of terrible *Isa 13:11*
the high fort of thy walls shall he lay *l.* *Isa 25:12*
the lofty city he layeth it *l.* to the ground *Isa 26:5*
thy speech shall be *l.* out of the dust *Isa 29:4*
and the city shall be *l.* in a *l.* place *Isa 32:19*
I called on thy name out of *l.* dungeon *La 3:55*
it became a spreading vine of *l.* stature *Eze 17:6*
trees shall know that I have exalted the *l.* tree *Eze 17:24*
exalt him that is *l.* abase him that is high *Eze 21:26*
shall set thee in the *l.* parts of the earth *Eze 26:20*
he regarded *l.* estate of his handmaiden *Lu 1:48*
he hath exalted them of *l.* degree *Lu 1:52*
but condescend to men of *l.* estate *Ro 12:16*
let the brother of *l.* degree rejoice *Jas 1:9*
but the rich in that he is made *l.* *Jas 1:10*

LOWBORN

l. against honorable (A) *Isa 3:5*
l. insignificant (A)(B)(N) *1Co 1:28*

LOWER

with *l.* second and third stories make ark *Ge 6:16*
lower (S) *Ex 19:17; De 24:6; Jos 15:19; 16:3; 18:13; J'g 1:15; 1Ki 9:17; 1Ch 7:24; 2Ch 8:5; Job 41:24; Eze 31:14, 16, 18; 32:18, 24*
if rising be in sight *l.* than the skin *Le 13:20*
and if it be no *l.* than the skin *Le 13:21; 13:26*
upper and *l.* springs (A)(B)(R) *Jos 15:19*
l. Beth-haron (A)(B)(R) *1Ki 9:17*
therefore I set in the *l.* places the people *Ne 4:13*
made him little *l.* than angels *Ps 8:5; Heb 2:7, 9*
shall go into the *l.* parts of the earth *Ps 63:9*
shouldest be put *l.* in presence of prince *Pr 25:7*
ye gathered the waters of the *l.* pool *Isa 22:9*
sing, O heavens, shout ye *l.* parts of earth *Isa 44:23*
death, to the *l.* world (A) *Eze 31:14*
from the bottom even to the *l.* settle *Eze 43:14*
no longer under *l.* nature (N) *Ro 8:4*
that he descended first into the *l.* parts *Eph 4:9*
keep clear of desires of *l.* nature (P) *1Pe 2:11*
foulness of *l.* nature (P) *2Pe 2:10*

LOWERING

offence in *l.* myself (N) *2Co 11:7*

LOWEST

and shall burn to the *l.* hell *De 32:22*
made priests *l.* *1Ki 12:31; 13:33; 2Ki 17:32*
hast delivered my soul from the *l.* hell *Ps 86:13*
thou hast laid me in the *l.* pit, in darkness *Ps 88:6*
curiously wrought in the *l.* parts of earth *Ps 139:15*
and so increased from the *l.* chamber *Eze 41:7*
the building was straitened more than the *l.* *Eze 42:6*
thou begin with shame to take *l.* room *Lu 14:9*
but go and sit down in the *l.* room *Lu 14:10*

LOWETH

wild ass bray, or *l.* the ox over his fodder *Job 6:5*

LOWING

the kine went along the highway *l.* *1Sa 6:12*
what meaneth then the *l.* of the oxen *1Sa 15:14*

LOWLAND

lowland (A)(E) *De 1:7; Jos 10:40; 1Ki 10:27; 2Ch 1:15; Jer 33:13*
the *l.* (B) *2Ch 1:15; Jer 33:13*

LOWLINESS

that ye walk with all *l.* and meekness *Eph 4:2*
but in *l.* of mind, let each esteem other *Ph'p 2:3*
lowliness (E)(R) *Col 3:12*

LOWLY

Lord high, yet hath he respect to *l.* *Ps 138:6*
the scorners, but he giveth grace to *l.* *Pr 3:34*
then cometh shame, but with *l.* is wisdom *Pr 11:2*
better to be of humble spirit with the *l.* *Pr 16:19*
better be of *l.* spirit (E)(R) *Pr 16:19*
l. in spirit obtains (B)(E)(R) *Pr 29:23*
take a *l.* seat (B)(R) *Jer 13:18*
he is just, *l.* and riding on an ass *Zec 9:9*
learn of me, for I am meek and *l.* *M't 11:29*
lifted up the *l.* (B)(N)(P) *Lu 1:52*
l. enough among you (A)(E) *2Co 10:1*

our *l.* body (S) *Ph'p 3:21*
give grace to the *l.* (A) *Jas 4:6*
take *l.* position (B) *Jas 4:10*

LOWRING

foul weather, for the sky is *M't 16:3*
red and *l.*
red, has a gloomy threatening *M't 16:3*
look (A)
red and cloudy (B) *M't 16:3*
red and threatening (P)(R) *M't 16:3*

LOYAL

my *l.* comrade (N)(P) *Ph'p 4:3*
truly *l.* (A) *Tit 2:10*

LOYALLY

deal *l.* with (A) *Ge 47:29; Jos 2:14*
the *l.* side rooms (B)(R)(S) *1Ki 6:6*
sensual pull of *l.* passions (P) *2Pe 2:18*

LOYALTY

know nothing of *l.* (B) *De 32:20*
maintaining *l.* (B) *1Ch 12:29*
no *l.* to parents (N) *Ro 1:30*
boldly confessed your *l.* (P) *1Ti 6:12*

LUBIM

Put and *L.* were thy helpers *Na 3:9*

LUBIMS

the *L.*, the Sukkims *2Ch 12:3*
Ethiopians and the *L.* *2Ch 16:8*

LUCAS

Marcus, Demas, *L.* thy *Ph'm 24*
fellow-labourers

LUCIFER

how art thou fallen from *Isa 14:12*
heaven, O *L.*
light-bringer and day-star *Isa 14:12*
(A)
shining gleam, son of the *Isa 14:12*
morning (B)
day-star, son of the morning *Isa 14:12*
(E)
Day Star, Son of Dawn (R) *Isa 14:12*

LUCIUS

L. of Cyrene was a teacher at *Ac 13:1*
Antioch
L., Jason, and Sosipater *Ro 16:21*
salute you

LUCRE

Samuel's sons turned after *l.* *1Sa 8:3*
took bribes
turned aside for money (B) *1Sa 8:3*
turned aside after gain (R) *1Sa 8:3*
a bishop not greedy of filthy *l.* *1Ti 3:3;*
3:8
not a lover of money *1Ti 3:3*
(A)(E)(N)(R)
not after money (B) *1Ti 3:3*
not fond of money grabbing *1Ti 3:3*
(P)
a bishop must not be given to *Tit 1:7*
filthy *l.*
not greedy of dishonest gain *Tit 1:7*
(B)
no money-grabber (N) *Tit 1:7*
or greedy of financial gain (P) *Tit 1:7*
or greedy for gain (R) *Tit 1:7*
teaching things they ought not *Tit 1:11*
for filthy *l.*
for base advantage, *Tit 1:11*
disreputable gain (A)
for dishonest gain (B) *Tit 1:11*
for sordid gain (N) *Tit 1:11*
for the sake of what they can *Tit 1:11*
get (P)
for base gain (R) *Tit 1:11*
feed flock not for filthy *l.* but *1Pe 5:2*
ready mind
not dishonorably motivated by *1Pe 5:2*
advantages and profits (A)
not out of greedy gain (B) *1Pe 5:2*
not for gain but sheer devotion *1Pe 5:2*
(N)

not for what you can make (P) *1Pe 5:2*
not for shameful gain (R) *1Pe 5:2*

LUCRE'S

for filthy *l.* sake *Tit 1:11*

LUD

Asshur, Arphaxad, and *L.* *Ge 10:22*
L. and Aram, and Uz *1Ch 1:17*
Pul and *L.* that draw the bow *Isa 66:19*
They of Persia and of *L.* *Eze 27:10*

LUDIM

Mizraim begat *L.* *Ge 10:13; 1Ch 1:11*
the *L.* that handle the shield *Jer 46:9*
(S)

LUGGAGE

we took up our *l.* (S) *Ac 21:15*

LUHITH

mounting up of *L.* with *Isa 15:5*
weeping
going up of *L.* continual *Jer 48:5*
weeping

LUKE

L. the beloved physician *Col 4:14*
greeteth you
only *L.* is with me, bring Mark *2Ti 4:11*
with thee

LUKEWARM

so then because thou art *l.* *Re 3:16*

LUMBER

of Lebanese *l.* (B) *1Ki 7:2*

LUMP

take a *l.* of figs and lay *2Ki 20:7;*
Isa 38:21
Take a cake of figs *2Ki 20:7;*
(A)(B)(E)(R) *Isa 38:21*
of the same *l.* one vessel to *Ro 9:21*
honour
if the first fruit be holy the *l.* *Ro 11:16*
is holy
so is the whole mass holy *Ro 11:16*
(A)(B)
so is the whole loaf holy (P) *Ro 11:16*
a little leaven leaveth the *l.* *1Co 5:6;*
Ga 5:9
the whole batch (B) *1Co 5:6*
leavens all the dough (N) *1Co 5:6*
purge out old leaven, that ye *1Co 5:7*
may be a new *l.*
that you may be fresh dough *1Co 5:7*
(A)(R)
you will be a fresh batch (B) *1Co 5:7*
bread of a new baking (N) *1Co 5:7*
be new unleavened bread (P) *1Co 5:7*

LUMPS

l. of fat on his flanks (S) *Job 15:27*

LUNATIC

and those which were *l.* he *M't 4:24*
healed
epileptics *M't 4:24;*
(A)(B)(E)(N)(R) *17:15*
the insane (P) *M't 4:24*
Lord have mercy on my son, *M't 17:15*
for he is *l.*

LUNCHEON

when you give a *l.* (P) *Lu 14:13*

LURE

l. with lustful desires (A) *2Pe 2:18*

LURED

be *l.* into imitating them (B) *De 12:30*

LURK

come, let us *l.* privily for the *Pr 1:11*
innocent

let us ambush the innocent *Pr 1:11;*
(A)(B)(R) *1:18*
they *l.* privily for their own *Pr 1:18*
lives

LURKING

take knowledge of all the *l.* *1Sa 23:23*
places
find all his hiding places (B) *1Sa 23:23*
he sitteth in the *l.* places of the *Ps 10:8*
villages
ambush in the villages *Ps 10:8*
(A)(B)(R)
as it were a young lion *l.* in *Ps 17:12*
secret places
lion waiting in ambush (B) *Ps 17:12*
disclosed his *l.* places (B) *Jer 49:10*

LURKS

l. as a lion (B) *De 33:20*

LUST

my *l.* shall be satisfied upon *Ex 15:9*
them
heart by asking meat for their *Ps 78:18*
l.
were not estranged from their *Ps 78:30*
l.
them up unto their own *Ps 81:12*
hearts' *l.*
L. not after her beauty in *Pr 6:25*
defiled her with *l.* (B)(R) *Eze 23:17*
l. and wine (B)(R) *Ho 4:11*
looketh on a woman to *l.* after *M't 5:28*
burned in their *l.* one toward *Ro 1:27*
for I had not known *l.* except *Ro 7:7*
not for *l.* (B)(N) *1Co 6:13*
should not *l.* after evil things *1Co 10:6*
shall not fulfil the *l.* of the flesh *Ga 5:16*
mortify *l.* (N) *Col 3:5*
Not in the *l.* of concupiscence *1Th 4:5*
he is drawn away of his own *l.* *Jas 1:14*
Then when *l.* hath conceived, it *Jas 1:15*
Ye *l.* and have not; ye kill, and *Jas 4:2*
meant sensuality, *l.* (P) *1Pe 4:3*
that is in the world through *l.* *2Pe 1:4*
the flesh in the *l.* of *2Pe 2:10*
uncleanness
l. of the flesh, and the *l.* of the *1Jo 2:16*
eyes
passeth away, and the *l.* *1Jo 2:17*
thereof
indulged in unnatural *l.* (R) *Jude 7*

LUSTED

there they buried the people *Nu 11:34*
that *l.*
But *l.* exceedingly in the *Ps 106:14*
wilderness
after evil things, as they also *1Co 10:6*
l.
the fruits that thy soul *l.* after *Re 18:14*

LUSTETH

eat whatsoever thy soul *l.* *De 12:15*
after
flesh, whatsoever thy soul *l.* *De 12:20*
after
gates whatsoever thy soul *l.* *De 12:21*
after
for whatsoever thy soul *l.* after *De 14:26*
For the flesh *l.* against the *Ga 5:17*
Spirit
that dwelleth in us *l.* to envy *Jas 4:5*

LUSTFUL

adulteries and *l.* cries (B) *Jer 13:27*
lure with *l.* desires *2Pe 2:18*

LUSTFULNESS

not repented of *l.* (P) *2Co 12:21*

LUSTING

that was among them fell a *l.* *Nu 11:4*

LUSTRE

add *l.* to the doctrine (N) *Tit 2:10*

LUSTS

lavished their *l.* (B) *Eze 23:8*
the *l.* of other things entering *M'k 4:19*

LUSTS

and the *l.* of your father ye — Joh 8:44
through the *l.* of their own — Ro 1:24
hearts, to
l. of own hearts to impurity — Ro 1:24;
(R) 6:19; 2Co 12:21; Ga 5:19;
Eph 5:3; Col 3:5
ye should obey it in the *l.* — Ro 6:12
for the flesh, to fulfil the *l.* — Ro 13:14
the flesh with the affections — Ga 5:24
and *l.*
in times past in the *l.* of our — Eph 2:3
flesh
corrupt according to the — Eph 4:22
deceitful *l.*
and into many foolish and — 1Ti 6:9
hurtful *l.*
Flee also youthful *l.*: but — 2Ti 2:22
follow
with sins led away with divers — 2Ti 3:6
l.
after their own *l.* shall they — 2Ti 4:3
heap
denying ungodliness and — Tit 2:12
worldly
serving divers *l.* and pleasures — Tit 3:3
your *l.* that war in your — Jas 4:1
members
ye may consume it upon your *l.* — Jas 4:3
to the former *l.* in your — 1Pe 1:14
ignorance
abstain from fleshly *l.*, which — 1Pe 2:11
war
time in the flesh to the *l.* of — 1Pe 4:2
men
walked in lasciviousness, *l.* — 1Pe 4:3
excess
indulging in unbridled *l.* (B) — 1Pe 4:3
follow their abominable *l.* — 2Pe 2:10
(N)
allure through the *l.* of the — 2Pe 2:18
flesh
entice in *l.* of the flesh — 2Pe 2:18
(E)(N)
scoffers, walking after their — 2Pe 3:3
own *l.*
followed unnatural *l.* (N) — Jude 7
walking after their own *l.* — Jude 16
walk after their own ungodly *l.* — Jude 18

LUSTY

men, all *l.* and all men of — J'g 3:29
valour

LUTE

the harp, and the *l.* (S) — Isa 5:12

LUTES

noise of the *l.* (S) — Isa 14:11

LUXURIOUS

in their *l.* palaces (B) — Isa 15:2
comely and *l.* (B) — Jer 6:2
enjoyed *l.* living (B) — Lu 16:19

LUXURIOUSLY

and lived *l.* (S) — Re 18:7; 18:9

LUXURY

lived in *l.* (A)(B)(N)(P)(R) — Lu 7:25
lead a life of daily *l.* (P) — Lu 16:19
excessive *l.* (A)(B) — Re 18:3

LUZ

the name of that city was — Ge 28:19
called *L.*
So Jacob came to *L.*, which is — Ge 35:6
Almighty appeared unto me at — Ge 48:3
L.
And goeth out from Beth-el to — Jos 16:2
L.
thence toward *L.* to the — Jos 18:13
side of *L.*
the name of the city before was — J'g 1:23
L.
and called the name thereof *L.* — J'g 1:26

LYCAONIA

Lystra and Derbe, cities of *L.* — Ac 14:6
voices, saying in the speech of — Ac 14:11
L.

LYCIA

we came to Myra, a city of *L.* — Ac 27:5

LYDDA

to the saints which dwelt at *L.* — Ac 9:32
And all that dwelt at *L.* and — Ac 9:35
Saron
forasmuch as *L.* was nigh to — Ac 9:38
Joppa

LYDIA

Ethiopia, and Libya, and *L.* — Eze 30:5
And a certain woman named — Ac 16:14
L.
and entered into the house of — Ac 16:40
L.

LYDIANS

L. that handle and bend the — Jer 46:9
bow

LYE

though thou wash with *l.* (S) — Jer 2:22

LYING

were three flocks of sheep *l.* by — Ge 29:2
Israel in *l.* with Jacob's — Ge 34:7
l. words (A)(E)(R) — Ex 5:9
hateth thee *l.* under his burden — Ex 23:5
hath known man by *l.* with — Nu 31:17
him
not known a man by *l.* with — Nu 31:18;
him 31:35
hurl at him by *l.* in wait (S) — Nu 35:20;
35:22
l. in the field, and it be not — De 21:1
known
a man be found *l.* with a — De 22:22
woman
were with him, from *l.* in wait — J'g 9:35
Now there were men *l.* in wait — J'g 16:9
lying (S) — J'g 16:12; Joh 5:6; 20:6
known no man by *l.* with any — J'g 21:12
male
l. down (S) — 1Sa 3:2;
3:3; M't 8:14; M'k 7:30
be a *l.* spirit in the mouth of — 1Ki 22:22
Lord hath put a *l.* spirit in — 1Ki 22:23
the mouth
be a *l.* spirit in the mouth of — 2Ch 18:21
Lord hath put a *l.* spirit in — 2Ch 18:22
the mouth
them that regard *l.* vanities — Ps 31:6
Let the *l.* lips be put to silence — Ps 31:18
and *l.* rather — Ps 52:3
than righteousness
and for cursing and *l.* which — Ps 59:12
against me with a *l.* tongue — Ps 109:2
Remove from me the way of — Ps 119:29
l.
I hate and abhor *l.*: but thy — Ps 119:163
law
Deliver my soul, O Lord, from — Ps 120:2
l. lips
Thou compassest my *l.* down — Ps 139:3
proud look, a *l.* tongue, and — Pr 6:17
hands
He that hideth hatred with *l.* — Pr 10:18
lips
but a *l.* tongue is but for a — Pr 12:19
moment
L. lips are abomination to the — Pr 12:22
Lord
A righteous man hateth *l.*: but — Pr 13:5
fool: much less do *l.* lips a — Pr 17:7
prince
getting of treasures by a *l.* — Pr 21:6
tongue
A *l.* tongue hateth those that — Pr 26:28
is a rebellious people, *l.* — Isa 30:9
children
to destroy the poor with *l.* — Isa 32:7
words
l. down loving to slumber — Isa 56:10
and *l.* against the Lord, and — Isa 59:13
Trust ye not in *l.* words, saying — Jer 7:4
ye trust in *l.* words, that cannot — Jer 7:8
have spoken *l.* words in my — Jer 29:23
name
He was unto me as a bear *l.* in — La 3:10
wait
have seen vanity and *l.* — Eze 13:6
divination

have ye not spoken a *l.* — Eze 13:7
divination
give *l.* prophecies (A) — Eze 13:9
l. divinations (B)(R) — Eze 13:9
by your *l.* to my people that — Eze 13:19
hear
l. divinations (R) — Eze 13:23
prepared *l.* and corrupt words — Eze 13:23
By swearing, and *l.* and killing — Ho 4:2
that observe *l.* vanities forsake — Jon 2:8
a man sick of the palsy *l.* on a — M't 9:2
bed
enterreth in where damsel — M'k 5:40
was *l.*
swaddling clothes, *l.* in a — Lu 2:12
manger
Joseph, and the babe, *l.* in a — Lu 2:16
manger
He then *l.* on Jesus' breast — Joh 13:25
saith
looking in, saw the linen — Joh 20:5
clothes *l.*
not *l.* with the linen clothes — Joh 20:7
l. in wait was known (S) — Ac 9:24
me by the *l.* in wait of the — Ac 20:19
Jews
sister's son heard of their *l.* in — Ac 23:16
wait
Wherefore putting away *l.* — Eph 4:25
speak
all power and signs and *l.* — 2Th 2:9
wonders

LYRE

l. with the harp (A)(B)(R) — Ps 81:2
my soul moans like a *l.* (R) — Isa 16:11
upon the *l.* (S) — Da 3:5; 3:7, 10, 15

LYRES

on *l.* harps (A)(B)(R) — 2Sa 6:5;
1Ki 10:12; 1Ch 13:8; 15:16, 28; 16:5;
25:1, 6; 2Ch 5:12; 9:11; 20:28; 29:25;
Ne 12:27
were to lead with *l.* (A)(R) — 1Ch 15:21

LYSANIAS

and *L.* the tetrarch of Abilene — Lu 3:1

LYSIAS

Claudius *L.* unto Felix — Ac 23:26
sendeth
the chief captain *L.* came — Ac 24:7
upon us
L. the chief captain shall — Ac 24:22
come

LYSTRA

fled unto *L.* and Derbe, cities — Ac 14:6
And there sat a certain man at — Ac 14:8
L.
they returned again to *L.* and — Ac 14:21
Then came he to Derbe and *L.* — Ac 16:1
by the brethren that were at *L.* — Ac 16:2
me at Antioch, at Iconium, at — 2Ti 3:11
L.

M

MAACAH

son of *M.* the daughter of — 2Sa 3:3
Talmai
and of king *M.* a thousand — 2Sa 10:6
men
and *M.*, were by themselves in — 2Sa 10:8

MAACHAH

and Gaham, and Thahash, — Ge 22:24
and *M.*
Achish son of *M.* king of — 1Ki 2:39
Gath
his mother's name was *M.* the — 1Ki 15:2
And also *M.* his mother, even — 1Ki 15:13
her
M., Caleb's concubine, bare — 1Ch 2:48
son of *M.* the daughter of — 1Ch 3:2
Talmai
whose sister's name was *M.* — 1Ch 7:15
M. the wife of Machir bare a — 1Ch 7:16
son

MAACHAH

whose wife's name was *M*.	1Ch 8:29
Jehiel, whose wife's name was *M*.	1Ch 9:35
Hanan the son of *M*., and	1Ch 11:43
and the king of *M*. and his people	1Ch 19:7
Shephatiah the son of *M*.	1Ch 27:16
took *M*. the daughter of Absalom	2Ch 11:20
Rehoboam loved *M*. the daughter	2Ch 11:21
Abijah the son of *M*. the chief	2Ch 11:22
concerning *M*. the mother of Asa	2Ch 15:16

MAACHATHI

the coasts of Geshuri and *M*.	De 3:14

MAACHATHITE

son of Ahasbai, the son of the *M*.	2Sa 23:34
Jaazaniah the son of a *M*.	2Ki 25:23
Garmite, and Eshtemoa the *M*.	1Ch 4:19
and Jezaniah the son of a *M*.	Jer 40:8

MAACHATHITES

of the Geshurites and the *M*.	Jos 12:5
border of the Geshurites and *M*.	Jos 13:11
not the Geshurites, nor the *M*.	Jos 13:13
M. dwell among the Israelites	Jos 13:13

MAADAI

of Bani; *M*., Amram, and Uel	Ezr 10:34

MAADIAH

Miamin, *M*., Bilgah	Ne 12:5

MAAI

Milalai, Gilalai, *M*., Nethaneel	Ne 12:36

MAALEH-ACRABBIM

went out to the south side to *M*.	Jos 15:3

MAARATH

And *M*., and Beth-anoth, and	Jos 15:59

MAASEIAH

Eliab, and Benaiah, and *M*.	1Ch 15:18
M. and Benaiah, with psalteries	1Ch 15:20
Obed, and *M*. the son of Adaiah	2Ch 23:1
Jeiel the scribe and *M*. the ruler	2Ch 26:11
a mighty man of Ephraim, slew *M*.	2Ch 28:7
and *M*. the governor of the city	2Ch 34:8
M. and Eliezer, and Jarib	Ezr 10:18
And of the sons of Harim; *M*.	Ezr 10:21
the sons of Pashur; Elioenai, *M*.	Ezr 10:22
Chelal, Benaiah, *M*., Mattaniah	Ezr 10:30
repaired Azariah the son of *M*.	Ne 3:23
and *M*. on his right hand; and	Ne 8:4
Hodijah, *M*., Kelita, Azariah	Ne 8:7
Rehum, Hashabnah, *M*.	Ne 10:25
And *M*. the son of Baruch, the son	Ne 11:5
the son of *M*., the son of Ithiel	Ne 11:7
the priests; Eliakim, *M*., Miniamin	Ne 12:41
M. and Shemaiah and Eleazar	Ne 12:42
Zephaniah the son of *M*. the priest	Jer 21:1
Zedekiah the son of *M*.	Jer 29:21
to Zephaniah the son of *M*.	Jer 29:25
the son of *M*., in the sight of	Jer 32:12
was above the chamber of *M*.	Jer 35:4
Zephaniah the son of *M*. the	Jer 37:3
the son of *M*., when he went	Jer 51:59

MAASIAI

and *M*. the son of Adiel, the son	1Ch 9:12

MAATH

Which was the son of *M*., which was	Lu 3:26

MAAZ

firstborn of Jerahmeel were *M*.	1Ch 2:27

MAAZIAH

the four and twentieth to *M*.	1Ch 24:18
M., Bilgai, Shemaiah: these	Ne 10:8

MACEDONIA

stood a man of *M*., and prayed	Ac 16:9
Come over into *M*. and help us	Ac 16:9
we endeavoured to go into *M*.	Ac 16:10
is the chief city of that part of *M*.	Ac 16:12
and Timotheus were come from *M*.	Ac 18:5
when he had passed through *M*.	Ac 19:21
and sent into *M*. two of them	Ac 19:22
men of *M*., Paul's companions in	Ac 19:29
and departed for to go into *M*.	Ac 20:1
he purposed to return through *M*.	Ac 20:3
it hath pleased them of *M*.	Ro 15:26
when I shall pass through *M*.	1Co 16:5
for I do pass through *M*.	1Co 16:5
to pass by you into *M*., and to	2Co 1:16
come again out of *M*. unto you	2Co 1:16
them, I went from thence into *M*.	2Co 2:13
when we were come into *M*.	2Co 7:5
bestowed on the churches of *M*.	2Co 8:1
I boast of you to them of *M*.	2Co 9:2
Lest haply if they of *M*. come	2Co 9:4
the brethren which came from *M*.	2Co 11:9
when I departed from *M*., no	Ph'p 4:15
ensamples to all that believe in *M*.	1Th 1:7
word of the Lord not only in *M*.	1Th 1:8
the brethren which are in all *M*.	1Th 4:10
at Ephesus, when I went into *M*.	1Ti 1:3

MACEDONIAN

Aristarchus, being with a *M*.	Ac 27:2

MACHBANAI

the tenth, *M*. the eleventh	1Ch 12:13

MACHBENAH

Sheva the father of *M*., and	1Ch 2:49

MACHI

tribe of Gad. Geuel the son of *M*.	Nu 13:15

MACHINERY

m. devised by inventors (A)(B)	2Ch 26:15

MACHIR

also of *M*. the son of Manasseh	Ge 50:23
of *M*., the family of the Machirites	Nu 26:29
M. begat Gilead: of Gilead come	Nu 26:29
son of *M*., the son of	Nu 27:1
children of *M*. the son of	Nu 32:39
unto *M*. the son of Manasseh	Nu 32:40
children of Gilead, the son of *M*.	Nu 36:1
And I gave Gilead unto *M*.	De 3:15
pertaining unto the children of *M*.	Jos 13:31
to the one half of the children of *M*.	Jos 13:31

MADE

(continued)

for *M*. the firstborn of Manasseh	Jos 17:1
son of *M*., the son of Manasseh	Jos 17:3
out of *M*. came down governors	J'g 5:14
he is in the house of *M*., the	2Sa 9:4
fetched him out of the house of *M*.	2Sa 9:5
M. the son of Ammiel of Lo-debar	2Sa 17:27
went in to the daughter of *M*.	1Ch 2:21
these belonged to the sons of *M*.	1Ch 2:23
concubine the Aramitess bare *M*.	1Ch 7:14
And *M*. took to wife the sister	1Ch 7:15
the wife of *M*. bare a son, and	1Ch 7:16
son of *M*., the son of	1Ch 7:17

MACHIRITES

of Machir, the family of the *M*.	Nu 26:29

MACHNADEBAI

M., Shashai, Sharai	Ezr 10:40

MACHPELAH

he may give me the cave of *M*.	Ge 23:9
field of Ephron, which was in *M*.	Ge 23:17
wife in the cave of the field of *M*.	Ge 23:19
buried him in the cave of *M*. in	Ge 25:9
In the cave that is in the field of *M*.	Ge 49:30
him in the cave of the field of *M*.	Ge 50:13

MAD

be *m*. for the sight of thine eyes	De 28:34
feigned himself *m*. in their hands	1Sa 21:13
servants, Lo, ye see the man is *m*.	1Sa 21:14
Have I need of *m*. men, that	1Sa 21:15
to lay the *m*. man in my presence	1Sa 21:15
came this *m*. fellow to thee	2Ki 9:11
m. against me are sworn	Ps 102:8
a *m*. man who casteth firebrands	Pr 26:18
I said of laughter, It is *m*.: and	Ec 2:2
oppression maketh a wise man *m*.	Ec 7:7
the liars, and maketh diviners *m*.	Isa 44:25
drink, and be moved, and be *m*.	Jer 25:16
every man that is *m*. and maketh	Jer 29:26
and they are *m*. upon their idols	Jer 50:38
wine; therefore the nations are *m*.	Jer 51:7
is a fool, the spiritual man is *m*.	Ho 9:7
said, He hath a devil, and is *m*.	Joh 10:20
they said unto her, Thou art *m*.	Ac 12:15
exceedingly *m*. against them	Ac 26:11
learning doth make thee *m*.	Ac 26:24
I am not *m*. most noble Festus	Ac 26:25
will they not say that ye are *m*.	1Co 14:23

MADAI

Magog, and *M*., and Javan	Ge 10:2; 1Ch 1:5

MADE

the arms of his hands were *m*. strong	Ge 49:24
who *m*. thee prince over us	Ex 2:14; Ac 7:27
L. said to him, Who hath *m*. man's mouth	Ex 4:11
m. his servants and cattle flee into the houses	Ex 9:20
after he had *m*. it a molten calf, they said	Ex 32:4
Aaron had *m*. them naked to their shame	Ex 32:25

and have *m.* them gods of   *Ex 32:31;*
gold   *Ho 8:4*
so the children of Israel *m.* all   *Ex 39:42*
the work
whereby he may *m.* be unclean   *Le 22:5*
they shall bear all that is *m.*   *Nu 4:26*
for them
he shall eat nothing that is *m.*   *Nu 6:4*
of the vine tree
why have ye *m.* us to come   *Nu 20:5*
from Egypt
I took your sin and calf which   *De 9:21*
he had *m.*
Joshua and Israel *m.* as if they   *Jas 8:15*
were beaten
went and *m.* as if they had been   *Jos 9:4*
ambassadors
they *m.* the heart of the people   *Jos 14:8*
melt
the pattern of the altar which   *Jos 22:28*
our fathers *m.*
she *m.* Samson sleep upon her   *J'g 16:19*
knees
Samson *m.* the Philistines   *J'g 16:25;*
sport   *16:27*
ye have taken away the gods   *J'g 18:24*
which I *m.*
his sons *m.* themselves vile,   *1Sa 3:13*
restrained not
that Samuel *m.* his sons judges   *1Sa 8:1*
over Israel
behold, I have *m.* a king over   *1Sa 12:1*
you
wast thou not *m.* the head of   *1Sa 15:17*
Israel
as thy sword hath *m.* women   *1Sa 15:33*
childless
David *m.* marks (S)   *1Sa 21:13*
Achish said, Whither have   *1Sa 27:10*
ye *m.* road to-day
m. it known (S)   *2Sa 11:22; Es 3:6*
Amnon lay down and *m.*   *2Sa 13:6*
himself sick
what supplication be *m.*   *1Ki 8:38;*
   2Ch 6:29
sacrificing the calves that he   *1Ki 12:32*
had *m.*
hast gone and *m.* thee other   *1Ki 14:9*
gods
he removed all idols which   *1Ki 15:12*
his fathers *m.*
she had *m.* an idol in a grove   *1Ki 5:13;*
   2Ch 15:16
shalt make streets as my   *1Ki 20:34*
father *m.* in Samaria
they *m.* him king and   *2Ki 11:12*
anointed him
as Ahaz sent, so Urijah the   *2Ki 16:11*
priest *m.* it
yet his father *m.* the   *1Ch 26:10*
chief
and had *m.* ready for the   *1Ch 28:2*
building
ears attend to prayer *m.* in   *2Ch 6:40*
this place
art thou *m.* of the king's   *2Ch 25:16*
counsel
for Ahaz *m.* Judah naked   *2Ch 28:19*
and transgressed
set the idol he had *m.* in the   *2Ch 33:7*
house of God
Josiah *m.* all present to serve   *2Ch 34:33*
the Lord
Shesh-bazzar whom he *m.*   *Ezr 5:14*
governor
let there be search *m.* in king's   *Ezr 5:17*
house
and search was *m.* in the house   *Ezr 6:1*
of the rolls
let his house be *m.* a dunghill   *Ezr 6:11*
for this
we *m.* our prayer unto our God   *Ne 4:9*
Ahasuerus *m.* her queen instead   *Es 2:17*
of Vashti
let a gallows be *m.* of fifty   *Es 5:14*
cubits high
they *m.* it day of feasting and   *Es 9:17*
gladness
I am *m.* to possess months of   *Job 7:3*
vanity
or wast thou *m.* before the   *Job 15:7*
hills
not his like on earth, who is   *Job 41:33*
m. without fear
he *m.* a pit, and is fallen into   *Ps 7:15*
pit he *m.*
the heathen are sunk into the   *Ps 9:15*
pit they *m.*

be not afraid when one is *m.*   *Ps 49:16*
rich
this is the man that *m.* not God   *Ps 52:7*
his strength
I am fearfully and   *Ps 139:14*
wonderfully *m.*
the way of the righteous is *m.*   *Pr 15:19*
plain
scorner is punished, the simple   *Pr 21:11*
is *m.* wise
that putteth trust in the Lord   *Pr 28:25*
shall be *m.* fat
what is crooked cannot be *m.*   *Ec 1:15*
straight
I *m.* me great works, I builded   *Ec 2:4*
houses
I *m.* me gardens   *Ec 2:5*
I *m.* me pools of water   *Ec 2:6*
for by sadness of countenance,   *Ec 7:3*
the heart is *m.* better
a feast is *m.* for laughter,   *Ec 10:19*
wine makes
they *m.* me the keeper of the   *Ca 1:6*
vineyards
he *m.* the pillars of silver,   *Ca 3:10*
bottom of gold
my soul *m.* me like chariots of   *Ca 6:12*
Amminadib
that which their own fingers   *Isa 2:8*
have *m.*
is this the man that *m.* earth   *Isa 14:16*
to tremble
for we have *m.* lies our   *Isa 28:15*
refuge and falsehood
shall work say of him that *m.*   *Isa 29:16*
it, He *m.* me not
which your hands have *m.*   *Isa 31:7*
unto you for a sin
they have *m.* them crooked   *Isa 31:8*
paths
the son of man, which shall   *Isa 51:12*
be *m.* as grass
shall earth be *m.* to bring forth   *Isa 66:8*
in one day
m. it a lie (R)   *Jer 8:8*
the gods that have not *m.* the   *Jer 10:11*
heavens
have *m.* my pleasant portion   *Jer 12:10*
a wilderness
vessel he *m.* was marred in   *Jer 18:4*
hand of potter, so he *m.*
again another vessel
a vessel that cannot be *m.*   *Jer 19:11*
whole again
the word of the Lord was *m.*   *Jer 20:8*
a reproach
for they had *m.* that the   *Jer 37:15*
prison
which Asa the king had *m.* for   *Jer 41:9*
fear of Baasha
Nebuchadnezzar *m.* me an   *Jer 51:34*
empty vessel
ye *m.* the heart of the   *Eze 13:22*
righteous sad
where the king dwelleth that   *Eze 17:16*
m. him king
there also they *m.* their sweet   *Eze 20:28*
savour
ye have *m.* your iniquity to   *Eze 21:24*
be remembered
waters *m.* him great, deep set   *Eze 31:4*
him upon high
thy father *m.* master of the   *Da 5:11*
magicians
thy heart was *m.* like the beasts   *Da 5:21*
ye *m.* we not our prayer before   *Da 9:13*
the Lord
the princes have *m.* him sick   *Ho 7:5*
with wine
the workman *m.* it, therefore it   *Ho 8:6*
is not God
the god which ye *m.* to   *Am 5:26*
yourselves
yea they *m.* their hearts as an   *Zec 7:12*
adamant
command that these stones be   *M't 4:3*
m. bread
and the rent is *m.* worse   *M't 9:16;*
   M'k 2:21
daughter, thy faith hath *m.*   *M't 9:22;*
thee whole   *M'k 5:34; 10:52; Lu 8:48;*
   17:19
have *m.* commandment of   *M't 15:6*
God of none effect
all to be sold, and payment   *M't 18:25*
to be *m.*
house of prayer, ye have *m.*   *M't 21:13;*
it a den of thieves   *M'k 11:17; Lu 19:46*

when he is *m.* ye make him   *M't 23:15*
twofold more
and at midnight there was a   *M't 25:6*
cry *m.*, Behold
traded and *m.* them other   *M't 25:16*
five talents
but that rather a tumult was   *M't 27:24*
m.
command that the sepulchre   *M't 27:64*
be *m.* sure
he said, The sabbath was *m.*   *M'k 2:27*
for man
man, who *m.* me a judge over   *Lu 12:14*
you
lest a recompence be *m.* thee   *Lu 14:12*
same day Pilate and Herod   *Lu 23:12*
were *m.* friends
all things were *m.* by him,   *Joh 1:3*
without him was not any thing
m. that was *m.*
was in the world, the world   *Joh 1:10*
was *m.* by him
the Word was *m.* flesh, and   *Joh 1:14*
dwelt among us
he should be *m.* manifest to   *Joh 1:31*
Israel
ruler had tasted the water that   *Joh 2:9*
was *m.* wine
wilt thou be *m.* whole   *Joh 5:6*
art *m.* whole   *Joh 5:14*
ye shall be *m.* free   *Joh 8:33*
might be *m.* blind   *Joh 9:39*
that they may be *m.* perfect   *Joh 17:23*
in one
his name hath *m.* this man   *Ac 3:16*
strong
distribution was *m.* to every   *Ac 4:35*
man as need
for Saul, he *m.* havock of the   *Ac 8:3*
church
but prayer was *m.* without   *Ac 12:5*
ceasing for Peter
promise which was *m.* to our   *Ac 13:32;*
fathers   *26:6*
we went where prayer was   *Ac 16:13*
wont to be *m.*
they be no gods which are *m.*   *Ac 19:26*
with hands
more than forty who had *m.*   *Ac 23:13*
this conspiracy
they hoisted sail, and *m.*   *Ac 27:40*
toward shore
Jesus who was *m.* of the seed of   *Ro 1:3*
David
being understood by the things   *Ro 1:20*
that are *m.*
thy circumcision is *m.*   *Ro 2:25*
uncircumcision
many were *m.* sinners, many   *Ro 5:19*
m. righteous
being *m.* free from sin, ye   *Ro 6:18;*
became   *6:22*
was then that which is good,   *Ro 7:13*
m. death to me
we had been *m.* like to Sodom   *Ro 7:29*
and Gomorrha
hath *m.* free from law of sin   *Re 8:2*
and death
with the mouth confession is   *Ro 10:10*
m. to salvation
let their table be *m.* a snare   *Ro 11:9*
and a trap
nor any thing whereby thy   *Ro 14:21*
brother is *m.* weak
lest cross of Christ be *m.* of   *1Co 1:17*
none effect
are in Christ, who of God is   *1Co 1:30*
m. to us wisdom
for we are *m.* a spectacle to   *1Co 4:9*
the world to angels
we are *m.* as filth of world   *1Co 4:13*
and offscouring
I am *m.* all things to all men,   *1Co 9:22*
that I might
have been all *m.* to drink   *1Co 12:13*
into one Spirit
even so in Christ shall all be   *1Co 15:22*
m. alive
m. alive (S)   *1Co 15:36;*
   Eph 2:1, 5; Col 2:13; 1Pe 3:18
it is written, the first man   *1Co 15:45*
Adam was a *m.* a living soul,
last Adam was *m.* a quickening
spirit
for even that which was *m.*   *2Co 3:10*
glorious
an house not *m.* with hands,   *2Co 5:1*
eternal in heavens

might be *m.* the righteousness 2Co 5:21
of God in him
my strength is *m.* perfect in 2Co 12:9
weakness
are ye now *m.* perfect by the Ga 3:3
flesh
Christ redeemed us, being *m.* a Ga 3:13
curse for us
to Abraham, and his seed Ga 3:16
were the promises *m.*
seed should come, to whom Ga 3:19
promise was *m.*
sent his Son, *m.* of a woman, *m.* Ga 4:4
under law
the circumcision in the flesh Eph 2:11
m. by hands
were far off, are *m.* nigh by Eph 2:13
the blood of Christ
whereof I was *m.* a minister Eph 3:7;
Col 1:23, 25
and was *m.* in the likeness of Ph'p 2:7
men
being *m.* conformable to his Ph'p 3:10
death
having *m.* peace thro' the Col 1:20
blood of his cross
with the circumcision *m.* Col 2:11
without hands
the law is not *m.* for a 1Ti 1:9
righteous man
concerning faith have *m.* 1Ti 1:19
shipwreck
and giving of thanks be *m.* for 1Ti 2:1
all men
justified by his grace, we should Tit 3:7
be *m.* heirs
being *m.* so much better than Heb 1:4
the angels
it behoved him to be *m.* like Heb 2:17
to his brethren
for we are *m.* partakers of Heb 3:14
Christ, if we hold
Christ glorified not himself Heb 5:5
to be *m.* high priest
being *m.* perfect, he became Heb 5:9
the Author of salvation
like to the Son of God, abideth Heb 7:3
a priest
there is *m.* of necessity a Heb 7:12
change of the law
m. not after law of a carnal Heb 7:16
commandment
for the law *m.* nothing perfect Heb 7:19
as not without an oath he was Heb 7:20
m. priest
for those priests were *m.* Heb 7:21
without an oath
Jesus was *m.* a surety of a Heb 7:22
better testament
there was tabernacle *m.* Heb 9:2
wherein was candlestick
a perfect tabernacle not *m.* Heb 9:11
with hands
not entered into holy places *m.* Heb 9:24
with hands
there is a remembrance *m.* of Heb 10:3
sins every year
expecting till his enemies be Heb 10:13
m. his footstool
partly whilst ye were *m.* a Heb 10:33
gazing stock
were not *m.* of things which Heb 11:3
do appear
who out of weakness were Heb 11:34
m. strong
that they without us should Heb 11:40
not be *m.* perfect
and to the spirits of just men Heb 12:23
m. perfect
but the rich, in that he is *m.* Jas 1:10
low
and by works was faith *m.* Jas 2:22
perfect
which are *m.* after the Jas 3:9
similitude of God
the same is *m.* head of the 1Pe 2:7
corner
but these *m.* to be taken and 2Pe 2:12
destroyed
he that believeth not, hath *m.* 1Jo 5:10
God a liar
m. them white in the blood of Re 7:14
the Lamb
waters, because they were *m.* Re 8:11
bitter
she *m.* all nations drink of the Re 14:8
wine
been *m.* drunk with wine of her Re 17:2
fornication

MADE with *GOD, LORD CHRIST*

God *m.* the firmament and Ge 1:7
divided
m. two great lights, he *m.* Ge 1:16;
stars Ps 136:7, 9
God *m.* the beast of the earth Ge 1:25
after his kind
God saw everything that he Ge 1:31
had *m.* was good
God rested from all his works Ge 2:2
he had *m.*
God *m.* the earth and heavens Ge 2:4;
Ex 20:11; 31:17; Ps 146:6; Isa 45:18;
Jer 10:12
m. to grow every tree Ge 2:9
m. he a woman Ge 2:22
in the likeness of God *m.* he Ge 5:1;
9:6
it repented the Lord he had *m.* Ge 6:6;
6:7
God *m.* a wind to pass over the Ge 8:1
earth
and Sarah said, God hath *m.* Ge 21:6
me to laugh
the Lord had *m.* his journey Ge 24:21
prosperous
now the Lord hath *m.* room Ge 26:22
for us
the Lord *m.* all Joseph did to Ge 39:3;
prosper 39:23
God hath *m.* me to forget all Ge 41:51
my toil
God hath *m.* me a father to Ge 45:8
Pharaoh
God hath *m.* me Lord of all Ge 45:9
Egypt
the midwives feared God, he Ex 1:21
m. houses
and the Lord *m.* the sea dry Ex 14:21
land
I *m.* Israel to dwell in booths Le 23:43
I am Lord your God and I Le 26:13
have *m.* you go upright
he *m.* them wander in the Nu 32:13
wilderness
for the Lord *m.* his heart De 2:30
obstinate
out of heaven he *m.* thee to De 4:36
hear his voice
the Lord hath *m.* thee as the De 10:22
stars
how he *m.* the water of the De 11:4
Red sea to overflow
thee above all nations which De 26:19
he hath *m.*
hath he not *m.* thee, and De 32:6
established thee
he *m.* him ride, *m.* him suck De 32:13
honey out of rock
then he forsook God which De 32:15
m. him, and rock
the Lord *m.* Jordan border Jos 22:25
between us
he *m.* him have dominion over J'g 5:13
mighty
the Lord had *m.* a breach in J'g 21:15
the tribes
and *m.* them dwell in this 1Sa 12:8
place
the Lord repented that he had 1Sa 15:35
m. Saul king
because the Lord had *m.* a 2Sa 6:8
breach upon
he *m.* darkness, pavilions 2Sa 22:12
round about him
thy gentleness hath *m.* me 2Sa 22:36;
great Ps 18:35
who hath *m.* me a house as 1Ki 2:24
promised
the Lord loved Israel, 1Ki 10:9;
therefore he *m.* thee king 14:7; 16:2;
2Ch 1:11
but the Lord *m.* the 1Ch 16:26;
heavens Ne 9:6; Ps 33:6; 96:5; 121:2;
124:8; 134:3
the Lord had *m.* them to 2Ch 20:27
rejoice
he sought the Lord, God *m.* 2Ch 26:5
him to prosper
Lord had *m.* them joyful Ezr 6:22;
Ne 12:43
thy hands have *m.* me and Job 10:8
fashioned me
he hath *m.* me weary, thou Job 16:7
hast *m.* desolate
he hath *m.* me by-word of the Job 17:6
people

when he *m.* a decree for the Job 28:26
rain, and a way
did not he that *m.* me in the Job 31:15
womb make
the Spirit of God *m.* me, and Job 33:4
gave me life
he that *m.* him can make his Job 40:19
sword approach
hast not *m.* my foes to rejoice Ps 30:1
over me
what desolations he hath *m.* in Ps 46:8
the earth
the sea is his and he *m.* it Ps 95:5
he sent darkness, and *m.* it Ps 105:28
this is the day the Lord hath Ps 118:24
m. will rejoice
thy hands have *m.* me and Ps 119:73
fashioned me
that by wisdom *m.* the Ps 136:5;
heavens Ac 14:15
and *m.* Israel to pass Ps 136:14
through the midst of it
he hath *m.* a decree which Ps 148:6
shall not pass
let Israel rejoice in him that Ps 149:2
m. him
the Lord *m.* all things for Pr 16:4
himself
the Lord hath *m.* even both of Pr 20:12
them
he hath *m.* every thing Ec 3:11
beautiful in time
I found that God hath *m.* man Ec 7:29
upright
he that *m.* them will not have Isa 27:11
mercy
he hath *m.* Tophet deep and Isa 30:33
large
thus saith the Lord that *m.* Isa 44:2
and formed thee
he *m.* intercession for the Isa 53:12
transgressors
all these things hath mine hand Isa 66:2
m.
lo, certainly in vain *m.* he it Jer 8:8
the Lord *m.* thee priest Jer 29:26
instead of Jehoiada
and hast *m.* thee a name as at Jer 32:20
this day
as the Lord liveth, that *m.* us Jer 38:16
this soul
he hath *m.* me desolate and La 1:13;
faint 3:11
the Lord hath *m.* my strength La 1:14
to fall
my flesh and my skin hath he *m.* La 3:4
hath *m.* my chain heavy La 3:7
m. my paths crooked La 3:9
he hath *m.* me drunken with La 3:15
wormwood
I *m.* nations to shake at the Eze 31:16
sound
I fear God who hath *m.* sea Jon 1:9
and dry land
I *m.* their streets waste, none Zep 3:6
passeth
he *m.* them male and female M't 19:4;
M'k 10:6
did not he that *m.* that which Lu 11:40
is without
without him was not any thing Joh 1:3
m.
Jesus *m.* more disciples; he *m.* Joh 4:1;
water wine 4:46
he that *m.* me whole said, Joh 5:11
Take up thy bed
he spat and *m.* clay of the Joh 9:6;
spittle 11:14
because he *m.* himself the Son Joh 19:7
of God
know that God hath *m.* that Ac 2:36
same Jesus
ye know that God *m.* choice Ac 15:7
among us
God that *m.* the world and all Ac 17:24
things therein
hath *m.* of one blood all Ac 17:26
nations of men
the Holy Ghost hath *m.* you Ac 20:28
overseers
m. foolish the wisdom of this 1Co 1:20
world
hath *m.* us able ministers of 2Co 3:6
New Testament
hath *m.* him to be sin for us 2Co 5:21
who knew no sin
liberty wherewith *Christ* hath Ga 5:1
m. us free
he hath *m.* us accepted in the Eph 1:6
beloved

God hath *m.* us sit together in *Eph 2:6* heavenly places
he is our peace who hath *m.* *Eph 2:14* both one
but *m.* himself of no *Ph'p 2:7* reputation
who hath *m.* us meet to be *Col 1:12* partakers
he *m.* a shew of them openly, *Col 2:15* triumphing
by whom also he *m.* the worlds *Heb 1:2*
for when *God m.* promise to *Heb 6:13* Abraham
and hath *m.* us kings and priests *Re 1:6* to God
and worship him that *m.* *Re 14:7* heaven and earth

MADE *HASTE*

Rebekah *m. haste* and let down *Ge 24:46* her pitcher
Joseph *m. haste* *Ge 43:30*
Moses *m. haste* *Ex 34:8*
Manoah's wife *m. haste* and *J'g 13:10* ran
David *m. haste* *1Sa 23:26*
Abigail *m. haste* *1Sa 25:18*
as Mephibosheth's nurse *m.* *2Sa 4:4* haste to flee
I *m. haste,* and delayed not *Ps 119:60* to keep thy
Zaccheus *m. haste* and came *Lu 19:6* down

MADE *MANIFEST*

nothing secret that shall not be *Lu 8:17* *m. manifest*
but that he should be *m.* *Joh 1:31* manifest to Israel
to the light, that his deeds *Joh 3:21* may be *m. manifest*
the works of God should be *Joh 9:3* *m. manifest* in him
I was *m. manifest* to them *Ro 10:20* that asked not
but now is *m. manifest* to all *Ro 16:26* nations for obedience
every man's work shall be *m.* *1Co 3:13* manifest
that they which are *1Co 11:19* approved may be *m. manifest*
thus are the secrets of his *1Co 14:25* heart *m. manifest*
life of Jesus should be *m.* *2Co 4:10;* manifest *4:11*
we have been thoroughly *m.* *2Co 11:6* manifest among you
are approved are *m. manifest* *Eph 5:13* by the light
but now is *m. manifest* to his *Col 1:26* saints
now *m. manifest* by the *2Ti 1:10* appearing of Christ
way into the holiest was not *Heb 9:8* yet *m. manifest*
went out that they might be *m.* *1Jo 2:19* manifest
for thy judgments are *m.* *Re 15:4* manifest

MADE *PEACE*

Joshua *m. peace* with them *Jos 9:15;* *10:1, 4*
there was not a city that *m.* *Jos 11:19* peace with Israel
m. peace with Israel *2Sa 10:19;* *1Ch 19:19*
Jehoshaphat *m. peace* with *1Ki 22:44* Israel

MADE *READY*

they *m. ready* the present *Ge 43:25* against noon
Joseph *m. ready* his chariot to *Ge 46:29* meet Israel
Pharaoh *m. ready* his chariot *Ex 14:6* and took
and Gideon went in and *m.* *J'g 6:19* ready a kid
Manoah said, till we have *m.* *J'g 13:15* ready a kid
m. ready before it was brought *1Ki 6:7* thither
and Joram's chariot was *m.* *2Ki 9:21* ready
and had *m. ready* for the *1Ch 28:2* building

afterward they *m. ready* for *2Ch 35:14* themselves
he hath bent his bow and *m.* it *Ps 7:12* ready
they have *m. ready* their heart *Ho 7:6* like an oven
the disciples *m. ready* the *M't 26:19;* passover *M'k 14:16; Lu 22:13*
while they *m. ready* Peter fell *Ac 10:10* into a trance
boast of things *m. ready* to *2Co 10:16* our hand
and his wife hath *m.* herself *Re 19:7* ready

MADE *SPEED*

Rehoboam *m. speed* to get *1Ki 12:18;* *2Ch 10:18*

MADE *VOID*

if her husband hath utterly *m.* *Nu 30:12* void
thou hast *m. void* covenant *Ps 89:39* of thy servant
time to work, for they have *Ps 119:126* *m. void* thy law
for if they of law be heirs, *Re 4:14* faith is *m. void*

I HAVE, HAVE I MADE

destroy every living substance *I Ge 7:4* have *m.*
lest thou say, *I have m.* *Ge 14:23* Abram rich
a father of nations have *I m.* *Ge 17:5;* thee *Ro 4:17*
Isaac said, Behold, *I have m.* *Ge 27:37* him thy Lord
see *I have m.* thee a god to *Ex 7:1* Pharaoh
I have m. thee a great name *2Sa 7:9;* *1Ch 17:8*
wherewith *I have m.* *1Ki 8:59* supplication
for the which *I have m.* *1Ch 29:19* provision
I Darius have m. a decree *Eze 6:11;* *6:12*
I have m. my bed in the *Job 17:13* darkness
if *I have m.* gold my hope, or *Job 31:24* have said
whose house *I have m.* the *Job 39:6* wilderness
I will speak of things which *I Ps 45:1* have *m.*
who can say, *I have m.* my *Pr 20:9* heart clean
I have m. their shouting to *Isa 16:10* cease
the sighing thereof have *I m.* *Isa 21:2* to cease
I have formed him, yea, *I Isa 43:7;* have *m.* him *46:4*
I have m. the earth, and *Isa 45:12;* created man *Jer 27:5*
and the souls which *I have m.* *Isa 57:16* should fail
behold *I have m.* thee a *Jer 1:18* defenced city
but *I have m.* Esau bare, and *Jer 49:10* uncovered
behold, *I have m.* thy face *Eze 3:8;* strong *3:9*
I have m. thee a watchman to *Eze 3:17* house of Israel
ye made heart sad, whom *I Eze 13:22* have not *m.* sad
and *I have m.* the dry tree to *Eze 17:24* flourish
therefore have *I m.* thee a *Eze 22:4* reproach
my river is mine, *I have m.* it *Eze 29:3;* for myself *29:9*
I have m. him fair by *Eze 31:9* multitude of his branches
worship the image which *I Da 3:15* have *m.*
I have m. the stink of camps *Am 4:10* to come up
I have m. thee small among the *Ob 2* heathen
therefore have *I m.* you *Mal 2:9* contemptible
because *I have m.* a man *Joh 7:23* every whit whole
yet have *I m.* myself servant *1Co 9:19* to all

THOU HAST MADE

plant them in the place which *Ex 15:17* thou hast *m.*
when *thou hast m.* an *Ex 29:36* atonement for it
this oath which *thou hast m.* *Jos 2:17;* us swear *2:20*
thou hast m. thy servant king *1Ki 3:7* instead of David
I have heard thy supplication *1Ki 9:3* that *thou hast m.*
O Lord God of Israel, thou *2Ki 19:15;* hast *m.* heaven and earth *Isa 37:16; Jer 32:17*
word came, saying *thou hast* *1Ch 22:8* *m.* great wars
thou hast m. an hedge about *Job 1:10* him and his house
remember that *thou hast m.* *Job 10:9* me as the clay
thou hast m. desolate all my *Job 16:7* company
thou hast m. him little lower *Ps 8:5* than angels
thou hast m. me the head of *Ps 18:43* the heathen
thou hast m. him most blessed *Ps 21:6* for ever
thou hast m. my mountain to *Ps 30:7* stand strong
behold, *thou hast m.* my days *Ps 39:5* as a hand breadth
thou hast m. the earth to *Ps 60:2* tremble, thou hast broken
thou hast m. us drink the wine *Ps 60:3* of astonishment
thou hast m. summer and *Ps 74:17* winter
all nations whom *thou hast m.* *Ps 86:9* shall worship
thou hast m. me an *Ps 88:8* abomination to them
thou hast m. all his enemies to *Ps 89:42* rejoice
thou hast m. his glory to cease, *Ps 89:44* and cast his throne
wherefore hast thou *m.* all *Ps 89:47* men in vain
because *thou hast m.* the Lord *Ps 91:9* thy habitation
thou, Lord, hast m. me glad *Ps 92:4* through thy work
thy works, in wisdom hast *Ps 104:24* thou *m.* them all
Leviathan, whom *thou hast* *Ps 104:26* *m.* to play therein
thou hast m. me wiser than *Ps 119:98* mine enemies
for *thou hast m.* of a city an *Isa 25:2* heap, a ruin
but *thou hast m.* me to serve *Isa 43:24* with thy sins
Lord why *thou hast m.* us to *Isa 63:17* err from thy ways
but where are thy gods that *Jer 2:28* *thou hast m.*
we wait on thee, for *thou hast Jer 14:22* *m.* all these things
thou hast m. us as the *La 3:45* offscouring and refuse
nor hast *thou m.* up the hedge *Eze 13:5* in the house
thou hast m. thee an high *Eze 16:24* place in every street
thou hast m. thy beauty to be *Eze 16:25* abhorred
at thy dishonest gain which *Eze 22:13* *thou hast m.*
at thy dishonest gain which *Eze 22:13* *thou hast m.* and blood
but one hour, and *thou hast* *M't 20:12* *m.* them equal to us
thing formed say, Why hast *Ro 9:20* *thou m.* me thus
thou hast m. us to our God *Re 5:10* kings and priests

MADEST

thou *m.* him to have dominion *Ps 8:6* over works
visit the branch that thou *m.* *Ps 80:15* strong for thyself
son of man, whom thou *m.* *Ps 80:17* strong for thyself
and *m.* to thyself images of *Eze 16:17* men

thou *m.* all their loins to be at *Eze 29:7*
a stand
neither *m.* it grow, which *Jon 4:10*
came up
art not that Egyptian which *Ac 21:38*
m. uproar
thou *m.* him a little lower than *Heb 2:7*
the angels

MADIAN

was a stranger in the land of *Ac 7:29*
M.

MADMAN

why did this *m.* come (B) *2Ki 9:11*

MADMANNAH

Ziklag, and *M.*, and *Jos 15:31*
Sansannah
bare also Shaaph the father *1Ch 2:49*
of *M.*

MADMEN

thou shalt be cut down, O *M.* *Jer 48:2*

MADMENAH

M. is removed; the *Isa 10:31*
inhabitants of

MADNESS

The Lord shall smite thee with *De 28:28*
m.
wisdom, and to know *m.* and *Ec 1:17*
folly
behold wisdom, and *m.* and *Ec 2:12*
folly
of folly, even of foolishness *Ec 7:25*
and *m.*
m. is in their heart while they *Ec 9:3*
live
end of his talk is mischievous *Ec 10:13*
m.
and his rider with *m.* *Zec 12:4*
And they were filled with *m.* *Lu 6:11*
voice forbad the *m.* of the *2Pe 2:16*
prophet

MADON

that he sent to Johab king of *Jos 11:1*
M.
The king of *M.*, one; the king *Jos 12:19*

MAGBISH

The children of *M.*, an *Ezr 2:30*
hundred

MAGDALA

and came into the coasts of *M't 15:39*
M.

MAGDALENE

Among which was Mary *M.* *M't 27:56*
there was Mary *M.*, and the *M't 27:61*
came Mary *M.* and the *M't 28:1*
other Mary
among whom was Mary *M.* *M'k 15:40*
Mary *M.* and Mary the *M'k 15:47*
Mary *M.*, and Mary the *M'k 16:1*
mother of
week, he appeared first to *M'k 16:9*
Mary *M.*
Mary called *M.*, out of whom *Lu 8:2*
It was Mary *M.*, and Joanna *Lu 24:10*
the wife of Cleophas, and *Joh 19:25*
Mary *M.*
day of the week cometh Mary *Joh 20:1*
M.
Mary *M.* came and *Joh 20:18*
told disciples

MAGDIEL

Duke *M.*, duke Iram: these be *Ge 36:43*
Duke *M.*, duke Iram. These *1Ch 1:54*

MAGIC

practiced *m.* arts (A)(B)(R) *Ac 8:9*
with his skill of *m.* arts *Ac 8:11*
(A)(B)(N)(R)

by your *m.* spells (A)(B) *Ac 18:23*
idolatry, *m.* (B) *Ga 5:20*
their *m.* arts (B) *Re 9:21*
practicers of *m.* (A)(B) *Re 21:8; 22:15*

MAGICAL

by *m.* practices (P) *Ac 8:11*
which used *m.* arts (S) *Ac 19:19*

MAGICIAN

skilful *m.*, expert in charms (R) *Isa 3:3*
that asked such things at any *Da 2:10*
a Jewish *m.* (B)(P)(R) *Ac 13:6; 13:8*

MAGICIANS

and called for all the *m.* of *Ge 41:8*
Egypt
sent for scribes and wise men *Ge 41:8*
(B)
I told this unto the *m.*; but *Ge 41:24*
related to the interpreters (B) *Ge 41:24*
now the *m.* of Egypt, they also *Ex 7:11*
and the *m.* (B) *Ex 7:11*
the *m.* of Egypt did so with *Ex 7:22*
their
m. did so with their *Ex 8:7;*
enchantments *8:18*
Then the *m.* said unto Pharaoh *Ex 8:19*
the scribes said to Pharaoh *Ex 8:19;*
(B) *9:11*
m. could not stand before *Ex 9:11*
Moses
the boil was upon the *m.* and *Ex 9:11*
upon
ten times better than all the *m.* *Da 1:20*
the king commanded to call the *Da 2:2*
m.
wise men, the astrologers, the *Da 2:27*
m.
came in the *m.* the astrologers *Da 4:7*
O Belteshazzar, master of the *Da 4:9*
m.
thy father made master of the *Da 5:11*
m.

MAGISTRATE

there was no *m.* in the land *J'g 18:7*
no ruler in the land (B) *J'g 18:7*
none in land possessing *J'g 18:7*
authority (E)
with thine adversary to the *m.* *Lu 12:58*

MAGISTRATES

set *m.* and judges, which may *Ezr 7:25*
appoint judges and officials *Ezr 7:25*
(B)
unto the synagogues, and unto *Lu 12:11*
m.
to rulers and authorities *Lu 12:11*
(B)(E)(R)
brought before state *Lu 12:11*
authorities (N)
brought them to the *m.*, *Ac 16:20*
saying
before the authorities (B)(P) *Ac 16:20*
and the *m.* rent off their *Ac 16:22*
rulers commanded they to be *Ac 16:22*
beaten (A)
the officials ordered them *Ac 16:22*
flogged (B)
the *m.* sent the serjeants, *Ac 16:35*
saying
The *m.* have sent to let you go *Ac 16:36*
told these words unto the *m.* *Ac 16:38*
to obey *m.* to be ready to every *Tit 3:1*
m. and authorities (A) *Tit 3:1*
subject to ruling authorities (B) *Tit 3:1*
subject to rulers and authorities *Tit 3:1*
(E)(R)
submissive to government *Tit 3:1*
authorities (N)
recognize the power of those *Tit 3:1*
who rule (P)

MAGNANIMITY

let your *m.* known (N) *Ph'p 4:5*

MAGNIFICAL

the Lord must be exceeding *1Ch 22:5*
m.
made most magnificent *1Ch 22:5*
(A)(B)(E)(R)

MAGNIFICENCE

feasted in *m.* (N) *Lu 16:19*
the *m.* of God (P) *Ac 2:11*
and her *m.* should be *Ac 19:27*
destroyed
glorious manificence be *Ac 19:27*
disregarded (A)
lose respect and magnificent *Ac 19:27*
glory (B)
cease to command respect *Ac 19:27*
(N)
come to be lightly regarded *Ac 19:27*
(P)

MAGNIFIED

and thou hast *m.* thy mercy *Ge 19:19*
you have shown wonderful *Ge 19:19*
kindness (B)
you have shown me great *Ge 19:19*
kindness (R)
m. Joshua in the sight of all *Jos 4:14*
Israel
revered him all his life (B) *Jos 4:14*
exalted Joshua in the sight of *Jos 4:14*
Israel (R)
And let thy name be *m.* for *2Sa 7:26*
ever
thy name may be forever great *2Sa 7:26*
(B)
that thy name may be *m.* for *1Ch 17:24*
ever
the Lord *m.* Solomon *1Ch 29:25*
exceedingly
with him, and *m.* him *2Ch 1:1*
exceedingly
was *m.* in the sight of all *2Ch 32:23*
nations
exalted in the eyes of many *2Ch 32:23*
nations (B)
Let the Lord be *m.*, which *Ps 35:27*
say continually, The Lord be *Ps 40:16*
m.
say continually, Let God be *m.* *Ps 70:4*
m. thy word above all thy *Ps 138:2*
name
for he *m.* himself against the *Jer 48:26*
Lord
hath *m.* himself against the *Jer 48:42*
Lord
for the enemy hath *m.* himself *La 1:9*
he *m.* himself even to the *Da 8:11*
prince
m. themselves against their *Zep 2:8*
border
exalted themselves against their *Zep 2:8*
(B)
made boasts against their *Zep 2:8*
territory (R)
m. themselves against the *Zep 2:10*
people
Lord will be *m.* from the *Mal 1:5*
border of
to them: but the people *m.* *Ac 5:13*
held them in high regard (A) *Ac 5:13*
people valued them highly (B) *Ac 5:13*
people spoke highly of them *Ac 5:13*
(N)
their general popularity was *Ac 5:13*
great (P)
people held them in high honor *Ac 5:13*
(R)
the name of the Lord Jesus *Ac 19:17*
was *m.*
name of Lord Jesus was *Ac 19:17*
highly praised (B)
name of Lord Jesus gained in *Ac 19:17*
honour (N)
name of Lord Jesus became *Ac 19:17*
highly respected (P)
name of Lord Jesus was *Ac 19:17*
highly extolled (R)
be *m.* in you (E) *2Co 10:15*
also Christ shall be *m.* in my *Ph'p 1:20*
body
honor of Christ be enhanced *Ph'p 1:20*
in my body (B)
greatness of Christ shine out *Ph'p 1:20*
in my (N)
Christ be honored in my *Ph'p 1:20*
body (R)

MAGNIFICENT

the house very *m.* *1Ch 22:5*
(A)(B)(E)(R)(S)
lose respect and *m.* glory (B) *Ac 19:27*

MAGNIFY

begin to *m.* thee in the sight of   Jos 3:7
begin to exalt you in the eyes of   Jos 3:7
Israel (B)
man, that thou shouldest *m.*   Job 7:17
him
ye will *m.* yourselves against   Job 19:5
you would assume a superior   Job 19:5
attitude (B)
Remember that thou *m.* his   Job 36:24
work
Remember to glorify his   Job 36:24
works (B)
Remember to extol his work   Job 36:24
(R)
O *m.* the Lord with me, and let   Ps 34:3
that *m.* themselves against me   Ps 35:26
who puff themselves up (B)   Ps 35:26;
  38:16
they *m.* themselves against me   Ps 38:16
me that did *m.* himself against   Ps 55:12
who vaunts himself against me   Ps 55:12
(B)
who deals insolently with me   Ps 55:12
(R)
and will *m.* him with   Ps 69:30
thanksgiving
the saw *m.* itself against him   Isa 10:15
saw vaunt itself over the one   Isa 10:15
who uses it (B)
he will *m.* the law, and make   Isa 42:21
Thus will I *m.* myself, and   Eze 38:23
sanctify
I will manifest my greatness   Eze 38:23
(B)
I will show my greatness (R)   Eze 38:23
he shall *m.* himself in his heart   Da 8:25
and *m.* himself above every   Da 11:36
god
for he shall *m.* himself above   Da 11:37
he shall exalt himself above   Da 11:37
all (B)
m. themselves against Judah   Zec 12:7
be not exalted over Judah (B)   Zec 12:7
said, My soul doth *m.* the Lord   Lu 1:46
my soul magnifies and extols   Lu 1:46
the Lord (A)
my soul magnifies the Lord   Lu 1:46
(B)(R)
Tell out, my soul, the greatness   Lu 1:46
of the Lord (N)
My heart is overflowing with   Lu 1:46
praise (P)
speak with tongues, and *m.*   Ac 10:46
God
extolling and magnifying God   Ac 10:46
(A)
declaring the greatness of   Ac 10:46
God (B)(N)
speaking foreign languages   Ac 10:46
glorifying (P)
speaking in tongues extolling   Ac 10:46
God (R)
of the Gentiles, I *m.* mine   Ro 11:13
office
I take pride in my ministry   Ro 11:13
(B)
I glorify my ministry (E)   Ro 11:13
I give all honor to that   Ro 11:13
ministry (N)

MAGOG

sons of Japheth; Gomer, and   Ge 10:2
M.
sons of Japheth; Gomer, and   1Ch 1:5
M.
face against Gog, the land of   Eze 38:2
M.
I will send a fire on *M.*, and   Eze 39:6
among
quarters of the earth, Gog and   Ro 20:8
M.

MAGOR-MISSABIB

called thy name Pashur, but   Jer 20:3
M.

MAGPIASH

M., Meshullam, Hezir   Ne 10:20

MAHALAH

bare Ishod, and   1Ch 7:18
Abiezer, and *M.*

MAHALALEEL

lived seventy years, and begat   Ge 5:12
M.
Cainan lived after he begat *M.*   Ge 5:13
And *M.* lived sixty and five   Ge 5:15
years
M. lived after he begat Jared   Ge 5:16
eight hundred thirty
And all the days of *M.* were   Ge 5:17
eight hundred ninety five
Kenan, *M.*, Jared
son of *M.*, of the children of   Ne 11:4
Perez

MAHALATH

had *M.* the daughter of   Ge 28:9
Ishmael
Rehoboam took him *M.* the   2Ch 11:18
To the chief Musician upon   Ps 53 title
M.
to the chief Musician upon   Ps 88 title
M.

MAHALI

sons of Merari; *M.* and Mushi   Ex 6:19

MAHANAIM

called the name of that place   Ge 32:2
M.
from *M.* unto the border of   Jos 13:26
Debir
And their coast was from *M.*   Jos 13:30
slayer; and *M.* with her   Jos 21:38
suburbs
Saul, and brought him over to   2Sa 2:8
M.
Saul, went out from *M.* to   2Sa 2:12
Gibeon
all Bithron, and they came to   2Sa 2:29
M.
Then David came to *M.* And   2Sa 17:24
pass, when David was come   2Sa 17:27
to *M.*
of sustenance while he lay at   2Sa 19:32
M.
in the day when I went to *M.*   1Ki 2:8
Ahinadab the son of Iddo had   1Ki 4:14
M.
suburbs, and *M.* with her   1Ch 6:80
suburbs
she dances the *M.* dance   Ca 6:13
(B)(E)

MAHANEH-DAN

they called that place *M.* unto   J'g 18:12

MAHARAI

the Ahohite, *M.* the   2Sa 23:28
Netophathite
M. the Netophathite, Heled   1Ch 11:30
the son
captain for the tenth month   1Ch 27:13
was *M.*

MAHATH

the son of *M.* the son of   1Ch 6:35
Amasai
arose. *M.* the son of   2Ch 29:12
Amasai
M., and Benaiah, were   2Ch 31:13
overseers

MAHAVITE

Eliel the *M.*, and Jeribai   1Ch 11:46

MAHAZIOTH

Mallothi, Hothir and *M.*   1Ch 25:4
three and twentieth to *M.*   1Ch 25:30

MAHER-SHALAL-HASH-BAZ

with a man's pen concerning *M.*   Isa 8:1
the Lord to me, Call his name   Isa 8:3
M.

MAHLAH

daughters of Zelophehad were   Nu 26:33
M.

M., Noah, and Hoglah, and   Nu 27:1
Milcah
For *M.*, Tirzah, and Hoglah   Nu 36:11
the names of his daughters, *M.*   Jos 17:3

MAHLI

of Merari by their families; *M.*   Nu 3:20
sons of Merari; *M.*, and   1Ch 6:19
Mushi
sons of Merari; *M.*, Libni his   1Ch 6:29
son
The son of *M.*, the son of   1Ch 6:47
sons of Merari; *M.* and   1Ch 23:21
Mushi
sons of Mushi; *M.* and Eder   1Ch 23:23
sons of Merari were *M* and   1Ch 24:26
Mushi
Of *M.* came Eleazar, who   1Ch 24:28
had no sons
sons also of Mushi; *M.* and   1Ch 24:30
Eder
understanding, of the sons of   Ezr 8:18
M.

MAHLITES

Merari was the family of the   Nu 3:33
M.
the family of the *M.*, the   Nu 26:58

MAHLON

of his two sons *M.* and Chilion   Ru 1:2
M. and Chilion died also both   Ru 1:5
Ruth the Moabitess, the wife   Ru 4:10
of *M.*

MAHLON'S

and all that was Chilion's and   Ru 4:9
M.

MAHOL

and Darda, the sons of *M.*   1Ki 4:31

MAID

I pray thee, go in unto my *m.*   Ge 16:2
took Hagar her *m.* the   Ge 16:3
Egyptian
I have given my *m.* into thy   Ge 16:5
bosom
Behold, thy *m.* is in thy hand   Ge 16:6
Sarai's *m.*, Whence camest   Ge 16:8
thou
Zilpah his *m.* for an   Ge 29:24
handmaid
Bilhah his handmaid to be   Ge 29:29
her *m.*
Behold my *m.* Bilhah, go in   Ge 30:3
Rachel's *m.* conceived again   Ge 30:7
she took Zilpah her *m.* and   Ge 30:9
gave
Zilpah Leah's *m.* bare Jacob a   Ge 30:10
son
Leah's *m.* bare Jacob a   Ge 30:12
second son
flags, she sent her *m.* to fetch it   Ex 2:5
the *m.* went and called the   Ex 2:8
child's
a man smite his servant, or   Ex 21:20
his *m.*
or the eye of his *m.* that it   Ex 21:26
perish
if a man entice a *m.* that is   Ex 22:16
if she bear a *m.* child, then she   Le 12:5
and for thy servant, and for thy   Le 25:6
m.
came to her, I found her not a   De 22:14
m.
found not thy daughter a *m.*   De 22:17
and the *m.* (B)   De 32:25
your *m.* a good-for-nothing   1Sa 1:16
(B)
of the land of Israel a little *m.*   2Ki 5:2
Thus and thus said the *m.* that   2Ki 5:4
is of Israel
and the *m.* was fair and   Es 2:7
beautiful
then should I think upon a *m.*   Job 31:1
and the way of a man with a   Pr 30:19
m.
master; as with the *m.* so with   Isa 24:2
her
Can a *m.* forget her   Jer 2:32
ornaments, or
pieces the young man and the   Jer 51:22
m.

father will go in unto the same *Am 2:7*
m.
the *m.* is not dead, but *M't 9:24*
sleepeth
her by the hand, and the *m.* *M't 9:25*
arose
damsel (S) *M't 26:69;*
Joh 18:17; Ac 12:13; 16:16
into the porch, another *m.* *M't 26:71*
saw him
a *m.* saw him again, and *M'k 14:69*
began to
hand, and called, saying, *M.* *Lu 8:54*
arise
a certain *m.* beheld him as he *Lu 22:56*
a *m.* (A)(N)(R) *Ac 12:13*

MAIDEN

the *m.* was (A) *Ge 24:43; Jer 31:13*
maiden (R) *Ge 24:55;*
34:3, 12; J'g 5:30; Ru 2:5, 6; 1Ki 1:4
have given my *m.* to my *Ge 30:18*
husband
Behold, here is my daughter *J'g 19:24*
a *m.*
a young *m.* (R) *1Ki 1:2; Jer 31:13*
compassion upon young man *2Ch 36:17*
or *m.*
let the *m.* which pleaseth the *Es 2:4*
king
m. pleased him, and she *Es 2:9*
obtained
thus came every *m.* unto the *Es 2:13*
king
eyes of a *m.* unto the hand of *Ps 123:2*
father and the mother of the *m.* *Lu 8:51*

MAIDENHOOD

you come to full *m.* (A)(R) *Eze 16:7*
seven years from *m.* (A) *Lu 2:31*

MAIDENS

her *m.* walked along by the *Ex 2:5*
river's
but abide here fast by my *m.* *Ru 2:8*
that thou go out with his *m.* *Ru 2:22*
So she kept fast by the *m.* of *Ru 2:23*
Boaz
kindred, with those *m.* thou *Ru 3:2*
wast
found young *m.* going out to *1Sa 9:11*
draw
all young *m.* (B) *Es 2:3; Ca 1:3*
all young *m.* (A) *Es 2:3;*
2:19; Ca 1:3; La 1:4, 18; 2:10, 21;
Ac 21:9; 1Co 7:25
many *m.* were gathered together *Es 2:8*
as belonged to her, and seven *m.* *Es 2:9*
I also and my *m.* will fast *Es 4:16*
likewise
or wilt thou bind him for thy *Job 41:5*
m.
m. were not given to *Ps 78:63*
marriage
Both young men, and *m.*; old *Ps 148:12*
men
She hath sent forth her *m.* she *Pr 9:3*
and for the maintenance for *Pr 27:27*
thy *m.*
household, and a portion to *Pr 31:15*
her *m.*
I got me servants and *m.* and *Ec 2:7*
the *m.* love (R) *Ca 1:3;*
6:8; La 1:4, 18; 2:10; 21; M't 25:1, 7, 11
they shall take *m.* of the seed *Eze 44:22*
to beat the menservants and *m.* *Lu 12:45*

MAIDS

Beside their servants and their *Ezr 2:65*
m.
he preferred her and her *m.* unto *Es 2:9*
So Esther's *m.* *Es 4:4*
and chamberlains
my *m.* count me for a *Job 19:15*
stranger
and the *m.* in the cities of *La 5:11*
Judah
utterly old and young, both *m.* *Eze 9:6*
her *m.* shall lead her as with the *Na 2:7*
cheerful, and new wine the *m.* *Zec 9:17*
one of the *m.* of the high *M't 14:66*
priest

MAID'S

when every *m.* turn was come *Es 2:12*

MAIDSERVANT

unto the firstborn of the *m.* *Ex 11:5*
that is
thy manservant, nor thy *m.* *Ex 20:10*
nor thy
his manservant, nor his *m.* *Ex 20:17*
nor his
a man sell his daughter to be a *Ex 21:7*
m.
ox shall push a manservant or *Ex 21:32*
a *m.*
nor thy manservant, nor thy *m.* *De 5:14*
and thy *m.* may rest as well as *De 5:14*
thou
or his manservant, or his *m.*, *De 5:21*
his ox
thy manservant, and thy *m.* *De 12:18*
unto thy *m.* thou shalt do *De 15:17*
likewise
thy manservant, and thy *m.* *De 16:11;*
and *16:14*
made Abimelech, the son of his *J'g 9:18*
m.
a *m.* went (A)(E)(R)(S) *2Sa 17:17*
cause of my manservant or *Job 31:13*
of my *m.*
manservant, and every man *Jer 34:9*
his *m.*
manservant, and every one *Jer 34:10*
his *m.*

MAIDSERVANTS

asses, and menservants, and *Ge 12:16*
m.
Abimelech, and his wife, and *Ge 20:17*
his *m.*
menservants, and *m.* and *Ge 24:35*
camels
cattle, and *m.* and menservants *Ge 30:43*
menservants, and your *m.* and *De 12:12*
menservants, and your *m.* and *1Sa 8:16*
of the *m.* which thou hast *2Sa 6:22*
spoken
oxen, and menservants, and *2Ki 5:26*
m.
their manservants and their *m.* *Ne 7:67*
men servants and *m.* (S) *Lu 12:45*

MAIDSERVANT'S

manservant's tooth, or his *m.* *Ex 21:27*
tooth

MAIDSERVANTS'

tent, and into the two *m.* tents *Ge 31:33*

MAIL

a coat of *m.* (S) *Ex 28:14; 39:23*
he was armed with a coat of *1Sa 17:5*
m.
also he armed him with a *1Sa 17:38*
coat of *m.*
coats of *m.* (S) *2Ch 26:14; Ne 4:16*

MAIMED

Blind, or broken, or *m.* or *Le 22:22*
having
that were lame, blind, dumb, *M't 15:30*
m.
dumb to speak, the *m.* to be *M't 15:31*
whole
thee to enter into life halt or *M't 18:8*
m.
better for thee to enter into *M'k 9:43*
life *m.*
a feast, call the poor, the *m.* *Lu 14:13*
bring in hither the poor, and *Lu 14:21*
the *m.*

MAINSAIL

lowered the *m.* (N) *Ac 27:17*
and hoisted up the *m.* to the *Ac 27:40*
wind

MAINTAIN

cannot *m.* himself (R) *Le 12:35*
supplication, and *m.* their *1Ki 8:45*
cause
dwelling place, and *m.* their *1Ki 8:49*
cause
that he *m.* the cause of his *1Ki 8:59*
servant
to *m.* the house of the Lord *1Ch 26:27*

supplication, and *m.* their *2Ch 6:35*
cause
supplications, and *m.* their *2Ch 6:39*
cause
I will *m.* mine own ways *Job 13:15*
before
m. the right of a man *Job 16:21*
(E)(R)
will *m.* the cause of the *Ps 140:12*
afflicted
m. the rights of (R) *Pr 31:9*
does not *m.* indignation (B) *Mic 7:18*
might be careful to *m.* good *Tit 3:8*
works
let ours also learn to *m.* good *Tit 3:14*
works

MAINTAINED

hast *m.* my right and my cause *Ps 9:4*
m. blameless (B) *1Th 5:23*

MAINTAINERS

makers and *m.* of peace (A) *M't 5:9*

MAINTAINEST

and of my cup: thou *m.* my lot *Ps 16:5*

MAINTENANCE

have *m.* from the king's palace *Ezr 4:14*
and for the *m.* for thy maidens *Pr 27:27*

MAJESTIC

make you *m.* for ever (R) *Isa 60:15*
made them as his *m.* horse *Zec 10:3*
(S)

MAJESTY

glory, and the victory, and *1Ch 29:11*
the *m.*
bestowed upon him such *1Ch 29:25*
royal *m.*
and the honour of his excellent *Es 1:4*
m.
the north: with God is *Job 37:22*
terrible *m.*
Deck thyself now with *m.* and *Job 40:10*
honour and *m.* hast thou laid *Ps 21:5*
the voice of the Lord is full *Ps 29:4*
of *m.*
mighty, with thy glory and thy *Ps 45:3*
m.
And in they *m.* ride *Ps 45:4*
prosperously
reigneth, he is clothed with *m.* *Ps 93:1*
Honour and *m.* are before him *Ps 96:6*
thou art clothed with honour *Ps 104:1*
and *m.*
of the glorious honour of. thy *Ps 145:5*
m.
the glorious *m.* of his kingdom *Ps 145:12*
Lord, and for the glory of his *Isa 2:10*
m.
Lord, and for the glory of *Isa 2:19;*
his *m.* *2:21*
shall sing for the *m.* of the *Isa 24:14*
Lord
will not behold the *m.* of the *Isa 26:10*
Lord
an everlasting *m.* (B) *Isa 60:15*
of his ornament, he set it in *Eze 7:20*
m.
and for the honour of my *m.* *Da 4:30*
excellent *m.* was added unto *Da 4:36*
me
and *m.* and glory, and honour *Da 5:18*
And for the *m.* that he gave him *Da 5:19*
in the *m.* of the name of the *Mic 5:4*
Lord
the right hand of the *M.* on *Heb 1:3*
high
throne of the *M.* in the heavens *Heb 8:1*
but were eyewitnesses of his *2Pe 1:16*
m.
be glory and *m.*, dominion and *Jude 25*

MAJORITY

punishment by the *m.* (R) *2Co 2:6*
your enthusiasm stimulated the *2Co 9:2*
m. (A)(P)

MAKAZ

The son of Dekar, in *M.*, and *1Ki 4:9*

MAKE

said, Let us *m.* man in our image — Ge 1:26
I will *m.* him an help meet for him — Ge 2:18
a tree to be desired to *m.* one wise — Ge 3:6
did the Lord *m.* coats of skins — Ge 3:21
M. thee an ark of gopher wood — Ge 6:14
rooms shalt thou *m.* in the ark, and — Ge 6:14
fashion which thou shalt *m.* it — Ge 6:15
window shalt thou *m.* to the ark — Ge 6:16
and third stories shalt thou *m.* — Ge 6:16
covenant which I *m.* between — Ge 9:12
let us *m.* brick, and burn them — Ge 11:3
and let us *m.* us name, lest we — Ge 11:4
I will *m.* of thee a great nation — Ge 12:2; 21:18; 46:3; Ex 32:10
I will *m.* thy seed as the dust — Ge 13:16
will *m.* my covenant between — Ge 17:2
I will *m.* thee exceeding fruitful — Ge 17:6
and I will *m.* nations of thee — Ge 17:6
him, and will *m.* him fruitful — Ge 17:20
and I will *m.* him a great nation — Ge 17:20
M. ready quickly three measures of — Ge 18:6
it, and *m.* cakes upon the hearth — Ge 18:6
let us *m.* our father drink wine — Ge 19:32
let us *m.* him drink wine this night — Ge 19:34
the bondwoman will I *m.* a nation — Ge 21:13
for I will *m.* him a great nation — Ge 21:18
And I will *m.* thee swear by the Lord — Ge 24:3
I will *m.* thy seed to multiply — Ge 26:4
let us *m.* a covenant between thee — Ge 26:28
m. me savoury meat, such as I — Ge 27:4
venison, and *m.* me savoury meat — Ge 27:7
I will *m.* them savoury meat for thy — Ge 27:9
bless thee, and *m.* thee fruitful — Ge 28:3
come thou, let us *m.* a covenant — Ge 31:44
m. thy seed as the sand of the — Ge 32:12
m. ye marriages with us, and — Ge 34:9
have troubled me to *m.* me to stink — Ge 34:30
and *m.* there an altar unto God — Ge 35:1
I will *m.* there an altar unto God — Ge 35:3
and *m.* mention of me unto Pharaoh — Ge 40:14
men home, and slay, and *m.* ready — Ge 43:16
there *m.* of thee a great nation — Ge 46:3
m. thy father and brethren to dwell — Ge 47:6
m. them rulers over my cattle — Ge 47:6
me, Behold, I will *m.* thee fruitful — Ge 48:4
m. of thee a multitude of people — Ge 48:4
God *m.* thee as Ephraim and — Ge 48:20
ye *m.* them rest from their burdens — Ex 5:5
give the people straw to *m.* brick — Ex 5:7
which they did *m.* heretofore — Ex 5:8
and they say to us, *M.* brick — Ex 5:16
shall *m.* your count for the lamb — Ex 12:4
m. them know the statutes of God — Ex 18:16
m. unto thee any graven image — Ex 20:4
shall not *m.* with me gods of silver — Ex 20:23
shall ye *m.* unto you gods of gold — Ex 20:23
An altar of earth thou shalt *m.* — Ex 20:24
thou wilt *m.* me an altar of stone — Ex 20:25
owner of the pit shall *m.* it good — Ex 21:34
for he should *m.* full restitution — Ex 22:3
vineyard, shall he *m.* restitution — Ex 22:5
the fire shall surely *m.* restitution — Ex 22:6

thereof, and he shall not *m.* it good — Ex 22:11
shall *m.* restitution unto the owner — Ex 22:12
he shall not *m.* good that which — Ex 22:13
with it, he shall surely *m.* it good — Ex 22:14
be with it, he shall not *m.* it good — Ex 22:15
m. no mention of the name of other — Ex 23:13
I will *m.* all thine enemies — Ex 23:27
Thou shalt *m.* no covenant — Ex 23:32
land, lest they *m.* thee sin against me — Ex 23:33
And let them *m.* me a sanctuary — Ex 25:8
thereof, even so shall ye *m.* it — Ex 25:9
shall *m.* an ark of shittim wood — Ex 25:10
thou shalt *m.* holy garments for Aaron — Ex 28:2
these are the garments which they shall *m.* — Ex 28:4; 28:4
for Aaron's sons thou shalt *m.* coats, girdles — Ex 28:40
thou shalt *m.* them linen breeches — Ex 28:42
thou shalt *m.* him an altar of shittim wood — Ex 30:1
thou shalt *m.* it an oil of holy ointment — Ex 30:25
as to perfume, you shall not *m.* like to it — Ex 30:37
that they *m.* all that I commanded — Ex 31:6; 35:10
up *m.* us gods to go before us — Ex 32:1; 32:23; Ac 7:40
I will *m.* of thee a great nation — Ex 32:10
I will *m.* my goodness pass before thee — Ex 33:19
and *m.* thy sons go a whoring after their gods — Ex 34:16
thou shalt not *m.* molten gods — Ex 34:17; Le 19:4
neither man nor woman *m.* any more — Ex 36:6
he shall *m.* amends for the harm done — Le 5:16
m. atonement (S) — Le 6:30
not *m.* yourselves abominable — Le 11:43; 20:25
not *m.* any cuttings in your flesh for dead — Le 19:28
they shall not *m.* baldness — Le 21:5; De 14:1
I will *m.* you fruitful, and multiply you — Le 26:9
I will *m.* your heaven as iron, earth as brass — Le 26:19
beasts, which shall *m.* you few in number — Le 26:22
when a man shall *m.* a singular vow — Le 27:2
the Lord *m.* thee a curse, *m.* thy thigh to rot — Nu 5:21
he shall not *m.* himself unclean for his father — Nu 6:7
the Lord *m.* his face to shine upon thee — Nu 6:25
let them wash, and so *m.* themselves clean — Nu 8:7
let us *m.* a captain, and return to Egypt — Nu 14:4
I will *m.* of thee a greater nation than they — Nu 14:12
except thou *m.* thyself a prince over us — Nu 16:13
if the Lord *m.* a new thing and the earth open — Nu 16:30
let them *m.* them broad plates for the altar — Nu 16:38
I will *m.* to cease from me the murmurings — Nu 17:5
m. thee a fiery serpent, and set it on a pole — Nu 21:8
he shall *m.* her vow of none effect — Nu 30:8
ye shall *m.* it go through fire and water — Nu 31:23
Lord *m.* you a thousand times more — De 1:11
and I will *m.* them rulers over you — De 1:13
I will *m.* them hear my words to fear me — De 4:10
lest ye *m.* you a graven image — De 4:16; 4:23

nor shalt thou *m.* marriages with them — De 7:3
m. thee know that man liveth not by bread — De 8:3
if it *m.* thee answer of peace, and open to — De 20:11
if it will *m.* no peace with thee, but war — De 20:12
to *m.* thee high above all nations he made — De 26:19
the Lord shall *m.* thee plenteous — De 28:11; 30:9
Lord shall *m.* thee the head, and not the tail — De 28:13
m. the remembrance of them to cease — De 32:26
I kill, and I *m.* alive, I wound, and I heal — De 32:39
thou shalt *m.* thy way prosperous — Jos 1:8
lest ye *m.* yourselves accursed, — Jos 6:18
and *m.* the camp of Israel a curse, and trouble it
and *m.* confession to him — Jos 7:19; Ezr 10:11
so shall your children *m.* our children cease — Jos 22:25
and shall *m.* marriages with them — Jos 23:12
Samson, that he may *m.* us sport — J'g 16:25
Lord *m.* the woman like Rachel and Leah — Ru 4:11
provoked her sore, to *m.* her fret — 1Sa 1:6
and to *m.* them inherit the throne of glory — 1Sa 2:8
ye *m.* the Lord's people to transgress — 1Sa 2:24
to *m.* yourselves fat with chiefest offerings — 1Sa 2:29
ye shall *m.* images of your emerods — 1Sa 6:5
m. a new cart — 1Sa 6:7
m. us a king to judge — 1Sa 8:5
hearken to them, and *m.* them a king — 1Sa 8:22
it hath pleased the Lord to — 1Sa 12:22; 1Ch 17:22
m. you his people
the Lord will *m.* my lord a sure house — 1Sa 25:28
m. thee keeper of mine head for ever — 1Sa 28:2
m. this fellow return that he may go again — 1Sa 29:4
that he will *m.* thee an house — 2Sa 7:11
hast done these things, to *m.* thy servant know — 2Sa 7:21
to *m.* him a name — 2Sa 7:23
and *m.* thyself sick — 2Sa 13:5
should I *m.* thee go up and down with us — 2Sa 15:20
all my desire, though he *m.* it not to grow — 2Sa 23:5
m. his throne greater than David's — 1Ki 1:37
God *m.* the name of Solomon better than — 1Ki 1:47
did I not *m.* thee to swear by the Lord — 1Ki 2:42
prayer which thy servant shall *m.* toward this place — 1Ki 8:29; 2Ch 6:21
confess thy name, pray, and *m.* supplication to thee — 1Ki 8:33; 8:47; 2Ch 6:24
I will *m.* him prince all days of his life — 1Ki 11:34
m. the yoke lighter — 1Ki 12:9; 12:10; 2Ch 10:10
m. thy house like the house of Jeroboam — 1Ki 16:3; 21:22; 2Ki 9:9
and after *m.* for thee and for thy son — 1Ki 17:13
if *m.* not thy life as the life of one of them — 1Ki 19:2
let us *m.* a little chamber on wall — 2Ki 4:10
am I God to kill and to *m.* alive — 2Ki 5:7
let us *m.* a place, where we may dwell — 2Ki 6:2
if Lord would *m.* windows in heaven — 2Ki 7:2; 7:19
m. him arise up, and anoint him king — 2Ki 9:2
we will not *m.* any king, do that is good — 2Ki 10:5
m. an agreement with me — 2Ki 18:31; Isa 36:16
nor will I *m.* feet of Israel move any more — 2Ki 21:8

no man *m.* son or daughter   *2Ki 23:10;*
pass through fire to Molech   *Eze 20:31*
all Israel to *m.* him king   *1Ch 11:10;*
     12:31, 38
to *m.* thee a name of   *1Ch 17:21*
greatness and terribleness
Lord *m.* his people 100 times   *1Ch 21:3*
so many more
he liked me to *m.* me king   *1Ch 28:4*
over Israel
O Lord, in thine hand it is to   *1Ch 29:12*
m. great
will *m.* it a proverb among all   *2Ch 7:20*
nations
for he thought to *m.* him   *2Ch 11:22*
king
God shall *m.* thee fall before   *2Ch 25:8*
the enemy
I *m.* a decree what ye shall do   *Ezr 6:8;*
     7:13, 21
fetch branches of thick trees to   *Ne 8:15*
m. booths
m. it known (S)   *Es 2:10*
go into king to *m.* supplication   *Es 4:8*
to him
Haman stood up to *m.* request   *Es 7:7*
for his life
should *m.* them days of feasting   *Es 9:22*
and joy
he woundeth and his hands *m.*   *Job 5:18*
whole
m. thy supplication to   *Job 8:5;*
Almighty   *22:27*
and if I *m.* my hands never so   *Job 9:30*
clean
should thy lies *m.* men hold   *Job 11:3*
their peace
m. me to know my   *Job 13:23*
transgression and sin
that ye *m.* yourselves strange   *Job 19:3*
to me
if it be not so now, who will   *Job 24:25*
m. me a liar
did not he that made me in   *Job 31:15*
womb *m.* him
he giveth quietness, who then   *Job 34:29*
can *m.* trouble
they *m.* the oppressed to cry,   *Job 35:9*
they cry out
can *m.* his sword to   *Job 40:19*
approach to him
will he *m.* many supplications   *Job 41:3*
to thee
the companions *m.* a banquet   *Job 41:6*
The arrow cannot *m.* him flee   *Job 41:28*
m. thy way straight before my   *Ps 5:8*
face
all the night *m.* I my bed to   *Ps 6:6*
swim
thou shalt *m.* them as a fiery   *Ps 21:9*
oven in anger
therefore thou shalt *m.* them   *Ps 21:12*
turn their back
thou didst *m.* me hope when on   *Ps 22:9*
That I may *m.* known (S)   *Ps 26:7*
m. thy face shine on thy   *Ps 31:16;*
servant   *119:135*
my soul shall *m.* her boast in   *Ps 34:2*
the Lord
Lord *m.* me to know mine end   *Ps 39:4*
m. me not the reproach of the   *Ps 39:8*
foolish
m. no tarrying   *Ps 40:17;*
     70:5
will *m.* all his bed   *Ps 41:3*
I will *m.* thy name to be   *Ps 45:17*
remembered
the streams shall *m.* glad the   *Ps 46:4*
city of God
in hidden part shalt *m.* me   *Ps 51:6*
know wisdom
m. me to hear joy and gladness,   *Ps 51:8*
that the bones
of thy wings, will I *m.* my   *Ps 57:1*
refuge
sing forth his name, *m.* his   *Ps 66:2*
praise glorious
ye people *m.* the voice of his   *Ps 66:8*
praise to be heard
for lo, thine enemies *m.* a   *Ps 83:2*
tumult
m. their nobles like Oreb and   *Ps 83:11*
Zeeb
O my God, *m.* them like a   *Ps 83:13*
wheel
through the valley of Baca, *m.*   *Ps 84:6*
it a well
also I will *m.* him my   *Ps 89:27*
firstborn

his seed also will I *m.* to   *Ps 89:29*
endure for ever
m. us glad, according to the   *Ps 90:15*
days afflicted
until I *m.* thine enemies thy   *Ps 110:1;*
footstool   *M't 22:44;*
  M'k 12:36; Lu 20:43; Ac 2:35; Heb 1:13
they that *m.* them are like   *Ps 115:8;*
unto them   *135:18*
m. me to understand the way   *Ps 119:27*
of thy precepts
m. me go in the path of thy   *Ps 119:35*
commandments
there will I *m.* the horn of   *Ps 132:17*
David to bud
if I *m.* my bed in hell, thou art   *Ps 139:8*
to the Lord did I *m.* my   *Ps 142:1*
supplication
go humble thyself, and *m.* sure   *Pr 6:3*
thy friend
fools *m.* a mock at sin, but   *Pr 14:9*
among righteous
and with good advice *m.* war   *Pr 20:18*
it is a snare after vows to *m.*   *Pr 20:25*
enquiry
that I might *m.* thee know the   *Pr 22:21*
certainty
m. no friendship with an   *Pr 22:24*
angry man
for riches certainly *m.*   *Pr 23:5*
themselves wings
my son, be wise, and *m.* my   *Pr 27:11*
heart glad
yet *m.* they their houses in the   *Pr 30:26*
rocks
who can *m.* that straight which   *Ec 7:13*
not righteous over much, nor   *Ec 7:16*
m. thyself over wise
we will *m.* haste (S)   *Ca 1:4*
when ye *m.* many prayers, I   *Isa 1:15*
will not hear
wash you, *m.* you clean   *Isa 1:16*
m. me not a ruler   *Isa 3:7*
m. the heart of this people fat,   *Isa 6:10*
ears heavy
and let us *m.* a breach therein   *Isa 7:6*
for us
Lord of hosts shall *m.* a   *Isa 10:23*
consumption
shall *m.* him of quick   *Isa 11:3*
understanding
and shall *m.* men go over dry   *Isa 11:15*
m. mention that his name is   *Isa 12:4*
exalted
I will *m.* a man more   *Isa 13:12*
precious than gold
m. thy shadow as the night in   *Isa 16:3*
noonday
Lord *m.* to all people a feast   *Isa 25:6*
of fat things
that he may *m.* peace with me   *Isa 27:5*
whom shall he *m.* to   *Isa 28:9*
understand doctrine
that *m.* a man an offender for   *Isa 29:21*
a word
to *m.* empty the soul of the   *Isa 32:6*
hungry
so wilt thou recover me and   *Isa 38:16*
m. me live
m. straight in the desert a   *Isa 40:3;*
highway for our God   *M't 3:3; M'k 1:3;*
     Lu 3:4
I will *m.* the wilderness a   *Isa 41:18*
pool of water
I will *m.* the rivers islands,   *Isa 42:15*
dry up pools
I will *m.* darkness light before   *Isa 42:16*
he will magnify and *m.* the   *Isa 42:21*
law honourable
I will even *m.* a way in the   *Isa 43:19*
wilderness
they that *m.* a graven image   *Isa 44:9*
are vanity
and *m.* the crooked places   *Isa 45:2*
straight
I *m.* peace and create evil, I   *Isa 45:7*
the Lord do all things
they shall *m.* supplication to   *Isa 45:14*
thee
to whom will ye *m.* me equal   *Isa 46:5*
and compare me
m. bare the leg, uncover the   *Isa 47:2*
thigh, pass over
and he shall *m.* his way   *Isa 48:15*
prosperous
and I will *m.* all my   *Isa 49:11*
mountains a way

behold I *m.* the rivers a   *Isa 50:2*
wilderness
I will *m.* my judgment to rest   *Isa 51:4*
for alight
they that rule over them, *m.*   *Isa 52:5*
them to howl
where thou shalt *m.* his soul   *Isa 53:10*
an offering
I will *m.* thy windows of   *Isa 54:12*
agates, thy gates
I will *m.* them joyful in my   *Isa 56:7*
house of prayer
against whom *m.* ye a wide   *Isa 57:4*
mouth
to *m.* your voice to be heard on   *Isa 58:4*
high
and the Lord shall *m.* fat   *Isa 58:11*
thy bones
I will *m.* the place of my feet   *Isa 60:13*
glorious
I will *m.* thee an eternal   *Isa 60:15*
excellency
I will *m.* also thy officers   *Isa 60:17*
peace and exactors
till he *m.* Jerusalem a praise in   *Isa 62:7*
the earth
and I will *m.* them drunk in   *Isa 63:6*
my fury
the water to *m.* himself an   *Isa 63:12*
everlasting name
lead thy people to *m.* thyself a   *Isa 63:14*
glorious name
to *m.* thy name known to thy   *Isa 64:2*
adversaries
as new earth which I will *m.*   *Isa 66:22*
shall remain
in vain shalt thou *m.* thyself   *Jer 4:30*
fair
I will *m.* my words in thy   *Jer 5:14*
mouth fire
m. thee mourning, as for an   *Jer 6:26*
only son
nor *m.* intercession to me for   *Jer 7:16*
this people
I will *m.* Jerusalem heaps   *Jer 9:11*
and den of dragons
he turn it, and *m.* it gross   *Jer 13:16*
darkness
I will *m.* thee a fenced brasen   *Jer 15:20*
wall
shall a man *m.* gods to   *Jer 16:20*
himself, and no gods
as seemed good to the potter   *Jer 18:4*
to *m.* it
I will *m.* void counsel of Judah   *Jer 19:7*
and Jerusalem
I will even *m.* this city as   *Jer 19:12*
Tophet
I will *m.* thee a terror to   *Jer 20:4*
thyself
yet surely I will *m.* thee a   *Jer 22:6*
wilderness
hearken not to the prophets,   *Jer 23:16*
they *m.* you vain
m. slaves of them (S)   *Jer 25:14*
then will I *m.* this house like   *Jer 26:6*
Shiloh
m. the bonds and yokes, put   *Jer 27:2*
them on thy neck
let them now *m.* intercession   *Jer 27:18*
to the Lord
behold, I will *m.* them like   *Jer 29:17*
vile figs
the Lord *m.* thee like   *Jer 29:22*
Zedekiah and Ahab
I will *m.* you be removed into   *Jer 34:17*
all kingdoms
did we *m.* her cakes to   *Jer 44:19*
worship her
m. ye him drunken, for he   *Jer 48:26*
magnified himself
I will *m.* thee small among the   *Jer 49:15*
heathen
I will *m.* thee a burnt   *Jer 51:25*
mountain
m. her springs dry   *Jer 51:36*
m. them drunken   *Jer 51:39*
I will *m.* drunk her princes   *Jer 51:57*
and wise men
m. bread thereof   *Eze 4:9*
m. a chain   *Eze 7:23*
I will *m.* him a sign and a   *Eze 14:8*
proverb, and cut off
I will *m.* my fury toward thee   *Eze 16:42*
to rest
and *m.* you a new heart, and   *Eze 18:31*
a new spirit
it is furbished, should we   *Eze 21:10*
then *m.* mirth

MAKE

842

MAKE *SPEED*

sought a man that should *m.*   *Eze 22:30*
up the hedge
m. no mourning for the dead,   *Eze 24:17*
bind the tire
and *m.* her like the top of a   *Eze 26:4;*
rock   *26:14*
I will *m.* thee a terror, thou   *Eze 26:21*
shalt be no more
I will *m.* the stars thereof dark *Eze 32:7;*
                         32:8
and I will *m.* them and   *Eze 34:26*
places a blessing
I will *m.* myself known   *Eze 35:11*
among them
m. them one stick, shall be   *Eze 37:19*
one in my hand
I will *m.* them one nation in *Eze 37:22*
the land
I will *m.* them keepers of   *Eze 44:14*
charge of house
shall *m.* thee eat grass as oxen *Da 4:25;*
                         4:32
m. this man to understand the *Da 8:16;*
vision   *10:14*
seventy weeks to *m.*   *Da 9:24*
reconciliation for iniquity
some shall fall to *m.* them   *Da 11:35*
white
he shall go utterly to purge   *Da 11:44*
and *m.* away many
lest I *m.* her as a wilderness,   *Ho 2:3*
and slay her
I will *m.* a wall, that she shall   *Ho 2:6*
not find her path
and I will *m.* them to lie down *Ho 2:18*
safely
they *m.* the king glad with their *Ho 7:3*
wickedness
I will *m.* Ephraim ride,   *Ho 10:11*
Judah shall plow
how shall *m.* thee as Admah? *Ho 11:8*
set thee as Zeboim
I will yet *m.* thee dwell in   *Ho 12:9*
tabernacles
nor will I *m.* you a reproach   *Joe 2:19*
any more
even to *m.* the poor of the land *Am 8:4*
to fail
they shall *m.* gardens, and   *Am 9:14*
eat fruit of them
the prophets that *m.* my people *Mic 3:5*
err
I will *m.* her that halted a   *Mic 4:7*
remnant
therefore I will *m.* thee sick in *Mic 6:13*
smiting thee
I will *m.* thy grave, for thou   *Na 1:14*
art vile
I will cast filth on thee, and *m.* *Na 3:6*
thee vile
m. thyself many as the   *Na 3:15*
cankerworm, or locusts
write the vision, and *m.* it   *Hab 2:2*
plain upon tables
he will *m.* my feet like hinds' *Hab 3:19*
feet
for he shall *m.* even a speedy *Zep 1:18*
riddance
for I will *m.* you a name and *Zep 3:20*
a praise
saith the Lord, I will *m.* thee a *Hag 2:23*
signet
so that Lord shall *m.* bright   *Zec 10:1*
clouds
I will *m.* Jerusalem a cup of   *Zec 12:2*
trembling
in that day will I *m.*   *Zec 12:3*
Jerusalem a burdensome stone
did not he *m.* one? yet had   *Mal 2:15*
the residue
in that day when I *m.* up my *Mal 3:17*
jewels
not willing to *m.* her a public *M't 1:19*
example
I will *m.* you fishers of men   *M't 4:19;*
                    M'k 1:17
thou canst not *m.* one hair   *M't 5:36*
white
leper said, If thou wilt, thou   *M't 8:2;*
canst *m.* me clean   *M'k 1:40; Lu 5:12*
m. the tree good, *m.* the tree *M't 12:33*
corrupt
Peter said, Let us *m.* here   *M't 17:4;*
three tabernacles   *M'k 9:5; Lu 9:33*
for pretence *m.* long prayers *M't 23:14;*
                 M'k 12:40
to *m.* one proselyte, and   *M't 23:15*
when he is made

ye *m.* clean the outside of   *M't 23:25;*
the cup   *Lu 11:39*
I will *m.* thee ruler over   *M't 25:21*
many things
go your way, *m.* it as sure as *M't 27:65*
ye can
why *m.* ye this ado and weep *M'k 5:39*
can ye *m.* children of   *Lu 5:34*
bride-chamber fast
did he not *m.* that which is   *Lu 11:40*
within also
all with one consent began to *Lu 14:18*
m. excuse
m. me as one of thy hired   *Lu 15:19*
servants
m. friends of the mammon of *Lu 16:9*
unrighteousness
m. straight the way of the   *Joh 1:23*
Lord
m. not my Father's house   *Joh 2:16*
house of merchandise
and take him by force to *m.*   *Joh 6:15*
him a king
know truth, and the truth   *Joh 8:32*
shall *m.* you free
if the Son *m.* you free, ye shall *Joh 8:36*
be free indeed
how long dost thou *m.* us to *Joh 10:24*
doubt
we will come and *m.* our   *Joh 14:23*
abode with him
m. me full of joy with thy   *Ac 2:28*
countenance
Peter said to him, Arise and *Ac 9:34*
m. thy bed
to *m.* thee a minister and a   *Ac 26:16*
witness
Paul, much learning doth *m.*   *Ac 26:24*
thee mad
m. the faith of God without   *Ro 3:3*
effect
do we then *m.* void the law   *Ro 3:31*
through faith
power to *m.* one vessel unto   *Ro 9:21*
honour
short work will the Lord *m.* on *Ro 9:28*
the earth
and *m.* not provision for the   *Ro 13:14*
flesh
for god is able to *m.* him stand *Ro 14:4*
follow the things which *m.* for *Ro 14:19*
peace
to *m.* a certain contribution   *Ro 15:26*
for the poor
and *m.* them the members of *1Co 6:15*
a harlot
if meat *m.* my brother to   *1Co 8:13*
offend
with temptation also *m.* a   *1Co 10:13*
way to escape
if I *m.* you sorry, who maketh *2Co 2:2*
glad
m. known to you (S)   *2Co 8:1*
and *m.* up beforehand your   *2Co 9:5*
bounty
and God is able to *m.* all grace *2Co 9:8*
abound
did I *m.* gain of you by any *2Co 12:17*
of them
I *m.* myself a transgressor   *Ga 2:18*
m. void grace (S)   *Ga 2:21*
that it should *m.* promise of *Ga 3:17*
none effect
as many as desire to *m.* fair   *Ga 6:12*
shew in flesh
to *m.* in himself to twain one *Eph 2:15*
new man
for whatsoever doth *m.*   *Eph 5:13*
manifest
Lord *m.* you to increase in   *1Th 3:12*
love
to *m.* ourselves an ensample to *2Th 3:9*
you
are able to *m.* thee wise to   *2Ti 3:15*
salvation
m. full proof of thy ministry *2Ti 4:5*
to *m.* Captain of salvation   *Heb 2:10*
perfect
to *m.* reconciliation for the   *Heb 2:17*
sins of people
he ever liveth to *m.*   *Heb 7:25*
intercession for them
m. all things according to   *Heb 8:5*
pattern shewed
could not *m.* him that did   *Heb 9:9*
service perfect
m. the comers thereunto   *Heb 10:1*
perfect
and *m.* straight paths for   *Heb 12:13*
your feet

m. perfect in every good   *Heb 13:21*
work to do will
is sown in peace, of them that *Jas 3:18*
m. peace
the God of all grace *m.* you   *1Pe 5:10*
perfect
m. your calling and election *2Pe 1:10*
sure
we *m.* him a liar, his word is *1Jo 1:10*
not in us
I will *m.* them worship before *Re 3:9*
thy feet
I will *m.* a pillar in the temple *Re 3:12*
of my God
eat it, and it shall *m.* thy belly *Re 10:9*
bitter
shall *m.* war against them, and *Re 11:7*
overcome
went to *m.* war with remnant *Re 12:17*
of her seed
saying, Who is able to *m.* war *Re 13:4*
with him
that they should *m.* an image *Re 13:14*
to the beast
in righteousness he doth judge *Re 19:11*
and *m.* war
behold, I *m.* all things   *Re 21:5*
new

MAKE HASTE

the things that come on them *De 32:35*
m. haste
said, *M.* haste and do as I   *J'g 9:48*
have done
he is before you, *m.* haste now *1Sa 9:12*
God commanded me to *m.*   *2Ch 35:21*
haste
king said, Cause Haman to *m.*   *Es 5:5;*
haste   *6:10*
cause me to answer, for this I *Job 20:2*
m. haste
m. haste to help me, O Lord, *Ps 38:22;*
my salvation   *40:13; 70:1; 71:12*
I am poor and needy, *m.* haste *Ps 70:5;*
unto me   *141:1*
they *m.* haste to shed blood   *Pr 1:16;*
                     Isa 59:7
m. haste, my beloved, and be *Ca 8:14*
like a roe
he that believeth shall not *m.* *Isa 28:16*
haste
children shall *m.* haste, thy   *Isa 49:17*
destroyers
let them *m.* haste, take up a   *Jer 9:18*
wailing
they shalt *m.* haste to the wall *Na 2:5*
thereof
Zaccheus, *m.* haste and come *Lu 19:5*
down
m. haste, get quickly out of   *Ac 22:18*
Jerusalem

MAKE MANIFEST

will *m.* manifest the counsels *1Co 4:5*
of the heart
whatsoever doth *m.* manifest *Eph 5:13*
is light
that I may *m.* it manifest as I *Col 4:4*
ought

MAKE READY

m. ready three measures of fine *Ge 18:6*
meal
m. ready, for these men shall *Ge 43:16*
dine with me
and Joram said, *M.* ready and *2Ki 9:21*
he went out
they *m.* ready their arrow on the *Ps 11:2*
string
when thou shalt *m.* ready   *Ps 21:12*
thine arrows
they have blown the trumpet   *Eze 7:14*
to *m.* ready
there *m.* ready for us   *M'k 14:15;*
                   Lu 22:12
m. ready a people prepared for *Lu 1:17*
Lord
rather say, *M.* ready,   *Lu 17:8*
wherewith I may sup
m. ready 200 soldiers to go to *Ac 23:23*
Cæsarea

MAKE SPEED

he cried, *M. speed,* haste,   *1Sa 20:38*
stay not
m. speed to depart, lest he   *2Sa 15:14*
overtake

that say, Let him *m. speed*   *Isa 5:19*
and hasten

MAKE *WASTE*

I will *m.* your cities *waste*   *Le 26:31*
I will *m. waste* mountains   *Isa 42:15*
and hills
moreover, I will *m.* Jerusalem *Eze 5:14*
waste
I will *m.* land of Egypt   *Eze 29:10;*
utterly *waste*   *30:12*

MAKER

shall a man be more pure than *Job 4:17*
his *M.*
in so doing my *M.* will soon *Job 32:22*
take me away
but none saith, Where is   *Job 35:10*
God my *M.*
I will ascribe righteousness to *Job 36:3*
my *M.*
let us kneel before the Lord our *Ps 95:6*
M.
oppresseth the poor,   *Pr 14:31*
reproacheth his *M.*
whoso mocketh the poor   *Pr 17:5*
reproacheth his *M.*
rich and poor, the Lord is the *Pr 22:2*
m. of them all
and the *m.* of it as a spark   *Isa 1:31*
at that day shall a man look to *Isa 17:7*
his *M.*
ye have not looked to the *m.* *Isa 22:11*
thereof
woe to him that striveth with *Isa 45:9*
his *M.*
saith the holy One of Israel   *Isa 45:11*
and his *M.*
forgettest the Lord thy *m.*   *Isa 51:13*
that stretched out
thy *M.* is thy husband, and thy *Isa 54:5*
Redeemer
thus saith the Lord the *m.*   *Jer 33:2*
thereof
for Israel hath forgotten his *M. Ho 8:14*
the graven image that the *m. Hab 2:18*
hath graven, *m.* of his work
as a mischief *m.* (P)   *Lu 23:14*
for a city, whose builder and *Heb 11:10*
m. is God

MAKERS

together that are *m.* of idols *Isa 45:16*
m. and maintainers of peace *M't 5:9*
(A)

MAKEST

and what *m.* thou in this place *J'g 18:3*
m. me possess the iniquities *Job 13:26*
of my youth
is it gain to him that thou *m. Job 22:3*
thy ways perfect
thou only *m.* me to dwell in   *Ps 4:8*
safety
thou *m.* his beauty to consume *Ps 39:11*
as a moth
thou *m.* us to turn back from *Ps 44:10*
the enemy
thou *m.* us a reproach to our *Ps 44:13*
neighbours
thou *m.* us a byword among   *Ps 44:14*
the heathen
thou *m.* the outgoings of   *Ps 65:8*
morning to rejoice
thou *m.* the earth soft with   *Ps 65:10*
showers
thou *m.* us a strife to our   *Ps 80:6*
neighbours
thou *m.* darkness, and it is   *Ps 104:20*
night
what is man, that thou *m.*   *Ps 144:3*
account of him
where thou *m.* thy flock to rest at *Ca 1:7*
noon
to him that fashioneth it,   *Isa 45:9*
what *m.* thou
Lebanon, that *m.* thy nest in *Jer 22:23*
cedars
thou *m.* this people to trust in *Jer 28:15*
a lie
m. thy high place in every   *Eze 16:31*
street
and *m.* men as the fishes of *Hab 1:14*
the sea
puttest thy bottle to him, *m.* *Hab 2:15*
him drunken
when thou *m.* a dinner or a   *Lu 14:12*
supper

but when thou *m.* a feast, call *Lu 14:13*
the poor
prophets are dead, whom *m.*   *Joh 8:53*
thou thyself
because thou being a man *m.* *Joh 10:33*
thyself God
art called a Jew, and *m.* thy   *Ro 2:17*
boast of God
thou that *m.* thy boast of the   *Ro 2:23*
law

MAKETH

who *m.* the dumb, or deaf, or   *Ex 4:11*
priest that *m.* atonement clean   *Le 7:7;*
                              14:11
it is the blood that *m.* an   *Le 17:11*
atonement
that *m.* his son pass through   *De 18:10*
the fire
against the city that *m.* war   *De 20:20*
with thee
when he *m.* his sons to inherit *De 21:16*
m. merchandise of him, or   *De 24:7*
selleth him
cursed be the man that *m.*   *De 27:15*
graven image
cursed be he that *m.* blind to *De 27:18*
wander
oath which Lord *m.* with thee *De 29:12*
this day
the Lord killeth and *m.* alive *1Sa 2:6*
Lord *m.* poor and *m.* rich, he *1Sa 2:7*
bringeth low
God *m.* my way perfect   *2Sa 22:33;*
                         Ps 18:32
he *m.* my feet like hinds feet *2Sa 22:34;*
                         Ps 18:33
for he *m.* sore, and bindeth   *Job 5:18*
up, he wounds
Lord *m.* Arcturus, Orion, and   *Job 9:9*
Pleiades
he *m.* judges fools   *Job 12:17*
he *m.* to stagger   *Job 12:25*
he *m.* collops of fat on his   *Job 15:27*
flanks
God *m.* my heart soft, and   *Job 23:16*
troubleth me
he *m.* peace in his high places *Job 25:2*
and as a booth that the keeper *Job 27:18*
m.
who *m.* us wiser than fowls   *Job 35:11*
of heaven
he *m.* small drops of water,   *Job 36:27*
they pour
he *m.* the deep to boil like a   *Job 41:31*
pot
he *m.* a path to shine after   *Job 41:32*
when he *m.* inquisition for   *Ps 9:12*
blood
he *m.* me to live down in green *Ps 23:2*
the voice of the Lord *m.* the *Ps 29:9*
hinds to calve
he *m.* the devices of people of *Ps 33:10*
none effect
blessed is the man that *m.* the *Ps 40:4*
Lord his trust
he *m.* wars to cease to the end *Ps 46:9*
of the earth
who *m.* the clouds his chariot *Ps 104:3*
who *m.* his angels spirits   *Ps 104:4;*
                         Heb 1:7
and wine that *m.* glad the   *Ps 104:15*
heart of man
he *m.* the storm a calm, the *Ps 107:29*
and there he *m.* the hungry to *Ps 107:36*
dwell
and *m.* him families like a   *Ps 107:41*
flock
he *m.* the barren woman to   *Ps 113:9*
keep house
he *m.* lightnings for rain, brings *Ps 135:7*
the wind
who *m.* grass to grow on the *Ps 147:8*
mountains
he *m.* peace in thy borders *Ps 147:14*
a wise son *m.* a glad father   *Pr 10:1;*
                         15:20
but the hand of the diligent *m. Pr 10:4*
rich
the blessing of the Lord, it *m. Pr 10:22*
rich
she that *m.* ashamed is as   *Pr 12:4*
rottenness in bones
heaviness in the heart of a   *Pr 12:25*
man *m.* it to stoop, but a
good word *m.* it glad
than *m.* himself rich, yet hath *Pr 13:7*
nothing, *m.* himself poor,
yet hath riches

hope deferred *m.* heart sick   *Pr 13:12*
merry heart *m.* cheerful   *Pr 15:13*
countenance
and a good report *m.* the   *Pr 15:30*
bones fat
he *m.* even enemies to be at   *Pr 16:7*
peace
a man's gift *m.* room for him *Pr 18:16*
wealth *m.* many friends, but *Pr 19:4*
poor is separated
she *m.* herself coverings of   *Pr 31:22*
tapestry
she *m.* fine linen, and selleth *Pr 31:24*
no man can find out the work *Ec 7:7*
that God *m.*
surely oppression *m.* a wise man *Ec 7:7*
mad
a man's wisdom *m.* his face to *Ec 8:1*
shine
thou knowest not works of   *Ec 11:5*
God, who *m.* all
behold, the Lord *m.* the earth *Isa 24:1*
empty
he *m.* the judges of the earth *Isa 40:23*
as vanity
saith the Lord, which *m.* a   *Isa 43:16*
way in the sea
he *m.* a god, and worshippeth *Isa 44:15*
it   *44:17; 46:6*
I am the Lord that *m.* all   *Isa 44:24*
things
he *m.* diviners mad; *m.*   *Isa 44:25;*
himself a prey   *59:15*
watereth earth, and *m.* it   *Isa 55:10*
bring forth
he *m.* lightnings with rain   *Jer 10:13;*
                         51:16
cursed be the man that *m.* flesh *Jer 17:5*
his arm
every man that *m.* himself a *Jer 29:26;*
prophet   *29:27*
and *m.* idols against herself to *Eze 22:3*
defile
but *m.* his petition three times *Da 6:13*
a day
place abomination that *m.*   *De 11:31;*
desolate   *12:11*
that *m.* the morning darkness *Am 4:13*
seek him that *m.* the seven   *Am 5:8*
stars and Orion
he rebuketh the sea, and *m.* it   *Na 1:4*
he *m.* his sun rise on the evil *M't 5:45*
and good
he *m.* both deaf to hear, and *M'k 7:37*
dumb speak
whosoever *m.* himself a king, *Joh 19:12*
speaketh
Æneas, Jesus Christ *m.* thee   *Ac 9:34*
whole
hope *m.* not ashamed, because *Ro 15:5*
love of God
the Spirit *m.* intercession for *Ro 8:26;*
us   *8:27, 34*
he *m.* intercession to God   *Ro 11:2*
against Israel
who *m.* thee to differ from   *1Co 4:7*
another
who is he that *m.* me glad but *2Co 2:2*
m. manifest the savour of his *2Co 2:14*
knowledge by us
whatsoever they were, it *m.* no *Ga 2:6*
matter
m. increase of the body to the *Eph 4:16*
edifying
law *m.* men high priests,   *Heb 7:28*
word of the oath since law *m.*
the Son
he *m.* fire come down from   *Re 13:13*
heaven
nor whatsoever *m.* a lie   *Re 21:27;*
                         22:15

MAKETH *HASTE*

that *m. haste* to be rich not   *Pr 28:20*
innocent

MAKHELOTH

pitched in *M.*   *Nu 33:25*
removed from *M.*   *Nu 33:26*

MAKING

m. confession to the Lord   *2Ch 30:22*
testimony of Lord is sure, *m.*   *Ps 19:7*
wise simple

of *m*. many books there is no *Ec 12:12*
end
walking and *m*. a tinkling with *Isa 3:16*
their feet
that brought tidings, *m*. him *Jer 20:15*
very glad
m. ephah small and the shekel *Am 8:5*
great
wares of thy *m*.   *Eze 27:16; 27:18*
m. the word of God of none *M'k 7:13*
effect
m. himself equal with God *Joh 5:18*
as poor, yet *m*. many rich *2Co 6:10*
m. mention of you in my *Eph 1:16;*
prayers   *1Th 1:2; Ph'm 4*
one new man, so *m*. peace *Eph 2:15*
m. melody in your heart to *Eph 5:19*
the Lord
in every prayer *m*. request *Ph'p 1:4*
with joy
m. them an ensample unto *2Pe 2:6*
those that
of some have compassion, *m*. a *Jude 22*
difference

MAKKEDAH

to Azekah, and unto *M*.   *Jos 10:10*
hid themselves in a cave of *Jos 10:16;*
M.   *10:17*
the camp to Joshua at *M*. *Jos 10:21;*
                                 10:28-29
the king of *M*., one   *Jos 12:16*
Naamah, and *M*.   *Jos 15:41*

MAKTESH

Howl, ye inhabitants of *M*.   *Zep 1:11*

MALACHI

word of the Lord to Israel by *Mal 1:1*
M.

MALCHAM

and Zibia, and Mesha, and *M*. *1Ch 8:9*
the Lord, and that swear by *M*. *Zep 1:5*

MALCHIAH

son of Baaseiah, the son of *1Ch 6:40*
M.
and Jeziah, and *M*., and *Ezr 10:25*
Miamin
Eliezer, Ishijah, *M*.,   *Ezr 10:31*
Shemaiah
the dung gate repaired *M*. the *Ne 3:14*
him repaired *M*. the   *Ne 3:31*
goldsmith's
Pedaiah, and Mishael, and *M*. *Ne 8:4*
the son of Pashur, the son of *Ne 11:12*
M.
and Pashur the son of *M*., *Jer 38:1*
heard
and cast him into the dungeon *Jer 38:6*

MALCHIEL

sons of Beriah; Heber, and *Ge 46:17*
M.
M., the family of the   *Nu 26:45*
Malchielites
sons of Beriah; Heber, and *1Ch 7:31*
M.

MALCHIELITES

Malchiel, the family of the *M*. *Nu 26:45*

MALCHIJAH

the son of Pashur, the son of *1Ch 9:12*
M.
The fifth to *M*., the sixth to *1Ch 24:9*
and Eleazar, and *M*., and *Ezr 10:25*
Benaiah
M. the son of Harim, and *Ne 3:11*
Hashub
Pashur, Amariah, *M*.   *Ne 10:3*
Jehohanan, and *M*., and *Ne 12:42*
Elam, and

MALCHIRAM

M. also, and Pedaiah, and *1Ch 3:18*

MALCHI-SHUA

Saul begat Jonathan, and *M*. *1Ch 8:33;*
                                 9:39
and Abinadab, and *M*., the *1Ch 10:2*
sons of

MALCHUS

ear. The servant's name was *Joh 18:10*
M.

MALE

m. and female created he them *Ge 1:27*
M. and female created he them *Ge 5:2*
thee; they shall be *m*. and *Ge 6:19*
female
by sevens, the *m*. and his female *Ge 7:2*
clean by two the *m*. and his *Ge 7:2*
female
by sevens, the *m*. and the female *Ge 7:3*
into the ark, the *m*. and the *Ge 7:9*
female
went in *m*. and female of all *Ge 7:16*
flesh
male (S)   *Ge 17:10;*
17:12, 14; Le 12:2; 1Sa 1:11; Job 3:3;
             Jer 20:15; Re 12:5, 13
every *m*. among the men of *Ge 17:23*
every *m*. of you be   *Ge 34:15*
circumcised
every *m*. among us be   *Ge 34:22*
circumcised
and every *m*. was circumcised *Ge 34:24*
m. babies (B)   *Ex 1:17*
m. children (S)   *Ex 1:17;*
                     1:18; 1Ki 21:13
blemish, a *m*. of the first year *Ex 12:5*
whether ox or sheep, that is *m*. *Ex 34:19*
him offer a *m*. without blemish *Le 1:3*
shall bring it a *m*. without *Le 1:10*
blemish
whether it be a *m*. or a female *Le 3:1*
Lord be of the flock; *m*. or *Le 3:6*
female
the goats, a *m*. without blemish *Le 4:23*
Every *m*. among the priests shall *Le 7:6*
her that hath born a *m*. or a *Le 12:7*
female
own will a *m*. without blemish *Le 22:19*
of the *m*. from twenty years old *Le 27:3*
shall be of the *m*. twenty *Le 27:5*
shekels
be of the *m*. five shekels of *Le 27:6*
silver
if it be a *m*. then thy estimation *Le 27:7*
names, every *m*. by their polls *Nu 1:2*
every *m*. from twenty years *Nu 1:20;*
old   *1:22*
every *m*. from a month old and *Nu 3:15*
Both *m*. and female shall be put *Nu 5:3*
every *m*. shall eat it: it shall *Nu 18:10*
kill every *m*. among the little *Nu 31:17*
ones
figure, the likeness of *m*. or *De 4:16*
female
be *m*. or female barren among *De 7:14*
you
shalt smite every *m*. thereof *De 20:13*
his *m*. organ severed (B)(R) *De 23:1*
m. children of Manasseh the *Jos 17:2*
son
Ye shall utterly destroy every *J'g 21:11*
m.
no man by lying with any *m*. *J'g 21:12*
every *m*. (A)(B)(R)   *1Sa 25:22;*
25:34; 1Ki 14:10; 16:11; 21:21; 2Ki 9:8
he had smitten every *m*. in *1Ki 11:15*
Edom
he had cut off every *m*. in *1Ki 11:16*
Edom
every *m*. (S)   *1Ki 16:11;*
1Sa 25:22; 25:34; 1Ki 14:10; 16:11;
                  21:21; 2Ki 9:8
which hath in his flock a *m*. *Mal 1:14*
made them *m*. and female *M't 19:4*
God made them *m*. and female *M'k 10:6*
Every *m*. that openeth the *Lu 2:23*
womb
free, there is neither *m*. nor *Ga 3:28*
female

MALEFACTOR

If he were not a *m*. we would *Joh 18:30*
not

MALEFACTORS

m. led with him to be put to *Lu 23:32*
death
they crucified him, and the *m*. *Lu 23:33*
one of the *m*. which were *Lu 23:39*
hanged

MALELEEL

which was the son of *M*.   *Lu 3:37*

MALES

the city boldly, and slew all *Ge 34:25*
the *m*.
let all his *m*. be circumcised *Ex 12:48*
hast; the *m*. shall be the *Ex 13:12*
Lord's
that openeth the matrix, being *Ex 13:15*
m.
all thy *m*. shall appear before *Ex 23:17*
your *m*. shall appear   *Ex 34:23*
(B)(E)(R)
All the *m*. among the children *Le 6:18*
the *m*. among the priests shall *Le 6:29*
eat
to the number of all the *m*. *Nu 3:22;*
from a   *3:34*
In the number of all the *m*. *Nu 3:28*
from a
m. from a month old and *Nu 3:39*
upward
Number all the firstborn of the *Nu 3:40*
m.
the firstborn *m*. by the number *Nu 3:43*
m. from a month old and *Nu 26:62*
upward
Moses; and they slew all the *Nu 31:7*
m.
firstling *m*. that come of thy *De 15:19*
herd
all thy *m*. appear before the *De 16:16*
Lord
came out of Egypt, that were *m*. *Jos 5:4*
from
to give portions to all the *m*. *2Ch 31:16*
among
reckoned by genealogy of the *Ezr 8:3*
m. an

MALICE

m. is in their hearts (B)   *Ps 28:3*
with contempt, *m*., spite *Eze 25:6*
(A)(B)(R)
perceived their *m*. (B)(R) *M't 22:18*
the leaven of *m*. and   *1Co 5:8*
wickedness
howbeit in *m*. be ye children, *1Co 14:20*
but in
continue to be babes in evil *1Co 14:20*
(A)(R)
although infants in   *1Co 14:20*
wickedness (B)
as innocent of evil as babes *1Co 14:20*
(N)(P)
be put away from you, with *Eph 4:31*
all *m*.
anger, wrath, *m*., blasphemy *Col 3:8*
living in *m*. and envy, hateful *Tit 3:3*
m. that hurries excess (N) *Jas 1:21*
laying aside all *m*. and   *1Pe 2:1*
all guile
every trace of wickedness *1Pe 2:1*
(A)(E)
lay aside all deceit (B) *1Pe 2:1*
have done with all evil and *1Pe 2:1*
deceit (P)

MALICIOUS

a *m*. witness (B)(R)   *Ex 23:1*
their *m*. plot (A)   *M't 22:18*
prating against us with *m*. *3Jo 10*
words

MALICIOUSNESS

wickedness, covetousness, *m*. *Ro 1:29*
using your liberty for a cloke *1Pe 2:16*
of *m*.
as a pretext of wickedness *1Pe 2:16*
(A)
to cover up wickedness (B) *1Pe 2:16*
for a cloak of wickedness (E) *1Pe 2:16*

to provide a screen for wrongdoing (N)   *1Pe 2:16*

as an excuse for doing wrong (P)   *1Pe 2:16*

as a pretext for evil (R)   *1Pe 2:16*

MALIGNANT

foul and *m.* sores (B)(N)(P)   *Re 16:2*

MALIGNING

m., criticising, judging law (A)   *Jas 4:11*

MALIGNITY

envy, murder, debate, deceit, *m.*   *Ro 1:29*

MALIGNS

m., criticizes the law (B)   *Jas 4:11*

MALLOTHI

Romamti-ezer, Joshbekashah, *M.*   *1Ch 25:4*

The nineteenth to *M.*, he, his sons   *1Ch 25:26*

MALLOWS

Who cut up *m.* by the bushes   *Job 30:4*

MALTREAT

not *m.* an alien (B)   *Ex 22:21*

and *m.* him (B)   *Le 19:33*

m. them (N)   *Ac 14:5*

MALTREATED

he was *m.* (B)   *Isa 53:7*

m. and spat upon (N)   *Lu 18:32*

maltreated (B)   *Heb 11:37*

the *m.* as suffering (B)(N)   *Heb 13:3*

MALTREATMENT

sharing *m.* (B)   *Heb 11:25*

MALLUCH

the son of Abdi, the son of *M.*   *1Ch 6:44*

the sons of Bani; Meshullam, *M.*   *Ezr 10:29*

Benjamin, *M.*, and Shemariah   *Ezr 10:32*

Hattush, Shebaniah, *M.*   *Ne 10:4*

M., Harim, Baanah   *Ne 10:27*

Amariah, *M.*, Hattush   *Ne 12:2*

MAMMON

Ye cannot serve God and *m.*   *M't 6:24*

friends of the *m.* of unrighteousness   *Lu 16:9*

to use deceitful wealth (B)   *Lu 16:9*

use your worldly wealth (N)   *Lu 16:9*

to use money (P)   *Lu 16:9*

been faithful in the unrighteous (N)   *Lu 16:11*

other. Ye cannot serve God and *m.*   *Lu 16:13*

MAMRE

came and dwelt in the plain of *M.*   *Ge 13:18*

in the plain of *M.* the Amorite   *Ge 14:13*

with me, Aner, Eshcol, and *M.*   *Ge 14:24*

unto him in the plains of *M.*   *Ge 18:1*

Machpelah, which was before *M.*   *Ge 23:17*

of the field of Machpelah before *M.*   *Ge 23:19*

the Hittite, which is before *M.*   *Ge 25:9*

came unto Isaac his father unto *M.*   *Ge 35:27*

Machpelah, which is before *M.*   *Ge 49:30*

of Ephron the Hittite, before *M.*   *Ge 50:13*

MAN

let us make *m.* in our image   *Ge 1:26; 1:27; 9:6*

Lord God formed *m.* of dust of ground   *Ge 2:7*

it is not good that *m.* should be alone   *Ge 2:18*

they were both naked, the *m.* and his wife   *Ge 2:25*

behold, the *m.* is become as one of us   *Ge 3:22*

my Spirit shall not always strive with *m.*   *Ge 6:3*

I will destroy *m.* whom I have created   *Ge 6:7*

blood, by *m.* shall his blood be shed   *Ge 9:6*

who have not known *m.*   *Ge 19:8; Nu 31:35*

restore the *m.* his wife, he is a prophet   *Ge 20:7*

m. wondering at her held his peace   *Ge 24:21*

Laban ran out to the *m.* to the well   *Ge 24:29*

what *m.* is this that walketh in the field   *Ge 24:65*

better than give her to another *m.*   *Ge 29:19*

by *m.* whose these are, am I with child   *Ge 38:25*

take your brother, arise, go again to the *m.*   *Ge 43:13*

m. in whose hand the cup is   *Ge 44:17*

why is it that ye have left the *m.*   *Ex 2:20*

Moses was content to dwell with the *m.*   *Ex 2:21*

the *m.* that brought us out of Egypt   *Ex 32:1; 32:23*

blood be imputed to that *m.* and that *m.*   *Le 17:4*

the *m.* bring his wife to priest   *Nu 5:15*

the *m.* that is clean, and not in a journey   *Nu 9:13*

the *m.* Moses was meek above all men   *Nu 12:3*

the *m.* shall be put to death   *Nu 15:35; De 22:25*

the *m.* whom Lord doth choose   *Nu 16:7*

but *m.* that shall be unclean   *Nu 19:20*

since the day that God created *m.*   *De 4:32*

God doth talk with *m.* and he liveth   *De 5:24*

m. doth not live by bread only, but by every word   *De 8:3; M't 4:4; Lu 4:4*

they shall come *m.* by *m.*   *Jos 7:14; 7:17-18*

but they let go the *m.* and all his family   *J'g 1:25*

I will shew thee the *m.* whom thou seekest   *J'g 4:22*

for as the *m.* is, so is his strength   *J'g 8:21*

wherewith by me they honour God and *m.*   *J'g 9:9*

my wine which cheereth God and *m.*   *J'g 9:13*

what *m.* will fight against Ammon   *J'g 10:18*

the *m.* hath appeared that came to me   *J'g 13:10*

art thou the *m.* spakest to the woman   *J'g 13:11*

I shall be weak, and as another *m.*   *J'g 16:7; 16:11, 17*

bring forth the *m.* that came into thy house   *J'g 19:22*

then the *m.* took her on an ass and rose   *J'g 19:28*

the name of the *m.* was Elimelech   *Ru 1:2; 2:19*

for the *m.* will not be in rest, till he hath finished   *Ru 3:18*

the *m.* of thine whom I shall not cut off   *1Sa 2:33*

the *m.* came in hastily, and told Eli   *1Sa 4:14*

a *m.* of God, and he is an honourable   *1Sa 9:6*

behold the *m.* whom I spake   *1Sa 9:17*

if the *m.* should yet come   *1Sa 10:22*

for the Lord seeth not as *m.*   *1Sa 16:7*

what be done to the *m.* that killeth him   *1Sa 17:26*

lo, ye see the *m.* is mad, wherefore then   *1Sa 21:14*

David's anger kindled against the *m.* said to Nathan, *m.* who did this   *2Sa 12:5*

Nathan said to David, Thou art the *m.*   *2Sa 12:7*

come out, come out, thou bloody *m.*   *2Sa 16:7; 16:8*

the *m.* thou seekest is as if all returned   *2Sa 17:3*

m. that consumed us, and devised against us   *2Sa 21:5*

the *m.* who was raised up on high   *2Sa 23:1*

and they slew every one his *m.*   *1Ki 20:20*

when *m.* turned again to meet thee   *2Ki 5:26*

I will bring you to the *m.* whom ye seek   *2Ki 6:19*

ye know the *m.* and his communication   *2Ki 9:11*

tell the *m.* that sent you   *2Ki 22:15; 2Ch 34:23*

the Levites *m.* by *m.* were 38,000   *1Ch 23:3*

the palace is not for *m.* but for the Lord God   *1Ch 29:1*

let not *m.* prevail against thee   *2Ch 14:11*

for ye judge not for *m.* but for the Lord   *2Ch 19:6*

what shall be done to the *m.* whom   *Es 6:6; 6:7, 9*

shall *m.* be more just than God   *Job 4:17*

yet *m.* is born to trouble, as sparks fly upwards   *Job 5:7*

happy is the *m.* whom God correcteth   *Job 5:17*

is there not an appointed time for *m.* on earth   *Job 7:1*

what is *m.* that thou shouldest magnify him   *Job 7:17; 15:14; Ps 8:4; 144:3; Heb 2:6*

but how should *m.* be just with God   *Job 9:2*

eyes of flesh? or seest thou as *m.* seeth   *Job 10:4*

are thy days as days of *m.*   *Job 10:5*

vain *m.* would be wise, tho' *m.* be born like   *Job 11:12*

m. that is born of a woman is of few days   *Job 14:1*

m. dieth and wasteth away, *m.* giveth up ghost   *Job 14:10*

so *m.* lieth down, and riseth not till heavens   *Job 14:12*

art thou the first *m.* that was born   *Job 15:7*

what is *m.* that he should be clean   *Job 15:14*

how much more abominable and filthy is *m.*   *Job 15:16*

since *m.* was first placed on the earth   *Job 20:4*

as for me is my complaint to *m.*   *Job 21:4*

how then can *m.* be justified with God   *Job 25:4*

how much less *m.* that is a worm, and son of *m.*   *Job 25:6*

there is a spirit in *m.* inspiration of Almighty   *Job 32:8*

God thrusteth him down, not *m.*   *Job 32:13*

I answer, that God is greater than *m.*   *Job 33:12*

God speaketh, yet *m.* perceiveth it not   *Job 33:14*

he opens the ears of men, that he may withdraw *m.* from purpose, and hide pride from *m.*   *Job 33:17*

if a messenger, to shew to *m.* his uprightness   *Job 33:23*

these things worketh God often with *m.*   *Job 33:29*

what *m.* is like Job who drinketh scorning   *Job 34:7*

if he set his heart upon *m.* if he gather to himself   *Job 34:13*

for he will not lay on *m.* more than right   *Job 34:23*

arise, O Lord, let not *m.* prevail   *Ps 9:19*

that the *m.* of earth may no   Ps 10:18
more oppress
what *m.* is he that feareth the   Ps 25:12
Lord
what *m.* is he that desireth life   Ps 34:12
when thou dost correct *m.* for   Ps 39:11
iniquity
m. being in honour abideth   Ps 49:12;
not   49:20
I will not be afraid what *m.*   Ps 56:11
can do to me
m. did eat angels' food, he   Ps 78:25
sent them meat
thy hand be on the *m.* of thy   Ps 80:17
right hand
what *m.* is he that liveth, and   Ps 89:48
not see death
thou turnest *m.* to destruction   Ps 90:3
that teacheth *m.* knowledge   Ps 94:10
shall not he know
as for *m.* his days are as   Ps 103:15
grass, as a flower
m. goeth forth to his work   Ps 104:23
I will not fear what *m.* can do   Ps 118:6
better trust in Lord, than put   Ps 118:8
confidence in *m.*
m. is like to vanity, his days   Ps 144:4
as a shadow
from *m.* that speaketh froward   Pr 2:12
and thy want come as an   Pr 6:11;
armed *m.*   24:34
the preparations of the heart in   Pr 16:1
m.
m. goings are of the Lord,   Pr 20:24
how can a *m.*
so is the *m.* that deceiveth his   Pr 26:19
neighbour
things full of labour *m.* cannot   Ec 1:8
utter it
what can the *m.* do that cometh   Ec 2:12
after king
for what hath *m.* of all his   Ec 2:22
labour
is named, and it is known that   Ec 6:10
it is *m.*
what is *m.* better   Ec 6:11
what is good for *m.*   Ec 6:12
because *m.* goeth to his long   Ec 12:5
home
cease from *m.* whose breath is   Isa 2:22
in his nostrils
I said, I shall behold *m.* no   Isa 38:11
more
the *m.* that executeth my   Isa 46:11
counsel
it is not in *m.* to direct his   Jer 10:23
steps
I am the *m.* that hath seen   La 3:1
affliction
hath executed judgment   Eze 18:8
between *m.* and *m.*
let his heart be changed from   Da 4:16
m.
said, O *m.* greatly beloved,   Da 10:19
fear not
for I am God, and not *m.* the   Ho 11:9
holy One
and declareth to *m.* what is   Am 4:13
his thought
that tarrieth not for *m.* nor   Mic 5:7
waiteth
he hath shewed thee, O *m.*   Mic 6:8
what is good
the *m.* of wisdom shall see thy   Mic 6:9
name
the wicked devoureth *m.*   Hab 1:13
more righteous
I will cut off the *m.* from the   Zep 1:3
land
the *m.* whose name is the   Zec 6:12
Branch
from *m.* taught me to keep   Zec 13:5
cattle from youth
awake, O sword, against *m.*   Zec 13:7
that is my fellow
Lord will cut off the *m.* that   Mal 2:12
doeth this
what *m.* if his son ask bread   M't 7:9;
will give him a stone   12:11; Lu 15:4
from the heart, and they   M't 15:18
defile the *m.*
let not *m.* put asunder   M't 19:6;
       M'k 10:9
he denied, I do not know   M't 26:2;
the *m.*   26:74
sabbath was made for *m.* not   M'k 2:27
m. for sabbath
shall find a colt tied, whereon   M'k 11:2
never *m.* sat

he said, M. thy sins are   Lu 5:20
forgiven thee
m. who made me a judge over   Lu 12:14
you
though I fear not God, nor   Lu 18:4
regard *m.*
thou art of them, Peter said,   Lu 22:58
M. I am not
Peter said, M. I know not   Lu 22:60
what thou sayest
he asked, whether the *m.* was   Lu 23:6
a Galilean
wherein never *m.* was laid   Lu 23:53;
       Joh 19:41
for he knew what was in *m.*   Joh 2:25
what *m.* is that which said unto   Joh 5:12
thee
but I received not testimony   Joh 5:34
from *m.*
the works which none other   Joh 15:24
m. did
Pilate said unto them, Behold   Joh 19:5
the *m.*
for the *m.* was above forty   Ac 4:22
years old
how can I, except some *m.*   Ac 8:31
should guide me
eunuch said of himself, or of   Ac 8:34
some other *m.*
the *m.* in whom the evil   Ac 19:16
spirit was
what *m.* is there that knoweth   Ac 19:35
not how that
so shall bind the *m.* that   Ac 21:11
owneth this girdle
how the Jews laid wait for the   Ac 23:30
m.
Agrippa said, I would also   Ac 25:22
hear the *m.* myself
inexcusable, O *m.*   Ro 2:1
thinkest thou, O *m.*   Ro 2:3
a *m.* justify himself (P)   Ro 3:20
I delight in law of God after   Ro 7:22
the inward *m.*
O wretched *m.* that I am,   Ro 7:24
who shall deliver me
but O *m.* who art thou that   Ro 9:20
repliest against God
the *m.* who doeth these things   Ro 10:5;
shall live by them   Ga 3:12
with the heart *m.* believeth   Ro 10:10
unto righteousness
m. of learning (N)   1Co 1:20
no mortal *m.* should boast (A)   1Co 1:29
what *m.* knoweth the things of   1Co 2:11
a *m.*
how knowest thou, O *m.*   1Co 7:16
whether thou
no temptation but such as is   1Co 10:13
common to *m.*
and the head of the woman is   1Co 11:3
the *m.*
m. is not of the woman   1Co 11:8
but woman for the *m.*   1Co 11:9
nor is the *m.* without the   1Co 11:11
woman, nor the woman
without the *m.* in the Lord
even so is the *m.* also by the   1Co 11:12
woman
since by *m.* came death, by   1Co 15:21
m. came resurrection
the first *m.* Adam was made   1Co 15:45
a living soul
first *m.* is of the earth,   1Co 15:47
earthy; the second *m.* is the
Lord from heaven
but though our outward *m.*   2Co 4:16
perish, yet the inward *m.*
is renewed day by day
an apostle, not of men, neither   Ga 1:1
by *m.*
the gospel I preached is not   Ga 1:11
after *m.*
for to make of twain one new   Eph 2:15
m.
with might by his Spirit in the   Eph 3:16
inner *m.*
that ye put on new *m.* created   Eph 4:24
in righteousness
have put on the new *m.* which   Col 3:10
is renewed
despiseth not *m.* but god, who   1Th 4:8
hath given
between God and men, the *m.*   1Ti 2:5
Christ Jesus
woman not to usurp authority   1Ti 2:12
over the *m.*
love of God our Saviour toward   Tit 3:4
m. appeared

for every house is built by   Heb 3:4
some *m.*
the tabernacle the Lord   Heb 8:2
pitched, and not *m.*
I will not fear what *m.* shall   Heb 13:6
do to me
a double-minded *m.* is unstable   Jas 1:8
in his ways
wilt thou know, O vain *m.* that   Jas 2:20
faith
let it be the hidden *m.* of the   1Pe 3:4
heart

MAN *CHILD*

every *m.* child shall be   Ge 17:10;
circumcised   17:12
the uncircumcised *m.* child   Ge 17:14
shall be cut off
if a woman have born a   Le 12:2
m. child then
if wilt give to thy handmaid a   1Sa 1:11
m. child
one *m.* child (E)   1Sa 25:22;
       25:34; 1Ki 14:10; 16:11; 21:21; 2Ki 9:8
let the night perish wherein it   Job 3:3;
was said, There is a *m.* child   Jer 20:15
conceived
she was delivered of a   Isa 66:7;
m. child   Re 12:5
persecuted woman brought   Re 12:13
forth a *m.* child

MAN *SERVANT*

not do work, thy *m.* servant   Ex 20:10;
       De 5:14
not covet thy neighbour's *m.*   Ex 20:17;
servant   De 5:21
and if he smite out his *m.*   Ex 21:27
servant's tooth
if the ox shall push a *m.*   Ex 21:32
servant, he shall give
must eat them, thou and thy   De 12:18
m. servant
shalt rejoice, thou and thy *m.*   De 16:11;
servant   16:14
if I did despise the cause of   Job 31:13
my *m.* servant
every man let his *m.* servant go   Jer 34:9;
free   34:10

MAN *OF GOD*

Moses the *m.* of God   De 33:1; Jos 14:6;
woman told, saying, A *m.* of   J'g 13:6
God came to me
let the *m.* of God come again   J'g 13:8
to us, and teach us
there came a *m.* of God to Eli,   1Sa 2:27
and said
behold now there is in this city   1Sa 9:6
a *m.* of God
there is not a present to bring   1Sa 9:7
the *m.* of God
that will I give to the *m.* of   1Sa 9:8
God to tell us
word came to Shemaiah the   1Ki 12:22
m. of God
and there came a *m.* of God   1Ki 13:1
out of Judah
it is the *m.* of God who was   1Ki 13:26
disobedient
what have I to do with thee,   1Ki 17:18
O *m.* of God
now by this I know that thou   1Ki 17:24
art a *m.* of God
there came a *m.* of God and   1Ki 20:28
spake to Ahab
Thou *m.* of God king said,   2Ki 1:9;
Come down   1:11
O *m.* of God I pray thee, let   2Ki 1:13
my life be precious
she came and told *m.* of God   2Ki 4:7
I perceive this is *m.* of God   2Ki 4:9
thou *m.* of God, do not lie to   2Ki 4:16
thine handmaid
that I may run to *m.* of God,   2Ki 4:22
and come again
she came unto the *m.* of God   2Ki 4:25;
to Carmel   4:27
O thou *m.* of God, there is   2Ki 4:40
death in the pot
brought the *m.* of God bread,   2Ki 4:42
of firstfruits
dipped, according to the   2Ki 5:14
saying of *m.* of God
Gehazi, servant of Elisha, the   2Ki 5:20;
m. of God   8:4

sent to place which the *m. of*   *2Ki 6:10*
God told him
when the servant of the *m. of*   *2Ki 6:15*
God was risen
a lord answered the *m. of* God   *2Ki 7:2;*
and said   *7:19*
people trod on him as the *m.*   *2Ki 7:17;*
of God said   *7:18*
the woman did after the saying   *2Ki 8:2*
of *m. of God*
m. of God is come hither   *2Ki 8:7*
m. of God wept   *2Ki 8:11*
take a present and go meet the   *2Ki 8:8*
m. of God
and the *m. of God* was wroth   *2Ki 13:19*
according to the word which   *2Ki 23:16*
the *m. of God*
it is the sepulchre of *m. of*   *2Ki 23:17*
God which came
Moses *m. of God*   *1Ch 23:14;*
      2Ch 30:16; Ezr 3:2
David the *m. of God*   *2Ch 8:14;*
      Ne 12:24, 36
but there came a *m. of God*   *2Ch 25:7*
to Amaziah
the *m. of God* answered, the   *2Ch 25:9*
Lord is able to give
Hanan the son of Igdaliah a   *Jer 35:4*
m. of God
but thou, O *m. of God* flee   *1Ti 6:11*
these things
that the *m.* of God may be   *2Ti 3:17*
perfect

MAN *OF WAR*

the Lord is a *m. of war*, Lord   *Ex 15:3*
is his name
Machir, son of Manasseh, was   *Jos 17:1*
a *m. of war*
David a *m. of war*   *1Sa 16:18;*
      2Sa 17:8; 1Ch 28:3
Goliath was a *m. of war* from   *Jos 17:33*
his youth
the Lord doth take away the *m.*   *Isa 3:2*
of war
he shall stir up jealousy like a   *Isa 42:13*
m. of war

MAN with *WOMAN*

the *m.* said, The *woman*   *Ge 3:12*
whom thou gavest me
dead *m.* for the *woman* thou   *Ge 20:3*
hast is man's wife
every *m.* and *woman* whose   *Ex 35:29*
heart made
let no *m.* nor *woman* make any   *Ex 36:6*
more work
if a *m.* or *woman* have the   *Le 13:29*
plague
if *m.* or *woman* have in the   *Le 13:38*
skin bright spots
the *woman* also with whom   *Le 15:18*
the *m.* shall lie
that hath an issue of the *m.*   *Le 15:33*
and *woman*
if *m.* lie with a *woman* having   *Le 20:18*
her sickness
a *m.* or *woman* that hath a   *Le 20:27*
familiar spirit
when *m.* or *woman* shall   *Nu 5:6*
commit any sin
when either *m.* or *woman* shall   *Nu 6:2*
separate themselves
kill *woman* that hath known   *Nu 31:17;*
m.   *J'g 21:11*
m. or *woman* that hath   *De 17:2*
wrought wickedness
bring forth that *m.* or *woman*,   *De 17:5*
and stone them
the *woman* shall not wear that   *De 22:5*
pertaineth to a *m.* nor shall *m.*
put on a woman's garment
if a *m.* be found lying with a   *De 22:22*
woman, both the *m.* that lay
with the *woman*, and the *woman*
lest there should be among   *De 29:18*
you, *m.* or *woman*
utterly destroyed both *m.* and   *Jos 6:21*
woman
but slay both *m.*, *woman* and   *1Sa 15:3*
infant
David left neither *m.* nor   *1Sa 27:9;*
woman alive   *27:11*
he dealt both to *m.* and   *1Ch 16:3*
woman a loaf
not seek Lord, *m.* or *woman*   *2Ch 15:13*
shall die

whether *m.* or *woman* come to   *Es 4:11*
the king
to cut off from you, *m.*, *woman*   *Jer 44:7*
and child
I will break in pieces *m.* and   *Jer 51:22*
woman
and the head of the *woman* is   *1Co 11:3*
the *m.*
but the *woman* is the glory of   *1Co 11:7*
the *m.*
the *m.* is not of the *woman*   *1Co 11:8*
but *woman* of the *m.*
nor is the *m.* without the   *1Co 11:11*
woman in the Lord
as *woman* is of the *m.* so is   *1Co 11:12*
the *m.* by the *woman*
if any *m.* or *woman* have   *1Ti 5:16*
widows

A MAN

there was not a *m.* to till the   *Ge 2:5*
ground
therefore shall a *m.* leave his   *Ge 2:24;*
father and mother   *M't 19:5; M'k 10:7;*
      Eph 5:31
I have gotten a *m.* from the   *Ge 4:1*
Lord
for I have slain a *m.* to my   *Ge 4:23*
wounding
if a *m.* can number the dust   *Ge 13:16*
of the earth
there is not a *m.* to come in   *Ge 19:31*
unto us
Esau a cunning hunter, a *m.*   *Ge 25:27*
of the field
there wrestled a *m.* with him   *Ge 32:24*
till breaking
let Pharaoh look out a *m.*   *Ge 41:33*
discreet and wise
a *m.* in whom the Spirit of   *Ge 41:38*
God is
wot ye not such a *m.* as I can   *Ge 44:15*
certainly divine
for in their anger they slew a   *Ge 49:6*
m.
face to face as a *m.* speaketh   *Ex 33:11*
to his friend
when the plague of leprosy is in   *Le 13:9*
a *m.*
judgments, which if a *m.* do he   *Le 18:5;*
shall live in them   *Ne 9:29; Eze 20:11,*
      13, 21
and a *m.* of Israel strove   *Le 24:10*
together in the camp
as he hath caused a blemish in   *Le 24:20*
a *m.*
no devoted thing a *m.* shall   *Le 27:28*
devote
there shall be a *m.* of every   *Nu 1:4*
tribe
of every tribe shall ye send a   *Nu 13:2*
m.
they found a *m.* that gathered   *Nu 15:32*
sticks
this is the law when a *m.*   *Nu 19:14*
dieth in a tent
God is not a *m.* that he   *Nu 23:19;*
should lie   *1Sa 15:29*
among these there was not a   *Nu 26:64*
m. of them
there was not left a *m.* save   *Nu 26:65*
Caleb and Joshua
set a *m.* over the congregation   *Nu 27:16*
take the Joshua a *m.* in   *Nu 27:18*
whom is the Spirit
Lord bare thee, as a *m.* doth his   *De 1:31*
son
the breadth of it, after the   *De 3:11*
cubit of a *m.*
consider, that as a *m.*   *De 8:5*
chasteneth his son
one witness shall not rise   *De 19:15*
against a *m.*
take ye out of every tribe a *m.*   *Jos 3:12;*
      4:2, 4
there stood a *m.* over against   *Jos 5:13*
him with sword
there shall not a *m.* of them   *Jos 10:8*
stand before thee
the Lord hearkened to the   *Jos 10:14*
voice of a *m.*
which Arba was a great *m.*   *Jos 14:15*
among Anakims
stood not a *m.* of all their   *Jos 21:44*
enemies before
the spies saw a *m.* come out of   *J'g 1:24*
the city
escaped not a *m.*   *J'g 3:29*

was not a *m.* left   *J'g 4:16*
there was a *m.* that told a   *J'g 7:13*
dream to his fellow
save the sword of Gideon a *m.*   *J'g 7:14*
of Israel
Tola a *m.* of Issachar   *J'g 10:1*
she called a *m.*   *J'g 16:19*
a *m.* plucked off his shoe and   *Ru 4:7*
gave it
I will send thee a *m.* out of   *1Sa 9:16*
Benjamin
there shall not a *m.* be put to   *1Sa 11:13*
death
the Lord hath sought him a   *1Sa 13:14*
m.
and let us not leave a *m.* of   *1Sa 14:36*
them
to seek out a *m.* who is a   *1Sa 16:16*
cunning player
provide me a *m.* that can   *1Sa 16:17*
play well
choose you a *m.* for you, let   *1Sa 17:8*
him come
give me a *m.* that we may   *1Sa 17:10*
fight together
he is such that a *m.* cannot   *1Sa 25:17*
speak to him
and there escaped not a *m.*   *1Sa 30:17*
as a *m.* falleth before wicked   *2Sa 3:34*
Abner a great *m.* is fallen in   *2Sa 3:38*
as if a *m.* inquired at the   *2Sa 16:23*
oracle of God
happened to be there a *m.* of   *2Sa 20:1*
Belial
be strong, and shew thyself a   *1Ki 2:2*
m.
not fail thee a *m.* on the   *1Ki 2:4;*
throne   *8:25*
a *m.* turned aside, and   *1Ki 20:39*
brought a *m.*
a *m.* whom I appointed to   *1Ki 20:42*
destruction
came a *m.* to meet us, and said   *2Ki 1:6*
there came a *m.* from   *2Ki 4:42*
Baal-shalisha
there was not a *m.* left that   *2Ki 10:21*
came not
as they were burying a *m.*   *2Ki 13:21*
they spied
a son born, who shall be a *m.*   *1Ch 22:9*
of rest
there shall not fail thee a *m.*   *2Ch 6:16;*
      7:18
come a *m.* to seek the welfare   *Ne 2:10*
of Israel
I said, Should such a *m.* as I   *Ne 6:11*
flee
all that a *m.* hath will he give   *Job 2:4*
for his life
why is light given to a *m.* whose   *Job 3:23*
way
shall a *m.* be more pure than   *Job 4:17*
his Maker
he is not a *m.* as I am, that I   *Job 9:32*
should answer
and should a *m.* full of talk be   *Job 11:2*
justified
he shutteth up a *m.*   *Job 12:14*
if a *m.* die   *Job 14:14*
O that one might plead for a   *Job 16:21*
m. with God, as a *m.*
pleadeth for his neighbour
can a *m.* be profitable to God   *Job 22:2*
as he that is wise
whether done against a nation   *Job 34:29*
or a *m.*
thy wickedness may hurt a *m.*   *Job 35:8*
as thou art
if a *m.* speak he shall be   *Job 37:20*
swallowed up
gird up now thy loins like a   *Job 38:3;*
m.   *40:7*
I was as a *m.* that heareth not   *Ps 38:14*
but it was thou a *m.* mine   *Ps 55:13*
equal
how long will ye imagine   *Ps 62:3*
mischief against a *m.*
a *m.* was famous according as   *Ps 74:5*
he lifted up
I am as a *m.* that hath no   *Ps 88:4*
strength
he sent a *m.* before them,   *Ps 105:17*
even Joseph
he taketh not pleasure in the   *Ps 147:10*
legs of a *m.*
strive not with a *m.* without   *Pr 3:30*
cause
for jealousy is the rage of a *m.*   *Pr 6:34*

a way that seemeth right to *a*   *Pr 14:12; m.*   *16:25*
all ways of *a m.* are clean in his   *Pr 16:2* own eyes
when *a m.* ways please the   *Pr 16:7* Lord he maketh
how can *a m.* understand his   *Pr 20:24* own way
if thou be *a m.* given to   *Pr 23:2* appetite
so *a* contentious *m.* to kindle   *Pr 26:21* strife
so is *a m.* that wandereth from   *Pr 27:8* his place
as the furnace, so is *a m.* to   *Pr 27:21* his praise
but when the wicked rise *a m.*   *Pr 28:12* is hidden
he that rebuketh *a m.* shall   *Pr 28:23* find more favour
seest thou *a m.* that is hasty in   *Pr 29:20* words
a m. whose labour is in wisdom,   *Ec 2:21* yet to *a m.* that hath not labour
God giveth to *a m.* that is good   *Ec 2:26* in his sight
for this *a m.* is envied of his   *Ec 4:4* neighbour
a m. to whom God hath given   *Ec 6:2* riches
who can tell *a m.* what shall be   *Ec 6:12*
a m. cannot tell what shall be   *Ec 10:14* after him
if *a m.* live many years, and   *Ec 11:8* rejoice
if *a m.* would give all his   *Ca 8:7* substance
because I am *a m.* of unclean   *Isa 6:5* lips
I will make *a m.* more   *Isa 13:12* precious than gold
at that day shall *a m.* look to   *Isa 17:7* his maker
than that *a m.* can stretch   *Isa 28:20* himself on it
that make *a m.* an offender   *Isa 29:21* for a word
a m. shall be an hiding place   *Isa 32:2* from the wind
and I will not meet thee as a   *Isa 47:3* *m.*
he is *a m.* of sorrows and   *Isa 53:3* acquainted with grief
a day for *a m.* to afflict his   *Isa 58:5* soul
he that killeth an ox, is as if he   *Isa 66:3* slew *a m.*
forsaken, and not *a m.* dwell   *Jer 4:29*
seek in broad places, if ye can   *Jer 5:1* find *a m.*
why shouldest thou be as *a m.*   *Jer 14:9* astonied
that thou hast borne me *a m.*   *Jer 15:10* of strife
shall *a m.* make gods to   *Jer 16:20* himself and no gods
a m. that shall not prosper in   *Jer 22:30* his days
I am like *a m.* whom wine   *Jer 23:9* hath overcome
see whether *a m.* doth travail   *Jer 30:6* with child
a woman shall compass *a m.*   *Jer 31:22*
David shall never want *a m.*   *Jer 33:17* to sit on throne
nor shall the priests want *a m.*   *Jer 33:18* before me
Jonadab shall not want *a m.*   *Jer 35:19* to stand before me
every man put in array like *a*   *Jer 50:42* *m.* to battle
it is good for *a m.* to hope and   *La 3:26*
it is good for *a m.* that he bear   *La 3:27* the yoke
complain, *a m.* for the   *La 3:39* punishment of his sins
I sought for *a m.* among   *Eze 22:30*
yet thou art *a m.* and not God   *Eze 28:2; 28:9*
if the people of the land take   *Eze 33:2* *a m.*
not *a m.* on earth that can   *Da 2:10* shew
I have found *a m.* of the   *Da 2:25* captives of Judah
there is *a m.* in thy kingdom in   *Da 5:11* stand as *a m.*   *Da 7:13*
he said, O Daniel, *a m.*   *Da 10:11* greatly beloved

as troops of robbers wait for *a*   *Ho 6:9* *m.*
there shall not be *a m.* left, woe   *Ho 9:12* to them
I drew them with cords of *a m.*   *Ho 11:4*
a m. and his father go in to one   *Am 2:7* maid
as if *a m.* did flee from a lion   *Am 5:19*
oppress *a m.* and his house,   *Mic 2:2* even *a m.*
if *a m.* walking in spirit and   *Mic 2:11* falsehood
as *a m.* spareth his own son   *Mal 3:17* that serveth him
I am *a m.* under authority   *M't 8:9; Lu 7:8*
I am come to set *a m.* at   *M't 10:35* variance
how much is *a m.* better than   *M't 12:12* a sheep
the unclean spirit is gone out   *M't 12:43* of *a m.*
cometh out of the mouth   *M't 15:11* defileth *a m.*
to eat with unwashen hands   *M't 15:20* defileth not *a m.*
is it lawful for *a m.* to put   *M't 19:3; M'k 10:2* away
if *a m.* die, having no   *M't 22:24* children
he said, Go into the city, to   *M't 26:18;* such *a m.* and say to him   *M'k 14:13; Lu 22:10*
how shall this be, seeing I   *Lu 1:34* know not *a m.*
depart, for I am a sinful *m.* O   *Lu 5:8* Lord
a m. took and cast into his   *Lu 13:19* garden
to be guest with *a m.* that is a   *Lu 19:7* sinner
there was *a m.* sent from God   *Joh 1:6* named John
after me cometh *a m.* who is   *Joh 1:30* preferred
except *a m.* be born again, he   *Joh 3:3;* cannot see   *3:5*
how can *a m.* be born when he   *Joh 3:4* is old
a m. can receive nothing,   *Joh 3:27* except given him
come, see *a m.* which told me   *Joh 4:29* all things
angry, because I have made a   *Joh 7:23* *m.* whole
a m. that hath told you the   *Joh 8:40* truth
a m. that is called Jesus made   *Joh 9:11* clay
how can *a m.* a sinner, do   *Joh 9:16* such miracles
thou being *a m.* makest   *Joh 10:33* thyself God
if *a m.* love me, he will keep   *Joh 14:23*
for joy that *a m.* is born into   *Joh 16:21* the world
Jesus, *a m.* approved of God   *Ac 2:22*
stand up, I myself also am *a m.*   *Ac 10:26*
I found David, *a m.* after mine   *Ac 13:22* own heart
not believe, though *a. m.*   *Ac 13:41* declare it to you
stood *a m.* of Macedonia,   *Ac 16:9* prayed him
I am *a m.* who am a Jew of   *Ac 21:39* Tarsus
that preachest *a m.* should not   *Ro 2:21* steal
sayest *a m.* should not commit   *Ro 2:22* adultery
I speak as *a m.*   *Ro 3:5*
dominion over *a m.*   *Ro 7:1*
let *a m.* so account of us as   *1Co 4:1* ministers
it is required, that *a m.* be   *1Co 4:2* found faithful
every sin that *a m.* doeth is   *1Co 6:18* without body
it is good for *a m.* not to touch   *1Co 7:1* a woman
I say that it is good for *a m.*   *1Co 7:26* so to be
say I these things as *a m.* or   *1Co 9:8* saith not law
a m. indeed ought not to   *1Co 11:7* cover his head
if *a m.* have long hair, it is a   *1Co 11:14* shame

let *a m.* examine himself and   *1Co 11:28* let him eat
when became *a m.* I put   *1Co 13:11* away childish
sufficient to such *a m.* is this   *2Co 2:6* punishment
it is accepted according to   *2Co 8:12* that *a m.* hath
if *a m.* bring into bondage, if   *2Co 11:20* *a m.* smite
I knew *a m.* in Christ caught   *2Co 12:2;* up to heaven   *12:3*
which it is not lawful for *a m.*   *2Co 12:4* to utter
a m. is not justified by works of   *Ga 2:16* the law
brethren, if *a m.* be overtaken   *Ga 6:1* in a fault
if *a m.* think himself to be   *Ga 6:3* something
and being found in fashion as   *Ph'p 2:8* *a m.*
the law is good, if *a m.* use it   *1Ti 1:8* lawfully
if *a m.* desire the office of a   *1Ti 3:1* bishop
if *a m.* know not how to rule   *1Ti 3:5* his house
if *a m.* also strive for masteries   *2Ti 2:5*
if *a m.* therefore purge himself   *2Ti 2:21*
a m. that is a heretic, reject   *Tit 3:10*
he is like *a m.* beholding his   *Jas 1:23* face
if there come *a m.* with a gold   *Jas 2:2* ring
what profit, though *a m.* say,   *Jas 2:14* he hath faith
a m. may say, Thou hast faith,   *Jas 2:18* I have works
ye see how that by works *a m.*   *Jas 2:24* is justified
Elias was *a m.* subject to like   *Jas 5:17* passions
if *a m.* for conscience toward   *1Pe 2:19* God
for of whom *a m.* is overcome   *2Pe 2:19*
if *a m.* say, I love God, and   *1Jo 4:20* hateth
the third beast had a face as a   *Re 4:7* *m.*
as torment of a scorpion, when   *Re 9:5* he striketh *a m.*

A CERTAIN MAN

a certain m. found him, and   *Ge 37:15* asked him
a certain m. saw it, and told   *2Sa 18:10* Joab, and said
a certain m. drew bow at   *1Ki 22:34;* venture   *2Ch 18:33*
a certain m. had two sons   *M't 21:28; Lu 15:11*
a certain m. went down from   *Lu 10:39* Jerusalem
ground of *a certain* rich *m.*   *Lu 12:16* brought forth
a certain m. had a fig tree   *Lu 13:6* planted in his vineyard
a certain m. made a great   *Lu 14:16* supper, and bade many
there was *a certain m.* which   *Lu 16:1* had a steward
a certain blind *m.* sat by the   *Lu 18:35* way side begging
a certain m. planted a   *Lu 20:9* vineyard, and let it out
nor *a certain m.* was sick,   *Joh 11:1* named Lazarus, of Bethany
a certain m. lame from his   *Ac 3:2* mother's womb
a certain m. named Ananias, sold   *Ac 5:1* a possession
a certain m. called Simeon, who   *Ac 8:9* used sorcery
and there he found *a certain*   *Ac 9:33* *m.* named Æneas
there was *a certain m.* in   *Ac 10:1* Cæsarea called Cornelius
there sat *a certain m.* at   *Ac 14:8* Lystra, impotent in his feet
entered into *a certain m.* house   *Ac 18:7* named Justus
a certain m. named   *Ac 19:24* Demetrius, a silversmith
there is *a certain m.* left in   *Ac 25:14* bonds by Felix

ANY MAN

a virgin, nor had *any m.* known her	Ge 24:16
if thou knowest *any m.* of activity among them	Ge 47:6
if *any m.* have any matters to	Ex 24:14
nor let *any m.* be seen through all the mount	Ex 34:3
nor shall *any m.* desire thy land, when go up	Ex 34:24
when *any m.* hath a running issue	Le 15:2
if *any m.* lie with her at all, he shall be unclean	Le 15:24
that killeth *any m.* shall surely be put to death	Le 24:17
whatsoever *any m.* giveth the priest	Nu 5:10
if *any m.* die very suddenly by him	Nu 6:9
that toucheth the dead body of *any m.*	Nu 19:11; 19:13
if a serpent had bitten *any m.* when beheld	Nu 21:9
if *any m.* hate his neighbour and smite him	De 19:11
if false witness rise up against *any m.* to testify	De 19:16
blood on thy house, if *any m.* fall from thence	De 22:8
there be *any m.* among you that is not clean	De 23:10
shall not *any m.* be able to stand before thee	Jos 1:5
nor did there remain courage in *any m.*	Jos 2:11
if *any m.* enquire, is there *any m.* here	J'g 4:20
I shall become weak and be like *any other m.*	J'g 16:17
and had no business with *any m.*	J'g 18:7; 18:28
that when *any m.* offered sacrifice	1Sa 2:13
if *any m.* said, fail not to burn the fat	1Sa 2:16
when *any m.* that had a controversy	2Sa 15:2
it was so, that when *any m.* came nigh to him	2Sa 15:5
shall *any m.* be put to death this day in Israel	2Sa 19:22
nor for us shalt thou kill *any m.* in Israel	2Sa 21:4
if *any m.* trespass against his neighbour	1Ki 8:31
supplication be made by *any m.*	1Ki 8:38; 2Ch 6:29
if thou meet *any m.* salute him not	2Ki 4:29
nor choose I *any m.* ruler over Israel	2Ch 6:5
nor told I *any m.* what God put in my heart	Ne 2:12
surely I am more brutish than *any m.*	Pr 30:2
his visage was more marred than *any m.*	Isa 52:14
no more named in mouth of *any m.*	Jer 44:26
come not near *any m.* on whom is the mark	Eze 9:6
shall ask a petition of *any god* or *m.*	Da 6:7; 6:12
if *any m.* sue thee at law, and take thy coat	M't 5:40
nor know, *any m.* the Father, save the Son	M't 11:27
nor shall *any m.* hear his voice in the streets	M't 12:19
if *any m.* will come after me	M't 16:24; Lu 9:23
if *any m.* will come after me	M't 16:24;
say, The Lord hath need of him	M'k 11:3; Lu 19:31
art true, nor carest thou for *any m.* for thou	M't 22:16
nor durst *any m.* from that day ask questions	M't 23:46
if *any m.* say, Lo here is Christ	M't 24:23; M'k 13:21
see thou say nothing to *any m.* but go	M'k 1:44
if *any m.* hath ears to hear	M'k 4:23; 7:16; Re 13:9

neither could *any m.* tame him	M'k 5:4
he would not that *any m.* should know it	M'k 9:30
if *any m.* desire to be first, the same shall be last	M'k 9:35
take heed, lest *any m.* deceive	M'k 13:5
nor said any thing to *any m.* they were afraid	M'k 16:8
when thou art bidden of *any m.* to a wedding	Lu 14:8
if *any m.* come to me, and hate not father	Lu 14:26
if I have taken any thing from *any m.*	Lu 19:8
hath *any m.* bought him ought to eat	Joh 4:33
not that *any m.* hath seen the Father	Joh 6:46
if *any m.* eat of this bread he shall live for ever	Joh 6:51
if *any m.* do his will he shall know of doctrine	Joh 7:17
if *any m.* thirst, let him come to me and drink	Joh 7:37
doth our law judge *any m.* before it hear him	Joh 7:51
and we were never in bondage to *any m.*	Joh 8:33
if *any m.* did confess that he was Christ	Joh 9:22
if *any m.* be a worshipper of God, him he hear	Joh 9:31
that *any m.* opened the eyes of one born blind	Joh 9:32
by me if *any m.* enter in, he shall be saved	Joh 10:9
nor shall *any m.* pluck them out of my hand	Joh 10:28
if *any m.* walk in the day, he stumbleth not	Joh 11:9
if *any m.* knew where he were, he should shew it	Joh 11:57
if *any m.* serve me, let him follow me	Joh 12:26
if *any m.* hear my words and believe not	Joh 12:47
needest not that *any m.* should ask thee	Joh 16:30
it is not lawful for us to put *any m.* to death	Joh 18:31
not call *any m.* common or unclean	Ac 10:28
can *any m.* forbid water, these be not baptized	Ac 10:47
if have a matter against *any m.*, law is open	Ac 19:38
neither found me disputing with *any m.*	Ac 24:12
not manner of Romans to deliver *any m.*	Ac 25:16
if *any m.* have not the Spirit of Christ	Ro 8:9
if *any m.* build on this foundation	1Co 3:12
if *any m.* defile the temple of God him destroy	1Co 3:17
if *any m.* among you seemeth to be wise	1Co 3:18
if *any m.* that is called a brother be a fornicator	1Co 5:11
is *any m.* called, being circumcised	1Co 7:18
if *any m.* think that he knoweth any thing	1Co 8:2
if *any m.* love God	1Co 8:3
if *any m.* see thee which hast knowledge	1Co 8:10
that *any m.* should make my glorying void	1Co 9:15
if *any m.* say that this is offered	1Co 10:28
but if *any m.* seem to be contentious	1Co 11:16
if *any m.* hunger, let him	1Co 11:34
if *any m.* speak in an unknown tongue	1Co 14:27
if *any m.* think himself to be a prophet	1Co 14:37
if *any m.* be ignorant, let him be ignorant	1Co 14:38
if *any m.* love not the Lord Jesus, let him be	1Co 16:22
if *any m.* be in Christ he is a new creature	2Co 5:17
if *any m.* trust to himself that he is Christ's	2Co 10:7
lest *any m.* should think of me above what	2Co 12:6
if *any m.* preach any other gospel	Ga 1:9

not of works, lest *any m.* should boast	Eph 2:9
know, that whatsoever good thing *any m.* doeth	Eph 6:8
lest *any m.* should beguile you with words	Col 2:4
beware lest *any m.* spoil you thro' philosophy	Col 2:8
if *any m.* have a quarrel against any	Col 3:13
that none render evil for evil to *any m.*	1Th 5:15
if *any m.* obey not our word, note that man	2Th 3:14
if *any m.* teach otherwise and consent	1Ti 6:3
lest *any m.* fall after the same example	Heb 4:11
but if *any m.* draw back, my soul shall have	Heb 10:38
lest *any m.* fail of the grace of God	Heb 12:15
God cannot be tempted, nor tempteth he *any m.*	Jas 1:13
if *any m.* among you seem to be religious	Jas 1:26
if *any m.* offend not in word, he is perfect	Jas 3:2
if *any m.* speak let him speak as oracles	1Pe 4:11
yet if *any m.* suffer as Christian, not be ashamed	1Pe 4:16
if *any m.* sin, we have an advocate	1Jo 2:1
if *any m.* love the world, the love of Father	1Jo 2:15
and ye need not that *any m.* teach you	1Jo 2:27
if *any m.* see his brother sin not unto death	1Jo 5:16
if *any m.* hear my voice, and open door	Re 3:20
if *any m.* will hurt them, fire proceedeth	Re 11:5
if *any m.* worship the beast and his image	Re 14:9
if *any m.* shall add to these things	Re 22:18
if *any m.* shall take away from the words	Re 22:19

EVERY MAN

all flesh died on earth, and *every m.*	Ge 7:21
his hand be against *every m.*	Ge 16:12
then they took down *every m.* his sack	Ge 44:11
and laded *every m.* his ass, and returned	Ge 44:13
Joseph cried, Cause *every m.* to go out from me	Ge 45:1
the Egyptians sold *every m.* his field	Ge 47:20
every m. and his household came with Jacob	Ex 1:1
for they cast down *every m.* his rod	Ex 7:12
let *every m.* borrow of his neighbour jewels	Ex 11:2
they shall take to them *every m.* a lamb	Ex 12:3
every m. according to his eating	Ex 12:4; 16:16; 18:21
save that which *every m.* must eat, that only	Ex 12:16
abide ye *every m.* in his place, let no man go	Ex 16:29
of *every m.* that giveth it willingly	Ex 25:2
shall give *every m.* a ransom for his soul	Ex 30:12
every m. a sword slay *every m.* his brother, *every m.* his	Ex 32:27
stood *every m.* at his tent door and looked	Ex 33:8
they worshipped *every m.* in his tent door	Ex 33:10
came *every m.* from his work that they made	Ex 36:4
a bekah for *every m.*, that is, half a shekel	Ex 38:26
fear *every m.* his mother and father	Le 19:3
ye shall return *every m.* to his family	Le 25:10; 25:13
pitch *every m.* by his standard	Nu 1:52; 2:2, 17

give to *every m.* according to   *Nu 7:5*
his service
take *every m.* his censer, and *Nu 16:17*
put incense in
they took *every m.* his censer *Nu 16:18*
and put fire in them
they looked and took *every m.* *Nu 17:9*
his rod
men of war had taken spoil *Nu 31:53*
every m. for himself
Israel inherited *every m.* his *Nu 32:18*
inheritance
servants will pass over *every Nu 32:27;*
m. armed   *32:29*
judge righteously between   *De 1:16*
every m.
shall ye return *every m.* to his *De 3:20*
possession
not do *every m.* what is right *De 12:8*
in his eyes
every m. shall give as he is *De 16:17*
able
every m. shall die for his own *De 24:16;*
sin   *2Ki 14:6; 2Ch 25:4*
take up *every m.* of you a stone *Jos 4:5*
ascend *every m.* straight   *Jos 6:5;*
before him   *6:20*
every m. to his inheritance *Jos 24:28;*
                         J'g 2:6
divided to *every m.* a damsel or *J'g 5:30*
two
let other people go *every m.* *J'g 7:7;*
unto his place   *7:8*
would give me *every m.* his *J'g 8:24;*
earrings   *8:25*
the people cut down *every m.* *J'g 9:49*
his bough
every m. did what was right in *J'g 17:6;*
his eyes   *21:25*
catch you *every m.* his wife *J'g 21:21*
of the daughters
every m. to his tribe, *every J'g 21:24*
m. to his inheritance
and they fled *every m.* into his *1Sa 4:10*
tent
Samuel said, Go ye *every m.* *1Sa 8:22*
into his city
bring hither *every m.* his ox, *1Sa 14:34*
every m. his sheep
that break away *every m.* *1Sa 25:10*
from his master
David said, Gird you on *every 1Sa 25:13*
m. his sword
Lord render to *every m.*   *1Sa 26:23;*
his righteousness   *2Ch 6:30*
grieved *every m.* for his sons *1Sa 30:6*
and daughters
save to *every m.* his wife and *1Sa 30:22*
children
and they went out *every m.* *2Sa 13:9*
from him
every m. gat him upon his *2Sa 13:29*
mule, and fled
that *every m.* which hath any *2Sa 15:4*
suit or cause
covered *every m.* his head, *2Sa 15:30*
and they went up
for Israel hath fled *every m.* to *2Sa 19:8*
his tent
Sheba said, *Every m.* to his *2Sa 20:1*
tents, O Israel
dwelt safely *every m.* under *1Ki 4:25*
his vine
which shall know *every m.* the *1Ki 8:38*
plague of heart
give to *every m.* according to *1Ki 8:39;*
his ways   *Job 34:11; Jer 17:10*
brought *every m.* his *1Ki 10:25;*
present   *2Ch 9:24*
return *every m.* to his house, *1Ki 12:24;*
for this thing is from me   *22:17, 36;*
                   2Ch 11:4
take the kings *every m.* out of *1Ki 20:24*
his place
let us go and take thence *every 2Ki 6:2*
m. a beam
every m. with his weapons in *2Ki 11:11*
his hand
Judah fled *every m.* to their *2Ki 14:12*
tents
and then eat ye *every m.* of *2Ki 18:31*
his own vine
so God shake out *every m.* *Ne 5:13*
from his house
every m. should bear rule in his *Es 1:22*
own house
and *every m.* shall draw after *Job 21:33*
him
he sealeth up the hand of *Job 37:7*
every m. that

every m. at his best state is   *Ps 39:5;*
vanity   *39:11*
surely *every m.* walketh in a   *Ps 39:6*
vain show
thou renderest to *every m.*   *Ps 62:12;*
according to his work   *Pr 24:12*
every m. is a friend to him   *Pr 19:6*
that giveth
every m. shall kiss his lips that *Pr 24:26*
giveth right answer
eat *every m.* the flesh of his   *Isa 9:20*
own arm
in that day *every m.* shall cast *Isa 31:7*
away his idols
every m. is brutish in   *Jer 10:14;*
knowledge   *51:17*
turn *every m.* from his evil   *Jer 26:3;*
way   *35:15; 36:3*
for *every m.* that is mad, and *Jer 29:26*
maketh himself
teach no more *every m.* his   *Jer 31:34;*
neighbour   *Heb 8:11*
in proclaiming liberty *every Jer 34:15;*
m. to his neighbour   *34:17*
they should rise up *every m.* in *Jer 37:10*
his tent
go out and deliver ye *every m.* *Jer 51:45*
his soul
with *every m.* his censer in his *Eze 8:1*
hand
every m. in the chambers of his *Eze 8:12*
imagery
every m. with his destroying   *Eze 9:1;*
weapon   *9:2*
cast away *every m.*   *Eze 20:7*
abominations of his eyes
they did not *every m.* cast   *Eze 20:8*
away abominations
every m. shall tremble for his *Eze 32:10*
own life
not scattered *every m.* from *Eze 46:18*
his possession
every m. that shall hear the   *Da 3:10*
sound fall down
that *every m.* that shall ask a   *Da 6:12*
petition
the mariners cried *every m.* to *Jon 1:5*
his god
they shall sit *every m.* under *Mic 4:4*
his vine
they hunt *every m.* his brother *Mic 7:2*
with a net
and ye run *every m.* to his own *Hag 1:9*
house
call *every m.* his neighbour *Zec 3:10*
under the vine
every m. with his staff in his *Zec 8:4*
hand for age
speak *every m.* truth to his *Zec 8:16;*
neighbour   *Eph 4:25*
why do we deal treacherously *M't 2:10*
every m.
shall reward *every m.*   *M't 16:27;*
according to his works *Ro 2:6; Re 22:12*
they received *every m.* a   *M't 20:9;*
penny   *20:10*
he gave to *every m.*   *M't 25:15*
according to his ability
he was restored, and saw   *M'k 8:25*
every m. clearly
and gave to *every m.* his   *M'k 13:34*
work, and commanded
casting lots what *every m.* *M'k 15:24*
should take
give to *every m.* that asketh of *Lu 6:30*
thee
is preached, and *every m.* *Lu 16:16*
presseth into it
how much *every m.* had *Lu 19:15*
gained by trading
the true light, which lighteth *Joh 1:9*
every m.
every m. at beginning doth set *Joh 2:10*
forth good wine
every m. that hath heard and *Joh 6:45*
learned of Father
ye shall be scattered *every m.* *Joh 16:32*
to his own
how hear we *every m.* in our   *Ac 2:8*
own tongue
parted to all men, as *every m.* *Ac 2:45;*
had need   *4:35*
every m. determined to send *Ac 11:29*
relief to brethren
peace to *every m.* that worketh *Ro 2:10*
good
yea, let God be true, but *every Ro 3:4*
m. a liar
as God dealt to *every m.* the   *Ro 12:3*
measure of faith

let *every m.* be fully persuaded *Ro 14:5*
in his own mind
even as the Lord gave to *every 1Co 3:5;*
m.   *7:17*
then shall *every m.* have praise *1Co 4:5*
of God
nevertheless, let *every m.* have *1Co 7:2*
his own wife
but *every m.* hath his proper *1Co 7:7*
gift of God
let *every m.* abide in the   *1Co 7:20;*
same calling   *7:24*
there is not in *every m.* that *1Co 8:7*
knowledge
but let *every m.* seek   *1Co 10:24*
another's wealth
know that the head of *every 1Co 11:3*
m. is Christ
Spirit is given to *every m.* to *1Co 12:7*
profit withal
but *every m.* in his order, *1Co 15:23*
Christ first fruits
I testify again to *every m.*   *Ga 5:3*
that is circumcised
let *every m.* prove his own work *Ga 6:4*
for *every m.* shall bear his own *Ga 6:5*
own burden
look not *every m.* on his own *Ph'p 2:4*
things
teaching *every m.* in all   *Col 1:28*
wisdom to present *every*
m. perfect in Christ
may know how ye ought to   *Col 4:6*
answer *every m.*
that he should taste death   *Heb 2:9*
for *every m.*
but *every m.* is tempted,   *Jas 1:14*
when he is drawn
let *every m.* be swift to hear, *Jas 1:19*
slow to speak
to give a reason to *every m.*   *1Pe 3:15*
that asketh of hope
as *every m.* hath received the *1Pe 4:10*
gift, even so
every m. that hath this hope in *1Jo 3:3*
him, purifies
judged *every m.* according to *Re 20:13*
their works
for I testify to *every m.* that *Re 22:18*
heareth the words

MIGHTY MAN

the Lord is with thee, thou   *J'g 6:12*
mighty m.
now Jephthah was a *mighty m.* *J'g 11:1*
of valour
Naaman was also a *mighty m.* *2Ki 5:1*
mighty m. of wealth
Kish a Benjamite, a *mighty m.* *1Sa 9:1*
of power
David *mighty m.* and man   *1Sa 16:18;*
of war   *2Sa 17:10*
the man Jeroboam was a   *1Ki 11:28*
mighty m.
Naaman was also a *mighty m.* *2Ki 5:1*
in valour
Ismaiah a *mighty m.* among *1Ch 12:4*
the thirty
of Benjamin Eliada a *mighty 2Ch 17:17*
m. of valour
Zichri, a *mighty m.* of   *2Ch 28:7*
Ephraim, slew Maaseiah
as for the *mighty m.* he had   *Job 22:8*
the earth
a *mighty m.* is not delivered *Ps 33:16*
by strength
why boastest thou in mischief, *Ps 52:1*
O *mighty m.*
then the Lord awaked like a   *Ps 78:65*
mighty m.
as arrows are in the hand of   *Ps 127:4*
a *mighty m.*
the Lord doth take away the   *Isa 3:2*
mighty m.
and the *mighty m.* shall be   *Isa 5:15*
humbled
shall fall with the sword, not   *Isa 31:8*
of a *mighty m.*
the Lord shall go forth as a   *Isa 42:13*
mighty m.
nor let the *mighty m.* glory in *Jer 9:23*
his might
shouldest be as a *mighty m.*   *Jer 14:9*
that cannot save
nor *mighty m.* escape   *Jer 46:6*
mighty m. stumbled   *Jer 46:12*
the *mighty m.* shall cry there   *Zep 1:14*
bitterly

have made thee as sword of a *Zec 9:13* mighty *m.*

they of Ephraim shall be like *Zec 10:7* a *mighty m.*

NO MAN

no m. is with us, see, God is *Ge 31:50* witness

without thee shall *no m.* lift *Ge 41:44* his hand

stood *no m.* while Joseph made *Ge 45:1* himself known

and when he saw that there *Ex 2:12* was *no m.*

let *no m.* leave of it till the *Ex 16:19* morning

let *no m.* go out of his place *Ex 16:29* on the seventh day

be hurt or driven away, no *Ex 22:10* *m.* seeing it

no m. did put on him his *Ex 33:4* ornaments

for there shall *no m.* see me *Ex 33:20* and live

and *no m.* shall come up with *Ex 34:3* thee

there shall be *no m.* in the *Le 16:17* tabernacle

no m. that hath a blemish shall *Le 21:21* come nigh

no m. shall sanctify it, it is the *Le 27:26* Lord's

if *no m.* hath lain with thee, be *Nu 5:19* thou free

no m. able to stand before *De 7:24;* thee 11:25

oppressed, and *no m.* shall *De 28:29;* save thee 28:68

but *no m.* knoweth of his *De 34:6* sepulchre

no m. hath been able to stand *Jos 23:9* before you

Jephthah's daughter knew no *J'g 11:39* *m.*

no m. that took them to his *J'g 19:15;* house 19:18

young virgins that had known *J'g 21:12* *no m.*

for by strength shall *no m.* *1Sa 2:9* prevail

and then if there be *no m.* to *1Sa 11:3* save us

let *no m.* know any thing of *1Sa 21:2* the business

and *no m.* saw nor knew it, *1Sa 26:12* nor awaked

no m. deputed of the king to *2Sa 15:3* hear thee

is *no m.* that sinneth not *1Ki 8:46;* 2Ch 6:36

behold, there was *no m.* in *2Ki 7:5;* camp 7:10

let him alone, let *no m.* move *2Ki 23:18* his bones

he suffered *no m.* to do *1Ch 16:21;* them wrong *Ps 105:14*

queen did let *no m.* come in *Es 5:12* with king

may *no m.* reverse *Es 8:8*

no m. could withstand *Es 9:2*

shall *no m.* make thee ashamed *Job 11:3*

in houses which *no m.* *Job 15:28* inhabiteth

therefore shall *no m.* look for *Job 20:21* his goods

he riseth, and *no m.* is sure *Job 24:22* of his life

where *no m.* is, wherein *Job 38:26* there is *no m.*

I am a worm, and *no m.* a *Ps 22:6*

there was *no m.* *Ps 142:4;* *Isa 41:28; 59:16; Jer 4:25*

in thy sight shall *no m.* be *Ps 143:2* justified

I stretched my hand, and *no m.* *Pr 1:24* regarded

the wicked flee when *no m.* *Pr 28:1* pursueth

shall flee to the pit, let *no m.* *Pr 28:17* stay him

no m. hath power over the spirit *Ec 8:8*

no m. knoweth either love or *Ec 9:1* hatred

no m. remembered that same *Ec 9:15* poor man

no m. shall spare his brother *Isa 9:19*

no m. may come in *Isa 24:10*

he regardeth *no m.* *Isa 33:8*

wherefore when I came, *Isa 50:2* was there *no m.*

and *no m.* layeth it to heart *Isa 57:1;* *Jer 12:11*

so that *no m.* went through *Isa 60:15* thee

and where *no m.* dwelt *Jer 2:6*

no m. repent *Jer 8:6*

for *no m.* of his seed shall *Jer 22:30* prosper

this is Zion, whom *no m.* *Jer 30:17* seeketh after

go hide, and let *no m.* know *Jer 36:19* where ye be

Zedekiah said, Let *no m.* *Jer 38:24* know of these words

and *no m.* shall know it *Jer 40:15*

no m. knew it *Jer 41:4*

and *no m.* dwelleth therein *Jer 44:2;* 51:43

no m. shall abide there *Jer 49:18;* 49:33; 50:4

ask bread, and *no m.* breaketh it *La 4:4* to them

that *no m.* may pass thro' for *Eze 14:15* the beasts

no m. shall enter in by this *Eze 44:2* gate

yet let *no m.* strive or reprove *Ho 4:4* another

is scattered, and *no m.* *Na 3:18* gathereth them

so that there is *no m.* none *Zep 3:6* inhabitant

so that *no m.* did lift up his *Zec 1:21* head

that *no m.* passed through nor *Zec 7:14* returned

no m. can serve two masters *M't 6:24;* *Lu 16:13*

tell *no m.* *M't 8:4* 16:20; M'k 7:36; Lu 5:14; 9:21

see that *no m.* know it *M't 9:30;* M'k 5:43; 7:24; 8:30; 9:9

no m. knoweth Son but *M't 11:27;* Father *Lu 10:22*

they saw *no m.* save Jesus *M't 17:8*

tell the vision to *no m.* till *M't 17:9* the Son be risen

no m. was able to answer *M't 22:46* him a word

call *no m.* father on the earth *M't 23:9*

that day and hour knoweth *M't 24:36;* *no m.* *M'k 13:32*

no m. that hath left house *M'k 10:29;* *Lu 18:29*

no m. eat fruit of thee *M'k 11:14* hereafter for ever

we know that thou carest for *M'k 12:14* *no m.*

do violence to *no m.* *Lu 3:14*

salute *no m.* *Lu 10:4*

with the husks, and *no m.* *Lu 15:16* gave unto him

no m. hath seen God *Joh 1:18; 1Jo 4:12*

no m. can do these miracles, *Joh 3:2* except God be

no m. hath ascended up to *Joh 3:13* heaven

for the Father judgeth *no m.* *Joh 5:22* but hath

no m. can come to me, except *Joh 6:44;* Father draw 6:65

but *no m.* laid hands on him *Joh 7:30;* 7:44; 8:20

she said, *No m.* Lord *Joh 8:11;* judge *no m.* 8:15

the night cometh when *no m.* *Joh 9:4* can work

no m. taketh it from me, I *Joh 10:18* lay it down

no m. is able to pluck them *Joh 10:29* out of my Father's

no m. at the table knew why *Joh 13:28* he spake this

no m. cometh to the Father *Joh 14:6* but by me

greater love hath *no m.* than *Joh 15:13* this

and your joy *no m.* taketh *Joh 16:22* from you

and let *no m.* dwell therein *Ac 1:20*

that they speak to *no m.* in this *Ac 4:17* name

of the rest durst *no m.* join *Ac 5:13* himself

we had opened, we found *no* *Ac 5:23* *m.* within

hearing a voice, but seeing *no* *Ac 9:7;* *m.* 9:8

no m. shall set on thee to *Ac 18:10* hurt thee

preaching kingdom of God *Ac 28:31*

no m. forbidding him

recompense to *no m.* evil for *Ro 12:17* evil

owe *no m.* any thing, but to *Ro 13:8* love one another

liveth to himself, and *no m.* *Ro 14:7* dieth to himself

that *no m.* put a *Ro 14:13* stumblingblock in his way

the things of God knoweth no *1Co 2:11* *m.*

yet he himself is judged of *no* *1Co 2:15* *m.*

for other foundation can *no* *1Co 3:11* *m.* lay than is laid

let *no m.* deceive himself *1Co 3:18; 3:21*

let *no m.* seek his own, but *1Co 10:24* another's wealth

henceforth know we *no m.* *2Co 5:16* after the flesh

we have wronged *no m.* have *2Co 7:2* corrupted *no m.*

but that *no m.* is justified by *Ga 3:11* the law

let *no m.* deceive you *Eph 5:6; 2Th 2:3*

for *no m.* ever yet hated his *Eph 5:29* own flesh

for I have *no m.* like-minded, *Ph'p 2:20* who will

let *no m.* beguile you of your *Col 2:18* reward

that *no m.* go beyond his *1Th 4:6* brother in any

lay hands suddenly on *no m.* *1Ti 5:22*

at my first answer *no m.* stood *2Ti 4:16* with me

put them in mind, to speak evil *Tit 3:2* of *no m.*

no m. taketh this honour to *Heb 5:4* himself

of which *no m.* gave *Heb 7:13* attendance at the altar

without which *no m.* shall *Heb 12:14* see the Lord

let *no m.* say when he is *Jas 1:13* tempted

the tongue can *no m.* tame, it is *Jas 3:8* unruly

little children, let *no m.* deceive *1Jo 3:7* you

a new name, which *no m.* *Re 2:17* knoweth

he that shutteth, and *no m.* *Re 3:7* openeth

and *no m.* can shut it *Re 3:8*

no m. take thy crown *Re 3:11*

and *no m.* was able to open the *Re 5:3;* book 5:4

and multitude which *no m.* *Re 7:9* could number

that *no m.* might buy or sell *Re 13:17* save he that

no m. could learn that song but *Re 14:3* the redeemed

no m. was able to enter into *Re 15:8* the temple

no m. buyeth their *Re 18:11* merchandise any more

he had a name written, that *Re 19:12* *no m.* knew

OF MAN

at the hand *of m.* will I require *Ge 9:5* life *of m.*

all the firstborn *of m.* *Ex 13:13;* *Nu 18:15*

ye shall not be afraid of the *De 1:17* face *of m.*

is this the manner *of m.* O *2Sa 7:19* Lord God

not fall into the hands *of m.* *2Sa 24:14;* *1Ch 21:13*

what manner *of m.* was he *2Ki 1:7* which came

there was no man there, nor *2Ki 7:10* voice *of m.*

are thy days as the days *of m.* *Job 10:5*

thou destroyest the hope *of* *Job 14:19* *m.*

for vain is the help *of m.* *Ps 60:11;* 108:12

the wrath *of m.* shall praise thee   *Ps 76:10*

the ways *of m.* are before the Lord   *Pr 5:21*

the spirit *of m.* will sustain his infirmity   *Pr 18:14*

the discretion *of m.* deferreth his anger   *Pr 19:11*

the desire *of m.* is his kindness   *Pr 19:22*

so the heart *of m.* answereth to man   *Pr 27:19*

the fear *of m.* bringeth a snare   *Pr 29:25*

and have not the understanding of *m.*   *Pr 30:2*

and the way *of* a *m.* with a maid   *Pr 30:19*

all the labour *of m.* is for his mouth   *Ec 6:7*

the misery *of m.* is great upon him   *Ec 8:6*

for this is the whole duty *of m.*   *Ec 12:13*

maketh it after the figure *of m.* according to the beauty *of* a *m.*   *Isa 44:13*

that thou shouldest be afraid *of* a *m.*   *Isa 51:12*

I know the way *of m.* is not in himself   *Jer 10:23*

to turn aside the right *of* a *m.*   *La 3:35*

they four had the face *of* a *m.*   *Eze 1:10; 10:14*

no foot *of m.* shall pass through it   *Eze 29:11*

neither shall the foot *of m.* trouble them   *Eze 32:13*

stood as the appearance *of* a *m.*   *Da 8:15; 10:18*

when eyes *of* a *m.* shall be toward Lord   *Zec 9:1*

who formeth the spirit *of m.* within him   *Zec 12:1*

what manner *of m.* is this   *M't 8:27; M'k 4:41; Lu 8:25*

if the case *of m.* be so with his wife   *M't 19:10*

he said, Come out of the *m.*   *M'k 5:8; Lu 8:29*

nor of the will *of m.* but of God   *Joh 1:13*

needed not that any should testify *of m.*   *Joh 2:25*

it is the voice of a god, not *of* a *m.*   *Ac 12:22*

upon ever soul *of m.* that doeth evil   *Ro 2:9*

David describeth the blessedness of the *m.*   *Ro 4:6*

neither hath entered into the heart *of m.*   *1Co 2:9*

what man knoweth things of *1Co 2:11* a *m.* save the spirit *of m.* which is in him

should be judged of you, or *of m.* judgment   *1Co 4:3*

but the woman is the glory *of*   *1Co 11:7* the *m.*

but the woman is of the *m.*   *1Co 11:8; 11:12*

for I neither received it *of m.*   *Ga 1:12*

wrath *of m.* worketh not righteousness   *Jas 1:20*

forgetteth what manner *of m.* he was   *Jas 1:24*

all glory *of m.* as flower of grass   *1Pe 1:24*

came not in old time by will *of m.*   *2Pe 1:21*

for it is the number *of* a *m.*   *Re 13:18*

according to the measure of a *m.*   *Re 21:17*

ONE MAN

they gathered two homers for one *m.*   *Ex 16:22*

if thou kill this people as one *m.*   *Nu 14:15*

shall one *m.* sin, and wilt thou be wroth   *Nu 16:22*

and there lacketh not one *m.* of us   *Nu 31:49*

one *m.* shall chase a thousand   *Jos 23:10*

smite the Midianites as one *m.*   *J'g 6:16*

to be a priest to the house of one *m.*   *J'g 18:19*

congregation was gathered as one *m.*   *J'g 20:1*

all the people arose as *one m.* saying   *J'g 20:6*

if *one m.* sin against another   *1Sa 2:25*

even as the heart of *one m.*   *2Sa 19:14*

there is yet one *m.* Micaiah   *1Ki 22:8; 2Ch 18:7*

gathered together as one *m.*   *Ezr 3:1; Ne 8:1*

as *one m.* mocketh another, do ye mock   *Job 13:9*

one *m.* among a thousand have I found   *Ec 7:8*

wherein *one m.* ruleth over another   *Ec 8:9*

seven women shall take hold of one *m.*   *Isa 4:1*

one *m.* was clothed with linen   *Eze 9:2*

one *m.* shall die for the people   *Joh 11:50; 18:14*

as by *one m.* sin entered into the world   *Ro 5:12*

the gift by grace, which is by one *m.* Jesus   *Ro 5:15*

one *m.* esteemeth one day above another   *Ro 14:5*

having been the wife of one *m.*   *1Ti 5:9*

SON OF MAN, MAN'S

nor *son of m.* that he should repent   *Nu 23:19*

and the *son of m.* which is a worm   *Job 25:6*

righteousness may profit the *son of m.*   *Job 35:8*

and *son of m.* that thou visitest him   *Ps 8:4; Heb 2:6*

and on *son of m.* whom thou madest strong   *Ps 80:17*

or *son of m.* that thou makest account of him   *Ps 144:3*

put not your trust in the son *of m.*   *Ps 146:3*

be not afraid of the son *of m.* which   *Isa 51:12*

blessed is the *son of m.* that layeth hold on it   *Isa 56:2*

nor shall *son of m.* dwell in it   *Jer 49:18; 49:33; 50:40*

neither doth any *son of m.* pass thereby   *Jer 51:43*

hast thou seen this, O *son of m.*   *Eze 8:15; 8:17*

sigh therefore, thou *son of m.* with bitterness   *Eze 21:6*

one like the *Son of m.* came   *Da 7:13*

with the clouds   *Re 1:13; 14:14*

Son of m. hath not where to lay   *M't 8:20; Lu 9:58*

Son of m. hath power on earth to forgive sins   *M't 9:6; Lu 5:24*

not gone over, till the Son of *m.* be come   *M't 10:23*

the *Son of m.* came eating   *M't 11:19; Lu 7:34*

for the *Son of m.* is Lord   *M't 12:8*

even of the sabbath   *M'k 2:28; Lu 6:5*

speaketh against Son of *m.*   *M't 12:32; Lu 12:10*

Son of m. be three days and nights   *M't 12:40*

that soweth good seed is the *Son of m.*   *M't 13:37*

the *Son of m.* shall send forth his angels   *M't 13:41*

whom do men say that I, the *Son of m.* am   *M't 16:13*

until the *Son of m.* be risen again   *M't 17:9; M'k 9:9*

the *Son of m.* shall be betrayed   *M't 17:22; 20:18; 26:2; M'k 14:41; Lu 9:44*

so shall also the coming of the *Son of m.* be   *M't 24:27; 24:37, 39; Lu 17:26*

shall see *Son of m.* coming   *M't 24:30; M'k 13:26; Lu 21:27*

hour ye think not *Son of m.* cometh   *M't 24:44; Lu 12:40*

when the *Son of m.* shall come in his glory   *M't 25:31*

the *Son of m.* goeth   *M't 26:24; M'k 14:21; Lu 22:22*

of him shall *Son of m.* be ashamed when he cometh in glory of Father   *M'k 8:38*

and how it is written of the *Son of m.*   *M'k 9:12*

the *Son of m.* is delivered   *M'k 9:31; 10:33; Lu 24:7*

Son of m. is as a man taking a far journey   *M'k 13:34*

reproach you for the *Son of m.* sake   *Lu 6:22*

the *Son of m.* must suffer many things   *Lu 9:22*

the *Son of m.* is not come to destroy men's lives   *Lu 9:56*

so shall *Son of m.* be to this generation   *Lu 11:30; 17:24*

him shall the *Son of m.* confess before angels   *Lu 12:8*

desire to see one of the days of the *Son of m.*   *Lu 17:22*

when the *Son of m.* cometh, shall he find faith   *Lu 18:8*

the *Son of m.* is come to seek and to save lost   *Lu 19:10*

be worthy to stand before the *Son of m.*   *Lu 21:36*

betrayest thou the *Son of m.* with a kiss   *Lu 22:48*

ascending and descending on *Son of m.*   *Joh 1:51*

even the *Son of m.* which is in heaven   *Joh 3:13*

even so must the *Son of m.* be lifted up   *Joh 3:14*

given authority, because he is the *Son of m.*   *Joh 5:27*

which the *Son of m.* shall give unto you   *Joh 6:27*

except ye eat the flesh of the *Son of m.*   *Joh 6:53*

what, and if ye shall see the *Son of m.* ascend   *Joh 6:62*

when ye have lift up the *Son of m.* then shall   *Joh 8:28*

that the *Son of m.* should be glorified   *Joh 12:23*

Son of m. must be lifted up, who is this *Son of m.*   *Joh 12:34*

Jesus said, Now is the *Son of m.* glorified   *Joh 13:31*

I see the *Son of m.* standing on right hand   *Ac 7:56*

THAT MAN

even *that m.* shall be cut off from his people   *Le 17:9*

I will set my face against *that m.*   *Le 20:3; 20:5; Eze 14:8*

brought not offering *that m.* shall bear his sin   *Nu 9:13*

stone *that m.* or woman till they die   *De 17:5; 17:12*

elders shall take *that m.* and chastise him   *De 22:18*

answer and say, So shall it be done to *that m.*   *De 25:9*

his jealousy shall smoke against *that m.*   *De 29:20*

that m. perisheth not alone in iniquity   *Jos 22:20*

and *that m.* was perfect and upright   *Job 1:1*

for the end of *that m.* is peace   *Ps 37:37*

blessed is *that m.* who maketh Lord his trust   *Ps 40:4*

he said, This and *that m.* was born in her   *Ps 87:5*

for bread *that m.* will transgress   *Pr 28:21*

let *that m.* be as cities Lord overthrew   *Jer 20:16*

I will even punish *that m.* and his house   *Jer 23:34*

last state of *that m.* is worse   *M't 12:45; Lu 11:26*

woe to *that m.* by whom the offence cometh   *M't 18:7*

woe to *that m.* by whom the *M't 26:24; M'k 14:21; Son of man is betrayed   Lu 22:22*

have thou nothing to do with *that* just *m.*   *M't 27:19*

by *that m.* whom he hath ordained   *Ac 17:31*

evil for *that m.* who eateth with offence   *Ro 14:20*

that m. of sin be revealed, son of perdition   *2Th 2:3*

note *that m.* and have no company with him   *2Th 3:14*

let not *that m.* think he shall receive   *Jas 1:7*

THIS MAN

wilt thou go with *this m.*? I   *Ge 24:58*
will go
he that toucheth *this m.* or his   *Ge 26:11*
wife
how long shall *this m.* be a   *Ex 10:7*
snare to us
I gave my daughter to *this m.*   *De 22:16*
to wife
seeing *this m.* is come to my   *J'g 19:23*
house
but to *this m.* do not so vile a   *J'g 19:24*
thing
this m. went up yearly to   *1Sa 1:3*
worship
but they said, How shall *this*   *1Sa 10:27*
m. save us
have you seen *this m.* that is   *1Sa 17:25*
come up
let not my lord regard *this m.*   *1Sa 25:25*
of Belial
see how *this m.* seeketh   *1Ki 20:7*
mischief
brought a man to me, and   *1Ki 20:39*
said, Keep *this m.*
this m. sends to me to   *2Ki 5:7*
recover a man
grant him mercy in sight of   *Ne 1:11*
this m.
for *this m.* Mordecai waxed   *Es 9:4*
greater and
this m. was the greatest of the   *Job 1:3*
men of east
lo, *this m.* made not God his   *Ps 52:7*
strength
shall be said, *this m.* was born   *Ps 87:4;*
there   *87:5, 6*
is *this* the *m.* that made earth   *Isa 14:16*
tremble
but to *this m.* will I look, even   *Isa 66:2*
is *this m.* Coniah a despised   *Jer 22:28*
broken idol
thus saith the Lord, Write ye   *Jer 22:30*
this m. childless
saying, *This m.* is worthy to   *Jer 26:11;*
die   *26:16*
let *this m.* be put to death,   *Jer 38:4*
this m. seeketh not welfare of
make *this m.* understand the   *Da 8:16*
vision
let us not perish for *this m.*   *Jon 1:14*
life
this m. shall be the peace   *Mic 5:5*
when Assyrian
I say to *this m.* Go, and he   *M't 8:9*
goeth, to another
scribes said, *This m.*   *M't 9:3;*
blasphemeth   *M'k 2:7*
whence had *this m.* this   *M't 13:54;*
wisdom   *M'k 6:2*
some said, *This m.* calleth   *M't 27:47*
for Elias
I know not *this m.* of whom   *M'k 14:71*
ye speak
truly *this m.* was the Son of   *M'k 15:30*
God
this m. if he were a prophet,   *Lu 7:39*
would have
come and say to thee, Give   *Lu 14:9*
this m. place
saying, *This m.* began to   *Lu 14:30*
build and was not able
this m. receiveth sinners, and   *Lu 15:2*
eateth with them
I tell you, *this m.* went down   *Lu 18:14*
justified rather
we will not have *this m.* to   *Lu 19:14*
reign over us
and said, *This m.* was also   *Lu 22:56*
with him
I find no fault in *this m.*   *Lu 23:4*
away with *this m.*   *Lu 23:18*
but *this m.* hath done nothing   *Lu 23:41*
amiss
this m. went to Pilate and   *Lu 23:52*
begged the body
how can *this m.* give us his   *Joh 6:52*
flesh to eat
how knoweth *this m.* letters,   *Joh 7:15*
having never
howbeit, we know *this m.*   *Joh 7:27*
whence he is
answered, Never man spake   *Joh 7:46*
like *this m.*
Master, who did sin, *this m.* or   *Joh 9:2*
his parents
neither hath *this m.* sinned, nor   *Joh 9:3*
his parents

this m. is not of God he   *Joh 9:16*
keepeth not the sabbath
praise God, we know that   *Joh 9:24*
this m. is a sinner
if *this m.* were not of God he   *Joh 9:33*
could do nothing
all that John spake of *this m.*   *Joh 10:41*
were true
could not *this m.* which   *Joh 11:37*
opened the eyes of blind,
caused that *this m.* should not
what do we? for *this m.*   *Joh 11:47*
doeth many miracles
art not thou one of *this m.*   *Joh 18:17*
disciples
what accusation bring ye   *Joh 18:29*
against *this m.*
not *this m.* but Barabbas,   *Joh 18:40*
now a robber
if let *this m.* go, art not   *Joh 19:12*
Caesar's friend
Peter saith, and what shall   *Joh 21:21*
this m. do
how *this m.* purchased a field   *Ac 1:18*
with reward
as though we had made this   *Ac 3:12;*
m. to walk   *3:16*
even by him doth *this m.* stand   *Ac 4:10*
and intend to bring *this m.*   *Joh 5:28*
blood upon us
after *this m.* rose up Judas of   *Ac 5:37*
Galilee
this m. ceaseth not to speak   *Ac 6:13*
blasphemous
saying, *This m.* is the great   *Ac 8:10*
power of God
I heard of *this m.* how much   *Ac 9:13*
evil hath done
of *this m.* seed hath God   *Ac 13:23*
raised Jesus
thro' *this m.* is preached to   *Ac 13:38*
you forgiveness of sins
this m. was instructed in way   *Ac 18:25*
of the Lord
this is the *m.* that teacheth   *Ac 21:28*
all men against law
this m. is a Roman   *Ac 22:26*
find no fault in *this m.*   *Ac 23:9*
this m. was taken of the   *Ac 23:27*
Jews, and should
for we have found *this m.* a   *Ac 24:5*
pestilent fellow
accuse *this m.* if there be any   *Ac 25:5*
wickedness
ye see *this m.* about whom   *Ac 25:24*
Jews dealt with me
this m. doeth nothing worthy   *Ac 26:31*
of death
this m. might have been set at   *Ac 26:32*
liberty
no doubt *this m.* is a   *Ac 28:4*
murderer, vengeance
this m. was counted worthy of   *Heb 3:3*
more glory
now consider how great *this m.*   *Heb 7:4*
was, to whom
but *this m.* because he   *Heb 7:24*
continueth ever
that *this m.* have somewhat also   *Heb 8:3*
to offer
this m. after he had offered   *Heb 10:12*
one sacrifice
this m. shall be blessed in his   *Jas 1:25*
deed

WICKED MAN

if the *wicked m.* be worthy to   *De 25:2*
be beaten
the *wicked m.* travaileth with   *Job 15:20*
pain
the portion of a *wicked m.*   *Job 20:29;*
from God   *27:13*
set thou a *wicked m.* over him   *Ps 109:6*
a *wicked m.* walketh with   *Pr 6:12*
froward mouth
he that rebuketh a *wicked m.*   *Pr 9:7*
getteth a blot
when a *wicked m.* dieth, his   *Pr 11:7*
expectation
a *wicked m.* is loathsome, and   *Pr 13:5*
cometh
a *wicked m.* taketh a gift out   *Pr 17:23*
of the bosom
wicked m. hardeneth his face,   *Pr 21:29*
but the upright
lay not wait, O *wicked m.*   *Pr 24:15*
against dwelling

a *wicked m.* that prolongeth   *Ec 7:15*
his days
the same *wicked m.* shall die   *Eze 3:18*
in iniquity
and doth that which the   *Eze 18:24*
wicked m. doeth
when a *wicked m.* turneth   *Eze 18:27*
from his wickedness
O *wicked m.* thou shalt surely   *Eze 33:8*
die, that *wicked m.* shall die

WISE MAN

look out a *m.* discreet and   *Ge 41:33*
wise, set him
Solomon was *wise m.* and knew   *1Ki 2:9*
what to do
Jonathan David's uncle, was   *1Ch 27:32*
a *wise m.*
should a *wise m.* utter vain   *Job 15:2*
knowledge
I cannot find one *wise m.*   *Job 17:10*
among you
and let a *wise m.* hearken to   *Job 34:34*
a *wise m.* will hear and increase   *Pr 1:5*
rebuke a *wise m.* and he will   *Pr 9:8*
love thee
give instruction to a *wise m.* he   *Pr 9:9*
will be wiser
a *wise m.* feareth, and   *Pr 14:16*
departeth from evil
a *wise m.* will pacify the wrath   *Pr 16:14*
of a king
a reproof entereth more into a   *Pr 17:10*
wise m.
a *wise m.* scaleth the city of   *Pr 21:22*
the mighty
seest thou a *m.* wise in his   *Pr 26:12*
own conceit
if a *wise m.* contendeth with a   *Pr 29:9*
foolish man
but a *wise m.* keepeth it in till   *Pr 29:11*
afterwards
and how dieth the *wise m.*? as   *Ec 2:16*
the fool
whether he shall be *wise m.* or   *Ec 2:19*
a fool?
surely oppression maketh a *wise*   *Ec 7:7*
m. mad
who is as the *wise m.* and who   *Ec 8:1*
knoweth
though a *wise m.* think to   *Ec 8:17*
know it, yet not able
now there was found in it a   *Ec 9:15*
poor *wise m.*
who is the *wise m.* that may   *Jer 9:12*
understand
let not the *wise m.* glory in his   *Jer 9:23*
wisdom
I will liken him to a *wise m.*   *M't 7:24*
who built
that there is not a *wise m.*   *1Co 6:5*
amongst you
who is a *wise m.* endued with   *Jas 3:13*
knowledge

YOUNG MAN

I have slain a *young m.* to my   *Ge 4:23*
hurt
Abraham gave it to a *young m.*   *Ge 18:7*
to dress it
the *young m.* deferred not to   *Ge 34:19*
do the thing
there was with us a *young m.*   *Ge 41:12*
an Hebrew
Joshua a *young m.* departed   *Ex 33:11*
not out
and there ran *young m.* and   *Nu 11:27*
told Moses
destroy both the *young m.*   *De 32:25*
and virgin
caught a *young m.* of the men   *J'g 8:14*
of Succoth
Abimelech called hastily to the   *J'g 9:54*
young m. and his *young m.*
thrust him through and he died
there was a *young m.* of   *J'g 17:7*
Bethlehem-Judah
the *young m.* became his   *J'g 17:12*
priest, and was in
knew the voice of the *young m.*   *J'g 18:3*
the Levite
Saul was a choice *young m.* and   *1Sa 9:2*
goodly
Jonathan said to the *young m.*   *1Sa 14:1*
that bare

and Saul said, Whose son art thou, *young m.*   *1Sa 17:58*

but if I say thus to the *young m.* Behold   *1Sa 20:22*

he said to David, I am *young m.* of Egypt   *1Sa 30:13*

David said to the *young m.* that told   *2Sa 1:5; 1:13*

go bring the *young m.* Absalom again   *2Sa 14:21*

deal gently for my sake with the *young m.*   *2Sa 18:5*

king said, Is the *young m.* Absalom safe   *2Sa 18:29; 18:32*

the enemies of my lord be as that *young m.* is   *2Sa 18:32*

Solomon seeing *young m.* industrious   *1Ki 11:28*

Lord opened the eyes of the *young m.*   *2Ki 6:17*

so the *young m.* even *young m.* went to Ramoth   *2Ki 9:4*

and Zadok, *young m.* mighty in valour   *1Ch 12:28*

and had no compassion on *young m.*   *2Ch 36:17*

wherewith shall *young m.* cleanse his way   *Ps 119:9*

to *young m.* knowledge and discretion   *Pr 1:4*

I discerned a *young m.* void of understanding   *Pr 7:7*

rejoice, O *young m.* in thy youth   *Ec 11:9*

for as *young m.* marrieth a virgin   *Isa 62:5*

break in pieces the *young m.* and maid   *Jer 51:22*

said to me, Run, speak to this *young m.*   *Zec 2:4*

the *young m.* said, All these have I kept   *M't 19:20*

there followed him a certain *young m.*   *M'k 14:51*

they saw a *young m.* sitting on the right side   *M'k 16:5*

he said, *Young m.* I say to thee, arise   *Lu 7:14*

sat in a window a *young m.* named Eutychus   *Ac 20:9*

and they brought the *young m.* alive   *Ac 20:12*

bring this *young m.* to the chief captain   *Ac 23:17; 23:18*

the chief captain then let the *young m.* depart   *Ac 23:22*

MANSLAYER

six cities ye shall appoint for *m.*   *Nu 35:6*

that the *m.* die not, till he stand before   *Nu 35:12*

MANSLAYERS

that the law was made for *m.*   *1Ti 1:9*

MANAEN

Lucius of Cyrene, and *M.*   *Ac 13:1*

MANAGER

the dishonest *m.* (A)(B)   *Lu 16:8*

MANAHATH

Alvan, and *M.*   *Ge 36:23; 1Ch 1:40*

they removed them to *M.*   *1Ch 8:6*

MANAHETHITES

half of the *M.*   *1Ch 2:52; 2:54*

MANASSEH

Joseph called the firstborn *M.*   *Ge 41:51*

thy two sons *M.* and Ephraim are mine   *Ge 48:5*

God make thee as Ephraim and *M.* and he set Ephraim before *M.*   *Ge 48:20*

of *M.* Gamaliel was prince   *Nu 1:10*

Gamaliel prince of *M.* offered on eighth day   *Nu 7:54*

these are the families of *M.*   *Nu 26:34; 27:1*

they were married into the family of *M.*   *Nu 36:12*

they are the thousands of *M.*   *De 33:17*

of Joseph were two tribes, *M.* Ephraim   *Jos 14:4*

these were the male children of *M.*   *Jos 17:2*

Zelophehad son of *M.* had no sons but daughters   *Jos 17:3*

there fell ten portions to *M.* beside Gilead   *Jos 17:5*

the daughters of *M.* had an inheritance   *Jos 17:6*

M. had in Issachar, Beth-shean and Ibleam   *Jos 17:11*

children of *M.* could not drive out inhabitants   *Jos 17:12*

behold my family is poor in *M.*   *J'g 6:15*

Jonathan son of Gershom, son of *M.* priest   *J'g 18:30*

M. his son reigned   *2Ki 20:21; 2Ch 32:33*

and *M.* seduced them to do more evil   *2Ki 21:9*

M. shed innocent blood, till he filled Jerusalem   *2Ki 21:16*

the altars *M.* made did Josiah beat down   *2Ki 23:12*

provocations that *M.* had provoked him withal   *2Ki 23:26*

for the sins of *M.* this came upon Judah   *2Ki 24:3*

in Jerusalem dwelt of the children of *M.*   *1Ch 9:3*

and there fell some of *M.* to David   *1Ch 12:19*

the strangers out of *M.* fell to Asa   *2Ch 15:9*

Hezekiah wrote letters to Ephraim and *M.*   *2Ch 30:1*

yet divers of *M.* humbled themselves   *2Ch 30:11*

all Israel cut down the groves in *M.*   *2Ch 31:1*

M. made Judah and Jerusalem to err   *2Ch 33:9*

the Lord spake to *M.* he would not hearken   *2Ch 33:10*

the captains took *M.* among the thorns   *2Ch 33:11*

than *M.* knew that the Lord he was God   *2Ch 33:13*

Amon humbled not himself, as *M.* had done   *2Ch 33:23*

so did Josiah in the cities of *M.* and Ephraim   *2Ch 34:6*

M. had taken strange wives   *Ezr 10:30; 10:33*

Gilead is mine, *M.* is mine   *Ps 60:7; 108:8*

before *M.* stir up thy strength, and save us   *Ps 80:2*

M. shall eat Ephraim, Ephraim *M.*   *Isa 9:21*

cause them to be removed, because of *M.*   *Jer 15:4*

to the west side a portion for *M.*   *Eze 48:4*

Ezekias begat *M.* and *M.* begat Amon   *M't 1:10*

MANASSEH'S

left hand upon *M.* head   *Ge 48:14; 48:17*

rest of *M.* sons had the   *Jos 17:6*

northward it was *M.*   *Jos 17:10*

MANASSES

begat *M.*, *M.* begat Amon   *M't 1:10*

the tribe of *M.*   *Re 7:6*

MANASSITES

Golan in Bashan, of the *M.*   *De 4:43*

and among the *M.*   *J'g 12:4*

Reubenites, and the *M.*   *2Ki 10:33*

MANDRAKES

found *m.* in the field, and brought   *Ge 30:14; 30:15-16*

found May-apples (B)   *Ge 30:14; 30:15-16*

The *m.* give a smell, and our gates   *Ca 7:13*

MANEH

fifteen shekels, shall be your *m.*   *Eze 45:12*

your mina shall be fifty shekels (B)(R)   *Eze 45:12*

MANGER

remain beside the *m.* (A)   *Job 39:9*

clothes, and laid him in a *m.*   *Lu 2:7*

in swaddling clothes, lying in a *m.*   *Lu 2:12*

and the babe lying in the *m.*   *Lu 2:16*

carry to the table *m.* (A)(B)   *Joh 2:8*

MANHOOD

to full *m.* (N)(R)   *Ga 3:3*

MANIFEST

let work be *m.* (R)   *Ps 90:16*

that God might *m.* them, and   *Ec 3:18*

causes them to see themselves (A)(B)(E)   *Ec 3:18*

show them that they are beasts (R)   *Ec 3:18*

I will *m.* my holiness (A)(R)   *Eze 20:41*

nothing hid except be *m.* (R)   *M'k 4:22*

secret, that shall not be made *m.*   *Lu 8:17*

he should be made *m.* to Israel   *Joh 1:31*

that his deeds may be made *m.*   *Joh 3:21*

works of God should be made *m.*   *Joh 9:3*

him, and will *m.* myself to him   *Joh 14:21*

show myself to him (A)(B)   *Joh 14:21*

disclose myself to him (N)   *Joh 14:21*

make myself known to him (P)   *Joh 14:21*

that thou wilt *m.* thyself unto   *Joh 14:22*

reveal yourself-make yourself real (A)   *Joh 14:22*

show yourself to us (B)   *Joh 14:22*

disclose yourself to us (N)   *Joh 14:22*

make yourself known to us (P)   *Joh 14:22*

great and *m.* day (R)   *Ac 2:20*

is *m.* to all them that dwell in   *Ac 4:16*

plain to all residents (A)   *Ac 4:16*

is obvious to all Jerusalem (B)   *Ac 4:16*

common knowledge to all Jerusalem (N)   *Ac 4:16*

evident to everyone living in (P)   *Ac 4:16*

be known of God is *m.* in them   *Ro 1:19*

is evident in them (A)(B)   *Ro 1:19*

God himself has disclosed it to them (N)   *Ro 1:19*

has made it plain to them (P)   *Ro 1:19*

God has shown it to them (R)   *Ro 1:19*

I was made *m.* unto them that   *Ro 10:20*

But now is made *m.* and by   *Ro 16:26*

man's work shall be made *m.*   *1Co 3:13*

make *m.* the counsels of the hearts   *1Co 4:5*

disclose and expose aims of hearts (A)   *1Co 4:5*

shall reveal the inner motives (B)   *1Co 4:5*

bring to light disclose inward motives (N)   *1Co 4:5*

expose the secret motives (P)   *1Co 4:5*

disclose purposes of the heart (R)   *1Co 4:5*

may be made *m.* among you   *1Co 11:19*

the secrets of his heart made *m.*   *1Co 14:25*

him, it is *m.* that he is excepted   *1Co 15:27*

evident that he is excepted (A)(E)   *1Co 15:27*

it is clear that the One is excepted (B)   *1Co 15:27*

it clearly means to exclude God (N)   *1Co 15:27*

quite obvious that God is 1Co 15:27
excepted (P)
it is plain that he is excepted 1Co 15:27
(R)
and maketh *m*. the savour 2Co 2:14
of his
makes evident the fragrance 2Co 2:14
of (A)
who evidences through us (B) 2Co 2:14
uses us to reveal and spread 2Co 2:14
abroad (N)
through us spreads the 2Co 2:14
fragrance (R)
of Jesus, be made *m*. in our 2Co 4:10
body
of Jesus might be made *m*. in 2Co 4:11
be *m*. before the judgment 2Co 5:10
(E)
but we are made *m*. unto 2Co 5:11
God; and
I trust also are made *m*. in 2Co 5:11
we have been thoroughly 2Co 11:6
made *m*.
Now the works of the flesh are Ga 5:19
m.
doings of flesh are Ga 5:19
clear-obvious (A)
works of flesh are in evidence Ga 5:19
(B)
Anyone can see the kind of Ga 5:19
behaviour (N)
activities of lower nature is Ga 5:19
obvious (P)
works of the flesh are plain Ga 5:19
(R)
reproved are made *m*. by Eph 5:13
the light
whatsoever doth make *m*. is Eph 5:13
light
my bonds in Christ are *m*. in Ph'p 1:13
but now is made *m*. to his Col 1:26
saints
I may make it *m*. as I ought to Col 4:4
proclaim it fully and make it Col 4:4
clear (A)
that I may make this clearly Col 4:4
known (B)(R)
that I may make the secret Col 4:4
plain (N)
a *m*. token of the righteous 2Th 1:5
judgment
God was *m*. in the flesh, 1Ti 3:16
justified
made visible in human flesh 1Ti 3:16
(A)
was revealed in the flesh (B) 1Ti 3:16
progress *m*. to (E)(R) 1Ti 4:15
the good works of some are *m*. 1Ti 5:25
is now made *m*. by the 2Ti 1:10
appearing
folly shall be *m*. unto all men as 2Ti 3:9
creature that is not *m*. in his Heb 4:13
sight
holiest of all was not yet made Heb 9:8
m.
was *m*. in these last times for 1Pe 1:20
they might be made *m*. that 1Jo 2:19
these not of us
In this the children of God are 1Jo 3:10
m.
children of God are 1Jo 3:10
distinguished (B)
distinction between the 1Jo 3:10
children (N)
By this may be seen who are 1Jo 3:10
the (R)
nakedness not be *m*. (E) 1Jo 3:18
for thy judgments are made *m*. Re 15:4

MANIFESTATION

for the *m*. of the sons of God Ro 8:19
revealing of the sons of God Ro 8:19
(A)(B)(E)(R)
God's sons to be revealed (N) Ro 8:19
But the *m*. of the Spirit is 1Co 12:7
given to
to each is granted evidence 1Co 12:7
of the (B)
to each the Spirit is 1Co 12:7
manifested (N)
by *m*. of the truth commending 2Co 4:2

MANIFESTED

nothing hid, which shall not M'k 4:22
be *m*.

nothing hidden except to be M'k 4:22
revealed (A)
nothing hidden except to be M'k 4:22
shown (B)
nothing put under cover M'k 4:22
unless it is to come out
into the open (N)
nothing hidden which is not M'k 4:22
meant to be made perfectly
plain (P)
nothing hid, except to be M'k 4:22
made manifest (R)
of Galilee, and *m*. forth his Joh 2:11
glory
displayed his greatness and Joh 2:11
power (A)
thereby displaying his Joh 2:11
greatness (B)
Jesus revealed his glory (N) Joh 2:11
he demonstrated his power Joh 2:11
(P)
I have *m*. thy name unto the Joh 17:6
men
made thy name known Joh 17:6
(B)(N)
of God without the law is *m*. Ro 3:21
God's righteousness been Ro 3:21
revealed (A)(B)
God's justice brought to light Ro 3:21
(N)
God's righteousness been Ro 3:21
declared (P)
to each the spirit is *m*. (N) 1Co 12:7
Christ be *m*. (E)(N) Col 3:4
But hath in due times *m*. his Tit 1:3
word
when chief Shepherd is *m*. 1Pe 5:4
(E)(R)
the life was *m*. and we have 1Jo 1:2
seen
the life was revealed (A)(B) 1Jo 1:2
the life was made visible (N) 1Jo 1:2
the Father, and was *m*. unto us 1Jo 1:2
that he was *m*. to take away our 1Jo 3:5
came in visible form to take 1Jo 3:5
away sin (A)(B)
Christ appeared to do away 1Jo 3:5
with sin (N)(R)
became man for purpose of 1Jo 3:5
removing sin (P)
purpose the Son of God was *m*. 1Jo 3:8
Son of God appeared to break 1Jo 3:8
up works (B)(N)
Son of God came to earth with 1Jo 3:8
express purpose of liquidating
devil's activities (P)
Son of God appeared to 1Jo 3:8
destroy works of (R)
In this was *m*. the love of 1Jo 4:9
God
love of God was revealed (B) 1Jo 4:9
his love was disclosed in this 1Jo 4:9
(N)

MANIFESTLY

m. declared to be the epistle of 2Co 3:3

MANIFOLD

thou in thy *m*. mercies Ne 9:19
forsookest
according to the *m*. mercies Ne 9:27
O Lord, how *m*. are thy Ps 104:24
works! in
how many and varied are thy Ps 104:24
works (A)
how innumerable are thy Ps 104:24
works (B)
I know your *m*. transgressions Am 5:12
Who shall not receive *m*. Lu 18:30
more in
return many times more in Lu 18:30
world (A)(B)(R)
the church the *m*. wisdom of Eph 3:10
God
many-sided wisdom of God Eph 3:10
(A)(B)
wisdom of God in all its Eph 3:10
varied forms (N)
the complex wisdom of God's Eph 3:10
plan (P)
through *m*. temptations 1Pe 1:6
distressed by various trials (B) 1Pe 1:6
under trials of many kinds (N) 1Pe 1:6

all kinds of trials and 1Pe 1:6
temptations (P)
suffer various trials (R) 1Pe 1:6
stewards of the *m*. grace of 1Pe 4:10
God
God's many sided grace (A) 1Pe 4:10
God's richly varied grace (B) 1Pe 4:10
grace of God in its varied 1Pe 4:10
forms (N)
varied grace of God (P)(R) 1Pe 4:10

MANKIND

Thou shalt not lie with *m*. as Le 18:22
If a man also lie with *m*. as he Le 20:13
thing, and the breath of all *m*. Job 12:1
nor abusers of themselves with 1Co 6:9
m.
them that defile themselves 1Ti 1:10
with *m*.
and hath been tamed of *m*. Jas 3:7

MANLY

lost their *m*. vigor (B)(R) Job 30:2

MANNA

it, said one to another, It is Ex 16:15
m.
Israel called the name thereof Ex 16:31
M.
and put an omer full of *m*. Ex 16:33
therein
children of Israel did eat *m*. Ex 16:35
forty
they did eat *m*. until they Ex 16:35
came
is nothing at all, besides this *m*. Nu 11:6
And the *m*. was as coriander Nu 11:7
seed
in the night, the *m*. fell upon it Nu 11:9
and fed thee with *m*. which thou De 8:3
fed thee in the wilderness with De 8:16
m.
And the *m*. ceased on the Jos 5:12
morrow
the children of Israel *m*. any Jos 5:12
more
withheldest not thy *m*. from Ne 9:20
their
rained down *m*. upon them to Ps 78:24
Our fathers did eat *m*. in the Joh 6:31
Your fathers did eat *m*. in the Joh 6:49
not as your fathers did eat *m*. Joh 6:58
was the golden pot that had *m*. Heb 9:4
will I give to eat of the hidden Re 2:17
m.

MANNER

two *m*. of people shall be Ge 25:23
separated
m. of women upon me (E) Ge 31:35
was of all *m*. of bake-meats Ge 40:17
for Pharaoh
made their lives bitter in all *m*. Ex 1:14
of service
no *m*. of work shall be done in Ex 12:16
all *m*. of trespass, any *m*. of lost Ex 22:9
thing
in wisdom, and in all *m*. of Ex 31:3;
workmanship 31:5; 35:31, 33, 35; 36:1;
1Ch 28:21
burnt offering according to *m*. Le 5:12;
Nu 9:14
shall eat no *m*. of fat of ox or Le 7:23
sheep
ye shall eat no *m*. of blood Le 7:26;
7:27; 17:10, 14
the law for all *m*. of the Le 14:54
plague of leprosy
ye shall do no *m*. of work, it Le 23:31
shall be a statute
ye shall have one *m*. of law Le 24:22;
Nu 15:16
neither she be taken with the Nu 5:13
m.
and his drink offering Nu 15:24
according to the *m*.
ye shall do no *m*. of servile Nu 28:18
work
for ye saw no *m*. of similitude De 4:15
in Horeb
and this is the *m*. of the release De 15:2

cursed be he that lieth with | *De 27:21*
any *m.* of beast
what *m.* of men were they ye | *J'g 8:18*
slew at Tabor
now this was the *m.* in former | *Ru 4:7*
time
and shew them the *m.* of the | *1Sa 8:9;*
king | *8:11*
Samuel told the people the | *1Sa 10:25*
m. of the kingdom
and the bread is in *m.* | *1Sa 21:5*
common
and so will be his *m.* all the | *1Sa 27:11*
while
is this the *m.* of man, O Lord | *2Sa 7:19*
God
what *m.* of man was he who told | *2Ki 1:7*
you
the king stood by a pillar, as | *2Ki 11:14*
the *m.* was
know not the *m.* of God | *2Ki 17:26*
of the land
let him teach them the *m.* of | *2Ki 17:27*
God of the land
for all *m.* of measure and | *1Ch 23:29*
size
for so was the king's *m.* toward | *Es 1:13*
m. of life (S) | *Ps 37:14;*
Ga 1:13; Eph 2:3; 4:22; Heb 13:5, 7;
1Pe 1:18; 3:16; 2Pe 2:7
their soul abhorreth all *m.* of | *Ps 107:18*
meat
garners be full, affording all | *Ps 144:13*
m. of store
at our gates are all *m.* of | *Ca 7:13*
pleasant fruits
then the lambs shall feed after | *Isa 5:17*
their *m.*
this hath been thy *m.* from thy | *Jer 22:21*
youth
and no *m.* of hurt was found | *Da 6:23*
on him
and the *m.* of Beer-sheba | *Am 8:14*
liveth
and healing all *m.* of sickness | *M't 4:23;*
| *10:1*
shall say all *m.* of evil against | *M't 5:11*
you falsely
what *m.* of man is this, that | *M't 8:27;*
winds and sea obey him | *M'k 4:41;*
| *Lu 8:25*
all *m.* of sin shall be forgiven | *M't 12:31*
to men
see what *m.* of stones are here | *M'k 13:1*
what *m.* of salutation this | *Lu 1:29*
should be
saying, What *m.* of child shall | *Lu 1:66*
this be
having known what *m.* of | *Lu 7:39*
woman this is
ye know not what *m.* of spirit | *Lu 9:55*
ye are of
ye tithe the mint, rue, and all *m.* | *Lu 11:42*
of herbs
what *m.* of communications | *Lu 24:17*
are these
in the same *m.* (S) | *Joh 5:19*
what *m.* of saying is this that | *Joh 7:36*
he said
as the *m.* of the Jews is to | *Joh 19:40*
bury
in this *m.* (S) | *Joh 21:1*
Paul, as his *m.* was, went in to | *Ac 17:2*
them
ye come after what *m.* I have | *Ac 20:18*
been with
taught according to the perfect | *Ac 22:3*
m. of the law
it is not *m.* of Romans to | *Ac 25:16*
deliver any to die
my *m.* of life from my youth, | *Ac 26:4*
know Jews
wrought in me all *m.* of | *Ro 7:8*
concupiscence
ye were made sorry after a | *2Co 7:9*
godly *m.*
former *m.* of life (A)(E)(N) | *Ga 1:13*
former *m.* of life (E)(R) | *Eph 4:13*
your *m.* of life (A)(E)(R) | *Ph'p 1:27*
as ye know what *m.* of men we | *1Th 1:5*
what *m.* of entering in we had | *1Th 1:9*
unto you
but thou hast known my *m.* of | *2Ti 3:10*
life
assembling, as the *m.* of | *Heb 10:25*
some is
consider their *m.* of living | *Heb 13:7*
(A)
forgetteth what *m.* of man he | *Jas 1:24*

what *m.* of time the Spirit of | *1Pe 1:11*
Christ
so be ye holy in all *m.* of | *1Pe 1:15*
conversation
vain *m.* of life (E) | *1Pe 1:18*
revile your good *m.* of life (E) | *1Pe 3:16*
what *m.* of persons ought ye | *2Pe 3:11*
to be
behold what *m.* of love the | *1Jo 3:1*
Father
he must in this *m.* be killed | *Re 11:5*
tree of life, which bare twelve | *Re 22:2*
m. of fruits

AFTER THE MANNER

to be with Sarah *after the m.* | *Ge 18:11*
of women
to come in to us *after the m.* | *Ge 19:31*
of all the earth
after the former *m.* when | *Ge 40:13*
thou wast his butler
deal with her *after the m.* of | *Ex 21:9*
daughters
according to the number, | *Nu 29:18*
after the m.
compassed the city *after the* | *Jos 6:15*
same *m.*
careless, *after the m.* of the | *J'g 18:7*
Zidonians
he turned and spake *after* | *1Sa 17:30*
the same *m.*
after the m. of the nations | *2Ki 17:33;*
| *2Ch 13:9*
and I answered them *after the* | *Ne 6:4*
same *m.*
after the m. of Egypt | *Isa 10:24;*
| *10:26; Am 4:10*
polluted *after the m.* of your | *Eze 20:30*
fathers
after the m. of the | *Eze 23:15*
Babylonians of Chaldea
after the m. of adulteresses, | *Eze 23:45*
and *after the m.* of women
after the m. of the purifying of | *Joh 2:6*
the Jews
ye be circumcised *after the m.* | *Ac 15:1*
of Moses
I speak *after the m.* of men | *Ro 6:19;*
| *1Co 15:32; Ga 3:15*
after the same *m.* also he | *1Co 11:25*
took the cup
being a Jew, livest *after the m.* | *Ga 2:14*
of the Gentiles

AFTER THIS MANNER

that be far from thee to do | *Ge 18:25*
after this m.
saying, *After this m.* did thy | *Ge 39:19*
servant to me
to his father he sent *after this* | *Ge 45:23*
m. ten asses
after this m. ye shall offer | *Nu 28:24*
daily
Ahithophel hath spoken *after* | *2Sa 17:6*
this m.
after this m. will I mar the | *Jer 13:9*
pride of Judah
after this m. therefore pray ye, | *M't 6:9*
Our Father
one *after this m.* and another | *1Co 7:7*
after that
after this m. in old time, | *1Pe 3:5*
women trusted

ON THIS MANNER

saying, *On this m.* shall ye | *Ge 32:19*
speak to Esau
told Saul, saying, *On this m.* | *1Sa 18:24*
spake David
on this m. did Absalom to all | *2Sa 15:6*
Israel
one said *on this m.* | *1Ki 2:20; 2Ch 18:19*
let not Hezekiah persuade | *2Ch 32:15*
you *on this m.*

MANNERS

shall not walk in the *m.* of the | *Le 20:23*
nations
they do after the former *m.* | *2Ki 17:34*
have done after the *m.* of the | *Eze 11:12*
heathen
forty years suffered he their | *Ac 13:18*
m.
evil communications corrupt | *1Co 15:33*
good *m.*
God in divers *m.* spake in | *Heb 1:1*
time past

MANOAH

the Danites, whose name was | *J'g 13:2;*
M. *13:8, 9, 11-13, 15-17, 19-22*
the burying place of *M.* his | *J'g 16:31*
father

MAN'S

the ground any more for *m.* | *Ge 8:21*
sake
I will not curse the ground for | *Ge 8:21*
m. sake
the imagination of *m.* heart is | *Ge 8:21*
evil
at the hand of every *m.* | *Ge 9:5*
brother will
Whoso sheddeth *m.* blood, by | *Ge 9:6*
man
hast taken; for she is a *m.* wife | *Ge 20:3*
We are all one *m.* sons; we are | *Ge 42:11*
true
to restore every *m.* money | *Ge 42:25*
into his
every *m.* bundle of money was | *Ge 42:35*
in his
every *m.* money was in the | *Ge 43:21*
mouth of
every *m.* money in his sack's | *Ge 44:1*
mouth
we may not see the *m.* face, | *Ge 44:26*
except
him, Who hath made *m.* mouth | *Ex 4:11*
But every *m.* servant that is | *Ex 12:44*
bought
if one *m.* ox hurt another's, | *Ex 21:35*
that he
and shall feed in another *m.* | *Ex 22:5*
field
and it be stolen out of the *m.* | *Ex 22:7*
house
Upon *m.* flesh shall it not be | *Ex 30:32*
that offereth any *m.* burnt | *Le 7:8*
offering
if any *m.* seed of copulation | *Le 15:16*
go out
adultery with another *m.* wife | *Le 20:10*
every *m.* hallowed things shall | *Nu 5:10*
be
If any *m.* wife go aside, and | *Nu 5:12*
commit
write every *m.* name upon | *Nu 17:2*
his rod
the *m.* rod, whom I shall choose | *Nu 17:5*
every *m.* inheritance shall be | *Nu 33:54*
in the
(for the tree of the field is *m.* | *De 20:19*
life
she may go and be another *m.* | *De 24:2*
wife
for he taketh a *m.* life to | *De 24:6*
pledge
he put a trumpet in every *m.* | *J'g 7:16*
hand
every *m.* sword against his | *J'g 7:22*
fellow
down at the door of the *m.* | *J'g 19:26*
house
The *m.* name with whom I | *Ru 2:19*
wrought
thou taken ought of any *m.* | *1Sa 12:4*
hand
every *m.* sword against his | *1Sa 14:20*
fellow
Let no *m.* heart fail because | *1Sa 17:32*
of him
took the poor *m.* lamb, and | *2Sa 12:4*
dressed
came to a *m.* house in | *2Sa 17:18*
Bahurim
which Amasa was a *m.* son, | *2Sa 17:25*
whose
cloud out of the sea, like a | *1Ki 18:44*
m. hand
money that cometh into any | *2Ki 12:4*
m. heart
which were on a *m.* left hand | *2Ki 23:8*
at the
great *m.* house burnt he with | *2Ki 25:9*
fire
do according to every *m.* | *Es 1:8*
pleasure
of man? are thy years as *m.* | *Job 10:5*
days
I pray you, accept any *m.* | *Job 32:21*
person
which strengtheneth *m.* heart | *Ps 104:15*
The rich *m.* wealth is his | *Pr 10:15*
strong city

recompence of a *m.* hands | *Pr 12:14*
shall be
ransom of a *m.* life are his | *Pr 13:8*
riches
When a *m.* ways please the | *Pr 16:7*
Lord, he
A *m.* heart deviseth his way | *Pr 16:9*
words of a *m.* mouth are as | *Pr 18:4*
deep
The rich *m.* wealth is his | *Pr 18:11*
strong city
A *m.* gift maketh room for | *Pr 18:16*
him, and
I have given cow's dung for | *Eze 4:15*
m. dung
a *m.* enemies of his own | *Mic 7:6*

MANSERVANT

thy son, nor thy daughter, thy | *Ex 20:10*
m.
thy neighbour's wife, nor his | *Ex 20:17*
m.
If the ox shall push a *m.* or a | *Ex 21:32*
son, nor thy daughter, nor thy | *De 5:14*
m.
that thy *m.* and thy maidservant | *De 5:14*
house, his field, or his *m.* or his | *De 5:21*
son, and thy daughter, and | *De 12:18*
thy *m.*
and thy daughter, and thy | *De 16:11;*
m. | *16:14*
If I did despise the cause of | *Job 31:13*
my *m.*
That every man should let his | *Jer 34:9*
m.
that every one should let his | *Jer 34:10*
m.

MANSERVANTS

Besides their *m.* and their | *Ne 7:67*

MANSERVANT'S

And if he smite out his *m.* | *Ex 2:27*
tooth

MANSIONS

my Father's house are many | *Joh 14:2*
m.

MANSLAYER

which ye shall appoint for the | *Nu 35:6*
m.
that the *m.* die not, until he | *Nu 35:12*
stand

MANSLAYERS

and murderers of mothers, for | *1Ti 1:9*
m.

MANTLE

like a hairy *m.* (R) | *Ge 25:25*
an attractive *m.* (A) | *Jos 7:21*
tent, she covered him with a *m.* | *J'g 4:18*
hold upon the skirt of his *m.* | *1Sa 15:27*
up; and he is covered with a | *1Sa 28:14*
m.
that he wrapped his face in | *1Ki 19:13*
his *m.*
by him, and cast his *m.* upon | *1Ki 19:19*
him
Elijah took his *m.* and wrapped | *2Ki 2:8*
it
He took up also the *m.* of | *2Ki 2:13*
Elijah that
took the *m.* of Elijah that fell | *2Ki 2:14*
from
I rent my garment and my *m.* | *Ezr 9:3*
rent my garment and my *m.* I | *Ezr 9:5*
Then Job arose, and rent his *m.* | *Job 1:20*
they rent every one his *m.*, and | *Job 2:12*
their own confusion, as with | *Ps 109:29*
a *m.*
stripped me of my *m.* | *Ca 5:7*
(B)(E)(R)
a *m.* of praise (B)(R) | *Isa 61:3*
m. of hair to deceive | *Zec 13:4*
(B)(E)(R)
a Babylonish *m.* (E)(R) | *Joh 7:21; 7:24*
turn back to get his *m.* | *M'k 13:16*
(A)(R)

sell *m.* and buy sword | *Lu 22:36*
(A)(R)
wrap *m.* around you (R) | *Ac 12:8*
as a *m.* (A)(B)(E)(P)(R) | *Heb 1:12*

MANTLES

suits of apparel, and the *m.* | *Isa 3:22*
their *m.* (B)(E)(R) | *Da 3:21; 3:27*

MANFACTURED

M. or invented (B) | *Ac 17:29*

MANUFACTURES

m. thoughts and plans (A) | *Pr 6:18*

MANUSCRIPTS

especially the *m.* (P) | *2Ti 4:13*

MANY

my covenant is with thee, thou | *Ge 17:4;*
shalt be a father of *m.* nations | *17:5;*
| *Ro 4:17-18*
he made him a coat of *m.* | *Ge 37:3;*
colours | *37:23, 32*
many (S) | *Ge 50:20;*
Nu 20:20; 21:6; Jos 11:4; 2Sa 13:34;
2Ch 30:13; Ps 35:18; Eze 17:15; 26:7;
M'k 5:21, 24; 6:34; Lu 7:11, 12; 8:4;
9:37; Joh 12:9, 12; Ac 5:37; 11:24, 26;
18:10; 19:26; Re 19:1
they gaze, and *m.* of them | *Ex 19:21*
perish
whatsoever hath *m.* feet (S) | *Le 11:42*
when the ark rested, Moses | *Nu 10:36*
said, Return, O Lord, to the
m. thousands
and see whether they be few | *Nu 13:18*
or *m.*
to *m.* thou shalt give more | *Nu 26:54*
inheritance
the possession be divided | *Nu 26:56*
between *m.* and few
from them that have *m.* cities, | *Nu 35:8*
shall give *m.*
hath cast out *m.* nations before | *De 7:1*
thou shalt lend to *m.* nations | *De 15:6;*
| *28:12*
and *m.* evils shall befall them | *De 31:17;*
| *28:21*
with horses and chariots very | *Jos 11:4*
m.
m. were overthrown and | *J'g 9:40*
wounded
the destroyer which slew *m.* | *J'g 16:24*
she that hath *m.* children is | *1Sa 2:5*
feeble
no restraint to the Lord to | *1Sa 14:6*
save by *m.* or few
Judah and Israel were *m.* as | *1Ki 4:20*
the sand
unweighed, because they were | *1Ki 7:47*
exceeding *m.*
and dress it first, for ye are | *1Ki 18:25*
m.
and her witchcrafts are so *m.* | *2Ki 9:22*
the sons of Rehabiah were | *1Ch 23:17*
very *m.*
for the Lord hath given me *m.* | *1Ch 28:5*
sons
Rehoboam desired *m.* wives | *2Ch 11:23*
nothing with thee to help | *2Ch 14:11*
with *m.* or few
there were *m.* in | *2Ch 30:17*
congregation not sanctified
m. of Ephraim, and | *2Ch 30:18*
Manasseh not cleansed
we are *m.* that have | *Ezr 10:13*
transgressed
we, our sons and our daughters | *Ne 5:2*
are *m.*
there were *m.* in Judah sworn | *Ne 6:18*
to Tobiah
he was faithful, and feared God | *Ne 7:2*
above *m.*
among *m.* nations was no | *Ne 13:26*
king like him
and *m.* lay in sackcloth and | *Es 4:3*
ashes
behold, thou hast instructed | *Job 4:3*
m.
yea, *m.* shall make suit unto | *Job 11:19*
thee
m. are they that rise up against | *Ps 3:1*
me
there be *m.* that say of my soul | *Ps 3:2;*
| *4:6*

consider mine enemies, they | *Ps 25:19;*
are *m.* | *56:2*
for I have heard the slander | *Ps 31:13*
of *m.*
m. sorrows shall be to the | *Ps 32:10*
wicked
m. are the afflictions of the | *Ps 34:19*
righteous
is better than the riches of *m.* | *Ps 37:16*
wicked
m. shall see it and fear, and | *Ps 40:3*
trust in the Lord
he delivered, for there were *m.* | *Ps 55:18*
with me
I am as a wonder to *m.* thou | *Ps 71:7*
art my refuge
m. are my persecutors and | *Ps 119:157*
enemies
and the years of thy life shall be | *Pr 4:10*
m.
for she hath cast down *m.* | *Pr 7:26*
wounded
the lips of the righteous feed | *Pr 10:21*
m.
but the rich hath *m.* friends | *Pr 14:20*
wealth maketh *m.* friends, but | *Pr 19:4*
the poor
for transgression *m.* are the | *Pr 28:2*
princes thereof
he that hideth his eyes, shall | *Pr 28:27*
have *m.* a course
the days of darkness shall be | *Ec 11:8*
m.
and trust in chariots because | *Isa 31:1*
they are *m.*
by his knowledge shall he | *Isa 53:11*
justify *m.*
he bare the sin of *m.* and | *Isa 53:12*
made intercession
and the slain of the Lord | *Isa 66:16*
shall be *m.*
because their transgressions are | *Jer 5:6*
m.
for our backslidings are *m.* we | *Jer 14:7*
sinned
pray for us, for we are left | *Jer 42:2*
but few of *m.*
he made *m.* to fall, one fell on | *Jer 46:16*
another
for my sighs are *m.* my heart is | *La 1:22*
faint
but we are *m.* the land is given | *Eze 33:24*
and by peace shall destroy *m.* | *Da 8:25*
there shall *m.* stand up | *Da 11:14*
against king
they that understand shall | *Da 11:33*
instruct *m.*
to destroy and utterly make | *Da 11:44*
away *m.*
m. that sleep in the dust shall | *Da 12:2*
awake
m. shall run to and fro, and | *Da 12:4*
knowledge be
Ephraim hath made *m.* altars | *Ho 8:11*
to sin
though they be quiet, and | *Na 1:12*
likewise *m.*
shall come inhabitants of *m.* | *Zec 8:20*
cities
but did turn *m.* away from | *Mal 2:6*
iniquity
and *m.* there be that go in | *M't 7:13*
thereat
m. will say to me in that day, | *M't 7:22*
Lord, Lord
m. shall come from the east | *M't 8:11*
and west
he did not *m.* mighty works | *M't 13:58*
there
m. that are first shall be last | *M't 19:30;*
| *M'k 10:31*
for *m.* be called but few | *M't 20:16;*
chosen | *22:14*
m. shall come in my name | *M't 24:5;*
and deceive *m.* | *M'k 13:6; Lu 21:8*
iniquity abound, love of *m.* | *M't 24:12*
wax cold
blood shed for *m.* | *M't 26:28*
they appear to *m.* | *M't 27:53*
name is Legion, for we are *m.* | *M'k 5:9;*
| *Lu 8:30*
m. shall he turn to the Lord | *Lu 1:16*
their God
this child for the fall and rising | *Lu 2:34*
of *m.* in Israel
m. widows | *Lu 4:25*
m. lepers were in Israel | *Lu 4:27*
and devils also came out of *m.* | *Lu 4:41*
crying out

her sins which are *m.* are   *Lu 7:47*
forgiven
certain man made   *Lu 14:16*
great supper, and bade *m.*
but what are they among so *m.* *Joh 6:9*
m. therefore of his disciples *Joh 6:60;*
        6:66
and *m.* resorted to him, and *Joh 10:41*
for all so *m.* the net was not *Joh 21:11*
broken
I have heard by *m.* of this man *Ac 9:13*
where *m.* were gathered   *Ac 12:12*
together
m. brought their books and *Ac 19:19*
burnt them
m. of the saints did I shut up *Ac 26:10*
in prison
if thro' offence of one *m.* be *Ro 5:15*
dead grace hath abounded to *m.*
m. made sinners, *m.* made *Ro 5:19*
righteous
so we, being *m.* are one body *Ro 12:5*
in Christ
she hath been a succourer of *m.* *Ro 16:2*
not *m.* wise, not *m.* mighty are *1Co 1:26*
called
yet have ye not *m.* fathers, for *1Co 4:15*
in Christ Jesus
as their be gods *m.* and lords *1Co 8:5*
m.
but with *m.* god was not well *1Co 10:5*
pleased
we being *m.* are one bread, *1Co 10:17*
and one body
but the profit of *m.* that they *1Co 10:33*
may be saved
for this cause *m.* are weak *1Co 11:30*
and *m.* sleep
the body is not one member, *1Co 12:14*
but *m.*
great door, and there are *m.* *1Co 16:9*
adversaries
that thanks may be given by *2Co 1:11*
m.
this punishment was inflicted *2Co 2:6*
of *m.*
by the *m.* (S)   *2Co 2:6*
we are not as *m.* which   *2Co 2:17*
corrupt the word
thro' thanksgiving of *m.*   *2Co 4:15*
redound to glory
as poor, yet making *m.* rich *2Co 6:10*
and your zeal hath provoked *2Co 9:2*
very *m.*
and profited above *m.* my *Ga 1:14*
equals
he saith not, and to seeds, as *Ga 3:16*
of *m.*
m. sided wisdom of God *Eph 3:10*
(A)(B)
m. waxing confident by my *Ph'p 1:14*
bonds
m. walk of whom I have told *Ph'p 3:18*
you often
in bringing *m.* sons to glory, *Heb 2:10*
to make
and they truly were *m.* priests *Heb 7:23*
Christ was once offered to *Heb 9:28*
bear sins of *m.*
sprang of one so *m.* as the *Heb 11:12*
stars of the sky
my brethren, be not *m.* masters *Jas 3:1*
God's *m.*-sided grace (A) *1Pe 4:10*
m. shall follow pernicious ways *2Pe 2:2*
even now are there *m.* *1Jo 2:18*
antichrists
m. false prophets are gone out *1Jo 4:1*
into

MANY PEOPLE

the *people* of the land now are *Ex 5:5*
m.
people great and *m.* and tall as *De 2:21*
Anakims
people are too *m.* for me *J'g 7:2*
yet *people* are too *m.* *J'g 7:4*
the Lord had smitten *m.* of *1Sa 6:19*
the *people*
and *m.* of the *people* are fallen *2Sa 1:4*
and dead
but the *people* are *m.* and *Ezr 10:13*
time of rain
m. people of land became Jews *Es 8:17*
for fear
m. people shall go and say, *Isa 2:3*
Come let us go
he shall judge and rebuke *m.* *Isa 2:4*
people

woe to the multitude of *m.* *Isa 17:12*
people which
not to *m. people* of a strange *Eze 3:6*
speech
shall wither without *m. people Eze 17:9*
to pluck it
I will also vex the hearts of *m. Eze 32:9*
people* when
I will make *m. people*   *Eze 32:10*
amazed at thee
thou, thy bands, and *m.*   *Eze 38:9;*
people with thee   *38:15*
he shall judge among *m. people Mic 4:3*
thou shalt beat in pieces *m.* *Mic 4:13*
people
remnant of Jacob shall be in *Mic 5:7*
midst of *m. people*
m. people shall come and seek *Zec 8:22*
the Lord
thou must prophesy before *m. Re 10:11*
people*

MANY THINGS

Job said, I have heard *m.* such *Job 16:2*
things
and *m.* such *things* are with *Job 23:14*
him
there be *m. things* that increase *Ec 6:11*
vanity
seeing *m. things*, but *Isa 42:20*
observest not
he spake *m. things* to them in *M't 13:3*
parables
suffer *m. things* of elders *M't 16:21;*
   M'k 8:31; 9:12; Lu 9:22; 17:25
make thee ruler over *m.* *M't 25:21;*
things   *25:23*
how *m. things* they witness *M'k 27:13;*
against thee   *M'k 15:4*
I have suffered *m. things* this *M't 27:19*
day in a dream
suffered *m. things* of many *M'k 5:26*
physicians
he did *m. things*, and heard *M'k 6:20*
him gladly
m. things there be, as washing *M'k 7:4;*
of cups   *7:8, 13*
chief priests accused him of *M'k 15:3*
m. things
thou art troubled about *m. Lu 10:41*
things*
to provoke him to speak of *m. Lu 11:53*
things*
I have *m. things* to say, and *Joh 8:26;*
judge   *16:12*
there are *m.* other *things* *Joh 21:25*
which Jesus did
that I ought to do *m. things* *Ac 26:9*
contrary to name of Jesus
we have proved diligent in *m. 2Co 8:22*
things*
have ye suffered so *m. things* in *Ga 3:4*
vain
in how *m. things* he ministered *2Ti 1:18*
to me
of whom we have *m. things* to *Heb 5:11*
say
for in *m. things* we offend all *Jas 3:2*
m. things to write to you *2Jo 12; 3Jo 13*

MANY A TIME

yea, *m. a time* turned he his *Ps 78:38*
anger away
m. a time have they *Ps 129:1;*
afflicted me   *129:2*

MANY TIMES

how *m. times* shall I adjure *1Ki 22:16*
thee
m. times didst deliver them *Ne 9:28;*
        Ps 106:43

MANY YEARS

if there be yet *m. years* behind *Le 25:51*
the house that was builded *m. Ezr 5:11*
years* ago
yet *m. years* didst thou forbear *Ne 9:30*
if a man beget children, and live *Ec 6:3*
m. years
if a man live *m. years*, and *Ec 11:8*
rejoice in them all
m. days and *years* shall ye be *Isa 32:10*
troubled
prophets, which prophesied *Eze 38:17*
m. years

weep, as I have done these so *Zec 7:3*
m. years
thou hast goods laid up for *m. Lu 12:19*
years*
he said, Lo, these *m. years* do *Lu 15:29*
I serve thee
thou hast been of *m. years* a *Ac 24:10*
judge
now after *m. years* I came to *Ac 34:17*
bring alms
a great desire *m. years* to *Ro 15:23*
come to you

AFTER MANY

speak in a cause to decline *Ex 23:2*
after *m.*

AS MANY AS

and *as m. as* were *Ex 35:22*
willing-hearted
as m. as had not known all the *J'g 3:1*
wars
as m. as came to the place *2Sa 2:23*
stood still
as m. as were of free heart *2Ch 29:31*
brought
as m. as ye find bid to the *M't 22:9*
marriage
gathered together *as m. as M't 22:10*
they found
as m. as touched him were *M'k 6:56*
made whole
will rise and give *as m. as* he *Lu 11:8*
needeth
but *as m. as* received him, to *Joh 1:12*
them gave he power
give eternal life to *as m. as Joh 17:2*
hast given him
even to *as m. as* the Lord shall *Ac 2:39*
call
as m. as have spoken have also *Ac 3:24*
foretold
fear came on *as m. as* heard *Ac 5:11*
these things
who was slain, and *as m. as Ac 5:36;*
obeyed him   *5:37*
were astonished, *as m. as Ac 10:45*
came with Peter
as m. as were ordained to life *Ac 13:48*
believed
as m. as have sinned without *Ro 2:12*
law, and *as m. as* have sinned
in the law
for *as m. as* are led by the *Ro 8:14*
Spirit of God
as m. as are of the works of *Ga 3:10*
the law
as m. as desire to make a fair *Ga 6:12*
shew in flesh
and *as m. as* walk according *Ga 6:16*
to this rule
as m. as be perfect be thus *Ph'p 3:15*
minded
and for *as m. as* have not seen *Col 2:1*
my face
as m. servants *as* are under the *1Ti 6:1*
yoke
but to *as m. as* have not this *Re 2:24*
doctrine
as m. as I love I rebuke and *Re 3:19*
chasten
as m. as would not worship *Re 13:15*
beast

MAOCH

the son of *M.*, king of Gath *1Sa 27:2*

MAON

M., Carmel, and Ziph, and *Jos 15:55*
Juttah
men were in the wilderness *1Sa 23:24*
of *M.*
and abode in the wilderness *1Sa 23:25*
of *M.*
after David in the wilderness *1Sa 23:25*
of *M.*
And there was a man in *M.*, *1Sa 25:2*
whose
And the son of Shammai was *1Ch 2:45*
M.
and *M.* was the father of *1Ch 2:45*
Beth-zur

MAONITES

and the *M.*, did oppress you *J'g 10:12*

MAR

thou *m.* the corners of thy   Le 19:27
beard
lest I *m.* mine own inheritance   Ru 4:6
of your mice that *m.* the land   1Sa 6:5
and *m.* every good piece of   2Ki 3:19
land
They *m.* my path, they set   Job 30:13
forward
will I *m.* the pride of Judah   Jer 13:9

MARA

Call me not Naomi, call me *M.* Ru 1:20

MARAH

when they came to *M.*   Ex 15:23
could not drink of the waters Ex 15:23
of *M.*
the name of it was called *M.* Ex 15:23
of Etham, and pitched in *M.*   Nu 33:8
they removed from *M.*, and   Nu 33:9

MARALAH

went up toward the sea, and Jos 19:11
M.

MARAN-ATHA

Christ, let him be Anathema 1Co 16:22
M.

MARBLE

and *m.* stones in abundance   1Ch 29:2
to silver rings and pillars of   Es 1:6
m.
and blue, and white, and black Es 1:6
m.
His legs are as pillars of *m.* set Ca 5:15
and of brass, and iron, and *m.* Re 18:12

MARCH

didst *m.* through the wilderness Ps 68:7
for they shall m. with an   Jer 46:22
army
they shall *m.* every one on his Joe 2:7
ways
shall *m.* through the breadth   Hab 1:6
Thou didst *m.* through the   Hab 3:12
land in

MARCHED

the Egyptians *m.* after them   Ex 14:10

MARCHEDST

thou *m.* out of the field of Edom J'g 5:4

MARCHING

sound of *m.* (S)   2Sa 5:24; 1Ch 14:15
m. at the words (A)   Lu 4:22;
       8:25; 11:14; 24:41
they *m.* (B)   Lu 8:25; 11:14; Re 17:6
they *m.* (S)   Lu 8:25; 9:43; 11:14
amazed and *m.* (E)   Ac 2:6

MARCUS

and *M.*, sister's son to   Col 4:10
Barnabas
M., Aristarchus, Demas,   Ph'm 24
Lucas
you; and so doth *M.* my son   1Pe 5:13

MARESHAH

And Keilah, and Achzib, and Jos 15:44
M
sons of *M.* the father of   1Ch 2:42
Hebron
and Laadah the father of *M.*   1Ch 4:21
And Gath, and *M.*, and Ziph   2Ch 11:8
chariots; and came unto *M.*   2Ch 14:9
in the valley of Zephathah at 2Ch 14:10
M.
Eliezer the son of Dodavah   2Ch 20:37
of *M.*
heir unto thee, O inhabitant   Mic 1:15
of *M.*

MARINERS

of Zidon, and Arvad were thy Eze 27:8
m.

---

the ships of the sea with their Eze 27:9
m.
thy *m.* and thy pilots, thy   Eze 27:27
calkers
the *m.* and all the pilots of   Eze 27:29
the sea
Then the *m.* were afraid, and Jon 1:5
cried

MARISHES

m. thereof shall not be healed Eze 47:11

MARK

the Lord set a *m.* upon Cain, Ge 4:15
lest
be a *m.* (R)   Ex 13:16; 2Th 3:17
ye shall *m.* out (S)   Nu 34:7; 34:8, 10
m. the place where he shall lie Ru 3:4
thereof, as though I shot at a 1Sa 20:20
m.
M. ye now when Amnon's   2Sa 13:28
heart
M. I pray you, and see how   1Ki 20:7
and *m.* and see what thou   1Ki 20:22
doest
thou set me as a *m.* against   Job 7:20
thee
pieces, and set me up for his   Job 16:12
m.
m. and afterwards we will   Job 18:2
speak
M. me, and be astonished, and Job 21:5
lay
M. well, O Job, hearken unto Job 33:31
thou *m.* when the hinds do   Job 39:1
calve
M. the perfect man, and   Ps 37:37
behold
M. ye well her bulwarks,   Ps 48:13
consider
they *m.* my steps, when they   Ps 56:6
wait
thou, Lord, shouldest *m.*   Ps 130:3
iniquities
and set me as a *m.* for the   La 3:12
arrow
m. upon the foreheads of the Eze 9:4
men
any man upon whom is the *m.* Eze 9:6
m. out, trace two ways   Eze 21:19
(A)(B)(R)(S)
Son of man, *m.* well, and   Eze 44:5
behold
m. well the entering in of the Eze 44:5
the *m.* of circumcision (A)(B) Ro 4:11
m. them which cause   Ro 16:17
divisions
press toward the *m.* for the Ph'p 3:14
prize
m. which walk so as ye   Ph'p 3:17
to receive a *m.* in their right Re 13:16
hand
save he that had the *m.* or the Re 13:17
and receive his *m.* in his   Re 14:9
forehead
receiveth the *m.* of his name Re 14:11
over his image, and over his *m.* Re 15:2
upon the men which had the   Re 16:2
m. of
had received the *m.* of the   Re 19:20
beast
had received his *m.* upon their Re 20:4

MARK a person

of John, whose surname was Ac 12:12
M.
John, whose surname was *M.* Ac 12:25;
                   15:37
and so Barnabas took *M.* and Ac 15:39
Take *M.*, and bring him with 2Ti 4:11
thee

MARKED

the Lord, and Eli *m.* her   1Sa 1:12
mouth
Hast thou *m.* the old way   Job 22:15
which
m. for themselves in the   Job 24:16
daytime
m. out the heavens   Isa 40:12
(A)(B)(R)
yet thine iniquity is *m.* before Jer 2:22
who hath *m.* his word,   Jer 23:18
and heard
when he *m.* how they chose out Lu 14:7
m. out, appointed (A)   Ro 11:2

---

m. with promised Holy Spirit Eph 1:13
(B)
m. for day of redemption   Eph 4:30
(B)(N)

MARKER

what *m.* is that (S)   2Ki 23:17

MARKEST

If I sin, then thou *m.* me   Job 10:14

MARKET

the *m.* city for the people (B) Eze 27:3
and vessels of brass in thy *m.* Eze 27:13
they traded in thy *m.* wheat   Eze 27:17
and calamus, were in thy *m.* Eze 27:19
Tarshish did sing of thee in   Eze 27:25
thy *m.*
the *m.* places (S)   M't 11:6;
           23:7; Lu 11:43; 20:46
And when they come from the M'k 7:4
come from the *m.* place (S)   M'k 7:4;
                 Ac 17:17
Father's house a *m.* (N)(P)   Joh 2:16
at Jerusalem by the sheep *m.* a Joh 5:2
pool
near the sheep gate   Joh 5:2
(A)(B)(E)(P)(R)
Now at the Sheep-Pool (N)   Joh 5:2
in the *m.* daily with them that Ac 17:17
met
sold in the meat *m.*   1Co 10:25
(A)(B)(N)(P)(R)(S)

MARKETH

in the stocks, he *m.* all my   Job 33:11
paths
m. it out with a line; he   Isa 44:13
fitteth it
m. it out with the compass   Isa 44:13

MARKETPLACE

saw others standing idle in the M't 20:3
m.
standing in the bazaar (B)   M't 20:3;
                 Lu 7:32
like unto children sitting in the Lu 7:32
m.
them into the *m.* unto the   Ac 16:19
rulers

MARKETPLACES

and love salutations in the *m.* M'k 12:38

MARKETS

like unto children sitting in   M't 11:16
greetings in the *m.* and to be M't 23:7
called
synagogues, and greetings in Lu 11:43
the *m.*
robes, and love greetings in   Lu 20:46
the *m.*

MARKS

dead, nor print any *m.* upon Le 19:28
you
my body the *m.* of the Lord   Ga 6:17
Jesus

MAROTH

inhabitant of *M.* waited   Mic 1:12
carefully

MARRED

his visage was so *m.* more   Isa 52:14
the girdle was *m.* it was   Jer 13:7
profitable
vessel that he made of clay was Jer 18:4
m.
out. and *m.* their vine branches Na 2:2
spilled, and the bottles will be M'k 2:22
m.

MARRIAGE

endowed with *m.* gift   Ge 30:20
(A)(E)(R)
in *m.* (S)   Ex 6:20;

6:23, 25; J'g 1:12, 13; 21:1, 7; 1Sa 18:17,
19, 27; 25:39, 40; 1Ki 2:17, 21; 11:19;
　2Ki 14:9; 1Ch 2:35; 2Ch 11:18; 25:18

her raiment, and her duty of m.	Ex 21:10
give m. present (R)	Ex 22:16
made a m. alliance (S)	2Ch 18:1
maidens were not given to m.	Ps 78:63
praised in a wedding song (A)	Ps 78:63
maidens were not serenaded (B)	Ps 78:63
maidens had no marriage song (E)(R)	Ps 78:63
bride her m. girdle (A)	Jer 2:32
mixed in m. (B)(R)	Da 2:43
king which made a m. for his son	M't 22:2
made a wedding banquet (A)(B)	M't 22:2
prepared a feast for son's wedding (N)	M't 22:2
arranged a wedding for his son (P)	M't 22:2
prepared a marriage feast (R)	M't 22:2
to the m. feast (E)(R)	M't 22:3
are ready: come unto the m.	M't 22:4
come to the wedding feast (A)(R)	M't 22:4
come to the wedding (B)(N)	M't 22:4
many as ye shall find, bid to the m.	M't 22:9
neither marry, nor are given in m.	M't 22:30
marrying and giving in m.	M't 24:38
ready went in with him to the m.	M't 25:10
went into the marriage feast (A)(E)(R)	M't 25:10
went into the banquet (B)	M't 25:10
went in with him to the wedding (N)	M't 25:10
went in with him to the festivities (P)	M't 25:10
neither marry, nor are given in m.	M'k 12:25; Lu 20:35
to the m. feast (A)(E)(R)	Lu 12:36; 14:8
they were given in m. until the world marry, and are given in m.	Lu 17:27 Lu 20:34
there was a m. in Cana of	Joh 2:1
there was a wedding (A)(B)(N)(P)	Joh 2:1; 2:2
called, and his disciples, to the m.	Joh 2:2
that giveth her in m. doeth well	1Co 7:38
giveth her not in m. doeth better	1Co 7:38
M. is honourable in all, and	Heb 13:4
for the m. of the Lamb is come	Re 19:7
the wedding banquet (B)	Re 19:7; 19:9
wedding day of the Lamb is come (N)(P)	Re 19:7
unto the m. supper of the Lamb	Re 19:9
wedding-supper of the Lamb (N)	Re 19:9
wedding-feast (R)	Re 19:9

MARRIAGES

make ye m. with us, and give	Ge 34:9
Neither shalt thou make m. with	De 7:3
shall make m. with them, and	Jos 23:12

MARRIED

in law, which m. his daughters	Ge 19:14
if he were m. then his wife	Ex 21:3
If the priest's daughter also be m.	Le 22:12
of the woman whom he had m.	Nu 12:1
he had m. an Ethiopian woman	Nu 12:1
And if they be m. to any of the sons	Nu 36:3
m. unto their father's brother's sons	Nu 36:11
were m. into the families of the sons	Nu 36:12
with a woman m. to an husband	De 22:22
hath taken a wife, and m. her	De 24:1
he m. when he was threescore	2Ch 13:21
mighty, and m. fourteen wives	2Ch 13:21
m. foreign women (S)	Ezr 10:2; 10:14, 17-18, 44
that had m. wives of Ashdod	Ne 13:23

odious woman when she is m.	Pr 30:23
than the children of the m. wife	Isa 54:1
in thee, and thy land shall be m.	Isa 62:4
the Lord; for I am m. unto you	Jer 3:14
m. the daughter of a strange god	Mal 2:11
the first, when he had m. a wife	M't 22:25
Philip's wife: for he had m.	M'k 6:17
husband, and be m. to another	M'k 10:12
another said, I have m. a wife	Lu 14:20
did eat, they drank, they m.	Lu 17:27
liveth, she be m. to another man	Ro 7:3
though she be m. to another man	Ro 7:3
that ye should be m. to another	Ro 7:4
unto the m. I command, yet not I	1Co 7:10
he that is m. careth for the things	1Co 7:33
she that is m. careth for the things	1Co 7:34
liberty to be m. to whom she will	1Co 7:39

MARRIETH

For as a young man m. a virgin	Isa 62:5
whoso m. her which is put away	M't 19:9
away his wife, and m. another	Lu 16:18
whosoever m. her that is put away	Lu 16:18

MARROW

his bones are moistened with m.	Job 21:24
my m. dried up (B)	Ps 32:4
satisfied as with m. and fatness	Ps 63:5
to thy navel and m. to thy bones	Pr 3:8
of fat things full of m. of wines	Isa 25:6
spirit, and of the joints and m.	Heb 4:12

MARRY

thy brother's wife, and m. her	Ge 38:8
them m. to whom they think best	Nu 36:6
tribe of their father shall they m.	Nu 36:6
not m. without unto a stranger	De 25:5
virgin, so shall thy sons m. thee	Isa 62:5
shall m. her that is divorced	M't 5:32
m. another, committeth adultery	M't 19:9
with his wife, it is not good to m.	M't 19:10
his brother shall m. his wife	M't 22:24
in the resurrection they neither m.	M't 22:30
put away his wife, and m. another	M'k 10:11
they neither m., nor are given	M'k 12:25
The children of this world m.	Lu 20:34
the dead, neither m. nor are given	Lu 20:35
they cannot contain, let them m.	1Co 7:9
for it is better to m. than to burn	1Co 7:9
if thou m. thou hast not sinned	1Co 7:28
if a virgin m. she hath not sinned	1Co 7:28
will, he sinneth not: let them m.	1Co 7:36
Forbidding to m. and commanding	1Ti 4:3
wanton against Christ, they will m.	1Ti 5:11
that the younger women m. bear	1Ti 5:14

MARRYING

refrain from m. (S)	Ru 1:13
our God in m. strange wives	Ne 13:27
m. and giving in marriage, until	M't 24:38

MARS'

Paul stood in the midst of M. hill | Ac 17:22

MARSENA

M., and Memucan, the seven | Es 1:14

MARSH

the m. hen (B)	Le 11:18
where there is no m. (A)(B)(R)	Job 8:11

MARSHAL

the m. (N) | Re 6:15

MART

and she is a m. of nations	Isa 23:3
became merchandise of the nations (A)	Isa 23:3
merchant trader of the nations (B)	Isa 23:3
the merchant of the nations (R)	Isa 23:3

MARTHA

and a certain woman named M.	Lu 10:38
But M. was cumbered about much	Lu 10:40
M. M., thou art careful and	Lu 10:41
the town of Mary and her sister M.	Joh 11:1
Jesus loved M. and her sister	Joh 11:5
the Jews came to M. and Mary, to	Joh 11:19
Then M. as soon as she heard	Joh 11:20
Then said M. unto Jesus, Lord, if	Joh 11:21
M. saith unto him, I know that he	Joh 11:24
in that place where M. met him	Joh 11:30
M. the sister of him that was dead	Joh 11:39
made him a supper; and M. served	Joh 12:2

MARTYR

blood of thy m. Stephen was shed	Ac 22:20
Antipas was my faithful m.	Re 2:13
Antipas my witness (A)(E)(R)	Re 2:13
my faithful Antipas, who witnessed (B)	Re 2:13
Antipas, my faithful witness (N)(P)	Re 2:13

MARTYRS

with the blood of the m. of Jesus	Re 17:6
blood of those who had borne testimony (N)	Re 17:6

MARVEL

I am a m. to money (B)	Ps 71:7; Ac 13:41
in a province, m. not at the matter	Ec 5:8
be not astonished at the matter (B)	Ec 5:8
do not be amazed at the matter (R)	Ec 5:8
done for him: and all men did m.	M'k 5:20
all were astonished (B)	M'k 5:20
they were all amazed (N)(P)	M'k 5:20
M. not that I said unto thee, Ye	Joh 3:7
Do not feel surprised (B)	Joh 3:7
You ought not be astonished (P)	Joh 3:7
works than these, that ye may m.	Joh 5:20
M. not at this: for the hour is	Joh 5:28
Be not surprised at this (A)(B)	Joh 5:28
Do not wonder at this (N)	Joh 5:28
have done one work, and ye all m.	Joh 7:21
this is the m. of it (B)(E)(R)	Joh 9:30
men of Israel, why m. ye at	Ac 3:12

why are you so surprised and   *Ac 3:12*
wondering (A)
why are you surprised at this   *Ac 3:12*
(B)(N)(P)
why do you wonder at this (R)   *Ac 3:12*
m. and perish (A)(B)   *Ac 13:41*
And no *m.*; for Satan himself   *2Co 11:14*
I *m.* that ye are so soon   *Ga 1:6*
removed
I am surprised and astonished   *Ga 1:6*
that (A)
I am amazed that you are so   *Ga 1:6*
readily (B)(P)
I am astonished to find you   *Ga 1:6*
(N)(R)
M. not, my brethren, if the   *1Jo 3:13*
world
Do not be surprised and   *1Jo 3:13*
wonder (A)(B)(N)(P)
Do not wonder, brethren (R)   *1Jo 3:13*
unto me, Wherefore didst thou   *Re 17:7*
m.
Why do you wonder (A)(E)   *Re 17:7*
Why are you amazed (B)(P)   *Re 17:7*
Why are you so astonished   *Re 17:7*
(N)
the earth shall *m.* (R)   *Re 17:8*

MARVELLED

and the men *m.* one at   *Ge 43:33*
another
looked at one another amazed   *Ge 43:33*
(A)
look at one another,   *Ge 43:33*
wondering (B)
looked at one another in   *Ge 43:33*
amazement (R)
They saw it, and so they *m.*   *Ps 48:5*
they were amazed (A)(B)(E)   *Ps 48:5*
they were astounded (R)   *Ps 48:5*
When Jesus heard it, he *m.*   *M't 8:10*
the men *m.*, saying, What   *M't 8:27*
manner
were stunned and bewildered   *M't 8:27*
(A)
amazed, the men exclaimed   *M't 8:27*
(B)
the men were astonished (N)   *M't 8:27*
men were filled with   *M't 8:27*
astonishment (P)
when the multitudes saw it,   *M't 9:8*
they *m.*
the multitudes *m.* saying, It   *M't 9:33*
when the disciples saw it, they   *M't 21:20*
m.
had heard these words, they   *M't 22:22*
m.
that the governor *m.* greatly   *M't 27:14*
to the governor's great   *M't 27:14*
surprise (B)
to the governor's great   *M't 27:14*
astonishment (N)
to the governor's amazement   *M't 27:14*
(P)
the governor wondered   *M't 27:14*
greatly (R)
he *m.* because of their unbelief   *M'k 6:6*
he wondered at their unbelief   *M'k 6:6*
(B)
taken aback by their want of   *M'k 6:6*
faith (N)
lack of faith astonished him   *M'k 6:6*
(P)
are God's. And they *m.* at   *M'k 12:17*
him
answered nothing; so that   *M'k 15:5*
Pilate *m.*
Pilate *m.* if he were already   *M'k 15:44*
dead
and *m.* that he tarried so long   *Lu 1:21*
in the
wondered at his delaying   *Lu 1:21*
(A)(R)
wondering why he delayed   *Lu 1:21*
(B)(P)
surprised at staying so long   *Lu 1:21*
(N)
name is John. And they *m.* all   *Lu 1:63*
they were all astonished (A)   *Lu 1:63*
which surprised them all (B)   *Lu 1:63*
to the astonishment of them all   *Lu 1:63*
(N)
neighbors were awestruck at   *Lu 1:63*
this (P)
And Joseph and his mother *m.*   *Lu 2:33*
wondering about the things   *Lu 2:33*
spoken (B)
were full of wonder (N)   *Lu 2:33*
amazed at what was said (P)   *Lu 2:33*

---

heard these things, he *m.* at him   *Lu 7:9*
he *m.* that he had not first   *Lu 11:38*
washed
Pharisee noticed and was   *Lu 11:38*
astonished (A)(R)
Pharisee noticed and wondered   *Lu 11:38*
(B)
Pharisee noticed with surprise   *Lu 11:38*
(N)(P)
and they *m.* at his answer,   *Lu 20:26*
and held
m. that he talked with the   *Joh 4:27*
woman
wondered to find him talking   *Joh 4:27*
with (A)
surprised that he was talking   *Joh 4:27*
(B)(P)
astonished to find him talking   *Joh 4:27*
(N)
the Jews *m.* saying, How   *Joh 7:15*
knoweth
they were astonished (A)(N)   *Joh 7:15*
Jews were surprised (B)   *Joh 7:15*
the Jews were amazed (P)   *Joh 7:15*
they were all amazed and *m.*   *Ac 2:7*
beside themselves with   *Ac 2:7*
amazement (A)
astounded and amazed (B)   *Ac 2:7*
they were amazed (N)(P)(R)   *Ac 2:7*
and ignorant men, they *m.*; and   *Ac 4:13*

MARVELLOUS

Remember his *m.* works that   *1Ch 16:12*
his *m.* works among all   *1Ch 16:24*
nations
m. things without number   *Job 5:9*
thou shewest thyself *m.* upon   *Job 10:16*
me
once more mighty against me   *Job 10:16*
(B)
work wonders against me   *Job 10:16*
(R)
I will shew forth all thy *m.*   *Ps 9:1*
works
Shew thy *m.* loving kindness, O   *Ps 17:7*
hath shewed me his *m.* kindness   *Ps 31:21*
shown me his lovingkindness   *Ps 31:21*
(B)
shown his stedfast love (R)   *Ps 31:21*
M. things did he in the sight   *Ps 78:12*
of
performed miracles before   *Ps 78:12*
(B)
in sight of fathers wrought   *Ps 78:12*
marvels (R)
for he hath done *m.* things: his   *Ps 98:1*
(B)
performed wondrous things   *Ps 98:1*
Remember his *m.* works that   *Ps 105:5*
he
Lord's doing; it is *m.* in our   *Ps 118:23*
eyes
m. are thy works; and that   *Ps 139:14*
my soul
I will proceed to do a *m.*   *Isa 29:14*
work
even a *m.* work and a   *Isa 29:14*
wonder
speak *m.* things against the   *Da 11:36*
God of
speak astonishing things   *Da 11:36*
(A)(R)
utter monstrous boasts (B)   *Da 11:36*
will I shew unto him *m.*   *Mic 7:15*
things
cause them to see wonders   *Mic 7:15*
(B)
it be *m.* in the eyes of the   *Zec 8:6*
remnant
should it also be *m.* in mine   *Zec 8:6*
eyes
doing, and it is *m.* in our   *M't 21:42;*
eyes   *M'k 12:11*
fills our eyes with wonder   *M't 21:42*
(B)
is wonderful in our eyes (N)   *M't 21:42*
Why herein is a *m.* thing, that   *Joh 9:30*
ye
this is astonishing (A)   *Joh 9:30*
This is the marvel of it   *Joh 9:30*
(B)(E)(R)
What an extraordinary thing   *Joh 9:30*
(N)
out of darkness into his *m.*   *1Pe 2:9*
light
sign in heaven, great and *m.*   *Re 15:1*
seven
Great and *m.* are thy works   *Re 15:3*

MARVELLOUSLY

for he was *m.* helped, till he   *2Ch 26:15*
he received exceptional help   *2Ch 26:15*
(B)
God thundereth *m.* with his   *Job 37:5*
voice
God thunders wondrously   *Job 37:5*
(B)(R)
and regard, and wonder *m.*! (A)   *Hab 1:5*
be astonished! Astonished! (A)   *Hab 1:5*
be astounded, be amazed (B)   *Hab 1:5*
wonder and be astounded (R)   *Hab 1:5*

MARVELOUS

Lord do *m.* things (B)   *Jos 3:5; Ps 96:3*
m. things (A)(E)(R)   *Ne 9:10; Ps 96:3*
all his *m.* deeds (A)   *Ps 105:2*
swamps and *m.* (A)(R)(S)   *Eze 47:11*
m. and pools (B)   *Eze 47:11*
reeds and *m.* (A)(R)   *Job 40:21*

MARVELS

before all thy people I will do   *Ex 34:10*
m.
I will work such wonders (B)   *Ex 34:10*
portents and *m.* (B)   *De 6:22*
fathers wrought *m.* (R)   *Ps 78:12*
and delusive *m.* (A)   *2Th 2:9*
performed *m.* (P)   *Re 19:20*

MARY

begat Joseph the husband of   *M't 1:16*
M.
his mother *M.* was espoused   *M't 1:18*
to Joseph
fear not to take unto thee *M.*   *M't 1:20*
thy
young child with *M.* his   *M't 2:11*
mother
son? is not his mother called   *M't 13:55*
M.
Among which was *M.*   *M't 27:56*
Magdalene
M. the mother of James and   *M't 27:56*
Joses
And there was *M.*   *M't 27:61*
Magdalene, and
the other *M.*, sitting over   *M't 27:61*
against
came *M.* Magdalene and the   *M't 28:1*
other
the other *M.* to see the   *M't 28:1*
sepulchre
this the carpenter, the son of   *M'k 6:3*
M.
among whom was *M.*   *M'k 15:40*
Magdalene
M. the mother of James the   *M'k 15:40*
less
M. Magdalene and the   *M'k 15:47*
mother of
and *M.* the mother of Joses   *M'k 15:47*
beheld
sabbath was past, *M.*   *M'k 16:1*
Magdalene
and *M.* the mother of James   *M'k 16:1*
he appeared first to *M.*   *M'k 16:9*
Magdalene
and the virgin's name was *M.*   *Lu 1:27*
angel said unto her, Fear not,   *Lu 1:30*
M.
Then said *M.* unto the angel,   *Lu 1:34*
How
And *M.* said, Behold the   *Lu 1:38*
handmaid
M. arose in those days, and   *Lu 1:39*
went
heard the salutation of *M.*, the   *Lu 1:41*
And *M.* said, My soul doth   *Lu 1:46*
magnify
and *M.* abode with her about   *Lu 1:56*
three
be taxed with *M.* his espoused   *Lu 2:5*
wife
haste, and found *M.* and   *Lu 2:16*
Joseph
But *M.* kept all these things   *Lu 2:19*
said unto *M.* his mother,   *Lu 2:34*
Behold
M. called Magdalene, out of   *Lu 8:2*
whom
And she had a sister called *M.*   *Lu 10:39*
and *M.* hath chosen that good   *Lu 10:42*
part
It was *M.* Magdalene, and   *Lu 24:10*
Joanna

M. the mother of James, and   *Lu 24:10*
town of M. and her sister   *Joh 11:1*
Martha
that M. which anointed the   *Joh 11:2*
Lord
the Jews came to Martha and   *Joh 11:19*
M.
him: but M. sat still in the   *Joh 11:20*
house
and called M. her sister   *Joh 11:28*
secretly
when they saw M. that she   *Joh 11:31*
rose up
M. was come where Jesus was   *Joh 11:32*
of the Jews which came to   *Joh 11:45*
M. and
Then took M. a pound of   *Joh 12:3*
ointment
M. the wife of Cleophas, and   *Joh 19:25*
wife of Cleophas, and M.   *Joh 19:25*
Magdalene
week cometh M. Magdalene   *Joh 20:1*
early
M. stood without at the   *Joh 20:11*
sepulchre
Jesus saith unto her, M. She   *Joh 20:16*
M. Magdalene came and told   *Joh 20:18*
and M. the mother of Jesus, and   *Ac 1:14*
house of M. the mother of   *Ac 12:12*
John
Greet M., who bestowed much   *Ro 16:6*

MASCHIL

A Psalm of David, M.   *Ps 32 title*
To the chief Musician, M.   *Ps 42 title*
for the sons of Korah, M.   *Ps 44 title*
for the sons of Korah, M.   *Ps 45 title*
A Song
To the chief Musician, M.   *Ps 52 title*
Musician upon Mahalath,   *Ps 53 title*
M.
chief Musician on   *Ps 54; 55 title*
Neginoth, M.
M. of Asaph   *Ps 74; 78 title*
M. of Heman the Ezrahite   *Ps 88 title*
M. of Ethan the Ezrahite   *Ps 89 title*
M. of David; A Prayer   *Ps 142 title*
when he

MASH

Uz, and Hul, and Gether, and   *Ge 10:23*
M.

MASHAL

M. with her suburbs and   *1Ch 6:74*
Abdon

MASKS

wearing m. of apostles (B)   *2Co 11:13*

MASONS

trees, and carpenters, and m.   *2Sa 5:11*
And to m. and hewers of   *2Ki 12:12*
stone
carpenters, and builders, and   *2Ki 22:6*
m.
with m. and carpenters, to   *1Ch 14:1*
he set m. to hew wrought   *1Ch 22:2*
stones
hired m. and carpenters to   *2Ch 24:12*
repair
They gave money also unto the   *Ezr 3:7*
m.

MASQUERADES

Satan m. as an angel   *2Co 11:14*
(A)(B)(N)(P)
m. as ministers (A)(B)(N)   *2Co 11:15*

MASQUERADING

m. as apostles (A)(N)   *2Co 11:13*

MASREKAH

Samlah of M. reigned in his   *Ge 36:36;*
stead   *1Ch 1:47*

MASS

m. of their transgression (B)   *Ps 5:10*
the whole m. is holy (A)(B)   *Ro 11:16*

MASSA

And Mishma, and Dumah,   *Ge 25:14*
and M.
Dumah, M., Hadad, and Tema   *1Ch 1:30*

MASSAH

called the name of the place M.   *Ex 17:7*
your God, as ye tempted him   *De 6:16*
in M.
at M. and at Kibroth-hattaavah   *De 9:22*
whom thou didst prove at M.   *De 33:8*

MASSES

m. of the slain (B)   *Na 3:3*

MAST

he that lieth upon the top of a   *Pr 23:34*
m.
not well strengthen their m.   *Isa 33:23*

MASTER

you must m. it (A)(B)(R)   *Ge 4:7*
this m. of dreams (A)(B)   *Ge 37:19*
Joseph's m. put him in prison   *Ge 39:20*
if she pleased not her m. who   *Ex 21:8*
betrothed
shall give to their m. thirty   *Ex 21:32*
shekels of silver
the m. of the house shall be   *Ex 22:8*
brought to judges
food offering from the m. (B)   *Le 2:3*
and spake to the m. of the   *J'g 19:22*
house
the m. of the house went out   *J'g 19:23*
unto them
David sent messengers to   *1Sa 25:14*
salute our m.
for evil is determined against   *1Sa 25:17*
our m.
because you have not kept   *1Sa 26:16*
your m.
for your m. Saul is dead and   *2Sa 2:7*
the house
these have no m.   *1Ki 22:17; 2Ch 18:16*
he cried, Alas m. for it was   *2Ki 6:5*
borrowed
they may eat and drink, and   *2Ki 6:22*
go to their m.
sent them away, and they   *2Ki 6:23*
went to their m.
thus shall ye say to your m.   *2Ki 19:6;*
  Isa 37:6
and Chenaniah, m. of the   *1Ch 15:27*
song
the m. as the (B)   *1Ch 25:8*
as with the servant, so with his   *Isa 24:2*
m.
m. of the flock (B)   *Jer 25:34*
the king spake to the m. of the   *Da 1:3*
eunuchs
O Belteshazzar, m. of the   *Da 4:9;*
magicians   *5:11*
and if I be a m. where is my   *Mal 1:6*
fear
the Lord will cut off the m.   *Mal 2:12*
and the scholar
m. I will follow thee   *M't 8:19*
whithersoever thou goest
why eateth your m. with   *M't 9:11*
publicans and sinners
if they have called the m.   *M't 10:25*
Beelzebub
m. we would see a sign from   *M't 12:38*
thee
they said, Doth not your m.   *M't 17:24*
pay tribute
m. we know that thou art   *M't 22:16;*
true   *M'k 12:14*
for one is your m. even Christ   *M't 23:8;*
  23:10
the m. saith, My time is at   *M't 26:18*
hand
m. is it   *M't 26:25*
hail m. and kissed *M't 26:49; M'k 14:45*
why troublest thou the m. any   *M'k 5:35*
more
m. it is good for us to be here   *M'k 9:5;*
  Lu 9:33
good m. what shall I do   *M'k 10:17;*
  Lu 10:25
for ye know not when the m.   *M'k 13:35*
cometh
the publicans said, M. what   *Lu 3:12*
shall we do

m. say on; saying, M. we   *Lu 7:40;*
perish   *8:24*
thy daughter is dead; trouble   *Lu 8:49*
not the m.
when once the m. of the house   *Lu 13:25*
is risen
take to the m. of ceremonies   *Joh 2:8*
(P)
art thou a m. in Israel, and   *Joh 3:10*
knowest not
the m. is come and calleth   *Joh 11:28*
for thee
ye call me m. and ye say   *Joh 13:13*
well, for so I am
if I then your m. have   *Joh 13:14*
washed your feet
m. of every form of deception   *Ac 13:10*
(A)(B)(R)
the centurion believed the m.   *Ac 27:11*
of the ship
sin not be your m. (B)(N)(P)   *Ro 6:14*
knowing your m. is in heaven   *Eph 6:9;*
  Col 4:1
makes him m. (P)   *Ph'p 3:21*
m. of himself, upright (R)   *Tit 1:8*

HIS MASTER

put his hand under the thigh of   *Ge 24:9*
his m.
took ten camels of his m.   *Ge 24:10*
goods of his m.
Joseph was in house of his m.   *Ge 39:2*
the Egyptian
when his m. heard the words   *Ge 39:19*
of his wife
if his m. have given him a wife   *Ex 21:4*
his m. shall bore his ear   *Ex 21:6*
through with an awl
not deliver to his m. the   *De 23:15*
servant escaped from his m.
the servant said to his m., Let   *J'g 19:11*
us lodge
gathered the arrows and   *1Sa 20:38*
came to his m.
servants break away every   *1Sa 25:10*
one from his m.
wherewith should reconcile   *1Sa 29:4*
himself to his m.
Naaman was a great man with   *2Ki 5:1*
his m.
Gehazi went in, and stood   *2Ki 5:25*
before his m.
Hazael departed and came to   *2Ki 8:14*
his m.
she said, Had Zimri peace,   *2Ki 9:31*
who slew his m.
his m. hath sent to reproach   *2Ki 19:4;*
God   *Isa 37:4*
saying, He will fall to his   *1Ch 12:19*
m. Saul
and the servant is free from   *Job 3:19*
his m.
so he that waiteth on his m.   *Pr 27:18*
shall be
accuse not a servant to his m.   *Pr 30:10*
lest he curse him
and a servant honoureth his m.   *Mal 1:6*
the disciple is not above his   *M't 10:24;*
m.   *Lu 6:46*
it is enough that the disciple   *M't 10:25*
be as his m.
every one perfect shall be as   *Lu 6:40*
his m.
to his own m. he standeth or   *Ro 14:4*
falleth

MY MASTER

O Lord god of my m.   *Ge 24:12;*
Abraham shew kindness to   *27:42, 48*
to my m. Abraham
know that thou hast shewed   *Ge 24:14*
kindness to my m.
the Lord hath blessed my m.   *Ge 24:35*
greatly
if you will deal truly and   *Ge 24:49*
kindly with my m.
and he said, Send me away   *Ge 24:54;*
to my m.   *24:56*
and the servant had said, It is   *Ge 26:65*
my m.
behold, my m. wotteth not   *Ge 39:8*
what is with me
if the servant shall say, I love   *Ex 21:5*
my m.
God forbid I should do this to   *1Sa 24:6*
my m.
my m. left me because I fell   *1Sa 30:13*
sick

nor deliver me into the hands *1Sa 30:15*
of *my m.*
my m. goeth into the house of *2Ki 5:18*
Rimmon
my m. hath spared Naaman *2Ki 5:20*
this Syrian
my m. hath sent me, saying, *2Ki 5:22*
Behold
and he said, Alas, *my m.* how *2Ki 6:15*
shall we do
behold I conspired against *2Ki 10:9*
my m. and slew
hath *my m.* sent me to thy *2Ki 18:27;*
master *Isa 36:12*
give pledges, I pray thee, to *Isa 36:8*
my m.

THY MASTER

Lord will take away *thy m.* *2Ki 2:3;*
to-day *2:5*
let them go, we pray thee, and *2Ki 2:16*
seek *thy m.*
thou shalt smite the house of *2Ki 9:7*
Ahab *thy m.*
my master sent me to *thy m.* *2Ki 18:27*
and to thee

MASTERBUILDER

as wise *m.* I have laid *1Co 3:10*
foundation

MASTERED

m. both of them (E)(R) *Ac 19:16*
not be enslaved, be *m.* *1Co 6:12*
(A)(B)(P)

MASTERING

m. the two of them (A) *Ac 19:16*

MASTERS

look unto the hand of their *m.* *Ps 123:2*
for he refresheth the soul of *Pr 25:13*
his *m.*
fastened by the *m.* of *Ec 12:11*
assemblies
command them to say unto *Jer 27:4*
their *m.*
Thus shall ye say unto your *m.* *Jer 27:4*
which say to their *m.* Bring *Am 4:1*
No man can serve two *m.:* *Mt 6:24*
Neither be ye called *m.:* for *M't 23:10*
one is
No servant can serve two *m.* *Lu 16:13*
which brought her *m.* much *Ac 16:16*
gain
when her *m.* saw that the hope *Ac 16:19*
obedient to them that are your *Eph 6:5*
m.
ye *m.* do the same things unto *Eph 6:9*
Servants, obey in all things *Col 3:22*
your *m.*
M., give unto your servants that *Col 4:1*
their own *m.* worthy of all *1Ti 6:1*
honour
And they that have believing *m.* *1Ti 6:2*
to be obedient unto their own *Tit 2:9*
m.
My brethren, be not many *m.* *Jas 3:1*
subject to your *m.* with all *1Pe 2:18*
fear

MASTER'S

me to the house of my *m.* *Ge 24:27*
brethren
And Sarah my *m.* wife bare a *Ge 24:36*
son to
hath appointed out for my *m.* *Ge 24:44*
son
to take my *m.* brother's *Ge 24:48*
daughter
and let her be thy *m.* son's *Ge 24:51*
wife
m. wife cast her eyes upon *Ge 39:7*
Joseph
said unto his *m.* wife, Behold *Ge 39:8*
and her children shall be her *Ex 21:4*
m.
thy *m.* servants that are come *1Sa 29:10*
have given unto thy *m.* son all *2Sa 9:9*
that
that thy *m.* son may have food *2Sa 9:10*
thy *m.* son shall eat bread *2Sa 9:10*
alway
I gave thee thy *m.* house, and *2Sa 12:8*

the *m.* wives into thy bosom *2Sa 12:8*
said, And where is thy *m.* son *2Sa 16:3*
the sound of his *m.* feet *2Ki 6:32*
behind him
seeing your *m.* sons are with *2Ki 10:2*
you
best and meetest of your *m.* *2Ki 10:3*
sons
throne, and fight for your *m.* *2Ki 10:3*
house
the heads of the men your *m.* *2Ki 10:6*
sons
of the least of my *m.* servants *2Ki 10:24*
his owner, and the ass his *m.* crib *Isa 1:3*
disgrace of *m.* palace (A)(B) *Isa 22:18*
of the least of my *m.* servants *Isa 36:9*
and meet for the *m.* use, and *2Ti 2:21*

MASTERS'

fill their *m.* houses with *Zep 1:9*
violence
which fall from their *m.* table *M't 15:27*

MASTERIES

And if a man also strive for *m.* *2Ti 2:5*

MASTERY

voice of them that shout for *Ex 32:18*
m.
and the lions had the *m.* of *Da 6:24*
them
every man that striveth for the *1Co 9:25*
m.

MASTS

cedars from Lebanon to make *Eze 27:5*
m.

MATE

gathered, every one with her *Isa 34:15*
m.
shall fail, none shall want her *Isa 34:16*
m.

MATERIAL

contribute *m.* things *Ro 15:27*
(A)(B)(N)(R)

MATHUSALA

Which was the son of *M.* which *Lu 3:37*

MATRED

Mehetabel, the daughter of *Ge 36:39;*
M. *1Ch 1:50*

MATRI

the family of *M.* was taken *1Sa 10:21*

MATRIX

the Lord all that openeth the *Ex 13:12;*
m. *13:15*
All that openeth the *m.* is *Ex 34:19*
mine
the firstborn that openeth the *Nu 3:12*
m.
that openeth the *m.* in all *Nu 18:15*
flesh

MATTAN

slew *M.* the priest of Baal *2Ki 11:18;*
before *2Ch 23:17*
Then Shephatiah the son of *M.* *Jer 38:1*

MATTANAH

the wilderness they went to *Nu 21:18*
M.
And from *M.* to Nahaliel *Nu 21:19*

MATTANIAH

made *M.* his father's *2Ki 24:17*
brother king
and *M.* the son of Micah, the *1Ch 9:15*
son of
the sons of Heman; Bukkiah, *1Ch 25:4*
M.
The ninth to *M.,* he, his *1Ch 25:16*
sons, and

the son of *M.,* a Levite of *2Ch 20:14*
the sons
sons of Asaph; Zechariah, *2Ch 29:13*
and *M.*
sons of Elam; *M.* Zechariah *Ezr 10:26*
of Zattu; Elioenai, Eliashib, *Ezr 10:27*
M.
M., Bezaleel, and Binnui, and *Ezr 10:30*
M., Mattenai, and Jaasau *Ezr 10:37*
M. the son of Micha, the son *Ne 11:17*
son of Hashabiah, the son of *Ne 11:22*
M.
Judah, and *M.,* which was *Ne 12:8*
over
M. and Bakbukiah, *Ne 12:25*
Obadiah
the son of *M.,* the son of *Ne 12:35*
Michaiah
the son of Zaccur, the son of *Ne 13:13*
M.

MATTATHA

which was the son of *M.* *Lu 3:31*

MATTATHAH

Mattenai, *M.,* Zabad, *Ezr 10:33*
Eliphelet

MATTATHIAS

Which was the son of *M.* *Lu 3:25*
of Maath, which was the son *Lu 3:26*
of *M.*

MATTENAI

sons of Hashum; *M.* *Ezr 10:33*
Mattathah
Mattaniah, *M.,* and Jaasau *Ezr 10:37*
And of Joiarib, *M.;* of *Ne 12:19*
Jedaiah

MATTER

and sware to him concerning *Ge 24:9*
that *m.*
is it a small *m.* that thou hast *Ge 30:15*
taken
when they have a *m.* they *Ex 18:16*
come to me
every great *m.* they shall bring *Ex 18:22*
to thee, but every small *m.*
but every small *m.* they *Ex 18:26*
judged themselves
keep thee far from false *m.* *Ex 23:7*
them that died about the *m.* *Nu 16:49*
of Korah
beguiled you in *m.* of Peor, in *Nu 25:18*
m. of Cozbi
to commit trespass in the *m.* *Nu 31:16*
of Peor
if there arise a *m.* too hard for *De 17:8*
thee
at mouth of three witnesses *De 19:15*
m. be established
till thou know how the *m.* will *Ru 3:18*
fall out
of the *m.* of the kingdom he *1Sa 10:16*
told not
touching the *m.* thou and I *1Sa 20:23*
have spoken of
only Jonathan and David *1Sa 20:39*
knew the *m.*
how went the *m.?* I pray thee *2Sa 1:4*
tell me
there is no *m.* hid from the *2Sa 18:13*
king
they ended the *m.;* the *m.* is *2Sa 20:18;*
not so *20:21*
at all times as the *m.* shall *1Ki 8:59*
require
save in the *m.* of Uriah the *1Ki 15:5*
Hittite
for every *m.* pertaining to *1Ch 26:32*
God
their officers that served the *1Ch 27:1*
king in any *m.*
departed not from command *2Ch 8:15*
in any *m.*
see ye hasten the *m.* they *2Ch 24:5*
hastened not
to cease, till the *m.* came to *Ezr 5:5*
Darius
and sat down to examine the *Ezr 10:16*
m.
they might have *m.* for evil *Ne 6:13*
report
when inquisition was made of *Es 2:23*
the *m.*

seeing the root of the *m.* is   *Job 19:28*
found in me
I will answer, for I am full of   *Job 32:18*
m.
my heart is inditing a good *m.*   *Ps 45:1*
they encourage themselves in   *Ps 64:5*
an evil *m.*
a faithful spirit concealeth the   *Pr 11:13*
m.
that handleth a *m.* wisely   *Pr 16:20*
shall find good
that repeateth a *m.* separateth   *Pr 17:9*
very friends
that answereth a *m.* before he   *Pr 18:13*
heareth it
the honour of kings is to search   *Pr 25:2*
out a *m.*
if seest oppression, marvel not   *Ec 5:8*
at the *m.*
that which hath wings shall   *Ec 10:20*
tell the *m.*
let us hear the conclusion of   *Ec 12:13*
the *m.*
for the *m.* was not perceived   *Jer 38:27*
he that had the inkhorn,   *Eze 9:11*
reported the *m.*
is this of thy whoredoms a   *Eze 16:20*
small *m.*
not a man can shew the king's   *Da 2:10*
m.
thou hast made known to us   *Da 2:23*
the king's *m.*
hitherto is the end of the *m.* I   *Da 7:28*
kept the *m.*
understand the *m.* and   *Da 9:23*
consider the vision
and began to blaze abroad the   *M'k 1:45*
m.
his disciples asked him again   *M'k 10:10*
the same *m.*
Peter rehearsed the *m.* from   *Ac 11:4*
beginning
the elders came to consider of   *Ac 15:6*
this *m.*
Gallio said, If it were a *m.*   *Ac 18:14*
of wrong
if Demetrius have a *m.* against   *Ac 19:38*
any
I will know the uttermost of   *Ac 24:22*
your *m.*
concerning the *m.* (E)   *Ac 25:16*
dare any of you having a *m.* go   *1Co 6:1*
to law
same might be ready as a *m.* of   *2Co 9:5*
bounty
whatsoever it were, it maketh   *Ga 2:6*
no *m.*
that no man defraud brother in   *1Th 4:6*
any *m.*
how great a *m.* little fire   *Jas 3:5*
kindleth

THIS MATTER

Lord said, Speak no more to   *De 3:26*
me of *this m.*
as a man slayeth his   *De 22:26*
neighbour, so is *this m.*
who will hearken to you in   *1Sa 30:24*
this m.
wherefore be ye angry for   *2Sa 19:42*
this m.
Darius returned answer   *Ezr 5:5*
concerning *this m.*
send his pleasure to us   *Ezr 5:17*
concerning *this m.*
arise, for *this m.* belongeth to   *Ezr 10:4*
the people sat trembling   *Ezr 10:9*
because of *this m.*
Jonathan, Asahel, were   *Ezr 10:15*
employed about *this m.*
they had seen concerning *this*   *Es 9:26*
m.
Melzar consented to them in   *Da 1:14*
this m.
we are not careful to answer   *Da 3:16*
thee in *this m.*
this m. is by the decree of the   *Da 4:17*
watchers
thou hast neither part nor lot   *Ac 8:21*
in *this m.*
we will hear thee again of *this*   *Ac 17:32*
m. others said
ye approved yourselves clear   *2Co 7:11*
in *this m.*

MATTERS

if any man have any *m.* to do,   *Ex 24:14*
let

---

m. of controversy within thy   *De 17:8*
gates
a man of war, and prudent in   *1Sa 16:18*
m.
an end of telling the *m.* of   *2Sa 11:19*
the war
See, thy *m.* are good and   *2Sa 15:3*
right
speakest thou any more of   *2Sa 19:29*
thy *m.*
is over you in all *m.* of the   *2Ch 19:11*
Lord
house of Judah, for all the   *2Ch 19:11*
king's *m.*
in all *m.* concerning the people   *Ne 11:24*
whether Mordecai's *m.* would   *Es 3:4*
stand
the *m.* of the fastings and their   *Es 9:31*
cry
confirmed these *m.* of Purim   *Es 9:32*
giveth not account of any of   *Job 33:13*
his *m.*
devise deceitful *m.* against   *Ps 35:20*
them
do I exercise myself in great   *Ps 131:1*
m.
m. of wisdom and   *Da 1:20*
understanding
dream, and told the sum of the   *Da 7:1*
m.
omitted the weightier *m.* of   *M't 23:23*
the law
to it; for I will be no judge of   *Ac 18:15*
such *m.*
enquire any thing concerning   *Ac 19:39*
other *m.*
and there be judged of these   *Ac 25:20*
m.
ye unworthy to judge the   *1Co 6:2*
smallest *m.*
spiritual *m.* (P)   *1Co 12:1*
or as a busybody in other   *1Pe 4:15*
men's *m.*

MATTHAN

Eleazar begat *M.*; and *M.*   *M't 1:15*
begat

MATTHAT

Which was the son of *M.,*   *Lu 3:24;*
which   *3:29*

MATTHEW

he saw a man, named *M.,*   *M't 9:9*
sitting
Thomas, and *M.* the publican   *M't 10:3*
Bartholomew, and *M.,* and   *M'k 3:18*
M. and Thomas, James the son   *Lu 6:15*
Thomas, Bartholomew, and   *Ac 1:13*
M.

MATTHIAS

was surnamed Justus, and *M.*   *Ac 1:23*
their lots; and the lot fell upon   *Ac 1:26*
M.

MATTITHIAH

M., one of the Levites, who   *1Ch 9:31*
was
And *M.,* and Elipheleh, and   *1Ch 15:18;*
    15:21
Shemiramoth, and Jehiel, and   *1Ch 16:5*
M.
Jeshaiah. Hashabiah, and *M.*   *1Ch 25:3*
fourteenth to *M.,* he, his   *1Ch 25:21*
sons, and
Jeiel, *M.,* Zabad, Zebina,   *Ezr 10:43*
Jadau
and beside him stood *M.,* and   *Ne 8:4*

MATTOCK

coulter, and his axe, and his   *1Sa 13:20*
m.
his ax or sickle (B)   *1Sa 13:20*
plowshare and his *m.* (S)   *1Sa 13:20*
that shall be digged with the   *Isa 7:25*
m.
tilled with a hoe (B)   *Isa 7:25*
which used to be hoed R   *Isa 7:25*

MATTOCKS

they had a file for the *m.* and   *1Sa 13:21*
with their *m.* round about   *2Ch 34:6*

MATURE

so that they never *m.*   *Isa 8:14*
(B)(R)
the spiritually *m.* (A)(B)(P)(R)   *1Co 2:6*
present every man *m.*   *Col 1:28*
(A)(N)(R)
stand firm and *m.* (A)(B)(R)   *Col 4:12*
may become *m.* Christians   *Col 4:12*
(P)
who are spiritually *m.*   *Ph'p 3:15*
(A)(B)(N)(R)

MATURING

m. for destruction (B)   *Ro 9:22*
m. of times, climax of the   *Eph 1:10*
ages (A)(B)
arrive at full *m.* (P)   *Eph 4:13*
every man to full *m.* (P)   *Col 1:28*
advance to *m.* (B)(P)(R)   *Heb 6:1*
love of God reach *m.* (B)   *1Jo 2:5*

MAUL

against his neighbour is a *m.*   *Pr 25:18*
like a heavy sledge hammer   *Pr 25:18*
(A)
As a scattering club (B)   *Pr 25:18*
is like a war club (R)   *Pr 25:18*

MAW

and the two cheeks, and the *m.*   *De 18:3*
both cheeks and the stomach   *De 18:3*
(B)(R)
filled his *m.* (E)   *Jer 51:34*

MAY, MAY BE

that it *m.* be well with   *Ge 12:13*
me for thy sake
it *m.* be that I may obtain   *Ge 16:2*
children
found *M.*-apples (B)   *Ge 30:14;*
    30:15-16
that the Lord's law *m.* be in   *Ex 13:9*
thy mouth
that his fear *m.* be before   *Ex 20:20*
your face
of all meat which *m.* be eaten   *Le 11:34*
for his sister a virgin he *m.* be   *Le 21:3*
defiled
that it *m.* be an holy   *Le 23:21*
convocation
they *m.* be for a memorial   *Nu 10:10*
before God
that the possession *m.* be ours   *Nu 32:32*
may live, and that it *m.* be well   *De 5:33;*
with you   *6:3, 18; 22:7; Ru 3:1; Jer 7:23*
he *m.* be to thee a God as he   *De 29:13*
hath said
that it *m.* be there for a   *De 31:26*
witness against
that it *m.* be for a witness   *Jos 22:27*
between
it *m.* be the Lord will work   *1Sa 14:6*
for us
she *m.* be a snare, Philistines   *1Sa 18:21*
m. be against him
it *m.* be that the king will   *2Sa 14:15*
perform
seeing I go whither I *m.*   *2Sa 15:20*
return thou
it *m.* be Lord will look on my   *2Sa 16:12*
affliction
m. be Lord thy God will hear   *2Ki 19:4;*
    Isa 37:4
that it *m.* be before thee for   *1Ch 17:27*
ever
that ye *m.* be strong, and eat   *Ezr 9:12*
the good
it *m.* be that my sons have   *Job 1:5*
sinned
consume them, that they *m.* not   *Ps 59:13*
be
that Israel *m.* be no more in   *Ps 83:4*
remembrance
that our sons *m.* be as plants   *Ps 144:12*
grown up
that our garners *m.* be full,   *Ps 144:13*
affording store
that our oxen *m.* be strong to   *Ps 144:14*
labour
that thy trust *m.* be in the   *Pr 22:19*
Lord
whereof it *m.* be said, See this   *Ec 1:10*
is new
that it *m.* be for the time to   *Isa 30:8*
come

the Lord waiteth that he *m.*   Isa 30:18
be gracious
that we *m. be* like; I *m. be*   Isa 46:5;
glorified   60:21
that his name *m. be* no   Jer 11:19
more remembered
it *m. be* the house of Judah   Jer 36:3
will hear
it *m. be* they will present their   Jer 36:7
supplication
that it *m. be* well with us when   Jer 42:6
we obey
take balm, if so be she *m. be*   Jer 51:8
healed
mouth in dust, if so be there *m.*   La 3:29
be hope
it *m. be* they will consider,   Eze 12:3
though they
that they *m. be* my people,   Eze 14:11
and I their God
it *m. be* a lengthening of   Da 4:27
tranquillity
they made idols, that they *m. be*   Ho 8:4
cut off
it *m. be* the Lord will be   Am 5:15
gracious
it *m. be* ye shall be hid in the   Zep 2:3
day
that ye *m. be* children of your   M't 5:45
Father
that thine alms *m. be* in secret,   M't 6:4
and thy Father
she said, If I *m. be* but touch   M't 9:21
his garment
if this cup *m.* not pass away   M't 26:42
from me
it *m. be* they will reverence   Lu 20:13
him
kill him, that the inheritance   Lu 20:14
m. be ours
that ye *m. be* the children of   Joh 12:36
light
that where I am, there ye *m.*   Joh 14:3
be also
that they *m. be* one, as we   Joh 17:11;
are one   21:22
that the love *m. be* in them,   Joh 17:26
and I in them
that he *m. be* wise; *m. be*   1Co 3:18;
new lump   5:7
that she *m. be* holy in body   1Co 7:34
and spirit
there are, it *m. be,* so many   1Co 14:10
kind of voices
Son be subject, that God *m.*   1Co 15:28
be all in all
and it *m. be* that I will winter   1Co 16:6
with you
see that he *m. be* with you   1Co 16:10
without fear
the excellency of the power *m.*   2Co 4:7
be of God
so there *m. be* a performance   2Co 8:11
also out of that
that your abundance *m. be* a   2Co 8:14
supply for want
that, as I said, you *m. be* ready   2Co 9:3
that it *m. be* well with thee   Eph 6:3
that ye *m. be* blameless and   Ph'p 2:15
harmless
that I *m. be* of good comfort   Ph'p 2:19
when I know
and that I *m. be* the less   Ph'p 2:28
sorrowful
give charge that they *m. be*   1Ti 5:7
blameless
that the man of God *m. be*   2Ti 3:17
perfect
that they *m. be* found in the   Tit 1:13
faith
and as I *m.* so say, Levi paid   Heb 7:9
tithes
that ye *m. be* perfect and entire   Jas 1:4
Yea, a man *m.* say, Thou hast   Jas 2:18
faith
horses' mouths, that they *m.*   Jas 3:3
obey us
ye *m.* consume it upon your   Jas 4:3
lusts
one for another, that ye *m. be*   Jas 5:16
healed
of the word that ye *m.* grow   1Pe 2:2
thereby
they *m. be* your good works   1Pe 2:12
with well doing ye *m.* put to   1Pe 2:15
silence
they also *m.* without the word   1Pe 3:1
be won
m. be ashamed that falsely   1Pe 3:16
accuse

m. suffice us to have wrought   1Pe 4:3
the will
that God in all things *m. be*   1Pe 4:11
glorified
ye *m. be* glad also with   1Pe 4:13
exceeding
God, that he *m.* exalt you in   1Pe 5:6
due time
about, seeking whom he *m.*   1Pe 5:8
devour
that ye *m. be* able after my   2Pe 1:15
decease
That ye *m. be* mindful of the   2Pe 3:2
words
be diligent that ye *m. be* found   2Pe 3:14
of him
ye also *m.* have fellowship with   1Jo 1:3
us
we unto you, that your joy *m.*   1Jo 1:4
be full
we *m.* have confidence, and   1Jo 2:28
not be
that we *m.* have boldness in   1Jo 4:17
the day of
ye *m.* know that ye have   1Jo 5:13
eternal life
ye *m.* believe on the name of   1Jo 5:13
the Son
that we *m.* know him that is   1Jo 5:20
true
face to face, that our joy *m.*   2Jo 12
be full
of you into prison, that ye *m.*   Re 2:10
be tried
that they *m.* rest from their   Re 14:13
labours
That ye *m.* eat the flesh of   Re 19:18
kings, and
they *m.* have right to the tree   Re 22:14
of life
m. enter in through the gates   Re 22:14
into the

MAYEST

tree of the garden thou *m.*   Ge 2:16
freely eat
but that thou *m.* bury thy dead   Ge 23:6
thou *m.* inherit the land   Ge 28:4
wherein thou
me, that thou *m.* come in   Ge 38:16
unto me
that thou *m.* bring forth my   Ex 3:10
people
m. know that there is none like   Ex 8:10
unto
thou *m.* know that I am the   Ex 8:22
Lord in
m. know that there is none like   Ex 9:14
me
m. know that the earth is the   Ex 9:29
Lord's
thou *m.* tell in the ears of thy   Ex 10:2
son
thou *m.* bring the causes unto   Ex 18:19
God
written; that thou *m.* teach   Ex 24:12
them
m. bring in thither within the   Ex 26:33
veil
m. thou offer for a free will   Le 22:23
offering
thou *m.* use them for the   Nu 10:2
calling of
place, from whence thou *m.*   Nu 23:13
see them
thou *m.* curse me them from   Nu 23:27
thence
possess, that thou *m.* inherit   De 2:31
his land
that thou *m.* prolong thy days   De 4:40
m. go in and possess the good   De 6:18
land
thou *m.* not consume them at   De 7:22
once
out of whose hills thou *m.* dig   De 8:9
brass
thou *m.* gather in thy corn   De 11:14
cattle that thou *m.* eat and be   De 11:15
full
thou *m.* kill and eat flesh in   De 12:15
all thy
Thou *m.* not eat within thy   De 12:17
gates
thou *m.* eat flesh, whatsoever   De 12:20
thy soul
thou *m.* not eat the life with   De 12:23
the flesh
eat it; or thou *m.* sell it unto   De 14:21
an alien

thou *m.* learn to fear the Lord   De 14:23
thy God
with all thy soul, that thou *m.*   De 30:6
live
and that thou *m.* cleave unto   De 30:20
do it
that thou *m.* live and   De 30:16
multiply: and
That thou *m.* love the Lord   De 30:20
thy God
and that thou *m.* obey his   De 30:20
voice, and
and that thou *m.* cleave unto   De 30:20
him
thou *m.* dwell in the land   De 30:20
which the
thou *m.* observe to do   Jos 1:7
according to all
m. prosper wheresoever thou   Jos 1:7
goest
m. observe to do according to   Jos 1:8
all that
with all thine heart, thou *m.*   Ac 8:37
m. take knowledge of all these   Ac 24:8
things
Because that thou *m.*   Ac 24:11
understand
but if thou *m.* be made free,   1Co 7:21
use
and thou *m.* live long on the   Eph 6:3
earth
that thou *m.* know how thou   1Ti 3:15
oughtest
that thou *m.* prosper and be in   3Jo 2
health
tried in the fire, that thou *m.*   Re 3:18
be rich
that thou *m.* be clothed, and   Re 3:18
that the
eyes with eyesalve, that thou   Re 3:18
m. see

MAYEST *BE*

that thou *m. be* a multitude of   Ge 28:3
people
thou *m. be* to us instead of   Nu 10:31
eyes
and that thou *m. be* an holy   De 26:19
people
buildest, that thou *m. be* their   Ne 6:6
king
condemn me, that thou *m. be*   Job 40:8
justified
forgiveness, that thou *m. be*   Ps 130:4
feared
sing songs, that thou *m. be*   Isa 23:16
remembered
that thou *m. be* my salvation   Isa 49:6
to end of earth
wash thy heart, that thou *m.*   Jer 4:14
be saved
none to plead, that thou *m.*   Jer 30:13
be bound up
for thou *m. be* no longer   Lu 16:2
steward

MAZZAROTH

canst thou bring forth *M.* in   Job 38:32
season

ME

the serpent beguiled *m.,* and I   Ge 3:13
did eat
put in ward both *m.* and the   Ge 41:10
chief baker
m. he restored, and him he   Ge 41:13
hanged
m. have ye bereaved of my   Ge 42:36
children
there is none like *m.* in all the   Ex 9:14
earth
not thee, but they have rejected   1Sa 8:7
m.
when Joab sent *m.* thy   2Sa 18:29
servant
but *m.* ever *m.* thy servant   1Ki 1:26
hast discovered thyself to   Isa 57:18
another than *m.*
be dismayed, but let not *m.*   Jer 17:18
be dismayed
who like *m.* and who will   Jer 50:44
appoint *m.* time
and thou shalt know no God   Ho 13:4
but *m.*
loveth father and mother   M't 10:37
more than *m.*
receiveth you receiveth *m.*   M't 10:40;
he that receiveth *m.*   M'k 9:37; Joh 13:20

why called thou *m.* good — M't 19:17; Lu 18:19

m. ye have not always — M't 26:11; M'k 14:7; Joh 2:8

that despiseth *m.* despiseth — Lu 10:16
him that sent *m.*

believed Moses. ye would have — Joh 5:46
believed *m.*

the world cannot hate you, but — Joh 7:7
m. it hateth

ye neither know *m.* nor my — Joh 8:19
Father

though ye believe not *m.* — Joh 10:38
believe the works

yet hast thou not known *m.* — Joh 14:9
Philip

he that hateth *m.* hateth my — Joh 15:23
Father

have seen and hated both *m.* — Joh 15:24
and my Father

they have not known the — Joh 16:3
Father nor *m.*

O Father, glorify thou *m.* with — Joh 17:5
thyself

why askest thou *m.?* ask them — Joh 18:21
who heard *m.*

but if well, why smitest thou — Joh 18:23
m.

he that delivered *m.* to thee — Joh 19:11
hath greater sin

Simon, son of Jonas, lovest — Joh 21:15; 16:17
thou *m.*

Saul, why persecutest thou *m.* — Ac 9:4; 22:7

what advantageth it *m.* if the — 1Co 15:32
dead

ABOVE ME

and honourest thy sons *above* — 1Sa 2:29
m.

ABOUT ME

like the nations that are *about* — De 17:14
m.

when my children were *about* — Job 29:5
m.

they came round *about m.* — Ps 88:17
daily like water

even the night shall be light — Ps 139:11
about m.

the earth with her bars was — Jon 2:6
about m.

there shone a great light *about* — Ac 22:6; *m.* 26:13

AFTER ME

thou hast so hotly pursued — Ge 31:36
after m.

he said unto them, Follow — J'g 3:28
after m.

said to armour-bearer, Come — 1Sa 14:12
after m.

that thou wilt not cut off my — 1Sa 24:21
seed *after m.*

Solomon shall reign *after m.* — 1Ki 1:13; 1:17, 30

hast said, Adonijah shall reign — 1Ki 1:24
after m.

unto the man that shall be *after* — Ec 2:18
m.

neither shall there be *after m.* — Isa 43:10

when wentest *after m.* in the — Jer 2:2
wilderness

he cometh *after m.* is mightier — M't 3:11;
than I — M'k 1:7; Joh 1:15, 27, 30

he that followeth not *after* — M't 10:38;
m. — Lu 14:27

that will come *after m.* — M't 16:24; M'k 8:34; Lu 9:23

there cometh one *after m.* — Ac 13:25
whose shoes

manifest to them that asked — Ro 10:20
not *after m.*

AGAINST ME

I withheld thee from sinning — Ge 20:6
against m.

all these things are *against m.* — Ge 42:36

but as for you, ye thought evil — Ge 50:20
against m.

lest they make thee sin — Ex 23:33
against m.

whoso hath sinned *against m.* — Ex 32:33
him will I blot

which they trespassed *against* — Le 26:40
m.

congregation which murmur — Nu 14:27;
against m.

that are gathered together — Nu 14:35
against m.

abide over *against m.* — Nu 22:5

thou stoodest *against m.* — Nu 22:34

trespassed *against m.* at — De 32:51;
Meribah — Eze 17:20; 20:27, 38; 39:23, 26

let not thine anger be hot — J'g 6:39
against m.

lest Israel vaunt themselves — J'g 7:2
against m.

but thou doest me wrong to — J'g 11:27
war *against m.*

hand of the Lord is gone out — Ru 1:13
against m.

witness *against m.* before the — 1Sa 12:3
Lord

when he arose *against m.* I — 1Sa 17:35
caught him by beard

that all of you have conspired — 1Sa 22:8;
against m. — 22:13

if the Lord hath stirred thee — 1Sa 26:19
up *against m.*

let thy hand, I pray thee, be — 2Sa 24:17
against m.

see how he seeketh a quarrel — 2Ki 5:7
against m.

thou renewest thy witnesses — Job 10:17
against m.

thou writest bitter things — Job 13:26
against m.

with wrinkles, which is a — Job 16:8
witness *against m.*

they whom I loved are turned — Job 19:19
against m. — 14:29

will he plead *against m.* with — Job 23:6
his great power

with thy hand thou opposest — Job 30:21
thyself *against m.*

if my land cry *against m.* or — Job 31:38
the furrows

behold, he findeth occasions — Job 33:10
against m.

are many that rise up *against* — Ps 3:1;
m. — 18:39, 48

false witnesses are risen up — Ps 27:12;
against m. — 54:3

they opened their mouth wide — Ps 35:21
against m.

against m. do they devise my — Ps 41:7
hurt, whisper *against m.*

they are mad *against m.* they — Ps 102:8
are sworn *against m.*

princes also did sit and speak — Ps 119:23
against m.

but he that sinneth *against m.* — Pr 8:36
wrongeth

have rebelled *against m.* — Isa 1:2;
Eze 2:3; 20:8

it crieth out *against m.* — Jer 12:8
therefore I hated

surely, *against m.* he is turned, — La 3:3
he turneth

hast seen all their imaginations — La 3:60
against m.

as they increased, so they — Ho 4:7
sinned *against m.*

they transgressed *against m.* — Ho 7:13
spoken lies *against m.*

and they assemble and rebel — Ho 7:14
against m.

yet do they imagine mischief — Ho 7:15
against m.

O my people, testify *against m.* — Mic 6:3

rejoice not *against m.,* O mine — Mic 7:8
enemy

your words have been stout — Mal 3:13
against m.

that is not with me is — M't 12:30;
against m. — Lu 11:23

how oft shall my brother sin — M't 18:21
against m.

hath lift up his heel *against* — Joh 13:18
m.

couldest have no power at all — Joh 19:11
against m.

and object, if they had aught — Ac 24:19
against m.

AT ME

thou hast thrust sore *at m.* to — Ps 118:13
fall

are ye angry *at m.* because I — Joh 7:23
made a man

BEFORE ME

the end of all flesh is come — Ge 6:13
before m.

for thee have I seen righteous — Ge 7:1
before m.

walk *before m.* — Ge 17:1;
1Sa 2:30; 1Ki 2:34; 8:25; 9:4; 2Ch 7:17

in my dream, behold a vine — Ge 40:9
was *before m.*

shalt have no other gods — Ex 20:3;
before m. — De 5:7

none shall appear *before m.* — Ex 23:15;
empty — 34:20

because thy way is perverse — Nu 22:32
before m.

go up *before m.* to the high — 1Sa 9:19
place

and thou shalt go down *before* — 1Sa 10:8
m. to Gilgal

let David, I pray thee, stand — 1Sa 16:22
before m.

go on *before m.* behold I — 1Sa 25:19
come after you

for all his judgments were — 2Sa 22:23;
before m. — Ps 18:22; 119:30

as thou hast walked *before* — 1Ki 8:25;
m. — 2Ch 6:16

David may have a light — 1Ki 11:36
before m. in Jerusalem

how Ahab humbleth himself — 1Ki 21:29
before m.

because hath wept *before* — 2Ki 22:19;
m. — 2Ch 34:27

letter hath been plainly read — Ezr 4:18
before m.

former governors that were — Ne 5:15
before m.

will he force the queen also — Es 7:8
before m.

who then is able to stand — Job 41:10
before m.

I have set the Lord always — Ps 16:8
before m.

thou preparest a table *before* — Ps 23:5
m. in presence

my sorrow is continually — Ps 38:17
before m.

keep my mouth while the — Ps 39:1
wicked is *before m.*

offerings to have been — Ps 50:8
continually *before m.*

my transgressions and my sin is — Ps 51:3
ever *before m.*

his throne shall endure as the — Ps 89:36
sun *before m.*

then all that have been *before* — Ec 1:16;
m. — 2:7, 9

my vineyard which is mine, is — Ca 8:12
before m.

when ye come to appear — Isa 1:12
before m. who

keep silence *before m.* O — Isa 41:1
islands

before m. there was no god — Isa 43:10
formed, nor after

behold thy walls are — Isa 49:16
continually *before m.*

for the spirit should fail — Isa 57:16
before m.

behold, it is written *before m.* — Isa 65:6
I will not

shall remain *before m.* saith — Isa 66:22
the Lord

yet thine iniquity is marked — Jer 2:22
before m.

before m. continually is grief — Jer 6:7
and wounds

and come and stand *before m.* — Jer 7:10
in this house

tho' Moses and Samuel stood — Jer 15:1
before m.

if thou return, thou shalt — Jer 15:19
stand *before m.*

prophets that have been *before* — Jer 28:8
m. and thee

for Israel have only done evil — Jer 32:30
before m.

priests shall not want a man — Jer 33:18;
before m. — 35:19

ye had made a covenant — Jer 34:15
before m. in the house

shepherd that will stand — Jer 49:19;
before m. — 50:44

and the elders of Judah sat — Eze 8:1
before m.

then the elders of Israel sat — Eze 14:1;
before m. — 20:1

their way was *before m.* as — Eze 36:17
the uncleanness

and they shall stand *before* — Eze 44:15
m. to offer

at the last Daniel came in — Da 4:8
before m.

their wickedness is come up   Jon 1:2
before m.
spoiling and violence are   Hab 1:3
before m.
so is this people and nation   Hag 2:14
before m.
shall prepare the way *before*   Mal 3:1;
m.   M't 11:10
bring hither and slay them   Lu 19:27
before m.
preferred *before m.* for he   Joh 1:15;
was *before m.*   27:30
I am coming, another steppeth   Joh 5:7
down *before m.*
all that ever came *before m.*   Joh 10:8
are robbers
there be judged of these things   Ac 25:9
before m.
who also were in Christ *before*   Ro 16:7
m.
to them which were apostles   Ga 1:17
before m.

BEHIND ME

Jehu said, Turn thee *behind*   2Ki 9:18;
m.   9:19
I heard *behind m.* a voice of   Eze 3:12
rushing
get *behind m.* Satan, thou art   M't 16:23
an offence   M'k 8:33; Lu 4:8

BESIDE, BESIDES ME

she arose and took my son   1Ki 3:20
from *beside m.*
besides m. there is no Saviour   Isa 43:11;
  Ho 13:4
and *besides m.* there is no   Isa 44:6;
God   45:5-6, 21
that sayest, I am, and none   Isa 47:8;
else *besides m.*   47:10

BETWEEN ME

covenant I make *between m.*   Ge 9:12;
and you   9:13
that is *between m.* and every   Ge 9:15;
living creature   9:17
let there be no strife *between*   Ge 13:8
m. and thee
Lord judge *between m.* and   Ge 16:5;
thee   1Sa 24:12, 15
I make my covenant *between*   Ge 17:2;
m. and thee   17:7, 10-11
what is that *between m.* and   Ge 23:15
thee? bury thy dead
let it be for a witness   Ge 31:44;
between m. and thee   31:48
Lord watch *between m.* and   Ge 31:49
thee when absent
see, God is witness *between*   Ge 31:50
m. and thee
sabbath shall keep for a sign   Ex 31:13;
between m. and   31:17; Eze 20:12, 20
cast lots *between m.* and   1Sa 14:42
Jonathan
there is but a step *between m.*   1Sa 20:3
and death
is a league *between m.* and   1Ki 15:19;
thee   2Ch 16:3
judge, I pray you, *between m.*   Isa 5:3
and my vineyard
and the wall *between m.* and   Eze 43:8
them

BY ME

Rachel died *by m.* in the land   Ge 48:7
of Canaan
behold, there is a place *by m.*   Ex 33:21
Edom said, Thou shalt not   Nu 20:18
pass *by m.*
as for thee, stand thou here *by*   De 5:31
m.
wherewith *by m.* they honour   J'g 9:9
God
Lord hath done, as he spake   1Sa 28:17
by m.
the Spirit of the Lord spake   2Sa 23:2
by m.
Lord not spoken *by m.*   1Ki 22:28;
  2Ch 18:27
he that sounded the trumpet   Ne 4:18
was *by m.*
lo, he goeth *by m.* and I see   Job 9:11
him not
by m. kings reign; *by m.*   Pr 8:15;
princes rule   8:16

by *m.* thy days shall   Pr 9:11
be multiplied
which are borne *by m.;* but   Isa 46:3;
not *by m.*   54:15
they have set up kings, but not   Ho 8:4
by *m.*
mightest be profited *by m.*   M't 15:5;
  M'k 7:11
that eateth me, even he shall   Joh 6:57
live *by m.*
I am the door, *by m.* if any   Joh 10:9
man enter in
no man cometh to the Father   Joh 14:6
but *by m.*
an angel stood *by m.* this   Ac 27:23
night
which Christ hath wrought *by*   Ro 15:18
m.
Son of God preached *by m.*   2Co 1:19
was not yea
but the same which is made   2Co 2:2
sorry *by m.*
that *by m.* preaching might be   2Ti 4:17
known

CONCERNETH, CONCERNING ME

Lord said to Moses *concerning*   Jos 14:6
m. and thee
Lord continue his word he   1Ki 2:4
spake *concerning m.*
for he doth not prophesy   1Ki 22:8;
good *concerning m.*   22:18
Lord will perfect that which   Ps 138:8
concerneth m.
cometh to a prophet to   Eze 14:7
inquire *concerning m.*
for the things *concerning m.*   Lu 22:37
have an end
which are written in the   Lu 24:44
Psalms *concerning m.*
not receive thy testimony   Ac 22:18
concerning m.

FOR ME

entreat *for m.* to Ephron   Ge 23:8;
  Ex 8:28
hast thou not reserved a   Ge 27:36
blessing *for m.*
if thou wilt do this thing *for*   Ge 30:31
m.
so shall my righteousness   Ge 30:33
answer *for m.*
in my grave which I have   Ge 50:5
digged *for m.*
take this child and nurse it *for*   Ex 2:9
m.
thou shalt take the Levites *for*   Nu 3:41
m.
not able, because it is too   Nu 11:14
heavy *for m.*
for they are too mighty *for m.*   Nu 22:6
this song may be a witness *for*   De 31:19
m.
as *for m.* and my house we   Jos 24:15
will serve Lord
people are too many *for m.* to   J'g 7:2
give
she said, Let this thing be   J'g 11:37
done *for m.*
now therefore get her *for m.*   J'g 14:2;
to wife   14:3
there is bread and wine also   J'g 19:19
for m.
as *for m.*   1Sa 12:23;
1Ch 22:7; 28:2; 29:17; Job 21:4; Ps 5:7;
  17:15; 35:13
only be thou valiant *for m.*   1Sa 18:17
and fight
till I know what God will do   1Sa 22:3
for m.
there is none of you that is   1Sa 22:8
sorry *for m.*
nothing better *for m.* than to   1Sa 27:1
escape
sons of Zeruiah be too hard   2Sa 3:39
for m.
shalt thou build an house *for*   2Sa 7:5
m. to dwell in
if Syrians be too strong *for*   2Sa 10:11;
m.   1Ch 19:12
good *for m.* to have been   2Sa 14:32
there still
then mayest thou *for m.*   2Sa 15:34
defeat counsel
they were too strong *for m.*   2Sa 22:18;
  Ps 18:17

pray *for m.* that my hand be   1Ki 13:6
restored
may go in and dress it *for m.*   1Ki 13:12
and my son
drive, slack not thy riding *for*   2Ki 4:24
m.
the brazen altar be *for m.* to   2Ki 16:15
inquire by
inquire of the Lord *for m.*   2Ki 22:13;
  2Ch 34:21
which was prepared *for m.*   Ne 5:18
daily
the graves are ready *for m.*   Job 17:1
performeth the thing   Job 23:14
appointed *for m.*
they waited *for m.* as for the   Job 29:23
rain
I uttered things too wonderful   Job 42:3
for m.
thou, O Lord, art a shield *for m.*   Ps 3:3
awake *for m.*   Ps 7:6
this I know, for God is *for m.*   Ps 56:9
the net they have laid privily   Ps 31:4;
for m. 35:7; 119:110; 140:5; 141:9; 142:3
as *for m.*   Ps 41:12;
55:16; 69:13; Isa 59:21; Jer 17:16; 26:14;
  40:10; Eze 9:10; Da 2:30; 7:28; 10:17
this I know, for God is   Ps 56:9
to God, that performeth all   Ps 57:2
things *for m.*
for thou hast been a shelter *for*   Ps 61:3
m.
to know this, it was too   Ps 73:16
painful *for m.*
rise up *for m.* who will stand   Ps 94:16
up *for m.*
but do thou *for m.* O God   Ps 109:21
the Lord
good *for m.;* the proud   Ps 119:71;
digged pits *for m.*   119:85
the wicked have waited *for*   Ps 119:95
m. to destroy me
or in things too high *for m.*   Ps 131:1
such knowledge is too   Ps 139:6
wonderful *for m.*
feed me with food convenient   Pr 30:8
for m.
there be three things too   Pr 30:18
wonderful *for m.*
I am oppressed, undertake   Isa 38:14
for m.
and who shall set it in order   Isa 44:7
for m.
the place is too strait *for m.*   Isa 49:20
they shall not be ashamed   Isa 49:23
that wait *for m.*
surely the isles shall wait *for m.*   Isa 60:9
I am sought of them that   Isa 65:1
asked not *for m.*
search *for m.* with all your   Jer 29:13
heart
is there any thing too hard   Jer 32:27
for m.
because they wrought *for m.*   Eze 29:20
thou shalt abide *for m.* many   Ho 3:3
days
better *for m.* to die than to live   Jon 4:3;
  4:8
until he execute judgment *for*   Mic 7:9
m.
when I have bent Judah *for*   Zec 9:13
m.
that take and give *for m.* and   M't 17:27
thee
weep not *for m.* but for   Lu 23:28
yourselves
Simon said, Pray ye to the   Ac 8:24
Lord *for m.*
for what intent ye have sent   Ac 10:29
for m.
strive in your prayers to God   Ro 15:30
for m.
all things are lawful *for m.*   1Co 6:12;
  10:23
it were better *for m.* to die,   1Co 9:15
than that
who loved me, and gave   Ga 2:20
himself *for m.*
and *for m.* that utterance may   Eph 6:19
be given me
laid up *for m.* a crown of   2Ti 4:8
righteousness

FROM ME

separate thyself, I pray thee,   Ge 13:9
from m.
hast not withheld thine only   Ge 22:12
son *from m.*

wherefore didst thou steal away *from m.* Ge 31:27

wouldest take by force thy daughters *from m.* Ge 31:31

nor hath he kept back any thing *from m.* Ge 39:9

the one went out *from m.* and he is torn Ge 44:28

if ye take this also *from m.* ye shall bring Ge 44:29

cause every man to go out *from m.* Ge 45:1

get thee *from m.* see my face no more Ex 10:28

tell me, hide it not *from m.* Jos 7:19; 1Sa 3:17

then my strength will go *from m.* J'g 16:17

why should my Father hide this *from m.* 1Sa 20:2

Amnon said, Have out all men *from m.* 2Sa 13:9

put this woman out *from m.;* far be it *from m.* 2Sa 13:17; 20:20

return, for this thing is *from m.* 1Ki 12:24

went Spirit of Lord *from m.* 1Ki 22:24; 2Ch 18:23

and the Lord hath hid it *from m.* 2Ki 4:27

saying, I have offended, return *from m.* 2Ki 18:14

therefore I chased him *from m.* Ne 13:28

and is wisdom driven quite *from m.* Job 6:13

let him take his rod away *from m.* Job 9:34

withdraw thine hand far *from m.* Job 13:21

he hath put my brethren far *from m.* Job 19:13

the counsel of the wicked is far *from m.* Job 21:16

I will not remove mine integrity *from m.* Job 27:5

how long wilt thou hide thy face *from m.* Ps 13:1

I did not put away his statutes *from m.* Ps 18:22

thou hast seen, O Lord, be not far *from m.* Ps 35:22

light of mine eyes, it is gone *from m.* Ps 38:10

remove thy stroke away *from m.* Ps 39:10

withhold not thy tender mercies *from m.* Ps 40:11

and take not thy Holy Spirit *from m.* Ps 51:11

nor hath turned his mercy *from m.* Ps 66:20

Lord, why hidest thou thy face *from m.* Ps 88:14

hide not thy face *from m.* in trouble Ps 102:2; 143:7

hide not thy commandments *from m.* Ps 119:19

the keepers took away my veil *from m.* Ca 5:7

turn away thine eyes *from m.* for they have Ca 6:5

look away *from m.* I will weep bitterly Isa 22:4

mine age is removed *from m.* as a tent Isa 38:12

give ear, for a law shall proceed *from m.* Isa 51:4

surely his anger shall turn *from m.* Jer 2:35

and shall not turn away *from m.* Jer 3:19

this is the portion of thy measures *from m.* Jer 13:25

I will ask thee, hide nothing *from m.* Jer 38:14

from m. shall spoilers come unto her Jer 51:53

and give them warning *from m.* Eze 3:17; 33:7

because they are all estranged *from m.* Eze 14:5

every one that separateth himself *from m.* Eze 14:7

that Judah may go no more astray *from m.* Eze 14:11

went astray *from m.* after their idols Eze 44:10

when children of Israel went astray *from m.* Eze 44:15

the king said, The thing is gone *from m.* Da 2:5; 2:8

I know Ephraim, Israel is not hid *from m.* Ho 5:3

woe unto them, for they have fled *from m.* Ho 7:13

my people are bent to backsliding *from m.* Ho 11:7

like a fir tree, *from m.* is thy fruit found Ho 14:8

take away *from m.* the noise of songs Am 5:23

if it be possible, let this cup pass *from m.* M't 26:39; M'k 14:36; Lu 22:22

if this cup may not pass away *from m.* M't 26:42

my lord taketh *from m.* the stewardship Lu 16:3

no man taketh it *from m.,* I lay it down Joh 10:18

all in Asia be turned away *from m.* 2Ti 1:15

IN ME

Joseph answered, It is not in *m.* Ge 41:16

if there be iniquity *in m.* 1Sa 20:8; 2Sa 14:32

because my life is yet whole in *m.* 2Sa 1:9

because he delighted in *m.* 2Sa 22:20; Ps 18:19

is not my help in *m.?* is wisdom driven Job 6:13

the root of the matter is found *in m.* Job 19:28

no, but he would put strength in *m.* Job 23:6

all the while my breath is in *m.* Job 27:3

the depth saith, It is not in *m.* Job 28:14

I am clean, nor is there iniquity in *m.* Job 33:9

according to mine integrity in *m.* Ps 7:8

for thine arrows stick fast in *m.* Ps 38:2

when I remember, I pour out my soul in *m.* Ps 42:4

and why art thou disquieted in *m.* Ps 42:5

see if there be any wicked way in *m.* Ps 139:24

fury is not in *m.* who would set briars Isa 27:4

that putteth trust in *m.* shall possess land Isa 57:13

what iniquity have fathers found in *m.* Jer 2:5

because thou hast put thy trust in *m.* Jer 39:18

and let thy widows trust in *m.* Jer 49:11

my soul is humbled in. *m.* La 3:20

before him innocency was found in *m.* Da 6:22

there remained no strength in *m.* Da 10:8; 10:17

they shall find none iniquity in *m.* Ho 12:8

hast destroyed thyself, but in *m.* is thy help Ho 13:19

shall not be offended in *m.* M't 11:6; Lu 7:23

little ones which believe in *m.* M't 18:6; M'k 9:42

must yet be accomplished in *m.* Lu 22:37

he dwelleth in *m.* and I in him Joh 6:56

he that believeth in *m.* shall live Joh 11:25; 11:26

believe also in *m.* Joh 14:1

but the Father that dwelleth in *m.* Joh 14:10

you in *m.* and I in you Joh 14:20

prince cometh, and that nothing in *m.* Joh 14:30

every branch in *m.;* abide in *m.* Joh 15:2; 15:4

he that abideth in *m.* Joh 15:5

if a man abide not in *m.* he is cast forth Joh 15:6

if ye abide in *m.* Joh 15:7

spoken, that in *m.* ye might have peace Joh 16:33

as thou, Father, art in *m.,* and I in thee Joh 17:21

in them, and thou in *m.,* that they may Joh 17:23

if they have found any evil doing in *m.* Ac 24:20

which are sanctified by faith that is in *m.* Ac 26:18

there was no cause of death in *m.* Ac 28:18

as much as in *m.* is, I am ready to preach Ro 1:15

wrought in *m.* all manner of concupiscence Ro 7:8

sin working death in *m.* by what is good Ro 7:13

no more I, but sin that dwelleth in *m.* Ro 7:17; 7:20

I know that in *m.* dwelleth no good thing Ro 7:18

as the truth of Christ is in *m.* 2Co 11:10

since ye seek a proof of Christ speaking in *m.* 2Co 13:3

it pleased God to reveal his Son in *m.* Ga 1:16

and they glorified God in *m.* Ga 1:24

the same was mighty in *m.* towards Gentiles Ga 2:8

yet not I, but Christ liveth in *m.* Ga 2:20

which ye saw in *m.* and now hear to be in *m.* Ph'p 1:30

the things ye have heard and seen in *m.* do Ph'p 4:9

working which worketh in *m.* mightily Col 1:29

that in *m.* Christ Jesus might shew 1Ti 1:16

OF ME

say *of m.,* He is my brother Ge 20:13

peradventure he will accept *of m.* Ge 32:20

men say not *of m.,* A woman slew him J'g 9:54

thou shouldest take knowledge *of m.* Ru 2:10

Saul shall despair *of m.* to seek me 1Sa 27:1

wherefore then dost thou ask *of m.* 1Sa 28:16

return, for this thing is done *of m.* 2Ch 11:4

not spoken *of m.* the thing that is right Job 42:7

ask *of m.* and I shall give thee the heathen Ps 2:8

in thy book it is written *of m.* Ps 40:7; Heb 10:7

mine enemies speak evil *of m.* Ps 41:5

Philistia, triumph thou because *of m.* Ps 60:8

and Israel would none *of m.* Ps 81:11

but doth not take counsel *of m.* Isa 30:1

from day, wilt thou make an end *of m.* Isa 38:12; 38:13

thou hast been weary *of m.* O Israel Isa 43:22

thou shalt not be forgotten *of m.* Isa 44:21

and their righteousness *of m.,* saith the Lord Isa 54:17

they ask *of m.* the ordinances of justice Isa 58:2

my children are gone forth *of m.* Jer 10:20

say to the king that sent you to enquire *of m.* Jer 37:7

and say, Are ye come to enquire *of m.* Eze 20:3

they say *of m.,* Doth he not speak parables Eze 20:49

more than me, is not worthy *of m.* M't 10:37; 10:38

and learn *of m.,* for I am meek and lowly M't 11:29

be offended, because *of m.* M't 26:31; M'k 14:27

whoso shall be ashamed of *m.* M'k 8:38; Lu 9:26

that can lightly speak evil *of m.* M'k 9:39

I perceive that virtue is gone out *of m.* Lu 8:46

saying, This do in remembrance *of m.* Lu 22:19

thou being a Jew, askest drink *of m.* Joh 4:9

another that beareth witness *of m.* Joh 5:32; 5:37

and they are they which testify *of m.* Joh 5:39

have believed me, for Moses   *Joh 5:46*
wrote *of m.*
this voice came not because   *Joh 12:30*
of *m.*
the Comforter come, he shall   *Joh 15:26*
testify *of m.*
or did others tell it thee *of*   *Joh 18:34*
m.
wait for the promise ye have   *Ac 1:4*
heard *of m.*
as thou hast testified *of m.* in *Ac 23:11*
Jerusalem
be ye followers *of m.*   *1Co 4:16;*
       11:1; Ph'p 3:17
this do in remembrance *of*   *1Co 11:24;*
m.   *11:25*
last of all he was seen *of m.*   *1Co 15:8*
the salutation *of m.* Paul   *1Co 16:21;*
               Col 4:18
lest any should think *of m.*   *2Co 12:6*
above that which he seeth
me or heareth *of m.*
that gospel which is preached *Ga 1:11*
of m.
your care *of m.* hath   *Ph'p 4:10*
flourished
the testimony *of m.* his prisoner *2Ti 1:8*
sound words, which thou hast *2Ti 1:13*
heard *of m.*
things that thou hast heard *of* *2Ti 2:2*
m. commit
he had compassion *of m.* in *Heb 10:34*
my bonds

ON ME, UPON ME

I have taken *upon m.* to speak *Ge 18:27;*
to Lord   *18:31*
that thou hast brought *on m.* a *Ge 20:9*
great sin
I shall bring a curse *upon m.* *Ge 27:12*
not a blessing
upon m. by thy curse, my son, *Ge 27:13*
only obey me
for the custom of women is   *Ge 31:35*
upon m.
think *on m.* when it shall be   *Ge 40:14*
well with thee
ye will not fall *upon m.*   *J'g 15:12*
yourselves
howsoever, let all thy wants *J'g 19:20*
lie *upon m.*
Philistines will come down   *1Sa 13:12*
upon m.
upon m., my lord, *upon m.,* *1Sa 25:24*
let this inquity be
the iniquity be *on m.* and   *2Sa 14:9*
father's house
that all Israel set their faces *on 1Ki 2:15*
m.
let thy hand, I pray thee, be *1Ch 21:17*
on *m.*
understand in writing by his *1Ch 28:19*
hand *upon m.*
hand of the Lord *upon m.*   *Ezr 7:28;*
             Ne 2:8, 18
think *upon m.* my God, for   *Ne 5:19*
good
which I greatly feared is come *Job 3:25*
upon m.
fear came *upon me.;* be   *Job 4:14;*
content, look *upon m.*   *6:28*
thine eyes are *upon m.,* and I *Job 7:8*
am not
thou shewest thyself   *Job 10:16*
marvellous *upon m.*
he runneth *upon m.* like a   *Job 16:14*
giant
have pity *upon m.,* O ye my *Job 19:21*
friends
have mercy *upon m.*   *Ps 4:1;*
  6:2; 9:13; 25:16; 27:7; 30:10; 31:9;
            51:1; 86:16
tell my bones, they look and   *Ps 22:17*
stare *upon m.*
for day and night thy hand was *Ps 32:4*
heavy *upon m.*
I am poor, yet the Lord   *Ps 40:17*
thinketh *upon m.*
they cast iniquity *upon m.,* and *Ps 55:3*
hate me
thy vows are *upon m.,* I will *Ps 56:12*
render praises
because he hath set his love *Ps 91:14*
upon m.
call *upon m.;* look thou *upon Ps 91:15;*
m.   *119:132*
and thou hast laid thine hand *Ps 139:5*
upon m.
look not *upon m.* sun hath   *Ca 1:6*
looked *upon m.*

thou hast not called *upon m.* *Isa 43:22*
O Jacob
the isles shall wait *upon m.*   *Isa 51:5*
and shall trust
Spirit of the Lord God is   *Isa 61:1;*
upon m.   *Lu 4:18*
wherefore come these things *Jer 13:22*
upon m.
and they have cast a stone *upon La 3:53*
m.
the hand of the Lord was   *Eze 3:14*
strong *upon m.*
was there *upon m.;* hand fell *Eze 3:22;*
there *upon m.*   *8:1*
the Spirit of the Lord fell *upon Eze 11:5*
m. and said
the hand of Lord was *upon Eze 33:22;*
m.   *37:1; 40:1*
therefore wait ye *upon m.* until *Zep 3:10*
the day
then cried he *upon m.* and   *Zec 6:8*
spake unto me
the poor of the flock that   *Zec 11:11*
waited *upon m.*
they shall look *upon m.*   *Zec 12:10*
whom they pierced
have mercy *upon m.,* thou   *M't 15:22;*
Son of David   *M'k 10:47-48; Lu 18:38-*
               39
wrought a good work *upon M't 26:10;*
m.   *M'k 14:6*
in the days wherein he looked *Lu 1:25*
on *m.*
he that believeth *on m.*   *Joh 6:35;*
    6:47; 7:38; 12:44, 46; 14:12
of sin, because they believe   *Joh 16:9*
not *on m.*
who shall believe *on m.*   *Joh 17:20*
through their word
that none of those things come *Ac 8:24*
upon m.
that reproached thee fell *on m.* *Ro 15:3*
for necessity is laid *upon m.* *1Co 9:16*
that which cometh *upon m.* *2Co 11:28*
daily
that the power of Christ may *2Co 12:9*
rest *upon m.*
but God had mercy *on m.*   *Ph'p 2:27*
also
he laid his right hand *upon m.,* *Re 1:17*
saying

OVER ME

Moses said to Pharaoh, Glory *Ex 8:9*
over m.
shalt say, I will set a king *over De 17:14*
m.
that thou settest a watch *over Job 7:12*
m.
shall mine enemy be exalted   *Ps 13:2*
over m.
let them not have dominion   *Ps 19:13;*
over m.   *119:133*
let not mine enemies triumph   *Ps 25:2*
over m.
mine enemy doth not triumph *Ps 41:11*
over m.
thy waves and billows are gone *Ps 42:7*
over m.
thy fierce wrath goeth *over m.* *Ps 88:16*
and his banner *over m.* was love *Ca 2:4*
thy billows and waves passed *Jon 2:3*
over m.

TO, UNTO ME

thy brother's blood crieth *unto* *Ge 4:10*
m.
behold, *to m.* thou hast given *Ge 15:3*
no seed
said he not *unto m.;* swear   *Ge 20:5;*
unto m. by God   *21:23*
saying, Thus spake the man *Ge 24:30*
unto m.
wherefore come ye *to m.,*   *Ge 26:27*
seeing ye hate
because the Lord hath   *Ge 27:20*
brought it *to m.*
what is this thou hast done   *Ge 29:25*
unto m.
thus God hath given them   *Ge 31:9*
to m.
Lord which saidst *unto m.,*   *Ge 32:9*
Return to thy country
what ye shall say *unto m.* I ·*Ge 34:11;*
will give   *34:12*
shew kindness, I pray thee, *Ge 40:14*
unto m.
and my father's house are   *Ge 46:31*
come *unto m.*

the cry of children of Israel is   *Ex 3:9*
come *unto m.*
surely a bloody husband art   *Ex 4:25*
thou *to m.*
may hold a feast *unto m.* in the *Ex 5:1*
wilderness
and I will take you *to m.* for a *Ex 6:7*
people
children of Israel have not   *Ex 6:12*
hearkened *unto m.*
sanctify *unto m.* all the   *Ex 13:2*
firstborn
wherefore criest thou *unto*   *Ex 14:15*
m.? speak to Israel
when they have a matter, they *Ex 18:16*
come *unto m.*
ye shall be a peculiar treasure *Ex 19:5*
unto m.
ye shall be *unto m.* a kingdom *Ex 19:6*
of priests
and they cry at all *unto m.* I *Ex 22:23;*
will hear   *19:27*
firstborn of thy sons shalt   *Ex 22:29*
thou give *unto m.*
and ye shall be holy men *unto Ex 22:31*
m., nor eat
                 Ex 28:1;
  28:3; 29:1; 30:30; 40:13; Jer 33:22;
             Eze 43:19
let him come *unto m.;* thou   *Ex 32:26;*
sayest *unto m.*   *33:12*
present thyself there to m. in *Ex 34:2*
the mount
for *unto m.* Israel are servants *Le 25:55*
of brethren like *unto m.*   *De 18:15;*
          Ac 3:22; 7:37
to m. belongeth vengeance   *De 32:35*
and recompence
why are ye come *unto m.* now *J'g 11:7*
as they did *unto m.,* so have I *J'g 15:11*
done to them
and be *unto m.* a father and a *J'g 17:10*
priest
Lord do so *to m.*   *Ru 1:17;*
   2Sa 3:35; 19:13; 1Ki 2:23
because their cry is come *unto 1Sa 9:16*
m.
anoint *unto m.* him whom I   *1Sa 16:3*
name unto thee
and *to m.* they ascribed but   *1Sa 18:8*
thousands
very pleasant hast thou been   *2Sa 1:26*
unto m.
go to him. but he shall not   *2Sa 12:23*
return *to m.*
that every man might come   *2Sa 15:4*
unto m.
thou knowest what Joab did *to 1Ki 2:5*
m.
so let the gods do *to m.* and   *1Ki 19:2;*
more   *20:10*
what Lord saith *unto m.* that *1Ki 22:14*
will I speak
send *unto m.* to recover a man *2Ki 5:7*
of leprosy
let him come now *to m.;* God *2Ki 5:8;*
do so *to m.*   *6:31*
thus and thus spake he *to m.* *2Ki 9:12*
and come *to m.* to Jezreel by *2Ki 10:6*
to-morrow
tell man that sent you *to m.* *2Ki 22:15;*
          2Ch 34:23
how bring ark of God home *1Ch 13:12*
to m.
he would not prophesy good *2Ch 18:17*
unto m.
and hath extended mercy *unto Ezr 7:28*
m.
then were assembled *unto m.* *Ezr 9:4*
every one that
but if ye turn *unto m.* and keep *Ne 1:9*
my commandments
that which I was afraid of is   *Job 3:25*
come *unto m.*
and wearisome nights are   *Job 7:3*
appointed *to m.*
only do not two things *unto Job 13:20*
m., then not hide
unto m. gave ear   *Job 29:21;*
               40:7
declare *unto m.*   *Job 42:4*
lines are fallen *unto m.* in   *Ps 16:6*
pleasant places
O God incline thine ear *unto Ps 17:6;*
m.   *31:2; 102:2*
turn *unto m.*   *Ps 25:16*
be merciful *unto m.*   *Ps 26:11;*
  41:4, 10; 56:1; 57:1; 86:3; 119:58, 132
be not silent to *m.*   *Ps 28:1*
he inclined *unto m.* and heard *Ps 40:1*
my cry   *77:1*

I will not fear what flesh can do *unto m.*   Ps 56:4

not be afraid what man can do *unto m.*   Ps 56:11; 118:6

O Israel, if thou wilt hearken *unto m.*   Ps 81:8

he shall cry *unto m.*, thou art my father   Ps 89:26

O when wilt thou come *unto m.*? I will walk   Ps 101:2

I was glad when they said *unto m.*   Ps 122:1

how precious are thy thoughts *unto m.*   Ps 139:17

Lord, I cry unto thee, make haste *unto m.*   Ps 141:1

whoso hearkeneth *unto m.* shall dwell   Pr 1:33

I will do so to him as he hath done *to m.*   Pr 24:29

as to fool, so it happeneth even *to m.*   Ec 2:15

bundle of myrrh is my beloved *unto m.*   Ca 1:13; 1:14

incense is an abomination *unto m.*   Isa 1:13

your new moons, they are a trouble *unto m.*   Isa 1:14

he calleth to me out of Seir, Watchman   Isa 21:11

and it shall be *unto m.* as Ariel   Isa 29:2

return *unto m.*, for I have redeemed thee   Isa 44:22

look *unto m.* and be ye saved, all the ends   Isa 45:22

unto me every knee shall bow, every tongue   Isa 45:23

mine adversary, let him come near *to m.*   Isa 50:8

for this is as the waters of Noah *unto m.*   Isa 54:9

come not near *to m.* I am holier than thou   Isa 65:5

if thou wilt return, return O Israel *unto m.*   Jer 4:1

tho' they shall cry *unto m.* I will not hear   Jer 11:11

mine heritage is *unto m.* as a lion   Jer 12:8; 12:9

that they might be *unto m.* for a people   Jer 13:11

thy word was *unto m.* joy of mine heart   Jer 15:16

wilt thou be altogether *unto m.* as a liar   Jer 15:18

they are all of them *unto m.* as Sodom   Jer 23:14

this city hath been *to m.* a provocation   Jer 32:31

it shall be *to m.* a name of joy   Jer 33:9

trusted, saying, Who shall come *unto m.*   Jer 49:4

the violence done *to m.* be upon Babylon   Jer 51:35

and they shall be like *unto m.*   La 1:21

and do to them as thou hast done *unto m.*   La 1:22

thy sons whom thou hast born *unto m.*   Eze 16:20

the house of Israel is *to m.* become dross   Eze 22:18

moreover this they have done *unto m.*   Eze 23:38

aha, she is broken, she is turned *unto m.*   Eze 26:2

to do the office of a priest *unto m.*   Eze 44:13

they shall come near *to m.* to minister *unto m.*   Eze 44:15

this secret is not revealed *to m.*   Da 2:30

my reason returned *unto m.*   Da 4:36

lords sought *unto m.*

I will betroth thee *unto m.* for ever   Ho 2:19

and I will sow her *unto m.* in the earth   Ho 2:23

so I bought her *to m.* for fifteen pieces   Ho 3:2

reject thee, thou shalt be no priest *to m.*   Ho 4:6

there is none among them that calleth *unto m.*   Ho 7:7

they have not cried *unto m.* with their hearts   Ho 7:14

Israel shall cry *unto m.*, My God, we know thee   Ho 8:2

are ye not as Ethiopians *unto m.*   Am 9:7

out of thee shall come forth *unto m.*   Mic 5:2

when in darkness, Lord shall be a light *unto m.*   Mic 7:8

I will watch to see what he will say *unto m.*   Hab 2:1

I smote you, yet ye turned not *to m.*   Hag 2:17

turn ye *unto m.* saith the Lord of hosts   Zec 1:3

did ye at all fast *unto m.* even *to m.*   Zec 7:5

baptized of thee, and comest thou *to m.*   M't 3:14

many will say *to m.* in that day, Lord, Lord   M't 7:22

come *unto m.* all ye that labour and are   M't 11:28

bring them *to m.*   M't 14:18; 17:17; 21:2; M'k 9:19

forbid them not to come *unto m.*   M't 19:14; M'k 10:14

and ye came *unto m.*; ye have done it *unto m.*   M't 25:36; 25:40

as ye did it not to these, ye did it not *to m.*   M't 25:45

all power is given *unto m.* in heaven   M't 28:18

let it be *unto m.* according to thy word   Lu 1:38

all this power, for that is delivered *unto m.*   Lu 4:6

whoso cometh *to m.* and heareth   Lu 6:47; 14:26

all things are delivered *to m.* of my Father   Lu 10:22

God be merciful *to m.* a sinner   Lu 19:13

ye will not come *to m.* to have life   Joh 5:40

he that cometh *to m.* shall never hunger   Joh 6:35; 6:37

no man can come *to m.*   Joh 6:44; 6:65

except Father draw

hath learned of the Father cometh *unto m.*   Joh 6:45

if any thirst, let him come *unto m.* and drink   Joh 7:37

if lifted up, I will draw all men *unto m.*   Joh 12:32

even as the Father said *unto m.*, so I speak   Joh 12:50

Pilate said, Speakest thou not *unto m.*   Joh 19:10

and ye shall be witnesses *unto m.*   Ac 1:8

hast made known *unto m.* the ways of life   Ac 2:28

go thy way, for he is a chosen vessel *to m.*   Ac 9:15

a vessel descend, and it came even *to m.*   Ac 11:5

I heard a voice speaking *unto m.*   Ac 26:14

was that which is good made death *unto m.*   Ro 7:13

through the grace given *unto m.*   Ro 12:3; 1Co 3:10

all things are lawful *unto m.* but all   1Co 6:12

that it should be so done *unto m.*   1Co 9:15

woe is *unto m.* if I preach not the gospel   1Co 9:16

dispensation of the gospel is committed *unto m.*   1Co 9:17

and he shall be a barbarian *unto m.*   1Co 14:11

an effectual door is open *unto m.*   1Co 16:9; 2Co 2:12

for that which was lacking *to m.*   2Co 11:9

what they were, it maketh no matter *to m.*   Ga 2:6

plucked out eyes, and have given them *to m.*   Ga 4:15

unto me who am less than least of all saints   Eph 3:8

for *to m.* to live is Christ, to die is gain   Ph'p 1:21

to m. indeed is not grievous, but for you safe   Ph'p 3:1

but what things were gain *to m.* those counted   Ph'p 3:7

which have been a comfort *unto m.*   Col 4:11

not *to m.* only; profitable *to m.*   2Ti 4:8; 4:11

but now profitable to thee and *to m.*   Ph'm 11

especially *to m.*; thou owest *to m.* thyself   Ph'm 16; 19

vengeance belongeth *unto m.*, saith Lord   Heb 10:30

I will not fear what man shall do *unto m.*   Heb 13:6

TOWARD ME

countenance is not *toward m.* as before   Ge 31:5

for great is thy mercy *toward m.*   Ps 86:13

render for all his benefits *toward m.*   Ps 116:12

I am my beloved's, his desire is *toward m.*   Ca 7:10

their fear *toward m.* is taught by men   Isa 29:13

sounding of bowels and mercies *toward m.*   Isa 63:15

that the high God hath wrought *toward m.*   Da 4:2

he told us your fervent mind *toward m.*   2Co 7:7

supply your lack of service *toward m.*   Ph'p 2:30

UNDER ME

enlarged my steps *under m.*   2Sa 22:37; Ps 18:36

thou hast subdued *under m.*   2Sa 22:40; Ps 18:39

bringeth down the people *under m.*   2Sa 22:48; Ps 18:47

for the beast that was *under m.* to pass   Ne 2:14

who subdueth my people *under m.*   Ps 144:2

having soldiers *under m.*   M't 8:9; Lu 7:8

WITH ME

that it may be well *with m.* for thy sake   Ge 12:13

if God will be *with m.* and keep me   Ge 28:20; Jos 14:12

thou knowest how thy cattle was *with m.*   Ge 30:29

the God of my father hath been *with m.*   Ge 31:5

discern thou what is thine *with m.* and take   Ge 31:32

and she said, Lie *with m.*   Ge 39:7; 39:12, 14; 2Sa 13:11

send lad *with m.*; lad be not *with m.*   Ge 43:8; 44:34

why chide ye *with m.* why tempt Lord   Ex 17:2

ye shall not make *with m.* gods of silver   Ex 20:23

if thy presence go not *with m.* carry us not   Ex 33:15

if thou deal thus *with m.*, kill me   Nu 11:15

is not this laid up in store *with m.*   De 32:34

that I, even I, am he, and there is no God *with m.*   De 32:39

I and all the people that are *with m.*   Jos 8:5

if thou wilt go *with m.* then I will go   J'g 4:8

I and all that are *with m.* then blow ye   J'g 7:18

saying, What hast thou to do *with m.*   J'g 11:12

I love thee, when thy heart is not *with m.*   J'g 16:15

behold, the silver is *with m.*; dwell *with m.*   J'g 17:2; 17:10

as ye have dealt *with m.*; why go *with m.*   Ru 1:8; 1:11

go up, for ye shall eat *with m.* to-day   1Sa 9:19

if he be able to fight *with m.* and to kill me   1Sa 17:9

but *with m.* thou shalt be in safeguard   1Sa 22:23

how that thou hast dealt well *with m.*   1Sa 24:18

to-morrow shalt thou and thy sons be *with m.*   1Sa 28:19

wherefore wentest not thou *with m.*   2Sa 19:25

I will feed thee *with m.* in Jerusalem   2Sa 19:33

hath made *with m.* an everlasting covenant   2Sa 23:5

that thine hand might be *with m.*   1Ch 4:10

even so deal *with m.;* are *with m.* in Judah   2Ch 2:3; 2:7

from meddling with God, who is *with m.*   2Ch 35:21

and not fear, but it is not so *with m.*   Job 9:35

and the sea saith, It is not *with m.*   Job 28:14

when the Almighty was yet *with m.*   Job 29:5

that was at peace *with m.;* thou art *with m.*   Ps 17:4; 23:4

in the night his song shall be *with m.*   Ps 42:8

those that have made a covenant *with m.*   Ps 50:5

he delivered, for there were many *with m.*   Ps 55:18

the faithful, that they may dwell *with m.*   Ps 101:6

thy commands, for they are ever *with m.*   Ps 119:98

riches and honour are *with m.,* yea, durable   Pr 8:18

come *with m.* from Lebanon, my spouse   Ca 4:8

and he shall make peace *with m.*   Isa 27:5

who will contend *with m.,* let us stand   Isa 50:8

of the people there was none *with m.*   Isa 63:3

the Lord is *with m.* as a mighty one   Jer 20:11

do *with m.* as seemeth good and meet to you   Jer 26:14

none holdeth *with m.* but Michael   Da 10:21

for then it was better *with m.* than now   Ho 2:7

yea, and what have ye to do *with m.*   Joe 3:4

he walked *with m.* in peace and equity   Mal 2:6

he that is not *with m.* is against me. he that gathereth not *with m.*   M't 12:30; Lu 11:23

Lord, have patience *with m.* I will pay   M't 18:26; 18:29

didst not thou agree *with m.* for a penny   M't 20:13

said, Tarry ye here, and watch *with m.*   M't 26:38; 26:40

and my children are *with m.* in bed   Lu 11:7

saying, Rejoice *with m.*   Lu 15:6; 15:9; Ph'p 2:18

son, thou art ever *with m.*   Lu 15:31

with m. on   Lu 22:21

ye are they which have continued *with m.*   Lu 22:28

to-day shalt thou be *with m.* in paradise   Lu 23:43

he that sent me is *with m.* the Father   Joh 8:29

if I wash thee not, thou hast no part *with m.*   Joh 13:8

he that eateth bread *with m.* hath lifted up   Joh 13:18

have been *with m.* from the beginning   Joh 15:27

am not alone, because the Father *with m.*   Joh 16:32

that they also be *with m.* where I am   Joh 17:24

ministered to them that were *with m.*   Ac 20:34

they that were *with m.* saw the light   Ac 22:9; 22:11

I would do good, evil is present *with m.*   Ro 7:21

strive *with m.* in your prayers to God   Ro 15:30

but *with m.* it is a very small thing   1Co 4:3

but the grace of God that was *with m.*   1Co 15:10

if it be meet that I go, they shall go *with m.*   1Co 16:4

that *with m.* there should be yea, yea   2Co 1:17

he hath served *with m.* in the gospel   Ph'p 2:22

so soon as I shall see how it will go *with m.*   Ph'p 2:23

women, who laboured *with m.* in the gospel   Ph'p 4:3

no church communicated *with m.* but ye only   Ph'p 4:15; 4:16

only Luke is *with m.;* none stood *with m.*   2Ti 4:11

the Lord stood *with m.* and strengthened me   2Ti 4:17

whom I would have retained *with m.*   Ph'm 13

they shall walk *with m.* in white, for they   Re 3:4

will come and sup with him, and he *with m.*   Re 3:20

will I grant to sit *with m.* in my throne   Re 3:21

I come quickly, and my reward is *with m.*   Re 22:12

WITHIN ME

the arrows of the Almighty are *within m.*   Job 6:4

though my reins be consumed *within m.*   Job 19:27

the spirit *within m.* constraineth me   Job 32:18

heart was hot *within m.* while musing   Ps 39:3

O my God, my soul is cast down *within m.*   Ps 42:6

why art thou disquieted *within m.*   Ps 42:11; 43:5

O God, renew a right spirit *within m.*   Ps 51:10

in the multitude of my thoughts *within m.*   Ps 94:19

and all that is *within m.* bless his holy name   Ps 103:1

spirit was overwhelmed *within m.*   Ps 142:3; 143:4

with my spirit *within m.* will I seek thee   Isa 26:9

my heart *within m.* is broken   Jer 23:9

my heart is turned *within m.* because of   La 1:20; Ho 11:8

when my soul fainted *within m.*   Jon 2:7

WITHOUT ME

without m. they shall bow down under   Isa 10:4

for *without m.* ye can do nothing   Joh 15:5

MEADOW

fatfleshed; and they fed in a *m.*   Ge 41:2

well favoured; and they fed in a *m.*   Ge 41:18

MEADOWS

even out of the *m.* of Gibeah   J'g 20:33

the *m.* by the Nile (A)(B)(E)   Isa 19:7

MEAH

the tower of *M.* they sanctified   Ne 3:1

the tower of *M.* even unto   Ne 12:39

MEAL

three measures of fine *m.*   Ge 18:6

meal (S)   Ex 29:41; 30:9; 40:29; Le 2:1, 3, 4, 5, 6, 7, 8, 9, 10, 11, 13, 14, 15; 5:13; 6:14, 15, 20, 21, 23; 7:9, 10, 37; 9:4, 17; 10:12; 14:10, 20, 21, 31; 23:13, 16, 18, 37; Nu 4:16, 6:15, 17; 7:13, 19, 25, 31, 37, 49, 55, 61, 67, 73, 79, 87; 8:8; 15:4, 6, 9, 24; 18:9; 28:5, 8, 9, 12, 13, 20, 26, 28, 31; 29:3, 6, 9, 11, 14, 16, 18, 19, 21, 22, 24, 25, 27, 28, 30, 31, 33, 34, 37, 38; Jos 22:23, 29; J'g 13:19, 23; 1Ki 8:64; 2Ki 3:20; 16:13, 15; 1Ch 21:23; 23:29; 2Ch 7:7; Ezr 7:17; Ne 10:33; 13:5, 9; Isa 57:6; Jer 17:26; 33:18; Eze 42:13; 44:29; 45:15, 17, 24, 25; 46:5, 7, 11, 14, 15, 20; Joe 1:9, 13; 2:14; Am 5:22

m. offering (E)   Ex 29:41; 40:29; Eze 42:13; 44:29

m. offering (B)(E)   Ex 30:9; Nu 4:16; 15:6; 28:8; 29:6; J'g 13:19, 23; Ne 10:33; Isa 57:6; Joe 1:9; 2:14

m. offering (E)   Le 2:1; 2:3; 6:14; 14:19; Nu 28:26

part of an ephah of barley *m.*   Nu 5:15

m. offering (E)   Nu 7:13

m. offering (B)(E)(R)   Nu 29:6

m. offerings (B)(E)   Nu 29:39

m. offering (E)   Jos 22:29

and threescore measures of *m.*   1Ki 4:22

m. offering (B)(E)   1Ki 8:64; Ne 13:5; Am 5:22

but an handful of *m.* in a barrel   1Ki 17:12

barrel of *m.* shall not waste   1Ki 17:14

the barrel of *m.* wasted not   1Ki 17:16

But he said, Then bring *m.*   2Ki 4:41

meat, *m.,* cakes of figs, and bunches   1Ch 12:40

Take the millstones and grind *m.*   Isa 47:2

m. offering (E)   Eze 45:17

stalk: the bud shall yield no *m.*   Ho 8:7

and hid in three measures of *m.*   M't 13:33; Lu 13:21

for a single *m.* sold (A)(B)(N)(R)   Heb 12:16

for one mess of *m.* sold (E)   Heb 12:16

MEALTIME

her. At *m.* come thou hither   Ru 2:14

MEAN

What *m.* these seven ewe lambs which   Ge 21:29

unto you, What *m.* ye by this service   Ex 12:26

What *m.* the testimonies, and saying, What *m.* ye by these stones   De 6:20; Jos 4:6

to come, saying, What *m.* these stones   Jos 21

came to pass in the *m.* while   1Ki 18:45

he shall not stand before *m.* men   Pr 22:29

the *m.* man boweth down, and   Isa 2:9

and ye that ye beat my people to pieces   Isa 3:15

the *m.* man shall be brought down   Isa 5:1

the sword, not of a *m.* man   Isa 31:8

know ye not what these things *m.*   Eze 17:12

What *m.* ye, that ye used this proverb   Eze 18:2

rising from the dead should *m.*   M'k 9:10

In the *m.* time, when there were   Lu 12:1

the *m.* while his disciples prayed   Joh 4:31

vision he had seen should *m.*   Ac 10:17

know what these things *m.*   Ac 17:20

What *m.* ye to weep and to break   Ac 21:13

in Cilicia, a citizen of no *m.* city   Ac 21:39

thoughts the *m.* while accusing   Ro 2:15

I *m.* not that other men be eased   2Co 8:13

MEANEST

What *m.* thou by all this drove   Ge 33:8

unto Ziba, What *m.* thou by these   2Sa 16:2

not shew us what thou *m.* by these   Eze 37:18

unto him, What *m.* thou, O sleeper   Jon 1:6

MEANETH

what *m.* the heat of this great anger   De 29:24

What *m.* the noise of this great shout   1Sa 4:6

What *m.* the noise of this tumult   1Sa 4:14

m. then this bleating of the sheep   1Sa 15:14

Howbeit he *m.* not so, neither   Isa 10:7

But go ye and learn what that *m.*   M't 9:13

But if ye had known what this *m.*   M't 12:7

one to another, What *m.* this   Ac 2:12

MEANING

dream with its own *m*. (R)   Ge 40:5
show its *m*. (B)   Da 2:4; 4:19; 7:16
the vision and sought for the   Da 8:15
m. to sail by the coasts of Asia Ac 27:2
if I know not the *m*. of the   1Co 14:11
voice

MEANINGLESS

m. word (B)   De 32:47;
                              Isa 1:13; Eph 5:6
come no more with *m*.   Isa 1:13
offerings (B)
m. words (B)   Eph 5:6

MEANS

that will by no *m*. clear the   Ex 34:7
guilty
and by no *m*. clearing the   Nu 14:18
guilty
broken by *m*. of the pransings J'g 5:22
by what *m*. we may prevail   J'g 16:5
against
by all *m*. (S)   1Sa 6:3
yet dcth he devise *m*. that his 2Sa 14:14
by no *m*. (S)   1Ki 3:26; 3:27
they bring them out by their 1Ki 10:29
m.
if by any *m*. he be missing,   1Ki 20:39
then shall
for the kings of Syria, by   2Ch 1:17
their *m*.
by this *m*. thou shalt have no Ezr 4:16
can by any *m*. redeem his   Ps 49:7
brother
For by *m*. of a whorish woman a Pr 6:26
the priests bear rule by their Jer 5:31
m.
this hath been by your *m*.: will Mal 1:9
Thou shalt by no *m*. come out M't 5:26
and they sought *m*. to bring Lu 5:18
him in
by what *m*. he that was   Lu 8:36
possessed
nothing shall by any *m*. hurt Lu 10:19
you
But by what *m*. he now seeth Joh 9:21
by what *m*. he is made whole Ac 4:9
I must by all *m*. keep this feast Ac 18:21
if by any *m*. they might attain Ac 27:12
to
if by any *m*. now at length I Ro 1:10
might
If by any *m*. I may provoke Ro 11:14
to
heed lest by any *m*. this liberty 1Co 8:9
of
that I might by all *m*. save 1Co 9:22
some
lest that by any *m*. when I 1Co 9:27
have
upon us by the *m*. of many 2Co 1:11
persons
lest by any *m*. as the serpent 2Co 11:3
lest by any *m*. I should run, or Ga 2:2
If by any *m*. I might attain Ph'p 3:11
unto
lest by some *m*. the tempter 1Th 3:5
have
no man deceive you by any *m*. 2Th 2:3
give you peace always by all 2Th 3:16
m.
testament, that by *m*. of death Heb 9:15
by the *m*. of those miracles Re 13:14
which he

MEANT

God *m*. it unto good, to bring Ge 50:20
to
and asked what these thing *m*. Lu 15:26
pass by, he asked what it *m*. Lu 18:36

MEARAH

M. that is beside the Sidonians Jos 13:4

MEASURE

they did *m*. it (S)   Ex 16:18
the curtains shall have one *m*. Ex 26:2
curtains shall be all of one *m*. Ex 26:8
a tenth of four (A)(R)   Ex 29:40
in *m*. of length (S)   Le 19:25
in meteyard, in weight, or in Le 19:35
m.

ye shall *m*. from without the   Nu 35:5
city
they shall *m*. unto the cities   De 21:2
which
and just *m*. shalt thou have   De 25:15
about two thousand cubits by Jos 3:4
m.
were of one *m*. and one size   1Ki 6:25
one casting, one *m*. and one   1Ki 7:37
size
shall a *m*. of fine flour be sold 2Ki 7:1
for
So a *m*. of fine flour was sold 2Ki 7:16
for a.
a *m*. of fine flour for a shekel 2Ki 7:18
and for all manner of *m*. and 1Ch 23:29
size
first *m*. was threescore cubits   2Ch 3:3
The *m*. thereof is longer than Job 11:9
he weigheth the waters by *m*. Job 28:25
and the *m*. of my days, what it Ps 39:4
is
m. the valley of Succoth (S)   Ps 60:6;
                                                  108:7
them tears to drink in great *m*. Ps 80:5
understanding beyond *m*. (R) Ps 147:5
opened her mouth without *m*. Isa 5:14
In *m*. when it shooteth forth Isa 27:8
the dust of the earth in a *m*. Isa 40:12
I *m*. their former work into Isa 65:7
their
but I will correct thee in *m*. Jer 30:11
end of thee, but correct thee Jer 46:28
in *m*.
and the *m*. of thy   Jer 51:13
covetousness
Thou shalt drink also water Eze 4:11
by *m*.
and they shall drink water by Eze 4:16
m.
side; they three were of one Eze 40:10
m.
the posts had one *m*. on this Eze 40:10
side
were after the *m*. of the first Eze 40:21
gate
were after the *m*. of the gate Eze 40:22
that
about within and without, by Eze 41:17
m.
and let them *m*. the pattern Eze 43:10
of this *m*. shalt thou *m*. the Eze 45:3
length
and the bath shall be of one Eze 45:11
m.
the *m*. thereof shall be after Eze 45:11
these four corners were of Eze 46:22
one *m*.
east side ye shall *m*. from Eze 47:18
Hauran
the scant *m*. that is   Mic 6:10
abominable
To *m*. Jerusalem, to see what is Zec 2:2
and with what *m*. ye mete, it M't 7:2;
shall   M'k 4:24
what *m*. you us. (S)   M't 7:2;
                              M'k 4:24; Lu 6:38
Fill ye up then the the *m*. of your M't 23:32
in themselves beyond *m*. and M'k 6:51
And were beyond *m*.   M'k 7:37
astonished
they were astonished out of M'k 10:26
m.
good *m*. pressed down, and Lu 6:38
For with the same *m*. that ye Lu 6:38
mete
put in a grain *m*. (B)   Lu 11:33
not the Spirit by *m*. unto him Joh 3:34
dealt to every man the *m*. of Ro 12:3
faith
we were pressed out of *m*.   2Co 1:8
not boast of things without 2Co 10:13
our *m*.
but according to the *m*. of 2Co 10:13
the rule
to us, a *m*. to reach even unto 2Co 10:13
you
stretch not ourselves beyond 2Co 10:14
our *m*.
boasting of things without our 2Co 10:15
m.
in stripes above *m*. in   2Co 11:23
prisons
lest I should be exalted above 2Co 12:7
m.
beyond *m*. I persecuted the Ga 1:13
to the *m*. of the gift of Christ Eph 4:7
the *m*. of the stature of the Eph 4:13
fulness

working in the *m*. of   Eph 4:16
every part
A *m*. of wheat for a penny, and Re 6:6
Rise, and *m*. the temple of God Re 11:1
temple leave out, and *m*. it not Re 11:2
had a golden reed to *m*. the Re 21:15
city
according to the *m*. of a man Re 21:17

MEASURED

it, he *m*. six measures of barley Ru 3:15
Moab, and *m*. them with a line 2Sa 8:2
even with two lines *m*. he to 2Sa 8:2
put to
a nation *m*. out   Isa 18:2; 18:7
hath *m*. the waters in the   Isa 40:12
hollow
m. the heaven with a span (S) Isa 40:12
m. the dust of the earth (S)   Isa 40:12
If heaven above can be *m*.   Jer 31:37
neither the sand of the sea *m*. Jer 33:22
he *m*. the breadth of the   Eze 40:5
building
and *m*. the threshold of the   Eze 40:6
gate
He *m*. also the porch of the   Eze 40:8
gate
Then *m*. he the porch of the   Eze 40:9
gate
And he *m*. the breadth of   Eze 40:11
the entry
He *m*. then the gate from the Eze 40:13
roof
Then he *m*. the breadth from Eze 40:19
he *m*. the length thereof, and Eze 40:20
m. from gate to gate an   Eze 40:23
hundred
and he *m*. the posts thereof   Eze 40:24
and he *m*. from gate to gate Eze 40:27
toward
and he *m*. the south gate   Eze 40:28
according
and he *m*. the gate according Eze 40:32
to
gate, and *m*. it according to Eze 40:35
these
So he *m*. the court, an   Eze 40:47
hundred
and *m*. each post of the   Eze 40:48
porch, five
and *m*. the posts, six cubits Eze 41:1
broad
and he *m*. the length thereof, Eze 41:2
forty
inward, and *m*. the post of the Eze 41:3
door
So he *m*. the length thereof, Eze 41:4
twenty
After he *m*. the wall of the   Eze 41:5
house
So he *m*. the house, an   Eze 41:13
hundred
And he *m*. the length of the   Eze 41:15
building
the east and *m*. it round   Eze 42:15
about
He *m*. the east side with the Eze 42:16
He *m*. the north side, five   Eze 42:17
hundred
He *m*. the south side, five   Eze 42:18
hundred
and *m*. five hundred reeds   Eze 42:19
with the
He *m*. it by the four sides: it Eze 42:20
eastward he *m*. a thousand   Eze 47:3
cubits
Again he *m*. a thousand cubits Eze 47:4
Again he *m*. a thousand, and Eze 47:4
Afterward he *m*. a thousand Eze 47:5
which cannot be *m*. nor   Ho 1:10
numbered
He stood, and *m*. the earth: he Hab 3:6
mete, it shall be *m*. to you   M't 7:2
again
ye mete, it shall be *m*. to you M'k 4:24
withal it shall be *m*. to you Lu 6:38
again
and he *m*. the city with the   Re 21:16
reed
he *m*. the wall thereof, an   Re 21:17
hundred

MEASURES

quickly three *m*. of fine meal Ge 18:6
bring three pecks of fine meal Ge 18:6
(B)
in *m*. of length (E)(R)   Le 19:35
I will take *m*. against you (B) Le 26:28

MEASURES

not have in thine house *De 25:14*
divers *m.*
he measured six *m.* of barley *Ru 3:15*
These six *m.* of barley gave he *Ru 3:17*
me
five *m.* of parched corn, and *1Sa 25:18*
two bushels of roasted grain *1Sa 25:18*
(B)
one day was thirty *m.* of fine *1Ki 4:22*
flour
195 bushels of fine flour, 390 *1Ki 4:22*
bushels of meal (B)
flour, and threescore *m.* of *1Ki 4:22*
meal
Hiram twenty thousand *m.* of *1Ki 5:11*
wheat
20,000 sacks of wheat (B) *1Ki 5:11*
and twenty *m.* of pure oil *1Ki 5:11*
to the *m.* of hewed stones *1Ki 7:9*
after the *m.* of hewed stones *1Ki 7:11*
as would contain two *m.* of *1Ki 18:32*
seed
two bushels of seed (B) *1Ki 18:32*
and two *m.* of barley for *2Ki 7:1;*
a shekel *7:16*
Two *m.* of barley for a shekel *2Ki 7:18*
thousand *m.* of beaten wheat *2Ch 2:10*
twenty thousand *m.* of barley *2Ch 2:10*
ten thousand *m.* of wheat, *2Ch 27:5*
and ten
and to an hundred *m.* of *Ezr 7:22*
wheat, and
1125 bushels of wheat (B) *Ezr 7:22*
Who hath laid the *m.* thereof *Job 38:5*
Divers weights, and divers *m.* *Pr 20:10*
the portion of thy *m.* from me *Jer 13:25*
thereof according to these *m.* *Eze 40:24;*
40:29
south gate according to these *Eze 40:28*
m.
the gate according to these *m.* *Eze 40:32*
thereof, were according to *Eze 40:33*
these *m.*
measured it according to *Eze 40:35*
these
these are the *m.* of the altar *Eze 43:13*
after
And these shall be the *m.* *Eze 48:16*
thereof
four thousand and five *Eze 48:30;*
hundred *m.* *48:33*
round about eighteen *Eze 48:35*
thousand *m.*
one came to an heap of twenty *Hag 2:16*
m.
a heap of twenty bushels (B) *Hag 2:16*
draw out fifty *m.* (R) *Hag 2:16*
took, and hid in three *m.* of *M't 13:33;*
meal *Lu 13:21*
in three portions of flour *M't 13:33*
(B)
half a hundredweight of flour *M't 13:33*
(N)
And he said, An hundred *m.* of *Lu 16:6*
oil
a hundred barrels of oil (B) *Lu 16:6*
a thousand gallons of olive oil *Lu 16:6*
(N)
he said, An hundred *m.* of *Lu 16:7*
wheat
a hundred sacks of wheat (B) *Lu 16:7*
a thousand bushels of wheat *Lu 16:7*
(N)(P)
three *m.* of barley for a penny *Re 6:6*

MEASURING

the *m.* line shall yet go forth *Jer 31:39*
over
of flax in his hand, and a *m.* *Eze 40:3*
reed
in the man's hand a *m.* reed of *Eze 40:5*
six
made an end of *m.* the inner *Eze 42:15*
house
the east side with the *m.* reed *Eze 42:16*
with the *m.* reed round *Eze 42:16;*
about *42:17*
hundred reeds, with the *m.* *Eze 42:18;*
reed *42:19*
a man with a *m.* line in his hand *Zec 2:1*
they *m.* themselves by *2Co 10:12*
themselves

MEAT

seed; to you it shall be for *m.* *Ge 1:29*
it shall be for food *Ge 1:29;*
(A)(B)(E)(R) *1:30; 9:3*

have given every green herb for *Ge 1:30*
m.
that liveth shall be *m.* for you *Ge 9:3*
there was set *m.* before him *Ge 24:33*
make me savoury *m.* such as I *Ge 27:4*
make me savoury *m.* that I *Ge 27:7*
make them savoury *m.* for thy *Ge 27:9*
and his mother made savoury *Ge 27:14*
m.
she gave the savoury *m.* and *Ge 27:17*
And he also had made savoury *Ge 27:31*
m.
laden with corn and bread *Ge 45:23*
and *m.*
of all *m.* which may be eaten *Le 11:34*
All edible food *Le 11:34;*
(A)(B)(E)(R) *22:11, 13; 25:6*
that is born in his house, shall *Le 22:11*
eat of his *m.*
she shall eat of her father's *m.* *Le 22:13*
the sabbath of the land shall *Le 25:6;*
be *m.* for you *25:7*
m. of the sacrifice made by fire *Nu 28:24*
ye shall buy *m.* of them for *De 2:6*
money
food (A)(B)(E)(R) *De 2:6;*
2:28; 1Ki 10:5; Job 6:7; 12:11; 20:14;
30:4; 33:20; 34:3; 36:31; 38:41; Ps 42:3;
59:15; 69:21 74:14; 78:25, 30; 79:2;
104:27; 107:18; 145:15; Pr 6:8; 23:3;
30:22 25; 31:15; Isa 62:8; 65:25;
La 1:11, 19; 4:10; Eze 4:10; 16:19; 29:5;
34:10; 47:12; Da 1:10; 4:12; Joe 1:16;
Hab 1:16; 3:17; Hag 2:12; Mal 1:12;
3:10
thou shalt sell me *m.* for *De 2:28*
money to eat
thou shalt destroy trees not *De 20:20*
for *m.*
m. offerings *Jos 22:29;*
1Ki 8:64; 2Ch 7:7; Ezr 7:17; 13:5;
Jer 17:26; 33:18; Eze 45:17; Am 5:22
kings gathered their *m.* under *J'g 1:7*
my table
out of the eater came forth *m.* *J'g 14:14*
and out of
not fail to sit with the king at *1Sa 20:5*
m.
the king sat him down to eat *1Sa 20:24*
m.
cometh not the son of Jesse *1Sa 20:27*
to *m.*
did eat no *m.* the second day *1Sa 20:34*
of the
to eat *m.* while it was yet day *2Sa 3:35*
him a mess of *m.* from the *2Sa 11:8*
king
it did eat of his own *m.* and *2Sa 12:3*
drank
Tamar come, and give me *m.* *2Sa 13:5*
dress the *m.* in my sight, that I *2Sa 13:5*
Amnon's house, and dress him *2Sa 13:7*
m.
Bring the *m.* into the *2Sa 13:10*
chamber
the *m.* of his table, and the *1Ki 10:5*
sitting
the strength of that *m.* forty *1Ki 19:8*
days
on oxen, and *m.* meal, cakes *1Ch 12:40*
And the *m.* of his table, and *2Ch 9:4*
to touch are as my sorrowful *Job 6:7*
m.
words? and the mouth taste *Job 12:11*
his *m.*
his *m.* in his bowels is *Job 20:14*
turned, it
There shall none of his *m.* be *Job 20:21*
left
and juniper roots for their *m.* *Job 30:4*
bread, and his soul dainty *m.* *Job 33:20*
words, as the mouth tasteth *m.* *Job 34:3*
people; he giveth *m.* in *Job 36:31*
abundance
God, they wander for lack of *Job 38:41*
m.
My tears have been my *m.* day *Ps 42:3*
us like sheep appointed for *m.* *Ps 44:11*
them wander up and down for *Ps 59:15*
m.
They gave me also gall for my *Ps 69:21*
m.
gavest him to be *m.* to the *Ps 74:14*
people
heart by asking *m.* for their *Ps 78:18*
lust

food: he sent them *m.* to the *Ps 78:25*
full
their *m.* was yet in their *Ps 78:30*
mouths
servants have they given to be *Ps 79:2*
m.
prey, and seek their *m.* from *Ps 104:21*
God
give them their *m.* in due *Ps 104:27;*
season *145:15*
soul abhorreth all manner of *Ps 107:18*
m.
hath given *m.* unto them that *Ps 111:5*
fear
Provideth her *m.* in the summer *Pr 6:8*
dainties: for they are deceitful *m.* *Pr 23:3*
and a fool when he is filled *Pr 30:22*
with *m.*
prepare their *m.* in the *Pr 30:25*
summer
giveth *m.* to her household *Pr 31:15*
no more give thy corn to be *m.* *Isa 62:8*
dust shall be the serpent's *m.* *Isa 65:25*
carcases of this people shall be *Jer 7:33*
m.
carcases shall be *m.* for the *Jer 16:4*
fowls
will I give to be *m.* for the *Jer 19:7*
fowls
dead bodies shall be for *m.* *Jer 34:20*
unto
given their pleasant things for *La 1:11*
m.
they sought their *m.* to relieve *La 1:19*
were their *m.* in the destruction *La 4:10;*
thy *m.* which thou shalt eat *Eze 4:10*
shall
My *m.* also which I gave thee *Eze 16:19*
given thee for, to be the beasts *Eze 29:5*
became *m.* to all the beasts of *Eze 34:5*
flock became *m.* to every beast *Eze 34:8*
that they may not be *m.* for *Eze 34:10*
there
shall grow all trees for *m.* *Eze 47:12*
the fruit thereof shall be for *Eze 47:12*
m.
a daily provision of the king's *Da 1:5*
m.
with the portion of the king's *Da 1:8*
m.
hath appointed your *m.* and *Da 1:10*
your
eat of the portion of the king's *Da 1:13;*
m. *1:15*
took away the portion of their *Da 1:16*
m.
much, and in it was *m.* for *Da 4:12;*
all *4:21*
feed of the portion of his *m.* *Da 11:26*
shall
their jaws, and I laid *m.* unto *Ho 11:4*
them
is fat, and their *m.* plenteous *Hab 1:16*
and the fields shall yield no *Hab 3:17*
m.
pottage, or wine, or oil, or *Hag 2:12*
any *m.*
even his *m.* is contemptible *Mal 1:12*
there may be *m.* in mine *Mal 3:10*
house
his *m.* was locusts and wild *M't 3:4*
honey
Is not the life more than *m.* *M't 6:25*
life greater than food *M't 6:25*
(A)(E)(N)(P)(R)
life more important than *M't 6:25*
nourishment (B)
as Jesus sat at *m.* in the house *M't 9:10*
the workman is worthy of his *M't 10:10*
m.
deserves his support-living, *M't 10:10*
food (A)
worker deserves his support *M't 10:10*
(B)
laborer is worthy of his food *M't 10:10*
(E)(R)
worker earns his keep *M't 10:10*
(N)(P)
and them which sat with him *M't 14:9*
at *m.*
broken *m.* that was left seven *M't 15:37*
baskets
to give them *m.* in due season *M't 24:45*
give to the others the food *M't 24:45*
(A)(E)(P)(R)
provide their sustenance (B) *M't 24:45*
issue their rations (N) *M't 24:45*

an hungered, and ye gave   *M't 25:35*
me *m.*
hungered, and ye gave me no   *M't 25:42*
m.
poured it on his head, as he   *M't 26:7*
sat at *m.*
as Jesus sat at *m.* in his house   *M'k 2:15*
broken *m.* that was left seven   *M'k 8:8*
baskets
as he sat at *m.* there came a   *M'k 14:3*
woman
unto the eleven as they sat at   *M'k 16:14*
m.
and he that hath *m.* let him do   *Lu 3:11*
Pharisee's house, and sat down   *Lu 7:36*
to *m.*
sat at *m.* in the Pharisee's   *Lu 7:37*
house
they that sat at *m.* with him   *Lu 7:49*
began to
and he commanded to give her   *Lu 8:55*
m.
go and buy *m.* for all this people   *Lu 9:13*
and he went in, and sat down   *Lu 11:37*
to *m.*
The life is more than *m.* and   *Lu 12:23*
and make them to sit down to   *Lu 12:37*
m.
their portion of *m.* in due   *Lu 12:42*
season
of them that sit at *m.* with   *Lu 14:10*
thee
them that sat at *m.* with him   *Lu 14:15*
heard
from the field, Go and sit   *Lu 17:7*
down to *m.*
is greater, he that sitteth at *m.*   *Lu 22:27*
or
serveth? is not he that sitteth   *Lu 22:27*
at *m.*
as he sat at *m.* with them, he   *Lu 24:30*
took
unto them, Have ye here any   *Lu 24:41*
m.
away unto the city to buy *m.*   *Joh 4:8*
gone off to buy food   *Joh 4:8*
(A)(B)(E)(N)(P)(R)
have *m.* to eat that ye know   *Joh 4:32*
not of
I have food to eat of   *Joh 4:32;*
(A)(N)(P)(R)   *4:34*
I have nourishment of which   *Joh 4:32;*
you (B)   *4:34*
My *m.* is to do the will of him   *Joh 4:34*
that
labour not for the *m.* which   *Joh 6:27*
perisheth
labor not for food   *Joh 6:27*
(A)(B)(E)(N)(P)(R)
m. which endureth unto   *Joh 6:27*
everlasting
For my flesh is *m.* indeed and   *Joh 6:55*
my
My flesh is genuine food   *Joh 6:55*
(A)(B)(N)(P)(R)
them, Children, have ye any *m.*   *Joh 21:5*
did eat their *m.* with gladness   *Ac 2:46*
received *m.* he was   *Ac 9:19*
strengthened
set *m.* before them, and   *Ac 16:34*
rejoiced
besought them all to take *m.*   *Ac 27:33*
I pray you to take some *m.*   *Ac 27:34*
cheer, and they also took   *Ac 27:36*
some *m.*
brother be grieved with thy   *Ro 14:15*
m.
Destroy not him with thy *m.*   *Ro 14:15*
the kingdom of God is not *m.*   *Ro 14:17*
not a matter of food and   *Ro 14:17*
drink (A)(R)
consist in eating and drinking   *Ro 14:17*
(B)(E)(N)
m. destroy not the work of   *Ro 14:20*
God
neither eat *m.* (S)   *Ro 14:21*
fed you with milk, and not with   *1Co 3:2*
m.
But *m.* commendeth us not to   *1Co 8:8*
God
food does not commend us   *1Co 8:8;*
(A)(B)(E)(N)(P)(R)   *8:10, 13*
sit at *m.* in the idol's temple   *1Co 8:10*
if *m.* make my brother to   *1Co 8:13*
offend
I will eat no *m.* while (S)   *1Co 8:13*
did all eat the same spiritual   *1Co 10:3*
m.
same spiritual food   *1Co 10:3*
(A)(B)(E)(N)(P)(R)

sold in the *m.* market   *1Co 10:25*
(A)(B)(N)(P)(R)
no man therefore judge you in   *Col 2:16*
m.
of milk, and not of strong *m.*   *Heb 5:12*
solid food   *Heb 5:12;*
(A)(B)(E)(N)(P)(R)   *5:14*
strong *m.* belongeth to them   *Heb 5:14*
that
morsel of *m.* sold his   *Heb 12:16*
birthright

MEAT *OFFERING*

according to *m. offering* of   *Ex 29:41*
the morning
cereal offering (A)(B)(R)   *Ex 29:41;*
40:29; Eze 42:13; 44:29; 45:17, 25; 46:5,
               7
meal-offering (S)   *Ex 29:41;*
     40:29; Eze 42:13; 44:29
shall offer no *m. offering* on   *Ex 30:9*
altar of incense
cereal offering (A)(R)   *Ex 30:9;*
Nu 4:16; 15:6; 28:8; 29:6; J'g 13:19, 23;
     Ne 10:33; Isa 57:6; Joe 1:9; 2:14
meal offering (B)(E)   *Ex 30:9;*
Nu 4:16; 15:6; 28:8; 29:6; J'g 13:19, 23;
     Ne 10:33; Isa 57:6; Joe 1:9; 2:14
on altar of burnt offering   *Ex 40:29*
offered *m. offering*
when any will offer a *m.*   *Le 2:1;*
offering   *2:4-5, 7, 14*
cereal offering (A)(R)   *Le 2:1;*
    2:3; 6:14; 14:10; Nu 28:26
food offering (B)   *Le 2:1;*
    2:3; 6:14; 14:10; Nu 28:26
meal-offering (E)   *Le 2:1;*
    2:3; 6:14; 14:10; Nu 28:26
remnant of *m. offering* shall be   *Le 2:3;*
Aaron's   *2:10; 5:13*
this is the law of the *m.*   *Le 6:14;*
offering   *7:37*
three tenth deals of flour for a   *Le 14:10*
m. offering
to Eleazar pertaineth daily *m.*   *Nu 4:16*
offering
mingled with oil for *m.*   *Nu 7:13;*
offering   *7:19; 28:12-13*
cereal offering (A)(R)   *Nu 7:13*
grain offering (B)   *Nu 7:13*
meal-offering (E)   *Nu 7:13*
for *m. offering* two tenth deals   *Nu 15:6;*
of flour   *28:9, 12*
as the *m. offering* of the   *Nu 28:8*
morning, offer it
when ye bring a new *m.*   *Nu 28:26*
offering to the Lord
besides his *m. offering* and   *Nu 29:6;*
burnt offering   *29:22, 25, 34*
cereal offering (A)   *Nu 29:6*
meal offering (B)(E)(R)   *Nu 29:6*
if altar to offer *m. offering*   *Jos 22:23*
save us not
Manoah took a kid with a *m.*   *J'g 13:19*
offering
not have received a *m.*   *J'g 13:23*
offering at our hands
when the *m. offering* was   *2Ki 3:20*
offered, behold
wheat for the *m. offering* I   *1Ch 21:23*
give it all
for continual *m. offering* and   *Ne 10:33*
burnt offering
to them hast thou offered a *m.*   *Isa 57:6*
offering
there shall they lay the *m.*   *Eze 42:13*
offering
they shall eat the *m. offering*   *Eze 44:29*
and sin offering
he shall prepare the *m.*   *Eze 45:17;*
offering   *45:24*
shall do the like according to   *Eze 45:25*
the *m. offering*
the *m. offering* shall be an   *Eze 46:5*
ephah for a ram
a *m. offering* and an ephah   *Eze 46:7;*
for a bullock   *46:11*
thus shall they prepare the *m.*   *Eze 46:15*
offering and oil
the *m. offering* and the drink   *Joe 1:9*
offering is cut off
the *m. offering* and drink   *Joe 1:13*
offering is withholden
leave a blessing, even a *m.*   *Joe 2:14*
offering to our God

MEAT *OFFERINGS*

these ye shall do for your *m.*   *Nu 29:39*
offerings
cereal offerings (A)(R)   *Nu 29:29*
meal offerings (B)(E)   *Nu 29:39*
turn to build an altar for *m.*   *Jos 22:29*
offerings
cereal offerings (A)(R)   *Jos 22:29*
food offerings (B)   *Jos 22:29*
meal-offerings (E)   *Jos 22:29*
Solomon offered *m. offerings*   *1Ki 8:64;*
altar too little to receive   *2Ch 7:7*
m. offerings
cereal offerings (A)(R)   *1Ki 8:64;*
    Ne 13:5; Am 5:22
meal offerings (B)(E)   *1Ki 8:64;*
    Ne 13:5; Am 5:22
buy speedily lambs with their   *Ezr 7:17*
m. offerings
chamber, where they laid their   *Ne 13:5*
m. offerings
come from Judah to bring *m.*   *Jer 17:26*
offerings
Levites not want a man to   *Jer 33:18*
kindle *m. offerings*
be the prince's part to give *m.*   *Eze 45:17*
offerings
cereal offerings (B)(R)   *Eze 45:17*
meal-offerings (E)   *Eze 45:17*
tho' ye offer *m. offerings* I   *Am 5:22*
will not accept you

MEATS

neither desire thou his dainty   *Pr 23:6*
m.
dainty foods (A)   *Pr 23:6*
neither desire his delicacies   *Pr 23:6*
(B)(R)
Neither desire his dainties (E)   *Pr 23:6*
into the draught. purging all *m.*   *M'k 7:19*
abstain from *m.* offered to   *Ac 15:29*
idols
abstain from what is offered   *Ac 15:29*
idols (A)(R)
abstain from food offered to   *Ac 15:29*
idols (B)
abstain from things offered to   *Ac 15:29*
idols (E)
m. for the belly, and the belly   *1Co 6:13*
for *m.*
Food for stomach, stomach   *1Co 6:13*
for food (A)(B)(N)(P)(R)
to abstain from *m.* God hath   *1Ti 4:3*
created
abstain from certain kinds of   *1Ti 4:3*
food (A)
prohibit enjoyment of foods   *1Ti 4:3*
(B)(N)(P)(R)
which stood only in *m.* and   *Heb 9:10*
drinks
food and drink   *Heb 9:10*
(B)(N)(P)(R)
the heart be established with   *Heb 13:9*
grace, not *m.*

MEBUNNAI

Anethothite, M. the   *2Sa 23:27*
Hushathite

MECHERATHITE

Hepher the M., Ahijah the   *1Ch 11:36*

MEDAD

and the name of the other M.   *Nu 11:26*
Eldad and M. do prophesy in   *Nu 11:27*

MEDAN

Zimran, and Jokshan, and M.   *Ge 25:2*
M. and Midian, and Ishbak   *1Ch 1:32*

MEDDLE

m. not with them of mount Seir   *De 2:5*
do not provoke or stir them up   *De 2:5*
(A)
Do not challenge them (B)   *De 2:5*
contend not with them (E)(R)   *De 2:5*
m. not with the children of   *De 2:19*
Ammon
why *m.* to thy hurt   *2Ki 14:10; 2Ch 25:19*
Why should you stir up   *2Ki 14:10*
trouble (B)
Why should you provoke   *2Ki 14:10*
trouble (R)

m. not with him that flattereth   *Pr 20:19*
do not associate with him   *Pr 20:19*
(A)(B)(R)
company not with him (E)   *Pr 20:19*
m. not with them that are   *Pr 24:21*
given to change
do not associate with those   *Pr 24:21*
(A)
do not mingle with those who   *Pr 24:21*
(B)
company not with them (E)   *Pr 24:21*

MEDDLED

leave off contention before it   *Pr 17:14*
be *m.* with
stop contention before it   *Pr 17:14*
becomes (A)(E)
quit before quarrel breaks out   *Pr 17:14*
(B)(R)

MEDDLETH

that *m.* with strife not   *Pr 26:17*
belonging to him
involves himself in a quarrel   *Pr 26:17*
(B)
vexed himself with strife (E)   *Pr 26:17*

MEDDLING

forbear thee from *m.* with   *2Ch 35:21*
God
Refrain from opposing God   *2Ch 35:21*
(A)
Quit interferring with God   *2Ch 35:21*
(B)
Cease opposing God (R)   *2Ch 35:21*
but every fool will be *m.*   *Pr 20:3*
every fool will be quarreling   *Pr 20:3*
(A)(B)(E)(R)

MEDE

Darius the *M.* (S)   *Da 5:31*
in the first year of Darius the   *Da 11:1*
M.

MEDEBA

Nophah, which reacheth unto   *Nu 21:30*
M.
and all the plain of *M.* unto   *Jos 13:9*
Dibon
the river, and all the plain by   *Jos 13:16*
M.
who came and pitched before   *1Ch 19:7*
M.
shall howl over Nebo, and over   *Isa 15:2*
M.

MEDES

Gozan, and in the cities of the   *2Ki 17:6;*
M.   *18:11*
that is in the province of the *M.*   *Ezr 6:2*
laws of the Persians and the *M.*   *Es 1:19*
I will stir up the *M.*   *Isa 13:17*
against them
Elam, and all the kings of the   *Jer 25:25*
M.
up the spirit of the kings of   *Jer 51:11*
the *M.*
nations with the kings of the   *Jer 51:28*
M.
is divided, and given to the *M.*   *Da 5:28*
according to the law of the   *Da 6:8;*
M.   *6:12*
O king, that the law of the *M.*   *Da 6:15*
Ahasuerus, of the seed of the *M.* *Da 9:1*
Parthians, and *M.,* and Elamites   *Ac 2:9*

MEDIA

power of Persia and *M.,* the   *Es 1:3*
nobles
the seven princes of Persia   *Es 1:14*
and *M.*
shall the ladies of Persia and *M.* *Es 1:18*
of the chronicles of the kings of   *Es 10:2*
M.
Go up, O Elam: besiege, O *M.*   *Isa 21:2*
two horns are the kings of *M.*   *Da 8:20*

MEDIAN

Darius the *M.* took the   *Da 5:31*
kingdom

MEDIATE

who shall *m.* for him (S)   *1Sa 2:25*
people *m.* a vain thing (E)   *Ps 2:1*
m. treachery and deceit   *Ps 38:12*
(A)(R)
m. deceits all day (E)   *Ps 38:12*
with my heart I *m.* (A)(B)(R)   *Ps 77:6*
m. on all your doings   *Ps 143:5*
(A)(B)(R)

MEDIATION

through *m.* of angels (B)   *Ac 7:53*

MEDIATIONS

for his twilight *m.* (B)   *Ge 24:6*

MEDIATES

habitually *m.,* ponders (A)   *Ps 1:2*
the covenant he *m.*   *Heb 8:6*
(B)(N)(P)(R)

MEDIATOR

by angels in the hand of a *m.*   *Ga 3:19*
a go-between-an intermediary   *Ga 3:19;*
person between God and man   *3:20*
(A)
by means of a go-between (B)   *Ga 3:19*
an intermediary (N)(P)(R)   *Ga 3:19;*
  3:20
is not a *m.* of one, but God is   *Ga 3:20*
one
and one *m.* between God and   *1Ti 2:5*
men
one go-between of God and of   *1Ti 2:5*
men (B)
one intermediary between God   *1Ti 2:5*
and man (P)
he is the *m.* of a better   *Heb 8:6*
covenant
the covenant he mediates   *Heb 8:6*
(B)(N)(P)(R)
he is the *m.* of the new   *Heb 9:15*
testament
administrator of new   *Heb 9:15*
agreement (P)
Jesus the *m.* of the new   *Heb 12:24*
covenant

MEDICINE

merry heart doeth good like a   *Pr 17:22*
m.
cheerful heart makes a good   *Pr 17:22*
cure (B)
meat, and the leaf thereof for   *Eze 47:12*
m.
their leaf for healing   *Eze 47:12*
(A)(B)(E)(R)

MEDICINES

up: thou hast no healing *m.*   *Jer 30:13*
no healing device, no binding   *Jer 30:13*
plaster (A)
in vain shalt thou use many *m.*   *Jer 46:11*

MEDITATE

went out to *m.* in the field at   *Ge 24:63*
for his twilight meditations   *Ge 24:63*
(B)
shalt *m.* therein day and night   *Jos 1:8*
his law doth he *m.* day. and night   *Ps 1:2*
habitually meditates, ponders,   *Ps 1:2*
and studies by day and night (A)
ponders day and night (B)   *Ps 1:2*
m. on thee in the night watches   *Ps 63:6*
I will *m.* also of all thy work   *Ps 77:12*
I will think of all thy works   *Ps 77:12*
(B)
I will *m.* in thy precepts, and   *Ps 119:15*
thy servant did *m.* in thy   *Ps 119:23*
statutes
loved; and I will *m.* in thy   *Ps 119:48*
statues
cause: but I will *m.* in thy   *Ps 119:78*
precepts
that I might *m.* in thy word   *Ps 119:148*
I *m.* on all thy works; I muse   *Ps 143:5*
on
I will think about all thy   *Ps 143:5*
dealings (B)
Thine heart shall *m.* terror.   *Isa 33:18*
Where
not to *m.* before what ye shall   *Lu 21:14*

not to premeditate your   *Lu 21:14*
defense (B)
make up your minds not to   *Lu 21:14*
prepare (N)
M. upon these things; give   *1Ti 4:15*
thyself
Cultivate these matters, live in   *1Ti 4:15*
them (B)
Be diligent in these things (E)   *1Ti 4:15*
Make these matters your   *1Ti 4:15*
business (N)
Give whole attention, energies   *1Ti 4:15*
to (P)
Practice these duties, devote   *1Ti 4:15*
to them (R)

MEDITATION

words, O Lord, consider my *m.*   *Ps 5:1*
the *m.* of my heart, be   *Ps 19:14*
acceptable
the thoughts of my heart (B)   *Ps 19:14;*
  49:3
m. of my heart be   *Ps 49:3*
understanding
My *m.* of him shall be sweet: *Ps 104:34*
I will
I thy law! it is my *m.* all the   *Ps 119:97*
day
for thy testimonies are my *m.*   *Ps 119:99*

MEDIUM

a *m.* or fortune teller (A)(B)   *Le 20:27*
consulter with a *m.*   *De 18:11*
(A)(B)(R)
who is a *m.* (A)(B)(R)   *1Sa 28:7*
is a *m.* (S)   *1Sa 28:7;*
  28:8-9; 1Ch 10:13; 2Ch 33:6; Isa 29:4
consulting a *m.* (A)(B)(R)   *1Ch 10:13*

MEDIUMS

do not turn to *m.,* wizards   *Le 19:31*
(B)(R)
who turns to *m.* and wizards   *Le 20:6*
(R)
mediums (S)   *De 18:11;*
1Sa 28:3; 2Ki 21:6; 23:24; Isa 8:19; 19:3
had put away *m.* (A)(B)(R)   *1Sa 28:3;*
  28:9
had dealt with *m.* (A)(R)   *2Ki 21:6*
Josiah put away *m.* (A)(R)   *2Ki 23:24*
encouraging *m.* and wizards   *2Ch 33:6*
(A)(B)(R)
consult *m.* and wizards   *Isa 8:19*
(A)(R)
to *m.* and wizards (A)(R)   *Isa 19:3*

MEEK

man Moses was very *m.* above   *Nu 12:3*
the desire of the *m.* (E)(R)   *Ps 10:17*
The *m.* shall eat and be   *Ps 22:26*
satisfied
The *m.* will he guide in   *Ps 25:9*
judgment
and the *m.* will he teach his   *Ps 25:9*
way
m. hear and be glad (E)   *Ps 34:2*
But the *m.* shall inherit the   *Ps 37:11*
earth
m. have seen it (E)   *Ps 69:32*
to save all the *m.* of the earth   *Ps 76:9*
The Lord lifteth up the *m.*: he   *Ps 147:6*
will beautify the *m.* with   *Ps 149:4*
salvation
with equity for the *m.* of the   *Isa 11:4*
earth
The *m.* also shall increase   *Isa 29:19*
their joy
preach good tidings unto the   *Isa 61:1*
m.
and turn aside the way of the *m.* *Am 2:7*
ye the Lord, all ye *m.* of the   *Zep 2:3*
earth
Blessed are the *m.*: for they shall   *M't 5:5*
for I am *m.* and lowly in   *M't 11:29*
heart
thee, *m.* and sitting upon an   *M't 21:5*
ass
so *m.* when face to face (B)   *2Co 10:1*
show his works in *m.* (R)   *Jas 3:13*
ornament of a *m.* and quiet   *1Pe 3:4*
spirit

MEEKNESS

truth and *m.* and righteousness   *Ps 45:4*
seek righteousness, seek *m.*: it   *Zep 2:3*

or in love, and in the spirit of *1Co 4:21*
m.
by the *m.* and gentleness of *2Co 10:1*
Christ
M. temperance: against such *Ga 5:23*
such an one in the spirit of *m.* *Ga 6:1*
With all lowliness and *m.* with *Eph 4:2*
of mind, *m.*, longsuffering *Col 3:12*
godliness faith, love, patience, *1Ti 6:11*
m.
In *m.* instructing those that *2Ti 2:25*
oppose
gentle, shewing all *m.* unto all *Tit 3:2*
men
and receive with *m.* the *Jas 1:21*
engrafted
his works with *m.* of wisdom *Jas 3:13*
that is in you with *m.* and fear *1Pe 3:15*

MEET

will make him an help *m.* for *Ge 2:18*
was not found an help *m.* for *Ge 2:20*
him
king of Sodom went out to *m.* *Ge 14:17*
him
he ran to *m.* them from the *Ge 18:2*
tent
seeing them rose up to *m.* them *Ge 19:1*
servant ran to *m.* her, and *Ge 24:17*
said, Let
that walketh in the field to *m.* *Ge 24:65*
us
he ran to *m.* him, and *Ge 29:13*
embraced
Leah went out to *m.* him, and *Ge 30:16*
and also he cometh to *m.* thee *Ge 32:6*
Esau ran to *m.* him, and *Ge 33:4*
embraced
went up to *m.* Israel his *Ge 46:29*
father, to
behold, he cometh forth to *m.* *Ex 4:14*
thee
Go into the wilderness to *m.* *Ex 4:27*
Moses
by river's brink to *m.* (S) *Ex 7:15*
Moses said, It is not *m.* so *Ex 8:26*
to do
went out to *m.* his father in *Ex 18:7*
law
out of the camp to *m.* with God *Ex 19:17*
If thou *m.* thine enemy's ox or *Ex 23:4*
there I will *m.* with thee, and I *Ex 25:22*
where I will *m.* you, to speak *Ex 29:42*
there
I will *m.* with the children of *Ex 29:43*
Israel
testimony, where I will *m.* *Ex 30:6*
thee
where I will *m.* with thee: it *Ex 30:36*
testimony, where I will *m.* with *Nu 17:4*
you
he went out to *m.* him unto a *Nu 22:36*
city
the Lord will come to *m.* me *Nu 23:3*
while I *m.* the Lord yonder *Nu 23:15*
to *m.* them without the camp *Nu 31:13*
Israel, all that are *m.* for the *De 3:18*
war
lest the pursuers *m.* you; and *Jos 2:16*
and go to *m.* them, and say *Jos 9:11*
Jael went out to *m.* Sisera, and *J'g 4:18*
Jael came out to *m.* him, and *J'g 4:22*
m. for the necks of them that *J'g 5:30*
take the
and they came up to *m.* them *J'g 6:35*
of the doors of my house to *J'g 11:31*
m. me
came out to *m.* him with *J'g 11:34*
timbrels
saw him, he rejoiced to *m.* him *J'g 19:3*
that they *m.* thee not in any *Ru 2:22*
other
and there shall *m.* thee three *1Sa 10:3*
men
that thou shalt *m.* a company *1Sa 10:5*
of
Saul went out to *m.* him, that *1Sa 13:10*
Samuel rose early to *m.* Saul *1Sa 15:12*
drew nigh to *m.* David, that *1Sa 17:48*
the army to *m.* the Philistine *1Sa 17:48*
to *m.* king Saul, with tabrets *1Sa 18:6*
which sent thee this day to *m.* *1Sa 15:32*
me
hadst hasted and come to *m.* *1Sa 25:34*
me
they went forth to *m.* David *1Sa 30:21*
m. the people that were with *1Sa 30:21*
him
of Saul came out to *m.* David *2Sa 6:20*

he sent to *m.* them, because *2Sa 10:5*
the Archite came to *m.* him *2Sa 15:32*
with his
came to Gilgal, to go to *m.* the *2Sa 19:15*
king
the men of Judah to *m.* king *2Sa 19:16*
David
to go down to *m.* my lord the *2Sa 19:20*
king
of Saul came down to *m.* the *2Sa 19:24*
king
come to Jerusalem to *m.* the *2Sa 19:25*
king
he came down to *m.* me at *1Ki 2:8*
Jordan
And the king rose up to *m.* *1Ki 2:19*
her, and
Obadiah went to *m.* Ahab, *1Ki 18:16*
and told
him: and Ahab went to *m.* *1Ki 18:16*
Elijah
go down to *m.* Ahab king of *1Ki 21:18*
Israel
go up to *m.* the messengers of *2Ki 1:3*
There came a man up to *m.* us *2Ki 1:6*
was he which came up to *m.* *2Ki 1:7*
you
they came to *m.* him, and *2Ki 2:15*
bowed
Run now, I pray thee, to *m.* *2Ki 4:26*
her
if thou *m.* any man, salute *2Ki 4:29*
him not
he went again to *m.* him, and *2Ki 4:31*
told
down from the chariot to *m.* *2Ki 5:21*
him
again from his chariot to *m.* *2Ki 5:26*
thee
hand, and go, *m.* the man of *2Ki 8:8*
God
Hazael went to *m.* him, and *2Ki 8:9*
took a
send to *m.* them, and let him *2Ki 9:17*
say
went one on horseback to *m.* *2Ki 9:18*
him
son of Rechab coming to *m.* *2Ki 10:15*
him
to Damascus to *m.* *2Ki 16:10*
Tiglath-pileser
and David went out to *m.* *1Ch 12:17*
them
he sent to *m.* them: for the *1Ch 19:5*
men
he went out to *m.* Asa, and *2Ch 15:2*
Hanani the seer went out to *2Ch 19:2*
m. him
was not *m.* for us to see the *Ezr 4:14*
king's
let us *m.* together in some one *Ne 6:2*
us *m.* together in the house *Ne 6:10*
of God
which were *m.* to be given her *Es 2:9*
They *m.* with darkness in the *Job 5:14*
it is *m.* to be said unto God, I *Job 34:31*
have
he goeth on to *m.* the armed *Job 39:21*
men
meet (S) *Ps 59:10; 79:8; Am 9:10*
came I forth to *m.* thee, *Pr 7:15*
diligently
that withholdeth more than is *Pr 11:24*
m.
robbed of her whelps *m.* a *Pr 17:12*
man
The rich and poor *m.* together *Pr 22:2*
and the deceitful man *m.* *Pr 29:13*
together
Isaiah, Go forth now to *m.* *Isa 7:3*
Ahaz
is moved for thee to *m.* thee at *Isa 14:9*
beasts of the desert shall also *Isa 34:14*
m.
and I will not *m.* thee as a man *Isa 47:3*
as seemeth good and *m.* unto *Jer 26:14*
you
unto whom it seemed *m.* unto *Jer 27:5*
me
forth from Mizpah to *m.* them *Jer 41:6*
One post shall run to *m.* *Jer 51:31*
another
and one messenger to *m.* *Jer 51:31*
another
burned. Is it *m.* for any work *Eze 15:4*
was whole, it was *m.* for no *Eze 15:5*
work
less shall it be *m.* yet for any *Eze 15:5*
work
I will *m.* them as a bear that is *Ho 13:8*

prepare to *m.* thy God, O *Am 4:12*
Israel
another angel went out to *m.* *Zec 2:3*
him
therefore fruits *m.* for *M't 3:8*
repentance
city came out to *m.* Jesus *M't 8:34*
not *m.* to take the children's *M't 15:26;*
bread *M'k 7:27*
forth to *m.* the bridegroom *M't 25:1*
cometh; go ye out to *m.* him *M't 25:6*
m. you a man bearing *M'k 14:13*
a pitcher of
to *m.* him that comest against *Lu 14:31*
him
m. that we should make merry *Lu 15:32*
a man *m.* you, bearing a *Lu 22:10*
pitcher
and went forth to *m.* him *Joh 12:13*
and do works *m.* for *Ac 26:20*
repentance
to *m.* us as far as Appii *Ac 28:15*
forum
that recompence which was *Ro 1:27*
m.
am not *m.* to be called an *1Co 15:9*
apostle
if it be *m.* that I go also they *1Co 16:4*
shall
is *m.* for me to think this of *Ph'p 1:7*
you
hath made us *m.* to be *Col 1:12*
partakers
to *m.* the Lord in the air *1Th 4:17*
always for you, brethren, as it *2Th 1:3*
is *m.*
and *m.* for the master's use *2Ti 2:21*
forth herbs *m.* for them by *Heb 6:7*
whom
I think it *m.* as long as I am *2Pe 1:13*

MEETEST

the best and *m.* of your *2Ki 10:3*
master's
Thou *m.* him that rejoiceth *Isa 64:5*

MEETETH

When Esau my brother *m.* thee *Ge 32:17*
when he *m.* him, he shall slay *Nu 35:19*
him
slay the murderer, when he *Nu 35:21*
m. him

MEETING

m. tent (A)(B) *Ex 29:10;*
29:44; *Le 3:8; 10:7; Nu 4:3; 8:9; 25:6;*
2Ch 1:3
hold a holy *m.* (B) *Le 23:27*
a sacred *m.* (B) *Nu 28:18;*
28:25-26; 29:1, 7, 12
have a sacred *m.* (B) *Nu 29:35*
was afraid at the *m.* of David *1Sa 21:1*
it is iniquity, even the solemn *Isa 1:13*
m.

MEGIDDO

one; the king of *M.* one *Jos 12:21*
inhabitants of *M.* and her *Jos 17:11;*
towns *J'g 1:27*
in Taanach by the waters of *M.* *J'g 5:19*
to him pertained Taanach and *1Ki 4:12*
M.
and Hazor, and *M.*, and *1Ki 9:15*
Gezer
And he fled to *M.* and died *2Ki 9:27*
there
slew him at *M.*, when he had *2Ki 23:29*
seen
him in a chariot dead from *2Ki 23:30*
M.
M. and her towns, Dor and *1Ch 7:29*
came to fight in the valley of *2Ch 35:22*
M.

MEGIDDON

mourning in the valley of *Zec 12:11*
M.

MEHETABEEL

son of Delaiah the son of *M.* *Ne 6:10*

MEHETABEL

wife's name was *M.* the *Ge 36:39;*
daughter *1Ch 1:50*

MEHIDA

of Bazluth, the children of M.   Ezr 2:52;
                                    Neh 7:54

MEHIR

the brother of Shuah begat M.   1Ch 4:11

MEHOLATHITE

given unto Adriel the M. to   1Sa 18:19
wife
Adriel the son of Barzillai the   2Sa 21:8
M.

MEHUJAEL

and Irad begat M.: and M.   Ge 4:18
begat

MEHUMAN

with wine, he commanded M.   Es 1:10

MEHUNIM

of Asnah, the children of M.   Ezr 2:50

MEHUNIMS

dwelt in Gur-baal, and the M.   2Ch 26:7

ME-JARKON

M. and Rakkon, with the   Jos 19:46
border

MEKONAH

and at M. and the villages   Ne 11:28

MELATIAH

them repaired M. the Gibeonite   Ne 3:7

MELCHI

which was the son of M.   Lu 3:24;
which   3:28

MELCHIAH

unto him Pashur the son of M.   Jer 21:1

MELCHISEDEC

for ever after the order of M.   Heb 5:6;
                                6:20; 7:17, 21
high priest after the order of   Heb 5:10
M.
For this M., king of Salem,   Heb 7:1
priest
of his father, when M. met   Heb 7:10
him
should rise after the order of   Heb 7:11
M.
for that after the similitude of Heb 7:15
M.

MELCHI-SHUA

Jonathan, and Ishui, and M.   1Sa 14:49
Jonathan and Abinadab, and   1Sa 31:2
M.

MELCHIZEDEK

M. king of Salem brought   Ge 14:18
forth
for ever after the order of M.   Ps 110:4

MELEA

Which was the son of M.   Lu 3:31

MELECH

of Micha were, Pithon, and   1Ch 8:35;
M.   9:41

MELICU

Of M., Jonathan; of   Ne 12:14
Shebaniah

MELITA

that the island was called M.   Ac 28:1

MELODY

make sweet m. sing many   Isa 23:16
songs
thanksgiving, and the voice of   Isa 51:3
m.
I will not hear the m. of thy   Am 5:23
viols
making m. in your heart to   Eph 5:19

MELONS

the m. and the leeks, and the   Nu 11:5
onions

MELT

inhabitants of Caanan shall   Ex 15:15
m.
made hearts m. (B)(E)(R)   De 1:28
these things, our hearts did m. Jos 2:11
made the heart of the people   Jos 14:8
m.
heart of a lion, shall utterly   2Sa 17:10
m.
Let them m. away as waters   Ps 58:7
which
gnash with his teeth, and m.   Ps 112:10
away
and every man's heart shall   Isa 13:7
m.
heart of Egypt shall m. in the   Isa 19:1
midst
I will m. them, and try them   Jer 9:7
they m. in fear (R)   Jer 49:23
every heart shall m. and all   Eze 21:7
hands
to blow the fire upon it, to m. Eze 22:20
it
I will leave you there, and m.   Eze 22:20
you
toucheth the land, and it shall Am 9:5
m.
wine and all the hills shall m. Am 9:13
the mountains shall m.   Mic 1:4
(A)(B)(R)
the hills m. and the earth is   Na 1:5
burned
elements shall m. with fervent   2Pe 3:10;
                                      3:12

MELTED

when the sun waxed hot, it m.   Ex 16:21
melted (S)   Ex 32:4;
32:8; 34:17; Le 19:4; Nu 33:53; De 9:12,
16; 27:15; J'g 17:3-4; 18:14, 17:18;
1Ki 7:23; 14:9; 2Ki 17:16; Ne 9:18;
Ps 106:19; Isa 30:22; 42:17; 48:5;
Jer 10:14; 51:17; Eze 24:11; Mic 1:4;
                        Na 1:14; Hab 2:18
that their heart m. neither was Jos 5:1
the hearts of the people m. and Jos 7:5
The mountains m. from before   J'g 5:5
the multitude m. away, and   1Sa 14:16
melted (S)   1Ki 7:16;
2Ch 4:2; 28:2; 34:3; Isa 41:29; 44:10;
                                      Ho 13:2
m. supports (S)   1Ki 7:30
is m. in the midst of my bowels Ps 22:14
he uttered his voice, the earth Ps 46:6
m.
hills m. like wax at the presence Ps 97:5
their soul is m. because of   Ps 107:26
trouble
mountains, m. with their   Isa 34:3
blood
m. and cast an image (S)   Isa 44:10
they m. in fear (B)(E)   Jer 49:23
and ye shall be m. in the   Eze 22:21
midst
As silver is m. in the midst of Eze 22:22
so shall ye be m. in the   Eze 22:22
midst
the mountains m. under him   Mic 1:4
(E)
As a snail which m., let every   Ps 58:8
one
as wax m. before the fire, so let Ps 68:2
My soul m. for heaviness   Ps 119:28
out this word, and m. them: he   Ps 147:18
The workman m. a graven   Isa 40:19
image
m. and casteth silver chains   Isa 40:19
(S)
the founder m. in vain: for the Jer 6:29
and the heart m. and the knees   Na 2:10

MELTING

As when the m. fire burneth, the Isa 64:2

MELZAR

Then said Daniel to M., whom   Da 1:11
M. took away the portion of   Da 1:16
their

MEM

mem   Ps 119:97-104 title

MEMBER

or hath his privy m. cut off,   De 23:1
shall not
For the body is not one m.   1Co 12:14
And if they were all one m.   1Co 12:19
where
And whether one m. suffer,   1Co 12:26
all the
or one m. be honoured, all   1Co 12:26
Even so the tongue is a little m. Jas 3:5

MEMBERS

and all my m. are as a shadow   Job 17:7
in thy book all my m. were   Ps 139:16
written
one of thy m. should   M't 5:29; 5:30
perish
Neither yield ye your m. as   Ro 6:13
and your m. as instruments of   Ro 6:13
as ye have yielded your m.   Ro 6:19
servants
so now yield your m. servants   Ro 6:19
to
did work in our m. to bring   Ro 7:5
forth
But I see another law in my m.   Ro 7:23
to the law of sin which is in   Ro 7:23
my m.
as we have many m. in one   Ro 12:4
body
all m. have not the same office Ro 12:4
and every one m. one of   Ro 12:5
another
your bodies are the m. of   1Co 6:15
Christ
shall I then take the m. of   1Co 6:15
Christ
and make them the m. of a   1Co 6:15
harlot
the body is one, and   1Co 12:12
hath many m.
and all the m. of that one   1Co 12:12
body
now hath God set the m.   1Co 12:18
every one
But now are they many m.   1Co 12:20
much more those m. of the   1Co 12:22
body
And those m. of the body,   1Co 12:23
which we
that the m. should have the   1Co 12:25
same
suffer, all the m. suffer with   1Co 12:26
it
honoured, all the m. rejoice   1Co 12:26
with it
body of Christ and m. in   1Co 12:27
particular
for we are m. one of another   Eph 4:25
For we are m. of his body, of   Eph 5:30
which
Mortify therefore your m.   Col 3:5
so is the tongue among our m.   Jas 3:6
of your lusts that war in your m. Jas 4:1

MEMORIAL

is my m. unto all generations   Ex 3:15
day shall be unto you for a m.   Ex 12:14
and for a m. between thine   Ex 13:9
eyes
Write this for a m. in a book   Ex 17:14
the ephod for stones of the   Ex 28:12
upon his two shoulders for a   Ex 28:12
m.
for a m. before the Lord   Ex 28:29
continually
it may be a m. unto the   Ex 30:16
children
stones for a m. to the children Ex 39:7
the priest shall burn the m. of it Le 2:2
from the meat offering a m.   Le 2:9;
thereof   2:16
even a m. thereof, and burn it   Le 5:12
on the
even the m. of it, unto the Lord Le 6:15
a m. of blowing of trumpets   Le 23:24
it may be on the bread for a m. Le 24:7

an offering of *m.*, bringing   *Nu 5:15*
iniquity
put the offering of *m.* in her   *Nu 5:18*
hands
the *m.* thereof, and burn it   *Nu 5:26*
upon
that they may be to you for a   *Nu 10:10*
m.
be a *m.* unto the children of   *Nu 16:40*
Israel
for a *m.* for the children of   *Nu 31:54*
Israel
these stones shall be for a *m.*   *Jos 4:7*
unto
nor right, nor *m.* in Jerusalem   *Ne 2:20*
the *m.* of them perish from   *Es 9:28*
their
their *m.* is perished with them   *Ps 9:6*
and thy *m.* O Lord,   *Ps 135:13*
throughout all
God of hosts; the Lord is his   *Ho 12:5*
m.
for a *m.* in the temple of the   *Zec 6:14*
Lord
hath done, be told for a *m.*   *M't 26:13*
of her
shall be spoken of for a *m.* of   *M'k 14:9*
her
thine alms are come up for a   *Ac 10:4*
m.

MEMORY

m. of them has vanished (B)   *Ps 9:6*
cut off the *m.* of them from   *Ps 109:15*
utter the *m.* of thy great   *Ps 145:7*
goodness
the *m.* of the just is blessed   *Pr 10:7*
for the *m.* of them is forgotten   *Ec 9:5*
and made all their *m.* to   *Isa 26:14*
perish
if ye keep in *m.* what I   *1Co 15:2*
preached unto

MEMPHIS

the princes of *M.* (S)   *Isa 19:13*
and at *M.* (S)   *Jer 44:1*
and publish at *M.* (S)   *Jer 46:14*
M. shall be waste (S)   *Jer 46:19*
images shall cease out of *M.*   *Eze 30:13*
(S)
M. shall have distresses daily   *Eze 30:16*
(S)
them up, *M.* shall bury them   *Ho 9:6*

MEMUCAN

Meres, Meresna, and *M.*   *Es 1:14*
M. answered before the king   *Es 1:16*
did according to the word of   *Es 1:21*
M.

MEN

then began *m.* to call on the   *Ge 4:26*
name of Lord
when *m.* began to multiply on   *Ge 6:1*
the earth
Abraham divided his *m.* (S)   *Ge 14:15*
he looked, and lo, three *m.*   *Ge 18:2*
stood by him
the *m.* of the city, *m.* of Sodom *Ge 19:4*
compassed
where are *m.* which came in   *Ge 19:5*
to thee this night
only to these *m.* do nothing;   *Ge 19:8;*
smote the *m.*   *19:11*
power with God and *m.*   *Ge 32:28*
and hast prevailed
these *m.* are peaceable with   *Ge 34:21*
us, let them
only herein will the *m.*   *Ge 34:22*
consent to us
we are true *m.*   *Ge 42:11; 42:31*
bring *m.* home   *Ge 43:16*
Joseph said, Up, follow after   *Ge 44:4*
the *m.*
m. are shepherds, for their   *Ge 46:32*
trade to feed cattle
but saved the *m.* children alive   *Ex 1:17;*
                                          1:18
go now, ye that are *m.* and   *Ex 10:11*
serve the Lord
thrice in the year shall *m.*   *Ex 34:23*
children appear
Moses and Aaron took these *m.*   *Nu 1:17*
all the people are *m.* of great   *Nu 13:32*
stature
those *m.* that did bring evil   *Nu 14:37*
report on land

wilt thou put out the eyes of   *Nu 16:14*
these *m.*
if these *m.* die the common   *Nu 16:29*
death of all men
God said, What *m.* are these   *Nu 22:9*
with thee
the angel said to Balaam,   *Nu 22:35*
Go with the *m.*
slay ye every one his *m.* that   *Nu 25:5*
were joined
pray which the *m.* of war had   *Nu 31:32*
not one of these *m.* shall see   *De 1:35*
good land
make remembrance to cease   *De 32:26*
from among *m.*
let Reuben live, let not his *m.* be *De 33:6*
few
there came *m.* in hither to-night   *Jos 2:2*
of Israel
bring forth the *m.* that   *Jos 2:3;*
come   *1Sa 11:12*
because he feared the *m.* of the   *J'g 6:27*
city
the *m.* of Penuel answered as *m.* *J'g 8:8*
of Succoth
should give bread to thy *m.*   *J'g 8:15*
that are weary
that *m.* say not of me, a   *J'g 9:54*
woman slew him
there were *m.* lying in wait in   *J'g 16:9*
the chamber
now therefore deliver us the *m.*   *J'g 20:13*
of Belial
was in favour with the Lord   *1Sa 2:26*
and *m.*
he smote the *m.* of city, small   *1Sa 5:9*
and great
m. that died not were smitten   *1Sa 5:12*
with emerods
but the *m.* were very good   *1Sa 25:15*
unto us
these *m.* the sons of Zeruiah   *2Sa 3:39*
too hard
and let us play the *m.* for our   *2Sa 10:12*
people
were but dead *m.* before my   *2Sa 19:28*
lord the king
hear any more the voice of   *2Sa 19:35*
singing *m.*
he that ruleth over *m.* must be   *2Sa 23:3*
just
slew two lionlike *m.* of   *2Sa 23:20;*
Moab   *1Ch 11:22*
happy thy *m.* that hear thy   *1Ki 10:8*
wisdom
there are *m.* come out of   *1Ki 20:17*
Samaria
now the *m.* did diligently   *1Ki 20:33*
observe whether
Lord, open the eyes of these   *2Ki 6:20*
m. to see
they reckoned not with *m.* of   *2Ki 12:15*
the money
the *m.* of Babylon made   *2Ki 17:30*
Succoth-benoth, *m.* of Cuth,
Nergal, *m.* of Hamath, Ashima
hath he not sent me to the   *2Ki 18:27;*
m.   *Isa 36:12*
said to Him, What said these   *2Ki 20:14;*
m.   *Isa 39:3*
shall I drink the blood of   *1Ch 11:19*
these *m.*
were *m.* that had   *1Ch 12:32*
understanding of
let *m.* say among the   *1Ch 16:31*
nations, Lord reigns
for the *m.* were greatly   *1Ch 19:5*
ashamed
will God in very deed dwell   *2Ch 6:18*
with *m.*
for the band of *m.* that came   *2Ch 22:1*
with the
the *m.* expressed by name   *2Ch 28:15*
took the captives
and the *m.* did the work   *2Ch 34:12*
faithfully
m. of his place help him with   *Ezr 1:4*
silver
two hundred singing *m.* and   *Ezr 2:65*
singing
give commandment to cause   *Ezr 4:21*
these *m.* cease
I decree that expences be given   *Ezr 6:8*
to these *m.*
together out of Israel chief *m.*   *Ezr 7:28*
to go
nor *m.* of the guard which   *Ne 4:23*
followed

other *m.* have our lands and   *Ne 5:5*
vineyards
There dwelt *m.* of Tyre also   *Ne 13:16*
therein
when deep sleep falleth on *m.*   *Job 4:13;*
                                          33:15
are dried up, they are gone   *Job 28:4*
away from *m.*
if the *m.* of my tabernacle said   *Job 31:31*
not
m. do therefore fear him, he   *Job 37:24*
respecteth not
they may know themselves to   *Ps 9:20*
be but *m.*
from *m.* which are thy hand,   *Ps 17:14*
from *m.*
m. will praise thee when thou   *Ps 49:18*
doest well
m. of low degree are vanity, *m.* *Ps 62:9*
of high a lie
ascended, thou hast received   *Ps 68:18*
gifts for *m.*
and *m.* shall be blessed in him,   *Ps 72:17*
all nations
they are not in trouble as other   *Ps 73:5*
m. neither are they plagued like
other *m.*
ye are gods, but ye shall die   *Ps 82:7*
like *m.*
that *m.* may know that thou   *Ps 83:18*
art over all
O that *m.* would praise the   *Ps 107:8;*
Lord   *107:15, 21, 31*
on our side, when *m.* rose up   *Ps 124:2*
against us
m. shall speak of the might of   *Ps 145:6*
thy acts
m. do not despise a thief, if he   *Pr 6:30*
steal
many *m.* have been slain by   *Pr 7:26*
her
to you, O *m.* I call; *m.* depart   *Pr 8:4;*
from evil   *16:6*
most *m.* proclaim each his own   *Pr 20:6*
goodness
which the *m.* of Hezekiah   *Pr 25:1*
copied out
so for *m.* to search their own   *Pr 25:27*
glory, not glory
when the wicked rise, *m.* hide   *Pr 28:28*
themselves
God doeth it that *m.* should   *Ec 3:14*
fear him
thy *m.* shall fall by the sword,   *Isa 3:25*
thy mighty
and the Lord have removed *m.*   *Isa 6:12*
far away
is it a small thing for you to   *Isa 7:13*
weary *m.*
now the Egyptians are *m.* and   *Isa 31:3*
not God
the wayfaring *m.* though fools   *Isa 35:8*
O Lord, by these things *m.* live   *Isa 38:16*
therefore will I give *m.* for   *Isa 43:4*
thee, and people
even to h:m shall *m.* come,   *Isa 45:24*
and all incensed
remember this, and shew   *Isa 46:8*
yourselves *m.*
that *m.* may bring to thee the   *Isa 60:11*
forces
m. shall call you the ministers   *Isa 61:6*
of our God
m. have not heard, nor   *Isa 64:4*
perceived by the ear
they set a trap, they catch *m.*   *Jer 5:26*
horses set in array, as *m.* for   *Jer 6:23*
war against thee
neither can *m.* hear the voice   *Jer 9:10*
of the cattle
and let their *m.* be put to   *Jer 18:21*
death
I will give the *m.* that   *Jer 34:18*
transgress my covenant
these *m.* have done evil to   *Jer 38:9*
prophet Jeremiah
then came to Gedaliah they   *Jer 40:8*
and their *m.*
then the *m.* shall cry and shall   *Jer 47:2*
howl
arise ye, and spoil the *m.* of   *Jer 49:28*
the east
surely I will fill thee with *m.*   *Jer 51:14*
as with caterpillars
that *m.* call the perfection of   *La 2:15*
beauty
these are the *m.* that devise   *Eze 11:2*
mischief
these *m.* set up their idols in   *Eze 14:3*
their heart

tho' these three *m.*, Noah,   *Eze* 14:14;
Daniel, Job   *Job* 14:16, 18
that ye have sent for *m.* to   *Eze* 23:40
come from far
I will deliver thee to the *m.* of *Eze* 25:4;
the east   25:10
ye, my flock of my pasture,   *Eze* 34:31
are *m.*
I will fill his mountains with   *Eze* 35:8
his slain *m.*
I will multiply *m.* upon you   *Eze* 36:10;
  36:37
these *m.* have not regarded   *Da* 3:12
thee
fire slew those *m.* that took up *Da* 3:22
Shadrach
m. on whose bodies fire had no *Da* 3:27
power
that they shall drive thee from *Da* 4:25;
m.   4:32
then said these *m.*, We shall   *Da* 6:5
not find occasion
that *m.* fear before the God of *Da* 6:26
Daniel
but they like *m.* transgressed *Ho* 6:7
the covenant
m. that were at peace deceived thee *Ob* 7
that pass securely, as *m.* averse *Mic* 2:8
from war
man's enemies are the *m.* of his *Mic* 7:6
own house
and makest *m.* as the fishes of *Hab* 1:14
the sea
thy fellows, they are *m.*   *Zec* 3:8
wondered at
had sent their *m.* to pray before *Zec* 7:2
the Lord
but lo, I will deliver the *m.* *Zec* 11:6
every one
let your light so shine before *M't* 5:16
m.
and shall teach *m.* so, shall be *M't* 5:19
called the least
take heed you do not your alms *M't* 6:1
before *m.*
their faces, that they may   *M't* 6:16
appear to *m.* to fast
anoint, that thou appear not *M't* 6:18
unto *m.* to fast
whatsoever ye would that *m.* *M't* 7:12;
should do to you, do ye   *Lu* 6:31
God who had given such power *M't* 9:8
to *m.*
shall confess me before *m.* *M't* 10:32;
  Lu 12:8
whoso shall deny me before *M't* 10:33;
m.   *Lu* 12:9
but while *m.* slept, his enemy *M't* 13:25
came
whom do *m.* say that I am *M't* 16:13;
  M'k 8:27
miserably destroy those   *M't* 21:41
wicked *m.*
outwardly ye appear   *M't* 23:28
righteous to *m.*
and said, I see *m.* as trees *M'k* 8:24
walking
with *m.* it is impossible   *M'k* 10:27;
  Lu 18:27
peace on earth, good will   *Lu* 2:14
toward *m.*
from henceforth thou shalt *Lu* 5:10
catch *m.*
shall rise up with the *m.* of *Lu* 11:31
this generation
to whom *m.* have committed *Lu* 12:48
much
I thank thee, I am not as other *Lu* 18:11
m. are
I receive not honour from *m.* *Joh* 5:41
I have manifested thy name to *Joh* 17:6
the *m.*
of these *m.* which have   *Ac* 1:21
companied with us
others said, These *m.* are full *Ac* 2:13
of new wine
saying, What shall we do to *Ac* 4:16
these *m.*
thou hast not lied unto *m.* but *Ac* 5:4
unto God
the *m.* ye put in prison are in *Ac* 5:25
the temple
we ought to obey God rather *Ac* 5:29
than *m.*
what ye intend to do, as   *Ac* 5:35
touching these *m.*
I say unto you, Refrain from *Ac* 5:38
these *m.*
the Spirit said, Behold three *Ac* 10:19
m. seek thee

we also are *m.* of like   *Ac* 14:15
passions with you
m. that hazarded their lives *Ac* 15:26
for Jesus
these *m.* are the servants of *Ac* 16:17
most high God
sent the serjeants, saying,   *Ac* 16:35
Let those *m.* go
for ye have brought hither   *Ac* 19:37
these *m.*
also of yourselves shall *m.*   *Ac* 20:30
arise speaking
conscience void of offence   *Ac* 24:16
toward God and *m.*
m. with *m.* working which is *Ro* 1:27
unseemly
but condescend to *m.* of low *Ro* 12:16
estate
we are made a spectacle to   *1Co* 4:9
angels and *m.*
for he speaketh not to *m.* but *1Co* 14:2
to God
not children, but in   *1Co* 14:20
understanding be *m.*
with *m.* of other tongues and *1Co* 14:21
lips will I speak
the terror of the Lord, we   *2Co* 5:11
persuade *m.*
for I mean not that other *m.* *2Co* 8:13
be eased
do I now persuade *m.*? or seek *Ga* 1:10
please *m.*
he led captive, and gave gifts *Eph* 4:8
to *m.*
so ought *m.* to love their   *Eph* 5:28
wives as their own
as to the Lord and not to *m.* *Eph* 6:7;
  Col 3:23
we speak not as pleasing *m.* *1Th* 2:4
but God
toward one another, and   *1Th* 3:12
toward all *m.*
I will that *m.* pray every where *1Ti* 2:8
and the younger *m.* as brethren *1Ti* 5:1
m. shall be lovers of   *2Ti* 3:2
themselves, proud
every high priest taken from *Heb* 5:1
among *m.*
for *m.* verily swear by the   *Heb* 6:16
greater, an oath
and here *m.* that die receive *Heb* 7:8
tithes
as it is appoined unto *m.*   *Heb* 9:27
once to die
to the spirits of just *m.* made *Heb* 12:23
perfect
that giveth to all *m.* liberally *Jas* 1:5
therewith curse we *m.* which *Jas* 3:9
are made
might be judged according to *1Pe* 4:6
m. in flesh
but holy *m.* of God spake as *2Pe* 1:21
moved
for there are certain *m.* crept in *Jude* 4
unawares
but only those *m.* which   *Re* 9:4
have not the seal
their power was to hurt *m.* five *Re* 9:10
months
these were redeemed from   *Re* 14:4
among *m.*
such as was not since *m.* were *Re* 16:18
on the earth
behold, the tabernacle of God *Re* 21:3
is with *m.*

MEN *OF WAR*

servants have taken sum of   *Nu* 31:49
m. of war
till all generation of *m. of war* *De* 2:14;
were consumed 2:16; *Jos* 5:6
ye shall compass the city, ye *m. Jos* 6:3
of war
drew sword, all these were *m.* *J'g* 20:17
of war
and Saul set him over the *m.* *1Sa* 18:5
of war
but they were *m. of war*, and *1Ki* 9:22;
the chief of his captains *2Ch* 8:9
and all the *m. of war* fled *2Ki* 25:4;
  Jer 52:7
took an officer set over *m.* of *2Ki* 25:19;
war   *Jer* 52:25
of Gadites *m. of war* came to *1Ch* 12:8
David
all these *m. of war* came to *1Ch* 12:38
Hebron to make
Abijah set battle in array   *2Ch* 13:8
with *m. of war*

and the *m. of war* were in *2Ch* 17:13
Jerusalem
thus he weakeneth the hands *Jer* 38:4
of *m. of war*
slew all the *m. of war*   *Jer* 41:3
Johanan took the *m. of war* *Jer* 41:16
and the women
all the *m. of war* shall be cut *Jer* 49:26;
off   50:30
m. of war are affrighted   *Jer* 51:32
they of Phut were thy *m. of Eze* 27:10
war
all thy *m. of war* that are in *Eze* 27:27
thee shall fall
shall be filled at my table   *Eze* 39:20
with *m. of war*
they shall climb the wall like *m. Joe* 2:7
of war
let all the *m. of war* draw near, *Joe* 3:9
let them come
Herod with his *m. of war* set *Lu* 23:11
him at nought

MEN with *WICKED*

but the *m.* of Sodom were   *Ge* 13:13
wicked
depart from tents of these   *Nu* 16:26
wicked *m.*
then answered all the   *1Sa* 30:22
wicked *m.*
as a man falleth before wicked *2Sa* 3:34
m.
how much more when wicked *2Sa* 4:11
m. have slain
marked old way that wicked *Job* 22:15
m. have trodden
and which walketh with wicked *Job* 34:8
m.
he striketh them as wicked *Job* 34:26
m. in open sight
because of his answers for *Job* 34:36
wicked *m.*
there be wicked *m.* to whom it *Ec* 8:14
happeneth
among my people are found *Jer* 5:26
wicked *m.*
will miserably destroy those *M't* 24:41
wicked *m.*
that we may be delivered from *2Th* 3:2
wicked *m.*

MEN with *WOMEN*

both *m.* and *women* brought *Ex* 35:22
bracelets
utterly destroyed *m.* and   *De* 2:34;
women of every city   *Jos* 8:25
died about a thousand *m.* and *J'g* 9:49
women
and thither fled all the *m.* and *J'g* 9:51
women
house full of *m.* and *women*, *J'g* 16:27
upon roof about 3000 *m.* and
women
he dealt as well to the *women* *2Sa* 6:19
as *m.*
brought the law before *m.* and *Ne* 8:2;
women   8:3
Jeremiah said to the *m.* and *Jer* 44:20
women
were added to Lord both *m.* and *Ac* 5:14
women
Saul, haling *m.* and *women*, *Ac* 8:3
committed them
they were baptized, both *m.* *Ac* 8:12
and *women*
whether *m.* or *women* he might *Ac* 9:2
bring them bound
delivering into prison both *m.* *Ac* 22:4
and *women*

ALL MEN

all the *m.* of his house were *Ge* 17:27
circumcised
all the *m.* are dead which sought *Ex* 4:19
thy life
if these die the common   *Nu* 16:29
death of all *m.*
all the *m.* that followed   *De* 4:3
Baal-peor
Ammon said, Have out all *m.* *2Sa* 13:9
from me
for Solomon was wiser than *1Ki* 4:31
all *m.*
that all *m.* may know his work *Job* 37:7
all *m.* shall fear, and shall *Ps* 64:9
declare
wherefore hast thou made all *Ps* 89:47
m. in vain

I said in my haste, *All m.* are   *Ps 116:11*
liars
for that is the end of *all m.* and *Ec 7:2*
living
so with *all* the *m.* that set   *Jer 42:17*
their faces
I set *all m.* every one against *Zec 8:10*
his neighbour
and ye shall be hated of *all* *M't 10:22;*
m. for my name's sake   *M'k 13:13;*
                      Lu 21:17
all m. cannot receive this *M't 19:11*
saying, save they
tho' *all m.* shall be offended, *M't 26:33*
yet will not I
all m. seek thee; *all m.* did *M'k 1:37;*
marvel   *5:20*
all m. counted John a   *M'k 11:32*
prophet indeed
woe to you when *all m.* speak *Lu 6:26*
well of you
sinners above *all m.* in   *Lu 13:41*
Jerusalem
that *all m.* through him might *Joh 1:7*
believe
not commit himself, because *Joh 2:24*
he knew *all m.*
the same baptizeth and *all m.* *Joh 3:26*
come to him
that *all m.* should honour the *Joh 5:23*
Son, even as
if we let alone, *all m.* will *Joh 11:48*
believe on him
I lifted up from earth, will *Joh 12:32*
draw *all m.* to me
by this shall *all m.* know ye *Joh 13:35*
are my disciples
Lord, who knowest the hearts of *Ac 1:24*
all m.
all m. glorified God for what *Ac 4:21*
was done
but now commandeth *all m.* *Joh 17:30*
to repent
whereof he hath given   *Joh 17:31*
assurance to *all m.*
and *all* the *m.* were about *Joh 19:7*
twelve
and burned their books   *Joh 19:19*
before *all m.*
that I am pure from blood of *Joh 20:26*
all m.
for thou shalt be his witness *Joh 22:15*
to *all m.*
and so death passed upon *all* *Ro 5:12*
m. for all
judgment came on *all m.* the *Ro 5:18*
free gift came on *all m.*
provide things honest in the *Ro 12:17*
sight of *all m.*
if it be possible, live   *Ro 12:18*
peaceably with *all m.*
your obedience is come   *Ro 16:19*
abroad to *all m.*
I would that *all m.* were even *1Co 7:7*
as I
for tho' I be free from *all m.* *1Co 9:19*
yet servant to all
I am made all things to *all m.* *1Co 9:22*
may save some
even as I please *all m.* in all *1Co 10:33*
things
we are of *all m.* most   *1Co 15:19*
miserable
our epistle known and read of *2Co 3:2*
all m.
let us do good to *all m.*   *Ga 6:10*
especially to
to make *all m.* see what is the *Eph 2:9*
fellowship
let your moderation be known *Ph'p 4:5*
to *all m.*
please not God and contrary *1Th 2:15*
to *all m.*
·make you to abound in love *1Th 3:12*
toward *all m.*
support weak, be patient   *1Th 5:14*
toward *all m.*
but ever follow that which is *1Th 5:15*
good to *all m.*
for *all m.* have not faith   *2Th 3:2*
that giving of thanks be made *1Ti 2:1*
for *all m.*
who will have *all m.* to be *1Ti 2:4*
saved and to come
we trust in God, who is   *1Ti 4:10*
Saviour of *all m.*
but be gentle to *all m.* apt to *2Ti 2:24*
teach
for their folly shall be made *2Ti 3:9*
manifest to *all m.*

no man stood with me, but *all 2Ti 4:16*
m. forsook me
the grace of God hath   *Tit 2:11*
appeared to *all m.*
be gentle, shewing all meekness *Tit 3:2*
to *all m.*
follow peace with *all m.* and *Heb 12:14*
holiness
let him ask of God, that giveth *Jas 1:5*
to *all m.*
honour *all m.* love the   *1Pe 2:17*
brotherhood
Demetrius hath good report of *3Jo 12*
all m.

IN MEN

therefore let no man glory in *1Co 3:21*
m.

LIKE MEN

quit yourselves *like m.*   *1Sa 4:9;*
                      1Co 16:13
ye are gods, but ye shall die *Ps 82:7*
like m.
but they *like m.* have   *Ho 6:7*
transgressed covenant
yourselves *like m.* that wait *Lu 12:36*
for their Lord

MIGHTY MEN

mighty m. which were of old, *Ge 6:4*
men of renown
mighty m. of Moab trembling *Ex 15:15*
shall take
the *mighty m.* of valour shall *Jos 1:14*
pass over
I have given thee Jericho and the *Jos 6:2*
mighty m.
Joshua chose out thirty   *Jos 8:3*
thousand *mighty m.*
all the *m.* of Gibeon were *Jos 10:2*
mighty
ascended from Gilgal with *Jos 10:7*
mighty m. of valour
the bows of the *mighty m.* were *1Sa 2:4*
broken
David sent Joab all host of *2Sa 10:7;*
mighty m.   20:7; *1Ch 19:8*
mighty m. were on his right *2Sa 16:6*
hand and left
and his *m.* that they be *mighty 2Sa 17:8*
and chafed
these be names of the *mighty 2Sa 23:8*
m. David had
Eleazar one of the three   *2Sa 23:9*
mighty m. with David
the three *mighty m.* brake *2Sa 23:16;*
thro' the host   *23:17*
Benaiah had the name   *2Sa 23:22*
among three *mighty m.*
the *mighty m.* were not with *1Ki 1:8*
Adonijah
the *mighty m.* and Solomon he *1Ki 1:10*
called not
exacted of all *mighty m.* of *2Ki 15:20*
wealth
he carried away all the   *2Ki 24:14*
mighty m. of valour
were *mighty m.* of valour *1Ch 5:24;*
               7:7, 9, 11, 40
the sons of Ulam were   *1Ch 8:40*
mighty m. of valour
these also are the chief of *1Ch 11:10;*
the *mighty m.*   *11:11*
they were among the   *1Ch 12:1*
mighty m. helpers
were all *mighty m.* of   *1Ch 12:21;*
valour   12:25, 30; 26:6, 31
mighty m. submitted   *1Ch 29:24*
themselves to Solomon
mighty m. of valour   *2Ch 13:3;*
         14:8; 17:13-14, 16
Amaziah hired an hundred *2Ch 25:6*
thousand *mighty m.*
Hezekiah took counsel with *2Ch 32:3*
his *mighty m.*
an angel cut off all the   *2Ch 32:21*
mighty m. of valour
and their brethren *mighty m.* *Ne 11:14*
of valour
he shall break in pieces   *Job 34:24*
mighty m.
wisdom strengtheneth more *Ec 7:19*
than ten *mighty m.*
hang bucklers, all shields of *Ca 4:4*
mighty m.
mighty m. of Kedar shall be *Isa 21:17*
diminished

an open sepulchre, they are all *Jer 5:16*
mighty m.
Jehoiakim the king, with all *Jer 26:21*
his *mighty m.*
Johanan recovered the *mighty Jer 41:16*
m. of war
let *mighty m.* come forth; we *Jer 46:9;*
are *mighty m.*   *48:14*
hearts of *mighty m.* of Moab *Jer 48:41*
as heart of woman
heart of *mighty m.* of Edom *Jer 49:22*
shall be as
a sword is upon her *mighty* *Jer 50:36*
m. and they shall
mighty m. of Babylon have *Jer 51:30*
forborne to fight
her *mighty m.* are taken, their *Jer 51:56*
bows are broken
I will make drunk her   *Jer 51:57*
captains and *mighty m.*
Lord hath trodden under foot *La 1:15*
my *mighty m.*
be filled at my table with *Eze 39:20*
mighty m.
commanded *mighty m.* to bind *Da 3:20*
Shadrach
trust in the multitude of thy *Ho 10:13*
mighty m.
they shall run like *mighty m.* *Joe 2:7*
and climb
prepare war, wake up the   *Joe 3:9*
mighty m.
thy *mighty m.* O Teman, shall be *Ob 9*
dismayed
the shield of his *mighty m.* is *Na 2:3*
made red
they shall be as *mighty m.* that *Zec 10:5*
tread
mighty m. hide themselves in *Re 6:15*
the dens
that ye may eat the flesh of *Re 19:18*
mighty m.

OF MEN

sons of God saw the daughters *Ge 6:2*
of m.
the sons of God came in to the *Ge 6:4*
daughters *of m.*
none devoted *of m.* shall be *Le 27:29*
redeemed
whether it be *of m.* or beasts, *Nu 18:15*
be thine
took all the prey both *of m.* *Nu 31:11*
and beasts
what manner *of m.* were they *J'g 8:18*
ye slew
there went with him a band *1Sa 10:26*
of m.
I will chasten him with the *2Sa 7:14*
rod *of m.*
behold they spied a band *of 2Ki 13:21*
m.
he filled their places with the *2Ki 23:14*
bones *of m.*
they took away *of m.* ten *1Ch 5:21*
thousand
the band *of m.* had slain all *2Ch 22:1*
the eldest
what shall I do, O thou   *Job 7:20*
Preserver *of m.*
then he openeth the ears *of Job 33:16*
m. and sealeth
concerning the works *of m.* *Ps 17:4*
but I am a reproach *of m.* and *Ps 22:6*
despised
the haughtiness *of m.* shall be *Isa 2:11*
bowed down
the haughtiness *of m.* shall be *Isa 2:17*
made low
their fear is taught by the *Isa 29:13*
precept *of m.*
and the workmen, they are *of Isa 44:11*
m.
fear ye not the reproach *of m.* *Isa 51:7*
nor be afraid
he is despised and rejected *of Isa 53:3*
m. a man of
carcases *of m.* shall fall as *Jer 9:22*
dung on field
to fill them with the dead *Jer 33:5*
bodies *of m.*
and madest to thyself images *Eze 16:17*
of m.
and eat not the bread *of m.* *Eze 24:17;*
                    24:22
they traded the persons *of Eze 27:13*
m. in market
thou shalt no more bereave *Eze 36:12*
them *of m.*

the waste cities be filled with   *Eze 36:38*
flocks *of m.*
they shall mingle with the seed   *Da 2:43*
of m.
the Most High ruleth in the   *Da 4:17;*
kingdom *of m.*   4:25, 32; 5:21
by reason of multitude *of m. Mic 2:12;*
     Zec 2:4
and I will make you fishers *of M't 4:19*
m.
to be cast out and trodden   *M't 5:13*
under foot *of m.*
they may have glory *of m.*   *M't 6:2*
seen *of m.*   *M't 6:5; 23:5*
beware *of m.*   *M't 10:17*
for doctrines, commandments   *M't 15:9;*
of m.   *M'k 7:7*
but the things that be *of m. M't 16:23;*
     M'k 8:38
shall be betrayed into the   *M't 17:22;*
hands *of m. M'k 9:31; Lu 9:44; 24:7*
made eunuchs *of m.*   *M't 19:12*
was John's baptism of   *M't 21:25*
heaven or *of m.*
if we say *of m.*   *M't 21:26;*
    M'k 11:30, 32; Lu 20:4, 6
regardest not persons *of m. M't 22:16;*
     M'k 12:14
love to be called *of m.* Rabbi, *M't 23:7*
Rabbi
out of the heart *of m.* proceed *M'k 7:21*
evil
and the life was the light *of m. Joh 1:4*
they loved the praise *of m. Joh 12:43*
more than
Judas having received a band *Joh 18:3*
of m.
to whom a number *of m.*   *Ac 5:36*
joined
if this work be *of m.* it will   *Ac 5:38*
come to nought
the gods are come down   *Ac 14:11*
in likeness *of m.*
the residue *of m.* might seek *Ac 15:17*
after God
honourable woman, and *of m.*   *Ac 17:12*
not a few
against all unrighteousness *of Ro 1:18*
m.
God shall judge the secrets *of Ro 2:16*
m.
whose praise is not *of m.* but *of Ro 2:29*
God
I speak after the manner *of m. Ro 6:19*
that serveth Christ is   *Ro 14:18*
approved *of m.*
faith not stand in the wisdom   *1Co 2:5*
of m.
ye might learn in us not to   *1Co 4:6*
think *of m.*
ye are bought, be not the   *1Co 7:23*
servants *of m.*
I speak with tongues *of m.*   *1Co 13:1*
and angels
if after the manner *of m.* I   *1Co 15:32*
have fought
honest things in the sight of   *2Co 8:21*
m.
Paul an apostle, not *of m.* but   *Ga 1:1*
by Christ
brethren, I speak after the   *Ga 3:15*
manner *of m.*
wind of doctrine, by sleight *of Eph 4:14*
m.
and was made in the likeness *Ph'p 2:7*
of m.
vain deceit, after the tradition *Col 2:8*
of m.
after commandments and   *Col 2:22*
doctrines *of m.*
ye know what manner *of m. 1Th 1:5*
we were
nor *of m.* sought we glory,   *1Th 2:6*
neither of you
ye received it not as the word *1Th 2:13*
of m.
disputings *of m.* of corrupt   *1Ti 6:5*
minds
commandments *of m.* that turn *Tit 1:14*
from truth
disallowed indeed *of m.* but   *1Pe 2:4*
chosen of God
may put to silence ignorance   *1Pe 2:15*
of foolish *m.*
he should no longer live to the *1Pe 4:2*
lusts *of m.*
if we receive the witness *of m. 1Jo 5:9*
their faces were as the faces *of Re 9:7*
m.

prepared to slay the third part *Re 9:15;*
of m.   *9:18*
in the earthquake were slain   *Re 11:13*
of m. 7000
maketh fire come down in   *Re 13:13*
sight *of m.*
merchandise of slaves and   *Re 18:13*
souls *of m.*

SONS OF MEN

Oh ye *sons of m.* how long   *Ps 4:2;*
will ye turn   *58:1*
that trust in thee before the   *Ps 31:19*
sons of m.
the Lord beholdeth all the   *Ps 33:13*
sons of m.
I lie among the *sons of m.*   *Ps 57:4*
whose teeth are
to make known to *sons of*   *Ps 145:12*
m. his mighty acts
and my delights were with the   *Pr 8:31*
sons of m.
travail God hath given to the   *Ec 1:13*
sons of m.
might see what was that good   *Ec 2:3*
for *sons of m.*
and I gat me the delights of the *Ec 2:8*
sons of men
travail which God hath given *Ec 3:10*
to *sons of m.*
I said concerning the estate of *Ec 3:18*
the *sons of m.*
for that which befalleth the   *Ec 3:19*
sons of m.
heart of *sons of m.* set in them *Ec 8:11*
to do evil
also the heart of the *sons of m.* is *Ec 9:3*
full of evil
so are the *sons of m.* snared in *Ec 9:12*
an evil time
and his form more than the   *Isa 52:14*
sons of m.
thine eyes are open upon the *Jer 32:19*
sons of m.
and he was driven from the   *Da 5:21*
sons of m.
one like the similitude of the *Da 10:16*
sons of m.
joy is withered away from the *Joe 1:12*
sons of m.
tarrieth not, nor waiteth for   *Mic 5:7*
the *sons of m.*
all sins shall be forgiven to   *M'k 3:28*
sons of m.
which was not made known to *Eph 3:5*
sons of m.

WISE MEN

Pharaoh called for all *wise*   *Ge 41:8;*
m.   *Ex 7:11*
all the *wise m.* that wrought *Ex 36:4*
the work
take ye *wise m.* and   *De 1:13*
understanding
I took the chief of your tribes, *De 1:15*
wise m.
king said to *wise m.* that knew *Es 1:13*
the times
then said Haman's *wise m.* and *Es 6:13*
Zeresh
which *wise m.* have told from *Job 15:18*
their fathers
hear my words, O ye *wise m. Job 34:2*
and give ear
he seeth that *wise m.* die, and *Ps 49:10*
the fool
wise m. lay up knowledge, but *Pr 10:14*
foolish
he that walketh with *wise m. Pr 13:20*
shall be wise
but *wise m.* turn away wrath   *Pr 29:8*
the words of *wise m.* are heard *Ec 9:17*
in quiet
where are thy *wise m.* let   *Isa 19:12*
them tell
the wisdom of their *wise m. Isa 29:14*
shall perish
that turneth *wise m.*   *Isa 44:25*
backward
the *wise m.* are ashamed and   *Jer 8:9*
dismayed
as among all the *wise m.* of the *Jer 10:7*
nations
sword is upon Babylon, and   *Jer 50:35*
on her *wise m.*
and I will make drunken her   *Jer 51:57*
wise m.
thy *wise m.* O Tyrus, were thy *Eze 27:8*
pilots

and the *wise m.* thereof were   *Eze 27:9*
thy calkers
to destroy all the *wise m.* of   *Da 2:12*
Babylon
cannot the *wise m.* shew unto *Da 2:27*
the king
I made a decree to bring in all   *Da 4:6*
the *wise m.*
Belshazzar the king spake to the *Da 5:7*
wise m.
even destroy the *wise m.* out of   *Ob 8*
Edom
came *wise m.* from the east to *M't 2:1*
Jerusalem
Herod, when he had privily   *M't 2:7*
called the *wise m.*
was mocked of *wise m.*;   *M't 2:16;*
I send *wise m.*   *23:34*
not many *wise m.* not noble, *1Co 1:26*
are called
speak as to *wise m.* judge ye *1Co 10:15*
what I say

YE MEN

hearken unto me, *ye m.* of   *J'g 9:7*
Shechem
hearken, *ye m.* of   *Job 34:10*
understanding
ye m. of Galilee; *ye m.* of   *Ac 1:11;*
Judæa   *2:14*
ye m. of Israel   *Ac 5:35*
ye m. and brethren, if ye have *Ac 13:15*
any word
ye m. of Athens   *Ac 17:22*
ye m. of Ephesus, what man *Ac 19:35*
is there

YOUNG MEN

that which the *young m.* have *Ge 14:24*
eaten
Moses sent *young m.* which   *Ex 24:5*
offered burnt
Joshua one of the *young m. Nu 11:28*
answered
the *young m.* that were spies   *Jos 6:23*
went in
for so used the *young m.* to do *J'g 14:10*
have I not charged the *young m. Ru 2:9*
inasmuch as thou followedst   *Ru 3:10*
not *young m.*
the sin of the *young m.* was   *1Sa 2:17*
very great
he will take your goodliest   *1Sa 8:16*
young m.
if the *young m.* kept themselves *1Sa 21:4*
from women
and the vessels of the *young m. 1Sa 21:5*
are holy
ask thy *young m.* and they will *1Sa 25:8*
shew thee
thine handmaid saw not the   *1Sa 25:25*
young m.
let one of the *young m.* come *1Sa 26:22*
over and fetch
save 400 *young m.* which rode *1Sa 30:17*
on camels
and David called one of the   *2Sa 1:15*
young m.
let the *young m.* arise and   *2Sa 2:14*
play before us
and lay thee hold on one of   *2Sa 2:21*
the *young m.*
not suppose they have slain *2Sa 13:32*
all the *young m.*
and ten *young m.* that bare *2Sa 18:15*
Joab's armour
Rehoboam consulted with   *1Ki 12:8*
young m.
spake after counsel of *young 1Ki 12:14;*
m.   *2Ch 10:8, 14*
by *young m.* of the princes of *1Ki 20:14*
the provinces
send, I pray thee, one of the   *2Ki 4:22*
young m.
there be come two *young m. 2Ki 5:22*
of the prophets
their *young m.* wilt thou slay *2Ki 8:12*
with the sword
who slew their *young m. 2Ch 36:17*
with sword
if fell upon the *young m.* they *Job 1:19*
are dead
the *young m.* saw me, and   *Job 29:8*
hid themselves
the fire consumed their *young Ps 78:63*
m.
praise the Lord, *young m.*   *Ps 148:12*
and maidens

the glory of *young m.* is their *Pr 20:29*
strength
Lord shall have no joy in their *Isa 9:17*
young m.
their bows also shall dash *Isa 13:18*
young m. to pieces
neither do I nourish up young *Isa 23:4*
m. nor virgins
and his *young m.* shall be *Isa 31:8*
discomfited
and the *young m.* shall utterly *Isa 40:30*
fall
will pour fury on assembly of *Jer 6:11*
young m.
to cut off the *young m.* from *Jer 9:21*
the streets
the *young m.* shall die by the *Jer 11:22*
sword
I brought against the mother of *Jer 15:8*
the *young m.*
let their *young m.* be slain by *Jer 18:21*
the sword
both *young m.* and old rejoice *Jer 31:13*
together
his chosen *young m.* are gone *Jer 48:15*
to slaughter
her *young m.* shall fall in her *Jer 49:26*
streets
therefore shall her *young m.* *Jer 50:30*
fall in the streets
spare ye not her *young m.* *Jer 51:3*
destroy utterly
called an assembly to crush my *La 1:15*
young m.
my virgins and *young m.* are *La 1:18*
gone into captivity
the *young m.* and old lie on the *La 2:21*
ground
they took the *young m.* to *La 5:13*
grind, children fell
the *young m.* have ceased from *La 5:14*
their music
all of them desirable young *Eze 23:6;*
m. 23:12, 23
young m. of Aven shall fall *Eze 30:17*
by the sword
your *young m.* shall see *Joe 2:28;*
visions *Ac 2:17*
and of your *young m.* for *Am 2:11*
Nazarites
your *young m.* have I slain *Am 4:10*
with the sword
and your *young m.* shall faint *Am 8:13*
for thirst
corn shall make the *young m.* *Zec 9:17*
cheerful
and the *young m.* laid hold *M'k 14:51*
on him
and the *young m.* arose, wound *Ac 5:6*
him up
the *young m.* came in and *Ac 5:10*
found her dead
young m. likewise exhort to be *Tit 2:6*
sober
I write to you *young m.* *1Jo 2:13;*
because *2:14*

MENACE

a *m.* to good fellowship (P) *Jude 12*

MENAHEM

M. the son of Gadi went up *2Ki 15:14*
from
M. smote Tiphsah, and all *2Ki 15:16*
that
began *M.* the son of Gadi *2Ki 15:17*
to reign
M. gave Pul a thousand *2Ki 15:19*
talents of
M. exacted the money of *2Ki 15:20*
Israel
the rest of the acts of *M.* and *2Ki 15:21*
And *M.* slept with his *2Ki 15:22*
father; and
the son of *M.* began to reign *2Ki 15:23*
over

MENAN

which was the son of *M.*, *Lu 3:31*
which

MENCHILDREN

the year shall all your *m.* *Ex 34:23*
appear

MEND

brass to *m.* the house of the *2Ch 24:12*
Lord
and *m.* the house (S) *2Ch 34:10*
M. your ways (N)(R) *2Co 13:11*
m. your faith (N) *1Th 3:10*

MENDING

with their father, *m.* their *M't 4:21*
nets
also were in the ship *m.* their *M'k 1:19*
nets

MENE

written, *M. M.* Tekel, *Da 5:25*
Upharsin
M.; God hath numbered thy *Da 5:26*

MENIAL

one for beauty, one for *m.* use *Ro 9:21*
(R)
some *m.* and ignoble *2Ti 2:20*
(A)(B)(R)
by unaided *m.* powers (B) *2Pe 1:20*

MENPLEASERS

Not with eyeservice, as *m.*; *Eph 6:6;*
but *Col 3:22*

MEN'S

and the *m.* feet that were with *Ge 24:32*
him
Fill the *m.* sacks with food, as *Ge 44:1*
much
serve gods, the work of *m.* *De 4:28*
hands
Wherefore hearest thou *m.* *1Sa 24:9*
words
forsook the old *m.* counsel *1Ki 12:13*
that they
m. bones shall be burnt upon *1Ki 13:2*
thee
no gods, but the work of *m.* *2Ki 19:18*
hands
and burned *m.* bones upon *2Ki 23:20*
them
and gold, the work of *m.* *Ps 115:4;*
hands *135:15*
no gods, but the work of *m.* *Isa 37:19*
hands
the mighty *m.* hearts in Moab *Jer 48:41*
at that
because of *m.* blood, and *Hab 2:8;*
for the *2:17*
and lay them on *m.* shoulders *M't 23:4*
but are within full of dead *m.* *M't 23:27*
bones
is not come to destroy *m.* lives *Lu 9:56*
M. hearts failing them for *Lu 21:26*
fear, and
Neither is worshiped with *m.* *Ac 17:25*
hands
measure, that is, of other *m.* *2Co 10:15*
labours
neither be partaker of other *1Ti 5:22*
m. sins
Some *m.* sins are open before- *1Ti 5:24*
hand
or as a busy body in other *m.* *1Pe 4:15*
matters
having *m.* persons in *Jude 16*
admiration

MENSERVANTS

and oxen, and he asses and *m.* *Ge 12:16*
took sheep, and oxen, and *m.* *Ge 20:14*
herds, and silver, and gold, *Ge 24:35*
and *m.*
cattle, and maidservants, and *Ge 30:43*
m.
oxen, and asses, flocks, and *m.* *Ge 32:5*
she shall not go out as the *m.* *Ex 21:7*
do
your *m.* and your *De 12:12*
maidservants
he will take your *m.* and your *1Sa 8:16*
and sheep, and oxen, and *m.* *2Ki 5:26*
shall begin to beat the *m.* and *Lu 12:45*

MENSTEALERS

with mankind, for *m.* for liars *1Ti 1:10*

MENSTRUATION

time of her *m.* (B)(R) *Le 12:2*

MENSTRUOUS

cast them away as a *m.* cloth *Isa 30:22*
Jerusalem is as a *m.* woman *La 1:17*
hath come near to a *m.* *Eze 18:6*
woman

MENTION

and make *m.* of me unto *Ge 40:14*
Pharaoh
make no *m.* of the name of *Ex 23:13*
other
make *m.* of the name of their *Jos 23:7*
gods
when he made *m.* of the ark *1Sa 4:18*
of God
No *m.* shall be made of coral *Job 28:18*
will make *m.* of thy *Ps 71:16*
righteousness
make *m.* of Rahab and Babylon *Ps 87:4*
make *m.* that his name is *Isa 12:4*
exalted
every one that maketh *m.* *Isa 19:17*
thereof
only will we make *m.* of thy *Isa 26:13*
name
and make *m.* of the God of *Isa 48:1*
Israel
hath he made *m.* of my name *Isa 49:1*
ye that make *m.* of the Lord, *Isa 62:6*
keep
m. the lovingkindness of the *Isa 63:7*
Lord
Make ye *m.* to the nations; *Jer 4:16*
behold
I said, I will not make *m.* of *Jer 20:9*
him
burden of the Lord shall ye *Jer 23:36*
m. no
make *m.* of the name of the *Am 6:10*
Lord
m. of you always in my prayers *Ro 1:9*
making *m.* of you in my *Eph 1:16*
prayers
making *m.* of you in our *1Th 1:2*
prayers
m. of thee always in my prayers *Ph'm 4*
died, made *m.* of the *Heb 11:22*
departing of

MENTIONED

mentioned (S) *Nu 1:17;*
1Ch 16:41; 2Ch 28:15; 31:19; Ezr 8:20
these cities which are here *m.* *Jos 21:9*
m. by their names were *1Ch 4:38*
princes
who is *m.* in the book of *2Ch 20:34*
the kings
For thy sister Sodom was not *Eze 16:56*
m.
they shall not be *m.* unto him *Eze 18:22*
that he hath done shall not *Eze 18:24*
be *m.*
hath committed shall be *m.* *Eze 33:16*
unto

MENTIONS

m., speaks of happiness (B)(N) *Ro 4:6*

MEONENIM

come along by the plain of *M.* *J'g 9:37*

MEONOTHAI

M. begat Ophrah: and *1Ch 4:14*
Seraiah

MEPHAATH

Jahaza, and Kedemoth, and *Jos 13:18*
M.
M. with her suburbs; four *Jos 21:37*
cities
suburbs, and *M.* with her *1Ch 6:79*
suburbs
and upon Jahazah, and upon *Jer 48:21*
M.

MEPHIBOSHETH

lame. And his name was *M.* *2Sa 4:4*
Now when *M.*, the son of *2Sa 9:6*
Jonathan

MEPHIBOSHETH (continued)

And David said, *M.* And he	2Sa 9:6
M. thy master's son shall eat bread	2Sa 9:10
As for *M.*, said the king, he shall	2Sa 9:11
M. had a young son, whose name	2Sa 9:12
of Ziba were servants unto *M.*	2Sa 9:12
So *M.* dwelt in Jerusalem: for	2Sa 9:13
Ziba the servant of *M.* met him	2Sa 16:1
are all that pertained unto *M.*	2Sa 16:4
M. the son of Saul came down to	2Sa 19:24
wentest not thou with me, *M.*	2Sa 19:25
M. said unto the king, Yea, let him	2Sa 19:30
But the king spared *M.*, the son of	2Sa 21:7
bare unto Saul, Armoni and *M.*	2Sa 21:8

MERAB

the name of the firstborn *M.*	1Sa 14:49
Behold my elder daughter *M.*	1Sa 18:17
pass at the time when *M.* Saul's	1Sa 18:19

MERAIAH

of the fathers: of Seraiah, *M.*	Ne 12:12

MERAIOTH

Zerahiah, and Zerahiah begat *M.*	1Ch 6:6
M. begat Amariah, and Amariah	1Ch 6:7
M. his son, Amariah his son	1Ch 6:52
the son of *M.*, the son of Ahitub	1Ch 9:11
the son of Azariah, the son of *M.*	Ezr 7:3
the son of Zadok, the son of *M.* the	Ne 11:11
Of Harim, Adna; of *M.*, Helkai	Ne 12:15

MERARI

Levi; Gershon, Kohath, and *M.*	Ge 46:11; Ex 6:16; Nu 3:17; 1Ch 6:1; 6:16
the sons of *M.*; Mahali and Mushi	Ex 6:19
the sons of *M.* by their families	Nu 3:20
M. was the family of the Mahlites	Nu 3:33
these are the families of *M.*	Nu 3:33
of the families of *M.* was Zuriel the	Nu 3:35
custody and charge of the sons of *M.*	Nu 3:36
the sons of *M.*, thou shalt number	Nu 4:29
the families of the sons of *M.*	Nu 4:33; 4:42, 45
oxen he gave unto the sons of *M.*	Nu 7:8
sons of *M.* set forward, bearing the	Nu 10:17
of *M.* the family of the Merarites	Nu 26:57
The children of *M.* by their families	Jos 21:7
the families of the children of *M.*	Jos 21:34
all the cities for the children of *M.*	Jos 21:40
The sons of *M.*; Mahli, and Mushi	1Ch 6:19; 23:21
The sons of *M.*: Mahli; Libni	1Ch 6:29
sons of *M.* stood on the left hand	1Ch 6:44
the son of Mushi, the son of *M.*	1Ch 6:47
Unto the sons of *M.* were given by	1Ch 6:63
Unto the rest of the children of *M.*	1Ch 6:77
of Hashabiah, of the sons of *M.*	1Ch 9:14
Of the sons of *M.*; Ashaiah the chief	1Ch 15:6
of the sons of *M.* their brethren	1Ch 15:17
namely, Gershon, Kohath, and *M.*	1Ch 23:6
sons of *M.* were Mahli and Mushi	1Ch 24:26
The sons of *M.* by Jaaziah; Beno	1Ch 24:27
Hosah, of the children of *M.*, had	1Ch 26:10
Kore, and among the sons of *M.*	1Ch 26:19
and of the sons of *M.*; Kish the son	2Ch 29:12
the Levites, of the sons of *M.*	2Ch 34:12
him Jeshaiah of the sons of *M.*	Ezr 8:19

MERARITES

of Merari, the family of the *M.*	Nu 26:57

MERATHAIM

Go up against the land of *M.*	Jer 50:12

MERCHANDISE

thou shalt not make *m.* of her	De 21:14
not sell for money or enslave her (B)(E)(R)	De 21:14
maketh *m.* of him, or selleth him	De 24:7
selling him (B)	De 24:7
or sell him (E)(R)	De 24:7
For the *m.* of it is better than	Pr 3:14
her profit is better (A)(B)(E)(R)	Pr 3:14
is better than the *m.* of silver	Pr 3:14
perceiveth that her *m.* is good	Pr 31:18
because the *m.* of nations (A)(S)	Isa 23:3
m. and her hire shall be holiness	Isa 23:18
her *m.* shall be for them that dwell	Isa 23:18
m. of Ethiopia and of the Sabeans	Isa 45:14
riches, and make a prey of thy *m.*	Eze 26:12
were in thee to occupy thy *m.*	Eze 27:9
handle your wares (B)	Eze 27:9
barter for your wares (R)	Eze 27:9
isles were the *m.* of thine hand	Eze 27:15
and made of cedar, among thy *m.*	Eze 27:24
and thy fairs, thy *m.* thy mariners	Eze 27:27
calkers, and the occupiers of the *m.*	Eze 27:27
multitude of thy riches and of thy *m.*	Eze 27:33
thy *m.* and all company in by the *m.* (S)	Eze 27:34
By the multitude of thy *m.*	Eze 28:5; 28:18
one to his farm, another to his *m.*	M't 22:5
my Father's house an house of *m.*	Joh 2:16
Father's house a sales shop (B)	Joh 2:16
Father's house into a market (N)(P)	Joh 2:16
Father's house a house of trade (R)	Joh 2:16
with feigned words make *m.* of you	2Pe 2:3
they will exploit you (A)(B)(P)(R)	2Pe 2:3
they will trade on your credulity (N)	2Pe 2:3
no man buyeth their *m.* any more	Re 18:11
no one buys freight, cargo (A)(B)(N)(P)(R)	Ro 18:11
m. of gold, silver, and precious	Re 18:12

MERCHANT

silver, current money with the *m.*	Ge 23:16
delivereth girdles unto the *m.*	Pr 31:24
with all powders of the *m.*	Ca 3:6
m. trader of nations (B)(R)	Isa 23:3
against the *m.* city, to destroy	Isa 23:11
a *m.* of the people for many isles	Eze 27:3
the market city for the peoples	Eze 27:3
Tarshish was thy *m.* by reason of	Eze 27:12
Syria was thy *m.* by reason of	Eze 27:16
Damascus was thy *m.* in the	Eze 27:18
Dedan was thy *m.* in precious	Eze 27:20

He is a *m.* the balances of deceit	Ho 12:7
for all the *m.* people are cut down	Zep 1:11
of heaven is like unto a *m.* man	M't 13:45

MERCHANTMEN

there passed by Midianites *m.*	Ge 37:28
Midianite traders (B)(R)	Ge 37:28
Besides that he had of the *m.*	1Ki 10:15

MERCHANTS

and of the traffick of the spice *m.*	1Ki 10:15
king's *m.* received the linen yarn	1Ki 10:28; 2Ch 1:16
which chapmen and *m.* brought	2Ch 9:14
of the Nethinims, and of the *m.*	Ne 3:31
repaired the goldsmiths and the *m.*	Ne 3:32
m. and sellers of all kind of ware	Ne 13:20
shall they part him among the *m.*	Job 41:6
the *m.* of Zidon, that pass over	Isa 23:2
crowning city, whose *m.* are princes	Isa 23:8
whose *m.* are the honorable (S)	Isa 23:8
thou hast laboured, even thy *m.*	Isa 47:15
traffick; he set it in a city of *m.*	Eze 17:4
m. to barter for (R)	Eze 27:9
and Mesech, they were thy *m.*	Eze 27:13
The men of Dedan were thy *m.*	Eze 27:15
land of Israel, they were thy *m.*	Eze 27:17
goats: in these were they thy *m.*	Eze 27:21
The *m.* of Sheba and Raamah	Eze 27:22
they were thy *m.*: they occupied in	Eze 27:22
Canneh, and Eden, the *m.* of Sheba	Eze 27:23
Asshur, and Chilmad, were thy *m.*	Eze 27:23
were thy *m.* in all sorts of things	Eze 27:24
m. among the people shall hiss at	Eze 27:36
and Dedan, and the *m.* of Tarshish	Eze 38:13
multiplied thy *m.* above the stars	Na 3:16
the *m.* of the earth are waxed rich	Re 18:3
the *m.* of the earth shall weep	Re 18:11
The *m.* of these things, which were	Re 18:15
m. were the great men of the earth	Re 18:23

MERCHANTS'

She is like the *m.* ships; she	Pr 31:14

MERCIES

worthy of the least of all the *m.*	Ge 32:10
least of all kindness (B)	Ge 32:10
least of lovingkindness (E)	Ge 32:10
least of all stedfast love (R)	Ge 32:10
of the Lord, for his *m.* are great	2Sa 24:14
the Lord: for very great are his *m.*	1Ch 21:13
remember the *m.* of David thy	2Ch 6:42
the acts of lovingkindness (B)(E)	2Ch 6:42
remember thy stedfast love (R)	2Ch 6:42
thou in thy manifold *m.* forsookest	Ne 9:19
according to thy manifold *m.* thou	Ne 9:27
deliver them according to thy *m.*	Ne 9:28
O Lord, thy tender *m.* and thy	Ps 25:6
not thou thy tender *m.* from me	Ps 40:11

unto the multitude of thy *Ps 51:1*
tender *m.*
greatness of thy compassion *Ps 51:1*
(B)
to the multitude of thy tender *Ps 69:16*
m.
he in anger shut up his tender *Ps 77:9*
m.
let thy tender *m.* speedily *Ps 79:8*
prevent
I will sing of the *m.* of the *Ps 89:1*
Lord
lovingkindness and tender *m.* *Ps 103:4*
not the multitude of thy *m.* *Ps 106:7*
endless tokens of *Ps 106:7;*
lovingkindness (A)(B)(E) *106:45*
abundance of thy stedfast *Ps 106:7;*
love (R) *106:45*
according to the multitude of *Ps 106:45*
his *m.*
thy *m.* come also unto me, O *Ps 119:41*
Lord
may thy lovingkindness come *Ps 119:41*
(B)(E)
let your stedfast love come *Ps 119:41*
(R)
Let thy tender *m.* come unto *Ps 119:77*
me
Great are thy tender *m.* O *Ps 119:156*
Lord
his tender *m.* are over all his *Ps 145:9*
works
tender *m.* of the wicked are *Pr 12:10*
cruel
with great *m.* will I gather *Isa 54:7*
thee
with great compassion will *Isa 54:7*
I gather (B)(R)
you, even the sure *m.* of David *Isa 55:3*
on them according to his *m.* *Isa 63:7*
of thy bowels and of thy *m.* *Isa 63:15*
toward
yearning pity and compassion *Isa 63:15*
(A)(B)(E)(R)
Lord, even lovingkindness *Jer 16:5*
and *m.*
even kindness and compassion *Jer 16:5*
(B)
thy stedfast love and mercy *Jer 16:5*
(R)
I will shew *m.* unto you, that *Jer 42:12*
ye may
I will grant you compassion *Jer 42:12*
(B)
It is of the Lord's *m.* that *La 3:22*
we are
according, the multitude of *La 3:32*
his *m.*
they would desire *m.* of the *Da 2:18*
God
To the Lord our God belong *m. Da 9:9*
righteousnesses for thy great *Da 9:18*
m.
thy great compassions (B) *Da 9:18*
and in lovingkindness, and in *Ho 2:19*
m.
I am returned to Jerusalem *Zec 1:16*
with *m.*
will give you the sure *m.* of *Ac 13:34*
David
by the *m.* of God, that ye *Ro 12:1*
present
the Father of *m.* and the God *2Co 1:3*
of all
tender *m.* of Christ *Ph'p 1:8*
(A)(E)(S)
of the Spirit, if any bowels *Ph'p 2:1*
and *m.*
depth of affection, passionate *Ph'p 2:1*
sympathy (A)
deep-felt affections and *Ph'p 2:1*
sympathies (B)
any warmth of affection or *Ph'p 2:1*
compassion (N)
kindness and deep sympathy *Ph'p 2:1*
(P)
any affection and sympathy *Ph'p 2:1*
(R)
bowels of *m.*, kindness, *Col 3:12*
humbleness
tenderhearted pity and mercy *Col 3:12*
(A)
tenderness of heart (B) *Col 3:12*
a heart of compassion (E) *Col 3:12*
merciful in action, kindly of *Col 3:12*
heart (P)

MERCIES'

Nevertheless for thy great *m.* *Ne 9:31*
sake

soul: oh save me for thy *m.* *Ps 6:4*
sake
servant: save me for thy *m.* *Ps 31:16*
sake
help, and redeem us for thy *Ps 44:26*
m. sake

MERCIFUL

the Lord being *m.* unto him *Ge 19:16*
The Lord God, *m.* and gracious *Ex 34:6*
(For the Lord thy God is a *m.* *De 4:31*
God
Be *m.*, O Lord, unto thy *De 21:8*
people
and will be *m.* unto his land *De 32:43*
With the *m.* thou wilt shew *2Sa 22:26*
thyself
wilt shew thyself *m.* and with *2Sa 22:26*
the house of Israel are *m.* *1Ki 20:31*
kings
Lord your God is gracious *2Ch 30:9*
and *m.*
ready to pardon, gracious and *Ne 9:17*
m.
for thou art a gracious and *m.* *Ne 9:31*
God
With the *m.* thou wilt shew *Ps 18:25*
thyself
shew thyself *m.*; with an *Ps 18:25*
upright
redeem me, and be *m.* unto me *Ps 26:11*
He is ever *m.* and lendeth; *Ps 37:26*
and his
Lord, be *m.* unto me: heal my *Ps 41:4*
But thou, O Lord, be *m.* unto *Ps 41:10*
me
Be *m.* unto me, O God: for *Ps 56:1*
man
Be *m.* unto me, O God, be *m.* *Ps 57:1*
unto
be not *m.* to wicked *Ps 59:5*
transgressors
God be *m.* unto us, and bless us *Ps 67:1*
the *m.* one forgone (B)(E) *Ps 78:38*
Be *m.* unto me, O Lord: for I *Ps 86:3*
cry
m. and gracious (A)(E)(R) *Ps 86:15*
the Lord is *m.* and gracious, *Ps 103:8*
slow
and righteous; yea, our God is *Ps 116:5*
m.
his *m.* kindness is great toward *Ps 117:2*
be *m.* unto me according to *Ps 119:58*
thy
m. kindness be for my *Ps 119:76*
comfort
be *m.* unto me, as thou usest *Ps 119:132*
to do
The *m.* man doeth good to his *Pr 11:17*
own
and *m.* man are taken away, *Isa 57:1*
none
for I am *m.* saith the Lord *Jer 3:12*
for he is gracious and *m.* slow *Joe 2:13*
to
art a gracious God, and *m.* *Jon 4:2*
slow to
Blessed are the *m.*: for they shall *M't 5:7*
m., as your Father also is *m.* *Lu 6:36*
saying, God be *m.* to me a *Lu 18:13*
sinner
be a *m.* and faithful high *Heb 2:17*
priest
be *m.* to their unrighteousness *Heb 8:12*

MERCILESS

against a *m.* people (B) *Ps 43:1*

MERCURIUS

Barnabas, Jupiter; and Paul *Ac 14:12*
M.

MERCY

not left destitute my master *Ge 24:27*
of *m.*
and God give you *m.* before *Ge 43:14*
the man
make a *m.* seat of gold *Ex 25:17*
the cherubims covering the *Ex 25:20*
m. seat
m. seat between the *Ex 25:22;*
cherubims *Le 16:2; Nu 7:89*
shall put the *m.* seat upon *Ex 26:34;*
the ark *40:20*
keeping *m.* for thousands *Ex 34:7;*
Da 9:4

make the *m.* seat of pure *Ex 37:6*
gold
toward the *m.* seat (S) *Ex 37:9*
Lord is longsuffering and of *Nu 14:18;*
great *m.* *Ps 103:11; 145:8*
incense may cover the *m.* *Le 16:13*
seat
who keepeth covenant and *m.* *De 7:9;*
7:12
but my *m.* shall not depart *2Sa 7:15;*
from him *1Ch 17:13; Ps 89:24*
return thou, *m.* and truth be *2Sa 15:20*
with thee
who keepest covenant and *m.* *1Ki 8:23;*
with thy servants *Ne 1:5; 9:32*
had *m.* on them (B) *2Ki 13:23*
his *m.* endureth for ever *1Ch 16:34;*
16:41; 2Ch 5:13; 7:3, 6; 20:21;
Ezr 3:11; Ps 106:1; 107:1; 118:1;
136:1-26; Jer 33:1
gave Solomon the pattern *1Ch 28:11*
of the *m.* seat
hath extended *m.* to me before *Ezr 7:28*
the king
extended *m.* to us in sight of *Ezr 9:9*
the kings of Persia
grant him *m.* in the sight of *Ne 1:11*
this man
appeal for *m.* (A)(B) *Job 9:15*
whether for correction or for *Job 37:13*
m.
and through the *m.* of the *Ps 21:7*
most High
surely goodness and *m.* shall *Ps 23:6*
follow me
all the paths of the Lord are *m. Ps 25:10*
and truth
that trusts in Lord *m.* shall *Ps 32:10*
compass him about
eye on Lord is on them that *Ps 33:18*
hope in his *m.*
I trust in the *m.* of God for *Ps 52:8*
ever and ever
God shall send forth his *m.* and *Ps 57:3*
truth
the God of my *m.* shall *Ps 59:10;*
prevent me *59:17*
O prepare *m.* and truth which *Ps 61:7*
may preserve
also unto thee, O Lord, *Ps 62:12*
belongeth *m.*
which hath not turned his *m.* *Ps 66:20*
from me
is his *m.* clean gone for ever? *Ps 77:8*
doth *m.* fail
bestows *m.* and honor (B) *Ps 84:11*
m. and truth are met together, *Ps 85:10*
righteousness
thou, Lord, art plenteous in *m.* *Ps 86:5;*
86:15; 103:8
I said, *M.* shall be built up for *Ps 89:2*
ever
m. and truth shall go before *Ps 89:14*
thy face
my *m.* will I keep for him *Ps 89:28*
for evermore
he hath remembered his *m.* *Ps 98:3*
toward Israel
the Lord is good, his *m.* is *Ps 100:5*
everlasting
I will sing of *m.* and *Ps 101:1*
judgment, to thee
the *m.* of the Lord is from *Ps 103:17*
everlasting
let there be none to extend *Ps 109:12*
m. to him
with the Lord there is *m.* *Ps 130:7*
and redemption
takes pleasure in those that *Ps 147:11*
hope in his *m.*
let not *m.* and truth forsake *Pr 3:3*
thee
he that hath *m.* on the poor, *Pr 14:21*
happy is he
m. and truth shall be to them *Pr 14:22*
that devise good
he that honoureth God hath *Pr 14:31*
m. on the poor
by *m.* and truth iniquity is *Pr 16:6*
purged
m. and truth preserve the *Pr 20:28;*
king, and his throne is *Isa 16:5*
upholden by *m.*
he that followeth after *m.* *Pr 21:21*
findeth life
he that hath *m.* on them *Isa 49:10*
shall lead them
saith the Lord that hath *m.* *Isa 54:10*
on thee

but in my favour have I had   *Isa 60:10*
m. on thee
they are cruel, and have no *m.*   *Jer 6:23*
because there is no truth, nor   *Jer 4:1*
m. in the land
for I desired *m.* and not   *Jer 6:6*
sacrifice
reap in *m.;* keep *m.* and wait   *Jer 10:12;*
on God   *12:6*
for in thee the fatherless   *Jer 14:3*
findeth *m.*
they forsake their own *m.*   *Jon 2:8*
but to do justly, and to love *m.*   *Mic 6:8*
retains not anger, because he   *Mic 7:18*
delighteth in *m.*
thou wilt perform the *m.* to   *Mic 7:20*
Abraham
O Lord, in wrath remember *m.*   *Hab 3:2*
show kindness and *m.* (R)   *Zec 7:9*
blessed are the merciful, shall   *M't 5:7*
obtain *m.*
should have *m.*   *M't 18:35*
(A)(B)(E)(R
and have omitted judgment   *M't 23:23*
and *m.*
m. on you   *M'k 5:19*
(A)(B)(E)(N)(R)
his *m.* is on them that fear him   *Lu 1:50*
holpen Israel in remembrance   *Lu 1:54*
of his *m.*
to perform the *m.* promised to   *Lu 1:72*
our fathers
by remission through the   *Lu 1:78*
tender *m.* of our God
made *m.* in splendor (A)   *Lu 16:19*
justified freely through *m.* (B)   *Ro 3:24*
the riches of his glory on vessels   *Ro 9:23*
of *m.*
have now obtained *m.* thro'   *Ro 11:30*
their unbelief
that through your *m.* they   *Ro 11:31*
also may obtain *m.*
that Gentiles might glorify   *Ro 15:9*
God for his *m.*
that hath obtained *m.* to be   *1Co 7:25*
faithful
as we have received *m.* we faint   *2Co 4:1*
not
peace be on them, and and *m.*   *Ga 6:16*
on Israel
God who is rich in *m.* hath   *Eph 2:4*
quickened us
was nigh to death, but God   *Ph'p 2:27*
had *m.* on him
m. from God our Father, and   *1Ti 1:2;*
Jesus Christ   *2Ti 1:2; Tit 1:4; 3Jo 3*
but I obtained *m.* because I did   *1Ti 1:13*
it ignorantly
howbeit, for this cause I   *1Ti 1:16*
obtained *m.*
Lord give *m.* to the house of   *2Ti 1:16*
Onesiphorus
that he may find *m.* of the   *2Ti 1:18*
Lord in that day
but according to his *m.* he saved   *Tit 3:5*
us
that we may obtain *m.* and   *Heb 4:16*
find grace
he that despised Moses' law   *Heb 10:28*
died without *m.*
judgment without *m.* that   *Jas 2:13*
shewed no *m.* and *m.* rejoiceth
the wisdom that is from above   *Jas 3:17*
is full of *m.*
the Lord is very pitiful and of   *Jas 5:11*
tender *m.*
according to his abundant *m.*   *1Pe 1:3*
hath begotten
had not obtained *m.* but now   *1Pe 2:10*
have obtained *m.*
m. to you, peace and love be   *Jude 2*
multiplied
looking for the *m.* of lord Jesus   *Jude 21*
to eternal life
have *m.* who waver and doubt   *Jude 22*
(A)

HAVE MERCY

have *m.* upon me   *Ps 4:1;*
6:2; 9:13; 25:16; 27:7; 30:10; 31:9; 51:1;
   86:16
shalt have *m.* on Zion;   *Ps 102:13;*
have *m.* on us   *123:2-3*
whoso forsaketh his sins shall   *Pr 28:13*
have *m.*
neither have *m.* on their   *Isa 9:17*
fatherless and widows
for Lord will have *m.* on   *Isa 14:1*
Jacob, and choose

he that made them will not   *Isa 27:11*
have *m.* on them
be exalted, that he may have   *Isa 30:18*
m. on you
for God will have *m.* upon his   *Isa 49:13*
afflicted
with everlasting kindness will I   *Isa 54:8*
have *m.* on thee
let him return, and he will   *Isa 55:7*
have *m.* on him
nor have *m.* but destroy them   *Jer 13:14;*
   21:7
and I will have *m.* on his   *Jer 30:18*
dwelling places
I will surely have *m.* on him   *Jer 31:20;*
   33:26; Eze 39:25; Ho 1:7; 2:23
that he may have *m.* on you,   *Jer 42:12*
and cause you
no more have *m.* on the   *Ho 1:6;*
house of Israel   *2:4*
O Lord, how long wilt thou   *Zec 1:12*
not have *m.*
I will bring them again, for I   *Zec 10:6*
have *m.* upon them
I will have *m.* and not   *M't 9:13;*
sacrifice   *12:7*
thou Son of David, have *m.*   *M't 9:27;*
on me   *15:22; 20:30-31; M'k 10:47-48;*
   Lu 18:38-39
Lord, have *m.* on my son, for   *M't 17:15*
he is lunatic
father Abraham, have *m.* on   *Lu 16:24*
me, and send
they said, Jesus, Master, have   *Lu 17:13*
m. on us
I will have *m.* on whom I will   *Ro 9:15;*
have *m.*   *9:18*
all in unbelief, that he might   *Ro 11:32*
have *m.* on all

SHEW, SHEWED, SHEWETH, SHEWING, MERCY

Lord was with Joseph, and   *Ge 39:21*
shewed him *m.*
shewing m. to thousands   *Ex 20:6;*
   De 5:10
I will *shew m.* on whom I will   *Ex 33:19*
shew m.
shalt make no covenant, nor   *De 7:2*
shew them *m.*
that the Lord may turn and   *De 13:17*
shew thee *m.*
shew us city, and we will *shew*   *J'g 1:24*
thee *m.*
sheweth m. to his anointed   *2Sa 22:51;*
   Ps 18:50
hast *shewed* to thy servant   *1Ki 3:6;*
David, my father, great *m.*   *2Ch 1:8*
and *shewest m.* to thy   *2Ch 6:14*
servants
but the righteous *sheweth m.*   *Ps 37:21*
and giveth
shew us thy *m.* O Lord, and   *Ps 85:7*
grant thy salvation
because he remembered not   *Ps 109:16*
to *shew m.*
and thou didst *shew* them no   *Isa 47:6*
m.
they are cruel, and will not   *Jer 50:42*
shew m.
break off thy sins, by *shewing*   *Da 4:27*
m.
execute true judgment, and   *Zec 7:9*
shew m.
how the Lord *shewed* great *m.*   *Lu 1:58*
on her
and he said, He that *shewed*   *Lu 10:37*
m. on him
not that runs, but of God that   *Ro 9:16*
sheweth m.
he that *sheweth m.* with   *Ro 12:8*
cheerfulness
judgment without mercy that   *Jas 2:13*
shewed no *m.*

THY MERCY

and thou hast magnified thy   *Ge 19:19*
m. to me
in thy *m.* hast led forth the   *Ex 15:13*
people
according to the greatness of   *Nu 14:19*
thy *m.*
spare me according to thy *m.*   *Ne 13:22*
into thy house, in multitude of   *Ps 5:7*
thy *m.*
I have trusted in thy *m.* my   *Ps 13:5*
heart shall rejoice

according to thy *m.* remember   *Ps 25:7*
thou me
I will be glad and rejoice in thy   *Ps 31:7*
m. for thou
let thy *m.* O Lord, be upon us,   *Ps 33:22*
as we hope
thy *m.* O Lord, is in the   *Ps 36:5*
heavens
for thy *m.* is great unto the   *Ps 57:10*
heavens
I will sing aloud of thy *m.* in   *Ps 59:16*
the morning
in the multitude of thy *m.*   *Ps 69:13*
hear me
shew us thy *m.* O Lord; great   *Ps 85:7;*
is thy *m.*   *86:13*
O satisfy us early with thy *m.*   *Ps 90:14*
to rejoice
my foot slippeth, thy *m.* O   *Ps 94:18*
Lord, held me up
for thy *m.* is great above the   *Ps 108:4*
heavens
because thy *m.* is good,   *Ps 109:21*
deliver thou me
O Lord my God, save me   *Ps 109:26*
according to thy *m.*
for thy *m.* and for thy truth's   *Ps 115:1*
sake
the earth, O Lord, is full of   *Ps 119:64*
thy *m.*
deal with thy servant   *Ps 119:124*
according to thy *m.*
thy *m.* endureth for ever,   *Ps 138:8*
forsake not
and of thy *m.* cut off mine   *Ps 143:12*
enemies

MERCYSEAT

of glory shadowing the *m.*   *Heb 9:5*

MERED

sons of Ezra were, Jether, and   *1Ch 4:17*
M.
daughter of Pharaoh, which   *1Ch 4:18*
M. took

MEREMOTH

by the hand of *M.* the son of   *Ezr 8:33*
Uriah
Vaniah, *M.,* Eliashib   *Ezr 10:36*
them repaired *M.* the son of   *Ne 3:4*
Urijah
him repaired *M.* the son of   *Ne 3:21*
Urijah
Harim, *M.,* Obadiah   *Ne 10:5*
Shechaniah, Rehum, *M.*   *Ne 12:3*

MERES

M., Marsena, and Memucan   *Es 1:14*

MERIBAH

name of the place Massah, and   *Ex 17:7*
M.
This is the water of *M.*   *Nu 20:13*
against my word at the water   *Nu 20:24*
of *M.*
that is the water of *M.* in   *Nu 27:14*
Kadesh
didst strive at the waters of *M.*   *De 33:8*
I proved thee at the waters of   *Ps 81:7*
M.

MERIBAH-KADESH

of Israel at the waters of *M.*   *De 32:51*

MERIB-BAAL

And the son of Jonathan was   *1Ch 8:34;*
M.   *9:40*
and *M.* begat Micah   *1Ch 8:34;*
   9:40

MERIBOTH-KADESH

waters of *M.* (S)   *Eze 47:19; 48:28*

MERIT

what is your *m.* (B)   *M't 5:46*

MERODACH

M. is broken in pieces   *Jer 50:2*

MERODACH-BALADAN

that time *M.*, the son of   *Isa 39:1*
Baladan

MEROM

together at the waters of *M.*   *Jos 11:5*
against them by the waters of *Jos 11:7*
M.

MERONOTHITE

the asses was Jehdeiah the   *1Ch 27:30*
M.
the Gibeonite, and Jadon   *Ne 3:7*
the *M.*

MEROZ

Curse ye *M.* said the angel of   *J'g 5:23*

MERRILY

then go thou in *m.* with the   *Es 5:14*
king

MERRY

they drank, and were *m.* with   *Ge 43:34*
him
drank and got hilarious (B)   *Ge 43:34*
trode the grapes, and made *m.*   *J'g 9:27*
pass, when their hearts were   *J'g 16:25*
m.
they were in high spirits (B)   *J'g 16:25*
all night, and let thine heart be   *J'g 19:6*
m.
here, that thine heart may be *m.* *J'g 19:9*
they were making their hearts   *J'g 19:22*
m.
while they were enjoying   *J'g 19:22*
themselves (B)
and drunk, and his heart was *m.*   *Ru 3:7*
felt happy at heart (B)   *Ru 3:7*
Nabal's heart was *m.* within   *1Sa 25:36*
him
Nabal was in a happy mood   *1Sa 25:36*
(B)
Amnon's heart is *m.* with   *2Sa 13:28*
wine
and drinking, and making *m.*   *1Ki 4:20*
ate, drank, and rejoiced (A)   *1Ki 4:20*
ate and drank and enjoyed life   *1Ki 4:20*
(B)
ate, drank, and were happy   *1Ki 4:20*
(R)
bread, and let thine heart be   *1Ki 21:7*
m.
let your heart be happy (A)   *1Ki 21:7*
eat and be of good cheer (B)   *1Ki 21:7*
let your heart be cheerful (R)   *1Ki 21:7*
their tents, glad and *m.* in   *2Ch 7:10*
heart
joyful and glad-hearted (B)   *2Ch 7:10*
joyful and glad of heart   *2Ch 7:10*
(E)(R)
when the heart of the king was   *Es 1:10*
m.
A *m.* heart maketh a cheerful   *Pr 15:13*
happy heart makes face look   *Pr 15:13*
sunny (B)
but he that is of a *m.* heart   *Pr 15:15*
hath a
glad heart has continual feast   *Pr 15:15*
(B)
cheerful heart has continual   *Pr 15:15*
feast (E)(R)
A *m.* heart doeth good like a   *Pr 17:22*
cheerful, happy heart   *Pr 17:22*
(A)(B)(E)(R)
to eat, and to drink, and to be   *Ec 8:15*
m.
eat, drink, and be joyful   *Ec 8:15*
(A)(B)(E)(R)
drink thy wine with a *m.* heart   *Ec 9:7*
drink wine with a cheerful heart   *Ec 9:7*
(A)
for laughter, and wine maketh   *Ec 10:19*
m.
those, who make *m.* (A)(E)   *Jer 15:17*
the voice of them that make   *Jer 30:19*
m.
in the dances of them that make   *Jer 31:4*
m.
thine ease, eat, drink, and be   *Lu 12:19*
m.
eat, drink, and enjoy thyself   *Lu 12:19*
(A)(B)(N)
eat, drink, and have a good   *Lu 12:19*
time (P)

and kill it; and let us eat, and   *Lu 15:23*
be *m.*
is found. And they began to   *Lu 15:24*
be *m.*
I might make *m.* with my   *Lu 15:29*
friends
was meet, that we should   *Lu 15:32*
make *m.*
Is any *m.*? let him sing psalms   *Jas 5:13*
Is any glad at heart (A)   *Jas 5:13*
Is anyone feeling cheerful   *Jas 5:13*
(B)(E)(R)
Is any one in good heart (N)   *Jas 5:13*
If anyone is flourishing (P)   *Jas 5:13*
rejoice over them, and make   *Re 11:10*
m.

MERRYHEARTED

languisheth, all the *m.* do sigh   *Isa 24:7*

MERRYMAKERS

assembly of *m.* (B)(R)   *Jer 15:17*

MESECH

Woe is me, that I sojourn in   *Ps 120:5*
M.

MESHA

And their dwelling was from   *Ge 10:30*
M.
M. of Moab was a   *2Ki 3:4*
sheepmaster
M. his firstborn, which was   *1Ch 2:42*
and Zibia, and *M.*, and   *1Ch 8:9*
Malcham

MESHACH

Shadrach; and to Mishael, of   *Da 1:7*
M.
set Shadrach, *M.*, and   *Da 2:49*
Abed-nego
Shadrach, *M.*, and Abed-nego   *Da 3:12;*
                                     3:16, 26
bring Shadrach, *M.*, and   *Da 3:13*
Abed-nego
O Shadrach, *M.*, and   *Da 3:14*
Abed-nego
was changed against Shadrach,   *Da 3:19*
M.
bind Shadrach, *M.*, and   *Da 3:20*
Abed-nego
men that took up Shadrach,   *Da 3:22*
Shadrach, *M.*, and Abed-nego,   *Da 3:23*
fell
spake, and said, Shadrach, *M.*   *Da 3:26*
be the God of Shadrach, *M.*   *Da 3:28*
against the God of Shadrach,   *Da 3:29*
M.
the king promoted Shadrach,   *Da 3:30*
M.

MESHECH

and Tubal, and *M.*, and Tiras   *Ge 10:2;*
                                     1Ch 1:5
Uz, and Hul, and Gether,   *1Ch 1:17*
and *M.*
and *M.*, they were thy   *Eze 27:13*
merchants
There is *M.*, Tubal, and all   *Eze 32:26*
her
the chief prince of *M.* and   *Eze 38:2;*
Tubal   *38:3; 39:1*

MESHELEMIAH

the son of *M.* was porter of   *1Ch 9:21*
Korhites was *M.* the son of   *1Ch 26:1*
Kore
the sons of *M.* were,   *1Ch 26:2*
Zechariah the
M. had sons and brethren,   *1Ch 26:9*
strong

MESHEZABEEL

son of Berechiah, the son of *M.*   *Ne 3:4*
M., Zadok, Juddua   *Ne 10:21*
And Pethahiah the son of *M.*   *Ne 11:24*

MESHILLEMITH

son of Meshullam, the son of   *1Ch 9:12*
M.

MESHILLEMOTH

Berechiah the son of *M.*, and   *2Ch 28:12*
the son of Ahasai, the son of   *Ne 11:13*
M.

MESHOBAB

And *M.*, and Jamlech, and   *1Ch 4:34*
Joshah

MESHULLAM

son of *M.*, the scribe, to the   *2Ki 22:3*
house
M., and Hananiah, and   *1Ch 3:19*
Shelomith
and *M.*, and Sheba, and Jorai   *1Ch 5:13*
And Zebadiah, and *M.*, and   *1Ch 8:17*
Hezeki
Sallu the son of *M.*, the son of   *1Ch 9:7*
M. the son of Shephathiah, the   *1Ch 9:8*
the son of Hilkiah, the son   *1Ch 9:11*;
of *M.*   *Ne 11:11*
son of *M.* the son of   *1Ch 9:12*
Meshillemith
M., of the sons of the   *2Ch 34:12*
Kohathites
and for Zechariah, and for *M.*,   *Ezr 8:16*
chief
and *M.* and Shabbethai the   *Ezr 10:15*
Levite
of the sons of Bani; *M.*,   *Ezr 10:29*
Malluch
And next unto them repaired *M.*   *Ne 3:4*
and *M.* the son of Besodeiah   *Ne 3:6*
repaired *M.* the son of   *Ne 3:30*
Berechiah
had taken the daughter of *M.*   *Ne 6:18*
Hashbadana, Zechariah, and *M.*   *Ne 8:4*
M., Abijah, Mijamin   *Ne 10:7*
Magpiash, *M.*, Hezir   *Ne 10:20*
Sallu the son of *M.*, the son of   *Ne 11:7*
Joed
Of Ezra, *M.*; of Amariah   *Ne 12:13*
Iddo, Zechariah; of   *Ne 12:16*
Ginnethon, *M.*
and Bakbukiah, Obadiah, *M.*   *Ne 12:25*
And Azariah, Ezra, and *M.*   *Ne 12:33*

MESHULLEMETH

And his mother's name was   *2Ki 21:19*
M.

MESOBAITE

Eliel, and Obed, and Jasiel   *1Ch 11:47*
the *M.*

MESOPOTAMIA

and he arose, and went to *M.*   *Ge 24:10*
the son of Beor of Pethor of   *De 23:4*
M.
of Cushan-rishathaim king of   *J'g 3:8;*
M.   *3:10*
chariots and horsemen out of   *1Ch 19:6*
M.
the dwellers in *M.* and in Judaea *Ac 2:9*
father Abraham, when he was   *Ac 7:2*
in *M.*

MESS

Benjamin's *m.* was five times   *Ge 43:34*
so
there followed him a *m.* of   *2Sa 11:8*
meat
for one *m.* of meat sold (E)   *Heb 12:16*

MESSAGE

heard this adverse *m.* (B)   *Ex 33:4*
I have a *m.* from God unto   *J'g 3:20*
thee
wrote a *m.* to Joab (N)   *2Sa 11:14*
when Ben-hadad heard this   *1Ki 20:12*
m. as
He that sendeth a *m.* by the   *Pr 26:6*
hand
see *m.* fulfilled (B)   *Eze 13:6*
preach to it the *m.* (B)(R)   *Jon 3:2*
in the Lord's *m.* unto the   *Hag 1:13*
people
him, and sent a *m.* after him   *Lu 19:14*
delivering the *m.*   *Ac 11:19*
(A)(B)(N)(P)
witnessed the *m.* (B)(N)   *Ac 14:3*

delivering the *m.* (N)(P)	Ac 16:6
the *m.* of the cross (A)(B)	1Co 1:18
simplemindedness of the gospel *m.* (P)	1Co 1:21
my language and my *m.* (A)(B)(R)	1Co 2:4
the good *m.* (B)	1Th 3:6
m. planted in hearts (N)(P)	Jas 1:21
preach his *m.* as from God (P)	1Pe 4:11
is the *m.* which we have heard of	1Jo 1:5
is the *m.* that ye heard from	1Jo 3:11

MESSAGES

God's *m.* were entrusted (P)	Ro 3:2

MESSENGER

And they sent a *m.* unto Joseph	Ge 50:16
the *m.* answered and said, Israel	1Sa 4:17
But there came a *m.* unto Saul	1Sa 23:27
And charged the *m.* saying, When	2Sa 11:19
So the *m.* went, and came and	2Sa 11:22
the *m.* said unto David, Surely	2Sa 11:23
David said unto the *m.* Thus shalt	2Sa 11:25
there came a *m.* to David, saying	2Sa 15:13
Jezebel sent a *m.* unto Elijah	1Ki 19:2
And the *m.* that was gone to call	1Ki 22:13
Elisha sent a *m.* unto him, saying	2Ki 5:10
ere the *m.* came to him, he said to	2Ki 6:32
when the *m.* cometh, shut the door	2Ki 6:32
the *m.* came down unto him	2Ki 6:33
The *m.* came to them, but he	2Ki 9:18
And there came a *m.* and told him	2Ki 10:8
the *m.* that went to call Micaiah	2Ch 18:12
And there came a *m.* unto Job, and	Job 1:14
If there be a *m.* with him, an	Job 33:23
A wicked *m.* falleth into mischief	Pr 13:17
a cruel *m.* shall be sent against	Pr 17:11
is a faithful *m.* to them that send	Pr 25:13
or deaf, as my *m.* that I sent	Isa 42:19
and one *m.* to meet another, to	Jer 51:31
unto whom a *m.* was sent	Eze 23:40
spake Haggai the Lord's *m.* in the	Hag 1:13
he is the *m.* of the Lord of hosts	Mal 2:7
I will send my *m.* and he shall	Mal 3:1
even the *m.* of the covenant	Mal 3:1
I send my *m.* before thy face, which	M't 11:10; M'k 1:2; Lu 7:27
m. of heaven (P)	Ro 8:38
the *m.* of Satan to buffet me, lest I	2Co 12:7
one of Satan's angels (P)	2Co 12:7
your *m.* and he that ministered	Ph'p 2:25

MESSENGERS

Jacob sent *m.* before him to Esau	Ge 32:3
the *m.* returned to Jacob, saying	Ge 32:6
And Moses sent *m.* from Kadesh	Nu 20:14
Israel sent *m.* unto Sihon king of	Nu 21:21
He sent *m.* therefore unto Balaam	Nu 22:5
Spake I not also to thy *m.* which	Nu 24:12
And I sent *m.* out of the wilderness	De 2:26
because he hid the *m.* that we sent	Jos 6:17
she hid the *m.* which Joshua sent	Jos 6:25
So Joshua sent *m.* and they ran	Jos 7:22
sent *m.* throughout all Manasseh	J'g 6:35

he sent *m.* unto Asher, and	J'g 6:35
And Gideon sent *m.* throughout all	J'g 7:24
he sent *m.* unto Abimelech privily	J'g 9:31
Jephthah sent *m.* unto the king	J'g 11:12
answered unto the *m.* of Jephthah	J'g 11:13
Jephthah sent *m.* again unto	J'g 11:14
Israel sent *m.* unto the king of	J'g 11:17
Israel sent *m.* unto Sihon king of	J'g 11:19
And they sent *m.* to the inhabitants	1Sa 6:21
may send *m.* unto all the coasts of	1Sa 11:3
Then came the *m.* to Gibeah	1Sa 11:4
coasts of Israel by the hands of *m.*	1Sa 11:7
they said unto the *m.* that came	1Sa 11:9
m. came and shewed it to the men	1Sa 11:9
Wherefore Saul sent *m.* unto Jesse	1Sa 16:19
also sent *m.* unto David's house	1Sa 19:11
when Saul sent *m.* to take David	1Sa 19:14; 19:20
Saul sent the *m.* again to see David	1Sa 19:15
when the *m.* were come in, behold	1Sa 19:16
Spirit of God was upon the *m.* of	1Sa 19:20
it was told Saul, he sent other *m.*	1Sa 19:21
Saul sent *m.* again the third time	1Sa 19:21
David sent *m.* out of the wilderness	1Sa 25:14
and she went after the *m.* of David	1Sa 25:42
And David sent *m.* unto the men	2Sa 2:5
And Abner sent *m.* to David on his	2Sa 3:12
And David sent *m.* to Ish-bosheth	2Sa 3:14
he sent *m.* after Abner, which	2Sa 3:26
king of Tyre sent *m.* to David	2Sa 5:11; 1Ch 14:1
And David sent *m.* and took her	2Sa 11:4
Joab sent *m.* to David, and said	2Sa 12:27
he sent *m.* to Ahab king of Israel	1Ki 20:2
And the *m.* came again, and said	1Ki 20:5
he said, unto the *m.* of Ben-hadad	1Ki 20:9
the *m.* departed, and brought	1Ki 20:9
he sent *m.* and said unto them, Go	2Ki 1:2
meet the *m.* of the king of Samaria	2Ki 1:3
when the *m.* turned back unto him	2Ki 1:5
as thou hast sent *m.* to enquire of	2Ki 1:16
the *m.* returned, and told the king	2Ki 7:15
Then Amaziah sent *m.* to Jehoash	2Ki 14:8
So Ahaz sent *m.* to Tiglath-pileser	2Ki 16:7
he had sent *m.* to So king of Egypt	2Ki 17:4
he sent *m.* again unto Hezekiah	2Ki 19:9
the letter of the hand of the *m.* and	2Ki 19:14
By thy *m.* thou hast reproached the	2Ki 19:23
And David sent *m.* to comfort him	1Ch 19:2
worse before Israel, they sent *m.*	1Ch 19:16
their father sent to them by his *m.*	2Ch 36:15
But they mocked the *m.* of God, and	2Ch 36:16
I sent *m.* unto them, saying, I am	Ne 6:3
wrath of a king is as *m.* of death	Pr 16:14

then answer the *m.* of the nation	Isa 14:32
saying, Go, ye swift *m.* to a nation	Isa 18:2
he heard it, he sent *m.* to Hezekiah	Isa 37:9
the letter from the hand of the *m.*	Isa 37:14
performeth the counsel of his *m.*	Isa 44:26
didst send thy *m.* far off, and	Isa 57:9
by the hand of the *m.* which come	Jer 27:3
and sent *m.* unto them into Chaldea	Eze 23:16
that day shall *m.* go forth from me	Eze 30:9
the voice of thy *m.* shall no more be	Na 2:13
when the *m.* of John were departed	Lu 7:24
And sent *m.* before his face	Lu 9:52
he sends *m.* (P)	Lu 14:32
they are the *m.* of the churches	2Co 8:23
extra-special *m.* (P)	2Co 11:5
she had received the *m.* and	Jas 2:25

MESSES

sent *m.* unto them from before	Ge 43:34

MESSIAH

and build Jerusalem unto the M.	Da 9:25
and two weeks shall M. be cut off	Da 9:26

MESSIAS

unto him, We have found the M.	Joh 1:41
I know that M. cometh, which is	Joh 4:25

MET

and the angels of God *m.* him	Ge 32:1
thou by all this drove which I *m.*	Ge 33:8
of the Hebrews hath *m.* with us	Ex 3:18
that the Lord *m.* him, and sought	Ex 4:24
and *m.* him in the mount of God	Ex 4:27
of the Hebrews hath *m.* with us	Ex 5:3
And they *m.* Moses and Aaron	Ex 5:20
And God *m.* Balaam: and he said	Nu 23:4
Lord *m.* Balaam, and put a word	Nu 23:16
they *m.* you not with bread and	De 23:4
How he *m.* thee by the way	De 25:18
all these kings were *m.* together	Jos 11:5
m. together in Asher on the north	Jos 17:10
a company of prophets *m.* him	1Sa 10:10
against her; and she *m.* them	1Sa 25:20
m. together by the pool of Gibeon	2Sa 2:13
servant of Mephibosheth *m.* him	2Sa 16:1
Absalom *m.* the servants of David	2Sa 18:9
a lion *m.* him by the way, and slew	1Ki 13:24
in the way, behold, Elijah *m.* him	1Ki 18:7
m. him in the portion of Naboth	2Ki 9:21
m. with the brethren of Ahaziah	2Ki 10:13
m. not the children of Israel with	Ne 13:2
Mercy and truth are *m.* together	Ps 85:10
m. him a woman with the attire	Pr 7:10
as he *m.* them, he said unto them	Jer 41:6
flee from a lion, and a bear *m.* him	Am 5:19
m. him two possessed with devils	M't 8:28
Jesus *m.* them, saying, All hail	M't 28:9
there *m.* him out of the tombs a man	M'k 5:2
in a place where two ways *m.*	M'k 11:4
m. him out of the city a certain	Lu 8:27
from the hill, much people *m.* him	Lu 9:37

m. him ten men that were   *Lu 17:12*
lepers
his servants *m.* him, and told   *Joh 4:51*
him
was coming, went and *m.*   *Joh 11:20*
him
in that place where Martha   *Joh 11:30*
m. him
this cause the people also *m.*   *Joh 12:18*
him
was coming in, Cornelius.   *Ac 10:25*
him
with a spirit of divination *m.*   *Ac 16:16*
us
daily with them that *m.* with   *Ac 17:17*
him
when he *m.* with us at Assos,   *Ac 20:14*
we
falling into a place where two   *Ac 27:41*
seas *m.*
who *m.* Abraham returning   *Heb 7:1*
from
father, when Melchisedec *m.*   *Heb 7:10*
him

METAL

no *m.* worker (A)   *1Sa 13:19*
heavy *m.* mirror (S)   *Job 37:18*
Alexander the *m.* worker (B)   *2Ti 4:14*

METE

when they did *m.* it with an   *Ex 16:18*
omer
Measuring with a six pint   *Ex 16:18*
vessel (B)
and *m.* out the valley of   *Ps 60:6*
Succoth
I will divide and portion out   *Ps 60:6*
(A)
portion out valley of Succoth   *Ps 60:6*
(R)
and *m.* out the valley of   *Ps 108:7*
Succoth
with what measure ye *m.* it   *M't 7:2;*
shall   *M'k 4:24*
with the measure you deal out   *M't 7:2*
(A)(N)(P)(R)
what yardstick you measure   *M't 7:2*
you will be measured (B)
with the same measure that ye   *Lu 6:38*
m.

METED

a nation *m.* out and trodden   *Isa 18:2;*
down   *18:7*
and *m.* out heaven with the   *Isa 40:12*
span
marked off the heavens   *Isa 40:12*
(A)(B)(R)

METEYARD

in *m.*, in weight, or in measure   *Le 19:35*
in measurements (B)   *Le 19:35*
in measures of length (E)(R)   *Le 19:35*

METHEG-AMMAH

David took *M.* out of the hand   *2Sa 8:1*
of

METHODS

his *m.* (P)   *2Co 2:11*
the devil's *m.* of attack (P)   *Eph 6:11*

METHUSAEL

Mehujael begat *M.*: and *M.*   *Ge 4:18*
begat

METHUSELAH

and five years, and begat *M.*   *Ge 5:21*
walked with God after he begat   *Ge 5:22*
M.
M. lived an hundred eighty and   *Ge 5:25*
M. lived after he begat Lamech   *Ge 5:26*
the days of *M.* were nine   *Ge 5:27*
hundred
Henoch, *M.*, Lamech   *1Ch 1:3*

MEUNIM

the children of *M.* the children   *Ne 7:52*

MEZAHAB

of Matred, the daughter of   *Ge 36:39;*
M.   *1Ch 1:50*

MIAMIN

Malchiah, and *M.* and   *Ezr 10:25*
Eleazar
M., Maadiah, Bilgah   *Ne 12:5*

MIBHAR

Nathan, *M.* the son of   *1Ch 11:38*
Haggeri

MIBSAM

and Kedar, and Adbeel, and   *Ge 25:13;*
M.   *1Ch 1:29*
Shallum his son, *M.* his son   *1Ch 4:25*

MIBZAR

Kenaz, duke Teman, duke *M.*   *Ge 36:42;*
   1Ch 1:53

MICAH

Ephraim, whose name was *M.*   *J'g 17:1*
and they were in the house of   *J'g 17:4;*
M.   *17:5, 8-10, 12-13; 18:2-4, 13,*
   15, 22-23, 26-27
M. his son, Reaia his son, Baal   *1Ch 5:5*
his
and Merib-baal begat *M.*   *1Ch 8:34;*
   9:40
the sons of *M.* were, Pithon   *1Ch 8:35;*
   9:41
Mattaniah the son of *M.* the   *1Ch 9:15*
Of the sons of Uzziel; *M.*:   *1Ch 23:20*
the first
Abdon the son of *M.* and   *2Ch 34:20*
Shaphan
M. the Morashite prophesied   *Jer 26:18*
in
word of the Lord that came to   *Mic 1:1*
M.

MICAH'S

And these went into *M.*   *J'g 18:18*
house, and
in the houses near to *M.*   *J'g 18:22*
house
they set them up *M.* graven   *J'g 18:31*
image

MICAIAH

yet one man, *M.* the son of   *1Ki 22:8;*
Imlah   *22:9, 13-15, 24-26, 28;*
   2Ch 18:7-8, 12-14, 23-25, 27

MICE

and five golden *m.* according   *1Sa 6:4*
to the
images of your *m.* that mar the   *1Sa 6:5*
the coffer with the *m.* of gold   *1Sa 6:11*
the golden *m.* according to the   *1Sa 6:18*
vermin and *m.* (B)   *Isa 66:17*

MICHA

young son, whose name was   *2Sa 9:12*
M.
M., Rehob, Hashabiah   *Ne 10:11*
And Mattaniah the son of *M.*   *Ne 11:17*
son of Mattaniah, the son of   *Ne 11:22*
M.

MICHAEL

of Asher, Sethur the son of   *Nu 13:13*
M.
house of their fathers, were,   *1Ch 5:13*
M.
the son of *M.*, the son of   *1Ch 5:14*
Jeshishai
son of *M.*, the son of   *1Ch 6:40*
Baaseiah, the
M., and Obadiah, and Joel,   *1Ch 7:3*
Ishiah
M., and Ispah, and Joha, the   *1Ch 8:16*
sons
M., and Jozabad, and Elihu   *1Ch 12:20*
of Issachar, Omri the son of   *1Ch 27:18*
M.

Zechariah, and Azariah, and   *2Ch 21:2*
M.
Zebadiah the son of *M.*, and   *Ezr 8:8*
M., one of the chief princes,   *Da 10:13*
came
in these things, but *M.* your   *Da 10:21*
prince
at that time shall *M.* stand up   *Da 12:1*
Yet *M.* the archangel, when   *Jude 9*
M. and his angels fought against   *Re 12:7*

MICHAH

Of the sons of Uzziel; *M.*: of   *1Ch 24:24*
of the sons of *M.*; Shamir   *1Ch 24:24*
The brother of *M.* was   *1Ch 24:25*
Isshiah: of

MICHAIAH

and Achbor the son of *M.*   *2Ki 22:12*
His mother's name also was   *2Ch 13:2*
M.
and to *M.*, to teach in the   *2Ch 17:7*
cities of
the son of *M.*, the son of   *Ne 12:35*
Zaccur
Eliakim, Maaseiah,   *Ne 12:41*
Miniamin, *M.*
When *M.* the son of   *Jer 36:11*
Gemariah
M. declared unto them all the   *Jer 36:13*

MICHAL

and the name of the younger   *1Sa 14:49*
M.
M. Saul's daughter loved   *1Sa 18:20*
David
Saul gave him *M.* his   *1Sa 18:27*
daughter to
that *M.* Saul's daughter loved   *1Sa 18:28*
him
M. David's wife told him,   *1Sa 19:11*
saying
So *M.* let David down   *1Sa 19:12*
through a
M. took an image, and laid it   *1Sa 19:13*
Saul said unto *M.*, Why hast   *1Sa 19:17*
thou
M. answered Saul, He said   *1Sa 19:17*
unto
Saul had given *M.* his   *1Sa 25:44*
daughter
first bring *M.* Saul's daughter   *2Sa 3:13*
Deliver me my wife *M.*, which   *2Sa 3:14*
M. Saul's daughter looked   *2Sa 6:16*
through
M. the daughter of Saul came   *2Sa 6:20*
out
David said unto *M.*, It was   *2Sa 6:21*
before
M. the daughter of Saul had   *2Sa 6:23*
no
sons of *M.* the daughter of   *2Sa 21:8*
Saul
M. the daughter of Saul   *1Ch 15:29*
looking

MICHMAS

The men of *M.* an hundred   *Ezr 2:27;*
   Ne 7:31

MICHMASH

thousand were with Saul in *M.*   *1Sa 13:2*
they came up, and pitched in   *1Sa 13:5*
M.
themselves together at *M.*   *1Sa 13:11*
the Philistines encamped in   *1Sa 13:16*
M.
went out to the passage of *M.*   *1Sa 13:23*
situate northward over   *1Sa 14:5*
against *M.*
the Philistines that day from   *1Sa 14:31*
M.
Benjamin from Geba dwelt at   *Ne 11:31*
M.
at *M.* he had laid up his   *Isa 10:28*
carriages

MICHMETHAH

went out toward the sea to *M.*   *Jos 16:6*
Manasseh was from Asher   *Jos 17:7*
to *M.*

MICHRI

the son of Uzzi, the son of *M.*   *1Ch 9:8*

MICHTAM

M. of David   Ps 16 title
M. of David when the   Ps 56 title
Philistines
M. of David, when he fled   Ps 57 title
from
Al-taschith M. of David   Ps 58 title
M. of David; when Saul sent   Ps 59 title
M. of David, to teach; when   Ps 60 title

MIDDAY

came to pass, when m. was   1Ki 18:29
past
from the morning until m.   Ne 8:3
it was about m. (P)   Joh 4:6
At m., O king, I saw in the   Ac 26:13

MIDDIN

the wilderness, Beth-arabah,   Jos 15:61
M.

MIDDLE

m. bar in the midst of the   Ex 26:28
boards
And he made the m. bar to   Ex 36:33
shoot
from the m. of the river, and   Jos 12:2
in the beginning of the m.   J'g 7:19
watch
people down by the m. of the   J'g 9:37
land
took hold of the two m. pillars   J'g 16:29
out, as out of the m. of a sling   1Sa 25:29
cut off their garments in the m.   2Sa 10:4
in the m. (S)   2Sa 23:20;
24:5; 1Ki 6:27; 8:51; 1Ch 19:4; Jer 41:7;
    Eze 15:4
and the m. was six cubits broad   1Ki 6:6
door for the m. chamber was in   1Ki 6:8
winding stairs into the m.   1Ki 6:8
chamber
and out of the m. into the third   1Ki 6:8
the king hallow the m. of the   1Ki 8:64
court
was gone out into the m. court   2Ki 20:4
hallowed the m. of the court   2Ch 7:7
came in, and sat in the m. gate   Jer 39:3
were a wheel in the m. of a   Eze 1:16
wheel
the m. one (S)   Eze 42:5
the m. ones (S)   Eze 42:6
hath broken down the m. wall   Eph 2:14
of

MIDDLEMOST

and than the m. of the building   Eze 42:5
lowest and the m. from the   Eze 42:6
ground

MIDIAN

but Moses dwelt in the land of   Ex 2:15
M.
Jethro priest of M. heard all   Ex 18:1
God had done
Moab said to the elders of M.   Nu 22:4
Cozbi daughter of Zur of a   Nu 25:15
chief house in M.
let them go and avenge the   Nu 31:3
Lord of M.
they slew the kings of M.   Nu 31:8
beside the rest
Israel took all the women of   Nu 31:9
M. captives
the Lord delivered them to M.   J'g 6:1;
    6:2
for into his hand hath God   J'g 7:14
delivered M.
thou hast delivered us from   J'g 8:22;
M.   9:17
thus was M. subdued before   J'g 8:28
Israel
some Edomites arose out of   1Ki 11:18
M.
thou hast broken the yoke, as in   Isa 9:4
day of M.
according to the slaughter of   Isa 10:26
M. at Oreb
the dromedaries of M. shall   Isa 60:6
cover thee
the curtains of the land of M.   Hab 3:7
did tremble

MIDIANITE

son of Raguel the M.   Nu 10:29

MIDIANITES

there passed by M.   Ge 37:28
merchant men
the M. sold him into Egypt to   Ge 37:36
Potiphar
vex the M.; avenge Israel of   Nu 25:17;
the M.   31:2
Israel cried to the Lord because   J'g 6:7
of M.
and thou shalt smite the M. as   J'g 6:16
one man
the men of Israel pursued after   J'g 7:23
the M.
they took two princes of the   J'g 7:25
M. Oreb, Zeeb
when thou wentest to fight with   J'g 8:1
the M.
do to them as to the M. as to   Ps 83:9
Sisera

MIDIANITISH

a M. woman in the sight of   Nu 25:6
Moses
that was slain with the M.   Nu 25:14
woman
the name of the M. woman   Nu 25:15
that

MIDNIGHT

About m. will I go out into   Ex 11:4
at m. the Lord smote all the   Ex 12:29
lay till m. and arose at m.   J'g 16:3
it came to pass at m. that the   Ru 3:8
she arose at m. and took my   1Ki 3:20
people shall be troubled at m.   Job 34:20
At m. I will rise to give thanks   Ps 119:62
at m. there was a cry made   M't 25:6
or at m. or at the   M'k 13:35
cockcrowing, or
and shall go unto him at m.   Lu 11:5
at m. Paul and Silas prayed   Ac 16:25
and continued his speech until   Ac 20:7
m.
about m. the shipmen deemed   Ac 27:27

MIDST

go on dry ground through m.   Ex 14:16
of sea   Nu 33:8; Ne 9:11; Ps 136:14
I will take sickness from the m.   Ex 23:25
of thee
the mountain burnt to the m.   De 4:11
of heaven
shalt put evil away from the   De 13:5
m. of thee
thy God will rise a Prophet   De 18:15
from m. of thee
from the m. of the furnace of   1Ki 8:51
iron
brook that ran thro' the m. of   2Ch 32:4
the land
the m. thereof being paved with   Ca 3:10
love
purged blood from the m. of   Isa 4:4
Jerusalem
breath shall reach to the m.   Isa 30:28
of the neck
take away from the m. of   Isa 58:9
thee the yoke
the governor proceed from   Jer 30:21
the m. of them
a flame shall come from the   Jer 48:45
m. of Sihon
go through the m. of the city   Eze 9:4
and set
the glory of Lord went up   Eze 11:23
from m. of city
I will cut him off from m. of   Eze 14:8;
my people   14:9
the m. of it is burnt, is it meet   Eze 15:4
for work
have filled the m. of thee   Eze 28:16
with violence
I will bring forth a fire from   Eze 28:18
the m. of thee
came forth of the m. of the fire   Da 3:26
I will cut off judge from the m.   Am 2:3
thereof
but he passing through the m.   Lu 4:30
of them
about the m. of the feast Jesus   Joh 7:14
went
going thro' the m. of them,   Joh 8:59
so passed by
an angel flying through the m.   Re 8:13
of heaven

IN THE MIDST

be a firmament in the m. of   Ge 1:6
heaven
the tree of life in the m. of the   Ge 2:9;
garden   3:3
and Abram divided them in   Ge 15:10
the m.
wonders I will do in the m.   Ex 3:20
thereof
I am the Lord in the m. of the   Ex 8:22
earth
overthrew Egyptians in the m.   Ex 14:27
of the sea
walked on dry land in the m.   Ex 14:29;
of the sea   15:19
for I will not go up in the m. of   Ex 33:3
thee,
in the m. of their uncleanness   Le 16:16
tabernacle set forward in the   Nu 2:17
m. of camp
defile not the camps in the m.   Nu 5:3
whereof I dwell
and the city shall be in the m.   Nu 35:5;
    Eze 48:15
acts which he did in the m. of   De 11:3
Egypt
swallowed them up in the m.   De 11:6
of all Israel
separate three cities in the m.   De 19:2
of thy land
God walketh in the m. of thy   De 23:14
camp
priests stood firm in m. of   Jos 3:17;
Jordan   4:10
set up twelve stones in the m. of   Jos 4:9
Jordan
there is an accursed thing in   Jos 7:13
the m. of thee
they are hid in the earth in the   Jos 7:21
m. of my tent
anointed him in the m. of   1Sa 16:13
brethren
he was yet alive in the m. of   2Sa 18:14
the oak
but he stood in the m. of the   2Sa 23:12
ground
slew a lion in the m. of a pit   2Sa 23:20
in time of snow
behold, they were in the m. of   2Ki 6:20
Samaria
and cut off their garments in   1Ch 19:4
the m.
nor see, till we come in the m.   Ne 4:11
among
it is melted in the m. of my   Ps 22:14
bowels
I will declare thy name, in the   Ps 22:22;
m. of the congregation   Heb 2:12
God is in the m. of her, she   Ps 46:5
shall not be moved
mischief in the m.   Ps 55:10;
    55:11
wickedness in the m.   Ps 74:4
enemies roar in the m. of thy
congregation
working salvation in the m. of   Ps 74:12
the earth
and he let it fall in the m. of   Ps 78:28
their camp
take me not away in the m.   Ps 102:24
of my days
rule thou in the m. of thine   Ps 110:2
enemies
pay vows in the m. of thee, O   Ps 116:19
Jerusalem
though I walk in the m. of   Ps 138:7
trouble, thou wilt
keep them in the m. of thine   Pr 4:21
heart
I was in all evil in the m. of the   Pr 5:14
congregation
I lead in the m. of the paths of   Pr 8:20
judgment
that which is in the m. of   Pr 14:33
fools is folly
as he that lieth down in the m.   Pr 23:34
of the sea
the way of a ship in the m. of   Pr 30:19
the sea
and I built a tower in the m.   Isa 5:2
of it
I dwell in the m. of a people of   Isa 6:5
unclean lips
be a great forsaking in the m.   Isa 6:12
of the land
set a king in the m. of it, the   Isa 7:6
son of Tabeal
great is the Holy One in the   Isa 12:6;
m. of thee   Ho 11:9

as the night *in the m.* of the   *Isa 16:3*
noon day
even a blessing *in the m.* of   *Isa 19:24*
the land
I will open fountains *in the m.*   *Isa 41:18*
of thee
she is wholly oppression *in the*   *Jer 6:6*
m. of her
thine habitation is *in the m.*   *Jer 9:6*
of deceit
thou, O Lord, art *in the m.* of   *Jer 14:9*
us, leave us not
he shall leave them *in the m.*   *Jer 17:11*
of his days
to separate himself *in the m.*   *Jer 37:12*
of the people
shed blood of the just *in the m.*   *La 4:13*
of her
I have set it *in the m.* of the   *Eze 5:5*
nations
I will execute judgment *in the*   *Eze 5:8*
m. of thee
the slain shall fall *in the m.* of   *Eze 6:7;*
you   *11:7*
in the m. of Babylon he shall   *Eze 17:16*
die
the city sheddeth blood *in the*   *Eze 22:3*
m. of it
and ye shall be melted *in the*   *Eze 22:21*
m. thereof
as silver is melted *in the m.*   *Eze 22:22*
of the furnace
they have made many widows   *Eze 22:25*
in the m. thereof
princes *in the m.* thereof are   *Eze 22:27*
like wolves
thus have they done *in the m.*   *Eze 23:39*
of my house
for spreading of nets *in the m.*   *Eze 26:5*
of the sea
O Zidon, I will be glorified *in*   *Eze 28:22*
the m. of thee
which ye have profaned *in*   *Eze 36:23*
the m. of them
will set my sanctuary *in the*   *Eze 37:26*
m. of them
when my sanctuary shall be   *Eze 37:28*
in the m. of them
where I will dwell *in the m.* of   *Eze 43:7;*
Israel   *43:9*
and the prince *in the m.* shall   *Eze 46:10*
go in
four men walking *in the m.* of   *Da 3:25*
the fire
in the m. of the week, oblation   *Da 9:27*
shall cease
spirit of whoredoms is *in the m.*   *Ho 5:4*
of them
ye shall know I am *in the m.*   *Joe 2:27*
of Israel
conspired *in the m.* of the   *Am 7:10*
house of
remnant be *in the m.* of many   *Mic 5:7;*
people   *7:8*
thy casting down shall be *in*   *Mic 6:14*
the m. of thee
thy people *in the m.* of thee are   *Na 3:13*
women
in the m. of the years revive thy   *Hab 3:2*
work
flocks shall lie down *in the m.*   *Zep 2:14*
of her
just Lord is *in the m.* thereof,   *Zep 3:5*
will not do
I will leave *in the m.* of thee a   *Zep 3:12*
poor people
king of Israel the Lord is *in*   *Zep 3:15;*
the m. of thee   *3:17*
I will be the glory *in the m.*   *Zec 2:5*
of her
rejoice, for I will dwell *in the*   *Zec 2:10;*
m. of thee   *2:11*
the curse shall remain *in the m.*   *Zec 5:4*
of his house
a woman that sitteth *in the m.*   *Zec 5:7*
of the ephah
and will dwell *in the m.* of   *Zec 8:3;*
Jerusalem   *8:8*
the mount of olives shall   *Zec 14:4*
cleave *in the m.*
I send you as sheep *in the m.*   *M't 10:16*
of wolves
ship was *in the m.* of the sea   *M't 14:24;*
   M'k 6:47
set a little child *in the m.* of   *M't 18:2;*
them   *M'k 9:36*
are gathered, there am I *in*   *M't 18:20*
the m. of them
found him sitting *in the m.* of   *Lu 2:46*
the doctors

rise, and stand forth *in the m.*   *Lu 6:8*
and he arose
in the m. of (S)   *Lu 17:21*
let them which are *in the m.* of   *Lu 21:21*
it depart
the veil of the temple was rent   *Lu 23:45*
in the m.
Jesus himself stood *in the m.*   *Lu 24:36;*
   Joh 20:19, 26
and when they had set her *in*   *Joh 8:3;*
the m.   *8:9*
on either side one, and Jesus   *Joh 19:18*
in the m.
Peter stood up *in the m.* of the   *Ac 1:15*
disciples
Judas falling burst asunder *in*   *Ac 1:18*
the m.
then Paul stood up *in the m.* of   *Ac 17:22*
of Mars' hill
blameless *in the m.* of a   *Ph'p 2:15*
crooked generation
in the m. of the seven   *Re 1:13;*
candlesticks   *2:1*
which is *in the m.* of the   *Re 2:7*
Paradise of God
and *in the m.* of the throne were   *Re 4:6*
four beasts
lo, *in the m.* of the throne stood   *Re 5:6*
a Lamb   *7:17*
in the m. of the four beasts   *Re 6:6*
in the m. of heaven   *Re 14:7; 19:17*
In the m. of the street of it   *Re 22:2*

INTO THE MIDST

Israel went *into the m.* of the   *Ex 14:22*
sea
and Moses went *into the m.* of   *Ex 24:18*
the cloud
I will come *into the m.* of   *Ex 33:5*
thee and consume
Aaron ran *into the m.* of   *Nu 16:47*
congregation
blood ran *into the m.* of the   *1Ki 22:35*
chariot
Mordeci went *into the m.* of city   *Es 4:1*
and cried
tho' mountains be carried *into*   *Ps 46:2*
the m. of sea
into the m. whereof they are   *Ps 57:6*
fallen themselves
I will assemble them *into the*   *Jer 21:4*
m. of this city
cast it *into the m.* of the river   *Jer 51:63*
Euphrates
cast them *into the m.* of the fire   *Eze 5:4*
and burn
I will gather you *into the m.*   *Eze 22:19*
of Jerusalem
shall be cast *into the m.* of a   *Da 3:6*
fiery furnace
and he cast it *into the m.* of the   *Zec 5:8*
ephah

OUT OF THE MIDST

sent Lot *out of the m.* of the   *Ge 19:29*
overthrow
angel appeared *out of the m.* of   *Ex 3:2*
a bush
God called to him *out of the m.*   *Ex 3:4;*
of bush   *24:16*
the Lord spake unto you *out*   *Ex 4:12;*
of the m. of the fire *4:15, 33, 36; 5:4, 22,*
   24
to take him a nation *out of the*   *De 4:34*
m. of another
take *out of the m.* of Jordan   *Jos 4:3;*
twelve stones   *4:8*
and they took them *out of the*   *Jos 7:23*
m. of the tent
and he that cometh *out of the*   *Isa 24:18*
m. of pit
depart, go *out of the m.* of   *Isa 52:11;*
her   *Jer 50:8; 51:6, 45*
I will bring you forth *out of*   *Eze 11:7*
the m. of it
I will bring thee *out of the m.*   *Eze 29:4*
of thy rivers
shall speak to him *out of the*   *Eze 32:21*
m. of hell
that eat calves *out of the m.* of   *Am 6:4*
the stall
I will cut off horses *out of*   *Mic 5:10;*
the m. of thee   *5:13*
pluck up grooves *out of the*   *Mic 5:14*
m. of thee
then I will take away *out of the*   *Zep 3:11*
m. of thee

MIDWIFE

labour, that the *m.* said unto   *Ge 35:17*
her
m. took and bound upon his   *Ge 38:28*
hand a
When ye do the office of a *m.*   *Ex 1:16*

MIDWIVES

of Egypt spake to the Hebrew   *Ex 1:15*
m.
the *m.* feared God, and did not   *Ex 1:17*
the king of Egypt called for the   *Ex 1:18*
m.
the *m.* said unto Pharaoh,   *Ex 1:19*
Because
ere the *m.* come in unto them   *Ex 1:19*
God dealt well with the *m.*   *Ex 1:20*
to pass because the *m.* feared   *Ex 1:21*
God

MIGDAL-EL

And Iron, and *M.*, Horem   *Jos 19:38*

MIGDAL-GAD

Zenan, and Hadashah, and   *Jos 15:37*
M.

MIGDOL

between *M.* and the sea, over   *Ex 14:2*
and they pitched before *M.*   *Nu 33:7*
land of Egypt, which dwelt at   *Jer 44:1*
M.
ye in Egypt, and publish in   *Jer 46:14*
M. and

MIGHT

Reuben, thou art my firstborn,   *Ge 49:3*
my *m.*
broughtest up this people in   *Nu 14:13*
thy *m.*
that can do according to thy   *De 3:24*
m.
thou shalt love thy God with all   *De 6:5*
thy *m.*
the *m.* of mine hand hath   *De 8:17*
gotten me wealth
there shall be no *m.* in thine   *De 28:32*
hand
as the sun goeth forth in his *m.*   *J'g 5:31*
go in this thy *m.*; bowed with   *J'g 6:14;*
his *m.*   *16:30*
might (R)   *1Sa 2:9;*
   Job 12:13; Ec 9:16; Da 2:37
David danced with all his *m.*   *2Sa 6:14*
the acts of Asa and all his *m.*   *1Ki 15:23*
Baasha his *m.*: Omri and his   *1Ki 16:5;*
m.   *16:27*
Jehoshaphat and his *m.* that   *1Ki 22:45*
he shewed
Jehu his *m.*; Jehoahaz his *m.*   *2Ki 10:34;*
   13:8
Joash; acts of Jehoash and   *2Ki 13:12;*
his *m.*   *14:15*
Jeroboam; Hezekiah and his   *2Ki 14:28;*
m.   *20:20*
Josiah turned to the Lord   *2Ki 23:25*
with all his *m.*
the king brought captive all   *2Ki 24:16*
the men of *m.*
men of *m.* came to David to   *1Ch 12:8*
the hold
seek the Lord and his *m.*   *1Ch 16:11*
(B)
glory and *m.* (B)   *1Ch 16:28;*
   Ne 12:13; Ps 20:6; 68:34
I prepared for the house with   *1Ch 29:2*
all my *m.*
in thine hand is power and   *1Ch 29:12;*
m.   *2Ch 20:6*
the acts of David with his   *1Ch 29:30*
reign and *m.*
thy *m.* (R)   *2Ch 6:41;*
Ps 54:1; 71:18; 74:13; 77:14; 80:2;
   Isa 63:15
we have no *m.* against this   *2Ch 20:12*
company
acts of Ahasuerus, his power   *Es 10:2*
and *m.*
might (R)   *Job 12:13;*
   38:19; Pr 8:14; 24:15
deliver by his *m.* (R)   *Ps 33:17*
thy *m.* (E)   *Ps 54:1; 80:2*
who by his *m.* (B)   *Ps 65:6; Isa 63:1*
none of the men of *m.* found   *Ps 76:5*
their hands

men shall speak of the *m.* — Ps 145:6
of thy acts
thy hand findeth to do, do it — Ec 9:10
with thy *m.*
the spirit of counsel and *m.* — Isa 11:2
shall rest on him
ye that are near, acknowledge — Isa 33:13
my *m.*
calleth them by the greatness — Isa 40:26
of his *m.*
to them that have no *m.* he — Isa 40:29
increaseth strength
nor let the mighty man glory in — Jer 9:23
his *m.*
thou art great, and thy name is — Jer 10:6
great in *m.*
behold, I will cause them to — Jer 16:21
know my *m.*
I will break the chief of their — Jer 49:35
m.
their *m.* hath failed, they — Jer 51:30
became as women
they are ashamed of their *m.* — Eze 32:30
blessed be God for wisdom — Da 2:20
and *m.* are his
I thank thee, O God, who — Da 2:23
hast given me *m.*
that I have built by the *m.* of — Da 4:30
my power
truly I am full of judgment and — Mic 3:8
of *m.*
nations shall be confounded — Mic 7:16
at all their *m.*
not by *m.* nor by power, but by — Zec 4:6
my Spirit
he showed his *m.* (N) — Lu 1:51
far above all *m.* power, and — Eph 1:21
dominion
to be strengthened with *m.* — Eph 3:16;
                                              Col 1:11
be strong in the Lord, and in — Eph 6:10
power of his *m.*
to him be honor and *m.* (N) — 1Ti 6:16
though I *m.* be much bold in — Ph'm 8
Christ
call to splendour and *m.* (N) — 2Pe 1:3
whereas angels that are — 2Pe 2:11
greater in *m.*
glory, honor and *m.* (N)(R) — Re 5:13
glory and *m.* be unto our God — Re 7:12
for ever

MIGHT BE

I would it *m. be* according to — Ge 30:34
thy word
to couple the tent, that it *m.* — Ex 36:18
be one
that it *m. be* above the — Ex 39:21
curious girdle
brought forth that I *m. be* — Le 26:45
their God
fear me, that it *m. be* well with — De 5:29
them
that he *m. be* the king's — 1Sa 18:27
son in law
that my name *m. be* put — 1Ki 18:16
therein
would make windows, *m.* — 2Ki 7:2
this thing *be*
gave silver, that his hand — 2Ki 15:19
m. be with him
an house, that my name *m. be* — 2Ch 6:5;
there   6:6
m. not *be* as their fathers, a — Ps 78:8
stubborn
that they *m. be* unto me a — Jer 13:11
people
in good soil that it *m. be* a — Eze 17:8
goodly vine
that ye *m. be* a possession to — Eze 36:3
the heathen
that my covenant *m. be* with — Mal 2:4
Levi
pray, that he *m. be* with him — M'k 5:18;
                                              Lu 8:38
asked, saying, What *m.* this — Lu 8:9
parable *be*
and that your joy *m. be* full — Joh 15:11
m. be the father of them that — Ro 4:11
believe
that it *m. be* of grace; *m. be* — Ro 4:16;
Lord of dead   14:9
m. not *be* chargeable to any of — 2Th 3:8
you
though I *m. be* much bold in — Ph'm 8
Christ
that he *m. be* a merciful — Heb 2:17
high priest

that we *m. .be* partakers of — Heb 12:10
his holiness
that your faith and hope *m.* — 1Pe 1:21
be in God

MIGHTEST

thou *m.* know that the Lord — De 4:35
That thou *m.* fear the Lord — De 6:2
thou *m.* be bound — J'g 16:6; 16:10, 13
that thou *m.* see the battle — 1Sa 17:28
that thou *m.* bring them again — Ne 9:29
that thou *m.* still the enemy — Ps 8:2
m. be justified when — Ps 51:4; Ro 3:4
thou *m.* answer words of truth — Pr 22:21
that thou *m.* know the — Da 2:30
thoughts
whatsoever *m.* be profited — M't 15:5;
                                              M'k 7:11
thou *m.* know the certainty of — Lu 1:4
that thou *m.* receive thy sight — Ac 9:17
m. overcome when judged — Ro 3:4
thou *m.* charge some that they — 1Ti 1:3
thou by them *m.* war a good — 1Ti 1:18

MIGHTIER

for thou art much *m.* than we — Ge 26:16
the childen of Israel are *m.* than — Ex 1:9
we
a greater nation and *m.* than — Nu 14:12;
they   14; 11:23
the Lord on high is *m.* than — Ps 93:4
many waters
neither contend with him that — Ec 6:10
is *m.*
he that cometh after me — M't 3:11;
is *m.* than I — M'k 1:7; Lu 3:16

MIGHTIES

Eleazar was one of the three — 1Ch 11:12
m.
Benaiah had a name among — 1Ch 11:24
the three *m.*

MIGHTIEST

did these three *m.* — 1Ch 11:19

MIGHTILY

observe to do it, that ye may — De 6:3
increase *m.*
Jabin *m.* oppressed Israel — J'g 4:3
twenty years
the Spirit of Lord came *m.* on — J'g 14:6;
Samson   15:14
he will do *m.* (A)(E) — Isa 42:13
the Lord shall *m.* roar on his — Jer 25:30
habitation
let man and beast cry *m.* unto — Jon 3:8
God
watch the way, fortify thy — Na 2:1
power *m.*
for he *m.* convinced the Jews — Ac 18:28
so *m.* grew the word of God, — Ac 19:20
and prevailed
his working, which worketh in — Col 1:29
me *m.*
he cried *m.* saying, Babylon is — Re 18:2
fallen

MIGHTY

he was a *m.* hunter before the — Ge 10:9
Lord
Abraham shall become a — Ge 18:18
great and *m.* nation
hear us, thou art a *m.* prince — Ge 23:6
amongst us
the children of Israel waxed *m.* — Ex 1:7;
                                              1:20
that there be no more *m.* — Ex 9:28
thunderings and hail
the Lord turned a *m.* strong — Ex 10:19
west wind
by a *m.* hand (B) — Ex 13:3
they sank as lead in the *m.* — Ex 15:10
waters
nor shall honour the person of — Le 19:15
the *m.*
curse this people, for they are — Nu 22:6
too *m.*
he brought thee out with *m.* — De 4:37;
power   9:29
shall destroy them with a *m.* — De 7:23
destruction
became there a great nation, — De 26:5
m. and populous

Lord made me have dominion — J'g 5:13
over the *m.*
they came not to help of the — J'g 5:23
Lord against the *m.*
m. men of courage (A) — J'g 6:12;
       1Ki 11:28; 1Ch 12:21; 2Ch 14:8; 17:13
m. hero (B) — J'g 6:12; 1Ch 26:6
m. warrior (A) — J'g 11:1;
       1Ch 7:9; 40; 8:40; 2Ch 32:21
m. warrior (R) — J'g 11:1; 2Ch 32:21
no human power renders one — 1Sa 2:9
m. (B)
out of the hand of these — 1Sa 4:8
m. gods
how are the *m.* fallen — 2Sa 1:19; 1:25
the shield of the *m.* is vilely — 2Sa 1:21
cast away
from the blood of the slain, — 2Sa 1:22
from fat of the *m.*
the *m.* of the land carried he — 2Ki 24:15
captive
Nimrod was *m.* — 1Ch 1:10
m. men of strength (A) — 1Ch 5:24
the *m.* men (S) — 1Ch 11:12; 11:19, 24
Zadok *m.* — 1Ch 12:28
m. men of ability (A) — 1Ch 26:6;
                                          26:30-32
m. warriors — 1Ch 26:31; 1Ch 13:3
Benaiah was *m.* — 1Ch 27:6
Abijah *m.* — 2Ch 13:21
army that made war with — 2Ch 26:13
m. power
so Jotham became *m.* because — 2Ch 27:6
he prepared
there have been *m.* kings over — Ezr 4:20
Jerusalem
hath extended mercy to me — Ezr 7:28
before *m.* princes
Nehemiah repaired to the — Ne 3:16
house of the *m.*
thou threwest a stone in the — Ne 9:11
m. waters
but he saveth the poor from — Job 5:15
the *m.*
or redeem me from the hand — Job 6:23
of the *m.*
he is wise in heart, and *m.* in — Job 9:4
strength
once more *m.* against me (B) — Job 10:16
he leadeth princes, and he — Job 12:19
overthroweth
wherefore are the wicked *m.* — Job 21:7
in power
he draweth also the *m.* with — Job 24:22
his power
the *m.* shall be taken away — Job 34:20
without hand
they cry out by reason of the — Job 35:9
arm of the *m.*
he raiseth himself, the *m.* are — Job 41:25
afraid
Lord strong and *m.* Lord *m.* in — Ps 24:8
battle
give to the Lord. O ye *m.* — Ps 29:1
glory and strength
gird thy sword on thy thigh, O — Ps 45:3
m. most
for lo, the *m.* are gathered — Ps 59:3
against me
doth send out his voice, and — Ps 68:33
that a *m.* voice
being mine enemies wrongfully — Ps 69:4
are *m.*
thou driedst up *m.* rivers, the — Ps 74:15
day is thine
God standeth in the — Ps 82:1
congregation of the *m.*
who among sons *m.* can be — Ps 89:6
likened to Lord
thou hast a *m.* arm, strong is — Ps 89:13
thy hand
I have laid help upon one that — Ps 89:19
is *m.*
I bear in my bosom the — Ps 89:50
reproach of the *m.*
the Lord is mightier than the — Ps 93:4
m. waves of sea
that he might make his *m.* — Ps 106:8
power known
his seed shall be *m.* upon the — Ps 112:2
earth
sharp arrows of the *m.* with — Ps 120:4
coals of juniper
who smote great nations, and — Ps 135:10
slew *m.* kings
that is slow to anger is better — Pr 16:32
than *m.*
the lot parteth between the *m.* — Pr 18:18

a wise man scaleth the city of *Pr 21:22*
the *m.*

their Redeemer is *m.* shall *Pr 23:11*
plead their cause

and thy *m.* shall fall in the war *Isa 3:25*

woe to them that are *m.* to *Isa 5:22*
drink wine

with his *m.* wind shall he *Isa 11:15*
shake his hand

a rushing like the rushing of *Isa 17:12*
m. waters

will carry thee away with a *Isa 22:17*
m. captivity

he proves himself *m.* (B)(R) *Isa 42:13*

shall the prey be taken from *Isa 49:24*
the *m.*

I that speak in righteousness, *Isa 63:1*
m. to save

it is a *m.* and an ancient *Jer 5:15*
nation, a nation

great in counsel and *m.* in *Jer 32:19*
work

and I will shew thee great and *Jer 33:3*
m. things

he hath also taken the *m.* of *Eze 17:13*
the land

by the swords of the *m.* will I *Eze 32:12*
make thee fall

the strong among the *m.* shall *Eze 32:21*
speak to him

they shall not lie with the *m.* *Eze 32:27*
that are fallen

thou shalt come with a great *Eze 38:15*
and *m.* army

ye shall eat the flesh of the *Eze 39:18*
m. and drink

how great and *m.* are his *Da 4:3*
wonders

his power shall be *m.* but not *Da 8:24*
by his own power

a *m.* king shall stand up that *Da 11:3*
shall rule

stirred up with a very great *Da 11:25*
and *m.* army

neither shall the *m.* deliver *Am 2:14*
himself

he that is courageous among *Am 2:16*
the *m.* shall flee

I know your *m.* sins; as a *m.* *Am 5:12;*
stream 5:24

there was a *m.* tempest in the *Jon 1:4*
sea

howl, because the *m.* *Zec 11:2*
are spoiled

where most of his *m.* works *M't 11:20*
were done

if the *m.* works which were *M't 11:21;*
done in you 11:23

whence hath this man these *M't 13:54*
m. works

he did not many *m.* works *M't 13:58;*
there *M'k 6:5*

m. works do shew forth *M't 14:2;*
themselves in him *M'k 6:14*

m. works are wrought by his *M'k 6:2*
hand

he that is *m.* hath done great *Lu 1:49*
things

he hath put down the *m.* from *Lu 1:52*
their seats

they were amazed at the *m.* *Lu 9:43*
power of God

there arose a *m.* famine in *Lu 15:14*
that land

praised God for the *m.* works *Lu 19:37*
they had seen

who was a prophet *m.* in deed *Lu 24:19*
and word

sound from heaven as of a *Ac 2:2*
rushing *m.* wind

Moses was *m.* in words and in *Ac 7:22*
deeds

Apollos was *m.* in the *Ac 18:24*
scriptures

the Gentiles obedient through *Ro 15:19*
m. signs

not many *m.* not many noble, *1Co 1:26*
are called

God hath chosen weak, to *1Co 1:27*
confound things *m.*

weapons of our warfare are *2Co 10:4*
m. thro' God

which to you is not weak, but *2Co 13:3*
m. in you

the same was *m.* in me *Ga 2:8*
toward the Gentiles

according to the working of *Eph 1:19*
his *m.* power

Jesus shall be revealed with his *2Th 1:7*
m. angels

when she is shaken of a *m.* *Re 6:13*
wind

I saw another *m.* angel come *Re 10:1;*
down 18:21

so *m.* an earthquake and so *Re 16:18*
great

that *m.* city; voice of *m.* *Re 18:10*
thunderings 19:6

MIGHTY *ONE*

Nimrod began to be a *m. one* *Ge 10:8*
in the earth

m. one of Israel *Isa 1:24*
30:29; 49:26; 60:16

and Lebanon shall fall by a *Isa 10:34*
m. one

behold, the Lord hath a *m.* *Isa 28:2*
and strong *one*

the Lord is with me as a *m.* *Jer 20:11*
terrible *one*

have delivered him into hand *Eze 31:11*
of *m. one*

MIGHTY *ONES*

broken by prancings of their *J'g 5:22*
m. ones

I have called my *m. ones* for *Isa 13:3*
mine anger

their *m. ones* are beaten down *Jer 46:5*
and fled

thither cause thy *m. ones* to *Joe 3:11*
come down

MIGRANT

a *m.* in the land of Ham (B) *Ps 105:25*

MIGRANTS

outsiders, exiles, *m.* (A) *Eph 2:19*

MIGRATED

as men *m.* in the east (R) *Ge 11:2*

MIGRON

pomegranate tree which is in *1Sa 14:2*
M.

come to Aiath, he is passed *Isa 10:28*
M.

MIJAMIN

fifth to Malchijah, the sixth to *1Ch 24:9*
M.

Meshullam, Abijah, M. *Ne 10:7*

MIKLOTH

And M. begat Shimeah, And *1Ch 8:32*
and Ahio, and Zechariah, and *1Ch 9:37*
M.

And M. begat Shimeam. And *1Ch 9:38*
his course was M. also the *1Ch 27:4*
ruler

MIKNEIAH

M. and Obed-edom, and *1Ch 15:18;*
Jeiel 15:21

MILALAI

and Azarael, M., Gilalai *Ne 12:36*

MILCAH

and the name of Nahor's *Ge 11:29*
wife, M.

the father of M. and the *Ge 11:29*
father of

M., she hath also borne *Ge 22:20*
children

these eight M. did bear to *Ge 22:23*
Nahor

who was born to Bethuel, son *Ge 24:15*
of M.

daughter of Bethuel the son of *Ge 24:24*
M.

son, whom M. bare unto him *Ge 24:47*

and Noah, Hoglah, M., and *Nu 26:33*
Tirzah

and Hoglah, and M., and *Nu 27:1;*
Tirzah *Jos 17:3*

Tirzah, and Hoglah, and M. *Nu 36:11*

MILCH

Thirty *m.* camels with their *Ge 32:15*
colts

new cart, and take two *m.* kine *1Sa 6:7*

two fresh cows (B) *1Sa 6:7*

took two *m.* kine, and *1Sa 6:10*
tied them to

MILCOM

after M. the abomination of *1Ki 11:5*

and M. the god of the *1Ki 11:33*
children of

M. the abomination of the *2Ki 23:13*
children

MILDEW

and with blasting, and with *De 28:22*
m.

if there be pestilence, blasting, *1Ki 8:37*
m.

pestilence, if there be *2Ch 6:28*
blasting or *m.*

smitten you with blasting and *Am 4:9*
m.

smote you with blasting and *Hag 2:17*
with *m.*

MILE

shall compel thee to go a *m.* *M't 5:41*

MILES

about seven *m.* *Lu 24:13*
(A)(B)(N)(P)(R)

rowed three or four *m.* *Joh 6:19*
(A)(B)(N)(P)(R)

about two *m.* *Joh 11:18*
(A)(B)(N)(P)(R)

about two hundred *m.* *Re 14:20*
(A)(B)(N)(P)

about fifteen hundred *m.* *Re 21:16*
(A)(B)

MILETUM

Trophimus have I left at M. *2Ti 4:20*
sick

MILETUS

and the next day we came *Ac 20:15*
to M.

from M. he sent to Ephesus *Ac 20:17*

MILITARY

m. fighting units (B) *1Ch 7:4*

the *m.* commandants, tribunes *Ac 25:23*
(A)(R)

MILK

he took butter, and *m.* and the *Ge 18:8*

wine, and his teeth white with *Ge 49:12*
m.

a land flowing with *m.* and *Ex 3:8;*
honey *Ex 3:17; 13:5; 33:3; Jer 11:5;*
32:22

not seethe a kid in his *Ex 23:19;*
mother's *m.* 34:26; De 14:21

that floweth with *m.* and *Le 20:24;*
honey 16:13, 14; De 6:3; 11:9;
26:9, 15; 27:3; 31:20; Jos 5:6

it floweth with *m.* and honey *Nu 13:27*

which floweth with *m.* and *Nu 14:8*
honey

Butter of kine, and *m.* of *De 32:14*
sheep

she opened a bottle of *m.* and *J'g 4:19*
gave

asked water, and she gave him *J'g 5:25*
m.

milk (S) *1Sa 6:7; 6:10*

thou not poured me out as *m.* *Job 10:10*

His breasts are full of *m.* and *Job 21:24*

have goats' *m.* enough for thy *Pr 27:27*
food

the churning of *m.* bringeth *Pr 30:33*
forth

honey and *m.* are under thy *Ca 4:11*
tongue

I have drunk my wine with my *Ca 5:1*
m.

rivers of waters, washed with *Ca 5:12*
m.

abundance of *m.* that they shall *Isa 7:22*

them that are weaned from the *Isa 28:9*
m.
buy wine and *m.* without *Isa 55:1*
money
also suck the *m.* of the *Isa 60:16*
Gentiles
that ye may *m.* out, and be *Isa 66:11*
than snow, they were whiter *La 4:7*
than *m.*
flowing with *m.* and honey *Eze 20:6;*
20:15
fruit, and they shall drink thy *Eze 25:4*
m.
and the hills shall flow with *m.* *Joe 3:18*
I have fed you with *m.* and not *1Co 3:2*
eateth not of the *m.* of the *1Co 9:7*
flock
become such as have need of *Heb 5:12*
m.
every one that useth *m.* is *Heb 5:13*
unskilful
desire the sincere *m.* of the *1Pe 2:2*
word

MILL

maidservant that is behind the *Ex 11:5*
m.
sound of the *m.* becomes law *Ec 12:4*
(B)
shall be grinding at the *m.* *M't 24:41*

MILLET

and lentiles, and *m.*, and fitches *Eze 4:9*

MILLION

a *m.* talents of silver (S) *1Ch 22:14*
with a *m.* men (S) *2Ch 14:9*

MILLIONS

the mother of thousands of *Ge 24:60*
m.

MILLO

together, and all the house of *M.* *J'g 9:6*
of Shechem, and the house of *J'g 9:20*
M.
and from the house of *M.* and *J'g 9:20*
David built round about from *2Sa 5:9*
M.
and *M.*, and the wall of *1Ki 9:15*
Jerusalem
built for her: then did he *1Ki 9:24*
build *M.*
Solomon built *M.*, and *1Ki 11:27*
repaired
and slew Joash in the house *2Ki 12:20*
of *M.*
about, even from *M.* round *1Ch 11:8*
about
repaired *M.* in the city of *2Ch 32:5*
David

MILLS

and ground it in *m.* or beat it *Nu 11:8*
in a

MILLSTONE

nether or the upper *m.* to *De 24:6*
pledge
of a *m.* upon Abimelech's head *J'g 9:53*
woman cast a piece of a *m.* *2Sa 11:21*
upon him
as hard as a piece of the *Job 41:24*
nether *m.*
a *m.* were hanged about his *M't 18:6;*
M'k 9:42; Lu 17:2
took up a stone like a great *Re 18:21*
m.
the sound of a *m.* shall be *Re 18:22*
heard no

MILLSTONES

Take the *m.* and grind meal *Isa 47:2*
sound of the *m.* and the light *Jer 25:10*
of

MINA

your *m.* shall be 50 shekels *Eze 45:12*
(B)(R)

MINCING

walking and *m.* as they go, and *Isa 3:16*

MIND

which were a grief of *m.* to *Ge 26:35*
Isaac
the *m.* of the Lord might be *Le 24:12*
shewed them
till will of Lord be declared *Le 24:12*
(A)(R)
awaiting revelation of Lord's *Le 24:12*
will (B)
declared at the mouth of *Le 24:12*
Jehovah (E)
change his *m.* (B) *Nu 23:19; 1Sa 15:29*
and come with all the desire of *De 18:6*
his *m.*
the Lord shall give thee *De 28:65*
sorrow of *m.*
Lord give sorrow of heart (B) *De 28:65*
Lord give a trembling heart *De 28:65*
(E)(R)
shalt call them to *m.* among *De 30:1*
the nations
of unsound *m.* (B) *De 32:28*
an understanding *m.* (A)(R) *1Ki 3:9*
an observant *m.* (B) *1Ki 3:9*
a discerning *m.* (A)(R) *1Ki 3:12*
wise and perceptive *m.* (B) *1Ki 3:12*
m. and heart (A) *1Ki 8:48; 1Ch 22:19*
and serve him with a willing *1Ch 28:9*
m.
for the people had a *m.* to work *Ne 4:6*
people had a will to work (B) *Ne 4:6*
but he is of one *m.* who can *Job 23:13*
turn him
does what he wants to do *Job 23:13*
(A)(B)
What he desires that he does *Job 23:13*
(R)
try my reins and my *m.* (S) *Ps 26:2*
am forgotten, as a dead man *Ps 31:12*
out of *m.*
I am lost to memory like one *Ps 31:12*
dead (B)
I hate men of double *m.* *Ps 119:113*
(E)(R)
a crafty *m.* (B) *Pr 7:10*
make your *m.* understand (B) *Pr 8:5*
calm, undisturbed *m.* and *Pr 14:30*
heart (A)
relaxed *m.* makes physical *Pr 14:30*
health (B)
m. of righteous ponders *Pr 15:28*
(A)(B)(R)
sweet to the *m.* (A) *Pr 16:24*
crooked *m.* finds no good *Pr 17:20*
(A)(B)(R)
many plans in man's *m.* *Pr 19:21*
(A)(R)
planning in man's *m.* is deep *Pr 19:21*
(B)(R)
he bringeth it with a wicked *Pr 21:27*
m.
he brings it with evil intention *Pr 21:27*
(A)
he brings it with evil intent *Pr 21:27*
(B)(R)
your *m.* utter things untrue *Pr 23:33*
(A)(B)
m. of kings is unsearchable *Pr 25:3*
(B)(R)
a fool uttereth all his *m.* but a *Pr 29:11*
wise man
my *m.* reels and wonders (A) *Isa 21:4*
keep in peace, whose *m.* is *Isa 26:3*
stayed on thee
bring it again to *m.* O ye *Isa 46:8*
transgressors
and the former shall not *Isa 65:17*
come into *m.*
the ark of covenant shall not *Jer 3:16*
come to *m.*
the heart and the *m.* (S) *Jer 11:20;*
20:12
sees the heart and *m.* *Jer 20:12*
(A)(B)(E)(R)
and came it not into his *m.* *Jer 44:21*
an animal *m.* be given (B)(R) *Da 4:16*
when his *m.* was hardened in *Da 5:20*
pride
God will change his *m.* (B) *Jon 3:9*
then shall his *m.* change, and *Hab 1:11*
he shall
sitting in his right *m.* *M'k 5:15; Lu 8:35*
dressed and sane (B) *M'k 5:15*
Peter called to *m.* the words *M'k 14:72*
of Jesus

Mary cast in her *m.* what *Lu 1:29*
salutation
reflected what sort of greeting *Lu 1:29*
(B)
wondered what this greeting *Lu 1:29*
might mean (N)
neither be ye of doubtful *m.* *Lu 12:29*
neither be anxious (B) *Lu 12:29*
you are not to worry (N)(P) *Lu 12:29*
they received word with all *Lu 17:11*
readiness of *m.*
serving the Lord with humility *Lu 20:19*
of *m.*
God gave them up to a *Ro 1:28*
reprobate *m.*
over to a condemned *m.* *Ro 1:28*
(A)(R)
conscious *m.* endorses (P) *Ro 7:22*
so then, with the *m.* I serve the *Ro 7:25*
law of God
with my heart I serve God (B) *Ro 7:25*
the carnal *m.* is enmity against *Ro 8:7*
God
worldly-mindedness is hostile to *Ro 8:7*
God (B)
lower nature is enmity to God *Ro 8:7*
(N)
carnal attitude is opposed to *Ro 8:7*
God (P)
he knoweth what is the *m.* of *Ro 8:27*
the Spirit
who hath known the *m.* of the *Ro 11:34*
Lord
be of the same *m.* one toward *Ro 12:16*
another
every man be fully persuaded *Ro 14:5*
in his own *m.*
that ye may with one *m.* *Ro 15:6*
glorify God
ye be joined together in the *1Co 1:10*
same *m.*
united in the same *m.* *1Co 1:10*
(B)(E)(R)
who hath known *m.* of Lord *1Co 2:16*
but we have the *m.* of Christ
my *m.* is unproductive *1Co 14:14*
(A)(B)
if in our right *m.* *2Co 5:13*
(A)(N)(R)(S)
when he told us your fervent *2Co 7:7*
m. toward me
for if there be first a willing *2Co 8:12*
m. it is accepted
brethren, be of one *m.* *2Co 13:11;*
Ph'p 1:27; 2:2
fulfilling the desires of the *Eph 2:3*
flesh and *m.*
as other Gentiles walk in *Eph 4:17*
vanity of their *m.*
in lowliness of *m.* let each *Ph'p 2:3*
esteem other
let this *m.* be in you which *Ph'p 2:5*
was in Christ Jesus
that they be of the same *m.* in *Ph'p 4:2*
the Lord
vainly puffed up by his fleshly *Col 2:18*
m.
put on kindness, humbleness *Col 3:12*
of *m.*
that they be not soon shaken in *2Th 2:2*
m.
his *m.* a morbid jumble of *1Ti 6:4*
disputation (P)
many agonies of *m.* (P) *1Ti 6:10*
God hath given us the spirit of *2Ti 1:7*
sound *m.*
power, love, and self-control *2Ti 1:7*
(B)(R)
power, love, and discipline (E) *2Ti 1:7*
inspire strength, love, *2Ti 1:7*
self-discipline (N)
men of corrupt *m.* (R) *2Ti 3:8*
but their *m.* and conscience is *Tit 1:15*
defiled
put them in *m.* to be subject to *Tit 3:1*
powers
I will put my laws into their *Heb 8:10*
m.
be ye all of one *m.* having *1Pe 3:8*
compassion
be harmonious (B) *1Pe 3:8*
be ye all likeminded (R) *1Pe 3:8*
be one in thought and feeling *1Pe 3:8*
(N)
have unity of spirit (R) *1Pe 3:8*
arm yourselves likewise with *1Pe 4:1*
the same *m.*
not for filthy lucre, but of a *1Pe 5:2*
ready *m.*

here is the *m.* which hath wisdom *Re 17:9*

these have one *m.* and shall give their power *Re 17:13*

MINE, MY MIND

I have not done them of *mine* own *m.* *Nu 16:28*
act of my own accord (A) *Nu 16:28*
not act on my own impulse (B) *Nu 16:28*
then Jehovah has not sent me (E)(R) *Nu 16:28*
I cannot do good or bad of *mine* own *m.* *Nu 24:13*
do good or bad of my own will (A)(R) *Nu 24:13*
do good or evil of my own accord (B) *Nu 24:13*
according to that which is in *my m.* *1Sa 2:35*
it was in *my m.* to build an house *1Ch 22:7*
my m. could not be toward this people *Jer 15:1*
neither came it into *my m.* *Jer 19:5; 32:35*
this I recall to *my m.* therefore hope *La 3:21*
another law warring against law of *my m.* *Ro 7:23*
battling against principles of reason (B) *Ro 7:23*
fighting against law of my reason (N) *Ro 7:23*

THY MIND

set not *thy m.* on asses, they are found *1Sa 9:20*
should it be according to *thy m.* *Job 34:33*
same time shall things come into *thy m.* *Eze 38:10*
O king, *thy* thoughts came into *thy m.* *Da 2:29*
thou shalt love the Lord thy *M't 22:37;* God with all *thy m. M'k 12:30; Lu 10:27*
without *thy m.* would I do nothing *Ph'm 14*

YOUR MIND

if it be *your m.* I should bury my dead *Ge 23:8*
and let Jerusalem come into *your m.* *Jer 51:50*
I know the things that come into *your m.* *Eze 11:5*
come into your hearts (B) *Eze 11:5*
and that which cometh into *your m.* *Eze 20:32*
be transformed by renewing of *your m.* *Ro 12:2*
and declaration of *your* ready *m.* *2Co 8:19*
for I know the forwardness of *your m.* *2Co 9:2*
and be renewed in the spirit of *your m.* *Eph 4:23*
renewed in your mental attitude (B) *Eph 4:23*
that were sometimes enemies in *your m.* *Col 1:21*
gird up the loins of *your m.* be sober *1Pe 1:13*

MINDED

she was stedfastly *m.* to go with her *Ru 1:18*
Joash was *m.* to repair the house *2Ch 24:4*
which are *m.* of their own free will *Ezr 7:13*
Joseph was *m.* to put her away privily *M't 1:19*
not willing to expose her (A)(E) *M't 1:19*
was fairminded (B) *M't 1:19*
wanting to save her from exposure (P) *M't 1:19*
did not want to see her disgraced (P) *M't 1:19*
unwilling to put her to shame (R) *M't 1:19*
were *m.* to slay them (E) *Ac 5:33*
to be carnally *m.* is death, but *Ro 8:6*
to be spiritually *m.* is life

to be worldly-minded means death (B) *Ro 8:6*
be not high *m.* but fear *Ro 11:20*
Do not become proud and conceited (A)(R) *Ro 11:20*
Do not be haughty, but feel awe (B) *Ro 11:20*
put away your pride, be on guard (N) *Ro 11:20*
grant you to be like *m.* one toward another *Ro 15:5*
in this confidence I was *m.* to come *2Co 1:15*
when I was thus *m.* did I use lightness *2Co 1:17*
that you will be no otherwise *m.* *Ga 5:10*
that ye be like *m.* having the same love *Ph'p 2:2*
no man like *m.* who will care for your state *Ph'p 2:20*
as many as be perfect, be thus *m.* if in any thing ye be otherwise *m.* *Ph'p 3:15*
brethren, comfort the feeble *m.* *1Th 5:14*
charge that the rich be not high *m.* *1Ti 6:17*
young men exhort to be sober *m.* *Tit 2:6*
a double-*m.* man is unstable in all his ways *Jas 1:8*
and purify your hearts, ye double *m.* *Jas 4:8*
you of divided interests (A)(B) *Jas 4:8*

MINDFUL

be ye *m.* always of his covenant *1Ch 16:15*
our fathers were not *m.* of thy wonders *Ne 9:17*
what is man thou art *m.* of him *Ps 8:4; Heb 2:6*
he will ever be *m.* of his covenant *Ps 111:5*
the Lord hath been *m.* of us, he will bless us *Ps 115:12*
not been *m.* of the rock of thy strength *Isa 17:10*
ye were also *m.* (S) *Ph'p 4:10*
being *m.* of thy tears, to be filled *2Ti 1:4*
if they had been *m.* of that country *Heb 11:15*
that ye may be *m.* of the words spoken *2Pe 3:2*

MINDING

Paul *m.* himself to go afoot *Ac 20:13*

MINDS

change your *m.* (A) *Ex 32:12*
consider of it, and speak your *m.* *J'g 19:30*
and they be chafed in their *m.* *2Sa 17:8*
if it be your *m.* let none go forth *2Ki 9:15*
m. and hearts (B)(R) *1Ch 22:19; 2Ch 6:38*
trieth the *m.* and hearts (E)(R)(S) *Ps 7:9*
treat my heart and *m.* (A)(E)(R) *Ps 26:2*
tests my heart and *m.* (A)(E)(R) *Jer 11:20*
that whereupon they set their *m.* *Eze 24:25*
with despiteful *m.* to cast it out for a prey *Eze 36:5*
argued in their *m.* (B) *M'k 2:6*
do not let *m.* be dull (N)(P) *Lu 12:34*
and made their *m.* evil affected *Ac 14:2*
they changed their *m.* said he was a god *Ac 28:6*
misguided *m.* plunged into darkness (N) *Ro 1:2*
stupid, silly *m.* (B)(P) *Ro 1:21*
slaves to degenerate *m.* (P) *Ro 1:28*
m. teemed with inventions (P) *Ro 1:30*
but their *m.* were blinded, veil untaken *2Co 3:14*
the god of this world hath blinded the *m.* *2Co 4:4*
so your *m.* should be corrupted from simplicity *2Co 11:3*
unsettle your *m.* (N) *Ga 1:7*
futility of their *m.* (R) *Eph 4:17*

the peace of God shall keep your *m.* *Ph'p 4:7*
set, app'y your *m.* (A)(B)(E)(R) *Col 3:2*
men of corrupt *m.* *1Ti 6:5; 2Ti 3:8*
depraved *m.* (B)(R) *1Ti 6:5; 2Ti 3:8*
warped *m.* (P) *1Ti 6:5*
their *m.* distorted (P) *2Ti 3:8*
and in their *m.* will I write them *Heb 10:16*
lest ye be wearied and faint in your *m.* *Heb 12:3*
stir up your pure *m.* by way of *2Pe 3:1*
he who searches *m.* *Re 2:23*
(A)(B)(P)(R)(S)

MINE

and all that thou seest is *m.* *Ge 31:43*
are *m.* as Reuben and Simeon shall be *m.* *Ge 48:5*
m. honour, be not thou united *Ge 49:6*
sanctify all firstborn of man and beast it is *m.* *Ex 13:2; 34:19; Nu 3:13*
for all the earth is *m.* *Ex 19:5; Ps 50:12*
that ye should be *m.* *Le 20:26; Isa 43:1*
the land is *m.* for ye are strangers *Le 25:23*
the Levites shall be *m.* *Nu 3:12; 3:45; 8:14*
the firstborn of children of Israel are *m.* *Nu 8:17*
Absalom said, See, Joab's field is near *m.* *2Sa 14:30*
knowest that the kingdom was *m.* *1Ki 2:15*
let it be neither *m.* nor thine, divide it *1Ki 3:26*
thy silver, and gold, and wives, are *m.* *1Ki 20:3*
if ye will be *m.* and if ye will hearken *2Ki 10:6*
my God put into *m.* heart to gather *Ne 7:5*
a *m.* of silver (A)(B)(E)(R) *Job 28:1*
whatsoever is under heaven is *m.* *Job 41:11*
I kept myself from *m.* iniquity *Ps 18:23*
for every beast of the forest is *m.* *Ps 50:10*
and the wild beasts of the field are *m.* *Ps 50:11*
apart from any fault of *m.* (S) *Ps 59:4*
Gilead is *m.* and Manasseh is *m.* *Ps 60:7; 108:8*
against the wrath of *m.* enemies *Ps 138:7*
counsel is *m.* and sound wisdom: I *Pr 8:14*
my beloved is *m.* and I am his *Ca 2:16; 6:3*
my vineyard, which is *m.* is before me *Ca 8:12*
whose word shall stand, *m.* or theirs *Jer 44:28*
I sware to thee, thou becamest *m.* *Eze 16:8*
behold, all souls are *m.* soul of son is *m.* *Eze 18:4*
and they were *m.* *Eze 23:4*
when she was *m.* *Eze 23:5*
the river is *m.* *Eze 29:9*
these countries be *m.* *Eze 35:10*
the silver is *m.* and the gold is *m.* *Hag 2:8*
they shall be *m.* saith the Lord *Mal 3:17*
that heareth sayings of *m.* and doeth them *M't 7:24*
heareth these sayings of *m.* and doeth them not *M't 7:26*
to sit on my right hand and on my left, is not *m.* to give *M't 20:23; M'k 10:40*
a friend of *m.* in his journey is come *Lu 11:6*
Jesus saith, *M.* hour is not yet *Joh 2:4*
my doctrine is not *m.;* am known of *Joh 7:16; 10:14*
the word which ye hear is not *m.* *Joh 14:24*
he shall receive of *m.* and shew it you *Joh 16:14*
all things that the Father hath are *m.* *Joh 16:15*
all *m.* are thine, and thine are *m.* *Joh 17:10*
vengeance is *m.* I will repay *Ro 12:19*
in every prayer of *m.* making request *Ph'p 1:4*

MINGLE

and men of strength to m. strong drink	Isa 5:22
mixing alcoholic drinks (A)	Isa 5:22
men mixing intoxicants (B)	Isa 5:22
mixing strong drinks (R)	Isa 5:22
they shall m. with the seed of men	Da 2:43
mixed in marriage (B)	Da 2:43
mix with one another in marriage (R)	Da 2:43

MINGLED

there was fire m. with the hail	Ex 9:24
mixed m. (A)(B)(E)(R)	Ex 29:2
shalt not sow thy field with m. seed	Le 19:19
garment of m. stuff (A)	De 22:11
holy seed have m. themselves with people	Ezr 9:2
and m. my drink with weeping	Ps 102:9
mixed tears with my drink (B)	Ps 102:9
but were m. among the heathen	Ps 106:35
associated with those pagans (B)	Ps 106:35
killed her beasts, she hath m. her wine	Pr 9:2
mixed her spiritual wine (A)	Pr 9:2; 9:5
and drink of the wine which I have m.	Pr 9:5
the Lord hath m. a perverse spirit	Isa 19:14
give the cup to all the m. people	Jer 25:20; 25:24
all the mixed foreign population (A)	Jer 25:20
all the mixed people (B)	Jer 25:20
all the foreign folk (R)	Jer 25:20
a sword on all the m. people	Jer 50:37; Eze 30:5
all the foreign troops (B)(R)	Jer 50:37
they gave him vinegar m. with gall	M't 27:34
they gave him wine m. with myrrh	M'k 15:23
wine flavored with myrrh (B)	M'k 15:23
offered drugged wine (N)(P)	M'k 15:23
whose blood Pilate had m. with sacrifice	Lu 13:1
blood mixed with sacrifices (A)(B)(N)(P)	Lu 13:1
there followed hail and fire m. with blood	Re 8:7
hail and fire mixed with blood (B)(P)	Re 8:7
I saw as it were a sea of glass m. with fire	Re 15:2
glassy sea blended with fire (A)	Re 15:2
glassy sea mixed with fire (B)	Re 15:2
sea of glass shot with fire (N)(P)	Re 15:2

MINIAMIN

were Eden, and M., and Jehsua	2Ch 31:15
Of Abijah, Zichri; of M., Moadiah	Ne 12:17
the priests; Eliakim, Maaseiah, M.	Ne 12:41

MINISH

not m. ought from your bricks	Ex 5:19
not diminish aught from your bricks (A)(E)	Ex 5:19
not reduce the daily number of bricks (B)	Ex 5:19
no means lessen the number of bricks (R)	Ex 5:19

MINISHED

they are m. and brought low	Ps 107:39
they are diminished (A)(E)(R)	Ps 107:39
they are become few and brought (B)	Ps 107:39

MINISTER

rose up, and his m. Joshua	Ex 24:13
Joshua his attendant (A)	Ex 24:13

Joshua, his assistant (B)	Ex 24:13; Jos 1:1
may m. unto me in the priest's office	Ex 28:1; 28:3, 4, 41; 30:30; 40:13, 15
to officiate as my priests (B)	Ex 28:1
to serve as priests (R)	Ex 28:1
And it shall be upon Aaron to m.	Ex 28:35
the altar to m. in the holy place	Ex 28:43
to m. unto me in the priest's office	Ex 29:1
cometh to m. in the holy place	Ex 29:30
sons, to m. to me in the priest's office	Ex 29:44; 31:10; 35:19; 39:41
to serve me as priests (B)(R)	Ex 29:44
they come near to the altar to m.	Ex 30:20
about the hem of the robe to m.	Ex 39:26
m. in to m. unto the Lord in the priest's	Le 7:35
consecrate to m. in the priest's office	Le 16:32
and they shall m. unto it, and shall	Nu 1:50
consecrated to m. in the priest's office	Nu 3:3
priest, that they may m. unto him	Nu 3:6
the sanctuary wherewith they m.	Nu 3:31
thereof, wherewith they m. unto it	Nu 4:9
wherewith they m. in the sanctuary	Nu 4:12
wherewith they m. about it	Nu 4:14
But shall m. with their brethren in	Nu 8:26
help their brethren (A)	Nu 8:26
assist their fellow workers (B)	Nu 8:26
the congregation to m. unto them	Nu 16:9
joined unto thee, and m. unto thee	Nu 18:2
thou and thy sons with thee shall m.	Nu 18:2
before the Lord to m. unto him	De 10:8
that standeth to m. there before the	De 17:12
stand to m. in the name of the Lord	De 18:5
he shall m. in the name of the Lord	De 18:7
God hath chosen to m. unto him	De 21:5
Joshua the son of Nun, Moses' m.	Jos 1:1
And the child did m. unto the Lord	1Sa 2:11
was in the Lord's service (B)	1Sa 2:11
the priests could not stand to m.	1Ki 8:11
of God, and to m. unto him for ever	1Ch 15:2
Levites to m. before the ark of	1Ch 16:4
to m. before ark continually	1Ch 16:37
before the Lord, to m. unto	1Ch 23:13
him, and to m. in the house of	1Ch 26:12
Lord the priests could not stand to m.	2Ch 5:14
m. by to praise and m. before the	2Ch 8:14
priests the priests, which m. unto the Lord	2Ch 13:10
and they that m. of the Levites	2Ch 23:6
even vessels to m. and to offer	2Ch 24:14
ye should m. unto him, and burn	2Ch 29:11
to m. and to give thanks, and	2Ch 31:2
that m. in the house of our God	Ne 10:36
priests that m. and the porters	Ne 10:39
shall m. judgment to the people	Ps 9:8
rams of Nebaioth m. unto thee	Isa 60:7
and their kings shall m. unto thee	Isa 60:10
and the Levites that m. unto me	Jer 33:22
near to the Lord to m. unto him	Eze 40:46
lay their garments wherein they m.	Eze 42:14

approach unto me, to m. unto me	Eze 43:19
stand before them to m. unto them	Eze 44:11
come near unto me to m. unto me	Eze 44:15
near to my table, to m. unto me	Eze 44:16
m. in the gates of the inner court	Eze 44:17
inner court, to m. in the sanctuary	Eze 44:27
shall come near to m. unto the Lord	Eze 45:4
among you, let him be your m.	M't 20:26
must be your servant (A)(N)(R)	M't 20:26
he must be your slave (P)	M't 20:26
to be ministered unto, but to m.	M't 20:28; M'k 10:45
not to be waited on, but to serve (A)	M't 20:28
not to be served, but serve (B)(N)(P)(R)	M't 20:28
prison, and did not m. unto thee	M't 25:44
were of no service to you (B)	M't 25:44
did nothing for you (N)	M't 25:44
failed to look after you (P)	M't 25:44
among you, shall be your m.	M'k 10:43
he gave it again to the m. and sat	Lu 4:20
gave it back to attendant (A)(E)(N)(P)(R)	Lu 4:20
gave it back to the custodian (B)	Lu 4:20
and they had also John to their m.	Ac 13:5
John as an attendant (A)(B)(E)	Ac 13:5
John with them as their assistant (N)(P)	Ac 13:5
John to assist them (R)	Ac 13:5
none to m. or come unto him	Ac 24:23
be discouraged from rendering aid (B)	Ac 24:23
making themselves useful to him (N)	Ac 24:23
to look after his needs (P)	Ac 24:23
prevented from attending to his needs (R)	Ac 24:23
make thee a m. and a witness	Ac 26:16
servant and a witness (N)(P)	Ac 26:16
to serve and bear witness (R)	Ac 26:16
is the m. of God to thee for good	Ro 13:4
he is God's servant (A)(P)(R)	Ro 13:4
he is God's agent (B)(N)	Ro 13:4
he is the m. of God, a revenger	Ro 13:4
a m. of the circumcision for	Ro 15:8
I should be the m. of Jesus Christ	Ro 15:16
Jerusalem to m. unto the saints	Ro 15:25
to m. unto them in carnal things	Ro 15:27
they which m. about holy things	1Co 9:13
employed in the temple services (A)(R)	1Co 9:13
conduct the temple service (B)(N)	1Co 9:13
sower both m. bread for your food	2Co 9:10
is therefore Christ the m. of sin	Ga 2:17
Whereof I was made a m., according	Eph 3:7; Col 1:25
it may m. grace unto the hearers	Eph 4:29
add a blessing to the listeners (B)	Eph 4:29
brings a blessing to those who hear (N)	Eph 4:29
a beloved brother and faithful m.	Eph 6:21
is for you a faithful m. of Christ	Col 1:7
whereof I Paul am made a m.	Col 1:23
a faithful m. and fellowservant in	Col 4:7
our brother, and m. of God, and our	1Th 3:2
m. questions, rather than godly	1Ti 1:4
shalt be a good m. of Jesus Christ	1Ti 4:6

sent forth to *m*. for them who shall | *Heb 1:14*
for the service of those who (A)(E) | *Heb 1:14*
for the assistance of those (B) | *Heb 1:14*
sent out to serve (N)(P)(R) | *Heb 1:14*
ministered to the saints, and do *m*. | *Heb 6:10*
A *m*. of the sanctuary, and of | *Heb 8:2*
as Administrator of things holy (A) | *Heb 8:2*
a ministrant in the real sanctuary (N) | *Heb 8:2*
but unto us they did *m*. the things | *1Pe 1:12*
the services they were rendering (A) | *1Pe 1:12*
were rendering their ministries (B) | *1Pe 1:12*
the matter they treated of (N) | *1Pe 1:12*
matters not meant for themselves (P) | *1Pe 1:12*
were not serving themselves, but you (R) | *1Pe 1:12*
even so *m*. the same one to another | *1Pe 4:10*
employ it for one another (A)(R) | *1Pe 4:10*
serve the group to measure of endowment (B) | *1Pe 4:10*
use it in service to one another (N) | *1Pe 4:10*
if any man *m*. let him do it as of | *1Pe 4:11*
who renders service (A)(N)(R) | *1Pe 4:11*
if serving, let it be with the (B) | *1Pe 4:11*
if any man serves the church (P) | *1Pe 4:11*

MINISTERED

Ithamar *m*. in the priest's office | *Nu 3:4*
served as priests (B)(R) | *Nu 3:4*
his son *m*. in the priest's office in | *De 10:6*
Samuel *m*. before the Lord | *1Sa 2:18*
the child Samuel *m*. unto the Lord | *1Sa 3:1*
called his servant that *m*. unto him | *2Sa 13:17*
called young man who served him (A)(R) | *2Sa 13:17*
called the attendant who waited on him (B) | *2Sa 13:17*
cherished the king, and *m*. to him | *1Ki 1:4*
waited on and nursed him (A) | *1Ki 1:4*
became king's nurse and served him (B) | *1Ki 1:4*
she *m*. to him (R) | *1Ki 1:4*
the Shunammite *m*. unto the king | *1Ki 1:15*
went after Elijah, and *m*. unto him | *1Ki 19:21*
served him (A) | *1Ki 19:21*
became his servant (B) | *1Ki 19:21*
vessels of brass wherewith they *m*. | *2Ki 25:14; Jer 52:18*
m. before the dwelling place of the | *1Ch 6:32*
companies that *m*. to the king | *1Ch 28:1*
of Ahaziah, that *m*. to Ahaziah, he | *2Ch 22:8*
king's servants that *m*. unto him | *Es 2:2; 6:3*
they *m*. unto them before their idols | *Eze 44:12*
their garments wherein they *m*. | *Eze 44:19*
thousand thousands *m*. unto him | *Da 7:10*
thousand thousands served him (B)(R) | *Da 7:10*
angels came and *m*. unto him | *M't 4:11*
angels came forward and waited on him (B)(N) | *M't 4:11*
angels took care of him (P) | *M't 4:11*
and she arose, and *m*. unto them | *M't 8:15; Lu 4:39*
she got up and began waiting on him (A) | *M't 8:15*
she got up and waited on him (B)(N) | *M't 8:15*
got up and began to see to their needs (P) | *M't 8:15*
she arose and served him (R) | *M't 8:15*
Son of man came not to be *m*. unto | *M't 20:28; M'k 10:45*

beasts; and the angels *m*. unto him | *M'k 1:13*
left her, and she *m*. unto them | *M'k 1:31*
followed him, and *m*. unto him | *M'k 15:41*
m. unto him of their substance | *Lu 8:3*
supported them out of their means (B) | *Lu 8:3*
provided for them out of their resources (N) | *Lu 8:3*
look after his comfort from own resources (A) | *Lu 8:3*
provided for them out of their means (R) | *Lu 8:3*
As they *m*. to the Lord, and fasted | *Ac 13:2*
were worshipping and fasting (A)(B)(P)(R) | *Ac 13:2*
keeping a fast and offering worship (N) | *Ac 13:2*
two of them that *m*. unto him | *Ac 19:22*
hands have *m*. unto my necessities | *Ac 20:34*
hands have supplied my needs | *Ac 20:34*
hands of mine earned enough for me and (N) | *Ac 20:34*
hands have provided for my own needs and (P) | *Ac 20:34*
to be the epistle of Christ *m*. by us | *2Co 3:3*
letter of Christ delivered by us (A)(B)(R) | *2Co 3:3*
letter from Christ, given to us to deliver (N) | *2Co 3:3*
letter of Christ we ourselves have written (P) | *2Co 3:3*
gift *m*. by us (E) | *2Co 8:20*
and he that *m*. to my wants | *Ph'p 2:25*
and bands having nourishments *m*. | *Col 2:19*
things he *m*. unto me at Ephesus | *2Ti 1:18*
might have *m*. unto me in the bonds | *Ph'm 13*
m. to the saints, and do minister | *Heb 6:10*
an entrance shall be *m*. unto you | *2Pe 1:11*
will be richly and abundantly provided (A) | *2Pe 1:11*
will be liberally provided for you (B) | *2Pe 1:11*
shall be richly supplied unto you (E) | *2Pe 1:11*
afforded full and free admission into (N) | *2Pe 1:11*
will open wide for you the gates of (P) | *2Pe 1:11*
richly provided for you an entrance (R) | *2Pe 1:11*

MINISTERETH

Now he that *m*. seed to the sower | *2Co 9:10*
who provides seed for the sower (A)(B) | *2Co 9:10*
supplieth seed to the sower (E)(R) | *2Co 9:10*
provides seed for sowing (N) | *2Co 9:10*
gives the seed to the sower (P) | *2Co 9:10*

MINISTERING

had the charge of the *m*. vessels | *1Ch 9:28*
serving utensils (A) | *1Ch 9:28*
were over the utensils of the service (B)(R) | *1Ch 9:28*
had charge of the vessels of service (E) | *1Ch 9:28*
women rendering him service (B) | *1Ch 27:55*
followed Jesus and waited on him (N) | *1Ch 27:55*
of the house, and *m*. to the house | *Eze 44:11*
Jesus from Galilee, *m*. unto him | *M't 27:55*
Or ministry, let us wait on our *m*. | *Ro 12:7*
give himself to serving (A) | *Ro 12:7*
If practical service, then in such service (B) | *Ro 12:7*
gift of administration, in administration (N) | *Ro 12:7*
if serving others, concentrate on service (P) | *Ro 12:7*

if service, in our serving (R) | *Ro 12:7*
the Gentiles *m*. the gospel of God | *Ro 15:16*
fellowship of the *m*. to the saints | *2Co 8:4*
this ministration for the saints (A) | *2Co 8:4*
this service for the saints (B) | *2Co 8:4*
this generous service to fellow-Christians (N) | *2Co 8:4*
share in the honor of supporting brothers (P) | *2Co 8:4*
taking part in the relief of saints (R) | *2Co 8:4*
gift we are *m*. (R) | *2Co 8:20*
as touching the *m*. to the saints | *2Co 9:1*
m. of this fund (A) | *2Co 9:12*
Are they not all *m*. spirits | *Heb 1:14*
every priest standeth daily *m*. and | *Heb 10:11*

MINISTERS

attendance of his *m*. and their | *1Ki 10:5*
standing at attention of his servants (A) | *1Ki 10:5*
servants (B) | *1Ki 10:5*
| *Ezr 7:24; Ps 103:21; 104:4; Isa 61:6*
attendance of his *m*. and their | *Ch 9:4*
or *m*. of this house of God | *Ezr 7:24*
that they should bring unto us *m*. | *Ezr 8:17*
ye *m*. of his, that do his pleasure | *Ps 103:21*
angels spirits; his *m*. a flaming fire | *Ps 104:4*
shall call you the M. of our God | *Isa 61:6*
with the Levites the priests, my *m*. | *Jer 33:21*
they shall be *m*. in my sanctuary | *Eze 44:11*
the priests the *m*. of the sanctuary | *Eze 45:4*
the Levites, the *m*. of the house | *Eze 45:5*
with the *m*. of the house shall boil | *Eze 46:24*
the priests, the Lord's *m*., mourn | *Joe 1:9*
howl, ye *m*. of the altar: come, lie | *Joe 1:13*
night in sackcloth, ye *m*. of my God | *Joe 1:13*
Let the priests, the *m*. of the Lord | *Joe 2:17*
eyewitnesses, and *m*. of the word | *Lu 1:2*
attendants of the Word (B) | *Lu 1:2*
servants of the Gospel (N) | *Lu 1:2*
teachers of the message (P) | *Lu 1:2*
for they are God's *m*. attending | *Ro 13:6*
official servants under God (A) | *Ro 13:6*
they are God's agents (B) | *Ro 13:6*
The authorities are in God's service (N) | *Ro 13:6*
civil authorities are appointed by God (P) | *Ro 13:6*
m. by whom ye believed, even as | *1Co 3:5*
supplies you with his marvelous Spirit (A) | *1Co 3:5*
endued you with the Spirit (B) | *1Co 3:5*
supplieth to you the Spirit (E) | *1Co 3:5*
when God gives you the Spirit (N)(P) | *1Co 3:5*
supplies the Spirit to you and works (R) | *1Co 3:5*
account of us, as of *m*. of Christ | *1Co 4:1*
servants of Christ (B)(R) | *1Co 4:1*
Christ's underlings (N) | *1Co 4:1*
hath made us able *m*. of the new | *2Co 3:6*
approving ourselves as *m*. of God | *2Co 6:4*
servants of God (A)(N)(R) | *2Co 6:4*
assistants of God (B) | *2Co 6:4*
thing if his *m*. also be transformed | *2Co 11:15*
as the *m*. of righteousness | *2Co 11:15*
servants of righteousness (B)(R) | *2Co 11:15*
agents of good (N) | *2Co 11:15*
Are they *m*. of Christ? (I speak as a | *2Co 11:23*
spirits, and his *m*. a flame of fire | *Heb 1:7*

MINISTRATION

days of his *m.* were accomplished   *Lu 1:23*
time of performing priestly functions (A)   *Lu 1:23*
time of service was over (B)(R)   *Lu 1:23*
When his period of duty was over (N)   *Lu 1:23*
his days of duty were over (P)   *Lu 1:23*
were neglected in the daily *m.*   *Ac 6:1*
widows overlooked in the daily charities (B)   *Ac 6:1*
overlooked in daily distribution (N)(P)(R)   *Ac 6:1*
varieties of *m.* (A)(E)   *1Co 12:5*
But if the *m.* of death, written   *2Co 3:7*
the dispensation of death (A)(R)   *2Co 3:7*
the ministry of death (B)   *2Co 3:7*
the administration of the law (P)   *2Co 3:7*
m. of the spirit be rather glorious   *2Co 3:8*
the dispensation of the Spirit (A)(N)(R)   *2Co 3:8*
the ministry of the Spirit (B)   *2Co 3:8*
administration of the Spirit (P)   *2Co 3:8*
if the *m.* of condemnation be glory   *2Co 3:9*
m. of righteousness exceed in glory   *2Co 3:9*
Whiles by the experiment of this *m.*   *2Co 9:13*

MINISTRIES

distinctive *m.* (B)   *1Co 12:5*

MINISTRY

take all the instruments of *m.*   *Nu 4:12*
utensils of the service (A)   *Nu 4:12*
the ministering utensils (B)   *Nu 4:12*
the vessels of the service (R)   *Nu 4:12*
came to do the service of the *m.*   *Nu 4:47*
service and of burden bearing (A)   *Nu 4:47*
the service for work (B)   *Nu 4:47*
the work of service (E)(R)   *Nu 4:47*
when David praised by their *m.*   *2Ch 7:6*
David gave praise through their service (B)   *2Ch 7:6*
by the *m.* of the prophets   *Ho 12:10*
parables acted out by the prophets (A)(B)(R)   *Ho 12:10*
and had obtained part of this *m.*   *Ac 1:17*
That he may take part of this *m.*   *Ac 1:25*
prayer, and to the *m.* of the word   *Ac 6:4*
when they had fulfilled their *m.*   *Ac 12:25*
and the *m.* which I have received   *Ac 20:24*
among the Gentiles by his *m.*   *Ac 21:19*
Or *m.* let us wait on ministering   *Ro 12:7*
addicted to the *m.* of the saints   *1Co 16:15*
the service of the saints (A)(B)(R)   *1Co 16:15*
to serve God's people (N)   *1Co 16:15*
devote lives looking after Christian brothers (P)   *1Co 16:15*
Therefore seeing we have this *m.*   *2Co 4:1*
given to us the *m.* of reconciliation   *2Co 5:18*
thing, that the *m.* be not blamed   *2Co 6:3*
for the work of the *m.* for the   *Eph 4:12*
Take heed to the *m.* which thou hast   *Col 4:17*
faithful, putting me into the *m.*   *1Ti 1:12*
appointed me to his service (B)(E)(N)(R)   *1Ti 1:12*
to appoint me his minister (P)   *1Ti 1:12*
evangelist, make full proof of thy *m.*   *2Ti 4:5*
for he is profitable to me for the *m.*   *2Ti 4:11*
helpful to me in service (B)   *2Ti 4:11*
helpful to me in ministering (E)   *2Ti 4:11*

I find him a useful assistant (N)   *2Ti 4:11*
I can certainly find a job for him here (P)   *2Ti 4:11*
he is very useful in serving me here (R)   *2Ti 4:11*
he obtained a more excellent *m.*   *Heb 8:6*
and all the vessels of the *m.*   *Heb 9:21*
sprinkled all the sacred vessels used in (A)   *Heb 9:21*
sprinkled all the service utensils with (B)   *Heb 9:21*
sprinkled all vessels of divine service (N)   *Heb 9:21*
sprinkled all the vessels used in worship (R)   *Heb 9:21*

MINNI

the kingdoms of Ararat, *M.*   *Jer 51:27*

MINNITH

Aroer, even till thou come to *M.*   *J'g 11:33*
traded in thy market wheat of *M.*   *Eze 27:17*

MINSTREL

But now bring me a *m.* And it came to pass, when the *m.* played   *2Ki 3:15*   *2Ki 3:15*

MINSTRELS

m. and the people making a noise   *M't 9:23*
harpers and *m.* (S)   *Re 18:22*

MINT

ye pay the tithe of *m.* and anise   *M't 23:23*
ye tithe *m.* and rue and all manner   *Lu 11:42*

MIPHKAD

over against the gate *M.*   *Ne 3:31*

MIRACLE

you, saying, Shew a *m.* for you   *Ex 7:9*
considered not the *m.* of the loaves   *M'k 6:52*
understand meaning of the loaves (B)   *M'k 6:52*
understand not concerning the loaves (E)   *M'k 6:52*
understood the incident of the loaves (N)   *M'k 6:52*
learn the lesson of the loaves (P)   *M'k 6:52*
understood about the loaves (R)   *M'k 6:52*
which shall do a *m.* in my name   *M'k 9:39*
hoped to have seen some *m.* done   *Lu 23:8*
again the second *m.* that Jesus did   *Joh 4:54*
second sign Jesus did (A)(B)(E)(N)(P)(R)   *Joh 4:54*
they had seen the *m.* that Jesus did   *Joh 6:14*
him, and said, John did no *m.*   *Joh 10:41*
John wrought no sign (B)(E)(P)(R)   *Joh 10:41*
John gave no miraculous sign (N)   *Joh 10:41*
heard that he had done this *m.*   *Joh 12:18*
notable *m.* hath been done by them   *Ac 4:16*
a notable sign has occurred (B)(R)   *Ac 4:16; 4:22*
this *m.* of healing was shewed   *Ac 4:22*

MIRACLES

all those *m.* (R)   *Ex 4:21; Ps 78:11, 43; 105:29*
all the *m.* (B)   *Nu 14:11*
and my *m.* which I did in Egypt   *Nu 14:22*
his *m.* and his acts, which he did   *De 11:3*
signs and deeds he performed (A)(B)(E)(R)   *De 11:3*

the signs, and those great *m.*   *De 29:3*
signs and great wonders (A)(B)(E)(R)   *De 29:3*
performed great *m.* (B)   *Jos 24:17*
and where be all his *m.* which   *J'g 6:13*
all his wondrous works (A)(B)(E)   *J'g 6:13*
all his wonderful deeds (R)   *J'g 6:13*
talk of all his *m.* (B)   *1Ch 16:9*
m. of old (B)   *Ps 77:11; 105:5, 27; 106:7; 2Th 2:9; Re 13:13*
performed *m.* before (B)   *Ps 78:12*
the *m.* (A)   *Ps 106:7; Re 13:13*
beginning of *m.* did Jesus in Cana   *Joh 2:11*
first of his signs (A)(B)(E)(N)(P)(R)   *Joh 2:11*
they saw the *m.* which he did   *Joh 2:23*
seeing his signs (A)(B)(E)(N)(P)(R)   *Joh 2:23*
can do these *m.* that thou doest   *Joh 3:2*
they saw his signs (A)(B)(E)(N)(P)(R)   *Joh 3:2*
because they saw his *m.* which   *Joh 6:2*
seek me, not because ye saw the *m.*   *Joh 6:26*
because you saw his signs (B)(E)(N)(P)(R)   *Joh 6:26*
will he do more *m.* than these   *Joh 7:31*
signs (B)(E)(P)(R)   *Joh 7:31; 11:47; 12:37; Ac 2:22; 6:8; 8:6, 13; 15:12*
signs (N)   *Joh 7:31; 9:16; 11:47; 12:37*
man that is a sinner do such *m.*   *Joh 9:16*
for this man doeth many *m.*   *Joh 11:47*
signs (A)   *Joh 11:47; Ac 2:22; 6:8*
though he had done so many *m.*   *Joh 12:37*
approved of God among you by *m.*   *Ac 2:22*
many *m.* (P)   *Ac 2:43; 14:3; Ro 15:19; 2Co 12:12; Heb 2:4*
did great wonders and *m.* among   *Ac 6:8*
had showed *m.* (N)   *Ac 7:36; 14:3; 2Th 2:9; Heb 2:4; Re 13:13*
and seeing the *m.* which he did   *Ac 8:6*
the *m.* and signs which were done   *Ac 8:13*
m. and wonders God had wrought   *Ac 15:12*
special *m.* by the hands of Paul   *Ac 19:11*
To another the working of *m.*; to   *1Co 12:10*
to another miraculous powers (B)(N)   *1Co 12:10*
power to do great deeds (P)   *1Co 12:10*
after that *m.*, then gifts of healings   *1Co 12:28*
wonder-workers (A)   *1Co 12:28*
workers of spiritual power (P)   *1Co 12:28*
all teachers? are all workers of *m.*   *1Co 12:29*
worketh *m.* among you, doeth he it   *Ga 3:5*
works powerfully and miraculously (A)   *Ga 3:5*
effects wonder-working power (B)   *Ga 3:5*
and wonders, and with divers *m.*   *Heb 2:4*
signs and wonders (A)(B)(E)(R)   *Heb 2:4*
those *m.* which he had power to do   *Re 13:14*
because of his signs (A)(E)(P)(R)   *Re 13:14*
by means of the wonders (B)   *Re 13:14*
the spirits of devils, working *m.*   *Re 16:14*
that perform signs (A)(E)(R)   *Re 16:14*
performing wonders (P)   *Re 16:14*
the false prophet that wrought *m.*   *Re 19:20*
wrought the signs (E)(R)   *Re 19:20*
performed marvels (P)   *Re 19:20*

MIRACULOUS

to another *m.* powers (B)(N)   *1Co 12:10*
variety of *m.* powers (B)(R)   *Heb 2:4*

MIRE

them as the *m.* of the street   *2Sa 22:43*
like dust (A)(B)(E)(R)   *2Sa 22:43*

Can the rush grow up | Job 8:11
without m.
where there is no marsh | Job 8:11
(A)(B)(R)
He hath cast me into the m. | Job 30:19
has thrown me in the mud | Job 30:19
(B)
sharp pointed things upon | Job 41:30
the m.
I sink in deep m., where | Ps 69:2
there is
Deliver me out of the m., | Ps 69:14
and let
down like the m. of the streets | Isa 10:6
whose waters cast up m. and | Isa 57:20
dirt
there was no water, but m. | Jer 38:6
so Jeremiah sunk in the m. | Jer 38:6
thy feet are sunk in the m. | Jer 38:22
sunk in the quicksand (B) | Jer 38:22
down as the m. of the streets | Mic 7:10
fine gold as the m. of the streets | Zec 9:3
like mud of the streets (B) | Zec 9:3
like dust of the streets (R) | Zec 9:3
enemies in the m. of the | Zec 10:5
streets in
washed to her wallowing in | 2Pe 2:22
the m.

MIRIAM

M. the prophetess, the sister | Ex 15:20
M. answered them, Sing ye to | Ex 15:21
M. and Aaron spake against | Nu 12:1
Moses
unto M., Come out ye | Nu 12:4
three unto
and called Aaron and M.: and | Nu 12:5
M. became leprous, white as | Nu 12:10
snow
Aaron looked upon M. and | Nu 12:10
M. was shut out from the | Nu 12:15
camp
not till M. was brought in | Nu 12:15
again
and M. died there, and was | Nu 20:1
buried
and Moses, and M. their | Nu 26:59
sister
what the Lord thy God did | De 24:9
unto M.
and she bare M., and | 1Ch 4:17
Shammai
Aaron, and Moses, and M. The | 1Ch 6:3
before thee Moses, Aaron, and | Mic 6:4
M.

MIRMA

And Jeuz, and Shachia, and | 1Ch 8:10
M.

MIRROR

heavy metal m. (S) | Job 37:18
in a m. (A)(B)(N)(P)(R) | 1Co 13:12
in a m. (S) | 1Co 13:12; 2Co 3:18;
| Jas 1:23

MIRRORS

The hand m. (S) | Isa 3:23

MIRTH

have sent thee away with m. | Ge 31:27
portions, and to make great m. | Ne 8:12
that wasted us required of us | Ps 137:3
m.
and the end of that m. is | Pr 14:13
heaviness
joy may eventuate in grief | Pr 14:13
(B)(R)
to now, I will prove thee | Ec 2:1
with m.
test you with gladness (B) | Ec 2:1
test of pleasure (R) | Ec 2:1
is mad: and of m. What doeth it | Ec 2:2
heart of fools is in the house of | Ec 7:4
m.
fools is in the house of gaiety | Ec 7:4
(B)
Then I commended m. | Ec 8:15
because
I commended enjoyment | Ec 8:15
(A)(B)(R)
The m. of tabrets ceaseth, the | Isa 24:8
the m. of the land is gone | Isa 24:11
the voice of m., and the voice | Jer 7:34

and in your days, the voice of | Jer 16:9
m.
will take from them the | Jer 25:10
voice of m.
glitter: should we then make | Eze 21:10
m.
will also cause all her m. to | Ho 2:11
cease
an end to all her gaiety (B) | Ho 2:11

MIRY

an horrible pit, out of the m. | Ps 40:2
clay
But the m. places thereof and | Eze 47:11
swamps and marshes | Eze 47:11
(A)(R)
marshes and pools (B) | Eze 47:11
the iron mixed with m. clay | Da 2:41
sawest iron mixed with m. clay | Da 2:43

MISCARRIAGE

so there is a m. (A)(R) | Ex 21:22
why was I not a m. (A)(B) | Job 3:16

MISCARRIES

so that she m. (B) | Ex 21:22

MISCARRYING

give them a m. womb and dry | Ho 9:14
wombs that miscarry (B) | Ho 9:14

MISCHIEF

Lest peradventure m. befall | Ge 42:4
him
some harm or injury (A) | Ge 42:4
some harm come to him | Ge 42:4
(B)(E)(R)
if m. befall him by the way in | Ge 42:38
this also from me, and m. | Ge 44:29
befall him
from her, and yet no m. | Ex 21:22
follow
any damage follows (A) | Ex 21:22
but is not otherwise injured | Ex 21:22
(B)
no harm follows (E)(R) | Ex 21:22
if any m. follow, then thou | Ex 21:23
shalt
For m. did he bring them out | Ex 32:12
for evil he did bring them | Ex 32:12
forth (A)(E)(R)
to their misfortune he brought | Ex 32:12
(B)
the people, that they are set | Ex 32:22
on m.
knowest they are set on evil | Ex 32:22
(A)(E)(R)
know this people and their | Ex 32:22
wickedness (B)
has not witnessed m. in (B) | Nu 23:21
when I do then m. (R) | J'g 15:31
secretly practised m. against | 1Sa 23:9
him
Saul was planning evil | 1Sa 23:9
(A)(B)(R)
thou art taken in thy m. | 2Sa 16:8
because
beside the m. that Hadad did | 1Ki 11:25
doing harm as Hadad did | 1Ki 11:25
(B)
and see how this man seeketh | 1Ki 20:7
m.
this man is seeking our | 1Ki 20:7
destruction (A)
this fellow is seeking trouble | 1Ki 20:7
(B)(R)
light, some m. will come upon | 2Ki 7:9
us
punishment will befall us | 2Ki 7:9
(A)(B)(E)(R)
But they thought to do me m. | Ne 6:2
they plan to harm me | Ne 6:2
(A)(B)(R)
tears to put away the m. of | Es 8:3
Haman
avert the evil plot (A) | Es 8:3
to frustrate the wicked plot (B) | Es 8:3
to avert the evil design (R) | Es 8:3
they saw trouble and m. (A) | Job 4:8
They conceive m. and bring | Job 15:35
forth
iniquity, and hath conceived m. | Ps 7:14
the wicked man conceives | Ps 7:14
iniquity (A)
has conceived wrongdoing (B) | Ps 7:14;
| 7:16

the wicked man conceives evil | Ps 7:14
(R)
His m. shall return upon his | Ps 7:16
own
under his tongue is m. and | Ps 10:7
vanity
under tongue are trouble and | Ps 10:7
sin (A)(B)
for thou beholdest m. and | Ps 10:14
spite, to
you note trouble, grief, | Ps 10:14
vexation (A)
you note trouble, grief, | Ps 10:14
(B)
dost note trouble and vexation | Ps 10:14
(R)
they devise m. (R) | Ps 21:11
in whose hands is m., and their | Ps 26:10
in whose hand is wickedness | Ps 26:10
(A)(B)(E)
in whose hands are evil | Ps 26:10
devices (R)
but m. is in their hearts | Ps 28:3
malice is in their hearts (B) | Ps 28:3
He deviseth m. upon his bed | Ps 36:4
Why boastest thou thyself in m. | Ps 52:1
m. also and sorrow are in the | Ps 55:10
midst
damage and trouble are in its | Ps 55:10
center (B)
will ye imagine m. against a | Ps 62:3
man
set up a man, may slay him | Ps 62:3
(A)(E)(R)
assail a person to break him | Ps 62:3
down (B)
thee, which frameth m. by a | Ps 94:20
law
hide unrighteous doings under | Ps 94:20
law (A)
organizes oppression under | Ps 94:20
the pretense of law (B)
draw nigh that follow after | Ps 119:150
m.
follow after wrong thinking | Ps 119:150
(A)
follow wickedness (B)(E) | Ps 119:150
persecute me with evil | Ps 119:150
purpose (R)
m. of their own lips cover | Ps 140:9
them
not, except they have done m. | Pr 4:16
unless they cause someone to | Pr 4:16
fall (A)(E)
unless they do evil (B) | Pr 4:16
unless they have made someone | Pr 4:16
stumble (R)
he deviseth m. continually; he | Pr 6:14
devises trouble, vexation, and | Pr 6:14
evil (A)
devising evil continually | Pr 6:14
(B)(E)(R)
feet that be swift in running to | Pr 6:18
m.
swift in running to evil | Pr 6:18
(A)(E)(R)
It is as sport to a fool to do m. | Pr 10:23
sport to a fool to do | Pr 10:23
wickedness (A)(E)
To a fool doing wickedness is | Pr 10:23
sport (B)
is like sport to a fool to do | Pr 10:23
wrong (R)
he that seeketh m. it shall | Pr 11:27
come
evil comes to him who | Pr 11:27
searches (A)(B)(E)(R)
the wicked shall be filled with | Pr 12:21
m.
wicked be filled with evil | Pr 12:21
(A)(B)(E)
wicked be filled with trouble | Pr 12:21
(R)
wicked messenger falleth into | Pr 13:17
m.
wicked messenger falls into | Pr 13:17
evil (A)(B)(E)
bad messenger plunges men | Pr 13:17
into trouble (R)
perverted tongue stumbles into | Pr 17:20
m.
wicked and contrary tongue | Pr 17:20
will fall into calamity (A)(R)
perverted tongue stumbles | Pr 17:20
into evil (B)
and their lips talk of m. | Pr 24:2
called a m.-maker | Pr 24:8
(A)(B)(E)(R)
but the wicked shall fall into | Pr 24:16
m.

wicked falls into calamity (A) *Pr 24:16*
wicked stumbles into adversity *Pr 24:16* (B)
wicked are overthrown by *Pr 24:16* calamity (E)(R)
his heart shall fall into *m.* *Pr 28:14*
m. shall fall upon thee; thou *Isa 47:11* shalt
shall evil come upon you *Isa 47:11* (A)(E)(R)
disaster shall come upon you *Isa 47:11* (B)
they conceive *m.* and bring *Isa 59:4* forth
M. shall come upon *m.* and *Eze 7:26*
Calamity upon calamity (A) *Eze 7:26*
disaster upon disaster (B)(R) *Eze 7:26*
these are the men that devise *Eze 11:2* *m.*
who devise iniquity *Eze 11:2* (A)(B)(E)(R)
king's hearts shall be to do *m.* *Da 11:27*
do they imagine *m.* against me *Ho 7:15*
they think and devise evil *Ho 7:15* (A)(B)(R)
devise *m.* against me (E) *Ho 7:15*
as a *m.* maker (P) *Lu 23:14*
O full of all subtilty and all *Ac 13:10* *m.*
master of every form of *Ac 13:10* deception, recklessness, unscrupulousness, and wickedness (A)
full of every deceit and *Ac 13:10* villainy (B)(R)
full of all guile and villainy *Ac 13:10* (E)
You utter imposter and *Ac 13:10* charlatan (N)
you enemy of all goodness, *Ac 13:10* you monster of trickery and evil (P)
invent new kinds of *m.* (N) *Ro 1:30*
an undisciplined *m.* (B) *Jas 3:8*

MISCHIEFS

I will heap *m.* upon them; I *De 32:23* will
I will heap evils upon them *De 32:23* (A)(E)(R)
I will heap evils upon them *De 32:23* them (B)
Thy tongue deviseth *m.;* like a *Ps 52:2*
your tongue devises wickedness *Ps 52:2* (A)(B)(E)
your tongue is like a sharp *Ps 52:2* razor (R)
Which imagine *m.* in their *Ps 140:2* hearts
devise *m.* in heart (A) *Ps 140:2*
hearts devise evil plots (B) *Ps 140:2*
plan evil things in their hearts *Ps 140:2* (R)

MISCHIEVOUS

my taste discern *m.* (E) *Job 6:30*
they imagined a *m.* device *Ps 21:11*
they conceived a *m.* plot (A) *Ps 21:11*
that seek my hurt speak *m.* *Ps 38:12* things
who seek my hurt talk *Ps 38:12* mischief (B)
who seek my hurt speak of *Ps 38:12* ruin (R)
listens to *m.* tongue *Pr 17:4* (A)(E)(R)(S)
evil shall be called a *m.* *Pr 24:8* person
will be called a mischief-maker *Pr 24:8* (A)(B)(E)(R)
the end of his talk is *m.* *Ec 10:13* madness
end of his talk is wicked *Ec 10:13* madness (A)(R)
end of speech is perverse *Ec 10:13* stupidity (N)
man, he uttereth his *m.* desire *Mic 7:3*
utters his evil desire *Mic 7:3* (A)(E)(R)
outstanding man seek own *Mic 7:3* satisfaction (B)

MISCONDUCT

every kind of *m.* (B) *Ex 22:9*
overtaken in a *m.* (A)(B) *Ga 6:1*

MISCONSTRUE

lest enemies *m.* (A)(R) *De 32:27*

MISDEEDS

vengeance on their *m.* (S) *Ps 99:8*
our *m.* (B)(N) *Lu 23:41*
death because of our *m.* *Ro 4:25* (A)(B)(N)
no longer holding *m.* (N) *2Co 5:19*

MISDEMEANOR

what is my *m.* (B) *Ge 31:36; 50:17*
deal according to *m.* (B) *Job 42:8*
m. or villainy (A)(E) *Ac 18:14*
crime or grave *m.* (N) *Ac 18:14*
their *m.* (B) *Ro 11:12*

MISERABLE

things: *m.* comforters are ye *Job 16:2* all
Christ, we are of all men *1Co 15:19* most *m.*
are most to be pitied *1Co 15:19* (B)(N)(P)(R)
are of all men most pitiable *1Co 15:19* (E)
made *m.* (N) *2Co 2:3*
into *m.* perishing (A) *1Ti 6:9*
m. women (N) *2Ti 3:6*
that thou art wretched, and *m.* *Re 3:17*
pitiable (A)(B)(P)(R) *Re 3:17*
you are a most pitiful wretch *Re 3:17* (N)

MISERABLY

m. tormented by a demon *M't 15:22* (A)
will *m.* destroy those wicked *M't 21:41* men
put to miserable death *M't 21:41* (A)(B)(R)
bring those bad men to a bad *M't 21:41* end (N)
kill those scoundrels without *M't 21:41* mercy (P)

MISERIES

calamities and *m.* (B) *1Sa 10:19*
days of her affliction and of her *La 1:7* *m.*
weep and howl for your *m.* that *Jas 5:1*

MISERY

saw my *m.* (B) *Ge 31:42;*
Ex 3:7; 2Sa 16:12; Job 10:15
was grieved for the *m.* of *J'g 10:16* Israel
is light given to him that is *Job 3:20* in *m.*
months of *m.* (B) *Job 7:3*
Because thou shalt forget thy *Job 11:16* *m.*
you will forget trouble (B) *Job 11:16*
in irons and *m.* (E) *Ps 107:10*
and remember his *m.* no more *Pr 31:7*
the *m.* of man is great upon him *Ec 8:6*
person's trouble rest heavily on *Ec 8:6* him (B)(R)
mine affliction and my the *La 3:19*
my affliction and my anguish *La 3:19* (B)
my affliction and my bitterness *La 3:19* (R)
be great *m.* (P) *M't 24:21;*
M'k 13:24
terrible distress and *m.* (P) *M't 26:37*
m. of those days (B)(P) *M'k 13:19*
getting deserts for *m.* (B)(N) *Lu 23:41*
grinding *m.* upon (N) *Ro 2:9*
and *m.* are in their ways *Ro 3:16*
fate is eternal *m.* (A) *Ph'p 3:19*
draw back to eternal *m.* (A) *Heb 10:39*
in misery (N) *Heb 11:37*
feel for your *m.* (B) *Jas 4:9*
their eternal *m.* has (A) *2Pe 2:9*
those that *m.* you (B)(N) *1Jo 2:26*
brought such *m.* (B) *Re 11:10*

MISFORTUNE

neither adversary or *m.* (R) *1Ki 5:4*
deliver him by *m.* (B) *Ps 41:1*
avoids *m.* (B) *Pr 14:16*
in the day of his *m.* (B)(R) *Ob 12*

MISGAB

M. is confounded and *Jer 48:1* dismayed

MISGIVING

without any *m.* (P) *Ac 11:12*

MISGIVINGS

go with any *m.* (N)(P) *Ac 10:20*
without hesitation, *m.,* or *Ac 11:12* discrimination (A)

MISGUIDED

m. minds plunged into darkness *Ro 1:2* (N)

MISHAEL

And the sons of Uzziel: *M.* and *Ex 6:22*
Moses called *M.* and Elzaphan *Le 10:4*
on his left hand, Pedaiah, and *Ne 8:4* *M.*
of Judah, Daniel, Hananiah, *M.* *Da 1:6*
and to *M.,* of Meshach; and to *Da 1:7*
had set over Daniel, Hananiah, *Da 1:11* *M.*
none like Daniel, Hananiah, *Da 1:19* *M.*
the thing known to Hananiah, *Da 2:17* *M.*

MISHAL

of Asher, *M.* with her *Jos 21:30* suburbs

MISHAM

and *M.* and Shamed, who built *1Ch 8:12*

MISHEAL

Alammelech, and Amad, and *Jos 19:26* *M.*

MISHMA

And *M.* and Dumah, and *Ge 25:14* Massa
M. and Dumah, Massa, *1Ch 1:30* Hadad
son, Mibsam his son, *M.* his *1Ch 4:25*
And the sons of *M.;* Hamuel *1Ch 4:26*

MISHMANNAH

M. the fourth, Jeremiah the *1Ch 12:10* fifth

MISHRAITES

and the Shumathites, and the *1Ch 2:53* *M.*

MISINTERPRET

ignorant and unstable *m.* (N) *2Pe 3:16*

MISLEAD

to *m.* God's chosen (N) *M'k 13:22*

MISLEADETH

when he *m.* you (S) *2Ki 18:32*

MISLED

Manasseh *m.* them (B) *2Ki 21:9*
m. by the wise men (A) *M't 2:16*

MISPERETH

Bilshan, *M.,* Bigvai, Nehum *Ne 7:7*

MISREPHOTH-MAIM

unto great Zidon, and unto *M.* *Jos 11:8*
country from Lebanon unto *Jos 13:6* *M.*

MISS

at an hair breadth, and not *m.* *J'g 20:16*
If thy father at all *m.* me, then *1Sa 20:6*
neither shall they *m.* it (S) *Jer 3:16*

MISSED

and thou shalt be *m.* because   *1Sa 20:18*
not hurt, neither *m.* we any   *1Sa 25:15*
thing
nothing was *m.* of all that   *1Sa 25:21*
pertained

MISSING

neither was there ought *m.*   *1Sa 25:7*
unto
if by any means he be *m.*   *1Ki 20:39*
then shall
let none be *m.* (S)   *2Ki 10:19*

MISSION

sent you on a *m.* (A)(R)   *1Sa 15:18*

MISSLES

flaming *m.* (A)(P)   *Eph 6:16*

MISSTEP

brought up a *m.* (B)   *2Sa 3:8*

MIST

there went up a *m.* from the   *Ge 2:6*
earth
but a vapor used to rise (B)   *Ge 2:6*
he distils his *m.* in rain (R)   *Job 36:27*
he makes *m.* arise (R)   *Jer 10:13; 51:16*
blood, fire, smoky *m.* (B)   *Ac 2:19*
fell on him a *m.;* and a   *Ac 13:11*
darkness
the *m.* of darkness is reserved   *2Pe 2:17*
whirl-wind-driven fogs (B)   *2Pe 2:17*
like changing shapes of   *2Pe 2:17*
whirling storm-clouds (P)
no more than a *m.* (N)(R)   *Jas 4:14*

MISTAKES

composure may remedy serious   *Ec 10:4*
m. (B)
we all make *m.* in all kinds of   *Jas 3:2*
ways (P)(R)

MISTREAT

suppress or *m.* him (A)   *Le 19:33*

MISTREATED

Egyptians *m.* us (B)   *Nu 20:15*

MISTRESS

her *m.* was despised in her eyes   *Ge 16:4*
flee from the face of my *m.*   *Ge 16:8*
Sarai
said unto her, Return to thy   *Ge 16:9*
m.
the *m.* of the house, fell sick   *1Ki 17:17*
And she said unto her *m.,*   *2Ki 5:3*
Would
maiden unto the hand of her   *Ps 123:2*
m.
handmaid that is heir to her *m.*   *Pr 30:23*
as with the maid, so with her   *Isa 24:2*
m.
the *m.* of witchcrafts, that   *Na 3:4*
selleth

MISTRUST

they *m.* me (B)   *Nu 14:11*

MISUSED

and *m.* his prophets, until   *2Ch 36:16*

MITE

till thou hast paid the very   *Lu 12:59*
last *m.*

MITES

and she threw in two *m.*   *M'k 12:42*
widow casting in thither two   *Lu 21:2*
m.

MITHCAH

from Tarah, and pitched in   *Nu 33:28*
M.
they went from *M.* and   *Nu 33:29*
pitched in

MITHNITE

Maachah, and Joshaphat the   *1Ch 11:43*
M.

MITHREDATH

by the hand of *M.* the   *Ezr 1:8*
treasurer
Artaxerxes wrote Bishlam, *M.*   *Ezr 4:7*

MITRE

broidered coat, a *m.* and a   *Ex 28:4*
girdle
a turban (A)(B)(R)   *Ex 28:4;*
     28:37; 29:6; Le 8:9; 16:4; Zec 3:5
lace, that it may be upon the   *Ex 28:37*
m.
the forefront of the *m.* it shall   *Ex 28:37*
shalt make the *m.* of fine   *Ex 28:39*
linen, and
shalt put the *m.* upon his   *Ex 29:6*
head
put the holy crown upon the *m.*   *Ex 29:6*
And a *m.* of fine linen, and   *Ex 39:28*
goodly
to fasten it on high upon the   *Ex 39:31*
m.
And he put the *m.* upon his head   *Le 8:9*
also upon the *m.* even upon his   *Le 8:9*
and with the linen *m.* shall he   *Le 16:4*
remove the *m.* (A)(E)   *Eze 21:26*
them set a fair *m.* upon his head   *Zec 3:5*
So they set a fair *m.* upon his   *Zec 3:5*
head

MITYLENE

we took him in, and came to   *Ac 20:14*
M.

MIX

to *m.* strong drink (S)   *Isa 5:22*

MIXED

a *m.* multitude went up also   *Ex 12:38*
m., mingled (A)(B)(E)(R)   *Ex 29:2*
mixed (S)   *Ex 29:40;*
Le 2:4-5; 7:10, 12; 9:4; 14:10, 21;
19:19; 23:13; Nu 6:15; 7:13, 19, 25, 31,
37, 43, 49, 55, 61, 73, 79; 8:8; 15:4, 6,
9; 28:5, 9, 12-13, 20, 28; 29:3, 9, 14;
Ezr 9:2; Pr 9:2, 5; Jer 25:20, 24; 50:37;
                            Re 8:7
mixed (A)(B)(R)   *Ex 30:35*
from Israel all the *m.*   *Ne 13:3*
multitude
wine; they that go to seek *m.*   *Pr 23:30*
wine
never lacks *m.* wine (B)(E)(R)   *Ca 7:2*
dross, thy wine *m.* with water   *Isa 1:22*
sawest the iron *m.* with miry   *Da 2:41;*
clay   *2:43*
m. in marriage (B)(R)   *Da 2:43*
he hath *m.* himself among the   *Ho 7:8*
not being *m.* with faith in   *Heb 4:2*
them

MIXT

the *m.* multitude that was   *Nu 11:4*
among them

MIXTURE

the wine is red; it is full of *m.*   *Ps 75:8*
brought a *m.* of myrrh and   *Joh 19:39*
aloes
is poured out without *m.* into   *Re 14:10*

MIZAR

the Hermonites, from the hill   *Ps 42:6*
M.

MIZPAH

M.; for he said, The Lord   *Ge 31:49*
watch
them Geba of Benjamin, and   *1Ki 15:22*
M.
there came to Gedaliah to   *2Ki 25:23*
M., even
Chaldees that were with   *2Ki 25:25*
him at *M.*
he built therewith Geba and   *2Ch 16:6*
M.

and of *M.,* unto the throne of   *Ne 3:7*
Col-hozeh, the ruler of part of   *Ne 3:15*
M.
the son of Jeshua, the ruler of   *Ne 3:19*
M.
Gedaliah the son of Ahikam to   *Jer 40:6*
M.
they came to Gedaliah to *M.*   *Jer 40:8*
for me, behold, I will dwell at   *Jer 40:10*
M.
land of Judah, to Gedaliah,   *Jer 40:12*
unto *M.*
the fields, came to Gedaliah   *Jer 40:13*
to *M.*
spake to Gedaliah in *M.*   *Jer 40:15*
secretly
Gedaliah the son of Ahikam   *Jer 41:1*
to *M.*
they did eat bread together in   *Jer 41:1*
M.
at *M.* and the Chaldeans that   *Jer 41:3*
were
went forth from *M.* to meet   *Jer 41:6*
them
of the people that were in *M.*   *Jer 41:10*
all the people that remained   *Jer 41:10*
in *M.*
had carried away captive   *Jer 41:14*
from *M.*
from *M.,* after that he had   *Jer 41:16*
ye have been a snare on *M.*   *Ho 5:1*

MIZPAR

Bilshan, *M.,* Bigvai, Rehum   *Ezr 2:2*

MIZPEH

under Hermon in the land of   *Jos 11:3*
M.
unto the valley of *M.* eastward   *Jos 11:8*
And Dilean, and *M.* and   *Jos 15:38*
Joktheel
M. and Chephirah, and   *Jos 18:26*
Mozah
together, and encamped in *M.*   *J'g 10:17*
all his words before the Lord   *J'g 11:11*
in *M.*
and passed over *M.* of Gilead   *J'g 11:29*
from *M.* of Gilead he passed   *J'g 11:29*
over
came to *M.* unto his house   *J'g 11:34*
land of Gilead, unto the   *J'g 20:1*
Lord in *M.*
of Israel were gone up to *M.*   *J'g 20:3*
the men of Israel had sworn   *J'g 21:1*
in *M.*
came not up to the Lord to *M.*   *J'g 21:5*
of Israel that came not up to   *J'g 21:8*
M.
said, Gather all Israel to *M.*   *1Sa 7:5*
they gathered together to *M.*   *1Sa 7:6*
Samuel judged of Israel in   *1Sa 7:6*
M.
were gathered together to *M.*   *1Sa 7:7*
the men of Israel went out of   *1Sa 7:11*
M.
and set it between *M.* and   *1Sa 7:12*
Shen
to Beth-el, and Gilgal, and *M.*   *1Sa 7:16*
together unto the Lord to *M.*   *1Sa 10:17*
David went thence to *M.* of   *1Sa 22:3*
Moab

MIZRAIM

sons of Ham; Cush, and *M.*   *Ge 10:6;*
                        1Ch 1:8
And *M.* begat Ludim, and   *Ge 10:13;*
Anamim   *1Ch 1:11*

MIZZAH

and Zerah, Shammah, and *M.*   *Ge 36:13*
Zerah, duke Shammah, duke   *Ge 36:17*
M.
Nahath, Zerah, Shammah, and   *1Ch 1:37*
M.

MNASON

with them one *M.* of Cyprus   *Ac 21:16*
an

MOAB

Lot's eldest daughter's son   *Ge 19:37*
was *M.*

MOAB

smote Midian in field of *M.* — Ge 36:35; 1Ch 1:46
trembling shall take hold on — Ex 15:15
men of *M.*
woe to thee, *M.* — Nu 21:29; Jer 48:46
M. was sore afraid, and *M.* — Nu 22:3
was distressed
a sceptre shall smite, the — Nu 24:17
corners of *M.*
people commit whoredom with — Nu 25:1
daughters of *M.*
thou art to pass thro' the — De 2:18
coast of *M.*
so Moses died there in the — De 34:5
land of *M.*
they slew of *M.* about 10,000 — J'g 3:29
men
so *M.* was subdued under the — J'g 3:30
hand of Israel
Israel served the gods of Syria — J'g 10:6
and *M.*
Israel took not away the land — J'g 11:15
of *M.*
Elimelech came into the country — Ru 1:2
of *M.*
his sons took them wives of the — Ru 1:4
women of *M.*
Saul fought against *M.* and — 1Sa 14:47
Ammon
David smote *M.* and measured — 2Sa 8:2
them
Benaiah slew two lionlike — 2Sa 23:20
men of *M.*
for Chemosh the — 1Ki 11:7
abomination of *M.*
then *M.* rebelled against Israel — 2Ki 1:1
wilt thou go with me against — 2Ki 3:7
M. to battle
the kings are slain, therefore — 2Ki 3:23
M. to the spoil
Saraph, who had the — 1Ch 4:22
dominion in *M.*
the silver and gold he — 1Ch 18:11
brought from *M.*
M. came against Jehoshaphat — 2Ch 20:1
behold, how the children of — 2Ch 20:10
M. reward us
Jews that had married wives — Ne 13:23
of *M.*
M. is my washpot — Ps 60:8; 108:9
M. is confederate against thee — Ps 83:6
they shall lay their hand upon — Isa 11:14
M.
the burden of *M.* Ar of *M.* — Isa 15:1;
laid waste 15:13; Jer 48:1; — Eze 25:8;
— Am 2:2
my heart shall cry out for *M.* — Isa 15:5
his fugitives
we have heard the pride of *M.* — Isa 16:6;
— Jer 48:29
my bowels shall sound like an — Isa 16:11
harp for *M.*
and the glory of *M.* shall be — Isa 16:14
contemned
M. shall be trodden down — Isa 25:10
under him
I will punish Egypt, Judah, — Jer 9:26
and *M.*
I made Edom an *M.* to drink — Jer 25:21
of the cup
all the Jews returned from *M.* — Jer 40:11
there shall be no more praise of — Jer 48:2
M.
give wings to *M.* that it may — Jer 48:9
flee
M. hath been at ease from his — Jer 48:11
youth
tell ye it in Arnon, that *M.* is — Jer 48:20
spoiled
M. shall wallow in his vomit, — Jer 48:26
be in derision
joy and gladness is taken — Jer 48:33
from the land of *M.*
how hath *M.* turned the back — Jer 48:39
with shame
yet will I bring again the — Jer 48:47
captivity of *M.*
but I will send a fire upon *M.* — Am 2:2
and devour
saith the Lord, Surely *M.* shall — Zep 2:9
be as Sodom

MOABITE

a *M.* not enter into — De 23:3;
congregation to tenth — Ne 13:1
Ithmah the *M.* a valiant man — 1Ch 11:46

MOABITES

the same is the father of the — Ge 19:37
M.
the Lord said, Distress not the — De 2:9
M.
the Lord hath delivered the *M.* — J'g 3:28
to you
so the *M.* became David's — 2Sa 8:2;
servants, and brought gifts — 1Ch 18:2
Solomon loved women of the — 1Ki 11:1
M.
they worshipped Chemosh — 1Ki 11:33
god of the *M.*
he will deliver the *M.* into — 2Ki 3:18
your hand
the Israelites rose up and — 2Ki 3:24
smote the *M.*
the bands of the *M.* invaded — 2Ki 13:20
the land
the Lord sent against him — 2Ki 24:2
bands of the *M.*
according to the abominations — Ezr 9:1
of the *M.*

MOABITESS

and Ruth the *M.* her daughter — Ru 1:22
And Ruth the *M.* said unto — Ru 2:2
Naomi
Ruth the *M.* said, He said unto — Ru 2:21
me
must buy it also of Ruth the *M.* — Ru 4:5
Moreover Ruth the *M.* the wife — Ru 4:10
of
the son of Shimrith a *M.* — 2Ch 24:26

MOABITISH

It is the *M.* damsel that came — Ru 2:6
back

MOADIAH

Zichri; of Miniamin, of *M.* — Ne 12:17

MOAN

in my complaint and just *m.* — Ps 55:2
(A)(E)
m. when the end comes (B) — Pr 5:11
m. like doves (A)(B)(E)(R) — Isa 59:11

MOANING

I was *m.* (B)(R) — Ps 77:3
multiplied *m.* and mourning (B) — La 2:5
m. like doves (A)(B)(R) — Na 2:7
be weeping and *m.* (B) — Joh 16:20
m. together in pains (A) — Ro 8:22

MOB

gathered a *m.* (A)(B) — Ac 17:5
no *m.* or disturbance (R) — Ac 24:18

MOBBED

m. Jason's house (N) — Ac 17:5
riots, mobbings, *m.* — 2Co 6:5
(A)(B)(P)(R)

MOBBINGS

riots, *m.*, mobbed — 2Co 6:5
A)(B)(P)(R)

MOBS

without *m.* or riots (B) — Ac 24:18

MOCK

in an Hebrew unto us to *m.* — Ge 39:14
us
unto us, came in unto me to — Ge 39:17
m. me
sent to *m.* living God (R) — 2Ki 19:4
mocketh another, do ye so *m.* — Job 13:9
him
after that I have spoken, *m.* on — Job 21:3
go on mocking (B) — Job 21:3
I will *m.* when your fear — Pr 1:26
cometh
I will deride when terror (B) — Pr 1:26
Fools make a *m.* at sin: but — Pr 14:9
into their hand, and they *m.* — Jer 38:19
me
they abuse me (B)(R) — Jer 38:19
her, and did *m.* at her sabbaths — La 1:7

mocked at her destruction — La 1:7
(A)(B)
mocking at her downfall (R) — La 1:7
be far from thee shall *m.* thee — Eze 22:5
deliver him to the Gentiles to — M't 20:19
m.
to be mocked — M't 20:19
(A)(B)(N)(R)
to ridicule (P) — M't 20:19
they shall *m.* him, and shall — M'k 10:34
scourge
all that behold it begin to *m.* — Lu 14:29
him
to say in ridicule (B) — Lu 14:29
onlookers will laugh at him — Lu 14:29
(N)
began to jeer at him (P) — Lu 14:29
making *m.* of his death (N) — Heb 6:6

MOCKED

one that *m.* unto his sons in — Ge 19:14
law
as if he were joking (A) — Ge 19:14
as one who jested (B) — Ge 19:14
to be jesting (R) — Ge 19:14
the ass, Because thou hast *m.* — Nu 22:29
me
ridiculed and provoked me — Nu 22:29
(A)
made me look ridiculous (B) — Nu 22:29
you have made sport of me — Nu 22:29
(R)
hast *m.* me, and told me — J'g 16:10;
lies — 16:13
you have deceived me (B) — J'g 16:10
thou hast *m.* me these three — J'g 16:15
times
pass at noon, that Elijah *m.* — 1Ki 18:27
them
Elijah began to taunt them — 1Ki 18:27
(B)
children out of the city, and — 2Ki 2:23
m. him
poked fun at him (B) — 2Ki 2:23
jeered at him (R) — 2Ki 2:23
m. and insulted (A)(R) — 2Ki 19:22;
— Isa 37:23
them to scorn, and *m.* them — 2Ch 30:10
But they *m.* the messengers — 2Ch 36:16
of God
great indignation, and *m.* the — Ne 4:1
Jews
I am as one *m.* of his — Job 12:4
neighbour
I am a laughingstock — Job 12:4
(A)(B)(N)(R)
they impiously *m.* (R) — Ps 35:16
m. and reviled (A)(R) — Isa 37:23; 37:24
that he was *m.* of the wise — M't 2:16
men
misled by the wise men (A) — M't 2:16
outwitted by the wise men (B) — M't 2:16
the astrologers and tricked — M't 2:16
him (N)
had been fooled by the wise — M't 2:16
men (P)
the knee before him, and *m.* — M't 27:29
him
made sport of him (A) — M't 27:29
they ridiculed him (B) — M't 27:29
they jeered at him (N)(P) — M't 27:29
after that they had *m.* him — M't 27:31
And when they had *m.* him — M'k 15:20
shall be *m.* and spitefully — Lu 18:32
entreated
made sport of, scoffed, — Lu 18:32
jeered at, insulted and spit
upon (A)
ridiculed, insulted, and spat — Lu 18:32
upon (B)
jeered at and insulted (P) — Lu 18:32
and the men that held Jesus *m.* — Lu 22:63
him
treated him with contempt, — Lu 22:63
scoffed at, ridiculed, and beat
him (A)
made sport of him (B) — Lu 22:63
made a great game of — Lu 22:63
knocking him about (P)
war set him at nought, and *m.* — Lu 23:11
him
treated him with contempt, — Lu 23:11
scoffed and ridiculed him (A)
made light of him and — Lu 23:11
mockingly put a bright robe on
him (B)
treated him with contempt, — Lu 23:11
ridicule (N)

scoffing and jeering at Jesus Lu 23:11
(P)
the soldiers also m. him Lu 23:36
coming
they m. him (B) Lu 23:39
resurrection of the dead, some Ac 17:32
m.
some scoffed (A)(B)(N) Ac 17:32
some of them laughed Ac 17:32
outright (P)
Be not deceived; God is not m. Ga 6:7
God is not to be fooled (N) Ga 6:7
you cannot make a fool of God Ga 6:7
(P)

MOCKER

Wine is m., strong drink is Pr 20:1
wine is a scorner (B) Pr 20:1

MOCKERS

Are there not m. with me? and Job 17:2
With hypocritical m. in feasts Ps 35:16
profane m. (A)(B)(E) Ps 35:16
therefore be ye not m. lest Isa 28:22
do not be scoffers (A)(E) Isa 28:22
scoff no more (B)(R) Isa 28:22
sat not in the assembly of the Jer 15:17
m.
assembly of those who make Jer 15:17
merry (A)(E)
in the assembly of Jer 15:17
merrymakers (B)(R)
there should be m. in the last Jude 18
time
there will be scoffers Jude 18
(A)(B)(R)
who pour scorn on religion Jude 18
(N)

MOCKERY

called to him in m. (P) M't 27:39
hope is no m. (N) Ro 5:5

MOCKEST

when thou m. shall no man Job 11:3
make

MOCKETH

or as one man m. another, do Job 13:9
ye so
one deceives a man Job 13:9
(A)(B)(E)(R)
He m. at fear, and is not Job 39:22
affrighted
He laughs at terror (B)(R) Job 39:22
Whoso m. the poor reproacheth Pr 17:5
The eye that m. at his father Pr 30:17
in derision daily, every one m. Jer 20:7
me
everyone ridicules me (B) Jer 20:7

MOCKING

she had born unto Abraham, Ge 21:9
m.
son of Hagar teasing (B) Ge 21:9
playing with her son Isaac (R) Ge 21:9
heathen, and a m. to all Eze 22:4
countries
Likewise also the chief M't 27:41
priests m.
made sport of him (A) M't 27:41
elders twitted him (B) M't 27:41
jeering at him (P) M't 27:41
Likewise also the chief M'k 15:31
priests m.
Others m. said, These men Ac 2:13
are full
made a joke of it (A) Ac 2:13
others said sneeringly (B) Ac 2:13
others said contemptuously Ac 2:13
(N)
others laughed mockingly (P) Ac 2:13

MOCKINGS

trial of cruel m. and Heb 11:36
scourgings

MOCKS

m. at innocent (B)(R) Job 9:23

MODERATELY

given you the former rain m. Joe 2:23

MODERATION

Let your m. be known unto all Ph'p 4:5
known for your unselfishness, Ph'p 4:5
considerateness, forbearing
spirit (A)
known by your Ph'p 4:5
considerateness (B)
your forbearance be known Ph'p 4:5
(E)(R)
Let your magnanimity be Ph'p 4:5
known (N)
have a reputation for Ph'p 4:5
gentleness (P)

MODEST

adorn themselves in m. apparel 1Ti 2:9
observe pure and m. way (A) 1Pe 3:2

MODESTLY

adorn themselves m. 1Ti 2:9
(A)(B)(N)(R)

MODESTY

with m., pious care (A) Heb 12:28

MODIFIED

cannot be m. (P) Ga 3:16

MOIST

nor eat m. grapes, or dried Nu 6:3
eat fresh or dried grapes Nu 6:3
(A)(B)(E)(R)

MOISTEN

to m. with the fine flour (S) Eze 46:14

MOISTENED

his bones are m. with Job 21:24
marrow
marrow of bones still fresh Job 21:24
(B)

MOISTURE

my m. is turned into the Ps 32:4
drought of
my marrow dried up as summer Ps 32:4
(B)
my strength is dried up as by Ps 32:4
(R)
it withered because it lacked Lu 8:6
m.

MOLADAH

Amam, and Shema, and M. Jos 15:26
Beer-sheba, and Sheba, and Jos 19:2
M.
they dwelt at Beer-sheba, and 1Ch 4:28
M.
And at Jeshua, and at M. and Ne 11:26

MOLDED

m. it into a calf (B) Ex 32:4
to be m. into image of (A) Ro 8:29

MOLDING

a golden m. (A)(B)(R) Ex 25:25
just below the m. (B)(R) Ex 30:4
ornamental m. (A) Jer 52:21

MOLE

lizard, and the snail, and the Le 11:30
m.

MOLECH

seed pass through the fire to Le 18:21
M.
that giveth any of his seed unto Le 20:2
M.
he hath given of his seed unto Le 20:3
M.
when he giveth of his seed unto Le 20:4
M.
to commit whoredom with M. Le 20:5
is before Jerusalem, and for 1Ki 11:7
M.
to pass through the fire to 2Ki 23:10;
M. Jer 32:35

MOLES

worship, to the m. and to the Isa 2:20
bats

MOLEST

insult, abuse, m. (A)(R) Ac 14:5

MOLID

and she bare him Ahban, and 1Ch 2:29
M.

MOLLIFIED

up, neither m. with ointment Isa 1:6
softened with oil (A)(B)(R) Isa 1:6

MOLOCH

borne the tabernacle of your Am 5:26
M.
ye took up the tabernacle of Ac 7:43
M.

MOLTEN

after he had made them a m. Ex 32:4
calf
molded it into a calf (B) Ex 32:4
they have made them a m. calf Ex 32:8
Thou shalt make thee no m. Ex 34:17
gods
nor make to yourselves m. Le 19:4
gods: I
and destroy all their m. Nu 33:52
images
they have made them a m. De 9:12
image
God, and had made you a m. De 9:16
calf
maketh any graven or m. De 27:15
image, an
make a m. image (B) De 27:15
a graven image and a m. J'g 17:3;
image 17:4; 18:14
the teraphim, and the m. J'g 18:17;
image 18:18
made two chapiters of m. 1Ki 7:16
brass
he made a m. sea, ten cubits 1Ki 7:23;
from 2Ch 4:2
the laver were undersetters 1Ki 7:30
m. at
and their spokes, were all m. 1Ki 7:33
other gods, and m. images 1Ki 14:9
made also m. images for 2Ch 28:2
Baalim
carved images, and the m. 2Ch 34:3;
images 34:4
they had made them a m. calf Ne 9:18
and brass is m. out of the Job 28:2
stone
strong, and as a m. looking Job 37:18
glass
and worshipped the m. image Ps 106:19
ornament of thy m. images of Isa 30:22
gold
m. images are wind and Isa 41:29
confusion
say to the m. images, Ye are Isa 42:17
our
god, or m. a graven image Isa 44:10
that is
my m. image, hath Isa 48:5
commanded
for his m. image is Jer 10:14;
falsehood, and 51:17
the filthiness of it may be m. Eze 24:11
in it
them m. images of their silver Ho 13:2
mountains shall be m. under Mic 1:4
him
(A)(B)(R)
the mountains shall melt Mic 1:4
mountains shall be melted Mic 1:4
under him (E)
graven image and the m. image Na 1:14
the m. image, and a teacher Hab 2:18
of lies

MOMENT

up into the midst of thee in a Ex 33:5
m.
that I may consume them in a Nu 16:21
m.

I may consume them as in *Nu 16:45* a *m*.
now for a *m*. grace hath been *Ezr 9:8* (S)
morning, and try him every *m*. *Job 7:18*
joy of the hypocrite but for a *Job 20:5* *m*.
and in a *m*. go down to the *Job 21:13* grave
In a *m*. shall they die, and *Job 34:20*
For his anger endureth but a *m*. *Ps 30:5*
brought into desolation, as in *Ps 73:19* a *m*.
but a lying tongue is but for *Pr 12:19* a *m*.
spoken at right *m*. (B) *Pr 25:11*
thyself as it were for a little *Isa 26:20* *m*.
I will water it every *m*.: lest *Isa 27:3* any
things shall come to thee in a *Isa 47:9* *m*. in
a small *m*. have I forsaken *Isa 54:7* thee
I hid my face from thee for a *Isa 54:8* *m*.
spoiled, and my curtains in a *Jer 4:20* *m*.
that was overthrown as in a *m*. *La 4:6*
and shall tremble at every *m*. *Eze 26:16*
shall tremble at every *m*. and *Eze 32:10* they
from that *m*. *M't 15:28* (A)(B)(N)(P)
from that exact *m*. (B)(N)(P) *M't 17:18*
kingdoms of the world in a *m*. *Lu 4:5*
In a *m*. in the twinkling of *1Co 15:52* an eye
affliction, which is but for a *2Co 4:17* *m*.

MONARCH

m. of earth (P) *Ro 8:38*

MONEY

or bought with *m*. of any *Ge 17:12* stranger
he that is bought with thy *m*. *Ge 17:13* must
all that were bought with his *Ge 17:23* *m*.
and bought with *m*. of the *Ge 17:27* stranger
for as much *m*. as it is worth he *Ge 23:9*
I will give thee *m*. for the field *Ge 23:13*
hath quite devoured also our *Ge 31:15* *m*.
enjoyed profits of our dowry *Ge 31:15* (B)
for an hundred pieces of *m*. *Ge 33:19*
to restore every man's *m*. into *Ge 42:25*
he espied his *m*.: for, behold, *Ge 42:27* it was
My *m*. is restored; and, lo, it *Ge 42:28*
man's bundle of *m*. was in his *Ge 42:35* sack
their father saw the bundles *Ge 42:35* of *m*.
And take double *m*. in your *Ge 43:12* hand
have double payments with *Ge 43:12* you (B)
the *m*. that was brought again *Ge 43:12*
they took double *m*. in their *Ge 43:15* hand
m. that was returned in our *Ge 43:18* sacks
m. was in the mouth of his *Ge 43:21* sack
of his sack, our *m*. in full *Ge 43:21* weight
other *m*. have we brought *Ge 43:22* down in
tell who put our *m*. in our *Ge 43:22* sacks
in your sacks: I had your *m*. *Ge 43:23*
every man's *m*. in his sack's *Ge 44:1* mouth
payment in mouth of sack (B) *Ge 44:1*
of the youngest, and his corn *Ge 44:2* *m*.
Behold, the *m*. which we found *Ge 44:8*
Joseph gathered up all the *m*. *Ge 47:14*
Joseph brought *m*. into *Ge 47:14* Pharaoh's
when *m*. failed in the land of *Ge 47:15* Egypt

in thy presence? for the *m*. *Ge 47:15* faileth
give you for your cattle, if *m*. *Ge 47:16* fail
my lord, how that our *m*. is *Ge 47:18* spent
man's servant that is bought *Ex 12:44* for *m*.
shall she go out free without *Ex 21:11* *m*.
free without reimbursement *Ex 21:11* (B)
not be punished: for he is his *Ex 21:21* *m*.
he is his property (A)(B) *Ex 21:21*
If there be laid on him a sum *Ex 21:30* of *m*.
give *m*. unto the owner of *Ex 21:34* them
the live ox, and divide the *m*. *Ex 21:35* of it
deliver unto his neighbour *m*. *Ex 22:7*
pay *m*. according to the *Ex 22:17* dowry
If thou lend *m*. to any of my *Ex 22:25* people
thou shalt take the atonement *Ex 30:16* *m*.
priest buy any soul with his *m*. *Le 22:11*
not give him thy *m*. upon *Le 25:37* usury
out of the *m*. that he was *Le 25:51* bought
fifth part of the *m*. of thy *Le 27:15;* estimation *27:19*
priest shall reckon unto him *Le 27:18* the *m*.
thou shalt give the *m*. *Nu 3:48* wherewith
Moses took the redemption *m*. *Nu 3:49*
silver for the redemption (B) *Nu 3:49*
children of Israel took he the *Nu 3:50*
And Moses gave the *m*. of them *Nu 3:51*
for the *m*. of five shekels, *Nu 18:16* after the
Ye shall buy meat of them for *De 2:6* *m*.
shall also buy water of them for *De 2:6* *m*.
Thou shalt sell me meat for *m*. *De 2:28*
give me water for *m*. that I *De 2:28* may
Then shalt thou turn it into *m*. *De 14:25*
and bind up the *m*. in thine *De 14:25* hand
And thou shalt bestow that *De 14:26* *m*. for
thou shalt not sell her at all *De 21:14* for *m*.
sell for *m*. enslave *De 21:14* (B)(E)(R)
usury of *m*. usury of victuals *De 23:19*
Megiddo; they took no gain of *J'g 5:19* *m*.
her, and brought *m*. in their *J'g 16:18* hand
he restored the *m*. unto his *J'g 17:4* mother
turned aside for *m*. (B)(S) *1Sa 8:3*
will give thee the worth of it *1Ki 21:2* in *m*.
reimburse you for it with cash *1Ki 21:2* (B)
him, Give me thy vineyard for *1Ki 21:6* *m*.
he refused to give thee for *m*. *1Ki 21:15*
Is it a time to receive *m*. and *2Ki 5:26*
All the *m*. of the dedicated *2Ki 12:4* thing
the *m*. of every one that *2Ki 12:4* passeth
the *m*. that ever man is set at *2Ki 12:4*
the *m*. that cometh into any *2Ki 12:4* man's
no more *m*. of your *2Ki 12:7* acquaintance
receive no more *m*. of the *2Ki 12:8* people
the *m*. that was brought into *2Ki 12:9*
there was much *m*. in the *2Ki 12:10* chest
the *m*. that was found in the *2Ki 12:10* house
And they gave the *m*. being *2Ki 12:11* told
m. that was brought into the *2Ki 12:13* house
the *m*. to be bestowed on *2Ki 12:15* workmen

The trespass *m*. and sin *m*. *2Ki 12:16* was not
Menahem exacted the *m*. of *2Ki 15:20* Israel
made with them of the *m*. *2Ki 22:7*
Thy servants have gathered *2Ki 22:9* the *m*.
but he taxed the land to give *2Ki 23:35* the *m*.
of all Israel *m*. to repair the *2Ch 24:5* house
they saw that there was *2Ch 24:11* much *m*.
and gathered *m*. in *2Ch 24:11* abundance
brought the rest of the *m*. *2Ch 24:14* before
delivered the *m*. that was *2Ch 34:9* brought
when they brought out the *2Ch 34:14* *m*. that
they have gathered together *2Ch 34:17* the *m*.
They gave *m*. also unto the *Ezr 3:7* masons
mayest buy speedily with this *Ezr 7:17* *m*.
have borrowed *m*. for the king's *Ne 5:4*
might exact of them *m*. and *Ne 5:10* corn
also the hundredth part of the *Ne 5:11* *m*.
the *m*. that Haman had *Es 4:7* promised
eaten the fruits thereof *Job 31:39* without *m*.
man also gave him a piece of *Job 42:11* *m*.
putteth not out his *m*. to usury *Ps 15:5*
I am a marvel to *m*. (B) *Ps 71:7;* *Ac 13:41*
hath taken a bag of *m*. with *Pr 7:20* him
is a defence, and *m*. is a *Ec 7:12* defence
merry: but *m*. answereth all *Ec 10:19* things
bought me no sweet cane *Isa 43:24* with *m*.
shall be redeemed without *m*. *Isa 52:3*
the waters, and he that hath *Isa 55:1* no *m*.
milk without *m*. and without *Isa 55:1* prices
do ye spend *m*. for that which *Isa 55:2* is not
weighed him the *m*. even *Jer 32:9* seventeen
weighed him the *m*. in the *Jer 32:10* balances
Buy thee the field for *m*. and *Jer 32:25* take
Men shall buy fields for *m*. *Jer 32:44*
We have drunken our water for *La 5:4* *m*.
the prophets thereof divine *Mic 3:11* for *m*.
cannot serve God and *m*. (S) *M't 6:24;* *Lu 16:13*
that received tribute *m*. came *M't 17:24* to
thou shalt find a piece of *m*. *M't 17:27*
you will find a shekel *M't 17:27* (A)(E)(R)
you will find a coin (B)(P) *M't 17:27*
you will find a silver coin *M't 17:27* (N)
Shew me the tribute *m*. And *M't 22:19*
show me the legal coin (B) *M't 22:19*
in the earth, and hid his *M't 25:18* lord's *m*.
have put my *m*. to the *M't 25:27* exchangers
they gave large *m*. unto the *M't 28:12* soldiers
So they took the *m*. and did *M't 28:15* as they
no bread, no *m*. in their purse *M'k 6:8*
the people cast *m*. into the *M'k 12:41* treasury
glad, and promised to give *M'k 14:11* him *m*.
nor scrip, neither bread, neither *Lu 9:3* *m*.
to use *m*. (P)(S) *Lu 16:9*
faithful in *m*. *Lu 16:11*
give *m*. away to poor (P) *Lu 18:22*
to whom he had given the *m*. *Lu 19:15*
not thou my *m*. into the *Lu 19:23* bank

glad, and covenanted to give him m.   *Lu 22:5*

and the changers of m. sitting   *Joh 2:14*

poured out the changers' m.   *Joh 2:15*

had a m. box (A)(R)   *Joh 13:29*

land, sold it, and brought the m.   *Ac 4:37*

Abraham bought for a sum of m. of   *Ac 7:16*

was given, he offered them m.   *Ac 8:18*

Thy m. perish with thee, because   *Ac 8:20*

of God may be purchased with m.   *Ac 8:20*

hoped also that m. should have   *Ac 24:26*

under some pretext after m. (B)   *1Th 2:5*

not a lover of m. (A)(B)(E)(N)(P)(R)   *1Ti 3:3*

the love of m. is the root of all evil   *1Ti 6:10*

no m.-grabber (N)   *Tit 1:7*

free from love of m. (A)(B)(E)(P)(R)   *Heb 13:5*

do not live for m. (N)   *Heb 13:5*

not with m. payment (P)   *1Pe 1:18*

MONEYCHANGERS

and overthrew the tables of the m.   *M't 21:12; M'k 11:15*

MONSTER

a sea m. (A)(E)(R)(S)   *Job 7:12*

slay the m. (A)(E)   *Isa 27:1*

the night m. (A)(B)(E)   *Isa 34:14*

pierce the m. (E)   *Isa 51:9*

like a m. (S)   *Jer 51:34; Eze 29:3*

the great m. (A)(E)   *Eze 29:3*

like a m. in the seas (E)(S)   *Eze 32:2*

the sea m. (A)(B)   *M't 12:40*

m. of trickery and evil (P)   *Ac 13:10*

MONSTERS

created great sea m. (A)(B)(E)(R)(S)   *Ge 1:21*

sea m. (A)(B)(E)(R)   *Ps 148:7*

the sea m. draw out the breast   *La 4:3*

jackals draw out the breast (A)(B)(E)(R)   *La 4:3*

MONSTROUS

utter m. boasts (B)   *Da 11:36*

MONTH

Jacob abode with Laban space of a m.   *Ge 29:14*

this day came ye out in the m. Abib   *Ex 13:4*

thou shalt keep the feast in the m. Abib   *Ex 23:15*

for in the m. Abib thou camest out from Egypt   *Ex 34:18; De 16:1; Jos 5:10*

if it be from a m. old to five years   *Le 27:6*

of Levi, every male from a m. old   *Nu 3:15; 3:22, 28, 34, 39-40, 43; 26:62*

or a m. or year that the cloud tarried   *Nu 9:22*

ye shall eat flesh, even a whole m.   *Nu 11:20; 11:21*

from a m. old shalt thou redeem   *Nu 18:16*

the burnt offering of every m.   *Nu 28:14; 29:6*

remain in thine house a full m.   *De 21:13*

each man his m. made provision   *1Ki 4:7; 4:27*

a m. they were in Lebanon, two at home   *1Ki 5:14*

in the m. Zif; in the m. Bul   *1Ki 6:37; 6:38*

feast in m. Ethanim; in m. Chisleu   *1Ki 8:2; Ne 1:1*

in m. Nisan   *Ne 2:1; Es 3:7*

m. Elul   *Es 6:15*

Jews gathered in m. Adar   *Es 9:15; 9:17, 19, 21*

m. which was turned from sorrow to joy   *Es 9:22*

in her m. they shall find her   *Jer 2:24*

now shall a m. devour them with portions   *Ho 5:7*

three shepherds I cut off in one m.   *Zec 11:8*

which were prepared for a day and a m.   *Re 9:15*

the tree of life yielded her fruit every m.   *Re 22:2*

SECOND MONTH

in second m. the fountains were broken up   *Ge 7:11*

and in the second m. was the earth dried   *Ge 8:14*

came to the wilderness of Sin in second m.   *Ex 16:1*

in second m. take sum of the congregation   *Nu 1:1*

on second m. shall keep passover   *Nu 9:11; 2Ch 30:2*

on second m. cloud was taken up from tabernacle   *Nu 10:11*

second m. Solomon began to build   *1Ki 6:1; 2Ch 3:2*

over the course of second m. was Dodai   *1Ch 27:4*

in second m. began Zerubbabel to appoint   *Ezr 3:8*

THIRD MONTH

in third m. came into wilderness of Sinai   *Ex 19:1*

third captain for third m. was Benaiah   *1Ch 27:5*

gathered at Jerusalem in the third m.   *2Ch 15:10*

in third m. they began to lay the foundation   *2Ch 31:7*

the king's scribes were called in third m.   *Es 8:9*

in third m. word of Lord came to Ezekiel   *Eze 31:1*

FOURTH MONTH

in the fourth m. the famine prevailed   *2Ki 25:3*

fourth captain for fourth m. was Asahel   *1Ch 27:7*

in the fourth m. the city was broken up   *Jer 39:2*

in fourth m. the famine was sore in the city   *Jer 52:6*

in fourth m. Ezekiel saw visions of God   *Eze 1:1*

the fast of the fourth m. shall be joy   *Zec 8:19*

SIXTH MONTH

the sixth captain for sixth m. was Ira   *1Ch 27:9*

in sixth m. the elders of Judah sat before me   *Eze 8:1*

in sixth m. word of Lord came by Haggai   *Hag 1:1*

in sixth m. they did work in house of the Lord   *Hag 1:15*

in sixth m. the angel Gabriel was sent   *Lu 1:26*

this is sixth m. with her that was called barren   *Lu 1:36*

EIGHTH MONTH

in eighth m. came the word to Zechariah   *Zec 1:1*

NINTH MONTH

in the ninth m. the people sat trembling   *Ezr 10:9*

in the ninth m. they proclaimed a fast   *Jer 36:9*

the king sat in winter house in the ninth m.   *Jer 36:22*

in ninth m. came word of Lord by Haggai   *Hag 2:10*

even from the ninth m. consider it   *Hag 2:18*

the word came to Zechariah in ninth m.   *Zec 7:1*

TENTH MONTH

the waters decreased until the tenth m.   *Ge 8:5*

and sat down in tenth m. to examine   *Ezr 10:16*

Esther was taken to the king in tenth m.   *Es 2:16*

tenth m. came Nebuchadazzar against Jerusalem   *Jer 39:1; 52:4*

in tenth m. came word of Lord to me   *Eze 24:1; 29:1*

in the tenth m. one that had escaped told me   *Eze 33:21*

ELEVENTH MONTH

in the eleventh m. Moses spake to Israel   *De 1:3*

in eleventh m. came the word to Zechariah   *Zec 1:7*

TWELFTH MONTH

cast lots before Haman to the twelfth m.   *Es 3:7*

on the thirteenth day of twelfth m.   *Es 3:13; 8:12; 9:1*

in twelfth m. Evil-merodach lifted head   *Jer 52:31*

in twelfth m. the word of Lord came to me   *Eze 32:1*

THIS MONTH

this m. shall be the beginning of months   *Ex 12:2*

this m. they shall take every man a lamb   *Ex 12:3*

keep this service in this m.   *Ex 13:5; Nu 9:3; 28:17*

on tenth day of this m. an holy convocation   *Nu 29:7*

this m. Israel assembled with fasting   *Ne 9:1*

MONTHLY

let the m. prognosticators stand up   *Isa 47:13*

MONTHS

in beginnings of your m. blow trumpets   *Nu 10:10*

in beginnings of m. offer a burnt offering   *Nu 28:11*

this is the burnt offering through the m.   *Nu 28:14*

let me alone two m. that I may bewail   *J'g 11:37*

at the end of two m. she returned to Jephthah   *J'g 11:39*

his concubine was with her father four m.   *J'g 19:2*

and abode in the rock Rimmon four m.   *J'g 20:47*

ark was in country of Philistines seven m.   *1Sa 6:1*

David was with Philistines a vear and four m.   *1Sa 27:7*

David reigned in Hebon seven years and six m.   *2Sa 2:11; 5:5; 1Ch 3:4*

the ark was with Obed-edom three m.   *2Sa 6:11*

they came to Jerusalem at the end of nine m.   *2Sa 24:8*

and two m. they were at home   *1Ki 5:14*

for six m. did Joab remain in Edom   *1Ki 11:16*

Zachariah reign over Israel six m.   *2Ki 15:8*

month by month thro' the m. of the year   *1Ch 27:1*

twelve m. purified, six m. with oil of myrrh, six m. with   *Es 2:12*

let it not come into the number of the m.   *Job 3:6*

so am I made to possess m. of vanity   *Job 7:3*

m. of misery (B)(E)   *Job 7:3*

the number of his m. are with thee   *Job 14:5*

when the number of his m. is cut off   *Job 21:21*

O that I were as in m. past, as in the days   *Job 29:2*

canst thou number the m. that they fulfil   *Job 39:2*

seven m. Israel shall be burying of Gog   *Eze 39:12*

after the end of seven m. shall they search   *Eze 39:14*

shall bring new fruit according to his m.   *Eze 47:12*

at the end of twelve *m.*   *Da 4:29*
Nebuchadnezzar walked
Elizabeth conceived and hid   *Lu 1:24*
herself five *m.*
when heaven was shut three   *Lu 4:25;*
years and six *m.*   *Jas 5:17*
are yet four *m.* then cometh   *Joh 4:35*
harvest
Paul continued there a year   *Ac 18:11*
and six *m.*
ye observe days, and *m.* and   *Ga 4:10*
times
they shall be tormented five *m.*   *Re 9:5;*
                     9:10
holy city they tread under foot *Re 11:2*
forty-two *m.*
power was given him to   *Re 13:5*
continue forty-two *m.*

MONUMENTS

the graves, and lodge in the *m.*   *Isa 65:4*

MOOD

Nabal was in a happy *m.* (B) *1Sa 25:36*
people in ugly *m.* (B)   *1Sa 30:6*

MOON

sun, the *m.* and the eleven   *Ge 37:9*
stars
the sun, and the *m.* and the   *De 4:19*
stars
either the sun, or *m.* or any of *De 17:3*
things put forth by the *m.*   *De 33:14*
thou, *M.* in the valley of   *Jos 10:12*
Ajalon
sun stood still, and the *m.*   *Jos 10:13*
stayed
Behold, to-morrow is the r   *1Sa 20:5*
m.
To-morrow is the new *m.*   *1Sa 20:18*
and when the new *m.* was   *1Sa 20:24*
come
it is neither new *m.* nor   *2Ki 4:23*
sabbath
to the sun, and to the *m.* and to *2Ki 23:5*
sun, *m.*, and constellations   *2Ki 23:5*
(A)(R)
even to the *m.* and it shineth   *Job 25:5*
not
or the *m.* walking in   *Job 31:26*
brightness
m. and the stars, which thou hast *Ps 8:3*
as long as the sun and *m.*   *Ps 72:5*
endure
of peace so long as the *m.*   *Ps 72:7*
endureth
Blow up the trumpet in the new *Ps 81:3*
m.
be established for ever as the *Ps 89:37*
m.
He appointed the *m.* for   *Ps 104:19*
seasons
thee by day, nor the *m.* by   *Ps 121:6*
night
The *m.* and stars to rule by   *Ps 136:9*
night
Praise ye him, sun and *m.*   *Ps 148:3*
m. or the stars, be not   *Ec 12:2*
darkened
fair as the *m.* clear as the sun   *Ca 6:10*
and their round tires like the   *Isa 3:18*
m.
the *m.* shall not cause her   *Isa 13:10*
light to
Then the *m.* shall be   *Isa 24:23*
confounded
light of the *m.* shall be as the *Isa 30:26*
light
shall the *m.* give light unto   *Isa 60:19*
thee
neither shall thy *m.* withdraw *Isa 60:20*
that from one new *m.* to   *Isa 66:23*
another
before the sun, and the *m.* and *Jer 8:2*
ordinances of the *m.* and of   *Jer 31:35*
the stars
and the *m.* shall not give her   *Eze 32:7*
light
in the day of the new *m.* it   *Eze 46:1;*
shall   *46:6*
the sun and the *m.* shall be   *Joe 2:10*
dark
darkness, and the *m.* into   *Joe 2:31*
blood
sun and the *m.* shall be   *Joe 3:15*
darkened
When will the new *m.* be gone   *Am 8:5*

The sun and *m.* stood still in *Hab 3:11*
their
and the *m.* shall not give   *M't 24:29;*
her light   *M'k 13:24*
build *m.* (B)   *Lu 11:47*
be signs in the sun, and in the *Lu 21:25*
m.
darkness, and the *m.* into   *Ac 2:20*
blood
sun, and another glory of the *1Co 15:41*
m.
or of the new *m.* or of the   *Col 2:16*
sabbath
hair, and the *m.* became as   *Re 6:12*
blood
and the third part of the *m.*   *Re 8:12*
the sun, and the *m.* under her   *Re 12:1*
feet
need of the sun, neither of the *Re 21:23*
m.

MOONS

the new *m.* and on the set   *1Ch 23:31*
feasts
on the new *m.* and on the   *2Ch 2:4;*
solemn   *8:13*
the new *m.* and for the set   *2Ch 31:3*
feasts
both of the new *m.* and of all   *Ezr 3:5*
the set
of the sabbaths, of the new *m.*   *Ne 10:33*
the new *m.* and sabbaths, the   *Isa 1:13*
new *m.* and your appointed   *Isa 1:14*
feasts
in the feasts, and in the new   *Eze 45:17*
m.
in the sabbaths and in the new   *Eze 46:3*
m.
her feast days, her new *m.* and *Ho 2:11*

MOORINGS

slip from your own *m.* (R)   *2Pe 3:17*

MORAL

purge of *m.* foulness (B)   *Eze 22:15*
lawlessness, *m.* anarchy (N)   *Ro 6:19*
he is a *m.* twist (P)   *Tit 3:11*
character or *m.* disposition   *Heb 13:5*
(A)

MORALS

discourse of *m.* (P)   *Ac 24:25*
corrupt good *m.* (S)   *1Co 15:33*

MORASTHITE

Micah the *M.* prophesied in   *Jer 26:18*
Lord that came to Micah the   *Mic 1:1*
M.

MORBID

m. fondness for controversy   *1Ti 6:4*
(A)(B)(P)(R)
m. cravings (P)   *2Ti 3:6*

MORBIDLY

m. keen on verbal questions   *1Ti 6:4*
(N)

MORDECAI

Nehemiah, Seraiah, Reelaiah,   *Ezr 2:2*
M.
Nahamani, *M.*, Bilshan,   *Ne 7:7*
Mispereth
a certain Jew, whose name was   *Es 2:5*
M.
whom *M.*, took for his own   *Es 2:7*
M. had charged her that she   *Es 2:10*
should
M. walked every day before the *Es 2:11*
daughter of Abihail the uncle   *Es 2:15*
of *M.*
then *M.* sat in the king's gate   *Es 2:19;*
                   2:21
her people; as *M.* had charged   *Es 2:20*
her
Esther did the commandment   *Es 2:20*
of *M.*
And the thing was known to *M.* *Es 2:22*
But *M.* bowed not, nor did him   *Es 3:2*
said unto *M.*, Why transgresseth *Es 3:3*
Haman saw that *M.* bowed not   *Es 3:5*

scorn to lay hands on *M.* alone   *Es 3:6*
had shewed him the people of   *Es 3:6*
M.
Ahasuerus, even the people of   *Es 3:6*
M.
M. perceived all that was done   *Es 4:1*
M. rent his clothes, and put on   *Es 4:1*
and she sent raiment to clothe   *Es 4:4*
M.
gave him a commandment to *M.*   *Es 4:5*
Hatach went forth to *M.* unto   *Es 4:6*
M. told him of all that had   *Es 4:7*
happened
and told Esther the words of *M.* *Es 4:9*
gave him commandment unto   *Es 4:10*
M.
And they told to *M.* Esther's   *Es 4:12*
words
M. commanded to answer   *Es 4:13*
Esther
bade them return *M.* this   *Es 4:15*
answer
M. went his way, and did   *Es 4:17*
according
Haman saw *M.* in the king's   *Es 5:9*
gate
was full of indignation against   *Es 5:9*
M.
so long as I see *M.* the Jew   *Es 5:13*
sitting
that *M.* may be hanged thereon   *Es 5:14*
that *M.* had told of Bigthana   *Es 6:2*
and dignity hath been done to   *Es 6:3*
M.
the king to hang *M.* on the   *Es 6:4*
gallows
and do even so to *M.* the Jew   *Es 6:10*
arrayed *M.* and brought him on *Es 6:11*
M. came again to the king's   *Es 6:12*
gate
If *M.* be of the seed of the Jews *Es 6:13*
which Haman had made for *M.*   *Es 7:9*
that he had prepared for *M.*   *Es 7:10*
And *M.* came before the king   *Es 8:1*
from Haman, and gave it unto   *Es 8:2*
M.
Esther set *M.* over the house of   *Es 8:2*
unto Esther and to *M.* the Jew   *Es 8:7*
that *M.* commanded unto the   *Es 8:9*
Jews
M. went out from the presence   *Es 8:15*
of
the fear of *M.* fell upon them   *Es 9:3*
M. was great in the king's house *Es 9:4*
man *M.* waxed greater and   *Es 9:4*
greater
M. wrote these things, and sent *Es 9:20*
and as *M.* had written unto   *Es 9:23*
them
and *M.* the Jew, wrote with all   *Es 9:29*
M. the Jew and Esther the   *Es 9:31*
queen
declaration of the greatness of   *Es 10:2*
M.
For *M.* the Jew was next unto   *Es 10:3*
king

MORDECAI'S

the king thereof in *M.* name   *Es 2:22*
whether *M.* matters would stand *Es 3:4*

MORE

Jacob loved Rachel *m.* than   *Ge 29:30*
Leah
riches *m.* than that they might *Ge 36:7*
dwell together
Israel loved Joseph *m.* than   *Ge 37:3*
all his children
and his brethren hated him   *Ge 37:5;*
yet the *m.*   *37:8*
the children of Israel are *m.*   *Ex 1:9*
than we
the *m.* they afflicted them, the   *Ex 1:12*
m. they grew
let there *m.* work be laid upon   *Ex 5:9*
the men
Pharaoh sinned yet *m.* and   *Ex 9:34*
hardened his heart
yet will I bring one plague *m.*   *Ex 11:1*
on Pharaoh
they gathered some *m.* some   *Ex 16:17*
less
the rich shall not give *m.* nor   *Ex 30:15*
poor less
and shall add the fifth part *m.*   *Le 5:5*
thereto
priest shall shut him seven   *Le 13:5;*
days *m.*   *13:33, 54*

I will punish you seven times *Le 26:18; m.* 26:21

firstborn which are *m.* than *Nu 3:46* Levites

sent again princes *m.* *Nu 22:15* honourable than they

beyond the word of the Lord, *Nu 22:18* to do less or *m.*

I may know what the Lord *Nu 22:19* will say to me *m.*

to many thou shalt give the *Nu 26:54; m.* 33:54

the Lord make you a thousand *De 1:11* times *m.*

Lord did not set his love on *De 7:7* you, because *m.*

if thou say, nations are *m.* *De 7:17;* than I 20:1

then shalt thou add three cities *De 19:9* *m.* for these

they were *m.* which died with *Jos 10:11* hail

they corrupted themselves *m.* *J'g 2:19* than

m. than they which he slew in *J'g 16:30* his life

ye are gone away, and what *J'g 18:24* have I *m.*

Lord do so to me and *m.* also *Ru 1:17; 1Sa 14:44; 2Sa 3:35; 19:13*

thou hast shewed *m.* kindness *Ru 3:10* in the latter end

God do so to thee and *m.* also *1Sa 3:17*

what can ye have *m.* but the *1Sa 18:8* kingdom

the Lord do so and much *m.* *1Sa 20:13* to Jonathan

thy servant knew nothing *1Sa 22:15* less or *m.*

he said, Thou art *m.* *1Sa 24:17* righteous than I

so and *m.* do God to the *1Sa 25:22* enemies of David

she told him nothing less or *1Sa 25:36* *m.* until morning

so do God to Abner, and *m.* *2Sa 3:9* also

David took him *m.* concubines *2Sa 5:13* and wives

and I will yet be *m.* vile than *2Sa 6:22* thus

and what can David say *m.* *2Sa 7:20* unto thee

we have also *m.* right in *2Sa 19:43* David than ye

God do so *m.* also *1Ki 2:23; 20:10; 2Ki 6:31*

Ahab did *m.* to provoke God *1Ki 16:33* to anger

so let the gods do to me, and *1Ki 19:2* *m.* also

he said, There is not a vessel *2Ki 4:6* *m.*

m. than they that be with *2Ki 6:16;* them *2Ch 32:7*

Manasseh seduced them to do *2Ki 21:9* *m.* evil

Lord make his people so *1Ch 21:3* many *m.*

and there were *m.* chief men *1Ch 24:4* found

I will put *m.* to your yoke *2Ch 10:11*

found *m.* spoil than they *2Ch 20:25* could carry away

the Lord is able to give thee *2Ch 25:9* *m.* than this

ye intend to add *m.* to our *2Ch 28:13* sins and trespass

Ahaz did trespass yet *m.* *2Ch 28:22* against the Lord

the Levites were *m.* upright *2Ch 29:34* in heart

his servants spake *m.* against *2Ch 32:16* the Lord

but Amon trespassed *m.* *2Ch 33:23* and *m.*

whatsoever *m.* shall be needful *Ezr 7:20*

yet ye bring *m.* wrath upon *Ne 13:18* Israel

Esther obtained favour *m.* than *Es 2:17* all

delight to do honour *m.* to *Es 6:6* myself

and dig for it *m.* than bid *Job 3:21* treasures

his words *m.* than my *Job 23:12* necessary food

nor regardeth the rich *m.* *Job 34:19* than the poor

for he will not lay on man *Job 34:23* *m.* than right

saidst, My righteousness is *Job 35:2* *m.* than God's

who teacheth us *m.* than the *Job 35:11* beasts of earth

Lord blessed the latter end of *Job 42:12* Job *m.* than

m. than when their corn and *Ps 4:7* wine increased

m. to be desired are they than *Ps 19:10* gold

thy thoughts are *m.* than can be *Ps 40:5* numbered

iniquities are *m.* than hairs of *Ps 40:12* mine head

thou lovest evil *m.* than good, *Ps 52:3* and lying

that hate me are *m.* than hairs *Ps 69:4* of mine head

and I will yet praise thee *m.* *Ps 71:14* and *m.*

they have *m.* than heart could *Ps 73:7* wish

and they sinned yet *m.* against *Ps 78:17* him

gates of Zion *m.* than all *Ps 87:2* dwellings of Jacob

the Lord shall increase you *Ps 115:14* *m.* and *m.*

I have *m.* understanding than *Ps 119:99* my teachers

I understand *m.* than the *Ps 119:100* ancients

m. than they that watch for *Ps 130:6* the morning

wisdom is *m.* precious than *Pr 3:15* rubies

that shineth *m.* and *m.* to the *Pr 4:18* perfect day

there is that withholdeth *m.* *Pr 11:24* than is meet

a reproof entereth *m.* into a *Pr 17:10* wise man

there is *m.* hope of a fool *Pr 26:12;* than of him 29:20

I increased *m.* than all before *Ec 2:9* me

there is no remembrance of *Ec 2:16* wise *m.* than fool

or who can hasten hereunto *m.* *Ec 2:25* than I

the dead *m.* than the living that *Ec 4:2* are yet alive

and be *m.* ready to hear than to *Ec 5:1* give sacrifice

we will remember thy love *m.* *Ca 1:4* than wine

what is thy beloved *m.* than *Ca 5:9* another

what could been done *m.* to my *Isa 5:4* vineyard

afterward did *m.* grievously *Isa 9:1* afflict her

for I will bring *m.* upon *Isa 15:9* Dimon, lions

his visage so marred *m.* than *Isa 52:14* any man

for *m.* are the children of the *Isa 54:1* desolate than

Israel justified herself *m.* than *Jer 3:11* Judah

because they are *m.* than the *Jer 46:23* grasshoppers

changed my judgments into *Eze 5:6* wicked, *m.*

because he multiplied *m.* than *Eze 5:7* the nations

corrupted *m.* than they *Eze 16:47; 16:51-52; 23:11*

not for any wisdom that I have *Da 2:30* *m.* than

they should heat the furnace *Da 3:19* seven times *m.*

he shall continue *m.* years than *Da 11:8* the king

knowledge of God *m.* than *Ho 6:6* burnt offering

now they sin *m.* and *m.* and I *Ho 13:2* have made idols

wicked devoureth man *m.* *Hab 1:13* righteous than

what is *m.* than these cometh *M't 5:37* of evil

brethren only, what do you *m.* *M't 5:47* than others

is not the life *m.* than meat *M't 6:25; Lu 12:23*

of *m.* value than many *M't 10:31;* sparrows *Lu 12:7*

he that loveth father or *M't 10:37* mother *m.* than me

I say unto you, and *m.* than a *M't 11:9* prophet

taketh seven spirits *m.* wicked *M't 12:45* than himself

and he shall have *m.* *M't 13:12* abundance

he rejoiceth *m.* of that sheep *M't 18:13* than of 99

then take with thee one or *M't 18:16* two *m.*

they supposed they should *M't 20:10* have received *m.*

but they cried the *m.*, Have *M't 20:31;* mercy on us 27:23; *M'k 10:48; 15:14; Lu 18:39*

give me *m.* than twelve *M't 26:53* legions of angels

to you that hear shall *m.* be *M'k 4:24* given

the *m.* he charged them, so *M'k 7:36* much the *m.*

poor widow cast in *m.* than *M'k 12:43;* all *Lu 21:3*

the ointment might have been *M'k 14:5* sold for *m.*

what thou spendest *m.* I will *Lu 10:35* repay

committed much, of him they *Lu 12:48* will ask *m.*

who shall not receive *Lu 18:30* manifold *m.*

many *m.* believed, because of *Joh 4:41* his word

the Jews sought the *m.* to kill *Joh 5:18* him

will he do *m.* miracles than *Joh 7:31* these

they loved the praise of men *Joh 12:43* *m.* than

purgeth it, that it may bring *Joh 15:2* forth *m.* fruit

Simon, lovest thou me *m.* *Joh 21:15* than these

to hearken to you *m.* than to *Ac 4:19* God

believers were the *m.* added to *Ac 5:14* the Lord

but Saul increased the *m.* in *Ac 9:22* strength

the *m.* part knew not why *Ac 19:32* they came

it is *m.* blessed to give, than *Ac 20:35* to receive

there were *m.* than forty who *Ac 23:13;* conspired 23:21

believed the master *m.* than *Ac 27:11* Paul

who served the creature *m.* *Ro 1:25* than Creator

if the truth of God hath *m.* *Ro 3:7* abounded

in all these we are *m.* than *Ro 8:37* conquerors

myself servant to all, that I *1Co 9:19* might gain the *m.*

I speak with tongues *m.* than *1Co 14:18* you all

so I rejoiced the *m.;* I boast *2Co 7:7;* the *m.* 10:8

I am *m.,* in prisons *m.* *2Co 11:23* frequent, in deaths oft

the desolate hath many *m.* *Ga 4:27* children

love may abound *m.* and *m.* *Ph'p 1:9; 1Th 4:10*

if he might trust in the flesh, *Ph'p 3:4* I *m.*

in pleasing God, abound *m.* *1Th 4:1* and *m.*

lovers of pleasure *m.* than *2Ti 3:4* lovers of God

that thou wilt also do *m.* that *Ph'm 21* I say

what shall I say *m.* time *Heb 11:32* would fail

much *m.* shall not we *Heb 12:25* escape, if we turn

yet once *m.* I shake not the *Heb 12:26;* earth only 12:27

he giveth *m.* grace, wherefore *Jas 4:6* saith

we have a *m.* sure word of *2Pe 1:19* prophecy

and the last to be *m.* than the *Re 2:19* first

behold, there come two woes *Re 9:12* *m.* hereafter

ANY MORE

the dove returned not again   Ge 8:12
any m.
I will not curse the ground *any* Ge 8:21;
m.   9:11
nor shall thy name *any m.* be   Ge 17:5
called Abram
not *any m.* be called Jacob, but Ge 35:10
Israel
let not Pharaoh deal deceitfully Ex 8:29
any m.
neither shall there be *any m.*   Ex 9:29
hail
nor shall there a cry be like   Ex 11:6
it *any m.*
let neither man nor woman   Ex 36:6
make *any m.*
it shall not be redeemed *any*   Le 27:20
m.
that there be no wrath *any m.* Nu 18:5
on Israel
if we hear the voice of the   De 5:25
Lord *any m.*
neither let me see this great   De 18:16
fire *any m.*
neither had Israel manna *any* Jos 5:12
neither will I be with you *any* Jos 7:12
m.
are there *any m.* sons in my   Ru 1:11
womb
Saul shall despair to seek me   1Sa 27:1
any m.
nor children of wickedness   2Sa 7:10
afflict *any m.*
feared to help Ammon *any*   2Sa 10:19;
m.   1Ch 19:19
why speakest thou *any m.* of 2Sa 10:29
thy matters
neither make feet of Israel   2Ki 21:8;
move *any m.*   2Ch 33:8
nor his place know him *any*   Job 7:10,
m.   20:9
it is meet to say, I will not   Job 34:31
offend *any m.*
neither have they *any m.* a   Ec 9:5
reward
why should ye be stricken *any* Isa 1:5
m.
nor shall they learn war *any m.* Isa 2:4;
     Mic 4:3
nor shall thy teachers be   Isa 30:20
removed *any m.*
nor shall thy land be termed   Isa 62:4
desolate *any m.*
neither shall that be done *any* Jer 3:16
m.
nor walk *any m.* after   Jer 3:17
imagination of heart
there is none to stretch forth Jer 10:20
my tent *any m.*
I said, I will not speak *any m.* Jer 20:9
in his name
he shall not return thither *any* Jer 22:11
m.
no man shall prosper, ruling   Jer 22:30
any m. in Judah
they shall not sorrow *any m.* Jer 31:12
at all
it shall not be thrown down   Jer 31:40
any m. for ever
should not serve themselves   Jer 34:10
of them *any m.*
whereunto I will not do *any m.* Eze 5:9
the like
none of my words be   Eze 12:28
prolonged *any m.*
thou also shalt give no hire   Eze 16:41
any m.
thou mayest never open thy   Eze 16:63
mouth *any m.*
my sword shall not return *any* Eze 21:5
m.
thou shalt not remember   Eze 23:27
Egypt *any m.*
not be purged from thy   Eze 24:13
filthiness *any m.*
be a terror, and never shalt   Eze 27:36;
be *any m.*   28:19
neither shall it exalt itself *any* Eze 29:15
m.
nor foot of man trouble them Eze 32:13;
any m.   37:23
but I have left none of them   Eze 39:28
any m. there
nor will I hide my face *any*   Eze 39:29
m. from them
nor say *any m.* to the work of Ho 14:3
our hands

what have I to do *any m.*   Ho 14:8
with idols
no strangers pass through her Joe 3:17
any m.
I will not again pass by them   Am 7:8;
any m.   8:2
but prophesy not again *any m.* Am 7:13
at Beth-el
thou shalt not see evil *any m.* Zep 3:15
nor durst any ask him *any m.* M't 22:46
questions
they had not *any m.* than one M'k 8:14
loaf
they saw no man *any m.* save M'k 9:8
Jesus only
neither can they die *any m.*   Lu 20:36
for they
I will not eat *any m.* thereof, Lu 22:16
until it be
let us not judge one another   Ro 14:13
any m.
word should not be spoken   Heb 12:19
to them *any m.*
neither shall they thirst *any m.* Re 7:16
nor was their place in heaven Re 12:8
found *any m.*
no man buyeth her   Re 18:11
merchandise *any m.*
neither shall there be *any m.* Re 21:4
pain

NO MORE

the waters shall *no m.* become Ge 9:15
a flood
thy name shall be called no   Ge 32:28
m. Jacob
and Judah knew her again no Ge 38:26
m.
ye shall see my face *no m.*   Ge 44:23;
     Ex 10:28
ye shall *no m.* give the people Ex 5:7
straw
he said, I will see thy face   Ex 10:29
again *no m.*
ye shall see them again *no m.* Ex 14:13
for ever
shall *no m.* offer their sacrifices Le 17:7
to devils
from age of fifty they shall   Nu 8:25
serve *no m.*
speak *no m.* to me of this   De 3:26
matter
these words the Lord spake,   De 5:22
and added *no m.*
circumcise, and be *no m.* stiff- De 10:16
necked
shall do *no m.* such   De 13:11;
wickedness   17:13
henceforth return *no m.* that De 17:16
way
thou shalt see it *no m.*   De 28:68
again, and be sold
I am 120 years, I can *no m.* go De 31:2
out and come in
God will *no m.* drive out   Jos 23:13
these nations
so they lifted up their heads no J'g 8:28
m.
wherefore I will deliver you J'g 10:13
no m.
her countenance was *no m.*   1Sa 1:18
sad
talk *no m.* so exceeding proudly 1Sa 2:3
they came *no m.* into the coast 1Sa 7:13
of Israel
and Samuel came *no m.* to   1Sa 15:35
see Saul
let him go *no m.* home to his 1Sa 18:2
father's house
return, for I will *no m.* do   1Sa 26:21
thee harm
and he sought *no m.* again for 1Sa 27:4
him
and answereth me *no m.* by   1Sa 28:15
prophets
and pursued after Israel *no m.* 2Sa 2:28
a place of their own, and   2Sa 7:10;
move *no m.*   1Ch 17:9
thou shalt go *no m.* out with 2Sa 21:17
us to battle
there was *no m.* spirit in her 1Ki 10:5;
     2Ch 9:4
and Elisha saw Elijah *no m.*   2Ki 2:12
the bands of Syria came *no m.* 2Ki 6:23
into the land
they found *no m.* of her than 2Ki 9:35
the skull
shall *no m.* carry the   1Ch 23:26
tabernacle

a reproach
they came *no m.* on the   Ne 13:21
sabbath
Vashti come *no m.* before the Es 1:19
king
she came *no m.* in to the king, Es 2:14
mine eyes shall *no m.* see good Job 7:7
shall see me *no m.;* shall come Job 7:8;
up *no m.*   7:9
he shall return *no m.* to his   Job 7:10
house
man riseth not, till the   Job 14:12
heavens be *no m.*
the eye that saw him shall see Job 20:9
him *no m.*
he shall be *no m.*   Job 24:20
remembered
were amazed, they answered Job 32:15;
no m.   32:16
if I have done iniquity, I will Job 34:32
do *no m.*
remember the battle, do *no* Job 41:8
m.
that man of earth may *no m.* Ps 10:18
oppress
spare me, before I go hence, Ps 39:13
and be *no m.*
now that he lieth, he shall rise Ps 41:8
up *no m.*
see not signs, there is *no m.* any Ps 74:9
prophet
will he cast off, and be   Ps 77:7
favourable *no m.*
that name of Israel be *no m.*   Ps 83:4
in remembrance
the slain whom thou   Ps 88:5
rememberest *no m.*
the place thereof shall know Ps 103:16
it *no m.*
and let the wicked be *no m.*   Ps 104:35
as the whirlwind, so is the   Pr 10:25
wicked *no m.*
and remember his misery *no m.* Pr 31:7
king, who will *no m.* be   Ec 4:13
admonished
bring *no m.* vain oblation   Isa 1:13
shall *no m.* stay on him that Isa 10:20
smote them
shall wither, be driven away, Isa 19:7
and be *no m.*
there is *no m.* strength; no   Isa 23:10;
m. rejoice   23:12
the earth shall *no m.* cover   Isa 26:21
her slain
shalt weep *no m.*   Isa 30:19
the vile person shall be *no m.* Isa 32:5
called liberal
behold man *no m.*   Isa 38:11
thou shalt *no m.* be called   Isa 47:1
tender and
shalt *no m.* be called the lady Isa 47:5
of kingdoms
thou shalt *no m.* drink it   Isa 51:22
again
no m. come into the   Isa 52:1
uncircumcised
violence shall *no m.* be heard Isa 60:18
in thy land
the sun shall be *no m.* thy   Isa 60:19
light by day
thy sun shall *no m.* go down Isa 60:20
thou shalt *no m.* be termed   Isa 62:4
Forsaken
I will *no m.* give thy corn to Isa 62:8
thine enemies
voice of weeping shall be no Isa 65:19
m. heard
shall be *no m.* thence an   Isa 69:20
infant of days
are lords, we will come *no m.* Jer 2:31
to thee
they shall say *no m.* the ark of Jer 3:16
the covenant
it shall *no m.* be called Tophet Jer 7:32;
     19:6
that his name may be *no m.*   Jer 11:19
remembered
shall be *no m.* said, The   Jer 16:14;
Lord liveth   23:7
shall return *no m.;* see this   Jer 22:10;
land *no m.*   22:12
they shall fear *no m.* nor be Jer 23:4
dismayed
the burden of the Lord shall Jer 23:36
ye mention *no m.*
fall, and rise *no m.* because Jer 25:27
of the sword

teach *no m.* every man and I | Jer 31:34
will remember their sin *no m.*
they should be *no m.* a nation | Jer 33:24
before them
and ye shall see this place no | Jer 42:18
m.
my name shall be *no m.* | Jer 44:26
named in Egypt
saith Lord, Is wisdom *no m.* | Jer 49:7
in Teman
it shall *no m.* be inhabited for | Jer 50:39
ever
law is *no m.* her prophets find no | La 2:9
vision
no m. carry thee away into | La 4:22
captivity
there shall be *no m.* any vain | Eze 12:24
vision
and my word shall be *no m.* | Eze 12:25
prolonged
the wall is *no m.* | Eze 13:15
and they shall be *no m.* in | Eze 13:21
your hand
therefore ye shall see *no m.* | Eze 13:23
vanity
go *no m.* astray | Eze 14:11
I will be quiet, and will be no | Eze 16:42
m. angry
that his voice should be *no m.* | Eze 19:9
heard
but pollute ye my holy name | Eze 20:39
no m.
it shall be *no m.* saith the | Eze 21:13;
Lord | 21:27
thou shalt be *no m.* | Eze 21:32
remembered
and thou shalt speak, and be | Eze 24:27
no m. dumb
thou shalt be *no m.* built; | Eze 26:14;
shall be *no m.* | 26:21
there shall be *no m.* a | Eze 28:24
pricking briar to Israel
they shall *no m.* rule over the | Eze 29:15
nations
shall be *no m.* the confidence | Eze 29:16
of Israel
there shall be *no m.* a prince | Eze 30:13
of Egypt
and they shall be *no m.* a | Eze 34:22;
prey | 34:28-29
therefore thou shalt devour | Eze 36:14
men *no m.*
and they shall be *no m.* two | Eze 37:22
nations
my name shall house of Israel | Eze 43:7
no m. defile
my princes shall *no m.* | Eze 45:8
oppress my people
I will *no m.* have mercy upon | Ho 1:6
Israel
and thou shalt call me *no m.* | Ho 2:16
Baali
they shall *no m.* be | Ho 2:17
remembered by their name
I will drive them out, I will | Ho 9:15
love them *no m.*
I will *no m.* make you a | Joe 2:19
reproach
the virgin is fallen, she shall no | Am 5:2
m. rise
they shall *no m.* be pulled out | Am 9:15
of their land
thou shalt have *no m.* | Mic 5:12
soothsayers
thou shalt *no m.* worship work | Mic 5:13
of thine hands
I will afflict thee *no m.* saith | Na 1:12
the Lord
a command that *no m.* of thy | Na 1:14
name be sown
the wicked shall *no m.* pass | Na 1:15
through thee
voice of thy messengers shall | Na 2:13
no m. be heard
and thou shalt *no m.* be | Zep 3:11
haughty
I will *no m.* pity the | Zec 11:6
inhabitants
and they shall *no m.* be | Zec 13:2
remembered
there shall be *no m.* utter | Zec 14:11
destruction
be *no m.* the Canaanite in | M't 14:21
the house of Lord
they are *no m.* twain, but one | M't 19:6;
| M'k 10:8
and ye suffer him *no m.* to do | M'k 7:12
ought
come out of him, and enter | M'k 9:25
no m. into him

I will drink *no m.* of the | M'k 14:25
fruit of the vine
exact *no m.* than that is | Lu 3:13
appointed
we have *no m.* but five loaves | Lu 9:13
and two fishes
after that have *no m.* that they | Lu 12:4
can do
thou art made whole, sin no | Joh 5:14;
m. | 8:11
many went back, and walked | Joh 6:66
no m. with him
a little while the world seeth | Joh 14:19
me *no m.*
no m. can ye, except ye abide | Joh 15:4
in me
I go to my Father, and ye see | Joh 16:10
me *no m.*
she remembereth *no m.* the | Joh 16:21
anguish, for joy
when I shall *no m.* speak in | Joh 16:25
parables
now I am *no m.* in the world, | Joh 17:11
but these are
that the eunuch saw him *no m.* | Ac 8:39
now *no m.* to return to | Ac 13:34
corruption
I know that ye shall see my | Ac 20:25;
face *no m.* | 20:38
dieth *no m.* death hath *no m.* | Ro 6:9
dominion
now then it is *no m.* I that do | Ro 7:17;
it, but sin | 7:20
it is *no m.* of works, else grace | Ro 11:6
is *no m.* grace, but if of works,
grace is *no m.* grace
yet henceforth know we him | 2Co 5:16
no m.
if of the law, it is *no m.* of | Ga 3:18
promise
thou art *no m.* a servant, but a | Ga 4:7
son
ve are *no m.* strangers and | Eph 2:19
foreigners
we be *no m.* children tossed | Eph 4:14
to and fro
let him that stole steal *no m.* | Eph 4:28
but labour
their iniquities I will | Heb 8:12;
remember *no m.* | 10:17
should have *no m.* conscience | Heb 10:2
of sins
there is *no m.* offering for | Heb 10:18;
sin | 10:26
he that overcometh shall go *no* | Re 3:12
m. out
shall hunger *no m.* neither | Re 7:16
thirst any more
thou shalt find them *no m.* at | Re 18:14
all
musicians shall be heard no | Re 18:22;
m. in thee | 18:23
that he should deceive the | Re 20:3
nations *no m.*
no m. sea; *no m.* death; *no m.* | Re 21:1;
curse | 21:4; 22:3

MUCH MORE

the people bring *much m.* than | Ex 36:5
enough
much m. the wicked and the | Pr 11:31
sinner
as this day, and *much m.* | Isa 56:12
abundant
shall he not *much m.* clothe | M't 6:30
you
so *much m.* went a fame of | Lu 5:15
him abroad
I say unto you, and *much m.* | Lu 7:26
than a prophet
much m. being now justified by | Ro 5:9
his blood
much m. being reconciled, we | Ro 5:10
shall be saved
much m. they that receive | Ro 5:17
abundance of grace
where sin abounded, grace | Ro 5:20
much m. abound
much m. doth ministration of | 2Co 3:9
righteousness
much m. that which | 2Co 3:11
remaineth is glorious
but we have we have proved | 2Co 8:22
much m. diligent
are *much m.* bold to speak | Ph'p 1:14
thereof
have obeyed, now *much m.* | Ph'p 2:12
in my absence

so *much m.* as you see day | Heb 10:25
approaching
much m. shall not we | Heb 12:25
escape, if we turn
being *much m.* precious than of | 1Pe 1:7
gold

MOREH

unto the plain of M. | Ge 12:6; De 11:30
by the hill of M. | J'g 7:1

MOREOVER

m. by them is thy servant | Ps 19:11
warned
he said, M. there shall be | Isa 39:8
peace and truth
thou hast *m.* multiplied | Eze 16:29
fornication
m. this is their resemblance | Zec 5:6
through earth
of mockings, *m.* of bonds | Heb 11:36
and imprisonment

MORESHETH-GATH

shalt give presents to M. | Mic 1:14

MORIAH

and get thee into the land of | Ge 22:2
M.
Solomon built the house of | 2Ch 3:1
Lord in M.

MORNING

when the *m.* arose, the angel | Ge 19:15
hastened Lot
Abraham and servants rose | Ge 24:54
up in the *m.*
they rose betimes in the *m.* | Ge 26:31
and sware
that in the *m.* behold it was | Ge 29:25
Leah
Joseph came unto them in the | Ge 40:6
m. were sad
in the *m.* he shall devour the | Ge 49:27
prey
get thee to Pharaoh in the *m.* | Ex 7:15
in the *m.* the east wind | Ex 10:13
brought locusts
the sea returned to his | Ex 14:27
strength in the *m.*
in the *m.* ye shall see the glory | Ex 16:7
of the Lord
shall give you in the *m.* bread | Ex 16:8;
to the full | 16:12
in the *m.* the dew lay round | Ex 16:13
about the host
one lamb thou shalt offer in | Ex 29:39;
m. | Nu 28:4
according to the meat offering | Ex 29:41
of the *m.*
be ready in the *m.* and come up | Ex 34:2
in the *m.*
nor shall the passover be left | Ex 34:25
to the *m.*
the burning on the altar all night | Le 6:9
to the *m.*
the cloud was taken up in the | Nu 9:21
m.
Balaam rose in the *m.* and | Nu 22:21;
saddled his ass | 22:22
in the *m.* would God it were | De 28:67
even
let him be put to death whilst | J'g 6:31
it is yet *m.*
in the *m.* when it is day, we | J'g 16:2
shall kill him
her lord rose in the *m.* and | J'g 19:27
opened the doors
the children of Israel rose up | J'g 20:19
in the *m.*
he shall be as the light of *m.,* | 2Sa 23:4
even a *m.* without clouds
for when David was up in | 2Sa 24:11
the *m.* word came
when I had considered it in | 1Ki 3:21
the *m.*
and called on name of Baal | 1Ki 18:26
from *m.* to noon
some laboured from *m.* till stars | Ne 4:21
appear
he read therein from *m.* to | Ne 8:3
midday
shalt seek me in *m.* but I | Job 7:21
shall not be

thou shalt shine forth, and be *Job 11:17*
as the *m.*
the *m.* is to them as shadow *Job 24:17*
of death
hast thou commanded *m.* *Job 38:12*
since thy days
his eyes are like eyelids of *Job 41:18*
the *m.*
voice shalt thou hear in *m.* in *m.* *Ps 5:3*
will I direct prayer to thee
weeping for a night, but joy *Ps 30:5*
cometh in the *m.*
shall have dominion over them *Ps 49:14*
in the *m.*
I will sing of thy mercy in the *Ps 59:16*
m.
in the *m.* shall my prayer *Ps 88:13*
prevent thee
in the *m.* they are like grass *Ps 90:5*
which grows up
in the *m.* it flourisheth and *Ps 90:6*
groweth up
I prevented the dawning of *Ps 119:147*
the *m.*
waits more than they that *Ps 130:6*
watch for the *m.*
if I take the wings of the *m.* *Ps 139:9*
and dwell
to hear thy lovingkindness in *Ps 143:8*
the *m.*
thy king, a child and princes *Ec 10:16*
eat in the *m.*
in *m.* sow thy seed, and in the *Ec 11:6*
evening
who is she that looketh forth *Ca 6:10*
as the *m.*
how art fallen, O Lucifer, son *Isa 14:12*
of the *m.*
and behold, before the *m.* he *Isa 17:14*
is not
the watchman said, The *m.* *Isa 21:12*
cometh
for *m.* by *m.* shall it pass *Isa 28:19*
over, by day and
he wakeneth *m.* by *m.* he *Isa 50:4*
wakeneth my ear
then shall thy light break forth *Isa 58:8*
as the *m.*
they were as fed horses in the *Jer 5:8*
m. every one
and let him hear the cry in *Jer 20:16*
the *m.*
execute judgment in the *m.* *Jer 21:12*
and deliver
the *m.* is come on thee, O thou *Eze 7:7*
that dwell
the *m.* is gone forth, the rod *Eze 7:10*
hath blossomed
in the *m.* came the world of *Eze 12:8*
the Lord
I spake to people in *m.* at *Eze 24:18*
even my wife died, I did
in *m.* as commanded
opened my mouth until came *Eze 33:22*
to me in the *m.*
his going forth is prepared as *Ho 6:3*
the *m.*
for your goodness is as a *m.* *Ho 6:4*
cloud, as early dew
in the *m.* it burneth as a flaming *Ho 7:6*
fire
in a *m.* shall the king of *Ho 10:15*
Israel be cut off
as the *m.* spread upon the *Joe 2:2*
mountains
that maketh the *m.* darkness *Am 4:13*
and treadeth
and turneth the shadow of *Am 5:8*
death into the *m.*
God prepared a worm when the *Jon 4:7*
m. rose
when the *m.* is light, they *Mic 2:1*
practice it
in the *m.* it will be foul *M't 16:3*
weather
when *m.* was come, the elders *M't 27:1*
took counsel
in the *m.* as they passed by, *M'k 11:20*
they saw
watch, or at the *M'k 13:35*
cockcrowing, or in *m.*

MORNING LIGHT

let us spoil them until *m.* *1Sa 14:36*
light
all that pertain to him by *m.* *1Sa 25:22*
light
Abigail told him nothing *1Sa 25:36*
until *m.* light

they passed over Jordan by *2Sa 17:22*
m. light
they said, If we tarry until *m.* *2Ki 7:9*
light

MORNING STAR, STARS

m. stars sang together, sons of *Job 38:7*
God
and I will give him the *m.* star *Re 2:28*
I Jesus am the bright and *m.* *Re 22:16*
star

MORNING *WATCH*

in *m.* watch the Lord said to *Ex 14:24*
Moses
came into middle of host in *1Sa 11:11*
m. watch

EARLY IN THE MORNING

Abraham gat up *early in m.* *Ge 19:27;*
21:14; 22:3
therefore Abimelech rose *early* *Ge 20:8*
in the m.
Jacob rose up *early in m.* and *Ge 28:18*
set up a pillar
Laban rose *early in the m.* *Ge 31:55*
kissed sons, daughters
Lord said, Rise up *early in m.* *Ex 8:21;*
stand *9:13*
Moses rose *early in m.* built *Ex 24:4;*
an altar *34:4*
Joshua rose *early in m.* *Jos 3:1;*
6:12; 7:16; 8:10
the men of the city rose *early* *J'g 6:28*
in the m.
Gideon rose *early in the m.* *J'g 6:38*
they arose *early in the m.* *J'g 19:5*
rose *early in the m.* *1Sa 1:19*
29:11; 2Ki 3:22; 19:35; 2Ch 20:20;
Isa 37:36
Samuel rose *early in the m.;* *1Sa 15:12;*
David rose *early in the m.* *17:20*
wherefore rise up *early in* *1Sa 29:10*
the m. and depart
Job rose *early in the m.* and *Job 1:5*
offered
blesseth his friend, rising *early* *Pr 27:14*
in the m.
woe to them that rise *early in* *Isa 5:11*
the m. to
arose *early in the m.* they *Isa 37:36*
were all dead corpses
then king Darius rose very *Da 6:19*
early in the m.
who went *early in the m.* to *M't 20:1*
hire labourers
early in the m. came to *M'k 6:2;*
sepulchre *Lu 24:1*
the people came *early in the* *Lu 21:38;*
m. *Joh 8:2*
they entered into the temple *Ac 5:21*
early in the m.

EVERY MORNING

and they gathered manna *Ex 16:21*
every m.
shalt burn thereon sweet *Ex 30:7*
incense *every m.*
brought unto him free offerings *Ex 36:3*
every m.
the priest shall burn wood on it *Le 6:12*
every m.
opening *every m.* pertaineth *1Ch 9:27*
to porters
to stand *every m.* to thank *1Ch 23:30*
and praise Lord
they burn to the Lord *every* *2Ch 13:11*
m.
that thou shouldest visit him *Job 7:18*
every m.
and I have been chastened *Ps 73:14*
every m.
O Lord, be thou our arm *every* *Isa 33:2*
m.
the Lord's mercies are new *La 3:23*
every m.
thou shalt prepare a lamb *Eze 46:13*
every m.
meat offering *every m.;* *Eze 46:14;*
every m. a burnt offering *46:15*
and bring your sacrifices *every* *Am 4:4*
m.
every m. doth he bring *Zep 3:5*
judgment to light

UNTIL THE MORNING

nothing remain *until the m.* *Ex 12:10;*
12:16, 19; 23:18; 29:34; Le 7:15; Nu 9:12
none of you shall go out at *Ex 12:22*
the door *until the m.*
but some of them left of it *Ex 16:20*
until the m.
lay up for you to be kept *until* *Ex 16:23*
the m.
the wages shall not abide *until* *Le 19:13*
the m.
nor any of the flesh remain *De 16:4*
until the m.
they abused her all night *until* *J'g 19:25*
the m.
lie down *until the m.;* she lay *Ru 3:13;*
until the m. *3:14*
and Samuel lay *until the m.* *1Sa 3:15*
and opened
therefore take heed to thyself *1Sa 19:2*
until the m.
lay heads of kings in two *2Ki 10:8*
heaps *until the m.*
let us take our fill of love *until* *Pr 7:18*
the m.
I reckoned *until the m.* that *Isa 38:13*
as a lion

MORROW

to *m.* shall this sign be, the *Ex 8:23*
Lord did so
to *m.* the Lord shall do this *Ex 9:5*
thing in the land
the Lord did that thing, on the *Ex 9:6*
m. cattle died
to *m.* is the rest of the holy *Ex 16:23*
sabbath to Lord
go, and sanctify them to day *Ex 19:10*
and to *m.*
Aaron said, To *m.* is a feast to *Ex 32:5*
the Lord
on *m.* the remainder shall be *Le 7:16;*
eaten *19:6*
ye shall leave none of it till *Le 22:30*
the *m.*
on *m.* after sabbath priest *Le 23:11*
shall wave it
ye shall count from the *m.* *Le 23:15*
after the sabbath
say people, sanctify *Nu 11:18;*
yourselves against to *m.* *Jos 7:13*
to *m.* the Lord will shew who *Nu 16:5*
are his
be thou, they and Aaron to *Nu 16:16*
m. before the Lord
on the *m.* the congregation *Nu 16:41*
murmured
to *m.* Lord will do wonders *Jos 3:5*
among you
manna ceased on the *m.* after *Jos 5:12*
they had eaten
to *m.* he will be wroth with *Jos 22:18*
congregation
to *m.* get you early on your *J'g 19:9*
way
go up, for to *m.* I will deliver *J'g 20:28*
them
to *m.* by that time the sun be *1Sa 11:9*
hot
behold, to *m.* is the new *1Sa 20:5;*
moon *20:18*
to *m.* shalt thou and thy sons *1Sa 28:19*
be with me
I will send my servants to thee *1Ki 20:6*
to *m.*
thy son to day, we will eat my *2Ki 6:28*
son to *m.*
to *m.* measure flour be sold for *2Ki 7:1*
shekel
on the *m.* he took a thick *2Ki 8:15*
cloth, and dipped
come to me to Jezreel by to *m.* *2Ki 10:6*
this time
to *m.* go ye down against *2Ch 20:16;*
them *20:17*
I will do to *m.* as the king hath *Es 5:8*
said
to *m.* am I invited to her with *Es 5:12*
the king
to *m.* I will give, when thou *Pr 3:28*
hast it by thee
boast not thyself to *m.* thou *Pr 27:1*
knowest not
let us eat, for to *m.* we die *Isa 22:13;*
1Co 15:32
and to *m.* shall be as this day, *Isa 56:12*
much more

they gnaw not the bones till the　Zec 3:3
m.
to m. is cast into the oven　M't 6:30;
　　　　　　　　　　　　　　　Lu 12:28
take no thought for the m. for　M't 6:34
the m. shall take thought for
and I do cures to day, and to　Lu 13:32
m.
nevertheless I must walk to　Lu 13:33
day and to m.
Paul preached; ready to depart　Ac 20:7
on m.
to m. said he, thou shalt hear　Ac 25:22
him
to day or to m. we will go into　Jas 4:13
such a city
ye know not what shall be on　Jas 4:14
the m.

MORSEL

And I will fetch a m. of bread　Ge 18:5
bite of bread (B)　　　　Ge 18:5; J'g 19:5
thine heart with a m. of bread　J'g 19:5
bread, and dip thy m. in the　Ru 2:14
vinegar
dip your bit of bread (B)　　　Ru 2:14
piece of silver and a m. of　　1Sa 2:36
bread
let me set a m. of bread　　　1Sa 28:22
before
Bring me, I pray thee, a m.　　1Ki 17:11
of bread
Or have eaten my m. myself　　Job 31:17
alone
Better is a dry m. and quietness　Pr 17:1
The m. which thou hast eaten　　Pr 23:8
shalt
the bit you have eaten (B)　　　Pr 23:8
one m. of meat sold his　　　Heb 12:16
birthright
for a single meal sold　　　Heb 12:16
(A)(B)(N)(R)
for one mess of meat sold　　Heb 12:16
his (E)
to satisfy momentary hunger　Heb 12:16
(P)

MORSELS

He casteth forth his ice like　Ps 147:17
m.
casts forth ice like crumbs　Ps 147:17
(A)
hurls down ice in fragments　Ps 147:17
(B)
are dainty m. (A)(B)(E)(R)　　Pr 18:8;
　　　　　　　　　　　　　　　26:22

MORTAL

m. man be more just than God　Job 4:17
no m. survive (B)　　　　　　M't 24:22
human beings, no less m. than　Ac 14:15
you (N)
resembling m. man　　　　　　Ro 1:23
(A)(B)(N)(P)(R)
therefore reign in your m. body　Ro 6:12
also quicken your m. bodies by　Ro 8:11
no m. man should boast (A)　　1Co 1:29
this m. must put on　　　　　1Co 15:53
immortality
m. shall have put on　　　　　1Co 15:54
immortality
be made manifest in our m.　　2Co 4:11
flesh
not from a m. origin (A)(N)　　1Pe 1:23

MORTALITY

m. might be swallowed up of　2Co 5:4
life

MORTALLY

smite him m. (B)(E)(R)　　　De 19:6
and smite him m. that he die　De 19:11
heart m. sick (A)　　　　　　Jer 17:6
m. grieved (B)　　　　　　　M't 26:38

MORTAR

or beat it in a m. and baked it　Nu 11:8
thou shouldest bray a fool in a　Pr 27:22
m.

MORTER

stone, and slime had they for　Ge 11:3
m.
hard bondage, in m. and in　Ex 1:14
brick

and he shall take other m. and　Le 14:42
and all the m. of the house　Le 14:45
come upon princes as upon　Isa 41:25
m.
others daubed it with　　　　Eze 13:10
untempered m.
which daub it with　　　　　Eze 13:11
untempered m.
ye have daubed with　　　　Eze 13:14;
untempered m.　　　　　　　　13:15
daubed them with　　　　　Eze 22:28
untempered m.
go into clay, and tread the m.　Na 3:14

MORTGAGED

We have m. our lands, vineyards　Ne 5:3

MORTIFY

the Spirit do m. the deeds of　Ro 8:13
you are habitually putting to　Ro 8:13
death (A)
put to death the practices of　Ro 8:13
(B)(E)(N)(R)
cut the nerve of instinctive　Ro 8:13
actions (P)
M. therefore your members　Col 3:5
which
kill the evil desire (A)　　　Col 3:5
Deaden your organs that tend　Col 3:5
earthward (B)
Put to death your members　Col 3:5
(E)(N)(R)
consider yourselves dead to (P)　Col 3:5

MOSERA

of the children of Jaakan to M.　De 10:6

MOSEROTH

Hashmonah encamped at M.　Nu 33:30
they departed from M. and　Nu 33:31
pitched

MOSES

Pharaoh's daughter called his　Ex 2:10
name M.
M. feared, and said, This thing　Ex 2:14
is known
Pharaoh sought to slay M. but　Ex 2:15
M. fled
the Lord called to him, and said,　Ex 3:4
M. M.
M. hid his face, he was afraid to　Ex 3:6
look
the Lord's anger was kindled　Ex 4:14
against M.
go to meet M.　　　　　　　Ex 4:27
M. returned unto the Lord and　Ex 5:22
said
according to word of M.　　　Ex 8:13;
　　　　　　　　8:31; 9:12, 35; 12:35
M. stretched forth his hand　　Ex 10:22
toward heaven
M. was very great　　　　　　Ex 11:3
people believed Lord and his　Ex 14:31
servant M.
the people murmured against　Ex 15:24;
M.　　　　　　　　　　　　　17:3
notwithstanding they　　　　Ex 16:20
hearkened not to M.
M. cried to the Lord; M. did so　Ex 17:4;
　　　　　　　　　　　　　　Nu 17:11
M. built an altar　　　　　　Ex 17:15
M. sat to judge; M. went up　Ex 18:43;
unto God　　　　　　　　　　19:3
M. returned the words of the　Ex 19:8
people to Lord
the Lord called M. up to　　　Ex 19:20
mount Sinai
M. drew near unto the thick　Ex 20:21
darkness
M. alone shall come near the　Ex 24:2
Lord
M. wrote all the words of the　Ex 24:4
Lord
and M. went into the midst of　Ex 24:18
the cloud
as for M. we wot not what　Ex 32:1;
become of him　　　　　　　32:23
M. besought the Lord　　　　Ex 32:11
the Lord talked with M.; M.　Ex 33:9;
went up　　　　　　　　　　34:4
M. put the veil upon his face　Ex 34:35
again

M. did look on all work; M.　Ex 39:43
blessed them
M. was not able to enter into　Ex 40:35
the tent
M. sought the goat of　　　　Le 10:16
sin offering
they brought the blasphemer　Le 24:11
to M.
as the Lord spake to M. so did　Nu 5:4
Israel
people cried to M. and M.　　Nu 11:2
prayed
M. heard people weep　　　　Nu 11:10
through their families
hath the Lord indeed spoken　Nu 12:2
only by M.
M. was meek above all men　Nu 12:3
upon earth
M. is not so, who is faithful in　Nu 12:7
all my house
ark and M. departed not out　Nu 14:44
of the camp
when M. heard it, he fell upon　Nu 16:4
his face
M. laid up the rods before the　Nu 17:7
Lord
the people chode with M.　　Nu 20:3
and spake
people spake against God and　Nu 21:5
against M.
M. made a serpent of brass　Nu 21:9
and put it on a pole
brought a Midianitish woman　Nu 25:6
in sight of M.
M. sent them to the war, and　Nu 31:6
Phinehas
M. was wroth with the　　　Nu 31:14
officers of the host
M. wrote their goings out by　Nu 33:2
command
M. charged people the same　De 27:11
day
M. wrote this law and delivered　De 31:9
it
M. wrote this song, and taught　De 31:22
it Israel
M. the man of God blessed　De 33:1
Israel
M. the servant of the Lord　De 34:5
died there
not a prophet since in Israel　De 34:10
like to M.
as I was with M. I will be with　Jos 1:5;
thee　　　　　　　　　　　　3:7
as we hearkened to M. so will　Jos 1:17
we to thee
people feared Joshua, as they　Jos 4:14
feared M.
ever since Lord spake this　Jos 14:10
word to M.
am as strong as I was in day　Jos 14:11
M. sent me
keep commandments in law of　1Ki 2:3;
M.　　2Ki 23:25; 2Ch 23:18; Ezr 3:2;
　　　　Da 9:11, 13; Lu 24:44; 1Co 9:9
save the two tables which M.　1Ki 8:9
put there
concerning M. man of God　1Ch 23:14
the son of M. was ruler of　1Ch 26:24
the treasures
he made known his ways unto　Ps 103:7
M.
he sent M. his servant, and　Ps 105:26
Aaron
they envied M. also in the　Ps 106:16
camp
had not M. stood before him　Ps 106:23
in the breach
so that it went ill with M. for　Ps 106:32
their sakes
that led them by the right　Isa 63:12
hand of M.
though M. and Samuel stood　Jer 15:1
before me
remember the law of M. my　Mal 4:4
servant
there appeared M. and Elias　M't 17:3;
　　　　　　　　　M'k 9:4; Lu 9:30
let us make one tabernacle　M't 17:4;
for M.　　　　　　　　　　M'k 9:5
why did M. command to give　M't 19:7
a writing
M. suffered you to put away　M't 19:8
your wives
he said, What did M.　　　　M'k 10:3
command you
M. wrote, If a man's　　　　M'k 12:19;
brother die　　　　　　　　Lu 20:28

they have *M.* and the prophets *Lu 16:29*
if they hear not *M.* and the *Lu 16:31*
prophets
that dead are raised *M.* *Lu 20:37*
shewed at bush
beginning at *M.* and all the *Lu 24:27*
prophets
law was given by *M.* grace by *Joh 1:17*
Jesus Christ
we have found him of whom *Joh 1:45*
M. did write
as *M.* lifted up serpent in *Joh 3:14*
wilderness
one accuseth you, even *M.* *Joh 5:45*
whom ye trust
had ye believed *M.* ye had *Joh 5:46*
believed me
M. gave you not that bread *Joh 6:32*
from heaven
M. give you the law? none *Joh 7:19*
keepeth it
not because it is of *M.* but of *Joh 7:22*
the fathers
that the law of *M.* should not *Joh 7:23*
be broken
we know that God spake unto *Joh 9:29*
M.
for *M.* truly said unto the *Ac 3:22*
fathers
heard him speak blasphemous *Ac 6:11*
words against *M.*
change customs which *M.* *Ac 6:14*
delivered us
in which time *M.* was born, *Ac 7:20*
and was fair
then *M.* trembled and durst *Ac 7:32*
not behold
this *M.* whom they refused did *Ac 7:35*
God send
this is that *M.* that said unto *Ac 7:37*
Israel
ye could not be justified by *Ac 13:39*
the law of *M.*
except ye be circumcised after *Ac 15:1*
manner of *M.*
to command them to keep the *Ac 15:5*
law of *M.*
M. hath in every city them *Ac 15:21*
that preach him
thou teachest the Jews to *Ac 21:21*
forsake *M.*
things which *M.* did say *Ac 26:22*
should come
out of the law of *M.* and the *Ac 28:23*
prophets
death reigned from Adam to *Ro 5:14*
M.
M. described the righteousness *Ro 10:5*
of the law
were all baptized to *M.* in the *1Co 10:2*
cloud
Israel could not behold the *2Co 3:7*
face of *M.*
not as *M.* who put a veil over *2Co 3:13*
his face
when *M.* is read, the veil is on *2Co 3:15*
their heart
as Jannes and Jambres *2Ti 3:8*
withstood *M.*
M. was faithful in all his *Heb 3:2;*
house *3:5*
counted worthy of more glory *Heb 3:3*
than *M.*
not all that came out of *Heb 3:16*
Egypt by *M.*
which tribe *M.* spake nothing *Heb 7:14*
of priesthood
for when *M.* had spoken every *Heb 9:19*
precept
by faith *M.* was hid three *Heb 11:23*
months
M. refused be called son of *Heb 11:24*
Pharaoh's daughter
M. said, I exceedingly fear *Heb 12:21*
and quake
he disputed about the body of *Jude 9*
M.
sing the song of *M.* and the *Re 15:3*
Lamb

MOSES'

M. hands were heavy *Ex 17:12*
M. father in law *Ex 18:1;*
18:2, 5, 12, 14, 17; Nu 10:29; J'g 1:16
M. anger waxed hot *Ex 32:19*
two tables of testimony in *M.* *Ex 34:29*
hand
skin of *M.* face shone *Ex 34:35*

ram of consecration it was *M.* *Le 8:29*
part
M. minister *Jos 1:1*
Pharisees sit in *M.* seat *M't 23:2*
we are *M.* disciples *Joh 9:28*
he that despised *M.* law *Heb 10:28*

MOST

the *m.* high God *Ge 14:18;*
14:19-20, 22; Nu 24:16; De 32:8;
2Sa 22:14; Ps 78:56; Da 3:26; 5:18, 21;
M'k 5:7; Ac 16:17; Heb 7:1
the *m.* holy place *Ex 26:33;*
26:34; Nu 18:10; 1Ki 6:16; 7:50 8:6;
1Ch 6:49; 2Ch 4:22; 5:7; Eze 41:4;
44:13; 45:3; Da 9:24
an altar *m.* holy *Ex 29:37; 40:10*
it is *m.* holy *Ex 30:10;*
30:29, 36; Le 2:3; 6:17, 25, 29; 7:1, 6;
10:12, 17; 14:13; 24:9; 27:28; Eze 43:12;
48:12
the *m.* holy things *Le 21:22;*
Nu 4:4, 19; 18:9; 1Ch 23:13; 2Ch 31:14;
Ne 7:65; Eze 42:13
Was he not *m.* honorable of *2Sa 23:19*
the three
he made the *m.* holy house *2Ch 3:8;*
3:10
one of the king's *m.* noble *Es 6:9*
princes
thou condemn him that is *m.* *Job 34:17*
just
the Lord *m.* high *Ps 7:17; 9:2; 47:2*
hast made him *m.* blessed for *Ps 21:6*
ever
the *m.* High *Ps 21:7;*
46:4; 50:14; 56:2; 73:11; 77:10; 78:17;
83:18; 91:1, 9; 107:11; Isa 14:14;
La 3:35, 38; Da 4:17, 24-25, 32, 34; 7:18,
22, 25, 27; Ho 7:16; 11:7; Ac 7:48
O *m.* mighty, high *Ps 45:3; 92:1*
I will cry unto God *m.* high *Ps 57:2;*
92:8
M. men will proclaim every one *Pr 20:6*
his own goodness
His head is as the *m.* fine gold *Ca 5:11*
His mouth is *m.* sweet *Ca 5:16*
which hath a *m.* vehement flame *Ca 8:6*
m. upright, dost weigh path of *Isa 26:7*
the just
m. bitter lamentation *Jer 6:26*
O thou *m.* proud *Jer 50:31; 50:32*
how is the *m.* fine gold changed *La 4:1*
they are *m.* rebellious *Eze 2:7*
rulers clothed *m.* gorgeously *Eze 23:12*
I will lay the land *m.* *Eze 33:28;*
desolate *33:29; 35:3, 7*
commanded the *m.* mighty *Da 3:20*
men
take the *m.* fenced cities *Da 11:15*
the *m.* strong holds *Da 11:39*
provoked him to anger *m.* *Ho 12:14*
bitterly
the *m.* upright is sharper than *Mic 7:4*
a thorn
m. of his mighty works were *M't 11:20*
done
are *m.* surely believed among us *Lu 1:1*
in order, *m.* excellent *Lu 1:3*
Theophilus
which of them will love him *m.* *Lu 7:42*
he, to whom he forgave *m.* *Lu 7:43*
Jesus, thou Son of God *m.* high *Lu 8:28*
unto the *m.* excellent governor *Ac 23:26*
in all places *m.* noble Felix *Ac 24:3*
after the *m.* straitest sect of *Ac 26:5*
our
I am not mad, *m.* noble *Ac 26:25*
Festus
let it be by two, or at the *m.* *1Co 14:27*
by three
we are of all men *m.* *1Co 15:19*
miserable
M. gladly therefore will I *2Co 12:9*
rather glory
yourselves on your *m.* holy *Jude 20*
faith
manner vessels of *m.* precious *Re 18:12*
wood
was like unto a stone *m.* *Re 21:11*
precious

MOTE

why beholdest thou *m.* in thy *M't 7:3;*
brother's eye *Lu 6:41*
let me pull out the *M.* out *M't 7:4*
of thine eye
then shalt see clearly to cast *M't 7:5;*
out *m.* out of thy brother's eye *Lu 6:42*

MOTH

in them which are crushed *Job 4:19*
before the *m.*
he buildeth his house as a *m.* *Job 27:18*
and booth
thou makest his beauty *Ps 39:11*
consume like a
the *m.* shall eat them up *Isa 50:9; 51:8*
therefore will I be to Ephraim *Ho 5:12*
as a *m.*
treasures, where *m.* and rust *M't 6:19*
doth corrupt
grows rusty and *m.*-eaten (N) *M't 6:19*
where neither *m.* nor rust *M't 6:20;*
corrupt *Lu 12:33*

MOTH *EATEN*

consumeth as garment that is *Job 13:28*
m. eaten
riches corrupted, your *Jas 5:2*
garments *m. eaten*

MOTHER

because she was the *m.* of all *Ge 3:20*
living
I will bless her, she shall be a *Ge 17:16*
m. of nations
gave her brother and *m.* *Ge 24:53*
precious things
be thou the *m.* of thousands *Ge 24:60*
of millions
lest he smite the *m.* with the *Ge 32:11*
children
maid went and called the child's *Ex 2:8*
m.
to take a wife and her *m.* is *Le 20:14*
wickedness
till that I Deborah arose a *m.* in *J'g 5:7*
Israel
the *m.* of Sisera looked out at *J'g 5:28*
a window
Abigail, sister to Zeruiah, *2Sa 17:25*
Joab's *m.*
thou seekest to destroy a *m.* *2Sa 20:19*
in Israel
caused a seat to be set for the *1Ki 2:19*
king's *m.*
give her the child, she is the *1Ki 3:27*
m. thereof
he carried away the king's *m.* *2Ki 24:15*
when my *m.* bore me (A)(E) *Job 3:11*
and to be a joyful *m.* of *Ps 113:9*
children
a generation doth not bless *Pr 30:11*
their *m.*
my dove, she is the only one of *Ca 6:9*
her *m.*
your *m.* shall be sore *Jer 50:12*
confounded
as is the *m.* so is the *Eze 16:44*
daughter
your *m.* was an Hittite, *Eze 16:45*
father an Amorite
were two women the *Eze 23:2*
daughters of one *m.*
plead with your *m.* for she is *Ho 2:2*
not my wife
for their *m.* hath played the *Ho 2:5*
harlot
m. was dashed in pieces upon *Ho 10:14*
her children
daughter riseth up against her *Mic 7:6;*
m. *M't 10:35; Lu 12:53*
saw Peter's wife's *m.* sick *M't 8:14;*
Lu 4:38
she being before instructed of *M't 14:8*
her *m.*
and she brought it to her *m.* *M't 14:11;*
M'k 6:28
then came the *m.* of *M't 20:20*
Zebedee's children
the *m.* of my Lord should come *Lu 1:43*
to me
the *m.* of Jesus was there *Joh 2:1;*
Ac 1:14
he came to house of Mary *m.* *Ac 12:12*
of John
Jerusalem which is the *m.* of *Ga 4:26*
us all
the *m.* of harlots and *Re 17:5*
abominations

MOTHER *IN LAW*

cursed be that lieth with his *De 27:23*
m. in law

and Orpah kissed her *m. in*   Ru 1:14
law
all that thou hast done to thy   Ru 2:11
m. in law
and Ruth dwelt with her   Ru 2:23
m. in law
according to all that her   Ru 3:6
m. in law bade her
for he said, Go not empty to   Ru 3:17
thy *m. in law*
daughter in law riseth up   Mic 7:6;
against *m. in law*   M't 10:35; Lu 12:53

HIS MOTHER

his m. took him a wife out of   Ge 21:21
Egypt
Isaac brought Rebekah into   Ge 24:67
his m. tent, comforted after
death of *his m.*
Jacob went and brought them   Ge 27:14
to *his m.*
Reuben brought mandrakes to   Ge 30:14
his m.
he alone is left of *his m.* his   Ge 44:20
father loves him
that lieth with the daughter of   De 27:22
his m.
he said to *his m.*; he restored   J'g 17:2;
it to *his m.*   17:3
his m. made him a little coat   1Sa 2:19
and *his m.* bare him after   1Ki 1:6
Absalom
his m. he removed from   1Ki 15:13
being queen
Elijah delivered him to *his*   1Ki 17:23
m. and said
Ahaziah walked in the way   1Ki 22:52
of *his m.*
he said to a lad, Carry him to   2Ki 4:19
his m.
his m. called his name Jabez   1Ch 4:9
his m. was his counsellor to   2Ch 22:3
do wickedly
as one that mourneth for *his*   Ps 35:14
m.
let not the sin of *his m.* be   Ps 109:14
blotted out
as a child that is weaned of   Ps 131:2
his m.
a foolish son is the heaviness   Pr 10:1
but a foolish man despiseth   Pr 15:20
his m.
a child left bringeth *his m.* to   Pr 29:15
shame
the prophecy that *his m.* taught   Pr 31:1
him
crown wherewith *his m.*   Ca 3:11
crowned him
as one whom *his m.*   Isa 66:13
comforteth
when *his m.* was espoused to   M't 1:18
Joseph
take the young child and *his*   M't 2:13;
m. and flee   2:20
his m. stood without   M't 12:46;
       M'k 3:31; Lu 8:19
carpenter's son, is not *his m.*   M't 13:55
called Mary
his m. said, He shall be called   Lu 1:60
John
but Joseph and *his m.* knew   Lu 2:43
not of it
but *his m.* kept these sayings in   Lu 2:51
her heart
the only son of *his m.* and she   Lu 7:12
was a widow
he sat up, and he delivered him   Lu 7:15
to *his m.*
his m. stood by the cross of   Joh 19:25
Jesus
when Jesus saw *his m.* he   Joh 19:26
saith to *his m.*
salute Rufus and *his m.* and   Ro 16:13
mine

MY MOTHER

she is not the daughter of *my*   Ge 20:12
m.
my brethren, even the sons of   J'g 8:19
my m.
the king said to her, Ask on,   1Ki 2:20
my m.
I have said to the worm,   Job 17:14
Thou art *my m.*
and in sin did *my m.* conceive   Ps 51:5
me
tender and beloved in the sight   Pr 4:3
of *my m.*

my brother that sucked the   Ca 8:1
breasts of *my m.*
the bowels of *my m.* he made   Isa 49:1
mention
woe is me *my m.* that thou   Jer 15:10
hast borne me
let not the day wherein *my m.*   Jer 20:14
bare me
or that *my m.* might have   Jer 20:17
been my grave
Jesus said, Who is *my m.*   M't 12:48;
           M'k 3:33
behold, *my m.* and my   M't 12:49;
brethren   M'k 3:34
my m. and my brethren are   Lu 8:21
these

THY MOTHER

shall I and *thy m.* come to   Ge 37:10
bow to thee
nakedness of *thy m.* shalt thou   Le 18:7
not uncover
not uncover nakedness of   Le 18:9
daughter of *thy m.*
not uncover nakedness of   Le 8:13;
sister of *thy m.*   20:19
brother, the son of *thy m.*   De 13:6
entice thee
so shall *thy m.* be childless   1Sa 15:33
among women
as whoredoms of *thy m.* are   2Ki 9:22
so many
and forsake not the law of *thy*   Pr 1:8;
m.   6:20
and despise not *thy m.* when   Pr 23:22
she is old
there *thy m.* brought thee forth   Ca 8:5
cast thee out, and *thy m.* that   Jer 22:26
bare thee
thy father an Amorite, *thy m.*   Eze 16:3
an Hittite
and say, What is *thy m.*? a   Eze 19:2
lioness
thy m. is like a vine in thy   Eze 19:10
blood, planted
thou shalt fall, and I will   Ho 4:5
destroy *thy m.*
one said to him, Behold *thy*   M't 12:47;
m. and thy brethren M'k 3:32; Lu 8:20;
                Joh 19:27
faith, which dwelt in *thy m.*   2Ti 1:5
Eunice

MOTHERS

and queens shall be thy   Isa 49:23
nursing *m.*
saith the Lord, concerning   Jer 16:3
their *m.*
we are fatherless, our *m.* are as   La 5:3
widows
receive an hundredfold   M'k 10:30
sisters, *m.*
the law is made for murderers   1Ti 1:9
of *m.*
but entreat the elder women as   1Ti 5:2
m. the younger

MOTHER'S

m. house   Ge 24:28; Ru 1:8; Ca 3:4; 8:2
m. death   Ge 24:67
m. sons   Ge 27:29
m. father   Ge 28:2; J'g 9:1
m. brother   Ge 28:2; 29:10
m. son   Ge 43:29; Ps 50:20
m. milk   Ex 23:19; 34:26; De 14:21
m. sister   Le 18:13; 20:19; Joh 19:25
m. daughter   Le 20:17; Eze 16:45
m. name   Le 24:11;
1Ki 11:26;   14:21;   15:2,   10; 22:42;
2Ki 8:26; 12:1; 14:2; 15:2, 33; 18:2; 21:1
19; 22:1; 23:21, 36; 24:8, 18; 2Ch 13:2;
13:2; 20:31; 22:2; 24:1; 25:1; 26:3; 27:1;
               29:1; Jer 52:1
m. womb   Nu 12:12;
   J'g 16:17; Job 1:21; 3:10; 31:18;
Ps 139:13; Ec 5:15; M't 19:12; Lu 1:15;
      Joh 3:4; Ac 3:2; 14:8; Ga 1:15
m. brethren   J'g 9:1; 9:3
m. nakedness   1Sa 20:30
m. breasts   Ps 22:9
m. belly   Ps 22:10
m. children   Ps 69:8; Ca 1:6
m. bowels   Ps 71:6
m. divorcement   Isa 50:1

MOTHERS'

poured out into *m.* bosom   La 2:12

MOTIONS

my *m.* stir (B)   Jer 31:20
the *m.* of sins did work in our   Ro 7:5

MOTIVE

members
any baneful *m.* (B)   Ps 139:24

MOTIVES

reveal inner *m.* (B)(N)(P)   1Co 4:5
with reverence, awe, and   Eph 6:5
unmixed *m.* (B)
nothing from factional *m.* (A)   Ph'p 2:3
with unmixed *m.* (B)   Col 3:22
conceal greedy *m.* (A)(P)   1Th 2:5

MOTTLED

striped, speckled, *m.* (B)(R)   Ge 31:10

MOULDY

the bread of provision was dry   Jos 9:5;
and *m.*   9:12

MOUND

cast up a *m.* (S)   2Sa 20:15; 2Ki 19:32
lay siege with a *m.* (S)   Isa 29:3;
Jer 6:6; Eze 4:2; 21:22; 26:8; Da 11:15

MOUNDS

siege *m.* (A)(B)(E)(R)(S)   Jer 32:24;
           33:4; Eze 17:17

MOUNT

Jacob offered sacrifice on the   Ge 31:54
m.
where he encamped at the *m.*   Ex 18:5
of God
whoso toucheth the *m.* shall   Ex 19:12
be put to death
Moses went down from the   Ex 19:14;
m.   32:15; 34:29
a thick cloud upon the *m.*   Ex 19:16;
                24:15
m. Sinai on a smoke; bounds   Ex 19:18;
about the *m.*   19:20
the glory of the Lord abode   Ex 24:16
upon *m.* Sinai
was like devouring fire on the   Ex 24:17
top of *m.*
the Lord gave Moses on *m.*   Ex 31:18
Sinai two tables
and Moses brake them   Ex 32:19
beneath the *m.*
and come up in the morning to   Ex 34:2
m. Sinai
nor let any man be seen   Ex 34:3
through all the *m.*
they departed from the *m.* of   Nu 10:33
the Lord
from Kadesh, and came unto   Nu 20:22
m. Hor
bring up to *m.* Hor; Aaron   Nu 20:25;
died in *m.* Hor   20:28
you shall point out for you *m.*   Nu 34:7
Hor
ye have dwelt long enough in   De 1:6
this *m.*
turn you, and go to the *m.* of   De 1:7
the Amorites
I came down, and the *m.*   De 9:15
burned with fire
and these shall stand upon *m.*   De 27:13
Ebal
get thee to *m.* Nebo, which is   De 32:49
Moab
the Lord shined forth from *m.*   De 33:2
Paran
go and draw towards *m.* Tabor   J'g 4:6
let him depart early from *m.*   J'g 7:3
Gilead
Abimelech gat him up to *m.*   J'g 9:48
Zalmon
David went up by the ascent   2Sa 15:30
of *m.*
the top of the *m.* where he   2Sa 15:32
worshipped God
Elijah went to Horeb, the *m.*   1Ki 19:8
of God
go and stand on the *m.*   1Ki 19:11
before the Lord

on right hand the *m.* of   *2Ki 23:13*
corruption
go to the *m.* and fetch olive   *Ne 8:15*
branches
thou camest down also on *m.*   *Ne 9:13*
Sinai
though his excellency *m.* up to   *Job 20:6*
the heavens
doth the eagle *m.* up at thy   *Job 39:27*
command
they *m.* up to heaven, they go   *Ps 107:26*
down
is as a flock of goats from *m.*   *Ca 4:1*
Gilead
they shall *m.* up as the lifting   *Isa 9:18*
up of smoke
the *m.* of the daughter of   *Isa 10:32;*
Zion   *16:1*
I will sit on the *m.* of the   *Isa 14:13*
congregation
shall worship in the holy *m.*   *Isa 27:13*
at Jerusalem
and will lay siege against thee   *Isa 29:3*
with a *m.*
they shall *m.* up with wings,   *Isa 40:31*
as eagles
hew ye down trees and cast a   *Jer 6:6;*
m. against Jerusalem   *Eze 4:2; 21:22;*
   26:8
though Babylon should *m.* up   *Jer 51:5*
to heaven
when the cherubims lift up   *Eze 10:16;*
to *m.* up   *10:19*
the king of the north shall   *Da 11:15*
cast up a *m.*
even destroy understanding out of   *Ob 8*
m. Esau
saviours shall come to judge the   *Ob 21*
m. of Esau
and the Holy One from *m.*   *Hab 3:3*
Paran
there appeared in wilderness of   *Ac 7:30*
m. Sinai
the one from the *m.* Sinai,   *Ga 4:24*
which is Agar
for this Agar is *m.* Sinai in   *Ga 4:25*
Arabia
not come to the *m.* might be   *Heb 12:18*
touched

MOUNT *OF OLIVES*

feet stand on the *m.* of   *Zec 14:4*
Olives, the *m. of Olives* shall
they were come to *m.* of   *M't 21:1;*
Olives   *Lu 19:29*
and as he sat upon *m.* of   *M't 24:3;*
Olives   *M'k 13:3*
when he had sung an hymn,   *M't 26:30;*
they went into *m. of Olives*   *M'k 14:26;*
   Lu 22:39
he was at the descent of *m. of*   *Lu 19:37*
Olives
at night he went out, and   *Lu 21:37*
abode in *m. of Olives*
Jesus went unto the *m.* of   *Joh 8:1*
Olives
then they returned from the *m.*   *Ac 1:12*
of Olives

BEFORE THE MOUNT

and there Israel camped *before*   *Ex 19:2*
the m.
neither let the flocks feed   *Ex 34:3*
before the m.

IN, INTO THE MOUNT

in the m. of the Lord it shall   *Ge 22:14*
be seen
and they overtook Jacob *in*   *Ge 31:23*
the m. Gilead
they did eat, and tarried all   *Ge 31:54*
night *in the m.*
he went and met him *in the m.*   *Ex 4:27*
of God
take heed ye go not up *into*   *Ex 19:12*
the m. or
Lord said to Moses, Come   *Ex 24:12;*
into m.   *De 10:1*
Moses went up *into the m.* of   *Ex 24:13;*
God   *24:15, 18*
Moses was *in the m.* forty   *Ex 24:18;*
days and forty nights   *De 9:9; 10:10*
make them after pattern   *Ex 25:40;*
shewed *in the m.*   *26:30; 27:8; Heb 8:5*
get thee up *into m.* Abarim,   *Nu 27:12*
and see
die *in the m.* as Aaron died *in*   *De 32:50*
m. Hor

Joshua built an altar to Lord   *Jos 8:30*
in m. Ebal
Josiah spied the sepulchres *in*   *2Ki 23:16*
the m.
to build the house of Lord *in*   *2Ch 3:1*
m. Moriah
for the Lord shall rise up as   *Isa 28:21*
in m. Perazim
the angel who spake to him *in*   *Ac 7:38*
m. Sinai
when we were with him *in the*   *2Pe 1:18*
holy *m.*

MOUNTAIN

and they that remained fled to   *Ge 14:10*
the *m.*
escape to the *m.*   *Ge 19:17*
I cannot escape to *m.*   *Ge 19:19*
and came to the *m.* of God even   *Ex 3:1*
to Horeb
people from Egypt, shall serve   *Ex 3:12*
God on this *m.*
the Lord called to him out of   *Ex 19:3*
the *m.* saying
all the people saw the *m.*   *Ex 20:18*
smoking
they gat them up into top of   *Nu 14:40*
the *m.*
ye are come to the *m.* of the   *De 1:20*
Amorites
ye have compassed this *m.* long   *De 2:3*
enough
let me see that goodly *m.* and   *De 3:25*
Lebanon
the *m.* burnt with fire to   *De 4:11;*
heaven   *5:23*
m. sheep (S)   *De 14:5*
they shall call the people to   *De 33:19*
the *m.*
get ye to the *m.* and hide   *Jos 2:16*
yourselves
Joshua took the plain and the   *Jos 11:16*
m. of Israel
give me this *m.*; the *m.* shall   *Jos 14:12;*
be thine   *17:18*
he drave out the inhabitants of   *J'g 1:19*
the *m.*
Amorites forced children of   *J'g 1:34*
Dan into the *m.*
Phi'istines stood on a *m.* and   *1Sa 17:3*
Israel stood on a *m.*
Saul went on this side of *m.*   *1Sa 23:26*
and David and his men on
that side of *m.*
hidden by the *m.*   *1Sa 25:20*
(A)(B)(R)(S)
the Spirit hath cast him on   *2Ki 2:16*
some *m.*
the *m.* was full of horses and   *2Ki 6:17*
chariots
surely the *m.* falling cometh   *Job 14:18*
to nought
how say ye, Flee as a bird to   *Ps 11:1*
your *m.*
thou hast made my *m.* to stand   *Ps 30:7*
strong
brought to this *m.* his right   *Ps 78:54*
hand purchased
the *m.* of Lord's house   *Isa 2:2;*
established   *Mic 4:1*
let us go up to the *m.* of the   *Isa 2:3;*
Lord   *Mic 4:2*
until ye be left as a beacon on   *Isa 30:17*
the top of a *m.*
as when one goeth with a   *Isa 30:29*
pipe to *m.* of Lord
every *m.* shall be made low   *Isa 40:4;*
   Lu 3:5
they shall hunt them from   *Jer 16:16*
every *m.*
O my *m.* in the field, I will give   *Jer 17:3*
thy substance
Zion plowed like a field, and   *Jer 26:18;*
the *m.* of the house as   *Mic 3:12*
my people have gone from *m.*   *Jer 50:6*
to hill
I am against thee, O   *Jer 51:25*
destroying *m.* and I will
make thee a burnt *m.*
our eyes are dim, because of *m.*   *La 5:18*
of Zion
the glory of the Lord stood   *Eze 11:23*
on the *m.*
I will cast thee as profane   *Eze 28:16*
out of *m.* of God
this is the law of the house   *Eze 43:12*
on top of the *m.*

---

and the stone became a great   *Da 2:35*
m.
the stone was cut out of the *m.*   *Da 2:45*
without hands
he shall come to thee from *m.*   *Mic 7:12*
to *m.*
go up to *m.* bring wood and   *Hag 1:8*
build house
who art thou, O great *m.*   *Zep 4:7*
before Zerubbabel
be called the *m.* of the Lord,   *Zep 8:3*
the holy *m.*
half of *m.* shall remove   *Zep 14:4*
towards the north
went up into *m.*   *M't 5:1;*
   14:23; 15:29; M'k 3:13; 6:46; Lu 6:12;
   9:28; Joh 6:3, 15
when he was come down from   *M't 8:1*
the *m.*
Jesus bringeth them into an   *M't 17:1*
high *m.* apart
and as they came down from   *M't 17:9*
the *m.*   *M'k 9:9*
shall say to this *m.*, Remove   *M't 17:20;*
hence   *21:21; M'k 11:23*
went into a *m.* where Jesus   *M't 28:16*
had appointed
an herd of many swine feeding   *Lu 8:32*
on *m.*
come down from the *m.* (S)   *Lu 9:37*
if so much as a beast touch   *Heb 12:20*
the *m.*
every *m.* and island were   *Re 6:14*
removed from
as it were a great *m.* burning   *Re 8:8*
with fire

HIGH MOUNTAIN

lift ye up a banner upon the   *Isa 13:2*
high m.
there shall be upon every high   *Isa 30:25*
m. rivers
O Zion, get thee up into the   *Isa 40:9*
high m.
on a lofty and *high m.* hast   *Isa 57:7*
thou set thy bed
Israel is gone up upon every   *Jer 3:6*
high m.
and I will plant it on a *high*   *Eze 17:22*
m.
he brought me, and set me on   *Eze 40:2*
a very *high m.*
the devil taketh him up into an   *M't 4:8;*
exceeding *high m.*   *Lu 4:5*
bringeth into an *high m.*   *M't 17:1;*
apart   *M'k 9:2*
he carried me in the Spirit to   *Re 21:10*
high m.

IN THE, IN THIS MOUNTAIN

Lot went from Zoar, and   *Ge 19:30*
dwelt *in the m.*
plant them *in the m.* of thine   *Ex 15:17*
inheritance
Moses said unto them, Go up   *Nu 13:17*
into the m.
get thee up *in this m.* Abarim,   *De 32:49*
to Nebo
he blew a trumpet *in the m.* of   *J'g 3:27*
Ephraim
D·vid remained *in a m.* of   *1Sa 23:14*
Ziph
Solomon told 80,000 to hew *in*   *2Ch 2:2*
the m.
God is to be praised *in the m.*   *Ps 48:1*
of holiness
in this m. shall the Lord make   *Isa 25:6*
a feast
he will destroy *in this m.* the   *Isa 25:7*
face of covering
in this m. shall the hand of the   *Isa 25:10*
Lord rest
in the m. of Israel I will   *Eze 17:23*
plant it
ye kine, that are *in the m.* of   *Am 4:1*
Samaria
woe to them that trust *in the*   *Am 6:1*
m. of Samaria
our fathers worshipped *in this*   *Joh 4:20*
m.
neither *in this m.* nor   *Joh 4:21*
Jerusalem, worship

MOUNTAINS

m. were covered   *Ge 7:20*
ark rested on the *m.*   *Ge 8:4*

in tenth month tops of the *m.* *Ge 8:5*
were seen
blessings of eternal *m.* (R) *Ge 49:26*
they departed from the *m.* of *Nu 33:48*
Abarim
ye shall destroy places on the *De 12:2*
high *m.*
Joshua cut off the Anakims *Jos 11:21*
from the *m.*
the *m.* melted from before the *J'g 5:5*
Lord
that I may go up and down *J'g 11:37*
on the *m.*
she bewailed her virginity on *J'g 11:38*
the *m.*
ye *m.* of Gilboa, let there be *2Sa 1:21*
no dew
a great and strong wind rent *1Ki 19:11*
the *m.*
were as swift as the roes on *1Ch 12:8*
the *m.*
I did see all Israel scattered *2Ch 18:16*
on the *m.*
which removeth the *m.* and they *Job 9:5*
know not
he overturneth the *m.* by the *Job 28:9*
roots
surely the *m.* bring him forth *Job 40:20*
food
thy righteousness is like the *Ps 36:6*
great *m.*
tho' the *m.* be carried into the *Ps 46:2*
midst of the sea
though the *m.* shake with the *Ps 46:3*
swelling thereof
by his strength setteth fast the *Ps 65:6*
m.
the *m.* shall bring peace to the *Ps 72:3*
people
thou art more glorious than the *Ps 76:4*
m. of prey
as the flames setteth the *m.* on *Ps 83:14*
fire
before the *m.* were brought *Ps 90:2*
forth
the waters stood above the *m.* *Ps 104:6*
they go up by the *m.* down by *Ps 104:8*
the valleys
m. skipped like rams, little *Ps 114:4;*
hills as lambs *114:6*
as the *m.* are round about *Ps 125:2*
Jerusalem
as the dew that descended on *Ps 133:3*
the *m.*
touch the *m.* and they shall *Ps 144:5*
smoke
who maketh grass to grow on *Ps 147:8*
the *m.*
m. and all hills praise the Lord *Ps 148:9*
before the *m.* were settled *Pr 8:25*
behold, he cometh leaping on *Ca 2:8*
the *m.*
turn, and be thou like a roe on *Ca 2:17;*
the *m.* *8:14*
look from Amana and *m.* of *Ca 4:8*
leopards
the day of the Lord shall be on *Isa 2:14*
high *m.*
and on my *m.* tread him *Isa 14:25*
under foot
when he lifeth up an ensign on *Isa 18:3*
the *m.*
the *m.* shall be melted with *Isa 34:3*
their blood
who hath weighed the *m.* in *Isa 40:12*
scales
thou shalt thresh the *m.* and *Isa 41:15*
beat small
and I will make waste *m.* and *Isa 42:15*
hills
break forth into singing, ye *Isa 44:23;*
m. *49:13*
and I will make all my *m.* a *Isa 49:11*
way
how beautiful on the *m.* are *Isa 52:7;*
feet *Na 1:15*
for the *m.* shall depart, the *Isa 54:10*
hills be removed
m. shall break forth before *Isa 55:12*
you into singing
the *m.* might flow down at thy *Isa 64:1;*
presence *64:3*
which have burnt incense on *Isa 65:7*
the *m.*
will bring out of Judah an *Isa 65:9*
inheritor of my *m.*
I beheld the *m.* and they *Jer 4:24*
trembled
for the *m.* will I take up a *Jer 9:10*
weeping

before your feet stumble on *Jer 13:16*
the dark *m.*
shall come from the *m.* *Jer 17:26*
bringing offerings
shall plant vines on the *m.* of *Jer 31:5*
Samaria
as Tabor among the *m.* so *Jer 46:18*
shall ye come
they have turned them away *Jer 50:6*
on the *m.*
our persecutors pursued us on *La 4:19*
the *m.*
set thy face toward the *m.* of *Eze 6:2*
Israel
and say, Ye *m.* of Israel, hear *Eze 6:3*
the word of Lord
they shall be on the *m.* of *Eze 7:16*
doves of valleys
and hath not eaten upon the *Eze 18:6;*
m. *18:15*
but hath eaten on the *m.* and *Eze 18:11*
defiled
his voice should no more be *Eze 19:9*
heard on the *m.*
and in thee they eat upon the *Eze 22:9*
m.
upon the *m.* his branches *Eze 31:12*
are fallen
I will lay thy flesh on the *m.* *Eze 32:5*
and fill valleys
the *m.* of Israel shall be *Eze 33:28*
desolate
my sheep wandered through *Eze 34:6*
all the *m.*
I will feed them on the *m.* of *Eze 34:13;*
Israel *34:14*
I will fill his *m.* with his slain *Eze 35:8*
men
which thou hast spoken *Eze 35:12*
against the *m.* of Israel
prophesy unto *m.* of Israel, *Eze 36:1;*
and say, Ye *m.* of Israel, hear *36:4*
O *m.* of Israel shall shoot *Eze 36:8*
forth branches
I will make one nation on *Eze 37:22*
the *m.* of Israel
and is gathered out against *Eze 38:8*
the *m.* of Israel
and the *m.* shall be thrown *Eze 38:20*
down
I will call a sword against *Eze 38:21*
him thro' all my *m.*
and I will bring thee on the *m.* *Eze 39:2*
of Israel
shalt fall on the *m.* of Israel, *Eze 39:4*
and all bands
even a great sacrifice on the *Eze 39:17*
m. of Israel
as the morning spread upon the *Joe 2:2*
m.
that the *m.* shall drop down *Joe 3:18*
new wine
assemble yourselves on the *m.* *Am 3:9*
of Samaria
he that formeth the *m.* the *Am 4:13*
Lord is his name
and the *m.* shall drop sweet *Am 9:13*
wine
the *m.* shall be molten under *Mic 1:4*
him
the *m.* shall melt *Mic 1:4*
(A)(B)(E)(R)
arise, contend thou before the *Mic 6:1*
m. let the hills
hear ye, O ye *m.* the Lord's *Mic 6:2*
controversy
the *m.* quake at him, the hills *Na 1:5*
melt
thy people is scattered on the *Na 3:18*
m. no man
the everlasting *m.* were *Hab 3:6*
scattered, the hills
the *m.* saw thee, and they *Hab 3:10*
trembled
I called for a drought on the *Hag 1:11*
m.
four chariots between the *m.* of *Zec 6:1*
brass
I hated Esau, and laid his *m.* *Mal 1:3*
waste
and goeth into the *m.* and *M't 18:12*
seeketh
let them which be in Judæa *M't 24:16*
flee into the *m.*
all faith, so that I could *1Co 13:2*
remove *m.*
every island, and *m.* were not *Re 16:20*
found
the seven heads are seven *m.* *Re 17:9*
on which

IN THE MOUNTAINS

bring the mount to slay them in *Ex 32:12*
the *m.*
pitched *in the m.* of *Nu 33:47*
Abarim, before Nebo
thou camest not to the cities *in De 2:37*
the *m.*
the kings that dwell *in the m.* *Jos 10:6*
are gathered
Israel made them dens *in the m.* *J'g 6:2*
and caves
as one doth hunt a partridge *1Sa 26:20*
in the m.
eighty thousand hewers *in the* *1Ki 5:15*
m.
he made high places *in the* *2Ch 21:11*
m. of Judah
Uzziah had vine dressers *in* *2Ch 26:10*
the m.
the noise of a multitude *in the* *Isa 13:4*
m. like
night and day he was *in the m.* *M'k 5:5*
and tombs
they wandered in deserts *Hab 11:38*
and *in the m.*

OF THE MOUNTAINS

offer him on one *of m.* I will *Ge 22:2*
tell thee of
Balak brought me out *of m.* of *Nu 23:7*
the east
set on fire the foundations *of De 32:22*
the m.
for the chief things *of the* *De 33:15*
ancient *m.*
set liers in wait for him in top *J'g 9:25*
of the m.
come people down from top *J'g 9:36*
of the m. thou seest shadow
of the m. as men
I am come up to height *of* *2Ki 19:23;*
m. *Isa 37:24*
they are wet with the showers *Job 24:8*
of the m.
the range *of the m.* is his *Job 39:8*
pasture
I know all the fowls *of the m.* *Ps 50:11*
and beasts
shall be an handful of corn on *Ps 72:16*
top *of the m.*
and herbs *of the m.* are *Pr 27:25*
gathered
shall be established in top *Isa 2:2;*
of the m. *Mic 4:1*
and shall be chased as the *Isa 17:13*
chaff *of the m.*
they shall be left to the fowls *Isa 18:6*
of the m.
let them shout from the top *of Isa 42:11*
the m.
hoped for from the multitude *Jer 3:23*
of the m.
shall take witnesses in the *Jer 32:44*
cities *of the m.*
in cities *of the m.* shall flocks *Jer 33:13*
pass again
their slain shall be in the *Eze 6:13*
tops *of the m.*
and not the sounding again *of* *Eze 7:7*
the m.
they sacrifice on the tops *of* *Ho 4:13*
the m.
like the noise of chariots on *Joe 2:5*
tops *of the m.*
I went down to the bottom *of* *Jon 2:6*
the m.
and ye shall flee to the valley *Zec 14:5*
of the m.
hid themselves in the rocks *of Re 6:15*
the m.

TO THE MOUNTAINS

I will get me *to the m.* of myrrh *Ca 4:6*
it is a day of trouble and *Isa 22:5*
crying *to the m.*
thus saith the Lord *to the m.* *Eze 6:3;*
and hills *36:4*
I will water with thy blood *Eze 32:6*
even *to the m.*
son of man, prophesy *to the* *Eze 36:1;*
m. of Israel *36:6*
and they shall say *to the m.,* *Ho 10:8*
Cover us
there was nigh *to the m.* a *M'k 5:11*
herd of swine

that be in Judæa flee *to*   M'k 13:14;
the m.   Lu 21:21
begin to say *to the m.,* Fall   Lu 23:30;
on us   Re 6:16

MOUNTED

m. up from the earth in my   Eze 10:19
sight

MOUNTING

by the *m.* up of Luhith with   Isa 15:5
made the ascent to Luhith's   Isa 15:5
(B)

MOUNTS

the *m.,* they are come unto   Jer 32:24
siege mounds   Jer 32:24;
(A)(B)(E)(R)   33:4; Eze 17:17
which are thrown down by the   Jer 33:4
m.
by casting up *m.,* and   Zec 17:17
building

MOURN

Abraham came to *m.* for Sarah   Ge 23:2
came to lament and weep (B)   Ge 23:2
how long wilt thou *m.* for Saul   1Sa 16:1
grieve over Saul (B)(R)   1Sa 16:1
rend clothes, and *m.* before   2Sa 3:31
Abner
old prophet came into the city   1Ki 13:29
to *m.*
all Israel shall *m.* for him,   1Ki 14:13
and bury him
All Israel shall bewail him   1Ki 14:13
(B)
this day is holy to the Lord, *m.*   Ne 8:9
not
he made an appointment to *m.*   Job 2:11
with him
to condole with him (A)(R)   Job 2:11
to sympathize with him (B)   Job 2:11
to bemoan him (E)   Job 2:11
that those which *m.* may be   Job 5:11
exalted to safety
and his soul within him shall   Job 14:22
m.
his soul bemoans himself (B)   Job 14:22
I *m.* in my complaint, and   Ps 55:2
make a noise
in my complaint and must   Ps 55:2
moan (A)(E)
in restlessness I groan (B)   Ps 55:2
I am overcome by my trouble   Ps 55:2
(R)
and thou *m.* at the last, when   Pr 5:11
thy flesh
moan when the end comes (B)   Pr 5:11
at the end of life you groan   Pr 5:11
(R)
when the wicked bear rule, the   Pr 29:2
people *m.*
the people groan and sigh   Pr 29:2
(A)(B)(R)
the people sigh (E)   Pr 29:2
a time to *m.* and a time to dance   Ec 3:4
and her gates shall lament and   Isa 3:26
m.
for foundations of   Isa 16:7
Kir-hareseth shall ye *m.*
fishers shall *m.;* I did *m.* as a   Isa 19:8;
dove   38:14
we roar like bears, we *m.* sore   Isa 59:11
like doves
moan like doves   Isa 59:11
(A)(B)(E)(R)
he hath sent me to comfort all   Isa 61:2
that *m.*
to appoint them that *m.* in   Isa 61:3
Zion beauty for ashes
rejoice for joy, all ye that *m.*   Isa 66:10
for her
for this shall earth *m.* and   Jer 4:28
heavens black
how long shall the land *m.*   Jer 12:4
herbs wither
my heart shall *m.* for men of   Jer 48:31
Kir-hereseth
ways of Zion do *m.* because   La 1:4
none come
the time is come, let not the   Eze 7:12
seller *m.*
the king shall *m.* and the   Eze 7:27
prince be clothed
yet neither shalt thou *m.* nor   Eze 24:16
weep

ye shall pine away and *m.*   Eze 24:23
one towards another
I caused Lebanon to *m.* for   Eze 31:15
him
therefore shall the land *m.* and   Ho 4:3
languish
for the people shall *m.* over   Ho 10:5
Samaria
the priests, the Lord's   Joe 1:7
ministers, *m.*
gird yourselves and *m.* (B)   Joe 1:13
the habitations of the   Am 1:2
shepherds shall *m.*
and every one *m.* that dwelleth   Am 8:8;
therein   9:5
and shall *m.* for him as one   Zec 12:10
mourneth
and the land shall *m.* every   Zec 12:12
family apart
blessed are they that *m.* for   M't 5:4
they shall
can the children of the   M't 9:15
bridechamber *m.*
then shall all the tribes of the   M't 24:30
earth *m.*
woe to you that laugh, for ye   Lu 6:25
shall *m.*
m. for many (E)(R)   2Co 12:21
be afflicted, and *m.* and weep   Jas 4:9
beat breasts, *m.,* lament (A)(E)   Re 1:7
the merchants shall weep and   Re 18:11
m.

MOURNED

Jacob *m.* for his son many   Ge 37:34
days
Egyptians *m.* for Jacob   Ge 50:3;
seventy days   50:10
bemoaned him 70 days (A)(B)   Ge 50:3
wept for him 70 days (E)(R)   Ge 50:3
people heard these evil   Ex 33:4;
tidings, they *m.*   Nu 14:39
the congregation *m.* for   Nu 20:29
Aaron
nevertheless Samuel *m.* for   1Sa 15:35
Saul
and they *m.* for Saul and   2Sa 1:12
Jonathan
Bath-sheba *m.* for Uriah her   2Sa 11:26
husband
David *m.* for his son   2Sa 13:37
Absalom every day
as one that had long time *m.*   2Sa 14:2
for the dead
and they *m.* over the man of   1Ki 13:30
God
all Israel *m.* for Jeroboam's   1Ki 14:18
son
Ephraim their father *m.* many   1Ch 7:22
days
and all Judah *m.* for Josiah   2Ch 35:24
he *m.* for the transgression of   Ezr 10:6
them
I sat down and *m.* certain days   Ne 1:4
m. with fasting (B)   Ps 69:10
when ye *m.* and fasted, did ye   Zec 7:5
fast to me
and saying, We have *m.*   M't 11:17;
unto you, and ye have not   Lu 7:32
lamented
you, and ye have not lamented   Lu 7:32
and she told them as they *m.*   M'k 16:10
and wept
are puffed up, and have not   1Co 5:2
rather *m.*

MOURNER

I pray thee, feign thyself to be   2Sa 14:2
a *m.*
play part of a *m.* (A)(B)(R)   2Sa 14:2

MOURNERS

I dwelt as one that   Job 29:25
comforteth the *m.*
and the *m.* go about the streets   Ec 12:5
I will restore comforts to him   Isa 57:18
and his *m.*
sacrifices shall be to them as   Ho 9:4
bread of *m.*

MOURNETH

behold, the king *m.* for   2Sa 19:1
Absalom
I bowed as one that *m.* for his   Ps 35:14
mother
mine eye *m.* by reason of   Ps 88:9
affliction

the earth *m.*   Isa 24:4; 33:9
the new wine *m.*   Isa 24:7
my vineyard being desolate   Jer 12:11
m. to me
Judah *m.* and the gates thereof   Jer 14:2
languish
for because of swearing the   Jer 23:10
land *m.*
the land *m.* for the corn is   Joe 1:10
wasted
as one that *m.* for his   Zec 12:10
firstborn

MOURNFULLY

what profit that we have   Mal 3:14
walked *m.*

MOURNING

the days of *m.* for my father   Ge 27:41
are at hand
will go down to the grave to   Ge 37:35
my son *m.*
and when the days of his *m.*   Ge 50:4
were past
he made a *m.* for his father   Ge 50:10
Jacob seven days
the Canaanites saw the *m.*   Ge 50:11
this is a grievous *m.*
I have not eaten thereof in   De 26:14
my *m.*
so the days of *m.* for Moses   De 34:8
were ended
when the *m.* was past David   2Sa 11:27
sent
I pray thee, put on *m.* apparel   2Sa 14:2
the victory that day was   2Sa 19:2
turned into *m.*
there was great *m.* among the   Es 4:3
Jews
but Haman hasted to his house   Es 6:12
m.
was turned to them from *m.*   Es 9:22
into a good day
who are ready to raise up their   Job 3:8
m.
I went *m.* without the sun. I   Job 30:28
stood up
my harp also is turned to *m.*   Job 30:31
and my organ
thou hast turned my *m.* into   Ps 30:11
dancing
I am troubled, I go *m.* all day   Ps 38:6
long
why go I *m.* because of   Ps 42:9;
oppression of enemy   43:2
widows made no *m.* (B)   Ps 78:64
it is better to go to the house of   Ec 7:2
m.
the heart of the wise is in the   Ec 7:4
house of *m.*
in that day the Lord did call   Isa 22:12
to *m.*
heaviness and *m.* (B)   Isa 29:2
and sorrow and *m.* shall flee   Isa 51:11
away
and the days of thy *m.* shall   Isa 60:20
be ended
to give to them the oil of joy   Isa 61:3
for *m.*
make thee *m.* as for an only   Jer 6:26
son
consider ye, and call for the *m.*   Jer 9:17
women
enter not into the house of *m.*   Jer 16:5
neither go
m. to comfort them for the   Jer 16:7
dead
for I will turn their *m.* into   Jer 31:13
joy
increased in the daughter of   La 2:5
Judah *m.*
multiplied moaning and *m.* (B)   La 2:5
joy is ceased, our dance is   La 5:15
turned into *m.*
was written lamentations, *m.*   Eze 2:10
and woe
all of them *m.* for their   Eze 7:16
iniquities
no *m.* for the dead I caused   Eze 24:17;
a *m.*   31:15
in those days I Daniel was   Da 10:2
m. three weeks
turn ye to me with weeping   Joe 2:12
and *m.*
they shall call the husbandmen   Am 5:16
to *m.*
and I will turn your feasts   Am 8:10
into *m.* and I will make it as
the *m.* of an only son

I will make a *m.* as the owls   *Mic 1:8*
came not forth in the *m.* of   *Mic 1:11*
Beth-ezel
m. in Jerusalem. as *m.* of   *Zec 12:11*
Hadadrimmon
was heard great *m.* Rachel   *M't 2:18*
weeping
weeping and *m.* (B)   *Joh 16:20*
grieved and *m.* (A)   *2Co 6:16*
when he told us your desire,   *2Co 7:7*
your *m.*
let your laughter be turned into   *Jas 4:9*
m.
so much *m.* give her (E)(R)   *Re 18:7;*
                    21:4
in one day death and *m.* and   *Re 18:8*
famine

MOUSE

the weasel and *m.* shall be   *Le 11:29*
unclean
eating the abomination, and   *Isa 66:17*
the *m.*

MOUTH

and lo, in her *m.* was an   *Ge 8:11*
olive leaf
call the damsel, and inquire at   *Ge 24:57*
her *m.*
and a great stone was upon the   *Ge 29:2*
well's *m.*
they rolled the stone from the   *Ge 29:3;*
well's *m.*   *29:10*
his money was in his sack's   *Ge 42:27;*
m.   *43:12, 21*
Lord said, Who hath made   *Ex 4:11*
man's *m.*
even he shall be to thee instead   *Ex 4:16*
of a *m.*
as a *m.* piece (A)(R)   *Ex 4:16*
with him will I speak *m* to *m.*   *Nu 12:8*
the earth open her *m.* and   *Nu 16:30*
swallow them up
the Lord put a word in   *Nu 23:5*
Balaam's *m.*
shall be put to death by the   *Nu 35:30;*
m. of witnesses   *De 17:6, 19:15*
open *m.* of cave, and bring   *Jos 10:22*
out the five kings
as she prayed, Eli marked her   *1Sa 1:12*
m.
so Joab put the words in her   *2Sa 14:3;*
m.   *14:19*
she spread a covering over   *2Sa 17:19*
the well's *m.*
every *m.* that hath not kissed   *1Ki 19:18*
him
declare good to the king with   *1Ki 22:13*
one *m.*
I will go forth and be a lying   *1Ki 22:22;*
spirit in the *m.* of his prophets   *22:23;*
               2Ch 18:21-22
hearkened not to Necho   *2Ch 35:22*
from *m.* of God
to fulfil the word of the   *2Ch 36:21;*
Lord by the *m.* of Jeremiah   *36:22;*
               Ezr 1:1
as the word went out of the   *Es 7:8*
king's *m.*
poor hath hope, iniquity   *Job 5:16*
stoppeth her *m.*
doth not the *m.* taste his *m.*   *Job 12:11;*
               34:3
there was no answer in the *m.*   *Job 32:5*
of these men
out of *m.* of babes hast ordained   *Ps 8:2*
strength
save me from the lion's *m.* for   *Ps 22:21*
thou heardest
whose *m.* must be held in with   *Ps 32:9*
bit and bridle
the *m.* of the righteous   *Ps 37:30*
speaketh wisdom
and in whose *m.* are no   *Ps 38:14*
reproofs
but *m.* that speaketh lies shall   *Ps 63:11*
be stopped
let not the pit shut her *m.*   *Ps 69:15*
upon me
and all iniquity shall stop her   *Ps 107:42*
m.
m. of wicked, *m.* of deceitful   *Ps 109:2*
are opened
then was our *m.* filled with   *Ps 126:2*
laughter
our bones are scattered at the   *Ps 141:7*
grave's *m.*
whose *m.* speaketh vanity   *Ps 144:8;*
               144:11

put away from thee a froward   *Pr 4:24*
m.
and her *m.* is smoother than oil   *Pr 5:3*
wicked man walketh with   *Pr 6:12;*
froward *m.*   *10:32*
proud, and the froward *m.* do I   *Pr 8:13*
hate
violence covereth the *m.* of the   *Pr 10:6;*
wicked   *10:11*
the *m.* of the foolish is near   *Pr 10:14*
destruction
the *m.* of the just bringeth   *Pr 10:31*
forth wisdom
the city is overthrown by *m.*   *Pr 11:11*
of the wicked
the *m.* of the upright shall   *Pr 12:6*
deliver them
in the *m.* of the foolish is a rod   *Pr 14:3*
of pride
the *m.* of fools poureth out   *Pr 15:2*
foolishness
the *m.* of fools feedeth on   *Pr 15:14*
foolishness
the *m.* of the wicked poureth   *Pr 15:28*
out evil things
the words of a man's *m.* are as   *Pr 18:4*
deep waters
a fool's *m.* is his destruction,   *Pr 18:7*
and his lips
the *m.* of the wicked   *Pr 19:28*
devoureth iniquity
the *m.* of a strange woman is   *Pr 22:14*
a deep pit
so is a parable in the *m.* of   *Pr 26:7;*
fools   *26:9*
and a flattering *m.* worketh   *Pr 26:28*
ruin
she eateth, and wipeth her *m.*   *Pr 30:20*
and saith
words of a wise man's *m.* are   *Ec 10:12*
gracious
they shall devour Israel with   *Isa 9:12*
open *m.*
an evil doer, and every *m.*   *Isa 9:17*
speaketh folly
against whom make ye a wide   *Isa 57:4*
m.
my Spirit not depart out of   *Isa 59:21*
m. of thy seed
shall speak with him *m.* to *m.*   *Jer 32:4;*
               34:3
Baruch wrote from *m.* of   *Jer 36:4;*
Jeremiah   *36:27, 32; 45:1*
what thing goeth forth out of   *Jer 44:17*
our *m.*
no more named in *m.* of any   *Jer 44:26*
man of Judah
out of the *m.* of most High   *La 3:38*
proceedeth
to open the *m.* in the   *Eze 21:22*
slaughter
I will give thee the opening   *Eze 29:21*
of the *m.*
came near to the *m.* of the   *Da 3:26*
furnace
while the word was in the   *Da 4:31*
king's *m.*
a stone brought, and laid on   *Da 6:17*
the *m.* of the den
it had three ribs in *m.* of it   *Da 7:5*
between teeth
there was a *m.* speaking great   *Da 7:8;*
things   *7:20*
take the names of Baalim out   *Ho 2:17*
of her *m.*
as a shepherd taketh out of   *Am 3:12*
the *m.*
shall even fall into the *m.* of   *Am 3:12*
the eater
cast the weight of lead on the   *Zec 5:8*
m. of it
that proceedeth out of the *m.*   *M't 4:4*
of God
abundance of the heart the   *M't 12:34*
m. speaketh
what goeth into the *m.*   *M't 15:11*
defileth not
m. of two or three witnesses   *M't 18:16;*
every word be established   *2Co 13:1*
out of the *m.* of babes hast   *M't 21:16*
perfected praise
as he spake by *m.* of his holy   *Lu 1:70*
prophets
for I will give you a *m.* and   *Lu 21:15*
wisdom
Holy Ghost spake by *m.* of   *Ac 1:16;*
David   *4:25*
God shewed by *m.* of all his   *Ac 3:18;*
prophets   *3:21*
who shall tell you the same   *Ac 15:27*
things by *m.*

commanded them to smite him   *Ac 23:2*
on the *m.*
whose *m.* is full of cursing and   *Ro 3:14*
bitterness
that every *m.* may be stopped,   *Ro 3:19*
and all world
with the *m.* confession is   *Ro 10:10*
made to salvation
that ye may with one *m.*   *Ro 15:6*
glorify God
thou shalt not muzzle the *m.* of   *1Co 9:9*
the ox
I was delivered out of *m.* of   *2Ti 4:17*
the lion
out of the same *m.* proceedeth   *Jas 3:10*
blessing
given to him a *m.* speaking   *Re 13:5*
blasphemies
the spirits came out of *m.* of   *Re 16:13*
the dragon

MOUTH *OPENED*

earth *opened m.* to receive   *Ge 4:11*
brother's blood
earth *opened* her *m.* and   *Nu 16:32;*
swallowed them up   *26:10; De 11:6*
Lord *opened m.* of ass, and   *Nu 22:28*
she said
I have *opened* my *m.* to the   *J'g 11:35;*
Lord   *11:36*
opened Job his *m.* and cursed   *Job 3:1*
his day
and they *opened* their *m.*   *Job 29:23;*
wide   *Ps 35:21*
I pray, hear, now I have   *Job 33:2*
opened my *m.*
I was dumb I *opened* not my   *Ps 39:9*
m.
m. of the deceitful are *opened*   *Ps 109:2*
against me
I *opened* my *m.* and panted   *Ps 119:131*
hell *opened* her *m.* without   *Isa 5:14*
measure
there was none that *opened*   *Isa 10:14*
m. or peeped
he was oppressed, yet he   *Isa 53:7*
opened not his *m.*
I *opened* my *m.* and he caused   *Eze 3:2*
me to eat
thy *m.* be *opened* to him   *Eze 24:27;*
which is escaped   *33:22*
then I *opened* my *m.* and   *Da 10:16*
spake
he *opened* his *m.* and taught   *M't 5:2*
them
when thou hast *opened* his   *M't 17:27*
m. thou shalt find
his *m.* was *opened*   *Lu 1:64*
immediately, and spake
like a lamb dumb, so *opened*   *Ac 8:32*
he not his *m.*
Philip *opened m.*; Peter   *Ac 8:35;*
opened m. said   *10:34*
O Corinthians, our *m.* is   *2Co 6:11*
opened to you
earth *opened* her *m.* and   *Re 12:16*
helped woman
he *opened* his *m.* in blasphemy   *Re 13:6*
against God

MOUTH *OPENETH*

as a dumb man that *openeth*   *Ps 38:13*
not his *m.*
a fool *openeth* not his *m.* in the   *Pr 24:7*
gate
she *openeth* her *m.* with   *Pr 31:26*
wisdom

HIS MOUTH

put words in *his m.* I will be   *Ex 4:15*
with *his m.*
God put a word in *his m.* and   *Nu 23:5*
said, Go
according to all that   *Nu 30:2*
proceedeth out of *his m.*
and I will put my words in *his*   *De 18:18*
m.
but no man put his hand to   *1Sa 14:26;*
his m.   *14:27*
I went and delivered it out of   *1Sa 17:35*
his m.
if he be alone, there is tidings   *2Sa 18:25*
in *his m.*
and fire out of *his m.*   *2Sa 22:9;*
devoured   *Ps 18:8*
spake with *his m.* to David   *1Ki 8:15;*
               2Ch 6:4

and he put *his* m. on *his* m.   2Ki 4:34
remember the judgments of   1Ch 16:12
his m.
by the breath of *his* m. he   Job 15:30
shall go away
though wickedness be sweet   Job 20:12
in *his* m.
though he keep it still within   Job 20:13
his m.
receive, I pray thee, the law   Job 22:22
from *his* m.
I have esteemed the words of   Job 23:12
his m. more
and the sound that goeth out   Job 37:2
of *his* m.
that he can draw up Jordan   Job 40:23
into *his* m.
out of *his* m. go burning   Job 41:19
lamps and sparks
and a flame goeth out of *his*   Job 41:21
m.
his m. is full of cursing and   Ps 10:7
deceit
the host of them made by   Ps 33:6
breath of *his* m.
the words of *his* m. are iniquity   Ps 36:3
and deceit
as a dumb man that openeth   Ps 38:13
not *his* m.
words of *his* m. are smoother   Ps 55:21
than butter
remember the judgments of   Ps 105:5
his m.
out of *his* m. cometh knowledge   Pr 2:6
hypocrite with *his* m.   Pr 11:9
destroyeth neighbour
satisfied with good by the fruit   Pr 12:14
of *his* m.
a man shall eat good by the   Pr 13:2
fruit of *his* m.
he that keepeth *his* m. keepeth   Pr 13:3
his life
a man hath joy by the answer   Pr 15:23
of *his* m.
his m. transgresseth not in   Pr 16:10
judgment
the heart of the wise teacheth   Pr 16:23
his m.
for himself, for *his* m. craveth   Pr 16:26
it of him
and *his* m. calleth for strokes   Pr 18:6
shall be satisfied with the fruit   Pr 18:20
of *his* m.
will not so much as bring it   Pr 19:24;
to *his* m.   26:15
but *his* m. shall be filled with   Pr 20:17
gravel
whoso keepeth *his* m. keepeth   Pr 21:23
his soul
all the labour of a man is for *his*   Ec 6:7
m.
beginning of words of *his* m.   Ec 10:13
is foolishness
let him kiss me with the kisses   Ca 1:2
of *his* m.
his m. is most sweet, this is my   Ca 5:16
beloved
smite the earth with the rod of   Isa 11:4
his m.
neither was any deceit in *his*   Isa 53:9
m.
one speaketh peaceably with *his*   Jer 9:8
m.
and let your ear receive the   Jer 9:20
word of *this* m.
how didst thou write all these   Jer 36:17
words at *his* m.
bring out of *his* m. that which   Jer 51:44
he swallowed
he putteth *his* m. in the dust, if   La 3:29
so be there
the tongue cleaveth to the roof   La 4:4
of *his* m.
I will take away his blood out   Zec 9:7
of *his* m.
the law of truth was in *his* m.   Mal 2:6
and they should seek the law at   Mal 2:7
his *m*.
and *his* m. was opened   Lu 1:64
immediately
gracious words proceeded out   Lu 4:22
of *his* m.
of the abundance of heart *his*   Lu 6:45
m. speaketh
seeking to catch somewhat   Lu 11:54
out of *his* m.
ourselves have heard of *his*   Lu 22:71
own *m*.
filled a spunge and put it to   Joh 19:29
his m.

and shouldest hear the voice   Ac 22:14
of *his* m.
shall consume with the spirit of   2Th 2:8
his m.
neither was guile found in *his*   1Pe 2:22
m.
out of *his* m. went a sharp   Re 1:16;
sword   9:15, 21
the serpent cast out of *his* m.   Re 12:15
water
the flood which the dragon   Re 12:16
cast out of *his* m.
and *his* m. was as the mouth of   Re 13:2
a lion

MINE, MY MOUTH

that it is *my* m. that speaketh   Ge 45:12
to you
the word God putteth in *my*   Nu 22:38;
m.   23:12
hear, O earth, the words of *my*   De 32:1
m.
my m. is enlarged over mine   1Sa 2:1
enemies
therefore I will not refrain *my*   Job 7:11
m.
mine own *m*. shall condemn   Job 9:20
me
I would strengthen you with   Job 16:5
my m.
I entreated my servant with   Job 19:16
my m.
I would fill *my* m. with   Job 23:4
arguments
or *my* m. hath kissed my   Job 31:27
hand
neither have I suffered *my* m.   Job 31:30
to sin
behold my tongue hath spoken   Job 33:2
in *my* m.
I am vile, I will lay my hand   Job 40:4
upon *my* m.
purposed *my* m. shall not   Ps 17:3
transgress
let the words of *my* m. be   Ps 19:14
acceptable
his praise shall continually be   Ps 34:1
in *my* m.
I said, I will keep *my* m. with a   Ps 39:1
bridle
he hath put a new song in *my*   Ps 40:3
m. even praise
hear this, *my* m. shall speak   Ps 49:3
of wisdom
and *my* m. shall shew forth thy   Ps 51:15
praise
hear and give ear to the words   Ps 54:2
of *my* m.
my m. shall praise thee with   Ps 63:5
joyful lips
my m. hath spoken when I   Ps 66:14
was in trouble
I cried to him with *my* m. he   Ps 66:17
was extolled
let *my* m. be filled with thy   Ps 71:8
praise
my m. shall shew forth thy   Ps 71:15
righteousness
incline your ears to the words   Ps 78:1
of *my* m.
I will open *my* m. in a parable,   Ps 78:2
I will utter
with *my* m. will I make known   Ps 89:1
thy faithfulness
I will greatly praise the Lord   Ps 109:30
with *my* m.
take not the word of truth   Ps 119:43
out of *my* m.
thy words are sweeter than   Ps 119:103
honey to *my* m.
accept the freewill   Ps 119:108
offerings of *my* m.
let my tongue cleave to the   Ps 137:6
roof of *my* m.
set a watch, O Lord, before   Ps 141:3
my m.
my m. shall speak the praise   Ps 145:21
of the Lord
nor decline from words of *my*   Pr 4:5;
m.   5:7
O children, attend to the words   Pr 7:24
of *my* m.
my m. shall speak truth, and   Pr 8:7
wickedness
the words of *my* m. are in   Pr 8:8
righteousness
and he laid the coal on *my* m.   Isa 6:7
and said
go to Egypt, and have not   Isa 30:2
asked at *my* m.

for *my* m. it hath commanded   Isa 34:16
word is gone out of *my* m. in   Isa 45:23
righteousness
the former things went forth   Isa 48:3
out of *my* m.
he hath made *my* m. like a   Isa 49:2
sharp sword
so shall my word be that   Isa 55:11
goeth out of *my* m.
put forth his hand and touched   Jer 1:9
my m.
shalt be as *my* m.; written   Jer 15:19;
from *my* m.   36:6
it was in *my* m. like honey for   Eze 3:3
sweetness
therefore hear the word at   Eze 3:17;
my m.   33:7
nor came there abominable   Eze 4:14
flesh into *my* m.
neither came flesh nor wine in   Da 10:3
my m.
I have slain them by the words   Ho 6:5
of *my* m.
I will open *my* m. in parables   M't 13:35
hath at any time entered into   Ac 11:8
my m.
Gentiles by *my* m. should hear   Ac 15:7
the word
praying that I may open *my*   Eph 6:19
m. boldly
I will fight with the sword of   Re 2:16
my m.
nor cold nor hot, I will spue   Re 3:16
thee out of *my* m.
the book was in *my* m. sweet   Re 10:10
as honey

THEIR MOUTH

lapped, putting their hand to   J'g 7:6
their m.
withheldest not manna from   Ne 9:20
their m.
but he saveth the poor from   Job 5:15
their m.
they have gaped upon me   Job 16:10
with *their* m.
the princes laid their hand on   Job 29:9
their m.
their tongue cleaved to the   Job 29:10
roof of *their* m.
there is no faithfulness in *their*   Ps 5:9
m.
with *their* m. they speak   Ps 17:10
proudly
break their teeth in *their* m.   Ps 58:6
behold they belch out with *their*   Ps 59:7
m.
sin of *their* m. and words of   Ps 59:12
their lips
bless with *their* m. but curse   Ps 62:4
inwardly
they set *their* m. against the   Ps 73:9
heavens
did flatter him with *their* m.   Ps 78:36
and lied
let the high praises of God be   Ps 149:6
in *their* m.
this people draw near me   Isa 29:13
with *their* m.
and truth is cut off from *their*   Jer 7:28
m.
thou art near in *their* m. far   Jer 12:2
from their reins
enemies opened *their* m.   La 2:16
against thee
with *their* m. they shew much   Eze 33:31
love
I will deliver my flock from   Eze 34:10
their m.
their tongue is deceitful in   Mic 6:12
their m.
they shall lay their hand on   Mic 7:16
their m.
nor a deceitful tongue found   Zep 3:13
in *their* m.
tongue shall consume away   Zec 14:12
in *their* m.
their m. speaketh great   Jude 16
swelling words
this people draweth nigh to me   M't 15:8
with *their* m.
their power is in *their* m. and   Re 9:19
tails
if any hurt them, fire   Re 11:5
proceedeth out of *their* m.
and in *their* m. was found no   Re 14:5
guile

THINE, THY MOUTH

I will be with *thy m.* and teach   *Ex 4:12;*
thee   *4:15*
that the Lord's law may be in   *Ex 13:9*
thy m.
no mention of other gods out   *Ex 23:13*
of *thy m.*
keep that hast promised with   *De 23:23*
thy m.
word is nigh to thee, in *thy*   *De 30:14;*
m.   *Ro 10:8*
book of law not depart out   *Jos 1:8*
of *thy m.*
then said Zebul, where is now   *J'g 9:38*
thy m.
if thou hast opened *thy m.* to   *J'g 11:36*
the Lord
lay thine hand upon *thy m.*   *J'g 18:19;*
   Pr 30:32
thy m. hath testified against   *2Sa 1:16*
thee
thou spakest with *thy m.*   *1Ki 8:24;*
   2Ch 6:15
the word of the Lord in *thy*   *1Ki 17:24*
m. is truth
the words of *thy m.* be like a   *Job 8:2*
strong wind
till he fill *thy m.* with   *Job 8:21*
laughing, and thy lips
for *thy m.* uttereth thine   *Job 15:5*
iniquity
thine own *m.* condemneth   *Job 15:6*
thee, and not I
that thou lettest such words   *Job 15:13*
go out of *thy m.*
shouldest take my covenant in   *Ps 50:16*
thy m.
thou givest *thy m.* to evil;   *Ps 50:19;*
open *thy m.*   *81:10*
who satisfieth *thy m.* with   *Ps 103:5*
good things
have declared all the   *Ps 119:13*
judgments of *thy m.*
the law of *thy m.* is better to   *Ps 119:72*
me than gold
so shall I keep the testimony   *Ps 119:88*
of *thy m.*
when they hear the words of   *Ps 138:4*
thy m.
thou art snared with the words   *Pr 6:2*
of *thy m.*
let another praise thee, and not   *Pr 27:2*
thine own *m.*
open *thy m.* for the dumb, in   *Pr 31:8*
the cause of all
open *thy m.* judge righteously   *Pr 31:9*
be not rash with *thy m.* to utter   *Ec 5:2*
any thing
suffer not *thy m.* to cause thy   *Ec 5:6*
flesh to sin
the roof of *thy m.* like the best   *Ca 7:9*
wine
I have put my words in *thy*   *Isa 51:16;*
m.   *Jer 1:9*
which I put in *thy m.* not   *Isa 59:21*
depart out of *thy m.*
I will make my words in *thy*   *Jer 5:14*
m. fire
open *thy m.* and eat that I give   *Eze 2:8*
thee
make my tongue cleave to   *Eze 3:26*
roof of *thy m.*
I will open *thy m.* and thou   *Eze 3:27*
shalt say
sister Sodom not mentioned   *Eze 16:56*
by *thy m.*
thou mayest never open *thy*   *Eze 16:63*
m. any more
set the trumpet to *thy m.* he   *Ho 8:1*
shall come
keep doors of *thy m.* from her   *Mic 7:5*
that lieth
out of *thine* own *m.* will I   *Lu 19:22*
judge thee
if confess with *thy m.* the Lord   *Ro 10:9*
Jesus
it shall be in *thy m.* sweet as   *Re 10:9*
honey

YOUR MOUTH

do that which proceeded out   *Nu 32:24*
of *your m.*
let not arrogancy come out of   *1Sa 2:3*
your m.
mark me, and lay your hand   *Job 21:5*
on *your m.*
thus with *your m.* ye have   *Eze 35:13*
boasted

for the wine is cut off from   *Joe 1:5*
your m.
communication proceed out   *Eph 4:29;*
of *your m.*   *Col 3:8*

MOUTHS

write this song, put it in their   *De 31:19*
m.
not be forgotten out of *m.* of   *De 31:21*
their seed
they gaped upon me with their   *Ps 22:13*
m.
while their meat was yet in   *Ps 78:30*
their *m.*
have *m.* but they speak not   *Ps 115:5;*
   135:16
neither is there any breath in   *Ps 135:17*
their *m.*
the kings shall shut their *m.*   *Isa 52:15*
at him
ye and wives have spoken   *Jer 44:25*
with your *m.*
our enemies opened their *m.*   *La 3:46*
against us
my God hath shut the lions' *m.*   *Da 6:22*
and he that putteth not into   *Mic 3:5*
their *m.*
deceivers, whose *m.* must be   *Tit 1:11*
stopped
who stopped the *m.* of lions   *Heb 11:33*
behold. we put bits in the   *Jas 3:3*
horses' *m.*
out of their *m.* issued fire and   *Re 9:17;*
smoke   *9:18*

MOVE

a dog *m.* his tongue against   *Ex 11:7*
man
of all that *m.* in the waters   *Le 11:10*
move (S)   *Nu 36:7;*
   Isa 46:7; Eze 12:3, 11; M't 17:20
not *m.* sickle into neighbour's   *De 23:25*
corn
and I will *m.* them to jealousy   *De 32:21*
with those
the Spirit of the Lord began   *J'g 13:25*
to *m.* him
may dwell and *m.* no more   *2Sa 7:10;*
   2Ki 21:8
let him alone, let no man *m.*   *2Ki 23:18*
his bones
they fasten it with nails that it   *Jer 10:4*
m. not
they shall *m.* out of holes like   *Mic 7:17*
worms
they themselves will not *m.*   *M't 23:4*
them
in him we live, *m.* have our   *Ac 17:28*
being
none of these things *m.* me,   *Ac 20:24*
nor count I

MOVEABLE

all *m.* property (B)   *Ge 31:18*
her ways are *m.* canst not know   *Pr 5:6*
them

MOVED

Spirit of God *m.* on face of the   *Ge 1:2*
waters
all flesh died that *m.* on the   *Ge 7:21*
earth, of fowl
they *m.* and stood far off (S)   *Ex 20:18*
have *m.* me to jealousy with   *De 32:21*
none *m.* his tongue against   *Jos 10:21*
Israel
m. him to ask of father a   *Jos 15:18;*
field   *J'g 1:14*
that all the city was *m.* about   *Ru 1:19*
them
she spake in her heart, only   *1Sa 1:13*
her lips *m.*
the king was much *m.* and   *2Sa 18:33*
wept
the foundations of heaven *m.*   *2Sa 22:8*
and shook
he *m.* David against them, to   *2Sa 24:1*
say, Go number
fear before him, that it be   *1Ch 16:30;*
not *m.*   *Ps 93:1; 96:10*
they shall dwell, and shall be   *1Ch 17:9*
m. no more
God *m.* them to depart from   *2Ch 18:31*
him

they have *m.* sedition of old   *Ezr 4:15*
time
Haman saw that Mordecai *m.*   *Ex 5:9*
not for him
at this my heart is *m.* out of   *Job 37:1*
his place
the flakes of his flesh, they   *Job 41:23*
cannot be *m.*
I shall not be *m.*   *Ps 10:6;*
   16:8; 30:6; 62:2, 6
those that trouble me rejoice   *Ps 13:4*
when I am *m.*
he that doeth these things shall   *Ps 15:5*
never be *m.*
foundations of hills *m.* and   *Ps 18:7*
were shaken
the king trusteth in Lord, and   *Ps 21:7*
shall not be *m.*
she shall not be *m.* God shall   *Ps 46:5*
help her
the heathen raged, the   *Ps 46:6*
kingdoms were *m.*
shall never suffer the righteous   *Ps 55:22*
to be *m.*
and sufferest not our feet to be   *Ps 66:9*
m.
Sinai was *m.* at the presence of   *Ps 68:8*
God
they *m.* him to jealousy with   *Ps 78:58*
graven images
the Lord reigneth, let the earth   *Ps 99:1*
be *m.*
surely he shall not be *m.* for   *Ps 112:6*
ever
he will not suffer thy foot to   *Ps 121:3*
be *m.*
the root of the righteous shall   *Pr 12:3*
not be *m.*
and my bowels were *m.* for him   *Ca 5:4*
posts of the door *m.* at the   *Isa 6:4*
voice of him
his heart was *m.* as trees are *m.*   *Isa 7:2*
with wind
and there was none that *m.*   *Isa 10:14*
the wing
hell from beneath is *m.* for   *Isa 14:9*
thee to meet thee
my feelings are *m.* for Moab   *Isa 16:11*
(B)
idols of Egypt shall be *m.* at   *Isa 19:1*
his presence
earth is broken down, and *m.*   *Isa 24:19*
exceedingly
a graven image that shall not   *Isa 40:20;*
be *m.*   *41:7*
they trembled, and all the hills   *Jer 4:24*
m. lightly
they shall drink, and be *m.*   *Jer 25:16*
and be mad
whose waters are *m.* as the   *Jer 46:7;*
rivers   *46:8*
the earth is *m.* at the noise of   *Jer 49:21*
Edom's fall
at the taking of Babylon the   *Jer 50:46*
earth is *m.*
he was *m.* with choler against   *Da 8:7*
him
the king of the south shall be   *Da 11:11*
m. with choler
he was *m.* with compassion   *M't 9:36;*
on them   *14:14; 18:27; M'k 1:41; 6:34*
were *m.* with indignation   *M't 20:24*
against brethren
all the city was *m.* saying,   *M't 21:10*
Who is this
but the chief priests *m.* the   *M'k 15:11*
people
Jesus had *m.* away (S)   *Joh 5:13*
was deeply *m.* (N)(P)   *Joh 11:33*
on my right hand, that I should   *Ac 2:25*
not be *m.*
were *m.* to the depths (B)   *Ac 2:27*
patriarchs, *m.* with envy, sold   *Ac 7:9*
Joseph into Egypt
but the Jews *m.* with envy,   *Ac 17:5*
took lewd fellows
the city was *m.* and people   *Ac 21:30*
ran together
be not *m.* from the hope of   *Col 1:23*
the gospel
that no man be *m.* by these   *1Th 3:3*
afflictions
Noah, *m.* with fear, prepared   *Heb 11:7*
an ark
we receiving a kingdom   *Heb 12:28*
which cannot be *m.*
they spake as *m.* by the Holy   *2Pe 1:21*
Ghost
every mountain and island *m.*   *Re 6:14*
out of place

MOVEDST

tho' thou *m.* me against him   *Job 2:3*
without cause

MOVER

have found this fellow a *m.* of   *Ac 24:5*
sedition

MOVETH

God created every living   *Ge 1:21*
creature that *m.*
dominion over every thing that   *Ge 1:28*
m. on earth
the fear of you shall be on all   *Ge 9:2*
that *m.* on earth
this is the law of every   *Le 11:46*
creature that *m.*
Behemoth *m.* his tail like a   *Job 40:17*
cedar
let every thing that *m.* praise   *Ps 69:34*
him
not on wine when it *m.* itself   *Pr 23:31*
aright
that *m.* whithersoever the   *Eze 47:9*
rivers come

MOVING

let the waters bring forth *m.*   *Ge 1:20*
creatures
every *m.* thing shall be meat for   *Ge 9:3*
you
the *m.* of my lips should   *Job 16:5*
assuage grief
m. his lips, he bringeth evil to   *Pr 16:30*
pass
m. to and fro (S)   *Isa 49:21*
blind, waiting for the *m.* of the   *Joh 5:3*
water

MOWED

m. down Amalek (R)   *Ex 17:13*

MOWER

wherewith the *m.* filleth not   *Ps 129:7*
his hand

MOWINGS

the latter growth after the   *Am 7:1*
king's *m.*

MOWN

come down like rain upon the   *Ps 72:6*
m. grass

MOZA

bare Haran, and *M.*   *1Ch 2:46*
Zimra begat *M.*   *1Ch 8:36; 9:42*
M. begat Binea   *1Ch 8:37; 9:43*

MOZAH

Chephirah, and *M.*   *Jos 18:26*

MUCH

very *m.* (S)   *Ge 20:8;*
Nu 22:3; Jos 9:24; J'g 10:9; 1Sa 17:24;
21:12; 28:15, 20-21; 31:4; 2Ki 20:3;
1Ch 10:4; 2Ch 28:19; Ne 13:8;
Ps 118:18; Eze 27:35; Da 6:14; M't 17:6;
M'k 6:51; 9:6; Lu 2:9
for as *m.* money as it is worth   *Ge 23:9*
he shall
for thou art *m.* mightier than   *Ge 26:16*
we
it is a night to be *m.* observed   *Ex 12:42*
he that gathered *m.*   *Ex 16:18; 2Co 8:15*
if the scab spread *m.* abroad   *Le 13:7;*
  22:27, 35
soul of the people was *m.*   *Nu 21:4*
discouraged
shall carry *m.* seed out into   *De 28:38*
the field
and how *m.* more after my   *De 31:27*
death
return with *m.* riches to your   *Jos 22:8*
tents
it grieveth me *m.* for your   *Ru 1:13*
sakes
had there been a *m.* greater   *1Sa 14:30*
slaughter

so that his name was *m.* set   *1Sa 18:30*
by
but Jonathan delighted *m.* in   *1Sa 19:2*
David
as thy life was *m.* set by, so   *1Sa 26:24*
let my life be *m.* set by
his servants wept very *m.* (S)   *2Sa 13:36*
Solomon had understanding   *1Ki 4:29*
exceeding *m.*
but Jehu shall serve him *m.*   *2Ki 10:18*
Ahab wrought *m.* wickedness   *2Ki 21:6*
in sight of Lord
on the wall of Ophel he built   *2Ch 27:3*
m.
Manasseh wrought *m.* evil in   *2Ch 33:6*
sight of Lord
and salt without prescribing   *Ezr 7:22*
how *m.*
and it is a time of *m.* rain,   *Ezr 10:13*
not able
I was *m.* afraid (S)   *Ne 2:2*
it yieldeth *m.* increase unto   *Ne 9:37*
the kings
because mine hand had   *Job 31:25*
gotten *m.*
m. less do lying lips become a   *Pr 17:7*
prince
m. less for a servant to have   *Pr 19:10*
rule over
sleep is sweet, whether he eat   *Ec 5:12*
little or *m.*
he hath *m.* sorrow and wrath   *Ec 5:17*
with sickness
but one sinner destroyeth *m.*   *Ec 9:18*
good
for though thou take thee *m.*   *Jer 2:22*
soap
how *m.* less shall it be meet   *Eze 15:5*
containeth *m.*; shew *m.* love   *Eze 23:32;*
  33:31
and the fruit thereof was *m.*   *Da 4:12;*
  4:21
ye have sown *m.*; ye looked   *Hag 1:6;*
for *m.*   *1:9*
I am *m.* displeased (S)   *Zec 1:15*
are ye not *m.* better than they   *M't 6:26*
this ointment might have been   *M't 26:9*
sold for *m.*
where it had not *m.* earth   *M'k 4:5;*
  M't 13:5
her many sins are forgiven, for   *Lu 7:47*
she loved *m.*
to whom *m.* is given, of him   *Lu 12:48*
shall *m.* be required, to whom
men have committed *m.*
he that is faithful also in *m.* is   *Lu 16:10*
unjust in *m.*
it bringeth forth *m.* fruit   *Joh 12:24; 15:5*
hereafter I will not talk *m.*   *Joh 14:30*
with you
which brought her masters *m.*   *Ac 16:16*
gain
who helped them *m.* which   *Ac 18:27*
had believed
Festus said, *M.* learning doth   *Ac 26:24*
make thee mad
m. every way; labour *m.* in   *Ro 3:2;*
Lord   *16:12*
out of *m.* affliction I wrote to   *2Co 2:4*
you
m. rather be in subjection   *Heb 12:9*
and live
m. more shall not we escape,   *Heb 12:25*
if we turn away
the prayer of the righteous   *Jas 5:16*
availeth *m.*
I wept *m.* because no man was   *Re 5:4*
found

AS MUCH

give it for *as m.* money as it is   *Ge 23:9*
worth
mess was five times *as m.* as   *Ge 43:34*
any of theirs
fill sacks with food *as m.* as   *Ge 44:1*
they can carry
twice *as m.* as they gather daily   *Ex 16:5;*
  16:22
Aaron's sons have one *as m.* as   *Le 7:10*
another
for *as m.* as the Lord hath   *Jos 17:14*
blessed me
then take *as m.* as thy soul   *1Sa 2:16*
desireth
cut wood *as m.* as thou shalt   *2Ch 2:16*
need
the Lord gave Job twice *as*   *Job 42:10*
m. as he had
joy in testimonies, *as m.* as in   *Ps 119:14*
all riches

sinners lend, to receive *as m.*   *Lu 6:34*
again
likewise of fishes *as m.* as they   *Joh 6:11*
would
as m. as in me is, I am ready   *Ro 1:15*
to preach
in *as m.* as I am the apostle   *Ro 11:13*
of the Gentiles
as m. as lieth in you, live   *Ro 12:18*
peaceably with all
in *as m.* as both in bonds, and   *Ph'p 1:7*
in defence
in *as m.* as he who builded the   *Heb 3:3*
house
in *as m.* as not without an   *Heb 7:20*
oath was priest
in *as m.* as ye are partakers of   *1Pe 4:13*
sufferings

SO MUCH

remained not *so m.* as one of   *Ex 14:28*
them
and of sweet cinnamon half   *Ex 30:23*
so m.
if he be poor and cannot get   *Le 14:21*
so m.
not give you *so m.* as a   *De 2:5*
foot breadth
none to be *so m.* praised as   *2Sa 14:25*
Absalom
there shall not be left *so m.*   *2Sa 17:12*
as one
in gathering the spoil, it was   *2Ch 20:25*
so m.
will not *so m.* as bring it to his   *Pr 19:24*
mouth
eat *so m.* as is sufficient for   *Pr 25:16*
thee, lest filled
why gaddest thou *so m.* to   *Jer 2:36*
change thy way
what have we spoken *so m.*   *Mal 3:13*
against thee
whence should we have *so m.*   *M't 15:33*
bread
was no room, no not *so m.* as   *M'k 2:2*
about door
so that they could not *so m.*   *M'k 3:20;*
as eat   *6:31*
so m. more a great deal they   *M'k 7:36*
published it
so m. the more went there a   *Lu 5:15*
fame abroad
have ye not read *so m.* as this   *Lu 6:3*
what David did
would not lift up *so m.* as his   *Lu 18:13*
eyes to heaven
he cried *so m.* the more, Have   *Lu 18:39*
mercy on me
if ye sold it for *so m.* she said,   *Ac 5:8*
Yea, for *so m.*
no inheritance, not *so m.* as to   *Ac 7:5*
set his foot on
not *so m.* as heard whether any   *Ac 19:2*
Holy Ghost
not *so m.* as named among the   *1Co 5:1*
Gentiles
being made *so m.* better than   *Heb 1:4*
the angels
by *so m.* Jesus made surety of   *Heb 7:22*
better testament
and *so m.* more, as ye see   *Heb 10:25*
day approaching
if *so m.* as a beast touch the   *Heb 12:20*
mountain
so m. torment and sorrow give   *Re 18:7*
her

TOO MUCH

the stuff was sufficient, and *too*   *Ex 36:7*
m.
said to them, Ye take *too m.*   *Nu 16:3;*
upon you   *16:7*
part of children of Judah was   *Jos 19:9*
too m.
too m. for you to go up to   *1Ki 12:28*
Jerusalem
thus shall there arise *too m.*   *Es 1:18*
contempt

VERY MUCH

Joseph gathered corn as sand,   *Ge 41:49*
very m.
very m. cattle went up with   *Ex 12:38*
them
remaineth *very m.* land to be   *Jos 13:1*
possessed
return with *very m.* cattle, *very*   *Jos 22:8*
m. raiment

queen of Sheba came with *very m.* gold   *1Ki 10:2*

Manasseh shed innocent blood. *very m.*   *2Ki 21:16*

from Chun brought David *very m.* brass   *1Ch 18:8*

they carried away *very m.* spoil   *2Ch 14:13*

for God hath given him substance *very m.*   *2Ch 32:29*

the priests and people transgressed *very m.*   *2Ch 36:14*

I am afflicted *very m.* quicken me   *Ps 119:107*

and gathered summer fruits *very m.*   *Jer 40:12*

MUD

like *m.* I trample them (B)   *2Sa 22:43*

has thrown me in the *m.* (B)   *Job 30:19*

like *m.* of the streets (B)   *Zec 9:3*

MUDDIED

like a *m.* fountain (A)(R)   *Pr 25:26*

MUFFLED

face *m.* in a handkerchief (P)   *Joh 11:44*

MUFFLERS

I will take away the chains, the *m.*   *Isa 3:19*

spangled face veils and scarfs (A)   *Isa 3:19*

and gauze veils (B)   *Isa 3:19*

and the scarfs (R)   *Isa 3:19*

MULBERRY *TREES*

come upon them over-against the *m. trees*   *2Sa 5:23;* *1Ch 14:14*

the balsam trees (B)(R)   *2Sa 5:23; 5:24*

when thou hearest the sound in tops of the *m. trees*   *2Sa 5:24;* *1Ch 14:15*

the *m.* trees (B)(E)(R)   *1Ch 27:28*

the *m.* tree (A)(B)   *Lu 17:6*

MULE

every man gat him upon his *m.*   *2Sa 13:29*

Absalom rode on a *m.* the *m.* went away   *2Sa 18:9*

cause Solomon to ride on my *m.*   *1Ki 1:33; 38:44*

be not as the horse or *m.* which have   *Ps 32:9*

so shall be plague of the horse, of the *m.*   *Zec 14:15*

MULES

Anah that found *m.* in the wilderness   *Ge 36:24*

discovered hot springs (A)(B)(E)(R)   *Ge 36:24*

brought *m.* a rate year by year   *1Ki 10:25; 2Ch 9:24*

we may find grass to save the *m.* alive   *1Ki 18:5*

be given to thy servant two *m.* burden   *2Ki 5:17*

brought bread on camels and on *m.*   *1Ch 12:40*

their *m.* were 245   *Ezr 2:66; Ne 7:68*

he sent letters by riders on *m.*   *Es 8:10; 8:14*

they shall bring your brethren on *m.*   *Isa 66:20*

Togarmah traded in thy fairs with *m.*   *Eze 27:14*

MULES'

two *m.* burden of the earth   *2Ki 5:17*

MULTIPLIED

Israel grew and *m.*   *Ge 47:27; Ex 1:7, 20*

the more afflicted, they *m.* and grew   *Ex 1:12*

that my wonders may be *m.* in Egypt   *Ex 11:9*

the Lord your God hath *m.* you   *De 1:10*

thy gold is *m.* and all that thou hast is *m.*   *De 8:13*

that your days may be *m.* in the land   *De 11:21*

I *m.* his seed, and gave him Isaac   *Jos 24:3*

because their cattle were *m.* in Gilead   *1Ch 5:9*

if his children be *m.* it is for sword   *Job 27:14*

if thy transgressions be *m.* what doest thou to him   *Job 35:6*

their sorrows shall be *m.* that hasten   *Ps 16:4*

troubles are *m.* (A)   *Ps 25:17*

they that hate me wrongfully are *m.*   *Ps 38:19*

he blesseth them, so that they are *m.*   *Ps 107:38*

for by me thy days shall be *m.*   *Pr 9:11*

when wicked are *m.* transgression increaseth   *Pr 29:16*

thou hast *m.* the nation, and not increased   *Isa 9:3*

for our transgressions are *m.* before thee   *Isa 59:12*

when ye be *m.* they shall say no more   *Jer 3:16*

ye *m.* more than the nations about you   *Eze 5:7*

ye have *m.* your slain in this city   *Eze 11:6*

thou hast *m.* thy whoredoms   *Eze 16:25; 23:19*

m. fornication   *Eze 16:29*

m. whoredom (E)   *Eze 16:29*

m. abominations   *Eze 16:51*

that their heart may faint, and ruins be *m.*   *Eze 21:15*

his boughs were *m.*; *m.* your words   *Eze 31:5; 35:13*

peace be *m.* to you   *Da 4:1; 6:25; 1Pe 1:2; 2Pe 1:2; Jude 2*

did not know that I *m.* her silver and gold   *Ho 2:8*

and Judah hath *m.* fenced cities   *Ho 8:14*

I have *m.* visions, and used similitudes   *Ho 12:10*

thou hast *m.* thy merchants above stars   *Na 3:16*

m. lewdness (A)   *M't 24:12*

iniquity *m.* (E)(R)   *M't 24:12*

when the number of disciples was *m.*   *Ac 6:1; 6:7*

the people grew and *m.* in Egypt   *Ac 7:17*

walking in the fear of the Lord were *m.*   *Ac 9:31*

but the word of God grew and *m.*   *Ac 12:24*

MULTIPLIEDST

their children also *m.* thou as the stars   *Ne 9:23*

MULTIPLIETH

he *m.* my wounds without cause   *Job 9:17*

he *m.* his words against God   *Job 34:37*

he *m.* words without knowledge   *Job 35:16*

MULTIPLY

be fruitful and *m.*   *Ge 1:22; 1:28; 8:17; 9:7; 35:11*

I will *m.* my sorrow and conception   *Ge 3:16*

when men began to *m.* on the face of the earth   *Ge 6:1*

I will *m.* Hagar's seed exceedingly   *Ge 16:10; 17:20*

they will be numerous (B)   *Ge 16:10*

and I will *m.* thee exceedingly   *Ge 17:2; 48:4*

I will *m.* thy seed   *Ge 22:17; 26:4, 24; Heb 6:14*

God Almighty bless thee, and *m.* thee   *Ge 28:3*

an association of people (B)   *Ge 28:3*

a company of peoples (E)(R)   *Ge 28:3*

let us deal wisely with them, lest they *m.*   *Ex 1:10*

I will *m.* my signs and wonders in Egypt   *Ex 7:3*

lest the beast of the field *m.* against thee   *Ex 23:29*

to whom thou saidst, I will   *Ex 32:13;*

m. your seed   *Le 26:9; De 7:13; 13:17; 28:63; 30:5*

that ye may live and *m.* and go in   *De 8:1; 30:16*

the king shall not *m.* horses to himself   *De 17:16*

neither shall he *m.* wives, nor silver, and gold   *De 17:17*

neither did all their family *m.*   *1Ch 4:27*

I shall *m.* my days as the sand   *Job 29:18*

I will *m.* them, they shall not be few   *Jer 30:19*

so will I *m.* the seed of David my servant   *Jer 33:22*

I have caused thee to *m.* as *m.* harlotry (A)(B)(R)   *Eze 16:7; Eze 16:29*

I will *m.* men   *Eze 36:10*

m. man and beast   *Eze 36:11*

I will *m.* the fruit of the tree, and increase   *Eze 36:30*

and I will place them and *m.* them   *Eze 37:26*

come to Beth-el, at Gilgal *m.* transgression   *Am 4:4*

to *m.* law breaking (N)   *Ro 5:20*

grace may *m.* (A)   *Ro 6:1*

and *m.* your seed sown, and increase   *2Co 9:10*

MULTIPLYING

in *m.* I will multiply   *Ge 22:17; Heb 6:14*

MULTITUDE

not numbered for *m.*   *Ge 16:10; 32:12; 1Ki 3:8*

God Almighty make thee a *m.* of people   *Ge 28:3*

and it is now increased unto a *m.*   *Ge 30:30*

has broadened to a great many (B)   *Ge 30:30*

has increased abundantly (R)   *Ge 30:30*

I will make of thee a *m.* of people   *Ge 48:4; 48:16, 19*

a mixed *m.* went up also with them   *Ex 12:38*

a motley throng (B)   *Ex 12:38*

thou shalt not follow a *m.* to do evil   *Ex 23:2*

according to the *m.* of years increase   *Le 25:16*

and the mixed *m.* fell a lusting   *Nu 11:4*

the alien rabble (B)(R)   *Nu 11:4*

this *m.* will (A)(B)(E)   *Nu 22:4*

behold, ye are the *m.* of the De *1:10;* stars for me   *10:22; 28:62; Heb 11:12*

as sand on sea shore for *m.*   *Jos 11:4; J'g 7:12; 1Sa 13:5; 2Sa 17:11; 1Ki 4:20*

Midianites as grasshoppers for *m.*   *J'g 6:5; 7:12*

behold, the *m.* melted away   *1Sa 14:16*

he dealt among the whole *m.* of Israel   *2Sa 6:19*

and oxen that could not be told for *m.*   *1Ki 8:5*

they are as all the *m.* that are left   *2Ki 7:13*

with the *m.* of my chariots I am come up   *2Ki 19:23; Isa 37:24*

over a people like the dust for *m.*   *2Ch 1:9*

in thy name we go against this *m.*   *2Ch 14:11*

this great *m.* (R)   *2Ch 20:12*

and behold, the *m.* were dead bodies   *2Ch 20:24*

for a *m.* had not cleansed themselves   *2Ch 30:18*

be not afraid of all the *m.* with him   *2Ch 32:7*

they separated from Israel the mixed *m.*   *Ne 13:3*

Haman told of the *m.* of his children   *Es 5:11*

Mordecai accepted of the *m.* of brethren   *Es 10:3*

should not the *m.* of words be answered   *Job 11:2*

a deluge of words (B)   *Job 11:2*

and *m.* of years should teach wisdom   *Job 32:7*

by reason of the *m.* of oppressions they make   *Job 35:9*

often repeated oppressions (B)   *Job 35:9*

he scorneth the *m.* of the city, nor regardeth   *Job 39:7*

I will come in the *m.* of thy   *Ps 5:7*
mercy
abundance of stedfast mercy   *Ps 5:7*
(A)
greatness of thy unfailing love   *Ps 5:7*
(B)
abundance of thy lovingkindness   *Ps 5:7*
(E)
abundance of thy stedfast love   *Ps 5:7*
(R)
cast them out in *m.* of their   *Ps 5:10*
transgressions
mass of their transgressions   *Ps 5:10*
(B)
their many transgressions (R)   *Ps 5:10*
there is no king saved by the   *Ps 33:16*
m. of an host
I had gone with the *m.* to the   *Ps 42:4*
house of God
walk on with the throng   *Ps 42:4*
(A)(B)(E)(R)
that boast themselves in *m.* of   *Ps 49:6*
their riches
abundance of their riches   *Ps 49:6*
(A)(B)(R)
according to the *m.* of thy   *Ps 51:1*
mercies b ot out
according to greatness of   *Ps 51:1*
compassion (B)
according to thy abundant   *Ps 51:1*
mercy (R)
rebuke the *m.* of bulls, with   *Ps 68:30*
calves
O God, in the *m.* of thy   *Ps 69:13*
mercy, hear me
turn to me, according to *m.* of   *Ps 69:16*
thy mercies
deliver me not to the *m.* of the   *Ps 74:19*
wicked
in the *m.* of my thoughts   *Ps 94:19*
within me
perplexing cares crowd within   *Ps 94:19*
me (B)
cares of my heart are many   *Ps 94:19*
(R)
they remembered not *m.* of   *Ps 106:7*
thy mercies
endless tokens of   *Ps 106:7*
lovingkindness (B)
abundance of thy stedfast love   *Ps 106:7*
(R)
and repented, according to   *Ps 106:45*
m. of his mercies
I will praise him among the   *Ps 109:30*
m.
in the *m.* of words wanteth   *Pr 10:19*
not sin
in the *m.* of counsellors is   *Pr 11:14;*
safety   *24:6*
abundance of counselors   *Pr 11:14*
(B)(R)
in the *m.* of people is the   *Pr 14:28*
king's honour
in *m.* of counsellors they are   *Pr 15:22*
established
there is gold, and a *m.* of   *Pr 20:15*
rubies
a dream cometh through *m.* of   *Ec 5:3*
business, a fool's voice is known
by *m.* of words
in the *m.* of dreams there are   *Ec 5:7*
divers vanities
to what purpose is the *m.* of   *Isa 1:11*
sacrifices
and their *m.* dried up with   *Isa 5:13*
thirst
their *m.* and pomp shall   *Isa 5:14*
descend into hell
woe to the *m.* of many people   *Isa 17:12*
which make noise
so *m.* of nations be that fight   *Isa 29:8*
against Zion
when *m.* of shepherds is called   *Isa 31:4*
against him
shall come on thee for *m.* of   *Isa 47:9*
thy sorceries
stand now with the *m.* of thy   *Isa 47:12*
sorceries
thou art wearied in the *m.* of   *Isa 47:13*
thy counsels
the *m.* of camels shall cover   *Isa 60:6*
thee
according to *m.* of his   *Isa 63:7*
lovingkindnesses
is a *m.* of waters in heavens   *Jer 10:13;*
  51:16
yea, they have called a *m.* after   *Jer 12:6*
thee
I have wounded thee for *m.*   *Jer 30:14*
of thine iniquity

behold, I will punish the *m.*   *Jer 46:25*
of No
afflicted her, for *m.* of her   *La 1:5*
transgressions
compassion according to *m.* of   *La 3:32*
his mercies
wrath is on all the *m.* thereof   *Eze 7:12;*
  7:14
for the vision is touching the   *Eze 7:13*
whole *m.* thereof
answer him according to the   *Eze 14:4*
m. of his idols
by reason of the *m.* of   *Eze 27:12;*
riches   *27:18, 33*
by reason of the *m.* of the   *Eze 27:16;*
wares   *27:18*
this is Pharaoh and all his   *Eze 32:18;*
m.   *32:32*
Elam and her *m.*; Tubal and   *Eze 32:24*
all her *m.*
they shall bury Gog, and all   *Eze 39:11*
his *m.*
voice of his words like the   *Da 10:6*
voice of a *m.*
the king of the north shall set   *Da 11:13*
forth a *m.*
days of recompence, for *m.* of   *Ho 9:7*
thine iniquity
thou didst trust in the *m.* of   *Ho 10:13*
mighty men
there is a *m.* of slain, they   *Na 3:3*
stumble
because of the *m.* of the   *Na 3:4*
whoredoms of harlot
put to death, he feared the   *M't 14:5;*
m.   *21:46*
I have compassion on the *m.*   *M't 15:32;*
  M'k 8:2
seest the *m.* thronging thee   *M'k 5:31;*
  Lu 8:45
there was with the angel a *m.*   *Lu 2:13*
of the host
great *m.* of disciples (E)   *Lu 6:17*
man from the *m.* (E)   *Lu 9:38*
were gathered together an   *Lu 12:1*
innumerable *m.*
many thousands of people   *Lu 12:1*
(A)(E)(N)(P)(R)
countless people were massed   *Lu 12:1*
(B)
to betray him in the absence   *Lu 22:6*
of the *m.*
and while he yet spake,   *Lu 22:47*
behold, a *m.*
whole *m.* of them arose, and   *Lu 23:1*
led him to Pilate
a *m.* being present in that   *Joh 5:13*
place
a vast *m.* (A)(E)(R)   *Joh 6:5*
not able to draw it for the *m.*   *Joh 21:6*
of fishes
the *m.* that believed were of   *Ac 4:32*
one heart
and the saying pleased the   *Ac 6:5*
whole *m.*
the *m.* rose up together   *Ac 16:22*
against them
the *m.* must needs come   *Ac 21:22*
together
shall hide a *m.* of sins   *Jas 5:20*
for charity shall cover the *m.* of   *1Pe 4:8*
sins

MULTITUDES

draw her and all her *m.*   *Eze 32:20*
m. m. in the valley of   *Joe 3:14*
decision
the dumb spake; and the *m.*   *M't 9:33*
marvelled
when he saw the *m.* he was   *M't 9:36*
moved
the *m.* cried, saying, Hosanna   *M't 21:9*
to Son of David
m. were added both of men   *Ac 5:14*
and women
Jews saw *m.* they were filled   *Ac 13:45*
with envy
countless *m.* of angels (A)   *Heb 12:22*
the waters are *m.* and nations   *Re 17:15*

MUNITION

all that fight against her and   *Isa 29:7*
her *m.*
her and her stronghold   *Isa 29:7*
(A)(E)(R)
with all its equipment (B)   *Isa 29:7*
keep the *m.* watch the way,   *Na 2:1*
fortify

keep the fortress and ramparts   *Na 2:1*
(A)
man the ramparts (B)(R)   *Na 2:1*

MUNITIONS

his defence shall be the *m.* of   *Isa 33:16*
rocks
will be fortresses of rocks   *Isa 33:16*
(A)(B)(R)

MUPPIM

Rosh, *M.*, and Huppim   *Ge 46:21*

MURDER

do not *m.* him (B)   *1Sa 26:9*
in secret doth he *m.* the   *Ps 10:8*
innocent
they slay the widow, and *m.* the   *Ps 94:6*
fatherless
will ye steal, *m.* and commit   *Jer 7:9*
adultery
so priests *m.* in the way by   *Ho 6:9*
consent
to *m.* him (B)   *M't 2:13*
Jesus said, Thou shalt do no   *M't 19:18*
m.
You shall not kill   *M't 19:18*
(A)(B)(E)(R)
one Barabbas, who had   *M'k 15:7*
committed *m.*
and for *m.* was cast into   *Lu 23:19;*
prison   *23:25*
threats and *m.* (B)(R)   *Ac 9:1*
undertook to *m.* him (B)(N)   *Ac 9:29*
full of envy, *m.*, debate, deceit   *Ro 1:29*

MURDERED

m. between altar and temple   *Lu 11:5*
(B)

MURDERER

if he smite him he is a *m.* the   *Nu 35:16;*
m. shall surely be put to death   *17:18, 21*
the revenger of blood shall   *Nu 35:19;*
slay the *m.*   *35:21*
m. shall be put to death by   *Nu 35:30*
mouth of witnesses
shall take no satisfaction for   *Nu 35:31*
the life of a *m.*
see how this son of *m.* hath   *2Ki 6:32*
sent to take
m. rising with the light,   *Job 24:14*
killeth the poor
Ephraim bring forth his   *Ho 9:13*
children to the *m.*
he was a *m.* from the   *Joh 8:44*
beginning
ye desired a *m.* to be granted   *Ac 3:14*
to you
they said, No doubt this man   *Ac 28:4*
a *m.*
but let none of you suffer as a   *1Pe 4:15*
m.
whoso hateth his brother is a   *1Jo 3:15*
m. no *m.* hath eternal life

MURDERERS

the children of the *m.* he slew   *2Ki 14:6*
not
righteousness lodged in it, but   *Isa 1:21*
now *m.*
for my soul is wearied,   *Jer 4:31*
because of *m.*
he sent forth and destroyed   *M't 22:7*
those *m.*
of whom ye have been now the   *Ac 7:52*
m.
and leddest out 4000 men that   *Ac 21:38*
were *m.*
law made for *m.* of fathers and   *1Ti 1:9*
mothers
m. shall have their part in the   *Re 21:8*
lake
for without are whoremongers   *Re 22:15*
and *m.*

MURDEROUS

threatening and *m.* desire   *Ac 9:1*
(A)(N)(P)

MURDERS

out of the heart proceed *m.*   *M't 15:19;*
  M'k 7:21

the works of the flesh are   *Ga 5:21*
envyings, *m.*

nor repented they of their *m.*   *Re 9:21*
nor fornication

MURMUR

what are we, that ye *m.* against   *Ex 16:7*
us

who hears you grumble (B)   *Ex 16:7*
Lord heareth murmurings, ye   *Ex 16:8;*
m.   *Nu 14:27*

hearing your complaints (B)   *Ex 16:8*
the spies made the   *Nu 14:36*
congregation to *m.*

prompted assembly to   *Nu 14:36*
grumble (B)

grumble and complain (A)   *Nu 14:36*
what is Aaron, that ye *m.*   *Nu 16:11*
against him

you complain against him   *Nu 16:11*
(B)

of Israel, whereby they *m.*   *Nu 17:5*
against you

relieve myself of the   *Nu 17:5*
complaints (B)

a general *m.* (N)   *Lu 19:7*
Jesus said, *M.* not among   *Joh 6:43*
yourselves

stop grumbling (A)   *Joh 6:43*
stop your mutual mutterings   *Joh 6:43*
(B)

Do not grumble among   *Joh 6:43*
yourselves (P)

neither *m.* as some of them   *1Co 10:10*
murmured

Nor discontentedly complain   *1Co 10:10*
(A)

Do not grumble against God   *1Co 10:10*
(B)(N)(R)

M. not against one another (S)   *Jas 5:9*

MURMURED

the people *m.* against Moses   *Ex 15:24;*
   17:3

the people complained (B)   *Ex 15:24*
the whole congregation of   *Ex 16:2;*
Israel *m.* against   *Nu 14:2; 16:41*

whole congregation grumbled   *Ex 16:2*
(B)

from twenty years old, which   *Nu 14:29*
have *m.*

you have grumbled against   *Nu 14:29*
me (B)

and ye *m.* in your tents, and   *De 1:27*
all the congregation *m.* against   *Jos 9:18*
princes

they believed not, but *m.* in   *Ps 106:25*
their tents

they complained in their   *Ps 106:25*
tents (B)

they that *m.* shall learn   *Isa 29:24*
doctrine

when they had received a   *M't 20:11*
penny, they *m.*

they grumbled   *M't 20:11*
(A)(B)(N)(P)(R)

and they *m.* against her   *M'k 14:5*
they censured and reproved   *M'k 14:5*
her (A)

they chided her (B)   *M'k 14:5*
they turned upon her with   *M'k 14:5*
fury (N)

they reproached her (R)   *M'k 14:5*
but the Scribes and Pharisees   *Lu 5:30*
m.

Pharisees were grumbling (A)   *Lu 5:30*
Pharisees grumbled (B)   *Lu 5:30*
complained to the disciples   *Lu 5:30*
(N)

kept muttering indignantly (P)   *Lu 5:30*
they *m.* saying, This man   *Lu 15:2*
receiveth sinners

kept muttering, indignantly   *Lu 15:2*
complaining (A)

Pharisees complained (B)(P)   *Lu 15:2*
began grumbling among   *Lu 15:2*
themselves (N)

m. that he was gone to be guest   *Lu 19:7*
to Zaccheus

people muttered, indignantly   *Lu 19:7*
complained (A)

all who looked upon   *Lu 19:7*
complained (B)

a general murmur of   *Lu 19:7*
disapproval (N)

bystanders muttered their   *Lu 19:7*
disapproval (P)

the Jews, *m.* at him, because   *Joh 6:41*
he said

Jews grumbled about him (B)   *Joh 6:41*
he knew that his disciples *m.*   *Joh 6:61*
at it

his disciples were complaining   *Joh 6:61*
(A)

his disciples were grumbling   *Joh 6:61*
(B)

the Pharisees heard that the   *Joh 7:32*
people *m.*

neither murmur as some of   *1Co 10:10*
them *m.*

MURMURERS

these are *m.* complainers,   *Jude 16*
walking after lusts

MURMURING

there was much *m.* among the   *Joh 7:12*
people

much whispered discussion   *Joh 7:12*
and hot disputing about him (A)

considerable dispute about   *Joh 7:12*
him (B)

much whispering about him   *Joh 7:12*
(N)

undercurrent of discussion   *Joh 7:12*
about him (P)

much muttering about him   *Joh 7:12*
(R)

a *m.* of Grecians against the   *Ac 6:1*
Hebrews

complaint was made by   *Ac 6:1*
Hellenists (A)(B)

a disagreement between those   *Ac 6:1*
(N)

the Greeks complained (P)   *Ac 6:1*

MURMURINGS

he heareth your *m.*   *Ex 16:7;*
   16:8-9, 19; Nu 14:27

who hears you grumble (B)   *Ex 16:7*
your *m.* are not against us, but   *Ex 16:8*
the Lord

I will make to cease the *m.* of   *Nu 17:5*
Israel

relieve myself of complaints   *Nu 17:5;*
(B)   *17:10*

thou shalt quite take away   *Nu 17:10*
their *m.* from me

groan because of heart *m.* (R)   *Ps 38:8*
do all things without *m.* and   *Ph'p 2:14*
disputings

without grumbling,   *Ph'p 2:14*
faultfinding, complaining,
questioning, doubting (A)

without grumbling and   *Ph'p 2:14*
objections (B)

without complaint or   *Ph'p 2:14*
wrangling (N)

without grumbling or arguing   *Ph'p 2:14*
(P)

without grumbling or   *Ph'p 2:14*
questioning (R)

MURRAIN

therefore there shall be a very   *Ex 9:3*
grievous *m.*

MUSCLE

the hip *m.* (B)   *Ge 32:32*

MUSCLES

m. of his body   *Job 40:16*
(B)(E)(R)(S)

MUSE

I *m.* on the work of thy hands   *Ps 143:5*
meditate on all your doings   *Ps 143:5*
(A)(B)(R)

MUSED

all men *m.* in their hearts of   *Lu 3:15*
John

in suspense, waiting   *Lu 3:15*
expectantly, reasoned,
questioned (A)

in suspense, debating in minds   *Lu 3:15*
(B)

reasoned in their hearts (E)   *Lu 3:15*
on tiptoe of expectation,   *Lu 3:15*
wondering (N)

great state of expectation and   *Lu 3:15*
inwardly discussing (P)

in expectation, questioned in   *Lu 3:15*
hearts (R)

MUSHI

Mahali and *M.*   *Ex 6:19;*
   Nu 3:20; 1Ch 6:19; 23:21; 24:26

the son of *M.*   *1Ch 6:47*
the sons of *M.*; Mahli, Eder   *1Ch 23:23;*
   24:30

MUSHITES

the family of the *M.*   *Nu 3:33; 26:58*

MUSICAL

with *m.* instruments of God   *1Ch 16:42*
with *m.* instruments of   *Ne 12:36*
David

as *m.* instruments, that of all   *Ec 2:8*
sorts

concubines very many (A)   *Ec 2:8*
mistresses galore (B)   *Ec 2:8*
concubines, man's delight (R)   *Ec 2:8*

MUSICIAN

In the titles of   *Ps 4, 5, 6, 8, 9, 11, 12,*
13, 14, 18, 19, 20, 21, 22, 31, 36, 40, 41,
42, 44, 45, 46, 47, 49, 51, 52, 53, 54, 55,
56, 57, 58, 59, 60, 61, 62, 64, 65, 66, 67,
68, 69, 70, 75, 76, 77, 80, 81, 84, 85, 88,
109, 139, 140

MUSICIANS

saw the *m.* and the people (S)   *M't 9:23*
of harpers, and *M.*   *Re 18:22*
harpers, and minstrels   *Re 18:22*
(A)(E)(N)(R)

MUSICK

with instruments of *m.*   *1Sa 18:6;*
   1Ch 15:16; 2Ch 5:13; 34:12; Da 6:18

instruments of *m.* of the Lord   *2Ch 7:6*
singers with instruments of   *2Ch 23:13*
m.

all daughters of *m.* shall be   *Ec 12:4*
their rising up; I am their *m.*   *La 3:63*
the young men from their *m.*   *La 5:14*
all kinds of   *Da 3:5; 3:7; 10, 15*
instruments of *m.* like David   *Am 6:5*
heard *m.* and dancing   *Lu 15:25*

MUSING

while I was *m.* the fire burned   *Ps 39:3*

MUST

m. needs be circumcised   *Ge 17:13*
m. I needs bring my son again   *Ge 24:5*
unto

it *m.* not be so done in our   *Ge 29:26*
country

thou *m.* come in to me; if it   *Ge 30:16;*
m. be so   *43:11*

it *m.* be put in water, so be   *Le 11:32*
cleansed

seven days ye *m.* eat   *Le 23:6*
unleavened bread

so he *m.* do after the law of   *Nu 6:21*
separation

m. we fetch you water out of   *Nu 20:10*
this rock

m. I not take heed to speak   *Nu 23:12*
that the Lord

all that the Lord speaketh   *Nu 23:26*
that I *m.* do

bring us word by what way we   *De 1:22*
m. go

I *m.* die in this land, I *m.* not   *De 4:22*
go over

thou *m.* eat them before the   *De 12:18*
Lord thy God

thy days approach that thou   *De 31:14*
m. die

may know the way by which ye   *Jos 3:4*
m. go

thou *m.* offer it to the Lord   *J'g 13:16*
there *m.* be an inheritance for   *J'g 21:17*
them

I did but taste a little, and lo   *1Sa 14:43*
I *m.* die

he that ruleth over men *m.* be   *2Sa 23:3*
just

that shall touch them *m.* be fenced with iron	*2Sa 23:7*
he sleepeth, and *m.* be awaked	*1Ki 18:27*
that thou *m.* go to be with thy fathers	*1Ch 17:11*
As thou hast said, so *m.* we do	*Ezr 10:12*
For precept *m.* be upon precept	*Isa 28:10*
they *m.* needs be borne, they cannot go	*Jer 10:5*
scriptures be fulfilled, that thus it *m.* be	*M't 26:54*
but new wine *m.* be put into new bottles	*M'k 2:22; Lu 5:38*
Son of man *m.* suffer many things	*M'k 8:31; 9:12*
why say the scribes that Elias *m.* first come	*M'k 9:11*
not troubled, for such things *m.* be	*M'k 13:7; Lu 21:9*
gospel *m.* first be published among all nations	*M'k 13:10*
I *m.* be about my Father's business	*Lu 2:49*
I *m.* preach kingdom of God, for I am sent	*Lu 4:43*
I bought ground, and *m.* go and see it	*Lu 14:18*
Zaccheus, to day I *m.* abide at thy house	*Lu 19:5*
the day when the passover *m.* be killed	*Lu 22:7*
the things written *m.* be accomplished	*Lu 22:37; 24:44*
he *m.* release one to them at the feast	*Lu 23:17*
Son of man *m.* be delivered to sinful men	*Lu 24:7*
marvel not I said, Ye *m.* be born again	*Joh 3:7*
the serpent, so *m.* the Son of man be lifted up	*Joh 3:14*
he *m.* increase, but I *m.* decrease	*Joh 3:30*
and he *m.* needs go through Samaria	*Joh 4:4*
God is a Spirit, *m.* worship him in spirit, truth	*Joh 4:24*
I *m.* work the works of him that sent me	*Joh 9:4*
other sheep I have, also I *m.* bring	*Joh 10:16*
knew not that he *m.* rise again from the dead	*Joh 20:9*
this scripture *m.* have been fulfilled	*Ac 1:16*
m. one be ordained to be a witness with us	*Ac 1:22*
none other name whereby we *m.* be saved	*Ac 4:12*
it shall be told thee what thou *m.* do	*Ac 9:6*
we *m.* thro' much tribulation enter kingdom	*Ac 14:22*
ye *m.* be circumcised and keep the law	*Ac 15:24*
said, Sirs, what *m.* I do to be saved	*Ac 16:30*
I *m.* by all means keep this feast in Jerusalem	*Ac 18:21*
the multitude *m.* needs come together	*Ac 21:22*
so *m.* thou bear witness also at Rome	*Ac 23:11*
fear not, thou, *m.* be brought before Cæsar	*Ac 27:24*
howbeit we *m.* be cast on a certain island	*Ac 27:26*
wherefore ye *m.* needs be subject	*Ro 13:5*
then *m.* ye needs go out of the world	*1Co 5:10*
there *m.* also be heresies among you	*1Co 11:19*
for he *m.* reign till he hath put under	*1Co 15:25*
for we *m.* all appear before the judgment	*2Co 5:10*
if I *m.* needs glory, I will glory of things	*2Co 11:30*
a bishop then *m.* be blameless	*1Ti 3:2; Tit 1:7*
he *m.* have a good report of them without	*1Ti 3:7*
likewise *m.* deacons be grave, not double tongued	*1Ti 3:8*
husbandman *m.* be first partaker of fruits	*2Ti 12:6*

the servant of the Lord *m.* not strive	*2Ti 2:24*
it remaineth that some *m.* enter therein	*Heb 4:6*
there *m.* be the death of the testator	*Heb 9:16*
he that cometh to God, *m.* believe that he is	*Heb 11:6*
they watch, as they that *m.* give account	*Heb 13:17*
shew thee things which *m.* be hereafter	*Re 4:1*
if any be hurt he *m.* in this manner be killed	*Re 11:5*
after that he *m.* be loosed a little season	*Re 20:3*
to shew things which *m.* shortly be done	*Re 22:6*

MUSTARD

heaven is like a grain of *m.* seed	*M't 13:31*
faith as a grain of *m.* seed	*M't 17:20; Lu 17:6*
like a grain of *m.* seed	*M'k 4:31; Lu 13:19*

MUSTERED

took the scribe which *m.*	*2Ki 25:19; Jer 52:25*

MUSTERETH

the Lord *m.* the host of the battle	*Isa 13:4*

MUTH-LABBEN

chief musician upon *M.*	*Ps 9 title*

MUTILATE

who *m.* the flesh (A)(R)	*Ph'p 3:2*

MUTILATION

the *m.* faction (B)(N)	*Ph'p 3:2*

MUTILATORS

would be *m.* of bodies (P)	*Ph'p 3:2*

MUTTER

to wizards that peep, and that *m.*	*Isa 8:19*
who chirp and *m.* (A)(B)(E)(R)	*Isa 8:19*

MUTTERED

your tongue hath *m.* perverseness	*Isa 59:3*
people *m.* (A)(P)	*Lu 19:7*

MUTTERING

kept *m.* (A)	*Lu 15:2*
much *m.* about him (R)	*Joh 7:12*

MUTTERINGS

stop your mutual *m.* (B)	*Joh 6:43*

MUTUAL

stop your *m.* mutterings (B)	*Joh 6:43*
I may be comforted by the *m.* faith	*Ro 1:12*
for *m.* building up (A)(R)	*Ro 14:19*
m. love increasing (B)(R)	*2Th 1:3*

MUTUALLY

became *m.* friendly (B)	*Lu 23:12*

MUZZLE

shalt not *m.* the ox when he treadeth out the corn	*De 25:4; 1Co 9:9; 1Ti 5:18*

MYRA

we came to *M.* a city of Lycia	*Ac 27:5*

MYRIAD

a *m.* of tutors in Christ (B)	*1Co 4:15*

MYRIADS

m. of angels (N)	*Heb 12:22*

MYRRH

Ishmaelites came bearing balm and *m.*	*Ge 37:25*
carry resin (B)	*Ge 37:25*
carry down the man a present, *m.* nuts	*Ge 43:11*
of pure *m.* five hundred shekels	*Ex 30:23*
to wit, six months with oil of *m.*	*Es 2:12*
thy garments smell of *m.* aloes and cassia	*Ps 45:8*
I have perfumed my bed with *m.*	*Pr 7:17*
a bundle of *m.* is my beloved to me	*Ca 1:13*
perfumed with *m.* and frankincense	*Ca 3:6*
I will get me to the mountain of *m.* and aloes	*Ca 4:6*
m. and aloes with all the chief spices	*Ca 4:14*
I have gathered my *m.* with my spice	*Ca 5:1*
my hands dropped with *m.* fingers with sweet *m.*	*Ca 5:5*
his lips like lilies, dropping sweet smelling *m.*	*Ca 5:13*
they presented to him gifts, gold and *m.*	*M't 2:11*
to drink wine mingled with *m.*	*M'k 15:23*
brought a mixture of *m.* and aloes	*Joh 19:39*

MYRTLE

go forth and fetch olive branches and *m.* branches	*Ne 8:15*
I will plant in the wilderness the *m.*	*Isa 41:19*
instead of brier shall come the *m.* tree	*Isa 55:13*

MYRTLE *TREES*

and he stood among the *m.*	*Zec 1:8; 1:10-11*

MYSELF

I hid *m.*	*Ge 3:10*
By *m.* have I sworn	*Ge 22:16*
wings, and brought you unto me.	*Ex 19:4*
I sanctified them for *m.*	*Nu 8:17*
I the Lord will make *m.* known	*Nu 12:6; Eze 35:11*
Am not able to bear you *m.*	*De 1:9; 1:12*
I forced *m.* and offered a	*1Sa 13:12*
bow *m.* in house of Rimmon	*1Ki 5:18*
Then I consulted with *m.* and I	*Ne 5:7*
I would harden *m.* in sorrow	*Job 6:10*
I am a burden to *m.*	*Job 7:20*
If I justify *m.* mine own mouth	*Job 9:20*
If I wash *m.* in snow water	*Job 9:30*
whom I shall see for *m.*	*Job 19:27*
I abhor *m.* and repent in dust	*Job 42:9*
I kept *m.* from iniquity	*Ps 18:23*
I behaved *m.* as though he	*Ps 35:14; 101:2; 132:2*
I would have hid *m.* from him	*Ps 55:12*
I *m.* will awake early	*Ps 57:8; 108:2*
I give *m.* unto prayer	*Ps 109:4*
I have sworn by *m.*	*Isa 45:28; Jer 22:5; 49:13*
make *m.* known unto them	*Eze 20:5; 20:9*
I will make *m.* known among them	*Eze 35:11*
will I magnify *m.*, sanctify *m.*	*Eze 38:23*
I *m.* worthy to come unto thee	*Lu 7:7*
hands and feet, that it is I *m.*	*Lu 24:39*
If I bear witness of *m.*	*Joh 5:31; 8:14, 18*
whether I speak of *m.*	*Joh 7:17*
I am not come of *m.*	*Joh 7:28; 8:42*
I do nothing of *m.*	*Joh 8:28*
I lay it down of *m.*	*Joh 10:18*
I have not spoken of *m.*	*Joh 12:49*
receive you unto *m.*	*Joh 14:3*
I speak not of *m.*	*Joh 14:10*
I sanctify *m.* that they also	*Joh 17:19*

I *m.* also am a man	*Ac 10:26*
I count not my life dear to *m.*	*Ac 20:24*
I think *m.* happy, king Agrippa	*Ac 26:2*
I *m.* serve the law of God	*Ro 7:25*
reserved to *m.* seven thousand	*Ro 11:4*
I know nothing by *m.*	*1Co 4:4*
I made *m.* a servant unto all men	*1Co 9:19*
I *m.* should be a castaway	*1Co 9:27*
kept *m.* from being burdensome	*2Co 11:9*
that I may boast *m.* a little	*2Co 11:16*
I make *m.* a transgressor	*Ga 2:18*
count not *m.* to have apprehended	*Ph'p 3:13*

MYSIA

come to M.	*Ac 16:7*
they passing by M.	*Ac 16:8*

MYSTERIES

who reveals *m.* (B)(R)	*De 2:28*
it is given to you to know *m.*	*M't 13:11;*
of kingdom	*Lu 8:10*
secrets of the kingdom (B)(N)(P)(R)	*M't 13:11*
and as stewards of the *m.* of God	*1Co 4:1*
secrets of God (N)(P)	*1Co 4:1*
and tho' I understand all *m.* and knowledge	*1Co 13:2*
see through every secret (B)	*1Co 13:2*
know every hidden truth (N)	*1Co 13:2*
know the very secrets of God (P)	*1Co 13:2*
howbeit, in the Spirit he speaketh *m.*	*1Co 14:2*
he utters secret truths, hidden things (A)	*1Co 14:2*
uttering secret matters (B)	*1Co 14:2*
speaking spiritual secrets (P)	*1Co 14:2*

MYSTERIOUS

deep and *m.* things (B)(R)	*Da 2:22*
m. purpose of God (P)	*Re 10:7*

MYSTERY

concerning this *m.* (B)(R)	*Da 2:18;*
	2:19, 27, 47
no *m.* is any trouble (B)(R)	*Da 4:9*
to you given to know the *m.*	*M'k 4:11*
of kingdom	
the secret of God's kingdom (B)(N)(P)(R)	*M'k 4:11*
that ye should be ignorant of this *m.*	*Ro 11:25*
be ignorant of this secret (B)	*Ro 11:25*
knowledge of God's secret plan (P)	*Ro 11:25*
according to the revelation of the *m.*	*Ro 16:25*
involves revealing of the secret (B)	*Ro 16:25*
revelation of that divine secret (N)	*Ro 16:25*
knowledge of God's secret plan (P)	*Ro 16:25*
we speak the wisdom of God in a *m.*	*1Co 2:7*
wisdom of God once hidden (A)	*1Co 2:7*
God's hidden wisdom, secret purpose (N)	*1Co 2:7*
mysterious secret wisdom of God (P)	*1Co 2:7*
a secret and hidden wisdom of God (A)	*1Co 2:7*
I shew you a *m.* we shall not all sleep	*1Co 15:51*
I am telling you a secret (B)(P)	*1Co 15:51*
made known to us the *m.* of his will	*Eph 1:9*
known the secret of his purpose (B)	*Eph 1:9*
known to us his hidden purpose (N)	*Eph 1:9*
know the secret of his plan (P)	*Eph 1:9*
how that he made known to me the *m.*	*Eph 3:3*
the secret was made known to me (B)(N)(P)	*Eph 3:3*
understand my knowledge in the *m.* of Christ	*Eph 3:4*
I understand the secret of Christ (N)	*Eph 3:4*

make all see what is the fellowship of the *m.*	*Eph 3:9*
hidden purpose put into effect (N)	*Eph 3:9*
meaning of that divine secret (P)	*Eph 3:9*
this is a great *m.* but I speak of Christ	*Eph 5:32*
great truth hidden here (N)	*Eph 5:32*
to make known the *m.* of the gospel	*Eph 6:19;* *Col 1:26-27; 4:3*
the secret truth of the gospel (B)	*Eph 6:19*
make known the hidden purpose (N)	*Eph 6:19*
the secret of the gospel (P)	*Eph 6:19*
to the acknowledgment of the *m.* of God	*Col 2:2*
that mystic secret of God (A)	*Col 2:2*
grasp God's secret (N)(P)	*Col 2:2*
the *m.* of iniquity doth already work	*2Th 2:7*
the hidden principle of lawlessness (B)	*2Th 2:7*
the secret power of wickedness (N)	*2Th 2:7*
holding *m.* of faith in pure conscience	*1Ti 3:9*
the mystic secret of faith (A)	*1Ti 3:9*
the hidden truth of faith (B)	*1Ti 3:9*
the deep truths of our faith (N)	*1Ti 3:9*
great is *m.* of godliness, God manifest	*1Ti 3:16*
hidden truth, mystic secret (A)	*1Ti 3:16*
hidden truth of godliness (B)	*1Ti 3:16*
the *m.* of the seven stars thou sawest	*Re 1:20*
the hidden meaning of seven stars (A)	*Re 1:20*
secret meaning of the seven stars (N)(P)	*Re 1:20*
the *m.* of God should be finished, as declared	*Re 10:7*
the hidden purpose of God (N)	*Re 10:7*
mysterious purpose of God (P)	*Re 10:7*
m. Babylon the great	*Re 17:5*
a symbolic title was inscribed (B)	*Re 17:5*
a name with a secret meaning (N)(P)	*Re 17:5*
m. of the woman	*Re 17:7*

MYSTIC

that *m.* secret of God (A)	*Col 2:2*
the *m.* secret of faith (A)	*1Ti 3:9*
hidden truth, *m.* secret (A)	*1Ti 3:16*

MYSTIFIED

completely *m.* as to (P)	*Joh 13:22*

MYSTIFYING

m. the people (P)	*Ac 8:9*

MYTHOLOGY

turn to *m.* (N)	*2Ti 4:4*
with his *m.* (B)(E)(N)(R)	*Jude 14*

MYTHS

hoary old *m.* (P)(R)	*1Ti 1:4*
avoid silly *m.* (A)(N)(R)	*1Ti 4:7*
m. man-made fictions (A)(B)(P)(R)	*2Ti 4:4*
Jewish *m.* (N)(R)	*Tit 1:14*
cleverly devised *m.* (R)	*2Pe 1:16*

N

NAAM

of Jephunneh; Iru, Elah, and N.	*1Ch 4:15*

NAAMAH

the sister of Tubal-cain was N.	*Ge 4:22*
Gederoth, Beth-dagon, and N.	*Jos 15:41*
And his mother's name was N.	*1Ki 14:21;* *14:31; 2Ch 12:13*

NAAMAN

N., Ehi, and Rosh, Muppim	*Ge 46:21*
the sons of Bela were Ard and N.	*Nu 26:40*
Ardites; and of N. the family	*Nu 26:40*
Now N., captain of the host of	*2Ki 5:1;* *5:6, 9, 11, 17, 20-21, 23, 27*
And Abishua, and N., and Ahoah	*1Ch 8:4*
And N., and Ahiab, and Gera	*1Ch 8:7*
cleansed, saving N. the Syrian	*Lu 4:27*

NAAMAN'S

maid; and she waited on N. wife	*2Ki 5:2*

NAAMATHITE

the Shuhite, and Zophar the N.	*Job 2:11;* *42:9*
Then answered Zophar the N.	*Job 11:1;* *20:1*

NAAMITES

of Naaman, the family of the N.	*Nu 26:40*

NAARAH

had two wives, Helah and N.	*1Ch 4:5*
and N. bare him Ahuzam, and	*1Ch 4:6*
These were the sons of N.	*1Ch 4:6*

NAARAI

Carmelite, N. the son of Ezbai	*1Ch 11:37*

NAARAN

eastward N., and westward Gezer	*1Ch 7:28*

NAARATH

and to N., and came to Jericho	*Jos 16:7*

NAASHON

Amminadab, sister of N., to wife	*Ex 6:23*

NAASSON

Aminadab begat N.; and N.	*M't 1:4*
Salmon, which was the son of N.	*Lu 3:32*

NABAL

Now the name of the man was N.	*1Sa 25:3;* *25:4-5, 9-10, 19, 25-26, 34, 36, 39*
the wife of N. the Carmelite	*1Sa 30:5;* *2Sa 3:3*

NABAL'S

young men told Abigail, N. wife	*1Sa 25:14*
N. heart was merry within him	*1Sa 25:36*
Abigail the Carmelitess, N. wife	*1Sa 27:3*
Abigail N. wife the Carmelite	*2Sa 2:2*

NABOTH

N. the Jezreelite had a vineyard	*1Ki 21:1;* *21:2-4, 6-9, 12-16, 19*
in the portion of N. the Jezreelite	*2Ki 9:21*
in the portion of the field of N. the	*2Ki 9:25*
seen yesterday the blood of N.	*2Ki 9:26*

NACHON'S

they came to N. threshingfloor	*2Sa 6:6*

NACHOR

Abraham, and the father of N.	*Jos 24:2*
Thara, which was the son of N.	*Lu 3:34*

NADAB

to wife; and she bare him *N.*   *Ex 6:23*
the Lord, thou, and Aaron, *N.*   *Ex 24:1*
went up Moses, and Aaron, *N.*   *Ex 24:9*
office, even Aaron, *N.* and   *Ex 28:1*
Abihu
N. and Abihu, the sons of   *Le 10:1*
Aaron
the names of the sons of Aaron;   *Nu 3:2*
N.
N. and Abihu died before the   *Nu 3:4*
Lord
And unto Aaron was born *N.*   *Nu 26:60*
And *N.* and Abihu died,   *Nu 26:61*
when they
N. his son reigned in his   *1Ki 14:20*
stead
N. the son of Jeroboam   *1Ki 15:25*
began to
for *N.* and all Israel laid   *1Ki 15:27*
siege to
the rest of the acts of *N.* and   *1Ki 15:31*
sons of Shammai; *N.*, and   *1Ch 2:28*
Abishur
sons of *N.*: Seled, and   *1Ch 2:30*
Appaim
sons also of Aaron; *N.* and   *1Ch 6:3*
Abihu
Zur, and Kish, and Baal, and   *1Ch 8:30*
N.
Kish, and Baal, and Ner, and   *1Ch 9:36*
N.
The sons of Aaron; *N.*, and   *1Ch 24:1*
Abihu
N. and Abihu died before their   *1Ch 24:2*

NAGGE

of Esli, which was the son of   *Lu 3:25*
N.

NAHALAL

N. with her suburbs; four   *Jos 21:35*
cities

NAHALIEL

And from Mattanah to *N.*   *Nu 21:19*
and from *N.* to Bamoth   *Nu 21:19*

NAHALLAL

Kattath, and *N.*, and   *Jos 19:15*
Shimron

NAHALOL

Kitron, nor the inhabitants of   *J'g 1:30*
N.

NAHAM

the sister of *N.*, the father of   *1Ch 4:19*

NAHAMANI

Azariah, Raamiah, *N.*,   *Ne 7:7*
Mordecai

NAHARAI

the Ammonite, *N.* the   *1Ch 11:39*
Berothite

NAHARI

N. the Beerothite,   *2Sa 23:37*
armourbearer

NAHASH

Then *N.* the Ammonite came   *1Sa 11:1*
up
the men of Jabesh said unto   *1Sa 11:1*
N.
N. the Ammonite answered   *1Sa 11:2*
them
that *N.* the king of the   *1Sa 12:12*
children of
kindness unto Hanun the son   *2Sa 10:2*
of *N.*
in to Abigail the daughter of   *2Sa 17:25*
N.
that Shobi the son of *N.* of   *2Sa 17:27*
Rabbah
that *N.* the king of the   *1Ch 19:1*
children of
kindness unto Hanun the son   *1Ch 19:2*
of *N.*

NAHATH

the sons of Reuel; *N.*, and   *Ge 36:13*
Zerah
duke *N.*, duke Zerah, duke   *Ge 36:17*
N., Zerah, Shammah, and   *1Ch 1:37*
Mizzah
Zophai his son, and *N.* his   *1Ch 6:26*
son
and Azaziah, and *N.* and   *2Ch 31:13*
Asahel

NAHBI

of Naphtali, *N.* the son of   *Nu 13:14*
Vophsi

NAHOR

lived thirty years, and begat   *Ge 11:22;*
N.   *11:23-27*
Abram and *N.* took them   *Ge 11:29*
wives
born children unto thy   *Ge 22:20*
brother *N.*
these eight Milcah did bear to   *Ge 22:23*
N.
Mesopotamia, unto the city of   *Ge 24:10*
N.
the wife of *N.*, Abraham's   *Ge 24:15*
brother
of Milcah which she bare   *Ge 24:24*
unto *N.*
Know ye Laban the son of *N.*   *Ge 29:5*
God of *N.* the God of their   *Ge 31:53*
father
Serug, *N.*, Terah   *1Ch 1:26*

NAHOR'S

and the name of *N.* wife,   *Ge 11:29*
Milcah
The daughter of Bethuel, *N.*   *Ge 24:47*
son

NAHSHON

N. the son of Amminadab   *Nu 1:7;*
  2:3; 7:17; 10:14
his offering the first day was *N.*   *Nu 7:12*
begat *N.* and *N.* begat Salmon   *Ru 4:20*
and Ammminadab begat *N.*,   *1Ch 2:10*
prince
N. begat Salma, and Salma   *1Ch 2:11*
begat

NAHUM

the vision of *N.*, the Elkoshite   *Na 1:1*

NAIL

Heber's wife took a *n.* of the   *J'g 4:21*
tent
took a tent-pin (A)(E)   *J'g 4:21;*
  4:22; 5:26
took a tent peg   *J'g 4:21; 4:22; 5:26*
(B)(R)
and smote the *n.* into his   *J'g 4:21*
temples
dead, and the *n.* was in his   *J'g 4:22*
temples
She put her hand to the *n.* and   *J'g 5:26*
her
to give us a *n.* in his holy place   *Ezr 9:8*
fasten him as a *n.* in a sure   *Isa 22:23*
place
like a peg (B)(R)   *Isa 22:23; 22:25*
n. that is fastened in the sure   *Isa 22:25*
place
out of him the *n.*, out of him   *Zec 10:4*
the tent peg (A)(B)(R)   *Zec 10:4*

NAILED

old self *n.* to cross (A)   *Ro 6:6*

NAILING

out of the way, *n.* it to his   *Col 2:14*
cross

NAILS

shave her head, and pare her   *De 21:12*
n.
iron in abundance for the *n.*   *1Ch 22:3*
weight of the *n.* was fifty   *2Ch 3:9*
shekels
as *n.* fastened by the masters   *Ec 12:11*

driven home like spikes (B)   *Ec 12:11*
and he fastened it with *n.* that   *Isa 41:7*
it with *n.* and with hammers   *Jer 10:4*
and his *n.* like birds' claws   *Da 4:33*
were of iron, and his *n.* of   *Da 7:19*
brass
in his hands the print of the   *Joh 20:25*
n.
my finger into the print of   *Joh 20:25*
the *n.*

NAIN

that he went into a city called   *Lu 7:11*
N.

NAIOTH

Samuel went and dwelt in *N.*   *1Sa 19:18*
Behold, David is at *N.* in   *1Sa 19:19*
Ramah
Behold, they be at *N.* in   *1Sa 19:22*
Ramah
he went thither to *N.* in   *1Sa 19:23*
Ramah
until he came to *N.* in   *1Sa 19:23*
Ramah
David fled from *N.* in Ramah   *1Sa 20:1*

NAKED

they were both *n.* the man and   *Ge 2:25*
knew that they were *n.*;   *Ge 3:7*
I was afraid, because I was *n.*   *Ge 3:10*
Who told thee that thou wast   *Ge 3:11*
n.
saw that the people were *n.*   *Ex 32:25*
people were unrestrained   *Ex 32:25*
(A)(B)
people were broken loose   *Ex 32:25*
(E)(R)
had made them *n.* unto their   *Ex 32:25*
shame
lay down *n.* all that day and   *1Sa 19:24*
took off his royal robes (A)   *1Sa 19:24*
stripped off his clothes   *1Sa 19:24*
(B)(R)
all that were *n.* among them   *2Ch 28:15*
Israel; for he made Judah *n.*   *2Ch 28:19*
dealt with reckless cruelty   *2Ch 28:19*
(A)
fostered lack of constraint in   *2Ch 28:19*
Judah (B)
dealt wantonly in Judah   *2Ch 28:19*
(E)(R)
N. came I out out of my   *Job 1:21*
mother's
and *n.* shall I return thither   *Job 1:21*
stripped the *n.* of their   *Job 22:6*
clothing
the *n.* to lodge without   *Job 24:7*
clothing
him to go *n.* without   *Job 24:10*
clothing, and
Hell is *n.* before him, and   *Job 26:6*
Sheol lies exposed before him   *Job 26:6*
(B)
n. shall he return to go as he   *Ec 5:15*
came
to be stripped *n.* (A)   *Isa 3:17*
he did so, walking *n.* and   *Isa 20:2*
barefoot
servant Isaiah hath walked *n.*   *Isa 20:3*
young and old, *n.* and barefoot   *Isa 20:4*
when thou seest the *n.*   *Isa 58:7*
and shalt make thyself *n.*   *La 4:21*
whereas thou wast *n.* and   *Eze 16:7*
bare
youth, when thou wast *n.* and   *Eze 16:22*
bare
jewels, and leave these *n.* and   *Eze 16:39*
bare
hath covered the *n.* with a   *Eze 18:7;*
garment   *18:16*
hath covered the *n.* with a   *Eze 18:16*
garment
and shall leave thee *n.* and   *Eze 23:29*
bare
Lest I strip her *n.* and set her as   *Ho 2:3*
the mighty shall flee away *n.*   *Am 2:16*
howl, I will go stripped and *n.*   *Mic 1:8*
of Saphir, having thy shame   *Mic 1:11*
n.
Thy bow was made quite *n.*   *Hab 3:9*
N., and ye clothed me: I was   *M't 25:36*
sick
thee in? Or *n.* and clothed   *M't 25:38*
thee
n. and ye clothed me not   *M't 25:43*
or *n.* or sick, or in prison,   *M't 25:44*
and did

linen cloth cast about his *n.* *M'k 14:51*
body
linen cloth, and fled from *M'k 14:52*
them *n.*
coat unto him, (for he was *n.*) *Joh 21:7*
he was stripped for work *Joh 21:7*
(A)(B)(N)(R)
out of that house *n.* and *Ac 19:16*
wounded
hunger, and thirst, and are *n.* *1Co 4:11*
clothed we shall not be found *2Co 5:3*
n.
be found coverless (B) *2Co 5:3*
all things are *n.* and opened *Heb 4:13*
unto
bare and exposed before him *Heb 4:13*
(B)
open and laid bare (R) *Heb 4:13*
If a brother or sister be *n.* and *Jas 2:15*
and poor, and blind, and *n.* *Re 3:17*
lest he walk *n.* and they see *Re 16:15*
and shall make her desolate *Re 17:16*
and *n.*
make her cheerless, strip her *Re 17:16*
(A)
render her isolated and *Re 17:16*
stripped (B)

NAKEDNESS

Canaan, saw the *n.* of his *Ge 9:22*
father
and covered the *n.* of their *Ge 9:23*
father
and they saw not their father's *Ge 9:23*
n.
to see the *n.* of the land ye are *Ge 42:9;*
                                              42:12
land lies exposed (B) *Ge 42:9*
see the weakness of the land *Ge 42:9*
thy *n.* be not discovered *Ex 20:26*
thereon
them linen breeches to cover *Ex 28:42*
their *n.*
of kin to him, to uncover their *Le 18:6*
n. of thy father, or the *n.* of *Le 18:7;*
          18:8-19; 20:11, 17-21
hunger, and in thirst, and in *De 28:48*
n.
the confusion of thy mother's *1Sa 20:30*
n.
Thy *n.* shall be uncovered, yea *Isa 47:3*
n. exposed (B) *Jer 13:26*
because they have seen her *n.* *La 1:8*
skirt over thee, and covered *Eze 16:8*
thy *n.*
and thy *n.* discovered *Eze 16:36*
through thy
and will discover thy *n.* unto *Eze 16:37*
them
them, that they may see all *Eze 16:37*
thy *n.*
they discovered their father's *Eze 22:10*
n.
These discovered her *n.*: they *Eze 23:10*
discovered her *n.*: then my *Eze 23:18*
mind
the *n.* of thy whoredoms *Eze 23:29*
shall be
and my flax given to cover her *Ho 2:9*
n.
and I will shew the nations thy *Na 3:5*
n.
that thou mayest look on *Hab 2:15*
their *n.*
famine, or *n.*, or peril, or *Ro 8:35*
sword
in fastings often, in cold and *2Co 11:27*
n.
the shame of thy *n.* do not *Re 3:18*
appear

NAME

what Adam called, that was *n.* *Ge 2:19*
thereof
call the *n.* of the city after the *Ge 4:17*
n. of his son
he blessed them, and called their *Ge 5:2*
n. Adam
let us make us a *n.* lest we be *Ge 11:4*
scattered
therefore the *n.* of the city is *Ge 19:22*
Zoar
the *n.* of the city was Luz at *Ge 28:19*
the first
shall be called after the *n.* of *Ge 48:6*
their brethren
the Lord, whose *n.* is Jealous, *Ex 34:14*
is jealous

neither profane the *n.* of *Le 18:21;*
thy God *19:12; 21:6; 22:2, 32*
n. of one Eldad, of the other *Nu 11:26*
Medad
write thou every man's *n.* upon *Nu 17:2*
his rod
the *n.* of the Israelite that *Nu 25:14*
was slain
n. of Midianitish woman *Nu 25:15*
slain was Cozbi
why should *n.* of our father be *Nu 27:4*
done away
and called it Nobah, after his *Nu 32:42*
own *n.*
destroy their *n.* from under *De 7:24*
heaven
and blot out their *n.* from *De 9:14*
under heaven
bring up an evil *n.* on her, *De 22:14*
and say
he hath brought up an evil *n.* *De 22:19*
on a virgin
firstborn succeed in *n.* of his *De 25:6*
brother
to raise up to his brother a *n.* *De 25:7*
in Israel
to make thee high in *n.* and in *De 26:19*
honour
mayest fear this glorious and *De 28:58*
fearful *n.*
nor make mention of *n.* of *Jos 23:7*
their gods
man's *n.* with whom I wrought *Ru 2:19*
is Boaz
to raise up the *n.* of the dead *Ru 4:5;*
                                                4:10
the women her neighbours *Ru 4:17*
gave it a *n.*
anoint to me him whom I *n.* *1Sa 16:3*
the *n.* of the man was Nabal *1Sa 25:3*
they spake to Nabal in the *n.* *1Sa 25:9*
of David
bring him up whom I shall *n.* *1Sa 28:8*
whose *n.* is called by the *n.* of *2Sa 6:2*
the Lord
called the *n.* of the place *2Sa 6:8*
Perez-uzzah
I have made thee a great *n.* *2Sa 7:9;*
like the *n.* of the great men *1Ch 17:8*
God redeemed to make him a *2Sa 7:23;*
n. *1Ch 17:21*
David gat him a *n.* when he *2Sa 8:13*
returned
shall not leave to my husband *2Sa 14:7*
neither *n.* nor
Abishai had the *n.* among *2Sa 23:18*
three
Benaiah, and had *n.* among *2Sa 23:22;*
three *1Ch 11:20, 24*
God make *n.* of Solomon *1Ki 1:47*
better than thy *n.* and
chose to put his *n.* there *1Ki 14:21;*
                                          2Ch 12:13
call ye on the *n.* of your *1Ki 18:24;*
gods *18:25*
so Jezebel wrote letters in *1Ki 21:8*
Ahab's *n.*
would not blot out the *n.* of *2Ki 14:27*
Israel
and was called after their *n.* *Ezr 2:61;*
                                          Ne 7:63
prophesied in the *n.* of the God *Ezr 5:1*
of Israel
and gavest him the *n.* of *Ne 9:7*
Abraham
so didst thou get thee a *n.* as it *Ne 9:10*
is this day
Esther certified the king in *Es 2:22*
Mordecai's *n.*
write ye also for the Jews in the *Es 8:8*
king's *n.*
he shall have no *n.* in the *Job 18:17*
street
thou hast put out their *n.* for *Ps 9:5*
ever
the *n.* of the God of Jacob *Ps 20:1*
defend thee
in the *n.* of God we will set up *Ps 20:5*
our banners
if we have forgotten the *n.* of *Ps 44:20*
our God
I will praise the *n.* of God *Ps 69:30*
with a song
the *n.* of Israel be no more in *Ps 83:4*
remembrance
whose *n.* alone is JEHOVAH, *Ps 83:18*
art most high
let them praise thy great *n.* for *Ps 99:3*
it is holy
and let their *n.* be blotted out *Ps 109:13*

the Lord's *n.* is to be praised *Ps 113:3*
but the *n.* of the wicked shall *Pr 10:7*
rot
the *n.* of the Lord is a strong *Pr 18:10*
tower
a good *n.* is rather to be chosen *Pr 22:1*
than riches
lest I take the *n.* of my God in *Pr 30:9*
vain
a good *n.* better than precious *Ec 7:1*
ointment
I will cut off from Babylon *Isa 14:22*
the *n.*
it shall be to the Lord for a *n.* *Isa 55:13*
for a sign
I will give them a *n.* an *Isa 56:5*
everlasting *n.*
whose *n.* is holy; called by a *Isa 57:15;*
new *n.* *62:2*
which the mouth of the Lord *Isa 62:2*
shall *n.*
to make himself an *Isa 63:12*
everlasting *n.*
lead thy people, to make *Isa 63:14*
thyself a glorious *n.*
leave your *n.* for a curse to *Isa 65:15*
my chosen, and call servants
by another *n.*
so shall your seed and your *n.* *Isa 66:22*
remain
that they might be to me for a *Jer 13:11;*
n. *33:9*
which hast made thee a *n.* *Jer 32:20*
this is the *n.* wherewith she *Jer 33:16*
shall be called
King, whose *n.* is the Lord *Jer 46:18;*
of hosts *48:15; 51:57*
and the *n.* thereof is called *Eze 20:29*
Bamah
son of man, write thee the *n.* *Eze 24:2*
of the day
the *n.* of the city shall be, *Eze 48:35*
The Lord is there
blessed be the *n.* of God for *Da 2:20*
ever and ever
Daniel came, according to the *Da 4:8*
n. of my God
God said to him, Call her *n.* *Ho 1:6*
Lo-ruhamah
they shall no more be *Ho 2:17*
remembered by their *n.*
saith Lord, whose *n.* is the *Am 5:27*
God of hosts
all people walk in the *n.* of his *Mic 4:5*
god, we will walk in *n.* of our
God
I will cut off the *n.* of the *Zep 1:4*
Chemarims
I will make you a *n.* and a *Zep 3:20*
praise
the man whose *n.* is the *Zec 6:12*
BRANCH
receiveth prophet in *n.* of a *M't 10:41*
prophet, a righteous man in
n. of a righteous man
shall give a cup of water only *M't 10:42*
in *n.* of disciple
baptizing them in the *n.* of *M't 28:19*
the Father
none of thy kindred is called *Lu 1:61*
by this *n.*
and he wrote, saying, His *n.* is *Lu 1:63*
John
blessed, when shall cast out *Lu 6:22*
your *n.* as evil
a man sent from God, whose *n.* *Joh 1:6*
was John
not believed in the *n.* of the *Joh 3:18*
only begotten
I am come in my Father's *n.* *Joh 5:43*
and ye receive
works that I do in my *Joh 10:25*
Father's *n.*
be baptized in the *n.* of the *Ac 2:38*
Lord Jesus
in the *n.* of Jesus Christ, rise up *Ac 3:6*
and walk
by what power or *n.* have ye *Ac 4:7*
done this
there is none other *n.* under *Ac 4:12*
heaven given
speak henceforth to no man in *Ac 4:17;*
this *n.* *4:18*
wonders may be done by the *n.* *Ac 4:30*
of Jesus
that you should not teach in *Ac 5:28;*
this *n.* *5:40*
preaching, concerning the *n.* *Ac 8:12*
of Jesus

that destroyed them that called   Ac 9:21
on this *n*.
he had preached boldly in the   Ac 9:27
n. of Jesus
hazarded their lives for *n*. of   Ac 15:26
Jesus
said, In the *n*. of Jesus come   Ac 16:18
out of her
they were baptized in the *n*. of   Ac 19:5
Jesus
to do contrary to *n*. of Jesus of   Ac 26:9
Nazareth
for the *n*. of God is   Ro 2:24
blasphemed
were ye baptized in the *n*. of   1Co 1:13
Paul
in the *n*. of our Lord Jesus   1Co 5:4;
     Eph 5:20
are justified in the *n*. of the   1Co 6:11
Lord Jesus
far above every *n*. that is   Eph 1:21
named
hath given him a *n*. above   Ph'p 2:9
every *n*.
at the *n*. of Jesus every knee   Ph'p 2:10
should bow
do all in the *n*. of the Lord   Col 3:17
Jesus
that the *n*. of God be not   1Ti 6:1
blasphemed
n. of Christ, depart from   2Ti 2:19
iniquity
he hath obtained a more   Heb 1:4
excellent *n*.
do not they blaspheme that   Jas 2:7
worthy *n*.
if reproached for the *n*. of   1Pe 4:14
Christ
should believe on *n*. of his   1Jo 3:23;
Son   5:13
a *n*. written, which no man   Re 2:17
knoweth
thou hast a *n*. that thou livest,   Re 3:1
and art dead
I will write on him the *n*. of   Re 3:12
my God
the *n*. of the star is called   Re 8:11
Wormwood
whose *n*. in Hebrew tongue is   Re 9:11
Abaddon
and on his heads the *n*. of   Re 13:1
blasphemy
his Father's *n*. written in their   Re 14:1
foreheads
and men blasphemed the *n*. of   Re 16:9
God
on her forehead was a *n*.   Re 17:5
written, Mystery
a *n*. written no man knew but   Re 19:12
himself
on his thigh a *n*. written, King   Re 19:16
of kings

BY NAME, BY THE NAME

I appeared *by the n*. of God   Ex 6:3
Almighty
I have called *by n*. Bezaleel   Ex 31:2;
     35:30
yet thou hast said, I know   Ex 33:12;
thee *by n*.   33:17
by n. ye shall reckon the   Nu 4:32
instruments
they gave these cities   Jos 21:9
mentioned *by n*.
Philistine of Gath, Goliath   1Sa 17:23
by n.
Sheba, son of Bichri *by n*.   2Sa 20:21
hath lifted
a child shall be born, Josiah   1Ki 13:2
by n.
these written *by n*. came and   1Ch 4:41
smote
expressed *by n*.   1Ch 12:31;
     16:41; 2Ch 28:15; 31:19
except that she were called *by n*.   Es 2:14
shall call himself *by the n*. of   Isa 44:5;
Jacob, and surname himself   48:1
by the n. of Israel
I the Lord which call thee *by*   Isa 45:3
thy *n*.
and he calleth his own sheep   Joh 10:3
by n.
by the n. of Jesus this man is   Ac 4:10
whole
I beseech you *by the n*. of our   1Co 1:10
Lord
our friends salute thee, great   3Jo 14
friends *by n*.

HIS NAME

shall say, What is *his n*.   Ex 3:13;
     Pr 30:4
the Lord is *his n*.   Ex 15:3;
     Jer 33:2; Am 5:8; 9:6
guiltless that taketh *his n*. in   Ex 20:7;
vain   De 5:11
every stone with *his n*. shall   Ex 28:21;
they be   39:14
Jair called them after *his* own   De 3:14
n.
shalt serve him, and shalt   De 6:13
swear by *his n*.
to bless in *his n*. to this day   De 10:8;
     1Ch 23:13
Lord choose to put *his n*.   De 12:5;
there   12:21; 1Ki 14:21; 2Ch 12:13
shall choose to cause *his n*. to   De 12:11
dwell there
choose to place *his n*. there   De 14:23;
     16:6, 11; 26:2
the Lord shall choose to set   De 14:24
his n. there
that *his n*. be not put out of   De 25:6
Israel
and *his n*. shall be called in   De 25:10
Israel
Lord shall blot out *his n*.   De 29:20
from under heaven
I asked not, neither told he me   J'g 13:6
his n.
that *his n*. may be famous in   Ru 4:14
Israel
so that *his n*. was much set   1Sa 18:30
by
as *his n*. is, so is he, Nabal is   1Sa 25:25
his n.
call upon *his n*.   1Ch 16:8;
     Ps 105:1; Isa 12:4
give the glory due to *his n*.   1Ch 16:29;
     Ps 29:2; 96:8
God that caused *his n*. dwell   Ezr 6:12
there
let us exalt *his n*. together   Ps 34:3; 66:2
when shall he die and *his n*.   Ps 41:5
perish
that rideth on the heavens by   Ps 68:4
his n.
they that love *his n*. shall   Ps 69:36
dwell therein
his n. shall endure for ever, as   Ps 72:17
long as sun
and blessed be *his* glorious *n*.   Ps 72:19
for ever
his n. is great in Israel   Ps 76:1
Samuel among them that call   Ps 99:6
on *his n*.
bless *his n*.   Ps 100:4
holy and reverend is *his n*.   Ps 111:9
sing praises to *his n*. for it is   Ps 135:3
pleasant
praise *his n*. for *his n*. alone   Ps 148:13
is excellent
let them praise *his n*. in the   Ps 149:3
dance
proud and haughty scorner is   Pr 21:24
his n.
his n. shall be covered with   Ec 6:4
darkness
shall call *his n*. Immanuel   Isa 7:14;
     M't 1:23
and *his n*. shall be called,   Isa 9:6
Wonderful
make mention that *his n*. is   Isa 12:4
exalted
Lord of hosts is *his n*.   Isa 47:4;
48:2; 51:15; 54:5; Jer 10:16; 31:35;
     32:18; 50:34; 51:19
his n. should not have been   Isa 48:19
cut off
his n. may be no more   Jer 11:19
remembered
I will not speak any more in   Jer 20:9
his n.
this is *his n*. whereby he shall   Jer 23:6
be called
all ye that know *his n*. say,   Jer 48:17
How is staff
the Lord, the God of hosts is   Am 4:13
his n.
they shall walk up and down   Zec 10:12
in *his n*.
in that day shall be one Lord,   Zec 14:9
and *his n*. one
for them that thought on *his*   Mal 3:16
n. a book
shalt call *his n*. Jesus   M't 1:23;
     Lu 1:31; 2:21

in *his n*. shall the Gentiles   M't 12:21
trust
for *his n*. was spread abroad   M'k 6:14
and thou shalt call *his n*. John   Lu 1:13
remission of sins should be   Lu 24:47
preached in *his n*.
even to them that believe on   Joh 1:12
his n.
many believed in *his n*. when   Joh 2:23
they saw
if another shall come in *his*   Joh 5:43
own *n*.
that believing ye might have   Joh 20:31
life thro' *his n*.
his n. through faith in *his n*.   Ac 3:16
hath made
they were counted worthy to   Ac 5:41
suffer for *his n*.
thro' *his n*. shall receive   Ac 10:43
remission of sins
Elymas the sorcerer, for so is   Ac 13:8
his n.
to take out of them a people   Ac 15:14
for *his n*.
to the faith among all nations   Ro 1:5
for *his n*.
of love which ye shewed   Heb 6:10
towards *his n*.
let us offer praise, giving   Heb 13:15
thanks to *his n*.
not blot out *his n*. but will   Re 3:5
confess *his n*.
and *his n*. that sat on him was   Re 6:8
Death
in the Greek tongue hath *his n*.   Re 9:11
Apollyon
to blaspheme *his n*.   Re 13:6
whosoever receiveth the mark   Re 14:11
of *his n*.
number of *his n*.   Re 15:2
and *his n*. shall be in their   Re 22:4
foreheads

MY NAME

why is it that thou dost ask   Ge 32:29
after *my n*.
let *my n*. be named on them,   Ge 48:16
let them grow
this is *my n*. for ever, and my   Ex 3:15
memorial
raised thee up, that *my n*. may   Ex 9:16
be declared
where I record *my n*. I will   Ex 20:24
come unto thee
provoke him not, for *my n*. is   Ex 23:21
in him
ye shall not swear by *my n*.   Le 19:12
falsely
his seed unto Molech, to   Le 20:3
profane *my* holy *n*.
put *my n*. on the children of   Nu 6:27
Israel
which he shall speak in *my n*.   De 18:19;
     18:20
why askest thou thus after *my*   J'g 13:18
n.
swear thou wilt not destroy   1Sa 24:21
my n.
and go to Nabal, and greet   1Sa 25:5
him in *my n*.
he shall build an house for   2Sa 7:13;
my n.   1Ki 5:5; 8:18-19; 1Ch 22:10
lest the city be called after   2Sa 12:28
my n.
I have no son to keep *my n*.   2Sa 18:18
in remembrance
that *my n*. might be therein   1Ki 8:16;
8:29; 11:36; 2Ki 21:4, 7; 2Ch 6:5-6;
     7:16; 33:4, 7
this house which I have   1Ki 9:7
hallowed for *my n*.
shall not build an house to   1Ch 22:8;
my n.   28:3
in heart to build an house for   2Ch 6:8
my n.
Solomon shall build the house   2Ch 6:9
for *my n*.
this house which I have   2Ch 7:20
sanctified for *my n*.
I have chosen to set *my n*. there   Ne 1:9;
     Jer 7:12
in *my n*. shall his horn be   Ps 89:24
exalted
because he hath known *my n*.   Ps 91:14
they shall sanctify *my n*. and   Isa 29:23
fear
from rising of the sun shall he   Isa 41:25
call on *my n*.

I am the Lord, that is *my n.*   *Isa 42:8*
and my glory
for how should *my n.* be   *Ps 48:11*
polluted
hath he made mention of *my*   *Isa 49:1*
n.
my n. continually every day is *Isa 52:5*
blasphemed
therefore my people shall   *Isa 52:6*
know *my n.*
they shall know that *my n.* is *Jer 16:21*
the Lord
they think to cause my people *Jer 23:27*
to forget *my n.* as their
fathers forgot *my n.*
they prophesy a lie in *my n.*   *Jer 27:15;*
               29:9, 21, 23
but ye turned and polluted *my Jer 34:16*
n.
sworn by *my* great *n. my n.*   *Jer 44:26*
no more named
I wrought for *my n.*   *Eze 20:9; 14:22, 44*
and I will sanctify *my* great *Eze 36:23*
n.
they shall call on *my n.* I will *Zec 13:9*
hear
to you, O priests, that despise *Mal 1:6*
my n.
my n. be great among   *Mal 1:11*
Gentiles, and in every place
incense be offered to *my n.*
my n. is dreadful among the *Mal 1:14*
heathen
lay it to heart, to give glory   *Mal 2:2*
unto *my n.*
he feared me, and was afraid *Mal 2:5*
before *my n.*
to you that fear *my n.* shall the *Mal 4:2*
sun of righteousness
receive a child in *my n.*   *M't 18:5;*
         M'k 9:37; Lu 9:48
two or three are gathered   *M't 18:20*
together in *my n.*
for many shall come in *my n. M't 24:5;*
and shall deceive many   *M'k 13:6;*
                 Lu 21:8
he answered, saying, *My n.* is *M'k 5:9*
Legion
no man which shall do a   *M'k 9:39*
miracle in *my n.*
give you a cup of water to   *M'k 9:41*
drink in *my n.*
in *my n.* shall they cast out *M'k 16:17*
devils
whatsoever ye shall ask in   *Joh 14:13;*
my n. that will I Do   *15:16; 16:23-24, 26*
the Comforter whom he will *Joh 14:26*
send in *my n.*
he is a chosen vessel to bear *Ac 9:15*
my n.
the Gentiles upon whom *my Ac 15:17*
n. is called
and that *my n.* might be   *Ro 9:17*
declared
lest any say, I baptized in   *1Co 1:15*
mine own *n.*
thou holdest fast *my n.* and   *Re 2:13*
hast not denied
hast kept my word, and hast not *Re 3:8*
denied *my n.*

THY NAME

I will bless thee, and make *thy Ge 12:2*
n. great
thy n. Abram, but *thy n.* shall *Ge 17:5*
be Abraham
said to him, What is *thy n.?*   *Ge 32:27;*
         32:29; J'g 13:17
he said, *Thy n.* shall be no   *Ge 32:28;*
more called Jacob   *35:10; 1Ki 18:34*
since came to Pharaoh to   *Ex 5:23*
speak in *thy n.*
what wilt thou do to *thy* great *Jos 7:9*
n.
let *thy n.* be magnified for ever *2Sa 7:26*
I will sing praise to *thy n.*   *2Sa 22:50;*
  Ps 9:2; 18:49; 61:8; 66:4; 92:1
name of Solomon better than *.1Ki 1:47*
thy n.
turn and confess *thy n.*   *1Ki 8:33;*
         2Ch 6:24, 26
for they shall hear of *thy* great *1Ki 8:42*
n.
all people of earth may know *1Ki 8:43;*
thy n., called by *thy n.*   *2Ch 6:33*
house I built for *thy n.*   *1Ki 8:44;*
       8:48; 2Ch 6:34, 38

thy n. may be magnified for   *1Ch 17:24*
ever
we thank and praise *thy n.*   *1Ch 29:13;*
               Ps 44:8
that thou wouldest put *thy n. 2Ch 6:20*
there
in *thy n.* we go against this   *2Ch 14:11*
multitude
have built thee a sanctuary   *2Ch 20:8*
for *thy n.*
before this house, for *thy n.* is *2Ch 20:9*
in this house
servants, who desire to fear *thy Ne 1:11*
n.
blessed be *thy* glorious *n.* which *Ne 9:5*
is exalted
let them that love *thy n.* be   *Ps 5:11*
joyful
how excellent is *thy n.* in all the *Ps 8:1;*
earth   *8:9*
they that know *thy n.* will trust *Ps 9:10*
in thee
I will declare *thy n.* to   *Ps 22:22;*
brethren   *Heb 2:12*
through *thy n.* will we tread   *Ps 44:5*
them under
I will make *thy n.* to be   *Ps 45:17*
remembered
according to *thy n.* so is thy   *Ps 48:10*
praise
I will wait on *thy n.;* save me *Ps 52:9;*
by *thy n.*   *54:1*
given the heritage of those that *Ps 61:5*
fear *thy n.*
will bless, I will lift up my   *Ps 63:4*
hands in *thy n.*
they have defiled the dwelling *Ps 74:7*
place of *thy n.*
shall the enemy blaspheme *thy Ps 74:10*
n. for ever
the foolish people have   *Ps 74:18*
blasphemed *thy n.*
let the poor and needy praise *Ps 74:21*
thy n.
for that *thy n.* is near thy   *Ps 75:1*
works declare
that have not called on *thy n. Ps 79:6;*
            Jer 10:25
help us for the glory of *thy n. Ps 79:9*
quicken us, and we will call   *Ps 80:18*
upon *thy n.*
that they may seek *thy n.* O   *Ps 83:16*
Lord
all nations shall come and   *Ps 86:9;*
glorify *thy n.*   *86:12*
teach me, unite my heart to   *Ps 86:11*
fear *thy n.*
Hermon shall rejoice in *thy n. Ps 89:12;*
            89:16
nor unto us, but unto *thy n.*   *Ps 115:1*
give glory
I have remembered *thy n.* in *Ps 119:55*
the night
as thou usest to do to those *Ps 119:132*
that love *thy n.*
thy n. O Lord, endureth for   *Ps 135:13*
ever
I will praise *thy n.* for thy   *Ps 138:2*
lovingkindness, hast magnified
word above all *thy n.*
and thine enemies take *thy n. Ps 139:20*
in vain
the righteous shall give   *Ps 140:13*
thanks to *thy n.*
out of prison, that I may   *Ps 142:7*
praise *thy n.*
I will bless *thy n.* for ever and *Ps 145:1;*
ever   *145:2*
I will praise *thy n.* for ever   *Ps 145:2;*
            Isa 25:1
thy n. is as ointment poured   *Ca 1:3*
forth
the desire of our soul is to *thy Isa 26:8*
n.
by thee we will make mention *Isa 26:13*
of *thy n.*
O Lord, *thy n.* is from   *Isa 63:16*
everlasting
make *thy n.* known to thine   *Isa 64:2*
adversaries
there is none that calleth on   *Isa 64:7*
thy n.
thou art great and *thy n.* is   *Jer 10:6*
great in might
the Lord calleth *thy n.* a   *Jer 11:16*
green olive tree
sent letters in *thy n.* to all   *Jer 29:25*
people at Jerusalem
I called upon *thy n.* out of the *La 3:55*
dungeon

the prophets spake in *thy n.* to *Da 9:6*
our kings
and the man of wisdom shall *Mic 6:9*
see *thy n.*
that no more of *thy n.* be sown *Na 1:14*
wherein have we despised *thy Mal 1:6*
n.
hallowed be *thy n.*   *M't 6:9; Lu 11:2*
in *thy n.* have we not cast out *M't 7:22*
devils
he asked him, What is *thy n. M'k 5:9;*
            Lu 8:30
casting out devils in *thy n.*   *M'k 9:38;*
            Lu 9:49
the devils are subject through *Lu 10:17*
thy n.
Father glorify *thy n.* then   *Joh 12:28*
came a voice
I have manifested *thy n.* to   *Joh 17:6;*
the men   *17:26*
holy Father, keep through   *Joh 17:11;*
thine own *n.*   *17:12*
authority to bind all that call *Ac 9:14*
on *thy n.*
I will confess, and sing unto   *Ro 15:9*
thy n.
give reward to them that fear *Re 11:18*
thy n.
who shall not fear and glorify *Re 15:4*
thy n.

NAMED

Abraham weighed silver   *Ge 23:16*
which he had *n.*
he said, Is not he rightly *n.*   *Ge 27:36*
Jacob
and let my name be *n.* on   *Ge 48:16*
them
she *n.* the child I-chabod,   *1Sa 4:21*
saying
the children of Jacob whom *2Ki 17:34*
he *n.* Israel
Moses' sons *n.* of the tribe of *1Ch 23:14*
Levi
what hath been, is *n.* already *Ec 6:10*
ye shall be *n.* the priests of the *Isa 61:6*
Lord
my name shall no more be *n. Jer 44:26*
in mouth
which are *n.* chief of the   *Am 6:1*
nations
O thou that art *n.* of the house *Mic 2:7*
of Jacob
Jesus was so *n.* of the angel   *Lu 2:21*
before conceived
he chose twelve, whom he *n.*   *Lu 6:13*
apostles
to preach, not where Christ   *Ro 15:20*
was *n.*
such fornication not *n.*   *1Co 5:1*
among Gentiles
far above every name that is *Eph 1:21*
n.
the whole family in heaven   *Eph 3:15*
and earth is *n.*
covetousness, let it not be once *Eph 5:3*
n. among you

NAMELESS

worthless, *n.* men (A)   *Job 30:8*

NAMELY

n., of the sheep   *Le 1:10*
n., the tent of the testimony   *Nu 9:15*
Of the tribe of Joseph, *n.,* of *Nu 13:11*
the tribe
N., Bezer in the wilderness   *De 4:43*
N., the gods of the people   *De 13:7*
n., the Hittites, and Amorites *De 20:17*
N., five lords of the Philistines *J'g 3:3*
n., Gideon, according to all the *J'g 8:35*
n., the thirteenth day of the   *Es 8:12*
the second is like, *n.* this   *M'k 12:31*
n. Judas surnamed Barsabas *Ac 15:22*
n., Thou shalt love thy   *Ro 13:9*
neighbour

NAMES

Adam gave *n.* to all cattle, and *Ge 2:20*
to fowl
called their *n.* after *n.* his   *Ge 26:18*
father called them
be circumcised and make no *Ex 23:13;*
mention of *n.* of other gods   *De 12:3*
grave on them the *n.* of   *Ex 28:9;*
children of Israel   *28:21*

NAMES

Aaron shall bear their *n.* *Ex 28:12;* before the Lord 28:29
the number of their *n.* by their *Nu 1:2* poll
the *n.* of the men that shall *Nu 1:5* stand with you
number of *n.* of the Levites *Nu 3:43* from a month old
the *n.* of the men which *Nu 13:16* Moses sent to spy
n. of men which shall divide *Nu 34:17* the land
the *n.* of mighty men whom *2Sa 23:8* David had
what are their *n.* who make this *Ezr 5:4* building
nor take up their *n.* into my *Ps 16:4* lips
they call their lands after their *Ps 49:11* own *n.*
the stars he calleth them by *n.* *Ps 147:4;* *Isa 40:26*
the *n.* of them were Aholah *Eze 23:4* the elder
for I will take away the *n.* of *Ho 2:17* Baalim
cut off the *n.* of the idols out *Zec 13:2* of the land
rejoice, your *n.* are written in *Lu 10:20* heaven
the number of the *n.* together *Ac 1:15* were 120
if it be a question of words *Ac 18:15* and *n.* look to it
whose *n.* are in the book of *Ph'p 4:3* life
thou hast a few *n.* in Sardis, not *Re 3:4* defiled
whose *n.* are not written in *Re 13:8;* book *17:8*
I saw a woman full of *n.* of *Re 17:3* blasphemy
n. written thereon, *n.* of the *Re 21:12* twelve tribes
in them the *n.* of twelve *Re 21:14* apostles of the Lamb

NAME'S

for his *n.* sake *1Sa 12:22;* *Ps 23:3; 106:8; 1Jo 2:12; 3Jo 7*
for thy *n.* sake *1Ki 8:41;* *2Ch 6:32; Ps 25:11; 31:3; 79:9; 109:21; 143:11; Jer 14:7, 21*
for my *n.* sake *Isa 48:9;* *66:5; Eze 20:9, 14, 22, 44; M't 10:22; 19:29; 24:9; M'k 13:13; Lu 21:12, 17; Joh 15:21; Ac 9:16; Re 2:3*
for mine holy *n.* sake *Eze 36:22*

NAMETH

one that *n.* the name of Christ *2Ti 2:19*

NAOMI

the name of Elimelech's wife *Ru 1:2* was *N.*
is this *N.;* call me not *N.* *Ru 1:19;* call me Mara *1:20*
N. had a kinsman of her *Ru 2:1* husband's, Boaz
what day thou buyest the field *Ru 4:5* of hand of *N.*
that I have bought all at the *Ru 4:9* hand of *N.*
the women said, There is a son *Ru 4:17* born to *N.*

NAOMI'S

Elimelech *N.* husband *Ru 1:3*

NAPHISH

Tema, Jetur, *N.* *Ge 25:15* Jetur, *N.,* and Kedemah *1Ch 1:31*

NAPHTALI

and Rachel called his name *N.* *Ge 30:8* sons of Bilhah Rachel's *Ge 35:25* handmaid, Dan, *N.*
sons of *N.* *Ge 46:24;* *Nu 1:42; 26:48; 1Ch 7:13*
N. is a hind let loose; he gives *Ge 49:21* goodly words
the sons of Israel, *N.* Gad, and *Ex 1:4* Asher

of *N.* Ahira was prince *Nu 1:15;* *2:29; 7:78*
on mount Ebal to curse; Dan, *De 27:13*
of *N.* he said, O *N.* satisfied *De 33:23* with favour
the sixth lot came out to *N.* *Jos 19:32*
appointed Kedesh in Galilee, *Jos 20:7* in mount *N.*
nor did *N.* drive out the *J'g 1:33* inhabitants
Barak called Zebulun and *N.* *J'g 4:10* to Kedesh
Zebu'lun and *N.* jeoparded *J'g 5:18* their lives
Gideon sent messengers to *N.* *J'g 6:35* and they came
Israel gathered themselves *J'g 7:23* together out of *N.*
Ahimaaz was officer in *N.* *1Ki 4:15*
Ben-hadad smote *N.* *1Ki 15:20;* *2Ch 16:4*
carried *N.* captive to Assyria *2Ki 15:29*
N. brought bread on asses *1Ch 12:40* and mules
the captain of *N.* was *1Ch 27:19* Jerimoth
Josiah in *N.* brake down the *2Ch 34:6* altars
there the princes of Zebulun *Ps 68:27* and *N.*
he lightly afflicted the land of *Isa 9:1* *N.*
a portion for *N.;* one gate of *Eze 48:3;* *N.* *48:34*
he dwelt in the borders of *N.* *M't 4:13*
the land of *N.* by the way of *M't 4:15* the sea

TRIBE OF NAPHTALI

numbered of the *tribe of N.* *Nu 1:43* 53,400
over the host of the *tribe of* *Nu 10:27* *N.* Ahira
of the *tribe of N.* Nahbi; *Nu 13:14;* Pedahel *34:28*
this is the inheritance of the *Jos 19:39* *tribe of N.*
cities out of *tribe of N.* *Jos 21:32;* *1Ch 6:62, 76*
Hiram a widow's son of *tribe* *1Ki 7:14* of *N.*
of the *tribe of N.* were sealed *Re 7:6* 12,000

NAPHTUHIM

Lehabim, and *N.* *Ge 10:13; 1Ch 1:11*

NAPKIN

thy pound which I have kept *Lu 19:20* in a *n.*
his face was bound about *Joh 11:44* with a *n.*
face wrapped in a towel (B) *Joh 11:44*
face wrapped in a cloth *Joh 11:44* (N)(R)
face muffled in a *Joh 11:44* handkerchief (A)
the *n.* that was about his head *Joh 20:7* not lying
also the handkerchief (B)(P) *Joh 20:7*

NARCISSUS

that be of household of *N.* *Ro 16:11*

NARD

my *n.* gave fragrance (R) *Ca 1:12*
henna and *n.* (R) *Ca 4:14*
jar of pure *n.* *M'k 14:3* (A)(B)(E)(N)(R)
pure liquid *n.* *Joh 12:3* (A)(B)(E)(N)(R)

NARRATED

n. and explained (A) *Ac 11:4*

NARRATIVE

the former *n.* (B) *Ac 1:1*

NARROW

angel of the Lord stood in a *n.* *Nu 22:26* way

cut down, if mount Ephraim *Jos 17:15* be too *n.*
for house he made windows of *1Ki 6:4* *n.* lights
and a strange woman is a *n.* *Pr 23:27* pit
the land of thy destruction *Isa 49:19* shall be too *n.*
narrow (S) *Isa 49:20;* *M't 7:13-14; Lu 13:24*
n. is the way which leadeth to *M't 7:14* life

NARROWED

in wall of house made *n.* rests *1Ki 6:6* round
the waters are *n.* (S) *Job 37:10*

NARROWER

the covering *n.* than he can *Isa 28:20* wrap himself
chambers were *n.* (S) *Eze 42:5*

NARROWLY

thou lookest *n.* to all my *Job 13:27* paths
that see thee, shall *n.* look *Isa 14:16* upon thee

NASTINESS

conversation not be *n.,* *Eph 5:4* silliness, flippancy (P)

NATHAN

son of David, *N.; N.* the *2Sa 5:14;* prophet *7:2*
so did *N.* speak; Lord sent *2Sa 7:17;* *12:1, 25*
Igal son of *N.* one of *2Sa 23:36* David's worthies
but *N.* the prophet he called *1Ki 1:10* not
while she talked with David, *1Ki 1:22* *N.* came in
let Zadok and *N.* anoint him *1Ki 1:34* king over Israel
Azariah son of *N.* was over the *1Ki 4:5* officers
Artai begat *N.* and *N.* begat *1Ch 2:36* Zabad
Joel the brother of *N.* a *1Ch 11:38* valiant man
David's acts written in the *1Ch 29:29* book of *N.*
acts of Solomon in the book *2Ch 9:29* of *N.*
I sent from Ahava for *N.* and *Ezr 8:16* Ariel
Shelemiah, *N.* had taken *Ezr 10:39* strange wives
the family of the house of *N.* *Zec 12:12* apart
Mattatha, which was the son *Lu 3:31* of *N.*

NATHANAEL

Philip findeth *N.* *Joh 1:45;* *1:46-49; 21:2*

NATHAN-MELECH

chamber of *N.* the *2Ki 23:11* chamberlain

NATION

and also that *n.* they serve *Ge 15:14* will I judge
Lord, wilt thou slay also a *Ge 20:4* righteous *n.*
slay a blameless people *Ge 20:4* (B)(R)
of the bondwoman I will *Ge 21:13* make a *n.*
a *n.* and kings shall come of *Ge 35:11* thee
in all Egypt, since it became a *Ex 9:24* *n.*
ye shall be unto me an holy *n.* *Ex 19:6;* *1Pe 2:9*
to sell her to a strange *n.* have *Ex 21:8* no power
to sell her to a foreign people *Ex 21:8* (A)(E)(R)

no right to sell her to outsiders *Ex 21:8* (B)

and consider that this *n.* is thy *Ex 33:13* people

have not been done in any *n.* *Ex 34:10* do with thee

nor any of your *n.* commit *Le 18:26* abominations

shall not walk in the manners *Le 20:23* of the *n.*

I will make of thee a great *n.* *Nu 14:12; De 9:14*

hath God assayed to take him *De 4:34* a *n.* from midst of another *n.* by wonders

the fruit of thy land shall a *n.* *De 28:33* eat up

the Lord shall bring thee and *De 28:36* thy king to a *n.*

Lord shall bring a *n.* against *De 28:49* thee from far

a *n.* of fierce countenance *De 28:50* shall not regard

are a *n.* void of counsel, no *De 32:28* understanding

what *n.* like thy people *2Sa 7:23; 1Ch 17:21*

no *n.* whither my Lord hath *1Ki 18:10* not sent to seek thee, he took oath of that *n.*

every *n.* made gods of their *2Ki 17:29* own

and when they went from *n.* *1Ch 16:20* to *n.*

n. was destroyed of *n.* and *2Ch 15:6* city of city

no god of any *n.* or kingdom *2Ch 32:15* was able

it be done against a *n.* or a *Job 34:29* man only

blessed is the *n.* whose God is *Ps 33:12* the Lord

O God plead my cause against *Ps 43:1* an ungodly *n.*

against a merciless people (B) *Ps 43:1* against an ungodly people (R) *Ps 43:1* come, let us cut them off from *Ps 83:4* being a *n.*

they went from one *n.* to *Ps 105:13* another

that I may rejoice in the *Ps 106:5* gladness of thy *n.*

he hath not dealt so with any *Ps 147:20* *n.*

righteousness exalteth a *n.* but *Pr 14:34* sin is

ah sinful *n.* a people laden with *Isa 1:4* iniquity

n. shall not lift up sword *Isa 2:4;* against *n.* *Mic 4:3*

thou hast multiplied the *n.* not *Isa 9:3* increased joy

I will send him against an *Isa 10:6* hypocritical *n.*

what answer the messengers *Isa 14:32* of the *n.*

go swift messengers, to *n.* *Isa 18:2;* scattered and peeled, a *n.* *18:7* meted out and trodden

to a people tall, a people *Isa 18:2* dreaded (B)

open that the righteous *n.* may *Isa 26:2* enter in

thou hast increased the *n.* O *Isa 26:15* Lord, the *n.*

saith the Lord to him whom *Isa 49:7* the *n.* abhorreth

hearken and give ear to me, O *Isa 51:4* my *n.*

thou shalt call a *n.* thou *Isa 55:5* knowest not

seek me, as a *n.* that did *Isa 58:2* righteousness

the *n.* that will not serve thee *Isa 60:12* shall perish

and a small one shall become *Isa 60:22* a strong *n.*

a *n.* that was not called by my *Isa 65:1* name

or shall a *n.* be born at once *Isa 66:8* hath a *n.* changed their gods *Jer 2:11* my soul be avenged on such a *Jer 5:9;* *n.* *5:29; 9:9*

I will bring a *n.* on you from *Jer 5:15* far, a mighty *n.* an ancient *n.*

a *n.* that obeyeth not the voice *Jer 7:28* of the Lord

I will utterly pluck up and *Jer 12:17* destroy that *n.*

speak concerning a *n.* to pluck *Jer 18:7;* it up *18:9*

if that *n.* against whom I have *Jer 18:8* pronounced

punish that *n.* for their *Jer 25:12;* iniquity *27:8*

behold, evil shall go forth *Jer 25:32* from *n.* to *n.*

n. which will not serve *Jer 27:8;* Nebuchadnezzar *27:13*

then Israel cease from being *Jer 31:36;* a *n.* *33:24*

let us cut off Moab from *Jer 48:2* being a *n.*

arise, get you up to the *Jer 49:31* wealthy *n.*

shall be no *n.* whither Elam *Jer 49:36* shall come

out of the north cometh a *n.* *Jer 50:3* against her

have watched for a *n.* that *La 4:17* could not save

I send thee to Israel, a *Eze 2:3* rebellious *n.*

I will make them one *n.* in *Eze 37:22* the land

four kingdoms shall stand up *Da 8:22* out of the *n.*

trouble, such as never was *Da 12:1* since was a *n.*

for a *n.* is come up upon my *Joe 1:6* land

behold, I will raise up *Am 6:14* against you a *n.*

I will make her that was cast *Mic 4:7* off a strong *n.*

the Chaldeans, that bitter and *Hab 1:6* hasty *n.*

gather together, O *n.* not *Zep 2:1* desired

woe to the *n.* of the Cherethites *Zep 2:5* so is this people and *n.* before *Hag 2:14* me

even this whole *n.* have robbed *Mal 3:9* me

the kingdom of God given to *M't 21:43* a *n.*

given to a people (A)(B)(P) *M't 21:43* *n.* shall rise against *n.* *M't 24:7; M'k 13:8; Lu 21:10*

for he loveth our *n.* and hath *Lu 7:5* built us

we found this fellow perverting *Lu 23:2* the *n.*

the Romans shall come and *Joh 11:48* take our *n.*

take away our place and *Joh 11:48* people (B)

one man die, that the whole *Joh 11:50* *n.* perish not

prophesied that Jesus should *Joh 11:51* die for that *n.*

and not for that *n.* only, but *Joh 11:52* that also

thine own *n.* hath delivered *Joh 18:35* thee to me

Jews, devout men out of every *Ac 2:5* *n.*

the *n.* to whom they shall be in *Ac 7:7* bondage

of good report among all the *Ac 10:22* *n.* of the Jews

it is unlawful to come to one *Ac 10:28* of another *n.*

but in every *n.* he that feareth *Ac 10:35* him

that very worthy deeds are *Ac 24:2* done to this *n.*

I know that thou hast been a *Ac 24:10* judge to this *n.*

I came to bring alms to my *n.* *Ac 24:17* and offerings

my life was at first *Ac 26:4* among mine own *n.*

not that I had aught to accuse *Ac 28:19* my *n.* of

profited above my equals in my *Ga 1:14* own *n.*

in midst of a crooked and *Ph'p 2:15* perverse *n.*

crooked and wicked *Ph'p 2:15* generation (A)(B)

crooked and perverse *Ph'p 2:15* generation (E)(R)

warped and crooked *Ph'p 2:15* generation (N)

warped and diseased world *Ph'p 2:15* (P)

thou hast redeemed us out of *Re 5:9* every *n.*

having the gospel to preach to *Re 14:6* every *n.*

NATIONS

nations (S) *Ge 10:5; Le 25:44; 26:33, 38, 45; De 4:27; J'g 4:2, 13, 16; 2Sa 22:44, 50; 2Ki 16:3; 17:8, 11, 15; 21:2; 1Ch 16:24, 35; 2Ch 20:6; 28:3; 33:2, 9; 36:14; Ezr 6:21; Ne 5:8, 9, 17; 6:6, 16; Ps 2:1, 8; 9:5, 15, 19; 10:16; 18:43, 49; 33:10; 44:2, 11, 14; 46:6, 10; 47:8; 59:5, 8; 78:55; 79:1, 6, 10; 80:8; 94:10; 96:3, 10; 98:2; 102:15; 105:44; 106:35, 41, 47; 110:6; 111:6; 115:2; 126:2; 135:15; 149:7; Isa 11:10; 16:8; 42:1, 6; 49:6, 22; 54:3; 60:3, 5, 11, 16; 61:6, 9; 62:2; 66:12, 19; Jer 4:7; 9:16; 10:2, 25; 14:22; 16:19; 18:13; 46:1; 49:14, 15; La 1:3, 10; 2:9; 4:15, 20; Eze 4:13; 7:24; 11:12, 16; 12:16; 16:14; 20:14, 22, 23, 32, 41; 22:4, 16; 23:30; 25:7, 8; 28:25; 30:3; 31:11, 17; 34:28, 29; 36:2, 4, 5, 6, 7, 15, 19, 20, 21, 22, 23, 24, 30, 36; 37:21, 28; 38:16; 39:7, 21, 23, 28; Ho 8:8; Joe 2:17, 19; 3:9, 11, 12; Am 9:12; Ob 1, 2, 15, 16; Mic 5:8, 15; Hab 1:5; 2:13; 3:12; Zep 2:11; Hag 2:2; Zec 1:15, 21; 8:13; 9:10; 12:3; 14:14, 18; Mal 1:11, 14; M't 4:15; Ac 4:25, 27; 7:45; 13:47; 15:14, 17; Ro 15:9, 10, 11, 12; 1Ti 3:16; Re 11:2)*

isles of the *n.* (E) *Ge 10:5* and by these were the *n.* *Ge 10:32* divided

Tidal king of *n.* made war *Ge 14:1;* with Bera *14:9*

shalt be a father of many *n.* *Ge 17:4; 17:5; Ro 4:17-18*

and I will make *n.* of thee *Ge 17:6; 35:11; 48:19*

I will bless Sarah, she shall be *Ge 17:16* a mother of *n.*

the Lord said, Two *n.* are in *Ge 25:23* thy womb

and let *n.* bow down to thee *Ge 27:29* all *n.* (B) *Ge 41:57*

I will cast out the *n.* before *Ge 34:24;* thee *De 4:38; 7:22; 8:20*

the *n.* are defiled; as it spued *Le 18:24;* out *n.* *18:28*

the *n.* (B)(E)(R) *Le 25:44; 26:45; 2Sa 22:44; 2Ki 16:3; 17:8, 11; 2Ch 20:6; 33:2, 9; Ezr 6:21; Ne 5:9; 6:16*

the *n.* (A)(B)(E)(R) *Le 26:33; 26:38; De 4:27; 2Sa 22:50; 1Ch 16:24 Ne 5:17; 6:6*

and shall not be reckoned *Nu 23:9* among the *n.*

Israel shall eat up the *n.* his *Nu 24:8* enemies

Amalek was the first of the *n.* *Nu 24:20* but latter end

I will put the fear of thee on *De 2:25* the *n.*

this is your wisdom in sight of *De 4:6* the *n.*

Lord shall scatter you among *De 4:27;* the *n.* *Ne 1:8*

Lord hath cast out many *n.* *De 7:1* before thee

to possess *n.* greater than *De 9:1;* thyself *11:23*

when God shall cut off the *n.* *De 12:29; 19:1*

thou shalt lend to many *n.* *De 15:6; 28:12*

the Lord will set thee on high *De 28:1* above all *n.*

Most High divided to the *n.* *De 32:8* their inheritance

rejoice, O ye *n.* with his *De 32:43* people, he will avenge

therefore the Lord left those *n.* *J'g 2:23* which thou redeemedst from *2Sa 7:23* the *n.*

of the *n.* concerning which the *1Ki 11:2* Lord said

served gods after the manner *2Ki 17:33* of *n.*

the gods of the *n.* *2Ki 18:33; 19:12; 2Ch 32:13-14; Isa 36:18*

say, among the *n.*, The Lord *1Ch 16:31* reigneth

deliver from the *n.* (E) *1Ch 16:35* by driving out *n.* from *1Ch 17:21* before thy people

made priests after the manner *2Ch 13:9* of *n.*

among many *n.* was no king   *Ne 13:26*
like him
he increaseth the *n.* he   *Job 12:23*
enlargeth the *n.*
the *n.* (A)(B)(E)(R)   *Ps 2:1;*
2:8; 9:5, 15, 19; 10:16; 33:10; 44:2; 46:6;
47:8; 59:5, 8; 78:55; 79:1; 94:10; 98:2;
102:15; 105:44; 106:41; 111:6; 135:15;
149:7; Isa 16:8; Jer 49:14; La 1:10;
Eze 7:24; 11:12; 20:9, 32, 41; 22:4, 16;
23:30; 25:7, 8; 30:3; 31:11, 17; 34:28, 29;
36:3, 4, 6, 20, 23; 39:21; Joe 2:17; 3:11,
                      12
that the *n.* may know   *Ps 9:20*
themselves
all the kindreds of *n.* shall   *Ps 22:27*
worship thee
the Lord is governor among   *Pr 22:28*
the *n.*
the *n.* (A)(B)(E)(R)   *Pr 44:11;*
44:14; 47:10; 96:10; 106:35, 47; 110:6;
126:2; Jer 18:13; 49:15; La 1:3; 4:15, 20;
Eze 11:6; 12:16; 16:14; 36:19, 21; 24:30;
39:21, 28; Joe 2:19; Ob 1, 2; Hab 1:5;
             Zec 8:13; Mal 1:11, 14
he shall subdue the *n.* under   *Ps 47:3*
our feet
I will sing to thee among the *n.* *Ps 57:9;*
                       108:3
his eyes behold the *n.*; let the   *Ps 66:7;*
n. be glad   *67:4*
the Gentile *n.* (A)   *Ps 79:6; 79:10;*
for all the gods of the *n.* are   *Ps 96:5*
idols
to overthrow their seed   *Ps 106:27*
among the *n.*
they did not destroy the *n.*   *Ps 106:34*
Lord commanded
the people curse, *n.* shall abhor   *Pr 24:24*
him
and he shall judge among the *n.* *Isa 2:4*
he will lift up an ensign for   *Isa 5:26*
n. from far
it is in his heart to cut off *n.*   *Isa 10:7*
not a few
the *n.* seek (A)(B)(E)(R)   *Isa 11:10*
he shall set up an ensign for   *Isa 11:12*
the *n.*
he that ruled the *n.* in anger, is *Isa 14:6*
persecuted
how cut down, which didst   *Isa 14:12*
weaken the *n.*
all the kings of the *n.* lie in   *Isa 14:18*
glory
the seed of Sihor, she is a mart *Isa 23:3*
of *n.*
at the lifting up the *n.* were   *Isa 33:3*
scattered
come near, ye *n.* to hear   *Isa 34:1;*
                     Jer 31:10
behold, the *n.* are as a drop   *Isa 40:15*
of a bucket
truth of the *n.* (A)(B)(R)   *Isa 42:1*
light of the *n.* (A)(R)   *Isa 42:6*
lift up my hand to n.   *Isa 49:22*
(B)(E)(R)
so shall he sprinkle many *n.*   *Isa 52:15*
possess the *n.* (A)(B)(E)(R)   *Isa 54:3*
n. that knew not thee, shall   *Isa 55:5*
(A)(B)(E)(R)
n. come to light   *Isa 60:3*
run to thee
yea, those *n.* shall be utterly   *Isa 60:12*
wasted
milk the *n.* (B)(E)(R)   *Isa 60:16*
eat wealth of *n.*   *Isa 61:6*
(A)(B)(E)(R)
known among *n.*   *Isa 61:9*
(A)(B)(E)(R)
the *n.* (A)(B)(E)(R)   *Isa 62:2;*
66:12, 19; Jer 4:7; 14:22; 16:19;
Eze 4:13; Ho 8:8; Joe 3:9; Mic 5:8;
            Zec 1:21; Mal 1:11
that the *n.* may tremble at thy *Isa 64:2*
presence
I will send those that escape   *Isa 66:19*
to the *n.*
the *n.* seek (A)(B)(E)(R)   *Isa 11:10*
and ordained thee a prophet to *Jer 1:5*
the *n.*
see, I have this day set thee   *Jer 1:10*
over the *n.*
n. shall bless themselves in him, *Jer 4:2*
and glory
make ye mention to *n.* publish *Jer 4:16*
against Jerusalem
therefore hear ye *n.* and know *Jer 6:18;*
                     31:10

who would not fear thee, O   *Jer 10:7*
King of *n.*
the *n.* not be able to abide his *Jer 10:10*
indignations
many *n.* shall pass by this city, *Jer 22:8*
and say
n. shall serve themselves of   *Jer 25:14;*
them   *27:7*
the Lord hath a controversy   *Jer 25:31*
with the *n.*
court case against all *n.*   *Jer 25:31*
(B)(R)
the *n.* have heard of thy   *Jer 46:12*
shame
declare ye among *n.* Babylon is *Jer 50:2*
taken
hindermost of the *n.* shall be *Jer 50:12*
a wilderness
and the cry is heard among   *Jer 50:46*
the *n.*
the *n.* have drunken of her   *Jer 51:7*
wine, *n.* are mad
with thee will I break in   *Jer 51:20*
pieces the *n.*
prepare the *n.* against her,   *Jer 51:27*
call together
Babylon is an astonishment   *Jer 51:41*
among the *n.*
the *n.* shall not flow together *Jer 51:44*
any more
the city that was great among   *La 1:1*
the *n.* (B)(R)   *Eze 5:5;*
5:6; 6:8, 11; 16:17; 25:7; 29:12; Zec 10:9
the *n.* (E)   *Eze 5:5;*
              5:6; 6:8; 11:16, 17
into wickedness, more than   *Eze 5:6;*
the *n.*   *5:7*
I will make thee a reproach   *Eze 5:14*
among the *n.*
the remnant shall escape   *Eze 6:8*
among the *n.*
that escape shall remember me *Eze 6:9*
among the *n.*
when I shall scatter them   *Eze 12:15*
among the *n.*
the *n.* also heard of him, he   *Eze 19:4*
was taken
then the *n.* set against him on *Eze 19:8*
every side
I will cause many *n.* to come *Eze 26:3*
against thee
and it shall become a spoil to *Eze 26:5*
the *n.*
I will bring strangers upon   *Eze 28:7;*
thee. the terrible of the *n.*   *30:11; 31:12*
I will scatter Egyptians   *Eze 29:12;*
among *n.*   *30:23*
that they shall no more rule *Eze 29:15*
over the *n.*
I cause *n.* shake at the sound *Eze 31:16*
of his fall
thou art like a lion of the *n.* as *Eze 32:2*
a whale
the daughters of the *n.* shall *Eze 32:16;*
lament her   *32:18*
reproach of *n.* (A)(B)(R)   *Eze 34:29;*
                     36:6
thou hast said, These two *n.* *Eze 35:10*
shall be mine
two *n.* (B)(E)(R)   *Eze 35:10*
thou land hast bereaved thy   *Eze 36:13*
n.
reproach of the *n.* (A)(B)   *Eze 36:15*
and they shall be no more   *Eze 37:22*
two *n.*
it is brought forth out of the *Eze 38:8;*
n.   *38:12*
I will be known in the eyes *Eze 38:23*
of many *n.*
and am sanctified in the sight *Eze 39:27*
of many *n.*
though they have hired among *Ho 8:10*
the *n.*
they shall be wanderers among *Ho 9:17*
the *n.*
whom they have scattered   *Joe 3:2*
among the *n.*
woe to them which are named *Am 6:1*
chief of *n.*
the *n.* (A)(B)(E)(R)   *Am 9:12;*
Ob 15-16; Mic 5:15; Hab 3:12; Zep 2:11;
     Hag 2:22; Zec 1:15; 9:10; 14:14, 18
many *n.* shall come and say,   *Mic 4:2*
Let us go
he shall rebuke strong *n.* afar *Mic 4:3*
off, and beat
now also many *n.* are   *Mic 4:11*
gathered against thee

the *n.* shall see, be   *Mic 7:16*
confounded at their might
that selleth *n.* through her   *Na 3:4*
whoredoms
I will shew the *n.* thy nakedness *Na 3:5*
and shame
shall they not spare   *Hab 1:17*
continually to slay *n.*
because thou hast spoiled   *Hab 2:8*
many *n.*
he beheld, and drove asunder *Hab 3:6*
the *n.*
I have cut off the *n.* their   *Zep 3:6*
towers desolate
for my determination is to   *Zep 3:8*
gather the *n.*
many *n.* shall be joined to the *Zec 2:11*
Lord
the isles of the *n.* (E)   *Zec 2:11*
the lands of the *n.* (R)   *Zec 2:11*
and strong *n.* shall come to   *Zec 8:22*
seek the Lord
take hold out of all the   *Zec 8:23*
languages of the *n.*
the *n.* (B)   *M't 4:15; 12:21; Ac 9:15*
these things do the *n.* seek   *Lu 12:30*
after
and upon the earth shall be   *Lu 21:25*
distress of *n.*
when he had destroyed seven *Ac 13:19*
n. in Chanaan
among the *n.* (B)   *Ro 1:13*
good-for-nothing *n.* (N)   *Eph 4:17*
world's crude elemental *n.*   *Col 2:20*
(A)
proclaimed among the *n.*   *1Ti 3:16*
(N)(P)
to him will I give power over *Re 2:26*
the *n.*
thou must prophesy before   *Re 10:11*
many *n.*
n. shall see their dead bodies *Re 11:9*
three days
and the *n.* were angry, thy   *Re 11:18*
wrath is come
and power was given him over *Re 13:7*
all *n.*
cities of the *n.* fell; waters   *Re 16:19;*
are *n.*   *17:15*
that he should deceive the *n.* *Re 20:3*
no more
the *n.* of them which are   *Re 21:24*
saved shall walk
they shall bring the honour of *Re 21:26*
the *n.* into it
the leaves were for the   *Re 22:2*
healing of the *n.*

ALL NATIONS

which the Lord hath divided to *De 4:19*
all n.
and to make thee high above *De 26:19;*
all n.   *28:1*
shall become a byword   *De 28:37*
among *all n.*
his fame was in *all n.* round   *1Ki 4:31*
about
brought the fear of David on *1Ch 14:17*
all n.
declare his marvellous works *1Ch 16:24*
among *all n.*
Hezekiah magnified in sight *2Ch 32:23*
of *all n.*
thy saving health among *all n.* *Ps 67:2*
kings fall down, *all n.* shall   *Ps 72:11*
serve him
men blessed in him, *all n.*   *Ps 72:17*
shall call him blessed
arise, O God, for thou shalt   *Ps 82:8*
inherit *all n.*
all n. shall come and worship *Ps 86:9*
before thee
Lord is high above *all n.* glory *Ps 113:4*
above heaven
praise the Lord, *all* ye *n.*   *Ps 117:1*
praise him
all n. compassed me about,   *Ps 118:10*
but in name
and *all n.* shall flow unto it   *Isa 12:2*
he will destroy the veil that is *Isa 25:7*
over *all n.*
the indignation of the Lord   *Isa 34:2*
is on *all n.*
all n. before him are as   *Isa 40:17*
nothing, and vanity
I will gather *all n.* and   *Isa 66:18;*
languages   *Joe 3:2*
they shall bring your brethren *Isa 66:20*
out of *all n.*

and *all n.* shall serve him   *Jer 27:7;*
                                Da 7:14
I will sift the house of Israel *Am 9:9*
among *all n.*
but gathereth to him *all n.* and *Hab 2:5*
people
I will shake *all n.* and the   *Hab 2:7*
desire of *all n.* shall come, and
I will gather *all n.* against *Zec 14:2*
Jerusalem
the punishment of *all n.* that *Zec 14:19*
come not up
and *all n.* shall call you   *Mal 3:12*
blessed
ye shall be hated of *all n.* for *M't 24:9*
my sake
this gospel of kingdom shall *M't 24:14;*
be preached to *all n.* *M'k 13:10;*
           Lu 24:47; Ro 16:26
before him shall be gathered *M't 25:32*
all n.
go, and teach *all n.*   *M't 28:19*
baptizing them
be called of *all n.* the house *M'k 11:17*
of prayer
shall be led away captive into *Lu 21:24*
all n.
who suffered *all n.* to walk in *Ac 14:16*
their ways
hath made of one blood *all n.* *Ac 17:26*
of men
for obedience to the faith   *Ro 1:5*
among *all n.*
made known to *all n.* for *Ro 16:26*
obedience of faith
saying, In thee shall *all n.* be *Ga 3:8*
blessed
a multitude of *all n.* stood   *Re 7:9*
before throne
a man-child, who was to rule *Re 12:5*
all n. with a rod
she made *all n.* drink of the *Re 14:8;*
wine   *18:3*
for *all n.* shall come and   *Re 15:4*
worship before thee
for by thy sorceries were *all n.* *Re 18:23*
deceived

ALL THE NATIONS

all the n. of earth be blessed *Ge 18:18;*
                      22:18; 26:4
chosen above *all the n.* on *De 14:2*
earth
set a king over me, as *all the De 17:14;*
n.*   *1Sa 8:5, 20*
thou shalt call them to mind *De 30:1*
among *all the n.*
the Lord will gather thee from *De 30:3*
all the n.
into hell, and *all the n.* that *Ps 9:17*
forget God
hand that is stretched out on *Isa 14:26*
all the n.
the multitude of *all the n.* that *Isa 29:7;*
fight   *29:8*
laid waste *all the n.* and their *Isa 37:18*
countries
let *all the n.* be gathered   *Isa 43:9*
together, and let
Lord made bare his holy arm *Isa 52:10*
in eyes of *all the n.*
cause praise to spring forth *Isa 61:11*
before *all the n.*
and *all the n.* shall be gathered *Jer 3:17*
unto it
Jeremiah prophesied against *Jer 25:13*
all the n.
cause *all the n.* to drink it; *Jer 25:15*
made *all the n.* drinks
make this city a curse to *all* *Jer 26:6*
the n. of the earth
I will gather you from *all the Jer 29:14*
n.* and places
a reproach among *all the n.* *Jer 29:18;*
of the earth   *44:8*
name of joy and honour before *Jer 33:9*
all the n.
for I will make a full end of *Jer 46:28*
all the n.
but I scattered them among *all Zec 7:14*
the n.*
destroy *all the n.* that come *Zec 12:9*
against Jerusalem
left of *all the n.* that came *Zec 14:6*
against Jerusalem

THESE NATIONS

if thou say, *These n.* are more *De 7:17*
than I

---

for wickedness of *these n.*   *De 9:4;*
Lord doth drive   *9:5*
then will the Lord drive out *De 11:23*
all *these n.*
saying, How did *these n.* *De 12:30*
serve their gods
these n. hearkened to   *De 18:14*
observers of times
thus do to the cities which *De 20:15*
are not of *these n.*
among *these n.* shalt thou find *De 28:65*
no ease
lest any among you serve the *De 29:18*
gods of *these n.*
the Lord will destroy *these n.* *De 31:3*
before thee
seen what the Lord hath done *Jos 23:3*
to *these n.*
I have divided to you by lot *Jos 23:4*
these n. that remain
that ye come not among *these Jos 23:7*
n.* that remain
if ye cleave to the remnant of *Jos 23:12*
these n.
God will no more drive out *Jos 23:13*
any of *these n.*
these n. the Lord left to prove *J'g 3:1*
Israel
so *these n.* feared Lord and *2Ki 17:41*
served images
for all *these n.* are   *Jer 9:26*
uncircumcised
bring them against *these n.* *Jer 25:9*
round about
these n. shall serve the king of *Jer 25:11*
Babylon
I have put yoke of iron on *Jer 28:14*
neck of *these n.*

NATIVE

in the *n.* land (B)   *Ge 11:28*
your *n.* land (B)   *Ru 2:11*
he shall no more see his *n.* *Jer 22:10*
country
in your *n.* land (B)   *Eze 21:30*
whose *n.* land is (A)(R)   *Eze 23:15*
our own *n.* speech (B)(N)   *Ac 2:8*
our own *n.* language (P)   *Ac 2:11*

NATIVES

when *n.* saw (A)(B)(P)(R)   *Ac 28:8*

NATIVITY

Haran died in the land of his *Ge 11:28*
n.
in the land of his birth   *Ge 11:28*
(A)(R)
in his native land (B)   *Ge 11:28*
how thou hast left the land of *Ru 2:11*
thy *n.*
in the land of your birth   *Ru 2:11*
(A)(B)
your native land (R)   *Ru 2:11*
arise, let us go the land of our *Jer 46:16*
n.
to the land of our birth   *Jer 46:16*
(A)(R)
thy *n.* is of the land of Canaan *Eze 16:3*
spiritual origin and birth are *Eze 16:3*
(A)
By origin and by birth you *Eze 16:3*
(B)(R)
as for thy *n.* in the day thou *Eze 16:4*
wast born
I will judge thee in the land *Eze 21:30*
of thy *n.*
in land of origin and birth *Eze 21:30*
(A)
in your native land (B)   *Eze 21:30*
the land of your origin (R) *Eze 21:30*
the manner of Chaldea, the *Eze 23:15*
land of their *n.*
whose native land is   *Eze 23:15*
Chaldea (A)(R)

NATURAL

eye not dim, nor his *n.* force *De 34:7*
abated
his vigor abated (B)   *De 34:7*
even women did change the *n.* *Ro 1:26*
use
also men leaving the *n.* use of *Ro 1:27*
the woman
without *n.* affection *Ro 1:31; 2Ti 3:3*
in *n.* descent (A)(N)   *Ro 9:5*
if God spared not the *n.* *Ro 11:21;*
branches   *11:24*

---

n. man receiveth not things of *1Co 2:14*
Spirit of God
still on a *n.* plane (N)   *1Co 3:3*
it is sown a *n.* body, there is *1Co 15:44*
a *n.* body
but that which is *n.* was first, *1Co 15:46*
and afterward
a man beholding his *n.* face in *Jas 1:23*
a glass
of the lower *n.* (P)   *Jas 3:13*
these as *n.* brute beasts speak *2Pe 2:12*
evil

NATURALLY

who will *n.* care for your   *Ph'p 2:20*
state
but what they know *n.* as brute *Jude 10*
beasts

NATURE

all *n.* (B)(E)(R)   *Ps 110:6*
let a beast's *n.* be given (A) *Da 4:16*
human beings of *n.* like your *Ac 14:15*
(A)(R)
women did change to that   *Ro 1:26*
against *n.*
do by *n.* the things contained *Ro 2:14*
in the law
shall not uncircumcision by *n.* *Ro 2:27*
judge thee
human *n.* under sin's   *Ro 7:25*
(B)(N)(P)
no longer over lower *n.* (N) *Ro 8:4*
lower *n.* is emmity beside (N) *Ro 8:7*
not to our earthly *n.*   *Ro 8:12*
(B)(N)(P)
olive tree wild by *n.* and *Ro 11:24*
wert graffed to
doth not even *n.* itself teach *1Co 11:14*
you
outer *n.* suffers decay   *2Co 4:16*
(B)(N)(R)
who are Jews by *n.* and not *Ga 2:15*
sinners of
did service unto them, which *Ga 4:8*
by *n.* are no gods
and were by *n.* children of *Eph 2:3*
wrath
former *n.* (A)(B)   *Eph 4:22*
divine *n.* was his (N)(P) *Ph'p 2:6*
the full *n.* of God (P)   *Col 1:19*
stamp of this *n.* (P)(R)   *Heb 1:3*
he took not on him the *n.* of *Heb 2:16*
angels
tongue setteth on fire the course *Jas 3:6*
of *n.*
keep clear of desires of lower *1Pe 2:11*
n. (P)
ye might be partakers of the *2Pe 1:4*
divine *n.*
foulness of lower *n.* (P)   *2Pe 2:10*

NAUGHT

water is *n.* and ground barren *2Ki 2:19*
It is *n.*, it is *n.*   *Pr 20:14*
shall labor for *n.* (R)   *Jer 51:58*

NAUGHTINESS

I know the *n.* of thy heart *1Sa 17:28*
presumption and evilness of *1Sa 17:28*
heart (A)
impudence and ugly heart *1Sa 17:28*
(B)
the evil of your heart (C) *1Sa 17:28*
transgressors be taken in their *Pr 11:6*
own *n.*
taken in their iniquity, greedy *Pr 11:6*
desire (A)
trapped by their own greediness *Pr 11:6*
(B)
taken in their own iniquity (E) *Pr 11:6*
taken captive by their own lust *Pr 11:6*
(R)
lay apart all filthiness and *Jas 1:21*
superfluity of *n.*
all uncleanness, and the   *Jas 1:21*
rampant outgrowth of
wickedness (A)
everything vile, outgrowth of *Jas 1:21*
evil (B)
all filthiness, overflowing of *Jas 1:21*
wickedness (E)
all that is sordid, the malice *Jas 1:21*
that hurries to excess (N)
impurity, every evil that   *Jas 1:21*
touches others (P)
all filthiness, and rank growth *Jas 1:21*
of wickedness (R)

NAUGHTY

a *n.* person walketh with froward mouth — Pr 6:12
worthless, wicked man walks (A)(B)(E)(R) — Pr 6:12
and a liar giveth ear to a *n.* tongue — Pr 17:4
listens to a mischievous tongue (A)(E)(R) — Pr 17:4
attention to a vicious tongue (B) — Pr 17:4
the other basket had very *n.* figs — Jer 24:2
very bad figs (A)(B)(E)(R) — Jer 24:2

NAUM

Amos, which as the son of *N.* — Lu 3:25

NAUSEA

overcome with *n.* of self-indulgence (A) — Lu 21:34

NAVEL

his force is in the *n.* of his belly — Job 40:16
power in the sinews of his belly (A)(P) — Job 40:16
force in muscles of his body (B)(E)(R) — Job 40:16
it shall be health to thy *n.* and marrow — Pr 3:8
health to your nerves and sinews (A) — Pr 3:8
healing to your body (B) — Pr 3:8
healing to your flesh (R) — Pr 3:8
thy *n.* is like a round goblet — Ca 7:2
n., like a rounded bowl (B)(R) — Ca 7:2
when thou wast born, thy *n.* was not cut — Eze 16:4

NAVES

their *n.* and spokes were all molten — 1Ki 7:33
spokes and hubs were all cast (A)(B)(R) — 1Ki 7:33

NAVY

Solomon made a *n.* of ships in Ezion-geber — 1Ki 9:26
built a fleet (A)(B)(R) — 1Ki 9:26; 9:27; 10:11, 22
Hiram sent in the *n.* his servants, shipmen — 1Ki 9:27
the *n.* of Hiram brought gold from Ophir — 1Ki 10:11
king Solomon had at sea a *n.* of Tarshish — 1Ki 10:22

NAY

And they said, *N.* but we will — Ge 19:2
speak, for he will not say thee *n.* — 1Ki 2:17
say me not *n.* for I will not say thee *n.* — 1Ki 2:20
but let your communication be yea, yea, *n. n.* — M't 5:37; Jas 5:12
I tell you *n.* but rather division — Lu 12:51
I tell you *n.* but except ye repent — Lu 13:3; 13:5
and he said, *N.* father Abraham, but if one — Lu 16:30
n. verily, but let them come and fetch — Ac 16:37
by law of works? *n.* but by law of faith — Ro 3:27
n. but O man, who art thou that repliest — Ro 9:20
with me there should be yea, yea, *n. n.* — 2Co 1:17
our word toward you was not yea and *n.* — 2Co 1:18
the Son of God Jesus Christ was not yea, *n.* — 2Co 1:19

NAZARENE

by the prophet, he shall be called a *N.* — M't 2:23
the *N.* heresy (B) — Ac 24:5

NAZARENES

a ringleader of the sect of the *N.* — Ac 24:5

NAZARETH

Joseph dwelt in a city called *N.* — M't 2:23
this is Jesus of *N.* — M't 21:11; M'k 1:24; 10:47; Lu 4:34; 18:37; 24:19
thou wast also with Jesus of *N.* — M'k 14:67
be not affrighted, ye seek Jesus of *N.* — M'k 16:6
the angel Gabriel was sent to *N.* — Lu 1:26
Jesus came to *N.* and was subject — Lu 2:51; 4:16
Jesus of *N.* — Joh 1:45; 18:5, 7; 19:19; Ac 2:22; 4:10; 6:14; 22:8
can there any good thing come out of *N.* — Joh 1:46
in the name of Jesus of *N.* rise up — Ac 3:6
how God anointed Jesus of *N.* with power — Ac 10:38
things contrary to the name of Jesus of *N.* — Ac 26:9

NAZARITE

a vow of a *N.* to separate themselves — Nu 6:2
and this is the law of the *N.* — Nu 6:13; 6:21
the *N.* shall shave the head of his separation — Nu 6:18
and shall put them on the hands of the *N.* — Nu 6:19
and after that the *N.* may drink wine — Nu 6:20
the child shall be a *N.* to God — J'g 13:5; 13:7; 16:17

NAZARITES

her *N.* purer than snow, whiter than milk — La 4:7
princes purer than snow (A)(B)(R) — La 4:7
nobles purer than snow (E) — La 4:7
I raised up of your young men for *N.* — Am 2:11
but ye gave the *N.* wine to drink, and prophets — Am 2:12

NEAH

out of Remmon-methoar to *N.* — Jos 19:13

NEAPOLIS

and the next day we came to *N.* — Ac 16:11

NEAR

this city is *n.* to flee to, it is a little one — Ge 19:20
Jacob went *n.* to Isaac his father — Ge 27:22
bring it *n.* he brought it *n.* and he did eat — Ge 27:25
Jacob went *n.* and rolled the stone — Ge 29:10
thou shalt be *n.* to me, thou and thy children — Ge 45:10
near (S) — Ge 47:29; Ex 3:5; 14:10; 24:2; 34:30, 32; Le 10:3; 21:3, 21, 23; 25:49; Nu 1:51; 3:10, 38; 8:19; 18:3, 4, 7, 22; 24:17; De 1:7; 2:19; 4:7; 13:7; 20:2, 10; 22:2; 30:14; Jos 8:11; 1Sa 17:48; 2Sa 10:13; 11:20, 21; 15:5; 1Ki 2:1; 8:59; 1Ch 12:40; 19:14; Ne 2:8; Es 9:20; Ps 34:18; 69:18; 85:9; 88:3; 91:10; 145:18; Pr 5:8; Ec 12:1; Isa 5:19; Eze 44:25; Joe 2:1; M't 15:8, 29; 21:1; 24:32; M'k 2:4; 5:11, 21; 11:1; 13:29; Lu 7:12; 10:9, 11; 15:25; 18:35; 19:11, 29, 37; 21:20, 28, 30, 31; 22:1; 24:28; Joh 6:4, 19, 23; 11:18, 55; 19:20, 42; Ac 7:17; 9:38; 10:9; 22:6; 27:8; Ro 10:8; Eph 2:13, 17; Ph'p 2:27, 30; Heb 6:8; 7:19; Jas 4:8; 5:8
he brought them *n.* and kissed them — Ge 48:10
the land of Philistines, altho' that was *n.* — Ex 13:17
not approach to any that is *n.* of kin — Le 18:6
she is thy father's *n.* kinswoman — Le 18:12
for she is thy mother's *n.* kinswoman — Le 18:13; 18:17
for he uncovereth his *n.* kin — Le 20:19
but for his kin *n.* to him he may be defiled — Le 21:2
being the tribe of Levi *n.* and present — Nu 3:6
bring her in *n.* set her before the Lord — Nu 5:16
to bring you *n.* to himself — Nu 16:9; 16:10
whoso cometh *n.* the tabernacle shall die — Nu 17:13
Moses spake in plains of Moab, *n.* Jericho — Nu 26:3
plains of Moab by Jordan *n.* Jericho — Nu 33:48; 35:1
go thou *n.* and hear all God shall say — De 5:27
not plant a grove of trees *n.* altar of Lord — De 16:21
the men *n.* Micah's house gathered — J'g 18:22
they knew not that evil was *n.* them — J'g 20:34
the man is *n.* of kin to us, next kinsman — Ru 2:20
spread skirt, for thou art a *n.* kinsman — Ru 3:9; 3:12
see, Joab's field is *n.* mine, set on fire — 2Sa 14:30
because the king is *n.* of kin to us — 2Sa 19:42
land of enemy far or *n.* — 1Ki 8:46; 2Ch 6:36
thy vineyard, because it is *n.* to my house — 1Ki 21:2
one is so *n.* another, no air can come — Job 41:16
for trouble is *n.*; thy name is *n.* — Ps 22:11; 75:1
thou art *n.* O Lord, thy commandments are truth — Ps 119:151
the horn of Israel, a people *n.* to him — Ps 148:14
passing through the street *n.* her corner — Pr 7:8
but the mouth of the foolish is *n.* destruction — Pr 10:14
better is a neighbour that is *n.* than a brother — Pr 27:10
ye that are *n.* acknowledge my might — Isa 33:13
tell ye, and bring them *n.* yea, let them — Isa 45:21
I bring *n.* my righteousness, not far off — Isa 46:13
he is *n.* that justifieth me, who will contend — Isa 50:8
my righteousness is *n.* my salvation — Isa 51:5
call upon the Lord while he is *n.* — Isa 55:6
my salvation is *n.* to come, and my righteousness — Isa 56:1
peace be to him that is *n.* saith the Lord — Isa 57:19
thou art *n.* in their mouth, and — Jer 12:2
all kings of the north far and *n.* shall drink — Jer 25:26
our end is *n.* our days are fulfilled — La 4:18
he that is *n.* shall fall by the sword — Eze 6:12
the time is come, the day of trouble is *n.* — Eze 7:7; 30:3
who say, It is not *n.* let us build houses — Eze 11:3
those that be *n.* and far shall mock thee — Eze 22:5
confusion belongs to Israel that are *n.* — Da 9:7
the day of the Lord is *n.* — Ob 15; Zec 1:14
know that it is *n.* even at the doors — M't 24:33
ye know that summer is *n.* — M'k 13:28
Cornelius called together his *n.* friends — Ac 10:24

NEARBY

into the village *n.* (S) — M'k 11:2

NEARER

howbeit, there is a kinsman *n.* than I — Ru 3:12
our salvation *n.* than when we believed — Ro 13:11

NEARIAH

Baraiah, and *N.*, and Shaphat *1Ch 3:22*
the sons of *N.*, Elieenai and *1Ch 3:23*
and *N.*, Rephaiah, and Uzziel *1Ch 4:42*

NEBAI

Hariph, Anathoth, *N.* *Ne 10:19*

NEBAIOTH

the son of Ishmael, *N.* *Ge 25:13;*
1Ch 1:29
the rams of *N.* shall *Isa 60:7*
minister to thee

NEBAJOTH

firstborn of Ishmael, *N.* *Ge 25:13*
the sister of *N.*, to be his wife *Ge 28:9*
Ishmael's daughter, sister of *N. Ge 36:3*

NEBALLAT

Hadid, Zeboim, *N.* *Ne 11:34*

NEBAT

Jeroboam the son of *N.* *1Ki 11:26;*
12:2, 15; 16:3, 26, 31; 21:22; 22:52;
2Ki 3:3; 9:9; 10:29; 13:2, 11; 14:24; 15:9,
18, 24, 28; 17:21; 23:15; 2Ch 9:29; 10:2,
15; 13:6

NEBO

Elealah and *N.* is a land for *Nu 32:3*
cattle
the children of Reuben built *Nu 32:38*
N.
get thee up unto mount *N.* *De 32:49;*
34:1
Bela dwelt in Aroer, even unto *1Ch 5:8*
N.
the children of *N.* *Ezr 2:29; 10:43*
the men of the other *N.* *Ne 7:33*
fifty-two
Moab shall howl over *N.* and *Isa 15:2*
Medeba
N. stoopeth; woe unto *N.* *Isa 46:1;*
Jer 48:1
judgment is come upon Dibon *Jer 48:22*
and *N.*

NEBUCHADNEZZAR

N. king of Babylon came *2Ki 24:1;*
24:10-11; 25:1, 8, 22
Jerusalem by the hand of *N.* *1Ch 6:15*
against him came *N.* *2Ch 36:6*
N. carried of the vessels of *2Ch 36:7*
N. sent and brought him to *2Ch 36:10*
he also rebelled against king *2Ch 36:13*
N.
which *N.* had brought forth out *Ezr 1:7*
of
whom *N.* king of Babylon had *Ezr 2:1*
gave them into the hand of *N. Ezr 5:12*
which *N.* took out of the *Ezr 5:14;*
temple *6:5*
N. king of Babylon had carried *Ne 7:6;*
Es 2:6
all these lands into the hand *Jer 27:6;*
of *N.* *27:8, 20; 28:3, 11, 14; 29:1, 3;*
34:1; 39:5
came *N.* king of Babylon *Da 1:1*
Eunuchs brought them in *Da 1:18*
before *N.*
second year of *N.*, *N.* dreamed *Da 2:1*
dreams
maketh known to the king *N.* *Da 2:28*
N. fell upon his face, and *Da 2:46*
N. made an image of gold *Da 3:1;*
3:2-3, 5, 7, 9, 13-14, 16, 19, 24, 26, 28
N. the king to all peoples *Da 4:1;*
4:4, 18
all this came upon *N.* *Da 4:18;*
4:28, 31, 33, 34, 37
which his father *N.* had taken *Da 5:2;*
out *5:11, 18*

NEBUCHADREZZAR

N. king of Babylon maketh *Jer 21:2;*
war *21:7; 22:25; 24:1, 9; 29:21; 32:1, 28*
when *N.* came up *Jer 35:11;*
37:1; 39:1, 11
I will send *N.* the king of *Jer 43:10*
Babylon

king of Judah into hand of *Jer 44:30;*
N. 46:2, 13, 26; 49:28, 30; 50:17; 51:34;
52:4, 12, 28-30
I will bring upon Tyre *N.* *Eze 26:7;*
29:18, 19; 30:10

NEBUSHASBAN

captain of guard sent, and *N. Jer 39:13*

NEBUZARADAN

came *N.* captain of the guard *2Ki 25:8;*
25:11, 20; Jer 39:9-11, 13; 40:1; 41:10;
43:6; 52:12, 15-16, 26, 30

NECESSARY

his mouth more than my *n.* *Job 23:12*
food
it was *n.* that the word of *Ac 13:46*
God
burden than these *n.* things *Ac 15:28*
such things as were *n.* *Ac 28:10*
seem to be more feeble, are *1Co 12:22*
n.
I thought it *n.* to exhort *2Co 9:5*
I supposed it *n.* to send to *Ph'p 2:25*
you
maintain good works for *n.* *Tit 3:14*
uses
was therefore *n.* that the *Heb 9:23*
patterns

NECESSITIES

hands have ministered unto *Ac 20:34*
my *n.*
much patience, in affliction, in *2Co 6:4*
n.
reproaches, in *n.*, in *2Co 12:10*
persecutions

NECESSITY

for of *n.* he must release one *Lu 23:17*
at the feast
distributing to the *n.* of *Ro 12:13*
saints
having no *n.* and hath so *1Co 7:37*
decreed
for *n.* is laid upon me, yea, *1Co 9:16*
woe is to me
so let him give, not grudgingly, *2Co 9:7*
or of *n.*
ye sent once and again to my *Ph'p 4:16*
n.
not be as it were of *n.* but *Ph'm 14*
willingly
there is made of *n.* a change *Heb 7:12*
of the law
it is of *n.* this man have *Heb 8:2*
somewhat to offer
there must of *n.* be the death *Heb 9:16*
of the testator

NECHO

N. king of Egypt came up *2Ch 35:20;*
35:22
N. took Jehoahaz his brother *2Ch 36:4*

NECK

put the skins on the smooth *Ge 27:16*
of his *n.*
thou shalt break the yoke *Ge 27:40*
from off thy *n.*
Esau fell on his *n.* and kissed *Ge 33:4*
him
Pharaoh put a gold chain *Ge 41:42;*
about Joseph's *n. Eze 16:11; Da 5:7, 16,*
29
Joseph fell on Benjamin's *n.* *Ge 45:14*
and wept
he fell on Jacob's *n.* he wept *Ge 46:29*
on his *n.*
thy hand shall be on the *n.* of *Ge 49:8*
thine enemies
if not redeem it, break his *n.* *Ex 13:13;*
34:20
and wring off his head from his *Le 5:8*
n.
n. ornament (A) *Nu 31:50*
strike off the heifer's *n.* in the *De 21:4*
valley
he shall put a yoke of iron *De 28:48*
upon thy *n.*
and his *n.* brake, and he died *1Sa 4:18*

Zedekiah stiffened his *n.* *2Ch 36:13*
hardened his heart
hardened their *n.* and would *Ne 9:29*
not hear
he runneth on him, even on *Job 15:26*
his *n.*
he hath taken me by the *n.* *Job 16:12*
and shaken me
hast thou clothed his *n.* with *Job 39:19*
thunder
in his *n.* remaineth strength, *Job 41:22*
and sorrow
lift not up, speak not with a *Ps 75:5*
stiff *n.*
for they shall be chains about *Pr 1:9*
thy *n.*
bind them about thy *n.* write *Pr 3:3;*
them *6:21*
so shall they be life and grace *Pr 3:22*
to thy *n.*
thy *n.* is comely with chains of *Ca 1:10*
gold
thy *n.* is like the tower of David *Ca 4:4*
hast ravished my heart with one *Ca 4:9*
chain of thy *n.*
thy *n.* is a tower of ivory, thine *Ca 7:4*
eyes
he shall reach even to the *n.* *Isa 8:8*
his yoke shall be taken from *Isa 10:27*
off thy *n.*
shall reach to the midst of the *Isa 30:23*
n.
thy *n.* is an iron sinew, thy *Isa 48:4*
brow brass
loose thyself from the bands *Isa 52:2*
of thy *n.*
that sacrificeth, as if he cut off *Isa 66:3*
a dog's *n.*
but they obeyed not, made *Jer 17:23*
their *n.* stiff
make thee yokes, and put them *Jer 27:2*
on thy *n.*
will not put *n.* under yoke of *Jer 27:8;*
king of Babylon *27:11*
took the yoke from off *Jer 28:10;*
Jeremiah's *n.* *28:12*
I have put a yoke on the *n.* of *Jer 28:14*
these nations
I will break his yoke from off *Jer 30:8*
thy *n.*
my transgressions are come *La 1:14*
upon my *n.*
but I passed over on her fair *Ho 10:11*
n.
discovering the foundation to *Hab 3:13*
the *n.*
better that a millstone were *M't 18:6;*
hanged about *n.* *M'k 9:42; Lu 17:2*
his father fell on his *n.* and *Lu 15:20*
kissed him
put a yoke on the *n.* of the *Ac 15:10*
disciples
they fell on Paul's *n.* and *Ac 20:37*
kissed him

NECKLACE

pride is their *n.* (R) *Ps 73:6*
jewel of *n.* (A)(B)(R) *Ca 4:9*

NECKLACES

necklaces (A)(B)(E)(R)(S) *Ex 35:22*
necklaces (B) *Nu 31:50*

NECKS

put your feet on the *n.* of *Jos 10:24*
these kings
for the *n.* of them that take the *J'g 15:30*
spoil
ornaments that were on their *J'g 8:21;*
camel's *n.* *8:26*
given me *n.* of enemies *2Sa 22:41;*
Ps 18:40
the nobles put not their *n.* to the *Ne 3:5*
work
and walk with stretched forth *Isa 3:16*
n.
bring your *n.* under yoke of *Jer 27:12*
Babylon
our *n.* are under persecution, *La 5:5*
we labour
to bring the on the *n.* of the *Eze 21:29*
slain
from which ye shall not *Mic 2:3*
remove your *n.*
who for my life laid down *Ro 16:4*
their own *n.*

NECROMANCER

there shall not be found   De 18:11
among you a n.

NECROMANCERS

provided n. and wizards (B)   2Ki 21:6
exterminated n., wizards (B)   2Ki 23:24
consult n., fortunetellers (B)   Isa 8:19

NEDABIAH

Hoshama, and N.   1Ch 3:18

NEED

thou shalt lend him sufficient   De 15:8
for his n.
have I n. of madmen, that ye   1Sa 21:15
brought
cut wood as much as thou   2Ch 2:16
shalt n.
ye shall not n. to fight in this   2Ch 20:17
battle
and let what they have n. of be   Ezr 6:9
given
so he shall have no n. of spoil   Pr 31:11
I have n. to be baptized of   M't 3:14
thee
your father knoweth what   M't 6:8;
things ye have n. of   6:32; Lu 12:30
they that be whole n. not a   M't 9:12;
physician   M'k 2:17; Lu 5:31
they n. not depart, give ye   M't 14:16
them to eat
Lord hath n. of them, and he   M't 21:3;
will send them   M'k 11:3; Lu 19:31, 34
what further n. have we of   M't 26:65;
witnesses   M'k 14:63; Lu 22:71
read what David did when he   M'k 2:25
had n.
and healed them that had n. of   Lu 9:11
healing
over just persons which n. no   Lu 15:7
repentance
buy those things we have n.   Joh 13:29
of
parted them as every man had   Ac 2:45;
n.   4:35
that ye assist her in what she   Ro 16:2
hath n.
if n. so require, let him do   1Co 7:36
what he will
cannot say to the hand, I   1Co 12:21
have no n. of thee
for our comely parts have no   1Co 12:24
n. but God
or n. we epistles of   2Co 3:1
commendation to you
that ministered to my n. (S)   Ph'p 2:25
I know how to abound and   Ph'p 4:12
to suffer n.
my God shall supply all your   Ph'p 4:19
n. by Christ Jesus
so that we n. not to speak any   1Th 1:8
thing
of brotherly love ye n. not that   1Th 4:9
I write
of the times ye have no n. that   1Th 5:1
I write
and find grace to help in time   Heb 4:16
of n.
n. one teach you, such as   Heb 5:12
have n. of milk
what n. that another priest   Heb 7:11
should rise
for ye have n. of patience,   Heb 10:36
that after
though now, if n. be, ye are in   1Pe 1:6
heaviness
ye n. not that any man teach   1Jo 2:27
you
whoso hath goods, and see his   1Jo 3:17
brother have n.
I am rich, and have n. of   Re 3:17
nothing
the city hath no n. of sun or   Re 21:23
moon
and they n. no candle, nor light   Re 22:5
of the sun

NEEDED

n. not that any should testify   Joh 2:25
hands, as though he n. any   Ac 17:25
thing

NEEDEST

n. not that any man should   Joh 16:30
ask

NEEDETH

And he said, What n. it? let   Ge 33:15
me find
and give him as many as he n.   Lu 11:8
n. not save to wash his feet   Joh 13:10
he may have to give to him   Eph 4:28
that n.
workman that n. not to be   2Ti 2:15
ashamed
Who n. not daily, as those   Heb 7:27
high

NEEDFUL

be n. for the house of thy God   Ezr 7:20
food n. for me (A)(E)(R)   Ps 30:8
But one thing is n.: and Mary   Lu 10:42
hath
That it was n. to circumcise   Ac 15:5
them
abide in the flesh is more n.   Ph'p 1:24
for you
things which are n. to the body   Jas 2:16
it was n. for me to write unto   Jude 3
you

NEEDLE

camel to go through the eye   M't 19:24;
of a n.   M'k 10:25

NEEDLE'S

for a camel to go through a   Lu 18:25
n. eye

NEEDLEWORK

linen, wrought with n.   Ex 26:36
fine twined linen, wrought   Ex 27:16
with n.
thou shalt make the girdle of   Ex 28:39
n.
scarlet and fine twined linen,   Ex 36:37
of n.
for the gate of the court was   Ex 38:18
n.
blue, and purple, and scarlet,   Ex 39:29
of n.
a prey of divers colours of n.   J'g 5:30
divers colours of n. on both   J'g 5:30
sides
unto the king in raiment of n.   Ps 45:14

NEEDS

money, must n. be   Ge 17:13
circumcised
and he will n. be a judge   Ge 19:9
must I n. bring thy son again   Ge 24:5
unto
though thou wouldest n. be   Ge 31:30
gone
For we must n. die, and are   2Sa 14:14
as waters
they must n. be borne,   Jer 10:5
because they
for it must n. be that offences   M't 18:7
for such things must n. be;   M'k 13:7
but the
and I must n. go and see it   Lu 14:18
he must n. go through Samaria   Joh 4:4
this scripture must n. have   Ac 1:16
been
that Christ must n. have   Ac 17:3
suffered
the multitude must n. come   Ac 21:22
ye must n. be subject, not only   Ro 13:5
then must ye n. go out of the   1Co 5:10
world
If I must n. glory, I will   2Co 11:30
glory of

NEEDY

to thy poor, and to thy n. in   De 15:11
thy land
an hired servant that is poor   De 24:14
and n.
They turn the n. out of the   Job 24:4
way
with the light killeth the poor   Job 24:14
and n.
the n. shall not alway be   Ps 9:18
forgotten
of the poor, for the sighing of   Ps 12:5
the n.
the n. from him that spoileth   Ps 35:10
him

to cast down the poor and n.   Ps 37:14
and to
But I am poor and n.; yet the   Ps 40:17
Lord
I am poor and n.; make haste   Ps 70:5
unto
he shall save the children of the   Ps 72:4
n.
shall deliver the n. when he   Ps 72:12
crieth
He shall spare the poor and n.   Ps 72:13
and shall save the souls of the   Ps 72:13
n.
let the poor and n. praise thy   Ps 74:21
name
do justice to the afflicted and n.   Ps 82:3
Deliver the poor and n.: rid   Ps 82:4
them
Lord, hear me: for I am poor   Ps 86:1
and n.
but persecuted the poor and   Ps 109:16
n. man
For I am poor and n. and my   Ps 109:22
heart
and lifteth the n. out of the   Ps 113:7
dunghill
earth, and the n. from among   Pr 30:14
men
plead the cause of the poor and   Pr 31:9
n.
forth her hands to the n.   Pr 31:20
turn aside the n. from   Isa 10:2
judgment
and the n. shall lie down in   Isa 14:30
safety
a strength to the n. in his   Isa 25:4
distress
the poor, and the steps of the   Isa 26:6
n.
even when the n. speaketh   Isa 32:7
right
When the poor and n. seek   Isa 41:17
water
the right of the n. do they not   Jer 5:28
judge
judged the cause of the poor   Jer 22:16
and n.
the hand of the poor and n.   Eze 16:49
Hath oppressed the poor and   Eze 18:12
n.
and have vexed the poor and   Eze 22:29
n.
oppress the poor, which crush   Am 4:1
the n.
this, O ye that swallow up the   Am 8:4
n.
and the n. for a pair of shoes   Am 8:6

NE'ER-DO-WELLS

good-for-nothing, n. (B)   2Ch 13:7

NEESINGS

By his n. a light doth shine   Job 41:18
His sneezings flash   Job 41:18
(A)(B)(E)(R)

NEGEV

Negev (S)   Ge 12:9;
13:1, 3; 20:1; 24:62; Nu 13:17, 22, 29;
21:1; 33:40; De 1:7; 34:3; Jos 10:40;
11:16; 12:8; 15:19, 21; 19:8; J'g 1:9, 15,
16; Ps 126:4; Isa 21:1; 30:6; Jer 13:19;
17:26; 32:44; 33:13; Eze 20:46-47;
               Ob 19-20; Zec 7:7

NEGINAH

To the chief Musician   Ps 61 title
upon N.

NEGINOTH

to the chief musician on N.   Ps 4,
       6, 54, 55, 67, 76 title

NEGLECT

and if he shall n. to hear   M't 18:17
them
but if he n. to hear the   M't 18:17
church, let
N. not the gift that is in thee   1Ti 4:14
escape, if we n. so great   Heb 2:3
salvation

NEGLECTED

were n. in the daily ministration   Ac 6:1

NEGLECTING

and humility, and n. of the   Col 2:23
body

NEGLIGENT

My sons, be not now n.: for   2Ch 29:11
I will not be n. to put you   2Pe 1:12
always

NEHELAMITE

also speak to Shemaiah the   Jer 29:24
N.
Lord concerning Shemaiah   Jer 29:31
the N.
I will punish Shemaiah the N.   Jer 29:32

NEHEMIAH

with Zerubbabel: Jeshua, N.   Ezr 2:2
words of N. the son of   Ne 1:1
Hachaliah
him repaired N. the son of   Ne 3:16
Azbuk
came with Zerubbabel, Jeshua,   Ne 7:7
N.
N. which is the Tirshatha, and   Ne 8:9
that sealed were, N. the   Ne 10:1
Tirshatha
and in the days of N. the   Ne 12:26
governor
in the days of N. gave the   Ne 12:47
portions

NEHILOTH

To the chief Musician upon   Ps 5 title
N.

NEHUM

Bilshan, Mispereth, Bigvai, N.   Ne 7:7

NEHUSHTA

And his mother's name was   2Ki 24:8
N.

NEHUSHTAN

incense to it: and he called it   2Ki 18:4
N.

NEIEL

and N., and goeth out to   Jos 19:27
Cabul

NEIGHBOR

why strike n. (B)   Ex 2:13
surety for thy n.   Pr 6:1;
(A)(B)(E)(R)   6:3
if thou come into the hand of   Pr 6:3
thy n. (S)
surety in presence of n.   Pr 17:18;
(A)(B)(E)(R)   27:14

NEIGHBORING

the n. cities (S)   Jer 49:18; 50:40

NEIGHBOUR

every woman borrow of her n.   Ex 3:22;
  11:2
and hath given it to a n. of   1Sa 15:28
thine
better is a n. that is near, than   Pr 27:10
a brother
the n. and his friends shall   Jer 6:21
perish
and teach every one her n.   Jer 9:20
lamentation
as in overthrow of Sodom   Jer 49:18;
and Gomorrah and n. cities   50:40
was n. to him that fell among   Lu 10:36
thieves

HIS NEIGHBOUR

let him and his n. take a lamb   Ex 12:4
but if a man come on his n. to   Ex 21:14
slay him

if a man deliver to his n.   Ex 22:7
money or stuff
whether he put his hand to his   Ex 22:8;
n. goods   22:11
if a man deliver to his n. an   Ex 22:10
ass or ox
if borrow ought of his n. and   Ex 22:14
it be hurt or die
go through the camp, slay   Ex 32:27
every man his n.
and lie unto or hath deceived his   Le 6:2
n.
and if a man cause a blemish   Le 24:19
in his n.
which should kill his n.   De 4:42;
unawares   19:4
aught to his n. not exact   De 15:2
of his n. or his brother
if any hate his n. and lie in   De 19:11
wait for him
a man riseth against his n.   De 22:26
and slayeth him
cursed be he that smiteth his   De 27:24
n. secretly
man plucked off his shoe, and   Ru 4:7
gave to his n.
if a man trespass against his   1Ki 8:31
n. an oath
if a man sin against his n. and   2Ch 6:22
an oath
I am as one mocked of his n.   Job 12:4
laughingstock to my friends   Job 12:4
(A)(B)(R)
plead with God as a man   Job 16:21
pleadeth for his n.
they speak vanity each with his   Ps 12:2
n.
nor doeth evil to his n. taketh   Ps 15:3
up a reproach
whoso privily slandereth his n.   Ps 101:5
will cut off
an hypocrite with mouth   Pr 11:9
destroyeth his n.
who is void of wisdom   Pr 11:12;
despiseth his n.   14:21
the righteous is more excellent   Pr 12:26
than his n.
the poor is hated even of his   Pr 14:20
n.
violent man enticeth his n.   Pr 16:29
and leadeth
but his n. cometh and   Pr 18:17
searcheth him
but the poor is separated from   Pr 19:4
his n.
his n. findeth no favour in his   Pr 21:10
eyes
beareth false witness against   Pr 25:18
his n.
so is the man that deceiveth   Pr 26:19
his n.
flattereth his n., spread a net   Pr 29:5
for his feet
that for this a man is envied of   Ec 4:4
his n.
shall be oppressed every one by   Isa 3:5
his n.
they shall fight every one   Isa 19:2
against his n.
they helped every one his n.   Isa 41:6
and said
execute judgment between a   Jer 7:5
man and his n.
take ye heed every one of his n.   Jer 9:4
trust not
and they will deceive every one   Jer 9:5
his n.
speak peaceably to his n. with   Jer 9:8
his mouth
they shall say every man to   Jer 22:8;
his n.   23:35
dreams they tell every one to   Jer 23:27
his n.
that steal my word, every one   Jer 23:30
from his n.
teach no more every man his   Jer 31:34;
n.   Heb 8:11
in proclaiming liberty to his   Jer 34:15;
n.   34:17
woe to him that giveth his n.   Hab 2:15
drink
call every man his n. under   Zec 3:10
the vine
for I set all men, every one   Zec 8:10
against his n.
speak ye every man the truth   Zec 8:16
to his n.
let none of you imagine evil   Zec 8:17
against his n.

to love his n. as himself, is   M'k 12:33
more
he that did his n. wrong thrust   Ac 7:27
him
love worketh no evil to his n.   Ro 13:10
let every one please his n. for   Ro 15:2
his good
speak every man truth with   Eph 4:25
his n.

MY NEIGHBOUR

but he said to Jesus, Who is   Lu 10:29
my n.

THY NEIGHBOUR

thou shalt not bear false   Ex 20:16;
witness against thy n.   De 5:20
shalt not defraud thy n. nor   Le 19:13
rob him
in righteousness shalt thou   Le 19:15
judge thy n.
nor shalt stand against blood   Le 19:16
of thy n.
thou shalt in any wise rebuke   Le 19:17
thy n.
but thou shalt love thy n. as   Le 19:18
thyself
if sell to, or buyest ought of   Le 25:14;
thy n.   25:15
rent kingdom, and given it   1Sa 28:17
to thy n.
take wives and give them to   2Sa 12:11
thy n.
say not to thy n. Go, and come   Pr 3:28
again
devise not evil against thy n.   Pr 3:29
seeing he dwells
be not witness against thy n.   Pr 24:28
without cause
when thy n. hath put thee to   Pr 25:8
shame
debate thy cause with thy n.   Pr 25:9
himself
thou shalt love thy n.   M't 5:43;
19:19;   22:39;   M'k 12:31;   Lu 10:27;
  Ro 13:9;   Ga 5:14;   Jas 2:8

NEIGHBOURS

they heard that they were   Jos 9:16
their n.
the women her n. gave it a   Ru 4:17
name
go borrow vessels abroad of all   2Ki 4:3
thy n.
who speak peace to their n. but   Ps 28:3
mischief
I was a reproach among all   Ps 31:11
my n.
thou makest us a reproach to   Ps 44:13
our n.
we are become a reproach to   Ps 79:4
our n.
render to our n. sevenfold   Ps 79:12
into their bosom
thou makest us a strife to our   Ps 80:6
n.
spoil him he is a reproach to   Ps 89:41
his n.
thus saith the Lord against   Jer 12:14
all my evil n.
his seed is spoiled and his n.   Jer 49:10
and he is not
commit fornication with   Eze 16:26
Egypt, thy n.
thou hast gained of thy n. by   Eze 22:12
extortion
she doted on the Assyrians   Eze 23:5;
her n.   23:12
her n. and her cousins heard   Lu 1:58
how Lord
when makest a supper, call   Lu 14:12
not thy rich n.
he calleth together his friends   Lu 15:6;
and n.   15:9
n. and they who before had   Joh 9:8
seen him blind

NEIGHBOUR'S

not covet n. house, wife, any   Ex 20:17;
thing that is thy n.   De 5:21
put hand to his n. goods   Ex 22:8; 22:11
If at all take thy n. raiment   Ex 22:26
not lie carnally with n. wife   Le 18:20
adultery with his n. wife   Le 20:10
buyest ought of thy n. hand   Le 25:14
not remove n. landmark   De 19:14;
  27:17

he hath humbled his *n.* wife   De 22:24
cometh into thy *n.* vineyard   De 23:24
sickle in thy *n.* standing corn   De 23:25
if ı have laid wait at *n.* door   Job 31:9
So he that goeth in to *n.* wife   Pr 6:29
thy foot from thy *n.* house   Pr 25:17
every one neighed after *n.* wife   Jer 5:8
useth his *n.* service without   Jer 22:13
wages
have committed adultery,   Jer 29:23
with their *n.* wives
neither hath defiled his *n.*   Eze 18:6;
wife   18:11, 15; 33:26
abomination with thy *n.* wife   Eze 22:11
every one into his *n.* hand   Zec 11:6

NEIGHBOURS'

adultery with their *n.* wives   Jer 29:23

NEIGHED

every one *n.* after his neigh-   Jer 5:8
bour's wife

NEIGHING

land trembled at the *n.* of his   Jer 8:16
strong ones

NEIGHINGS

I have seen thine adulteries   Jer 13:27
and *n.*
adulteries and lustful cries   Jer 13:27
(B)

NEITHER

nor eat of it *n.* shall ye touch it   Ge 3:3
n. will I again smite any more   Ge 8:21
every
n. shall all flesh be cut off any   Ge 9:11
more
n. shall there any more be a   Ge 9:11
flood
N. shall thy name any more be   Ge 17:5
thee, *n.* stay thou in all the   Ge 19:17
plain
this thing: *n.* didst thou tell   Ge 21:26
me
me, *n.* yet heard I of it, but to   Ge 21:26
day
n. do thou any thing unto him   Ge 22:12
n. had any man known her   Ge 24:16
n. is it time that the cattle   Ge 29:7
should
n. hath he kept back anything   Ge 39:9
from
there shall *n.* be earing nor   Ge 45:6
harvest
n. hearken to the voice of the   Ex 4:8
first
signs, *n.* hearken unto thy voice   Ex 4:9
n. heretofore, nor since thou   Ex 4:10
hast
Lord, *n.* will I let Israel go   Ex 5:2
n. hast thou delivered thy   Ex 5:23
people
n. did he hearken unto them   Ex 7:22
n. did he set his heart to this   Ex 7:23
also
also *n.* would he let the people   Ex 8:32
go
n. shall there be any more hail   Ex 9:29
n. would he let the children of   Ex 9:35
n. thy fathers, nor thy fathers   Ex 10:6
as they *n.* after them shall be   Ex 10:14
such
n. rose any from his place for   Ex 10:23
three
n. had prepared victual   Ex 12:39
n. shall ye break a bone   Ex 12:46
thereof
n. shall there be leaven seen   Ex 13:7
with
n. was there any worm   Ex 16:24
n. shall ye make unto you   Ex 20:23
gods of
N. shalt thou go up by steps   Ex 20:26
unto
n. vex a stranger, nor oppress   Ex 22:21
him
n. shalt thou lay upon him   Ex 22:25
usury
n. shall ye eat any flesh that is   Ex 22:31
torn
n. shalt thou speak in a cause   Ex 23:2
to
N. shalt thou countenance a   Ex 23:2
poor

n. let it be heard out of thy   Ex 23:13
mouth
n. shall the fat of my sacrifice   Ex 23:18
n. shall the people go up with   Ex 24:2
him
n. shall ye pour drink offering   Ex 30:9
n. shall ye make any other   Ex 30:32
like it
n. is it the voice of them that   Ex 32:18
cry for
n. let any man be seen   Ex 34:3
throughout
n. let the flocks nor herds feed   Ex 34:3
n. shall any man desire thy   Ex 34:24
land
n. shall the sacrifice of the   Ex 34:25
feast
he did *n.* eat bread, nor drink   Ex 34:28
water
Let *n.* man nor woman make   Ex 36:6
any
n. shalt thou suffer the salt of   Le 2:13
that ye eat *n.* fat nor blood   Le 3:17
n. shall he put any frankincense   Le 5:11
n. shall it be imputed unto him   Le 7:18
n. rend your clothes; lest ye   Le 10:6
die, and
n. shall ye make yourselves   Le 11:43
unclean
n. shall ye defile yourselves   Le 11:44
with
n. shall any stranger eat   Le 17:12
blood
n. shall ye walk in their   Le 18:3
ordinances
n. shalt thou take her son's   Le 18:17
N. shalt thou take a wife   Le 18:18
to her
N. shalt thou profane   Le 18:21
the name of
N. shalt thou lie with   Le 18:23
any beast to
n. shall any woman stand   Le 18:23
before a
n. any of your own nation,   Le 18:26
nor any
n. shalt thou gather the   Le 19:9
gleanings of
n. shalt thou gather every   Le 19:10
grape of
Ye shall not steal, *n.* deal   Le 19:11
falsely
deal falsely, *n.* lie one to   Le 19:11
another
n. shalt thou profane the   Le 19:12
name of the
not defraud thy neighbour *n.*   Le 19:13
rob
n. shalt thou stand against the   Le 19:16
n. shall a garment mingled of   Le 19:19
linen
n. shall ye use enchantment   Le 19:26
n. shalt thou mar the corners   Le 19:27
of thy
n. seek after wizards, to be   Le 19:31
defiled
n. shall they shave off the   Le 21:5
corner
n. shall they take a woman put   Le 21:7
away
N. shall he go in to any dead   Le 21:11
body
N. shall he go out of the   Le 21:12
sanctuary
N. shall he profane his seed   Le 21:15
among
n. shall ye make any offering   Le 22:24
N. from a stranger's hand shall   Le 22:25
ye
N. shall ye profane my holy   Le 22:32
name
ye shall eat *n.* bread, nor   Le 23:14
parched
n. shalt thou gather any   Le 23:22
gleaning
thou shalt *n.* sow thy field, nor   Le 25:4
n. gather the grapes of thy vine   Le 25:5
n. reap that which groweth of   Le 25:11
itself
n. rear you up a standing image   Le 26:1
n. shall ye set up any image of   Le 26:1
n. shall the sword go through   Le 26:6
your
n. shall the trees of the land   Le 26:20
yield
them away *n.* will I abhor   Le 26:44
them
good or bad, *n.* shall he change   Le 27:33
it

n. take the sum of them among   Nu 1:49
n. she be taken with the   Nu 5:13
manner
n. shall he drink any liquor of   Nu 6:3
days, *n.* ten days, nor twenty   Nu 11:19
days
n. fear ye the people of   Nu 14:9
the land
n. shall any of them that   Nu 14:23
provoked
them, *n.* have I hurt one of   Nu 16:15
them
that *n.* they, nor ye also, die   Nu 18:3
n. shalt thou have any part   Nu 18:20
among
N. must the children of   Nu 18:22
Israel
n. shall ye pollute the holy   Nu 18:32
things
n. is there any water to drink   Nu 20:5
n. will we drink of the water   Nu 20:17
of thy
is no bread, *n.* is there any   Nu 21:5
water
n. the son of man, that he   Nu 23:19
should
n. hath he seen perverseness in   Nu 23:21
n. is there any divination   Nu 23:23
against
N. curse them at all, nor bless   Nu 23:25
not his enemy, *n.* sought his   Nu 35:23
harm
N. shall the inheritance   Nu 36:9
remove
thee; fear not, *n.* be   De 1:21
discouraged
Dread not, *n.* be afraid of   De 1:29
them
unto them, Go not up, *n.* fight   De 1:42
n. contend with them in battle   De 2:9
I will *n.* turn unto the right   De 2:27
hand
n. shall ye diminish ought from it   De 4:2
n. see, nor hear, nor eat, nor   De 4:28
smell
not forsake thee, *n.* destroy   De 4:31
thee
N. shalt thou commit   De 5:18
adultery
N. shalt thou steal   De 5:19
N. shalt thou bear false witness   De 5:20
N. shalt thou covet thy   De 5:21
neighbour's
n. shalt thou make marriages   De 7:3
with
them: *n.* shalt thou serve their   De 7:16
gods
N. shalt thou bring an   De 7:26
abomination
not *n.* did thy fathers know   De 8:3
old upon thee, *n.* did thy foot   De 8:4
swell
I *n.* did eat bread nor drink   De 9:9
water
I did *n.* eat bread, nor drink   De 9:18
water
n. shall thine eye pity him   De 13:8
eye pity him, *n.* shalt thou   De 13:8
spare
spare, *n.* shalt thou conceal   De 13:8
him
n. shall there any thing of the   De 16:4
flesh
not respect persons, *n.* take a   De 16:19
gift
N. shalt thou set thee up any   De 16:22
image
N. shall he multiply   De 17:17
wives to
n. shall he greatly multiply   De 17:17
silver
n. let me see this great fire   De 18:16
any more
n. be ye terrified because of   De 20:3
them
valley, which is *n.* eared nor   De 21:4
sown
this blood, *n.* have our eyes   De 21:7
seen it
n. shall a man put on a   De 22:5
woman's
n. shall he be charged with any   De 24:5
n. shall the sun go down upon   De 24:15
it
n. shall the children be put to   De 24:16
death
commandments, *n.* have I   De 26:13
forgotten
n. have I taken away ought   De 26:14
thereof

n. thou nor thy fathers have known   *De 28:36*

n. drink of the wine, nor gather the   *De 28:39*

n. thou nor thy fathers have known   *De 28:64*

n. shall sole of thy foot have rest   *De 28:65*

n. have ye drunk wine or strong   *De 29:6*

N. with you only do I make this   *De 29:14*

not hidden from thee, n. is it far off   *De 30:11*

N. is it beyond the sea, that thou   *De 30:13*

he will not fail thee, n. forsake thee   *De 31:8*

thee: fear not, n. be dismayed   *De 31:8*

n. is there any understanding in   *De 32:28*

n. is there any that can deliver out of   *De 32:39*

n. did acknowledge his brethren   *De 33:9*

be not afraid, n. be thou dismayed   *Jos 1:9*

n. did remain any more courage   *Jos 2:11*

n. was there spirit in them any more   *Jos 5:1*

n. had the children of Israel manna   *Jos 5:12*

n. shall any word proceed out of your   *Jos 6:10*

n. will I be with you any more   *Jos 7:12*

Fear not, n. be thou dismayed   *Jos 8:1*

them, n. left they any to breathe   *Jos 11:14*

n. make mention of the name of   *Jos 23:7*

n. serve them, nor bow yourselves   *Jos 23:7*

N. did Manasseh drive out the   *J'g 1:27*

N. did Ephraim drive out the   *J'g 1:29*

N. did Zebulun drive out the   *J'g 1:30*

N. did Asher drive out the   *J'g 1:31*

N. did Naphtali drive out the   *J'g 1:33*

n. delivered he them into the hand   *J'g 2:23*

for Israel, n. sheep, nor ox, nor ass   *J'g 6:4*

you, n. shall my son rule over you   *J'g 8:23*

N. shewed they kindness to the   *J'g 8:35*

her he had n. son nor daughter   *J'g 11:34*

he was, n. told he me his name   *J'g 13:6*

drink, n. eat any unclean thing   *J'g 13:7*

n. let her drink wine or strong drink   *J'g 13:14*

n. would he have shewed us all   *J'g 13:23*

n. will we any of us turn into his   *J'g 20:8*

n. go from hence, but abide   *Ru 2:8*

I have drunk n. wine nor strong   *1Sa 1:15*

n. is there any rock like our God   *1Sa 2:2*

n. was the word of the Lord yet   *1Sa 3:7*

answered not, n. did she regard it   *1Sa 4:20*

n. the priests of Dagon, nor any   *1Sa 5:5*

n. hast thou taken ought of any   *1Sa 12:4*

was n. sword nor spear found in the   *1Sa 13:22*

N. hath the Lord chosen   *1Sa 16:8; 16:9*

to meat, n. yesterday, nor to-day   *1Sa 20:27*

n. brought my sword nor my   *1Sa 21:8*

is n. evil nor transgression in mine   *1Sa 24:11*

n. was there ought missing unto   *1Sa 25:7*

not hurt, n. missed we any thing   *1Sa 25:15*

man saw it, nor knew it, n. awaked   *1Sa 26:12*

and left n. man nor woman alive   *1Sa 27:9*

n. by dreams, nor by Urim, nor by   *1Sa 28:6*

saved n. man nor woman alive   *1Sa 27:11*

n. by prophets, nor by dreams   *1Sa 28:15*

that thou wilt n. kill me, nor deliver   *1Sa 30:15*

n. small nor great, n. sons   *1Sa 30:19*

n. spoil, nor anything that they had   *1Sa 30:19*

dew, n. let there be rain, upon you   *2Sa 1:21*

no more, n. fought they any more   *2Sa 2:28*

n. shall the children of wickedness   *2Sa 7:10*

n. is there any God beside thee   *2Sa 7:22*

not, n. did he eat bread with them   *2Sa 12:17*

his brother Amnon n. good nor bad   *2Sa 13:22*

n. name nor remainder upon   *2Sa 14:7*

n. doth God respect any person   *2Sa 14:14*

n. if half of us died, will they care   *2Sa 18:3*

regardest n. princes nor servants   *2Sa 19:6*

n. do thou remember that which thy   *2Sa 19:19*

n. dressed his feet, nor trimmed   *2Sa 19:24*

n. have we inheritance in the son of   *2Sa 20:1*

n. for us shalt thou kill any man in   *2Sa 21:4*

n. the birds of the air to rest on   *2Sa 21:10*

n. will I offer burnt offerings unto   *2Sa 24:24*

n. hast asked riches for thyself   *1Ki 3:11*

n. after thee shall any arise like   *1Ki 3:12*

Let it be n. mine nor thine   *1Ki 3:26*

that there is n. adversary nor evil   *1Ki 5:4*

there was n. hammer nor axe   *1Ki 6:7*

n. was the weight of the brass found   *1Ki 7:47*

n. shall they come in unto you   *1Ki 11:2*

n. have we inheritance in the son of   *1Ki 12:16*

n. will I eat bread nor drink water   *1Ki 13:8; 13:16*

n. of his kinsfolks, nor of his friends   *1Ki 16:11*

waste, n. shall the cruse of oil fail   *1Ki 17:14*

not, n. did the cruse of oil fail   *1Ki 17:16*

was n. voice, nor any to answer   *1Ki 18:29*

Fight n. with small nor great, save   *1Ki 22:31*

not see wind, n. shall ye see rain   *2Ki 3:17*

it is n. new moon, nor sabbath   *2Ki 4:23*

but there was n. voice, nor hearing   *2Ki 4:31*

offer n. burnt offering nor sacrifice   *2Ki 5:17*

is not the way, n. is this the city   *2Ki 6:19*

was no man there, n. voice of man   *2Ki 7:10*

forty men; n. left he any of them   *2Ki 10:14*

n. to repair the breaches of   *2Ki 12:8*

N. did he leave of the people to   *2Ki 13:7*

n. cast he them from his presence   *2Ki 13:23*

n. do they after their statutes, or   *2Ki 17:34*

forget: n. shall ye fear other gods   *2Ki 17:38*

N. let Hezekiah make you trust in   *2Ki 18:30*

N. will I make the feet of Israel   *2Ki 21:8*

n. after him arose there any like   *2Ki 23:25*

n. did all their family multiply like   *1Ch 4:27*

n. shall the children of wickedness   *1Ch 17:9*

n. is there any God beside thee   *1Ch 17:20*

n. would the Syrians help the   *1Ch 19:19*

n. was the number put in the   *1Ch 27:24*

enemies, n. yet has asked long life   *2Ch 1:11*

n. shall there any after thee have   *2Ch 1:12*

n. chose I any man to be a ruler   *2Ch 6:5*

n. was there any such spice as   *2Ch 9:9*

N. did Jeroboam recover strength   *2Ch 13:20*

n. know we what to do: but our   *2Ch 20:12*

n. shall the children die for   *2Ch 25:4*

n. shall it be for thine honour from   *2Ch 26:18*

n. had the people gathered on this manner, n. yet   *2Ch 30:3*

believe him   *2Ch 32:15*

N. will I any more remove the foot   *2Ch 33:8*

declined n. to the right hand, nor   *2Ch 34:2*

n. shall mine eyes see all the evil   *2Ch 34:28*

n. did all the kings of Israel keep   *2Ch 35:18*

n. take their daughters unto your   *Ezr 9:12*

n. is this a work of one day or two   *Ezr 10:13*

n. told I any man what my God had   *Ne 2:12*

n. was there any beast with me   *Ne 2:12*

n. had I as yet told it to the Jews   *Ne 2:16*

They shall not know, n. see, till we   *Ne 4:11*

So n. I, nor my brethren, nor my   *Ne 4:23*

n. is it in our power to redeem them   *Ne 5:5*

this wall, n. bought we any land   *Ne 5:16*

n. be ye sorry; for the joy of   *Ne 8:10*

for the day is holy; n. be ye grieved   *Ne 8:11*

n. were mindful of thy wonders   *Ne 9:17*

n. the pillar of fire by night, to shew   *Ne 9:19*

N. have our kings, our princes   *Ne 9:34*

n. turned they from their   *Ne 9:35*

for she had n. father nor mother   *Es 2:7*

people; n. keep they the king's laws   *Es 3:8*

n. eat nor drink three days, night   *Es 4:16*

n. let the light shine upon it   *Job 3:4*

n. let it see the dawning of the day   *Job 3:9*

I was not in safety, n. had I rest   *Job 3:26*

n. was I quiet; yet trouble came   *Job 3:26*

n. is there any to deliver them   *Job 5:4*

n. doth trouble spring out of   *Job 5:6*

n. shalt be afraid of destruction   *Job 5:21*

n. shall thou be afraid of the beasts   *Job 5:22*

n. shall his place know him any   *Job 17:10*

man, n. will he help the evil doers   *Job 8:20*

N. is there any daysman betwixt   *Job 9:33*

n. shall his substance continue   *Job 15:29*

n. shall he prolong the perfection   *Job 15:29*

He shall n. have son nor nephew   *Job 18:19*

n. shall his place any more behold   *Job 20:9*

n. is the rod of God upon them   *Job 21:9*

N. have I gone back from the   *Job 23:12*

n. hath he covered the darkness   *Job 23:17*

n. is it found in the land of   *Job 28:13*

n. shall silver be weighed for   *Job 28:15*

n. shall it be valued with pure gold   *Job 28:19*

N. have I suffered my mouth to sin   *Job 31:30*

n. do the aged understand judgment   *Job 32:9*

n. answer him with speeches   *Job 32:14*

n. let me give flattering titles unto   *Job 32:21*

n. shall my hand be heavy upon   *Job 33:7*

innocent; n. is there iniquity in me   *Job 33:9*

n. the Almighty pervert judgment   *Job 34:12*

n. will the Almighty regard it   *Job 35:13*

n. can the number of his *Job 36:26*
years be
n. regardeth he the crying of *Job 39:7*
n. imparted to her *Job 39:17*
understanding
n. turneth he back from the *Job 39:22*
sword
n. believeth he that it is the *Job 39:24*
sound
n. shall evil dwell with thee *Ps 5:4*
thine anger, *n.* chasten me in thy *Ps 6:1*
n. wilt thou suffer thine Holy *Ps 16:10*
One
n. did I turn again till they *Ps 18:37*
were
n. hath he hid his face from *Ps 22:24*
him
n. will I go in with dissemblers *Ps 26:4*
leave me not, *n.* forsake me, O *Ps 27:9*
God
n. deliver any by great *Ps 33:17*
strength
n. let them wink with the eye *Ps 35:19*
n. be thou envious against the *Ps 37:1*
n. chasten me in thy hot *Ps 38:1*
displeasure
n. is there any rest in my bones *Ps 38:3*
n. did their own arm save them *Ps 44:3*
my bow, *n.* shall my sword save *Ps 44:6*
me
n. have we dealt falsely in thy *Ps 44:17*
n. have our steps declined *Ps 44:18*
from thy
n. was it he that hated me that *Ps 55:12*
n. let the deep swallow me up *Ps 69:15*
n. are they plagued like other *Ps 73:5*
men
n. is there among us any that *Ps 74:9*
promotion cometh *n.* from the *Ps 75:6*
east
n. were steadfast in his *Ps 78:37*
covenant
n. shalt thou worship any *Ps 81:9*
strange
know not, *n.* will they *Ps 82:5*
understand
n. are there any works like unto *Ps 86:8*
n. shall any plague come nigh *Ps 91:10*
not; *n.* doth a fool understand *Ps 92:6*
this
n. shall the God of Jacob *Ps 94:7*
regard it
n. will he forsake his *Ps 94:14*
inheritance
n. will he keep his anger for *Ps 103:9*
ever
n. let there be any to favour *Ps 109:12*
his
n. speak they through their *Ps 115:7*
throat
n. any that go down into *Ps 115:17*
silence
Israel shall *n.* slumber nor *Ps 121:4*
sleep
N. do they which go by say, *Ps 129:8*
The
n. do I exercise myself in great *Ps 131:1*
n. is there any breath in their *Ps 135:17*
n. take they hold of the paths *Pr 2:19*
of life
n. be weary of his correction *Pr 3:11*
n. of the desolation of the *Pr 3:25*
wicked
n. decline from the words of my *Pr 4:5*
n. let her take thee with her *Pr 6:25*
eyelids
n. will he rest content, though *Pr 6:35*
him; *n.* will he go unto the *Pr 15:12*
wise
n. oppress the afflicted in the *Pr 22:22*
gate
n. desire thou his dainty meats *Pr 23:6*
evil men, *n.* desire to be with *Pr 24:1*
them
n. be thou envious at the *Pr 24:19*
wicked
n. go into thy brother's house *Pr 27:10*
in the
I *n.* learned wisdom, nor have *Pr 30:3*
give me *n.* poverty nor riches; *Pr 30:8*
feed
n. shall there be any *Ec 1:11*
remembrance
he hath *n.* child nor brother *Ec 4:8*
n. is his eye satisfied with riches *Ec 4:8*
n. saith he, For whom do I *Ec 4:8*
labour
n. say thou before the angel *Ec 5:6*

n. may he contend with him *Ec 6:10*
that
much; *n.* make thyself over *Ec 7:16*
wise
much wicked, *n.* be thou *Ec 7:17*
foolish
n. hath power in the day of *Ec 8:8*
death
n. shall wickedness deliver those *Ec 8:8*
n. shall he prolong his days, *Ec 8:13*
which
there is that *n.* day nor night *Ec 8:16*
n. have they any more a reward *Ec 9:5*
n. have they any more a portion *Ec 9:6*
n. yet bread to the wise, nor yet *Ec 9:11*
love, *n.* can the floods drown it *Ca 8:7*
n. bound up, *n.* mollified with *Isa 1:6*
n. doth the cause of the widow *Isa 1:23*
n. shall they learn war any more *Isa 2:4*
n. is there end of their *Isa 2:7*
treasures
n. is there any end of their *Isa 2:7*
chariots
my house is *n.* bread nor *Isa 3:7*
clothing
n. consider the operation of *Isa 5:12*
his
n. shall the girdle of their loins *Isa 5:27*
be
n. be fainthearted for the two *Isa 7:4*
tails
stand, *n.* shall it come to pass *Isa 7:7*
not ask, *n.* will I tempt the *Isa 7:12*
Lord
n. fear ye their fear, nor be *Isa 8:12*
afraid
n. do they seek the Lord of *Isa 9:13*
hosts
n. have mercy on their *Isa 9:17*
fatherless
not so, *n.* doth his heart think *Isa 10:7*
so
n. reprove after the hearing of *Isa 11:3*
his
n. shall it be dwelt in from *Isa 13:20*
n. shall the Arabian pitch tent *Isa 13:20*
n. shall the shepherds make *Isa 13:20*
their
singing, *n.* shall there be *Isa 16:10*
shouting
N. shall there be any *Isa 19:15*
work for
n. had respect unto him that *Isa 22:11*
n. do I nourish up young men, *Isa 23:4*
nor
n. have the inhabitants of the *Isa 26:18*
n. is a cart wheel turned about *Isa 28:27*
upon
n. shall his face now wax pale *Isa 29:22*
One of Israel, *n.* seek the Lord *Isa 31:1*
n. shall any of the cords *Isa 33:20*
thereof
n. shall gallant ship pass *Isa 33:21*
thereby
N. let Hezekiah make you *Isa 36:15*
trust in
earth, fainteth not, *n.* is *Isa 40:28*
weary
n. my praise to graven images *Isa 42:8*
n. were they obedient unto *Isa 42:24*
his law
n. shall the flame kindle upon *Isa 43:2*
thee
formed, *n.* shall there be after *Isa 43:10*
me
things, *n.* consider the things *Isa 43:18*
of old
n. hast thou honoured me *Isa 43:23*
with
n. hast thou filled me with the *Isa 43:24*
fat
Fear ye not, *n.* be afraid: have *Isa 44:8*
not
heart, *n.* is there knowledge *Isa 44:19*
nor
n. didst remember the latter *Isa 47:7*
end
n. shall I know the loss of *Isa 47:8*
children
n. shall the heat nor sun smite *Isa 49:10*
not rebellious, *n.* turned away *Isa 50:5*
back
n. be ye afraid of their *Isa 51:7*
revilings
n. is there any that taketh her *Isa 51:18*
by
n. was any deceit in his mouth *Isa 53:9*
n. be thou confounded; for *Isa 54:4*
thou

n. shall the covenant of my *Isa 54:10*
peace
n. are your ways my ways *Isa 55:8*
N. let the son of the strangers *Isa 56:3*
n. let the eunuch say, Behold, I *Isa 56:3*
am
n. will I be always wroth: for *Isa 57:16*
n. his ear heavy, that it cannot *Isa 59:1*
hear
n. shall they cover themselves *Isa 59:6*
with
from us, *n.* doth justice *Isa 59:9*
overtake us
n. for brightness shall the *Isa 60:19*
moon
n. shall thy moon withdraw *Isa 60:20*
itself
n. thy land any more be *Isa 62:4*
termed
n. hath the eye seen, O God, *Isa 64:4*
besides
n. remember iniquity for ever *Isa 64:9*
my fame, *n.* have seen my *Isa 66:19*
glory
die, *n.* shall their fire be *Isa 66:24*
quenched
N. said they, Where is the Lord *Jer 2:6*
the Lord: *n.* shall it come to *Jer 3:16*
mind
n. shall they remember it *Jer 3:16*
n. shall they visit it *Jer 3:16*
n. shall that be done any more *Jer 3:16*
n. shall they walk any more *Jer 3:17*
after
repent, *n.* will I turn back *Jer 4:28*
from it
not he; *n.* shall evil come upon *Jer 5:12*
us
n. shall we see sword nor *Jer 5:12*
famine
n. understandest what they say *Jer 5:15*
N. say they in their heart, Let *Jer 5:24*
us
ashamed, *n.* could they blush *Jer 6:15*
n. walk after other gods to your *Jer 7:6*
n. lift up cry nor prayer for *Jer 7:16*
them
them, *n.* make intercession to *Jer 7:16*
me
them not, *n.* came it into my *Jer 7:31*
heart
all ashamed, *n.* could they *Jer 8:12*
blush
n. can men hear the voice of *Jer 9:10*
obeyed my voice, *n.* walked *Jer 9:13*
therein
n. they nor their fathers have *Jer 9:16*
n. let the mighty man glory in *Jer 9:23*
his
n. also is it in them to do good *Jer 10:5*
n. lift up a cry or prayer for *Jer 11:14*
them
sword, *n.* shall ye have famine *Jer 14:13*
not, *n.* have I commanded *Jer 14:14*
them
them, *n.* spake unto them *Jer 14:14*
I have *n.* lent on usury, nor *Jer 15:10*
men
a wife, *n.* shalt thou have sons *Jer 16:2*
or
lamented; *n.* shall they be *Jer 16:4*
buried
n. go to lament nor bemoan *Jer 16:5*
them
n. shall men lament for them, *Jer 16:6*
N. shall men tear *Jer 16:7*
themselves for
n. shall men give them the cup *Jer 16:7*
of
know not, *n.* ye nor your *Jer 16:13*
fathers
n. is their iniquity hid from *Jer 16:17*
mine
n. shall cease from yielding *Jer 17:8*
fruit
n. have I desired the woeful *Jer 17:16*
day
N. carry forth a burden out *Jer 17:22*
of your
the sabbath day, *n.* do ye any *Jer 17:22*
work
obeyed not, *n.* inclined their *Jer 17:23*
ear
n. blot out their sin from thy *Jer 18:23*
sight
n. they nor their fathers have *Jer 19:4*
spake it, *n.* came it into my *Jer 19:5*
mind

them, *n.* have pity, nor have mercy — Jer 21:7
n. shed innocent blood in this place — Jer 22:3
ye not for the dead, *n.* bemoan him — Jer 22:10
n. shall they be lacking, saith — Jer 23:4
lamented, *n.* gathered, nor buried — Jer 25:33
n. hearken to your dreams — Jer 29:8
n. shall he behold the good that I — Jer 29:32
n. be dismayed, O Israel: for lo, I — Jer 30:10
thy voice, *n.* walked in thy law — Jer 32:23
them not, *n.* came it into my mind — Jer 32:35
N. shall the priests the Levites — Jer 33:18
n. the sand of the sea measured — Jer 33:22
not unto me, *n.* inclined their ear — Jer 34:14
drink no wine, *n.* ye nor your sons — Jer 35:6
N. shall ye build house, nor sow — Jer 35:7
n. have we vineyard, nor field, nor — Jer 35:9
n. the king, nor any of his servants — Jer 36:24
n. he, nor his servants, nor the — Jer 37:2
n. will I give thee into the hand of — Jer 38:16
n. obey the voice of the Lord your — Jer 42:13
knew not *n.* they, ye, nor your father — Jer 44:3
n. have they feared, nor walked in — Jer 44:10
n. hath he gone into captivity — Jer 48:11
n. shall a son of man dwell in it — Jer 49:18
which have *n.* gates nor bars — Jer 49:31
n. shall it be dwelt in from — Jer 50:39
n. shall any son of man dwell — Jer 50:40
n. doth any son of man pass — Jer 51:43
remain in it, *n.* man nor beast — Jer 51:62
them, *n.* be afraid of their words — Eze 2:6
not, *n.* be dismayed at their looks — Eze 3:9
n. came there abominable flesh into — Eze 4:14
n. have kept my judgments — Eze 5:7
n. have done according to the — Eze 5:7
thee; *n.* shall mine eye spare — Eze 5:11
eye spare, *n.* will I have any pity — Eze 5:11
not spare thee, *n.* will I have pity — Eze 7:4
shall not spare, *n.* will I have pity — Eze 7:9
n. shall there be wailing for them — Eze 7:11
n. shall any strengthen himself in — Eze 7:13
their souls, *n.* fill their bowels — Eze 7:19
shall not spare, *n.* will I have pity — Eze 8:18
not your eye spare, *n.* have ye pity — Eze 9:5
shall not spare, *n.* will I have pity — Eze 9:10
n. shall ye be the flesh in the midst — Eze 11:11
n. executed my judgments — Eze 11:12
n. made up the hedge for the house — Eze 13:5
n. shall they be written in the — Eze 13:9
n. shall they enter into the land of — Eze 13:9
is no more, *n.* they that daubed it — Eze 13:15
n. be polluted any more with — Eze 14:11
shall deliver *n.* sons nor daughters — Eze 14:16; 14:18
shall deliver *n.* son nor daughter — Eze 14:20
n. wast thou washed in water — Eze 16:4
shall not come, *n.* shall it be — Eze 16:16
n. did she strengthen the hand — Eze 16:49
N. hath Samaria committed half of — Eze 16:51
N. shall Pharaoh with his mighty — Eze 17:17
n. hath lifted up his eyes to the — Eze 18:6
n. hath defiled his neighbour's — Eze 18:6
n. hath come near to a menstruous — Eze 18:6

usury, *n.* hath taken any increase — Eze 18:8
n. hath lifted up his eyes to — Eze 18:15
N. hath oppressed any, hath not — Eze 18:16
pledge, *n.* hath spoiled by violence — Eze 18:16
n. shall the father bear the iniquity — Eze 18:20
n. did they forsake the idols of — Eze 20:8
n. did I make an end of them in the — Eze 20:17
n. observe their judgments — Eze 20:18
n. kept my judgments to do them — Eze 20:21
n. have they shewed difference — Eze 22:26
N. left she her whoredoms brought — Eze 23:8
n. will I spare, *n.* will I repent — Eze 24:14
yet *n.* shalt thou mourn nor weep — Eze 24:16
weep, *n.* shall thy tears run down — Eze 24:16
n. shall it be inhabited forty years — Eze 29:11
n. shall it exalt itself any more — Eze 29:15
n. shoot up their top among — Eze 31:14
n. their trees stand up in their — Eze 31:14
n. shall the foot of man trouble — Eze 32:13
n. shall the righteous be able to live — Eze 33:12
n. have ye healed that which was — Eze 34:4
n. have ye bound up that which was — Eze 34:4
n. have ye brought again that which — Eze 34:4
n. have ye sought that which was — Eze 34:4
n. did my shepherds search for my — Eze 34:8
flock; *n.* shall the shepherds feed — Eze 34:10
n. shall the beast of the land devour — Eze 34:28
n. bear the shame of the heathen — Eze 34:29
n. bereave thy nations any more — Eze 36:14
N. will I cause men to hear in thee — Eze 36:15
n. shalt thou bear the reproach of — Eze 36:15
n. shalt thou cause thy nations to — Eze 36:15
n. shall they be divided into two — Eze 37:22
N. shall they defile themselves any — Eze 37:23
walls, and having *n.* bars nor gates — Eze 38:11
n. cut down any out of the forests — Eze 39:10
N. will I hide my face any more — Eze 39:29
more defile, *n.* they, nor their kings — Eze 43:7
N. shall they save their heads — Eze 44:20
N. shall any priest drink wine — Eze 44:21
N. shall they take for their wives a — Eze 44:22
fade, *n.* shall the fruit thereof be — Eze 47:12
they shall not sell of it, *n.* exchange — Eze 48:14
n. were their coats changed, nor — Da 3:27
n. was there any error or fault found — Da 6:4
n. were instruments of musick — Da 6:18
n. was there any that could deliver — Da 8:4
N. have we hearkened unto thy — Da 9:6
N. have we obeyed the voice of — Da 9:10
n. came flesh nor wine in my mouth — Da 10:3
n. did I anoint myself at all, till — Da 10:3
in me, *n.* is there breath left in me — Da 10:17
n. he stand, nor his arm withstand, *n.* his chosen people — Da 11:6
— Da 11:15
n. shall there be any strength to — Da 11:15

not stand on his side, *n.* be for him — Da 11:17
destroyed, *n.* in anger, nor in battle — Da 11:20
N. shall he regard the God of his — Da 11:37
not my wife, *n.* am I her husband — Ho 2:2
Gilgal, *n.* go ye up to Beth-aven — Ho 4:15
n. shall they be pleasing unto him — Ho 9:4
n. will we say any more to the work — Ho 14:3
like, *n.* shall be any more after it — Joe 2:2
N. shall one thrust another — Joe 2:8
n. shall the mighty deliver himself — Am 2:14
N. shall he stand that handleth — Am 2:15
n. shall he that rideth the horse — Am 2:15
n. will I regard the peace offerings — Am 5:22
prophet, *n.* was I a prophet's son — Am 7:14
n. shouldest thou have rejoiced — Ob 12
n. shouldest thou have spoken — Ob 12
N. shouldest thou have stood in — Ob 14
n. shouldest thou have delivered up — Ob 14
Let *n.* man nor beast, herd nor — Jon 3:7
not laboured, *n.* madest it grow — Jon 4:10
your necks; *n.* shall ye go haughtily — Mic 2:3
n. shall they learn war any more — Mic 4:3
n. understand they his counsel — Mic 4:12
a proud man, *n.* keepeth at home — Hab 2:5
n. shall fruit be in the vines — Hab 3:17
will not do good, *n.* will he do evil — Zep 1:12
N. their silver nor their gold shall — Zep 1:18
n. shall a deceitful tongue be found — Zep 3:13
n. was there any peace to him that — Zec 8:10
n. shall seek the young one — Zec 11:16
n. shall they wear a rough garment — Zec 13:4
n. do ye kindle fire on mine altar — Mal 1:10
n. will I accept an offering at your — Mal 1:10
n. shall your vine cast her fruit — Mal 3:11
shall leave them *n.* root nor branch — Mal 4:1
N. do men light a candle, and put — M't 5:15
n. by heaven; for it is God's throne — M't 5:34
n. by Jerusalem; for it is the city — M't 5:35
N. shalt thou swear by thy head — M't 5:36
n. will your Father forgive your — M't 6:15
n. moth nor rust doth corrupt — M't 6:20
n. do they reap, nor gather into — M't 6:26
grow; they toil not, *n.* do they spin — M't 6:28
n. cast ye your pearls before swine — M't 7:6
n. can a corrupt tree bring forth — M't 7:18
N. do men put new wine into old — M't 9:17
Provide *n.* gold, nor silver, nor — M't 10:9
your journey, *n.* two coats, *n.* shoes — M't 10:10
John came *n.* eating nor drinking — M't 11:18
n. knoweth any man the Father — M't 11:27
n. for them which were with him — M't 12:4
n. shall any man hear his voice in — M't 12:19
be forgiven him, *n.* in this world — M't 12:32
world, *n.* in the world to come — M't 12:32
hear not, *n.* do they understand — M't 13:13

n. remember the five loaves of the	*M't 16:9*	Christ, nor Elias, *n.* that prophet	*Joh 1:25*
N. the seven loaves of the four	*M't 16:10*	light, *n.* cometh to the light	*Joh 3:20*
N. tell I you by what authority I do	*M't 21:27*	thirst not, *n.* come hither to draw	*Joh 4:15*
n. carest thou for any man	*M't 22:16*	shall *n.* in this mountain, nor yet	*Joh 4:21*
n. marry, nor given in marriage	*M't 22:30; Lu 20:35*	*n.* heard his voice at any time, nor	*Joh 5:37*
n. durst any man from that day	*M't 22:46*	was not there, *n.* his disciples	*Joh 6:24*
N. be ye called masters: for one	*M't 23:10*	*n.* did his brethren believe in him	*Joh 7:5*
men: for ye *n.* go in yourselves	*M't 23:13*	N. do I condemn thee: go, and sin	*Joh 8:11*
n. suffer ye them that are entering	*M't 23:13*	Ye *n.* know me, nor my Father: if	*Joh 8:19*
N. let him which is in the field	*M't 24:18*	*n.* came I of myself, but he sent	*Joh 8:42*
the winter, *n.* on the sabbath day	*M't 24:20*	N. hath this man sinned, nor his	*Joh 9:3*
ye know *n.* the day nor the hour	*M't 25:13*	*n.* shall any man pluck them	*Joh 10:28*
n. was any thing kept secret	*M'k 4:22*	*n.* he that is sent greater than he	*Joh 13:16*
n. could any man tame him	*M'k 5:4*	it seeth him not, *n.* knoweth him	*Joh 14:17*
n. had they in the ship with	*M'k 8:14*	be troubled, *n.* let it be afraid	*Joh 14:27*
perceive ye not yet, *n.* understand	*M'k 8:17*	N. pray I for these alone, but for	*Joh 17:20*
N. go into the town, nor tell it to	*M'k 8:26*	*n.* wilt thou suffer thine Holy One	*Ac 2:27*
n. will your Father which is in	*M'k 11:26*	*n.* his flesh did see corruption	*Ac 2:31*
N. do I tell you by what authority	*M'k 11:33*	N. is there salvation in any	*Ac 4:12*
her, and died, *n.* left he any seed	*M'k 12:21*	*n.* said any of them that ought of	*Ac 4:32*
scriptures, *n.* the power of God	*M'k 12:24*	N. was there any among them	*Ac 4:34*
shall speak, *n.* do ye premeditate	*M'k 13:11*	Thou hast *n.* part nor lot in this	*Ac 8:21*
n. enter therein, to take any thing	*M'k 13:15*	sight, and *n.* did eat nor drink	*Ac 9:9*
unto this time, *n.* shall be	*M'k 13:19*	*n.* our fathers nor we were able	*Ac 15:10*
heaven, *n.* the Son, but the Father	*M'k 13:32*	us to receive, *n.* to observe, being	*Ac 16:21*
n. wist they what to answer	*M'k 14:40*	N. is worshipped with men's	*Ac 17:25*
But *n.* so did their witness agree	*M'k 14:59*	which are *n.* robbers of churches	*Ac 19:37*
n. understand I what thou sayest	*M'k 14:68*	*n.* count I my life dear unto	*Ac 20:24*
n. said they any thing to any	*M'k 16:8*	*n.* to walk after the customs	*Ac 21:21*
residue: *n.* believed they them	*M'k 16:13*	resurrection, *n.* angel, nor spirit	*Ac 23:8*
n. wine nor strong drink	*Lu 1:15*	they would *n.* eat nor drink till	*Ac 23:12*
to no man, *n.* accuse any falsely	*Lu 3:14*	they will *n.* eat nor drink till they	*Ac 23:21*
n. doth a corrupt tree bring forth	*Lu 6:43*	they *n.* found me in the temple	*Ac 24:12*
n. thought I myself worthy to come	*Lu 7:7*	any man, *n.* raising up the people	*Ac 24:12*
came *n.* eating bread nor drinking	*Lu 7:33*	*n.* in the synagogue, nor in the	*Ac 24:12*
n. any thing hid, that shall not be	*Lu 8:17*	N. can they prove the things	*Ac 24:13*
n. abode in any house, but in	*Lu 8:27*	in the temple, *n.* with multitude	*Ac 24:18*
n. could be healed of any	*Lu 8:43*	N. against the law of the Jews	*Ac 25:8*
journey, *n.* staves, nor scrip, *n.*	*Lu 9:3*	*n.* against the temple, nor yet	*Ac 25:8*
n. scrip, *n.* bread, *n.* money	*Lu 9:3*	when *n.* sun nor stars in many	*Ac 27:20*
money; *n.* have two coats apiece	*Lu 9:3*	We *n.* received letters out of Judæa	*Ac 28:21*
Carry *n.* purse, nor scrip, nor	*Lu 10:4*	*n.* any of the brethren that came	*Ac 28:21*
secret place, *n.* under a bushel	*Lu 11:33*	him not as God, *n.* were thankful	*Ro 1:21*
n. hid, that shall not be known	*Lu 12:2*	*n.* is that circumcision, which is	*Ro 2:28*
n. for the body, what ye shall put	*Lu 12:22*	*n.* yet the deadness of Sarah's womb	*Ro 4:19*
ravens: for they *n.* sow nor reap	*Lu 12:24*	N. yield ye your members as	*Ro 6:13*
which *n.* have storehouse nor barn	*Lu 12:24*	to the law of God, *n.* indeed can be	*Ro 8:7*
drink, *n.* be ye of doubtful mind	*Lu 12:29*	*n.* death, nor life, nor angels, nor	*Ro 8:38*
approacheth, *n.* moth corrupteth	*Lu 12:33*	N. because they are the seed of	*Ro 9:7*
n. did according to his will	*Lu 12:47*	*n.* having done any good or	*Ro 9:11*
thy brethren, *n.* thy kinsmen, nor	*Lu 14:12*	It is good *n.* to eat flesh, nor	*Ro 14:21*
It is *n.* fit for the land, nor yet	*Lu 14:34*	*n.* have entered into the heart	*1Co 2:9*
n. transgressed I at any time thy	*Lu 15:29*	*n.* can they know them, because	*1Co 2:14*
n. can they pass to us, that would	*Lu 16:26*	bear it, *n.* yet now are ye able	*1Co 3:2*
n. will they be persuaded, though	*Lu 16:31*	*n.* is he that planteth any thing	*1Co 3:7*
N. shall they say, Lo here! or	*Lu 17:21*	*n.* he that watereth; but God that	*1Co 3:7*
feared not God, *n.* regarded man	*Lu 18:2*	*n.* with the leaven of malice	*1Co 5:8*
n. knew they the things which	*Lu 18:34*	*n.* fornicators, nor idolaters, nor	*1Co 6:9*
N. tell I you by what authority I	*Lu 20:8*	for *n.* if we eat, are we the better	*1Co 8:8*
n. acceptest thou the person	*Lu 20:21*	*n.* if we eat not, are we the worse	*1Co 8:8*
N. can they die any more: for	*Lu 20:36*	*n.* have I written these things, that	*1Co 9:15*
		N. be ye idolaters, as were some	*1Co 10:7*
N. let us commit fornication, as	*1Co 10:8*		
N. let us tempt Christ, as some of	*1Co 10:9*		
N. murmur ye, as some of them	*1Co 10:10*		
n. to the Jews, nor to the Gentiles	*1Co 10:32*		
N. was the man created for	*1Co 11:9*		
n. is the man without the woman	*1Co 11:11*		
n. the woman without the man	*1Co 11:11*		
custom, *n.* the churches of God	*1Co 11:16*		
of God; *n.* doth corruption inherit	*1Co 15:50*		
n. by man, but by Jesus Christ	*Ga 1:1*		
For I *n.* received it of man	*Ga 1:12*		
n. was I taught it, but by the Lord	*Ga 1:12*		
N. went I up to Jerusalem to	*Ga 1:17*		
N. Titus, who was with me, being a	*Ga 2:3*		
There is *n.* Jew nor Greek, there	*Ga 3:28*		
there is *n.* bond nor free, there	*Ga 3:28*		
there is *n.* male nor female: for ye	*Ga 3:28*		
n. circumcision availeth any thing	*Ga 5:6*		
For *n.* they themselves who are	*Ga 6:13*		
n. circumcision availeth any thing	*Ga 6:15*		
N. give place to the devil	*Eph 4:27*		
N. filthiness, nor foolish	*Eph 5:4*		
n. is there respect of persons	*Eph 6:9*		
run in vain, *n.* laboured in vain	*Ph'p 2:16*		
Where there is *n.* Greek nor Jew	*Col 3:11*		
n. at any time used we flattering	*1Th 2:5*		
glory, *n.* of you, nor yet of others	*1Th 2:6*		
n. by spirit, nor by word, nor	*2Th 2:2*		
N. did we eat any man's bread	*2Th 3:8*		
would not work, *n.* should he eat	*2Th 3:10*		
N. give heed to fables and endless	*1Ti 1:4*		
understanding *n.* what they say	*1Ti 1:7*		
n. be partaker of other men's sins	*1Ti 5:22*		
N. is there any creature that	*Heb 4:13*		
n. beginning of days, nor end	*Heb 7:3*		
N. by the blood of goats and	*Heb 9:12*		
n. the first testament was dedicated	*Heb 9:18*		
not, *n.* hadst pleasure therein	*Heb 10:8*		
evil, *n.* tempteth he any man	*Jas 1:13*		
variableness, *n.* shadow of turning	*Jas 1:17*		
brethren, swear not, *n.* by heaven	*Jas 5:12*		
n. by earth, *n.* by any other oath	*Jas 5:12*		
n. was guile found in his mouth	*1Pe 2:22*		
of their terror, *n.* be troubled	*1Pe 3:14*		
N. as being lords over God's	*1Pe 5:3*		
shall *n.* be barren nor unfruitful	*2Pe 1:8*		
n. the things that are in the world	*1Jo 2:15*		
hath not seen him, *n.* known	*1Jo 3:6*		
God, *n.* he that loveth not his brother	*1Jo 3:10*		
us not love in word, *n.* in tongue	*1Jo 3:18*		
your house, *n.* bid him God speed	*2Jo 10*		
n. doth he himself receive the	*3Jo 10*		
works, that thou art *n.* cold nor hot	*Re 3:15*		
art lukewarm, and *n.* cold nor hot	*Re 3:16*		
nor in earth, *n.* under the earth	*Re 5:3*		
to open the book, *n.* to look thereon	*Re 5:3*		
read the book, *n.* to look thereon	*Re 5:4*		
Hurt not the earth, *n.* the sea, nor	*Re 7:3*		
no more, *n.* thirst any more	*Re 7:16*		
n. shall the sun light on them, nor	*Re 7:16*		

NEITHER (continued)

n. any green thing, *n.* any tree — Re 9:4
which *n.* can see, nor hear, nor — Re 9:20
N. repented they of their — Re 9:21
n. was there place found any more — Re 12:8
worshipped the beast, *n.* his image — Re 20:4
n. received his mark upon — Re 20:4
more death, *n.* sorrow, nor crying — Re 21:4
n. shall there be any more pain: for — Re 21:4
sun, *n.* of the moon, to shine in it — Re 21:23
n. whatsoever worketh abomination — Re 21:27
need no candle, *n.* light of the sun — Re 22:5

NEKEB

N. and Jabneel, unto Lahum — Jos 19:33

NEKODA

children of *N.* — Ezr 2:48; 2:60; Ne 7:50, 62

NEMUEL

sons of Eliab; *N.* and Dathan — Nu 26:9
of *N.*, the family of Nemuelites — Nu 26:12
sons of Simeon, *N.* and Jamin — 1Ch 4:24

NEMUELITES

the family of the *N.* — Nu 26:12

NEPHEG

sons of Izhar; Koran, and *N.* — Ex 6:21
and Elishua, and *N.* — 2Sa 5:15
Nogah, and *N.* — 1Ch 3:7; 14:6

NEPHEW

he shall neither have son nor *n.* — Job 18:19
son or grandson (A)(E) — Job 18:19
no offspring or descendant (B)(R) — Job 18:19
I will cut off from Babylon son and *n.* — Isa 14:22
son or son's son (A)(B)(E) — Isa 14:22
offspring and posterity (R) — Isa 14:22

NEPHEWS

Abdon had forty sons and thirty *n.* — J'g 12:14
thirty grandsons (B)(E)(R) — J'g 12:14
if any widow have children or *n.* — 1Ti 5:4
children or grandchildren (A)(B)(E)(N)(P)(R) — 1Ti 5:4

NEPHISH

Hagarites, with Jetur, and *N.* — 1Ch 5:19

NEPHISHESIM

the children of *N.* — Ne 7:52

NEPHTHALIM

the borders of Zabulon and *N.* — M't 4:13
the land of *N.*, by the way of — M't 4:15
N. were sealed twelve thousand — Re 7:6

NEPHTOAH

fountain of the water of *N.* — Jos 15:9
out of well of waters of *N.* — Jos 18:15

NEPHUSIM

the children of *N.* — Ezr 2:50

NER

Abner the son of *N.* — 1Sa 14:50; 14:51; 26:5, 14; 2Sa 2:8, 12; 3:23, 25, 28, 37; 1Ki 2:5, 32; 1Ch 8:33; 9:36, 39; 26:28

NEREUS

Salute Philologus, and Julia, *N.* — Ro 16:15

NERGAL

the men of Cuth made *N.* — 2Ki 17:30

NERGAL-SHAREZER

in the middle gate, even *N.* — Jer 39:3; 39:13

NERI

which was the son of *N.* — Lu 3:27

NERIAH

Baruch the son of *N.* — Jer 32:12; 32:16; 36:4, 8, 14, 32; 43:3, 6; 45:1
commanded Seraiah the son of *N.* — Jer 51:59

NERVES

health to *n.* and sinews (A) — Pr 3:8
cut the *n.* of instinctive action (P) — Ro 8:13

NEST

and thou puttest thy *n.* in a rock — Nu 24:21
if a bird's *n.* chance to be before thee — De 22:6
as an eagle stirreth up her *n.* — De 32:11
then I said, I shall die in my *n.* — Job 29:18
doth eagle at thy command make *n.* on high — Job 39:27
the swallow hath found a *n.* for herself — Ps 84:3
as a bird that wandereth from her *n.* — Pr 27:8
hath found as a *n.* the riches of the peop.e — Isa 10:14
as a wandering bird cast out of the *n.* — Isa 16:2
there shall the great owl make her *n.* — Isa 34:15
that makest thy *n.* in the cedars — Jer 22:23
one nestling among the cedars (B) — Jer 22:23
nested among the cedars (R) — Jer 22:23
the dove makes her *n.* in the sides of holes — Jer 48:28
tho' thou make thy *n.* as high as the eagle — Jer 49:16
though thou set thy *n.* among the stars — Ob 4
that he may set his *n.* on high — Hab 2:9
set his seat on high (B) — Hab 2:9

NESTED

n. among the cedars (R) — Jer 22:23

NESTLING

n. among the cedars (B) — Jer 22:23

NESTS

where the birds make their *n.* — Ps 104:17
all the fowls of heaven made their *n.* — Eze 31:6
and the birds of the air have *n.* — M't 8:20
birds have their lodging places (A) — Lu 9:58
wild birds have their roosts (B)(N) — M't 8:20

NET

upon the *n.* shalt thou make four — Ex 27:4
the *n.* may be even to the midst of — Ex 27:5
he is cast into a *n.* by his own feet — Job 18:8
hath compassed me with his *n.* — Job 19:6
in the *n.* which they hid is their — Ps 9:15
when he draweth him into his *n.* — Ps 10:9
he shall pluck my feet out of the *n.* — Ps 25:15
me out of the *n.* that they have laid — Ps 31:4
they hid for me their *n.* in a pit — Ps 35:7
n. that he hath hid catch himself — Ps 35:8

have prepared a *n.* for my steps — Ps 57:6
Thou broughtest us into the *n.* — Ps 66:11
have spread a *n.* by the wayside — Ps 140:5
n. is spread in the sight of any bird — Pr 1:17
wicked desireth the *n.* of evil men — Pr 12:12
spreadeth a *n.* for his feet — Pr 29:5
fishes that are taken in an evil *n.* — Ec 9:12
the streets, as a wild bull in a *n.* — Isa 51:20
he hath spread a *n.* for my feet — La 1:13
My *n.* also will I spread upon him — Eze 12:13
And I will spread my *n.* upon him — Eze 17:20
and spread their *n.* over him — Eze 19:8
I will therefore spread out my *n.* — Eze 32:3
they shall bring thee up in my *n.* — Eze 32:3
and a *n.* spread upon Tabor — Ho 5:1
go, I will spread my *n.* upon them — Ho 7:12
every man his brother with a *n.* — Mic 7:2
they catch them in their *n.* — Hab 1:15
they sacrifice unto their *n.* — Hab 1:16
Shall they therefore empty their *n.* — Hab 1:17
brother, casting a *n.* into the sea — M't 4:18
the kingdom of heaven is like a *n.* — M't 13:47
like a dragnet (A) — M't 13:47
like a seine (B) — M't 13:47
brother, casting a *n.* into the sea — M'k 1:16
at thy word I will let down the *n.* — Lu 5:5
of fishes: and their *n.* break — Lu 5:6
Cast the *n.* on the right side of — Joh 21:6
cubits,) dragging the *n.* with fishes — Joh 21:8
drew the *n.* to the land full of fishes — Joh 21:11
many, yet was not the *n.* broken — Joh 21:11

NETHANEEL

of Issachar; *N.* the son of Zuar — Nu 1:8; 2:5; 7:18, 23; 10:15
N. the fourth, Raddai the fifth — 1Ch 2:14
N., and Amasai, and Zechariah — 1Ch 15:24
Shemaiah the son of *N.* the scribe — 1Ch 24:6
Sacar the fourth, and *N.* the fifth — 1Ch 26:4
to *N.*, and to Michaiah, to teach in — 2Ch 17:7
and Shemaiah and *N.*, his brethren — 2Ch 35:9
Ishmael, *N.*, Jozabad, and Elasah — Ezr 10:22
Hashabiah; of Jedaiah, *N.* — Ne 12:21
N. and Judah, Hanani, with — Ne 12:36

NETHANIAH

even Ishmael the son of *N.* — 2Ki 25:23
month, that Ishmael the son of *N.* — 2Ki 25:25
and *N.*, and Asarelah, the sons of — 1Ch 25:2
The fifth to *N.*, he, his sons — 1Ch 25:12
Levites, even Shemaiah, and *N.* — 2Ch 17:8
princes sent Jehudi the son of *N.* — Jer 36:14
Mizpah, even Ishmael the son of *N.* — Jer 40:8
Ishmael the son of *N.* to slay — Jer 40:14
I will slay Ishmael the son of *N.* — Jer 40:15
Ishmael the son of *N.* the son of — Jer 41:1
arose Ishmael the son *N.*, and the — Jer 41:2; 41:6-7, 9-12, 15-16, 18

NETHER

stood at the *n.* part of the mount — Ex 19:17
at the foot of the mountain (A) — Ex 19:17

at the base of the mountain *Ex 19:17* (B)
take the *n.* or the upper *De 24:6* millstone
upper springs, and the *n.* *Jos 15:19;* springs *J'g 1:15*
upper and lower springs *Jos 15:19* (A)(B)(R)
the coast of Beth-horon the *n.* *Jos 16:3*
the south side of the *n.* *Jos 18:13* Beth-horon
Gezer, and Beth-horon, the *n.* *1Ki 9:17*
lower Beth-horon (A)(B)(R) *1Ki 9:17*
who built Beth-horon the *1Ch 7:24*
the upper, and Beth-horon the *2Ch 8:5* *n.*
hard as a piece of the *n.* *Job 41:24* millstone
death, to the *n.* parts of the *Eze 31:14* earth
death, to the lower world *Eze 31:14* (A)
in the *n.* parts of the earth *Eze 31:16*
Eden unto the *n.* parts of the *Eze 31:18* earth
unto the *n.* parts of the earth *Eze 32:18*
into the *n.* parts of the earth *Eze 32:24*

NETHERMOST

n. chamber was five cubits *1Ki 6:6* broad
the first story side chambers *1Ki 6:6* (A)
the lowest side rooms (B) *1Ki 6:6*
the lowest story (R) *1Ki 6:6*

NETHINIMS

the priests, Levites, and the *N.* *1Ch 9:2*
the temple servants (B)(R) *1Ch 9:2*
The *N.*: the children of Ziha *Ezr 2:43;* *Ne 7:46*
The temple attendants (B) *Ezr 2:43;* 2:58; 7:7, 24; 8:17, 20; Ne 3:26; 10:28; 11:21
The temple servants (R) *Ezr 2:43;* 2:58; 7:7, 24; 8:17, 20; Ne 3:26; 10:28; 11:21
All the *N.*, and the children *Ezr 2:58;* of *Ne 7:60*
and the *N.*, dwelt in their *Ezr 2:70* cities
and the *N.* unto Jerusalem, in *Ezr 7:7*
N., or ministers of this house *Ezr 7:24*
his brethren the *N.*, at the *Ezr 8:17* place
Also of the *N.*, whom David *Ezr 8:20*
two hundred and twenty *N.* *Ezr 8:20*
Moreover the *N.* dwelt in *Ne 3:26* Ophel
Malchiah unto the place of *Ne 3:31* *N.*
people, and the *N.*, and all *Ne 7:73* Israel
the porters, the singers, the *Ne 10:28* *N.*
and the *N.* and the children of *Ne 11:3*
But the *N.* dwelt in Ophel *Ne 11:21*
Ziha and Gispa were over the *Ne 11:21* *N.*

NETOPHAH

The men of *N.* fifty and six *Ezr 2:22*
The men of Beth-lehem and *N.* *Ne 7:26*

NETOPHATHI

and from the village of *N.* *Ne 12:28*

NETOPHATHITE

the Ahohite, Maharai the *N.* *2Sa 23:28*
Heleb the son of Baanah, a *2Sa 23:29* *N.*
the son of Tanhumeth the *N.* *2Ki 25:23*
Maharai the *N.*, Heled the *1Ch 11:30* son
Heled the son of Baanah the *1Ch 11:30* *N.*
tenth month was Maharai *1Ch 27:13* the *N.*
twelfth month was Heldai *1Ch 27:15* the *N.*
sons of Ephai the *N.* and *Jer 40:8* Jezaniah

NETOPHATHITES

of Salma: Beth-lehem, and *1Ch 2:54* the *N.*
dwelt in the villages of the *N.* *1Ch 9:16*

NETS

n. of checker work, and *1Ki 7:17* wreaths
the wicked fall into their own *Ps 141:10* *n.*
whose heart is snares and *n.* *Ec 7:26*
that spread *n.* upon the waters *Isa 19:8*
be a place for the spreading of *Eze 26:5* *n.*
shalt be a place to spread *n.* *Eze 26:14* upon
shall be a place to spread *Eze 47:10* forth *n.*
they straightway left their *n.* *M't 4:20*
their father, mending their *n.* *M't 4:21*
straightway they forsook their *M'k 1:18* *n.*
were in the ship mending *M'k 1:19* their *n.*
them, and were washing their *n.* *Lu 5:2*
and let down your *n.* for a *Lu 5:4* draught

NETTLES

under the *n.* they were *Job 30:7* gathered
n. have covered the face *Pr 24:31* thereof
n. and brambles in the *Isa 34:13* fortresses
their silver, *n.* shall possess *Ho 9:6* them
the breeding of *n.* and saltpits *Zep 2:9*

NETWORK

for it a grate of *n.* of brass *Ex 27:4*
for the altar a brasen grate of *Ex 38:4* *n.*
rows round about upon the *1Ki 7:18* one *n.*
the belly which by the *n.* *1Ki 7:20*
rows of pomegranates for one *1Ki 7:42* *n.*
on each *n.* (A)(B)(E)(R) *2Ch 4:13;* *2Ki 25:17; 2Ch 4:12*
n. and pomegranates upon the *Jer 52:22*
all the pomegranates upon the *Jer 52:23* *n.*

NETWORKS

the two *n.* to cover the two *1Ki 7:41* bowls
pomegranates for the two *n.* *1Ki 7:42* even
the two *n.* (S) *2Ch 4:12; 4:13*
and they that weave *n.* shall be *Isa 19:9*

NEUTRALIZE

n. the one (B) *Heb 2:14*

NEVER

kine, such as I *n.* saw in all *Ge 41:19* Egypt
the fire on the altar shall *n.* go *Le 6:13* out
a red heifer, upon which *n.* *Nu 19:2* came yoke
the poor shall *n.* cease out of *De 15:11* the land
I will *n.* break my covenant with *J'g 2:1* you
is there *n.* a woman among all *J'g 14:3* my people
with seven green withs that *J'g 16:7* were *n.* dried
if bind with new ropes that *n.* *J'g 16:11* were occupied
the sword shall *n.* depart *2Sa 12:10* from thy house
he *n.* prophesied good unto *2Ch 18:7* me
there was *n.* a son left him, *2Ch 21:17* save Jehoahaz
as infants which *n.* saw light *Job 3:16*
and if I make my hands *n.* so *Job 9:30* clean
another *n.* eateth with *Job 21:25* pleasure
hath said, For I shall *n.* be in *Ps 10:6* adversity
he hideth his face, he will *n.* *Ps 10:11* see it
he that doeth these things shall *Ps 15:5* *n.* be moved

in prosperity I said, I shall *n.* *Ps 30:6* be moved
in thee do I trust, let me *n.* be *Ps 31:1* ashamed
shall go up to fathers; they *Ps 49:19* shall *n.* see
Lord will *n.* suffer the *Ps 55:22* righteous to be moved
O Lord, let me *n.* be put to *Ps 71:1* confusion
I will *n.* forget thy precepts, *Ps 119:93* for with them
the righteous shall *n.* be *Pr 10:30* removed
hell and destruction are *n.* *Pr 27:20* full, so the eyes of a man are *n.*
there are three things that are *Pr 30:15* *n.* satisfied
Babylon *n.* be inhabited nor *Isa 13:20* dwelt in
the seed of evil doers shall *n.* *Isa 14:20* be renowned
to be no city, it shall *n.* be *Isa 25:2* built
are greedy dogs which can *n.* *Isa 56:11* have enough
watchmen that shall *n.* hold *Isa 62:6* their peace
we are thine, thou *n.* barest *Isa 63:19* rule over them
their confusion shall *n.* be *Jer 20:11* forgotten
David shall *n.* want a man to *Jer 33:17* sit on throne
and *n.* open thy mouth any *Eze 16:63* more
Tyrus shall *n.* be found *Eze 26:21* again, saith Lord
a terror and *n.* shalt be any *Eze 27:36;* more *28:19*
a kingdom that shall *n.* be *Da 2:44* destroyed
there shall be trouble, such as *Da 12:1* *n.* was
and my people shall *n.* be *Joe 2:26;* ashamed *2:27*
I will *n.* forget any of their *Am 8:7* works
even they shall fall and *n.* rise *Am 8:14* up again
and judgment doth *n.* go forth *Hab 1:4*
I will profess unto them I *n.* *M't 7:23* knew you
saying, It was *n.* so seen in *M't 9:33* Israel
have ye *n.* read, Out of the *M't 21:16;* mouth of babes *21:42; M'k 2:25*
Peter said, Yet will I *n.* be *M't 26:33* offended
and he answered him to *n.* a *M't 27:14* word
saying, We *n.* saw it on this *M'k 2:12* fashion
shall blaspheme against Holy *M'k 3:29* Ghost, hath *n.* forgiveness
into fire that *n.* shall be *M'k 9:43;* quenched *9:45*
colt tied, whereon *n.* man sat *M'k 11:2;* *Lu 19:30*
good for that man if he had *M'k 14:21* *n.* been born
yet thou *n.* gavest me a kid to *Lu 15:29* make
blessed are the wombs that *n.* *Lu 23:29* bare
wherein *n.* man before was *Lu 23:53;* laid *Joh 19:41*
who drinks of water I give, *Joh 4:14* shall *n.* thirst
he that cometh to me shall *n.* *Joh 6:35* hunger, and he that believeth on me shall *n.* thirst
how knoweth this man, having *Joh 7:15* *n.* learned
the officers said, *N.* man spake *Joh 7:46* like this man
and we were *n.* in bondage to *Joh 8:33* any
he shall *n.* see death *Joh 8:51;* *8:52; 10:28; 11:26*
Peter saith, Thou shalt *n.* *Joh 13:8* wash my feet
I have *n.* eaten any thing *Ac 10:14* common
being a cripple, who *n.* had *Ac 14:8* walked
charity *n.* faileth, but whether *1Co 13:8* prophecies
n. able to come to knowledge of *2Ti 3:7* truth

can *n.* with those sacrifices *Heb 10:1*
make perfect
the same sacrifices which can *Heb 10:11*
n. take away sins
I will *n.* leave thee, nor *Heb 13:5*
forsake thee
if ye do these things, ye shall *2Pe 1:10*
n. fall

NEVER SO

to charmers, charming *n. so* *Ps 58:5*
wisely

NEVER SO MUCH

ask me *n. so much* dowry, *Ge 34:12*
and I will give

NEVERTHELESS

n. in the day when I visit, I *Ex 32:34*
will visit
n. these ye shall not eat *Le 11:4;*
De 14:7
n. a fountain or pit shall be *Le 11:36*
clean
n. the people be strong that *Nu 13:28*
dwell
n. the ark of the covenant *Nu 14:44*
departed not
n. the firstborn of man shalt *Nu 18:15*
thou redeem
n. the Kenite shall be wasted, *Nu 24:22*
until Asshur
n. it shall be purified with *Nu 31:23*
water of separation
n. the Lord thy God would not *De 23:5*
hearken
n. children of Israel expelled *Jos 13:13*
not Geshur
n. my brethren that went up *Jos 14:8*
with me
n. the inhabitants of *J'g 1:33*
Beth-shemesh
n. the Lord raised up judges to *J'g 2:16*
deliver them
n. the people refused to obey *1Sa 8:19*
Samuel
to see Saul, *n.* Samuel *1Sa 15:35*
mourned for Saul
n. Saul spake not any thing *1Sa 20:26*
that day
said to David, *N.* the lords *1Sa 29:6*
favour thee not
n. David took the strong hold *2Sa 5:7*
of Zion
n. a lad saw them, and told *2Sa 17:18*
Absalom
n. he would not drink *2Sa 23:16*
thereof, poured out
n. thou shalt not build the *1Ki 8:19*
house
n. for David's sake did the *1Ki 15:4*
Lord give
n. Asa his heart was perfect *1Ki 15:14*
with the Lord
n. in his old age he was *1Ki 15:23*
diseased in his feet
n. the high places were not *1Ki 22:43*
taken away
n. if thou see me when I am *2Ki 2:10*
taken
n. he cleaved to the sins of *2Ki 3:3*
Jeroboam
n. they departed not from the *2Ki 13:6*
sins of Jeroboam
n. the priests of the high *2Ki 23:9*
places came not
n. David took the castle of *1Ch 11:5*
Zion
n. the king's word prevailed *1Ch 21:4*
against Joab
n. they shall be his servants *2Ch 12:8*
n. the heart of Asa was *2Ch 15:17*
perfect all his days
n. there are good things found *2Ch 19:3*
in thee
n. divers of Asher humbled *2Ch 30:11*
themselves
n. the people did sacrifice in *2Ch 33:17*
the high places
n. Josiah would not turn *2Ch 35:22*
from him
n. we made our prayer to our *Ne 4:9*
God
n. they were disobedient and *Ne 9:26*
rebelled against thee
n. for thy mercies' sake thou *Ne 9:31*
didst not consume

n. him did outlandish women *Ne 13:26*
cause to sin
n. Haman refrained himself *Es 5:10*
n. thou heardest my *Ps 31:22*
supplication
n. man being in honour, *Ps 49:12*
abideth not
n. I am continually with thee, *Ps 73:23*
hast holden
n. they did flatter him with *Ps 78:36*
their mouth
n. my lovingkindness not take *Ps 89:33*
from him
n. he saved them for his *Ps 106:8*
name's sake
n. he regarded their affliction, *Ps 106:44*
heard their cry
n. the counsel of the Lord *Pr 19:21*
shall stand
n. the poor man's wisdom is *Ec 9:16*
despised
n. the dimness shall not be such *Isa 9:1*
as was
n. in those days I will make a *Jer 5:18*
full end
n. in the hand of Ahikam was *Jer 26:24*
with Jeremiah
n. hear thou this word that I *Jer 28:7*
speak in thy ears
n. Elnathan and Delaiah *Jer 36:25*
made intercession
n. if thou warn the righteous *Eze 3:21*
man
n. I will remember my *Eze 16:60*
covenant with thee
n. mine eye spared them *Eze 20:17*
from destroying
n. I withdrew my hand, and *Eze 20:22*
wrought for my
n. leave the stump of his roots *Da 4:15*
in earth
n. the man rowed hard to *Jon 1:13*
bring to land
n. for the oath's sake he *M't 14:9*
commanded it
from me, *n.* not as I will, but *M't 26:39*
as thou wilt
n. hereafter ye shall see the *M't 26:64*
Son of man coming
n. not what I will *M'k 14:36; Lu 22:42*
n. at thy word I will let down *Lu 5:5*
the net
n. I must walk to-day and *Lu 13:33*
to-morrow
n. when Son of man cometh *Lu 18:8*
shall he find faith
nevertheless (S) *Joh 6:23; 16:13*
Lazarus is dead, *n.* let us go *Joh 11:15*
to him
n. among the chief rulers *Joh 12:42*
many believed
n. I tell you the truth, it is *Joh 16:7*
expedient for you
n. he left not himself without *Ac 14:17*
witness
n. the centurion believed the *Ac 27:11*
master of ship
n. death reigned from Adam to *Ro 5:14*
Moses
n. I have written more boldly *Ro 15:15*
to you
n. to avoid fornication let *1Co 7:2*
every man have
n. such shall have trouble in *1Co 7:28*
the flesh
n. he that standeth stedfast in *1Co 7:37*
his heart
n. we have not used this *1Co 9:12*
power
n. neither is the man without *1Co 11:11*
the woman
n. when it shall turn to the *2Co 3:16*
Lord
n. God that comforteth those *2Co 7:6*
that are cast down
n. being crafty, I caught you *2Co 12:16*
with guile
n. I live, yet not I, but Christ *Ga 2:20*
in me
n. what saith scripture, cast out *Ga 4:30*
bondwoman
n. let every man so love his *Eph 5:33*
wife as himself
n. to abide in the flesh is *Ph'p 1:24*
more needful
n. whereto we have already *Ph'p 3:16*
attained

n. I am not ashamed, for I *2Ti 1:12*
know whom
n. the foundation of God *2Ti 2:19*
standeth sure
n. it yieldeth peaceable fruit *Heb 12:11*
of righteousness
n. we look for new heavens *2Pe 3:13*
and earth
n. I have somewhat against thee *Re 2:4*

NEW

changes of *n.* suits (B) *Ge 45:22*
there arose up a *n.* king over *Ex 1:8*
Egypt
offer a *n.* meat offering *Le 23:16;*
Nu 28:26
shall bring forth the old, *Le 26:10*
because of the *n.*
but if the Lord make a *n.* *Nu 16:30*
thing
what man hath built a *n.* *De 20:5;*
house *22:8*
when taken a *n.* wife, he shall *De 24:5*
not go to war
they sacrificed to devils, to *n.* *De 32:17*
gods
and these bottles of wine were *Jos 9:13*
n.
they chose *n.* gods, then was war *J'g 5:8*
in gates
they bound him with *n.* cords *J'g 15:13;*
16:11-12
make a *n.* cart, and take two *1Sa 6:7*
kine
set the ark on a *n.* cart *2Sa 6:3;*
1Ch 13:7
he being girded with a *n.* *2Sa 21:16*
sword thought
Jeroboam clad with a *n.* *1Ki 11:29*
garment
Ahijah caught the *n.* garment, *1Ki 11:30*
and rent it
bring a *n.* cruse, and put salt *2Ki 2:20*
therein
Jehoshaphat stood in the *n.* *2Ch 20:5*
court
it is ready to burst like *n.* *Job 32:19*
bottles
sing to him a *n.* song *Ps 33:3;*
96:1; 98:1; 144:9; 149:1; Isa 42:10
he hath put a *n.* song in my *Ps 40:3*
mouth, even praise
there is no *n.* thing under the *Ec 1:9*
sun
is any thing whereof may be *Ec 1:10*
said, this is *n.*
are all pleasant fruits, *n.* and *Ca 7:13*
old
behold, *n.* things do I declare *Isa 42:9;*
48:6
behold, I will do a *n.* thing, *Isa 43:19*
make a way
and thou shalt be called by a *Isa 62:2*
n. name
I create *n.* heavens and a *n.* *Isa 65:17;*
earth *66:22*
the *n.* gate of the Lord's *Jer 26:10;*
house *36:10*
the Lord hath created a *n.* *Jer 31:22*
thing in the earth
the Lord's mercies are *n.* every *La 3:23*
morning
I will put a *n.* spirit within *Eze 11:19;*
you *36:26*
and make you a *n.* heart and *Eze 18:31*
a *n.* spirit
trees which shall bring forth *Eze 47:12*
n. fruit
putteth piece of *n.* cloth to an *M't 9:16;*
old garment *M'k 2:21; Lu 5:36*
put *n.* wine into *n.* bottles *M't 9:17;*
M'k 2:22; Lu 5:38
bringeth out of his treasure *M't 13:52*
things *n.* and old
this is my blood of the *n.* *M't 26:28;*
testament *M'k 14:24; Lu 22:20;*
1Co 11:25
until I drink it *n.* with you *M't 26:29;*
M'k 14:25
Joseph laid the body in his *M't 27:60*
own *n.* tomb
saying, What *n.* doctrine is *M'k 1:27*
this
they shall speak with *n.* *M'k 16:17*
tongues
a *n.* commandment I give *Joh 13:34*
unto you
a *n.* sepulchre, wherein was *Joh 19:41*
never man laid

may we know what this *n.*   *Ac 17:19*
doctrine is
but either to tell or to hear   *Ac 17:21*
some *n.* thing
purge out, that ye may be a *n.*   *1Co 5:7*
lump
made us able ministers of the   *2Co 3:6*
n. testament
if any man be in Christ, he is   *2Co 5:17*
a *n.* creature, all things are *n.*
nor uncircumcision, but a *n.*   *Ga 6:15*
creature
of twain, one *n.* man, so   *Eph 2:15*
making peace
and that ye put on the *n.* man *Eph 4:24;*
   Col 3:10
he is the Mediator of the *n.*   *Heb 9:15*
testament
by a *n.* and living way hath *Heb 10:20*
consecrated
we look for *n.* heavens and a *2Pe 3:13*
n. earth
I write no *n.* commandment   *1Jo 2:7*
unto you
a *n.* commandment I write unto *1Jo 2:8*
you
not as though I wrote a *n.*   *2Jo 5*
commandment
n. name written, which no man *Re 2:17*
knoweth
n. Jerusalem   *Re 3:12; 21:2*
write my *n.* name   *Re 3:12*
and they sung a *n.* song, saying *Re 5:9;*
   14:3
I saw a *n.* heaven and a *n.*   *Re 21:1*
earth
he said, Behold, I make all   *Re 21:5*
things *n.*

NEW WINE

shall bring offering of the *n.*   *Ne 10:39*
wine
prepare chamber where *n.* wine *Ne 13:5*
was laid
brought tithe of *n.* wine unto *Ne 13:12*
the treasuries
thy presses shall burst out with *Pr 3:10*
n. wine
n. wine mourneth, the vine   *Isa 24:7*
languisheth
as the *n.* wine is found in the *Isa 65:8*
cluster
wine and *n.* wine take away   *Ho 4:11*
the heart
and the *n.* wine shall fail in her *Ho 9:2*
the *n.* wine is cut off; *n.* wine *Joe 1:5;*
is dried up   *1:10*
mountains shall drop *n.* wine *Joe 3:18*
I called for a drought on the *Hag 1:11*
n. wine
n. wine shall make the maids *Zec 9:17*
cheerful
put *n.* wine into old bottles;   *M't 9:17;*
n. wine into new bottles   *M'k 2:22;*
   Lu 5:37
others said, These men are full *Ac 2:13*
of *n.* wine

NEWBORN

As *n.* babes desire the sincere *1Pe 2:2*

NEWLY

sacrificed to new gods that   *De 32:17*
came *n.* up
they had but *n.* set the watch *J'g 7:19*

NEWESS

even so we also should walk in *Ro 6:4*
n. of life
we should serve in *n.* of spirit, *Ro 7:6*
not oldness

NEWS

told the *n.* (A)   *1Sa 11:4;*
2Sa 4:4; 18:20, 25-26, 31; 1Ki 2:28;
   1Ch 10:9; Jer 37:5
to carry good *n.* (R)   *1Sa 31:9*
when the *n.* (R)   *2Sa 4:4;*
   18:20
the good *n.* (A)   *2Sa 4:10;*
1Ki 1:42; 2Ki 7:9; Isa 41:27; Lu 1:19;
   2:10; 8:1; Ac 13:32; 1Th 3:6
the good *n.* (B)   *2Sa 4:10;*
18:19, 31; 1Ki 1:42; 2Ki 7:9; 1Ch 10:9;
   Isa 41:27; Lu 2:10; 8:1

good *n.* (R)   *2Sa 4:10*
1Ki 1:42; 2Ki 7:9; 1Ch 10:9; Lu 1:19;
2:10; 8:1; Ac 13:32; Ro 10:15; 1Th 3:6
the *n.* (B)   *2Sa 18:20;*
   18:22, 25-26; Jer 20:15; 37:5
the heavy *n.* (A)(B)   *1Ki 14:6*
who hear the *n.* (A)(R)   *Ne 3:19*
told the good *n.* (R)   *Ps 40:9*
proclaimed the good *n.* (B)   *Ps 68:11*
so is good *n.* from a far   *Pr 25:25*
country
the *n.* (R)   *Jer 20:15; 35:5; Ac 11:22*
the bad *n.* (A)   *Jer 49:23*
announcing good *n.* (B)   *M't 4:23; 4:24*
proclaiming good *n.* (A)(P)   *M't 9:35*
poor hearing good *n.* (N)   *M't 11:5*
proclaim good *n.* (N)(P)   *M't 16:15*
believe the good *n.* (B)(P)   *M'k 1:15*
spread the good *n.* (N)   *M'k 5:20*
the good *n.* (N)   *Lu 1:19;*
2:10; 8:1; Ro 10:15; 1Th 3:6
the good *n.* (P)   *Lu 1:19; 8:1;*
   Ac 13:32
the glorious *n.* (P)   *Lu 2:10*
announce good *n.* (N)   *Lu 4:18*
proclaimed good *n.* (P)   *Ac 8:12*
announcing good *n.* (A)   *Ac 10:36*
n. of this reached (N)   *Ac 11:22*
to bring good *n.* (N)(P)   *Ac 16:10*
to attest the good *n.* (A)   *Ac 20:24*
publish good *n.* (B)(N)   *Ro 10:15*
carrying out good *n.* (A)   *Ro 15:19*
the definite *n.* (P)   *1Th 3:6*

NEXT

Sarah shall bear at this set   *Ge 17:21*
time *n.* year
let him and his neighbour *n.*   *Ex 12:4*
take a lamb
stood up all the *n.* day and   *Nu 11:32*
gathered
ye shall give inheritance to   *Nu 27:11*
his kinsman *n.*
the city which is *n.* to the slain *De 21:3*
man
the elders of the city *n.* to the *De 21:6*
slain man
the man is one of our *n.*   *Ru 2:20*
kinsmen
next (S)   *1Sa 5:4; 18:10; 2Sa 11:12*
thou king, and I shall be *n.*   *1Sa 23:17*
to thee
David smote them to the   *1Sa 30:17*
evening of *n.* day
Elkanah that was *n.* to the   *2Ch 28:7*
king
Mordecai was *n.* to king   *Es 10:3*
Ahasuerus
shall be *n.* to the oblation   *Eze 48:18*
(S)
a worm the *n.* day smote the   *Jon 4:7*
gourd
the *n.* day that followed the *M't 27:62*
preparation
he said, Let us go into the *n.*   *M'k 1:38*
towns
the *n.* day John seeth Jesus   *Joh 1:29*
coming
they put them in hold unto the *Ac 4:3*
n. day
the *n.* day Moses shewed   *Ac 7:26*
himself to them
that these words be preached *Ac 13:42;*
n. sabbath   *13:44*
whose house was *n.* to (S)   *Ac 18:7*

NEZIAH

children of N.   *Ezr 2:54; Ne 7:56*

NEZIB

and Ashnah, and N.   *Jos 15:43*

NIBHAZ

the Avites made N. and   *2Ki 17:31*
Tartak

NIBSHAN

And N., and the city of Salt *Jos 15:62*

NICANOR

they chose Stephen, Philip, and *Ac 6:5*
N.

NICODEMUS

N. a ruler of the Jews came to   *Joh 3:1*
Jesus
N. came to Jesus by night   *Joh 7:50;*
   19:39

NICOLAITANES

that thou hatest the deeds of the *Re 2:6*
N.
hast them that hold the   *Re 2:15*
doctrine of the N.

NICOLAS

N. a proselyte of Antioch   *Ac 6:5*

NICOPOLIS

be diligent to come unto me to *Tit 3:12*
N.

NIGER

at Antioch, Simeon who was   *Ac 13:1*
called N.

NIGH

time drew *n.* that Israel must *Ge 47:29*
die
Draw not *n.* hither: put off thy *Ex 3:5*
when Pharaoh drew *n.* the   *Ex 14:10*
children
Lord: but they shall not come *Ex 24:2*
n.
soon as he came *n.* unto the   *Ex 32:19*
camp
they were afraid to come *n.*   *Ex 34:30*
all the children of Israel came *Ex 34:32*
n.
be sanctified in them that come *Le 10:3*
n.
sister a virgin, that is *n.* unto   *Le 21:3*
him
shall come *n.* to offer the   *Le 21:21*
offerings
not come *n.* to offer the bread *Le 21:21*
of
nor come *n.* unto the altar   *Le 21:23*
any that is *n.* of kin unto him *Le 25:49*
stranger that cometh *n.* shall   *Nu 1:51;*
be   *3:10; 3:38*
children of Israel come *n.* unto *Nu 8:19*
they shall not come *n.* the   *Nu 18:3*
vessels
a stranger shall not come *n.*   *Nu 18:4*
unto
stranger that cometh *n.* shall   *Nu 18:7*
be
come *n.* the tabernacle of the *Nu 18:22*
I shall behold him, but not   *Nu 24:17*
n.: there
unto all the places *n.* thereunto *De 1:7*
when thou comest *n.* over   *De 2:19*
against
who hath God so *n.* unto them *De 4:7*
n. unto thee, or far off from   *De 13:7*
thee
when ye are come *n.* unto the *De 20:2*
battle
thou comest *n.* unto a city to *De 20:10*
fight
if thy brother be not *n.* unto   *De 22:2*
thee
But the word is very *n.* unto *De 30:14*
thee
went up, and drew *n.* and   *Jos 8:11*
came
came and drew *n.* to meet   *1Sa 17:48*
David
Joab drew *n.* and the people *2Sa 10:13*
approached ye so *n.* unto the *2Sa 11:20*
city
why went ye *n.* the wall? then *2Sa 11:21*
say
any man came *n.* to him to do *2Sa 15:5*
him
the days of David drew *n.* that   *1Ki 2:1*
be *n.* unto the Lord our God   *1Ki 8:59*
day and
Moreover they that were *n.* *1Ch 12:40*
them
drew *n.* before the Syrians *1Ch 19:14*
unto
king Ahasuerus, both *n.* and far *Es 9:20*
they shall not come *n.* unto him *Ps 32:6*
n. unto them that are of a   *Ps 34:18*
broken

Draw *n.* unto my soul, and	Ps 69:18
gone; my steps had well *n.*	Ps 73:2
slipped	
his salvation is *n.* them that	Ps 85:9
fear	
my life draweth *n.* unto the	Ps 88:3
grave	
but it shall not come *n.* thee	Ps 91:7
any plague come *n.* thy	Ps 91:10
dwelling	
draw *n.* that follow after	Ps 119:150
mischief	
n. unto all them that call	Ps 145:18
upon him	
come not *n.* the door of her	Pr 5:8
house	
nor the years draw *n.* when	Ec 12:1
thou	
of the Holy One of Israel draw	Isa 5:19
n.	
Lord cometh, for it is *n.* at	Joe 2:1
hand	
draweth *n.* unto me with their	M't 15:8
came *n.* unto the sea of	M't 15:29
Galilee	
when they drew *n.* unto	M't 21:1
Jerusalem	
ye know that summer is *n.*	M't 24:32
not come *n.* unto him for the	M'k 2:4
press	
there was *n.* unto the	M'k 5:11
mountains	
him: and he was *n.* unto the	M'k 5:21
sea	
And when they came *n.* to	M'k 11:1
Jerusalem	
come to pass, know that it is	M'k 13:29
n.	
when he came *n.* to the gate of	Lu 7:12
kingdom of God is come *n.*	Lu 10:9;
unto	10:11
as he came and drew *n.* to the	Lu 15:25
house	
as he was come *n.* unto	Lu 18:35
Jericho	
because he was *n.* to	Lu 19:11
Jerusalem	
when he was come *n.* to	Lu 19:29
Bethphage	
when he was come *n.* even now	Lu 19:37
that the desolation thereof is	Lu 21:20
n.	
for your redemption draweth	Lu 21:28
n.	
that summer is now *n.* at	Lu 21:30
hand	
the kingdom of God is *n.* at	Lu 21:31
hand	
feast of unleavened bread drew	Lu 22:1
n.	
And they drew *n.* unto the	Lu 24:28
village	
a feast of the Jews, was *n.*	Joh 6:4
sea, and drawing *n.* unto the	Joh 6:19
ship	
n. unto the place where they	Joh 6:23
Bethany was *n.* unto	Joh 11:18
Jerusalem	
the Jews' passover was *n.* at	Joh 11:55
hand	
Jesus was crucified *n.* to the	Joh 19:20
city	
for the sepulchre was *n.* at	Joh 19:42
hand	
the time of the promise drew *n.*	Ac 7:17
as Lydda was *n.* to Joppa, and	Ac 9:38
drew *n.* unto the city, Peter	Ac 10:9
went	
was come *n.* unto Damascus	Ac 22:6
about	
n. whereunto was the city of	Ac 27:8
Lasea	
The word is *n.* thee, even in	Ro 10:8
thy	
are made *n.* by the blood of	Eph 2:13
Christ	
afar off, and to them that	Eph 2:17
were *n.*	
indeed he was sick *n.* unto	Ph'p 2:27
death	
work of Christ he was *n.*	Ph'p 2:30
unto death	
rejected, and is *n.* unto cursing	Heb 6:8
by the which we draw *n.* unto	Heb 7:19
God	
Draw *n.* to God, and he will	Jas 4:8
draw *n.*	
the coming of the Lord draweth	Jas 5:8
n.	

NIGHT

the light day, and the darkness	Ge 1:5
he called *n.*	
let there be lights, to divide the	Ge 1:14
day from *n.*	
he made the lesser light to rule	Ge 1:16
the *n.*	
tarry all *n.*	Ge 19:2;
	Nu 22:19; J'g 19:6, 9
where are men which came in	Ge 19:5
to thee this *n.*	
they made him drink wine	Ge 19:33;
that *n.*	19:34-35
tarried all *n.*	Ge 24:54;
	28:11; 31:54; 32:13, 21
the Lord appeared to Isaac	Ge 26:24
the same *n.*	
Rachel said, He shall lie	Ge 30:15;
with thee to-*n.*	30:16
dreamed each man his dream	Ge 40:5;
in one *n.*	41:11
God spake to Israel in visions	Ge 46:2
of the *n.*	
and at *n.* he shall divide the	Ge 49:27
spoil	
eat the flesh in that *n.* roast	Ex 12:8
with fire	
I will pass through the land of	Ex 12:12
Egypt this *n.*	
a *n.* to be much observed, this	Ex 12:42
is that *n.* of the	
the one came not near the	Ex 14:20
other all *n.*	
the burning on the altar all *n.*	Le 6:9
the wages shall not abide with	Le 19:13
thee all *n.*	
the people stood up all that *n.*	Nu 11:32
and the people wept that *n.*	Nu 14:1
and murmured	
he said to them, Lodge here	Nu 22:8;
this *n.*	22:19
God came to Balaam at *n.*	Nu 22:20
and said to him	
there shall no leavened bread	De 16:4
remain all *n.*	
his body shall not remain all	De 21:23
n. on the tree	
there came men in hither to-*n.*	Jos 2:2
of Israel	
God did so that *n.* for it was	J'g 6:40
dry on fleece	
laid wait for him all *n.* and	J'g 16:2
were quiet all *n.*	
but the man would not tarry	J'g 19:10
that *n.*	
and abused her all the *n.* until	J'g 19:25
the morning	
if I should have an husband	Ru 1:12
also to-*n.*	
behold, Boaz winnoweth barley	Ru 3:2
to *n.*	
and Samuel cried to the Lord	1Sa 15:11
all *n.*	
tell what the Lord hath said	1Sa 15:16
to me this *n.*	
and David fled and escaped	1Sa 19:10
that *n.*	
saying, If thou save not thy	1Sa 19:11
life to *n.*	
Saul rose up and went away	1Sa 28:25
that *n.*	
the men of Jabesh went all *n.*	1Sa 31:12
and took	
Abner and his men walked all	2Sa 2:29
n.	
Joab and his men went all *n.*	2Sa 2:32
and came	
and gat them away through the	2Sa 4:7
plain all *n.*	
David went and lay all *n.* on	2Sa 12:16
the earth	
I will arise and pursue after	2Sa 17:1
David this *n.*	
saying, Lodge not this *n.* in	2Sa 17:16
the plain	
there will not tarry one with	2Sa 19:7
thee this *n.*	
that *n.* the angel of the Lord	2Ki 19:35
smote	
that *n.* did God appear to	2Ch 1:7
Solomon	
on that *n.* could not the king	Es 6:1
sleep	
let the *n.* perish in which it was	Job 3:3
said	
let that *n.* be solitary; the	Job 3:7;
visions of the *n.*	4:13
when shall I arise, and the *n.*	Job 7:4
be gone	

and the dew lay all *n.* on my	Job 29:19
branch	
desire not the *n.* when people	Job 36:20
are cut off	
all the *n.* make I my bed to swim	Ps 6:6
and *n.* unto *n.* sheweth	Ps 19:2
knowledge	
weeping may endure for a *n.*	Ps 30:5
but joy	
and meditate on thee in the *n.*	Ps 63:6
watches	
he led them all *n.* with a light	Ps 78:14
of fire	
to shew forth thy faithfulness	Ps 92:2
every *n.*	
thou makest darkness, and it	Ps 104:20
is *n.*	
even the *n.* shall be light	Ps 139:11
about me	
passing in the black and dark *n.*	Pr 7:9
she ariseth also while it is yet	Pr 31:15
n.	
he shall lie all *n.* between my	Ca 1:13
breasts	
and my locks with the drops of	Ca 5:2
the *n.*	
continue until *n.* till wine	Isa 5:11
inflame them	
take counsel, make thy shadow	Isa 16:3
as the *n.*	
the *n.* of my pleasure he turned	Isa 21:4
into fear	
watchman, what of the *n.*?	Isa 21:11
what of the *n.*	
the morning cometh, and also	Isa 21:12
the *n.*	
shall be as a dream of a *n.*	Isa 29:7
vision	
the *n.* monster (A)(B)(E)	Isa 34:14
the *n.* hag (R)	Isa 34:14
that turneth aside to tarry for	Jer 14:8
a *n.*	
the secret was revealed in a *n.*	Da 2:19
vision	
in that *n.* was Belshazzar the	Da 5:30
king slain	
then the king passed the *n.*	Da 6:18
fasting	
their baker sleepeth all the *n.*	Ho 7:6
howl, come, lie all *n.* in	Joe 1:13
sackcloth	
that maketh the day dark with	Am 5:8
n.	
which came up in a *n.*	Jon 4:10
perished in a *n.*	
therefore *n.* shall be to you,	Mic 3:6
shall be dark	
in fourth watch of *n.* Jesus	M't 14:25;
went to them walking on sea	M'k 6:48
all ye shall be offended,	M't 26:31;
because of me this *n.*	M'k 14:27
this *n.* before cock crow,	M't 26:34
thou shalt deny me	
we have toiled all *n.* and taken	Lu 5:5
nothing	
he continued all *n.* in prayer to	Lu 6:12
God	
this *n.* thy soul shall be	Lu 12:20
required of thee	
in that *n.* two shall be in one	Lu 17:34
bed	
at *n.* he went out and abode	Lu 21:37
in mount	
the *n.* cometh when no man	Joh 9:4
can work	
he immediately went out, and	Joh 13:30
it was *n.*	
and that *n.* they caught	Joh 21:3
nothing	
the same *n.* Peter was sleeping,	Ac 12:6
bound	
he took them the same hour	Ac 16:33
of the *n.*	
the *n.* following the Lord	Ac 23:11
stood by him	
make ready soldiers at third	Ac 23:23
hour of the *n.*	
stood by me this *n.* the angel	Ac 27:23
of God	
the *n.* is far spent, the day is	Ro 13:12
at hand	
the same *n.* in which he was	1Co 11:23
betrayed	
we are not of the *n.* nor of	1Th 5:5
darkness	
there shall be no *n.* there	Re 21:25; 22:5

NIGHT *HAWK*

owl and *n. hawk* ye shall not	Le 11:16;
eat	De 4:15

NIGHT *WATCHES*

when I meditate on thee in the *Ps 63:6*
n. watches
mine eyes prevent the n. *Ps 119:148*
watches to meditate

BY NIGHT

God came to Abimelech in a *Ge 20:3*
dream by n.
God came to Laban in a *Ge 31:24*
dream by n.
whether stolen by day, or *Ge 31:39*
stolen by n.
the drought consumed me, *Ge 31:40*
and the frost by n.
he called for Moses and *Ex 12:31*
Aaron by n.
Lord went before them by n. *Ex 13:21;*
in a pillar of fire *13:22; 14:20; 40:38;*
Ne 9:12
and the appearance of fire by *Nu 9:16*
n.
whether cloud was taken up by *Nu 9:21*
day or by n.
in fire by n. to shew you the *De 1:33*
way
God brought you forth out of *De 16:1*
Egypt by n.
by uncleanness that chanceth *De 23:10*
him by n.
and Joshua sent them away by *Jos 8:3*
n.
and so it was that he did it by *J'g 6:27*
n.
up by n. thou and thy people *J'g 9:32*
with thee
and beset the house round *J'g 20:5*
about by n.
go down after the Philistines *1Sa 14:36*
by n.
David and Abishai came to *1Sa 26:7*
the people by n.
Saul came to the woman by n. *1Sa 28:8*
and said
nor the beasts of the field by *2Sa 21:10*
n.
Lord appeared to Solomon by *1Ki 3:5;*
n. *2Ch 7:12*
came by n. and compassed the *2Ki 6:14*
city
rose by n. and smote *2Ki 8:21;*
Edomites *2Ch 21:9*
all the men of war fled by n. *2Ki 25:4;*
Jer 52:7
thou shalt not be afraid of *Ps 91:5*
terror by n.
nor shall the moon smite thee *Ps 121:6*
by n.
that by n. stand in the house *Ps 134:1*
of the Lord
moon and stars to rule by n. *Ps 136:9;*
Jer 31:35
her candle goeth not out by n. *Pr 31:18*
by n. on my bed I sought him *Ca 3:1*
whom
the shining of a flaming fire by *Isa 4:5*
n.
let us go by n. and destroy her *Jer 6:5*
palaces
they fled, and went forth out *Jer 39:4*
of the city by n.
if thieves by n. they will *Jer 49:9*
destroy till have
I saw in my vision by n. and *Da 7:2*
behold
if thieves came to thee, if robbers *Ob 5*
by n.
took the young child and his *M't 2:14*
mother by n.
lest his disciples come by n. *M't 27:64;*
and steal *28:13*
keeping watch over their flock *Lu 2:8*
by n.
Nicodemus came to Jesus by *Joh 3:2;*
n. *19:39*
the angel by n. opened the *Ac 5:19*
prison doors
they took Paul by n. and let *Ac 9:25*
him down
sent away Paul and Silas by *Ac 17:10*
n. to Berea

IN THE NIGHT

Pharaoh and his servants rose *Ex 12:30*
in the n.

when the dew fell on the camp *Nu 11:9*
in the n.
and this woman's child died in *1Ki 3:19*
the n.
and the king arose in the n. *2Ki 7:12*
and said
I arose in the n.; I went up in *Ne 2:12;*
the n. *2:15*
that in the n. they may be a *Ne 4:22*
guard to us
yea, in the n. will they come to *Ne 6:10*
slay thee
and grope in the noonday, as *Job 5:14*
in the n.
in the n. the murderer is as a *Job 24:14*
thief
a tempest stealeth him away *Job 27:20*
in the n.
and he overturneth them in *Job 34:25*
the n.
where is God, who giveth *Job 35:10*
songs in the n.
my reins instruct me in the n. *Ps 16:7*
seasons
thou hast visited me in the n. *Ps 17:3*
and tried me
I cry in the n. season, and am *Ps 22:2*
not silent
and in the n. his song shall be *Ps 42:8*
with me
my sore ran in the n. and *Ps 77:2*
ceased not
I call to remembrance my song *Ps 77:6*
in the n.
a thousand years are but as a *Ps 90:4*
watch in the n.
he spread a fire to give light *Ps 105:39*
in the n.
I have remembered thy name *Ps 119:55*
in the n.
his heart taketh not rest in the *Ec 2:23*
n.
hath his sword because of fear *Ca 3:8*
in the n.
in the n. Ar and Kir of Moab *Isa 15:1*
is laid waste
with my soul have I desired *Isa 26:9*
thee in the n.
ye shall have a song as in the *Isa 30:29*
n.
we stumble at noonday as in *Isa 59:10*
shall be cast out in the n. to *Jer 36:30*
the frost
she weepeth sore in the n.; cry *La 1:2;*
out in the n. *2:19*
the prophet shall fall with thee *Ho 4:5*
in the n.
if a man walk in the n. he *Joh 11:10*
stumbleth
a vision appeared to Paul in *Ac 16:9;*
the n. *18:9*
day cometh as a thief in the n. *1Th 5:2;*
2Pe 3:10
they that sleep, sleep in the n. *1Th 5:7*
are drunken in the n.

NIGHTS

forty days and forty n. *Ge 7:4;*
7:12; Ex 24:18; 34:28; De 9:9, 11, 18,
25; 10:10; 1Ki 19:8; M't 4:2
three days and three n. *1Sa 30:12;*
Jon 1:17; M't 12:40
ground seven days and seven n. *Job 2:1*
wearisome n. are appointed to *Job 7:3*
me
I am set in my ward whole n. *Isa 21:8*

NILE

rises like the N. *Jer 46:7;*
(A)(B)(E)(R) *46:8; Am 8:8; 9:5*

NIMRAH

N., and Heshbon *Nu 32:3*

NIMRIM

the waters of N. *Isa 15:6; Jer 48:34*

NIMROD

Cush begat N.; he began *Ge 10:8*
N. the mighty hunter before *Ge 10:9*
land of N. in the entrances *Mic 5:6*
thereof

NIMSHI

the son of N., shalt thou *1Ki 19:16*
anoint
Jehoshaphat the son of N. *2Ki 9:2; 9:14*
the driving of Jehu the son of *2Ki 9:20*
N.
against Jehu the son of N. *2Ch 22:7*

NINE

on fifth day n. bullocks, two *Nu 29:26*
rams
which the Lord commanded *Nu 34:13;*
to give n. tribes *Jos 13:7; 14:2*
Og's bedstead was n. cubits in *De 3:11*
length
Joab came to Jerusalem at *2Sa 24:8*
end of n. months
and n. parts to dwell in other *Ne 11:1*
cities
ten cleansed, but where are *Lu 17:17*
the n.
at n. tonight (A)(B)(N)(P) *Ac 23:23*

NINETEEN

there lacked of David's *2Sa 2:30*
servants n. men

NINETEENTH

in n. year of Nebuchadnezzar *2Ki 25:8;*
the house of *Jer 52:12*

NINETY

Enos lived n. years, and begat *Ge 5:9*
Cainan
shall Sarah, that is n. years *Ge 17:17*
old, bear
the length of the building n. *Eze 41:12*
cubits

NINETY-FIVE

the children of Gibbar n. *Ezr 2:20*
the children of Gibeon n. *Ne 7:25*

NINETY-SIX

offered for all Israel n. rams *Ezr 8:35*
were n. pomegranates on a *Jer 52:23*
side

NINETY-EIGHT

now Eli was n. years old *1Sa 4:15*
the children of Ater n. *Ezr 2:16;*
Ne 7:21

NINETY-NINE

Abram was n. years old, Lord *Ge 17:1*
appeared
was n. years old when he *Ge 17:24*
was circumcised
doth he not leave the n. and *M't 18:12;*
seeketh that *18:13; Lu 15, 4, 7*

NINEVE

men of N. shall rise up in *Lu 11:32*

NINEVEH

Asher went and builded N. *Ge 10:11*
Sennacherib dwelt at N. *2Ki 19:36;*
Isa 37:37; Jon 1:2
go to N. *Jon 3:2*
now N. was an exceeding great *Jon 3:3*
city
should not I spare N. *Jon 4:11*
the burden of N.; N. is like a *Na 1:1;*
pool *2:8*
N. is laid waste, who will *Na 3:7*
bemoan her
he will make N. a desolation, *Zep 2:13*
and dry
men of N. rise up in *M't 12:41;*
judgment and condemn *Lu 11:32*

NINEVITES

as Jonas was a sign unto the *Lu 11:30*
N.

NINTH

ye shall eat of old fruit till the *Le 25:22*
n. year

in *n*. year of Hoshea Samaria   *2Ki 17:6;*
taken   *18:10*
in the *n*. year of Zedekiah,   *2Ki 25:1;*
Nebuchadnezzar came   *Jer 39:1; 52:4;*
  Eze 24:1
Elzabad the *n*. captain of the   *1Ch 12:12*
Gadites
the *n*. lot came forth to   *1Ch 24:11*
Jeshuah
n. captain for the *n*. month   *1Ch 27:12*
was Abiezer
he went out about the sixth   *M't 20:5*
and *n*. hour
darkness over all the land   *M't 27:45;*
unto the *n*. hour   *M'k 15:33*
n. hour Jesus gave up the   *M't 27:46;*
ghost   *M'k 15:34*
at the hour of prayer, being the   *Ac 3:1*
n. hour
Cornelius saw a vision about   *Ac 10:3;*
the *n*. hour   *10:30*
the *n*. foundation was a topaz   *Re 21:20*

NIPPLES

bosom pressed, *n*. strapped   *Eze 23:3*
(B)

NISAN

in the month *N*.   *Ne 2:1; Es 3:7*

NISROCH

worshipping in the house of   *2Ki 19:37;*
N. his god   *Isa 37:38*

NITRE

as vinegar upon *n*. so is he   *Pr 25:20*
singing songs
though thou wash thee with *n*.   *Jer 2:22*
and soap

NO

let there be *no* strife between   *Ge 13:8*
me and thee
behold, to me thou hast given   *Ge 15:3*
no seed
be an oath that thou wilt do   *Ge 26:29*
us *no* hurt
shed *no* blood, and lay *no*   *Ge 37:22*
hand upon him
there was *no* harlot in this   *Ge 38:21;*
place   *38:22*
no interpreter; we are *no* spies   *Ge 40:8;*
  40:31, 34; 41:11
thy servants have *no* pasture   *Ge 47:4;*
  La 1:6
is *no* straw given to thy servants   *Ex 5:16*
that *no* swarms of flies shall be   *Ex 8:22*
there
no work shall be done   *Ex 12:16;*
Le 16:29; 23:3, 7, 21, 28, 31; Nu 29:1;
  De 16:8
seven days *no* leaven shall be   *Ex 12:19;*
found   *13:3, 7*
because there were *no* graves   *Ex 14:11*
in Egypt
he that gathered little had *no*   *Ex 16:18*
lack
hurt a woman, and *no*   *Ex 21:22*
mischief follow
there shall *no* blood be shed   *Ex 22:2*
for him
thou shalt take *no* gift, gift   *Ex 23:8*
blindeth the wise
thou shalt make *no* covenant   *Ex 23:32*
with them
ye shall offer *no* strange   *Ex 30:9*
incense thereon
that there be *no* plague   *Ex 30:12*
amongst them
for thou shalt worship *no*   *Ex 34:14*
other god
thou shalt make thee *no*   *Ex 34:17*
molten gods
ye shall kindle *no* fire in your   *Ex 35:3*
habitations
ye shall burn *no* leaven in any   *Le 2:11*
offering
put *no* oil upon it; ye shall eat   *Le 5:11;*
no fat   *7:23*
ye shall eat *no* manner of   *Le 7:26;*
blood   *17:12, 14*
ye shall touch *no* hallowed   *Le 12:4*
thing
and there be *no* white hairs   *Le 13:21;*
therein   *13:26*

no black hair; there be *no*   *Le 13:31;*
yellow hair   *13:32*
do *no* unrighteousness in   *Le 19:15;*
judgment   *19:35*
that there be *no* wickedness   *Le 20:14*
among you
but there shall *no* stranger eat   *Le 22:13*
thereof
there shall be *no* blemish   *Le 22:21*
therein
the houses which have *no*   *Le 23:31*
walls round about
take thou *no* usury of him, or   *Le 23:36*
increase
ye shall make you *no* idols nor   *Le 26:1*
graven image
no devoted thing shall be sold   *Le 27:28*
or redeemed
if the man have *no* kinsman to   *Nu 5:8*
recompense
and there be *no* witness   *Nu 5:13*
against her
and shall drink *no* vinegar of   *Nu 6:3*
wine
there shall *no* razor come upon   *Nu 6:5*
his head
he shall come at *no* dead body   *Nu 6:6*
that *no* stranger come near to   *Nu 16:40*
offer incense
was *no* water for the   *Nu 20:2*
congregation
Zelophehad had *no* sons, but   *Nu 26:33;*
daughters   *27:3-4; Jos 17:3; 1Ch 23:22;*
  24:28
if a man die and have *no* son   *Nu 27:8*
then cause
and if he have *no* daughter, ye   *Nu 27:9*
shall give
as sheep that have *no*   *Nu 27:17;*
shepherd   *Eze 34:5; M't 9:36*
no satisfaction for the life of   *Nu 35:31;*
a murderer   *35:32*
ye heard, but saw *no*   *De 4:12*
similitude   *4:15*
thine eye shall have *no* pity on   *De 7:16*
them
Levi hath *no* part with his   *De 10:9;*
brethren   *14:27, 29; 18:1; Jos 14:4; 18:7*
when there shall be *no* poor   *De 15:4*
among you
if it will make *no* peace with   *De 20:12*
thee
there shall be *no* might in thy   *De 28:32*
hand
among these nations thou   *De 28:65*
shalt find *no* ease
they are children in whom is   *De 32:20*
no faith
there was *no* day like that   *Jos 10:14*
before
ye have *no* part in the Lord   *Jos 22:25;*
  22:27
there was *no* king in Israel   *J'g 17:6;*
  18:1; 21:25
there was *no* magistrate   *J'g 18:7*
where there is *no* want of   *J'g 18:10;*
any thing   *19:19*
no deliverer   *J'g 18:28*
for it is *no* good report that I   *1Sa 2:24*
hear
word was precious, there was   *1Sa 3:1*
no open vision
take it, for there is   *1Sa 21:9*
no other, save that here
shall restore, because he had   *2Sa 12:6*
no pity
no such thing ought to be   *2Sa 13:12*
done in Israel
if he say, I have *no* delight in   *2Sa 15:26*
thee
I have *no* son to keep my   *2Sa 18:18*
name in remembrance
Sheba said, We have *no* part   *2Sa 20:1*
in David
no (S)   *1Ki 2:30;*
Jer 4:22; Eze 16:5; Mic 3:11; Ob 7;
  Na 2:9 3:3; Zep 3:6
there is *no* God like thee in   *1Ki 8:23*
heaven
he would prophesy *no* good   *1Ki 22:18*
concerning me
is it not because there is *no*   *2Ki 1:16*
God in Israel
because Ahaziah had *no* son   *2Ki 1:17*
Jehu took *no* heed to walk in   *2Ki 10:31*
the law
now Sheshan had *no* sons, but   *1Ch 2:34*
daughters

do my prophets *no* harm   *1Ch 16:22;*
  Ps 105:15
that have *no* shepherd   *2Ch 18:16;*
  Zec 10:2
there is *no* iniquity with the   *2Ch 19:7*
Lord
we have *no* might against   *2Ch 20:12*
this company
his people made *no* burning   *2Ch 21:19*
for him
there was *no* passover like to   *2Ch 35:18*
that
they mocked till there was   *2Ch 36:16*
no remedy
so that there should be *no*   *Ezr 9:14*
remnant
ye have *no* portion in   *Ne 2:20*
Jerusalem
there was *no* king like   *Ne 13:26*
Solomon
he put *no* trust in his servants   *Job 4:18*
in seven there shall *no* evil   *Job 5:19*
touch thee
see *no* good; that *no* eye had   *Job 9:25;*
seen me   *10:18*
he shutteth, and there can be   *Job 12:14*
no opening
causeth to wander where   *Job 12:24*
there is *no* way
ye are all physicians of *no*   *Job 13:4*
value
O earth, let my cry have *no*   *Job 16:18*
place
he shall have *no* name in the   *Job 18:17*
street
I called my servant, he gave   *Job 19:16*
me *no* answer
no eye shall see me; have *no*   *Job 24:15;*
helper   *30:13*
is a path which *no* fowl   *Job 28:7*
knoweth
there is *no* help for him in God   *Ps 3:2*
in whose spirit there is *no* guile   *Ps 32:2*
there is *no* want to them that   *Ps 34:9*
fear him
there is *no* fear of God before   *Ps 36:1*
his eyes
they were in fear where *no* fear   *Ps 53:5*
was
because they have *no* changes   *Ps 55:19*
no good will he withhold from   *Ps 84:11*
them
there shall *no* evil befall thee   *Ps 91:10*
there is *no* unrighteousness in   *Ps 92:15*
him
they do *no* iniquity, they walk   *Ps 119:3*
in his ways
son of man, in whom there is   *Ps 146:3*
no he'p
there shall *no* evil happen to   *Pr 12:21*
the just
to get wisdom, seeing he hath   *Pr 17:16*
no heart to it
there is *no* wisdom against the   *Pr 21:30*
Lord
were oppressed, and they had *no*   *Ec 4:1*
comforter
for there is *no* work in the   *Ec 9:10*
grave
my love, there is *no* spot in thee   *Ca 4:7*
we have a little sister, and she   *Ca 8:8*
hath *no* breasts
there is *no* soundness in it, but   *Isa 1:6*
wounds
join field to field, till there be *no*   *Isa 5:8*
place
it is because there is *no* light in   *Isa 8:20*
them
of his government there shall be   *Isa 9:7*
no end
no one of these shall fail,   *Isa 34:16*
none shall want
and to them that have *no*   *Isa 40:29*
might
and besides me there is *no*   *Isa 43:11*
Saviour
there is *no* peace to the   *Isa 48:22;*
wicked   *57:21*
that walketh in darkness, and   *Isa 50:10*
hath *no* light
he hath *no* form, nor   *Isa 53:2*
comeliness, nor beauty
no weapon formed against   *Isa 54:17*
thee shall prosper
and he that hath *no* money,   *Isa 55:1*
come ye, buy
thou saidst not, There is *no*   *Isa 57:10;*
hope   *Jer 2:25*
there is *no* judgment in their   *Isa 59:8*
goings

he wondered that there was *no* intercessor — Isa 59:16

changed their gods, which are yet *no* gods — Jer 2:11

your children received *no* correction — Jer 2:30

peace, peace, when there is *no* peace — Jer 6:14; 8:11

they are cruel, and have *no* mercy — Jer 6:23

we looked for peace, but *no* good came — Jer 8:15; 14:19

and there is *no* breath in them — Jer 10:14; 51:17

a vessel wherein is *no* pleasure — Jer 22:28; 48:38

provoke me not, I will do you *no* hurt — Jer 25:6

do him *no* harm; shall see *no* war — Jer 39:12; 42:14

spoiler shall come, and *no* city shall escape — Jer 48:8

hath Israel *no* sons? hath he *no* heir — Jer 49:1

she came down, she had *no* comforter — La 1:9

peace, and there was *no* peace — Eze 13:10; 13:16

I have *no* pleasure in death of him — Eze 18:32; 33:11

yet had he *no* wages, nor his army — Eze 29:18

because there is *no* other god can deliver — Da 3:29

because there is *no* truth nor mercy — Ho 4:1

reject thee, that thou shalt be *no* priest to me — Ho 4:6

now they shall say, We have *no* king — Ho 10:3

I was *no* prophet, neither prophet's son — Am 7:14

their lips, for there is *no* answer of God — Mic 3:7

why dost thou cry out? is there *no* king in thee — Mic 4:9

there is *no* healing of thy bruise — Na 3:19

as the creeping things that have *no* ruler — Hab 1:14

but the unjust knoweth *no* shame — Zep 3:5

love *no* false oath; *no* oppressor — Zec 8:17; 9:8

I have *no* pleasure in you, saith the Lord — Mal 1:10

ye shall in *no* case enter into heaven — M't 5:20

thou shalt by *no* means come out thence — M't 5:26

take therefore *no* thought for the morrow — M't 6:34; 10:19; M'k 13:11; Lu 12:11, 22

which say that there is *no* resurrection — M't 22:23; M'k 12:18; Ac 23:8; 1Co 15:12-13

shortened those days, *no* flesh be saved — M'k 13:20

just persons, which need *no* repentance — Lu 15:7

I find *no* fault in him — Lu 23:4; 23:14; Joh 18:38; 19:4, 6

I have *no* husband; ye have *no* life — Joh 4:17; 6:53

search, for out of Galilee ariseth *no* prophet — Joh 7:52

if ye were blind, ye should have *no* sin — Joh 9:41

he stumbleth, because there is *no* light in him — Joh 11:10

if I wash thee not, thou hast *no* part with me — Joh 13:8

now they have *no* cloak for their sin — Joh 15:22

we have *no* king but Caesar — Joh 19:15

put *no* difference between us and them — Ac 15:9

for I will be *no* judge of such matters — Ac 18:15

written that they observe *no* such thing — Ac 21:25

to the Jews have I done *no* wrong — Ac 25:10

the people shewed us *no* little kindness — Ac 28:2

all that believe, for there is *no* difference — Ro 3:22

for where *no* law is, *no* transgression — Ro 4:15

sin is not imputed where there is *no* law — Ro 5:13

that in my flesh dwelleth *no* good thing — Ro 7:18

to jealousy by them that are *no* people — Ro 10:19

love worketh *no* ill to his neighbour — Ro 13:10

that *no* flesh glory in his presence — 1Co 1:29

and have *no* certain dwelling place — 1Co 4:11

I will eat *no* flesh while the world standeth — 1Co 8:13

there hath *no* temptation taken you but such — 1Co 10:13

we have *no* such custom, nor the churches — 1Co 11:16

I have *no* need of thee; *no* charity — 1Co 12:21; 13:2

if there be *no* interpreter, let him keep — 1Co 14:28

made him sin for us, who knew *no* sin — 2Co 5:21

giving *no* offence in any thing, that ministry — 2Co 6:3

now I pray to God that ye do *no* evil — 2Co 13:7

meekness, against such there is *no* law — Ga 5:23

have *no* fellowship with works of darkness — Eph 5:11

but made himself of *no* reputation — Ph'p 2:7

and have *no* confidence in the flesh — Ph'p 3:3

even as others which have *no* hope — 1Th 4:13

and have *no* company with him — 2Th 3:14

but they shall proceed *no* further — 2Ti 3:9

because he could swear by *no* greater — Heb 6:13

no place have been sought for the second — Heb 8:7

without shedding of blood is *no* remission — Heb 9:22

my soul shall have *no* pleasure in him — Heb 10:38

no chastening for the present seemeth joyous — Heb 12:11

for he found *no* place of repentance, though he — Heb 12:17

here have we *no* continuing city, but seek — Heb 13:14

with whom is *no* variableness, nor shadow — Jas 1:17

who did *no* sin, nor was guile found — 1Pe 2:22

no prophecy of private interpretation — 2Pe 1:20

and in him is *no* darkness at all — 1Jo 1:5

if we say, we have *no* sin, we deceive ourselves — 1Jo 1:8

in him is *no* sin; there is *no* fear in love — 1Jo 3:5; 4:18

I have *no* greater joy than to hear — 3Jo 1:4

in their mouth was found *no* guile — Re 14:5

which have received *no* kingdom as yet — Re 17:12

I am *no* widow, and shall see *no* sorrow — Re 18:7

and there was found *no* place for them — Re 20:11

no temple therein; *no* need of the sun — Re 21:22; 21:23

no night there, they need *no* candle — Re 21:25; 22:5

NO, a city

I will punish *N*. — Jer 46:25; Eze 30:14-16

art thou better than populous *N*. — Na 3:8

NO RAIN

shut up heaven, that there be *no rain* — De 11:17; 2Ch 6:26; 7:13

no rain in the land — 1Ki 8:35; 1Ki 17:7; Jer 14:4

clouds, that they rain *no rain* upon it — Isa 5:6

and there hath been *no* latter *rain* — Jer 3:3

even upon them there shall be *no rain* — Zec 14:17

and if Egypt that have *no rain* come not — Zec 14:18

NO REST

but the dove found *no rest* for her foot — Ge 8:9

and my sinews take *no rest* — Job 30:17

whether he rage or laugh there is *no rest* — Pr 29:9

there also shalt thou have *no rest* — Isa 23:12

and give him *no rest* till he establish Jerusalem — Isa 62:7

I fainted in sighing, and find *no rest* — Jer 45:3

among the heathen she findeth *no rest* — La 1:3

give thyself *no rest*, we have *no rest* — La 2:18; 5:5

I had *no rest* in my spirit, because — 2Co 2:13

when come into Macedonia, our flesh had *no rest* — 2Co 7:5

they have *no rest* day nor night — Re 14:11

NO STRENGTH

and there was *no strength* in Saul — 1Sa 28:20

how savest thou arm that hath *no strength* — Job 26:2

I am as a man that hath *no strength* — Ps 88:4

and there remained *no strength* in me — Da 10:8; 10:17

are turned on me. I have retained *no strength* — Da 10:16

otherwise it is of *no strength* at all — Heb 9:17

NOADIAH

N. the son of Binnui, a Levite — Ezr 8:33

my God, think on the prophetess *N*. — Ne 6:14

NOAH

N. saying, This same shall comfort us — Ge 5:29

Lamech begat *N*.; *N*. found grace — Ge 5:30; 6:8

these are generations of *N*. — Ge 6:9; 10:1, 32; 1Ch 1:4

N. only remained alive, and they in the ark — Ge 7:23

God remembered *N*. and every living thing — Ge 8:1

N. opened the window of the ark he had made — Ge 8:6

N. builded an altar to the Lord, and offered — Ge 8:20

N. awoke from his wine; the days of *N*. — Ge 9:24; 9:29

names of daughters of Zelophehad were *N*., Tirzah — Nu 26:33; 27:1; 36:11; Jos 17:3

this is as the waters of *N*. unto me — Isa 54:9

tho' these three, *N*., Daniel, Job — Eze 14:14; 14:20

as it was in the days of *N*. — M't 24:37; Lu 17:26

Shem, which was the son of *N*. — Lu 3:36

by faith *N*. being warned of God — Heb 11:7

when God waited in the days of *N*. — 1Pe 3:20

God spared not old world, but saved *N*. — 2Pe 2:5

NOAH'S

six hundredth year of *N*. life — Ge 7:11

N. wife and the three wives of — Ge 7:13

NOB

David came to *N*. to Ahimelech — 1Sa 21:1

Doeg said, I saw son of Jesse coming to *N*. — 1Sa 22:9

the king sent to call the priests in *N*. — 1Sa 22:11

Doeg smote *N*. the city of the priests — 1Sa 22:19

the children of Benjamin dwelt at *N*. — Ne 11:32

as yet shall he remain at *N*. that day — Isa 10:32

NOBAH

N. went and took Kenath	Nu 32:42
called it N. after his own name	Nu 32:42
dwelt in tents on east of N.	J'g 8:11

NOBLE

whom the n. Asnapper brought over	Ezr 4:10
one of the king's most n. princes	Es 6:9
no mare called n. (A)(B)(E)(R)(S)	Isa 32:5
I had planted thee a n. vine	Jer 2:21
the Bereans more n. than Thessalonians	Ac 17:11
we accept it always most n. Felix	Ac 24:3; 26:25
one for n. use, one for ignoble (A)(B)	Ro 9:21
what is n. in sight of all (R)	Ro 12:17
how that not many n. are called	1Co 1:26
by his n. living show (A)	Jas 3:13

NOBLEMAN

A certain n. went into a far	Lu 19:12
there was a certain n.	Joh 4:46
The n. saith unto him, Sir, come	Joh 4:49

NOBLES

on the n. of Israel he laid not his hand	Ex 24:11
the n. of the people digged it	Nu 21:18
dominion over the n. among the people	J'g 5:13
Jezebel sent letters to the n. in his city	1Ki 21:8
Jehoiada took the n. of the people	2Ch 23:20
nor had I as yet told it to the n.	Ne 2:16
the n. put not their necks to the work	Ne 3:5
and I rebuked the n. and the rulers	Ne 5:7
the n. of Judah sent letters to Tobiah	Ne 6:17
God put into mine heart to gather the n.	Ne 7:5
they clave to their brethren, their n.	Ne 10:29
I contended with the n. of Judah	Ne 13:17
the n. held their peace	Job 29:10
make their n. like Oreb and Zeeb	Ps 83:11
to bind their n. with fetters of iron	Ps 149:8
by me princes rule, and n. all judges	Pr 8:16
when thy king is the son of n.	Ec 10:17
they may go into the gates of the n.	Isa 13:2
they shall call the n. to the kingdom	Isa 34:12
and have brought down all their n.	Isa 43:14
the n. sent their little ones to the waters	Jer 14:3
Nebuchadnezzar carried captive n. of Judah	Jer 27:20
and their n. shall be of themselves	Jer 30:21
the king of Babylon slew all the n. of Judah	Jer 39:6
Her n. were purer than snow (S)	La 4:7
by the decree of the king and his n.	Jon 3:7
recount his n. (E)(S)	Na 2:5
Assyria, thy n. shall dwell in the dust	Na 3:18

NOBLY

daughters have done n. (B)	Pr 31:29
confessed your faith n. (N)	1Ti 6:12

NOD

dwelt in the land of N.	Ge 4:16

NODAB

and Nephish, and N.	1Ch 5:19

NOE

as in the days of N.	M't 24:37; 24:38; Lu 17:26-27
which was the son of N.	Lu 3:36

NOGAH

N. and Nepheg	1Ch 3:7; 14:6

NOHAH

N. the fourth	1Ch 8:2

NOISE

people heard the n. or the trumpet	Ex 20:18
he said, There is a n. of war in the camp	Ex 32:17
but the n. of them that sing do I hear	Ex 32:18
ye shall not shout nor make any n.	Jos 6:10
are delivered from the n. of archers	J'g 5:11
what meaneth the n. of this shout	1Sa 4:6; 4:14
the n. in the host of Philistines increased	1Sa 14:19
wherefore is this n. of the city	1Ki 1:41
this is the n. that ye have heard	1Ki 1:45
the n. of chariots, and a n. of horses	2Ki 7:6
Athaliah heard n. of guard	2Ki 11:13; 2Ch 23:12
making a n. with psalteries	1Ch 15:28
not discern n. of joy, from n. of weeping	Ezr 3:13
any understand the n. of his tabernacle	Job 36:29
the n. thereof sheweth concerning it	Job 36:33
hear attentively the n. of his voice	Job 37:2
play skilfully with a loud n.	Ps 33:3
deep calleth at the n. of thy waterspouts	Ps 42:7
I mourn in my complaint, and make a n.	Ps 55:2
they make a n. like a dog	Ps 59:6; 59:14
who stilleth the n. of the seas, n. of waves	Ps 65:7
make a joyful n. to God, all ye lands	Ps 66:1; 81:1; 95:1-2; 98:4, 6; 100:1
the Lord is mightier than the n. of waters	Ps 93:4
for every battle is with confused n.	Isa 9:5
n. of multitude in mountains, a tumultuous n. of kingdoms of	Isa 13:4
the n. of thy viols is brought down	Isa 14:11
which make a n. like the n. of the seas	Isa 17:12
the n. of them that rejoice endeth	Isa 24:8
he who fleeth from the n. of fear	Isa 24:18
thou shalt bring down the n. of strangers	Isa 25:5
shall be visited of the Lord with great n.	Isa 29:6
nor abase himself for the n. of them	Isa 31:4
daunted at their n. (A)(B)(R)	Isa 31:4
at the n. of the tumult the people fled	Isa 33:3
a voice of n. from the city and temple	Isa 66:6
my heart maketh a n. in me	Jer 4:19
the city shall flee for the n. of horsemen	Jer 4:29
behold, the n. of the bruit is come	Jer 10:22
with the n. of great tumult he kindled	Jer 11:16
a n. shall come to the ends of the earth	Jer 25:31
Pharaoh king of Egypt is but a n.	Jer 46:17
at the n. of the stamping of his horses	Jer 47:3
earth is moved at n. of their fall, at cry the n. was heard in	Jer 49:21
at the n. of taking of Babylon	Jer 50:46
a n. of their voice is uttered	Jer 51:55

NONE (right column continuation and NON)

the enemy made n. in house of the Lord	La 2:7
I heard the n. of their wings, like the n. of great waters	Eze 1:24; 43:2
n. of the wheels, the n. of a great rushing	Eze 3:13
land was desolate by n. of his roaring	Eze 19:7
thy walls shall shake at the n. of horsemen	Eze 26:10
I will cause the n. of my songs to cease	Eze 26:13
and as I prophesied, there was a n.	Eze 37:7
like the n. of chariots, like the n. of fire	Joe 2:5
take from me the n. of thy songs	Am 5:23
shall make a great n. by reason	Mic 2:12
n. of a whip, n. of rattling wheels	Na 3:2
the n. of a cry from the fish gate	Zep 1:10
they shall drink and make a n.	Zec 9:15
he saw the people making a n.	M't 9:23
heavens shall pass away with great n.	2Pe 3:10
I heard as it were the n. of thunder	Re 6:1

NOISED

Joshua, his fame was n. throughout country	Jos 6:27
it was n. that he was in the house	M'k 2:1
all these sayings were n. abroad	Lu 1:65
now when this was n. abroad	Ac 2:6

NOISOME

shall deliver thee from the n. pestilence	Ps 91:3
I send sword and n. beast	Eze 14:21
fell a n. and grievous sore on the men	Re 16:2

NON

N. his son, Jehoshuah his son	1Ch 7:27

NONE

this is n. other but the house of God	Ge 28:17
n. of you shall go out at the door	Ex 12:22
I will put n. of these diseases upon thee	Ex 15:26
on the seventh day, in it there shall be n.	Ex 16:26
some went to gather, and they found n.	Ex 16:27
shalt have n. other gods before me	Ex 20:3; De 5:7
n. shall appear before me empty	Ex 23:15; 34:20
n. shall approach to any near of kin	Le 18:6
there shall n. be defiled for the dead	Le 21:1
shall leave n. of it until morrow	Le 22:30; Nu 9:12
and if the man have n. to redeem it	Le 25:26
shall lie down, and n. shall make you afraid	Le 26:6
ye shall flee when n. pursueth	Le 26:17; 26:36-37
but to the sons of Kohath he gave n.	Nu 7:9
n. that came out of Egypt shall see the land	Nu 32:11
we destroyed and left n. to remain	De 2:34; Jos 8:22; 10:28, 30, 33; 11:8
will put n. of the diseases of Egypt on you	De 7:15
thy sheep shall be given, and n. to rescue	De 28:31
thou shalt have n. assurance of thy life	De 28:66
n. went out of Jericho, n. came in	Jos 6:1
n. of you be freed from being bondmen	Jos 9:23
n. moved his tongue against any of Israel	Jos 10:21
there came n. to the camp from Jabesh	J'g 21:8

there is n. holy as the Lord | 1Sa 2:2
let n. of his words fall to the | 1Sa 3:19
ground
beware that n. touch the | 2Sa 18:12
young man
n. were of silver | 1Ki 10:21; 2Ch 9:20
Asa made a proclamation, n. | 1Ki 15:22
was exempted
as the Lord liveth, I will | 2Ki 5:16
receive n.
n. but Elisha tells the king of | 2Ki 6:12
Israel
and there shall be n. to bury | 2Ki 9:10
Jezebel
let n. go forth or escape out | 2Ki 9:15;
of the city | 10:25
till Jehu left Ahab n. | 2Ki 10:11
remaining
the prophets of Baal, let n. | 2Ki 10:19
be wanting
look there be n. of the | 2Ki 10:23
servants of God there
n. ought to carry ark of God | 1Ch 15:2
but Levites
honour, such as n. of the | 2Ch 1:12
kings have
he might let n. go out or come | 2Ch 16:1
in to Asa
so that n. is able to withstand | 2Ch 20:6
thee
they were dead bodies fallen, | 2Ch 20:24
n. escaped
n. which was unclean should | 2Ch 23:19
enter in
I found there n. of the sons of | Ezr 8:15
Levi
n. of us put off our clothes, | Ne 4:23
saving that
drinking according to law, n. did | Es 1:8
compel
n. might enter the king's gate in | Es 4:2
sackcloth
sat down, and n. spake a word | Job 2:13
to him
let it look for light but have n. | Job 3:9
shalt lie down, and n. shall | Job 11:19
make thee afraid
in his tabernacle, because it | Job 18:15
is n. of his
there shall n. of his meat be | Job 20:21
left
delivered him that had n. to | Job 29:12
help him
but n. saith, Where is God | Job 35:10
my Maker
there they cry, but n. giveth | Job 35:12
answer
seek out his wickedness till | Ps 10:15
thou find n.
and n. can keep alive his own | Ps 22:29
soul
let n. that wait on thee be | Ps 25:3
ashamed
n. that trust in him shall be | Ps 34:22
desolate
law in his heart, n. of his steps | Ps 37:31
shall slide
n. of them can redeem his | Ps 49:7
brother
lest I tear you, and there be n. | Ps 50:22
to deliver
I looked for comforters, but | Ps 69:20
found n.
and let n. dwell in their tents | Ps 69:25
n. of the men of might found | Ps 76:5
their hands
not hearken, Israel would n. | Ps 81:11
of me
let there be n. to extend | Ps 109:12
mercy to him
as yet there was n. of them | Ps 139:16
and ye would n. of my reproof | Pr 1:25
they would n. of my counsel, | Pr 1:30
they despised
n. that go unto her return | Pr 2:19
again, nor take
envy not, and choose n. of his | Pr 3:31
ways
bear twins, and n. is barren | Ca 4:2
among them
they shall burn, and n. shall | Isa 1:31
quench them
n. shall be weary, n. shall | Isa 5:27
slumber
carry it away safe, and n. shall | Isa 5:29
deliver it
he is persecuted, and n. | Isa 14:6
hindereth
n. shall be alone in his | Isa 14:31
appointed times

n. shall make them afraid | Isa 17:2; Zep 3:13
he shall open, and n. shall | Isa 22:22
shut, n. open
n. shall pass through it for | Isa 34:10
ever and ever
they shall call the nobles but | Isa 34:12
n. shall be there
no one shall fail, n. shall | Isa 34:16
want her mate
n. delivereth, and n. saith, | Isa 42:22
Restore
n. considereth in his heart, | Isa 44:19
nor is there
that sayest, I am, and n. else | Isa 47:8
besides me
n. seeth me | Isa 47:10
n. shall save thee | Isa 47:15
n. considering that righteous is | Isa 57:1
taken away
n. calleth for justice, nor | Isa 59:4
pleadeth for truth
because when I called, n. did | Isa 66:4
answer
and burn, that n. can quench it | Jer 4:4; 21:12
for the beasts, and n. shall fray | Jer 7:33
them away
burnt up, so that n. can pass | Jer 9:10
through them
burnt like a wilderness that n. | Jer 9:12
passeth through
shall fall as dung, and n. shall | Jer 9:22
gather them
cities shall be shut, and n. | Jer 13:19
shall open them
cast out, and shall have n. to | Jer 14:16
bury them
that n. doth return from his | Jer 23:14
wickedness
and n. shall make him afraid | Jer 30:10; 46:27
that n. should serve himself of | Jer 34:9
them
that n. should serve | Jer 34:10
themselves of them
to this day they drink n. but | Jer 35:14
obey father's
have n. to sit on the throne of | Jer 36:30
David
n. shall remain or escape | Jer 42:17
n. shall return, but such as | Jer 44:14
escape
n. shall tread with shouting, | Jer 48:33
no shouting
n. shall gather up him that | Jer 49:5
wandereth
land desolate, and n. shall | Jer 50:3
dwell therein
their arrows, n. shall return in | Jer 50:9
vain
iniquity sought for, and there | Jer 50:20
shall be n.
camp against it, let n. thereof | Jer 50:29
escape
the proud shall fall, and n. | Jer 50:32
shall raise him up
that n. shall remain in it | Jer 51:62; Eze 7:11
she hath n. to comfort her | La 1:2; 1:17
because n. come to the solemn | La 1:4
feasts
when her people fell, and n. did | La 1:7
help her
heard that I sigh, there is n. to | La 1:21
comfort me
but n. goeth to the battle | Eze 7:14
they shall seek peace, and | Eze 7:25
there shall be n.
n. of my words shall be | Eze 12:28
prolonged
n. followeth thee to commit | Eze 16:34
whoredoms
hath spoiled n. by violence, | Eze 18:7
given bread
I sought for a man, but I | Eze 22:30
found n.
n. of his sins shall be | Eze 33:16
mentioned to him
mountains desolate, that n. | Eze 33:28
shall pass through
and n. did search or seek after | Eze 34:6
them
safely, and n. shall make | Eze 34:28;
them afraid | 39:26; Mic 4:4; Na 2:11
and have left n. of them any | Eze 39:28
more there
n. found like Daniel among | Da 1:19
them all

n. stay hand, or say to him, | Da 4:35
What doest thou
astonished at the vision, but n. | Da 8:27
understood it
n. shall stand before him, he | Da 11:16
shall stand
shall come to his end, and n. | Da 11:45
shall help him
n. of the wicked shall | Da 12:10
understand, but the wise
n. shall deliver her out of my | Ho 2:10; 5:14
hands
though they called, n. at all | Ho 11:7
would exalt him
I am the Lord your God, and | Joe 2:27
n. else
there be n. to quench it in | Am 5:6
Bethel
shalt have n. that shall cast a | Mic 2:5
cord by lot
they will say, N. evil can | Mic 3:11
come upon us
he teareth in pieces, and n. can | Mic 5:8
deliver
they cry, Stand, but n. shall | Na 2:8
look back
let n. of you imagine evil | Zec 7:10; 8:17
let n. deal treacherously | Mal 2:15
against the wife
dry places seeking rest and | M't 12:43; Lu 11:24
findeth n.
witnesses came, yet found n. | M't 26:60; M'k 14:55
let him impart to him that hath | Lu 3:11
n.
to n. of them was Elias sent, | Lu 4:26
save to Sarepta
n. of them was cleansed save | Lu 4:27
Naaman the Syrian
n. of them shall taste of my | Lu 14:24
supper
n. is good, save one, that is | Lu 18:19
God
and yet n. of you keepeth the | Joh 7:19
law
if I had not done the works | Joh 15:24
n. other did
n. is lost but the son of | Joh 17:12
perdition
of them thou gavest me, I | Joh 18:9
have lost n.
Peter said, Silver and gold have | Ac 3:6
I n.
for as yet he was fallen on n. | Ac 8:16
of them
pray, that n. of these things | Ac 8:24
come on me
preaching the word to n. but | Ac 11:19
to the Jews
Gallio cared for n. of these | Ac 18:17
things
but n. of these things move | Ac 20:24
me
he should forbid n. of his | Ac 24:23
acquaintance
if there be n. of these things | Ac 25:11
they accuse
saying n. other than the | Ac 26:22
prophets did say
if any have not the Spirit, he is | Ro 8:9
n. of his
n. of us liveth, and n. dieth to | Ro 14:7
himself
I thank God, I baptized n. of | 1Co 1:14
you
whom n. of the princes of this | 1Co 2:8
world knew
they that have wives be as | 1Co 7:29
tho' they had n.
but I have used n. of these | 1Co 9:15
things
give n. offence to the Jews | 1Co 10:32
nor Gentiles
and n. of them is without | 1Co 14:10
signification
but other of the apostles saw I | Ga 1:19
n.
see that n. render evil for evil | 1Th 5:15
give n. occasion to the | 1Ti 5:14
adversary
let n. of you suffer as a | 1Pe 4:15
murderer
fear n. of these things thou | Re 2:10
shalt suffer

THERE IS NONE

there is n. greater in this house | Ge 39:9
than I
and *there is n.* that can | Ge 41:15
interpret it

there is *n*. so discreet and   Ge 41:39
wise as thou art
the Lord is God, there is *n*.   De 4:35;
else   4:39; 1Ki 8:60; Isa 45:5-6, 14, 18,
22; 46:9; M'k 12:32
for *there is n*. to redeem it   Ru 4:4
besides thee
there is *n*. holy as the Lord   1Sa 2:2
there is *n*. besides
there is *n*. sheweth me, there   1Sa 22:8
is *n*. that is sorry
days are as a shadow, there   1Ch 29:15
is *n*. abiding
there is *n*. that can deliver   Job 10:7;
Ps 7:2; 71:11
they are corrupt, *there is n*.   Ps 14:1;
that doeth good   14:3; 53:1, 3; Ro 3:12
for trouble is near, for *there is*   Ps 22:11
n. to help
there is *n*. on earth I desire   Ps 73:25
beside thee
when the needy seek water,   Isa 41:17
there is *n*.
there is *n*. sheweth, there is   Isa 41:26
that declareth
there is *n*. that can deliver out   Isa 43:13
of my hand
and *there is n*. to guide her   Isa 51:18
among her sons
we look for judgment, but   Isa 59:11
there is n.
and *there is n*. that calleth on   Isa 64:7
thy name
there is *n*. to stretch forth my   Jer 10:20
tent
there is *n*. to plead thy cause,   Jer 30:13
that thou
there is *n*. that doth deliver us   La 5:8
from hand
there is *n*. that holdeth with   Da 10:21
me in these
there is *n*. of them that calleth   Ho 7:7
on me
she is forsaken, *there is n*. to   Am 5:2
raise her up
there is *n*. upright among men,   Mic 7:2
they all lie
that said, I am, and *there is n*.   Zep 2:15
besides me
ye clothe you, but *there is n*.   Hag 1:6
warm
there is *n*. good but one   M't 19:17;
M'k 10:18
there is *n*. other   M'k 12:31
commandment greater
there is *n*. of thy kindred that is   Lu 1:6
called
there is *n*. other name under   Ac 4:12
heaven given
there is *n*. righteous, no, not   Ro 3:10
one
there is *n*. understandeth, there   Ro 3:11
is *n*. seeketh God
and *there is n*. other God but   1Co 8:4
one

THERE WAS NONE

there was *n*. of men of the   Ge 39:11
house within
there was *n*. that could   Ge 41:8
interpret them
but *there was n*. that could   Ge 41:24
declare it to me
until *there was n*. left him   Nu 21:35
alive
damsel cried, and *there was n*.   De 22:27
to save
they strove, and *there was n*.   2Sa 14:6
to part them
there was *n*. to be so much   2Sa 14:25
praised as Absalom
looked, but *there was n*. to   2Sa 22:42;
save   Ps 18:41
there was *n*. followed the   1Ki 12:20;
house of David but   2Ki 17:18
looked some to have pity, but   Ps 69:20
there was n.
shed their blood, and *there was*   Ps 79:3
n. to bury them
they fell down, and *there was*   Ps 107:12
n. to help
when as yet *there was n*. of   Ps 139:16
them
there was *n*. moved the wing   Isa 10:14
or peeped
when I called, *there was n*. to   Isa 50:2
answer
alone, and of people *there*   Isa 63:3
was n. with me

I wondered that *there was n*.   Isa 63:5
to uphold
there was *n*. that could deliver   Da 8:7
the ram

NON-JEWISH

to the *n*. world (P)   Ga 1:16

NONPLUSED

n. the Jews (B)   Ac 9:22

NONSENSE

shall utter *n*. (R)   Zec 10:2
reports seemed *n*. to (B)(N)   Lu 24:11
make *n*. of faith (P)   Ro 4:14
n. to dying world (P)   1Co 1:18
utterly unphilosophical *n*.   1Co 1:23
(A)(P)
spoils faith through high   Col 2:8
sounding *n*. (P)
utter arrogant *n*. (B)(P)   2Pe 2:18

NOON

these men shall dine with me   Ge 43:16
at *n*.
the present against Joseph   Ge 43:25
came at *n*.
and they tarried until after *n*.   J'g 19:8
Ish-bosheth, who lay on a bed   2Sa 4:5
at *n*.
they called on Baal even until   1Ki 18:26
n.
at *n*. Elijah mocked them,   1Ki 18:27
and said
he numbered them, and they   1Ki 20:16
went out at *n*.
he sat on her knees till *n*. and   2Ki 4:20
died
at *n*. will I pray, and he shall   Ps 55:17
hear
thou makest thy flock to rest at   Ca 1:7
n.
prepare war, arise, let us go up   Jer 6:4
at *n*.
I will cause the sun to go down   Am 8:9
at *n*.
it was about *n*. (A)(B)(N)   Joh 4:6
about *n*. there shone great light   Ac 22:6
round me

NOONDAY

thou shalt grope at *n*. as the   De 28:29
blind
they grope in the *n*. as in the   Job 5:14
night
thine age shall be clearer   Job 11:17
than the *n*.
he shall bring forth judgment   Ps 37:6
as *n*.
for the destruction that wasteth   Ps 91:6
at *n*.
shadow as the night, in midst   Isa 16:3
of *n*.
thy darkness shall be as the   Isa 58:10
n.
we stumble at *n*. as in the   Isa 59:10
night
I have brought a spoiler at   Jer 15:8
n.
they shall drive out Ashdod at   Zep 2:4
n.

NOONTIDE

let him hear the shouting at   Jer 20:16
n.

NOONTIME

about *n*. (A)(B)(N)(P)   Ac 10:9

NOOSE

like a trap or a *n*. (A)   Lu 21:34

NOPH

the princes of N. are deceived   Isa 19:13
the children of N. have broken   Jer 2:16
the crown
publish in N,; for N. shall   Jer 46:14;
be waste   46:19
will cause their images to   Eze 30:13
cease out N.
and N. shall have distresses   Eze 30:16
daily

NOPHAH

them waste even unto N.   Nu 21:30

NOR

when she lay down, *n*. when   Ge 19:35
she arose
n. my son, *n*. my son's son   Ge 21:23
n. a lawgiver from between   Ge 49:10
his feet
n. thy son, *n*. thy daughter, *n*.   Ex 20:10;
manservant, *n*. maidservant,   De 5:9, 14
n. thy cattle, *n*. ox, *n*. any thing
Do not drink wine *n*. strong   Le 10:9
drink
did eat bread, *n*. drink water   De 9:9;
9:18
Levi hath no part *n*.   De 10:9
inheritance with
Fear not, *n*. be dismayed   Jos 10:25;
1Ch 28:20; 2Ch 20:17
by dreams, *n*. Urim, *n*. by   1Sa 28:6;
prophets   28:15
n. for the arrow; *n*. for   Ps 91:5;
pestilence, *n*. for the   91:6
n. rewarded us according to   Ps 103:10
our iniquities
n. device, *n*. knowledge, *n*.   Ec 9:10
wisdom
n. awake my love, till he please   Ca 2:7;
3:5; 8:4
not hurt *n*. destroy in all my   Isa 11:9;
holy mountain   65:25
not fail *n*. be discouraged   Isa 42:4
have not known *n*. understood   Isa 44:18
they shall not hunger *n*.   Isa 49:10;
thirst, *n*. sun smite them   Re 7:16
he hath no form *n*. comeliness   Isa 53:2
Not by might, *n*. by power, but   Zec 4:6
marry, *n*. are given in   M't 22:30;
marriage   M'k 12:25; Lu 20:35
this time, no *n*. ever shall be   M't 24:21
day *n*. the hour the Son of   M't 25:13
man cometh
not be able to gainsay *n*. resist   Lu 21:15
not of blood, *n*. of the will of   Joh 1:13
the flesh, *n*. of the will of man
voice at any time, *n*. seen his   Joh 5:37
shape
neither know me, *n*. my   Joh 8:19;
Father   16:3
neither angel, *n*. spirit   Ac 23:8
neither death, *n*. life, *n*. angels,   Ro 8:38
n. principalities, *n*. powers,
n. things present, *n*. things to
come, *n*. height, *n*. depth, *n*. any
n. idolaters, *n*. adulterers, *n*.   1Co 6:9
effeminate, *n*. abusers, *n*. thieves,
n. covetous, *n*. drunkards, *n*.
revilers, *n*. extortioners
Jews, *n*. Gentiles, *n*. church   1Co 10:32
of God
n. handling the word of God   2Co 4:2
deceitfully
Jew, *n*. Greek, *n*. free, *n*.   Ga 3:28;
female   Col 3:11
filthiness, *n*. foolish talking, *n*.   Eph 5:4
jesting, *n*. unclean person, *n*.
covetous man
not of deceit, *n*. of   1Th 2:3
uncleanness, *n*. of guile, *n*. a
cloke of covetousness
spirit, *n*. by word, *n*. by letter   2Th 2:2
as from us
neither cold *n*. hot   Re 3:15; 3:16
neither see, *n*. hear, *n*. walk   Re 9:20
murders, *n*. sorceries, *n*.
fornication, *n*. thefts   Re 9:21
death, neither sorrow, *n*. crying   Re 21:4

NORTH

thou shalt spread abroad to   Ge 28:14
the *n*.
molten sea upon twelve oxen,   1Ki 7:25;
three oxen looking toward *n*.   2Ch 4:4
the porters were toward the   1Ch 9:24
n.
he stretcheth out the *n*. over   Job 26:7
empty place
and cold cometh out of the *n*.   Job 37:9
fair weather cometh out of   Job 37:22
the *n*. with
on the sides of *n*. the city of   Ps 48:2
great King
n. and south, thou hast   Ps 89:12
created them
the wind turneth about to the *n*.   Ec 1:6

if the tree fall toward the *n.* — *Ec 11:3*
there it shall be
I will sit in the sides of the *n.* — *Isa 14:13*
I will say to the *n.,* Give up; — *Isa 43:6*
and to the south
the pot's face is toward the *n.* — *Jer 1:13*
out of the *n.* an evil break forth — *Jer 1:14; 4:6; 46:20*
all the families of the — *Jer 1:15*
kingdoms of the *n.*
go and proclaim these words — *Jer 3:12*
toward the *n.*
shall come together out of the — *Jer 3:18*
land of the *n.*
for evil appeareth out of the *n.* — *Jer 6:1*
and great
which led Israel out of the *n.* — *Jer 23:8; 31:8*
country
I will send and take all the — *Jer 25:9*
families of the *n.*
all the kings of the *n.* far and — *Jer 25:26*
near, shall drink
they shall stumble and fall — *Jer 46:6*
toward the *n.*
Lord of hosts hath a sacrifice — *Jer 46:10*
in the *n.* country
she shall be delivered to the — *Jer 46:24*
people of the *n.*
behold, waters rise up out of — *Jer 47:2*
the *n.*
out of the *n.* cometh up a — *Jer 50:3*
nation against her
behold, a whirlwind came out — *Eze 1:4*
of the *n.*
so I lifted up mine eyes the way — *Eze 8:5*
toward the *n.*
toward the *n.* sat women — *Eze 8:14*
weeping for Tammuz
all faces from south to *n.* — *Eze 20:47*
shall be burnt
all flesh from south to *n.* will I — *Eze 21:4*
cut off
the princes of the *n.* all of — *Eze 32:30*
them be there
having the prospect toward — *Eze 40:44; 40:46*
the *n.*
one door was toward the *n.* — *Eze 41:11; 42:4*
brought into court and — *Eze 42:1*
building toward the *n.*
their doors *n.;* chambers — *Eze 42:4; 42:11, 13*
toward the *n.*
the holy chambers looked — *Eze 46:19*
toward the *n.*
for priests be this holy — *Eze 48:10*
oblation toward *n.*
the suburbs of the city shall — *Eze 48:17*
be toward the *n.*
of south shall come to the king — *Da 11:6*
of the *n.*
continue more years than the — *Da 11:8*
king of the *n.*
shall come and fight with the — *Da 11:11*
king of the *n.*
for the king of the *n.* shall — *Da 11:13*
return and set
the king of the *n.* shall cast — *Da 11:15; 11:40*
up a mount
but tidings out of the *n.* shall — *Da 11:44*
trouble him
he will stretch his hand — *Zep 2:13*
against the *n.*
black horses go into the *n.* — *Zec 6:6*
country
have quieted my spirit in the *n.* — *Zec 6:8*
country
the mountain shall remove — *Zec 14:4*
toward the *n.*
and on the *n.* were three gates — *Re 21:13*

NORTH BORDER

and this shall be your *n.* — *Nu 34:7; 34:9*
border

NORTH QUARTER

Judah's border in *n.* quarter — *Jos 15:5*
was from sea
Togarmah of *n.* quarter and — *Eze 38:6*
his bands

NORTH SIDE

tabernacle on the *n.* side — *Ex 26:20*
twenty boards
thou shalt put the table on the — *Ex 26:35*
n. side
for *n.* side hangings of 100 — *Ex 27:11; 38:11*
cubits

the camp of Dan shall be on — *Nu 2:25*
the *n.* side
people of war pitched on the — *Jos 8:11*
n. side of Ai
Midianites were on the *n.* side — *J'g 7:1*
of them
there is a feast on the *n.* side — *J'g 21:19*
of Beth-el
put brasen altar on *n.* side of — *2Ki 16:14*
altar
he measured the *n.* side 500 — *Eze 42:17*
reeds
the goings out of the city on — *Eze 48:30*
the *n.* side

FROM THE NORTH

gathered *from the n.* and the — *Ps 107:3;*
south — *Isa 49:12; Jer 16:15; 23:8*
for there shall come *from the* — *Isa 14:31*
n. a smoke
I raised up one *from the n.* he — *Isa 41:25*
shall come
I will bring evil *from the n.* — *Jer 4:6; 6:22; 10:22; 50:9, 41; 51:48*
I will bring a king of kings — *Eze 26:7*
from the n.
I will cause thee to come up — *Eze 39:2*
from the n. parts
they shall wander *from the n.* — *Am 8:12*
to the east
and flee *from the* land of *the n.* — *Zec 2:6*
come *from the n.* and sit — *Lu 13:29*
down in kingdom

NORTHERN

break the *n.* iron, and the — *Jer 15:12*
steel
I will remove from you, the *n.* — *Joe 2:20*
army

NORTHWARD

look *n.* and eastward — *Ge 13:14; De 3:27*
tabernacle *n.* without the veil — *Ex 40:22*
kill it on the side of the altar *n.* — *Le 1:11*
ye compassed mountain, turn — *De 2:3*
you *n.*
front of one rock was situate — *1Sa 14:5*
n.
Zecharias' lot came out *n.* — *1Ch 26:14*
and *n.* were four Levites a — *1Ch 26:17*
day
n. was this image of jealousy — *Eze 8:5*
then he brought me out of the — *Eze 47:2*
gate *n.*
three gates *n.* one gate of — *Eze 48:31*
Reuben

NOSE

that hath a flat *n.* shall not — *Le 21:18*
offer
put my hook in thy *n.* — *2Ki 19:28; Isa 37:29*
his *n.* pierceth through snares — *Job 40:24*
canst thou put a hook into his — *Job 41:2*
n.
the wringing of the *n.* bringeth — *Pr 30:33*
blood
thy *n.* is as the tower of — *Ca 7:4*
Lebanon
and the smell of thy *n.* like — *Ca 7:8*
apples
the rings, and *n.* jewels — *Isa 3:21*
these are a smoke in my *n.* a — *Isa 65:5*
fire that burns
they put the branch to their *n.* — *Eze 8:17*
put a jewel in thy *n.* (S) — *Eze 16:12*
they shall take away thy *n.* — *Eze 23:25*
and ears

NOSES

n. have they, but they smell — *Ps 115:6*
not
it shall stop the *n.* of the — *Eze 39:11*
passengers

NOSTRIL

put ring on *n.* — *Eze 16:12*
(A)(B)(E)(R)

NOSTRILS

God breathed into man's *n.* the — *Ge 2:7*
breath
all in whose *n.* was breath of — *Ge 7:22*
life, died

with blast of thy *n.* waters — *Ex 15:8*
gathered
eat till it come out at your *n.* — *Nu 11:20*
went a smoke of his *n.* — *2Sa 22:9; Ps 18:8*
the blast of the breath of his — *2Sa 22:16; Ps 18:15*
n.
by breath of his *n.* they are — *Job 4:9*
consumed
and the Spirit of God is in my — *Job 27:3*
n.
the glory of his *n.* is terrible — *Job 39:20*
out of his *n.* goeth smoke, as — *Job 41:20*
out of a pot
from man, whose breath is in — *Isa 2:22*
his *n.*
the breath of our *n.* was taken — *La 4:20*
stink of your camps to come — *Am 4:10*
into your *n.*

NOT

I will afflict, but *n.* for ever — *1Ki 11:39*
thine eyes are upon me, and I — *Job 7:8*
am *n.*
come to honour, he knoweth — *Job 14:21; 35:15*
it *n.*
n. unto us, O Lord, *n.* to us be — *Ps 115:1*
glory
to thy testimonies, and *n.* to — *Ps 119:36*
covetousness
the wicked are *n.;* sell it *n.* — *Pr 12:7; 23:23*
for riches are *n.* for ever, — *Pr 27:24*
doth crown endure
I will *n.* be an healer, make me — *Isa 3:7*
n. a ruler
shall I *n.* as I have done to — *Isa 10:11*
Samaria, so do
pride of Moab, but his lies — *Isa 16:6*
shall *n.* be so
take counsel, but *n.* of me, *n.* — *Isa 30:1*
of my Spirit
I have chosen thee, and *n.* cast — *Isa 41:9*
thee away
thou shalt *n.* be forgotten of — *Isa 44:21*
me
let go my captives, *n.* for a — *Isa 45:13*
price nor reward
but *n.* in truth and — *Isa 48:1*
righteousness
they may forget, yet will I *n.* — *Isa 49:15*
forget thee
I held my peace, and thou — *Isa 57:11*
fearest me *n.*
I am found of them that — *Isa 65:1*
sought me *n.*
a wind, *n.* to fan; and they are — *Jer 4:11; 10:20*
n.
I commanded, but they did — *Jer 11:8*
them *n.*
leave us *n.* — *Jer 14:9*
I sent them *n.* neither have — *Jer 14:14;*
commanded them — *14:15; 23:32; 29:9, 31; Eze 13:6*
n. for good — *Jer 21:10; 39:16*
and *n.* out of the mouth of — *Jer 23:16*
the Lord
of peace, and *n.* of evil; *n.* of — *Jer 29:11; 30:5*
peace
because they were *n.* — *Jer 31:15; M't 2:18*
brought into darkness, but *n.* — *La 3:2*
into light
our fathers have sinned, and — *La 5:7*
are *n.*
the like things shall *n.* come — *Eze 16:16*
I will give them, but *n.* by — *Eze 16:61*
thy covenant
n. according to your wicked — *Eze 20:44*
ways
yet thou art a man, and *n.* — *Eze 28:2*
God
they hear, but they will *n.* do — *Eze 33:31; 33:32*
them
I do *n.* this for your sakes, — *Eze 36:22; 36:32*
O Israel
shall be mighty but *n.* by his — *Da 8:24*
power
but *n.* for himself; shall *n.* — *Da 9:26; 11:25*
stand
ye are *n.* my people, I will *n.* be — *Ho 1:9*
your God
they return, but *n.* to the most — *Ho 7:16*
High
it shall *n.* be, saith the Lord — *Am 7:3; 7:6*
at the end it shall speak, and — *Hab 2:3*
n. he
be ye *n.* as your fathers, to — *Zec 1:4*
whom

n. by might nor power, but by　*Zec 4:6*
my Spirit
for I am the Lord, I change *n*.　*Mal 3:6*
be *n*. like the hypocrites　*M't 6:5; 6:8, 16*
and it fell *n*.; and doeth them　*M't 7:25;*
n.　　　　*7:26*
for he taught *n*. as the scribes　*M't 7:29;*
　　　　M'k 1:22
I will have mercy, and *n*.　*M't 9:13;*
sacrifice　　　*12:7*
shall *n*. be forgiven to men　*M't 12:31;*
　　　12:32; Lu 12:10
saying, Lord, this shall *n*. be　*M't 16:22*
unto thee
but it shall *n*. be so among　*M't 20:26*
you, whoso will
the Son of man came, *n*. to　*M't 20:28*
be ministered unto
the second said, I go, sir, and　*M't 21:30*
went *n*.
but do *n*. ye after their works　*M't 23:3*
to have done, and *n*. to leave　*M't 23:23*
the other undone
the end is *n*. yet; let him *n*.　*M't 24:6;*
come down　　*24:17*
ye clothed me *n*. ye visited　*M't 25:43*
me *n*.
did it *n*. to one of these, did　*M't 25:45*
it *n*. to me
n. on the feast day, lest there　*M't 26:5*
be an uproar
n. as I will, but as thou wilt　*M't 26:39;*
　　　　M'k 14:36
see ye *n*.? hear ye *n*.? do ye *n*.　*M'k 8:18*
remember
but so it shall *n*. be among　*M'k 10:43*
you
the poor ye have, but me ye　*M'k 14:7*
have *n*. always
whether he were the Christ or　*Lu 3:15*
n.
be healed, and *n*. on the　*Lu 13:14*
sabbath day
that I am *n*. as other men are　*Lu 18:11*
woman, I know him *n*.; man,　*Lu 22:57;*
I am *n*.　　　*22:58*
he confessed, I am *n*. the　*Joh 1:20;*
Christ　　　*3:28*
we believe, *n*. because of thy　*Joh 4:42*
saying
ye will *n*. come to me, that ye　*Joh 5:40*
might have life
I know ye have *n*. the love of　*Joh 5:42*
God in you
ye seek me *n*. because ye saw　*Joh 6:26*
the miracles
I came down, *n*. to do mine　*Joh 6:38*
own will
my judgment is true, for I am　*Joh 8:16;*
n. alone　　　*16:32*
I am *n*. of this world; *n*. the　*Joh 8:23;*
shepherd　　　*10:12*
ye believe *n*. because ye are　*Joh 10:26*
n. of my sheep
said I *n*. unto thee, if thou　*Joh 11:40*
wouldest believe
this spake he, *n*. of himself,　*Joh 11:51*
but being high priest
and *n*. for that nation only,　*Joh 11:52*
but that also
this he said, *n*. that he cared　*Joh 12:6*
for the poor
I judge him *n*. for I came *n*.　*Joh 12:47*
to judge world
Lord, *n*. my feet only, but also　*Joh 13:9*
my hands
ye are clean, but *n*. all: if　*Joh 13:10;*
it were *n*. so　　*14:2*
Judas, *n*. Iscariot, and *n*. to　*Joh 14:22*
the world
n. as the world giveth, give I　*Joh 14:27*
unto you
I call you *n*. servants, but　*Joh 15:15*
friends
if I go *n*. away, the Comforter　*Joh 16:7*
will *n*. come
for he shall *n*. speak of　*Joh 16:13*
himself
saying, N. this man; touch　*Joh 18:40;*
me *n*.　　　*20:17*
n. to speak at all in the name　*Ac 4:18*
of Jesus
have *n*. kept it; he opened *n*.　*Ac 7:53;*
his mouth　　　*8:32*
and shewed him, *n*. to all the　*Ac 10:41*
people
it is the voice of a god, and *n*.　*Ac 12:22*
of a man
I am *n*. the　　　*Ac 13:25*
though he be *n*. far from　*Ac 17:27*
every one of us

hold *n*. thy peace　*Ac 18:9*
n. knowing the things that　*Ac 20:22*
shall befall
shall wolves enter in, *n*.　*Ac 20:29*
sparing the flock
for I am ready *n*. to be bound　*Ac 21:13*
only
I wist *n*. that he was the　*Ac 23:5*
high priest
n. the hearers of the law are　*Ro 2:13*
just
these having *n*. the law, are a　*Ro 2:14*
law to themselves
and *n*. in the letter; but *n*.　*Ro 2:29,*
before God　　　*4:2*
but to him that worketh *n*. but　*Ro 4:5*
believeth
n. in circumcision, but　*Ro 4:10*
uncircumcision
and *n*. as it was by one that　*Ro 5:16*
sinned
I allow *n*. what I would, that　*Ro 7:15*
do I *n*.
but ye are *n*. in the flesh, but in　*Ro 8:9*
the Spirit
how shall he *n*. with him give　*Ro 8:32*
us all things
n. of the Jews only, but of the　*Ro 9:24*
Gentiles
where it was said, Ye are *n*.　*Ro 9:26*
my people
have they *n*. heard? yes, verily　*Ro 10:18*
n. to think of himself more　*Ro 12:3*
highly than
ought to bear, and *n*. to please　*Ro 15:1*
ourselves
to preach, *n*. where Christ　*Ro 15:20*
was named
to whom *n*. only I give thanks,　*Ro 16:4*
but also
hath chosen the things which　*1Co 1:28*
are *n*.
eye hath *n*. seen, nor ear heard,　*1Co 2:9*
nor entered
n. with meat　　*1Co 3:2*
are ye *n*. carnal, and walk　*1Co 3:3;*
as men　　　*5:4*
n. to think of men above that　*1Co 4:6*
is written
and I will know, *n*. the speech　*1Co 4:19*
of them which
n. with old leaven; *n*. before　*1Co 5:8;*
the saints　　　*6:1*
yet *n*. I, but the Lord　*1Co 7:10*
but to the rest speak I, *n*. the　*1Co 7:12*
Lord
am I *n*. an apostle? am I *n*.　*1Co 9:1*
free? have I *n*. seen
I therefore so run, *n*. as　*1Co 9:26*
uncertainly
conscience, I say, *n*. thine　*1Co 10:29*
own, but of others
have ye *n*. houses to eat and　*1Co 11:22*
drink in
because *n*. the eye, I am *n*.　*1Co 12:16*
of the body
yet *n*. I, but the grace of　*1Co 15:10*
God with me
for we are *n*. as many, which　*2Co 2:17*
corrupt
n. with ink, *n*. in tables of　*2Co 3:3*
stone
n. that we are sufficient of　*2Co 3:5*
ourselves
n. as Moses, which put a veil　*2Co 3:13*
over his face
we faint *n*.　　*2Co 4:1*
n. forsaken, cast down, but *n*.　*2Co 4:9*
destroyed
we have an house *n*. made with　*2Co 5:1*
hands
we walk by faith, *n*. by sight;　*2Co 5:7;*
n. in heart　　　*5:12*
God comforteth us, *n*. by his　*2Co 7:7*
coming only
I rejoice, *n*. that ye were made　*2Co 7:9*
sorry
I did it *n*. for his cause that　*2Co 7:12*
had done wrong
and this they did, *n*. as we　*2Co 8:5*
hoped, but first
and *n*. according to that he　*2Co 8:12*
hath *n*.
we dare *n*. make ourselves of　*2Co 10:12*
the number
walked we *n*. in the same　*2Co 12:18*
spirit, same steps
may be of God, and *n*. of us　*2Co 16:7*
Paul an apostle, *n*. of men, nor　*Ga 1:1*
by man

I live, yet *n*. I; and *n*. in　*Ga 2:20;*
another　　　*6:4*
through faith, and that *n*. of　*Eph 2:8*
yourselves
n. of works; *n*. as fools, but as　*Eph 2:9;*
wise　　　*5:15*
doing service as to the Lord,　*Eph 6:7*
and *n*. to men
for we wrestle *n*. against flesh　*Eph 6:12*
and blood
it is given to you, *n*. only to　*Ph'p 1:29*
believe
have obeyed, *n*. as in my　*Ph'p 2:12*
presence only
and *n*. on him only, but on　*Ph'p 2:27*
me also
found in him, *n*. having mine　*Ph'p 3:9*
own righteousness
n. as tho' I had already　*Ph'p 3:12*
attained, or perfect
n. holding the head, from　*Col 2:19*
which the body
touch *n*. taste *n*. handle *n*. all　*Col 2:21*
to perish
on things above, *n*. on things　*Col 3:2*
on the earth
do heartily, as to the Lord,　*Col 3:23*
and *n*. to men
our entrance, that it was *n*. in　*1Th 2:1*
vain
ye received it, *n*. as word of　*1Th 2:13*
men, but
therefore let us *n*. sleep, as do　*1Th 5:6*
others
for all men have *n*. faith　*2Th 3:2*
n. because we have *n*. power,　*2Th 3:9*
but to make
n. given to wine, *n*. greedy of　*1Ti 3:3*
lucre
n. according to our works　*2Ti 1:9;*
　　　　Tit 3:5
and *n*. to me only, but to them　*2Ti 4:8*
that love
to please them, *n*. answering　*Tit 2:9*
again
n. now as a servant, but above　*Ph'm 16*
a servant
n. without an oath, he was　*Heb 7:20*
made priest
which the Lord pitched, and *n*.　*Heb 8:2*
man
n. without blood, which he　*Heb 9:7*
offered for himself
n. made with hands, *n*. of this　*Heb 9:11*
building
faith is the evidence of things　*Heb 11:1*
n. seen
died, *n*. having received the　*Heb 11:13*
promises
they without us should *n*. be　*Heb 11:40*
made perfect
bastards, *n*. sons; *n*. with　*Heb 12:8;*
grief　　　*13:7*
if any man be a hearer, and *n*.　*Jas 1:23*
a doer
and have *n*. works, can faith　*Jas 2:14*
save him
n. by faith only; offend *n*. in　*Jas 2:24;*
word　　　*3:2*
yet ye have *n*.; and doeth it *n*.　*Jas 4:2;*
it is sin　　　*4:17*
n. a people, had *n*. obtained　*1Pe 2:10*
mercy
be subject, *n*. only to the good　*1Pe 2:18*
and gentle
who reviled *n*. again, he　*1Pe 2:23*
threatened *n*.
better for them *n*. to have　*2Pe 2:21*
known
the same hath *n*. the Father　*1Jo 2:23*
as Cain; *n*. that we loved　*1Jo 3:12;*
God　　　*4:10*
he that hath *n*. the Son, hath　*1Jo 5:12*
n. life
and there is a sin *n*. unto　*1Jo 5:17*
death
these be sensual, having *n*. the　*Jude 19*
Spirit
which say they are apostles,　*Re 2:2;*
and are *n*.　　　*2:9*
he said unto me, See thou do　*Re 19:10;*
it *n*.　　　*22:9*

IF NOT

I will go down, and *if n*. I will　*Ge 18:21*
know
and *if n*., tell me, that I may　*Ge 24:49*
know
if n. blot me, I pray, out of　*Ex 32:32*
thy book

if *n.* let fire come out of   *J'g* 9:15;
bramble   9:20
and *if n.* I will take it by force *1Sa* 2:16
but *if n.* then we shall know *1Sa* 6:9
that it is not
if *n.* let Amnon go; *if n.* *2Sa* 13:26;
speak   17:6
but *if n.* it shall not be so *2Ki* 2:10
if *n.* where, and who is he *Job* 9:24
if *n.* hearken to me, hold thy *Job* 33:33
peace
give me my price, and *if n.* *Zec* 11:12
forbear
if *n.* it shall turn to you again *Lu* 10:6
and *if n.* then thou shalt cut it *Lu* 13:9
down

OR NOT

Lord made his journey   *Ge* 24:21
prosperous, *or n.*
saying, Is the Lord among us, *Ex* 17:7
or n.
whether my word come to *Nu* 11:23
pass, *or n.*
whether there be wood *Nu* 13:20
therein, *or n.*
as their fathers did keep it, *or* *J'g* 2:22
n.

NOTABLE

the goat had a *n.* horn between *Da* 8:5
his eyes
had a conspicuous, remarkable *Da* 8:5
horn (A)
grew a prominent horn (B) *Da* 8:5
a conspicuous horn (R) *Da* 8:5
for it came up four *n.* ones, *Da* 8:8
toward four winds
in its place four good-sized *Da* 8:8
horns (B)
four conspicuous horns (R) *Da* 8:8
and they had then a *n.* *M't* 27:16
prisoner
a notorious prisoner *M't* 27:16
(A)(B)(P)(R)
a man of some notoriety (N) *M't* 27:16
before that *n.* day of the Lord *Ac* 2:20
come
great and conspicuous day (B) *Ac* 2:20
that great, resplendent day (N) *Ac* 2:20
great and manifest day (R) *Ac* 2:20
a *n.* miracle hath been done by *Ac* 4:16
them

NOTE

n. it in a book   *Isa* 30:8
who are of *n.* among apostles *Ro* 16:7
n. that man, have no company *2Th* 3:14
with

NOTEBOOKS

above all the *n.* (N)   *2Ti* 4:13

NOTED

n. in the scripture of truth *Da* 10:21

NOTHING

now *n.* will be restrained from *Ge* 11:6
them
only unto these men do *n.* for *Ge* 19:8
they came
as we have done to thee *n.* *Ge* 26:29
but good
nothing (S)   *Ge* 29:15;
De 13:17; 15:9; 28:63; *Jos* 21:45;
Ne 4:15; *Job* 1:9; 8:22; 14:18; 22:6;
Ps 44:12; *Pr* 20:14; *Isa* 29:20-21; 49:4;
52:3, 5; *Am* 5:5; 6:13; *Hab* 2:13;
Mal 1:10; *M't* 18:28; *Ac* 5:36, 38;
  1Co 1:28; 2:6; *2Th* 3:8; *Re* 18:17
and here also have I done *n.* *Ge* 40:15
to put me
n. die that is the children's of *Ex* 9:4
Israel
let *n.* of it remain until *Ex* 12:10
morning
ye shall eat *n.* leavened in *Ex* 12:20
your habitations
gathered much, had *n.* over *Ex* 16:18;
  2Co 8:15
if he have *n.* then he shall be *Ex* 22:3
sold for his theft
there shall *n.* cast their young *Ex* 23:26
eat *n.* that is made of the *Nu* 6:4
vine tree

touch *n.* of theirs, lest ye be *Nu* 16:26
consumed
let *n.* hinder thee from *Nu* 22:16
coming
thou hast lacked *n.* *De* 2:7; *Ne* 9:21
thou shalt save alive *n.* that *De* 20:16
breatheth
to the damsel thou shalt do *n.* *De* 22:26
because he hath *n.* left him in *De* 28:55
the siege
Joshua left *n.* commanded *Jos* 11:15
undone
at least such as before knew *n.* *J'g* 3:2
thereof
he rent him, and had *n.* in his *J'g* 14:6
hand
Samuel told, and hid *n.* from *1Sa* 3:18
him
my father will do *n.* but will *1Sa* 20:2
shew it me
thy servant knew *n.* of all *1Sa* 22:15
this
so that *n.* was missed of all *1Sa* 25:21;
  30:19
she told him *n.* less or more *1Sa* 25:36
until morning
the poor man had *n.* save one *2Sa* 12:3
ewe lamb
not offer of that which doth *2Sa* 24:24
cost me *n.*
provided victuals, they lacked *1Ki* 4:27
n.
there was *n.* in the ark save the *1Ki* 8:9
two tables
silver was *n.* accounted of in *1Ki* 10:21
days of Solomon
and he answered *n.* *1Ki* 11:22; *Lu* 22:35
tell me *n.* but truth *1Ki* 22:16;
  2Ch 18:15
fall *n.* to earth of word of the *2Ki* 10:10
Lord
n. in his house that he *2Ki* 20:13
shewed not
be carried away, *n.* shall be *2Ki* 20:17;
left   *Isa* 39:2, 6
n. hid from Solomon which *2Ch* 9:2
he told her not
said, Lord, it is *n.* with thee *2Ch* 14:11
to help
ye have *n.* to do with us in *Ezr* 4:3
building
then they found *n.* to answer *Ne* 5:8
we will restore, and require *n.* *Ne* 5:12
of them
send portions for whom *n.* is *Ne* 8:10
prepared
sustained them, so that they *Ne* 9:21
lacked *n.*
now Esther required *n.* but *Es* 2:15
what
yet all this availeth me *n.* so *Es* 5:13
long as I see
let *n.* fail of all that thou hast *Es* 6:10
spoken
they go to *n.* and perish; for *Job* 6:18;
ye are *n.*   6:21
we are but of yesterday, and *Job* 8:9
know *n.*
who will make my speech *n.* *Job* 24:25
worth
and he hangeth the earth upon *Job* 26:7
n.
he hath said, It profiteth man *Job* 34:9
n. that he delight himself
thou hast tried me and shalt *Ps* 17:3
find *n.*
and mine age is as *n.* before *Ps* 39:5
thee
when he dieth, he shall carry *Ps* 49:17
n. away
who love thy law, and *n.* *Ps* 119:165
shall offend them
a foolish woman is simple, and *Pr* 9:13
knoweth *n.*
treasures of wickedness profit *Pr* 10:2
n.
wicked comes to *n.* (B) *Pr* 10:28
the sluggard desireth, and hath *Pr* 13:4;
n.   20:4
there is that maketh himself *Pr* 13:7
rich, yet hath *n.*
shall reap *n.* (B)   *Pr* 22:8
if thou hast *n.* to pay, why *Pr* 22:27
should he take
whatsoever God doeth, *n.* can *Ec* 3:14
be put to it
and he shall take *n.* of his *Ec* 5:15
labour
so that he wanteth *n.* for his *Ec* 6:2
soul of all

to the end that man should find *Ec* 7:14
n. after him
none there, and all her *Isa* 34:12
princes shall be *n.*
all nations before him are as *Isa* 40:17;
n. they are counted less than *n.* 41:29
that bringeth the princes to *Isa* 40:23;
n.   41:11-12
Seek ye me for *n.* (A) *Isa* 45:19;
  Ro 13:3
not in anger, lest thou bring *Jer* 10:24
me to *n.*
done *n.* of all that thou *Jer* 32:23
commandest me
I will ask thee a thing, hide *n.* *Jer* 38:14
from me
left of the poor which had *n.* *Jer* 39:10
in Judah
I will keep *n.* back from you *Jer* 42:4
destroy her utterly, let *n.* of *Jer* 50:26
her be left
is it *n.* to you, all ye that pass *La* 1:12
by
woe to the prophets that have *Eze* 13:3
seen *n.*
all the inhabitants of earth *Da* 4:35
reputed as *n.*
a wilderness, yea, and *n.* shall *Joe* 2:3
escape them
will young lion cry if he have *Am* 3:4
taken *n.*
taken up snare, and taken *n.*; *Am* 3:5;
Lord will do *n.*   3:7
it is not in comparison of it as *Hag* 2:3
n.
they have *n.* to eat *M't* 15:32;
  M'k 6:36; 8:1-2
n. shall be impossible to you *M't* 17:20;
  Lu 1:37
he found *n.* thereon but *M't* 21:19;
leaves   *M'k* 11:13
answerest thou *n.*? what is it *M't* 26:62
these witness
he answered *n.*   *M't* 27:12;
  M'k 14:60-61; 15:3-5
have thou *n.* to do with that *M't* 27:19
just man
when Pilate saw that he *M't* 27:24
could prevail *n.*
see thou say *n.* to any man, *M'k* 1:44
but go
and had spent all, and was *n.* *M'k* 5:26
bettered
they should take *n.* for their *M'k* 6:8;
journey   *Lu* 9:3
this kind can come forth by *n.* *M'k* 9:29
but by prayer
and in those days he did eat *n.* *Lu* 4:2
have toiled all night and taken *Lu* 5:5;
n.   *Joh* 21:3
they had *n.* to pay, he frankly *Lu* 7:42
forgave them
and *n.* shall by any means *Lu* 10:19
hurt you
and I have *n.* to set before him *Lu* 11:6
and lo, *n.* worthy of death is *Lu* 23:15;
done to him *Ac* 23:29; 25:25; 26:31
but this man hath done *n.* *Lu* 23:41
amiss
man can receive *n.* except it *Joh* 3:27
be given him
verily the Son can do *n.* of *Joh* 5:19;
himself   5:30
gather, that *n.* be lost; I *Joh* 6:12;
should lose *n.*   6:39
the Spirit quickeneth, the flesh *Joh* 6:63
profiteth *n.*
they say *n.*; I do *n.* of myself *Joh* 7:26;
  8:28
he could do *n.*; ye know *n.* at *Joh* 9:33;
all   9:49
perceive ye how ye prevail *Joh* 12:19
n.? behold
the prince of this world hath *Joh* 14:30
n. in me
I am the vine, for without me *Joh* 15:5
ye can do *n.*
and in that day ye shall ask *Joh* 16:23
me *n.*
hitherto have ye asked *n.* in *Joh* 16:24
my name
I spake openly, in secret have *Joh* 18:20
I said *n.*
they could say *n.* against it *Ac* 4:14
finding *n.* how they might *Ac* 4:21
punish them
and go with them, doubting *Ac* 10:20;
n.   11:12
ye ought to be quiet, and do *Ac* 19:36
n. rashly

I kept back *n.* that was Ac 20:20
profitable to you
all may know, that those Ac 21:24
things are *n.*
we will eat *n.* until we have Ac 23:14
slain Paul
ye have continued fasting, Ac 27:33
having taken *n.*
bring to *n.* the understanding 1Co 1:19
of prudent
I know *n.* by myself; judge *n.* 1Co 4:4;
before the time 4:5
he knoweth *n.* yet as he ought 1Co 8:2
to know
for though I preach, I have *n.* 1Co 9:16
to glory of
and have no charity, I am *n.* 1Co 13:2;
2Co 12:11
and have not charity, it 1Co 13:3
profiteth me *n.*
as having *n.* yet possessing all 2Co 6:10
things
for we can do *n.* against the 2Co 13:8
truth
they in conference added *n.* to Ga 2:6
me
then Christ died for *n.* (N)(P) Ga 2:21
heir when a child, differeth *n.* Ga 4:1
from a servant
I say unto you, Christ shall Ga 5:2
profit you *n.*
let *n.* be done through strife Ph'p 2:3
or vainglory
made himself *n.* (N) Ph'p 2:7
every creature is good, *n.* to be 1Ti 4:4
refused
doing *n.* by partiality; proud, 1Ti 5:21;
knowing *n.* 6:4
for we brought *n.* and we can 1Ti 6:7
carry *n.* out
that *n.* be wanting unto them Tit 3:13
without thy mind would I do Ph'm 14
n.
he left *n.* that is not put under Heb 2:8
him
Moses spake *n.* concerning Heb 7:14
priesthood
for the law made *n.* perfect, Heb 7:19
but bringing in
be perfect and entire, wanting Jas 1:4
n.
but let him ask in faith, *n.* Jas 1:6
wavering
they went forth, taking *n.* of the 3 Jo 7
Gentiles

FOR NOTHING

in the seventh he shall go out Ex 21:2
free *for n.*
an image that is profitable *for* Isa 44:10
n.
the girdle was profitable *for* Jer 13:7;
n. 13:10
unsavoury salt is good *for n.* M't 5:13
to be cast out
do good and lend, hoping *for* Lu 6:35
n. again
be careful *for n.* but by prayer Ph'p 4:6
and supplication

IN NOTHING

Athenians spent their time *in* Ac 17:21
n. else
ye might receive damage by us 2Co 7:9
in n.
in n. am I behind chiefest, 2Co 12:11
though I be nothing
and my hope, that *in n.* I Ph'p 1:20
shall be ashamed
and *in n.* terrified by your Ph'p 1:28
adversaries

IS NOTHING

there *is n.* at all besides this Nu 11:6
manna
this *is n.* else save the sword of J'g 7:14
Gideon
there *is n.* better than to go to 1Sa 27:1
Philistines
he looked, and said, There *is* 1Ki 18:43
n.
there *is n.* among my 2Ki 20:15;
treasures Isa 39:4
it *is n.* with thee to help with 2Ch 14:11
many
this *is n.* else but sorrow of Ne 2:2
heart

they said, There *is n.* done for Es 6:3
him
there *is n.* hid from the heat Ps 19:6
thereof
there *is n.* froward or perverse in Pr 8:8
them
there *is n.* better for a man Ec 2:24;
3:22
begetteth a son, and there *is n.* Ec 5:14
in his hand
there *is n.* too hard for thee Jer 32:17
for there *is n.* covered that M't 10:26;
shall not be revealed M'k 4:22; Lu 12:2
whoso shall swear by the M't 23:16
temple, it *is n.*
whoso shall swear by the M't 23:18
altar, it *is n.*
there *is n.* from without a M'k 7:15
man defileth
if I honour myself, my honour Joh 8:54
is n.
that there *is n.* unclean of Ro 14:14
itself
circumcision *is n.* 1Co 7:19
uncircumcision *is n.*
we know that an idol *is n.* in 1Co 8:4
the world
when he *is n.* he deceiveth Ga 6:3
himself
to them that are defiled *is n.* Tit 1:15
pure

OF NOTHING

behold, ye are *of n.* your Isa 41:24
work nought
and that ye may have lack *of* 1Th 4:12
n.
I am rich, increased, and have Re 3:17
need *of n.*

NOTHINGNESS

all that cometh is *n.* (B) Ec 11:8;
Zec 10:2

NOTHINGS

mere *n.* idols (B) 1Sa 25:21
contemptible, *n.* (B)(N) 1Co 1:28

NOTICE

all the people took *n.* of it 2Sa 3:36
bounty, ye had *n.* before 2Co 9:5

NOTICED

n. and wondered (B)(N)(P) Lu 11:38
n. a boy (A)(B)(N)(R) Ac 27:39

NOTIONS

avoid contradictory *n.* (P) 1Ti 6:20

NOTORIETY

a man of some *n.* (N) M't 27:16

NOTORIOUS

n. prisoner (A)(B)(P)(R) M't 27:16

NOTWITHSTANDING

n. they hearkened not to Ex 16:20;
Moses 1Sa 2:25; 2Ki 17:14
n. if he continue a day or two Ex 21:21
not punished
n. ye would not go up, but De 1:26
rebelled
n. in thy days I will not do it 1Ki 11:12
n. I have spoken unto you, Jer 35:14
rising early
n. being warned of God in a M't 2:22
dream
n. he that is least in kingdom M't 11:11
is greater
n. lest we should offend, go M't 17:27
to the sea
n. be sure of this that Lu 10:11
kingdom is come
n. in this rejoice not, that Lu 10:20
spirits are subject
n. whether in pretence or Ph'p 1:18
truth Christ is
n. have well done, that ye Ph'p 4:14
communicate with
n. she shall be saved in 1Ti 2:15
childbearing

n. Lord stood with me, and 2Ti 4:17
strengthened
n. ye give them not those Jas 2:16
things needful
n. I have a few things against Re 2:20
thee

NOUGHT

shouldest thou therefore Ge 29:15
serve me for *n.*
shall cleave *n.* of the cursed De 13:17
thing
thy poor brother, and thou De 15:9
givest him *n.*
the Lord will rejoice to bring De 28:63
you to *n.*
the city is pleasant, but the 2Ki 2:19
water *n.*
God brought their counsel to Ne 4:15
n.
Satan said, Doth Job fear God Job 1:9
for *n.*
the place of the wicked shall Job 8:22
come to *n.*
surely the mountain falling Job 14:18
cometh to *n.*
hast taken a pledge from thy Job 22:6
brother for *n.*
Lord bringeth counsel of Ps 33:10
heathen to *n.*
thou sellest thy people for *n.* Ps 44:12
but ye have set at *n.* all my Pr 1:25
counsel
it is *n.* it is *n.* saith the buyer Pr 20:14
take counsel, it shall come to Isa 8:10
n.
for the terrible one is brought Isa 29:20
to *n.*
that turn aside the just for a Isa 29:21
thing of *n.*
they shall be as nothing, as a Isa 41:12
thing of *n.*
ye are of nothing, and your Isa 41:24
work of *n.*
I have spent my strength for *n.* Isa 49:4
and in vain
saith the Lord, Ye have sold Isa 52:3
yourselves for *n.*
that my people is taken away Isa 52:5
for *n.*
a false vision, and a thing of Jer 14:14
n.
and Beth-el shall come to *n.* Am 5:5
ye which rejoice in a thing of Am 6:13
n. who say
would shut the doors for *n.* Mal 1:10
neither kindle fire on mine altar
for *n.*
must suffer, and be set at *n.* M'k 9:12;
Lu 23:11
this is the stone set at *n.* of you Ac 4:11
builders
all were scattered and brought Ac 5:36
to *n.*
if this work be of men, it will Ac 5:38
come to *n.*
our craft is in danger to be set Ac 19:27
at *n.*
why dost thou set at *n.* thy Ro 14:10
brother
to bring to *n.* things that are 1Co 1:28
the wisdom of this world that 1Co 2:6
cometh to *n.*
nor did we eat any man's 2Th 3:8
bread for *n.*
in one hour so great riches Re 18:17
is come to *n.*

NOURISH

and there, will I *n.* thee Ge 45:11; 50:21
I will sustain and provide for Ge 45:11
you (A)
I will support you (B) Ge 45:11
I will provide for you (R) Ge 45:11
that man shall *n.* young cow Isa 7:21
and two sheep
shall keep alive a young cow Isa 7:21
(A)(B)(E)(R)
nor do I *n.* up young men, nor Isa 23:4
bring up virgins
he planteth an ash, the rain Isa 44:14
doth *n.* it
and rain made it grow (B) Isa 44:14

NOURISHED

Joseph *n.* his father and Ge 47:12
brethren
supplied his father (A) Ge 47:12

supported his father and brothers (B)   *Ge 47:12*

provided for father and brothers (R)   *Ge 47:12*

a lamb which he bought and *n*. up   *2Sa 12:3*

he brought it up (A)(R)   *2Sa 12:3*

he had bought and nurtured (B)   *2Sa 12:3*

I have *n*. and brought up children and they   *Isa 1:2*

nurtured and brought up children (B)   *Isa 1:2*

reared and brought up (R)   *Isa 1:2*

she *n*. her whelps among young lions   *Eze 19:2*

and *n*. in his father's house three months   *Ac 7:20*

nurtured in his father's house (A)(B)   *Ac 7:20*

nursed in his father's house (N)   *Ac 7:20*

brought up in his father's house (P)(R)   *Ac 7:20*

Pharaoh's daughter *n*. him for her own son   *Ac 7:21*

their country was *n*. by the king's country   *Ac 12:20*

n. up in words of faith and good doctrine   *1Ti 4:6*

ever nourishing your own self (A)   *1Ti 4:6*

nurturing on messages of faith (B)   *1Ti 4:6*

bred in the precepts of our faith (N)   *1Ti 4:6*

have *n*. your hearts as in day of slaughter   *Jas 5:5*

n. for a time, times, and half a time   *Re 12:14*

kept safe and fed (A)   *Re 12:14*

cared for during a period (B)   *Re 12:14*

she was to be sustained (N)   *Re 12:14*

NOURISHER

women said, He shall be *n*. of thy old age   *Ru 4:15*

He will rejuvenate, support you in (B)   *Ru 4:15*

NOURISHETH

but *n*. his flesh, as the Lord the church   *Eph 5:29*

NOURISHING

so *n*. them three years to stand before king   *Da 1:5*

ever *n*. your own self (A)   *1Ti 4:6*

NOURISHMENT

left no *n*. (A)   *J'g 6:4*

feed me my portion of *n*. (B)   *Ps 30:8*

more than *n*. (B)   *M't 6:25*

I have *n*. of which (B)   *Joh 4:32; 4:34*

left no *n*. (B)   *Ac 7:11*

all the body by joints and bands having *n*.   *Col 2:19*

NOVICE

not a *n*. lest being lifted up with pride   *1Ti 3:6*

not a new convert (A)(B)(N)(R)   *1Ti 3:6*

NOW

Adam said, This is *n*. bone of my bones   *Ge 2:23*

I will go down, *n*. and see whether they   *Ge 18:21*

n. will we deal worse with thee than   *Ge 19:9*

Take *n*. thy son, thine only son for *n*. I know that thou fearest God   *Ge 22:2; Ge 22:12*

if *n*. thou do prosper my way   *Ge 24:42*

thou art *n*. the blessed of the Lord   *Ge 26:29*

he said, Behold *n*., I am old   *Ge 27:2*

what shall I do *n*. to thee, my son   *Ge 27:37*

she said, *N*. will I praise the Lord   *Ge 29:35*

sojourned with Laban, and stayed there till *n*.   *Ge 32:4*

Israel said to them, If it be so *n*. do this   *Ge 43:11*

so *n*. it was not you that sent me hither   *Ge 45:8*

trade hath been about cattle from youth till *n*.   *Ge 46:34*

If *n*. I have found grace in thy sigh   *Ge 47:29*

n. the magicians of Egypt, they   *Ex 7:11*

not such hail been in Egypt even till *n*.   *Ex 9:18*

go *n*. ye that are men, and serve the Lord   *Ex 10:11*

yet *n*. if thou wilt forgive their sin   *Ex 32:32*

heal her *n*. O God, I beseech thee   *Nu 12:13*

has forgiven this people from Egypt till *n*.   *Nu 14:19*

I shall see him, but not *n*.   *Nu 24:17*

shall behold him but as captain of Lord's host am I *n*. come   *Jos 5:14*

tell me *n*. what thou hast done, hide it not   *Jos 7:19*

why are ye come to me *n*. in distress   *J'g 11:7*

I know that the Lord will do me good   *J'g 17:13*

nay, but thou shalt give it me *n*.   *1Sa 2:16*

but *n*. the Lord saith, be it far from me   *1Sa 2:30*

to pass: *n*. let us go thither   *1Sa 9:6*

honour me *n*. I pray thee, before the elders   *1Sa 15:30*

what have I *n*. done? is there not a cause   *1Sa 17:29*

Therefore *n*. let it please thee   *2Sa 7:29*

nay, my son, let us not all *n*. go   *2Sa 13:25*

so will I *n*. also be thy servant   *2Sa 15:34*

let us *n*. fall into the hand of the Lord   *2Sa 24:14*

And *n*., O God of Israel, let thy   *1Ki 8:26*

who shall cut off, but what? even *n*.   *1Ki 14:14*

it is enough, *n*. O Lord, take away my life   *1Ki 19:4*

he said, Why are ye *n*. turned back   *2Ki 1:5*

restore all that was hers since she went till *n*.   *2Ki 8:6*

know *n*. there shall fall to earth nothing   *2Ki 10:10*

N. the rest of the acts of Jehoahaz   *2Ki 13:8*

am I *n*. come up without Lord   *2Ki 18:25; Isa 36:10*

n. have I brought it to pass   *2Ki 19:25; Isa 37:26*

remember *n*. how I have walked   *2Ki 20:3; Isa 38:3*

be it *n*. known to the king, if city built   *Ezr 4:13*

even till *n*. hath it been building, not finished   *Ezr 5:16*

n. for little space grace been shewed from Lord   *Ezr 9:8*

n. there is hope in Israel concerning this thing   *Ezr 10:2*

put forth thy hand, *n*. and touch   *Job 1:11; 2:5*

n. it is come upon thee, and thou faintest   *Job 4:5*

for *n*. ye are nothing, ye see my casting down   *Job 6:21*

lay down *n*.; and if it be not so *n*.   *Job 17:3; 24:25*

where is *n*. my hope; *n*. I am their song   *Job 17:15; 30:9*

have heard of thee, but *n*. my eye seeth thee   *Job 42:5*

n. will I arise, saith the Lord   *Ps 12:5*

n. know I that the Lord saveth his anointed   *Ps 20:6*

n. Lord, what wait I for, my hope is in thee   *Ps 39:7*

why heathen say, Where is *n*. their God   *Ps 115:2*

save *n*. I beseech thee, O Lord, send now   *Ps 118:25*

but *n*. have I kept thy word   *Ps 119:67*

do this *n*. my son, and deliver thyself   *Pr 6:3*

n. she is without, *n*. in the streets, and lieth   *Pr 7:12*

go to *n*.   *Ec 2:1*

that which *n*. is shall all be forgotten   *Ec 2:16*

what hath been is *n*.   *Ec 3:15*

I will rise *n*. and go about the city   *Ca 3:2*

n. go to, I will tell you what I will do   *Isa 5:5*

said, Hear ye *n*. O house of David   *Isa 7:13*

but *n*. the Lord hath spoken, saying   *Isa 16:14*

thy wise men, let them tell thee *n*.   *Isa 19:12*

what aileth thee *n*. that thou art wholly gone   *Isa 22:1*

n. will I rise, *n*. will I lift up myself   *Isa 33:10*

n. have I brought it to pass   *Isa 37:26*

but *n*. O Lord, thou art our Father   *Isa 64:8*

n. what hast thou to do in way of Egypt   *Jer 2:18*

n. will I give sentence against them   *Jer 4:12*

the word of the Lord let it *n*. come   *Jer 17:15*

turn *n*. every one from his evil way   *Jer 25:5*

N. therefore why hast thou not   *Jer 29:27*

ask ye *n*. and see whether a man doth travail   *Jer 30:6*

ye were *n*. turned, and had done right   *Jer 34:15*

return ye *n*. every man from his evil way   *Jer 35:15*

woe is me *n*. the Lord hath added grief   *Jer 45:3*

even till *n*. have I not eaten of that   *Eze 4:14*

O Daniel, to thee am I *n*. sent   *Da 10:11*

for then was it better with me than *n*.   *Ho 2:7*

and *n*. they sin more and more, and made   *Ho 13:2*

Therefore also *n*. saith the Lord   *Joe 2:12*

turn ye *n*. from your evil ways and doings   *Zec 1:4*

for *n*. have I seen with mine eyes   *Zec 9:8*

prove me *n*. herewith, saith the Lord   *Mal 3:10*

n. all this was done, that it might be   *M't 1:22*

from the days of John the Baptist, till *n*.   *M't 11:12*

sleep on *n*.   *M't 26:45*

thinkest that I cannot *n*. pray to my Father   *M't 26:53*

let him *n*. come down from the cross   *M't 27:42*

let him deliver *n*.   *M't 27:43*

so that the ship was *n*. full of waves   *M'k 4:37*

Lord, *n*. lettest thy servant depart in peace   *Lu 2:29*

which *n*. these three was neighbour to him   *Lu 10:36*

come, for all things are *n*. ready   *Lu 14:17*

but *n*. he that hath a purse, let him take it   *Lu 22:36*

draw out *n*. and bear to governor of feast   *Joh 2:8*

but thou hast kept the good wine until *n*.   *Joh 2:10*

he whom thou *n*. hast is not thy husband   *Joh 4:18*

but the hour cometh, and *n*. is   *Joh 4:23; 5:25*

who was born blind, how then doth he *n*. see   *Joh 9:19*

what I do thou knowest not *n*. but shalt know   *Joh 13:7*

many things, but ye cannot *n*. bear them   *Joh 16:12*

ye *n*. therefore have sorrow, but I will see you   *Joh 16:22*

lo, *n*. speakest thou plainly, and no proverb   *Joh 16:29*

n. we are sure; do ye *n*. believe   *Joh 16:30; 16:31*

I kept them, and *n*. come I to thee   *Joh 17:13*

this is *n*. the third time that Jesus shewed   *Joh 21:14*

shed forth this which ye *n*. see and hear   *Ac 2:33*

n. when they heard this, were pricked in heart   *Ac 2:37*

and *n.* Lord, behold their   *Ac 4:29*
threatenings
n. I know of a surety Lord   *Ac 12:11*
sent his angel
n. as soon as it was day, there   *Ac 12:13*
was a stir
N. they had gone throughout   *Ac 16:6*
and *n.* why tarriest thou,   *Ac 22:16*
arise, be baptized
the Gentiles, to whom *n.* I   *Ac 26:17*
send thee
N. if we be dead with Christ, we   *Ro 6:8*
but *n.* being made free from   *Ro 6:22*
sin
n. then it is no more I that do   *Ro 7:17*
it, but sin
n. it is high time to awake out   *Ro 13:11*
of sleep
n. ye are full, *n.* ye are rich   *1Co 4:8*
n. are they holy   *1Co 7:14*
N. concerning virgins I have   *1Co 7:25*
no
n. I know in part   *1Co 13:12*
for I will not see you *n.* by   *1Co 16:7*
the way
as we said before, so say I *n.*   *Ga 1:9*
again
for do I *n.* persuade men or   *Ga 1:10*
God
the life which I *n.* live in the   *Ga 2:20*
flesh, I live by
are ye *n.* made perfect by the   *Ga 3:3*
flesh
I desire to be present with you   *Ga 4:20*
n. and change
but as then, even so it is *n.*   *Ga 4:29*
to the intent that *n.* to   *Eph 3:10*
principalities
were darkness, but *n.* are ye   *Eph 5:8*
light in the Lord
your fellowship from the first   *Ph'p 1:5*
day until *n.*
obeyed, but *n.* much more in   *Ph'p 2:12*
my absence
but *n.* ye also put off all these,   *Col 3:8*
anger
n. we live, if ye stand fast in   *1Th 3:8*
the Lord
having the promise of the life   *1Ti 4:8*
that *n.* is
for I am *n.* ready to be offered   *2Ti 4:6*
not *n.* as a servant, but above   *Ph'm 16*
a servant
n. we see not yet all things put   *Heb 2:8*
under him
N. if thou commit no adultery   *Jas 2:11*
go to, *n.* ye that say, to-day or   *Jas 4:13*
to-morrow
go to, *n.* rich men, weep and   *Jas 5:1*
howl for miseries
though *n.* ye see him not, yet   *1Pe 1:8*
believing
but are *n.* the people of God   *1Pe 2:10*
had not obtained
because the true light *n.* shineth   *1Jo 2:8*
n. are we the sons of God, it   *1Jo 3:2*
doth not appear
and even *n.* already is it in the   *1Jo 4:3*
world

NOW *THEREFORE*

n. therefore restore the man   *Ge 20:7*
his wife
n. therefore my husband will   *Ge 29:32*
love me
come *n. therefore* and let us   *Ge 37:20*
slay him, and cast
n. therefore fear Lord, and   *Jos 24:14*
serve him
n. therefore behold king ye   *1Sa 12:13*
have chosen
n. therefore stand and see   *1Sa 12:16*
this great thing
shall I not *therefore n.* require   *2Sa 4:11*
his blood
n. therefore let my life be   *2Ki 1:14*
precious
n. therefore advise thyself   *1Ch 21:12*
what word
send me *n. therefore* man   *2Ch 2:7*
cunning to work
n. therefore O God, strengthen   *Ne 6:9*
my hands
n. therefore be content, look   *Job 6:28*
upon me
be wise, *n. therefore* O ye   *Ps 2:10*
kings, be instructed
n. therefore be not mockers,   *Isa 28:22*
lest your bands

n. therefore what have I here,   *Isa 52:5*
saith the Lord
n. therefore amend your   *Jer 26:13*
ways and doings
n. therefore why hast thou   *Jer 29:27*
not reproved
n. therefore know certainly   *Jer 42:22*
that ye shall die
n. therefore O our God, hear   *Da 9:17*
the prayer
therefore also *n.* saith the   *Joe 2:12*
Lord, turn ye
therefore n. shall they go   *Am 6:7*
captive first
n. therefore hear thou word of   *Am 7:16*
the Lord
n. therefore are we all present   *Ac 10:33*
before God
n. therefore why tempt ye   *Ac 15:10*
God to put a yoke
n. therefore depart, and go in   *Ac 16:36*
peace
n. therefore there is a fault   *1Co 6:7*
among you
n. therefore perform the   *2Co 8:11*
doing of it
n. therefore ye are no more   *Eph 2:19*
strangers

NULL

faith is *n.* (R)   *Ro 4:14*
preaching is *n.* and void (N)   *1Co 15:14*
cannot render *n.* and void (P)   *Ga 3:17*

NULLIFIES

n. them (B)   *Nu 30:12; 30:13*

NULLIFY

n. them (A)   *Nu 30:15*
not *n.* grace (N)(R)   *Ga 2:21*

NUMBER

if a man can *n.* the dust of   *Ge 13:16*
the earth
tell the stars, if thou be able to   *Ge 15:5*
n. them
I being few in *n.* they shall   *Ge 34:30*
slay me
very much, for it was without   *Ge 41:49*
n.
number (S)   *Ex 5:8;*
   5:18; 1Sa 18:27; Ps 48:12
take the lamb according to *n.*   *Ex 12:4*
of souls
gather manna, according to *n.*   *Ex 16:16*
of persons
nothing barren, *n.* of thy days   *Ex 23:26*
I will fulfil
he shall *n.* seven days for his   *Le 15:13*
cleansing
then she shall *n.* to herself   *Le 15:28*
seven days
after the seventh sabbaths   *Le 23:16*
shall ye *n.* fifty days
thou shalt *n.* seven sabbaths of   *Le 25:8*
years to thee
the *n.* of years after the   *Le 25:15;*
jubilee, the *n.* of years   *25:16, 50*
beasts, which shall make you   *Le 26:22*
few in *n.*
with the *n.* of their names   *Nu 1:2;*
   18:22
Aaron shall *n.* them by their   *Nu 1:3*
armies
only thou shalt not *n.* the tribe   *Nu 1:49*
of Levi
n. the children of Levi from a   *Nu 3:15*
month old
n. of males from a month old   *Nu 3:22;*
   3:28, 34, 40, 43
until fifty years old shalt   *Nu 4:23;*
thou *n.* them   *4:30*
as for the sons of Merari thou   *Nu 4:29*
shalt *n.* them
which Moses and Aaron did   *Nu 4:37*
n.
your whole *n.* from twenty   *Nu 14:29*
years old
after the *n.* of days ye   *Nu 14:34*
searched the land
according to *n.* ye shall   *Nu 15:12*
prepare, so shall ye do to
every one according to their *n.*
who can count the *n.* of   *Nu 23:10*
fourth part of Israel

offerings according to *n.*   *Nu 29:18;*
   21:24, 27, 30, 33, 37
the half of their portion was   *Nu 31:36*
in *n.*
left few in *n.* among heathen   *De 4:27;*
   28:62
because ye were more in *n.* than   *De 7:7*
any people
seven weeks shalt thou *n.* begin   *De 16:9*
to *n.*
judge cause him to be beaten   *De 25:2*
by a certain *n.*
he set bounds according to the   *De 32:8*
n. of Israel
every man of you a stone   *Jos 4:5;*
according to *n.*   *4:8*
they and their camels without   *J'g 6:5;*
n.   *7:12*
the *n.* of them that lapped were   *J'g 7:6*
300 men
according to the *n.* of them   *J'g 21:23*
that danced
the *n.* of the lords of the   *1Sa 6:4*
Philistines
to the *n.* of all the cities of the   *1Sa 6:18*
Philistines
n. and see who is gone from   *1Sa 14:17*
us
there arose and went over by   *2Sa 2:15*
n. twelve
had fingers and toes   *2Sa 21:20*
twenty-four in *n.*
to say, Go *n.* Israel and Judah   *2Sa 24:1*
that I may know the *n.* of the   *2Sa 24:2*
people
Joab gave up the sum of the *n.*   *2Sa 24:9*
of the people
Elijah took twelve stones   *1Ki 18:31*
according to *n.*
whose *n.* was in the days of   *1Ch 7:2*
David
the *n.* of them after their   *1Ch 7:9;*
genealogy   *7:40*
the *n.* of mighty men whom   *1Ch 11:11*
David had
n. thee an army like the army   *1Ch 20:25*
lost
Satan provoked David to *n.*   *1Ch 21:1*
Israel
of the gold and silver there is   *1Ch 22:16*
no *n.*
their *n.* by their polls, man by   *1Ch 23:3*
man
set feasts by *n.*; *n.* of the   *1Ch 23:31;*
workman   *25:1*
the *n.* that were instructed in   *1Ch 25:7*
the songs
but David took not the *n.* of   *1Ch 27:23*
them
Joab began to *n.* but he   *1Ch 27:24*
finished not
the people were without *n.*   *2Ch 12:3*
that came
the whole *n.* of the chief of   *2Ch 26:12*
the fathers
the *n.* of the burnt offerings,   *2Ch 29:32*
bullocks
a great *n.* of priests   *2Ch 30:24*
sanctified themselves
and this is the *n.* of the vessels   *Ezr 1:9*
the *n.* of the men of the people   *Ezr 2:2*
of Israel
and offered the daily burnt   *Ezr 3:4*
offerings by *n.*
twelve he goats, according to   *Ezr 6:17*
the *n.* of tribes
by *n.* and by weight of every   *Ezr 8:34*
one
the *n.* of those slain in Shushan   *Es 9:11*
the palace
Job offered according to the *n.*   *Job 1:5*
of them all
let it not come into the *n.* of   *Job 3:6*
the months
marvellous things without *n.*   *Job 5:9;*
   9:10
the *n.* of his months are with   *Job 14:5*
thee
the *n.* of years is hidden to   *Job 15:20*
the oppressor
is there any *n.* of his armies   *Job 25:3*
I would declare to him the *n.*   *Job 31:37*
of my steps
shall break in pieces mighty   *Job 34:24*
men without *n.*
neither can the *n.* of his   *Job 36:26*
years be searched
because the *n.* of thy days is   *Job 38:21*
great
who can *n.* the clouds in   *Job 38:37*
wisdom

canst thou *n.* the months that *Job 39:2*
they fulfil
so teach us to *n.* our days, *Ps 90:12*
that we may
when they were but a few *Ps 105:12*
men in *n.*
caterpillars, and that without *Ps 105:34*
n.
they are more in *n.* than the *Ps 139:18*
sand
he telleth the *n.* of the stars, *Ps 147:4*
calleth them
there are queens and virgins *Ca 6:8*
without *n.*
the residue of the *n.* of *Isa 21:17*
archers, mighty men
that bringeth out their host *Isa 40:26*
by *n.*
that furnish the drink offering *Isa 65:11*
to that *n.*
therefore will I *n.* you to the *Isa 65:12*
sword
as *n.* of thy cities are thy gods, *Jer 2:28*
O Judah
my people have forgotten me *Jer 2:32*
days without *n.*
according to the *n.* of thy *Jer 11:13*
cities, O Judah
yet a small *n.* that escape *Jer 44:28*
sword shall return
according to the *n.* of the days *Eze 4:4;*
4:5, 9
thou shalt take a few in *n.* and *Eze 5:3*
bind them
I understand by books the *n.* of *Da 9:2*
years
n. of Israel shall be as the *Ho 1:10;*
sand *Ro 9:27*
a nation is come up strong and *Joe 1:6*
without *n.*
there is a great *n.* of carcases, *Nu 3:3*
they stumble
Judas, being of the *n.* of the *Lu 22:3*
twelve
the men sat down, in *n.* 5000 *Joh 6:10;*
Ac 4:4
the *n.* of the names together *Ac 1:15*
were 120
to Theudas a *n.* of men joined *Ac 5:36*
when the *n.* of disciples was *Ac 6:1;*
multiplied *6:7*
large *n.* of priests (A) *Ac 6:7*
a great *n.* believed and turned *Ac 11:21*
to the Lord
from among their *n.* (A) *Ac 15:22*
the churches were increased in *Ac 16:5*
n. daily
for we dare not make *2Co 10:12*
ourselves of the *n.*
let not a widow be taken into *1Ti 5:9*
the *n.*
the *n.* of them was 10,000 times *Re 5:11*
10,000
I heard the *n.* of them which *Re 7:4*
were sealed
a great multitude which no man *Re 7:9*
could *n.*
the *n.* of the army of the *Re 9:16*
horsemen
n. of his name *Re 13:17*
count the *n.* *Re 13:18*
it is the *n.* of a man, and his *Re 13:18*
n. is 666
I saw them that had victory *Re 15:2*
over *n.* beast
n. of Gog is as the sand of the *Re 20:8*
sea

NUMBERED

then shall thy seed also be *n.* *Ge 13:16*
it shall not be *n.* for *Ge 16:10;*
multitude *32:12*
that passeth among them that *Ex 30:13*
are *n.*
them that were *n.* of the *Ex 38:25;*
congregation *38:26*
he *n.* them in the wilderness of *Nu 1:19*
Sinai
those that were *n.* of them *Nu 1:21;*
1:23, 44, 46; 2:4, 13, 15, 19, 21, 23, 26,
28, 30
the Levites were not *n.* among *Nu 1:47;*
them *2:33*
all that were *n.* in the camp of *Nu 2:9*
Judah
were *n.* in camp of Reuben; *n.* *Nu 2:16;*
of Ephraim *2:24*
n. in camp of Dan; Moses *n.* *Nu 2:31;*
them *3:16, 42*

all that were *n.* of the Levites *Nu 3:39*
were 22,000
they *n.* of the sons of the *Nu 4:34;*
Kohathites *4:37*
those that were *n.* of the *Nu 4:38;*
Gershonites *4:41*
those that were *n.* of the sons *Nu 4:42;*
of Merari *4:45*
these whom Moses and *Nu 4:45;*
Aaron *n.* *4:46*
who were princes and over *Nu 7:2*
them that were *n.*
carcases fell in wilderness, all *Nu 14:29*
that were *n.*
these were *n.* of the children *Nu 26:51*
of Israel
n. of the Levites; Moses and *Nu 26:57;*
Eleazar *n.* *26:53*
Joshua rose early and *n.* the *Jos 8:10*
people
the children of Benjamin were *J'g 20:15*
n.
and when he *n.* them in Bezek *1Sa 11:8*
Saul *n.* people in Telaim, *1Sa 15:4*
200,000 footmen
David *n.* the people that were *2Sa 18:1*
with him
David's heart smote him *2Sa 24:10*
after he had *n.*
a great people that cannot be *n.* *1Ki 3:8*
sheep and oxen that could not *1Ki 8:5;*
be *n.* *2Ch 5:6*
then he *n.* the princes of the *1Ki 20:15*
provinces
at return of the year *1Ki 20:26*
Ben-hadad *n.* the Syrians
Israel were *n.* and were like *1Ki 20:27*
two flocks
and king Jehoram *n.* all Israel *2Ki 3:6*
I commanded the people to *1Ch 21:17*
be *n.*
now the Levites were *n.* from *1Ch 23:3;*
thirty years *23:27*
Solomon *n.* all the strangers *2Ch 2:17*
in Israel
he *n.* them from twenty years *2Ch 25:5*
old and
Cyrus *n.* the vessels to *Ezr 1:8*
Sheshbazzar
they are more than can be *n.* *Ps 40:5*
too many to be *n.* (A)(B)(R) *Ps 40:5*
that which is wanting cannot *Ec 1:15*
be *n.*
ye have *n.* the houses of *Isa 22:10*
Jerusalem
he was *n.* with transgressors *Isa 53:12;*
M'k 15:28
as the host of heaven, cannot *Jer 33:22*
be *n.*
God hath *n.* thy kingdom, and *Da 5:26*
finished it
as the sand of the sea, which *Ho 1:10*
cannot be *n.*
hairs of your head are all *n.* *M't 10:30;*
Lu 12:7
for he was *n.* with us, and *Ac 1:17*
obtained part
Matthias was *n.* with the *Ac 1:26*
eleven apostles

NUMBEREST

when thou *n.* that be no *Ex 30:12*
plague when thou *n.*
for now thou *n.* my steps, *Job 14:16*
dost not thou

NUMBERING

Joseph gathered corn until he *Ge 41:49*
left *n.*
after the *n.* wherewith David *2Ch 2:17*
numbered

NUMBERS

the *n.* of the bands that were *1Ch 12:23*
the *n.* of them according to *2Ch 17:14*
for I know not the *n.* thereof *Ps 71:15*

NUN

Joshua, the son of *N.* *Ex 33:11;*
Nu 11:28; 13:8, 16; 14:6, 30, 38; 26:65;
27:18; 32:12, 28; 34:17; De 1:28; 31:33;
34:44; 34:9; Jos 1:1; 2:1, 23; 6:6;
14:1; 17:4; 19:49, 51; 21:1; 24:29;
J'g 2:8; 1Ki 16:34; Ne 8:17

NURSE

given children *n.* (A) *Ge 21:7;*
1Ki 3:21; Isa 66:11
Rebekah their sister, and her *Ge 24:59*
n.
But Deborah Rebekah's *n.* *Ge 35:8*
died, and
to thee a *n.* of the Hebrew *Ex 2:7*
women
that she may *n.* the child for *Ex 2:7*
thee
this child away, and *n.* it for me *Ex 2:9*
her bosom, and became *n.* *Ru 4:16*
unto it
and his *n.* took him up, and *2Sa 4:4*
fled
they hid him, even him and *2Ki 11:2*
his *n.*
him and his *n.* in a *2Ch 22:11*
bedchamber
nurse (S) *Isa 46:11;*
1Ki 3:21; La 4:3; Joe 2:16; M't 24:19
Lu 21:23
as a *n.* cherisheth her children *1Th 2:7*
like a devoted mother nursing *1Th 2:7*
her (A)
like a nursing mother tenderly *1Th 2:7*
fostering (B)

NURSED

nursed (S) *Ge 21:7;*
1Sa 1:23; Ca 8:1; Isa 66:12; Lu 11:2;
23:29
woman took the child, and *n.* it *Ex 2:9*
n. her son (A) *1Sa 1:23;*
Isa 66:12; Lu 23:29
waited on and *n.* him (A) *1Ki 1:4*
n. from the breast (A) *Ca 8:1*
daughters shall be *n.* at thy *Isa 60:4*
side
daughters are carried on the *Isa 60:4*
hip (B)
daughters carried in the arms *Isa 60:4*
(E)(R)
have *n.* (A) *La 2:22*
n. in father's house (N) *Ac 7:20*

NURSING

as a *n.* father beareth the *Nu 11:12*
sucking
nursing (S) *Nu 11:12;*
Isa 11:8; 49:15; La 4:4; M'k 13:17
And kings shall be thy *n.* *Isa 49:23*
fathers
kings be foster fathers and *Isa 49:23*
guardians (A)(B)(R)
and their queens thy *n.* *Isa 49:23*
mothers
who have *n.* babes (A) *M't 24:19;*
M'k 13:17; Lu 21:23
like a devoted mother *n.* *1Th 2:7*
(A)(B)

NURTURE

n. and admonition of the Lord *Eph 6:4*
rear them (tenderly) in *Eph 6:4*
training (A)
bring them up in instruction *Eph 6:4*
and admonition (B)
give them instruction and *Eph 6:4*
correction (N)
Bring them up with Christian *Eph 6:4*
teaching (P)

NURTURED

bought and *n.* (B) *2Sa 12:3*
n. and brought up (B) *Isa 1:2*
n. in father's house (A)(B) *Ac 7:20*

NURTURING

n. on messages of faith (B) *1Ti 4:6*

NUTS

spices, and myrrh, *n.* and *Ge 43:11*
almonds
went down into the garden of *Ca 6:11*
n. to

NYMPHAS

which are in Laodicea, and *N.* *Col 4:15*

O

OAK

the *o*. (S)   *Ge 12:6;*
   J'g 4:11; 9:6, 37; 1Sa 10:3
Jacob hid the gods under the *o*.   *Ge 35:4*
buried beneath the terebinth   *Ge 35:4*
(B)
Deborah was buried under an   *Ge 35:8*
o.
and set it up there under an   *Jos 24:26*
o.
an angel of the Lord sat under   *J'g 6:11*
an *o*.
Absalom's mule went under   *2Sa 18:9*
an *o*.
Absalom, hanged in an *o*.;   *2Sa 18:10;*
alive in the *o*.   *18:14*
he found the man of God   *1Ki 13:14*
under an *o*.
buried their bones under *o*.   *1Ch 10:12*
in Jabesh
ye shall be as an *o*. whose leaf   *Isa 1:30*
fadeth
as teil tree, or *o*. whose   *Isa 6:13*
substance is in them
he taketh the cypress and *o*.   *Isa 44:14*
to make a god
among their idols under every   *Eze 6:13*
thick *o*.

OAKS

by the *o*. (S)   *Ge 13:18; 14:13; 18:1*
be ashamed of the *o*. which ye   *Isa 1:29*
desire
day of the Lord on all *o*. of   *Isa 2:13*
Bashan
of *o*. of Bashan have they   *Eze 27:6*
made thine oars
and burn incense upon the   *Ho 4:13*
hills under *o*.
the Amorite was strong as the   *Am 2:9*
o.
howl, fir tree, howl, O ye *o*.   *Zec 11:2*
of Bashan

OAR

all that handle the *o*. shall   *Eze 27:29*
cry

OARS

wherein shall go no galley   *Isa 33:21*
with *o*.
of the oaks of Bashan they   *Eze 27:6*
made thy *o*.

OATH

made an *o*. (B)   *Ge 21:31;*
  24:7; De 4:31; 1Sa 19:6; 2Ch 15:14
thou shalt be clear from this   *Ge 24:8;*
my *o*.   *24:4*
perform the *o*. I swear to   *Ge 26:3;*
Abraham   *De 7:8; Ps 105:9; Jer 11:5*
let there be now an *o*. betwixt   *Ge 26:28*
us and thee
Joseph took an *o*. of the   *Ge 50:25*
children of Israel
had demanded an *o*. (B)   *Ex 13:19*
an *o*. of Lord shall be between   *Ex 22:11*
sin by an *o*. (S)   *Le 5:1; 5:4*
that a man shall pronounce with   *Le 5:4*
an *o*.
the priest shall charge her by   *Nu 5:19*
an *o*.
Lord make thee a curse and   *Nu 5:21*
an *o*. among people
promised an *o*. (B)   *Nu 14:23;*
32:11; De 6:18, 23; 7:13; 8:1; 31:21;
   J'g 2:1
if a man swear an *o*. to bind   *De 30:2;*
his soul   *30:10*
vow, and every binding *o*. to   *De 30:13*
afflict soul
his *o*. which the Lord maketh   *De 29:12*
with thee
neither with you only do I   *De 29:14*
make this *o*.
we will be blameless of this   *Jos 2:17*
thine *o*.
sware by *o*. (B) *Jos 9:15; 9:20; Lu 1:73*
lest wrath be on us, because of   *Jos 9:20*
the *o*.
Moses said under *o*. (B)   *Jos 14:9*
for Israel had made a great *o*.   *J'g 21:5*

for the people feared the *o*.   *1Sa 14:26*
when Saul charged them   *1Sa 14:27;*
with the *o*.   *14:28*
David asserted with an *o*. (B)   *1Sa 20:5*
David gave his *o*. (A)   *1Sa 24:22;*
   2Sa 19:23
took an *o*. (A)   *2Sa 3:35;*
  1Ki 1:29; 2Ch 15:14; Ezr 10:5
confirmed it with an *o*. (B)   *2Sa 19:23*
king spared Mephibosheth,   *2Sa 21:7*
because of *o*.
why then hast thou not kept   *1Ki 2:43*
the *o*.
an *o*. be laid on him, and the   *1Ki 8:31;*
o. come before thine altar   *2Ch 6:22*
he took an *o*. of the kingdom   *1Ki 18:10*
and nation
Jehoiada took an *o*. of them   *2Ki 11:4*
in house
be mindful of his *o*. to Isaac   *1Ch 16:16*
all Judah rejoiced at the *o*.   *2Ch 15:15*
and Nehemiah took an *o*. of   *Ne 5:12*
the priests
they entered into an *o*. to   *Ne 10:29*
walk in God's law
and that in regard of the *o*. of   *Ec 8:2*
God
he that sweareth, as he that   *Ec 9:2*
feareth an *o*.
which hast despised the *o*.   *Eze 16:59;*
   17:18-19
a covenant, and hath taken   *Eze 17:13*
an *o*. of him
that made him king, whose *o*.   *Eze 17:16*
he despised
curse is poured on us, and *o*.   *Da 9:11*
written in law
love no false *o*. for this I hate   *Zec 8:17*
he promised with an *o*. to give   *M't 14:7*
her
again he denied with an *o*. I   *M't 26:72*
know not man
put himself under *o*. (A)   *M'k 6:23*
the *o*. which he sware to our   *Lu 1:73*
father
sealed by an *o*. (A)   *Lu 1:73*
that God hath sworn with an   *Ac 2:30*
o. to him
which have bound themselves   *Ac 23:21*
with an *o*.
an *o*. for confirmation is an   *Heb 6:16*
end of all strife
God confirmed it by an *o*.   *Heb 6:17*
that by two things
as not without an *o*. he was   *Heb 7:20;*
made priest   *7:21*
the *o*. which was since the   *Heb 7:28*
law, maketh the Son
swear not by the earth, nor   *Jas 5:12*
any other *o*.

OATHS

and took *o*. (A)   *Ge 26:31*
divination to them that have   *Eze 21:23*
sworn *o*.
false, empty, *o*. (B)(R)   *Ho 10:4*
the bow made naked,   *Hab 3:9*
according to the *o*.
shalt perform to the Lord   *M't 5:33*
thine *o*.

OATH'S

nevertheless, for the *o*. sake   *M't 14:9;*
   M'k 6:26

OBADIAH

Ahab called *O*. Now *O*. feared   *1Ki 18:3*
the Lord
O. took an hundred prophets,   *1Ki 18:4*
and hid them
as *O*. was in the way, behold   *1Ki 18:7*
Elijah met him
so *O*. went to meet Ahab,   *1Ki 18:16*
and told him
sons of *O*.   *1Ch 3:21*
son of Izrahiah, *O*.; *O*. son   *1Ch 7:3;*
of Azel   *8:38; 9:44*
O. the son of Shemaiah, the   *1Ch 9:16*
son of Galal
of Gadites men of might, *O*.   *1Ch 12:9*
the second
Ishmaiah son of *O*.   *1Ch 27:19*
he sent to his princes, to *O*. to   *2Ch 17:7*
teach
the overseers were Jahath   *2Ch 34:12*
and *O*.
O. son of Jehiel went up with   *Ezr 8:9*
Ezra

O. sealed; *O*. was a porter   *Ne 10:5;*
   12:25
the vision of *O*. thus saith the   *Ob 1*
Lord

OBED

and they called his name *O*.   *Ru 4:17*
Boaz begat *O*.   *Ru 4:21;*
   1Ch 2:12; M't 1:5
Ephlal begat *O*.   *1Ch 2:37*
O. one of David's valiant   *1Ch 11:47*
men
Shemaiah; and *O*.   *1Ch 26:7*
took Azariah son of *O*. into   *2Ch 23:1*
covenant
Jesse, which was the son of *O*.   *Lu 3:32*

OBED-EDOM

David carried the ark into   *2Sa 6:10;*
the house of *O*.   *6:11; 1Ch 13:13-14*
Lord blessed the house of *O*.   *2Sa 6:11;*
   6:12; 1Ch 13:14
brought ark from house of *O*.   *2Sa 6:12;*
into the city of David   *1Ch 15:25*
O. a porter; *O*. with harp   *1Ch 15:18;*
   15:21, 24
O. and Jeiel with psalteries   *1Ch 16:5*
and harps
O. with their brethren, *O*.   *2Sa 16:38*
also son of Jeduthun
sons of *O*.; sons of *O*. fit for   *1Ch 26:4;*
service   *26:8*
the lot southward fell to *O*.   *1Ch 26:15*
and his sons
Joash took the vessels found   *2Ch 25:24*
with *O*.

OBEDIENCE

show *o*. to ordinances   *De 7:12*
o. to establish tradition (N)   *M'k 7:3*
for *o*. to the faith among all   *Ro 1:5*
nations
by the *o*. of one shall many be   *Ro 5:19*
made righteous
of sin to death, or of *o*. unto   *Ro 6:16*
righteousness
render *o*. (B)   *Ro 13:1*
your *o*. is come abroad unto   *Ro 16:19*
all men
made known to all nations   *Ro 16:26*
for the *o*. of faith
women are commanded to   *1Co 14:34*
be under *o*.
he remembereth the *o*. of you   *2Co 7:15*
all
bringing every thought to the   *2Co 10:5*
o. of Christ
all disobedience, when your *o*.   *2Co 10:6*
is fulfilled
having confidence in thy *o*. I   *Ph'm 21*
wrote
yet learned he *o*. by the things   *Heb 5:8*
he suffered
through santification of the   *1Pe 1:2*
Spirit to *o*.

OBEDIENT

Lord hath said, We will do,   *Ex 24:7*
and be *o*.
put honour on him, that   *Nu 27:20*
Israel may be *o*.
if turn to Lord and shall be *o*.   *De 4:30*
to his voice
ye shall perish, because ye   *De 8:20*
would not be *o*.
strangers shall be *o*. unto me   *2Sa 22:45*
so is a wise reprover upon an   *Pr 25:12*
o. ear
if *o*. ye shall eat the good of   *Isa 1:19*
the land
neither were they *o*. to his   *Isa 42:24*
law
o. unto them (A)(P)(R)   *Lu 2:51*
the priests were *o*. to the faith   *Ac 6:7*
to make Gentiles *o*. by word   *Ro 15:18*
and deed
might know whether ye be *o*.   *2Co 2:9*
in all things
servants, be *o*. to your masters   *Eph 6:5;*
   Tit 2:9
Christ became *o*. unto death   *Ph'p 2:8*
of the cross
wives, be *o*.; children, be *o*.   *Tit 2:5;*
   1Pe 1:14

OBEISANCE

your sheaves made o. to my | Ge 37:7
sheaf
bowed down (A)(B)(R) | Ge 37:7; 37:9
the sun, moon, and eleven stars | Ge 37:9
made o. to me
they bowed and made o. to | Ge 43:28
Joseph
bending their bodies (B) | Ge 43:28
Moses did o. to his | Ex 18:7
father in law
bowed in homage and kissed | Ex 18:7
(A)
bowed deeply and kissed him | Ex 18:7
(B)
the Amalekite did o. to David | 2Sa 1:2
bowed to the ground and | 2Sa 1:2
fell on face and did o. | 2Sa 9:6
(A)(E)(R)
did o. (S) | 2Sa 9:6; 1Ki 1:31; Es 3:2, 5
prostrated himself (B)
the woman of Tekoah did o. | 2Sa 14:4
to the king
face to the ground and | 2Sa 14:4
prostrated herself (B)
when any man came nigh to | 2Sa 15:5
do him o.
approached to prostrate | 2Sa 15:5
himself (B)
I do o. (A)(E)(R) | 2Sa 16:4
Bath-sheba did o. to king | 1Ki 1:16
David
fell upon her knees and did | 1Ki 1:16
homage (B)
bowed and did o. (A)(E)(R) | 1Ki 1:31
princes of Judah made o. to | 2Ch 24:17
the king
bowed down to the king (B) | 2Ch 24:17
nor did o. (R) | Es 3:2; 3:5

OBELISKS

pillars, o. (A) | 2Ki 10:26
o. of Heliopolis (A)(R) | Jer 43:13
o. of Bethshemesh (B) | Jer 43:13
goodly pillars or o. (A) | Ho 10:1

OBEY

therefore, my son, o. my voice | Ge 27:8;
27:13, 43
who is the Lord, that I should o. | Ex 5:2
him
now if ye will o. my voice | Ex 19:5
indeed
o. his voice; if shalt indeed o. | Ex 23:21;
his voice | 28:22
a blessing, if ye o. commands | De 11:27
of Lord
o. his voice | De 13:4;
27:10; 30:2, 8; 1Sa 12:14
and that thou mayest o. his | De 30:20
voice
be careful to o. (B) | Jos 22:5; De 6:17
the Lord's voice will we o. | Jos 24:24
the people refused to o. voice | 1Sa 8:19
of Samuel
behold, to o. is better than | 1Sa 15:22
sacrifice
and refused to o. neither were | Ne 9:17
mindful
it they o. and serve him they | Job 36:11
shall spend
as soon as they hear, they | Ps 18:44
shall o. me
the eye that despiseth, to o. | Pr 30:17
his mother
the children of Ammon shall | Isa 11:14
o. them
o. my voice, and I will be | Jer 7:23;
your God | 11:4, 7
amend your ways, and o. | Jer 26:13;
voice of the Lord | 38:20; Zec 6:15
Rechabites o. their father's | Jer 35:14
commandment
we will o. the voice of Lord | Jer 42:6
our God, that it may be well
with us when we o. the Lord
and all dominions shall serve | Da 7:27
and o. him
even winds and sea, o. him | M't 8:27;
M'k 4:41; Lu 8:25
he ought to o. (A) | M't 13:6
even the unclean spirits o. | M'k 1:27
him
devils o. (P) | Lu 10:17
be thou plucked up, and it | Lu 17:6
shall o. you
we ought to o. God rather than | Ac 5:29
men

whom God hath given to them | Ac 5:32
that o. him
but to them that o. | Ro 2:8
unrighteousness
that ye should o. it in the lusts | Ro 6:12
thereof
to o. his servants ye are to | Ro 6:16
whom ye o.
children, o. your parents | Eph 6:1;
Col 3:20
servants, o. in all things your | Col 3:22
matters
put them in mind to o. | Tit 3:1
magistrates
author of eternal salvation to | Heb 5:9
all that o. him
o. them that have the rule | Heb 13:17
over you
put bits in horses' mouths, that | Jas 3:3
they may o.

NOT OBEY, OBEY NOT

a curse, if ye will not o. the | De 11:28;
commandments | 28:62; 1Sa 12:15;
Job 36:12; Jer 12:17; 18:10
who will not o. the voice of | De 21:18;
his father | 21:20
wherefore then didst thou | 1Sa 15:19
not o.
but if ye say, We will not o. | Jer 42:13
the Lord
that they might not o. thy | Da 9:11
voice
to whom our fathers would not | Ac 7:39
o.
that are contentious, and do not | Ro 2:8
o. truth
who bewitcheth you, that | Ga 3:1;
should not o. | 5:7
taking vengance on them that | 2Th 1:8
o. not gospel
if any man o. not our word, | 2Th 3:14
note that man
if any o. not the word, they | 1Pe 3:1
may be won
what shall end be of them that | 1Pe 4:17
o. not gospel

OBEYED

be blessed, because thou hast | Ge 22:18;
o. | 26:5
that Jacob o. his father and his | Ge 28:7
mother
have o. my voice in all I | Jos 22:2
commanded you
Saul said, I have o. the voice | 1Sa 15:20
of Lord
because I feared the people, | 1Sa 15:24
and o. their voice
behold, thine handmaid hath | 1Sa 28:21
o. thy voice
then all Israel o. Solomon | 1Ch 29:23
they o. the words of the Lord | 2Ch 11:4
then they o. and let them go | Jer 34:10
thus have we o. the voice of | Jer 35:8;
Jonadab | 35:10
because ye o. the | Jer 35:18
commandment of your fathers
neither have we o. the voice of | Da 9:10
the Lord
the people o. the voice of the | Hag 1:12
Lord
many as o. Theudas were | Ac 5:36;
scattered | 5:37
have o. from heart that form | Ro 6:17
of doctrine
ye have o. not in my presence | Ph'p 2:12
only
by faith Abraham o. and | Heb 11:8
went out
Sarah o. Abraham, calling him, | 1Pe 3:6
Lord

NOT OBEYED

were consumed, because they o. | Jos 5:6
not
but ye have not o. my voice | J'g 2:2;
6:10
thou hast not o. the voice of | 1Ki 20:36
Lord
because they o. not the voice | 2Ki 18:12
of Lord
and have not o. the voice of my | Pr 5:13
teachers
ye have not o. my voice, saith | Jer 3:13;
the Lord | 3:25; 42:21; 43:4, 7; 44:23
they have not o. my voice | Jer 9:13;
11:8; 17:23; 32:23; 40:3; Da 9:10

she o. not the voice, she drew | Zep 3:2
not near
but they have not all o. the | Ro 10:16
gospel

OBEYEDST

because thou o. not the voice | 1Sa 28:18
of Lord
thy manner that thou o. not | Jer 22:21
my voice

OBEYETH

who that o. the voice of his | Isa 50:10
servant
this is a nation that o. not the | Jer 7:28
Lord
cursed be the man that o. not | Jer 11:3
the words of

OBEYING

your fathers o. but they did not | J'g 2:17
so
in sacrifice, as in o. the voice | 1Sa 15:22
have purified your souls in o. | 1Pe 1:22
the truth

OBIL

over the camels also was O. | 1Ch 27:30

OBJECT

an o. of scorn (A)(E)(R) | Ps 69:11
o. of scorn to accusers (R) | Ps 109:25;
Jer 6:10
and o. if they had ought | Ac 24:19
against me

OBJECTION

came I without o. (S) | Ac 10:29

OBJECTIONABLE

do not consider it o. (B) | Ge 21:12
who finds nothing o. (B) | M't 11:6

OBJECTIONS

without o. (B) | Ph'p 2:14
those who raise o. (B) | Tit 1:9

OBJECTORS

confute o. (N) | Tit 1:9

OBJECTS

all sorts of gold o. (R) | Ex 35:22
o. of worship (A)(B)(E)(R) | Ac 17:23
o. of retribution (N) | Ro 9:22

OBLATION

an o. of a meat offering baken | Le 2:4;
2:5, 7, 13
an offering (A)(B)(R) | Le 2:4;
2:12; 3:1; 7:14, 29; 22:18; Nu 18:9;
31:50; Isa 19:21; 40:20; 66:3; Jer 14:12;
Eze 44:30; 45:1, 13, 16; Da 2:46; 9:27
as for o. of the firstfruits, ye | Le 2:12
shall offer them
if his o. be a sacrifice of peace | Le 3:1
offering
he shall offer one out of the | Le 7:14
whole o.
he shall bring his o. to the | Le 7:14
Lord, of sacrifices
that will offer his o. for all his | Le 22:18
vows
every o. of theirs shall be most | Nu 18:9
holy
we have brought an o. for the | Nu 31:50
Lord
the Egyptians shall do o. to | Isa 19:21
the Lord
that is so impoverished that | Isa 40:20
he hath no o.
that offereth an o. as if he | Isa 66:3
offered swine's flesh
when they offer an o. I will | Jer 14:12
not accept
and every o. shall be the | Eze 44:30
priest's
when ye shall divide the land, | Eze 45:1
offer an o.

OBLATION (continued)

this is the *o*. ye shall offer   Eze 45:13; 48:9, 20-21
shall give this *o*. for the   Eze 45:16
prince in Israel
that they should offer an *o*.   Da 2:46
to Daniel
time of the evening *o*.; shall   Da 9:21;
cause *o*. to cease   9:27
time of evening sacrifice   Da 9:21
(A)(B)(R)

OBLATIONS

he commanded Israel to offer   Le 7:38
their *o*.
their sacrifices (A)   Le 7:38
their offerings (B)(R)   Le 7:38
to distribute the *o*. of the   2Ch 31:14
Lord
apportion the contributions   2Ch 31:14
(A)(B)(R)
bring no more vain *o*. unto me   Isa 1:13
bring no more offerings of   Isa 1:13
vanity (A)
Come no more with   Isa 1:13
meaningless offerings (B)
Bring no more vain offerings   Isa 1:13
(R)
presented offensive *o*. (B)   Eze 20:28
the firstfruits of your *o*.   Eze 20:40
firstfruits of choicest   Eze 20:40
contributions
contributions and choicest of   Eze 20:40
gifts (B)(R)
every sort of your *o*.   Eze 44:30
all kinds from all your   Eze 44:30
offerings (A)(R)

OBLIGATION

a perpetual *o*. (B)   Ex 29:28
I am under *o*. (A)(N)(P)(R)   Ro 1:14;
   Ga 5:3
no *o*. to honor (P)   Ro 1:31
wages not a favor, but an *o*.   Ro 4:4
(B)

OBLITERATED

to be *o*. (B)   Es 7:4

OBNOXIOUS

o. ways of nations (B)   De 18:9
o. and disgusting (A)   2Sa 10:6

OBOTH

set forward and pitched in   Nu 21:10;
O.   33:43
they journeyed from O.   Nu 21:11; 33:44

OBSCENITIES

full of *o*. (N)   Re 17:4

OBSCENITY

of every *o*. (N)   Re 17:5

OBSCURE

shall be put out in *o*. darkness   Pr 20:20
be put out in complete   Pr 20:20
darkness (A)
put out in utter darkness   Pr 20:20
(B)(R)
put out in blackness of   Pr 20:20
darkness (E)
an *o*. speech (A)(B)(E)(R)   Isa 33:19

OBSCURITY

eyes of the blind see out of *o*.   Isa 29:18
blind see in spite of dimness   Isa 29:18
and darkness (B)
out of their gloom and   Isa 29:18
darkness (R)
then shall thy light rise out of   Isa 58:10
o.
your gloom shall become like   Isa 58:10
noonday (B)(R)
we wait for light, but behold *o*.   Isa 59:9
wait for light, but see only   Isa 59:9
darkness (A)(B)(E)(R)

OBSERVANT

an *o*. mind (B)   1Ki 3:9

OBSERVATION

at my *o*. post (B)   Isa 21:8
kingdom of God cometh not   Lu 17:20
with *o*.
does not come with signs to   Lu 17:20
be observed or visible display
(A)
does not come with eye   Lu 17:20
appeal (B)
never comes by watching for   Lu 17:20
it (P)
not coming with signs to be   Lu 17:20
observed (R)

OBSERVE

o. the feast of unleavened   Ex 12:17;
bread   12:24; De 16:1
o. the sabbath   Ex 31:16
o. thou that which I   Ex 34:11;
command thee this day   De 12:28;
   24:8
o. feast of weeks   Ex 34:22
nor shall ye use enchantments,   Le 19:26
o. times
ye shall *o*. all my statutes   Le 19:37;
   2Ch 7:17; Ne 1:5; Ps 105:45; Eze 37:24
my sacrifice shall ye *o*. to offer   Nu 28:2
me
o. the feast of tabernacles   De 16:13
seven days
now the men did diligently *o*.   1Ki 20:33
whoso is wise, and will *o*.   Ps 107:43
these things
I shall *o*. it with my whole   Ps 119:34
heart
and let thine eyes *o*. my ways   Pr 23:26
the crane and swallow *o*. the   Jer 8:7
time
neither *o*. their judgments   Eze 20:18
nor defile
as a leopard by the way will I   Ho 13:7
o. them
that *o*. lying vanities, forsake   Jon 2:8
their mercies
teaching them to *o*. all things   M't 28:20
whatever
customs not lawful to *o*. being   Ac 16:21
Romans
o. the old customs   Ac 21:21
(A)(P)(R)
concluded that the Gentiles *o*.   Ac 21:25
no such thing
ye *o*. days, and months, and   Ga 4:10
times
then *o*. these things without   1Ti 5:21
preferring
o. pure and modest way (A)   1Pe 3:2

OBSERVED

but his father *o*. the saving   Ge 37:11
he *o*. an Egyptian smiting (S)   Ex 2:11
it is a night to be much *o*. to   Ex 12:42
the Lord
have erred, and not *o*.   Nu 15:22
commandments
Levi *o*. thy word, kept thy   De 33:9
covenant
Eli *o*. her mouth (S)   1Sa 1:12
when Joab *o*. city, he   2Sa 11:16
assigned Uriah
Manasseh *o*. times   2Ki 21:6; 2Ch 33:6
Lord, *o*., felt compassion   1Ch 21:15
(B)
my heart *o*. abundance (B)   Ec 1:16
I have heard him, and *o*. him   Ho 14:8
for Herod feared John and *o*.   M'k 6:20
him
all these have I *o*. from my   M'k 10:20
youth

OBSERVER

there shall not be found an *o*.   De 18:10
of times

OBSERVERS

these nations hearkened to *o*.   De 18:14
of times

OBSERVEST

seeing many things, but thou   Isa 42:20
o. not

OBSERVETH

he that *o*. the wind shall not   Ec 11:4
sow

OBSERVING

o. tradition of elders (B)(R)   M'k 7:3

OBSOLETE

is *o*. (A)(B)   Heb 8:13

OBSTACLE

an *o*. to the Jews (B)   1Co 1:23
every proud *o*. to (P)   2Co 10:5

OBSTACLES

keep an eye on those who   Ro 16:17
cause splits and *o*. (B)

OBSTINACY

my eye dwells on their *o*. (A)   Job 17:2
detestable *o*. disqualifies them   Tit 1:16
(N)

OBSTINATE

are wilfully *o*. (A)   Nu 22:32
the Lord thy God made his   De 2:30
heart *o*.
because I knew that thou art   Isa 48:4
o.
o. to wisdom of just (B)   Lu 1:17

OBSTRUCTION

o. before them (B)   Le 19:14

OBTAIN

it may be I may *o*. children by   Ge 16:2
her
and shall *o*. favour of the Lord   Pr 8:35
they shall *o*. joy and   Isa 35:10;
gladness   51:11
he shall *o*. the kingdom by   Da 11:21
flatteries
be accounted worthy to *o*.   Lu 20:35
that world
thro' your mercy they may *o*.   Ro 11:31
mercy
so run that ye may *o*.   1Co 9:24
they do it to *o*. a corruptible   1Co 9:25
crown, but we
but to *o*. salvation by our   1Th 5:9
Lord Jesus Christ
may *o*. salvation which is in   2Ti 2:10
Christ Jesus
that we may *o*. mercy, and   Heb 4:16
find grace
that they might *o*. a better   Heb 11:35
resurrection
ye kill, ye desire to have, and   Jas 4:2
cannot *o*.

OBTAINED

after certain days I *o*. leave of   Ne 13:6
the king
Esther *o*. kindness; she *o*.   Es 2:9;
grace   2:12
o. favor and kindness (E)   Es 2:17
have mercy on her that had   Ho 2:23
not *o*. mercy
and had *o*. part of this ministry   Ac 1:17
with a great sum *o*. I this   Ac 22:28
freedom
having *o*. help of God I   Ac 26:22
continue to this day
supposing that they had *o*.   Ac 27:13
their purpose
Israel hath not *o*. what he   Ro 11:7
seeketh for, election hath *o*. it
ye have now *o*. mercy through   Ro 11:30
their unbelief
as one that hath *o*. mercy of   1Co 7:25
the Lord
in whom we have *o*. an   Eph 1:11
inheritance
I *o*. mercy, because I did it   1Ti 1:13;
ignorantly   1:16
o. a more excellent name than   Heb 1:4
they
he had patiently endured, he   Heb 6:15
o. the promises
he hath *o*. a more excellent   Heb 8:6
ministry than they
having *o*. eternal redemption   Heb 9:12
for us
by it the elders *o*. a good   Heb 11:2;
report   11:39

Abel *o.* witness that he was *Heb 11:4*
righteous
who *o.* promises, stopped *Heb 11:33*
mouths of lions
which had not *o.* mercy, but *1Pe 2:10*
now have *o.*
that have *o.* like precious faith *2Pe 1:1*
with us

OBTAINETH

gracious woman *o.* honor (E) *Pr 11:16*
a good man *o.* favor of the *Pr 12:2*
Lord
a good thing, and *o.* favor of *Pr 18:22*
Lord

OBTAINING

to *o.* of the glory of our Lord *2Th 2:14*
Jesus Christ

OBVIOUS

o. God is excepted (P) *1Co 15:27*
doings of flesh are *o.* (A)(P) *Ga 5:19*
shallowness be *o.* (B) *2Ti 3:9*

OCCASION

that he may seek *o.* against us *Ge 43:18*
and fall
mayest do as thou shalt find *o.* *J'g 9:33;*
1Sa 10:7
Samson sought *o.* against the *J'g 14:4*
Philistines
given great *o.* to enemies to *2Sa 12:14*
blaspheme
which thou shalt have *o.* to *Ezr 7:20*
bestow
in her *o.* who can turn her *Jer 2:24*
away
shall not have *o.* any more to *Eze 18:3*
use proverb
sought to find *o.* and could find *Da 6:4;*
none *o.* *6:5*
no o. of stumbling in me (E) *M't 11:6*
whoever is an *o.* for stumbling *M't 18:6*
(B)
find in me an *o.* of stumbling *M't 26:31*
(B)
sin taking *o.* by the *Ro 7:8;*
commandment *7:11*
put not an *o.* to fall in his *Ro 14:13*
brother's way
we give you *o.* to glory on our *2Co 5:12*
behalf
I speak by *o.* of the *2Co 8:8*
forwardness of others
that I may cut off *o.* from *2Co 11:12*
them which desire *o.*
only use not liberty for an *o.* to *Ga 5:13*
the flesh
younger give none *o.* to the *1Ti 5:14*
adversary
not give opponents *o.* *1Ti 5:14*
(A)(B)(N)(R)
there is none *o.* of stumbling *1Jo 2:10*
in him

OCCASIONED

I have *o.* the death of all the *1Sa 22:22*
persons

OCCASIONS

and give *o.* of speech against *De 22:14;*
her *22:17*
behold, he findeth *o.* against *Job 33:10*
me
because of *o.* of stumbling *M't 18:7*
(B)(E)(N)
mark them causing divisions *Ro 16:17*
and *o.* of stumbling (B)

OCCUPANTS

fair without *o.* (B) *Isa 5:9*

OCCUPATION

shall say, What is your *o.* *Ge 46:33;*
47:3; Jon 1:8
their *o.* was (A) *Ge 46:52*
for by *o.* they were tentmakers *Ac 18:3*
of the same *o.* (A)(B) *Ac 18:3*
whom he called, with the *Ac 19:25*
workmen of like *o.*
men of similar trades *Ac 19:25*
(A)(B)(N)(P)

OCCUPIED

the gold that was *o.* for the *Ex 38:24*
work
if bind with new ropes that *J'g 16:11*
never were *o.*
Syria *o.*; Dan and Javan *o.* *Eze 27:16;*
27:19
Arabia *o.*; Sheba *o.* in thy *Eze 27:21;*
fairs *27:22*
meats not profited them that *Heb 13:9*
have *o.*

OCCUPIERS

the *o.* of thy merchandise *Eze 27:27*
shall fall
dealers in merchandise *Eze 27:27*
(A)(E)(R)
experts in bargaining (B) *Eze 27:27*

OCCUPIETH

he that *o.* the room of the *1Co 14:16*
unlearned

OCCUPY

with mariners to *o.* thy *Eze 27:9*
merchandise
mariners were in you to deal *Eze 27:9*
in (A)(E)
mariners came to handle thy *Eze 27:9*
wares (B)
merchants to barter for (R) *Eze 27:9*
said to servants, O. till I come *Lu 19:13*
buy and sell with these (A) *Lu 19:13*
trade with this *Lu 19:13*
(B)(E)(N)(P)(R)

OCCURRENCE

nor evil *o.* (E) *1Ki 5:4*

OCCURRENT

there is neither adversary nor *1Ki 5:4*
evil *o.*
nor evil confronting me (A) *1Ki 5:4*
neither adversary or opposition *1Ki 5:4*
(B)
nor evil occurrence (E) *1Ki 5:4*
neither adversary or misfortune *1Ki 5:4*
(R)

OCCURS

when war, *o.* (S) *Ex 1:10*

OCEAN

the *o.* surrounding me (B) *Jon 2:5*

O'CLOCK

about nine *o.* (A)(B)(P) *M't 20:3*
about twelve *o.* *M't 27:45*
(A)(B)(N)(P)
about three *o.* *M't 27:46*
(A)(B)(N)(P)
it was nine *o.* *M'k 15:25*
(A)(B)(N)(P)
about four *o.* (A)(B)(N)(P) *Joh 1:39*
about one *o.* (A)(B)(N)(P) *Joh 4:52*
it is only nine *o.* *Ac 2:15*
(A)(B)(N)(P)
the three *o.* hour *Ac 3:1; 10:3*
(A)(B)(N)(P)

OCRAN

of Asher; Pagiel the son of O. *Nu 1:13;*
2:27; 7:72, 77, 10:26

ODD

the *o.* number of them is to be *Nu 3:48*
redeemed

ODED

Spirit of God came on *2Ch 15:1*
Azariah son of O.
a prophet of the Lord was *2Ch 28:9*
there, called O.

ODIOUS

making me *o.* (B)(E)(R)(S) *Ge 34:30*
became *o.* (B)(R) *1Sa 13:4*
became *o.* to David (E)(R) *2Sa 10:6*

made yourself *o.* (R) *2Sa 16:21*
the Ammonites made *1Ch 19:6*
themselves *o.*
made themselves hateful (A) *1Ch 19:6*
how serious they had *1Ch 19:6*
antagonized (B)
For an *o.* woman *Pr 30:23*
An unloved and repugnant *Pr 30:23*
woman (A)
an unloved woman (B)(R) *Pr 30:23*

ODOR

as *o.* of the field (A) *Ge 27:27*
river never have such an *o.* (R) *Ex 7:18*
an acceptable *o.* (B) *Ex 29:18*
send forth a vile *o.* (A)(B)(E) *Ec 10:1*
o. of garments, *o.* of Lebanon *Ca 4:11*
(A)
instead of sweet *o.* (A) *Isa 3:24*
throws off offensive *o.* *Joh 11:39*
(A)(B)(R)
a fragrant *o.* (R) *Eph 5:2*
fragrant *o.* of an offering *Ph'p 4:18*
(A)

ODORS

pleasant *o.* (B) *Le 26:31*
they make soothing *o.* (R) *Eze 20:28*

ODOUR

house filled with *o.* of the *Joh 12:3*
ointment
filled with fragrance of *Joh 12:3*
perfume (A)
filled with fragrance of the *Joh 12:3*
ointment (B)
an *o.* of a sweet smell *Ph'p 4:18*
a fragrant perfume (B) *Ph'p 4:18*
a fragrant offering (R) *Ph'p 4:18*

ODOURS

smell the savour of your sweet *Le 26:31*
o.
laid in a bed of sweet *o.* *2Ch 16:14*
on a bed filled with sweet *2Ch 16:14*
spices (B)(R)
six months with oil of myrrh *Es 2:12*
and sweet *o.*
six months with sweet spices *Es 2:12*
and perfumes (A)
six months with balms and *Es 2:12*
perfumes (B)
six months with spices and *Es 2:12*
ointments (R)
so shall they burn *o.* *Jer 34:5*
with burnings of spices and *Jer 34:5*
perfumes (A)
shall burn incense for you (B) *Jer 34:5*
shall make burning for you *Jer 34:5*
(E)
shall burn spices for you (R) *Jer 34:5*
They should offer sweet *o.* *Da 2:46*
offering and incense be offered *Da 2:46*
(A)
an offering of incense be *Da 2:46*
offered (R)
having golden vials full of *o.* *Re 5:8*
had golden bowls full of incense *Re 5:8*
(A)(B)(E)(N)(P)(R)
no man buyeth their *o.* and *Re 18:13*
ointments
incense, ointment, and *Re 18:13*
perfume (A)(B)(E)(N)(P)(R)

OF

darkness upon face *o.* the deep *Ge 1:2*
Spirit *o.* God moved upon the *Ge 1:2*
deep
firmament in midst *o.* the *Ge 1:6*
waters
finished, and all the host *o.* *Ge 2:1*
them
book *o.* the generations *o.* *Ge 5:1*
Adam
multiply on face *o.* the earth *Ge 6:1*
make ark *o.* gopher wood *Ge 6:14*
Get out *o.* thy country *Ge 12:1*
make *o.* thee a great nation *Ge 12:2*
Abram went up out *o.* Egypt *Ge 13:1*
father *o.* many nations *Ge 17:4; 17:5-6*
mother *o.* many *Ge 17:16*
nations, kings *o.* thee
I know not the day *o.* my *Ge 27:2*
death
dwelt in the land *o.* Canaan *Ge 37:1*

two *o*. officers, *o*. butlers, *o*.   *Ge 40:2* bakers
names *o*. the children of Israel   *Ex 1:1*
man *o*. the house of Levi   *Ex 2:1*
beginning *o*. months of the   *Ex 12:2* year
Lord spake out *o*. the tabernacle *Le 1:1*
trees *o*. field yield their fruit   *Le 26:4*
these are the names *o*. the men *Nu 1:5*
take *o*. every one them, *o*.   *Nu 17:2* all princes
son *o*. Machir, *o*. Manasseh, *o*. *Nu 36:1* Joseph
on the first day *o*. the month   *De 1:3*
Hew two tables *o*. stone   *De 10:1*
a dreamer *o*. dreams   *De 13:1*
voice *o*. the Lord, nations *o*.   *De 28:1* earth
Moses the servant *o*. the Lord *Jos 1:1*
Joshua the son *o*. Nun sent out *Jos 2:1* *o*. Shittim
dwelt on other side *o*. the flood *Jos 24:2*
Jacob bought *o*. the sons of   *Jos 24:32* Hamor
drive out inhabitants *o*. the   *J'g 1:19* valley
an angel *o*. the Lord   *J'g 2:1; 2Ki 1:3*
all the wars *o*. Canaan   *J'g 3:1*
gods *o*. Syria, *o*. Zidon, *o*.   *J'g 10:6* Moab, *o*. Ammon, and *o*. the Philistines
took wives *o*. the women of   *Ru 1:4* Moab
a mighty man *o*. wealth   *Ru 2:1*
went up out *o*. his city, priests *1Sa 1:3* *o*. the Lord
the Spirit *o*. the Lord   *1Sa 10:6*
name *o*. one was Bozez, *o*.   *1Sa 14:4* the other Seneh
after the death *o*. Saul, a man *2Sa 1:1*
came out *o*. the camp from Saul
David enquired *o*. the Lord   *2Sa 2:1*
house *o*. David, house *o*. Saul *2Sa 3:1*
Lord God *o*. my lord the king *1Ki 1:36*
Go, enquire *o*. Baalzebub, god *2Ki 1:3*
o. Ekron, recover *o*. this disease
I dwell in an house *o*. cedar *1Ch 17:1*
build an house for name *o*. the *2Ch 2:1* Lord
a prophet of the Lord was   *2Ch 28:9*
greatest *o*. all men *o*. the east *Job 1:3*
the sons *o*. God   *Job 1:6; 2:1*
answered Job out *o*. the   *Job 40:6* whirlwind
heard *o*. thee by hearing *o*. the *Job 42:5* ear
Lord turned captivity *o*. Job *Job 42:10*
counsel *o*. ungodly, seat *o*.   *Ps 1:1* scornful
give thee the desires *o*. thine *Ps 37:4* heart
dwelleth in secret place *o*. most *Ps 91:1* High, shadow *o*. the Almighty
I will say *o*. the Lord, He is *Ps 91:2*
fear *o*. the Lord is beginning *o*. *Pr 1:7* wisdom
walk in the way *o*. good men *Pr 2:20*
curse of Lord in house *o*. the *Pr 3:33* wicked
Hear the word *o*. the Lord   *Isa 1:10; Jer 7:2*
chastisement *o*. our peace was *Isa 53:5* upon him
laid on him iniquity *o*. us all *Isa 53:6*
shall see the travail *o*. his soul *Isa 53:11*
Stand in gate *o*. Lord's house *Jer 7:2*
slain *o*. Lord from one end *o*. *Jer 25:33* earth to the other end *o*. earth
a whirlwind out *o*. the north *Eze 1:4*
name *o*. the city from that   *Eze 48:35* day
children of the king's seed   *Da 1:3*
God *o*. heaven set up a   *Da 2:44* kingdom
And *o*. the ten horns, and *o*. *Da 7:20* the other
seal book to time *o*. the end *Da 12:4*
beginning *o*. word *o*. the Lord *Ho 1:2* to Hosea
before great and terrible day *Jol 2:31* *o*. Lord
The virgin *o*. Israel is fallen *Am 5:2*
Ask *o*. Lord in time *o*. latter *Zec 10:1* rain
every one that is left *o*. the *Zec 14:16* nations
book *o*. generation *o*. Jesus *M't 1:1* Christ
birth *o*. Jesus Christ was on *M't 1:18* this

after tribulation *o*. those   *M't 24:29* days
in the name *o*. the Father, *o*. *M't 28:19* the Son, and *o*. the Holy Ghost
with you, even unto end *o*.   *M't 28:20* the world
receive gift *o*. the Holy Ghost *Ac 2:38*
perfect soundness in presence *Ac 3:16* *o*. all
preaching the kingdom *o*.   *Ac 28:31* God
made *o*. the seed *o*. David   *Ro 1:3*
not ashamed *o*. the gospel   *Ro 1:16*
became servants *o*.   *Ro 6:18* righteousness
beseech by the mercies *o*. God *Ro 12:1*
But *o*. him are ye in Christ *1Co 1:30*
manifest the saviour *o*. his *2Co 2:14* knowledge
live by faith *o*. the Son *o*. God *Ga 2:20*
Now the works *o*. the flesh *Ga 5:19*
the fruit *o*. the Spirit is love, *Ga 5:22* joy
in dispensation *o*. fulness *o*. *Eph 1:10* time
I press toward mark *o*. the   *Ph'p 3:14* prize
Blotting out handwriting *o*.   *Col 1:14* ordinances
this is the will *o*. God in   *1Th 5:18*
For the love *o*. money is   *1Ti 6:10*
Not by works *o*. righteousness *Tit 3:5*
partakers *o*. the heavenly   *Heb 3:1* calling
hold fast profession *o*. faith *Heb 10:23*
river *o*. water *o*. life   *Re 22:1*

OFF

from *o*. the face of the earth   *Ge 7:4*
waters returned from *o*. the   *Ge 8:3* earth
were dried up from *o*. the earth *Ge 8:7*
from *o*. the face of the ground *Ge 8:8*
mouth was an olive leaf   *Ge 8:11* pluckt *o*.
were abated from *o*. the earth *Ge 8:11*
were dried up from *o*. the earth *Ge 8:13*
shall all flesh be cut *o*. any *Ge 9:11* more by
and they left *o*. to build the *Ge 11:8* city
soul shall be cut *o*. from his *Ge 17:14* people
he left *o*. talking with him, and *Ge 17:22* God
down over against him a good *Ge 21:16* way *o*.
up his eyes, and saw the place *Ge 22:4* afar *o*.
saw Isaac, she lighted *o*. the *Ge 24:64* camel
break his yoke from *o*. thy *Ge 27:40* neck
And when thy saw him afar *o*. *Ge 37:18* even
her widow's garments *o*. from *Ge 38:14* her
lift up thy head from *o*. thee *Ge 40:19*
shall eat thy flesh from *o*. thee *Ge 40:19*
took *o*. his ring from his hand *Ge 41:42*
out of the city, and not   *Ge 44:4* yet far *o*.
his sister stood afar *o*. to wit *Ex 2:4* what
put *o*. thy shoes from *o*. thy *Ex 3:5* feet; for
and cut *o*. the foreskin of her *Ex 4:25* son
thou shalt be cut *o*. from the *Ex 9:15* earth
that soul shall be cut *o*. from *Ex 12:15* Israel
shall be cut *o*. from the   *Ex 12:19* congregation
And took *o*. their chariot   *Ex 14:25* wheels that
saw it, they removed, and stood *Ex 20:18* afar *o*.
the people stood afar *o*. and *Ex 20:21*
the Jebusites; and I will cut *Ex 23:23* them *o*.
of Israel; and worship ye afar *Ex 24:1* *o*. Lord
shall even be cut *o*. from his *Ex 30:33; 30:38* people
shall be cut *o*. from among his *Ex 31:14* people

Break *o*. the golden earrings, *Ex 32:2* which are
people brake *o*. the golden   *Ex 32:3* earrings
hath any gold, let them break *Ex 32:24* it *o*.
now put *o*. thy ornaments from *Ex 33:5* thee
the camp, afar *o*. from the   *Ex 33:7* camp
he took the veil *o*. until he   *Ex 34:34* came out
and wring *o*. his head and   *Le 1:15* burn it on
he take *o*. hard by the backbone *Le 3:9*
take *o*. from it the fat of the *Le 4:8* bullock
As it was taken *o*. from the *Le 4:10* bullock
fat is taken away from *o*. the *Le 4:31* sacrifice
and wring *o*. his head from his *Le 5:8* neck
And he shall put *o*. his   *Le 6:11* garments, and
soul shall be cut *o*. from his *Le 7:20; 7:21, 27* people
it shall be cut *o*. from his   *Le 7:25* people
from *o*. the sacrifices of their *Le 7:34* peace
took them from *o*. their hands *Le 8:28*
man whose hair is fallen *o*. his *Le 13:40* head
hair fallen *o*. from the part of *Le 13:41* his head
shave *o*. all his hair, and wash *Le 14:8* himself
he shall save all his hair *o*. his *Le 14:9* head
even all his hair he shall shave *Le 14:9* *o*.
that they scrape *o*. without the *Le 14:41* city
coals of fire from *o*. the altar *Le 16:12*
shall put *o*. the linen   *Le 16:23* garments, which
shall be cut *o*. from among his *Le 17:4; 17:9; 18:5; 23:9; Nu 9:13; 15:30*
people
will cut him *o*. from among   *Le 17:10; 20:4, 26* his people
whosoever eateth it shall be *Le 17:14* cut *o*.
be cut *o*. from among their *Le 18:29; 20:18* people
against his family, and will cut *Le 20:5* him *o*.
be cut *o*. in the sight of their *Le 20:17* people
they shave *o*. the corner of *Le 21:5* their beard
shall be cut *o*. from my   *Le 22:3* presence
far *o*. about the tabernacle of *Nu 2:2*
Cut ye not *o*. the tribe of the *Nu 4:18* families
unto him from *o*. the mercy seat *Nu 7:89*
or be in a journey afar *o*. yet *Nu 9:10* he shall
taken up from *o*. the   *Nu 10:11* tabernacle
departed from *o*. the   *Nu 12:10* tabernacle
that soul shall utterly be cut *Nu 15:31* *o*.
put fire therein from *o*. the *Nu 16:46* altar
that soul shall be cut *o*. from *Nu 19:13* Israel
cut *o*. from among the   *Nu 19:20* congregation
utterly perish from *o*. the land *De 4:26*
thee from *o*. the face of the *De 6:15* earth
ye perish from *o*. the good   *De 11:17* land
shall cut *o*. the nations from *De 12:29* before
nigh unto thee, or far *o*. from *De 13:7* thee
Lord thy God hath cut *o*. the *De 19:1* nations
cities which are very far *o*. *De 20:15* from thee
strike *o*. the heifer's neck there *De 21:4*
of her captivity from *o*. her *De 21:13*
or hath his privy member cut *De 23:1* *o*.
loose his shoe from *o*. his foot *De 25:9*

Then thou shalt cut *o.* her hand, thine   *De 25:12*

consumed thee from *o.* the land   *De 28:21*

shall be plucked from *o.* the land   *De 28:63*

hidden from thee, neither is it far *o.*   *De 30:11*

the waters of Jordan shall be cut *o.*   *Jos 3:13*

the salt sea, failed, and were cut *o.*   *Jos 3:16*

the waters of Jordan were cut *o.*   *Jos 4:7*

the reproach of Egypt from *o.* you   *Jos 5:9*

loose thy shoe from *o.* thy foot; for   *Jos 5:15*

and cut *o.* our name from the earth   *Jos 7:9*

they took them down from the trees   *Jos 10:27*

and cut *o.* the Anakims from   *Jos 11:21*

and she lighted *o.* her ass   *Jos 15:18; J'g 1:14*

with all the nations that I have cut *o.*   *Jos 23:4*

ye perish from *o.* this good land   *Jos 23:13*

you from *o.* this good land which   *Jos 23:15*

quickly from *o.* the good land   *Jos 23:16*

caught him, and cut *o.* his thumbs   *J'g 1:6*

thumbs and their great toes cut *o.*   *J'g 1:7*

lighted down from *o.* his chariot   *J'g 4:15*

smote Sisera, she smote *o.* his head   *J'g 5:26*

toward heaven from *o.* the altar   *J'g 13:20*

his bands loosed from *o.* his hands   *J'g 15:14*

from *o.* his arms like a thread   *J'g 16:12*

caused him to shave *o.* the seven locks   *J'g 16:19*

is one tribe cut *o.* from Israel this day   *J'g 21:6*

Lord, who hath not left *o.* his kindness   *Ru 2:20*

a man plucked *o.* his shoe, and gave it   *Ru 4:7*

it for thee. So he drew *o.* his shoe   *Ru 4:8*

that the name of the dead be not cut *o.*   *Ru 4:10*

come, that I will cut *o.* thine arm   *1Sa 2:31*

I shall not cut *o.* from mine altar   *1Sa 2:33*

fell from *o.* the seat backward by   *1Sa 4:18*

hands were cut *o.* upon the threshold   *1Sa 5:4*

will lighten his hand from *o.* you   *1Sa 6:5*

and from *o.* your gods   *1Sa 6:5*

and from *o.* your land   *1Sa 6:5*

them. And David put them *o.* him   *1Sa 17:39*

him, and cut *o.* his head therewith   *1Sa 17:51*

And he stripped *o.* his clothes also   *1Sa 19:24*

cut *o.* thy kindness from my house   *1Sa 20:15*

when the Lord hath cut *o.* the enemies   *1Sa 20:15*

and cut *o.* the skirt of Saul's robe   *1Sa 24:4*

because he had cut *o.* Saul's skirt   *1Sa 24:5*

for in that I cut *o.* the skirt of thy robe   *1Sa 24:11*

thou wilt not cut *o.* my seed after me   *1Sa 24:21*

lighted *o.* the ass, and fell before   *1Sa 25:23*

and stood on the top of an hill afar *o.*   *1Sa 26:13*

hath cut *o.* those that have familiar   *1Sa 28:9*

And they cut *o.* his head, and   *1Sa 31:9*

and stripped *o.* his armour   *1Sa 31:9*

and cut *o.* their hands and their feet   *2Sa 4:12*

have cut *o.* all thine enemies out of   *2Sa 7:9*

shaved *o.* the one half of their beards   *2Sa 10:4*

cut *o.* their garments in the middle   *2Sa 10:4*

that David arose from *o.* his bed   *2Sa 11:2*

shooters shot from *o.* the wall upon   *2Sa 11:24*

their king's crown from *o.* his head   *2Sa 12:30*

and tarried in a place that was far *o.*   *2Sa 15:17*

over, I pray thee, and take *o.* his head   *2Sa 16:9*

cut *o.* the head of Sheba the son of   *2Sa 20:22*

will I cut *o.* Israel out of the land   *1Ki 9:7*

he had cut *o.* every male in Edom   *1Ki 11:16*

house of Jeroboam, even to cut it *o.*   *1Ki 13:34*

it from *o.* the face of the earth   *1Ki 13:34*

will cut *o.* from Jeroboam him that   *1Ki 14:10*

cut *o.* the house of Jeroboam that day   *1Ki 14:14*

that he left *o.* building of Ramah, and   *1Ki 15:21*

Jezebel cut *o.* the prophets of the Lord   *1Ki 18:4*

boast himself as he that putteth it *o.*   *1Ki 20:11*

and will cut *o.* from Ahab him that   *1Ki 21:21*

shalt not come down *o.* that bed on   *2Ki 1:16*

went, and stood to view far *o.*   *2Ki 2:7*

man of God saw her afar *o.* that he   *2Ki 4:25*

and I will cut *o.* from Ahab him that   *2Ki 9:8*

Ahaz cut *o.* the borders of the bases   *2Ki 16:17*

removed the layer from *o.* them   *2Ki 16:17*

the sea from *o.* the brasen oxen   *2Ki 16:17*

cut *o.* the gold from the doors of the   *2Ki 18:16*

and will cast *o.* this city Jerusalem   *2Ki 23:27*

have cut *o.* all thine enemies from   *1Ch 17:8*

and cut *o.* their garments in the midst   *1Ch 19:4*

of their king from *o.* his head   *1Ch 20:2*

forsake him, he will cast thee *o.* for ever   *1Ch 28:9*

captives unto a land far *o.* or near   *2Ch 6:36*

cast them *o.* from executing   *2Ch 11:14*

he left *o.* building of Ramah, and let   *2Ch 16:5*

which they stripped *o.* for themselves   *2Ch 20:25*

anointed to cut *o.* the house of Ahab   *2Ch 22:7*

was cut *o.* from the house of the Lord   *2Ch 26:21*

angel, which cut *o.* all the mighty men   *2Ch 32:21*

and the noise was heard afar   *Ezr 3:13*

plucked *o.* the hair of my head and of   *Ezr 9:3*

none of us put *o.* our clothes, saving   *Ne 4:23*

every one put them *o.* for washing   *Ne 4:23*

I pray you, let us leave *o.* this usury   *Ne 5:10*

joy of Jerusalem, was heard afar *o.*   *Ne 12:43*

and plucked *o.* their hair, and made   *Ne 13:25*

And the king took *o.* his ring, which   *Es 8:2*

lifted up their eyes afar *o.*, and knew   *Job 2:12*

or where were the righteous cut *o.*   *Job 4:7*

let loose his hand, and cut me *o.*   *Job 6:9*

Whose hope shall be cut *o.* and whose   *Job 8:14*

I will leave *o.* my heaviness   *Job 9:27*

If he cut *o.* and shut up, or gather   *Job 11:10*

Yea, thou castest *o.* fear, and   *Job 15:4*

shake *o.* his unripe grape as the vine   *Job 15:33*

shall cast *o.* his flower as the olive   *Job 15:33*

my purposes are broken *o.* even the   *Job 17:11*

and above shall his branch be cut *o.*   *Job 18:16*

of his months is cut *o.* in the midst   *Job 21:21*

I was not cut *o.* before the darkness   *Job 23:17*

cut *o.* as the tops of the ears of corn   *Job 24:24*

no more: they left *o.* speaking   *Job 32:15*

when people are cut *o.* in their place   *Job 36:20*

may see it; man may behold it afar *o.*   *Job 36:25*

and he smelleth the battle afar *o.*   *Job 39:25*

the prey, and her eyes behold afar *o.*   *Job 39:29*

Why standest thou afar *o.* O Lord   *Ps 10:1*

Lord shall cut *o.* all flattering lips   *Ps 12:3*

thou hast put *o.* my sackcloth   *Ps 30:11*

I am cut *o.* from before thine eyes   *Ps 31:22*

cut *o.* the remembrance of them from   *Ps 34:16*

he hath left *o.* to be wise, and to do   *Ps 36:3*

For evildoers shall be cut *o.* but   *Ps 37:9*

that be cursed of him shall be cut *o.*   *Ps 37:22*

the seed of the wicked shall be cut *o.*   *Ps 37:28*

when the wicked are cut *o.* thou shalt   *Ps 37:34*

the end of the wicked shall be cut *o.*   *Ps 37:38*

sore; and my kinsman stand afar *o.*   *Ps 38:11*

why dost thou cast me *o.?* why go I   *Ps 43:2*

But thou hast cast *o.* and put us to   *Ps 44:9*

O Lord? arise, cast us not *o.* for ever   *Ps 44:23*

enemies: cut them *o.* in thy truth   *Ps 54:5*

Lo, then would I wander far *o.*   *Ps 55:7*

O God, thou hast cast us *o.* thou hast   *Ps 60:1*

thou, O God, which hadst cast us *o.*   *Ps 60:10*

of them that are afar *o,* upon the sea   *Ps 65:5*

Cast me not *o.* in the time of old age   *Ps 71:9*

why hast thou cast us *o.* for ever   *Ps 74:1*

horns of the wicked also will I cut *o.*   *Ps 75:10*

He shall cut *o.* the spirit of princes   *Ps 76:12*

Will the Lord cast *o.* for ever? and will   *Ps 77:7*

let us cut them *o.* from being a nation   *Ps 83:4*

and they are cut *o.* from thy hand   *Ps 88:5*

why castest thou *o.* my soul? why   *Ps 88:14*

over me; thy terrors have cut me *o.*   *Ps 88:16*

But thou hast cast *o.* and abhorred   *Ps 89:38*

for it is soon cut *o.* and we fly away   *Ps 90:10*

the Lord will not cast *o.* his people   *Ps 94:14*

cut them *o.* in their wickedness   *Ps 94:23*

the Lord our God shall cut them *o.*   *Ps 94:23*

his neighbour, him will I cut *o.*   *Ps 101:5*

I may cut *o.* all the wicked doers from   *Ps 101:8*

not thou, O God, who hast cast us *o.*   *Ps 108:11*

Let his posterity be cut *o.*; and in the   *Ps 109:13*

he may cut *o.* the memory of them   *Ps 109:15*

but the proud he knoweth afar *Ps 138:6*
o.
understandest my thought afar *Ps 139:2*
o.
of thy mercy out o. mine *Ps 143:12*
enemies
wicked shall be cut o. from the *Pr 2:22*
earth
leave o. contention, before it *Pr 17:14*
be
thine expectation shall not be *Pr 23:18*
cut o.
and thy expectation shall not *Pr 24:14*
be cut o.
the hand of a fool cutteth o. *Pr 26:6*
the feet
that is near than a brother far *Pr 27:10*
o.
to devour the poor from o. the *Pr 30:14*
earth
That which is far o. and *Ec 7:24*
exceeding
I have put o. my coat; how shall *Ca 5:3*
I put
with the tongs from o. the altar *Isa 6:6*
will cut o. from Israel head *Isa 9:14*
and tail
heart to destroy and cut o. *Isa 10:7*
nations
taken away from o. thy *Isa 10:27*
shoulder
and his yoke from o. thy neck *Isa 10:27*
adversaries of Judah shall be *Isa 11:13*
cut o.
cut o. from Babylon the name *Isa 14:22*
shall his yoke depart from o. *Isa 14:25*
them
depart from o. their shoulders *Isa 14:25*
be baldness, and every beard *Isa 15:2*
cut o.
rebuke them, and they shall *Isa 17:13*
flee far o.
cut o. the sprigs with pruning *Isa 18:5*
hooks
the sackcloth from o. thy loins *Isa 20:2*
and put o. thy shoe from thy *Isa 20:2*
foot
that was upon it shall be cut *Isa 22:25*
o.
feet, shall carry her afar o. to *Isa 23:7*
sojourn
wipe away tears from o. all *Isa 25:8*
faces
he take away from o. all the *Isa 25:8*
earth
withered, they shall be broken *Isa 27:11*
o.
beat o. from the channel of *Isa 27:12*
the river
all that watch for iniquity are *Isa 29:20*
cut o.
and Carmel shake o. their *Isa 33:9*
fruits
Hear, ye that are far o. what *Isa 33:13*
I have
behold the land that is very *Isa 33:17*
far o.
as the leaf falleth o. from the *Isa 34:4*
vine, and
I said in the cutting o. of my *Isa 38:10*
days
cut o. like a weaver my life: *Isa 38:12*
he will
he will cut me o. with pining *Isa 38:12*
sickness
it shall not be far o. and *Isa 46:13*
salvation
thou shalt not be able to put *Isa 47:11*
it o.
refrain for thee, that I cut thee *Isa 48:9*
not o.
his name should not have *Isa 48:19*
been cut o.
to them that plucked o. the *Isa 50:6*
hair
for he was cut o. out of the *Isa 53:8*
land of the
everlasting sign shall not be *Isa 55:13*
cut o.
everlasting name shall not be *Isa 56:5*
cut o.
and didst send thy messengers *Isa 57:9*
far o.
Peace, peace to him that is *Isa 57:19*
far o. and
for salvation, but it is far o. *Isa 59:11*
from us
backward, and justice *Isa 59:14*
standeth afar o.

a lamb, as if he cut o. a dog's *Isa 66:3*
neck
to the isles afar o. that have *Isa 66:19*
not heard
perished is cut o. from their *Jer 7:28*
mouth
Cut o. thine hair, O *Jer 7:29*
Jerusalem
to cut o. the children from *Jer 9:21*
without
cut him o. from the land of *Jer 11:19*
the living
saith the Lord, and not a God *Jer 23:23*
afar o.
they be consumed from o. the *Jer 24:10*
land
o. the prophet Jeremiah's *Jer 28:10*
neck
o. the neck of the prophet *Jer 28:12*
Jeremiah
thee from o. the face of the *Jer 28:16*
earth
break his yoke from o. thy *Jer 30:8*
neck
and declare it in the isles afar *Jer 31:10*
o. and
I will also cast o. all the seed *Jer 31:37*
of Israel
he hath even cast them o. *Jer 33:24*
thus they
So they left o. speaking with *Jer 38:27*
him; for
to cut o. from you man and *Jer 44:7*
woman
that ye might cut yourselves o. *Jer 44:8*
you for evil, and to cut o. all *Jer 44:11*
Judah
since we left o. to burn *Jer 44:18*
incense to the
behold, I will save thee from *Jer 46:27*
afar o.
And to cut o. from Tyrus and *Jer 47:4*
Zidon
Askelon is cut o. with the *Jer 47:5*
remnant of
let us cut it o. from being a *Jer 48:2*
nation
The horn of Moab is cut o. *Jer 48:25*
and his
men of war shall be cut o. in *Jer 49:26*
that day
Flee, get you far o. dwell *Jer 49:30*
deep, O ye
Cut o. the sower from *Jer 50:16*
Babylon, and
men of war shall be cut o. in *Jer 50:30*
that day
be not cut o. in her iniquity; *Jer 51:6*
for this is
remember the Lord afar o. *Jer 51:50*
and let
to cut it o. that none shall *Jer 51:62*
remain in
He hath cut o. in his fierce *La 2:3*
anger all
The Lord hath cast o. his altar *La 2:7*
removed my soul far o. from *La 3:17*
peace
For the Lord will not cast o. *La 3:31*
for ever
have cut o. my life in the *La 3:53*
dungeon
mine head; then I said, I am *La 3:54*
cut o.
that is far o. shall die of the *Eze 6:12*
pestilence
I should go far o. from my *Eze 8:6*
sanctuary
departed from o. the *Eze 10:18*
threshold of
cast them far o. among the *Eze 11:16*
heathens
of the times that are afar o. *Eze 12:27*
will cut him o. from the midst *Eze 14:8*
of my
and will cut o. man and beast *Eze 14:13*
from it
so that I cut o. man and *Eze 14:17*
beast from it
blood, to cut o. from it man *Eze 14:19*
and beast
to cut o. from it man and *Eze 14:21*
beast
cropped o. the top of his *Eze 17:4*
young twigs
and cut o. the fruit thereof, *Eze 17:9*
that it
building forts, to cut o. many *Eze 17:17*
persons

I will crop o. from the top of *Eze 17:22*
his young
hath taken o. his hand from *Eze 18:17*
the poor
will cut o. from thee the *Eze 21:3*
righteous and
I will cut o. from thee the *Eze 21:4*
righteous
the diadem, and take o. the *Eze 21:26*
crown
thereof pluck o. thine own *Eze 23:34*
breasts
and I will cut thee o. from the *Eze 25:7*
people
and will cut o. man and beast *Eze 25:13*
from it
and I will cut o. the *Eze 25:16*
Cherethims, and
and put o. their broidered *Eze 26:16*
garments
and cut o. man and beast out *Eze 29:8*
of thee
and I will cut o. the *Eze 30:15*
multitude of No
terrible of the nations, have *Eze 31:12*
cut him o.
will cut o. from him that *Eze 35:7*
passeth out
is lost: we are cut o. for our *Eze 37:11*
parts
shall put o. their garments *Eze 44:19*
wherein
down the tree, and cut o. his *Da 4:14*
branches
and break o. thy sins by *Da 4:27*
righteousness
that are near, and that are far *Da 9:7*
o.
two weeks shall Messiah be cut *Da 9:26*
o.
have left o. to take heed to the *Ho 4:10*
Lord
hath cast o. the thing that is *Ho 8:3*
good
them idols, that they may be cut *Ho 8:4*
o.
Thy calf, O Samaria, hath cast *Ho 8:5*
thee o.
Samaria, her king is cut o. as *Ho 10:7*
the foam
the king of Israel utterly be *Ho 10:15*
cut o.
take o. the yoke on their jaws *Ho 11:4*
wine; for it is cut o. from your *Joe 1:5*
mouth
is cut o. from the house of the *Joe 1:9*
Lord
Is not the meat cut o. before *Joe 1:16*
our eyes
far o. from you the northern *Joe 2:20*
army
to the Sabeans, to a people far *Joe 3:8*
o.
cut o. the inhabitant from the *Am 1:5*
plain of
cut o. the inhabitant from *Am 1:8*
Ashdod
and did cast o. all pity, and *Am 1:11*
his anger
I will cut o. the judge from the *Am 2:3*
midst
the horns of the altar shall be *Am 3:14*
cut o.
leave o. righteousness in the *Am 5:7*
earth
it from o. the face of the earth *Am 9:8*
(how art thou cut o.!) would *Ob 5*
they not
of Esau may be cut o. by *Ob 9*
slaughter
and thou shalt be cut o. for ever *Ob 10*
to cut o. those of his that did *Ob 14*
escape
ye pull o. the robe with the *Mic 2:8*
garment
who pluck o. the skin from o. *Mic 3:2*
them
their flesh from o. their bones *Mic 3:2*
and flay their skin from o. *Mic 3:3*
them
rebuke strong nations afar o. *Mic 4:3*
that was cast far o. a strong *Mic 4:7*
nation
and all thine enemies shall be *Mic 5:9*
cut o.
cut o. thy horses out of the *Mic 5:10*
midst of
And I will cut o. the cities of *Mic 5:11*
thy land

cut *o.* witchcrafts out of thine *Mic 5:12* hand

Thy graven images also will I *Mic 5:13* cut *o.*

will I break his yoke from *o.* *Na 1:13* thee

thy gods will I cut *o.* the *Na 1:14* graven image

through thee; he is utterly cut *Na 1:15* *o.*

I will cut *o.* thy prey from the *Na 2:13* earth

the sword shall cut thee *o.* it *Na 3:15* shall eat

thy house by cutting *o.* many *Hab 2:10* people

the flock shall be cut *o.* from *Hab 3:17* the fold

all things from *o.* the land *Zep 1:2*

cut *o.* man from *o.* the land *Zep 1:3*

I will cut *o.* the remnant of *Zep 1:4* Baal from

all they that bear silver are *Zep 1:11* cut *o.*

I have cut *o.* the nations: their *Zep 3:6* towers

their dwelling should not be cut *Zep 3:7* *o.*

every one that stealeth shall be *Zec 5:3* cut *o.*

every one that sweareth shall *Zec 5:3* be cut *o.*

that are far *o.* shall come and *Zec 6:15* build

will cut *o.* the pride of the *Zec 9:6* Philistines

I will cut *o.* the chariot from *Zec 9:10* Ephraim

and the battle bow shall be cut *Zec 9:10* *o.*

be as though I had not cast *Zec 10:6* them *o.*

Three shepherds also I cut *o.* *Zec 11:8* in one

that is to be cut *o.* let it be cut *Zec 11:9* *o.*

shall not visit those that be *Zec 11:16* cut *o.*

cut *o.* the names of the idols *Zec 13:2* out of the

parts therein shall be cut *o.* *Zec 13:8* and die

shall not be cut *o.* from the *Zec 14:2* city

will cut *o.* the man that doeth *Mal 2:12* this

thy right hand offend thee, cut *M't 5:30* it *o.*

a good way *o.* from them a *M't 8:30* herd

city, shake *o.* the dust of *M't 10:14* your feet

or thy foot offend thee, cut *M't 18:8;* them *o.* *M'k 9:45*

high priest's, and smote *o.* *M't 26:51* his ear

Peter followed him afar *o.* *M't 26:58* unto the

they took the robe *o.* from *M't 27:31* him

women were beholding afar *M't 27:55* *o.*

when he saw Jesus afar *o.* he *M'k 5:6* ran

shake *o.* the dust under your *M'k 6:11* feet

And if thy hand offend thee, *M'k 9:43* cut it *o.*

cut down branches *o.* the *M'k 11:8* trees

seeing a fig tree afar *o.* *M'k 11:13* having leaves

of the high priest, and cut *o.* *M'k 14:47* his ear

Peter followed him afar *o.* *M'k 14:54* even

they took *o.* the purple from *M'k 15:20* him

were also women looking on *M'k 15:40* afar *o.*

shake *o.* the very dust from your *Lu 9:5*

on us, we do wipe *o.* against *Lu 10:11* you

while the other is yet a great *Lu 14:32* way *o.*

But when he was yet a great *Lu 15:20* way *o.*

and seeth Abraham afar *o.* *Lu 16:23*

that were lepers, which stood *Lu 17:12* afar *o.*

publican, standing afar *o.* *Lu 18:13* would not

high priest, and cut *o.* his *Lu 22:50* right ear

house. And Peter followed *Lu 22:54* afar *o.*

him from Galilee, stood afar *Lu 23:49* *o.*

Jerusalem, about fifteen *Joh 11:18* furlongs *o.*

servant, and cut *o.* his right *Joh 18:10* ear

his kinsman whose ear Peter *Joh 18:26* cut *o.*

to all that are far *o.* even as *Ac 2:39* many

Put *o.* thy shoes from thy feet *Ac 7:33*

his chains fell *o.* from his *Ac 12:7* hands

shook *o.* the dust of their feet *Ac 13:51*

the magistrates rent *o.* their *Ac 16:22* clothes

cried out, and cast *o.* their *Ac 22:23* clothes

soldiers cut *o.* the ropes of the *Ac 27:32* boat

ropes of the boat, and let her *Ac 27:32* fall *o.*

he shook *o.* the beast into the *Ac 28:5* fire

if some of the branches be *Ro 11:17* broken *o.*

The branches were broken *o.* *Ro 11:19* that I

of unbelief they were broken *Ro 11:20* *o.*

otherwise thou also shalt be *Ro 11:22* cut *o.*

let us cast *o.* the works of *Ro 13:12* darkness

I may cut *o.* occasion from *2Co 11:12* them

were even cut *o.* which trouble *Ga 5:12* you

were far *o.* are made nigh by *Eph 2:13*

peace to you which were afar *Eph 2:17* *o.*

ye put *o.* concerning the *Eph 4:22* former

putting *o.* the body of the sins *Col 2:11* of the

But now ye also put *o.* all these *Col 3:8*

put *o.* the old man with his *Col 3:9* deeds

they have cast *o.* their first *1Ti 5:12* faith

but having seen them afar *o.* *Heb 11:13* and were

things is blind, and cannot see *2Pe 1:9* afar *o.*

I must put *o.* this my *2Pe 1:14* tabernacle

Standing afar *o.* for the fear *Re 18:10* of her

shall stand afar *o.* for the fear *Re 18:15* of

many as trade by sea, stood *Re 18:17* afar *o.*

OFFENCE

what is my *o.* (R) *Ge 31:36*

o. to Egyptians (B) *Ge 43:32; 8:26*

this shall be no *o.* of heart to *1Sa 25:31*

This shall be no staggering *1Sa 25:31* grief (A)

your heart will suffer no *1Sa 25:31* self-accusation (B)

no grief or pangs of *1Sa 25:31* conscience *o* (R)

a rock of *o.* to both houses of *Isa 8:14* Israel

an *o.* is he (B) *Isa 41:24*

till they acknowledge their *o.* *Ho 5:15*

until they acknowledge their *Ho 5:15* guilt (B)(R)

they took *o.* at him (A)(R) *M't 13:57*

have taken great *o.* (N) *M't 15:12*

Satan, thou art an *o.* unto me *M't 16:23*

Satan, you are a snare to me *M't 16:23* (B)

Satan, thou art a *M't 16:23* stumblingblock unto me (E)(N)

Satan! You stand right in my *M't 16:23* path (P)

Satan! You are a hindrance to *M't 16:23* me (R)

do not want to give *o.* (P)(R) *M't 17:37*

a conscience void of *o.* *Ac 24:16* towards God

keep at all times a clear *Ac 24:16* conscience (N)(P)(R)

committed no *o.* (N)(P) *Ac 25:8*

ιso also is the free gift, *Ro 5:15;* ιfor if through the *o.* of one *5:18* many be dead

God's free gift is not to be *Ro 5:15* compared to the trespass

many be dead through man's *Ro 5:15* falling (A)(E)(R)

the free gift by no means is as *Ro 5:15* with the fall, through the

lapsing of one many die (B) *Ro 5:15*

God's act of grace is out of *Ro 5:15* proportion to Adam's wrongdoing, wrongdoing of

one man brought death (N) *Ro 5:15*

Nor is the effect of God's gift *Ro 5:15* the same as the effect of

man's sins, man's sin brought judgment (P)

if by one man's *o.* death *Ro 5:17* reigned

because of one man's trespass *Ro 5:17* death (A)(E)(R)

due to one person's fall, death *Ro 5:17* is king (B)

by the wrongdoing of one *Ro 5:17* death reigned (N)

one act of sin exposed the *Ro 5:17* whole race to God's judgment and condemnation (P)

law entered that the *o.* might *Ro 5:20* abound

law came to increase the *Ro 5:20* trespass (A)(B)(E)(R)

law intruded to multiply *Ro 5:20* law-breaking (N)

law keeps slipping into the *Ro 5:20* picture to point the vast extent of sin (P)

I lay in Sion a rock of *o.* *Ro 9:33*

laying in Zion a Rock that will *Ro 9:33* make them fall (A)(R)

I place in Zion a tripping stone *Ro 9:33* (B)

I lay in Zion a rock to trip *Ro 9:33* them up (N)

it is evil for that man who *Ro 14:20* eateth with *o.*

wrong for anyone to hurt the *Ro 14:20* conscience of others to make them fall (A)(N)(R)

wrong to eat what means a *Ro 14:20* stumbling block (B)

give no *o.* in any thing *1Co 10:32;* *2Co 6:3*

behave that you cause *1Co 10:32* (none) to stumble (B)(P)

give no occasion of *1Co 10:32* stumbling (E)

love is not quick to take *o.* *1Co 13:5* (N)

have I committed an *o.* in *2Co 11:7* abasing myself

did I make a mistake and do *2Co 11:7* you wrong (A)

have I erred by humbling *2Co 11:7* myself (B)

did I commit a sin in *2Co 11:7* humbling myself (E)(R)

Perhaps I made a mistake in *2Co 11:7* cheapening myself (P)

then is the *o.* of the cross *Ga 5:11* ceased

In that case the cross has *Ga 5:11* ceased to be a stumbling block and is made meaningless (A)

the offensiveness of the *Ga 5:11* cross has been made meaningless (B)

then hath the stumblingblock *Ga 5:11* of the cross been done away (E)(R)

In that case, my preaching of *Ga 5:11* the cross is a stumblingblock no more (N)

the hostility which the *Ga 5:11* preaching of the cross provokes would disappear (P)

may be without *o.* till the day *Ph'p 1:10* of Christ

not stumbling or causing *Ph'p 1:10* others to stumble (A)

may be unsullied and *Ph'p 1:10* blameless (B)

be flawless and without *Ph'p 1:10* blame (N)

live sincere and blameless *Ph'p 1:10* lives (P)

may be pure and blameless *Ph'p 1:10* (R)
a rock of *o.* to them that   *1Pe 2:8* stumble
a rock to stumble over (B)(N) *1Pe 2:8*
a rock that will make them fall *1Pe 2:8* (R)

OFFENCES

I am reminded of my *o.* (B)   *Ge 41:9*
commit these *o.* (B)   *Le 18:26*
for yielding pacifieth great *o.* *Ec 10:4*
composure may remedy serious *Ec 10:4* mistakes (B)
woe to the world because of *M't 18:7;*
o. for it must needs be   *Lu 17:1* that *o.* come
Woe to the world for such   *M't 18:7* temptations to sin and influences to do wrong! It is necessary that temptation come (A)(R)
Alas for the world because of *M't 18:7* occasions of stumbling. The occasions have to come (B)(E)(N)
Alas for the world with its *M't 18:7* pitfalls! In the nature of things there must be pitfalls (P)
forgive *o.* (A)   *M't 18:35*
who was delivered for our *o.* *Ro 4:25* and raised for our
who was betrayed and put to *Ro 4:25* death because of our misdeeds and was raised (A)(B)(N)
who was delivered up for our *Ro 4:25* trespasses (A)
who was delivered to death for *Ro 4:25* our sins (P)
who was put to death for our *Ro 4:25* trespasses (R)
free gift is of many *o.* to *Ro 5:16* justification
free gift following many   *Ro 5:16* transgressions (A)
divine grace led to justification *Ro 5:16* out of many lapses (B)
free gift came of many   *Ro 5:16* trespasses into justification (E)(R)
countless men's sins are met *Ro 5:16* with the free gift of grace, and result in justification (P)
mark them which cause *o.* *Ro 16:17*
keep an eye on those who *Ro 16:17* cause splits and obstacles (B)
mark them that are causing *Ro 16:17* divisions and occasions of stumbling (E)
keep an eye on those who stir *Ro 16:17* up quarrels and lead others astray (N)
keep a watchful eye on those *Ro 16:17* who cause trouble and make difficulties (P)
take note of those who create *Ro 16:17* dissensions and difficulties (R)
full of accursed *o.* (A)(B)   *Re 17:4*

OFFEND

do not *o.* him (B)   *Ex 23:21*
it is meet to say, I will not *o. Job 34:31* any more
I should *o.* against the   *Ps 73:15* generation of children
been untrue and dealt   *Ps 73:15* treacherously (A)(E)
played false to thy children *Ps 73:15* (B)
been untrue to the generation *Ps 73:15* of (R)
love thy law, nothing shall *Ps 119:165* *o.* them
no stumblingblock is in   *Ps 119:165* their path (B)
they have no occasion of *Ps 119:165* stumbling (E)
nothing can make them   *Ps 119:165* stumble (R)
all that devour him shall *o.* *Jer 2:3*
all who ate of it (injuring   *Jer 2:3* Israel offended and became guilty (A)
all those devouring him shall be *Jer 2:3* punished (B)
all that devour him shall be *Jer 2:3* guilty (E)
all who ate of it became guilty *Jer 2:3* (R)

adversaries said, We *o.* not *Jer 50:7*
adversaries said, We are not *Jer 50:7* guilty (A)(B)(E)(R)
tho' Israel played harlot let *Ho 4:15* not Judah *o.*
let not Judah be guilty (B)(R) *Ho 4:15*
he shall pass over and *o.* *Hab 1:11* imputing
if right eye *o.* thee pluck it out *M't 5:29*
if right eye serves as a trap *M't 5:29* (A)
if right eye would entice you to *M't 5:29* sin (B)
if right eye causes you to *M't 5:29* stumble (E)
if right eye leads you astray *M't 5:29* (N)(P)
if right eye causes you to sin *M't 5:29* (R)
if right hand *o.* thee cut it off *M't 5:30;*   *18:8-9; M'k 9:43, 45, 47* (A)
if right hand serves as a trap *M't 5:30* (B)
if right hand entices you to sin *M't 5:30* (B)
if right hand causes you to *M't 5:30* stumble (E)
if right hand is your undoing *M't 5:30* (N)
if right hand leads you astray *M't 5:30* (P)
if right hand causes you to sin *M't 5:30* (R)
they shall gather all things *M't 13:41* that *o.*
gather all causes of offense - *M't 13:41* persons by whom others are drawn into sin - all who do iniquity and act wickedly (A)(N)
gather all stumbling blocks *M't 13:41* and those practicing lawlessness (B)
gather all things that cause *M't 13:41* stumbling and those that do iniquity (E)
uproot from the kingdom *M't 13:41* everything that is spoiling it, and all those who live in defiance of its laws (P)
gather all causes of sin and *M't 13:41* all evildoers (R)
lest we should *o.* them, go to *M't 17:27* the sea
lest we cause them to   *M't 17:27* stumble (E)
we do not want to give   *M't 17:27* offense to (P)(R)
who shall *o.* one of these *M't 18:6;*   *M'k 9:42; Lu 17:2*
causes one to stumble and sin *M't 18:6* (A)(E)
whoever is an occasion for *M't 18:6* stumbling (B)
if a man is a cause of   *M't 18:6* stumbling to (N)
if anyone leads astray one of *M't 18:6* these (P)
whoever causes one of these *M't 18:6* to sin (R)
doth this *o.* you   *Joh 6:61*
Is this a stumbling block and *Joh 6:61* an offense, does it upset, displease, shock, and scandalize you (A)
Doth this cause you to   *Joh 6:61* stumble (E)
Does this shock you (N) *Joh 6:61*
Is this too much for you (P) *Joh 6:61*
Do you take offense at this *Joh 6:61* (R)
if meat make thy brother *o.* *1Co 8:13* lest he *o.*
if eating cause my brother's *1Co 8:13* falling, or is hindering his spiritual progress (A)
if eating causes my brother to *1Co 8:13* stumble (B)(E)
if food be the downfall of my *1Co 8:13* brother (N)
if any possibility of injuring *1Co 8:13* my brother (P)
if food is the cause of my *1Co 8:13* brother's falling (R)
yet *o.* in one point, he is guilty *Jas 2:10* of all
slips in cne point (B)   *Jas 2:10*
yet stumble in one point (E) *Jas 2:10*
keeps whole law but for a *Jas 2:10* single exception (P)

fails in one point has become *Jas 2:10* guilty of all (R)
in many things we *o.* all, if any *Jas 3:2* man *o.* not
we all make many a slip, who *Jas 3:2* makes no slip (A)
in many things we all stumble *Jas 3:2* (E)
all of us often go wrong. The *Jas 3:2* man who never says a wrong thing is a perfect character (N)
We all make mistakes in all *Jas 3:2* kinds of ways (P)(R)

OFFENDED

what have I *o.* thee, that thou *Ge 20:9*
wherein have I sinned against *Ge 20:9* thee (E)(R)
baker had *o.* their lord the king *Ge 40:1*
I have *o.*; return from me *2Ki 18:14*
I have done wrong; depart *2Ki 18:14* from me (A)(B)(R)
have *o.* against the Lord *2Ch 28:13* already
we are guilty before the Lord *2Ch 28:13* already (A)
our guilt is already great *2Ch 28:13* (B)(R)
our trespass is great (E) *2Ch 28:13*
will you be *o.* (A)(R)   *Job 4:2*
A brother *o.* is harder to be *Pr 18:19* won
o. and became guilty (A) *Jer 2:3*
What have I *o.* against thee *Jer 37:18*
what have I sinned against *Jer 37:18* you (A)(E)
What wrong have I done *Jer 37:18* against you (B)(R)
and hath greatly *o.*, and *Eze 25:12* revenged
Edom hath acted wrongfully *Eze 25:12* (B)
Edom acted revengefully (R) *Eze 25:12*
but when he *o.* in Baal, he died *Ho 13:1*
he fell into sin through Baal *Ho 13:1* (B)
he incurred guilt through Baal *Ho 13:1* (R)
whosoever shall not be *o.* in *M't 11:6;* me   *Lu 7:23*
he who takes no offense in *M't 11:6* (A)(R)
who finds nothing   *M't 11:6* objectionab'e (B)
find no occasion of stumbling *M't 11:6* in me (E)
who does not find me a   *M't 11:6* stumbling-block (N)
who never loses his faith in *M't 11:6* me (P)
of the word, by and by he is *M't 13:21;* *o.*   *M'k 4:17*
he is caused to stumble - he *M't 13:21* is repelled and begins to distrust and desert him whom he ought to trust and obey, and he falls away (A)
at once he feels scandalized *M't 13:21* (B)
straightway he stumblest (E) *M't 13:21*
he falls away at once   *M't 13:21* (N)(R)
he gives up his faith at once *M't 13:21* (P)
they were *o.* in him *M't 13:57; M'k 6:3*
they took offense at him *M't 13:57* (A)(R)
So they fell foul of him (N) *M't 13:57*
Knowest thou the Pharisees *M't 15:12* were *o.*
were shocked at hearing you *M't 15:12* say this (B)
have taken great offense (N) *M't 15:12*
And then many shall be *o.*, *M't 24:10* and shall
Many then shall fall away *M't 24:10* (B)(R)
And then many shall stumble *M't 24:10* (E)
Many will lose their faith *M't 24:10* (N)(P)
All ye shall be *o.* because of *M't 26:31;* me   *M'k 14:27, 29*
find in me an occasion of *M't 26:31* stumbling (B)
Tonight you shall all fall *M't 26:31* from your faith (N)
every one shall lose his faith *M't 26:31* (P)

You will all fall away   *M't 26:31*
because of me (R)
Though all men shall be *o.*   *M't 26:33*
because of thee, yet will I never
be *o.*
though all are offended and   *M't 26:33*
stumble and fall away because
of you and distrust and desert
you, I will never do so (A)
Though they all fall away   *M't 26:33*
scandalized on your account,
I never (B)
Everyone else may fall away   *M't 26:33*
on your account, but I never
will (N)
Even if everyone should lose   *M't 26:33*
his faith in you, I never will (P)
Though they all fall away   *M't 26:33*
because of you, I will never
fall away (R)
unto you, that ye should not   *Joh 16:1*
be *o.*
so that you may not be   *Joh 16:1*
trapped (B)
that ye should not be caused   *Joh 16:1*
to stumble (E)
to guard you against the   *Joh 16:1*
breakdown of your faith (N)
that your faith in me might   *Joh 16:1*
not be shaken (P)
to keep you from falling away   *Joh 16:1*
(R)
have I *o.* any thing at all   *Ac 25:8*
I have committed nothing   *Ac 25:8*
whatever wrong (B)
neither have I sinned at all (E)   *Ac 25:8*
I have committed no offence   *Ac 25:8*
(N)(P)
brother stumbleth, or is *o.*   *Ro 14:21*
if it makes him stumble *o.*   *Ro 14:21*
offends (B)
make your brother stumble   *Ro 14:21*
(B)(E)
do anything where by your   *Ro 14:21*
brother stumbleth (E)
doing anything which causes   *Ro 14:21*
your brother's downfall (N)
be willing to be both   *Ro 14:21*
vegetarians and teetotalers if
by so doing otherwise we
impede a brother's progress (P)
who is *o.,* and I burn not   *2Co 11:29*
who is made to stumble and   *2Co 11:29*
fall and have his faith hurt,
and I am not on fire (with
sorrow or indignation) (A)
who is caused to stumble,   *2Co 11:29*
and I burn not (E)
If anyone is made to   *2Co 11:29*
stumble, does my heart not
blaze with indignation (N)
Does anyone have his faith   *2Co 11:29*
upset without my longing to
restore him (R)

OFFENDER

That make a man an *o.* for a   *Isa 29:21*
word
who for a word declare a   *Isa 29:21*
person guilty (B)
if I be an *o.,* or have   *Ac 25:11*
committed
If then I am a wrongdoer   *Ac 25:11*
(A)(E)(R)
In case I am guilty (B)   *Ac 25:11*
If I am guilty of any capital   *Ac 25:11*
crime (N)
If I were a criminal (P)   *Ac 25:11*
retribution of the *o.* (N)   *Ro 13:4*

OFFENDERS

son Solomon shall be counted   *1Ki 1:21*
o.
will be considered criminals   *1Ki 1:21*
(B)
were first *o.* (B)   *Ezr 9:2*
convicted as violaters and *o.*   *Jas 2:9*
(A)

OFFENDS

makes him stumble or *o.* (A)   *Ro 14:21*
if a brother *o.* you (P)   *Lu 17:3*

OFFENSE

is this an *o.* (A)(R)   *Joh 6:61*
he who takes no *o.* in me   *M't 11:6*
(A)(R)

OFFENSIVE

made us *o.* (R)(S)   *Ex 5:21*
o., repulsive (B)   *Le 11:10*
extremely *o.* (A)   *Pr 11:1;*
   11:20; 12:22; 13:19; 15:26; 16:5; 20:10
grossly *o.* thoughts (A)   *Jer 4:4*
o. impurities (B)   *Eze 11:18*
presented *o.* oblations (B)   *Eze 20:28*
throws off *o.* odor   *Joh 11:39*
(A)(B)(R)

OFFER

o. him there for a burnt   *Ge 22:2*
offering
not delay to *o.* the first of thy   *Ex 22:29*
ripe
not *o.* the blood of my   *Ex 23:18*
sacrifice
thou shalt *o.* every day a   *Ex 29:36*
bullock
which thou shalt *o.* upon the   *Ex 29:38*
altar
lamb thou shalt *o.* in the   *Ex 29:39*
morning
other lamb thou shalt *o.* at   *Ex 29:39;*
even   *29:41*
o. no strange incense thereon   *Ex 30:9*
not *o.* the blood of my   *Ex 34:25*
sacrifice
that did *o.* an offering of   *Ex 35:24*
silver
him *o.* a male without blemish   *Le 1:3*
shall *o.* it of his own voluntary   *Le 1:3*
will
when any will *o.* a meat offering   *Le 2:1*
ye shall *o.* them unto the Lord   *Le 2:12*
thine offerings thou shalt *o.* salt   *Le 2:12*
o. a meat offering of thy   *Le 2:14*
firstfruits
thou shalt *o.* for the meat   *Le 2:14*
offering
offering, if he *o.* it of the herd   *Le 3:1*
he shall *o.* it without blemish   *Le 3:1;*
before   *3:6*
shall *o.* of the sacrifice of the   *Le 3:3*
peace
If he *o.* a lamb for his offering,   *Le 3:7*
then
then shall he *o.* it before the   *Le 3:7;*
Lord   *3:12*
o. of the sacrifice of the peace   *Le 3:9*
he shall *o.* thereof his   *Le 3:14*
offering
shall *o.* a young bullock for the   *Le 4:14*
sin
who shall *o.* that which is for   *Le 5:8*
the sin
o. the second for a burnt   *Le 5:10*
offering
Aaron shall *o.* it before the   *Le 6:14*
Lord
which they shall *o.* unto the   *Le 6:20*
Lord in
shalt thou *o.* for a sweet savour   *Le 6:21*
is anointed in his stead shall *o.*   *Le 6:22*
it
he shall *o.* of it all the fat thereof   *Le 7:3*
which he shall *o.* unto the Lord   *Le 7:11*
If he *o.* it for a thanksgiving,   *Le 7:12*
then
o. with the sacrifice of   *Le 7:12*
thanksgiving
o. for his offering leavened   *Le 7:13*
bread
o. one out of the whole oblation   *Le 7:14*
men *o.* an offering made by fire   *Le 7:25*
unto
to *o.* their oblations unto the   *Le 7:38*
Lord
and *o.* them before the Lord   *Le 9:2*
o. his sin offering, and thy burnt   *Le 9:7*
o. the offering of the people, and   *Le 9:7*
Who shall *o.* it before the Lord   *Le 12:7*
him for a trespass offering   *Le 14:12*
the priest shall *o.* the sin   *Le 14:19*
offering
priest shall *o.* the burnt   *Le 14:20*
offering
shall *o.* the one of the turtle   *Le 14:30*
doves
And the priest shall *o.* them   *Le 15:15*
shall *o.* the one for a sin   *Le 15:30*
o. his bullock of the sin   *Le 16:6*
offering
fell, and *o.* him for a sin   *Le 16:9*
offering
forth, and *o.* his burnt offering   *Le 16:24*

to *o.* an offering unto the Lord   *Le 17:4*
which they *o.* in the open field   *Le 17:5*
o. them for peace offerings   *Le 17:5*
unto
o. their sacrifices unto devils   *Le 17:7*
to *o.* it unto the Lord; even   *Le 17:9*
ye *o.* a sacrifice of peace   *Le 19:5*
offerings
Lord, ye shall *o.* it at your own   *Le 19:5*
will
be eaten the same day ye *o.* it   *Le 19:6*
bread of their God, they do *o.*   *Le 21:6*
approach to *o.* the bread of   *Le 21:17*
his God
nigh to *o.* the offerings of the   *Le 21:21*
Lord
nigh to *o.* the bread of his   *Le 21:21*
God
Israel, which they *o.* unto the   *Le 22:15*
Lord
that will *o.* his oblation for all   *Le 22:18*
his
will *o.* unto the Lord for a   *Le 22:18*
burnt
Ye shall *o.* at your own will a   *Le 22:19*
male
a blemish, that shall ye not *o.*   *Le 22:20*
ye shall not *o.* these unto the   *Le 22:22*
Lord
thou *o.* for a freewill offering   *Le 22:23*
not *o.* unto the Lord that   *Le 22:24*
which
shall ye *o.* the bread of your   *Le 22:25*
God
when ye will *o.* a sacrifice of   *Le 22:29*
the Lord, *o.* it at your own   *Le 22:29*
will
shall *o.* an offering made by fire   *Le 23:8*
ye shall *o.* that day when ye   *Le 23:12*
wave
shall *o.* a new meat offering   *Le 23:16*
unto
shall *o.* with the bread seven   *Le 23:18*
lambs
o. an offering by fire   *Le 23:25;*
        23:27, 36-37
do not *o.* a sacrifice unto the   *Le 27:11*
the Lord, and *o.* it upon the   *Nu 5:25*
altar
shall *o.* the one for a sin   *Nu 6:11*
offering
shall *o.* his offering unto the   *Nu 6:14*
Lord
shall *o.* his sin offering, and his   *Nu 6:16*
shall *o.* the ram for a sacrifice   *Nu 6:17*
shall *o.* also his meat offering   *Nu 6:17*
They shall *o.* their offering,   *Nu 7:11*
each
of Zuar, prince of Issachar,   *Nu 7:18*
did *o.*
of the children of Zebulun, did   *Nu 7:24*
o.
of the children of Reuben, did   *Nu 7:30*
o.
of the children of Simeon did   *Nu 7:36*
o.
Aaron shall *o.* the Levites   *Nu 8:11*
before *o.*
shalt *o.* the one for a sin   *Nu 8:12*
offering
o. them for an offering unto the   *Nu 8:13*
them, and *o.* them for an   *Nu 8:15*
offering
not *o.* an offering of the Lord in   *Nu 9:7*
o. the third part of an hin of   *Nu 15:7*
wine
will *o.* an offering made by   *Nu 15:14*
fire
ye shall *o.* up an heave   *Nu 15:19*
o. up a cake of the first of   *Nu 15:20*
your
shall *o.* one young bullock for   *Nu 15:24*
come near to *o.* incense   *Nu 16:40*
before
which they shall *o.* unto the   *Nu 18:12*
Lord
children of Israel *o.* unto the   *Nu 18:19*
Lord
they *o.* as an heave offering   *Nu 18:24*
unto
shall *o.* up an heave offering   *Nu 18:26*
of it
ye also shall *o.* an heave   *Nu 18:28*
offering
ye shall *o.* every heave   *Nu 18:29*
offering of
o. unto me in their due season   *Nu 28:2*
which ye shall *o.* unto the Lord   *Nu 28:3*

lamb shalt thou *o.* in the morning	*Nu 28:4*
other lamb shalt thou *o.* at even	*Nu 28:4; 28:8*
thou shalt *o.* it, a sacrifice made by	*Nu 28:8*
ye shall *o.* a burnt offering unto	*Nu 28:11*
ye shall *o.* a sacrifice made by fire	*Nu 28:19*
tenth deals shall ye *o.* for a bullock	*Nu 28:20*
A several tenth deal shalt thou *o.* for	*Nu 28:21*
o. these beside the burnt offering	*Nu 28:23*
this manner ye shall *o.* daily	*Nu 28:24*
ye shall *o.* the burnt offering for	*Nu 28:27*
shall *o.* them beside the continual	*Nu 28:31*
shall *o.* a burnt offering for a sweet	*Nu 29:2*
shall *o.* a burnt offering unto	*Nu 29:8*
And ye shall *o.* a burnt offering, a	*Nu 29:13*
shall *o.* twelve young bullocks, two	*Nu 29:17*
But ye shall *o.* a burnt offering	*Nu 29:36*
thou *o.* not thy burnt offerings in	*De 12:13*
thou shalt *o.* thy burnt offerings	*De 12:14; 12:27*
from them that *o.* a sacrifice	*De 18:3*
o. burnt offerings thereon unto	*De 27:6*
thou shalt *o.* peace offerings	*De 27:7*
shall *o.* sacrifices of righteousness	*De 33:19*
o. thereon burnt offering or meat	*Jos 22:23*
if to *o.* peace offerings thereon, let	*Jos 22:23*
made an end to *o.* the present	*J'g 3:18*
o. a burnt sacrifice with the wood	*J'g 6:26*
I will *o.* it up for a burnt offering	*J'g 11:31*
if thou wilt *o.* a burnt offering	*J'g 13:16*
thou must *o.* it unto the Lord	*J'g 13:16*
o. a great sacrifice unto Dagon	*J'g 16:23*
went up to *o.* unto the yearly	*1Sa 1:21*
husband was to *o.* the yearly sacrifice	*1Sa 2:19*
to *o.* upon mine, altar, to burn	*1Sa 2:28*
unto thee, to *o.* burnt offerings	*1Sa 10:8*
the Lord, I *o.* thee three things	*2Sa 24:12*
take and *o.* up what seemeth good	*2Sa 24:22*
will I *o.* burnt offerings unto	*2Sa 24:24*
did Solomon *o.* upon that altar	*1Ki 3:4*
did Solomon *o.* burnt offerings	*1Ki 9:25*
upon thee shall he *o.* the priests	*1Ki 13:2*
o. neither burnt offering nor	*2Ki 5:17*
to *o.* sacrifices and burnt offerings	*2Ki 10:24*
o. burnt offerings unto the Lord	*1Ch 16:40*
the Lord, I *o.* thee three things	*1Ch 21:10*
nor *o.* burnt offerings without	*1Ch 21:24*
o. all burnt sacrifices unto	*1Ch 23:31*
should be able to *o.* so willingly	*1Ch 29:14*
here, to *o.* willingly unto thee	*1Ch 29:17*
o. the burnt offerings of the Lord	*2Ch 23:18*
to minister, and to *o.* withal	*2Ch 24:14*
to *o.* them on the altar of the Lord	*2Ch 29:21*
to *o.* the burnt offering upon	*2Ch 29:27*
o. unto the Lord, as it is written	*2Ch 35:12*
o. burnt offerings upon the altar	*2Ch 35:16*
to *o.* burnt offerings thereon, as it	*Ezr 3:2*
o. burnt offerings unto the Lord	*Ezr 3:6*
may *o.* sacrifices of sweet savours	*Ezr 6:10*
and *o.* them upon the altar of	*Ezr 7:17*
and *o.* up for yourselves a burnt	*Job 42:8*
O. the sacrifices of righteousness	*Ps 4:5*
offerings of blood will I not *o.*	*Ps 16:4*

o. in his tabernacle sacrifices of	*Ps 27:6*
O. unto God thanksgiving	*Ps 50:14*
they *o.* bullocks upon thine altar	*Ps 51:19*
will *o.* unto thee burnt sacrifices	*Ps 66:15*
I will *o.* bullocks with goats	*Ps 66:15*
Sheba and Seba shall *o.* gifts	*Ps 72:10*
I will *o.* to thee the sacrifice of	*Ps 116:17*
wentest thou up to *o.* sacrifice	*Isa 57:7*
gods unto whom they *o.* incense	*Jer 11:12*
o. burnt offering and an oblation	*Jer 14:12*
before me to *o.* burnt offerings	*Jer 33:18*
where they did *o.* sweet savour	*Eze 6:13*
For when ye *o.* your gifts, when	*Eze 20:31*
o. burnt offerings thereon, and to	*Eze 43:18*
second day thou shalt *o.* a kid	*Eze 43:22*
thou shalt *o.* a young bullock	*Eze 43:23*
thou shalt *o.* them before the Lord	*Eze 43:24*
o. them up for a burnt offering	*Eze 43:24*
o. my bread, the fat and the blood	*Eze 44:7*
o. unto me the fat and the blood	*Eze 44:15*
he shall *o.* his sin offering, saith	*Eze 44:27*
shall *o.* an oblation unto the Lord	*Eze 45:1*
is the oblation that ye shall *o.*	*Eze 45:13*
ye shall *o.* the tenth part of a bath	*Eze 45:14*
offering that the prince shall *o.*	*Eze 46:4*
be the offering which ye shall *o.*	*Eze 48:8*
oblation that ye shall *o.* unto	*Eze 48:9*
o. the holy oblation foursquare	*Eze 48:20*
o. an oblation and sweet odours	*Da 2:46*
not *o.* wine offerings to the Lord	*Ho 9:4*
And *o.* a sacrifice of thanksgiving	*Am 4:5*
Though ye *o.* me burnt offerings	*Am 5:22*
which they *o.* there is unclean	*Hag 2:14*
Ye *o.* polluted bread upon mine	*Mal 1:7*
if ye *o.* the blind for sacrifice, is it	*Mal 1:8*
if ye *o.* the lame and sick, is it not	*Mal 1:8*
o. it now unto thy governor; will	*Mal 1:8*
may *o.* unto the Lord an offering	*Mal 3:3*
and then come and *o.* thy gift	*M't 5:24*
o. the gift that Moses commanded	*M't 8:4*
o. for thy cleansing those things	*M'k 1:44*
to *o.* a sacrifice according to that	*Lu 2:24*
o. for thy cleansing, according as	*Lu 5:14*
on the one cheek *o.* also the other	*Lu 6:29*
an egg, will he *o.* him a scorpion	*Lu 11:12*
o. both gifts and sacrifices	*Heb 5:1*
so also for himself, to *o.* for sins	*Heb 5:3*
to *o.* up sacrifice, first for his own	*Heb 7:27*
ordained to *o.* gifts and sacrifices	*Heb 8:3*
man have somewhat also to *o.*	*Heb 8:3*
that *o.* gifts according to the law	*Heb 8:4*
that he should *o.* himself often	*Heb 9:25*
let us *o.* the sacrifice of praise to	*Heb 13:15*
to *o.* up spiritual sacrifices	*1Pe 2:5*
o. it with the prayers of all saints	*Re 8:3*

OFFERED

o. burnt offerings on the altar	*Ge 8:20*
and *o.* him up for a burnt offering	*Ge 22:13*

o. sacrifice upon the mount	*Ge 31:54*
and *o.* sacrifices unto the God of his	*Ge 46:1*
of Israel, which *o.* burnt offerings	*Ex 24:5*
o. burnt offerings and brought	*Ex 32:6*
man that *o.* an offering of gold	*Ex 35:22*
every man *o.* an offering of gold	*Ex 35:22*
o. upon it the burnt offering	*Ex 40:29*
he slew the goat, and *o.* it for sin	*Le 9:15*
o. strange fire, and fire	*Le 10:1;*
devoured them and they died	*16:1; Nu 3:4; 26:61*
the princes *o.* for the dedication	*Nu 7:2; 7:10*
Aaron *o.* them as an offering before the Lord	*Nu 8:21*
two hundred and fifty men that *o.* incense	*Nu 16:35*
Balak *o.* oxen and sheep	*Nu 22:40; 23:2, 4, 14, 30*
the people willingly *o.* themselves	*J'g 5:2; 5:9*
Manoah took a kid and *o.* it on a rock	*J'g 13:19*
when the time was that Elkanah *o.*	*1Sa 1:4*
when any *o.* the priest's servant came	*2Sa 2:13*
David *o.* peace offerings	*2Sa 6:17; 24:25*
Solomon and all Israel *o.*	*1Ki 8:62; 8:63*
Jeroboam *o.* in Beth-el to the calves	*1Ki 12:32; 12:33*
the people *o.* yet in the high places	*1Ki 22:43*
when meat offering was *o.* came water	*2Ki 3:20*
Ahaz approached to the altar and *o.*	*2Ki 16:12*
the captains with the rulers *o.*	*1Ch 29:6*
the people rejoiced for that they *o.* willingly	*1Ch 29:9*
Asa *o.* to the Lord of the spoil	*2Ch 15:11*
Amaziah willingly *o.* himself to the Lord	*2Ch 17:16*
besides all that was willingly *o.*	*Ezr 1:6*
some of fathers *o.* freely for the house of God	*Ezr 2:68*
o. at the dedication of this house of God	*Ezr 6:17*
his counsellors freely *o.* to the God of Israel	*Ezr 7:15*
the king and all Israel there present had *o.*	*Ezr 8:25*
they *o.* a ram of the flock for their trespass	*Ezr 10:19*
willingly *o.* themselves to dwell at Jerusalem	*Ne 11:2*
that day they *o.* great sacrifices	*Ne 12:43*
to them thou hast *o.* a meat offering	*Isa 57:6*
offereth an oblation, as if he *o.* swine's blood	*Isa 66:3*
they have *o.* incense unto Baal	*Jer 32:29*
they *o.* there their sacrifices	*Eze 20:28*
cause the reproach *o.* by him to cease	*Da 11:18*
have ye *o.* to me sacrifices and offerings	*Am 5:25*
the men feared, and *o.* a sacrifice to Lord	*Jon 1:16*
in every place incense be *o.* to my name	*Mal 1:11*
Simon *o.* them money, saying, Give me	*Ac 8:18*
abstain from meats *o.* to idols	*Ac 15:29; 21:25*
an offering should be *o.* for every one of them	*Ac 21:26*
things *o.* to idols	*1Co 8:1; 8:4, 7, 10; 10:19, 28*
if I be *o.* on the service of your faith	*Ph'p 2:17*
for I am now ready to be *o.* the time	*2Ti 4:6*
when he had *o.* up prayers and supplications	*Heb 5:7*
this he did once, when he *o.* up himse'f	*Heb 7:27*
not without blood, which he *o.* for himself	*Heb 9:7*
were *o.* gifts	*Heb 9:9*
o. himself without spot to God	*Heb 9:14*

Christ was once *o*. to bear the   Heb 9:28
sins of many
by faith Abel *o*. to God a   Heb 11:4
more excellent sacrifice
by faith Abraham, when   Heb 11:17
tried, *o*. up Isaac
Abraham justified by works   Jas 2:21
when he *o*.

OFFERETH

the priest that *o*. it for sin shall   Le 6:26
eat it
neither shall it be imputed to   Le 7:18
him that *o*. it
for he *o*. the bread of thy God,   Le 21:8
shall be holy
whoso *o*. praise glorifieth me,   Ps 50:23
to him
he that *o*. oblation as if offered   Isa 66:3
swine's flesh

OFFERING

Cain brought an *o*. unto the   Ge 4:3
Lord
the Lord had respect to Abel   Ge 4:4
and to his *o*.
bring me an *o*. of every man,   Ex 25:2
take my *o*.
this is the *o*. which ye shall   Ex 25:3;
take   35:5
an half shekel shall be the *o*.   Ex 30:13
of the Lord
an *o*. to the Lord to make   Ex 30:15
atonement for your souls
ye shall bring your *o*. of the   Le 1:2
cattle
o. to Lord be of fowls; *o*. of   Le 1:14;
fine flour   2:1
an *o*. (A)(B)(R)   Le 2:4;
2:12; 3:1; 7:14, 29; 22:18; Nu 18:9;
31:50; Isa 19:21; 40:20; 66:3; Jer 14:12;
Eze 44:30; 45:1, 13, 16; Da 2:46; 9:27
no meat *o*. shall be made with   Le 2:11
leaven
he shall lay his hand on the   Le 3:2;
head of his *o*.   3:8
if he offer a lamb for his *o*.   Le 3:7;
   Nu 6:14
and if his *o*. be a goat Le 3:12; 4:23, 28
this is the *o*. of Aaron and of   Le 6:20
his sons
if his *o*. be a vow, or a   Le 7:16
voluntary *o*.
an *o*. of jealousy, an *o*. of   Nu 5:15
memorial
the princes offered their *o*.   Nu 7:10
before the altar
they shall offer their *o*. each   Nu 7:11
prince on his day
shall offer Levites before the   Nu 8:11;
Lord for an *o*.   8:21
the *o*. of the Lord in his   Nu 9:13
appointed season
Moses said, Respect not thou   Nu 16:15
their *o*.
wherefore kick ye at mine *o*.   1Sa 2:29
shall not be purged with   1Sa 3:14
sacrifice nor *o*.
as Samuel was *o*. the burnt   1Sa 7:10
offering
if the Lord have stirred thee 1Sa 26:19
up against me, accept an *o*.
David made an end of *o*.   2Sa 6:18;
   1Ch 16:2
prophesied till *o*. of evening 1Ki 18:29
sacrifice
as soon as Jehu had made an 2Ki 10:25
end of *o*.
bring an *o*. and come   1Ch 16:29;
   Ps 96:8
o. according to   2Ch 8:13
commandment of Moses
made an end of *o*. the king, 2Ch 29:29
and all bowed
they did eat seven days *o*. 2Ch 30:22
peace offerings
the sons of Aaron were   2Ch 35:14
busied in *o*.
priests *o*. willingly for the   Ezr 7:16
house of God
Israel shall bring the *o*. of the Ne 10:39
corn
I have not caused thee to   Isa 43:23
serve with an *o*.
thou shalt make his soul an *o*. Isa 53:10
for sin
they shall bring your brethren Isa 66:20
for an *o*.

to provoke me to anger in *o*.   Jer 11:17
to Baal
they presented provocation   Eze 20:28
of their *o*.
the daughter of my dispersed   Zep 3:10
bring my *o*.
nor will I accept an *o*. at your   Mal 1:10
hand
thus ye brought an *o*. should I   Mal 1:13
accept this
that he regardeth not the *o*.   Mal 2:13
any more
offer to the Lord an *o*. in   Mal 3:3
righteousness
coming to him and *o*. him   Lu 23:36
vinegar
a fragrant *o*. (A)(N)(R)   Ph'p 4:18
a fragrant *o*. (B)   Eph 5:2
every priest *o*. often the   Heb 10:11
same sacrifices
that the *o*. up of Gentiles be   Ro 15:16
acceptable
an *o*. and a sacrifice to God   Eph 5:2
for us
sacrifice and *o*. thou   Heb 10:5;
wouldest not   10:8
through the *o*. of the body   Heb 10:10
of Jesus once for all
by one *o*. he hath perfected   Heb 10:14
for ever sanctified
where remission is, there is   Heb 10:18
no more *o*. for sin

HEAVE OFFERING

sanctify the shoulder of the   Ex 29:27
heave *o*.
out of the whole oblation for   Le 7:14
an heave *o*.
ye shall offer up an heave *o*.   Nu 15:19;
   15:20
of the first dough give an   Nu 15:21
heave *o*. to the Lord
the tithes which they offer as Nu 18:24
an heave *o*.
give the Lord's heave *o*. to   Nu 18:28
Aaron the priest
give it to Eleazar for an   Nu 31:29
heave *o*. of the Lord
the tribute which was the   Nu 31:41
Lord's heave *o*.

PEACE OFFERING

if oblation be sacrifice of peace Le 3:1;
o.   3:3, 6, 9

SIN OFFERING

the flesh of bullock shalt thou Ex 29:14;
burn it is a sin *o*. Le 4:21, 24; 5:9, 11-12
the blood of the sin *o*. of   Ex 30:10
atonements
let him bring a young bullock Le 4:3;
without blemish for a sin *o*. 16:3, 27;
   Nu 8:8
the priest shall take of the   Le 4:25;
blood of sin *o*.   5:9
shall lay his hand on the head Le 4:29;
of the sin *o*.   4:33
slay the sin *o*. in the place of Le 4:29
the burnt offering
if he bring a lamb for a sin *o*.   Le 4:32;
   Nu 6:14
he shall bring a lamb or a kid Le 5:6;
of goats for a sin *o*. 9:3; 16:5, 15, 27;
   23:19
priest shall offer that which is   Le 5:8
for the sin *o*. first
he shall bring fine flour for a   Le 5:11
sin *o*.
saying, This is the law of the   Le 6:25;
sin *o*.   7:37
as the sin *o*. is so is trespass Le 7:7;
offering   14:13
take thee a young calf for a sin Le 9:2
o. and a ram
Moses sought the goat of the   Le 10:16
sin *o*.
why have ye not eaten sin *o*. Le 10:17
in the holy place
she shall bring a turtledove   Le 12:6
for a sin *o*.
fat of the sin *o*. shall be burnt Le 16:25
on the altar
one kid of the goats for a sin Nu 7:16;
o.   7:22, 28; 15:24; 28:15; 29:5
the sin *o*. should be made for 2Ch 29:24
all Israel
offered twelve he goats for a   Ezr 8:35
sin *o*.

and sin *o*. hast thou not required Ps 40:6
give the priest a bullock for a Eze 43:19
sin *o*.
on the second day offer a kid Eze 43:22
for a sin *o*.
prepare every day a goat for   Eze 43:25
a sin *o*.
into sanctuary he shall offer Eze 44:27
his sin *o*.
they shall eat the meat   Eze 44:29
offering and sin *o*.
this is the place where priest Eze 46:20
shall boil sin *o*.

TRESPASS OFFERING

he shall bring his trespass *o*. to   Le 5:6
the Lord
shall bring lamb without   Le 5:15
blemish for trespass *o*.
atonement with ram trespass Le 5:16;
   5:18; 6:6; 19:21-22
he shall give it in the day of his Le 6:5
trespass *o*.
law of trespass *o*.   Le 7:37
he lamb for trespass *o*.   Le 14:12;
   14:21, 24, 25; Nu 6:12
trespass *o*. is most holy   Le 14:13
but in any wise return him a 1Sa 6:3
trespass *o*.
they said, What shall be the   1Sa 6:4;
trespass *o*.   8:17
two tables to slay the   Eze 40:39;
trespass *o*. on   42:13
eat the trespass *o*. and every Eze 44:29
dedicated thing
where the priests shall boil Eze 46:20
the trespass *o*.

WAVE OFFERING

wave them for a wave *o*.   Ex 29:24;
29:26; Le 7:30; 8:27, 29; 9:21; 10:15;
   14:12, 24; 23:20; Nu 6:20
thou shalt sanctify the breast   Ex 6:27
of the wave *o*.
ye brought the sheaf of the   Le 23:15
wave *o*.

WOOD OFFERING

cast lots for the wood *o*. to   Ne 10:34
bring it
and for the wood *o*. at the   Ne 13:31
times appointed

OFFERINGS

o. of grains and vines (B)   Ex 22:29
if his *o*. be of the flocks, sheep Le 1:10
or goats
with all thy *o*. thou shalt offer   Le 2:13
salt
offer their *o*. (B)(R)   Le 7:38
to make fat with chief of all 1Sa 2:29
the *o*.
let there be no dew nor fields 2Sa 1:21
of *o*.
the people brought in the *o*. 2Ch 31:12
people gave to the priests for 2Ch 35:8
passover, *o*.
but the other holy *o*. sod   2Ch 35:13
they in pots
should bring the firstfruits   Ne 10:37;
of *o*.   12:44
the Lord remember all thy *o*.   Ps 20:3
bring no more *o*. (A)(B)(R)   Isa 1:13
with *o*. and incense in their   Jer 41:5
hands
there will I require your *o*.   Eze 20:40
all kinds of *o*. (A)(R)   Eze 44:30
they sacrifice flesh for my *o*.   Ho 8:13
have ye offered me *o*. forty   Am 5:25
years
then *o*. of Judah and Jerusalem Mal 3:4
be pleasant
wherein have we robbed thee? Mal 3:8
in tithes and *o*.
of their abundance cast in unto Lu 21:4
the *o*.
I came to bring alms to my   Ac 24:17
nations and *o*.

OFFERINGS *MADE BY FIRE*

o. made by fire   Le 2:3;
2:10; 4:35; 5:12; 6:17, 18; 7:30, 35;
10:12, 15; 21:6, 21; 24:9; De 18:1;
   1Sa 2:28

OFFERINGS *OF THE LORD*

for men abhorred the *o. of the*   *1Sa 2:17*
Lord

BURNT OFFERINGS

burnt o.   *Ge 8:20;*
Ex 10:25;   20:24;   24:5;   32:6;   Nu
10:10; 29:39; De 12:6,   11,   13,   14,   27;
27:6; Jos 8:31; 22:27, 28, 29; J'g 20:26;
21:4; 1Sa 6:15; 10:8; 15:22; 2Sa 6:17,
18; 24:24, 25; 1Ki 3:4, 15; 8:64; 9:25;
2Ki 10:24; 1Ch 16:2, 40; 30:15; 31:2, 3;
35:12, 14, 16; Ezr 3:2, 3, 4, 6; 6:9, 8:35;
Job 1:5; Ps 50:8; 43:18, 27; 45:15, 17;
46:2,   12;   Ho 6:6;   Am 5:22;   Mic 6:6;
M'k 12:33;   Heb 10:6,   8

DRINK OFFERINGS

drink o.   *Le 23:18;*
23:37; Nu 6:15; 28:14, 31; 29:6, 11, 18,
19, 21, 24, 27, 30, 33, 37, 39; 22:38;
2Ki 16:13; 1Ch 29:21; Ezr 7:17; Ps 16:4;
Jer 19:13; 32:39; 44:17, 18, 19, 25; 45:17

FREEWILL OFFERINGS

freewill o.   *Ex 36:1; Le 23:38;*
Le 23:38; Nu 29:39; De 12:6, 17;
2Ch 31:14;   Am 4:5

HEAVE OFFERINGS

given the charge of mine *heave*   *Nu 18:8*
o.
thither ye shall bring your   *De 12:6*
heave o.

MEAT OFFERINGS

meat o.   *Nu 29:39; Jos 22:29; 1Ki 8:64;*
2Ch 7:7;   Ezr 7:17;   13:5;   Jer 33:18;
Eze 45:17; Am 5:22

PEACE OFFERINGS

shalt sacrifice thereon thy   *Ex 20:24*
peace o.
sacrificed *peace o.* of oxen to   *Ex 24:5*
the Lord
it is an heave offering of the   *Ex 29:28*
peace o.
people brought *peace o.* and   *Ex 32:6*
sat down to eat
as taken from the bullock of   *Le 4:10*
peace o.
shall burn as fat of *peace o.*   *Le 4:26;*
4:31, 35; 6:12
this is the law of sacrifice of   *Le 7:11;*
peace o.   *7:13, 37*
also a bullock and ram for   *Le 9:4;*
peace o.   *9:18*
are given out of the sacrifice   *Le 10:14*
of *peace o.*
offer them for *peace o.* to the   *Le 17:5;*
Lord   *23:19*
if ye offer a sacrifice of *peace*   *Le 19:5;*
o.   *22:21*
a lamb for *peace o.*; a ram for *Nu 6:14;*
peace o.   *6:17*
for sacrifice of *peace o.* two   *Nu 7:17;*
oxen   *7:23, 29, 35, 41; 29:39*
blow over the sacrifice of   *Nu 10:10*
your *peace o.*
Joshua sacrificed *peace o.* to   *Jos 8:31*
the Lord
if to offer *peace o.* let the   *Jos 22:23*
Lord require it
all Israel offered *peace o.*   *J'g 20:26;*
                   21:4
I will come and offer *peace o.* *1Sa 10:8;*
                 11:15
David offered *peace o.*   *2Sa 6:17;*
       24:25; 1Ch 21:26
Solomon offered *peace o.* *1Ki 3:15; 8:63*
thrice in a year Solomon   *1Ki 9:25*
offered *peace o.*
Hezekiah appointed priests   *2Ch 31:2*
for *peace o.*
Manasseh offered *peace o.*   *2Ch 33:16*
on the altar
she said to him, I have *peace o.*   *Pr 7:14*
with me
peace o. to make   *Eze 45:15;*
reconciliation   *45:17*
priest prepare *peace o.*;   *Eze 46:2;*
prince his *peace o.*   *46:12*
not regard *peace o.* of your   *Am 5:22*
fat things

SIN OFFERINGS

sin *o.* to make an atonement   *Ne 10:33*
for Israel

THANK OFFERINGS

come near and bring *thank*   *2Ch 29:31*
o. to house
the altar, and sacrified   *2Ch 33:16*
thereon *thank o.*

WAVE OFFERINGS

all the *wave o.* I have given to *Nu 18:11*
thee

WINE OFFERINGS

not offer *wine o.* to be pleasing *Ho 9:4*
to God

OFFICE

me he restored unto mine *o.*   *Ge 41:13*
the *o.* of a midwife to the   *Ex 1:16*
Hebrew
minister unto me in the priest's *Ex 28:1;*
o.   *29:1, 44; 30:30; 40:13, 15*
unto me in the priest's *o.*   *Ex 28:3;*
               28:4, 41
and the priest's *o.* shall be   *Ex 29:9*
theirs for
sons, to minister in the   *Ex 31:10;*
priest's *o.*   *35:19, 41; Nu 3:3*
unto the Lord in the priest's *o.* *Le 7:35*
in the priest's *o.* in his father's *Le 16:32*
ministered in the priest's *o.* in   *Nu 3:4*
they shall wait on their priest's *Nu 3:10*
o.
And to the *o.* of Eleazar the   *Nu 4:16*
son of
keep your priest's *o.* for   *Nu 18:7*
everything
I have given your priest's *o.*   *Nu 18:7*
unto you
in the priest's *o.* in his stead   *De 10:6*
priest's *o.* in the temple that   *1Ch 6:10*
waited on their *o.* according   *1Ch 6:32*
the seer did ordain in their set *1Ch 9:22*
o.
were in their set *o.* and were *1Ch 9:26*
over
had the set *o.* over the things *1Ch 9:31*
that
their *o.* was to wait on the *1Ch 23:28*
sons of
Ithamar executed the priest's *1Ch 24:2*
o.
from executing the priest's   *2Ch 11:14*
o. unto
was brought unto the king's *2Ch 24:11*
o. by
the cities of the priests, in *2Ch 31:15*
their set *o.*
for in their set *o.* they   *2Ch 31:18*
sanctified
and their *o.* was to distribute *Ne 13:13*
unto
few; and let another take his   *Ps 109:8*
o.
to do the *o.* of a priest unto *Eze 44:13*
me
tax *o.* (S)   *M't 9:9; M'k 2:14; Lu 5:27*
while he executed the priest's *o.* *Lu 1:8*
to the custom of the priest's *o.* *Lu 1:9*
o. let another take (E)(P)(R)   *Ac 1:20*
of the Gentiles, I magnify   *Ro 11:13*
mine *o.*
all members have not the same *Ro 12:4*
o.
according to divine *o.* (R)   *Col 1:25*
If a man desire the *o.* of a   *1Ti 3:1*
bishop
let them use the *o.* of a deacon *1Ti 3:10*
that have used the *o.* of a   *1Ti 3:13*
deacon
receive the *o.* of the   *Heb 7:5*
priesthood

OFFICER

unto Potiphar, an *o.* of   *Ge 37:36*
Pharaoh's
and Potiphar, an *o.* of   *Ge 39:1*
Pharaoh
of Jerubbaal? and Zebul his *o.* *J'g 9:28*
the son of Nathan was   *1Ki 4:5*
principal *o.*

the only *o.* which was in the   *1Ki 4:19*
land
the king of Israel called an *o.* *1Ki 22:9*
appointed unto her a certain *o.* *2Ki 8:6*
he took an *o.* that was set   *2Ki 25:19*
over the
priest's *o.* came and emptied *2Ch 24:11*
the
the judge deliver thee to the   *M't 5:25;*
o.   *Lu 12:58*
and the *o.* cast thee into   *Lu 12:58*
prison
o. commanding the cohort (N) *Ac 21:31*
every legitimate *o.* is (P)   *Ro 13:4*

OFFICERS

was wroth against two of his *o.* *Ge 40:2*
asked Pharaoh's *o.* that were   *Ge 40:7*
with
let him appoint *o.* over the   *Ge 41:34*
land
of the people, and their *o.*   *Ex 5:6*
saying
of the people went out, and   *Ex 5:10*
their *o.*
And the *o.* of the children of   *Ex 5:14*
Israel
the *o.* of the children of Israel *Ex 5:15*
came
the *o.* of the children of Israel *Ex 5:19*
did
of the people, and *o.* over   *Nu 11:16*
them
was wroth with the *o.* of the *Nu 31:14*
host
o. which were over thousands *Nu 31:48*
of
tens, and *o.* among your tribes *De 1:15*
Judges and *o.* shalt thou make *De 16:18*
thee
the *o.* shall speak unto the   *De 20:5*
people
the *o.* shall speak further unto *De 20:8*
when the *o.* have made an end *De 20:9*
of
your *o.* with all the men of   *De 29:10*
Israel
elders of your tribes, and your *De 31:28*
o.
Joshua commanded the *o.* of   *Jos 1:10*
that the *o.* went through the   *Jos 3:2*
host
all Israel, and their elders, and *Jos 8:33*
o.
for their judges, and for their *Jos 23:2;*
o.   *24:1*
give to his *o.* and to his   *1Sa 8:15*
servants
the son of Nathan was over the *1Ki 4:1*
o.
had twelve *o.* over all Israel   *1Ki 4:7*
those *o.* provided victual for *1Ki 4:27*
king
they unto the place where the *1Ki 4:28*
o.
the chief of Solomon's *o.*   *1Ki 5:16*
which
o. that were over Solomon's   *1Ki 9:23*
work
the *o.* of the guard (S)   *1Ki 14:27*
the hundreds, the *o.* of the *2Ki 11:15*
host
priest appointed, *o.* over the *2Ki 11:18*
house
and his princes, and his *o.*   *2Ki 24:12*
king's wives, and his *o.* and   *2Ki 24:15*
six thousand were *o.* and   *1Ch 23:4*
judges
over Israel, for *o.* and judges *1Ch 26:29*
o. among them of Israel on *1Ch 26:30*
this
their *o.* that served the king in *1Ch 27:1*
with the *o.* and with the   *1Ch 28:1*
mighty
the chief of king Solomon's *o.* *2Ch 8:10*
of Israel called for one of his *2Ch 18:8*
o.
the Levites shall be *o.* before *2Ch 19:11*
you
there were scribes, and *o.*   *2Ch 34:13*
to all the *o.* of his house, that   *Es 1:8*
king appoint *o.* in all the   *Es 2:3*
provinces
o. of the king, helped the Jews *Es 9:3*
I will also make thy *o.* peace *Isa 60:17*
be *o.* in the house of the Lord *Jer 29:26*
recount his *o.* (B)(R)   *Na 2:5*
chief priests sent *o.* to take *Joh 7:32*
him

OFFICERS

came the *o.* of the chief priests and   *Joh 7:45*
The *o.* answered, Never man spake   *Joh 7:46*
received a band of men and *o.* from   *Joh 18:3*
and *o.* of the Jews took Jesus, and   *Joh 18:12*
the servants and *o.* stood there   *Joh 18:18*
one of the *o.* which stood by struck   *Joh 18:22*
priests therefore and *o.* saw him   *Joh 19:6*
But when the *o.* came, and found   *Ac 5:22*
Then went the captain with the *o.*   *Ac 5:26*
magistrates sent *o.* (N)   *Ac 16:35; 16:38*

OFFICES

pray thee, into one of the priests' *o.*   *1Sa 2:36*
according to their *o.* in their   *1Ch 24:3*
And the priests waited on their *o.*   *2Ch 7:6*
Levites to their *o.* (S)   *2Ch 8:14*
the *o.* of the house of the Lord   *2Ch 23:18*
of my God, and for the *o.* thereof   *Ne 13:14*

OFFICIAL

700 *o.* wives (B)   *1Ki 11:3*
o. servants under God (A)   *Ro 13:6*

OFFICIALS

o. who supervised (B)   *1Ki 9:23*
appoint judges and *o.* (B)   *Ezr 7:25*
o. ordered them flogged (B)   *Ac 16:22*

OFFICIATE

to *o.* as priests (B)   *Ex 28:1*

OFFSCOURING

made us as the *o.* and refuse in   *La 3:45*
the *o.* of all things unto this day   *1Co 4:13*

OFFSPRING

offspring (A)   *Ge 3:15; 17:12; 21:13; 48:11; 2Sa 7:12; 2Ki 5:27; Isa 43:5; 44:3; 54:3; 66:22*
offspring (B)   *Ge 3:15; 12:7; 15:5; 17:12; 21:13; 22:18; 48:11; Le 18:21; 21:17; 22:3; Nu 18:19; De 30:6; Job 5:25; Ps 89:4; Isa 43:5; 44:3; Ga 3:16*
offspring (A)   *Ge 15:3; 38:8; Le 21:21; 22:4; Ru 4:12; 1Ch 16:13; Le 6:13; Job 21:8; Ps 21:10; 22:23; 37:28; Isa 1:4; 45:25; 57:3; 61:9; Jer 23:8; 31:37; 33:22; Eze 20:5; 43:19; 44:22; Da 9:1; Mal 2:15; Joh 7:42; Ro 9:8*
offspring (B)   *Ge 15:3; 38:9; Le 22:4; Nu 16:40; Ru 4:12; 1Sa 2:20; 2Ki 11:1; 25:25; Ezr 9:2; Ps 21:10; 37:28; 69:36; 102:28; 106:27; Pr 11:21; Isa 45:25; 57:3; Jer 7:15; 23:8; Mal 2:15; M'k 12:20; Joh 7:42; Ac 13:23; Ro 9:8, 29; Ga 3:19; Re 12:17*
offspring (B)   *Ge 15:3; 19:32; 38:8, 9; 1Ch 16:13; Job 21:8; Ps 21:10; Isa 1:4; 45:19, 25; 57:3, 4; 65:23; Jer 7:15; Mal 2:15; Ga 3:19; Re 12:17*
offspring (R)   *Ge 17:12; 21:13; Nu 18:19; Isa 43:5; Ga 3:16*
offspring (R)   *Ge 46:6; Jos 24:3; Isa 53:10; Jer 22:30; 36:31*
offspring (B)   *Ge 48:19; Nu 24:7; Jos 24:3; 2Sa 4:8; 22:51; Ps 35:13; 37:26; 89:29; 112:2; Isa 53:10; Jer 22:28, 30; 29:32; 36:31; 49:10*
offspring (B)   *Le 20:2; 21:15; Nu 24:7; Jos 24:3; 2Sa 22:51; Ps 25:13; 37:25, 26; 9:29; 112:2; Jer 22:28; 30; 36:31; 49:10; Ac 7:5, 8*
own *o.* assassinated (A)(B)   *2Ch 32:21*
thine *o.* as the grass of the earth   *Job 5:25*

no *o.* or descendant (B)(R)   *Job 18:19*
and their *o.* before their eyes   *Job 21:8*
o. shall not be satisfied with bread   *Job 27:14*
eat; yea, let my *o.* be rooted out   *Job 31:8*
their *o.* you will destroy (A)(B)(R)   *Ps 21:10*
should *o.* be dispersed (A)   *Pr 5:16*
o. and posterity (R)   *Isa 14:22*
o. and the issue, all vessels of small   *Isa 22:24*
and my blessing upon thine *o.*   *Isa 44:3*
the *o.* of thy bowels like the gravel   *Isa 48:19*
o. of deceit (R)   *Isa 57:4*
and their *o.* among the people   *Isa 61:9*
the Lord, and their *o.* with them   *Isa 65:23*
you *o.* of vipers (E)   *M't 3:7*
have said, For we are also his *o.*   *Ac 17:28*
then as we are the *o.* of God, we   *Ac 17:29*
I am the root and the *o.* of David   *Re 22:16*

OFT

as *o.* as he passed by, he turned   *2Ki 4:8*
How *o.* is the candle of wicked put out   *Job 21:17*
how *o.* cometh their destruction upon   *Job 21:17*
How *o.* did they provoke him   *Ps 78:40*
do we and the Pharisees fast *o.*   *M't 9:14*
into the fire, and *o.* into the water   *M't 17:15*
how *o.* shall my brother sin against   *M't 18:21*
they wash their hands *o.*, eat not   *M'k 7:3*
And I punished them *o.* in every   *Ac 26:11*
this do ye, as *o.* as ye drink it, in   *1Co 11:21*
more frequent, in deaths *o.*   *2Co 11:23*
he *o.* refreshed me, and was not   *2Ti 1:16*
in the rain that cometh *o.* upon it   *Heb 6:7*

OFTEN

He, that being *o.* reproved hardeneth   *Pr 29:1*
that feared the Lord spake *o.* one   *Mal 3:16*
often (S)   *M't 9:14; 17:15; 18:21; M'k 7:3; 9:22; Lu 8:29; Ac 26:11*
how *o.* would I have gathered thy   *M't 23:37; Lu 13:34*
been *o.* bound with fetters and   *M'k 5:4*
the disciples of John fast *o.*   *Lu 5:33*
For as *o.* as ye eat this bread   *1Co 11:26*
In journeyings *o.* in perils of   *2Co 11:26*
watchings *o.*, in hunger and thirst   *2Co 11:27*
fastings *o.* in cold and nakedness   *2Co 11:27*
walk, of whom I have told you *o.*   *Ph'p 3:18*
sake and thine *o.* infirmities   *1Ti 5:23*
that he should offer himself *o.* as   *Heb 9:25*
For then must he *o.* have suffered   *Heb 9:26*
with all plagues, as *o.* as they will   *Re 11:6*

OFTENER

wherefore he sent for him the *o.*   *Ac 24:26*

OFTENTIMES

these things worketh God *o.*   *Job 33:29*
For *o.* also thine own heart   *Ec 7:22*
o. it had caught him: and he   *Lu 8:29*
o. I purposed to come unto you   *Ro 1:13*
o. proved diligent in many things   *2Co 8:22*
and offering *o.* the same sacrifices   *Heb 10:11*

OFTTIMES

for *o.* he falleth into the fire   *M't 17:15*
o. it hath cast him into the fire   *M'k 9:22*
Jesus *o.* resorted thither with his   *Joh 18:2*

OG

O. the king of Bashan went out   *Nu 21:33; De 1:4; 3:1, 3, 4, 11; 4:47; 29:7; 31:4; Jos 2:10; 9:10; 12:4; 1Ki 4:19; Ne 9:22; Ps 135:11; 136:20*
the kingdom of *O.* king of   *Nu 32:33*
Bashan   *De 3:10, 13; Jos 3:12, 30-31*

OGLING

with *o.* eyes (B)   *1Sa 3:16*

OH

O. let not the Lord be angry   *Ge 18:30; 18:32*
unto them, *O.*, not so, my Lord   *Ge 19:18*
O. let me escape thither, (is it not   *Ge 19:20*
O. my lord, let thy servant, I pray   *Ge 44:18*
O. this people have sinned a great   *Ex 32:31*
O. my Lord, if the Lord be with us   *J'g 6:13*
O. my Lord, wherewith shall I save   *J'g 6:15*
O. my lord, as thy soul liveth, my   *1Sa 1:26*
O. that I were made judge in the land   *2Sa 15:4*
O. that one would give me drink of the   *2Sa 23:15; 1Ch 11:17*
O. that thou wouldest bless me   *1Ch 4:10*
O. that my grief were thoroughly   *Job 6:2*
O. that I might have my request; and   *Job 6:8*
o. that I had given up the ghost, and   *Job 10:18*
o. that God would speak, and open his   *Job 11:5*
O. that my words were now written   *Job 19:23*
o. that they were printed in a book   *Job 19:23*
O. that I knew where I might find him   *Job 23:3*
O. that I were as in months past, as in   *Job 29:2*
O. that we had of his flesh! we cannot   *Job 31:31*
O. that one would hear me! behold   *Job 31:35*
o. save me for thy mercies' sake   *Ps 6:4*
O. let the wickedness of the   *Ps 7:9*
O. that the salvation of Israel were   *Ps 14:7; 53:6*
O. how great is thy goodness, which   *Ps 31:19*
O. that I had wings like a dove! for   *Ps 55:6*
O. that my people had hearkened   *Ps 81:13*
O. that men would praise   *Ps 107:8; 107:15, 21, 31*
O. that thou wouldest rend the   *Isa 64:1*
O. that my head were waters   *Jer 9:1*
O. that I had in the wilderness a   *Jer 9:2*
O. do not this abominable thing   *Jer 44:4*

OHAD

Jemuel, and Jamin, and *O.*   *Ge 46:10; Ex 6:15*

OHEL

And Hashubah, and *O.*, and   *1Ch 3:20*

OIL

and poured *o.* upon the top of   *Ge 28:18*
thereon, and he poured *o.* thereon   *Ge 35:14*
O. for the light   *Ex 25:6;*

27:20; 35:8, 14, 28; 39:27; Le 24:2;
  Nu 4:16
spices for the anointing o. Ex 25:6
cakes, wafers anointed with Ex 29:2;
o. Le 2:4-5
the anointing o. Ex 29:7;
29:21; 30:25, 31; 31:11; 35:8, 15, 28;
39:38; 40:9; Le 8:2, 10, 12, 30; 10:7;
 21:12; Nu 4:16
fourth part of an hin of o. Ex 29:40;
 Nu 15:4, 6, 9; 28:5
olive o. Ex 30:24; De 8:8; 2Ki 18:32
he made the holy anointing o. Ex 37:29
he shall pour o. upon it Le 2:1;
 2:6, 15; 14:26; 21:10; Nu 5:15
be made with fine flour with o. Le 2:7;
 2:16; 6:15, 21
he shall put no o. upon it Le 5:11
meat offering mingled with o. Le 7:10;
7:12; 9:4; 14:10, 21; 23:13; Nu 6:15;
7:13, 19, 25, 31, 37, 43, 49, 55, 61, 67, 73,
79; 8:8; 28:9, 12, 13, 20, 28; 29:3, 9, 14
a log of o. Le 14:12; 14:15, 21, 24
dip finger in o. Le 14:16
all the o. vessels Nu 4:9
of it was the taste of fresh o. Nu 11:8
best of the o. Nu 18:12
was anointed with the holy o. Nu 35:25
wine, and o. De 7:13;
11:14; 12:17; 14:23; 18:4; 28:51;
1Ch 9:29; 12:40; 2Ch 2:15; 11:11; 31:5;
32:28; Ezr 3:7; 6:9; 7:22; Ne 5:11; 10:37,
 39; 13:5, 12
not anoint thyself with the o. De 28:40;
 2Sa 14:2
o. out of the flinty rock De 32:13
let him dip his foot in o. De 33:24
anointing kings with o. 1Sa 10:1;
16:1, 13; 2Sa 1:21; 1Ki 1:39; 2Ki 9:1, 3,
 6
twenty measures of pure o. 1Ki 5:11
a cruse of o. 1Ki 17:12; 17:14, 16
a pot of o. 2Ki 4:2
a vessel more. And the o. 2Ki 4:6
stayed
Go, sell the o. and pay thy debt 2Ki 4:7
over the cellars of o. was 1Ch 27:28
Joash
twenty thousand baths of o. 2Ch 2:10
six months with o. of myrrh Es 2:12
Which make o. within their Job 24:11
walls
rock poured me out rivers of Job 29:6
o.
thou anointest my head with o. Ps 23:5
anointed thee with o. of Ps 45:7
gladness
his words were softer than o. Ps 55:21
yet
with my holy o. have I Ps 89:20
anointed him
I shall be anointed with fresh Ps 92:10
o.
o. to make his face to shine Ps 104:15
water, and like o. into his Ps 109:18
bones
it shall be an excellent o. Ps 141:5
which
and her mouth is smoother than Pr 5:3
o.
he that loveth wine and o. Pr 21:17
shall not
and o. in the dwelling of the Pr 21:20
wise
right hand encountereth o. Pr 27:16
(E)(R)
and the myrtle, and the o. Isa 41:19
tree
ashes, the o. of joy for Isa 61:3
mourning
for wine, and for o. and for Jer 31:12
wine, and summer fruits, and Jer 40:10
o.
of barley, and of o. and of Jer 41:8
honey
thee, and I anointed thee with Eze 16:9
o.
eat fine flour, and honey, and Eze 16:13
o.
hast set mine o. and mine Eze 16:18
incense
thee, fine flour, and o. and Eze 16:19
honey
hast set mine incense and Eze 23:41
mine o.
and honey, and o. and balm Eze 27:17
and cause their rivers to run Eze 32:14
like o.
the ordinance of o., the bath Eze 45:14
of o.

ram, and an hin of o. for an Eze 45:24
ephah
offering, and according to Eze 45:25
the o.
and an hin of o. to an ephah Eze 46:5;
 46:7, 11
and the third part of an hin Eze 46:14
of o. to
and the meat offering, and Eze 46:15
the o.
and my flax, mine o. and my Ho 2:5
drink
I gave her corn, and wine, and Ho 2:8
o.
the corn, and the wine, and the Ho 2:22
o.
and o. is carried into Egypt Ho 12:1
is dried up, the o. languisheth Joe 1:10
send you corn, and wine, and Joe 2:19
o.
shall overflow with wine and Joe 2:24
with ten thousands of rivers of Mic 6:7
o.
thou shalt not anoint with Mic 6:15
thee o.
the new wine and upon the o. Hag 1:11
bread or pottage, or wine, or Hag 2:12
o. or
empty the golden o. out of Zec 4:12
themselves
lamps, and took no o. with M't 25:3
them
wise took o. in their vessels M't 25:4
Give us of your o.; for our M't 25:8
lamps
anointed with o. many that M'k 6:13
were
My head with o. thou didst not Lu 7:46
his wounds, pouring in o. and Lu 10:34
wine
he said, An hundred measures Lu 16:6
of o.
anointed thee with o. of Heb 1:9
gladness
anointing him with o. in the Jas 5:14
name
thou hurt not the o. and the Re 6:6
wine
and wine, and o. and fine Re 18:13
flour, and

OILED

bread, and one cake of o. Ex 29:23
bread
a cake of o. bread, and one Le 8:26
wafer

OINTMENT

shalt make it an oil of holy o. Ex 30:25
an o.
an o. compound after the art Ex 30:25
the spices, and the precious 2Ki 20:13
o.
sons of the priests made the o. 1Ch 9:30
of
he maketh the sea like a pot Job 41:31
of o.
like the precious o. upon the Ps 133:2
head
O. and perfume rejoice the Pr 27:9
heart
and the o. of his right hand Pr 27:16
name is better than precious o. Ec 7:1
white; and let thy head lack no Ec 9:8
o.
flies cause the o. of the Ec 10:1
apothecary
putrify perfume's o. (R) Ec 10:1
thy name is as o. poured forth Ca 1:3
bound up, neither mollified with Isa 1:6
o.
and the spices, and the Isa 39:2
precious o.
thou wentest to the king with Isa 57:9
o.
alabaster box of very M't 26:1
precious o.
For this o. might have been M't 26:9
sold for
she hath poured this o. on M't 26:12
my body
alabaster box of o. M'k 14:3
spikenard
Why was this waste of the o. M'k 14:4
made
brought an alabaster box of o. Lu 7:37
feet, and anointed them with Lu 7:38
the o.

hath anointed my feet with o. Lu 7:46
which anointed the Lord with Joh 11:2
o.
Mary a pound of o. of Joh 12:3
spikenard
was filled with the odour of Joh 12:3
the o.
Why was not this o. sold for Joh 12:5
three
o. for your eyes (N) Re 3:18

OINTMENTS

with spices and o. (R) Es 2:12
of the savour of thy good o. thy Ca 1:3
the smell of thine o. than all Ca 4:10
spices
anoint themselves with the Am 6:6
chief o.
and prepared spices and o. Lu 23:56
cinnamon, and odours, and o. Re 18:13

OLD

Noah was 500 years o. and Ge 5:32
begat Shem
Noah was 600 years o. when the Ge 7:6
flood came
Shem was 100 years o. and Ge 11:10
begat Arphaxad
Abraham 75 years o. when Ge 12:4
departed from Haran
take a heifer and a ram of Ge 15:9
three years o.
Abram was fourscore and six Ge 16:16
years o. when Hagar
he that is eight days o. shall Ge 17:12
be circumcised
child born to him that is Ge 17:17
hundred years o.
Abraham 99 years o. when he Ge 17:24
was circumcised
Ishmael thirteen years o. Ge 17:25
when circumcised
now Abraham and Sarah were Ge 18:11
o.
after I am waxed o. my Lord Ge 18:12
being o. also
Sarah said, Shall of surety Ge 18:13
bear child, who am o.
men of city compassed the Ge 19:4
house, o. and young
our father is o. Ge 19:31
Abraham circumcised Isaac Ge 21:4
when eight days o.
Abraham 100 years o. when Ge 21:5
Isaac was born
Sarah was 127 years o. the Ge 23:1
years of her life
Abraham was o. Ge 24:1
Isaac 40 years o. when took Ge 25:20
Rebekah to wife
Isaac was 60 years o. when Ge 25:26
she bare them
Esau 40 years o. when he Ge 26:34
took Judith
it came to pass when Isaac Ge 27:1;
was o. 27:2; 35:29
Joseph being 17 years o. was Ge 37:2
feeding flock
Pharaoh said to Jacob, How Ge 47:8
o. art thou
couch, as an o. lion who shall Ge 49:9
rouse him up
Joseph died, being 110 years Ge 50:26
o.
Moses was eighty years o. and Ex 7:7
Aaron eighty three years o.
when spake to Pharaoh
we will go with our young our Ex 10:9
o. with sons
every one numbered from Ex 30:14;
twenty years o. and above 38:26;
Nu 1:3, 18; 14:29; 1Ch 23:27; 2Ch 23:5;
 31:17; Ezr 3:8
it is an o. leprosy in the skin Le 13:11
of his flesh
shall eat o. fruit; shall eat o. Le 25:22;
store 26:10
the male from 20 years o. even Le 27:3
to 60 years
and if it be from five even to Le 27:5
twenty years o.
if it be from a month o. to five Le 27:6
years o.
every male from a month o. Nu 3:15;
and upward shalt thou number 3:22, 28,
 34, 39-40, 43
from thirty years o. to fifty Nu 4:3;
from among the sons of Levi 4:23, 30;
 1Ch 23:3

the Levites from twenty-five *Nu 8:24*
years *o.* and upward
to be redeemed, from month *Nu 18:16*
o. shalt redeem
numbered 23,000 from a *Nu 26:62*
month *o.* and upward
Aaron was 123 years *o.* when *Nu 33:39*
he died
thy raiment waxed not *o.* *De 8:4;*
29:5; Ne 9:21
which shall not regard the *De 28:50*
person of the *o.*
Moses said, I am 120 years *o.* *De 31:2*
this day
Moses was an 120 years *o.* *De 34:7*
when he died
and they did eat of the *o.* *Jos 5:11;*
corn *5:12*
utterly destroyed men and *Jos 6:21*
women young and *o.*
they took *o.* sacks; *o.* shoes on *Jos 9:4;*
their feet *9:5, 13*
Joshua was *o.* and stricken in *Jos 13:1;*
years *23:1-2*
forty years *o.* was I, when *Jos 14:7*
Moses sent me
and now, lo, I am this day *Jos 14:10*
eighty-five years *o.*
Joshua died, being 110 years *Jos 24:29;*
o. *J'g 2:8*
for I am too *o.* to have a *Ru 1:12*
husband
now Eli was very *o.* and heard *1Sa 2:22*
all
Eli was ninety and eight years *1Sa 4:15*
o. his eyes
when Samuel was *o.* he made *1Sa 8:1;*
8:5; 12:2
Saul's son was forty years *o.* *2Sa 2:10*
when
Mephibosheth was lame, and *2Sa 4:4*
five years *o.*
David thirty years *o.* when he *2Sa 5:4*
began to reign
now Barzillai was eighty *2Sa 19:32;*
years *o.* *19:35*
king David was *o.* *1Ki 1:1;*
1:15; 1Ch 23:1
when Solomon was *o.* his *1Ki 11:4*
wives turned his heart
there dwelt an *o.* prophet in *1Ki 13:11*
Beth-el
she hath no child, and her *2Ki 4:14*
husband is *o.*
Hezron married when sixty *1Ch 2:21*
years *o.*
males from three years *o.* *2Ch 31:16*
and upward
who were *o.* men (S) *Ezr 3:12*
from of *o.* (S) *Ezr 4:15; 4:19*
sent to destroy all the Jews, *Es 3:13*
young and *o.*
why do the wicked live, *Job 21:7*
become *o.*
Elihu said, I am young, and ye *Job 32:6*
are very *o.*
my bones waxed *o.* through my *Ps 32:3*
roaring
I have been young, and now *Ps 37:25*
am *o.*
now when I am *o.* O God, *Ps 71:18*
forsake me not
when *o.* he will not depart from *Pr 22:6*
it
remove not *o.* landmark, *Pr 23:10*
enter not fields
and despise not thy mother *Pr 23:22*
when she is *o.*
better is a wise child than an *Ec 4:13*
king
all manner of pleasant fruits *Ca 7:13*
new and *o.*
an heifer of three years *o.* *Isa 15:5;*
Jer 48:34
captives, young and *o.* naked *Isa 20:4*
and barefoot
they shall wax *o.* as garment, *Isa 50:9*
moth eat them
they shall build the *o.* waste *Isa 58:12;*
places *64:1*
child shall die 100 years *o.* *Isa 65:20*
but sinner being 100 years *o.*
Lord said, See and ask for the *Jer 6:16*
o. paths
Ebedmelech took thence *o.* *Jer 38:11;*
clouts, *o.* rags *38:12*
with thee I will break in *Jer 51:22*
pieces young and *o.*
the young and *o.* lie on the *La 2:21*
ground

my flesh and my skin that he *La 3:4*
made *o.*
slay utterly *o.* and young, *Eze 9:6*
maids and children
then I said to her that was *o. Eze 23:43*
in adulteries
vengeance to destroy it for *Eze 25:15*
the *o.* hatred
I will settle you after your *o. Eze 36:11*
estates
spoken of *o.* time (S) *Eze 38:17*
Darius took kingdom, being 62 *Da 5:31*
years *o.*
shall I come before him with *Mic 6:6*
calves of year *o.*
Herod slew the children from *M't 2:16*
two years *o.*
no man putteth new cloth *M't 9:16*
on *o.* garment
neither do men put new wine *M't 9:17;*
into *o.* bottles *M'k 2:21-22; Lu 5:36-37*
bringeth forth of treasure *M't 13:52*
things new and *o.*
Jesus twelve years *o.* went to *Lu 2:42*
Jerusalem
for he saith, The *o.* wine is *Lu 5:39*
better
it was said, that one of the *o.* *Lu 9:8*
prophets is risen
how can a man be born when *Joh 3:4*
he is *o.*
thou art not yet fifty years *o.* *Joh 8:57*
hast seen Abraham
when thou shalt be *o.* *Joh 21:18*
another shall lead thee
the man was above forty years *Ac 4:22*
o.
when Moses was full forty *Ac 7:23*
years *o.*
brought Mnason of Cyprus, *Ac 21:16*
an *o.* disciple
Abraham when about 100 *Ro 4:19*
years *o.*
purge out therefore the *o.* leaven *1Co 5:7*
let us keep the feast, not with *1Co 5:8*
o. leaven
in the reading of the *O.* *2Co 3:14*
Testament
o. things are past away, all *2Co 5:17*
things are new
refuse profane and *o.* wives' *1Ti 4:7*
fables
unholy and *o.*-womanish tales *1Ti 4:7*
(B)
widow not be taken under sixty *1Ti 5:9*
years *o.*
a new covenant, he hath *Heb 8:13*
made the first *o.* and wax *o.*
that he was purged from his *o.* *2Pe 1:9*
sins
if God spared not the *o.* world, *2Pe 2:5*
but saved Noe
o. commandment is word *1Jo 2:7*
from beginning
that *o.* serpent, called the devil *Re 12:9*
and Satan
he laid hold on the dragon, *Re 20:2*
that *o.* serpent

OLD *AGE*

thou shalt be buried in a good *Ge 15:15*
o. age
Sarah bare Abraham a son of *Ge 21:2;*
his *o. age* *21:7*
Abraham died in a good *o.* *Ge 25:8*
age, an old man
Joseph was the son of his *o.* *Ge 37:3;*
age *44:20*
and Gideon died in a good *o.* *J'g 8:32*
age
he shall be a nourisher in thine *Ru 4:15*
o. age
Asa in *o. age* was diseased in *1Ki 15:23*
his feet
David died in good *o. age,* *1Ch 29:28*
full of days
in whom *o. age* was perished *Job 30:2*
cast me not off in the time of *o. Ps 71:9*
age
they shall bring forth fruit in *Ps 92:14*
o. age
and even to your *o. age* I am *Isa 46:4*
he
Elizabeth conceived a son in *Lu 1:36*
her *o. age*

OLD *MAN*

Abraham died an *o. man* full *Ge 25:8*
of years

the *o. man* of whom ye *Ge 43:27*
spake, is he alive
and we said, We have a *Ge 44:20*
father, an *o. man*
thou shalt honour the face of *Le 19:32*
the *o. man*
there came an *o. man* from *J'g 19:16*
his work
the *o. man* said; spake to the *J'g 19:17;*
o. man *19:20, 22*
not be an *o. man* in thy *1Sa 2:31;*
house *2:32*
Eli was an *o. man*; Jesse *1Sa 4:18;*
was an *o. man* *17:12*
an *o. man* cometh up, and is *1Sa 28:14*
covered
had no compassion on *o.* *2Ch 36:17*
man
o. man that hath not filled his *Isa 65:20*
days
I am an *o. man*, my wife in *Lu 1:18*
years
our *o. man* is crucified with him *Ro 6:6*
put off the *o. man* which is *Eph 4:22*
corrupt
have put off *o. man* with his *Col 3:9*
deeds

OLD MEN

Rehoboam consulted with the *1Ki 12:6*
o. men
forsook counsel of *o. men* *1Ki 12:8;*
12:13; 2Ch 10:6, 8, 13
o. men and children, praise *Ps 148:12*
the Lord
children's children the crown of *Pr 17:6*
o. men
the beauty of *o. men* is the *Pr 20:29*
grey head
rejoice in the dance, young *Jer 31:13*
men and *o.*
hear this ye *o. men*, and give *Joe 1:2*
ear all ye
o. men shall dream dreams *Joe 2:28;*
Ac 2:17
o. men and women dwell in the *Zec 8:4*
streets

OLD *TIME*

giants dwelt there in *o. time* *De 2:20*
Zamzummims
they of *o. time* set in thy *De 19:14*
inheritance
your fathers dwelt on other *Jos 24:2*
side in *o. time*
they were wont to speak in *2Sa 20:18*
o. time
they have moved sedition of *o. Ezr 4:15*
time
it hath been already of *o. time* *Ec 1:10*
for of *o. time* I have broken *Jer 2:20*
thy yoke
bring thee down with people *Eze 26:20*
of *o. time*
he of whom I have spoken in *Eze 38:17*
o. time
it was said by them of *o. time* *M't 5:21;*
5:27, 33
Moses of *o. time* hath in *Ac 15:21*
every city
in *o. time* holy women also *1Pe 3:5*
adorned
prophecy came not in *o. time* *2Pe 1:21*
by man

OLD *WAY*

the *o. way* which wicked *Job 22:15*
men have trodden

OF OLD

which were *of o.* men of renown *Ge 6:4*
those nations were *of o.* *1Sa 27:8*
inhabitants
they of Ham had dwelt there *1Ch 4:40*
of o.
of o. there were chief of the *Ne 12:46*
singers
knowest thou not this *of o.* *Job 20:4*
since man
tender mercies have been ever *Ps 25:6*
of o.
what work thou didst in the *Ps 44:1*
times *of o.*
afflict them, even he that *Ps 55:19*
abideth *of o.*
heavens of heavens which *Ps 68:33*
were *of o.*

congregation which hast purchased *of o.* — Ps 74:2
God is my king *of o.* working salvation — Ps 74:12
I have considered the days *of o.* — Ps 77:5
surely I will remember thy wonders *of o.* — Ps 77:11
I will utter dark sayings *of o.* — Ps 78:2
throne is established *of o.* from everlasting — Ps 93:2
of o. hast laid the foundation of earth — Ps 102:25
I remembered thy judgments *of o.* O Lord — Ps 119:52
thy testimonies I have known *of o.* — Ps 119:152
I remember the days *of o.* — Ps 143:5; Isa 63:11
Lord possessed me before his works *of o.* — Pr 8:22
counsels *of o.* are faithfulness and truth — Isa 25:1
Tophet is ordained *of o.* he hath made — Isa 30:33
neither consider the things *of o.* — Isa 43:18
remember the former things *of o.* — Isa 46:9
awake, awake, as in the generations *of o.* — Isa 51:9
have not I held my peace even *of o.* — Isa 57:11
and carried them all the days *of o.* — Isa 63:9
the prophets before me and thee *of o.* — Jer 28:8
the Lord hath appeared *of o.* to me — Jer 31:3
afterwards be inhabited as in day *of o.* — Jer 46:26
pleasant things she had in days *of o.* — La 1:7
word that he commanded in days *of o.* — La 2:17
set me in dark places, as they that be dead *of o.* — La 3:6
turn us, O Lord, renew our days as *of o.* — La 5:21
shall bring thee down with people *of o.* — Eze 26:20
I will build it as in the days *of o.* — Am 9:11
whose goings forth have been from *of o.* — Mic 5:2
let them feed in Bashan, as in days *of o.* — Mic 7:14
hast sworn to our fathers from the days *of o.* — Mic 7:20
Nineveh is *of o.* like a pool of water — Na 2:8
be pleasant to the Lord, as in days *of o.* — Mal 3:4
by word of God heavens were *of o.* — 2Pe 3:5
who were *of o.* ordained to condemnation — Jude 4

OLDEN

were wont to speak in *o.* times (S) — 2Sa 20:18

OLDER

they were *o.* (S) — Job 15:10; 32:4

OLDNESS

that we should not serve in *o.* of the letter — Ro 7:6

OLIVE

and lo, in her mouth was an *o.* leaf — Ge 8:11
for thine *o.* shall cast her fruit — De 28:40
go to mount, and fetch *o.* branches — Ne 8:15
he shall cast off his flower as the *o.* — Job 15:33
children like *o.* plants round thy table — Ps 128:3
although labour of the *o.* shall fail — Hab 3:17
I said, What be these two *o.* branches — Zec 4:12
can fig tree, my brethren, bear *o.* berries — Jas 3:12

OLIVE *TREE*

when thou beatest thine *o.* tree — De 24:20
they said to the *o.* tree, Reign over us — J'g 9:8
the *o.* tree said, Should I leave my fatness — J'g 9:9
he made two cherubims of *o.* tree — 1Ki 6:23
two doors were of *o. tree*; posts of *o. tree* — 1Ki 6:31; 6:32-33
like a green *o. tree* in the house of God — Ps 52:8
as the shaking of an *o. tree* — Isa 17:6; 24:13
the Lord called thy name a green *o. tree* — Jer 11:16
his beauty shall be as the *o. tree* — Ho 14:6
as yet the *o. tree* hath not brought forth — Hag 2:19
thou partakest of the fatness of *o. tree* — Ro 11:17
cut out of the *o. tree*, graffed in a good *o. tree* — Ro 11:24

OLIVE *TREES*

and *o. trees*, which thou plantest not — De 6:11
thou shalt have *o. trees*, but shalt not anoint — De 28:40
over the *o. trees* was Baal-hanan — 1Ch 27:28
o. trees increased, palmerworm — Am 4:9
two *o. trees* by it on the right and left — Zec 4:3
these are the two *o. trees* standing before — Re 11:4

WILD OLIVE *TREE*

thou being *wild o. tree* wert graffed in — Ro 11:17

OLIVE *YARD*

thus shalt thou do with thy *o. yard* — Ex 23:11

OLIVE *YARDS*

vineyards and *o. yards* ye planted not — Jos 24:13; Ne 9:25
the king shall take your *o. yards* — 1Sa 8:14
a time to receive money and *o. yards* — 2Ki 5:26
restore, I pray, to them their *o. yards* — Ne 5:11

OLIVES

corn, with the vineyards and *o.* — J'g 15:5
thou shalt tread the *o.* but — Mic 6:15
in that day upon the mount of *O.* — Zec 14:4
the mount of *O.* shall cleave in — Zec 14:4
Bethphage, unto the mount of *O.* — M't 21:1
And as he sat upon the mount of *O.* — M't 24:3; M'k 13:3
they went out into the mount of *O.* — M't 26:30; M'k 14:26
and Bethany, at the mount of *O.* — M'k 11:1
the mount called the mount of *O.* — Lu 19:29
at the descent of the mount of *O.* — Lu 19:37
that is called the mount of *O.* — Lu 21:37
as he was wont, to the mount of *O.* — Lu 22:39
Jesus went unto the mount of *O.* — Joh 8:1

OLIVET

up by the ascent of mount *O.* — 2Sa 15:30
from the mount called *O.* — Ac 1:12

OLYMPAS

and *O.* and all the saints which — Ro 16:15

OMAR

sons of Eliphaz were Teman, *O.* — Ge 36:11; 1Ch 1:36
duke Teman, duke *O.* duke Zepho — Ge 36:15

OMEGA

I am Alpha and *O.* — Re 1:8; 1:11; 21:6; 22:13

OMEN

a sign or *o.* (A)(R) — Zec 3:8
a clear *o.* of destruction (B) — Ph'p 1:20

OMENS

confounds *o.* of soothsayers (B)(R) — Isa 44:25

OMER

an *o.* for every man, according to — Ex 16:16
when they did mete it with an *o.* — Ex 16:18
Fill an *o.* of it to be kept for your — Ex 16:32
a pot, and put an *o.* full of manna — Ex 16:33
an *o.* is the tenth part of an ephah — Ex 16:36

OMERS

much bread, two *o.* for one man — Ex 16:22

OMITTED

o. weightier matters of the law — M't 23:23

OMNIPOTENT

for the Lord God *o.* reigneth — Re 19:6

OMRI

made *O.* captain of the host — 1Ki 16:16; 16:17, 21-23, 25, 27-30
Athaliah, the daughter of *O.* — 2Ki 8:26; 2Ch 22:2
and *O.* and Jerimoth, and Abiah — 1Ch 7:8
the son of Ammihud, the son of *O.* — 1Ch 9:4
of Issachar, *O.* the son of Michael — 1Ch 27:18
the statutes of *O.* are kept, and all — Mic 6:16

ON

o. the seventh day God ended his work — Ge 2:2
he rested *o.* the seventh day from all — Ge 2:2
Cain, vengeance shall be taken *o.* him — Ge 4:15
in the land of Nod, *o.* the east of Eden — Ge 4:16
multiply *o.* the face of the earth — Ge 6:1
that he had made man *o.* the earth — Ge 6:6
o. the seventeenth day of the month — Ge 8:4
month, *o.* the first day of the month — Ge 8:5
o. the face of the whole earth — Ge 8:9
o. the altar — Ge 8:20; 22:9; Ex 24:6; Le 1:9, 15; 2:12; 3:5; 5:12; 6:10; 8:28; 9:14
o. journey, journeys — Ge 13:3; 29:1; 1Sa 15:18
called *o.* the name of the Lord — Ge 13:4; 21:33; J'g 15:18; 1Ki 18:24; Ac 2:21; Ro 10:14
fell *o.* face, faces — Ge 17:3; Le 9:24; Nu 14:5; 22:31; Jos 5:14; J'g 13:20; 1Sa 20:41; 2Sa 9:6; 14:4, 22, 33; 1Ki 18:7; 39:2; 2Ki 8:15; M't 17:6
o. the way — Ge 18:16; 32:1; 33:16; J'g 19:9, 14
o. the morrow — Ge 19:34; 18:13; 32:30; Le 19:6; 23:11; Nu 17:8; 22:41; 33:3; De 4:15; Jos 5:11-12; J'g 6:38; 9:42; 21:4; 1Sa 5:3-4; 11:11; 20:27; 31:8;

1Ki 2:37, 42; *2Ki* 8:15; *1Ch* 10:8; 29:21; *Jer* 20:3
o. the shoulder   *Ge* 21:14; 24:45
o. the earth   *Ge* 28:12;
Le 11:2; *De* 4:17; *1Sa* 28:20; *2Sa* 13:31;
1Ki 8:27; *M't* 16:19; 18:18; *Re* 5:10, 13;
7:1; 10:2; 11:10; 13:13-14; 14:6, 16; 17:8
o. the third day   *Ge* 32:22;
34:25; *Ex* 19:16; *Le* 7:17-18;   19:7;
Nu 7:24; 19:12, 19; 29:20; 31:19,
Jos 9:17; *1Sa* 30:1; *2Sa* 1:2; *2Ki* 20:5;
Ezr 5:1
o. his neck   *Ge* 33:4; 44:34; 46:29
o. the ground   *Ge* 38:9;
44:14; *Ex* 4:3; 14:16; 16:14; 20:25;
De 4:18; 22:6; *M't* 10:29; 15:35; *Joh* 8:6,
8; 9:6
o. the garment, garments   *Ge* 38:19;
Le 6:10-11; 16:24; 21:10
o. the head   *Ge* 40:16;
49:26; *J'g* 13:5; *2Sa* 13:19; *2Ki* 9:3, 6
o. a tree   *Ge* 40:19
De 21:22; *Jos* 8:29; *Ac* 5:30; 10:39;
Ga 3:13; *1Pe* 2:24
compassion *o.*   *Ex* 2:6;
1Sa 23:21; *1Ki* 8:50; *2Ki* 13:23; *M't* 9:36;
15:32 20:34; *Ro* 9:15; *Heb* 5:2
o. the day   *Ex* 6:28;
Nu 3:13; 7:1; 8:17; 9:15; 30:12; *De* 27:2;
Jos 9:12; 10:35
o. feet   *Ex* 12:11;
Nu 20:19; *J'g* 4:15, 17; *2Ki* 13:21;
2Ch 3:13
o. his throne   *Ex* 12:29;
1Ki 2:19; 3:6; 8:20, 25; 10:9; 16:11;
22:19; *2Ki* 15:12; *1Ch* 29:23; *2Ch* 9:8;
Ac 2:30
o. right hand   *Ex* 22:29;
1Ki 2:19; *M't* 20:21, 23; 22:44; 25:33-34;
26:64; *Ac* 2:25, 34; 7:55-56; *Col* 3:1;
Heb 1:3, 13; 10:12; *1Pe* 3:22
o. sixth day   *Ex* 16:5;
16:22, 29; *Nu* 7:42; 29:29
o. seventh day   *Ex* 16:26;
16:27, 29; 23:12; 34:21; 35:2; *Le* 13:5-6,
51; 14:9; *Nu* 6:9; 7:48; 19:12, 19; 28:25;
29:32;   31:24;   *De* 16:8;   *Jos* 6:15;
J'g 14:15, 18; *2Sa* 12:18
bare you *o.* eagles' wings   *Ex* 19:4;
De 32:11
o. eighth day   *Ex* 22:30;
Le 9:1;   14:10;   15:14, 29;   23:36, 39;
Nu 6:10;   7:54;   29:35;   *1Ki* 8:66
o. first day   *Ex* 40:2;
40:17; *Le* 23:35, 39-40; *Nu* 1:1, 18; 7:11;
29:1; *De* 1:3
o. the fire   *Le* 1:8; 1:12; 3:5
o. the plague   *Le* 13:3;
13:31-32, 55; 14:37
bring them *o.* the eighth day   *Le* 14:23
o. second day   *Nu* 7:18;
29:17; *Jos* 10:32; *Es* 7:2
o. fourth day   *Nu* 7:30; 29:23; *J'g* 19:5
o. fifth day   *Nu* 7:36;
29:26; *J'g* 19:8
o. that day   *Nu* 9:6;
Jos 4:14;   5:15;   14:9;   *J'g* 5:1;   6:32;
1Sa 7:6, 10; *1Ch* 29:22; *Ne* 13:1
o. the sabbath   *Ne* 10:31; *2Ch* 2:4; 8:13;
Ne 13:15, 19, 21; *Jer* 17:21-22, 24, 27;
M't 12:1, 5, 11-12; 24:20; *Joh* 5:9, 16;
7:22-23; 19:31; *Ac* 16:13
husband disallowed her *o.* the   *Nu* 30:8
day
set *o.* high   *De* 28:1;
Ps 69:29; 91:14; 107:41
o. dry ground   *Jos* 3:17; 4:22; *2Ki* 2:8
look not *o.* his countenance   *1Sa* 16:7
o. stature, *o.* outward
appearance, but *o.* the heart
o. the solemn feasts of the   *2Ch* 2:4;
Lord   *2Ch* 8:13
To cause it to rain *o.* the   *Job* 38:26
earth
o. the wilderness, wherein   *Job* 38:26
there
cherubims stood *o.* the right   *Eze* 10:3
side of
o. the one side and *o.* the   *Eze* 48:21
other of the
o. a pinnacle of the temple   *M't* 4:5
o. the sea, *o.* the water   *M't* 14:25;
14:26, 28-29; *Joh* 6:19
o. these two commandments   *M't* 22:11
hang
and he laid his hands *o.* every   *Lu* 4:40
one
as a snare shall it come *o.* all   *Lu* 21:35
them

believe *o.*   *Joh* 1:12;
2:11; 3:18, 36; 4:39; 5:24: 6:40; 7:31, 38-
39, 48, 8:30-31; 9:35-36; 10:42; 11:45,
48; 12:37, 42, 44; 14:12; 16:2; 17:20;
Ac 11:17; 16:31; 18:8; 19:4; *Ro* 4:5, 24;
9:33; 10:11; *Ph'p* 1:29; *1Ti* 1:16; 3:16;
1Pe 2:6; *1Jo* 3:23; 5:10, 13
with the laying *o.* of the hands *1Ti* 4:14
sat *o.* the throne   *Re* 4:2;
4:9-10; 5:1; 6:16; 7:15; 19:4
reign *o.* the earth   *Re* 5:10

ON, a person

daughter of Poti-pherah   *Ge* 41:45;
priest of *O.*   41:50; 46:20
and *O.* the son of Peleth, sons *Nu* 16:1
of

ONAM

and Ebal, Shepho, and *O.*   *Ge* 36:23
and Ebal, Shephi, and *O.*   *1Ch* 1:40
Atarah; she was the mother   *1Ch* 2:26
of *O.*
the sons of *O.* were,   *1Ch* 2:28
Shammai, and

ONAN

a son; and she called his name *Ge* 38:4
O.
Judah said unto *O.*, Go in unto *Ge* 38:8
thy
O. knew that the seed should *Ge* 38:9
not be
the sons of Judah; Er, and *O.* *Ge* 46:12;
Nu 26:19; *1Ch* 2:3
and *O.* died in the land of   *Ge* 46:12;
Canaan   *Nu* 26:19

ONCE

and I will speak yet but this   *Ge* 18:32
o.
I pray thee, my sin only this   *Ex* 10:17
o.
upon the horns of it *o.* in a   *Ex* 30:10
year
o. in the year shall he make   *Ex* 30:10
of Israel for all their sins *o.* a *Le* 16:34
year
Let us go up at *o.* and possess *Nu* 13:30
it
mayest not consume them at *o.* *De* 7:22
and go round about the city *o.* *Jos* 6:3
compassed the city, going   *Jos* 6:11
about it *o.*
day they compassed the city *o.* *Jos* 6:14
me, and I will speak but this *o.* *J'g* 6:39
prove but this *o.* with the   *J'g* 6:39
fleece
Come up this *o.* for he hath   *J'g* 16:18
shewed
me, I pray thee, only this *o.* O *J'g* 16:28
God
be at *o.* avenged of the   *J'g* 16:28
Philistines
spear even to the earth at *o.*   *1Sa* 26:8
o. in three years came the   *1Ki* 10:22
navy of
saved himself there, not *o.* nor *2Ki* 6:10
twice
every three years *o.* came the *2Ch* 9:21
ships
and *o.* in ten days store of all *Ne* 5:18
sorts
lodged without Jerusalem *o.*   *Ne* 13:20
For God speaketh *o.* yea   *Job* 33:14
twice, yet
O. have I spoken; but I will   *Job* 40:5
not
God hath spoken *o.*; twice   *Ps* 62:11
have I
carved work thereof at *o.* with *Ps* 74:6
axes
in thy sight when *o.* thou art   *Ps* 76:7
angry
O. have I sworn by my   *Ps* 89:35
holiness that
perverse in his ways shall fall *Pr* 28:18
at *o.*
I will destroy and devour at   *Isa* 42:14
o.
or shall a nation be born at *o.* *Isa* 66:8
inhabitants of the land at this *Jer* 10:18
o.
made clean? when shall it *o.*   *Jer* 13:27
be
I will this *o.* cause them to   *Jer* 16:21
know

Yet *o.*, it is a little while, and *Hag* 2:6
I will
When *o.* the master of the   *Lu* 13:25
house is risen
they cried out all at *o.* saying *Lu* 23:18
that he died, he died unto sin *Ro* 6:10
o.
I was alive without the law *o.* *Ro* 7:9
above five hundred brethren *1Co* 15:6
at *o.*
I beaten with rods, *o.* was I *2Co* 11:25
stoned
the faith which *o.* he destroyed *Ga* 1:23
let it not be *o.* named among *Eph* 5:3
you
o. and again unto my necessity *Ph'p* 4:16
unto you, even I Paul, *o.* and *1Th* 2:18
again
for those who were *o.*   *Heb* 6:4
enlightened
for this he did *o.* when he   *Heb* 7:27
offered
the high priest alone *o.* every *Heb* 9:7
year
he entered in *o.* into the holy *Heb* 9:12
place
o. in the end of the world   *Heb* 9:26
hath he
it is appointed unto men *o.* to *Heb* 9:27
die
So Christ was *o.* offered to   *Heb* 9:28
bear the
worshippers *o.* purged should *Heb* 10:2
have
the body of Jesus Christ *o.*   *Heb* 10:10
for all
o. more I shake not the   *Heb* 12:26
earth only
this word, Yet *o.* more,   *Heb* 12:27
signifieth the
Christ also hath *o.* suffered   *1Pe* 3:18
for sins
when *o.* the longsuffering of   *1Pe* 3:20
God
faith which was *o.* delivered   *Jude* 3
unto the
though ye *o.* knew this, how   *Jude* 5
that the

ONE

man cleave to wife, and they *Ge* 2:24;
be *o.* flesh *M't* 19:5; *M'k* 10:8; *1Co* 6:16
if they give not thee *o.* thou   *Ge* 24:41
shalt
hast thou but *o.* blessing, my *Ge* 27:38
father
not give our sister to *o.* that is *Ge* 34:14
uncircumcised
o. is not; *o.* went out   *Ge* 42:13;
from me   44:28
yet will bring *o.* plague more *Ex* 11:1
on Pharaoh
in *o.* house shall it be eaten, *Ex* 12:46
not carry forth
o. law to him that is   *Ex* 12:49;
homeborn   *Le* 24:22; *Nu* 15:16, 29
I will not drive them out in *o.* *Ex* 23:29
year
every curtain shall have *o.*   *Ex* 26:2;
measure   36:9, 15
and it shall be *o.* tabernacle *Ex* 26:6;
36:13
o. loaf of bread, *o.* cake, and *Ex* 29:23
o. wafer
he shall be guilty in *o.* of these *Le* 5:4;
5:5, 13
every *o.* that toucheth them   *Le* 11:26
shall be
whether *o.* of your own   *Le* 16:29;
country   17:15
take of every *o.* of them a rod *Le* 17:2
ten women bake your bread   *Le* 26:26
on *o.* oven
if they blow but with *o.*   *Nu* 10:4
trumpet
I have not taken *o.* as   *Nu* 16:15
from them
o. rod shall be for the head of *Nu* 17:3
the house
to every *o.* shall his   *Nu* 26:54
inheritance be
of the tribe shall be wife to *o.* *Nu* 36:8
of the family
I took twelve men, *o.* of a tribe *De* 1:23
that fleeing to *o.* of these cities *De* 4:42;
19:5, 11
o. witness shall not rise up   *De* 19:15
against a man

if *o.* be found slain in the land *De 21:1*
but he shall be free at home *o.* *De 24:5*
year
from *o.* end of the earth even *De 28:64*
unto
how should *o.* chase a *De 32:30*
thousand
all these Joshua took at *o.* *Jos 10:42*
time
the king of Jericho, *o.* the king *Jos 12:9*
of Ai *o.*
the king of Jerusalem *o.* king *Jos 12:10*
of Hebron *o.*
why hast given me but *o.* lot *Jos 17:14*
and *o.* portion
a great people, thou shalt not *Jos 12:17*
have *o.* lot only
whether is better, that *o.* reign *J'g 9:2*
over you
what *o.* is there of the tribes of *J'g 21:8*
Israel
for *o.* plague was on you all *1Sa 6:4*
and lords
for Ashdod *o.* for Gaza *o.* for *1Sa 6:17*
Ashkelon *o.*
and they came out with *o.* *1Sa 11:7*
consent
this day my son in law in *o.* *1Sa 18:21*
of the twain
as when *o.* doth hunt a *1Sa 26:20*
partridge in
what *o.* nation is like *2Sa 7:23*
the people
and with *o.* full line to keep *2Sa 8:2*
alive
there will not tarry *o.* with *2Sa 19:7*
thee this night
whom he slew at *o.* time *2Sa 23:8;*
1Ch 11:11
O that *o.* would give me *2Sa 23:15;*
drink of water of well *1Ch 11:17*
given me *o.* to sit on my *1Ki 1:48*
throne
I ask *o.* petition of thee, deny *1Ki 2:16*
me not
the cherubims were of *o.* *1Ki 6:25*
measure, *o.* size
there hath not failed *o.* word *1Ki 8:56*
of his promise
I will give *o.* tribe to thy son *1Ki 11:13;*
11:32, 36
words of prophets declare *1Ki 22:13;*
good to king with *o.* mouth *2Ch 18:12*
carry thither *o.* of the priests *2Ki 17:27*
o. of the priests came and *2Ki 17:28*
dwelt in Beth-el
will turn away face of *o.* *2Ki 18:24;*
captain *Isa 36:9*
even against the Holy *O.* of *2Ki 19:22*
Israel
for asking counsel of *1Ch 10:13*
o. that had fame
o. of the least was over an *1Ch 12:14*
hundred
he shall worship before *o.* *2Ch 32:12*
altar
Hanani, *o.* of my brethren, came *Ne 1:2*
bring *o.* of ten to dwell in *Ne 11:1*
Jerusalem
and *o.* of the sons of Joiada, *Ne 13:28*
the son of
he cannot answer him *o.* of a *Job 9:3*
thousand
o. dieth in his full strength, *Job 21:23*
at ease
he is in *o.* mind, and who *Job 23:13*
can turn him
if an interpreter, *o.* among a *Job 33:23*
thousand
my only *o.* (S) *Ps 22:20; 35:17*
be not afraid when *o.* is made *Ps 49:16*
rich
and shall fall like *o.* of the *Ps 82:7*
princes
I have laid help on *o.* that is *Ps 89:19*
mighty
the holy *o.* (A)(B)(R) *Ps 106:16;*
Da 8:13
saying, Sing us *o.* of the songs *Ps 137:3*
of Zion
cast in thy lot, let us all have *o.* *Pr 1:14*
purse
is like *o.* that taketh a dog by *Pr 26:17*
the ears
o. generation passeth away *Ec 1:4*
another cometh
I perceived that *o.* event *Ec 2:14*
happened to them all

yea, they have all *o.* breath, all *Ec 3:19*
is vanity
all go unto *o.* place, all are *Ec 3:20;*
dust *6:6*
two better than *o.;* how can *o.* *Ec 4:9;*
be warm *4:11*
if *o.* prevail against him, two *Ec 4:12*
shall withstand
counting *o.* by *o.* to find out *Ec 7:27*
the account
but *o.* sinner destroyeth much *Ec 9:18*
good
words, which are given from *Ec 12:11*
o. shepherd
with *o.* of thy eyes, with *o.* *Ca 4:9*
chain of neck
my undefiled is but *o.* she is the *Ca 6:9*
only *o.*
ten acres of vineyard shall *Isa 5:10*
yield *o.* bath
and as *o.* gathereth eggs that *Isa 10:14*
are left
what shall *o.* answer *Isa 14:32*
messengers of nation
o. shall be called the city of *Isa 19:18*
destruction
according to the days of *o.* *Isa 23:15*
king
ye shall be gathered *o.* by *o.* O *Isa 27:12*
Israel
o. thousand shall flee at the *Isa 30:17*
rebuke of *o.*
no *o.* of these shall fail, none *Isa 34:16*
want her mate
I have raised up *o.* from the *Isa 41:25*
north
I will give Jerusalem *o.* that *Isa 41:27*
bringeth good tidings
o. shall say, I am the Lord's, *Isa 44:5*
and another
surely shall *o.* say, In Lord *Isa 45:24*
have I righteousness
o. saith, Destroy it not, a *Isa 65:8*
blessing is in it
thine adversaries, every *o.* of *Jer 30:16*
them
they four had *o.* likeness, and *Eze 1:16*
a wheel
she brought up *o.* of her *Eze 19:3*
whelps, it became
both twain shall come forth *Eze 21:19*
out of *o.* land
then I saw that they took *Eze 23:13*
both *o.* way
that *o.* that had escaped *Eze 33:21*
came unto me
Abraham was *o;* as a lovely *Eze 33:24;*
song of *o.* *33:32*
I will set up *o.* shepherd *Eze 34:23;*
over them *37:24*
and they shall become *o.* in *Eze 37:17*
thy hand
make them *o.* stick; *o.* *Eze 37:19;*
nation *o.* king *37:22*
as *o.* goeth up to the entry of *Eze 40:40*
the north
o. gate of Reuben; *o.* gate of *Eze 48:31;*
Joseph *48:32*
there is but *o.* decree for you *Da 2:9*
then Daniel was astonied for *Da 4:19*
o. hour
behold, *o.* like the Son of man *Da 7:13;*
10:16, 18
he shall confirm the covenant *Da 9:27*
for *o.* week
out of a branch of her roots *Da 11:7*
shall *o.* stand
o. shall come and overflow, *Da 11:10*
and pass
shall speak lies at *o.* table, *Da 11:27*
not prosper
Israel shall appoint themselves *Ho 1:11*
o. head
faithful Holy *O.* *Ho 11:12*
(A)(B)(E)(R)
two or three cities wandered to *Am 4:8*
o. city
if there remain ten men in *o.* *Am 6:9*
house
to serve the Lord with *o.* *Zep 3:9*
consent
behold, on *o.* stone shall be *Zec 3:9*
seven eyes
I will cut off three shepherds *Zec 11:8*
in *o.* month
there shall be *o.* Lord, and his *Zec 14:9*
name *o.*
did he not make *o.* and *Mal 2:15*
wherefore *o.*

voice of *o.* crying in wilderness *M't 3:3;*
M'k 1:3; Lu 3:4; Joh 1:23
o. jot, or *o.* tittle shall not *M't 5:18*
pass from the law
whoso break *o.* of least *M't 5:19*
commandments
that *o.* of thy members should *M't 5:29;*
perish *5:30*
thou canst not make *o.* hair *M't 5:36*
white or black
which of you can add *o.* cubit *M't 6:27*
to his stature
was not arrayed like *o.* of *M't 6:29;*
these *Lu 12:27*
shall give to drink to *o.* of *M't 10:42*
these little ones
what man among you shall *M't 12:11*
have *o.* sheep
Elias, Jeremias, or *o.* of the *M't 16:14;*
prophets *M'k 6:15; 8:28; Lu 9:8, 19*
tabernacles, *o.* for thee, *o.* for *M't 17:4;*
Moses and *o.* for *M'k 9:6; Lu 9:33*
Elias
offend *o.* of these *M't 18:6;*
M'k 9:42; Lu 17:2
take heed ye despise not *o.* of *M't 18:10*
these little ones
that *o.* of these little ones *M't 18:14*
should perish
if not hear, then take with *M't 18:16*
thee, *o.* or two more
none good but *o.* *M't 19:17;*
M'k 10:18; Lu 18:19
saying, These last have *M't 20:12*
wrought but *o.* hour
they beat *o.* and killed *M't 21:35*
another, and stoned
they went their ways, *o.* to his *M't 22:5*
farm, another
they themselves will not move *M't 23:4;*
them with *o.* finger *Lu 11:46*
for *o.* is your Master, even *M't 23:8;*
Christ *23:10*
o. is your Father *M't 23:9*
he gave to *o.* five talents, to *M't 25:15*
another two
but he that had received the *M't 25:18;*
o. *25:24*
as ye have done it to *o.* *M't 25:40*
as ye did it not to *o.* of the *M't 25:45*
least of these
Jesus said, *O.* of you shall *M't 26:21;*
betray me *M'k 14:18; Joh 13:21*
could ye not watch *o.* hour *M't 26:40;*
M'k 14:37
nor had they more than *o.* *M'k 8:14*
loaf
whoever shall receive *o.* of *M'k 9:37*
such children
we saw *o.* casting out devils *M'k 9:38;*
Lu 9:49
I will also ask of you *o.* *M'k 11:29*
question
having yet *o.* son, he sent him *M'k 12:6*
also to them
and they began to say, *O.* by *M'k 14:19*
o. It is I
at the feast he released *o.* *M'k 15:6;*
Lu 23:17
John said, But *o.* mightier than *Lu 3:16*
I cometh
I say to *o.* Go, and he goeth, and *Lu 7:8*
to another
he had *o.* only daughter, and *Lu 8:42*
she lay a dying
there shall be five in *o.* house *Lu 12:52*
divided
joy in heaven over *o.* sinner *Lu 15:7;*
that repenteth *15:10*
to pass, than *o.* tittle of the *Lu 16:17*
law to fail
nay, but if *o.* went from the *Lu 16:30;*
dead *16:31*
to see *o.* of the days of the *Lu 17:22*
Son of man
let him sell his garment, and *Lu 22:36*
buy *o.*
but there standeth *o.* among *Joh 1:26*
you
o. of you is a evil; have done *Joh 6:70;*
o. works *7:21*
went out *o.* by *o.* beginning at *Joh 8:9*
the eldest
I am *o.* that bear witness of *Joh 8:18*
myself
they said, We have *o.* Father, *Joh 8:41*
even God
and there shall be *o.* fold, and *Joh 10:16*
o. shepherd
I and my Father are *o.* *Joh 10:30*

should gather in *o.* the   Joh 11:52
children of God
he hath *o.* that judgeth him,   Joh 12:48
the word
that they may be *o.* so we are   Joh 17:11;
                          17:21-22
that they may be made perfect   Joh 17:23
in *o.*
art not thou *o.* of this man's   Joh 18:17;
disciples   18:25
must *o.* be ordained to be   Ac 1:22
witness of resurrection
believed, were of *o.* heart and   Ac 4:32
of *o.* soul
go and enquire for *o.* Saul of   Ac 9:11
Tarsus
there cometh *o.* after me,   Ac 13:25
whose shoes
saying, that there is another   Ac 17:7
king, *o.* Jesus
God hath made of *o.* blood all   Ac 17:26
nations
except it be for this *o.* voice,   Ac 24:21
of resurrection
had questions of *o.* Jesus,   Ac 25:19
who was dead
after that Paul had spoken *o.*   Ac 28:25
word
scarcely for a righteous man   Ro 5:7
will *o.* die
if through the offence of *o.*   Ro 5:15
many be dead
not as by *o.* that sinned, for   Ro 5:16
judgment was by *o.* to
death reigned by *o.* shall reign   Ro 5:17
in life by *o.* Jesus Christ
by the offence of *o.* so by   Ro 5:18
righteousness of *o.*
so by obedience of *o.* shall   Ro 5:19
many be righteous
but when Rebekah also had   Ro 9:10
conceived by *o.*
For *o.* believeth that he may   Ro 14:2
eat all
for while *o.* saith, I am Paul   1Co 3:4
now he that planteth and that   1Co 3:8
watereth are *o.*
such fornication, that *o.* have   1Co 5:1
his father's wife
and that there is none other   1Co 8:4
God but *o.*
to us there is but *o.* God and a   1Co 8:6
Lord Jesus
all run, but *o.* receiveth the   1Co 9:24
prize
we being many are *o.* bread   1Co 10:17
and *o.* body
o. is hungry   1Co 11:21
to *o.* is given by Spirit the   1Co 12:8
word of wisdom
by *o.* Spirit we are baptized   1Co 12:13
into *o.* body
there come in *o.* that   1Co 14:24
believeth not, or *o.* unlearned
let *o.* interpret   1Co 14:27
for ye may all prophesy *o.* by   1Co 14:31
o. that all may
was seen of me as of *o.* born   1Co 15:8
out of due time
To the *o.* we are the savour of   2Co 2:16
if *o.* died for all, then were   2Co 5:14
all dead
for I have espoused you to *o.*   2Co 11:2
husband
five times received I forty   2Co 11:24
stripes save *o.*
be perfect, be of good   2Co 13:11;
comfort, be of *o.* mind   Ph'p 2:2;
               1Pe 3:8; Re 17:13
but as of *o.* ye are all *o.* in   Ga 3:16;
Christ   3:28
for all the law is fulfilled in *o.*   Ga 5:14
word
he might gather together in *o.*   Eph 1:10
all things
who hath made both *o.; o.*   Eph 2:14;
new man   2:15
through him we both have   Eph 2:18
access by *o.* Spirit
as ye are called in *o.* hope of   Eph 4:4
your calling
o. faith, *o.* Lord, *o.* baptism;   Eph 4:5;
o. God   4:6
that stand fast with *o.* spirit,   Ph'p 1:27
with *o.* mind
the husband of *o.* wife   1Ti 3:2; Tit 1:6
a bishop, *o.* that ruleth well his   1Ti 3:4
own house

the deacons be the husbands   1Ti 3:12
of *o.* wife
o. of themselves, even a   Tit 1:12
prophet, said
but *o.* in a certain place   Heb 2:6
testifieth
they that are sanctified are all   Heb 2:11
of *o.*
ye have need that *o.* teach   Heb 5:12
you again
but this man after he had   Heb 10:12
offered *o.* sacrifice
for by *o.* offering he hath   Heb 10:14
perfected for ever
therefore sprang there even   Heb 11:12
of *o.* so many
for *o.* morsel of meat sold his   Heb 12:16
birthright
here we have no city, but we   Heb 13:14
seek *o.* to come
yet offend in *o.* point, he is   Jas 2:10
guilty of all
if any of you err, and *o.*   Jas 5:19
convert him
these three are *o.; * these agree   1Jo 5:7;
in *o.*   5:8
o. woe is past, there come two   Re 9:12
woes more
I saw *o.* of his heads as   Re 13:3
wounded to death
on the cloud *o.* sat like unto   Re 14:14
the Son of man
receive power as kings *o.* hour   Re 17:12
with the beast
for in *o.* hour is thy judgment   Re 18:10
come
in *o.* hour so great riches   Re 18:17
come to nought
that great city, for in *o.* hour   Re 18:19
is she made desolate
every several gate was of *o.*   Re 21:21
pearl

ONE OF THEM

as *o.* of them opened his sack   Ge 42:27
in the inn
there remained not so much   Ex 14:28
as *o.* of them
neither have I hurt *o.* of them   Nu 16:15
if *o.* of them die, and have   De 25:5
no child
thou art *o.* of them that   J'g 11:35
trouble me
this Philistine shall be as *o.*   1Sa 17:36
of them
lacked not *o.* of them was not   2Sa 17:22
over Jordan
I am *o.* of them that are   2Sa 20:19
peaceable in Israel
three things choose *o.* of   2Sa 24:12;
them   1Ch 21:10
prophets of Baal, let not *o.* of   1Ki 18:40
them escape
if I make not thy life as the   1Ki 19:2
life of *o.* of them
let thy word be like the word   1Ki 22:13
of *o.* of them
keep, his bones, not *o.* of them   Ps 34:20
is broken
every *o.* of them is gone back,   Ps 53:3
none doth good
as a snail let every *o.* of them   Ps 58:8
pass away
inward thought of every *o.* of   Ps 64:6
them is deep
every *o.* of them in Zion   Ps 84:7
appeareth before God
their enemies, there was not   Ps 106:11
o. of them left
be not thou *o.* of them that   Pr 22:26
strike hands
labour of foolish wearieth   Ec 10:15
every *o.* of them
yet every *o.* of them doth   Jer 15:10
for I know the things, every   Eze 11:5
o. of them
out of *o.* of them came forth a   Da 8:9
little horn
and cast lots, even thou wast as   Ob 11
o. of them
o. of them sold for a   M't 10:29;
farthing   Lu 12:6
have sheep, *o.* of them be   M't 18:12;
gone astray   Lu 15:4
surely thou art *o.* of them   M't 26:73;
               M'k 14:69-70
o. of them when he saw that   Lu 17:15
he was healed

that every *o.* of them may take   Joh 6:7
a little
that came to Jesus by night,   Joh 7:50
being *o.* of them
Lazarus was *o.* of them that   Joh 12:2
sat at the table
and seeing *o.* of them suffer   Ac 7:24
wrong
and there stood up *o.* of them   Ac 11:28
named Agabus

ONE, *OTHER*

name of *o.* was Adah, of *other*   Ge 4:19
Zillah
they separated the *o.* from the   Ge 13:11
other
from the *o.* end of Egypt to   Ge 47:21
the *other*
name of *o.* Shiphrah, of the   Ex 1:15
other Puah
so that the *o.* came not near   Ex 14:20
the *other*
stayed up his hands on *o.*   Ex 17:12
side, and the *other*
name of the *o.* Gershom, of the   Ex 18:3
other Eliezer
pigeons, *o.* for sin offering,   Le 5:7;
other for burnt offering   12:8; Nu 6:11;
                8:12
o. lot for the Lord, *other* for   Le 16:8
the scapegoat
name of the *o.* Eldad, the   Nu 11:26
other Medad
o. lamb in the morning, the   Nu 28:4
other at even
ask from *o.* side of heaven to   De 4:32
the *other*
from the *o.* end of the earth to   De 13:7;
other   28:64
took hold of *o.* pillar and of   J'g 16:29
the *other*
name of the *o.* was Orpah, of   Ru 1:4
other Ruth
name of *o.* Hannah, the *other*   1Sa 1:2
Peninnah
name of *o.* Baanah, of the   2Sa 4:2
other Rechab
there were two men, *o.* rich,   2Sa 12:1
the *other* poor
o. saith, This is my son, the   1Ki 3:23
other saith
give half to the *o.* and half to   1Ki 3:25
the *other*
they pitched *o.* against the   1Ki 20:29
other seven days
o. hand wrought, with *other*   Ne 4:17
held weapon
as the *o.* dieth, so dieth the   Ec 3:19
other
God hath set *o.* over against   Ec 7:14
the *other*
sword of Lord shall devour   Jer 12:12;
from *o.* end of land to the   25:33
o. basket had good figs, *other*   Jer 24:2
basket had bad
go the *o.* way or *other* on   Eze 21:16
right or left
but *o.* horn was higher than the   Da 8:3
other
o. on this side of river, *other* on   Da 12:5
that side
the *o.* I called Beauty, the   Zec 11:7
other Bands
hate *o.* and love the *other,* or   M't 6:24;
hold to *o.* and despise   Lu 16:13
the *other*
two sons may sit, *o.* on right   M't 20:21;
hand, and *other* on left   M'k 10:37
gather from *o.* end of heaven   M't 24:31
to the *other*
o. taken, the *other* left   M't 24:40;
              24:41; Lu 17:34-36
crucify two thieves, *o.* on   M'k 15:27;
right hand, *other* on left   Lu 23:33
if smite thee on *o.* cheek, offer   Lu 6:29
other
the *o.* owed 500 pence, the   Lu 7:41
other fifty
lightning out of *o.* part,   Lu 17:24
shineth to *other*
the *o.* a Pharisee, the *other* a   Lu 18:10
publican
o. angel at the head, *other* at   Joh 20:12
the feet
that they departed asunder *o.*   Ac 15:39
from *other*
the *o.* part Sadducees, the   Ac 23:6
other Pharisees
defraud ye not *o.* the *other,*   1Co 7:5
except it be

to *o.* the savour of life, to   2Co 2:16
other of death
o. by bondmaid, *other* by a   Ga 4:22
freewoman
and these are contrary, the *o.* to Ga 5:17
the *other*
and *o.* is, the *other* is not yet Re 17:10
come

ONE *THING*

not *o.* thing hath failed of all Jos 23:14
the good
this is *o.* thing, therefore I   Job 9:22
said it
o. thing have I desired of the   Ps 27:4
Lord
even *o. thing* befalleth them   Ec 3:19
I will ask you *o. thing*   M't 21:24;
       Lu 6:9; 20:3
o. thing thou lackest   M'k 10:21;
       Lu 18:22
thou art careful, but *o. thing* Lu 10:42
is needful
o. thing I know that whereas I Joh 9:25
was blind
some cried *o. thing* some   Ac 19:32;
another   21:34
but this *o. thing* I do, I press Ph'p 3:13
toward mark
but be not ignorant of this *o.* 2Pe 3:8
thing

AS ONE

behold, the man is become *as* Ge 3:22
o. of us
but he seemed *as o.* that   Ge 19:14
mocked to his sons
Dan shall judge *as o.* of the   Ge 49:16
tribes of Israel
he shall be *as o.* that is born Ex 12:48;
in the land   Le 19:34; 24:22
let her not be *as o.* dead, of Nu 12:12
whom
Gibeon a great city, as *o.* of Jos 10:2
royal cities
young man was to him *as o.* J'g 17:11
of his sons
Philistine be *as o.* of them 1Sa 17:36
as when *o.* doth hunt a   1Sa 26:20
partridge in mountain
uncovered *as o.* of the vain 2Sa 6:20
fellows
he shall eat at my table *as o.* 2Sa 9:11
of king's sons
thou shalt be *as o.* of the   2Sa 13:13
fools in Israel
the king speaketh this *as o.* 2Sa 14:13
that is faulty
there shall not be left so   2Sa 17:12
much *as o.*
but *as o.* was felling a beam, 2Ki 6:5
axe head fell
the trumpeters and singers 2Ch 5:13
were *as o.*
thou speakest *as o.* of the   Job 2:10
foolish women
I am *as o.* mocked of his   Job 12:4
neighbour
he counteth me to him *as o.* Job 19:11
of his enemies
as o. that mourneth for his   Ps 35:14
mother
then the Lord awaked *as o.* Ps 78:65
out of sleep
thou hast broken Rahab, *as o.* Ps 89:10
that is slain
I rejoice *as o.* that findeth Ps 119:162
great spoil
thy poverty *as o.* that travaileth Pr 6:11;
       24:3
as the *o.* dieth, so dieth the Ec 3:19
other
for why should I be *as o.*   Ca 1:7
turneth aside
then I was in his eyes *as o.* that Ca 8:10
found favour
as o. that gathereth eggs that Isa 10:14
are left
thy voice *as o.* that hath a   Isa 29:4
familiar spirit
as. o. whom his mother   Isa 66:13
comforteth
I will break *as o.* breaketh Jer 19:11
potter's vessel
mourn *as o.* in bitterness for Zec 12:10
firstborn
as o. having authority   M't 7:29;
       M'k 1:22

or *as o.* of the prophets;   M'k 6:15;
as o. dead   9:26
make me *as o.* of thy hired Lu 15:19
servants
this man *as o.* that perverteth Lu 23:14
the people
as o. that hath obtained   1Co 7:25
mercy of Lord
so fight !, not *as o.* that   1Co 9:26
beateth the air

IS ONE

the people *is o.;* the   Ge 11:6;
dream *is o.*   11:26; 41:25
this *is o.* of the Hebrew children Ex 2:6
the Lord our God *is o.* Lord De 6:4;
       M'k 12:29
Boaz *is o.* of our next kinsmen Ru 2:20
in this place *is o.* greater than M't 12:6
the temple
it *is o.* of the twelve that   M'k 14:20
dippeth
he is not a Jew that *is o.*   Ro 2:28
outwardly
but he is a Jew who *is o.*   Ro 2:29
inwardly
seeing it *is o.* God who shall Ro 3:30
justify
that is joined to the Lord *is o.* 1Co 6:17
spirit
for as body *is o.* and hath   1Co 12:2
many members
but the glory of the celestial 1Co 15:40
is o. and glory
is not a mediator of one, but Ga 3:20
God *is o.*
with Onesimus, who *is o.* of Col 4:9;
you   4:12

NOT ONE

if they give *not* the *o.* shall be Ge 24:41
clear
there remained *not o.*   Ex 8:31; 10:19
but of the cattle of Israel died Ex 9:6;
not o.   9:7
not a house where there was Ex 12:30
not o. dead
not o. of these men see that De 1:35
good land
there was *not o.* city too strong De 2:36
for us
and there is *not o.* of them 2Sa 13:30
left
till there be *not o.* small stone 2Sa 17:13
found there
he left him *not o.* that pisseth 1Ki 16:11
against wall
a clean thing out of an   Job 14:4
unclean, *not o.*
and did *not o.* fashion us in Job 31:15
the womb
not o. be cast down at the   Job 41:9
sight of him
altogether filthy, none that   Ps 14:3;
doeth good, *not o.*   53:3; Ro 3:12
there was *not o.* feeble   Ps 105:37
person among them
for that he is strong in power, Isa 40:26
not o. faileth
take heed ye despise *not o.* M't 18:10
of these little ones
there is none righteous, no *not* Ro 3:10
o.
no *not o.* that shall be able to 1Co 6:5
judge
for the body is *not o.*   1Co 12:14
member, but many

THERE IS ONE

trespass offering, *there is o.* law Le 7:7
for them
there is o. tribe cut off from J'g 21:6
Israel
there is o. law of his to put him Es 4:11
to death
there is o. alone, and there is Ec 4:8
not a second
there is o. event to righteous and Ec 9:2
the wicked
this is an evil, that *there is o.* Ec 9:3
event to all
if ye will not, *there is o.* decree Da 2:9
for you
there is o. come out of thee   Na 1:11
imagineth evil
there is o. God   M'k 12:32;
       1Ti 2:5; Jas 2:19

there is *o.* that accuseth you, Joh 5:45
even Moses
there is *o.* that seeketh and   Joh 8:50
judgeth
there is *o.* kind of flesh of   1Co 15:39
men
there is *o.* glory of sun,   1Co 15:41
another of moon
there is *o.* lawgiver, who is   Jas 4:12
able to save

WICKED ONE

then cometh the *wicked o.* M't 13:19
and catcheth
the tares are the children of M't 13:38
the *wicked o.*
because ye have overcome   1Jo 2:13;
wicked o.   2:14
not as Cain, who was of that 1Jo 3:12
wicked o.
and that *wicked o.* toucheth 1Jo 5:18
him not

ONENESS

attain to *o.* in the faith (A)   Eph 4:13

ONES

all their little *o.* and their   Ge 34:29
wives took
we, and thou, and also our little Ge 43:8
o.
the land of Egypt for your   Ge 45:19
little *o.*
their little *o.* and their wives Ge 46:5
and for food for your little *o.* Ge 47:24
only their little *o.* and their Ge 50:8
flocks
I will nourish you, and your Ge 50:21
little *o.*
as I will let you go, and your Ex 10:10
little *o.*
let your little *o.* also go with Ex 10:24
you
But your little *o.* which ye   Nu 14:31
said should
of Midian captives, and their Nu 31:9
little *o.*
kill every male among the   Nu 31:17
little *o.*
our cattle, and cities for our Nu 32:16
little *o.*
little *o.* shall dwell in the   Nu 32:17
fenced cities
Build your cities for your   Nu 32:24
little *o.* and
Our little *o.,* our wives, our Nu 32:26
flocks, and
your little *o.* which ye said De 1:39
should be a
women, and the little *o.* of De 2:34
every city
But your wives, and your little De 3:19
o. and
But the women, and the little De 20:14
o. and
whether they be young *o.,* or De 22:6
eggs, and
Your little *o.* your wives, and De 29:11
thy
holy *o.* (A)(B)(E)(R)   De 33:2;
1Sa 2:9; Job 5:1; 15:15; Ps 50:5; 89:5;
       97:10; Zec 14:5
Your wives, your little *o.* and Jos 1:14
your
with the women, and the little Jos 8:35
o. and
the pransings of their mighty *o.* J'g 5:22
and put the little *o.* and the J'g 18:21
cattle
and all the little *o.* that were 2Sa 15:22
with him
ye children of Jacob, his   1Ch 16:13
chosen *o.*
all their little *o.* their wives, 2Ch 31:18
and their
and for our little *o.* and for all Ezr 8:21
our
assault them, both little *o.* and Es 8:11
women
send forth their little *o.* like a Job 21:11
flock
when his young *o.* cry unto Job 38:41
God, they
bring forth their young *o.* they Job 39:3
cast
Their young *o.* are in good Job 39:4
liking, they

She is hardened against her   *Job 39:16*
young *o.*
Her young *o.* also suck up   *Job 39:30*
blood: and
that the poor may fall by his   *Ps 10:10*
strong *o.*
and consulted against thy   *Ps 83:3*
hidden *o.*
dasheth thy little *o.* against the   *Ps 137:9*
stones
How long, ye simple *o.* will ye   *Pr 1:22*
love
among the simple *o.* I discerned   *Pr 7:7*
the waste places of the fat *o.*   *Isa 5:17*
shall
hosts, send among his fat *o.*   *Isa 10:16*
leanness
high *o.* of stature shall be   *Isa 10:33*
hewn down
their young *o.* shall lie down   *Isa 11:7*
together
I have commanded my   *Isa 13:3*
sanctified *o.*
called my mighty *o.* for mine   *Isa 13:3*
anger
thee, even all the chief *o.* of   *Isa 14:9*
the earth
shall punish the host of the   *Isa 24:21*
high *o.*
the blast of the terrible *o.* is as   *Isa 25:4*
a storm
of the terrible *o.* shall be   *Isa 25:5*
brought low
of the terrible *o.* shall be as   *Isa 29:5*
chaff that
be troubled, ye careless *o.*   *Isa 32:11*
strip you
valiant *o.* shall cry without: *Isa 33:7*
their
to revive the heart of the   *Isa 57:15*
contrite *o.*
also taught the wicked *o.* thy   *Jer 2:33*
ways
sound of the neighing of his   *Jer 8:16*
strong *o.*
have sent their little *o.* to the   *Jer 14:3*
waters
and their mighty *o.* are beaten   *Jer 46:5*
down
her little *o.* have caused a   *Jer 48:4*
cry to be
of the head of the tumultuous   *Jer 48:45*
o.
they give suck to their young *o.*   *La 4:3*
the demand by the word of the   *Da 4:17*
holy *o.*
for it came up four notable *o.*   *Da 8:8*
shall he
and upright *o.* with him; thus   *Da 11:17*
cause thy mighty *o.* to come   *Joe 3:11*
down
These are the two anointed *o.*   *Zec 4:14*
will turn mine hand upon the   *Zec 13:7*
little *o.*
of these little *o.* a cup of cold   *M't 10:42*
water
shall offend one of these little   *M't 18:6*
o. which
ye despise not one of these   *M't 18:10*
little *o.*
one of these little *o.* should   *M't 18:14*
perish
shall offend one of these little   *M'k 9:42*
o. that
their great *o.* exercise   *M'k 10:42*
authority upon
he should offend one of these   *Lu 17:2*
little *o.*

ONE'S

day of death than the day of *o.*   *Ec 7:1*
birth
and every *o.* bands were   *Ac 16:26*
loosed

ONESIMUS

O. a faithful and beloved   *Col 4:9*
brother
I beseech thee for my son *O.*   *Ph'm 10*

ONESIPHORUS

give mercy unto the house of   *2Ti 1:16*
O.
Aquila, and the household of   *2Ti 4:19*
O.

ONIONS

leeks and the *o.* and the garlick   *Nu 11:5*

ONLY

thoughts of his heart are *o.* evil   *Ge 6:5*
continually
Noah *o.* remained alive, and   *Ge 7:23*
those in the ark
Save *o.* that which the young   *Ge 14:24*
men
eyes: *o.* unto these men do   *Ge 19:8*
nothing
take now thy son, thine *o.* son   *Ge 22:2*
Isaac
thou hast not withheld thy   *Ge 22:12;*
son, thine *o.* son   *22:16*
o. bring not my son thither   *Ge 24:8*
again
o. obey my voice, and go   *Ge 27:13*
fetch me them
o. herein will the men   *Ge 34:22;*
consent to us   *34:23*
o. in the throne will I be   *Ge 41:40*
greater than thou
o. the land of priests bought   *Ge 47:22;*
he not   *47:26*
they may remain in the river *o.*   *Ex 8:9;*
  8:11
I will let you go, *o.* you shall   *Ex 8:28*
not go far away
forgive sin *o.* this once take   *Ex 10:17*
away from me this death *o.*
o. let your flocks and your   *Ex 10:24*
herds be stayed
man must eat, that *o.* may   *Ex 12:16*
be done of you
o. he shall pay for the loss of   *Ex 21:19*
his time
that sacrificeth to any, save to   *Ex 22:20*
the Lord *o.*
for that is his covering, it is *o.*   *Ex 22:27*
his raiment
o. he shall not go in unto the   *Le 21:23*
veil
o. the firstling of the beasts, it   *Le 27:26*
is the Lord's
o. thou shalt not number tribe   *Nu 1:49*
of Levi
hath the Lord indeed *o.*   *Nu 12:2*
spoken by Moses
rebel not ye against the Lord   *Nu 14:9*
o.
o. they shall not come nigh   *Nu 18:3*
the vessels
I will *o.* go through on my   *Nu 20:19;*
feet   *De 2:28*
o. the word that I shall speak   *Nu 22:35*
to thee
o. the gold and the silver, the   *Nu 31:22*
brass
o. marry to the family of their   *Nu 36:6*
father's tribe
o. take heed to thyself, keep thy   *De 4:9*
soul
ye saw no similitude, *o.* ye   *De 4:12*
heard a voice
know that man doth not live by   *De 8:3*
bread *o.*
o. the Lord had a delight in   *De 10:15*
thy fathers
o. ye shall not eat the blood   *De 12:16;*
  12:23; 15:23
the man *o.* that lay with her   *De 22:25*
shall die
thou shalt be above *o.* not be   *De 28:13*
beneath
thou shalt be *o.* oppressed   *De 28:29;*
and spoiled   *28:33*
nor with you *o.* do I make   *De 29:14*
this covenant
o. be thou strong and very   *Jos 1:7;*
courageous   *1:18*
o. Lord thy God be with thee   *Jos 1:17*
as with Moses
o. that day compassed the city   *Jos 6:15*
seven times
o. Rahab shall live; burned   *Jos 6:17;*
Hazor *o.*   *11:13*
thou shalt not have one lot *o.*   *Jos 17:17*
they might *o.* know to teach   *J'g 3:2*
them war
if dew be on the fleece *o.* and   *J'g 6:37*
dry on earth
let it not be dry *o.* upon the   *J'g 6:39;*
fleece   *6:40*
deliver us *o.* we pray thee,   *J'g 10:15*
this day

came to meet him, and she   *J'g 11:34*
was his *o.* child
strengthen me, I pray thee, *o.*   *J'g 16:28*
this once
the man said, *O.* lodge not in   *J'g 19:20*
the street
Hannah *o.* moved her lips,   *1Sa 1:13*
voice not heard
o. the Lord establish his word   *1Sa 1:23*
o. the stump of Dagon was left   *1Sa 5:4*
to him
and serve him *o.*   *1Sa 7:3;*
  7:4; M't 4:10; Lu 4:8
o. fear the Lord, and serve   *1Sa 12:24*
him in truth
o. be thou valiant for me,   *1Sa 18:17*
and fight battles
not *o.* while I live, shew me   *1Sa 20:14*
kindness
o. Jonathan and David knew   *1Sa 20:39*
the matter
Jonadab said, *O.* Ammon is   *2Sa 13:32;*
dead   *13:33*
the people flee, and I will   *2Sa 17:2*
smite the king *o.*
deliver him *o.* and I will   *2Sa 20:21*
depart from city
the people returned after him   *2Sa 23:10*
o. to spoil
o. the people sacrificed in high   *1Ki 3:2;*
places   *3:3*
Gebar was the *o.* officer who   *1Ki 4:19*
was in the land
o. let me go (S)   *1Ki 11:22*
none followed David, but   *1Ki 12:20*
Judah *o.*
David did that *o.* which was   *1Ki 14:8*
right in my eyes
he *o.* of Jeroboam shall come   *1Ki 14:13*
to grave
save *o.* in the matter of Uriah   *1Ki 15:5*
the Hittite
I *o.* am left, and they seek   *1Ki 19:10;*
my life   *19:14*
fight not, save *o.* with the king   *1Ki 22:31*
of Israel
but the worshippers of Baal   *2Ki 10:23*
o.
there was none left but the   *2Ki 17:18*
tribe of Judah *o.*
thou art the Lord, even thou   *2Ki 19:19;*
o.   *Isa 37:20*
o. the Lord give thee wisdom   *1Ch 22:12*
save *o.* to burn sacrifice before   *2Ch 2:6*
him
thou *o.* knowest the hearts of   *2Ch 6:30*
children of men
did sacrifice, yet to the Lord   *2Ch 33:17*
their God *o.*
the queen hath not done wrong   *Es 1:16*
to king *o.*
o. on himself put not forth thy   *Job 1:12*
hand
I *o.* am escaped to tell thee   *Job 1:15;*
  1:16-17, 19
o. do not two things to me,   *Job 13:20*
then will I not
whether done against a   *Job 34:29*
nation, or a man *o.*
thou Lord, *o.* makest me dwell   *Ps 4:8*
in safety
my *o.* one (S)   *Ps 22:20; 35:17*
against thee, thee *o.* have I   *Ps 51:4*
sinned
he *o.* is my rock and my   *Ps 62:2;*
salvation   *62:6*
o. consult to cast him down   *Ps 62:4*
from excellency
my soul, wait thou *o.* upon God   *Ps 62:5*
mention thy righteousness,   *Ps 71:16*
even thine *o.*
God of Israel *o.* doth   *Ps 72:18*
wondrous things
o. with thine eyes shalt thou   *Ps 91:8*
behold and see
tender and *o.* beloved in sight of   *Pr 4:3*
mother
let them be *o.* thine own, and   *Pr 5:17*
not strangers
the desire of the righteous is *o.*   *Pr 11:23*
good
o. by pride cometh contention   *Pr 13:10*
the talk of the lips tendeth *o.*   *Pr 14:23*
to penury
an evil man seeketh *o.*   *Pr 17:11*
rebellion
tend *o.* to plenteousness, *o.* to   *Pr 21:5*
want
this *o.* have I found, that God   *Ec 7:29*
made man

she is the o. one of her mother *Ca 6:9*
o. let us be called by thy name *Isa 4:1*
we will o. make mention of *Isa 26:13*
thy name
it shall be a vexation o. to *Isa 28:19*
understand report
o. acknowledge thine iniquity *Jer 3:13*
make mourning as for an o. *Jer 6:26;*
son *Am 8:10*
o. done evil, o. provoked me *Jer 32:30*
to anger
and evil, an o. evil, behold is *Eze 7:5*
come
they o. shall be delivered *Eze 14:16;*
 14:18
they shall o. poll their heads *Jer 44:20*
you o. have I known of all *Am 3:2*
families of earth
if ye salute your brethren o. *M't 5:47*
what do you
the centurion said, Lord, speak *M't 8:8*
the word o.
shall give a cup of cold water *M't 10:42*
o. in name
not lawful for him to eat, but *M't 12:4*
o. for priests
they might o. touch hem of *M't 14:36*
his garment
they saw no man, save Jesus *M't 17:8;*
o. *M'k 9:8*
they found nothing thereon *M't 21:19*
but leaves o.
shall not o. do this which is *M't 21:21*
done to fig tree
not the angels in heaven, but *M't 24:36*
my Father o.
who can forgive sins, but God *M'k 2:7*
o.
Jesus saith, Be not afraid, o. *M'k 5:36;*
believe *Lu 8:50*
should take nothing for *M'k 6:8*
journey, save a staff o.
was a dead man, o. son of his *Lu 7:12*
mother
one o. daughter he is my o. *Lu 8:42;*
child *9:38*
art thou o. a stranger in *Lu 24:18*
Jerusalem not known
not o. because he had broken *Joh 5:18*
sabbath
and seek not honour that *Joh 5:44*
cometh from God o.
that Jesus should die, not for *Joh 11:52*
that nation o.
came not for Jesus' sake o. *Joh 12:9*
but to see Lazarus
Lord, not my feet o. but also *Joh 13:9*
my hands
that they might know thee the *Joh 17:3*
o. true God
o. they were baptized in name *Ac 8:16*
of Jesus
preaching the word to none *Ac 11:19*
but Jews o.
Apollos taught, knowing o. *Ac 18:25*
baptism of John
not o. our craft is in danger *Ac 19:27*
to be at nought
ready to not be bound o. but *Ac 21:13*
to die for Jesus
o. that they keep themselves *Ac 21:25*
from things offered
I would to God that not o. *Ac 26:29*
thou, but all
not o. do same, but have *Ro 1:32*
pleasure in them
is he God of Jews o.? is he not *Ro 3:29*
of Gentiles
cometh this blessedness on *Ro 4:9;*
circumcision o. *4:12*
not to that o. which is of law, *Ro 4:16*
but to faith
not o. so *Ro 5:3; 5:11*
not o. they, but ourselves *Ro 8:23*
whom he called, not of Jews o. *Ro 9:24*
but of Gentiles
ye must be subject, not o. for *Ro 13:5*
wrath, but also
to whom not o. I give thanks, *Ro 16:4*
but churches
to God o. wise be glory *Ro 16:27;*
 1Ti 1:17; Jude 25
o. in the Lord; I o. and *1Co 7:39;*
Barnabas *9:6*
came word of God from you *1Co 14:36*
o. or to you o.
if in this life o. we have *1Co 15:19*
hope, most miserable
God comforted us, not by his *2Co 7:7*
coming o.

have begun not o. to do; not *2Co 8:10;*
that o. *8:19*
not o. in sight of Lord, but in *2Co 8:21*
sight of men
heard o. he who persecuted in *Ga 1:23*
times past
o. would that we should *Ga 2:10*
remember gospel
this o. would I learn of you, *Ga 3:2*
received ye Spirit
and not o. when I am present *Ga 4:18*
with you
o. use not liberty for an *Ga 5:13*
occasion to the flesh
o. lest they should suffer *Ga 6:12*
persecution for Christ
every name named, not o. in *Eph 1:21*
this world
o. let your conversation be as *Ph'p 1:27*
becomes gospel
is given not o. to believe on *Ph'p 1:29*
him, but to suffer
obeyed, not in presence o. *Ph'p 2:12*
but in absence
God had mercy not on him o. *Ph'p 2:27*
but on me
no church communicated *Ph'p 4:15*
with me, but ye o.
these o. are my fellow-workers *Col 4:11*
to kingdom
gospel came not in word o. but *1Th 1:5*
in power
to have imparted to you not *1Th 2:8*
gospel of God o.
o. he who now letteth will let, *2Th 2:7*
till taken
not o. idle, but tattlers and *1Ti 5:13*
busybodies
is blessed and o. Potentate, *1Ti 6:15*
King of kings
who o. hath immortality, *1Ti 6:16*
dwelling in light
not to me o; o. Luke is with *2Ti 4:8;*
me *4:11*
which stood o. in meats and *Heb 9:10*
drinks
once more I shake not earth *Heb 12:26*
o. but heaven
be ye doers of word, and not *Jas 1:22*
hearers o.
a man is justified by works, *Jas 2:24*
and not faith o.
not o. to good and gentle, but *1Pe 2:18*
froward
not for our sins o; not by *1Jo 2:2;*
water *5:6*
whom I love in the truth, and not *2Jo 1*
I o.
denying the o. Lord God *Jude 4*
and our Lord Jesus
but o. those which have not seal *Re 9:4*
of God
who shall not fear thee? for *Re 15:4*
thou o. art holy

ONO

who built O. and Lod, with *1Ch 8:12*
the children of Lod, Hadid, *Ezr 2:33;*
and O. *Ne 7:37*
one of the villages in the plain *Ne 6:2*
of O.
Lod, and O. the valley of *Ne 11:35*
craftsmen

ONWARD

of Israel went o. in all their *Ex 40:36*
journeys
onward (S) *1Sa 16:13;*
 18:9; 30:25; Eze 43:27

ONYCHA

stacte, and o. and galbanum *Ex 30:34*

ONYX

there is bdellium and the o. *Ge 2:12*
stone
O. stones, and stones to be set *Ex 25:7;*
in *1Ch 29:2*
And thou shalt take two o. *Ex 28:9*
stones
the fourth row a beryl, and an *Ex 28:20*
o.
o. stones, and stones to be set *Ex 35:9*
for
And the rulers brought o. *Ex 35:27*
stones

they wrought o. stones inclosed *Ex 39:6*
in
row, a beryl, an o., and a *Ex 39:13*
jasper
gold of Ophir, with the *Job 28:16*
precious o.
the beryl, the o. and the *Eze 28:13*
jasper

OPEN

in the o. firmament of heaven *Ge 1:20*
sat in an o. place, which is *Ge 38:14*
by the
if a man shall o. a pit, or if a *Ex 21:33*
man
living bird loose into the o. *Le 14:7*
field
bird out of the city into the o. *Le 14:53*
fields
which they offer in the o. field *Le 17:5*
instead of such as o. every *Nu 8:16*
womb
and the earth o. her mouth *Nu 16:30*
And every o. vessel, which *Nu 19:15*
hath no
slain with a sword in the o. *Nu 19:16*
fields
man whose eyes are o. hath *Nu 24:3;*
said *24:15; 24:16*
a trance, but having his eyes o. *Nu 24:4*
shalt o. thine hand wide unto *De 15:8*
him
shalt o. thine hand wide unto *De 15:11*
thy
answer of peace, and o. unto *De 20:11*
thee
shall o. unto thee his good *De 28:12*
treasure
they left the city o. and pursued *Jos 8:17*
O. the mouth of the cave, and *Jos 10:22*
bring
those days, there was no o. *1Sa 3:1*
vision
lord, are encamped in the o. *2Sa 11:11*
fields
carved with knops and o. *1Ki 6:18*
flowers
palm trees and o. flowers, *1Ki 6:29*
within
and palm trees and o. flowers *1Ki 6:32;*
 6:35
thine eyes may be o. toward *1Ki 8:29*
this
That thine eyes may be o. *1Ki 8:52*
unto the
Lord, I pray thee, o. his eyes, *2Ki 6:17*
that
Lord, o. the eyes of these men *2Ki 6:20*
Then o. the door, and flee, and *2Ki 9:3*
he said, O. the window *2Ki 13:17*
eastward
o. Lord, thine eyes, and see *2Ki 19:16*
That thine eyes may be o. *2Ch 6:20*
upon
let, I beseech thee, thine eyes *2Ch 6:40*
be o.
Now mine eyes shall be o. and *2Ch 7:15*
in an o. place (S) *2Ch 18:9*
and thine eyes o. that thou *Ne 1:6*
mayest
time with an o. letter in his *Ne 6:5*
hand
speak, and o. his lips against *Job 11:5*
thee
dost thou o. thine eyes upon *Job 14:3*
such
I will o. my lips and answer *Job 32:20*
men in the o. sight of others *Job 34:26*
doth Job o. his mouth in vain *Job 35:16*
in the o. field (S) *Job 39:4*
Who can o. the doors of his *Job 41:14*
face
their throat is an o. sepulchre *Ps 5:9;*
 Ro 3:13
and his ears are o. unto their *Ps 34:15*
cry
I will o. my dark saying upon *Ps 49:4*
O Lord, o. thou my lips; and *Ps 51:15*
my
I will o. my mouth in a parable *Ps 78:2*
o. thy mouth wide, and I will *Ps 81:10*
fill it
O. the gates of righteousness *Ps 118:19*
O. thou mine eyes, that I *Ps 119:18*
may
but a fool layeth o. his folly *Pr 13:16*
o. thine eyes, and thou shalt be *Pr 20:13*
O. rebuke is better than secret *Pr 27:5*
O. thy mouth for the dumb in *Pr 31:8*

O. thy mouth, judge righteously *Pr 31:9*
O. to me, my sister, my love, my *Ca 5:2*
I rose up to o. to my beloved *Ca 6:5*
shall devour Israel with o. *Isa 9:12*
mouth
so he shall o. and none shall *Isa 22:22*
shut
and he shall shut, and none *Isa 22:22*
shall o.
the windows from on high are *Isa 24:18*
o.
O. ye the gates, that the *Isa 26:2*
righteous
doth he o. and break the *Isa 28:24*
clods of
o. thine eyes, O Lord, and *Isa 37:17*
see: and
I will o. rivers in high places *Isa 41:18*
To o. the blind eyes, to bring *Isa 42:7*
out
to o. before him the two leaved *Isa 45:1*
let the earth o. and let them *Isa 45:8*
bring
thy gates shall be o. *Isa 60:11*
continually
Their quiver is as an o. *Jer 5:16*
sepulchre
fall as dung upon the o. field *Jer 9:22*
shut up, and none shall o. *Jer 13:19*
them
custom, and that which was o. *Jer 32:11*
and this evidence which is o. *Jer 32:14*
thine eyes are o. upon all the *Jer 32:19*
ways
utmost border, o. her *Jer 50:26*
storehouses
o. thy mouth, and eat that I *Eze 2:8*
give
I will o. thy mouth, and thou *Eze 3:27*
shalt
thou wast cast out in the o. *Eze 16:5*
field
and never o. thy mouth any *Eze 16:63*
more
to o. the mouth in the *Eze 21:22*
slaughter
I will o. the side of Moab *Eze 25:9*
from the
thou shalt fall upon the o. *Eze 29:5*
fields
cast thee forth upon the o. *Eze 32:4*
field
him that is in the o. field will *Eze 33:27*
I give
were very many in the o. *Eze 37:2*
valley
I will o. your graves, and *Eze 37:12*
cause
Thou shalt fall upon the o. *Eze 39:5*
field
the o. space (S) *Eze 45:2*
one shall then o. him the *Eze 46:12*
gate that
the o. fields (S) *Eze 48:15*
and his windows being o. in *Da 6:10*
his
o. thine eyes, and behold our *Da 9:18*
set wide o. unto thine enemies *Na 3:13*
O. thy doors, O Lebanon, that *Zec 11:1*
I will o. mine eyes upon the *Zec 12:4*
house
I will not o. you the windows *Mal 3:10*
of
I will o. my mouth in *M't 13:35*
parables; I
virgins, saying, Lord, Lord, *M't 25:11*
o. to us
they may o. unto him *Lu 12:36*
immediately
door, saying, Lord, Lord, o. *Lu 13:25*
unto us
Hereafter ye shall see heaven *Joh 1:51*
o.
Can a devil o. the eyes of the *Joh 10:21*
blind
sleep, and seeing the prison *Ac 16:27*
doors o.
Paul was now about to o. his *Ac 18:14*
mouth
the law is o. and there are *Ac 19:38*
deputies
To o. their eyes, and to turn *Ac 26:18*
them
with o. face beholding as in a *2Co 3:18*
glass
we speak quite frank and o. *2Co 5:12*
(P)
our mouth is o. unto you, our *2Co 6:11*
heart
that I may o. my mouth boldly *Eph 6:19*

that God would o. unto us a *Col 4:3*
door
men's sins are o. beforehand *1Ti 5:24*
o. and laid bare (R) *Heb 4:13*
afresh, and put him to an o. *Heb 6:6*
shame
and his ears are o. unto their *1Pe 3:12*
prayers
I have set before thee an o. door *Re 3:8*
man hear my voice, and o. the *Re 3:20*
door
Who is worthy to o. the book, *Re 5:2*
and to
no man was able to o. the *Re 5:3*
book
worthy to o. and to read the *Re 5:4*
book
hath prevailed to o. the book *Re 5:5*
the book, and to o. the seals *Re 5:9*
thereof
he had in his hand a little book *Re 10:2*
o.
and take the little book which is *Re 10:8*
o.

OPENED

thereof, then your eyes shall be *Ge 3:5*
o.
And the eyes of them both *Ge 3:7*
were o.
which hath o. her mouth to *Ge 4:11*
receive
the windows of heaven were o. *Ge 7:11*
that Noah o. the window of the *Ge 8:6*
ark
God o. her eyes, and she saw *Ge 21:19*
Leah was hated, he o. her *Ge 29:31*
womb
hearkened to her, and o. her *Ge 30:22*
womb
Joseph o. all the storehouses *Ge 41:56*
as one of them o. his sack to *Ge 42:27*
give
we o. our sacks, and, behold, *Ge 43:21*
every
ground, and o. every man his *Ge 44:11*
sack
she had o. it, she saw the child *Ex 2:6*
earth o. her mouth, and *Nu 16:32*
swallowed
the Lord o. the mouth of the *Nu 22:28*
ass
the Lord o. the eyes of *Nu 22:31*
Balaam
earth o. her mouth, and *Nu 26:10;*
swallowed *De 11:6*
he o. not the doors of the *J'g 3:25*
parlour
they took a key, and o. them *J'g 3:25*
she o. a bottle of milk, and *J'g 4:19*
gave
I have o. my mouth unto the *J'g 11:35*
Lord
hast o. thy mouth unto the *J'g 11:36*
Lord
o. the doors of the house, and *J'g 19:27*
o. the doors of the house of *1Sa 3:15*
the Lord
times, and the child o. his eyes *2Ki 4:35*
Lord o. the eyes of the young *2Ki 6:17*
man
Lord o. their eyes, and they *2Ki 6:20*
saw
And he o. the door and fled *2Ki 9:10*
window eastward. And he o. *2Ki 13:17*
it
because they o. not to him *2Ki 15:16*
o. the doors of the house of *2Ch 29:3*
the Lord,
Let not the gates of Jerusalem *Ne 7:3*
be o.
Ezra o. the book in the sight of *Ne 8:5*
all
when he o. it, all the people *Ne 8:5*
stood
that they should not be o. till *Ne 13:19*
after
After this o. Job his mouth, and *Job 3:1*
they o. their mouth wide as *Job 29:23*
for the
but I o. my doors to the *Job 31:32*
traveller
Behold, now I have o. my *Job 33:2*
mouth
Have the gates of death been *Job 38:17*
o.
they o. their mouth wide *Ps 35:21*
against

I was dumb, I o. not my mouth *Ps 39:9*
mine ears hast thou o.: burnt *Ps 40:6*
above, and o. the doors of *Ps 78:23*
heaven
He o. the rock, and the *Ps 105:41*
waters
earth o. and swallowed up *Ps 106:17*
Dathan
the mouth of the deceitful are *Ps 109:2*
o.
I o. my mouth, and panted *Ps 119:131*
I o. to my beloved; but my *Ca 5:6*
beloved
o. her mouth without measure *Isa 5:14*
moved the wing, or o. the *Isa 10:14*
mouth
o. not the house of his *Isa 14:17*
prisoners
the eyes of the blind shall be o. *Isa 35:5*
time that thine ear was not o. *Isa 48:8*
The Lord God hath o. mine *Isa 50:5*
ear
afflicted, yet he o. not his *Isa 53:7*
mouth
for unto thee have I o. my *Jer 20:12*
cause
The Lord hath o. his armoury *Jer 50:25*
enemies have o. their mouths *La 2:16*
our enemies have o. their *La 3:46*
mouths
the heavens were o. and I saw *Eze 1:1*
I o. my mouth, and he caused *Eze 3:2*
me
and hast o. thy feet to every *Eze 16:25*
one
In that day shall thy mouth *Eze 24:27*
be o.
had o. my mouth, until he *Eze 33:22*
came to
and my mouth was o. and I *Eze 33:22*
was no
when I have o. your graves, *Eze 37:13*
O my
gate shall be shut, it shall not *Eze 44:2*
be o.
on the sabbath it shall be o. *Eze 46:1*
and in
day of the new moon it shall *Eze 46:1*
be o.
was set, and the books were o. *Da 7:10*
then I o. my mouth, and *Da 10:16*
spake
The gates of the rivers shall be *Na 2:6*
o.
shall be a fountain o. to the *Zec 13:1*
house
when they had o. their *M't 2:11*
treasures
the heavens were o. unto him *M't 3:16*
he o. his mouth, and taught *M't 5:2*
them
knock, and it shall be o. unto *M't 7:7;*
you *Lu 11:9*
to him that knocketh it shall *M't 7:8;*
be o. *Lu 11:10*
their eyes were o; and Jesus *M't 9:30*
straitly
and when thou hast o. his *M't 17:27*
mouth
him, Lord, that our eyes may *M't 20:33*
be o.
graves were o.; and many *M't 27:52*
bodies
he saw the heavens o. and the *M'k 1:10*
him, Ephphatha, that is, Be o. *M'k 7:34*
straightway his ears were o. *M'k 7:35*
his mouth was o. immediately *Lu 1:64*
and praying, the heaven was o. *Lu 3:21*
And when he had o. the *Lu 4:17*
book, he
their eyes were o. and they *Lu 24:31*
knew
while he o. to us the *Lu 24:32*
scriptures
Then o. he their *Lu 24:45*
understanding
unto him, How were thine *Joh 9:10*
eyes o.
Jesus made the clay, and o. *Joh 9:14*
his eyes
of him, that he hath o. thine *Joh 9:17*
eyes
who hath o. his eyes, we know *Joh 9:21*
not
did he to thee? how o. he thine *Joh 9:26*
eyes
he is, and yet he hath o. mine *Joh 9:30*
eyes
that any man o. the eyes of *Joh 9:32*
one that

man, which o. the eyes of the *Joh 11:37*
blind
Lord by night o. the prison *Ac 5:19*
doors
when we had o. we found no *Ac 5:23*
man
Behold, I see the heavens o. *Ac 7:56*
his shearer, so o. he not his *Ac 8:32*
mouth
Then Philip o. his mouth, and *Ac 8:35*
began
when his eyes were o. he saw no *Ac 9:8*
she o. her eyes: and when she *Ac 9:40*
saw
saw heaven o. and a certain *Ac 10:11*
vessel
Then Peter o. his mouth, and *Ac 10:34*
said
which o. to them of his own *Ac 12:10*
accord
she o. not the gate for *Ac 12:14*
gladness, but
and when they had o. the *Ac 12:16*
door, and
o. the door of faith unto the *Ac 14:27*
Gentiles
whose heart the Lord o. that *Ac 16:14*
she
immediately all the doors *Ac 16:26*
were o.
door and effectual is o. unto *1Co 16:9*
me
a door was o. unto me of the *2Co 2:12*
Lord
all things are naked and o. *Heb 4:13*
unto
behold, a door was o. in heaven *Re 4:1*
when the Lamb o. one of the *Re 6:1*
seals
And when he had o. the second *Re 6:3*
seal
And when he had o. the third *Re 6:5*
seal
And when he had o. the fourth *Re 6:7*
seal
And when he had o. the fifth *Re 6:9*
seal
when he had o. the sixth seal *Re 6:12*
And when he had o. the seventh *Re 8:1*
seal
And he o. the bottomless pit *Re 9:2*
the temple of God was o. in *Re 11:19*
heaven
earth o. her mouth, and *Re 12:16*
swallowed
o. his mouth in blasphemy *Re 13:6*
against
of the testimony in heaven was *Re 15:5*
o.
And I saw heaven o. and *Re 19:11*
behold a
before God; and the books *Re 20:12*
were o.
another book was o. which is *Re 20:12*

OPENEST

thou o. thine hand, they are *Ps 104:28*
filled
Thou o. thine hand, and *Ps 145:16*
satisfiest

OPENETH

whatsoever o. the womb among *Ex 13:2*
unto the Lord all that o. the *Ex 13:12;*
matrix *13:15*
All that o. the matrix is mine *Ex 34:19*
all the firstborn that o. the *Nu 3:12*
matrix
thing that o. the matrix in all *Nu 18:15*
flesh
he o. his eyes and he is not *Job 27:19*
he o. the ears of men, and *Job 33:16*
sealeth
He o. also their ear to *Job 36:10*
discipline
and o. their ears in *Job 36:15*
oppression
dumb man that o. not his *Ps 38:13*
mouth
The Lord o. the eyes of the *Ps 146:8*
blind
he that o. wide his lips shall *Pr 13:3*
have
he o. not his mouth in the gate *Pr 24:7*
She o. her mouth with wisdom *Pr 31:26*
is dumb, so he o. not his *Isa 53:7*
mouth

the fire all that o. the womb *Eze 20:26*
Every male that o. the womb *Lu 2:23*
shall
To him the porter o.; and the *Joh 10:3*
sheep
he that o. and no man shutteth *Re 3:7*
and shutteth, and no man o. *Re 3:7*

OPENING

o. in the ark all around (B) *Ge 6:16*
and the o. thereof every *1Ch 9:27*
morning
up a man, and there can be *Job 12:14*
no o.
o. of my lips shall be right things *Pr 8:6*
o. the ears, but he heareth not *Isa 42:20*
o. of the prison to them that *Isa 61:1*
are
will give thee the o. of *Eze 29:21*
the mouth
O. and alleging, that Christ *Ac 17:3*
must

OPENINGS

concourse, in the o. of the gates *Pr 1:21*

OPENLY

that was o. by the way side *Ge 38:21*
righteousness hath he o. shewed *Ps 98:2*
secret shall reward thee o. *M't 6:4;*
6:6, 18
I will say to them o. (A) *M't 7:23*
no more o. enter into the city *M'k 1:45*
And he spake that saying o. *M'k 8:32*
himself seeketh to be known o. *Joh 7:4*
not o. but as it were in secret *Joh 7:10*
no man spake o. of him for *Joh 7:13*
fear of
walked no more o. among *Joh 11:54*
the Jews
I spake o. to the world; I *Joh 18:20*
ever
spoken o. to the world *Joh 18:20*
(A)(B)(E)(N)(P)(R)
the third day, and shewed him *Ac 10:40*
o.
have beaten us o. *Ac 16:37*
uncondemned
with boldness o. (A) *Ac 28:31*
o. without hindrance *Ac 28:31*
(B)(N)(R)
we speak freely, o. (A) *2Co 5:12*
Christ hath been o. set forth *Ga 3:1*
(S)
he made a shew of them o. *Col 2:15*

OPERATION

the Lord, nor the o. of his *Ps 28:5*
hands
nor the work of his hands *Ps 28:5*
(B)(R)
neither consider the o. of his *Isa 5:12*
hands
the works of his hands (B)(R) *Isa 5:12*
through the faith of the o. of *Col 2:12*
God
through faith in the working *Col 2:12*
of God (A)(E)(R)
through the faith wrought of *Col 2:12*
God (B)
faith in the active power of *Col 2:12*
God (N)
faith in the tremendous power *Col 2:12*
of God (P)

OPERATIONS

there are diversities of o. but *1Co 12:6*
it is
are varieties of things *1Co 12:6*
accomplished (B)
are diversities of workings *1Co 12:6*
(E)
are many forms of work (N) *1Co 12:6*
are different ways of serving *1Co 12:6*
God (P)
are varieties of working (R) *1Co 12:6*

OPHEL

on the wall of O. he built *2Ch 27:3*
much
and compassed about O. and *2Ch 33:14*
raised
the Nethinims dwelt in O. unto *Ne 3:26*
lieth out, even unto the wall of *Ne 3:27*
O.
But the Nethinims dwelt in O. *Ne 11:21*

OPHIR

And O. and Havilah, and *Ge 10:29;*
Jobab *1Ch 1:23*
they came to O. and fetched *1Ki 9:28*
from
Hiram, that brought gold *1Ki 10:11*
from O.
brought in from O. great *1Ki 10:11*
plenty of
ships of Tharshish to go to *1Ki 22:48*
O. for
talents of gold, of the gold of *1Ch 29:4*
O.
with the servants of Solomon *2Ch 8:18*
to O.
which brought gold from O. *2Ch 9:10*
brought
the gold of O. as the stones of *Job 22:24*
cannot be valued with the *Job 28:16*
gold of O.
did stand the queen in gold of *Ps 45:9*
O.
man than the golden wedge of *Isa 13:12*
O.

OPHNI

Chephar-haammonai, and O. *Jos 18:24*

OPHRAH

And Avim, and Parah, and *Jos 18:23*
O.
sat under an oak which was in *J'g 6:11*
O.
it is yet in O. of the Abi-ezrites *J'g 6:24*
and put it in his city, even in *J'g 8:27*
O.
sepulchre of Joash his father, *J'g 8:32*
in O.
went unto his father's house at *J'g 9:5*
O.
unto the way that leadeth to *1Sa 13:17*
O.
And Meonothai begat O.; and *1Ch 4:14*

OPINION

and durst not shew you mine *Job 32:6*
o.
dared not show you my views *Job 32:6*
(B)
to me; I also will shew mine *Job 32:10*
o.
I too will show you what I *Job 32:10*
think (B)
my part, I also will shew *Job 32:17*
mine o.
I will tell you what I know *Job 32:17*
(B)
it is my o. that (A)(B)(P) *Ac 15:19*
sharp clash of o. (P) *Ac 15:39*
I give my o. and advice *1Co 7:25*
(A)(B)(P)(R)

OPINIONS

How long halt ye between *1Ki 18:21*
two o.
How long will you lean to *1Ki 18:21*
both sides (B)(E)
revealing personal o. *Pr 18:2*
(A)(B)(R)
not criticize his o. (A)(R) *Ro 14:1*

OPPONENT

o. to your opponents (B) *Ex 23:22*
caught his o. (A)(B)(R) *2Sa 2:16*
come to terms with o. (B)(P) *M't 5:25*
go with your o. (B)(N)(P) *Lu 12:58*
do justice to my o. (B)(N) *Lu 18:3*
o. incentive for slandering *1Ti 5:14*
(B)(N)

OPPONENTS

not give o. occasion *1Ti 5:14*
(A)(B)(N)
must correct his o. (A) *2Ti 2:25*

OPPORTUNITY

time he sought o. to betray *M't 26:16*
him
watched for a chance to *M't 26:16;*
betray him (B) *Lu 22:6*
sought o. to betray him unto *Lu 22:6*
them

have o. to answer (S) *Ac 25:16*
As we have therefore o. let us *Ga 6:10* do
use present o. (A)(N) *Eph 5:16; Col 4:5*
were also careful, but ye *Ph'p 4:10* lacked o.
have had o. to have returned *Heb 11:15*
abuse grace as an o. of *Jude 4* immorality (P)

OPPOSE

began to o. him (S) *Lu 11:53*
instructing those that o. *2Ti 2:25* themselves
He must correct his opponents *2Ti 2:25* (A)(R)
discipline those in opposition *2Ti 2:25* (B)
tolerant, and gentle when *2Ti 2:25* discipline is needed (N)
contradict and o. (A) *Tit 1:9*

OPPOSED

show thyself o. (S) *Ps 18:26*
And when they o. themselves *Ac 18:6*
o. to purpose of God (P) *Ro 8:7*

OPPOSERS

to convince the o. (S) *Tit 1:9*

OPPOSEST

hand thou o. thyself against *Job 30:21* me

OPPOSETH

Who o. and exalteth himself *2Th 2:4* above

OPPOSING

cease o. God (A)(R) *2Ch 35:21*

OPPOSITE

opposite (S) *De 1:1; Ne 3:10, 16, 23, 25, 26, 28, 29, 30, 31; 7:3; 12:9, 24, 37; Es 5:1; Eze 40:23; 41:15, 16; 42:1, 3, 10; 46:9; 48:15; M't 21:2; M'k 12:41; 13:3; Lu 8:26; 19:30; Ac 20:15*
portion o. the great tower (S) *Ne 3:27; 3:19*

OPPOSITION

behave in o. to me (B) *Le 26:27*
neither adversary or o. (B) *1Ki 5:4*
in o. to each other (B)(R) *Ga 5:17*
discipline those in o. (B) *2Ti 2:25*
confute o. (P)(R) *Tit 2:9*

OPPOSITIONS

and o. of science falsely so *1Ti 6:20* called
subtleties and contradictions *1Ti 6:20* in what is falsely called knowledge and spiritual illumination (A)
irreligious and empty *1Ti 6:20* discussions and contradictions of what is falsely called knowledge (B)
profane babblings and *1Ti 6:20* opposition to knowledge which is falsely so called (E)
empty and worldly chatter, *1Ti 6:20* and contradictions of so-called knowledge (N)
godless mixture of *1Ti 6:20* contradictory notions which is falsely known as knowledge (P)
godless chatter and *1Ti 6:20* contradictions of what is falsely called knowledge (R)

OPPRESS

they shall o. them (B)(R) *Ge 15:13*
wherewith the Egyptians o. *Ex 3:9* them
neither vex a stranger, nor o. *Ex 22:21* him
Also thou shalt not o. a *Ex 23:9* stranger

neither o. neighbor (E)(R) *Le 19:13*
hand, ye shall not o. one *Le 25:14* another
shall not therefore o. one *Le 25:17* another
him best: thou shalt not o. *De 23:16* him
Thou shalt not o. an hired *De 24:14* servant
and the Maonites, did o. you *J'g 10:12*
unto thee that thou shouldest *Job 10:3* o.
man of the earth may no more *Ps 10:18* o.
From the wicked that o. me *Ps 17:9*
for good; let not the proud *Ps 119:122* o. me
neither o. the afflicted in the *Pr 22:22* gate
I will feed them that o. thee *Isa 49:26* with
o. all your employees (B)(R) *Isa 58:3*
If ye o. not the stranger, the *Jer 7:6*
and I will punish all that o. *Jer 30:20* them
shall no more o. my people *Eze 45:8*
are in his hand: he loveth to o. *Ho 12:7*
which o. the poor, which crush *Am 4:1*
so they o. a man and his house *Mic 2:2*
o. not the widow, nor the *Zec 7:10* fatherless
that o. the hireling in his wages *Mal 3:5*
Do not rich men o. you, and *Jas 2:6* draw

OPPRESSED

more they were o. (A)(R) *Ex 1:12*
thou shalt be only o. and *De 28:29* spoiled
thou shalt be only o. and *De 28:33* crushed
by reason of them that o. them *J'g 2:18*
mightily o. the children of Israel *J'g 4:3*
out of the hand of all that o. *J'g 6:9* you
and o. the chidren of Israel *J'g 10:8*
crushed and o. them (R) *J'g 10:8*
kingdoms, and of them that *1Sa 10:18* o. you
whom have I o.? or of whose *1Sa 12:3* hand
hast not defrauded us, nor o. *1Sa 12:4* us
because the king of Syria o. *2Ki 13:4* them
But Hazael king of Syria o. *2Ki 13:22* Israel
And Asa o. some of the *2Ch 16:10* people
o. and hath forsaken the poor *Job 20:19*
they make the o. to cry: they *Job 35:9* cry
also will be refuge for the o. *Ps 9:9*
To judge the fatherless and the *Ps 10:18* o.
o. see and be glad (R) *Ps 69:32*
O let not the o. return *Ps 74:21* ashamed
and judgment for all that are *Ps 103:6* o.
Their enemies also o. them *Ps 106:42*
executeth judgment for the o. *Ps 146:7*
the tears of such as were o. *Ec 4:1*
seek judgment, relieve the *Isa 1:17* o.
And the people shall be o. every *Isa 3:5*
no more rejoice, O thou o. *Isa 23:12* virgin
O Lord, I am o.; undertake *Isa 38:14* for me
Assyrian o. them without *Isa 52:4* cause
He was o. and he was afflicted *Isa 53:7*
to let the o. go free, and that *Isa 58:6* ye
and the children of Judah *Jer 50:33* were o.
hath not o. any, but hath *Eze 18:7* restored
Hath o. the poor and needy, *Eze 18:12*
Neither hath o. any, hath not *Eze 18:16*
because he cruelly o. spoiled *Eze 18:18* his
o. the fatherless (A)(B)(R) *Eze 22:7*
have o. the stranger *Eze 22:29* wrongfully
Ephraim is o. and broken in *Ho 5:11*
and the o. in the midst thereof *Am 3:9*
those o., downtrodden (A) *Lu 4:18*
and avenged him that was o. *Ac 7:24*

all that were o. of the devil *Ac 10:38*
o. in every way (A) *2Co 4:8*
utterly destitute, o. *Heb 11:37* (A)(B)(N)

OPPRESSETH

against the enemy that o. you *Nu 10:9*
me up; he fighting daily o. me *Ps 56:1*
He that o. the poor *Pr 14:31* reproacheth
He that o. the poor to increase *Pr 22:16* his
A poor man that o. the poor is *Pr 28:3* like

OPPRESSING

our nativity from the o. *Jer 46:16* sword
for fear of the o. sword they *Jer 50:16* shall
filthy and polluted, to the o. *Zep 3:1* city

OPPRESSION

the o. wherewith the Egyptians *Ex 3:9*
and our labour, and our o. *De 26:7*
he saw the o. of Israel, because *2Ki 13:4*
and openeth their ears in *Job 36:15*
opens their ears in and by *Job 36:15* adversity (A)(R)
through their distress he *Job 36:15* opens their ears (B)
For the o. of the poor, for the *Ps 12:5*
because of the o. of the enemy *Ps 42:9; 43:2*
forgettest our affliction and *Ps 44:24* our o.
because of the o. of the wicked *Ps 55:3*
because of threatenings of the *Ps 55:3* wicked (B)
Trust not in o. and become *Ps 62:10* not
and speak wickedly concerning *Ps 73:8* o.
scoff and wickedly mention *Ps 73:8* depression (B)
brought low through o. *Ps 107:39* affliction
bowed through o. *Ps 107:39* (A)(B)(E)(R)
Deliver me from the o. of *Ps 119:134* man
minds plot o. (A)(E) *Pr 24:2*
If thou seest the o. of the poor *Ec 5:8*
Surely o. maketh a wise man *Ec 7:7* mad
extortion maddens the wise man *Ec 7:7* (B)(E)
for judgment, but behold o. *Isa 5:7*
looked for justice, but see, *Isa 5:7* bloodshed (B)(R)
despise this word, and trust *Isa 30:12* in o.
thou shalt be far from o.; for *Isa 54:14* thou
speaking o. and revolt, *Isa 59:13* concerning
she is wholly o. in the midst of *Jer 6:6* her
and for o. and for violence, to *Jer 22:17* do it
death by o. (E) *Eze 22:5; 22:29*
they dealt by o. with the *Eze 22:7* stranger
foreigner suffers extortion *Eze 22:7; 22:29* among you (B)(R)
people of the land have used *Eze 22:29* o.
violence and o. (R) *Eze 45:9*
of the people's inheritance by *Eze 46:18* o.
wrest property from (B) *Eze 46:18*
thrusting them out of their *Eze 46:18* property (E)(R)
full of o. (B) *Mic 6:12*
o. and violence (B) *Hab 1:3*
share o. (A) *Heb 11:25*
come through great o. (P) *Re 7:14*

OPPRESSIONS

By reason of the multitude of *Job 35:9* o.
the o. that are done under the *Ec 4:1* sun
he that despiseth the gain of *Isa 33:15* o.

OPPRESSIVE

they are an *o.* burden	Isa 1:14
(A)(B)(R)	
afflict, *o.*, torment (A)	Ac 12:1
orders not *o.* (A)	1Jo 5:3

OPPRESSOR

An *o.*, an enemy (B)	Es 9:6
they hear not the voice of the *o.*	Job 3:18
hear not the taskmaster's voice (A)(B)	Job 3:18
hear not the voice of the taskmaster (E)(R)	Job 3:18
number of years is hidden to the *o.*	Job 15:20
the tyrant during years granted him (B)	Job 15:20
years laid up for the ruthless (R)	Job 15:20
and shall break in pieces the *o.*	Ps 72:4
Envy thou not the *o.* and	Pr 3:31
Do not resentfully envy and be jealous of an unscrupulous grasping man (A)	Pr 3:31
Do not envy a violent man (B)	Pr 3:31
Envy not the man of violence (E)(R)	Pr 3:31
understanding is also a great *o.*	Pr 28:16
prince who lacks understanding is cruelly oppressive (B)	Pr 28:16
of his shoulder, the rod of his *o.*	Isa 9:4
his slaveholder's rod (B)	Isa 9:4
and say, How hath the *o.* ceased	Isa 14:4
How the tyrant has stopped (B)	Isa 14:4
the *o.* has met his end (B)(R)	Isa 16:4
day because of the fury of the *o.*	Isa 51:13
and where is the fury of the *o.*	Isa 51:13
spoiled out of the hand of the *o.*	Jer 21:12; 22:3
because of the fierceness of the *o.*	Jer 25:38
no *o.* shall pass through them	Zec 9:8
bow, out of him every *o.* together	Zec 10:4

OPPRESSORS

and the heritage of *o.* which they	Job 27:13
and *o.* seek after my soul: they	Ps 54:3
violent and ruthless seek my life (A)	Ps 54:3
violent men seek my life (B)(R)	Ps 54:3
ruthless men seek my life (R)	Ps 54:3
justice: leave me not to mine *o.*	Ps 119:121
side of their *o.* there was power	Ec 4:1
children are their *o.* and women	Isa 3:12
their ruling tyrants are children (B)(R)	Isa 3:12
and they shall rule over their *o.*	Isa 14:2
o. are consumed out of the land	Isa 16:4
unto the Lord because of the *o.*	Isa 19:20

OPTION

I had no *o.* but to appeal (N)	Ac 28:19

OR

cannot speak good *o.* bad	Ge 24:50
o. deaf, *o.* the seeing, *o.* the blind	Ex 4:11
o. if your soul abhor my judgments	Le 26:15
man *o.* woman shall commit	Nu 5:6
God is there in heaven *o.* earth	De 3:24
to the right hand, *o.* to the left	Jos 1:7
whether poor *o.* rich	Ru 3:10
o. kettle, *o.* caldron, *o.* pot	1Sa 2:14
man hath any suit *o.* cause	2Sa 15:4
to battle, *o.* shall I forbear	1Ki 22:6; 22:15
O. as an hidden untimely birth	Job 3:16
o. who is a rock save our God	Ps 18:31
as the horse, *o.* as the mule	Ps 32:9

up into heaven, *o.* descended	Pr 30:4
O. ever the silver cord be loosed	Ec 12:6
o. shall a nation be born at once	Isa 66:8
sons *o.* daughters in	Jer 16:2
for father *o.* for the mother	Jer 16:7
o. for son, *o.* for daughter	Eze 44:25
destroy the law, *o.* the prophets	M't 5:17
Lo here is Christ, *o.* there	M't 24:23
o. distress, *o.* persecution, *o.* sword	Ro 8:35
o. extortioners, *o.* covetous	1Co 5:10
o. respect for an holyday	Col 2:16
o. else I will come unto thee	Re 2:15
right hand, *o.* in the foreheads	Re 13:16
abomination, *o.* maketh a lie	Re 21:27

ORACLE

had enquired at the *o.* of God	2Sa 16:23
had consulted the word of God (A)(B)	2Sa 16:23
both of the temple and of the *o.*	1Ki 6:5
both of the temple and the holies (A)	1Ki 6:5
both of the temple and the inner room (B)	1Ki 6:5
both the nave and the inner sanctuary (R)	1Ki 6:5
for it within, even for the *o.*	1Ki 6:16
built it within for the sanctuary, the holy of holies (A)	1Ki 6:16
made for himself an inner room, a sanctuary (B)	1Ki 6:16
built within an inner sanctuary, most holy place (R)	1Ki 6:16
the *o.* he prepared in the house	1Ki 6:19
he prepared the holy of holies in the inner room (A)	1Ki 6:19
prepared a sanctuary in the innermost part (B)(R)	1Ki 6:19
the *o.* in the forepart was twenty	1Ki 6:20
the holy of holies was twenty cubits (A)	1Ki 6:20
sanctuary was 30 square (B)	1Ki 6:20
the inner sanctuary was 20 cubits (R)	1Ki 6:20
by the chains of gold before the *o.*	1Ki 6:21
chains of gold in front of holy of holies (A)	1Ki 6:21
chains in front of the sanctuary (B)(R)	1Ki 6:21
altar that was by the *o.* he overlaid	1Ki 6:22
altar that belonged to the holy of holies (A)	1Ki 6:22
altar of the sanctuary (B)(R)	1Ki 6:22
the *o.* he made two cherubims	1Ki 6:23
entering of the *o.* he made doors	1Ki 6:31
For the holy of holies he made doors (A)	1Ki 6:31
for entrance of the holy place (B)	1Ki 6:31
For entrance of the inner sanctuary (R)	1Ki 6:31
five on the left, before the *o.*	1Ki 7:49
in front of the holy of holies (A)	1Ki 7:49
five to the left of the sanctuary (B)	1Ki 7:49
before the inner sanctuary (R)	1Ki 7:49
into the *o.* of the house	1Ki 8:6
in the holy of holies (A)	1Ki 8:6
in the sanctuary (B)	1Ki 8:6
in the inner sanctuary (R)	1Ki 8:6
before the *o.*	1Ki 8:8
before the holy of holies (A)	1Ki 8:8
in front of the sanctuary (B)	1Ki 8:8
before the inner sanctuary (R)	1Ki 8:8
he made chains, as in the *o.*	2Ch 3:16
after the manner before the *o.*	2Ch 4:20
burn before the inner sanctuary (A)(B)	2Ch 4:20
in front of the inner room (B)	2Ch 4:20
to the *o.* of the house	2Ch 5:7
to the sanctuary of the house (A)	2Ch 5:7
in Holy of Holies, the inner chamber (B)	2Ch 5:7
in the inner sanctuary (R)	2Ch 5:7

seen from the ark before the *o.*	2Ch 5:9
from the front of the holy of holies (A)	2Ch 5:9
at the front of the inner room (B)	2Ch 5:9
from the holy place before the inner sanctuary (R)	2Ch 5:9
up my hands toward thy holy *o.*	Ps 28:2
toward your inner most sanctuary (A)	Ps 28:2
toward thy inner sanctuary (B)	Ps 28:2
toward thy most holy sanctuary (R)	Ps 28:2

ORACLES

the lively *o.* to give unto us	Ac 7:38
he received the living word (B)	Ac 7:38
received the living utterances of God (N)	Ac 7:38
received words, living words (P)	Ac 7:38
were committed the *o.* of God	Ro 3:2
entrusted with the utterances of God (B)	Ro 3:2
God's messages were entrusted (P)	Ro 3:2
the first principles of the *o.* of God	Heb 5:12
first principles of God's word (A)(R)	Heb 5:12
the elementary beginnings of God's lessons (B)	Heb 5:12
the ABC of God's revelation to men (P)	Heb 5:12
let him speak as the *o.* of God	1Pe 4:11
let it be as God's suggestions (B)	1Pe 4:11
preach his message as from God (P)	1Pe 4:11

ORACULAR

an *o.* spirit (N)	Ac 16:16

ORATION

made an *o.* unto them	Ac 12:21
made a public address unto them (B)	Ac 12:21
Herod harangued them (N)	Ac 12:21
made a speech to them (P)	Ac 12:21

ORATOR

I am no *o.* (B)	Ex 4:10
artificer, and the eloquent *o.*	Isa 3:3
expert craftsman and skillful enchanter (A)(E)	Isa 3:3
skilful craftsman and expert charmer (B)	Isa 3:3
skilful magician, the expert in charms (R)	Isa 3:3
with a certain *o.* named Tertullus	Ac 24:1
a certain forensic advocate Tertullus (A)	Ac 24:1
an advocate name Tertullus (N)	Ac 24:1
a lawyer by the name of Tertullus (P)	Ac 24:1
a spokesman, one Tertullus (R)	Ac 24:1

ORCHARD

plants are an *o.* of pomegranates	Ca 4:13

ORCHARDS

I made me gardens and *o.*	Ec 2:5
I laid out gardens and parks (B)(E)(R)	Ec 2:5

ORDAIN

o. Aaron and sons (A)(B)(R)	Ex 29:9
seven days *o.* them (A)(B)	Ex 29:35
today you *o.* yourselves (R)	Ex 32:29
the seer did *o.* in their set office	1Ch 9:22
the seer had established (A)(R)	1Ch 9:22
the seer had appointed (B)	1Ch 9:22
I will *o.* a place for my people	1Ch 17:9
I will appoint a place (A)(E)(R)	1Ch 17:9
I have established a place (B)	1Ch 17:9
thou wilt *o.* peace for us	Isa 26:12
thou wilt establish peace (B)	Isa 26:12
And so *o.* I in all churches	1Co 7:17

This is my order in all churches (A) — 1Co 7:17
This is my ruling in all churches (B) — 1Co 7:17
This is what I teach in all congregations (N) — 1Co 7:17
This is the rule I lay down in all (P)(R) — 1Co 7:17
o. elders in every city — Tit 1:5
appoint elders and set them over (A)(B)(E)(P)(R) — Tit 1:5
institute elders in every town (N) — Tit 1:5

ORDAINED

o. to minister (A)(R) — Nu 3:3
o. in mount Sinai for a sweet — Nu 28:6
instituted in mount Sinai (B) — Nu 28:6
Jeroboam o. a feast — 1Ki 12:32
Jeroboam appointed a feast (A)(R) — 1Ki 12:32
Jeroboam set a festival (B) — 1Ki 12:32
o. a feast to the children of Israel — 1Ki 12:33
he appointed a feast for Israelites (A) — 1Ki 12:33
he made a festival for (B) — 1Ki 12:33
had o. to burn incense in high places — 2Ki 23:5
he appointed to burn incense (B) — 2Ki 23:5
as o. for ever (A)(B)(R) — 2Ch 2:4
he o. him priests for high places — 2Ch 11:15
he appointed his own priests (A)(E)(R) — 2Ch 11:15
with singing, as it was o. by David — 2Ch 23:18
singing, ordered by David (A)(B) — 2Ch 23:18
singing, according to the order of (E)(R) — 2Ch 23:18
instruments o. by David — 2Ch 29:27
Jews o. and took upon them — Es 9:27
o. strength because of thine anointed — Ps 8:2
established strength because of foes (A)(E) — Ps 8:2
founded a bulwark because of foes (R) — Ps 8:2
the stars which thou hast o. — Ps 8:3
stars which thou has established (B)(R) — Ps 8:3
This is o. in Joseph for a testimony — Ps 81:5
assigned it in Joseph for a testimony (B) — Ps 81:5
appointed in Joseph a testimony (E) — Ps 81:5
made it a decree in Joseph (R) — Ps 81:5
o. a lamp for mine anointed — Ps 132:17
prepared a lamp for my anointed (R) — Ps 132:17
Tophet is o. of old — Isa 30:33
Tophet is long ago prepared (A)(B)(E)(R) — Isa 30:33
I o. thee a prophet unto the nations — Jer 1:5
I appointed you a prophet (A)(E)(R) — Jer 1:5
I designated you a prophet (B) — Jer 1:5
whom the king had o. to destroy the — Da 2:24
appointed to destroy wisemen (A)(B)(E)(R) — Da 2:24
hast o. them for judgment — Hab 1:12
have appointed to execute your judgment (B) — Hab 1:12
o. twelve, that they should be — M'k 3:14
appointed twelve to continue (A)(E)(N)(P)(R) — M'k 3:14
chosen, and o. you that you should — Joh 15:16
I have appointed you (A)(B)(E)(N)(P)(R) — Joh 15:16
must one be o. to be a witness — Ac 1:22
join us and become a witness (A)(E)(R) — Ac 1:22
o., set in order (A)(E) — Ac 7:53
was o. of God to be the Judge — Ac 10:42
He is a God-appointed Judge (B) — Ac 10:42
designated by God as Judge (N) — Ac 10:42
appointed by God to be judge (P) — Ac 10:42
as were o. to eternal life believed — Ac 13:48

as many as were destined to eternal life (A)(P) — Ac 13:48
appointed for eternal life (B) — Ac 13:48
marked out for eternal life believed (N) — Ac 13:48
when they had o. them elders — Ac 14:23
chose elders for them (B) — Ac 14:23
appointed for them elders (E)(N)(P)(R) — Ac 14:23
were o. of the apostles — Ac 16:4
regulations decided upon by apostles (A)(B) — Ac 16:4
decisions taken by the apostles (N)(P)(R) — Ac 16:4
by that man whom he hath o. — Ac 17:31
whom he has destined and appointed (A) — Ac 17:31
through a man destined for the task (B) — Ac 17:31
by a man of his choosing (N) — Ac 17:31
by a man whom he has — Ac 17:31
which was o. to life, I found to be — Ro 7:10
was designed and intended to bring (A) — Ro 7:10
command that was aimed to give life (B) — Ro 7:10
commandment which promised life (R) — Ro 7:10
the powers that be are o. of God — Ro 13:1
that exist do so by God's appointment (A) — Ro 13:1
those in charge are divinely constituted (B) — Ro 13:1
existing authorities are instituted by him (N)(R) — Ro 13:1
existing authority is appointed under God (P) — Ro 13:1
God o. before the world unto — 1Co 2:7
God devised and decreed (A) — 1Co 2:7
God designed for our glory (B) — 1Co 2:7
God foreordained before the worlds (E) — 1Co 2:7
framed from the very beginning (N) — 1Co 2:7
God planned before the Creation (P) — 1Co 2:7
God decreed before the ages (R) — 1Co 2:7
Lord o. that they which preach — 1Co 9:14
Lord directed that those who (A)(B) — 1Co 9:14
Lord gave instructions that those (N) — 1Co 9:14
Lord has ordered that those who (P) — 1Co 9:14
Lord has commanded that those who (R) — 1Co 9:14
was o. by angels in the hand of — Ga 3:19
It was promulgated through angels (N) — Ga 3:19
the law was inaugurated in the (P) — Ga 3:19
o. that we should walk in them — Eph 2:10
works which God predestined for us (A) — Eph 2:10
works God previously prepared (B)(E)(R) — Eph 2:10
good deeds which God has designed us (N) — Eph 2:10
good deeds which God planned (P) — Eph 2:10
Whereunto I am o. a preacher — 1Ti 2:7
I was appointed a preacher (A)(B)(E)(N)(P)(R) — 1Ti 2:7
o. for men in things pertaining to — Heb 5:1
is appointed to act (A)(B)(E)(N)(P)(R) — Heb 5:1
every high priest is o. to offer gifts — Heb 8:3
appointed to offer gifts (A)(B)(E)(N)(P)(R) — Heb 8:3
when these things were thus o. — Heb 9:6
These things having thus been made (A) — Heb 9:6
With these things so arranged (B) — Heb 9:6
these things having been prepared (E) — Heb 9:6
Under this arrangement (N)(P) — Heb 9:6
These preparations having thus been made (R) — Heb 9:6

who were before of old o. to this — Jude 4
their doom was predicted long ago (A) — Jude 4
long ago this condemnation was set forth (B)(P) — Jude 4
written of beforehand unto this condemnation (E) — Jude 4
Scripture long ago marked down for the doom (N) — Jude 4
designated for this condemnation (R) — Jude 4

ORDAINETH

he o. his arrows against the — Ps 7:13
He makes His arrows fiery shafts (A)(B)(E)(R) — Ps 7:13

ORDAINING

o. whom he wished (B) — 1Ki 13:33

ORDEAL

what is good of the o. (P) — 1Co 15:32
passed through great o. (N) — Re 7:14

ORDER

there, and laid the wood in o. — Ge 22:9
the o. of their birth (A)(B) — Ex 6:16
set in o. one against another — Ex 26:17
dovetailing and fitting together (A) — Ex 26:17
each frame to fit tightly to next frame (B) — Ex 26:17
board, joined one to another (E) — Ex 26:17
each frame, for fitting together (R) — Ex 26:17
Aaron and sons shall o. it from evening to — Ex 27:21
Aaron and sons shall keep it burning from (A) — Ex 27:21
Aaron and sons shall keep it supplied from (B) — Ex 27:21
Aaron and sons shall tend it (R) — Ex 27:21
even with the lamps to be set in o. — Ex 39:37
lampstand with its arrangement of lamps (B) — Ex 39:37
set in o. the things upon the table — Ex 40:4
set the bread in o. upon it — Ex 40:23
arranging upon it the bread (B) — Ex 40:23
lay the wood in o. upon the fire — Le 1:7
arrange the wood on the fire (B) — Le 1:7
the fat in o. upon the wood — Le 1:8
the fat on top of the wood (B) — Le 1:8
the priest shall lay them in o. — Le 1:12
priest arrange them upon the wood (B) — Le 1:12
lay the burnt offering in o. upon it — Le 6:12
arranged the burnt sacrifice upon it (B) — Le 6:12
Aaron o. it from the evening to — Le 24:3
Aaron shall keep it continually (B) — Le 24:3
shall o. the lamps upon the — Le 24:4
shall continually supply the lamps — Le 24:4
every sabbath he shall set it in o. — Le 24:8
he shall arrange it anew (B) — Le 24:8
she laid in o. upon the roof — Jos 2:6
How shall we o. the child — J'g 13:12
how shall we manage the child (B) — J'g 13:12
what way of life and his activites (R) — J'g 13:12
what is to be the boy's manner of life (R) — J'g 13:12
put his household in o. — 2Sa 17:23
made arangements for his household (B) — 2Sa 17:23
he put the wood in o. — 1Ki 18:33
he arranged the wood (B) — 1Ki 18:33
Who shall o. the battle — 1Ki 20:14
who shall attack (B) — 1Ki 20:14
Who shall begin the battle (E)(R) — 1Ki 20:14
Set thine house in o. — 2Ki 20:1
the priests of the second o. — 2Ki 23:4
the priests of the second rank (A)(B) — 2Ki 23:4

their office according to their *1Ch 6:32*
o.
officiated as prescribed from *1Ch 6:32*
them (B)
we sought him not after the *1Ch 15:13*
due *o.*
did not seek him in way *1Ch 15:13*
ordained (A)(R)
failed to seek him the proper *1Ch 15:13*
way (B)
not according to the *1Ch 15:13*
ordinance (E)
according to the *o.* *1Ch 23:31*
commanded
according to the ordinance *1Ch 23:31*
(A)(E)
in such number as was *1Ch 23:31*
prescribed (B)
according to the number *1Ch 23:31*
required (R)
according to the *o.* of the king *1Ch 25:2*
under the direction of the *1Ch 25:2;*
king (B)(R) *25:6*
according to the *o.* of David *2Ch 8:14*
as ordered by David (A) *2Ch 8:14*
according to the ordinance of *2Ch 8:14*
David (B)(E)(R)
shewbread set they in *o.* *2Ch 13:11*
upon
according to the *o.* of David *2Ch 23:18*
(E)(R)
set the house of God in *o.* *2Ch 24:13*
(S)
house of the Lord was set in *2Ch 29:35*
o.
service of temple was *2Ch 29:35*
re-established (B)
service of the house was *2Ch 29:35*
restored (R)
after the *o.* of David (A)(E) *Ezr 3:10*
shadow of death, without *Job 10:22*
any *o.*
only chaos, and light is *Job 10:22*
gloom (B)(R)
I would *o.* my cause before *Job 23:4*
him
I would lay my cause before *Job 23:4*
him (A)(R)
present my case before him *Job 23:4*
(B)
set thy words in *o.* before me *Job 33:5*
marshal your words; take *Job 33:5*
your stand (B)
o. your speech by reason of *Job 37:19*
darkness
we cannot state our case *Job 37:19*
(A)(B)(R)
he reckoned up in *o.* unto the *Ps 40:5*
they are too many to be *Ps 40:5*
numbered (A)(B)(R)
set them in *o.* before thine *Ps 50:21*
eyes
lay the charge before thee (R) *Ps 50:21*
ever after the *o.* of *Ps 110:4;*
Melchisedek *Heb 5:6, 10; 6:20; 7:11,*
17, 21

O. my steps in thy word *Ps 119:133*
Establish my steps and *Ps 119:133*
direct them (A)(E)
Keep steady my steps *Ps 119:133*
according to thy promise (R)
set in *o.* many proverbs *Ec 12:9*
he made many proverbs (B) *Ec 12:9*
weighing, studying, and *Ec 12:9*
arranging many (R)
kingdom, to *o.* it, and to *Isa 9:7*
establish it
to establish it and to uphold it *Isa 9:7*
(A)(E)(R)
in that it is firmly established *Isa 9:7*
(B)
Set thine house in *o.* *Isa 38:1*
declare it, set it in *o.* for me *Isa 44:7*
declare it and state proofs *Isa 44:7*
before me (B)
declare it and set it forth *Isa 44:7*
before me (R)
fixed *o.* of the moon (A)(R) *Jer 31:35;*
31:36
O. ye the buckler and shield *Jer 46:3*
Set in line the buckler and *Jer 46:3*
shield (B)
Prepare the buckler and shield *Jer 46:3*
(E)(R)
thirty in *o.* *Eze 41:6*
thirty in each story *Eze 41:6*
(A)(B)(R)
in *o.* a declaration of those *Lu 1:1*
things

draw up a narrative of those *Lu 1:1*
matters (B)(E)
draw up an account of the *Lu 1:1*
events (N)
written an account of the events *Lu 1:1*
(P)
compile a narrative of the things *Lu 1:1*
(R)
to write unto thee in *o.* most *Lu 1:3*
to write an orderly account *Lu 1:3*
(A)(B)(R)
the whole course of these events *Lu 1:3*
(N)(P)
before God in the *o.* of his *Lu 1:8*
course
in the sequence of his series (B) *Lu 1:8*
it was the turn of his division *Lu 1:8*
(N)
performing his priestly functions *Lu 1:8*
(P)
his division was on duty (R) *Lu 1:8*
expounded it by *o.* unto them *Lu 11:4*
explained to them step by step *Lu 11:4*
(A)
undertook to put the whole *Lu 11:4*
matter plainly (B)
laying before them the facts *Lu 11:4*
(N)
explain how the situation had *Lu 11:4*
actually arisen (P)
place to place in an orderly *Lu 18:23*
manner (A)(R)
made his way successively *Lu 18:23*
through country (B)
went through the region *Lu 18:23*
(E)(N)
visit systematically *Lu 18:23*
throughout Galatia (P)
ordained, set in *o.* (A)(E) *Ac 7:53*
explained them in *o.* (B) *Ac 11:4*
went over all the country of *Ac 18:23*
Galatia and Phrygia in *o.*
my *o.* in all churches (A) *1Co 7:17*
rest will I set in *o.* when I *1Co 11:34*
come
I will give you directions *1Co 11:34*
when (A)(R)
I will arrange on my arrival *1Co 11:34*
(B)(N)
I will settle in person when *1Co 11:34*
(P)
things be done decently and *1Co 14:40*
in *o.*
in an orderly fashion *1Co 14:40*
(A)(B)
every man in his own *o.* *1Co 15:23*
each one in his own rank *1Co 15:23*
and turn (A)
in his turn (B) *1Co 15:23*
each one in his own proper *1Co 15:23*
place (N)
as I have given *o.* to the *1Co 16:1*
churches
as I directed the churches *1Co 16:1*
(A)(R)
as I suggested to the churches *1Co 16:1*
(B)
follow my directions to (N) *1Co 16:1*
follow the same rule that I *1Co 16:1*
gave (P)
joying and beholding your *o.* *Col 2:5*
at the sight of your orderly *Col 2:5*
array (A)(N)
enjoying your well-ordered *Col 2:5*
condition (B)
set in *o.* things that are wanting *Tit 1:5*
set right what was defective *Tit 1:5*
(A)(R)
straighten out unfinished *Tit 1:5*
business (B)
set right matters that needed *Tit 1:5*
attention (P)
dare to *o.* you to do (P) *Ph'm 8*
after the *o.* of Melchisedec *Heb 5:6;*
5:10; 6:20; 7:11, 17, 21
the A B C of God's *o.* *Heb 5:12*
(N)(P)

ORDERED

he *o.* (S) *Ge 43:17; 2Sa 1:18; 14:19*
top of this rock, in the *o.* place *J'g 6:26*
arrange it properly (B) *J'g 6:26*
in orderly manner (E) *J'g 6:26*
covenant *o.* in all things *2Sa 23:5*
singing *o.* by David (A)(B) *2Ch 23:18*
I have *o.* my cause *Job 13:18*
I have prepared my case *Job 13:18*
(A)(B)(R)

steps of good man are *o.* by *Ps 37:23*
Lord
are directed and established *Ps 37:23*
by (A)
are confirmed by the Lord (B) *Ps 37:23*
going are established by (E) *Ps 37:23*
he establishes him (R) *Ps 37:23*
Lord *o.* that those (P) *1Co 9:14*

ORDERETH

to him that *o.* his conversation *Ps 50:23*
aright
he who orders his way aright *Ps 50:23*
(A)(R)
he who prepares his way (B) *Ps 50:23*

ORDERINGS

the *o.* of them in their service *1Ch 24:19*

ORDERLIES

magistrates sent *o.* (B) *Ac 16:35*

ORDERLY

made him his *o.* (B) *Ge 39:4*
cleaned and *o.* (B)(P) *M't 12:44*
that thou thyself walketh *o.* *Ac 21:24*
you yourself walk in *Ac 21:24*
observance of the law (A)(B)(R)
you are a practicing Jew and *Ac 21:24*
keep the law (N)
you yourself observe the law *Ac 21:24*
(P)

ORDERS

my *o.*, my rules (B) *Ge 26:5*
there are legal *o.* (B) *Ex 21:1*
I will give *o.* (S) *2Sa 14:8; 18:5*
o. not oppressive (A) *1Jo 5:3*

ORDINANCE

keep it a feast by an *o.* for *Ex 12:14*
ever
your generations by an *o.* for *Ex 12:17*
ever
observe this thing for an *o.* to *Ex 12:24*
thee
This is the *o.* of the passover *Ex 12:43*
therefore keep this *o.* in his *Ex 13:10*
season
for them a statute and an *o.* *Ex 15:25*
a perpetual *o.* (B) *Ex 28:43;*
Le 3:17; 10:15; 16:29, 34; 23:14, 41;
Da 6:7
Therefore shall ye keep mine *Le 18:30*
o.
They shall therefore keep mine *Le 22:9*
o.
according to the *o.* of the *Nu 9:14*
passover
ye shall have one *o.* both for *Nu 9:14*
ordinance (S) *Nu 9:14;*
15:16, 24; 29:6, 18, 21, 24, 27, 30, 33, 37;
2Ch 4:20; Ne 8:18
shall be to you for an *o.* for *Nu 10:8*
ever
One *o.* shall be both for you *Nu 15:15*
of the
an *o.* for ever in your *Nu 15:15*
generations
and to thy sons, by an *o.* for *Nu 18:8*
ever
This is the *o.* of the law which *Nu 19:2*
statute and *o.* (A)(E)(R) *Nu 27:11*
This is the *o.* of the law *Nu 31:21*
which the
a statute and an *o.* in *Jos 24:25*
Shechem
it a statute and an *o.* for *1Sa 30:25*
Israel
according to the *o.* (A)(E) *1Ch 23:31*
This is an *o.* for ever to Israel *2Ch 2:4*
as ordained for ever *2Ch 2:4*
(A)(B)(R)
according to the *o.* *2Ch 8:14*
(B)(E)(R)
with fire according to the *o.* *2Ch 35:13*
made them an *o.* in Israel *2Ch 35:25*
made them a standing *2Ch 35:25*
custom (B)
according to the *o.* (A)(E)(R) *Ezr 3:4*
after the *o.* of David *Ezr 3:10*
after the order of David *Ezr 3:10*
(A)(E)

in accordance with direction _Ezr 3:10_
of David (B)(R)
_o_. of God (A)(B)(E)(R) _Ps 81:4_
the _o_. that he gave them _Ps 99:7_
the statute he gave them _Ps 99:7_
(A)(E)(R)
injunctions and statutes he gave _Ps 99:7_
(B)
changed the _o_. _Isa 24:5_
disregarded the statutes _Isa 24:5_
(A)(B)(E)(R)
forsook not the _o_. of their God _Isa 58:2_
Concerning the _o_. of oil _Eze 45:14_
as to the set portion of oil _Eze 45:14_
(A)(E)
as to the set portion of oil _Eze 45:14_
(B)(R)
by a perpetual _o_. unto the _Eze 46:14_
Lord
is it that we have kept his _o_. _Mal 3:14_
we have kept this charge _Mal 3:14_
(B)(E)(R)
knowing God's _o_. (B)(E) _Ro 1:32_
the power, resisteth the _o_. of _Ro 13:2_
God
resists what God has _Ro 13:2_
appointed (A)
resisting God's appointment _Ro 13:2_
(B)
resisting a divine institution _Ro 13:2_
(N)
existing authority is appointed _Ro 13:2_
under God (P)
Submit to every _o_. of man _1Pe 2:13_
Be submissive to every human _1Pe 2:13_
institution (A)(B)(N)(R)
Obey every man-made _1Pe 2:13_
authority (P)

ORDINANCES

teach them _o_. and laws _Ex 18:20_
Teaching them decrees and _Ex 18:20_
laws (A)
make clear rules and laws (B) _Ex 18:20_
teach them statutes and laws _Ex 18:20_
(E)
teach them statutes and _Ex 18:20_
decisions (R)
these are the _o_. (A)(E)(R) _Ex 21:1_
all the _o_. (A)(E)(R) _Ex 24:3_
ordinances (S) _Ex 24:3;_
_Le 18:4-5, 26; 19:37; 20:22; 25:18; 26:15,_
_43, 46; Nu 35:24; 36:13; De 4:1, 5, 8,_
_14, 45; 5:1, 31; 6:1, 20; 7:11, 12; 8:11;_
_11:1, 32; 12:1; 26:16-17; 30:16; 33:10,_
_21; 2Sa 22:23; 1Ki 2:3; 6:12; 8:58; 9:4;_
_11:33; 1Ch 22:13; 28:7; 2Ch 7:17; 19:10;_
Ezr 7:10; Ne 1:7; 9:13, 29; 10:29;
_Ps 18:22; 19:9; 89:30; 119:13, 20, 30, 39,_
_43, 52, 62, 102, 106, 149, 156, 160, 164,_
175; 147:19-20; Eze 5:6-7; 7:5; 11:12;
_18:9, 17; 20:11, 13, 16, 18-19, 21, 24-_
_25; 36:27; 37:24; 44:24; Da 9:5_
teach all _o_. (B) _Le 10:11_
neither walk in their _o_. _Le 18:3_
neither shall ye walk in their _Le 18:3_
statutes (A)(E)(R)
you will not follow their rules _Le 18:3_
(B)
keep mine _o_. to walk therein _Le 18:4_
practice my regulations (B) _Le 18:4_
mine _o_. you shall do (E)(R) _Le 18:4_
keep my law and _o_. _Le 18:5;_
(B)(E)(R) _19:37; 26:46_
soul abhor my _o_. (E)(R) _Le 26:15_
they despised my _o_. _Le 26:43_
(B)(E)(R)
all the _o_. of the passover they _Nu 9:12_
shall
all the statute of the passover _Nu 9:12_
(A)(E)(R)
every regulation of the _Nu 9:12_
passover (B)
according to these _o_. (E)(R) _Nu 35:24_
the commands and _o_. _Nu 36:13_
(A)(E)(R)
laws and _o_. (A)(B)(E)(R) _De 4:1;_
_4:5, 14; 5:31; 6:20; 8:11_
show obedience to _o_. _De 7:12_
(B)(E)(R)
or after their _o_., or after the _2Ki 17:34_
law
they follow the statutes and _2Ki 17:34;_
judgments (B) _17:37_
the _o_. by the hand of Moses _2Ch 33:8_
regulations and judgments by _2Ch 33:8_
(B)
Also we made _o_. for us _Ne 10:32_
we pledged ourselves (A) _Ne 10:32_

we imposed upon ourselves _Ne 10:32_
(B)
we lay upon ourselves _Ne 10:32_
obligation (R)
Knowest thou the _o_. of _Job 38:33_
heaven
know the laws of the heaven _Job 38:33_
ordinances (A)(B)(E)(R) _Ps 119:13;_
_119:20, 30, 39, 43, 62, 102, 106, 108;_
_147:20_
this day according to thine _Ps 119:91_
_o_.
by thy appointments they _Ps 119:91_
stand (R)
according to thy _o_. (B)(E) _Ps 119:149_
they ask of me the _o_. of justice _Isa 58:2_
they ask of me righteous _Isa 58:2_
judgments (A)(E)(R)
the _o_. of the moon, and stars _Jer 31:35_
fixed order of the moon _Jer 31:35;_
(A)(R) _31:36_
appointed the _o_. of heaven _Jer 33:25_
rebelled against my _o_. _Eze 5:6;_
(B)(E)(R) _5:7_
_o_. of the emotions _Eze 5:7_
(A)(B)(E)(R)
keep mine _o_. and do them _Eze 11:20_
observe my _o_. (B)(E)(R) _Eze 36:27_
all the _o_. thereof, all the _Eze 43:11_
forms
These are the _o_. of the altar _Eze 43:18_
These are the regulations _Eze 43:18_
(A)(B)
concerning all the _o_. of the _Eze 44:5_
house
according to my _o_. (E) _Eze 44:24_
swerved from _o_. _Da 9:5_
(A)(B)(E)(R)
ye are gone away from mine _o_. _Mal 3:7_
turned away from my statutes _Mal 3:7_
(B)(R)
_o_. of the Lord blameless _Lu 1:6_
blamelessly in all _Lu 1:6_
commandments and requirements
of the Lord (A)(P)
walking in agreement with all _Lu 1:6_
the commandments and injunctions
of the Lord (B)
keep the _o_. as I delivered _1Co 11:2_
them
keep firm possession of the _1Co 11:2_
traditions (A)(E)(N)(P)(R)
observing the suggestions (B) _1Co 11:2_
commandments contained in _Eph 2:15_
_o_.
demolished the law of _Eph 2:15_
commandments with regulations
(B)
annulled the law with its rules _Eph 2:15_
and regulations (N)
By his sacrifice he removed _Eph 2:15_
the hostility of the Law with all
its commandments and rules (P)
Blotting out the handwriting _Col 2:14_
or _o_.
Having cancelled and blotted _Col 2:14_
out and wiped away the
handwriting of the note with its
legal decrees and demands (A)
cancelled our red ledger of _Col 2:14_
regulations (B)
cancelled decrees of the law _Col 2:14_
(N)
utterly wiped out the damning _Col 2:14_
evidence of broken laws (P)
cancelled legal demands (R) _Col 2:14_
in the world, are ye subject to _Col 2:20_
_o_.
Why submit to rules and _Col 2:20_
regulations (A)(R)
why allow regulations be _Col 2:20_
imposed on you (B)
Why let people dictate to you _Col 2:20_
(N)
slightest notice to purely _Col 2:20_
human prohibitions (P)
had also _o_. of divine service _Heb 9:1_
rules and regulations for _Heb 9:1_
divine worship (A)(R)
its worship regulations (B) _Heb 9:1_
rules for the service of God (P) _Heb 9:1_
divers washings, and carnal _o_. _Heb 9:10_
external rules and regulations _Heb 9:10_
(A)
various ablutions-physical _Heb 9:10_
regulations (B)
rules for bodily conduct (P) _Heb 9:10_
various ablutions, regulations _Heb 9:10_
for the body (R)

ORDINARY

have diminished thine _o_. _Eze 16:27_
food
take interest in _o_. people (P) _Ro 12:16_
behaving like _o_. men (R) _1Co 3:3_

ORDINATION

_o_. ram (B)(R) _Ex 29:31_
_o_ offering (A)(B)(R) _Le 8:28; 8:31_

OREB

of the Midianites, _O_. and Zeeb _J'g 7:25;_
_8:2_
Make their nobles like _O_. _Ps 83:11_
slaughter of Midian at the _Isa 10:26_
rock _O_..

OREN

Bunah, and _O_., and Ozem _1Ch 2:25_

ORGAN

such as handle the harp and _o_. _Ge 4:21_
who play the lyre and pipe _Ge 4:21_
(A)(R)
players on harp and flute (B) _Ge 4:21_
such as handle the harp and _Ge 4:21_
pipe (E)
his male _o_. severed (B)(R) _De 23:1_
rejoice at the sound of the _o_. _Job 21:12_
rejoice at the sound of the _Job 21:12_
pipe (A)(E)(R)
make merry to the sound of _Job 21:12_
the flute (B)
my _o_. into the voice of them _Job 30:31_
who weep
my pipe into the voice of _Job 30:31_
those who weep (A)(E)(R)
my flute to bitter lamentation _Job 30:31_
(B)

ORGANIZATIONS

against _o_. and spiritual _Eph 6:12_
powers (P)

ORGANIZERS

organizers (P) _1Co 12:28_

ORGANIZED

_o_. into sections (A) _1Ch 23:6_

ORGANS

with stringed instruments and _Ps 150:4_
_o_.
with wind instruments or _Ps 150:4_
flutes (A)(B)
with stringed instruments and _Ps 150:4_
pipe (E)
with strings and pipe (R) _Ps 150:4_
deaden your _o_. that (B) _Col 3:5_

ORGIES

_o_. and the like (N)(P) _Ga 5:21_

ORIGIN

spiritual _o_. and birth _Eze 16:3_
(A)(B)(R)
in land of _o_. (A)(R) _Eze 21:30_
not from mortal _o_. (A) _1Pe 1:23_

ORION

made Arcturus, _O_., and _Job 9:9_
Pleiades
made Kesil and Kimah, the _Job 9:9_
Pleiades (B)
Pleiades, or loose the bands _Job 38:31_
of _o_.
maketh the seven stars and _O_. _Am 5:8_

ORNAMENT

be an _o_. of grace unto thy head _Pr 1:9_
a chaplet of grace upon your _Pr 1:9_
head (A)(E)
a fair garland upon your head _Pr 1:9_
(B)(R)
give to thine head an _o_. or grace _Pr 4:9_
give your head a wreath of _Pr 4:9_
gracefulness (A)

a fair garland upon your head   *Pr 4:9*
(B)(R)
give to thy head a chaplet of   *Pr 4:9*
grace (E)
an *o.* of fine gold   *Pr 25:12*
o. of thy molten images of   *Isa 30:22*
gold
thee with them all, as with an   *Isa 49:18*
o.
As for the beauty of his *o.*   *Eze 7:20*
the *o.* of a meek and quiet   *1Pe 3:4*
spirit

ORNAMENTAL

o. molding (A)   *Jer 52:21*

ORNAMENTS

no man put on his *o.*   *Ex 33:4; 33:5-6*
neck *o.* (A)   *Nu 31:50*
took away the *o.*   *J'g 8:21*
took crescents from camels   *J'g 8:21;*
(B)(E)(R)   *8:26*
put on *o.* of gold upon your   *2Sa 1:24*
apparel
tinkling *o.* about their feet   *Isa 3:18*
anklets, ancle chains   *Isa 3:18;*
(A)(B)(E)(R)   *3:20*
decketh himself with *o.*   *Isa 61:10*
decks himself with a garland   *Isa 61:10*
(A)(E)(R)
his priestlike crown (B)   *Isa 61:10*
Can a maid forget her *o.*   *Jer 2:32*
thou deckest thee with *o.* of   *Jer 4:30*
gold
thou art come to excellent *o.*   *Eze 16:7*
you came to full maidenhood   *Eze 16:7*
(A)(R)
I decked thee also with *o.*   *Eze 16:11;*
   23:40

ORNAN

threshingfloor of *O.*   *1Ch 21:15;*
   21:18, 28; 2Ch 3:1
O. saw the angel, *O.*   *1Ch 21:20*
threshing wheat
David came to *O.*   *1Ch 21:21;*
   21:22, 24-25

ORPAH

name of one was *O.*   *Ru 1:4; 1:14*

ORPHAN

any *o.* (B)(R)   *Ex 22:22*

ORPHANS

leave you *o.* (A)(B)   *Job 14:18*

OSPRAY

eagle, ossifrage, and *o.*   *Le 11:13;*
   De 14:12
eagle, the fish hawk, the black   *Le 11:13*
eagle (B)

OSSIFRAGE

eagle, *o.*, and ospray   *Le 11:13; De 14:12*
eagle, fish hawk (B)   *Le 11:13*

OSTRICH

the *o.*, the night hawk   *Le 11:16*
(A)(R)(S)   *De 14:16*
wings and feathers unto the   *Job 39:13*
o.
wings of the *o.*   *Job 39:13*
(A)(B)(E)(R)

OSTRICHES

the *o.* (S)   *Job 30:29;*
   Isa 13:12; 34:13; 43:20; Jer 50:39;
   Mic 1:8
abode of *o.* (A)(B)(R)   *Isa 34:13*
cruel, like the *o.* in the   *La 4:3*
wilderness

OTHER

Noah stayed yet *o.* seven days   *Ge 8:10*
that are with thee, and with   *Ge 20:16*
all *o.*
shall be stronger than the *o.*   *Ge 25:23*
people

this is none *o.* but the house of   *Ge 28:17*
God
serve with me yet *o.* seven   *Ge 29:27;*
years   *29:30*
if shalt take *o.* wives besides   *Ge 31:50*
my daughters
the *o.* company that is left   *Ge 32:8*
shall escape
seven *o.* kine came up   *Ge 41:3; 41:19*
he may send away your *o.*   *Ge 43:14*
brother
o. money have we brought   *Ge 43:22*
down to buy food
it was turned again as his *o.*   *Ex 4:7*
flesh
they asked each *o.* of their   *Ex 18:7*
welfare
the *o.* lamb offer thou at even   *Ex 29:41;*
   Nu 28:8
ye shall not make any *o.* like   *Ex 30:32*
that oil
put off his garments, and put   *Le 6:11;*
on *o.* garments   *Eze 42:14; 44:19*
the fat may be used in any *o.*   *Le 7:24*
use
they shall take *o.* stones and   *Le 14:42*
o. mortar
nor take a wife besides the *o.*   *Le 18:18*
in her life
I have separated you from *o.*   *Le 20:24;*
people   *20:26*
the *o.* did set up the   *Nu 10:21*
tabernacle
went not as at *o.* times to seek   *Nu 24:1*
enchantment
gave *o.* names to the cities   *Nu 32:38*
they built
if they be married to any of   *Nu 36:3*
the *o.* tribes
all *o.* cities they took in battle   *Jos 11:19*
the man that came to me the   *J'g 13:10*
o. day
be like any *o.* man; as at *o.*   *J'g 16:17;*
times   *16:20*
they began to kill as at *o.*   *J'g 20:31*
times
the Lord called as at *o.* times   *1Sa 3:10*
David played with his hand   *1Sa 18:10*
as at *o.* times
Saul sat on his seat as at *o.*   *1Sa 20:25*
times by wall
take it, for there is no *o.* save   *1Sa 21:9*
that here
this evil is greater than *o.*   *2Sa 13:16*
thou didst
took counsel, to keep *o.*   *2Ch 30:23*
seven days
Lord saved Hezekiah from   *2Ch 32:22*
hand of all *o.*
the *o.* half of them held both   *Ne 4:16*
spears
for *o.* men have our lands and   *Ne 5:5*
vineyards
and with *o.* things for the   *Es 2:12*
purifying
the flag withereth before any   *Job 8:12*
o. herb
they are taken out of the   *Job 24:24*
way, as all *o.*
wicked not in trouble as *o.*   *Ps 73:5*
men, neither plagued like *o.* men
righteousness and peace kissed   *Ps 85:10*
each *o.*
this hath more rest than the *o.*   *Ec 6:5*
o. lords have had dominion   *Isa 26:13*
over us
shalt have, after thou hast   *Isa 49:20*
lost the *o.*
the land even to the *o.* end of   *Jer 12:12*
the land
contrary is in thee from *o.*   *Eze 16:34*
women
none *o.* can shew it before the   *Da 2:11*
king
the kingdom shall not be left   *Da 2:44*
to *o.* people
rejoice not for joy, as *o.* people   *Ho 9:1*
where is any *o.* to save thee   *Ho 13:10*
going on he saw *o.* two   *M't 4:21*
brethren
on the right cheek, turn to   *M't 5:39*
him the *o.* also
restored whole as *o.*   *M't 12:13;*
   M'k 3:5; Lu 6:10
then he taketh seven *o.*   *M't 12:45;*
spirits   *Lu 11:26*
o. fell into good ground   *M't 13:8;*
   M'k 4:8; Lu 8:8
again he sent *o.* servants   *M't 21:36*
more   *22:4*

let out his vineyard to *o.*   *M't 21:41*
husbandmen
not to leave *o.* undone   *M't 23:23;*
   Lu 11:42
afterward came also *o.* virgins   *M't 25:11*
he traded, and made them *o.*   *M't 25:16*
five talents
the lusts of *o.* things entering   *M'k 4:19*
in
many *o.* things there be   *M'k 7:4;*
they hold   *7:8*
none *o.* commandments is   *M'k 12:31*
greater than these
there is one God, and there   *M'k 12:32*
is none *o.*
must preach kingdom of God   *Lu 4:43*
to *o.* cities
Lord appointed *o.* seventy also,   *Lu 10:1*
and sent
else while the *o.* is yet a great   *Lu 14:32*
way off
I thank thee, that I am not as   *Lu 18:11*
o. men
he went down justified rather   *Lu 18:14*
than the *o.*
o. things blasphemously spake   *Lu 22:65*
they against him
o. men laboured; *o.* sheep I   *Joh 4:38;*
have   *10:16*
if I had not done works none   *Joh 15:24*
o. man did
went out that *o.* disciple,   *Joh 18:16*
spake to her
are many *o.* things which   *Joh 21:25*
Jesus did
they began to speak with *o.*   *Ac 2:4*
tongues
and with many *o.* words did he   *Ac 2:40*
testify
neither is salvation in any *o.*   *Ac 4:12*
none *o.* name whereby we must
speaketh he of himself, or of   *Ac 8:34*
some *o.* man
nor *o.* creature shall be able to   *Ro 8:39*
separate
if there be any *o.*   *Ro 13:9*
commandment, it is
I know not whether I   *1Co 1:16*
baptized any *o.*
o. foundation can no man lay   *1Co 3:11*
than is laid
power to lead about sister   *1Co 9:5*
well as *o.* apostles
in eating every one taketh   *1Co 11:21*
before *o.*
givest thanks, but the *o.* is   *1Co 14:17*
not edified
with men of *o.* tongues and   *1Co 14:21*
o. lips I will speak
let the prophets speak, and   *1Co 14:29*
let the *o.* judge
it may chance of wheat, or   *1Co 15:37*
some *o.* grain
for I mean not that *o.* men be   *2Co 8:13*
eased
not boasting of *o.* men's   *2Co 10:15*
labours
I robbed *o.* churches to do   *2Co 11:8*
you service
I write to them and to all *o.*   *2Co 13:2*
that if I come
o. apostles saw I none, save   *Ga 1:19*
James
the *o.* Jews dissembled likewise   *Ga 2:13*
with him
which in *o.* ages was not made   *Eph 3:5*
known
that ye walk not as *o.*   *Eph 4:17*
Gentiles walk
but the *o.* preach Christ of   *Ph'p 1:17*
love
let each esteem *o.* better than   *Ph'p 2:3*
themselves
if any *o.* thinketh that he   *Ph'p 3:4*
might trust in flesh
with Clement and *o.* my   *Ph'p 4:3*
fellow-labourers
charity toward each *o.*   *2Th 1:3*
aboundeth
charge that they teach no *o.*   *1Ti 1:3*
doctrine
be any *o.* thing contrary to   *1Ti 1:10*
sound doctrine
neither be partaker of *o.*   *1Ti 5:22*
men's sins
neither swear by any *o.* oath,   *Jas 5:12*
but let
as a busybody in *o.* men's   *1Pe 4:15*
matters

they wrest, as they do *o.*   *2Pe 3:16*
scriptures
I will put on you none *o.*   *Re 2:24*
burden
by reason of *o.* the *o.* voices of   *Re 8:13*
the trumpet

OTHERS

and out of the earth shall *o.*   *Job 8:19*
grow
and let *o.* bow down upon   *Job 31:10*
her
and he shall set *o.* in their   *Job 34:24*
stead
he striketh them in the open   *Job 34:26*
sight of *o.*
they die, and leave their   *Ps 49:10*
wealth to *o.*
lest thou give thine honour to *o.*   *Pr 5:9*
that thou thyself likewise has   *Ec 7:22*
cursed *o.*
yet will I gather *o.* to him,   *Isa 56:8*
besides those
their houses shall be turned to   *Jer 6:12*
o.
I will give their wives unto *o.*   *Jer 8:10*
and fields
and they have made *o.* to hope   *Eze 13:6*
and *o.* daubed it with   *Eze 13:10*
untempered mortar
fourth beast which was diverse   *Da 7:19*
from all *o.*
for his kingdom shall be   *Da 11:4*
plucked up for *o.*
there stood two *o.* (S)   *Da 12:5*
what do ye more than *o.*   *M't 5:47*
o. say thou art Jeremias   *M't 16:14;*
   M'k 6:15; 8:28; Lu 9:8, 19
he saw *o.* standing idle in the   *M't 20:3*
market
o. cut down branches from   *M't 21:8;*
trees   *M'k 11:8*
o. smote him with the palms   *M't 26:67*
of their hands
will give vineyard to *o.*   *M'k 12:9;*
   Lu 20:16
saved *o.* himself he cannot   *M'k 15:31;*
   Lu 23:35
and many *o.* which ministered to   *Lu 8:3*
him
or did *o.* tell it thee of me   *Joh 18:34*
if I be not an apostle to *o.* yet   *1Co 9:2*
to you
if *o.* be partakers of this   *1Co 9:12*
power over you
lest when I have preached to   *1Co 9:27*
o. I be castaway
conscience, not thine own,   *1Co 10:29*
but of the *o.*
that by my voice I might   *1Co 14:19*
teach *o.* also
need we, as some *o.* epistles   *2Co 3:1*
of commendation
but by occasion of the   *2Co 8:8*
forwardness of *o.*
we were children of wrath,   *Eph 2:3*
even as *o.*
but every man also on the   *Ph'p 2:4*
things of *o.*
neither of you, nor yet of *o.*   *1Th 2:6*
sought we
that ye sorrow not as *o.* which   *1Th 4:13*
have no hope
let us not sleep as do *o.* but let   *1Th 5:6*
us watch
them that sin rebuke, that *o.*   *1Ti 5:20*
may fear
who shall be able to teach *o.*   *2Ti 2:2*
also
entered every year with the   *Heb 9:25*
blood of *o.*
o. were tortured, not   *Heb 11:35*
accepting deliverance
o. had trial of cruel   *Heb 11:36*
mockings and scourgings
o. save with fear, pulling them   *Jude 23*
out of fire

OTHERWISE

O. I should have wrought   *2Sa 18:13*
O. it shall come to pass, when   *1Ki 1:21*
passover *o.* than it was   *2Ch 30:18*
written
lest *o.* they should rejoice over   *Ps 38:16*
me
o. ye have no reward of your   *M't 6:1*
if *o.* then both the new maketh   *Lu 5:36*
works: *o.* grace is no more   *Ro 11:6*
grace

grace: *o.* work is no more work   *Ro 11:6*
o. thou also shalt be cut off   *Ro 11:22*
if *o.* yet as a fool receive me   *2Co 11:16*
that ye will be none *o.*   *Ga 5:10*
minded
if in any thing ye be *o.*   *Ph'p 3:15*
minded
and they that are *o.* cannot be   *1Ti 5:25*
hid
If any man teach *o.* and   *1Ti 6:3*
consent
o. it is of no strength at all   *Heb 9:17*
while

OTHNI

The sons of Shemaiah; *O.*   *1Ch 26:7*

OTHNIEL

O. the son of Kenaz, the   *Jos 15:17*
brother
And *O.* the son of Kenaz,   *J'g 1:13*
Caleb's
even *O.* the son of Kenaz,   *J'g 3:9*
Caleb's
and *O.* the son of Kenaz died   *J'g 3:11*
And the sons of Kenaz; *O.*   *1Ch 4:13*
and the sons of *O.*; Hathath   *1Ch 4:13*
Heldai the Netophathite, of   *1Ch 27:15*
O.

OUCHES

make them to be set in *o.* of   *Ex 28:11;*
gold   *28:13, 25*
set in sockets or rosettes of   *Ex 28:11;*
gold (A)   *28:13, 25*
set in sockets of gold (B)   *Ex 28:11;*
   28:13, 25
enclosed in settings of gold   *Ex 28:11;*
(E)(R)   *28:13, 25*
wreathen chains to the *o.*   *Ex 28:14*
chains to the settings (A)   *Ex 28:14*
chains to the sockets (B)   *Ex 28:14*
inclosed in *o.* of gold   *Ex 39:6;*
enclosed in settings of gold   *Ex 39:6;*
(A)(E)(R)   *39:13*
set in plaited gold work (B)   *Ex 39:6*
inclosed in *o.* of gold   *Ex 39:13*
set in gold enclosures (B)   *Ex 39:13*
inclosed in inclosings of gold   *Ex 39:13*
in their settings (E)
enclosed in settings of gold   *Ex 39:13*
filigree (R)
they made two *o.* of gold   *Ex 39:16*
made two settings of gold   *Ex 39:16*
filigree (A)
two gold clasps (B)   *Ex 39:16*
made two settings of gold   *Ex 39:16*
(E)
made two settings of gold   *Ex 39:16*
filigree (R)
chains they fastened in the   *Ex 39:18*
two *o.*
chains of gold they put on the   *Ex 39:18*
two settings (A)
chains they fastened in the   *Ex 39:18*
clasps (B)
chains they put on the two   *Ex 39:18*
settings (E)
cords to two settings of   *Ex 39:18*
filigree (R)

OUGHT

hast done deeds unto me that   *Ge 20:9*
o. not to
which thing *o.* not to be done   *Ge 34:7*
he knew not *o.* he had, save   *Ge 39:6*
there is not *o.* left in the sight   *Ge 47:18*
of my
ye shall not diminish *o.* thereof   *Ex 5:8*
yet not *o.* of your work shall be   *Ex 5:11*
shall not minish *o.* from your   *Ex 5:19*
bricks
shalt not carry forth *o.* of the   *Ex 12:46*
flesh
if a man borrow *o.* of his   *Ex 22:14*
neighbour
o. of the flesh of the   *Ex 29:34*
consecrations
things which *o.* not to be done   *Le 4:2; 4:27*
whosoever beareth *o.* of the   *Le 11:25*
carcase
and if *o.* remain until the third   *Le 19:6*
day
if thou sell *o.* unto thy   *Le 25:14*
neighbour

or buyest *o.* of thy neighbour's   *Le 25:14*
hand
man will all redeem *o.* of   *Le 27:31*
his tithes
if *o.* be committed by   *Nu 15:24*
ignorance
the soul that doeth *o.*   *Nu 15:30*
presumptuous
vowed, or uttered *o.* out of her   *Nu 30:6*
lips
neither shall ye diminish *o.*   *De 4:2*
from it
that lendeth *o.* unto his   *De 15:2*
neighbour
neither have I taken away *o.*   *De 26:14*
there
nor given *o.* thereof for the   *De 26:14*
dead
failed not *o.* of any good   *Jos 21:45*
thing
if *o.* but death part thee and   *Ru 1:17*
taken *o.* of any man's hand   *1Sa 12:4*
have not found *o.* in my hand   *1Sa 12:5*
there *o.* missing unto them   *1Sa 25:7*
we will not give them *o.* of   *1Sa 30:22*
the spoil
if I taste bread, or *o.* else   *2Sa 3:35*
no such thing *o.* to be done   *2Sa 13:12*
in Israel
said, Whosoever saith *o.*   *2Sa 14:10*
unto thee
o. that my lord the king hath   *2Sa 14:19*
spoken
times, to know what Israel   *1Ch 12:32*
o. to do
None *o.* to carry the ark of   *1Ch 15:2*
God but
O. ye not to know that the   *2Ch 13:5*
Lord God
o. ye not to walk in the fear of   *Ne 5:9*
God
presents unto him that *o.* to be   *Ps 76:11*
feared
thy brother hath *o.*   *M't 5:23*
against thee
And if any man say *o.* unto   *M't 21:3*
you
these *o.* ye to have done, and   *Mt 23:23*
not
do *o.* for his father or his   *M'k 7:12*
mother
him, he asked him if he saw   *M'k 8:23*
o.
forgive, if ye have *o.* against   *M'k 11:25*
any
prophet, standing where it *o.*   *M'k 13:14*
not
these *o.* ye to have done, and   *Lu 11:42*
not to
in the same hour what we   *Lu 12:12*
o. to say
six days in which men *o.* to   *Lu 13:14*
work
o. not this woman, being   *Lu 13:16*
a daughter
that men *o.* always to pray,   *Lu 18:1*
and not
O. not Christ to have suffered   *Lu 24:26*
the place where men *o.* to   *Joh 4:20*
worship
any man brought him *o.* to eat   *Joh 4:33*
also *o.* to wash one another's   *Joh 13:14*
feet
a law, and by our law he *o.* to   *Joh 19:7*
die
o. of the things which he   *Ac 4:32*
possessed
o. to obey God rather than   *Ac 5:29*
men
o. not to think that the   *Ac 17:29*
Godhead
ye *o.* to be quiet, and to do   *Ac 19:36*
nothing
labouring ye *o.* to support the   *Ac 20:35*
weak
o. not to circumcise their   *Ac 21:21*
children
Who *o.* to have been here   *Ac 24:19*
before
object, if they had *o.* against   *Ac 24:19*
me
seat, where I *o.* to be judged   *Ac 25:10*
that he *o.* not to live any   *Ac 25:24*
longer
I *o.* to do many things contrary   *Ac 26:9*
to
I had *o.* to accuse my nations   *Ac 28:19*
of

what we should pray for as we *Ro 8:26*
o.
more highly than he *o.* to think *Ro 12:3*
strong *o.* to bear the infirmities *Ro 15:1*
of
nothing yet as he *o.* to know *1Co 8:2*
indeed *o.* not to cover his *1Co 11:7*
head
cause *o.* the woman to have *1Co 11:10*
power
from them of whom I *o.* to *2Co 2:3*
rejoice
ye *o.* rather to forgive him, and *2Co 2:7*
for I *o.* to have been *2Co 12:11*
commended
o. not to lay up for the *2Co 12:14*
parents
So *o.* men to love their wives *Eph 5:28*
may speak boldly, as I *o.* to *Eph 6:20*
speak
make it manifest, as I *o.* to *Col 4:4*
speak
how ye *o.* to answer every man *Col 4:6*
how ye *o.* to walk and to *1Th 4:1*
please God
know how ye *o.* to follow us *2Th 3:7*
speaking things which they *o. 1Ti 5:13*
not
teaching things which they *o. Tit 1:11*
not
wronged thee, or oweth thee *o. Ph'm 18*
o. to give the more earnest *Heb 2:1*
heed
by reason hereof he *o.* as for *Heb 5:3*
for the time ye *o.* to be *Heb 5:12*
teachers
these things *o.* not so to be *Jas 3:10*
For that ye *o.* to say, If the *Jas 4:15*
Lord
what manner of persons *o.* ye *2Pe 3:11*
to be
o. himself also so to walk, even *1Jo 2:6*
as
we *o.* to lay down our lives for *1Jo 3:16*
us, we *o.* also to love one *1Jo 4:11*
another
We therefore *o.* to receive such *3Jo 8*

OUGHTEST

knowest what thou *o.* to do *1Ki 2:9*
unto him
o. therefore to have put my *M't 25:27*
money
shall tell thee what thou *o.* to *Ac 10:6*
do
know how thou *o.* to behave *1Ti 3:15*
thyself

OUR

in *o.* image, *o.* likeness *Ge 1:26*
concerning *o.* work, toil of *o. Ge 5:29*
hands
O. father *Ge 19:31;*
19:32, 34; 31:1, 14, 16
o. brethren *Ge 31:32;*
Nu 20:3; De 1:28; 2:8
o. journey *Ge 33:12; De 2:1*
o. daughter *Ge 34:9;*
34:16-17, 21; Ex 10:9
o. sister *Ge 34:14; Ca 8:8; Ro 16:1*
o. brother *Ge 37:27;*
42:21; 43:4; Nu 36:2
o. dreams; *o.* state *Ge 41:12 43:7*
o. kindred *Ge 43:7;*
Ru 2:20; 3:2; Ac 7:19
o. little ones *Ge 43:8; Nu 32:16-17*
o. asses *Ge 43:18; J'g 19:19*
o. sacks *Ge 43:21; 43:22; 44:8*
o. money *Ge 43:21; 43:22; 47:18*
o. hand, hands *Ge 43:21;*
43:22; De 3:3; 21:7
o. fathers *Ge 46:34; Nu 20:15; 36:3-4*
o. lands *Ge 47:18*
47:19; Ne 5:4; Ps 85:12
o. lives *Ge 47:25; Jos 2:10*
o. enemies *Ex 1:10; De 32:31; 1Sa 4:3*
o. God *Ex 3:18;*
5:3, 8; 8:10, 27; 10:25; De 1:6, 19
o. sons, son *Ex 10:9; De 21:20*
o. flocks *Ex 10:9; 32:26; Ne 10:36*
o. herds *Ex 10:9; Ne 10:36*
o. cattle *Ex 10:26;*
17:3 Nu 20:4; 32:16, 26
o. houses *Ex 12:27;*
Nu 32:18; Jos 9:12; Pr 1:13
o. children *Ex 17:3; Nu 14:3; De 29:9*
o. iniquity *Ex 34:9;*
Ps 90:8; 103:10; Isa 53:5

o. sin, sins *Ex 34:9;*
1Sa 12:19; Ps 90:8; 103:10
o. soul *Nu 11:6;*
21:5; 31:50; Ps 33:20; 44:25
o. eyes *Nu 11:6;*
De 6:22; 20:12; Ps 118:23
o. own sight; *o.* charge *Nu 13:33; 31:49*
o. wives *Nu 14:3; 32:26*
o. voice *Nu 20:16; De 26:7; 2Sa 12:18*
o. inheritance *Nu 32:19;*
36:3; Ps 47:4; Eph 1:14
o. heart, hearts *De 1:28;*
Jos 2:11; 1Ki 9:58
o. good; *o.* labour *De 6:24; 26:7*
o. affliction *De 26:7; 2Ch 20:9; Ps 44:24*
o. oppression *De 26:7; Ps 44:24*
o. Rock *De 32:31; 2Sa 22:32; Ps 18:31*
o. life *Jos 2:14;*
9:24; Isa 38:20; Col 3:4
o. business; *o.* name *Jos 2:14;*
2:20; 7:9
o. head *Jos 2:19; J'g 11:8; Ezr 9:6*
o. adversaries *Jos 5:13; Ne 4:11*
o. country *Jos 9:11*
o. bread *Jos 9:12;*
Isa 4:1
o. provision; *o.* garments *Jos 9:12;*
9:13
o. shoes; *o.* generations *Jos 9:13;*
22:27-28
o. peace offerings *Jos 22:27*
o. father's house; *o.* captain *J'g 11:2;*
11:6; 2Ch 13:12
o. way *J'g 18:5;*
1Sa 9:6, 8
o. sakes *J'g 21:22; 1Co 9:10*
o. people *1Sa 5:10;*
5:11; 2Sa 10:12
o. king *1Sa 8:20; Ps 47:6*
o. vessels *1Sa 9:7*
o. lord *1Sa 9:7; 1Ki 1:11, 43, 47*
o. servants; *o.* family *1Sa 17:9; 20:29*
o. part *1Sa 23:20; M'k 9:40*
o. master *1Sa 25:14; 25:17*
o. ears *2Sa 7:22;*
1Ch 17:20; Job 28:25
o. hearing *2Sa 18:12*
o. yoke *1Ki 12:4; 12:10; 2Ch 10:4, 10*
o. loins *1Ki 20:31; Ps 66:11*
o. peace *2Ki 7:9; Eph 2:14*
o. heads *1Ch 12:19; Ps 66:12*
o. salvation *1Ch 16:35;*
Ps 68:19; 79:9; 85:4; 95:1; Ro 13:11
o. substance *Ezr 8:21; Job 22:20*
o. king *Ezr 9:7; Ne 9:32, 34; Isa 33:22*
o. priests *Ezr 9:7; Ne 9:32, 34*
o. trespasses *Ezr 9:15*
o. rulers *Ezr 10:14; Isa 3:6; Lu 24:20*
o. prayer *Ne 4:9; La 3:44; Da 9:17*
o. princes *Ne 9:32;*
9:34; Da 9:6, 8
o. prophets *Ne 9:32*
o. ground; *o.* dough; *o. Ne 10:35;*
offerings *10:37*
o. days *Job 8:9;*
Ps 90:9, 14; La 4:18; 5:21
o. rest; *o.* speech *Job 17:16; 37:19*
o. tongue *Ps 12:4; 126:2*
o. steps *Ps 17:11; 44:10*
o. banners; *o.* armies *Ps 20:5;*
44:9; 60:10
o. neighbours *Ps 44:13; 79:4, 12; 80:6*
o. belly; *o.* help *Ps 44:25;*
124:8
o. refuge and strength *Ps 46:1; 46:7, 11*
o. feet *Ps 47:3; 66:9; 122:2; Lu 1:79*
o. guide; *o.* shield *Ps 48:14; 59:11; 84:9*
o. signs; *o.* sight *Ps 74:9; 79:10*
o. solemn feast; *o.* strength *Ps 81:1;*
81:3
o. horn *Ps 89:17*
o. defence; *o.* dwelling place *Ps 89:18;*
90:1
o. years; *o.* maker *Ps 90:9; 90:10; 95:6*
o. transgressions *Ps 103:12; Isa 59:12*
o. frame; *o.* hosts *Ps 103:14; 108:11*
o. side; *o.* mouth *Ps 124:1;*
124:2; 126:2; Jer 44:17
o. captivity *Ps 126:4; Eze 33:21; 40:1*
o. low estate; *o.* harps *Ps 136:23; 137:2*
o. bones, *o.* hope *Ps 141:7; Eze 37:11*
o. garners; *o.* sheep *Ps 144:13*
o. oxen *Ps 144:13; 144:14*
o. streets *Ps 144:13;*
144:14; Jer 4:18; Lu 13:26
o. fill of love *Pr 7:18*
o. bed; *o.* rafters *Ca 1:16; 1:17*
o. walls *Ca 2:9*
o. vines; *o.* gates *Ca 2:15; 7:13*

o. reproach *Isa 4:1; La 5:1*
o. works *Isa 26:12*
o. expectation *Isa 26:6*
o. solemnities *Isa 33:20*
o. judge; *o.* judges *Isa 33:22; Da 9:12*
o. lawgiver *Isa 33:22*
o. redeemer *Isa 47:4; 63:16*
o. griefs *Isa 53:4*
o. peace *Isa 53:5; Eph 2:14*
o. unrighteousness *Isa 64:6; Da 9:18*
o. pleasant things *Isa 64:11*
o. shame; *o.* confusion; *o. Jer 3:25*
youth
o. eyelids *Jer 9:18*
o. windows; *o.* palaces *Jer 9:21;*
Mic 5:5
o. last end *Jer 12:4; La 4:18*
o. backslidings; *o.* wickedness *Jer 14:7;*
14:20
o. sanctuary; *o.* own *Jer 17:12;*
devices *18:12*
O. revenge; *o.* habitations *Jer 20:10;*
21:13
o. supplication; *o.* vows *Jer 42:2; 44:25*
o. righteousness *Jer 51:10*
o. faces *Jer 51:51*
o. ways; *o.* doings *La 3:40; Zec 1:6*
o. persecutors; *o.* nostrils *La 4:19; 4:20*
o. mothers; *o.* necks *La 5:3; 5:5*
o. skin; *o.* dance *La 5:10;*
5:15
o. countenances; *o. Da 1:13*
supplications
o. desolations *Da 9:18*
o. lips; *o.* gods *Ho 14:2; 14:3*
o. fields; *o.* borders *Mic 2:4;*
5:6
O. Father; *o.* debts; *o.* debtors *M't 6:9;*
6:12
o. infirmities, *o.* sickness *M't 8:17;*
Ro 8:26
O. lamps; *o.* nation *M't 25:8; Lu 7:5*
o. deeds; *o.* company *Lu 23:41; 24:22*
o. duty *Lu 17:10*
o. witness; *o.* law *Joh 3:11;*
7:51; 19:7; 24:6
o. friend; *o.* abode *Joh 11:11; 14:23*
o. own tongue *Ac 2:8; 2:11*
o. Lord Jesus Christ *Ac 15:26;*
20:21; Ro 1:3; 6:23
o. city; *o.* being *Ac 16:20; 17:28*
o. wealth *Ac 19:25*
o. craft; *o.* leave; *o.* course *Ac 19:27;*
21:6-7
o. carriages; *o.* religion *Ac 21:15; 26:5*
o. unrighteousness; *o. Ro 3:5;*
justification *4:25*
o. old man; *o.* members *Ro 6:6; 7:5*
o. spirit; *o.* body *Ro 8:16; 8:23*
o. report *Ro 10:16; Isa 53:1*
o. ministering; *o.* learning *Ro 12:7;*
15:4
o. helper *Ro 16:9*
o. glory; *o.* passover *1Co 2:7; 5:7*
o. admonition *1Co 10:11*
o. uncomly parts; *o.* comely *1Co 12:23;*
parts *12:24*
o. preaching *1Co 15:14*
o. tribulation; *o.* consolation *2Co 1:4;*
1:5
o. hope; *o.* trouble *2Co 1:7; 1:8*
o. rejoicing; *o.* conscience; *o. 2Co 1:12*
conversation
o. word; *o.* epistle *2Co 1:18; 3:2*
o. sufficiency *2Co 3:5*
o. gospel; *o.* mortal flesh *2Co 4:3; 4:11*
o. outward man *2Co 4:16*
o. light affliction; *o.* earthly *2Co 4:17;*
house *5:1-2*
o. flesh; *o.* boasting *2Co 7:5;*
7:14; 8:24; 9:3
o. warfare; *o.* authority *2Co 10:4; 10:8*
o. measure *2Co 10:13; 10:14-15*
o. liberty; *o.* schoolmaster *Ga 2:4;*
3:24
o. conversation *Eph 2:3; Ph'p 3:20*
o. affairs *Eph 6:22*
o. vile body *Ph'p 3:21*
o. prayers; *o.* exhortation *1Th 1:3; 2:3*
o. labour and travail *1Th 2:9; 3:5*
o. testimony *2Th 1:10*
o. Saviour *1Ti 2:3;*
2Ti 1:10; Tit 2:10, 13; 3:4, 6
o. profession *Heb 3:1;*
4:14
o. confidence; *o.* faith *Heb 3:14; 10:23;*
12:2
o. profit *Heb 12:10*
o. love made perfect *1Jo 4:17*

o. joy may be full   2Jo 12
o. record is true   3Jo 12
o. blood on them that dwell   Re 6:10

OURS

herdmen, saying, The water is   Ge 26:20
o.
hath taken from our father,   Ge 31:16
that is o.
and every beast of theirs be o.   Ge 34:23
on this side Jordan may be o.   Nu 32:32
Know ye that Ramoth in   1Ki 22:3
Gilead is o.
even the ancient high places   Eze 36:2
are o.
and the inheritance shall be o.   M'k 12:7
that the inheritance may be o.   Lu 20:14
Christ our Lord, both theirs   1Co 1:2
and o.
as ye also are o. in the day of   2Co 1:14
let o. also learn to maintain   Tit 3:14
good
and not for o. only, but also for   1Jo 2:2

OURSELVES

to bow down o. to thee to the   Ge 37:10
earth
we speak? or how shall we   Ge 44:16
clear o.
we o. will go ready armed   Nu 32:17
before
we took cattle for a prey unto   De 2:35
o.
of the cities, we took for a prey   De 3:7
to o.
and we will discover o. unto   1Sa 14:8
them
and let us behave o.   1Ch 19:13
valiantly for the
but we o. together will   Ezr 4:3
build unto
we might afflict o. before   Ezr 8:21
our God
to charge o. yearly with the   Ne 10:32
third
let us know among o. what is   Job 34:4
good
for o. what is right; among o.   Job 34:4
what is good (S)
Let us take to o. the houses of   Ps 83:12
God
that hath made us, and not we   Ps 100:3
o.
morning; let us solace o. with   Pr 7:18
loves
and under falsehood have we   Isa 28:15
hid o.
and we will fill o. with strong   Isa 56:12
drink
Come, and let us join o. to the   Jer 50:5
Lord
we o. have heard of his own   Lu 22:71
mouth
for we have heard him o. and   Joh 4:42
know
will give o. continually to prayer   Ac 6:4
have bound o. under a great   Ac 23:14
curse
but o. also which have the first   Ro 8:23
fruits
of the Spirits, even we o. groan   Ro 8:23
groan with o. waiting for the   Ro 8:23
of the weak, and not to please   Ro 15:1
o.
For if we would judge o. we   1Co 11:31
should
we o. are comforted of God   2Co 1:4
we had the sentence of death   2Co 1:9
in o.
that we should not trust in o.   2Co 1:9
have conducted o. (A)   2Co 1:12
Do we begin again to   2Co 3:1
commend o.
that we are sufficient of o. to   2Co 3:5
think
to think any thing as of o.; but   2Co 3:5
commending o. to every man's   2Co 4:2
For we preach not o. but   2Co 4:5
Christ
o. your servants for Jesus'   2Co 4:5
sake
we commend not o. again   2Co 5:12
unto you
whether we be beside o. it is   2Co 5:13
to God
approving o. as the ministers of   2Co 6:4
let us cleanse o. from all   2Co 7:1
filthiness

we dare not make o. of   2Co 10:12
the number
or compare o. with some   2Co 10:12
that
stretch not o. beyond our   2Co 10:14
measure
think ye that we excuse o.   2Co 12:19
unto you
if we o. also are found   Ga 2:17
sinners, is
we behaved o. among you   1Th 2:10
that believe
we o. glory in you in the   2Th 1:4
churches
behaved not o. disorderly   2Th 3:7
among you
to make o. an ensample unto   2Th 3:9
you
we o. also were sometimes   Tit 3:3
foolish
the assembling of o. together   Heb 10:25
we deceive o. and the truth is   1Jo 1:8

OUT

o. of the ground made to grow   Ge 2:9
came o. of the loins of Jacob   Ex 1:5
o. of the tabernacle   Le 1:1
o. of Egypt   Nu 11:20; De 6:12
o. of the house of bondage   De 7:8
law not depart o. of thy mouth   Jos 1:8
angel departed o. of his sight   J'g 7:21
seek o. a man who is cunning   1Sa 16:16
came a man of God o. of   1Ki 13:1
Judah
naked came I o. of mother's   Job 1:20
womb
neither doth trouble spring o.   Job 5:6
of ground
O. of the south cometh   Job 37:9
whirlwind
Lord answered o. of   Job 38:1;
whirlwind   40:6
O. of mouth of babes and   Ps 8:2
sucklings
o. of ivory palaces   Ps 45:8
eyes stand o. with fatness   Ps 73:7
pour o. my spirit   Pr 1:23; Ac 2:17-18
presses burst o. with new wine   Pr 3:10
o. of it are the issues of life   Pr 4:23
o. of Zion shall go forth the law   Isa 2:3
cut off o. of land of living   Isa 53:8
root o. and pull down   Jer 1:10
waters issued o. from temple   Eze 47:1
stone cut o. without hands   Da 2:34;
                            2:45
four beasts rise o. of the earth   Da 7:17
wear o. saints of most High   Da 7:25
hidden things sought o. (S)   Ob 6
O. of Egypt have I called my   M't 1:15
Son
lightning cometh o. of the   M't 24:27
east
I will in no wise cast o.   Joh 6:37
o. of his belly rivers of living   Joh 7:38
water
neither shall any man pluck   Joh 10:28;
o. of my hand; o. of Father's   10:29
hand
gavest me o. of the world   Joh 17:6
that sins may be blotted o.   Ac 3:19
poured o. gift of Holy Ghost   Ac 10:45
take o. of Gentiles a people   Ac 15:14
for his name
time to awake o. of sleep   Ro 13:11
Purge o. the old leaven   1Co 5:7
as of one born o. of due time   1Co 15:8
commanded light to shine o. of   2Co 4:6
darkness
come o. from among them   2Co 6:17
work o. own salvation   Ph'p 2:12
Blotting o. handwriting of   Col 2:14
ordinances
o. of darkness into marvelous   1Pe 2:9
light
deliver godly o. of temptation   2Pe 2:9
perfect love castest o. fear   1Jo 4:18
remove candlestick o. of place   Re 2:5
not blot name o. of book of life   Re 3:5
proceeding o. of the throne of   Re 22:1
God

OUTCAST

they called thee an O. saying   Jer 30:17

OUTCASTS

gathereth together the o. of   Ps 147:2
Israel

gathering together the exiles   Ps 147:2
(A)(B)
and shall assemble the o. of   Isa 11:12
Israel
hide the o.; bewray not him   Isa 16:3
that
hide the hunted (B)   Isa 16:3
Let mine o. dwell with thee,   Isa 16:4
Moab
and the o. in the land of   Isa 27:13
Egypt
which gathereth the o. of   Isa 56:8
Israel
gathers the exiled of Israel (B)   Isa 56:8
the o. of Elam shall not come   Jer 49:36

OUTCRY

no o. in our streets (A)(E)   Ps 144:14

OUTER

o. court (S)   Es 6:4;
           Eze 40:17, 20, 34; 44:1
was heard even to the o. court   Eze 10:5
on the o. side (S)   Eze 40:19
the o. court (S)   Eze 40:31;
40:37; 42:1, 3, 7-8, 14; 44:19; 46:20-21;
                      47:2
shall be cast out into o.   M't 8:12
darkness
and cast him into o. darkness   M't 22:13
servant into o. darkness   M't 25:30
our o. man is decaying   2Co 4:16
(A)(B)(E)(N)(P)

OUTERMOST

his servant to the o. part (S)   J'g 7:11

OUTFLOW

o. of grape juice   Ex 22:29
(A)(E)(R)(S)

OUTGOINGS

and the o. of it were at the sea   Jos 17:9
and the o. of it shall be thine   Jos 17:18
o. of the border were at the   Jos 18:19
north
the o. thereof are in the   Jos 19:14
valley of
o. of their border were at   Jos 19:22
Jordan
the o. thereof are at the sea   Jos 19:29
from
and the o. thereof were at   Jos 19:33
Jordan
the o. of the morning and   Ps 65:8
evening

OUTGROWTH

o. of wickedness (A)(B)   Jas 1:21

OUTLANDISH

him did o. women cause to   Ne 13:26
sin
strange women caused him to   Ne 13:26
sin (A)
caused to sin by foreign wives   Ne 13:26
(B)(E)(R)
divers o. teachings (N)   Heb 13:9

OUTLAW

o. you and insult you (N)   Lu 6:22

OUTLAWS

counted with o. (A)(B)(N)   M'k 15:28;
                     Lu 23:37
counted among o. (N)   Lu 22:37

OUTLINE

our o. of sound teaching (N)   2Ti 1:13

OUTLIVED

elders that o. Joshua (S)   Jos 24:31
the elders that o. Joshua   J'g 2:7

OUTLOOK

change your whole o. (P)   M't 18:3

OUTMOST

curtain that is *o*. in the   *Ex 26:10*
coupling
outmost (S)   *Ex 36:11; 36:17; 1Ki 6:24*
o. coast of the salt sea   *Nu 34:3*
eastward
out unto the *o*. parts of heaven   *De 30:4*
in the *o*. fruitful branches   *Isa 17:6*
thereof

OUTRAGE

persecution and *o*. (N)   *1Ti 1:13*

OUTRAGED

if brother is *o*. (N)   *Ro 14:15*

OUTRAGEOUS

Wrath is cruel, and anger is *o*.   *Pr 27:4*
anger is an overwhelming flood   *Pr 27:4*
(A)(B)(E)(R)

OUTRAGING

o. the Holy Spirit   *Heb 10:29*
(A)(B)(R)

OUTRAN

and *o*. Cushi (S)   *2Sa 18:23*

OUTRUN

the other disciple did *o*. Peter   *Joh 20:4*

OUTSIDE

outside (S)   *Ge 9:22*
19:16; 24:11, 31; Ex 26:35; 27:21; 29:14;
33:7; 40:22; Le 4:12, 21; 6:11; 8:17;
9:11; 13:46; 14:40, 41; 16:27; Nu 5:3, 4;
15:35, 36; 19:3, 9; 31:13, 19; 35:5, 26,
27; De 23:12; Jos 6:23; 1Ki 6:6; 8:8;
Ezr 10:13; Ne 13:20; Pr 1:20; 7:12;
22:13; 24:27; Ca 8:1; Isa 33:7; Jer 9:21;
21:4; Eze 40:40, 44; 41:9, 17, 25;
42:7; 43:21; 46:2; 47:2; M't 12:46, 47;
26:69; M'k 3:31, 32; 4:11; 7:18; 11:4;
Lu 1:10; 8:20; 13:25; Joh 18:16; 20:11;
Ac 5:23; 1Co 5:12, 13; 6:18; Col 4:5;
1Th 4:12; 1Ti 3:7; Heb 13:11, 12, 13;
Re 11:2; 14:20; 22:15
unto the *o*. of the armed men   *J'g 7:11*
when I come to the *o*. of the   *J'g 7:17*
camp
came unto the *o*. of the camp   *J'g 7:19*
in the
on the *o*. toward the great   *1Ki 7:9*
court
behold a wall on the *o*. of the   *Eze 40:5*
house
ye make clean the *o*. of the   *M't 23:25;*
cup   *Lu 11:39*
the *o*. of them may be clean   *M't 23:26*
also
God judges those *o*. (R)   *1Co 5:13*

OUTSIDER

outsider (B)(R)   *Ex 29:33;*
          30:33; Le 22:12-13
outsider (A)   *Ex 30:33;*
Le 22:10, 12; Nu 16:40; Pr 5:20; 11:15
married unto an *o*. (S)   *Le 22:12*
living as an *o*. (B)   *J'g 19:1*
an *o*. (R)   *1Co 14:16; 14:23-24*

OUTSIDERS

outsiders (B)   *Ge 31:15; Pr 18:44*
sell her to *o*. (B)(R)   *Ex 21:8*
o., exiles, migrants (A)(P)   *Eph 2:19*
command respect of *o*. (N)   *1Th 4:12*

OUTSTRETCHED

with an *o*. arm (S)   *Ex 6:6;*
De 4:34; 5:15; 7:19; 9:29; 11:2;
1Ki 8:42; 2Ki 17:36; 2Ch 6:32;
Ps 136:12; Jer 32:17, 21; Eze 20:33-34
a mighty hand, and with an *o*.   *De 26:8*
arm
fight against you with an *o*.   *Jer 21:5*
hand
by my great power by my *o*.   *Jer 27:5*
arm

OUTWARD

from the wall of the city and *o*.   *Nu 35:4*
man looketh on the *o*.   *1Sa 16:7*
appearance
for the *o*. business over   *1Ch 26:29*
Israel
had the oversight of the *o*.   *Ne 11:16*
business
Haman was come into the *o*.   *Es 6:4*
court
despise their *o*. show (A)   *Ps 73:20*
brought he me into the *o*.   *Eze 40:17*
court
the gate of the *o*. court that   *Eze 40:20*
looked
arches were toward the *o*.   *Eze 40:34*
court
way of the gate of the *o*.   *Eze 44:1*
sanctuary
which indeed appear   *M't 23:27*
beautiful *o*.
which is *o*. in the flesh   *Ro 2:28*
though our *o*. man perish, yet   *2Co 4:16*
on things after the *o*.   *2Co 10:7*
appearance
o. adorning of plaiting the hair   *1Pe 3:3*

OUTWARDLY

so ye also *o*. appear righteous   *M't 23:28*
o. seem just (A)(B)   *M't 23:28*
is not a Jew, which is one *o*.   *Ro 2:28*

OUTWENT

out of all cities, and *o*. them   *M'k 6:33*

OUTWITTED

Jacob *o*. Laban (R)   *Ge 31:20*
o. by the wise men (B)   *M't 2:16*

OVEN

a smoking *o*. (A)(B)   *Ge 15:17*
of a meat offering baken in the   *Le 2:4*
o.
offering that is baken in the *o*.   *Le 7:9*
whether it be *o*. or ranges for   *Le 11:35*
pots
shall bake your bread in one   *Le 26:26*
o.
Thou shalt make them as a   *Ps 21:9*
fiery *o*.
skin was black like an *o*.   *La 5:10*
because
as an *o*. heated by the baker   *Ho 7:4*
made ready their heart like an   *Ho 7:6*
o.
They are all hot as an *o*. and   *Ho 7:7*
have
cometh, that shall burn as an *o*.   *Mal 4:1*
and to-morrow is cast into the   *M't 6:30;*
o.   *Lu 12:28*

OVENS

and into thine *o*. and into thy   *Ex 8:3*

OVER

first red, all *o*. like an hairy   *Ge 25:25*
garment
be lord *o*. thy brethren, let   *Ge 27:29*
them bow to thee
Pharaoh said, Thou shalt be   *Ge 41:40*
o. my house
gathered much had nothing   *Ex 16:18;*
o.   *2Co 8:15*
what remaineth *o*. lay up   *Ex 16:23*
until the morning
the mercyseat, *o*. the   *Ex 30:6;*
testimony   *Heb 9:5*
the cherubims covered *o*. the   *Ex 37:9*
mercy seat
the cloud was taken up from   *Ex 40:36*
o. the tabernacle
one be killed *o*. running water   *Le 14:5;*
           14:6, 50
thou shalt appoint Levites *o*.   *Nu 1:50*
tabernacle
o. and above them that were   *Nu 3:49*
redeemed
blow with trumpets *o*. the   *Nu 10:10*
burnt offerings
let the Lord set a man *o*. the   *Nu 27:16*
congregation
dominion *o*. the nobles, *o*. the   *J'g 5:13*
mighty

and go to be promoted *o*. the   *J'g 9:9;*
trees   *11:13*
o. Saul and Jonathan his son   *2Sa 1:17;*
           1:24
he made Ish-bosheth king *o*.   *2Sa 2:9*
Gilead, *o*. Ashurites, *o*. Jezreel,
o. Ephraim, and *o*. Benjamin
Edom made a king *o*.   *2Ki 8:20*
themselves
o. and above all I have   *1Ch 29:3*
prepared
our iniquities are increased *o*.   *Ezr 9:6*
our heads
dost thou not watch *o*. my sin   *Job 14:16*
he is a king *o*. the children of   *Job 41:34*
pride
anointest my head, my cup   *Ps 23:5*
runneth *o*.
deliver me not *o*. to will of   *Ps 27:12*
enemies
but he hath not given me *o*.   *Ps 118:18*
to death
his tender mercies are *o*. all   *Ps 145:9*
his works
winter is past, rain is *o*. and   *Ca 2:11*
gone
set thee *o*. the nations and *o*.   *Jer 1:10*
kingdoms
he setteth up *o*. it the basest of   *Da 4:17*
men
king thought to set him *o*. the   *Da 6:3*
whole realm
people shall mourn *o*. it and   *Ho 10:5*
priest
and the day shall be dark *o*.   *Mic 3:6*
them
I will make thee ruler *o*.   *M't 25:21;*
many   *25:23*
measure shaken together, and   *Lu 6:38*
running *o*.
more joy *o*. one sinner that   *Lu 15:7;*
repenteth   *15:10*
we will not have this man to   *Lu 19:14*
reign *o*. us
been faithful, have authority   *Lu 19:17*
o. ten cities
come near, he beheld city,   *Lu 19:41*
and wept *o*. it
we may appoint *o*. this business   *Ac 6:3*
that the law hath dominion *o*. a   *Ro 7:1*
man
hath not the potter power *o*.   *Ro 9:21*
the clay
given themselves *o*. to   *Eph 4:19*
lasciviousness
not usurp authority *o*. the man   *1Ti 2:12*
eyes of the Lord are *o*.   *1Pe 3:12*
the righteous
to him will I give power *o*.   *Re 2:26*
the nations

OVER *AGAINST*

candlestick *o*. *against* table   *Ex 26:35;*
          40:24
lamps give light *o*. *against*   *Nu 8:2;*
candlestick   *8:3*
fetch compass behind them *o*.   *2Sa 5:23;*
against mulberry trees   *1Ch 14:14*
they pitched one *o*. *against*   *1Ki 20:29*
the other
appoint every one to be *o*.   *Ne 7:3*
against house
God hath set one *o*. *against* the   *Ec 7:14*
other
the line shall yet go forth *o*.   *Jer 31:39*
against it
go into village *o*. *against* you   *M't 21:2;*
       M'k 11:2; Lu 19:30
and Mary sitting *o*. *against*   *M't 27:61*
the sepulchre

OVERBEARING

not *o*., short-tempered (N)   *Tit 1:7*

OVERBURDENED

hearts *o*. and depressed (A)   *Lu 21:34*

OVERCAME

darkness *o*. it not (S)   *Joh 1:5*
o. them, and prevailed against   *Ac 19:16*
mastering the two of them   *Ac 19:16*
(A)
overpowered them all   *Ac 19:16*
(B)(N)(P)
mastered both of them   *Ac 19:16*
(E)(R)

o. kingdoms (B)   *Heb 11:33*
even as I also *o.* and am set   *Re 3:21*
down
I also conquered (B)(R)   *Re 3:21*
I myself was victorious (N)   *Re 3:21*
I myself have won the victory   *Re 3:21*
(P)
o. him by the blood of the   *Re 12:11*
Lamb
they have conquered him   *Re 12:11*
(B)(N)(P)(R)

OVERCAST

the sky is red and *o.* (S)   *M't 16:3*

OVERCHARGE

in part: that I may not *o.*   *2Co 2:5*
you all

OVERCHARGED

your hearts be *o.* with   *Lu 21:34*
surfeiting
hearts be overburdened and   *Lu 21:34*
depressed (A)
hearts be overloaded (B)   *Lu 21:34*
do not let your minds be dull   *Lu 21:34*
(N)
see that your minds are never   *Lu 21:34*
clouded (P)
hearts be weighed down (R)   *Lu 21:34*

OVERCOAT

have your *o.* also (P)   *M't 5:40*

OVERCOME

Gad, a troop shall *o.* him   *Ge 49:19*
but he shall *o.* at the last   *Ge 49:19*
of them that cry for being *o.*   *Ex 32:18*
it; for we are well able to *o.* it   *Nu 13:30*
I shall be able to *o.* them   *Nu 22:11*
o. with fear (B)   *J'g 20:41*
Ahaz, but could not *o.* him   *2Ki 16:5*
o. cities (B)   *2Ch 14:14*
from me, for they have *o.* me   *Ca 6:5*
of them that are *o.* with wine   *Isa 28:1*
they will not *o.* you (B)   *Jer 1:19*
we shall *o.* him (B)(R)   *Jer 20:10*
like a man whom wine hath *o.*   *Jer 23:9*
o. with fear (N)   *Lu 1:12*
shall come upon him, and *o.*   *Lu 11:22*
him
has not *o.* it (R)   *Joh 1:5*
of good cheer; I have *o.* the   *Joh 16:33*
world
mightest *o.* when thou art   *Re 3:4*
judged
Be not *o.* of evil   *Re 12:21*
but *o.* evil with good   *Re 12:21*
for of whom a man is *o.* of   *2Pe 2:19*
again entangled therein, and   *2Pe 2:20*
o.
because ye have *o.* the wicked   *1Jo 2:13;*
one   *2:14*
little children, and have *o.* them   *1Jo 4:4*
has *o.* and conquered (A)(E)   *Re 5:5*
and shall *o.* them, and kill   *Re 11:7*
them
with the saints, and to *o.* them   *Re 13:7*
Lamb, and the Lamb shall *o.*   *Re 17:14*
them

OVERCOMETH

is born of God *o.* the world   *1Jo 5:4*
is the victory that *o.* the world   *1Jo 5:4*
Who is he that *o.* the world   *1Jo 5:5*
To him that *o.* will give to eat   *Re 2:7;*
of   *2:17*
He that *o.* shall not be hurt of   *Re 2:11*
He that *o.* and keepeth my   *Re 2:26*
works
He that *o.* the same shall be   *Re 3:5*
Him that *o.* will I make a   *Re 3:12*
pillar in
To him that *o.* will I grant to   *Re 3:21*
sit
He that *o.* shall inherit all   *Re 21:7*
things

OVERDRIVE

if men should *o.* them one day   *Ge 33:13*

OVERFLOW

water of the Red sea to *o.*   *De 11:4*
them
waters, where the floods *o.* me   *Ps 69:2*
Let not the waterflood *o.* me   *Ps 69:15*
he shall *o.* and go over, he shall   *Isa 8:8*
decreed shall *o.* with   *Isa 10:22*
righteousness
waters shall *o.* the hiding   *Isa 28:17*
places
the rivers, they shall not *o.*   *Isa 43:2*
thee
shall *o.* the land, and all that is   *Jer 47:2*
one shall certainly come, and   *Da 11:10*
o.
destroy him, and his army   *Da 11:26*
shall *o.*
and shall *o.* and pass over   *Da 11:40*
the fats shall *o.* with wine and   *Joe 2:24*
for the press is full, the fats *o.*   *Joe 3:13*
did grace (A)(B)(P)   *Ro 5:15; 5:20*
o. with thanksgiving   *Col 2:7*
(A)(B)(N)(P)
o. with love (A)(N)   *1Th 3:12*

OVERFLOWED

gushed out, and the streams *o.*   *Ps 78:20*
was, being *o.* with water,   *2Pe 3:6*
perished

OVERFLOWETH

Jordan *o.* all his banks all the   *Jos 3:15*
heart *o.* with (E)   *Ps 45:1*

OVERFLOWING

He bindeth the floods from *o.*   *Job 28:11*
watercourse for the *o.* of   *Job 38:25*
waters
My heart is *o.* (S)   *Ps 45:1*
a flood of mighty waters *o.*   *Isa 28:2*
shall
when the *o.* scourge shall   *Isa 28:15;*
pass   *28:18*
And his breath, as an *o.*   *Isa 30:28*
stream
and shall be an *o.* flood, and   *Jer 47:2*
shall
there shall be an *o.* shower   *Eze 13:11*
be an *o.* shower in mine   *Eze 13:13*
anger
an *o.* rain, and great   *Eze 38:22*
hailstones
with an *o.* flood (R)   *Na 1:8*
the *o.* of the water passed by   *Hab 3:10*
increasing, *o.* love (P)   *1Th 3:12*
o. of wickedness (E)   *Jas 1:21*

OVERFLOWN

when it had *o.* all his   *1Ch 12:15*
banks; and
foundation was *o.* with a   *Job 22:16*
flood
shall they be *o.* from before   *Da 11:22*
him

OVERFLOWS

heart *o.* with (A)(B)(R)   *Ps 45:1*
cup of suffering *o.* (N)   *2Co 1:5*

OVERGROWN

members *o.* or shrunk (B)   *Le 22:23*

OVERLAID

of shittim wood *o.* with gold   *Ex 26:32*
he *o.* the boards with gold   *Ex 36:34*
the bars, and *o.* the bars with   *Ex 36:34*
gold
wood, and *o.* them with gold   *Ex 36:36; 37:4; 28*
and he *o.* their chapiters and   *Ex 36:38*
their
And he *o.* it with pure gold   *Ex 37:2*
within
he *o.* it with pure gold, and   *Ex 37:11*
made
o. them with gold, to bear the   *Ex 37:15*
table
And he *o.* it with pure gold,   *Ex 37:26*
both
the same: and he *o.* it with   *Ex 38:2*
brass
wood, and *o.* them with brass   *Ex 38:6*

o. their chapiters, and filleted   *Ex 38:28*
them
in the night; because she *o.*   *1Ki 3:19*
it
and he *o.* it with pure gold   *1Ki 6:20*
Solomon *o.* the house within   *1Ki 6:21*
the oracle; and he *o.* it   *1Ki 6:21*
with gold
the whole house he *o.* with   *1Ki 6:22*
gold
altar, by the oracle he *o.*   *1Ki 6:22*
with gold
And he *o.* the cherubims   *1Ki 6:28*
with gold
floor of the house he *o.* with   *1Ki 6:30*
gold
flowers, and *o.* them with gold   *1Ki 6:32*
o. with gold (R)   *1Ki 6:35*
ivory, and *o.* it with the best   *1Ki 10:18*
gold
Hezekiah king of Judah had   *2Ki 18:16*
o.
and he *o.* it within with pure   *2Ch 3:4*
gold
which he *o.* with fine gold,   *2Ch 3:5*
and set
He *o.* also the house, the   *2Ch 3:7*
beams
cubits: and he *o.* it with fine   *2Ch 3:8*
gold
o. the upper chambers with   *2Ch 3:9*
gold
work, and *o.* them with gold   *2Ch 3:10*
and *o.* the doors of them with   *2Ch 4:9*
brass
of ivory, and *o.* it with pure   *2Ch 9:17*
gold
as bright ivory *o.* with   *Ca 5:14*
sapphires
covenant *o.* round about with   *Heb 9:4*
gold

OVERLAY

thou shalt *o.* it with pure gold   *Ex 25:11*
within and without shalt thou   *Ex 25:11; 25:24*
o. it
wood and *o.* them with   *Ex 25:13; 25:28; 30:5*
gold
thou shalt *o.* the boards with   *Ex 26:29*
gold
thou shalt *o.* the bars with gold   *Ex 26:29*
o. them with gold and their   *Ex 26:37*
hooks
and thou shalt *o.* it with brass   *Ex 27:2*
wood, and *o.* them with brass   *Ex 27:6*
shalt *o.* it with pure gold, the   *Ex 30:3*
top
to *o.* the walls of the houses   *1Ch 29:4*

OVERLAYING

the *o.* of their chapiters of   *Ex 38:17*
silver
the *o.* of their chapiters and   *Ex 38:19*
their

OVERLIVED

the elders that *o.* Joshua   *Jos 24:31*

OVERLOADED

hearts be *o.* (B)   *Lu 21:34*

OVERLOOKED

ignorance God *o.*   *Ac 17:30*
(E)(N)(P)(R)
o. sins of the past (N)   *Ro 3:25*

OVERMUCH

be swallowed up with *o.*   *2Co 2:7*
sorrow

OVERPASS

they *o.* the deeds of the wicked   *Jer 5:28*

OVERPAST

until these calamities be *o.*   *Ps 57:1*
until the indignation be *o.*   *Isa 26:20*

OVERPAYMENT

restore the *o.* (S)   *Le 25:27*

OVERPLUS

and restore the *o.* unto the man to — Le 25:27

OVERPOWER

may *o.* him (A)(B)(R) — J'g 16:6
gates of hades not *o.* it (A)(N) — M't 16:18

OVERPOWERED

overpowered (B) — 1Sa 13:3; 2Ch 16:4
I have *o.* him (B) — Ps 13:4
darkness never *o.* it (A) — Joh 1:5
o. them all (B)(N)(P) — Ac 19:16

OVERPOWERS

horror *o.* me (B) — Ps 55:5

OVERRAN

way of the plain, and *o.* Cushi — 2Sa 18:23

OVERRUNNING

But with an *o.* flood he will make — Na 1:8
with an overwhelming flood (B) — Na 1:8
with an overflowing flood (R) — Na 1:8
o. love (B) — 1Th 3:12

OVERSEE

also were appointed to *o.* the vessels — 1Ch 9:29
and six hundred to *o.* them — 2Ch 2:2
3,600 overseers (A) — 2Ch 2:2
3600 foremen (B) — 2Ch 2:2

OVERSEER

he made him *o.* over his house — Ge 39:4
made him supervisor (A) — Ge 39:4; 39:5
made him his orderly (B) — Ge 39:4
he had made him *o.* in his house — Ge 39:5
made him his superintendent (B) — Ge 39:5
the son of Zichri was their *o.* — Ne 11:9
their *o.* was Zabdiel, the son of one — Ne 11:14
o. also of the Levites at Jerusalem — Ne 11:22
sang loud, with Jezrahiah their *o.* — Ne 12:42
Jezrahiah as leader (A)(R) — Ne 12:42
having no guide, *o.* or ruler — Pr 6:7

OVERSEERS

3,600 *o.* (A) — 2Ch 2:2
o. to set the people a work — 2Ch 2:18
3600 foremen (B) — 2Ch 2:18
o. under the hand of Cononiah — 2Ch 31:13
the *o.* of them were Jahath — 2Ch 34:12
o. of all that wrought the work in — 2Ch 34:13
over them as foreman (B) — 2Ch 34:13
it into the hand of the *o.* and — 2Ch 34:17
over to the supervisors (B) — 2Ch 34:17
the Holy Ghost hath made you *o.* — Ac 20:28
appointed you bishops and guardians (A) — Ac 20:28
made you bishops (E) — Ac 20:28
as shepherds of the church (N)(P) — Ac 20:28
made you guardians (R) — Ac 20:28

OVERSHADOW

power of the Highest shall *o.* thee — Lu 1:35
Peter passing by might *o.* some — Ac 5:15

OVERSHADOWED

behold, a bright cloud *o.* them — M't 17:5
there was a cloud that *o.* them — M'k 9:7
there came a cloud, and *o.* them — Lu 9:34

OVERSHADOWING

cherub with *o.* wings (A)(B) — Eze 28:14
the *o.* cherub (B) — Eze 28:16

OVERSIGHT

hand; peradventure it was an *o.* — Ge 43:12
o. of them that keep the charge of — Nu 3:32
the *o.* of all the tabernacle, and of — Nu 4:16
the *o.* of the house of the Lord — 2Ki 12:11; 22:5, 9; 2Ch 34:10
had the *o.* of the gates of the house — 1Ch 9:23
had the *o.* of the outward business — Ne 11:16
having the *o.* of the chamber of — Ne 13:4
among you, taking the *o.* thereof — 1Pe 5:2

OVERSPREAD

of them was the whole earth *o.* — Ge 9:19

OVERSPREADING

and for the *o.* of abominations he — Da 9:27
upon the wing or pinnacle of abominations (A) — Da 9:27
on a wing of horrors (B) — Da 9:27
upon the wing of abominations (E)(R) — Da 9:27

OVERTAKE

some evil *o.* thee (S) — Ge 19:19
when thou dost *o.* them, say unto — Ge 44:4
enemy said, I will pursue, I will *o.* — Ex 15:9
while his heart is hot, and *o.* him — De 19:6
shall come on thee, and *o.* thee — De 28:2
shall come upon thee, and *o.* thee — De 28:15
and shall pursue thee, and *o.* thee — De 28:45
them quickly; for ye shall *o.* them — Jos 2:5
after this troop? shall I *o.* them — 1Sa 30:8
for thou shalt surely *o.* them — 1Sa 30:8
lest he *o.* us suddenly, and bring — 2Sa 15:14
from us, neither doth justice *o.* us — Isa 59:9
sword, which ye feared, shall *o.* you — Jer 42:16
lovers, but she shall not *o.* them — Ho 2:7
children of iniquity did not *o.* them — Ho 10:9
evil shall not *o.* nor prevent us — Am 9:10
the plowman shall *o.* the reaper — Am 9:13
darkness did not *o.* it (B) — Joh 1:5
that day should *o.* you as a thief — 1Th 5:4

OVERTAKEN

affliction has *o.* me (B) — Job 30:27
mine enemies, and *o.* them — Ps 18:37
Brethren, if a man be *o.* in a fault — Ga 6:1

OVERTAKETH

sword of thine enemies *o.* thee — 1Ch 21:12

OVERTHREW

And he *o.* those cities, and all — Ge 19:25
he *o.* the cities in which Lot dwelt — Ge 19:29
and the Lord *o.* the Egyptians — Ex 14:27
which the Lord *o.* in his anger — De 29:23
But *o.* Pharaoh and his host in the — Ps 136:15
God *o.* Sodom and Gomorrah — Isa 13:19
be as the cities which the Lord *o.* — Jer 20:16
Lord *o.* without pity (R) — Jer 20:16
As God *o.* Sodom and Gomorrah — Jer 50:40; Am 4:11
o. the tables of moneychangers — M't 21:12; M'k 11:15
changers' money, and *o.* the tables — Joh 2:15

OVERTHROW

also, that I will not *o.* this city — Ge 19:21
sent Lot out of the midst of the *o.* — Ge 19:29
but thou shalt utterly *o.* them — Ex 23:24
ye shall *o.* their altars, and break — De 12:3
therein, like the *o.* of Sodom — De 29:23
and to spy it out, and to *o.* it — 2Sa 10:3
strong against the city, and *o.* it — 2Sa 11:25
and to *o.* and to spy out the land — 1Ch 19:3
to *o.* them in the wilderness — Ps 106:26
To *o.* their seed also among — Ps 106:27
o. me wrongfully (E) — Ps 119:78
have purposed to *o.* my goings — Ps 140:4
hunt the violent man to *o.* him — Ps 140:11
to *o.* the righteous in judgment — Pr 18:5
in the *o.* of Sodom and Gomorrah — Jer 49:18
I will *o.* the throne of kingdoms — Hag 2:22
I will *o.* the chariots, and those — Hag 2:22
if it be of God, ye cannot *o.* it — Ac 5:39
o. work of God (E) — Ro 14:20
already; and *o.* the faith of some — 2Ti 2:18
condemned them with an *o.* — 2Pe 2:6

OVERTHROWETH

away spoiled, and *o.* the mighty — Job 12:19
but wickedness *o.* the sinner — Pr 13:6
but God *o.* the wicked for their — Pr 21:12
o. the words of the transgressor — Pr 22:12
but he that receiveth gifts *o.* it — Pr 29:4

OVERTHROWN

hast *o.* them that rose up against — Ex 15:7
and many were *o.* and wounded — J'g 9:40
some of them be *o.* at the first — 2Sa 17:9
and the Ethiopians were *o.* that — 2Ch 14:13
Know now that God hath *o.* me — Job 19:6
judges are *o.* in stony places — Ps 141:6
it is *o.* by the mouth of the wicked — Pr 11:11
The wicked are *o.* and are not — Pr 12:7
house of the wicked shall be *o.* — Pr 14:11
it is desolate, as *o.* by strangers — Isa 1:7
but let them be *o.* before thee — Jer 18:23
that was *o.* as in a moment, and — La 4:6
and many countries shall be *o.* — Da 11:41
I have *o.* some of you, as God *o.* — Am 4:11
days, and Nineveh shall be *o.* — Jon 3:4
for they were *o.* in the wilderness — 1Co 10:5

OVERTOOK

they *o.* him in the mount Gilead — Ge 31:23
Then Laban *o.* Jacob. Now — Ge 31:25
And he *o.* them, and he spake unto — Ge 44:6
and *o.* them encamping by the sea — Ex 14:9
and *o.* the chidren of Dan — J'g 18:22
but the battle *o.* them; and — J'g 20:42
and *o.* him in the plains of Jericho — 2Ki 25:5
o. Zedekiah in the plains of Jericho — Jer 39:5; 52:8
o. her between the straits — La 1:3

OVERTURN

them out, and they *o.* the earth — Job 12:15
overwhelm the land (A)(B)(R) — Job 12:15
I will *o., o., o.* it: and it shall be — Eze 21:27
I will overthrow, overthrow, overthrow it (A) — Eze 21:27
Ruin, ruin I will make it (B)(R) — Eze 21:27

OVERTURNED

and *o*. it, that the tent lay along　　　*J'g 7:13*

OVERTURNETH

not: which *o*. them in his anger　　*Job 9:5*
he *o*. the mountains by the roots　　*Job 28:9*
and he *o*. them in the night　　*Job 34:25*

OVERWHELM

Yea, ye *o*. the fatherless, and ye　　*Job 6:27*
ye cast lots over the fatherless　*Job 6:27*
(A)(B)(E)(R)
they *o*. him (B)　　　　　*Job 15:24*
o. me with waves (R)　　　*Ps 88:7*
o. the land (B)(R)　　　　*Eze 21:27*

OVERWHELMED

upon me, and horror hath *o*. me　　*Ps 55:5*
horror overpowers me (B)　　*Ps 55:5*
unto thee, when my heart is *o*.　*Ps 61:2*
and my spirit was *o*.　　　*Ps 77:3*
my spirit was faint (B)(R)　*Ps 77:3*
not: but the sea *o*. their enemies　　*Ps 78:53*
enemies he covered with the sea (B)　　*Ps 78:53*
by wrath *o*. (R)　　　　　*Ps 90:7*
of the afflicted, when he is *o*.　*Ps 102 title*
Then the waters had *o*. us, the　*Ps 124:4*
When my spirit was *o*. within me　　*Ps 142:3*
my spirit weakens (B)　　　*Ps 142:3*
my spirit is faint (R)　　*Ps 142:3*
is my spirit *o*. within me; my　*Ps 143:4*
my spirit is losing hope (B)　*Ps 143:4*
my spirit faints (R)　　　*Ps 143:4*
remained *o*. among them (S)　*Eze 3:15*
be *o*. before him (E)　　*Da 11:22*
o. with grief (A)　　　　*M't 14:34*

OVERWHELMING

it was *o*. to me (B)　　　*Ps 75:16*
anger is an *o*. flood　　*Pr 27:4*
(A)(B)(E)(R)
end shall come *o*. (B)　　*Da 9:26*
with an *o*. flood (B)　　*Na 1:8*

OWE

O. no man any thing, but to love　　*Ro 13:8*

OWED

o. him ten thousand talents　*M't 18:24*
which *o*. him an hundred pence　　*M't 18:28*
the one *o*. five hundred pence　*Lu 7:41*

OWEST

saying, Pay me that thou *o*.　*M't 18:28*
How much *o*. thou unto my lord　　*Lu 16:5*
another, And how much *o*. thou　*Lu 16:7*
o. unto me even thine own self　*Ph'm 19*

OWETH

wronged thee, or *o*. thee ought　*Ph'm 18*

OWL

the *o*. and the night hawk　*Le 11:16; De 14:15*
The ostrich, the nighthawk　*Le 11:16; De 14:15*
(A)(R)
the little *o*. and the cormorant　*Le 11:17*
the cormorant, and the great *o*.　*Le 11:17*
the little *o*. and the swan　*De 14:16*
and the great *o*. and the swan　*De 14:16*
I am like an *o*. of the desert　*Ps 102:6*
the *o*. also and the raven shall　*Isa 34:11*
screech *o*. also shall rest there　*Isa 34:14*
shall the great *o*. make her nest　*Isa 34:15*

OWLS

and a companion to *o*.　　*Job 30:29*
and *o*. shall dwell there, and　*Isa 13:21*

dragons, and a court for *o*.　*Isa 34:13*
me, the dragons and the *o*.　*Isa 43:20*
and the *o*. shall dwell therein　*Jer 50:39*
and mourning as the *o*.　　*Mic 1:8*

OWN

God created man in his *o*. image　　*Ge 1:27*
Adam begat a son in his *o*. likeness　　*Ge 5:3*
trained servants, born in his *o*. house　　*Ge 14:14*
shall come of thine *o*. bowels shall be heir　　*Ge 15:4*
send me, that I may go to mine *o*. place　　*Ge 30:25*
four parts shall be your *o*. for seed of field　　*Ge 47:24*
ox for ox, and dead shall be his *o*.　　*Ex 21:36*
of best of his *o*. field, shall make restitution　　*Ex 22:5*
he shall offer it of his *o*. voluntary will　　*Le 1:3*
his *o*. hands shall bring offering of Lord　　*Le 7:30*
pour it into palm of his *o*. left hand　　*Le 14:15; 14:26*
for theirs is thine *o*. nakedness　*Le 18:10*
nor any of your *o*. nation, nor strangers　　*Le 18:26*
that which groweth of its *o*. accord　　*Le 25:5*
and he shall return to his *o*. family　　*Le 25:41*
each by his *o*. camp, by his *o*. standard　　*Nu 1:52*
have not done them of mine *o*. mind　　*Nu 16:28; 24:13*
censers of sinners against their *o*. souls　　*Nu 16:38*
he called it after his *o*. name　*Nu 32:42; De 3:14*
shall keep himself to his *o*. inheritance　　*Nu 36:9*
mayest eat grapes at thine *o*. pleasure　　*De 23:24*
he may sleep in his *o*. raiment, and bless　　*De 24:13*
man shall be put to death for his *o*. sin　　*De 24:16; 2Ki 14:6; 2Ch 25:4*
thou shall eat the fruit of thine *o*. body　　*De 28:53*
nor knew he his *o*. children　*De 33:9*
they have put it even among their *o*. stuff　　*Jos 7:11*
they ceased not from their *o*. doings　　*J'g 2:19*
saying, Mine *o*. hand hath saved me　　*J'g 7:2*
and they went to their *o*. home　*1Sa 2:20*
let the ark go again to his *o*. place　　*1Sa 5:11*
when thou wast little in thine *o*. sight　　*1Sa 15:17*
from avenging with thine *o*. hand　　*1Sa 25:26*
I will be base in mine *o*. sight　*2Sa 6:22*
that they may dwell in a place of their *o*.　　*2Sa 7:10*
did eat of his *o*. meat, and drink of his *o*. cup　　*2Sa 12:3*
that thou go to battle in thine *o*. person　　*2Sa 17:11*
have wrought falsehood against mine *o*. life　　*2Sa 18:13*
spoken this word against his *o*. life　　*1Ki 2:23*
shall return his blood on his *o*. head　　*1Ki 2:32; 2:37*
she turned and went to her *o*. country　　*1Ki 10:13*
he laid his carcase in his *o*. grave　　*1Ki 13:30*
and Elijah laid him upon his *o*. bed　　*1Ki 17:19*
he took hold of his *o*. clothes, and rent　　*2Ki 2:12*
every nation made gods of their *o*.　　*2Ki 17:29*
and of thine *o*. have we given thee　　*1Ch 29:14*
all this store we prepared, is all thine *o*.　　*1Ch 29:16*
recompensing his way on his *o*. head　　*2Ch 6:23*
his *o*. servants conspired against him　　*2Ch 24:25*

turn their reproach on their *o*. head　　*Ne 4:4*
wicked devise should return on *o*. head　　*Es 9:25*
he shall perish for ever like his *o*. dung　　*Job 20:7*
let them fall by their *o*. counsel　*Ps 5:10*
our lips are our *o*. who is lord over us　　*Ps 12:4*
They are inclosed in their *o*. fat; with　　*Ps 17:10*
God, even our *o*. God, shall bless us　　*Ps 67:6*
were filled, for he gave them their *o*. desire　　*Ps 78:29*
I gave them up to their *o*. hearts' lust　　*Ps 81:12*
he shall bring on them their *o*. iniquity, and shall cut them off in their *o*. wickedness　*Ps 94:23*
Let the wicked fall into their *o*. nets　　*Ps 141:10*
Let them be only their *o*. and not　　*Ps 5:17*
Thine *o*. friend, and thy father's friend　　*Pr 27:10*
lie in glory, every one in his *o*. house　　*Isa 14:18*
for mine *o*. sake　*Isa 37:35; 43:25; 48:11*
have turned every one to his *o*. way　　*Isa 53:6*
not finding thine *o*. pleasure, nor *o*. words　　*Isa 58:13*
worshipped the works of their *o*. hands　　*Jer 1:16*
which hath said, My river is mine *o*.　　*Eze 29:3*
if he trust to his *o*. righteousness　　*Eze 33:13*
now their *o*. doings have beset them about　　*Ho 7:2*
they forsake their *o*. mercy　*Jon 2:8*
lawful to do what I will with mine *o*.　　*M't 20:15*
if any man hate not his *o*. life also　　*Lu 14:26*
who shall give you that which is your *o*.　　*Lu 16:12*
he came to his *o*. his *o*. received him not　　*Joh 1:11*
when he speaketh a lie, he speaketh of his *o*.　　*Joh 8:44*
an hireling, whose *o*. the sheep are not　　*Joh 10:12*
having loved his *o*. that were in the world　　*Joh 13:1*
if of the world, world would love his *o*.　　*Joh 15:19*
ye shall be scattered every man to his *o*.　　*Joh 16:32*
as though by our *o*. power or holiness　　*Ac 3:12*
was it not thine *o*.? was it not in thine *o*. power　　*Ac 5:4*
which he purchased with his *o*. blood　　*Ac 20:28*
he considered not his *o*. body now dead　　*Ro 4:19*
he that spared not his *o*. Son, but delivered　　*Ro 8:32*
to his *o*. master he standeth or falleth　　*Ro 14:4*
ye are not your *o*. for ye are bought　　*1Co 6:19*
nevertheless, let every man have his *o*. wife　　*1Co 7:2*
let no man seek his *o*. but another's wealth　　*1Co 10:24*
conscience, I say, not thine *o*. but others　　*1Co 10:29*
charity seeketh not her *o*. is not easily　　*1Co 13:5*
for all seek their *o*. things, not Christ's　　*Ph'p 2:21*
found in him, not having mine *o*. righteousness　　*Ph'p 3:9*
but if any provide not for his *o*. his *o*.　　*1Ti 5:8*
a prophet of their *o*. said, The Cretians　　*Tit 1:12*
but by his *o*. blood he entered in once　　*Heb 9:12*
washed us from our sins in his *o*. blood　　*Re 1:5*

OWNER

but the *o*. of the ox shall be quit　　*Ex 21:28*
and it hath been testified to his *o*.　　*Ex 21:29*

and his *o.* also shall be put to *Ex 21:29*
death
The *o.* of the pit shall make it *Ex 21:34*
good
give money unto the *o.* of *Ex 21:34*
them
and his *o.* hath not kept him *Ex 21:36*
in
and the *o.* of it shall accept *Ex 22:11*
thereof
shall make restitution unto *Ex 22:12*
the *o.*
the *o.* thereof being not with *Ex 22:14*
it, he
the *o.* thereof be with it, he *Ex 22:15*
shall not
the name of Shemer, *o.* of *1Ki 16:24*
the hill
The ox knoweth his *o.* and the *Isa 1:3*
o. of the house (S) *M'k 14:14;*
Lu 12:39; 22:11
the master and the *o.* of the *Ac 27:11*
ship

OWNERS

the *o.* thereof to lose their *Job 31:39*
life
taketh away the life of the *o.* *Pr 1:19*
good is there to the *o.* thereof *Ec 5:11*
riches kept for the *o.* thereof to *Ec 5:13*
the *o.* thereof said unto them *Lu 19:33*

OWNETH

And he that *o.* the house shall *Le 14:35*
come
bind the man that *o.* this *Ac 21:11*
girdle

OX

they disabled an *o.* (A)(B)(E) *Ge 49:6*
nor his *o.* nor his ass, nor any *Ex 20:17*
If an *o.* gore a man or a *Ex 21:28*
woman
then the *o.* shall be surely *Ex 21:28*
stoned
the owner of the *o.* shall be *Ex 21:28*
quit
o. were wont to push with his *Ex 21:29*
horn
the *o.* shall be stoned, and his *Ex 21:29*
If the *o.* shall push a *Ex 21:32*
manservant
silver, and the *o.* shall be *Ex 21:32*
stoned
and an *o.* or an ass fall *Ex 21:33*
therein
And if one man's *o.* hurt *Ex 21:35*
another's
then they shall sell the live *o.* *Ex 21:35*
the dead *o.* also they shall *Ex 21:35*
divide
the *o.* hath used to push in *Ex 21:36*
time
in; he shall surely pay *o.* for *Ex 21:36*
o.
If a man shall steal an *o.* or a *Ex 22:1*
he shall restore five oxen for an *Ex 22:1*
o.
whether it be *o.* or ass, or *Ex 22:4*
sheep
whether it be for *o.* for ass, for *Ex 22:9*
his neighbor an ass, or an *o.* *Ex 22:10*
meet thine enemy's *o.* or his ass *Ex 23:4*
that thine *o.* and thine ass may *Ex 23:12*
thy cattle, whether *o.* or sheep *Ex 34:19*
shall eat no manner of fat, of *Le 7:23*
o.
that killeth an *o.*, or lamb, or *Le 17:3*
goat
whether it be *o.* or sheep: it is *Le 27:26*
princes, and for each one an *o.* *Nu 7:3*
as the *o.* licketh up the grass *Nu 22:4*
of the
the wild *o.* (A)(E)(R) *Nu 23:22;*
24:8; Job 39:9-10; Ps 29:6; 92:10
thine *o.*, nor thine ass, nor any *De 5:14*
of
his *o.*, or his ass, or any thing *De 5:21*
that
ye shall eat; the *o.*, the sheep *De 14:4*
the wild *o.*, and the chamois *De 14:5*
sacrifice, whether it be *o.* or *De 18:3*
sheep
brother's *o.* or his sheep go *De 22:1*
astray
thy brother's ass or his *o.* fall *De 22:4*
down
not plow with an *o.* and an *De 22:10*
ass

shalt not muzzle the *o.* when he *De 25:4*
Thine *o.* shall be slain before *De 28:31*
thine
the wild *o.* (A)(B)(E)(R) *De 33:17;*
Ps 22:21; Isa 34:7
and *o.* and sheep, and ass, *Jos 6:21*
with the
hundred men with an *o.* goad *J'g 3:31*
for Israel, neither sheep, nor *o.* *J'g 6:4*
whose *o.* have I taken? or *1Sa 12:3*
whose ass
Bring me hither every man *1Sa 14:34*
his *o.*
brought every man his *o.* with *1Sa 14:34*
him
infant and suckling, *o.* and *1Sa 15:3*
sheep
was one *o.* and six choice *Ne 5:18*
sheep
or loweth the *o.* over his fodder *Job 6:5*
take the widow's *o.* for a *Job 24:3*
pledge
the wild *o.* (B) *Job 39:9;*
Ps 92:10
thee; he eateth grass as an *o.* *Job 40:15*
o.
please the Lord better than an *Ps 69:31*
o.
similitude of an *o.* that *Ps 106:20*
eateth grass
as an *o.* goeth to the slaughter *Pr 7:22*
increase is by the strength of *Pr 14:4*
the *o.*
a stalled *o.* and hatred *Pr 15:17*
therewith
The *o.* knoweth his owner, and *Isa 1:3*
the lion shall eat straw like the *Isa 11:7*
o.
the feet of the *o.* and the ass *Isa 32:20*
He that killeth an *o.* is as if he *Isa 66:3*
slew
I was like a lamb or an *o.* *Jer 11:19*
that is
they four had the face of an *o.* *Eze 1:10*
the sabbath loose his *o.* or his *Lu 13:15*
ass
an ass or an *o.* fallen into a pit *Lu 14:5*
not muzzle the mouth of the *o.* *1Co 9:9*
not muzzle the *o.* that treadeth *1Ti 5:18*
out

OXEN

and he had sheep, and *o.* and *Ge 12:16*
Abimelech took sheep, and *o.* *Ge 20:14*
And Abraham took sheep and *Ge 21:27*
o.
And I have *o.* and asses, flocks *Ge 32:5*
took their sheep, and their *Ge 34:28*
o. and
in wantonness hamstring *o.* *Ge 49:6*
(R)
upon the *o.* and upon the sheep *Ex 9:3*
offerings, thy sheep, and thine *Ex 20:24*
he shall restore five *o.* for an ox *Ex 22:1*
shalt thou do with thine *o.* *Ex 22:30*
peace offerings of *o.* unto the *Ex 24:5*
Lord
oxen (S) *Le 22:19;*
22:21; Nu 31:28, 30, 33, 38, 44
six covered wagons, and twelve *Nu 7:3*
o.
Moses took the wagons and the *Nu 7:6*
o.
Two wagons and four *o.* *Nu 7:7*
he gave
four wagons and eight *o.* he *Nu 7:8*
gave
two *o.*; five rams, five he *Nu 7:17;*
goats *7:23, 29, 35, 41, 47, 53, 59, 65,*
71,77
all the *o.* for the sacrifice of *Nu 7:88*
Balak offered *o.* and sheep, *Nu 22:40*
and sent
and prepare me here seven *Nu 23:1*
for *o.* or for sheep, or for *De 14:26*
wine, or
and his *o.* and his asses, and *Jos 7:24*
he took a yoke of *o.* and *1Sa 11:7*
hewed
so shall it be done unto his *o.* *1Sa 11:7*
land, which a yoke of *o.* *1Sa 14:14*
might plow
took sheep and *o.* and calves *1Sa 14:32*
the best of the sheep, and of *1Sa 15:9*
the *o.*
the lowing of the *o.* which I *1Sa 15:14*
hear

the best of the sheep and *1Sa 15:15*
of the *o.*
took of the spoil, sheep and *1Sa 15:21*
o. the
o. and asses, and sheep, with *1Sa 22:19*
took away the sheep, and the *1Sa 27:9*
o.
took hold of it; for the *o.* *2Sa 6:6*
shook it
paces, he sacrificed *o.* and *2Sa 6:13*
fatlings
here be *o.* for burnt sacrifice *2Sa 24:22*
instruments of the *o.* for *2Sa 24:22*
wood
and the *o.* for fifty shekels of *2Sa 24:24*
silver
Adonijah slew sheep and *o.* *1Ki 1:9*
and fat
And he hath slain *o.* and fat *1Ki 1:19*
cattle
hath slain *o.* and fat cattle *1Ki 1:25*
and sheep
Ten fat *o.* and twenty *o.* out *1Ki 4:23*
of
It stood upon twelve *o.*, *1Ki 7:25*
three
were lions, *o.* and cherubims *1Ki 7:29*
and beneath the lions and *o.* *1Ki 7:29*
were
sea, and twelve *o.* under the *1Ki 7:44*
sea
sacrificing sheep and *o.* that *1Ki 8:5*
could
two and twenty thousand *o.* *1Ki 8:63*
was plowing with twelve *1Ki 19:19*
yoke of *o.*
And he left the *o.* and ran *1Ki 19:20*
after
took a yoke of *o.* and slew *1Ki 19:21*
them
flesh with the instruments of *1Ki 19:21*
the *o.*
vineyards, and sheep, and *o.* *2Ki 5:26*
the brasen *o.* that were under *2Ki 16:17*
it
and on mules, and on *o.* and *1Ch 12:40*
meat
and wine, and oil, and *o.* *1Ch 12:40*
and sheep
hold the ark; for the *o.* *1Ch 13:9*
stumbled
thee the *o.* also for burnt *1Ch 21:23*
offerings
under it was the similitude of *2Ch 4:3*
Two rows of *o.* were cast, *2Ch 4:3*
when it
It stood upon twelve *o.* three *2Ch 4:4*
One sea, and twelve *o.* under *2Ch 4:15*
it
sacrificed sheep and *o.* which *2Ch 5:6*
could
of twenty and two thousand *o.* *2Ch 7:5*
had brought, seven hundred *2Ch 15:11*
o. and
Ahab killed sheep and *o.* for *2Ch 18:2*
him in
six hundred *o.* and three *2Ch 29:33*
thousand
brought in the tithe of *o.* and *2Ch 31:6*
sheep
small cattle, and three *2Ch 35:8*
hundred *o.*
small cattle, and five hundred *2Ch 35:9*
o.
Moses. And so did they with *2Ch 35:12*
the *o.*
camels, and five hundred yoke *Job 1:3*
of *o.*
The *o.* were plowing, and the *Job 1:14*
asses
camels, and a thousand yoke *Job 42:12*
of *o.*
All sheep and *o.* yea, and the *Ps 8:7*
beasts
our *o.* may be strong to *Ps 144:14*
labour
Where no *o.* are, the crib is *Pr 14:4*
clean
shall be for the sending forth *Isa 7:25*
of *o.*
joy and gladness, slaying *o.* *Isa 22:13*
The *o.* likewise and the young *Isa 30:24*
asses
the husbandman and his yoke *Jer 51:23*
of *o.*
make thee to eat grass as *o.* *Da 4:25;*
4:32
and did eat grass as *o.* and his *Da 4:33*
they fed him with grass like *o.* *Da 5:21*

OXEN

rock? will one plow there with *o*.	*Am 6:12*
my *o*. and my fatlings are killed	*M't 22:4*
I have bought five yoke of *o*.	*Lu 14:19*
that sold *o*. and sheep and doves	*Joh 2:14*
temple, and the sheep, and the *o*.	*Joh 2:15*
o. and garlands unto the gates	*Ac 14:13*
corn. Doth God take care for *o*.	*1Co 9:9*

OZEM

O. the sixth, David the seventh	*1Ch 2:15*
and Oren, and *o*. and Ahijah	*1Ch 2:25*

OZIAS

begat Joram, and Joram begat *O*.	*M't 1:8*
And *O*. begat Joatham; and	*M't 1:9*

OZNI

of *O*. the family of the Oznites	*Nu 26:16*

OZNITES

Of Ozni, the family of the *O*.	*Nu 26:16*

P

PAARAI

the Carmelite, *P*. the Arbite	*2Sa 23:35*

PACES

ark of the Lord had gone six *p*.	*2Sa 6:13*
ark advanced six steps (B)	*2Sa 6:13*

PACK

like the immoral *p*. in Israel (B)	*2Sa 13:13*
no *p*. (N)	*M't 10:10; M'k 6:8; Lu 9:3*
nor *p*. (N)	*Lu 10:4; 22:35-36*

PACIFIED

Then was the king's wrath *p*.	*Es 7:10*
the king's anger calmed down (B)	*Es 7:10*
the anger of the king abated (R)	*Es 7:10*
when I am *p*. toward thee for all	*Eze 16:63*

PACIFIETH

A gift in secret *p*. anger: and a	*Pr 21:14*
for yielding *p*. great offences	*Ec 10:4*

PACIFY

death: but a wise man will *p*. it	*Pr 16:14*

PADAN

as for me, when I came from *P*.	*Ge 48:7*

PADAN-ARAM

of Bethuel the Syrian of *P*.	*Ge 25:20*
go to *P*. to the house of Bethuel	*Ge 28:2*
he went to *P*. unto Laban, son of	*Ge 28:5*
Jacob and sent him away to *P*.	*Ge 28:6*
his mother, and was gone to *P*.	*Ge 28:7*
which he had gotten in *P*. for to go	*Ge 31:18*
of Canaan, when he came from *P*.	*Ge 33:18*
again when he came out of *P*.	*Ge 35:9*
which were born to him in *P*.	*Ge 35:26*
which she bare unto Jacob in *P*.	*Ge 46:15*

PADDLE

a *p*. or spade (A)(B)	*Nu 35:18*
shalt have a *p*. upon thy weapon	*De 23:13*

PADON

of Siaha, the children of *P*.	*Ezr 2:44*
children of Sia, the children of *P*.	*Ne 7:47*

PAGAN

a *p*. man and a (A)(B)(N)(P)	*M't 18:17*
before a *p*. court (B)(N)(R)	*1Co 6:1*

PAGANS

associated with *p*. (B)	*Ps 106:35*
as the *p*. do (B)(P)(S)	*M't 6:7*
perils from *p*. (P)	*2Co 11:26*
giving way to lust like *p*. (N)	*1Th 4:5*

PAGES

p. of the human heart (N)	*2Co 3:3*

PAGIEL

Of Asher; *P*. the son of Ocran	*Nu 1:13*
Asher shall be *P*. the son of Ocran	*Nu 2:27*
eleventh day *P*. the son of Ocran	*Nu 7:72*
the offering of *P*. the son of Ocran	*Nu 7:77*
of Asher was *P*. the son of Ocran	*Nu 10:26*

PAHATH-MOAB

children of *P*. of the children	*Ezr 2:6; Ne 7:11*
Of the sons of *P*.; Elihoenai the	*Ezr 8:4*
And of the sons of *P*.; Adna	*Ezr 10:30*
and Hashub the son of *P*. repaired	*Ne 3:11*
The chief of the people; Parosh, *P*.	*Ne 10:14*

PAI

and the name of his city was *P*.	*1Ch 1:50*

PAID

they *p*. the carpenters (S)	*2Ki 12:11*
and custom, was *p*. unto them	*Ezr 4:20*
so he *p*. the fare thereof, and went	*Jon 1:3*
thou hast *p*. the uttermost farthing	*M't 5:26*
they have been *p*. in full (B)	*M't 6:5*
till thou hast *p*. the very last mite	*Lu 12:59*
repay her what she *p*. (A)(B)	*Re 18:6*

PAILS

gathered good into *p*. (N)	*M't 13:48*

PAIN

in *p*. bring forth children (E)(R)	*Ge 3:16*
I hear him with *p*. (A)(B)(R)	*1Ch 4:9; Jer 30:15*
no *p*. assails me (B)	*1Ch 4:10*
own plague and *p*. (B)	*1Ch 6:29*
his flesh upon him shall have *p*.	*Job 14:22*
his body shall grieve (A)	*Job 14:22*
the wicked man travaileth with *p*.	*Job 15:20*
The wicked man suffers torment (A)	*Job 15:20*
The wicked man is tormented (B)	*Job 15:20*
would assuage your *p*. (R)	*Job 16:5; 16:6*
He is chastened also with *p*. upon	*Job 33:19*
multitude of his bones with strong *p*.	*Job 33:19*
bear *p*. in my soul (R)	*Ps 13:2*
upon mine affliction and my *p*.	*Ps 25:18*
and *p*. as of a woman in travail	*Ps 48:6; Jer 6:24; 22:23*

PAINED

gossip of *p*. of pierced ones (B)	*Ps 69:26*
in *p*. (B)(R)	*Ps 69:29*
sustain him in bodily *p*. (A)	*Pr 18:14*
in *p*. as a woman that travaileth	*Isa 13:8*
desperate *p*. (B)	*Isa 17:11; Jer 30:15*
my loins filled with *p*.:	*Isa 21:3*
my loins filled with anguish (A)(B)(E)(R)	*Isa 21:3*
the time of her delivery, is in *p*.	*Isa 26:17*
been with child, we have been in *p*.	*Isa 26:18*
before her *p*. came, she was travail	*Isa 66:7*
pangs as of a woman (A)(E)	*Jer 6:24*
they have put themselves to *p*.	*Jer 12:13*
They have worn themselves out (A)	*Jer 12:13*
they have uselessly exhausted themselves (E)	*Jer 12:13*
they have tired themselves out (R)	*Jer 12:13*
Why is my *p*. perpetual, and my	*Jer 15:18*
p. is (E)	*Jer 30:15; 51:29*
fall with *p*. upon the head of	*Jer 30:23*
take balm for her *p*. if so be she	*Jer 51:8*
great *p*. shall be upon Ethiopia	*Eze 30:4*
great sorrow shall be upon Ethiopia (A)	*Eze 30:4*
anguish upon Ethiopia (B)(E)(R)	*Eze 30:4*
great *p*. upon them	*Eze 30:9*
great sorrow upon them (A)	*Eze 30:9*
anguish shall seize them (B)(E)(R)	*Eze 30:9*
Sin shall have great *p*.	*Eze 30:16*
Pelusium shall have great anguish (A)	*Eze 30:16*
pour out my fury on Sin (B)	*Eze 30:16*
Sin shall have great anguish (E)	*Eze 30:16*
Pelusium shall be in great agony (R)	*Eze 30:16*
Be in *p*., and labour to bring forth	*Mic 4:10*
Writhe and cry out like a woman (A)	*Mic 4:10*
Writhe and groan like a woman (R)	*Mic 4:10*
much *p*. in all loins	*Na 2:10*
anguish in all loins (A)(B)(E)(R)	*Na 2:10*
racked with *p*. (N)(P)	*M't 8:6*
your *p*. shall be (P)	*Joh 16:20*
travaileth in *p*. together	*Ro 8:22*
sighing and in throes in unison (A)	*Ro 8:22*
groans as if in pangs of childbirth (N)	*Ro 8:22*
groans in a sort of universal travail (P)	*Ro 8:22*
groaning in travail (R)	*Ro 8:22*
p. of childbirth (P)	*Ga 4:19*
p. of unjust suffering (B)	*1Pe 2:19*
they gnawed their tongues for *p*.	*Re 16:10*
gnawed their tongues for the torment (A)	*Re 16:10*
gnawed their tongues in agony (N)(P)	*Re 16:10*
gnawed their tongues in anguish (R)	*Re 16:10*
neither shall there be any more *p*.	*Re 21:4*

PAINED

My heart is sore *p*. within me	*Ps 55:4*
My heart is distressed within me (B)	*Ps 55:4*
My heart is in anguish within me (R)	*Ps 55:4*
be sorely *p*. at the report of Tyre	*Isa 23:5*
be in anguish over the report of Tyre (R)	*Isa 23:5*
I am *p*. at my very heart	*Jer 4:19*
I writhe in pain (A)(B)(R)	*Jer 4:19*
the people shall be much *p*.	*Joe 2:6*
the people are in anguish (A)(B)(E)(R)	*Joe 2:6*
be sore *p*. (E)	*Zec 9:5*
if brother is *p*. (A)(B)	*Ro 14:15*
made you *p*. (A)	*2Co 7:9*

in birth, and *p.* to be delivered *Re 12:2*
in the anguish of her delivery *Re 12:2* (A)(N)
pangs of her delivery (B) *Re 12:2*
in the pains of bringing forth *Re 12:2* (P)
in the pangs of birth (R) *Re 12:2*

PAINFUL

it was too *p.* for me *Ps 73:16*
it was too overwhelming for *Ps 73:16* me (R)
it seemed to me a wearisome *Ps 73:16* task (R)
p. briers (B) *Pr 28:24*
not joyful, but *p.* *Heb 12:11* (B)(N)(R)
foul and *p.* ulcers (A)(S) *Re 16:2*

PAINFULNESS

In weariness and *p.*, in *2Co 11:27* watchings
In toil and hardship, *2Co 11:27* watching (A)(R)
In wearying work and *2Co 11:27* hardship (B)
In labour and travail (E) *2Co 11:27*

PAINS

travailed; for her *p.* came *1Sa 4:19* upon her
for the birth-pains came upon *1Sa 4:19* her (B)
they cast their *p.* (A)(E)(R) *Job 39:3*
the *p.* of hell gat hold upon me *Ps 116:3*
the terrors of Sheol had laid *Ps 116:3* hold (A)
the terrors of the grave had *Ps 116:3* laid (B)
the pangs of Sheol laid hold *Ps 116:3* on me (R)
all his days are *p.* (B) *Ec 2:23*
p. and agonies seize (B) *Isa 13:8*
p. are turned (R) *Da 10:16*
p. of a woman (A) *Ho 13:13*
p. have taken you (A) *Mic 4:9*
distressed with intense *p.* (A) *M't 8:6* (A)(B)
early *p.* of birth pangs *M't 24:8;* (A)(B)   *M'k 13:8*
loosed the *p.* of death *Ac 2:24*
liberating him from pangs of *Ac 2:24* death (A)(E)(N)(R)
unfastening the cords of death *Ac 2:24* (B)
once more suffer birth *p.* (B) *Ga 4:19*
labor *p.* of a woman (A) *1Th 5:3*
because of their *p.* and their *Re 16:11* sores
because of their anguish and *Re 16:11* ulcers (A)
for their sufferings and sores *Re 16:11* (B)

PAINTED

she *p.* her face, and tired her *2Ki 9:30* head
with cedar, and *p.* with *Jer 22:14* vermillion

PAINTEDST

p. thy eyes, and deckedst *Eze 23:40* thyself

PAINTING

thou rentest thy face with *p.* in *Jer 4:30*

PAIR

silver, and the poor for a *p.* of *Am 2:6* shoes
and the needy for a *p.* of shoes *Am 8:6*
A *p.* of turtledoves, or two *Lu 2:24* young
had a *p.* of balances in his hand *Re 6:5*

PALACE

into the *p.* of the king's *1Ki 16:18* house
stronghold of the king's house *1Ki 16:18* (A)
the citadel of the king's palace *1Ki 16:18* (B)(R)
castle of the king's house *1Ki 16:18* (E)

hard by the *p.* of Ahab *1Ki 21:1*
in the *p.* of the king's house *2Ki 15:25*
in citadel of king's house *2Ki 15:25* (A)(B)(R)
in the castle of the king's *2Ki 15:25* house (E)
in the *p.* of the king of *2Ki 20:18* Babylon
p. is not for man, but for the *1Ch 29:1* Lord
the edifice is not for man (B) *1Ch 29:1*
these things, and to build the *1Ch 29:19* *p.*
to erect the edifice (B) *1Ch 29:19*
the king's *p.* *2Ch 9:11; Ezr 4:14; 6:2*
I was in Shushan the *p.* *Ne 1:1*
I was in the castle of Shushan *Ne 1:1* (A)
I was in Susa the capital (R) *Ne 1:1*
make beams for the gates of the *Ne 2:8* *p.*
beams for the gates of the *Ne 2:8* fortress(A)(B)(R)
beams for the gates of the castle *Ne 2:8* (E)
the ruler of the *p.* *Ne 7:2*
the ruler of the castle *Ne 7:2* (A)(E)(R)
commandant of the fortress (B) *Ne 7:2*
which was in Shushan the *p.* *Es 1:2*
in Susa the capital (R) *Es 1:2*
present in Shushan the *p.* *Es 1:5*
present in Shushan the capital *Es 1:5* (A)
of the Shushan stronghold (B) *Es 1:5*
in Susa the capital (R) *Es 1:5*
virgins unto Shushan the *p.* *Es 2:3*
virgins to the capital in Shushan *Es 2:3* (A)
virgins to harem in Susa the *Es 2:3* capital (R)
Now in Shushan the *p.* *Es 2:5;* *2:8; 3:15; 7:7-8; 8:14; 9:6, 11-12*
in Shushan the capital (A) *Es 2:5;* *2:8; 3:15; 8:14; 9:6,11-12*
in the Shushan stronghold (B) *Es 2:5;* *3:15; 9:6, 12*
in Susa the capital (R) *Es 2:5;* *2:8; 3:15; 8:14; 9:6, 11-12*
into the *p.* garden *Es 7:7*
they shall enter into the king's *Ps 45:15* *p.*
after the similitude of a *p.* *Ps 144:12*
after a palatial pattern (B) *Ps 144:12*
will build upon her a *p.* of silver *Ca 8:9*
build upon her a turret of silver *Ca 8:9* (A)(B)(E)
build upon her a battlement of *Ca 8:9* silver (A)
disgrace ot master's *p.* *Isa 22:18* (A)(B)
a *p.* of strangers to be no city *Isa 25:2*
castle of foreigners is no more *Isa 25:2* a city (B)
the *p.* of the king of Babylon *Isa 39:7*
p. shall remain after the *Jer 30:18* manner
in them to stand in the king's *Da 1:4;* *p.*   *4:4, 29; 5:5; 6:18*
I was at Shushan in the *p.* *Da 8:2*
in the Susan stronghold (B) *Da 8:2*
in Susa the capital (R) *Da 8:2*
shall plant the tabernacles of *Da 11:45* his *p.*
shall pitch his palatial tents *Da 11:45* (A)(B)(R)
he shall cast them into the *p.* *Am 4:3*
he shall cast forth into *Am 4:3* Harmon (A)(E)(R)
shall be driven to the fortress *Am 4:3* (B)
the *p.* shall be dissolved *Na 2:6*
unto the *p.* of the high priest *M't 26:3;* *M'k 14:54; Joh 18:15*
afar off unto the high priest's *M't 26:58* *p.*
courtyard of the high priest's *M't 26:58* home (A)(B)(E)(P)(R)
into the court of the high *M't 26:58* priest (E)
Peter sat without in the *p.* *M't 26:69;* *M'k 14:66*
sitting outside in courtyard *M't 26:69* (A)(B)(N)(P)(R)
sitting without in the court *M't 26:69* (E)
strong man armed keepeth his *Lu 11:21* *p.*
armed guards his own *Lu 11:21* dwelling (A)

armed guards his own *Lu 11:21* residence (B)
guardeth his own court (E) *Lu 11:21*
guard over his castle (N) *Lu 11:21*
guards his own house (P) *Lu 11:21*
into the *p.* (P) *Joh 18:28*
entered the *p.* again (B)(P) *Joh 18:33*
again he entered the *p.* *Joh 19:9* (B)(P)
into Herod's *p.* - the *Ac 23:35* praetorium (A)(E)(N)(P)(R)
in Christ are manifest in all *Ph'p 1:13* the *p.*
throughout the whole *Ph'p 1:13* imperial guard (A)(B)
throughout the whole *Ph'p 1:13* praetorian guard (E)(R)
became common to all at *Ph'p 1:13* headquarters (N)
witness before the palace *Ph'p 1:13* guards (P)

PALACES

burnt all the *p.* thereof with *2Ch 36:19* fire
and cassia, out of the ivory *p.* *Ps 45:8*
is known in her *p.* for a refuge *Ps 48:3*
well her bulwarks, consider *Ps 48:13* her *p.*
he built his sanctuary like high *Ps 78:69* *p.*
walls, and prosperity within *Ps 122:7* thy *p.*
with her hands, and is in *Pr 30:28* kings' *p.*
and dragons in their *Isa 13:22* pleasant *p.*
they raised up the *p.* *Isa 23:13* thereof; and
Because the *p.* shall be *Isa 32:14* forsaken
And thorns shall come up in *Isa 34:13* her *p.*
by night, and let us destroy her *Jer 6:5* *p.*
and is entered into our *p.* to cut *Jer 9:21* off
it shall devour the *p.* of *Jer 17:27* Jerusalem
shall consume the *p.* of *Jer 49:27* Ben-hadad
he hath swallowed up all her *p.* *La 2:5*
of the enemy the walls of her *p.* *La 2:7*
he knew their desolate *p.* and *Eze 19:7* he laid
and they shall set their *p.* in *Eze 25:4* thee
and it shall devour the *p.* *Ho 8:14* thereof
shall devour the *p.* of *Am 1:4* Ben-hadad
which shall devour the *p.* *Am 1:7;* thereof   *1:10, 14*
which shall devour the *p.* of *Am 1:12* Bozrah
and it shall devour the *p.* of *Am 2:2* Kirioth
it shall devour the *p.* of *Am 2:5* Jerusalem
Publish in the *p.* at Ashdod *Am 3:9*
and in the *p.* in the land of *Am 3:9* Egypt
up violence and robbery in *Am 3:10* their *p.*
thee, and thy *p.* shall be *Am 3:11* spoiled
I abhor Jacob, and hate his *Am 6:8* *p.*
and when he shall tread in our *Mic 5:5* *p.*

PALAL

P. the son of Uzai, over *Ne 3:25* against

PALATIAL

after a *p.* pattern (B) *Ps 144:12*
pitch his *p.* tents (A)(B)(R) *Da 11:45*

PALE

neither shall his face now *Isa 29:22* wax *p.*
I looked, and behold a *p.* horse *Re 6:8*
an ashy pale horse (A) *Re 6:8*
an ash-colored horse (B) *Re 6:8*
another horse, sickly pale (N) *Re 6:8*
a horse sickly green in color (P) *Re 6:8*

PALED

king's face *p.* (B)   *Da 5:6*

PALENESS

and all faces are turned into *p.* *Jer 30:6*

PALESTINA

hold on the inhabitants of *P.*	*Ex 15:14*
Rejoice not thou, whole *P.* because	*Isa 14:29*
city; thou, whole *P.* art dissolved	*Isa 14:31*

PALESTINE

Zidon, and all the coasts of *P.*   *Joe 3:4*

PALLOR

turned to *p.* (A)   *Da 10:8*

PALLU

Hanoch, and *P.,* Hezron, and	*Ex 6:14;* *1Ch 5:3*
of *P.* the family of the Palluites	*Nu 26:5*
And the sons of *P.*; Eliab	*Nu 26:8*

PALLUITES

of Pallu, the family of the *P.*   *Nu 26:5*

PALM

and threescore and ten *p.* trees	*Ex 15:27;* *Nu 33:9*
into the *p.* of his own left hand	*Le 14:15;* *14:26*
branches of *p.* trees, goodly trees	*Le 23:40*
Jericho, the city of *p.* trees	*De 34:3;* *2Ch 28:15*
went up out of the city of *p.* trees	*J'g 1:16*
and possessed the city of *p.* trees	*J'g 3:13*
under the *p.* tree of Deborah	*J'g 4:5*
cherubims and *p.* trees and open	*1Ki 6:29;* *6:32; 6:35*
cherubims, and upon the *p.* trees	*1Ki 6:32*
cherubims, lions, and *p.* trees	*1Ki 7:36*
and set thereon *p.* trees and chains	*2Ch 3:5*
myrtle branches, and *p.* branches	*Ne 8:15*
shall flourish like the *p.* tree	*Ps 92:12*
This thy stature is like to a *p.* tree	*Ca 7:7*
I said, I will go up to the *p.* tree	*Ca 7:8*
They art upright as the *p.* tree	*Jer 10:5*
and upon each post were *p.* trees	*Eze 40:16*
and their arches, and their *p.* trees	*Eze 40:22*
and it had *p.* trees, one on this side	*Eze 40:26*
p. trees were upon the posts	*Eze 40:31;* *40:34, 37*
made with cherubims and *p.* trees	*Eze 41:18*
that a *p.* tree was between a cherub	*Eze 41:18*
toward the *p.* tree on the one side	*Eze 41:19*
toward the *p.* tree on the other side	*Eze 41:19*
were cherubims and *p.* trees made	*Eze 41:20*
cherubims and *p.* trees, like as were	*Eze 41:25*
were narrow windows and *p.* trees	*Eze 41:26*
the *p.* tree also, and the apple tree	*Joe 1:12*
Took branches of *p.* trees, and	*Joh 12:13*
struck Jesus with the *p.* of his	*Joh 18:22*

PALMERWORM

That which the *p.* hath left hath	*Joe 1:4*
What the crawling locust left (A)(B)	*Joe 1:4*
What the cutting locust left (R)	*Joe 1:4*
the caterpillar, and the *p.*	*Joe 2:25*

the crawling locust (A)	*Joe 2:25*
the hopper, stripper, and shearer (B)	*Joe 2:25*
the hopper, destroyer, and cutter (R)	*Joe 2:25*
the *p.* devoured them	*Am 4:9*
the locusts are eating (B)(R)	*Am 4:9*

PALMS

both the *p.* of his hands were cut	*1Sa 5:4*
the feet, and the *p.* of her hands	*2Ki 9:35*
graven upon the *p.* of my hands	*Isa 49:16*
knees and upon the *p.* of my hands	*Da 10:10*
smote him with *p.* of their hands	*M't 26:67;* *M'k 14:65*
robes, and *p.* in their hands	*Re 7:9*

PALPABLE

they are *p.* frauds (P)   *Tit 1:16*

PALSIED

are *p.* by terror (A)(R)   *Eze 7:27*

PALSIES

and many taken with *p.* and that   *Ac 8:7*

PALSY

lunatick, and those that had *p.*	*M't 4:24*
epileptics, and paralyzed (A)(E)(N)(P)	*M't 4:24*
epileptics and paralytics (B)(R)	*M't 4:24*
servant lieth at home sick of the *p.*	*M't 8:6*
lieth at home paralyzed (A)(B)(N)(P)(R)	*M't 8:6*
brought to him a man sick of the *p.*	*M't 9:2;* 9:6; M'k 2:3, 5, 9, 10; Lu 5:18, 24; Ac 9:33
a paralyzed man (A)(B)(E)(N)(P)(R)	*M't 9:2;* 9:6; M'k 2:3, 5, 9-10; Lu 5:18, 24; Ac 9:33

PALTI

of Benjamin, *P.* the son of Raphu   *Nu 13:9*

PALTIEL

of Issachar, *P.* the son of Azzan   *Nu 34:26*

PALTITE

Helez the *P.* Ira the son of   *2Sa 23:26*

PAMPERS

p. his servant (A)(B)(R)   *Pr 29:21*

PAMPHYLIA

Phrygia, and *P.* in Egypt, and	*Ac 2:10*
Paphos, they came to Perga in *P.*	*Ac 13:13*
Pisidia, they came to *P.*	*Ac 14:24*
who departed from them from *P.*	*Ac 15:38*
sailed over the sea of Cilicia and *P.*	*Ac 27:5*

PAN

be a meat offering baken in a *p.*	*Le 2:5;* *6:21; 7:9*
baked on a griddle (A)(B)(R)	*Le 2:5;* *6:21; 7:9*
offering of the baking-pan (E)	*Le 2:5;* *6:21; 7:9*
pan (B)	*Nu 7:14;* 7:20, 26, 32, 38, 44, 50, 56, 62, 68, 74, 80
he struck it into the *p.*	*1Sa 2:14*
thrust into the pot (B)	*1Sa 2:14*
she took a *p.* and poured	*2Sa 13:9*
that which he baked in a *p.*	*1Ch 23:29*
baked on the griddle (A)	*1Ch 23:29*
those from the baking-pans (B)	*1Ch 23:29*

the baked offering (R)	*1Ch 23:29*
take thou unto thee an iron *p.*	*Eze 4:3*
take a plate of iron (A)(B)(R)	*Eze 4:3*

PANELED

p. with cedar (S)   *Jer 22:14;* *Eze 41:16; Hab 1:4*

PANELS

panels (S)   *1Ki 7:28; 7:29, 31-32, 35-36*

PANGS

multiply *p.* of childbearing (A)	*Ge 3:16*
Rachel felt birth *p.* (B)	*Ge 35:16*
p. take hold (A)(E)(R)	*Ex 15:14*
all adversity and birth *p.* (A)	*Nu 20:14*
no *p.* of conscience (R)	*1Sa 25:31*
many *p.* (R)	*Ps 32:10;* *Jer 13:21; Ho 13:13; 1Ti 6:10*
no. *p.* in their death (S)	*Ps 73:4*
p. and sorrows shall take hold of	*Isa 13:8*
p. have taken hold upon me, as	*Isa 21:3*
the *p.* of a woman that travaileth	*Isa 21:3*
in pain, and crieth out in her *p.*	*Isa 26:17*
p. as of a woman (A)(E)	*Jer 6:24*
p. take thee (A)(B)	*Jer 13:21*
thou be when *p.* come upon thee	*Jer 22:23*
as the heart of a woman in her *p.*	*Jer 48:41;* *49:22*
and *p.* as of a woman in travail	*Jer 50:43*
p. have taken thee as a woman in	*Mic 4:9*
pains have taken you like a woman in (A)	*Mic 4:9*
early pains of birth *p.* (A)(N)	*M't 24:8;* *M'k 13:8*
liberating from *p.* of death (A)(E)(N)(R)	*Ac 2:24*
groans as if in *p.* of (N)	*Ro 8:22*
am again suffering *p.* (A)	*Ga 4:19*
birth *p.* upon a woman (B)(P)(R)	*1Th 5:3*
many acute (mental) *p.* (A)	*1Ti 6:10*
p. of her delivery (B)(R)	*Re 12:2*

PANIC

brought on *p.* (B)	*Ex 14:24*
threw all the army into *p.* (R)	*J'g 8:12*
city of resultant *p.* (A)(B)(R)	*1Sa 5:9*
deadly *p.* in city (A)(R)	*1Sa 5:11*
p. seized her (A)	*Jer 49:24*
soldiers are in *p.* (R)	*Jer 51:32*
cause to be *p.* - stricken (A)	*Zec 1:21*
day of great *p.* (E)	*Zec 14:13*

PANICKY

men of war *p.* (B)   *Jer 51:32*

PANNAG

market wheat of Minnith, and *P.*   *Eze 27:17*

PANS

make his *p.* to receive ashes	*Ex 27:3*
make pots to take away ashes (A)(E)(R)	*Ex 27:3*
make ashpans for it (B)	*Ex 27:3*
pans (B)	*Nu 7:84; 7:86; 1Ki 7:50*
baked it in *p.* and made cakes	*Nu 11:8*
boiled it in pots, made cakes (A)(B)(E)(R)	*Nu 11:8*
things that were made in *p.*	*1Ch 9:31*
from the baking *p.* (B)	*1Ch 23:29*
in caldrons, and in *p.*	*2Ch 35:13*

PANT

| gasp and *p.* together (A)(B)(E)(R) | *Isa 42:14* |
| that *p.* after the dust of the earth | *Am 2:7* |

PANTED

| I opened my mouth and *p.* | *Ps 119:131* |
| My heart *p.*, fearfulness | *Isa 21:4* |

My mind reels and wanders (A) — Isa 21:4
My heart reels (B)(R) — Isa 21:4
My heart fluttereth (E) — Isa 21:4

PANTETH

set him in safety he p. for (E) — Ps 12:5
My heart p. — Ps 38:10
My heart throbs (A)(E)(R) — Ps 38:10
My heart beats fast (B) — Ps 38:10
As the hart p. after the water brooks — Ps 42:1
As the hart longs for flowing streams (R) — Ps 42:1

PANTOMINE

like a shadow in a p. (A) — Ps 39:6

PANTS

in salvation for which he p. (A) — Ps 12:5

PAPER

The p. reeds by the brooks — Isa 19:7
The meadows by the Nile (A)(B)(E) — Isa 19:7
would not write with p. and ink — 2Jo 12

PAPHOS

gone through the isle unto P. — Ac 13:6
his company loosed from P. — Ac 13:13

PAPS

Egyptians for the p. of thy youth — Eze 23:21
Egypt handled your bosom on (A)(R) — Eze 23:21
Egyptians handled your breasts (B) — Eze 23:21
the handling of thy bosom (E) — Eze 23:21
the p. which thou hast sucked — Lu 11:27
breasts that gave you suck (A)(B)(E)(N)(R) — Lu 11:27
the p. which never gave suck — Lu 23:29
breasts that never gave suck (A)(B)(E)(N)(R) — Lu 23:29
about the p. a golden girdle — Re 1:13
girdle of gold about his breast (A)(B)(E)(N)(P)(R) — Re 1:13

PARABLE

And he took up his p. and said — Nu 23:7
Balaam took up his figurative speech (A) — Nu 23:7
Balaam began his discourse (B)(R) — Nu 23:7; 24:3; 24:20
he took up his p. and said — Nu 23:18
Balaam took up his figurative discourse (A) — Nu 23:18; 23:3, 15
Balaam announced his discourse (B)(R) — Nu 23:18
He took up his oracles (B) — Nu 24:3
he took up discourse (B)(R) — Nu 24:15; 24:20, 23
he took up his prophetic utterance (A) — Nu 24:20; 24:21, 23
Moreover Job continued his p. — Job 27:1
Job again took up his discourse (A)(B)(R) — Job 27:1
Job continued his p. — Job 29:1
Job again took up his — Job 29:1
discussion (A)
Job again took up his discourse (B)(R) — Job 29:1
I will incline mine ear to a p. — Ps 48:4
I will incline my ear to a proverb (A) — Ps 48:4
I will open my mouth in a p. — Ps 78:2
so is a p. in mouth of fools — Pr 26:7; 26:9
so is a proverb in the mouth of fools (B)(R) — Pr 26:7
take up this taunting p. (A)(E) — Isa 14:4
speak a p. unto the house of Israel — Eze 17:2
propound a riddle and speak an allegory (R) — Eze 17:2
utter a p. unto the rebellious house — Eze 24:3
propound also an allegory (B)(R) — Eze 24:3

shall one take up a p. against you — Mic 2:4
take up against you a proverb (B) — Mic 2:4
take up a taunt song against you (R) — Mic 2:4
all these take up a p. against him — Hab 2:6
take up a taunt against him (A)(R) — Hab 2:6
take up a taunt song (B) — Hab 2:6
take up a p. (E) — Hab 2:6
the p. of the sower — M't 13:18; M'k 4:13; Lu 8:11
another p. — M't 13:24; 13:31, 33-34, 36; 21-33
Declare unto us this p. — M't 15:15
Explain this proverb (A) — M't 15:15
Now learn a p. of the fig tree — M't 24:32; Lu 21:29
From the fig tree learn its lesson (A)(B)(N)(R) — M'k 24:32
the twelve asked him the p. — M'k 4:10; 4:13; 7:17; Lu 8:8
without a p. spake he not unto them — M'k 4:34
he had spoken this p. against them — M'k 12:12; Lu 20:19
he spake also a p. unto them — Lu 5:36; 6:39; 8:4; 12:16; 13:6; 14:7; 15:3; 18:1, 9; 19:11; 20:9; 21:29; Joh 10:6
speakest this p. unto us — Lu 12:41

PARABLES

Doth he not speak p. — Eze 20:49
Is he not an inventor of allegories (B)(R) — Eze 20:49
p. acted out by prophets (A)(B)(R) — Ho 12:10
many things to them in p. — M't 13:3; 13:10, 13, 34, 53; 22:1; M'k 3:23; 4:2, 11, 13, 33; 12:1
I will open my mouth in p. — M't 13:35
Pharisees had heard his p. — M't 21:45
but to others in p.; that seeing they — Lu 8:10
told you in p. (A)(P) — Joh 16:25
speaking not in p. (A)(P) — Joh 16:29

PARADISE

To-day shalt thou be with me in p. — Lu 23:43
How that he was caught up into p. — 2Co 12:4
is in the midst of the p. of God — Re 2:7

PARAH

And Avim, and P. — Jos 18:23

PARALLEL

p. to the oblation (S) — Eze 48:18

PARALYZED

p. by fear (B) — Eze 7:27
epilentics, p. (A)(B)(E)(N)(P)(R) — M't 4:24
lieth at home p. (A)(B)(N)(P)(R) — M't 8:6
a p. man (A)(B)(E)(N)(P)(R) — M't 9:2; 9:6; M'k 2:3, 5, 9-10; Lu 5:18, 24; Ac 9:33
paralyzed (S) — M'k 3:1; Lu 6:6; Joh 5:3

PARAMOUR

beloved of a p. (A)(B)(R) — Ho 3:1

PARAMOURS

she doted upon their p. — Eze 23:20

PARAN

he dwelt in the wilderness of P. — Ge 21:21
cloud rested in the wilderness of P. — Nu 10:12
and pitched in the wilderness of P. — Nu 12:16
them from the wilderness of P. — Nu 13:3
unto the wilderness of P. to — Nu 13:26
Red sea, between P. and Tophel — De 1:1
he shined forth from mount P. — De 33:2
went down to the wilderness of P. — 1Sa 25:1

arose out of Midian, and came to P. — 1Ki 11:18
they took men with them out of P. — 1Ki 11:18
and the Holy One from mount P. — Hab 3:3

PARAPET

thou make a p. (S) — De 22:8
the p. of the temple (N) — M't 4:5; 4:9

PARBAR

At P. westward, four at the — 1Ch 26:18
at the causeway, and two at P. — 1Ch 26:18

PARCEL

he bought a p. of a field, where he — Ge 33:19
bought a piece of land (A)(R) — Ge 33:19
he bought the lot (B) — Ge 33:19
in a p. of land Jacob bought — Job 24:32
in the portion of land (A)(B)(R) — Jos 24:32
selleth a p. of ground — Ru 4:3
the tract of land (B) — Ru 4:3
was a p. of land full of barley — 1Ch 11:13
the plot of ground full of barley (A)(E)(R) — 1Ch 11:13; 11:14
a section of the field that was full (B) — 1Ch 11:13; 11:14
the p. of ground that Jacob gave — Joh 4:5
the tract of land that Jacob gave (A)(B) — Joh 4:5
the plot of ground which Jacob gave (N)(P) — Joh 4:5
near the field that Jacob gave (R) — Joh 4:5

PARCHED

eat neither bread, nor p. corn — Le 23:14
and p. corn in the selfsame day — Jos 5:11
he reached her p. corn, and she — Ru 2:14
brethren an ephah of this p. corn — 1Sa 17:17
and five measures of p. corn, and an — 1Sa 25:18
and barley, and flour, and p. corn — 2Sa 17:28
beans, and lentiles, and p. pulse — 2Sa 17:28
p. peas and beans (A)(B) — 2Sa 17:28
p. ground shall become a pool — Isa 35:7
shall inhabit the p. places in — Jer 17:6

PARCHMENTS

the books, but especially the p. — 2Ti 4:13
books, but above all my notebooks (N) — 2Ti 4:13
the books, especially the manuscripts (P) — 2Ti 4:13

PARDON

will not p. your transgressions — Ex 23:21
and p. our iniquity and our sin — Ex 34:9
P., I beseech thee, the iniquity — Nu 14:19
Forgive, I beseech thee (B) — Nu 14:19
I pray thee, p. my sin — 1Sa 15:25
the Lord p. thy servant — 2Ki 5:18
forgive your servant (B) — 2Ki 5:18
blood, which the Lord would not p. — 2Ki 24:4
The good Lord p. every one — 2Ch 30:18
thou art a God ready to p. — Ne 9:17
dost thou not p. my transgression — Job 7:21
O Lord, p. mine iniquity — Ps 25:11
our God, for he will abundantly p. — Isa 55:7
seeketh the truth; and I will p. it — Jer 5:1
How shall I p. thee for this — Jer 5:7
I will p. all their iniquities — Jer 33:8
for I will p. them whom I receive — Jer 50:20

PARDONED

I have p. according to thy word — Nu 14:20
that her iniquity is p.: for she — Isa 40:2
have rebelled: thou hast not p. — La 3:42

PARDONETH

like unto thee, that *p.* iniquity Mic 7:18

PARE

shave her head, and *p.* her De 21:12
nails

PARENT

p.- despisers (B) Ro 1:30

PARENTAGE

not from mortal *p.* (N) 1Pe 1:23

PARENTAL

in her *p.* home (B) Ge 38:11
lamb for his *p.* family (B) Ex 12:3

PARENTS

shall rise up against their M't 10:21;
p. M'k 13:12
the *p.* brought in the child Lu 2:27
Jesus
his *p.* went to Jerusalem every Lu 2:41
year
And her *p.* were astonished: Lu 8:56
but he
hath left house, or *p.* or Lu 18:29
brethren
ye shall be betrayed both by Lu 21:16
p.
who did sin, this man, or his *p.* Joh 9:2
hath this man sinned, nor his *p.* Joh 9:3
until they called the *p.* of him Joh 9:18
that
His *p.* answered them and Joh 9:20
said, We
These words spake his *p.* Joh 9:22
because
Therefore said his *p.*, He is Joh 9:23
of age
of evil things, disobedient to *p.* Ro 1:30
no loyalty to *p.* (N)(P) Ro 1:30
ought not to lay up for the *p.* 2Co 12:14
but the *p.* for the children 2Co 12:14
Children, obey your *p.* in the Eph 6:1
Lord
obey your *p.* in all things: for Col 3:20
at home, and to requite their *p.* 1Ti 5:4
disobedient to *p.*, unthankful 2Ti 3:2
was hid three months of his Heb 11:23
p.

PARKS

I laid out gardens and *p.* Ec 2:5
(B)(E)(R)

PARLOUR

and he was sitting in a summer J'g 3:20
p.
shut the doors of the *p.* upon J'g 3:23
him
the doors of the *p.* were locked J'g 3:24
he opened not the doors of the J'g 3:25
p.
and brought them into the *p.* 1Sa 9:22

PARLOURS

and of the inner *p.* thereof 1Ch 28:11

PARMASHTA

And *P.* and Arisai, and Aridai Es 9:9

PARMENAS

and Timon, and *P.*, and Ac 6:5
Nicolas a

PARNACH

Zebulun, Elizaphan the son of Nu 34:25
P.

PAROSH

The children of *P.* two Ezr 2:3
thousand
of the sons of *P.* Ramiah Ezr 10:25
After him Pedaiah the son of Ne 3:25
P.
The children of *P.* two thousand Ne 7:8
The chief of the people; *P.* Ne 10:14

PARSHANDATHA

P., and Dalphon, and Aspatha Es 9:7

PART

they stood at nether *p.* of Ex 19:17
mountain
thou shalt take the breast, it Ex 29:26
shall be thy *p.*
part (S) Ex 29:40;
Le 14:21; Nu 15:4; 28:13, 21, 29; 29:4,
10, 15
p. of the beaten corn, *p.* of oil Le 2:16
thereof
he shall have the right shoulder Le 7:33
for his *p.*
the breast of consecration was Le 8:29
Moses' *p.*
if any *p.* of their carcase fall Le 11:37;
thereon 11:38
his hair fallen off from the *p.* Le 13:41
of his head
neither shalt thou have any Nu 18:20;
p. among them De 10:9; 12:21; 14:27,
29; 18:1; Jos 14:3; 18:7
I am thy *p.* and thine Nu 18:20
inheritance in Israel
might see utmost *p.* of the Nu 22:41;
people 23:13
he provided the first *p.* for De 33:21
himself
the *p.* of Judah was too much Jos 19:9
for them
ye have no *p.* in the Jos 22:25;
Lord 22:27
her hap was to light on a *p.* of Ru 2:3
the field
perform to thee *p.* of a kinsman Ru 3:13
Saul tarried in the utmost *p.* 1Sa 14:2
of the camp
our *p.* to deliver him into 1Sa 23:20
king's hand
as his *p.* is that goeth down 1Sa 30:24
to battle, so shall his *p.* be that
Sheba said, We have no *p.* in 2Sa 20:1
David
the lepers were come to 2Ki 7:5;
uttermost *p.* 7:8
cut off a *p.* of Israel (S) 2Ki 10:32
if able on thy *p.* to set 2Ki 18:23;
riders Isa 36:8
greatest *p.* had kept house of 1Ch 12:29
Saul
the priests went into the 2Ch 29:16
inner *p.*
cast out to the uttermost *p.* of Ne 1:9
heaven
restore the hundredth *p.* of the Ne 5:11
money
I will answer my *p.* will shew Job 32:17
my opinion
neither *p.* like potsherds (B) Job 41:30
their inward *p.* is very Ps 5:9
wickedness
in hidden *p.* shalt make me Ps 51:6
know wisdom
Lord takes my *p.* with them Ps 118:7
that help me
nor highest *p.* of the dust of the Pr 8:26
world
rejoicing in the habitable *p.* of Pr 8:31
his earth
shall have *p.* of inheritance Pr 17:2
among brethren
hiss for the fly that is in the Isa 7:18
utmost *p.*
from utmost *p.* of earth we Isa 24:16
heard songs
he burneth *p.* thereof in the Isa 44:16;
fire, with *p.* thereof he eateth 44:19
thou shalt drink the sixth *p.* of Eze 4:11
an hin
cut off on our *p.* (S) Eze 37:11
leave not the sixth *p.* of thee, Eze 39:2
and cause thee
sixth *p.* of an ephah of an Eze 45:13
homer of wheat
it shall be the prince's *p.* to Eze 45:17
give offerings
a meat offering the sixth *p.* Eze 46:14
of an ephah
his feet *p.* of iron, and *p.* of Da 2:33;
clay 41:42
the king saw *p.* of the hand Da 5:5;
that wrote 5:24
arms shall stand on his *p.* they Da 11:31
shall pollute
it devoured great deep, did eat Am 7:4
up a *p.*

he was in the hinder *p.* of the M'k 4:38
ship
he that is not against us, is on M'k 9:40
our *p.*
and Mary hath chosen that Lu 10:42
good *p.*
your inward *p.* is full of Lu 11:39
ravening and wickedness
as lightning that lighteneth Lu 17:24
out of one *p.* shining to other
p. under heaven
if I wash thee not, hast no *p.* Joh 13:8
with me
soldiers made four parts, Joh 19:23
every soldier a *p.*
and had obtained *p.* of this Ac 1:17
ministry
that he may take *p.* of this Ac 1:25
ministry
Ananias kept back *p.* of price, Ac 5:2;
and brought *p.* and laid it at 5:3
thou hast neither *p.* nor lot in Ac 8:21
this matter
p. held with the Jews, *p.* with Ac 14:4
the apostles
the chief city of that *p.* of Ac 16:12
Macedonia
more *p.* knew not wherefore Ac 19:32
they came
perceived that the one *p.* were Ac 23:6
Sadducees
the more *p.* advised to depart Ac 27:12
thence
honour to that *p.* which 1Co 12:24
lacked
of whom the greater *p.* 1Co 15:6
remain to this day
what was lacking on your *p.* 1Co 16:17
they supplied
what *p.* he that believeth with 2Co 6:15
infidel
the working in the measure of Eph 4:16
every *p.*
that he of the contrary *p.* may Tit 2:8
be ashamed
himself likewise took *p.* of Heb 2:14
the same
on their *p.* he is evil spoken 1Pe 4:14
of, but on your *p.* he is glorified
and the third *p.* of trees was Re 8:7
burnt up
holy that hath *p.* in the first Re 20:6
resurrection
all liars shall have their *p.* in Re 21:8
the lake
God shall take away his *p.* out Re 22:19
of book

IN PART

blindness *in p.* is happened to Ro 11:25
Israel
we know *in p.* and we 1Co 13:9
prophesy *in p.*
then that which is *in p.* shall 1Co 13:10
be done away
I know *in p.* but then shall I 1Co 13:12
know as I am
as also ye have acknowledged 2Co 1:14
us *in p.*
caused grief, it hath not 2Co 2:5
grieved me but *in p.*

THIRD PART

for a ram, flour mingled with Nu 15:6;
the *third p.* of an hin of oil 28:14;
Eze 46:14
thou shalt offer the *third p.* of Nu 15:7
an hin of wine
David sent a *third p.* of the 2Sa 18:2
people
a *third p.* that enter in on the 2Ki 11:5
sabbath
a *third p.* of you shall be 2Ch 23:4
porters
charge ourselves with *third p.* Ne 10:32
of shekel
burn with fire a *third p.* a Eze 5:2;
third p. smite a *third p.* scatter 5:12
in wind
but the *third p.* shall be left Zec 13:8
therein
I will bring the *third p.* Zec 13:9
through the fire
third p. of the trees was burnt Re 8:7
up
and the *third p.* of the sea Re 8:8
became blood
third p. of the creatures died, Re 8:9
third p. of ships

and it fell upon the *third p.* of   *Re 8:10*
the rivers
the *third p.* of the waters   *Re 8:11*
became wormwood
the *third p.* of the sun, moon,   *Re 8:12*
and stars, was smitten, the day
shone not for a *third p.* of it
were prepared for to slay   *Re 9:15*
the *third p.* of men
by these three was the *third p.*   *Re 9:18*
of men killed
his tail drew *third p.* of the   *Re 12:4*
stars of heaven

FOURTH PART

flour mingled with *fourth p.*   *Ex 29:40;*
of an hin of oil   *Nu 15:4; 28:15*
fourth p. of an hin of wine   *Ex 29:40;*
for a drink offering   *Le 23:13; Nu 15:5;*
   28:7, 14
I have here the *fourth p.* of a   *1Sa 9:8*
shekel
posts of olive tree *fourth p.* of   *1Ki 6:33*
wall
the *fourth p.* of a cab of   *2Ki 6:25*
doves' dung
read one *fourth p.* another   *Ne 9:3*
fourth p. they
power was given over *fourth p.*   *Re 6:8*
of earth

FIFTH PART

take up *fifth p.* of the land of   *Ge 41:34*
Egypt
ye shall give the *fifth p.* to   *Ge 47:24;*
Pharaoh   *47:26*
and shall add the *fifth p.*   *Le 5:16;*
thereto   *6:5; 22:14; 27:13, 19, 27, 31;*
   Nu 5:7
lintel and side posts were a   *1Ki 6:31*
fifth p.

TENTH PART

an homer is the *tenth p.* of an   *Ex 16:36*
ephah
bring for offering *tenth p.* of   *Le 5:11;*
an ephah of fine flour   *6:20; Nu 28:5*
the *tenth p.* of an ephah of   *Nu 5:15*
barley meal
ye shall offer even the *tenth p.*   *Nu 18:26*
of the tithe
bath and ephah may contain   *Eze 45:11*
tenth p.
ye shall offer the *tenth p.* of a   *Eze 45:14*
bath of oil
to whom Abraham gave a   *Heb 7:2*
tenth p. of all

PARTAKER

and hast been *p.* with   *Ps 50:18*
adulterers
have taken part with   *Ps 50:18*
adulterers (A)(B)
keep company with adulterers   *Ps 50:18*
(R)
in hope should be *p.* of his   *1Co 9:10*
hope
hope of a share in the crop   *1Co 9:10*
(B)(P)(R)
I might be *p.* with you   *1Co 9:23*
I may become a participator   *1Co 9:23*
in (A)
I may have a share in it   *1Co 9:23*
(B)(R)
I want to play my part in (P)   *1Co 9:23*
if I by grace be a *p.* why   *1Co 10:30*
am I evil
If I partake with   *1Co 10:30*
thankfulness (A)(B)(E)(N)(R)
neither be *p.* of other men's   *1Ti 5:22*
sins
nor share or participate in   *1Ti 5:22*
another (A)
make no common cause with   *1Ti 5:22*
sins (B)
be thou *p.* of the afflictions of   *2Ti 1:8*
take your share of sufferings   *2Ti 1:8*
(A)(B)(N)(R)
suffer hardship with the gospel   *2Ti 1:8*
(E)
accept all hardship the gospel   *2Ti 1:8*
entails (P)
husbandman must be first *p.* of   *2Ti 2:6*
fruits
farmer must first share of the   *2Ti 2:6*
produce (B)(P)(R)

his labour has first claim on his   *2Ti 2:6*
crop (N)
a *p.* of the glory that shall be   *1Pe 5:1*
revealed
a sharer in the glory (A)(B)   *1Pe 5:1*
will share with you the glories   *1Pe 5:1*
(P)
bid God speed is *p.* of his evil   *2Jo 11*
deeds

PARTAKERS

we would not have been *p.*   *M't 23:30*
with them
we would not have aided   *M't 23:30*
them (A)
would not have been their   *M't 23:30*
associates (B)
never had taken part with   *M't 23:30*
them (N)(R)
never have joined in the   *M't 23:30*
killing of (P)
made *p.* of their spiritual   *Ro 15:27*
things
come to share spiritual   *Ro 15:27*
blessings (A)(P)(R)
shared in their spiritual things   *Ro 15:27*
(B)(N)
be *p.* of this power over you   *1Co 9:12*
share in this rightful claim (A)   *1Co 9:12*
if you allow others these   *1Co 9:12*
rights (N)
we have never exercised this   *1Co 9:12*
right (P)(R)
at the altar are *p.* with the   *1Co 9:13;*
altar   *10:18*
tend the altar share with the   *1Co 9:13*
altar (A)(B)(P)(R)
we are all *p.* of that one bread   *1Co 10:17*
we all participate in that one   *1Co 10:17*
bread (B)
we all share one bread (P)   *1Co 10:17*
cannot be *p.* of the Lord's   *1Co 10:21*
table and
cannot partake of Lord's   *1Co 10:21*
table (A)(E)(N)(R)
cannot participate in Lord's   *1Co 10:21*
table (B)
cannot be a guest at Lord's   *1Co 10:21*
table and (P)
as ye are *p.* of the sufferings   *2Co 1:7*
you share and are partners in   *2Co 1:7*
(A)
sharing as well in the sufferings   *2Co 1:7*
(B)
have part in the sufferings (N)   *2Co 1:7*
as you share in our sufferings   *2Co 1:7*
(R)
p. of his promise in Christ   *Eph 3:6*
participants of the promise   *Eph 3:6*
(B)
sharers together of the promise   *Eph 3:6*
(N)
equal partners of the promise   *Eph 3:6*
(P)
Be not *p.* with them   *Eph 5:7*
do not associate or be sharers   *Eph 5:7*
with them (A)
be not their companions (B)   *Eph 5:7*
Have no part or lot with them   *Eph 5:7*
(N)
Have nothing to do with men   *Eph 5:7*
like that (P)
do not associate with them   *Eph 5:7*
(R)
ye are all *p.* of my grace   *Ph'p 1:7*
you share with me in divine   *Ph'p 1:7*
grace (B)
you all share in the privilege   *Ph'p 1:7*
that (N)
we shared together the grace   *Ph'p 1:7*
of God (P)
meet to be *p.* of the   *Col 1:12*
inheritance
share the portion which is the   *Col 1:12*
(A)
share in the inheritance   *Col 1:12*
(B)(R)
share the heritage of God's   *Col 1:12*
people (N)
share the lot of those who are   *Col 1:12*
(P)
p. of the benefit   *1Ti 6:2*
the children are *p.* of flesh   *Heb 2:14*
children share flesh and blood   *Heb 2:14*
(A)(B)(N)(R)
children are sharers of flesh   *Heb 2:14*
and (E)
children have a common   *Heb 2:14*

physical nature as human beings
(P)
p. of the heavenly calling   *Heb 3:1*
who share in the heavenly   *Heb 3:1*
calling (A)(N)(P)(R)
sharers in the heavenly calling   *Heb 3:1*
(B)
made *p.* of Christ, if we hold   *Heb 3:14*
confidence
become fellows with Christ   *Heb 3:14*
and share in all he has for us,
if only we hold (A)
become sharers with Christ, if   *Heb 3:14*
(B)(R)
become Christ's partners if   *Heb 3:14*
only (N)
continue to share so long as   *Heb 3:14*
we maintain (P)
made *p.* of the Holy Ghost   *Heb 6:4*
become sharers of the Holy   *Heb 6:4*
Spirit (A)
participants of the Holy Spirit   *Heb 6:4*
(B)
share in the Holy Spirit (N)   *Heb 6:4*
becoming *p.* with them (E)   *Heb 10:33*
whereof all are *p.*, then are ye   *Heb 12:8*
bastards
discipline which all share   *Heb 12:8*
(A)(B)(N)
correction which all sons   *Heb 12:8*
have to bear (P)
discipline which all have   *Heb 12:8*
participated (R)
might be *p.* of his holiness   *Heb 12:10*
become sharers in his own   *Heb 12:10*
holiness (A)
might share in his holiness   *Heb 12:10*
(B)(N)(R)
to teach us his holiness (P)   *Heb 12:10*
ye are *p.* of Christ's suffering   *1Pe 4:13*
sharing in Christ's sufferings   *1Pe 4:13*
(A)(B)
share in Christ's sufferings   *1Pe 4:13*
(N)(P)(R)
might be *p.* of the divine nature   *2Pe 1:4*
become sharers of the divine   *2Pe 1:4*
nature (A)(B)
share in the very being of God   *2Pe 1:4*
(N)
share in God's essential nature   *2Pe 1:4*
(P)
that ye be not *p.* of her sins   *Re 18:4*
may not share in her sins (A)   *Re 18:4*
not participate in her sins (B)   *Re 18:4*
have no fellowship with her sins   *Re 18:4*
(E)
lest you take part in her sins   *Re 18:4*
(N)(R)
lest you become accomplices in   *Re 18:4*
her sins (P)

PARTAKEST

them *p.* of the root and   *Ro 11:17*
fatness of
to share the richness of the   *Ro 11:17*
olive tree (A)(R)
sharing the rich sap of the   *Ro 11:17*
olive tree (B)
share the same root and sap   *Ro 11:17*
of (N)
share like a natural branch   *Ro 11:17*
(P)

PARTED

and from thence it was *p.* and   *Ge 2:10*
of fire, and *p.* them both   *2Ki 2:11*
asunder
waters, they *p.* hither and   *2Ki 2:14*
thither
By what way is the light *p.*   *Job 38:24*
among the nations, and *p.*   *Joe 3:2*
my land
and *p.* his garments, casting   *M't 27:35;*
lots   *M'k 15:24*
They *p.* my garments among   *M't 27:35*
then
they *p.* his raiment, and cast   *Lu 23:34*
lots
he was *p.* from them, and   *Lu 24:51*
carried
they *p.* my raiment among   *Joh 19:24*
them
p. them to all men, as every   *Ac 2:45*
man
after we were *p.* from them   *Ac 21:1*
(S)

PARTETH

Whatsoever p. the hoof, and is	Le 11:3
And every beast that p. the hoof	De 14:6
cease, and p. between the mighty	Pr 18:18

PARTHIANS

P. and Medes, and Elamites	Ac 2:9

PARTIAL

not be p. (A)(R)	De 1:17; 16:19
not p. and take no bribe (A)(R)	De 10:17
but have been p. in the law	Mal 2:9
shown favoritism to persons in	Mal 2:9
your administration of the law (A)	
you have shown partiality in the law (B)	Mal 2:9
had respect of persons in the law (E)	Mal 2:9
shown partiality in your instruction (R)	Mal 2:9
Are ye not become p. in yourselves	Jas 2:4
Are ye not discriminating among your own (A)(B)	Jas 2:4
Do you not make distinctions among yourselves (E)	Jas 2:4
do you not see that you are inconsistent (N)	Jas 2:4
making class distinctions in your mind (P)(R)	Jas 2:4

PARTIALITY

show no p. (B)	De 1:17
no p., nor can be bribed (B)	De 10:17
shall not show p. (R)(S)	De 16:19
p. in judging is not good (R)	Pr 24:23
respecting persons showing p. (A)(R)	Isa 3:9
shown p. in law (B)(R)	Mal 2:9
God shows no p. (R)	Ac 10:34
God shows no p. (A)(R)	Ro 2:11
there† is no p. (B)(R)	Eph 6:9
there is no p. (A)(B)(R)	Col 3:25
doing nothing by p.	1Ti 5:21
observe these things without discrimination (N)	1Ti 5:21
act with strict impartiality (N)(P)	1Ti 5:21
show no p. (A)(B)(R)	Jas 2:1
if you show p. (B)(R)	Jas 2:9
of mercy and good fruits, without p.	Jas 3:17
impartial and unfeigned (A)(B)	Jas 3:17
without variance (E)	Jas 3:17
without uncertainty or insincerity (R)	Jas 3:17

PARTICIPANTS

p. of the promise (B)	Eph 3:6
p. of Holy Spirit (B)	Heb 6:4

PARTICIPATE

do not p. in (B)	Eph 5:11

PARTICIPATION

p. in the blood of (R)	1Co 10:16

PARTICULAR

body of Christ, members in p.	1Co 12:27
Christ's body, members of it, each part severally and distinct (A)	1Co 12:27
Christ's body, members with assigned parts (B)	1Co 12:27
every one of you in p. so love	Eph 5:33

PARTICULARLY

he declared p. what	Ac 21:19
we cannot now speak p.	Heb 9:5

PARTIES

cause of both p. shall come before	Ex 22:9
have to be p. (A)	1Co 11:19

PARTING

Babylon stood at the p. of the way	Eze 21:21

PARTITION

made a p. by the chains of gold	1Ki 6:21
broken down the middle wall of p.	Eph 2:14
abolished the hostile dividing wall (A)	Eph 2:14
broken down the enmity which stood (N)	Eph 2:14
breaking down the barrier which lay (P)	Eph 2:14
broken down the middle wall of hostility (R)	Eph 2:14

PARTLY

shall be p. strong, and p. broken	Da 2:42
you; and I p. believe it	1Co 11:18
P. whilst ye were made a	Heb 10:33
p. whilst ye became companions	Heb 10:33

PARTNER

Whoso is p. with a thief hateth his	Pr 29:24
he is my p. and fellowhelper	2Co 8:23
Titus my p. (N)(R)	2Co 8:23
If thou count me therefore a p.	Ph'm 17

PARTNERS

And they beckoned unto their p.	Lu 5:7
Zebedee, which were p. with Simon	Lu 5:10
are p. in (A)	2Co 1:7
equal p. of the promise (P)	Eph 3:6
p. with me (E)(N)	Ph'p 4:15
become Christ's p. (N)	Heb 3:14
p. with those so treated (R)	Heb 10:33

PARTNERSHIP

what p. have (A)(R)	2Co 6:14
p. with me (A)(B)	Ph'p 4:1

PARTOOK

p. with glad and generous hearts (R)	Ac 2:46

PARTRIDGE

as when one doth hunt a p. in the	1Sa 26:20
the p. sitteth on eggs, and hatcheth	Jer 17:11

PARTS

four p. shall be your own, for seed	Ge 47:24
hand, and thou shalt see my back p.	Ex 33:23
Aaron's sons, shall lay the p. the parts (S)	Le 1:8
	Le 14:10; 23:13, 17; 24:5-6, 9; 28:9, 12, 20, 28; 29:3, 9, 14
thing superfluous or lacking in his p.	Le 22:23
lie on the east p. shall go forward	Nu 10:5
were in the uttermost p. of the camp	Nu 11:1
divide the prey into two p.; between	Nu 31:27
giveth thee to inherit, into three p.	De 19:3
by the private p. (A)(B)(R)	De 25:11
out unto the outmost p. of heaven	De 30:4
they shall divide it into seven p.	Jos 18:5
describe the land into seven p.	Jos 18:6
it by cities into seven p. in a book	Jos 18:9
they had emerods in their secret p.	1Sa 5:9
and said, We have ten p. in the king	2Sa 19:43
throughout all the p. thereof	1Ki 6:38
and all their hinder p. were inward	1Ki 7:25; 2Ch 4:4
of Israel divided into two p.	1Ki 16:21
two p. of all you that go forth	2Ki 11:7
nine p. to dwell in other cities	Ne 11:1
these are p. of his ways: but how	Job 26:14

hath put wisdom in the inward p.	Job 38:36
I will not conceal his p. nor his	Job 41:12
uttermost p. of the earth for thy	Ps 2:8
the inward p. (S)	Ps 31:9
thou desirest truth in the inward p.	Ps 51:6
shall go into the lower p. of the earth	Ps 63:9
dwell in the uttermost p. are afraid	Ps 65:8
he smote his enemies in the hinder p.	Ps 78:66
which divided the Red sea into p.	Ps 136:13
dwell in the uttermost p. of the sea	Ps 139:9
wrought in the lowest p. of the earth	Ps 139:15
into the innermost p. of the belly	Pr 18:8; 26:22
searching all the inward p. of the belly	Pr 20:27
so do stripes the inward p. of the belly	Pr 20:30
the Lord will discover their secret p.	Isa 3:17
and mine inward p. for Kir-haresh	Isa 16:11
shout, ye lower p. of the earth	Isa 44:23
I will put my law in their inward p.	Jer 31:33
and passed between the p. thereof	Jer 34:18
passed between the p. of the calf	Jer 34:19
set thee in the low p. of the earth	Eze 26:20
their inward p. to shake (S)	Eze 29:7
death, to the nether p. of the earth	Eze 31:14
comforted in the nether p. of the earth	Eze 31:16
Eden unto the nether p. of the earth	Eze 31:18
unto the nether p. of the earth, with	Eze 32:18
into the nether p. of the earth, which	Eze 32:24
we are cut off for our p.	Eze 37:11
from thy place out of the north p.	Eze 38:15
thee to come up from the north p.	Eze 39:2
in length as one of the other p.	Eze 48:8
two p. therein shall be cut off	Zec 13:8
he turned aside into the p. of Galilee	M't 2:22
from the uttermost p. of the earth to	M't 12:42
came into the p. of Dalmanutha	M'k 8:10
came from the utmost p. of the earth	Lu 11:31
his garments, and made four p.	Joh 19:23
and in the p. of Libya about Cyrene	Ac 2:10
when he had gone over those p.	Ac 20:2
having no more place in these p.	Ro 15:23
our uncomely p. have more abundant	1Co 12:23
For our comely p. have no need: but	1Co 12:24
first into the lower p. of the earth	Eph 4:9
great city was divided into three p.	Re 16:19

PARTY

be with the p. (N)	Lu 2:44
when you give a p. (N)	Lu 14:13
p. of the Sadducees (A)(B)(N)(P)(R)	Ac 5:17
the Pharisee p. (B)(N)(P)(R)	Ac 15:5
the Pharisees' p. arose (S)	Ac 23:9
strictest p. of our religion (R)	Ac 26:5
divisions, p. spirit (A)(P)(R)	Ga 5:20

PARUAH

Jehoshaphat the son of P. in	1Ki 4:17

PARVAIM

and the gold was gold of P.	2Ch 3:6

PASACH

sons of Japhlet; *P*. and Bimhal   *1Ch 7:33*

PAS-DAMMIM

He was with David at *P*. and *1Ch 11:13*

PASEAH

Eshton begat Beth-rapha, and *1Ch 4:12*
P.

children of Uzza, the children *Ezr 2:49*
of *P*.

repaired Jehoiada the son of *P*. *Ne 3:6*

PASHUR

the son of Jeroham, the son *1Ch 9:12*
of *P*.
The children of *P*. a thousand *Ezr 2:38*;
two   *Ne 7:41*
And of the sons of *P*.;   *Ezr 10:22*
Elioenai
P., Amariah, Malchijah   *Ne 10:3*
the son of *P*. the son of   *Ne 11:12*
Malchiah
P. the son of Immer the priest *Jer 20:1*
P. smote Jeremiah the prophet *Jer 20:2*
P. brought forth Jeremiah out *Jer 20:3*
of
Lord hath not called thy name *Jer 20:3*
P.
P., all that dwell in thine *Jer 20:6*
house
king Zedekiah sent unto him *P*. *Jer 21:1*
and Gedaliah the son of *P*. and *Jer 38:1*
and *P*. the son of Malchiah *Jer 38:1*

PASS

and it came to *p*. when they *Ge 4:8*
were in the
And it shall come to *p*. when I *Ge 9:14*
bring a
And it came to *p*. when he *Ge 12:11*
was come
Therefore it shall come to *p*. *Ge 12:12*
when the
And it came to *p*. that, when *Ge 12:14*
Abram
it came to *p*. in the days of *Ge 14:1*
Amraphel
And it came to *p*. that, when *Ge 15:17*
the sun
will fetch bread, after that ye *Ge 18:5*
shall *p*. on
it came to *p*. when they had *Ge 19:17*
brought
it came to *p*. when God had *Ge 19:29*
destroyed
And it came to *p*. on the *Ge 19:34*
morrow, that
And it came to *p*. at that *Ge 21:22*
time, that
And it came to *p*. after *Ge 22:1*;
these things   *22:20*
And let it come to *p*. that the *Ge 24:14*
damsel
And it came to *p*. before he *Ge 24:15*
had done
And it came to *p*. as the *Ge 24:22*
camels had
And it came to *p*. when he saw *Ge 24:30*
it shall come to *p*. that when *Ge 24:43*
the virgin
And it came *to p*. the same *Ge 26:32*
day
And it came to *p*. when she *Ge 35:17*
was in
and god will shortly bring it to *Ge 41:32*
p.
I will make my goodness *p*. *Ex 33:19*
before thee
p. through the boards (S) *Ex 36:33*
it came to *p*. on the twentieth *Nu 10:11*
day of
inheritance of their father to *Nu 27:7*;
p. to them   *27:8*
ye shall *p*. before your *Jos 1:14*
brethren armed
he said to people, *P*. on, and *Jos 6:7*
compass the city
and it came to *p*. on the *J'g 14:17*
seventh day
bid the servants *p*. on before *1Sa 9:27*
us
And all those sighs came to *p*. *1Sa 10:9*
that day

went out to the *p*. (S) *1Sa 13:23*
Jesse made Abinadab *p*. *1Sa 16:8*
before Samuel
Jesse, made seven of his sons *1Sa 16:10*
p. before him
a mountain *p*. (B) *1Sa 25:20*
And it came to *p*. after forty *2Sa 15:7*
years, that
let me *p*. through (S) *Ne 2:7*
there was no place for the *Ne 2:14*
beast to *p*.
as a stream of brooks they *p*. *Job 6:15*
away
and remember it as waters *Job 11:16*
that *p*. away
and people shall be troubled, *Job 34:20*
and *p*. away
as snail which melteth let them *Ps 58:8*
p. away
those who *p*. by (S) *Pr 9:15*
moving his lips he bringeth *Pr 16:30*
evil to *p*.
the simple *p*. on and are *Pr 22:3*;
punished   *27:12*
idols *p*. away (E)(R) *Isa 2:18*
gone out to the *p*. (S) *Isa 10:29*
in every place where *Isa 30:32*
grounded staff shall *p*.
no galley nor gallant ship *Isa 33:21*
shall *p*. thereby
dried up rivers, now have I *Isa 37:26*
brought it to *p*.
they *p*. over the deeds of the *Jer 5:28*
wicked (S)
the things I have given shall *p*. *Jer 8:13*
away
come to *p*. after that I have *Jer 12:15*
plucked
shall come to *p*. if they will *Jer 12:16*
diligently
I will make thee to *p*. with *Jer 15:14*
thine enemies
flocks shall *p*. again under the *Jer 33:13*
hands of him that telleth them
nor doth any son of man *p*. *Jer 51:43*
thereby
cause a barber's razor to *p*. on *Eze 5:1*
thine head
And it came to *p*. in the *Eze 20:1*
seventh year
I will cause you to *p*. under *Eze 20:37*
rod, and bring
whom dost thou *p*. in *Eze 32:19*
beauty? go down
p. ye unto Calneh and see, go *Am 6:2*
to Hamath
p. ye away, thou inhabitant of *Mic 1:11*
Saphir
and their king shall *p*. before *Mic 2:13*
them
before decree bring forth, the *Zep 2:2*
day *p*. as
I have caused thy iniquity to *p*. *Zec 3:4*
from thee
but it shall come to *p*. that at *Zec 14:7*
evening
heaven and earth shall *p*. one *M't 5:18*
tittle not *p*.
Father, let this cup *p*. from *M't 26:39*;
me   *M'k 14:35*
they which would *p*. from *Lu 16:26*
hence to you cannot; nor can
they *p*. to us from you
he ran to see him, for he was *Lu 19:4*
to *p*. that way
if she *p*. the flower of her age, *1Co 7:36*
and need
as flower of the grass he shall *Jas 1:10*
p. away
p. time of your sojourning *1Pe 1:17*
here in fear
in which the heavens shall *p*. *2Pe 3:10*
away

PASS BY

cover thee with my hand *Ex 33:22*
while I *p*. by
Sihon would not let us *p*. by *De 2:30*
him
then Jesse made Shammah to *1Sa 16:9*
p. by
all they that *p*. by the way do *Ps 80:12*
pluck her
all that *p*. by the way spoil *Ps 89:41*
him, he is at
many nations shall *p*. by this *Jer 22:8*
city

all ye that *p*. by behold and see *La 1:12*
all that *p*. by clap their hands *La 2:15*
at thee
a reproach in sight of all that *Eze 5:14*
p. by
and caused me to *p*. by them *Eze 37:2*
round about
caused me to *p*. by four *Eze 46:21*
corners of the earth
I will not again *p*. by them *Am 7:8*;
any more   *8:2*
ye pull off garments of them *Mic 2:8*
that *p*. by
that no man might *p*. by that *M't 8:28*
way
hearing the multitude *p*. by he *Lu 18:36*
asked
and to *p*. by you into *2Co 1:16*
Macedonia

PASS *NOT*

my lord, *p*. *not* away from thy *Ge 18:3*
servant
beware that thou *p*. *not* such a *2Ki 6:9*
place
avoid it, *p*. *not* by it, turn aside *Pr 4:15*
seek not Beth-el, *p*. *not* to *Am 5:5*
Beer-sheba

PASS *OVER*

God made a wind to *p*. *over* *Ge 8:1*
the earth
that I will not *p*. *over* this *Ge 31:52*
heap to thee
p. *over* before me, and put a *Ge 32:16*
space betwixt
let my lord *p*. *over* before thy *Ge 33:14*
servant
when I see blood, I will *p*. *Ex 12:13*;
over you   *12:23*
as still as a stone, till thy *Ex 15:16*
people *p*. *over*
but thy servants will *p*. *over* *Nu 32:27*;
  32:29, 32
if they will not *p*. *over* with *Nu 32:30*
you armed
thou art to *p*. *over* through Ar *De 2:18*
this day
p. *over* Arnon *De 2:24*
until I shall *p*. *over* Jordan *De 2:29*
ye shall *p*. *over* armed before *De 3:18*
your brethren
thou art to *p*. *over* Jordan this *De 9:1*;
day   *11:31; 27:2; Jos 1:11; 3:6, 14; 4:5*
then *p*. *over* into the land of *Jos 22:19*
possession
and suffered not a man to *p*. *J'g 3:28*
over
his master said, We will *p*. *J'g 19:12*
over to Gibeah
behold, we will *p*. *over* to *1Sa 14:8*
these men
David said to Ittai, Go and *p*. *2Sa 15:22*
over
lodge not in plains, but *2Sa 17:16*
speedily *p*. *over*
set a bound, that they may not *Ps 104:9*
p. *over*
it is a glory to *p*. *over* a *Pr 19:11*
transgression
p. *over* to Tarshish, howl ye *Isa 23:6*
inhabitants
p. *over* to Chittim; by *Isa 23:12*;
morning shall *p*. *over*   *28:19*
he shall *p*. *over* to his *Isa 31:9*
stronghold for fear
the way of holiness, unclean *Isa 35:8*
shall not *p*. *over*
uncover the thigh, *p*. *over* the *Isa 47:2*
rivers
the depths, a way for *Isa 51:10*
ransomed to *p*. *over*
for *p*. *over* the isles of Chittim *Jer 2:10*
and see
though they roar, yet can they *Jer 5:22*
not *p*. *over* it
it was a river that I could not *Eze 47:5*
p. *over*
and let seven times *p*. *over* *Da 4:16*;
him   *4:25*
the king of the north shall *p*. *Da 4:40*
over
his mind shall change, he *Hab 1:11*
shall *p*. *over*
and *p*. *over* judgment, and *Lu 11:42*
love of God

PASS *THROUGH*

I will *p. through* all thy flock *Ge 30:32* to-day
I will *p. through* land of Egypt *Ex 12:12* this night
the Lord will *p. through* to *Ex 12:23* smite the Egyptians
not let any of thy seed *p.* *Le 18:21;* through fire to Molech *De 18:10;* *2Ki 17:17*
let us I pray thee *p. through* *Nu 20:17* thy country
let me *p. through* thy land *Nu 21:22;* *De 2:27*
Sihon not suffer Israel to *p.* *Nu 21:23;* through *J'g 11:20*
ye are to *p. through* the coasts *De 2:4* of Edom
water to drink, only I will *p.* *De 2:28* through on my feet
p. through the host and *Jos 1:11* command the people
and made them *p. through* *2Sa 12:31* brickkiln
they divided the land to *p.* *1Ki 18:6* through it
to *p. through* the fire *2Ki 16:3;* 21:6; 23:10; 2Ch 33:6; *Jer 32:35;* *Eze 20:26, 31*
caused them to *p. through* the *Ps 78:13;* sea *136:14*
he shall *p. through* Judah, and *Isa 8:8* go over
shall *p. through* it hardly *Isa 8:21* bestead and hungry
as whirlwinds in the south *p.* *Isa 21:1* through so it
p. through thy land as a *Isa 23:10* river, O Tarshish
the overflowing scourge shall *Isa 28:15;* *p. through* *28:18*
none shall *p. through* it for *Isa 34:10* ever and ever
burnt up, so that none can *p.* *Jer 9:10* through them
that our prayers should not *p.* *La 3:44* through
the cup also shall *p. through* to *La 4:21* thee
pestilence and blood shall *p.* *Eze 5:17* through thee
beasts *p. through* land *Eze 14:15;* that no man may *p.* 29:11; 33:28 through for beasts
the passengers that *p.* *Eze 39:15* through the land
one shall come, *p. through* *Da 11:10* and overflow
no stranger shall *p. through* *Joe 3:17* her any more
I will *p. through* thee, saith *Am 5:17* the Lord
shall be cut down, when he *Na 1:12* shall *p. through*
the wicked shall no more *p.* *Na 1:15* through thee
and no oppressor shall *p.* *Zec 9:8* through them
when I shall *p. through* *1Co 16:5* Macedonia

NOT, CANNOT PASS

we will *not p.* through the *Nu 20:17* fields or vineyards
and Edom said, Thou shalt *Nu 20:18* *not p.* by me
hast appointed his bounds he *Job 14:5* *cannot p.*
he hath fenced my way, that I *Job 19:8* *cannot p.*
he made a decree, which shall *Ps 148:6* *not p.*
waters should *not p.* his *Pr 8:29* commandment
by a perpetual decree, that it *Jer 5:22* *cannot p.*
everlasting dominion that shall *Da 7:14* *not p.* away
this generation shall *not p.* *M't 24:31;* away, till *M'k 13:30; Lu 21:32*
heaven and earth pass away, *M't 24:35;* my word shall *not p.* away *M'k 13:31;* *Lu 21:33*

PASSAGE

Edom refused to give Israel *p.* *Nu 20:21*
at the *p.* of the children of *Jos 22:11* Israel

went out to the *p.* of *1Sa 13:23* Michmash
They are gone over the *p.* *Isa 10:29*
was a *p.* way (B)(R) *Eze 42:4*

PASSAGES

Gileadites took the *p.* of *J'g 12:5* Jordan
and slew him at the *p.* of *J'g 12:6* Jordan
between the *p.* by which *1Sa 14:4* Jonathan
cry from the *p.;* for all thy *Jer 22:20* lovers
And that the *p.* are stopped *Jer 51:32*

PASSED

a lamp that *p.* between those *Ge 15:17* pieces
until we have *p.* thy borders *Nu 20:17*
ye have not *p.* this way *Jos 3:4* heretofore
the seven priests *p.* on before *Jos 6:8* and blew
God preserved us among all *Jos 24:17* people through whom we *p.*
Ehud escaped and *p.* beyond *J'g 3:26* quarries
Saul is gone about and *p.* on *1Sa 15:12*
the lords of Philistines *p.* on *1Sa 29:2* by hundreds
David's servants *p.* on beside *2Sa 15:18* him
until all the people had *p.* *2Sa 15:24* (S)
it fell, that Elisha *p.* to Shunem *2Ki 4:8*
Gehazi *p.* on before them, and *2Ki 4:31* laid the staff
Solomon *p.* all the kings in *2Ch 9:22* wisdom
then a spirit *p.* before my face *Job 4:15*
my days are *p.* away, as the *Job 9:26* swift ships
and no stranger *p.* among *Job 15:19* them
at the brightness, his thick *Ps 18:12* clouds *p.*
yet he *p.* away, and lo, he was *Ps 37:36* not
calamities *p.* by (S) *Ps 57:1*
p. through river on foot *Ps 66:6* (A)(B)(E)(R)
all our days are *p.* away in thy *Ps 90:9* wrath
it was but a little that I *p.* from *Ca 3:4* them
he is come to Aiath, he is *p.* *Isa 10:28* to Migron
justice due me is *p.* away (S) *Isa 40:27*
he pursued them, and *p.* safely *Isa 41:3*
and the holy flesh is *p.* from *Jer 11:15* thee
and *p.* between the parts *Jer 34:18;* thereof *34:19*
he hath *p.* the time appointed *Jer 46:17*
nor the smell of fire and *p.* on *Da 3:27* them
the king went and *p.* the night *Da 6:18* fasting
hath not thy wickedness *p.* *Na 3:19* continually
a desert place, now the time *M'k 6:35* is far *p.*
but is *p.* from death to life *Joh 5:24;* *1Jo 3:14*
p. over former sins (R) *Ro 3:25*
so death *p.* on all men, all have *Ro 5:12* sinned
great high priest that is *p.* *Heb 4:14* into heavens
first heaven and first earth were *Re 21:1* *p.* away
for the former things are *p.* *Re 21:4* away

PASSED BY

there *p.* by Midianites, *Ge 37:28* merchantmen
Lord *p.* by before him, and *Ex 34:6* proclaimed
through the nations which ye *De 29:16* *p.* by
behold, men *p.* by and saw *1Ki 13:25* the lion
the Lord *p.* by; Elijah *p.* by *1Ki 19:11;* Elisha *19:19*
as the king *p.* by he cried to *1Ki 20:39* the king

that as oft as he *p.* by he *2Ki 4:8* turned in
the king *p.* by on the wall, *2Ki 6:30* people looked
and there *p.* by a wild beast *2Ki 14:9;* *2Ch 25:18*
nor hath the fierce lion *p.* by it *Job 28:8*
for lo, the kings *p.* by together *Ps 48:4*
when I *p.* by and saw thee *Eze 16:6;* polluted *16:8*
poured fornication on every *Eze 16:15;* one that *p.* by *16:25*
it lay desolate in sight of all *Eze 36:34* that *p.* by
the overflowing of the waters *Hab 3:10* *p.* by
when heard they Jesus *p.* by *M't 20:30* they cried
they that *p.* by reviled him *M'k 27:39;* *M'k 15:29*
as he *p.* by he saw Levi sitting *M'k 2:14* at receipt
he cometh, and would have *M'k 6:48* *p.* by them
in morning as they *p.* by *M'k 11:20* they saw fig tree
they compel one Simon who *M'k 15:21* *p.* by to bear
he *p.* by on the other side *Lu 10:31;* *10:32*
going thro' midst of them, and *Joh 8:59* so *p.* by
as I *p.* by and beheld your *Ac 17:23* devotion

PASSED *OVER*

Jacob rose up, and *p.* over the *Ge 31:21* river
for with my staff I *p.* over this *Ge 31:21* Jordan
who *p.* over houses of Israel *Ex 12:27* in Egypt
when ye are *p.* over Jordan *Nu 33:51;* *De 27:2*
they *p.* over right against *Jos 3:16* Jericho
all the Israelites *p.* over on dry *Jos 3:17* ground
when all people were clean *p.* *Jos 4:1;* over *4:11*
people hasted and *p.* over; the *Jos 4:10;* ark *p.* over *4:11*
Reubenites and Gadites *p.* *Jos 4:12* over armed before
Gideon *p.* over and 300 men *J'g 8:4* with him
the children of Ammon *p.* over *J'g 10:9* Jordan
Jephthah *p.* over to fight with *J'g 11:29;* Ammon *11:32*
the battle *p.* over to *1Sa 14:23* Beth-aven
David *p.* over with 600 men *1Sa 27:2* unto Achish
Abner and his men *p.* over *2Sa 2:29* Jordan
Ittai *p.* over; king and *2Sa 15:22;* people *p.* over *15:23*
my judgment is *p.* over from *Isa 40:27* my God
a river that could not be *p.* *Eze 47:5* over
but I *p.* over upon her fair *Ho 10:11* neck
all thy billows and waves *p.* *Jon 2:3* over me

PASSED *THROUGH*

Abram *p. through* the land to *Ge 12:6* Sichem
land which we *p. through* to *Nu 14:7* search is good
they *p. through* midst of the *Nu 33:8* sea into wilderness
Saul *p. through* mount *1Sa 9:4* Ephraim and Shalisha
posts *p. through* country of *2Ch 30:10* Ephraim
breaker is come, they *p.* *Mic 2:13* through the gate
land was desolate, that no man *Zec 7:14* *p. through*
that he *p. through* the midst *Lu 17:11* of Samaria
as Peter *p. through* all *Ac 9:32* quarters, came down
they went out, and *p. through* *Ac 12:10* one street

all our fathers *p. through* the   *1Co 10:1*
sea
by faith they *p. through* the   *Heb 11:29*
Red sea

PASSEDST

why *p.* thou over to fight   *J'g 12:1*
against Ammon

PASSENGERS

she standeth to call *p.* who go   *Pr 9:15*
right on
give Gog valley of *p.* it shall   *Eze 39:11*
stop noses of *p.* there shall bury
to bury with *p.* those that   *Eze 39:14*
remain on earth
when *p.* see a man's bone,   *Eze 39:15*
they set a sign by it

PASSERBY

they forced a *p.* to (A)(B)   *M'k 15:21*

PASSES

between the *p.* (S)   *1Sa 14:4*
cry from the *p.* (S)   *Jer 22:20*

PASSEST

so Lord do to all kingdoms   *De 3:21*
whither thou *p.*
on land whither thou *p.* over   *De 30:18*
to possess
if *p.* on, thou shalt be a   *2Sa 15:33*
burden
day thou *p.* over the brook   *1Ki 2:37*
Kidron
when *p.* thro' waters, I will be   *Isa 43:2*
with thee

PASSETH

every one that *p.* among them   *Ex 30:13;*
  30:14
I will cover thee, while my   *Ex 33:22*
glory *p.* by
whatsoever *p.* under the rod,   *Le 27:32*
the tenth
even the Lord *p.* over before   *Jos 3:11*
you
at this house every one that *p.*   *1Ki 9:8;*
by it shall hiss   *2Ch 7:21*
is an holy man of God, which   *2Ki 4:9*
p. by us
money of every one that *p.* the   *2Ki 12:4*
account
he *p.* on also, but I perceive   *Job 9:11*
him not
thou prevailest against him,   *Job 14:20*
and he *p.*
and my welfare *p.* away as a   *Job 30:15*
cloud
but the wind *p.* and cleanseth   *Job 37:21*
them
dominion over whatever *p.* thro'   *Ps 8:8*
the seas
are a wind that *p.* away,   *Ps 78:39*
comes not again
for the wind *p.* over it, and it   *Ps 103:16*
is gone
his days are as a shadow that   *Ps 144:4*
p. away
as whirlwind *p.* so is wicked   *Pr 10:25*
no more
he that *p.* by and meddleth   *Pr 26:17*
with strife
one generation *p.* away, and   *Ec 1:4*
another cometh
the terrible shall be as chaff   *Isa 29:5*
that *p.* away
a land that no man *p.* through   *Jer 2:6;*
  9:12
scatter them as stubble that *p.*   *Jer 13:24*
away
every one that *p.* shall be   *Jer 18:16;*
astonished   *19:8*
I will cut off from it him that   *Eze 35:7*
p. out
they shall be as early dew that   *Ho 13:3*
p. away
God that *p.* by transgression   *Mic 7:18*
of remnant
every one that *p.* by her shall   *Zep 2:15*
hiss
I made their streets waste, that   *Zep 3:6*
none *p.* by
I will encamp, because of him   *Zec 9:8*
that *p.* by

they told him that Jesus *p.* by   *Lu 18:37*
fashion of this world *p.* away   *1Co 7:31;*
  1Jo 2:17
the love of Christ which *p.*   *Eph 3:19*
knowledge
the peace of God which *p.*   *Ph'p 4:7*
understanding

PASSING

We are *p.* from   *J'g 19:18*
Beth-lehem-judah
was wonderful, *p.* the love of   *2Sa 1:26*
women
people had done *p.* out of the   *2Sa 15:24*
city
king of Israel was *p.* by upon   *2Ki 6:26*
Who *p.* through the valley of   *Ps 84:6*
Baca
P. through the street near her   *Pr 7:8*
beauty is *p.* (B)   *Pr 31:30*
and *p.* over he will preserve it   *Isa 31:5*
p. through the land to bury   *Eze 39:14*
with
he *p.* through the midst of them   *Lu 4:30*
the shadow of Peter *p.* by   *Ac 5:15*
might
p. through he preached in all   *Ac 8:40*
p. by Mysia came down to   *Ac 16:8*
Troas
hardly *p.* it, came unto a place   *Ac 27:8*
that which is *p.* away (E)   *2Co 3:13*

PASSION

shewed himself alive after his *p.*   *Ac 1:3*
after his suffering (B)(P)   *Ac 1:3*
after his death (N)   *Ac 1:3*
mortify *p.* (B)(E)(P)(R)   *Col 3:5*
p. of lust (A)(B)(E)(R)   *1Th 4:5*
lusts of defiling *p.* (R)   *2Pe 2:10*
wine of her impure *p.* (R)   *Re 14:8;*
  18:3

PASSIONATE

p. sympathy (A)   *Ph'p 2:1*
p. and unprincipled (P)   *2Ti 3:3*
wine of her *p.* unchastity   *Re 14:8*
(A)(B)
wine of her *p.* unfaithfulness   *Re 14:8;*
(P)   *18:3*
wine of her *p.* unchastity (B)   *Re 18:3*

PASSIONATELY

I *p.* hope (N)   *Ph'p 1:20*

PASSIONS

We also are men of like *p.*   *Ac 14:15*
with you
human beings, of nature like   *Ac 14:15*
your own (A)
human, with emotions as   *Ac 14:15*
yourselves (B)
human beings, no less mortal   *Ac 14:15*
than you (N)
human beings with feelings   *Ac 14:15*
like yours (P)
men, of like nature with you   *Ac 14:15*
(R)
control of *p.* (A)(B)   *Ac 24:25*
shameful, vile, disgraceful,   *Ro 1:26*
dishonorable *p.* (B)(E)(N)(P)(R)
cannot restrain *p.* (B)   *1Co 7:9*
p., appetites, desires   *Ga 5:24*
(A)(B)(N)(R)
p., lusts (E)   *Ga 5:24*
p. of all sorts (B)(N)   *Tit 3:3*
spend it on your *p.* (R)   *Jas 4:3*
a man subject to like *p.* as we   *Jas 5:17*
are
abstain from *p.* of the flesh   *1Pe 2:11*
living in licentiousness, *p.* (R)   *1Pe 4:3*
lust of polluting *p.* (A)(B)   *2Pe 2:10*
lower *p.* to attract (P)(R)   *2Pe 2:18*
the impious *p.* (B)(R)   *Jude 18*

PASSOVER

eat it in haste: it is the Lord's   *Ex 12:11*
p.
to your families, and kill the   *Ex 12:21*
p.
It is the sacrifice of the Lord's   *Ex 12:27*
p.
This is the ordinance of the *p.*   *Ex 12:43*
and will keep the *p.* to the   *Ex 12:48*
Lord   *Nu 9:14*
of the *p.* be left unto   *Ex 34:25*
the morning

first month at even is the   *Le 23:5*
Lord's *p.*
keep the *p.* at his appointed   *Nu 9:2*
season
Israel, that they should keep the   *Nu 9:4*
p.
kept the *p.* on the fourteenth   *Nu 9:5*
day
could not keep the *p.* on that   *Nu 9:6*
day
he shall keep the *p.* unto the   *Nu 9:10*
Lord
ordinances of the *p.* they shall   *Nu 9:12*
keep
and forbeareth to keep the *p.*   *Nu 9:13*
according to the ordinance of   *Nu 9:14*
the *p.*
first month is the *p.* of the   *Nu 28:16*
Lord
morrow after the *p.* the   *Nu 33:3*
children
keep the *p.* unto the Lord thy   *De 16:1*
God
shalt therefore sacrifice the *p.*   *De 16:2*
Thou mayest not sacrifice the   *De 16:5*
p.
thou shalt sacrifice the *p.* at   *De 16:6*
even
kept the *p.* on the fourteenth   *Jos 5:10*
day
land on the morrow after   *Jos 5:11*
the *p.*
Keep the *p.* unto the Lord   *2Ki 23:21*
your God
there was not holden such a   *2Ki 23:22*
p. from
this *p.* was holden to the   *2Ki 23:23*
Lord in
to keep the *p.* unto the Lord   *2Ch 30:1*
God
to keep the *p.* in the second   *2Ch 30:2;*
month   *30:5, 15, 18; 35:1, 6-9, 11, 13,*
  16-19
children of the captivity kept   *Ezr 6:19*
the *p.*
killed the *p.* for all the   *Ezr 6:20*
children of
of the month, ye shall have   *Eze 45:21*
the *p.*
after two days is the feast of   *M't 26:2*
the *p.*
we prepare for thee to eat   *M't 26:17*
the *p.*
I will keep the *p.* at thy   *M't 26:18*
house with
them; and they made ready   *Ezr 26:19*
the *p.*
two days was the feast of the   *M'k 14:1*
p.
when they killed the *p.* his   *M'k 14:12*
disciples
prepare that thou mayest eat   *M'k 14:12*
the *p.*
I shall eat the *p.* with my   *M'k 14:14;*
disciples   *Lu 22:11*
them: and they made ready   *M'k 14:16*
the *p.*
every year at the feast of the *p.*   *Lu 2:41*
drew nigh, which is called the   *Lu 22:1*
P.
bread, when the *p.* must be   *Lu 22:7*
killed
Go and prepare us the *p.* that   *Lu 22:8*
we
them: and they made ready   *Lu 22:13*
the *p.*
I have desired to eat this *p.*   *Lu 22:15*
with you
And the Jews' *p.* was at hand   *Joh 2:13*
when he was in Jerusalem at   *Joh 2:23*
the *p.*
the *p.* a feast of the Jews, was   *Joh 6:4*
nigh
And the Jews' *p.* was nigh at   *Joh 11:55*
hand
went up to Jerusalem   *Joh 11:55*
before the *p.*
Jesus six days before the *p.*   *Joh 12:1*
came to
Now before the feast of the *p.*   *Joh 13:1*
when
but that they might eat the *p.*   *Joh 18:28*
release unto you one at the *p.*   *Joh 18:39*
and it was the preparation   *Joh 19:14*
of the *p.*
Christ our *p.* is sacrificed for   *1Co 5:7*
us
Through faith he kept the   *Heb 11:8*
p. and

PASSOVERS

the charge of the killing of the *p.*   *2Ch 30:17*

PAST

the days of his mourning were *p.*   *Ge 50:4*
to push with his horn in time *p.*   *Ex 21:29*
the ox hath used to push in time *p.*   *Ex 21:36*
way, until we be *p.* thy borders   *Nu 21:22*
Emims dwelt therein in times *p.*   *De 2:10*
ask now of the days that are *p.*   *De 4:32*
and hated him not in times *p.*   *De 4:42*
whom he hated not in time *p.*   *De 19:4*
as he hated him not in time *p.*   *De 19:6*
Surely the bitterness of death is *p.*   *1Sa 15:32*
was in his presence, as in times *p.*   *1Sa 19:7*
for David in times *p.* to be king   *2Sa 3:17*
in time *p.* when Saul was king over   *2Sa 5:2*
And when the mourning was *p.*   *2Sa 11:27*
when David was a little *p.* the top   *2Sa 16:1*
came to pass when midday was *p.*   *1Ki 18:29*
was the ruler over them in time *p.*   *1Ch 9:20*
time *p.* even when Saul was king   *1Ch 11:2*
doeth great things *p.* finding out   *Job 9:10*
me secret, until thy wrath be *p.*   *Job 14:13*
My days are *p.* my purposes are   *Job 17:11*
Oh that I were as in months *p.*   *Job 29:2*
are but as yesterday when it is *p.*   *Ps 90:4*
God requireth that which is *p.*   *Ec 3:15*
the winter is *p.* the rain is over   *Ca 2:11*
until the indignation be *p.* (S)   *Isa 26:20*
harvest is *p.* the summer is ended   *Jer 8:20*
place, and the time is now *p.*   *M't 14:15*
when the sabbath was *p.,* Mary   *M'k 16:1*
the voice was *p.* Jesus was found   *Lu 9:36*
p. the first and the second ward   *Ac 12:10*
in times *p.* suffered all nations   *Ac 14:16*
because the fast was already *p.*   *Ac 27:9*
the remission of sins that are *p.*   *Ro 3:25*
in times *p.* have not believed God   *Ro 11:30*
and his ways *p.* finding out   *Ro 11:33*
heard of my conversation in time *p.*   *Ga 1:13*
he which persecuted us in times *p.*   *Ga 1:23*
as I have also told you in time *p.*   *Ga 5:21*
Wherein in time *p.* ye walked   *Eph 2:2*
all had our conversation in times *p.*   *Eph 2:3*
that ye, being in time *p.* Gentiles   *Eph 2:11*
Who being *p.* feeling have given   *Eph 4:19*
that the resurrection is *p.* already   *2Ti 2:18*
in time *p.* was to thee unprofitable   *Ph'm 11*
spake in time *p.* unto the fathers   *Heb 1:1*
of a child when she was *p.* age   *Heb 11:11*
Which in time *p.* were not a people   *1Pe 2:10*
the time *p.* of our life may suffice   *1Pe 4:3*
because the darkness is *p.* and   *1Jo 2:8*
One woe is *p.;* and, behold, there   *Re 9:12*
The second woe is *p.;* and   *Re 11:14*

PASTOR

have not hastened from being a *p.*   *Jer 17:16*
escape from being a shepherd after you (A)(E)   *Jer 17:16*

PASTORS

p. also transgressed against me   *Jer 2:8*
shepherds (A)(B)(E)(R)   *Jer 2:8; 3:15; 10:21; 12:10; 22:22; 23:1-2*
will give you *p.* according to mine   *Jer 3:15*
p. are become brutish, and have   *Jer 10:21*
Many *p.* destroyed my vineyard   *Jer 12:10*
The wind shall eat up all thy *p.*   *Jer 22:22*
Woe be unto the *p,* that destroy   *Jer 23:1*
against the *p.* that feed my people   *Jer 23:2*
and some, *p.* and teachers   *Eph 4:11*

PASTURE

servants have no *p.* for their flocks   *Ge 47:4*
the *p.* lands (S)   *Le 25:34; Nu 35:2, 4-5; Jos 14:4; 21:2-3, 8, 11, 13-19, 21-36, 38-39, 41-42; 1Ch 13:2; 2Ch 31:19; Eze 27:28; 48:17*
valley, to seek *p.* for their flocks   *1Ch 4:39*
And they found fat *p.* and good, and   *1Ch 4:40*
there was *p.* there for their flocks   *1Ch 4:41*
range of the mountains is his *p.*   *Job 39:8*
smoke against the sheep of thy *p.*   *Ps 74:1*
we, thy people and sheep of thy *p.*   *Ps 79:13*
the people of his *p.* and the sheep   *Ps 95:7*
his people, and the sheep of his *p.*   *Ps 100:3*
a joy of wild asses, a *p.* of flocks   *Isa 32:14*
and scatter the sheep of my *p.*   *Jer 23:1*
for the Lord hath spoiled their *p.*   *Jer 25:36*
become like harts that find no *p.*   *La 1:6*
I will feed them in a good *p.*   *Eze 34:14*
and in a fat *p.* shall they feed upon   *Eze 34:14*
you to have eaten up the good *p.*   *Eze 34:18*
ye my flock, the flock of my *p.*   *Eze 34:31*
According to their *p.* so were they   *Ho 13:6*
perplexed, because they have no *p.*   *Joe 1:18*
shall go in and out, and find *p.*   *Joh 10:9*

PASTURES

and twenty oxen out of the *p.*   *1Ki 4:23*
in all the *p.* (S)   *1Ch 5:16; 6:55, 57-60, 64, 67, 81*
maketh me to lie down in green *p.*   *Ps 23:2*
drop upon the *p.* of the wilderness   *Ps 65:12*
The *p.* are clothed with flocks   *Ps 65:13*
day shall thy cattle feed in large *p.*   *Isa 30:23*
their *p.* shall be in all high places   *Isa 49:9*
your feet the residue of your *p.*   *Eze 34:18*
hundred, out of the fat *p.* of Israel   *Eze 45:15*
devoured the *p.* of the wilderness   *Jos 1:19; 1:20*
the *p.* of the wilderness do spring   *Joe 2:22*

PATARA

Rhodes, and from hence unto *P.*   *Ac 21:1*

PATCH

p. an old coat (B)(N)(P)   *M't 9:16*

PATCHED

and *p.* shoes (S)   *Jos 9:5*

PATE

shall come down upon his own *p.*   *Ps 7:16*

PATH

an adder in the *p.* that biteth   *Ge 49:17*
angel of the Lord stood in a *p.* of   *Nu 22:24*
is a *p.* which no fowl knoweth, and   *Job 28:7*
They mar my *p.* they set forward   *Job 30:13*
He maketh a *p.* to shine after him   *Job 41:32*
Thou wilt shew me the *p.* of life   *Ps 16:11*
O Lord, and lead me in a plain *p.*   *Ps 27:11*
sea, and thy *p.* in the great waters   *Ps 77:19*
Make me to go in the *p.* of   *Ps 119:35*
my feet, and a light unto my *p.*   *Ps 119:105*
no stumbling block in their *p.* (B)   *Ps 119:165*
Thou compassest my *p.* and   *Ps 139:3*
me, then thou knewest my *p.*   *Ps 142:3*
them; refrain thy foot from their *p.*   *Pr 1:15*
and equity; yea, every good *p.*   *Pr 2:9*
Enter not into the *p.* of the wicked   *Pr 4:14*
the *p.* of the just is as the shining   *Pr 4:18*
Ponder the *p.* of thy feet, and let   *Pr 4:26*
shouldest ponder the *p.* of life   *Pr 5:6*
dost weigh the *p.* of the just   *Isa 26:7*
of the way, turn aside out of the *p.*   *Isa 30:11*
taught him in the *p.* of judgment   *Isa 40:14*
and a *p.* in the mighty waters   *Isa 43:16*
shall walk ever one in his *p.*   *Joe 2:8*
set feet on new *p.* of life (N)   *Ro 6:4*

PATHLESS

the *p.* wastes (B)   *Ps 136:16*

PATHROS

and from Egypt, and from *P.*   *Isa 11:11*
at Noph, and in the country of *P.*   *Jer 44:1*
dwelt in the land of Egypt, in *P.*   *Jer 44:15*
them to return into the land of *P.*   *Eze 29:14*
And I will make *P.* desolate   *Eze 30:14*

PATHRUSIM

And *P.* and Casluhim, (out of   *Ge 10:14*
and *P.* and Casluhim, (of whom   *1Ch 1:12*

PATHS

p. of their way are turned aside   *Job 6:18*
So are the *p.* of all that forget God   *Job 8:13*
lookest narrowly unto all my *p.*   *Job 13:27*
and he hath set darkness in my *p.*   *Job 19:8*
thereof, nor abide in the *p.* thereof   *Job 24:13*
the stocks, he marketh all my *p.*   *Job 33:11*
know the *p.* to the house thereof   *Job 38:20*
passeth through the *p.* of the seas   *Ps 8:8*
me from the *p.* of the destroyer   *Ps 17:4*
Hold up my goings in thy *p.* that   *Ps 17:5*
me in the *p.* of righteousness   *Ps 23:3*
thy ways, O Lord; teach me thy *p.*   *Ps 25:4*

All the *p.* of the Lord are mercy   *Ps 25:10*
goodness; and thy *p.* drop fatness   *Ps 65:11*
He keepeth the *p.* of judgment   *Pr 2:8*
leave the *p.* of uprightness, to walk   *Pr 2:13*
and they froward in their *p.*   *Pr 2:15*
death, and her *p.* unto the dead   *Pr 2:18*
take they hold of the *p.* of life   *Pr 2:19*
and keep the *p.* of the righteous   *Pr 2:20*
him, and he shall direct thy *p.*   *Pr 3:6*
and all her *p.* are peace   *Pr 3:17*
wisdom; I have led thee in right *p.*   *Pr 4:11*
her ways, go not astray in her *p.*   *Pr 7:25*
by the way in the places of the *p.*   *Pr 8:2*
in the midst of the *p.* of judgment   *Pr 8:20*
his ways, and we will walk in his *p.*   *Isa 2:3*
err, and destroy the way of thy *p.*   *Isa 3:12*
in *p.* that they have not known   *Isa 42:16*
The restorer of *p.* to dwell in   *Isa 58:12*
and destruction are in their *p.*   *Isa 59:7*
they have made them crooked *p.*   *Isa 59:8*
and ask for the old *p.* where is the   *Jer 6:16*
in their ways from the ancient *p.*   *Jer 18:15*
walk in *p.* in a way not cast up   *Jer 18:15*
be unto them as slippery *p.* (S)   *Jer 23:12*
stone, he hath made my *p.* crooked   *La 3:9*
wall, that she shall not find her *p.*   *Ho 2:6*
ways, and we will walk in his *p.*   *Mic 4:2*
of the Lord, make his *p.*   *M't 3:3*
straight   *M'k 1:3; Lu 3:4*
making crooked straight *p.* of Lord (R)   *Ac 13:10*
made straight *p.* for your feet, lest   *Heb 12:13*

PATHWAY

in the *p.* thereof is no death   *Pr 12:28*

PATIENCE

Lord, have *p.* with me, and I will   *M't 18:26*
Have *p.* with me, and I will pay   *M't 18:29*
it, and bring forth fruit with *p.*   *Lu 8:15*
In your *p.* possess ye your souls   *Lu 21:19*
strain the *p.* of God (P)   *Ac 15:10*
that tribulation worketh *p.*   *Ro 5:3*
And *p.* experience; and experience   *Ro 5:4*
not, then do we with *p.* wait for it   *Ro 8:25*
p. and comfort of the scriptures   *Ro 15:4*
Now the God of *p.* and consolation   *Ro 15:5*
the ministers of God, in much *p.* in   *2Co 6:4*
were wrought among you in all *p.*   *2Co 12:12*
unto all *p.* and longsuffering with   *Col 1:11*
and *p.* of hope in our Lord Jesus   *1Th 1:3*
for your *p.* and faith in all your   *2Th 1:4*
godliness, faith, love, *p.*, meekness   *1Ti 6:11*
faith, longsufferng, charity, *p.*   *2Ti 3:10*
sound in faith, in charity, in *p.*   *Tit 2:2*
faith and *p.* inherit the promises   *Heb 6:12*
For ye have need of *p.* that, after   *Heb 10:36*
let us run with *p.* the race that is   *Heb 12:1*
the trying of your faith worketh *p.*   *Jas 1:3*
But let *p.* have her perfect work   *Jas 1:4*
and hath long *p.* for it, until he   *Jas 5:7*
of suffering affliction, and of *p.*   *Jas 5:10*
Ye have heard of the *p.* of Job   *Jas 5:11*
temperance *p.*; and to *p.* godliness   *2Pe 1:6*

the kingdom and *p.* of Jesus Christ   *Re 1:9*
works, and thy labour, and thy *p.*   *Re 2:2*
hast *p.* and for my name's sake   *Re 2:3*
faith, and thy *p.* and thy works   *Re 2:19*
thou hast kept the word of my *p.*   *Re 3:10*
it the *p.* and the faith of the saints   *Re 13:10*
Here is the *p.* of the saints   *Re 14:12*

PATIENT

p. in spirit is better than the proud   *Ec 7:8*
God's generosity, *p.* mercy (P)   *Ro 2:4*
by *p.* continuance in well doing   *Ro 2:7*
p. persistence in (A)(N)   *Ro 2:7*
in hope; *p.* in tribulation   *Ro 12:12*
the weak, be *p.* toward all men   *1Th 5:14*
and into the *p.* waiting for Christ   *2Th 3:5*
p. not a brawler, not covetous   *1Ti 3:3*
gentle unto all men, apt to teach, *p.*   *2Ti 2:24*
Be *p.* therefore, brethren, unto   *Jas 5:7*
Be ye also *p.*; stablish your hearts   *Jas 5:8*

PATIENTLY

in the Lord, and wait *p.* for him   *Ps 37:7*
I waited *p.* for the Lord; and he   *Ps 40:1*
I beseech thee to hear me *p.*   *Ac 26:3*
p. doing good (P)   *Ro 2:7*
bear *p.* with ignorant (N)   *Heb 5:2*
And so, after he had *p.* endured   *Heb 6:15*
for your faults, ye shall take it *1Pe 2:20*
ye take it *p.* this as acceptable with   *1Pe 2:20*

PATMOS

was in the isle that is called *P.*   *Re 1:9*

PATRIARCH

speak unto you of the *p.* David   *Ac 2:29*
the *p.* Abraham gave the tenth of   *Heb 7:4*

PATRIARCHS

and Jacob begat the twelve *p.*   *Ac 7:8*
And the *p.* moved with envy, sold   *Ac 7:9*

PATRIMONY

which cometh of the sale of his *p.*   *De 18:8*

PATROBAS

P., Hermes, and the brethren   *Ro 16:14*

PATROL

p. the earth (A)(R)   *Zec 1:10; 6:7*

PATROLLED

p. the earth (B)(R)   *Zec 1:11*

PATTERN

after the *p.* of the tabernacle   *Ex 25:9*
the *p.* of all the instruments thereof   *Ex 25:9*
p. shewed thee in the mount   *Ex 25:40*
the *p.* which the Lord had shewed   *Nu 8:4*
the *p.* of the altar of the Lord   *Jos 22:28*
fashion of the altar, and the *p.* of it   *2Ki 16:10*
p. of the porch, and of the houses   *1Ch 28:11*
the *p.* of all that he had by the spirit   *1Ch 28:12*
and gold for the *p.* of the chariot of   *1Ch 28:18*
me, even all the works of this *p.*   *1Ch 28:19*

after a palatial *p.* (B)   *Ps 144:12*
full *p.* of exactness (A)   *Eze 28:12*
and let them measure the *p.*   *Eze 43:10*
p. of teaching (N)   *Ro 6:17*
p. to them which should hereafter   *1Ti 1:16*
p. of teaching (A)(B)(E)(R)   *2Ti 1:13*
showing thyself a *p.* of good works   *Tit 2:7*
the *p.* shewed to thee in the mount   *Heb 8:5*
p. of the true (E)   *Heb 9:24*

PATTERNS

p. of things in the heavens should   *Heb 9:23*

PAU

and the name of his city was *P.*   *Ge 36:39*

PAUL

then Saul, called *P.* filled with Holy Ghost   *Ac 13:9*
many Jews and religious proselytes followed *P.*   *Ac 13:43*
P. waxed bold   *Ac 13:46*
Jews raised persecution against *P.* and Barnabas   *Ac 13:50*
the same heard *P.*   *Ac 14:9*
called *P.* Mercurius, he was chief speaker   *Ac 14:12*
having stoned *P.* drew him out of the city   *Ac 14:19*
P. thought not good to take him with them   *Ac 15:38*
P. chose Silas   *Ac 15:40*
him would *P.* have to go forth with him   *Ac 16:3*
and a vision appeared to *P.* in the night   *Ac 16:9*
Lydia attended to the things spoken of *P.*   *Ac 16:14*
followed *P.*; but *P.* being grieved   *Ac 16:17; 16:18*
P. and Silas prayed, and sang praises to God   *Ac 16:25*
but *P.* cried, saying, Do thyself no harm   *Ac 16:28*
P. as his manner was, went in unto them   *Ac 17:2*
some believed and consorted with *P.* and Silas   *Ac 17:4*
brethren sent *P.* away   *Ac 17:10; 17:14*
now while *P.* waited for them at Athens   *Ac 17:16*
P. was pressed in spirit, and testified to Jews   *Ac 18:5*
the Lord spake to *P.* in the night by a vision   *Ac 18:9*
God wrought miracles by the hands of *P.*   *Ac 19:11*
P. I know   *Ac 19:15*
P. purposed in spirit to go to Jerusalem   *Ac 19:21*
this *P.* hath persuaded and turned away   *Ac 19:26*
P. preached unto them, ready to depart   *Ac 20:7*
P. went down, and embracing him, said   *Ac 20:10*
who said to *P.* through the Spirit, not go up   *Ac 21:4*
the day following *P.* went in with us to James   *Ac 21:18*
they took *P.* and drew him out of the temple   *Ac 21:30*
when they saw soldiers, they left beating *P.*   *Ac 21:32*
P. stood on the stairs; *P.* beholding   *Ac 21:40; 23:1*
fearing lest *P.* should have been pulled   *Ac 23:10*
P. be of good cheer   *Ac 23:11*
they would not eat till they had killed *P.*   *Ac 23:12; 23:14*
P. prayed me to bring this young man to thee   *Ac 23:18*
the soldiers brought *P.* to Antipatris   *Ac 23:31*
who informed the governor against *P.*   *Ac 24:1*
that money should have been given him of *P.*   *Ac 24:26*
Felix left *P.* bound   *Ac 24:27*
one Jesus, whom *P.* affirmed to be alive   *Ac 25:19*

Festus said, *P.* thou art beside   *Ac 26:24*
thyself
and Julius courteously   *Ac 27:3*
entreated *P.*
saying, Fear not, *P.*   *Ac 27:24*
P. besought them all to take   *Ac 27:33*
meat, saying
the centurion, willing to save   *Ac 27:43*
P. kept them
but *P.* was suffered to dwell   *Ac 28:16*
by himself
I am of *P.*   *1Co 1:12*
is Christ divided? was *P.*   *1Co 1:13*
crucified for you
who then is *P.*   *1Co 3:5*
whether *P.* or Apollos, or   *1Co 3:22*
Cephas, or world
the salutation of me *P.* with   *1Co 16:21;*
mine own hand   *Col 4:18; 2Th 3:17*
we would have come to you,   *1Th 2:18*
even I *P.*
being such a one as *P.* the aged   *Ph'm 9*
as our beloved brother *P.*   *2Pe 3:15*
wrote

PAUL'S

P. companions in travel, they   *Ac 19:29*
fell on *P.* neck, and kissed   *Ac 20:37*
him
that were of *P.* company   *Ac 21:8*
departed
took *P.* girdle, and bound his   *Ac 21:11*
own
And when *P.* sister's son   *Ac 23:16*
heard of
declared *P.* cause unto the   *Ac 25:14*
king

PAULUS

deputy of the country, Sergius   *Ac 13:7*
P.

PAVED

were a *p.* work of a sapphire   *Ex 24:10*
stone
midst thereof being *P.* with   *Ca 3:10*
love

PAVEMENT

it, and put it upon a *p.* of   *2Ki 16:17*
stones
faces to the ground upon the *p.*   *2Ch 7:3*
a *p.* of red, and blue, and white   *Es 1:6*
p. made for the court round   *Eze 40:17*
about
thirty chambers were upon the   *Eze 40:17*
p.
And the *p.* by the side of the   *Eze 40:18*
gates
of the gates was the lower *p.*   *Eze 40:18*
p. which was for the utter   *Eze 42:3*
court
in a place that is called the *P.*   *Joh 19:13*

PAVILION

noise of his *p.* (S)   *Job 36:29*
his *p.* round about him were   *Ps 18:11*
dark
he shall hide me in his *p.;* in the   *Ps 27:5*
shalt keep them secretly in a   *Ps 31:20*
p.
p. as a shade by day (B)(E)   *Isa 4:6*
shall spread his royal *p.* over   *Jer 43:10*
them

PAVILIONS

he made darkness *p.* round   *2Sa 22:12*
about
drinking, he and the kings in   *1Ki 20:12*
the *p.*
drinking himself drunk in the   *1Ki 20:16*
p.

PAW

delivered me out of *p.* of   *1Sa 17:37*
the lion
and out of the *p.* of the bear   *1Sa 17:37*

PAWETH

He *p.* in the valley, and   *Job 39:21*
rejoiceth

PAWS

And whatsoever goeth upon   *Le 11:27*
his *p.*

PAY

will *p.* us back (A)(R)   *Ge 50:15*
he shall *p.* for the loss of his   *Ex 21:19*
time
he shall *p.* as the judges   *Ex 21:22*
determine
he shall surely *p.* ox for ox   *Ex 21:36*
thief be found, let him *p.*   *Ex 22:7*
double
p. double unto his neighbour   *Ex 22:9*
p. money according to the   *Ex 22:17*
dowry
thy water, then I will *p.* for it   *Nu 20:19*
thou shalt not slack to *p.* it   *De 23:21*
let me go and *p.* my vow,   *2Sa 15:7*
which I
else thou shalt *p.* a talent of   *1Ki 20:39*
silver
Go, sell the oil, and *p.* thy debt   *2Ki 4:7*
make to *p.* tribute until this   *2Ch 8:8*
day
children of Ammon *p.* unto   *2Ch 27:5*
him
will they not *p.* toll, tribute   *Ezr 4:13*
will *p.* ten thousand talents of   *Es 3:9*
silver
that Haman had promised to *p.*   *Es 4:7*
to
p. a bribe on my account   *Job 6:22*
(A)(B)(R)
thee, and thou shalt *p.* thy   *Job 22:27*
vows
p. my vows before them that   *Ps 22:25*
fear
and *p.* thy vows unto the most   *Ps 50:14*
High
p. back evil to enemies (A)   *Ps 54:5*
offerings; I will *p.* thee my   *Ps 66:13*
vows
Vow, and *p.* unto the Lord   *Ps 76:11*
your God
p. my vows unto the Lord   *Ps 116:14;*
now   *116:18*
fools *p.* attention (R)   *Pr 8:5*
he hath given will he *p.* him   *Pr 19:17*
again
If thou hast nothing to *p.* why   *Pr 22:27*
a vow unto God, defer not to *p.*   *Ec 5:4*
it
p. that which thou hast vowed   *Ec 5:4*
thou shouldest vow and not *p.*   *Ec 5:5*
I will *p.* that that I have vowed   *Jon 2:9*
Doth not your master *p.*   *M't 17:24*
tribute
forasmuch as he had not to   *M't 18:25*
p. his
with me, and I will *p.* thee   *M't 18:26*
all
saying, *P.* me that thou owest   *M't 18:28*
with me, and I will *p.* thee all   *M't 18:29*
prison, till he should *p.* the   *M't 18:30*
debt
should *p.* all that was due   *M't 18:34*
him
for ye *p.* tithe of mint and   *M't 23:23*
anise and
when they had nothing to *p.* he   *Lu 7:42*
For this cause *p.* ye tribute   *Ro 13:6*
also
receive his own *p.* (B)(N)   *1Co 3:8*
p. attention, weigh, discern   *1Co 14:29*
(A)(B)
worker earns his *p.* (N)   *1Ti 5:18*
Lord will *p.* him back (A)(B)   *2Ti 4:14*
I will *p.* back (B)(N)(R)   *Heb 10:30*
p. her back in her own coin   *Re 18:6*
(N)(P)

PAYED

me; this day have I *p.* my vows   *Pr 7:14*
tithes, *p.* tithes in Abraham   *Heb 7:9*

PAYETH

borroweth, and *p.* not again   *Ps 37:21*

PAYING

p. the price in misdeeds (N)   *Lu 23:41*

PAYMENT

each one's *p.* in sack (B)   *Ge 44:1*
took a heavy *p.* (B)   *Ex 12:36*

you may press for *p.* (B)   *De 15:3*
mortar under the *p.* (B)   *Jer 43:9*
that he had, and *p.* to be   *M't 18:25*
made

PAYMENTS

have double *p.* (B)   *Ge 43:12*

PAYS

p. no attention to their   *Job 24:12*
prayers (R)
see she *p.* husband all respect   *Eph 5:33*
(N)

PEACE

God will give Pharaoh an   *Ge 41:16*
answer of *p.*
I will give *p.* in land, none   *Le 26:6*
make afraid
Lord lift up countenance and   *Nu 6:26*
give thee *p.*
I give to him my covenant of   *Nu 25:12*
p.
sent a messenger to Sihon with   *De 2:26*
words of *p.*
when comest nigh city,   *De 20:10*
proclaim *p.* to it
if it make thee answer of *p.*   *De 20:11*
and open
if it will make no *p.* with   *De 20:12*
thee, then besiege
thou shalt not seek their *p.* nor   *De 23:6*
prosperity
I shall have *p.* though walk in   *De 29:19*
there was *p.* between Jabin and   *J'g 4:17*
Heber
if he say, It is well, servant   *J'g 20:7*
shall have *p.*
for there is *p.* to thee, no hurt   *J'g 20:21*
but on his throne shall there   *1Ki 2:33*
be *p.*
Solomon had *p.* on all sides   *1Ki 4:24*
round about
there was *p.* between Hiram   *1Ki 5:12*
and Solomon
whether they be come for *p.*   *1Ki 20:18*
take them
and let him say, Is it *p.* Jehu   *2Ki 9:17;*
  9:18
what hast thou to do with   *2Ki 9:19*
p.? turn
what *p.* so long as her   *2Ki 9:22*
witchcrafts are many
had Zimri *p.* who slew his   *2Ki 9:31*
master
is it not good, if *p.* be in my   *2Ki 20:19;*
days   *Isa 39:8*
I will give *p.* to Israel in his   *1Ch 22:9*
days
in those times there was no *p.*   *2Ch 15:5*
to him
and to the rest beyond the   *Ezr 4:17*
river, *p.*
to Darius king, all *p;* to Ezra   *Ezr 5:7;*
perfect *p.*   *7:12*
nor seek their *p.* or their   *Ezr 9:12*
wealth for ever
Mordecai sent letters with   *Es 9:30*
words of *p.* and truth
Mordecai speaking *p.* to all his   *Es 10:3*
seed
beasts of field shall be at *p.*   *Job 5:23*
with thee
acquaint thyself with him,   *Job 22:21*
and be at *p.*
he maketh *p.* in his high   *Job 25:2*
places
if I have evil to him that was at   *Ps 7:4*
p. with me
which speak *p.* to neighbours,   *Ps 28:3*
but mischief
the Lord will bless his people   *Ps 29:11*
with *p.*
do good, seek *p.* and pursue it   *Ps 34:14;*
  1Pe 3:11
they speak not *p.* but they   *Ps 35:20*
devise matters
meek delight themselves in   *Ps 37:11*
abundance of *p.*
for the end of the upright man   *Ps 37:37*
is *p.*
put forth against such as be at   *Ps 55:20*
p. with him
the mountains shall bring *p.* to   *Ps 72:3*
the people
in days abundance of *p.* so long   *Ps 72:7*
as moon endureth

he will speak *p.* to his people *Ps 85:8* and saints
righteousness and *p.* have *Ps 85:10* kissed each other
great *p.* have they which *Ps 119:165* love thy law
I am for *p.* but they are *Ps 120:7* for war
pray for *p.* of Jerusalem, *Ps 122:6* prosper that love
but *p.* shall be upon Israel *Ps 125:5*
yea, thou shalt see *p.* upon *Ps 128:6* Israel
he maketh *p.* in thy borders, *Ps 147:14* filleth
wisdom's ways pleasantness, *Pr 3:17* and paths *p.*
but to the counsellors of *p.* is *Pr 12:20* joy
maketh his enemies to be at *p.* *Pr 16:7* with him
a time of war, and a time of *p.* *Ec 3:8*
Prince of *p.;* increase of his *p.* *Isa 9:6;* no end *9:7*
Lord, thou wilt ordain *p.* for *Isa 26:12* us, for thou
he make *p.* with me, and he *Isa 27:5* shall make *p.*
the work of righteousness *Isa 32:17* shall be *p.*
the ambassadors of *p.* shall *Isa 33:7* weep bitterly
behold, for *p.* I had great *Isa 38:17* bitterness
make *p.* and create evil, I do *Isa 45:7* all these things
then had thy *p.* been as river, *Isa 48:18* righteousness
there is no *p.* to the wicked *Isa 48:22; 57:21*
feet of him that publisheth *p.* *Isa 52:7; Na 1:15*
the chastisement of our *p.* was *Isa 53:5* upon him
punishment procurred our *p.* *Isa 53:5* (B)
nor shall covenant of my *p.* *Isa 54:10* be removed
and great shall be the *p.* of *Isa 54:13* thy children
ye shall go out with joy, led *Isa 55:12* forth with *p.*
he shall enter into *p.* they shall *Isa 57:2* rest in beds
I create the fruit of the lips, *Isa 57:19* *p. p.* to him
the way of *p.* they know not *Isa 59:8; Ro 3:17*
I will make thine officers *p.* *Isa 60:17* and exactors
I will extend *p.* to her like *Isa 66:12* river
ye shall have *p.* whereas sword *Jer 4:10* reaches
saying, *P. p.* when there is *Jer 6:14;* no *p.* *8:11*
we looked for *p.* but no good *Jer 8:15;* came *14:19*
if in land of *p.* they wearied *Jer 12:5* thee, then
sword shall devour, no flesh *Jer 12:12* shall have *p.*
I will give you assured *p.* in *Jer 14:13* this place
I have taken away my *p.* from *Jer 16:5* this people
the prophet which prophesied *Jer 28:9* of *p.*
and seek *p.* of the city whither *Jer 29:7* I caused
I think toward you thoughts *Jer 29:11* of *p.* not evil
we have heard a voice of fear, *Jer 30:5* and not of *p.*
reveal to them abundance of *p.* *Jer 33:6* and truth
thou hast removed my soul far *La 3:17* from *p.*
they shall seek *p.* there shall *Eze 7:25* be none
saying *p.* and there was no *Eze 13:10;* *p.* *13:16*
will make with them a *Eze 34:25;* covenant of *p.* *37:26*
and by *p.* he shall destroy many *Da 8:25*
men at *p.* with thee have *Ob 7* deceived thee
that bite with their teeth and *Mic 3:5* cry *p.*

this man shall be *p.* when *Mic 5:5* Assyrian come
and in this place I will give *p.* *Hag 2:9* saith Lord
the counsel of *p.* be between *Zec 6:13* them both
nor was there any *p.* to him *Zec 8:10* that came in
execute judgment of truth and *Zec 8:16* *p.*
love *p.* *Zec 8:19*
and he shall speak *p.* to the *Zec 9:10* heathen
my covenant was with him of *Mal 2:5* life and *p.*
p. and uprightness (A)(B) *Mal 2:6*
make *p.* with brother *M't 5:24* (A)(N)(P)
if house be worthy, let *p.* *M't 10:13* come upon it; if not, let *p.*
think not that I am come to *M't 10:34* send *p.* on earth
said to the sea, *P.* be still *M'k 4:39*
and have *p.* one with another *M'k 9:50*
to guide our feet into the way *Lu 1:79* of *p.*
on earth *p.* good will toward *Lu 2:14* men
if son of *p.* be there, your *p.* *Lu 10:6* shall rest
property is in *p.* (P) *Lu 11:21*
that I am come to give *p.* on *Lu 12:51* the earth
he sendeth and desireth *Lu 14:32* conditions of *p.*
p. in heaven, and glory in the *Lu 19:38* highest
if known the things that *Lu 19:42* belong to thy *p.*
p. I leave with you, my *p.* I *Joh 14:27* give you
that in me ye might have *p.* *Joh 16:33* in world tribulation
preaching *p.* by Jesus Christ *Ac 10:36* the Lord of all
having made Blastus their *Ac 12:20* friend desired (B)
pleaded for *p.* (B) *Ac 12:20*
a pestilential disturber of *p.* *Ac 24:5* (P)
p. from God the Father *Ro 1:7;* *1Co 1:3; 2Co 1:2; Ga 1:3;* *Eph 1:2; Ph'p 1:2*
but *p.* to every man that *Ro 2:10* worketh good
justified, we have *p.* with God, *Ro 5:1* through Christ
but to be spiritually minded is *Ro 8:6* life and *p.*
feet of them that preach the *Ro 10:15* gospel of *p.*
for the kingdom of God is joy *Ro 14:17* and *p.*
let us follow the things that *Ro 14:19* make for *p.*
for another's *p.* and *Ro 14:19* development (B)(N)
fill you with all joy and *p.* in *Ro 15:13* believing
but God hath called us to *p.* *1Co 7:15*
but author of *p.* as *1Co 14:33* in churches of saints
the fruit of the Spirit is love, *Ga 5:22* joy, *p.*
for he is our *p;* so making *p.* *Eph 2:14; 2:15*
Christ came and preached *p.* *Eph 2:17* to you afar off
to keep unity of the Spirit in *Eph 4:3* the bond of *p.*
feet shod with preparation of *Eph 6:15* gospel of *p.*
p. of God, which passeth *Ph'p 4:7* understanding
grace and *p.* from God our *Col 1:2;* Father *1Th 1:1; 2Th 1:2; 1Ti 1:2; 2Ti 1:2; Tit 1:4; Ph'm 3; 2Jo 3*
let the *p.* of God rule in your *Col 3:15* hearts
for when they shall say *p.* and *1Th 5:3* safety
and be at *p.* among yourselves *1Th 5:13*
now Lord of *p.* give you *p.* *2Th 3:16* always
follow *p.* with all men *2Ti 2:22; Heb 12:14*
the king of Salem, that is, *Heb 7:2* king of *p.*
Rahab believed and received *Heb 11:31* spies in *p.*

is sown in *p.* of them that *Jas 3:18* make *p.*
p. from him that is, was, and is *Re 1:4* to come
power was given to take *p.* from *Re 6:4* earth

PEACE *BE*

and he said, *P.* be to you, fear *Ge 43:23* not
the Lord said, *P.* be to thee, *J'g 6:23* fear not
and the old man said, *P.* be *J'g 19:20* with thee
p. be to thee, *p.* be to house, *p.* *1Sa 25:6* be to all
p. be to thee, and *p.* be to *1Ch 12:18* thy helpers
p. be within thy walls, and *Ps 122:7* prosperity
I will now say, *P.* be within *Ps 122:8* thee
p. be multiplied to you *Da 4:1* *6:25; 1Pe 1:2; 2Pe 1:2; Jude 2*
p. be to thee, be strong, yea, *Da 10:19* be strong
first say, *P.* be to this house *Lu 10:5*
he saith, *P.* be to you *Lu 24:36; Joh 20:19, 21, 26*
p. be on them, and mercy on *Ga 6:16* Israel of God
p. be to brethren, and love *Eph 6:23* with faith
p. be with you all that are in *1Pe 5:14* Christ
p. be to thee, our friends salute *3Jo 14* thee

GOD *OF* PEACE

the *God of p.* be with you all, *Ro 15:33* amen
the *God of p.* shall bruise *Ro 16:20* Satan shortly
God of p. shall be with you *2Co 13:11; Ph'p 4:9*
very *God of p.* sanctify you *1Th 5:23* wholly
now the *God of p.* make you *Heb 13:20* perfect

IN PEACE

and we have sent thee away *Ge 26:29* *in p.*
and they departed from Isaac *Ge 26:31* *in p.*
so that I come to my father's *Ge 28:21* house *in p.*
as for you, get you up *in p.* to *Ge 44:17* your father
came to Joshua, at *Jos 10:21* Makkedah, *in p.*
when I come again *in p.* will *J'g 8:9* break down
when I return *in p.* *J'g 11:31* whatever meet me
Abner went *in p.;* he is gone *2Sa 3:21;* *in p.* *3:22-23*
return to the city *in p.* and *2Sa 15:27* your two sons
so all the people shall be *in p.* *2Sa 17:3*
king departed, until the day *2Sa 19:24* he came *in p.*
as my lord the king is come *2Sa 19:30* again *in p.*
Joab shed the blood of war *in* *1Ki 2:5* *p.*
return every man *in p.* *1Ki 22:17; 2Ch 18:16*
in prison until I come *in p.* *1Ki 22:27; 2Ch 18:26*
if thou return at all *in p.* *2Ki 22:28; 2Ch 18:27*
shalt be gathered to thy *2Ki 22:20* grave *in p.* not see evil *2Ch 34:28*
and Jehoshaphat returned *in* *2Ch 19:1* *p.*
shalt know thy tabernacle shall *Job 5:24* be *in p.*
I will lay me down *in p.* and *Ps 4:8* sleep
he hath delivered my soul *in p.* *Ps 51:18* from the battle
thou wilt keep him *in* perfect *Isa 26:3* *in p.*
in the *p.* thereof shall ye have *Jer 29:7* peace
but thou shalt die *in p.* they *Jer 34:5* will lament

he walked with me in *p.* and equity   *Mal 2:6*

now lettest thou thy servant depart in *p*   *Lu 2:29*

keepeth his palace his goods are in *p.*   *Lu 11:21*

but conduct him forth in *p.* may come   *1Co 16:11*

be perfect, be of one mind, live in *p.*   *2Co 13:11*

depart in *p.* be ye warmed and filled   *Jas 2:16*

the fruit of righteousness is sown in *p.*   *Jas 3:18*

that ye may be found of him in *p.*   *2Pe 3:14*

PEACEABLE

These men are *p.* with us   *Ge 34:21*

that are *p.* and faithful in Israel   *2Sa 20:19*

land was wide, and quiet, and *p.*   *1Ch 4:40*

shall dwell in a *p.* habitation   *Isa 32:18*

the *p.* habitations are cut down   *Jer 25:37*

we may lead a quiet and *p.* life   *1Ti 2:2*

the *p.* fruit of righteousness unto   *Heb 12:11*

first pure, then *p.*, gentle, and easy   *Jas 3:17*

PEACEABLY

and could not speak *p.* unto him   *Ge 37:4*

now restore those lands again *p.*   *J'g 11:13*

Rimmon, and to call *p.* unto them   *J'g 21:13*

coming, and said, Comest thou *p.*   *1Sa 16:4*

And he said, *P.*: I am come to   *1Sa 16:5*

And she said, Comest thou *p.*   *1Ki 2:13*

And he said, *P.*   *1Ki 2:13*

If ye be come *p.* unto me to help me   *1Ch 12:17*

one speaketh *p.* to his neighbour   *Jer 9:8*

he shall come in *p.* and obtain   *Da 11:21*

He shall enter *p.* even upon   *Da 11:24*

lieth in you, live *p.* with all men   *Ro 12:18*

PEACEMAKERS

Blessed are the *p.*: for they shall   *M't 5:9*

makers and maintainers of peace (A)   *M't 5:9*

PEACOCKS

and silver, ivory, and apes, and *p.*   *1Ki 10:22; 2Ch 9:21*

thou the goodly wings unto the *p.*   *Job 39:13*

wings of the ostrich (A)(B)(E)(R)   *Job 39:13*

PEAK

perch on a craggy *p.* (B)   *Job 39:28*

PEALS

p. of thunder (S)   *Re 19:6*

PEARL

he had found one *p.* of great price   *M't 13:46*

every several gate was of one *p.*   *Re 21:21*

PEARLS

shall be made of coral, or of *p.*   *Job 28:18*

wisdom is above *p.* (B)(R)   *Job 28:18*

multitude of *p.* (A)   *Pr 20:15*

cast ye your *p.* before swine   *M't 7:6*

a merchant man, seeking goodly *p.*   *M't 13:45*

hair, or gold, or *p.*, or costly array   *1Ti 2:9*

gold and precious stones and *p.*   *Re 17:4; 18:16*

and precious stones, and of *p.*   *Re 18:12*

the twelve gates were twelve *p.*   *Re 21:21*

PEAS

parched *p.* and beans (A)   *2Sa 17:28*

PECKS

three *p.* of fine meal (B)   *Ge 18:6*

PECULIAR

ye shall be a *p.* treasure unto me   *Ex 19:5*

thee to be a *p.* people unto himself   *De 14:2*

thee this day to be his *p.* people   *De 26:18*

and Israel for his *p.* treasure   *Ps 135:4*

the *p.* treasure of kings and   *Ec 2:8*

a *p.* people, zealous of good works   *Tit 2:14*

p. teachings (P)   *Heb 13:9*

an holy nation, a *p.* people   *1Pe 2:9*

PEDAHEL

Naphtali, *P.* the son of Ammihud   *Nu 34:28*

PEDAHZUR

Manasseh; Gamaliel the son of *P.*   *Nu 1:10*

shall be Gamaliel the son of *P.*   *Nu 2:20*

day offered Gamaliel the son of *P.*   *Nu 7:54*

offering of Gamaliel the son of *P.*   *Nu 7:59*

was Gamaliel the son of *P.*   *Nu 10:23*

PEDAIAH

the daughter of *P.* of Rumah   *2Ki 23:36*

Malchiram also, and *P.* and   *1Ch 3:18*

the sons of *P.* were, Zerubbabel   *1Ch 3:19*

of Manasseh, Joel the son of   *1Ch 27:20*

After him *P.* the son of Parosh   *Ne 3:25*

on his left hand, *P.* and Mishael   *Ne 8:4*

the son of Joed, the son of *P.*   *Ne 11:7*

the scribe, and of the Levites, *p.*   *Ne 13:13*

PEDESTAL

there was a *p.* (S)   *1Ki 7:29*

the work of the *p.* (S)   *1Ki 7:31*

PEDIGREE

without *p.* (B)   *Heb 7:3; 7:6*

PEDIGREES

they declared their *p.* after their   *Nu 1:18*

PEELED

p. white streaks (A)(B)(E)(R)(S)   *Ge 30:37; 30:38*

to a nation scattered and *p.* to   *Isa 18:2*

nation tall and polished (A)   *Isa 18:2; 18:7*

people tall and smooth (B)(E)(R)   *Isa 18:2; 18:7*

of a people scattered and *p.*   *Isa 18:7*

bald, and every shoulder was *p.*   *Eze 29:18*

PEEP

and unto wizards that *p.* and   *Isa 8:19*

who chirp and mutter (A)(B)(E)(R)   *Isa 8:19*

PEEPED

wing, or opened the mouth, or *p.*   *Isa 10:14*

opened the mouth, and chirped (A)(B)(E)(R)   *Isa 10:14*

PEG

took a tent *p.* (B)(R)   *J'g 4:21; 4:22; 5:26*

like a *p.* (B)(R)   *Isa 22:23; 22:25*

take a *p.* to hang (A)(B)(E)   *Eze 15:3*

the tent *p.* (A)(B)(E)   *Zec 10:4*

PEKAH

But *P.* the son of Remaliah   *2Ki 15:25; 15:27, 29-32, 37*

In the seventeenth year of *P.*   *2Ki 16:1*

P. son of Remaliah king of Israel   *2Ki 16:5*

For *P.* the son of Remaliah slew in   *2Ch 28:6*

P. the son of Remaliah, king of   *Isa 7:1*

PEKAHIAH

P. his son reigned in his stead   *2Ki 15:22*

P. the son of Menahem began to   *2Ki 15:23*

And the rest of the acts of *P.*   *2Ki 15:26*

PEKOD

and against the inhabitants of *P.*   *Jer 50:21*

all the Chaldeans, *P.* and Shoa   *Eze 23:23*

PELAIAH

and Eliashib, and *P.* and Akkub   *1Ch 3:24*

P. and the Levites, caused the   *Ne 8:7*

Shebaniah, Hodijah, Kelita, *P.*   *Ne 10:10*

PELALIAH

the son of Jeroham, the son of *P.*   *Ne 11:12*

PELATIAH

the sons of Hananiah; *P.* and   *1Ch 3:21*

having for their captains *P.*   *1Ch 4:42*

P., Hanan, Anaiah   *Ne 10:22*

and *P.* the son of Benaiah, princes   *Eze 11:1*

that *P.* the son of Benaiah died   *Eze 11:13*

PELEG

two sons: the name of one was *P.*   *Ge 10:25*

four and thirty years, and begat *P.*   *Ge 11:16*

And Eber lived after he begat *P.*   *Ge 11:17*

P. lived thirty years, and begat   *Ge 11:18*

P. lived after he begat Reu   *Ge 11:19*

two sons: the name of the one was *P.*   *1Ch 1:19*

Eber, *P.*, Reu   *1Ch 1:25*

PELET

Gesham, and *P.* and Ephah   *1Ch 2:47*

and *P.* the sons of Azmaveth   *1Ch 12:3*

PELETH

and On, the son of *P.* sons of   *Nu 16:1*

the sons of Jonathan; *P.* and   *1Ch 2:33*

PELETHITES

both the Cherethites and the *P.*   *2Sa 8:18*

and all the *P.* and all the Gittites   *2Sa 15:18*

the *P.*, and all the mighty men   *2Sa 20:7*

the Cherethites and over the *P.*   *2Sa 20:23*

and the *P.* went down, and caused   *1Ki 1:38*

the Cherethites, and the *P.*   *1Ki 1:44*

over the Cherethites and the *P.*   *1Ch 18:17*

PELICAN

and the *p.* and the gier eagle	*Le 11:18;*
	De 14:17
I am like a *p.* of the	*Ps 102:6*
wilderness	
the *p.* and porcupine	*Isa 34:11*
(A)(B)(E)	
the *p.* and hedgehog (A)	*Zep 2:14*

PELONITE

the Harorite, Helez the *P.*	*1Ch 11:27*
the Mecherathite, Ahijah	*1Ch 11:36*
the *P.*	
seventh month was Helez the	*1Ch 27:10*
P.	

PELUSIUM

P. shall have anguish (A)	*Eze 30:16*

PEN

they that handle the *p.* of the	*J'g 5:14*
they were graven with an	*Job 19:24*
iron *p.*	
tongue is a *p.* of a ready	*Ps 45:1*
writer	
roll, and write in it with a	*Isa 8:1*
man's *p.*	
it; the *p.* of the scribes is in vain	*Jer 8:8*
Judah is written with a *p.* of	*Jer 17:1*
iron	
with ink and *p.* write unto thee	*3Jo 13*

PENALTY

there is one *p.,* execution (B)	*Es 4:11*
p. suffered in hell (A)	*M't 23:33*
the *p.* due them (A)	*Ro 13:2*
p. of everlasting ruin (P)	*2Th 1:9*
received and appropriate *p.*	*Heb 2:2*
(A)	
more severe *p.* (N)	*Heb 10:29*
p. of eternal fire (N)	*Jude 7*

PENCE

which owed him an hundred	*M't 18:28*
p.	
a hundred denarii	*M't 18:28*
(A)(B)(R)	
a hundred shillings (E)	*M't 18:28*
a few pounds (N)	*M't 18:28*
owed him a few dollars (P)	*M't 18:28*
for more than three hundred	*M'k 14:5*
p.	
for more than three hundred	*M'k 14:5*
denarii (A)(B)(E)(R)	
the one owed five hundred *p.*	*Lu 7:41*
owed him five hundred denarii	*Lu 7:41*
(A)(B)(E)(R)	
he took out two *p.* and	*Lu 10:35*
gave them to	
he took out two denarii	*Lu 10:35*
(A)(B)(E)(R)	
ointment sold for three	*Joh 12:5*
hundred *p.*	
perfume sold for three hundred	*Joh 12:5*
denarii (A)(B)(E)(R)	

PENDANTS

the *p.* (A)(B)(E)(S)	*Isa 3:19*

PENIEL

called the name of the place	*Ge 32:30*
P.	

PENINNAH

and the name of the other *P.*	*1Sa 1:2*
and *P.* had children, but	*1Sa 1:2*
Hannah	
offered, he gave to *P.* his wife	*1Sa 1:4*

PENITENT

thine heart was *p.* (B)(R)	*2Ki 22:19*
heart was *p.* (R)	*2Ch 34:27*
a *p.* heart (B)	*Ps 51:17*
a *p.* spirit (A)	*Isa 57:15*
be deeply *p.* (A)	*Jas 4:9*

PENKNIFE

leaves, he cut it with the *p.*	*Jer 36:23*

PENNY

with labourers for a *p.* a day	*M't 20:2*
laborers for a denarius	*M't 20:2;*
(A)(R)	*20:9-10, 13; 22:19; M'k 12:15;*
	Lu 20:24
agreeing on a quarter a day	*M't 20:2;*
(B)	*20:9-10, 13*
agreed on a shilling a day	*M't 20:2;*
(E)	*20:9-10, 13*
agreeing to pay a full day's	*M't 20:2;*
wage (N)	*20:10, 13*
a silver coin a day (P)	*M't 20:2; 20:13*
not a *p.* in their belt	*M'k 6:8*
(A)(B)(N)(R)	
a measure of wheat for a *p.*	*Re 6:6*
(A)(R)	
a quart of wheat for a denarius	*Re 6:6*
(A)(R)	
a quart of wheat for a day's	*Re 6:6*
wage (B)(N)	
a measure of wheat for a	*Re 6:6*
shilling (E)	
a quart of wheat for a quarter	*Re 6:6*
(P)	

PENNYWORTH

buy two hundred *p.* of bread	*M'k 6:37*
two hundred denarii (A)(R)	*M'k 6:37*
fifty dollars worth of bread	*M'k 6:37;*
(B)	*Joh 6:7*
two hundred shillings (E)	*M'k 6:37;*
	Joh 6:7
spend twenty pounds (N)	*M'k 6:37;*
	Joh 6:7
spend ten dollars (P)	*M'k 6:37; Joh 6:7*
Two hundred *p.* of bread is not	*Joh 6:7*

PENTECOST

the day of *P.* was fully come	*Ac 2:1*
to be at Jerusalem the day of	*Ac 20:16*
P.	
I will tarry at Ephesus until *P.*	*1Co 16:8*

PENUEL

as he passed over *P.* the sun	*Ge 32:31*
rose	
he went up thence to *P.* and	*J'g 8:8*
spake	
and the men of *P.* answered him	*J'g 8:8*
he spake also unto the men of	*J'g 8:9*
P.	
And he beat down the tower of	*J'g 8:17*
P.	
went out from thence, and	*1Ki 12:25*
built *P.*	
and *P.* the father of Gedor	*1Ch 4:4*
and *P.* the sons of Shashak	*1Ch 8:25*

PENURY

talk of the lips tendeth only to	*Pr 14:23*
p.	
leads only to poverty (A)	*Pr 14:23*
leads only to want (B)(R)	*Pr 14:23*
but she of her *p.* hath cast in	*Lu 21:4*
all	
contributed of her lack and	*Lu 21:4*
want (A)	
she from her shortage (B)	*Lu 21:4*
she of her want did cast in	*Lu 21:4*
(E)	
she, with less than enough (N)	*Lu 21:4*
she in her poverty did (P)(R)	*Lu 21:4*

PEOPLE

slay a blameless *p.* (B)(R)	*Ge 20:4*
let *p.* serve thee, nations bow	*Ge 27:29*
to thee	
he also shall become a *p.* and	*Ge 48:19*
be great	
take you for a *p.* be to you a	*Ex 6:7*
God	*De 4:20; 2Sa 7:24;*
the *p.* change their purpose	*Ex 13:17*
(A)	
thou art a stiffnecked *p.*	*Ex 33:3;*
	33:5; 34:9; De 9:6
the *p.* (B)(E)	*Le 10:17;*
	Nu 14:27; 16:47
I separated you from other *p.*	*Le 20:24;*
	20:26
thou art undone, O *p.* of	*Nu 21:29*
Chemosh	
behold, there is a *p.* come out	*Nu 22:5;*
from Egypt	*25:11*
he was head over a *p.* in	*Nu 25:15*
Midian	
ever *p.* hear voice of God out	*De 4:33*
of fire	
God hath chosen thee to be a	*De 7:6*
special *p.*	
Lord hath chosen thee to be a	*De 14:2*
peculiar *p.*	
a *p.* more than thou, be not	*De 20:1*
afraid	
thy sons shall be given to	*De 28:32*
another *p.*	
he may establish thee for *p.* to	*De 29:13*
himself	
move them with those that	*De 32:21*
are not a *p.*	
who is like to thee O *p.* saved	*De 33:29*
by Lord	
thy sister is gone back to her *p.*	*Ru 1:15*
ye make the Lord's *p.* to	*1Sa 2:24*
transgress	
brought ark to us to slay our	*1Sa 5:10*
p.	
let it go, that it slay us not,	*1Sa 5:11*
and our *p.*	
whom God went to redeem for	*2Sa 7:23*
a *p.*	
afflicted *p.* thou wilt save	*2Sa 22:28;*
	Ps 18:27
a *p.* I knew not shall serve	*2Sa 22:44;*
me	*Ps 18:43*
hearken, O *p.* every one of	*1Ki 22:28*
you	
shalt be Lord's *p.*	*2Ki 11:17; 2Ch 23:16*
from one kingdom to	*1Ch 16:20;*
another *p.*	*Ps 105:13*
behave ourselves valiantly	*1Ch 19:13*
for our *p.*	
thou hast made me king over a	*2Ch 1:9*
p.	
for he sent letters to every *p.*	*Es 1:22;*
	3:12; 8:9; Ne 13:24
Esther had not shewed her *p.*	*Es 2:10*
there is a certain *p.* scattered	*Es 3:8*
abroad	
go in make request for her *p.*	*Es 4:8*
when *p.* are cut off in their	*Job 36:20*
place	
p. plot in vain (R)	*Ps 2:1*
frustrated purposes of *p.* (B)	*Ps 33:10*
ye *p.* pour out your hearts	*Ps 62:8*
before him	
bless our God, ye *p.;* a *p.* that	*Ps 66:8;*
do err	*95:10*
went out from a *p.* of a	*Ps 114:1*
strange language	
happy is that *p.;* a *p.* near	*Ps 144:15;*
to him	*148:14*
but sin is a reproach to any *p.*	*Pr 14:34*
so is a wicked ruler over the	*Pr 28:15*
poor *p.*	
ants are a *p.* not strong, yet	*Pr 30:25*
prepare	
a *p.* laden with iniquity, a seed	*Isa 1:4*
of evil doers	
give ear to the law, ye *p.* of	*Isa 1:10*
Gomorrah	
Ephraim shall be broken, that it	*Isa 7:8*
be not a *p.*	
should not a *p.* seek unto their	*Isa 8:19*
God	
for it is a *p.* of no	*Isa 27:11*
understanding, therefore	
write, That this is a rebellious	*Isa 30:9;*
p.	*65:2*
therefore I will give *p.* for thy	*Isa 43:4*
life	
bring forth the blind *p.* that	*Isa 43:8*
have eyes	
a *p.* that provoketh me to	*Isa 65:3*
anger to my face	
I create Jerusalem a	*Isa 65:18*
rejoicing, and her *p.* a joy	
a *p.* cometh from the north	*Jer 6:22;*
	50:41
Moab shall be destroyed from	*Jer 48:42*
being a *p.*	
her *p.* fell into the hand of the	*La 1:7*
enemy	
there shall be like *p.* like priest	*Ho 4:9*
repoice not, O Israel, for joy	*Ho 9:1*
as other *p.*	
tell us, of what *p.* art thou	*Jon 1:8*
be exalted, and *p.* shall flow	*Mic 4:1*
unto it	
there shall come *p.* and	*Zec 8:20*
inhabitants	
given to a *p.* (A)(B)(P)	*M't 21:43*
to make ready a *p.* prepared	*Lu 1:17*
for Lord	

p. of this world (A)(N) Lu 20:34
take away our place and p. Joh 11:48
(B)
the p. begged (B) Ac 13:48
to take out of them a p. for Ac 15:14
his name
provoke to jealousy by them Ro 10:19
that are no p.
he might purify to himself a Tit 2:14
peculiar p.
to them a God, and they shall Heb 8:10
be to me a p.
but ye are a peculiar p. to shew 1Pe 2:9
forth
p. of God in time past were not 1Pe 2:10
a p. now
foolishness of thoughtless p. 1Pe 2:15
(B)
thou hast redeemed us out of Re 5:9
every p.

PEOPLE *OF GOD*

presently in assembly of the p. J'g 20:2
of God
thought such a thing against 2Sa 14:13
p. of God
even p. of the God of Ps 47:9
Abraham, gathered
there remaineth a rest to the Heb 4:9
p. of God
choosing to suffer affliction Heb 11:25
with p. of God
was not a people, but are 1Pe 2:10
now p. of God

PEOPLE *OF THE LAND*

Abraham bowed himself to p. Ge 23:7;
of the land 23:12
Joseph that sold to all p. of Ge 42:6
the land
p. of the land are many Ex 5:5
p. of the land shall stone him Le 20:2
with stones
if p. of the land do hide their Le 20:4
eyes
rebel not, neither fear ye p. of Nu 14:9
the land
all p. of the land rejoiced 2Ki 11:14;
and blew 11:20
Jotham judged p. of the land 2Ki 15:5;
2Ch 26:21
p. of the land slew and p. of 2Ki 21:24;
the land made Josiah king 2Ch 33:25
p. of land took Jehoahaz 2Ki 23:30;
his son 2Ch 36:1
there was no bread for p. of 2Ki 25:3;
the land Jer 52:6
took him that mustered p. 2Ki 25:19;
of the land and sixty men Jer 52:25
of p. of the land
went after the gods of p. of 1Ch 5:25
the land
p. of the land weakened hands Ezr 4:4
of builders
taken strange wives of the p. Ezr 10:2
of the land
separate yourselves from p. Ezr 10:11
of the land
not give our daughters to p. Ne 10:30
of the land
if the p. of the land bring Ne 10:31
ware, or victuals
the p. of the land became Jews Es 8:17
made an iron pillar against p. Jer 1:18
of the land
all the p. of the land which Jer 34:19
passed between
hands of p. of the land shall Eze 7:27
be troubled
p. of the land have used Eze 22:29
oppression and robbery
if p. of the land take man to Eze 33:2
be a watchman
all the p. of the land shall Eze 39:13
bury them
all p. of the land shall give Eze 45:16
oblation
the prince prepare for p. of Eze 45:22
the land
p. of the land shall worship Eze 46:3
at door of this gate
when p. of the land shall Eze 46:9
come in solemn
prophets which spake to the p. Da 9:6
of the land
be strong, all ye p. of the Hag 2:4
land, and work
speak to all the p. of the land Zec 7:5
and priests

PEOPLES

his marvelous works among 1Ch 16:24
the p. (S)
scatter you among the p. (S) Ne 1:8
disgrace of the p. (R) Eze 36:15
thou must prophesy before Re 10:11
many p.
waters thou sawest are p. Re 17:15
and multitudes

PEOPLE'S

And he brought the p. offering Le 9:15
shall not take of the p. Eze 46:18
inheritance
For this p. heart is waxed M't 13:15
gross
his own sins, and then for Heb 7:27
the p.

ALL PEOPLE

be a peculiar treasure above Ex 19:5;
all p. De 7:6, 14; 10:15; Ps 99:2
for ye were the fewest of all p. De 7:7
the Lord shall scatter thee De 28:64
among all p.
came of all p. to hear wisdom 1Ki 4:34
of Solomon
all p. may know thy name 1Ki 8:43;
2Ch 6:33
shall be a proverb and byword 1Ki 9:7
among all p.
and their laws are diverse from Es 3:8
all p.
copy of writing was published Es 3:14;
to all p. 8:13
for the fear of them fell upon all Es 9:2
p.
O clap your hands, all ye p. Ps 47:1
shout to God
declare his wonders among all Ps 96:3
p.
praise him, all ye p. for his Ps 117:1;
kindness 148:11; Ro 15:11
Lord make to all p. a feast of Isa 25:6
fat things
the face of the covering cast Isa 25:7
over all p.
be called house of prayer for Isa 56:7
all p.
all her p. sigh, they seek bread La 1:11
hear, I pray you, all p. behold La 1:18;
Mic 1:2
all p. and nations feared Da 5:19
before him
that all p. and nations should Da 7:14
serve him
all p. will walk in name of his Mic 4:5
god
because he heapeth unto him Hab 2:5
all p.
make you a praise among all Zep 3:20
p. of earth
make Jerusalem a burdensome Zec 12:3
stone for all p.
tidings of joy, which shall be to Lu 2:10
all p.
hast prepared before the face Lu 9:31
of all p.

ALL THE PEOPLE

all the p. of Sodom compassed Ge 19:4
Lot's
came to Luz, he and all the p. Ge 35:6
with him
he it was that sold to all the p. Ge 42:6
get thee out, and all the p. that Ex 11:8
follow thee
all the p. stand by thee from Ex 18:14
morning to
shalt provide out of all the p. Ex 18:21
able men
all the p. answered together Ex 19:8;
and said 24:3
Lord will come down in sight Ex 19:11
of all the p.
all the p. saw thunderings and Ex 20:18
lightnings
glory of the Lord appeared to Le 9:23
all the p.
before all the p. I will be Le 10:3
glorified
that all the Lord's p. were Nu 11:29
prophets
all the p. we saw are men of Nu 13:32
great stature

seeing all the p. were in Nu 15:26
ignorance
afterwards the hands of all the De 13:9;
17:7
all the p. shall hear and fear, De 17:13
and do no more
all the p. say, Amen De 27:15; 27:16-26
all the p. of the earth shall see De 28:10
that thou
that all the p. of the earth Jos 4:24
might know
all the p. that came out were Jos 5:4;
circumcised 5:5
all the p. shall shout; Jos 6:5;
let not all the p. go 7:3
Lord drave out from before us Jos 24:18
all the p.
the house fell upon all the p. J'g 16:30
therein
all the p. arose as one man, J'g 20:8
saying
there is none like him among 1Sa 10:24
all the p.
all the p. wept; all the p. 1Sa 11:4;
feared greatly 12:18
because the soul of all the p. 1Sa 30:6
was grieved
all the p. stood, and pursued 2Sa 2:28
no more
wept at Abner's grave, and 2Sa 3:32;
all the p. wept 3:34
all the p. took notice of it, it 2Sa 3:36
pleased
bring back all the p. unto 2Sa 17:3
thee, so all the p. shall be in peace
all the p. were at strife 2Sa 19:9
through all Israel
woman went to all the p. in 2Sa 20:22
her wisdom
didst separate them from all 1Ki 8:53
the p.
that all the p. of the earth 1Ki 8:60
may know that
not suffice for handfuls for 1Ki 20:10
all the p.
all the p. stood to the 2Ki 23:3
covenant
all the p. said, Amen, and 1Ch 16:36
praised
all the p. will be wholly at 1Ch 28:21
thy command
king and all the p. offered 2Ch 7:4
sacrifices
set judges, which may judge Ezr 7:25
all the p.
in sight of all the p. for he was Ne 8:5
above all the p.
so the Levites stilled all the p. Ne 8:11
saying
O God, let all the p. praise Ps 67:3;
thee 67:5
heavens declare righteousness Ps 97:6
and all the p. see his glory
let all the p. say, Amen Ps 106:48
there is no end of all the p. Ec 4:16
even of all
Lord commanded him to Jer 26:8
speak to all the p.
all the p. were gathered against Jer 26:9
Jeremiah
and all the p. fought against Jer 34:1
Jerusalem
Zedekiah made a covenant Jer 34:8;
with all the p. 34:10
thus he weakeneth the hands Jer 38:4
of all the p.
all the p. obeyed not the voice Jer 43:4
of the Lord
all the p. are gone from his Eze 31:12
shadow
when all the p. heard the sound Da 3:7
of cornet
break my covenant I made Zec 11:10
with all the p.
Jerusalem a cup of trembling Zec 12:2
to all the p.
the Lord will smite all the p. Zec 14:12
that fought
I also made you base before all Mal 2:9
the p.
she declared unto him before Lu 8:47
all the p.
all the p. rejoiced for the Lu 13:17
glorious things
all the p. when they saw, gave Lu 18:43
praise to God
all the p. were very attentive Lu 19:48
to hear him
if we say, Of men, all the p. Lu 20:6
will stone us

and having favour with *all the*   *Ac 2:47*
p.
Gamaliel had reputation   *Ac 5:34*
among *all the p.*
not to *all the p.* but unto   *Ac 10:41*
witnesses chosen
the baptism of repentance to   *Ac 13:24*
all the p.
stirred up *all the p.* and laid   *Ac 21:27*
hands on him
Moses spoke every precept to   *Heb 9:19*
all the p.; sprinkled book and
all the p.

AMONG THE **PEOPLE**

shall be cut off from *among*   *Le 18:29*
the p.
woman shall be a curse *among*   *Nu 5:27*
the p.
disperse yourselves *among*   *1Sa 14:34*
the p.
understand, ye brutish *among*   *Ps 94:8*
the p.
all that know thee *among the*   *Eze 28:19*
p. shall be
they that understand *among*   *Da 11:33*
the p.
wherefore should they say   *Joe 2:17*
among the p.
and I will sow them *among*   *Zec 10:9*
the p.
all manner of disease *among*   *M't 4:23;*
the p.   *9:35*
lest there be an uproar *among*   *M't 26:5*
the p.
there was much murmuring   *Joh 7:12*
among the p.
was a division *among the p.*   *Joh 7:43*
because of him
shall be destroyed from *among*   *Ac 3:23*
the p.
that it spread no further   *Ac 4:17*
among the p.
many wonders wrought *among*   *Ac 5:12;*
the p.   *6:8*
Barnabas and Paul ran in   *Ac 14:14*
among the p.
there were false prophets also   *2Pe 2:1*
among the p.

HIS **PEOPLE**

be cut off from *his p.*   *Ge 17:14;*
Ex 30:33, 38; 31:14; Le 7:20-21, 25, 27;
17:4, 9; 19:8; 23:29; Nu 9:13; 15:30
then Abraham was gathered to   *Ge 25:8*
his p.
Ishmael was gathered to *his*   *Ge 25:17,*
p.; Isaac   *35:29*
Dan shall judge *his p.* as one   *Ge 49:16;*
of tribes   *49:33*
that flies may depart from *his*   *Ex 8:29;*
p.   *8:31*
Joshua discomfited Amalek   *Ex 17:13*
and *his p.*
done for Moses and for Israel   *Ex 18:1*
his p.
blood, I will cut him off from   *Le 17:10;*
among *his p.*   *20:3, 6; 23:30*
none be defiled for the dead   *Le 21:1*
among *his p.*
nor shall he profane his seed   *Le 21:15*
among *his p.*
Aaron shall be gathered to   *Nu 20:24;*
his p.   *20:26*
I have delivered him into thy   *Nu 21:34;*
hand, and all *his p.*   *21:35; De 2:33*
I will deliver Og and all *his p.*   *De 3:2;*
  3:3
Lord avouched thee to be his   *De 26:18*
peculiar *p.*
for Lord's portion is *his p.*   *De 32:9*
Jacob the lot
the Lord shall judge *his p.*   *De 32:36;*
  Ps 131:14
rejoice with *his p.* he will be   *De 32:43;*
merciful to *his p.*   *Ro 15:10*
Aaron died was gathered to   *De 32:50*
his p.
hear, Lord, and bring Judah to   *De 33:7*
his p.
given thee Ai, the king and *his*   *Jos 8:1*
p.
dispossessed Amorites before   *J'g 11:23*
his p.
heard how the Lord had visited   *Ru 1:6*
his p.
Lord will not forsake *his p.*   *1Sa 12:22*
for it pleased the Lord to
make you *his p.*

to anoint thee to be king over   *1Sa 15:1*
all *his p.*
made *his p.* Israel utterly to   *1Sa 27:12*
abhor him
David executed justice to all   *2Sa 8:15;*
his p.   *1Ch 18:14*
and thy people shall go for   *1Ki 20:42*
his p.
the Lord make *his p.* a   *1Ch 21:3*
hundred times so many more
land is subdued before Lord   *1Ch 22:18*
and *his p.*
God of Israel hath given rest   *1Ch 23:25*
to *his p.*
because the Lord hath loved   *2Ch 2:11*
his p.
for the Lord hath blessed *his*   *2Ch 31:10*
p.
who was there that could   *2Ch 32:14;*
deliver *his p.*   *32:15*
the Lord spake to Manasseh   *2Ch 33:10*
and *his p.*
because he had compassion   *2Ch 36:15*
on *his p.*
mocked, until wrath rose   *2Ch 36:16*
against *his p.*
who among you of all *his p.*   *2Ch 36:23;*
go up   *Ezr 1:3*
Mordecai seeking the wealth of   *Es 10:3*
his p.
not have son nor nephew   *Job 18:19*
among *his p.*
bringeth back captivity of *his*   *Ps 14:7;*
p.   *53:6*
Lord will give strength to *his*   *Ps 29:11;*
p. the Lord will bless *his p.*   *68:35*
he shall call, that he may judge   *Ps 50:4*
his p.
his p. return hither, and   *Ps 73:10*
waters
they said, Can he provide   *Ps 78:20*
flesh for *his p.*
he gave *his p.* over also to the   *Ps 78:62*
sword
he brought him to feed Jacob   *Ps 78:71*
his p.
he will speak peace to *his p.*   *Ps 85:8*
and saints
for the Lord will not cast off   *Ps 94:14*
his p.
we are *his p.*   *Ps 100:3*
he increased *his p.* greatly,   *Ps 105:24*
made them
he turned their heart to hate   *Ps 105:25*
his p. to deal
brought forth *his p.*   *Ps 105:43*
wrath of Lord kindled   *Ps 106:40;*
against *his p.* that he   *Isa 5:25*
he shewed *his p.* the power of   *Ps 111:6*
his works
he sent redemption to *his p.*   *Ps 111:9*
holy is his name
set him with the princes of *his*   *Ps 113:8*
p.
now in the presence of all   *Ps 116:14;*
his p.   *116:18*
so is the Lord round about *his*   *Ps 125:2*
p.
led *his p.* through the   *Ps 136:16*
wilderness
he also exalteth the horn of   *Ps 148:14*
his p.
Lord taketh pleasure in *his p.*   *Ps 149:4*
into judgment with the   *Isa 3:14*
ancients of *his p.*
his heart was moved, and the   *Isa 7:2*
heart of *his p.*
to recover the remnant of *his*   *Isa 11:11*
p. left
be an highway for the   *Isa 11:16*
remnant of *his p.*
the poor of *his p.* shall trust   *Isa 14:32*
in him
the rebuke of *his p.* shall he   *Isa 25:8*
take away
for a diadem of beauty to   *Isa 28:5*
residue of *his p.*
in day Lord bindeth up   *Isa 30:26*
breach of *his p.*
for God hath comforted *his*   *Isa 49:13;*
p.   *52:9*
thy God that pleadeth the   *Ps 51:22*
cause of *his p.*
the Lord hath separated me   *Ps 56:3*
from *his p.*
remembered days of old,   *Ps 63:11*
Moses and *his p.*
and serve him and *his p.* and   *Jer 27:12*
live

they shall return every one to   *Jer 50:16*
his p.
did what is not good among   *Eze 18:18*
his p.
he and *his p.* with him shall   *Eze 30:11*
be brought
Lord be jealous and pity *his p.*   *Joe 2:18*
the Lord will answer and say   *Joe 2:19*
to *his p.*
the Lord will be the hope of   *Joe 3:16*
his p.
Lord hath a controversy with   *Mic 6:2*
his p.
Lord shall save them as flock   *Zec 9:16*
of *his p.*
he shall save *his p.* from their   *M't 1:21*
sins
for he hath visited and   *Lu 1:68*
redeemed *his p.*
give knowledge of salvation to   *Lu 1:77*
his p.
prophet risen, and God visited   *Lu 7:16*
his p.
hath God cast away *his p.?*   *Ro 11:1*
God forbid
God hath not cast away *his p.*   *Ro 11:2*
he foreknew
again the Lord shall judge   *Heb 10:30*
his p.
they shall be *his p.* God himself   *Re 21:3*
their God

MUCH **PEOPLE**

Edom came out against him   *Nu 20:20*
with *much p.*
they went with *much p.* even   *Jos 11:4*
as the sand
there came *much p.* by way   *2Sa 13:34*
of the hill
there assembled at Jerusalem   *2Ch 30:13*
much p.
so there was gathered *much p.*   *2Ch 32:4*
together
I will praise thee among *much*   *Ps 35:18*
p.
much p. gathered unto him   *M'k 5:21*
nigh the sea
much p. followed him   *M'k 5:24*
saw *much p.* was moved with   *M'k 6:34*
compassion
much p. of Jews knew he was   *Joh 12:9*
there
much p. took branches of   *Joh 12:12*
palm trees
and drew away *much p.* after   *Ac 5:37*
him
and *much p.* was added unto   *Ac 11:24*
the Lord
I am with thee, I have *much p.*   *Ac 18:10*
in this city
this Paul hath turned away   *Ac 19:26*
much p.
I heard a voice of *much p.* in   *Re 19:1*
heaven

MY **PEOPLE**

in presence of the sons of   *Ge 23:11*
my p. give I
to thy word shall all *my p.* be   *Ge 41:40*
ruled
I am to be gathered to *my p.*   *Ge 49:29*
bury me
I have seen affliction of *my p.*   *Ex 3:7;*
  Ac 7:34
that thou mayest bring forth   *Ex 3:10;*
my p.   *7:4*
let *my p.* go   *Ex 5:1;*
7:16; 8:1, 20; 9:1, 13; 10:3
take away frogs from *my p.*   *Ex 8:8*
else if thou wilt not let *my p.*   *Ex 8:21;*
go   *10:4*
sever the land in which *my p.*   *Ex 8:22;*
are   *8:23*
as yet exaltest thou thyself   *Ex 9:17*
against *my p.*
Lord is righteous, I and *my p.*   *Ex 9:27*
are wicked
and get you forth from among   *Ex 12:31*
my p.
if thou lend money to any of   *Ex 22:25*
my p.
ye shall be *my p.*   *Le 26:12;*
  Jer 11:4; 30:22
and now behold I go unto *my*   *Nu 24:14*
p.
I and *my p.* were at great strife   *J'g 12:2*
is there never a woman among   *J'g 14:3*
all *my p.*

put forth a riddle to children *J'g 14:16*
of *my p.*
thy people shall be *my p.* God *Ru 1:16*
my God
for all the city of *my p.* doth *Ru 3:11*
know that
anoint him captain over *my p. 1Sa 9:16*
to serve *my p.* I looked on *my p.*
by the hand of David I will *2Sa 3:18*
save *my p.*
took thee to be a ruler over *my 2Sa 7:8;*
p. *2Ch 6:5*
my p. as they people, my *1Ki 22:4;*
horses as thy horses *2Ki 3:7; 2Ch 18:3*
tell Hezekiah, the captain of *2Ki 20:5*
my p.
whom I commanded to feed *1Ch 17:6*
my p.
David stood and said, Hear *1Ch 28:2*
me, *my p.*
who am I, and what *my p.* to *1Ch 29:14*
be able
wisdom, that thou mayest *2Ch 1:11*
judge *my p.*
I brought forth *my p.* out of *2Ch 6:5*
Egypt
or if I send pestilence among *2Ch 7:13*
my p.
if *my p.* shall humble *2Ch 7:14*
themselves and pray
let *my p.* be given me at my *Es 7:3*
request
we are sold, I and *my p.* to be *Es 7:4*
destroyed
endure to see evil shall come to *Es 8:6*
my p.
who eat up *my p.* as they eat *Ps 14:4;*
bread *53:4*
hear, O *my p.* I will speak and *Ps 50:7;*
testify *81:8*
slay them not, least *my p. Ps 59:11*
forget
I will bring *my p.* again from *Ps 68:22*
Bashan
give ear, O *my p.* to my law, *Ps 78:1*
incline
but *my p.* would not hearken *Ps 81:11*
to my voice
O that *my p.* had hearkened *Ps 81:13*
unto me
who subdueth *my p.* under me *Ps 144:2*
Israel not know, *my p.* doth not *Isa 1:3*
consider
as for *my p.* children are their *Isa 3:12*
oppressors, O *my p.*
what mean ye that ye beat *my Isa 3:15*
p.
my p. are gone into captivity, *Isa 5:13*
because
to take away the right from *Isa 10:2*
poor of *my p.*
O *my p.* that dwellest in Zion *Isa 10:24*
blessed be Egypt, *my p.* and *Isa 19:25*
Assyria
come, *my p.* enter thou into *Isa 26:20*
thy chambers
my p. shall dwell in a *Isa 32:18*
peaceable habitation
comfort ye, comfort ye *my p. Isa 40:1*
saith God
to give drink to *my p.* my *Isa 43:20*
chosen
I was wroth with *my p.* I have *Isa 47:6*
polluted
hearken unto me, *my p.* and *Isa 51:4*
give ear
and say to Zion, Thou art *Isa 51:16*
my p.
my p. went down into Egypt *Isa 52:4*
to sojourn
that *my p.* is taken away for *Isa 52:5*
nought
therefore *my p.* shall know *Isa 52:6*
my name
transgression of *my p.* was he *Isa 53:8*
stricken
take stumblingblock out of *Isa 57:14*
way of *my p.*
shew *my p.* their *Isa 58:1*
transgression, and Jacob
surely they are *my p.,* children *Isa 63:8*
Sharon a fold for *my p.* that *Isa 65:10*
have sought
rejoice in Jerusalem, and joy *Isa 65:19*
in *my p.*
as the days of a tree are *Isa 65:22*
days of *my p.*
but *my p.* have changed their *Jer 2:11*
glory for

for *my p.* have committed two *Jer 2:13*
evils, forsaken
why say *my p.* we are lords, *Jer 2:31*
will come
yet *my p.* have forgotten me *Jer 2:32;*
18:15
my p. is foolish, they have not *Jer 4:22*
known
for among *my p.* are found *Jer 5:26*
wicked men
my p. love to have it so, what *Jer 5:31*
will ye do
I have set thee for a fortress *Jer 6:27*
among *my p.*
obey my voice, and ye shall be *Jer 7:23*
my p.
my p. know not the judgment *Jer 8:7*
of the Lord
that I might leave *my p.* and go *Jer 9:2*
from them
diligently learn the ways of *Jer 12:16*
my p. as they taught *my p.* to
I will destroy *my p.* since they *Jer 15:7*
return not
saith Lord against the pastors *Jer 23:2*
that feed *my p.*
if they had caused *my p.* to *Jer 23:22*
hear my words
who think to cause *my p.* to *Jer 23:27*
forget my name
cause *my p.* to err by their *Jer 23:32*
lies and lightness
they shall be *my p.* *Jer 24:7;*
31:1, 33; 32:38; Eze 11:20; 36:28; 37:23,
27; Zec 8:8
nor behold good that I will *Jer 29:32*
do for *my p.*
my p. shall be satisfied with *Jer 31:14*
my goodness
thus they have despised *my p. Jer 33:24*
not a nation
my p. hath been lost sheep, *Jer 50:6*
they have gone
my p. go ye out of midst of *Jer 51:45;*
her *Re 18:4*
I was a derision to all *my p.* *La 3:14*
and song
they shall not be in assembly *Eze 13:9*
of *my p.*
have seduced *my p.;* hunt *Eze 13:10;*
souls of *my p.* *13:18*
ye pollute me among *my p. Eze 13:19*
by lying to *my p.*
I will deliver *my p.* out of *Eze 13:21;*
your hand *13:23*
I will cut him off from the *Eze 14:8*
midst of *my p.*
but that they may be *my p. Eze 14:11*
and I their God
terrors by the sword shall be *Eze 21:12*
upon *my p.*
even house of Israel are my *Eze 34:30*
p. saith Lord
behold, O *my p.* I will open *Eze 37:12;*
your graves *37:13*
thou shalt come up against *Eze 38:16*
my p. Israel
they shall teach *my p.* the *Eze 44:23*
difference
my princes shall no more *Eze 45:8*
oppress *my p.*
take away your exactions from *Eze 45:9*
my p.
that *my p.* be not scattered *Eze 46:18*
then said God, Are ye not *my Ho 1:9;*
p. *1:10*
say to them which were not *Ho 2:23*
my p.
my p. are destroyed for lack *Ho 4:6*
of knowledge
they eat up the sin of *my p. Ho 4:8*
and they set
my p. ask counsel at their *Ho 4:12*
stocks
when I returned the captivity *Ho 6:11*
of *my p.*
my p. are bent to *Ho 11:7*
backsliding from me
my p. shall never be ashamed *Joe 2:26;*
2:27
and will plead with them there *Joe 3:2*
for *my p.*
and they have cast lots for *my Joe 3:3*
p. and sold
sinners of *my p.* shall die by *Am 9:10*
the sword
not have entered into the gate *Ob 13*
of *my p.*
he is come to the gate of *my Mic 1:9*
p. even

he hath changed the portion *Mic 2:4*
of *my p.*
of late *my p.* is risen up as an *Mic 2:8*
enemy
the women of *my p.* have ye *Mic 2:9*
cast out
who also eat the flesh of *my Mic 3:3*
p. and flay
concerning prophets that make *Mic 3:5*
my p. err
O *my p.* what have I done *Mic 6:3;*
unto thee *6:5*
therefore ye shall bear the *Mic 6:16*
reproach of *my p.*
whereby they reproached *my Zep 2:8*
p.
the residue of *my p.* shall spoil *Zep 2:9*
them
and many nations shall be *my Zec 2:11*
p.
I will save *my p.* from the east *Zec 8:7*
country
I will say, It is *my p.* and *Zec 13:9*
they shall say
call them *my p.* which were *Ro 9:25*
not *my p.*
where it was said, Ye are not *Ro 9:26*
my p.
I will be their God, they *2Co 6:16*
shall be *my p.*

OF THE PEOPLE

two manner *of the p.* be *Ge 25:23*
separated
one *of the p.* might lightly *Ge 26:10*
have lien
to him shall the gathering of *Ge 49:10*
the p. be
take all the heads *of the p. Nu 25:4*
and hang
take the sum *of the p.* from *Nu 26:4*
twenty years old
take you twelve men out *of the Jos 4:2*
p.
he was higher than any *of the 1Sa 9:2;*
p. *10:23*
for there is a sacrifice *of the 1Sa 9:12*
p. to-day
so none *of the p.* tasted any *1Sa 14:24*
food
then answered one *of the p. 1Sa 14:28*
and said
there came one *of the p.* to *1Sa 26:15*
destroy king
nor did he leave *of the p.* to *2Ki 13:7*
Jehoahaz
because *of the p.* of those *Ezr 3:3*
countries
great cry *of the p.* and their *Ne 5:1*
wives
some *of the p.* dwelt in their *Ne 7:73*
cities
which stilleth the tumult *of the Ps 65:7*
p.
he shall judge the poor *of the Ps 72:4*
p. and save
I have exalted one chosen out *Ps 89:19*
of the p.
a present *of a p.* scattered and *Isa 18:7*
peeled
I will give thee for a covenant *Isa 42:6*
of the p.
my judgment to rest for a *Isa 51:4*
light *of the p.*
and *of the p.* there was none *Isa 63:3*
with me
prince not take *of the p. Eze 46:18*
inheritance
ministers shall boil the *Eze 46:24*
sacrifice *of the p.*
many *of the p.* believed on *Joh 7:31*
him
because *of the p.* that stand *Joh 11:42*
by I said it
how they might punish, *Ac 4:21*
because *of the p.*
he offered for himself, and *Heb 9:7*
errors *of the p.*
they *of the p.* shall see their *Re 11:9*
dead bodies

ONE PEOPLE

one *p.* shall be stronger than *Ge 25:23*
the other
we will dwell with you, and *Ge 34:16*
become one *p.*
will consent to dwell with us, *Ge 34:22*
to be *one p.*

OWN PEOPLE

but the fault is in thine *own p.* Ex 5:16
he shall take a virgin of his *own p.* Le 21:14
God went to redeem to be 1Ch 17:21 his *own p.*
that could not deliver their 2Ch 25:15 *own p.*
O daughter, forget also thy Ps 45:10 *own p.*
made his *own p.* to go forth Ps 78:52 like sheep
shall every man turn to his Isa 13:14 *own p.*
arise, let us go again to our Jer 46:16 *own p.*

THE PEOPLE

the Lord said, Behold *the p.* is Ge 11:6 one
why do ye let *the p.* from work Ex 5:4
behold, *the p.* of the land now Ex 5:5 are many
and *the p.* bowed the head Ex 12:27 and worshipped
God led *the p.;* was told that Ex 13:18; *the p.* fled 14:5
the p. feared Lord, and Ex 14:31 believed the Lord
the p. shall hear and be Ex 15:14 afraid, sorrow take
till *the p.* pass over which Ex 15:16 thou hast purchased
the p. murmured, saying, Ex 15:24 What shall we drink
so *the p.* rested on the Ex 16:30 seventh day
there was no water for *the p.* to Ex 17:1 drink
the p. did chide with Moses Ex 17:2; Nu 20:3
shall come water out of it, that Ex 17:6 *the p.* may drink
be thou for *the p.* to Ex 18:19 God-ward, to bring
that *the p.* may hear when I Ex 19:9 speak with thee
Moses brought forth *the p.* Ex 19:17 out of the camp
charge *the p.* let not *the p.* Ex 19:21; break through 19:24
when *the p.* saw it, they Ex 20:18; stood afar off 20:21
neither shall *the p.* go up with Ex 24:2 him
Moses took blood and Ex 24:8 sprinkled it on *the p.*
make an atonement for thyself Le 9:7 and *the p.*
the sin offering for *the p.* Le 9:15; 9:18; 16:15
blessed *the p.;* *the p.* Le 9:23; complained Nu 11:1
the p. cried to Moses, and he Nu 11:2 prayed
and see *the p.* that dwelleth Nu 13:18 therein
the p. be strong; Caleb stilled Nu 13:28 *the p.* 13:30
the p. wept that night; *the p.* Nu 14:1; mourned 14:39
the p. spake against God and Nu 21:5 against Moses
lo, *the p.* shall dwell alone, Nu 23:9 not reckoned
behold, *the p.* shall rise up as Nu 23:24 a great lion
the Lord said, Gather me the De 4:10 *p.* together
this shall be the priest's due De 18:3 from *the p.*
yea, he loved *the p.;* he shall De 33:3; push *the p.* 33:17
they shall call *the p.* to the De 33:19 mountain
and *the p.* hasted and passed Jos 4:10 over
so *the p.* shouted; let *the p.* Jos 6:20; depart 24:28
the p. that are with thee are J'g 7:2; too many 7:4
up thou, and *the p.* that are J'g 9:32 with thee
the priest's custom with the 1Sa 2:13 *p.* was
so *the p.* sent to Shiloh to 1Sa 4:4 bring the ark

did they not let *the p.* go, and 1Sa 6:6 they departed
the p. refused to obey the 1Sa 8:19 voice of Samuel
for *the p.* will not eat until he 1Sa 9:13 come
the p. said to Saul, Shall 1Sa 14:45 Jonathan die? so *the p.* rescued Jonathan
for *the p.* spared the best of 1Sa 15:15 the sheep
but *the p.* took of the spoil 1Sa 15:21 sheep and oxen
the p. answered after this 1Sa 17:27; manner 17:30
David distressed, for *the p.* 1Sa 30:6 spake of stoning him
that *the p.* are fled from the 2Sa 1:4 battle
it is because *the p.* have 2Sa 14:15 made me afraid
for *the p.* increased with 2Sa 15:12 Absalom
and *the p.* piped with pipes 1Ki 1:40 and rejoiced
for *the p.* went to worship 1Ki 12:30 before the one
the p. that followed Omri 1Ki 16:22 prevailed against *the p.* that followed Tibni
and *the p.* answered him not 1Ki 18:21 a word
pour out for *the p.* that they 2Ki 4:41 may eat
he said, Give *the p.* that they 2Ki 4:43 may eat
and *the p.* trode upon him in 2Ki 7:17 the gate
made a covenant between 2Ki 11:17 king and *the p.*
as yet *the p.* did sacrifice 2Ki 12:3; 14:4; 15:4, 35
the p. held their peace, and 2Ki 18:36 answered not
inquire of the Lord for me 2Ki 22:13 and for *the p.*
the p. were without number 2Ch 12:3 that came
as yet *the p.* had not 2Ch 20:33; prepared 30:3
and *the p.* did yet corruptly 2Ch 27:2
hearkened to Hezekiah and 2Ch 30:20 healed *the p.*
since *the p.* began to bring 2Ch 31:10 offerings
the p. rested on the words of 2Ch 32:8 Hezekiah
and *the p.* transgressed 2Ch 36:14 very much
but *the p.* are many, and it Ezr 10:13 is rain
for *the p.* had a mind to work Ne 4:6
and *the p.* did according to this Ne 5:13 promise
city was large, but *the p.* were Ne 7:4 few therein
and *the p.* stood in their place Ne 8:7
so *the p.* went and brought Ne 8:16 palm branches
the p. blessed all that offered Ne 11:2 willingly
they had shewed him *the p.* of Es 3:6 Mordecai
the p. also, to do with them as Es 3:11 seemeth
the p. of the king's provinces Es 4:11 do know
Job said, No doubt but ye are Job 12:2 *the p.*
hypocrite reign not, lest the Job 34:30 *p.* be
why do *the p.* imagine a vain Ps 2:1 thing
blessed are *the p.* whom he Ps 33:12 hath chosen
we heard, how thou didst Ps 44:2 afflict *the p.*
arrows, whereby *the p.* fall Ps 45:5 under thee
therefore shall *the p.* praise Ps 45:17 thee for ever
in thine anger cast down *the p.* Ps 56:7 O God
let *the p.* praise thee, O God Ps 67:3; 67:5
blessed is *the p.* that know Ps 89:15 joyful sound
and we are *the p.* of his Ps 95:7 pasture

he shall judge *the p.* with his Ps 96:13 truth
and he shall judge *the p.* with Ps 98:9 equity
the Lord reigneth, let *the p.* Ps 99:1 tremble
make known his deeds among Ps 105:1 *the p.*
where no counsel is *the p.* fall Pr 11:14
withholds corn, *the p.* shall Pr 11:26; curse him 24:24
in authority, *the p.* rejoiced, Pr 29:2 *the p.* mourn
where there is no vision, the Pr 29:18 *p.* perish
the p. shall be oppressed, every Isa 3:5 one by
the p. that walked in darkness Isa 9:2 have seen
the p. turneth not to him that Isa 9:13 smiteth them
and *the p.* shall be as the fuel Isa 9:19 of the fire
against *the p.* of my wrath Isa 10:6 will I give
and *the p.* shall take them Isa 14:2 and bring them
it shall be as with *the p.* so Isa 24:2 with the priest
the p. shall dwell in Zion at Isa 30:19 Jerusalem
the p. shall be forgiven their Isa 33:24 iniquity
sword shall come on *the p.* of Isa 34:5 my curse
surely *the p.* is grass, the Isa 40:7 grass withereth
the p. in whose heart is my Isa 51:7 law, fear
I will tread down *the p.* in Isa 63:6 mine anger
the p. of thy holiness have Isa 63:18 possessed it
the p. that shall say, The Jer 23:34 burden of
the p. which were left of Jer 31:2 sword found grace
came in and went out among Jer 37:4 *the p.*
him home, so he dwelt Jer 39:14 among *the p.*
dwell with him among *the p.* Jer 40:5; 40:6
woe to thee, O Moab the Jer 48:46 *p.* of Chemosh
the p. shall labour in vain, Jer 51:58 and be weary
I will even gather you from Eze 11:17 *the p.*
I will bring you out from Eze 20:34; *the p.* 34:13
and I will cut thee off Eze 25:7 from *the p.*
will bring thee down with Eze 26:20 *the p.*
see sword come, and *the p.* Eze 33:6 be not warned
and they come unto thee as Eze 33:31 *the p.* cometh
they said, These are *the p.* of Eze 36:20 the Lord
thou shalt fall, and *the p.* Eze 39:4 that is with thee
approach to those things Eze 42:14 which are for *the p.*
they shall slay the sacrifice Eze 44:11 for *the p.*
sanctify *the p.* with their Eze 44:19 garments
the p. of the prince that shall Da 9:26 come
the p. that know their God Da 11:32 shall be strong
the p. that doth not Ho 4:14 understand
for *the p.* thereof shall mourn Ho 10:5 over it
and *the p.* shall be gathered Ho 10:10 against them
before them *the p.* shall be Joe 2:6 much pained
the p. of Syria shall go into Am 1:5 captivity
shall trumpet be blown, and Am 3:6 *the p.* not afraid
so *the p.* of Nineveh believed Jon 3:5 God
that *the p.* shall labour in the Hab 2:13 fire, and *the p.* shall

magnified themselves against *the p.* of Lord — Zep 2:10

and *the p.* did fear before the Lord — Hag 1:12

the p. against whom Lord hath indignation — Mal 1:4

the p. that sat in darkness saw light — M't 4:16

if we shall say, Of men, we — M't 21:26;

fear *the p.* for all hold — M'k 11:32

and *the p.* waited for Zacharias — Lu 1:21

as *the p.* were in expectation and all men mused — Lu 3:15

the p. sought him; *the p.* pressed on — Lu 4:42; 5:1

when returned, *the p.* gladly received him — Lu 8:40

he asked them, Whom say the *p.* that I am — Lu 9:18

feared *the p.* — Lu 20:19; 22:2

stirreth up *the p.* — Lu 23:5

this man, one that perverteth *the p.* — Lu 23:14

the p. saw that Jesus was not there — Joh 6:24

others said, Nay, but he deceiveth *the p.* — Joh 7:12

one man should die for *the p.* — Joh 11:50; 18:14

but *the p.* magnified them — Ac 5:13

the p. with one accord gave heed — Ac 8:6

the p. gave shout, saying, It is voice of God — Ac 12:22

and when *the p.* saw what Paul had done — Ac 14:11

with these sayings scarce restrained they *the p.* — Ac 14:18

who persuaded *the p.* and stoned Paul — Ac 14:19

delivering thee from *the p.* and Gentiles — Ac 26:17

though I committed nothing against *the p.* — Ac 28:17

as for *the p.* so also for himself — Heb 5:3; 7:27

for under it *the p.* received the law — Heb 7:11

might sanctify *the p.* with his blood — Heb 13:12

how that the Lord having saved *the p.* — Jude 5

THIS PEOPLE

I will give *this p.* favour in sight of — Ex 3:21

why hast thou so evil entreated *this p.* — Ex 5:22

for Pharaoh hath done evil to *this p.* — Ex 5:23

Moses cried, saying, What shall I do to *this p.* — Ex 17:4

thou wilt wear away, both thou and *this p.* — Ex 18:18

all *this p.* shall also go to their place in peace — Ex 18:23

I have seen *this p.*; what did — Ex 32:9; 32:21

oh, *this p.* have sinned a great sin — Ex 32:31

see, thou sayest to me, ring up *this p.* — Ex 33:12

layest the burden of all *this p.* — Nu 11:11

I conceived all *this p.* flesh to *this p.* — Nu 11:12; 11:13

I am not able to bear all *this p.* alone — Nu 11:14

how long will *this p.* provoke me — Nu 14:11

they heard that thou art among *this p.* — Nu 14:14

if thou shalt kill all *this p.* as one man — Nu 14:15

was not able to bring *this p.* into the land — Nu 14:16

pardon *this p.* as thou hast forgiven *this p.* — Nu 14:19

if thou wilt indeed deliver *this p.* — Nu 21:2

come now, I pray thee, curse *this p.* — Nu 22:6; 22:17

what *this p.* shall do to thy people — Nu 24:14

and ye shall destroy all *this p.* — Nu 32:15

Joshua shall go over before *this p.* — De 3:28

I have heard voice of the words of *this p.* — De 5:28

Lord spake, saying, I have seen *this p.* — De 9:13

look not to the stubbornness of *this p.* — De 9:27

be strong, for thou must go with *this p.* — De 31:7

this p. go whoring after gods — De 31:16

to *this p.* thou shalt divide the land — Jos 1:6

because *this p.* have transgressed — J'g 2:20

would to God *this p.* were under my hand — J'g 9:29

is not *this p.* thou hast despised — J'g 9:38

I hear of your evil doings by *this p.* — 1Sa 2:23

but whom Lord and *this p.* choose — 2Sa 16:18

that I may answer *this p.* — 1Ki 12:6; 12:9; 2Ch 10:6, 9

if thou wilt be a servant to *this p.* this day — 1Ki 12:7

if *this p.* go up to do sacrifice; then *this p.* shall turn again to Rehoboam — 1Ki 12:27

told me I should be king over *this p.* — 1Ki 14:2

hear me, O Lord, that *this p.* may know — 1Ki 18:37

I pray, smite *this p.* with blindness — 2Ki 6:18

I may go out and come in before *this p.* — 2Ch 1:10

the bondage was heavy on *this p.* — Ne 5:18

accord, to all that I have done for *this p.* — Ne 5:19

go and tell *this p.*, Hear ye indeed, but not — Isa 6:9

make the heart of *this p.* fat — Isa 6:10; M't 13:15; Ac 28:26-27

this p. refuseth the waters of Shiloah — Isa 8:6

I should not walk in the way of *this p.* — Isa 8:11

to whom *this p.* shall say, a confederacy — Isa 8:12

the leaders of *this p.* cause them to err — Isa 9:16

this p. was not till the Assyrian founded it — Isa 23:13

with another tongue will speak to *this p.* — Isa 28:11

hear, ye scornful men that rule *this p.* — Isa 28:14

this p. draw near me with their mouth — Isa 29:13

to do a marvellous work among *this p.* — Isa 29:14

but *this p.* is a *p.* robbed and spoiled — Isa 42:22

this p. have I formed for myself — Isa 43:21

thou hast greatly deceived *this p.* — Jer 4:10

will make my words fire, and *this p.* wood — Jer 5:14

but *this p.* hath a revolting heart — Jer 5:23

behold, I will bring evil on *this p.* — Jer 6:19

I will lay stumblingblocks before *this p.* — Jer 6:21

pray not thou for *this p.* — Jer 7:16; 11:14; 14:11

carcasses of *this p.* meat for fowls — Jer 7:33

why is *this p.* of Jerusalem slidden back — Jer 8:5

I will feed even *this p.* with wormwood — Jer 9:15

this evil *p.* who refuse to hear my words — Jer 13:10

yet my mind could not be toward *this p.* — Jer 15:1

I have taken away my peace from *this p.* — Jer 16:5

will I break *this p.* and this city — Jer 19:11

they shall not profit *this p.* at all — Jer 23:32

and when *this p.* shall ask thee, saying — Jer 23:33

thou makest *this p.* to trust in a lie — Jer 28:15

not have a man to dwell among *this p.* — Jer 29:32

brought all this great evil upon *this p.* — Jer 32:42

considerest not what *this p.* have spoken — Jer 33:24

but *this p.* have not hearkened unto me — Jer 35:16

great is anger pronounced against *this p.* — Jer 36:7

what have I offended against *this p.* — Jer 37:18

this man seeketh not welfare of *this p.* — Jer 38:4

he shall be the prophet of *this p.* — Mic 2:11

this p. say, The time is not come — Hag 1:2

Haggai said, So is *this p.* before me — Hag 2:14

in the eyes of the remnant of *this p.* — Zec 8:6

I will not be to *this p.* as in former days — Zec 8:11

I will cause the remnant of *this p.* draweth nigh with — Zec 8:12

this p. draweth nigh with their mouth — M't 15:8

this p. honoureth me with their lips — M'k 7:6

except we should buy meat for *this p.* — Lu 9:13

for there shall be wrath upon *this p.* — Lu 21:23

but *this p.* who knoweth not the law — Joh 7:49

the God of *this p.* chose our fathers — Ac 13:17

with other lips I will speak to *this p.* — 1Co 14:21

THY PEOPLE

neither hast thou delivered *thy p.* — Ex 5:23

frogs on *thy p.* — Ex 8:3; 8:4

swarms of flies on *thy p.* — Ex 8:3; 8:21

for I will send all my plagues on *thy p.* — Ex 9:14

smite thee and *thy p.* with pestilence — Ex 9:15

they shall be still, till *thy p.* pass over — Ex 15:16

nor shalt curse ruler of *thy p.* — Ex 22:28; Ac 23:5

that the poor of *thy p.* may eat — Ex 23:11

and consider that this nation is *thy p.* — Ex 33:13

I and *thy p.* have found grace in thy sight — Ex 33:16

I make a covenant before all *thy p.* — Ex 34:10

not go as a talebearer among *thy p.* — Le 19:16

make thee a curse among *thy p.* — Nu 5:21

this people shall do *thy p.* in latter days — Nu 24:14

be gathered to *thy p.* — Nu 27:13; 31:2; De 32:50

for *thy p.* have corrupted themselves — De 9:12

destroy not *thy p.* — De 9:26

yet they are *thy p.* and inheritance — De 9:29; Ne 1:10

we will return with thee to *thy p.* — Ru 1:10

thy p. my people — Ru 1:16

what nation like *thy p.* — 2Sa 7:23; 1Ch 17:21

thy p. thou redeemedst from Egypt — 2Sa 7:23

thy servant is in the midst of *thy p.* — 1Ki 3:8

understanding heart to judge *thy p.* — 1Ki 3:9; 2Ch 1:10

if *thy p.* go out to battle, and shall pray — 1Ki 8:44

forgive *thy p.* that have sinned — 1Ki 8:50; 2Ch 6:34, 39

they be *thy p.*; *thy p.* for his people — 1Ki 8:51; 20:42

I am as thou art, my people as thy *p.* — 1Ki 22:4; 2Ch 18:3

but let not thy hand be on *thy p.* — 1Ch 21:17

keep in thoughts of heart of *thy p.* — 1Ch 29:18

with a plague will the Lord   2Ch 21:14
smite *thy p.* thy children
thy blessing is upon *thy p.*   Ps 3:8
save *thy p.* and bless thine   Ps 28:9;
    Jer 31:7
thou sellest *thy p.* for nought   Ps 44:12
thou hast shewed *thy p.* hard   Ps 60:3
things
when thou wentest forth   Ps 68:7
before *thy p.*
he shall judge *thy p.* with   Ps 72:2
righteousness
thou hast with thine arm   Ps 77:15
redeemed *thy p.*
leddest *thy p.* as flock by   Ps 77:20
Moses
so we *thy p.* will give thee   Ps 79:13
thanks
how long be angry against   Ps 80:4
prayer of *thy p.*
they have taken crafty counsel   Ps 83:3
against *thy p.*
thou hast forgiven the iniquity   Ps 85:2
of *thy p.*
revive us, that *thy p.* may   Ps 85:6
rejoice in thee
they break in pieces *thy p.* O   Ps 94:5
Lord
the favour that thou bearest   Ps 106:4
to *thy p.*
thy p. be willing in day of   Ps 110:3
power
therefore thou hast forsaken   Isa 2:6
thy p.
Lord shall bring on thee and   Isa 7:17
thy p.
thou hast destroyed thy land   Isa 14:20
and *thy p.*
thy p. shall be all righteous,   Isa 60:21
shall inherit
so didst thou lead, *thy p.*;   Isa 63:14;
we are *thy p.*   64:9
hear, thou and *thy p.* that   Jer 22:2
enter in
why will ye die, thou and *thy*   Jer 27:13
p. by sword
get thee to *thy p.* and speak   Eze 3:11
to them
set thy face gainst the   Eze 13:17
daughters of *thy p.*
he shall slay *thy p.* with the   Eze 26:11
sword
speak to the children of *thy p.*   Eze 33:2;
and say   33:12
children of *thy p.* say, way   Eze 33:17
is not equal
the children of *thy p.* still   Eze 33:30
are talking
when the children of *thy p.*   Eze 37:18
shall speak
thy p. are become a reproach   Da 9:16
to all
thy city and *thy p.* are called   Da 9:19
by thy name
seventy weeks are determined   Da 9:24
upon *thy p.*
to understand what shall   Da 10:14
befall *thy p.*
Michael standeth for children   Da 12:1
of *thy p.* and *thy p.* delivered
thy p. as they that strive with   Ho 4:4
the priest
shall a tumult arise among   Ho 10:14
thy p.
spare *thy p.*; feed *thy p.*   Joe 2:17;
    Mic 7:14
thy p. in the midst of thee are   Na 3:13
women
thy p. is scattered on the   Na 3:18
mountains
then wentest forth for   Hab 3:13
salvation of *thy p.*

TO, UNTO THE PEOPLE

and he shall be spokesman to   Ex 4:16
the *p.*
Jethro saw all that he did to   Ex 18:14
the *p.* what is this thou doest
to the *p.*
go to the *p.*; set bounds to   Ex 19:10;
the *p.*   19:12
Moses went down from   Ex 19:14;
mount to the *p.*   19:25
that the priest shall speak to   De 20:2
the *p.*
and the officers shall speak to   De 20:5;
the *p.*   20:8
give, I pray, loaves of bread to   J'g 8:5
the *p.*

when ye go, ye shall come to   J'g 18:10;
a *p.* secure   18:27
and art come to a *p.* thou   Ru 2:11
knewest not
Samuel told all the words to   1Sa 8:10
the *p.*
David and Abishai came to   1Sa 26:7
the *p.* by night
David cried to the *p.* and to   1Sa 26:14
Abner
when David came near to   1Sa 30:21
the *p.* he saluted
now the Lord thy God add to   2Sa 24:3
the *p.*
the king hearkened not to   1Ki 12:15
the *p.*
Elijah came to the *p.* and   1Ki 18:21
said, How long
Elisha gave to the *p.* and   1Ki 19:21
they did eat
he said, Give to the *p.* that   2Ki 4:42
they may eat
Athaliah came to the *p.*   2Ki 11:13;
    2Ch 23:12
Philistines sent to carry   1Ch 10:9
tidings to the *p.*
Josiah gave to the *p.* lambs   2Ch 35:7
and kids
gave willingly to the *p.*   2Ch 35:8
at the same time said I to the   Ne 4:22
p.
former governors were   Ne 5:15
chargeable to the *p.*
he shall minister judgment to   Ps 9:8
the *p.*
the mountains shall bring peace   Ps 72:3
to the *p.*
he that giveth breath to the *p.*   Isa 42:5
upon it
and I will set up my   Isa 49:22
standard to the *p.*
given him for a witness to the   Isa 55:4
p. a leader and commander to
the *p.*
so I spake to the *p.* in the   Eze 24:18
morning
kingdom be given to the *p.* of   Da 7:27
the saints
they shall sell them to the *p.*   Joe 3:8
far off
when he cometh up to the   Hab 3:16
p. he will invade
I will turn to the *p.* a pure   Zep 3:9
language
then spake Haggai to the *p.*   Hag 1:13
while he yet talked to the *p.*   M't 12:46
behold
was wont to release to the *p.*   M't 27:15
a prisoner
he began to speak to the *p.*   Lu 7:24
concerning John
as they spake to the *p.* the   Ac 4:1
priests came
speak in the temple to the *p.*   Ac 5:20
all the words
which gave alms to the *p.* and   Ac 10:2
prayed to God
and he commanded us to   Ac 10:42
preach to the *p.*
intending to bring Peter forth   Ac 12:4
to the *p.*
seen of them who are his   Ac 13:31
witnesses to the *p.*
the Jews sought to bring them   Ac 17:5
out to the *p.*
when Paul would have   Ac 19:30
entered in to the *p.*
and would have made his   Ac 19:33
defence to the *p.*
I beseech thee suffer me to   Ac 21:39
speak to the *p.*
Paul beckoned with the hand   Ac 21:40
to the *p.*
Christ should suffer, and shew   Ac 26:23
light to the *p.*

PEOR

Balaam unto the top of *P.*   Nu 23:28
beguiled you in the matter of   Nu 25:18
P.
against the Lord in the   Nu 31:16
matter of *P.*
Is the iniquity of *P.* too little   Jos 22:17
for us

PEOR'S

the day of the plague for *P.*   Nu 25:18
sake

PERADVENTURE

P. there be fifty righteous   Ge 18:24;
within   18:28-32; 31:31;
    32:20; 38:11; 42:12; 44:34; 50:15
Suppose (A)(R)   Ge 18:24;
    18:29-32; 31:31
perhaps (B)   Ge 18:24; 18:30
perchance (B)   Ge 18:28; 18:29, 31-32
P. the woman will not be   Ge 24:5
willing to
P. the woman will not follow   Ge 24:39
me
my father *p.* will feel me, and   Ge 27:12
I shall
perhaps (A)   Ge 32:20;
    39:11; 42:4; 50:15
he may accept (B)   Ge 32:20
Suppose (B)   Ge 50:15
Lest *p.* the people repent   Ex 13:17
p. I shall make an atonement   Ex 32:30
for them
perhaps I can make an   Ex 32:30
atonement (A)(B)(R)
p. I shall prevail   Nu 22:6
perhaps I may be able   Nu 22:6
(A)(B)(R)
P. I shall be able to overcome   Nu 22:11
them
perhaps I may be able   Nu 22:11
(A)(B)(R)
p. the Lord will come to meet   Nu 23:3
me
perhaps the Lord will come   Nu 23:3
p. it will please God   Nu 23:27
perhaps it will please God   Nu 23:27
(A)(B)(R)
P. ye dwell among us   Jos 9:7
Perhaps you live among us   Jos 9:7
(A)(B)(R)
p. he will lighten his hand from   1Sa 6:5
off
Perhaps he will lighten (A)(R)   1Sa 6:5
possibly he will lighten (B)   1Sa 6:5
p. he can shew us our way   1Sa 9:6
Perhaps he can show us   1Sa 9:6
(A)(B)(R)
p. we might find grass   1Ki 18:5
perhaps we may find grass   1Ki 18:5
(A)(B)(R)
p. he sleepeth, and must be   1Ki 18:27
awakened
perhaps he is asleep   1Ki 18:27
(A)(B)(R)
p. he will save thy life   1Ki 20:31
perhaps he will save your life   1Ki 20:31
(A)(B)(R)
lest *p.* the Spirit of the Lord   2Ki 2:16
hath
it may be that the Spirit   2Ki 2:16
(A)(R)
Perhaps the Spirit of the Lord   2Ki 2:16
(B)
P. he will be enticed   Jer 20:10
Perhaps he will be persuaded   Jer 20:10
(A)(B)(R)
yet *p.* for a good man some   Ro 5:7
would
perhaps for a   Ro 5:7
noble benefactor (A)(B)(R)
if God will *p.* give them   2Ti 2:25
repentance
God may grant that he will   2Ti 2:25
repent (A)(B)
God may perhaps grant   2Ti 2:25
repentance (R)

PERAZIM

Lord rise up as in mount *P.*   Isa 28:21

PERCEIVE

not given you a heart to *p.*   De 29:4
not given you a heart to   De 29:4
understand (A)(B)(R)
not given you a heart to know   De 29:4
(E)
day we *p.* that the Lord is   Jos 22:31
among
Today we know the Lord is   Jos 22:31
among us (A)(B)(E)(R)
that your wickedness is great   1Sa 12:17
know that your wickedness is   1Sa 12:17
(A)(E)(R)
understand how great an evil   1Sa 12:17
(B)
this day I *p.* that Absalom   2Sa 19:6

PERCEIVE

today I see that if Absalom | 2Sa 19:6
(A)
I know that if Absalom had | 2Sa 19:6
(B)
I *p.* that this an holy man | 2Ki 4:9
passeth on, and I *p.* him not | Job 9:11
he goes by me, I see him not | Job 9:11
(A)
but I cannot *p.* him | Job 23:8
but I cannot see him (A)(B) | Job 23:8
to *p.* the words of understanding | Pr 1:2
discern and comprehend words | Pr 1:2
(A)
to understand discerning words | Pr 1:2
(B)
to discern words of | Pr 1:2
understanding (E)
understand the words of insight | Pr 1:2
(R)
i *p.* that here is nothing better | Ec 3:22
I saw there is nothing better | Ec 3:22
(A)(B)(E)(R)
see ye indeed, but, *p.* not | Isa 6:9;
  M't 13:14; M'k 4:12; Ac 28:26
see continually, but do not | Isa 6:9
comprehend (A)
deeper speech than thou canst | Isa 33:19
p.
too deep and obscure to | Isa 33:19
comprehend (A)
an obscure speech of an | Isa 33:19
unintelligible barbarous
language (B)
Do ye not *p.* that whatsoever | M'k 7:18
thing
Do ye not discern (A) | M'k 7:18; 8:17
do you not see (N)(R) | M'k 7:18
Can't you see (P) | M'k 7:18
I *p.* that virtue has gone out | Lu 8:46
of me
I am conscious of power | Lu 8:46
having gone (B)
I felt that power had gone out | Lu 8:46
(N)(R)
I *p.* that thou art a prophet | Joh 4:19
I see and understand that you | Joh 4:19
(A)(N)(P)
P. ye how we prevail nothing | Joh 12:19
See! The whole world has | Joh 12:19
gone (A)(P)(R)
Look! the world is running | Joh 12:19
after him (N)

PERCEIVED

he *p.* not when she lay down | Ge 19:33;
  | 19:35
he was not aware when | Ge 19:33;
(A)(B) | 19:35
he knew not when (E) | Ge 19:33 19:35
he did not know when (R) | Ge 19:33;
  | 19:35
Gideon *p.* that he was an angel | J'g 6:22
Gideon realized that he was (B) | J'g 6:22
Gideon saw that he was an | J'g 6:22
angel (E)
Eli *p.* that the Lord had called | 1Sa 3:8
it dawned on Eli (B) | 1Sa 3:8
Saul *p.* that it was Samuel | 1Sa 28:14
Saul then understood (B) | 1Sa 28:14
Saul knew that it was Samuel | 1Sa 28:14
(R)
David *p.* Lord had | 2Sa 5:12;
established kingdom | 1Ch 14:2
David recognized that (B) | 2Sa 5:12
David *p.* that the child was | 2Sa 12:19
dead
realized that the boy had | 2Sa 12:19
died (A)
p. that the king's heart was | 2Sa 14:1
toward
knew that king's heart was | 2Sa 14:1
toward (A)(B)
p. that it was not the king of | 1Ki 22:33;
Israel | 2Ch 18:32
saw that it was not the king | 1Ki 22:33
(A)(B)(E)(R)
I *p.* that God had not sent him | Ne 6:12
I saw that God had not sent | Ne 6:12
(A)
I realized that God had not | Ne 6:12
sent (B)
I discerned that God had not | Ne 6:12
sent (E)
I understood and saw that God | Ne 6:12
had (R)
p. that this work was wrought | Ne 6:16
by God
saw that this work was done | Ne 6:16
by God (A)

understood that this work was | Ne 6:16
(B)
p. that the portions of the | Ne 13:10
Levites
I discovered that (B) | Ne 13:10
I found out that (R) | Ne 13:10
Mordecai *p.* all that was done | Es 4:1
Mordecai learned all that was | Es 4:1
done (A)(R)
Mordecai ascertained everything | Es 4:1
(B)
Mordecai knew all that was | Es 4:1
done (E)
thou *p.* the breadth of the | Job 38:18
earth
you comprehended the | Job 38:18
breadth (A)(E)(R)
your grasp taken in the | Job 38:18
breadth (B)
I *p.* among youths (A)(B)(R) | Pr 7:7
I *p.* that this also is vexation of | Ec 1:17
I discovered that this was (B) | Ec 1:17
I myself *p.* also that one event | Ec 2:14
plank (N)
I myself know that (B) | Ec 2:14
have not heard, nor *p.* by the | Isa 64:4
ear
hath *p.* and heard his word | Jer 23:18
for the matter was not *p.* | Jer 38:27
conversation was not | Jer 38:27
discovered (A)
matter had not been | Jer 38:27
overheard (B)(R)
when Jesus *p.*, he said unto | M't 16:8
But Jesus aware of this asked | M't 16:8
(A)(B)(R)
Knowing what was in their | M't 16:8
minds (N)
when Jesus saw this (P) | M't 16:8
p. that he spake of them | M't 21:45;
  | Lu 20:19
knew he was talking about | M't 21:45
them (B)
saw he was referring to them | M't 21:45
(E)
they realized he was talking | M't 21:45
about (P)
Jesus *p.* their wickedness | M't 22:18;
  | Lu 20:23
aware of their malicious plot | M't 22:18
(A)(N)(R)
saw through their malice (B) | M't 22:18
knowing their evil intention | M't 22:18
(P)
when Jesus *p.* in his spirit | M'k 2:8
becoming fully aware in his | M'k 2:8
spirit (A)
Jesus knew in his own mind | M'k 2:8
(N)
Jesus realized instantly (P) | M'k 2:8
they *p.* that he had a vision | Lu 1:22
they recognized he had seen | Lu 1:22
(B)
they realized that he had seen | Lu 1:22
(N)(R)
when Jesus *p.* their thoughts | Lu 5:22
Jesus knowing their thoughts | Lu 5:22
(A)
Jesus aware of their reasonings | Lu 5:22
(B)
Jesus knew their thoughts (N) | Lu 5:22
realized what was going on in | Lu 5:22
minds (P)
hid from them, they *p.* it not | Lu 9:45
kept hidden so they could not | Lu 9:45
grasp it and understand (A)
they did not understand | Lu 9:45
(B)(P)
it was concealed from them | Lu 9:45
(E)
p. they would come and make | Joh 6:15
him
knowing that they meant to | Joh 6:15
make (A)
aware that they intended | Joh 6:15
(B)(N)
realizing that they were going | Joh 6:15
to (P)
p. that they were unlearned | Ac 4:13
men
p. one part were Pharisees | Ac 23:6
aware that one party was | Ac 23:6
(B)(N)
realizing that one part (P) | Ac 23:6
I *p.* to be accused of | Ac 23:29
questions of
I found he was charged with | Ac 23:29
(A)(B)(E)(N)(R)
I discovered that he was | Ac 23:29
charged (P)
p. a bay (E) | Ac 27:39

p. the grace that was given | Ga 2:9
when they knew the grace (A) | Ga 2:9
acknowledging the grace (B) | Ga 2:9
recognizing the favor bestowed | Ga 2:9
(E)
saw how God had given me his | Ga 2:9
grace (P)

PERCEIVEST

p. not in him lips of knowledge | Pr 14:7
will not find knowledge in his | Pr 14:7
lips (A)
will not discern words of | Pr 14:7
knowledge (E)
p. not the beam in thine own | Lu 6:41
eye
do not notice or consider beam | Lu 6:41
(A)
aware of the beam in your own | Lu 6:41
eye (B)
considerest not the beam (E) | Lu 6:41
never a thought for the great | Lu 6:41
plank (N)
fail to notice the plank in | Lu 6:41
your eye (P)
do not see the log in own eye | Lu 6:41
(R)

PERCEIVETH

brought low, but he *p.* it not | Job 14:21
of them
are humbled, but he does not | Job 14:21
notice (A)
once, yea twice, yet man *p.* | Job 33:14
it not
more than once, even though | Job 33:14
men do not regard it (A)
man regardeth it not (E) | Job 33:14
p. that her merchandise is | Pr 31:18
good
she tastes and sees that (A) | Pr 31:18
she sees that her merchandise | Pr 31:18
is (B)

PERCEIVING

p. that he had answered | M'k 12:28
them well
noticing that Jesus had | M'k 12:28
answered (A)(P)
aware that he had | M'k 12:28
answered them (B)
knowing he had answered | M'k 12:28
them (E)
noted how well he had | M'k 12:28
answered (N)
seeing that he answered | M'k 12:28
them well (R)
Jesus *p.* thought of their heart | Lu 9:47
Jesus aware of the | Lu 9:47
deliberations (B)
Jesus saw the reasoning of | Lu 9:47
their hearts (A)
Knew what was passing in | Lu 9:47
their minds (N)
Jesus knowing what they were | Lu 9:47
arguing (P)
p. that he had faith to be | Ac 14:9
healed
observing he had faith (A) | Ac 14:9
noticing that he had faith (B) | Ac 14:9
seeing that he had faith | Ac 14:9
(E)(P)(R)
saw that he had faith (N) | Ac 14:9

PERCEPTIVE

wise and *p.* mind (B) | 1Ki 3:12

PERCH

p. on a craggy peak (B) | Job 39:28

PERCHANCE

p. there be (B) | Ge 18:28; 18:29, 31-32

PERDITION

a son of *p.* (B) | M't 23:15
the sentence of *p.* (B) | M't 23:33
of them is lost, but the son of | Joh 17:12
p.
except the son of destruction | Joh 17:12
(P)
your money go to *p.* (B) | Ac 8:20
those on way to *p.* (N) | 2Co 2:15
is to them an evident token | Ph'p 1:28
of *p.*

a clear sign to them of destruction (A)(B)(R) — *Ph'p 1:28*
a sign that their doom is sealed (N) — *Ph'p 1:28*
is plain proof that they are lost to God (P) — *Ph'p 1:28*
whose end is *p.* (E) — *Ph'p 3:19*
of sin be revealed, the son of *p.* — *2Th 2:3*
man of lawlessness, the son of doom (A)(B) — *2Th 2:3*
drown men in destruction and *p.* — *1Ti 6:9*
into ruin, destruction, miserable perishing (A) — *1Ti 6:9*
into destruction and ruin (B)(R) — *1Ti 6:9*
not of them who draw back into *p.* — *Heb 10:39*
draw back to eternal misery (A) — *Heb 10:39*
who shrink back so as to perish (B) — *Heb 10:39*
shrink back and are lost (N) — *Heb 10:39*
who cower back and are lost (P) — *Heb 10:39*
who shrink back and are destroyed (R) — *Heb 10:39*
of judgment and *p.* of ungodly men — *2Pe 3:7*
day of judgment and destruction (A)(B)(E)(P)(R) — *2Pe 3:7*
judgment when the godless are destroyed (N) — *2Pe 3:7*
of bottomless pit, and go into *p.* — *Re 17:8; 17:11*
from abyss and go into destruction (B)(P) — *Re 17:8*

PERES

P.; Thy kingdom is divided — *Da 5:28*

PERESH

a son, and she called his name *P.* — *1Ch 7:16*

PEREZ

Of the children of *P.* was the chief — *1Ch 27:3*
of Mahalaleel, of the children of *P.* — *Ne 11:4*
sons of *P.* that dwelt at Jerusalem — *Ne 11:6*

PEREZ-UZZA

that place is called *P.* to this day — *1Ch 13:11*

PEREZ-UZZAH

name of the place *P.* to this day — *2Sa 6:8*

PERFECT

Noah was a just man and *p.* in his generation — *Ge 6:9*
righteous man, and blameless (A)(B)(R) — *Ge 6:9*
walk before me, and be thou *p.* — *Ge 17:1*
live in my presence and be upright (B) — *Ge 17:1*
walk before me and be blameless (R) — *Ge 17:1*
sheep, it shall be *p.* to be accepted — *Le 22:21*
it must be flawless to be pleasing (B) — *Le 22:21*
be *p.* with the Lord thy God — *De 18:13*
be blameless (absolutely true) to (A) — *De 18:13*
be blameless before the Lord (B)(R) — *De 18:13*
have a *p.* and just weight — *De 25:15*
a full and just weight (B)(R) — *De 25:15*
He is the Rock, his work is *p.* — *De 32:4*
Lord God of Israel, Give a *p.* lot — *1Sa 14:41*
God of Israel, Give Urim (R) — *1Sa 14:41*
hast been *p.* (E) — *2Sa 22:24; Ps 18:23, 25*
As for God, his way is *p.* — *2Sa 22:31; Ps 18:30*
how complete his way (B) — *2Sa 22:31*
he maketh my way *p.* — *2Sa 22:33; Ps 18:32*

he guides the blameless in his way (A) — *2Sa 22:33*
he levels for me his good way (B) — *2Sa 22:33*
has made my way safe (R) — *2Sa 22:33*
Let your heart be *p.* — *1Ki 8:61*
heart be blameless and wholly true (A) — *1Ki 8:61*
be of one mind with the Lord (B) — *1Ki 8:61*
be wholly true to the Lord (R) — *1Ki 8:61*
his heart was not *p.* with the Lord — *1Ki 11:4*
his heart was no longer true (B)(R) — *1Ki 11:4*
his heart was not *p.* with the Lord — *1Ki 15:3*
his heart was not blameless (A) — *1Ki 15:3*
his mind was not one with the Lord (B) — *1Ki 15:3*
heart was not wholly true (R) — *1Ki 15:3*
Asa's heart was *p.* — *1Ki 15:14; 2Ch 15:17*
Asa's heart was blameless (A) — *1Ki 15:14*
his heart was at one with the Lord (B) — *1Ki 15:14*
heart was wholly true to the Lord (R) — *1Ki 15:14*
thee in truth with a *p.* heart — *2Ki 20:3*
with a whole heart devoted to you (A) — *2Ki 20:3*
walked faithfully and wholeheartedly (B) — *2Ki 20:3*
walked in faithfulness with whole heart (R) — *2Ki 20:3*
with *p.* heart — *1Ch 12:38; 29:9; 2Ch 19:9; 25:2*
with a blameless heart (A) — *1Ch 12:38; 29:9; 2Ch 19:9; 25:2*
was of one mind (B)(R) — *1Ch 12:38*
with a *p.* heart — *1Ch 28:9*
serve him wholeheartedly (B) — *1Ch 28:9*
serve him with a whole heart (R) — *1Ch 28:9*
with perfect heart they offered willingly — *1Ch 29:9*
offered wholeheartedly (B) — *1Ch 29:9*
with a whole heart (R) — *1Ch 29:9*
unto Solomon my son a *p.* heart — *1Ch 29:19*
to Solomon a blameless heart (A) — *1Ch 29:19*
a heart of integrity (B) — *1Ch 29:19*
that with a whole heart (R) — *1Ch 29:19*
made he of gold, and that *p.* gold — *2Ch 4:21*
tongs of purest gold (A)(R) — *2Ch 4:21*
them whose heart is *p.* toward him — *2Ch 16:9*
whose heart is blameless before him (A)(R) — *2Ch 16:9*
whose heart is full of integrity (B) — *2Ch 16:9*
Ezra the priest *p.* peace — *Ezr 7:12*
that man was *p.* and upright — *Job 1:1; 1:8; 2:3*
blameless and upright (A)(R) — *Job 1:1; 1:8; 2:3*
a man of integrity and upright (B) — *Job 1:1; 1:8; 2:3*
God will not cast away a *p.* man — *Job 8:20*
never cast away a blameless man (A)(R) — *Job 8:20*
not cast off an upright man (B) — *Job 8:20*
if I say, I am *p.* it shall also prove — *Job 9:20*
thought I am blameless (A)(R) — *Job 9:20*
though I were upright (B) — *Job 9:20*
Though I were *p.* yet would I not — *Job 9:21*
Though I am blameless — *Job 9:21*
I am upright (B) — *Job 9:21*
destroyeth the *p.* with the wicked — *Job 9:22*
destroys the blameless with the wicked (A)(R) — *Job 9:22*
destroys the upright with the wicked (B) — *Job 9:22*
that thou makest thy way *p.* — *Job 22:23*
make your ways blameless (R) — *Job 22:23*
he that is *p.* in knowledge is with — *Job 36:4; 37:16*
with a *p.* man (B) — *Ps 18:25*

law of Lord is *p.*, converting the soul — *Ps 19:7*
mark the *p.* man, and behold — *Ps 37:37*
mark the blameless man (A)(R) — *Ps 37:37*
Watch the upright (B) — *Ps 37:37*
they shoot in secret at the *p.* — *Ps 64:4*
shoot from ambush at the blameless (A)(R) — *Ps 64:4*
shoot from ambush at the innocent (B) — *Ps 64:4*
a *p.* way, a *p.* heart — *Ps 101:2; 102:6*
blameless way, blameless heart (A)(R) — *Ps 101:2*
heart be *p.* in statutes (E) — *Ps 119:80*
will *p.* that which concerneth me — *Ps 138:8*
fulfill his purpose on my behalf (B)(R) — *Ps 138:8*
I hate them with *p.* hatred — *Ps 139:22*
I hate them with complete hatred (B) — *Ps 139:22*
the *p.* shall remain in the land — *Pr 2:21*
blameless and complete shall remain (A) — *Pr 2:21*
the upright shall inhabit (B)(R) — *Pr 2:21*
more and more unto the *p.* day — *Pr 4:18*
brighter until the full day (R) (B) — *Pr 4:18*
brighter until the full day (R) — *Pr 4:18*
righteousness of the *p.* shall direct — *Pr 11:5*
righteousness of the blameless (A)(B)(R) — *Pr 11:5*
when the bud is *p.* — *Isa 18:5*
flower becomes a ripening grape (A)(B)(E)(R) — *Isa 18:5*
wilt keep him in *p.* peace — *Isa 26:3*
thee in truth and with a *p.* heart — *Isa 38:3*
with a whole heart devoted to you (A)(R) — *Isa 38:3*
in sincerity of heart (B) — *Isa 38:3*
who is blind as he that is *p.* — *Isa 42:19*
blind as he who is at peace with me (A)(E) — *Isa 42:19*
blind as my devoted one (B) — *Isa 42:19*
blind as my dedicated one (R) — *Isa 42:19*
it was *p.* through my comeliness — *Eze 16:14*
p. beauty — *Eze 27:3; 27:11; 28:12*
p. in thy ways from the day created — *Eze 28:15*
blameless in your ways (A)(R) — *Eze 28:15*
Be ye therefore *p.* even as your Father in heaven is *p.* — *M't 5:48*
be all goodness, as your heavenly Father is all good (N) — *M't 5:48*
If thou wilt be *p.*, go sell that thou hast — *M't 19:21*
if thou wilt be complete (B) — *M't 19:21*
If you wish to go the whole way (N) — *M't 19:21*
having had a *p.* understanding — *Lu 1:3*
searched out diligently and followed all things closely and traced accurately the course from the highest to the minutest detail (A) — *Lu 1:3*
accurately acquainted with everything (B) — *Lu 1:3*
traced the course of all things accurately (E) — *Lu 1:3*
gone over the whole course of these events in detail (N) — *Lu 1:3*
traced the course of these happenings carefully from the beginning (P) — *Lu 1:3*
having followed all things closely (R) — *Lu 1:3*
that is *p.* shall be as his master — *Lu 6:40*
every one completely trained (A) — *Lu 6:40*
every well-trained student shall be (B) — *Lu 6:40*
when his training is complete, will (N) — *Lu 6:40*
when he is fully trained shall be (P) — *Lu 6:40*
when he is fully taught will be (R) — *Lu 6:40*
that they may be made *p.* in one — *Joh 17:23*
may become one and perfectly united (A) — *Joh 17:23*
may be completed in one (B) — *Joh 17:23*
may be perfected in one (E) — *Joh 17:23*

may be perfectly one (N)(R)	*Joh 17:23*
may grow complete into one	*Joh 17:23*
(P)	
hath given him this *p.*	*Ac 3:16*
soundless	
made him completely well (N)	*Ac 3:16*
gave this man perfect health	*Ac 3:16*
(P)(R)	
p. manner of the law of the	*Ac 22:3*
fathers	
according to the strictest care	*Ac 22:3*
(A)	
educated with exacting care	*Ac 22:3*
(B)	
according to the strict manner	*Ac 22:3*
of law (E)(R)	
Thoroughly trained in every	*Ac 22:3*
point of (N)	
schooled in strictest observance	*Ac 22:3*
of law (P)	
a *p.* pest (A)(N)	*Ac 24:5*
more *p.* knowledge of that	*Ac 24:22*
way	
having rather accurate	*Ac 24:22*
understanding (A)	
understood teachings of the	*Ac 24:22*
Way (B)	
exact knowledge concerning	*Ac 24:22*
the Way (E)	
well about the Christian	*Ac 24:22*
movement (N)	
better acquainted with the	*Ac 24:22*
Way (P)	
rather accurate knowledge of	*Ac 24:22*
the Way (R)	
acceptable and *p.* will of God	*Ro 12:2*
in *p.* harmony (A)	*1Co 1:10*
wisdom among them that are	*1Co 2:6*
p.	
the full grown-spiritually	*1Co 2:6*
mature (A)	
among the mature (B)(R)	*1Co 2:6*
among them that are full grown	*1Co 2:6*
(E)	
to those who are ripe for it	*1Co 2:6*
(N)	
among those who are spiritually	*1Co 2:6*
mature (P)	
when that which is *p.* is	*1Co 13:10*
come	
when the complete comes	*1Co 13:10*
(P)	
strength is made *p.* in	*2Co 12:9*
weakness	
strength comes to perfection	*2Co 12:9*
where (B)	
power comes to full strength	*2Co 12:9*
in weakness (N)	
power shown where there is	*2Co 12:9*
weakness (P)	
Be *p.*, be of good comfort	*2Co 13:11*
Be strengthened, perfected,	*2Co 13:11*
completed (A)	
Be adjusted (B)	*2Co 13:11*
Mend your ways (N)(R)	*2Co 13:11*
Straighten yourselves out	*2Co 13:11*
(P)	
are ye now made *p.* by the flesh	*Ga 3:3*
are you reaching perfection on	*Ga 3:3*
flesh (A)	
would now compete with the	*Ga 3:3*
flesh (B)	
are you perfected in the flesh	*Ga 3:3*
(E)	
completes (life) by reverting to	*Ga 3:3*
outward observances (P)	
unto a *p.* man, unto the	*Eph 4:13*
measure of	
brings completeness of	*Eph 4:13*
personality (B)	
unto a full grown man (E)	*Eph 4:13*
to full manhood (N)(R)	*Eph 4:13*
arrive at full maturity (P)	*Eph 4:13*
either were already *p.*	*Ph'p 3:12*
or already reached perfection	*Ph'p 3:12*
(B)(N)	
as many as be *p.* be thus	*Ph'p 3:15*
minded	
those who are spiritually	*Ph'p 3:15*
mature (A)(B)(N)(R)	
all who are spiritually adult	*Ph'p 3:15*
(P)	
present every man *p.* in Christ	*Col 1:28*
present every man mature	*Col 1:28*
(A)(N)(R)	
present every man complete	*Col 1:28*
(B)	
bring every man to full	*Col 1:28*
maturity (P)	

that ye may stand *p.* and	*Col 4:12*
complete	
stand firm and mature	*Col 4:12*
(A)(B)(R)	
that you may stand fast (N)	*Col 4:12*
may become mature	*Col 4:12*
Christians (P)	
might *p.* that which is lacking	*1Th 3:10*
mend and make good the	*1Th 3:10*
imperfect (A)	
adjust what needs	*1Th 3:10*
advancement (B)	
mend your faith (N)	*1Th 3:10*
complete whatever is	*1Th 3:10*
imperfect (R)	
supply what is lacking in your	*1Th 3:10*
faith (R)	
That the man of God may be	*1Th 3:17*
p.	
man of God may be complete	*1Th 3:17*
(A)(E)(R)	
man of God may be	*1Th 3:17*
well-fitted (B)	
man of God may be efficient	*1Th 3:17*
(N)	
fit him fully (P)	*1Th 3:17*
make captain of their	*Heb 2:10*
salvation (P)	
being made *p.* he became the	*Heb 5:9*
author	
when perfected, he became	*Heb 5:9*
(B)	
the law made nothing *p.*	*Heb 7:19*
made *p.* forever	*Heb 7:28*
(A)(B)(E)(N)(P)(R)	
make him that did the service	*Heb 9:9;*
p.	*10:1*
greater and more *p.*	*Heb 9:11*
tabernacle	
offered himself a *p.* sacrifice	*Heb 9:14*
(P)	
without us should not be	*Heb 11:40*
made *p.*	
spirits of just men made *p.*	*Heb 12:23*
make you *p.* in every good	*Heb 13:21*
work	
patience have *p.* work, ye may	*Jas 1:4*
be *p.*	
endurance and stedfastness and	*Jas 1:4*
patience have full play be	
perfectly developed (A)	
every *p.* gift is from above	*Jas 1:17*
looketh into the *p.* law of	*Jas 1:25*
liberty	
looks into the flawless law (A)	*Jas 1:25*
by works was faith made *p.*	*Jas 2:22*
his faith was completed (A)	*Jas 2:22*
faith reached its supreme	*Jas 2:22*
expression (B)	
faith was fully proved (N)	*Jas 2:22*
faith was completed by works	*Jas 2:22*
(R)	
offend not in word is a *p.* man	*Jas 3:2*
who never say a wrong is a *p.*	*Jas 3:2*
character (N)	
suffered awhile make you *p.*	*1Pe 5:10*
will himself make you	*1Pe 5:10*
complete (A)	
personally equip, stabilize (B)	*1Pe 5:10*
restore, establish (N)(R)	*1Pe 5:10*
will make you whole (P)	*1Pe 5:10*
love made *p.*; *p.* in love	*1Jo 4:17:*
	4:18
love is brought to completion	*1Jo 4:17*
(A)(B)	
have not found thy works *p.*	*Re 3:2*
none of your works meeting	*Re 3:2*
requirements (B)	
not found work completed	*Re 3:2*
(N)(P)	

PERFECTED

house of the Lord was *p.*	*2Ch 8:16*
house of the Lord was	*2Ch 8:16*
completed (A)(E)(R)	
house of the Lord was	*2Ch 8:16*
finished (B)	
the work was *p.* by them	*2Ch 24:13*
they restored the house of	*2Ch 24:13*
God (B)	
thy builders have *p.* thy beauty	*Eze 27:4*
sucklings thou hast *p.* praise	*M't 21:16*
the third day I shall be *p.*	*Lu 13:32*
third day I finish my course	*Lu 13:32*
(A)(R)	
third day I complete my work	*Lu 13:32*
(B)	
third day I reach my goal (N)	*Lu 13:32*

third day my work will be	*Lu 13:32*
finished (P)	
be *p.* together in the same	*1Co 1:10*
mind (E)	
by one suffering he hath *p.*	*Heb 10:14*
for ever	
in him is the love of God *p.*	*1Jo 2:5*
love of God reached maturity	*1Jo 2:5*
(B)	
love has come to its perfection	*1Jo 2:5*
(N)	
his love is *p.* in us	*1Jo 4:12*

PERFECTING

p. holiness in the fear of God	*2Co 7:1*
bring consecration to	*2Co 7:1*
completeness (A)	
complete our dedication (B)	*2Co 7:1*
complete our consecration	*2Co 7:1*
(N)	
consecrating ourselves to him	*2Co 7:1*
completely (P)	
make holiness perfect (R)	*2Co 7:1*
For the *p.* of the saints	*Eph 4:12*
to make the saints fit (B)	*Eph 4:12*
to equip God's people for	*Eph 4:12*
work (N)	
Christians might be properly	*Eph 4:12*
equipped (P)	
for the equipment of saints	*Eph 4:12*
(R)	

PERFECTION

find out the Almighty unto *p.*	*Job 11:7*
compass the limits of the	*Job 11:7*
Almighty (B)(R)	
shall he prolong the *p.*	*Job 15:29*
thereof	
and searcheth out all *p.*	*Job 28:3*
Out of Zion, the *p.* of beauty	*Ps 50:2;*
	La 2:15
I have seen the end of all *p.*	*Ps 119:96*
that everything has its limits	*Ps 119:96*
and end (A)	
I have seen limits to all things	*Ps 119:96*
(B)	
come upon thee in their *p.*	*Isa 47:9*
come upon you in full measure	*Isa 47:9*
(A)(B)(E)(R)	
the signet of *p.* (R)	*Eze 28:12*
bring no fruit to *p.*	*Lu 8:14*
so that they never mature (B)	*Lu 8:14*
bring nothing to maturity (N)	*Lu 8:14*
they produce nothing (P)	*Lu 8:14*
their fruit does not mature (R)	*Lu 8:14*
this also we wish, your *p.*	*2Co 13:9*
your all around perfecting of	*2Co 13:9*
soul (A)	
your all-around completeness	*2Co 13:9*
(B)	
that all might be put right	*2Co 13:9*
(N)	
we pray for your	*2Co 13:9*
improvement (R)	
let us go on to *p.*	*Heb 6:1*
advance toward maturity	*Heb 6:1*
(B)(R)	
go forward to adult	*Heb 6:1*
understanding (P)	
if *p.* were by the Levitical	*Heb 7:11*
priesthood	
if anything final had come by	*Heb 7:11*
(B)	
if possible to bring men to	*Heb 7:11*
spiritual maturity (P)	
love has come to *p.* (N)	*1Jo 2:5*

PERFECTLY

latter days ye shall consider it	*Jer 23:20*
p.	
as touched were made *p.*	*M't 14:36*
whole	
were completely healed (B)	*M't 14:36*
were made whole (E)	*M't 14:36*
was completely cured (N)	*M't 14:36*
were made well (R)	*M't 14:36*
unto him the way of God	*Ac 18:26*
more *p.*	
more definitely and accurately	*Ac 18:26*
(A)	
explained more accurately	*Ac 18:26*
(B)(E)(P)(R)	
expounded in greater detail	*Ac 18:26*
(N)	
would enquire something	*Ac 23:20;*
more *p.*	*23:15*

examine him more exactly (A)(E) — Ac 23:20

investigate more particularly (B) — Ac 23:20

on the pretext of obtaining more precise information (N) — Ac 23:20

enquire more carefully (P) — Ac 23:20

enquire more closely (R) — Ac 23:20

that ye be p. joined together — 1Co 1:10

be in perfect harmony and full agreement (A) — 1Co 1:10

be agreeable mutually in mind and attitude (B) — 1Co 1:10

be perfected together in the same mind (E) — 1Co 1:10

be firmly joined in unity of mind and thought (N) — 1Co 1:10

achieving unity in thought and judgment (P) — 1Co 1:10

united in the same mind and judgment (R) — 1Co 1:10

I am p. frank with you (N) — 2Co 7:4

know p., that the day of the Lord — 1Th 5:2

you yourselves are keenly aware (B) — 1Th 5:2

you are well aware of (P) — 1Th 5:2

you yourselves know well that the day (R) — 1Th 5:2

be p. composed (B)(N) — 1Pe 1:13

PERFECTNESS

put on charity, which is the bond of p. — Col 3:14

love, which is the perfect bond of union (B) — Col 3:14

love, to bind all together and complete the whole (N) — Col 3:14

love is the golden chair of all virtues (P) — Col 3:14

love, which binds everything together in perfect harmony (R) — Col 3:14

PERFORM

I will p. the oath which I sware — Ge 26:3

I will make good the oath (B) — Ge 26:3

I will establish the oath (E) — Ge 26:3

I will fulfill the oath (R) — Ge 26:3

art not able to p. it thyself alone — Ex 18:18

you cannot handle it alone (B) — Ex 18:18

all that enter in to p. the service — Nu 4:23

qualify to enter the service for work (B) — Nu 4:23

all that enter to wait upon service (E) — Nu 4:23

who can enter the service (R) — Nu 4:23

p. the work (A)(R) — Nu 8:24

which he commanded you to p. — De 4:13

which he ordered you to keep (B) — De 4:13

may p. the word which the Lord — De 9:5

he may fulfill the promise (A) — De 9:5

to establish the word (B)(E) — De 9:5

that he may confirm the word (R) — De 9:5

of thy lips thou shalt keep and p. it — De 23:23

of thy lips thou shalt observe and do (E) — De 23:23

p. the duty of an husband's brother — De 25:5; 25:7

p. unto thee the part of a kinsman — Ru 3:13

if he wants to redeem you (B) — Ru 3:13

if he will not do the part of a kinsman (E) — Ru 3:13

if he will do the part of a kinsman (R) — Ru 3:13

day I will p. against Eli all things — 1Sa 3:12

carry out from start to finish against (A) — 1Sa 3:12

fulfill against Eli all that I have spoken (R) — 1Sa 3:12

p. the request of his handmaid — 2Sa 14:15

then will I p. my word with thee — 1Ki 6:12

then will I fulfill my promises (A)(E) — 1Ki 6:12

then will I establish my word (E)(R) — 1Ki 6:12

that he might p. his saying — 1Ki 12:15

that he might fulfill his word (A) — 1Ki 12:15

establish his word (B)(E) — 1Ki 12:15

he might fulfill his word (R) — 1Ki 12:15

to p. the words of his covenant — 2Ki 23:3; 2Ch 34:31

to confirm the words of this covenant (A)(E) — 2Ki 23:3

uphold the words of this covenant (B) — 2Ki 23:3

might p. the words of the law — 2Ki 23:24

might establish the words of the law (A)(R) — 2Ki 23:24

to carry out the words of the law (B) — 2Ki 23:24

to confirm the words of the law (E) — 2Ki 23:24

the Lord might p. his word — 2Ch 10:15

might carry out his word (B) — 2Ch 10:15

might establish his word (E) — 2Ch 10:15

might fulfill his word (R) — 2Ch 10:15

to p. my request — Es 5:8

in granting my request (B) — Es 5:8

to fulfill my request (R) — Es 5:8

hands cannot p. their enterprise — Job 5:12

their hands achieve no success (B)(R) — Job 5:12

which they are not able to p. — Ps 21:11

unable to put into practice (B) — Ps 21:11

they will not succeed (R) — Ps 21:11

that I may daily p. my vows — Ps 61:8

paying my vows day by day (A) — Ps 61:8

I may daily pay my vows (B)(R) — Ps 61:8

I have sworn, and will p. it — Ps 119:106

sworn, and have confirmed it (A)(B)(E)(R) — Ps 119:106

heart to p. thy statutes alway — Ps 119:112

practicing thy statutes (B) — Ps 119:112

zeal of Lord of hosts will p. it — Isa 9:7

zeal of Lord of hosts will do it (B)(R) — Isa 9:7

vow a vow unto the Lord, and p. it — Isa 19:21

shall p. all my pleasure — Isa 44:28

shall fulfill all my pleasure (B)(R) — Isa 44:28

I will hasten my word and p. it — Jer 1:12

awake over my word to fulfill it (B) — Jer 1:12

p. the oath which I sware — Jer 11:5

may fulfill my agreement (B) — Jer 11:5

may establish my oath (E) — Jer 11:5

Lord p. thy words which thou hast — Jer 28:6

fulfill your words which you (B) — Jer 28:6

words you prophesied come true (R) — Jer 28:6

p. my good word toward you — Jer 29:10

keep my good promise (A) — Jer 29:10

fulfill my promise (B)(R) — Jer 29:10

will p. that good thing which I have — Jer 33:14

fulfill the good promise (A)(B)(R) — Jer 33:14

p. our vows, p. your vows — Jer 44:25

I say the word, and will p. it — Eze 12:25

word I speak will come to pass (B) — Eze 12:25

Thou wilt p. the truth to Jacob — Mic 7:20

show faithfulness to Jacob (B)(R) — Mic 7:20

thy solemn feasts, p. thy vows — Na 1:15

pay your vows (B) — Na 1:15

fulfill your vows (R) — Na 1:15

shall p. unto the Lord thine oaths — M't 5:33

Oaths sworn to the Lord must be kept (N) — M't 5:33

p. the mercy promised to our — Lu 1:72

show the mercy promised (A)(E) — Lu 1:72

To make true the mercy promised (B) — Lu 1:72

that he would deal mercifully (N) — Lu 1:72

p. unmentionable deeds (P) — Ro 1:28

promised, he was able also to p. — Ro 4:21

God was able to and mighty to keep (A) — Ro 4:21

he was able to make good (B) — Ro 4:21

to do what he had promised (N) — Ro 4:21

God was able to implement his promise (P) — Ro 4:21

he was able to do what he had (R) — Ro 4:21

how to p. that which is good I find — Ro 7:18

Now therefore p. the doing of it — 2Co 8:11

will p. it until the day of Jesus Christ — Ph'p 1:6

PERFORMANCE

there shall be a p. of those things — Lu 1:45

be a fulfillment of the things (A)(E)(R) — Lu 1:45

shall be accomplished (B) — Lu 1:45

Lord's promise would be fulfilled (N) — Lu 1:45

he does make his promises come true (P) — Lu 1:45

so there may be a p. also out of — 2Co 8:11

So now finish doing it (A) — 2Co 8:11

complete the enterprise (B) — 2Co 8:11

now complete the doing also (E) — 2Co 8:11

go on and finish it (N) — 2Co 8:11

Finish it, then, as well as you can (P) — 2Co 8:11

PERFORMED

hath not p. my commandments — 1Sa 15:11

hath not carried out my orders (B) — 1Sa 15:11

hath p. the commandments of the Lord — 1Sa 15:13

I have carried out the Lord's (B) — 1Sa 15:13

p. all that the king commanded — 2Sa 21:14

did all the king commanded (A)(R) — 2Sa 21:14

the Lord hath p. his word — 1Ki 8:20; 2Ch 6:10

hath fulfilled his promise (A)(E)(R) — 1Ki 8:20

hath established his word (E) — 1Ki 8:20

hast p. thy words: for thou art — Ne 9:8

you have fulfilled your promise (A)(B)(R) — Ne 9:8

she hath not p. the commandment — Es 1:15

she has not done the bidding (A)(E) — Es 1:15

she has failed to carry out orders (B) — Es 1:15

half of the kingdom it shall be p. — Es 5:6; 7:2

it shall be met, if it were half (B) — Es 5:6

it shall be fulfilled (R) — Es 5:6

unto thee shall the vow be p. — Ps 65:1

the vow shall be fulfilled (B) — Ps 65:1

Lord hath p. his whole work — Isa 10:12

Lord has completed all his work (A) — Isa 10:12

Lord has finished all his work (B)(R) — Isa 10:12

have p. the thoughts of his heart — Jer 23:20; 30:24

has executed and accomplished the thoughts — Jer 23:20; 30:24

and intents of his mind (A)(R) — Jer 23:20

not p. the words of the covenant — Jer 34:18

did not keep terms of covenant (A)(B)(R) — Jer 34:18

words of Jonadab are p. — Jer 35:14; 35:16

command has been carried out (A) — Jer 35:14

has been observed (B) — Jer 35:14

kept all his precepts (E)(R) — Jer 35:14

purpose of the Lord shall be p. — Jer 51:29

Lord have spoken it, and p. — Eze 37:14

I have said it and done it (B)(R) — Eze 37:14

day these things shall be p. — Lu 1:20

day these things take place (A)(B)(E) — Lu 1:20

day these things happen (N)(P) — Lu 1:20

day these things come to pass (R) — Lu 1:20

p. all things according to the | Lu 2:39
law
done everything according to | Lu 2:39
the law (A)(N)
finished everything according | Lu 2:39
to law (B)
accomplished everything | Lu 2:39
according (E)
completed all requirements of | Lu 2:39
the law (P)
p. on the sick | Joh 6:2
(A)(B)(E)(N)(P)
When therefore I have p. this | Ro 15:28
When I have completed this | Ro 15:28
mission (A)(P)(R)
This finished, and that | Ro 15:28
donation (B)
When I have accomplished | Ro 15:28
this (E)
when I have finished this | Ro 15:28
business (N)

PERFORMETH

that p. not this promise | Ne 5:13
who does not keep this promise | Ne 5:13
(A)
who does not fulfill this | Ne 5:13
promise (B)
p. the thing that is appointed | Job 23:14
he will not carry what he has | Job 23:14
planned (B)
he will not complete what he | Job 23:14
appoints (R)
unto God that p. all things for | Ps 57:2
me
who completes all things for | Ps 57:2
me (B)
who fulfills his purpose for me | Ps 57:2
(R)
p. the counsel of his | Isa 44:26
messengers
who confirms the word of his | Isa 44:26
servants (A)(B)(E)(R)

PERFORMING

a sacrifice in p. a vow | Nu 15:3;
 | 15:8
to fulfill a special vow (A) | Nu 15:3;
 | 15:8
fulfilling a special vow (B) | Nu 15:3;
 | 15:8
to accomplish a vow (E) | Nu 15:3;
 | 15:8
p. their service (A)(R) | 1Ch 6:32
p. priestly function (P) | Lu 1:8

PERFUME

thou shalt make it a p. | Ex 30:35; 30:37
p., an ointment (A)(B)(E) | Ex 30:35
make an incense (R) | Ex 30:35; 30:37
make a p. (S) | Ex 30:35
Ointment and p. rejoice the | Pr 27:9
heart
p. boxes (A)(B)(E)(R)(S) | Isa 3:2
instead of p. (R) | Isa 3:24
p. your head (A) | M't 6:17
jar of pure nard p. (B) | M'k 14:3
pound of costly p. (B)(N)(P) | Joh 12:3
a fragrant p. (B) | Ph'p 4:18

PERFUMED

p. incense (B) | Ex 25:6;
 | 30:7; 31:11; 35:15, 28; 39:38
have p. my bed with myrrh, | Pr 7:17
aloes
p. with myrrh and frankincense | Ca 3:6

PERFUMER

incense blended by p. (R) | Ex 30:25
after the art of the p. (S) | Ex 30:25;
 | 30:35; 37:29
the ointment of the p. (S) | Ec 10:1

PERFUMERS

daughters to be p. (S) | 1Sa 8:13
son of one of the p. (S) | Ne 3:8
sweet spices and p. (A)(B) | Es 2:12

PERFUMER'S

p. ointment (B)(R) | Ec 10:1

PERFUMERS'

prepared by the p. art (S) | 2Ch 16:14

PERFUMES

didst increase thy p. | Isa 57:9

PERGA

they came to P. in Pamphylia | Ac 13:13
when they departed from P. | Ac 13:14
they
they had preached the word | Ac 14:25
in P.

PERGAMOS

and unto P. and unto Thyatira | Re 1:11
angel of the church in P. write | Re 2:12

PERGAMUM

Pergamum (S) | Re 1:11; 2:12

PERHAPS

p. there are fifty (B) | Ge 18:24; 18:30
perhaps (S) | Ge 27:12;
 | 31:31; 32:20; 38:11; 42:4; 43:12; 44:34;
 | 50:15; Ex 32:30; Nu 22:6, 11; 23:3, 27;
 | 1Sa 6:5; 9:6; 1Ki 18:5, 27; 20:31;
 | 2Ki 2:16; Jer 20:10; Ro 5:7; 2Ti 2:25
p. he will (A) | Ge 32:20;
 | 39:11; 42:4; 50:15
the p. they had obtained | Ge 46:15;
(B) | 46:18, 26; Le 18:29; Eze 13:19
p. I can make atonement | Ex 32:30
(A)(B)(R)
p. I am able (A)(B)(R) | Nu 22:6; 22:11
p. the Lord will (A)(B)(R) | Nu 23:3
p. it will please God | Nu 23:27
(A)(B)(R)
p. you live among us | Jos 9:7
(A)(B)(R)
p. he will lighten (A)(B) | 1Sa 6:5
p. he can show us (A)(B) | 1Sa 9:6
p. he is asleep (A)(B)(R) | 1Ki 18:2
p. we may find grass | 1Ki 18:5
(A)(B)(R)
p. he will save your life | 1Ki 20:31
(A)(B)(R)
p. the Spirit (B) | 2Ki 2:16
p. he will be (A)(B)(R) | Jer 20:10
perhaps (S) | M'k 11:13;
 | Lu 14:29; Ac 5:39; 17:27
if p. the thought of thine | Ac 8:22
heart may
p. for a noble (A)(B)(R) | Ro 5:7
lest p. such should be | 2Co 2:7
swallowed
For p. he departed for a | Ph'm 15
season

PERIDA

of Sophereth, the children of | Ne 7:57
P.

PERIL

gat our bread with the p. of our | La 5:9
lives
or nakedness, or p. or sword | Ro 8:35
Or danger? Or sword (B) | Ro 8:35
danger to life and limb (P) | Ro 8:35

PERILOUS

in last days p. times shall come | 2Ti 3:1
troublous times impending (B) | 2Ti 3:1
grievous times shall come (E) | 2Ti 3:1
to be a time of troubles (N) | 2Ti 3:1
times will be full of danger | 2Ti 3:1
(P)
will come in times of stress (R) | 2Ti 3:1

PERILS

p. of waters, p. of robbers, | 2Co 11:26
p. by countrymen, p. by
heathen, p. in city, p. in
wilderness, p. in the sea, and
p. among false brethren
in dangers of rivers, robbers, | 2Co 11:26
Jews, Gentiles, city, desert, sea,
dangers among sham brothers
(B)(N)(P)(R)

PERIOD

p. of women upon me (B) | Ge 31:35
custody for a p. (B) | Ge 40:4

her p. of uncleanness (B) | Le 15:25
and the p. we came from (S) | De 2:14
relates to the final p. (B) | Da 8:17
 | 11:35; 12:4, 9
a p., periods and half p. (B) | Da 12:7;
 | Re 12:7, 14

PERIODS

a period, p. and half period | Da 12:7;
(B) | Re 12:7, 14
appointing pre-established p. | Ac 17:26
(B)
relative to p. and dates (B) | 1Th 5:1

PERISH

land p. not through famine | Ge 41:36
land not be ruined and cut | Ge 41:36
off by (A)
land not be ruined by famine | Ge 41:36
(B)
people gaze, and many p. | Ex 19:21
lest the Lord break forth upon | Ex 19:21
(B)
on eye of his maid, that it p. | Ex 21:26
eye of maid so it is destroyed | Ex 21:26
(A)
eye and destroys it | Ex 21:26
(B)(E)(R)
ye shall p. among the heathen | Le 26:38
we die, we p., we all p. | Nu 17:12
latter end that he p. for ever | Nu 24:20
latter end come to | Nu 24:20;
destruction (A)(B)(E)(R) | 24:24
soon utterly p. from the land | De 4:26
ye shall surely p. | De 8:19
ye shall go down to ruin (B) | De 8:19
so shall ye p.; because ye | De 8:20
would not
be destroyed, because you | De 8:20
would (B)
ye p. quickly from off the | De 11:17;
land | 28:20, 22; 30:18; Jos 23:13, 16
A Syrian ready to p. was my | De 26:5
father (B)(R)
A wandering Aramean was my | De 26:5
father (B)(R)
let all thine enemies p., O Lord | J'g 5:31
descend in battle and p. | 1Sa 26:10; 27:1
go to battle and be wiped out | 1Sa 26:10
(B)
the whole house of Ahab shall | 2Ki 9:8
p.
whole house of Ahab be | 2Ki 9:8
destroyed (B)
cause to p. all Jews | Es 3:13
to destroy all Jews | Es 3:13
(A)(B)(E)(R)
to annihilate all Jews (R) | Es 3:13
if I p., I p. | Es 4:16
be destroyed, be slain, and to p. | Es 7:4;
 | 8:11
and wiped out of existence (A) | Es 7:4
to be obliterated (B) | Es 7:4
and to be annihilated (R) | Es 7:4
to slay, and cause to p. | Es 8:11
to slay and to wipe out (A) | Es 8:11
kill, and exterminate (B) | Es 8:11
slay, and to annihilate (R) | Es 8:11
nor a memorial of them | Es 9:28
from
Purim should never cease (A) | Es 9:28
Purim days may not lapse | Es 9:28
among Jews (B)
Purim not fail among Jews (E) | Es 9:28
Purim never fall into disuse | Es 9:28
(R)
Let the day p. wherein I was | Job 3:3
born
By the blast of God they p. and | Job 4:9
p. for ever without any | Job 4:20
regarding it
aside; they go to nothing, and | Job 6:18
p.
and the hypocrite's hope shall | Job 8:13
p.
His remembrance shall p. | Job 18:17
from the
he shall p. for ever like his | Job 20:7
own dung
blessing of him that was | Job 29:13
ready to p.
have seen any p. for want | Job 31:19
of clothing
All flesh shall p. together, | Job 34:15
and man
they shall p. by the sword | Job 36:12
but the way of the ungodly | Ps 1:6
shall p.

ungodly shall end in ruin (B) Ps 1:6
lest he be angry, and ye p. from Ps 2:12
they shall fall and p. at thy Ps 9:3
presence
expectation of the poor shall Ps 9:18
not p.
the wicked shall p. and the Ps 37:20
enemies
When shall he die, and his Ps 41:5
name p.
his name vanish (B) Ps 41:5
the fool and the brutish Ps 49:10
person p.
not: he is like the beasts that Ps 49:12
p.
not, is like the beasts that p. Ps 49:20
let the wicked p. at presence Ps 68:2
of God
they that are far from thee Ps 73:27
shall p.
p. at the rebuke of thy Ps 80:16
countenance
let them be put to shame and Ps 83:17
p.
Lord, for, lo, thine enemies Ps 92:9
shall p.
They shall p. but thou shalt Ps 102:26
endure
the desire of the wicked shall Ps 112:10
p.
in that very day his thoughts Ps 146:4
p.
expectation of the wicked Pr 10:28
shall p.
the wicked comes to nothing Pr 10:28
(B)
man dieth, his expectation shall Pr 11:7
p.
the wicked p. there is shouting Pr 11:10
and he that speaketh lies shall p. Pr 19:9
A false witness shall p.: but Pr 21:28
the man
when they p. the righteous Pr 28:28
increase
there is no vision, the people Pr 29:18
p.
no vision the people run wild Pr 29:18
(B)
drink unto him that is ready to Pr 31:6
p.
But those riches p. by evil Ec 5:14
travail
wealth is lost in a bad venture Ec 5:14
(B)
and made all their memory to Isa 26:14
p.
ready to p. in the land of Isa 27:13
Assyria
wisdom of their wise men Isa 29:14
shall p.
they that strive with thee Isa 41:11
shall p.
that will not serve thee shall Isa 60:12
p.
that the heart of the king shall Jer 4:9
p.
neighbour and his friend shall Jer 6:21
p.
they shall p. from the earth Jer 10:11
time of their visitation they Jer 10:15
shall p.
the law shall not p. from the Jer 18:18
priest
drive you out, and ye should Jer 27:10
p.
drive you out, and that ye Jer 27:15
might p.
and the remnant in Judah p. Jer 40:15
the valley also shall p. and the Jer 48:8
plain
time of their visitation they Jer 51:18
shall p.
but the law shall p. from the Eze 7:26
priest
priest shall be devoid of Eze 7:26
instruction (B)
cause thee to p. out of the Eze 25:7
countries
eliminate you from the Eze 25:7
countries (B)
Daniel and his fellows should Da 2:18
not p.
the remnant of the Philistines Am 1:8
shall p.
the flight shall p. from the Am 2:14
swift
the houses of ivory shall p. Am 3:15
the day when they p. (B) Ob 12
will think upon us, that we p. Jon 1:6
not

let us not p. for this man's Jon 1:14
life, and
from his fierce anger, that we Jon 3:9
p. not
and the king shall p. from Gaza Zec 9:5
one of thy members should p. M't 5:29;
5:30
better to lose one of members M't 5:29;
(A)(B)(N)(P)(R) 5:30
Lord, save us, we p. M't 8:25;
M'k 4:38; Lu 8:24
Lord, save, we are lost (B) M't 8:25
Lord, we are sinking (N) M't 8:25
Lord, we are drowning (P) M't 8:25
wine runneth out, and the M't 9:17;
bottles. Lu 5:37
the skins are ruined M't 9:17
(A)(B)(P)
the skins are spoilt (N) M't 9:17
the skins are destroyed (R) M't 9:17
one of these little ones M't 18:14
should p.
little ones should be lost M't 18:14
(B)(N)(P)
the sword shall p. with the M't 26:52
sword
will die by the sword M't 26:52
(A)(N)(P)
shall be destroyed by the M't 26:52
sword (B)
Repent, ye shall likewise p. Lu 13:3;
13:5
I p. with hunger Lu 15:17
I am starving (B)(N) Lu 15:17
I am dying of hunger (P) Lu 15:17
shall not an hair of your head Lu 21:18
p.
not a hair of your head be Lu 21:18
lost (B)(N)
believeth in him should not p. Jon 3:16;
3:15
may not die (N) Joh 3:16
should not be lost (P) Joh 3:16
they shall never p. Joh 10:28
they shall never die (P) Joh 10:28
that the whole nations p. not Joh 11:50
the whole nation ruined (B) Joh 11:50
whole nation be destroyed Joh 11:50
(N)(P)
Thy money p. with thee Ac 8:20
Destruction overtake your Ac 8:20
money (A)
May your money go to Ac 8:20
perdition (B)
To hell with you and your Ac 8:20
money (P)
ye despisers, and wonder, and Ac 13:41
p.
marvel, and vanish (B) Ac 13:41
wonder, and begone (N) Ac 13:41
law shall also p. without law Ro 2:12
shall be lost without law (B) Ro 2:12
will die without reference to Ro 2:12
(P)
cross to them that p. 1Co 1:18
foolishness
folly to those on way to 1Co 1:18
destruction (B)
folly to those on way to ruin 1Co 1:18
(N)
nonsense to those involved in 1Co 1:18
dying world (P)
utter disaster to the weak 1Co 8:11
this weak man is ruined 1Co 8:11
(A)(B)
shall the weak brother p. 1Co 8:11
(N)(P)
weak man be destroyed (R) 1Co 8:11
in them that p. 2Co 2:15
those on the way to perdition 2Co 2:15
(N)
who are heading for death 2Co 2:15
(P)
though our outward man p. 2Co 4:16
our outer man is decaying 2Co 4:16
(A)(E)
outer nature suffer decay 2Co 4:16
(B)(N)
outer man suffers wear and 2Co 4:16
tear (P)
outer nature is wasting away 2Co 4:16
(R)
all are to p. with using Col 2:22
destined to be ruined by wear Col 2:22
(B)
all pass away after use (P) Col 2:22
unrighteousness in them that 2Th 2:10
p.
are going to destruction (B) 2Th 2:10

on those doomed to 2Th 2:10
destruction (N)
to those involved in dying (P) 2Th 2:10
They shall p.; but thou Heb 1:11
remainest
they all shall wear out (B) Heb 1:11
shrink back so as to p. (B) Heb 10:39
utterly p. in own corruption 2Pe 2:12
be destroyed by their own 2Pe 2:12
corruption (B)
shall surely be destroyed 2Pe 2:12
(E)(P)(R)
they shall p. (N) 2Pe 2:12
not willing that any should p. 2Pe 3:9
not his will that any be lost 2Pe 3:9
(N)
not wish that any be destroyed 2Pe 3:9
(P)

PERISHABLE

receive p. crown (B)(R) 1Co 9:25
is p. and decays (A)(B)(R) 1Co 15:42
p. inherit imperishable 1Co 15:50
(A)(B)(R)
this p. nature 1Co 15:53
(A)(B)(N)(P)(R)
no p. stuff (N)(R) 1Pe 1:18
not from p. sperm (B) 1Pe 1:23
not from p. seed (R) 1Pe 1:23

PERISHABLES

not with p. (B) 1Pe 1:18

PERISHED

p. from the congregation Nu 16:33
vanished from the community Nu 16:33
(B)
Heshbon is p. even unto Nu 21:30
Dibon
Heshbon is lost even to Nu 21:30
Dibon (B)
the men of war were p. (S) De 2:14
man p. not alone in his Jos 22:20
iniquity
die alone because of his Jos 22:20
wickedness (B)
the weapons of war p. 2Sa 1:27
weapons of war destroyed (B) 2Sa 1:27
who ever p. being innocent Job 4:7
profit me, in whom old age p. Job 30:2
men who lost their manly Job 30:2
vigor (B)(R)
their memorial is p. with them Ps 9:6
memory of them has vanished Ps 9:6
(B)
heathen are p. out of the land Ps 10:16
Which p. at En-dor Ps 83:10
who were destroyed at En-dor Ps 83:10
(B)(R)
should then have p. in my Ps 119:92
affliction
their envy is now p. Ec 9:6
jealousy long since vanished (B) Ec 9:6
truth is p. and is cut off Jer 7:28
riches that he hath gotten are Jer 48:36
p.
is counsel p. from the prudent Jer 49:7
is counsel vanished (A) Jer 49:7
my hope is p. from the Lord La 3:18
the harvest of the field is p. Joe 1:11
the harvest of the field is Joe 1:11
ruined (B)
up in a night, and p. in a night Jon 4:10
is thy counsellor p. Mic 4:9; 7:2
in the sea, and p. in the water M't 8:32
into the sea, and died in the M't 8:32
water (A)
into the lake and were M't 8:32
drowned (P)
p. between the altar and Lu 11:51
temple
slain between altar and Lu 11:51
sanctuary (A)
murdered between altar and Lu 11:51
temple (B)
died between altar and Lu 11:51
sanctuary (P)
he also p. and all with him Ac 5:37
scattered
p. by serpents (E) 1Co 10:9
are fallen asleep in Christ are 1Co 15:18
p.
fallen asleep in Christ are 1Co 15:18
lost (B)(N)
are utterly dead and gone 1Co 15:18
(P)

By faith the harlot Rahab p. *Heb 11:31*
not
was not destroyed along *Heb 11:31*
with (A)
escaped the doom of *Heb 11:31*
unbelievers (N)
did not share fate of *Heb 11:31*
disobedient (N)
being overflowed with water p. *2Pe 3:6*
world was destroyed, deluged *2Pe 3:6*
with (B)(N)(P)
and p. in the gainsaying of *Jude 11*
Core
share his doom (N) *Jude 11*
destroyed themselves by *Jude 11*
rebelling (P)

PERISHETH

old lion p. for lack of food *Job 4:11*
the hope of unjust men p. *Pr 11:7*
just man that p. in his *Ec 7:15*
righteousness
righteous p., and no man *Isa 57:1*
layeth
the land p. and is burned up *Jer 9:12*
the land ruined and laid waste *Jer 9:12*
(A)(B)(R)
the people of Chemosh p. *Jer 48:46*
people of Chemosh are *Jer 48:46*
undone (A)(B)(E)(R)
Labour not for the meat *Joh 6:27*
which p.
work for food that must *Joh 6:27*
decompose (B)
for food which does not last *Joh 6:27*
(P)
the grace of the fashion of it p. *Jas 1:11*
its beauty fades away (A) *Jas 1:11*
is ruined (B) *Jas 1:11*
what was lovely to look at is *Jas 1:11*
lost (N)
that lovely sight is destroyed *Jas 1:11*
(P)
more precious than gold that p. *1Pe 1:7*

PERISHING

his life from p. with the *Job 33:18*
sword

PERIZZITE

the P. dwelled then in the land *Ge 13:7*
and the Hittite, and the P. *Ex 33:2;*
Ex 34:11
Amorite, the Canaanite, the P. *Jos 9:1*
P. and Jebusite in the *Jos 11:3*
mountain

PERIZZITES

Hittites, and the P. and the *Ge 15:20*
among the Canaanites and *Ge 34:30*
the P.
the P. and the Hivites, and the *Ex 3:8;*
3:17; De 7:1; 20:17; Jos 12:8; 2Ch 8:7
and the Hittites, and the P. *Ex 23:33*
and the P. and the Girgashites *Jos 3:10*
in the land of the P. and the *Jos 17:15*
the Amorites, and the P. *Jos 24:11*
Canaanites and the P. into their *J'g 1:4*
slew the Canaanite and the P. *J'g 1:5*
Hittites, and Amorites, and P. *J'g 3:5;*
Ne 9:8
P., Hivites, and Jebusites, *1Ki 9:20*
the Canaanites, the Hittites, the *Ezr 9:1*
P.

PERJURE

Thou shalt not p. thyself (S) *M't 5:33*

PERJURED

for liars, for p. persons, and if *1Ti 1:10*

PERMANENT

p. solid reward (P) *2Co 4:17*
are really p. (P) *2Co 4:18*
p. house in heaven (P) *2Co 5:1*
p. warning of fire of judgment *Jude 7*
(P)

PERMISSION

when he had given p. (S) *Acts 21:40*

given p. to (P) *M't 19:8*
give p. (B) *Lu 8:32*
But I speak this by p. and not *1Co 7:6*

PERMIT

did not p. (A) *Ge 31:7;*
M'k 5:19; Lu 4:41; Ac 16:7; 19:30
did not p. (R) *Ge 31:7; 31:28*
permit (S) *Ex 12:23;*
Nu 21:23; Jos 10:19; J'g 16:25; 2Sa 14:
11; M't 3:15; 8:21, 31; 19:14; 23:13;
M'k 7:12; 10:14; Lu 9:59; 22:51; Ac 21:
39; 1Co 10:13; 1Ti 2:12; Re 11:9
not p. (R) *Ex 22:18;*
1Ki 15:17; Ps 55:22; M't 23:13;
M'k 7:12; 1Ti 2:12
permit (S) *Jos 10:19;*
M't 3:15; 19:14; M'k 10:14; Lu 22:51
let (B) *J'g 16:26;*
Job 9:18; Pr 10:3; Ec 5:12; Eze 44:20;
Ac 21:39
let (R) *J'g 16:26;*
Ps 16:10; Eze 44:20; M't 3:15; 8:21;
19:14; M'k 10:14; Lu 8:32; 9:59; 18:16;
Ac 2:27; 13:35; 1Co 10:13; Re 11:9
p. them *1Sa 24:7*
p. it (A) *M't 3:15 M'k 11:16; Lu 9:59*
let (N) *M't 3:15;*
8:21; 19:14; M'k 10:14; Lu 8:32; 9:59;
18:16; 22:51; Ac 2:27; 13:35
let (P) *M't 3:15; Lu 8:32; 12:39*
permit (B) *M't 8:21;*
Ac 2:27; 1Co 10:13
permit (B)(R) *M'k 1:34;*
Ac 16:7; 19:30
wind did not p. (A) *Ac 27:7*
a while with you, if the Lord *1Co 16:7*
p.
do not p. (N) *1Ti 2:12*
And this will we do, if God p. *Heb 6:3*

PERMITTED

permitted (B) *Ge 31:7*
De 18:14; J'g 3:28; M't 19:8; M'k 5:37;
10:4; Lu 8:32; 12:39
permitted (S) *Ge 31:28;*
De 18:14; J'g 3:28; 1Sa 24:7; Ps 105:14;
M't 19:8; M'k 1:34; 5:19, 37; 10:4;
Lu 8:32; 12:39; Ac 19:30; 27:7; 28:16
p. not (A) *J'g 3:28;*
M't 16:8; M'k 8:51; Lu 12:39; Ac 14:16;
28:16
no longer p. (N) *M'k 7:12*
Moses (N) *M'k 10:4*
he p. no man (R) *Lu 8:51*
Thou art p. to speak for thyself *Ac 26:1*
p. not to live (A) *Ac 28:4*
it is not p. to them to speak *1Co 14:34*

PERMITTETH

p. not their cattle to decrease *Ps 107:38*
(S)

PERNICIOUS

many shall follow their p. ways *2Pe 2:2*

PERPETUAL

is with you, for p. generations *Ge 9:12*
a p. ordinance (B) *Ex 28:43;*
Le 3:17; 10:15; 16:29, 31, 34; 23:14, 41;
Da 6:7
shall be theirs for a p. statute *Ex 29:9*
a p. obligation (B) *Ex 29:28*
a p. incense before the Lord *Ex 30:8*
generations, for a covenant *Ex 31:16*
a p. statute for your *Le 3:17*
generations
fine flour for a meat offering p. *Le 6:20*
Lord made by fire by a p. *Le 24:9*
statute
sold; for it is their p. *Le 25:34*
possession
it shall be a p. statute unto *Nu 19:21*
them
destructions are come to a p. *Ps 9:6*
end
thy feet unto the p. desolations *Ps 74:3*
he put them to a p. reproach *Ps 78:66*
bound of the sea by a p. decree *Jer 5:22*
slidden back by a p. backsliding *Jer 8:5*
turned away in p. backsliding *Jer 8:5*
(B)(R)
Why is my pain p. and my *Jer 15:18*
wound
land desolate, and a p. hissing *Jer 18:16*

and a p. shame, which shall *Jer 23:40*
not
and an hissing, and p. *Jer 25:9*
desolations
and will make it p. *Jer 25:12*
desolations
the cities thereof shall be p. *Jer 49:13*
wastes
to the Lord in a p. covenant *Jer 50:5*
that
and sleep a p. sleep, and not *Jer 51:39*
wake
shall sleep a p. sleep, and not *Jer 51:57*
wake
Because thou hast had a p. *Eze 35:5*
hatred
will make thee p. desolations *Eze 35:9*
by a p. ordinance unto the *Eze 46:14*
Lord
scattered, the p. hills did bow *Hab 3:6*
and saltpits, and a p. *Zep 2:9*
desolation
p. contention (A)(B) *1Ti 6:5*
exhibit of p. punishment (A) *Jude 7*

PERPETUALLY

mine heart shall be there p. *1Ki 9:3;*
2Ch 7:16
all pity, and his anger did tear *Am 1:11*
p.

PERPETUATE

to p. our family (B) *Ge 19:32*

PERPLEX

p. with discussions (A) *Ro 14:1*

PERPLEXED

drink; but the city Shushan was *Es 3:15*
Daniel was p. (S) *Da 4:19*
rulers were p. (B)(E)(R)(S) *Da 5:9*
the herds of cattle are p. *Joe 1:18*
because
And he was p. because that it *Lu 9:7*
was
as they were much p. *Lu 24:4*
thereabout
perplexed *Ac 2:12; 5:24; 10:17; 25:20*
we are p. but not in despair *2Co 4:8*

PERPLEXITY

and of p. by the Lord God of *Isa 22:5*
hosts
cometh; now shall be their p. *Mic 7:4*
earth distress of nations, with *Lu 21:25*
p.

PERSECUTE

Why do ye p. me as God, *Job 19:22*
and are
Why p. we him, seeing the *Job 19:28*
root of
save me from them that p. me *Ps 7:1*
from all who pursue me *Ps 7:1*
(B)(E)(R)
Let the enemy p. my soul *Ps 7:5*
Let the enemy pursue *Ps 7:5*
(A)(B)(E)(R)
in his pride doth p. the poor *Ps 10:2*
pursue the afflicted (B)(R) *Ps 10:2*
the poor are hotly pursued (E) *Ps 10:2*
from them that p. me *Ps 31:15;*
35:3; 119:84, 86; Jer 17:18
pursue me (A)(B) *Ps 31:15; 35:3*
my persecutors (R) *Ps 31:15*
let angel of the Lord p. them *Ps 35:6*
pursuing and afflicting them *Ps 35:6*
(A)(B)(E)(R)
they p. him whom thou hast *Ps 69:26*
smitten
P. and take him *Ps 71:11*
chase and seize him (B) *Ps 71:11*
pursue and take him (E) *Ps 71:11*
pursue and seize him (R) *Ps 71:11*
So p. them with thy tempest *Ps 83:15*
pursue and afflict them *Ps 83:15*
(A)(B)(E)(R)
I will p. them with the sword *Jer 29:18*
pursue with sword *Jer 29:18*
(A)(B)(E)(R)
P. and destroy them in anger *La 3:66*
pursue and afflict them *La 3:66*
(A)(B)(E)(R)

PERSECUTE

men shall revile and *p.* you   *M't 5:11;*
  5:44; 10:23; Lu 21:12; Joh 15:20;
  Ro 12:14
p. them from city to city   *M't 23:34;*
  Lu 11:49
therefore did Jews *p.* Jesus   *Joh 5:16*

PERSECUTED

that hate thee, which *p.* thee   *De 30:7*
but *p.* the poor and needy   *Ps 109:16*
man
have *p.* me without a cause   *Ps 119:161*
For the enemy hath *p.* my   *Ps 143:3*
soul; he
ruled the nations in anger,   *Isa 14:6*
is *p.*
covered with anger, and *p.* us   *La 3:43*
are *p.* for righteousness' sake   *M't 5:10*
so *p.* they the prophets which   *M't 5:12*
were
If they have *p.* me, they will   *Joh 15:20*
also
prophets have not your fathers   *Ac 7:52*
p.
p. those who called (P)   *Ac 9:21*
And I *p.* this way unto the   *Ac 22:4*
death
I *p.* them even unto strange   *Ac 26:11*
cities
we bless; being *p.* we suffer it   *1Co 4:12*
because I *p.* the church of   *1Co 15:9*
God
P. but not forsaken; cast down   *2Co 4:9*
measure I *p.* the church of God   *Ga 1:13*
he which *p.* us in times past   *Ga 1:23*
p. him that was born after the   *Ga 4:29*
own prophets, and have *p.* us   *1Th 2:15*
p. and insulted (P)(R)   *1Ti 1:13*
p. the woman which brought   *Re 12:13*
forth

PERSECUTEST

him, Saul, Saul, why *p.* thou me   *Ac 9:4*
said, I am Jesus whom thou *p.*   *Ac 9:5;*
  26:15
me, Saul, Saul, why *p.* thou me   *Ac 22:7*
Jesus of Nazareth, whom thou   *Ac 22:8*
p.
Saul, Saul, why *p.* thou me? it   *Ac 26:14*
is

PERSECUTING

Concerning zeal, *p.* the church   *Ph'p 3:6*

PERSECUTION

Our necks are under *p.*: we   *La 5:5*
or *p.* ariseth because of the   *M'k 13:21*
word
or *p.* ariseth for the word's   *M'k 4:17*
sake
p. ariseth   *M'k 4:17*
(A)(B)(E)(N)(P)(R)
was a great *p.* against the   *Ac 8:1*
church
the *p.* that arose about   *Ac 11:19*
Stephen
and raised *p.* against Paul and   *Ac 13:50*
p.
shall tribulation, or distress, or   *Ro 8:35*
circumcision, why do   *Ga 5:11*
I suffer *p.*
suffer *p.* for the cross of Christ   *Ga 6:12*
much *p.* (A)(P)   *1Th 1:6*
p. an outrage (N)   *1Ti 1:13*
godly in Christ Jesus shall   *2Ti 3:12*
suffer *p.*

PERSECUTIONS

and children, and lands, with   *M'k 10:30*
p.
p. in distresses for Christ's   *2Co 12:10*
sake
faith in all your *p.* and   *2Th 1:4*
tribulations
p. and distresses (B)(E)(R)   *2Th 1:4*
P., afflictions, which came   *2Ti 3:11*
unto me
at Lystra; what *p.* I endured   *2Ti 3:11*

PERSECUTOR

before a blasphemer, and a *p.*   *1Ti 1:13*
p. and an oppressor (B)   *1Ti 1:13*

PERSECUTORS

p. thou threwest into the deeps   *Ne 9:11*
his arrows against the *p.*   *Ps 7:13*
are my *p.* and mine enemies   *Ps 119:157*
very low: deliver me from my   *Ps 142:6*
p.
me, and revenge me of my *p.*   *Jer 15:15*
therefore my *p.* shall stumble   *Jer 20:11*
all her *p.* overtook her between   *La 1:3*
Our *p.* are swifter than the   *La 4:19*
eagles

PERSEVERANCE

with all *p.* and supplication   *Eph 6:18*
for

PERSIA

the reign of the kingdom of   *2Ch 36:20*
P.
the first year of Cyrus king   *2Ch 36:22;*
of *P.*   *Ezr 1:1*
up the spirit of Cyrus king   *2Ch 36:22;*
of *P.*   *Ezr 1:1*
Thus saith Cyrus king of *P.,*   *2Ch 36:23*
All the
saith Cyrus king of *P.* The Lord   *Ezr 1:2*
did Cyrus king of *P.* bring   *Ezr 1:8*
forth
that they had of Cyrus king of   *Ezr 3:7*
P.
the king of *P.* hath commanded   *Ezr 4:3*
us
all the days of Cyrus king of *P.*   *Ezr 4:5*
the reign of Darius king of *P.*   *Ezr 4:5*
wrote unto Artaxerxes king   *Ezr 4:7*
of *P.*
of the reign of Darius king   *Ezr 4:24;*
of *P.*   *7:1*
Darius, and Artaxerxes king   *Ezr 6:14*
of *P.*
us in the sight of the kings of   *Ezr 9:9*
P.
the power of *P.* and Media, the   *Es 1:3*
the seven princes of *P.* and   *Es 1:14*
Media
shall the ladies of *P.* and Media   *Es 1:18*
say
of the kings of Media and *P.*   *Es 10:2*
They of *P.* and of Lud and of   *Eze 27:10*
Phut
P., Ethiopia, and Libya with   *Eze 38:5*
them
are the kings of Media and *P.*   *Da 8:20*
the third year of Cyrus king of   *Da 10:1*
P.
But the prince of the   *Da 10:13*
kingdom of *P.*
remained with the kings of   *Da 10:13*
P.
to fight with the prince of *P.*   *Da 10:20*
stand up yet three kings in *P.*   *Da 11:2*

PERSIAN

the *P.* commander (A)   *Ezr 4:8*
to the reign of Darius the *P.*   *Ne 12:22*
and in the reign of Cyrus the   *Da 6:28*
P.

PERSIANS

the laws of the *P.* and the   *Es 1:19*
Medes
and given to the Medes and *P.*   *Da 5:28*
to the law of the Medes and   *Da 6:8;*
P.   *6:12*
that the law of the Medes and   *Da 6:15*
P.

PERSIS

Salute the beloved *P.* which   *Ro 16:12*

PERSIST

if we *p.* in sin after (N)   *Heb 10:26*

PERSISTENCE

his shameless *p.* (A)   *Lu 11:8*
patient *p.* in (A)(N)   *Ro 2:7*

PERSISTS

yet if he *p.* (P)   *Lu 11:8*

PERSON

that *p.* (B)   *Ge 17:14;*
  Ex 12:15, 19; Le 17:10; 22:3; 23:30;
  Nu 15:31
Joseph was a goodly *p.* and   *Ge 39:6*
well
that *p.* (R)   *Ge 12:15;*
  12:19; Le 17:10; 22:3; 23:30; Nu 15:31
no uncircumcised *p.* shall eat   *Ex 12:48*
thereof
person (B)   *Le 4:2;*
  5:1, 4, 17; 6:2; 22:11; 23:30; Nu 9:13;
  Pr 19:15; Ro 13:1
not respect the *p.* of the poor   *Le 19:15*
nor honour the *p.* of the   *Le 19:15*
mighty
if a *p.* turns to mediums   *Le 20:6*
(B)(N)(P)
if a priest buy any *p.* (S)   *Le 22:11*
person (R)   *Le 23:30;*
  Nu 9:13; Ro 13:1
when commit any sin that *p.* be   *Nu 5:6*
guilty
p. does anything wilfully (A)   *Nu 15:20*
for an unclean *p.* shall take of   *Nu 19:17*
the ashes
clean *p.* shall take hyssop and   *Nu 19:18*
dip it in water
And the clean *p.* shall sprinkle   *Nu 19:19*
upon
whatsoever unclean *p.*   *Nu 19:22*
toucheth, be unclean
whosoever hath killed any *p.*   *Nu 31:19;*
or touched any slain   *35:11, 15, 30;*
  Jos 20:3, 9
one witness shall not testify   *Nu 35:30*
against any *p.*
unclean and clean *p.* shall eat   *De 15:22*
it alike
that taketh reward to slay an   *De 27:25*
innocent *p.*
shall not regard the *p.* of old   *De 28:50*
or young
that killeth any *p.* unawares   *Jos 20:3*
that whosoever killeth any *p.*   *Jos 20:9*
of Israel a goodlier *p.* than he   *1Sa 9:2*
prudent in matters, and a   *1Sa 16:18*
comely *p.*
voice, and have accepted thy   *1Sa 25:35*
p.
men have slain a righteous *p.*   *2Sa 4:11*
in
neither doth God respect any   *2Sa 14:14*
p.
thou go to battle in thine   *2Sa 17:11*
own *p.*
Will ye accept his *p.*? will ye   *Job 13:8*
up; and he shall save the   *Job 22:29*
humble *p.*
I pray you, accept any man's   *Job 32:21*
p.
In whose eyes a vile *p.* is   *Ps 15:4*
contemned
converting the whole *p.* (A)   *Ps 19:7*
the fool and the brutish *p.*   *Ps 49:10*
perish
from me: I will not know a   *Ps 101:4*
wicked *p.*
not one feeble *p.* among their   *Ps 105:37*
tribes
A naughty *p.* a wicked man   *Pr 6:12*
person (A)   *Pr 11:25;*
  19:15; Jer 31:25; Ro 13:1
to accept the *p.* of the wicked   *Pr 18:5*
shall be called a mischievous *p.*   *Pr 24:8*
violence to the blood of any *p.*   *Pr 28:17*
The vile *p.* shall be no more   *Isa 32:5*
called
the vile *p.* will speak villainy,   *Isa 32:6*
and his
every *p.* that Nebuzar-adan the   *Jer 43:6*
them that were near the   *Jer 52:25*
king's *p.*
to the lothing of thy *p.* in the   *Eze 16:5*
day
and take any *p.* from among   *Eze 33:6*
them
shall come at no dead *p.* to   *Eze 44:25*
defile
in his estate shall stand up a   *Da 11:21*
vile *p.*
or accept thy *p.*? saith the   *Mal 1:8*
Lord
thou regardest not the *p.* of   *M't 22:16;*
men   *M'k 12:14*
innocent of the blood of this   *M't 27:24*
just *p.*
neither acceptest thou the *p.*   *Lu 20:21*
of any

no *p.* justified (A) | Ro 3:20
every *p.* be subject (N) | Ro 13:1
from among yourselves that | 1Co 5:13
wicked (A)
forgave I it in the *p.* of Christ | 2Co 2:10
a new *p.* altogether (P) | 2Co 5:17
to me: God accepteth no man's | Ga 2:6
p.
nor unclean *p.* nor covetous | Eph 5:5
man
a factious *p.* (B)(E)(R) | Tit 3:10
such a *p.* is distorted (B) | Tit 3:11
and the express image of his *p.* | Heb 1:3
any fornicator, or profane *p.* | Heb 12:16
as Esau
but saved Noah the eighth *p.* a | 2Pe 2:5

PERSONAL

dream with *p.* significance (B) | Ge 40:5
my *p.* possession (B)(E)(R) | Ex 19:5;
 | Ps 135:4
p. contribution (A) | 2Ch 31:3
revealing *p.* opinions | Pr 18:2
(A)(B)(R)
property and *p.* belongings (A) | Lu 8:2
his *p.* attendant's (A)(B)(P) | Ac 10:7
p. pledge of redemption (P) | Eph 4:30
p. or special interpretation | 2Pe 1:20
(A)
made *p.* atonement for our | 1Jo 2:2;
sins (P) | 4:10

PERSONALLY

p. decide right (B)(P) | Lu 12:57
p. implemented promises (P) | Ro 15:9

PERSONNEL

the *p.* they had obtained (B) | Ge 12:5

PERSONS

said unto Abram, Give me the | Ge 14:21
p.
and all the *p.* of his house, and | Ge 36:6
his
according to the number of | Ex 16:16
your *p*
the *p.* shall be for the Lord by | Le 27:2
thy
and upon the *p.* that were | Nu 19:18
there
soul of five hundred, both of | Nu 31:28
the *p.*
take one portion of fifty, of | Nu 31:30
the *p.*
and two thousand *p.* in all | Nu 31:35
the *p.* were sixteen thousand | Nu 31:40
tribute was thirty and two *p.* | Nu 31:40
And sixteen thousand *p.* | Nu 31:46
shall not respect *p.* in judgment | De 1:17
which regardeth not *p.* nor | De 10:17
taketh
Egypt with threescore and | De 10:22
ten *p.*
thou shalt not respect *p.* | De 16:19
neither
which are threescore and ten *p.* | J'g 9:2
Abimelech hired vain and light | J'g 9:4
p.
being threescore and ten *p.* upon | J'g 9:5
threescore and ten *p.* upon one | J'g 9:18
of the men of Israel about | J'g 20:39
thirty *p.*
bidden, which were about | 1Sa 9:22
thirty *p.*
five *p.* that did wear a linen | 1Sa 22:18
ephod
of all the *p.* of thy father's | 1Sa 22:22
house
the king's sons, being seventy | 2Ki 10:6
p.
slew seventy *p.* and put their | 2Ki 10:7
heads
nor respect of *p.* nor taking of | 2Ch 19:7
you, if ye do secretly accept | Job 13:10
p.
that accepteth not the *p.* of | Job 34:19
princes
I have not sat with vain *p.* | Ps 26:4
neither
and accept the *p.* of the wicked | Ps 82:2
he that followeth vain *p.* is | Pr 12:11
void of
not good to have respect of *p.* | Pr 24:23
after vain *p.* shall have | Pr 28:19
poverty
To have respect of *p.* is not | Pr 28:21
good

respecting *p.* showing partiality | Isa 3:9
(A)(R)
eight hundred thirty and two | Jer 52:29
p.
seven hundred forty and five | Jer 52:30
p.
the *p.* were four thousand and | Jer 52:30
six
respected not the *p.* of the | La 4:16
priests
building forts, to cut off | Eze 17:17
many *p.*
traded the *p.* of men and | Eze 27:13
vessels
are more than sixscore | Jon 4:11
thousand *p.*
are light and treacherous *p.* | Zep 3:4
means: will he regard your *p.* | Mal 1:9
than over ninety and nine just | Lu 15:7
p.
that God is no respecter of *p.* | Ac 10:34
with the Jews, and with the | Ac 17:17
devout
there is no respect of *p.* with | Ro 2:11
God
upon us by the means of | 2Co 1:11
many *p.*
is there respect of *p.* with him | Eph 6:9
done: and there is no respect | Col 3:25
of *p.*
for liars, for perjured *p.* and if | 1Ti 1:10
Lord of glory, with respect of *p.* | Jas 2:1
if ye have respect to *p.* ye | Jas 2:9
commit
who without respect of *p.* | 1Pe 1:17
judgeth
what manner of *p.* ought ye to | 2Pe 3:11
be in
having men's *p.* in admiration | Jude 16

PERSUADE

Who shall *p.* Ahab, that he | 1Ki 22:20
may
the Lord, and said, I will *p.* | 1Ki 22:21
him
Thou shalt *p.* him, and | 1Ki 22:22
prevail
Doth not Hezekiah *p.* you to | 2Ch 32:11
give
you, nor *p.* you on | 2Ch 32:15
this manner
Beware lest Hezekiah *p.* you | Isa 36:18
tried to *p.* king (A) | Jer 36:25
we will *p.* him, and secure | M't 28:14
you
the terror of the Lord, we *p.* | 2Co 5:11
men
For do I now *p.* men, or God | Ga 1:10

PERSUADED

p. him to stay (B) | 2Ki 4:8
and *p.* him to go up with him | 2Ch 18:2
By long forbearing is a prince | Pr 25:15
p.
and elders *p.* the multitude | M't 27:20
that
neither will they be *p.* though | Lu 16:31
one
they be *p.* that John was a | Lu 20:6
prophet
p. them to continue in the | Ac 13:43
grace of
who *p.* the people, and, having | Ac 14:19
and *p.* the Jews and the Greeks | Ac 18:4
p. and turned away much | Ac 19:26
people
And when he would not be *p.* | Ac 21:14
I am *p.* that none of these | Ac 26:26
things
And being fully *p.* that, what | Ro 4:21
he
For I am *p.* that neither death | Ro 8:38
man be fully *p.* in his own | Ro 14:5
mind
and am *p.* by the Lord Jesus | Ro 14:14
also am *p.* of you, my | Ro 15:14
brethren
and I am *p.* that in thee, also | 2Ti 1:5
and am *p.* that he is able to | 2Ti 1:12
keep
we are *p.* better things of you | Heb 6:9
were *p.* of them, and | Heb 11:13
embraced

PERSUADEST

thou *p.* me to be a Christian | Ac 26:28

PERSUADETH

unto Hezekiah, when he *p.* | 2Ki 18:32
you
This fellow *p.* men to worship | Ac 18:13
God

PERSUADING

and *p.* the things concerning | Ac 19:8
spoke boldly, *p.*, pleading | Ac 19:8
(A)(E)(R)
p. them concerning Jesus, | Ac 28:23
both out

PERSUASION

using argument and *p.* (N)(P) | Ac 19:8
p. cometh not of him that | Ga 5:8
calleth

PERSUASIVELY

p. discussing kingdom of God | Ac 19:8
(B)

PERTAIN

peace offerings, that *p.* unto the | Le 7:20
Lord
offerings, which *p.* unto the | Le 7:21
Lord
if I leave of all that *p.* to him | 1Sa 25:22
in those things which *p.* to | Ro 15:17
God
much more things that *p.* to | 1Co 6:3
this life
unto us all things that *p.* unto | 2Pe 1:3
life

PERTAINED

half that *p.* unto the | Nu 31:43
congregation
in a hill that *p.* to Phinehas | Jos 24:33
his son
that *p.* unto Joash the | J'g 6:11
Abi-ezrite
was missed of all that *p.* unto | 1Sa 25:21
him
which *p.* to Ish-bosheth the | 2Sa 2:15
son of
p. to Saul and to all his house | 2Sa 9:9
are all that *p.* unto | 2Sa 16:4
Mephibosheth
to him *p.* Sochoh, and all the | 1Ki 4:10
land of
to him *p.* Taanach and | 1Ki 4:12
Megiddo, and
to him *p.* the towns of Jair | 1Ki 4:13
son of
to him also *p.* the region of | 1Ki 4:13
Argob
all the vessels that *p.* unto the | 1Ki 7:48
house
all that *p.* to the king of Egypt | 2Ki 24:7
thereof every morning *p.* to | 1Ch 9:27
them
that *p.* to the children of | 1Ch 11:31
Benjamin
the fenced cities which *p.* to | 2Ch 12:4
Judah
that *p.* to the children of | 2Ch 34:33
Israel

PERTAINETH

got that which *p.* to his | Le 14:32
cleansing
the priest *p.* the oil for the | Nu 4:16
light
wear that which *p.* unto a man | De 22:5
Ziklag *p.* unto the kings of | 1Sa 27:6
Judah
Obed-edom, and all that *p.* | 2Sa 6:12
unto him
to whom *p.* the adoption, and | Ro 9:4
are spoken *p.* to another tribe | Heb 7:13

PERTAINING

were *p.* unto the children | Jos 13:31
of Machir
every matter *p.* to God, and | 1Ch 26:32
affairs
things *p.* to the kingdom of God | Ac 1:3
as *p.* to the flesh, hath found | Ro 4:1
judgments of things *p.* to this | 1Co 6:4
life
high priest in things *p.* to | Heb 2:17
God

PERTAINING

ordained for men in things *p.*   *Heb 5:1*
to God
perfect, as *p.* to the conscience *Heb 9:9*

PERTURBED

he was *p.* (N)(R)   *M't 2:3;*
           Lu 24:28; 1Pe 3:14
Mary was greatly *p.* (P)   *Lu 1:29*

PERUDA

of Sophereth, the children of   *Ezr 2:55*
P.

PERVERSE

it is *p.* (B)   *Le 18:2; 20:13*
because thy way is *p.* before   *Nu 22:32*
me
are wilfully obstinate and   *Nu 22:32*
contrary (A)
your road leads headlong into *Nu 22:32*
destruction (B)
are a *p.* and crooked   *De 32:5*
generation
a twisted and crooked race   *De 32:5*
(B)
son of the *p.* rebellious   *1Sa 20:30*
woman
son of rebellious,   *1Sa 20:30*
undisciplined woman (B)
p. way servant acted (B)   *2Sa 19:19*
show thyself *p.* (R)(S)   *2Sa 22:27*
Cannot my taste discern *p.*   *Job 6:30*
things
Cannot my taste discern   *Job 6:30*
mischievous (E)
Cannot my taste discern   *Job 6:30*
calamity (R)
it shall also prove me *p.*   *Job 9:20*
p. nature be absent (B)(S)   *Ps 101:4*
speaketh *p.* things (S)   *Pr 2:12*
p. in their paths (S)   *Pr 2:15*
the *p.* is an abomination (S)   *Pr 3:32*
p. lips put far from me   *Pr 4:24*
willful and contrary talk put   *Pr 4:24*
away (A)
put devious talk far away (R)   *Pr 4:24*
walketh with a *p.* mouth (S)   *Pr 6:12;*
           8:13
is nothing forward or *p.* in them *Pr 8:8*
nothing contrary to truth or   *Pr 8:8*
crooked in (A)
nothing twisted or crooked in   *Pr 8:8*
them (B)(R)
the *p.* tongue shall be cut out *Pr 10:31*
(S)
the *p.* heart an abomination   *Pr 11:20*
(S)
a *p.* heart shall be despised   *Pr 12:8*
a man with twisted thought   *Pr 12:8*
shall be (B)
is *p.* in his ways despiseth him *Pr 14:2*
contrary and devious in his   *Pr 14:2*
ways (A)
A *p.* man soweth strife (S)   *Pr 16:28*
shutteth his eyes to *p.* things   *Pr 16:30*
(B)(R)(S)
a *p.* tongue falleth into   *Pr 17:20*
mischief
a willful and contrary tongue   *Pr 17:20*
will (A)
a perverted tongue fall into   *Pr 17:20*
trouble (B)
a *p.* heart findeth no good (S) *Pr 17:20*
he that is *p.* in his lips, and a *Pr 19:1*
fool
snares are in the way of the *p.* *Pr 22:5*
(S)
thine heart shall utter *p.* things *Pr 23:33*
your mind will utter things   *Pr 23:33*
turned the wrong way, untrue,
incorrect, petulant (A)
your mind will utter   *Pr 23:33*
upside-down things (B)
he that is *p.* in his ways   *Pr 28:6; 28:18*
willfully goes in double and   *Pr 28:6*
wrong ways (A)
Lord hath mingled and *p.*   *Isa 19:14*
spirit
mingled a spirit of   *Isa 19:14*
perverseness (B)
mingled a spirit of error (B)   *Isa 19:14*
mingled with a spirit of   *Isa 19:14*
confusion (R)
heart exceedingly *p.* (A)   *Jer 17:9*
faithless and *p.* generation   *M't 17:17;*
           Lu 9:41

unbelieving and rebellious   *M't 17:17*
generation (B)
an unbelieving and difficult   *M't 17:17*
people (P)
p. generation (A)(P)   *Ac 2:4*
men arise, speaking *p.* things *Ac 20:30*
teach distorted things (B)   *Ac 20:30*
will distort truth to induce   *Ac 20:30*
disciples (N)
speaking perversions of truth *Ac 20:30*
(P)
midst of crooked and *p.*   *Ph'p 2:15*
nation
crooked and wicked   *Ph'p 2:15*
generation (A)
crooked and distorted   *Ph'p 2:15*
generation (B)
warped and crooked   *Ph'p 2:15*
generation (N)
warped and diseased world   *Ph'p 2:15*
(P)
p. and wicked men (A)   *2Th 3:2*
P. disputings of men of corrupt *1Ti 6:5*
mind
protracted wrangling, wearing *1Ti 6:5*
discussion, and perpetual friction
among men (A)
perpetual contention between *1Ti 6:5*
(B)
wranglings of men corrupted *1Ti 6:5*
(E)
slander, base suspicions, endless *1Ti 6:5*
wrangles (N)(R)
insults, continual wrangling (P) *1Ti 6:5*
but also to the *p.* (S)   *1Pe 2:18*

PERVERSELY

that which thy servant did *p.* *2Sa 19:19*
the perverse way your   *2Sa 19:19*
servant acted (B)
your servant did wrong (R)   *2Sa 19:19*
have sinned and done *p.*   *1Ki 8:47*
have sinned and done wrong *1Ki 8:47*
(B)
we have done *p.* (R)   *1Ki 8:47*
we have done *p.* (B)(E)(R)   *2Ch 6:37*
They have dealt *p.* with me *Ps 119:78*
have distorted my cause   *Ps 119:78*
deceitfully (B)
have overthrown me   *Ps 119:78*
wrongfully (E)
have subverted me with guile *Ps 119:78*
(R)
he deals *p.* (A)   *Isa 26:10*

PERVERSENESS

hath he seen *p.* in Israel   *Nu 23:21*
has not witnessed mischief in *Nu 23:21*
(B)
has he seen trouble in Israel *Nu 23:21*
(R)
delight in *p.* of evil (A)(E)(S) *Pr 2:14*
the wicked speak *p.* (S)   *Pr 10:32*
p. of transgressors shall destroy *Pr 11:3*
contrariness, crookedness of *Pr 11:3*
treacherous (B)
glibness of the treacherous   *Pr 11:3*
destroys (B)
crookedness of the treacherous *Pr 11:3*
(R)
p. therein is a breach in the *Pr 15:4*
spirit
willful contrariness breaks (A) *Pr 15:4*
perversity in tongue breaks (B) *Pr 15:4*
a spirit of *p.* (A)(B)   *Isa 19:14*
trust in oppression and *p.*   *Isa 30:12*
trusted in oppression and   *Isa 30:12*
crookedness (B)
your tongue hath muttered *p.* *Isa 59:3*
tongue utters wickedness   *Isa 59:3*
(A)(E)
tongue muttered injustice (B) *Isa 59:3*
lips have spoken lies (R)   *Isa 59:3*
the city full of *p.*   *Eze 9:9*
city full of injustice (B)(R)   *Eze 9:9*
city full of wresting of   *Eze 9:9*
judgment (E)
cause me to see *p.* (A)(B)(E) *Hab 1:3*

PERVERSION

it is *p.* (B)(R)   *Le 18:23*
no *p.* of justice with God (R) *2Ch 19:7*
to sexual immorality and *p.* (P) *Jude 7*

PERVERSIONS

speaking *p.* of truth (P)   *Ac 22:30*

PERVERSITY

p. is in his heart (S)   *Pr 6:14*
p. in tongue breaks (B)   *Pr 15:4*
gave themselves to sexual *p.* (A) *Jude 7*

PERVERT

p. the words of the righteous *De 16:19*
subverts cause of the innocent *De 16:19*
(B)
p. the judgment of the   *De 24:17*
stranger
violate rights of the   *De 24:17*
immigrant (B)
wrest justice of the sojourner *De 24:17*
(E)
Doth God *p.* judgment; *p.*   *Job 8:3;*
justice   *34:12*
will not *p.* justice (B)   *Job 37:22*
to *p.* ways of judgment   *Pr 17:23; 31:5*
p. all equity   *Mic 3:9*
twist everything that is right *Mic 3:9*
(B)
to *p.* the right ways of the   *Ac 13:10*
Lord
plotting against saving   *Ac 13:10*
purposes of God (B)
falsifying straight ways of the *Ac 13:10*
Lord (N)
making crooked straight   *Ac 13:10*
paths of Lord (R)
would *p.* the gospel of Christ *Ga 1:7*
distort the gospel (B)(N)   *Ga 1:7*
upsetting faith with travesty of *Ga 1:7*
gospel (P)
p. grace into lawlessness   *Jude 4*
(A)(B)(N)(R)

PERVERTED

had *p.* their way (B)   *Ge 6:12*
certain *p.* men (B)   *J'g 19:22*
the *p.* fellows (B)   *J'g 20:13*
took bribes, and *p.* judgment *1Sa 8:3*
sinned, and *p.* that which   *Job 33:27*
was right
twisted that which was right *Job 33:27*
(B)
a *p.* tongue fall into trouble *Pr 17:20*
(B)
thy knowledge, it hath *p.* me *Isa 47:10*
your knowledge led you   *Isa 47:10*
astray (A)(R)
knowledge has seduced you *Isa 47:10*
(B)
they have *p.* their way   *Jer 3:21*
they have distorted their way *Jer 3:21*
(B)
p. the words of the living God *Jer 23:36*
justice goeth forth *p.* (S)   *Hab 1:4*
over to *p.* tendencies (B)   *Ro 1:28*
sexually uncontrolled, *p.* (P) *1Ti 1:10*
is *p.* and corrupted   *Tit 3:11*
(A)(E)(R)
bent on *p.* sensuality (B)   *Jude 8*

PERVERTETH

p. the words of the righteous *Ex 23:8*
thwarts the just man's   *Ex 23:8*
testimony (B)
subverts the cause of the right *Ex 23:8*
(R)
cursed is he that *p.* judgment *De 27:19*
that *p.* his ways shall be known *Pr 10:9*
who takes a crooked way (A) *Pr 10:9*
who takes a crooked course (B) *Pr 10:9*
foolishness of man *p.* his way *Pr 19:3*
foolishness of man subverts his *Pr 19:3*
way (A)(E)
foolishness of man ruins his *Pr 19:3*
affairs (B)
folly brings his way to ruin (R) *Pr 19:3*
as one that *p.* the people   *Lu 23:14*
inducing people to rebellion   *Lu 23:14*
(B)
a charge of subversion (N)   *Lu 23:14*
as a mischief maker (P)   *Lu 23:14*

PERVERTING

violent *p.* of judgment   *Ec 5:8*
violent taking away justice   *Ec 5:8*
(A)(E)(R)
seizure of justice (B)   *Ec 5:8*
We found this fellow *p.* the *Lu 23:2*
nation
subverting our nation (N)   *Lu 23:2*
corrupting our people (P)   *Lu 23:2*

PERVERTS

for sexual *p.* (B)(N)   *1Ti 1:10*

PEST

a perfect *p.* (A)(N)   *Ac 24:5*

PESTILENCE

he fall upon us with *p.* or with	*Ex 5:3*
smite thee and thy people with	*Ex 9:15*
p.	
I will send the *p.* among you	*Le 26:25*
I will smite them with the *p.*	*Nu 14:12*
shall make the *p.* cleave unto	*De 28:21*
thee	
every sickness and *p.* (B)	*De 28:61*
deadly *p.* (A)(B)(R)	*De 32:24*
there be three days' *p.* in thy	*2Sa 24:13*
land	
So the Lord sent *p.* upon	*2Sa 24:15*
Israel	
be in the land famine, if there	*1Ki 8:37*
be *p.*	
even the *p.* in the land, and	*1Ch 21:12*
So the Lord sent *p.* upon	*1Ch 21:14*
Israel	
if there be *p.* if there be	*2Ch 6:28*
blasting	
or if I send *p.* among my	*2Ch 7:13*
people	
sword, judgment, or *p.* or	*2Ch 20:9*
famine	
but gave their life over to the	*Ps 78:50*
p.	
fowler, and from the noisome	*Ps 91:3*
p.	
for the *p.* that walketh in	*Ps 91:6*
darkness	
and by the famine, and by the	*Jer 14:12*
p.	
die of the *p.* (E)	*Jer 16:4*
they shall die of a great *p.*	*Jer 21:6*
as are left in this city from the	*Jer 21:7*
p.	
and by the famine, and by the	*Jer 21:9;*
	32:36
famine, and the *p.* among	*Jer 24:10*
them	
with the famine, and with the	*Jer 27:8*
p.	
sword, by the famine, and by	*Jer 27:13;*
the *p.*	*38:2; 42:17; 22; 44:13;*
	Eze 6:11
of war, and of evil, and of *p.*	*Jer 28:8*
the sword, the famine, and	*Jer 29:17*
the *p.*	
the famine, and with the *p.*	*Jer 29:18*
famine, and of the *p.:* and	*Jer 32:24*
sword, to the *p.* and to the	*Jer 34:17*
famine	
A third part shall die with	*Eze 5:12*
the *p.*	
p. and blood shall pass	*Eze 5:17*
through	
He that is far off shall die of	*Eze 6:12*
the *p.*	
and the *p.* and the famine	*Eze 7:15*
within	
famine and *p.* shall devour	*Eze 7:15*
him	
from the famine, and from	*Eze 12:16*
the *p.*	
Or if I send a *p.* into that	*Eze 14:19*
land, and	
the noisome beast, and the *p.*	*Eze 14:21*
I will send into her *p.* and	*Eze 28:23*
blood	
and in the caves shall die of	*Eze 33:27*
the *p.*	
against him with *p.* and with	*Eze 38:22*
blood	
I have sent among you the *p.*	*Am 4:10*
after	
Before him went the *p.* and	*Hab 3:5*

PESTILENCES

p. and earthquakes, in divers	*M't 24:7*
divers places, and famines,	*Lu 21:11*
and *p.*	

PESTILENT

have found this man a *p.*	*Ac 24:5*
fellow	
a perfect pest-a real plague-an	*Ac 24:5*
agitator and source of	
disturbance to all Jews (A)	
a vertible plague (B)	*Ac 24:5*

a perfect pest, a fomenter of	*Ac 24:5*
discord (N)	
a pestilential disturber of peace	*Ac 24:5*
(P)	
a *p.* fellow, an agitator (R)	*Ac 24:5*

PESTILENTIAL

a *p.* disturber of peace (P)   *Ac 24:5*

PESTLE

a mortar among wheat with a   *Pr 27:22*
p.

PETER

when *P.* was come down out	*M't 14:29*
of the ship	
I say also to thee that thou	*M't 16:18*
art *P.*	
he said to *P.* Get thee	*M't 16:23;*
behind me	*M'k 8:33*
he taketh *P.* James and John	*M't 17:1;*
26:37; M'k 5:37; 9:2; 14:33; Lu 8:51;	
	9:28
they that received	*M't 17:24*
tribute money came to *P.*	
P. followed him to the high	*M't 26:58*
priest's palace	
P. remembered words of	*M't 26:75;*
Jesus	*M'k 14:72*
go your way, tell his disciples	*M'k 16:7*
and *P.*	
the Lord turned and looked	*Lu 22:61*
upon *P.*	
Bethsaida, the city of Andrew	*Joh 1:44*
and *P.*	
being his kinsman, whose ear	*Joh 18:26*
P. cut off	
P. was grieved because he	*Joh 21:17*
said unto him	
in those days *P.* stood up in	*Ac 1:15*
the midst	
seeing *P.* and John about to go	*Ac 3:3*
into the temple	
P. filled with the Holy Ghost,	*Ac 4:8*
said to them	
when they saw the boldness of	*Ac 4:13*
P. and John	
at least the shadow of *P.* might	*Ac 5:15*
overshadow	
the apostles sent unto them *P.*	*Ac 8:14*
and John	
the disciples had heard that *P.*	*Ac 9:38*
was there	
P. put them all forth, and	*Ac 9:40*
kneeled down	
there came a voice, Rise, *P.*	*Ac 10:13;*
kill and eat	*11:7*
while *P.* spake these words,	*Ac 10:44*
Holy Ghost fell	
were astonished, as many as	*Ac 10:45*
came with *P.*	
he proceeded further to take	*Ac 12:3*
P. also	
P. was sleeping between two	*Ac 12:6*
soldiers in chains	
the angel of the Lord smote *P.*	*Ac 12:7*
on the side	
as *P.* knocked at the door of	*Ac 12:13*
the gate	
there was no small stir what	*Ac 12:18*
was become of *P.*	
then I went up to Jerusalem to	*Ga 1:18*
see *P.*	
the gospel of circumcision was	*Ga 2:7*
committed to *P.*	
for he that wrought effectually	*Ga 2:8*
in *P.* to the apostleship	
I said unto *P.* before them all,	*Ga 2:14*
If thou be a Jew	

SIMON PETER

Jesus walking, saw *Simon*	*M't 4:18*
called *P.*	
the first *Simon,* who is called	*M't 10:2*
P. and Andrew	
to cast out devils, *Simon* he	*M'k 3:16*
surnamed *P.*	
Simon P. fell down at Jesus'	*Lu 5:8*
knees	
he chose *Simon,* whom he also	*Lu 6:14*
named *P.*	
then cometh he to *Simon P.*	*Joh 13:6*
he saith	
then she runneth and cometh	*Joh 20:2*
to *Simon P.*	
Jesus saith to *Simon P.,*	*Joh 21:15*
Simon son of Jonas	

send men to Joppa, and call	*Ac 10:5;*
for one *Simon,* whose	*10:32; 11:13*
surname is *P.*	

PETER'S

Jesus was come into *P.* house	*M't 8:14*
him, was Andrew, Simon *P.*	*Joh 1:40*
brother	
Andrew, Simon *P.* brother,	*Joh 6:8*
saith	
And when she knew *P.* voice,	*Ac 12:14*
she	

PETHAHIAH

nineteenth to *P.* the	*1Ch 24:16*
twentieth	
Kelaiah, (the same is	*Ezr 10:23*
Kelita,) *P.*	
Hodijah, Shebaniah, and *P.*	*Ne 9:5*
And *P.* the son of	*Ne 11:24*
Meshezabeel, of	

PETHOR

unto Balaam the son of   *Nu 22:5*
Beor to *P.*
Balaam the son of Beor of *P.*   *De 23:4*

PETUEL

that come to Joel the son of *P.* *Joe 1:1*

PETITION

God of Israel grant thee thy *p.*	*1Sa 1:17*
Lord hath given me my *p.*	*1Sa 1:27*
which I	
I ask one *p.* of thee, deny me	*1Ki 2:16*
not	
said, I desire one small *p.* of	*1Ki 2:20*
thee	
What is thy *p.?* and it shall be	*Es 5:6*
and said, My *p.* and my request	*Es 5:7*
is	
if it please the king to grant my	*Es 5:8*
p.	
What is thy *p.* queen Esther	*Es 7:2*
let my life be given me at my *p.*	*Es 7:3*
now that is thy *p.?* and it shall	*Es 9:12*
be	
hide not from my *p.* (B)	*Ps 55:1;*
	119:170
shall ask a *p.* of any God or	*Da 6:7*
man	
making humble *p.* (B)	*Da 6:11*
that shall ask a *p.* of any God	*Da 6:12*
or man	
maketh his *p.* three times a	*Da 6:13*
day	
prayer and *p.* (A)(N)	*Ph'p 4:6*
to make *p.* to God (A)	*Heb 7:25*

PETITIONED

p. the Lord (B)   *J'g 13:8*

PETITIONING

p. judicial hearing (A)   *Ac 25:15*

PETITIONS

does not fear *p.* (B)	*Job 24:12*
banners: the Lord fulfill all thy	*Ps 20:5*
p.	
heed their *p.* (B)	*Isa 19:22*
present our *p.* (B)	*Da 9:18;*
	9:23; 1Ti 2:1; 5:5; Heb 5:7
p., prayers (A)(N)	*1Ti 2:1*
have the *p.* that we desired of	*1Jo 5:15*
him	
the *p.* we asked (E)	*1Jo 5:15*

PETULANT

mind utter things *p.* (A)   *Pr 23:33*

PEULTHAI

the seventh, *P.* the eighth   *1Ch 26:5*

PHALEC

which was the son of *P.* which   *Lu 3:35*

PHALLU

sons of Reuben; Hanoch, and   *Ge 46:9*
P.

PHALTI

his daughter, David's wife,   1Sa 25:44
to P.

PHALTIEL

even from P. the son of Laish   2Sa 3:15

PHANTOMS

despise their. p. (R)   Ps 73:20

PHANUEL

a prophetess, the daughter of   Lu 2:36
P.

PHARAOH

princes commended Sarai   Ge 12:15
before P.
the Lord plagued P. and his   Ge 12:17
house
Potiphar an officer of P.   Ge 39:1
bought Joseph
P. was wroth against two of   Ge 40:2
his officers
P. shall lift up thine head   Ge 40:13;
and restore thee   40:19
make mention of me to P.   Ge 40:14
and bring me out
P. dreamed so P. awoke   Ge 41:1;
                                  41:4
Joseph said, God shall give P. Ge 41:16
answer of peace
let P. do this   Ge 41:34
I am P. and without thee   Ge 41:44
people cried to P. by the life Ge 41:55;
of P.   42:15-16
thou art as P.; made me a   Ge 44:18;
father to P.   45:8
Joseph said, I will go up and   Ge 46:31
shew P.
Jacob blessed P. and went out   Ge 47:10
from P.
speak, I pray you, in the ears Ge 50:4
of P. saying
when P. heard, he sought to   Ex 2:15
slay Moses
come now, and I will send thee Ex 3:10
to P.
see thou do all those wonders   Ex 4:21
before P.
P. said, Who is the Lord that I Ex 5:2
should obey him
then the officers came and   Ex 5:15
cried unto P.
since I came to P. to speak in Ex 5:23
thy name
now shalt thou see what I will Ex 6:1
do to P.
Moses spake, How then shall   Ex 6:12;
P. hear me   6:30
Lord said, See, I have made   Ex 7:1
thee a god to P.
stand before P.; P. sent for   Ex 8:20;
Moses   9:13, 27
yet will I bring one plague   Ex 11:1
more upon P.
Moses and Aaron did all these   Ex 11:10
wonders before P.
from the firstborn of P. on   Ex 12:29
the throne
when P. had let people go   Ex 13:17
God led them not
and I will be honoured upon   Ex 14:4;
P.   14:17
the waters covered all the host Ex 14:28
of P.
Solomon made affinity with P.   1Ki 3:1
Hadad found favour in the   1Ki 11:19
sight of P.
Lord, who brought them   2Ki 17:7
from under P.
so is P. to all that trust in   2Ki 18:21;
him   Isa 36:6
according to the   2Ki 23:35
commandment of P.
thou shewedst signs and   Ne 9:10
wonders on P.
who sent tokens and wonders   Ps 135:9
on P.
but overthrew P. and his host   Ps 136:15
in Red sea
how say ye to P. I am the son   Isa 19:11
of wise
to strengthen themselves in   Isa 30:2
strength of P.
the strength of P. shall be your Isa 30:3
shame

I made P. and his servants to   Jer 25:19
drink
did cry, P. king of Egypt is   Jer 46:17
but a noise
word that came, before that P. Jer 47:1
smote Gaza
P. with his army not make   Eze 17:17
for him
set thy face against P. king of Eze 29:2
Egypt
I am against thee, P. king of   Eze 29:3;
Egypt   30:22
I have broken the arm of P.   Eze 30:21;
                                30:24-25
this is P. and his multitude,   Eze 31:18
saith the Lord
son of man, take up a   Eze 32:2
lamentation for P.
Joseph's kindred made known   Ac 7:13
to P.
for scripture saith to P. I   Ro 9:17
raised thee up

PHARAOH-HOPHRA

will give P. into hand of   Jer 44:30
enemies

PHARAOH-NECHO

P. went against Assyria   2Ki 23:29
P. put Jehoahaz in bands at   2Ki 23:33
Riblah
P. made Eliakim son of   2Ki 23:34
Josiah king
he taxed the land to give   2Ki 23:35
money to P.
word came to Jeremiah against   Jer 46:2
P.

PHARAOH'S

woman was taken into P.   Ge 12:15
house
unto Potiphar, an officer of P. Ge 37:36
he asked P. officers that were Ge 40:7
with
P. cup was in my hand: and I   Ge 40:11
took
and pressed them into P. cup   Ge 40:11
and I gave the cup into P.   Ge 40:11
hand
shalt deliver P. cup into his   Ge 40:13
hand
third day, which was P.   Ge 40:20
birthday
and he gave the cup into P.   Ge 40:21
hand
fame thereof was heard in P.   Ge 45:16
house
brought the money into P.   Ge 47:14
house
over them: so the land   Ge 47:20
became P.
my lord, and we will be P.   Ge 47:25
servants
priests only, which became   Ge 47:26
not P.
Then said his sister to P.   Ex 2:7
daughter
And P. daughter said unto her, Ex 2:8
Go
P. daughter said unto her, Take Ex 2:9
she brought him unto P.   Ex 2:10
daughter
P. taskmasters had set over   Ex 5:14
them
And I will harden P. heart, and Ex 7:3
And he hardened P. heart, that Ex 7:13
P. heart was hardened, he   Ex 7:14
refuseth
P. heart was hardened, neither Ex 7:22
and P. heart was hardened, and Ex 8:19
P. servants said, How long   Ex 10:7
were driven out from P.   Ex 10:11
presence
the Lord hardened p. heart   Ex 10:20;
                                10:27
Egypt, in the sight of P.   Ex 11:3
servants
the Lord hardened P. heart,   Ex 11:10
so that
I will harden P. heart, that he Ex 14:4
shall
sea, even all P. horses, his   Ex 14:23
chariots
P. chariots and hosts hath he   Ex 15:4
cast
We were P. bondmen in Egypt   De 6:21
they were in Egypt in P. house 1Sa 2:27

and took P. daughter, and   1Ki 3:1
brought
made also an house for P.   1Ki 7:8
daughter
P. daughter came up out of   1Ki 9:24
the city
Tahpenes weaned in P. house   1Ki 11:20
and Genubath was in P.   1Ki 11:20
household
company of horses in P.   Ca 1:9
chariots
P. army was come out of   Jer 37:5
Egypt
P. army, which has come forth   Jer 37:7
Jerusalem for fear of P.   Jer 37:11
army, from
which is at the entry of P.   Jer 43:9
house
but I will break P. arms, and   Eze 30:24
P. daughter took him up, and   Ac 7:21
be called the son of   Heb 11:24
daughter

PHARES

And Judas begat P. and Zara   M't 1:3
P. begat Esrom; and Esrom   M't 1:3
begat
Esrom, which was the son of P. Lu 3:33

PHAREZ

therefore his name was called   Ge 38:29
P.
and Shelah, and P. and Zarah   Ge 46:12
sons of P. were Hezron and   Ge 46:12
Hamul
of P., the family of the   Nu 26:20
Pharzites
sons of P. were; of Hezron   Nu 26:21
thy house be like the house of Ru 4:12
P.
the generations of P.: P. begat Ru 4:18
his daughter in law bare him   1Ch 2:4
P.
sons of P.; Hezron, and Hamul   1Ch 2:5
P., Hezron, and Carmi, and   1Ch 4:1
Hur
children of P. the son of Judah 1Ch 9:4

PHARISEE

Thou blind P. cleanse first   M't 23:26
that
the P. which had bidden him   Lu 7:39
saw it
P. besought him to dine with   Lu 11:37
him
when the P. saw it, he   Lu 11:38
marveled
one a P. and the other a   Lu 18:10
publican
The P. stood and prayed thus   Lu 18:11
with
a P. named Gamaliel, a doctor   Ac 5:34
the P. party (B)(N)(P)(R)   Ac 15:5
Men and brethren, I am a P.   Ac 23:6
the son of a P.: of the hope   Ac 23:6
sect of our religion I lived a P. Ac 26:5
as touching the law, a P.   Ph'p 3:5

PHARISEES

exceed the righteousness of   M't 5:20
the P.
why do we and the P. fast oft   M't 9:14;
                                M'k 2:18
P. said, He casteth out devils M't 9:34
by prince of devils
knowest thou that the P.   M't 15:12
were offended
beware of the leaven of the P. M't 16:6;
and Sadducees 16:11; M'k 8:15; Lu 12:1
the P. also came to him   M't 19:3
tempting him
saying, The scribes and P. sit M't 23:2
in Moses' seat
woe to you scribes and P.,   M't 23:13;
hypocrites   23:14-15, 23, 25, 27, 29;
                                Lu 11:42-44
the scribes and P. murmured   Lu 5:20;
                                15:2
the scribes and P. watched him, Lu 6:7
whether
but the P. rejected the counsel Lu 7:30
of God
now do ye P. make clean   Lu 11:39
outside of the cup
P. who were covetous, heard   Lu 16:14
these things

they which were sent were of   Joh 1:24
the P.
there was a man of the P.   Joh 3:1
named Nicodemus
the P. and priests sent officers   Joh 7:32
to take him
have any of the rulers or P.   Joh 7:48
believed on him
then the P. gathered a   Joh 11:47
council, and said
now the P. had given a   Joh 11:57
commandment
there rose up certain of sect of   Ac 15:5
the P.
there arose a dissension   Ac 23:7
between P. and Sadducees
there is no resurrection, but   Ac 23:8
the P. confess both

PHARISEE'S

he went into the P. house, and   Lu 7:36
sat
Jesus sat at meat in the P.   Lu 7:37
house

PHARISEES'

scribes that were of the P. part   Ac 23:9

PHAROSH

of Shechaniah, of the sons of P.   Ezr 8:3

PHARPAR

and P., rivers of Damascus   2Ki 5:12

PHARZITES

of Pharez, the family of the   Nu 26:20
P.

PHASEAH

of Uzza, the children of P.   Ne 7:51

PHEBE

I commend unto you P. our   Ro 16:1
sister

PHENICE

Stephen travelled as far as P.   Ac 11:19
passed through P. and Samaria   Ac 15:3
means they might attain to P.   Ac 27:12

PHENICIA

finding a ship sailing unto P.   Ac 21:2

PHICHOL

P. the chief captain of his   Ge 21:22;
host   21:32
P. the chief captain of his   Ge 26:26
army

PHILADELPHIA

and unto Sardis, and unto P.   Re 1:11
angel of the church of P. write   Re 3:7

PHILEMON

unto P. our dearly beloved, and   Ph'm 1

PHILETUS

of whom is Hymenæus and P.   2Ti 2:17

PHILIP

P. and Bartholomew,   M't 10:3;
Thomas and Matthew   M'k 3:18;
    Lu 6:14; Ac 1:13
his brother P. tetrarch of Iturea   Lu 3:1
Jesus findeth P. and saith,   Joh 1:43
Follow me
now P. was of Bethsaida, the   Joh 1:44
city of Andrew
P. findeth Nathanael, and   Joh 1:45
saith to him
the same came to P. and   Joh 12:21
desired him
telleth Andrew, Andrew and   Joh 12:22
P. told Jesus
and yet hast thou not known   Joh 14:9
me, P.

P. the deacon   Ac 6:5
P. went down to Samaria, and   Ac 8:5
preached Christ
gave heed to those things which   Ac 8:6
P. spoke
but when they believed P.   Ac 8:12
preaching things
Simon continued with P. and   Ac 8:13
wondered
the Spirit said to P.   Ac 8:29
P. ran to him, heard the   Ac 8:30
eunuch read Esaias
the Spirit of the Lord caught   Ac 8:39
away P.
we entered into the house of P.   Ac 21:8
the evangelist

PHILIPPI

into the coasts of Cæsarea   M't 16:13
P.
into the towns of Cæsarea P.   M'k 8:27
And from thence to P. which   Ac 16:12
is
And we sailed away from P.   Ac 20:6
after
in Christ Jesus which are at P.   Ph'p 1:1
as ye know, at P., we were   1Th 2:2
bold in

PHILIPPIANS

Now ye P. know also, that in   Ph'p 4:15

PHILIP'S

Herodias' sake, his brother P.   M't 14:3;
wife   M'k 6:17
for Herodias his brother P.   Lu 3:19
wife

PHILISTIA

the inhabitants of P. (S)   Ex 15:14
P. triumph thou because of me   Ps 60:8
behold P., and Tyre, with   Ps 87:4
Ethiopia
my shoe; over P. will I   Ps 108:9
triumph
rejoice O P. (S)   Isa 14:29; 14:31
all the coasts of P. (S)   Joe 3:4

PHILISTIM

Casluhim, (out of whom   Ge 10:14
came P.

PHILISTINE

am not I a P.   1Sa 17:8
17:10-11, 16, 23, 26, 32-33, 36-37, 40-
    45, 48-51, 54-55, 57
from the slaughter of the P.   1Sa 18:6
life in his hand, and slew the   1Sa 19:5
P.
The sword of Goliath the P.   1Sa 21:9
whom
him the sword of Goliath the   1Sa 22:10
P.
and smote the P. and killed   2Sa 21:17
him

PHILISTINES

out of whom came the P. (S)   Ge 10:14
Isaac had flocks, and the P.   Ge 26:14
envied him
P. stopped the wells Abraham   Ge 26:15;
digged   26:18
God led them not thro' the   Ex 13:17
land of P.
the borders of P. not yet   Jos 13:2
conquered
from Sihor to Ekron, five   Jos 13:3;
lords of the P.   J'g 3:3
Shamgar slew of the P. 600   J'g 3:31
men
and Israel served the gods of   J'g 10:6
the P.
he sold them into the hands of   J'g 10:7;
the P.   13:1
did not I deliver you from   J'g 10:11
Egyptians and P.
Samson sought an occasion   J'g 14:4
against the P.
now shall I be more blameless   J'g 15:3
than the P.
the P. came up and burnt her   J'g 15:6
and her father
knowest thou not that the P.   J'g 15:11
are rulers over us

Samson judged Israel in the   J'g 15:20
days of the P.
the P. be upon thee, Samson   J'g 16:9;
    16:12, 14, 20
the P. took Samson and put   J'g 16:21
out his eyes
that I may be at once avenged   J'g 16:28
of the P.
Samson said, Let me die with   J'g 16:30
the P. bowed him
now Israel went out against the   1Sa 4:1
P.
why hath the Lord smitten us   1Sa 4:3
before the P.
be strong, quit yourselves like   1Sa 4:9
men, O ye P.
the P. took the ark of God and   1Sa 5:1
brought it
the ark was in the land of P.   1Sa 6:1
seven months
P. have brought again the ark   1Sa 6:21
of the Lord
he will save us out of the hand   1Sa 7:8
of the P.
the P. drew near to battle   1Sa 7:10
against Israel
so the P. were subdued, and   1Sa 7:13
came no more
the P. will come down upon   1Sa 13:12
me to Gilgal
Israelites went down to the P.   1Sa 13:20
to sharpen
noise that was in the host of   1Sa 14:19
the P. went on
was sore war against the P.   1Sa 14:52
all the days of Saul
the P. saw their champion   1Sa 17:51
was dead
Israel returned from chasing   1Sa 17:53
after the P.
but let the hand of the P. be   1Sa 18:17;
on him   18:21
then the princes of the P.   1Sa 18:30
went forth
David fought with the P.   1Sa 19:8;
    23:5; 2Sa 21:15
Saul returned from following   1Sa 24:1
the P.
than that I should escape into   1Sa 27:1
land of the P.
for the P. make war against   1Sa 28:15
me, God departed
that thou displease not the   1Sa 29:7
lords of the P.
P. followed hard upon Saul   1Sa 31:2;
    1Ch 10:2
sent into land of the P. round   1Sa 31:9
about to publish it
all the P. came up to seek   2Sa 5:17
David
shall I go up to the P.? wilt   2Sa 5:19
thou deliver
David smote the P.; gold got   2Sa 5:25;
from P.   8:1, 12
Eleazar smote the P.   2Sa 23:10
Shammah slew P.   2Sa 23:12
mighty men brake through   2Sa 23:16
the host of the P.
the woman sojourned in land   2Ki 8:2
of the P.
stirred up against Jehoram   2Ch 21:16
spirit of P.
God helped Uzziah against   2Ch 26:7
the P. and Arabians
P. had invaded the cities of   2Ch 28:18
the low country
the P. with the inhabitants of   Ps 83:7
Tyre
they are soothsayers like the P.   Isa 2:6
the Syrians before, and the P.   Isa 9:12
behind
they shall fly on the shoulders   Isa 11:14
of the P.
the kings of the P. shall drink   Jer 25:20
the cup
the word of the Lord came   Jer 47:1
against the P.
for the Lord will spoil the P.   Jer 47:4
the remnant
delivered thee to the   Eze 16:27
daughter of P.
because the P. have dealt by   Eze 25:15
revenge
I will stretch out mine hand   Eze 25:16
upon the P.
the remnant of the P. shall   Am 1:8
perish
then go down to Gath of the P.   Am 6:2

PHILISTINES

have not I brought the *P.* from   *Am 9:7*
Caphtor
they of the plain shall possess   *Ob 19*
the *P.*
O land of the *P.* I will destroy   *Zep 2:5*
thee
I will cut off the pride of the *P.*   *Zec 9:6*

PHILISTINES'

Abraham sojourned in the *P.*   *Ge 21:34*
land
let us go over to the *P.*   *1Sa 14:1*
garrison
to go over unto the *P.* garrison   *1Sa 14:4*
P. garrison was then at   *1Ch 11:16*
Beth-lehem

PHILOLOGUS

Salute *P.* and Julia, Nereus   *Ro 16:15*

PHILOSOPHER

philosopher (B)(P)   *1Co 1:20*

PHILOSOPHERS

Then certain *p.* of the   *Ac 17:18*
Epicureans

PHILOSOPHY

words of human *p.* (A)   *1Co 2:1*
spoil you through *p.* and   *Col 2:8*
deceit

PHINEHAS

she bare him *P.:* these are the   *Ex 6:25*
and when *P.* the son of   *Nu 25:7*
Eleazar
P. the son of Eleazar, the   *Nu 25:11;*
son of   *J'g 20:28*
P. the son of Eleazar the   *Nu 31:6;*
priest   *Jos 22:13; 22:31-32*
when *P.* the priest, and the   *Jos 22:30*
princes
a hill that pertained to *P.* his   *Jos 24:33*
son
the two sons of Eli, Hophni   *1Sa 1:3;*
and *P.*   *4:4*
thy two sons, on Hophni and   *1Sa 2:34*
P.
of Eli, Hophni and *P.* were   *1Sa 4:11*
slain
sons also, Hophni and *P.* are   *1Sa 4:17*
dead
Ichabod's brother, the son of   *1Sa 14:3*
P.
Eleazar begat *P., P.* begat   *1Ch 6:4*
Abishua
Aaron; Eleazar his son, *P.* his   *1Ch 6:50*
son
P. the son of Eleazar was the   *1Ch 9:20*
ruler
The son of Abishua, the son of   *Ezr 7:5*
P.
Of the sons of *P.*; Gershom: of   *Ezr 8:2*
with him was Eleazar the son   *Ezr 8:33*
of *P.*
stood up *P.*, executed   *Ps 106:30*
judgment

PHINEHAS'

And his daughter in law, *P.*   *1Sa 4:19*
wife

PHLEGON

Salute Asyncritus, *P.*, Hermas   *Ro 16:14*

PHRASES

heap up empty *p.* (A)(R)   *M't 6:7*

PHRYGIA

P. and Pamphylia, in Egypt   *Ac 2:10*
when they had gone   *Ac 16:6*
throughout *P.*
all the country of Galatia and   *Ac 18:23*
P.

PHURAH

go thou with *P.* thy servant   *J'g 7:10*
down
went he down with *P.* his   *J'g 7:11*
servant

PHUT

and Mizraim, and *P.*, and   *Ge 10:6*
Canaan
of Persia and of Lud and of   *Eze 27:10*
P.

PHUVAH

sons of Issachar; Tola, and *P.*   *Ge 46:13*

PHYGELLUS

of whom are *P.* and   *2Ti 1:15*
Hermogenes

PHYLACTERIES

they make broad their *p.* and   *M't 23:5*

PHYSICAL

relaxed mind makes *p.* health   *Pr 14:30*
(B)
moral weakness and *p.*   *Heb 5:2*
infirmity (A)
gained *p.* vitality (P)   *Heb 11:11*

PHYSICIAN

in Gilead; is there no *p.* there   *Jer 8:22*
They that be whole need not   *M't 9:12;*
a *p.*   *Lu 5:31*
are whole have no need of the   *M'k 2:17*
p.
me this proverb. *P.*, heal   *Lu 4:23*
thyself
Luke, the beloved *p.* and   *Col 4:14*
Demas

PHYSICIANS

commanded his servants the *p.*   *Ge 50:2*
and the *p.* embalmed Israel   *Ge 50:2*
sought not to the Lord, but   *2Ch 16:12*
to the *p.*
of lies, ye are all *p.* of no value   *Job 13:4*
suffered many things of many   *M'k 5:26*
p.
had spent all her living upon *p.*   *Lu 8:43*

PI-BESETH

The young men of Aven and   *Eze 30:17*
of *P.*

PICK

ravens of the valley shall *p.* it   *Pr 30:17*
out

PICKED

p. representatives (P)   *Col 3:12*

PICTURE

a *p.* of the present age (A)(P)   *Heb 9:9*

PICTURES

destroy all their *p.* and   *Nu 33:52*
destroy
is like apples of gold in *p.* of   *Pr 25:11*
silver
Tarshish, upon all pleasant   *Isa 2:16*
p.
p. of Chaldeans (A)   *Eze 23:14*

PIECE

he laid one *p.* against another   *Ge 15:10*
made two cherubims beaten   *Ex 37:7*
out of one *p.*
make thee two trumpets of   *Nu 10:2*
a whole *p.*
a certain woman cast a *p.* of a   *J'g 9:53;*
millstone upon   *2Sa 11:21*
come and crouch to him for a   *1Sa 2:36*
p. of silver, that I may eat a *p.*
of bread
they gave him a *p.* of a cake   *1Sa 30:12*
of figs
to every one a *p.* of flesh   *2Sa 6:19;*
   1Ch 16:3
where was a *p.* of ground full   *2Sa 23:11*
of lentiles
and mar every good *p.* of   *2Ki 3:19;*
land   *3:25*

and Hashub repaired the other   *Ne 3:11*
p.
next Ezer another *p.*   *Ne 3:19;*
   3:20-21, 24, 27, 30
as hard as a *p.* of the nether   *Job 41:24*
millstone
every man also gave him a *p.*   *Job 42:11*
of money
a man is brought to a *p.* of   *Pr 6:26*
bread
for a *p.* of bread that man will   *Pr 28:21*
transgress
thy temples are a *p.* of   *Ca 4:3;*
pomegranate   *6:7*
should give him daily a *p.* of   *Jer 37:21*
bread
every good *p.* the thigh and   *Eze 24:4*
the shoulder
bring it out *p.* by *p.* let no lot   *Eze 24:6*
fall upon it
out of the mouth of lion a *p.*   *Am 3:12*
of an ear
one *p.* was rained on, and the   *Am 4:7*
p. whereon
no man putteth a *p.* of new   *M't 9:16;*
cloth to an old garment   *M'k 2:21;*
   Lu 5:36
thou shalt find a *p.* of money,   *M't 17:27*
that take
I have bought a *p.* of ground   *Lu 14:18*
if she lose one *p.* she doth light   *Lu 15:8*
a candle
for I have found that *p.* that I   *Lu 15:9*
had lost
they gave him a *p.* of a   *Lu 24:42*
broiled fish

PIECES

a burning lamp passed   *Ge 15:17*
between those *p.*
I have given thy brother 1000   *Ge 20:16*
p. of silver
bought for 100 *p.* of money   *Ge 33:19;*
   Jos 24:32
they sold Joseph for twenty *p.*   *Ge 33:28*
of silver
Joseph without doubt is rent   *Ge 33:33;*
in *p.*   *44:28*
he gave to Benjamin thirty *p.*   *Ge 45:22*
of silver
if it be torn in *p.* let him bring   *Ex 22:13*
it
the ephod shall have the two   *Ex 28:7*
shoulder *p.*
put two chains on the   *Ex 28:25;*
shoulder *p.*   *39:4, 18*
thou shalt part the meat offering   *Le 2:6*
in *p.*
Moses burnt the *p.* and fat of   *Le 8:20*
the ram
they presented burnt offering   *Le 9:13*
with the *p.*
they gave Abimelech seventy *p.*   *J'g 9:4*
of silver
we will give thee 1100 *p.* of   *J'g 16:5*
silver
he divided his concubine into   *J'g 19:29*
twelve *p.*
Saul hewed a yoke of oxen in   *1Sa 11:7*
p.
Samuel hewed Agag in *p.*   *1Sa 15:33*
before the Lord
Ahijah rent new garment in   *1Ki 11:30*
twelve *p.*
Ahijah rent to Jeroboam,   *1Ki 11:31*
Take thee ten *p.*
a strong wind brake in *p.* the   *1Ki 19:11*
rocks
Elisha rent his clothes in two   *2Ki 2:12*
p.
Naaman took with him 6000 *p.*   *2Ki 5:5*
of gold
an ass's head was sold for   *2Ki 6:25*
eighty *p.* of silver
and brake the images of   *2Ki 11:18;*
Baal in *p.*   *23:14*
brake in *p.* the brasen serpent   *2Ki 18:4*
Moses made
went to house of Baal, and   *2Ch 23:17;*
brake the images in *p.*   *38:1; 34:4;*
   Mic 1:7
and he hath also shaken me   *Job 16:12*
in *p.*
bones as strong *p.* of brass,   *Job 40:18*
as bars of iron
rending in *p.* while none to   *Ps 7:2*
deliver
consider this, lest I tear you in   *Ps 50:22*
p.

till every one submit with *p.* of silver	*Ps 68:30*	

PIECES (continued)

till every one submit with *p.* of *Ps 68:30*
silver
thou brakest the heads of *Ps 74:14*
Leviathan in *p.*
every one for the fruit bring *Ca 8:11*
1000 *p.*
what mean ye that ye beat my *Isa 3:15*
people to *p.*
every one that goeth out shall *Jer 5:6*
be torn in *p.*
a hammer that breaketh the *Jer 23:29*
rock in *p.*
he hath turned aside and pulled *La 3:11*
me in *p.*
have not eaten that which is *Eze 4:14*
torn in *p.*
and will ye pollute me for *p.* *Eze 13:19*
of bread
gather the *p.* thereof into the *Eze 24:4*
pot
which brake the image in *p.* *Da 2:34;*
    2:45
forasmuch as iron breaketh in *Da 2:40*
p. and subdueth
the lions brake all their bones *Da 6:24*
in *p.*
the fourth beast devoured and *Da 7:7;*
brake in *p.* *7:19*
I bought her to me for fifteen *p.* *Ho 3:2*
of silver
who chop my people in *p.* as *Mic 3:3*
for the pot
and thou shalt beat in *p.* *Mic 4:13*
many people
as a lion teareth in *p.* and none *Mic 5:8*
can deliver
lion did tear in *p.* enough for *Na 2:12*
his whelps
they weighed for my price *Zec 11:12*
thirty *p.*
I took the thirty *p.* of silver *Zec 11:13;*
    M't 27:6, 9
took up of the broken *p.* (S) *M't 15:37;*
    M'k 8:8
what woman having ten *p.* of *Lu 15:8*
silver
they found the price 50,000 *p.* *Ac 19:19*
of silver
lest Paul should be pulled in *Ac 23:10*
p. of them
and some on broken *p.* of the *Ac 27:44*
ship

PIERCE

he shall *p.* them through with *Nu 24:8*
arrows
on which if a man lean, it will *2Ki 18:21*
go into his hand and *p.* it *Isa 36:6*
p. him through (B)(R) *Job 20:24;*
    Heb 3:14
p. the dragon (E)(R) *Isa 51:9*
a sword shall *p.* through thy *Lu 2:35*
own soul

PIERCED

when she had *p.* through his *J'g 5:26*
temples
my bones are *p.* in me in the *Job 30:17*
night
they *p.* my hands and my feet *Ps 22:16*
gossip of pain of *p.* ones (B) *Ps 69:26*
I was *p.* deep within (B) *Ps 73:21*
heart *p.* (B) *Ps 109:22; Isa 51:9; 53:5*
they shall look on me whom *Zec 12:10;*
they have *p.* and *Joh 19:37*
one of the soldiers *p.* his side *Joh 19:34*
and *p.* themselves with many *1Ti 6:10*
sorrows
they also which *p.* him shall see *Re 1:7*
him

PIERCETH

Behemoth's nose . through *Job 40:24*
snares

PIERCING

the Lord shall punish the *p.* *Isa 27:1*
serpent
word of God is quick, *p.* to *Heb 4:12*
the dividing

PIERCINGS

that speaketh like the *p.* of a *Pr 12:18*
sword

PIETY

producing *p.* before men (R) *M't 6:1*
through our own *p.* *Ac 3:12*
(A)(B)(P)(R)
let them learn to shew *p.* at *1Ti 5:4*
home

PIGEON

and a turtledove, and a young *p.* *Ge 15:9*
and a young *p.* or a turtledove *Le 12:6*

PIGEONS

of turtledoves, or of young *p.* *Le 1:14*
two turtledoves, or two *Le 5:7;*
young *p.* *5:11; 14:22; 15:14*
bring two turtles, or two *Le 12:8;*
young *p.* *Nu 6:10*
the turtledoves, or of the *Le 14:30*
young *p.*
her two turtles, or two young *Le 15:29*
p.
of turtledoves, or two young *p.* *Lu 2:24*

PI-HAHIROTH

they turn and encamp before *P.* *Ex 14:2*
sea, beside *P.* before *Ex 14:9*
Baal-zephon
Etham and turned again unto *Nu 33:7*
P.
And they departed from before *Nu 33:8*
P.

PILATE

delivered him to Pontius *P.* *M't 27:2;*
    M'k 15:1
P. saw he could prevail *M't 27:24*
nothing
so that *P.* marvelled *M'k 15:5; 15:44*
P. willing to content the *M'k 15:15*
people released
Pontius *P.* being governor of *Lu 3:1*
Judæa
whose blood *P.* had mingled *Lu 13:1*
with sacrifices
same day *P.* and Herod were *Lu 23:12*
made friends
this man went to *P.* and *Lu 23:52*
begged the body
P. then went out to them and *Joh 18:29*
said
then *P.* entered into the *Joh 18:33*
judgment hall
when *P.* heard that he was the *Joh 19:8*
more afraid
from thenceforth *P.* sought to *Joh 19:12*
release him
P. wrote a title, and put it on *Joh 19:19*
the cross
Joseph besought *P.* and *P.* *Joh 19:38*
gave him leave
ye denied him in the presence *Ac 3:13*
of *P.*
against Jesus Herod and *P.* *Ac 4:27*
were gathered
yet desired they *P.* that he *Ac 13:28*
should be slain
who before *P.* witnessed a *1Ti 6:13*
good confession

PILDASH

and Hazo, and *P.,* and *Ge 22:22*
Jidlaph

PILE

p. thereof is fire and much *Isa 30:33*
wood
pyre made deep and large *Isa 30:33*
(A)(R)
will even make the *p.* for fire *Eze 24:9*
great

PILEHA

Hallohesh, *P.* Shobek *Ne 10:24*

PILFER

not to *p.* (N)(R) *Tit 2:10*

PILGRIMAGE

they had *p.* (B) *Ge 35:27*
The days of the years of my *p.* *Ge 47:9*

my fathers in the days of their *Ge 47:9*
p.
years of my sojourning (R) *Ge 47:9*
land of Canaan, the land of *Ex 6:4*
their *p.*
land of temporary residence (A) *Ex 6:4*
where they lived temporarily *Ex 6:4*
(B)
land of their sojournings (E) *Ex 6:4*
dwelt as sojourners (R) *Ex 6:4*
my songs in the house of my *Ps 119:54*
p.
during your *p.* (B) *1Pe 1:17*

PILGRIMS

p. in it (B) *1Ch 16:19; 1Pe 1:1*
strangers and *p.* on the earth *Heb 11:13*
strangers, temporary *Heb 11:13*
residents, exiles (A)
guests and visitors on earth *Heb 11:13*
(B)
strangers and travellers on *Heb 11:13*
earth (N)
lived on earth as exiles and *Heb 11:13*
foreigners (P)
strangers and exiles on earth *Heb 11:13*
(R)
I beseech you as strangers and *1Pe 2:11*
p.
as sojourners, strangers, and *1Pe 2:11*
exiles (A)
as visitors and travelers (B) *1Pe 2:11*
as aliens in a foreign land (N) *1Pe 2:11*
as strangers and temporary *1Pe 2:11*
residents (P)
as aliens and exiles (R) *1Pe 2:11*

PILLAGE

pillage (B) *Isa 17:14; Eze 26:5*

PILLAGED

pillaged (A) *Isa 24:3*

PILLAR

him, and she became a *p.* of *Ge 19:26*
salt
his pillows, and set it up for a *Ge 28:18*
p.
this stone, which I have set *Ge 28:22*
for a *p.*
where thou anointedst the *p.* *Ge 31:13*
took a stone, and set it up for *Ge 31:45*
a *p.*
this heap, and behold this *p.* *Ge 31:51*
this *p.* be witness, that I will *Ge 31:52*
not
not pass over this heap and *Ge 31:52*
this *p.*
And Jacob set up a *p.* in the *Ge 35:4*
place
talked with him, even a *p.* of *Ge 35:14*
And Jacob set a *p.* upon her *Ge 35:20*
grave
that is the *p.* of Rachel's *Ge 35:20*
grave
them by day in a *p.* of a *Ex 13:21*
cloud, to
by night in a *p.* of fire, to give *Ex 13:21*
them
took not away the *p.* of the *Ex 13:22*
cloud
by day, nor the *p.* of fire by *Ex 13:22*
night
the *p.* of the cloud went from *Ex 14:19*
before
through the *p.* of fire and of *Ex 14:24*
the cloudy *p.* descended, and *Ex 33:9*
stood
the people saw the cloudy *p.* *Ex 33:10*
stand
Lord came down in the *p.* of *Nu 12:5*
them, by day time in a *p.* of a *Nu 14:14*
cloud
and in a *p.* of fire by night *Nu 14:14*
the tabernacle in a *p.* of a *De 31:15*
cloud
p. of the cloud stood over the *De 31:15*
door
of the *p.* that was in Sechem *J'g 9:6*
out of the city with a *p.* of *J'g 20:40*
smoke
and reared up for himself a *2Sa 18:18*
he called the *p.* after his own *2Sa 18:18*
name
set up the right *p.* and called *1Ki 7:21*

he set up the left *p.* and called *1Ki 7:21*
out the *p.* of Baal (B)(E)(R) *2Ki 10:26*
the king stood by a *p.* as the *2Ki 11:14*
the king stood by a *p.* and *2Ki 23:3*
made a
the one *p.* was eighteen *2Ki 25:17*
cubits
the second *p.* with wreathen *2Ki 25:17*
work
the king stood at his *p.* at *2Ch 23:13*
them in the day by a cloudy *p.* *Ne 9:12*
and in the night by a *p.* of fire *Ne 9:12*
p. of the cloud departed not *Ne 9:19*
from
neither the *p.* of fire by night *Ne 9:19*
spake unto them in the cloudy *Ps 99:7*
p.
a *p.* at the border thereof to *Isa 19:19*
defenced city, and an iron *p.* *Jer 1:18*
of one *p.* was eighteen cubits *Jer 52:21*
The second *p.* also and the *Jer 52:22*
without an idolatrous *p.* *Ho 3:4*
(A)(B)(E)(R)
the *p.* and ground of the truth *1Ti 3:15*
a *p.* in the temple of my God *Re 3:12*

PILLARS

break worship *p.* (B)(E)(R) *Ex 23:24*
p. according to the twelve *Ex 24:4*
tribes
it upon four *p.* of shittim *Ex 26:32*
wood
hanging five *p.* of shittim *Ex 26:37*
wood
twenty *p.* thereof and their *Ex 27:10*
twenty
the hooks of the *p.* and their *Ex 27:10;*
fillets *38:10-11*
twenty *p.* and their twenty *Ex 27:11*
sockets
hooks of the *p.* and their *Ex 27:11;*
fillets *38:12, 17*
their *p.* ten, and their sockets *Ex 27:12;*
38:12
their *p.* three, and their *Ex 27:14;*
sockets *27:15; 38:14-15*
p. shall be four, and their *Ex 27:16*
sockets
All the *p.* round about the *Ex 27:17*
court
his bars, his *p.* and his *Ex 35:11;*
sockets *39:33*
his *p.* and their sockets, and *Ex 35:17*
thereunto four *p.* of shittim *Ex 36:36*
wood
the five *p.* of it with their *Ex 36:38*
hooks
Their *p.* were twenty, and *Ex 38:10*
their *p.* were twenty, and their *Ex 38:11*
the sockets for the *p.* were of *Ex 38:17*
brass
all the *p.* of the court were *Ex 38:17*
filleted
their *p.* were four, and their *Ex 38:19*
sockets
shekels he made hooks for the *Ex 38:28*
p.
his *p.* and his sockets, and the *Ex 39:40*
bars thereof, and reared up *Ex 40:18*
his *p.*
and the *p.* thereof, and the *Nu 3:36*
sockets
the *p.* of the court round *Nu 3:37;*
about *4:32*
bars thereof, and the *p.* thereof *Nu 4:31*
break their *p.* burn their groves *De 12:3*
and they set him between the *J'g 16:25*
p.
Suffer me that I may feel the *J'g 16:26*
p.
took hold of the two middle *J'g 16:29*
p.
the *p.* of the earth are the *1Sa 2:8*
Lord's
upon four rows of cedar *p.* *1Ki 7:2*
with cedar beams upon the *p.* *1Ki 7:2*
lay on forty five *p.* fifteen in a *1Ki 7:3*
row
And he made a porch of *p.;* the *1Ki 7:6*
the other *p.* and the thick beam *1Ki 7:6*
he cast two *p.* of brass, of *1Ki 7:15*
eighteen
to set upon the tops of the *p.* *1Ki 7:16*
which were upon the top of *1Ki 7:17*
the *p.*
And he made the *p.* and two *1Ki 7:18*
rows

the top of the *p.* were of lily *1Ki 7:19;*
work *7:22*
And the chapiters upon the *1Ki 7:20*
two *p.*
the *p.* in the porch of the *1Ki 7:21*
temple
so was the work of the *p.* *1Ki 7:22*
finished
The two *p.* and the two bowls *1Ki 7:41*
that were on the top of *1Ki 7:41*
the two *p.*
which were upon the top of *1Ki 7:41*
the *p.*
the chapiters that were upon *1Ki 7:42*
the *p.*
king made of the almug trees *1Ki 10:12*
p.
high places, *p.,* Asherim *1Ki 14:23*
(A)(B)(E)(R)
p. or obelisks (A) *2Ki 10:26*
p. which Hezekiah king of *2Ki 18:16*
Judah
p. of brass that were in the *2Ki 25:13*
house
The two *p.* one sea, and the *2Ki 25:16*
bases
made the brasen sea, and the *1Ch 18:8*
p.
he made before the house two *2Ch 3:15*
p.
put them on the heads of the *2Ch 3:16*
p.
reared up the *p.* before the *2Ch 3:17*
temple
the two *p.* and the pommels *2Ch 4:12*
were on the top of the two *p.* *2Ch 4:12*
which were on the top of the *2Ch 4:12*
p.
chapiters which were upon *2Ch 4:13*
the *p.*
p. and Asherim (A) *2Ch 14:3*
shattered *p.,* Asherahs *2Ch 14:3*
(B)(E)(R)
to silver rings and *p.* of marble *Es 1:6*
place, and the *p.* thereof *Job 9:6*
tremble
The *p.* of heaven tremble and *Job 26:11*
are dissolved: I bear up the *p.* *Ps 75:3*
of it
she hath hewn out her seven *p.* *Pr 9:1*
of the wilderness like *p.* of *Ca 3:6*
smoke
He made the *p.* thereof of *Ca 3:10*
silver
His legs are as *p.* of marble, set *Ca 5:15*
concerning the *p.* and *Jer 27:19*
p. of brass that were in the *Jer 52:17*
house
The two *p.* one sea, and *Jer 52:20*
twelve
concerning the *p.* the height *Jer 52:21*
of
and there were *p.* by the *Eze 40:49*
posts, one
had not a *p.* as the *p.* of the *Eze 42:6*
courts
goodly *p.* or obelisks (A) *Ho 10:1*
he made his sacred *p.* *Ho 10:1*
(B)(E)(R)
destroy idolatrous *p.* *Ho 10:2*
(A)(E)(R)
blood, and fire, and *p.* of *Joe 2:30*
smoke
and John, who seemed to be *p.* *Ga 2:9*
the sun, and his feet as *p.* of *Re 10:1*
fire

PILLED

and *p.* white strakes in them *Ge 30:37*
peeled white streaks in them *Ge 30:37;*
(A)(B)(E)(R) *30:38*
rods which he had *p.* before *Ge 30:38*

PILLOW

a *p.* of goats' hair for his *1Sa 19:13;*
bolster *19:16*
part of the ship, asleep on a *M'k 4:38*
p.

PILLOWS

that place, and put them for *Ge 28:11*
his *p.*
the stone that he had put for *Ge 28:18*
his *p.*
women that sew *p.* in all *Eze 13:18*
armholes
I am against your *p.* *Eze 13:20*
wherewith ye

PILOT

where the *p.* willeth (S) *Jas 3:4*
the *p.* directs (R) *Jas 3:4*

PILOTS

that were in thee, were thy *p.* *Eze 27:8*
thy mariners, and thy *p.* thy *Eze 27:27*
at the sound of the cry of thy *Eze 27:28*
p.
all the *p.* of the sea, shall *Eze 27:29*
come

PILTAI

of Miniamin, of Moadiah, P. *Ne 12:17*

PIN

she fastened it with the *p.* and *J'g 16:14*
went away with the *p.* of the *J'g 16:14*
beam
p. David to the wall *1Sa 18:11*
(A)(B)(R)
take a *p.* of it to hang any *Eze 15:3*
vessel
take a peg on which to hang *Eze 15:3*
(A)(B)(R)

PINE

makes soul *p.* away *Le 26:16*
(A)(E)(R)
that are left of you shall *p.* *Le 26:39*
away
shall they *p.* away with them *Le 26:39*
fetch olive branches, and *p.* *Ne 8:15*
they will *p.* away (B) *Isa 19:8*
the desert the fir tree, and the *Isa 41:19*
p.
unto thee the fir tree, the *p.* *Isa 60:13*
tree
p. away (B) *Jer 31:12*
these *p.* away, stricken through *La 4:9*
p. away for their iniquity (S) *Eze 4:17*
shall *p.* away for your *Eze 24:23*
iniquities
upon us, and we *p.* away in *Eze 33:10*
them

PINES

the *p.* of Cyprus (B) *Eze 27:6*

PINETH

with his teeth, and *p.* away *M'k 9:18*

PINING

p. of soul (E) *De 28:65*
he will cut me off with *p.* *Isa 38:12*
sickness

PINNACLE

the wing or *p.* of (A) *Da 9:27*
setteth him on a *p.* of the *M't 4:5;*
temple *Lu 4:9*
turret of the temple (A) *M't 4:5*
loftiest point of the temple (B) *M't 4:5*
parapet of the temple (N) *M't 4:5*
the highest ledge of the temple *M't 4:5*
(P)
and set him on a *p.* of the *Lu 4:9*
temple
on a gable of the temple (A) *Lu 4:9*
the summit of the temple (B) *Lu 4:9*
the parapet of the temple (N) *Lu 4:9*
highest ledge of the temple (P) *Lu 4:9*

PINNACLES

p. of agates (B)(E)(R) *Isa 54:12*

PINNED

he *p.* his faith (P) *Lu 11:22*

PINON

Aholibamah, duke Elah, *Ge 36:41;*
duke P. *1Ch 1:52*

PINS

thereof, and all the *p.* thereof *Ex 27:19*
the *p.* of the court shall be of *Ex 27:19*
brass
The *p.* of the tabernacle, and *Ex 35:18*
the *p.* of the court, and their *Ex 35:18*
cords

all the *p.* of the tabernacle   *Ex 38:20;*
                                    38:31
all the *p.* of the court round   *Ex 38:31*
about
his cords, and his *p.* and all   *Ex 39:40*
and their *p.* and their cords   *Nu 3:37;*
                                    4:32
the wimples, and the crisping   *Isa 3:22*
p.

PINT

measuring with a six *p.* vessel   *Ex 16:18*
(B)
with 2½ *p.* of oil (B)   *Ex 29:40*
three *p.* of oil (B)   *Le 23:13*
three *p.* of wine (B)   *Nu 15:5*
two *p.* of water (B)   *Eze 4:11*

PINTS

six *p.* of fine flour (A)   *Ex 29:40*

PIOUS

with modesty, *p.* care (A)   *Heb 12:28*

PIPE

play the lyre and *p.*   *Ge 4:21*
(A)(E)(R)(S)
with a tabret, and a *p.* and a   *1Sa 10:5*
harp
flute   (A)(B)(R)   *1Sa 10:5;*
        Isa 5:12; 30:29; 1Co 14:7
rejoice at sound of the *p.*   *Job 21:12*
(A)(E)(R)
with strings and *p.* (E)(R)   *Ps 150:4*
viol, the tabret, and *p.* and   *Isa 5:12*
wine
one goeth with a *p.* to come   *Isa 30:29*
into the
the *p.* (A)(B)(R)(S)   *Da 3:5;*
                                   3:7, 10, 15
giving sound, whether *p.* or   *1Co 14:7*
harp

PIPED

and the people *p.* with pipes   *1Ki 1:40*
playing flutes (B)   *1Ki 1:40;*
      M't 11:17; Lu 7:32; 1Co 14:7
We have *p.* unto you, and   *M't 11:17;*
ye   *Lu 7:32*
it be known what is *p.* or   *1Co 14:7*
harped

PIPERS

harpers, and musicians, and   *Re 18:22*
of *p.*
flute players   *Re 18:22*
(A)(B)(E)(N)(P)(R)

PIPES

and the people piped with *p.*   *1Ki 1:40*
flutes (B)   *1Ki 1:40; Jer 48:36*
heart shall sound for Moab   *Jer 48:36*
like *p.*
flute (A)(R)   *Jer 48:36*
mine heart shall sound like *p.*   *Jer 48:36*
of thy tabrets and of thy *p.*   *Eze 28:13*
seven *p.* to the seven lamps   *Zec 4:2*
seven ducts (B)   *Zec 4:2*
two golden *p.* empty the   *Zec 4:12*
golden
two golden tubes or spouts   *Zec 4:12*
(A)(B)(E)

PIRAM

and unto *P.* king of Jarmuth   *Jos 10:3*

PIRATHON

was buried in *P.* in the land   *J'g 12:15*
of

PIRATHONITE

son of Hillel, a *P.* judged   *J'g 12:13*
Israel
Abdon the son of Hillel the *P.*   *J'g 12:15*
died
Benaiah the *P.* Hiddai of the   *2Sa 23:30*
of Benjamin, Benaiah the *P.*   *1Ch 11:31*
month was Benaiah the *P.* of   *1Ch 27:14*

PISGAH

top of *P.* which looketh   *Nu 21:20*
toward
field of Zophim, to the top of   *Nu 23:14*
P.
the slopes of *P.* (S)   *De 3:17;*
                                Jos 12:3; 13:20
Get thee up into the top of *P.*   *De 3:27*
the plain, under the springs of   *De 4:49*
P.
the top of *P.* that is over against *De 34:1*

PISIDIA

they came to Antioch in *P.*   *Ac 13:14*
they had passed throughout *P.*   *Ac 14:24*

PISON

The name of the first is *P.*   *Ge 2:11*

PISPAH

Jephunneh, and *P.* and Ara   *1Ch 7:38*

PISS

and drink their own *p.* with   *2Ki 18:27;*
you   *Isa 36:12*

PISSETH

any that *p.* against the wall   *1Sa 25:22;*
25:34; 1Ki 14:10; 16:11; 21:21; 2Ki 9:8
every male (A)(B)(R)   *1Sa 25:22;*
25:34; 1Ki 14:10; 16:11; 21:21; 2Ki 9:8
one man-child (E)   *1Sa 25:22;*
25:34; 1Ki 14:10; 16:11; 21:21; 2Ki 9:8

PIT

him, and cast him into some   *Ge 37:20*
p.
but cast him into this *p.* that   *Ge 37:22*
is in
took him, and cast him into   *Ge 37:24*
a *p.*
p. was empty, there was no   *Ge 37:24*
water
and lifted up Joseph out of   *Ge 37:28*
the *p.*
And Reuben returned unto   *Ge 37:29*
the *p.*
behold, Joseph was not in the   *Ge 37:29*
p.
And if a man shall open a *p.*   *Ex 21:33*
if a man shall dig a *p.* and not *Ex 21:33*
cover
owner of the *p.* shall make it   *Ex 21:34*
good
Nevertheless a fountain or *p.*   *Le 11:36*
a spring, cistern, or reservoir   *Le 11:36*
(A)
fountain, cistern, or reservoir   *Le 11:36*
(B)
a spring or cistern (R)   *Le 11:36*
they go down quick into the   *Nu 16:30*
p.
go down alive into Sheol   *Nu 16:30*
(A)(B)(E)(R)
went down alive into the *p.*   *Nu 16:33*
he is hid now in some *p.* or in   *2Sa 17:9*
cast him into a great *p.* in   *2Sa 18:17*
the wood
and slew a lion in the midst   *2Sa 23:20*
of a *p.*
slew them at the *p.* of the   *2Ki 10:14*
shearing
slew them at the cistern of   *2Ki 10:14*
(A)
slew a lion in a *p.* in a snowy   *1Ch 11:22*
day
and ye dig a *p.* for your friend *Job 6:27*
plunge me into a *p.* (R)   *Job 9:31*
go down to the bars of the *p.*   *Job 17:16*
go down to the bars of Sheol   *Job 17:16*
(A)(E)(R)
descend with me into Sheol   *Job 17:16*
(R)
keepeth back his soul from   *Job 33:18*
the *p.*
draweth near unto the *p.* (S)   *Job 33:22*
him from going down to the   *Job 33:24*
p.
his soul from going into the   *Job 33:28*
p.
To bring back his soul from   *Job 33:30*
the *p.*
He made a *p.* and digged it   *Ps 7:15*

heathen are sunk down in the   *Ps 9:15*
p.
like them that go down into the   *Ps 28:1*
p.
that I should not go down to   *Ps 30:3*
the *p.*
them that go down to the   *Ps 30:3;*
grave (B)   *30:9*
blood, when I go down to the   *Ps 30:9*
p.
they hid for me their net in a *p.*   *Ps 35:7*
me up also out of an horrible *p.*   *Ps 40:2*
down into the *p.* of   *Ps 55:23*
destruction
they have digged a *p.* before me *Ps 57:6*
let not the *p.* shut her   *Ps 69:15*
mouth upon
with them that go down into   *Ps 88:4*
the *p.*
Thou hast laid me in the lowest   *Ps 88:6*
p.
the *p.* be digged for the   *Ps 94:13*
wicked
life from the *p.* (R)   *Ps 103:4*
unto them that go down into   *Ps 143:7*
the *p.*
as those that go down into the   *Pr 1:12*
p.
of strange women is a deep *p.*   *Pr 22:14*
a strange woman is a narrow   *Pr 23:27*
p.
harlot is a deep *p.* (B)(R)   *Pr 23:27*
Whoso diggeth a *p.* shall fall   *Pr 26:27*
shall fall himself into his own   *Pr 28:10*
p.
doeth violence shall flee to   *Pr 28:17*
the *p.*
He that diggeth a *p.* shall fall *Ec 10:8*
into
down to hell, to the sides of   *Isa 14:15*
the *p.*
that go down to the stones of   *Isa 14:19*
the *p.*
Fear, and the *p.* and the snare   *Isa 24:17*
noise of fear shall fall into   *Isa 24:18*
the *p.*
cometh up out of the midst of   *Isa 24:18*
the *p.*
as prisoners are gathered in   *Isa 24:22*
the *p.*
to take water withal out of   *Isa 30:14*
the *p.*
dip water from a cistern   *Isa 30:14*
(A)(B)(E)(R)
it from the *p.* of corruption   *Isa 38:17*
that go down into the *p.*   *Isa 38:18*
cannot hope
hole of the *p.* whence ye are   *Isa 51:1*
digged
the quarry from which you   *Isa 51:1*
were digged (A)(B)(R)
that he should not die in the   *Isa 51:14*
p.
they have digged a *p.* for my   *Jer 18:20*
soul
have digged a *p.* to take me   *Jer 18:22*
cast them into the midst of the   *Jer 41:7*
p.
cast into a cistern (A)(B)(R)   *Jer 41:7;*
                                   41:9
the *p.* where Ishmael had   *Jer 41:9*
cast all
Fear, and the *p.* and the snare   *Jer 48:43*
from the fear shall fall into   *Jer 48:44*
the *p.*
and he that getteth up out of   *Jer 48:44*
the *p.*
pit (B)(R)   *La 3:55*
he was taken in their *p.* and   *Eze 19:4*
over him: he was taken in   *Eze 19:8*
their *p.*
with them that descend into   *Eze 26:20;*
the *p.*   *31:16*
with them that go down to   *Eze 26:20;*
the *p.*   *31:14; 32:18, 24-25, 29, 30*
shall bring thee down to the *p.* *Eze 28:8*
graves are set in the sides of   *Eze 32:23*
the *p.*
out of the *p.* wherein is no   *Zec 9:11*
water
it fall into a *p.* on the   *M't 12:11*
sabbath day
fall into a *p.* (B)(E)(R)   *M't 15:14*
an ass or an ox fallen into a *p.* *Lu 14:5*
to *p.* of nether gloom (R)   *2Pe 2:4*
given the key of the bottomless   *Re 9:1*
p.
key of the shaft of the abyss   *Re 9:1*
(A)(N)(R)

key to the pit of the abyss (B)(E) — Re 9:1
key of the fathomless pit (P) — Re 9:1
And he opened the bottomless p. — Re 9:2
there arose a smoke out of the p. — Re 9:2
by reason of the smoke of the p. — Re 9:2
he opened the long shaft of the abyss (A)(N)(R) — Re 9:2
he opened the pit of the abyss (B)(E) — Re 9:2
is the angel of the bottomless p. — Re 9:11
the angel of the abyss (A)(B)(E)(N) — Re 9:11
ascendeth out of the bottomless p. — Re 11:7
comes out of the abyss (A)(B)(E)(N) — Re 11:7; 17:8
ascend out of the bottomless p. — Re 17:8
having the key of the bottomless p. — Re 20:1
key of the abyss (A)(B)(E)(N) — Re 20:1
And cast him into the bottomless p. — Re 20:3
hurled him into the abyss (A)(B)(E)(N) — Re 20:3
hurled him into the pit (P)(R) — Re 20:3

PITCH

shalt p. it within and without — Ge 6:14
it within and without with p. — Ge 6:14
daubed it with slime and with p. — Ex 2:3
of Israel shall p. their tents — Nu 1:52
the Levites shall p. round about — Nu 1:53
shall p. by his own standard — Nu 2:2
of the congregation shall they p. — Nu 2:2
Judah p. throughout their armies — Nu 2:3
And those that do p. next unto him — Nu 2:5
And those which p. by him shall be — Nu 2:12
shall p. behind the tabernacle — Nu 3:23
p. on the side of the tabernacle — Nu 3:29; 3:35
you out a place to p. your tents in — De 1:33
of Jordan, did Joshua p. in Gilgal — Jos 4:20
neither shall the Arabian p. tent — Isa 13:20
thereof shall be turned into p. — Isa 34:9
thereof shall become burning p. — Isa 34:9
shall p. their tents against her — Jer 6:3

PITCHED

east of Beth-el, and p. his tent — Ge 12:8
and p. his tent toward Sodom — Ge 13:12
p. his tent in the valley of Gerar — Ge 26:17
an altar, and p. his tent there — Ge 26:25
Jacob had p. his tent in the mount — Ge 31:25
Laban p. in the mount of Gilead — Ge 31:25
and p. his tent before the city — Ge 33:18
p. in Rephidim; and there was no — Ex 17:1
and had p. in the wilderness — Ex 19:2
and p. it without the camp — Ex 33:7
when the tabernacle is to be p. — Nu 1:51
so they p. by their standard — Nu 2:34
children of Israel p. their tents — Nu 9:17
commandment of the Lord they p. — Nu 9:18
and p. in the wilderness of Paran — Nu 12:16
Israel set forward, and p. in Oboth — Nu 21:10
p. at Ije-abarim, in the wilderness — Nu 21:11
and p. in the valley of Zared — Nu 21:12
and p. on the other side of Arnon — Nu 21:13; J'g 11:18
and p. in the plains of Moab on this — Nu 22:1
from Rameses, and p. in — Nu 33:5; 33:6-9, 15-16, 18-23, 25-29, 31, 33, 36-37, 41-45, 47-49
and p. on the north side of Ai — Jos 8:11
p. together at the waters of Merom — Jos 11:5

and p. his tent unto the plain of — J'g 4:11
and p. in the valley of Jezreel — J'g 6:33
and p. beside the well of Harod — J'g 7:1
and p. in Jahaz, and fought against — J'g 11:20
the Philistines p. in Judah — J'g 15:9
and p. in Kirjath-jearim, in Judah — J'g 18:12
battle, and p. beside Eben-ezer — 1Sa 4:1
and the Philistines p. in Aphek — 1Sa 4:1
they came up, and p. in Michmash — 1Sa 13:5
p. between Shochoh and Azekah — 1Sa 17:1
p. by the valley of Elah, and set — 1Sa 17:2
And Saul p. in the hill of Hachilah — 1Sa 26:3
to the place where Saul had p. — 1Sa 26:5
and the people p. round about him — 1Sa 26:5
and came and p. in Shunem — 1Sa 28:4
together, and they p. in Gilboa — 1Sa 28:4
p. by a fountain which is in Jezreel — 1Sa 29:1
tabernacle that David had p. for it — 2Sa 6:17
Absalom p. in the land of Gilead — 2Sa 17:26
p. in the valley of Rephaim — 2Sa 23:13
passed over Jordan, and p. in Aroer — 2Sa 24:5
children of Israel p. before them — 1Ki 20:27
they p. one over against the other — 1Ki 20:29
Jerusalem, and p. against it — 2Ki 25:1
the ark of God, and p. it for a tent — 1Ch 15:1
of the tent that David had p. for it — 1Ch 16:1
who came and p. before Medeba — 1Ch 19:7
had p. a tent for it at Jerusalem — 2Ch 1:4
Jerusalem, and p. against it — Jer 52:4
which the Lord p. and not man — Heb 8:2

PITCHER

Let down thy p. I pray thee, that — Ge 24:14
with her p. upon her shoulder — Ge 24:15; 24:16-18, 20, 43, 45-46
water jar (A)(R) — Ge 24:15; 24:16-18, 20, 43, 45, 46
or the p. be broken at the fountain — Ec 12:6
you a man bearing a p. of water — M'k 14:13
meet you, bearing a p. of water — Lu 22:10

PITCHERS

every man's hand, with empty p. — J'g 7:16
and lamps within the p. — J'g 7:16
and brake the p. that were in their — J'g 7:19
brake the p. and held the lamps — J'g 7:20
p. of heaven (B) — Job 38:37
are they esteemed as earthern p. — La 4:2
bowls to p. (B) — Isa 22:24

PITFALL

dug p. for me (A)(B)(R) — Ps 119:85
made a p. (A)(R) — Ro 11:9
a p. to the weak (N) — 1Co 8:9

PITFALLS

the world with its p. (P) — M't 18:7

PITHOM

treasure cities, P. and Raamses — Ex 1:11

PITHON

sons of Micah were P. and — 1Ch 8:35; 9:41

PITIABLE

of all men most p. (E) — 1Co 15:19
wretched and p. — Re 3:17
(A)(B)(P)(R)

PITIED

she p. him (A)(B)(R) — Ex 2:6
He made them also to be p. of all — Ps 106:46
of Jacob, and hath not p. — La 2:2
hath thrown down, and hath not p. — La 2:17
anger; thou hast killed, and not p. — La 2:21
thou hast slain, thou hast not p. — La 3:43
None eye p. thee, to do any of — Eze 16:5
are most to be p. — 1Co 15:19
(B)(N)(P)

PITIETH

Like as a father p. his children — Ps 103:13
so the Lord p. them that fear — Ps 103:13
eyes, and that which your soul p. — Eze 24:21

PITIFUL

The hands of the p. women have — La 4:10
the Lord is very p. and of tender — Jas 5:11
love as brethren, be p. be — 1Pe 3:8
a most p. wretch (N) — Re 3:17

PITS

fall of tar p. (B) — Ge 14:10
rocks, and in high places, and in p. — 1Sa 13:6
The proud have digged p. for me — Ps 119:85
dug pitfalls for me — Ps 119:85
(A)(B)(R)
be cast into the fire: into deep p. — Ps 140:10
be cast into trenches (B) — Ps 140:10
through a land of deserts and p. — Jer 2:6
they came to the p. and found — Jer 14:3
came to the cisterns — Jer 14:3
(A)(E)(N)
came to the wells (B) — Jer 14:3
the Lord, was taken in their p. — La 4:20
taken in their snares (A) — La 4:20
p. of gloom (A)(R) — 2Pe 2:4
p. of darkness (E) — 2Pe 2:4
p. of hell (N) — 2Pe 2:4

PITY

eye shall have no p. upon them — De 7:16
neither shall thine eye p. him — De 13:8
Thine eye shall not p. him, but thou — De 19:13
thine eye shall not p.; but the life shall — De 19:21
her hand, thine eye shall not — De 25:12
Lord moved with p. (R) — J'g 2:18
thing, and because he had no p. — 2Sa 12:6
is afflicted p. should be shewed — Job 6:14
Have p. upon me, have p. upon me — Job 19:21
I looked for some to take p. — Ps 69:20
I looked for p. (A)(E)(R) — Ps 69:20
He that hath p. upon the poor — Pr 19:17
it for him that will p. the poor — Pr 28:8
no p. on the fruit of the womb — Isa 13:18
and in his p. he redeemed them — Isa 63:9
your yearning p. — Isa 63:15
(A)(B)(E)(R)
I will not p. nor spare, nor have — Jer 13:14
For who shall have p. upon thee — Jer 15:5
Lord crushed without p. — Jer 20:16
(B)(R)
neither have p. nor have mercy — Jer 21:7
spare, neither will I have any p. — Eze 5:11
spare thee, neither will I have p. — Eze 7:4
not spare, neither will I have p. — Eze 7:9; 8:18; 9:10
your eye spare, neither have ye — Eze 9:5
But I had p. for mine holy name — Eze 36:21

for his land, and *p*. his people *Joe 2:18*
the sword, and did cast off all *Am 1:11*
p.
Thou hast had *p*. on the gourd *Jon 4:10*
their own shepherds *p*. them *Zec 11:1*
not
no more *p*. the inhabitants of *Zec 11:6*
moved with *p*. and sympathy *M't 9:36*
(A)(N)(P)
filled with *p*. over them (B) *M't 9:36*
in *p*. for that agent *M't 18:27*
(B)(N)(P)(R)
fellowservant, I had *p*. on *M't 18:33*
thee
had *p*. and mercy *M't 18:35*
(A)(B)(N)(P)
Jesus in *p*. (A)(B)(P)(R) *M't 20:34*
moved with *p*. and sympathy *M'k 1:41*
(A)
filled with *p*. for him (P)(R) *M'k 1:41*
moved with *p*., sympathy *Lu 10:33*
(A)(B)(N)(P)
moved with *p*., tenderness *Lu 15:20*
(A)
tenderhearted *p*. and mercy *Col 3:12*
(A)
doubting souls need your *p*. *Jude 22*
(N)
you can feel *p*. (P) *Jude 22*

PLACE

Lord said, Look from *p*. *Ge 13:14*
where thou art
wilt thou destroy and not *Ge 18:24*
spare the *p*.
I will spare the *p*. for their *Ge 18:26*
sakes
the kindness thou shalt shew *Ge 20:13*
at every *p*.
the third day Abraham saw the *Ge 22:4*
p. afar off
send me away, I may go to *Ge 30:25*
mine own *p*.
the *p*. where Joseph was bound *Ge 40:3*
p. where thou standest is holy *Ex 3:5;*
Jos 5:15
thy holy dwelling *p*. (B) *Ex 15:13*
this people shall go to their *p*. *Ex 18:23*
in peace
to bring thee into the *p*. I *Ex 23:20*
have prepared
when he goeth in unto the *Ex 28:29*
holy *p*.
he shall cast it by the *p*. of the *Le 1:16*
ashes
in the first *p*. went standard *Nu 10:14*
of Judah
eat in every *p*. ye and *Nu 18:31*
households
every *p*. the soles of your feet *De 11:24;*
shall tread shall be yours *Jos 1:3*
p. the Lord God shall choose *De 12:5;*
12:14; 16:16
offer not thy burnt offering in *De 12:13*
every *p*.
if the *p*. be too far from thee *De 12:21;*
14:24
let us pass through thy land to *J'g 11:19*
my *p*.
men of Israel gave *p*. to the *J'g 20:36*
Benjamites
thou shalt mark the *p*. where he *Ru 3:4*
lieth
and one of the same *p*. *1Sa 10:12*
answered
the Philistines went to their *1Sa 14:46*
own *p*.
and David's *p*. was empty *1Sa 20:25;*
20:27
he fell down and died in same *2Sa 2:23*
p.
in what *p*. my lord, the king *2Sa 15:21*
shall be
he is hid in some pit, or in *2Sa 17:9*
some other *p*.
so shall we come upon him *2Sa 17:12*
in some *p*.
it is called to this day *2Sa 18:18*
Absalom's *p*.
place (S) *2Sa 19:13;*
M't 2:22; Lu 12:17; 14:9, 10; Ac 24:27;
1Co 14:16
thine eyes may be open *1Ki 8:29*
toward *p*.
and strike his hand over the *p*. *2Ki 5:11*
behold *p*. where we dwell is too *2Ki 6:1*
strait for us
a covered *p*. for the (S) *2Ki 16:18*
grant me the *p*. of *1Ch 21:22*
threshingfloor

David gave to Ornan for the *1Ch 21:25*
p. 600 shekels
the priests stood in their *p*. *2Ch 30:16;*
35:10
singers, sons of Asaph, were *2Ch 35:15*
in their *p*.
p. of my father's sepulchre lieth *Ne 2:3*
waste
there was no *p*. for beast under *Ne 2:14*
me to pass
in what *p*. ye hear sound of the *Ne 4:20*
trumpet
I set singers and Levites in *Ne 13:11*
their *p*.
Esther and her maids to the best *Es 2:9*
p.
shall deliverance arise from *Es 4:14*
another *p*.
they are consumed out of their *Job 6:17*
p.
pulled out of his *p*. (B) *Job 8:18*
which shake the earth out of *Job 9:6*
her *p*.
cover not my blood, let my *Job 16:18*
cry have no *p*.
where is the *p*. of *Job 28:12;*
understanding *28:20*
and he knoweth the *p*. *Job 28:23*
thereof
when people are cut off in *Job 36:20*
their *p*.
as for darkness, where is the *Job 38:19*
p. thereof
and tread down the wicked *Job 40:12*
in their *p*.
the *p*. where thine honour *Ps 26:8*
dwelleth
my foot standeth in an even *p*. *Ps 26:12*
thou art my hiding *p*. *Ps 32:7; 119:114*
from the *p*. of his habitation *Ps 33:14*
he looketh
profaned dwelling *p*. (A)(B) *Ps 74:7;*
Eze 7:24
the *p*. thereof shall know it *Ps 103:16*
no more
the *p*. of judgment the *p*. of *Ec 3:16*
righteousness
all go to one *p*. all are of the *Ec 3:20;*
dust *6:6*
profane my precious *p*. (R) *Ec 7:22*
that lay field to field, till there *Isa 5:8*
be no *p*.
the earth shall remove out of *Isa 13:13*
her *p*.
shall take them, and bring *Isa 14:2*
them to their *p*.
full of filthiness, so that there *Isa 28:8*
is no *p*. clean
the appointed barley and rye *Isa 28:25*
in their *p*.
in every *p*. where grounded *Isa 30:32*
staff shall pass
the *p*. is too strait for me, *Isa 49:20*
give *p*. to me
enlarge the *p*. of thy tent, *Isa 54:2*
spare not
I will make the *p*. of my feet *Isa 60:13*
glorious
and where is the *p*. of my rest *Isa 66:1*
go to my *p*.; till there be no *p*. *Jer 7:12;*
7:32; 19:11
glorious throne is the *p*. of *Jer 17:12*
our sanctuary
the flowing waters come from *Jer 18:14*
another *p*.
into the burial *p*. of common *Jer 26:23*
people (S)
there slain be on *p*. where they *Eze 6:13*
offered
p. of my throne shall Israel no *Eze 43:7*
more defile
he shall burn it in the *Eze 43:21*
appointed *p*. of house
that no *p*. was found for them *Da 2:35*
the *p*. of his sanctuary was *Da 8:11*
cast down
I will go and return to my *p*. *Ho 5:15*
till they
there shall be many dead bodies *Ho 8:3*
in every *p*.
their *p*. is not known where *Na 3:17*
they are
and *p*. shall not be found for *Zec 10:10*
them
shall be inhabited again in *Zec 12:6;*
her own *p*. *14:10*
incense shall be offered in *Mal 1:11*
every *p*.
see the *p*. where Lord lay *M't 28:6;*
M'k 16:6

in what *p*. soever ye enter *M'k 6:10*
into an house
in the market *p*. (S) *M'k 7:4; Ac 17:17*
he found the *p*. where it was *Lu 4:17*
written
Lord sent them two and two *Lu 10:1*
unto every *p*.
a Levite, when he was at the *Lu 10:32*
p. passed by
and say to thee, Give this man *Lu 14:9*
p.
Jerusalem is the *p*. of worship *Joh 4:20*
because my word hath no *p*. *Joh 8:37*
in you
he abode two days still in the *Joh 11:6*
same *p*.
Romans shall take away our *Joh 11:48*
p. and nation
take away our *p*. and people *Joh 11:48*
(B)
Judas which betrayed him, *Joh 18:2*
knew the *p*.
they were with one accord in *Ac 2:1*
one *p*.
purpose preordained to take *p*. *Ac 4:28*
(B)(E)
when they had prayed, the *p*. *Ac 4:31*
was shaken
the *p*. whereon thou standest is *Ac 7:33*
holy
or what is the *p*. of my rest *Ac 7:49*
the *p*. of scripture which he *Ac 8:32*
read was this
avenge not, but rather give *p*. *Ro 12:19*
to wrath
but now having no more *p*. in *Ro 15:23*
these parts
with all that in every *p*. call on *1Co 1:2*
Jesus Christ
no *p*. for human pride (N) *1Co 1:29*
when ye come together into *1Co 11:20*
one *p*.
the whole church be come *1Co 14:23*
into one *p*.
the savour of his knowledge *2Co 2:14*
in every *p*.
to whom gave *p*. by subjection *Ga 2:5*
not an hour
neither give *p*. to the devil *Eph 4:27*
things are out of *p*. (P) *Eph 5:4*
he might have first *p*. (B) *Col 1:18*
in every *p*. your faith *1Th 1:8*
God-ward is spread
as he saith also in another *p*. *Heb 5:6*
Thou art a priest
no. *p*. should have been sought *Heb 8:7*
for the second
he found no *p*. of repentance *Heb 12:17*
though sought
at the same *p*. sweet water and *Jas 3:11*
bitter
abandoned proper dwelling *p*. *Jude 6*
(A)(B)(R)
nor was there *p*. found any *Re 12:8*
more in heaven
that she might fly into *Re 12:14*
wilderness to her *p*.
and there was found no *p*. for *Re 20:11*
them

PLACE (verb)

and *p*. such over them to be *Ex 18:21*
rulers
in the place which he shall *De 14:23;*
choose, to *p*. his name there *16:2, 6, 11;*
26:2
and *p*. them in the house of *Ezr 6:5*
God
and I will *p*. salvation in Zion *Isa 46:13*
for Israel
I shall *p*. you in your own *Eze 37:14;*
land *37:26*
and they shall *p*. the *Da 11:31*
abomination
I will *p*. them in their houses, *Ho 11:11*
saith Lord
I will bring them again to *p*. *Zec 10:6*
them

A PLACE

a *p*. where king's prisoners *Ge 39:20*
were bound
then I will appoint thee a *p*. *Ex 21:13*
to flee
the Lord said, Behold, there is *Ex 33:21*
a *p*. by me
behold, the place was a *p*. for *Nu 32:1*
cattle
search you out a *p*. to pitch *De 1:33*
your tents in

thou shalt have *a p.* without   *De 23:12* the camp
they shall give him *a p.* in the   *Jos 20:4* city
to sojourn where he could find   *J'g 17:8;* *a p.*   *17:9*
a p. where is no want of any   *J'g 18:10* thing
Saul set him up *a p.* and is   *1Sa 15:12* gone
I have appointed my servants   *1Sa 21:2* to such *a p.*
let them give me *a p.* in some   *1Sa 27:5* town
I will appoint *a p.* for Israel,   *2Sa 7:10;* they may dwell in *a p.*   *1Ch 17:9*
Joab assigned Uriah to *a p.*   *2Sa 11:16* where valiant
I set there *a p.* for ark   *1Ki 8:21;*   *1Ch 15:1*
let us make *a p.* where we may   *2Ki 6:2* dwell
in such and such *a p.*   *2Ki 6:8*
shall be my camp
man of God said, Beware thou   *2Ki 6:9* pass not such *a p.*
I have built *a p.* for thy   *2Ch 6:2* dwelling
there is *a p.* for gold where   *Job 28:1* they fine it
until I find out *a p.* for the   *Ps 132:5* Lord
and his children have *a p.* of   *Pr 14:26* refuge
shall be for *a p.* of refuge from   *Isa 4:6* rain
the Lord will be to us *a p.* of   *Isa 33:21* broad rivers
and find for herself *a p.* of   *Isa 34:14* rest
and within my walls *a p.* and a   *Isa 56:5* name
Achor *a p.* for the herds to lie   *Isa 65:10* down in
a p. for the spreading of nets   *Eze 26:5;*   *26:14*
I will give to Gog, *a p.* of   *Eze 39:11* graves in Israel
she is become *a p.* for beasts   *Zep 2:15* to lie down
that is *a p.* of a skull   *M't 27:33;*   *Joh 19:17*
found colt in *a p.* where two   *M'k 11:4* ways met
I go to prepare *a p.* for you   *Joh 14:2;*   *14:3*
one in *a certain p.* testified,   *Heb 2:6* saying
he spake in *a certain p.* of the   *Heb 4:4* seventh day
when called to go out into *a*   *Heb 11:8* *p.* he obeyed
where she hath *a p.* prepared   *Re 12:6* of God
gathered them into *a p.* called   *Re 16:16* Armageddon

HIGH PLACE

and Balaam went up to an   *Nu 23:3* high *p.*
there is a sacrifice to-day in   *1Sa 9:12* high *p.*
shalt meet prophets coming   *1Sa 10:5* from high *p.*
when had made an end, Saul   *1Sa 10:13* came to high *p.*
that was great high *p.*   *1Ki 3:4;*   *1Ch 16:39*
Solomon built an high *p.* for   *1Ki 11:7* Chemosh
high *p.* Jeroboam made,   *2Ki 23:15* Josiah brake down high *p.* burnt high *p.*
so Solomon went to the high *p.*   *2Ch 1:3* come from his journey to   *2Ch 1:13* high *p.* at Gibeon
that Moab is weary on the   *Isa 16:12* high *p.*
made high *p.* in every street   *Eze 16:24;*   *16:25, 31*
what is the high *p.*   *Eze 20:29* whereunto ye go

HIS PLACE

and Abraham returned to his   *Ge 18:33* *p.*
Laban rose up and returned   *Ge 31:55* to *his p.*

neither rose from *his p.* for   *Ex 10:23* three days
abide every man in *his p.*   *Ex 16:29* none go out of *his p.*
but if the bright spot stay in   *Le 13:23* *his p.*
every man in *his p.* by their   *Nu 2:17* standards
Balaam rose up and returned   *Nu 24:25* to *his p.*
and bring him to the gate of   *De 21:19* *his p.*
name of dead be not cut off   *Ru 4:10* from *his p.*
when Eli was laid down in his   *1Sa 3:2* *p.*
so Samuel went and lay down   *1Sa 3:9* in *his p.*
and they set Dagon in *his p.*   *1Sa 5:3*
let the ark go down to *his*   *1Sa 5:11;* own *p.*   *6:2*
go and see *his p.* where his   *1Sa 23:22* haunt is
David went on, Saul   *1Sa 26:25* returned to *his p.*
send David, that he may go   *1Sa 29:4* again to *his p.*
they set the ark of the Lord in   *2Sa 6:17* *his p.*
Barzillai returned to his own   *2Sa 19:39* *p.*
priests brought ark to *his p.*   *1Ki 8:6;*   *2Ch 5:7*
take kings away, every man   *1Ki 20:24* out of *his p.*
to bring the ark of the Lord   *1Ch 15:3* to *his p.*
strength and gladness are in   *1Ch 16:27* *his p.*
carried the chest to *his p.*   *2Ch 24:11* again
king stood in *his p.* and   *2Ch 34:31* made a covenant
let men of *his p.* help him with   *Ezr 1:4* silver
for house of God to set it   *Ezr 2:68;* in *his p.*   *5:15; 6:7*
they came every one from his   *Job 2:11* own *p.*
neither shall *his p.* know him   *Job 7:10* any more
if he destroy him from *his p.*   *Job 8:18* it shall deny
and the rock is removed out   *Job 14:18* of *his p.*
and shall the rock be removed   *Job 18:4* out of *his p.*
nor shall *his p.* any more   *Job 20:9* behold him
and as a storm hurleth him   *Job 27:21* out of *his p.*
men shall clap hands and   *Job 27:23* hiss him out of *his p.*
and my heart is removed out   *Job 37:1* of *his p.*
and caused the dayspring to   *Job 38:12* know *his p.*
thou shalt diligently consider   *Ps 37:10* *his p.*
so is a man that wandereth   *Pr 27:8* from *his p.*
the sun hasteth to *his p.* where   *Ec 1:5* he arose
Lord cometh out of *his p.* to   *Isa 26:21* punish
his p. of defence shall be   *Isa 33:16* munition of rocks
set him in *his p.* shall not   *Isa 46:7* remove from *his p.*
he is gone from *his p.* to make   *Jer 4:7* desolate
they shall feed every one in his   *Jer 6:3* *p.*
blessed be the glory of Lord   *Eze 3:12* from *his p.*
behold, the Lord cometh out of   *Mic 1:3* *his p.*
men shall worship every one   *Zep 2:11* from *his p.*
and he shall grow up out of   *Zec 6:12* *his p.*
put up again thy sword into   *M't 26:52* *his p.*
that he might go to *his own p.*   *Ac 1:25*
remove thy candlestick out of   *Re 2:5* *his p.*

IN THE PLACE

Joseph said, Fear not, I am   *Ge 50:19* in *the p.* of God

plant them in *the p.* thou hast   *Ex 15:17* made
kill it in *the p.* where they kill   *Le 4:24;* burnt offering   *4:29, 33; 6:25; 7:2*
in *the p.* of the boil there be   *Le 13:19* white rising
in *the p.* where cloud abode,   *Nu 9:17* there Israel
inheritance be in *the p.* where   *Nu 33:54* his lot falleth
Joshua set up twelve stones in   *Jos 4:9* *the p.*
because hast drunk water in   *1Ki 13:22* *the p.*
in *the p.* where dogs licked   *1Ki 21:19* blood of Naboth
in *the p.* that David had   *2Ch 3:1* prepared
hast sore broken us in *the p.*   *Ps 44:19* of dragons
and stand not in *the p.* of great   *Pr 25:6* men
in *the p.* where the tree falleth   *Ec 11:3* it shall be
but he shall die in *the p.*   *Jer 22:12;*   *38:9; 42:22*
in *the p.* where the king   *Eze 17:16* dwelleth
judge thee in *the p.* where   *Eze 21:30* thou wast created
that in *the p.* where it was   *Ho 1:10;* said   *Ro 9:26*
not stay long in *the p.* of   *Ho 13:13* breaking forth
in *the p.* where crucified, was   *Joh 19:41* a garden

OF THE PLACE

men *of p.* asked him, lest men   *Ge 26:7* of *the p.* kill
Laban gathered all the men *of*   *Ge 29:22* *the p.*
Jacob called the name *of the*   *Ge 32:30* *p.* Peniel
name *of the p.* Succoth;   *Ge 33:17;* name *of the p.* Beth-el   *35:15*
and he called name *of the p.*   *Ex 17:7* Massah
name *of the p.* Taberah   *Nu 11:3*
name *of the p.* Hormah   *Nu 21:3*
take ye out *of the p.* twelve   *Jos 4:3* stones
name *of the p.* Gilgal   *Jos 5:9*
name *of the p.* was called   *Jos 7:26* Valley of Achor
the men *of the p.* were   *J'g 19:16* Benjamites
Naomi went forth out *of the p.*   *Ru 1:7* where
David called name *of the p.*   *2Sa 6:8* Perez-uzzah
pattern *of the p.* of the   *1Ch 28:11* mercy seat
name *of the p.* valley of   *2Ch 20:26* Berachah
breadth *of the p.* left was five   *Eze 41:11* cubits
raise them out *of the p.* whither   *Joe 3:7* ye sold
make an utter end *of the p.*   *Na 1:8* thereof

THAT PLACE

Abraham called *that p.*   *Ge 21:31* Beer-sheba
that p. Jehovah-jireh   *Ge 22:14*
that p. Beth-el   *Ge 28:19*
that p. Mahanaim   *Ge 32:2*
asked men of *that p.*   *Ge 38:21*
name of *that p.*   *Nu 11:34* Kibroth-hattaavah
destroy names of them out of   *De 12:3* *that p.*
the sentence they of *that p.*   *De 17:10* shall shew
they called name of *that p.*   *J'g 2:5* Bochim
that p. Ramath-lehi   *J'g 15:17*
called *that p.* Mahaneh-dan   *J'g 18:12*
called *that p.*   *1Sa 23:28* Selah-hammah-lekoth
that p. was called   *2Sa 2:16* Helkath-hazzurim
called *that p.* Baal-perazim   *2Sa 5:20;*   *1Ch 14:11*
that p. is called Perez-uzzah   *1Ch 13:11*
men of *that p.* had knowledge   *M't 14:35* of him

there abide till ye depart from   *M'k 6:10*
that p.
a multitude being in *that p.*   *Joh 5:13*
but was in *that p.* where   *Joh 11:30*
Martha met him
both we and they of *that p.*   *Ac 21:12*
besought

THIS PLACE

thy sons bring them out of   *Ge 19:12*
this p.
we will destroy *this p.*; get   *Ge 19:13;*
out of *this p.*   *19:14*
surely the fear of God is not   *Ge 20:11*
in *this p.*
Lord is in *this p.*; dreadful is   *Ge 28:16;*
this p.   *28:17*
there was no harlot in *this p.*   *Ge 38:21;*
  38:22
are sons, whom God hath   *Ge 48:9*
given me in *this p.*
the Lord brought you out from   *Ex 13:3*
this p.
to bring us unto *this* evil *p.*   *Nu 20:5*
bare thee till ye come to *this*   *De 1:31;*
p.   *9:7; 11:5*
and he hath brought us into   *De 26:9*
this p.
when ye came unto *this p.*   *De 29:7*
Sihon came out
and what makest thou in *this p.* *J'g 18:3*
hearken to prayer toward *this* *1Ki 8:29;*
p.   *8:30; 2Ch 6:20-21, 26, 40; 7:15*
nor eat bread, nor drink   *1Ki 13:8;*
water in *this p.*   *13:16*
come not without Lord   *2Ki 18:25*
against *this p.*
I will bring evil on *this p.*   *2Ki 22:16;*
  26:17, 20; 2Ch 34:24-25, 28
and have chosen *this p.* to   *2Ch 7:12*
myself
this the *p.* of him that knows *Job 18:21*
not God
and shed not innocent blood in   *Jer 7:6*
this p.
my fury shall be poured out on   *Jer 7:20*
this p.
I will give you assured peace *Jer 14:13*
in *this p.*
neither have sons nor   *Jer 16:2*
daughters in *this p.*
cause to cease out of *this p.*   *Jer 16:9*
the voice of mirth
behold, I will bring evil upon   *Jer 19:3*
this p.
they estranged *this p.* filled   *Jer 19:4*
this p. with blood
that *this p.* shall no more be   *Jer 19:6*
called Tophet
thus will I do to *this p.* saith   *Jer 19:12;*
the Lord   *40:2*
which went forth out of *this* *Jer 22:11;*
p.   *24:5*
and I will restore them to   *Jer 27:22;*
this p.   *32:37*
I will bring to *this p.* all the   *Jer 28:3;*
vessels   *28:6*
I will bring again to *this p.*   *Jer 28:4*
Jeconiah
in causing you to return to   *Jer 29:10*
this p.
again be heard in *this p.* the   *Jer 33:10*
voice of joy
and ye shall see *this p.* no   *Jer 42:18*
more
that I will punish you in *this* *Jer 44:29*
p.
O Lord, thou hast spoken   *Jer 51:62*
against *this p.*
this is *p.* where the priests   *Eze 46:20*
shall boil
cut off the remnant of Baal   *Zep 1:4*
from *this p.*
in *this p.* will I give peace,   *Hag 2:9*
saith the Lord
in *this p.* one greater than the   *M't 12:6*
temple
lest they come into *this p.* of   *Lu 16:28*
torment
teaching, beginning from   *Lu 23:5*
Galilee to *this p.*
Jesus of Nazareth shall destroy   *Ac 6:14*
this p.
they shall come forth and serve   *Ac 7:7*
me in *this p.*
that teacheth against the law   *Ac 21:28*
and *this p.*
and in *this p.* again, if they   *Heb 4:5*
shall enter

THY PLACE

Pharaoh shall restore thee to   *Ge 40:13*
thy p.
therefore now flee thou to *thy*   *Nu 24:11*
p.
return to *thy p.* and abide   *2Sa 15:19*
with king
if ruler rise against thee, leave   *Ec 10:4*
not *thy p.*
thou shalt remove from *thy p.*   *Eze 12:3;*
  38:15

TO, UNTO THE PLACE

Abram went *unto the p.*   *Ge 13:3;*
where his tent   *13:4*
went *unto the p.* of which God *Ge 22:3;*
told him   *22:9*
to bring you *unto the p.* of the   *Ex 3:8*
Canaanite
lead people *unto the p.* of   *Ex 32:34*
which I spake
we are journeying *to the p.* of *Nu 10:29*
which
go up *to the p.* which Lord   *Nu 14:40*
hath promised
carried stones *to the p.* where   *Jos 4:8*
they lodged
come *to the p.* where thou   *1Sa 20:19*
hide thyself
as many as came *to the p.*   *2Sa 2:23*
stood still
sent *to the p.* which man of   *2Ki 6:10*
God told
bring ark *to the p.* that I   *1Ch 15:12*
prepared
I will bring them *to the p.* I   *Ne 1:9*
have chosen
they go *to the p.* that thou   *Ps 104:8*
hast founded
present brought *to the p.* of   *Isa 18:7*
name of Lord
I will do *to the p.* which I gave *Jer 7:14*
to you
will bring you again *to the p.* *Jer 29:14*
whence I caused
and was entered *into the p.* of *Ac 25:23*
hearing

PLACED

God *p.* at east of the garden   *Ge 3:24*
cherubims
Joseph *p.* his father and his   *Ge 47:11*
brethren
Jeroboam *p.* in Beth-el the   *1Ki 12:32*
priests
and *p.* them in Halah and in   *2Ki 17:6*
Habor
and *p.* them in the cities of   *2Ki 17:24;*
Samaria   *17:26*
which he *p.* in the chariot   *2Ch 1:14*
cities
he made tables, *p.* them in the   *2Ch 4:8*
temple
he *p.* forces in all the fenced   *2Ch 17:2*
cities of Judah
of old, since man was *p.* upon   *Job 20:4*
earth
the tent which he had *p.*   *Ps 78:60*
among men
that they may be *p.* alone in the   *Isa 5:8*
midst
which *p.* sand for the bound of *Jer 5:22*
the sea
the eagle *p.* it by the great   *Eze 17:5*
waters
thrones were *p.* (S)   *Da 7:9*

PLACES

I am with thee, will keep thee   *Ge 28:15*
in all *p.*
in all *p.* where I record my   *Ex 20:24*
name
shall utterly destroy all the *p.*   *De 12:2*
wherein
abode in their *p.* till they were   *Jos 5:8*
whole
delivered in the *p.* of drawing   *J'g 5:11*
water
let us draw near to one of   *J'g 19:13*
these *p.* to lodge
Samuel judged Israel in all   *1Sa 7:16*
those *p.*
David sent presents to all the *1Sa 30:31*
p.

in all the *p.* spake I a word   *2Sa 7:7*
with any
high *p.*, pillars, Asherim   *1Ki 14:23*
(A)(B)(E)(R)
places (S)   *1Ki 20:24;*
  M't 23:6; M'k 12:39; Lu 14:7; 20:46
put down priests in *p.* about   *2Ki 23:5*
Jerusalem
he filled their *p.* with the   *2Ki 23:14*
bones of men
from all *p.* whence ye shall   *Ne 4:12*
return
I set the people in lower *p.* and   *Ne 4:13*
on higher *p.*
they sought Levites out of all   *Ne 12:27*
their *p.*
where are dwelling *p.* of the   *Job 21:28*
wicked
beasts go into dens and   *Job 37:8*
remain in their *p.*
he sitteth in lurking *p.* of the   *Ps 10:8*
villages
the lines are fallen to me in   *Ps 16:6*
pleasant *p.*
and be afraid out of their   *Ps 18:45*
close *p.*
thou didst set them in slippery *Ps 73:18*
p.
the dark *p.* of the earth are   *Ps 74:20*
full of cruelty
bless the Lord, all his works, *Ps 103:22*
in all *p.*
they ran in the dry *p.* like a   *Ps 105:41*
river
he shall fill the *p.* with the   *Ps 110:6*
dead bodies
she standeth in the *p.* of the   *Pr 8:2*
paths
O my dove, that art in the   *Ca 2:14*
secret *p.*
my people shall dwell in quiet *Isa 32:18*
resting *p.*
crooked made straight, and   *Isa 40:4*
rough *p.* plain
I will make the crooked *p.*   *Isa 45:2*
straight
a wind from those *p.* shall   *Jer 4:12*
come to me
in all *p.* whither I have driven *Jer 8:3;*
them   *29:14*
they shall come from *p.* about *Jer 17:26*
Jerusalem
to be a taunt and a curse in all *Jer 24:9*
p. I drive
take witnesses in the *p.* about *Jer 32:44*
Jerusalem
all the Jews returned out of   *Jer 40:12*
all *p.* whither
thy life I will give for a prey in *Jer 45:5*
all *p.*
uncovered his hidden *p.*   *Jer 49:10*
(A)(B)(R)
he hath destroyed his *p.* of the   *La 2:6*
assembly
as a lion in hidden *p.* (B)   *La 3:10*
I will deliver them out of all   *Eze 34:12*
I will make the *p.* round my   *Eze 34:26*
hill a blessing
he said, These are the *p.* of   *Eze 46:24*
them that boil
but the miry *p.* thereof shall   *Eze 47:11*
not be healed
and want of bread in all your   *Am 4:6*
p.
I will give thee *p.* to walk   *Zec 3:7*
among these
in the market *p.* (S)   *M't 11:16;*
  23:7; Lu 11:43; 20:46
he walketh through dry *p.*   *M't 12:43;*
  Lu 11:24
some fell on stony *p.* and   *M't 13:5;*
sprung up   *13:20*
and there shall be famines   *M't 24:7;*
and earthquakes in divers *p.* *M'k 13:8;*
  Lu 21:11
we accept it in all *p.* most   *Ac 24:3*
noble Felix
who hath blessed us in   *Eph 1:3*
heavenly *p.*
set him at his own right hand *Eph 1:20*
in heavenly *p.*
made us sit together in   *Eph 2:6*
heavenly *p.* in Christ Jesus
to powers in heavenly *p.*   *Eph 3:10*
might be known
my bonds in Christ are   *Ph'p 1:13*
manifest in all *p.*
mountain and island moved   *Re 6:14*
out of their *p.*

HIGH PLACES

I will destroy your *high p.* and   *Le 26:30*
images
consumed lords of *high p.* of   *Nu 21:28*
Arnon
brought him up into the *high*   *Nu 22:41*
p. of Baal
and quite pluck down all   *Nu 33:52*
their *high p.*
made him ride on *high p.* of   *De 32:13*
the earth
and thou shalt tread upon   *De 33:29*
their *high p.*
jeoparded their lives in the   *J'g 5:18*
high p.
the people hide themselves in   *1Sa 13:6*
high p.
the beauty of Israel slain in   *2Sa 1:19*
high p.
Jonathan, thou wast slain in   *2Sa 1:25*
thy *high p.*
and setteth me on my *high*   *2Sa 22:34;*
p.   *Ps 18:33*
only the people sacrificed in   *1Ki 3:2;*
high p.   *2Ki 17:32; 2Ch 33:17*
burnt incense in *high p.*   *1Ki 3:3;*
   22:43; 2Ki 12:3; 15:4, 35; 16:4; 17:11
Jeroboam made an house of   *1Ki 12:31*
high p.
he placed in Beth-el the   *1Ki 12:32*
priests of *high p.*
he shall offer the priests of the   *1Ki 13:2*
high p.
he cried against all the   *1Ki 13:32*
houses of the *high p.*
made of lowest of people   *1Ki 13:33;*
priests of *high p.*   *2Ki 17:32*
the *high p.* were not   *1Ki 15:14;*
removed   *22:43; 2Ki 12:3; 14:4; 15:4, 35*
put their gods in houses of   *2Ki 17:29*
high p.
Hezekiah removed the *high p.*   *2Ki 18:4;*
  18:22
had ordained to burn incense   *2Ki 23:5*
in the *high p.*
defi.ed *high p.* and brake   *2Ki 23:8;*
down *high p.*   *23:13; 2Ch 31:1; 32:12;*
  Isa 36:7
priests of *high p.* came not up   *2Ki 23:9*
to altar of Lord
he slew all the priests of the   *2Ki 23:20*
high p.
Rehoboam ordained priests   *2Ch 11:15*
for *high p.*
Asa took away the *high p.*   *2Ch 14:3;*
and images   *14:5*
the *high p.* were not taken   *2Ch 15:17;*
away   *20:33*
Jehoshaphat took away the   *2Ch 17:6*
high p.
Jehoram made *high p.*;   *2Ch 21:11;*
Ahaz *high p.*   *28:25*
Josiah did purge Jerusalem   *2Ch 34:3*
from the *high p.*
he maketh peace in his *high p.*   *Job 25:2*
they provoked him with their   *Ps 78:58*
high p.
she standeth on the top of the   *Pr 8:2*
high p.
sitteth on a seat in the *high p.*   *Pr 9:14*
of the city
he is gone up to the *high p.* to   *Isa 15:2*
weep
I will open rivers in *high p.*   *Isa 41:18*
and fountains
their pastures shall be in all   *Isa 49:9*
high p.
cause thee to ride on *high p.*   *Isa 58:14*
of the earth
lift up thine eyes to the *high p.*   *Jer 3:2*
and see
a voice was heard on the *high*   *Jer 3:21*
p. weeping
a dry wind in the *high p.* of the   *Jer 4:11*
wilderness
and take up a lamentation in   *Jer 7:29*
the *high p.*
the spoilers are come up on   *Jer 12:12*
all the *high p.*
the wild asses did stand in the   *Jer 14:6*
high p.
I will give thy *high p.* for sin,   *Jer 17:3*
thro' borders
and the mountain of the   *Jer 26:18;*
house shall become as the   *Mic 3:12*
high p. of the forest
to cease in Moab him that   *Jer 48:35*
offereth in *high p.*
behold, I will destroy your *high*   *Eze 6:3*
p.

deckedst thy *high p.* with   *Eze 16:16*
divers colours
and they shall break down   *Eze 16:39*
thy *high p.*
the ancient *high p.* are ours in   *Eze 36:2*
possession
the *high p.* of Aven shall be   *Ho 10:8*
destroyed
treadeth on *high p.* of earth   *Am 4:13;*
  Mic 1:3
the *high p.* of Isaac shall be   *Am 7:9*
desolate
and what are the *high p.* of   *Mic 1:5*
Judah
will make me to walk on   *Hab 3:19*
mine *high p.*
against spiritual wickedness   *Eph 6:12*
in *high p.*

WASTE PLACES

waste p. of fat ones shall   *Isa 5:17*
strangers eat
the Lord will comfort all her   *Isa 51:3*
waste p.
sing together, ye *waste p.* of   *Isa 52:9*
Jerusalem
and they shall build the old   *Isa 58:12*
waste p.

PLAGUE

p. country with frogs (R)   *Ex 8:2*
a dreadful *p.* (A)(B)(R)(S)   *Ex 9:3*
yet I will bring one *p.* on   *Ex 11:1*
Pharaoh
the *p.* shall not be on you to   *Ex 12:13*
destroy you
that there be no *p.* among   *Ex 30:12*
them
when hair in the *p.* is turned   *Le 13:3;*
white   *13:17*
if the *p.* spread not in the skin   *Le 13:5;*
  13:6; 14:48
disease (A)   *Le 13:5;*
  13:30, 44, 50, 57-58
if a man or woman hath a *p.*   *Le 13:30;*
then priest shall see the *p.*   *13:31-32,*
  13:50-51, 55; 14:37
he is a leprous man; his *p.* is   *Le 13:44*
in his head
and shut up it that hath the *p.*   *Le 13:50*
seven days
if it appear in warp or woof,   *Le 13:57*
it is a spreading *p.*
if *p.* be departed from them, it   *Le 13:58*
be washed
there is as it were a *p.* in the   *Le 14:35*
house
that there be no *p.* among   *Nu 8:19*
Israel
Lord smote people with a   *Nu 11:33*
very great *p.*
destroy with a *p.*   *Nu 14:12*
those men died by the *p.*   *Nu 14:37*
before the Lord
wrath is gone out, the *p.* is   *Nu 16:46;*
begun   *16:47*
and the *p.* was stayed   *Nu 16:48;*
  16:50; 25:8
now they that died in the *p.*   *Nu 16:49;*
were   *25:9*
every *p.* which is not written   *De 28:61*
in book
every sickness and affliction   *De 28:61*
(A)(R)
every sickness and pestilence   *De 28:61*
(B)
we are not cleaned, altho'   *Jos 22:17*
there was *p.*
one *p.* was on you all and your   *1Sa 6:4*
lords
that *p.* may be stayed   *2Sa 24:21;*
  1Ch 21:22
whatever *p.* or sickness there   *1Ki 8:37*
be
shall know every man the *p.*   *1Ki 8:38*
of his own heart
whatsoever *p.* or sickness (S)   *2Ch 6:28;*
  6:29
own *p.* and pain (B)   *2Ch 6:29*
with a great *p.* will the Lord   *2Ch 21:14*
smite
fatal *p.* is poured out (B)   *Ps 41:8*
I will *p.* them that hate him   *Ps 89:23*
nor any *p.* come nigh thy   *Ps 91:10*
dwelling
and the *p.* brake in upon   *Ps 106:29*
them
Phinehas executed judgment,   *Ps 106:30*
so *p.* was stayed

burning *p.* followed (A)(R)   *Hab 3:5*
this shall be *p.* the Lord will   *Zec 14:12;*
smite   *14:18*
she felt that she was healed of   *M'k 5:29*
that *p.*
her ailment (A)   *M'k 5:29*
her affliction (B)   *M'k 5:29*
cured of her trouble (N)   *M'k 5:29*
the hemorrhage (P)(R)   *M'k 5:29*
go in peace, and be whole of   *M'k 5:34*
thy *p.*
be healed of your disease   *M'k 5:34*
(A)(R)
be healed of your affliction   *M'k 5:34*
(B)
be free from your trouble   *M'k 5:34*
(N)(P)
a real *p.* (A)(B)   *Ac 24:5*
blasphemed because of the *p.*   *Re 16:21*
of hail

PLAGUED

the Lord *p.* Pharaoh and his   *Ge 12:17*
house
the Lord scourged Pharaoh   *Ge 12:17*
(A)
the Lord struck Pharaoh (B)   *Ge 12:17*
the Lord afflicted Pharaoh   *Ge 12:17*
(R)
Lord *p.* the people for making   *Ex 32:35*
calf
p. Egypt, and afterwards   *Jos 24:5*
brought you
were *p.* (B)   *1Sa 5:12*
God *p.* them (B)   *1Ch 15:6*
not on people, that they   *1Ch 21:17*
should be *p.*
nor are they *p.* like other men   *Ps 73:5*
all the day have I been *p.* and   *Ps 73:14*
chastened

PLAGUES

Lord plagued Pharaoh with   *Ge 12:17*
I will at this time send all my   *Ex 9:14*
p.
I will bring seven times more   *Le 26:21*
p. on you
the Lord will make thy *p.*   *De 28:59*
wonderful
when they see the *p.* of that   *De 29:22*
land
gods that smote the Egyptians   *1Sa 4:8*
with *p.*
own *p.* and sorrow (E)   *2Ch 6:29*
hiss, because of the *p.*   *Jer 19:8;*
  49:17; 50:13
O death, I will be thy *p.* O   *Ho 13:14*
grave
pressed to touch him as many   *M'k 3:10*
as had *p.*
same hour he cured many of   *Lu 7:21*
their *p.*
cured of diseases, *p.* (N)(R)   *Lu 7:21*
rest which were not killed by   *Re 9:20*
these *p.*
these have power to smite   *Re 11:6*
earth with *p.*
name of God, who hath power   *Re 16:9*
over these *p.*
and that ye receive not of her   *Re 18:4*
p.
therefore shall her *p.* come in   *Re 18:8*
one day, death
God shall add to him the *p.*   *Re 22:18*
written

PLAIN

they found a *p.* in the land of   *Ge 11:2*
Shinar
and Lot beheld all the *p.* of   *Ge 13:10*
Jordan
then Lot chose him all the *p.*   *Ge 13:11*
of Jordan
Lot dwelled in cities of the *p.*   *Ge 13:12*
toward Sodom
Abram came and dwelt in   *Ge 13:18;*
the *p.*   *14:13*
nor stay thou in all *p.* escape   *Ge 19:17*
to mountain
he overthrew those cities in   *Ge 19:25*
all the *p.*
Jacob was a *p.* man, dwelling   *Ge 25:27*
in tents
dwell in the *p.* (B)   *De 11:30*
Joshua took the valley and   *Jos 11:16*
the *p.*

made Abimelech king by *p.* of   *J'g 9:6*
pillar
Jephthah smote the   *J'g 11:33*
Ammonites to the *p.*
thou shalt come to the *p.* of   *1Sa 10:3*
Tabor
David and his men were in   *1Sa 23:24*
the *p.*
the *p.* (B)   *1Sa 23:25;*
    Joe 1:19; 2:22; Eze 34:25
Abner and his men walked   *2Sa 2:29*
through *p.*
Baanah and Rechab gat them   *2Sa 4:7*
through the *p.*
I will tarry in the *p.* till I   *2Sa 15:28*
hear from you
then Ahimaaz ran by the way   *2Sa 18:23*
of the *p.*
in *p.* of Jordan did king cast   *1Ki 7:46*
them
let us fight against them in   *1Ki 20:23;*
the *p.*   *20:25*
king went towards the *p.*   *2Ki 25:4;*
    Jer 52:7
after him repaired the priests   *Ne 3:22*
of the *p.*
teach me, and lead me in a *p.*   *Ps 27:11*
path
they are *p.* to him that   *Pr 8:9*
understandeth
but the way of the righteous is *Pr 15:19*
made *p.*
when he made *p.* the face   *Isa 28:25*
thereof
Sharon is like a *p.* (S)   *Isa 33:9*
crooked made straight, and   *Isa 40:4*
rough places *p.*
shall come from *p.* bringing   *Jer 17:26*
offerings
I am against thee, O rock of   *Jer 21:13*
the *p.*
p. shall be destroyed, as Lord   *Jer 48:8*
hath spoken
judgment is come on the *p.*   *Jer 48:21*
country
he said, Arise, go forth in the   *Eze 3:22;*
p.   *3:23*
according to the vision that I   *Eze 8:4*
saw in the *p.*
write the vision, make it *p.*   *Hab 2:2*
upon tables
tongue was loosed, and he   *M'k 7:35*
spake *p.*
works of flesh are *p.* (R)   *Ga 5:19*
made the secret *p.* (N)(P)   *Col 4:4*

PLAINLY

if the servant shall *p.* say I love *Ex 21:5*
I speak *p.,* not obscurely   *Nu 12:8*
(B)(S)
all the words of this law very   *De 27:8*
p.
p. appear unto the house of   *1Sa 2:27*
He told us *p.* that the asses   *1Sa 10:16*
were
sent unto us hath been *p.* read *Ezr 4:18*
shall be ready to speak *p.*   *Isa 32:4*
I shall tell them *p.* (P)   *M't 7:23*
If thou be the Christ, tell us   *Joh 10:24*
p.
Then said Jesus unto them *p.*   *Joh 11:14*
I shall shew you *p.* of the   *Joh 16:25*
Father
him, Lo, now speakest thou   *Joh 16:29*
p.
put the whole matter *p.* (B)   *Ac 11:4*
declare *p.* that they seek a   *Heb 11:14*
country

PLAINNESS

hope, we use great *p.* of speech *2Co 3:12*

PLAINS

unto him in the *p.* of Mamre   *Ge 18:1*
and pitched in the *p.* of Moab   *Nu 22:1;*
    33:48
spake with them in the *p.* of   *Nu 26:3*
Moab
children of Israel in the *p.* of   *Nu 26:63*
Moab by
unto the camp at the *p.* of   *Nu 31:12*
Moab
unto Abel-shittim in the *p.* of *Nu 33:49*
Moab
spake unto Moses in the *p.*   *Nu 33:50;*
of Moab   *35:1*
children of Israel in the *p.* of   *Nu 36:13*
Moab

Gilgal, beside the *p.* of Moreh *De 11:30*
Moses went up from the *p.* of   *De 34:1*
Moab
wept for Moses in the *p.* of   *De 34:8*
Moab
unto battle, to the *p.* of   *Jos 4:13*
Jericho
month at even in the *p.* of   *Jos 5:10*
Jericho
and of the *p.* south of   *Jos 11:2*
Chinneroth
and in the *p.* and in the   *Jos 12:8*
springs
for inheritance in the *p.* of   *Jos 13:32*
Moab
night in the *p.* of the   *2Sa 17:16*
wilderness
overtook him in the *p.* of   *2Ki 25:5*
Jericho
trees that were in the low *p.* *1Ch 27:28*
trees that are in the low *p.* in *2Ch 9:27*
in the low country, and in   *2Ch 26:10*
the *p.*
Zedekiah in the *p.* of Jericho *Jer 39:5;*
    52:8

PLAISTER

morter, and shall *p.* the house *Le 14:42*
great stones, and *p.* them with *De 27:2*
Ebal, and thou shalt *p.* them   *De 27:4*
with
and lay it for a *p.* upon the   *Isa 38:21*
boil
p. of the wall of the king's   *Da 5:5*
palace

PLAISTERED

the house, and after it is *p.*   *Le 14:43*
the house, after the house was *Le 14:48*
p.

PLAITED

they *p.* a crown of thorns (S) *M't 27:29*

PLAITING

outward adorning of *p.* the hair *1Pe 3:3*
with interweaving and knotting *1Pe 3:3*
of the hair (A)
braided hair (B)(E)(N)(R)   *1Pe 3:3*
elaborate coiffure (P)   *1Pe 3:3*

PLANE

the *p.* trees (B)(E)(R)   *Ge 30:37*
the *p.* trees   *Eze 31:8*
(A)(B)(E)(R)(S)

PLANES

he fitteth it with *p.* and he   *Isa 44:13*

PLANETS

and to the *p.* and to all the   *2Ki 23:5*
hosts
the sun, moon, and the   *2Ki 23:5*
constellations (A)(R)
sun, moon, and signs of the   *2Ki 23:5*
Zodiac (B)

PLANKS

floor of the house with *p.* of   *1Ki 6:15*
fir
made all the ship *p.* (S)   *Eze 27:5*
thick *p.* upon the face   *Eze 41:25*
of porch
of the house, and thick *p.*   *Eze 41:26*

PLAN

nothing they *p.* to do (B)   *Ge 11:6*
p. designs of gold (B)   *Ex 31:4*
listened to their *p.* (B)   *1Ki 20:25*
every *p.* and thought (R)   *1Ch 28:9*
p. my hurt (A)   *Ps 35:4*
p. harm against me (B)   *Ps 41:7*
a well-devised *p.* (A)   *Ps 64:6*
p. evil things in hearts (R)   *Ps 140:2*
do not *p.* evil (R)   *Pr 3:29*
who *p.* evil (B)   *Pr 12:20*
plot mischief, *p.* good (B)   *Pr 14:22*
p. perverse things (B)   *Pr 16:30*
devise a *p.* (A)(B)(R)(S)   *Jer 18:11*
the *p.* of the Lord (A)(R)   *Jer 49:20*
his *p.* regarding Babylon (B) *Jer 51:11*

p. strategies (B)   *Da 11:24*
devise some cunning *p.* (N)   *M'k 14:1*
the counsel's *p.* (B)   *Lu 23:51*
fixed purpose, settled *p.* (A)   *Ac 2:23*
deliberate will and *p.* of God   *Ac 2:23*
(N)
determined *p.* of God (P)(R)   *Ac 2:23*
rebel against God's *p.* of love   *Ro 2:8*
(P)
their fulfilling God's *p.*   *Ro 11:12*
knowledge of God's secret *p.* *Ro 11:25;*
(P)   *16:25; Eph 1:9*
the secret of his *p.* (P)   *Eph 1:9*
p. for fulness of time (R)   *Eph 1:10*
complex wisdom of God's *p.* *Eph 3:10*
(P)
unchangeableness of purpose *Heb 6:17*
and *p.* (A)(B)(P)

PLANNED

this has been *p.* (B)   *2Sa 13:32*
p. to prevent us (A)(B)(R)   *2Sa 21:5*
purposes *p.* of old (A)   *Isa 25:1*
p. evil against her (A)(R)   *Jer 48:2*
P. and done (R)   *Jer 51:12*
thy hand and will *p.* (P)(R)   *Ac 4:28*
God *p.* before creation (P)   *1Co 2:7*
he *p.* in his purpose of love   *Eph 1:5*
(P)
good deeds God *p.* (P)   *Eph 2:10*

PLANNING

p. of the wicked (B)   *Job 21:16*
p. of the afflicted (B)   *Ps 14:6*

PLANS

p. of the poor (A)(R)   *Ps 14:6*
fulfill all your *p.* (A)(B)(R)   *Ps 20:4*
thoughts and *p.* (R)   *Ps 33:10*
p. wrongdoing on bed (A)   *Ps 36:4*
carries out wicked *p.* (B)   *Ps 37:7*
did not wait his *p.* (A)   *Ps 106:13*
wicked thoughts and *p.*   *Pr 6:18*
(A)(R)
p. go wrong (B)(R)   *Pr 15:22*
man's mind *p.* his ways   *Pr 16:9*
(A)(B)(R)
many *p.* in man's mind   *Pr 19:21*
(A)(B)(R)
p. to do evil (A)(B)(R)   *Pr 24:8*
p. determined long ago   *Isa 25:1*
(B)(R)
exhausted due to many *p.* (B) *Isa 47:13*
follow own *p.* (R)(S)   *Jer 18:12*
devise *p.* (A)(R)   *Da 11:24*
keep *p.* in my soul (B)   *Da 13:2*
p. in man's mind is deep   *Pr 19:21*
(B)(R)

PLANT

every *p.* of the field before it   *Ge 2:5*
was
shalt bring them in, and *p.*   *Ex 15:17*
them
shalt not *p.* thee a grove of   *De 16:21*
any
thou shalt *p.* a vineyard, and *De 28:30*
shalt
Thou shalt *p.* vineyards, and *De 28:39*
dress
my people Israel, and will *p.*   *2Sa 7:10*
them
sow ye, and reap, and *p.*   *2Ki 19:29*
vineyards
my people Israel, and will *p.*   *1Ch 17:9*
them
and bring forth boughs like a *Job 14:9*
p.
sow the fields, and *p.*   *Ps 107:37*
vineyards
a time to *p.* and a time to pluck *Ec 3:2*
up
the men of Judah his pleasant   *Isa 5:7*
p.
shalt thou *p.* pleasant plants *Isa 17:10*
shalt thou make thy *p.* to   *Isa 17:11*
grow
ye, and reap, and *p.*   *Isa 37:30*
vineyards
will *p.* in the wilderness the   *Isa 41:19*
cedar
that I may *p.* the heavens,   *Isa 51:16*
and lay
grow up before him as a   *Isa 53:2*
tender *p.*
they shall *p.* vineyards, and   *Isa 65:21*
eat

they shall not *p.* and another   *Isa 65:22* eat
to throw down, to build, and   *Jer 1:10* to *p.*
art turned into the degenerate   *Jer 2:21* *p.*
a kingdom, to build and to *p.*   *Jer 18:9* it
and I will *p.* them, and not   *Jer 24:6* pluck
p. gardens, and eat the fruit   *Jer 29:5;* of them   *29:28*
yet *p.* vines upon the   *Jer 31:5* mountains
the planters shall *p.* and shall   *Jer 31:5* eat
over them, to build, and to *p.*   *Jer 31:28* I will *p.* them in this land   *Jer 32:41* assuredly
nor sow seed, nor *p.* vineyard   *Jer 35:7* I will *p.* you and not pluck   *Jer 42:10* you up
p. it upon an high mountain   *Eze 17:22* of the height of Israel will I   *Eze 17:23* *p.* it
build houses, and *p.*   *Eze 28:26* vineyards
raise up for them a *p.* of   *Eze 34:29* renown
and *p.* that that was desolate   *Eze 36:36* *p.* the tabernacles of his   *Da 11:45* palace
and they shall *p.* vineyards   *Am 9:14* and I will *p.* them upon their   *Am 9:15* land
and they shall *p.* vineyards,   *Zep 1:13* but not
p. which my heavenly Father   *M't 15:13*

PLANTATION

water it by the furrows of her   *Eze 17:7* *p.*

PLANTED

Lord God *p.* a garden eastward   *Ge 2:8* husbandman, and he *p.* a   *Ge 9:20* vineyard
Abraham *p.* a grove in   *Ge 21:33* Beer-sheba
shall have *p.* all manner of   *Le 19:23* trees
lign aloes which the Lord hath   *Nu 24:6* *p.*
man is he that hath *p.* a   *De 20:6* vineyard
oliveyards which ye *p.* not do   *Jos 24:13* ye eat
shall be like a tree *p.* by the   *Ps 1:3* rivers
cast out the heathen, and *p.* it   *Ps 80:8* which thy right hand hath *p.*   *Ps 80:15* that he *p.* in the house of the   *Ps 92:13* He that *p.* the ear, shall he not   *Ps 94:9* of Lebanon, which he hath *p.*   *Ps 104:16* me houses; I *p.* me vineyards   *Ec 2:4* and I *p.* trees in them of all   *Ec 2:5* kinds of
a time to pluck up that which is   *Ec 3:2* *p.*
p. it with the choicest vine, and   *Isa 5:2* they shall not be *p.*; yea, they   *Isa 40:24* shall
I had *p.* thee a noble vine,   *Jer 2:21* wholly
the Lord of hosts, that *p.*   *Jer 11:17* thee, hath
Thou hast *p.* them, yea, they   *Jer 12:2* have
shall be as a tree *p.* by the   *Jer 17:8* waters
which I have *p.* I will pluck up   *Jer 45:4* of the land, and *p.* it in a   *Eze 17:5* fruitful field
It was *p.* in a good soil by   *Eze 17:8* great
behold, being *p.* shall it   *Eze 17:10* prosper
in thy blood, *p.* by the waters   *Eze 19:10* And now she is *p.* in the   *Eze 19:13* wilderness
Tyrus, is *p.* in a pleasant place   *Ho 9:13* ye have *p.* pleasant vineyards   *Am 5:11* my heavenly Father hath not   *M't 15:13* *p.*
which *p.* a vineyard, and   *M't 21:33* hedged it

A certain man *p.* a vineyard   *M'k 12:1;*   *Lu 20:9*
had a fig tree *p.* in his vineyard   *Lu 13:6* the root, and be thou *p.* in the   *Lu 17:6* sea
they sold, they *p.*, they   *Lu 17:28* builded
p. together in the likeness of his   *Ro 6:5* I have *p.*, Apollos watered;   *1Co 3:6* but
message *p.* in hearts (N)   *Jas 1:21*

PLANTEDST

and olive trees, which thou *p.*   *De 6:11* not
with thy hand, and *p.* them   *Ps 44:2*

PLANTERS

the *p.* shall plant, and shall eat   *Jer 31:5*

PLANTETH

of her hands she *p.* a vineyard   *Pr 31:16* he *p.* an ash, and the rain   *Isa 44:14* doth
neither is he that *p.* any thing   *1Co 3:7* Now he that *p.* and he that   *1Co 3:8* watereth
who *p.* a vineyard, and eateth   *1Co 9:7* not

PLANTING

the branch of my *p.* the work   *Isa 60:21* of
the *p.* of the Lord, that he   *Isa 61:3* might

PLANTINGS

the field, and as *p.* of a   *Mic 1:6* vineyard

PLANTS

that dwelt among *p.* and   *1Ch 4:23* hedges
children like olive *p.* round   *Ps 128:3* about
our sons may be as *p.* grown   *Ps 144:12* up
p. are orchard of   *Ca 4:13* pomegranates
broken down the principal *p.*   *Isa 16:8* shalt thou plant pleasant *p.*   *Isa 17:10* thy *p.* are gone over the sea   *Jer 48:32* rivers running round about *p.*   *Eze 31:4*

PLAT

I will requite thee in this *p.*   *2Ki 9:26* saith
cast him into the *p.* of ground   *2Ki 9:26* the plot of ground (A)(R)   *2Ki 9:26* on the property (B)   *2Ki 9:26*

PLATE

thou shalt make a *p.* of pure   *Ex 28:36* gold
they made the *p.* of the holy   *Ex 39:30* crown
forefront, did he put the golden   *Le 8:9* *p.*
take a *p.* of iron (A)(B)(R)   *Eze 4:3* cup and *p.* (B)(R)   *M't 23:25; 23:26* cup and *p.* (A)(B)(N)   *Lu 11:39*

PLATES

they did beat the gold into thin   *Ex 39:3* *p.*
let them make them broad *p.*   *Nu 16:38* were made broad *p.* for a   *Nu 16:39* covering
brasen wheels, and *p.* of brass   *1Ki 7:30* For on the *p.* of the ledges   *1Ki 7:36* thereof
Silver spread into *p.* is brought   *Jer 10:9* from

PLATFORM

on a wooden *p.* (B)   *Ne 8:4*

PLATTED

they had *p.* a crown of thorns   *M't 27:29* *p.* a crown of thorns, and   *M'k 15:17* put it
the soldiers *p.* a crown of   *Joh 19:2* thorns

PLATTER

one silver *p.* (S)   *Nu 7:13;*   *7:19, 25, 31, 37, 43, 49, 55, 61, 67, 73, 79*   *85; M't 14:8, 11; M'k 6:25, 28*
outside of the cup and of   *M't 23:25;* the *p.*   *Lu 11:39*
cup and plate (B)(R)   *M't 23:25; 23:26* that which is within the cup   *M't 23:26* and *p.*
cup and dish (N)(P)   *M't 23:26* cup and plate (A)(B)(N)   *Lu 11:39* cups and dishes (A)   *Lu 11:39* cup and dish (R)   *Lu 11:39*

PLATTERS

silver *p.* (S)   *Nu 7:84; Ezr 1:9*

PLAUSIBLE

p., attractive arguments (P)   *Ro 16:18*

PLAY

p. the lyre and pipe   *Ge 4:21* (A)(E)(R)
and to drink, and rose up to *p.*   *Ex 32:6* *p.* the harlot with (S)   *Ex 34:15;*   *34:16; Le 17:7; 20:5-6; Nu 15:39;*   *De 31:16; J'g 2:17; 8:33; 1Ch 5:25;*   *2Ch 21:13; Ps 73:27; 106:39; Eze 23:30;*   *Ho 4:12; 9:1*
to *p.* the whore in her father's   *De 22:21* house
he shall *p.* with his hand, and   *1Sa 16:16* me now a man that can *p.*   *1Sa 16:17* well
to *p.* the mad man in my   *1Sa 21:15* presence
men now arise, and *p.* before   *2Sa 2:14* us
therefore will I *p.* before the   *2Sa 6:21* Lord
and let us *p.* the men for our   *2Sa 10:12* people
where all the beasts of the   *Job 40:20* field *p.*
thou *p.* with him as with a   *Job 41:5* bird
p. skillfully with a loud noise   *Ps 33:3* thou hast made to *p.* therein   *Ps 104:26* shall *p.* on the hole of the asp   *Isa 11:8* and can *p.* well on an   *Eze 33:32* instrument
thou shalt not *p.* the harlot, and   *Ho 3:3* *p.* the harlot, yet let not Judah   *Ho 4:15* offend
eat and drink, and rose up to   *1Co 10:7* *p.*

PLAYED

daughter in law hath *p.* the   *Ge 38:24* harlot
concubine *p.* the whore against   *J'g 19:2* him
an harp, and *p.* with his hand   *1Sa 16:23* answered one another as they   *1Sa 18:7* *p.*
David *p.* with his hand, as at   *1Sa 18:10* other
and David *p.* with his hand   *1Sa 19:9* I have *p.* the fool, and have   *1Sa 26:21* erred
house of Israel *p.* before the   *2Sa 6:5* Lord
and *p.* on flutes (S)   *1Ki 1:40* came to pass, when the   *2Ki 3:15* minstrel *p.*
David and all Israel *p.* before   *1Ch 13:8* God
p. false to thy children (B)   *Ps 73:15* *p.* harlot in doings (E)(R)   *Ps 106:39* thou hast *p.* the harlot with   *Jer 3:1* many
tree, and there hath *p.* the   *Jer 3:6* harlot
not, but went, and *p.* the harlot   *Jer 3:8* also
Thou hast *p.* the whore also   *Eze 16:28* with the

PLAYED

yea, thou hast *p.* the harlot with them — *Eze 16:28*
Aholah *p.* the harlot when she was — *Eze 23:5*
had *p.* the harlot in the land of Egypt — *Eze 23:19*
For their mother hath *p.* the harlot — *Ho 2:5*

PLAYEDST

p. the harlot because of thy renown — *Eze 16:15*
p. the harlot thereupon: the like — *Eze 16:16*

PLAYER

who is a cunning *p.* on a harp — *1Sa 16:16*

PLAYERS

p. on instruments followed after — *Ps 68:25*
p. on instruments shall be there — *Ps 87:7*
and flute *p.* (S) — *Re 18:22*

PLAYETH

go in unto a woman that *p.* the harlot — *Eze 23:44*

PLAYFELLOW

made evil their *p.* (P) — *2Th 2:12*

PLAYING

she profane herself by *p.* the whore — *Le 21:9*
p. the harlot with (S) — *J'g 8:27*
Beth-lehemite that is cunning in *p.* — *1Sa 16:18*
saw king David dancing and *p.* — *1Ch 15:29*
were the damsels *p.* with timbrels — *Ps 68:25*
tree thou wanderest *p.* the harlot — *Jer 2:20*
cause thee to cease from *p.* the harlot — *Eze 16:41*
boys and girls *p.* in the streets — *Zec 8:5*
p. with sex (P) — *Ro 13:13*

PLAYMATES

call to *p.* (A)(B)(R) — *M't 11:16*

PLAYTHINGS

p. of own desires (P) — *Ro 1:24*

PLEA

between *p.* and *p.* and between — *De 17:8*

PLEAD

I shall *p.* for you (B) — *Ex 8:9*
Will ye *p.* for Baal? will ye save — *J'g 6:31*
will you contend for Baal (A)(E)(R) — *J'g 6:31*
will you strive for Baal (B) — *J'g 6:31*
he that will *p.* for him, let him be — *J'g 6:31*
let him *p.* for himself, because one — *J'g 6:31*
Let Baal *p.* against him, because — *J'g 6:32*
may *p.* with you (A) — *1Sa 12:7*
and *p.* my cause, and deliver me — *1Sa 24:15*
be my Advocate, do me justice (B) — *1Sa 24:15*
p. with the Lord (B) — *1Ki 13:6*
beg for mercy and *p.* (B) — *Es 4:8*
p. for mercy (B) — *Job 9:15*
who shall set me a time to *p.* — *Job 9:19*
who will summon me (A)(E)(R) — *Job 9:19*
Who will challenge me (B) — *Job 9:19*
Who is he that will *p.* with me — *Job 13:19*
who will argue against and refute me (A) — *Job 13:19*
who will refute me (B) — *Job 13:19*
who will contend with me (E)(R) — *Job 13:19*

one might *p.* for a man with God — *Job 16:21*
do man justice between him and God (B) — *Job 16:21*
maintain the right of a man (E)(R) — *Job 16:21*
and *p.* against me my reproach — *Job 19:5*
Will he *p.* against me with his — *Job 23:6*
contend with me (B)(E)(R) — *Job 23:6*
P. my cause, O Lord, with them — *Ps 35:1*
Contend with those who contend (A)(B)(R) — *Ps 35:1*
Strive with them that strive with me (E) — *Ps 35:1*
Judge me, O God, and *p.* my cause — *Ps 43:1*
Arise, O God, *p.* thine own — *Ps 74:22*
P. my cause, and deliver me — *Ps 119:154*
the Lord will *p.* their cause — *Pr 22:23*
he shall *p.* their cause with thee — *Pr 23:11*
defend their cause (B) — *Pr 23:11*
p. the cause of the poor and needy — *Pr 31:9*
administer justice (A)(E) — *Pr 31:9*
defend the rights of the poor (B) — *Pr 31:9*
maintain the rights of (R) — *Pr 31:9*
the fatherless, *p.* for the widow — *Isa 1:17*
defend the widow (B) — *Isa 1:17*
The Lord standeth up to *p.* — *Isa 3:13*
Lord stands up to contend (A)(E)(R) — *Isa 3:13*
Lord stands up to hold court (B) — *Isa 3:13*
remembrance: let us *p.* together — *Isa 43:26*
let us judge together (B) — *Isa 43:26*
let us argue together (R) — *Isa 43:26*
will the Lord *p.* with all flesh — *Isa 66:16*
the Lord will execute judgment (A)(B)(E)(R) — *Isa 66:16*
I will yet *p.* with you, saith — *Jer 2:9*
your children's children will I *p.* — *Jer 2:9*
Wherefore will ye *p.* with me — *Jer 2:29*
why will you complain (A)(B)(R) — *Jer 2:29*
will you contend with me (E) — *Jer 2:29*
I will *p.* with thee, because thou — *Jer 2:35*
thou, O Lord, when I *p.* with thee — *Jer 12:1*
p. and reason with you (A)(E)(R) — *Jer 12:1*
he will *p.* with all flesh; he will — *Jer 25:31*
enter into judgment with mankind (A)(E) — *Jer 25:31*
has a court case against all nations (B) — *Jer 25:31*
has an indictment against all nations (R) — *Jer 25:31*
let them *p.* with Lord (B) — *Jer 27:18*
There none to *p.* thy cause — *Jer 30:13*
he shall thoroughly *p.* their cause — *Jer 50:34*
he will defend their cause (B) — *Jer 50:34; 51:36*
Behold, I will *p.* thy cause, and take — *Jer 51:36*
and will *p.*: with him there for his — *Eze 17:20*
enter into judgment with (A)(E)(R) — *Eze 17:20; 38:22*
conduct a court case with him (B) — *Eze 17:20*
will I *p.* with you face to face — *Eze 20:35*
so will I *p.* with you, saith the Lord — *Eze 20:36*
will *p.* against him with pestilence — *Eze 38:22*
P. with your mother, *p.*: for she — *Ho 2:2*
p. with them there for my people — *Joe 3:2*
enter into judgment with (A)(B)(E)(R) — *Joe 3:2*
people, and he will *p.* with Israel — *Mic 6:2*
has an accusation against his — *Mic 6:2*
has a controversy with (E)(R) — *Mic 6:2*
until he *p.* my cause, and execute — *Mic 7:9*
to *p.* with him (A)(N) — *Lu 15:28*
living to *p.* on behalf (N) — *Heb 7:25*
one to *p.* our cause (N) — *1Jo 2:1*

PLEADED

the Lord that hath *p.* the cause — *1Sa 25:39*
thou hast *p.* the causes of my soul — *La 3:58*
Like as I *p.* with your fathers in — *Eze 20:36*
p. for peace (B) — *Ac 12:20*
p. with God on behalf (P) — *Ro 11:2*

PLEADETH

as a man *p.* for his neighbour — *Job 16:21*
that *p.* the cause of his people — *Isa 51:22*
for justice, nor any *p.* for truth — *Isa 59:4*
p. with God against (E) — *Ro 11:2*

PLEADING

p. to thee (B) — *Job 41:3*
weeping and *p.* (A) — *Jer 3:21*
through groans the Spirit is *p.* (N) — *Ro 8:26*
spoke boldly, persuading, *p.* (A)(R) — *Ac 19:8*
prayer and *p.* (B) — *Ph'p 4:6*

PLEADINGS

and hearken to the *p.* of my lips — *Job 13:6*
listen to my *p.* (B) — *Job 13:6*

PLEADS

spirit *p.* with unspeakable yearnings and groanings (A)(N) — *Ro 8:26*
how he *p.* with God (A) — *Ro 11:2*

PLEAS

rely on empty *p.* (R) — *Isa 59:4*

PLEASANT

every tree that is *p.* to the sight — *Ge 2:9*
pleasing to the eyes (A)(B) — *Ge 2:9*
it was *p.* to the eyes, and a tree — *Ge 3:6*
delightful to look at (A)(B)(E)(R) — *Ge 3:6*
good, and the land that it was *p.* — *Ge 49:15*
and Jonathan were lovely and *p.* — *2Sa 1:23*
were beloved and lovely (A)(B)(R) — *2Sa 1:23*
very *p.* hast thou been unto me — *2Sa 1:26*
whatsoever is *p.* in thine eyes — *1Ki 20:6*
all the desire of your eyes (A) — *1Ki 20:6*
everything dear to you (B) — *1Ki 20:6*
whatever pleases them (R) — *1Ki 20:6*
situation of this city is *p.*, as — *2Ki 2:19*
location of city is excellent (B) — *2Ki 2:19*
and for all manner of *p.* jewels — *2Ch 32:27*
all kinds of attractive vessels (A) — *2Ch 32:27*
all sorts of precious articles (B) — *2Ch 32:27*
all manner of goodly vessels (E) — *2Ch 32:27*
all kinds of costly vessels (R) — *2Ch 32:27*
are fallen unto me in *p.* places — *Ps 16:6*
the *p.* harp with the psaltery — *Ps 81:2*
sweet lyre with the harp (A)(R) — *Ps 81:2*
lovely lyre with the harp (B) — *Ps 81:2*
they despised the *p.* land, they — *Ps 106:24*
spurned the desirable land (B) — *Ps 106:24*
how *p.* it is for brethren to dwell — *Ps 133:1*
praises unto his name; for it is *p.* — *Ps 135:3*
name is gracious and lovely (A) — *Ps 135:3*
his name, for it is sweet (B) — *Ps 135:3*
his name, for he is gracious (R) — *Ps 135:3*
praises unto our God; for it is *p.* — *Ps 147:1*
praise is becoming and appropriate (A) — *Ps 147:1*
song of praise is so befitting (B) — *Ps 147:1*
song of praise is seemly (R) — *Ps 147:1*

and knowledge is *p.* to thy soul *Pr 2:10*
be as the loving hind and *p.* *Pr 5:19*
roe
a lovely hind, a graceful doe *Pr 5:19*
(B)(R)
and bread eaten in secret is *p. Pr 9:17*
the words of the pure are *p.* *Pr 15:26*
words
words of the pure are pleasing *Pr 15:26*
(A)(R)
kindly words are pure (B) *Pr 15:26*
P. words are as an honeycomb *Pr 16:24*
p. thing if thou keep them *Pr 22:18*
within
with all precious and *p.* riches *Pr 24:4*
a *p.* thing it is for the eyes to *Ec 11:7*
thou art fair, my beloved, yea, *Ca 1:16*
p.
you are delightful (A) *Ca 1:16*
you are very handsome (B) *Ca 1:16*
you are truly lovely (R) *Ca 1:16*
of pomegranates, with *p.* fruits *Ca 4:13*
his garden, and eat his *p.* fruits *Ca 4:16*
How fair and how *p.* art thou, O *Ca 7:6*
gates and all manner of *p.* fruits *Ca 7:13*
Tarshish, and upon all *p.* *Isa 2:16*
pictures
the men of Judah his *p.* plant *Isa 5:7*
his cherished planting (B) *Isa 5:7*
and dragons in their *p.* *Isa 13:22*
palaces
luxurious palaces (B) *Isa 13:22*
shalt thou plant *p.* plants, and *Isa 17:10*
for the teats, for the *p.* fields *Isa 32:12*
and all thy borders of *p.* *Isa 54:12*
stones
precious stones, gems *Isa 54:12*
(A)(B)(E)(R)
all our *p.* things are laid *Isa 64:11*
waste
cherished place laid waste *Isa 64:11*
(B)
and give thee a *p.* land, a *Jer 3:19*
goodly
p. portion a desolate *Jer 12:10*
wilderness
p. places of the wilderness are *Jer 23:10*
and ye shall fall like a *p.* *Jer 25:34*
vessel
like a choice vessel (A)(B) *Jer 25:34*
like a goodly vessel (E) *Jer 25:34*
like choice rams (R) *Jer 25:34*
my dear son? is he a *p.* child *Jer 31:20*
he is a darling child *Jer 31:20*
(A)(B)(E)(R)
sleep was *p.* (R) *Jer 31:26*
all her *p.* things that she had in *La 1:7*
the treasures in days of old (B) *La 1:7*
precious things (R) *La 1:7; 1:10*
his hand upon all her *p.* things *La 1:10*
have given their *p.* things for *La 1:11*
meat
slew all that were *p.* to the eye *La 2:4*
walls, and destroy thy *p.* *Eze 26:12*
houses
song of one that hath a *p.* *Eze 33:32*
voice
beautiful voice (B)(R) *Eze 33:32*
the east, and toward the *p.* land *Da 8:9*
precious, blessed land of Israel *Da 8:9*
(A)
the Glory-land (B) *Da 8:9*
the glorious land (E)(R) *Da 8:9*
I ate no *p.* bread, neither came *Da 10:3*
no appetizing food (B) *Da 10:3*
I ate no delicacies (R) *Da 10:3*
precious stones and jewelry *Da 11:38*
(B)
precious stones and costly *Da 11:38*
gifts (R)
p. places for their silver, nettles *Ho 9:6*
previous things of silver *Ho 9:6*
(A)(R)
strongbox of their silver (B) *Ho 9:6*
Tyrus, is planted in a *p.* place *Ho 9:13*
the treasure of all *p.* vessels *Ho 13:15*
every precious vessel (A) *Ho 13:15*
every precious thing (B)(R) *Ho 13:15*
all goodly vessels (E) *Ho 13:15*
temples my goodly *p.* things *Joe 3:5*
my precious treasures *Joe 3:5*
(A)(B)(E)(R)
ye have planted *p.* vineyards *Am 5:11*
desirable vineyards (B) *Am 5:11*
ye cast out from their *p.* houses *Mic 2:9*
happy homes (B) *Mic 2:9*
glory out of all the *p.* furniture *Na 2:9*
precious furnishings (A) *Na 2:9*
all kinds of precious things *Na 2:9*
(B)(R)

all goodly furniture (E) *Na 2:9*
for they laid the *p.* land *Zec 7:14*
desolate
a desirable land to desolation *Zec 7:14*
(B)
of Judah and Jerusalem be *p.* *Mal 3:4*
Jerusalem pleasing to Lord *Mal 3:4*
(A)(B)(R)
various desires and *p.* feelings *Tit 3:3*
(P)

PLEASANTLY

when he speaketh *p.* (S) *Pr 26:25*
speak *p.* to them (P) *Col 4:6*

PLEASANTNESS

Her ways are ways of *p.* and all *Pr 3:17*

PLEASE

If she *p.* not her master, who *Ex 21:8*
peradventure it will *p.* God *Nu 23:27*
if it *p.* my father to do thee *1Sa 20:13*
evil
p. thee to bless the house of *2Sa 7:29*
thy
p. to give you (B) *1Ki 10:9*
else, if it *p.* thee, I will give *1Ki 21:6*
thee
p. thee to bless the house of *1Ch 17:27*
thy
kind to this people, and *p.* *2Ch 10:7*
them
If it *p.* the king, and if thy *Ne 2:5*
servant
If it *p.* the king, let letters be *Ne 2:7*
it *p.* the king, let there go a *Es 1:19*
royal
If it *p.* the king, let it be written *Es 3:9*
if it *p.* the king to grant my *Es 5:8*
petition
if it *p.* the king, let my life be *Es 7:3*
given
if it *p.* the king, and if I have *Es 8:5*
found
If it *p.* the king, let it be *Es 9:13*
granted
it would *p.* God to destroy me *Job 6:9*
children shall seek to *p.* the *Job 20:10*
poor
shall *p.* the Lord better than an *Ps 69:31*
ox
When a man's ways *p.* the Lord *Pr 16:7*
up, nor awake my love, till he *Ca 2:7;*
p. *3:5; 8:4*
p. themselves in the children of *Isa 2:6*
shall accomplish that which I *Isa 55:11*
p.
and choose the things that *p.* *Isa 56:4*
me
do always those things that *p.* *Joh 8:29*
him
that are in the flesh cannot *p.* *Ro 8:8*
God
the weak, and not to *p.* *Ro 15:1*
ourselves
Let every one of us *p.* his *Ro 15:2*
neighbour
the Lord, how he may *p.* the *1Co 7:32*
Lord
the world, how he may *p.* his *1Co 7:33*
wife
world, how she may *p.* her *1Co 7:34*
husband
Even as I *p.* all men in all *1Co 10:33*
things
men, or God? or do I seek to *Ga 1:10*
p. men
they *p.* not God, and are *1Th 2:15*
contrary
how ye ought to walk and to *p.* *1Th 4:1*
God
he may *p.* him who hath chosen *2Ti 2:4*
him
to *p.* them well in all things *Tit 2:9*
faith it is impossible to *p.* *Heb 11:6*
him

PLEASED

daughters of Canaan *p.* not *Ge 28:8*
of God, and thou wast *p.* with *Ge 33:10*
me
And their words *p.* Hamor *Ge 34:18*
and it *p.* Pharaoh well and *Ge 45:16*
Balaam saw that it *p.* the Lord *Nu 24:1*

And the saying *p.* me well *De 1:23*
of Manasseh spake, it *p.* them *Jos 22:30*
thing *p.* the children of Israel *Jos 22:33*
If the Lord was *p.* to kill us *J'g 13:23*
and she *p.* Samson well *J'g 14:7*
hath *p.* the Lord to make you *1Sa 12:22*
his
Saul, and the thing *p.* him *1Sa 18:20*
it *p.* David well to be the *1Sa 18:26*
king's
notice of it, and it *p.* them *2Sa 3:36*
whatsoever the king did *p.* all *2Sa 3:36*
the saying *p.* Absalom well *2Sa 17:4*
day, then it had *p.* thee well *2Sa 19:6*
the speech *p.* the Lord, that *1Ki 3:10*
desire which he was *p.* to do *1Ki 9:1*
him; and they *p.* him not *1Ki 9:12*
the thing *p.* the king and all *2Ch 30:4*
So it *p.* the king to send me *Ne 2:6*
p. the king and the princess *Es 1:21*
And the thing *p.* the king *Es 2:4*
And the maiden *p.* him, and *Es 2:9*
And the thing *p.* Haman; and *Es 5:14*
Be *p.* O Lord, to deliver me *Ps 40:13*
shalt thou be *p.* with the *Ps 51:19*
sacrifices
hath done whatsoever he hath *Ps 115:3*
p.
Whatsoever the Lord *p.* that *Ps 135:6*
did
Lord is well *p.* for his *Isa 42:21*
righteousness
Yet it *p.* the Lord to bruise *Isa 53:10*
him
It *p.* Darius to set over the *Da 6:1*
O Lord, hast done as it *p.* thee *Jon 1:14*
Lord be *p.* with thousands of *Mic 6:7*
rams
will he be *p.* with thee, or *Mal 1:8*
accept
beloved Son, in whom I am *M't 3:17;*
well *p.* *17:5; M'k 1:11; Lu 3:22;*
2Pe 1:17
beloved, in whom my soul is *M't 12:18*
well *p.*
danced before them, and *p.* *M't 14:6*
Herod
done to him as they *p.* *M't 17:12*
(B)(R)
came in, and danced, and *p.* *M'k 6:22*
Herod
the saying *p.* the whole *Ac 6:5*
multitude
And because he saw it *p.* the *Ac 12:3*
Jews
Then *p.* it the apostles and *Ac 15:22*
elders
it *p.* Silas to abide there still *Ac 15:34*
For even Christ *p.* not himself *Ro 15:3*
For it hath *p.* them of *Ro 15:26*
Macedonia
It hath *p.* them verily; and *Ro 15:27*
their
it *p.* God by the foolishness of *1Co 1:21*
and she be *p.* to dwell with *1Co 7:12*
him
if he be *p.* to dwell with her, *1Co 7:13*
let
many of them God was not *1Co 10:5*
well *p.*
in the body, as it hath *p.* him *1Co 12:18*
giveth it a body as it hath *p.* *1Co 15:38*
him
for if I yet *p.* men, I should *Ga 1:10*
not be
But when it *p.* God, who *Ga 1:15*
separated
it *p.* the Father that in him *Col 1:19*
should
had this testimony, that he *p.* *Heb 11:5*
God
with such sacrifices God is *Heb 13:16*
well *p.*

PLEASETH

hand; do to her as it *p.* thee *Ge 16:6*
thee: dwell where it *p.* thee *Ge 20:15*
where it *p.* him best (S) *De 23:16;*
Es 8:8
for me; for she *p.* me well *J'g 14:3*
the maiden which *p.* the king *Es 2:4*
whoso *p.* God shall escape *Ec 7:26*
for he doeth whatsoever *p.* him *Ec 8:3*

PLEASES

whatever *p.* him (R) *1Ki 20:6*
wind blows where it *p.* (B) *Joh 3:8*

PLEASING

p. in the eyes (A)(B)   Ge 2:9
Lord smelled a p. (A)(B)   Ge 8:21
p. odor (R)   Ge 8:21;
29:18, 25, 41; Le 1:9; 2:2, 9, 12; 3:5, 16;
4:31; 6:15, 21; 28; 17:6; 23:13, 18;
26:31; Nu 15:3, 7, 10, 14, 24; 18:17
p. fragrance (B)   Le 1:9;
2:9, 12; 3:5 17:6; 23:13, 18; Nu 15:3, 7,
10, 14, 24; 18:17; 28:2, 6, 8, 13, 24, 27;
29:2, 6, 8, 13, 36
the king, and I be p. in his eyes   Es 8:5
my meditation p. (R)   Ps 104:34
neither shall they be p. unto   Ho 9:4
him
walk worthy of the Lord unto   Col 1:10
all p.
not as p. men, but God, which   1Th 2:4
trieth
those things that are p. in his   1Jo 3:22
sight

PLEASURE

I am waxed old shall I have p.   Ge 18:12
eat grapes thy fill at thine p.   De 23:24
my father took p. in me (S)   1Ch 28:4
heart, and hast p. in   1Ch 29:17
uprightness
test you with p. (R)   Ec 2:1
and let the king send his p. to   Ezr 5:17
us
God of your fathers, and do   Ezr 10:11
his p.
and over our cattle, at their p.   Ne 9:37
do according to every man's p.   Es 1:8
For what p. hath he in his   Job 21:21
house
soul, and never eateth with p.   Job 21:25
Is it any p. to the Almighty   Job 22:3
God that hath p. in wickedness   Ps 5:4
p. in the prosperity of his   Ps 35:27
servant
Do good in thy good p. unto   Ps 51:18
Zion
thy servants take p. in her   Ps 102:14
stones
ye ministers of his, that do   Ps 103:21
his p.
To bind his princes at his p.   Ps 105:22
of all them that have p.   Ps 111:2
therein
taketh not p. in the legs of a   Ps 147:10
man
Lord taketh p. in them that   Ps 147:11
fear
the Lord taketh p. in his   Ps 149:4
people
that loveth p. shall be a poor   Pr 21:17
man
therefore enjoy p.: and, behold   Ec 2:1
pay it; for he hath no p. in fools   Ec 5:4
thou shalt say, I have no p. in   Ec 12:1
them
the night of my p. hath he   Isa 21:4
turned
and shall perform all my p.   Isa 44:28
shall stand, and I will do all   Isa 46:10
my p.
he will do his p. on Babylon   Isa 48:14
p. of the Lord shall prosper   Isa 53:10
in his
in the day of your fast ye find   Isa 58:3
p.
from doing thy p. on my holy   Isa 58:13
day
own ways, nor finding thine   Isa 58:13
own p.
snuffeth up the wind at her p.   Jer 2:24
is he a vessel wherein is no p.   Jer 22:28
he had set at liberty at their   Jer 34:16
p.
like a vessel wherein is no p.   Jer 48:38
with whom thou hast taken   Eze 16:37
p.
Have I any p. at all that the   Eze 18:23
wicked
no p. in the death of him   Eze 18:32
that dieth
no p. in the death of the   Eze 33:11
wicked
as a vessel wherein is no p.   Ho 8:8
I will take p. in it, and I will   Hag 1:8
be
I have no p. in you, saith the   Mal 1:10
your Father's good p. to give   Lu 12:32
you
willing to shew the Jews a p.   Ac 24:27

Festus, willing to do the Jews a   Ac 25:9
p.
but have p. in them that do   Ro 1:32
them
have a double p. (R)   2Co 1:15
Therefore I take p. in   2Co 12:10
infirmities
according to the good p. of his   Eph 1:5
will
according to his good p. which   Eph 1:9
he
both to will and to do of his   Ph'p 2:13
good p.
all the good p. of his goodness   2Th 1:11
but had p. in unrighteousness   2Th 2:12
But she that liveth in p. is dead   1Ti 5:6
sacrifices thou hast, had no   Heb 10:6
p.
not, neither hadst p. therein   Heb 10:8
my soul shall have no p. in   Heb 10:38
him
chastened after their own   Heb 12:10
p.
Ye have lived in p. on the earth   Jas 5:5
count it p. to riot in the day   2Pe 2:13
time
and for thy p. they are and   Re 4:11
were

PLEASURES

in prosperity, and their years   Job 36:11
in p.
hand there are p. for evermore   Ps 16:11
them drink of the river of thy   Ps 36:8
p.
thou that art given to p. that   Isa 47:8
cares and riches and p. of this   Lu 8:14
life
lovers of p. more than lovers of   2Ti 3:4
serving divers lusts and p.   Tit 3:3
living
to enjoy the p. of sin for a   Heb 11:25
season
spend it in sensual p. (A)   Jas 4:3

PLEDGE

Wilt thou give me a p. till   Ge 38:17
thou
he said, What p. shall I give   Ge 38:18
thee
his p. from the woman's hand   Ge 38:20
thy neighbour's raiment to p.   Ex 22:26
nether or the upper millstone   De 24:6
to p.
for he taketh a man's life to p.   De 24:6
go into his house to fetch his   De 24:10
p.
bring out the p. abroad unto   De 24:11
thee
thou shalt not sleep with his   De 24:12
p.
shalt deliver him the p. again   De 24:13
take the widow's raiment to   De 24:17
p.
brethren fare, and take their   1Sa 17:18
p.
taken a p. from thy brother   Job 22:6
they take the widow's ox for a   Job 24:3
p.
breast, and take a p. of the   Job 24:9
poor
a p. of him for a strange   Pr 20:16;
woman   27:13
hath restored to the debtor his   Eze 18:7
p.
hath not restored the p. and   Eze 18:12
hath not withholden the p.   Eze 18:16
neither
If the wicked restore the p.   Eze 32:15
give
clothes laid to p. by every altar   Am 2:8
a p. of what is to come (N)   2Co 1:22
p. deposit of our legacy   Eph 1:14
(B)(N)
personal p. of redemption   Eph 4:30
(P)

PLEDGES

give p. to my lord king of   2Ki 18:23
Assyria
give p. I pray thee, to my   Isa 36:8
master

PLEIADES

maketh Arcturus, Orion, and P.   Job 9:9
bind the sweet influences of   Job 38:31
P.
stars called P. (A)(B)(E)(R)   Am 5:8

PLENTEOUS

of Egypt in the seven p. years   Ge 41:34;
     41:47
seven abundant years (B)   Ge 41:34;
     41:47
Lord shall make thee p. in   De 28:11
goods
make you have a surplus of   De 28:11
prosperity (A)
grant you an abundance of   De 28:11
good things (B)
make you abound in   De 28:11
prosperity (R)
make thee p. in every work   De 30:9
make you abundantly   De 30:9
prosperous (A)(R)
God will prosper you   De 30:9
abundantly (B)
gold in Jerusalem as p. as   2Ch 1:15
stones
gold as common as stones   2Ch 1:15
(A)(B)(R)
in p. righteousness (S)   Job 37:23
p. in mercy to all that call upon   Ps 86:5
him
abundant in mercy (A)   Ps 86:5
rich in loving-kindness (B)   Ps 86:5
abundant in loving-kindness   Ps 86:5
(E)
abundant in steadfast love (R)   Ps 86:5
p. in mercy and truth   Ps 86:15
abounding in mercy,   Ps 86:15
loving-kindness, and truth (A)
rich in loving-kindness and   Ps 86:15
truth (B)
abundant in loving-kindness   Ps 86:15
and truth (E)
abounding in steadfast love   Ps 86:15
(R)
slow to anger, and p. in mercy   Ps 103:8
abounding in mercy (B)   Ps 103:8
abundant in loving-kindness   Ps 103:8
(E)
abounding in steadfast love   Ps 103:8
(R)
with him is p. redemption   Ps 130:7
with him is abundant   Ps 130:7
redemption (B)
it shall be fat and p.   Isa 30:23
it will be rich and plentiful   Isa 30:23
(A)
portion is fat, and their meat   Hab 1:16
p.
his food plentiful and rich (A)   Hab 1:16
his food is rich (B)(R)   Hab 1:16
The harvest is p.,   M't 9:37
labourers
harvest is abundant, but   M't 9:37
workers (B)
The crop is heavy, but   M't 9:37
labourers (N)
the harvest is great enough,   M't 9:37
but (P)

PLENTEOUSNESS

the seven years of p. that was   Ge 41:53
in
of the diligent tend only to p.   Pr 21:5

PLENTIFUL

Thou, O God, didst send a p.   Ps 68:9
rain
away, and joy out of the p.   Isa 16:10
field
it will be rich and p. (A)   Isa 30:23
I brought you into a p. country   Jer 2:7
gladness is taken from the p.   Jer 48:33
field
his food p. and rich (A)   Hab 1:16
grace become more p. (B)   Ro 6:1

PLENTIFULLY

hast thou p. declared the thing   Job 26:3
and p. rewardeth the proud   Ps 31:23
doer
certain rich man brought   Lu 12:16
forth p.

PLENTY

the earth, and p. of corn and   Ge 27:28
wine
come seven years of great p.   Ge 41:29
the p. shall be forgotten in the   Ge 41:30
land

p. shall not be known in the land — Ge 41:31
pit, wherein there is *p.* of water — Le 11:36
Ophir great *p.* of almug trees — 1Ki 10:11
enough to eat, and have left *p.* — 2Ch 31:10
and thou shalt have *p.* of silver — Job 22:25
in judgment, and in *p.* of justice — Job 37:23
So shall thy barns be filled with *p.* — Pr 3:10
his land shall have *p.* of bread — Pr 28:19
for then had we *p.* of victuals — Jer 44:17
And ye shall eat in *p.* and be — Joe 2:26
how to enjoy *p.* (A)(B) — Ph'p 4:12

PLIGHT

knew their *p.* (S) — Ex 2:25
because of their *p.* (A) — Ps 107:26

PLIGHTED

p. my troth (A)(B) — Eze 16:8

PLOT

do not share in their *p.* (B) — Ge 49:6
plot (S) — Jos 24:32; Ru 4:3; 1Ch 11:13-14; Joh 4:5
the *p.* of ground (S) — 2Sa 23:11
center of the *p.* (S) — 2Sa 23:12
on the *p.* of ground (A)(B)(S) — 2Ki 9:26
a *p.* of ground (A)(E)(R) — 1Ch 11:13; 11:14
avert the evil *p.* (A)(B)(S) — Es 8:3
wicked *p.* schemed (B)(R) — Es 9:25
people *p.* in vain (R) — Ps 2:1
they conceived a mischievous *p.* (A)(B) — Ps 21:11
p. treacheries (B) — Ps 35:20
a cunningly conceived *p.* (R) — Ps 64:6
do not further his evil *p.* (R) — Ps 140:8
p. mischief, plan good (B) — Pr 14:22
attempt to *p.* against (A)(R) — M't 22:18
their malicious *p.* (A) — M'k 3:6
went out to *p.* against (N) — Joh 4:5
the *p.* of ground (N)(P) — Ac 9:23
hatched a *p.* (N)(P)

PLOTTED

had *p.* against the Jews (S) — Es 9:24
they *p.* together (A)(B)(R) — Ps 31:13
have *p.* evil (B) — Isa 7:5
p. evil against Lord (R) — Na 1:11
Thou hast *p.* shame (S) — Hab 2:10
p. to kill him (R) — Ac 9:23

PLOTTER

a *p.* of evil against (B) — Na 1:11

PLOTTETH

The wicked *p.* against the just — Ps 37:12

PLOTS

from secret *p.* of wicked (R) — Ps 64:2
devise evil *p.* (B) — Ps 140:2
concocted *p.* against me (B)(S) — Jer 11:19
make *p.* (R) — Jer 18:18
p. be devised (R) — Da 11:25
p. evil against the Lord (A) — Na 1:11
lay *p.* in vain (N) — Ac 4:25

PLOTTING

was *p.* rebellion (B) — 2Ki 17:4
know all their *p.* (A)(R) — Isa 18:23
your *p.* is against (B) — Na 1:9
began *p.* against (N) — M'k 3:6
p. against sowing purposes of God (B) — Ac 10:10

PLOTTINGS

the *p.* of the wily (B) — Job 5:13

PLOUGH

man, having put his hand to the *p.* — Lu 9:62

PLOW

Thou shalt not *p.* with an ox — De 22:10
set them to *p.* his ground (S) — 1Sa 8:12
land, which a yoke of oxen might *p.* — 1Sa 14:14
I have seen, they that *p.* iniquity — Job 4:8
sluggard will not *p.* by reason of — Pr 20:4
the plowman *p.* all day to sow — Isa 28:24
Judah shall *p.* and Jacob shall — Ho 10:11
rock? will one *p.* there with oxen — Am 6:12
he that ploweth should *p.* in hope — 1Co 9:10

PLOWED

neither *p.* nor sown (S) — De 21:4
If ye had not *p.* with my heifer — J'g 14:18
The plowers *p.* upon my back — Ps 129:3
Zion shall be *p.* like a field — Jer 26:18
Ye have *p.* wickedness, ye have — Ho 10:13
Zion for your sake be *p.* as a field — Mic 3:12

PLOWERS

The *p.* plowed upon my back — Ps 129:3

PLOWETH

he that *p.* should plow in hope — 1Co 9:10

PLOWING

neither *p.* nor harvest (S) — Ge 45:6; Ex 34:21
was *p.* with twelve yoke of oxen — 1Ki 19:19
The oxen were *p.* and the asses — Job 1:14
and the *p.* of the wicked, is sin — Pr 21:4
having a servant *p.* or feeding — Lu 17:7

PLOWMAN

Doth the *p.* plow all day to sow — Isa 28:24
call the *p.* to mourning (B) — Am 5:16
the *p.* shall overtake the reaper — Am 9:13

PLOWMEN

vinedressers and *p.* (R) — 2Ki 25:12
p. and vinedressers (R) — 2Ch 26:10
sons of the alien shall be your *p.* — Isa 61:5
p. were ashamed, they covered their — Jer 14:4

PLOWSHARES

shall beat their swords into *p.* — Isa 2:4; Mic 4:3
Beat your *p.* into swords, and your — Joe 3:10

PLUCK

p. away his crop with his feathers — Le 1:16
p. down all their high places — Nu 33:52
thou mayest *p.* the ears with thine — De 23:25
will I *p.* them up by the roots — 2Ch 7:20
p. the fatherless from the breast — Job 24:9
he shall *p.* my feet out of the net — Ps 25:15
p. thee out of thy dwelling place — Ps 52:5
right hand? *p.* it out of thy bosom — Ps 74:11
which pass by the way do *p.* her — Ps 80:12
time to *p.* up that which is planted — Ec 3:2
I will *p.* them out of their land — Jer 12:14
and *p.* out the house of Judah from — Jer 12:14
p. up and destroy that nation — Jer 12:17
to *p.* up, and to pull down, and — Jer 18:7
hand, yet would I *p.* thee thence — Jer 22:24

plant them, and not *p.* them up — Jer 24:6
to *p.* up, and to break down — Jer 31:28
will plant you, and not *p.* you up — Jer 42:10
plant you, and not pull you down (A)(B)(R) — Jer 42:10
which I have planted I will *p.* up — Jer 45:4
which I have planted I am plucking up (A)(R) — Jer 45:4
what I have planted I will pull up (B) — Jer 45:4
to *p.* it up by the roots — Eze 17:9
Will he not pull up its roots (E)(R) — Eze 17:9
p. off thine own breasts — Eze 23:34
tear your own breasts (A)(B)(E)(R) — Eze 23:34
p. off their skin from off them — Mic 3:2
strip the skin off the people (B) — Mic 3:2
tear the skin off (R) — Mic 3:2
I will *p.* up thy groves — Mic 5:14
I will root out your Asherim (A)(R) — Mic 5:14
I will root out your shame-images (B) — Mic 5:14
right eye offend thee *p.* it out — M't 5:29; M'k 9:47
tear it out and fling it away (N) — M't 5:29
began to *p.* the ears of corn — M't 12:1; M'k 2:23
pick off the spikes of grain (A) — M't 12:1
began picking ears of wheat (P) — M't 12:1
any man *p.* them out of my hand — Joh 10:28; 10:29
no one able to snatch them out (A)(B)(E)(N)(P)(R) — Joh 10:28

PLUCKED

p. it out of his bosom — Ex 4:7
he took it out of his bosom (A)(B)(E)(R) — Ex 4:7
ye shall be *p.* from off the land — De 28:63
shall be torn away from off (B) — De 28:63
a man *p.* off his shoe, and gave it — Ru 4:7
a man pulled off his sandal (A)(B) — Ru 4:7
a man drew off his shoe (E)(R) — Ru 4:7
p. spear out of Egyptian's hand — 2Sa 23:21; 1Ch 11:23
snatched the spear out of (A)(B)(R) — 2Sa 23:21
p. off the hair of the head — Ezr 9:3
I pulled hair from my head (A)(B)(R) — Ezr 9:3
I *p.* off their hair — Ne 13:25
I pulled out their hair (A)(R) — Ne 13:25
I contended, pulling out their hair (B) — Ne 13:25
and *p.* the spoil out of his teeth — Job 29:17
forced them to drop their prey (B)(R) — Job 29:17
cheeks to them that *p.* off the hair — Isa 50:6
who pulled out the beard (R) — Isa 50:6
the wicked are not *p.* away — Jer 6:29
wicked are not removed (A)(B)(R) — Jer 6:29
I have *p.* them out — Jer 12:15
it shall not be *p.* up, nor thrown — Jer 31:40
it shall not be uprooted (R) — Jer 31:40
she was *p.* up in fury, she was cast — Eze 19:12
till the wings thereof were *p.* — Da 7:4
first horns *p.* up by the roots — Da 7:8
horns were uprooted (B) — Da 7:8
his kingdom shall be *p.* up — Da 11:4
his kingdom shall be torn out and uprooted (A) — Da 11:4
his realm shall be rooted up (B) — Da 11:4
firebrand *p.* out of the burning — Am 4:11; Zec 3:2
had been *p.* asunder by him — M'k 5:4
chains he wrenched apart (A)(R) — M'k 5:4
chains lay shattered (B) — M'k 5:4
chains had been rent asunder (E) — M'k 5:4

snapped his chains (N)(P)	M'k 5:4
disciples p. the ears of corn	Lu 6:1
disciples picked some of the spikes (A)(B)	Lu 6:1
disciples began picking ears of corn (P)	Lu 6:1
Be thou p. up by the root	Lu 17:6
Be pulled up by the roots (A)	Lu 17:6
Be uprooted (B)	Lu 17:6
Be rooted up (E)(N)(R)	Lu 17:6
Pull yourself up by the roots (P)	Lu 17:6
would have p. out your eyes	Ga 4:15
would have torn out your own eyes (A)(N)	Ga 4:15
twice dead, p. up by the roots	Jude 12
twice dead and uprooted (B)(R)	Jude 12
twice dead and pulled up by the roots (N)	Jude 12
doubly dead no roots either (P)	Jude 12

PLUCKETH

foolish p. it down with her hands	Pr 14:1
foolish one tears it down (A)(B)(R)	Pr 14:1

PLUCKING

I am p. up (A)(R)	Isa 45:4

PLUCKT

her mouth was an olive leaf p. off	Ge 8:11

PLUMBLINE

made by a p. with a p. in his hand	Am 7:7
what seest thou? And I said, A p.	Am 7:8
I will set a p. in the midst of my	Am 7:8

PLUMMET

and the p. of the house of Ahab	2Ki 21:13
line, and righteousness to the p.	Isa 28:17
shall see the p. in the hand of	Zec 4:10

PLUNDER

plunder (B)	Ex 15:9; 1Sa 14:36; 30:16, 22; 2Sa 3:22; 12:30; 2Ki 21:14; 1Ch 20:2; 2Ch 14:13; 15:11; 20:25; 24:23; Ezr 9:7; Es 3:13; Ps 44:10; 89:41; 109:11; Pr 16:19; Isa 3:14; 11:14; 33:4; Jer 50:10; Eze 7:21; 26:12; Da 11:33; Zec 2:9; 14:1; M'k 3:27
plunder (A)	1Sa 14:36; 15:19; 2Ch 14:14; 28:8; Ps 109:11; Pr 1:13; Jer 20:5; Da 11:33; Ho 13:15; Hab 2:8; Zec 2:9; M't 12:29; M'k 3:2
divided his p. (B)	1Ch 26:27; Lu 11:22
plunder (R)	2Ch 14:14; Es 3:13; 8:11; 9:10; Ps 109:11; Isa 11:14; Jer 20:5; 50:10; Da 11:33; Na 2:9; Hab 2:8; Zep 2:9; Zec 2:9; M't 12:29; M'k 3:21
plunder (E)	Ezr 9:7; Eze 39:10; Hab 2:8
who p. my heritage (A)(B)(E)	Jer 50:11
p. your wealth (B)	Eze 26:12
p., spoil, goods (A)(B)	Da 11:24
divided his p. (A)(N)	Lu 11:22

PLUNDERED

plundered (A)	Ge 34:27; 1Sa 14:48; 17:53; 2Ki 7:16; 2Ch 14:14; Isa 13:16; 42:22; Jer 9:19; 10:20; Am 3:11; Hab 2:8; Zec 2:8
plundered (B)	Ge 34:27; J'g 2:14, 16; 1Sa 17:53; 2Ki 7:16; 2Ch 14:14; Isa 42:22; Jer 2:3; Am 3:11; Zec 2:8
plundered (E)	Ge 34:27; 1Sa 17:53; 2Ki 7:16; Isa 42:22; Jer 39:10; Am 3:11; Hab 2:8; Zec 2:8
plundered (R)	Ge 34:27; J'g 2:14, 16; 1Sa 14:48; 17:53; 2Ch 14:14; Isa 13:16; 42:22; Am 3:11; Hab 2:8
p. their camp (S)	1Sa 17:53

PLUNDERERS

plunderers (A)(B)(R)	J'g 2:14
plunderers (B)	1Sa 14:48
plunderers (B)	2Ki 17:20
p. of my heritage (R)	Jer 50:11

PLUNDERING

p. of belongings (A)(B)(R)	Heb 10:34

PLUNDERS

plunders (R)	Isa 21:2

PLUNGE

Yet shalt thou p. me in the ditch	Job 9:31
p. me into a pit (R)	Job 9:31

PLUNGED

minds, p. into darkness (N)	Ro 1:21

POCHERETH

the children of P. of Zebaim	Ezr 2:57; Ne 7:59

POCKETS

no money in their p. (P)	M'k 6:8

PODS

with carob p. (A)(P)	Lu 15:16
with bean p. (B)(R)	Lu 15:16

POEM

take up this p. (B)	Isa 14:4

POETS

also of your own p. have said	Ac 17:28

POINT

said, Behold, I am at the p. to die	Ge 25:32
ye shall p. out for you mount Hor	Nu 34:7
mount Hor, ye shall p. out your	Nu 34:8
ye shall p. out your east border	Nu 34:10
and with the p. of a diamond	Jer 17:1
have set the p. of the sword against	Eze 21:15
loftiest p. of the temple (B)	M't 4:5
daughter lieth at the p. of death	M'k 5:23
son: for he was at the p. of death	Joh 4:47
yet offend in one p. he is guilty	Jas 2:10

POINTED

sharp p. things upon the mire	Job 41:30
prophecies p. to thee (S)	1Ti 1:18

POINTLESS

arguing with p. talk (B)	Job 15:3

POINTS

in all p. as he came, so shall he	Ec 5:16
was in all p. tempted like as we are	Heb 4:15
tempted in every respect (A)(B)	Heb 4:15
tested every way (N)(R)	Heb 4:15
shared fully in our experience of temptation (P)	Heb 4:15

POISON

such p. and wormwood (B)	De 29:18
with the p. of serpents the dust	De 32:24
venom of creatures (B)	De 32:24; 32:33; Ps 58:4; 140:3
grapes of p. (B)(R)	De 32:32
Their wine is the p. of dragons, and	De 32:33
p. whereof drinketh up my spirit	Job 6:4

He shall suck the p. of asps	Job 20:16
Their p. is like the p. of a serpent	Ps 58:4
adders' p. is under their lips	Ps 140:3
justice into p. (R)	Am 6:12
the p. of the asps is under their lips	Ro 3:13
venom of asps (A)(B)(N)(R)	Ro 3:13
p. our whole being (P)	Jas 3:6
an unruly evil, full of deadly p.	Jas 3:8
deadly venom (N)	Jas 3:8

POISONED

p. earth with lewdness (A)	Re 19:2

POISONOUS

bearing p. bitter fruit (R)	De 29:18
given us p. drink (B)(R)	Jer 8:14; 9:15

POKED

p. fun at him (B)	2Ki 2:23

POLE

fiery serpent, and set it upon a p.	Nu 21:8
of brass, and put it upon a p. (R)	Nu 21:9

POLES

make p. (A)(B)(R)	Ex 25:13; 25:14; 37:15; 40:20; Nu 4:6; 1Ch 15:15

POLICE

magistrates sent p. (R)	Ac 16:35; 16:38

POLICEMEN

magistrates sent p. (A)	Ac 16:35; 16:38

POLICY

through his p. shall cause craft	Da 8:25
their p. and action (N)	Lu 23:51

POLISH

p. the spears (S)	Jer 46:4

POLISHED

of p. brass (S)	2Ch 4:16
p. after the similitude of a palace	Ps 144:12
nation tall and p. (A)	Isa 18:2; 18:7
hid me, and made me a p. shaft	Isa 49:2
sword is p. (S)	Eze 21:9; 21:10-11, 28
his feet like in colour to p. brass	Da 10:6
feet like glowing burnished bronze (A)(E)(R)	Da 10:6
not a p. speaker (P)	2Co 11:6

POLISHES

p. with hammer (B)	Isa 41:7

POLISHING

rubies, their p. was of sapphire	La 4:7

POLL

take five shekels apiece by the p.	Nu 3:47
they shall only p. their heads	Eze 44:20
cut short or trim the hair (A)(B)(E)(R)	Eze 44:20
p. thee for thy delicate children	Mic 1:16
cut your hair for the children (A)(B)(E)(R)	Mic 1:16

POLLED

And when he p. his head, (for it	2Sa 14:26
at every year's end that he p. it	2Sa 14:26
heavy on him, therefore he p. it	2Sa 14:26
cut the hair (A)(B)(E)(R)	2Sa 14:26

POLLS

names, every male by their *p.*   *Nu 1:2*
head by head (A)(R)   *Nu 1:2;*
     1:18, 20, 22
name by name (B)   *Nu 1:2; 1:18, 22*
years old and upward, by their   *Nu 1:18*
p.
number of the names, by their   *Nu 1:20;*
p.   *1:22*
their number by their *p.* man   *1Ch 23:3*
by number of names by their   *1Ch 23:24*
p.

POLLUTE

neither shall ye *p.* the holy   *Nu 18:32*
things
neither shall he have polluted   *Nu 18:32*
holy (A)
you are not to desecrate holy   *Nu 18:32*
(B)
ye shall not profane holy   *Nu 18:32*
things (E)(R)
ye shall not *p.* the land   *Nu 35:33*
not *p.* the land (A)(E)(R)   *Nu 35:33*
not to desecrate the land (B)   *Nu 35:33*
is called by thy name, to *p.* it   *Jer 7:30*
my name, to defile it   *Jer 7:30*
(A)(E)(R)
they shall *p.* it   *Eze 7:21*
they shall profane it   *Eze 7:21*
(A)(E)(R)
to defile it (B)   *Eze 7:21*
they shall *p.* my secret place   *Eze 7:22;*
     44:7; Da 11:31
They shall profane it   *Eze 7:22*
(A)(B)(E)(R)
will ye *p.* me among the   *Eze 13:19*
people
you have profaned me   *Eze 13:19*
(A)(E)(R)
you are profaning my name   *Eze 13:19*
(B)
ye *p.* yourselves with all your   *Eze 20:31*
idols
defile yourselves with your   *Eze 20:31*
idols (A)(B)(R)
p. ye my holy name no more   *Eze 20:39*
profane my holy name   *Eze 20:39;*
(A)(B)(E)(R)   *39:7*

POLLUTED

thou hast *p.* it   *Ex 20:25;*
     2Ki 23:16
profane it by applying tools to   *Ex 20:25*
it (B)(R)
p. father's couch (A)(R)   *1Ch 5:1*
p. the house of the Lord   *2Ch 36:14*
have desecrated the Lord's   *2Ch 36:14*
temple (B)
as *p.* put from the priesthood   *Ezr 2:62;*
     Ne 7:64
excluded as unclean (A)(R)   *Ezr 2:62;*
     Ne 7:64
a *p.* and godless man   *Job 13:16*
(A)(B)(E)(R)
the godless and *p.* (A)   *Job 17:8; 27:8*
the land was *p.* with blood   *Ps 106:38*
p. spring (A)(B)(R)   *Pr 25:26*
lies *p.* by (B)(E)(R)   *Isa 24:5*
have *p.* mine inheritance   *Isa 47:6*
I ordered my inheritance be   *Isa 47:6*
profaned (A)(B)(E)(R)
how should my name be *p.*   *Isa 48:11;*
     Jer 34:16
how my name is profaned   *Isa 48:11*
(B)(E)(R)
How canst thou say, I am not   *Jer 2:23*
p.
I am not defiled (A)(E)(R)   *Jer 2:23*
I have not followed after Baals   *Jer 2:23*
(B)
the land is greatly *p.*   *Jer 3:1; 3:2*
he hath *p.* the kingdom   *La 2:2*
have *p.* themselves with blood   *La 4:14;*
     Ho 6:8
soul hath not been *p.*   *Eze 4:14*
I have never defiled myself   *Eze 4:14*
(A)(B)(R)
neither be *p.* any more with   *Eze 14:11*
all
neither defile themselves   *Eze 14:11*
(A)(B)(E)(R)
saw thee *p.* in your own blood   *Eze 16:6;*
     16:22
rolling about in your own   *Eze 16:6;*
blood (A)   *16:22*
weltering in your blood   *Eze 16:6*
(B)(E)(R)

should not be *p.* before   *Eze 20:9;*
heathen   *20:14, 22*
profaned in sight of heathen   *Eze 20:9*
(A)(B)(E)(R)
my sabbaths *p.*   *Eze 20:13; 20:16, 21, 24*
profaned my sabbaths   *Eze 20:13;*
(A)(B)(E)(R)   *20:16, 21, 24*
p. them in their own gifts   *Eze 20:26*
I defiled them through gifts   *Eze 20:26*
(B)(R)
Are ye *p.* after the manner of   *Eze 20:30*
your
defile yourselves after the   *Eze 20:30*
manner (A)(B)(R)
been *p.* (B)(E)(R)   *Eze 20:43*
she was *p.* with them   *Eze 23:17*
they defiled her   *Eze 23:17*
(A)(B)(E)(R)
thou art *p.* with their idols   *Eze 23:30;*
     36:18
have defiled yourself with   *Eze 23:30*
idols (A)
all that eat shall be *p.*   *Ho 9:4*
shall be defiled (A)(B)(R)   *Ho 9:4*
thou shalt die in a *p.* land   *Am 7:17*
die in a defiled land (A)   *Am 7:17*
upon unclean ground you will   *Am 7:17*
die (B)
die in a land that is unclean   *Am 7:17*
(E)
die in an unclean land (R)   *Am 7:17*
because it is *p.* it shall destroy   *Mic 2:10*
because of uncleanness   *Mic 2:10*
(A)(B)(E)(R)
Woe to her that is filthy and *p.*   *Zep 3:1*
Woe to her that is rebellious   *Zep 3:1*
and defiled (R)
her priests have *p.* the   *Zep 3:4*
sanctuary
her priests have profaned the   *Zep 3:4*
sanctuary (A)(E)(R)
priests defiled the sanctuary   *Zep 3:4*
(B)
Ye offer *p.* bread   *Mal 1:7; 1:12*
does not *p.* (B)   *M't 15:11; 15:20*
avoid anything *p.* (A)(N)(P)   *Ac 15:20*
hath *p.* this holy place   *Ac 21:28*
hath defiled this place   *Ac 21:28*
(B)(E)(R)
clothing *p.* by sensuality   *Jude 23*
(B)(N)
the *p.* (R)   *Re 21:8*

POLLUTES

p. our whole being (N)   *Jas 3:6*

POLLUTING

keepeth the sabbath from *p.*   *Isa 56:2*
sabbath so as not to profane it   *Isa 56:2*
(A)(B)(E)(R)
no foul, *p.* language (B)   *Eph 4:29*
lust of *p.* passions (A)(B)   *2Pe 2:10*

POLLUTION

her that was set apart for *p.*   *Eze 22:10*
women unclean from their   *Eze 22:10*
impurity (B)(E)(R)
bodily *p.* (N)   *1Pe 3:21*

POLLUTIONS

p. of the people (A)(R)   *Ezr 6:21;*
     9:11
that they abstain from *p.* of   *Ac 15:20*
idols
avoid anything that has been   *Ac 15:20*
polluted (A)(N)(P)
abstain from what has been   *Ac 15:20*
contaminated (B)
have escaped the *p.* of this   *2Pe 2:20*
world
contaminations of the world   *2Pe 2:20*
(B)(P)
defilements of the world   *2Pe 2:20*
(E)(N)(R)

POLLUX

whose sign was Castor and P.   *Ac 28:11*

POMEGRANATE

bell and a *p.* a golden bell and   *Ex 28:34*
a *p.*
A bell and a *p.* a bell and a *p.*   *Ex 39:26*
under a *p.* tree which is in   *1Sa 14:2*
Migron
thy temples are like a piece   *Ca 4:3*
of a *p.*

As a piece of a *p.* are thy   *Ca 6:7*
temples
spiced wine of the juice of my *p.*   *Ca 8:2*
the *p.* tree, the palm tree also   *Joe 1:12*
the *p.* and the olive tree, hath   *Hag 2:19*
not

POMEGRANATES

thou shalt make *p.* of blue   *Ex 28:33*
upon the hems of the robe *p.*   *Ex 39:24*
of blue
and put the bells between the   *Ex 39:25*
p.
robe, round about between   *Ex 39:25*
the *p.*
they brought of the *p.* and of   *Nu 13:23*
or of figs, or of vines, or of *p.*   *Nu 20:5*
and vines, and fig trees, and *p.*   *De 8:8*
that were upon the top, with   *1Ki 7:18*
p.
upon the two pillars had *p.*   *1Ki 7:20*
also
and the *p.* were two hundred   *1Ki 7:20*
in
And four hundred *p.* for the   *1Ki 7:42*
two
two rows of *p.* for one   *1Ki 7:42*
network
p. upon the chapiter round   *2Ki 25:17*
about
and made an hundred *p.* and   *2Ch 3:16*
put
hundred *p.* on the two   *2Ch 4:13*
wreaths
two rows of *p.* on each   *2Ch 4:13*
wreath
Thy plants are an orchard of *p.*   *Ca 4:13*
vine flourished, and the *p.*   *Ca 6:11*
budded
grape appear, and the *p.* bud   *Ca 7:12*
forth
p. upon the chapiters round   *Jer 52:22*
about
and the *p.* were like unto   *Jer 52:22*
these
were ninety and six *p.* on a   *Jer 52:23*
side
and all the *p.* upon the   *Jer 52:23*
network

POMMELED

they *p.* him (B)   *Lu 10:30*

POMMELS

and the *p.* and the chapiters   *2Ch 4:12;*
     4:13
the bowls (A)(B)(E)(R)   *2Ch 4:12;*
     4:13

POMP

their multitude and their *p.*   *Isa 5:14*
thy *p.* is brought down to   *Isa 14:11*
make the *p.* of the strong to   *Eze 7:24*
cease
the *p.* of her strength shall   *Eze 30:18;*
cease   *33:28*
they shall spoil the *p.* of   *Eze 32:12*
Egypt
come, and Bernice with great   *Ac 25:23*
p.

POMPOUS

a *p.* ignoramus (N)   *1Ti 6:4*

PONDER

P. the path of thy feet   *Pr 4:26*
Consider well the path (A)(B)   *Pr 4:26*
Make level the path of (E)   *Pr 4:26*
Take heed to the path of (R)   *Pr 4:26*
p. the path of life   *Pr 5:6*
path of life she does not   *Pr 5:6*
consider (B)
findeth not the level path of life   *Pr 5:6*
(E)
not take heed to path of life (R)   *Pr 5:6*

PONDERED

and *p.* them in her heart   *Lu 2:19*
thought them over in her heart   *Lu 2:19*
(B)
turned them over in her mind   *Lu 2:19*
(P)

PONDERETH

the Lord, and he *p.* all his   *Pr 5:21*
goings
eyes; but the Lord *p.* the hearts *Pr 21:2*
not he that *p.* the heart   *Pr 24:12*
consider it

PONDERS

p. day and night (A)(B)   *Ps 1:2*
mind of righteous *p.*   *Pr 15:28*
(A)(B)(R)

PONDS

upon their rivers, and upon   *Ex 7:19*
their *p.*
over the rivers, and over the *p.*   *Ex 8:5*
all that make sluices and *p.*   *Isa 19:10*
for fish

PONTIUS

him to *P.* Pilate the governor   *M't 27:2*
P. Pilate being governor of   *Lu 3:1*
Judaea
both Herod and *P.* Pilate, with   *Ac 4:27*
before *P.* Pilate witnessed a   *1Ti 6:13*
good

PONTUS

and Cappadocia, in *P.* and Asia   *Ac 2:9*
Jew named Aquila, born in *P.*   *Ac 18:2*
strangers scattered throughout   *1Pe 1:1*
P.

POOL

met together by the *p.* of   *2Sa 2:13*
Gibeon
the one on the one side of the   *2Sa 2:13*
p.
other on the other side of the   *2Sa 2:13*
p.
them up over the *p.* in Hebron   *2Sa 4:12*
the chariot in the *p.* of   *1Ki 22:38*
Samaria
by the conduit of the upper   *2Ki 18:17*
p.
how he made a *p.* and a   *2Ki 20:20*
conduit
the fountain, and to the king's   *Ne 2:14*
p.
p. of Siloah by the king's   *Ne 3:15*
garden
and to the *p.* that was made   *Ne 3:16*
wilderness into a *p.* (S)   *Ps 107:35;*
  114:8
end of the conduit of the upper   *Isa 7:3*
p.
together the waters of the   *Isa 22:9*
lower *p.*
two walls for the water of the   *Isa 22:11*
old *p.*
parched ground shall become a   *Isa 35:7*
p.
by the conduit of the upper *p.*   *Isa 36:2*
make the wilderness a *p.* of   *Isa 41:18*
water
Nineveh is like a *p.* of water   *Na 2:8*
there is by the sheep market a   *Joh 5:2*
p.
at the sheep-*p.* (N)   *Joh 5:2*
down at a certain season into   *Joh 5:4*
the *p.*
is troubled, to put me into the   *Joh 5:7*
p.
him, Go, wash in the *p.* of   *Joh 9:7*
Siloam
Go to the *p.* of Siloam, and   *Joh 9:11*
wash

POOLS

and upon all their *p.* of water   *Ex 7:19*
a well; the rain also filleth the   *Ps 84:6*
p.
I made me *p.* of water, to water   *Ec 2:6*
for the bittern, and *p.* of   *Isa 14:23*
water
islands, and I will dry up the   *Isa 42:15*
p.
marshes and *p.* (B)   *Eze 47:11*

POOR

came up after them seven *p.*   *Ge 41:19*
kine

---

that the *p.* of thy people may   *Ex 23:11*
eat
p. shall not give less than half   *Ex 30:15*
a shekel
if he be *p.* and cannot get so   *Le 14:21*
much
shalt leave them for the *p.* and   *Le 19:10*
stranger
thou shalt not respect the   *Le 19:15*
person of the *p.*
if thy brother be waxen *p.*   *Le 25:25;*
  25:35, 39, 47
save when there be no *p.*   *De 15:4*
among you
for the *p.* shall never cease   *De 15:11*
out of the land
followedst not young men, *p.*   *Ru 3:10*
or rich
the Lord maketh *p.* and maketh   *1Sa 2:7*
rich
he raiseth up the *p.* out of the   *1Sa 2:8;*
dust   *Ps 113:7*
two men, one rich, and the   *2Sa 12:1*
other *p.*
captain of guard left of *p.* of   *2Ki 25:12;*
land   *Jer 39:10; 40:7; 52:15-16*
but he saveth the *p.* from the   *Job 5:15*
sword
so the *p.* hath hope, and   *Job 5:16*
iniquity stoppeth
his children shall seek to   *Job 20:10*
please the *p.*
he hath oppressed and   *Job 20:19*
forsaken the *p.*
p. of the earth hide themselves   *Job 24:4*
together
and they take a pledge of the   *Job 24:9*
p.
the murderer killeth the *p.*   *Job 24:14*
and needy
because I delivered the *p.*   *Job 29:12*
that cried
was not my soul grieved for   *Job 30:25*
the *p.*
if I withheld the *p.* from   *Job 31:16*
their desire
or if I have seen any *p.*   *Job 31:19*
without covering
nor regardeth the rich more   *Job 34:19*
than the *p.*
they cause the cry of the *p.*   *Job 34:28*
to come to him
he delivereth the *p.* in   *Job 36:15;*
affliction   *Ps 72:12*
cry of the *p.* (E)   *Ps 9:12; 10:12*
the expectation of the *p.* shall   *Ps 9:18*
not perish
the wicked in his pride doth   *Ps 10:2*
persecute the *p.*
his eyes are privily set against   *Ps 10:8*
the *p.*
he lieth in wait secretly to catch   *Ps 10:9*
the *p.*
that the *p.* may fall by his   *Ps 10:10*
strong ones
the *p.* committeth himself to   *Ps 10:14*
thee, thou art
for the oppression of the *p.* I   *Ps 12:5*
will arise
ye have shamed the counsel of   *Ps 14:6*
the *p.*
plans of the *p.* (A)(R)   *Ps 14:6*
who deliverest the *p.* from him   *Ps 35:10*
that spoileth
have bent their bow to cast   *Ps 37:14*
down the *p.*
but I am *p.*   *Ps 40:17;*
  69:29; 70:5; 86:1; 109:22
blessed is he that considereth   *Ps 41:1*
the *p.*
both low and high, rich and *p.*   *Ps 49:2*
together
hast prepared of thy goodness   *Ps 68:10*
for the *p.*
Lord heareth *p.* and despiseth   *Ps 69:33*
not prisoners
he shall judge the *p.* of the   *Ps 72:4*
people
he shall spare the *p.*   *Ps 72:13*
let the *p.* and needy praise   *Ps 74:21*
thy name
defend the *p.*   *Ps 82:3*
deliver the *p.* and needy, rid   *Ps 82:4*
them out of
yet setteth he *p.* on high from   *Ps 107:41*
affliction
he shall stand at the right   *Ps 109:31*
hand of the *p.*
will satisfy her *p.* with bread,   *Ps 132:15*
will clothe

---

and will maintain the right of   *Ps 140:12*
the *p.*
he becometh *p.* that dealeth   *Pr 10:4*
with a slack
the destruction of the *p.* is   *Pr 10:15*
their poverty
there is that maketh himself *p.*   *Pr 13:7*
hath riches
his riches, but the *p.* heareth   *Pr 13:8*
not rebuke
much food is in the tillage of   *Pr 13:23*
the *p.* but there
the *p.* is hated even of his   *Pr 14:20*
neighbour
he that hath mercy on the *p.*   *Pr 14:21*
happy is he
oppresseth *p.* reproacheth his   *Pr 14:31*
Maker; honoureth him hath
mercy on the *p.*
days of *p.* are unfortunate (B)   *Pr 15:15*
whoso mocketh the *p.*   *Pr 17:5*
reproacheth his Maker
the *p.* useth entreaties, but the   *Pr 18:23*
rich
the *p.* is separated from his   *Pr 19:4*
own neighbour
all brethren of the *p.* do hate   *Pr 19:7*
him, how much
whoso stoppeth his ears at the   *Pr 21:13*
cry of the *p.*
the rich and *p.* meet together,   *Pr 22:2*
Lord is maker
the rich ruleth over the *p.* and   *Pr 22:7*
the borrower is
he that oppresseth the *p.* to   *Pr 22:16*
increase his riches
shall gather it for him that will   *Pr 28:8*
pity the *p.*
the *p.* that hath understanding   *Pr 28:11*
searcheth him
so is a wicked ruler over the *p.*   *Pr 28:15*
people
righteous considereth the   *Pr 29:7;*
cause of the *p.*   *29:13*
the king that faithfully judgeth   *Pr 29:14*
the *p.*
lest I be *p.* and steal, and take   *Pr 30:9*
name of God
whose teeth are as swords, to   *Pr 30:14*
devour the *p.*
and plead the cause of the *p.*   *Pr 31:9*
and needy
that is born in his kingdom,   *Ec 4:14*
becometh *p.*
if thou seest the oppression of   *Ec 5:8*
the *p.*
what hath the *p.* that knoweth   *Ec 6:8*
to walk
the spoil of the *p.* is in your   *Isa 3:14*
houses
what mean ye that ye grind   *Isa 3:15*
faces of the *p.*
and to take away the right   *Isa 10:2*
from the *p.*
cause it to be heard to Laish,   *Isa 10:30*
O *p.* Anathoth
with righteousness shall he   *Isa 11:4*
judge the *p.*
the firstborn of the *p.* shall   *Isa 14:30*
feed in it
and the *p.* of his people shall   *Isa 14:32*
trust in it
even the feet of the *p.* shall   *Isa 26:6*
tread it down
even *p.* among men shall   *Isa 29:19*
rejoice in Holy One
to destroy the *p.* with lying   *Isa 32:7*
words
when the *p.* and needy seek   *Isa 41:17*
water
that thou bring the *p.* that are   *Isa 58:7*
cast out
is found the blood of the *p.*   *Jer 2:34*
innocents
I said, Surely these are *p.* they   *Jer 5:4*
are foolish
for he hath delivered the soul   *Jer 20:13*
of the *p.*
he judged the cause of the *p.*   *Jer 22:16*
and needy
nor did she strengthen hand   *Eze 16:49*
of the *p.*
hath oppressed *p.* and needy,   *Eze 18:12*
hath spoiled
that hath taken off his hand   *Eze 18:17*
from the *p.*
and they have vexed the *p.*   *Eze 22:29*
and needy
they sold the *p.* for a pair of   *Am 2:6*
shoes

that pant after the dust on the   *Am 2:7*
head of the *p.*
which oppress the *p.* and crush *Am 4:1*
the needy
forasmuch as your treading is *Am 5:11*
on the *p.*
and they turn aside the *p.* in *Am 5:12*
the gate
even to make the *p.* of the land *Am 8:4*
to fail
that we may buy the *p.* for   *Am 8:6*
silver, and needy
their rejoicing was to devour *Hab 3:14*
the *p.*
the *p.* people shall trust in the *Zep 3:12*
Lord
and oppress not the widow   *Zec 7:10*
nor *p.*
I will feed even you, O *p.* of *Zec 11:7*
the flock
the *p.* of the flock that waited *Zec 11:11*
upon me
blessed are the *p.* in spirit, for *M't 5:3*
theirs is
a *p.* tree bad fruit (N)(P)(R) *M't 7:17*
the *p.* have the gospel   *M't 11:5*
preached to them
the *p.* always with you, but *M't 26:11;*
me ye have not always   *M'k 14:7;*
  Joh 12:8
there came a certain *p.*   *M'k 12:42*
widow
this *p.* widow cast more in *M'k 12:43;*
  Lu 21:3
blessed be ye *p.* yours is the *Lu 6:20*
kingdom
call the *p.* the maimed, the *Lu 14:13;*
lame   *14:21*
this he said, not that he cared *Joh 12:6*
for the *p.*
to make a contribution for *Ro 15:26*
the *p.*
as *p.* yet making many rich *2Co 6:10*
though rich, yet for your sakes *2Co 8:9*
he become *p.*
that we should remember the *Ga 2:10*
p.
hath not God chosen the *p.* *Jas 2:5*
of this world
but ye have despised the *p.* rich *Jas 2:6*
oppress you
and knowest not that thou art *Re 3:17*
p.
he causeth rich and *p.* to *Re 13:16*
receive a mark

POOR *MAN*

nor countenance a *p.* man in *Ex 23:3*
his cause
if a *p. man,* harden not thy *De 15:7*
heart
if a *p. man* sleep not with his *De 24:12*
pledge
to be king's son, seeing I am *1Sa 18:23*
a *p. man*
p. man had nothing, save one *2Sa 12:3*
ewe lamb
but took the *p. man's*   *2Sa 12:4*
ewe lamb and dressed it
this *p. man* cried, and the Lord *Ps 34:6*
heard
but persecuted the *p.* and *Ps 109:16*
needy *man*
and a *p. man* is better than a *Pr 19:22*
liar
he that loveth pleasure shall *Pr 21:17*
be a *p. man*
a *p. man* that oppresseth the *Pr 28:3*
poor is like
the *p.* and deceitful *man* meet *Pr 29:13*
together
found in it a *p.* wise *man,* yet *Ec 9:15*
no man remembered that same
p. man
the *p. man's* wisdom is despised *Ec 9:16*
and not heard
there come in a *p. man* in vile *Jas 2:2*
raiment

IS POOR

if lend to any of my people *Ex 22:25*
that *is p.*
shalt not oppress hired servant *De 24:14*
that *is p.*
for he *is p.* and setteth his *De 24:15*
heart upon it
behold, my family *is p.* in *J'g 6:15*
Manasseh

better *is* the *p.* that walketh in *Pr 19:1;*
his integrity   *28:6*
rob not poor because he *is p.* *Pr 22:22*
nor oppress
better *is* a *p.* and wise child, *Ec 4:13*
than an old
to him that *is p.* and of a *Isa 66:2*
contrite heart

TO THE POOR

thou shalt leave them *to the p.* *Le 23:22*
and stranger
make them days of sending *Es 9:22*
gifts *to the p.*
I was a father *to the p.* and *Job 29:16*
feet to lame
of the wicked, but he giveth *Job 36:6*
right *to the p.*
he hath given *to the p.* *Ps 112:9;*
  2Co 9:9
for he giveth of his bread *to the* *Pr 22:9*
p.
he that giveth *to the p.* shall *Pr 28:27*
not lack
she stretcheth out her hand *to* *Pr 31:20*
the p.
thou hast been a strength *to* *Isa 25:4*
the p.
break off sins, by shewing *Da 4:27*
mercy *to the p.*
sell all, and give *to the p.* *M't 19:21;*
  M'k 10:21
ointment might have been *M't 26:9;*
sold and given *to the p.* *M'k 14:5;*
  Joh 12:5
to preach the gospel *to the p.* *Lu 4:18;*
  7:22
sell all thou hast and *Lu 18:22*
distribute *to the p.*
behold, the half of my goods I *Lu 19:8*
give *to the p.*
that he should give *Joh 13:29*
something *to the p.*
I bestow all my goods *to* feed *1Co 13:3*
the p.
and say *to the p.* Stand thou *Jas 2:3*
there, or sit here

THY POOR

shalt not wrest the judgment of *Ex 23:6*
thy p.
nor shut thine hand from *thy* *De 15:7*
p. brother
and thine eye be evil against *De 15:9*
thy p. brother
thou shalt open thine hand *De 15:11*
wide to *thy p.*
he shall judge *thy p.* with *Ps 72:2*
judgment
forget not the congregation of *Ps 74:19*
thy p. for ever

POORER

if he be *p.* than thy estimation *Le 27:8*

POOREST

p. sort of the people of the *2Ki 24:14*
land

POPLAR

Jacob took him rods of green *Ge 30:37*
p.

POPLARS

hills, under oaks and *p.* and *Ho 4:13*
elms

POPULAR

there is a *p.* saying (N) *1Ti 3:1*

POPULARITY

their *p.* was great (P) *Ac 5:13*
a possession for the *p.* (S) *Isa 14:23*
the pelican and *p.* *Isa 34:11*
(A)(B)(E)
the hawk and *p.* (R)(S) *Isa 34:11*
the cormorant and the *p.* (S) *Zep 2:14*

POPULATE

p. the earth (B) *Ge 9:1*

POPULOUS

a nation, great, mighty, and *p.* *De 26:5*
Art thou better than *p.* No, that *Na 3:8*

PORATHA

And *P.* and Adalia, and *Es 9:8*
Aridatha

PORCH

Ehud went forth through the *p.* *J'g 3:23*
went out into the vestibule *J'g 3:23*
(A)(R)
p. before the temple *1Ki 6:3; 6:2*
vestibule in front of temple *1Ki 6:3*
(A)(R)
made a *p.* of pillar *1Ki 7:6; 7:19, 21*
made a Hall of Pillars (A)(R) *1Ki 7:6*
made a vestibule of pillars (B) *1Ki 7:7*
even the *p.* of judgment *1Ki 7:7; 7:8*
the hall of judgment (R) *1Ki 7:7*
the *p.* of the house *1Ki 7:12*
the vestibule of the house (R) *1Ki 7:12*
the pattern of the *p.* *1Ch 28:11*
plan of the vestibule of *1Ch 28:11*
temple (A)(R)
p. in front of the house *2Ch 3:4*
the vestibule in front of the *2Ch 3:4*
house (R)
which he had built before the *2Ch 8:12*
p.
built before the vestibule (R) *2Ch 8:12*
that was before the *p.* of the *2Ch 15:8*
Lord
in front of the vestibule (R) *2Ch 15:8*
shut the doors of the *p.* *2Ch 29:7*
the doors of the vestibule (R) *2Ch 29:7*
the *p.* of the Lord *2Ch 29:17*
the vestibule of the Lord *2Ch 29:17*
(R)
between the *p.* and the altar *Eze 8:16;*
  Joe 2:17
between the vestibule and *Eze 8:16*
Altar (R)
the *p.* of the gate *Eze 40:7;*
  40:8-9; 39-40, 48
the vestibule of the gate *Eze 40:7*
(B)(R)
the *p.* of the house *Eze 40:48*
the vestibule of the temple *Eze 40:48*
(B)
the length of the *p.* 20 cubits *Eze 40:49*
the length of the vestibule *Eze 40:49*
(B)(R)
planks upon the face of the *Eze 41:25*
p.
canopy of wood over front of *Eze 41:25*
vestibule (B)(R)
on the sides of the *p.* *Eze 41:26*
on sides of the vestibule *Eze 41:26*
(B)(R)
shall enter by way of the *p.* *Eze 44:3;*
  46:2, 8
entering by the vestibule *Eze 44:3*
(B)(R)
has gone out into *p.* *M't 26:71;*
  M'k 14:68
gone out into the vestibule *M't 26:71*
(B)
went out to the gateway (N) *M't 26:71*
in the temple of Solomon's *Joh 10:23;*
p.   *Ac 3:11; 5:12*
temple of Solomon's *Joh 10:23;*
vestibule (B)   *Ac 3:11; 5:12*
in Solomon's Cloister (N) *Joh 10:23;*
  Ac 3:11; 5:12
in the portico of Solomon *Joh 10:23*
(R)

PORCHES

the *p.* of the court *Eze 41:15*
the outer vestibule *Eze 41:15*
(A)(B)(R)
Bethesda, having five *p.* *Joh 5:2*
with five entrances (B) *Joh 5:2*
with five colonades (N) *Joh 5:2*
pool surrounded by five arches *Joh 5:2*
(P)
which has five porticoes (R) *Joh 5:2*

PORCIUS

after two years *P.* Festus *Ac 24:27*
came

PORT

dragon well, and to the dung *p.* *Ne 2:13*
Dragon's well, and Dung Gate *Ne 2:13*
(A)(B)(E)(R)

PORTENT

I am a *p.* to many (R) *Ps 71:7; Isa 20:3*
a great *p.* (B)(N)(R) *Re 12:1;*
　　　　　　　　　　　12:3
another *p.* in heaven *Re 15:10*
(B)(N)(R)

PORTENTS

by *p.* and marvels (B) *De 6:22*
signs and *p.* (B)(R) *Isa 8:18; Joe 2:30*
ye see *p.* (N) *Joh 4:48; Ac 2:19, 22*

PORTER

watchman called unto the *p.* *2Sa 18:26*
watchman called to *2Sa 18:26*
gatekeeper (A)(B)
watchman called to the gate *2Sa 18:26*
(R)
called unto the *p.* of the city *2Ki 7:10;*
　　　　　　　　　1Ch 9:21; 2Ch 31:14
gatekeeper, doorkeeper *2Ki 7:10;*
(A)(B)(R) *1Ch 9:21; 2Ch 31:14*
commanded the *p.* to watch *M'k 13:34*
the doorkeeper *M'k 13:34*
(A)(N)(P)(R)
the sentinel (B) *M'k 13:34*
To him the *p.* openeth *Joh 10:3*
The watchman opens (A) *Joh 10:3*
The doorkeeper opens *Joh 10:3*
(B)(N)(P)
The gatekeeper opens (R) *Joh 10:3*

PORTERS

he called the *p.*: and they told *2Ki 7:11*
it
the gatekeepers (A)(B)(R) *2Ki 7:11*
the *p.* were *1Ch 9:17; 16:42; 23:5*
the gatekeepers (A)(B)(R) *1Ch 9:17;*
　　　　　　　　　　　　23:5
the *p.* in the companies *1Ch 9:18;*
9:22, 24, 26; 15:18; 16:38; 2Ch 23:4
　　　　　　　　　　　　　　34:13
the gatekeepers, doorkeepers *1Ch 9:18;*
(A)(B)(R) *9:22, 24, 26; 15:18; 16:38;*
　　　　　　　　　　2Ch 23:4; 34:13
divisions of the *p.* *1Ch 26:1*
　　　　　　26:12, 19; 2Ch 8:14
gatekeepers (A)(B)(R) *1Ch 26:1*
　　　　　　26:12, 19; 2Ch 8:14
set *p.* at the gates *2Ch 23:19; 35:15*
gatekeepers (A)(B)(R) *2Ch 23:19*
　　　　　　　　　　　35:15
children of the *p.* (A)(B)(R) *Ezr 2:42;*
　　　　　　　　　　　　Ne 7:45
singers, the *p.* *Ezr 2:70;*
7:7, 24; 10:24; Ne 7:1, 73; 10:28, 39;
　　11:19; 12:25, 45, 47; 13:5
gatekeepers, doorkeepers *Ezr 2:70;*
(A)(B)(R) *7:7, 24; 10:24; Ne 7:1, 73;*
10:28, 39; 11:19; 12:25, 45, 47; 13:5

PORTICOES

pool with five *p.* (R) *Joh 5:2*
the *p.* of Solomon (R) *Joh 10:23*

PORTION

the *p.* of the men which went *Ge 14:24*
with
and Mamre: let them take *Ge 14:24*
their *p.*
yet any *p.* or inheritance for *Ge 31:14*
us in
bought a *p.* of the field (S) *Ge 33:19*
the priests had a *p.* assigned *Ge 47:22*
them
did eat their *p.* which *Ge 47:22*
Pharaoh gave
to thee one *p.* above thy *Ge 48:22*
brethren
given it unto them for their *p.* *Le 6:17*
of
This is the *p.* of the anointing *Le 7:35*
of Aaron
thou shalt take one *p.* of fifty *Nu 31:30*
p. of them that went out to *Nu 31:36*
war
Moses took one *p.* of fifty, *Nu 31:47*
both of
a double *p.* of all that he hath *De 21:17*
For the Lord's *p.* is his people *De 32:9*
in a *p.* of the lawgiver, was he *De 33:21*
portion (S) *Jos 14:4;*
　15:13; 18:5-7, 9; 19:9; 22:25, 27
but one lot and one *p.* to *Jos 17:14*
inherit

of the *p.* of the children of *Jos 19:9*
Judah
Come up with me into my *p.* *J'g 1:3*
(S)
violated dedicated *p.* (B) *J'g 7:1*
p. of land (A)(B)(R) *J'g 24:32*
she happened to come to a *p.* of *Ru 2:3*
field (S)
unto Hannah he gave a worthy *1Sa 1:5*
p.
Bring the *p.* which I gave thee *1Sa 9:23*
What *p.* have we in David? *1Ki 12:16*
neither
double *p.* of thy spirit be upon *2Ki 2:9*
me
eat Jezebel in the *p.* of Jezreel *2Ki 9:10*
met him in the *p.* of Naboth *2Ki 9:21*
him in the *p.* of the field of *2Ki 9:25*
Naboth
In the *p.* of Jezreel shall dogs *2Ki 9:36*
eat
face, of the field in the *p.* of *2Ki 9:37*
Jezreel
saying, What *p.* have we in *2Ch 10:16*
David
For Ahaz took away a *p.* out *2Ch 18:21*
of the
also the king's *p.* of his *2Ch 31:3*
substance
p. of the priests and the *2Ch 31:4*
Levites
his daily *p.* for their service *2Ch 31:16*
have no *p.* on this side the *Ezr 4:16*
river
but ye have no *p.* nor right, nor *Ne 2:20*
portion (S) *Ne 3:11;*
　　　　　3:19-21, 24, 27, 30
a certain *p.* should be for the *Ne 11:23*
singers
and the porters, every day his *Ne 12:47*
p.
the *p.* of a wicked man from *Job 20:29*
God
their *p.* is cursed in the *Job 24:18*
earth: he
but how little a *p.* is heard of *Job 26:14*
him
the *p.* of a wicked man with *Job 27:13*
God
what *p.* of God is there from *Job 31:2*
above
this shall be the *p.* of their cup *Ps 11:6*
Lord is the *p.* of mine *Ps 16:5*
inheritance
which have their *p.* in this life *Ps 17:14*
p. out the valley (A)(R) *Ps 60:6*
sword: they shall be *p.* for *Ps 63:10*
foxes
of my heart, and my *p.* for *Ps 73:26*
ever
Thou art my *p.* O Lord: I *Ps 119:57*
have
and my *p.* in the land of the *Ps 142:5*
living
feed me my *p.* of nourishment *Pr 30:8*
(B)
and a *p.* to her maidens *Pr 31:15*
this was my *p.* of all my labour *Ec 2:10*
therein shall he leave it for his *Ec 2:21*
in his own works; for that is *Ec 3:22*
his *p.*
God giveth him: for it is his *p.* *Ec 5:18*
to eat thereof, and to take his *p.* *Ec 5:19*
neither have they any more a *p.* *Ec 9:6*
for that is thy *p.* in this life, and *Ec 9:9*
Give a *p.* to seven, and also to *Ec 11:2*
eight
This is the *p.* of them that *Isa 17:14*
spoil us
I divide him a *p.* with the *Isa 53:12*
great
stones of the stream is thy *p.* *Isa 57:6*
they shall rejoice in their *p.* *Isa 61:7*
p. of Jacob is not like them: *Jer 10:16*
for he
have trodden my *p.* under *Jer 12:10*
foot
pleasant *p.* a desolate *Jer 12:10*
wilderness
the *p.* of thy measures from *Jer 13:25*
me
The *p.* of Jacob is not like *Jer 51:19*
them
day a *p.* until the day of his *Jer 52:34*
death
The Lord is my *p.* saith my *La 3:24*
soul

unto the Lord, an holy *p.* of *Eze 45:1*
the land
The holy *p.* of the land shall *Eze 45:4*
be for
against the oblation of the *Eze 45:6;*
holy *p.* *48:18*
And a *p.* shall be for the *Eze 45:7*
prince on the
other side of the oblation of *Eze 45:7*
the holy *p.*
before the oblation of the holy *Eze 45:7*
p. and
are his sides east and west, a *Eze 48:1*
p. for Dan
side unto the west side, a *p.* *Eze 48:2*
for Asher
unto the west side, a *p.* for *Eze 48:3*
Naphtali
unto the west side, a *p.* for *Eze 48:4*
Manasseh
unto the west side, a *p.* for *Eze 48:5*
Ephraim
unto the west side, a *p.* for *Eze 48:6*
Reuben
unto the west side, a *p.* for *Eze 48:7*
Judah
west side, Benjamin shall *Eze 48:23*
have a *p.*
the west side, Simeon shall *Eze 48:24*
have a *p.*
side unto the west side, *Eze 48:25*
Issachar a *p.*
side unto the west side, *Eze 48:26*
Zebulun a *p.*
east side unto the west side, *Eze 48:27*
Gad a *p.*
with the *p.* of the king's meat, *Da 1:8*
nor
eat of the *p.* of the king's meat *Da 1:13*
did eat the *p.* of the king's *Da 1:15*
meat
took away the *p.* of their meat *Da 1:16*
let his *p.* be with the beasts in *Da 4:15*
let his *p.* be with the beasts of *Da 4:23*
they that feed of the *p.* of his *Da 11:26*
meat
hath changed the *p.* of my *Mic 2:4*
people
by them their *p.* is fat, and *Hab 1:16*
their
Lord shall inherit Judah his *p.* *Zec 2:12*
him his *p.* with the *M't 24:51*
hypocrites
their *p.* of meat in due season *Lu 12:42*
him his *p.* with the *Lu 12:46*
unbelievers
give me the *p.* of goods that *Lu 15:12*
falleth
considerable *p.* of (P) *Ac 6:7*

PORTIONS

shall have like *p.* to eat, *De 18:8*
besides
fell ten *p.* to Manasseh, *Jos 17:5*
besides
her sons and her daughters, *p.* *1Sa 1:4*
give *p.* to all the males *2Ch 31:19*
among the
and send *p.* unto them for *Ne 8:10*
whom
and to send *p.* and to make *Ne 8:12*
great
p. of the law for the priests *Ne 12:44*
gave the *p.* of the singers and *Ne 12:47*
the *p.* of the Levites had not *Ne 13:10*
been
and of sending *p.* one to *Es 9:19;*
another *9:22*
shall be over against one of *Eze 45:7*
two *p.*
Israel: Joseph shall have *Eze 47:13*
two *p.*
over against the *p.* for the *Eze 48:21*
prince
these are their *p.* saith the *Eze 48:29*
Lord
month devour them with their *Ho 5:7*
p.
three *p.* of flour (B) *M't 13:33*

PORTRAY

and *p.* it upon the city, even *Eze 4:1*

PORTRAYED

p. upon the wall round about *Eze 8:10*
she saw men *p.* upon the wall *Eze 23:14*
the Chaldeans *p.* with *Eze 23:14*
vermilion

POSITION

p. or overseership (A)   *Ac 1:20*

POSSESS

know I shall *p.* it (R)   *Ge 15:8*
shall *p.* the gate of his   *Ge 22:17*
enemies
let thy seed *p.* the gate of   *Ge 24:60*
those
shall *p.* it forever (B)   *Ex 32:13*
give it unto you to *p.* it, a land *Le 20:24*
Let us go up at once, and *p.* it *Nu 13:30*
he went; and his seed shall *p.*   *Nu 14:24*
it
of his family, and he shall *p.*   *Nu 27:11*
it
I have given you the land to   *Nu 33:53*
p. it
p. the land which the Lord   *De 1:8*
sware
go up and *p.* it, as the Lord   *De 1:21*
God of
will I give it, and they shall   *De 1:39*
p. it
begin to *p.* it, and contend with *De 2:24*
begin to *p.* that thou mayest   *De 2:31*
hath given you this land to *p.* it *De 3:18*
until they also *p.* the land   *De 3:20*
which
go in and *p.* the land which the *De 4:1*
in the land whither ye go to *p.* it *De 4:5*
the land whither ye go over to   *De 4:14*
p. it
shall go over, and *p.* that good *De 4:22*
land
ye go over Jordan to *p.* it; ye   *De 4:26*
shall
the land which I give them to   *De 5:31*
p. it
days in the land which ye shall *De 5:33*
p.
in the land whither ye go to *p.* it *De 6:1*
mayest go in and *p.* the good   *De 6:18*
land
the land whither thou goest to   *De 7:1;*
p. it   11:29; 23:20; 28:21, 63; 30:16
and go in and *p.* the land which *De 8:1*
p. nations greater and mightier *De 9:1*
hath brought me in to *p.* this   *De 9:4*
land
heart, dost thou go to *p.* their   *De 9:5*
land
land to *p.* it for thy   *De 9:6*
righteousness
and *p.* the land which I have   *De 9:23*
given
they may go in and *p.* the   *De 10:11*
land
be strong, and go in and *p.* the *De 11:8*
land
the land, whither ye go to *p.* it *De 11:8*
whither thou goest in to *p.* it *De 11:10*
the land, whither ye go to *p.*,   *De 11:11*
it is a
p. greater nations and   *De 11:23*
mightier
over Jordan to go into the   *De 11:31*
land
you, and ye shall *p.* it, and   *De 11:31*
dwell
of thy fathers giveth thee to *p.* *De 12:1*
it
nations which ye shall *p.*   *De 12:2*
served
whither thou goest to *p.* them *De 12:29*
thee for an inheritance to *p.* it *De 15:4*
shalt *p.* it, and shalt dwell   *De 17:14*
therein
these nations, which thou   *De 18:14*
shalt *p.*
Lord thy God giveth thee to *p.* *De 19:2;*
it   19:14; 21:1
giveth thee an inheritance to *De 25:19*
p. it
possessed, and thou shalt *p.* it *De 30:5*
passest over Jordan to go to   *De 30:18*
p. it
before thee, and thou shalt *p.* *De 31:3*
them
whither ye go over Jordan to   *De 31:13;*
p. it   32:47
p. thou the west and the south *De 33:23*
this Jordan, to go in to *p.* the *Jos 1:11*
land
Lord your God giveth you to *Jos 1:11*
p. it

long are ye slack to go to *p.*   *Jos 18:3*
the land
ye shall *p.* their land, as the   *Jos 23:5*
Lord
gave unto Esau mount Seir, to *Jos 24:4*
p. it
hand, that ye might *p.* their   *Jos 24:8*
land
unto his inheritance to *p.* the   *J'g 2:6*
land
Israel, and shouldest thou *p.*   *J'g 11:23*
Wilt not thou *p.* that which   *J'g 11:24*
Chemosh thy god giveth thee   *J'g 11:24*
to *p.*
out from before us, them will   *J'g 11:24*
we *p.*
to go, and to enter to *p.*   *J'g 18:9*
the land
whither he is gone down to   *1Ki 21:18*
p. it
that ye may *p.* this good land *1Ch 28:8*
The land, unto which ye go to *Ezr 9:11*
p. it
they should go in to *p.* the land *Ne 9:15*
that they should go in to *p.* it *Ne 9:23*
I made to *p.* months of vanity *Job 7:3*
to *p.* the iniquities of my   *Job 13:26*
youth
house of Israel shall *p.* them in *Isa 14:2*
do not rise, nor *p.* the land   *Isa 14:21*
and the bittern shall *p.* it; the *Isa 34:11*
owl
they shall *p.* it forever, from   *Isa 34:17*
his trust in me shall *p.* the   *Isa 57:13*
land
their land they shall *p.* double *Isa 61:7*
their fathers, and they shall *p.* *Jer 30:3*
it
and they shall *p.* their houses *Eze 7:24*
blood: and shall ye *p.* the   *Eze 33:25*
land
wife: and shall ye *p.* the land *Eze 33:26*
shall be mine, and we will *p.*   *Eze 35:10*
it
and they shall *p.* thee, and   *Eze 36:12*
thou
p. the kingdom for ever, even *Da 7:18*
for
their silver, nettles shall *p.* them *Ho 9:6*
to *p.* the land of the Amorite *Am 2:10*
they may *p.* the remnant of   *Am 9:12*
Edom
of Jacob shall *p.* their   *Ob 17*
possessions
south shall *p.* the mount of Esau *Ob 19*
they shall *p.* the fields of   *Ob 19*
Ephraim
and Benjamin shall *p.* Gilead *Ob 19*
shall *p.* that of the Canaanites *Ob 20*
shall *p.* the cities of the south *Ob 20*
p. the dwellingplaces that are *Hab 1:6*
not
remnant of my people shall *p.* *Zep 2:9*
this people to *p.* all these   *Zec 8:12*
things
I give tithes of all that I *p.*   *Lu 18:12*
In your patience *p.* ye your   *Lu 21:19*
souls
dispose of all I *p.* (P)   *1Co 13:3*
cannot *p.* immortality (N)   *1Co 15:50*
transitory never *p.* the   *1Co 15:50*
everlasting (P)
p. his vessels in sanctification *1Th 4:4*
p. the mystic secret of faith   *1Ti 3:9*
(A)

POSSESSED

and *p.* his land from Arnon   *Nu 21:24*
unto
them alive and they *p.* his   *Nu 21:35*
land
this land which we *p.* at that *De 3:12*
time
they *p.* his land, and the land *De 4:47*
of Og
the land which thy fathers *p.* *De 30:5*
they also have *p.* the land   *Jos 1:15*
which
p. their land on the other side *Jos 12:1*
yet very much land to be *p.*   *Jos 13:1*
the edge of the sword, and *p.* *Jos 19:47*
it
and they *p.* it, and dwelt   *Jos 21:43*
therein
possession, whereof they were *Jos 22:9*
p.
and *p.* the city of palm trees *J'g 3:13*
p. all the land of the Amorites *J'g 11:21*

p. all the coasts of the   *J'g 11:22*
Amorites
p. Samaria, and dwelt in the *2Ki 17:24*
cities
so they *p.* the land of Sihon   *Ne 9:22*
children went in and *p.* the   *Ne 9:24*
land
p. houses full of all goods, wells *Ne 9:25*
For thou hast *p.* my reins: *Ps 139:13*
thou
Lord *p.* me in the beginning of *Pr 8:22*
people of thy holiness have *p.* *Isa 63:18*
it
shall be *p.* again in this land *Jer 32:15*
And they came in, and *p.* it *Jer 32:23*
that the saints *p.* the kingdom *Da 7:22*
those which were *p.* with   *M't 4:24*
devils
many that were *p.* with devils *M't 8:16*
there met him two *p.* with   *M't 8:28*
devils
befallen to the *p.* of the devils *M't 8:33*
him a dumb man *p.* with a   *M't 9:32*
devil
one *p.* with a devil, blind, and *M't 12:22*
badly demon *p.* (B)(R)   *M't 15:22;*
                          17:15
and them that were *p.* with   *M'k 1:32*
devils
see him that was *p.* with the *M'k 5:15*
devil
to him that was *p.* with the   *M'k 5:16*
devil
had been *p.* with the devil   *M'k 5:18*
prayed
was *p.* of the devils was healed *Lu 8:36*
aught of the things which he *p.* *Ac 4:32*
of many that were *p.* with them *Ac 8:7*
damsel *p.* with a spirit of   *Ac 16:16*
divination
that buy, as though they *p.*   *1Co 7:30*
not
p. by faith (B)   *1Ti 1:19*

POSSESSEST

and *p.* it, and dwellest therein *De 26:1*

POSSESSETH

daughter, that *p.* an   *Nu 36:8*
inheritance
abundance of things which   *Lu 12:15*
he *p.*

POSSESSING

nothing, and yet *p.* all things *2Co 6:10*

POSSESSION

Canaan, for an everlasting *p.* *Ge 17:8*
me a *p.* of a buryingplace with *Ge 23:4*
you
p. of a buryingplace amongst *Ge 23:9*
you
Unto Abraham for a *p.* in the *Ge 23:18*
Abraham for a *p.* of a   *Ge 23:20*
buryingplace
had *p.* of flocks, and *p.* of   *Ge 26:14*
herds
habitations in the land of   *Ge 36:43*
their *p.*
them a *p.* in the land of Egypt *Ge 47:11*
seed after thee for an   *Ge 48:4*
everlasting *p.*
Hittite for a *p.* of a burying *Ge 49:30*
place
the field for a *p.* of a   *Ge 50:13*
buryingplace
give it to you as a *p.* (R)   *Ex 6:8*
my personal *p.* (B)(E)(R)   *Ex 19:5;*
                       Ps 135:4
Canaan, which I give to you   *Le 14:34*
for a *p.*
in a house of the land of your *Le 14:34*
p.
shall return every man unto   *Le 25:10;*
his *p.*   *25:13*
all the land of your *p.* ye shall *Le 25:24*
grant
and hath sold away some of   *Le 25:25*
his *p.*
it; that he may return unto his *Le 25:27*
p.
and he shall return unto his *p.* *Le 25:28*
the houses of the cities of   *Le 25:32*
their *p.*
the city of his *p.* shall go out *Le 25:33*
in the

p. among the children of Israel	Le 25:33	ourselves the houses of God in *p.*	Ps 83:12	**POSSESSOR**		
be sold; for it is their perpetual *p.*	Le 25:34	shall have good things in *p.*	Pr 28:10	high God *p.* of heaven and earth	Ge 14:19	
unto their *p.* of his fathers shall he	Le 25:41	also make it a *p.* for the bittern	Isa 14:23	God, the *p.* of heaven and earth	Ge 14:22	
your land; and they shall be your *p.*	Le 25:45	unto us is this land given in *p.*	Eze 11:15	**POSSESSORS**		
after you, to inherit them for a *p.*	Le 25:46	to the men of the east for a *p.*	Eze 25:4	Whose *p.* slay them, and hold	Zec 11:5	
some part of a field of his *p.* then	Le 27:16	and will give them in *p.* that	Eze 25:10	*p.* of lands or houses sold them	Ac 4:34	
the *p.* thereof shall be the priest's	Le 27:21	ancient high places are ours in *p.*	Eze 36:2	**POSSIBLE**		
which is not of the fields of his *p.*	Le 27:22	might be a *p.* unto the residue of	Eze 36:3	but with God all things are *p.*	M't 19:26	
whom the *p.* of the land did belong	Le 27:24	appointed my land into their *p.*	Eze 36:5	if it were *p.* they shall deceive	M't 24:24	
his *p.* shall be sold or redeemed	Le 27:28	them no *p.* in Israel: I am their *p.*	Eze 44:28	if it be *p.* let this cup pass from me	M't 26:39	
And Edom shall be a *p.*, Seir also	Nu 24:18	for a *p.* for twenty chambers	Eze 45:5	things are *p.* to him that believeth	M'k 9:23	
Seir also shall be a *p.* for his	Nu 24:18	ye shall appoint the *p.* of the city	Eze 45:6	God: for with God all things are *p.*	M'k 10:27	
According to the lot shall the *p.*	Nu 26:56	and of the *p.* of the city, before the	Eze 45:7	seduce, if it were *p.* even the elect	M'k 13:22	
Give unto us therefore a *p.* among	Nu 27:4	before the *p.* of the city, from	Eze 45:7	if it were *p.* the hour might pass	M'k 14:35	
shalt surely give them a *p.* of an	Nu 27:7	In the land shall be his *p.* in Israel	Eze 45:8	Father, all things are *p.* unto thee	M'k 14:36	
be given unto thy servants for a *p.*	Nu 32:5	it shall be their *p.* by inheritance	Eze 46:16	impossible with men are *p.* with God	Lu 18:27	
fallen heir to our *p.* (B)	Nu 32:19	to thrust them out of their *p.*; but	Eze 46:18	not *p.* that he should be holden	Ac 2:24	
shall be your *p.* before the Lord	Nu 32:22	sons inheritance out of his own *p.*	Eze 46:18	it were *p.* for him, to be at Jerusalem	Ac 20:16	
them the land of Gilead for a *p.*	Nu 32:29	not scattered every man from his *p.*	Eze 46:18	if it were *p.* to thrust in the ship	Ac 27:39	
p. of our inheritance on this side	Nu 32:32	foursquare, with the *p.* of the city	Eze 48:20	If it be *p.* as much as lieth in you	Ro 12:18	
the inheritance of their *p.*	Nu 35:2	and of the *p.* of the city, over	Eze 48:21	if it had been *p.* would have	Ga 4:15	
cities to of the *p.* of the children of Israel	Nu 35:8	Moreover, from the *p.* of the Levites	Eze 48:22	it is not *p.* that the blood of bulls	Heb 10:4	
shall return into the land of his *p.*	Nu 35:28	Levites, and from the *p.* of the city	Eze 48:22	**POST**		
mount Seir unto Esau for a *p.*	De 2:5	*p.* of nettles (A)(B)(E)(R)(S)	Zep 2:9	on the upper door *p.* of the houses	Ex 12:7	
not give thee of their land for a *p.*	De 2:9	my special *p.* (B)(E)(R)	Mal 3:17	to the door, or unto the door *p.*	Ex 21:6	
unto the children of Lot for a *p.*	De 2:9	with Sapphira his wife, sold a *p.*	Ac 5:1	upon a seat by a *p.* of the temple	1Sa 1:9	
land of his *p.* which the Lord gave	De 2:12	he would give it to him for a *p.*	Ac 7:5	Now my days are swifter than a *p.*	Job 9:25	
of the children of Ammon any *p.*	De 2:19	Jesus into the *p.* of the Gentiles	Ac 7:45	I am set at my post (S)	Isa 21:8	
unto the children of Lot for a *p.*	De 2:19	redemption of the purchased *p.*	Eph 1:14	One *p.* shall run to meet another	Jer 51:31	
ye return every man unto his *p.*	De 3:20	**POSSESSIONS**		the *p.* of the court round about the	Eze 40:14	
the substance that was in their *p.*	De 11:6	possessions (A) Ge 12:5; 13:6; 15:14; 34:23; 36:6; Jos 14:4; 2Ch 21:17; 32:29; 35:7; Ezr 8:21; Job 1:10; Pr 12:27; 28:8; Ob 13; Heb 10:34		and upon each *p.* were palm trees	Eze 40:16	
unto the children of Israel for a *p.*	De 32:49	possessions (R) Ge 12:5; 13:6; 15:14; 34:23; 2Ch 21:17; 31:3; 32:29; 35:7; Job 1:10; Ps 105:21		and measured each *p.* of the porch	Eze 40:48	
return unto the land of your *p.*	Jos 1:15	therein, and get you *p.* therein	Ge 34:10	and measured the *p.* of the door, two	Eze 41:3	
gave it for a *p.* unto the Rubenites	Jos 12:6	property (B) Ge 34:23; 36:6; 1Ch 27:31; 28:1; Ezr 10:8; Lu 15:13; Heb 10:34		their *p.* by my posts, and the wall	Eze 43:8	
for a *p.* according to their divisions	Jos 12:7	property (R) Ge 34:23; 36:6; 1Ch 27:31; 28:1; Ezr 10:8; Lu 15:13; Heb 10:34		and shall stand by the *p.* of the gate	Eze 46:2	
this was the *p.* of the half tribe of	Jos 13:29	all the *p.* (E)	Ge 36:6	**POSTERITY**		
the son of Jephunneh for his *p.*	Jos 21:12	their *p.* were more (B)(R)	Ge 36:7	posterity (A) Ge 21:2; Nu 18:19; Jer 30:10		
the *p.* of the children of Israel were	Jos 21:41	and they had *p.* therein, and grew	Ge 47:27	to preserve you a *p.* in the earth	Ge 45:7	
unto the land of your *p.* which	Jos 22:4	with all *p.* (B)	Nu 16:30	you or of your *p.* shall be unclean	Nu 9:10	
Moses had given *p.* in Bashan	Jos 22:7	have *p.* among you in the land	Nu 32:30	posterity (A) 2Sa 7:12; Jer 30:10		
to the land of their *p.* whereof they	Jos 22:9	the *p.* before them (S)	J'g 18:21	I will take away the *p.* of Baasha	1Ki 16:3	
had taken *p.* (S)	Jos 22:9	Maon, whose *p.* were in Carmel	1Sa 25:2	and the *p.* of his house; and	1Ki 16:3	
if the land of your *p.* be unclean	Jos 22:19	And their *p.* and habitations were	1Ch 7:28	will take away thy *p.* and will cut	1Ki 21:21	
unto the land of the *p.* of the Lord	Jos 22:19	that dwelt in their *p.* in their cities	1Ch 9:2	yet their *p.* approve their sayings	Ps 49:13	
dwelleth, and take *p.* among us	Jos 22:19	not asked *p.* (R)	2Ch 1:11	Let his *p.* be cut off; and in	Ps 109:13	
p. of the vineyard of Naboth	1Ki 21:15	cities, and *p.* of flocks and herds in	2Ch 32:29	and not to his *p.* nor according to	Da 11:4	
the Jezreelite, to take *p.* of it	1Ki 21:16	great *p.* of great and small cattle	Ec 2:7	hooks, and your *p.* with fishhooks	Am 4:2	
Hast thou killed, and also taken *p.*	1Ki 21:19	God has given wealth and *p.* (R)	Ec 5:19; 6:2	**POSTPONED**		
p. of the king, and of his sons	1Ch 28:1	re-inherit the desolate *p.* (B)	Isa 49:8	I have *p.* my anger (B)	Isa 48:9	
left their suburbs and their *p.*	2Ch 11:14	of Jacob shall possess their *p.*	Ob 17	**POSTS**		
to come to cast us out of thy *p.*	2Ch 20:11	sorrowful: for he had great *p.*	M't 19:22	and strike it on the two side *p.*	Ex 12:7	
every man to his *p.* into their *p.*	2Ch 31:1	over his *p.* (A)(R)	M't 24:47	and the two side *p.* with the blood	Ex 12:22	
every one in his *p.* in their cities	Ne 11:3	grieved: for he had great *p.*	M'k 10:22	the lintel, and on the two side *p.*	Ex 12:23	
parts of the earth for thy *p.*	Ps 2:8	who have great *p.* (P)	M'k 10:23			
got not the land in *p.* by their own	Ps 44:3	his *p.* are safe (N)	Lu 11:21			
may dwell there, and have it in *p.*	Ps 69:35	squandering his *p.* (A)	Lu 16:1			
		half of *p.* to poor (N)(P)	Lu 19:8			
		And sold their *p.* and goods	Ac 2:45			
		sold *p.* and property (A)(B)	Ac 2:45			
		quarters were *p.* of the chief man	Ac 28:7			
		seizure of *p.* (N)	Heb 10:34			

write them upon the *p.* of thy   *De 6:9*
house
write them upon the door *p.* of   *De 11:20*
gate of the city, and the two *p.*   *J'g 16:3*
lintel and side *p.* were a fifth   *1Ki 6:31*
part
for the door of the temple *p.*   *1Ki 6:33*
of olive
all the doors and *p.* were   *1Ki 7:5*
square
beams, and *p.* and walls   *2Ch 3:7*
thereof
stood at their *p.* (S)   *2Ch 7:6*
p. went with the letters from   *2Ch 30:6*
the *p.* passed from city to   *2Ch 30:10*
city
the letters were sent by *p.* into   *Es 3:13*
all
The *p.* went out, being   *Es 3:15*
hastened by
and sent letters by *p.* on   *Es 8:10*
horseback
So the *p.* that rode upon mules   *Es 8:14*
waiting at the *p.* of my doors   *Pr 8:34*
He made the *p.* thereof (S)   *Ca 3:10*
the *p.* of the door moved at the   *Isa 6:4*
Behind the doors also and the   *Isa 57:8*
p.
and the *p.* thereof, two cubits   *Eze 40:9*
p. had one measure on this   *Eze 40:10*
side and
made also *p.* of threescore   *Eze 40:14*
cubits
p. within the gate round   *Eze 40:16*
about
the *p.* thereof and the arches   *Eze 40:21*
thereof
he measured the *p.* thereof   *Eze 40:24*
and the
on that side, upon the *p.*   *Eze 40:26*
thereof
chambers thereof, and the *p.*   *Eze 40:29;*
thereof   *40:33, 36*
palm trees were upon the *p.*   *Eze 40:31;*
thereof   *40:34, 37*
p. thereof were toward the   *Eze 40:37*
utter
thereof were by the *p.* of the   *Eze 40:38*
gates
there were pillars by the *p.*   *Eze 40:49*
one on
measured the *p.* six cubits   *Eze 41:1*
broad on
door *p.* and the narrow   *Eze 41:16*
windows
The *p.* of the temple were   *Eze 41:21*
squared
their post by my *p.* and   *Eze 43:8*
the wall
and put it upon the *p.* of the   *Eze 45:19*
house
upon the *p.* of the gate of the   *Eze 45:19*
inner
the door, that the *p.* may shake   *Am 9:1*

POT

smoking fire *p.*, flaming torch   *Ge 15:17*
(R)
Take a *p.* and put an omer   *Ex 16:33*
full
if it be sodden in a brasen *p.* it   *Le 6:28*
in an earthen *p.* (B)   *Le 14:5*
and he put the broth in a *p.*   *J'g 6:19*
pan, or kettle, or caldron, or   *1Sa 2:14*
p.
thrust into the *p.* (B)   *1Sa 2:14*
thing in the house, save a *p.* of   *2Ki 4:2*
oil
his servant, Set on the great *p.*   *2Ki 4:38*
shred them into the *p.* of   *2Ki 4:39*
pottage
man of God, there is death in   *2Ki 4:40*
the *p.*
meal. And he cast it into the   *2Ki 4:41*
p.
And there was no harm in the   *2Ki 4:41*
p.
as out of a seething *p.* or   *Job 41:20*
caldron
maketh the deep to boil like   *Job 41:31*
a *p.*
the sea like a *p.* of ointment   *Job 41:31*
The fining *p.* is for silver, and   *Pr 17:3*
As the fining *p.* for silver, and   *Pr 27:21*
the crackling of thorns under a   *Ec 7:6*
p.
I said, I see a seething *p.*; and   *Jer 1:13*
Set on a *p.* set it on, and also   *Eze 24:3*
to the *p.* whose scum is   *Eze 24:6*
therein

chop them in pieces, as for the   *Mic 3:3*
p.
every *p.* in Jerusalem and in   *Zec 14:21*
Judah
was the golden *p.* that had   *Heb 9:4*
manna

POTENCY

p. or conception (B)   *Heb 11:11*

POTENTATE

who is the blessed and only *P.*   *1Ti 6:15*
blessed, only Sovereign   *1Ti 6:15*
(A)(B)(R)
God who is eternal felicity   *1Ti 6:15*
alone (N)
the blessed controller of all   *1Ti 6:15*
things (P)

POTIPHAR

sold him into Egypt unto *P.*   *Ge 37:36*
P. an officer of Pharaoh,   *Ge 39:1*
captain

POTI-PHERAH

the daughter of *P.* priest of   *Ge 41:45*
On
the daughter of *P.* priest of   *Ge 41:50;*
On bare   *46:20*

POTS

when we sat by the flesh *p.* and   *Ex 16:3*
make *p.* to take away ashes   *Ex 27:3*
(A)(E)(R)
p. and the shovels, and the   *Ex 38:3*
basons
whether it be oven, or ranges   *Le 11:35*
for‹p.
boiled in *p.* (A)(B)(E)(R)   *Nu 11:8*
the *p.* and the shovels, and   *1Ki 7:45;*
the   *2Ki 25:14*
And Huram made the *p.* and   *2Ch 4:11*
The *p.* also, and the shovels,   *2Ch 4:16*
and the
other holy offerings sod they   *2Ch 35:13*
in *p.*
Before your *p.* can feel the   *Ps 58:9*
thorns
Though ye have lien among   *Ps 68:13*
the *p.*
hands were delivered from the   *Ps 81:6*
p.
of the Rechabites *p.* full ·of   *Jer 35:15*
wine
p. in the Lord's house shall   *Zec 14:20*
be like
p. brasen vessels, and of tables   *M'k 7:4*
men, as the washing of *p.* and   *M'k 7:8*
cups
carry water *p.* (P)   *M'k 11:16*
p. of earthenware (N)   *2Co 4:7; Re 2:27*
as earthen *p.* are broken   *Re 2:27*
(A)(R)

POTSHERD

he took him a *p.* to scrape   *Job 2:8*
himself
took a piece of broken pottery   *Job 2:8*
(A)(B)
My strength is dried up like a   *Ps 22:15*
like a fragment of clay pottery   *Ps 22:15*
(A)
and a wicked heart are like a   *Pr 26:23*
p.
like an earthen vessel covered   *Pr 26:23*
with scum of molten silver (A)
like a vessel overlaid with   *Pr 26:23*
silver dross (B)(E)
like glaze covering on an   *Pr 26:23*
earthen vessel (R)
Let the *p.* strive with the   *Isa 45:9*
potsherds
a worthless piece of broken   *Isa 45:9*
pottery (A)
an earthen vessel with the   *Isa 45:9*
potter (R)

POTSHERDS

nether part like *p.* (B)   *Job 41:30*
Let the potsherd strive with   *Isa 45:9*
the *p.*

POTTAGE

And Jacob sod *p.*: and Esau   *Ge 25:29*
came
I pray thee, with that same   *Ge 25:30*
red *p.*
red lentil stew (A)   *Ge 25:30; 25:34*
gave Esau bread and *p.* of   *Ge 25:34*
lentiles
and see the *p.* for the sons of   *2Ki 4:38*
boil stew (B)   *2Ki 4:38*
and shred them into the pot of   *2Ki 4:39*
p.
pass, as they were eating of   *2Ki 4:40*
the *p.*
they could not eat the *p.* (S)   *2Ki 4:40*
with his skirt do touch bread,   *Hag 2:12*
or *p.*

POTTER

morter, and as the *p.* treadeth   *Isa 41:25*
clay
we are the clay, and thou our   *Isa 64:8*
p.
was marred in the hand of the   *Jer 18:4*
p.
as seemed good to the *p.* to   *Jer 18:4*
make it
cannot I do with you as this *p.*   *Jer 18:6*
the work of the hands of the *p.*   *La 4:2*
said unto me, Cast it unto   *Zec 11:13*
the *p.*
cast them to the *p.* in the   *Zec 11:13*
house of
not the *p.* power over the clay   *Ro 9:21*
as the vessels of a *p.* shall they   *Re 2:27*
be

POTTERS

These were the *p.* and those   *1Ch 4:23*
that

POTTER'S

them in pieces like a *p.* vessel   *Ps 2:9*
shall be esteemed as the *p.*   *Isa 29:16*
clay
Arise, and go down to the *p.*   *Jer 18:2*
house
I went down to the *p.* house   *Jer 18:3*
Behold, as the clay is in the *p.*   *Jer 18:6*
hand
Go and get a *p.* earthen bottle   *Jer 19:1*
city, as one breaketh a *p.*   *Jer 19:11*
vessel
part of *p.* clay, and part of   *Da 2:41*
iron
brought with them the *p.* field   *M't 27:7*
And gave them for the *p.*   *M't 27:10*
field, as

POTTERS'

p. vessel that is broken in   *Isa 30:14*
pieces

POTTERY

the earthen *p.* (B)   *2Sa 17:28*
took broken *p.* (A)(B)   *Job 2:8*
like a fragment of *p.* (A)   *Ps 22:15*
like broken *p.* (A)   *Isa 45:9*

POUND

three *p.* of gold went to one   *1Ki 10:17*
shield
five thousand *p.* of silver, and   *Ezr 2:69*
one
and two hundred *p.* of silver   *Ne 7:71*
gold, and two thousand *p.* of   *Ne 7:72*
silver
p. a fool in a mortar (A)   *Pr 27:22*
battering rams shall *p.*   *Eze 26:9*
(B)(R)
thy *p.* hath gained ten pounds   *Lu 19:16*
thy *p.* hath gained five pounds   *Lu 19:18*
here is thy *p.* which I have   *Lu 19:20*
kept
Take from him the *p.* and   *Lu 19:24*
give it to
a *p.* of ointment of spikenard   *Joh 12:3*
aloes, about a hundred *p.*   *Joh 19:39*
weight

POUNDS

a few *p.* (N)   *M't 18:28*
twenty *p.* (N)   *M'k 6:37; Joh 6:7*

servants, and delivered them *Lu 19:13*
ten *p.*
Lord, thy pound hath gained *Lu 19:16*
ten *p.*
Lord, thy pound hath gained *Lu 19:18*
five *p.*
and give it to him that hath *Lu 19:24*
ten *p.*
said unto him, Lord, he hath *Lu 19:25*
ten *p.*

POUR

river, and *p.* it upon the dry *Ex 4:9*
land
with which to *p.* (S) *Ex 25:29*
and *p.* it upon his head, and *Ex 29:7*
anoint
p. all the blood beside the *Ex 29:12*
bottom
shall ye *p.* drink offering *Ex 30:9*
thereon
and he shall *p.* oil upon it, and *Le 2:1*
put
part it in pieces, and *p.* oil *Le 2:6*
thereon
shall *p.* all the blood of the *Le 4:7*
bullocks
p. out all the blood at the *Le 4:18*
bottom
shall *p.* out his blood at the *Le 4:25*
bottom
p. out all the blood thereof at *Le 4:30*
shall *p.* out all the blood *Le 4:34*
thereof at
p. it into the palm of his own *Le 14:15*
left
he shall *p.* upon the head of *Le 14:18*
him
priest shall *p.* of the oil into *Le 14:26*
they shall *p.* out the dust that *Le 14:41*
they
shall even *p.* out the blood *Le 17:13*
thereof
he shall *p.* no oil upon it, nor *Nu 5:15*
put
p. the water out of his buckets *Nu 24:7*
shall *p.* it upon the earth as *De 12:16*
water
shalt *p.* it upon the earth as *De 12:24*
water
shalt *p.* it upon the ground as *De 15:23*
water
this rock, and *p.* out the broth *J'g 6:20*
and *p.* it on the burnt *1Ki 18:33*
sacrifice
p. out into all those vessels, and *2Ki 4:4*
P. out for the people, that they *2Ki 4:41*
may
the box of oil, and *p.* it on his *2Ki 9:3*
head
they *p.* down rain according *Job 36:27*
to the
who can *p.* out the bottles of *Job 38:37*
heaven (S)
things, I *p.* out my soul in me *Ps 42:4*
p. out your heart before him: *Ps 62:8*
God
P. out thine indignation upon *Ps 69:24*
them
P. out thy wrath upon the *Ps 79:6*
heathen
I will *p.* out my spirit unto you *Pr 1:23*
p. water upon him that is *Isa 44:3*
thirsty
I will *p.* my spirit upon thy *Isa 44:3*
seed
the skies *p.* down righteousness *Isa 45:8*
p. it out upon the children *Jer 6:11*
abroad
to *p.* out drink offerings unto *Jer 7:18*
other
P. out thy fury upon the *Jer 10:25*
heathen
will *p.* their wickedness upon *Jer 14:16*
them
p. out their blood by the force *Jer 18:21*
of
p. out drink offerings unto *Jer 44:17;*
44:18-19, 25
p. out thine heart like water *La 2:19*
I shortly *p.* out my fury upon *Eze 7:8*
thee
and *p.* out my fury upon it in *Eze 14:19*
blood
I will *p.* out my fury upon *Eze 20:8*
p. out my fury upon them in *Eze 20:13*
I would *p.* out my fury upon *Eze 20:21*
them

p. out mine indignation upon *Eze 21:31*
thee
set it on, and also *p.* water *Eze 24:3*
into it
And I will *p.* my fury upon *Eze 30:15*
Sin, the
p. out my wrath upon them *Ho 5:10*
like
will *p.* out my spirit upon all *Joe 2:28*
flesh
those days will I *p.* out my *Joe 2:29*
spirit
I will *p.* down the stones *Mic 1:6*
thereof
to *p.* upon them mine *Zep 3:8*
indignation
I will *p.* upon the house of *Zec 12:10*
David
heaven, and *p.* you out a *Mal 3:10*
blessing
p. out of my Spirit upon all *Ac 2:17*
flesh
p. out in those days of my *Ac 2:18*
Spirit
p. out the vials of the wrath of *Re 16:1*
God

POURED

pillar, and *p.* oil upon the top *Ge 28:18*
of it
and he *p.* a drink offering *Ge 35:14*
thereon
and he *p.* oil thereon *Ge 35:14*
the rain was not *p.* upon the *Ex 9:33*
earth
Upon man's flesh shall it not *Ex 30:32*
be *p.*
place, where the ashes are *p.* *Le 4:12*
out
where the ashes are *p.* out shall *Le 4:12*
he
And he *p.* of the anointing oil *Le 8:12*
upon
p. the blood at the bottom of *Le 8:15*
p. out the blood at the bottom *Le 9:9*
of
whose head the anointing oil *Le 21:10*
was *p.*
cause the strong wine to be *p.* *Nu 28:7*
p. out upon the altar of the *De 12:27*
Lord
p. out my soul before the Lord *1Sa 1:15*
water, and *p.* it out before the *1Sa 7:6*
Lord
vial of oil, and *p.* it upon his *1Sa 10:1*
head
a pan, and *p.* them out before *2Sa 13:9*
him
thereof, but *p.* it out unto *2Sa 23:16*
the Lord
that are upon it shall be *p.* out *1Ki 13:3*
and the ashes *p.* out from the *1Ki 13:5*
altar
p. water on the hands of *2Ki 3:11*
Elijah
the vessels to her; and she *p.* *2Ki 4:5*
out
So they *p.* out for the men to *2Ki 4:40*
eat
he *p.* the oil on his head, and *2Ki 9:6*
said
p. his drink offering, and *2Ki 16:13*
sprinkled
drink of it, but *p.* it out to *1Ch 11:18*
the Lord
my wrath shall not be *p.* out *2Ch 12:7*
upon
wrath of the Lord that is *p.* *2Ch 34:21*
out upon
my wrath shall be *p.* out upon *2Ch 34:25*
this
roarings are *p.* out like the *Job 3:24*
waters
groanings *p.* out *Job 3:24*
(A)(B)(E)(R)
Hast thou not *p.* me out as *Job 10:10*
milk
p. out as a stream (A) *Job 22:16*
the rock *p.* me out rivers of oil *Job 29:6*
now my soul is *p.* out upon *Job 30:16*
me
I am *p.* out like water, and all *Ps 22:14*
my
grace is *p.* into thy lips *Ps 45:2*
therefore
The clouds *p.* out water: the *Ps 77:17*
skies
p. out my complaint before *Ps 142:2*
him

thy name is as ointment *p.* forth *Ca 1:3*
they *p.* out a prayer when thy *Isa 26:16*
hath *p.* out upon you the *Isa 29:10*
spirit
spirit be *p.* upon us from on *Isa 32:15*
high
p. upon him the fury of his *Isa 42:25*
anger
hath *p.* out his soul unto *Isa 53:12*
death
hast thou *p.* a drink offering *Isa 57:6*
thou
my fury shall be *p.* out upon *Jer 7:20*
this
p. out drink offering unto *Jer 19:13;*
other *32:29*
and my fury hath been *p.* *Jer 42:18*
forth
so shall my fury be *p.* forth *Jer 42:18*
upon
fury and mine anger was *p.* *Jer 44:6*
forth
p. out drink offerings unto *Jer 44:19*
her
Zion: he *p.* out his fury like fire *La 2:4*
my liver is *p.* upon the earth *La 2:11*
p. out into their mothers' *La 2:12*
bosom
p. out in the top of every street *La 4:1*
he hath *p.* out his fierce anger *La 4:11*
Because thy filthiness was *p.* *Eze 16:36*
out
p. out there their drink *Eze 20:28*
offerings
with fury *p.* out, will I rule *Eze 20:33*
over
out arm, and with fury *p.* *Eze 20:34*
out
Lord have *p.* out my fury *Eze 22:22*
upon you
I *p.* out mine indignation *Eze 22:31*
upon
and *p.* their whoredom upon *Eze 23:8*
her
she *p.* it not upon the ground, *Eze 24:7*
to
Wherefore I *p.* my fury upon *Eze 36:18*
them
p. out my spirit upon the *Eze 39:29*
house
therefore the curse is *p.* upon *Da 9:11*
us
shall be *p.* upon the desolate *Da 9:27*
waters that are *p.* down a steep *Mic 1:4*
his fury is *p.* out like a fire, and *Na 1:6*
blood shall be *p.* out as dust *Zep 1:17*
ointment, and *p.* it on his *M't 26:7*
head
hath *p.* this ointment on my *M't 26:12*
body
the box, and *p.* it on his head *M'k 14:3*
and *p.* out the changers' *Joh 2:15*
money
p. out the gift of the Holy *Ac 10:45*
Ghost
p. out upon us wisdom (B) *Eph 1:8*
p. out without mixture into *Re 14:10*
p. out his vial upon the earth *Re 16:2*
angel *p.* out his vial upon the *Re 16:3*
sea
p. out his vial upon the rivers *Re 16:4*
angel *p.* out his vial upon the *Re 16:8*
sun
angel *p.* out his vial upon the *Re 16:10*
seat
p. out his vial upon the great *Re 16:12*
river
angel *p.* out his vial into the *Re 16:17*
air

POUREDST

p. out thy fornications on *Eze 16:15*
every

POURETH

He *p.* contempt upon princes *Job 12:21*
p. out my gall upon the *Job 16:13*
ground
mine eye *p.* out tears unto *Job 16:20*
God
p. out of the same: but the *Ps 75:8*
dregs
p. out his complaint before *Ps 102 title*
He *p.* contempt upon princes *Ps 107:40*

mouth of fools *p.* out foolishness *Pr 15:2*
of the wicked *p.* out evil things *Pr 15:28*
p. them out upon the face of *Am 5:8; Am 9:6*
After that he *p.* water into a bason *Joh 13:5*

POURING

p. out of thy fury upon Jerusalem *Eze 9:8*
p. in oil and wine, and set him on his *Lu 10:34*

POVERTY

and all that thou hast, come to *p.* *Ge 45:11*
thy *p.* come as one that travelleth *Pr 6:11; 28:19*
destruction of the poor is their *p.* *Pr 10:15*
than is meet, but it tendeth to *p.* *Pr 11:24*
P. and shame shall be to him that *Pr 13:18*
leads only to *p.* (A) *Pr 14:23*
not sleep, lest thou come to *p.* *Pr 20:13*
and the glutton shall come to *p.* *Pr 23:21*
vain persons shall have *p.* enough *Pr 28:19*
not that *p.* shall come upon him *Pr 28:22*
give me neither *p.* nor riches *Pr 30:8*
Let him drink, and forget his *p.* *Pr 31:7*
she in her *p.* did (P)(R) *Lu 21:4*
deep *p.* abounded unto the riches *2Co 8:2*
ye through his *p.* might be rich *2Co 8:9*
thy works, and tribulation, and *p.* *Re 2:9*

POWDER

it in the fire, and ground it to *p.* *Ex 32:20*
the rain of thy land *p.* and dust *De 28:24*
and stamped it small to *p.* and *2Ki 23:6*
the *p.* thereof upon the graves of *2Ki 23:6*
stamped it small to *p.* and burned *2Ki 23:15*
beaten the graven images into *p.* *2Ch 34:7*
shall fall, it will grind him to *p.* *M't 21:44; Lu 20:18*

POWDERS

with all *p.* of the merchant *Ca 3:6*

POWER

filled with lust and *p.* (B) *Ge 6:11; 6:13*
as a prince hast thou *p.* with God *Ge 32:28*
have striven with God and won (B) *Ge 32:28*
striven with God and hast prevailed (E)(R) *Ge 32:28*
the excellency of dignity, excellency of *p.* *Ge 49:3*
prominent in prowess (B) *Ge 49:3*
I will break the pride of your *p.* *Le 26:19*
break down the pride of your might (B) *Le 26:19*
have I now any *p.* to say any thing *Nu 22:38*
am I at liberty to say anything (B) *Nu 22:38*
brought thee with his mighty *p.* out of Egypt *De 4:37*
it is he that giveth thee *p.* to get wealth *De 8:18*
when he seeth that their *p.* is gone *De 32:36*
he sees their strength is gone (B) *De 32:36*
so is his *p.* (B) *J'g 8:21; Ps 68:34*
power (B) *1Sa 2:9; 2:10; 1Ch 16:27; 2Ch 13:20; Ps 68:34; Isa 25:4; Eze 30:18; 1Co 15:5; Re 12:10; 17:13*
God is my strength and *p.* *2Sa 22:33*
God is my Tower and Strength (B) *2Sa 22:33*
God is my strong refuge (R) *2Sa 22:33*
the inhabitants were of small *p.* *2Ki 19:26*
their citizens impotent (B) *2Ki 19:26*
inhabitants shorn of strength (R) *2Ki 19:26*
his *p.* by the river Euphrates (B) *1Ch 18:3*
Joab led forth the *p.* of the army *1Ch 20:1*
led forth the strength of the army (B) *1Ch 20:1*
thine is the *p.* and the glory *1Ch 29:11; M't 6:13*
in thine hand is *p.* and might *1Ch 29:12; 2Ch 20:6*
power (R) *2Ch 13:20; Ps 68:34; 1Co 15:56; Heb 11:11; Re 3:8; 5:12; 12:10; 17:13*
God hath *p.* to help, and cast down *2Ch 25:8*
Sennacherib laid siege, and all his *p.* with him *2Ch 32:9*
with all his forces (A)(R) *2Ch 32:9*
with all his imperial force (B) *2Ch 32:9*
and made them cease by force and *p.* *Ezr 4:23*
by strength and by force (B) *Ezr 4:23*
his *p.* and wrath against all that forsake him *Ezr 8:22*
nor is it in our *p.* to redeem them *Ne 5:5*
helpless to better ourselves (B) *Ne 5:5*
he made a feast to *p.* of Persia and Media *Es 1:3*
to cause to perish the *p.* of the people *Es 8:11*
the Jews hoped to have *p.* over them *Es 9:1*
Jews had rule over them (A)(E) *Es 9:1*
Jews gained the upper hand (B) *Es 9:1*
Jews should get the mastery over them (R) *Es 9:1*
redeem in war from the *p.* of the sword *Job 5:20*
he draweth also the mighty with his *p.* *Job 24:22*
how hast thou helped him that is without *p.* *Job 26:2*
sustained arm without strength (A) *Job 26:2*
sustained the feeble arm (B) *Job 26:2*
saved the arm that has no strength (R) *Job 26:2*
he divided the sea with his *p.* *Job 26:12*
the thunder of his *p.* who can understand *Job 26:14*
behold, God exalteth by his *p.* *Job 36:22*
God is exalted in his might (B) *Job 36:22*
I will not conceal his parts nor his *p.* *Job 41:12*
nor his mighty strength (A)(B)(E)(R) *Job 41:12*
my darling from the *p.* of the dog *Ps 22:20*
deliver by his *p.* (E) *Ps 33:17*
redeem my soul from the *p.* of the grave *Ps 49:15*
from the hand of Sheol (B) *Ps 49:15*
judge me by thy *p.* (B) *Ps 54:1; 71:18; 74:13; 77:14*
I heard, that *p.* belongeth unto God *Ps 62:11*
strength belongs to God (B) *Ps 62:11*
who setteth fast mountains girded with *p.* *Ps 65:6*
he ruleth by his *p.* for ever, his eyes behold *Ps 66:7*
ascribe *p.* to God (R) *Ps 68:34; 78:61*
he giveth strength and *p.* to his people *Ps 68:35*
he gives strength and fulness of might (A)(B) *Ps 68:35*
declared your *p.* (A) *Ps 77:14*
by his *p.* he brought in the south wind *Ps 78:26*
in his might he brought a south wind (B) *Ps 78:26*
from the *p.* of Sheol (S) *Ps 89:48*
who knoweth the *p.* of thine anger *Ps 90:11*
Who knows the force of thy anger (B) *Ps 90:11*
might make his mighty *p.* to be known *Ps 106:8*
he shewed his people the *p.* of his works *Ps 111:6*
praise him in the firmament of his *p.* *Ps 150:1*
praise him in his mighty firmament (B)(R) *Ps 150:1*
on the side of oppressors there was *p.* *Ec 4:1*
and hath given him *p.* to eat thereof *Ec 5:19*
God giveth him not *p.* to eat thereof *Ec 6:2*
ability to enjoy it (B) *Ec 6:2*
where the word of a king is, there is *p.* *Ec 8:4*
there is no man hath *p.* over the spirit *Ec 8:8*
their inhabitants were of small *p.* *Isa 37:27*
residents shorn of their strength (B)(R) *Isa 37:27*
he giveth *p.* to the faint, and to them *Isa 40:29*
imparts vigor to the fainting (B) *Isa 40:29*
which bringeth forth the army and *p.* *Isa 43:17*
shall not deliver from the *p.* of the flame *Isa 47:14*
he made the earth by his *p.* *Jer 10:12; 51:15*
were in thee to their *p.* to shed blood *Eze 22:6*
excellency of your *p.* (E)(R) *Eze 24:21*
and the pride of her *p.* shall come down *Eze 30:6*
her vaunted strength shall come down (B) *Eze 30:6*
her proud might shall come down (R) *Eze 30:6*
power (E) *Eze 30:15; 1Co 15:56; Heb 11:11; Re 3:8; 5:8; 12:10; 17:13*
God hath given thee *p.* and glory *Da 2:37*
who delivered Daniel from the *p.* of lions *Da 6:27*
ran in fury of his *p.*; but not in his *p.* *Da 8:6; 8:22*
his *p.* shall be mighty, but not by his *p.* *Da 8:24*
but she shall not retain the *p.* of the arm *Da 11:6*
effectiveness of her might (B) *Da 11:6*
the strength of her arm (R) *Da 11:6*
he shall stir up his *p.* and his courage *Da 11:25*
he will direct his strength (B) *Da 11:25*
but he shall have *p.* over the treasures of gold *Da 11:43*
he shall gain control over (B) *Da 11:43*
he shall become ruler of (R) *Da 11:43*
to scatter the *p.* of the holy people *Da 12:7*
by his strength he had *p.* with God *Ho 12:3*
in his manly strength he strove (B)(R) *Ho 12:3*
yea, he had *p.* over the angel, and prevailed *Ho 12:4*
wrestled with the angel and prevailed (B)(R) *Ho 12:4*
I will ransom them from the *p.* of the grave *Ho 13:14*
because it is in the *p.* of their hand *Mic 2:1*
I am full of *p.* by the Spirit of the Lord *Mic 3:8*
imputing this his *p.* to his god *Hab 1:11*
their might is their god (B)(R) *Hab 1:11*
that he may be delivered from the *p.* of evil *Hab 2:9*
and there was the hiding of his *p.* *Hab 3:4*
not by might, nor by my *p.* but by my Spirit *Zec 4:6*
behold, the Lord will smite her *p.* in the sea *Zec 9:4*
Son of man hath *p.* on earth to forgive sins *M't 9:6; M'k 2:10; Lu 5:24*
authority to forgive (A)(B)(E)(P)(R) *M't 9:6*
has the right to forgive sins (N) *M't 9:6*

glorified God, who had given *M't 9:8*
such *p.* to men
give *p.* against unclean spirits *M't 10:1;*
Lu 9:1
coming in the clouds with *p. M't 24:30;*
Lu 21:27
sitting on right hand with *p. M't 26:64;*
M'k 14:62
all *p.* is given to me in *M't 28:18*
heaven and earth
all authority *M't 28:18*
(A)(B)(E)(N)(R)
and to have *p.* to heal *M'k 3:15*
sicknesses
p. had gone out of him *M'k 5:30;*
(A)(B)(E)(N)(P)(R) *Lu 6:19; 8:46*
power (S) *M'k 5:30; Lu 6:19; 8:46*
have seen the kingdom of God *M'k 9:1*
come with *p.*
p. of the Highest shall *Lu 1:35*
overshadow thee
the devil said, All this *p.* will I *Lu 4:6*
give thee
they were astonished for his *Lu 4:32*
word was with *p.*
his word was with authority *Lu 4:32*
(A)(B)(E)(N)(P)(R)
with *p.* he commandeth *Lu 4:36*
unclean spirits
the *p.* of the Lord was present *Lu 5:17*
to heal them
I give you *p.* to tread on *Lu 10:19*
serpents, and over all the
p. of the enemy
authority to tread on serpents *Lu 10:19*
(B)(E)(R)
fear him that hath *p.* to cast *Lu 12:5*
into hell
they might deliver him to *p. Lu 20:20*
of governor
this is your hour, and the *p. Lu 22:53*
of darkness
until ye be endued with *p. Lu 24:49*
from on high
to them gave he *p.* to become *Joh 1:12*
sons of God
he gave authority to become *Joh 1:12*
(A)
he granted ability to become *Joh 1:12*
(B)
gave he the right to become *Joh 1:12*
(E)(N)
I have *p.* to lay it down, and *Joh 10:18*
p. to take it
authority to lay it down (B) *Joh 10:18*
I have the right to (N) *Joh 10:18*
thou hast given him *p.* over all *Joh 17:2*
flesh
authority over all flesh *Joh 17:2*
(A)(B)(E)(P)
made him sovereign over all *Joh 17:2*
mankind (N)
I have *p.* to crucify thee, *p. Joh 19:10*
to release thee
seasons the Father hath put in *Ac 1:7*
his own *p.*
under his personal authority *Ac 1:7*
(B)(E)
set within his own control *Ac 1:7*
(N)(R)
the Father's sole authority (P) *Ac 1:7*
shall receive *p.* after Holy *Ac 1:8*
Ghost is come on you
as though by our own *p.* or *Ac 3:12*
holiness we made
they asked, By what *p.* have ye *Ac 4:7*
done this
after it was sold, was it not in *Ac 5:4*
thine own *p.*
Stephen full of faith and *p.* did *Ac 6:8*
great wonders
saying, Give me also this *p.* on *Ac 8:19*
whom lay hand
how God anointed Jesus *Ac 10:38*
with Holy Ghost and *p.*
grew in *p.* and influence (P) *Ac 19:20*
to turn them from the *p.* of *Ac 26:18*
Satan to God
from authority of Satan to *Ac 26:18*
God (B)
from the dominion of Satan *Ac 26:18*
(N)
declared to be the Son of God *Ro 1:4*
with *p.*
even his eternal *p.* and *Ro 1:20*
Godhead
death no longer has *p.* (A)(P) *Ro 6:9*
legal claims have *p.* (A) *Ro 7:14*
hath not the potter *p.* over the *Ro 9:21*
clay

what if God, willing to make *Ro 9:22*
his *p.* known
whosoever resisteth the *p. Ro 13:2*
resisteth
Authority, authorities *Ro 13:2;*
(A)(B)(N)(P)(R) *13:3*
wilt thou then not be afraid *Ro 13:3*
of the *p.*
abound in hope, thro' *p.* of *Ro 15:13*
Holy Ghost
wonders, by the *p.* of the *Ro 15:19*
Spirit of God
now to him that is of *p.* to *Ro 16:25*
establish you
able to establish, strengthen *Ro 16:25*
(A)(B)(E)(N)(P)(R)
in demonstration of the Spirit *1Co 2:4*
and *p.*
I will not know their speech, *1Co 4:19*
but the *p.*
speech, but the force (A)(B) *1Co 4:19*
with the *p.* of our Lord Jesus *1Co 5:4*
Christ
I will not be brought under *1Co 6:12*
the *p.* of any
not be a slave, be mastered *1Co 6:12*
(A)(B)(P)
be enslaved by anything (R) *1Co 6:12*
and will also raise us up by *1Co 6:14*
his own *p.*
the wife and husband have not *1Co 7:4*
p. of their body
have exclusive control over *1Co 7:4*
(A)(B)
no longer has full rights over *1Co 7:4*
(P)
does not rule own body (R) *1Co 7:4*
but hath *p.* over his own will *1Co 7:37*
so decreed
have we not *p.* to eat and to *1Co 9:4*
drink
have the right *1Co 9:4;*
(A)(B)(E)(N)(R) *9:5*
have we not *p.* to lead about a *1Co 9:5*
wife
have we not *p.* to forbear *1Co 9:6*
working
if others be partakers of this *1Co 9:12*
p. over you, not used this *p.*
the woman ought to have *p. 1Co 11:10*
on her head
taken of authority *1Co 11:10*
(A)(B)(E)(N)(P)(R)
p. to do great deeds (B) *1Co 12:10*
p. to guide them (N) *1Co 12:28*
he hath put down all *1Co 15:24*
authority and *p.*
the excellency of *p.* may be of *2Co 4:7*
God
to their *p.* yea, and beyond *2Co 8:3*
their *p.*
according to ability (A) *2Co 8:3*
that the *p.* of Christ may rest *2Co 12:9*
upon me
my *p.* made perfect *2Co 12:9*
(E)(N)(P)(R)
according to the *p.* God hath *2Co 13:10*
given me
effects wonder-working *p.* (B) *Ga 3:5*
p. of a new birth (P) *Ga 6:15*
exceeding greatness of his *p. Eph 1:19*
according to working of
mighty *p.*
far above all principality, *p. Eph 1:21*
and might
according to the prince of the *Eph 2:2*
p. of the air
given to me, by the effectual *Eph 3:7*
working of his *p.*
according to the *p.* that *Eph 3:20*
worketh in us
know the *p.* of his *Ph'p 3:10*
resurrection
strengthened according to his *Col 1:11*
glorious *p.*
who delivered us from *p.* of *Col 1:13*
darkness
who is head of all principality *Col 2:10*
and *p.*
head of all rule and authority *Col 2:10*
(A)(B)(R)
faith in the active power of *Col 2:12*
God (N)(P)
be punished from the glory of *2Th 1:9*
his *p.*
and fulfil the work of faith *2Th 1:11*
with *p.*
after the working of Satan *2Th 2:9*
with all *p.*

not because we have not *p.* but *2Th 3:9*
to make
whom be honour and *p. 1Ti 6:16*
everlasting
To him be honor and *1Ti 6:16*
dominion (B)(R)
To him be honor and might *1Ti 6:16*
almighty (N)
God hath given us spirit of *p. 2Ti 1:7*
and love
form of godliness, but denying *2Ti 3:5*
the *p.*
lost the *p.* to reason (N) *2Ti 3:8*
upholding all things by word *Heb 1:3*
of his *p.*
sustains universe by his word *Heb 1:3*
(B)
spiritual *p.* (N)(P) *Heb 2:4*
he might destroy him that *Heb 2:14*
had *p.* of death
but after the *p.* of an endless *Heb 7:16*
life
quenched *p.* of fire (B)(E) *Heb 11:34*
divine *p.* hath given us all *2Pe 1:3*
things
when we made known the *p. 2Pe 1:16*
of our Lord
to only wise God our Saviour *Jude 25*
be glory and *p.*
to him will I give *p.* over the *Re 2:26*
nations
authority over the Gentiles (B) *Re 2:26*
authority over the nations *Re 2:26*
(E)(N)(P)
you have little *p.* (P) *Re 3:8*
thou art worthy to receive *Re 4:11;*
honour and *p.* *5:12*
glory, honor, and dominion *Re 4:11*
(A)(B)
blessing, glory, honour, and *p. Re 5:13*
be to him
honor, glory, and dominion *Re 5:13*
(B)(E)
honor, glory, and might *Re 5:13*
(N)(R)
p. was given to him that sat on *Re 6:4*
the red horse
empowered to take peace from *Re 6:4*
(A)(B)
permitted to take peace from (R) *Re 6:4*
p. was given them over fourth *Re 6:8*
part of earth
Authority was granted him *Re 6:8*
(B)(E)
honour, *p.* and might be given *Re 7:12*
to our God
to them was given *p.* as *Re 9:3*
scorpions have *p.*
and their *p.* was to hurt men *Re 9:10*
five months
for their *p.* is in their mouth *Re 9:19*
and their tails
I will give *p.* to my two *Re 11:3*
witnesses
these have *p.* to shut heaven, *p. Re 11:6*
over waters
now is the *p.* of his Christ *Re 12:10*
come
the dragon gave him *p.* and *Re 13:2;*
his seat *13:4*
p. was given to him to *Re 13:5;*
continue *13:7*
he exerciseth all the *p.* of the *Re 13:12*
first beast
to exercise full authority *Re 13:12*
(A)(E)(N)(P)(R)
had *p.* to give life; had *p.* over *Re 13:15;*
fire *14:18*
the temple was filled with *Re 15:8*
smoke from his *p.*
p. was given him to scorch men *Re 16:8*
with fire
blasphemed God who hath *p. Re 16:9*
over these plagues
but receive *p.* as kings one *Re 17:12*
hour with beast
receive royal authority with *Re 17:12*
(B)(E)(N)(P)
shall give their *p.* and strength *Re 17:13*
to the beast
glory, honour, and *p.* to the *Re 19:1*
Lord our God

POWER *OF GOD*

ye do err, not knowing *M't 22:29;*
scriptures, nor *p. of God M'k 12:24*
all amazed at the mighty *p. of Lu 9:43*
God
Son sit on the right hand of *p. Lu 22:69*
of God

this man is the great *p. of God* *Ac 8:10*
gospel is the *p. of God* to *Ro 1:16*
salvation
to us which are saved, it is *1Co 1:18*
the *p. of God*
Christ the *p. of God,* and *1Co 1:24*
wisdom of God
faith should not stand but by *1Co 2:5*
the *p. of God*
by word of truth, by *p. of God* *2Co 6:7*
crucified thro' weakness, he *2Co 13:4*
liveth by *p. of God* but we shall
live with him by *p. of God*
partaker of afflictions of the *2Ti 1:8*
gospel, according to the *p. of God*
who are kept by the *p. of God* *1Pe 1:5*

IN POWER

it is *in p.* of my hand to do *Ge 31:29*
you hurt
thy right hand is become *Ex 15:6*
glorious *in p.*
why are the wicked mighty *in* *Job 21:7*
p.
the wicked increase in *Job 21:7*
strength (B)
he is excellent *in p.* and in *Job 37:23*
judgment
when it is *in p.* of thy hand to *Pr 3:27*
do it
death and life are *in* the *p.* of *Pr 18:21*
the tongue
that he is strong *in p.* not one *Isa 40:26*
faileth
the Lord is slow to anger, great *Na 1:3*
in p.
shall go before him *in* the *p.* of *Lu 1:17*
Elias
Jesus returned *in* the *p.* of the *Lu 4:14*
Spirit
kingdom of God not in word, *1Co 4:20*
but *in p.*
it is sown in weakness, it is *1Co 15:43*
raised *in p.*
be strong in Lord and *p.* of *Eph 6:10*
his might
but our gospel came in word, *1Th 1:5*
and also *in p.*
angels greater *in p.* and might *2Pe 2:11*

MY POWER

with all *my p.* I have served *Ge 31:6*
I raised thee to shew in thee *Ex 9:16*
my p.
my p. hath gotten me this *De 8:17*
wealth
Babylon built by the might of *Da 4:30*
my p.
that I might shew *my p.* in thee *Ro 9:17*
that I abuse not *my p.* in the *1Co 9:18*
gospel

NO POWER

to sell her, he shall have *no p.* *Ex 21:8*
have *no p.* to stand before *Le 26:37*
enemies
men of Ai had *no p.* to flee *Jos 8:20*
this way
David and people had *no p.* to *1Sa 30:4*
weep
to help with them that have *2Ch 14:11*
no p.
Ahaziah had *no p.* to keep *2Ch 22:9*
kingdom
have I *no p.* to deliver *Isa 50:2*
on whose bodies the fire had *Da 3:27*
no p.
there was *no p.* in the ram to *Da 8:7*
stand
no p. against me except it *Joh 19:11*
were
for there is *no p.* but of God *Ro 13:1*
no authority (A)(B)(N)(R) *Ro 13:1*
on such the second death hath *Re 20:6*
no p.

THY POWER

broughtest out by *thy mighty p.* *De 9:29*
all that he hath is in *thy p.* *Job 1:12*
so will we sing, and praise *thy* *Ps 21:13*
p.
scatter them by *thy p.;* *Ps 59:11;*
will sing of *thy p.* *59:16*
to see *thy p.* and thy glory, as I *Ps 63:2*
have seen
greatness of *thy p.* enemies *Job 66:3*
submit

and *thy p.* to every one that is *Ps 71:18*
to come
according to the greatness of *Ps 79:11*
thy p.
people shall be willing in day *Ps 110:3*
of *thy p.*
and they shall talk of *thy p.* *Ps 145:11*
watch the way, fortify *thy p.* *Na 2:1*
mightily

POWERFUL

a *p.* man (B) *2Sa 17:10*
p. heroes (B) *1Ch 7:2; 7:5*
p. heroes (B) *1Ch 7:11;*
  8:40; 12:21, 25, 28, 30
The voice of the Lord is *p.;* the *Ps 29:4*
p.
his letters are weighty and *2Co 10:10*
p.
the word of God is quick, *Heb 4:12*
and *p.*
a good man's prayer is *p.* (N) *Jas 5:16*

POWERFULLY

p. confuted Jews (R) *Ac 18:28*
works *p.* and miraculously (A) *Ga 3:5*

POWERLESS

you are *p.* against them (B) *Es 6:13*
when *p.,* Christ died (A) *Ro 5:6*

POWERS

men of *p.* (B) *1Ch 26:32*
p. of the heavens shall be *M't 24:29*
shaken
forces of heaven be shaken *M't 24:29*
(B)
the *p.* that are in heaven *M'k 13:25*
shall be
heavenly hosts be shaken *M'k 13:25*
(B)
unto magistrates, and *p.* take *Lu 12:11*
ye
magistrates and authorities *Lu 12:11*
(A)(B)(E)(N)(P)(R)
the *p.* of heaven shall be *Lu 21:26*
shaken
angels, nor principalities, nor *Ro 8:38*
p.
soul be subject unto the higher *Ro 13:1*
p.
the *p.* that be are ordained of *Ro 13:1*
God
authorities (A)(B)(N)(P)(R) *Ro 13:1;*
  Eph 3:10; Col 1:16; Tit 3:1
extraordinary *p.* of healing *1Co 12:9*
(A)
to another miraculous *p.* *1Co 12:10*
(B)(N)
and *p.* in heavenly places *Eph 3:10*
might be
against principalities, against *Eph 6:12*
p.
dominions, or principalities, *Col 1:16*
or *p.*
having spoiled principalities *Col 2:15*
and *p.*
reasoning *p.* atrophied (N) *1Ti 6:5*
be subject to principalities and *Tit 3:1*
p.
miraculous *p.* (B)(E) *Heb 2:4*
and the *p.* of the world to *Heb 6:5*
come
p. being made subject unto *1Pe 3:22*
him
by one's unaided mental *p.* *2Pe 1:20*
(B)

PRACTICE

p. my regulations (B) *Le 18:4*
p. profaneness (E) *Isa 32:6*
mighty in *p.* (B) *Lu 24:19*
p. cunning (N)(R) *2Co 4:2*
p. these duties (R) *1Ti 4:15*

PRACTICED

p. sorcery (S) *2Ch 33:6*
have *p.* hospitality *1Ti 5:10*
(A)(B)(E)(N)(R)

PRACTICES

abominable *p.* (A) *De 18:9;*
  20:18; 2Ki 16:3; 21:2
destestable *p.* (B) *2Ch 36:8; 36:14*

wicked *p.* (B) *Ezr 9:1; 9:11*
make the pay for evil *p.* (B) *Ps 99:8*
angry with *p.* (A)(B) *Ps 106:29*
p. true judgment (B) *Eze 18:8*
p. shown up (N) *Joh 3:20*
exposing their *p.* *Ac 19:18*
(A)(B)(P)(R)
old self with evil *p.* (A)(B)(R) *Col 3:9*
they have exercised with *2Pe 2:14*
covetous *p.*
p. lawbreaking (B) *1Jo 3:4*
repent of *p.* (B) *Re 2:22; 16:11*

PRACTICING

set heart on *p.* (B) *Ps 119:112*
those *p.* lawlessness (B) *M't 13:4*
I was still a *p.* Jew (N) *Ga 1:13*

PRACTISE

to *p.* wicked works with men *Ps 141:4*
that
to *p.* hypocrisy, and to utter *Isa 32:6*
error
and shall prosper, and *p.* and *Da 8:24*
shall
when the morning is light, they *Mic 2:1*
p. it

PRACTISED

Saul secretly *p.* mischief *1Sa 23:9*
against
ground; and it *p.* and *Da 8:12*
prospered

PRAETORIAN

into the *p.* (A)(B)(E)(R) *Joh 18:28*
into the *p.* (E)(R) *Joh 18:33*
entered the *p.* again (E)(R) *Joh 19:9*
into Herod's palace - the *p.* *Ac 23:35*
(A)(E)(N)(P)(R)
the whole *p.* guard (E)(R) *Ph'p 1:13*

PRAETORIUM

him away into the hall, *M'k 15:16*
called *P.*

PRAISE

he whom thy brethren shall *p.* *Ge 49:8*
the fruit thereof holy to *p.* the *Le 19:24*
Lord
he is thy *p.* and he is thy God *De 10:21*
to make thee high in *p.* and in *De 26:19*
name
I will sing *p.* to the Lord *J'g 5:3;*
  Ps 7:17; 9:2; 57:7; 61:8; 104:33
deliver, that we may glory in *1Ch 16:35*
thy *p.*
instruments I made to *p.* *1Ch 23:5*
therewith
we thank and *p.* thy glorious *1Ch 29:13*
name
Levites to *p.* before the priests *2Ch 8:14*
that should *p.* the beauty of *2Ch 20:21*
holiness
and when they began to sing *2Ch 20:22*
and to *p.*
and such as taught to sing *p.* *2Ch 23:13*
and to *p.* in the gates of the *2Ch 31:2*
tents of Lord
exalted above all blessing and *p.* *Ne 9:5*
in the days of David were *Ne 12:46*
songs of *p.*
p. you because (B) *Job 40:14*
that I may shew forth all thy *p.* *Ps 9:14*
so will we sing and *p.* thy *Ps 21:13*
power
ye that fear the Lord, *p.* him *Ps 22:23*
my *p.* shall be of thee in *Ps 22:25*
congregation
when I go to pit, shall dust *p.* *Ps 30:9*
thee
that is my glory may sing *p.* to *Ps 30:12*
thee
for *p.* is comely for the upright *Ps 33:1*
his *p.* shall be continually in my *Ps 34:1*
mouth
my tongue shall speak of thy *Ps 35:28*
p. all day
even *p.* to our God; with voice *Ps 40:3;*
of *p.* *42:4*
hope in God, for I shall yet *p.* *Ps 42:5;*
him *42:11; 43:5*
in God we boast, and *p.* thy *Ps 44:8*
name for ever

therefore shall the people *p.* *Ps 45:17* thee

so is thy *p.* to the ends of the *Ps 48:10* earth

men will *p.* thee, when doest *Ps 49:18* well

whoso offereth *p.* glorifieth me *Ps 50:23*

and my mouth shall shew *Ps 51:15* forth thy *p.*

my lips shall *p.*; mouth *p.* thee *Ps 63:3; 63:5*

p. waiteth for thee, O God, in *Ps 65:1* Sion

sing forth his honour, make his *Ps 66:2* *p.* glorious

and make the voice of his *p.* to *Ps 66:8* be heard

let people *p.* thee *Ps 67:3; 67:5*

let the heaven and earth *p.* *Ps 69:34* him

my *p.* shall be continually of *Ps 71:6* thee

let my mouth be filled with thy *Ps 71:8* *p.*

I will yet *p.* thee more and *Ps 71:14* more

let the poor and needy *p.* thy *Ps 74:21* name

surely the wrath of man shall *Ps 76:10* *p.* thee

we will shew forth thy *p.* *Ps 79:13*

shall the dead arise and *p.* *Ps 88:10* thee

heavens shall *p.* thy wonders *Ps 89:5*

sing *p.* *Ps 98:4*

let them *p.* thy great and *Ps 99:3* terrible name

and enter into his courts with *Ps 100:4* *p.*

and to declare his *p.* in *Ps 102:21* Jerusalem

who can shew forth all his *p.* *Ps 106:2*

then they sang his *p.*; *Ps 106:12; 106:47* triumph in thy *p.*

p. him in the assembly of the *Ps 107:32* elders

I will sing and give *p.* with my *Ps 108:1* glory

O God of my *p.*; his *p.* *Ps 109:1; 111:10* endureth

p. him, O ye servants of the *Ps 113:1; 135:1* Lord

the dead *p.* not the Lord, nor *Ps 115:17* any that

seven times a day do I *p.* *Ps 119:164* thee

lips shall utter *p.* when thou *Ps 119:171* hast taught

let my soul live and it shall *Ps 119:175* *p.* thee

before the gods will I sing *p.* *Ps 138:1* to thee

I will *p.* thy name for loving *Ps 138:2* kindness

all the kings of the earth shall *Ps 138:4* *p.* thee

bring out of prison that I may *Ps 142:7* *p.* thy

one generation *p.* thy works to *Ps 145:4* another

all thy works shall *p.* thee, O *Ps 145:10* Lord

my mouth shall speak the *p.* *Ps 145:21* of the Lord

p. is comely; sing *p.* on the *Ps 147:1; 147:7* harp

p. the Lord Jerusalem, *p.* thy *Ps 147:12* God, O Zion

p. ye the Lord, *p.* him in the *Ps 148:1* heights

p. him, all his angels, *p.* him, *Ps 148:2* ye his hosts

p. him, sun and moon, *p.* him, *Ps 148:3* all ye stars

p. him, ye heavens of heavens, *Ps 148:4* and waters

he exalteth the *p.* of all his *Ps 148:14* saints

sing his *p.* in the congregation *Ps 149:1* of saints

let them *p.* his name in the *Ps 149:3* dance

p. God in his sanctuary, *p.* *Ps 150:1* him in firmament

p. him for his mighty acts, *p.* *Ps 150:2* him for greatness

p. him with trumpet; *p.* him *Ps 150:3; 150:4* with timbrel

p. him upon the high *Ps 150:5* sounding cymbals

let another man *p.* thee, a *Pr 27:2* stranger

as the furnace, so is a man to *Pr 27:21* his *p.*

they that forsake the law *p.* the *Pr 28:4* wicked

let her own works *p.* her in the *Pr 31:31* gates

grave cannot *p.* thee, death *Isa 38:18* cannot

the living he shall *p.* thee, as I *Isa 38:19* do this day

I will not give my *p.* to graven *Isa 42:8* images

sing his *p.* from the end of *Isa 42:10* the earth

let them declare his *p.* in the *Isa 42:12* islands

this people, they shall shew *Isa 43:21* forth my *p.*

and for my *p.* will I refrain for *Isa 48:9* thee

but thou shalt call thy gates *Isa 60:18* *P.*

garment of *p.* for spirit of *Isa 61:3* heaviness

Lord will cause righteousness *Isa 61:11* and *p.* to spring

till he make Jerusalem a *p.* in *Isa 62:7* the earth

that they might be to me for a *Jer 13:11* *p.*

save me, O Lord, for thou art *Jer 17:14* my *p.*

bringing sacrifices of *p.* to *Jer 17:26; 33:11* house of Lord

p. ye and say, O Lord save *Jer 31:7* people

it shall be to me a joy, a *p.* and *Jer 33:9* an honour

there shall be no more *p.* of *Jer 48:2* Moab

how is the city of *p.* not left, *Jer 49:25* city of joy

how is the *p.* of whole earth *Jer 51:41* surprised

I thank and *p.* thee, O God *Da 2:23*

I *p.* extol, and honour the king *Da 4:37* of heaven

p. the name of the Lord your *Joe 2:26* God

and the earth was full of his *p.* *Hab 3:3*

I will get them *p.* and fame *Zep 3:19*

make you a *p.* among all *Zep 3:20* people of earth

of sucklings, thou hast *M't 21:16* perfected *p.*

people. when they saw it, gave *Lu 18:43* *p.* to God

disciples began to *p.* God with *Lu 19:37* loud voice

give God the *p.* this man is a *Joh 9:24* sinner

loved *p.* of men more than *p.* *Joh 12:43* of God

whose *p.* is not of men, but of *Ro 2:29* God

do good, thou shalt have *p.* of *Ro 13:3* same

give *p.* to God (R) *Ro 14:11*

p. you among Gentiles *Ro 15:9* (A)(B)(E)(N)(R)

let all people *p.* him *Ro 15:11* (A)(E)(N)(P)(R)

then shall every man have *p.* of *1Co 4:5* God

now I *p.* you that ye *1Co 11:2* remember me

in this that I declare, I *p.* *1Co 11:17; 11:22* you not

the brother, whose *p.* is in the *2Co 8:18* gospel

predestined to *p.* of glory of *Eph 1:6* his grace

to *p.* of glory who first *Eph 1:12; 1:14* trusted in Christ

by Jesus Christ, to *p.* and *Ph'p 1:11* glory of God

if there be any *p.* think on *Ph'p 4:8* these things

worthy of *p.* (R) *Ph'p 4:8*

in midst of the church will I *Heb 2:12* sing *p.*

by him let us offer sacrifice *Heb 13:15* of *p.* continually

trial of your faith might be *1Pe 1:7* found to *p.*

and for the *p.* of them that do *1Pe 2:14* well

to whom be *p.* and dominion *1Pe 4:11* for ever

saying, *P.* our God, all ye his *Re 19:5* servants

PRAISE YE, PRAISE
THE LORD

p. ye the Lord, for the avenging *J'g 5:2* of Israel

he appointed Levites to *p.* the *1Ch 16:4* Lord

to stand every morning to *p.* *1Ch 23:30* the Lord

who prophesied with a harp *1Ch 25:3* to *p.* the Lord

the Levites stood up to *p.* the *2Ch 20:19* Lord

p. the Lord, for his mercy *2Ch 20:21* endureth for ever

set Levites with cymbals to *p.* *Ezr 3:10* the Lord

they shall *p.* the Lord that *Ps 22:26* seek him

p. the Lord with harp, sing *Ps 33:2* unto him

people that shall be created *Ps 102:18* shall *p.* the Lord

p. ye the Lord *Ps 104:35; 106:1, 48; 111:1; 112:1; 113:1, 9; 115:18; 116:19; 117:2; 135:1; 146:1, 10; 147:20; 148:1, 14; 149:1, 9; 150:1, 6; Jer 20:13*

oh that men would *p.* the *Ps 107:8; 107:15, 21, 31* Lord

I will greatly *p.* the Lord *Ps 109:30* with my mouth

I will *p.* the Lord: *p.* Lord *Ps 118:19; 135:3* for he is good

while I live will I *p.* the Lord, *Ps 146:2* I will sing

p. ye the Lord for it is good to *Ps 147:1* sing praise

p. the Lord O Jerusalem, *Ps 147:12* praise thy God, O Zion

p. the Lord from the earth, ye *Ps 148:7* dragons

shall say, *P.* the Lord, call *Isa 12:4* upon his name

but they shall eat it, and *p.* the *Isa 62:9* Lord

p. the Lord of hosts, for the *Jer 33:11* Lord is good

and again, *P.* the Lord, all ye *Ro 15:11* Gentiles

I WILL, WILL I PRAISE

Leah said, Now *will I p.* the *Ge 29:35* Lord

I will *p.* Lord according to his *Ps 7:17* righteousness

I will *p.* thee, O Lord, with my *Ps 9:1; 111:1; 138:1* whole heart

in midst of the congregation *Ps 22:22* *will I p.* thee

therefore with my song *will I p.* *Ps 28:7* him

I will give thee thanks, I will *Ps 35:18; 57:9; 108:3; 109:30* *p.* thee among

on the harp *will I p.* thee, O *Ps 43:4* God

I will *p.* thee for ever, because *Ps 52:9* thou hast done

I will *p.* thy name, O Lord for *Ps 54:6* it is good

in God I will *p.* his word, in *Ps 56:4* God I trust

I will *p.* the name of God with *Ps 69:30* a song

I will also *p.* thee with the *Ps 71:22* psaltery

I will *p.* thee, O Lord my God *Ps 86:12* with my heart

I will go into them, and will *p.* *Ps 118:19* the Lord

I will *p.* thee, for thou hast *Ps 118:21* heard me

thou art my God, and *I will* *Ps 118:28* *p.* thee

I will *p.* thee with uprightness *Ps 119:7* of heart

I will *p.* thee, for I am *Ps 139:14* wonderfully made

I will *p.* thy name for ever and *Ps 145:2* ever

I will *p.* thee, though thou *Isa 12:1* wast angry

I will *p.* thy name, thou hast *Isa 25:1* done wonders

PRAISED

people saw him, they *p.* their   *J'g 16:24*
god
none to be so much *p.* as   *2Sa 14:25*
Absalom
on the Lord, who is worthy to   *2Sa 22:4*
be *p.*
is the Lord, and greatly to be   *1Ch 16:25*
p.
people said, Amen, and *p.*   *1Ch 16:36*
the Lord
four thousand *p.* the Lord   *1Ch 23:5*
with the
p. the Lord, saying, For he is   *2Ch 5:13*
good
and worshipped, and *p.* the   *2Ch 7:3*
Lord
when David *p.* by their   *2Ch 7:6*
ministry
Levites and the priests *p.* the   *2Ch 30:21*
Lord
great shout, when they *p.* the   *Ezr 3:11*
Lord
said, Amen, and *p.* the Lord   *Ne 5:13*
the Lord, who is worthy to be   *Ps 18:3*
p.
greatly to be *p.* in the city of   *Ps 48:1*
our
continually; daily shall he be   *Ps 72:15*
p.
Lord is great, and greatly to be   *Ps 96:4*
p.
same the Lord's name is to be   *Ps 113:3*
p.
is the Lord, and greatly to be   *Ps 145:3*
p.
feareth the Lord, she shall be   *Pr 31:30*
p.
I *p.* the dead which are already   *Ec 4:2*
the concubines, and they *p.* her   *Ca 6:9*
house, where our fathers *p.*   *Isa 64:11*
thee
I *p.* and honoured him that   *Da 4:34*
liveth
drank wine, and *p.* the gods of   *Da 5:4*
gold
thou hast *p.* the gods of silver   *Da 5:23*
loosed, and he spake, and *p.*   *Lu 1:64*
God
Jesus was highly *p.* (B)   *Ac 19:17*

PRAISES

fearful in *p.* doing wonders   *Ex 15:11*
and I will sing *p.* unto thy   *2Sa 22:50*
name
And they sang *p.* with   *2Ch 29:30*
gladness
Sing *p.* to the Lord, which   *Ps 9:11*
heathen sing *p.* unto thy   *Ps 18:49*
name
that inhabitest the *p.* of Israel   *Ps 22:3*
yea, I will sing *p.* unto the Lord   *Ps 27:6*
Sing *p.* to God, sing *p.*   *Ps 47:6*
sing ye *p.* with understanding   *Ps 47:7*
O God: I will render *p.* unto   *Ps 56:12*
thee
unto God, sing *p.* to his name   *Ps 68:4*
the earth; O sing *p.* unto the   *Ps 68:32*
Lord
I will sing *p.* to the God of   *Ps 75:9*
Jacob
p. of the Lord, and his strength   *Ps 78:4*
to sing *p.* unto thy name, O   *Ps 92:1*
most
I will sing *p.* unto thee among   *Ps 108:3*
Lord is good: sing *p.* unto his   *Ps 135:3*
name
ten strings will I sing *p.* unto   *Ps 144:9*
thee
I will sing *p.* unto my God   *Ps 146:2*
while I
it is good to sing *p.* unto our   *Ps 147:1*
God
sing *p.* unto him with the   *Ps 149:3*
timbrel
the high *p.* of God be in their   *Ps 149:6*
mouth
p. his neighbor (A)   *Pr 27:14*
shew forth the *p.* of the Lord   *Isa 60:6*
and the *p.* of the Lord,   *Isa 63:7*
according
prayed, and sang *p.* unto God   *Ac 16:25*
greatly sing his *p.* (B)   *Ro 15:11*
shew forth the *p.* of him who   *1Pe 2:9*
hath

PRAISETH

her husband also, and he *p.*   *Pr 31:28*
her

PRAISING

heard in *p.* and thanking the   *2Ch 5:13*
Lord
the people running and *p.*   *2Ch 23:12*
the king
p. and giving thanks unto the   *Ezr 3:11*
Lord
thy house, they will be still *p.*   *Ps 84:4*
thee
heavenly host, *p.* God, and   *Lu 2:13*
saying
glorifying and *p.* God for all   *Lu 2:20*
in the temple, *p.* and blessing   *Lu 24:53*
God
P. God, and having favour   *Ac 2:47*
with all
walking, and leaping, and *p.*   *Ac 3:8*
God
people saw him walking and *p.*   *Ac 3:9*
God

PRAISEWORTHY

anything *p.* (B)(P)   *Ph'p 4:8*

PRANSING

the *p.* horses, and of the   *Na 3:2*
jumping

PRANSINGS

broken by the means of the *p.*   *J'g 5:22*
the *p.* of their mighty ones   *J'g 5:22*

PRATING

but a *p.* fool shall fall   *Pr 10:8*
sorrow; but a *p.* fool shall fall   *Pr 10:10*
p. against us with malicious   *3Jo 10*

PRAY

I *p.* thee (used of man to   *Ge 12:13;*
man) *13:8, 9; 16:2; 19:7, 8; 23:13; 25:30;*
27:19, 21; 30:14, 27; 33:10-11, 14;
34:8; 37:6, 14, 16; 38:16; 40:8, 14; 44:33;
45:4; 47:4, 29; 50:4, 5, 17; Ex 4:18;
5:3; 10:17; Nu 10:31; 16:8; 20:17; 22:6,
16-17, 19; 23:13, 27; Jos 2:12; 7:19;
J'g 4:19; 6:18, 39; 8:5; 9:2; 9:38; 10:15;
11, 23; Ru 2:7; 1Sa 2:36; 3:17; 9:18;
10:15; 12:23; 14:29; 15:25, 30; 16:22;
19:2; 20:29; 22:3; 23:22; 25:8, 24, 25;
26:8, 11, 19; 28:8, 22; 30:7; 2Sa 1:4, 9;
13:5, 6, 13, 26; 14:2, 11, 12, 18; 15:7;
16:9; 18:22; 19:37; 20:16; 24:17;
1Ki 1:12; 2:17, 20; 14:2; 17:10, 11;
19:20; 20:7, 31, 32, 37; 22:5, 13;
2Ki 1:13; 2:2, 4, 6, 9, 19; 4:10, 22, 26;
5:7, 15, 17, 22; 6:2, 17, 18; 7:13; 8:4;
18:23; 2Ch 18:4, 12; Ne 1:6, 11; 5:10,
11; Job 6:29; 8:8; 22:22; 33:1; Isa 29:11;
36:8, 11; Jer 21:2; 32:8; 40:15; La 1:18;
Mal 1:9
I *p.* thee (men to God)   *Ge 18:3;*
18:4; 32:11; Ex 4:13; 32:32; 33:13; 34:9;
Nu 11:15; De 3:25; J'g 13:15; 16:28;
1Ki 8:26; 17:21; 1Ch 21:17; Job 32:21;
Jon 4:2
Put I *p.* thee, thy hand under   *Ge 24:2*
my
I *p.* thee, send me good speed   *Ge 24:12*
this
Let down thy pitcher, I *p.*   *Ge 24:14*
thee, that
Let me, I *p.* thee, drink a   *Ge 24:17*
little water
daughter art thou? tell me, I   *Ge 24:23*
p. thee
Give me, I *p.* thee, a little   *Ge 24:43*
water of
unto her, Let me drink, I *p.*   *Ge 24:45*
thee
take, I *p.* thee, thy weapons   *Ge 27:3*
I *p.* thee (God to men)   *Ge 32:29;*
Nu 16:26; J'g 13:4; Isa 5:3; Mic 3:1, 9;
Hag 2:15
Discern, I *p.* thee, whose are   *Ge 38:25*
these
let thy servant, I *p.* thee,   *Ge 44:18*
speak a

Bring them, I *p.* thee, unto me   *Ge 48:9*
p. to the Lord (B)   *Ex 8:8*
unto the Lord, that he take   *Nu 21:7*
we *p.* thee   *J'g 1:24; Ex 5:3*
I will *p.* for you unto the Lord   *1Sa 7:5*
P. for thy servants unto the   *1Sa 12:19*
Lord
I *p.* thee, forgive the trespass   *1Sa 25:28*
in his heart to pray this prayer   *2Sa 7:27*
O Lord, I *p.* thee, turn the   *2Sa 15:31*
counsel
they shall *p.* toward this place   *1Ki 8:30;*
8:35, 42, 44; 2Ch 6:26, 34
confess thy name and *p.*   *1Ki 8:33;*
2Ch 6:24
p. unto thee toward this land   *1Ki 8:48;*
2Ch 6:37-38
p. for me, that thy hand may   *1Ki 13:6*
be
Smite me, I *p.* thee. And the   *1Ki 20:35*
man
let them go, we *p.* thee, and   *2Ki 2:16*
seek thy
Be content, I *p.* thee, and go   *2Ki 6:3*
with
Speak, I *p.* thee to thy   *2Ki 18:26*
servants in
humble themselves and *p.* and   *2Ch 7:14*
seek
p. for the life of the king   *Ezr 6:10*
I *p.* before thee now, day and   *Ne 1:6*
night
Remember, I *p.* thee, whoever   *Job 4:7*
should we have, if we *p.* unto   *Job 21:15*
him
he shall *p.* unto God, and he   *Job 33:26*
will
my servant Job shall *p.* for   *Job 42:8*
you
my King, my God, for to thee   *Ps 5:2*
will I *p.*
evening, morning, and at noon   *Ps 55:17*
will I *p.*
Let, I *p.* thee, thy merciful   *Ps 119:76*
kindness
p. for peace of Jerusalem   *Ps 122:6*
prosper that love thee
he shall come to his sanctuary   *Isa 16:12*
to *p.*
saying, Read this, I *p.* thee   *Isa 29:11*
and *p.* to a god that cannot   *Isa 45:20*
save
p. not thou for this people   *Jer 7:16;*
11:14; 14:11
seek peace of the city, *p.* to the   *Jer 29:7*
Lord for it
ye shall *p.* to me, and I will   *Jer 29:12*
hearken to you
p. now to the Lord our God   *Jer 37:3;*
42:2, 20
for us
behold, I will *p.* to the Lord   *Jer 42:4*
your God
those who *p.* for me (A)   *Zep 3:10*
they sent men to *p.* before the   *Zec 7:2*
Lord
go speedily to *p.* before the   *Zec 8:21;*
8:22
Lord
p. for them which despitefully   *M't 5:44;*
Lu 6:28
use
to *p.* standing in the   *M't 6:5*
synagogues
p. to thy Father which is in   *M't 6:6*
secret
when ye *p.* use not vain   *M't 6:7*
repetitions
After this manner therefore *p.*   *M't 6:9*
ye
P. ye therefore the Lord of   *M't 9:38;*
Lu 10:2
the
up into a mountain apart to   *M't 14:23*
p.
put his hands on them and *p.*   *M't 19:13*
professing that you *p.* long   *M't 23:14*
(B)
p. ye that your flight be not   *M't 24:20;*
in the   *M'k 13:18*
ye here, while I go and *p.*   *M't 26:36*
yonder
Watch and *p.* that ye enter   *M't 26:41*
not into
that I cannot now *p.* to my   *M't 26:53*
Father
they began to *p.* him to   *M'k 5:17*
depart out
I *p.* thee, come and lay thy   *M'k 5:23*
hands on
he departed into a mountain   *M'k 6:46*
to *p.*

things ye desire, when ye *p.*   *M'k 11:24*
believe
watch and *p.*: for ye know   *M'k 13:33*
not
disciples, Sit ye here, while I   *M'k 14:32*
shall *p.*
Watch ye and *p.* lest ye enter   *M'k 14:38*
into
he went out into a mountain to   *Lu 6:12*
p.
and went up into a mountain   *Lu 9:28*
to *p.*
unto him, Lord, teach us to *p.*   *Lu 11:1*
When ye *p.* say, Our Father   *Lu 11:2*
which
see it: I *p.* thee have me   *Lu 14:18*
excused
them: I *p.* thee have me   *Lu 14:19*
excused
I *p.* thee therefore, father,   *Lu 16:27*
that thou
men ought always to *p.* and not   *Lu 18:1*
went up into the temple to *p.*   *Lu 18:10*
ye therefore, and *p.* always,   *Lu 21:36*
that
P. that ye enter not into   *Lu 22:40*
and *p.* lest ye enter into   *Lu 22:46*
temptation
I will *p.* the Father, and he   *Joh 14:16*
shall
that I will *p.* the Father for   *Joh 16:26*
you
I *p.* for them: I *p.* not for the   *Joh 17:9*
I *p.* not that thou shouldest   *Joh 17:15*
take
Neither *p.* I for these alone,   *Joh 17:20*
but
this thy wickedness, and *p.*   *Ac 8:22*
God
P. ye to the Lord for me, that   *Ac 8:24*
I *p.* thee, of whom speaketh   *Ac 8:34*
went up upon the housetop to   *Ac 10:9*
p.
I *p.* thee that thou wouldest   *Ac 24:4*
hear
I *p.* you to take some meat: *Ac 27:34*
for
we should *p.* for as we ought   *Ro 8:26*
comely that a woman *p.*   *1Co 11:13*
unto God
tongue *p.* that he may   *1Co 14:13*
interpret
if I *p.* in an unknown   *1Co 14:14*
tongue, my
it then? I will *p.* with the   *1Co 14:15*
spirit
will *p.* with the   *1Co 14:15*
understanding also
we *p.* you in Christ's stead, be   *2Co 5:20*
ye
Now *p.* to God that ye do no   *2Co 13:7*
evil
And this I *p.* that your love   *Ph'p 1:9*
may
do not cease to *p.* for you, and   *Col 1:9*
to
P. without ceasing   *1Th 5:17*
I *p.* God your whole spirit   *1Th 5:23*
and soul
Brethren, *p.* for us   *1Th 5:25*
we *p.* always for you, that our   *2Th 1:11*
God
brethren, *p.* for us, that the   *2Th 3:1*
word
therefore that men *p.* every   *1Ti 2:8*
where
I *p.* God that it may not be   *2Ti 4:16*
laid to
P. for us: for we trust we   *Heb 13:18*
have
among you afflicted? let him *p.*   *Jas 5:13*
let them *p.* over him, anointing   *Jas 5:14*
p. one for another, that ye may   *Jas 5:16*
I do not say that he shall *p.*   *1Jo 5:16*
for it

PRAYED

So Abraham *p.* unto God: and   *Ge 20:17*
p. to the Lord (A)(B)(R)   *Ge 25:21;*
  Ex 8:30
when Moses *p.* unto the Lord   *Nu 11:2*
us. And Moses *p.* for the   *Nu 21:7*
people
I *p.* for Aaron also the same   *De 9:20*
time
I *p.* therefore unto the Lord   *De 9:26*
p. unto the Lord, and wept   *1Sa 1:10*
sore

For this child I *p.*; and the   *1Sa 1:27*
Lord
Hannah *p.* and said, My   *1Sa 2:1*
heart
us. And Samuel *p.* unto the   *1Sa 8:6*
Lord
I have *p.* (B)   *1Sa 13:12; 1Ki 8:59*
p. for the Lord (A)   *2Sa 21:14*
them twain, and *p.* unto the   *2Ki 4:33*
Lord
Elisha *p.* and said, Lord, I   *2Ki 6:17*
pray
Elisha *p.* unto the Lord and   *2Ki 6:18*
said
Hezekiah *p.* before the Lord   *2Ki 19:15*
That which thou hast *p.* to   *2Ki 19:20*
me
to the wall, and *p.* unto the   *2Ki 20:2*
Lord
But Hezekiah *p.* for them,   *2Ch 30:18*
saying
of Amoz, *p.* and cried to   *2Ch 32:20*
heaven
the death, and *p.* unto the   *2Ch 32:24*
Lord
p. unto him: and he was   *2Ch 33:13*
intreated
Now when Ezra had *p.* and   *Ezr 10:1*
when
and *p.* before the God of heaven   *Ne 1:4*
So I *p.* to the God of heaven   *Ne 2:4*
Job, when he *p.* for his   *Job 42:10*
friends
Hezekiah *p.* unto the Lord,   *Isa 37:15*
saying
Whereas thou hast *p.* to me   *Isa 37:21*
the wall, and *p.* unto the Lord   *Isa 38:2*
Neriah, I *p.* unto the Lord,   *Jer 32:16*
saying
fell on his face, and *p.*,   *M't 26:39*
saying, O
away the second time, and *p.*   *M't 26:42*
p. the third time, saying the   *M't 26:44*
same
a solitary place, and there *p.*   *M'k 1:35*
p. him that he might be with   *M'k 5:18*
him
and *p.* that, if it were   *M'k 14:35*
possible
went away, and *p.* and spake   *M'k 14:39*
p. him that he would thrust out   *Lu 5:3*
a
himself into the wilderness,   *Lu 5:16*
and *p.*
And as he *p.* the fashion of his   *Lu 9:29*
stood, and *p.* thus with   *Lu 18:11*
himself
p. for thee, that thy faith fail   *Lu 22:32*
not
cast, and kneeled down and *p.*   *Lu 22:41*
in an agony he *p.* more   *Lu 22:44*
earnestly
his disciples *p.* him, saying   *Joh 4:31*
And they *p.* and said, Thou,   *Ac 1:24*
Lord
And when they had *p.*, the   *Ac 4:31*
place
when they had *p.* they laid their   *Ac 6:6*
p. that he might find   *Ac 7:46*
(A)(B)(P)
p. for them, that they might   *Ac 8:15*
receive
forth, and kneeled down, and   *Ac 9:40*
p.
to the people, and *p.* to God   *Ac 10:2*
alway
the ninth hour I *p.* in my   *Ac 10:30*
house
p. they him to tarry certain   *Ac 10:48*
days
when they had fasted and *p.*   *Ac 13:3*
p. with fasting, they   *Ac 14:23*
commended
man of Macedonia, and *p.* him   *Ac 16:9*
Paul and Silas *p.*, and sang   *Ac 16:25*
kneeled down, and *p.* with   *Ac 20:36*
them all
kneeled down on the shore,   *Ac 21:5*
and *p.*
while I *p.* in the temple, I was   *Ac 22:17*
in a
p. me to bring this young man   *Ac 23:18*
Paul entered in, and *p.*, and   *Ac 28:8*
laid

p. it might stop speaking   *Heb 12:19*
(P)
he *p.* earnestly that it might   *Jas 5:17*
not
he *p.* again, and the heaven   *Jas 5:18*
gave

PRAYER

heart to pray this *p.* unto thee   *2Sa 7:27*
thou respect unto the *p.* of thy   *1Ki 8:28*
hearken unto the cry and to   *1Ki 8:28*
the *p.*
p. which thy servant shall   *1Ki 8:29*
make
hear my *p.* (A)   *1Ki 8:30*
p. and supplication soever be   *1Ki 8:38*
made
hear thou in heaven their *p.*   *1Ki 8:45*
Then hear thou their *p.* and   *1Ki 8:49*
their
made an end of praying all   *1Ki 8:54*
this *p.*
him, I have heard thy *p.* and   *1Ki 9:3*
thy
lift up thy *p.* for the remnant   *2Ki 19:4*
that
I have heard thy *p.* I have   *2Ki 20:5*
seen
Have respect therefore to the   *2Ch 6:19*
p.
to the *p.* which thy servant   *2Ch 6:19*
prayeth
to hearken unto the *p.* which   *2Ch 6:20*
thy
p. or what supplication soever   *2Ch 6:29*
hear thou from the heavens   *2Ch 6:35*
their *p.*
their *p.* and their supplications   *2Ch 6:39*
attent unto the *p.* that is made   *2Ch 6:40*
I have heard thy *p.* and   *2Ch 7:12*
have
unto the *p.* that is made in   *2Ch 7:15*
this
and their *p.* came up to his   *2Ch 30:27*
holy
Manasseh, and his *p.* unto   *2Ch 33:18*
his God
His *p.* also, and how God   *2Ch 33:19*
was
hear the *p.* of thy servant, which   *Ne 1:6*
attentive to the *p.* of thy   *Ne 1:11*
servant
and to the *p.* of thy servants,   *Ne 1:11*
who
Nevertheless we made our *p.*   *Ne 4:9*
unto
begin the thanksgiving in *p.*   *Ne 11:17*
and restrainest *p.* before God   *Job 15:4*
mine hands: also my *p.* is   *Job 16:17*
pure
Thou shalt make thy *p.* unto   *Job 22:27*
him
mercy upon me, and hear my *p.*   *Ps 4:1*
will I direct my *p.* unto thee, and   *Ps 5:3*
the Lord will receive my *p.*   *Ps 6:9*
A *p.* of David   *Ps 17, 86 title*
give ear unto my *p.* that goeth   *Ps 17:1*
p. returned into mine own   *Ps 35:13*
bosom
Hear my *p.*, O Lord, and give   *Ps 39:12*
ear
p. unto the God of my life   *Ps 42:8*
Hear my *p.* O God give ear to   *Ps 54:2*
Give ear to my *p.* O God; and   *Ps 55:1*
hide
my cry, O God; attend unto my   *Ps 61:1*
p.
Hear my voice, O God, in my   *Ps 64:1*
p.
O thou that hearest *p.* unto   *Ps 65:2*
thee
attended to the voice of my *p.*   *Ps 66:19*
which hath not turned away   *Ps 66:20*
my *p.*
for me, my *p.* is unto thee, O   *Ps 69:13*
Lord
p. also shall be made for him   *Ps 72:15*
against the *p.* of thy people   *Ps 80:4*
O Lord God of hosts, hear my   *Ps 84:8*
p.
Give ear, O Lord, unto my *p.*   *Ps 86:6*
Let my *p.* come before thee: *Ps 88:2*
incline
morning shall my *p.* prevent   *Ps 88:13*
thee
A *p.* of Moses the man of   *Ps 90 title*
God

A p. of the afflicted, when   *Ps 102 title*
he is
Hear my p. O Lord, and let   *Ps 102:1*
my
will regard the p. of the   *Ps 102:17*
destitute
and not despise their p.   *Ps 102:17*
but I give myself unto p.   *Ps 109:4*
and let his p. become sin   *Ps 109:7*
Let my p. be set forth before   *Ps 141:2*
thee
yet my p. also shall be in their   *Ps 141:5*
David; A P. when he was   *Ps 142 title*
Hear my p. O Lord, give ear   *Ps 143:1*
to my
the p. of the upright is his   *Pr 15:8*
delight
he heareth the p. of the   *Pr 15:29*
righteous
his p. shall be an abomination   *Pr 28:9*
poured out a p. when   *Isa 26:16*
chastening
thy p. for the remnant that is   *Isa 37:4*
left
I have heard thy p. I have seen   *Isa 38:5*
them joyful in my house of p.   *Isa 56:7*
house shall be called an house   *Pr 56:7*
of p.
neither lift up cry nor p. for   *Jer 7:16;*
them   *11:14*
and shout, he shutteth out my p.   *La 3:8*
that our p. should not pass   *La 3:44*
through
seek by p. and supplications,   *Da 9:3*
with
we not our p. before the Lord   *Da 9:13*
our
God, hear the p. of thy servant   *Da 9:17*
whiles I was speaking in p.   *Da 9:21*
even
my p. came in unto thee, into   *Jon 2:7*
thine
A p. of Habakkuk the prophet   *Hab 3:1*
not out but by p. and fasting   *M't 17:21*
shall be called the house of   *M't 21:13*
p.; but
whatsoever ye shall ask in p.   *M't 21:22*
and for a pretence make long   *M't 23:14*
p.
by nothing, but by p. and   *M'k 9:29*
fasting
called of all nations the   *M'k 11:17*
house of p.
not, Zacharias: for thy p. is   *Lu 1:13*
heard
continued all night in p. to   *Lu 6:12*
God
My house is the house of p.:   *Lu 19:46*
but ye
when he rose up from p. and   *Lu 22:45*
was
one accord in p. and   *Ac 1:14*
supplication
the hour of p. being the ninth   *Ac 3:1*
hour
will give ourselves continually to   *Ac 6:4*
p.
And said, Cornelius, thy p. is   *Ac 10:31*
heard
but p. was made without   *Ac 12:5*
ceasing of
where p. was wont to be made   *Ac 16:13*
as we went to p. a certain   *Ac 16:16*
damsel
desire and p. to God for Israel   *Ro 10:1*
is
continuing instant in p.   *Ro 12:12*
give yourselves to fasting and   *1Co 7:5*
p.
also helping together by p. for   *2Co 1:11*
us
by their p. for you, which   *2Co 9:14*
long after
Praying always with all p. and   *Eph 6:18*
Always in every p. of mine for   *Ph'p 1:4*
you
to my salvation through your   *Ph'p 1:19*
p.
every thing by p. and   *Ph'p 4:6*
supplication
Continue in p. and watch in the   *Col 4:2*
sanctified by word of God and   *1Ti 4:5*
p.
the p. of faith shall save the   *Jas 5:15*
sick
fervent p. of a righteous man   *Jas 5:16*
a good man's p. is powerful   *Jas 5:16*
(N)
therefore sober, and watch   *1Pe 4:7*
unto p.

PRAYERS

answered p. of the land (B)   *2Sa 21:14;*
  24:25; 1Ch 5:2
pays no attention to their p.   *Job 24:12*
(R)
p. of David the son of Jesse   *Ps 72:20*
are
when ye make many p. I will   *Isa 1:15*
not
beginning of our p. (A)   *Da 9:23*
and for a pretence make   *M'k 12:40*
long p.
with fastings and p. night and   *Lu 2:37*
day
of John fast often, and make p.   *Lu 5:33*
and for a shew make long p.   *Lu 20:47*
and in breaking of bread, and   *Ac 2:42*
in p.
Thy p. and thine alms are   *Ac 10:4*
come up
mention of you always in my p.   *Ro 1:9*
with me in your p. to God   *Ro 15:30*
for me
making mention of you in my   *Eph 1:16*
p.
p. and petition (A)(B)(N)   *Ph'p 4:6*
labouring fervently for you in   *Col 4:12*
p.
making mention of you in our   *1Th 1:2*
p.
supplications, p., intercessions   *1Ti 2:1*
petitions, p. (A)(N)   *1Ti 2:1*
continueth in supplications and   *1Ti 5:5*
p.
have remembrance of thee in   *2Ti 1:3*
my p.
mention of thee always in my   *Ph'm 4*
p.
through your p. I shall be   *Ph'm 22*
given
he had offered up   *Heb 5:7*
p. supplications
life; that your p. be not   *1Pe 3:7*
hindered
and his ears are open unto   *1Pe 3:12*
their p.
our p. will be answered (P)   *1Jo 5:15*
odours, which are the p. of   *Re 5:8*
saints
offer it with the p. of all saints   *Re 8:3*
upon
came with the p. of the saints   *Re 8:4*

PRAYEST

when thou p. thou shalt not be   *M't 6:5*
as
when thou p. enter into thy   *M't 6:6*
closet

PRAYETH

thy servant p. before thee to   *1Ki 8:28*
day
which thy servant p. before   *2Ch 6:19*
thee
thy servant p. toward this   *2Ch 6:20*
place
and worshippeth it, and p.   *Isa 44:17*
unto it
Saul, of Tarsus: for, behold, he   *Ac 9:11*
p.
every woman that p. or   *1Co 11:5*
prophesieth
my spirit p. but my   *1Co 14:14*
understanding

PRAYING

she continued p. before the   *1Sa 1:12*
Lord
stood by thee here, p. unto the   *1Sa 1:26*
Lord
Solomon had made an end   *1Ki 8:54;*
of p. all   *2Ch 7:1*
and found Daniel p. and   *Da 6:11*
making
And whiles I was speaking,   *Da 9:20*
and p.
And when ye stand p.   *M'k 11:25*
forgive, if ye
people were p. without at the   *Lu 1:10*
time
Jesus also being baptized, and   *Lu 3:21*
p.
it came to pass, as he was   *Lu 9:18*
alone p.
as he was p. in a certain place   *Lu 11:1*
I was in the city of Joppa p.:   *Ac 11:5*
and in

many were gathered together   *Ac 12:12*
p.
Every man p. or prophesying   *1Co 11:4*
P. us with much intreaty that   *2Co 8:4*
we
P. always with all prayer and   *Eph 6:18*
Lord Jesus Christ, p. always for   *Col 1:3*
you
p. also for us, that God would   *Col 4:3*
open
Night and day p. exceedingly   *1Th 3:10*
that
holy faith, p. in the Holy Ghost   *Jude 20*

PRAYS

p. hard for you (N)(R)   *Col 4:12*

PREACH

prophets to p. of thee at   *Ne 6:7*
Jerusalem
set up prophets to announce   *Ne 6:7*
(A)
prophets to spread about (B)   *Ne 6:7*
prophets to proclaim about you   *Ne 6:7*
(R)
anointed me to p. good tidings   *Isa 61:1*
p. unto it the preaching that I   *Jon 3:2*
bid
p. to it the message (B)   *Jon 3:2*
From that time Jesus began to   *M't 4:17*
p.
as ye go, p. saying, The   *M't 10:7*
kingdom of
ear, that p. ye upon the   *M't 10:27*
housetops
proclaim upon the housetops   *M't 10:27*
(A)(E)(P)(R)
herald from the housetops   *M't 10:27*
(B)
shout from the housetops   *M't 10:27*
(N)
to teach and to p. in their   *M't 11:1*
cities
p. the baptism of repentance   *M'k 1:4*
for the
next towns, that I may p.   *M'k 1:38*
there also
that he might send them forth   *M'k 3:14*
to p.
and p. the gospel to every   *M'k 16:15*
creature
proclaim the good news   *M'k 16:15*
(N)(P)
me to p. the gospel to the poor   *Lu 4:18*
to p. deliverance to the   *Lu 4:18*
captives
to announce good news (N)   *Lu 4:18*
p. the acceptable year of the   *Lu 4:19*
Lord
proclaim the acceptable year   *Lu 4:19*
(A)(B)(E)(P)
I must p. the kingdom of God   *Lu 4:43*
to
he sent them to p. the kingdom   *Lu 9:2*
of
to announce the kingdom (B)   *Lu 9:2*
to proclaim the kingdom (N)   *Lu 9:2*
thou and p. the kingdom of   *Lu 9:60*
God
not to teach and p. Jesus   *Ac 5:42*
Christ
he commanded us to p. unto   *Ac 10:42*
bear solemn testimony   *Ac 10:42*
(A)(B)
proclaim to the people (N)   *Ac 10:42*
and p. unto you that ye   *Ac 14:15*
should turn
hath in every city them that p.   *Ac 15:21*
him
in every town his preachers   *Ac 15:21*
(A)(P)
every city those proclaiming   *Ac 15:21*
him (B)
spokesmen in every town (N)   *Ac 15:21*
Holy Ghost to p. the word in   *Ac 16:6*
Asia
proclaim the word (A)   *Ac 16:6*
speak the word in Asia   *Ac 16:6*
(B)(E)(R)
delivering the message (N)   *Ac 16:6*
speaking God's message (P)   *Ac 16:6*
us for to p. the gospel unto   *Ac 16:10*
them
proclaim the glad tidings (A)   *Ac 16:10*
to evangelize there (B)   *Ac 16:10;*
  2Co 10:16
to bring them good news (N)   *Ac 16:10*
to give the good news (P)   *Ac 16:10*

this Jesus, whom I *p.* unto you   Ac 17:3
Jesus whom we proclaim   Ac 17:3
(A)(E)(R)
proclaiming the Messiah   Ac 17:3
(N)(P)
I am ready to *p.* the gospel to   Ro 1:15
you
is, the word of faith, which we   Ro 10:8
p.
shall they *p.* except they be   Ro 10:15
sent
of them that *p.* the gospel of   Ro 10:15
peace
who publish the good news   Ro 10:15
(B)
bring glad tidings of good   Ro 10:15
things (E)(P)
the messengers of good news   Ro 10:15
(N)
so have I strived to *p.* the   Ro 15:20
gospel
not to baptize, but to *p.* the   1Co 1:17
gospel
But we *p.* Christ crucified,   1Co 1:23
unto the
they which *p.* the gospel   1Co 9:14
should
For though I *p.* the gospel, I   1Co 9:16
have
woe is unto me, if I *p.* not the   1Co 9:16
gospel
when I *p.* the gospel, I may   1Co 9:18
make
they, so we *p.* and so ye   1Co 15:11
believed
I came to Troas, to *p.* Christ's   2Co 2:12
gospel
For we *p.* not ourselves, but   2Co 4:5
Christ
p. the gospel in the regions   2Co 10:16
beyond
p. any other gospel unto you   Ga 1:8
than
man *p.* any other gospel unto   Ga 1:9
you
evangelizes you with the gospel   Ga 1:9
(B)
I might *p.* him among the   Ga 1:16
heathen
which I *p.* among the Gentiles   Ga 2:2
if I yet *p.* circumcision, why   Ga 5:11
do I
I should *p.* among the Gentiles   Eph 3:8
Some indeed *p.* Christ even   Ph'p 1:15
of envy
The one *p.* Christ of   Ph'p 1:16
contention
we *p.* warning every man,   Col 1:28
Whom
Him we proclaim   Col 1:28
(B)(E)(N)(P)(R)
P. the word; be instant in   2Ti 4:2
season
Herald the message (B)   2Ti 4:2
Proclaim the message (N)   2Ti 4:2
to *p.* unto them that dwell on   Re 14:6
to proclaim   Re 14:6
(B)(E)(N)(P)(R)

PREACHED

have *p.* righteousness in the   Ps 40:9
great
I have proclaimed glad tidings   Ps 40:9
(A)(B)(E)
I have told the glad news (R)   Ps 40:9
the poor have the gospel *p.* to   M't 11:5
them
the poor are evangelized (B)   M't 11:5
the poor are hearing the good   M't 11:5
news (N)
be *p.* in all the world for a   M't 24:14
witness
this gospel shall be *p.* in the   M't 26:13
whole
And *p.* saying, There cometh   M'k 1:7
one
And he *p.* in their synagogues   M'k 1:39
and he *p.* the word unto them   M'k 2:2
and *p.* that men should repent   M'k 6:12
this gospel shall be *p.*   M'k 14:9
throughout
they went forth, and *p.*   M'k 16:20
every where
exhortation *p.* he unto the   Lu 3:18
people
And he *p.* in the synagogues of   Lu 4:44
raised, to the poor the gospel is   Lu 7:22
p.
that time the kingdom of God   Lu 16:16
is *p.*

in the temple, and *p.* the gospel   Lu 20:1
should be *p.* in his name   Lu 24:47
among all
which before was *p.* unto you   Ac 3:20
Christ who was designated and   Ac 3:20
appointed (A)(B)
Christ who has been appointed   Ac 3:20
(E)(N)(R)
your long-heralded Christ (P)   Ac 3:20
p. through Jesus the resurrection   Ac 4:2
proclaiming Jesus the   Ac 4:2
resurrection (A)(E)(N)(R)
Samaria, and *p.* Christ unto   Ac 8:5
them
proclaimed the Christ   Ac 8:5
(A)(E)(R)
proclaiming the Messiah (N)   Ac 8:5
testified and *p.* the word of the   Ac 8:25
p. the gospel in many villages   Ac 8:25
of
scripture, and *p.* unto him   Ac 8:35
Jesus
he *p.* in all the cities, till he   Ac 8:40
came
he *p.* Christ in the synagogues   Ac 9:20
how he had *p.* boldly at   Ac 9:27
Damascus
after the baptism which John   Ac 10:37
p.
the baptism John heralded   Ac 10:37
(B)
the baptism John proclaimed   Ac 10:37
(N)(P)
they *p.* the word of God in the   Ac 13:5
John had first *p.* before his   Ac 13:24
coming
p. unto you the forgiveness of   Ac 13:38
sins
removal of sins now   Ac 13:38
proclaimed (A)(E)(N)(P)(R)
forgiveness of sins announced   Ac 13:38
(B)
be *p.* to them the next   Ac 13:42
sabbath
And there they *p.* the gospel   Ac 14:7
they had *p.* the gospel to that   Ac 14:21
city
they had *p.* the word in Perga   Ac 14:25
where we have *p.* the word of   Ac 15:36
that the word of God was *p.*   Ac 17:13
of Paul
word of God being   Ac 17:13
proclaimed (B)(E)(N)(P)(R)
because he *p.* unto them Jesus   Ac 17:18
Paul *p.* unto them, ready to   Ac 20:7
depart
discoursed with them   Ac 20:7
(A)(B)(E)
addressed them (N)   Ac 20:7
talked with them (R)   Ac 20:7
have fully *p.* the gospel of   Ro 15:19
Christ
carrying out to the full the   Ro 15:19
good news (A)
what I said and *p.* (P)   1Co 2:4
when I have *p.* to others, I   1Co 9:27
myself
after proclaiming to others   1Co 9:27
(A)
while heralding to others (B)   1Co 9:27
you the gospel which I *p.*   1Co 15:1
unto you
gospel proclaimed to you   1Co 15:1;
(A)   Ga 1:11; 3:8
keep in memory what I *p.*   1Co 15:2
unto you
if Christ be *p.* that he rose   1Co 15:12
from the
who was *p.* among you by us,   2Co 1:19
even
Jesus, whom we have not *p.*   2Co 11:4
I have *p.* to you the gospel of   2Co 11:7
God
that which we have *p.* unto you   Ga 1:8
the gospel which was *p.* of me   Ga 1:11
is not
p. before the gospel unto   Ga 3:8
Abraham
I *p.* the gospel unto you at the   Ga 4:13
came and *p.* peace to you   Eph 2:17
which
pretence, or in truth, Christ   Ph'p 1:18
is *p.*
which was *p.* to every   Col 1:23
creature
we *p.* unto you the gospel of   1Th 2:9
God
we proclaimed the glad tidings   1Th 2:9
(A)(N)

we heralded to you God's   1Th 2:9
gospel (B)
p. unto the Gentiles, believed   1Ti 3:16
on in
heralded among Gentiles (B)   1Ti 3:16
proclaimed among the nations   1Ti 3:16
(N)(P)
For unto us was the gospel *p.*   Heb 4:2
glad tidings proclaimed (A)   Heb 4:2
but the word *p.* did not profit   Heb 4:2
them
and they to whom it was first   Heb 4:6
p.
them that have *p.* the gospel   1Pe 1:12
unto
which by the gospel is *p.* unto   1Pe 1:25
you
and *p.* unto the spirits in   1Pe 3:19
prison
made his proclamation to   1Pe 3:19
spirits (N)
for this cause was the gospel *p.*   1Pe 4:6

PREACHER

words of the *P.* the son of David   Ec 1:1
Vanity of vanities, saith the *P.*   Ec 1:2;
    12:8
I the *P.* was king over Israel in   Ec 1:12
this have I found, saith the *p.*   Ec 7:27
because the *p.* was wise, he still   Ec 12:9
p. sought to find out   Ec 12:10
acceptable
appeared a *p.* (N)   M't 3:1
how shall they hear without a   Ro 10:14
p.
I am ordained a *p.* and an   1Ti 2:7
apostle
I am appointed a *p.* and an   2Ti 1:11
apostle
eighth person, a *p.* of   2Pe 2:5
righteousness

PREACHEST

the *p.* a man should not steal   Ro 2:21

PREACHETH

you by Jesus whom Paul *p.*   Ac 19:13
if he that cometh *p.* another   2Co 11:4
Jesus
now *p.* the faith which once he   Ga 1:23

PREACHING

unto it the *p.* that I bid thee   Jon 3:2
preach to it the message which   Jon 3:2
(B)
proclaim to it the message (R)   Jon 3:2
p. in the wilderness of Judaea   M't 3:1
proclaiming in the desert (B)   M't 3:1
appeared as a preacher in the   M't 3:1
wilderness (N)
and *p.* the gospel of the   M't 4:23;
kingdom   9:35; M'k 1:14
announcing the good news   M't 4:23
(B)
proclaiming the good news   M't 9:35
(A)(P)
announcing the gospel (B)(N)   M't 9:35
they repented at the *p.* of   M't 12:41;
Jonas   Lu 11:32
p. the baptism of repentance for   Lu 3:3
p. and shewing the glad tidings   Lu 8:1
of
p. the gospel, and healing every   Lu 9:6
went every where *p.* the word   Ac 8:4
believed Philip *p.* the things   Ac 8:12
he told the glad tidings (B)   Ac 8:12
proclaimed the good news (P)   Ac 8:12
Israel, *p.* peace by Jesus   Ac 10:36
Christ
announcing the good news   Ac 10:36
(A)
made known the good news   Ac 10:36
(B)
p. the word to none but unto   Ac 11:19
delivering the message (A)   Ac 11:19
telling the message (B)   Ac 11:19
speaking the word (E)(R)   Ac 11:19
bringing the message (N)   Ac 11:19
giving the message (P)   Ac 11:19
the Grecians, *p.* the Lord   Ac 11:20
Jesus
and *p.* the word of the Lord   Ac 15:35
proclaiming the word (A)   Ac 15:35
as Paul was long *p.* he sunk   Ac 20:9
down
Paul kept talking on   Ac 20:9
(B)(N)(R)

Paul discoursed yet longer (E) | Ac 20:9
Paul's address became longer | Ac 20:9
and longer (P)
have gone p. the kingdom of | Ac 20:25
God
proclaiming the kingdom | Ac 20:25
(A)(N)
gone in and out as a herald of | Ac 20:25
the kingdom (B)
P. the kingdom of God, and | Ac 28:31
gospel, and the p. of Jesus | Ro 16:25
Christ
For the p. of the cross is to | 1Co 1:18
them
the message of the cross | 1Co 1:18
(A)(B)
the word of the cross (E)(R) | 1Co 1:18
the doctrine of the cross (N) | 1Co 1:18
by the foolishness of p. to | 1Co 1:21
save
through the folly of the | 1Co 1:21
proclamation (B)
by the folly of the gospel (N) | 1Co 1:21
by the simplemindedness of | 1Co 1:21
the gospel message (P)
my p. was not with enticing | 1Co 2:4
word
my language and my message | 1Co 2:4
(A)(R)
the gospel I proclaimed (N) | 1Co 2:4
What I said and preached (P) | 1Co 2:4
my message and p. (B) | 1Co 2:4
be not risen, then is our p. | 1Co 15:14
vain
to you also in p. the gospel | 2Co 10:14
of Christ
me the p. might be fully | 2Ti 4:17
known
manifested his word through p. | Tit 1:3

PRECEDE

p. those asleep | 1Th 4:15
(A)(E)(P)(R)(S)

PRECEPT

p. must be upon p. p. upon p. | Isa 28:10
unto them p. upon p. p. upon | Isa 28:13
p.
me is taught by the p. of men | Isa 29:13
your heart he wrote you this | M'k 10:5
p.
Moses had spoken every p. to | Heb 9:19
all

PRECEPTS

hearken to these p. (A) | De 7:12
and commandedst them p. | Ne 9:14
p. of the Lord (A)(B) | Ps 19:8
commanded us to keep thy p. | Ps 119:4
I will meditate in thy p. and | Ps 119:15
have
to understand the way of thy | Ps 119:27
p.
I have longed after thy p.: | Ps 119:40
quicken
walk at liberty: for I seek thy | Ps 119:45
p.
This I had, because I kept | Ps 119:56
thy p.
thee, and of them that keep | Ps 119:63
thy p.
keep thy p. with my whole | Ps 119:69
heart
cause: but I will meditate in | Ps 119:78
thy p.
earth; but I forsook not thy | Ps 119:87
p.
I will never forget thy p.: for | Ps 119:93
with
save me; for I have sought | Ps 119:94
thy p.
the ancients, because I keep | Ps 119:100
thy p.
thy p. I get understanding | Ps 119:104
for me: yet I erred not from | Ps 119:110
thy p.
I esteem all thy p. | Ps 119:128
concerning all
of man: so will I keep thy | Ps 119:134
p.
despised: yet do not I forget | Ps 119:141
thy p.
Consider how I love thy p. | Ps 119:159
kept thy p. and thy | Ps 119:168
testimonies

help me; for I have chosen | Ps 119:173
thy p.
and kept all his p. and done | Jer 35:18
even by departing from thy p. | Da 9:5

PRECINCTS

which was in the p. (S) | 2Ki 23:11

PRECIOUS

and to her mother p. things | Ge 24:53
for the p. things of heaven | De 33:13
p. fruits brought forth by the | De 33:14
sun
p. things put forth by the | De 33:14
moon
for the p. things of the lasting | De 33:15
hills
for the p. things of the earth | De 33:16
of the Lord was p. in those | 1Sa 3:1
days
my soul was p. in thine eyes | 1Sa 26:21
this
a talent of gold with the p. | 2Sa 12:30
stones
and very much gold, and p. | 1Ki 10:2
stones
very great store, and p. | 1Ki 10:10
stones
plenty of almug trees, and p. | 1Ki 10:11
stones
thy servants, be p. in thy sight | 2Ki 1:13
let my life now be p. in thy | 2Ki 1:14
sight
all the house of his p. things | 2Ki 20:13
the spices, and the p. | 2Ki 20:13
ointment
and there were p. stones in it | 1Ch 20:2
all manner of p. stones, and | 1Ch 29:2
marble
they with whom p. stones | 1Ch 29:8
were found
garnished the house with p. | 2Ch 3:6
stones
gold in abundance, and p. | 2Ch 9:1
stones
great abundance, and p. | 2Ch 9:9
stones
brought algum trees and p. | 2Ch 9:10
stones
the dead bodies, and p. | 2Ch 20:25
jewels
and of gold, and of p. things | 2Ch 21:3
and for gold, and for p. | 2Ch 32:27
stones
all sorts of p. articles (B) | 2Ch 32:27
with the p. vessels (S) | 2Ch 36:10; 36:19
with beasts, and with p. things | Ezr 1:6
vessels of fine copper, p. as | Ezr 8:27
gold
and his eyes seeth every p. | Job 28:10
thing
gold of Ophir, with the p. | Job 28:16
onyx
the redemption of their soul is | Ps 49:8
p.
and p. shall their blood be in | Ps 72:14
his
P. in the sight of the Lord is | Ps 116:15
and weepeth, bearing p. seed | Ps 126:6
It is like the p. ointment upon | Ps 133:2
How p. also are thy thoughts | Ps 139:17
We shall find all p. substance, | Pr 1:13
we
She is more p. than rubies: and | Pr 3:15
all
adulteress will hunt for the p. | Pr 6:26
life
substance of a diligent man is | Pr 12:27
p.
A gift is a p. stone in the eyes | Pr 17:8
lips of knowledge are a p. | Pr 20:15
jewel
with all p. and pleasant riches | Pr 24:4
name is better than p. ointment | Ec 7:1
profane my p. place (R) | Ec 7:22
a man more p. than fine gold | Isa 13:12
a tried stone, a p. corner | Isa 28:16
stone
them the house of his p. things | Isa 39:2
the spices, and the p. ointment | Isa 39:2
Since thou wast p. in my sight | Isa 43:4
p. productions (B) | Isa 44:9
p. stones, gems | Isa 54:12
(A)(B)(E)(R)
take forth the p. from the | Jer 15:19
vile
and all the p. things thereof | Jer 20:5
p. things (B)(R) | La 1:7; 1:10

The p. sons of Zion, | La 4:2
comparable
taken the treasure and p. | Eze 22:25
things
Dedan thy merchant in p. | Eze 27:20
clothes
and with all p. stones, and | Eze 27:22
gold
every p. stone was thy | Eze 28:13
covering
p., blessed land (A) | Da 8:9
p. vessels of silver and of gold | Da 11:8
and silver, and with p. stones | Da 11:38
over all the p. things of | Da 11:43
Egypt
p. things of silver (A)(R) | Ho 9:6
every p. vessel | Ho 13:15
(A)(B)(R)
my p. treasures | Joe 3:5
(A)(B)(E)(R)(S)
p. furnishings (A) | Na 2:9
p. things (B)(R) | Na 2:9
alabaster box of very p. | M't 26:7
ointment
of ointment of spikenard | M'k 14:3
very p.
silver, p. stones, wood, hay | 1Co 3:12
waiteth for the p. fruit of the | Jas 5:7
earth
awaits p. produce (B) | Jas 5:7
more p. than of gold that | 1Pe 1:7
perisheth
But with the p. blood of | 1Pe 1:19
Christ, as
of men, but chosen of God, | 1Pe 2:4
and p.
Sion a chief corner stone, | 1Pe 2:6
elect, p.
therefore which believe he is | 1Pe 2:7
p.
that have obtained like p. faith | 2Pe 1:1
exceeding great and p. | 2Pe 1:4
promises
decked with gold and p. stones | Re 17:4
silver, and p. stones, and of | Re 18:12
pearls
all manner vessels of most p. | Re 18:12
wood
decked with gold, and p. | Re 18:16
stones and
light was like unto a stone | Re 21:11
most p.
with all manner of p. stones | Re 21:19

PRECIOUSNESS

a vase of p. (A) | Pr 20:15

PREDESTINATE

also did p. to be conformed to | Ro 8:29
whom he did p. them he also | Ro 8:30

PREDESTINATED

Having p. us unto the | Eph 1:5
adoption
He foreordained us (destined | Eph 1:5
us, planned in his love for us)
to be adopted (A)(E)
he destined us (N)(R) | Eph 1:5
he planned in his purpose of | Eph 1:5
love (P)
being p., according to the | Eph 1:11
purpose
been foreordained | Eph 1:11
(chosen and appointed
beforehand) in accordance (A)
foreordained according to his | Eph 1:11
purpose (B)(E)
we were long ago destined | Eph 1:11
for this (P)
been destined and appointed | Eph 1:11
to live (R)
God p. for us (A) | Eph 2:10

PREDESTINED

purpose has p. to (A)(R) | Ac 4:28
p. before world (N) | 1Pe 1:20

PREDETERMINED

p. plan and foreknowledge | Ac 2:23
(P)
joy in their p. | Ac 2:28
(A)(B)(N)(R)

PREDICTED

p. this present time (N)   *Ac 3:24*
p. suffering of Christ   *1Pe 1:11*
(A)(B)(N)(P)(R)
their doom *p.* long ago (A)   *Jude 4*

PRE-EMINENCE

not return *p.* (B)(E)(R)   *Ge 49:4*
got the *p.* (B)   *1Ch 29:11*
man hath no *p.* above the   *Ec 3:19*
beast
advantage of man over a beast   *Ec 3:19*
amounts to nothing (B)(R)
in all things he might have   *Col 1:18*
the *p.*
in every respect he might   *Col 1:18*
have first place (B)
in all things alone supreme   *Col 1:18*
(N)
the Lord of all (P)   *Col 1:18*
he might be pre-eminent (R)   *Col 1:18*
loveth to have the *p.* among   *3Jo 9*
brethren
who likes to take the lead (A)   *3Jo 9*
who loves to be prominent (B)   *3Jo 9*
who would be leader (N)(P)   *3Jo 9*
who likes to put himself first   *3Jo 9*
(R)

PRE-EMINENT

he might be *p.* (R)   *Col 1:18*

PRE-ESTABLISHED

appointing *p.* periods (B)   *Ac 17:26*

PREFER

If I *p.* not Jerusalem above   *Ps 137:6*
my

PREFERENTIAL

no *p.* treatment with God (P)   *Ro 2:11*

PREFERRED

he *p.* her and her maids unto   *Es 2:9*
this Daniel was *p.* above the   *Da 6:3*
cometh after me is *p.* before   *Joh 1:15*
me
coming after me is *p.* before   *Joh 1:27*
me
a man which is *p.* before me   *Joh 1:30*

PREFERRING

love; in honour *p.* one   *Ro 12:10*
another
without *p.* one before another   *1Ti 5:21*

PREGNANT

a *p.* woman (A)(B)   *Ex 21:22;*
     1Sa 4:19; 2Ki 8:12
their *p.* women (A)(R)   *Ho 13:16*
found to be *p.* (A)(R)   *M't 1:18*
shall become *p.* (A)   *M't 1:23*
women who are *p.* (A)(P)   *M't 24:19*
she was *p* (N)   *Lu 2:5*
she was *p.* (A)(B)(N)(P)   *Re 12:2*

PREGNANCY

increase *p.* troubles (A)(B)   *Ge 3:16*
whose *p.* was advanced (B)(P)   *Lu 2:5*

PREMEDITATE

ye shall speak, neither do ye   *M'k 13:11*
p.
to *p.* your defense (B)   *Lu 21:14*

PREMEDITATION

without *p.* (B)(S)   *Jos 20:3; 20:5*

PREORDAINED

purpose *p.* to take place   *Ac 4:28*
(B)(E)

PREPARATION

made *p.* for them (S)   *1Ch 12:39*
will therefore now make *p.*   *1Ch 22:5*
for it

flaming torches in the day of   *Na 2:3*
his *p.*
that followed the day of the   *M't 27:62*
p.
was come, because it was   *M'k 15:42*
the *p.*
And that day was the *p.* and   *Lu 23:54*
And it was the *p.* of the   *Joh 19:14*
passover
because it was the *p.* that   *Joh 19:31*
because of the Jews' *p.* day   *Joh 19:42*
with the *p.* of the gospel of   *Eph 6:15*
peace

PREPARATIONS

The *p.* of the heart in man   *Pr 16:1*
p. been made (R)   *Heb 9:6*

PREPARE

God, and I will *p.* him an   *Ex 15:2*
habitation
they shall *p.* that which they   *Ex 16:5*
bring
a drink offering shalt thou *p.*   *Nu 15:5*
with
thou shalt *p.* for a meat   *Nu 15:6*
offering
to the number that ye shall   *Nu 15:12*
p. so
p. me here seven oxen and   *Nu 23:1*
seven
and *p.* me here seven bullocks   *Nu 23:29*
Thou shalt *p.* thee a way, and   *De 19:3*
people, saying, *P.* you victuals   *Jos 1:11*
Let us now *p.* to build us an   *Jos 22:26*
altar
p. your hearts unto the Lord   *1Sa 7:3*
I pray you, *p.* ye, and know   *1Sa 23:22*
and
prepare (S)   *2Sa 12:4;*
   13:5, 7; 1Ki 17:12; 18:23, 25
Ahab, *P.* thy chariot, and   *1Ki 18:44*
get
shewbread, to *p.* it every   *1Ch 9:32*
sabbath
and *p.* their heart unto   *1Ch 29:18*
thee: and
to *p.* me timber in abundance   *2Ch 2:9*
to *p.* chambers in the   *2Ch 31:11*
house of
p. yourselves by the houses   *2Ch 35:4*
of your
yourselves, and *p.* your   *2Ch 35:6*
brethren
banquet that I shall *p.* for them   *Es 5:8*
p. thyself to the search of their   *Job 8:8*
If thou wilt *p.* thine heart, and   *Job 11:13*
stretch
dust, and *p.* raiment as the   *Job 27:16*
clay
He may *p.* it, but the just   *Job 27:17*
shall put
thou wilt *p.* their heart, thou   *Ps 10:17*
wilt
p. themselves without my   *Ps 59:4*
fault
O *p.* mercy and truth, which   *Ps 61:7*
may
they may *p.* a city for   *Ps 107:36*
habitation
P. thy work without, and   *Pr 24:27*
make it
they *p.* their meat in the   *Pr 30:25*
summer
P. slaughter for his children   *Isa 14:21*
P. the table, watch in the   *Isa 21:5*
P. ye the way the Lord,   *Isa 40:3*
make
to *p.* a graven image, that   *Isa 40:20*
shall
ye up, *p.* the way, take up the   *Isa 57:14*
p. ye the way of the people;   *Isa 62:10*
cast
that *p.* a table for that troop   *Isa 65:11*
P. ye war against her; arise   *Jer 6:4*
p. them for the day of   *Jer 12:3*
slaughter
I will *p.* destroyers against   *Jer 22:7*
thee
Stand fast, and *p.* thee; for   *Jer 46:14*
the watchmen, *p.* the   *Jer 51:12*
ambushes
p. the nations against her,   *Jer 51:27*
call
P. against her the nations   *Jer 51:28*
with the

thou shalt *p.* thy bread   *Eze 4:15*
therewith
man, *p.* thee stuff for   *Eze 12:3*
removing
I will *p.* thee unto blood, and   *Eze 35:6*
blood
and *p.* for thyself thou, and   *Eze 38:7*
all thy
thou *p.* every day a goat for   *Eze 43:25*
a sin
they shall also *p.* a young   *Eze 43:25*
bullock
he shall *p.* the sin offering,   *Eze 45:17*
and the
day shall the prince *p.* for   *Eze 45:22*
himself
p. a burnt offering to the   *Eze 45:23*
Lord
shall *p.* a meat offering of   *Eze 45:24*
an ephah
priests shall *p.* his burnt   *Eze 46:2*
offering
And he shall *p.* a meat   *Eze 46:7*
offering, an
shall *p.* a voluntary burnt   *Eze 46:12*
offering
he shall *p.* his burnt offering   *Eze 46:12*
Thou shalt daily *p.* a burnt   *Eze 46:13*
offering
thou shalt *p.* it every   *Eze 46:13*
morning
thou shalt *p.* a meat offering   *Eze 46:14*
for it
Thus shall they *p.* the lamb   *Eze 46:15*
P. war, wake up the mighty   *Joe 3:9*
men
p. to meet thy God, O   *Am 4:12*
Israel
they even *p.* war against him   *Mic 3:5*
and he shall *p.* the way before   *Mal 3:1*
me
P. ye the way of the Lord,   *M't 3:3;*
make   *M'k 1:3; Lu 3:4*
which shall *p.* thy way   *M't 11:10;*
before thee   *M'k 1:2; Lu 7:27*
p. for thee to eat the   *M't 26:17*
passover
Where wilt thou that we go   *M'k 14:12*
and *p.*
face of the Lord to *p.* his   *Lu 1:76*
ways
Go and *p.* us the passover,   *Lu 22:8*
that we
him, Where wilt thou that we   *Lu 22:9*
p.
told you. I go to *p.* a place   *Joh 14:2*
for you
And if I go and *p.* a place   *Joh 14:3*
for you
who shall *p.* himself to the   *1Co 14:8*
battle
p. our way to you (B)   *1Th 3:11*
p. me also a lodging: for I   *Ph'm 22*
trust

PREPARED

I have *p.* the house, and room   *Ge 24:31*
for
and the bread, which she had   *Ge 27:17*
p.
neither had they *p.* for   *Ex 12:39*
themselves
into the place which I have   *Ex 23:20*
p.
the city of Sihon be built and   *Nu 21:27*
p.
unto him, I have *p.* seven   *Nu 23:4*
altars
he had *p.* of the children of   *Jos 4:4*
Israel
forty thousand *p.* for war   *Jos 4:13*
passed
p. it for the man (S)   *2Sa 12:4*
Absalom *p.* him chariots and   *2Sa 15:1*
he *p.* him chariots and   *1Ki 1:5*
horsemen
so they *p.* timber and stones   *1Ki 5:18*
the oracle he *p.* in the house   *1Ki 6:19*
within
he *p.* great provision for   *2Ki 6:23*
them
they *p.* it (S)   *2Ki 18:26*
for their brethren had *p.* for   *1Ch 12:39*
them
and *p.* a place for the ark of   *1Ch 15:1*
God
his place, which he had *p.*   *1Ch 15:3*
for it

unto the place that I have *p.* for it	*1Ch 15:12*	
And David *p.* iron in abundance for	*1Ch 22:3*	
So David *p.* abundantly before his	*1Ch 22:5*	
I have *p.* for the house of the Lord	*1Ch 22:14*	
timber also and stone have I *p.*	*1Ch 22:14*	
Now I have *p.* with all my might for	*1Ch 29:2*	
all that I have *p.* for the holy house	*1Ch 29:3*	
we have *p.* to build thee an house	*1Ch 29:16*	
the place which David had *p.* for it	*2Ch 1:4*	
in the place that David had *p.* in	*2Ch 3:1*	
Now all the work of Solomon was *p.*	*2Ch 8:16*	
he *p.* not his heart to seek the Lord	*2Ch 12:14*	
spices *p.* by the apothecaries' art	*2Ch 16:14*	
thousand ready *p.* for the war	*2Ch 17:18*	
hast *p.* thine heart to seek God	*2Ch 19:3*	
people had not *p.* their hearts unto	*2Ch 20:33*	
Uzziah *p.* for them throughout all	*2Ch 26:14*	
p. his ways before the Lord his God	*2Ch 27:6*	
his transgression, have we *p.* and	*2Ch 29:19*	
people, that God had *p.* the people	*2Ch 29:36*	
of the Lord; and they *p.* them	*2Ch 31:11*	
the service was *p.* and the priests	*2Ch 35:10*	
the Levites *p.* for themselves	*2Ch 35:14*	
brethren the Levites *p.* for them	*2Ch 35:15*	
So all the service of the Lord was *p.*	*2Ch 35:16*	
this when Josiah had *p.* the temple	*2Ch 35:20*	
Ezra had *p.* his heart to seek the law	*Ezr 7:10*	
was *p.* for me daily was one ox	*Ne 5:18*	
also the fowls were *p.* for me	*Ne 5:18*	
unto them for whom nothing is *p.*	*Ne 8:10*	
had *p.* for him a great chamber	*Ne 13:5*	
the banquet that I have *p.* for him	*Es 5:4*	
to the banquet that Esther had *p.*	*Es 5:5; 6:14*	
banquet that she had *p.* but myself	*Es 5:12*	
the gallows that he had *p.* for him	*Es 6:4*	
the gallows that he had *p.* for	*Es 7:10*	
it; he *p.* it, yea, and searched it out	*Job 28:27*	
city, when I *p.* my seat in the street	*Job 29:7*	
also *p.* for him the instruments	*Ps 7:13*	
he hath *p.* his throne for judgment	*Ps 9:7*	
They have *p.* a net for my steps	*Ps 57:6*	
God, hast *p.* of thy goodness for	*Ps 68:10*	
thou hast *p.* the light and the sun	*Ps 74:16*	
hath *p.* his throne in the heavens	*Ps 103:19*	
p. a lamp for his anointed (R)	*Ps 132:17*	
When he *p.* the heavens, I was	*Pr 8:27*	
Judgments are *p.* for scorners, and	*Pr 19:29*	
The horse is *p.* against the day of	*Pr 21:31*	
of old; yea, for the king it is *p.*	*Isa 30:33*	
Tophet *p.* language (A)(B)(E)(R)	*Isa 30:33*	
p. for him that waiteth for him	*Isa 64:4*	
bed, and a table *p.* before it	*Eze 23:41*	
thy pipes was *p.* in thee in the day	*Eze 28:13*	

Be thou *p.* and prepare for thyself	*Eze 38:7*
have *p.* lying and corrupt words	*Da 2:9*
and gold, which they *p.* for Baal	*Ho 2:8*
going forth is *p.* as the morning	*Ho 6:3*
p. a great fish to swallow up	*Jon 1:17*
And the Lord God *p.* a gourd	*Jon 4:6*
God *p.* a worm when the morning	*Jon 4:7*
that God *p.* a vehement east wind	*Jon 4:8*
and the defence shall be *p.*	*Na 2:5*
the Lord hath *p.* a sacrifice, he hath	*Zep 1:7*
for whom it is *p.* of my Father	*M't 20:23*
Behold, I have *p.* my dinner: my	*M't 22:4*
inherit the kingdom *p.* for you from	*M't 25:34*
fire, *p.* for the devil and his angels	*M't 25:41*
be given to them for whom it is *p.*	*M'k 10:40*
upper room furnished and *p.*	*M'k 14:15*
ready a people *p.* for the Lord	*Lu 1:17*
p. before the face of all people	*Lu 2:31*
his lord's will, and *p.* not himself	*Lu 12:47*
and *p.* spices and ointments	*Lu 23:56*
the spices which they had *p.*	*Lu 24:1*
which he had afore *p.* unto glory	*Ro 9:23*
hath *p.* for them that love him	*1Co 2:9*
works previously *p.* (B)(E)(R)	*Eph 2:10*
use, and *p.* unto every good work	*2Ti 2:21*
having been *p.* (E)	*Heb 9:6*
these things were thus *p.* (S)	*Heb 9:6*
not, but a body hast thou *p.* me	*Heb 10:5*
p. an ark to the saving of his house	*Heb 11:7*
God: for he hath *p.* for them a city	*Heb 11:16*
trumpets *p.* themselves to sound	*Re 8:6*
like unto horses *p.* unto battle	*Re 9:7*
which were *p.* for an hour, and a	*Re 9:15*
where she hath a place *p.* of God	*Re 12:6*
the kings of the east might be *p.*	*Re 16:12*
p. as a bride adorned for her	*Re 21:2*

PREPAREDST

Thou *p.* room before it, and didst	*Ps 80:9*

PREPARES

p. his way (A)(B)	*Ps 50:23*

PREPAREST

thou *p.* a bullock for a burnt	*Nu 15:8*
Thou *p.* a table before me in	*Ps 23:5*
thou *p.* them corn, when thou	*Ps 65:9*

PREPARETH

That *p.* his heart to seek God, the	*2Ch 30:19*
vanity, and their belly *p.* deceit	*Job 15:35*
who *p.* rain for the earth, who	*Ps 147:8*

PREPARING

in *p.* him a chamber in the courts	*Ne 13:7*
while the ark was a *p.* wherein	*1Pe 3:20*

PRESBYTERY

laying on of the hands of the	*1Ti 4:14*
when elders laid hands upon you (A)(N)(P)(R)	*1Ti 4:14*

PRESCRIBED

as is *p.* (B)	*Ezr 3:4*
who has *p.* his way (R)	*Job 36:23*

grievousness which they have	*Isa 10:1*
Moses *p.* (B)(P)	*M't 8:4; M'k 1:44; Lu 5:14*

PRESCRIBING

and salt without *p.* how much	*Ezr 7:22*

PRESENCE

from the *p.* of the Lord God	*Ge 3:8*
Cain went out from the *p.* of	*Ge 4:16*
dwell in the *p.* of all his brethren	*Ge 16:12*
live in my *p.* (B)	*Ge 17:1*
in the *p.* of the sons of my people	*Ge 23:11*
in *p.* of the people (A)	*Ge 23:13*
in the *p.* of the children of Heth	*Ge 23:18*
died in the *p.* of all his brethren	*Ge 25:18*
out from the *p.* of Isaac his father	*Ge 27:30*
went out from the *p.* of Pharaoh	*Ge 41:46*
for they were troubled at his *p.*	*Ge 45:3*
for why should we die in thy *p.*	*Ge 47:15*
driven out from Pharaoh's *p.* I	*Ex 10:11*
My *p.* shall go with thee, and	*Ex 33:14*
If thy *p.* go not with me, carry us	*Ex 33:15*
departed from the *p.* of Moses	*Ex 35:20*
soul shall be cut off from my *p.*	*Le 22:3*
Moses and Aaron went from the *p.*	*Nu 20:6*
unto him in the *p.* of the elders	*De 25:9*
the priests, in the *p.* of the people	*Jos 4:11*
in the *p.* of the children of Israel	*Jos 8:32*
David avoided out of his *p.* twice	*1Sa 18:11*
he was in his *p.* as in times past	*1Sa 19:7*
he slipped away out of Saul's *p.*	*1Sa 19:10*
to play the mad man in my *p.*	*1Sa 21:15*
I not serve in the *p.* of his son	*2Sa 16:19*
as I have served in thy father's *p.*	*2Sa 16:19*
so will I be in thy *p.*	*2Sa 16:19*
went out from the *p.* of the king, to	*2Sa 24:4*
And she came into the king's *p.*	*1Ki 1:28*
in the *p.* of all the congregation	*1Ki 8:22*
fled from the *p.* of king Solomon	*1Ki 12:2*
against Naboth in the *p.* of	*1Ki 21:13*
that I regard the *p.* of Jehoshaphat	*2Ki 3:14*
his *p.* a leper as white as snow	*2Ki 5:27*
cast he them from his *p.* as yet	*2Ki 13:23*
he had cast them out from his *p.*	*2Ki 24:20*
of them that were in the king's *p.*	*2Ki 25:19*
Glory and honour are in his *p.*	*1Ch 16:27*
wood sing out at the *p.* of the Lord	*1Ch 16:33*
recorded them in the *p.* of (S)	*1Ch 24:6*
Aaron in the *p.* of David the king	*1Ch 24:31*
the *p.* of all the congregation of	*2Ch 6:12*
earth sought the *p.* of Solomon	*2Ch 9:23*
from the *p.* of Solomon the king	*2Ch 10:2*
and in thy *p.* (for thy name is in	*2Ch 20:9*
down the altars of Baalim in his *p.*	*2Ch 34:4*
not been beforetime sad in his *p.*	*Ne 2:1*

in the *p.* of Ahasuerus the   Es 1:10
king
went out from the *p.* of the   Es 8:15
king
went forth from the *p.* of the   Job 1:12
Lord
Satan forth from the *p.* of the   Job 2:7
Lord
Therefore am I troubled at   Job 23:15
his *p.*
they shall fall and perish at thy   Ps 9:3
p.
of life: in thy *p.* is fulness of   Ps 16:11
joy
sentence come forth from thy   Ps 17:2
p.
joy by the *p.* (A)(B)(E)(R)   Ps 21:6
me in the *p.* of mine enemies   Ps 23:5
hide them in the secret of thy   Ps 31:20
p.
Cast me not away from thy   Ps 51:11
p.; and
the wicked perish at the *p.* of   Ps 68:2
God
also dropped at the *p.* of God   Ps 68:8
itself was moved at the *p.* of   Ps 68:8
God
before his *p.* with thanksgiving   Ps 95:2
like wax at the *p.* of the Lord   Ps 97:5
p. of the Lord of the whole   Ps 97:5
earth
come before his *p.* with   Ps 100:2
singing
thou earth, at the *p.* of the   Ps 114:7
Lord
at the *p.* of the God of Jacob   Ps 114:7
Lord now in the *p.* of all   Ps 116:14;
his people   116:18
whither shall I flee from thy *p.*   Ps 139:7
the upright shall dwell in thy   Ps 140:13
p.
Go from the *p.* of a foolish   Pr 14:7
man
surety in the *p.* of his friend   Pr 17:18
forth thyself in the *p.* of the   Pr 25:6
king
be put lower in the *p.* of the   Pr 25:7
prince
strangers devour it in your   Isa 1:7
p. and
of Egypt shall be moved at   Isa 19:1
his *p.*
and the angel of his *p.* saved   Isa 63:9
them
mountains might flow at thy   Isa 64:1
p.
the nations may tremble at   Isa 64:2
thy *p.*
mountains flowed down at thy   Isa 64:3
p.
broken down at the *p.* of the   Jer 4:26
Lord
will ye not tremble at my *p.*   Jer 5:22
which
fathers, and cast you out of   Jer 23:39
my *p.*
the *p.* of the priests and of all   Jer 28:1
Hananiah in the *p.* of the   Jer 28:5
priests
and in the *p.* of all the people   Jer 28:5
that
spake in the *p.* of all the   Jer 28:11
people
and in the *p.* of the witnesses   Jer 32:12
that
he had cast them out from his   Jer 52:3
p.
of the earth, shall shake at   Eze 38:20
my *p.*
answered in the *p.* of the king   Da 2:27
Tarshish from the *p.* of the   Jon 1:3
Lord
he fled from the *p.* of the   Jon 1:10
Lord
and the earth is burned at his   Na 1:5
p.
thy peace at the *p.* of the Lord   Zep 1:7
God
that stand in the *p.* of God   Lu 1:19
We have eaten and drunk in   Lu 13:26
thy *p.*
in the *p.* of them that sit at   Lu 14:10
meal
there is joy in the *p.* of the   Lu 15:10
angels
did Jesus in the *p.* of his   Joh 20:30
disciples
and denied him in the *p.* of   Ac 3:13
Pilate
soundness in the *p.* of you all   Ac 3:16

come from the *p.* of the Lord   Ac 3:19
departed from the *p.* of the   Ac 5:41
council
thanks to God in the *p.* of   Ac 27:35
them
That no flesh should glory in   1Co 1:29
his *p.*
who in *p.* am base among   2Co 10:1
you
but his bodily *p.* is weak,   2Co 10:10
and his
always obeyed, not as in my   Ph'p 2:12
p. only
from you for a short time in   1Th 2:17
p.
in the *p.* of our Lord Jesus   1Th 2:19
Christ
from the *p.* of the Lord, and   2Th 1:9
from
to appear in the *p.* of God   Heb 9:24
for us
faultless before the *p.* of his   Jude 24
glory
shelter with his *p.* (A)(E)(R)   Re 7:15
in the *p.* of the holy angels,   Re 14:10
and in
angels, and in the *p.* of the   Re 14:10
Lamb

PRESENT

Ephron *p.* among sons of   Ge 23:10
Heth (A)
came to his hand a *p.* for   Ge 32:13
Esau
it is a *p.* sent unto my lord   Ge 32:18
Esau
I will appease him with the   Ge 32:20
p. that
So went the *p.* over before   Ge 32:21
him: and
then receive my *p.* at my   Ge 33:10
hand; for
carry down the man a *p.* a   Ge 43:11
little
the men took that *p.* and   Ge 43:15
they took
made ready the *p.* against   Ge 43:25
Joseph
brought him the *p.* which   Ge 43:26
was in
give a marriage *p.* (R)   Ex 22:16
Sinai, and *p.* thyself there to   Ex 34:2
me
p. the man that is to be made   Le 14:11
goats, and *p.* them before the   Le 16:7
Lord
shall *p.* himself before the   Le 27:8
priest
shall *p.* the beast before the   Le 27:11
priest
p. them before Aaron the   Nu 3:6
priest
p. yourselves in the   De 31:14
tabernacle of
sent a *p.* unto Eglon the king   J'g 3:15
of
he brought the *p.* unto Eglon   J'g 3:17
king
he had made an end to offer   J'g 3:18
the *p.*
away the people that bare the   J'g 3:18
p.
bring forth my *p.* and set it   J'g 6:18
before
is not a *p.* to bring to the man   1Sa 9:7
of
p. yourselves before the   1Sa 10:19
Lord by
the people that were *p.* with   1Sa 13:15
him
the people that were *p.* with   1Sa 13:16
in mine hand, or what there   1Sa 21:3
is *p.*
a *p.* for you of the spoil of   1Sa 30:26
a *p.* from the king (S)   2Sa 11:8
three days, and be thou here   2Sa 20:4
p.
a *p.* unto his daughter,   1Ki 9:16
Solomon's
they brought every man his   1Ki 10:25
p.
unto thee a *p.* of silver and   1Ki 15:19
gold
were numbered and were all   1Ki 20:27
p.
Take a *p.* in thine hand, and   2Ki 8:8
go

took a *p.* with him, even of   2Ki 8:9
every
it for a *p.* to the king of   2Ki 16:8
Assyria
no *p.* to the king of Assyria,   2Ki 17:4
as he
an agreement with me by a   2Ki 18:31
p.
letters and a *p.* unto   2Ki 20:12
Hezekiah
joy thy people, which are *p.*   1Ch 29:17
here
all the priests *p.* were   2Ch 5:11
sanctified
they brought every man his   2Ch 9:24
p.
all that were *p.* with him   2Ch 29:29
bowed
that were *p.* at Jerusalem   2Ch 30:21
kept the
all Israel that were *p.* went   2Ch 31:1
out to
all that were *p.* in Jerusalem   2Ch 34:32
all that were *p.* in Israel to   2Ch 34:33
serve
for all that were *p.* to the   2Ch 35:7
number
that were *p.* kept the   2Ch 35:17
passover at
all Judah and Israel that   2Ch 35:18
were *p.*
all Israel there *p.* had offered   Ezr 8:25
the people that were *p.* in   Es 1:5
Shushan
all the Jews that are *p.* in   Es 4:16
Shushan
to *p.* themselves before the   Job 1:6;
Lord   2:1
them to *p.* himself before the   Job 2:1
Lord
offer a *p.* for me (E)   Job 6:22
strength, a very *p.* help in   Ps 46:1
trouble
the *p.* be brought unto the   Isa 18:7
Lord of
an agreement with me by a   Isa 36:16
p.
sent letters and a *p.* to   Isa 39:1
Hezekiah
p. their supplication before the   Jer 36:7
ye sent me to *p.* your   Jer 42:9
supplication
for a *p.* horns of ivory and   Eze 27:15
ebony
p. our supplications before   Da 9:18
thee
p. our petitions (B)   Da 9:18;
   9:23; 1Ti 2:1; 5:5; Heb 5:7
Assyria for a *p.* to king Jareb   Ho 10:6
Jerusalem, to *p.* him to the   Lu 2:22
Lord
of the Lord was *p.* to heal   Lu 5:17
them
There were *p.* at that season   Lu 13:1
some
receive manifold more in this   Lu 18:30
p. time
unto you, being yet *p.* with   Joh 14:25
you
predicted this *p.* time (N)   Ac 3:24
are we all here *p.* before   Ac 10:33
God, to
James; and all the elders   Ac 21:18
were *p.*
all men which are here *p.*   Ac 25:24
with us
because of the *p.* rain, and   Ac 28:2
because
for to will is *p.* with me; but   Ro 7:18
how
would do good, evil is *p.* with   Ro 7:21
me
sufferings of this *p.* time are   Ro 8:18
not
nor things *p.* nor things to   Ro 8:38
come
then at this *p.* time also there   Ro 11:5
is a
ye *p.* your bodies a living   Ro 12:1
sacrifice
or things *p.* or things to   1Co 3:22
come
unto this *p.* hour we both   1Co 4:11
hunger
as absent in body, but *p.* in   1Co 5:3
spirit
have judged as though I   1Co 5:3
were *p.*
that this is good for the *p.*   1Co 7:26
distress

greater part remain unto this *1Co 15:6*
p.
by Jesus, and shall *p.* us with *2Co 4:14*
you
body, and to be *p.* with the *2Co 5:8*
Lord
that, whether *p.* or absent, we *2Co 5:9*
may
when I am *p.* with that *2Co 10:2*
confidence
we be also in deed when we *2Co 10:11*
are *p.*
I may *p.* you as a chaste *2Co 11:2*
virgin to
And when I was *p.* with you *2Co 11:9*
as if I were *p.* the second *2Co 13:2*
time
being *p.* I should use *2Co 13:10*
sharpness
deliver us from this *p.* evil *Ga 1:4*
world
not only when I am *p.* with *Ga 1:18*
you
I desire to be *p.* with you *Ga 4:20*
now, and
p. it to himself a glorious *Eph 5:27*
church
p. you holy and unblameable *Col 1:22*
may *p.* every man perfect in *Col 1:28*
Christ
that the day of Christ is *p.* *2Th 2:2*
(S)
me, having loved this *p.* world *2Ti 4:10*
and godly, in this *p.* world *Tit 2:12*
was a figure for the time then *Heb 9:9*
p.
a picture of the *p.* age (A)(P) *Heb 9:9*
no chastening for the *p.* *Heb 12:11*
seemeth
and be established in the *p.* *2Pe 1:12*
truth
and to *p.* you faultless before *Jude 24*

PRESENTED

p. me with rich dowry (B) *Ge 30:20*
Goshen, and *p.* himself unto *Ge 46:29*
him
men, and *p.* them unto *Ge 47:2*
Pharaoh
when it is *p.* unto the priest, he *Le 2:8*
p. them to minister unto the *Le 7:35*
Lord
sons *p.* unto him the blood *Le 9:12*
they *p.* the burnt offering unto *Le 9:13*
him
sons *p.* unto him the blood *Le 9:18*
be the scapegoat, shall be *p.* *Le 16:10*
alive
p. themselves in the *De 31:14*
tabernacle of
and they *p.* themselves before *Jos 24:1*
God
unto him under the oak, and *J'g 6:19*
p. it
p. themselves in the assembly *J'g 20:2*
of
evening, and *p.* himself forty *1Sa 17:16*
days
I *p.* my supplication before *Jer 38:26*
they *p.* the provocation of *Eze 20:28*
their
p. offering that provoked *Eze 20:28*
(A)
treasures, they *p.* unto him *M't 2:11*
gifts
saints and widows, *p.* her alive *Ac 9:41*
governor, *p.* Paul also before *Ac 23:33*
him

PRESENTING

p. my supplication before the *Da 9:20*
Lord

PRESENTLY

Let them not fail to burn the *1Sa 2:16*
fat *p.*
A fool's wrath is *p.* known: *Pr 12:16*
but a
And *p.* the fig tree withered *M't 21:19*
away
shall *p.* give me more than *M't 26:53*
twelve
Him therefore I hope to send *Ph'p 2:23*
p.

PRESENTS

accepted *p.*; trusted justice *1Sa 8:3*
(B)
him, and brought him no *p.* *1Sa 10:27*
brought *p.* and served *1Ki 4:21*
Solomon
his servant, and gave him *p.* *2Ki 17:3*
Judah brought to *2Ch 17:5*
Jehoshaphat *p.*
brought Jehoshaphat *p.* and *2Ch 17:11*
and *p.* to Hezekiah king of *2Ch 32:23*
Judah
shall kings bring *p.* unto thee *Ps 68:29*
and of the isles shall bring *p.* *Ps 72:10*
bring *p.* unto him that ought *Ps 76:11*
to be
thou give *p.* to *Mic 1:14*
Moresheth-gath

PRESERVE

we may *p.* seed of our *Ge 19:32;*
father *19:34*
to perpetuate our family (B) *Ge 19:32*
did send me before you to *p.* *Ge 45:5*
life
to save your life (B) *Ge 45:5*
to *p.* you a posterity in the *Ge 45:7*
earth
to assure you continuance on *Ge 45:7*
earth (B)
to *p.* a remnant (E)(R) *Ge 45:7*
that he might *p.* us alive, as it *De 6:24*
is
that he might keep us alive *De 6:24*
(B)
may *p.* your life (B) *1Ki 1:12*
p. them from this generation *Ps 12:7*
for
guard them from this *Ps 12:7*
generation (B)(R)
P. me, O God: for in thee do *Ps 16:1*
I put
Keep and protect me (A) *Ps 16:1*
integrity and uprightness *p.* *Ps 25:21*
me
thou shalt *p.* me from trouble *Ps 32:7*
and thy truth continually *p.* *Ps 40:11*
me
The Lord will *p.* him, and *Ps 41:2*
keep
and truth, which may *p.* him *Ps 61:7*
p. my life from fear of the *Ps 64:1*
enemy
guard my life (B) *Ps 64:1*
p. thou those that are *Ps 79:11*
appointed to
P. my soul: for I am holy: O *Ps 86:2*
thou
keep my life (B) *Ps 86:2*
The Lord shall *p.* thee from *Ps 121:7*
all evil
Lord will keep from all evil *Ps 121:7*
(A)(B)(E)(R)
he shall *p.* thy soul *Ps 121:7*
Lord shall *p.* thy going out *Ps 121:8*
and thy
Lord will keep your going out *Ps 121:8*
(A)(E)(R)
Lord will shield your going *Ps 121:8*
out (B)
man: *p.* me from the violent *Ps 140:1*
man
wicked: *p.* me from the violent *Ps 140:4*
man
protect me from violent men *Ps 140:4*
(B)
Discretion shall *p.* thee *Pr 2:11*
Discretion shall watch over *Pr 2:11*
you (A)(E)(R)
discretion will protect you (B) *Pr 2:11*
her not, and she shall *p.* thee *Pr 4:6*
she will keep, defend, and *Pr 4:6*
protect (A)
she shall protect you (B) *Pr 4:6*
she will keep you (R) *Pr 4:6*
the lips of the wise shall *p.* *Pr 14:3*
them
Mercy and truth *p.* the king *Pr 20:28*
The eyes of the Lord *p.* *Pr 22:12*
knowledge
eyes of Lord keep guard over *Pr 22:12*
knowledge (A)
eyes of the Lord protect *Pr 22:12*
knowledge (B)
eyes of Lord keep watch over *Pr 22:12*
knowledge (R)
it; and passing over he will *p.* *Isa 31:5*
it

and I will *p.* thee, and give *Isa 49:8*
thee
I will protect you and make *Isa 49:8*
(B)
I have kept you and given you *Isa 49:8*
(R)
children, I will *p.* them alive *Jer 49:11*
shall lose his life shall *p.* it *Lu 17:33*
whoever loses it shall *Lu 17:33*
revitalize it (B)
whoever loses it shall save it *Lu 17:33*
(N)
p. me unto his heavenly *2Ti 4:18*
kingdom
he will save me for his *2Ti 4:18*
kingdom (B)(E)(R)
keep me safe until his *2Ti 4:18*
kingdom (N)(P)

PRESERVED

God face to face, and my life *Ge 32:30*
is *p.*
my life is spared (A) *Ge 32:30*
p. us in all the way wherein *Jos 24:17*
we
protecting us through our *Jos 24:17*
whole journey (B)
who hath *p.* us, and *1Sa 30:23*
delivered the
p. David whithersoever he *2Sa 8:6;*
8:14; 1Ch 18:6, 13
gave David victory every where *2Sa 8:6;*
he went (B)(E)(R) *8:14; 1Ch 18:6, 13*
thy visitation hath *p.* my *Job 10:12*
spirit
as in the days when God *p.* *Job 29:2*
me
When his lamp shone above *Job 29:2*
my head (A)(E)
days when God protected me *Job 29:2*
(B)
days when God watched over *Job 29:2*
me (R)
they are *p.* for ever; but the *Ps 37:28*
seed
and to restore the *p.* of Israel *Isa 49:6*
Egypt, and by a prophet was *Ho 12:13*
he *p.*
by a prophet he was *Ho 12:13*
shepherded (B)
into new bottles, and both *M't 9:17;*
are *p.* *Lu 5:38*
be *p.* blameless unto the *1Th 5:23*
coming
maintained blameless (B) *1Th 5:23*
keep you sound in spirit (N) *1Th 5:23*
be kept in spotless integrity *1Th 5:23*
(P)
kept sound and blameless *1Th 5:23*
(R)
and *p.* in Jesus Christ, and *Jude 1*
called
kept for Jesus Christ *Jude 1*
(A)(B)(E)(P)(R)
safe keeping of Jesus Christ *Jude 1*
(N)

PRESERVER

I do unto thee, O thou *p.* of *Job 7:20*
men
you watcher and keeper of *Job 7:20*
men (A)
thou watcher of men *Job 7:20*
(B)(E)(R)

PRESERVEST

is therein, and thou *p.* them all *Ne 9:6*
O Lord, thou *p.* man and beast *Ps 36:6*
does not prolong life of *Ps 36:6*
wicked (A)(B)
does not keep the wicked alive *Ps 36:6*
(R)

PRESERVETH

He *p.* not the life of the *Job 36:6*
wicked
for the Lord *p.* the faithful *Ps 31:23*
he *p.* the souls of his saints; *Ps 97:10*
he
The Lord *p.* the simple: I *Ps 116:6*
was
Lord takes care of the *Ps 116:6*
helpless (B)
The Lord *p.* all them that *Ps 145:20*
love him
Lord protects those who *Ps 145:20*
love him (B)

The Lord *p.* the strangers; he   *Ps 146:9*
Lord protects the immigrants   *Ps 146:9*
(B)
Lord watches over the   *Ps 146:9*
sojourners (R)
and *p.* the way of his saints   *Pr 2:8*
protects the way of his saints   *Pr 2:8*
(B)
he that keepeth his way *p.* his   *Pr 16:17*
soul
guards his life takes heed to   *Pr 16:17*
his way (B)

PRESIDENTS

And over these three *p.*; of   *Da 6:2*
whom
preferred above the *p.* and   *Da 6:3*
princes
the *p.* and princes sought to   *Da 6:4*
find
these *p.* and princes assembled   *Da 6:6*
All the *p.* of the kingdom, the   *Da 6:7*

PRESS

you may *p.* for payment (B)   *De 15:3*
the *p.* of the battle (R)   *Isa 21:15*
for the *p.* is full, the vats   *Joe 3:13*
overflow
draw out fifty vessels out of   *Hag 2:16*
the *p.*
not come nigh unto him for   *M'k 2:4*
the *p.*
came in the *p.* behind, and   *M'k 5:27*
touched
him, turned him about in the   *M'k 5:30*
p.
could not come at him for the   *Lu 8:19*
p.
multitude throng thee and *p.*   *Lu 8:45*
thee
could not for the *p.* because   *Lu 19:3*
he
I *p.* toward the mark for the   *Ph'p 3:14*
prize

PRESSED

And he *p.* upon them greatly   *Ge 19:3*
they *p.* sore upon the man,   *Ge 19:9*
even
and *p.* them into Pharaoh's   *Ge 40:11*
cup
hand of Israel *p.* heavier (B)   *J'g 4:24*
p. him greatly (S)   *J'g 14:17*
she *p.* him daily with her   *J'g 16:16*
words
he *p.* him: howbeit he   *2Sa 13:25*
would not
But Absalom *p.* him, that he   *2Sa 13:27*
let
p. on the king's   *Es 8:14*
commandment
there were their breasts *p.*   *Eze 23:3*
Behold, I am *p.* under you, as   *Am 2:13*
a
as a cart is *p.* that is full of   *Am 2:13*
sheaves
p. him into service (N)   *M't 27:32*
they *p.* upon him for to   *M'k 3:10*
touch him
they *p.* him into service (N)   *M'k 15:21*
people *p.* upon him to hear the   *Lu 5:1*
good measure, *p.* down, and   *Lu 6:38*
shaken
they *p.* him (N)   *Lu 24:29*
Paul was *p.* in the spirit, and   *Ac 18:5*
that we were *p.* out of   *2Co 1:8*
measure
hard *p.* on every side (E)(N)   *2Co 4:8*

PRESSES

thy harvest and *p.*   *Ex 22:29*
(E)(R)(S)
treading wine *p.* on the   *Ne 13:15*
sabbath
p. shall burst out with new   *Pr 3:10*
wine
vats be overflowing with new   *Pr 3:10*
wine (A)(B)(E)(R)
shall tread out no wine in   *Isa 16:10*
their *p.*
wine in the pressing trough   *Isa 16:10*
(B)

PRESSETH

in me, and thy hand *p.* me   *Ps 38:2*
sore

---

preached, and every man *p.*   *Lu 16:16*
into it
strives violently to go in (A)   *Lu 16:16*
everyone forces into it   *Lu 16:16*
(B)(N)
every man enters violently   *Lu 16:16*
into it (E)(R)
men are forcing their way   *Lu 16:16*
into it (P)

PRESSFAT

one came to the *p.* for to   *Hag 2:16*
draw
gone to the winevat   *Hag 2:16*
(A)(B)(E)(R)

PRESUME

shall *p.* to speak a word in   *De 18:20*
my
that durst *p.* in his heart to do   *Es 7:5*
so
p. to ask him (B)   *M't 22:46*
p. upon riches (A)(R)   *Ro 2:4*
did not *p.* to condemn (N)(R)   *Jude 9*

PRESUMED

they *p.* to go up unto the hill   *Nu 14:44*
top

PRESUMPTION

p. and evilness (A)   *1Sa 17:28*

PRESUMPTUOUS

thy servant also from *p.* sins   *Ps 19:13*
P. are they, selfwilled, they   *2Pe 2:10*
are
headstrong as they are (B)   *2Pe 2:10*
Daring, self-willed (E)   *2Pe 2:10*
reckless, self-willed (N)   *2Pe 2:10*
Bold and wilfull (R)   *2Pe 2:10*

PRESUMPTUOUSLY

man come *p.* upon his   *Ex 21:14*
neighbour
comes wilfully upon another   *Ex 21:14*
(A)(R)
resentful against his neighbor   *Ex 21:14*
(B)
But the soul that doeth   *Nu 15:30*
ought *p.*
person who does anything   *Nu 15:30*
wilfully (A)
who defiantly rebels (B)   *Nu 15:30*
doeth aught with a high   *Nu 15:30*
hand (E)(R)
and went *p.* up into the hill   *De 1:43*
you rebelled against the Lord   *De 1:43*
(B)
And the man that will do *p.*   *De 17:12*
and fear, and do no more *p.*   *De 17:13*
never again act so recklessly   *De 17:13*
(B)
the prophet hath spoken it *p.*   *De 18:22*

PRETENCE

and for a *p.* make long   *M't 23:14*
prayer
professing that you pray   *M't 23:14*
long (B)
for a *p.* make long prayers;   *M'k 12:40*
these
whether in *p.* or in truth,   *Ph'p 1:18*
Christ is

PRETEND

p. that thou art sick (S)   *2Sa 13:5*
p. to be a mourner (S)   *2Sa 14:2;*
   1Ki 14:5
why *p.* to be another   *1Ki 14:6*
(A)(B)(R)

PRETENDED

p. that he was sick (S)   *2Sa 13:6*

PRETENDERS

nor fellowship with *p.* (A)(B)   *Ps 26:4*

PRETENDEST

why *p.* thou to be another   *1Ki 14:6*
(S)

PRETENDS

p. with his lips (A)(B)   *Pr 26:24*

PRETENSE

returned in *p.* (B)(R)   *Jer 3:10*
full of *p.* (A)(P)   *M't 23:28*
stand without *p.* before   *2Co 5:10*
Christ (P)

PRETENTIONS

p. of liars (R)   *1Ti 4:2*

PRETEXT

some *p.* after money (B)   *1Th 2:5*
as a *p.* for wickedness (A)   *1Pe 2:16*
a *p.* for evil (R)   *1Pe 2:16*

PRETEXTS

seeks *p.* against sound wisdom   *Pr 18:1*
(B)

PREVAIL

cubits upward did the waters   *Ge 7:20*
p.
became higher arose (A)(B)   *Ge 7:20*
peradventure I shall *p.* that   *Nu 22:6*
we
what means we may *p.* against   *J'g 16:5*
him
may overpower him   *J'g 16:5*
(A)(B)(R)
for by strength shall no man *p.*   *1Sa 2:9*
no human power renders   *1Sa 2:9*
mighty (B)
but if I *p.* against him, and   *1Sa 17:9*
kill him
great things, and also shalt   *1Sa 26:25*
still *p.*
you will succeed (B)(R)   *1Sa 26:25*
shalt persuade him, and *p.*   *1Ki 22:22*
also
God; let not man *p.* against   *2Ch 14:11*
thee
entice him, and thou shalt   *2Ch 18:21*
also *p.*
entice him, and also succeed   *2Ch 18:21*
(A)(B)(R)
thou shalt not *p.* against him   *Es 6:13*
you are powerless against him   *Es 6:13*
(B)
they shall *p.* against him, as   *Job 15:24*
a king
they overwhelm him (B)   *Job 15:24*
the robber shall *p.* against   *Job 18:9*
him
Arise, O Lord; let not man *p.*:   *Ps 9:19*
let
With our tongue will we *p.*   *Ps 12:4*
Iniquities *p.* against me: as for   *Ps 65:3*
Iniquities got the better of me   *Ps 65:3*
(B)
if one *p.* against him, two   *Ec 4:12*
shall
it, but could not *p.* against it   *Isa 7:1*
could not conquer it   *Isa 7:1*
(A)(B)(R)
to pray; but he shall not *p.*   *Isa 16:12*
it shall avail him nothing (B)   *Isa 16:12*
he shall *p.* against his   *Isa 42:13*
enemies
he will do mightily (A)(E)   *Isa 42:13*
he proves himself mighty   *Isa 42:13*
(B)(R)
to profit, if so be thou   *Isa 47:12*
mayest *p.*
perhaps you will be able to   *Isa 47:12*
profit (A)(B)(E)
perhaps you will be able to   *Isa 47:12*
succeed (R)
but they shall not *p.* against   *Jer 1:19*
thee
they shall not overcome you   *Jer 1:19*
(B)
themselves, yet can they not *p.*   *Jer 5:22*
they shall not *p.* against   *Jer 15:20*
thee: for I
enticed, and we shall *p.*   *Jer 20:10*
against him
we shall overcome him   *Jer 20:10*
(B)(R)
stumble, and they shall not   *Jer 20:11*
p.
deal against them, and shall *p.*   *Da 11:7*

active against him and   *Da 11:7*
conquer (B)
gates of hell shall not *p.*   *M't 16:18*
against
gates of hades shall not   *M't 16:18*
overpower it (A)(N)
gates of hell shall not hold   *M't 16:18*
out against her (B)
Pilate saw he could *p.*   *M't 27:24*
nothing
saw he was getting nowhere   *M't 27:24*
(A)(B)
saw nothing was being   *M't 27:24*
gained (N)
realized nothing more could   *M't 27:24*
be done (P)
saw he was gaining nothing   *M't 27:24*
(R)
may *p.* to escape (E)   *Lu 21:36*
Perceive ye how ye *p.*   *Joh 12:19*
nothing
how you accomplish nothing   *Joh 12:19*
(A)
how you are getting nowhere   *Joh 12:19*
(B)
you are doing no good at all   *Joh 12:19*
(N)
There is nothing one can do   *Joh 12:19*
(P)
you see you can do nothing   *Joh 12:19*
(R)

PREVAILED

the waters *p.* and were   *Ge 7:18*
increased
waters became mighty (A)   *Ge 7:18*
waters keep mounting (B)   *Ge 7:18*
the waters *p.* exceedingly upon   *Ge 7:19*
And the waters *p.* upon the   *Ge 7:24*
earth
with my sister, and I have *p.*   *Ge 30:8*
I have won out (B)   *Ge 30:8;*
    32:28
he saw that he *p.* not against   *Ge 32:25*
him
with God and with men, and   *Ge 32:28*
has *p.*
because the famine *p.* over   *Ge 47:20*
them
blessings of thy father have   *Ge 49:26*
p.
held up his hand, that Israel   *Ex 17:11*
p.
gained the upper hand (B)   *Ex 17:11*
he let down his hand,   *Ex 17:11*
Amalek *p.*
the hand of the house of   *J'g 1:35*
Joseph *p.*
p. against Chushan-rishathaim   *J'g 3:10*
and *p.* against Jabin the king   *J'g 4:24*
of
hand of Midian *p.* against   *J'g 6:2*
Israel
So David *p.* over the   *1Sa 17:50*
Philistine
David did conquer the   *1Sa 17:50*
Philistine (B)
Surely the men *p.* against us   *2Sa 11:23*
the king's word *p.* against   *2Sa 24:4*
Joab
the people that followed   *1Ki 16:22*
Omri *p.*
the famine *p.* in the city, and   *2Ki 25:3*
there
For Judah *p.* above his   *1Ch 5:2*
brethren
the king's word *p.* against   *1Ch 21:4*
Joab
to Hamath-zobah, and *p.*   *2Ch 8:3*
against it
children of Judah *p.*   *2Ch 13:18*
because they
Ammonites, and *p.* against   *2Ch 27:5*
them
enemy say, I have *p.* against   *Ps 13:4*
him
I have overpowered him (B)   *Ps 13:4*
yet they have not *p.* against   *Ps 129:2*
me
art stronger than I, and   *Jer 20:7*
hast *p.*
thee on, and have *p.* against   *Jer 38:22*
thee
desolate, because the enemy *p.*   *La 1:16*
the saints, and *p.* against them   *Da 7:21*
had power over the angel, and   *Ho 12:4*
p.
deceived thee, and *p.* against   *Ob 7*
thee

---

them and of the chief priests   *Lu 23:23*
she *p.* upon us (R)   *Ac 16:15*
p. against them, so that they   *Ac 19:16*
fled
grew the word of God, and   *Ac 19:20*
p.
word of the Lord extend and   *Ac 19:20*
intensify (B)
spreading widely and   *Ac 19:20*
effectively (N)
grow irresistibly in power and   *Ac 19:20*
influence (P)
David hath *p.* to open the book   *Re 5:5*
has overcome and conquered   *Re 5:5*
(A)
has conquered to open the   *Re 5:5*
book (B)(R)
hath overcome to open the   *Re 5:5*
book (E)
has won the right to open (N)   *Re 5:5*
has won the victory to open (P)   *Re 5:5*
p. not; neither was their   *Re 12:8*
place
they were defeated (A)(R)   *Re 12:8*
they were not strong enough   *Re 12:8*
(B)
they had not the strength to   *Re 12:8*
win (N)

PREVAILEST

Thou *p.* for ever against him   *Job 14:20*

PREVAILETH

my bones, and it *p.* against   *La 1:13*
them

PREVENT

planned to *p.* us (A)(B)(R)   *2Sa 21:5*
Why did the knees *p.* me? or   *Job 3:12*
why
Why did the knees receive me   *Job 3:12*
(A)(B)(E)(R)
The God of my mercy shall   *Ps 59:10*
p. me
God will meet me   *Ps 59:10*
(A)(B)(E)(R)
thy tender mercies speedily *p.*   *Ps 79:8*
us
mercies come to meet us   *Ps 79:8*
(A)(B)(E)(R)
morning shall my prayer *p.*   *Ps 88:13*
thee
my eyes *p.* the night   *Ps 119:148*
watches
My eyes anticipate the   *Ps 119:148*
night watches (A)(E)
My eyes waited for the   *Ps 119:148*
night watches (B)
my eyes are awake before   *Ps 119:148*
the night (R)
evil shall not overtake nor *p.*   *Am 9:10*
us
evil not overtake or meet us   *Am 9:10*
(A)(E)(R)
harm will not soon approach   *Am 9:10*
(B)
shall not *p.* them which are   *1Th 4:15*
asleep
in no way precede those   *1Th 4:15*
asleep (A)
not at all take precedence   *1Th 4:15*
over those (B)
precede fallen asleep   *1Th 4:15*
(E)(P)(R)
shall not forestall those who   *1Th 4:15*
have died (N)

PREVENTED

about; the snares of death *p.*   *2Sa 22:6*
me
I encountered the snares of   *2Sa 22:6,*
death (A)   *18:5*
snares of death blocked me   *2Sa 22:6;*
(B)   *18:18*
snares of death came upon   *2Sa 22:6*
me (E)
snares of death confronted   *2Sa 22:6*
me (R)
p. me in the day of my   *2Sa 22:19*
calamity
They came upon me in the   *2Sa 22:19*
day (A)(E)(R)
blocked me when I was   *2Sa 22:19*
distressed (B)
not: the days of affliction *p.*   *Job 30:27*
me

---

days of affliction came to   *Job 30:27*
meet me (A)(R)
affliction has overtaken me   *Job 30:27*
(B)
affliction came upon me (E)   *Job 30:27*
Who hath *p.* me, that I should   *Job 41:11*
about: the snares of death *p.*   *Ps 18:5*
me
They *p.* me in the day of my   *Ps 18:18*
I *p.* the dawning of the   *Ps 119:147*
morning
I anticipated the dawning   *Ps 119:147*
(A)(E)
I was up before dawn   *Ps 119:147*
(B)(R)
p. with their bread him that   *Isa 21:14*
fled
meet the fugitive with bread   *Isa 21:14*
(A)(B)(E)(R)
come into the house, Jesus   *M't 17:25*
p. him
Jesus spoke to him first   *M't 17:25*
(A)(E)(R)
Jesus forestalled him   *M't 17:25*
(B)(N)
Jesus anticipated what he   *M't 17:25*
was going to say (P)
I was *p.* thus far (S)   *Ro 1:13*

PREVENTEST

thou *p.* him with the blessings   *Ps 21:3*

PREVIOUS

p. career in Judaism (B)(R)   *Ga 1:13;*
    1:14

PREVIOUSLY

previously (S)   *1Sa 9:9;*
    10:11; Ac 8:9
where *p.* they laid the meat   *Ne 13:5*
(S)
as he did *p.* (S)   *Da 6:10*
works *p.* prepared   *Eph 2:19*
(B)(E)(R)

PREY

from the *p.* my son, thou art   *Ge 49:9*
gone
morning he shall devour the   *Ge 49:27*
p.
and our children should be a   *Nu 14:3*
p.
ones, which ye said should be   *Nu 14:31*
a *p.*
not lie down until he eat of   *Nu 23:24*
the *p.*
prey (E)   *Nu 31:9;*
    Job 29:17; Jer 20:5; Zep 2:9
took all the spoil, and all the   *Nu 31:11*
p.
brought the captives, and the   *Nu 31:12*
Take the sum of the *p.* that   *Nu 31:26*
was
And divide the *p.* into two   *Nu 31:27*
parts
the *p.* which the men of war   *Nu 31:32*
had
ones, which ye said, should be   *De 1:39*
a *p.*
we took for a *p.* unto ourselves   *De 2:35*
cities, we took for a *p.* to   *De 3:7*
ourselves
ye take for a *p.* unto   *Jos 8:2*
yourselves
Israel look for a *p.* unto   *Jos 8:27;*
themselves   *11:14*
have they not divided the *p.*;   *J'g 5:30*
to
to Sisera a *p.* of divers colours   *J'g 5:30*
p. of divers colours of   *J'g 5:30*
needlework
every man the earrings of his   *J'g 8:24;*
p.   *8:25*
they shall become a *p.* and a   *2Ki 21:14*
spoil
for a *p.* in the land of captivity   *Ne 4:4*
to take the spoil of them for a   *Es 3:13;*
p.   *8:11*
on the *p.* they laid not their   *Es 9:15*
hand
they laid not their hands on   *Es 9:16*
the *p.*
old lion perisheth for lack of   *Job 4:11*
p.

as the eagle that hasteth to the *p*.   *Job 9:26*

work; rising betimes for a *p*.   *Job 24:5*

prey (A)(B)(R)(S)   *Job 29:17;*
   Jer 50:10; Zep 2:9

Wilt thou hunt the *p*. for the lion   *Job 38:39*

provideth for the raven his *p*. (S)   *Job 38:31*

thence she seeketh the *p*. and her   *Job 39:29*

as a lion that is greedy of his *p*.   *Ps 17:12*

excellent than the mountains of *p*.   *Ps 76:4*

The young lions roar after their *p*.   *Ps 104:21*

not given us as a *p*. to their teeth   *Ps 124:6*

She also lieth in wait as for a *p*,   *Pr 23:28*

lay hold of the *p*. and shall carry   *Isa 5:29*

that widows may be their *p*.   *Isa 10:2*

to take the *p*. and to tread them   *Isa 10:6*

the young lion roaring on his *p*.   *Isa 31:4*

is the *p*. of a great spoil divided   *Isa 33:23*

spoil divided; the lame take the *p*.   *Isa 33:23*

any beast of *p*. (B)   *Isa 35:9*

they are for a *p*. and none   *Isa 42:22*

calling a bird of *p*. (R)   *Isa 46:11*

the *p*. be taken from the mighty   *Isa 49:24*

p. of the terrible shall be delivered   *Isa 49:25*

from evil maketh himself a *p*.   *Isa 59:15*

a captive and a *p*. (A)(R)   *Jer 2:14*

his life shall be unto him for a *p*.   *Jer 21:9*

p. upon thee will I give for a *p*.   *Jer 30:16*

he shall have his life for a *p*.   *Jer 38:2*

thy life shall be for a *p*. unto thee   *Jer 39:18*

life will I give unto thee for a *p*. in   *Jer 45:5*

shall be a *p*. (E)(S)   *Jer 50:10; Eze 7:21*

the hands of the strangers for a *p*.   *Eze 7:21*

and it learned to catch the *p*.   *Eze 19:3*

lion, and learned to catch the *p*.   *Eze 19:6*

like a roaring lion ravening the *p*.   *Eze 22:25*

like wolves ravening the *p*. to shed   *Eze 22:27*

and make a *p*. of thy merchandise   *Eze 26:12*

and take her spoil, and take her *p*.   *Eze 29:19*

because my flock became a *p*.   *Eze 34:8*

and they shall no more be a *p*.   *Eze 34:22*

shall no more be a *p*. to the heathen   *Eze 34:28*

became a *p*. and derision to   *Eze 36:4*

minds, to cast it out for a *p*.   *Eze 36:5*

To take a spoil, and to take a *p*.   *Eze 38:12*

gathered thy company to take a *p*.   *Eze 38:13*

give you to birds of *p*. (B)(R)   *Eze 39:4*

he shall scatter among them the *p*.   *Da 11:24*

in the forest, when he hath no *p*.   *Am 3:4*

filled his holes with *p*. and his dens   *Na 2:12*

I will cut off thy *p*. from the earth   *Na 2:13*

robbery; the *p*. departeth not   *Na 3:1*

the day that I rise up to the *p*.   *Zep 3:8*

PRICE

thou shalt increase the *p*. thereof   *Le 25:16*

thou shalt diminish the *p*. of it   *Le 25:16*

p. of his sale shall be according   *Le 25:50*

give again the *p*. of his redemption   *Le 25:51*

him again the *p*. of his redemption   *Le 25:52*

the *p*. of a dog, into the house of   *De 23:18*

I will surely buy it of thee at a *p*.   *2Sa 24:24*

received the linen yarn at a *p*.   *1Ki 10:28; 2Ch 1:16*

shalt grant it me for the full *p*.   *1Ch 21:22*

I will verily buy it for the full *p*.   *1Ch 21:24*

Man knoweth not the *p*. thereof   *Job 28:13*

be weighed for the *p*. thereof   *Job 28:15*

the *p*. of wisdom is above rubies   *Job 28:18*

increase thy wealth by their *p*.   *Ps 44:12*

a *p*. in the hand of a fool to get   *Pr 17:16*

the goats are the *p*. of the field   *Pr 27:26*

for her *p*. is far above rubies   *Pr 31:10*

my captives, not for *p*. nor reward   *Isa 45:13*

without money and without *p*.   *Isa 55:1*

will I give to the soil without *p*.   *Jer 15:13*

If you think good, give me my *p*.   *Zec 11:12*

for my *p*. thirty pieces of silver   *Zec 11:12*

a goodly *p*. that I was prised at   *Zec 11:13*

had found one pearl of great *p*.   *M't 13:46*

because it is the *p*. of blood   *M't 27:6*

the *p*. of him that was valued   *M't 27:9*

the *p*. of villainy (N)   *Ac 1:18*

kept back part of the *p*. his wife   *Ac 5:2*

keep back part of the *p*. of the land   *Ac 5:3*

and they counted the *p*. of them   *Ac 19:19*

For ye are bought with a *p*.   *1Co 6:20*

Ye are bought with a *p*. be not ye   *1Co 7:23*

is in the sight of God of great *p*.   *1Pe 3:4*

PRICES

p. of the things that were sold   *Ac 4:34*

PRICK

a brier to *p*. (A)(R)   *Eze 28:24*

PRICKED

grieved, and I was *p*. in my reins   *Ps 73:21*

I was pierced deep within (B)   *Ps 73:21*

p. horns (B)   *Pr 28:24*

they were *p*. in their heart   *Ac 2:37*

they were stung to the heart (A)   *Ac 2:37*

were moved to the depths of their hearts (B)   *Ac 2:37*

were cut to the heart (N)(R)   *Ac 2:37*

were cut to the quick (P)   *Ac 2:37*

PRICKING

shall be no more a *p*. brier unto   *Eze 28:24*

PRICKS

be *p*. in your eyes, and thorns   *Nu 33:55*

shall be as barbs in your eyes (B)   *Nu 33:55*

for thee to kick against the *p*.   *Ac 9:5; 26:14*

kicking against the goad (A)   *Ac 9:5; 26:14*

for thee to kick against the *p*.   *Ac 26:14*

PRIDE

I will break the *p*. of your power   *Le 26:19*

I know thy *p*. and the   *1Sa 17:28*

humbled himself for the *p*. of his   *2Ch 32:26*

purpose, and hide *p*. from man   *Job 33:17*

because of the *p*. of evil men   *Job 35:12*

His scales are his *p*. shut up   *Job 41:15*

a king over all the children of *p*.   *Job 41:34*

wicked in his *p*. doth persecute   *Ps 10:2*

through the *p*. of his countenance   *Ps 10:4*

thy presence from the *p*. of man   *Ps 31:20*

the foot of *p*. come against me   *Ps 36:11*

them even, be taken in their *p*.   *Ps 59:12*

p. compasseth them about as a   *Ps 73:6*

p. and arrogancy, and the evil   *Pr 8:13*

p. cometh, then cometh shame   *Pr 11:2*

Only by *p*. cometh contention: but   *Pr 13:10*

mouth of the foolish is a rod   *Pr 14:3*

P. goeth before destruction   *Pr 16:18*

man's *p*. shall bring him low   *Pr 29:23*

in the *p*. and stoutness of heart   *Isa 9:9*

the *p*. of the arrogant (R)   *Isa 13:11*

We have heard of the *p*. of Moab   *Isa 16:6*

even of his haughtiness, and his *p*.   *Isa 16:6*

it, to stain the *p*. of all glory   *Isa 23:9*

he shall bring down their *p*.   *Isa 25:11*

Woe to the crown of *p*. to the   *Isa 28:1*

The crown of *p*. the drunkards of   *Isa 28:3*

will I mar the *p*. of Judah   *Jer 13:9*

and the great *p*. of Jerusalem   *Jer 13:9*

weep in secret places for your *p*.   *Jer 13:17*

We have heard the *p*. of Moab   *Jer 48:29*

and his arrogancy, and his *p*.   *Jer 48:29*

thee, and the *p*. of thine heart   *Jer 49:16*

hath blossomed, *p*. hath budded   *Eze 7:10*

Sodom, *p*. fulness of bread   *Eze 16:49*

thy mouth in the day of thy *p*.   *Eze 16:56*

and the *p*. of her power shall come   *Eze 30:6*

those that walk in *p*. he is able   *Da 4:37*

his mind hardened in *p*. he was   *Da 5:20*

the *p*. of Israel doth testify to his   *Ho 5:5*

the *p*. of Israel testifieth to his   *Ho 7:10*

p. of thine heart hath deceived   *Ob 3*

This shall they have for their *p*.   *Zep 2:10*

them that rejoice in thy *p*.   *Zep 3:11*

cut off the *p*. of the Philistines   *Zec 9:6*

the *p*. of Assyria shall be brought   *Zec 10:11*

for the *p*. of Jordan is spoiled   *Zec 11:3*

eye, blasphemy, *p*.,   *M'k 7:22*

foolishness

I take *p*. in my ministry (B)   *Ro 11:13*

put away your *p*. (N)   *Ro 11:20*

no place for human *p*. (N)   *1Co 1:29*

told him my *p*. in you (N)(P)(R)   *2Co 7:14*

our *p*. and joy (P)   *1Th 2:19*

being lifted up with *p*. he fall into   *1Ti 3:6*

lust of the eyes, and the *p*. of life   *1Jo 2:16*

PRIEST

the *p*. of the most high God   *Ge 14:18; Heb 7:1*

the *p*. of Midian had seven daughters   *Ex 2:16*

that son that is *p*. in his stead   *Ex 29:30; Le 16:32*

p. burn it all on the altar   *Le 1:9; 1:13, 17; 2:2, 9, 16; 3:11, 16; 4:10, 30, 35; 7:5, 31*

p. shall lay them in order on the wood   *Le 1:12*

when presented to the *p*. he shall bring it   *Le 2:8*

if the *p*. that is anointed do sin as people   *Le 4:3*

p. shall dip his finger in the blood   *Le 4:6; 4:17*

p. shall make an atonement   *Le 4:20;*

for them *4:26; 5:6; 6:7; 12:8; 15:15, 30;*
16:30; 19:22
the *p.* shall take of the blood   *Le 4:25;*
4:30, 34
shall bring them to the *p.* who *Le 5:8*
shall offer
the *p.* shall put on his linen   *Le 6:10*
garment
p. shall have to himself the   *Le 7:8*
skin
it shall be the *p.* that offereth it *Le 7:9;*
7:14; 14:13
p. shall look on the plague in *Le 13:3;*
the skin *13:5-6, 17, 20-21; 25-27, 30-32*
the *p.* shall shut him up seven *Le 13:4;*
days *13:5, 31, 33*
p. shall pronounce him clean   *Le 13:6;*
17:23, 28, 34
brought to the *p.*; come to the *Le 13:9;*
p. *13:16; 14:2*
p. that maketh him clean   *Le 14:11*
shall present
the *p.* shall dip his right   *Le 14:16*
finger in the oil
that owneth the house shall *Le 14:35*
come and tell *p.*
the *p.* shall pronounce the   *Le 14:48*
house clean
if the daughter of a *p.* profane *Le 21:9*
herself
if the *p.* buy any soul with his *Le 22:11*
money
bring a sheaf of firstfruits to *Le 23:10*
the *p.*
the *p.* shall wave it before the *Le 23:11*
Lord
p. shall value him, according *Le 27:8*
to ability
let the trespass be recompensed *Nu 5:8*
to the *p.*
then the man shall bring his *Nu 5:15*
wife to the *p.*
the *p.* shall execute upon her *Nu 5:30*
all this law
this is holy for the *p.* with the *Nu 6:20*
wave breast
p. shall wash and be unclean *Nu 19:7*
until even
shall not dwell in land till *Nu 35:32*
death of high *p.*
the man that will not   *De 17:12*
hearken to *p.*
come nigh to battle, the *p.*   *De 20:2*
shall approach
thou shalt go to the *p.* in those *De 26:3*
days
one of his sons, who became *J'g 17:5*
his *p.*
be to me a father and a *p.*   *J'g 17:10*
do me good, seeing I have   *J'g 17:13*
Levite to my *p.*
Micah hath hired me, I am   *J'g 18:4*
his *p.*
be to us a *p.* and a father,   *J'g 18:19*
better be a *p.*
all that the *p.* took for   *1Sa 2:14*
himself
and said, Give flesh to roast *1Sa 2:15*
for the *p.*
did I choose him out of   *1Sa 2:28*
Israel to be my *p.*
and I will raise me up a   *1Sa 2:35*
faithful *p.*
while Saul talked to the *p.*   *1Sa 14:19*
the noise
then said the *p.*, Let us draw *1Sa 14:36*
near to God
p. answered, There is no   *1Sa 21:4*
common bread
so the *p.* gave him hallowed *1Sa 21:6*
bread
Solomon thrust Abiathar   *1Ki 2:27*
from being *p.*
the *p.* had said, Let her not *2Ki 11:15*
be slain
the same may be a *p.* of them *2Ch 13:9*
that are no gods
Israel hath been without a *2Ch 15:3*
teaching *p.*
till there stood up a *p.*   *Ezr 2:63;*
Ne 7:65
Lord hath sworn, thou art a *p. Ps 110:4;*
for ever after the order of   *Heb 5:6;*
Melchisedec *7:17, 21*
I took faithful witnesses, Uriah *Isa 8:2*
the *p.*
as with the people, so with   *Isa 24:2*
the *p.*
p. and the prophet have erred *Isa 28:7*
thro' wine

to the *p.* every one dealeth   *Jer 6:13;*
falsely *8:10*
prophet and *p.* go to a land *Jer 14:18*
they know not
the law shall not perish from *Jer 18:18*
the *p.*
for both prophet and *p.* are *Jer 23:11*
profane
when a prophet and a *p.* shall *Jer 23:33;*
ask thee *23:34*
Lord made thee *p.* instead of *Jer 29:26*
Jehoiada
and hath despised the king and *La 2:6*
the *p.*
shall the *p.* and prophet be   *La 2:20*
slain in
but the law shall perish from *Eze 7:26*
the *p.*
shall not come near to do   *Eze 44:13*
the office of a *p.*
nor shall any *p.* drink wine *Eze 44:21*
when they enter
or shall take a widow that   *Eze 44:22*
had a *p.* before
ye give to the *p.* the first of *Eze 44:30*
your dough
p. shall not eat of any thing *Eze 44:31*
that is torn
this people, as they that strive *Ho 4:4*
with the *p.*
I will reject thee, thou shalt be *Ho 4:6*
no *p.* to me
and there shall be like people *Ho 4:9*
like *p.*
the *p.* of Beth-el sent to   *Am 7:10*
Jeroboam
and he shall be a *p.* on his *Zec 6:13*
throne
the *p.* lips should keep   *Mal 2:7*
knowledge
tell no man, but go shew   *M't 8:4;*
thyself to the *p.*   *M'k 1:44; Lu 5:14*
certain *p.* named Zacharias,   *Lu 1:5*
and his wife
by chance there came down a *Lu 10:31*
certain *p.*
p. of Jupiter brought oxen   *Ac 14:13*
and garlands
like Son of God, abideth a *p. Heb 7:3*
continually
what need another *p.* should *Heb 7:11*
rise after order
after similitude Melchisedec *Heb 7:15*
ariseth another *p.*
as not without an oath he   *Heb 7:20*
was made *p.*
if he were on earth, he should *Heb 8:4*
not be a *p.*
every *p.* standeth daily   *Heb 10:11*
ministering

HIGH PRIEST

high *p.* shall not uncover his *Le 21:10*
head
abide in city of refuge till   *Nu 35:25;*
the death of the *high p.*   *Jos 20:6*
when much money in chest, *2Ki 12:10;*
the *high p.* came and   *2Ch 24:11*
go to Hilkiah the *high p.* that *2Ki 22:4*
he may sum
Eliashib the *high p.* rose up   *Ne 3:1*
with brethren
Joshua the *high p.* standing   *Zec 3:1;*
3:8; 6:11
to the palace of the *high p.*   *M't 26:3;*
Lu 22:54
struck a servant of the *high p. M't 26:51*
and smote off his ear   *Lu 22:50;*
Joh 18:10
led him to Caiaphas the *high M't 26:57;*
p.   *Joh 18:24*
the *high p.* rent his clothes *M't 26:65;*
M'k 14:63
in the days of Abiathar the   *M'k 2:26*
high p.
Caiaphas being *high p.*   *Joh 11:49;*
11:51; 18:13
that disciple was known to   *Joh 18:15*
the *high p.*
saying, Answerest thou the   *Joh 18:22*
high p. so
as many as were of the kindred *Ac 4:6*
of *high p.*
then said the *high p.*, Are these *Ac 7:1*
things so
Saul went to the *high p.* and *Ac 9:1*
desired letters
as also the *high p.* doth bear *Ac 22:5*
me witness

they said, Revilest thou God's *Ac 23:4*
high p.
that he might be a faithful   *Heb 2:17*
high p.
consider Apostle and *High P.* of *Heb 3:1*
our profession
high p. of religion we profess *Heb 3:1*
(N)
we have great *high p.* passed *Heb 4:14*
into heaven
we have not a *high p.* which *Heb 4:15*
cannot be touched
for every *high p.* taken from *Heb 5:1*
among men
Christ glorified not himself to *Heb 5:5*
be a *high p.*
called an *high p.* after order *Heb 5:10;*
of Melchisedec *6:20*
such an *high p.* became us, *Heb 7:26*
who is holy
we have such an *high p.* who *Heb 8:1*
is set on
every *high p.* is ordained to *Heb 8:3*
offer gift
but into the second went the *Heb 9:7*
high p. alone
Christ being come an *high p. Heb 9:11*
of good things
as the *high p.* entereth into *Heb 9:25*
the holy place
having a *high p.* over the   *Heb 10:21*
house of God
blood brought into   *Heb 13:11*
sanctuary by *high p.*

PRIESTHOOD

shall surely be an everlasting *Ex 40:15*
p.
with thee; and seek ye the *p. Nu 16:10*
also
shall bear the iniquity of your *Nu 18:1*
p.
the covenant of an   *Nu 25:13*
everlasting *p.*
p. of the Lord is their   *Jos 18:7*
inheritance
they, as polluted, put from   *Ezr 2:62;*
the *p.*   *Ne 7:64*
because they have defiled the *Ne 13:29*
p.
and the covenant of the *p.*   *Ne 13:29*
and of
who receive the office of the *Heb 7:5*
p.
perfection were by the   *Heb 7:11*
Levitical *p.*
For the *p.* being changed,   *Heb 7:12*
there is
Moses spake nothing   *Heb 7:14*
concerning *p.*
ever, hath an unchangeable *Heb 7:24*
p.
up a spiritual house, an holy *1Pe 2:5*
p.
a chosen generation, a royal *p. 1Pe 2:9*

PRIESTLY

installed in *p.* office (B)   *Nu 3:3*
division of *p.* (N)(P)(R)   *Lu 1:5*
performing *p.* function (P)   *Lu 1:8*

PRIESTS

land of *p.* bought he not, for *Ge 47:22*
p. had a portion assigned them
except the land of the *p.*   *Ge 47:26*
only, not Pharaoh's
ye shall be to me a kingdom *Ex 19:6*
of *p.*
the *p.* shall sprinkle the blood *Le 1:11;*
3:2
all the males among the *p.*   *Le 6:29*
shall eat thereof
or brought to one of his sons *Le 13:2*
the *p.*
he shall make an atonement *Le 16:33*
for the *p.*
a sojourner of the *p.* shall   *Le 22:10*
not eat
shall stand before *p.* and   *Le 19:17*
judges
the *p.* that bare the ark stood *Jos 3:17*
firm
p. bare seven trumpets of   *Jos 6:4;*
rams' horns *6:13*

and the *p.* took up the ark of *Jos 6:12* the Lord
Hophni and Phinehas *p.* were *1Sa 1:3* there
nor the *p.* of Dagon tread on *1Sa 5:5* the threshold
Philistines called for the *p.* *1Sa 6:2* and diviners
king said, Turn and slay the *p.* *1Sa 22:17*
said to Doeg, Turn thou and *1Sa 22:18* fall on the *p.*
shewed David, that Saul had *1Sa 22:21* slain Lord's *p.*
elders and the *p.* took up the *1Ki 8:3* ark
Jeroboam made *p.* of the *1Ki 12:31;* lowest of people *13:33*
on thee shall he offer the *p.* *1Ki 13:2* of high
Jehu slew Ahab's *p.* he left *2Ki 10:11* him none
call all Baal's *p.* let none be *2Ki 10:19* wanting
p. had not repaired breaches *2Ki 12:6* of the house
carry thither one of the *p.* *2Ki 17:27* ye brought
put down idolatrous *p.* of *2Ki 23:5* king of Judah
and he slew all the *p.* of the *2Ki 23:20* high places
the sea was for the *p.* to wash *2Ch 4:6* in
hundred twenty *p.* sounding *2Ch 5:12* with trumpets
p. could not stand to *2Ch 5:14* minister for the cloud
let thy *p.* be clothed with *2Ch 6:41* salvation
he appointed the courses of *2Ch 8:14* the *p.*
he ordained him *p.* for the *2Ch 11:15* high places
have ye not cast out the *p.* of *2Ch 13:9* the Lord
and his *p.* with trumpets to *2Ch 13:12* cry alarm
none came into the house of *2Ch 23:6* Lord save the
with him fourscore of the *2Ch 26:17* Lord
while Uzziah was wroth *2Ch 26:19* with the *p.*
the *p.* were too few, they *2Ch 29:34* could not slay
p. had not sanctified *2Ch 30:3* themselves
Josiah burnt the bones of the *2Ch 34:5* *p.*
Josiah set the *p.* in their *2Ch 35:2* charges
gave it to the *p.* for the *2Ch 35:8* passover offerings
they set the *p.* in their *Ezr 6:18* divisions
p. purified, and killed the *Ezr 6:20* passover for *p.*
of the people and *p.* offering *Ezr 7:16* willingly
our *p.* been delivered into *Ezr 9:7* hand of kings
nor had I as yet told it to the *Ne 2:16* *p.*
after him repaired the *p.* men *Ne 3:22* of the plain
trouble that hath come on us *Ne 9:32* and our *p.*
neither have we nor our *p.* *Ne 9:34* kept thy law
where they laid the offerings *Ne 13:5* of the *p.*
their *p.* fell by the sword, *Ps 78:64* their widows
Moses and Aaron among his *Ps 99:6* *p.* and Samuel
let thy *p.* be clothed with *Ps 132:9* righteousness
I will clothe her *p.* with *Ps 132:16* salvation
he sent elders of *p.* covered *Isa 37:2* with sackcloth
but ye shall be named the *p.* *Isa 61:6* of the Lord
against *p.* thereof and people of *Jer 1:18* land
the *p.* said not, Where is the *Jer 2:8* Lord
their *p.* ashamed; their *p.* *Jer 2:26;* astonished *4:9*

and the *p.* bare rule by their *Jer 5:31* means
the bones of the *p.* they shall *Jer 8:1* bring out
I will fill the *p.* with *Jer 13:13* drunkenness
I will satiate souls of *p.* with *Jer 31:14* fatness
to provoke me to anger, they *Jer 32:32* and their *p.*
shall go into captivity with *Jer 48:7;* his *p.* *49:3*
her *p.* sigh, her virgins are *La 1:4* afflicted
my *p.* and mine elders gave up *La 1:19* the ghost
the iniquities of her *p.* that *La 4:13* shed blood
they respected not the persons *La 4:16* of the *p.*
her *p.* violated my law, and *Eze 22:26* profaned
he said, This chamber is for *Eze 40:45* the *p.*
shall be for the *p.* *Eze 44:30;* *45:4; 48:10-11*
hear this, O *p.* and hearken, O *Ho 5:1* Israel
company of *p.* murder in the *Ho 6:9* way by consent
p. the Lord's ministers mourn *Joe 1:9;* *1:13; 2:17*
p. thereof teach for hire *Mic 3:11*
I will cut off the names of the *Zep 1:4*
her *p.* have polluted the *Zep 3:4* sanctuary
ask now the *p.* concerning *Hag 2:11* the law
to you, O *p.* that despise my *Mal 1:6* name
now, O *p.* this commandment *Mal 2:1* is for you
not lawful but only for the *p.* *M't 12:4* to eat
p. in the temple profane the *M't 12:5;* sabbath *M'k 2:26; Lu 6:4*
which is not lawful to eat *M'k 2:26* but for *p.*
go shew yourselves to the *p.* *Lu 17:14*
the *p.* and captain came upon *Ac 4:1* them
a company of *p.* were obedient *Ac 6:7* to the faith
the sons of Sceva chief of the *Ac 19:14* *p.* did so
those *p.* were made without *Heb 7:21* an oath
were many *p.* not suffered to *Heb 7:23* continue
seeing there are *p.* that offer *Heb 8:4* gifts by law
the *p.* went always into the *Heb 9:6* first tabernacle
hath made us kings and *p.* to *Re 1:6;* God *5:10*
be *p.* of God and of Christ, *Re 20:6* and reign

HIGH PRIESTS

Annas and Caiaphas were *high* *Lu 3:2* *p.*
needeth not daily as those *Heb 7:27* *high p.* to offer
the law maketh men *high p.* *Heb 7:28* which have

PRIEST'S

minister in *p.* office *Ex 28:1;* *28:3-4, 41; 29:1, 9, 44; 30:30; 31:10; 35:19; 39:41; 40:13, 15; Le 7:35; 16:32; Nu 3:3-4, 10; 18:7; De 10:6; 1Ch 6:10; 24:2; 2Ch 11:14; Lu 1:8-9*
the remnant shall be the *p.* as *Le 5:13* a
pan, shall be the *p.* that *Le 7:9* offereth it
shall be the *p.* that sprinkleth *Le 7:14*
for as the sin offering is the *Le 14:13*
oil that is in the *p.* hand he *Le 14:18;* shall *14:29*
the *p.* daughter also be *Le 22:12* married
if the *p.* daughter be a *Le 22:13* widow, or
possession thereof shall be the *Le 27:21* *p.*

be the *p.* due from the people *De 18:3*
And the *p.* heart was glad, *J'g 18:20* and he
the *p.* custom with the people *1Sa 2:13* was
the *p.* servant came, while the *1Sa 2:13* flesh
p. servant came, and said to *1Sa 2:15* the
into one of the *p.* offices, that *1Sa 2:36* I
and the high *p.* officer came *2Ch 24:11*
of your oblations, shall be *Eze 44:30* the *p.*
the *p.* lips should keep *Mal 2:7* knowledge
struck a servant of the high *M't 26:51* *p.*
him afar off unto the high *p.* *M't 26:58* palace
brought him into the high *p.* *Lu 22:54* house
it, and smote the high *p.* *Joh 18:10* servant

PRIESTS'

place where the *p.* feet stood *Jos 4:3* firm
the soles of the *p.* feet were *Jos 4:18* lifted
house of the Lord: it was *2Ki 12:16* the *p.*
and one hundred *p.* garments *Ezr 2:69*
hundred and thirty *p.* *Ne 7:70* garments
threescore and seven *p.* *Ne 7:72* garments
of the *p.* sons with trumpets *Ne 12:35*

PRINCE

thou art a mighty *p.* amongst *Ge 23:6* us
as a *p.* hast thou power with *Ge 32:28* God
when Shechem, *p.* of the *Ge 34:2* country, saw her
who made thee a man, a *p.* *Ex 2:14* over us
p. of father's houses (E) *Nu 3:24;* *3:30, 35; 25:14*
each *p.* shall offer on his day *Nu 7:11*
except make thyself *Nu 16:13* altogether a *p.* over us
for each *p.* a rod, even twelve *Nu 17:6* rods
Cozbi the daughter of a *p.* of *Nu 25:18* Midian
take one *p.* of every tribe to *Nu 34:18* divide the land
of each chief house a *p.* *Jos 22:14* through all Israel
know ye not there is a *p.* *2Sa 3:38* fallen in Israel
I will make him *p.* all his *1Ki 11:34* days
and made thee a *p.* over my *1Ki 14:7;* people *16:2*
of him came the *p.* (S) *1Ch 5:2*
anointed him to be *p.* *1Ch 29:22* (E)(R)(S)
numbered to Sheshbazzar the *Ezr 1:8* *p.* of Judah
for ye say, Where is the *Job 21:28* house of the *p.*
as a *p.* would I go near to *Job 31:37* him
but in want of people is *Pr 14:28* destruction of *p.*
much less do lying lips become *Pr 17:7* a *p.*
shouldest be put lower in *Pr 25:7* presence of the *p.*
by long forbearing is a *p.* *Pr 25:15* persuaded
p. that wanteth understanding *Pr 28:16* is an oppressor
the P. of peace *Isa 9:6*
p. be one of themselves *Jer 30:21* (A)(B)(E)(R)
and this Seraiah was a quiet *Jer 51:59* *p.*
the *p.* shall be clothed with *Eze 7:27* desolation
this burden concerneth the *Eze 12:10* *p.* in Jerusalem
and *p.* shall bear on his *Eze 12:12* shoulder in twilight
thou profane wicked *p.* of *Eze 21:25* Israel day is come

son of man, say to the *p.* of   *Eze 28:2*
Tyrus

be no more a *p.* of the land   *Eze 30:13*
of Egypt

and my servant David a *p.*   *Eze 34:24*
among them

my servant David shall be   *Eze 37:25*
their *p.* for ever

son of man, prophesy   *Eze 38:2;*
against Gog, Magog,   *38:3; 39:1*
the chief *p.* of

this gate is for the *p.* the *p.*   *Eze 44:3*
shall sit in it

and a portion shall be for the   *Eze 45:7*
p. on one side

on that day shall the *p.*   *Eze 45:22*
prepare a bullock

the *p.* shall enter by the way   *Eze 46:2*
of the porch

the burnt offering that the *p.*   *Eze 46:4*
shall offer

and when the *p.* shall enter   *Eze 46:8*
he shall go in

and the *p.* in the midst of   *Eze 46:10*
them, shall go in

when *p.* prepares a   *Eze 46:12*
voluntary burnt offering

if the *p.* give a gift to any of   *Eze 46:16*
his sons

after, it shall return to the   *Eze 46:17*
p. but inheritance

p. shall not take of the   *Eze 46:18*
people's inheritance

residue shall be for the *p.* on   *Eze 48:21*
the one side

to whom *p.* of the eunuchs   *Da 1:7*
gave names

he requested of *p.* of the   *Da 1:8*
eunuchs not to defile

Daniel in favour with the *p.* of   *Da 1:9*
the eunuchs

he magnified himself even to   *Da 8:11*
p. of the host

he shall also stand up against   *Da 8:25*
the *p.* of princes

to build Jerusalem, unto the   *Da 9:25*
Messiah, the *P.*

people of the *p.* that shall   *Da 9:26*
come shall destroy

but the *p.* of Persia   *Da 10:13*
withstood me

to fight with *p.* of Persia, *p.*   *Da 10:20*
of Grecia come

none holdeth with me, but   *Da 10:21*
Michael your *p.*

but a *p.* for his own behalf   *Da 11:18*
shall cause

shall be broken, also the *p.*   *Da 11:22*
of the covenant

then shall Michael stand up   *Da 12:1*
the great *p.*

Israel shall abide many days   *Ho 3:4*
without a *p.*

the *p.* and the judge ask for a   *Mic 7:3*
reward

Pharisees said, He casteth out   *M't 9:3;*
devils by the *p.* of devils   *12:24; M'k 3:22*

through the *p.* of demons   *Lu 11:15*
(A)(B)(E)(N)(R)

the *p.* of this world shall be   *Joh 12:31*
cast out

for the *p.* of this world   *Joh 14:30*
cometh, and hath

because the *p.* of this world   *Joh 16:11*
is judged

and killed *P.* of life whom   *Ac 3:15*
God raised

him hath God exalted to be a   *Ac 5:31*
P. and Saviour

according to *p.* of the power   *Eph 2:2*
of the air

Jesus Christ the *P.* of kings of   *Re 1:5*
the earth

PRINCEDOM

call *p.* and authority (B)   *Col 2:1*

PRINCES

the *p.* also of Pharaoh saw   *Ge 12:15*
Sarai

twelve *p.* shall Ishmael beget   *Ge 17:20;*
  25:16

a wagon for two *p.*   *Nu 7:3*
the *p.* offered   *Nu 7:10*
rose up 250 *p.*; the *p.* digged   *Nu 16:2;*
a well   *21:18*
and the *p.* of Moab abode   *Nu 22:8*
with Balaam

Balak sent yet again *p.* more   *Nu 22:15*
honourable than

p. of the congregation sware   *Jos 9:15*
to them

Moses smote with the *p.* of   *Jos 13:21*
Midian

with Phinehas ten *p.* sent to   *Jos 22:14*
Reuben

hear, O ye kings give ear O ye   *J'g 5:3*
p.

the *p.* of Issachar were with   *J'g 5:15*
Deborah

they took the two *p.* of the   *J'g 7:25*
Midianites

he described to him the *p.* of   *J'g 8:14*
Succoth

he raiseth poor to set them   *1Sa 2:8*
among *p.*

the *p.* of the Philistines were   *1Sa 29:4*
wroth

even by the young men of   *1Ki 20:14*
the *p.*

these were *p.* in their families   *1Ch 4:38*
p. and people will be at thy   *1Ch 28:21*
command

the *p.* of the fathers (S)   *2Ch 5:2*
armed men left spoil before   *2Ch 28:14*
the *p.*

one heart to do   *2Ch 30:12*
commandment of *p.*

and the *p.* gave a thousand   *2Ch 30:24*
bullocks

his *p.* gave willingly to the   *2Ch 35:8*
people

treasures of his *p.* brought to   *2Ch 36:18*
Babylon

and before all the king's   *Ezr 7:28*
mighty *p.*

yea the hand of the *p.* hath   *Ezr 9:2*
been chief

come according to the   *Ezr 10:8*
counsel of the *p.*

neither have our *p.* kept thy   *Ne 9:34*
law

our *p.* Levites and priests seal   *Ne 9:38*
to it

he made a feast to all his *p.*   *Es 1:3;*
  2:18
to the *p.* of every people (S)   *Es 3:12;*
  8:9; 9:3
how he had advanced him   *Es 5:11*
above the *p.*

hand of one of the king's noble   *Es 6:9*
p.

been at rest with *p.* that had   *Job 3:15*
gold

leadeth *p.* away spoiled,   *Job 12:19*
overthrows mighty

he poureth contempt on *p.*   *Job 12:21*
and weakeneth

p. refrained talking and laid   *Job 29:9*
their hands

is it fit to say to *p.*, Ye are   *Job 34:18*
ungodly

to him that accepteth not   *Job 34:19*
the persons of *p.*

thou mayest make *p.* in all   *Ps 45:16*
the earth

the *p.* of the people are   *Ps 47:9*
gathered

the *p.* of Zebulun the *p.* of   *Ps 68:27*
Naphtali

p. come out of Egypt   *Ps 68:31*
Ethiopia stretch

cut off the spirit of *p.* he is   *Ps 76:12*
terrible

die like men and fall like one   *Ps 82:7*
of the *p.*

to bind his *p.* at his pleasure   *Ps 105:22*
he poureth contempt upon *p.*   *Ps 107:40*
he may set him with *p.* even   *Ps 113:8*
with the *p.*

trust in Lord than to put   *Ps 118:9*
confidence in *p.*

p. also did sit and speak   *Ps 119:23*
against me

p. have persecuted me   *Ps 119:161*
without a cause

put not trust in *p.* nor in son   *Ps 146:3*
of man

p. and all judges of the   *Ps 148:11*
earth praise

by me *p.* decree justice: *p.*   *Pr 8:15;*
rule   *8:16*
it is not good to strike *p.* for   *Pr 17:26*
equity

much less for a servant to   *Pr 19:10*
rule over *p.*

for transgression many are the   *Pr 28:2*
p. thereof

it is not for *p.* to drink strong   *Pr 31:4*
drink

p. walking as servants on the   *Ec 10:7*
earth

O land when thy *p.* eat in   *Ec 10:16*
the morning

blessed art thou when thy *p.*   *Ec 10:17*
eat in due

thy *p.* are rebellious and   *Isa 1:23*
thieves

I will give children to be   *Isa 3:4*
their *p.*

the Lord will enter into   *Isa 3:14*
judgment with the *p.*

are not my *p.* altogether kings   *Isa 10:8*
p. of Zoan fools, *p.* of Noah   *Isa 19:11;*
deceived   *19:13*
arise, ye *p.* and anoint the   *Isa 21:5*
shield

against Tyre whose merchants   *Isa 23:8*
are *p.*

his *p.* were at Zoan his   *Isa 30:4*
ambassadors

his *p.* shall be afraid of the   *Isa 31:9*
ensign

and *p.* shall rule in judgment   *Isa 32:1*
and all her *p.* shall be   *Isa 34:12*
nothing

that bringeth the *p.* to   *Isa 40:23*
nothing

he shall come upon *p.* as on   *Isa 41:25*
mortar

I have profaned the *p.* of the   *Isa 43:28*
sanctuary

p. also shall worship because   *Isa 49:7*
of the Lord

made thee brasen walls   *Jer 1:18*
against the *p.*

they, their kings and *p.* are   *Jer 2:26*
ashamed

the heart of the *p.* shall be   *Jer 4:9*
astonished

they shall bring out the bones   *Jer 8:1*
of his *p.*

kings and *p.* sitting on   *Jer 17:25*
throne of David

will I give king of Judah and   *Jer 24:8*
his *p.*

p. said, This man is not   *Jer 26:16*
worthy to die

they and their kings and *p.*   *Jer 32:32*
provoke me

his *p.* I will give to their   *Jer 34:21*
enemies

the *p.* were wroth with   *Jer 37:15*
Jeremiah

if thou go forth to king of   *Jer 38:17*
Babylon's *p.*

if the *p.* hear that I have   *Jer 38:25*
talked with thee

the incense that ye and your   *Jer 44:21*
p. burn

Chemosh and his *p.* go into   *Jer 48:7;*
captivity   *49:3*
I will destroy from thence   *Jer 49:38*
the *p.*

a sword is on her *p.* and her   *Jer 50:35*
wise men

I will make drunk her *p.* and   *Jer 51:57*
wise men

her *p.* are become like harts   *La 1:6*
that find

polluted the kingdom and *p.*   *La 2:2*
thereof

her kings and *p.* are among the   *La 2:9*
Gentiles

p. are hanged up by their   *La 5:12*
hand

her *p.* like wolves ravening   *Eze 22:27*
the prey

in dyed attire all of them *p.*   *Eze 23:15*
to look to

Edom and her *p.* with their   *Eze 32:29*
might

there the *p.* of the north all   *Eze 32:30*
of them

and ye shall drink the blood   *Eze 39:18*
of the *p.*

my *p.* shall no more oppress   *Eze 45:8*
my people

the king sent to gather together   *Da 3:2*
the *p.*

pleased to set over the   *Da 6:1*
kingdom 120 *p.*

this Daniel was preferred   *Da 6:3*
above the *p.*

the *p.* sought occasion against   *Da 6:4*
Daniel

he shall stand up against the   *Da 8:25*
prince of *p.*

prophets who spake in thy *Da 9:6*
name to our *p.*
confusion of face to our *p.* and *Da 9:8*
fathers
Michael one of the chief *p.* *Da 10:13*
came to me
one of his *p.* shall be strong *Da 11:5*
above him
they make *p.* glad with their lies *Ho 7:3*
the *p.* have made him sick with *Ho 7:5*
wine
their *p.* shall fall by the sword *Ho 7:16*
for rage
they have made *p.* and I knew *Ho 8:4*
it not
shall sorrow for the burden *Ho 8:10*
of the king of *p.*
I love them no more all their *Ho 9:15*
p. are revolters
of whom thou saidst, Give *Ho 13:10*
me a king and *p.*
all your *p.* besides (B)(R) *Ho 13:10*
their king go into captivity, *Am 1:15*
he and his *p.*
hear, ye *p.* of the house of *Mic 3:1;*
Israel   *3:9*
eight *p.* among men *Mic 5:5*
(A)(B)(R)
The *p.* are as the locusts (S) *Na 3:17*
the *p.* shall be a scorn unto *Hab 1:10*
them
I will punish the *p.* and king's *Zep 1:8*
children
her *p.* within her are roaring *Zep 3:3*
lions
the *p.* of Gentiles exercise *M't 20:25*
dominion
nor the wisdom of the *p.* of *1Co 2:6*
this world
which none of the *p.* of this *1Co 2:8*
world knew

PRINCES OF JUDAH

then I brought up *p. of* *Ne 12:31*
Judah on wall
there is *p. of Judah*, and their *Ps 68:27*
counsel
he slew all the *p. of Judah* in *Jer 52:10*
Riblah
p. of Judah are like to them *Ho 5:10*
that remove
thou art not the least among *M't 2:6*
p. of Judah

ALL THE PRINCES

carried away *all the p.* and *2Ki 24:14*
mighty men
and *all the p.* submitted *1Ch 29:24*
themselves
and destroyed *all the p.* of *2Ch 24:23*
people
hath done wrong to *all the p.* *Es 1:16*
and people
set his seat above *all the p.* that *Es 3:1*
were with him
all the p. as Zebah and *Ps 83:11*
Zalmunna
Jeremiah spake to *all the p.* *Jer 26:12*
and people
Jehudi read it in the ears *Jer 36:21*
of *all the p.*
then *all the p.* of the sea *Eze 26:16*
came down
and will slay *all the p.* thereof *Am 2:3*
with him

PRINCE'S

thy feet with shoes, O *p.* *Ca 7:1*
daughter
the *p.* part to give burnt *Eze 45:17*
offerings
in the midst of that which is *Eze 48:22*
the *p.*

PRINCESS

she that was *p.* among the *La 1:1*
provinces

PRINCESSES

Solomon had 700 wives *p.* *1Ki 11:3*
700 official wives (B) *1Ki 11:3*

PRINCIPAL

take thou also unto thee *p.* *Ex 30:23*
spices

the best spices (A) *Ex 30:23*
the choicest spices (B) *Ex 30:23*
the chief spices (E) *Ex 30:23*
the finest spices (R) *Ex 30:23*
he shall even restore it in the *p.* *Le 6:5*
restore it in full *Le 6:5*
(A)(B)(E)(R)
recompense his trespass with *Nu 5:7*
the *p.*
make restitution in full *Nu 5:7*
(A)(B)(R)
the *p.* fathers of the *Nu 31:26;*
congregation (S) *36:1*
Zabud son of Nathan was *p.* *1Ki 4:5*
officer
the *p.* scribe of the host *2Ki 25:19;*
       Jer 52:25
one *p.* household taken for *1Ch 24:6*
Eleazar
the priests even *p.* fathers *1Ch 24:31*
cast lots
Mattaniah *p.* to begin *Ne 11:17*
thanksgiving
wisdom is the *p.* thing, *Pr 4:7*
therefore get wisdom
have broken down the *p.* *Isa 16:8*
plants thereof
and cast in the *p.* wheat and *Isa 28:25*
barley
wallow in the ashes, ye *p.* of *Jer 25:34*
the flock
masters of the flock (B) *Jer 25:34*
lords of the flock (R) *Jer 25:34*
no way to fly, nor the *p.* of *Jer 25:35*
the flock escape
keepers of the flocks (B) *Jer 25:35*
lords of the flock (R) *Jer 25:35*
there we shall rise against *Mic 5:5*
him eight *p.* men
eight princes among men *Mic 5:5*
(A)(B)(R)
p. men of the city entered *Ac 25:23*
with Agrippa
prominent citizens *Ac 25:23*
(A)(B)(N)(P)(R)

PRINCIPALITIES

your *p.* shall come down, *Jer 13:18*
even
your beautiful crown *Jer 13:18*
(A)(R)
your crown of beauty (B) *Jer 13:18*
your headtires (E) *Jer 13:18*
nor *p.* nor powers, nor things *Ro 8:38*
mighty ones (B) *Ro 8:38*
realm of spirits or *Ro 8:38*
superhuman powers (N)
messenger of heaven or *Ro 8:38*
monarch of earth (P)
now unto the *p.* and powers *Eph 3:10*
in
angelic rulers and authorities *Eph 3:10*
(A)(N)
rulers and authorities in *Eph 3:10*
heavenly spheres (B)
angelic powers (P) *Eph 3:10*
but against *p.* against powers *Eph 6:12*
against despotisms (A) *Eph 6:12*
against cosmic powers *Eph 6:12*
(B)(N)
against organizations and *Eph 6:12*
powers that are spiritual (P)
or dominions, or *p.* or powers *Col 1:16*
ruler or authorities (A)(B) *Col 1:16*
sovereignties, authorities (N) *Col 1:16*
And having spoiled *p.* and *Col 2:15*
powers
princes and authorities (B) *Col 2:15*
cosmic powers and *Col 2:15*
authorities (N)
mind to be subject to *p.* and *Tit 3:1*
powers
magistrates and authorities *Tit 3:1*
(A)
the ruling authorities (B) *Tit 3:1*
rulers and authorities (E)(R) *Tit 3:1*
government and authorities (N) *Tit 3:1*

PRINCIPALITY

Far above all *p.* and power *Eph 1:21*
Far above all rule and *Eph 1:21*
authority (A)(E)(R)
above all government and *Eph 1:21*
authority (B)(N)
is the head of all *p.* and *Col 2:10*
power
head of all princedom and *Col 2:10*
authority (B)

every power and authority *Col 2:10*
(N)
authority over all authorities *Col 2:10*
(P)
head of all rule and authority *Col 2:10*
(R)

PRINCIPLE

being a man of *p.* (N) *M't 1:19*
showed lack of *p.* (N) *Ga 2:13*
live by this *p.* (N)(P) *Ga 6:16*

PRINCIPLES

not arguing over *p.* (P) *Ro 14:1*
world's elemental *p.* *Col 2:8*
(B)(N)(P)(R)
neither *p.* nor self-control (P) *1Ti 1:9*
the first *p.* of the oracles of *Heb 5:12*
God
elementary beginnings (B) *Heb 5:12*
the ABC of God's oracles *Heb 5:12*
(N)(P)
leaving the *p.* of the doctrine *Heb 6:1*
of
the elementary stage *Heb 6:1*
(A)(B)(P)(R)
rudiments of Christianity (N) *Heb 6:1*
from *p.* invisible (P) *Heb 11:3*

PRINT

dead, nor *p.* any marks upon *Le 19:28*
you
a *p.* upon the heels of my *Job 13:27*
feet
in his hands the *p.* of the *Joh 20:25*
nails
my finger into the *p.* of the *Joh 20:25*
nails

PRINTED

oh that they were *p.* in a *Job 19:23*
book

PRISCA

Salute *P.* and Aquila, and the *2Ti 4:19*

PRISCILLA

come from Italy, with his wife *Ac 18:2*
P.
and with him *P.* and Aquila *Ac 18:18*
when Aquila and *P.* had *Ac 18:26*
heard
Greet *P.* and Aquila my *Ro 16:3*
helpers
Aquila and *P.* salute you *1Co 16:19*
much

PRISED

price that I was *p.* at of *Zec 11:13*
them

PRISON

and put him into the *p.* a *Ge 39:20*
and he was there in the *p.* *Ge 39:20*
sight of the keeper of the *p.* *Ge 39:21*
the keeper of the *p.* committed *Ge 39:22*
prisoners that were in the *p.* *Ge 39:22*
keeper of the *p.* looked not to *Ge 39:23*
into the *p.* the place where *Ge 40:3*
prison (N)   *Ge 40:3;*
40:4, 7; 41:10; 42:17; *Le 24:12;*
       Nu 15:34
which were bound in the *p.* *Ge 40:5*
ye shall be kept in *p.* that *Ge 42:16*
your
be bound in the house of *Ge 42:19*
your *p.*
and he did grind in the *p.* *J'g 16:21*
house
for Samson out of the *p.* *J'g 16:25*
house
Put this fellow in the *p.* *1Ki 22:27;*
and   *2Ch 18:26*
him up, and bound him in *p.* *2Ki 17:4*
king of Judah out of *p.* *2Ki 25:27*
And changed his *p.* *2Ki 26:29*
garments
seer, and put him in a *p.* *2Ch 16:10*
house
that was by the court of the *p.* *Ne 3:25*
and they stood still in the *p.* *Ne 12:39*
gate

Bring my soul out of *p*. that I   *Ps 142:7*
out of *p*. he cometh to reign   *Ec 4:14*
and shall be shut up in the   *Isa 24:22*
bring out the prisoners from   *Isa 42:7*
the *p*.
in darkness out of the *p*. house   *Isa 42:7*
and they are hid in *p*. houses   *Isa 42:22*
He was taken from *p*. and   *Isa 53:8*
from
opening of the *p*. to them that   *Isa 61:1*
are
thou shouldest put him in *p*.   *Jer 29:26*
was shut up in the court of the   *Jer 32:2*
p.
came to me in the court of the   *Jer 32:8*
p.
Jews that sat in the court of   *Jer 32:12*
the *p*.
yet shut up in the court of the   *Jer 33:1*
p.
they had not put him into *p*.   *Jer 37:4*
in *p*. in the house of Jonathan   *Jer 37:15*
for they had made that the *p*.   *Jer 37:15*
that ye have put me in *p*.   *Jer 37:18*
Jeremiah into the court of the   *Jer 37:21*
remained in the court of the   *Jer 37:21*
p.
that was in the court of the *p*.   *Jer 38:6*
remained in the court of the   *Jer 38:13*
p,
abode in the court of the *p*.   *Jer 38:28*
until
Jeremiah out of the court of   *Jer 39:14*
the *p*.
was shut up in the court of   *Jer 39:15*
the *p*.
in *p*. till the day of his death   *Jer 52:11*
brought him forth out of *p*.   *Jer 52:31*
And changed his *p*. garments   *Jer 52:33*
heard that John was cast into   *M't 4:12*
officer, and thou be cast into   *M't 5:25*
p.
John had heard in the *p*. the   *M't 11:2*
works
put him in *p*. for Herodias'   *M't 14:3*
sake
sent, and beheaded John in   *M't 14:10*
the *p*.
went and cast him into *p*. till   *M't 18:30*
he
I was in *p*. and ye came unto   *M't 25:36*
me
when saw we thee sick, or in   *M't 25:39*
p.
sick, and in *p*. and ye visited   *M't 25:43*
me
or sick, or in *p*. and did not   *M't 25:44*
after that John was put in *p*.   *M'k 1:14*
bound him in *p*. for Herodias'   *M'k 6:17*
sake
went, and beheaded him in the   *M'k 6:27*
p.
all, that he shut up John in *p*.   *Lu 3:20*
and the officer cast thee into   *Lu 12:58*
p.
ready to go with thee, both   *Lu 22:33*
into *p*.
and for murder, was cast into   *Lu 23:19*
p.
and murder was cast into *p*.   *Lu 23:25*
For John was not yet cast into   *Joh 3:24*
p.
and put them in the common *p*.   *Ac 5:18*
Lord by night opened the *p*.   *Ac 5:19*
doors
to the *p*. to have them brought   *Ac 5:21*
and found them not in the *p*.   *Ac 5:22*
The *p*. truly found we shut   *Ac 5:23*
with
the men whom ye put in *p*. are   *Ac 5:25*
women committed them to *p*.   *Ac 8:3*
he put him in *p*. and delivered   *Ac 12:4*
Peter therefore was kept in *p*.   *Ac 12:5*
keepers before the door kept   *Ac 12:6*
the *p*.
and a light shined in the *p*.:   *Ac 12:7*
and he
had brought him out of the *p*.   *Ac 12:17*
they cast them into *p*.   *Ac 16:23*
charging
thrust them into the inner *p*.   *Ac 16:24*
foundations the *p*. were   *Ac 16:26*
shaken
keeper of the *p*. awaking out   *Ac 16:27*
of
and seeing the *p*. doors open,   *Ac 16:27*
he

keeper of the *p*. told this   *Ac 16:36*
saying to
Romans, and have cast us   *Ac 16:37*
into *p*.
And they went out of the *p*.   *Ac 16:40*
of the saints did I shut up in   *Ac 26:10*
preached unto the spirits in *p*.   *1Pe 3:19*
devil shall cast some of you   *Re 2:10*
into *p*.
Satan shall be loosed out of his   *Re 20:7*
p.

PRISONER

the sighing of the *p*. come   *Ps 79:11*
before
To hear the groaning of the   *Ps 102:20*
p.
to release unto the people a   *M't 27:15*
p.
they had then a notable *p*.   *M't 27:16*
called
he released unto them one *p*.   *M'k 15:6*
Paul the *p*. called me unto   *Ac 23:18*
him, and
to me unreasonable to send a   *Ac 25:27*
was I delivered *p*. from   *Ac 28:17*
Jerusalem
Paul, the *p*. of Jesus Christ for   *Eph 3:1*
you
I therefore, the *p*. of the Lord   *Eph 4:1*
of our Lord, nor of me his *p*.   *2Ti 1:8*
Paul, a *p*. of Jesus Christ, and   *Ph'm 1*
and now also a *p*. of Jesus   *Ph'm 9*
Christ

PRISONERS

where the king's *p*. were   *Ge 39:20*
bound
all the *p*. that were in the   *Ge 39:22*
prison
Israel, and took some of them   *Nu 21:1*
p.
There the *p*. rest together;   *Job 3:18*
they
the poor, and despiseth not his   *Ps 69:33*
p.
hungry. The Lord looseth the   *Ps 146:7*
they shall bow down under   *Isa 10:4*
the *p*.
that opened not the house of   *Isa 14:17*
his *p*.
Assyria lead away Egyptians   *Isa 20:4*
p.
as *p*. are gathered in the pit   *Isa 24:22*
to bring out the *p*. from the   *Isa 42:7*
prison
That thou mayest say to the *p*.,   *Isa 49:9*
Go
his feet all the *p*. of the earth   *La 3:34*
have sent forth thy *p*. out of   *Zec 9:11*
the pit
to the strong hold, ye *p*. of   *Zec 9:12*
hope
unto God: and the *p*. heard   *Ac 16:25*
them
supposing that the *p*. had   *Ac 16:27*
been fled
delivered Paul and certain   *Ac 27:1*
other *p*.
soldiers' counsel was to kill   *Ac 27:42*
the *p*.
delivered the *p*. to the captain   *Ac 28:16*
p. of disobedience (N)(P)   *Ro 11:32*
p. in subjection to sin (N)   *Ga 3:22*
shared sufferings with *p*.   *Heb 10:34*
(N)

PRISONS

up to the synagogues, and   *Lu 21:12*
into *p*.
delivering into *p*. both men and   *Ac 22:4*
in *p*. more frequent, in   *2Co 11:23*
deaths oft

PRIVATE

by the *p*. parts (A)(B)(R)   *De 25:11*
have a *p*. chat (B)(R)   *1Sa 18:22*
enter *p*. room (B)   *M't 6:6*
within a *p*. room (B)(R)(S)   *Lu 12:3*
is of any *p*. interpretation   *2Pe 1:20*
personal or private or special   *2Pe 1:20*
interpretation (A)
explained by one's unaided   *2Pe 1:20*
mental powers (B)

interpret any prophecy by   *2Pe 1:20*
himself (P)
no prophecy arose from an   *2Pe 1:20*
individual's interpretation (R)

PRIVATELY

speak *p*. (A)   *1Sa 18:22*
privately (S)   *M't 1:19; 2:7; Ac 16:37*
came the disciples to Jesus *p*.   *M't 17:19*
(S)
disciples came unto him *p*.   *M't 24:3*
into a desert place by ship *p*.   *M'k 6:32*
his disciples asked him *p*.   *M'k 9:28*
Why
John and Andrew asked him   *M'k 13:3*
p.
aside *p*. into a desert place   *Lu 9:10*
and said *p*., Blessed are the   *Lu 10:23*
eyes
and went with him aside *p*.   *Ac 23:19*
but *p*. to them which were of   *Ga 2:2*

PRIVILEGE

p. as a wife not diminish (A)   *Ex 21:10*

PRIVILEGES

stripped himself of all *p*. and   *Ph'p 2:7*
rightful dignity (A)(P)

PRIVILY

messengers unto Abimelech *p*.   *J'g 9:31*
cut off the skirt of Saul's robe   *1Sa 24:4*
p.
his eyes are *p*. set against the   *Ps 10:8*
poor
p. shoot at the upright in heart   *Ps 11:2*
net that they have laid *p*. for   *Ps 31:4*
me
they commune of laying snares   *Ps 64:5*
Whoso *p*. slandereth his   *Ps 101:5*
neighbour
have they *p*. laid a snare for   *Ps 142:3*
me
let us lurk *p*. for the innocent   *Pr 1:11*
without
blood; they lurk *p*. for their   *Pr 1:18*
own lives
was minded to put her away   *M't 1:19*
when he had *p*. called the wise   *M't 2:7*
men
and now do they thrust us out   *Ac 16:37*
came in *p*. to spy out our liberty   *Ga 2:4*
who *p*. shall bring in damnable   *2Pe 2:1*

PRIVY

or hath his *p*. member cut off   *De 23:1*
wounded in his testicles, or has   *De 23:1*
been made a eunuch (A)
testicles crushed or male organ   *De 23:1*
severed (B)
testicles crushed or male   *De 23:1*
member cut off (R)
which thine heart is *p*. to, that   *1Ki 2:44*
house of Baal a *p*. (A)   *2Ki 10:27*
entereth into their *p*.   *Eze 21:14*
chambers
entered into inner chambers   *Eze 21:14*
(A)
price, his wife also being *p*. to it   *Ac 5:2*

PRIZE

this is David's *p*. (B)   *1Sa 30:20*
prize (S)   *Jer 21:9;*
   38:2; 39:8; 45:5
run all, but one receiveth the   *1Co 9:24*
p.
mark for the *p*. of the high   *Ph'p 3:14*
calling
disqualifying you for the *p*.   *Col 2:18*
(A)(B)(E)

PRIZED

I was *p*. at of them (S)   *Zec 11:13*

PROBLEMS

give explanations and solve *p*.   *Da 5:16*
(B)

PROCEED

that *p.* out of the candlestick *Ex 25:35*
any word *p.* out of your mouth *Jos 6:10*
which shall *p.* out of thy bowels *2Sa 7:12*
yea, twice; but I will *p.* no further; *Job 40:5*
I will *p.* to do a marvellous work *Isa 29:14*
for a law shall *p.* from me, and I *Isa 51:4*
for they *p.* from evil to evil, and *Jer 9:3*
out of them shall *p.* thanksgiving *Jer 30:19*
shall *p.* from the midst of them *Jer 30:21*
their dignity shall *p.* of themselves *Hab 1:7*
things which *p.* out of the mouth *M't 15:18*
out of the heart *p.* evil thoughts *M't 15:19*
the heart of men, *p.* evil thoughts *M'k 7:21*
communication *p.* out your mouth *Eph 4:29*
they shall *p.* no further: for their *2Ti 3:9*

PROCEEDED

then whatsoever *p.* out of her lips *Nu 30:12*
which hath *p.* out of your mouth *Nu 32:24*
which hath *p.* out of thy mouth *J'g 11:36*
Elihu also *p.* and said, *Job 36:1*
words which *p.* out of his mouth *Lu 4:22*
for I *p.* forth and came from God *Joh 8:42*
he *p.* further to take Peter also *Ac 12:3*
out of the throne *p.* lightnings *Re 4:5*
which sword *p.* out of his mouth *Re 19:21*

PROCEEDETH

The thing *p.* from the Lord: we *Ge 24:50*
to all that *p.* out of his mouth *Nu 30:2*
word that *p.* out of the mouth of *De 8:3; M't 4:4*
Wickedness *p.* from the wicked *1Sa 24:13*
as an error which *p.* from the ruler *Ec 10:5*
most High *p.* not evil and good *La 3:38*
therefore wrong judgment *p.* *Hab 1:4*
truth, which *p.* from the Father *Joh 15:26*
mouth *p.* blessing and cursing *Jas 3:10*
fire *p.* out of their mouth, and *Re 11:5*

PROCEEDING

crystal, *p.* out of the throne of God *Re 22:1*

PROCEEDS

the *p.* of infamy (P) *Ac 1:18*

PROCESS

And in *p.* of time it came to pass *Ge 4:3*
p. of time the daughter of Shuah *Ge 38:12*
it came to pass in *p.* of time, that *Ex 2:23; J'g 11:4*
it came to pass, that in *p.* of time *2Ch 21:19*

PROCESSION

bind festal *p.* with branches (R) *Ps 118:27*

PROCHORUS

Phillip, and *P.* and Nicanor, and *Ac 6:5*

PROCLAIM

and I will *p.* the name of the Lord *Ex 33:19*
ye shall *p.* to be holy convocations *Le 23:2*
which ye shall *p.* in their seasons *Le 23:4*
shall broadcast at appointed times (B) *Le 23:4; 23:21*
And ye shall *p.* on the selfsame day *Le 23:21*
make proclamation (A)(E)(R) *Le 23:21*
ye shall *p.* to be holy convocations *Ac 23:37*
p. liberty throughout all the land *Ac 25:10*
against it, then *p.* peace unto it *De 20:10*
I will *p.* the name (A)(B)(E)(R) *De 32:3*
p. in the ears of the people, saying *J'g 7:3*
announce in the hearing of the people (B) *J'g 7:3*
P. a fast, and set Naboth on high *1Ki 21:9*
P. a solemn assembly for Baal *2Ki 10:20*
Sanctify a solemn assembly (A)(B)(E)(R) *2Ki 10:20*
prophets to *p.* (R) *Ne 6:7*
publish, and *p.* in all their cities *Ne 8:15*
of the city, and *p.* before him *Es 6:9*
will *p.* every one his own goodness *Pr 20:6*
p. liberty to the captives *Isa 61:1*
p. the acceptable year of the Lord *Isa 61:2*
Go and *p.* these words toward *Jer 3:12*
Go, announce these words (B) *Jer 3:12*
p. to the house of Judah (B)(R) *Jer 5:20*
p. there this word, and say, Hear *Jer 7:2*
P. all these words in the cities of *Jer 11:6*
p. there the words that I shall tell *Jer 19:2*
Jerusalem, to *p.* liberty unto them *Jer 34:8*
make a proclamation of liberty (B) *Jer 34:8*
I *p.* a liberty for you, saith the Lord *Jer 34:17*
P. ye this among the Gentiles *Joe 3:9*
p. and publish the free offerings *Am 4:5*
p. to it the message (R) *Jon 3:2*
p. upon housetops *M't 10:27*
(A)(E)(P)(R)
p. in Decapolis (A)(R) *M'k 5:20*
p. the good news (N)(P) *M'k 16:15*
p. the acceptable year (A)(B)(E)(P) *Lu 4:18*
to *p.* the kingdom (N) *Lu 9:2*
p. to the people (N) *Ac 10:42*
p. the word (A) *Ac 16:6*
p. the glad tidings (A) *Ac 16:10*
Jesus whom we *p.* (A)(E)(R) *Ac 17:3*
him we *p.* (B)(E)(N)(P)(R) *Col 1:28*
p. it fully (A) *Col 4:4*
p. the message (N) *2Ti 4:2*
to *p.* (B)(E)(N)(P)(R) *Re 14:6*

PROCLAIMED

there, and *p.* the name of the Lord *Ex 34:5*
Lord passed by before him, and *p.* *Ex 34:6*
it to be *p.* throughout the camp *Ex 36:6*
broadcast in all the camp (B) *Ex 36:6*
They *p.* a fast, and set Naboth on *1Ki 21:12*
assembly for Baal. And they *p.* it *2Ki 10:20*
man of God *p.*, who *p.* these words *2Ki 23:16*
p. these things that thou hast done *2Ki 23:17*
and *p.* a fast throughout all Judah *2Ch 20:3*
Then I *p.* a fast there, at the river *Ezr 8:21*
p. throughout (A)(R) *Es 1:20*
p. before him, Thus shall it be done *Es 6:11*
I have *p.* glad tidings (A)(B)(E) *Ps 40:9*
p. the good news (B) *Ps 68:11*
the Lord hath *p.* unto the end of *Isa 62:11*
that they *p.* a fast before the Lord *Jer 36:9*
and *p.* a fast, and put on sackcloth *Jon 3:5*
he caused it to be *p.* and published *Jon 3:7*
more zealously *p.* (A)(R) *M'k 7:36*
shall be *p.* upon the housetops *Lu 12:3*
p. these days (R) *Ac 3:24*
p. the Christ (A)(E)(R) *Ac 8:5*
p. good news (P) *Ac 8:12*
p. through Judea (A)(N)(P)(R) *Ac 10:37*
removal of sins now *p.* (A)(E)(N)(P)(R) *Ac 13:38*
word of God *p.* (B)(E)(N)(P)(R) *Ac 17:13*
the gospel 1 *p.* (N) *1Co 2:4*
gospel *p.* (A) *1Co 15:1; Ga 1:11; 3:8*
we *p.* glad tidings (A)(N) *1Th 2:9*
p. among nations (N)(P) *1Ti 3:16*
glad tidings *p.* (A) *Heb 4:2*

PROCLAIMETH

the heart of fools *p.* foolishness *Pr 12:23*

PROCLAIMING

in *p.* liberty every man to his *Jer 34:15*
p. liberty, every one to his brother *Jer 34:17*
p. in the desert (B) *M't 3:1*
p. good news (A)(P) *M't 9:35*
p. Jesus the resurrection (A)(E)(N)(R) *Ac 4:2*
p. the Messiah (N) *Ac 8:5*
every city *p.* him (B) *Ac 15:21*
p. the word (A) *Ac 15:35*
p. the Messiah (N)(P) *Ac 17:3*
p. the kingdom (A)(N) *Ac 20:25*
p. Jesus Christ (B) *Ac 20:25*
after *p.* to others (A) *1Co 9:27*
strong angel *p.* with a loud voice *Re 5:2*

PROCLAMATION

and Aaron made *p.* and said, To *Ex 32:5*
make *p.* (A)(E)(R) *Le 23:4*
king Asa made a *p.* throughout *1Ki 15:22*
went a *p.* throughout the host *1Ki 22:36*
they made a *p.* through Judah *2Ch 24:9*
make *p.* throughout all *2Ch 30:5; 36:22; Ezr 1:1*
they made *p.* throughout *Ezr 10:7*
a *p.* to all people (A)(R) *Es 8:13*
make a *p.* of liberty (B) *Jer 34:8*
and made a *p.* concerning him *Da 5:29*
p. of Jesus Christ (N) *Ac 20:25*
the folly of the *p.* (B) *1Co 1:21*
made *p.* to spirits (N) *1Pe 3:9*

PROCURE

we *p.* great evil against our souls *Jer 26:19*
all the prosperity that I *p.* unto it *Jer 33:9*

PROCURED

p. wives for them (R) *2Ch 11:23*
punishment *p.* our peace (B) *Isa 53:5*
Hast thou not *p.* this unto thyself *Jer 2:17*
way and thy doings have *p.* these *Jer 4:18*
p. wrangling (A) *1Ti 6:5*

PROCURETH

diligently seeketh good *p.* favour *Pr 11:27*

PRODUCE

p. of the ground (B) *Ge 4:3; Le 25:3; Ps 105:35*
it may *p.* (A) *Le 19:25; Isa 5:10*
produce (B) *Le 19:25; 26:20; De 11:17; Ps 11:7; 85:12; Isa 5:10; Ho 8:7; Jas 3:12*
sold the *p.* (A) *Ne 13:15*
cover face of earth with *p.* (B) *Isa 26:6*
P. your cause, saith the Lord *Isa 41:21*
p. witnesses to justify them (B)(R) *Isa 43:9*

PRODUCE

p. tool for work (B) — Isa 54:16
when p. comes in (R) — Jer 25:22
p. of the vine (B) — M't 26:29
store my p. (N) — Lu 12:17
store my p. (B) — Lu 12:18
first share of p. (B)(P) — 2Ti 2:6
awaits precious p. (B) — Jas 5:7

PRODUCED

land p. its crops (A) — Jas 5:18

PRODUCES

p. weapon for (A)(E)(R) — Isa 54:16
inevitable disintegration lust p. — 2Pe 1:4
(P)

PRODUCING

p. piety before men (R) — M't 6:1

PRODUCT

eat p. of own hands (B) — Ps 128:1
the p. of her hands (B) — Pr 31:31

PRODUCTIONS

precious p. (B) — Isa 44:9

PRODUCTIVE

may be p. for God (P) — Ro 7:4
become p. for death (P) — Ro 7:5

PRODUCTS

p. of the land (A)(B) — Ge 43:11

PROFANE

p. it by applying tools (B)(R) — Ex 20:25
who p. it (A)(B)(E) — Ex 31:14
shalt thou p. the name of thy — Le 18:21;
thy God — 19:12
dishonor the name of God — Le 19:12;
(B) — 20:3
sanctuary, and to p. my holy — Le 20:3
name
among his people, to p. himself — Le 21:4
and not p. the name of their — Le 21:6
God
not desecrate the name of the — Le 21:6
Lord (B)
take a wife that is a whore, or — Le 21:7
p.
p. herself by playing the whore — Le 21:9
nor p. the sanctuary of his — Le 21:12
God
widow, or a divorced woman, — Le 21:14
or p.
he p. his seed among his — Le 21:15
people
not dishonor his offspring (B) — Le 21:15
that he p. not my sanctuaries — Le 21:23
that they p. not my holy name — Le 22:2
in
desecrate my holy name (B) — Le 22:2;
— 22:32
it, and die therefore, if they p. — Le 22:9
it
they shall not p. the holy — Le 22:15
things of
desecrate the holy gifts (B) — Le 22:15
Neither shall ye p. my holy — Le 22:32
name
not p. holy things (E)(R) — Nu 18:32
make you abound in p. (R) — De 28:11
that ye do, and p. the sabbath — Ne 13:17
day
defiling the sabbath (B) — Ne 13:17
the p. man destroys (B) — Pr 11:9
p. the name of God (A)(R) — Pr 30:9
p. my jewel (B)(R) — Ec 7:22
is p. (A)(E) — Isa 9:17
a p. nation (E)(R) — Isa 10:6
both prophet and priest are p. — Jer 23:11
they shall p. it (A)(E)(R) — Eze 7:21
they shall p. it — Eze 7:22
(A)(B)(E)(N)(R)
p. my holy name — Eze 20:39;
(A)(B)(E)(R) — 39:7
thou p. wicked prince of — Eze 21:25
Israel
between the holy and p. — Eze 22:26
neither
day into my sanctuary to p. it — Eze 23:39
Behold, I will p. my sanctuary — Eze 24:21
desecrate my sanctuary (B) — Eze 24:21
cast thee as p. out of the — Eze 28:16
mountain

the sanctuary and the p. — Eze 42:20
place
difference between the holy — Eze 44:23
and p.
shall be a p. place for the — Eze 48:15
city, for
same maid, to p. my holy name — Am 2:7
priests in the temple p. the — M't 12:5
sabbath
violate the sanctity of the — M't 12:5
sabbath (A)
break the sabbath (B)(N)(P) — M't 12:5
hath gone about to p. the — Ac 24:6
temple
desecrate and defile the temple — Ac 24:6
(A)(B)
and for sinners, for unholy and — 1Ti 1:9
p.
But refuse p. and old wives' — 1Ti 4:7
fables
unholy and old womanish tales — 1Ti 4:7
(B)
godless myths, fit only for old — 1Ti 4:7
women (N)
godless and silly myths (R) — 1Ti 4:7
avoid p., impure godless — 1Ti 4:7
fictions (A)
avoiding p. and vain — 1Ti 6:20
babblings, and
But shun p. and vain — 2Ti 2:16
babblings
be any fornicator, or p. — Heb 12:16
person
p., godless, sacrilegious — Heb 12:16
(A)(B)

PROFANED

hath p. the hallowed thing of — Le 19:8
p. dwelling place (A)(B) — Ps 74:7;
— Eze 7:24
thou hast p. his crown by — Ps 89:39
casting
defiled his crown in the dust — Ps 89:39
(B)(R)
I have p. the princes of the — Isa 43:28
I p. my heritage (A)(B)(E)(R) — Isa 47:6
my name is p. (B)(E)(R) — Isa 48:11
you have p. me (A)(E)(R) — Eze 13:19
p. in sight of heathen — Eze 20:9
p. my sabbaths — Eze 20:13;
(A)(B)(E)(R) — 20:16, 21, 24
things, and hast p. my — Eze 22:8
sabbaths
law, and have p. mine holy — Eze 22:26
things
sabbaths, and I am p. among — Eze 22:26
them
day, and have p. my sabbaths — Eze 23:38
my sanctuary, when it was p. — Eze 25:3
they went, they p. my holy — Eze 36:20
name
Israel had p. among the — Eze 36:21
heathen
ye have p. among the heathen — Eze 36:22
which was p. among the — Eze 36:23
heathen
ye have p. in the midst of — Eze 36:23
them
p. my holy name (A) — Eze 48:3
priests p. my sanctuary — Zep 3:4
(A)(E)(R)
But ye have p. it, in that ye — Mal 1:12
say
hath p. the holiness of the — Mal 2:11
Lord
p. the blood (N)(R) — Heb 10:29

PROFANELY

take name p. (B)(R) — Ex 20:7; De 5:11

PROFANENESS

practice p. (E) — Isa 32:6
the prophets of Jerusalem is — Jer 23:15
p.

PROFANETH

the whore, she p. her father; she — Le 21:9
she defiles her father (B) — Le 21:9

PROFANING

upon Israel by p. the sabbath — Ne 13:18
p. my name (B) — Eze 13:19
by p. the covenant of our — Mal 2:10
fathers

PROFESS

him, I p. this day unto the — De 26:3
Lord
I give thanks this day (A) — De 26:3
I here declare to the Lord — De 26:3
(B)(R)
then will I p. unto them, I — M't 7:23
never
I will say to them openly (A) — M't 7:23
I will frankly say to them (B) — M't 7:23
I will tell them to their face — M't 7:23
(N)
I shall tell them plainly (P) — M't 7:23
then will I declare to them — M't 7:23
(R)
They p. that they know God — Tit 1:16
high priest of religion we p. — Heb 3:1
(N)
hold fast religion we p. (N) — Heb 4:14

PROFESSED

for your p. subjection unto — 2Co 9:13
hast p. a good profession — 1Ti 6:12
before
boldly p. your loyalty (P) — 1Ti 6:12

PROFESSING

p. that you pray long (B) — M't 23:14
P. themselves to be wise, they — Ro 1:22
Claiming to be wise — Ro 1:22
(A)(B)(R)
They boast of their wisdom — Ro 1:22
(N)
becometh women p. godliness — 1Ti 2:10
some p. have erred concerning — 1Ti 6:21
making such profession some — 1Ti 6:21
(A)
some people have claimed (B) — 1Ti 6:21
many who lay claim to (N) — 1Ti 6:21

PROFESSION

who makes no p. (P) — 1Ti 5:8
good p. before many witnesses — 1Ti 6:12
confessed a good confession — 1Ti 6:12
(A)(B)(E)
confessed your faith nobly — 1Ti 6:12
(N)
boldly professed your loyalty — 1Ti 6:12
(P)
made a good confession (R) — 1Ti 6:12
making such p. some (A) — 1Ti 6:21
Apostle and High Priest of our — Heb 3:1
p.
high priest of our confession — Heb 3:1
(B)(E)(R)
high priest of the religion we — Heb 3:1
profess (N)
high priest of the faith we hold — Heb 3:1
(P)
Son of God, let us hold fast — Heb 4:14
our p.
hold fast our confession — Heb 4:14
(A)(B)(E)(R)
hold fast to the religion we — Heb 4:14
profess (N)
hold firmly to our faith (P) — Heb 4:14
Let us hold fast the p. of our — Heb 10:23
faith

PROFIT

what p. shall this birthright — Ge 25:32
do to
What p. is it if we slay our — Ge 37:26
brother
nor lend him for p. (S) — Le 25:37
which cannot p. nor deliver — 1Sa 12:21
cannot benefit (A) — 1Sa 12:21
for the king's p. to suffer them — Es 3:8
what p. should we have, if we — Job 21:15
the strength of their hands p. — Job 30:2
me
and, What p. shall I have, — Job 35:3
if I be
righteousness may p. the son — Job 35:8
of
What p. is there in my blood — Ps 30:9
of wickedness p. nothing; but — Pr 10:2
p. of wicked further sin (A) — Pr 10:16
Riches p. not in the day of — Pr 11:4
wrath
her p. is better — Pr 13:14
(A)(B)(E)(R)
In all labour there is p.: but — Pr 14:23
never lack p., gain — Pr 31:11
(B)(E)(R)

PROFIT

What *p.* hath a man of all his	Ec 1:3
and there was no *p.* under the sun	Ec 2:11
What *p.* hath he that worketh in	Ec 3:9
the *p.* of the earth is for all: the	Ec 5:9
and what *p.* hath he that hath	Ec 5:16
is *p.* to them that see the sun	Ec 7:11
a people that could not *p.* them	Isa 30:5
nor be an help nor *p.* but a shame	Isa 30:5
to a people that shall not *p.* them	Isa 30:6
their delectable things shall not *p.*	Isa 44:9
if so be thou shalt be able to	Isa 47:12
p. if	
you will be able to *p.*	Isa 47:12
(A)(B)(E)	
thy God which teacheth thee to *p.*	Isa 48:17
works; for they shall not *p.* thee	Isa 57:12
walked after things that do not *p.*	Jer 2:8
glory for that which doth not *p.*	Jer 2:11
trust in lying words, that cannot *p.*	Jer 7:8
themselves to pain, but shall not *p.*	Jer 12:13
and things wherein there is no *p.*	Jer 16:19
they shall not *p.* this people at all	Jer 23:32
what *p.* is it that we have kept his	Mal 3:14
For what shall it *p.* a man, if he	M'k 8:36
what does it *p.* (A)(R)	Lu 9:25; 1Co 15:32
p. each had made (N)(P)	Lu 19:15
what *p.* is there of circumcision	Ro 3:1
And this I speak for your own *p.*	1Co 7:35
things, not seeking mine own *p.*	1Co 10:33
p. of many, that they may be saved	1Co 10:33
is given to every man to *p.* withal	1Co 12:7
what shall I *p.* you, except I shall	1Co 14:6
what doth it *p.* if (S)	1Co 15:32
Christ shall *p.* you nothing	Ga 5:2
strive not about words to no *p.*	2Ti 2:14
word preached did not *p.* them	Heb 4:2
he for our *p.* that we might be	Heb 12:10
What doth it *p.*, my brethren	Jas 2:14
to the body; what doth it *p.*	Jas 2:16

PROFITABLE

Can a man be *p.* unto God, as he	Job 22:2
is wise may be *p.* unto himself	Job 22:2
but wisdom is *p.* to direct	Ec 10:10
image that is *p.* for nothing	Isa 44:1
was marred, it was *p.* for nothing	Jer 13:7
it is *p.* for thee that one of thy	M't 5:29; 5:30
back nothing that was *p.* unto you	Ac 20:20
godliness is *p.* unto all things	1Ti 4:8
and is *p.* for doctrine, for reproof	2Ti 3:16
for he is *p.* to me for the ministry	2Ti 4:11
things are good and *p.* unto men	Tit 3:8
but now *p.* to thee and to me	Ph'm 11

PROFITED

which was right, and it *p.* me not	Job 33:27
thou mightest be *p.* by me	M't 15:5
For what is a man *p.* if he shall	M't 16:26
thou mightest be *p.* by me; he	M'k 7:11
what is a man *p.* if (S)	Lu 9:25
And *p.* in the Jews' religion above	Ga 1:14
p. them that have been occupied	Heb 13:9

PROFITETH

It *p.* a man nothing that he	Job 34:9
What *p.* the graven image that	Hab 2:18

the flesh *p.* nothing: the words — Joh 6:63
circumcision verily *p.* if thou keep — Ro 2:25
have not charity, it *p.* me nothing — 1Co 13:3
For bodily exercise *p.* little — 1Ti 4:8

PROFITING

that thy *p.* may appear to all	1Ti 4:15

PROFITS

enjoyed *p.* of our dowry (B)	Ge 31:15
who despise unfair *p.* (B)	Ex 18:21
p. from trade (B)	1Ki 10:15

PROFLIGACY

accused of *p.* or unruly (S)	Tit 1:6
run not with them to the same *p.* (S)	1Pe 4:4

PROFLIGATE

being *p.* or insubordinate (R)	Tit 1:6

PROFOUND

revolters are *p.* to make slaughter	Ho 5:2
seized with *p.* dread (A)	Lu 8:25

PROGENITORS

blessings of my *p.* unto the utmost	Ge 49:26
blessings of my forefathers (A)	Ge 49:26
blessings of my forebears (B)	Ge 49:26
blessings of the eternal mountains (R)	Ge 49:26

PROGNOSTICATORS

stargazers, the monthly *p.* stand	Isa 47:13

PROGRESSED

how the war *p.* (A)(R)	2Sa 11:7

PROHIBITIONS

to purely human *p.* (P)	Col 2:20

PROJECTING

p. tower (S)	Ne 3:25; 3:26-27

PROJECTION

over against the rounded *p.* (S)	1Ki 7:20

PROLONG

shall not *p.* your days upon it	De 4:26
mayest *p.* thy days upon the earth	De 4:40
ye may *p.* your days in the land	De 5:33; 11:9
he may *p.* his days in his kingdom	De 17:20
and that thou mayest *p.* thy days	De 22:7
shall not *p.* your days upon the land	De 30:18
ye shall *p.* your days in the land	De 32:47
mine end, that I should *p.* my life	Job 6:11
neither shall he *p.* the perfection	Job 15:29
does not *p.* life of wicked (A)(B)	Job 36:6
Thou wilt *p.* the king's life	Ps 61:6
covetousness shall *p.* his days	
neither shall he *p.* his days, which	
seed, he shall *p.* his days, and the	

PROLONGED

that thy days may be *p.* and that	De 5:16
life; and that thy days may be *p.*	De 6:2

the state thereof shall be *p.* — Pr 28:2
his days be *p.* yet surely I know — Ec 8:12
come, and her days shall not be *p.* — Isa 13:22
The days are *p.* and every vision — Eze 12:22
it shall be no more *p.*: for in your — Eze 12:25
shall none of my words be *p.* any — Eze 12:28
lives were *p.* for a season and — Da 7:12

PROLONGETH

The fear of the Lord *p.* days	Pr 10:27
a wicked man that *p.* his life in	Ec 7:15
evil that I have *p.* against them	Jer 35:17
Lord hath *p.* against this people	Jer 36:7
He *p.* all these words unto me	Jer 36:18
evil that I have *p.* against them	Jer 36:31
hath *p.* this evil upon this place	Jer 40:2

PROMINENT

grew a *p.* horn (B)	Da 8:5
p. Ammonites escape (B)	Da 11:41
the *p.* woman (B)	Ac 17:4
p. citizens (A)(B)(N)(P)(R)	Ac 25:23
who likes to be *p.* (B)	3Jo 9

PROMISCUITY

sexual *p.* (P)	1Co 6:13

PROMISE

and ye shall know my breach of *p.*	Nu 14:34
hath fulfilled his *p.* (A)(B)(R)	1Ki 8:20
failed one word of all his good *p.*	1Ki 8:56
let thy *p.* unto David my father be	2Ch 1:9
should do according to this *p.*	Ne 5:12
performeth not this *p.* even thus	Ne 5:13
the people did according to this *p.*	Ne 5:13
fulfilled your *p.* (A)(B)(R)	Ne 9:8
doth his *p.* fail for ever more	Ps 77:8
he remembered his holy *p.*	Ps 105:42
the *p.* of my Father upon you	Lu 24:49
but wait for the *p.* of the Father	Ac 1:4
Father, the *p.* of the Holy Ghost	Ac 2:33
For the *p.* is unto you, and to your	Ac 2:39
when the time of the *p.* drew nigh	Ac 7:17
according to his *p.* raised unto	Ac 13:23
p. which was made unto the fathers	Ac 13:32
ready, looking for a *p.* from thee	Ac 23:21
for the hope of the *p.* made of God	Ac 26:6
Unto which *p.* our twelve tribes	Ac 26:7
For the *p.* that he should be to all	Ro 4:13
and the *p.* made of none effect	Ro 4:14
the end the *p.* might be sure to all	Ro 4:16
He staggered not at the *p.* of God	Ro 4:20
children of the *p.* are counted for	Ro 9:8
this is the word of *p.* At this time	Ro 9:9
the *p.* of the Spirit through faith	Ga 3:14
should make the *p.* of none effect	Ga 3:17
be of the law, it is no more of *p.*	Ga 3:18
but God gave it to Abraham by *p.*	Ga 3:18
come to whom the *p.* was made	Ga 3:19
that the *p.* by faith of Jesus Christ	Ga 3:22

and heirs according to the *p.*   *Ga 3:29*
he of the freewoman was by   *Ga 4:23*
p.
as Isaac was, are the children   *Ga 4:28*
of *p.*
sealed with that holy Spirit   *Eph 1:13*
of *p.*
from the covenants of *p.*   *Eph 2:12*
having
partakers of his *p.* in Christ   *Eph 3:6*
by the
participants of the *p.* (B)(P)   *Eph 3:6*
is the first commandment with   *Eph 6:2*
p.
having *p.* of the life that now   *1Ti 4:8*
is
the *p.* of life which is in Christ   *2Ti 1:1*
a *p.* being left us of entering   *Heb 4:1*
into
when God made *p.* to   *Heb 6:13*
Abraham
endured, he obtained the *p.*   *Heb 6:15*
to shew unto the heirs of *p.*   *Heb 6:17*
the *p.* of eternal inheritance   *Heb 9:15*
of God, ye might receive   *Heb 10:36*
the *p.*
faith he sojourned in the   *Heb 11:9*
land of *p.*
the heirs with him of the   *Heb 11:9*
same *p.*
through faith, received not   *Heb 14:39*
the *p.*
While they *p.* them liberty,   *2Pe 2:19*
they
Where is the *p.* of his coming   *2Pe 3:4*
is not slack concerning his *p.*   *2Pe 3:9*
according to his *p.* look for   *2Pe 3:13*
new
the *p.* that he hath promised   *1Jo 2:25*
us

PROMISED

according as he hath *p.* that   *Ex 12:25*
ye
you *p.* by thine own (R)   *Ex 32:13*
land you *p.* (B)   *Nu 11:12; De 26:15*
place which the Lord hath *p.*   *Nu 14:40*
and bless you, as he hath *p.*   *De 1:11*
you
Lord God of thy fathers hath   *De 6:3*
p.
into the land which he *p.*   *De 9:28*
them
as the Lord thy God *p.* him   *De 10:9*
thy border, as he hath *p.*   *De 12:20*
thee, and
God blesseth thee, as he *p.*   *De 15:6*
thee
land which he *p.* to give unto   *De 19:8*
thy
thou hast *p.* with thy mouth   *De 23:23*
peculiar people, as he hath *p.*   *De 26:18*
thee
God of thy fathers hath *p.*   *De 27:3*
thee
as the princes had *p.* them   *Jos 9:21*
unto your brethren, as he *p.*   *Jos 22:4*
them
Lord your God hath *p.* unto   *Jos 23:5*
you
fighteth for you, as he hath   *Jos 23:10*
p. you
the Lord your God *p.* you;   *Jos 23:15*
which
p. this goodness unto thy   *2Sa 7:28*
servant
hath made me an house, as   *1Ki 2:24*
he *p.*
Solomon wisdom, as he *p.*   *1Ki 5:12*
him
throne of Israel, as the Lord   *1Ki 8:20*
p.
Israel, according to all that he   *1Ki 8:56*
p.
which he *p.* by the hand of   *1Ki 8:56*
Moses
as I *p.* to David thy father,   *1Ki 9:5*
saying
as he *p.* him to give him   *2Ki 8:19*
alway a
p. this goodness unto thy   *1Ch 17:26*
servant
throne of Israel, as the Lord   *2Ch 6:10*
p.
that which thou hast *p.* him   *2Ch 6:15*
which thou hast *p.* him,   *2Ch 6:16*
saying
as he *p.* to give a light to   *2Ch 21:7*
him and

which thou hadst *p.* to their   *Ne 9:23*
fathers
money that Haman had *p.* to   *Es 4:7*
pay
all the good that I have *p.*   *Jer 32:42*
them
that good thing which I have   *Jer 33:14*
p.
he *p.* with an oath to give her   *M't 14:7*
glad, and *p.* to give him   *M'k 14:11*
money
perform the mercy *p.* to our   *Lu 1:72*
fathers
he *p.* and sought opportunity   *Lu 22:6*
to
yet he *p.* that he would give   *Ac 7:5*
it him
he had *p.* afore by his prophets   *Ro 1:2*
what he had *p.* he was able   *Ro 4:21*
also
commandment *p.* life (R)   *Ro 7:10*
God, that cannot lie, *p.* before   *Tit 1:2*
wavering; (he is faithful   *Heb 10:23*
that *p.*)
judged him faithful who   *Heb 11:11*
had *p.*
now he hath *p.* saying, Yet   *Heb 12:26*
once
Lord hath *p.* to them that   *Jas 1:12*
love him
kingdom which he hath *p.* to   *Jas 2:5*
them
promise that he hath *p.* us,   *1Jo 2:25*
even

PROMISEDST

David my father that thou *p.*   *1Ki 8:24;*
him   *8:25*
p. them that they should go in   *Ne 9:15*
to

PROMISER

regarded the *P.* trustworthy   *Heb 11:11*
(B)

PROMISES

does make his *p.* come true   *Lu 1:45*
(P)
and the service of God, and the   *Ro 9:4*
the *p.* made unto the fathers   *Ro 15:8*
personally implemented *p.* (P)   *Ro 15:9*
For all the *p.* of God in   *2Co 1:20*
are yea
Having therefore these *p.*   *2Co 7:1*
dearly
and his seed were the *p.* made   *Ga 3:16*
the law then against the *p.* of   *Ga 3:21*
God
faith and patience inherit the   *Heb 6:12*
p.
and blessed him that had the   *Heb 7:6*
p.
was established upon better *p.*   *Heb 8:6*
faith, not having received the   *Heb 11:13*
p.
he that had received the *p.*   *Heb 11:17*
offered
obtained *p.* stopped the   *Heb 11:33*
mouths of
exceeding great and precious   *2Pe 1:4*
p.

PROMISING

his wicked way, by *p.* him   *Eze 13:22*
life

PROMOTE

I will *p.* thee unto very great   *Nu 22:17*
able indeed to *p.* thee to   *Nu 22:37*
honour
to *p.* thee unto great honour   *Nu 24:11*
did king Ahasuerus *p.* Haman   *Es 3:1*
nor *p.* their schemes (B)   *Ps 140:8*
Exalt her, and she shall *p.* thee   *Pr 4:8*

PROMOTED

go to be *p.* over the trees   *J'g 9:9;*
   9:11, 13
p. Haman (A)(B)(E)(R)   *Es 3:1; 5:11*
wherein the king had *p.* him   *Es 5:11*
Then the king *p.* Shadrach   *Da 3:30*

PROMOTION

p. cometh neither from the   *Ps 75:6*
east
but shame shall be the *p.* of   *Pr 3:35*
fools
will find *p.* (P)   *M't 23:12*

PROMPTED

p. by her mother (A)(N)(P)(R)   *M't 14:8*
nothing *p.* by conceit (A)   *Ph'p 2:3*

PROMPTINGS

obeyed *p.* of instincts (N)   *Eph 2:3*

PROMULGATED

it was *p.* through angels (N)   *Ga 3:19*

PROMULGATING

p. ways of behavior (B)   *Ac 16:21*

PRONE

p. to human weakness (P)   *Heb 5:2*

PRONOUNCE

that a man shall *p.* with an   *Le 5:4*
oath
look on him, and *p.* him   *Le 13:3;*
unclean *3:8, 11, 15, 20, 22, 25, 27, 30,*
   44, 59
priest shall *p.* him clean   *Le 13:6;*
   13:13, 17, 23, 28, 34, 37; 14:7
the priest shall *p.* the house   *Le 14:48*
clean
he could not frame to *p.*   *J'g 12:6*
it right
do not *p.* reviling judgment   *2Pe 2:11*
(R)

PRONOUNCED

p. sentence upon him   *2Ki 25:6*
(A)(B)(R)(S)
he *p.* this prophecy against me   *Ne 6:12*
hath *p.* evil against thee, for   *Jer 11:17*
p. all this great evil against   *Jer 16:10*
us
nation, against whom I have   *Jer 18:8*
p.
the evil that I have *p.*   *Jer 19:15*
against it
words which I have *p.*   *Jer 25:13*
against it
evil that he hath *p.* against   *Jer 26:13*
you
evil which he had *p.* against   *Jer 26:19*
them
for I have *p.* the word, saith   *Jer 34:5*
God who *p.* her doom (N)   *Re 18:8*

PRONOUNCEMENT

aware of God's *p.* (P)   *Ro 1:32*

PRONOUNCES

p. a blessing (A)(E)(R)   *Ro 4:6*
God who *p.* the acquittal (N)   *Ro 8:33*

PRONOUNCING

swear, *p.* with his lips to do evil   *Le 5:4*
person unthinkingly utters an   *Le 5:4*
oath (B)
one swear rashly with his lips   *Le 5:4*
(E)
utters with his lips a rash oath   *Le 5:4*
(R)

PROOF

for a *p.* (P)   *M't 8:4; M'k 1:44; Lu 5:14*
p. is ground of hope (N)   *Ro 5:4*
that I might know the *p.* of   *2Co 2:9*
you
p. of your love, and of our   *2Co 8:24*
a *p.* of Christ speaking in me   *2Co 13:3*
But ye know the *p.* of him,   *Ph'p 2:22*
that
make full *p.* of thy ministry   *2Ti 4:5*
let right conduct give *p.* (N)   *Jas 3:13*
you have put to *p.* (N)   *Re 2:2*

PROOFS

p. of her virginity (B)   De 22:15
his passion by many infallible   Ac 1:3
p.

PROPER

it is not p. so to do (S)   Ex 8:26
sought him not the p. way   1Ch 15:13
(S)
I have of mine own p. good,   1Ch 29:3
of
meat in p. time (B)   Ps 145:15
feast in p. time (B)   Ec 10:17
at the p. time (A)(R)   M't 24:45
fulfilled in p. time (A)   Lu 1:20
at the p. time   Lu 12:42
(B)(N)(P)(R)
field is called in their p.   Ac 1:19
tongue
things not p. or decent   Ro 1:28
(A)(B)
every man hath his p. gift of   1Co 7:7
God
when p. time had come   Ga 4:4
(A)(P)
they saw he was a p. child   Heb 11:23
abandoned p. dwelling place   Jude 6
(A)(B)(R)
abandoned p. home (N)(P)   Jude 6

PROPERLY

conduct yourselves p. (A)   1Pe 2:12

PROPERTY

all moveable p. (B)   Ge 31:10
their p. which God (R)   Ge 31:16
acquire p. (B)   Ge 34:10
he is his p. (A)(B)   Ex 21:21
on the p. (B)   2Ki 9:26
all his p. forfeited (A)   Ezr 10:8
take the p. (S)   Es 3:13; 8:11
took over their p. (B)   Es 8:11
snatched from his p. (A)   Job 8:18
spoil, booty, p. (B)   Da 11:24
steal his p. (P)   M't 12:29
charge of his p. (B)(N)(P)   M't 24:47
p. and personal belongings (A)   Lu 8:3
p. is in peace (P)   Lu 11:21
share of p.   Lu 15:12
(A)(B)(N)(P)(R)
wasted his p. (N)(P)   Lu 15:13
squandering his p. (N)   Lu 16:1
sold possessions and p. (A)(B)   Ac 2:45
plundering your p. (B)(R)   Heb 10:34

PROPHECIES

whether there be p. they shall   1Co 13:8
the p. which went before on   1Ti 1:18
thee

PROPHECY

in the p. of Ahijah the   2Ch 9:29
Shilonite
and the p. of Oded the   2Ch 15:8
prophet
he pronounced this p. against   Ne 6:12
me
the son of Jakeh, even the p.   Pr 30:1
the p. that his mother taught   Pr 31:1
him
to seal up the vision and p.   Da 9:24
them is fulfilled the p. of   M't 13:14
Esaias
that is given to us, whether p.   Ro 12:6
working of miracles: to   1Co 12:10
another p.
though I have the gift of p.   1Co 13:2
in thee, which was given thee   1Ti 4:14
by p.
have also a more sure word   2Pe 1:19
of p.
that no p. of the scripture is   2Pe 1:20
of any
no one can interpret any p.   2Pe 1:20
by (N)
For the p. came not in old   2Pe 1:21
time by
they that hear the words of this   Re 1:3
p.
it rain not in the days of their   Re 11:6
p.
testimony of Jesus is the   Re 19:10
spirit of p.

the sayings of the p. of this   Re 22:7;
book   22:10
the words of the p. of this   Re 22:18
book
the words of the book of this   Re 22:19
p.

PROPHESIED

spirit rested upon them, they   Nu 11:25
tabernacle: and they p. in   Nu 11:26
the camp
upon him, and he p. among   1Sa 10:10
them
he p. among the prophets,   1Sa 10:11
that the
and he p. in the midst of the   1Sa 18:10
house
of Saul, and they also p.   1Sa 19:20
messengers, and they p.   1Sa 19:21
likewise
the third time, and they p.   1Sa 19:21
also
he went on, and p. until he   1Sa 19:23
came
p. before Samuel in like   1Sa 19:24
manner
and they p. until the time of   1Ki 18:29
all the prophets p. before   1Ki 22:10
them
all the prophets p. so,   1Ki 22:12
saying, Go
p. according to the order of   1Ch 25:2
also p. with a harp, to give   1Ch 25:3
thanks
for he never p. good unto   2Ch 18:7
me, but
all the prophets p. before   2Ch 18:9
them
And all the prophets p. so,   2Ch 18:11
saying
p. Eliezer against   2Ch 20:37
Jehoshaphat
p. unto the Jews that were in   Ezr 5:1
and the prophets p. by Baal   Jer 2:8
that Jeremiah p. these things   Jer 20:1
friends, to whom thou hast p.   Jer 20:6
lies
they p. in Baal, and caused   Jer 23:13
my
not spoken to them, yet they   Jer 23:21
p.
hath p. against all the   Jer 25:13
nations
thou p. in the name of the   Jer 26:9
Lord
for he hath p. against this   Jer 26:11
city, as
Micah the Morasthite p. in   Jer 26:18
the days
man that p. in the name of   Jer 26:20
the Lord
who p. against this city and   Jer 26:20
against
thy words which thou hast p.   Jer 28:6
old p. both against many   Jer 28:8
countries
that Shemaiah hath p. unto   Jer 29:31
you
your prophets which p. unto   Jer 37:19
you
to pass, when I p. that   Eze 11:13
Pelatiah
So I p. as I was commanded   Eze 37:7
and as I p. there was a noise   Eze 37:7
So I p. as he commanded   Eze 37:10
me, and
which p. in those days many   Eze 38:17
years
one of his vision, when he   Zec 13:4
hath p.
Lord, have we not p. in thy   M't 7:22
name
prophets and the law p.   M't 11:13
until John
Well hath Esaias p. of you   M'k 7:6
the Holy Ghost, and p. saying   Lu 1:67
he p. that Jesus should die   Joh 11:51
for that
p. through the Spirit (A)   Ac 11:28
and they spake with tongues,   Ac 19:6
and p.
with tongues, but rather that   1Co 14:5
ye p.
who p. of the grace that   1Pe 1:10
should
Adam, p. of these, saying,   Jude 14
Behold

PROPHESIETH

The prophet which p. of peace   Jer 28:9
he p. of the times that are   Eze 12:27
far off
thrust him through when he   Zec 13:3
p.
or p. with her head   1Co 11:5
uncovered
But he that p. speaketh unto   1Co 14:3
men
but he that p. edifieth the   1Co 14:4
church
greater is he that p. than he   1Co 14:5
that

PROPHESY

and Medad do p. in the   Nu 11:27
camp
before them; and they shall p.   1Sa 10:5
thou shalt p. with them, and   1Sa 10:6
shalt
he doth not p. good   1Ki 22:8
concerning me
would p. no good   1Ki 22:18
concerning me
who should p. with harps,   1Ch 25:1
with
he would not p. good unto   2Ch 18:17
me, but
P. not unto us right things,   Isa 30:10
speak
unto us smooth things, p.   Isa 30:10
deceits
The prophets p. falsely, and   Jer 5:31
P. not in the name of the   Jer 11:21
Lord
The prophets p. lies in my   Jer 14:14
name
they p. unto you a false   Jer 14:14
vision and
the prophets that p. in my   Jer 14:15
name
the people to whom they p.   Jer 14:16
shall be
whither the Lord had sent   Jer 19:14
him to p.
words of the prophets that p.   Jer 23:16
unto
said, that p. lies in my name   Jer 23:25
heart of the prophets, that p.   Jer 23:26
lies
against them that p. false   Jer 23:32
dreams
p. thou against them all these   Jer 25:30
sent me to p. against this   Jer 26:12
house
For they p. a lie unto you, to   Jer 27:10
remove
Babylon: for they p. a lie   Jer 27:14;
unto you   27:16
Lord, yet they p. a lie in my   Jer 27:15
name
and the prophets that p. unto   Jer 27:15
you
of your prophets that p. unto   Jer 27:16
you
p. falsely unto you in my   Jer 29:9
name
p. a lie unto you in my name   Jer 29:21
Wherefore dost thou p. and   Jer 32:3
say
and thou shalt p. against it   Eze 4:7
of Israel, and p. against them   Eze 6:2
p. against them, p. O son of   Eze 11:4
man
p. against the prophets of   Eze 13:2
Israel
the prophets of Israel that p.   Eze 13:2
unto them that p. out of their   Eze 13:2
own
the prophets of Israel which   Eze 13:16
p.
daughters of thy people,   Eze 13:17
which p.
heart; and p. thou against   Eze 13:17
them
p. against the forest of the   Eze 20:46
south
and p. against the land of   Eze 21:2
Israel
Son of man, p. and say, Thus   Eze 21:9;
saith   21:28; 30:2
son of man, p. and smite   Eze 21:14
thine
Ammonites, and p. against   Eze 25:2
them
against Zidon, and p.   Eze 28:21
against it

king of Egypt, and *p.* against *Eze 29:2*
him

p. against the shepherds of *Eze 34:2*
Israel

p. and say unto them, Thus *Eze 34:2*
saith

mount Seir, and *p.* against it *Eze 35:2*

p. unto the mountains of *Eze 36:1*
Israel

Therefore *p.* and say, Thus *Eze 36:3*
saith

P. therefore concerning the *Eze 36:6*
land of

P. upon these bones, and say *Eze 37:4*
unto

P. unto the wind, *p.*, son of *Eze 37:9*
man

Therefore *p.* and say unto *Eze 37:12*
them

and Tubal, and *p.* against *Eze 38:2*
him

son of man, *p.* and say unto *Eze 38:14*
Gog

thou son of man, *p.* against *Eze 39:1*
Gog

sons and your daughters shall *Joe 2:28;*
p.   *Ac 2:17*

the prophets, saying, *P.* not *Am 2:12*

God hath spoken, who can but *Am 3:8*
p.

and there eat bread, and *p.* *Am 7:12*
there

p. not again any more at *Am 7:13*
Beth-el

me, Go, *p.* unto my people *Am 7:15*
Israel

Thou sayest, *P.* not against *Am 7:16*
Israel

P. ye not, say they to them *Mic 2:6*
that

say they to them that *p:* they *Mic 2:6*
shall

they shall not *p.* to them, that *Mic 2:6*
they

I will *p.* unto thee of wine *Mic 2:11*
and of

that when any shall yet *p.* *Zec 13:3*
then

well did Esaias *p.* of you, *M't 15:7*
saying

P. unto us, thou Christ, *M't 26:68*
Who is he

him, and to say unto him, *M'k 14:65*
P.

P. who is it that smote thee *Lu 22:64*

of my Spirit; and they shall *p.* *Ac 2:18*

daughters, virgins, which did *Ac 21:9*
p.

let us *p.* according to the *Ro 12:6*
proportion

we know in part, and we *p.* *1Co 13:9*
in part

gifts, but rather that we may *1Co 14:1*
p.

if all *p.* and there come in *1Co 14:24*
one that

For ye may all *p.* one by *1Co 14:31*
one, that

covet to *p.* and forbid not *1Co 14:39*
to speak

Thou must *p.* again before *Re 10:11*
many

shall *p.* a thousand two *Re 11:3*
hundred

PROPHESYING

when he had made an end *1Sa 10:13*
of *p.*

the company of the prophets *1Sa 19:20*
p.

prospered through the *p.* of *Ezr 6:14*
Haggai

Every man praying or *p.* *1Co 11:4*
having

or by knowledge, or by *p.* or *1Co 14:6*
but *p.* serveth not for them *1Co 14:22*
that

PROPHESYINGS

Despise not *p.*   *1Th 5:20*

PROPHET

and Aaron thy brother shall be *Ex 7:1*
thy *p.*

but the *p.* which shall *De 18:20;*
presume   *18:22*

the *p.* Gad said to David, *1Sa 22:5*
Abide not

the word of the Lord came *2Sa 24:11*
to the *p.*

the *p.* God (A)(B) *2Sa 24:11*

David said, Call me Nathan *1Ki 1:32*
the *p.*

the king hath sent with him *1Ki 1:44*
Nathan the *p.*

Ahijah the *p.* found *1Ki 11:29*
Jeroboam in the way

there dwelt an old *p.* in *1Ki 13:11;*
Beth-el   *13:25*

for the *p.* whom he had *1Ki 13:23*
brought back

p. took up the carcase of *1Ki 13:29*
man of God and the old *p.*
came to mourn

by hand of the *p.* Jehu came *1Ki 16:7;*
the word   *16:12*

Elijah *p.* came near and *1Ki 18:36*
said, God

p. came to king of Israel, *1Ki 20:22*
and said

would God my lord were with *2Ki 5:3*
the *p.*

if the *p.* had bid thee do *2Ki 5:13*
some great thing

Elisha the *p.* telleth what *2Ki 6:12*
thou speakest

young man the *p.* went to *2Ki 9:4*
Ramoth

Isaiah the *p.* cried to Lord, *2Ki 20:11*
he brought

with bones of *p.* that came *2Ki 23:18*
out of Samaria

came Shemaiah the *p.* to *2Ch 12:5*
Rehoboam

are written in the story of *2Ch 13:22*
the *p.* Iddo

Asa heard the prophecy of *2Ch 15:8*
the *p.* Oded

there came a writing from *2Ch 21:12*
Elijah the *p.*

then the *p.* forbare, and *2Ch 25:16*
said, I know

p. Isaiah prayed and cried *2Ch 32:20*
to heaven

none like it from days of *2Ch 35:18*
Samuel the *p.*

humbled not himself before *2Ch 36:12*
Jeremiah the *p.*

then Haggai the *p.* prophesied *Ezr 5:1*

through the prophesying of *Ezr 6:14*
Haggai the *p.*

there is no more any *p.* among *Ps 74:9*
you

Lord doth take away the *p.* *Isa 3:2*

the *p.* that teacheth lies, he is *Isa 9:15*
the tail

priest and *p.* erred thro' *Isa 28:7*
strong drink

from *p.* to the priests deal *Jer 6:13;*
falsely   *8:10*

nor shall the word perish *Jer 18:18*
from the *p.*

for both *p.* and priests are *Jer 23:11*
profane

the *p.* that hath a dream let *Jer 23:28*
him tell

the *p.* Jeremiah said, Amen, *Jer 28:6*
the Lord do so

p. prophesieth of peace, when *Jer 28:9*
word of *p.* come to pass
then *p.* be known

so Hananiah the *p.* died the *Jer 28:17*
same year

to take Baruch and Jeremiah *Jer 36:26*
the *p.*

nor he nor his servants *Jer 37:2*
hearken to the *p.*

take up Jeremiah the *p.* out *Jer 38:10*
of dungeon

shall the *p.* be slain in the *La 2:20*
sanctuary

then shall they seek a vision *Eze 7:26*
of *p.*

cometh to the *p.* I will *Eze 14:4*
answer him

if *p.* be deceived, I have *Eze 14:9*
deceived that *p.*

punishment of the *p.* shall *Eze 14:10*
be even as

p. also shall fall with thee in *Ho 4:5*
the night

the *p.* is a fool; *p.* is a snare *Ho 9:7;*
of a fowler   *9:8*

then he said, I was no *p.* nor *Am 7:14*
prophet's son

a prayer of Habakkuk the *p.* *Hab 3:1*

he shall say, I am no *p.* *Zec 13:5*

behold, I will send you Elijah *Mal 4:5*
the *p.*

spoke by the *p.* Isaiah *M't 1:22;*
   2:15; 3:3; 4:14; 8:17; 21:4; Lu 3:4;
         Joh 1:23; 12:38; Ac 28:25

in Bethlehem, it is written by *M't 2:5*
the *p.*

which was spoken by Jeremy *M't 2:17;*
p.   *27:9*

but the sign of the *p.* Jonas *M't 12:39;*
     Lu 11:29

which was spoken by *p.* *M't 13:35;*
David   *27:35*

this is Jesus the *p.* of *M't 21:11*
Nazareth

spoken of by Daniel the *p.* *M't 24:15;*
     M'k 13:14

thou child be called *p.* of the *Lu 1:76*
Highest

delivered to him the book of *Lu 4:17*
p. Esaias

no *p.* is accepted in his own *Lu 4:24*
country

many lepers in the time of *Lu 4:27*
Eliseus the *p.*

not a greater *p.* than John the *Lu 7:28*
Baptist

people said, Of a truth this is *Joh 7:40*
the *p.*

look, for out of Galilee *Joh 7:52*
ariseth no *p.*

this is what was spoken by the *Ac 2:16*
p. Joel

not in temples made with *Ac 7:48*
hands, as saith *p.*

in his chariot he read Esaias *Ac 8:28;*
the *p.*   *8:30*

I pray thee, of whom speaketh *Ac 8:34*
the *p.* this

he gave them judges until *Ac 13:20*
Samuel the *p.*

ass forbade the madness of *2Pe 2:16*
the *p.*

A PROPHET

now restore man his wife, for *Ge 20:7*
he is a *p.*

if there be *a p.* among you, I *Nu 12:6*
the Lord

if there arise *a p.* or dreamer *De 13:1*
of dreams

raise up *a p.* from among *De 18:15;*
brethren   *18:18; Ac 3:22; 7:37*

when a *p.* speaketh in the *De 18:22*
name of the Lord

there arose not *a p.* in Israel *De 34:10*
like Moses

Lord sent *a p.* to children of *J'g 6:8*
Israel

Samuel was established to be *1Sa 3:20*
a p.

he that is now called *a p.* was *1Sa 9:9*
called a seer

he said, I am *a p.* also as *1Ki 13:18*
thou art

I, even I only remain *a p.* of *1Ki 18:22*
the Lord

anoint Elisha to be *a p.* in *1Ki 19:16*
thy room

there came *a p.* unto Ahab, *1Ki 20:13*
saying

is there not here *a p.* of the *1Ki 22:7;*
Lord besides *2Ki 3:11; 2Ch 18:6*

he shall know there is *a p.* in *2Ki 5:8*
Israel

the Lord sent *a p.* to *2Ch 25:15*
Amaziah

but *a p.* of the Lord was *2Ch 28:9*
there, Oded

I ordained thee *a p.* to the *Jer 1:5*
nation

that is mad and maketh *Jer 29:26;*
himself *a p.*   *29:27*

there hath been *a p.* among *Eze 2:5;*
them   *33:33*

cometh to *a p.* to inquire of *Eze 14:7*
him about me

by *a p.* Lord brought Israel *Ho 12:13*
out of Egypt, and by
a p. was preserved

he shall even be the *p.* of his *Mic 2:11*
people

he that receiveth *a p.* in the *M't 10:41*
name of *a p.* shall receive

but what went ye out for to *M't 11:9*
see? *a p.*

a p. is not without honour *M't 13:57;*
save in his own country *M'k 6:4;*
     Joh 4:44

feared multitude, they   *M't 14:5;*
accounted   *21:26; M'k 11:32; Lu 20:6*
him as *a p.*
multitude, they took him for   *M't 21:46*
a p.
that it is *a p.* or as one of   *M'k 6:15*
the prophets
a great *p.* is risen up among   *Lu 7:16*
us
if he were *a p.* would have   *Lu 7:39*
known
it cannot be that *a p.* perish   *Lu 13:33*
out of Jerusalem
concerning Jesus, who was *a*   *Lu 24:19*
p. mighty
I perceive that thou art *a p.*   *Joh 4:19*
the blind man said, He is *a p.*   *Joh 9:17*
David being *a p.* and knowing   *Ac 2:30*
that God
there came *a* certain *p.*   *Ac 21:10*
named Agabus
if any man think himself to   *1Co 14:37*
be *a p.*
one, even *a p.* of their own   *Tit 1:12*
land

FALSE PROPHET

found a *false p.* a Jew named   *Ac 13:6*
Bar-jesus
like frogs out of mouth of   *Re 16:13*
false p.
the beast was taken, with   *Re 19:20*
him the *false p.*
devil was cast where beast   *Re 20:10*
and *false p.*

THAT PROPHET

not hearken to the words of   *De 13:3*
that p.
and *that p.* or that dreamer   *De 13:5;*
shall die   *18:20*
I the Lord have deceived *that*   *Eze 14:9*
p.
they asked him, Art thou *that*   *Joh 1:21;*
p.   *1:25*
this is of a truth *that p.* that   *Joh 6:14*
should come
every soul which will not hear   *Ac 3:23*
that p.

PROPHETESS

Miriam the *p.,* the sister of   *Ex 15:20*
Aaron
Deborah, a *p.,* the wife of   *J'g 4:4*
Lapidoth
went unto Huldah, the *p.,*   *2Ki 22:14*
the wife
appointed, went to Huldah   *2Ch 34:22*
the *p.*
and on the *p.* Noadiah, and   *Ne 6:14*
the rest
And I went unto the *p.;* and   *Isa 8:3*
she
was one Anna, a *p.,* the   *Lu 2:36*
daughter
Jezebel, which calleth herself a   *Re 2:20*
p.

PROPHETIC

took up *p.* utterance (A)   *Nu 24:20;*
   24:21, 23
confirm the *p.* vision (B)   *Da 10:24*
no *p.* scripture can be   *2Pe 1:20*
explained by (B)

PROPHETS

that all the Lord's people   *Nu 11:29*
were *p.*
thou shalt meet a company of   *1Sa 10:5*
p.
p. met him; prophesied   *1Sa 10:10;*
among the *p.*   *10:11*
is Saul also among the *p.*   *1Sa 10:12;*
   19:24
the Lord answered him not   *1Sa 28:6;*
by *p.*   *28:15*
Obadiah hid 100 *p.* by 50 in   *1Ki 18:4*
a cave
Jezebel slew the *p.;* of   *1Ki 18:13;*
Baal 450   *18:19, 22*
take the *p.* of Baal, let none   *1Ki 18:40*
of them escape
Israel have forsaken thy   *1Ki 19:10;*
covenant, have slain   *19:14; Ne 9:26*
thy *p.*

the king of Israel gathered the   *1Ki 22:6*
p. together
I will be a lying spirit in *p.*   *1Ki 22:22;*
   2Ch 18:21
to *p.* of thy father, and *p.* of   *2Ki 3:13*
mother
Josiah went and the *p.* to the   *2Ki 23:2*
house of Lord
believe his *p.* so shall ye   *2Ch 20:20*
prosper
he sent *p.;* they misused his   *2Ch 24:19;*
p.   *36:16*
with them were the *p.* of God   *Ezr 5:2*
helping
thou hast appointed *p.* to   *Ne 6:7*
preach
p. to proclaim (R)   *Ne 6:7*
thou testifiedst by thy Spirit in   *Ne 9:30*
thy *p.*
the trouble that hath come on   *Ne 9:32*
our *p.*
the *p.* and seers hath he   *Isa 29:10*
covered
say to the *p.* Prophesy not   *Isa 30:10;*
   Am 2:12
p. prophesied by Baal, and   *Jer 2:8*
walked
their princes, their priests and   *Jer 2:26*
p. are ashamed
your own sword hath   *Jer 2:30*
devoured your *p.*
the *p.* shall wonder; *p.* become   *Jer 4:9;*
wind   *5:13*
p. prophesy falsely, and   *Jer 5:31*
priests bear rule
they shall bring out the bones   *Jer 8:1*
of the *p.*
I will fill the *p.* with   *Jer 13:13*
drunkenness
the *p.* say, Ye shall not see   *Jer 14:13*
the sword
p. prophesy lies in my name,   *Jer 14:14*
sent them not
by sword and famine shall   *Jer 14:15*
those *p.* be consumed
I have seen folly in the *p.* of   *Jer 23:13*
Samaria
I have seen in the *p.* an   *Jer 23:14*
horrible thing
from *p.* is profaneness gone   *Jer 23:15*
forth into land
I have not sent these *p.* yet   *Jer 23:21*
they ran
I have heard what the *p.*   *Jer 23:25*
said, that prophesy
they are *p.* of the deceit of   *Jer 23:26*
their own heart
I am against the *p.* that   *Jer 23:30;*
steal my word   *23:31*
so priests and *p.* heard   *Jer 26:7*
Jeremiah speaking
the *p.* and all the people took   *Jer 26:8*
Jeremiah
then spake the *p.* this man is   *Jer 26:11*
worthy to die
therefore hearken not to your   *Jer 27:9;*
p.   *27:16*
and that ye and the *p.* might   *Jer 27:15*
perish
if they be *p.* and word of   *Jer 27:18*
Lord be with them
p. that have been before me   *Jer 28:8*
and thee
words of the letter Jeremiah   *Jer 29:1*
sent to the *p.*
saith Lord, Let not your *p.*   *Jer 29:8*
deceive you
the Lord hath raised us up *p.*   *Jer 29:15*
in Babylon
they and their *p.* provoke me   *Jer 32:32*
to anger
where are now your *p.* which   *Jer 37:19*
prophesied
her *p.* also find no vision from   *La 2:9*
the Lord
thy *p.* have seen vain things for   *La 2:14*
thee
for the sins of her *p.* that hath   *La 4:13*
shed blood
prophesy against the *p.* of   *Eze 13:2*
Israel
thus saith the Lord, Woe unto   *Eze 13:3*
the foolish *p.*
O Israel, thy *p.* are like foxes   *Eze 13:4*
in deserts
my hand shall be upon the *p.*   *Eze 13:9*
that see vanity
there is a conspiracy of her   *Eze 22:25*
p. in midst

her *p.* daubed them with   *Eze 22:28*
untempered mortar
I have hewed them by the *p.*   *Ho 6:5*
have slain
I have spoken by *p.* and   *Ho 12:10*
multiplied visions
parables acted out by *p.*   *Ho 12:10*
(A)(B)(R)
I have raised up of your sons   *Am 2:11*
p.
commanded the *p.* saying,   *Am 2:12*
Prophesy not
the sun shall go down over the   *Mic 3:6*
p.
the *p.* thereof divine for   *Mic 3:11*
money
her *p.* are light and   *Zep 3:4*
treacherous persons
to whom the former *p.* have   *Zec 1:4*
cried
and the *p.* do they live for   *Zec 1:5*
ever
the words the Lord hath cried   *Zec 7:7*
by former *p.*
word Lord sent in his Spirit   *Zec 7:12*
by former *p.*
I will cause the *p.* to pass out   *Zec 13:2*
of land
p. shall be ashamed, each of   *Zec 13:4*
his vision
so persecuted they the *p.*   *M't 5:12;*
   Lu 6:23
think not that I am come to   *M't 5:17*
destroy *p.*
do so to them, for this is the   *M't 7:12*
law and the *p.*
many *p.* have desired to see   *M't 13:17;*
   Lu 10:24
on these two hang all the   *M't 22:40*
law and the *p.*
the children of them who   *M't 23:31*
killed the *p.*
I send unto you *p.* and wise   *M't 23:34;*
men   *Lu 11:49*
O Jerusalem, thou that   *M't 23:37*
killest the *p.*
as it is written in the *p.*   *M'k 1:2;*
   Lu 18:31; 24:25; Joh 6:45
as he spake by his holy *p.*   *Lu 1:70;*
   2Pe 3:2
the law and the *p.* were until   *Lu 16:16*
John
Abraham said, They have   *Lu 16:29;*
Moses and *p.*   *16:31*
slow to believe what the *p.*   *Lu 24:25*
have spoken
we found him of whom the *p.*   *Joh 1:45*
did write
Abraham and the *p.* are   *Joh 8:52;*
dead   *8:53*
God shewed by the mouth of   *Ac 3:18;*
his *p.*   *3:21*
p. came from Jerusalem to   *Ac 11:27*
Antioch
in church at Antioch certain   *Ac 13:1*
p. and teachers
after the reading of the law   *Ac 13:15*
and the *p.*
that come on you which is   *Ac 13:40*
spoken in the *p.*
Judas and Silas being *p.* also   *Ac 15:32*
themselves
believing all things written in   *Ac 24:14*
the *p.*
saying none other things than   *Ac 26:22*
p. did say
king Agrippa, believest thou   *Ac 26:27*
the *p.*
which he promised afore by his   *Ro 1:2*
p.
being witnessed by the law   *Ro 3:21*
and the *p.*
Lord, they have killed *p.* and   *Ro 11:3*
digged down
secondarily, *p.* thirdly,   *1Co 12:28*
teachers
are all *p.;* let *p.* speak two   *1Co 12:29;*
or three   *14:29*
built on the foundation of   *Eph 2:20*
the *p.*
as now revealed to his *p.* by   *Eph 3:5*
the Spirit
and he gave some *p.* and   *Eph 4:11*
teachers
killed the Lord and their own   *1Th 2:15*
p.
who spake to the fathers by   *Heb 1:1*
the *p.*
take, my brethren, *p.* who   *Jas 5:10*
have spoken

of which salvation the *p.* inquired — *1Pe 1:10*

because these two *p.* tormented them — *Re 11:10*

rejoice over her, ye holy apostles and *p.* — *Re 18:20*

in her was found blood of *p.* and of saints — *Re 18:24*

do it not, for I am of thy brethren the *p.* — *Re 22:9*

ALL THE PROPHETS

told Jezebel how he had slain all the *p.* — *1Ki 19:1*

all the *p.* prophesied — *1Ki 22:10; 22:12; 2Ch 18:9, 11*

now call to me all the *p.* of Baal — *2Ki 10:19*

Lord testified against Israel by all the *p.* — *2Ki 17:13*

all the *p.* prophesied until John — *M't 11:13*

that blood of all the *p.* may be required — *Lu 11:50*

when ye see all the *p.* in kingdom of God — *Lu 13:28*

beginning at all the *p.* he expounded — *Lu 24:27*

all the *p.* from Samuel foretold — *Ac 3:24*

to him give all the *p.* witness thro' his name — *Ac 10:43*

FALSE PROPHETS

beware of false *p.* in sheep's clothing — *M't 7:15*

many false *p.* shall rise — *M't 24:11; 24:24; M'k 13:22*

for so did their fathers to the false *p.* — *Lu 6:26*

there were false *p.* also among them — *2Pe 2:1*

because many false *p.* are gone out — *1Jo 4:1*

MY PROPHETS

do *my p.* no harm — *1Ch 16:22; Ps 105:15*

OF THE PROPHETS

behold, a company of the *p.* met him — *1Sa 10:10*

when they saw the company of the *p.* — *1Sa 19:20*

a certain man of the sons of the *p.* — *1Ki 20:35*

the king discerned him that he was of the *p.* — *1Ki 20:41*

words of the *p.* declare good — *1Ki 22:13; 2Ch 18:12*

sons of the *p.* that were at Beth-el — *2Ki 2:3*

the sons of the *p.* at Jericho came to Elisha — *2Ki 2:5*

fifty sons of the *p.* went to view afar off — *2Ki 2:7*

the sons of the *p.* said, The spirit of Elijah — *2Ki 2:15*

a woman of the wives of sons of the *p.* cried — *2Ki 4:1*

and seethe pottage for the sons of the *p.* — *2Ki 4:38*

my God, think thou of the rest of the *p.* — *Ne 6:14*

because of the *p.* all my bones shake — *Jer 23:9*

hearken not to the words of the *p.* — *Jer 23:16; 27:14*

how long shall this be in the heart of the *p.* — *Jer 23:26*

used similitudes by ministry of the *p.* — *Ho 12:10*

that hear these by the mouth of the *p.* — *Zec 8:9*

Elias or one of the *p.* — *M't 16:14; M'k 6:15; 8:28*

ye build the tombs of the *p.* — *M't 23:29; Lu 11:47*

partakers with them in the blood of the *p.* — *M't 23:30*

that scriptures of the *p.* might be fulfilled — *M't 26:56*

that one of the *p.* was risen again — *Lu 9:8; 9:19*

children of the *p.* and of covenant — *Ac 3:25*

as it is written in the book of the *p.* — *Ac 7:42*

which of *p.* have not fathers persecuted — *Ac 7:52*

after the reading of the law and the *p.* — *Ac 13:15*

because they knew not the voice of the *p.* — *Ac 13:27*

and to this agree the words of the *p.* — *Ac 15:15*

persuading them of Jesus out of the *p.* — *Ac 28:23*

made manifest by scriptures of the *p.* — *Ro 16:26*

spirits of the *p.* are subject to the — *1Co 14:32*

built on the foundation of the *p.* — *Eph 2:20*

time would fail me to tell of the *p.* — *Heb 11:32*

for they have shed the blood of the *p.* — *Re 16:6*

Lord God of the holy *p.* sent his angel — *Re 22:6*

SERVANTS THE PROPHETS

I may avenge blood of my servants the *p.* — *2Ki 9:7*

law which I sent to you by my servants the *p.* — *2Ki 17:13*

as Lord said by all his servants the *p.* — *2Ki 17:23*

and Lord spake by his servants the *p.* — *2Ki 21:10; 24:2*

which thou hast commanded by servants the *p.* — *Ezr 9:11*

sent you my servants the *p.* — *Jer 7:25; 25:4; 29:19; 35:15*

hearken to the words of my servants the *p.* — *Jer 26:5*

have spoken by my servants the *p.* — *Eze 38:17*

neither have we hearkened to servants the *p.* — *Da 9:6*

laws which he set before us by his servants the *p.* — *Da 9:10*

he revealeth his secret to his servants the *p.* — *Am 3:7*

words which I commanded my servants the *p.* — *Zec 1:6*

he finished, as he declared to his servants the *p.* — *Re 10:7*

give reward to servants the *p.* — *Re 11:18*

PROPHET'S

neither was I a *p.* son; but I was — *Am 7:14*

prophet shall receive a *p.* reward — *M't 10:41*

PROPITIATION

a *p.* through faith in his blood — *Ro 3:25*

a reconciling sacrifice in his blood (B) — *Ro 3:25*

expiating sin by his sacrificial death (N) — *Ro 3:25*

an expiation by his blood (R) — *Ro 3:25*

make *p.* for sins (A)(E) — *Heb 2:17*

he is the *p.* for our sins: and not — *1Jo 2:2*

an atoning sacrifice for our sins (B) — *1Jo 2:2*

a remedy for the defilement of our sins (N) — *1Jo 2:2*

made personal atonement for our sins (P) — *1Jo 2:2*

the expiation for our sins (R) — *1Jo 2:2*

his Son to be the *p.* for our sins — *1Jo 4:10*

an atoning sacrifice for our sins (B) — *1Jo 4:10*

remedy for the defilement of sin (N) — *1Jo 4:10*

personal atonement for our sins (P) — *1Jo 4:10*

the expiation for our sins (R) — *1Jo 4:10*

PROPORTION

according to the *p.* of every one — *1Ki 7:36*

nor his power, nor his comely *p.* — *Job 41:12*

according to the *p.* of faith — *Ro 12:6*

PROPORTIONS

love reached such *p.* (P) — *2Th 1:3*

PROPOSE

nothing they *p.* to do (R) — *Ge 11:6*

PROPOSED

p. nominated two men (A) — *Ac 1:23*

PROSELYTE

sea and land to make one *p.* — *M't 23:15*

to win one convert (N)(P) — *M't 23:15*

and Nicolas a *p.* of Antioch — *Ac 6:5*

a former convert to Judaism (N)(P) — *Ac 6:5*

PROSELYTES

strangers of Rome, Jews and *p.* — *Ac 2:10*

and religious *p.* followed Paul and — *Ac 13:43*

PROSPECT

and their *p.* was toward the south — *Eze 40:44*

facing, looking toward (A)(B)(R) — *Eze 40:44*

having the *p.* toward the north — *Eze 40:44*

whose *p.* is toward the south — *Eze 40:45*

with its view toward the south (A) — *Eze 40:45; 40:46*

chamber facing south (B)(R) — *Eze 40:45; 40:46*

whose *p.* is toward the north — *Eze 40:46*

gate whose *p.* is toward the east — *Eze 42:15; 43:4*

gate which faces east (A)(B)(R) — *Eze 42:15; 43:4*

PROSPECTS

spoiling *p.* with Pharaoh (B) — *Ex 5:21*

PROSPER

p. me this day (B) — *Ge 24:12*

angel with thee, and *p.* thy way — *Ge 24:40*

trip successful (B) — *Ge 24:40*

if now thou do *p.* my way which I — *Ge 24:42*

made all that he did to *p.* in his — *Ge 39:3*

made all to flourish and succeed (A) — *Ge 39:3*

he did, the Lord made it to *p.* — *Ge 39:23*

gave him success (B) — *Ge 39:23*

of the Lord? but it shall not *p.* — *Nu 14:41*

It will not succeed (A)(R) — *Nu 14:41*

It will get you nowhere (B) — *Nu 14:41*

and thou shalt not *p.* in thy ways — *De 28:29*

that ye may *p.* in all that ye do — *De 29:9*

p. you abundantly (B) — *De 30:9*

p. whithersoever thou goest — *Jos 1:7*

mayest *p.* in all that thou doest — *1Ki 2:3*

succeed in everything (B) — *1Ki 2:3*

Go up to Ramoth-gilead, and *p.* — *1Ki 22:12; 2Ch 18:11*

Go, and *p.* for the Lord shall — *1Ki 22:15*

p. thou, and build the house of the — *1Ch 22:11*

Then shalt thou *p.* if thou takest — *1Ch 22:13*

of your fathers; for ye shall not *p.* — *2Ch 13:12*

you will not win (B) — *2Ch 13:12*

you cannot succeed (R) — *2Ch 13:12*

Go ye up, and *p.* and they shall be — *2Ch 18:14*

believe his prophets, so shall ye *p.* — *2Ch 20:20*

you will succeed (B)(R) — *2Ch 20:20*

that ye cannot *p.*? because ye have — *2Ch 24:20*

you cannot succeed (B) — *2Ch 24:20*

the Lord, God made him to *p.* — *2Ch 26:5*

he made him thrive (B) — *2Ch 26:5*

and *p.* I pray thee, thy servant this — *Ne 1:11*

The God of heaven, he will *p.* us — *Ne 2:20*

The tabernacles of robbers *p.* *Job 12:6*
and whatsoever he doeth shall *Ps 1:3*
p.
the ungodly, who *p.* in the *Ps 73:12*
world
they shall *p.* that love thee *Ps 122:6*
covereth his sins shall not *p.* *Pr 28:13*
knowest not whether shall *p.* *Ec 11:6*
of the Lord shall *p.* in his *Isa 53:10*
hand
that is formed against thee *Isa 54:17*
shall *p.*
p. in the thing whereto I *Isa 55:11*
sent it
and thou shalt not *p.* in them *Jer 2:37*
cause of the fatherless, yet *Jer 5:28*
they *p.*
cause of the orphan will *Jer 5:28*
succeed (B)
therefore they shall not *p.* *Jer 10:21*
and all
doth the way of the wicked *p.* *Jer 12:1*
for they shall not *p.*: their *Jer 20:11*
man that shall not *p.* in his *Jer 22:30*
days
for no man of his seed shall *Jer 22:30*
p.
a King shall reign and *p.* and *Jer 23:5*
the Chaldeans, ye shall not *p.* *Jer 32:5*
are the chief, her enemies *p.* *La 1:5*
and thou didst *p.* into a *Eze 16:13*
kingdom
Shall it *p.?* shall he not pull *Eze 17:9*
up
being planted, shall it *p.?* *Eze 17:10*
shall it
Shall he *p.?* shall he escape *Eze 17:15*
that
shall *p.* and practise, and shall *Da 8:24*
shall cause craft to *p.* in his *Da 8:25*
hands
make deceit *p.* (A)(R) *Da 8:25*
it shall not *p.*: for yet the *Da 11:27*
end shall
shall *p.* till the indignation be *Da 11:36*
thou mayest *p.* and be in health *3Jo 2*

PROSPERED

seeing the Lord hath *p.* my *Ge 24:56*
way
made my journey successful *Ge 24:56*
(B)
hand of the children of Israel *J'g 4:24*
p.
Hand of Israel pressed ever *J'g 4:24*
heavier (B)
Israel bore harder and harder *J'g 4:24*
on Jabin (R)
people did, and how the war *2Sa 11:7*
p.
how the war progressed *2Sa 11:7*
(A)(R)
asked about the success of *2Sa 11:7*
fighting (B)
and he *p.* whithersoever he *2Ki 18:7*
went
made him succeed in every *2Ki 18:7*
venture (B)
of David his father, and *p.* *1Ch 29:23*
every side. So they built and *2Ch 14:7*
p.
they built and thrived (B) *2Ch 14:7*
he did it with all his heart, *2Ch 31:21*
and *p.*
with all his heart and was *2Ch 31:21;*
successful (B) *32:30*
And Hezekiah prospered in *2Ch 32:30*
all his works
they *p.* through the *Ezr 6:14*
prophesying
continued to build, and was *Ezr 6:14*
helped greatly (B)
himself against him, and hath *Job 9:4*
p.
Daniel *p.* in the reign of *Da 6:28*
Darius
ground; and it practised, and *Da 8:12*
p.
whatever it did succeeded (B) *Da 8:12*
him in store, as God hath *p.* *1Co 16:2*
him
p. and grown wealthy *Re 3:17*
(A)(B)(P)(R)

PROSPERETH

fast on, and *p.* in their hands *Ezr 5:8*
because of him who *p.* in his *Ps 37:7*
way

whithersoever it turneth, it *p.* *Pr 17:8*
be in health, even as thy soul *p.* *3Jo 2*

PROSPERITY

not seek their peace nor their *De 23:6*
p.
surplus of *p.* (A)(R) *De 28:11*
shall ye say to him that *1Sa 25:6*
liveth in *p.*
and *p.* exceedeth the fame *1Ki 10:7*
which
in *p.* the destroyer shall *Job 15:21*
come
they shall spend their days *Job 36:11*
in *p.*
in my *p.* I said, I shall never *Ps 30:6*
be
pleasure in the *p.* of his *Ps 35:27*
servant
when I saw the *p.* of the *Ps 73:3*
wicked
p. and welfare are (A) *Ps 112:3*
Lord, I beseech thee, send *Ps 118:25*
now *p.*
walls, and *p.* within thy palaces *Ps 122:7*
the *p.* of fools shall destroy *Pr 1:32*
them
In the day of *p.* be joyful, but *Ec 7:14*
I spake unto thee in thy *p.* *Jer 22:21*
all the *p.* that I procure unto *Jer 33:9*
it
far off from peace: I forgat *p.* *La 3:17*
My cities through *p.* shall yet *Zec 1:17*
be
was inhabited and in *p.* and *Zec 7:7*

PROSPEROUS

had made his journey *p.* or *Ge 24:21*
not
Joseph, and he was a *p.* man *Ge 39:2*
make you abundantly *p.* *De 30:9*
(A)(R)
then thou shalt make thy way *Jos 1:8*
p.
our way which we go shall be *J'g 18:5*
p.
habitation of thy righteousness *Job 8:6*
p.
him, and he shall make his *Isa 48:15*
way *p.*
For the seed shall be *p.*; the *Zec 8:12*
vine
I might have a *p.* journey by *Ro 1:10*

PROSPEROUSLY

in his own house, he *p.* *2Ch 7:11*
effected
majesty ride *p.* because of *Ps 45:4*
truth

PROSTITUTE

Do not *p.* thy daughter, to *Le 19:29*
cause
a prostitute (B) *Le 19:29; 21:7*
a temple *p.* (A)(B)(E)(R) *De 23:17*
the brow of a *p.* (A) *Jer 3:3*
unites with a *p.* (B) *1Co 6:16*

PROSTITUTES

alone with *p.* (A) *Ho 4:14*

PROSTITUTING

p. your beauty (B)(R) *Eze 16:25*

PROSTITUTION

not in *p.* and debauchery *Ro 13:13*
(B)

PROSTRATE

approached to *p.* himself (B) *2Sa 15:5*
p. myself (B) *2Sa 16:4*

PROSTRATED

p. himself (B) *2Sa 1:2; 14:14*
he *p.* himself (B) *2Sa 9:6*

PROTECT

discretion will *p.* you (B) *Ps 2:11*
he shall keep, defend, *p.* *Ps 4:6*
(A)(B)

keep and *p.* me (A) *Ps 16:1*
eyes of Lord *p.* knowledge *Ps 22:12*
(B)
p. me from violent men (B) *Ps 140:4*
p. the orphan (B) *Isa 1:17; 1:23*
I will *p.* you (B) *Isa 49:8*
an holy, and *p.* him (S) *M'k 6:20*

PROTECTED

when God *p.* me (B) *Job 29:2*

PROTECTING

p. us our whole journey (B) *Jos 24:17*

PROTECTION

up and help you, and be your *De 32:38*
p.
the rock of your *p.* (B) *Isa 17:10*

PROTECTS

Lord *p.* those who love (B) *Ps 145:20*
Lord *p.* immigrants (B) *Ps 146:9*
p. way of his saints (B) *Pr 2:8*
carefully *p.* it (B) *Eph 5:29*

PROTEST

The man did solemnly *p.* unto *Ge 43:3*
us
howbeit yet *p.* solemnly unto *1Sa 8:9*
them
as a *p.* (P) *M'k 6:11; Lu 9:5*
I *p.* by your rejoicing which *1Co 15:31*
I have

PROTESTED

by the Lord, and *p.* unto thee *1Ki 2:42*
I earnestly *p.* unto your *Jer 11:7*
fathers in
angel of the Lord *p.* unto *Zec 3:6*
Joshua
he *p.* violently (P) *M'k 14:31*

PROTESTING

rising early and *p.* saying, *Jer 11:7*
Obey

PROTRACTED

p. wrangling among men (A) *1Ti 6:5*

PROUD

the *p.* helpers do stoop under *Job 9:13*
him
beneath him Rahab's helpers *Job 9:13*
tremble (B)(E)(R)
he smiteth through the *p.* *Job 26:12*
here shall thy *p.* waves be *Job 38:11*
stayed
and behold every one that is *Job 40:11*
p.
Look on every one that is *p.* *Job 40:12*
tongue that speaketh *p.* things *Ps 12:3*
plentifully rewarded the *p.* *Ps 31:23*
doer
respecteth not the *p.* nor such *Ps 40:4*
as
the *p.* are risen against me *Ps 86:14*
arrogant men have risen up *Ps 86:14*
against me (B)
insolent men have risen up *Ps 86:14*
against me (R)
earth: render a reward to the *Ps 94:2*
p.
look and a *p.* heart will not I *Ps 101:5*
suffer
one who is conceited and *Ps 101:5*
arrogant (B)
haughty looks and arrogant *Ps 101:5*
heart (R)
rebuked the *p.* that are *Ps 119:21*
cursed
the arrogant (B) *Ps 119:21;*
119:51, 69, 78, 122; 123:4
Thou dost rebuke the *Ps 119:21*
insolent (R)
p. have had me greatly in *Ps 119:51*
derision
Godless men utterly deride *Ps 119:51;*
me (R) *119:69, 78, 85, 122*
p. have forged a lie against *Ps 119:69*
me

PROUD

Let the *p.* be ashamed; for *Ps 119:78* they
The *p.* have digged pits for *Ps 119:85* me
good: let not the *p.* oppress *Ps 119:122* me
and with the contempt of the *Ps 123:4* *p.*
p. waters have gone over our *Ps 124:5* soul
but the *p.* he knoweth afar *Ps 138:6* off
p. have hid a snare for me *Ps 140:5* (B)
Conceited men have hidden *Ps 140:5* (R)
Arrogant men have hidden *Ps 140:5* (R)
A *p.* look, a lying tongue, and *Pr 6:17* haughty eyes (B)(E)(R) *Pr 6:17; 21:4*
will destroy the house of the *Pr 15:25* *p.*
Every one that is *p.* in heart is *Pr 16:5* an
to divide the spoil with the *p. Pr 16:19*
high look, and a *p.* heart, and *Pr 21:4*
P. and haughty scorner is his *Pr 21:24* name, who dealeth in *p. Pr 21:24* wrath
He that is of a *p.* heart *Pr 28:25* stirreth up
The greedy man stirs up *Pr 28:25* (A)(B)(E)(R)
is better than the *p.* in spirit *Ec 7:8*
P. looks of man (A)(B) *Isa 2:11*
upon every one that is *p.* and *Isa 2:12* lofty
the arrogancy of the *p.* to *Isa 13:11* cease
the pride of Moab; he is very *Isa 16:6* *p.*
hear me, and give ear; be *Jer 13:15* not *p.*
and all the *p.* men, saying *Jer 43:2* unto
the arrogant men (B)(R) *Jer 43:2;*
Mal 3:15; 4:1
the insolent men (R) *Jer 43:2*
of Moab (he is exceeding *p.) Jer 48:29*
hath been *p.* against the *Jer 50:29* Lord
am against thee, O thou *Jer 50:31* most *p.*
the most *p.* shall stumble and *Jer 50:32* fall
he is a *p.* man, neither *Hab 2:5* keepeth
now we call the *p.* happy; *Mal 3:15* yea
we call the arrogant happy *Mal 3:15;* (B)(R) *4:1*
all the *p.*, yea, and all that do *Mal 4:1*
the *p.* in the imagination of *Lu 1:51* their
of God, despiteful, *p.*, boasters *Ro 1:30*
do not be *p.* and conceited *Ro 11:20* (A)(R)
you are *p.* and arrogant *1Co 5:2* (A)(N)(P)
He is *p.* knowing nothing, but *1Ti 6:4*
stupified with conceit (A) *1Ti 6:4*
he is conceited (B) *1Ti 6:4*
he is puffed up with conceit *1Ti 6:4* (E)(R)
I call him a pompous *1Ti 6:4* ignoramus (N)
he is a conceited idiot (P) *1Ti 6:4*
p. blasphemers, disobedient to *2Ti 3:2*
God resisteth the *p.* but giveth *Jas 4:6;*
1Pe 5:5
God opposes the arrogant *1Pe 5:5* (B)(N)

PROUDLY

the thing wherein they dealt *Ex 18:11* *p.*
Talk no more so exceedingly *p. 1Sa 2:3* let
that they dealt *p.* against them *Ne 9:10*
But they and our fathers dealt *Ne 9:16* *p.*
yet they dealt *p.* and *Ne 9:29* hearkened
with their mouth they speak *Ps 17:10* *p.*
which speak grievous things *Ps 31:18* *p.*
the child shall behave himself *Isa 3:5* *p.*
spoken *p.* in the day of distress *Ob 12*

PROVE

that I may *p.* them, whether *Ex 16:4* they
Fear not: for God is come to *Ex 20:20* *p.* you
to humble thee, and to *p.* thee *De 8:2*
thee, and that he might *p. De 8:16* thee
whom thou didst *p.* at Massah *De 33:8*
through them I may *p.* Israel *J'g 2:22*
to *p.* Israel by them, even as *J'g 3:1* many
they were to *p.* Israel by them *J'g 3:4*
let me *p.* I pray thee, but this *J'g 6:39* once
came to *p.* him with hard *1Ki 10:1* questions
to *p.* Solomon with hard *2Ch 9:1* questions
perfect, it shall also *p.* me *Job 9:20* perverse
the wicked *p.* (R) *Ps 12:8; La 5:18*
Examine me, O Lord, and *p. Ps 26:2* me
Go to now, I will *p.* thee with *Ec 2:1* mirth
P. thy servants, I beseech *Da 1:12* thee, ten
p. me now herewith, saith *Mal 3:10* the Lord
yoke of oxen, and I go to *p. Lu 14:19* them
And this he said to *p.* him: *Joh 6:6* for he
Neither can they *p.* the things *Ac 24:13*
Paul, which they could not *p. Ac 25:7*
that ye may *p.* what is that *Ro 12:2* good
and to *p.* the sincerity of your *2Co 8:8* love
be in the faith; *p.* your own *2Co 13:5* selves
But let every man *p.* his own *Ga 6:4* work
P. all things; hold fast that *1Th 5:21* which
p. you worthy of kingdom *2Th 1:5* (N)

PROVED

Hereby shall ye be *p.:* By the *Ge 42:15* life
prison, that your words may *Ge 42:16* be *p.*
ordinance, and there he *p. Ex 15:25* them
assayed to go: for he had *1Sa 17:39* not *p.* it
with these: for I have not *p. 1Sa 17:39* them
Thou hast *p.* mine heart; thou *Ps 17:3* hast
the word of the Lord is *p. Ps 18:30* (S)
thou, O God, hast *p.* us; thou *Ps 66:10* hast
I *p.* thee at the waters of *Ps 81:7* Meribah
me, *p.* me and saw my work *Ps 95:9*
All this have I *p.* by wisdom: *Ec 7:23* I
this matter, and *p.* them ten *Da 1:14* days
wisdom is *p.* right by (N) *M't 11:19*
we have before *p.* both Jews *Ro 3:9* and
ye have *p.* yourselves (S) *2Co 7:11*
p. diligent in many things *2Co 8:22*
let these also first be *p.;* then *1Ti 3:10*
your fathers tempted me, *p. Heb 3:9* me
faith was fully *p.* (N) *Jas 2:22*
p. by fire (E) *1Pe 1:7*

PROVENDER

have both straw and *p. Ge 24:25* enough
straw and fodder (B) *Ge 24:25; 24:32*
gave straw and *p.* for the *Ge 24:32* camels
opened his sack to give his *Ge 42:27* ass *p.* in
give his ass fodder (A) *Ge 42:27*
feet; and he gave their asses *Ge 43:24* *p.*
foddered their donkeys (B) *Ge 43:24*
is both straw and *p.* for our *J'g 19:19* asses

straw and fodder for *J'g 19:19;* donkeys (B) *19:21*
house, and gave *p.* unto the *J'g 19:21* asses
gather *p.* from the field (B)(E) *Job 24:6*
ear the ground shall eat clean *Isa 30:24* *p.*

PROVERB

become an astonishment, a *p. De 28:37*
Therefore it became a *p.* Is *1Sa 10:12* Saul
it became a saying (B) *1Sa 10:12*
As saith the *p.* of the *1Sa 24:13* ancients
Israel shall be a *p.* and a *1Ki 9:7* byword
but be a *p.* and a byword *2Ch 7:20* among all
incline mine ear to a *p.* (R) *Ps 48:4*
and I became a *p.* to them *Ps 69:11*
I became a byword—an *Ps 69:11* object of scorn (A)(E)(R)
I became a laughingstock (B) *Ps 69:11*
To understand a *p.* and the *Pr 1:6*
so is a *p.* in the mouth of *Pr 26:7* fools (B)(R)
take up this *p.* against the *Isa 14:4* king of
take up this taunting parable *Isa 14:4* (A)(E)
take up this poem (B) *Isa 14:4*
take up this taunt (R) *Isa 14:4*
to be a reproach and a *p.* a *Jer 24:9* taunt
that *p.* that ye have in the *Eze 12:22* land of
I will make this *p.* to cease, *Eze 12:23* and they
no more use it as a *p.* in *Eze 12:23* Israel
and will make him a sign and *Eze 14:8* a *p.*
a sign and a byword *Eze 14:8* (A)(B)(R)
shall use this *p.* against thee *Eze 16:44*
ye use this *p.* concerning the *Eze 18:2* land
any more to use this *p.* in *Eze 18:3* Israel
take up a *p.* (B) *Mic 2:4*
and a taunting *p.* against him *Hab 2:6*
take up a taunt (A)(R) *Hab 2:6*
take up a taunt-song (B) *Hab 2:6*
take up a parable (E) *Hab 2:6*
explain this *p.* (A) *M't 15:15*
Ye will surely say unto me *Lu 4:23* this *p.*
thou plainly, and speakest *Joh 16:29* no *p.*
speaking plainly and not in *Joh 16:29* parables (A)(P)
speaking plainly and not in *Joh 16:29* figures (B)(N)(R)
speakest thou no dark saying (E) *Joh 16:29*
unto them according to the *2Pe 2:22* true *p.*

PROVERBS

Wherefore they that speak in *Nu 21:27* *p.*
those who sing ballads *Nu 21:27* (A)(B)(R)
And he spake three thousand *1Ki 4:32* *p.*
The *p.* of Solomon the son of *Pr 1:1* David
The *p.* of Solomon. A wise son *Pr 10:1*
These are also *p.* of Solomon, *Pr 25:1* which
out, and set in order many *p. Ec 12:9*
every one that useth *p.* shall *Eze 16:44* use
have I spoken unto you in *p. Joh 16:25*
told you these things in *Joh 16:25* parables (A)(P)
told you these things in *Joh 16:25* illustrations (B)
spoken to you in dark *Joh 16:25* sayings (E)
I have been using figures of *Joh 16:25* speech (N)(R)
shall no more speak unto *Joh 16:25* you in *p.*

PROVETH

for the Lord your God *p.* you, *De 13:3* to

PROVIDE

God will *p.* himself a lamb for   Ge 22:8
shall I *p.* for mine own   Ge 30:30
house also
p. out of all the people able   Ex 18:21
men
P. me now a man that can   1Sa 16:17
play
woman to *p.* for thee (A)   1Ki 17:9
whom David my father did *p.*   2Ch 2:7
can he *p.* flesh for his people   Ps 78:20
I will *p.* for you (A)(R)   Isa 45:11
P. neither gold, nor silver,   M't 10:9
nor
p. yourselves bags which wax   Lu 12:33
not
p. purses   Lu 12:33
(A)(B)(E)(N)(P)(R)
And *p.* them beasts, that they   Ac 23:24
P. things honest in the sight of   Ro 12:17
But if any *p.* not his own, and   1Ti 5:8

PROVIDED

p. for father (R)   Ge 47:12
And he *p.* the first part for   De 33:21
himself
have *p.* me a king among his   1Sa 16:1
sons
he had *p.* the king of   2Sa 19:32
sustenance
which *p.* victuals for the king   1Ki 4:7
p. victual for king Solomon   1Ki 4:27
p. necromancers and wizards   2Ki 21:6
(B)
he *p.* him cities, and   2Ch 32:29
possessions
corn, when thou that so *p.* for   Ps 65:9
it
p. for them out of (N)   Lu 8:3
things be, which thou hast *p.*   Lu 12:20
God having *p.* some better   Heb 11:40
thing

PROVIDENCE

your *p.* hath (A)   Job 10:12
done unto this nation by thy   Ac 24:2
p.

PROVIDES

p. and cares for it (N)   Eph 5:29

PROVIDETH

Who *p.* for the raven his   Job 38:41
food
P. her meat in the summer, and   Pr 6:8

PROVIDING

P. for honest things, not only   2Co 8:21
in

PROVINCE

the children of the *p.* that   Ezr 2:1
went up
that we went into the *p.* of   Ezr 5:8
Judaea
that is in the *p.* of the Medes   Ezr 6:2
canst find in all the *p.* of   Ezr 7:16
Babylon
The remnant that are left in   Ne 1:3
the *p.*
These are the children of the *p.*   Ne 7:6
are the chief of the *p.* that   Ne 11:3
dwelt in
into every *p.* according to the   Es 1:22
governors that were over every   Es 3:12
p.
rulers of every people of every   Es 3:12
p.
commandment given in every   Es 3:14;
p.   8:13
And in every *p.* whithersoever   Es 4:3
unto every *p.* according to the   Es 8:9
the power of the people and *p.*   Es 8:11
that
And in every *p.* and in every   Es 8:17
city
family, every *p.* and every city   Es 9:28
of judgment and justice in a *p.*   Ec 5:8
ruler over the whole *p.* of   Da 2:48
Babylon
over the affairs of the *p.* of   Da 2:49;
Babylon   3:12

plain of Dura in the *p.* of   Da 3:1
Babylon
Abed-nego, in the *p.* of   Da 3:30
Babylon
the palace, which is the *p.* of   Da 8:2
Elam
upon the fattest places of the   Da 11:24
p.
letter, he asked of what *p.* he   Ac 23:34
was
when Festus was come into   Ac 25:1
the *p.*

PROVINCES

young men of the princes of   1Ki 20:14;
the *p.*   20:15
princes of the *p.* went out   1Ki 20:17
first
of the princes of the *p.*   1Ki 20:19
came out
and hurtful unto kings and *p.*   Ezr 4:15
hundred and seven and twenty *p.*   Es 1:1
the nobles and princes of the *p.*   Es 1:3
in all the *p.* of the king   Es 1:16;
Ahasuerus   9:2, 20
he sent letters into all the   Es 1:22
king's *p.*
in all the *p.* of his kingdom   Es 2:3
and he made a release to the   Es 2:18
p. and
people in all the *p.* of thy   Es 3:8
kingdom
sent by posts into all the   Es 3:13
king's *p.*
the people of the king's *p.* do   Es 4:11
know
Jews which are in all the   Es 8:5
king's *p.*
and rulers of the *p.* which are   Es 8:9
from
hundred twenty and seven *p.*   Es 8:9
unto
day in all the *p.* of king   Es 8:12
Ahasuerus
And all the rulers of the *p.*   Es 9:3
and the
went out throughout all the *p.*   Es 9:4
done in the rest of the king's   Es 9:12
p.
Jews that were in the king's *p.*   Es 9:16
and seven *p.* of the kingdom   Es 9:30
of
treasure of kings and of the *p.*   Ec 2:8
nations, and princess among   La 1:1
the *p.*
him on every side from the *p.*   Eze 19:8
the rulers of the *p.* to come to   Da 3:2
and all the rulers of the *p.*   Da 3:3
were

PROVING

p. that this is very Christ   Ac 9:22
showing and *p.* by   Ac 18:28
(A)(B)(E)
by the *p.* of this ministration   2Co 9:13
(S)
P. what is acceptable   Eph 5:10
unto Lord

PROVISION

and to give them *p.* for the   Ge 42:25
way
and gave them *p.* for the way   Ge 45:21
of their *p.* was dry and mouldy   Jos 9:5
our bread we took hot for   Jos 9:12
our *p.*
man his month in a year made   1Ki 4:7
Solomon's *p.* for one day was   1Ki 4:22
he prepared great *p.* for them   2Ki 6:23
for the which I have made   1Ch 29:19
p.
I will abundantly bless her   Ps 132:15
p.
them a daily *p.* of the king's   Da 1:5
meat
and make not *p.* for the   Ro 13:14
flesh, to

PROVISIONS

provisions (A)   Ge 14:11;
Jos 1:11;   9:11; J'g 7:8;   1Sa 22:10;
  1Ki 4:7;   11:18
provisions (B)   Ge 14:11;
Jos 1:11;   9:11, 14; J'g 7:8;   1Sa 22:10;
  1Ki 11:18

provisions (R)   Ge 14:11;
Jos 1:11;   9:11, 14;   1Sa 22:10;   Lu 9:12
  Lu 9:12
prepared *p.* (R)   Ex 2:39;
  J'g 20:10; 1Ki 4:27; 2Ch 11:23
take *p.* (E)   Jos 9:11; 9:14; Lu 9:12
bring *p.* (A)   J'g 20:10
he gave them *p.* (S)   2Ch 11:23
no *p.* bag (A)   Lu 10:4; 22:35-36
this nation by thy *p.* (S)   Ac 24:2

PROVOCATION

p. of the enemy (A)(E)(R)   De 32:27
bitter *p.* (A)(B)(E)   1Sa 1:16
Israel sin, by his *p.*   1Ki 15:30
wherewith he
for the *p.* wherewith thou   1Ki 21:22
hast
because you irritated me   1Ki 21:22
(B)
you have provoked me (R)   1Ki 21:22
not mine eye continue in   Job 17:2
their *p.*
my eye dwells on their   Job 17:2
obstinacy and insults and
resistance (A)
my eye gazes on their   Job 17:2
contention (B)
not your heart, as in the *p.*   Ps 95:8
For this city hath been to me   Jer 32:31
as a *p.*
presented the *p.* of their   Eze 20:28
offering
presented their offering that   Eze 20:28
provoked me (A)
presented their offensive   Eze 20:28
oblations (B)
not your hearts, as in the *p.*   Heb 3:8
in
harden not your hearts, as in   Heb 3:15
the *p.*
provoked and irritated and   Heb 3:15
embittered God (A)
grow stubborn as in days of   Heb 3:15
rebellion (B)(R)

PROVOCATIONS

of all the *p.* that Manasseh   2Ki 23:26
had
Egypt, and had wrought great   Ne 9:18
p.
to thee, and they wrought   Ne 9:26
great *p.*

PROVOKE

and obey his voice, *p.* him   Ex 23:21
not
do not offend him (B)   Ex 23:21
do not rebel against him (R)   Ex 23:21
How long will this people *p.*   Nu 14:11
me
they mistrust me (B)   Nu 14:11
they despise me (R)   Nu 14:11;
  De 31:20
do not *p.* or stir them up (A)   De 2:5
Lord thy God, to *p.* him to   De 4:25
anger
of the Lord, to *p.* him to   De 9:18
anger
gods, and serve them, and *p.*   De 31:20
me
to *p.* him to anger through   De 31:29
vexing him with your   De 31:29
handiwork (B)(R)
I will *p.* them to anger with   De 32:21
molten images, to *p.* me to   1Ki 14:9
anger
to irritate me (B)   1Ki 14:9
to *p.* me to anger with their   1Ki 16:2
sins
angering me with their sins   1Ki 16:2;
(B)   16:26, 33; 2Ki 23:19
sin, to *p.* the Lord God of   1Ki 16:26;
Israel to anger   16:33
things to *p.* the Lord to   2Ki 17:11
anger
of the Lord, to *p.* him to   2Ki 17:17;
anger   21:6; 2Ch 33:6
they might *p.* me to anger   2Ki 22:17
with all
had made to *p.* the Lord to   2Ki 23:19
anger
that they might *p.* me to   2Ch 34:25
anger
and they that *p.* God are   Job 12:6
secure
did they *p.* him in the   Ps 78:40
wilderness

defied and rebelled in   *Ps 78:40*
wilderness (A)(E)(R)
disobeyed him in the   *Ps 78:40*
wilderness (B)
Lord, to *p.* the eyes of his   *Isa 3:8*
glory
that they may *p.* me to anger   *Jer 7:18*
Do they *p.* me to anger? saith   *Jer 7:19*
not *p.* themselves to the   *Jer 7:19*
confusion
p. me to anger in offering   *Jer 11:17*
incense
p. me not to anger with the   *Jer 25:6*
works
ye might *p.* me to anger with   *Jer 25:7*
unto other gods, to *p.* me to   *Jer 32:29*
anger
they have done to *p.* me to   *Jer 32:32*
anger
to vex me (B)   *Jer 32:32; 44:3, 8*
have committed to *p.* me to   *Jer 44:3*
anger
p. me unto wrath with the   *Jer 44:8*
works
have returned to *p.* me to   *Eze 8:17*
anger
adding to my vexation (B)   *Eze 8:17*
thy whoredoms, to *p.* me to   *Eze 16:26*
anger
to *p.* him to speak of many   *Lu 11:53*
things
saith, I will *p.* you to   *Ro 10:19*
jealousy by
Gentiles, for to *p.* them to   *Ro 11:11*
jealousy
arouse them to jealousy   *Ro 11:11;*
(A)(B)(R)   *11:14*
to stir Israel to emulation   *Ro 11:11;*
(N)   *11:14*
any means I may *p.* to   *Ro 11:14*
emulation
Do we *p.* the Lord to   *1Co 10:22*
jealousy? are
p. not your children to wrath   *Eph 6:4*
do not arouse your children's   *Eph 6:4*
anger (B)
not goad your children to   *Eph 6:4*
resentment (N)
p. not your children to anger   *Col 3:21*
do not irritate your children   *Col 3:21*
(B)
do not exasperate your   *Col 3:21*
children (N)
when they had heard, did *p.*   *Heb 3:16*
to *p.* unto love and to good   *Heb 10:24*
works
studying how we may stir   *Heb 10:24*
up (A)(R)
stimulate one another to   *Heb 10:24*
love (B)
arouse others to love (N)   *Heb 10:24*
how we can encourage one   *Heb 10:24*
another to love (P)

PROVOKED

any of them that *p.* me see it   *Nu 14:23*
despised, spurned me (B)   *Nu 14:23;*
  16:30
that these men have *p.* the   *Nu 16:30*
Lord
in Horeb ye *p.* the Lord to   *De 9:8*
wrath
ye *p.* the Lord to wrath   *De 9:22*
p. him to jealousy with   *De 32:16*
strange
abominations *p.* they him to   *De 32:16*
anger
p. me to anger with their   *De 32:21*
vanities
them, and *p.* the Lord to   *J'g 2:12*
anger
angered the Lord (B)   *J'g 2:12;*
  1Ki 22:53; 2Ki 21:15
And her adversary also *p.* her   *1Sa 1:6*
sore
so she *p.* her; therefore she   *1Sa 1:7*
wept
they *p.* him to jealousy with   *1Ki 14:22*
their sins
exciting his ardent anger   *1Ki 14:22*
(B)
p. the Lord God of Israel to   *1Ki 15:30*
anger
thou hast *p.* me to anger   *1Ki 21:22*
irritated me (B)   *1Ki 21:22*
you *p.* me (R)   *1Ki 21:22*
p. to anger the Lord God of   *1Ki 22:53*
Israel
do not provoke trouble (R)   *2Ki 14:10*

have *p.* me to anger, since   *2Ki 21:15*
the day
that Manasseh had *p.* him   *2Ki 23:26*
withal
and *p.* David to number   *1Ch 21:1*
Israel
aroused David to number   *1Ch 21:1*
Israel (B)
and *p.* to anger the Lord   *2Ch 25:15*
God of his
p. the God of heaven unto   *Ezr 5:12*
wrath
have *p.* thee to anger before   *Ne 4:5*
tempted and *p.* the most high   *Ps 78:56*
p. him to anger with their   *Ps 78:58*
high
but *p.* him at the sea, even at   *Ps 106:7*
they *p.* him to anger   *Ps 106:29*
with their
made angry, aroused his   *Ps 106:29;*
temper (B)   *106:33*
p. Lord with doings (E)(R)   *Ps 106:29*
Because they *p.* his spirit, so   *Ps 106:33*
that
but they *p.* him with their   *Ps 106:43*
counsel
repeatedly reverted to   *Ps 106:43*
rebellious ways (B)
were rebellious in their   *Ps 106:43*
purposes (R)
have *p.* to anger the Holy One of Israel   *Isa 1:4*
shown contempt for the Holy   *Isa 1:4*
One (B)
have despised the Holy One of   *Isa 1:4*
Israel (E)(R)
p. me to anger with their   *Jer 8:19*
graven
Israel have only *p.* me to   *Jer 32:30*
anger
Israel only vexed me (B)   *Jer 32:30*
presented offering that *p.* (A)   *Eze 20:28*
Ephraim *p.* him to anger   *Ho 12:14*
most
when your fathers *p.* me to   *Zec 8:14*
wrath
your fathers have angered me   *Zec 8:14*
(B)
p. to jealousy (E)   *Ro 11:14*
is not easily *p.*, thinketh no   *1Co 13:5*
evil
love is not touchy, fretful,   *1Co 13:5*
resentful (A)
love is not irritable, resentful   *1Co 13:5*
(B)(R)
love is not quick to take   *1Co 13:5*
offence (N)
love is not touchy (P)   *1Co 13:5*
and your zeal hath *p.* very   *2Co 9:2*
many
your enthusiasm has stimulated   *2Co 9:2*
the majority (A)(P)
your zeal has stirred up a   *2Co 9:2*
goodly number (B)(E)(R)
most of them have been fired   *2Co 9:2*
by your zeal (N)
I was *p.* with (A)(R)   *Heb 3:10*
p., irritated, embittered God   *Heb 3:15*
(A)

PROVOKEDST

thou *p.* the Lord thy God to   *De 9:7*
wrath

PROVOKETH

whoso *p.* him to anger sinneth   *Pr 20:2*
A people that *p.* me to anger   *Isa 65:3*
of jealousy, which *p.* to   *Eze 8:3*
jealousy

PROVOKING

because of the *p.* of his sons   *De 32:19*
their groves, *p.* the Lord to   *1Ki 14:15*
anger
in *p.* him to anger with the   *1Ki 16:7*
work of
p. the Lord God of Israel to   *1Ki 16:13*
anger
by *p.* the most High in the   *Ps 78:17*
p. one another, 'envying one   *Ga 5:26*

PROWLING

a *p.* bear (B)   *Pr 28:15*

PRUDENCE

a wise son, endued with *p.*   *2Ch 2:12*
to give *p.* (S)   *Pr 1:4*

I wisdom dwell with *p.* and   *Pr 8:12*
find
I, wisdom, dwell with insight   *Pr 8:12*
(B)
full of *p.* (A)(R)   *Da 2:14*
toward us in all wisdom and   *Eph 1:8*
p.
gift of greatest wisdom and   *Eph 1:8*
insight (B)(N)(R)

PRUDENT

an intelligent and *p.* man   *Ge 41:33*
(B)
a man of war, and *p.* in   *1Sa 16:18*
matters
of sound judgment (B)   *1Sa 16:18*
but a *p.* man covereth shame   *Pr 12:16*
the discerning man ignores an   *Pr 12:16*
insult (B)
A *p.* man concealeth   *Pr 12:23*
knowledge
a man of insight (B)   *Pr 12:23;*
  13:16; 14:8, 15, 18
p. man dealeth with   *Pr 13:16*
knowledge
wisdom of the *p.* is to   *Pr 14:8*
understand
but the *p.* man looketh well   *Pr 14:15*
to his
the *p.* are crowned with   *Pr 14:18*
knowledge
he that regardeth reproof is *p.*   *Pr 15:5*
wise in heart shall be called   *Pr 16:21*
p.
a discerning man (B)   *Pr 16:21; 18:15*
heart of the *p.* getteth   *Pr 18:15*
knowledge
p. for man to restrain (B)   *Pr 19:11*
and a *p.* wife is from the   *Pr 19:14*
Lord
A *p.* man foreseeth the evil   *Pr 22:3;*
  27:12
and the *p.* and the ancient   *Isa 3:2*
eyes and *p.* in their own sight   *Isa 5:21*
for I am *p.* and I have   *Isa 10:13*
removed
the understanding of their *p.*   *Isa 29:14*
men
is counsel perished from the   *Jer 49:7*
p.? is
p. and he shall know them?   *Ho 14:9*
for the
p. shall keep silence in that   *Am 5:13*
time
these things from the wise   *M't 11:25*
and *p.*
from the wise, clever, and   *M't 11:25*
learned (A)
hiding from the learned and   *M't 11:25*
intelligent (B)
from the wise and   *M't 11:25*
understanding (E)(R)
from the learned and wise   *M't 11:25*
(N)
from the clever and   *M't 11:25*
intelligent (P)
faithful and *p.* servant (B)   *M't 24:45;*
  25:2, 4, 8-9
these things from the wise   *Lu 10:21*
and *p.*
country, Sergius Paulus, a *p.*   *Ac 13:7*
man
an intelligent and sensible   *Ac 13:7*
man of sound understanding (A)
an intelligent man   *Ac 13:7*
(B)(N)(P)(R)
a man of understanding (E)   *Ac 13:7*
the understanding of the *p.*   *1Co 1:19*
the discernment of the   *1Co 1:19*
discerning (A)(E)
set aside keenness of the   *1Co 1:19*
sagacious (B)
cleverness of the clever   *1Co 1:19*
(N)(R)

PRUDENTLY

my servant shall deal *p.*, he   *Isa 52:13*
shall
acting shrewdly and *p.*   *Lu 16:8*
(A)(R)
to behave *p.* (A)(B)   *Tit 2:6*

PRUNE

years thou shalt *p.* thy   *Le 25:3*
vineyard
sow thy field, nor *p.* thy   *Le 25:4*
vineyard

PRUNED

it shall not be *p*. nor digged   Isa 5:6

PRUNING

cut off the sprigs with *p*.   Isa 18:5
hooks

PRUNINGHOOKS

and their spears into *p*.   Isa 2:4;
    Mic 4:3
pruning shears (B)   Isa 2:4; Mic 4:3
swords, and your *p*. into   Joe 3:10
spears

PSALM

David delivered first this *p*.   1Ch 16:7
to that
Take up a *p*. and bring hither   Ps 81:2
the harp, and the voice of a *p*.   Ps 98:5
it is also written in the   Ac 13:33
second *p*.
Wherefore he saith also in   Ac 13:35
another *p*.
every one of you hath a *p*.   1Co 14:26
hath a

PSALMIST

Jacob, and the sweet *p*. of   2Sa 23:1
Israel

PSALMS

Sing unto him, sing *p*. unto   1Ch 16:9;
him   Ps 105:2
a joyful noise unto him with *p*.   Ps 95:2
himself saith in the book of   Lu 20:42
P.
and in the *p*. concerning me   Lu 24:44
it is written in the book of *P*.   Ac 1:20
Speaking to yourselves in *p*.   Eph 5:19
admonishing one another in   Col 3:16
p.
Is any merry? let him sing *p*.   Jas 5:13

PSALTERIES

even on harps, and on *p*. and   2Sa 6:5
lyres, harps (A)(B)(R)   2Sa 6:5;
1Ki 10:12; 1Ch 13:8; 15:16, 28, 16:5;
25:1, 6; 2Ch 5:12; 9:11; 20:28; 29:25;
    Ne 12:27
harps also and *p*. for   1Ki 10:12
singers: there
and with harps, and with *p*.   1Ch 13:8
musick, *p*. and harp and   1Ch 15:16
cymbals
and Benaiah, with *p*. on   1Ch 15:20
Alamoth
making a noise with *p*. and   1Ch 15:28
harps
and Jeiel with *p*. and with   1Ch 16:5
harps
prophesy with harps, with *p*.   1Ch 25:1
with cymbals, *p*. and harps   1Ch 25:6
having cymbals and *p*. and   2Ch 5:12
harps
and harps and *p*. for singers   2Ch 9:11
they came to Jerusalem with   2Ch 20:28
p. and
with *p*. and with harps,   2Ch 29:25
according
with cymbals, *p*. and with   Ne 12:27
harps

PSALTERY

from the high place with a *p*.   1Sa 10:5
sing unto him with the *p*. and   Ps 33:2
awake, *p*. and harp: I myself   Ps 57:8
will
also praise thee with the *p*.   Ps 71:22
even
the pleasant harp with the *p*.   Ps 81:2
of ten strings, and upon the *p*.   Ps 92:3
Awake, *p*. and harp: I myself   Ps 108:2
will
upon a *p*. and an instrument   Ps 144:9
of ten
praise him and with the *p*.   Ps 150:3
and harp
p., dulcimer, and all kinds of   Da 3:5;
    3:10; 3:15
p. and all kinds of musick   Da 3:7

PTOLEMAIS

from Tyre, we came to *P*. and   Ac 21:7

PUA

of *P*., the family of the   Nu 26:23
Punites

PUAH

and the name of the other *P*.   Ex 1:15
Tola the son of *P*. the son of   J'g 10:1
sons of Issachar were, Tola,   1Ch 7:1
and *P*.

PUBLICAN

Thomas, and Matthew the *p*.   M't 10:3
the tax collector (A)(B)(P)(R)   M't 10:3;
    18:17; Lu 5:27; 18:10, 11, 13
tax gatherer (N)   M't 10:3;
    18:17; Lu 5:27; 18:10, 11, 13
thee as an heathen man and   M't 18:17
a *p*.
and saw a *p*. named Levi,   Lu 5:27
sitting
one a Pharisee and the other   Lu 18:10
a *p*.
adulterers, or even as this *p*.   Lu 18:11
And the *p*. standing afar off,   Lu 18:13
would

PUBLICANS

ye? do not even the *p*. the   M't 5:46
same
tax collectors   M't 5:46;
(A)(B)(P)(R)   9:10-11; 11:19; 21:31-
    32; M'k 2:15-16; Lu 3:12; 5:29-30;
    7:29, 34; 15:1; 19:2
tax gatherers (N)   M't 5:46;
9:10-11; 11:19; 21:31-32; M'k 2:15-16;
    Lu 3:12; 5:29-30; 7:29, 34; 15:1; 19:2
others? do not even the *p*. so   M't 5:47
many *p*. and sinners came   M't 9:10
and sat
Why eateth your Master with   M't 9:11
p. and
a friend of *p*. and sinners   M't 11:19
That the *p*. and the harlots   M't 21:31
go into
the *p*. and the harlots   M't 21:32
believed him
house, many *p*. and sinners   M'k 2:15
sat also
saw him eat with *p*. and   M'k 2:16
sinners
and drinketh with *p*. and   M'k 2:16
sinners
Then came also *p*. to be   Lu 3:12
baptized
there was a great company of   Lu 5:29
eat and drink with *p*. and   Lu 5:30
sinners
the *p*., justified God, being   Lu 7:29
baptized
a friend of *p*. and sinners   Lu 7:34
Then drew near unto him all   Lu 15:1
the *p*.
which was the chief among   Lu 19:2
the *p*.

PUBLICK

willing to make her a *p*.   M't 1:19
example

PUBLICKLY

convinced the Jews, and that   Ac 18:28
p.
shewed you, and have taught   Ac 20:20
you *p*.

PUBLICLY

p. refuted Jews (P)   Ac 18:28

PUBLISH

I will *p*. the name of the Lord   De 32:3
I will proclaim the name   De 32:3
(A)(B)(E)(R)
to *p*. it in the house of their   1Sa 31:9
idols
broadcast the news (B)   1Sa 31:9
to carry the tidings (E)   1Sa 31:9
to carry the good news (R)   1Sa 31:9

p. it not in the streets of   2Sa 1:20
Askelon
announce it in the streets (A)   2Sa 1:20
p. and proclaim in all their   Ne 8:15
cities
That I may *p*. with the voice   Ps 26:7
of
and *p*. in Jerusalem; and say,   Jer 4:5
Blow
behold, *p*. against Jerusalem,   Jer 4:16
that
house of Jacob, and *p*. it in   Jer 5:20
Judah
Proclaim to the house of   Jer 5:20
Judah (B)(R)
p. ye, praise ye, and say, O   Jer 31:7
Lord
Declare ye in Egypt, and *p*. in   Jer 46:14
Migdol
and *p*. in Noph and in   Jer 46:14
Tahpanhes
ye among the nations, and *p*.   Jer 50:2
up a standard; *p*. and conceal   Jer 50:2
not
P. in the palaces at Ashdod,   Am 3:9
and in
proclaim and *p*. the free   Am 4:5
offerings
went out, and began to *p*. it   M'k 1:45
much
began to *p*. in Decapolis how   M'k 5:20
great
proclaim in Decapolis   M'k 5:20
(A)(R)
announce in Decapolis (B)   M'k 5:20
spread the good news (N)   M'k 5:20
who *p*. the good news (B)   Ro 10:15

PUBLISHED

be *p*. throughout all his empire   Es 1:20
proclaimed throughout   Es 1:20
(A)(R)
that it should be *p*. according   Es 1:22
to
province was *p*. unto all   Es 3:14;
people   8:13
a proclamation to all people   Es 8:13
(A)(R)
the company of those that *p*.   Ps 68:11
it
proclaimed the good news (B)   Ps 68:11
p. through Nineveh by the   Jon 3:7
decree
the more a great deal they *p*.   M'k 7:36
it
the more zealously they   M'k 7:36
proclaimed it (A)(R)
the more they broadcast it   M'k 7:36
(B)(P)
must first be *p*. among all   M'k 13:10
nations
and *p*. throughout the whole   Lu 8:39
city
which was *p*. throughout all   Ac 10:37
Judaea
proclaimed throughout all   Ac 10:37
Judea (A)(R)
And the word of the Lord   Ac 13:49
was *p*.
Word of the Lord scattered   Ac 13:49
and spread (A)
word of the Lord was carried   Ac 13:49
all over (B)
word of the Lord spread far   Ac 13:49
and wide (N)
word of the Lord spread all   Ac 13:49
over (P)
word of the Lord spread   Ac 13:49
throughout the region (R)

PUBLISHETH

good tidings, that *p*. peace   Isa 52:7;
    Na 1:15
tidings of good, that *p*.   Isa 52:7
salvation
p. affliction from mount   Jer 4:15
Ephraim

PUBLIUS

of the island, whose name was   Ac 28:7
P.
the father of *P*. lay sick   Ac 28:8
of a fever

PUDENS

Eubulus greeteth thee, and *P*.   2 Ti 4:21

PUFF

who *p.* themselves up (B)   Ps 35:26;
38:16

PUFFED

that no one of you be *p.* up   1Co 4:6
for one
so you may not be arrogantly   1Co 4:6
(B)
may not be inflated with pride   1Co 4:6
(N)
exalting one teacher above   1Co 4:6
another (P)
Now some are *p.* up, as   1Co 4:18
though
some are conceited and   1Co 4:18
arrogant (A)
grown inflated with pride   1Co 4:18
(B)
filled with self-importance   1Co 4:18
(N)
grown conceited (P)   1Co 4:18
Some are arrogant (R)   1Co 4:18
the speech of them which are   1Co 4:19
p. up
these conceited persons (B)   1Co 4:19
these self-important people   1Co 4:19
(N)
these pretentious ones (P)   1Co 4:19
these arrogant people (R)   1Co 4:19
ye are *p.* up, and have not   1Co 5:2
rather
you are proud and arrogant   1Co 5:2
(A)
you are still proud of   1Co 5:2
yourselves (N)
Are you still proud of your   1Co 5:2
church (P)
you are arrogant (R)   1Co 5:2
vaunteth not itself, is not *p.*   1Co 13:4
up
does not display itself   1Co 13:4
haughtily (A)
love is not out for display   1Co 13:4
(B)
love is not conceited or rude   1Co 13:4
(N)
love does not cherish inflated   1Co 13:4
ideas of its own importance (P)
love is not arrogant and rude   1Co 13:4
(R)
p. up, much elated (A)   2Co 12:7
vainly *p.* up by his fleshly   Col 2:18
mind
inflated by his worldly   Col 2:18
mind (B)
bursting with futile conceit of   Col 2:18
worldly minds (N)
inflated by an unspiritual   Col 2:18
imagination (P)

PUFFETH

for all his enemies he *p.* at   Ps 10:5
them
he sniffs and sneers at them   Ps 10:5
(A)(B)
in safety from him that *p.* at   Ps 12:5
him
I will set him in safety and in   Ps 12:5
the salvation for which he pants
(A)
I will grant him the   Ps 12:5
safekeeping for which he longs
(B)
set him in safety he panteth   Ps 12:5
for (E)
set him in safety for which he   Ps 12:5
longs (R)
Knowledge *p.* up, but charity   1Co 8:1
edifieth
knowledge breeds conceit (N)   1Co 8:1
knowledge may make a man   1Co 8:1
look big (P)

PUHITES

the Ithrites, and the *P.* and   1Ch 2:53

PUL

And *P.* the king of Assyria   2Ki 15:19
came
gave *P.* a thousand talents of   2Ki 15:19
stirred up the spirit of *P.*   1Ch 5:26
king of
nations, to Tarshish, *P.*   Isa 66:19
and Lud

PULL

he could not *p.* it in again   1Ki 13:4
to him
P. me out of the net that they   Ps 31:4
thy state shall be *p.* thee   Isa 22:19
down
I will *p.* up (B)   Isa 45:4
to root out, and to *p.* down,   Jer 1:10
and to
p. them out like sheep for the   Jer 12:3
and to *p.* down, and to   Jer 18:7
destroy it
them, and not *p.* them down   Jer 24:6
build you, and not *p.* you   Jer 42:10
down
not *p.* you down (A)(B)(R)   Jer 42:10
shall he not *p.* up the roots   Eze 17:9
p. off the robe with the   Mic 2:8
garment
p. out the mote out of thine   M't 7:4
eye
p. down the temple (N)(P)   M't 27:40
p. out the mote that is in   Lu 6:42
thine eye
to *p.* out the mote that is in   Lu 6:42
thy
I will *p.* down my barns, and   Lu 12:18
build
p. him out on the sabbath day   Lu 14:5

PULLED

p. her in unto him into the ark   Ge 8:9
and *p.* Lot into the house to   Ge 19:10
them
timber be *p.* down from his   Ezr 6:11
house
p. hair out (A)(B)(R)   Ezr 9:3;
Ne 13:25
p. out of his place (B)   Job 8:18
p. out the beard (R)   Isa 50:6
long robe *p.* aside (A)   Jer 13:22
my ways, and *p.* me in pieces   La 3:11
no more be *p.* up out of their   Am 9:15
land
and *p.* away the shoulder   Zec 7:11
be *p.* up by the roots (A)   Lu 17:6
Paul should have been *p.* in   Ac 23:10
pieces

PULLING

to the *p.* down of strong   2Co 10:4
holds
with fear, *p.* them out of the   Jude 23
fire

PULPIT

the scribe stood upon a *p.* of   Ne 8:4
wood
on a wooden platform (B)   Ne 8:4

PULSE

beans, and lentiles, and   2Sa 17:28
parched *p.*
parched peas and beans (A)   2Sa 17:28
parched lentils (B)   2Sa 17:28
and let them give up *p.* to eat   Da 1:12
vegetables (A)(B)(R)   Da 1:12; 1:16
should drink; and gave them *p.*   Da 1:16

PUNISH

I will *p.* that nation (B)   Ge 15:14
punish (B)   Le 18:25;
Jer 6:15; 9:9; 14:10; 49:8; Ho 9:9;
Am 3:14
punish (R)   Le 18:25;
Ps 59:5; 89:32; Jer 5:9, 29; 6:15; 9:9;
14:10; 49:8; 50:31; Ho 2:13; 8:13; 9:9;
Am 3:14
I will *p.* you seven times   Le 26:18
more for
p. you yet seven times for   Le 26:24
your
p. you sevenfold (B)   Le 26:28
to *p.* his house (A)   1Sa 3:13
punish (A)   Ps 89:32;
Jer 5:9, 29; 6:15; 9:9; 14:10; 49:8; 50:31;
La 4:22; Ho 8:13; 9:9; Am 3:14
shall he not *p.* (A)   Ps 94:10
Also to *p.* the just is not   Pr 17:26
good, nor
to impose a fine on the   Pr 17:26
righteous (B)(R)
will *p.* the fruit of the stout   Isa 10:12
heart

I will *p.* the world for their   Isa 13:11
evil, and
shall *p.* the host of the high   Isa 24:21
ones
to *p.* the inhabitants of the   Isa 26:21
earth
p. leviathan the piercing   Isa 27:1
serpent
punish (S)   Jer 5:9;
5:29; 9:9; 14:10; 49:8; 50:31; La 4:22
when I *p.* them (R)   Jer 8:12
that I will *p.* all them which   Jer 9:25
are
of hosts, Behold, I will *p.*   Jer 11:22
them
thou say, when he shall *p.*   Jer 13:21
thee
I will *p.* you according to the   Jer 21:14
fruit
I will even *p.* that man and   Jer 23:34
his
that I will *p.* the king of   Jer 25:12
Babylon
that nation will I *p.* saith the   Jer 27:8
Lord
I will *p.* Shemaiah the   Jer 29:32
Nehelamite
and I will *p.* all that oppress   Jer 30:20
them
I will *p.* him and his seed   Jer 36:31
and his
I will *p.* them that dwell in   Jer 44:13
the land
I will *p.* you in this place,   Jer 44:29
that ye
I will *p.* the multitude of No   Jer 46:25
I will *p.* the king of Babylon   Jer 50:18
And I will *p.* Bel in Babylon   Jer 51:44
I will *p.* them for their ways   Ho 4:9
I will not *p.* your daughters,   Ho 4:14
when
I will *p.* them (B)   Ho 7:12
will *p.* Jacob according to his   Ho 12:2
ways
I will *p.* you for all your   Am 3:2
iniquities
I will *p.* the princes, and the   Zep 1:8
king's
day also will I *p.* all those that   Zep 1:9
leap
p. the men that are settled on   Zep 1:12
their
As I thought to *p.* you, when   Zec 8:14
your
how they might *p.* them,   Ac 4:21
because
readiness to *p.* all   2Co 10:6
disobedience (S)

PUNISHED

his hand; he shall be surely   Ex 21:20
p.
a day or two, he shall not be   Ex 21:21
p.
he shall be surely *p.*   Ex 21:22
according to
hast *p.* us less than our   Ezr 9:13
iniquities
it is an iniquity to be *p.* by   Job 31:11
the judges
were an iniquity to be *p.* by   Job 31:28
the judge
p. in his anger (A)   Job 35:15
When the scorner is *p.* the   Pr 21:11
simple
but the simple pass on, and   Pr 22:3;
are *p.*   27:12
shall they be *p.* (R)   Isa 24:22; Jer 6:6
devouring him shall be *p.* (B)   Jer 2:3
city must be *p.* (A)(B)   Jer 6:6
as I have *p.* Jerusalem, by   Jer 44:13
as I have *p.* the king of   Jer 50:18
Assyria
not be cut off, howsoever I *p.*   Zep 3:7
them
the shepherds, and I *p.* the   Zec 10:3
goats
unto Jerusalem, for to be *p.*   Ac 22:5
I *p.* them oft in every   Ac 26:11
synagogue
bound to be *p.* (R)   Ro 13:2
p., yet not killed (R)   2Co 6:9
p. everlasting destruction   2Th 1:9
unto the day of judgment to   2Pe 2:9
be *p.*

PUNISHER

p. in such cases (B)(N)(P)   1Th 4:6

PUNISHMENT

My *p.* is greater than I can bear	Ge 4:13
accept of the *p.* of their iniquity	Le 26:41; 26:43
there shall no *p.* happen to thee for	1Sa 28:10
strange *p.* to the workers of iniquity	Job 31:3
man of great wrath shall suffer *p.*	Pr 19:19
in the day of *p.* (R)	Isa 10:3
p. was upon them (B)	Isa 26:16
p. procurred our peace (B)	Isa 53:5
time of *p.* (A)	Jer 8:12; 10:15; 11:23; 51:18; Mic 7:4
punishment (R)	Jer 10:15; 11:23; 23:12; 48:44; 51:18; Ho 9:7
punishment (R)	Jer 10:15; 11:23; 23:12; 46:21; 48:44; 50:27; 51:18; Ho 9:7; Mic 7:4
a man for the *p.* of his sins	La 3:39
p. of the iniquity of the daughter	La 4:6
than the *p.* of the sin of Sodom	La 4:6
p. of thine iniquity accomplished	La 4:22
shall bear the *p.* of their iniquity	Eze 14:10
the *p.* of the prophet shall be even	Eze 14:10
as the *p.* of him that seeketh unto	Eze 14:10
God relented of *p.* (B)	Jon 3:10
I will not turn away the *p.*	Am 1:3; 1:6, 9, 11, 13
will not turn away the *p.* thereof	Am 2:1; 2:4, 6
This shall be the *p.* of Egypt, and	Zec 14:19
the *p.* of all nations that come not	Zec 14:19
escape *p.* by the court (A)	M't 5:21
shall go away into everlasting *p.* (A)	M't 25:46
suffering the same *p.* (B)(P)	Lu 21:23
p. they will receive (N)	Lu 23:40
Sufficient to such a man is this *p.*	Ro 13:2
	2Co 2:6
p. by the majority (R)	2Co 2:6
what cruel *p.* (S)	2Co 7:11
eternal *p.* (B)	Heb 6:2
Of how much sorer *p.* suppose ye	Heb 10:29
sent by him for the *p.* of evildoers	1Pe 2:14
fear hath *p.* (A)(E)(N)(R)(S)	1Jo 4:18
exhibit of perpetual *p.* (A)(B)(E)(R)	Jude 7
fear of *p.* (P)	Re 18:15

PUNISHMENTS

bringeth the *p.* of the sword	Job 19:29
upon the heathen, and *p.* upon the	Ps 149:7
carry out *p.* (B)	Eze 25:17

PUNITES

of Pua, the family of the *P.*	Nu 26:23

PUNON

Zalmonah, and pitched in *P.*	Nu 33:42
they departed from *P.* and pitched	Nu 33:43

PUPIL

kept as the *p.* of his eye (A)	De 32:10
pupil (B)(N)	M't 10:24; 10:25

PUPS

little *p.* eat crumbs (A)(B)	M't 15:27

PUR

they cast *P.* that is, the lot	Es 3:7
and had cast *P.*, that is, the lot, to	Es 9:24
days Purim after the name of *P.*	Es 9:26

PURCHASE

The *p.* of the field, and of the cave	Ge 49:32

if a man *p.* of the Levites, then the	Le 25:33
p., a linen girdle (S)	Jer 13:1
So I took the evidence of the *p.*	Jer 32:11
I gave the evidence of the *p.* unto	Jer 32:12
that subscribed the book of the *p.*	Jer 32:12
evidences, this evidence of the *p.*	Jer 32:14
the evidence of the *p.* unto Baruch	Jer 32:16
releasing our deed of *p.* (B)	Eph 1:14
p. to themselves a good degree	1Ti 3:13

PURCHASED

Abraham *p.* of the sons of Heth	Ge 25:10
pass over, which thou hast *p.*	Ex 15:16
of Mahlon, have I *p.* to be my wife	Ru 4:10
which thou hast *p.* of old; the rod of	Ps 74:2
which his right hand had *p.*	Ps 78:54
man *p.* a field with the reward of	Ac 1:18
gift of God may be *p.* with money	Ac 8:20
he hath *p.* with his own blood	Ac 20:28
Christ *p.* our freedom (A)	Ga 3:13
redemption of the *p.* possession	Eph 1:4
with blood *p.* men (A)(E)(N)(P	Re 5:9
p. from the earth (B)(E)	Re 14:3

PURE

thou shalt overlay it with *p.* gold	Ex 25:11; 25:24
shalt make a mercy seat of *p.* gold	Ex 25:17
of *p.* gold shalt thou make them	Ex 25:29
shalt make a candlestick of *p.* gold	Ex 25:31
shall be one beaten work of *p.* gold	Ex 25:36
thereof, shall be of *p.* gold	Ex 25:38
a talent of *p.* gold shall he make it	Ex 25:39
p. oil olive beaten for the light	Ex 27:20
two chains of *p.* gold at the ends	Ex 28:14
ends of wreathen work of *p.* gold	Ex 28:22
thou shalt make a plate of *p.* gold	Ex 28:36
shalt overlay it with *p.* gold, the top	Ex 30:3
of *p.* myrrh five hundred shekels	Ex 30:23
sweet spices with *p.* frankincense	Ex 30:34
tempered together, *p.* and holy	Ex 30:35
and the *p.* candlestick with all his	Ex 31:8
he overlaid it with *p.* gold within	Ex 37:2
he made the mercy seat of *p.* gold	Ex 37:6
And he overlaid it with *p.* gold, and	Ex 37:11
covers to cover withal, of *p.* gold	Ex 37:16
made the candlestick of *p.* gold; of	Ex 37:17
.t was one beaten work of *p.* gold	Ex 37:22
and his snuffdishes, of *p.* gold	Ex 37:23
Of a talent of *p.* gold, made he it	Ex 37:24
he overlaid it with *p.* gold, both	Ex 37:26
and the *p.* incense of sweet spices	Ex 37:29
ends, of wreathen work of *p.* gold	Ex 39:15
they made bells of *p.* gold, and put	Ex 39:25
plate of the holy crown of *p.* gold	Ex 39:30
The *p.* candlestick, with the lamps	Ex 39:37

bring unto thee *p.* oil olive beaten	Le 24:2
the lamps upon the *p.* candlestick	Le 24:4
upon the *p.* table before the Lord	Le 24:6
p. frankincense upon each row	Le 24:7
drink the *p.* blood of the grape	De 32:14
the *p.* thou wilt shew thyself *p.*	2Sa 22:27; Ps 18:26
and twenty measures of *p.* oil	1Ki 5:11
he overlaid it with *p.* gold; and so	1Ki 6:20
the house within with *p.* gold	1Ki 6:21
candlesticks of *p.* gold, five on	1Ki 7:49
spoons, and the censers of *p.* gold	1Ki 7:50
forest of Lebanon were of *p.* gold	1Ki 10:21; 2Ch 9:20
Also *p.* gold for the fleshhooks	1Ch 28:17
he overlaid it within with *p.* gold	2Ch 3:4
before the oracle, of *p.* gold	2Ch 4:20
spoons, and the censers, of *p.* gold	2Ch 4:22
ivory, and overlaid it with *p.* gold	2Ch 9:17
they in order upon the *p.* table	2Ch 13:11
all of them were *p.* and killed	Eze 6:20
a man be more *p.* than his Maker	Job 4:17
can man be *p.* (A)(B)	Job 4:17
If thou wert *p.* and upright; surely	Job 8:6
thou hast said, My doctrine is *p.*	Job 11:4
in mine hands: also my prayer is *p.*	Job 16:17
the stars are not *p.* in his sight	Job 25:5
shall it be valued with *p.* gold	Job 28:19
words of the Lord are *p.* words	Ps 12:6
commandment of the Lord is *p.*	Ps 19:8
settest a crown of *p.* gold on his	Ps 21:3
hath clean hands, and a *p.* heart	Ps 24:4
Thy word is very *p.*: therefore	Ps 119:140
the words of the *p.* are pleasant	Pr 15:26
heart clean, I am *p.* from my sin	Pr 20:9
whether his work be *p.* and	Pr 20:11
but as for the *p.* his work is right	Pr 21:8
Every word of God is *p.*; he is	Pr 30:5
a generation that are *p.* in their	Pr 30:12
hair of his head like the *p.* wool	Da 7:9
until they are *p.* (B)(R)	Ho 8:5
Shall I count them *p.* with the	Mic 6:11
turn to the people a *p.* language	Zep 3:9
unto my name, and a *p.* offering	Mal 1:11
Blessed are the *p.* in heart: for	M't 5:8
I am *p.* from the blood of all men	Ac 20:26
All things indeed are *p.*; but it is	Ro 14:20
a *p.* virgin (B)(E)(R)	2Co 11:2
p. and blameless (R)	Ph'p 1:10
are just, whatsoever things are *p.*	Ph'p 4:8
p., fair, irreproachable (B)	1Th 2:10
is charity out of a *p.* heart, and	1Ti 1:5
of the faith in a *p.* conscience	1Ti 3:9
of other men's sins: keep thyself *p.*	1Ti 5:22
my forefathers with *p.* conscience	2Ti 1:3
call on the Lord out of a *p.* heart	2Ti 2:22
Unto the *p.* all things are *p.*	Tit 1:15
and unbelieving is nothing *p.*	Tit 1:15
our bodies washed with *p.* water	Heb 10:22
P. religion and undefiled before	Jas 1:27
wisdom that is from above is first *p.*	Jas 3:17
love one another with a *p.* heart	1Pe 1:22

PURE (continued)

desire the *p.* milk of the word   *1Pe 2:2*
(A)(E)(R)(S)
p. and modest way (A)(P)   *1Pe 3:2*
I stir up your *p.* minds by way   *2Pe 3:1*
purifieth himself, even as he is   *1Jo 3:3*
p.
clothed in *p.* and white linen   *Re 15:6*
and the city was *p.* gold, like   *Re 21:18*
unto
street of the city was *p.* gold,   *Re 21:21*
as it
he shewed me a *p.* river of   *Re 22:1*
water

PURELY

and *p.* purge away the dross   *Isa 1:25*

PURENESS

delivered by the *p.* of thine   *Job 22:30*
hands
He that loveth *p.* of heart, for   *Pr 22:11*
By *p.*, by knowledge, by   *2Co 6:6*

PURER

Her Nazarites were *p.* than   *La 4:7*
snow
art of *p.* eyes than to behold   *Hab 1:13*
evil

PUREST

from the *p.* motives (B)   *2Co 2:17*

PURGE

year he began to *p.* Judah and   *2Ch 34:3*
he began to clean up Judah   *2Ch 34:3*
(B)
P. me with hyssop, and I shall   *Ps 51:7*
be
thou shalt *p.* them away   *Ps 65:3*
deliver us, and *p.* away our   *Ps 79:9*
sins
and purely *p.* away thy dross   *Isa 1:25*
p. out from among you the   *Eze 20:38*
rebels
p. of moral foulness (B)   *Eze 22:15*
thus shalt thou cleanse and *p.*   *Eze 43:20*
it
Seven days shall they *p.* the   *Eze 43:26*
altar
to *p.* and to make them white   *Da 11:35*
and *p.* them as gold and silver   *Mal 3:3*
he will throughly *p.* his floor   *M't 3:12;*
   Lu 3:17
P. out therefore the old leaven   *1Co 5:7*
If a man therefore *p.* himself   *2Ti 2:21*
from
p. your conscience from dead   *Heb 9:14*

PURGED

shall not be *p.* with sacrifice   *1Sa 3:14*
nor
when he had *p.* the land, and   *2Ch 34:8*
mercy and truth iniquity is *p.*   *Pr 16:6*
have *p.* the blood of Jerusalem   *Isa 4:4*
is taken away, and thy sin *p.*   *Isa 6:7*
iniquity shall not be *p.* from   *Isa 22:14*
you
shall the iniquity of Jacob be   *Isa 27:9*
p.
lewdness: because I have *p.*   *Eze 24:13*
thee
not *p.* thou shalt not be *p.*   *Eze 24:13*
from
had by himself *p.* our sins   *Heb 1:3*
are by the law *p.* with blood   *Heb 9:22*
worshippers once *p.* should   *Heb 10:2*
have
that he was *p.* from his old sins   *2Pe 1:9*

PURGETH

he *p.* it, that it may bring   *Joh 15:2*
forth

PURGING

into the draught, *p.* all meats   *M'k 7:19*

PURIFICATION

of separation: it is a *p.* for sin   *Nu 19:9*
of the burnt heifer of *p.* for   *Nu 19:17*
sin
to the *p.* of the sanctuary   *2Ch 30:19*

---

their God, and the ward of   *Ne 12:45*
the *p.*
their things for *p.* be given them   *Es 2:3*
speedily gave her her things for   *Es 2:9*
p.
And when the days of her *p.*   *Lu 2:22*
accomplishment of the days   *Ac 21:26*
of *p.*

PURIFICATIONS

days of their *p.* accomplished   *Es 2:12*

PURIFIED

with his finger, and *p.* the altar   *Le 8:15*
And the Levites were *p.* and   *Nu 8:21*
they
nevertheless it shall be *p.* with   *Nu 31:23*
she was *p.* from her   *2Sa 11:4*
uncleanness
priests and the Levites were *p.*   *Ezr 6:20*
and the Levites *p.* themselves   *Ne 12:30*
p. the people, and the gates   *Ne 12:30*
furnace of earth, *p.* seven times   *Ps 12:6*
p. in an earthen furnace (B)   *Ps 12:6*
Many shall be *p.* and made   *Da 12:10*
Asia found me *p.* in the   *Ac 24:18*
temple
those consecrated, *p.* (A)   *1Co 1:2*
heavens should be *p.* with   *Heb 9:23*
these
ye have *p.* your souls in   *1Pe 1:22*
obeying

PURIFIER

sit as a refiner and *p.* of silver   *Mal 3:3*

PURIFIETH

and *p.* not himself, defileth   *Nu 19:13*
hath this hope in him *p.* himself   *1Jo 3:3*

PURIFY

p. the Israelites (B)   *Le 15:21*
p. himself with it on the third   *Nu 19:12*
day
if he *p.* not himself the third   *Nu 19:12*
day
the seventh day he shall *p.*   *Nu 19:19*
himself
unclean, and shall not *p.*   *Nu 19:20*
himself
p. both yourselves and your   *Nu 31:19*
p. all your raiment, and all   *Nu 31:20*
that is
to *p.* and hallow them (A)   *Job 1:5*
of breakings they *p.*   *Job 41:25*
themselves
and *p.* themselves in the   *Isa 66:17*
gardens
p. your hearts (B)   *Jer 4:4*
shall they purge the altar and   *Eze 43:26*
p. it
and he shall *p.* the sons of Levi   *Mal 3:3*
the passover, to *p.* themselves   *Joh 11:55*
take, and *p.* thyself with them   *Ac 21:24*
p. unto himself a peculiar   *Tit 2:14*
people
p. your hearts, ye double   *Jas 4:8*
minded

PURIFYING

blood of her *p.* three and thirty   *Le 12:4*
the days of her *p.* be fulfilled   *Le 12:4*
blood of her *p.* three score and   *Le 12:5*
the days of her *p.* are fulfilled   *Le 12:6*
Sprinkle water of *p.* upon them   *Nu 8:7*
and in the *p.* of all holy   *1Ch 23:28*
things
things for the *p.* of the women   *Es 2:12*
manner of the *p.* of the Jews   *Joh 2:6*
disciples and the Jews about   *Joh 3:25*
p.
them, *p.* their hearts by faith   *Ac 15:9*
the next day *p.* himself with   *Ac 21:26*
them
sanctifieth to the *p.* of the   *Heb 9:13*
flesh

PURIM

called these days *P.* after the   *Es 9:26*
these days of *P.* should not fail   *Es 9:28*
confirm this second letter of *P.*   *Es 9:29*
To confirm these days of *P.* in   *Es 9:31*
confirmed these matters of *P.*   *Es 9:32*

PURITY

until they attain *p.* (A)   *Ho 8:5*
discussed *p.* of life (B)   *Ac 24:25*
to most through *p.* (A)(P)   *1Th 4:7*
charity, in spirit, in faith, in *p.*   *1Ti 4:12*
the younger as sisters, with all   *1Ti 5:2*
p.

PURLOINING

Not *p.* but shewing all good   *Tit 2:10*
nor steal by taking things of   *Tit 2:10*
small value (A)
to evidence complete   *Tit 2:10*
reliability (B)
not to pilfer (N)(R)   *Tit 2:10*
not answer back, or be   *Tit 2:10*
light-fingered (P)

PURPLE

And blue, and *p.* and scarlet   *Ex 25:4;*
   26:1
shalt make a veil of blue, and   *Ex 26:31*
p.
door of the tent, of blue, and   *Ex 26:36*
p.
of twenty cubits, of blue, and   *Ex 27:16*
p.
gold, and blue, and *p.* and   *Ex 28:5*
scarlet
ephod of gold, of blue, and of   *Ex 28:6*
p.
even of gold, of blue, and *p.*   *Ex 28:8*
make it; of gold, of blue, and   *Ex 28:15*
of *p.*
pomegranates of blue, and of   *Ex 28:33*
p.
And blue, and *p.* and scarlet   *Ex 35:6*
with whom was found blue,   *Ex 35:23*
and *p.*
had spun, both of blue, and of   *Ex 35:25*
p.
in blue and in *p.* in scarlet   *Ex 35:35*
twined linen, and blue, and *p.*   *Ex 36:8*
he made a veil of blue, and *p.*   *Ex 36:35*
tabernacle door, of blue, and   *Ex 36:37*
p. and
was needlework, of blue, and   *Ex 38:18*
p.
an embroiderer in blue, and in   *Ex 38:23*
p.
of the blue, and *p.* and scarlet   *Ex 39:1*
and *p.* and scarlet, and fine   *Ex 39:2;*
twined   *39:8*
work it in the blue, and in the   *Ex 39:3*
p.
of gold, blue, and *p.* and scarlet   *Ex 39:5*
robe pomegranates of blue,   *Ex 39:24*
and *p.*
fine twined linen, and blue,   *Ex 39:29*
and *p.*
and spread a *p.* cloth thereon   *Nu 4:13*
p. raiment that was on the   *J'g 8:26*
kings of
and in iron, and in *p.* and   *2Ch 2:7*
crimson
in *p.* in blue, and in fine linen   *2Ch 2:14*
veil of blue, and *p.* and   *2Ch 3:14*
crimson
with cords of fine linen and *p.*   *Es 1:6*
a garment of fine linen and *p.*   *Es 8:15*
tapestry; her clothing is silk   *Pr 31:22*
and *p.*
the covering of it of *p.* the   *Ca 3:10*
midst
and the hair of the head like *p.*   *Ca 7:5*
blue and *p.* is their clothing: *Jer 10:9*
they
blue and *p.* from the isles of   *Eze 27:7*
Elishah
emeralds, *p.* and broidered   *Eze 27:16*
work
they clothed him with *p.* and   *M'k 15:17*
they took off the *p.* from   *M'k 15:20*
him, and
was clothed in *p.* and fine   *Lu 16:19*
linen
and they put on him a *p.* robe   *Joh 19:2*
crown of thorns, and the *p.*   *Joh 19:5*
robe
Lydia, a seller of *p.* of the city   *Ac 16:14*
of
arrayed in *p.* and scarlet colour   *Re 17:4*
and fine linen, and *p.* and silk   *Re 18:12*
was clothed in fine linen, and   *Re 18:16*
p.

PURPOSE

nothing they *p.* to do (E) — Ge 11:6
the people change their *p.* (A) — Ex 13:17
change your *p.* (B) — Ex 32:12
Israelites changed their *p.* (A) — J'g 21:6
of the handfuls of *p.* for her — Ru 2:16
I *p.* to build an house unto the — 1Ki 5:5
ye *p.* to keep under the — 2Ch 28:10
children
against them, to frustrate their — Ezr 4:5
p.
which they had made for the *p.* — Ne 8:4
may withdraw man from his — Job 33:17
p.
obscures *p.* by words (B) — Job 38:2
p. is established by counsel — Pr 20:18
to every *p.* under the heaven — Ec 3:1
a time there for every *p.* and — Ec 3:17
for
Because to every *p.* there is time — Ec 8:6
To what *p.* is the multitude of — Isa 1:11
your
the *p.* of the Holy One (B) — Isa 5:19
is the *p.* that is purposed — Isa 14:26
upon
p. against Egypt — Isa 19:17
(A)(B)(E)(R)
shall help in vain, and to no *p.* — Isa 30:7
To what *p.* cometh there to me — Jer 6:20
incense
which I *p.* to do unto them — Jer 26:3
because
evil which I *p.* to do unto them — Jer 36:3
hath conceived a *p.* against — Jer 49:30
you
his *p.* is against Babylon (S) — Jer 51:11
p. of the Lord shall be — Jer 51:29
performed
that the *p.* might not be — Da 6:17
changed
saying, To what *p.* is this — M't 26:8
waste
brought to nothing God's *p.* — Lu 7:30
(A)(B)(N)(P)(R)
not agreed to *p.* (A)(R) — Lu 23:51
fixed *p.*, settled plan (A) — Ac 2:23
with united *p.* (A)(B) — Ac 2:46
your will and *p.* predestined — Ac 4:28
(A)(B)(E)(R)
with *p.* of heart they would — Ac 11:23
cleave
I have appeared unto thee for — Ac 26:16
this *p.*
whole *p.* of God (B)(N) — Ac 26:27
that they had obtained their — Ac 27:13
p.
Paul, kept them from their *p.* — Ac 27:43
opposed to *p.* of God (P) — Ro 8:7
are the called according to his — Ro 8:28
p.
the *p.* of God according to — Ro 9:11
election
Even for this same *p.* have I — Ro 9:17
raised
the secret *p.* (N) — 1Co 2:7;
— Eph 1:9; 6:19
lightness? or the things that I — 2Co 1:17
p.
do I *p.* according to the flesh, — 2Co 1:17
that
he planned in his *p.* of love (P) — Eph 1:5
the hidden *p.* (N) — Eph 1:9;
— 3:9; 1Co 2:7; Re 10:7
p. of him who worketh all — Eph 1:11
things
p. in sovereign will (P) — Eph 1:11
the eternal *p.* which he — Eph 3:11
purposed
I have sent unto you for the — Eph 6:22
same *p.*
Christ died to no *p.* — Ga 2:21
(A)(B)(R)
in simplicity of *p.* (A) — Col 3:22
I have sent unto you for the — Col 4:8
same *p.*
but according to his own *p.* and — 2Ti 1:9
doctrine, manner of life, *p.*, — 2Ti 3:10
faith
unchangeableness of *p.* — Heb 6:17
(A)(B)(N)(R)
for the *p.* of removing sin (P) — 1Jo 3:5
For this *p.* the Son was — 1Jo 3:8
manifested

PURPOSED

that he was *p.* to fight against — 2Ch 32:2
I am *p.* that my mouth shall — Ps 17:3
not

have *p.* to overthrow my — Ps 140:4
goings
have *p.* evil (A)(E) — Isa 7:5
as I have *p.* so shall it stand — Isa 14:24
that is *p.* upon the whole — Isa 14:26
earth
For the Lord of hosts hath *p.* — Isa 14:27
Lord of hosts hath *p.* upon — Isa 19:12
Egypt
The Lord of hosts hath *p.* it, to — Isa 23:9
pass; I have *p.* it, I will also — Isa 46:11
do it
I have *p.* it, and will not repent — Jer 4:28
hath *p.* against the — Jer 49:20
inhabitants
that he hath *p.* against the — Jer 50:45
land of
p. and done (A)(S) — Jer 51:12
The Lord hath *p.* to destroy the — La 2:8
Daniel *p.* in his heart that he — Da 1:8
Paul *p.* in the spirit, when he — Ac 19:21
had
he *p.* to return through — Ac 20:3
oftentimes I *p.* to come unto — Ro 1:13
you
which he hath *p.* in himself — Eph 1:9
which he *p.* in Christ Jesus — Eph 3:11
our

PURPOSELESS

discussions, *p.* talk (A) — 1Ti 1:6
futile and *p.* (B) — Tit 3:9

PURPOSES

p. they were forming (R) — De 31:21
my *p.* are broken off, even — Job 17:11
deviseth wicked *p.* (E) — Ps 6:18
frustrated *p.* of people (B) — Ps 33:10
Without counsel *p.* are — Pr 15:22
p. are frustrated (A) — Pr 15:22
shall be broken in the *p.* — Isa 19:10
thereof
p. planned of old (A) — Isa 25:1
and his *p.* that he hath — Jer 49:20;
purposed — 50:45
plotting against sowing *p.* of — Ac 13:10
God (B)
disclose *p.* of the heart (R) — 1Co 4:5

PURPOSETH

according as he *p.* in his heart — 2Co 9:7

PURPOSING

doth comfort himself, *p.* to — Ge 27:42
kill thee

PURSE

among us: let us all have one *p.* — Pr 1:14
no bread, no money in their *p.* — M'k 6:8
not a penny in their belt — M'k 6:8
(A)(B)(N)(R)
no money in their pockets (P) — M'k 6:8
Carry neither *p.* nor scrip, nor — Lu 10:4
I sent you without *p.* and — Lu 22:35
scrip
he that hath a *p.* let him take — Lu 22:36
it

PURSES

purses (A)(B)(R) — Isa 3:22
nor silver, nor brass in your *p.* — M't 10:9
provide *p.* — Lu 12:33
(A)(B)(E)(N)(P)(R)

PURSUE

did not *p.* after the sons of — Ge 35:5
Jacob
The enemy said, I will *p.* I will — Ex 15:9
avenger of the blood *p.* the — De 19:6
slayer
they shall *p.* thee until thou — De 28:22
perish
shall *p.* thee, and overtake — De 28:45
thee
p. after them quickly; for ye — Jos 2:5
shall
called together to *p.* after them — Jos 8:16
p. after your enemies, and — Jos 10:19
smite
the avenger of blood *p.* after — Jos 20:5
him
after whom dost thou *p.*? — 1Sa 24:14
after a

Yet a man is risen to *p.* thee — 1Sa 25:29
my lord thus *p.* after his — 1Sa 26:18
servant
Shall I *p.* after this troop? — 1Sa 30:8
shall I
P.: for thou shalt surely — 1Sa 30:8
overtake
I will arise and *p.* after David — 2Sa 17:1
lord's servants, and *p.* after — 2Sa 20:6
him
p. after Sheba the son of — 2Sa
Bichri — 20:13
thine enemies, while they *p.* — 2Sa 24:13
thee
and wilt thou *p.* the dry — Job 13:25
stubble
they *p.* my soul as the wind — Job 30:15
a'l who *p.* me (B)(E)(R) — Ps 7:1
let the enemy *p.* (A)(B)(E)(R) — Ps 7:5
p. the afflicted (B)(R) — Ps 10:2
p. me (A)(E) — Ps 31:15; 35:3
and do good; seek peace, and — Ps 34:14
p. it
p. and seize them (E)(R) — Ps 71:11
p. and afflict them — Ps 83:15;
(A)(B)(E)(R) — La 3:66
shall they that *p.* you be swift — Isa 30:16
they *p.* evil (B) — Jer 23:10
p. with the sword — Jer 29:18
(A)(B)(E)(R)
Madmen; the sword shall *p.* — Jer 48:2
thee
blood, and blood shall *p.* thee — Eze 35:6
blood, even blood shall *p.* thee — Eze 35:6
is good: the enemy shall *p.* him — Ho 8:3
did *p.* his brother with the — Am 1:11
sword
and darkness shall *p.* his — Na 1:8
enemies
seek peace and *p.* it (S) — 1Pe 3:11

PURSUED

eighteen, and *p.* them unto — Ge 14:14
Dan
and *p.* them unto Hobah, — Ge 14:15
which
p. after him seven days' — Ge 31:23
journey
thou hast so hotly *p.* after me — Ge 31:36
he *p.* after the children of — Ex 14:8
Israel
But the Egyptians *p.* after them — Ex 14:9
And the Egyptians *p.* and — Ex 14:23
went in
overflow them as they *p.* after — De 11:4
you
the men *p.* after them the way — Jos 2:7
to
they which *p.* after them were — Jos 2:7
gone
and they *p.* after Joshua, and — Jos 8:16
were
the city open, and *p.* after — Jos 8:17
Israel
the Egyptians *p.* after your — Jos 24:6
fathers
they *p.* after him, and caught — J'g 1:6
him
Barak *p.* after the chariots, and — J'g 4:16
as Barak *p.* Sisera, Jael came — J'g 4:22
out
and *p.* after the Midianites — J'g 7:23
and *p.* Midian, and brought the — J'g 7:25
he *p.* after them, and took the — J'g 8:12
two
p. hard after them unto — J'g 20:45
Gidom
and *p.* the Philistines, and — 1Sa 7:11
smote
shouted, and *p.* the — 1Sa 17:52
Philistines
he *p.* after David in the — 1Sa 23:25
wilderness
David *p.* he and four — 1Sa 30:10
hundred
And Asahel *p.* after Abner; — 2Sa 2:19
and in
also and Abishai *p.* after — 2Sa 2:24
Abner
and *p.* after Israel no more, — 2Sa 2:28
Abishai his brother *p.* after — 2Sa 20:10
Sheba
I have *p.* mine enemies, and — 2Sa 22:38
Syrians fled; and Israel *p.* — 1Ki 20:20
them
of the Chaldees *p.* after the — 2Ki 25:5
king

Aijbah *p.* after Jeroboam, 2Ch 13:19
and took
were with him *p.* them unto 2Ch 14:13
Gerar
poor are hotly *p.* (E) Ps 10:2
I have *p.* mine enemies, and Ps 18:37
He *p.* them, and passed safely Isa 41:3
the Chaldeans' army *p.* after Jer 39:5
them
the Chaldeans *p.* after the king Jer 52:8
they *p.* us upon the mountains La 4:19

PURSUER

without strength before the *p.* La 1:6

PURSUERS

mountain, lest the *p.* meet you Jos 2:16
days, until the *p.* be returned Jos 2:16
days, until the *p.* were Jos 2:22
returned
p. sought them throughout all Jos 2:22
turned back upon the *p.* Jos 8:20

PURSUETH

ye shall flee when none *p.* you Le 26:17
and they shall fall when none Le 26:36
p.
were before a sword, when Le 26:37
none *p.*
tendeth to life: so he that *p.* Pr 11:19
evil
p. it to his own death Pr 11:19
Evil *p.* sinners: but to the Pr 13:21
he *p.* them with words, yet they Pr 19:7
The wicked flee when no man Pr 28:1
p.

PURSUING

were with him, faint, yet *p.* them J'g 8:4
I am *p.* after Zebah and J'g 8:5
Zalmunna
Saul returned from *p.* after 1Sa 23:28
David
David and Joab came from *p.* 2Sa 3:22
a troop
returned from *p.* after Israel 2Sa 18:16
he is talking, or he is *p.* or he 1Ki 18:27
is
that they turned back from 1Ki 22:33
p. him
turned back again from *p.* 2Ch 18:32
him
p. and afflicting them Ps 35:6
(A)(B)(E)(R)

PURSUITS

worthless *p.* (A)(R) Pr 12:11

PURTENANCE

his legs, and with the *p.* thereof Ex 12:9
its innerparts (A)(R) Ex 12:9
heart and liver (B) Ex 12:9
the inwards thereof (E) Ex 12:9

PUSH

ox were wont to *p.* with his Ex 21:29
horn
ox shall *p.* a manservant or a Ex 21:32
ox hath used to *p.* in time past Ex 21:36
p. the people together to the De 33:17
ends
these shalt thou *p.* the 1Ki 22:11
Syrians
p. Syria until they be 2Ch 18:10
consumed
they *p.* away my feet, and Job 30:12
they
thee will we *p.* down our Ps 44:5
enemies
the king of the south *p.* at Da 11:40
him

PUSHED

p. all the diseased with your Eze 34:21
horns

PUSHING

I saw the ram *p.* westward and Da 8:4
northward

PUT

there God *p.* the man he had Ge 2:8;
formed 2:15
I will *p.* enmity between thee Ge 3:15
and woman
p. thy hand under my thigh Ge 24:2;
24:9; 47:29
and I *p.* the earring upon her Ge 24:47
face
p. them upon Jacob her Ge 27:15
younger son
she *p.* the skins of the kids Ge 27:16
upon his hands
Jacob *p.* the stones for his Ge 28:11
pillows
p. the stone again on the well's Ge 29:3
mouth
he *p.* his own flocks by Ge 30:40
themselves
when cattle were feeble, he *p.* Ge 30:42
not the rods
Rachel *p.* them in the camels' Ge 31:34
furniture
p. space betwixt drove and Ge 32:16
drove
Tamar *p.* off her widow's Ge 38:14
garments
all he had he *p.* into Joseph's Ge 39:4
hand
that they should *p.* me into Ge 40:15
the dungeon
he *p.* them altogether in ward Ge 42:17
p. them in prison (R) Ge 42:17
Joseph shall *p.* his hand on Ge 46:4
thine eyes
p. thy right hand upon his Ge 48:18
head
Joseph was *p.* in a coffin in Ge 50:26
Egypt
draw not nigh hither, *p.* off thy Ex 3:5;
shoes Isa 20:2; Ac 7:33
ye shall *p.* them on your sons Ex 3:22
and daughters
Lord said, *P.* now thy hand in Ex 4:6
thy bosom
speak to him, and *p.* words in Ex 4:15
his mouth
to *p.* a sword in their hand to Ex 5:21
slay us
I will *p.* a division between my Ex 8:23
people
may know the Lord doth *p.* a Ex 11:7
difference
I will *p.* none of these diseases Ex 15:26
on thee
p. an homer full of manna Ex 16:33
therein
p. the Lord to the test (S) Ex 17:2
and *p.* in his beast in another Ex 22:5
man's field
to see whether he have *p.* in his Ex 22:8
hand
an oath that he hath not *p.* his Ex 22:11
hand
p. not thine hand with the Ex 23:1
wicked
thou shalt *p.* all in the hands Ex 29:24
of Aaron
p. of the perfume before the Ex 30:36
testimony
p. every man his sword by his Ex 32:27
side
now *p.* off thy ornaments from Ex 33:5
thee
I will *p.* thee in a cleft of the Ex 33:22
rock
he *p.* all on Aaron's and his Le 8:27
sons' hands
the vessel, it must be *p.* into Le 11:32
water
but if any water be *p.* on seed, Le 11:38
be unclean
she shall be *p.* apart seven Le 15:19
days
shalt not approach as long as Le 18:19
she *p.* apart
nor *p.* a stumblingblock Le 19:14
before the blind
and they *p.* the blasphemer in Le 24:12
ward
p. ten thousand to flight Le 26:8;
De 32:30
shall *p.* my name on the Nu 6:27
children of Israel
of spirit which is on thee, Nu 11:17
and *p.* upon them
the Lord would *p.* his Spirit Nu 11:29
on them
p. me to the test (S) Nu 14:22; Heb 3:9

Moses made a serpent of Nu 21:9
brass, and *p.* it on a
the Lord *p.* a word in Nu 23:5;
Balaam's mouth 23:16
p. the Lord your God to the De 6:16;
test (S) M't 4:7; Lu 4:12; Ac 15:10
thou shalt *p.* them in the ark De 10:2
I *p.* the tables in the ark De 10:5
which I had made
thou shalt *p.* the blessing on De 11:29
mount Gerizim
the place he shall choose to *p.* De 12:5;
his name 12:21
ye shall rejoice in all ye *p.* your De 12:7
hand to
and will *p.* my words in his De 18:18
mouth
but thou shalt not *p.* any De 23:24
grapes in thy vessel
p. it even among their own Jos 7:11
stuff
I *p.* my life in my hands, and J'g 12:3
passed
p. me into one of the priest's 1Sa 2:36
offices
your king, he will *p.* your 1Sa 8:16
asses to work
but no man *p.* his hand to his 1Sa 14:26
mouth
and David *p.* them off him 1Sa 17:39
put he *p.* Goliath's armour in 1Sa 17:54
his tent
for he did *p.* his life in his 1Sa 19:5
hand
I have *p.* my life in my hand 1Sa 28:21
hands not bound, nor feet *p.* 2Sa 3:34
in fetters
Joab's garment that he had *p.* 2Sa 20:8
on
Lord *p.* them under the soles of 1Ki 5:3
his feet
to *p.* my name there 1Ki 9:3;
11:36; 14:21
the other of the calves he *p.* 1Ki 12:29
in Dan
lay it on wood, and *p.* no fire 1Ki 18:23
under
the kings having *p.* on their 1Ki 22:10
robes
saith the king, *P.* this fellow 1Ki 22:27
in prison
he *p.* his mouth upon his 2Ki 4:34
mouth
the king's son, they *p.* the 2Ki 11:12
crown on him
p. thine hand upon the bow, 2Ki 13:16
he *p.* his hand
Judah was *p.* to worse before 2Ki 14:12
Israel
I will *p.* hook in thy nose 2Ki 19:28;
Isa 37:29
in this house will I *p.* my 2Ki 21:7;
name for ever 2Ch 6:20; 12:13; 33:7
that have *p.* their lives in 1Ch 11:19
jeopardy
because he *p.* his hand to the 1Ch 13:10
ark
the Syrians *p.* to the worse 1Ch 19:16;
19:19
and the angel *p.* up his 1Ch 21:27
sword again
neither was the number *p.* in 1Ch 27:24
the account
to find out every device shall 2Ch 2:14
be *p.*
and in the house have I *p.* the 2Ch 6:11
ark
if thy people Israel be *p.* to 2Ch 6:24
the worse
p. away the Asheroth 2Ch 19:3;
(A)(B) 33:3
Judah was *p.* to the worse 2Ch 25:22
before Israel
the king of Egypt *p.* him 2Ch 36:3
down at Jerusalem
Cyrus *p.* the decree in 2Ch 36:22;
writing Ezr 1:1
destroy kings that *p.* their Ezr 6:12
hand to alter
hath *p.* such a thing in the Ezr 7:27
king's heart
what God had *p.* in my heart Ne 2:12
to do
their nobles *p.* not their necks to Ne 3:5
the work
that every one *p.* them off for Ne 4:23
washing
Tobiah would have *p.* me in Ne 6:14;
fear 6:19

his decree drew near to be *p.* in *Es 9:1*
execution
behold, he *p.* no trust in his *Job 4:18*
servants
wherefore do I *p.* my life in *Job 13:14*
mine hand
lay down, *p.* me in a surety *Job 17:3*
with thee
he hath *p.* my brethren far *Job 19:13*
from me
no, but he would *p.* strength *Job 23:6*
in me
who *p.* wisdom in the inward *Job 38:36*
parts
canst thou *p.* an hook into his *Job 41:2*
nose
thou hast *p.* gladness in my *Ps 4:7*
heart
thou hast *p.* all things under his *Ps 8:6;*
feet *1Co 15:25, 27; Eph 1:22; Heb 2:8*
p. in fear, O Lord, that nations *Ps 9:20*
may know
thou hast *p.* off my sackcloth *Ps 30:11*
and girded me
let the lying lips be *p.* to *Ps 31:18*
silence
let them be *p.* to shame that *Ps 35:4;*
seek after my soul *83:17*
he hath *p.* a new song in my *Ps 40:3*
mouth
and *p.* to shame, that wish *Ps 40:14;*
me evil *44:7; 53:5*
but thou hast cast off and *p.* us *Ps 44:9*
to shame
p. thou my tears into thy bottle *Ps 56:8*
and *p.* to confusion, that desire *Ps 70:2*
my hurt
in thee I trust, let me never be *Ps 71:1*
p. to confusion
he *p.* them to a perpetual *Ps 78:66*
reproach
lover and friend hast thou *p.* *Ps 88:18*
far from me
better to trust in Lord than to *Ps 118:8*
p. confidence in man
better to trust in Lord than to *Ps 118:9*
p. confidence in princes
O Lord, *p.* me not to shame *Ps 119:31*
and *p.* a knife to thy throat *Pr 23:2*
than that thou shouldest be *p.* *Pr 25:7*
lower
when thy neighbour hath *p.* *Pr 25:8*
thee to shame
lest he that heareth it *p.* thee *Pr 25:10*
to shame
what God doeth, nothing can *Ec 3:14*
be *p.* to it
then must he *p.* to more *Ec 10:10*
strength
I have *p.* off my coat, how shall *Ca 5:3*
I *p.* it on
my beloved *p.* in his hand by *Ca 5:4*
hole of the door
woe to them that *p.* darkness *Isa 5:20*
for light
I have *p.* down the inhabitants *Isa 10:13*
weaned child *p.* his hand on *Isa 11:8*
cockatrice' den
I have *p.* my Spirit upon him *Isa 42:1;*
M't 12:18
p. me in remembrance, let us *Isa 43:26*
plead
thou shalt not be able to *p.* it *Isa 47:11*
off
I have *p.* words in thy mouth *Isa 51:16;*
Jer 1:9
p. it into the hand of them *Isa 51:23*
that afflict thee
to bruise him, he hath *p.* him *Isa 53:10*
to grief
for thou shalt not be *p.* to *Isa 54:4*
shame
the words I *p.* in thy mouth *Isa 54:21*
shall not depart
where is he that *p.* his Holy *Isa 63:11*
Spirit within him
how shall I *p.* thee among the *Jer 3:19*
children
for the Lord our God hath *p.* *Jer 8:14*
us to silence
they have *p.* themselves to *Jer 12:13*
pain, but not profit
I will *p.* my law in their *Jer 31:33*
inward parts
I will *p.* my fear in their *Jer 32:40*
hearts
O sword, *p.* up thyself into thy *Jer 47:6*
scabbard

they shall ride, everyone *p.* in *Jer 50:42*
array
they *p.* the branch to their *Eze 8:17*
nose
heart, I will *p.* a new spirit *Eze 11:19;*
within you *36:26-27; 37:14*
through my comeliness I had *Eze 16:14*
p. upon thee
her priests have *p.* no *Eze 22:26*
difference
I will *p.* hooks in thy jaws *Eze 29:4;*
38:4
I will *p.* a fear in the land of *Eze 30:13*
Egypt
and *p.* breath in you, and ye *Eze 37:6*
shall live
and whom he would he *p.* *Da 5:19*
down
p. in the sickle, for the harvest *Joe 3:13*
is ripe
I will *p.* them together as *Mic 2:12*
sheep of Bozrah
trust not a friend, *p.* ye not *Mic 7:5*
confidence in a guide
where they have been *p.* to *Zep 3:19*
shame
earneth wages to *p.* it in a bag *Hag 1:6*
with holes
nor light candle and *p.* it *M't 5:15*
under a bushel
for that which is *p.* in to fill it *M't 9:16*
up
nor do men *p.* new wine into *M't 9:17*
old bottles
p. up with (B)(P) *M't 17:17; M'k 9:19*
let not man *p.* asunder *M't 19:6;*
M'k 10:9
that he had *p.* the Sadducees *M't 22:34*
to silence
oughtest to *p.* my money to *M't 25:27*
exchangers
p. up again thy sword *M't 26:52;*
Joh 18:11
not lawful to *p.* them into the *M't 27:6*
treasury
now after that John was *p.* in *M'k 1:14*
prison
new wine *p.* into new bottles *M'k 2:22;*
Lu 5:38
hath *p.* down mighty from *Lu 1:52*
their seats
no man having *p.* his hand to *Lu 9:62*
plough
p. his hands on them, and *Lu 10:16*
blessed them
bring best robe, *p.* it on him, *Lu 15:22*
and *p.* a ring
I have none to *p.* me into the *Joh 5:7*
pool
he *p.* clay upon mine eyes, and *Joh 9:15*
I do see
Judas bare what was *p.* in the *Joh 12:6*
bag
devil having now *p.* into the *Joh 13:2*
heart of Judas
p. it upon hyssop, and *p.* it to *Joh 19:29*
his mouth
unless I *p.* my finger into the *Joh 20:25*
print of nails
p. on his clothes (R) *Joh 21:7*
the father hath *p.* in his own *Ac 1:7*
power
they *p.* the apostles in hold unto *Ac 4:3*
next day
and *p.* them in the common *Ac 5:18*
prison
behold, the men whom ye *p.* in *Ac 5:25*
prison
p. the whole matter plainly (B) *Ac 11:4*
seeing ye *p.* the word of God *Ac 13:46*
from you
and *p.* no difference between us *Ac 15:9*
and them
to *p.* a yoke upon the neck of *Ac 15:10*
the disciples
they *p.* to sea (S) *Ac 21:1; 27:2,*
p. them off (A)(R) *Ac 24:22*
p. away your pride (N) *Ro 11:20*
that no man *p.* a stumbling- *Ro 14:13*
block
p. Christ to the test (S) *1Co 10:9*
he shall have *p.* down *1Co 15:24*
authority
till he hath *p.* all his enemies *1Co 15:25*
under his feet
God, which *p.* the same *2Co 8:16*
earnest care in Titus
p. up with it (N) *2Co 11:19; 11:20*
that ye *p.* off the old man *Eph 4:22;*
Col 3:9

ye also *p.* off these, anger, *Col 3:8*
wrath
if thou *p.* the brethren in *1Ti 4:6;*
remembrance, shalt be *2Ti 2:14*
wherefore I *p.* thee in *2Ti 1:6*
remembrance
p. them in mind to be subject to *Tit 3:1*
powers
if he oweth, *p.* that on my *Ph'm 18*
account
to angels, hath he not *p.* in *Heb 2:5*
subjection
he left nothing that is not *p.* *Heb 2:8*
under him, but now we see not
yet all things *p.* under him
and *p.* him to open shame *Heb 6:6*
I will *p.* my laws into their *Heb 8:10*
mind, and write
I will *p.* my laws into their *Heb 10:16*
hearts
p. away all filthiness (S) *Jas 1:21*
we *p.* bits in the horses' mouths *Jas 3:3*
ye may *p.* to silence the *1Pe 2:15*
ignorance
to *p.* you always in *2Pe 1:12*
remembrance
knowing that I must *p.* off this *2Pe 1:14*
tabernacle
I will *p.* you also in *Jude 5*
remembrance
you have *p.* to proof (N) *Re 2:2*
I will *p.* on you none other *Re 2:24*
burden
not suffer dead bodies to be *p.* *Re 11:9*
in graves
God hath *p.* in their hearts to *Re 17:17*
fulfil his will

PUT *AWAY*

p. away the strange gods *Ge 35:2*
among you
p. away the leaven out of your *Ex 12:15*
houses
nor take a woman *p. away* *Le 21:7*
from her husband
p. away guilt of innocent *De 19:13;*
blood *21:9*
he may not *p.* her *away* all *De 22:19;*
his days *22:29*
p. away the strange gods *Jos 24:14;*
your fathers served *24:23; J'g 10:16;*
1Sa 7:3
Eli said, *P. away* thy wine *1Sa 1:14*
from thee
Saul had *p. away* wizards out *1Sa 28:3*
of the land
Saul whom I *p. away* before *2Sa 7:15*
thee
Nathan said, The Lord hath *2Sa 12:13*
p. away thy sin
Jehoram *p. away* the image of *2Ki 3:2*
Baal
all the abominations did *2Ki 23:24*
Josiah *p. away*
Asa *p. away* the abominable *2Ch 15:8*
idols
make a covenant to *p. away* *Ezr 10:3*
the wives
they gave their hands to *p.* *Ezr 10:19*
away their wives
if iniquity be in thine hand, *Job 11:14*
p. it *away*
p. away iniquity from thy *Job 22:23*
tabernacle
I did not *p. away* his statutes *Ps 18:22*
from me
p. not thy servant *away* in *Ps 27:9*
anger
thou hast *p. away* mine *Ps 88:8*
acquaintance
p. away from thee a froward *Pr 4:24*
mouth
whom I have *p. away* your *Isa 50:1*
mother, *p. away*
if a man *p. away* his wife, will *Jer 3:1*
he return
I had *p.* her *away*, and given *Jer 3:8*
her a bill of divorce
if thou wilt *p. away* thine *Jer 4:1*
abominations
let them *p. away* their *Eze 43:9*
whoredom
nor shall priest take her that *Eze 44:22*
is *p. away*
let her *p. away* her whoredoms *Ho 2:2*
ye that *p.* far *away* the evil day *Am 6:3*
Joseph was minded to *p.* her *M't 1:19*
away privily
it hath been said, Whoso shall *M't 5:31;*

p. away his wife 5:32; 19:9; *M'k* 10:11;
Lu 16:18
is it lawful for man to *p.* *M'k* 10:2
away his wife
if a woman shall *p. away* her *M'k* 10:12
husband
p. away from you that wicked 1Co 5:13
person
let not the husband *p. away* 1Co 7:11;
his wife 7:12
when a man, I *p. away* 1Co 13:11
childish things
let anger and evil speaking be *Eph* 4:31
p. away
which some having *p. away* 1Ti 1:19
p. away sin by sacrifice of *Heb* 9:26
himself

PUT *FORTH*

lest he *p. forth* and take of tree *Ge* 3:22
of life
Noah *p. forth* his hand and *Ge* 8:9
took the dove
the men *p. forth* their hand *Ge* 19:10
and pulled Lot
p. forth thine hand and take it *Ex* 4:4
by the tail
precious things *p. forth* by the *De* 33:14
moon
and Ehud *p. forth* his left hand *J'g* 3:21
the angel *p. forth* the end of *J'g* 6:21
the staff
I will now *p. forth* a riddle to *J'g* 14:12;
you 12:13
Samson *p. forth* and took the *J'g* 15:15
jawbone
Jonathan *p. forth* the rod and 1Sa 14:27
dipped it
the servants not *p. forth* to 1Sa 22:17
slay the priests
not *p. forth* mine hand 1Sa 24:10
against Lord's anointed
Uzzah *p. forth* his hand to ark 2Sa 6:6;
1Ch 13:9
to do Absalom obeisance, he 2Sa 15:5
p. forth his hand
yet not *p. forth* my hand 2Sa 18:12
against king's son
Jeroboam *p. forth* his hand, 1Ki 13:4
and he *p. forth*
p. forth thy hand and touch *Job* 1:11;
all 2:5
only upon himself *p. not forth* *Job* 1:12
thy hand
he *p. forth* hands against him *Ps* 55:20
at peace
lest the righteous *p. forth* their *Ps* 125:3
hands
doth not understanding, *p. forth* *Pr* 8:1
her voice
p. not forth thyself in presence *Pr* 25:6
of the king
Lord *p. forth* his hand and *Jer* 1:9
touched my mouth
he *p. forth* form of an hand *Eze* 8:3
and took me
son of man, *p. forth* a riddle *Eze* 17:2
and speak
Jesus *p. forth* his hand and *M't* 8:3;
touched him *M'k* 1:41; *Lu* 5:13
but when people were *p. forth*, *M't* 9:25
he went in
another parable *p.* he *forth* *M't* 13:24;
13:31; *Lu* 14:7
commanded to *p.* the apostles *Ac* 5:34
forth
but Peter *p.* them all *forth*, and *Ac* 9:40
kneeled

PUT *ON*

bread to eat, and raiment to *Ge* 28:20
p. on
Tamar *p. on* garments of her *Ge* 38:19
widowhood
his son that is priest, shall *p.* *Ex* 29:30
them *on*
no man did *p. on* him his *Ex* 33:4
ornaments
the priest shall *p. on* his linen *Le* 6:10
garment
he shall *p. on* other garments, *Le* 6:11
and carry forth
he shall *p. on* the holy linen *Le* 16:4
coat
he shall *p. on* his garments *Le* 16:24
and come forth
high priest consecrated to *p.* *Le* 21:10
on the garment

p. on incense, and go quickly *Nu* 16:46
to congregation
nor a man *p. on* a woman's *De* 22:5
garment
weep for Saul, who *p. on* 2Sa 1:24
ornaments
I pray *p. on* now mourning 2Sa 14:2
apparel
Joab's garment he had *p. on* 2Sa 20:8
was girded
but *p.* thou *on* thy robes 1Ki 22:30;
2Ch 18:29
all that were able to *p. on* 2Ki 3:21
armour
Mordecai *p. on* sackcloth with *Es* 4:1
ashes
Esther *p. on* her royal apparel *Es* 5:1
and stood
may prepare it, but the just *Job* 27:17
shall *p.* it *on*
I *p. on* righteousness, and it *Job* 29:14
clothed me
I put off my coat, how shall I *p.* *Ca* 5:3
it *on*
awake, awake, *p. on* strength *Isa* 51:9;
52:1
p. on thy beautiful garments, *Isa* 52:1
O Jerusalem
he *p. on* righteousness as a *Isa* 59:17
breastplate, he *p. on* garments
take a girdle and *p.* it on thy *Jer* 13:1;
loins 13:2
furbish the spears, and *p. on* *Jer* 46:4
the brigandines
and *p. on* thy shoes upon thy *Eze* 24:17
feet
and shall *p. on* other *Eze* 42:14;
garments 44:19
the people of Nineveh *p. on* *Jon* 3:5
sackcloth
nor what ye shall *p. on* *M't* 6:25;
Lu 12:22
they *p. on* the ass and colt *M't* 21:7
their clothes
they stripped him and *p. on* *M't* 27:28
him scarlet robe
crown of thorns, they *p.* it *M't* 27:29;
on his head *Joh* 19:2
one of them *p.* a sponge on *M't* 27:48;
a reed *M'k* 15:36
be shod with sandals, not *p. on* *M'k* 6:9
two coats
bring and *p. on* him the best *Lu* 15:22
robe
Pilate wrote a title and *p.* it *Joh* 19:19
on cross
and let us *p. on* armour of *Ro* 13:12
light
but *p.* ye *on* the Lord Jesus *Ro* 13:14
Christ
this corruptible must *p. on* 1Co 15:53
incorruption
this mortal shall have *p. on* 1Co 15:54
immortality
baptized into Christ, have *p.* *Ga* 3:27
on Christ
that ye *p. on* the new man *Eph* 4:24;
Col 3:10
p. on the whole armour of *Eph* 6:11
God, ye may be able
p. on therefore bowels of *Col* 3:12
mercies and kindness
p. on charity, which is the *Col* 3:14
bond of perfectness

PUT *OUT*

when she travailed one *p. out* *Ge* 38:28
his hand
p. out the remembrance of *Ex* 17:14
Amalek
the fire on the altar shall not be *Le* 6:12
p. out
p. out of the camp every leper *Nu* 5:2;
5:4
both male and female shall ye *Nu* 5:3
p. out
wilt thou *p. out* the eyes of *Nu* 16:14
these men
the Lord will *p. out* those *De* 7:22
nations
that his name be not *p. out* of *De* 25:6
Israel
the Philistines *p. out* *J'g* 16:21
Samson's eyes
p. now this woman *out* from 2Sa 13:17
me
he *p. out* his hand and took the 2Ki 6:7
axe
and they *p. out* the eyes of 2Ki 25:7;

Zedekiah and *Jer* 39:7; 52:11
also they have *p. out* the 2Ch 29:7
lamps
the light of the wicked shall be *Job* 18:5
p. out
the light shall be dark, and *Job* 18:6;
his candle be *p. out* 21:17; *Pr* 13:9;
20:20; 24:20
thou hast *p. out* their name for *Ps* 9:5
ever
when I *p.* thee *out* I will cover *Eze* 32:7
heaven
when he had *p.* them all *out* *M'k* 5:40;
Lu 8:54
when I am *p. out* of the *Lu* 16:4
stewardship
he should be *p. out* of the *Joh* 9:22
synagogue
lest they should be *p. out* of *Joh* 12:42
the synagogue
they shall *p.* you *out* of the *Joh* 16:2
synagogues

PUT *TRUST*

come and *p.* your *trust* in my *J'g* 9:15
shadow
p. thy *trust* on Egypt 2Ki 18:24;
Isa 36:9
because they *p.* their *trust* in 1Ch 5:20
him
and *p.* your *trust* in the Lord *Ps* 4:5
let all that *p.* their *trust* in thee *Ps* 5:11
rejoice
O Lord God in thee I *p. trust* *Ps* 7:1;
16:1; 25:20; 71:1
that know thy name, will *p.* *Ps* 9:10
trust in thee
in the Lord *p.* I my *trust* *Ps* 11:1;
31:1; 71:1
that savest them which *p.* their *Ps* 17:7
trust in thee
p. their *trust* under the shadow *Ps* 36:7
of thy wings
in God I have *p.* my *trust*, I *Ps* 56:4
will not fear
I have *p.* my *trust* in the Lord *Ps* 73:28
God
p. not your *trust* in princes, *Ps* 146:3
nor son of man
shield to them that *p.* their *Pr* 30:5
trust in him
because thou hast *p.* thy *trust* *Jer* 39:18
in me
to be *p.* in *trust* with gospel 1Th 2:4
and again, I will *p.* my *trust* *Heb* 2:13
in him

PUT a name

sons of Ham; Cush, Mizraim, 1Ch 1:8
P.
P. and Lubim were thy helpers *Na* 3:9

PUTEOLI

and we came the next day to *Ac* 28:13
P.

PUTIEL

one of the daughters of *P.* to *Ex* 6:25
wife

PUTRIFY

p. perfumer's ointment (B) *Ec* 10:1

PUTRIFYING

wounds, and bruises, and *p.* *Isa* 1:6
sores
fresh and bleeding stripes *Isa* 1:6
(A)(E)
bruises, welts, and raw wounds *Isa* 1:6
(B)
bruises, sores, and bleeding *Isa* 1:6
wounds (R)

PUTTEST

and thou *p.* thy nest in a rock *Nu* 24:21
all that thou *p.* thine hands *De* 12:18
unto
in all that thou *p.* thine hand *De* 15:10
unto
which thou *p.* on me will I 2Ki 18:14
bear
Thou *p.* my feet also in the *Job* 13:27
stocks

Thou *p.* away all the wicked *Ps 119:119*
of
that *p.* thy bottle to him, and *Hab 2:15*

PUTTETH

p. any of it upon a stranger, *Ex 30:33*
shall
word that God *p.* in my *Nu 22:38*
mouth
and *p.* forth her hand, and *De 25:11*
taketh
and *p.* it in a secret place *De 27:15*
boast himself as he that *p.* it *1Ki 20:11*
off
Behold, he *p.* no trust in his *Job 15:15*
saints
p. forth his hand upon the *Job 28:9*
rock
He *p.* my feet in the stocks, *Job 33:11*
he
He that *p.* not out his money to *Ps 15:5*
he *p.* down one, and setteth up *Ps 75:7*
he that *p.* his trust in the Lord *Pr 28:25*
whoso *p.* his trust in the Lord *Pr 29:25*
fig tree *p.* forth her green figs *Ca 2:13*
he that *p.* his trust in me shall *Isa 57:13*
as a shepherd *p.* on his *Jer 43:12*
garment
He *p.* his mouth in the dust; if *La 3:29*
so
p. the stumblingblock of his *Eze 14:4;*
                                           14:7
he that *p.* not into their mouths *Mic 3:5*
p. a piece of new cloth unto *M't 9:16*
an old
is yet tender, and *p.* forth *M't 24:32*
leaves
no man *p.* new wine into old *M'k 2:22;*
bottles   *Lu 5:37*
immediately he *p.* in the *M'k 4:29*
sickle
is yet tender, and *p.* forth *M'k 13:28*
leaves
p. a piece of a new garment *Lu 5:36*
upon
with a vessel, or *p.* it under a *Lu 8:16*
bed
a candle, *p.* it in a secret place *Lu 11:33*
Whosoever *p.* away his wife *Lu 16:18*
when he *p.* forth his own *Joh 10:4*
sheep

PUTTING

p. it on her shoulder, and the *Ge 21:14*
p. them the head of the goat *Le 16:21*
lapped, *p.* their hand to their *J'g 7:6*
mouth
p. forth of the finger, and *Isa 58:9*
speaking
Israel, saith that he hateth *p.* *Mal 2:16*
away
coming in, *p.* his hand on him *Ac 9:12*
p. his hands on him said, *Ac 9:17*
Brother
the Jews *p.* him forward. And *Ac 19:33*
as *p.* you in mind, because of *Ro 15:15*
p. your love to the test (N) *2Co 8:8*
Wherefore *p.* away lying, *Eph 4:25*
speak
p. off the body of the sins of *Col 2:11*
p. on the breastplate of faith *1Th 5:8*
faithful, *p.* me into the *1Ti 1:12*
ministry
in thee by the *p.* on of my *2Ti 1:6*
hands
of gold, or of *p.* on of apparel *1Pe 3:3*
the *p.* away of the filth of the *1Pe 3:21*
flesh
you up by *p.* you in *2Pe 1:13*
remembrance

PUZZLED

were utterly *p.* (A) *M't 19:25*
p. as to whom could mean *Joh 13:22*
(A)

PYGARG

the wild goat, and the *p.* and *De 14:5*
the ibex (A)(R) *De 14:5*
the chamois (B)(E) *De 14:5*

PYRE

the *p.* made deep and large *Isa 30:33*
(A)(R)

Q

pass, that at even the *q.* came *Ex 16:13*
up
brought *q.* from the sea, and *Nu 11:31*
let
next day, and they gathered *Nu 11:32*
the *q.*
people asked, and he brought *Ps 105:40*
q.

QUAILS

QUAKE

the land to *q.* (B)(R) *Ps 60:2*
the mountains *q.* (B)(R) *Isa 5:25*
The earth shall *q.* before them *Joe 2:10*
The mountains *q.* at him, and *Na 1:5*
and the earth did *q.* and the *M't 27:51*
rocks
said, I exceedingly fear and *Heb 12:21*
q.

QUAKED

and the whole mount *q.* *Ex 19:18*
greatly
also trembled, and the earth *1Sa 14:15*
q.

QUAKING

Son of man, eat thy bread *Eze 12:18*
with *q.*
but a great *q.* fell upon them, *Da 10:7*
so

QUAKES

the earth *q.* (B)(R) *Jer 10:10*

QUALMS

no *q.* of conscience (B)(P) *Ro 14:22*
doubts and *q.* of others (P) *Ro 15:1*

QUANTITY

in weight or in *q.* (S) *Le 19:35*
and the issue, all vessels of *Isa 22:24*
small *q.*

QUARREL

did *q.* with (A)(R) *Ge 26:20; 26:22*
if men *q.* together (A) *Ex 21:18;*
                                           Pr 25:8
if men *q.* (B) *Ex 21:18; 21:22; 2Ti 2:24*
avenge the *q.* of my covenant *Le 26:25*
execute vengeance of my *Le 26:25*
covenant (A)(E)(R)
administer retribution for the *Le 26:25*
covenant (B)
see how he seeketh a *q.* against *2Ki 5:7*
me
consider how he is trying to stir *2Ki 5:7*
up trouble (B)
quit before *q.* breaks out *Pr 17:14*
(B)(R)
involves himself in a *q.* (B) *Pr 26:17*
you *q.* and fight (R) *Isa 58:4*
he shall not *q.* (B) *M't 12:19*
Herodias had a *q.* against him *M'k 6:19*
Herodias held a grudge *M'k 6:19*
against him (A)(B)(N)(R)
Herodias set herself against *M'k 6:19*
him (E)
Herodias was furious against *M'k 6:19*
him (P)
q., quarreling (E)(R) *Ac 7:26*
if any man have a *q.* against *Col 3:13*
any
if one has a difference against *Col 3:13*
another (A)(P)
one feels a grievance against *Col 3:13*
another (B)
if any man has a complaint *Col 3:13*
against (E)(N)(R)

QUARRELED

they *q.* (A)(R) *Ge 26:20;*
                                           26:21; 2Sa 14:6
q. with Moses (B) *Ex 17:2*
q. together (B) *Le 24:10*
q. with him (A) *J'g 8:1*

QUARRELING

q. and fighting (A)(B) *Ex 2:13;*
                                           Ac 7:26
q. of Israel (B) *Ex 17:7*
every fool will be *q.* *Pr 20:3*
(A)(B)(E)(R)
quarrel, *q.* (E)(R) *Ac 7:26*
envy, murder, *q.* (B) *Ro 1:29*
quarrels, *q.* (N)(P) *Ro 13:13;*
                                           Ga 5:20
jealousy and *q.* (B) *1Co 3:3*
q. and jealousy (N)(R) *2Co 12:20*
q., quarrels (N)(P) *Ga 5:20*
without *q.* (A)(R) *1Ti 2:8*
jealousy, *q.*, slander (N)(P) *1Ti 6:4*

QUARRELS

keep an eye on those who *Ro 16:17*
stir up *q.* (E)
q. quarreling (N)(P) *Ro 13:13;*
                                           Ga 5:20
q., dissension, abuse (A) *1Ti 6:4*
quarrels (B)(N)(R) *2Ti 2:23*

QUARRELSOME

disagreeing, *q.*, scolding (A) *Pr 25:28*
must not be *q.* (A)(N)(R) *2Ti 2:24*

QUARRELSOMENESS

envy, murder, *q.* (P) *Ro 1:29*

QUARRIES

from the *q.* that were by Gilgal *J'g 3:19*
and passed beyond the *q.* and *J'g 3:26*

QUARRY

the *q.* from which you *Isa 51:1*
(A)(B)(R)

QUART

a *q.* of wheat for a denarius *Re 6:6*
(A)(B)(N)(P)(R)

QUARTER

all the people from every *q.* *Ge 19:4*
a *q.* ounce ring (B) *Ge 24:22*
q. shall be from the wilderness *Nu 34:3*
north *q.* was from the bay of *Jos 15:5*
the sea
of Judah: this was the west *q.* *Jos 18:14*
the south *q.* was from the end *Jos 18:15*
of
I have a silver *q.* (B) *1Sa 9:8*
the second *q.* (B)(E)(R)(S) *2Ki 22:14*
shall wander every one to his *Isa 47:15*
q.
every one for his gain, from *Isa 56:11*
his *q.*
a *q.* a day (B) *M't 20:2; 20:9-10, 13*
they came to him from every *M'k 1:45*
q.

QUARTERS

leaven seen with thee in all thy *Ex 13:7*
q.
upon the four *q.* of thy *De 22:12*
vesture
In four *q.* were the porters *1Ch 9:24*
winds from the four *q.* of *Jer 49:36*
heaven
of Togarmah of the north *q.* *Eze 38:6*
as Peter passed throughout all *Ac 9:32*
q.
the Jews which were in those *q.* *Ac 16:3*
In the same *q.* were *Ac 28:7*
possessions
are in the four *q.* of the earth *Re 20:8*

QUARTS

six *q.* of olive oil (B) *Ex 30:24*
six *q.* of fine flour (B) *Le 14:10*
two *q.* of oil (B) *Nu 15:6*
three *q.* of oil (B) *Nu 15:9*
three *q.* of fine flour (B) *Nu 28:13*
nine *q.* with a full (B) *Nu 28:20;*
                                           29:3, 9, 14

QUARTUS

saluteth you, and *Q.* a brother *Ro 16:23*

QUATERNIONS

delivered him to four *q.* of soldiers   *Ac 12:4*

QUEEN

the *q.* of Sheba heard of the fame   *1Ki 10:1; 2Ch 9:1*
when the *q.* of Sheba had seen all   *1Ki 10:4*
which the *q.* of Sheba gave to king   *1Ki 10:10*
unto the *q.* of Sheba all her desire   *1Ki 10:13*
wife, the sister of Tahpenes the *q.*   *1Ki 11:19*
even her he removed from being *q.*   *1Ki 15:13*
the king and the children of the *q.*   *2Ki 10:13*
q. of Sheba had seen the wisdom of   *2Ch 9:3*
the *q.* of Sheba gave king Solomon   *2Ch 9:9*
Solomon gave to the *q.* of Sheba all   *2Ch 9:12*
he removed her from being *q.*   *2Ch 15:16*
me, (the *q.* also sitting by him   *Ne 2:6*
Vashti the *q.* made a feast for   *Es 1:9*
bring Vashti the *q.* before the king   *Es 1:11*
the *q.* Vashti refused to come at the   *Es 1:12*
do unto the *q.* Vashti according to   *Es 1:15*
Vashti the *q.* hath not done wrong   *Es 1:16*
deed of the *q.* shall come abroad   *Es 1:17*
Vashti the *q.* to be brought in   *Es 1:17*
have heard of the deed of the *q.*   *Es 1:18*
which pleaseth the king be *q.*   *Es 2:4*
and made her *q.* instead of Vashti   *Es 2:17*
who told it unto Esther the *q.*   *Es 2:22*
was the *q.* exceedingly grieved   *Es 4:4*
Esther the *q.* standing in the court   *Es 5:2*
her, What wilt thou, *q.* Esther   *Es 5:3*
the *q.* did let no man come in with   *Es 5:12*
came to banquet with Esther the *q.*   *Es 7:1*
What is thy petition, *q.* Esther   *Es 7:2*
Esther the *q.* answered, and said   *Es 7:3*
said unto Esther the *q.,* Who is he   *Es 7:5*
afraid before the king and the *q.*   *Es 7:6*
request for his life to Esther the *q.*   *Es 7:7*
Will he force the *q.* also before me   *Es 7:8*
Jews' enemy unto Esther the *q.*   *Es 8:1*
Ahasuerus said unto Esther the *q.*   *Es 8:7*
the king said unto Esther the *q.*   *Es 9:12*
Then Esther the *q.* the daughter of   *Es 9:29*
Esther the *q.* had enjoined them   *Es 9:31*
right hand did stand the *q.* in gold   *Ps 45:9*
to make cakes to the *q.* of heaven   *Jer 7:18*
Say unto the king and to the *q.*   *Jer 13:18*
king, and the *q.* and the eunuchs   *Jer 29:2*
incense unto the *q.* of heaven   *Jer 44:17*
to burn incense to the *q.* of heaven   *Jer 44:18; 44:25*
burned incense to the *q.* of heaven   *Jer 44:19*
the *q.* by reason of the words of   *Da 5:10*
the *q.* spake and said, O king, live   *Da 5:10*
the *q.* of the south shall rise up in   *M't 12:42; Lu 11:31*
under Candace *q.* of the Ethiopians   *Ac 8:27*
for she saith in her heart, I sit a *q.*   *Re 18:7*

QUEENS

are threescore *q.* and fourscore   *Ca 6:8*
yea, the *q.* and the concubines   *Ca 6:9*

and their *q.* thy nursing mothers   *Isa 49:23*

QUEER

think it very *q.* (A)(P)   *1Pe 4:4*

QUENCH

they shall *q.* my coal which is left   *2Sa 14:7*
that thou *q.* not the light of Israel   *2Sa 21:17*
the wild asses *q.* their thirst   *Ps 104:11*
Many waters cannot *q.* love   *Ca 8:7*
together, and none shall *q.* them   *Isa 1:31*
the smoking flax shall he not *q.*   *Isa 42:3; M't 12:20*
fire, and burn that one can *q.* it   *Jer 4:4; 21:12*
there be none to *q.* it in Beth-el   *Am 5:6*
q. all the fiery darts of the wicked   *Eph 6:16*
Q. not the Spirit   *1Th 5:19*

QUENCHED

unto the Lord, the fire was *q.*   *Nu 11:2*
this place, and shall not be *q.*   *2Ki 22:17; 2Ch 34:25*
they are *q.* as the fire of thorns   *Ps 118:12*
It shall not be *q.* night nor day   *Isa 34:10*
they are extinct, they are *q.* as tow   *Isa 43:17*
q. like a lamp wick (A)(B)   *Isa 43:17*
die, neither shall their fire be *q.*   *Isa 66:24*
it shall burn, and shall not be *q.*   *Jer 7:20*
of Jerusalem, and it shall not be *q.*   *Jer 17:27*
the flaming flame shall not be *q.*   *Eze 20:47*
have kindled it: it shall not be *q.*   *Eze 20:48*
into the fire that never shall be *q.*   *M'k 9:43; 9:45*
dieth not, and the fire is not *q.*   *M'k 9:44; 9:46, 48*
darkness never *q.* it (N)   *Joh 1:5*
Q. the violence of fire, escaped the   *Heb 11:34*

QUESTION

which was a lawyer, asked him a *q.*   *M't 22:35*
began to *q.* with him, seeking of   *M'k 8:11*
the scribes, What *q.* ye with them   *M'k 9:16*
I will also ask of you one *q.*   *M'k 11:29*
man after that durst ask him any *q.*   *M'k 12:34*
they durst not ask him any *q.* at all   *Lu 20:40*
there arose a *q.* between some of   *Joh 3:25*
apostles and elders about this *q.*   *Ac 15:2*
if it be a *q.* of words and names   *Ac 18:15*
we are in danger to be called in *q.*   *Ac 19:40*
of the dead I am called in *q.*   *Ac 23:6*
I am called in *q.* by you this day   *Ac 24:21*
asking no *q.* for conscience sake   *1Co 10:25; 10:27*

QUESTIONED

Hezekiah *q.* with the priests   *2Ch 31:9*
that they *q.* among themselves   *M'k 1:27*
q. within themselves (R)   *M'k 2:8*
reasoned, *q.* in hearts (A)   *Lu 3:15*
he *q.* with him in many words   *Lu 23:9*

QUESTIONING

q. one with another what the   *M'k 9:10*
them, and the scribes *q.* with them   *M'k 9:14*

QUESTIONS

came to prove him with hard *q.*   *1Ki 10:1*

And Solomon told her all her *q.*   *1Ki 10:3; 2Ch 9:2*
to prove Solomon with hard *q.*   *2Ch 9:1*
the day forth ask him any more *q.*   *M't 22:46*
q. in their hearts (R)   *M'k 2:6*
assail him with *q.* (N)   *M'k 11:53*
hearing them, and asking them *q.*   *Lu 2:46*
dissension and *q.* (E)   *Ac 15:2*
had been much *q.* (E)   *Ac 15:7*
to be accused of *q.* of their law   *Ac 23:29*
But had certain *q.* against him of   *Ac 25:19*
I doubted of such manner of *q.*   *Ac 25:20*
to be expert in all customs and *q.*   *Ac 26:3*
without *q.* (A)(E)(R)   *Ph'p 2:14*
genealogies, which minister *q.*   *1Ti 1:4*
useless speculations and *q.* (A)   *1Ti 1:4*
minister *q.* (E)   *1Ti 1:4*
about *q.* and strifes of words   *1Ti 6:4*
But foolish and unlearned *q.* avoid   *2Ti 2:23*
avoid foolish *q.* and genealogies   *Tit 3:9*

QUICK

there be *q.* raw flesh in the rising   *Le 13:10*
q. flesh that burneth have a white   *Le 13:24*
the raw flesh (B)(R)   *Le 13:24*
and they go down *q.* into the pit   *Nu 16:30*
and let them go down *q.* into hell   *Ps 55:15*
they had swallowed us up *q.* when   *Ps 124:3*
shall make him of *q.* understanding   *Isa 11:3*
to be the Judge of *q.* and dead   *Ac 10:42*
the living and the dead   *Ac 10:42; 1Pe 4:5*
  (A)(B)(E)(N)(P)(R)
shall judge the *q.* and the dead   *2Ti 4:1*
not *q.* tempered (A)(R)   *Tit 1:7*
the word of God is *q.* and powerful   *Heb 4:12*
ready to judge the *q.* and the dead   *1Pe 4:5*

QUICKEN

sore troubles, shalt *q.* me again   *Ps 71:20*
wilt revive me again (B)(R)   *Ps 71:20*
q. us, and we will call upon thy   *Ps 80:18*
revive me (A)(B)   *Ps 80:18*
give us life (B)   *Ps 80:18*
q. thou me according to thy word   *Ps 119:25*
revive and stimulate me   *Ps 119:25*
  (A)(B)(R)
vanity; and *q.* thou me in thy way   *Ps 119:37*
restore me (A)   *Ps 119:37*
revive me (B)   *Ps 119:37*
give me life (R)   *Ps 119:37*
q. me in thy righteousness   *Ps 119:40*
give me life (A)(B)(R)   *Ps 119:40*
Q. me after thy lovingkindness: so   *Ps 119:88*
give life to me (A)   *Ps 119:88*
Revive me (B)   *Ps 119:88; 119:107, 149, 154, 156, 159*
spare my life (R)   *Ps 119:88*
q. me, O Lord, according unto thy   *Ps 119:107; 119:159*
q. me according to thy judgment   *Ps 119:149*
me; *q.* me according to thy word   *Ps 119:154*
revive me (A)   *Ps 119:154; 119:159*
q. me according to thy judgments   *Ps 119:156*
give me life (A)(R)   *Ps 119:156*
Q. me, O Lord, for thy name's sake   *Ps 143:11*
Save my life (A)   *Ps 143:11*
preserve my life (B)(R)   *Ps 143:11*
also *q.* your mortal bodies by his   *Ro 8:11*
restore to life (A)   *Ro 8:11*
make your mortal bodies live (B)   *Ro 8:11*
give life to your mortal bodies   *Ro 8:11*
  (E)(R)

give new life to your mortal   Ro 8:11
bodies (N)
bring to your whole being new   Ro 8:11
strength (P)

QUICKENED

affliction: for thy word hath   Ps 119:50
q. me
revived me and given me life   Ps 119:50
(A)(B)(R)
for with them thou hast q.   Ps 119:93
me
granted me life (B)(R)   Ps 119:93
that which thou sowest is   1Co 15:36
not q.
does not come to life   1Co 15:36
(A)(B)(N)(R)
does not germinate (P)   1Co 15:36
you hath he q. who were dead   Eph 2:1
he made alive (A)(E)(R)   Eph 2:1;
  2:5
hath q. us together with Christ   Eph 2:5
flesh, hath he q. together with   Col 2:13
him
brought to life (A)   Col 2:13
made to live (B)(E)(N)(R)   Col 2:13
in the flesh, but q. by the   1Pe 3:18
Spirit
made alive in the spirit   1Pe 3:18
(A)(E)(R)
made alive spiritually (B)   1Pe 3:18
came to life again in the spirit   1Pe 3:18
(P)

QUICKENETH

raiseth up the dead, and q.   Joh 5:21
them
even so the Son q. whom he   Joh 5:21
will
makes alive (A)(B)(N)(P)(R)   Joh 5:21;
  6:63; Ro 4:17
It is the spirit that q.; the flesh   Joh 6:63
even God, who q. the dead   Ro 4:17
the sight of God, who q. all   1Ti 6:13
things

QUICKENING

last Adam was made a q.   1Co 15:45
spirit

QUICKLY

Make ready q. three measures   Ge 18:6
of
is it that thou hast found it so   Ge 27:20
q.
turned aside q. out of the way   Ex 32:8
go q. unto the congregation   Nu 16:46
them out, and destroy them q.   De 9:3
get thee down q. from hence   De 9:12
they are q. turned aside out of   De 9:12
had turned aside q. out of the   De 9:16
way
lest ye perish q. from off the   De 11:17
good
and until thou perish q.;   De 28:20
because
pursue after them q.; for ye   Jos 2:5
shall
the ambush arose q. out of   Jos 8:19
their
come up to us q. and save us   Jos 10:6
ye shall perish q. from off the   Jos 23:16
good
they turned q. out of the way   J'g 2:17
then thou shalt go down q.   1Sa 20:19
Now therefore send q. and   2Sa 17:16
tell
they went both of them away   2Sa 17:18
q.
Arise, and pass q. over the   2Sa 17:21
water
hath the king said, Come   2Ki 1:11
down q.
Fetch q. Micaiah the son of   2Ch 18:8
Imla
answer me q. (B)   Ps 143:7
a threefold cord is not q.   Ec 4:12
broken
Agree with thine adversary   M't 5:25
q.
And go q. and tell his disciples   M't 28:7
departed q. from the sepulchre   M't 28:8
they went out q. and fled   M'k 16:8
from the
Go out q. into the streets and   Lu 14:21
and sit down q. and write fifty   Lu 16:6

she arose q. and came unto   Joh 11:29
him
unto him, That thou doest,   Joh 13:27
do q.
him up, saying, Arise up q.   Ac 12:7
get thee q. out of Jerusalem   Ac 22:18
or else I will come unto thee   Re 2:5;
q.   2:16
Behold, I come q.; hold that   Re 3:11
fast
behold, the third woe cometh   Re 11:14
q.
Behold, I come q.; blessed is   Re 22:7
he
I come q.; and my reward is   Re 22:12
with
saith, Surely I come q. Amen   Re 22:20

QUICKSAND

sank in the q. (B)   Jer 38:22

QUICKSANDS

lest they should fall into the q.   Ac 27:17

QUIET

Jacob was a q. man (S)   Ge 25:27
were q. all the night, saying, In   J'g 16:2
of the Zidonians, q. and secure   J'g 18:7
a people that were at q. and   J'g 18:27
secure
rejoiced, and the city was in   2Ki 11:20
q.
the land was wide, and q. and   1Ch 4:40
his days the land was q. ten   2Ch 14:1
years
the kingdom was q. before   2Ch 14:5
him
the realm of Jehoshaphat   2Ch 20:30
was q.
the city was q. after that   2Ch 23:21
they had
should I have lain still and   Job 3:13
been q.
had I rest, neither was I q.   Job 3:26
being wholly at ease and q.   Job 21:23
them that are q. in the land   Ps 35:20
are they glad because they be   Ps 107:30
q.
and shall be q. from fear of evil   Pr 1:33
man of understanding keeps q.   Pr 11:12
(A)
of wise men are heard in q.   Ec 9:17
more
Take heed, and be q.; fear   Isa 7:4
not
whole earth is at rest, and is q.   Isa 14:7
dwellings, and in q. resting   Isa 32:18
places
shall see Jerusalem a q.   Isa 33:20
habitation
shall be in rest, and be q. and   Jer 30:10
how long will it be ere thou be   Jer 47:6
q.
How can it be q. seeing the   Jer 47:7
Lord
sorrow on the sea; it cannot   Jer 49:23
be q.
And this Seraiah was a q.   Jer 51:59
prince
be q. and will be no more   Eze 16:42
angry
Though they be q. and likewise   Na 1:12
ye ought to be q. and to do   Ac 19:36
that ye study to be q. and to   1Th 4:11
do
may lead a q. and peaceable life   1Ti 2:2
ornament of a meek and q.   1Pe 3:4
spirit

QUIETED

I have behaved, and q. myself   Ps 131:2
have q. my spirit in the north   Zec 6:8

QUIETETH

he q. the earth by the south   Job 37:17
wind

QUIETLY

in the gate to speak with him   2Sa 3:27
q.
q. wait for the salvation of the   La 3:26
Lord

QUIETNESS

the country was in q. forty   J'g 8:28
years
will give peace and q. unto   1Ch 22:9
Israel
he shall not feel q. in his   Job 20:20
belly
When he giveth q. who then   Job 34:29
can
is a dry morsel, and q.   Pr 17:1
therewith
Better is an handful with q. than   Ec 4:6
in q. and in confidence shall   Isa 30:15
be
q. and assurance for ever   Isa 32:17
that by thee we enjoy great q.   Ac 24:2
that with q. they work, and   2Th 3:12
eat

QUIT

shall he that smote him be q.   Ex 21:19
the owner of the ox shall be q.   Ex 21:28
then we will be q. of thine   Jos 2:20
oath
q. interfering with God (B)   2Ch 35:21
q. before quarrel breaks out   Pr 17:14
(B)(R)
faith, q. you like men, be   1Co 16:13
strong

QUITE

and hath q. devoured also our   Ge 31:15
money
and q. break down their   Ex 23:24
images
q. take away their   Nu 17:10
murmurings
q. plucked down all their high   Nu 33:52
places
hast sent him away, and he is   2Sa 3:24
q. gone
and is wisdom driven q. from   Job 6:13
me
Thy bow was made q. naked   Hab 3:9
q. obvious God is excepted   1Co 15:27
(P)

QUIVER

thy weapons, thy q. and thy   Ge 27:3
bow
The q. rattleth against him   Job 39:23
Happy is the man that hath   Ps 127:5
his q.
Elam bare the q. with chariots   Isa 22:6
of
shaft; in his q. hath he hid me   Isa 49:2
Their q. is as an open   Jer 5:16
sepulchre
their faces q. (A)   Eze 27:35
of his q. to enter into my reins   La 3:13

QUIVERED

trembled; my lips q. at the   Hab 3:16
voice

R

RAAMAH

and Havilah, and Sabtah, and   Ge 10:7
R.
the sons of R.; Sheba, and   Ge 10:7;
Dedan   1Ch 1:9
and Havilah, and Sabta, and   1Ch 1:9
R.
The merchants of Sheba and   Eze 27:22
R.

RAAMIAH

Azariah, R., Nahamani,   Ne 7:7
Mordecai

RAAMSES

treasure cities, Pithom, and R.   Ex 1:11

RABBAH

unto Aroer that is before R. *Jos 13:25*
which is Kirjath-jearim, and *Jos 15:60*
R.
children of Ammon besieged *2Sa 11:1*
R.
And Joab fought against R. *2Sa 12:26*
of the
I have fought against R. and *2Sa 12:27*
have
went to R. and fought *2Sa 12:29*
against it
that Shobi the son of Nahash *2Sa 17:27*
of R.
Ammon, and came and *1Ch 20:1*
besieged R.
Joab smote R. and destroyed *1Ch 20:1*
it
an alarm of war to be heard in *Jer 49:2*
R.
cry, ye daughter's of R. gird *Jer 49:3*
you
I will make R. a stable for *Eze 25:5*
camels
will kindle a fire in the wall of *Am 1:14*
R.

RABBATH

in R. of the children of *De 3:11*
Ammon
that the sword may come to *Eze 21:20*
R.

RABBI

and to be called of men, R., R. *M't 23:7*
But be not ye called R.: for *M't 23:8*
one is
They said unto him, R, *Joh 1:38*
(which is
him, R. thou art the Son of *Joh 1:49*
God
R. we know thou art a teacher *Joh 3:2*
R. he that was with thee *Joh 3:26*
beyond
R. when camest thou hither *Joh 6:25*

RABBITH

And R. and Kishion, and *Jos 19:20*
Abez

RABBLE

the alien r. (B)(R) *Nu 11:4*
fellows of the r. (E)(N)(R) *Ac 17:5*

RABBONI

herself, and saith unto him, *Joh 20:16*
R.

RAB-MAG

Rab-saris, Nergal-sharezer, R. *Jer 39:3*
R. and all the king of *Jer 39:13*
Babylon's

RAB-SARIS

of Assyria sent Tartan and *2Ki 18:17*
R.
R., Nergal-sharezer, Rab-mag *Jer 39:3;*
                                 39:13

RAB-SHAKEH

and R. from Lachish to king *2Ki 18:17*
R. said unto them, Speak ye *2Ki 18:19*
now
unto R. Speak, I pray thee, *2Ki 18:26*
to thy
R. said unto them, Hath my *2Ki 18:27*
master
Then R. stood and cried with *2Ki 18:28*
a loud
and told him the words of R. *2Ki 18:37*
God will hear all the words of *2Ki 19:4*
R.
So R. returned, and found the *2Ki 19:8*
king
R. from Lachish to Jerusalem *Isa 36:2*
R. said unto them, Say ye now *Isa 36:4*
to
R. Speak, I pray thee, unto *Isa 36:11*
thy
R. said, Hath my master sent *Isa 36:12*
me

R. stood, and cried with a *Isa 36:13*
loud
rent, and told him the words *Isa 36:22*
of R.
thy God will hear the words of *Isa 37:4*
R.
So R. returned, and found the *Isa 37:8*
king

RACA

shall say to his brother, R. *M't 5:22*
shall
speaks contemptuously and *M't 5:22*
insultingly (A)(P)
calls his brother a simpleton *M't 5:22*
(B)
abuses his brother *M't 5:22*
(N)
insults his brother (R) *M't 5:22*

RACE

a trusted and crooked r. (B) *De 32:5*
the ruin of my r. (B) *Es 8:6*
as a strong man to run a r. *Ps 19:5*
the r. of the upright (B) *Ps 112:2*
the r. is not to the swift, nor *Ec 9:11*
r., family (A)(B) *Ac 13:26;*
they which run in a r. run all *1Co 9:24*
finished the r. (A)(B)(N)(R) *2Ti 4:7*
patience the r. that is set *Heb 12:1*
before us
a chosen r. (A)(B)(E)(N)(R) *1Pe 2:9*

RACES

r. of every tongue (B) *Da 3:4*

RACHAB

Salmon begat Booz of R. *M't 1:5*

RACHAL

And to them which were in *1Sa 30:29*
R.

RACHEL

R. his daughter cometh with *Ge 29:6*
R. came with her father's *Ge 29:9*
sheep
Jacob saw R. the daughter of *Ge 29:10*
Laban
Jacob kissed R. and lifted up *Ge 29:11*
his
And Jacob told R. that he *Ge 29:12*
was her
the name of the younger was *Ge 29:16*
R.
R. was beautiful and well *Ge 29:17*
favoured
And Jacob loved R.; and said *Ge 29:18*
will serve thee seven years for *Ge 29:18*
R.
Jacob served seven years for *Ge 29:20*
R.
did I not serve with thee for *Ge 29:25*
R.
gave him R. his daughter to *Ge 29:28*
wife
And Laban gave to R. his *Ge 29:29;*
daughter *46:25*
he went in also unto R. and *Ge 29:30*
he
he loved also R. more than *Ge 29:30*
Leah
her womb, but R. was barren *Ge 29:31*
when R. saw that she bare *Ge 30:1*
Jacob
R. envied her sister; and said *Ge 30:1*
unto
Jacob's anger kindled against *Ge 30:2*
R.
R. said, God hath judged me *Ge 30:6*
And R. said, With great *Ge 30:8*
wrestlings
R. said to Leah, Give me, I *Ge 30:14*
pray
And R. said, Therefore he *Ge 30:15*
shall lie
And God remembered R. and *Ge 30:22*
God
pass, when R. had borne *Ge 30:25*
Joseph
Jacob sent and called R. and *Ge 31:4*
Leah
R. and Leah answered and *Ge 31:14*
said

and R. had stolen the images *Ge 31:19*
that
knew not that R. had stolen *Ge 31:32*
them
Now R. had taken the images *Ge 31:34*
children unto Leah, and unto *Ge 33:1*
R.
and R. and Joseph hindermost *Ge 33:2*
after came Joseph near and R. *Ge 33:7*
and R. travailed, and she had *Ge 35:16*
hard
R. died, and was buried in *Ge 35:19*
the way
sons of R.; Joseph, and *Ge 35:24*
Benjamin
The sons of R. Jacob's wife *Ge 46:19*
These are the sons of R. *Ge 46:22*
which
R. died by me in the land of *Ge 48:7*
Canaan
thine house like R. and like *Ru 4:11*
Leah
R. weeping for her children *M't 2:18*

RACHEL'S

Bilhah R. maid conceived *Ge 30:7*
again
tent, and entered into R. tent *Ge 31:33*
that is the pillar of R. *Ge 35:20*
grave unto
the sons of Bilhah, R. *Ge 35:25*
handmaid
shalt find two men by R. *1Sa 10:2*
sepulchre

RADDAI

Nethaneel the fourth, R. the *1Ch 2:14*
fifth

RADIANCE

eternal exclusion from r. of *2Th 1:9*
(P)

RADIANT

looked unto him and were r. *Ps 34:5*
(S)

RAFTERS

house are cedar, and our r. of *Ca 1:17*
fir

RAGAU

Saruch, which was the son of *Lu 3:35*
R.

RAGE

he turned, and went away in a *2Ki 5:12*
r.
coming in, and thy r. against *2Ki 19:27*
me
Because thy r. against me *2Ki 19:28*
and thy
for he was in a r. with him *2Ch 16:10*
because
slain them in a r. that *2Ch 28:9*
reacheth
angry, in a great r. (A) *Ne 4:1*
the ground with fierceness *Job 39:24*
and r.
Cast abroad the r. of thy *Job 40:11*
wrath
Why do the heathen r. and the *Ps 2:1*
because of the r. of mine *Ps 7:6*
enemies
For jealousy is the r. of a man *Pr 6:34*
whether he r. or laugh, there is *Pr 29:9*
coming in, and thy r. against *Isa 37:28*
me
Because thy r. against me, *Isa 37:29*
and thy
ye horses; and r., ye chariots *Jer 46:9*
Nebuchadnezzar in his r. and *Da 3:13*
burn with r. (B) *Da 11:30*
sword for the r. of their tongue *Ho 7:16*
The chariots shall r. in the *Na 2:4*
streets
filled with r. (A) *Lu 4:28*
Why did the heathen r. and the *Ac 4:25*

RAGED

The heathen r. the kingdoms *Ps 46:6*
the sea r. (S) *Jon 1:11; 1:13*
the heathen r. *Re 11:18*
(A)(B)(N)(R)

RAGETH

but the fool r. and is confident　Pr 14:16
r. against sound wisdom (E)　　Pr 18:1

RAGGED

into the tops of the r. rocks,　Isa 2:21
for fear

RAGING

Thou rulest the r. of the sea　Ps 89:9
is a mocker, strong drink is r.　Pr 20:1
and the sea ceased from her r.　Jon 1:15
the wind and the r. of the　Lu 8:24
water
extinguishing r. fire (A)　　Heb 11:34
R. waves of the sea, foaming　Jude 13
out

RAGS

shall clothe a man with r.　Pr 23:21
righteousnesses are as filthy r.　Isa 64:6
old cast clouts and old rotten　Jer 38:11
r.
and rotten r. under thine　Jer 38:12
armholes

RAGUEL

unto Hobab, the son of R. the　Nu 10:29

RAHAB

into an harlot's house, named　Jos 2:1
R.
the king of Jericho sent unto R.　Jos 2:3
only R. the harlot shall live,　Jos 6:17
she
spies went in, and brought out　Jos 6:23
R.
Joshua saved R. the harlot　Jos 6:25
alive
make mention of R. and　　Ps 87:4
Babylon
Thou hast broken R. in pieces,　Ps 89:10
as
Art thou not it that hath cut　Isa 51:9
R.
By faith the harlot R.　　Heb 11:31
perished
was not R. the harlot justified　Jas 2:25
by

RAHAB'S

R. helpers tremble (B)(E)(R)　Job 9:13

RAHAM

And Shema begat R. the　　1Ch 2:44
father of

RAHEL

R. weeping for her children　Jer 31:15

RAID

made a r. today (S)　　　1Sa 27:10
ravage and r. (A)(B)(R)　　Ho 7:1

RAIDERS

raiders (A)(B)(R)　　2Sa 13:17; 14:15
hand of r. (A)(B)(R)　　　1Ch 12:21

RAIL

also letters to r. on the Lord　2Ch 32:17
God

RAILED

our master; and he r. on　　1Sa 25:14
them
he scoffed at them (B)　　1Sa 25:14
r. on him (E)　　　　　M't 27:39
And they that passed by r.　M'k 15:29
on him
reviling and reproaching him　M'k 15:29
(A)
they derided him (B)(R)　　M'k 15:29
hurled abuse at him (N)　　M'k 15:29
made fun of him (P)　　　M'k 15:29
which were hanged r. on him　Lu 23:39
mocked him (B)　　　　Lu 23:39
taunted him (N)　　　　Lu 23:39
covered him with abuse (P)　Lu 23:39

RAILER

idolater, or a r., or a　　1Co 5:11
drunkard
person with a foul tongue　1Co 5:11
(A)(P)
abusive (B)　　　　　1Co 5:11
a reviler (E)(R)　　　　1Co 5:11
a slanderer (N)　　　　1Co 5:11

RAILING

rendering evil for evil, or r. for　1Pe 3:9
r.
insult for insult (A)(P)　　1Pe 3:9
vituperaton for vituperation　1Pe 3:9
(B)
reviling for reviling (E)(R)　1Pe 3:9
abuse with abuse (N)　　　1Pe 3:9
bring not r. accusation against　2Pe 2:11
do not bring a defaming　　2Pe 2:11
charge against (A)(B)
employ no insults in seeking　2Pe 2:11
(N)
do not bring insulting　　2Pe 2:11
criticisms (P)
do not pronounce reviling　2Pe 2:11
judgment (R)
bring against him a r.　　Jude 9
accusation
dared not bring abusive　　Jude 9
condemnation against (A)
did not presume to condemn in　Jude 9
insulting words (N)
dare not to condemn him with　Jude 9
mockery (P)
did not presume to announce a　Jude 9
reviling judgment (R)

RAILINGS

whereof cometh envy, strife, r.　1Ti 6:4
quarrels, dissension, abuse,　1Ti 6:4
insults, slander (A)
result in envy, wrangling,　1Ti 6:4
slander (B)
give rise to jealousy,　　1Ti 6:4
quarreling, slander (P)
produce envy, dissension,　1Ti 6:4
slander (R)

RAIMENT

of gold, and r. and gave them　Ge 24:53
to
garments (A)　　　　　Ge 24:53
clothes (B)　　　　　Ge 24:53;
　　27:15, 27; 28:20; 41:14; J'g 3:16;
　　1Sa 28:8; 2Ki 5:5; Es 4:4
goodly r. of her eldest son　Ge 27:15
Esau
and he smelled the smell of his　Ge 27:27
r.
me bread to eat, and r. to put　Ge 28:20
on
changed his r. and came in　Ge 41:14
unto
he gave each man changes of　Ge 45:22
r.
changes of new suits (B)　Ge 45:22
of silver, and five changes of　Ge 45:22
r.
of silver, and jewels of gold,　Ex 3:22;
and r.　　　　　　　12:35
her food, her r. and her duty　Ex 21:10
of
clothing (B)　　　　　Ex 21:10;
　　Le 11:32; De 8:4; 10:18; J'g 8:26
for ass, for sheep, for r. or for　Ex 22:9
any
take thy neighbour's r. to　Ex 22:26
pledge
coat (N)　　　Ex 22:26; De 24:13
only, it is his r. for his skin　Ex 22:27
it be any vessel of wood, or r.　Le 11:32
purify all your r. and all that　Nu 31:20
is
Thy r. waxed not old upon thee　De 8:4
stranger, in giving him food　De 10:18
and r.
the r. of her captivity from off　De 21:13
her
and so shalt thou do with his r.　De 22:3
that he may sleep in his own　De 24:13
r.
nor take a widow's r. to　De 24:17
pledge
dress (B)　　　　　De 24:17
with iron, and with very much　Jos 22:8
r.

garments (B)　　　　　Jos 22:8;
　　2Ki 7:8; Job 27:16; Zec 3:4
under his r. upon his right　J'g 3:16
thigh
purple r. that was on the kings　J'g 8:26
of
changes of r. (A)　　　J'g 14:12
thee, and put thy r. upon thee　Ru 3:3
and put on other r. and he　1Sa 28:8
went
pieces of gold, and ten changes　2Ki 5:5
of r.
gold, and r. and went and hid it　2Ki 7:8
vessels of gold, and r.,　　2Ch 9:24
harness
robes (B)　　　2Ch 9:24; Re 3:5
and she sent r. to clothe　　Es 4:4
Mordecai
dust, and prepare r. as the　Job 27:16
clay
unto the king in r. of　　Ps 45:14
needlework
as r. he covereth (E)　　Ps 109:19
as the r. of those that are　Isa 14:19
slain
and I will stain all my r.　Isa 63:3
thy r. was of fine linen, and　Eze 16:13
silk
r. white as snow (E)　　Da 7:9
will clothe thee with change of　Zec 3:4
r.
garments (A)　　　　Zec 3:4;
　　11:8; 27:31; 28:3; M'k 9:3; Lu 7:25;
　　23:34; Joh 19:24; Ac 22:20; Re 3:5
clothes (B)　　　　　Zec 3:4;
　　11:8; 27:31; M'k 9:3; Lu 23:34;
　　Joh 19:24; Ac 22:20
John had his r. of camel's hair　M't 3:4
than meat, and the body than　M't 6:25
r.
And why take ye thought for　M't 6:28
r.
clothing (A)　　　　　M't 6:28;
　　17:2; Ac 18:6; 1Ti 6:8; Re 4:4
clothes (B)　　　　　M't 6:28;
　　17:2; Ac 22:20; Jas 2:2; Re 3:18
for to see? A man clothed in　M't 11:8;
soft r.　　　　　　　Lu 7:25
and his r. was white as the　M't 17:2
light
put his own r. on him, and　M't 27:31
led him
and his r. white as snow　M't 28:3
his r. became shining,　　M'k 9:3
exceeding
his r. was white and glistering　Lu 9:29
thieves, which stripped him of　Lu 10:30
his r.
clothes (A)　　Lu 10:30; 12:23; Re 3:18
meat, and the body is more　Lu 12:23
than r.
they parted his r. and cast lots　Lu 23:34
They parted my r. among　Joh 19:24
them
he shook his r. and said unto　Ac 18:6
them
garments (B)　　　　　Ac 18:6
kept the r. of them that slew　Ac 22:20
him
And having food and r. let us　1Ti 6:8
be
covering (B)　　　　　1Ti 6:8
come in also a poor man in vile　Jas 2:2
apparel (A)　　　　　Jas 2:2
name shall be clothed in white r.　Re 3:5
and white r. that thou mayest　Re 3:18
be
elders sitting, clothed in white r.　Re 4:4
robes (B)　　　　　Re 4:4

RAIN

not caused it to r. upon the　Ge 2:5
earth
I will cause it to r. upon the　Ge 7:4
earth
the r. was upon the earth forty　Ge 7:12
the r. from heaven was　　Ge 8:2
restrained
the r. was checked (A)(B)　Ge 8:2
cause it to r. a very grievous　Ex 9:18
hail
r. was not poured upon the　Ex 9:33
earth
when Pharaoh saw that the r.　Ex 9:34
will r. bread from heaven for　Ex 16:4
you
I will give you r. in due season　Le 26:4
drinketh water of the r. of　De 11:11
heaven

I will give you the *r*. of your   *De 11:14*
land
in his due season, the first *r*.   *De 11:14*
and the latter *r*. that thou   *De 11:14*
mayest
up the heaven, that there be   *De 11:17*
no *r*.
the *r*. unto thy land in his   *De 28:12*
season
make the *r*. of thy land   *De 28:24*
powder and
My doctrine shall drop as the   *De 32:2*
r. my
the small *r*. upon the tender   *De 32:2*
herb
and he shall send thunder   *1Sa 12:17*
and *r*.
the Lord sent thunder and *r*.   *1Sa 12:18*
that
neither let there be *r*. upon   *2Sa 1:21*
you
the earth by clear shining   *2Sa 23:4*
after *r*.
is shut up, and there is no *r*.   *1Ki 8:35*
and give *r*. upon thy land,   *1Ki 8:36*
which
shall not be dew nor *r*. these   *1Ki 17:1*
years
there had been no *r*. in the   *1Ki 17:7*
land
the Lord sendeth *r*. upon the   *1Ki 17:14*
earth
and I will send *r*. upon the   *1Ki 18:1*
earth
is a sound of abundance of *r*.   *1Ki 18:41*
thee down, that the *r*. stop   *1Ki 18:44*
thee not
and wind, and there was a   *1Ki 18:45*
great *r*.
see wind, neither shall ye see   *2Ki 3:17*
r.
is shut up, and there is no *r*.   *2Ch 6:26*
send *r*. upon thy land, which   *2Ch 6:27*
thou
shut up heaven that there be   *2Ch 7:13*
no *r*.
of this matter, and for the   *Ezr 10:9*
great *r*.
it is a time of much *r*. and we   *Ezr 10:13*
are
Who giveth *r*. upon the earth   *Job 5:10*
r. it upon him while he is   *Job 20:23*
eating
When he made a decree for   *Job 28:26*
the *r*.
they waited for me as for the   *Job 29:23*
r.
mouth wide as for the latter   *Job 29:23*
r.
they pour down *r*. according   *Job 36:27*
to the
to the small *r*. and to the great   *Job 37:6*
r.
To cause it to *r*. on the earth   *Job 38:26*
Hath the *r*. a father? or who   *Job 38:28*
hath
Upon the wicked he shall *r*.   *Ps 11:6*
snares
didst send a plentiful *r*.   *Ps 68:9*
whereby
come down like *r*. upon the   *Ps 72:6*
mown
a well; the *r*. also filleth the   *Ps 84:6*
pools
He gave them hail for *r*. and   *Ps 105:32*
he maketh lightnings for the *r*.   *Ps 135:7*
who prepareth *r*. for the earth   *Ps 147:8*
favour is as a cloud of the   *Pr 16:15*
latter *r*.
is like clouds and wind   *Pr 25:14*
without *r*.
The north wind driveth away   *Pr 25:23*
r.
and as *r*. in harvest, so honour   *Pr 26:1*
is
sweeping *r*. which leaveth no   *Pr 28:3*
food
If the clouds be full of *r*. they   *Ec 11:3*
nor the clouds return after the   *Ec 12:2*
r.
is past, the *r*. is over and gone   *Ca 2:11*
a covert from storm and from *r*.   *Isa 4:6*
the clouds that they *r*. no   *Isa 5:6*
clouds that they no *r*. upon it   *Isa 5:6*
shall he give the *r*. of thy seed   *Isa 30:23*
an ash, and the *r*. doth   *Isa 44:14*
nourish it
For as the *r*. cometh down   *Isa 55:10*
and there hath been no latter *r*.   *Jer 3:3*

the Lord our God, that giveth   *Jer 5:24*
r.
he maketh lightnings with *r*.   *Jer 10:13;*
   51:16
for there was no *r*. in the earth   *Jer 14:4*
of the Gentiles that can cause   *Jer 14:22*
is in the cloud in the day of *r*.   *Eze 1:28*
I will *r*. upon him, and upon   *Eze 38:22*
his
an overflowing *r*. and great   *Eze 38:22*
and he shall come unto us as   *Ho 6:3*
the *r*.
as the latter and former *r*. unto   *Ho 6:3*
and *r*. righteousness upon you   *Ho 10:12*
you the former *r*. moderately   *Joe 2:23*
cause to come down for you   *Joe 2:23*
the *r*.
down for you the former *r*.   *Joe 2:23*
the latter *r*. in the first month   *Joe 2:23*
have withholden the *r*. from   *Am 4:7*
you
I caused it to *r*. upon one city   *Am 4:7*
it not to *r*. upon another city   *Am 4:7*
Ask ye of the Lord *r*. in the   *Zec 10:1*
time
of the latter *r*. so the Lord   *Zec 10:1*
shall
and give them showers of *r*. to   *Zec 10:1*
even upon them shall be no *r*.   *Zec 14:17*
not up, and come not, that   *Zec 14:18*
have no *r*.
sendeth *r*. on the just and on   *M't 5:45*
And the *r*. descended, and the   *M't 7:25;*
   7:27
and gave us *r*. from heaven   *Ac 14:17*
because of the present *r*. and   *Ac 28:2*
the earth which drinketh in the   *Heb 6:7*
r.
he receive the early and latter *r*.   *Jas 5:7*
earnestly that it might not *r*.   *Jas 5:17*
again, and the heaven gave *r*.   *Jas 5:18*
it *r*. not in the days of their   *Re 11:6*

RAINBOW

was a *r*. round about the throne   *Re 4:3*
a *r*. was upon his head, and his   *Re 10:1*

RAINED

r. upon Sodom and Gomorrah   *Ge 19:24*
r. hail upon the land of Egypt   *Ex 9:23*
r. down manna upon them to   *Ps 78:24*
eat
He *r*. flesh also upon them as   *Ps 78:27*
dust
r. upon in the day of   *Eze 22:24*
indignation
one piece was *r*. upon, and the   *Am 4:7*
whereupon it *r*. not withered   *Am 4:7*
r. fire and brimstone from   *Lu 17:29*
heaven
r. not on the earth for the   *Jas 5:17*
space of

RAINY

r. day and contentious woman   *Pr 27:15*
are

RAISE

her, and *r*. up seed to thy   *Ge 38:8*
brother
Thou shalt not *r*. a false report   *Ex 23:1*
God will *r*. up unto thee a   *De 18:15*
Prophet
I will *r*. them up a Prophet   *De 18:18*
from
to *r*. up unto his brother a   *De 25:7*
name
r. thereon a great heap of   *Jos 8:29*
stones
r. up the name of the dead   *Ru 4:5;*
upon   *4:10*
will *r*. me up a faithful priest,   *1Sa 2:35*
that
I will *r*. up evil against thee   *2Sa 12:11*
out of
him, to *r*. him up from the   *2Sa 12:17*
earth
Lord shall *r*. him up a king   *1Ki 14:14*
over
that I will *r*. up thy seed   *1Ch 17:11*
after thee
ready to *r*. up their mourning   *Job 3:8*
and *r*. up their way against   *Job 19:12*
me
they *r*. up against me the   *Job 30:12*
ways of

merciful unto me, and *r*. me   *Ps 41:10*
up
shall *r*. up a cry of destruction   *Isa 15:5*
and I will *r*. forts against thee   *Isa 29:3*
and I will *r*. up the decayed   *Isa 44:26*
places
servant to *r*. up the tribes of   *Isa 49:6*
Jacob
thou shalt *r*. up the   *Isa 58:12*
foundation
shall *r*. up the former   *Isa 61:4*
desolations
r. unto David a righteous   *Jer 23:5*
Branch
king, whom I will *r*. up unto   *Jer 30:9*
them
I will *r*. and cause to come up   *Jer 50:9*
fall, and none shall *r*. him up   *Jer 50:32*
I will *r*. up against Babylon   *Jer 51:1*
will *r*. up thy lovers against   *Eze 23:22*
thee
I will *r*. up for them a plant   *Eze 34:29*
of
in the third day he will *r*. us up   *Ho 6:2*
I will *r*. them out of the place   *Joe 3:7*
land; there is none to *r*. her up   *Am 5:2*
I will *r*. up against you a   *Am 6:14*
nation
day will I *r*. up the tabernacle   *Am 9:11*
of
I will *r*. up his ruins, and I   *Am 9:11*
will
we *r*. against him seven   *Mic 5:5*
shepherds
that *r*. up strife and contention   *Hab 1:3*
lo, I *r*. up the Chaldeans, that   *Hab 1:6*
will *r*. up a shepherd in the   *Zec 11:16*
land
to *r*. up children into   *M't 3:9;*
Abraham   *Lu 3:8*
sick, cleanse the lepers, *r*. the   *M't 10:8*
dead
and *r*. up seed unto his   *M't 22:24;*
brother   *M'k 12:19; Lu 20:28*
and in three days I will *r*. it up   *Joh 2:19*
wilt thou *r*. it up in three days   *Joh 2:20*
(S)
r. it up again at the last day   *Joh 6:39*
will *r*. him up at the last day   *Joh 6:40;*
   6:44, 54
r. up Christ to sit on his   *Ac 2:30*
throne
shall the Lord your God *r*. up   *Ac 3:22;*
unto   *7:37*
you, that God should *r*. the   *Ac 26:8*
dead
will also *r*. up us by his own   *1Co 6:14*
power
Jesus shall *r*. up us also by   *2Co 4:14*
Jesus
that God was able to *r*. him   *Heb 11:19*
up
sick, and the Lord shall *r*. him   *Jas 5:15*
up

RAISED

for this cause have I *r*. thee up   *Ex 9:16*
whom he *r*. up in their stead   *Jos 5:7*
r. over him a great heap of   *Jos 7:26*
stones
Nevertheless the Lord *r*. up   *J'g 2:16*
judges
when the Lord *r*. them up   *J'g 2:18*
judges
r. up a deliverer to the children   *J'g 3:9*
of
the Lord *r*. them up a deliverer   *J'g 3:15*
the man who was *r*. up on   *2Sa 23:1*
high
Solomon *r*. a levy out of all   *1Ki 5:13*
Israel
the levy which king of   *1Ki 9:15*
Solomon *r*.
and *r*. it up to the towers, and   *2Ch 32:5*
and *r*. it up a very great   *2Ch 33:14*
height
all them whose spirit God had   *Ezr 1:5*
r.
awake, nor be *r*. out of their   *Job 14:12*
sleep
I *r*. thee up under the apple tree   *Ca 8:5*
r. above the hills (B)(R)   *Isa 2:2*
r. up from their thrones all the   *Isa 14:9*
they *r*. up the palaces thereof   *Isa 23:13*
Who *r*. up the righteous man   *Isa 41:2*
from
have *r*. up one from the   *Isa 41:25*
north, and

I have *r.* him up in | *Isa 45:13*
righteousness
a great nation shall be *r.* from | *Jer 6:22*
a great whirlwind shall be *r.* | *Jer 25:32*
from
The Lord hath *r.* us by | *Jer 29:15*
prophets
many kings shall be *r.* up | *Jer 50:41*
from
the Lord hath *r.* up the spirit | *Jer 51:11*
of
and it *r.* up itself on one side | *Da 7:5*
I *r.* up of your sons for | *Am 2:11*
prophets
is *r.* up in his holy | *Zec 2:13*
habitation
and *r.* up thy sons, O Zion, | *Zec 9:13*
against
Joseph being *r.* from sleep did | *M't 1:24*
as
the deaf hear, the dead are *r.* | *M't 11:5*
up
raised (S) | *M't 14:2;*
17:9; 26:32; M'k 6:16; 14:28; Lu 7:16
and be *r.* again the third day | *M't 16:21*
the third day he shall be *r.* | *M't 17:23*
again
r. to honor (A) | *M't 23:12*
bodies of saints were *r.* (S) | *M't 27:52*
r. up an horn of salvation for | *Lu 1:69*
us
the deaf hear, the dead are *r.* | *Lu 7:22*
to
be slain, and be *r.* the third day | *Lu 9:22*
Now that the dead are *r.* even | *Lu 20:37*
dead, whom he *r.* from the | *Joh 12:1*
dead
whom he had *r.* from the dead | *Joh 12:9*
r. him from the dead, bare | *Joh 12:17*
record
Whom God hath *r.* up, having | *Ac 2:24*
This Jesus hath God *r.* up | *Ac 2:32*
r. to right hand (P) | *Ac 2:33*
whom God hath *r.* from the | *Ac 3:15*
dead
God, having *r.* up his Son Jesus | *Ac 3:26*
whom God *r.* from the dead, | *Ac 4:10*
even
God of our fathers *r.* up Jesus | *Ac 5:30*
Him God *r.* up the third day | *Ac 10:40*
r. him up, saying, Arise up | *Ac 12:7*
quickly
he *r.* up unto them David to be | *Ac 13:22*
r. unto Israel a Saviour, Jesus | *Ac 13:23*
But God *r.* him from the dead | *Ac 13:30*
in that he hath *r.* up Jesus | *Ac 13:33*
again
that he *r.* him up from the | *Ac 13:34*
dead
he, whom God *r.* again, saw | *Ac 13:37*
no
r. persecution against Paul | *Ac 13:50*
that he hath *r.* him from the | *Ac 17:31*
dead
believe on him that *r.* up Jesus | *Ro 4:24*
was *r.* again for our | *Ro 4:25*
justification
as Christ was *r.* up from the | *Ro 6:4*
dead
Christ being *r.* from the dead | *Ro 6:9*
dieth
to him who is *r.* from the dead | *Ro 7:4*
him that *r.* up Jesus from the | *Ro 8:11*
dead
he that *r.* up Christ from the | *Ro 8:11*
dead
same purpose have I *r.* thee up | *Ro 9:17*
God hath *r.* him from the dead | *Ro 10:9*
God hath both *r.* up the Lord | *1Co 6:14*
of God that he *r.* up Christ | *1Co 15:15*
whom he *r.* not up, if so be | *1Co 15:15*
that the
dead rise not, then is not | *1Co 15:16*
Christ *r.*
Christ be not *r.* your faith is | *1Co 15:17*
vain
will say, How are the dead *r.* | *1Co 15:35*
up
corruption, it is *r.* in | *1Co 15:42*
incorruption
sown in dishonour, it is *r.* in | *1Co 15:43*
glory
sown in weakness; it is *r.* in | *1Co 15:43*
power
body; it is *r.* a spiritual body | *1Co 15:44*
dead shall be *r.* | *1Co 15:52*
incorruptible, and
that he which *r.* up the Lord | *2Co 4:14*
Father, who *r.* him from the | *Ga 1:1*
dead

when he *r.* him from the | *Eph 1:20*
dead, and
hath *r.* us up together, and | *Eph 2:6*
made
who hath *r.* him from the dead | *Col 2:12*
whom he *r.* from the dead, | *1Th 1:10*
even
seed of David was *r.* from the | *2Ti 2:8*
dead
received their dead *r.* to life | *Heb 11:35*
again
God, that *r.* him up from the | *1Pe 1:21*
dead

RAISER

up in his estate a *r.* of taxes | *Da 11:20*

RAISETH

He *r.* up the poor out of the | *1Sa 2:8*
dust
When he *r.* up himself, the | *Job 41:25*
and *r.* the stormy wind, | *Ps 107:25*
which
r. up the poor out of the dust | *Ps 113:7*
r. up all those that be bowed | *Ps 145:14*
down
r. them that are bowed down | *Ps 146:8*
For as the Father *r.* up the | *Joh 5:21*
dead
but in God which *r.* the dead | *2Co 1:9*

RAISIN

love *r.* cakes (A)(B)(E)(R) | *Ho 3:1*

RAISING

from *r.* after he hath kneaded | *Ho 7:4*
for *r.* a riot (A)(B)(P) | *Lu 23:19*
neither *r.* up the people | *Ac 24:12*

RAISINS

an hundred clusters of *r.* and | *1Sa 25:18*
two
cake of figs, and two clusters | *1Sa 30:12*
of *r.*
a cake of *r.* (S) | *2Sa 6:19;*
1Ch 16:3; Ca 2:5; Ho 3:1
an hundred bunches of *r.* and | *2Sa 16:1*
cakes of figs, and bunches of | *1Ch 12:40*
r. and
sustain me with *r.* (A)(E)(R) | *Ca 2:5*

RAKEM

and his sons were Ulam and | *1Ch 7:16*
R.

RAKKATH

Hammath, R. and Chinnereth | *Jos 19:35*

RAKKON

And Me-jarkon, and R. with | *Jos 19:46*

RAM

and a *r.* of three years old, and | *Ge 15:9*
r. caught in a thicket by his | *Ge 22:13*
horns
Abraham went and took the | *Ge 22:13*
r. and
Thou shalt also take one *r.* | *Ex 29:15*
their hands upon the head of | *Ex 29:15*
the *r.*
And thou shalt slay the *r.* and | *Ex 29:16*
thou
thou shalt cut the *r.* in pieces | *Ex 29:17*
burn the whole *r.* upon the | *Ex 29:18*
altar
And thou shalt take the other | *Ex 29:19*
r.
their hands upon the head of | *Ex 29:19*
the *r.*
Then shalt thou kill the *r.* and | *Ex 29:20*
take
thou shalt take of the *r.* the | *Ex 29:22*
fat and
for it is a *r.* of consecration | *Ex 29:22*
of the *r.* of Aaron's | *Ex 29:26*
consecration
of the *r.* of the consecration, | *Ex 29:27*
even of
shalt take the *r.* of the | *Ex 29:31*
consecration
his sons shall eat the flesh of | *Ex 29:32*
the *r.*

unto the Lord a *r.* without | *Le 5:15*
blemish
with the *r.* of the trespass | *Le 5:16;*
offering | *19:22*
he shall bring a *r.* without | *Le 5:18*
blemish
r. without blemish out of the | *Le 6:6*
flock
the *r.* for the burnt offering | *Le 8:18*
their hands upon the head of | *Le 8:18;*
the *r.* | *8:22*
And he cut the *r.* into pieces | *Le 8:20*
burnt the whole *r.* upon the | *Le 8:21*
altar
the other *r.* the *r.* of | *Le 8:22*
consecration
the *r.* of consecration it was | *Le 8:29*
Moses
a *r.* for a burnt offering, without | *Le 9:2*
bullock, and a *r.* for peace | *Le 9:4*
offerings
bullock and the *r.* for a | *Le 9:18*
sacrifice of
the fat of the bullock and of | *Le 9:19*
the *r.*
and a *r.* for a burnt offering | *Le 16:3*
and one *r.* for a burnt offering | *Le 16:5*
even a *r.* for a trespass | *Le 19:21*
offering
the *r.* of the atonement, | *Nu 5:8*
whereby an
one *r.* without blemish for | *Nu 6:14*
peace
he shall offer the *r.* for a | *Nu 6:17*
sacrifice of
take the sodden shoulder of | *Nu 6:19*
the *r.*
One young bullock, one *r.* one | *Nu 7:15;*
7:21, 27, 33, 39, 45, 51, 57, 63, 69, 75, 81
Or for a *r.* thou shalt prepare | *Nu 15:6*
for a
or for one *r.* or for a lamb, or | *Nu 15:11*
a kid
on every altar a bullock and a | *Nu 23:2;*
r. | *23:4*
a bullock and a *r.* on every | *Nu 23:14;*
altar | *23:30*
two young bullocks, and one | *Nu 28:11;*
r. | *28:19*
mingled with oil, for one *r.* | *Nu 28:12*
the third part of an hin unto | *Nu 28:14*
a *r.*
bullock, and two tenth deals | *Nu 28:20;*
for a *r.* | *29:3*
two young bullocks, one *r.* | *Nu 28:27*
seven
bullock, two tenth deals unto | *Nu 28:28*
one *r.*
one young bullock, one *r.* and | *Nu 29:2;*
seven | *29:8*
and two tenth deals to one *r.* | *Nu 29:9*
two tenth deals to each *r.* of | *Nu 29:14*
the two
one bullock, one *r.*, seven | *Nu 29:36*
lambs of
offerings for the bullock, for | *Nu 29:37*
the *r.*
a *r.* of the flock for their | *Ezr 10:19*
trespass
a *r.* out of the flock without | *Eze 43:23*
blemish
and a *r.* out of the flock, | *Eze 43:25*
without
and an ephah for a *r.* and an | *Eze 45:24*
hin of
blemish, and a *r.* without | *Eze 46:4*
blemish
offering shall be an ephah for | *Eze 46:5*
a *r.*
blemish, and six lambs, and a | *Eze 46:6*
r.
an ephah for a *r.* and for the | *Eze 46:7*
lambs
an ephah to a *r.* and to the | *Eze 46:11*
lambs
the river a *r.* which had two | *Da 8:3*
horns
I saw the *r.* pushing westward | *Da 8:4*
came to the *r.* that had two | *Da 8:6*
horns
I saw him come close unto the | *Da 8:7*
r.
and smote the *r.* and brake his | *Da 8:7*
two
and there was no power in the | *Da 8:7*
r. to
could deliver the *r.* out of his | *Da 8:7*
hand
The *r.* which thou sawest | *Da 8:20*
having

RAM, a name

Hezron begat R. and R. begat   *Ru 4:19*
Jerahmeel, and R. and Chelubai *1Ch 2:9*
And R. begat Amminadab   *1Ch 2:10*
of Hezran were, R. the   *1Ch 2:25*
firstborn
And the sons of R. the   *1Ch 2:27*
firstborn
the Buzite, of the kindred of   *Job 32:2*
R.

RAMA

in R. was there a voice heard   *M't 2:18*

RAMAH

Gibeon, and R. and Beeroth   *Jos 18:25*
And then the coast turneth to   *Jos 19:29*
R.
And Adamah, and R. and   *Jos 19:36*
Hazor
between R. and Beth-el in   *J'g 4:5*
mount
lodge all night, in Gibeah, or   *J'g 19:13*
in R.
and came to their house to R.   *1Sa 1:19*
Elkanah went to R. to his   *1Sa 2:11*
house
And his return was to R.; for   *1Sa 7:17*
and came to Samuel unto R.   *1Sa 8:4*
Then Samuel went to R.; and   *1Sa 15:34*
Saul
So Samuel rose up, and went   *1Sa 16:13*
to R.
came to Samuel to R. and   *1Sa 19:18*
told him
Behold, David is at Naioth   *1Sa 19:19*
in R.
Then went he also to R. and   *1Sa 19:22*
came
Behold, they be at Naioth in   *1Sa 19:22*
R.
he went thither to Naioth in   *1Sa 19:23*
R.: and
until he came to Naioth in R.   *1Sa 19:23*
David fled from Naioth in R.   *1Sa 20:1*
abode in Gibeah under a tree   *1Sa 22:6*
in R.
and buried him in his house at   *1Sa 25:1*
R.
buried him in R. even in his   *1Sa 28:3*
own
up against Judah, and built   *1Ki 15:17*
R.
that he left off building of R.   *1Ki 15:21*
and they took away the   *1Ki 15:22*
stones of R.
the Syrians had given him at   *2Ki 8:29*
R.
up against Judah, and built R.   *2Ch 16:1*
to
he left off building of R. and   *2Ch 16:5*
let his
they carried away the stones   *2Ch 16:6*
of R.
wounds which were given him   *2Ch 22:6*
at R.
The children of R. and Gaba,   *Ezr 2:26*
six
men of R. and Gaba, six   *Ne 7:30*
hundred
Hazor, R., Gittaim   *Ne 11:33*
R. is afraid; Gibeah of Saul   *Isa 10:29*
is fled
the Lord; A voice was heard   *Jer 31:15*
in R.
the guard had let him go from   *Jer 40:1*
R.
in Gibeah, and the trumpet in   *Ho 5:8*
R.

RAMATH

to Baalath-beer, R. of the   *Jos 19:8*
south

RAMATHAIM-ZOPHIM

there was a certain man of R.   *1Sa 1:1*
of

RAMATHITE

the vineyards was Shimei the   *1Ch 27:27*
R.

RAMATH-LEHI

his hand, and called that   *J'g 15:17*
place R.

RAMATH-MIZPEH

And from Heshbon unto R.   *Jos 13:26*

RAMESES

best of the land, in the land of   *Ge 47:11*
R.
journeyed from R. to Succoth   *Ex 12:37*
And they departed from R. in   *Ex 33:3*
children of Israel removed   *Ex 33:5*
from R.

RAMIAH

sons of Parosh; R. and Jeziah   *Ezr 10:25*

RAMOTH

and R. in Gilead, of the   *De 4:43*
Gadites
R. in Gilead out of the tribe of   *Jos 20:8*
Gad
R. in Gilead with her   *Jos 21:38*
suburbs, to be
to them which were in south   *1Sa 30:27*
R.
Know ye that R. in Gilead is   *1Ki 22:3*
ours
And R. with her suburbs, and   *1Ch 6:73*
Anem
R. in Gilead with her suburbs   *1Ch 6:80*
Adaiah, Jashub, and Sheal,   *Ezr 10:29*
and R.

RAMOTH-GILEAD

The son of Geber, in R.; to   *1Ki 4:13*
him
thou go with me to battle to   *1Ki 22:4*
R.
Shall I go against R. to battle,   *1Ki 22:6*
or
saying, Go up to R. and   *1Ki 22:12*
prosper
shall we go against R. to   *1Ki 22:15*
battle, or
that he may go on and fall at   *1Ki 22:20*
R.
the king of Judah went up to   *1Ki 22:29*
R.
against Hazael king of Syria   *2Ki 8:28;*
in R.   *2Ch 22:5*
of oil in thine hand, and go to   *2Ki 9:1*
R.
young man the prophet, went   *2Ki 9:4*
to R.
(Now Joram had kept R. he   *2Ki 9:14*
and all
him to go up with him to R.   *2Ch 18:2*
Judah, Wilt thou go with me   *2Ch 18:3*
to R.
Shall we go to R. to battle, or   *2Ch 18:5;*
shall   *18:14*
saying, Go up to R. and   *2Ch 18:11*
prosper
that he may go up and fall at   *2Ch 18:19*
R.
the king of Judah went up to   *2Ch 18:28*
R.

RAMPANT

r. outgrowth of wickedness (A)   *Jas 1:21*

RAMPART

it stood in the r. (S)   *2Sa 20:15*
the r. and the wall to lament   *La 2:8*
whose r. was the sea, and her   *Na 3:8*
wall

RAMPARTS

keep fortress and r. (A)(B)(R)   *Na 2:1*

RAMS

r. which leaped upon the   *Ge 31:10*
cattle
r. which leap upon the cattle   *Ge 31:12*
and the r. of the flock have I   *Ge 31:38*
not
two hundred ewes, and twenty   *Ge 32:14*
r.
and two r. without blemish   *Ex 29:1*
with the bullock, and the two   *Ex 29:3*
r.
red skins of r. and badgers'   *Ex 35:23*
skins
for the sin offering, and two r.   *Le 8:2*

and one young bullock, and   *Le 23:18;*
two r.   *Nu 7:17, 23, 29, 35, 41, 47, 53,*
  59, 65, 71, 77
five r. five he goats, five lambs   *Nu 7:83*
were twelve bullocks, the r.   *Nu 7:87*
twelve
and four bullocks, the r. sixty   *Nu 7:88*
me here seven oxen and seven   *Nu 23:1*
r.
here seven bullocks and seven   *Nu 23:29*
r.
thirteen young bullocks, two   *Nu 29:13*
r. and
deals to each ram of the two   *Nu 29:14*
r.
offer twelve young bullocks,   *Nu 29:17*
two r.
offerings for the bullocks, for   *Nu 29:18*
the r.
third day eleven bullocks, two   *Nu 29:20*
offerings for the bullocks,   *Nu 29:21*
for the r.   *29:27, 30, 33*
the fourth day ten bullocks,   *Nu 29:23*
two r.
offerings for the bullocks, for   *Nu 29:24*
the r.
the fifth day nine bullocks,   *Nu 29:26*
two r.
eight bullocks, two r. and   *Nu 29:29*
fourteen
seven bullocks, two r. and   *Nu 29:32*
fourteen
and r. of the breed of Bashan   *De 32:14*
and to hearken than the fat   *1Sa 15:22*
of r.
an hundred thousand r. with   *2Ki 3:4*
seven r.
offered seven bullocks and   *1Ch 15:26*
seven r.
a thousand bullocks, a   *1Ch 29:21*
thousand r.
with a young bullock and   *2Ch 13:9*
seven r.
thousand and seven hundred   *2Ch 17:11*
r.
brought seven bullocks, and   *2Ch 29:21*
seven r.
when they had killed the r.   *2Ch 29:22*
they
an hundred r. and two   *2Ch 29:32*
hundred
of, both young bullocks, and r.   *Ezr 6:9*
two hundred r. four hundred   *Ezr 6:17*
with this money bullocks, r.   *Ezr 7:17*
ninety and six r. seventy and   *Ezr 8:35*
now seven bullocks, and seven   *Job 42:8*
r.
of fatlings, with the incense of   *Ps 66:15*
r.
The mountains skipped like r.   *Ps 114:4*
mountains, that ye skipped   *Ps 114:6*
like r.
am full of the burnt offerings   *Isa 1:11*
of r.
with the fat of the kidneys of   *Isa 34:6*
r.
the r. of Nebaioth, shall   *Isa 60:7*
minister
like choice r. (R)   *Jer 25:34*
slaughter, like r. with he goats   *Jer 51:40*
set battering r. against it round   *Eze 4:2*
battering r. against the gates   *Eze 21:22*
battering r. shall pound   *Eze 26:9*
(B)(R)
occupied with thee in lambs,   *Eze 27:21*
and r.
between the r. and the he   *Eze 34:17*
goats
of r. of lambs, and of goats   *Eze 39:18*
and seven r. without blemish,   *Eze 45:23*
daily
be pleased with thousands of r.   *Mic 6:7*

RAM'S

make a long blast with the r.   *Jos 6:5*
horn

RAMS'

and r. skins dyed red, and   *Ex 25:5;*
badgers'   *35:7*
for the tent of r. skins dyed   *Ex 26:14;*
red   *36:19*
the covering of r. skins dyed   *Ex 39:34*
red
ark seven trumpets of r. horns   *Jos 6:4*
bear seven trumpets of r. horns   *Jos 6:6*
the seven trumpets of r. horns   *Jos 6:8*
bearing seven trumpets of r.   *Jos 6:13*
horns

RAN

he *r.* to meet them from the *Ge 18:2*
tent
Abraham *r.* unto the herd, and *Ge 18:7*
And the servants *r.* to meet her *Ge 24:17*
and *r.* again unto the well to *Ge 24:20*
draw
the damsel *r.* and told them of *Ge 24:28*
her
Laban *r.* out unto the man, *Ge 24:29*
unto
son: and she *r.* and told her *Ge 29:12*
father
son that he *r.* to meet him *Ge 29:13*
Esau *r.* to meet him, and *Ge 33:4*
embraced
the fire *r.* along upon the *Ex 9:23*
ground
there *r.* a young man, and told *Nu 11:27*
and *r.* into the midst of the *Nu 16:47*
and they *r.* unto the tent; and *Jos 7:22*
they *r.* as soon as he had *Jos 8:19*
stretched
and all the host *r.* and cried *J'g 7:21*
And Jotham *r.* away, and fled *J'g 9:21*
other companies *r.* upon all the *J'g 9:44*
the woman made haste, and *r.* *J'g 13:10*
And he *r.* unto Eli, and said, *1Sa 3:5*
Here
And there *r.* a man of *1Sa 4:12*
Benjamin
they *r.* and fetched him *1Sa 10:23*
thence: and
and *r.* into the army, and *1Sa 17:22*
came and
and *r.* toward the army to *1Sa 17:48*
meet the
Therefore David *r.* and stood *1Sa 17:51*
upon
And as the lad *r.* he shot an *1Sa 20:36*
arrow
bowed himself unto Joab, *2Sa 18:21*
and *r.*
Ahimaaz *r.* by the way of the *2Sa 18:23*
plain
of the servants of Shimei *r.* *1Ki 2:39*
away
the water *r.* round about the *1Ki 18:35*
altar
r. before Ahab to the *1Ki 18:46*
entrance of
left the oxen, and *r.* after *1Ki 19:20*
Elijah
the blood *r.* out of the wound *1Ki 22:35*
into
the brook that *r.* through the *2Ch 32:4*
my sore *r.* in the night, and *Ps 77:2*
r. in the dry places like a *Ps 105:41*
river
that *r.* down upon the beard, *Ps 133:2*
even
sent these prophets, yet they *Jer 23:21*
r.
living creatures *r.* and returned *Eze 1:14*
r. out waters on the right side *Eze 47:2*
r. unto him in the fury of his *Da 8:6*
swine *r.* violently down a steep *M't 8:32*
straightway one of them *r.* *M't 27:48*
afar off, he *r.* and worshipped *M'k 5:6*
him
r. violently down a steep *M'k 5:13;*
place *Lu 8:33*
r. afoot thither out of all *M'k 6:33*
cities
And *r.* through that whole *M'k 6:55*
region
one *r.* and filled a sponge *M'k 15:36*
full of
r. and fell on his neck, and *Lu 15:20*
kissed
he *r.* before, and climbed up *Lu 19:4*
into
Peter, and *r.* unto the *Lu 24:12*
sepulchre
So they *r.* both together; and *Joh 20:4*
people *r.* together unto them in *Ac 3:11*
and *r.* upon him with one *Ac 7:57*
accord
And Philip *r.* thither to him *Ac 8:30*
the gate for gladness, but *r.* in *Ac 12:14*
r. in among the people, crying *Ac 14:14*
out
and the people *r.* together *Ac 21:30*
centurions, and *r.* down unto *Ac 27:32*
them
they *r.* the ship aground; and *Ac 27:41*
and *r.* greedily after the error *Jude 11*
of

RANCID

grew wormy and *r.* (B) *Ex 16:20*
neither *r.* or wormy (R) *Ex 16:24*

RANG

shout, so that the earth *r.* again *1Sa 4:5*
rejoicing, so that the city *r.* *1Ki 1:45*
again
word of Lord *r.* out (N) *1Th 1:8*

RANGE

The *r.* of the mountains is his *Job 39:8*

RANGES

whether it be oven, or *r.* for *Le 11:35*
pots
or hearth for pots (A) *Le 11:35*
or baking pan (B) *Le 11:35*
or stove (R) *Le 11:35*
he that cometh within the *r.* *2Ki 11:8*
let
anyone who breaks into the *2Ki 11:8*
ranks (A)(B)(E)(R)
Have her forth without the *2Ki 11:8*
r. and
Take her forth outside the *2Ki 11:15*
ranks (A)(B)(E)(R)
Have her forth of the *r.:* and *2Ch 23:14*
Bring her forth between the *2Ch 23:14*
ranks (A)(B)(E)(R)

RANGING

As a roaring lion, and a *r.* *Pr 28:15*
bear
a charging bear (A)(R) *Pr 28:15*
a prowling bear (B) *Pr 28:15*

RANK

up upon one stalk, *r.* and good *Ge 41:5*
devoured the seven *r.* and full *Ge 41:7*
ears
they shall set forth in the *Nu 2:16*
second *r.*
they shall go forward in the *Nu 2:24*
third *r.*
thousand, which could keep *1Ch 12:33*
r.
men of war, that could keep *1Ch 12:38*
r.
first in *r.* *M'k 10:44*
(A)(B)(E)(N)(P)(R)
r. the highest (P) *Lu 22:24*
r. growth of wickedness (R) *Jas 1:21*

RANKS

was against light in three *r.* *1Ki 7:4;*
 7:5
breaks into the *r.* *2Ki 11:8;*
(A)(B)(E)(R)(S) *11:15; 2Ch 23:14*
beyond the *r.* (S) *2Ki 11:15*
and they shall not break their *r.* *Joe 2:7*
And they sat down in *r.* by *M'k 6:40*

RANSACK

r. his house (N)(P) *M't 12:29;*
 M'k 3:27
r. his household (A) *M't 12:29;*
 M'k 3:27

RANSOM

the *r.* of his life whatsoever is *Ex 21:30*
the redemption of his life *Ex 21:30*
(B)(R)
give every man a *r.* for his *Ex 30:12*
soul
ye shall make no *r.* (S) *Nu 35:31; 35:32*
taken a *r.* (E) *1Sa 12:3*
r. me from brigands (B)(R) *Job 6:23*
down to the pit: I have found *Job 33:24*
a *r.*
then a great *r.* cannot deliver *Job 36:18*
thee
nor give to God a *r.* for him *Ps 49:7*
He will not regard any *r.;* *Pr 6:35*
neither
r. of a man's life are his *Pr 13:8*
riches
The wicked shall be a *r.* for *Pr 21:18*
I gave Egypt for thy *r.* *Isa 43:3*
Ethiopia
I will *r.* them from the power *Ho 13:14*
of

(continued) RANSOM

save them from the hand of *Ho 13:14*
Sheol (A)
and to give his life a *r.* for *M't 20:28;*
many *M'k 10:45*
through the *r.* of Christ (B) *Ro 3:24*
Who gave himself a *r.* for all, *1Ti 2:6*
to be
didst *r.* men (R) *Re 5:9*

RANSOMED

r. by justice (B) *Isa 1:27*
the *r.* of the Lord shall return *Isa 35:10*
sea a way for the *r.* to pass *Isa 51:10*
over
the redeemed to pass over *Isa 51:10*
(A)(B)(E)(R)
r. of the Lord (B) *Isa 51:11*
r. him from the hand of him *Jer 31:11*
that
Lord has *r.* Jacob *Jer 31:11*
(A)(B)(R)
I have *r.* them (B) *Zec 10:8*
r. us from useless ways *1Pe 1:18*
(B)(P)(R)
r. from the earth (A)(N) *Re 14:3; 14:4*

RANTING

enemies are *r.* (B) *Ps 83:2*

RAPACITY

rapacity (R) *M't 23:25*

RAPHA

Nohah the fourth, and *R.* the *1Ch 8:2*
fifth
R. was his son, Eleasah his *1Ch 8:37*
son

RAPHAH

descendents of *R.* (B) *2Sa 21:16*

RAPHU

of Benjamin, Palti the son of *Nu 13:9*
R.

RARE

the word of the Lord was *r.* *1Sa 3:1*
(S)
make a man more *r.* than *Isa 13:12*
gold (S)
a *r.* thing that the king *Da 2:11*
requireth

RASCALLY

the *r.* steward (P) *Lu 16:8*

RASCALS

two scoundrels, *r.* (B) *1Ki 21:13*

RASE

R. it, *r.* it, even to the *Ps 137:7*
foundation
Down, down to the ground *Ps 137:7*
with her (A)
lay her bare to her *Ps 137:7*
foundations (B)

RASH

utters with lips a *r.* oath (R) *Le 5:4*
Be not *r.* with thy mouth, and *Ec 5:2*
let
r. shall understand knowledge *Isa 32:4*

RASHLY

one swear *r.* with lips (E) *Le 5:4*
to be quiet, and to do *Ac 19:36*
nothing *r.*

RASOR

shall not *r.* come upon his head *Nu 6:5;*
 1Sa 1:11
shall no *r.* come on his head *Nu 6:5*
hath not come a *r.* upon mine *J'g 16:17*
head
like a sharp *r.* working *Ps 52:2*
deceitfully

Lord shave with a *r.* that is *Isa 7:20*
hired
take thee a barber's *r.* and *Eze 5:1*
cause it

RATE

and gather a certain *r.* every *Ex 16:4*
day
horses, and mules, a *r.* year *1Ki 10:25;*
by year *2Ch 9:24*
of the king, a daily *r.* for *2Ki 25:30*
every day
Even after a certain *r.* every *2Ch 8:13*
day

RATED

every man is *r.* (S) *2Ki 12:4*

RATES

r. one day greater (B) *Ro 14:5*

RATHER

have not *r.* done it for fear of *Jos 22:24*
this
hath not David *r.* sent his *2Sa 10:3*
servants
how much *r.* then, when he *2Ki 5:13*
saith to
strangling, and death *r.* than *Job 7:15*
my life
he justified himself *r.* than *Job 32:2*
God
hast thou chosen *r.* than *Job 36:21*
affliction
lying *r.* than to speak *Ps 52:3*
righteousness
I had *r.* be a doorkeeper in the *Ps 84:10*
and knowledge *r.* than choice *Pr 8:10*
gold
understanding *r.* to be chosen *Pr 16:16*
than
man, *r.* than a fool in his folly *Pr 17:12*
A good name is *r.* to be chosen *Pr 22:1*
than
loving favour *r.* than silver and *Pr 22:1*
gold
And death shall be chosen *r.* *Jer 8:3*
than life
But go *r.* to the lost sheep of *M't 10:6*
r. fear him which is able to *M't 10:28*
destroy
r. than having two hands or *M't 18:8*
two
r. than having two eyes to be *M't 18:9*
cast
go ye *r.* to them that sell, and *M't 25:9*
buy
but that *r.* a tumult was *M't 27:24*
made, he
nothing bettered, but *r.* grew *M'k 5:26*
worse
should *r.* release Barabbas *M'k 15:11*
unto
but *r.* rejoice, because your *Lu 10:20*
names
Yea *r.* blessed are they that *Lu 11:28*
hear
r. give alms of such things as *Lu 11:41*
ye
But *r.* seek ye the kingdom of *Lu 12:31*
God
I tell you, Nay; but *r.* division *Lu 12:51*
And will not *r.* say unto him, *Lu 17:8*
Make
to his house justified *r.* than *Lu 18:14*
the other
men loved darkness *r.* than *Joh 3:19*
light
We ought to obey God *r.* than *Ac 5:29*
men
And not *r.* (as we be *Ro 3:8*
slanderously
died, yea, *r.* that is risen again *Ro 8:34*
r. through their fall salvation *Ro 11:11*
is come
but *r.* give place unto wrath: *Ro 12:19*
for
but judge this *r.* that no man *Ro 14:13*
put
puffed up, and have not *r.* *1Co 5:2*
mourned
Why do ye not *r.* take wrong? *1Co 6:7*
why
r. suffer yourselves to be *1Co 6:7*
defrauded
thou mayest be made free, use *1Co 7:21*
it *r.*

this power over you, are not *1Co 9:12*
we
gifts, but *r.* that ye may *1Co 14:1*
prophesy
tongues, but *r.* that ye *1Co 14:5*
prophesied
I had *r.* speak five words *1Co 14:19*
with my
ye ought *r.* to forgive him, and *2Co 2:7*
of the spirit be *r.* glorious *2Co 3:8*
r. to be absent from the body *2Co 5:8*
will I *r.* glory in my infirmities *2Co 12:9*
known God, or *r.* are known of *Ga 4:9*
God
but *r.* let him labour, working *Eph 4:28*
with
convenient; but *r.* giving of *Eph 5:4*
thanks
of darkness, but *r.* reprove *Eph 5:11*
them
fallen out *r.* unto the *Ph'p 1:12*
furtherance of
r. than godly edifying which is *1Ti 1:4*
in
exercise thyself *r.* unto *1Ti 4:7*
godliness
but *r.* do them service, because *1Ti 6:2*
Yet for love's sake I *r.* beseech *Ph'm 9*
thee
Choosing *r.* to suffer *Heb 11:25*
affliction with
r. be in subjection unto the *Heb 12:9*
Father
of the way; but let it *r.* be *Heb 12:13*
healed
But I beseech you the *r.* to *Heb 13:19*
do this
Wherefore the *r.* brethren, *2Pe 1:10*
give

RATIFIED

has been *r.* (B)(R) *Ga 3:15*
convenant *r.* by God (B)(R) *Ga 3:17*
inaugurated and *r.* *Heb 9:18*
(A)(B)(N)(R)

RATIONS

issue their *r.* (N) *M't 24:45*

RATTLE

r. off long prayers like pagan *M't 6:7*
(P)

RATTLETH

The quiver *r.* against him *Job 39:23*

RATTLING

the noise of the *r.* of the wheels *Na 3:2*

RAVAGE

they *r.* it (A)(B)(E)(R) *Eze 14:15*
r., ravageth (A)(B)(E)(R) *Ho 7:1*

RAVAGED

we have *r.* them (B) *Nu 21:30*
ravaged (B) *Jos 11:12; 19:47*
r. the country (R) *1Ch 20:1*

RAVAGETH

ravage, *r.* (A)(E) *Ho 7:1*

RAVAGING

r. those in Jerusalem (B) *Ac 9:21*

RAVEN

And he sent forth a *r.* which *Ge 8:7*
went
Every *r.* after his kind *Le 11:15*
And every *r.* after his kind *De 14:14*
Who provideth for the *r.* his *Job 38:41*
food
locks are bushy, and black as a *Ca 5:11*
r.
owl also and the *r.* shall dwell *Isa 34:11*
in it

RAVENING

mouths, as a *r.* and a roaring *Ps 22:13*
lion

like a *r.* lion (R) *Jer 2:30*
like a roaring lion *r.* the *Eze 22:25*
prey; they
are like wolves *r.* the prey, to *Eze 22:27*
shed
but inwardly they are *r.* *M't 7:15*
wolves
part is full of *r.* and *Lu 11:39*
wickedness

RAVENOUS

there, nor any *r.* beast shall go *Isa 35:9*
up
any beast of prey (B) *Isa 35:9*
Calling a *r.* bird from the *Isa 46:11*
east, the
calling a bird of prey (R) *Isa 46:11*
give thee unto the *r.* birds of *Eze 39:4*
every
give you to birds of prey *Eze 39:4*
(B)(R)
they are *r.* wolves (S) *M't 7:15*

RAVENS

the *r.* to feed thee there *1Ki 17:4*
the *r.* brought him bread and *1Ki 17:6*
flesh
food, and to the young *r.* *Ps 147:9*
which cry
the *r.* of the valley shall pick it *Pr 30:17*
out
Consider the *r.:* for they *Lu 12:24*
neither

RAVIN

Benjamin shall *r.* as a wolf: *Ge 49:27*
in the
Benjamin, a tearing wolf (B) *Ge 49:27*
with prey, and his dens with *r.* *Na 2:12*
(B)
his dens with plenty of booty *Na 2:12*
(B)
his dens with torn flesh (R) *Na 2:12*

RAVISH

r. them (B)(R) *J'g 19:24*

RAVISHED

he *r.* her (B) *Ge 34:5*
be thou *r.* always with her love *Pr 5:19*
transported with delight in her *Pr 5:19*
love (A)
always infatuated with her love *Pr 5:19*
(B)(R)
son, be *r.* with a strange woman *Pr 5:20*
infatuated with a loose woman *Pr 5:20*
(A)(B)(R)
Thou hast *r.* my heart, my sister *Ca 4:9*
thou hast *r.* my heart with one *Ca 4:9*
of
shall be spoiled, and their *Isa 13:16*
wives *r.*
They *r.* the woman in Zion *La 5:11*
houses rifled, and the women *Zec 14:2*
r.

RAW

Eat not of it *r.* nor sodden at *Ex 12:9*
all
be quick *r.* flesh in the rising *Le 13:10*
But when *r.* flesh appeareth in *Le 13:14*
him
the priest shall see the *r.* flesh *Le 13:15*
for the *r.* flesh is unclean: it is *Le 13:15*
Or if the *r.* flesh turn again, *Le 13:16*
and be
the *r.* flesh (B)(R) *Le 13:24*
have sodden flesh of thee, but *1Sa 2:15*
r.
welts and *r.* wounds (B) *Isa 1:6*
and every shoulder was *Eze 29:18*
rubbed *r.* (S)

RAZE

R. it, *r.* it (S) *Ps 137:7*

REACH

tower, whose top may *r.* unto *Ge 11:4*
heaven
boards shall *r.* from end to *Ex 26:28*
end
even unto the thighs shall they *Ex 28:42*
r.

threshing shall *r.* unto the | Le 26:5
vintage
vintage shall *r.* unto sowing | Le 26:5
time
shall *r.* unto the side of the | Nu 34:11
sea of
shall *r.* from the wall of the | Nu 35:4
city
and his head *r.* unto the | Job 20:6
clouds
over, he shall *r.* even to the | Isa 8:8
neck
overflowing stream, shall *r.* | Isa 30:28
they *r.* even to the sea of | Jer 48:32
Jazer: the
the mountains shall *r.* unto | Zec 14:5
Azal
R. hither thy finger, and | Joh 20:27
behold
r. hither thy hand, and thrust | Joh 20:27
failed to *r.* the goal (P) | Ro 9:31
us, a measure to *r.* even unto | 2Co 10:13
you

REACHED

and the top of it *r.* to heaven | Ge 28:12
Maralah, and *r.* to | Jos 19:11
Dabbasheth
r. to the river before | Jos 19:11
Jokneam
and he *r.* her parched corn | Ru 2:14
the height thereof *r.* unto | Da 4:11
heaven
whose height *r.* unto the | Da 4:20
heaven
as though we *r.* not unto | 2Co 10:14
you: for
For her sins have *r.* unto | Re 18:5
heaven

REACHETH

unto Nophah, which *r.* unto | Nu 21:30
Medeba
And the coast *r.* to Tabor | Jos 19:22
and *r.* to Carmel westward | Jos 19:26
and *r.* to Zebulun, and to the | Jos 19:27
valley
and *r.* to Zebulun on the south | Jos 19:34
side
and *r.* to Asher on the west | Jos 19:34
side
in a rage that *r.* up unto | 2Ch 28:9
heaven
thy faithfulness *r.* unto the | Ps 36:5
clouds
and thy truth *r.* unto the | Ps 108:4
clouds
r. forth her hands to the needy | Pr 31:20
the sword *r.* unto the soul | Jer 4:10
because it *r.* unto thine heart | Jer 4:18
for her judgment *r.* unto | Jer 51:9
heaven
is grown, and *r.* unto heaven | Da 4:22

REACHING

cubits, *r.* to the wall of the | 2Ch 3:11
house
r. to the wing of the other | 2Ch 3:11
cherub
cubits, *r.* to the wall of the | 2Ch 3:12
house
r. forth unto those things | Ph'p 3:13
which

READ

r. in the audience of the people | Ex 24:7
r. therein all the days of his | De 17:19
life
shalt *r.* this law before all | De 31:11
Israel
he *r.* all the words of the law | Jos 8:34
which Joshua *r.* not before all | Jos 8:35
the king of Israel had *r.* the | 2Ki 5:7
letter
hand of the messengers, and | 2Ki 19:14
r. it
the book to Shaphan, and he | 2Ki 22:8
r. it
And Shaphan *r.* it before the | 2Ki 22:10
king
which the king of Judah hath | 2Ki 22:16
r.
he *r.* in their ears all the | 2Ki 23:2
words of
And Shaphan *r.* it before the | 2Ch 34:18
king

have *r.* before the king of | 2Ch 34:24
Judah
he *r.* in their ears all the | 2Ch 34:30
words of
hath been plainly *r.* before me | Ezr 4:18
Artaxerxes' letter was *r.* before | Ezr 4:23
And he *r.* therein before the | Ne 8:3
street
they *r.* in the book in the law of | Ne 8:8
God
he *r.* in the book of the law of | Ne 8:18
God
r. in the book of the law of the | Ne 9:3
Lord
day they *r.* in the book of | Ne 13:1
Moses
and they were *r.* before the king | Es 6:1
R. this, I pray thee: and he | Isa 29:11;
saith | 29:12
out of the book of the Lord, | Isa 34:16
and *r.*
hand of the messengers, and | Isa 37:14
r. it
Zephaniah the priest *r.* this | Jer 29:29
letter
Therefore go thou, and *r.* in | Jer 36:6
the roll
shalt *r.* them in the ears of all | Jer 36:6
Judah
r. Baruch in the book the | Jer 36:10
words of
when Baruch *r.* the book in | Jer 36:13
the ears
roll wherein thou hast *r.* in | Jer 36:14
the ears
Sit down now, and *r.* it in our | Jer 36:15
ears
ears. So Baruch *r.* it in their | Jer 36:15
ears
Jehudi *r.* it in the ears of the | Jer 36:21
king
Jehudi had *r.* three or four | Jer 36:23
leaves
see, and shalt *r.* all these | Jer 51:61
words
Whosoever shall *r.* this writing | Da 5:7
but they could not *r.* the writing | Da 5:8
that they should *r.* this writing | Da 5:15
now if thou canst *r.* the writing | Da 5:16
I will *r.* the writing unto the | Da 5:17
king
Have ye not *r.* what David | M't 12:3
did
Or have ye not *r.* in the law, | M't 12:5
how
Have ye not *r.* that he which | M't 19:4
made
have ye never *r.*, Out of the | M't 21:16
mouth
Did ye never *r.* in the | M't 21:42
scriptures
have ye not *r.* that which was | M't 22:31
spoken
Have ye never *r.* what David | M'k 2:25
did
And have ye not *r.* this | M'k 12:10
scripture
have ye not *r.* in the book of | M'k 12:26
Moses
sabbath day, and stood up for | Lu 4:16
to *r.*
Have ye not *r.* so much as this, | Lu 6:3
what
This title then *r.* many of the | Joh 19:20
Jews
in his chariot *r.* Esaias the | Ac 8:28
prophet
heard him *r.* the prophet | Ac 8:30
Esaias
the scripture which he *r.* was | Ac 8:32
prophets which are *r.* every | Ac 13:27
sabbath
being *r.* in the synagogues | Ac 15:21
every
when they had *r.* they rejoiced | Ac 15:31
when the governor had *r.* the | Ac 23:34
letter
than what ye *r.* or | 2Co 1:13
acknowledge
our hearts, known and *r.* of all | 2Co 3:2
men
even unto this day, when | 2Co 3:15
Moses is *r.*
when ye *r.* ye may understand | Eph 3:4
my
when this epistle is *r.* among | Col 4:16
you
that it be *r.* also in the church | Col 4:16
r. the epistle from Laodicea | Col 4:16

be *r.* unto all the holy | 1Th 5:27
brethren
worthy to open and to *r.* the | Re 5:4
book

READEST

is written in the law? how *r.* | Lu 10:26
thou
Understandest thou what thou | Ac 8:30
r.

READETH

tables, that he may run that *r.* | Hab 2:2
(whoso *r.* let him understand | M't 24:15
(let him that *r.* understands,) | M'k 13:14
then
Blessed is he that *r.* and they | Ro 1:3

READINESS

received the word with all *r.* | Ac 17:11
by the *r.* of others (B) | 2Co 8:8
that as there was a *r.* to will | 2Co 8:11
I know your *r.* (E)(R)(S) | 2Co 9:2
a *r.* to revenge all | 2Co 10:6
disobedience

READING

caused them to understand the | Ne 8:8
r.
r. in the book words of the | Jer 36:8
Lord
hast made an end of *r.* this | Jer 51:63
book
the *r.* of the law and the | Ac 13:15
prophets
away in the *r.* of the old | 2Co 3:14
testament
Till I come, give attendance to | 1Ti 4:13
r.

READY

Make *r.* quickly three measures | Ge 18:6
men home, and slay, and | Ge 43:16
make *r.*
made *r.* the present against | Ge 43:25
Joseph
And Joseph made *r.* his | Ge 46:29
chariot
he made *r.* his chariot, and | Ex 14:6
took
they be almost *r.* to stone me | Ex 17:4
And be *r.* against the third | Ex 19:11
people. Be *r.* against the third | Ex 19:15
day
And be *r.* in the morning, and | Ex 34:2
come
But we ourselves will go *r.* | Nu 32:17
armed
ye were *r.* to go up into the hill | De 1:41
Syrian *r.* to perish was my | De 26:5
father
far from the city, but be ye all | Jos 8:4
r.
Gideon went in, and made *r.* a | J'g 6:19
kid
we shall have made *r.* a kid | J'g 13:15
for thee
and five sheep *r.* dressed, and | 1Sa 25:18
five
thy servants are *r.* to do | 2Sa 15:15
whatsoever
that thou hast no tidings *r.* | 2Sa 18:22
was built of stone made *r.* | 1Ki 6:7
before
And Joram said, Make *r.* | 2Ki 9:21
And his chariot was made *r.* | 2Ki 9:21
bands that were *r.* armed to | 1Ch 12:23
the war
eight hundred, *r.* armed to | 1Ch 12:24
the war
and had made *r.* for the | 1Ch 28:2
building
thousand *r.* prepared for the | 2Ch 17:18
war
they made *r.* for themselves | 2Ch 35:14
a *r.* scribe in the law of Moses | Ezr 7:6
but thou art a God *r.* to | Ne 9:17
pardon
they should be *r.* against that | Es 3:14
day
Jews should be *r.* against that | Es 8:13
day
are *r.* to raise up their | Job 3:8
mourning

He that is *r.* to slip with his feet   Job 12:5
day of darkness is *r.* at his hand   Job 15:23
him, as a king *r.* to the battle   Job 15:24
which are *r.* to become heaps   Job 15:28
are extinct, the graves are *r.* for me   Job 17:1
destruction shall be *r.* at his side   Job 18:12
ruin *r.* for his stumbling (B)   Job 18:12
blessing of him that was *r.* to perish   Job 29:13
it is *r.* to burst like new bottles   Job 32:19
hath bent his bow, and made it *r.*   Ps 7:12
make *r.* their arrow upon the string   Ps 11:2
thou shalt make *r.* thine arrows   Ps 21:12
I am *r.* to halt, and my sorrow   Ps 38:17
tongue is the pen of a *r.* writer   Ps 45:1
Lord, art good, and *r.* to forgive   Ps 86:5
and *r.* to die from my youth up   Ps 88:15
and those that are *r.* to be slain   Pr 24:11
drink unto him that is *r.* to perish   Pr 31:6
be more *r.* to hear, than to give   Ec 5:1
r. to perish in the land of Assyria   Isa 27:13
shall be to you as a breach *r.* to fall   Isa 30:13
shall be *r.* to speak plainly   Isa 32:4
The Lord was *r.* to save me   Isa 38:20
saying, It is *r.* for the soldering   Isa 41:7
as if he were *r.* to destroy   Isa 51:13
· the trumpet, even to make all *r.*   Eze 7:14
if ye be *r.* that at what time ye   Da 3:15
made *r.* their heart like an oven   Ho 7:6
are killed, and all things are *r.*   M't 22:4
The wedding is *r.* but they which   M't 22:8
Therefore be ye also *r.*: for   M't 24:44
in such
they that were *r.* went in with him   M't 25:10
and they made *r.* the passover   M't 26:19
prepared: there make *r.* for us   M'k 14:15
and they made *r.* the passover   M'k 14:16
The spirit truly is *r.* but the flesh   M'k 14:38
r. a people prepared for the Lord   Lu 1:17
unto him, was sick, and *r.* to die   Lu 7:2
Samaritans, to make *r.* for him   Lu 9:52
Be ye therefore *r.* also: for   Lu 12:40
Come; for all things are now *r.*   Lu 14:17
Make *r.* wherewith I may sup   Lu 17:8
room furnished: there make *r.*   Lu 22:12
and they made *r.* the passover   Lu 22:13
Lord, I am *r.* to go with thee, both   Lu 22:33
come: but your time is alway *r.*   Joh 7:6
they made *r.* he fell into a trance   Ac 10:10
r. to depart on the morrow   Ac 20:7
I am *r.* not to be bound only, but   Ac 21:13
he come near, are *r.* to kill him   Ac 23:15
now are they *r.* looking for a   Ac 23:21
Make *r.* two hundred soldiers   Ac 23:23
am *r.* to preach the gospel to you   Ro 1:15
and declaration of your *r.* mind   1Co 8:19
Achaia was *r.* a year ago; and   1Co 9:2
that, as I said, ye may be *r.*   1Co 9:3
that the same might be *r.* as a   1Co 9:5
line of things made *r.* to our hand   1Co 10:16
third time I am *r.* to come to you   1Co 12:14
in good works, *r.* to distribute   1Ti 6:18
For I am now *r.* to be offered   2Ti 4:6
to be *r.* to every good work   Tit 3:1
waxeth old is *r.* to vanish away   Heb 8:13
r. to be revealed in the last time   1Pe 1:5

and be *r.* always to give an answer   1Pe 3:15
r. to judge the quick and the dead   1Pe 4:5
for filthy lucre, but of a *r.* mind   1Pe 5:2
which remain, that are *r.* to die   Re 3:2
the woman *r.* to be delivered   Re 12:4
and his wife hath made herself *r.*   Re 19:7

REAFFIRM

r. your love for him (R)   2Co 2:8

REAIA

Micah his son, R. his son, Baal   1Ch 5:5

REAIAH

And R. the son of Shobal begat   1Ch 4:2
of Gahar, the children of R.   Ezr 2:47
The children of R. the children   Ne 7:50

REAL

r. riches (N)   Lu 16:11
Joh 1:9; 4:23; 6:32; 15:1; Ac 12:9; Heb 8:2; 1Jo 5:20
reveal yourself - make yourself *r.* (A)   Joh 14:22
I am the *r.* vine (P)   Joh 15:1
r. tabernacle (B)(P)   Heb 8:2; 9:24
the *r.* God and *r.* eternal life   1Jo 5:20

REALITY

prove the *r.* of your love (P)   2Co 8:8
symbol of *r.* (N)   Heb 9:24

REALIZE

r. what it means (B)   Nu 14:34

REALIZED

Gideon *r.* he was an angel (E)   J'g 6:22
I *r.* that God had not (B)   Ne 6:12
they *r.* he was talking (P)   M't 21:45
Jesus *r.* instantly (P)   M'k 2:8
they *r.* he had seen (N)(P)   Lu 1:22
r. what was going on (P)   Lu 5:22

REALLY

will God *r.* dwell with men (S)   2Ch 6:18

REALM

in all his *r.* (A)(R)   2Ki 20:13
the *r.* of Jehoshaphat was quiet   2Ch 20:30
his priests and Levites, in my *r.*   Ezr 7:13
wrath against the *r.* of the king   Ezr 7:23
astrologers that were in all his *r.*   Da 1:20
to set him over the whole *r.*   Da 6:3
king over the *r.* of the Chaldeans   Da 9:1
stir up all against the *r.* of Grecia   Da 11:2
r. of spirits (N)   Ro 8:38
thoughts dwell on higher *r.* (N)   Col 3:2

REAP

ye *r.* the harvest of your land   Le 19:9
shalt not wholly *r.* the corners   Le 19:9
and shall *r.* the harvest thereof   Le 23:10
ye *r.* the harvest of your land   Le 23:22
of thy harvest thou shalt not *r.*   Le 25:5
neither *r.* that which groweth   Le 25:11
eyes be on the field that they do *r.*   Ru 2:9
his ground, and to *r.* his harvest   1Sa 8:12
in the third year sow ye, and *r.*   2Ki 19:29
and sow wickedness, *r.* the same   Job 4:8
r. every one his corn in the field   Job 24:6
that sow in tears shall *r.* in joy   Ps 126:5
soweth iniquity shall *r.* vanity   Pr 22:8
regardeth the clouds shall not *r.*   Ec 11:4
in the third year sow ye, and *r.*   Isa 37:30

sown wheat, but shall *r.* thorns   Jer 12:13
and they shall *r.* the whirlwind   Ho 8:7
in righteousness, *r.* in mercy   Ho 10:12
shalt sow, but thou shalt not *r.*   Mic 6:15
neither do they *r.* nor gather   M't 6:26
I *r.* where I sowed not, and gather   M't 25:26
ravens: for they neither sow nor *r.*   Lu 12:24
to *r.* that whereon ye bestowed no   Joh 4:38
r. some harvest among you (B)(R)   Ro 1:13
what harvest did you *r.* (P)   Ro 6:21
if we shall *r.* your carnal things   1Co 9:11
sparingly shall *r.* also sparingly   2Co 9:6
bountifully shall *r.* bountifully   2Co 9:6
man soweth, that shall he also *r.*   Ga 6:7
shall of the flesh *r.* corruption   Ga 6:8
of the Spirit *r.* life everlasting   Ga 6:8
for in due season we shall *r.* if   Ga 6:9
Thrust in thy sickle, and *r.*   Ro 14:15
for the time is come for thee to *r.*   Ro 14:15

REAPED

wickedness, ye have *r.* iniquity   Ho 10:13
who have *r.* down your fields   Jas 5:4
the cries of them which have *r.*   Jas 5:4
the earth; and the earth was *r.*   Ro 14:16

REAPER

as when the *r.* gathereth corn (S)   Isa 17:5
the plowman shall overtake the *r.*   Am 9:13

REAPERS

gleaned in the field after the *r.*   Ru 2:3
said unto the *r.*, The Lord be   Ru 2:4
his servant that was set over the *r.*   Ru 2:5
the servant that was set over the *r.*   Ru 2:6
after the *r.* among the sheaves   Ru 2:7
And she sat beside the *r.*: and he   Ru 2:14
he went out to his father to the *r.*   2Ki 4:18
I will say to the *r.* Gather ye   M't 13:30
world; and *r.* are the angels   M't 13:39

REAPEST

corners of thy field when thou   Le 23:22
and *r.* that thou didst not sow   Lu 19:21

REAPETH

and *r.* the ears with his arm   Isa 17:5
he that *r.* receiveth wages, and   Joh 4:36
he that *r.* may rejoice together   Joh 4:36
true, One soweth, and another *r.*   Joh 4:37

REAPING

were *r.* their wheat harvest in   1Sa 6:13
r. where thou hast not sown   M't 25:24
down, and *r.* that I did not sow   Lu 19:22

REAR

thou shalt *r.* up the tabernacle   Ex 26:30
neither *r.* you up a standing image   Le 26:1
the *r.* guard (S)   Nu 10:25; Jos 6:9, 13; Isa 52:12; 58:8
those in the *r.* (S)   De 25:18
smite the *r.* of them (S)   Jos 10:19
passed on in the *r.* (S)   1Sa 29:2
Go up, *r.* an altar unto the Lord in   2Sa 24:18
the *r.* sections (S)   1Ki 7:25; 2Ch 4:4
his *r.* part toward the sea (S)   Joe 2:20
wilt thou *r.* it up in three days   Joh 2:20

REARED

that the tabernacle was r. up	Ex 40:17
Moses r. up the tabernacle	Ex 40:18
bars thereof, and r. up his pillars	Ex 40:18
And he r. up the court round about	Ex 40:33
day that the tabernacle was r. up	Nu 9:15
and r. up for himself a pillar	2Sa 18:18
And he r. up an altar for Baal in	1Ki 16:32
and he r. up altars for Baal	2Ki 21:3
And he r. up the pillars before the	2Ch 3:17
and he r. up altars for Baalim, and	2Ch 33:3
r. and brought up (R)	Isa 1:2

REASON

in the land by r. of that famine	Ge 41:31
because of (A)	Ge 41:31; Ex 2:23; De 5:5; Jos 9:13
Canaan fainted by r. of the famine	Ge 47:13
Israel sighed by r. of the bondage	Ex 2:23
on account of (B)	Ex 2:23
up unto God by r. of the bondage	Ex 2:23
cry by r. of their taskmasters	Ex 3:7
corrupted by r. of the swarm of flies	Ex 8:24
shall be unclean by r. of a dead body	Nu 9:10
I given them by r. of the anointing	Nu 18:8
And ye shall bear no sin by r.	Nu 18:32
for ye were afraid by r. of the fire	De 5:5
that is not clean by r. of uncleanness	De 23:10
this is the r. why Joshua (S)	Jos 5:4
old by r. of the very long journey	Jos 9:13
by r. of them that oppressed them	J'g 2:18
may r. with you before the Lord	1Sa 12:7
plead with (A)	1Sa 12:7
this is the r. of the levy which	1Ki 9:15
for his eyes were set by r. of his age	1Ki 14:4
stand to minister by r. of the	2Ch 5:14
by r. of this great multitude	2Ch 20:15
fall out by r. of the sickness day	2Ch 21:15
fell out by r. of his sickness	2Ch 21:19
which are blackish by r. of the ice	Job 6:16
choose out of my words to r. with him	Job 9:14
and I desire to r. with God	Job 13:3
argue my case with God (B)(R)	Job 13:3
Should he r. with unprofitable talk	Job 15:3
arguing with pointless talk (B)	Job 15:3
argue with unprofitable talk (R)	Job 15:3
Mine eye also is dim by r. of sorrow	Job 17:7
and by r. of his highness I could not	Job 31:23
By r. of the multitude of oppressions	Job 35:9
because of (A)(B)(R)	Job 35:9; 37:19
cry out by r. of the arm of the mighty	Job 35:9
our speech by r. of darkness	Job 37:19
by r. of breakings purify themselves	Job 41:25
have roared by r. of the disquietness	Ps 38:8
because of (B)(R)	Ps 38:8
by r. of the enemy and avenger	Ps 44:16
because of (A)(B)	Ps 44:16; 88:9
man that shouteth by r. of wine	Ps 78:65
eye mourneth by r. of affliction	Ps 88:9
if by r. of strength they be fourscore	Ps 90:10
By r. of the voice of my groaning my	Ps 102:5
because of (A)(B)(R)	Ps 102:5
will not plow by r. of the cold	Pr 20:4
seven men that can render a r.	Pr 26:16
out wisdom, and the r. of things	Ec 7:25
Come now, and let us r. together	Isa 1:18
let us adjudge the matter (B)	Isa 1:18
too narrow by r. of the inhabitants	Isa 49:19
plead and r. with you (A)(E)(R)	Jer 12:1
full of branches by r. of many waters	Eze 19:10
terrors by r. of the sword shall be	Eze 21:12
By r. of the abundance of his horses	Eze 26:10
thy merchant by r. of the multitude	Eze 27:12; 27:16
wisdom by r. of thy brightness	Eze 28:17
time my r. returned unto me	Da 4:36
by r. of the words of the king	Da 5:10
because of (B)(R)	Da 5:10
daily sacrifice by r. of transgression	Da 8:12
I cried by r. of mine affliction unto	Jon 2:2
noise by r. of the multitude of men	Mic 2:12
why r. ye among yourselves	M't 16:8
discussing among yourselves (A)(B)(R)	M't 16:8
why all this argument (P)	M't 16:8
Why r. ye these things in your	M'k 2:8
Why r. ye, because ye have no	M'k 8:17
and the Pharisees began to r.	Lu 5:21
them, What r. ye in your hearts	Lu 5:22
sea arose by r. of a great wind	Joh 6:18
by r. of him many of the Jews	Joh 12:11
on his account (A)(B)(N)(R)	Joh 12:11
It is not r. that we should leave	Ac 6:2
r. would that I should bear with	Ac 18:14
up to depraved r. (N)	Ro 1:28
battling principles of r. (B)(N)	Ro 7:23
I r. that the sufferings (B)	Ro 8:18
by r. of him who hath subjected	Ro 8:20
the sword without r. (B)	Ro 13:4
by r. of the glory that excelleth	2Co 3:10
lost the power to r. (N)	2Ti 3:8
by r. hereof he ought, as for	Heb 5:3
who by r. of use have their senses	Heb 5:14
suffered to continue by r. of death	Heb 7:23
willing to yield to r. (A)(N)(R)	Jas 3:17
a r. of the hope that is in you	1Pe 3:15
by r. of whom the way of truth	2Pe 2:2
because of them (A)(R)	2Pe 2:2
on whose account (B)	2Pe 2:2
earth by r. of the other voices	Re 8:13
because of (A)(B)	Re 8:13
by r. of the smoke of the pit	Re 9:2
in the sea by r. of her costliness	Re 18:19

REASONABLE

unto God, which is your r. service	Ro 12:1

REASONED

they r. among themselves, saying	M't 16:7
discussed it among themselves (R)	M't 16:7; Lu 20:5
they argued among themselves (B)	M't 16:7; 21:25; M'k 11:31; Lu 20:5, 14
they r. among themselves, saying	M't 21:25
they argued among themselves (N)(P)(R)	M't 21:25
that they so r. among themselves (A)	M'k 2:8
debated within themselves (A)	M'k 2:8
questioned within themselves (R)	M'k 2:8
they r. among themselves, saying	M'k 8:16
they r. with themselves, saying. If	M'k 11:31
r., questioned in hearts (A)(E)	Lu 3:15
they r. with themselves, saying, If	Lu 20:5
they r. among themselves, saying	Lu 20:14
they argued with themselves (A)	Lu 20:14
talked it all over together (N)	Lu 20:14
they communed together and r.	Lu 24:15
conversing and discussing together (A)	Lu 24:15
r. with them out of the scriptures	Ac 17:2
discussed with them out of the scriptures (B)	Ac 17:2
argued with them from the scriptures (N)(P)(R)	Ac 17:2
r. with Jews (A)(E)	Ac 17:17
r. in the synagogue every sabbath	Ac 18:4
discoursed and argued (A)(B)(R)	Ac 18:4
he held discussions in the synagogue (P)	Ac 18:4
synagogue, and r. with the Jews	Ac 18:19
And as he r. of righteousness	Ac 24:25
continued to argue about uprightness (A)	Ac 24:25
discussed purity of life (B)	Ac 24:25
talking about goodness (N)	Ac 24:25
discourse turned to the question of morals (P)	Ac 24:25
argued about justice (R)	Ac 24:25

REASONING

Hear now my r. and hearken to	Job 13:6
listen to my pleadings (B)	Job 13:6
sitting there, and r. in their hearts	M'k 2:6
holding a dialogue (A)	M'k 2:6
argued in their minds (B)	M'k 2:6
silently asking themselves (N)	M'k 2:6
they thought to themselves (P)	M'k 2:6
questioning in their hearts (R)	M'k 2:6
r. on way (E)	M'k 9:33
having heard them r. together	M'k 12:28
listened to them disputing (A)	M'k 12:28
listened to the discussions (B)(N)(P)	M'k 12:28
disputing with one another (R)	M'k 12:28
Then there arose a r. among them	Lu 9:46
there arose a controversy (A)	Lu 9:46
there came a discussion (B)	Lu 9:46
an argument arose (N)(R)	Lu 9:46
a dispute arose (P)	Lu 9:46
had great r. among themselves (A)	Ac 28:29
arguing and disputing among (A)	Ac 28:29
had considerable discussion (B)	Ac 28:29
r. powers atrophied (N)	1Ti 6:5

REASONINGS

became vain in r. (E)	Ro 1:21
refute arguments, theories, r. (A)	2Co 10:5

REASONS

I gave ear to your r. whilst ye	Job 32:11
bring forth your strong r. saith the	Isa 41:21

REASSURING

r. and encouraging (B)(N)	Ac 14:22

REBA

Hur, and R. five kings of Midian	Nu 31:18
and R. which were dukes of Sihon	Jos 13:21

REBECCA

R. also had conceived by one, even	Ro 9:10

REBEKAH

Bethuel begat R.; these eight	Ge 22:23
R. came out, who was born to	Ge 24:15

REBEKAH

R. had a brother, and his name was   *Ge 24:29*
he heard the words of *R.* his sister   *Ge 24:30*
R. came forth with her pitcher on   *Ge 24:45*
R. is before thee, take her, and go   *Ge 24:51*
and raiment, and gave them to *R.*   *Ge 24:53*
they called *R.* and said unto   *Ge 24:58*
they sent away *R.* their sister   *Ge 24:59*
they blessed *R.* and said unto her   *Ge 24:60*
R. arose, and her damsels, and they   *Ge 24:61*
servant took *R.* and went his way   *Ge 24:61*
R. lifted up her eyes, and when she   *Ge 24:64*
took *R.* and she became his wife   *Ge 24:67*
years old when he took *R.* to wife   *Ge 25:20*
of him, and *R.* his wife conceived   *Ge 25:21*
of his venison: but *R.* loved Jacob   *Ge 25:28*
of the place should kill me for *R.*   *Ge 26:7*
was sporting with *R.* his wife   *Ge 26:8*
grief of mind unto Isaac and to *R.*   *Ge 26:35*
R. heard when Isaac spake to Esau   *Ge 27:5*
And *R.* spake unto Jacob her son   *Ge 27:6*
Jacob said to *R.* his mother, Behold   *Ge 27:11*
And *R.* took goodly raiment of her   *Ge 27:15*
Esau her elder son were told to *R.*   *Ge 27:42*
R. said to Isaac, I am weary of my   *Ge 27:46*
the Syrian, the brother of *R.*   *Ge 28:5*
they buried Isaac and *R.* his wife   *Ge 49:31*

REBEKAH'S

brother, and that he was *R.* son   *Ge 29:12*
But Deborah *R.* nurse died, and   *Ge 35:8*

REBEL

do not *r.* against him (R)   *Ex 23:21*
Only *r.* not ye against the Lord   *Nu 14:9*
doth *r.* against thy commandment   *Jos 1:18*
r. this day against the Lord   *Jos 22:16*
seeing ye *r.* to-day against the Lord   *Jos 22:18*
but *r.* not against the Lord, nor   *Jos 22:19*
against the Lord, nor *r.* against us   *Jos 22:19*
God forbid that we should *r.* against   *Jos 22:29*
not *r.* against the commandment   *1Sa 12:14*
but *r.* against the commandment   *1Sa 12:15*
ye do? will ye *r.* against the king   *Ne 2:19*
that thou and the Jews think to *r.*   *Ne 6:6*
of those that *r.* against the light   *Job 24:13*
But if ye refuse and *r.* ye shall be   *Isa 1:20*
and wine, and they *r.* against me   *Ho 7:14*
r. against God's plan of life (P)   *Ro 2:8*

REBELLED

and in the thirteenth year they *r.*   *Ge 14:4*
because ye *r.* against my word   *Nu 20:24*
ye *r.* against my commandment in   *Nu 27:14*
r. against the commandment   *Nu 27:14*
but *r.* against the commandment   *De 1:26; 1:43*
you *r.* against the Lord (B)   *De 1:43*
ye *r.* against the commandment of   *De 9:23*
So Israel *r.* against the house of   *1Ki 12:19*

because thou hast *r.* (B)   *1Ki 13:21*
Then Moab *r.* against Israel after   *2Ki 1:1*
Moab *r.* against the king of Israel   *2Ki 3:5*
king of Moab hath *r.* against me   *2Ki 3:7*
he *r.* against the king of Assyria   *2Ki 18:7*
then he turned and *r.* against him   *2Ki 24:1*
Zedekiah *r.* against the king of   *2Ki 24:20*
And Israel *r.* against the house of   *2Ch 10:19*
up, and hath *r.* against his lord   *2Ch 13:6*
r. against king Nebuchadnezzar   *2Ch 36:13*
disobedient, and *r.* against thee   *Ne 9:26*
for they have *r.* against thee   *Ps 5:10*
defied and *r.* in (A)(E)(R)   *Ps 78:40*
and they *r.* not against his word   *Ps 105:28*
they *r.* against the words of God   *Ps 107:11*
and they have *r.* against me   *Isa 1:2*
r. against me (B)   *Isa 43:27; 66:24; Jer 2:8, 29; 3:13*
they *r.* and vexed his holy Spirit   *Isa 63:10*
r. against me (R)   *Isa 66:24; Jer 2:29; 3:13; Eze 2:3; Ho 7:13; Eph 3:11*
r. and revolted against me (A)(R)   *Jer 2:29*
Zedekiah *r.* against the king of   *Jer 52:3*
r. against his commandment   *La 1:18*
for I have grievously *r.*: abroad   *La 1:20*
We have transgressed and have *r.*   *La 3:42*
nation that hath *r.* against me   *Eze 2:3*
he *r.* against him in sending his   *Eze 17:15*
they *r.* against me, and would not   *Eze 20:8*
r. against me in the wilderness   *Eze 20:13*
the children *r.* against me: they   *Eze 20:21*
have *r.* even by departing from   *Da 9:5*
though we have *r.* against him   *Da 9:9*
for she hath *r.* against her God   *Ho 13:16*

REBELLEST

trust, that thou *r.* against me   *2Ki 18:20; Isa 36:15*

REBELLING

destroyed themselves by *r.* (P)   *Jude 11*

REBELLION

I know thy *r.* and thy stiff neck   *De 31:27*
if it be in *r.* or if in transgression   *Jos 22:22*
if it was in *r.* (R)   *Jos 22:22*
For *r.* is as the sin of witchcraft   *1Sa 15:23*
his *r.* (B)   *2Ch 33:19*
r. and sedition have been made   *Ezr 4:19*
r. and revolution made (B)   *Ezr 4:19*
in their *r.* appointed a captain to   *Ne 9:17*
For he addeth *r.* unto his sin, he   *Job 34:37*
An evil man seeketh only *r.*   *Pr 17:11*
hast taught *r.* against the Lord   *Jer 28:16*
he hath taught *r.* against the Lord   *Jer 29:32*
final *r.* comes first (N)(R)   *2Th 2:3*
grow stubborn as in *r.* (B)(R)   *Heb 3:15*
r. of Korah (A)(N)(P)(R)   *Jude 11*

REBELLIONS

not forgive your *r.* (B)   *Jos 24:19; Jer 5:6*

REBELLIOUS

ye have been *r.* against the Lord   *De 9:7*
Ye have been *r.* against the Lord   *De 9:24*

a man have a stubborn and *r.* son   *De 21:18*
This our son is stubborn and *r.* he   *De 21:20*
ye have been *r.* against the Lord   *De 31:27*
son of the perverse *r.* woman, do   *1Sa 20:30*
son of *r.* woman (B)   *1Sa 20:30*
building the *r.* and the bad city   *Ezr 4:12*
and know that this city is a *r.* city   *Ezr 4:15*
let not the *r.* exalt themselves   *Ps 66:7*
but the *r.* dwell in a dry land   *Ps 68:6*
yea, for the *r.* also, that the Lord   *Ps 68:18*
a stubborn and *r.* generation; a   *Ps 78:8*
repeatedly reverted to *r.* ways   *Ps 106:43 (B)*
were *r.* in their purpose (R)   *Ps 106:43*
princes are *r.* and companions of   *Isa 1:23*
Woe to the *r.* children, saith   *Isa 30:1*
this is a *r.* people, lying children   *Isa 30:9*
I was not *r.* neither turned away   *Isa 50:5*
hands all the day unto a *r.* people   *Isa 65:2*
she hath been *r.* against me, saith   *Jer 4:17*
hath a revolting and a *r.* heart   *Jer 5:23*
to a *r.* nation that hath rebelled   *Eze 2:3*
(for they are a *r.* house,) yet shall   *Eze 2:5*
looks, though they be a *r.* house   *Eze 2:6*
will forbear; for they are most *r.*   *Eze 2:7*
Be not thou *r.* like that *r.* house   *Eze 3:9*
looks, though they be a *r.* house   *Eze 3:9*
a reprover: for they are a *r.* house   *Eze 3:26*
forbear: for they are a *r.* house   *Eze 3:27*
dwellest in the midst of a *r.* house   *Eze 12:2*
hear not: for they are a *r.* house   *Eze 12:2*
consider, though they be a *r.* house   *Eze 12:3*
the house of Israel, the *r.* house   *Eze 12:9*
O *r.* house, will I say the word, and   *Eze 12:25*
Say now to the *r.* house, Know ye   *Eze 17:12*
utter a parable unto the *r.* house   *Eze 24:3*
thou shalt say to the *r.* even to   *Eze 44:6*
defiant, *r.* (A)(B)(E)(R)   *Zep 3:1*
unbelieving and *r.* generation (B)   *M't 17:17*

REBELS

who defiantly *r.* (B)   *Nu 15:30*
kept for a token against the *r.*   *Nu 17:10*
Hear now, ye *r.*; must we fetch   *Nu 20:10*
r. and sinners (A)(R)   *Isa 1:28; 46:8*
purge out from among you the *r.*   *Eze 20:38*
in custody with *r.* (N)   *M'k 15:7*

REBIRTH

saved through water of *r.* (N)   *Tit 3:5*

REBUKE

in any wise *r.* thy neighbour   *Le 19:17*
upon thee cursing, vexation *r.*   *De 28:20*
may glean them, and *r.* her not   *Ru 2:16*
day is a day of trouble, and of *r.*   *2Ki 19:3*
our fathers look thereon, and *r.* it   *1Ch 12:17*
r. that putteth to shame (S)   *Job 20:3*
O Lord, *r.* me not in thine anger   *Ps 6:1*
were discovered at thy *r.* O Lord   *Ps 18:15*
O Lord, *r.* me not in thy wrath   *Ps 38:1*
R. the company of spearmen   *Ps 68:30*
At thy *r.*, O God of Jacob, both   *Ps 76:6*
perish at the *r.* of thy countenance   *Ps 80:16*

At thy *r.* they fled; at the voice   *Ps 104:7*
r. a wise man, and he will love   *Pr 9:8*
but a scorner heareth not *r.*   *Pr 13:1*
riches: but the poor heareth   *Pr 13:8*
not *r.*
them that *r.* him shall be   *Pr 24:25*
delight
Open *r.* is better than secret   *Pr 27:5*
love
is better to hear the *r.* of the   *Ec 7:5*
wise
and shall *r.* many people   *Isa 2:4*
God shall *r.* them, and they   *Isa 17:13*
shall
r. of his people shall he take   *Isa 25:8*
away
shall flee at the *r.* of one; at   *Isa 30:17*
at the *r.* of five shall ye flee: *Isa 30:17*
till ye
day is a day of trouble, and of   *Isa 37:3*
r.
behold, at my *r.* I dry up the   *Isa 50:2*
sea, I
fury of the Lord, the *r.* of thy   *Isa 51:20*
God
be wroth with thee nor *r.* thee   *Isa 54:9*
fury, and his *r.* with flames of   *Isa 66:15*
fire
for thy sake I have suffered *r.*   *Jer 15:15*
shall be desolate in the day of *r.*   *Ho 5:9*
and *r.* strong nations afar off   *Mic 4:3*
The Lord *r.* thee, O Satan;   *Zec 3:2*
even
hath chosen Jerusalem *r.* thee   *Zec 3:2*
I will *r.* your seed (A)(E)(R)   *Mal 2:3*
r. the devourer for your sakes   *Mal 3:11*
took him, and began to *r.*   *M't 16:22;*
him   *M'k 8:32*
trespass against thee, *r.* him   *Lu 17:3*
unto him, Master *r.* thy   *Lu 19:39*
disciples
the sons of God, without *r.*   *Ph'p 2:15*
in the
R. not an elder, but intreat him   *1Ti 5:1*
Them that sin *r.* before all   *1Ti 5:20*
r. exhort with all longsuffering   *2Ti 4:2*
Wherefore *r.* them sharply,   *Tit 1:13*
that
exhort, and *r.* with all   *Tit 2:15*
authority
but said, The Lord *r.* thee   *Jude 9*
many as I love, I *r.* and chasten   *Re 3:19*

REBUKED

my hands, and *r.* thee   *Ge 31:42*
yesternight
and his father *r.* him, and   *Ge 37:10*
said
and I *r.* the nobles, and the   *Ne 5:7*
rulers
those I *r.* (B)   *Ne 13:15*
Thou hast *r.* the heathen, thou   *Ps 9:5*
He *r.* the Red sea also, and it   *Ps 106:9*
was
hast *r.* the proud that are   *Ps 119:21*
cursed
and *r.* the winds and the sea   *M't 8:26*
And Jesus *r.* the devil; and he   *M't 17:18*
pray: and the disciples *r.*   *M't 19:13*
them
the multitude *r.* them,   *M't 20:31*
because they
And Jesus *r.* him, saying,   *M'k 1:25*
Hold thy
he arose, and *r.* the wind, and   *M'k 4:39*
said
he *r.* Peter, saying, Get thee   *M'k 8:33*
behind
he *r.* the foul spirit, saying   *M'k 9:25*
r. unclean spirit   *M'k 9:25*
(A)(B)(E)(N)
his disciples *r.* those that   *M'k 10:13*
brought
And Jesus *r.* him, saying, Hold   *Lu 4:35*
thy
and *r.* the fever; and it left her   *Lu 4:39*
he arose, and *r.* the wind and   *Lu 4:39*
Jesus *r.* the unclean spirit, and   *Lu 9:42*
he turned, and *r.* them, and   *Lu 9:55*
said
his disciples saw it, they *r.*   *Lu 18:15*
them
they which went before *r.* him   *Lu 18:39*
But the other answering *r.*   *Lu 23:40*
him
nor faint when thou art *r.* of   *Heb 12:5*
him
But was *r.* for his iniquity: the   *2Pe 2:16*

REBUKER

I have been a *r.* of them all   *Ho 5:2*

REBUKES

When thou with *r.* dost correct   *Ps 39:11*
and in fury and in furious *r.*   *Eze 5:15*
upon them with furious *r.*   *Eze 25:17*

REBUKETH

he that *r.* a wicked man getteth   *Pr 9:7*
He that *r.* a man afterwards   *Pr 28:23*
shall
They hate him that *r.* in the   *Am 5:10*
gate
He *r.* the sea, and maketh it dry   *Na 1:4*

REBUKING

discovered, at the *r.* of the   *2Sa 22:16*
Lord
he *r.* them suffered them not to   *Lu 4:41*

RECALCITRANT

unruly, *r.* people (N)   *Ro 10:21*

RECALL

This I *r.* to my mind, therefore   *La 3:21*

RECAPTURED

r. all the loot (B)   *Ge 14:16*

RECEDED

waters *r.* (A)   *Ge 8:3*

RECEIPT

Matthew, sitting at *r.* of   *M't 9:9*
custom
sitting at tax collector's office   *M't 9:9;*
(A)(B)(N)(R)   *M'k 2:14; Lu 5:27*
sitting at the place of toll (E)   *M't 9:9*
at his seat in the custom-house   *M't 9:9*
(P)
Alphæus sitting at the *r.* of   *M'k 2:14*
custom
Levi, sitting at the *r.* of custom   *Lu 5:27*

RECEIVE

mouth to *r.* thy brother's blood   *Ge 4:11*
then *r.* my present at my hand   *Ge 33:10*
to *r.* his pledge from the   *Ge 38:20*
woman's
make his pans to *r.* his ashes   *Ex 27:3*
thou shalt *r.* them of their   *Ex 29:25*
hands
ye *r.* of the children of Israel   *Nu 18:28*
the mount to *r.* the tables of   *De 9:9*
stone
every one shall *r.* of thy words   *De 33:3*
which thou shalt *r.* of their   *1Sa 10:4*
hands
r. a thousand shekels of   *2Sa 18:12*
silver in
there and thou shalt *r.* them   *1Ki 5:9*
too little to *r.* the burnt   *1Ki 8:64*
offerings
whom I stand, I will *r.* none   *2Ki 5:16*
to *r.* money, and to *r.*   *2Ki 5:26*
garments
r. no more money of your   *2Ki 12:7*
to *r.* no more money of the   *2Ki 12:8*
people
not able to *r.* the burnt   *2Ch 7:7*
offerings
we *r.* good at the hand of God   *Job 2:10*
of God, and shall we not *r.*   *Job 2:10*
evil
Why did the knees *r.* me (S)   *Job 3:12*
R. I pray thee, the law from   *Job 22:22*
his
they shall *r.* of the Almighty   *Job 27:13*
the Lord will *r.* my prayer   *Ps 6:9*
r. the blessing from the Lord   *Ps 24:5*
of the grave: for he shall *r.* me   *Ps 49:15*
and afterward *r.* me to glory   *Ps 73:24*
When I shall *r.* the   *Ps 75:2*
congregation I

To *r.* the instruction of wisdom   *Pr 1:3*
My son, if thou wilt *r.* my words   *Pr 2:1*
Hear, O my son, and *r.* my   *Pr 4:10*
sayings
R. my instruction and not   *Pr 8:10*
silver
The wise will *r.*   *Pr 10:8*
commandments
Hear counsel, and *r.*   *Pr 19:20*
instruction
Should I *r.* comfort in these   *Isa 57:6*
they have refused to *r.*   *Jer 5:3*
correction
your ear *r.* the word of his   *Jer 9:20*
mouth
might not hear, nor *r.*   *Jer 17:23*
instruction
have not hearkened to *r.*   *Jer 32:33*
instruction
Will ye not *r.* instruction to   *Jer 35:13*
hearken
speak unto thee *r.* in thine   *Eze 3:10*
heart
when thou shalt *r.* thy sisters,   *Eze 16:61*
thine
shall *r.* no more reproach of   *Eze 36:30*
famine
ye shall *r.* of me gifts and   *Da 2:6*
rewards
Ephraim shall *r.* shame, and   *Ho 10:6*
all iniquity, and *r.* us   *Ho 14:2*
graciously
he shall *r.* of you his standing   *Mic 1:11*
fear me, thou wilt *r.* instruction   *Zep 3:7*
shall not be room enough to   *Mal 3:10*
r. it
whosoever shall not *r.* you,   *M't 10:14*
nor
shall *r.* a prophet's reward   *M't 10:41*
shall *r.* a righteous man's   *M't 10:41*
reward
blind *r.* their sight, and the   *M't 11:5*
lame
if ye will *r.* it, this is Elias,   *M't 11:14*
which
whoso shall *r.* one such little   *M't 18:5*
child
All men cannot *r.* this saying,   *M't 19:11*
save
that is able to *r.* it, let him *r.*   *M't 19:12*
it
shall *r.* an hundredfold, and   *M't 19:29*
shall
is right, that shall ye *r.*   *M't 20:7*
ask in prayer, believing, ye   *M't 21:22*
shall *r.*
that they might *r.* the fruits   *M't 21:34*
of it
ye shall *r.* the greater   *M't 23:14*
damnation
there was no room to *r.* them   *M'k 2:2*
immediately *r.* it with   *M'k 4:16*
gladness
such as hear the word, and *r.*   *M'k 4:20*
it
whosoever shall not *r.* you,   *M'k 6:11*
nor
shall *r.* one of such children   *M'k 9:37*
in
whosoever shall *r.* me,   *M'k 9:37*
receiveth not
shall not *r.* the kingdom of   *M'k 10:15*
God as
he shall *r.* an hundredfold   *M'k 10:30*
now in
Lord, that I might *r.* my   *M'k 10:51*
sight
ye pray, believe that ye *r.*   *M'k 11:24*
them
he might *r.* from the   *M'k 12:2*
husbandmen
these shall *r.* greater   *M'k 12:40*
damnation
to them of whom ye hope to *r.*   *Lu 6:34*
lend to sinners, to *r.* as much   *Lu 6:34*
again
they hear, *r.* the word with joy   *Lu 8:13*
whosoever will not *r.* you,   *Lu 9:5*
when ye
shall *r.* this child in my name   *Lu 9:48*
whosoever shall *r.* me receiveth   *Lu 9:48*
they did not *r.* him, because his   *Lu 9:53*
city ye enter, and they *r.* you,   *Lu 10:8*
eat
they *r.* you not, go your ways   *Lu 10:10*
out
they may *r.* me into their   *Lu 16:4*
houses

they may r. you into everlasting *Lu 16:9*
shall not r. the kingdom of *Lu 18:17*
God as
not r. manifold more in this *Lu 18:30*
present
said, Lord, that I may r. my *Lu 18:41*
sight
Jesus said unto him, R. thy *Lu 18:42*
sight
to r. for himself a kingdom *Lu 19:12*
same shall r. greater *Lu 20:47*
damnation
for we r. the due reward of *Lu 23:41*
our
seen; and ye r. not our witness *Joh 3:11*
A man can r. nothing, except *Joh 3:27*
it be
But I r. not testimony from *Joh 5:34*
man
I r. not honour from men *Joh 5:41*
Father's name, and ye r. me *Joh 5:43*
not
in his own name, him ye will *Joh 5:43*
r.
which r. honour, one of *Joh 5:44*
another
the sabbath day r. *Joh 7:23*
circumcision
they that believe on him *Joh 7:39*
should r.
again, and r. you unto myself *Joh 14:3*
whom the world cannot r. *Joh 14:17*
because
for he shall r. of mine, and *Joh 16:14*
shall
ask, and ye shall r. that your *Joh 16:24*
joy
unto them, R. ye the Holy *Joh 20:22*
Ghost
But ye shall r. power, after that *Ac 1:8*
shall r. the gift of the Holy *Ac 2:38*
Ghost
expecting to r. something of *Ac 3:5*
them
Whom the heaven must r. until *Ac 3:21*
and saying, Lord Jesus, r. my *Ac 7:59*
spirit
that they might r. the Holy *Ac 8:15*
Ghost
hands, he may r. the Holy *Ac 8:19*
Ghost
on him, that he might r. his *Ac 9:12*
sight
that thou mightest r. thy sight *Ac 9:17*
in him shall r. remission of *Ac 10:43*
sins
which are not lawful for us to *Ac 16:21*
r.
exhorting the disciples to r. *Ac 18:27*
him
is more blessed to give than to *Ac 20:35*
r.
unto me, Brother Saul, r. *Ac 22:13*
thy sight
r. thy testimony concerning *Ac 22:18*
me
they may r. forgiveness of sins *Ac 26:18*
they which r. abundance of *Ro 5:17*
grace
shall r. to themselves *Ro 13:2*
damnation
that is weak in the faith r. ye *Ro 14:1*
r. ye one another, as Christ *Ro 15:7*
also
That ye r. her in the Lord, as *Ro 16:2*
man shall r. his own reward *1Co 3:8*
thereupon, he shall r. a *1Co 3:14*
reward
hast thou that thou didst not r. *1Co 4:7*
thou didst r. it why dost thou *1Co 4:7*
glory
that the church may r. *1Co 14:5*
edifying
r. the things done in his body *2Co 5:10*
ye r. not the grace of God in *2Co 6:1*
vain
unclean thing; and I will r. *2Co 6:17*
you
R. us; we have wronged no *2Co 7:2*
man
might r. damage by us in *2Co 7:9*
nothing
intreaty that we would r. the *2Co 8:4*
gift
or if ye r. another spirit, *2Co 11:4*
which ye
as a fool r. me, that I may *2Co 11:16*
boast

might r. the promise of the *Ga 3:14*
Spirit
we might r. the adoption of *Ga 4:5*
sons
the same shall he r. of the Lord *Eph 6:8*
R. him therefore in *Ph'p 2:29*
the Lord with
r. the reward of the *Col 3:24*
inheritance
r. recompense of inheritance *Col 3:24*
(E)
r. for the wrong which he hath *Col 3:25*
if he come unto you, r. him *Col 4:10*
an elder r. not an accusation *1Ti 5:19*
thou therefore r. him, that is *Ph'm 12*
that thou shouldest r. him for *Ph'm 15*
ever .
a partner, r. him as myself *Ph'm 17*
who r. the office of the *Heb 7:5*
priesthood
And here men that die r. tithes *Heb 7:8*
might r. the promise of *Heb 9:15*
eternal
of God, ye might r. the *Heb 10:36*
promise
r. witness (S) *Heb 11:2; 11:39*
should after r. for an *Heb 11:8*
inheritance
he shall r. any thing of the Lord *Jas 1:7*
is tried, he shall r. the crown *Jas 1:12*
of life
r. with meekness the engrafted *Jas 1:21*
shall r. the greater *Jas 3:1*
condemnation
Ye ask, and r. not, because ye *Jas 4:3*
ask amiss
until he r. the early and latter *Jas 5:7*
rain
r. a crown of glory that fadeth *1Pe 5:4*
not
r. the reward of *2Pe 2:13*
unrighteousness
whatsoever we ask, we r. of *1Jo 3:22*
him
If we r. the witness of men, the *1Jo 5:9*
but that we r. a full reward *2Jo 8*
r. him not into your house, *2Jo 10*
neither
We therefore ought to r. such, *3Jo 8*
that
doth he himself r. the brethren *3Jo 10*
to r. glory and honour, and *Re 4:11*
power
Lamb that was slain to r. *Re 5:12*
power
to r. a mark in their right *Re 13:16*
hand
r. his mark in his forehead, or *Re 14:9*
but r. power as kings one *Re 17:12*
hour with
r. royal authority *Re 17:12*
(B)(E)(N)(P)
and that ye r. not of her *Re 18:4*
plagues

RECEIVED

land, and r. in the same year *Ge 26:12*
And he r. them at their hand *Ex 32:4*
they r. of Moses all the offering *Ex 36:3*
after that let her be r. in *Nu 12:14*
again
I have r. commandment to *Nu 23:20*
bless
fathers, have r. their *Nu 34:14*
inheritance
have r. their inheritance *Nu 34:14*
half tribe have r. their *Nu 34:15*
inheritance
the tribe whereunto they are r. *Nu 36:3; 36:4*
Gadites have r. their *Jos 13:8*
inheritance
had not yet r. their inheritance *Jos 18:2*
have r. their inheritance *Jos 18:7*
beyond
would not have r. a burnt *J'g 13:23*
offering
of whose hand have I r. any *1Sa 12:3*
bribe
So David r. of her hand that *1Sa 25:35*
which
merchants r. the linen yarn at *1Ki 10:28*
Hezekiah r. the letter of the *2Ki 19:14*
hand
David r. them, and made *1Ch 12:18*
them
merchants r. the linen yarn at *2Ch 1:16*

r. and held three thousand *2Ch 4:5*
baths
and the priests r. the blood *2Ch 29:22*
they r. at the hand of the *2Ch 30:16*
Levites
from him: but he r. it not *Es 4:4*
and mine ear r. a little thereof *Job 4:12*
thou hast r. gifts for men; yea *Ps 68:18*
looked upon it, and r. *Pr 24:32*
instruction
And Hezekiah r. the letter *Isa 37:14*
from the
for she hath r. of the Lord's *Isa 40:2*
hand
children; they r. no correction *Jer 2:30*
hath not r. usury nor increase *Eze 18:17*
she r. not correction: she *Zep 3:2*
trusted
freely ye have r., freely give *M't 10:8*
he which r. seed by the way *M't 13:19*
side
that r. the seed into stony *M't 13:20*
places
also that r. seed among the *M't 13:22*
thorns
that r. seed into the good *M't 13:23*
ground
they that r. tribute money *M't 17:24*
came to
hour, they r. every man a *M't 20:9*
penny
that they should have r. more *M't 20:10*
they likewise r. every man a *M't 20:10*
penny
And when they had r. it, they *M't 20:11*
and immediately their eyes r. *M't 20:34*
sight
he that had r. the five talents *M't 25:16*
went
And likewise he that had r. *M't 25:17*
two
But he that had r. one went *M't 25:18*
so he that had r. five talents *M't 25:20*
came
also that had r. two talents *M't 25:22*
came
which had r. the one talent *M't 25:24*
came
have r. mine own with usury *M't 25:27*
which they have r. to hold, as *M'k 7:4*
And immediately he r. his *M'k 10:52*
sight
with myrrh: but he r. it not *M'k 15:23*
he was r. up into heaven *M'k 16:19*
and sat
for ye have r. your consolation *Lu 6:24*
returned, the people gladly r. *Lu 8:40*
him
he r. them, and spake unto *Lu 9:11*
them
was come that he should be r. *Lu 9:51*
up
Martha r. him into her house *Lu 10:38*
he hath r. him safe and sound *Lu 15:27*
And immediately he r. his *Lu 18:43*
sight
came down, and r. him joyfully *Lu 19:6*
returned, having r. the *Lu 19:15*
kingdom
his own, and his own r. him *Joh 1:11*
not
as many as r. him, to them *Joh 1:12*
gave
And of his fulness have all we *Joh 1:16*
r.
He that hath r. his testimony *Joh 3:33*
hath
the Galilæans r. him, having *Joh 4:45*
seen
they willingly r. him into the *Joh 6:21*
ship
I went and washed, and I r. *Joh 9:11*
sight
asked him how he had r. his *Joh 9:15*
sight
he had been blind, and r. his *Joh 9:18*
sight
parents of him that had r. his *Joh 9:18*
sight
This commandment have I r. *Joh 10:18*
of
He then having r. the sop *Joh 13:30*
went
they have r. them, and have *Joh 17:8*
known
then, having r. a band of men *Joh 18:3*

Jesus therefore had *r*. the vinegar — *Joh 19:30*
a cloud *r*. him out of their sight — *Ac 1:9*
and having *r*. of the Father the — *Ac 2:33*
gladly *r*. his word were baptized — *Ac 2:41*
feet and ankle bones *r*. strength — *Ac 3:7*
r. the lively oracles to give unto us — *Ac 7:38*
r. the law by the disposition of — *Ac 7:53*
Samaria had *r*. the word of God — *Ac 8:14*
them and they *r*. the Holy Ghost — *Ac 8:17*
he *r*. sight forthwith, and arose — *Ac 9:18*
And when he had *r*. meat he was — *Ac 9:19*
vessel was *r*. up again into heaven — *Ac 10:16*
r. the Holy Ghost as well as we — *Ac 10:47*
Gentiles had also *r*. the word of — *Ac 11:1*
they were *r*. of the church, and — *Ac 15:4*
Who, having *r*. such a charge — *Ac 16:24*
Whom Jason hath *r*.: and these — *Ac 17:7*
they *r*. the word with all readiness — *Ac 17:11*
Have ye *r*. the Holy Ghost since ye — *Ac 19:2*
which I have *r*. of the Lord Jesus — *Ac 20:24*
the brethren *r*. us gladly — *Ac 21:17*
from whom also I *r*. letters unto — *Ac 22:5*
r. authority from the chief priests — *Ac 26:10*
fire, and *r*. us every one, because — *Ac 28:2*
who *r*. us, and lodged us three days — *Ac 28:7*
We neither *r*. letters out of Judæa — *Ac 28:21*
and *r*. all that came in unto him — *Ac 28:30*
we have *r*. grace and apostleship — *Ro 1:5*
And he *r*. the sign of circumcision — *Ro 4:11*
we have now *r*. the atonement — *Ro 5:11*
ye have not *r*. the Spirit of bondage — *Ro 8:15*
ye have *r*. the Spirit of adoption — *Ro 8:15*
that eateth: for God hath *r*. him — *Ro 14:3*
as Christ also *r*. us to the glory of — *Ro 15:7*
Now we have *r*. not the spirit of — *1Co 2:12*
glory, as if thou hadst not *r*. it — *1Co 4:7*
I have *r*. of the Lord that which — *1Co 11:23*
which also ye have *r*. and wherein — *1Co 15:1*
you first of all that which I also *r*. — *1Co 15:3*
as we have *r*. mercy, we faint not — *2Co 4:1*
with fear and trembling ye *r*. him — *2Co 7:15*
which ye have not *r*. or another — *2Co 11:4*
times *r*. I forty stripes save one — *2Co 11:24*
unto you than that ye have *r*. — *Ga 1:9*
For I neither *r*. it of man, neither — *Ga 1:12*
R. ye the Spirit by the works of — *Ga 3:2*
but *r*. me as an angel of God, even — *Ga 4:14*
ye have both learned, and *r*. — *Ph'p 4:9*
having *r*. of Epaphroditus the — *Ph'p 4:18*
ye have therefore *r*. Christ Jesus — *Col 2:6*
whom ye *r*. commandments: if — *Col 4:10*
which thou hast *r*. in the Lord — *Col 4:17*
r. the word in much affliction — *1Th 1:6*
when ye *r*. the word of God which — *1Th 2:13*
ye *r*. it not as the word of men — *1Th 2:13*
as ye have *r*. of us how ye ought — *1Th 4:1*
they *r*. not the love of the truth — *2Th 2:10*
the tradition which he *r*. of us — *2Th 3:6*
on in the world, *r*. up into glory — *1Ti 3:16*

which God hath created to be *r*. — *1Ti 4:3*
if it be *r*. with thanksgiving — *1Ti 4:4*
r. a just recompense of reward — *Heb 2:2*
r. just retribution (A)(B)(N)(P)(R) — *Heb 2:2*
from them *r*. tithes of Abraham — *Heb 7:6*
for under it the people *r*. the law — *Heb 7:11*
r. the knowledge of the truth — *Heb 10:26*
Sara herself *r*. strength to conceive — *Heb 11:11*
not having *r*. the promises — *Heb 11:13*
he that had *r*. the promises offered — *Heb 11:17*
whence also he *r*. him in a figure — *Heb 11:19*
she had *r*. the spies with peace — *Heb 11:31*
Women *r*. their dead raised to life — *Heb 11:35*
through faith, *r*. not the promise — *Heb 11:39*
when she had *r*. the messengers — *Jas 2:25*
vain conversation *r*. by tradition — *1Pe 1:18*
As every man hath *r*. the gift, even — *1Pe 4:10*
he *r*. from God the Father honour — *2Pe 1:17*
anointing which ye have *r*. of him — *1Jo 2:27*
we have *r*. a commandment from — *2Jo 4*
shivers: even as I *r*. of my Father — *Re 2:27*
how thou hast *r*. and heard, and — *Re 3:3*
which have *r*. no kingdom as yet — *Re 17:12*
that had *r*. the mark of the beast — *Re 19:20*
r. his mark upon their foreheads — *Re 20:4*

RECEIVEDST

in thy lifetime *r*. thy good things — *Lu 16:25*

RECEIVER

is the scribe? where is the *r*. — *Isa 33:18*

RECEIVETH

is no man that *r*. me to house — *J'g 19:18*
him? or what *r*. he of thine hand — *Job 35:7*
wise is instructed, he *r*. knowledge — *Pr 21:11*
but he that *r*. gifts overthroweth it — *Pr 29:4*
Lord their God, nor *r*. correction — *Jer 7:28*
or *r*. it with good will at your hand — *Mal 2:13*
For every one that asketh *r*. — *M't 7:8*
He that *r*. you, *r*. me, and he — *M't 10:40*
that *r*. me *r*. him that sent me — *M't 10:40*
He that *r*. a prophet in the name — *M't 10:41*
he that *r*. a righteous man in — *M't 10:41*
the word, and anon with joy *r*. it — *M't 13:20*
such little child in my name *r*. me — *M't 18:5*
little children in my name, *r*. me — *M'k 9:37*
shall receive me, *r*. not me — *M'k 9:37*
receive this child in my name *r*. — *Lu 9:48*
receive me *r*. him that sent me — *Lu 9:48*
every one that asketh *r*.: and — *Lu 11:10*
This man *r*. sinners, and eateth — *Lu 15:2*
And no man *r*. his testimony — *Joh 3:32*
And he that reapeth *r*. wages — *Joh 4:36*
and *r*. not my words, hath one that — *Joh 12:48*
that *r*. whomsoever I send *r*. me — *Joh 13:20*
he that *r*. me *r*. him, that sent me — *Joh 13:20*
the natural man *r*. not the things — *1Co 2:14*
race run all, but one *r*. the prize — *1Co 9:24*
it is dressed, *r*. blessing from God — *Heb 6:7*

but there he *r*. them, of whom it is — *Heb 7:8*
Levi also, who *r*. tithes, payed — *Heb 7:9*
scourgeth every son whom he *r*. — *Heb 12:6*
among them, *r*. us not — *3Jo 9*
man knoweth saving he that *r*. it — *Re 2:17*
whosoever *r*. the mark of his name — *Re 14:11*

RECEIVING

not *r*. at his hands that which he — *2Ki 5:20*
r. a commandment unto Silas — *Ac 17:15*
r. in themselves that recompence — *Ro 1:27*
what shall the *r*. of them be — *Ro 11:15*
me as concerning giving and *r*. — *Ph'p 4:15*
Wherefore we *r*. a kingdom which — *Heb 12:28*
R. the end of your faith, even — *1Pe 1:9*

RECEPTION

a big *r*. (N)(P) — *Lu 5:29*

RECESSED

the building was *r*. (S) — *Eze 42:6*

RECHAB

and the name of the other *R*. — *2Sa 4:2*
sons of Rimmon *R*. and Baanah — *2Sa 4:5*
R. and Baanah his brother escaped — *2Sa 4:6*
R. and Baanah his brother, the — *2Sa 4:9*
the son of *R*. coming to meet him — *2Ki 10:15*
went, and Jehonadab the son of *R*. — *2Ki 10:23*
the father of the house of *R*. — *1Ch 2:55*
repaired Malchiah the son of *R*. — *Ne 3:14*
of *R*. our father commanded us — *Jer 35:6*
the voice of Jonadab the son of *R*. — *Jer 35:8*
words of Jonadab the son of *R*. — *Jer 35:14*
the son of *R*. have performed — *Jer 35:16*
the son of *R*. shall not want a man — *Jer 35:19*

RECHABITES

Go unto the house of the *R*. — *Jer 35:2*
and the whole house of the *R*. — *Jer 35:3*
house of the *R*. pots full of wine — *Jer 35:5*
said unto the house of the *R*. — *Jer 35:18*

RECHAH

These are the men of *R*. — *1Ch 4:12*

RECKLESS

worthless and *r*. men (R) — *J'g 9:4*
dealt with *r*. cruelty (A) — *2Ch 28:19*
r. and self willed (N) — *2Pe 2:10*

RECKLESSLY

never again act so *r*. (B) — *De 17:12*

RECKLESSNESS

master of *r*. (A) — *Ac 13:10*

RECKON

he shall *r*. with him that bought — *Le 25:50*
he shall count from the year (B) — *Le 25:50*
priest shall *r*. unto him the money — *Le 27:18*
priest shall count the money — *Le 27:18*
priest shall compute the money (B)(R) — *Le 27:18*
priest shall *r*. unto him the worth — *Le 27:23*
priest shall compute the money (A)(B)(R) — *Le 27:23*

name ye shall *r.* the instruments *Nu 4:32*
you shall assign the articles (A)(R) *Nu 4:32*
point out to each the article (B) *Nu 4:32*
appoint the instruments of service (E) *Nu 4:32*
they shall *r.* unto him seven days *Eze 44:26*
he shall count seven days (R) *Eze 44:26*
r. to them their doings (B) *Ho 4:9*
And when he had begun to *r.* one *M't 18:24*
began the accounting (A) *M't 18:24*
he started the settlement (B) *M't 18:24*
started calling in his accounts (P) *M't 18:24*
Lord will not *r.* (A)(E)(P)(R) *Ro 4:8*
r. ye also yourselves to be dead *Ro 6:11*
consider yourselves also dead (A)(B)(R) *Ro 6:11*
regard yourselves as dead (N) *Ro 6:11*
look upon yourselves as dead (P) *Ro 6:11*
For I *r.* that the sufferings of this *Ro 8:18*
I consider that the sufferings (A)(R) *Ro 8:18*
I reason that the sufferings (B) *Ro 8:18*
In my opinion whatever we go through (P) *Ro 8:18*
r. other better (N) *Ph'p 2:3*
r. the number of the beast (R) *Re 13:18*

RECKONED

offering shall be *r.* unto you *Nu 18:27*
shall be credited to you (A)(B) *Nu 18:27*
shall not be *r.* among the nations *Nu 23:9*
cast not their lot among other nations (B) *Nu 23:9*
Beeroth also was *r.* to Benjamin *2Sa 4:2*
counted as part of Benjamin (B) *2Sa 4:2*
they *r.* not with the men, into *2Ki 12:15*
require an accounting (A)(B)(R) *2Ki 12:15*
and the genealogy is not to be *r.* *1Ch 5:1*
registered (B) *1Ch 5:1;*
5:7, 17; 9:22; 2Ch 31:19
of their generations was *r.* were *1Ch 5:7*
All these were *r.* by genealogies in *1Ch 5:17*
r. in all by their genealogies *1Ch 7:5*
and were *r.* by their genealogies *1Ch 7:7*
all Israel were *r.* by genealogies *1Ch 9:1*
These were *r.* by their genealogy in *1Ch 9:22*
to all that were *r.* by genealogies *2Ch 31:19*
those that were *r.* by genealogy *Ezr 2:62*
and with him were *r.* by genealogy *Ezr 8:3*
that they might be *r.* by genealogy *Ne 7:5*
those that were *r.* by genealogy *Ne 7:64*
cannot be *r.* up in order unto thee *Ps 40:5*
to many to be numbered (A)(B)(R) *Ps 40:5*
I *r.* till morning, that, as a lion *Isa 38:13*
was *r.* among the transgressors *Lu 22:37*
counted and classed among the wicked (A) *Lu 23:37*
rated among the criminals (B) *Lu 22:37*
counted among outlaws (N) *Lu 22:37*
r. as circumcision (E) *Ro 2:26; 4:5*
is the reward not *r.* of grace, but *Ro 4:4*
wages are not counted as a gift (A)(N)(P) *Ro 4:4*
wages are not credited as a (B) *Ro 4:4*
say that faith was *r.* to Abraham *Ro 4:9*
faith was credited to Abraham (A) *Ro 4:9;*
4:10

faith was accounted to Abraham (B) *Ro 4:9;*
4:10
Abraham's faith was counted for (N)(P) *Ro 4:9;*
4:10
How was it then *r.?* when he was *Ro 4:10*
righteousness *r.* to them (E) *Ro 4:11*
it was *r.* to him (E)(P)(R) *Ro 4:22;*
4:23
shall be *r.* (E)(P)(R) *Ro 4:24*
r. to him for righteousness (E)(R) *Ga 3:6*
r. worthy (N) *1Ti 5:17*

RECKONETH

cometh, and *r.* with them *M't 25:19*
came and settled accounts (A)(B)(N)(P)(R) *M't 25:19*
God *r.* righteousness (E) *Ro 4:6*

RECKONING

there was no *r.* made with them *2Ki 22:7*
no accounting required (A)(R) *2Ki 22:7*
not required to give an account (B) *2Ki 22:7*
they were in one *r.* according to *1Ch 23:11*
they were together as one (A) *1Ch 23:11*
according to number of *r.* (E)(S) *2Ch 26:11*
no *r.* is kept of sin (N) *Ro 5:13*
nor *r.* unto them (E) *2Co 5:19*

RECKONS

whom God *r.* righteousness (R) *Ro 4:6*

RECLINED

as he *r.* (N) *Joh 13:25*

RECLINING

was *r.* with him (B) *Joh 12:2*
r. on Jesus' bosom (A) *Joh 13:23*
was *r.* next to Jesus (B) *Joh 13:23*
was *r.* close beside Jesus (N) *Joh 13:23*

RECOGNIZE

did not *r.* him (R)(S) *Ge 27:23*
recognize (S) *Ge 37:33;*
J'g 18:3; Lu 24:31; Ac 27:39
recognize (S) *Ru 3:14; Lu 24:16*
r. what is justice (B)(E) *1Ki 3:11*
it anyone does not *r.* (N)(R) *1Co 14:38*

RECOGNIZED

king *r.* him (B)(R) *1Ki 20:41*
r. as governing (A) *M'k 10:32*
should not be *r.* (N)(R) *1Co 14:38*

RECOMMENDED

had been *r.* to the grace of God *Ac 14:26*
being *r.* by the brethren unto *Ac 15:40*

RECOMPENCE

me belongeth vengeance, and *r.* *De 32:35*
vengeance and retribution (B) *De 32:35*
vanity: for vanity shall be his *r.* *Job 15:31*
futility shall be his reward (B) *Job 15:31*
the *r.* of a man's hands shall be *Pr 12:14*
vengeance, even God with a *r.;* he *Isa 35:4*
his adversaries, *r.* to his enemies *Isa 59:18*
to the islands he will repay *r.* *Isa 59:18*
that rendereth *r.* to his enemies *Isa 66:6*
he will render unto her a *r.* *Jer 51:6*
Render unto them a *r.* O Lord *La 3:64*
the days of *r.* are come; Israel *Ho 9:7*
days of punishment, time of retribution (B) *Ho 9:7*
will ye render me a *r.?* and if ye *Joe 3:4*

return your *r.* upon your own head *Joe 3:4*
thee again, and a *r.* be made thee *Lu 14:12*
invite you in return and pay you back (A) *Lu 14:12*
invite you in turn and so repay you (B) *Lu 14:12*
ask you back again you will be repaid (N)(R) *Lu 14:12*
you will be fully repaid (P) *Lu 14:12*
r. of their error which was meet *Ro 1:27*
stumblingblock a *r.* unto them (A)(B)(N)(R) *Ro 11:9*
for retribution to them (A)(B)(N)(R) *Ro 11:9*
Now for a *r.* in the same, (I speak *2Co 6:13*
received a just *r.* of reward *Heb 2:2*
received an appropriate penalty (A) *Heb 2:2*
received just retribution (B)(N)(P)(R) *Heb 2:2*
which hath great *r.* of reward *Heb 10:35*
great and glorious compensation of reward (A) *Heb 10:35*
carries a rich reward (B)(P) *Heb 10:35*
which has a great reward (R) *Heb 10:35*
respect unto the *r.* of the reward *Heb 11:26*

RECOMPENCES

year of *r.* for the controversy of *Isa 34:8*
for the Lord God of *r.* shall surely *Jer 51:56*

RECOMPENSE

he shall *r.* his trespass with the *Nu 5:7*
if the man have no kinsman to *r.* *Nu 5:8*
r. those who hate me (A)(E) *De 32:41*
The Lord *r.* thy work, and a full *Ru 2:12*
king *r.* it me with such a reward *2Sa 19:36*
he will repay you (B) *Job 34:33;*
he will *r.* it, whether thou refuse *Job 34:33*
Pr 20:22; Eze 7:3, 8, 9; 11:21; Ho 12:2
Lord will *r.* me (A) *2Sa 16:12*
Say not thou, I will *r.* evil; but *Pr 20:22*
but will *r.* even *r.* into their bosom *Isa 65:6*
And first I will *r.* their iniquity *Jer 16:18*
r. them according to their deeds *Jer 25:14*
r. her according to her work *Jer 50:29*
and will *r.* upon thee all thine *Eze 7:3*
I will *r.* thy ways upon thee *Eze 7:4*
and will *r.* thee for all thine *Eze 7:8*
I will *r.* thee according to thy ways *Eze 7:9*
will *r.* their way upon their head *Eze 9:10*
r. their way upon their own heads *Eze 11:21*
will *r.* thy way upon thine head *Eze 16:43*
even it will I *r.* upon his own head *Eze 17:19*
they shall *r.* your lewdness upon *Eze 23:49*
to his doings will he *r.* him *Ho 12:2*
if ye *r.* me, swiftly and speedily *Joe 3:4*
your *r.* will be great (A) *Lu 6:35*
they cannot *r.* thee: for thou shalt *Lu 14:14*
R. to no man evil for evil. Provide *Ro 12:17*
Repay no one evil for evil (A)(R) *Ro 12:17*
In no case paying back evil for evil (B) *Ro 12:17*
Render to no man evil for evil (E) *Ro 12:17*
Don't pay back a bad turn for a bad turn (P) *Ro 12:17*
receive *r.* of inheritance (E) *Col 3:24*
with God to *r.* tribulation to them *2Th 1:6*

RECOMPENSE (continued)

unto me, I will r. saith the Lord	Heb 10:30
I will pay back (B)(N)(R)	Heb 10:30
time for r. for servants (N)	Re 11:18
bringing my r. with me (N)(R)	Re 22:12

RECOMPENSED

the trespass be r. unto the Lord	Nu 5:8
of my hands hath he r. me	2Sa 22:21
Lord hath r. me according to my	2Sa 22:25
of my hands hath he r. me	Ps 18:20
the Lord r. me according to	Ps 18:24
righteous shall be r. in the earth	Pr 11:31
Shall evil be r. for good? for they	Jer 18:20
way have I r. upon their heads	Eze 22:31
thou shalt be r. at the resurrection	Lu 14:14
and it shall be r. unto him again	Ro 11:35

RECOMPENSEST

and r. the iniquity of the fathers	Jer 32:18

RECOMPENSING

by r. his way upon his own head	2Ch 6:23

RECONCILE

to r. withal in the holy place	Le 6:30
he r. himself unto his master	1Sa 29:4
simple: so shall ye r. the house	Eze 45:20
r. both unto God in one body by	Eph 2:16
him to r. all things unto himself	Col 1:20

RECONCILED

first be r. to thy brother, and then	M't 5:24
make peace with your brother (A)(N)(P)	M't 5:24
have an understanding with your brother (B)	M't 5:24
r. to God by the death of his Son	Ro 5:10
much more, being r. we shall be	Ro 5:10
unmarried, or be r. to her husband	1Co 7:11
of God, who hath r. us to himself by	2Co 5:18
in Christ's stead, be ye r. to God	2Co 5:20
wicked works, yet now hath he r.	Col 1:21

RECONCILIATION

Sanctified it, to make r. upon it	Le 8:15
to make atonement for it (A)(B)(E)(R)	Le 8:15
made r. with their blood upon the	2Ch 29:24
made sin offering with their blood (A)(B)(E)(R)	2Ch 29:24
offerings, to make r. for them	Eze 45:15
to make atonement for them (A)(B)(E)(R)	Eze 45:15
to make r. for the house of Israel	Eze 45:17
and to make r. for iniquity	Da 9:24
to atone for the guilt, iniquity (B)(R)	Da 9:24
we have now received r. (S)	Ro 5:11
hath given to us the ministry of r.	2Co 5:18
committed unto us the word of r.	2Co 5:19
make r. for the sins of the people	Heb 2:17
make atonement and propitiation for sins (A)	Heb 2:17
for the atonement for people's sins (B)(P)	Heb 2:17
make propitiation for the sins of (E)	Heb 2:17

to expiate the sins of the people (N)	Heb 2:17
make expiation for the sins of (R)	Heb 2:17

RECONCILING

made an end of r. the holy place	Le 16:20
completed the atonement (A)(B)(E)(R)	Le 16:20
a r. sacrifice in his blood (B)	Ro 3:25
of them be the r. of the world	Ro 11:15
Christ, r. the world unto himself	2Co 5:19

RECORD

Jacob's family r. (B)	Ge 37:2
where I r. my name I will come	Ex 20:24
heaven and earth to r. this day	De 30:19
heaven and earth to r. against	De 31:28
and to r. and to thank and praise	1Ch 16:4
and therein was a r. thus written	Ezr 6:2
in heaven, and my r. is on high	Job 16:19
unto me faithful witnesses to r.	Isa 8:2
And this is the r. of John, when	Joh 1:19
John bare r. saying, I saw the	Joh 1:32
bare r. that this is the Son of God	Joh 1:34
him, Thou bearest r. of thyself	Joh 8:13
of thyself; thy r. is not true	Joh 8:13
Though I bear r. of myself, yet	Joh 8:14
of myself, yet my r. is true	Joh 8:14
raised him from the dead, bare r.	Joh 12:17
And he that saw it bare r. and	Joh 19:35
his r. is true: and he knoweth	Joh 19:35
I take you to r. this day, that I am	Ac 20:26
bear them r. that they have a zeal	Ro 10:2
I call God for a r. upon my soul	2Co 1:23
I bear r. yea, and beyond their	2Co 8:3
for I bear you r. that, if it had	Ga 4:15
For God is my r. how greatly I	Ph'p 1:8
For I bear him r. that he hath a	Col 4:13
without r. of (A)	Heb 7:3
are three that bear r. in heaven	1Jo 5:7
the r. that God gave of his Son.	1Jo 5:10
this is the r. that God hath given	1Jo 5:11
itself: yea, and we also bear r.	3Jo 12
and ye know that our r. is true	3Jo 12
Who bare r. of the word of God	Re 1:2

RECORDED

r. them in the presence of (S)	1Ch 24:6
number not r. (A)	1Ch 27:24; 2Ch 26:11
were r. chief of the fathers	Ne 12:22

RECORDER

the son of Ahilud was r.	2Sa 8:16; 20:24
the son of Ahilud, the r.	1Ki 4:3
and Joah the son of Asaph the r.	2Ki 18:18; 18:37
Jehoshaphat the son of Ahilud, r.	1Ch 18:15
and Joah the son of Joahaz the r.	2Ch 34:8
and Joah, Asaph's son, the r.	Isa 36:3
and Joah, the son of Asaph, the r.	Isa 36:22

RECORDS

may be made in the book of the r.	Ezr 4:15
thou find in the book of the r.	Ezr 4:15
the book of r. of the chronicles	Es 6:1
these were ancient r. (S)	1Co 4:22

RECOUNT

He shall r. his worthies: they	Na 2:5
he remembers and summons his bravest men (A)	Na 2:5
he summons his officers (B)(R)	Na 2:5
he remembereth his nobles (E)	Na 2:5

RECOVER

did ye not r. them within that	J'g 11:26
them, and without fail r. all	1Sa 30:8
went to r. his border at the river	2Sa 8:3
whether I shall r. of this disease	2Ki 1:2
for he would r. him of his leprosy	2Ki 5:3
thou mayest r. him of his leprosy	2Ki 5:6
unto me to r. a man of his leprosy	2Ki 5:7
hand over the place, and r. the leper	2Ki 5:11
saying, Shall I r. of this disease	2Ki 8:8; 8:9
him, Thou mayest certainly r.	2Ki 8:10
me that thou shouldest surely r.	2Ki 8:14
Neither did Jeroboam r. strength	2Ch 13:20
that they could not r. themselves	2Ch 14:13
spare me, that I may r. strength	Ps 39:13
to r. the remnant of his people	Isa 11:11
so wilt thou r. me and make me to	Isa 38:16
upon the boil, and he shall r.	Isa 38:21
will r. my wool and my flax	Ho 2:9
on the sick, and they shall r.	M'k 16:18
may r. themselves out of the snare	2Ti 2:26

RECOVERED

r. all that the Amalekites had	1Sa 30:18
had taken to them: David r. all	1Sa 30:19
ought of the spoil that we have r.	1Sa 30:22
him, and r. the cities of Israel	2Ki 13:25
how he r. Damascus, and Hamath	2Ki 14:28
time Rezin king of Syria r. Elath	2Ki 16:6
and laid it on the boil, and he r.	2Ki 20:7
sick, and was r. of his sickness	Isa 38:9
that he had been sick, and was r.	Isa 39:1
of the daughter of my people r.	Jer 8:22
whom he had r. from Ishmael	Jer 41:16

RECOVERING

r. of sight to the blind, to set at	Lu 4:18

RECTIFICATION

until time of r. (B)	Heb 9:10

RED

And the first came out r. all over	Ge 25:25
thee, with that same r.	Ge 25:30
His eyes shall be r. with wine	Ge 49:12
rams' skins dyed r. and badgers	Ex 25:5
for the tent of rams' skins dyed r.	Ex 26:14
rams' skins dyed r. and badgers'	Ex 35:7
r. skins of rams, and badgers' skins	Ex 35:23
for the tent of rams' skins dyed r.	Ex 36:19
the covering of rams' skins dyed r.	Ex 39:34
bring thee a r. heifer without spot	Nu 19:2
on the other side as r. as blood	2Ki 3:22
upon a pavement of r. and blue	Es 1:6

r. swollen with weeping   Job 16:16
(A)(B)(E)(R)
there is a cup, and the wine is   Ps 75:8
thou upon the wine when it is   Pr 23:31
r.
though they be r. like crimson   Isa 1:18
unto her, A vineyard of r. wine   Isa 27:2
art thou r. in thine apparel, and   Isa 63:2
of his mighty men is made r.   Na 2:3
behold a man riding upon a r.   Zec 1:8
horse
behind him were there r. horses   Zec 1:8
In the first chariot were r.   Zec 6:2
horses
be fair weather: for the sky is   M't 16:2
r.
today: for the sky is r. and   M't 16:3
lowring
r. ledger of regulations   Col 2:14
out another horse that was r.   Re 6:4
behold a great r. dragon,   Re 12:3
having

RED SEA

and cast them into the R.   Ex 10:19
sea
way the wilderness of the R.   Ex 13:18
sea
also are drowned in the R.   Ex 15:4
sea
brought Israel from the R. sea   Ex 15:22
will set thy bounds from the   Ex 23:31
R. sea
wilderness by the way of the   Nu 14:25
R. sea
mount Hor by the way of the   Nu 21:4
R. sea
What he did in the R. sea   Nu 21:14
Elim, and encamped by the R.   Nu 33:10
sea
And they removed from the   Nu 33:11
R. sea
the plain over against the R.   De 1:1
sea
wilderness by way of the R.   De 1:40
sea
wilderness by the way of the R.   De 2:1
sea
the water of the R. sea to   De 11:4
overflow
dried up the water of the R.   Jos 2:10
sea
Lord your God did to the R.   Jos 4:23
sea
and horsemen unto the R. sea   Jos 24:6
the wilderness unto the R. sea   J'g 11:16
on the shore of the R. sea, in   1Ki 9:26
heardest their cry by the R. sea   Ne 9:9
him at the sea, even at the R.   Ps 106:7
sea
He rebuked the R. sea also   Ps 106:9
and terrible things by the R.   Ps 106:22
sea
which divided the R. sea into   Ps 136:13
parts
Pharaoh and his host in the   Ps 136:15
R. sea
noise was heard in the R.   Jer 49:21
sea
land of Egypt, and in the R.   Ac 7:36
sea
passed through the R. sea   Heb 11:29
as by dry

REDDISH

spot, white, and somewhat r.   Le 13:19
bright spot, somewhat r. or   Le 13:24
white
a white r. sore; it is a leprosy   Le 13:42
if the rising of the sore be   Le 13:43
white
be greenish or r. in the   Le 13:49
garment
with hollow strakes, greenish   Le 14:37
or r.
greenish, or r. cavities (R)   Le 14:37

REDEEM

r. you with a stretched out arm   Ex 6:6
firstling of an ass thou shalt r.   Ex 13:13
if thou wilt not r. it then thou   Ex 13:13
shalt
firstborn of man shalt thou r.   Ex 13:13
all the firstborn of my   Ex 13:15
children I r.
firstling of an ass thou shalt r.   Ex 34:20

if thou r. him not, then shalt   Ex 34:20
thou
firstborn of thy sons thou   Ex 34:20
shalt r.
and if any of his kin come to   Le 25:25
r. it
buy back that which was sold   Le 25:25;
(B)   27:13, 15, 19, 20, 27, 31
he r. that which his brother   Le 25:25
sold
And if the man have none to   Le 25:26
r. it
and himself be able to r. it   Le 25:26
he may r. it within a whole   Le 25:29
year
within a full year may he r. it   Le 25:29
may the Levites r. at any time   Le 25:32
one of his brethren may r.   Le 25:48
him
or his uncle's son, may r. him   Le 25:49
unto him of his family may r.   Le 25:49
him
or if he be able, he may r.   Le 25:49
himself
But if he will at all r. it, then   Le 27:13
he
that sanctified it will r. his   Le 27:15
house
that sanctified the field will r.   Le 27:19
it
And if he will not r. the field,   Le 27:20
or if
he shall r. it according to   Le 27:27
thine
will at all r. ought of his tithes   Le 27:31
firstborn of man shalt   Nu 18:15
thou r.
of unclean beasts shalt thou   Nu 18:15
r.
from a month old shalt thou   Nu 18:16
r.
firstling of a goat, thou shalt   Nu 18:17
not r.
If thou wilt r. it, r. it: but   Ru 4:4
if thou wilt not r. it, then tell   Ru 4:4
me
there is none to r. it beside thee   Ru 4:4
after thee. And he said, I will r.   Ru 4:4
it
I cannot r. it for myself, lest I   Ru 4:6
mar
r. thou my right to thyself   Ru 4:6
for I cannot r. it   Ru 4:6
whom God went to r. for a   2Sa 7:23
people
God went to r. to be his own   1Ch 17:21
people
neither is it in our power to r.   Ne 5:5
them
famine he shall r. thee from   Job 5:20
death
R. me from the hand of the   Job 6:23
mighty
Ransom me from brigands   Job 6:23
(B)(R)
R. Israel, O God, out of all his   Ps 25:22
r. me, and be merciful unto   Ps 26:11
me
and r. us for thy mercies'   Ps 44:26
sake
deliver us for mercy's sake   Ps 44:26
(A)(B)(R)
can by any means r. his brother   Ps 49:7
God will r. my soul from the   Ps 49:15
power
Draw nigh unto my soul, and   Ps 69:18
r. it
He shall r. their soul from   Ps 72:14
deceit
r. Israel from all his iniquities   Ps 130:8
shortened at all, that it cannot   Isa 50:2
r.
I will r. thee out of the hand   Jer 15:21
of
grave; I will r. them from   Ho 13:14
death
shall r. thee from the hand of   Mic 4:10
thine
To r. them that were under the   Ga 4:5
purchase freedom of those   Ga 4:5
subject to law (A)(N)
in order to buy those under the   Ga 4:5
law (B)
he might r. us from all iniquity   Tit 2:14

REDEEMED

Angel which r. me from all   Ge 48:16
evil

led forth the people thou   Ex 15:13
hast r.
then shall he let her be r.   Ex 21:8
not at all r. nor freedom given   Le 19:20
her
r. within the space of a full   Le 25:30
year
they may be r. and they shall   Le 25:31
go
After that he is sold he may   Le 25:48
be r.
And if he be not r. in these   Le 25:54
years
man, it shall not be r. any   Le 27:20
more
if it be not r. then it shall be   Le 27:27
sold
devoted thing shall be sold   Le 27:28
or r.
None devoted shall be r.   Le 27:29
shall be holy; it shall not be r.   Le 27:33
And for those that are to be r.   Nu 3:46
ransom (B)   Nu 3:46; 3:48, 51
the odd number of them is to   Nu 3:48
be r.
them that were r. by the   Nu 3:49
Levites
the money of them that were r.   Nu 3:51
that are to be r. from a   Nu 18:16
month old
r. you out of the house of   De 7:8
bondmen
delivered you out of house of   De 7:8
bondage (B)
thou hast r. through thy   De 9:26
greatness
r. you out of the house of   De 13:5
bondage
and the Lord thy God r. thee   De 15:15
people Israel, whom thou hast   De 21:8
r.
the Lord thy God r. thee   De 24:18
thence
hath r. my soul out of all   2Sa 4:9
adversity
saved me out of every trouble   2Sa 4:9
(B)
hath r. my soul out of all   1Ki 1:29
distress
whom thou hast r. out of   1Ch 17:21
Egypt
thou hast r. by thy great power   Ne 1:10
have r. our brethren the Jews   Ne 5:8
hast r. me, O Lord God of   Ps 31:5
truth
and my soul, which thou hast   Ps 71:23
r.
inheritance, which thou hast r.   Ps 74:2
hast with thine arm r. thy   Ps 77:15
people
r. them from the hand of the   Ps 106:10
enemy
Let the r. of the Lord say so,   Ps 107:2
whom
hath r. from the hand of the   Ps 107:2
enemy
And hath r. us from our   Ps 136:24
enemies
rescued us from our enemies   Ps 136:24
(A)(R)
freed us from our adversaries   Ps 136:24
(B)
Zion shall be r. with judgment   Isa 1:27
ransomed by justice (B)   Isa 1:27
saith the Lord, who r.   Isa 29:22
Abraham
there; but the r. shall walk   Isa 35:9
there
Fear not: for I have r. thee, I   Isa 43:1
have
return unto me; for I have r.   Isa 44:22
thee
for the Lord hath r. Jacob   Isa 44:23
The Lord hath r. his servant   Isa 48:20
Jacob
the r. to pass over   Isa 51:10
(A)(B)(E)(R)
the r. of the Lord shall return   Isa 51:11
ransomed of the Lord shall   Isa 51:11
(B)
and ye shall be r. without   Isa 52:3
money
his people he hath r. Jerusalem   Isa 52:9
The holy people, The r. of the   Isa 62:12
Lord
and the year of my r. is come   Isa 63:4

his love and in his pity he r. *Isa 63:9* them
For the Lord hath r. Jacob *Jer 31:11*
Lord has ransomed Jacob *Jer 31:11* (A)(B)(R)
of my soul; thou hast r. my life *La 3:58*
though I have r. them, yet they *Ho 7:13*
r. thee out of the house of *Mic 6:4* servants
for I have r. them: and they *Zec 10:8* shall
I have ransomed them (B) *Zec 10:8*
hath visited and r. his people *Lu 1:68*
brought deliverance and *Lu 1:68* redemption (A)(B)(E)
saved them and set them free *Lu 1:68* (N)
he which should have r. Israel *Lu 24:21*
who would deliver Israel (B) *Lu 24:21*
the man to deliver Israel (N) *Lu 24:21*
Christ hath r. us from the *Ga 3:13* curse
purchased our freedom (A) *Ga 3:13*
bought us free from the curse *Ga 3:13* of the law (B)
bought us freedom from the *Ga 3:13* curse (N)
not r. with corruptible things *1Pe 1:18*
ransomed us from useless *1Pe 1:18* ways (B)(R)
and hast r. us to God by thy *Re 5:9* blood
with your blood you purchased *Re 5:9* men (A)(E)(N)(P)
thou wert sacrificed and hast *Re 5:9* bought (B)
didst ransom men (R) *Re 5:9*
which were r. from the earth *Re 14:3*
ransomed from the earth *Re 14:3;* (A)(N) *14:4*
purchased from the earth *Re 14:3;* (B)(E) *14:4*
These were r. from among men *Re 14:4*

REDEEMEDST

which thou r. to thee from *2Sa 7:23* Egypt

REDEEMER

I know that my r. liveth, and *Job 19:25*
O Lord, my strength, and my *Ps 19:14* r.
rock, and the high God their r. *Ps 78:35*
For their r. is mighty; he shall *Pr 23:11*
saith the Lord, and thy r. the *Isa 41:14* Holy
Thus saith the Lord, your r. *Isa 43:14*
Israel, and his r. the Lord of *Isa 44:6* hosts
Thus saith the Lord, thy r. *Isa 44:24* and he
As for our r. the Lord of hosts *Isa 47:4* is his
Thus saith the Lord, thy R. *Isa 48:17*
the R. of Israel, and his Holy *Isa 49:7* One
Lord am thy Saviour and thy *Isa 49:26* R.
and thy R. the Holy One of *Isa 54:5* Israel
on thee, saith the Lord thy *Isa 54:8* R.
And the R. shall come to *Isa 59:20* Zion, and
Lord am thy Saviour and thy *Isa 60:16* R.
thou, O Lord, art our father, *Isa 63:16* our r.
Their R. is strong; The Lord *Jer 50:34*

REDEEMETH

Lord r. the soul of his servants *Ps 34:22*
Who r. thy life from *Ps 103:4* destruction

REDEEMING

concerning r. and concerning *Ru 4:7*
R. the time, because the days *Eph 5:16* are
buying up each opportunity *Eph 5:16* (A)
make the best possible use of *Eph 5:16* time (B)(P)
use the present opportunity to *Eph 5:16* the full (N)

making the most of your time *Eph 5:16* (R)
them that are without, r. the *Col 4:5* time
making the most of your time *Col 4:5* (A)(R)
using time to best possible *Col 4:5* advantage (B)
use the present opportunity to *Col 4:5* the full (N)
make best possible use of your *Col 4:5* time (P)

REDEEMS

r. transgressions under *Heb 9:15* (P)(R)

REDEMPTION

the r. of his life (B)(R) *Ex 21:30*
ye shall grant a r. for the land *Le 25:24*
shall give again the price of *Le 25:51* his r.
give him again the price of his *Le 25:52* r.
Moses took the r. money of *Nu 3:49* them
(For the r. of their soul is *Ps 49:8* precious
He sent r. unto his people: he *Ps 111:9*
mercy, and with him is *Ps 130:7* plenteous r.
the right of r. is thine to buy it *Jer 32:7*
the r. is thine; buy it for *Jer 32:8* thyself
brought deliverance and r. *Lu 1:68* (A)(B)(E)
that looked for r. in Jerusalem *Lu 2:38*
heads; for your r. draweth *Lu 21:28* nigh
your deliverance is near (B) *Lu 21:28*
your liberation is near (N) *Lu 21:28*
you will soon be free (P) *Lu 21:28*
through the r. that is in Christ *Ro 3:24* Jesus
through the ransom that Christ *Ro 3:24* (B)
through the act of liberation in *Ro 3:24* (N)
adoption, to wit, the r. of our *Ro 8:23* body
and sanctification, and r. *1Co 1:30*
whom we have r. through his *Eph 1:7* blood
the r. of the purchased *Eph 1:14* possession
releasing of our deed of *Eph 1:14* purchase (B)
ye are sealed unto the day of *Eph 4:30* r.
whom we have r. through his *Col 1:14* blood
having obtained eternal r. for *Heb 9:12* us
for the r. of the *Heb 9:15* transgressions that
for atonement of the *Heb 9:15* transgressions (B)
deliverance from sins *Heb 9:15* committed under (N)
redeems transgressions under *Heb 9:15* (P)(R)

REDNESS

cause? who hath r. of eyes *Pr 23:29*
humiliated and has no r. (N) *Ac 8:33*

REDOUND

of many r. to the glory of *2Co 4:15* God
may increase to the glory of *2Co 4:15* God (A)(R)
may abound to the glory of *2Co 4:15* God (B)(E)

REDUCED

r. Israelites to severe slavery *Ex 1:13* (A)

REED

as a r. is shaken in the water *1Ki 14:15*
upon the staff of this bruised *2Ki 18:21* r.

r. grass grows without water *Job 8:11* (B)(R)
shady trees, in the covert of *Job 40:21* the r.
in the staff of this broken r. on *Isa 36:6*
A bruised r. shall he not break *Isa 42:3*
a staff of r. to the house of *Eze 29:6* Israel
in his hand, and a measuring *Eze 40:3* r.
a measuring r. of six cubits *Eze 40:5* long
the breadth of the building, *Eze 40:5* one r.
and the height, one r. *Eze 40:5*
of the gate, which was one r. *Eze 40:6* broad
the gate, which was one r. *Eze 40:6* broad
was one r. long, and one r. *Eze 40:7* broad
porch of the gate within was *Eze 40:7* one r.
the porch of the gate within, *Eze 40:8* one r.
were a full r. of six great *Eze 41:8* cubits
east side with the measuring *Eze 42:16* r.
the measuring r. round *Eze 42:16;* about *42:17*
reeds, with the measuring r. *Eze 42:18*
reeds with the measuring r. *Eze 42:19*
to see? A r. shaken with the *M't 11:7* wind
A bruised r. shall he not *M't 12:20* break, and
head, and a r. in his right *M't 27:29* hand
took the r. and smote him on *M't 27:30*
it with vinegar, and put it on *M't 27:48* a r.
smote him on the head with *M'k 15:19* a r.
full of vinegar, and put it on *M'k 15:36* a r.
to see? A r. shaken with the *Lu 7:24* wind
was given me a r. like unto a *Re 11:1* rod
talked with me had a golden *Re 21:15* r. to
he measured the city with the *Re 21:16* r.

REEDS

set it among the r. (B)(R) *Ex 2:3; 2:5*
up: the r. and flags shall wither *Isa 19:6*
r. and rushes shall wither *Isa 19:6* (A)(B)(R)
The paper r. by the brooks, by *Isa 19:7*
shall be grass with r. and *Isa 35:7* rushes
the r. they have burned with *Jer 51:32* fire
measuring reed, five hundred *Eze 42:16* r.
the north side, five hundred r. *Eze 42:17*
the south side, five hundred r. *Eze 42:18*
side, and measured five *Eze 42:19* hundred r.
round about, five hundred r. *Eze 42:20* long
length of five and twenty *Eze 45:1* thousand r.
five and twenty thousand r. in *Eze 48:8* breadth

REEFS

hidden r. in your feasts (A) *Jude 12*

REEL

They r. to and fro, and *Ps 107:27* stagger
earth shall r. to and fro like a *Isa 24:20*

REELAIAH

Seraiah, R., Mordecai, Bilshan *Ezr 2:2*

REELS

my heart r. (B)(R) *Isa 21:4*

REFINE

a place for gold where they *r.*   *Job 28:1*
it (S)
will *r.* them as silver is   *Zec 13:9*
refined
I will *r.* them (E)(R)   *Zec 13:9*

REFINED

most *r.* man (B)   *De 28:54*
for the altar of incense   *1Ch 28:18*
r. gold
seven thousand talents of   *1Ch 29:4*
r. silver
of wines on the lees well *r.*   *Isa 25:6*
I have *r.* thee, but not with   *Isa 48:10*
silver
and be *r.* (E)(R)   *Da 12:10*
and will refine them as silver   *Zec 13:9*
is *r.*
gold *r.* in fire (E)(N)(R)   *Re 3:18*

REFINER

a vessel for the *r.* (S)   *Pr 25:4*
he shall sit as a *r.* and purifier   *Mal 3:3*
of

REFINER'S

for he is like a *r.* fire, and like   *Mal 3:2*

REFINING

a *r.* pot for silver (S)   *Pr 17:3; 27:21*

REFLECTED

r. what this greeting (N)   *Lu 1:29*

REFORMATION

on them until the time of *r.*   *Heb 9:10*
until the time of rectification   *Heb 9:10*
(B)
until Christ should establish   *Heb 9:10*
truth (P)

REFORMED

if ye will not be *r.* by me by   *Le 26:23*
these
die without *r.* to law (P)   *Ro 2:12*

REFRACTORY

lawless and *r.* (B)   *1Ti 1:9*
r., senseless talkers (B)   *Tit 1:10*

REFRAIN

Joseph could not *r.* himself   *Ge 45:1*
before
r. from (A)(B)(R)   *Ex 23:5*
r. from marrying (S)   *Ru 1:13*
r. from opposing God (R)   *2Ch 31:21*
I will not *r.* my mouth; I will   *Job 7:11*
if I *r.* from speaking (A)   *Job 6:6*
them; *r.* thy foot from their   *Pr 1:15*
path
and a time to *r.* from embracing   *Ec 3:5*
for my praise will I *r.* for thee   *Isa 48:9*
Wilt thou *r.* thyself for these   *Isa 64:12*
things
I could not *r.* (S)   *Jer 20:9*
R. thy voice from weeping   *Jer 31:16*
R. from these men, and let   *Ac 5:38*
them
r. from manual labor   *1Co 9:6*
(A)(B)(R)
I will *r.* (B)(N)(R)   *2Co 12:6*
r. from sensual urges (B)   *1Pe 2:11*
let him *r.* his tongue from evil   *1Pe 3:10*

REFRAINED

r. himself, and said, Set on   *Ge 43:31*
bread
Nevertheless Haman *r.* himself   *Es 5:10*
The princes *r.* talking, and   *Job 29:9*
laid
I have not *r.* my lips O Lord,   *Ps 40:9*
thou
r. my feet from every evil   *Ps 119:101*
way
I have been still, and *r.*   *Isa 42:14*
myself
they have not *r.* their feet   *Jer 14:10*

REFRAINETH

sin: but he that *r.* his lips is   *Pr 10:19*
wise

REFRESH

home with me, and *r.* thyself,   *1Ki 13:7*
unto his friends to *r.* himself   *Ac 27:3*
the Lord: *r.* my bowels in the   *Ph'm 20*
Lord

REFRESHED

and the stranger, may be *r.*   *Ex 23:12*
seventh day he rested, and   *Ex 31:17*
was *r.*
So Saul was *r.* and was well   *1Sa 16:23*
weary, and *r.* themselves   *2Sa 16:14*
there.
I will speak, that I may be *r.*   *Job 32:20*
of God, and may with you be   *Ro 15:32*
r.
they have *r.* my spirit and   *1Co 16:18*
yours
because his spirit was *r.* by   *2Co 7:13*
you all
he oft *r.* me, and was not   *2Ti 1:16*
ashamed
bowels of the saints are *r.* by   *Ph'm 7*
thee

REFRESHETH

for he *r.* the soul of his   *Pr 25:13*
masters

REFRESHING

weary to rest; and this is the   *Isa 28:12*
r.
the times of *r.* shall come from   *Ac 3:19*

REFUGE

took *r.* in (A)(B)(E)(R)   *Ge 32:37*
there shall be six cities for *r.*   *Nu 35:6*
you cities to be cities of *r.* for   *Nu 35:11*
you
shall be unto you cities for *r.*   *Nu 35:12*
from
give six cities shall ye have   *Nu 35:13*
for *r.*
Canaan, which shall be cities   *Nu 35:14*
of *r.*
These six cities shall be a *r.*   *Nu 35:15*
both
shall restore him to the city   *Nu 35:25*
of his *r.*
out the border of the city of   *Nu 35:26*
his *r.*
the borders of the city of his   *Nu 35:27*
r.
remained in the city of his   *Nu 35:28*
r. until
him that is fled to the city of   *Nu 35:32*
his *r.*
The eternal God is thy *r.* and   *De 33:27*
Appoint out for you cities of   *Jos 20:2*
r.
your *r.* from the avenger of   *Jos 20:3*
blood
city of *r.* for the slayer   *Jos 21:13;*
  21, 27, 32, 38
take *r.* in (B)   *J'g 9:15;*
Ps 2:12; 5:11; 11:1; 16:1; 17:7; 18:2;
31:1, 19; 34:22; 36:7; 61:4; 71:1; 73:28;
144:2, Pr 30:5; Isa 14:32; 30:2; 57:13;
  Zep 3:12
take *r.* in (E)   *J'g 9:15;*
Ru 2:12; 2Sa 22:3, 31; Ps 2:12; 5:11; 7:1;
11:1; 16:1; 17:7; 18:2, 30; 25:20; 31:1,
19; 34:22; 36:7; 37:40; 61:4; 62:8; 64:10;
71:1; 73:28; 91:2, 4; 118:8, 9; 141:2;
Pr 30:5; Isa 14:32; 30:2; 57:13; Na 1:7;
  Zep 3:12
take *r.* in (R)   *J'g 9:15;*
Ru 2:12; 2Sa 22:3, 31; Ps 2:12; 5:11; 7:1;
16:1; 17:7; 18:2, 30; 25:20; 31:1, 19;
34:22; 36:7; 37:40; 64:10; 71:1; 73:28
91:2, 4; 118:8, 9; 141:2; Pr 30:5;
Isa 14:32; 30:2; 57:13; Na 1:7; Zep 3:12
my high tower, and my *r.* my   *2Sa 22:3*
Hebron, the city of *r.* and   *1Ch 6:57*
Libnah
gave unto them of the cities of   *1Ch 6:67*
r.
also will be a *r.* for the   *Ps 9:9*
oppressed

oppressed, a *r.* in times of   *Ps 9:9*
trouble
poor, because the Lord is his *r.*   *Ps 14:6*
you are my *r.* (R)   *Ps 31:4; 43:2*
takes *r.* in (E)(R)   *Ps 34:8; 57:1*
he is their *r.* (R)   *Ps 37:39*
God is our *r.* and strength, a   *Ps 46:1*
us; the God of Jacob is our *r.*   *Ps 46:7;*
  46:11
is known in her palaces for a *r.*   *Ps 48:3*
of thy wings will I make my *r.*   *Ps 57:1*
takes *r.* in (A)(B)   *Ps 57:1*
and *r.* in the day of my trouble   *Ps 59:16*
my strength, and my *r.* is in   *Ps 62:7*
God
before him: God is a *r.* for us   *Ps 62:8*
many: but thou art my strong   *Ps 71:7*
r.
Lord, He is my *r.* and my   *Ps 91:2*
fortress
hast made the Lord, which is   *Ps 91:9*
my *r.*
and my God is the rock of my   *Ps 94:22*
r.
high hills are a *r.* for the wild   *Ps 104:18*
goats
r. failed me; no man cared for   *Ps 142:4*
Thou art my *r.* and my   *Ps 142:5*
portion in
his children shall have a place   *Pr 14:26*
of *r.*
for a place of *r.* and for a   *Isa 4:6*
covert
be a *r.* to them (R)   *Isa 16:4*
the rock of your *r.* (R)   *Isa 17:10*
a *r.* from the storm, a shadow   *Isa 25:4*
from
for we have made lies our *r.*   *Isa 28:15*
hail shall sweep away   *Isa 28:17*
the *r.* of lies
and my *r.* in the day of   *Jer 16:19*
affliction
have fled for *r.* to lay hold   *Heb 6:18*
upon the

REFUGEES

r. among Greeks (P)   *Joh 7:35*

REFUND

he shall *r.* double (B)   *Ex 22:4; Le 24:21*
he shall make a *r.* (B)   *Ex 22:5*

REFUSE

if thou *r.* to let him go,   *Ex 4:23*
behold, I
if thou *r.* to let them go, behold   *Ex 8:2*
I
if thou *r.* to let them go, and   *Ex 9:2*
wilt
long wilt thou *r.* to humble   *Ex 10:3*
thyself
if thou *r.* to let my people go   *Ex 10:4*
r. ye to keep my   *Ex 16:28*
commandments
utterly *r.* to give her unto him   *Ex 22:17*
refuse (S)   *1Sa 2:8;*
1Ki 14:10; 2Ki 9:37; 18:27; Ne 3:13, 14;
Ps 83:10; Jer 8:2; 9:22; 16:4; 25:33;
  Da 2:5; 3:29; Ph'p 3:8
every thing that was vile and   *1Sa 15:9*
r.
he will not *r.* thee (S)   *1Ki 2:17; 2:20*
I pray thee *r.* me not (S)   *1Ki 2:20*
whether thou *r.* or whether   *Job 34:33*
thou
and be wise, and *r.* it not   *Pr 8:33*
because they *r.* to do judgment   *Pr 21:7*
him; for his hands *r.* to labour   *Pr 21:25*
would be scornfully *r.* (B)   *Ca 8:7*
But if ye *r.* and rebel, ye shall   *Isa 1:20*
that he may know to *r.* the   *Isa 7:15*
evil
the child shall know to *r.* the   *Isa 7:16*
evil
r. of silver (B)(E)(R)   *Jer 6:30*
hold fast deceit, they *r.* to   *Jer 8:5*
return
through deceit they *r.* to know   *Jer 9:6*
me
people, which *r.* to hear my   *Jer 13:10*
words
r. to take the cup at thine   *Jer 25:28*
hand to
But if thou *r.* to go forth,   *Jer 38:21*
this is

let him *r.* (R)   *Eze 3:27*
and *r.* in the midst of the   *La 3:45* people
yea, and sell the *r.* of the   *Am 8:6* wheat
r. to follow ancient customs   *M'k 7:5* (P)
worthy of death, I *r.* not to   *Ac 25:11* die
r. of the world (R)   *1Co 4:13*
r. to stultify grace (P)   *Ga 2:27*
r. profane and old wives'   *1Ti 4:7* fables
But the younger widows *r.*   *1Ti 5:11*
that ye *r.* not him that   *Heb 12:25* speaketh
r. them burial (N)(P)   *Re 11:9*

REFUSED

but he *r.* to be comforted   *Ge 37:35* and he
he *r.* and said unto his   *Ge 39:8* master's
his father *r.* and said, I know   *Ge 48:19*
Edom *r.* to give Israel   *Nu 20:21* passage
the people *r.* to obey the   *1Sa 8:19* voice of
stature; because I have *r.* him   *1Sa 16:7* eat
But he *r.* and said, I will not   *1Sa 28:23* eat
Howbeit he *r.* to turn aside   *2Sa 2:23*
out before him; but he *r.* to   *2Sa 13:9* eat
thee. And the man *r.* to   *1Ki 20:35* smite him
which he *r.* to give thee for   *1Ki 21:15* money
he urged him to take it; but   *2Ki 5:16* he *r.*
r. to obey, neither were   *Ne 9:17* mindful of
Vashti *r.* to come at the   *Es 1:12* king's
things that my soul *r.* to touch   *Job 6:7* are
not: my soul *r.* to be   *Ps 77:2* comforted
of God, and *r.* to walk in his   *Ps 78:10* law
he *r.* the tabernacle of Joseph   *Ps 78:67*
The stone which the builders   *Ps 118:22* *r.* is
Because I have called, and ye   *Pr 1:24* *r.*
wife of youth, when thou wast   *Isa 54:6* *r.*
they have *r.* to receive   *Jer 5:3* correction
a rock; they have *r.* to return   *Jer 5:3*
which *r.* to hear my words   *Jer 11:10*
r. to be comforted for her   *Jer 31:15* children
them fast; they *r.* to let them   *Jer 50:33* go
they have *r.* my judgments and   *Eze 5:6*
king, because they *r.* to return   *Ho 11:5*
But they *r.* to hearken, and   *Zec 7:11* pulled
Moses whom they *r.* saying,   *Ac 7:35* Who
God is good, and nothing to   *1Ti 4:4* be *r.*
r. to be called the son of   *Heb 11:24* Pharaoh's
escaped not who *r.* him that   *Heb 12:25* spake

REFUSEDST

forehead, thou *r.* to be   *Jer 3:3* ashamed

REFUSES

neither *r.* or reproaches anyone   *Jas 1:5* (N)

REFUSETH

hardened, he *r.* to let the   *Ex 7:14* people go
the Lord *r.* to give me leave   *Nu 22:13* to go
said, Baalam *r.* to come with   *Nu 22:14* us
My husband's brother *r.* to   *De 25:7* raise up

but he that *r.* reproof erreth   *Pr 10:17*
shall be to him that *r.*   *Pr 13:18* instruction
He that *r.* instruction   *Pr 15:32* despiseth
people *r.* the waters of Shiloah   *Isa 8:6*
incurable, which *r.* to be   *Jer 15:18* healed

REFUTE

arguments, theories,   *2Co 10:5* reasonings (A)
r. those who raise objections   *Tit 1:9* (B)

REFUTED

publicly *r.* Jews (P)   *Ac 18:28*

REGARD

Lord had *r.* for Abel (R)   *Ge 4:4*
he had no *r.* for Cain (R)   *Ge 4:5*
not *r.* with favor (R)   *Ge 31:2*
Also *r.* not your stuff   *Ge 45:20*
and let them not *r.* vain words   *Ex 5:9*
R. not them that   *Le 19:31* have familiar
will have *r.* for you (R)   *Le 26:9*
shall not *r.* the person of the   *De 28:50* old
answered not, neither did she   *1Sa 4:20* *r.* it
I pray thee, *r.* this man of   *1Sa 25:25* Be.ial
is thy brother: *r.* not this   *2Sa 13:20* thing
I *r.* the presence of   *2Ki 3:14* Jehoshaphat
let not God *r.* it from above   *Job 3:4*
neither will the Almighty *r.*   *Job 35:13* it
Take heed, *r.* not iniquity: *Job 36:21* for
does not *r.* wise (R)   *Job 37:24*
they *r.* not the works of the   *Ps 28:5* Lord
hated them that *r.* lying   *Ps 31:6* vanities
If I *r.* iniquity in my heart   *Ps 66:18*
have *r.* for the covenant   *Ps 74:20* (A)(R)
neither shall the God of Jacob   *Ps 94:7* *r.* it
will *r.* the prayer of the   *Ps 102:17* destitute
have *r.* for your statutes   *Ps 119:117* (A)(R)
That thou mayest *r.* discretion   *Pr 5:2*
He will not *r.* any ransom   *Pr 6:35*
that in *r.* of the oath of God   *Ec 8:2*
they *r.* not the work of the   *Isa 5:12* Lord
which shall not *r.* silver; and   *Isa 13:17* as
men will *r.* their maker (R)   *Isa 17:7*
he will no more *r.* them: they   *La 4:16*
shall he *r.* the God of his   *Da 11:37* fathers
desire of women, nor *r.* any   *Da 11:37*
will I *r.* the peace offerings of   *Am 5:22*
and *r.* and wonder   *Hab 1:5* marvellously
means: will he *r.* your persons   *Mal 1:9*
I fear not God, nor *r.* man   *Lu 18:4*
held in high *r.* (A)   *Ac 5:13*
to him they had *r.* because   *Ac 8:11* that
r. yourselves as dead (N)   *Ro 6:11*
day, to the Lord he doth not   *Ro 14:6* *r.* it
r. with contempt (A)   *Ga 4:14*
r. others as better, superior   *Ph'p 2:3* (A)(B)
r. as waste, consider as   *Ph'p 3:8* rubbish (B)(P)
with *r.* to a feast day   *Col 2:16* (A)(B)(R)
hold lovingly in highest *r.*   *1Th 5:13* (B)
r. masters as deserving (B)(R)   *1Ti 6:1*
if you show servile *r.* (A)   *Jas 2:9*

REGARDED

that *r.* not the word of the   *Ex 9:21* Lord

r. with contempt (B)   *Nu 15:31*
r. as Rephaim (B)   *De 2:11*
r. as the land of the Rephaim   *De 2:20* (B)
nor any to answer, nor any   *1Ki 18:29* that *r.*
r. me according to the   *1Ch 17:17* estate of a
Nevertheless he *r.* their   *Ps 106:44* affliction
out my hand, and no man *r.*   *Pr 1:24*
potter *r.* as clay (R)   *Isa 29:16*
be *r.* as a forest (R)   *Isa 29:17*
r. him as stricken (R)   *Isa 53:4*
no longer *r.* them (A)(E)(R)   *La 4:16*
men, O king, have not *r.* thee   *Da 3:12*
r. John as a prophet (A)   *M't 14:5*
r. him as a prophet (S)   *M't 21:46*
he hath *r.* the low estate of his   *Lu 1:48*
feared not God, neither *r.* man   *Lu 18:2*
r. the greatest (R)   *Lu 22:24*
r. as circumcision (R)   *Ro 2:26*
r. and counted as sheep   *Ro 8:36* (A)(R)
be *r.* as fools (N)   *2Ti 3:9*
and I *r.* them not, saith the   *Heb 8:9* Lord
she *r.* the promiser   *Heb 11:11* trustworthy (B)

REGARDEST

thou *r.* neither princes nor   *2Sa 19:6* servants
I stand up, and thou *r.* me   *Job 30:20* not
for thou *r.* not the person of   *M't 22:16;*   *M'k 12:14*

REGARDETH

r. not persons, nor taketh   *De 10:17* reward
nor *r.* the rich more than   *Job 34:19* the poor
r. he the crying of the driver   *Job 39:7*
man *r.* the life of his beast   *Pr 12:10*
that *r.* reproof shall be   *Pr 13:18* honoured
but he that *r.* reproof is   *Pr 15:5* prudent
but the wicked *r.* not to know   *Pr 29:7* it
that is higher than the highest   *Ec 5:8* *r.*
that *r.* the clouds shall not   *Ec 11:4* reap
despised the cities, he *r.* no   *Isa 33:8* man
of Judah, *r.* not thee, O king   *Da 6:13*
he *r.* not the offering any   *Mal 2:13* more
r. the day, *r.* it unto the Lord   *Ro 14:6*
he that *r.* not the day, to the   *Ro 14:6* Lord

REGARDING

perish for ever without any *r.*   *Job 4:20* it
nigh unto death, not *r.* his   *Ph'p 2:30* life

REGARDS

he *r.* the lowly (R)   *Ps 138:6*
r. one day more highly (N)   *Ro 14:5*

REGEM

sons of Jahdai; *R.* and   *1Ch 2:47* Jotham

REGEM-MELECH

Sherezer and *R.* and their men   *Zec 7:2*

REGENERATION

the *r.* when the Son of man   *M't 19:28* shall
in the new-age the Messianic   *M't 19:28* rebirth of the world (A)
in the new age (B)(R)   *M't 19:28*
in the world that is to be   *M't 19:28* (N)
in the next world (P)   *M't 19:28*
he saved us, by the washing of   *Tit 3:5* *r.*
by cleansing of the new birth   *Tit 3:5* (A)

REGENERATION (cont.)

through the water of rebirth (N)   *Tit 3:5*
by the cleansing power of a new birth (P)   *Tit 3:5*

REGION

desolate *r.*, the desert (B)   *Le 16:22*
all the *r.* of Argob, the kingdom of   *De 3:4*
the *r.* of Argob, with all Bashan   *De 3:13*
of Abinadab, in all the *r.* of Dor   *1Ki 4:11*
r. of Argob, which is in Bashan   *1Ki 4:13*
over all the *r.* on this side the river   *1Ki 4:24*
and all the *r.* round about Jordan   *M't 3:5*
sat in the *r.* and shadow of death   *M't 4:16*
all the *r.* round about Galilee   *M'k 1:28*
through that whole *r.* round about   *M'k 6:55*
and of the *r.* of Trachonitis   *Lu 3:1*
through all the *r.* round about   *Lu 4:14*
throughout all the *r.* round about   *Lu 7:17*
published throughout all the *r.*   *Ac 13:49*
unto the *r.* that lieth round about   *Ac 14:6*
Phyrgia and the *r.* of Galatia   *Ac 16:6*

REGIONS

throughout the *r.* of Judaea   *Ac 8:1*
preach the gospel in the *r.* beyond   *2Co 10:16*
this boasting in the *r.* of Achaia   *2Co 11:10*
I came into the *r.* of Syria   *Ga 1:21*

REGISTER

sought their *r.* among those that   *Ezr 2:62*
I found a *r.* of the genealogy of   *Ne 7:5*
sought their *r.* among those that   *Ne 7:64*

REGISTERED

genealogy *r.* (B)   *1Ch 5:1; 5:7, 17; 9:22; 2Ch 31:19*
registered (S)   *Lu 2:1; 2:3, 5*

REGISTRATION

registration (S)   *Ezr 2:62; Ne 7:5, 64; Lu 2:2; Ac 5:37*

REGRET

people might feel *r.* (B)   *Ex 13:17*
I *r.* I made Saul king (A)   *1Sa 15:11*
I will *r.* the calamity (B)   *Jer 42:10*
not *r.* it or change (A)(R)   *Heb 7:21*

REGRETFUL

makes me *r.* that (A)   *Ge 6:7*

REGRETTED

Lord *r.* he made man (A)   *Ge 6:6*
he *r.* and relented of evil (A)   *1Ch 21:15*

REGULAR

his allowance was a *r.*   *2Ki 25:30*
allowance (S)
resolved in *r.* assembly (P)   *Ac 19:39*

REGULARLY

eat bread at my table *r.* (S)   *2Sa 9:7; 9:13*
which passeth by *r.* (S)   *2Ki 4:9*
he did eat bread *r.* before him (S)   *2Ki 25:29*

REGULATION

established as a *r.* (B)   *Ge 47:26*
practice my *r.* (B)   *Le 18:4*
an everlasting *r.* (B)   *Le 24:3; 19:10; Nu 19:21*

every *r.* of the passover (B)   *Nu 9:12*
previous *r.* set aside (B)(R)   *Heb 7:18*

REGULATIONS

practice my *r.* (B)   *Le 18:4*
regulations (B)   *Nu 30:16; 2Ch 33:8*
according to these *r.* (B)   *Nu 35:24*
the commands and *r.* (B)   *Nu 36:13*
r. and judgments (B)   *2Ch 33:8*
the *r.* for women (S)   *Es 2:12*
these are the *r.* (A)(B)   *Eze 43:18*
not under old code of written *r.* (A)   *Ro 7:6*
external observations, *r.* (A)   *Ga 4:3*
commandments with *r.* (B)(N)   *Eph 2:15*
red ledger of *r.* (B)   *Col 2:14*
why submit to rules and *r.* (A)(B)(R)   *Col 2:20*
rules and *r.* of divine worship (A)(R)   *Heb 9:1*
its worship *r.* (B)   *Heb 9:1*
external rules and *r.* (A)(B)(R)   *Heb 9:10*

REHABIAH

sons of Eliezer were, R. the chief   *1Ch 23:17*
but the sons of R. were very many   *1Ch 23:17*
Concerning R.: of the sons of R.   *1Ch 24:21*
R. his son, and Jeshaiah his son   *1Ch 26:25*

REHEARSE

and *r.* it in the ears of Joshua   *Ex 17:14*
shall they *r.* the righteous acts   *J'g 5:11*

REHEARSED

he *r.* them in the ears of the Lord   *1Sa 8:21*
spake, they *r.* them before Saul   *1Sa 17:31*
But Peter *r.* the matter from   *Ac 11:4*
they *r.* all that God had done with   *Ac 14:27*

REHOB

from the wilderness of Zin unto R.   *Nu 13:21*
Hebron, and R. and Hammon, and   *Jos 19:28*
Ummah also, and Aphek, and R.   *Jos 19:30*
suburbs, and R. with her suburbs   *Jos 21:31; 1Ch 6:75*
of Helbah, nor of Aphik, nor of R.   *J'g 1:31*
also Hadadezer, the son of R.   *2Sa 8:3*
king
spoil of Hadadezer, the son of R.   *2Sa 8:12*
Syrians of Zobah, and of R.   *2Sa 10:8*
suburbs, and R. with her suburbs   *1Ch 6:75*
Micha, R., Hashabiah   *Ne 10:11*

REHOBOAM

R. the son of Solomon   *1Ki 11:43; 14:21; 2Ch 9:31*
reigned
R. consulted with the old men   *1Ki 12:6; 2Ch 10:6*
R. reigned over them   *1Ki 12:17; 2Ch 10:17*
to bring the kingdom again to R.   *1Ki 12:21; 2Ch 11:1*
then their heart shall turn again to R.   *1Ki 12:27*
was war between R. and Jeroboam   *1Ki 14:30; 15:6*
R. was Solomon's son   *1Ch 3:10; M't 1:7*
they made R. strong three years   *2Ch 11:17*
R. loved Maachah daughter of Absalom   *2Ch 11:21*
R. made Abijah the son of Maachah the chief   *2Ch 11:22*
Jeroboam strengthened himself against R. when R. was young   *2Ch 13:7*

REHOBOTH

Nineveh, and the city R. and R.   *Ge 10:11*
and he called the name of it R.   *Ge 26:22*
Saul of R. by the river reigned in   *Ge 36:37*
Shaul of R. by the river reigned in   *1Ch 1:48*

REHUM

Mizpar, Bigvai, R. Baanah   *Ezr 2:2*
R. the chancellor and Shimshai   *Ezr 4:8*
Then wrote R. the chancellor   *Ezr 4:9*
an answer unto R. the chancellor   *Ezr 4:17*
letter was read before R. and   *Ezr 4:23*
the Levites, R. the son of Bani   *Ne 3:17*
R., Hashabnah, Maaseiah   *Ne 10:25*
Shechaniah, R., Meremoth   *Ne 12:3*

REI

the prophet, and Shimei, and R.   *1Ki 1:8*

REIGN

him, Shalt thou indeed *r.* over us   *Ge 37:8*
are you going to *r.* over us (R)   *Ge 37:8*
The Lord shall *r.* for ever and ever   *Ex 15:18*
that hate you shall *r.* over you   *Le 26:17*
thou shalt *r.* over many nations   *De 15:6*
but they shall not *r.* over thee   *De 15:6*
threescore and ten persons, *r.* over   *J'g 9:2*
you, or that one *r.* over you   *J'g 9:2*
the olive tree, R. thou over us   *J'g 9:8*
fig tree, Come thou, and *r.* over us   *J'g 9:10*
the vine, Come thou, and *r.* over us   *J'g 9:12*
bramble, Come thou, and *r.* over us   *J'g 9:14*
Philistines had *r.* (E)   *J'g 14:4*
me, that I should not *r.* over them   *1Sa 8:7*
of the king that shall *r.* over them   *1Sa 8:9*
of the king that shall *r.* over you   *1Sa 8:11*
this same shall *r.* over my people   *1Sa 9:17*
that said, Shall Saul *r.* over us   *1Sa 11:12*
Nay; but a king shall *r.* over us   *1Sa 12:12*
forty years old when he began to *r.*   *2Sa 2:10*
r. over all that thine heart desireth   *2Sa 3:21*
thirty years old when he began to *r.*   *2Sa 5:4*
not heard that Adonijah doth *r.*   *1Ki 1:11*
Solomon thy son shall *r.* after me   *1Ki 1:13*
throne? why then doth Adonijah *r.*   *1Ki 1:13*
Solomon thy son shall *r.* after me   *1Ki 1:17*
Adonijah shall *r.* after me, and he   *1Ki 1:24*
Solomon thy son shall *r.* after me   *1Ki 1:30*
their faces on me, that I should *r.*   *1Ki 2:15*
year of Solomon's *r.* over Israel   *1Ki 6:1*
r. according to all that thy soul   *1Ki 11:37*
one years old when he began to *r.*   *1Ki 14:21*
And Nadab began to *r.* over Israel   *1Ki 15:25*
began Baasha to *r.* over all Israel   *1Ki 15:33*
began Elah to *r.* over Israel   *1Ki 16:8*
came to pass, when he began to *r.*   *1Ki 16:15*
did Zimri *r.* seven days in Tirzah   *1Ki 16:15*
began Omri to *r.* over Israel, twelve   *1Ki 16:23*

began Ahab to *r.* over   *1Ki 16:29*
Israel
Jehoshaphat, to *r.* over   *1Ki 22:41*
Judah
five years old when he began *1Ki 22:42*
to *r.*
Ahaziah began to *r.* over   *1Ki 22:51*
Israel
Jehoram began to *r.* over   *2Ki 3:1*
Israel
Jehoram the son began to *r.*   *2Ki 8:16*
old was he when he began to   *2Ki 8:17*
r.
did Ahaziah begin to *r.*   *2Ki 8:25*
was Ahaziah when he began   *2Ki 8:26*
to *r.*
began Ahaziah to *r.* over   *2Ki 9:29*
Judah
And Athaliah did *r.* over   *2Ki 11:3*
the land
was Jehoash when he began   *2Ki 11:21*
to *r.*
year of Jehu Jehoash began   *2Ki 12:1*
to *r.*
son of Jehu began to *r.* over   *2Ki 13:1*
Israel
began Jehoash to *r.* over   *2Ki 13:10*
Israel in
five years old when he began   *2Ki 14:2*
to *r.*
Jeroboam began to *r.* in   *2Ki 14:23*
Samaria
son of Amaziah king of Judah *2Ki 15:1*
to *r.*
old was he when he began to   *2Ki 15:2*
r.
did Zachariah *r.* over Israel   *2Ki 15:8*
in
Shallum son of Jabesh   *2Ki 15:13*
began to *r.*
the son of Gadi to *r.* over   *2Ki 15:17*
Israel
Pekahiah began to *r.* over   *2Ki 15:23*
Israel
Pekah began to *r.* over   *2Ki 15:27*
Israel
son of Uzziah king of Judah   *2Ki 15:32*
to *r.*
old was he when he began   *2Ki 15:33*
to *r.*
Ahaz son of Jotham began   *2Ki 16:1*
to *r.*
old was Ahaz when he began   *2Ki 16:2*
to *r.*
began Hoshea to *r.* in   *2Ki 17:1*
Samaria
that Hezekiah began to *r.*   *2Ki 18:1*
old was he when he began to   *2Ki 18:2*
r.
twelve years old he began to   *2Ki 21:1*
r.
two years old when he   *2Ki 21:19*
began to *r.*
eight years old when he   *2Ki 22:1*
began to *r.*
years old when he began to   *2Ki 23:31*
r.
that he might not *r.* in   *2Ki 23:33*
Jerusalem
five years old when he began   *2Ki 23:36*
to *r.*
years old when he began to *r.* *2Ki 24:8*
him in the eighth year of his   *2Ki 24:12*
r.
one years old when he began   *2Ki 24:18*
to *r.*
to pass in the ninth year of   *2Ki 25:1*
his *r.*
in the year that he began to   *2Ki 25:27*
r. did
their cities unto the *r.* of   *1Ch 4:31*
David
the fortieth year of the *r.* of *1Ch 26:31*
David
With all his *r.* and his   *1Ch 29:30*
might, and
hast made me to *r.* in his   *2Ch 1:8*
stead
month, in the fourth year of   *2Ch 3:2*
his *r.*
years old when he began to   *2Ch 12:13*
r.
began Abijah to *r.* over   *2Ch 13:1*
Judah
the fifteenth year of the *r.*   *2Ch 15:10*
of Asa
and thirtieth year of the *r.*   *2Ch 15:19;*
of Asa   *2Ch 16:1*
the thirty and ninth year of   *2Ch 16:12*
his *r.*

the one and fortieth year of   *2Ch 16:13*
his *r.*
third year of his *r.* he sent to *2Ch 17:7*
his
five years old when he   *2Ch 20:31*
began to *r.*
two years old when he began   *2Ch 21:5*
to *r.*
old was he when he began   *2Ch 21:20*
to *r.*
was Ahaziah when he began   *2Ch 22:2*
to *r.*
Behold, the king's son shall   *2Ch 23:3*
r. as
seven years old when he   *2Ch 24:1*
began to *r.*
five years old when he began   *2Ch 25:1*
to *r.*
was Uzziah when he began   *2Ch 26:3*
years old when he began to *r.* *2Ch 27:8;*
               28:1
Hezekiah began to *r.* when   *2Ch 29:1*
he was
He in the first year of his *r.*   *2Ch 29:3*
king Ahaz in his *r.* did cast *2Ch 29:19*
away
years old when he began to   *2Ch 33:1;*
r.   *33:21*
eight years old when he   *2Ch 34:1*
began to *r.*
in the eighth year of his *r.*   *2Ch 34:3*
while
the eighteenth year of his   *2Ch 34:8*
r. when
eighteenth year of the *r.* of *2Ch 35:19*
Josiah
years old when he began to *r.* *2Ch 36:2*
five years old when he began *2Ch 36:5*
to *r.*
eight years old when he   *2Ch 36:9*
began to *r.*
years old when he began to   *2Ch 36:11*
r.
the *r.* of the kingdom of   *2Ch 36:20*
Persia
the *r.* of Darius king of Persia *Ezr 4:5*
And in the *r.* of Ahasuerus, in *Ezr 4:6*
in the beginning of his *r.* wrote *Ezr 4:6*
the second year of the *r.* of *Ezr 4:24*
Darius
in the sixth year of the *r.* of *Ezr 6:15*
Darius
in the *r.* of Artaxerxes king of *Ezr 7:1*
in the *r.* of Artaxerxes the king *Ezr 8:1*
to the *r.* of Darius the   *Ne 12:22*
Persian
In the third year of his *r.* he   *Es 1:3*
made
in the seventh year of his *r.*   *Es 2:16*
That the hyprocrite *r.* not,   *Job 34:30*
lest the
The Lord shall *r.* for ever,   *Ps 146:10*
even thy
By me kings *r.* and princes   *Pr 8:15*
decree
For out of prison he cometh   *Ec 4:14*
to *r.*
the Lord of hosts shall *r.* in *Isa 24:23*
mount
a king shall *r.* in righteousness *Isa 32:1*
in the thirteenth year of his *r.* *Jer 1:2*
Shalt thou *r.* because thou   *Jer 22:15*
closest
and a King shall *r.* and   *Jer 23:5*
prosper
beginning of the *r.* of   *Jer 26:1;*
Jehoiakim   *27:1*
the beginning of the *r.* of   *Jer 28:1*
Zedekiah
have a son to *r.* upon his   *Jer 33:21*
throne
the *r.* of Zedekiah king of   *Jer 49:34*
Judah
in the fourth year of his *r.*   *Jer 51:59*
years old when he began to *r.* *Jer 52:1*
to pass in the ninth year of   *Jer 52:4*
in the first year of his *r.*   *Jer 52:31*
lifted up
third year of the *r.* of   *Da 1:1*
Jehoiakim
year of the *r.* of   *Da 2:1*
Nebuchadnezzar
this Daniel prospered in the *r.* *Da 6:28*
of
and in the *r.* of Cyrus the   *Da 6:28*
Persian

year of the *r.* of king   *Da 8:1*
Belshazzar
In the first year of his *r.* I   *Da 9:2*
Daniel
shall *r.* over them in mount   *Mic 4:7*
Zion
that Archelaus did *r.* in   *M't 2:22*
Judaea in
r. over the house of Jacob for *Lu 1:33*
ever
year of the *r.* of Tiberius   *Lu 3:1*
Caesar
not have this man to *r.* over *Lu 19:14*
us
would not that I should *r.*   *Lu 19:27*
over them
shall *r.* in life by one, Jesus *Ro 5:17*
Christ
grace *r.* through righteousness *Ro 5:21*
unto
Let not sin *r.* in your mortal *Ro 6:12*
body
shall rise to *r.* over the   *Ro 15:12*
Gentiles
us: and I would to God ye   *1Co 4:8*
did *r.*
that we also might *r.*   *1Co 4:8*
with you
For he must *r.* till he hath *1Co 15:25*
put all
suffer, we shall also *r.* with *2Ti 2:12*
him
and we shall *r.* on the earth *Re 5:10*
and he shall *r.* for ever and *Re 11:15*
shall *r.* with him a thousand *Re 20:6*
years
and they shall *r.* for ever and *Re 22:5*
ever

REIGNED

kings that *r.* in the land of   *Ge 36:31*
Edom
before there *r.* any king   *Ge 36:31*
over the
Bela the son of Beor *r.*   *Ge 36:32*
in Edom
and Jobah *r.* in his stead   *Ge 36:33*
and Husham *r.* in his stead   *Ge 36:34*
and Hadad *r.* in his stead   *Ge 36:35*
Samlah of Masrekah *r.* in his *Ge 36:36*
stead
died, and Saul *r.* in his   *Ge 36:37*
stead
the son of Achbor *r.* in his   *Ge 36:38*
stead
died, and Hadar *r.* in his   *Ge 36:39*
stead
And *r.* in mount Hermon, and *Jos 12:5*
Amorites, which *r.* in   *Jos 13:10*
Heshbon
which *r.* in Ashtaroth and in *Jos 13:12*
Edrei
the Amorites, which *r.* in   *Jos 13:21*
Heshbon
king of Canaan, that *r.* in   *J'g 4:2*
Hazor
Abimelech had *r.* three years *J'g 9:22*
over
Saul *r.* one year; and when *1Sa 13:1*
he had
he had *r.* two years over   *1Sa 13:1*
Israel
reign over Israel, and *r.* two *2Sa 2:10*
years
to reign, and he *r.* forty years *2Sa 5:4*
he *r.* over Judah seven years *2Sa 5:5*
he *r.* thirty and three years *2Sa 5:5*
over
And David *r.* over all Israel *2Sa 8:15*
and Hanun his son *r.* in his *2Sa 10:1*
stead
Saul, in whose stead thou   *2Sa 16:8*
hast *r.*
that David *r.* over Israel were *1Ki 2:11*
forty
seven years *r.* he in Hebron *1Ki 2:11*
and three years *r.* he in   *1Ki 2:11*
Jerusalem
And Solomon *r.* over all   *1Ki 4:21*
kingdoms
dwelt therein, and *r.* in   *1Ki 11:24*
Damascus
abhorred Israel, and *r.* over *1Ki 11:25*
Syria
Solomon *r.* in Jerusalem   *1Ki 11:42*
over all
Rehoboam his son *r.* in his *1Ki 11:43*
stead

of Judah, Rehoboam r. over them	1Ki 12:17	Israel, and r. ten years in Samaria	2Ki 15:17	And Jehoshaphat r. over Judah: he	2Ch 20:31
how he warred, and how he r.	1Ki 14:19	Pekahiah his son r. in his stead	2Ki 15:22	he r. twenty and five years in	2Ch 20:31
the days which Jeroboam r. were	1Ki 14:20	Israel in Samaria, and r. two years	2Ki 15:23	Jehoram his son r. in his stead	2Ch 21:1
and Nadab his son r. in his stead	1Ki 14:20	he killed him, and r. in his room	2Ki 15:25	and he r. eight years in Jerusalem	2Ch 21:5
And Rehoboam r. in Judah	1Ki 14:21	in Samaria, and r. twenty years	2Ki 15:27	and he r. in Jerusalem eight years	2Ch 21:20
he r. seventeen years in Jerusalem	1Ki 14:21	and slew him, and r. in his stead	2Ki 15:30	son of Jehoram king of Judah r.	2Ch 22:1
And Abijam his son r. in his stead	1Ki 14:31	he r. sixteen years in Jerusalem	2Ki 15:33	and he r. one year in Jerusalem	2Ch 22:2
son of Nebat r. Abijam over Judah	1Ki 15:1	and Ahaz his son r. in his stead	2Ki 15:38	and Athaliah r. over the land	2Ch 2:12
Three years r. he in Jerusalem	1Ki 15:2	and r. sixteen years in Jerusalem	2Ki 16:2	and he r. forty years in Jerusalem	2Ch 24:1
and Asa his son r. in his stead	1Ki 15:8	Hezekiah his son r. in his stead	2Ki 16:20	Amaziah his son r. in his stead	2Ch 24:27
king of Israel r. Asa over Judah	1Ki 15:9	and he r. twenty and nine years in	2Ki 18:2	and he r. twenty and nine years in	2Ch 25:1
and one years r. he in Jerusalem	1Ki 15:10	Esarhaddon his son r. in his stead	2Ki 19:37	r. fifty and two years in Jerusalem	2Ch 26:3
Jehoshaphat his son r. in his stead	1Ki 15:24	Manasseh his son r. in his stead	2Ki 20:21	and Jotham his son r. in his stead	2Ch 26:23
Judah, and r. over Israel two years	1Ki 15:25	r. fifty and five years in Jerusalem	2Ki 21:1	he r. sixteen years in Jerusalem	2Ch 27:1
slay him, and r. in his stead	1Ki 15:28	and Amon his son r. in his stead	2Ki 21:18	and r. sixteen years in Jerusalem	2Ch 27:8
it came to pass, when he r. that he	1Ki 15:29	and he r. two years in Jerusalem	2Ki 21:19	and Ahaz his son r. in his stead	2Ch 27:9
and Elah his son r. in his stead	1Ki 16:6	and Josiah his son r. in his stead	2Ki 21:26	he r. sixteen years in Jerusalem	2Ch 28:1
king of Judah, and r. in his stead	1Ki 16:10	and he r. thirty and one years in	2Ki 22:1	Hezekiah his son r. in his stead	2Ch 28:27
so Tibni died, and Omri r.	1Ki 16:22	he r. three months in Jerusalem	2Ki 23:31	and he r. nine and twenty years in	2Ch 29:1
years: six years r. he in Tirzah	1Ki 16:23	he r. eleven years in Jerusalem	2Ki 23:36	Manassah his son r. in his stead	2Ch 32:33
and Ahab his son r. in his stead	1Ki 16:28	Jehoiachin his son r. in his stead	2Ki 24:6	and he r. fifty and five years in	2Ch 33:1
Ahab the son of Omri r. over Israel	1Ki 16:29	he r. in Jerusalem three months	2Ki 24:8	and Amon his son r. in his stead	2Ch 33:20
Ahaziah his son r. in his stead	1Ki 22:40	he r. eleven years in Jerusalem	2Ki 24:18	and r. two years in Jerusalem	2Ch 33:21
and he r. twenty and five years in	1Ki 22:42	kings that r. in the land of Edom	1Ch 1:43	he r. in Jerusalem one and thirty	2Ch 34:1
Jehoram his son r. in his stead	1Ki 22:50	before any king r. over the children	1Ch 1:43	he r. three months in Jerusalem	2Ch 36:2
Judah, and r. two years over Israel	1Ki 22:51	Jobab the son r. in his stead	1Ch 1:44	he r. eleven years in Jerusalem	2Ch 36:5
And Jehoram r. in his stead in the	2Ki 1:17	Husham r. in his stead	1Ch 1:45	Jehoiachin his son r. in his stead	2Ch 36:8
king of Judah, and r. twelve years	2Ki 3:1	Hadad the son r. in his stead	1Ch 1:46	he r. three months and ten days in	2Ch 36:9
that should have r. in his stead	2Ki 3:27	Samlah of Masrekah r. in his stead	1Ch 1:47	and r. eleven years in Jerusalem	2Ch 36:11
he died: and Hazael r. in his stead	2Ki 8:15	Shaul of Rehoboth r. in his stead	1Ch 1:48	(this is Ahasuerus which r. from	Es 1:1
and he r. eight years in Jerusalem	2Ki 8:17	the son of Achbor r. in his stead	1Ch 1:49	Esar-haddon his son r. in his	Isa 37:38
and Ahaziah his son r. in his stead	2Ki 8:24	was dead, Hadad r. in his stead	1Ch 1:50	r. instead of Josiah his father	Jer 22:11
and he r. one year in Jerusalem	2Ki 8:26	he r. seven years and six months	1Ch 3:4	Zedekiah r. instead of Coniah	Jer 37:1
Jehoahaz his son r. in his stead	2Ki 10:35	he r. thirty and three years	1Ch 3:4	he r. eleven years in Jerusalem	Jer 52:1
the time that Jehu r. over Israel	2Ki 10:36	So David r. over all Israel	1Ch 18:14	death r. from Adam to Moses, even	Ro 5:14
and forty years r. he in Jerusalem	2Ki 12:1	died, and his son r. in his stead	1Ch 19:1	one man's offence death r. by one	Ro 5:17
Amaziah his son r. in his stead	2Ki 12:21	David the son r. over all Israel	1Ch 29:26	as sin hath r. unto death, even so	Ro 5:21
in Samaria, and r. seventeen years	2Ki 13:1	he r. over Israel was forty years	1Ch 29:27	ye have r. as kings without us	1Co 4:8
and Joash his son r. in his stead	2Ki 13:9	seven years r. he in Hebron	1Ch 29:27	thee thy great power, and hast r.	Re 11:17
in Samaria, and r. sixteen years	2Ki 13:10	and three years r. he in Jerusalem	1Ch 29:27	and r. with Christ a thousand years	Re 20:4
Ben-hadad his son r. in his stead	2Ki 13:24	and Solomon his son r. in his stead	1Ch 29:28		
r. Amaziah the son of Joash king	2Ki 14:1	congregation, and r. over Israel	2Ch 1:13	**REIGNEST**	
and r. twenty and nine years in	2Ki 14:2	And he r. over all the kings from	2Ch 9:26	come of thee, and thou r. over all	1Ch 29:12
Jeroboam his son r. in his stead	2Ki 14:16	Solomon r. in Jerusalem over all	2Ch 9:30		
Samaria, and r. forty and one years	2Ki 14:23	Rehoboam r. in his stead	2Ch 9:31	**REIGNETH**	
Zachariah his son r. in his stead	2Ki 14:29	of Judah, Rehoboam r. over them	2Ch 10:17	and also the king that r. over you	1Sa 12:14
and he r. two and fifty years in	2Ki 15:2	himself in Jerusalem, and r.: for	2Ch 12:13	shall say, Absalom r. in Hebron	2Sa 15:10
and Jotham his son r. in his stead	2Ki 15:7	he r. seventeen years in Jerusalem	2Ch 12:13	now, behold, Adonijah r.; and now	1Ki 1:18
and slew him, and r. in his stead	2Ki 15:10	and Abijah his son r. in his stead	2Ch 12:16	among the nations, The Lord r.	1Ch 16:31
and he r. a full month in Samaria	2Ki 15:13	He r. three years in Jerusalem	2Ch 13:2	God r. over the heathen: God	Ps 47:8
and slew him, and r. in his stead	2Ki 15:14	and Asa his son r. in his stead	2Ch 14:1	The Lord r. he is clothed, with	Ps 93:1
		Jehoshaphat his son r. in his stead	2Ch 17:1	the heathen that the Lord r.	Ps 96:10
				The Lord r.; let the earth rejoice	Ps 97:1
				The Lord r.; let the people	Ps 99:1
				For a servant when he r.; and	Pr 30:22
				that saith unto Zion, Thy God r.	Isa 52:7

REIGNETH

which r. over the kings of	Re 17:18
for the Lord God omnipotent r.	Re 19:6

REIGNING

rejected him from r. over Israel	1Sa 16:1

REIMBURSEMENT

free without r. (B)	Ex 21:11

REINS

he cleaveth my r. asunder	Job 16:13
he slashes open my vitals (A)	Job 16:13
he slashes open my kidneys (R)	Job 16:13
my r. be consumed within me	Job 19:27
my heart pines away and is consumed (A)(E)	Job 19:27
my heart faints within me (R)	Job 19:27
God trieth the hearts and r.	Ps 7:9
who try the hearts and emotions (A)(B)	Ps 7:9
who trieth the minds and hearts (E)(R)	Ps 7:9
my r. also instruct me in the night	Ps 16:7
my heart instructs me (A)(E)(R)	Ps 16:7
my emotions admonish me (B)	Ps 16:7
prove me: try my r. and my heart	Ps 26:2
test my heart and my mind (A)(E)(R)	Ps 26:2
test my soul and my attitude (B)	Ps 26:2
grieved, and I was pricked in my r.	Ps 73:21
I was pricked in my heart (A)(E)(R)	Ps 73:21
I was pierced deep within (B)	Ps 73:21
For thou hast possessed my r.	Ps 139:13
you did form my inward parts (A)(E)(R)	Ps 139:13
you did possess my inward parts (B)	Ps 139:13
my r. shall rejoice, when thy lips	Pr 23:16
my heart will rejoice (A)(B)(E)	Pr 23:16
my soul will rejoice (R)	Pr 23:16
faithfulness the girdle of his r.	Isa 11:5
faithfulness the girdle of his loins (A)(B)(E)(R)	Isa 11:5
that triest the r. and the heart	Jer 11:20
Who tests the heart and the mind (A)(E)(R)	Jer 11:20
their mouth, and far from their r.	Jer 12:2
near mouth, and far from their heart (A)(E)(R)	Jer 12:2
far from their inmost selves (B)	Jer 12:2
Lord search the heart, I try the r.	Je 17:10
I search the mind, I try the heart (A)(E)(R)	Jer 17:10
I search the heart and try the inner self (B)	Jer 17:10
and seest the r. and the heart, let	Jer 20:12
Who sees the heart and mind (A)(B)(E)(R)	Jer 20:12
of his quiver to enter into my r.	La 3:13
arrows of his quiver to enter my heart (A)(R)	La 3:13
arrows to enter my inmost parts (B)	La 3:13
which searcheth the r. and hearts	Re 2:23
he who searches minds and hearts (N)	Re 2:23
searcher of men's hearts and thoughts (N)	Re 2:23

REINSTATE

r. him in affection (B)	2Co 2:8

REINSTATEMENT

their full r. (A)	Ro 11:12

REJECT

my soul not r. you (A)(B)	Le 26:11
does not r. or despise evil (A)	Ps 36:4
do not r. the throne (B)	Jer 14:21
I will also r. thee, and thou shalt	Ho 4:6
sat with him, he would not r. her	M'k 6:26
well ye r. the commandment of God	M'k 7:9
first and second admonition r.	Tit 3:10

REJECTED

despised and r. (A)	Le 26:43
r. Jehovah (E)(R)	Nu 11:20
you have r. (B)(E)	Nu 14:31
spurned and r. them (A)	De 32:19
they have not r. thee, but they	1Sa 8:7
they have r. me, that I should not	1Sa 8:7
And ye have this day r. your God	1Sa 10:19
thou hast r. the word of the Lord	1Sa 15:23
hath also r. thee from being king	1Sa 15:23
thou hast r. the word of the Lord	1Sa 15:26
Lord hath r. thee from being king	1Sa 15:26
r. him from reigning over Israel	1Sa 16:1
And they r. his statutes, and his	2Ki 17:15
the Lord r. all the seed of Israel	2Ki 17:20
God has r. them (A)(B)(E)(R)	Ps 53:5
utterly r. Israel (R)	Ps 78:59
cast off and r. (A)(R)	Ps 89:38
it would utterly be r. (S)	Ca 8:7
He is despised and r. of men	Isa 53:3
the Lord hath r. thy confidences	Jer 2:37
my words, nor to my law, but r. it	Jer 6:19
because the Lord hath r. them	Jer 6:30
the Lord hath r. and forsaken	Jer 7:29
they have r. the word of the Lord	Jer 8:9
Hast thou utterly r. Judah	Jer 14:19
thou hast utterly r. us; thou art	La 5:22
because thou hast r. knowledge, I	Ho 4:6
The stone which the builders r.	M't 21:42
and be r. of the elders, and of the	M'k 8:31
The stone which the builders r. is	M'k 12:10
and lawyers r. the counsel of God	Lu 7:30
be r. of the elders and chief priests	Lu 9:22
things, and be r. of this generation	Lu 17:25
The stone which the builders r.	Lu 20:17
in my flesh ye despised not, nor r.	Ga 4:14
beareth thorns and briers is r.	Heb 6:8
r. and set at nought (A)(B)(E)	Heb 10:28
inherited the blessing, he was r.	Heb 12:17
r. by men (B)(E)(N)(P)(R)	1Pe 2:4
builders r. (A)(B)(E)(N)(P)	1Pe 2:7

REJECTETH

He that r. me, and receiveth not	Joh 12:48
r. not man but God (E)	1Th 4:8

REJECTION

a definite r. of God (N)	2Th 2:3

REJECTS

soul despises and r. (A)	Le 26:15
r. me, r. you (B)(E)(N)(R)	Lu 10:16

REJOICE

shall r. before the Lord your God	Le 23:40
shall r. in all that ye put your hand	De 12:7
shall r. before the Lord your God	De 12:12
shalt r. before the Lord your God	De 12:18
and thou shalt r. thou, and thine	De 14:26
shalt r. before the Lord thy God	De 16:11
thou shalt r. in thy feast, thou, and	De 16:14
therefore thou shalt surely r.	De 16:15
thou shalt r. in every good thing	De 26:11
and r. before the Lord thy God	De 27:7
Lord will r. over you to destroy	De 38:63
will again r. over thee for good	De 30:9
R., O ye nations, with his people	De 32:43
R., Zebulun, in thy going out	De 33:18
this day, then r. ye in Abimelech	J'g 9:19
and let him also r. in you	J'g 9:19
unto Dagon their god, and to r.	J'g 16:23
because I r. in thy salvation	1Sa 2:1
thou sawest it and didst r.	1Sa 19:5
the daughters of the Philistines r.	2Sa 1:20
heart of them r. that seek the Lord	1Ch 16:10
be glad, and let the earth r.	1Ch 16:31
let the fields r. and all that is	1Ch 16:32
and let thy saints r. in goodness	2Ch 6:41
made them to r. over their enemies	2Ch 20:27
had made them r. with great joy	Ne 12:43
Which r. exceedingly, and are glad	Job 3:22
be, and he shall not r.	Job 20:18
and r. at the sound of the organ	Job 21:12
with fear, and r. with trembling	Ps 2:11
that put their trust in thee r.	Ps 5:11
I will be glad and r. in thee: I will	Ps 9:2
of Zion: I will r. in thy salvation	Ps 9:14
trouble me r. when I am moved	Ps 13:4
my heart shall r. in thy salvation	Ps 13:5
Jacob shall r. and Israel shall be	Ps 14:7
We will r. in thy salvation, and in	Ps 20:5
salvation how greatly shall he r.	Ps 21:1
not made my foes to r. over me	Ps 30:1
I will be glad and r. in thy mercy	Ps 31:7
Be glad in the Lord, and r. ye	Ps 32:11
R. in the Lord, O ye righteous	Ps 33:1
For our heart shall r. in him	Ps 33:21
Lord: it shall r. in his salvation	Ps 35:9
enemies wrongfully r. over me	Ps 35:19
and let them not r. over me	Ps 35:24
together that r. at mine hurt	Ps 35:26
otherwise they should r. over me	Ps 38:16
Let all those that seek thee r.	Ps 40:16
Let mount Zion r. let the	Ps 48:11
bones thou hast broken may r.	Ps 51:8
Jacob shall r. and Israel shall be	Ps 53:6
righteous shall r. when he seeth	Ps 58:10
I will r., I will divide Shechem	Ps 60:6
the shadow of thy wings will I r.	Ps 63:7
But the king shall r. in God	Ps 63:11
outgoings of the morning to r.	Ps 65:8
the little hills r. on every side	Ps 65:12
on foot: there did we r. in him	Ps 66:6
be glad; let them r. before God	Ps 68:3

yea, let them exceedingly r.	Ps 68:3
name JAH, and r. before him	Ps 68:4
Let all those that seek thee r.	Ps 70:4
My lips shall greatly r. when I sing	Ps 71:23
that thy people may r. in thee	Ps 85:6
R. the soul of thy servant: for unto	Ps 86:4
and Hermon shall r. in thy name	Ps 89:12
thy name shall they r. all the day	Ps 89:16
hast made all his enemies to r.	Ps 89:42
we may r. and be glad all our days	Ps 90:14
Let the heavens r. and let the	Ps 96:11
shall all the trees of the wood r.	Ps 96:12
Lord reigneth; let the earth r.	Ps 97:1
R. in the Lord, ye righteous	Ps 97:12
make a loud noise, and r. and	Ps 98:4
the Lord shall r. in his works	Ps 104:31
heart of them r. that seek the Lord	Ps 105:3
may r. in the gladness of thy nation	Ps 106:5
The righteous shall see it, and r.	Ps 107:42
I will r., I will divide Shechem	Ps 108:7
ashamed; but let thy servant r.	Ps 109:28
made; we will r. and be glad in it	Ps 118:24
I r. at thy word, as one that	Ps 119:162
Israel r. in him that made him	Ps 149:2
Who r. to do evil, and delight	Pr 2:14
and r. with the wife of thy youth	Pr 5:18
wise, my heart shall r. even mine	Pr 23:15
Yea, my reins shall r. when thy	Pr 23:16
father of the righteous shall r.	Pr 23:24
and she that bare thee shall r.	Pr 23:25
R. not when thine enemy falleth	Pr 24:17
Ointment and perfume r. the heart	Pr 27:9
When righteous men do r. there	Pr 28:12
are in authority, the people r.	Pr 29:2
but the righteous doth sing and r.	Pr 29:6
and she shall r. in time to come	Pr 31:25
but for a man to r. and to do good	Ec 3:12
a man should r. in his own works	Ec 3:22
that come after shall not r. in him	Ec 4:16
his portion, and to r. in his labour	Ec 5:19
live many years, and r. in them all	Ec 11:8
R. O young man, in thy youth	Ec 11:9
we will be glad and r. in thee we	Ca 1:4
r. in Rezin and Remaliah's son	Isa 8:6
men r. when they divide the spoil	Isa 9:3
they r. before thee (S)	Isa 9:3
even them that r. in my highness	Isa 13:3
Yea, the fir trees r. at thee	Isa 14:8
R. not thou, whole Palestina	Isa 14:29
Thou shalt no more r. O thou	Isa 23:12
the noise of them that r. endeth	Isa 24:8
will be glad and r. in his salvation	Isa 25:9
poor among men shall r. in	Isa 29:19
and the desert shall r. and blossom	Isa 35:1
and r. even with joy and singing	Isa 35:2
thou shalt r. in the Lord, and shalt	Isa 41:16
they shall r. in their portion	Isa 61:7
I will greatly r. in the Lord, my	Isa 61:10
bride, so shall thy God r. over thee	Isa 62:5
my servants shall r. but ye shall	Isa 65:13

But be ye glad and r. for ever in	Isa 65:18
And I will r. in Jerusalem, and joy	Isa 65:19
R. ye with Jerusalem, and be glad	Isa 66:10
r. for joy with her, all ye that	Isa 66:10
your heart shall r. and your bones	Isa 66:14
shall the virgin r. in the dance	Jer 31:13
make them r. from their sorrow	Jer 31:13
I will r. over them to do them good	Jer 32:41
them drunken, that they may r.	Jer 51:39
caused thine enemy to r. over thee,	La 2:17
R. and be glad, O daughter of	La 4:21
let not the buyer r. nor the seller	Eze 7:12
As thou didst r. at the inheritance	Eze 35:15
R. not, O Israel, for joy, as other	Ho 9:1
Fear not, O land; be glad and r.	Joe 2:21
Zion, and r. in the Lord your God	Joe 2:23
Ye which r. in a thing of nought	Am 6:13
R. not against me, O mine enemy	Mic 7:8
therefore they r. and are glad	Hab 1:15
Yet I will r. in the Lord, I will joy	Hab 3:18
of thee them that r. in thy pride	Zep 3:11
be glad and r. with all the heart	Zep 3:14
save, he will r. over thee with joy	Zep 3:17
Sing and r. O daughter of Zion	Zec 2:10
for they shall r. and shall see	Zec 4:10
R. greatly, O daughter of Zion	Zec 9:9
heart shall r. as through wine	Zec 10:7
their heart shall r. in the Lord	Zec 10:7
R. and be exceeding glad: for	M't 5:12
and many shall r. at his birth	Lu 1:14
R. ye in that day, and leap for joy	Lu 6:23
Notwithstanding in this r. not	Lu 10:20
but rather r. because your names	Lu 10:20
R. with me; for I have found my sheep	Lu 15:6
R. with me; for I have found the piece	Lu 15:9
began to r. and praise God with a	Lu 19:37
and he that reapeth may r. together	Joh 4:36
willing for a season to r. in his light	Joh 5:35
If ye loved me, ye would r.	Joh 14:28
and lament, but the world shall r.	Joh 16:20
you again, and your heart shall r.	Joh 16:22
Therefore did my heart r. and	Ac 2:26
and r. in hope of the glory of God	Ro 5:2
R. with them that do r. and weep	Ro 12:15
R. ye Gentiles, with his people	Ro 15:10
and they that r. as though they	1Co 7:30
all the members r. with it	1Co 12:26
from them of whom I ought to r.	2Co 2:3
I r. not that ye were made sorry	2Co 7:9
I r. therefore that I have confidence	2Co 7:16
R. thou barren that bearest not	Ga 4:27
I therein do r., yea, and will r.	Ph'p 1:18
that I may r. in the day of Christ	Ph'p 2:16
faith, I joy, and r. with you all	Ph'p 2:17
cause also do ye joy, and r. with me	Ph'p 2:18

when ye see him again, ye may r.	Ph'p 2:28
Finally, my brethren, r. in the Lord	Ph'p 3:1
the spirit, and r. in Christ Jesus	Ph'p 3:3
Who now r. in my sufferings for	Col 1:24
R. evermore	1Th 5:16
Let the brother of low degree r.	Jas 1:9
But now ye r. in your boastings	Jas 4:16
Wherein ye greatly r. though	1Pe 1:6
ye r. with joy unspeakable and full	1Pe 1:8
r. inasmuch as ye are partakers	1Pe 4:13
upon the earth shall r. over them	Re 11:10
r. ye heavens, and ye that dwell	Re 12:12
R. over her, thou heaven, and ye	Re 18:20
Let us be glad and r. and give	Re 19:7

REJOICE
BEFORE THE LORD

ye shall r. before the Lord seven days	Le 23:40
ye shall r. before the Lord your God	De 12:12
shalt r. before the Lord thy God	De 12:28; 16:11; 27:7

REJOICE
IN THE LORD

r. in the Lord, O ye righteous	Ps 33:1; 97:12
r. in the Lord, glory in the Holy One	Isa 41:16
I will greatly r. in the Lord, and be joyful	Isa 61:10
ye children of Zion, r. in the Lord	Joe 2:23
yet I will r. in the Lord, I will joy	Hab 3:18
their heart shall r. in the Lord	Zec 10:7
finally, my brethren, r. in the Lord	Ph'p 3:1
r. in the Lord alway, and again, I say, rejoice	Ph'p 4:4

REJOICED

And Jethro r. for all the goodness	Ex 18:9
Lord r. over you to do you good	De 28:63
for good, as he r. over thy fathers	De 30:9
saw him, he r. to meet him	J'g 19:3
and saw the ark, and r. to see it	1Sa 6:13
and all the men of Israel r. greatly	1Sa 11:15
with pipes, and r. with great joy	1Ki 1:40
ate, drank, and r. (A)	1Ki 4:20
words of Solomon he r. greatly	1Ki 5:7
and all the people of the land r.	2Ki 11:14
And all the people of the land r.	2Ki 11:20
the people r. for that they offered	1Ch 29:9
David also r. with great joy	1Ch 29:9
And all Judah r. at the oath: for	2Ch 15:15
and all the people of the land r.	2Ch 23:13
and all the people of the land r.	2Ch 23:21
the princes and all the people r.	2Ch 24:10
And Hezekiah r. and all the people	2Ch 29:36
Israel, and that dwelt in Judah, r.	2Ch 30:25
offered great sacrifices, and r.	Ne 12:43
the wives also and the children r.	Ne 12:43

for Judah *r*. for the priests   *Ne 12:44*
city of Shushan *r*. and was   *Es 8:15*
glad
I *r*. because my wealth was   *Job 31:25*
great
If I *r*. at the destruction of   *Job 31:29*
him
r. at the ruin of him (R)   *Job 31:29*
But in mine adversity they *r*.   *Ps 35:15*
and the daughters of Judah *r*.   *Ps 97:8*
r. in the way of thy   *Ps 119:14*
testimonies
for my heart *r*. in all my   *Ec 2:10*
labour
assembly of the mockers nor   *Jer 15:17*
r.
Because ye were glad,   *Jer 50:11*
because ye *r*.
r. in heart with all thy despite   *Eze 25:6*
the priests thereof that *r*. on   *Ho 10:5*
it
thou have *r*. over the children   *Ob 12*
of
they *r*. with exceeding great   *M't 2:10*
joy
my spirit hath *r*. in God my   *Lu 1:47*
Saviour
upon her; and they *r*. with her   *Lu 1:58*
In that hour Jesus *r*. in spirit   *Lu 10:21*
people *r*. for all the glorious   *Lu 13:17*
things
father Abraham *r*. to see my   *Joh 8:56*
day
r. in the works of their own   *Ac 7:41*
hands
read, they *r*. for the   *Ac 15:31*
consolation
he set meat before them, and   *Ac 16:34*
r.
that rejoice, as though they *r*.   *1Co 7:30*
not
toward me; so that I *r*. the   *2Co 7:7*
more
But I *r*. in the Lord greatly,   *Ph'p 4:10*
that care had flourished
I *r*. greatly that I found of thy   *2Jo 4*
For I *r*. greatly, when the   *3Jo 3*
brethren testified of truth

REJOICES

r. in the right (R)   *1Co 13:6*

REJOICEST

when thou doest evil, then   *Jer 11:15*
thou *r*.

REJOICETH

and said, My heart *r*. in the   *1Sa 2:1*
Lord
the valley, and *r*. in his   *Job 39:21*
strength
my heart is glad, and my glory   *Ps 16:9*
r.
r. as a strong man to run a   *Ps 19:5*
race
therefore my heart greatly *r*.   *Ps 28:7*
with the righteous, the city *r*.   *Pr 11:10*
The light of the righteous *r*.   *Pr 13:9*
The light of the eyes *r*. the   *Pr 15:30*
heart
Whoso loveth wisdom *r*. his   *Pr 29:3*
father
he that *r*. shall descend into it   *Isa 5:14*
the bridegroom *r*. over the   *Isa 62:5*
bride
meetest him that *r*. and   *Isa 64:5*
worketh
When the whole earth *r*. I   *Eze 35:14*
will
he *r*. more of that sheep, than   *M't 18:13*
of
r. because of the   *Joh 3:29*
bridegroom's
R. not in iniquity   *1Co 13:6*
but *r*. in the truth   *1Co 13:6*
and mercy *r*. against judgment   *Jas 2:13*

REJOICING

they are come up from thence   *1Ki 1:45*
r.
with *r*. and with singing, as   *2Ch 23:18*
it was
laughing, and thy lips with *r*.   *Job 8:21*
of the Lord are right, *r*. the   *Ps 19:8*
heart
and *r*. shall they be brought   *Ps 45:15*

and declare his works with   *Ps 107:22*
r.
The voice of *r*. and salvation   *Ps 118:15*
is in
for they are the *r*. of my   *Ps 119:111*
heart
doubtless come again with *r*.   *Ps 126:6*
his delight, *r*. always before   *Pr 8:30*
him
R. in the habitable part   *Pr 8:31*
of his
I create Jerusalem a *r*. and   *Isa 65:18*
her
me the joy and *r*. of mine   *Jer 15:16*
heart
their *r*. was as to devour the   *Hab 3:14*
poor
is the *r*. city that dwelt   *Zep 2:15*
carelessly
he layeth it on his shoulders,   *Lu 15:5*
r.
r. that they were counted   *Ac 5:41*
worthy
more: and he went on his way   *Ac 8:39*
r.
R. in hope: patient in   *Ro 12:12*
tribulation
by your *r*. which I have in   *1Co 15:31*
Christ
For our *r*. is this, the   *2Co 1:12*
testimony of
that we are your *r*. even as   *2Co 1:14*
ye also
As sorrowful, yet always *r*.;   *2Co 6:10*
as
shall he have *r*. in himself   *Ga 6:4*
alone
your *r*. may be more   *Ph'p 1:26*
abundant in
is our hope, or joy, or crown   *1Th 2:19*
of *r*.
r. of the hope firm unto the   *Heb 3:6*
end
your boastings: all such *r*. is   *Jas 4:16*
evil

REJUVENATE

he will *r*. (B)   *Ru 4:15*

REKEM

were slain; namely, Evi, and   *Nu 31:8*
R.
the princes of Midian, Evi   *Jos 13:21*
and *R*.
And *R*. and Irpeel, and   *Jos 18:27*
Taralah
and Tappuah and *R*. and   *1Ch 2:43*
Shema
Jorkoam; and *R*. begat   *1Ch 2:44*
Shemmai

RELATED

r. by marriage (A)   *Ne 13:4*

RELATIONS

had sexual *r*. (B)   *Nu 5:19*
illicit *r*. (B)   *Nu 25:1*

RELATIONSHIP

not in old *r*. of literalness (B)   *Ro 7:6*

RELATIVE

your *r*. (A)   *Lu 1:36*

RELATIVES

brothers and *r*. (B)   *J'g 16:31*
we are *r*. (B)   *2Ki 10:13*
his *r*. heard of it (A)(B)   *M'k 3:21*
her *r*. (A)(N)(R)   *Lu 1:58*

RELAX

R. not thy hand from thy   *Jos 10:6*
servants (S)

RELAXED

r. mind makes physical health   *Pr 14:30*
(B)

RELEASE

seven years thou shalt make a   *De 15:1*
r.

And this is the manner of the   *De 15:2*
r.
unto his neighbour shall *r*. it   *De 15:2*
because it is called the Lord's   *De 15:2*
r.
thy brother thine hand shall *r*.   *De 15:3*
year, the year of *r*. is at hand   *De 15:9*
in the solemnity of the year   *De 31:10*
of *r*.
and he made a *r*. to the   *Es 2:18*
provinces
until the year of *r*. (B)   *Eze 46:17*
to *r*. unto the people a   *M't 27:15*
prisoner
will ye that I *r*. unto you?   *M't 27:17*
Barabbas
the twain will ye that I *r*.   *M't 27:21*
unto you
I *r*. unto you the King of the   *M'k 15:9*
Jews
rather *r*. Barabbas unto   *M'k 15:11*
them
therefore chastise him, and *r*.   *Lu 23:16*
him
must *r*. one unto them at the   *Lu 23:17*
feast
this man, and *r*. unto us   *Lu 23:18*
Barabbas
Pilate therefore, willing to *r*.   *Lu 23:20*
Jesus
r. unto you one at the   *Joh 18:39*
passover
I *r*. unto you the King of   *Joh 18:39*
the Jews
thee, and have power to *r*.   *Joh 19:10*
thee
thenceforth Pilate sought to   *Joh 19:12*
r. him

RELEASED

Then *r*. he Barabbas unto   *M't 27:26*
them
feast he *r*. unto them one   *M'k 15:6*
prisoner
the people, *r*. Barabbas unto   *M'k 15:15*
them
And he *r*. unto them him   *Lu 23:25*
that for

RELEASING

accustomed to *r*. one (S)   *M't 27:15*
r. the deed of purchase (B)   *Eph 1:14*

RELENT

Lord was moved to *r*. (A)   *J'g 2:18*
Lord did not *r*. (A)   *Jer 20:16; 26:19*
r. and reverse my decision   *Jer 26:3*
(A)(B)
did not Lord *r*. of evil (A)   *Jer 26:19*
r., ease myself (A)   *Jer 42:10*
neither will I *r*. (A)(B)(S)   *Eze 24:14*
I did not *r*. your sentence   *Zec 8:14*
(A)(B)(R)

RELENTED

Lord *r*. that he had (A)   *1Sa 15:35*
Lord *r*. of the evil (A)   *2Sa 24:16*
he regretted and *r*. of evil   *1Ch 21:15*
(A)
r. of the evil (A)(R)   *Ps 106:45*
Lord *r*. and revoked his   *Am 7:3;*
sentence   *7:6*
God *r*. of punishment (B)   *Jon 3:10*

RELENTING

I am weary of *r*. (A)(R)   *Jer 15:6*
r. and compassion are hid   *Ho 13:14*
(A)(B)

RELENTLESSLY

provoked her *r*. (S)   *1Sa 1:6*

RELIABLE

testimony is *r*. (B)   *Joh 5:31*
entirely *r*. (A)(B)   *Tit 2:10*
r., genuine (A)   *Re 22:6*

RELIED

they *r*. on (A)   *1Ch 5:20*
they *r*. upon the Lord God of   *2Ch 13:18*
their
thou hast *r*. on the king of   *2Ch 16:7*
Syria

and not r. on the Lord thy God   2Ch 16:7
on whom I r. (B)   Ps 41:9
r. on him (B)   Isa 30:12
armour wherein he r. (A)(R)   Lu 11:22
adhered to and r. on (A)   Eph 1:13

RELIEF

then shall r. come another place (S)   Es 4:14
given r. in distress (B)   Ps 4:1
to send r. unto the brethren   Ac 11:29
part in r. of saints (R)   2Co 8:4

RELIEVE

then thou shalt r. him: yea   Le 15:35
r. trouble of my heart (R)   Ps 25:17
seek judgment, r. the oppressed   Isa 1:17
things for meat to r. the soul   La 1:11
comforter that should r. my soul is   La 1:16
sought their meat to r. their souls   La 1:19
let them r. them, and let not   1Ti 5:16
that it may r. them that are widows   1Ti 5:16

RELIEVED

feet, if she have r. the afflicted   1Ti 5:10

RELIEVETH

he r. the fatherless and widow   Ps 146:9

RELIGION

questions of their own r. (S)   Ac 25:19
sect of our r. I lived a Pharisee   Ac 26:5
time past in the Jews' r. how   Ga 1:13
my previous career in Judaism (B)(R)   Ga 1:13; 1:14
I was still a practising Jew (N)   Ga 1:13
profited in the Jews' r. above many   Ga 1:14
own heart, this man's r. is vain   Jas 1:26
this person's religious service is worthless (A)   Jas 1:26
Pure r. and undefiled before God   Jas 1:27
External religious worship that is pure (A)   Jas 1:27
High priest of r. we profess (N)   Heb 3:1; 4:14

RELIGIOUS

many of the Jews and r. proselytes   Ac 13:43
you are very r. (S)   Ac 17:22
any man among you seem to be r.   Jas 1:26
r. service is worthless (A)   Jas 1:26
external r. worship (A)   Jas 1:27

RELISH

live simply, r. plenty (B)   Ph'p 4:12

RELUCTANCE

reproached them for r. to believe (P)   M't 16:14

RELUCTANT

r. to display his knowledge (A)   Pr 12:23

RELY

to r. on (B)   2Ki 18:20; 18:21; Ph'p 3:4
to r. on (R)   2Ki 18:20; 18:21-22, 24, 30; Isa 36:5-7, 9, 15; 59:4; 2Co 1:9
because thou didst r. on the Lord   2Ch 16:8
better r. upon the Lord (B)   Ps 118:8; 118:9
and r. thereon (S)   Isa 30:12; 31:1

REMAIN

not forever r. in man (B)   Ge 6:3
R. a widow at thy father's house   Ge 38:11
that they may r. in the river only   Ex 8:9
they shall r. in the river only   Ex 8:11
nothing of it r. until the morning   Ex 12:10
shall the fat of my sacrifice r.   Ex 23:18
of the bread, r. unto the morning   Ex 29:34
ought r. until the third day, it shall   Le 19:6
r. in the hand of him that bought   Le 25:28
r. but few years unto the year of   Le 25:52
according to the years that r.   Le 27:18
those which ye let r. of them shall   Nu 33:55
of every city, we left none to r.   De 2:34
r. all night until the morning.   De 16:4
which r. shall hear, and fear   De 19:20
and shall r. in thine house   De 21:13
His body shall not r. all night   De 21:23
shall r. in the land which Moses   Jos 1:14
r. any more courage in any man   Jos 2:11
they let none of them r. or escape   Jos 8:22
mouth, which r. until this very day   Jos 10:27
that were therein; he let none r.   Jos 10:28
were therein; he let none r. in it   Jos 10:30
you by lot these nations that r.   Jos 23:4
nations, these that r. among you   Jos 23:7
even these that r. among you, and   Jos 23:12
and why did Dan r. in ships   J'g 5:17
do for wives for them that r.   J'g 21:7; 21:16
remain (A)   Ru 3:13; 1Sa 1:23; 2Sa 11:12; 19:7; M'k 14:34; Lu 24:49; Joh 4:40; Ac 18:20; 1Co 16:7-8
remain (B)   Ru 3:13; Joh 21:22; Ac 18:20; 1Co 16:8
remain (R)   Ru 3:13; 2Sa 10:5; 11:12; 15:28; 1Ch 19:5; M't 26:38; M'k 14:34; Joh 21:22; Ac 10:48
hand, and shalt r. by the stone Ezel   1Sa 20:19
For six months did Joab r. there   1Ki 11:16
I only r. a prophet of the Lord   1Ki 18:22
thee five of the horses that r.   2Ki 7:13
for we r. yet escaped as it is this   Ezr 9:15
grave, and shall r. in the tomb   Job 21:32
that r. of him shall be buried in   Job 27:15
go into dens, and r. in their places   Job 37:8
far off, and r. in the wilderness   Ps 55:7
land, and the perfect shall r. in it   Pr 2:21
r. in the congregation of the dead   Pr 21:16
yet shall he r. at Nob that day: he   Isa 10:32
righteousness r. in the fruitful   Isa 32:16
man; that it may r. in the house   Isa 44:13
Which r. among the graves   Isa 65:4
I will make, shall r. before me   Isa 66:22
shall your seed and your name r.   Isa 66:22
a residue that r. of this evil family   Jer 8:3
r. in all the places whither I have   Jer 8:3
and this city shall r. for ever   Jer 17:25
of Jerusalem, that r. in this land   Jer 24:8
will I let r. still in their own land   Jer 27:11

of the vessels that r. in this city   Jer 27:19
the vessels that r. in the house of   Jer 27:21
palace shall r. after the manner   Jer 30:18
the men of war that r. in this city   Jer 38:4
none of them shall r. or escape   Jer 42:17
Judah, to leave you none to r.   Jer 44:7
shall escape or r. that they should   Jer 44:14
that none shall r. in it, neither   Jer 51:62
none of them shall r. nor of their   Eze 7:11
and they that r. shall be scattered   Eze 17:21
all the fowls of the heaven to r.   Eze 31:13
all the fowls of the heaven to r.   Eze 32:4
that r. upon the face of the earth   Eze 39:14
if there r. ten men in one house   Am 6:9
that did r. in the day of distress   Ob 14
shall r. in the midst of his house   Zec 5:4
All the families that r. every   Zec 12:14
And in the same house r. eating   Lu 10:7
Gather up the fragments that r.   Joh 6:12
r. with you forever (A)   Joh 14:16
r. in me (B)   Joh 15:4; 15:6-7, 10
that my joy might r. in you   Joh 15:11
fruit, and that your fruit should r.   Joh 15:16
r. in darkness (B)(N)(P)(R)   Joh 16:46
bodies should not r. upon the cross   Joh 19:31
if she depart, let her r. unmarried   1Co 7:11
the greater part r. unto this present   1Co 15:6
and r. unto the coming of the Lord   1Th 4:15
are alive and r. shall be caught up   1Th 4:17
which cannot be shaken may r.   Heb 12:27
from the beginning shall r. in you   1Jo 2:24
how can love r. in (A)   1Jo 3:17
we r. in him (B)   1Jo 4:13
strengthen the things which r.   Re 3:2

REMAINDER

the r. (A)   Ex 10:5;
Isa 21:17; 38:10; 44:19; Jer 27:19; Eze 48:18; Hag 2:2
thou shalt burn the r. with fire   Ex 29:34
the r. thereof shall Aaron and his   Le 6:16
also the r. of it shall be eaten   Le 7:15
the r. of the flesh of the sacrifice   Le 7:17
name nor r. upon the earth   2Sa 14:7
the r. of wrath shalt thou restrain   Ps 76:10

REMAINED

Noah only r. alive, and they that   Ge 7:23
they that r. fled to the mountain   Ge 14:10
from his peple; there r. not one   Ex 8:31
there r. not any green thing in   Ex 10:15
r. not one locust in all the coasts   Ex 10:19
there r. not so much as one of them   Ex 14:28
r. two of the men in the camp   Nu 11:26
have r. in the city of his refuge   Nu 35:28
their inheritance r. in the tribe   Nu 36:12
only Og king of Bashan r. of   De 3:11
ye shall have r. long in the land   De 4:25
the rest which r. of them entered   Jos 10:20

in Gath, and in Ashdod,   *Jos 11:22*
there r.
who r. of the remnant of the   *Jos 13:12*
giants
r. among the children of   *Jos 18:2*
Israel
which r. of the children of   *Jos 21:20*
Kohath
of the children of Kohath   *Jos 21:26*
that r.
and there r. ten thousand   *J'g 7:3*
they which r. were scattered,   *1Sa 11:11*
so that
r. in a mountain in the   *1Sa 23:14*
wilderness
his men r. in the sides of the   *1Sa 24:3*
cave
Tamar r. desolate in her   *2Sa 13:20*
brother
r. stedfast toward (S)   *2Sa 20:2*
which r. in the days of his   *1Ki 22:46*
father
Jehu slew all that r. of the   *2Ki 10:11*
house
he slew all that r. unto   *2Ki 10:17*
Ahab in
there r. the grove also in   *2Ki 13:6*
Samaria
none r. save the poorest sort   *2Ki 24:14*
of
as for the people that r. in   *2Ki 25:22*
the land
ark of God r. with the   *1Ch 13:14*
family of
also my wisdom r. with me   *Ec 2:9*
cities r. of the cities of Judah   *Jer 34:7*
there r. but wounded men   *Jer 37:10*
among
Jeremiah had r. there many   *Jer 37:16*
days
Thus Jeremiah r. in the court   *Jer 37:21*
of the
and Jeremiah r. in the court   *Jer 38:13*
of the
of the people that r. in the   *Jer 39:9*
city
with the rest of the people that   *Jer 39:9*
r.
all the people that r. in   *Jer 41:10*
Mizpah
therefore his taste r. in him   *Jer 48:11*
fight, they have r. in their   *Jer 51:30*
holds
of the people that r. in the   *Jer 52:15*
city
Lord's anger none escaped nor   *La 2:22*
r.
r. there astonished among   *Eze 3:15*
them
and there r. no strength in me   *Da 10:8*
I r. there with the kings of   *Da 10:13*
Persia
there r. no strength in me   *Da 10:17*
it would have r. until this   *M't 11:23*
day
fragments that r. twelve   *M't 14:20*
baskets
unto them, and r. speechless   *Lu 1:22*
that r. to them twelve baskets   *Lu 9:17*
which r. over and above unto   *Joh 6:13*
them
Whiles it r. was it not thine   *Ac 5:4*
own
stuck fast, and r. unmovable   *Ac 27:41*
r. two whole years (B)   *Ac 28:30*

REMAINEST

Thou O Lord, r. for ever; thy   *La 5:19*
They shall perish; but thou r.   *Heb 1:11*

REMAINETH

While the earth r. seedtime   *Ge 8:22*
which r. unto you from the   *Ex 10:5*
hail
which r. of it until the   *Ex 12:10*
morning
that which r. over lay up for   *Ex 16:23*
you
the remnant that r. of the   *Ex 26:12*
curtains
the half curtain that r. shall   *Ex 26:12*
hang
r. in the length of the   *Ex 26:13*
curtains of
And that which r. of the flesh   *Le 8:32*
Take the meat offering that r.   *Le 10:12*
that r. among them in the   *Le 16:16*
midst

shall destroy him that r. of   *Nu 24:19*
city
heap of stones, that r. unto   *Jos 8:29*
this
there r. yet very much land to   *Jos 13:1*
be
This is the land that yet r.:   *Jos 13:2*
all the
made him that r. have   *J'g 5:13*
dominion
which stone r. unto this day   *1Sa 6:18*
in the
There r. yet the youngest   *1Sa 16:11*
the covenant of the Lord r.   *1Ch 17:1*
under
whosoever r. in any place where   *Ezr 1:4*
erred, mine error r. with   *Ezr 19:4*
myself
your answers there r.   *Job 21:34*
falsehood
In his neck r. strength, and   *Job 41:22*
he that r. in Jerusalem, shall be   *Isa 4:3*
He that r. in this city shall die   *Jer 38:2*
by
and Zidon every helper that r.   *Jer 47:4*
he that r. and is besieged   *Eze 6:12*
shall die
so my spirit r. among you: *Hag 2:5*
fear ye
he that r. even he, shall be for   *Zec 9:7*
say, We see; therefore your   *Joh 9:41*
sin r.
it r. that both they that have   *1Co 7:29*
more that which r. is glorious   *2Co 3:11*
for until this day r. the same   *2Co 3:14*
veil
poor: his righteousness r. for   *2Co 9:9*
ever
it r. that some must enter   *Heb 4:6*
therein
r. therefore a rest to the people   *Heb 4:9*
of
there r. no more sacrifice   *Heb 10:26*
for sins
his seed r. in him: and he   *1Jo 3:9*
cannot

REMAINING

upon the tabernacle, r.   *Nu 9:22*
thereon
him until none was left to him   *De 3:3*
r.
until he had left him none r.   *Jos 10:33*
he left none r. according to   *Jos 10:37*
all that
he left none r.: as he had   *Jos 10:39*
done to
left none r. but utterly   *Jos 10:40*
destroyed
them, until they left them   *Jos 11:8*
none r.
r. of the families of the   *Jos 21:40*
Levites
r. in any of the coasts of   *2Sa 21:5*
Israel
priests, until he left him   *2Ki 10:11*
none r.
who r. in the chambers were   *1Ch 9:33*
free
people, nor any r. in his   *Job 18:19*
dwellings
not be any r. of the house of   *Ob 18*
Esau
Spirit descending, and r. on   *Joh 1:33*
him

REMAINS

r. of curtains (A)(R)   *Ex 26:12*
earth r. for ever (A)(B)(R)   *Ec 1:4*
r. with you (B)   *Joh 14:17*
God r. in us (B)   *1Jo 4:12*

REMALIAH

Pekah the son of R., a   *2Ki 15:25*
captain of
Pekah the son of R. began   *2Ki 15:27*
to reign
against Pekah the son of R.   *2Ki 15:30*
Pekah the son of R. king of   *2Ki 15:32*
Israel
of Syria, and Pekah the son   *2Ki 15:37*
of R.
year of Pekah the son of R.   *2Ki 16:1*
and Pekah son of R. king of   *2Ki 16:5*
Israel
Pekah the son of R. slew in   *2Ch 28:6*
Judah
Pekah the son of R. king of   *Isa 7:1*
Israel

with Syria and of the son of R.   *Isa 7:4*
Syria, Ephraim, and the son of   *Isa 7:5*
R.

REMALIAH'S

and the head of Samaria is R.   *Isa 7:9*
son
and rejoice in Rezin and R.   *Isa 8:6*
son

REMARKABLE

a conspicuous, r. horn (A)   *Da 8:5*

REMEDY

his people till there was no   *2Ch 36:16*
shall he be broken without r.   *Pr 6:15*
be destroyed, and that without   *Pr 29:1*
r.
composure may r. serious   *Ec 10:4*
mistakes (B)
the r. (R)   *Isa 21:17; Eze 48:18*
a r. for the defilement of our   *1Jo 2:2;*
sins (N)   *4:10*

REMEMBER

yet did not the butler r.   *Ge 40:23*
Joseph
Moses said to the people, R.   *Ex 13:3*
this day
r. the sabbath day to keep it   *Ex 20:8*
holy
r. Abraham, Isaac, and   *Ge 32:13;*
Israel   *De 9:27*
we r. the fish which we did   *Nu 11:5*
eat in Egypt
r. all the commandments of   *Nu 15:39*
the Lord
that ye may r. and do my   *Nu 15:40*
commandments
r. thou wast a servant in the   *De 5:15;*
land of Egypt   *15:15; 16:12; 24:18, 22*
thou shalt r. what the Lord   *De 7:18*
did to Pharaoh
thou shalt r. all the way the   *De 8:2*
Lord led thee
r. the Lord giveth thee power   *De 8:18*
to get wealth
r. how thou provokedst the   *De 9:7*
Lord thy God
r. that thou wast a bondman   *De 15:15;*
in Egypt   *16:12; 24:18, 22*
r. the day when thou camest   *De 16:3*
out of Egypt
r. what the Lord thy God did   *De 24:9*
to Miriam
r. what Amalek did to thee   *De 25:17*
by the way
r. the days of old, consider the   *De 32:7*
years of many
r. word which Moses   *Jos 1:13*
commanded you
r. also that I am your bone and   *J'g 9:2*
flesh
Abigail said, Then r. thine   *1Sa 25:31*
handmaid
let the king r. the Lord thy   *2Sa 14:11*
God
neither do thou r. what thy   *2Sa 19:19*
servant did
r. when I and thou rode after   *2Ki 9:25*
Ahab
r. how I have walked before   *2Ki 20:3;*
thee   *Isa 38:3*
r. his marvellous works   *1Ch 16:12;*
  Ps 101:5
r. the mercies of David thy   *2Ch 6:42*
servant
r. the word thou commandedst   *Ne 1:8*
Moses
r. the Lord, which is great   *Ne 4:14*
and terrible
r. them that have defiled the   *Ne 13:29*
priesthood
r. who ever perished, being   *Job 4:7*
innocent
O r. my life is wind, eye shall   *Job 7:7*
no more see good
that thou hast made me as   *Job 10:9*
the clay
and r. it as waters that pass   *Job 11:16*
away
r. that thou magnify his work   *Job 36:24*
lay thine hand upon him, r.   *Job 41:8*
the battle
r. all thy offerings and accept   *Ps 20:3*
sacrifice

but we will r. the name of the   Ps 20:7
Lord our God
all ends of world shall r. and   Ps 22:27
turn to Lord
r. thy mercies, they have been   Ps 25:6
ever of old
r. not the sins of my youth, r.   Ps 25:7
thou me
r. thy congregation thou hast   Ps 74:2
purchased
r. this, that the enemy hath   Ps 74:18
reproached
r. how the foolish man   Ps 74:22
reproacheth thee daily
O r. not against us former   Ps 79:8
iniquities
r. how short my time is   Ps 89:47
r. Lord the reproach of thy   Ps 89:50
servants
and to those that r. his   Ps 103:18
commandments
r. the word unto thy servant,   Ps 119:49
upon which
Lord, r. David, and all his   Ps 132:1
afflictions
r. O Lord, the children of   Ps 137:7
Edom
let him drink, and r. his   Pr 31:7
misery no more
he shall not much r. days of   Ec 5:20
his life
yet let him r. the days of   Ec 11:8
darkness
r. now thy Creator in the days   Ec 12:1
of thy youth
we will r. thy love more than   Ca 1:4
wine
Lord will r. Tyre (A)   Isa 23:17
r. ye not the former things   Isa 43:18;
                    46:9
for mine own sake I will not r.   Isa 43:25
thy sins
r. these, O Jacob and Israel   Isa 44:21
thou my servant
r. this, and shew yourselves   Isa 46:8
men
neither didst r. the latter end   Isa 47:7
shalt not r. the reproach of   Isa 54:4
thy widowhood
thou meetest those that r. thee   Isa 64:5
in thy ways
be not wroth, neither r.   Isa 64:9
iniquity for ever
neither shall they r. it, neither   Jer 3:16
visit it
they shall r. it (E)(R)   Jer 3:16
he will now r. their iniquity,   Jer 14:10
and visit
r. break not thy covenant   Jer 14:21
with us
whilst their children r. their   Jer 17:2
altars and groves
r. that I stood before thee to   Jer 18:20
speak good
the day I r. them (B)   Jer 27:22
since I spake I do earnestly   Jer 31:20
r. him still
and the people did not the   Jer 44:21
Lord r. them
ye that have escaped, r. the   Jer 51:50
Lord afar off
r. O Lord, what is come upon   Lam 5:1
us, consider
then shalt r. thy ways   Eze 16:61;
            20:43; 36:31
that thou mayest r. and be   Eze 16:63
confounded
so that thou shalt not r.   Eze 23:27
Egypt any more
now will he r. their iniquity,   Ho 8:13
and visit
therefore he will r. iniquity,   Ho 9:9
and visit their sins
O my people, r. now what   Mic 6:5
Balak consulted
O Lord revive thy work, in   Hab 3:2
wrath r. mercy
r. the law of Moses my   Mal 4:4
servant
neither r. the five loaves   M't 16:9;
            M'k 8:18
sir, we r. that deceiver said,   M't 27:63
I will rise again
the mercy, and to r. his holy   Lu 1:72
covenant
r. that thou in thy lifetime   Lu 16:25
receivedst
r. Lot's wife   Lu 17:32
r. how he spake to you   Lu 24:6

r. the word that I said unto   Joh 15:20
you
that when the time shall   Joh 16:4
come, ye may r.
r. that by the space of three   Ac 20:31
years
r. the words of the Lord   Ac 20:35
Jesus, how he said
they would that we should r.   Ga 2:10
the poor
r. that ye being in time past   Eph 2:11
Gentiles
r. my bonds, grace be with   Col 4:18
you, amen
for ye r. brethren our labour   1Th 2:9
and travail
r. ye not that I told you these   2Th 2:5
things
r. that Jesus Christ was raised   2Ti 2:8
from dead
r. them that are in bonds, as   Heb 13:3
bound
r. them which have the rule   Heb 13:7
over you
r. the words spoken of the   Jude 17
apostles
r. from whence thou art fallen,   Re 2:5
and repent
r. how thou hast received, and   Re 3:3
hold fast

REMEMBER ME

r. me that I may be at once   J'g 16:28
avenged
look on thine handmaid, and   1Sa 1:11
r. me
r. me O God, concerning   Ne 13:14;
this   13:22, 31
appoint me a set time, and   Job 14:13
r. me
r. me for thy goodness' sake,   Ps 25:7
O Lord
r. me with the favour that   Ps 106:4
thou bearest
O Lord, thou knowest, r. me,   Jer 15:15
and visit
and they that escape of you   Eze 6:9
shall r. me
and they shall r. me in far   Zec 10:9
countries
Lord r. me when thou comest   Lu 23:42
to thy kingdom
that ye r. me in all things,   1Co 11:2
and keep

I REMEMBER

saying, I do r. my faults this   Ge 41:9
day
I r. that which Amalek did to   1Sa 15:2
Israel
even when I r. I am afraid,   Job 21:6
and trembling
when I r. these I pour out my   Ps 42:4
soul
when I r. thee upon my bed,   Ps 63:6
and meditate
if I do not r. thee, let my   Ps 137:6
tongue cleave
I r. the days of old, I muse   Ps 143:5
on thy works
I r. thee the kindness of thy   Jer 2:2
youth
consider not that I r. all their   Ho 7:2
wickedness

I WILL REMEMBER

I will r. my covenant between   Ge 9:15;
me   9:16
I will r. my covenant with   Le 26:42
Abraham
I will for their sakes r. the   Le 26:45
covenant
therefore will I r. thee from   Ps 42:6
Jordan
but I will r. the years of the   Ps 77:10
right hand
I will r. the works, I will r.   Ps 77:11
thy wonders of old
I will r. their sins no more, I   Jer 31:34;
will forgive their iniquity   Heb 8:12;
                   10:17
I will r. my covenant with   Eze 16:60
thee
I will r. his deeds which he   3Jo 10
doeth

REMEMBERED

And God r. Noah, and every   Ge 8:1
living
that God r. Abraham, and   Ge 19:29
sent Lot
And God r. Rachel, and God   Ge 30:22
And Joseph r. the dreams   Ge 42:9
which he
God r. his covenant with   Ex 2:24
Abraham
and I have r. my covenant   Ex 6:5
shall ye be r. before the Lord   Nu 10:9
your God
children of Israel r. not the   J'g 8:34
Lord
Hannah his wife; and the   1Sa 1:19
Lord r.
Joash the king r. not the   2Ch 24:22
kindness
r. Vashti, and what she had   Es 2:1
done
these days should be r. and   Es 9:28
kept
he shall be no more r.; and   Job 24:20
name to be r. in all   Ps 45:17
generations
I r. God, and was troubled: I   Ps 77:3
they r. that God was their   Ps 78:35
rock
For he r. that they were but   Ps 78:39
flesh
They r. not his hand, nor the   Ps 78:42
day
He hath r. his mercy and his   Ps 98:3
truth
He hath r. his covenant for   Ps 105:8
ever
For he r. his holy promise   Ps 105:42
r. not the multitude of thy   Ps 106:7
mercies
And he r. for them his   Ps 106:45
covenant
Let the iniquity of his   Ps 109:14
fathers be r.
that he r. not to shew   Ps 109:16
mercy, but
made his wonderful works to   Ps 111:4
be r.
I r. thy judgments of old, O   Ps 119:52
Lord
I have r. thy name, O Lord   Ps 119:55
Who r. us in our low estate   Ps 136:23
yea, we wept, when we r.   Ps 137:1
Zion
yet no man r. that same poor   Ec 9:15
man
many songs, that thou   Isa 23:16
mayest be r.
thou hast lied, and hast not   Isa 57:11
r. me
Then he r. the days of old,   Isa 63:11
Moses
and the former shall not be   Isa 65:17
r. nor
that his name may be no   Jer 11:19
more r.
Jerusalem r. in the days of her   La 1:7
r. not his footstool in the day   La 2:1
of his
which he hath done shall not   Eze 3:20
be r.
hast not r. the days of thy   Eze 16:22;
youth   16:43
ye have made your iniquity   Eze 21:24
to be r.
thou shalt be no more r.:   Eze 21:32
for I the
that the Ammonites may not   Eze 25:10
be r.
his righteousnesses shall not   Eze 33:13
be r.
shall no more be r. by their   Ho 2:17
name
and r. not the brotherly   Am 1:9
covenant
soul fainted within me I r. the   Jon 2:7
Lord
land, and they shall no more   Zec 13:2
be r.
And Peter r. the word of   M't 26:75
Jesus
And Peter r. the word of the   Lu 22:61
Lord
And they r. his words   Lu 24:8
his disciples r. that it was   Joh 2:17
written
his disciples r. that he had   Joh 2:22
said this
then r. they that these things   Joh 12:16

Then *r.* I the word of the   *Ac 11:16*
Lord, how
and God hath *r.* her iniquities *Re 18:15*

REMEMBEREST

the grave, whom thou *r.* no   *Ps 88:5*
more
and there *r.* that thy brother *M't 5:23*
hath

REMEMBERETH

inquisition for blood, he *r.*   *Ps 9:12*
them
our frame: he *r.* that we are *Ps 103:14*
dust
she *r.* not her last end;   *La 1:9*
therefore
child, she *r.* no more the   *Joh 16:21*
anguish
he *r.* the obedience of you *2Co 7:15*
all, how

REMEMBERING

R. mine affliction and my   *La 3:19*
misery
R. without ceasing your work *1Th 1:3*

REMEMBERS

he *r.* and summons his bravest *Na 2:5*
men (A)(B)(R)

REMEMBRANCE

utterly put out the *r.* of   *Ex 17:14*
Amalek
memorial, bringing iniquity to *Nu 5:15*
r.
shalt blot out the *r.* of   *De 25:19*
Amalek
I would make the *r.* of them *De 32:26*
to cease
have no son to keep my   *2Sa 18:18*
name in *r.*
come unto me to call my sin *1Ki 17:18*
to *r.*
His *r.* shall perish from the *Job 18:17*
earth
the *r.* of him (S)   *Job 18:17*
For in death there is no *r.* of *Ps 6:5*
thee
thanks at the *r.* of his   *Ps 30:4*
holiness
to cut off the *r.* of them from *Ps 34:16*
A Psalm of David, to bring *Ps 38 title*
to *r.*
A Psalm of David, to bring *Ps 70 title*
to *r.*
I call to *r.* my song in the   *Ps 77:6*
night
name of Israel may be no   *Ps 83:4*
more in *r.*
thanks at the *r.* of his   *Ps 97:12*
holiness
and thy *r.* unto all   *Ps 102:12*
generations
righteous shall be in   *Ps 112:6*
everlasting *r.*
There is no *r.* of former things *Ec 1:11*
any *r.* of things that are to *Ec 1:11*
come
there is no *r.* of the wise more *Ec 2:16*
than
thy name, and to the *r.* of *Isa 26:8*
thee
Put me in *r.*: let us plead *Isa 43:26*
together
the posts hast thou set up thy *Isa 57:8*
r.
My soul hath them all in *r.*   *La 3:20*
but he will call to *r.* the   *Eze 21:23*
iniquity
because that ye are come to *Eze 21:24*
r.
calling to *r.* the days of her *Eze 23:19*
youth
thou calledst to *r.* the   *Eze 23:21*
lewdness of
which bringeth their iniquity *Eze 29:16*
to *r.*
a book of *r.* was written   *Mal 3:16*
before
Peter calling to *r.* saith unto *M'k 11:21*
him
servant Israel in *r.* of his   *Lu 1:54*
mercy
given for you: this do in *r.* of *Lu 22:19*

and bring all things to your   *Joh 14:26*
r.
and thine alms are had in *r.* *Ac 10:31*
shall bring you into *r.* of my *1Co 4:17*
ways
broken for you: this do in *r.* *1Co 11:24*
of me
do ye, as oft as ye drink it, *1Co 11:25*
in *r.* of me
thank God upon every *r.* of *Ph'p 1:3*
you
that ye have good *r.* of us   *1Th 3:6*
always.
the brethren in *r.* of these *1Ti 4:6*
things
I have *r.* of thee in my prayers *2Ti 1:3*
I call to *r.* the unfeigned faith *2Ti 1:5*
I put thee in *r.* that thou stir *2Ti 1:6*
up
Of these things put them in *2Ti 2:14*
r.
there is a *r.* again made of *Heb 10:3*
sins
But call to *r.* the former   *Heb 10:32*
days, in
you always in *r.* of these *2Pe 1:12*
things
stir you up by putting you in *2Pe 1:13*
r.
to have these things always in *2Pe 1:15*
r.
up your pure minds by way of *2Pe 3:1*
r.
I will therefore put you in *r.*   *Jude 5*
Babylon came in *r.* before *Re 16:19*
God

REMEMBRANCES

Your *r.* are like unto ashes, *Job 13:12*
your

REMETH

And *R.* and En-gannim, and *Jos 19:21*

REMINDER

song be a living *r.* (B)   *De 31:21*

REMISSION

is shed for many for the *r.* *M't 26:28*
of sins
forgiveness of sins   *M't 26:28;*
(A)(B)(N)(R)   *M'k 1:4; Lu 3:3; 24:47;*
  Ac 2:39; 10:43
set many free from sins (P) *M't 26:28*
of repentance for the *r.* of *M'k 1:4*
sins
forgiveness of sins   *M'k 1:4;*
  Lu 3:3; 24:47
his people by the *r.* of their *Lu 1:77*
of repentance for the *r.* of sins *Lu 3:3*
and *r.* of sins should be   *Lu 24:47*
preached
of Jesus Christ for the *r.* of *Ac 2:38*
sins
have your sins forgiven (P)   *Ac 2:38*
in him shall receive *r.* of sins *Ac 10:43*
for the *r.* of sins that are past *Ro 3:25*
in forgiving the sins   *Ro 3:25*
previously committed (B)
overlooked the sins of the   *Ro 3:25*
past (N)
wiping out the sins of the past *Ro 3:25*
(P)
he had passed over former   *Ro 3:25*
sins (R)
without shedding of blood is *Heb 9:22*
no *r.*
no forgiveness of sins   *Heb 9:22*
(B)(N)(R)
Now where *r.* of these is, *Heb 10:18*
there is no
where sins have been   *Heb 10:18*
forgiven (B)(N)
where there is forgiveness of *Heb 10:18*
these (R)

REMIT

Whose soever sins ye *r.* they *Joh 20:23*
are
if you forgive the sins of any *Joh 20:23*
(A)(B)(N)(P)(R)

REMITTED

ye remit, they are *r.* unto   *Joh 20:23*
them

REMMON

R. and Ether, and Ashan;   *Jos 19:7*
four

REMMON-METHOAR

and goeth out to *R.* to   *Jos 19:13*
Neah

REMNANT

to preserve a *r.* (E)(R)   *Ge 45:7*
r. that remaineth of the   *Ex 26:12*
curtains
the remains of the tent   *Ex 26:12*
curtains (A)
the left over portion of   *Ex 26:12*
curtains (B)
the overhanging part that   *Ex 26:12*
remaineth (E)
the part that remains of the *Ex 26:12*
curtains (R)
r. of the meat offering shall be *Le 2:3*
what is left (A)(E)(R)   *Le 2:3*
the remainder (B)   *Le 2:3; 5:13*
the *r.* shall be the priest's, as a *Le 5:13*
r. of the oil that is in the   *Le 14:18*
priest's
the rest of the oil   *Le 14:18*
(A)(B)(E)(R)
remained of the *r.* of giants *De 3:11*
the surviving Rephaim (B) *De 3:11;*
  Jos 12:4; 13:12
r. of his children which he   *De 28:54*
shall
which was of the *r.* of the   *Jos 12:4*
giants
remained of the *r.* of the   *Jos 13:12*
giants
cleave unto the *r.* of these *Jos 23:12*
nations
rest of the nations (B)   *Jos 23:12*
but of the *r.* of the Amorites *2Sa 21:2*
survivors (B)   *2Sa 21:2; 2Ki 19:30*
to the *r.* of the people,   *1Ki 12:23*
saying
the rest of (B)(E)(R)   *1Ki 12:23;*
  1Ch 6:70; Ezr 3:8
the *r.* of the house of   *1Ki 14:10*
Jeroboam
the *r.* of the sodomites,   *1Ki 22:46*
which
the remaining (B)   *1Ki 22:46*
lift up thy prayer for the *r.* *2Ki 19:4*
r. that is escaped of the   *2Ki 19:30*
house of
of Jerusalem shall go forth a *2Ki 19:31*
r.
forsake the *r.* of mine   *2Ki 21:14*
inheritance
with the *r.* of the multitude, *2Ki 25:11*
did
the rest of the people (R)   *2Ki 25:11*
of the *r.* of the sons of   *1Ch 6:70*
Kohath
and he will return to the *r.* *2Ch 30:6*
of you
the remainder (B)   *2Ch 30:6*
and of all the *r.* of Israel *2Ch 34:9*
r. of their brethren the priests *Ezr 3:8*
our God, to leave us a *r.* to *Ezr 9:8*
escape
should be no *r.* nor escaping *Ezr 9:14*
r. that are left of the captivity *Ne 1:3*
the *r.* of them the fire   *Job 22:20*
consumeth
had left unto us a very small *r.* *Isa 1:9*
the few survivors (B)   *Isa 1:9; 10:20*
in that day, that the *r.* of   *Isa 10:20*
Israel
The *r.* shall return, even the *Isa 10:21*
r. of
sea yet a *r.* of them shall   *Isa 10:22*
return
time to recover the *r.* of his *Isa 11:11*
people
an highway for the *r.* of his *Isa 11:16*
people
the name, and *r.* and son   *Isa 14:22*
famine, and he shall slay thy *Isa 14:30*
r.
Moab, and upon the *r.* of the *Isa 15:9*
land
r. shall be very small and   *Isa 16:14*
people
from Damascus, and the *r.* of *Isa 17:3*
Syria
the remnant (B)   *Isa 28:5;*
  Jer 8:3; 41:10; Hag 2:2; Zec 8:11

the remnant (R)   *Isa 28:5;*
Jer 8:3; 24:8; Zep 2:9; Hag 2:2; Zec 8:11
lift up thy prayer for the r.   *Isa 37:4*
that is
r. that is escaped of the   *Isa 37:31*
house of
of Jerusalem shall go forth a *Isa 37:32*
r.
the r. (A)   *Isa 38:10;*
              Zep 2:9; Zec 8:11
and all the r. of the house of *Isa 46:3*
Israel
glean the r. of Israel as a vine *Jer 6:9*
there shall be no r. of them   *Jer 11:23*
Verily it shall be well with   *Jer 15:11*
thy r.
will gather the r. of my flock *Jer 23:3*
out
and Ekron, and the r. of   *Jer 25:20*
Ashdod
save thy people, the r. of   *Jer 31:7*
Israel
captive, the r. of the people   *Jer 39:9*
of Babylon had left a r. of   *Jer 40:11*
Judah
and the r. in Judah perish   *Jer 40:15*
the r. of the people whom he *Jer 41:16*
had
Lord thy God, even for all   *Jer 42:2*
this r.
word of the Lord ye r. of   *Jer 42:15*
Judah
concerning you, O ye r. of   *Jer 42:19*
Judah
took all the r. of Judah, that *Jer 43:5*
were
I will take the r. of Judah,   *Jer 44:12*
that
none of the r. of Judah,   *Jer 44:14*
which are
all the r. of Judah, that are *Jer 44:28*
gone
the r. of the country of   *Jer 47:4*
Caphtor
cut off with the r. of their   *Jer 47:5*
valley
whole r. of thee will I scatter *Eze 5:10*
into
Yet will I leave a r. that ye   *Eze 6:8*
may
make a full end of the r. of *Eze 11:13*
Israel
therein shall be left a r. that *Eze 14:22*
shall
thy r. shall fall by the   *Eze 23:25*
sword: they
and destroy the r. of the sea *Eze 25:16*
coast
in the r. whom the Lord shall *Joe 2:32*
call
r. of the Philistines shall   *Am 1:8*
perish
be gracious unto the r. of   *Am 5:15*
Joseph
they may possess the r. of   *Am 9:12*
Edom
will surely gather the r. of   *Mic 2:12*
Israel
I will make her that halted a *Mic 4:7*
r.
r. of his brethren shall return *Mic 5:3*
r. of Jacob shall be in the   *Mic 5:7*
midst
the r. of Jacob shall be among *Mic 5:8*
of the r. of his heritage   *Mic 7:18*
all the r. of the people shall *Hab 2:8*
spoil
I will cut off the r. of Baal   *Zep 1:4*
for the r. of the house of   *Zep 2:7*
Judah
the r. of my people shall   *Zep 2:9*
possess
r. of Israel shall not do   *Zep 3:13*
iniquity
with all the r. of the people, *Hag 1:12*
obeyed
spirit of all the r. of the   *Hag 1:14*
people
in the eyes of the r. of this   *Zec 8:6*
people
the r. of this people to possess *Zec 8:12*
all
And the r. took his servants *M't 22:6*
of the sea, a r. shall be saved *Ro 9:27*
is a r. according to the   *Ro 11:5*
election of
the r. were affrighted and   *Re 11:13*
gave

make war with the r. of her   *Re 12:17*
seed
the r. were slain with the   *Re 19:21*
sword of

REMOLD

God r. minds (P)   *Ro 12:2*

REMORSE

troubled with r.   *M't 27:3*
(A)(B)(N)(P)

REMOVE

to r. it from Ephraim's head *Ge 48:17*
unto
of Israel r. from tribe to tribe *Nu 36:7*
the inheritance r. from one   *Nu 36:9*
tribe
not r. thy neighbour's   *De 19:14*
landmark
then ye shall r. from your   *Jos 3:3*
place
hand! then would I r.   *J'g 9:29*
Abimelech
So David would not r. the   *2Sa 6:10*
ark of
will r. Judah also out of my *2Ki 23:27*
sight
to r. them out of his sight   *2Ki 24:3*
r. the shame images (B)   *2Ch 17:6;*
       19:3; 31:1; 33:3; 34:3, 7
will I any more r. the foot of *2Ch 33:8*
Israel
Some r. the landmarks; they *Job 24:2*
not r. mine integrity from me *Job 27:5*
not the hand of the wicked r. *Ps 36:11*
me
R. thy stroke away from me *Ps 39:10*
R. from me   *Ps 119:22*
reproach, contempt
R. from me the way   *Ps 119:29*
of lying; and
nor to the left: r. thy foot   *Pr 4:27*
from evil
R. thy way far from her,   *Pr 5:8*
and come
R. not the ancient landmark *Pr 22:28*
R. not the old landmark; and *Pr 23:10*
R. far from me vanity and lies *Pr 30:8*
r. sorrow from thy heart, and *Ec 11:10*
the earth shall r. out of her *Isa 13:13*
place
from his place shall he not r. *Isa 46:7*
my sight, then shalt thou not r. *Jer 4:1*
you, to r. you far from your *Jer 27:10*
land
should r. it from before my *Jer 32:31*
face
they shall r. they shall depart *Jer 50:3*
R. out of the midst of   *Jer 50:8*
Babylon, and
r. by day in their sight; and *Eze 12:3*
thou
r. from thy place to another *Eze 12:3*
place
they shall r. and go into   *Eze 12:11*
captivity
R. the diadem, and take off *Eze 21:26*
r. violence, and spoil, and   *Eze 45:9*
execute
were like them that r. the   *Ho 5:10*
bound
r. far off from you the   *Joe 2:20*
northern
r. them far from their border *Joe 3:6*
which ye shall not r. your   *Mic 2:3*
necks
I will r. the iniquity of that *Zec 3:9*
land in
mountain shall r. toward the *Zec 14:4*
north
R. hence to yonder place   *M't 17:20*
to yonder place; and it shall *M't 17:20*
r.
be willing, r. this cup from *Lu 22:42*
me
faith, so that I could r.   *1Co 13:2*
mountains
r. with the breath (B)   *2Th 2:8*
r. thy candlestick out of his   *Re 2:5*
place

REMOVED

Noah r. the covering of the   *Ge 8:13*
ark
he r. from thence unto a   *Ge 12:8*
mountain

Then Abram r. his tent, and *Ge 13:18*
came
he r. from thence, and digged *Ge 26:22*
he r. that day the he goats   *Ge 30:35*
he r. them to cities from one *Ge 47:21*
end
and he r. the swarms of flies *Ex 8:31*
from
angel r. and went behind   *Ex 14:19*
them
when the people saw it, they *Ex 20:18*
r.
the people r. from Hazeroth *Nu 12:16*
From thence they r. and   *Nu 21:12;*
pitched   *21:13*
children of Israel r. from   *Nu 33:5*
Rameses
they r. from Etham, and   *Nu 33:7*
turned
they r. from Marah, and came *Nu 33:9*
unto
they r. from Elim, and   *Nu 33:10*
encamped
And they r. from the Red   *Nu 33:11*
sea, and
they r. from Alush, and   *Nu 33:14*
encamped
they r. from the desert of   *Nu 33:16*
Sinai
they r. from Libnah, and   *Nu 33:21*
pitched
they r. from mount Shapher *Nu 33:24*
they r. from Haradah, and   *Nu 33:25*
pitched
And they r. from Makheloth *Nu 33:26*
they r. from Tarah, and   *Nu 33:28*
pitched in
And they r. from   *Nu 33:32*
Bene-jaakan, and
And they r. from Jotbathah *Nu 33:34*
And they r. from   *Nu 33:36*
Ezion-gaber, and
they r. from Kadesh, and   *Nu 33:37*
pitched
And they r. from Dibon-gad *Nu 33:46*
they r. from   *Nu 33:47*
Almon-diblathaim
be r. into all the kingdoms of *De 28:25*
they r. from Shittim, and came *Jos 3:1*
to
when the people r. from their *Jos 3:14*
tent
why his hand is not r. from   *1Sa 6:3*
you
Saul r. him from him, and   *1Sa 18:13*
made
he r. Amasa out of the   *2Sa 20:12*
highway
he was r. out of the highway *2Sa 20:13*
r. all the idols that his   *1Ki 15:12*
fathers
even her he r. from being   *1Ki 15:13*
queen
Save that high places were   *2Ki 15:14*
not r.
Howbeit high places were   *2Ki 15:35*
not r.
and r. the laver from off   *2Ki 16:17*
them
and r. them out of his sight: *2Ki 17:18*
there
the Lord r. Israel out of his *2Ki 17:23*
sight
The nations which thou hast *2Ki 17:26*
r.
He r. the high places, and   *2Ki 18:4*
brake
as I have r. Israel and will   *2Ki 23:27*
cast off
and they r. them to Manahath *1Ch 8:6*
and Ahiah, and Gera, he r.   *1Ch 8:7*
them
king, he r. her from being   *2Ch 15:16*
queen
And they r. the burnt   *2Ch 35:12*
offerings
and he r. her (S)   *Es 2:9*
and the rock is r. out of his   *Job 14:18*
place
shall the rock be r. out of his *Job 18:4*
place
mine hope hath he r. like a *Job 19:10*
tree
would he have r. thee out of *Job 36:16*
we fear, though the earth be r. *Ps 46:2*
I r. his shoulder from the   *Ps 81:6*
burden
far hath he r. our   *Ps 103:12*
transgressions
that it should not be r. for   *Ps 104:5*
ever

as mount Zion, which cannot   *Ps 125:1*
be *r*.
The righteous shall never be   *Pr 10:30*
r.
the Lord have *r*. men far   *Isa 6:12*
away
I have *r*. the bounds of the   *Isa 10:13*
people
Madmenah is *r*.; the   *Isa 10:31*
inhabitants
r. covering of Judah   *Isa 22:8*
(A)(B)(E)(R)
fastened in the sure place be   *Isa 22:25*
r.
and shall be *r*. like a cottage   *Isa 24:20*
r. it far unto all the ends of   *Isa 26:15*
but have *r*. their heart far   *Isa 29:13*
from me
yet shall not thy teachers be   *Isa 30:20*
r.
the stakes thereof shall ever   *Isa 33:20*
be *r*.
r. from me as a shepherd's   *Isa 38:12*
tent
shall depart, and the hills be   *Isa 54:10*
r.
covenant of my peace be *r*.   *Isa 54:10*
thou shalt not be *r*. (S)   *Jer 4:1*
them to be *r*. into all   *Jer 15:4*
kingdoms of
them to be *r*. into all the   *Jer 24:9*
kingdoms
them to be *r*. to all the   *Jer 29:18*
kingdoms
you to be *r*. into all the   *Jer 34:17*
kingdoms
sinned; therefore she is *r*.   *La 1:8*
hast *r*. my soul far off from   *La 3:17*
peace
streets, and their gold shall   *Eze 7:19*
be *r*.
give them to be *r*. and   *Eze 23:46*
spoiled
the uncleanness of a *r*.   *Eze 36:17*
woman
stretched themselves shall be *r*.   *Am 6:7*
how hath he *r*. it from me   *Mic 2:4*
in that day shall the decree   *Mic 7:11*
be far *r*.
Be thou *r*. and be thou cast   *M't 21:21;*
into   *M'k 11:23*
was dead, he *r*. him into this   *Ac 7:4*
land
when he had *r*. him, he   *Ac 13:22*
raised up
I marvel that ye are so soon *r*.   *Ga 1:6*

REMOVETH

that *r*. his neighbour's   *De 27:17*
landmark
r. the mountains, and they   *Job 9:5*
know
r. away the speech of the   *Job 12:20*
trusty
Whoso *r*. stones shall be hurt   *Ec 10:9*
he *r*. kings, and setteth up   *Da 2:21*
kings

REMOVING

r. from thence all the   *Ge 30:32*
speckled
a captive, and *r*. to and fro   *Isa 49:21*
of man, prepare thee stuff for   *Eze 12:3*
r.
day in their sight, as stuff for   *Eze 12:4*
r.
r. of those things that are   *Heb 12:27*
shaken

REMOVES

r. shame from Israel (B)   *1Sa 17:26*

REMPHAN

the star of your god R. figures   *Ac 7:43*

REMUNERATION

your *r*. for services (B)   *Ge 18:31*
inheritance as your *r*. (B)   *Col 3:24*
return *r*. to (B)   *1Ti 5:4*

REND

about the hole, that it should   *Ex 39:23*
not *r*.
neither *r*. your clothes; lest ye   *Le 10:6*

he shall *r*. it out of the   *Le 13:56*
garment
his head, nor *r*. his clothes   *Le 21:10*
R. your clothes, and gird you   *2Sa 3:31*
with
surely *r*. the kingdom from   *1Ki 11:11*
thee
will *r*. it out of the hand of   *1Ki 11:12*
thy son
I will not *r*. away all the   *1Ki 11:13*
kingdom
r. the kingdom out of the   *1Ki 11:31*
hand of
and didst *r*. thy clothes, and   *2Ch 34:27*
weep
A time to *r*. and a time to sew   *Ec 3:7*
that thou wouldest *r*. the   *Isa 64:1*
heavens
fall; and a stormy wind shall   *Eze 13:11*
r. it
r. it with a stormy wind in   *Eze 13:13*
my fury
break and *r*. all their   *Eze 29:7*
shoulder
and will *r*. the caul of their   *Ho 13:8*
heart
And *r*. your heart, and not   *Joe 2:13*
your
feet, and turn again and *r*. you   *M't 7:6*
Let us not *r*. it, but cast lots   *Joh 19:24*
for it

RENDER

which they shall *r*. unto me,   *Nu 18:9*
shall
will *r*. vengeance to mine   *De 32:41*
enemies
r. vengeance to his   *De 32:43*
adversaries
did God *r*. upon their heads   *J'g 9:57*
r. to every man his   *1Sa 26:23*
righteousness
Lord will *r*. me good (B)   *2Sa 16:12*
r. unto every man according   *2Ch 6:30*
unto
r. unto man his   *Job 33:26*
righteousness
work of a man shall he *r*.   *Job 34:11*
unto him
hands; *r*. to them their desert   *Ps 28:4*
r. due reward (R)   *Ps 28:4*
They also that *r*. evil for   *Ps 38:20*
good are
God: I will *r*. praises unto   *Ps 56:12*
thee
r. unto our neighbours   *Ps 79:12*
sevenfold
earth: *r*. a reward to the   *Ps 94:2*
proud
What shall I *r*. unto the   *Ps 116:12*
Lord for
not he *r*. to every man   *Pr 24:12*
according to
r. to the man according to his   *Pr 24:29*
work
seven men that can *r*. a   *Pr 26:16*
reason
to *r*. his anger with fury, and   *Isa 66:15*
his
he will *r*. unto her a   *Jer 51:6*
recompence
I will *r*. unto Babylon and to   *Jer 51:24*
all
R. unto them a recompence, O   *La 3:64*
so will we *r*. the calves of our   *Ho 14:2*
lips
will ye *r*. me a recompence?   *Joe 3:4*
and if
r. true judgment (A)(B)(R)   *Zec 8:16*
that I will *r*. double unto thee   *Zec 9:12*
r. him the fruits in their   *M't 21:41*
seasons
R. therefore unto Caesar the   *M't 22:21*
things
R. to Caesar the things that   *M'k 12:17*
are
R. therefore unto Caesar the   *Lu 20:25*
things
will *r*. to every man according   *Ro 2:6*
to his
r. no man evil for evil (E)   *Ro 12:17*
R. therefore to all their dues   *Ro 13:7*
Let the husband *r*. unto the   *1Co 7:3*
wife due
what thanks can we *r*. to God   *1Th 3:9*
again
that none *r*. evil for evil unto   *1Th 5:15*
any
Lord will *r*. to him (E)   *2Ti 4:14*
r. as she has rendered (E)(R)   *Re 18:6*

RENDERED

r. the wickedness of   *J'g 9:56*
Abimelech
and *r*. unto the king of Israel   *2Ki 3:4*
Hezekiah *r*. not again   *2Ch 32:25*
according to
man's hands shall be *r*. unto   *Pr 12:14*
him
render as she has *r*. (E)(R)   *Re 18:6*

RENDEREST

r. to every man according to   *Ps 62:12*
his

RENDERETH

that *r*. recompence to his   *Isa 66:6*
enemies

RENDERING

r. service (B)   *1Ch 6:32*
not *r*. evil for evil, or railing   *1Pe 3:9*

RENDERS

no human power *r*. one mighty   *1Sa 2:9*
(B)

RENDING

my soul like a lion, *r*. it in   *Ps 7:2*
pieces

RENEGADES

r. lined up with him (B)   *J'g 11:3*

RENEW

Gilgal, and *r*. the kingdom   *1Sa 11:14*
there
and *r*. a right spirit within me   *Ps 51:10*
the Lord shall *r*. their   *Isa 40:31*
strength
and let the people *r*. their   *Isa 41:1*
strength
be turned; *r*. our days as of   *La 5:21*
old
to *r*. them again unto   *Heb 6:6*
repentance

RENEWED

and *r*. the altar of the Lord   *2Ch 15:8*
and my bow was *r*. in my   *Job 29:20*
hand
thy youth is *r*. like the eagle's   *Ps 103:5*
the inward man is *r*. day by   *2Co 4:16*
day
inner self being *r*.   *2Co 4:16*
(A)(B)(N)(R)
be *r*. in the spirit of your   *Eph 4:23*
mind
which is *r*. in knowledge after   *Col 3:10*

RENEWEST

Thou *r*. thy witnesses   *Job 10:17*
against me
and thou *r*. the face of the   *Ps 104:30*
earth

RENEWING

transformed by the *r*. of your   *Ro 12:2*
mind
regeneration, *r*. of the Holy   *Tit 3:5*
Ghost

RENOUNCE

wicked *r*. God (R)   *Ps 10:13*

RENOUNCED

r. the covenant (A)(R)   *Ps 89:39*
But have *r*. the hidden things   *2Co 4:2*

RENOWN

men which were of old, men of   *Ge 6:4*
r.
in the congregation, men of *r*.   *Nu 16:2*
thy *r*. went forth   *Eze 16:14*
among heathen
the harlot because of thy *r*.   *Eze 16:15*
I will raise up for them a   *Eze 34:29*
plant of *r*.

it shall be to them a *r.* the   *Eze 39:13*
day that
hast gotten thee *r.* as at this   *Da 9:15*
day

RENOWNED

were the *r.* of the   *Nu 1:16*
congregation
seed of evildoers shall never   *Isa 14:20*
be *r.*
and rulers great lords and *r.*   *Eze 23:23*
all
the *r.* city, which wast   *Eze 26:17*
strong in

RENT

in the pit: and he *r.* his   *Ge 37:29*
clothes
is without doubt *r.* in pieces   *Ge 37:33*
And Jacob *r.* his clothes, and   *Ge 37:34*
put
they *r.* their clothes, and   *Ge 44:13*
laded
of an habergeon, that it be   *Ex 28:32*
not *r.*
his clothes shall be *r.* and his   *Le 13:45*
searched the land, *r.* their   *Nu 14:6*
clothes
Joshua *r.* his clothes, and fell   *Jos 7:6*
and wine bottles, old and *r.*   *Jos 9:4*
were new; and behold, they be   *Jos 9:13*
r.
he saw her, that he *r.* his   *J'g 11:35*
clothes
him, and he *r.* him as he   *J'g 14:6*
would
as he would have *r.* a kid, and   *J'g 14:6*
the same day with his clothes   *1Sa 4:12*
r.
the skirt of his mantle, and   *1Sa 15:27*
it *r.*
The Lord hath *r.* the   *1Sa 15:28*
kingdom of
Lord hath *r.* the kingdom   *1Sa 28:17*
out of
camp from Saul with his   *2Sa 1:2*
clothes *r.*
hold on his clothes, and *r.*   *2Sa 1:11*
them
r. her garment of divers   *2Sa 13:19*
colours
stood by with their clothes *r.*   *2Sa 13:31*
came to meet him with his   *2Sa 15:32*
coat *r.*
earth *r.* with the sound of   *1Ki 1:40*
them
on him, and *r.* it in twelve   *1Ki 11:30*
pieces
the altar shall be *r.* and the   *1Ki 13:3*
ashes
the altar also was *r.* and the   *1Ki 13:5*
ashes
And *r.* the kingdom away   *1Ki 14:8*
from the
and strong wind *r.* the   *1Ki 19:11*
mountains
those words, that he *r.* his   *1Ki 21:27*
clothes
clothes, and *r.* them in two   *2Ki 2:12*
pieces
the letter, that he *r.* his clothes   *2Ki 5:7*
the king of Israel had *r.* his   *2Ki 5:8*
clothes
Wherefore hast thou *r.* thy   *2Ki 5:8*
clothes
the woman, that he *r.* his   *2Ki 6:30*
clothes
Athaliah *r.* her clothes, and   *2Ki 11:14*
cried
r. Israel from the house of   *2Ki 17:21*
David
to Hezekiah with their   *2Ki 18:37*
clothes *r.*
heard it, that he *r.* his clothes   *2Ki 19:1*
of the law, that he *r.* his   *2Ki 22:11*
clothes
hast *r.* thy clothes, and wept   *2Ki 22:19*
before
Then Athaliah *r.* her   *2Ch 23:13*
clothes and
of the law, that he *r.* his   *2Ch 34:19*
clothes
I *r.* my garment and my   *Ezr 9:3*
mantle
and having *r.* my garment and   *Ezr 9:5*
Mordecai *r.* his clothes, and put   *Es 4:1*
Then Job arose and *r.* his   *Job 1:20*
mantle

they *r.* every one his mantle   *Job 2:12*
the cloud is not *r.* under them   *Job 26:8*
and instead of a girdle a *r.*   *Isa 3:24*
to Hezekiah with their   *Isa 36:22*
clothes *r.*
heard it, that he *r.* his clothes   *Isa 37:1*
not afraid, nor *r.* their   *Jer 36:24*
garments
beards shaven, and their   *Jer 41:5*
clothes *r.*
and No shall be *r.* asunder   *Eze 30:16*
garment, and the *r.* is made   *M't 9:16*
worse
Then the high priest *r.* his   *M't 26:65*
clothes
veil of the temple was *r.* in   *M't 27:51*
twain
earth did quake, and the   *M't 27:51*
rocks *r.*
the old, and the *r.* is made   *M'k 2:21*
worse
the spirit cried, and *r.* him   *M'k 9:26*
sore
Then the high priest *r.* his   *M'k 14:63*
clothes
veil of the temple was *r.* in   *M'k 15:38*
twain
then both the new maketh a *r.*   *Lu 5:36*
the veil of the temple was *r.*   *Lu 23:45*
they *r.* their clothes, and ran   *Ac 14:14*
the magistrates *r.* off their   *Ac 16:22*
clothes

RENTEST

thou *r.* thy face with painting   *Jer 4:30*

REPAID

r. evil for good (B)   *Ge 44:4; Ps 109:5*
so God has *r.* me (A)   *J'g 1:7;*
  1Sa 25:21

REPAIR

them *r.* the breaches of the   *2Ki 12:5*
house
Why *r.* ye not the breaches of   *2Ki 12:7*
to *r.* the breaches of the   *2Ki 12:8*
house
hewed stone to *r.* the   *2Ki 12:12*
breaches of
was laid out for the house   *2Ki 12:12*
to *r.* it
to *r.* the breaches of the   *2Ki 22:5*
house
and hewn stone to *r.* the house   *2Ki 22:6*
Joash was minded to *r.* the   *2Ch 24:4*
house
money to *r.* the house of   *2Ch 24:5*
your God
and carpenters to *r.* the   *2Ch 24:12*
house of
to *r.* the house of the Lord   *2Ch 34:8*
Lord, to *r.* and amend the   *2Ch 34:10*
house
and to *r.* the desolations   *Ezr 9:9*
thereof
and they shall *r.* the waste   *Isa 61:4*
cities

REPAIRED

r. the cities, and dwelt in   *J'g 21:23*
them
and *r.* the breaches of the   *1Ki 11:27*
city of
r. the altar of the Lord that   *1Ki 18:30*
was
not *r.* the breaches of the   *2Ki 12:6*
house
r. therewith the house of the   *2Ki 12:14*
Lord
and Joab *r.* the rest of the   *1Ch 11:8*
city
and *r.* the altar of the Lord   *2Ch 15:8*
(S)
house of the Lord, and *r.*   *2Ch 29:3*
r. Millo in the city of David   *2Ch 32:5*
be *r.* the altar of the Lord   *2Ch 33:16*
r. the foundations   *Ezr 4:12*
(A)(E)(R)
next unto them *r.*   *Ne 3:4;*
  3:5-24, 27-32

REPAIRER

The *r.* of the breach. The   *Isa 58:12*
restorer

REPAIRING

and the *r.* of the house of   *2Ch 24:27*
God

REPAY

r. with the choicest (B)   *Ex 22:5*
him, he will *r.* him to his face   *De 7:10*
do you thus *r.* the Lord (A)   *De 32:6*
r. those who hate me (R)   *De 32:41*
Lord *r.* the evildoer (A)(B)   *2Sa 3:39*
Lord will *r.* me with good   *2Sa 16:12*
(R)
I will *r.* you on this plot   *2Ki 9:26*
(A)(B)
shall *r.* him what he hath   *Job 21:31*
done
r. them (B)   *Job 34:33;*
Pr 20:22; Eze 7:3, 8, 9; 11:21; Ho 12:2
prevented me, that I should   *Job 41:11*
r. him
r. them (B)   *Ps 28:4*
let me *r.* them (B)   *Ps 41:10*
thou mayest *r.* it (B)   *Pr 10:14*
accordingly he will *r.* fury to   *Isa 59:18*
the islands he will *r.*   *Isa 59:18*
recompence
he will surely *r.* (B)   *Jer 51:56*
r. them for their doings (A)   *Ho 4:9*
when I come again, I will *r.*   *Lu 10:35*
thee
r. no one evil for evil   *Ro 12:17*
(A)(R)
is mine; I will *r.* saith the   *Ro 12:19*
Lord
r. parents and grandparents (R)   *1Ti 5:4*
with mine own hand, I will *r.*   *Ph'm 19*
r. her what she paid (A)(B)   *Re 18:6*

REPAYED

to the righteous good shall be   *Pr 13:21*
r.

REPAYETH

r. them that hate him to their   *De 7:10*

REPAYING

r. parents for (P)   *1Ti 5:4*

REPAYMENT

is this *r.* to the Lord (B)   *De 32:6*

REPEAT

r. and *r.* like pagans (B)   *M't 6:7*

REPEATEDLY

r. reverted to rebellious ways   *Ps 106:43*
(B)

REPEATETH

he that *r.* a matter separateth   *Pr 17:9*

REPELLED

he is *r.* (A)   *M't 13:21*

REPENT

the people *r.* when they see   *Ex 13:17*
war
people change their purpose   *Ex 13:17*
(A)
people might feel regret (B)   *Ex 13:17*
r. of this evil against thy   *Ex 32:12*
people
change your mind (A)   *Ex 32:12*
change your purpose (B)   *Ex 32:12*
the son of man, that he   *Nu 23:19*
should *r.*
change his mind (B)   *Nu 23:19;*
  1Sa 15:29
and *r.* himself for his   *De 32:36*
servants
Strength of Israel will not   *1Sa 15:29*
lie nor *r.*
he is not a man, that he   *1Sa 15:29*
should *r.*
and *r.* and make supplication   *1Ki 8:47*
myself, and *r.* in dust and   *Job 42:6*
ashes
it *r.* thee concerning thy   *Ps 90:13*
servants

Lord hath sworn, and will not *r*.   *Ps 110:4*
will not revoke or change it (A)   *Ps 110:4*
and will not change (B)   *Ps 110:4*
and will not change his mind (R)   *Ps 110:4*
r. himself concerning his servants   *Ps 135:14*
will take into favor his servants (A)   *Ps 135:14*
will have compassion on servants (B)(R)   *Ps 135:14*
they *r*. and be healed (B)   *Isa 6:10*
I have purposed it, and will not *r*.   *Jer 4:28*
r. of the evil that I thought to do   *Jer 18:8*
my voice, then I will *r*. of the good   *Jer 18:10*
then will I change from the good (B)   *Jer 18:10*
that I may *r*. me of the evil   *Isa 26:3*
relent and reverse my decision (A)(B)   *Isa 26:3*
and the Lord will *r*. him of the evil   *Jer 26:13*
I *r*. me of the evil that I have done   *Jer 42:10*
relent, comfort, and ease myself   *Jer 42:10*
I will regret the calamity (B)   *Jer 42:10*
R. and turn from your idols   *Eze 14:6*
R. and turn yourselves from all   *Eze 18:30*
will I spare, neither will I *r*.   *Eze 24:14*
neither will I relent (A)(B)   *Eze 24:14*
knoweth if he will return and *r*.   *Joe 2:14*
Who can tell if God will turn and *r*.   *Jon 3:9*
God will turn and revoke his sentence (A)   *Jon 3:9*
who knows God will change his mind (B)   *Jon 3:9*
R. ye: for the kingdom of heaven   *M't 3:2*
R.: for the kingdom of heaven is at   *M't 4:17*
unless you *r*. (A)   *M't 18:3*
hand: *r*. ye, and believe the gospel   *M'k 1:15*
and preached that men should *r*.   *M'k 6:12*
except ye *r*. ye shall all likewise   *Lu 13:3; 13:5*
them from the dead, they will *r*.   *Lu 16:30*
him; and if he *r*. forgive him   *Lu 17:3*
saying, I *r*.; thou shalt forgive him   *Lu 17:4*
r. and I should heal (B)   *Joh 12:40*
R. and be baptized every one of you   *Ac 2:38*
R. ye therefore, and be converted   *Ac 3:19*
r. and turn to God (B)   *Ac 3:19*
R. therefore of this thy wickedness   *Ac 8:22*
all men every where to *r*.   *Ac 17:30*
that they should *r*. and turn to God   *Ac 26:20*
I do not *r*., though I did *r*.: for I   *2Co 7:8*
The Lord sware and will not *r*.   *Heb 7:21*
will not regret it or change his mind (A)(R)   *Heb 7:21*
has sworn and he will not rue it (B)   *Heb 7:21*
will not go back on his word (N)   *Heb 7:21*
whence thou art fallen, and *r*.   *Re 2:5*
out of his place, except thou *r*.   *Re 2:5*
R.; or else I will come unto thee   *Re 2:16*
her space to *r*. of her fornication   *Re 2:21*
except they *r*. of their deeds   *Re 2:22*
and heard, and hold fast, and *r*.   *Re 3:3*
be zealous therefore, and *r*.   *Re 3:19*

REPENTANCE

r. shall be hid from mine eyes   *Ho 13:14*
relenting and compassion are hid (A)   *Ho 13:14*
relenting is hid from my eyes (B)   *Ho 13:14*

compassion is hid from my eyes (R)   *Ho 13:14*
Bring forth fruits meet for *r*.   *M't 3:8*
baptize you with water unto *r*.   *M't 3:11*
the righteous, but sinners to *r*.   *M't 9:13*
and preach the baptism of *r*. for the   *M'k 1:4*
the righteous, but sinners to *r*.   *M'k 2:17*
preaching the baptism of *r*. for   *Lu 3:3*
Bring forth fruits worthy of *r*.   *Lu 3:8*
call the righteous, but sinners to *r*.   *Lu 5:32*
nine just persons, which need no *r*.   *Lu 15:7*
And that *r*. and remission of sins   *Lu 24:47*
to give *r*. to Israel, and forgiveness   *Ac 5:31*
to the Gentiles granted *r*. unto life   *Ac 11:18*
the baptism of *r*. to all the people   *Ac 13:24*
baptized with the baptism of *r*.   *Ac 19:4*
r. toward God, and faith toward   *Ac 20:21*
to God, and do works meet for *r*.   *Ac 26:20*
goodness of God leadeth thee to *r*.   *Ro 2:4*
and calling of God are without *r*.   *Ro 11:29*
sorry, but that ye sorrowed to *r*.   *2Co 7:9*
godly sorrow worketh *r*.   *2Co 7:10*
God peradventure will give them *r*.   *2Ti 2:25*
laying again the foundation of *r*.   *Heb 6:1*
to renew them again unto *r*.   *Heb 6:6*
but that all should come to *r*.   *2Pe 3:9*

REPENTED

r. the Lord that he had made man   *Ge 6:6*
Lord regretted that he had made man (A)   *Ge 6:6*
it was grief to the Lord ever having made (B)   *Ge 6:6*
Lord was sorry that he had made man (R)   *Ge 6:6*
Lord *r*. of the evil which he thought   *Ex 32:14*
Lord turned from the evil he thought (A)   *Ex 32:14*
the Lord felt grieved regarding the (B)   *Ex 32:14*
for it *r*. the Lord because of their   *J'g 2:18*
Lord was moved to relent (A)   *J'g 2:18*
Lord was moved with compassion (B)   *J'g 2:18*
Lord was moved to pity (R)   *J'g 2:18*
children of Israel *r*. for   *J'g 21:6*
Benjamin
Israelites changed their purpose (A)   *J'g 21:6*
Israelites felt grieved about Benjamin (B)   *J'g 21:6*
Israel had compassion for Benjamin   *J'g 21:6*
the people *r*. them for Benjamin   *J'g 21:15*
people had compassion on Benjamin (A)(R)   *J'g 21:15*
people felt grieved concerning (B)   *J'g 21:15*
Lord *r*. that he had made Saul king   *1Sa 15:35*
Lord relented that he had made Saul (A)   *1Sa 15:35*
it grieved God that he had made (B)   *1Sa 15:35*
the Lord *r*. him of the evil   *2Sa 24:16*
Lord relented of the evil (A)   *2Sa 24:16*
Lord felt grieved regarding (B)   *2Sa 24:16*
beheld, and he *r*. him of the evil   *1Ch 21:15*
He regretted and relented of the evil (A)   *1Ch 21:15*
Lord observed, felt compassion (B)   *1Ch 21:15*
r. according to the multitude of his   *Ps 106:45*

relented and revoked their sentence of evil (A)   *Ps 106:45*
felt grieved according to his (B)   *Ps 106:45*
Lord relented according to his (R)   *Ps 106:45*
no man *r*. him of his wickedness   *Jer 8:6*
the Lord overthrew, and *r*. not   *Jer 20:16*
Lord overthrew and did not relent (A)   *Jer 20:16*
Lord crushed without pity (B)   *Jer 20:16*
Lord overthrew without pity (R)   *Jer 20:16*
the Lord *r*. him of the evil which   *Jer 26:19*
did not the Lord relent of the evil (A)   *Jer 26:19*
did not the Lord feel grief about (B)   *Jer 26:19*
Surely after that I was turned, I *r*.   *Jer 31:19*
Lord *r*. for this: It shall not be   *Am 7:3*
Lord relented and revoked his sentence (A)   *Am 7:3; 7:6*
Lord had compassion on account of this (B)   *Am 7:3; 7:6*
Lord *r*. for this: This also shall not be   *Am 7:6*
God *r*. of the evil, that he had said   *Jon 3:10*
God revoked his sentence (A)   *Jon 3:10*
God relented of the punishment (B)   *Jon 3:10*
saith the Lord of hosts, and I *r*. not   *Zec 8:14*
I did not relent or revoke your sentence (A)   *Zec 8:14*
I did not relent (B)(R)   *Zec 8:14*
were done, because they *r*. not   *M't 11:20*
would have *r*. long ago in sackcloth   *M't 11:21*
they *r*. at the preaching of Jonas   *M't 12:41*
not: but afterward he *r*. and went   *M't 21:29*
ye had seen it, *r*. not afterward   *M't 21:32*
that he was condemned, *r*. himself   *M't 27:3*
troubled with remorse (A)(B)(N)(P)   *M't 27:3*
they had a great while ago *r*.   *Lu 10:13*
they *r*. at the preaching of Jonas   *Lu 11:32*
worketh repentance not to be *r*. of   *2Co 7:10*
and have not *r*. of the uncleanness   *2Co 12:21*
of her fornication; and she *r*. not   *Re 2:21*
r. not of the works of their hands   *Re 9:20*
Neither *r*. they of their murders   *Re 9:21*
and they *r*. not to give him glory   *Re 16:9*
sores, and *r*. not of their deeds   *Re 16:11*

REPENTEST

kindness, and *r*. thee of the evil   *Jon 4:2*
revoke the sentence of evil (A)   *Jon 4:2*
grieved at calamity (B)   *Jon 4:2*

REPENTETH

it *r*. me that I have made them   *Ge 6:7*
it grieves and makes me regretful that (A)   *Ge 6:7*
it is grief to me that I have made (B)   *Ge 6:7*
I am sorry that I have made them (R)   *Ge 6:7*
It *r*. me that I have set up   *1Sa 15:11*
I regret that I have made Saul king (A)   *1Sa 15:11*
I am grieved ever to have made Saul (B)   *1Sa 15:11*
kindness, and *r*. him of the evil   *Joe 2:13*
he revokes his sentence of evil (A)   *Joe 2:13*

feels grieved over punishment   Joe 2:13
(B)
in heaven over one sinner that   Lu 15:7
r.
angels, over one sinner that   Lu 15:10
r.

REPENTING

destroy thee; I am weary with   Jer 15:6
r.
I am weary of relenting   Jer 15:6
(A)(R)
I am weary of grieving (B)   Jer 15:6

REPENTINGS

me, my r. are kindled together   Ho 11:8
my compassions are kindled   Ho 11:8
together (A)(B)(E)
my compassion grows warm   Ho 11:8
and tender (R)

REPETITIONS

But when ye pray, use not   M't 6:7
vain r.

REPHAEL

sons of Shemaiah; Othni,   1Ch 26:7
and R.

REPHAH

And R. was his son, also   1Ch 7:25
Resheph

REPHAIAH

the sons of R., the sons of   1Ch 3:21
Arnan
and Neariah, and R. and   1Ch 4:42
Uzziel
sons of Tola; Uzzi, and R.   1Ch 7:2
Moza begat Binea; and R.   1Ch 9:43
his son
them repaired R. the son of   Ne 3:9
Hur

REPHAIM

regarded as R. (B)(E)(R)   De 2:11
regarded as the land of the R.   De 2:20
(B)
the surviving R. (B)   De 3:11;
     Jos 12:4; 13:12
last of the R. (E)(R)   De 3:11
land of R. (B)(E)(R)   De 3:13
the surviving R. (B)(E)(R)   Jos 12:4
valley of R. (B)(E)(R)   Jos 15:8;
     18:16
Perizzites and R. (B)(E)(R)   Jos 17:15
themselves in the valley of R.   2Sa 5:18;
     5:22
pitched in the valley of R.   2Sa 23:13
encamped in the valley of   1Ch 11:15
R.
themselves in the valley of R.   1Ch 14:9
descendents of R. (B)   1Ch 20:6
gathereth ears in the valley of   Isa 17:5
R.

REPHAIMS

and smote the R. in Ashteroth   Ge 14:5
and the Perizzites, and the R.   Ge 15:20

REPHIDIM

of the Lord, and pitched in R.   Ex 17:1
and fought with Israel in R.   Ex 17:8
For they were departed from   Ex 19:2
R.
and encamped at R. where   Nu 33:14
was no water
And they departed from R.   Nu 33:15

REPLACE

r. every man's money (R)   Ge 42:25
he shall r. it (A)   Le 24:21

REPLENISH

and multiply, and r. the earth   Ge 1:28
fill the earth (A)(B)(E)(R)   Ge 1:28
and multiply, and r. the earth   Ge 9:1
fill the earth (A)(R)   Ge 9:1
populate the earth (B)   Ge 9:1

REPLENISHED

because they be r. from the   Isa 2:6
east
filled with customs from the   Isa 2:6
east (A)(E)
influenced from the east (B)   Isa 2:6
full of diviners from the east   Isa 2:6
(R)
that pass over the sea, have r.   Isa 23:2
and I have r. every sorrowful   Jer 31:25
soul
I shall be r. now she is laid   Eze 26:2
waste
wast r. and made very   Eze 27:25
glorious

REPLIEST

who art thou that r. against   Ro 9:20
God

REPORT

brought unto his father their   Ge 37:2
evil r.
the r. was heard (S)   Ge 45:16; Jer 6:24
Thou shalt not raise a false r.   Ex 23:1
brought up an evil r. of the   Nu 13:32
land
bringing an evil r. (E)(R)   Nu 14:36
bring up the evil r. upon the   Nu 14:37
land
who shall hear r. of thee, and   De 2:25
report (S)   De 13:12; Isa 37:9
for it is no good r. that I   1Sa 2:24
hear
heard the r. (B)   1Sa 4:19; 2Sa 4:4
was a true r. that I heard in   1Ki 10:6
mine
was a true r. which I heard in   2Ch 9:5
mine
might have matter for an evil   Ne 6:13
r.
the evil r. (B)   Ps 112:7
a good r. maketh the bones   Pr 15:30
fat
As at the r. concerning Egypt   Isa 23:5
be sorely pained at the r. of   Isa 23:5
Tyre
a vexation to understand   Isa 28:19
the r.
Who hath believed our r.   Isa 53:1
R. say they, and we will r. it   Jer 20:10
king of Babylon hath heard   Jer 50:43
the r.
the evil r. of (E)   Eze 36:3
who hear the r. (B)(E)(S)   Na 3:19
r. from the east (B)   Da 11:44
Lord, who hath believed our   Joh 12:38
r.
among you seven men of   Ac 6:3
honest r.
men of good r. (E)   Ac 6:3
and of good r. among all the   Ac 10:22
nation
the r. reached the   Ac 21:31
(B)(N)(P)
having a good r. of all the   Ac 22:12
Jews
Lord, who hath believed our   Ro 10:16
r.
and r. that God is in you of   1Co 14:25
a truth
By honour and dishonour, by   2Co 6:8
evil r.
and good r.: as deceivers, and   2Co 6:8
whatsoever things are of good   Ph'p 4:8
r.
he must have a good r. of   1Ti 3:7
them
it the elders obtained a good   Heb 11:2
obtained a good r. through   Heb 11:39
faith
Demetrius hath good r. of all   3Jo 12
men

REPORTED

he r. them (S)   1Sa 8:21; 17:31
It is r. among the heathen, and   Ne 6:6
and now shall it be r. to the   Ne 6:7
king
they r. his good deeds before   Ne 6:19
me
in their eyes, when it shall be   Es 1:17
r.
inkhorn by his side, r. the   Eze 9:11
matter

commonly r. among the   M't 28:15
Jews is
it was r. that he was in the   M'k 2:1
house (S)
and r. all that the chief priests   Ac 4:23
was well r. of by the brethren   Ac 16:2
as we be slanderously r. and as   Ro 3:8
It is r. commonly that there is   1Co 5:1
Well r. of for good works; if   1Ti 5:10
which are now r. unto you by   1Pe 1:12
them

REPORTS

the good r. (B)   2Sa 18:27
r. seemed like nonsense   Lu 24:11
(B)(N)

REPRESENTATIVES

choose r. (N)(P)   Ac 15:22
picked r. (P)   Col 3:12

REPRIMANDED

Jacob r. Laban (B)   Ge 31:36

REPROACH

I have rolled away the r. of   Jos 5:9
Egypt
saying, Let her glean, and r.   Ru 2:15
her not
and taketh away the r. from   1Sa 17:26
Israel
removes the shame from   1Sa 17:26
Israel (B)
king of Assyria hath sent to   2Ki 19:4;
r. the living God   19:16; Isa 37:4, 17
sent to ridicule the living   2Ki 19:4
God (B)
sent to defy the living God   2Ki 19:4
(E)
sent to mock the living God   2Ki 19:4
(R)
the remnant are in great   Ne 1:3
affliction and r.
and turn their r. upon their   Ne 4:4
own head
turn their taunt upon own   Ne 4:4
heads (A)(R)
Return their contempt upon   Ne 4:4
heads (B)
because of the r. of the heathen   Ne 5:9
our enemies
have matter that they might r.   Ne 6:13
me
bring accusation against me   Ne 6:13
(B)
in order to taunt me (R)   Ne 6:13
my heart shall not r. me so   Job 27:6
long as I live
my conscience does not   Job 27:6
accuse me (B)
as with a sword, mine   Ps 42:10
enemies r. me
my r. faces me (B)   Ps 44:15
he shall save me from the r. of   Ps 57:3
him
save me from the slanders (B)   Ps 57:3
because for thy sake I have   Ps 69:7
borne r.
I have been humiliated for thy   Ps 69:7
sake (B)
r. hath broken my heart, I   Ps 69:20
am full of heaviness
let them be covered with r.   Ps 71:13
that seek
how long shall the adversary   Ps 74:10
r. me
he put them to a perpetual r.   Ps 78:66
caused them unending   Ps 78:66
disgrace (B)
put them to everlasting shame   Ps 78:66
(R)
their r. wherewith they   Ps 79:12
reproached thee
remember the r. of thy   Ps 89:50
servants, how I bear in my
bosom the r. of
mine enemies r. me all the   Ps 102:8
day
my enemies insult me (B)   Ps 102:8
my enemies taunt me (R)   Ps 102:8
remove from me r. and   Ps 119:22
contempt
and his r. shall not be wiped   Pr 6:33
away
his disgrace will not be wiped   Pr 6:33
away (B)(R)

and with ignominy cometh r.   *Pr 18:3*
folly and a r. (B)   *Pr 18:13*
is a son that causeth shame   *Pr 19:26*
and r.
acts shamefully and   *Pr 19:26*
disgracefully (B)
cast out scorner, strife and r.   *Pr 22:10*
shall cease
strife and abuse will cease   *Pr 22:10*
(A)
contention and abuse shall   *Pr 22:10*
cease (B)
strife and ignominy shall   *Pr 22:10*
cease (E)
quarrelling and abuse shall   *Pr 22:10*
cease (R)
called by thy name to take   *Isa 4:1*
away our r.
to take away our stigma (B)   *Isa 4:1*
Egypt be your r. (B)   *Isa 30:3*
fear ye not the r. of men nor   *Isa 51:7*
be afraid
not remember the r. of thy   *Isa 54:4*
widowhood
instead of r. (A)(B)   *Pr 61:7*
I will bring an everlasting r.   *Jer 23:40*
on you
an everlasting r. (A)(B)   *Jer 23:40*
because I did bear the r. of   *Jer 31:19*
my youth
a desolation, curse, r. (B)   *Jer 42:18*
we are confounded, because   *Jer 51:51*
we have heard r.
he is filled full with r.   *La 3:30*
thou hast heard their r. O   *La 3:61*
Lord, against me
remember, consider and behold   *La 5:1*
our r.
discovered, as at the time of   *Eze 16:57*
thy r.
concerning the r. of   *Eze 21:28*
Ammonites
r. of nations (A)(B)(R)   *Eze 34:29;*
  36:6, 7
nor shalt thou bear r. of the   *Eze 36:15*
people any more
that ye shall receive no more   *Eze 36:30*
of famine
prince shall cause the r.   *Da 11:18*
offered by him to cease,
without his own r.
his r. shall his Lord return to   *Ho 12:14*
him
and give not thine heritage to   *Joe 2:17*
r.
therefore ye shall bear r. of   *Mic 5:16*
my people
I have heard the r. of Moab   *Zep 2:8*
and Ammon
to whom the r. of it was a   *Zep 3:18*
burden
began to r. the cities (B)   *M't 11:20*
when men shall r. you for my   *Lu 6:22*
sake
revile, denounce, defame your   *Lu 6:22*
name (A)
denounce and defame your   *Lu 6:22*
name (B)
ban your name as infamous   *Lu 6:22*
(N)
slander and detest all you stand   *Lu 6:22*
for (P)
revile you and cast out your   *Lu 6:22*
name (R)
acquit himself of r. (A)   *Lu 10:29*
I speak as concerning r. as   *2Co 11:21*
though weak
must have a good report lest   *1Ti 3:7*
fall into r.
lest he be involved in slander   *1Ti 3:7*
(A)(B)
may not be exposed to scandal   *1Ti 3:7*
(N)
therefore we both labour and   *1Ti 4:10*
suffer r.
without spot, without r.   *1Ti 6:14*
(E)(P)(R)
esteeming r. of Christ   *Heb 11:26*
greater riches
he considered the contempt   *Heb 11:26*
(A)(B)
he considered the stigma   *Heb 11:26*
(N)
he considered the abuse   *Heb 11:26*
suffered (R)
let us go without the camp,   *Heb 13:13*
bearing his r.
bearing the contempt (A)   *Heb 13:13*
bearing his disgrace (B)   *Heb 13:13*
bearing the stigma that he   *Heb 13:13*
bore (N)

bearing abuse for him (R)   *Heb 13:13*
unblemished, above r. (N)   *2Pe 3:14*
jubilant and above r. (N)   *Jude 24*
beyond r. (P)   *Re 14:5*

A REPROACH

we cannot do this, that were   *Ge 34:14*
a. r. to us
a disgrace (A)(B)(R)   *Ge 34:14;*
  1Sa 11:2; Isa 30:5
and lay it for a r. upon all   *1Sa 11:2*
Israel
let us build, that we be no   *Ne 2:17*
more a r.
he that taketh not up a r.   *Ps 15:3*
against neighbour
does not carry a scandal   *Ps 15:3*
against (B)
a r. of men, and despised of   *Ps 22:6*
the people
I was a r. among all mine   *Ps 31:11*
enemies
the scorn of all my   *Ps 31:11*
adversaries (R)
make me not the r. of the   *Ps 39:8*
foolish
the taunt of the simpleton (B)   *Ps 39:8*
the scorn to the fool (R)   *Ps 39:8*
thou makest us a r. to our   *Ps 44:13*
neighbours
a taunt of our neighbors   *Ps 44:13*
(A)(B)(R)
we are become a r. to our   *Ps 79:4*
neighbours
a taunt to our neighbors (R)   *Ps 79:4*
all spoil him: he is a r. to his   *Ps 89:41*
neighbour
the scorn of all his neighbors   *Ps 89:41*
(B)(R)
I became also a r. to them,   *Ps 109:25*
they shaked
became a laughingstock to   *Ps 109:25*
others (B)
an object of scorn to my   *Ps 109:25;*
accusers (R)   *Jer 6:10*
but sin is a r. to any people   *Pr 14:34*
all ashamed of a people that   *Isa 30:5*
were a r.
the word of the Lord is to   *Jer 6:10*
them a r.
the word of the Lord was   *Jer 20:8*
made a r.
become a laughingstock (B)   *Jer 20:8*
I will deliver them for their   *Jer 24:9;*
hurt to be a r.   *29:18; 42:18; 44:8, 12*
Bozrah shall become a r. and   *Jer 49:13*
a curse
I will make thee a r. among   *Eze 5:14*
the nations
Jerusalem shall be a r. and a   *Eze 5:15*
taunt
I have made a r. unto the   *Eze 22:4*
heathen
because thy people are   *Da 9:16*
become a r.
become a disdain (B)   *Da 9:16*
and I will no more make you   *Joe 2:19*
a r.

MY REPROACH

she said, God hath taken   *Ge 20:23*
away my r.
that hath pleaded the cause   *1Sa 25:39*
of my r.
if indeed ye plead against me   *Job 19:5*
my r.
I have heard the check of my   *Job 20:3*
r.
when I wept, that was my r.   *Ps 69:10*
thou hast known my r. and   *Ps 69:19*
my shame
turn away my r. which I   *Ps 119:39*
fear
to take away my r. among   *Lu 1:25*
men

REPROACHED

hast thou r. and blasphemed   *2Ki 19:22*
mocked and insulted   *2Ki 19:22;*
(A)(R)   *19:23*
defied and blasphemed (E)   *2Ki 19:22;*
  19:23
messengers thou hast r. the   *2Ki 19:23*
Lord
These ten times have ye r.   *Job 19:3*
me: ye
ten times derided me (B)   *Job 19:3*

it was not an enemy that r.   *Ps 55:12*
me
an enemy who taunts me (R)   *Ps 55:12*
reproaches of them that r.   *Ps 69:9*
thee are
insults of those who insult thee   *Ps 69:9*
(R)
this, that the enemy hath r., O   *Ps 74:18*
Lord
the enemy scoffs (B)(R)   *Ps 74:18*
wherewith they have r. thee,   *Ps 79:12*
O Lord
the taunts with which they   *Ps 79:12*
have r.
Wherewith thine enemies   *Ps 89:51*
have r.
the enemies have taunted   *Ps 89:51*
(A)(B)(R)
they have r. the footsteps of   *Ps 89:51*
thine
hast thou r. and blasphemed   *Isa 37:23*
mocked and reviled (A)(R)   *Isa 37:23;*
  37:24
thy servants hast thou r. the   *Isa 37:24*
Lord
whereby they have r. my   *Zep 2:8*
people
have taunted my people (R)   *Zep 2:8*
have r. and magnified   *Zep 2:10*
themselves
have scoffed and boasted (R)   *Zep 2:10*
r. them for reluctance to   *M't 16:14*
believe (P)
they r. her (R)   *M'k 14:5*
r. him too (B)(E)   *M'k 15:32*
reproved and r. them   *M'k 16:14*
(A)(N)(P)
reproaches of them that r.   *Ro 15:3*
thee
the abuses of those who   *Ro 15:3*
abused (B)
If ye be r. for the name of   *1Pe 4:14*
Christ
be censured and suffer abuse   *1Pe 4:14*
(A)
be defamed for the name of   *1Pe 4:14*
Christ (B)

REPROACHES

the r. of them that reproached   *Ps 69:9*
thee
Jacob to the curse, and   *Isa 43:28*
Israel to r.
The r. of them that   *Ro 15:3*
reproached thee
take pleasure in infirmities,   *2Co 12:10*
in r.
in insults (A)(B)(R)   *2Co 12:10;*
  Heb 10:33
both by r. and afflictions   *Heb 10:33*
neither refuses or r. anyone   *Jas 1:5*
(N)

REPROACHEST

Master, thus saying thou r.   *Lu 11:45*
us also
you insult us, too (B)   *Lu 11:45*
you are insulting us (N)(P)   *Lu 11:45*

REPROACHETH

a stranger, the same r. the   *Nu 15:30*
Lord
is a blasphemer against the   *Nu 15:30*
Lord (B)
the same blasphemeth   *Nu 15:30*
Jehovah (E)
reviles the Lord (R)   *Nu 15:30*
For the voice of him that r.   *Ps 44:16*
words of the taunter and   *Ps 44:16*
reviler (A)(R)
voice of the scoffer and   *Ps 44:16*
scorner (B)
how the foolish man r. thee   *Ps 74:22*
daily
insults fools have hurled at   *Ps 74:22*
thee (B)
how the impious scoff at thee   *Ps 74:22*
(R)
to answer him that r. me   *Ps 119:42*
an answer to those who   *Ps 119:42*
taunt me (R)
oppresseth the poor r. his   *Pr 14:31*
Maker
oppresses poor insults his   *Pr 14:31;*
Maker (B)(R)   *17:5*
mocketh the poor r. his Maker   *Pr 17:5*
that I may answer him that r.   *Pr 27:11*
me

REPROACHFULLY

smitten me upon the cheek r.	Job 16:10
struck the cheek insolently (A)(B)(R)	Job 16:10
spoke r., abusively, jeered (A)	M't 27:39
to the adversary to speak r.	1Ti 5:14
opponent no incentive for slandering (B)	1Ti 5:14
no occasion to adversary for reviling (E)	1Ti 5:14
no opponent occasion for slander (N)	1Ti 5:14
give the enemy no occasion to revile (R)	1Ti 5:14

REPROACHING

without r. and faultfinding (A)(R)	Jas 1:5
began r. the cities (P)	M't 11:20
reviling and r. him (A)	M'k 15:29
who gives generously without r. (R)	Jas 1:5

REPROBATE

a r. person (B)(E)(R)	Ps 15:4
R. silver shall men call them	Jer 6:30
called refuse of silver (B)(E)(R)	Jer 6:30
God gave them over to a r. mind	Ro 1:28
over to a base and condemned mind (A)	Ro 1:28
over to perverted tendencies (B)	Ro 1:28
given them up to their own depraved reason (N)	Ro 1:28
slaves to their degenerate minds (P)	Ro 1:28
gave them up to a base mind (R)	Ro 1:28
minds, r. concerning the faith	2Ti 3:8
counterfeits as far as faith is concerned (B)	2Ti 3:8
lost the power to reason (N)	2Ti 3:8
their minds distorted (P)	2Ti 3:8
men of corrupt mind and counterfeit faith (R)	2Ti 3:8
and unto every good work r.	Tit 1:16
unfit and worthless for good work (A)	Tit 1:16
unfit for any good enterprise (B)(R)	Tit 1:16
detestable obstinacy disqualifies them (N)	Tit 1:16
they are palpable frauds (P)	Tit 1:16

REPROBATES

Christ is in you, except ye be r.	2Co 13:5
unless you are counterfeits (A)(B)	2Co 13:5; 13:6-7
ye shall know that we are not r.	2Co 13:6
which is honest, though we be as	2Co 13:7

REPRODUCTION

r. of things (P)	Heb 8:5

REPROOF

and are astonished at his r.	Job 26:11
Turn you at my r.: behold, I will	Pr 1:23
counsel, and would none of my r.	Pr 1:25
my counsel: they despised all r.	Pr 1:30
his r. (A)(B)(E)(R)	Pr 3:11
and my heart despised r.	Pr 5:12
but he that refuseth r. erreth	Pr 10:17
but he that hateth r. is brutish	Pr 12:1
that regardeth r. shall be honoured	Pr 13:18
but he that regardeth r. is prudent	Pr 15:5
way: and he hath hateth r. shall die	Pr 15:10
The ear that heareth the r. of life	Pr 15:31
heareth r. getteth understanding	Pr 15:32
A r. entereth more into a wise	Pr 17:10

The rod and r. give wisdom for doctrine, for r. for correction	Pr 29:15 2Ti 3:16

REPROOFS

and in whose mouth are no r.	Ps 38:14
r. of instruction are the way of life	Pr 6:23

REPROVE

will r. the words which the Lord	2Ki 19:4
but what doth your arguing r.	Job 6:25
Do ye imagine to r. words	Job 6:26
He will surely r. you, if ye do	Job 13:10
Will he r. thee for fear of thee	Job 22:4
I will not r. thee for thy sacrifices	Ps 50:8
I will r. thee, and set them in order	Ps 50:21
and let him r. me: it shall be	Ps 141:5
R. not a scorner, lest he hate thee	Pr 9:8
and r. one that hath understanding	Pr 19:25
lest he r. thee and thou be found a	Pr 30:6
r. after the hearing of his ears	Isa 11:3
r. with equity for the meek of	Isa 11:4
will r. the words which the Lord	Isa 37:4
and thy backslidings shall r. thee	Jer 2:19
let no man strive, nor r. another	Ho 4:4
is come, he will r. the world of sin	Joh 16:8
of darkness, but rather r. them	Eph 5:11
r. rebuke, exhort with all	2Ti 4:2

REPROVED

with all other: thus she was r.	Ge 20:16
Abraham r. Abimelech because	Ge 21:25
yea, he r. kings for their sakes	1Ch 16:21; Ps 105:14
being often r. hardeneth his neck	Pr 29:1
why hast thou not r. Jeremiah	Jer 29:27
what I shall answer when I am r.	Hab 2:1
r. and reproached them (A)(N)(P)	M'k 16:14
being r. by him for Herodias his	Lu 3:19
light lest his deeds should be r.	Joh 3:20
r., convicted (A)	1Co 14:24
that are r. are made manifest by	Eph 5:13

REPROVER

is a wise r. upon an obedient ear	Pr 25:12
dumb, and shalt not be to them a r.	Eze 3:26

REPROVES

whom God r. (A)(R)	Job 5:17

REPROVETH

he that r. God, let him answer it	Job 40:2
He that r. a scorner getteth to him	Pr 9:7
scorner loveth not one that r.	Pr 15:12
a snare for him that r. in the gate	Isa 29:21

REPUDIATED

he r. holy place (B)	La 2:7

REPUGNANT

an unloved r. woman (B)(R)	Pr 30:23

REPULSIVE

r. loathsome (B)	Le 7:18; 11:10
I am r. to my wife (A)(R)	Job 19:17

wounds r. and festering (R)(S)	Ps 38:5

REPUTATION

gives her an evil r. (A)	De 22:14
is in r. for wisdom and honour	Ec 10:1
had in r. among all the people	Ac 5:34
men of r. (B)(N)(P)	Ac 6:3
privately to them which were of r.	Ga 2:2
enjoyed a r. (B)(N)	Ga 2:6
But made himself of no r.	Ph'p 2:7
stripped himself of all privileges, and rightful dignity (A)(P)	Ph'p 2:7
emptied himself (B)(E)(R)	Ph'p 2:7
made himself nothing (N)	Ph'p 2:7
gladness; and hold such in r.	Ph'p 2:29

REPUTE

poor man of no r. (R)	1Sa 18:23
brought in bad r. (B)	1Sa 27:12
men of good r. (R)	Ac 6:3

REPUTED

as beasts, and r. vile in your sight	Job 18:3
of the earth are r. as nothing	Da 4:35
r. greatest (A)(B)(P)	Lu 22:24

REPTILES

reptiles (A)(B)(R)	Ro 1:23

REQUEST

r. for me of Ephron (B)	Ge 23:8
them, I would desire a r. of you	J'g 8:24
perform the r. of his handmaid	2Sa 14:15
hath fulfilled the r. of his servant	2Sa 14:22
the king granted him all his r.	Ezr 7:6
me, For what dost thou make r.	Ne 2:4
make r. before him for her people	Es 4:8
queen Esther? and what is thy r.	Es 5:3
and what is thy r.? even to the half	Es 5:6
and said, My petition and my r. is	Es 5:7
my petition, and to perform my r.	Es 5:8
and what is thy r.? and it shall be	Es 7:2
petition, and my people at my r.	Es 7:3
Haman stood up to make r. for his	Es 7:7
what is thy r. further? and it shall	Es 9:12
Oh that I might have my r.	Job 6:8
not withholden the r. of his lips	Ps 21:2
he gave them their r.; but sent	Ps 106:15
r. for sentence against him (B)(E)(R)	Ac 25:15
Making r. if by any means now at	Ro 1:10
for you all making r. with joy	Ph'p 1:4
the r. made of him (A)(B)(R)	1Jo 5:15

REQUESTED

just as you r. (B)	De 18:16
of the golden earrings that he r.	J'g 8:26
he r. for himself that he might die	1Ki 19:4
God granted him that which he r.	1Ch 4:10
he r. the prince of the eunuchs	Da 1:8
Then Daniel r. of the king	Da 2:49
whom they r. (A)(B)(E)(N)(R)	M'k 15:6
r. a murderer (B)	Ac 3:14
r. Philip to come (A)	Ac 8:31

REQUESTS

let your r. be made known unto God	Ph'p 4:6

REQUIRE

your blood of your lives will I *Ge 9:5*
r.
the hand of every beast will I *Ge 9:5*
r. it
brother will I r. the life of man *Ge 9:5*
of it; of my hand didst thou *Ge 31:39*
r. it
of my hand shalt thou r. him *Ge 43:9*
doth the Lord thy God r. of *De 10:12*
thee
in my name, I will r. it of *De 18:19*
him
thy God will surely r. it of *De 23:21*
thee
thereon, let the Lord himself *Jos 22:23*
r. it
the Lord even r. it at the *1Sa 20:16*
hand of
but one thing I r. of thee *2Sa 3:13*
now r. his blood of your *2Sa 4:11*
hand, and
whatsoever thou shalt r. of *2Sa 19:38*
me
at all times, as the matter *1Ki 8:59*
shall r.
r. an accounting (A)(B)(R) *2Ki 12:15*
then doth my lord r. this *1Ch 21:3*
thing
The Lord look upon it, and *2Ch 24:22*
r. it
the God of heaven, shall r. of *Ezr 7:21*
you
ashamed to r. of the king a *Ezr 8:22*
band
them, and will r. nothing of *Ne 5:12*
them
in his heart, Thou wilt not r. *Ps 10:13*
it
blood will I r. at thine hand *Eze 3:18;*
3:20
there will I r. your offerings *Eze 20:40*
blood will I r. at the *Eze 33:6*
watchman's
his blood will I r. at thine *Eze 33:8*
hand
I will r. my flock at their *Eze 34:10*
hand
and what doth the Lord r. of *Mic 6:8*
thee
the Jews r. a sign, and the *1Co 1:22*
Greeks
and need so r. let him do *1Co 7:36*
what he

REQUIRED

behold, also his blood is r. *Ge 42:22*
lent unto them such things *Ex 12:36*
as they r.
the king's business r. haste *1Sa 21:8*
when he r. they set bread *2Sa 12:20*
before
continually, as every day's *1Ch 16:37*
work r.
As the duty of every day r. *2Ch 8:13*
(S)
priests, as the duty of every *2Ch 8:14*
day r.
hast thou not r. of the *2Ch 24:6*
Levites to
as the duty of every day r. *Ezr 3:4*
r. not I the bread of the *Ne 5:18*
governor
she r. nothing but what Hegai *Es 2:15*
and sin offering hast thou not *Ps 40:6*
r.
us away captive r. of us a *Ps 137:3*
song
they that wasted us r. of us *Ps 137:3*
mirth
Two things have I r. of thee; *Pr 30:7*
deny
who hath r. this at your hand *Isa 1:12*
world, may be r. of this *Lu 11:50*
generation
It shall be r. of this *Lu 11:51*
generation
night thy soul shall be r. of *Lu 12:20*
thee
is given, of him shall be much *Lu 12:48*
r.
have r. mine own with usury *Lu 19:23*
that it should be as they r. *Lu 23:24*
r. letters (E)(R) *Ac 9:2*
Moreover it is r. in stewards, *1Co 4:2*
that

REQUIREMENTS

all these r. (B) *De 6:24*
blamelessly in all r. (A)(P) *Lu 1:6*

REQUIRES

r. full restitution (B) *Ge 50:15*

REQUIREST

I will do to thee all that thou *Ru 3:11*
r.

REQUIRETH

and God r. that which is past *Ec 3:15*
it is a rare thing that the king *Da 2:11*
r.

REQUIRING

voice, r. that he might be *Lu 23:23*
crucified

REQUITE

and will certainly r. us all the *Ge 50:15*
evil
will pay us back (A)(R) *Ge 50:15*
requires full restitution (B) *Ge 50:15*
Do ye thus r. the Lord, O *De 32:6*
foolish
Do you thus repay the Lord *De 32:6*
(A)
Is this your repayment to the *De 32:6*
Lord (B)
and I will also r. you this *2Sa 2:6*
kindness
I will also do well by you (A) *2Sa 2:6*
So I will deal with you (B) *2Sa 2:6*
I will do good to you (R) *2Sa 2:6*
Lord r. the evildoer (R) *2Sa 3:39*
the Lord will r. me good for *2Sa 16:12*
his
Lord will recompense me *2Sa 16:12*
good (A)
Lord will render me good *2Sa 16:12*
(B)
Lord will repay me with *2Sa 16:12*
good (R)
I will r. thee in this plat, *2Ki 9:26*
saith the
I will repay you on this plot *2Ki 9:26*
(A)(B)
and spite, to r. it with thy *Ps 10:14*
hand
thou mayest repay it (B) *Ps 10:14*
thou mayest take it unto thy *Ps 10:14*
hands (R)
raise me up, that I may r. *Ps 41:10*
me
let me repay them (B) *Ps 41:10*
r. evil unto enemies (E)(R) *Ps 54:5*
God of recompences shall *Jer 51:56*
surely r.
I will surely repay (B) *Jer 51:56*
r. them for their doings *Ho 4:9*
(E)(R)
at home and to r. their *1Ti 5:4*
parents
make return to their parents *1Ti 5:4*
(A)
return a remuneration to those *1Ti 5:4*
(B)
repay parents and *1Ti 5:4*
grandparents (E)
repaying parents for (P) *1Ti 5:4*
make some return to their *1Ti 5:4*
parents (R)
the Lord will r. him (R) *2Ti 4:14*

REQUITED

as I have done, so God hath r. *J'g 1:7*
me
so God has repaid me (A) *J'g 1:7*
and he hath r. me evil for *1Sa 25:21*
good
he has repaid me evil for *1Sa 25:21*
good (A)
he is returning evil for good *1Sa 25:21*
(B)(E)(R)

REQUITING

by r. the wicked, by *2Ch 6:23*
recompensing

REREWARD

which was the r. of all the *Nu 10:25*
camps

and the r. came after the ark *Jos 6:9*
but the r. came after the ark *Jos 6:13*
of the
passed on in the r. with *1Sa 29:2*
Achish
the God of Israel will be *Isa 52:12*
your r.
the glory of the Lord shall be *Isa 58:5*
thy r.

RESCUE

no one to r. her (R) *De 22:27*
no one to r. her (B) *De 28:29*
thou shalt have none to r. *De 28:31*
them
r. my people (B) *2Sa 3:18*
look on? r. my soul from *Ps 35:17*
their
take away, and none shall r. *Ho 5:14*
him

RESCUED

So the people r. Jonathan, *1Sa 14:45*
that he
away: and David r. his two *1Sa 30:18*
wives
r. us from our enemies *Ps 136:24*
(A)(R)
came I with an army, and r. *Ac 23:27*
him

RESCUETH

he delivereth and r. and he *Da 6:27*

RESCUING

a righteous and r. God *Isa 45:21*
(B)(R)

RESEMBLANCE

is their r. through all the earth *Zec 5:6*

RESEMBLE

like? and whereunto shall I *Lu 13:18*
r. it

RESEMBLED

each one r. the children of a *J'g 8:18*
king

RESEMBLES

r. Melchizedek (B) *Heb 7:15*

RESEMBLING

r. a human form (B) *Da 10:16*
r. mortal man *Ro 1:23*
(A)(B)(N)(P)(R)

RESEN

R. between Nineveh and *Ge 10:12*
Calah

RESENTFULLY

do not r. envy (A) *Pr 3:31*

RESENTMENT

the idol of r. (B) *Eze 8:3*
not good children to r. (N) *Eph 6:14*
without r. (A)(P) *1Ti 2:8*

RESERVATIONS

trusts God with inward r. (P) *Jas 1:6*

RESERVE

Will he r. his anger for ever *Jer 3:5*
for I will pardon them whom *Jer 50:20*
I r.
without r., faultfinding (B) *Jas 1:5*
to r. the unjust unto the day *2Pe 2:9*

RESERVED

thou not r. a blessing for me *Ge 27:36*
most holy things, r. from the *Nu 18:9*
fire
we r. not to each man his *J'g 21:22*
wife

gave to her that she had r.   *Ru 2:18*
after
r. of them for an hundred   *2Sa 8:4*
chariots
but r. of them an hundred   *1Ch 18:4*
chariots
is r. to the day of   *Job 21:30*
destruction
Which I have r. against the   *Job 38:23*
time of
be r. unto the hearing of   *Ac 35:21*
Augustus
I have r. to myself seven   *Ro 11:4*
thousand
not away, r. in heaven for you   *1Pe 1:4*
darkness, to be r. unto   *2Pe 2:4*
judgment
the mist of darkness is r. for   *2Pe 2:17*
ever
r. unto fire against the day of   *2Pe 3:7*
hath r. in everlasting chains   *Jude 6*
under
to whom is r. the blackness of   *Jude 13*

RESERVETH

r. unto us the appointed   *Jer 5:24*
weeks
and he r. wrath for his enemies   *Na 1:2*

RESHEPH

Rephah was his son, also R.   *1Ch 7:25*

RESIDENCE

a residence (B)   *2Ch 6:2*
to r. city they sought (B)   *Ps 107:7*
guards his own r. (B)   *Lu 11:21*
let his r. be deserted (A)   *Ac 1:20*
your temporary r. (A)   *1Pe 1:17*

RESIDENT

temporary r. (A)   *Le 25:6;*
    25:35, 40; Nu 15:15; 35:15; Ps 39:12
a temporary r. (B)   *Le 25:35*
a temporary r. (A)   *De 18:6; Heb 11:9*
an alien r. (B)   *Eze 14:7*

RESENTFUL

r. against his neighbor (B)   *Ex 21:14*
the king of Israel went r. (S)   *1Ki 20:43*

RESERVOIR

spring, cistern, r. (A)(B)   *Le 11:36*
r. between two walls   *Isa 22:11*
(A)(B)(E)(R)

RESIDE

strangers r. among you   *Eze 47:22*
(A)(B)

RESIDENTS

temporary r. (A)   *Le 25:23*
all r. (B)   *Nu 15:15*
r. up to this day (B)   *2Sa 4:3*
mere tenants, temporary r.   *1Ch 29:15*
(B)
ruins without r. (B)   *Isa 6:11;*
    9:9; 12:6; 33:24
temporary r. (A)   *Jer 35:7*

RESIDING

temporarily been r. (B)   *De 18:6*

RESIDES

stranger who r. in Israel (B)   *Le 20:2;*
    Nu 9:14
the foreigner r. (A)   *Eze 47:23*

RESIDUE

eat the r. of that which is   *Ex 10:5*
escaped
eat the remainder of what is   *Ex 10:5*
left (A)
devour the left-overs that   *Ex 10:5*
survived (B)
eat what is left to you (R)   *Ex 10:5*
And the r. of the families of   *1Ch 6:66*
the sons
the r. of Israel, of the   *Ne 11:20*
priests, and

the r. of Israel, of the   *Ne 11:20*
(B)(R)
the r. of the number of   *Isa 21:17*
archers, the
the remainder of the archers   *Isa 21:17*
(A)(R)
those that are left of the   *Isa 21:17*
archers (B)
of beauty, unto the r. of his   *Isa 28:5*
people
the remnant (A)(B)(R)   *Isa 28:5*
am deprived of the r. of my   *Isa 38:10*
years
the remainder of my years   *Isa 38:10*
(A)
the rest of my years (B)(R)   *Isa 38:10*
the r. thereof he maketh a   *Isa 44:17*
god
what is left of the log (A)   *Isa 44:17*
the rest of it (B)(R)   *Isa 44:17*
the r. thereof an   *Isa 44:19*
abomination
the remainder of it (A)(B)   *Isa 44:19*
r. of them that remain of this   *Jer 8:3*
evil
the remnant that remains   *Jer 8:3*
(B)(R)
the r. of them will I deliver to   *Jer 15:9*
the rest of them (A)(R)   *Jer 15:9*
the remainder of them (B)   *Jer 15:9*
the r. of Jerusalem, that   *Jer 24:8*
remain in
the remainder of Jerusalem   *Jer 24:8*
(B)
the remnant of Jerusalem (R)   *Jer 24:8*
concerning the r. of the   *Jer 27:19*
vessels
the remainder of the vessels   *Jer 27:19*
(A)(B)
the rest of the vessels (R)   *Jer 27:19*
Jerusalem unto the r. of the   *Jer 29:1*
elders
the r. of the princes of the   *Jer 39:3*
king of
the rest of the officers   *Jer 39:3*
(A)(B)(R)
all the r. of the people that   *Jer 41:10*
were
the rest of the people   *Jer 41:10*
(A)(R)
the whole remnant of the   *Jer 41:10*
people (B)
r. of the people that   *Jer 52:15*
remained in
wilt thou destroy all the r. of   *Eze 9:8*
Israel
wilt thou destroy all that is   *Eze 9:8*
left (A)(B)
wilt thou destroy all that   *Eze 9:8*
remains (R)
thy r. shall be devoured by   *Eze 23:25*
the fire
those who are left (A)   *Eze 23:25*
what remains of you (B)   *Eze 23:25*
your survivors shall be   *Eze 23:25*
devoured (R)
your feet the r. of your   *Eze 34:18*
pastures
ye must foul the r. with your   *Eze 34:18*
feet
unto the r. of the heathen   *Eze 36:3*
derision to the r. of the   *Eze 36:4*
heathen
against the r. of the heathen   *Eze 36:5*
the rest of the nations   *Eze 36:5*
(A)(R)
the remaining nations (B)   *Eze 36:5*
And the r. in length over   *Eze 48:18*
against
the remainder of the length   *Eze 48:18*
(A)(B)(R)
And the r. shall be for the   *Eze 48:21*
prince
what is left unallotted (A)   *Eze 48:21*
what remains shall belong to   *Eze 48:21*
(B)(R)
stamped the r. with the feet of   *Da 7:7*
it
what was left with its feet (A)   *Da 7:7;*
    7:19
stamped the remaining portions   *Da 7:7*
with (B)
and stamped the r. with his   *Da 7:19*
feet
what remained of the victim   *Da 7:19*
(B)
r. of my people shall spoil   *Zep 2:9*
them
the remnant of my people   *Zep 2:9*
(A)(R)

the remainder of my people   *Zep 2:9*
(B)
and to the r. of the people   *Hag 2:2*
saying
the remainder of my people   *Hag 2:2*
(A)
the remnant of my people   *Hag 2:2*
(B)(R)
be unto the r. of this people   *Zec 8:11*
as in former days
the remnant of my people   *Zec 8:11*
(A)(B)(R)
r. of the people shall not be   *Zec 14:2*
cut off
rest of the people (A)(B)(R)   *Zec 14:2*
Yet had he the r. of the   *Mal 2:15*
spirit
they went and told it unto   *M'k 16:13*
the r.
r. of the men might seek   *Ac 15:17*
after the

RESIGN

r. yourself to him (B)   *Ps 37:7*

RESIN

carry r. (B)   *Ge 37:25*

RESINOUS

ark of r. wood (B)   *Ge 6:14*

RESIST

at his right hand to r. him   *Zec 3:1*
I say unto you, That ye r. not   *M't 5:39*
evil
shall not be able to gainsay   *Lu 21:15*
nor r.
were not able to r. the wisdom   *Ac 6:10*
ears, ye do always r. the Holy   *Ac 7:51*
Ghost
and they that r. shall receive   *Ro 13:2*
Moses, so do these also r. the   *2Ti 3:8*
truth
R. the devil, and he will flee   *Jas 4:7*
from
the just; and he doth not r.   *Jas 5:6*
you
Whom r. stedfast in the faith   *1Pe 5:9*

RESISTANCE

my eye dwell on their r. (A)   *Job 17:2*

RESISTED

find fault? For who hath r.   *Ro 9:19*
his will

RESISTETH

Whosoever therefore r. the   *Ro 13:2*
power
r. the ordinance of God: and   *Ro 13:2*
they
God r. the proud, but giveth   *Jas 4:6;*
grace   *1Pe 5:5*

RESISTING

r. God's appointment (B)(N)   *Ro 13:2*

RESISTS

r. what God appointed (A)(R)   *Ro 13:2*

RESOLUTION

issued our r. (B)   *Ac 21:25*

RESOLVED

I am r. what to do, that, when   *Lu 16:4*
r. in regular assembly (P)   *Ac 19:39*
r. in his heart (A)   *1Co 7:37*

RESORT

trumpet, r. ye thither unto us   *Ne 4:20*
whereunto I may continually r.   *Ps 71:3*
and the people r. unto him   *M'k 10:1*
again
whither the Jews always r.   *Joh 18:20*
a r. of demons (B)   *Re 18:2*

RESORTED

r. to him out of all their   2Ch 11:13
coasts
and all the multitude r. unto   M'k 2:13
him
many r. unto him, and said,   Joh 10:41
John
Jesus ofttimes r. thither with   Joh 18:2
his
unto the women which r.   Ac 16:13
thither

RESOUND

made voices r. (B)   Jer 2:15

RESPECT

And the Lord had r. unto Abel   Ge 4:4
The Lord approved of Abel   Ge 4:4
(B)
the Lord had regard for Abel   Ge 4:4
(R)
and to his offering he had not   Ge 4:5
r.
The Lord did not approve of   Ge 4:5
Cain (B)
for Cain and offering he had   Ge 4:5
no regard (R)
Israel, and God had r. unto   Ex 2:25
them
concerned himself about them   Ex 2:25
(A)(B)
God took knowledge of them   Ex 2:25
(E)
God knew their condition (R)   Ex 2:25
not r. the person of the poor   Le 19:15
not partial to poor or show   Le 19:15
reference (A)(R)
neither favor poor nor show   Le 19:15
deference (B)
For I will have r. unto you   Le 26:9
will be leaning toward you   Le 26:9
(A)(B)
will have regard for you (R)   Le 26:9
Lord, R. not thou their   Nu 16:15
offering
Pay no attention to their   Nu 16:15
offering (B)
shall not r. persons in   De 1:17
judgment
not be partial (A)(R)   De 1:17; 16:19
show no partiality (B)   De 1:17
thou shalt not r. persons,   De 16:19
neither
you must be impartial (B)   De 16:19
shall not show partiality (R)   De 16:19
neither doth God r. any   2Sa 14:14
person
have thou r. unto the prayer   1Ki 8:28
had r. unto them, because of   2Ki 13:23
his
Have r. therefore to the   2Ch 6:19
prayer of
Lord our God, nor r. of   2Ch 19:7
persons
there is no injustice with   2Ch 19:7
God (A)(B)
no perversion of justice with   2Ch 19:7
God (R)
Have r. unto the covenant   Ps 74:20
have regard for the covenant   Ps 74:20
(A)(R)
Remember the covenant (B)   Ps 74:20
have r. unto all thy   Ps 119:6
commandments
my eyes fixed (R)   Ps 119:6; 119:15
precepts, and have r. unto   Ps 119:15
thy ways
r. unto thy statutes   Ps 119:117
continually
have regard for your   Ps 119:117
statutes (A)(R)
yet hath he r. unto the lowly   Ps 138:6
looks upon the lowly (B)   Ps 138:6
He regards the lowly (R)   Ps 138:6
have r. of persons in   Pr 24:23
judgment
partiality in judging is not   Pr 24:23
good (R)
To have r. of persons is not   Pr 28:21
good
To show partiality is not   Pr 28:21
good (B)(R)
have r. to the Holy One of   Isa 17:7
Israel
his eyes look to the Holy One   Isa 17:7
(B)(E)

men will regard their Maker   Isa 17:7
(R)
r. that which his fingers have   Isa 17:8
made
r. unto him that fashioned it   Isa 22:11
long
not look to the Maker   Isa 22:11
(A)(B)
they will r. my son   M't 21:37;
(A)(B)(N)(P)(R)   M'k 12:6; Lu 20:13
there is no r. of persons with   Ro 2:11
God
God shows no partiality   Ro 2:11
(A)(R)
God shows no favoritism (B)   Ro 2:11
God has no favourites (N)   Ro 2:11
No preferential treatment with   Ro 2:11
God (P)
glorious had no glory in this   2Co 3:10
r.
see she pays husband all r.   Eph 5:33
(N)
proper r. and responsibility   Eph 6:5
(P)
is there r. of persons with   Eph 6:9
him
there is no partiality (B)(R)   Eph 6:9
he has no favourites (N)   Eph 6:9
who makes no distinction   Eph 6:9
between (P)
Not that I speak in r. of   Ph'p 4:11
want
or in r. of an holyday, or of   Col 2:16
with regard to a feast day   Col 2:16
(A)(B)(R)
take you to task for (N)   Col 2:16
worry you by criticizing (P)   Col 2:16
and there is no r. of persons   Col 3:25
there is no partiality   Col 3:25
(A)(B)(R)
he has no favourites (N)   Col 3:25
command r. of children (P)   1Ti 3:4
treat masters with r. (P)   1Ti 6:1
had r. unto the recompence   Heb 11:26
looked forward and away   Heb 11:26
to reward (A)
fixed his eyes on final   Heb 11:26
recompense (B)
he looked unto the   Heb 11:26
recompense (E)
his eyes fixed upon the   Heb 11:26
coming day (N)
looked steadily at the   Heb 11:26
ultimate (P)
looked to the reward (R)   Heb 11:26
we paid r. to fathers (N)   Heb 12:9
Lord of glory, with r. of   Jas 2:1
persons
show to prejudice, no partiality   Jas 2:1
(A)
do not combine faith with   Jas 2:1
partiality (B)
you must not show snobbery   Jas 2:1
(N)
don't combine snobbery with   Jas 2:1
faith (P)
show no partiality (R)   Jas 2:1
r. to him that weareth the   Jas 2:3
gay
But if ye have r. to persons, ye   Jas 2:9
if you show servile regard   Jas 2:9
(prejudice, favoritism) for
people you commit sin (A)
if you show partiality (B)(R)   Jas 2:9
if you show snobbery (N)   Jas 2:9
once you allow any invidious   Jas 2:9
distinctions (P)
who without r. of persons   1Pe 1:17
judgeth
who judges each one   1Pe 1:17
impartially (A)(B)(N)(R)
judges without the slightest   1Pe 1:17
favoritism (P)

RESPECTED

r. not the persons of the   La 4:16
priests
no longer regarded them   La 4:16
(A)(E)(R)
no longer looks favorably   La 4:16
upon (B)
Jesus became highly r. (P)   Ac 19:17
we yielded and r. them   Heb 12:9
(A)(B)(P)(R)

RESPECTER

That God is no r. of persons   Ac 10:34
God is not partial (B)   Ac 10:34

God has no favourites (N)   Ac 10:34
God shows no partiality (R)   Ac 10:34

RESPECTETH

r. not any that are wise of   Job 37:24
heart
does not regard wise   Job 37:24
in own conceit (R)
and r. not the proud, nor such   Ps 40:4
turns not to the proud (A)(R)   Ps 40:4
does not turn to those defiant   Ps 40:4
(B)

RESPECTFUL

children submissive and r. (R)   1Ti 3:4
chaste r. behaviour   1Pe 3:16
(A)(E)(N)(P)(R)

RESPECTS

see she r. her husband (R)   Eph 5:33

RESPITE

Pharaoh saw that there was r.   Ex 8:15
saw that there was relief   Ex 8:15
(A)(B)
Give us seven days' r. that we   1Sa 11:3
give us seven days time (A)   1Sa 11:3
Allow us seven days (B)   1Sa 11:3

RESPLENDANT

that great r. day (N)   Ac 2:20

RESPONDED

r. to impact of teaching (P)   Ro 6:17

RESPONSIBLE

live r. lives (P)   Tit 2:12

RESPONSIBILITY

a sacred r. (P)   1Co 9:17
a due sense of r. (P)   Eph 5:15
proper respect and r. (P)   Eph 6:5

REST

dove found no r. for the sole of   Ge 8:9
and r. yourselves under the   Ge 18:4
tree
Jacob fed the r. of Laban's   Ge 30:36
flock
he saw that r. was good, and   Ge 49:15
make them r. from their   Ex 5:5
burdens
is the r. of the holy sabbath   Ex 16:23
unto
thou shalt let it r. and lie still   Ex 23:11
on the seventh day thou shalt   Ex 23:12
r.
thine ox and thine ass may r.   Ex 23:12
names of the r. on the other   Ex 28:10
stone
the seventh is the sabbath of   Ex 31:15
r.
with thee, and I will give   Ex 33:14
thee r.
on the seventh day thou shalt   Ex 34:21
r.
time and in harvest thou shalt   Ex 34:21
r.
day, a sabbath of r. to the   Ex 35:2
Lord
r. of the blood shall be wrung   Le 5:9
out
r. of the oil that is in his   Le 14:17
hand
the r. of the oil   Le 14:18
(A)(B)(E)(R)
r. of the oil that is in the   Le 14:29
priest's
shall be a sabbath of r. unto   Le 16:31
you
seventh day is the sabbath of   Le 23:3
r.
shall be unto you a sabbath   Le 23:32
of r.
be a sabbath of r. unto the   Le 25:4
land
for it is a year of r. unto the   Le 25:5
land
then shall the land r. and   Le 26:34
enjoy
long as it lieth desolate it   Le 26:35
shall r.
it did not r. in your sabbaths   Le 26:35

beside the *r.* of them that were slain — Nu 31:8

r. of the prey which the men — Nu 31:32

the *r.* of Gilead, and all Bashan — De 3:13

have given *r.* unto your brethren — De 3:20

maidservant may *r.* as well as thou — De 5:14

ye are not as yet come to the *r.* — De 12:9

he giveth you *r.* from all your — De 12:10

God hath given thee *r.* from — De 25:19

shall the sole of thy foot have *r.* — De 28:65

Lord your God hath given you *r.* — Jos 1:13

Lord have given your brethren *r.* — Jos 1:15

shall *r.* in the waters of Jordan — Jos 3:13

the *r.* which remained of them — Jos 10:20

the *r.* of the kingdom of Sihon — Jos 13:27

And the land had *r.* from war — Jos 14:15

the *r.* of the children of Manasseh — Jos 17:2

the *r.* of Manasseh's sons had — Jos 17:6

the *r.* of the children of Kohath — Jos 21:5

the *r.* of the Levites, out of — Jos 21:34

Lord gave them *r.* round about — Jos 21:44

hath given *r.* unto your brethren — Jos 22:4

the Lord had given *r.* unto Israel — Jos 23:1

And the land had *r.* forty years — J'g 3:11

the land had *r.* fourscore years — J'g 3:30

And the land had *r.* forty years — J'g 5:31

the *r.* of the people bowed down — J'g 7:6

he sent all the *r.* of Israel every man — J'g 7:8

grant you that ye may find *r.* — Ru 1:9

shall I not seek *r.* for thee, that — Ru 3:1

the man will not be in *r.* until he — Ru 3:18

the *r.* of the people he sent every — 1Sa 13:2

the *r.* we have utterly destroyed — 1Sa 15:15

Let it *r.* on the head of Joab — 2Sa 3:29

the Lord had given him *r.* round — 2Sa 7:1

thee to *r.* from all thine enemies — 2Sa 7:11

the *r.* of the people he delivered — 2Sa 10:10

gather the *r.* of the people together — 2Sa 12:28

the birds of the air to *r.* on them — 2Sa 21:10

the Lord my God hath given me *r.* — 1Ki 5:4

that hath given *r.* unto his people — 1Ki 8:56

the *r.* of the acts — 1Ki 11:41; 14:19, 29; 15:7, 23, 31; 16:5, 14, 20, 27; 22:39, 45; 2Ki 1:18; 8:23; 10:34; 12:19; 13:8, 12; 14:15, 18, 28; 15:6, 11, 15, 21, 26, 31, 36; 16:19; 20:20; 21:17, 25; 23:28; 24:5; 2Ch 9:29; 13:22; 20:34; 25:26; 26:22; 27:7; 28:26; 32:32; 33:18; 35:26; 36:8

But the *r.* fled to Aphek, into the — 1Ki 20:30

spirit of Elijah doth *r.* on Elisha — 2Ki 2:15

thou and thy children of the *r.* — 2Ki 4:7

r. of the people that were left in — 2Ki 25:11

smote the *r.* of the Amalekites — 1Ch 4:43

Lord, after that the ark had *r.* — 1Ch 6:31

r. of the children of Merari — 1Ch 6:77

Joab repaired the *r.* of the city — 1Ch 11:8

r. also of Israel were of one heart — 1Ch 12:38

and the *r.* that were chosen, who — 1Ch 16:41

r. of the people he delivered unto — 1Ch 19:11

to thee, who shall be a man of *r.* — 1Ch 22:9

give him *r.* from all his enemies — 1Ch 22:9

he not given you *r.* on every side — 1Ch 22:18

hath given *r.* unto his people, that — 1Ch 23:25

r. of the sons of Levi were these — 1Ch 24:20

build an house of *r.* for the ark of — 1Ch 28:2

for the land had *r.* and he had no — 2Ch 14:6

because the Lord had given him *r.* — 2Ch 14:6

he hath given us *r.* on every side — 2Ch 14:7

for we *r.* on thee, and in thy — 2Ch 14:11

Lord gave them *r.* round about — 2Ch 15:15

his God gave him *r.* round about — 2Ch 20:30

they brought the *r.* of the money — 2Ch 24:14

the *r.* of the chief of the fathers — Ezr 4:3

and the *r.* of their companions — Ezr 4:7; 4:9

r. of the nations, whom the great — Ezr 4:10

r. that are on this side the river — Ezr 4:10

r. of their companions that dwell — Ezr 4:17

and unto the *r.* beyond the river — Ezr 4:17

r. of the children of the captivity — Ezr 6:16

the *r.* of the silver, and the gold — Ezr 7:18

nor to the *r.* that did the work — Ne 2:16

to the *r.* of the people — Ne 4:14; 4:19

and the *r.* of our enemies, heard that I had built — Ne 6:1

and the *r.* of the prophets, that — Ne 6:14

which the *r.* of the people gave — Ne 7:72

But after they had *r.* they did evil — Ne 9:28

the *r.* of the people, the priests — Ne 10:28

the *r.* of the people also cast lots — Ne 11:1

the rest (B) — Ne 11:20; Isa 38:10; 44:17; Jer 39:3; Zec 14:2

the rest (R) — Ne 11:20; 1Sa 38:10; 44:17; Jer 15:9; 27:19; 39:3; 41:10; Eze 36:5; Zec. 14:2

in the *r.* of the king's provinces — Es 9:12

and had *r.* from their enemies — Es 9:16

have slept: then had I been at *r.* — Job 3:13

and there the weary be at *r.* — Job 3:17

There the prisoners *r.* together — Job 3:18

was not in safety, neither had I *r.* — Job 3:26

thou shalt take thy *r.* in safety — Job 11:18

Turn from him, that he may *r.* — Job 14:6

when our *r.* together is in the dust — Job 17:16

season: and my sinews take no *r.* — Job 30:17

my flesh also shall *r.* in hope — Ps 16:9

leave the *r.* of their substance — Ps 17:14

R. in the Lord, and wait patiently — Ps 37:7

neither is there any *r.* in my bones — Ps 38:3

then would I fly away, and be at *r.* — Ps 55:6

r. from the days of adversity — Ps 94:13

they should not enter into my *r.* — Ps 95:11

Return unto thy *r.* O my soul — Ps 116:7

the rod of the wicked shall not *r.* — Ps 125:3

Arise, O Lord, into thy *r.* — Ps 132:8

This is my *r.* for ever: here will I — Ps 132:14

neither will he *r.* content, though — Pr 6:35

he rage or laugh, there is no *r.* — Pr 29:9

thy son, and he shall give thee *r.* — Pr 29:17

his heart taketh not *r.* in the night — Ec 2:23

this hath more *r.* than the other — Ec 6:5

makest thy flock to *r.* at noon — Ca 1:7

shall *r.* all of them in the desolate — Isa 7:19

the *r.* of the trees of his forest — Isa 10:19

spirit of the Lord shall *r.* upon — Isa 11:2

seek; and his *r.* shall be glorious — Isa 11:10

shall give thee *r.* from thy sorrow — Isa 14:3

whole earth is at *r.* and is quiet — Isa 14:7

I will take my *r.* and I will — Isa 18:4

there also shalt thou have no *r.* — Isa 23:12

shall the hand of the Lord *r.* — Isa 25:10

said, This is the *r.* wherewith — Isa 28:12

ye may cause the weary to *r.* — Isa 30:12

returning and *r.* shall ye be saved — Isa 30:15

screech owl also shall *r.* there — Isa 34:14

and find for herself a place of *r.* — Isa 34:14

my judgment to *r.* for a light — Isa 51:4

they shall *r.* in their beds, each — Isa 57:2

troubled sea when it cannot *r.* — Isa 57:20

for Jerusalem's sake I will not *r.* — Isa 62:1

give him no *r.* till he establish — Isa 62:7

Spirit of the Lord caused him to *r.* — Isa 63:14

and where is the place of my *r.* — Isa 66:1

and ye shall find *r.* for your souls — Jer 6:16

the rest (A) — Jer 15:9; 39:3; 41:10; Eze 36:5; Zec 14:2

shall return, and shall be in *r.* — Jer 30:10

when I went to cause him to *r.* — Jer 31:2

the *r.* of the people that remained — Jer 39:9

in my sighing, and I find no *r.* — Jer 45:3

return, and be in *r.* and at ease — Jer 46:27

into thy scabbard, *r.* and be still — Jer 47:6

that he may give *r.* to the land — Jer 50:34

and the *r.* of the multitude — Jer 52:15

the heathen, she findeth no *r.* — La 1:3

day and night: give thyself no *r.* — La 2:18

we labour, and have no *r.* — La 5:5

cause my fury to *r.* upon them — Eze 5:13

make my fury toward thee to *r.* — Eze 16:42

and I will cause my fury to *r.* — Eze 21:17

caused my fury to *r.* upon — Ez 24:13

I will go to them that are at *r.* — Eze 38:11

the blessing to *r.* in thine house — Eze 44:30

r. of the land shall they give to the — Eze 45:8

As for the *r.* of the tribes, from the — Eze 48:23

the *r.* of the wise men of Babylon — Da 2:18

Nebuchadnezzar was at *r.* in mine — Da 4:4

As concerning the *r.* of the beasts — Da 7:12

thou shalt *r.* and stand in thy lot — Da 12:13

depart; for this is not your *r.* — Mic 2:10

I might *r.* in the day of trouble — Hab 3:16

he will *r.* in his love, he will joy — Zep 3:17

the earth sitteth still, and is at *r.* — Zec 1:11

Damascus shall be the *r.* thereof — Zec 9:1

let the *r.* eat every one the flesh — Zec 11:9

heavy laden, and I will give you *r.* — M't 11:28

and ye shall find *r.* unto your souls — M't 11:29

places, seeking r. and finding *M't 12:43*
none
Sleep on now, and take your *M't 26:45*
r.
The r. said, Let be, let us *M't 27:49*
see
into a desert place, and r. a *M'k 6:31*
while
Sleep on now, and take your *M'k 14:41*
r.
told it to the r. (S) *M'k 16:13*
there, your peace shall r. upon *Lu 10:6*
through dry places, seeking r. *Lu 11:24*
why take ye thought for the *Lu 12:26*
r.
unto the eleven and to all the *Lu 24:9*
r.
had spoken of taking of r. *Joh 11:13*
in sleep
also my flesh shall r. in hope *Ac 2:26*
Peter and to the r. of the *Ac 2:37*
apostles
of the r. durst no man join *Ac 5:13*
himself
or what is the place of my r. *Ac 7:49*
had the churches r. throughout *Ac 9:31*
And the r. some on boards *Ac 27:44*
obtained it, and the r. were *Ro 11:7*
blinded
But to the r. speak I, not *1Co 7:12*
the Lord
r. will I set in order when I *1Co 11:34*
come
I had no r. in my spirit, *2Co 2:13*
because I
Macedonia, our flesh had no *2Co 7:5*
r.
power of Christ may r. upon *2Co 12:9*
me
to you who are troubled r. *2Th 1:7*
with us
They shall not enter into *Heb 3:11*
my r.
they should not enter into *Heb 3:18*
his r.
being left us of entering into *Heb 4:1*
his r.
which have believed do enter *Heb 4:3*
into r.
if they shall enter into my r. *Heb 4:3*
God did r. the seventh day *Heb 4:4*
from
If they shall enter into my r. *Heb 4:5*
For if Jesus had given them r. *Heb 4:8*
therefore a r. to the people of *Heb 4:9*
God
For he that is entered into *Heb 4:10*
his r.
labour therefore to enter into *Heb 4:11*
that r.
live the r. of his time in the *1Pe 4:2*
flesh
I say, and unto the r. in *Re 2:24*
Thyatira
and they r. not day and night *Re 4:8*
should r. yet for a little season *Re 6:11*
r. of the men which were not *Re 9:20*
killed
and they have no r. day nor *Re 14:11*
night
that they may r. from their *Re 14:13*
labours
the r. of the dead lived not *Re 20:5*
again

RESTED

he r. on the seventh day from *Ge 2:2*
all
that in it he had r. from all his *Ge 2:3*
work
the ark r. in the seventh month *Ge 8:4*
and r. in all the coasts of *Ex 10:14*
Egypt
the people r. on the seventh *Ex 16:30*
day
in them is, and r. the seventh *Ex 20:11*
day
and on the seventh day he r. *Ex 31:17*
tabernacle they r. in their *Nu 9:18*
tents
of the Lord they r. in the *Nu 9:23*
tents
the cloud r. in the wilderness *Nu 10:12*
when it r. he said, Return, O *Nu 10:36*
Lord
when the spirit r. upon them *Nu 11:25*
Medad: and the spirit r. *Nu 11:26*
upon them
tribes. And the land r. from *Jos 11:23*
war

they r. on the house with *1Ki 6:10*
timber
r. themselves upon the words *2Ch 32:8*
fourteenth day of the same r. *Es 9:17*
they
fifteenth day of the same they *Es 9:18*
r.
the Jews r. from their enemies *Es 9:22*
My bowels boiled, and r. *Job 30:27*
not: the
and r. the sabbath day *Lu 23:56*
according

RESTEST

art called a Jew, and r. in the *Ro 2:17*
law

RESTETH

him to be in safety, whereon *Job 24:23*
he r.
Wisdom r. in the heart of *Pr 14:33*
him that
for anger r. in the bosom of *Ec 7:9*
fools
spirit of glory and of God r. *1Pe 4:14*
upon

RESTING

to search out a r. place for *Nu 10:33*
them
O Lord God, into thy r. *2Ch 6:41*
place, thou
righteous; spoil not his r. *Pr 24:15*
place
dwellings, and in quiet r. *Isa 32:18*
places

RESTINGPLACE

hill, they have forgotten their *Jer 50:6*
r.

RESTLESS

why so r. within me (B) *Ps 42:5*
a r. evil (A)(E)(R) *Jas 3:8*

RESTLESSNESS

in r. I groan (B) *Ps 55:2*

RESTITUTION

requires full r. (B) *Ge 50:15*
he should make full r.; if he *Ex 22:3*
have
his own vineyard, shall he *Ex 22:5*
make r.
he shall repay with the choicest *Ex 22:5*
(B)
kindled, fire shall surely make *Ex 22:6*
r.
who started fire shall make a *Ex 22:6*
refund (B)
he shall make r. unto the *Ex 22:12*
owner
he must repay the owner (B) *Ex 22:12*
make r. in full (A)(B)(R) *Nu 5:7*
to his substance shall the r. *Job 20:18*
until the times of r. of all *Ac 3:21*
things
time of the complete *Ac 3:21*
restoration (A)
times of universal restoration *Ac 3:21*
(B)(N)(P)
times of restoration of all *Ac 3:21*
things (E)
time of establishing all that *Ac 3:21*
God spoke (R)

RESTORATION

bring r. and health (B) *Isa 33:6*
time of complete r. *Ac 3:21*
(A)(B)(E)(N)(P)

RESTORE

r. the man his wife; for he is a *Ge 20:7*
return (B) *Ge 20:7; 42:25*
if thou r. her not, know thou *Ge 20:7*
that
head and r. thee unto thy *Ge 40:13*
place
r. every man's money into his *Ge 42:25*
sack
replace (R) *Ge 42:25*
he shall r. five oxen for an ox *Ex 22:1*

ass, or sheep; he shall r. *Ex 22:4*
double
refund r. (B) *Ex 22:4; Le 24:21*
r. that which he took violently *Le 6:4*
he shall even r. it in the *Le 6:5*
principal
that killeth a beast, he shall *Le 24:21*
r. it
replace it (A) *Le 24:21*
make it good (R) *Le 24:21*
r. the overplus unto the man *Le 25:27*
pay back (B)(R) *Le 25:27*
But if he be not able to r. it *Le 25:28*
to him
r. him to the city of his *Nu 35:25*
refuge
return him to his city (B) *Nu 35:25*
and thou shalt r. it to him *De 22:2*
again
God will r. your fortune *De 30:3*
(A)(B)(R)
r. those lands again *J'g 11:13*
peaceably
now therefore I will r. it unto *J'g 17:3*
thee
eyes therewith? and I will r. *1Sa 12:3*
it you
will r. thee all the land of Saul *2Sa 9:7*
And he shall r. the lamb *2Sa 12:6*
fourfold
make good four times over *2Sa 12:6*
(B)
r. me the kingdom of my *2Sa 16:3*
father
took from thy father, I will *1Ki 20:34*
r.
I will return (B) *1Ki 20:34*
R. all that was hers, and all *2Ki 8:6*
Return all her property (B) *2Ki 8:6*
R. I pray you, to them, even *Ne 5:11*
this
Then said they, We will r. *Ne 5:12*
them
and his hands shall r. their *Job 20:10*
goods
give back his wealth *Job 20:10*
(A)(B)(E)(R)
which he laboured for shall *Job 20:18*
he r.
shall he give back (A)(R) *Job 20:18*
he must give up (B) *Job 20:18*
R. unto me the joy of thy *Ps 51:12*
r. heritage (B)(R) *Ps 68:9*
r. us again (A)(B)(R) *Ps 80:3;
80:19; 85:4*
R. us again (S) *Ps 85:4; 80:3, 7, 19*
r. me in the way (A) *Ps 119:37*
he be found, he shall r. *Pr 6:31*
sevenfold
I will r. thy judges as at the *Isa 1:26*
first
I am able to r. (B) *Isa 3:7*
so wilt thou r. me (S) *Isa 38:16*
for a spoil, and none saith, R. *Isa 42:22*
Give back (B) *Isa 42:22*
and to r. the preserved of *Isa 49:6*
Israel
r. comforts unto him and to *Isa 57:18*
his
them up, and r. them to this *Jer 27:22*
place
For I will r. health unto *Jer 30:17*
thee, and
If the wicked r. the pledge, *Eze 33:15*
give
to r. and to build Jerusalem *Da 9:25*
unto
I will r. to you the years that *Joe 2:25*
shall first come, and r. all *M't 17:11*
things
false accusation, I r. him *Lu 19:8*
fourfold
r. again the kingdom of Israel *Ac 1:6*
r. such an one in the spirit of *Ga 6:1*
set him straight (B) *Ga 6:1*
set him right again (N) *Ga 6:1*
set him back on the right path *Ga 6:1*
(P)

RESTORED

and r. him Sarah his wife *Ge 20:14*
returned (B) *Ge 20:14; 42:28*
And he r. the chief butler *Ge 40:21*
unto his
me he r. unto mine office *Ge 41:13*
and him
My money is r.; and, lo, it is *Ge 42:28*
even
money put back (R) *Ge 42:28*

and shall not be *r.* to thee | *De 28:31*
not returned (B) | *De 28:31*
had *r.* the eleven hundred | *J'g 17:3*
shekels
he *r.* the money unto his | *J'g 17:4*
mother
taken from Israel were *r.* to | *1Sa 7:14*
Israel
that my hand may be *r.* me | *1Ki 13:6*
again
the king's hand was *r.* him | *1Ki 13:6*
again
whose son he had *r.* to life | *2Ki 8:1*
how he had *r.* a dead body to | *2Ki 8:5*
life
woman, whose son he had *r.* | *2Ki 8:5*
to life
is her son, whom Elisha *r.* to | *2Ki 8:5*
life
He built Elath, and *r.* it to | *2Ki 14:22*
Judah
He *r.* the coast of Israel | *2Ki 14:25*
from the
Joab *r.* the rest of the city | *1Ch 11:8*
(S)
which Huram had *r.* to | *2Ch 8:2*
Solomon
He built Eloth, and *r.* it to | *2Ch 26:2*
Judah
be *r.* and brought again unto | *Ezr 6:5*
I *r.* that which I took not | *Ps 69:4*
away
turn back and I shall be *r.* | *Jer 31:18*
(S)
but hath *r.* to the debtor his | *Eze 18:7*
pledge
hath not *r.* the pledge, and | *Eze 18:12*
it was *r.* whole, like as the | *M't 12:13*
other
his hand was *r.* whole as the | *M'k 3:5*
other
and he was *r.* and saw every | *M'k 8:25*
man
his hand was *r.* whole as the | *Lu 6:10*
other
that I may be *r.* to you the | *Heb 13:19*
sooner

RESTORER

shall be unto thee a *r.* of thy | *Ru 4:15*
life
breach, The *r.* of paths do | *Isa 58:12*
dwell in

RESTORETH

He *r.* my soul: he leadeth me | *Ps 23:3*
cometh first, and *r.* all things | *M'k 9:12*

RESTRAIN

restrain (S) | *Job 7:11;*
| *Isa 64:12; Jer 31:16*
dost thou *r.* wisdom to thyself | *Job 15:8*
he will not *r.* them (S) | *Job 37:4*
remainder of wrath shalt thou | *Ps 76:10*
r.
good sense makes a man *r.* | *Pr 19:11*
(A)(B)(R)
master wind to *r.* wind (B) | *Ec 8:8*
cannot *r.* in passions (B) | *1Co 7:9*

RESTRAINED

and the rain from heaven was | *Ge 8:2*
r.
rain was checked (A)(B) | *Ge 8:2*
now nothing will be *r.* from | *Ge 11:6*
them
the Lord hath *r.* me from | *Ge 16:2*
bearing
prevented me from bearing | *Ge 16:2*
(B)(R)
r. you (B) | *Ge 20:6; 1Sa 24:7*
the people were *r.* from | *Ex 36:6*
bringing
vile, and he *r.* them not | *1Sa 3:13*
David *r.* his servants (S) | *1Sa 24:7*
restrained (S) | *Ex 5:10;*
| *Ps 40:9; 119:101; Isa 42:14; Jer 14:10*
mercies toward me? are they | *Isa 63:15*
r.
I am *r.* (S) | *Jer 36:5*
and I *r.* the floods thereof | *Eze 31:15*
would have *r.* him (S) | *Lu 4:42*
sayings scarce *r.* they the | *Ac 14:18*
people

RESTRAINEST

off fear, and *r.* prayer before | *Job 15:4*
God

RESTRAINETH

that *r.* his hands from | *Isa 33:15*
holding bribes (S)
you know what *r.* (S) | *2Th 2:6*

RESTRAINT

allowed them to cast off *r.* | *Ex 32:25*
(B)
there is no *r.* to the Lord to | *1Sa 14:6*
save
where there is no *r.* (S) | *Job 36:16*

RESTRICTED

r. himself because of Saul | *1Ch 12:1*
(S)

RESTS

he made narrowed *r.* round | *1Ki 6:6*
about

RESULTS

wisdom is proved by *r.* (N) | *M't 11:19*
some *r.* among you (P) | *Ro 1:13*

RESURRECTION

which say that there is no *r.* | *M't 22:23*
in the *r.* whose wife shall | *M't 22:28*
she be of
For in the *r.* they neither | *M't 22:30*
marry
But as touching the *r.* of the | *M't 22:31*
dead
came out the graves after | *M't 27:53*
his *r.*
Sadducees, which say there | *M'k 12:18*
is no *r.*
In the *r.* therefore, when | *M'k 12:23*
they shall
be recompensed at the *r.* of | *Lu 14:14*
the just
which deny that there is any | *Lu 20:27*
r.
in the *r.* whose wife of them | *Lu 20:33*
is she
that world, and the *r.* from | *Lu 20:35*
the dead
of God, being the children of | *Lu 20:36*
the *r.*
have done good, unto the *r.* | *Joh 5:29*
of life
done evil, unto the *r.* of | *Joh 5:29*
damnation
rise again in the *r.* at the | *Joh 11:24*
last day
unto her, I am the *r.* and | *Joh 11:25*
the life
to be a witness with us of his | *Ac 1:22*
r.
this before spake of the *r.* of | *Ac 2:31*
Christ
through Jesus the *r.* from the | *Ac 4:2*
dead
witness of the *r.* of the Lord | *Ac 4:33*
Jesus
preached unto them Jesus | *Ac 17:18*
and *r.*
when they heard of the *r.* of | *Ac 17:32*
the dead
of the hope and *r.* of the dead | *Ac 23:6*
I am
Sadducees say that there is no | *Ac 23:8*
r.
that there shall be a *r.* of the | *Ac 24:15*
dead
Touching the *r.* of the dead I | *Ac 24:21*
am
of holiness, by the *r.* from the | *Ro 1:4*
dead
be also in the likeness of his | *Ro 6:5*
r.
you that there is no *r.* of the | *1Co 15:12*
dead
But if there be no *r.* of the | *1Co 15:13*
dead, then
by man came also the *r.* of | *1Co 15:21*
the dead
So also is the *r.* of the dead | *1Co 15:42*
know him, and the power of | *Ph'p 3:10*
his *r.*

attain unto the *r.* of the | *Ph'p 3:11*
dead
saying that the *r.* is past | *2Ti 2:18*
already
of *r.* of the dead, and of | *Heb 6:2*
eternal
that they might obtain a | *Heb 11:35*
better *r.*
lively hope by the *r.* of Jesus | *1Pe 1:3*
Christ
God,) by the *r.* of Jesus | *1Pe 3:21*
Christ
were finished. This is the first | *Re 20:5*
r.
he that hath part in the first | *Re 20:6*
r.

RETAIN

Dost thou still *r.* thine | *Job 2:9*
integrity
do you still hold fast | *Job 2:9*
(A)(B)(E)(R)
Let thine heart *r.* my words | *Pr 4:4*
let your heart hold fast my | *Pr 4:4*
words (A)(B)(R)
honour; and strong men *r.* | *Pr 11:16*
riches
violent men win riches (A) | *Pr 11:16*
violent men gain wealth (B) | *Pr 11:16*
violent men obtain riches (E) | *Pr 11:16*
over the spirit to *r.* the spirit | *Ec 8:8*
master over the wind to | *Ec 8:8*
restrain wind (B)
shall not *r.* the power of the | *De 11:6*
arm
whose soever sins ye *r.* they | *Joh 20:23*
are
like to *r.* God in their | *Ro 1:28*
knowledge
see fit to acknowledge God | *Ro 1:28*
(A)(B)(N)(P)(R)
refused to have God in their | *Ro 1:28*
knowledge (E)

RETAINED

and *r.* those three hundred men | *J'g 7:8*
the damsel's father, *r.* him | *J'g 19:4*
girl's father detained him | *J'g 19:4*
(A)(B)
girl's father made him stay | *J'g 19:4*
(R)
corruption, and I *r.* no | *Da 10:8*
strength
upon me, and I have *r.* no | *Da 10:16*
strength
soever sins ye retain, they | *Joh 20:23*
are *r.*
whom I would have *r.* with | *Ph'm 13*
me

RETAINETH

and happy is every one that *r.* | *Pr 3:18*
her
every one who holds her fast | *Pr 3:18*
(A)(B)(R)
A gracious woman *r.* honour | *Pr 11:16*
gracious woman wins honor | *Pr 11:16*
(A)
gracious woman gets honor | *Pr 11:16*
(B)(R)
gracious woman obtaineth | *Pr 11:16*
honor (E)
he *r.* not his anger for ever | *Mic 7:18*
does not maintain his | *Mic 7:18*
indignation (B)

RETINUE

with a great *r.* (R) | *1Ki 10:2*
a large *r.* (B)(R) | *2Ch 9:1*

RETIRE

r. from service (B) | *Nu 8:25*
and *r.* ye from him, that he | *2Sa 11:15*
may be
r. stay not: for I will bring | *Jer 4:6*

RETIRED

the men of Israel *r.* in the | *J'g 20:39*
battle
they *r.* from the city, every | *2Sa 20:22*
man

RETRACT

r. and repent (B) | *Job 42:6*

RETRIBUTION

administer r. (B)	Le 26:25
vengeance and r. (B)	De 32:35
thou god of r. (B)	Ps 94:1
time of r. (B)	Ho 9:7
a time of r. (N)	Lu 21:22
r. on this people (A)	Lu 21:23
to bring r. (N)	Ro 3:5
for r. to them (A)(B)(N)(R)	Ro 11:9
place to divine r. (B)	Ro 12:19
for r. an offender (N)	Ro 13:4
r. will fall upon him (N)	2Ti 4:14
received just r.	Heb 2:2
(B)(N)(P)(R)	

RETURN

bread, till thou r. unto the ground	Ge 3:19
art, and unto dust shalt thou r.	Ge 3:19
after his r. from the slaughter	Ge 14:17
R. to thy mistress, and submit	Ge 16:9
said, I will certainly r. unto thee	Ge 18:10
time appointed I will r. unto thee	Ge 18:14
r. the man his wife (B)	Ge 20:7; 42:25
R. unto the land of thy fathers	Ge 31:3
r. unto the land of thy kindred	Ge 31:13
R. unto thy country, and to thy	Ge 32:9
r. unto my brethren which are in Midian, Go, r. into Egypt	Ex 4:18
When thou goest to r. into Egypt	Ex 4:21
they see war, and they r. to Egypt	Ex 13:17
r. every man unto his possession	Le 25:10
shall r. every man unto his family	Le 25:10
r. every man unto his possession	Le 25:13
that he may r. unto his possession	Le 25:27
he shall r. unto his possession	Le 25:28
and shall r. unto his own family	Le 25:41
of his fathers shall he r.	Le 25:41
the field shall r. unto him of whom	Le 27:24
said, R., O Lord, unto the many	Nu 10:36
not better for us to r. into Egypt	Nu 14:3
captain and let us r. into Egypt	Nu 14:4
I will r. again (S)	Nu 22:34
R. unto Balak, and thus thou shalt	Nu 23:5
We will not r. unto our houses	Nu 32:18
then afterward ye shall r. and be	Nu 32:22
r. him to his city (B)	Nu 35:25
slayer shall r. into the land of his	Nu 35:28
r. every man unto his possession	De 3:20
nor cause the people to r. to Egypt	De 17:16
henceforth r. no more that way	De 17:16
let him go and r. to his house	De 20:5
let him also go and r. unto his house	De 20:6
him go and r. unto his house	De 20:7; 20:8
shalt r. unto the Lord thy God, and	De 30:2
will r. and gather thee from all the	De 30:3
thou shalt r. and obey the voice of	De 30:8
r. unto the land of your possession	Jos 1:15
then shall the slayer r. and come	Jos 20:6
therefore now r. ye, and get you	Jos 22:4
R. with much riches unto your	Jos 22:8
let him r. and depart early from	J'g 7:3
I r. in peace from the children	J'g 11:31
might r. from the country of Moab	Ru 1:6
way to r. unto the land of Judah	Ru 1:7

Go, r. each to her mother's house	Ru 1:8
will r. with thee unto thy people	Ru 1:10
gods: r. thou after thy sister in law	Ru 1:15
or to r. from following after thee	Ru 1:16
any wise r. him a trespass offering	1Sa 6:3
offering which we shall r. to him	1Sa 6:4
ye r. him for a trespass offering	1Sa 6:8
If ye do r. unto the Lord with all	1Sa 7:3
and his r. was to Ramah; for	1Sa 7:17
with him, Come, and let us r.	1Sa 9:5
unto Saul, I will not r. with thee	1Sa 15:26
r. my son David: for I will	1Sa 26:21
Make this fellow r. that he may	1Sa 29:4
Wherefore now r. and go in peace	1Sa 29:7
to r. into the land of the Philistines	1Sa 29:11
r. from following their brethren	2Sa 2:26
Then said Abner unto him, Go, r.	2Sa 3:16
your beards be grown, and then r.	2Sa 10:5
him, but he shall not r. to me	2Sa 12:23
r. to thy place, and abide with the	2Sa 15:19
r. thou, and take back thy brethren	2Sa 15:20
r. into the city in peace, and your	2Sa 15:27
if thou r. to the city, and say unto	2Sa 15:34
R. thou, and all thy servants	2Sa 19:14
I shall r. to him that sent me	2Sa 24:13
r. his blood upon his own head	1Ki 2:32
blood r. upon the head of Joab	1Ki 2:33
r. thy wickedness upon thine own	1Ki 2:44
r. unto thee with all their heart	1Ki 8:48
kingdom r. to the house of David	1Ki 12:26
I may not r. with thee, nor go in	1Ki 13:16
r. on thy way to the wilderness of	1Ki 19:15
r. of the year the king of Syria	1Ki 20:22
came to pass at the r. of the year	1Ki 20:26
I will r. it (B)	1Ki 20:34
r. every man to his house in peace	1Ki 22:17
If thou r. at all in peace the Lord	1Ki 22:28
r. again (S)	2Ki 1:6; 20:5
r. all her property (B)	2Ki 8:6
I have offended; r. from me: that	2Ki 18:14
and shall r. to his own land; and I	2Ki 19:7
he came, by the same shall he r.	2Ki 19:33
shadow r. backward ten degrees	2Ki 20:10
your beards be grown, and then r.	1Ch 19:5
shall r. and confess thy name, and	2Ch 6:24
they r. to thee with all their heart	2Ch 6:38
give ye me to r. answer to this	2Ch 10:6
we may r. answer to this people	2Ch 10:9
r. every man to his house: for this	2Ch 11:4
let them r. every man to his house	2Ch 18:16
of affliction, until I r. in	2Ch 18:26
If thou certainly r. in peace	2Ch 18:27
he will r. to the remnant of you	2Ch 30:6
face from you, if ye r. unto him	2Ch 30:9
be? and when wilt thou r.	Ne 2:6

From all places whence ye shall r.	Ne 4:12
a captain to r. to their bondage	Ne 9:17
Esther bade them r. Mordecai this	Es 4:15
Jews, should r. upon his own head	Es 9:25
and naked shall I r. thither	Job 1:21
R. I pray you, let it not be iniquity	Job 6:29
yea, r. again, my righteousness is	Job 6:29
He shall r. no more to his house	Job 7:10
Before I go whence I shall not r.	Job 10:21
believeth not that he shall r. out of	Job 15:22
go the way whence I shall r.	Job 16:22
for you all, do ye r. and come now	Job 17:10
If thou r. to the Almighty, thou	Job 22:23
shall r. to the days of his youth	Job 33:25
that they r. from iniquity	Job 36:10
go forth, and r. not unto them	Job 39:4
R., O Lord, deliver my soul	Ps 6:4
them r. and be ashamed suddenly	Ps 6:10
sakes therefore r. thou on high	Ps 7:7
His mischief shall r. upon his own	Ps 7:16
r. damage upon enemies (B)	Ps 54:5
They r. at evening: they make	Ps 59:6
And at evening let them r.	Ps 59:14
Therefore his people r. hither	Ps 73:10
let not the oppressed r.	Ps 74:21
R. we beseech thee, O God of	Ps 80:14
and sayest, R. ye children of men	Ps 90:3
R., O Lord, how long? and let	Ps 90:13
shall r. unto righteousness	Ps 94:15
they die, and r. to their dust	Ps 104:29
R. unto thy rest O my soul	Ps 116:7
None that go unto her r. again	Pr 2:19
rolleth a stone, it will r. upon him	Pr 26:27
rivers come, thither they r. again	Ec 1:7
shall he r. to go as he came	Ec 5:15
nor the clouds r. after the rain	Ec 12:2
the dust r. to the earth as it	Ec 12:7
shall r. unto God who gave it	Ec 12:7
R., r., O Shulamite	Ca 6:13
r., r., that we may look upon thee	Ca 6:13
it shall be a tenth, and it shall r.	Isa 6:13
The remnant shall r., even the	Isa 10:21
yet a remnant of them shall r.	Isa 10:22
r. and I would heal (B)	Isa 13:15
and they shall r. even to the Lord	Isa 19:22
will enquire, enquire ye: r. come	Isa 21:12
the ransomed of the Lord shall r.	Isa 35:10
a rumour, and r. to his own land	Isa 37:7
he came, by the same shall he r.	Isa 37:34
r. unto me; for I have redeemed	Isa 44:22
in righteousness, and shall not r.	Isa 45:23
the redeemed of the Lord shall r.	Isa 51:11
and let him r. unto the Lord	Isa 55:7
it shall not r. unto me void, but it	Isa 55:11
R. for thy servants' sake, the tribes	Isa 63:17
man's shall be r. unto her again	Jer 3:1
r. again unto me, saith the Lord	Jer 3:1
R. thou backsliding Israel, saith	Jer 3:12
R. ye backsliding children, and I	Jer 3:22
If thou wilt r., O Israel, saith	Jer 4:1
Lord, r. unto me: and if thou wilt	Jer 4:1

than a rock; they have refused | Jer 5:3
to r.
shall he turn away, and not r. | Jer 8:4
hold fast deceit, they refuse to | Jer 8:5
r.
I have plucked them out I | Jer 12:15
will r.
since they r. not from their | Jer 15:7
ways
If thou r. then will I bring | Jer 15:19
thee
my mouth: let them r. unto | Jer 15:19
thee
but r. not thou unto them | Jer 15:19
r. ye now every one from his | Jer 18:11
evil
for he shall r. no more, nor | Jer 22:10
see his
He shall not r. thither any | Jer 22:11
more
land whereunto they desire | Jer 22:27
to r.
thither shall they not r. | Jer 22:27
none doth r. from his | Jer 23:14
wickedness
the anger of the Lord shall | Jer 23:20
not r.
r. unto me with their whole | Jer 24:7
heart
in causing you to r. to this | Jer 29:10
place
I will cause them to r. to the | Jer 30:3
land
Jacob shall r. and shall be in | Jer 30:10
rest
fierce anger of the Lord shall | Jer 30:24
not r.
a great company shall r. | Jer 31:8
thither
for I will cause their | Jer 32:44
captivity to r.
and the captivity of Israel to | Jer 33:7
r.
cause to r. the captivity of | Jer 33:11
the land
for I will cause their | Jer 33:26
captivity to r.
whom they had let go free, | Jer 34:11
to r.
set at liberty at their | Jer 34:16
pleasure, to r.
and cause them to r. to this | Jer 34:22
city
R. ye now every man from | Jer 35:15
his evil
may r. every man from his | Jer 36:3
evil way
will r. every one from his evil | Jer 36:7
way
shall r. to Egypt into their | Jer 37:7
own land
not to r. to the house of | Jer 37:20
Jonathan
cause me to r. to Jonathan's | Jer 38:26
house
cause you to r. to your own | Jer 42:12
land
should r. into the land of | Jer 44:14
Judah
have a desire to r. to dwell | Jer 44:14
there
shall r. but such as shall | Jer 44:14
escape
shall r. out of the land of | Jer 44:28
Egypt
and Jacob shall r. and be in | Jer 46:27
rest
expert man; none shall r. in | Jer 50:9
vain
the seller shall not r. to that | Eze 7:13
which
multitude which shall not r. | Eze 7:13
should not r. from his | Eze 13:22
wicked way
shall r. to their former | Eze 16:55
estate
not that he should r. from | Eze 18:23
his ways
sheath: it shall not r. any | Eze 21:5
more
Shall I cause it to r. into his | Eze 21:30
sheath
to r. into the land of | Eze 29:14
Pathros
and thy cities shall not r. | Eze 35:9
shall not r. by the way of the | Eze 46:9
gate
after it shall r. to the | Eze 46:17
prince: but
me to r. to the brink of the | Eze 47:6
river

now will I r. to the fight with | Da 10:20
and shall r. into his own land | Da 11:9
then shall he r. and be | Da 11:10
stirred up
For the king of the north | Da 11:13
shall r.
r. into his land with great | Da 11:28
riches
do exploits, and r. to his | Da 11:28
own land
At the time appointed he | Da 11:29
shall r.
he shall be grieved, and r. | Da 11:30
shall even r. and have | Da 11:30
intelligence
I will go and r. to my first | Ho 2:7
husband
Therefore will I r. and take | Ho 2:9
away
shall the children of Israel r. | Ho 3:5
I will go and r. to my place, | Ho 5:15
till they
Come, and let us r. unto the | Ho 6:1
Lord
do not r. to the Lord their God | Ho 7:10
They r. but not to the most | Ho 7:16
High
their sins: they shall r. to | Ho 8:13
Egypt
but Ephraim shall r. to Egypt | Ho 9:3
shall not r. into the land of | Ho 11:5
Egypt
his king, because they refused | Ho 11:5
to r.
I will not r. to destroy | Ho 11:9
Ephraim
reproach shall his Lord r. | Ho 12:14
unto him
O Israel, r. unto the Lord thy | Ho 14:1
God
dwell under his shadow shall | Ho 14:7
r.
knoweth if he will r. and | Joe 2:14
repent
speedily will I r. your | Joe 3:4
recompence
and will r. your recompence | Joe 3:7
upon
thy reward shall r. upon thine | Ob 15
own
they shall r. to the hire of an | Mic 1:7
harlot
the remnant of his brethren | Mic 5:3
shall
r. and build the desolate | Mal 1:4
places
R. unto me, and I will r. unto | Mal 3:7
you
But ye said, Wherein shall we | Mal 3:7
Then shall ye r. and discern | Mal 3:18
that they should not r. to | M't 2:12
Herod
not worthy, let your peace r. | M't 10:13
to you
will r. into my house from | M't 12:44
whence
let him which is in the field | M't 24:18
r. back
your r. will be rich (B) | Lu 6:35
R. to thine own house, and | Lu 8:39
shew
r. unto my house whence I | Lu 11:24
came
when he will r. from the | Lu 12:36
wedding
field, let him likewise not r. | Lu 17:31
back
to receive a kingdom, and | Lu 19:12
to r.
when you r. to me (B) | Lu 22:32
r. and I should heal (E) | Joh 12:40
now no more to r. to | Ac 13:34
corruption
After this I will r. and will | Ac 15:16
build
but I will r. again unto you, | Ac 18:21
if God
purposed to r. through | Ac 20:3
Macedonia
what r. did you get (R) | Ro 6:21
make r. to their parents | 1Ti 5:4
(A)(B)(R)

RETURNED

the waters r. from off the earth | Ge 8:3
and she r. unto him into the | Ge 8:9
ark
dove: which r. not again unto | Ge 8:12
him

they r. and came to | Ge 14:7
En-mishpat
and Abraham r. unto his | Ge 18:33
place
r. his wife (B) | Ge 20:14; 42:28
r. into the land of the | Ge 21:32
Philistines
So Abraham r. unto his | Ge 22:19
young men
departed, and r. unto his | Ge 31:55
place
the messengers r. to Jacob, | Ge 32:6
saying
So Esau r. that day on his | Ge 33:16
way unto
And Reuben r. unto the pit | Ge 37:29
he r. unto his brethren, and | Ge 37:30
said
he r. to Judah, and said, I | Ge 38:22
cannot
r. to them again, and | Ge 42:24
communed
now we had r. this second | Ge 43:10
time
the money that was r. in our | Ge 43:18
sacks
every man his ass, and r. to | Ge 44:13
the city
And Joseph r. into Egypt, he | Ge 50:14
And Moses went and r. to | Ex 4:18
Jethro his
ass, and he r. to the land of | Ex 4:20
Egypt
And Moses r. unto the Lord | Ex 5:22
and the sea r. to his strength | Ex 14:27
when
And the waters r. and | Ex 14:28
covered the
Moses r. the words of the | Ex 19:8
people
And Moses r. unto the Lord | Ex 32:31
all the rulers of the | Ex 34:31
congregation r.
and is r. unto her father's | Le 22:13
house, as
they r. from searching of the | Nu 13:25
land
sent to search the land, who | Nu 14:36
r.
Aaron r. unto Moses unto the | Nu 16:50
door
he r. unto him, and, lo, he | Nu 23:6
stood
up, and went and r. to his | Nu 24:25
place:
And ye r. and wept before the | De 1:45
Lord
not r. to thee (B) | De 28:31
three days, until the pursuers | Jos 2:16
be r.
days, until the pursuers were | Jos 2:22
r.
So the two men r. and | Jos 2:23
descended
waters of Jordan r. unto their | Jos 4:18
place
the city once, and r. into the | Jos 6:14
camp
And they r. to Joshua, and | Jos 7:3
that all the Israelites r. unto | Jos 8:24
Ai
And Joshua r. and all Israel | Jos 10:15
And all the people r. to the | Jos 10:21
camp
Joshua r. and all Israel with | Jos 10:38;
10:43
and the half tribe of | Jos 22:9
Manasseh r.
r. from the children of | Jos 22:32
Reuben
they r. and corrupted | J'g 2:19
themselves
her, yea, she r. answer to | J'g 5:29
herself
r. of the people twenty and | J'g 7:3
two
r. into the host of Israel, and | J'g 7:15
said
the son of Joash r. from battle | J'g 8:13
that she r. unto her father, | J'g 11:39
who did
And after a time he r. to take | J'g 14:8
her
went and r. unto their | J'g 21:23
inheritance
So Naomi r., Ruth the | Ru 1:22
Moabitess
r. out of the country of Moab | Ru 1:22
worshipped before the Lord, | 1Sa 1:19
and r.

it, they *r.* to Ekron the same   *1Sa 6:16*
day
Philistines *r.* for a trespass   *1Sa 6:17*
offering
David went and *r.* from Saul   *1Sa 17:15*
to feed
r. from chasing after   *1Sa 17:53*
Philistines
r. from the slaughter of   *1Sa 17:57;*
Philistine   *1Sa 18:6*
Saul *r.* from pursuing after   *1Sa 23:28*
David
r. from following the   *1Sa 24:1*
Philistines
hath *r.* the wickedness of   *1Sa 25:39*
Nabal
on his way, and Saul *r.* to   *1Sa 26:25*
his place
apparel and *r.* and came to   *1Sa 27:9*
Achish
David was *r.* from the   *2Sa 1:1*
slaughter of
and the sword of Saul *r.* not   *2Sa 1:22*
empty
And Joab *r.* from following   *2Sa 2:30*
Abner
unto him, Go, return. And he   *2Sa 3:16*
r.
when Abner was *r.* to   *2Sa 3:27*
Hebron, Joab
David *r.* to bless his   *2Sa 6:20*
household
he *r.* from smiting of the   *2Sa 8:13*
Syrians
So Joab *r.* from the children   *2Sa 10:14*
and she *r.* unto her house   *2Sa 11:4*
all the people *r.* unto   *2Sa 12:31*
Jerusalem
So Absalom *r.* to his own   *2Sa 14:24*
house
hath *r.* upon thee all the   *2Sa 16:8*
blood of
whom thou seekest is as if all   *2Sa 17:3*
r.
not find them, they *r.* to   *2Sa 17:20*
Jerusalem
the people *r.* from pursuing   *2Sa 18:16*
after
So the king *r.* and came to   *2Sa 19:15*
Jordan
him; and he *r.* unto his own   *2Sa 19:39*
place
Joab *r.* to Jerusalem unto   *2Sa 20:22*
the king
people *r.* after him only to   *2Sa 23:10*
spoil
r. to depart, according to   *1Ki 12:24*
the word
r. not by the way that he   *1Ki 13:10*
came to
Jeroboam *r.* not from his   *1Ki 13:33*
evil way
And he *r.* back from him,   *1Ki 19:21*
and took
the messengers *r.* (S)   *2Ki 1:5*
and from thence he *r.* to   *2Ki 2:25*
Samaria
from him, and *r.* to their own   *2Ki 3:27*
land
he *r.* and walked in the house   *2Ki 4:35*
And he *r.* to the man of God,   *2Ki 5:15*
he and
And the messengers *r.* and   *2Ki 7:15*
told the
that the woman *r.* out of the   *2Ki 8:3*
land
king Joram was *r.* to be   *2Ki 9:15*
healed in
and hostages, and *r.* to   *2Ki 14:14*
Samaria
Rab-shakeh *r.* and found the   *2Ki 19:8*
king
and went and *r.* and dwelt   *2Ki 19:36*
at
upon them, and *r.* to   *2Ki 23:20*
Jerusalem
and David *r.* to bless his   *1Ch 16:43*
house
and all the people *r.* to   *1Ch 20:3*
Jerusalem.
it, that Jeroboam *r.* out of   *2Ch 10:2*
Egypt
r. from going against   *2Ch 11:4*
Jeroboam
in abundance, and *r.* to   *2Ch 14:15*
Jerusalem
Jehoshaphat the king of   *2Ch 19:1*
Judah *r.*
when they *r.* to Jerusalem   *2Ch 19:8*
Then they *r.* every man of   *2Ch 20:27*
Judah

And he *r.* to be healed in   *2Ch 22:6*
Jezreel
and they *r.* home in great   *2Ch 25:10*
anger
hostages also, and *r.* to   *2Ch 25:24*
Samaria
brethren: then they *r.* to   *2Ch 28:15*
Samaria
Then all the children of   *2Ch 31:1*
Israel *r.*
he *r.* with shame of face to   *2Ch 32:21*
his own
land of Israel, he *r.* to   *2Ch 34:7*
Jerusalem
Benjamin they *r.* to   *2Ch 34:9*
Jerusalem
and then they *r.* answer by   *Ezr 5:5*
letter
thus they *r.* us answer, saying,   *Ezr 5:11*
We
the gate of the valley, and so   *Ne 2:15*
r.
we *r.* all of us to the wall,   *Ne 4:15*
every one
yet when they *r.* and cried   *Ne 9:28*
unto
the morrow she *r.* into the   *Es 2:14*
second
the king *r.* out of the palace   *Es 7:8*
garden
my prayer *r.* into mine own   *Ps 35:13*
bosom
when Joab *r.* and smote of   *Ps 60 title*
Edom
r. and enquired early after   *Ps 78:34*
God
So I *r.* and considered all the   *Ec 4:1*
Then I *r.* and I saw vanity   *Ec 4:7*
under
I *r.* and saw under the sun,   *Ec 9:11*
that
So Rabshakeh *r.* and found   *Isa 37:8*
went and *r.* and dwelt at   *Isa 37:37*
Nineveh
So the sun *r.* ten degrees, by   *Isa 38:8*
which
Turn thou unto me. But she *r.*   *Jer 3:7*
not
they *r.* with their vessels   *Jer 14:3*
empty
Even all the Jews *r.* out of   *Jer 40:12*
all places
from Mizpah cast about and   *Jer 41:14*
r.
that were *r.* from all nations   *Jer 43:5*
And the living creatures ran   *Eze 1:14*
and *r.*
have *r.* to provoke me to   *Eze 8:17*
anger
Now when I had *r.* behold, at   *Eze 47:7*
mine understanding *r.* unto   *Da 4:34*
me
same time my reason *r.* unto   *Da 4:36*
me
honour and brightness *r.* unto   *Da 4:36*
me
I *r.* the captivity of my people   *Ho 6:11*
have ye not *r.* unto me   *Am 4:6;*
  4:8-11
and they *r.* and said, Like as   *Zec 1:6*
I am *r.* to Jerusalem with   *Zec 1:16*
mercies
that no man passed through   *Zec 7:14*
nor *r.*
I am *r.* unto Zion, and will   *Zec 8:3*
dwell in
as he *r.* into the city, he   *M't 21:18*
hungered
when he *r.* he found them   *M'k 14:40*
asleep
months, and *r.* to her own   *Lu 1:56*
house
the shepherds *r.* glorifying and   *Lu 2:20*
they *r.* into Galilee, to their   *Lu 2:39*
own
as they *r.,* the child Jesus   *Lu 2:43*
tarried
of the Holy Ghost *r.* from   *Lu 4:1*
Jordan
Jesus *r.* in the power of the   *Lu 4:14*
Spirit
up into the ship, and *r.* back   *Lu 8:37*
again
to pass, that, when Jesus was   *Lu 8:40*
r.
the apostles, when they were *r.*   *Lu 9:10*
And the seventy *r.* again with   *Lu 10:17*
joy
found that *r.* to give glory to   *Lu 17:18*
God

came to pass, that when he   *Lu 19:15*
was *r.*
done, smote their breasts,   *Lu 23:48*
and *r.*
And they *r.* and prepared   *Lu 23:56*
spices
r. from the sepulchre, and told   *Lu 24:9*
all
the same hour, and *r.* to   *Lu 24:33*
Jerusalem
and *r.* to Jerusalem with   *Lu 24:52*
great joy
Then *r.* they unto Jerusalem   *Ac 1:12*
from
not in the prison, they *r.* and   *Ac 5:22*
r. to Jerusalem, and preached   *Ac 8:25*
when
and Saul *r.* from Jerusalem,   *Ac 12:25*
told
John departing from them *r.*   *Ac 13:13*
they *r.* again to Lystra and to   *Ac 14:21*
took ship; and they *r.* home   *Ac 21:6*
again
to go with him, and *r.* to the   *Ac 23:32*
castle
and *r.* again unto Damascus   *Ga 1:17*
have had opportunity to   *Heb 11:15*
have *r.*
but are not *r.* unto the   *1Pe 2:25*
Shepherd

RETURNETH

goeth forth, he *r.* to his earth   *Ps 146:4*
As a dog *r.* to his vomit   *Pr 26:11*
so a fool *r.* to his folly   *Pr 26:11*
the wind *r.* again according to   *Ec 1:6*
his
from heaven and *r.* not   *Isa 55:10*
thither
that passeth out and him that   *Eze 35:7*
by, and because of him that *r.*   *Zec 9:8*

RETURNING

he is *r.* evil (B)(E)(R)   *1Sa 25:21*
In *r.* and rest shall ye be   *1Sa 30:15*
saved
r. to the house, found the   *Lu 7:10*
servant
Was *r.* and sitting in his   *Ac 8:28*
chariot
r. from the slaughter of the   *Heb 7:1*
kings

REU

lived thirty years, and begat   *Ge 11:18*
R.
Peleg lived after he begat R.   *Ge 11:19*
two
And R. lived two and thirty   *Ge 11:20*
years
R. lived after he begat Serug   *Ge 11:21*
two
Eber, Peleg, R.   *1Ch 1:25*

REUBEN

she bare a son, and called his   *Ge 29:32*
name R.
R. went in the days of   *Ge 30:14*
wheat-harvest
that R. went and lay with   *Ge 35:22*
Bilhah
sons of Leah, R. Jacob's   *Ge 35:23;*
firstborn   *46:8; 49:3; Nu 26:5;*
  1Ch 5:1
R. said unto them, shed no   *Ge 37:22*
blood
R. returned to the pit, Joseph   *Ge 37:29*
was not in it
the sons of R.   *Ge 46:9;*
  Ex 6:14; Nu 16:1; 32:1, 37; De 11:6;
  Jos 4:12; 1Ch 5:3, 18
as R. and Simeon, they shall   *Ge 48:5*
be mine
the standard of the camp of   *Nu 2:10;*
R.   *10:18*
all that were numbered of the   *Nu 2:16*
camp of R.
Elizur prince of the children   *Nu 7:30*
of R. did offer
Moses gave to children of   *Nu 32:33;*
R.   *Jos 13:23*
these on mount Ebal to curse   *De 27:13*
R.
let R. live, and let not his men   *De 33:6*
be few

to the stone of Bohan the | Jos 15:6;
son of R. | 18:17
Israel sent to the children of | Jos 22:13
R. and Gad
for divisions of R. great | J'g 5:15;
thoughts | 5:16
a portion for R. | Eze 48:6
one gate of R. | Eze 48:31

TRIBE OF REUBEN

of the *tribe of R.*, Elizur was | Nu 1:5
prince
of the *tribe of R.* were | Nu 1:21
numbered 46,500
of the *tribe of R.* Shammua | Nu 13:4
to spy land
the *tribe of R.* have received | Nu 34:14
inheritance
out of *tribe of R.* Gad and | Jos 20:8;
Manasseh | 1Ch 6:63, 78
of the *tribe of R.* were sealed | Re 7:5
12,000

REUBENITE

Adina the son of Shiza the | 1Ch 11:42
R. a

REUBENITES

These are the families of the | Nu 26:7
R.
cities thereof, gave I unto the | De 3:12
R.
unto the R. and unto the | De 3:16
Gadites
in the plain country, of the | De 4:43
R.
it for an inheritance unto the | De 29:8
R.
And to the R. and to the | Jos 1:12
Gadites,
it for a possession unto the R. | Jos 12:6
With whom the R. and the | Jos 13:8
Gadites
Then Joshua called the R. | Jos 22:1
the Gadites, and the R. and | 2Ki 10:33
captive: he was prince of the | 1Ch 5:6
R.
he carried them away even | 1Ch 5:26
the R.
a captain of the R. and | 1Ch 11:42
thirty with
the other side of Jordan, of | 1Ch 12:37
the R.
king David made rulers over | 1Ch 26:32
the R.
the ruler of the R. was | 1Ch 27:16
Eliezer the

REUEL

Eliphaz; and Bashemath bare | Ge 36:4
R.
R. the son of Bashemath the | Ge 36:10
wife of
these are the sons of R.; | Ge 36:13
Nahath
these are the sons of R., | Ge 36:17
Esau's son
these are the dukes that | Ge 36:17
came of R.
when they came to R. their | Ex 2:18
father
shall be Eliasaph the son of | Nu 2:14
R.
The sons of Esau; Eliphaz, | 1Ch 1:35
R. and
The sons of R.; Nahath, | 1Ch 1:37
Zerah
the son of R. the son of | 1Ch 9:8
Ibnijah

REUMAH

his concubine, whose name | Ge 22:24
was R.

REVEAL

we will not r. ourselves to | 1Sa 14:8
them (S)
The heaven shall r. his | Job 20:27
iniquity
heart may r. itself (E) | Pr 18:2
will r. unto them the | Jer 33:6
abundance of
reveal (S) | Da 2:10; 2:11, 24, 27

seeing thou couldest r. this | Da 2:47
secret
to whomsoever the Son will | M't 11:27
r. him
and he to whom the Son will | Lu 10:22
r. him
r. yourself - make yourself | Joh 14:22
real (A)
shall r. inner motives | 1Co 4:5
(B)(N)(P)
To r. his Son in me, that I | Ga 1:16
might
God shall r. even this unto | Ph'p 3:15
you

REVEALED

those things which are r. | De 29:29
belong
word of the Lord yet r. unto | 1Sa 3:7
him
for the Lord r. himself to | 1Sa 3:21
Samuel
hast r. to thy servant, saying, | 2Sa 7:27
I will
revealed (S) | Es 2:10; 2:20; Pr 26:26
gates of death been r. (S) | Job 38:17
let work be r. (A)(B) | Ps 90:16
it was r. in mine ears by the | Isa 22:14
Lord
the land of Chittim, it is r. to | Isa 23:1
them
the glory of the Lord shall be | Isa 40:5
r.
to whom is the arm of the | Isa 53:1
Lord r.
and my righteousness to be r. | Isa 56:1
for unto thee have I r. my | Jer 11:20
cause
was the secret r. unto Daniel | Da 2:19
in a
is not r. to me for any | Da 2:30
wisdom
Persia a thing was r. unto | Da 10:1
Daniel
covered, that shall not be | M't 10:26
r.; and
and hast r. them unto babes | M't 11:25
and blood hath not r. it | M't 16:17
unto thee
nothing hidden, except be r. | M'k 4:22
(A)
r. unto him by the Holy Ghost | Lu 2:26
thoughts of many hearts may | Lu 2:35
be r.
and hast r. them unto babes | Lu 10:21
nothing covered, that shall not | Lu 12:2
be r.
the day when the Son of man | Lu 17:30
is r.
r. his glory (N) | Joh 2:11
hath the arm of the Lord | Joh 12:38
been r.
r. by the Spirit (B) | Ac 11:28
righteousness of God r. from | Ro 1:17
faith
the wrath of God is r. from | Ro 1:18
heaven
righteousness been r. (A)(B) | Ro 3:21
the glory which shall be r. in | Ro 8:18
God's sons to be r. (N) | Ro 8:19
hath r. them unto us by his | 1Co 2:10
Spirit
it, because it shall be r. by | 1Co 3:13
fire
If any thing be r. to another | 1Co 14:30
faith which should afterwards | Ga 3:23
be r.
as it is now r. unto his holy | Eph 3:5
apostles
r. in human shape (N) | Ph'p 2:7
when the Lord Jesus shall be | 2Th 1:7
r. from
and that man of sin be r. the | 2Th 2:3
son
that he might be r. in his time | 2Th 2:6
then shall that Wicked be r. | 2Th 2:8
whom
r. in the flesh (B) | 1Ti 3:16
ready to be r. in the last time | 1Pe 1:5
when Christ is r. | 1Pe 1:7
(A)(B)(N)(P)
Unto whom it was r. that not | 1Pe 1:12
unto
when his glory shall be r. ye | 1Pe 4:13
may
of the glory that shall be r. | 1Pe 5:1
when Chief Shepherd is r. | 1Pe 5:4
(A)(P)
the life was r. (A)(B) | 1Jo 1:2
love of God was r. (B) | 1Jo 4:9

REVEALER

and a r. of secrets, seeing | Da 2:47
thou

REVEALETH

A tablebearer r. secrets: but he | Pr 11:13
about as a talebearer r. | Pr 20:19
secrets
and r. it not (S) | Pr 29:24
He r. the deep and secret | Da 2:22
things
is a God in heaven that r. | Da 2:28
secrets
he that r. secrets maketh | Da 2:29
known
he r. his secret unto his | Am 3:7
servants

REVEALING

r. personal opinions | Pr 18:2
(A)(B)(R)
and r. hard sentences (S) | Da 5:12
r. the sons of God | Ro 8:19
(A)(B)(E)(R)

REVEL

count it pleasure to r. (S) | 2Pe 2:13

REVELATION

awaiting r. of Lord's will (B) | Le 24:12
and r. of the righteous | Ro 2:5
judgment of
according to the r. of the | Ro 16:25
mystery
I shall speak to you either by | 1Co 14:6
r. or
doctrine, hath a tongue, | 1Co 14:26
hath a r.
it, but by the r. of Jesus | Ga 1:12
Christ
And I went up by r. and | Ga 2:2
unto you the spirit of | Eph 1:17
wisdom and r.
How that by r. he made | Eph 3:3
known unto
A B C of God's r. (P) | Heb 5:12
at r. of Jesus (E)(R) | 1Pe 1:7
unto you at the r. of Jesus | 1Pe 1:13
Christ
The R. of Jesus Christ, which | Re 1:1
God

REVELATIONS

come to visions and r. of | 2Co 12:1
through the abundance of the | 2Co 12:7
r.
in many separate r. (A) | Heb 1:1

REVELLING

not in r. and drunkenness | Ro 13:13
(S)
r. in their deception | 2Pe 2:13
(A)(R)(S)

REVELLINGS

drunkenness, r. and such like | Ga 5:21
carousing and the like | Ga 5:21
(A)(R)
carousings and everything of | Ga 5:21
the kind (B)
orgies and the like (N)(P) | Ga 5:21
r., banquetings, and | 1Pe 4:3
abominable

REVENGE

when he takes r. (N) | Pr 6:34
me, and r. me of my | Jer 15:15
persecutors
and we shall take our r. on | Jer 20:10
him
the Philistines hath dealt by | Eze 25:15
r.
desire, yea, what zeal, yea, | 2Co 7:11
what r.
readiness to r. all | 2Co 10:6
disobedience

REVENGED

and r. himself upon them | Eze 25:12

REVENGEFUL

enemy and the r. (B)	Ps 8:2
enemy and the r. (A)	Ps 44:16

REVENGEFULLY

Edom acted r. (R)	Eze 35:12

REVENGER

The r. of blood himself shall slay	Nu 35:19
r. of blood shall slay the murderer	Nu 35:21
between the slayer and r. cf blood	Nu 35:24
out of the hand of the r. of blood	Nu 35:25
the r. of blood find him without	Nu 35:27
and the r. of blood kill the slayer	Nu 31:27
a r. to execute wrath upon him	Ro 13:4

REVENGERS

suffer the r. of blood to destroy	2Sa 14:11

REVENGES

beginning of r. upon the enemy	De 32:42

REVENGETH

God is jealous, and the Lord r.	Na 1:2
the Lord r. and is furious; the	Na 1:2

REVENGING

r. of the blood of thy servants	Ps 79:10

REVENUE

shalt endamage the r. of the kings	Ezr 4:13
gold; and my r. than choice silver	Pr 8:19
my increase than choice silver (A)(B)	Pr 8:19
my yield than choice silver (R)	Pr 8:19
the harvest of the river is her r.	Isa 23:3
r. to whom r. (A)(R)	Ro 13:7

REVENUES

in the r. of the wicked is trouble	Pr 15:6
with the income of the wicked (A)(B)(R)	Pr 15:6
than great r. without right	Pr 16:8
than a large income (B)	Pr 16:8
shall be ashamed of your r.	Jer 12:13
be ashamed of their harvests (B)(R)	Jer 12:13

REVERE

r. my sanctuary (B)	Le 19:30; 26:2
they shall r. the Holy One (A)	Isa 29:23
wife may r. her husband (B)	Eph 5:33
r. Christ in your hearts (B)	1Pe 3:15

REVERED

I will be r. (B)	Le 22:32
r. him all his life (B)	Jos 4:14
to be worshipfully r. (A)(B)	Ps 89:7

REVERENCE

sabbaths, and r. my sanctuary	Le 19:30
revere my sanctuary (B)	Le 19:30; 26:2
my sabbaths, and r. my sanctuary	Le 26:2
he fell on his face, and did r.	2Sa 9:6
fell on his face and did obeisance (A)(E)(R)	2Sa 9:6
he prostrated himself (B)	2Sa 9:6
and did r. to the king, and	1Ki 1:31
bowed and did obeisance (A)(E)(R)	1Ki 1:31

fell on knees and paid homage (B)	1Ki 1:31
conduct yourselves in r. (A)	Ne 5:9
Mordecai bowed not, nor did him r.	Es 3:2
neither bowed deeply, nor knelt to him (B)	Es 3:2
neither bowed down, nor did obeisance (R)	Es 3:2
Mordecai bowed not, nor did him r.	Es 3:5
neither bowed nor knelt (B)	Es 3:5
did not bow down nor did obeisance (R)	Es 3:5
to be had in r. of all them that	Ps 89:7
to be feared and worshipfully revered (A)	Ps 89:7
revered above all (B)	Ps 89:7
to be feared above all (E)(R)	Ps 89:7
awesome, r. inspiring (A)	Ps 99:3
inspiring r. and godly fear (A)	Ps 111:9
son, saying, They will r. my son	M't 21:37
they will respect my son	M't 21:37;
(A)(B)(N)(P)(R)	M'k 12:6; Lu 20:13
them, saying, They will r. my son	M'k 12:6
they will r. him when they see him	Lu 20:13
eat without proper r. (P)	1Co 11:27
wife see that she r. her husband	Eph 5:33
so the wife may revere her husband (B)	Eph 5:33
see that she fear her husband (E)	Eph 5:33
see that she pays her husband all respect (N)	Eph 5:33
see that she respects her husband (R)	Eph 5:33
with r. awe, unmixed motives (B)	Eph 6:5
us, and we gave them r.	Heb 12:9
we yielded and respected them (A)(B)(P)(R)	Heb 12:9
we paid due respect to earthly fathers (N)	Heb 12:9
acceptably with r. and godly fear	Heb 12:28
with modesty, pious care, godly fear (A)	Heb 12:28
hold Christ in r. in (N)(R)	1Pe 3:15

REVERENCED

king's gate, bowed, and r. Haman	Es 3:2

REVEREND

ever: holy and r. is his name	Ps 111:9
inspiring reverence and godly fear (A)	Ps 111:9
awe-inspiring is his name	Ps 111:9
terrible is his name (R)	Ps 111:9

REVERENT

seized with r. dread (A)	Lu 8:25

REVERSE

hath blessed; and I cannot r.	Nu 23:20
to r. the letters devised by Haman	Es 8:5
the king's ring, may no man r.	Es 8:8

REVERT

relent and r. my decision (A)(B)	Jer 26:3

REVERTED

repeatedly r. to rebellious ways (B)	Ps 106:43

REVILE

Thou shalt not r. the gods	Ex 22:28
heap no abuse upon judges (B)	Ex 22:28
are ye, when men shall r. you	M't 5:11
r., denounce, defame (A)(R)	Lu 6:22
no occasion to r. (R)	1Ti 5:14
r. your right behavior (A)(R)	1Pe 3:16
r. your good manner of life (E)	1Pe 3:16
r. dignitaries (A)	2Pe 2:10

REVILED

mocked and r. (A)(R)	Isa 37:23; 37:24
And they that passed by r. him	M't 27:39
spoke reproachfully, abusively, jeered him (A)	M't 27:39
scoffed at him (B)	M't 27:39
railed on him (E)	M't 27:39
hurled abuse at him (N)	M't 27:39
called out to him in mockery (P)	M't 27:39
derided him (R)	Mt 27:39
were crucified with him r. him	M'k 15:32
reproached him too (B)(E)	M'k 15:32
taunted him (N)	M'k 15:32
hurled abuse at him (P)	M'k 15:32
Then they r. him, and said, Thou	Joh 9:28
They abused him (B)(N)	Joh 9:28
they turned on them furiously (P)	Joh 9:28
being r. we bless; being	1Co 4:12
being slandered, we bless (B)	1Co 4:12
he once r., set out to ruin (A)	Ga 1:23
Who, when he was r. r. not again	1Pe 2:23

REVILER

words of the r. (A)(B)(R)	Ps 44:16
a r., or drunkard (E)(R)	1Co 5:11

REVILERS

nor r. nor extortioners, shall	1Co 6:10

REVILES

r. the Lord (R)	Nu 15:30

REVILEST

said R. thou God's high priest	Ac 23:4

REVILING

r. and reproaching him (A)	M'k 15:29
no occasion for r. (E)	1Ti 5:14
r. for reviling (E)(R)	1Pe 3:9
do not pronounce r. judgment (R)	2Pe 2:11

REVILINGS

neither be ye afraid of their r.	Isa 51:7
the r. of the children of Ammon	Zep 2:8

REVITALIZE

who loses it shall r. it (B)	Lu 17:33

REVIVE

r. the stones out of the heaps of	Ne 4:2
wilt r. me again (A)(B)(R)	Ps 71:20; 80:18
revive (S)	Ps 71:20; 80:18; 119:25; 37; 88, 107, 149, 154, 156, 159
Wilt thou not r. us again: that thy	Ps 85:6
r. and stimulate me (A)(B)(R)	Ps 119:25
r. me in the way (B)	Ps 119:37
r. me (B)	Ps 119:88; 119:107, 149, 154, 156, 159
r. me (A)	Ps 119:154; 119:159
midst of trouble thou wilt r. me	Ps 138:7
to r. the spirit of the humble	Isa 57:15
r. the heart of the contrite ones	Isa 57:15
after two days will he r. us: in	Ho 6:2
They shall r. as the corn, and grow	Ho 14:7
r. thy work in the midst of	Hab 3:2

REVIVED

the spirit of Jacob their father r.	Ge 45:27
his spirit came again, and he r.	J'g 15:19

came into him again, and he 1Ki 17:22
r.
touched the bones of Elisha, 2Ki 13:21
he r.
r. me and given life Ps 119:50
(A)(B)(R)
purified, made white, r. (B) Da 12:10
the commandment came, sin r. Ro 7:9
Christ both died, and rose, Ro 14:9
and r.

REVIVING

give us a little r. in our Ezr 9:8
bondage
to give us a r. to set up the Ezr 9:9
house

REVOKE

will not r. or change it (A) Ps 110:4
I did not r. your sentence Zec 8:14
(A)
God will r. his sentence (A) Jon 3:9

REVOKED

r. their sentence of evil (A) Ps 106:45
Lord relented and r. his Am 7:3;
sentence (A) 7:6
he r. the matter (S) Ac 11:4; 14:27

REVOKING

know the r. of my promise Nu 14:34
(A)

REVOLT

did Libnah r. from under 2Ch 21:10
his hand
more? ye will r. more and Isa 1:5
more
God, speaking oppression Isa 59:13
and r.
the Karah r. (B) Jude 11

REVOLTED

Edom r. from under the hand 2Ki 8:20
Yet Edom r. from under the 2Ki 8:22
hand
Then Libnah r. at the same 2Ki 8:22
time
In his days the Edomites r. 2Ch 21:8
from
r. from the rule of Judah 2Ch 21:8
(A)(R)
So the Edomites r. from 2Ch 21:10
under the
continually r. (B) Ezr 4:15
children of Israel have deeply Isa 31:6
r.
rebelled and r. against me Jer 2:29
(A)(R)
heart: they are r. and gone Jer 5:23
shrink or be r. by (P) Ga 4:14

REVOLTERS

They are all grievous r. Jer 6:28
walking
the r. are profound to make a Ho 5:2
no more: all their princes are Ho 9:15
r.

REVOLTING

hath a r. and a rebellious Jer 5:23
heart

REVOLUTION

rebellion and r. made (B) Ezr 4:19

REWARD

shield and thy exceeding great Ge 15:1
r.
r. for your service in the Nu 18:31
tabernacle
your remuneration for Nu 18:31
services (B)
not persons, nor taketh r. De 10:17
not partial and take no bribe De 10:17
(A)(R)
no partiality nor can he be De 10:17
bribed (B)
r. to slay an innocent person De 27:25
who takes a bribe De 27:25
(A)(B)(E)(R)

and will r. them that hate me De 32:41
recompense those who hate De 32:41
me (A)(E)
repay those who hate me (B) De 32:41
requite those who hate me De 32:41
(R)
a full r. be given thee of the Ru 2:12
Lord
will richly r. (B) 1Sa 17:25
Lord r. thee good for that 1Sa 24:19
the Lord shall r. the doer of 2Sa 3:39
evil
Lord repay the evildoer 2Sa 3:39
(A)(B)
Lord requite the evildoer (R) 2Sa 3:39
have given him a r. for his 2Sa 4:10
tidings
recompense it me with such 2Sa 19:36
a r.
thyself, and I will give thee a 1Ki 13:7
r.
Behold, I say, how they r. 2Ch 20:11
us, to
a r. for me of your substance Job 6:22
Pay a bribe on my account Job 6:22
(A)(B)(R)
Offer a present for me (E) Job 6:22
hireling looketh for the r. of Job 7:2
laborer longs for his wages Job 7:2
(B)(E)(R)
taketh r. against the innocent Ps 15:5
who will not take a bribe Ps 15:5
(A)(B)(R)
keeping of them there is great Ps 19:11
r.
render due r. (R) Ps 28:4
then be desolate for a r. of Ps 40:15
their
shall r. evil unto mine enemies Ps 54:5
pay back evil to enemies (A) Ps 54:5
return the damage upon Ps 54:5
enemies (B)
requite the evil unto enemies Ps 54:5
(E)(R)
there is a r. for the righteous Ps 58:11
for a r. of their shame that say Ps 70:3
and see the r. of the wicked Ps 91:8
earth: render a r. to the proud Ps 94:2
this be the r. of mine Ps 109:20
adversaries
the fruit of the womb is his r. Ps 127:3
righteousness shall be a sure Pr 11:18
r.
a r. in the bosom strong wrath Pr 21:14
then there shall be a r. and Pr 21:14
shall be no r. to the evil man Pr 24:20
head, and the Lord shall r. Pr 25:22
have a good r. for their labour Ec 4:9
neither have they any more a r. Ec 9:5
r. of his hands shall be given Isa 3:11
him
what hands have done be Isa 3:11
done to him (A)(E)(R)
result of his hands be paid Isa 3:11
him (B)
Which justify the wicked for Isa 5:23
aquit the guilty for a bribe Isa 5:23
(A)(B)(E)(R)
behold, his r. is with him, Isa 40:10
and his
not for price nor r. saith the Isa 45:13
Lord
his r. is with him, and his Isa 62:11
work
guard gave him victuals and a Jer 40:5
r.
allowance of food and a Jer 40:5
present (A)(B)(E)(R)
and in that thou givest a r. Eze 16:34
and no r. is given unto thee Eze 16:34
ways, and r. them their doings Ho 4:9
repay them for their doings Ho 4:9
(A)
reckon to them their doings Ho 4:9
(B)
requite them for their doings Ho 4:9
(E)(R)
loved a r. upon every cornfloor Ho 9:1
loved a harlot's hire Ho 9:1
(A)(B)(E)(R)
thy r. shall return upon thine Ob 15
own
heads thereof judge for r. Mic 3:11
deal out judgment for a bribe Mic 3:11
(B)(R)
and the judge asketh for a r. Mic 7:3
judge ask for a bribe Mic 7:3
(A)(B)(R)
for great is your r. in heaven M't 5:12

which love you, what r. have M't 5:46
ye
what is your merit (B) M't 5:46
are you doing anything M't 5:46
exceptional (P)
what more are you doing M't 5:46
than others (R)
ye have no r. of your Father M't 6:1
I say unto you, They have M't 6:2
their r.
secret himself shall r. M't 6:4
thee openly
say unto you, They have their M't 6:5
r.
they have been paid in full M't 6:5
(B)
seeth in secret shall r. thee M't 6:6
openly
I say unto you, They have M't 6:16
their r.
seeth in secret, shall r. thee M't 6:18
openly
shall receive a prophet's r. M't 10:41
shall receive a righteous M't 10:41
man's r.
you, he shall in no wise lose M't 10:42
his r.
he shall r. every man M't 16:27
according
unto you, he shall not lose M'k 9:41
his r.
behold, your r. is great in Lu 6:23
heaven
your r. shall be great, and ye Lu 6:35
shall
your recompense will be great Lu 6:35
your return will be rich (B) Lu 6:35
we receive the due r. of our Lu 23:41
deeds
getting our deserts for our Lu 23:41
misdeeds (B)
paying the price for our Lu 23:41
misdeeds (N)
we got what we deserve (P) Lu 23:41
a field with the r. of iniquity Ac 1:18
the wages of crime (B) Ac 1:18
the price of his villainy (N) Ac 1:18
the proceeds of his infamy Ac 1:18
(P)
worketh is the r. not reckoned Ro 4:4
wages not counted as a favor Ro 4:4
(A)(B)(N)(P)(R)
every man shall receive his 1Co 3:8
own r.
receive his own pay (B)(N) 1Co 3:8
receive his own wages (R) 1Co 3:8
thereupon, he shall receive a 1Co 3:14
he will receive pay 1Co 3:14
do this thing willingly, I have 1Co 9:17
a r.
What is my r. then? Verily 1Co 9:18
that
Let no man beguile you of Col 2:18
your r.
disqualifying you for the Col 2:18
prize (A)
defraud you of salvation's Col 2:18
victory prize (B)
rob you of your prize (E) Col 2:18
disqualified by the decision of Col 2:18
people (N)
cheat of your joy in Christ Col 2:18
(P)
Let no one disqualify you Col 2:18
(R)
receive the r. of the Col 3:24
inheritance
the inheritance as your Col 3:24
remuneration (B)
receive the recompense of Col 3:24
inheritance (E)
The laborer is worthy of his 1Ti 5:18
r.
The laborer is worthy of his 1Ti 5:18
hire (A)(E)(P)
the worker deserves his wage 1Ti 5:18
(B)
the workman earns his pay 1Ti 5:18
(N)
the workman deserves his 1Ti 5:18
wages (R)
the Lord r. him according to 2Ti 4:14
his
The Lord will pay him back 2Ti 4:14
(A)(B)
Lord will render to him 2Ti 4:14
according (E)
retribution will fall upon him 2Ti 4:14
(N)

the Lord will requite him (R) *2Ti 4:14*
received a just recompence of *Heb 2:2*
r.
received an appropriate *Heb 2:2*
penalty (A)
received its just retribution *Heb 2:2*
(B)(R)
met with due retribution (N) *Heb 2:2*
received an appropriate *Heb 2:2*
retribution (P)
a great recompence of r. *Heb 10:35*
the recompence of the r. *Heb 11:26*
fixed eye on the final *Heb 11:26*
recompense (B)(N)
receive the r. of *2Pe 2:13*
unrighteousness
suffering wrong as the hire of *2Pe 2:13*
wrong-doing (E)
suffering hurt for the hurt *2Pe 2:13*
they inflicted (N)
suffering wrong for the *2Pe 2:13*
wrong-doing (R)
but that we receive a full r. *2Jo 8*
after the error of Balaam for *Jude 11*
r.
for the sake of gain (A)(R) *Jude 11*
by the error of Balaam's wage *Jude 11*
(B)
in the error of Balaam for *Jude 11*
hire (E)
plunged into Balaam's error *Jude 11*
for hire (N)
shouldest give r. unto thy *Re 11:18*
servants
time for recompense for thy *Re 11:18*
servants (N)
R. her even as she rewarded *Re 18:6*
you
Repay to her what she has *Re 18:6*
paid (A)(B)
Render to her as she has *Re 18:6*
rendered (E)(R)
Pay her back in her own coin *Re 18:6*
(N)(P)
my r. is with me to give *Re 22:12*
every
bringing my recompense with *Re 22:12*
me (N)(R)

REWARDED

Wherefore have we r. evil for *Ge 44:4*
good
repaid evil for good (B) *Ge 44:4;*
 Ps 109:5
thou hast r. me good, *1Sa 24:17*
whereas
whereas I have r. thee evil *1Sa 24:17*
The Lord r. me according to *2Sa 22:21;*
my *Ps 18:20*
weak: for your work shall be *2Ch 15:7*
r.
I have r. evil unto him that was *Ps 7:4*
They r. me evil for good to *Ps 35:12*
r. us according to our *Ps 103:10*
iniquities
And they have r. me evil for *Ps 109:5*
good
the commandment shall be r. *Pr 13:13*
they have r. evil unto *Isa 3:9*
themselves
for thy work shall be r. saith *Jer 31:16*
Reward her even as she r. you *Re 18:6*

REWARDER

a r. of them that diligently *Heb 11:6*
seek

REWARDETH

he r. him and he shall know *Joh 21:19*
and plentifully r. the proud *Ps 31:23*
doer
r. thee as thou hast served us *Ps 137:8*
Whoso r. evil for good, evil *Pr 17:13*
shall
formed all things both r. the *Pr 26:10*
fool
the fool, and r. transgressors *Pr 26:10*

REWARDS

the r. of divination in their *Nu 22:7*
hand
gifts, and followeth after r. *Isa 1:23*
loves bribes (A)(B)(E)(R) *Isa 1:23*
ye shall receive of me gifts and *Da 2:6*
r.

thyself, and give thy r. to *Da 5:17*
another
These are my r. that my *Ho 2:12*
lovers

REZEPH

as Gozan, and Haran, and *2Ki 19:12;*
R. and *Isa 37:12*

REZIA

Ulla; Arah, and Haniel, and *1Ch 7:39*
R.

REZIN

against Judah, R., king of *2Ki 15:37*
Syria
Then R. king of Syria and *2Ki 16:5*
Pekah
At that time R. king of Syria *2Ki 16:6*
people, captive to Kir, and *2Ki 16:9*
slew R.
The children of R. the *Ezr 2:48*
children of
of Reaiah, the children of R. *Ne 7:50*
that R. the king of Syria and *Isa 7:1*
Pekah
the fierce anger of R. with *Isa 7:4*
Syria
and the head of Damascus is *Isa 7:8*
R.
rejoice in R. and Remaliah's *Isa 8:6*
son
shall set up the adversaries of *Isa 9:11*
R.

REZON

adversary, R. the son of *1Ki 11:23*
Eliadah

RHEGIUM

fetched a compass, and came *Ac 28:13*
to R.

RHESA

which was the son of R. *Lu 3:27*

RHETORIC

if I lack skill in r. (B) *2Co 11:6*

RHODA

damsel came to hearken, *Ac 12:13*
named R.

RHODES

and the day following unto R. *Ac 21:1*

RIB

And the r. made he a woman *Ge 2:22*
spear smote him under the *2Sa 2:23*
fifth r.
smote him there under the *2Sa 3:27*
fifth r.
they smote him under the fifth *2Sa 4:6*
r.
smote him therewith in the *2Sa 20:10*
fifth r.

RIBAI

Ittai the son of R. out of *2Sa 23:29*
Gibeah
Ithai the son of R. of *1Ch 11:31*
Gibeah that

RIBBAND

fringe of the borders a r. of *Nu 15:38*
blue
a cord of blue (A)(E)(R) *Nu 15:38*
a blue thread (B) *Nu 15:38*

RIBLAH

go down from Shepham to *Nu 34:11*
R.
put him in bands at R. in *2Ki 23:33*
the land
up to the king of Babylon to *2Ki 25:6*
R.
them to the king of Babylon *2Ki 25:20*
to R.

and slew them at R. in the *2Ki 25:21*
land of
to R. in the land of Hamath *Jer 39:5*
slew the sons of Zedekiah in *Jer 39:6*
R.
to R. in the land of Hamath *Jer 52:9*
slew the princes of Judah in *Jer 52:10*
R.
them to the king of Babylon *Jer 52:26*
to R.
and put them to death in R. *Jer 52:27*

RIBS

took one of his r. and closed *Ge 2:21*
up
it had three r. in the mouth of *Da 7:5*

RICH

And Abram was very r. in *Ge 13:2*
cattle
shouldest say, I made *Ge 14:23*
Abram r.
The r. shall not give more *Ex 30:15*
a sojourner or stranger wax r. *Le 25:47*
young men, whether poor or r. *Ru 3:10*
Lord maketh poor, and *1Sa 2:7*
maketh r.
the one r. and the other poor *2Sa 12:1*
r. man had exceeding many *2Sa 12:2*
flocks
came a traveller unto the r. *2Sa 12:4*
man
they found r. pasture (S) *1Ch 4:40;*
 Eze 34:14
He shall not be r. neither *Job 15:29*
shall
The r. man shall lie down, *Job 27:19*
but he
nor regardeth the r. more *Job 34:19*
than
r. among the people shall *Ps 41:12*
intreat
low and high, r. and poor *Ps 49:2*
together
thou afraid when one is made *Ps 49:16*
r.
r. in loving-kindness (B) *Ps 86:5*
the hand of the diligent *Pr 10:4*
maketh r.
r. man's wealth is his strong *Pr 10:15*
city
blessing of the Lord, it *Pr 10:22*
maketh r.
There is that maketh himself r. *Pr 13:7*
but the r. hath many friends *Pr 14:20*
r. man's wealth is his strong *Pr 18:11*
city
but the r. answereth roughly *Pr 18:23*
loveth wine and oil shall not *Pr 21:17*
be r.
The r. and poor meet together *Pr 22:2*
The r. ruleth over the poor *Pr 22:7*
he that giveth to the r. shall *Pr 22:16*
surely
Labour not to be r.: cease *Pr 23:4*
from
is perverse though he be r. *Pr 28:6*
r. man is wise in his own *Pr 28:11*
conceit
he that maketh haste to be r. *Pr 28:20*
shall
hasteth to be r. hath an evil *Pr 28:22*
eye
abundance of the r. will not *Ec 5:12*
suffer
dignity, and the r. sit in low *Ec 10:6*
place
curse not the r. in thy *Ec 10:20*
bedchamber
a r. robe, sackcloth *Isa 3:24*
(A)(B)(E)(R)
it will be r. and plentiful *Isa 30:23*
(A)
wicked, and with the r. in his *Isa 53:9*
death
are become great, and waxen *Jer 5:27*
r.
not the r. man glory in his *Jer 9:23*
riches
in chests of r. apparel, *Eze 27:24*
bound with
making kings r. (B) *Eze 27:33*
Ephraim said, Yet I am *Ho 12:8*
become r.
the r. men are full of *Mic 6:12*
violence
his food r. (A)(B)(R) *Hab 1:16*
Blessed be the Lord; for I am *Zec 11:5*
r.

a r. man shall hardly enter   M't 19:23
into
than for a r. man to enter   M't 19:24
into the
there came a r. man of   M't 27:57
Arimathaea
than for a r. man to enter   M'k 10:25
into the
many that were r. cast in   M'k 12:41
much
the r. he hath sent empty   Lu 1:53
away
But woe unto you that are r.   Lu 6:24
your return will be r. (B)   Lu 6:35
The ground of a certain r.   Lu 12:16
man
himself, and is not r. toward   Lu 12:21
God
kinsmen, nor thy r.   Lu 14:12
neighbours
There was a certain r. man   Lu 16:1;
  16:19
which fell from the r. man's   Lu 16:21
table
r. man also died, and was   Lu 16:22
buried
very sorrowful: for he was   Lu 18:23
very r.
than for a r. man to enter   Lu 18:25
into the
among the publicans, and he   Lu 19:2
was r.
saw the r. men casting their   Lu 21:1
gifts
is r. unto all that call upon   Ro 10:12
him
Now we are full, now ye are r.   1Co 4:8
as poor, yet making many r.   2Co 6:10
so r. in everything (N)   2Co 8:7
though he was r. yet for your   2Co 8:9
through his poverty might be   2Co 8:9
r.
God, who is in mercy, for   Eph 2:4
that will be r. fall into   1Ti 6:9
temptation
Charge them that are r. in   1Ti 6:17
that they be r. in good works   1Ti 6:18
r. in good deeds (R)   1Ti 6:18
carries a r. reward (B)(P)   Heb 10:35
But the r. in that he is made   Jas 1:10
low
So also shall the r. man fade   Jas 1:11
away
the poor of this world r. in   Jas 2:5
faith
Do not r. men oppress you   Jas 2:6
Go to now, ye r. men, weep   Jas 5:1
and poverty, (but thou art r.)   Re 2:9
Because thou sayest, I am r.   Re 3:17
in the fire, that thou mayest be   Re 3:18
r.
the r. men, and the chief   Re 6:15
captains
great r. and poor, free and   Re 13:16
bond
merchants of the earth waxed   Re 18:3
r.
r. with wealth   Re 18:3
(A)(B)(E)(N)(P)(R)
things, which were made r.   Re 18:15
by her
were made r. all that had   Re 18:19
ships

RICHER

fourth shall be far r. than   Da 11:2
they all
love grows r. and r. (B)(N)   Ph'p 1:9

RICHES

the r. which God hath taken   Ge 31:16
wealth (B)   Ge 31:16;
Jos 22:8;   1Ki 10:23;   1Ch 29:12;
2Ch 32:27;   Es 1:4;   5:11;   Job 36:19;
  Ps 52:7
property (R)   Ge 31:16
their r. were more than that   Ge 36:7
they
possessions (B)(R)   Ge 36:7
Return with much r. unto   Jos 22:8
your
wealth (B)   Jos 22:8
king will enrich him with   1Sa 17:25
great r.
neither hast asked, r. for   1Ki 3:11
thyself
hast not asked, both r. and   1Ki 3:13
honour

exceeded kings of the earth   1Ki 10:23
for r.
Both r. and honour come of   1Ch 29:12
thee
wealth (B)   1Ch 29:12
old age, full of days, r. and   1Ch 29:28
honour
not asked r., wealth, or   2Ch 1:11
honour
possessions (R)   2Ch 1:11
I will give thee r. and wealth   2Ch 1:12
passed the kings of the   2Ch 9:22
earth in r.
he had r. and honour in   2Ch 17:5
abundance
Jehoshaphat had r. and   2Ch 18:1
honour in
both r. with the dead   2Ch 20:25
bodies, and
much cattle, garments,   2Ch 20:25
precious things (A)(R)
Hezekiah had exceeding   2Ch 32:27
much r.
great wealth (A)   2Ch 32:27
the r. of his glorious kingdom   Es 1:4
told them of the glory of his r.   Es 5:11
He hath swallowed down r.   Job 20:15
Will he esteem thy r.? no,   Job 36:19
not gold
better than the r. of many   Ps 37:16
wicked
the abundance of many   Ps 37:16
wicked (E)(R)
he heapeth up r. and knoweth   Ps 39:6
boast in the multitude of   Ps 49:6
their r.
trusted in the abundance of his   Ps 52:7
r.
if r. increase, set not your   Ps 62:10
heart
in the world; they increase in   Ps 73:12
r.
the mall: the earth is full of   Ps 104:24
thy r.
earth is full of well-made   Ps 104:24
creations (B)
earth is full of thy creatures   Ps 104:24
(R)
and r. shall be in his house   Ps 112:3
prosperity and welfare are in   Pr 112:3
his house (A)
testimonies, as much as in   Ps 119:14
all r.
in her left hand r. and honour   Pr 3:16
R. and honour are with me   Pr 8:18
yea, durable r. and   Pr 8:18
righteousness
R. profit not in the day of   Pr 11:4
wrath
honour: and strong men   Pr 11:16
retain r.
He that trusteth in his r. shall   Pr 11:28
fall
himself poor, yet hath great r.   Pr 13:7
hath great wealth (E)   Pr 13:7
ransom of a man's life are his   Pr 13:8
r.
The crown of the wise is   Pr 14:24
their r.
crown of wise is their wealth   Pr 14:24
(A)(B)
crown of the wise is their   Pr 14:24
wisdom (R)
house and wealth are   Pr 19:14
the inheritance
house and wealth are   Pr 19:14
inherited (B)(R)
rather to be chosen than great   Pr 22:1
r.
and the fear of the Lord are r.   Pr 22:4
oppresseth the poor to   Pr 22:16
increase his r.
r. certainly make themselves   Pr 23:5
wings
with all precious and pleasant   Pr 24:4
r.
For r. are not for ever: and   Pr 27:24
doth
give me neither poverty nor r.   Pr 30:8
neither is his eye satisfied with   Ec 4:8
r.
satisfied with wealth (B)   Ec 4:8
r. kept for the owners thereof   Ec 5:13
wealth retained by the owner   Ec 5:13
(B)
But those r. perish by evil   Ec 5:14
travail
wealth is lost in a bad venture   Ec 5:14
(B)
whom God hath given r. and   Ec 5:19
wealth

God has given wealth and   Ec 5:19
possessions (R)
A man to whom God hath   Ec 6:2
given r.
God gives wealth, possessions,   Ec 6:2
honor (R)
nor yet r. to men of   Ec 9:11
understanding
r. of Damascus and the spoil   Isa 8:4
the wealth of Damascus (R)   Isa 8:4
found as a nest the r. of the   Isa 10:14
people
the wealth of the people   Isa 10:14
(A)(B)(R)
carry their r. upon the   Isa 30:6
shoulders of
and hidden r. of secret places   Isa 45:3
hoarded wealth in secret   Isa 45:3
places (B)
ye shall eat the r. of the   Isa 61:6
Gentiles
eat the wealth of the nations   Isa 61:6
(A)(B)(E)(R)
not the rich man glory in his   Jer 9:23
r.
he that getteth r. and not by   Jer 17:11
right
r. he hath gotten are   Jer 48:36
perished
they shall make a spoil of   Eze 26:12
thy r.
plunder your wealth (B)   Eze 26:12
of the multitude of all kind   Eze 27:12
of r.
because of your great wealth   Eze 27:12
(B)(R)
making, for the multitude of   Eze 27:18
all r.
immense wealth of every   Eze 27:18
kind (A)(B)(R)
r. and thy fairs, thy   Eze 27:27
merchandise
your wealth and your wares   Eze 27:27
(B)
earth with the multitude of   Eze 27:33
thy r.
with your abundant wealth   Eze 27:33
(A)(B)(R)
thou hast gotten thee r. and   Eze 28:4
won for yourself great wealth   Eze 28:4
(B)(R)
traffick hast thou increased   Eze 28:5
thy r.
heart is lifted up because of   Eze 28:5
thy r.
through his r. he shall stir up   Da 11:2
all
through his wealth he has   Da 11:2
become (B)
by his r. he shall (E)   Da 11:2
a great army and with much   Da 11:13
r.
much substance and   Da 11:13
equipment (A)(E)
army amply equipped (B)   Da 11:13
great army and abundant   Da 11:13
supplies (R)
them the prey, and spoil, and   Da 11:24
r.
plunder, spoil and goods   Da 11:24
(A)(R)
distribute spoil, booty and   Da 11:24
property (B)
scatter prey, spoil and   Da 11:24
substance (E)
return into his land with   Da 11:28
great r.
return into his land with   Da 11:28
much booty (A)
return to his land loaded   Da 11:28
with loot (B)
return to his land with great   Da 11:28
substance (E)(R)
world, and the deceitfulness   M't 13:22
of r.
the enjoyment of wealth (B)   M't 13:22
the false glamour of wealth   M't 13:22
(N)
the illusions of wealth (P)   M't 13:22
world, and the deceitfulness   M'k 4:19
of r.
they that have r. enter into   M'k 10:23
those who possess wealth   M'k 10:23
(A)(B)
for the wealthy to enter   M'k 10:23
(N)
those who have great   M'k 10:23
possessions (P)
that trust in r. to enter into   M'k 10:24
put trust in wealth (B)   M'k 10:24

are choked with cares and r. *Lu 8:14*
wealth (B) *Lu 8:14;*
18:24; Ro 2:4; 9:23; 11:33; *2Co 8:2;*
Eph 1:7; 2:7; 3:8, 16; *Ph'p 4:19;*
          Col 1:27
will commit to your trust the *Lu 16:11*
true r.
faithful in deceitful r. (B) *Lu 16:11*
real r. (N) *Lu 16:11;*
Joh 1:9; 4:23; 15:1; Ac 12:9; *Heb 8:2;*
          1Jo 5:20
they that have r. enter into *Lu 18:24*
shared in his r. (P) *Joh 1:16*
Or despisest thou the r. of his *Ro 2:4*
make known the r. of his *Ro 9:23*
glory on
fall of them be the r. of the *Ro 11:12*
world
diminishing of them the r. of *Ro 11:12*
the
depth of the r. both of the *Ro 11:33*
wisdom
unto the r. of their liberality *2Co 8:2*
according to the r. of his *Eph 1:7*
grace
r. of the glory of his *Eph 1:18*
inheritance in
shew the exceeding r. of his *Eph 2:7*
grace
the unsearchable r. of Christ *Eph 3:8*
according to the r. of· his *Eph 3:16*
glory, to
to his r. in glory by Christ *Ph'p 4:19*
Jesus
the r. of the glory of this *Col 1:27*
mystery
unto all r. of the full assurance *Col 2:2*
nor trust in uncertain r. but *1Ti 6:17*
reproach of Christ greater than *Heb 11:26*
Your r. are corrupted, and *Jas 5:2*
your
was slain to receive power, *Re 5:12*
and r.
hour so great r. is come to *Re 18:17*
nought

RICHLY

will r. reward (B) *1Sa 17:25*
pour out on you r. (B)(N) *2Co 9:8*
the word of Christ dwell in *Col 3:16*
you r.
who giveth us r. all things to *1Ti 6:17*
enjoy

RID

he might r. him out of their *Ge 37:22*
hands
I will r. you out of their *Ex 6:6*
bondage
will r. evil beasts out of the *Le 26:6*
land
needy: r. them out of the hand *Ps 82:4*
r. me, and deliver me out of *Ps 144:7*
great
R. me, and deliver me from *Ps 144:11*
the
I will r. myself of mine *Isa 1:24*
adversaries (S)

RIDDANCE

not make clean r. of the *Le 23:22*
corners
for he shall make even a *Zep 1:18*
speedy r.

RIDDEN

ass, upon which thou hast r. *Nu 22:30*

RIDDLE

I will now put forth a r. unto *J'g 14:12*
you
Put forth thy r. that we may *J'g 14:13*
hear
not in three days expound *J'g 14:14*
the r.
could not solve the r. *J'g 14:14;*
          14:19
(A)(B)(E)(R)
that he may declare unto us *J'g 14:15*
the r.
thou hast put forth a r. unto *J'g 14:16*
she told the r. to the children *J'g 14:17*
of her
heifer, ye had not found out *J'g 14:18*
my r.

unto them which expounded *J'g 14:19*
the r.
Son of man, put forth a r. *Eze 17:2*
propound a r. (R) *Eze 17:2*

RIDDLES

solve r., knotty problems *Da 5:12*
(A)(B)(R)
who understands r. (R) *Da 8:23*

RIDE

he made him to r. in the *Ge 41:43*
second
He made him r. on the high *De 32:13*
places
Speak, ye that r. on white *J'g 5:10*
asses, ye
be for the king's household to *2Sa 16:2*
r. on
me an ass, that I may r. *2Sa 19:26*
thereon
cause Solomon my son to r. *1Ki 1:33*
upon
Solomon to r. upon king *1Ki 1:38*
David's
caused him to r. upon the *1Ki 1:44*
king's
So they made him r. in his *2Ki 10:16*
chariot
thou causest me to r. upon it *Job 30:22*
And in thy majesty r. *Ps 45:4*
prosperously
caused men to r. over our *Ps 66:12*
heads
We will r. upon the swift, *Isa 30:16*
therefore
and I will cause thee to r. *Isa 58:14*
upon the
they r. upon horses, set in *Jer 6:23*
they shall r. upon horses, *Jer 50:42*
every one
I will make Ephraim to r. *Ho 10:11*
save us; we will not r. upon *Ho 14:3*
horses
thou didst r. upon thine horses *Hab 3:8*
chariots, and those that r. in *Hag 2:22*
them

RIDER

so that this r. shall fall *Ge 49:17*
backward
horse and his r. hath he *Ex 15:1, 21*
thrown
she scorneth the horse and *Job 39:18*
his r.
break in pieces the horse and *Jer 51:21*
his r.
in pieces the chariot and his *Jer 51:21*
r.
and his r. with madness: and I *Zec 12:4*

RIDERS

on thy part to set r. upon *2Ki 18:23*
them
r. on mules, camels, and young *Es 8:10*
on thy part to set r. upon them *Isa 36:8*
and their r. shall come down *Hag 2:22*
r. on horses shall be *Zec 10:5*
confounded

RIDETH

what saddle soever he r. upon *Le 15:9*
who r. upon the heaven in thy *De 33:26*
help
and the horse that the king r. *Es 6:8*
upon
r. upon the heavens by his *Ps 68:4*
name
r. upon the heavens of heavens *Ps 68:33*
the Lord r. upon a swift cloud *Isa 19:1*
he that r. the horse deliver *Am 2:15*
himself

RIDGES

Thou waterest the r. thereof *Ps 65:10*

RIDICULE

sent to r. living God (B) *2Ki 19:4*
r. every stronghold (A) *Hab 1:10*
to r. and (P) *M't 20:19*
to say in r. (B) *Lu 14:29*

RIDICULED

do not want to be r. (B) *Ge 38:23*
r. or provoked me (A) *Nu 22:29*
they r. him (A) *M't 27:29;*
          Lu 23:11
r., insulted (B) *Lu 18:32*
scoffed at and r. (A) *Lu 22:63*

RIDICULES

everyone r. me (B) *Jer 30:7*

RIDICULOUS

made me r. (B) *Nu 22:29*
it seems r. (P) *Ac 25:27*

RIDING

Now he was r. upon his ass *Nu 22:22*
slack not thy r. for me, except *2Ki 4:24*
I bid
r. in chariots and on horses *Jer 17:25*
r. in chariots and on horses, he *Jer 22:4*
men, horsemen r. upon horses *Eze 23:6*
horsemen r. upon horses, all *Eze 23:12*
of them
all of them r. upon horses *Eze 23:23*
all of them r. upon horses, a *Eze 38:15*
great
behold a man r. upon a red *Zec 1:8*
horse
lowly, and r. upon an ass, and *Zec 9:9*

RIE

wheat and the r. were not *Ex 9:32*
smitten
barley and the r. in their *Isa 28:25*
place

RIFLED

shall be taken, and the houses *Zec 14:2*
r.

RIGHT

r. hand of man *Ge 13:9;*
24:49; 48:13, 14, 17, 18; Ex 14:22, 29;
Nu 20:17; 22:26; De 2:27; 5:32; 17:11,
20; 28:14; Jos 1:7; 17:7; 23:6; J'g 5:36;
7:20; 16:29; 1Sa 6:12; 2Sa 2:19, 21;
14:19; 16:6; 1Ki 2:19; 23:13; 1Ch 6:39;
12:2; 2Ch 3:17; 4:6, 7; 18:18; 34:2;
Ne 8:4; 12:31; Job 30:12; Ps 142:4;
144:8; Pr 4:27; 27:16; Ca 2:6; 8:3;
Isa 30:21; 41:13; 44:20; 45:1; 54:3;
63:12; Jon 4:11; Zec 3:1; 12:6; M't 5:29,
30; M'k 15:27; Ac 3:7
doing what is r. and fair (B) *Ge 18:19*
the judge of all the earth do r. *Ge 18:25*
wilt thou slay a r. and just *Ge 20:4;*
nation (A) *38:26; Job 15:14*
the Lord is r. (A)(R) *Ex 9:27*
r. hand of God *Ex 15:6;*
15:12; 1Ki 22:19; Ps 16:8, 17; 17:7;
18:35; 20:6; 21:8; 44:3; 48:10; 60:5;
63:8; 74:11; 77:10; 80:15, 17; 89:13;
91:7; 98:1; 108:6; 110:1, 5; 118:15, 16;
138:7; 139:10; Isa 41:10; 48:13; 62:8;
22:24; La 2:3; Hab 2:16; M't 22:44;
26:64; M'k 12:36; 14:62; 16:19;
Lu 20:42; 22:69; Ac 2:25, 33, 34; 5:31;
7:55, 56; Ro 8:34; Eph 1:20; Col 3:1;
Heb 1:3, 13; 8:1; 10:12; 12:2; 1Pe 3:22;
          Re 5:1, 7
tip of the r. ear *Ex 29:20;*
    Le 8:23, 24; 14:17, 25, 28
on thumb of r. hand *Ex 29:20;*
    Le 8:23, 24; 14:14, 17, 25, 28
upon great toe of r. foot *Le 8:23;*
    8:24; 14:14, 17, 25, 28
the r. shoulder *Le 8:25;*
    8:26; 9:21; Nu 18:18
dip his r. finger in oil *Le 14:16; 14:27*
daughters of Zelophehad speak *Nu 27:7*
r.
that which is r. *De 12:28; 13:18; 21:19*
the r. of the firstborn is his *De 21:17*
just and r. is he *De 32:4*
from his r. hand went a fiery *De 33:2*
law
people passed over r. against *Jos 3:16*
Jericho
seemed good and r. unto thee *Jos 9:25*
r. thigh *J'g 3:16; 3:21*
could not frame to pronounce *J'g 12:6*
it r.

every man did that which was *J'g 17:6;*
r. in his own eyes   *21:25; Pr 21:2*
I may thrust out your r. eyes   *1Sa 11:2*
teach you the good and r.   *1Sa 12:23*
See, thy matters are good   *2Sa 15:3*
and r.
we have more r. in David   *2Sa 19:43*
beard with the r. hand to kiss *2Sa 20:9*
him
r. side of the city   *2Sa 24:5*
to discern what is r. (R)   *1Ki 3:11*
r. side of the house   *1Ki 6:8; 7:39*
he set up the r. pillar   *1Ki 7:2*
five on the r. side *1Ki 7:49; 2Ch 4:7, 8*
do that which is r.   *1Ki 11:33;*
                          11:38; 14:8
did that which was r.   *1Ki 15:5;*
15:11; 22:43; 2Ki 12:2; 14:3; 15:3, 34;
16:2; 18:3; 22:2; 2Ch 14:2; 20:32; 24:2;
25:2; 26:4; 27:2; 28:1; 29:2; 31:30; 34:2
Is thine heart r. as my heart *2Ki 10:15*
r. corner of the temple   *2Ki 11:11*
things that were not r.   *2Ki 17:9*
the thing that was r. in the *1Ch 13:4*
eyes of all
set the sea on the r. side of the *2Ch 4:10*
gavest them r. judgments   *Ne 9:13*
for thou hast done r.   *Ne 9:33*
How forcible are r. words   *Job 6:25*
right (S)   *Job 8:3;*
27:2; 34:5; Ps 35:23; Jer 26:14; 27:5;
M't 15:26; M'k 7:27; 1Co 9:4, 5, 6, 12,
                        18; Ph'p 1:7
should man be r. before God   *Job 9:2*
(A)(E)
maintain the r. of a man   *Job 16:21*
(E)(R)
he hideth himself on the r.   *Job 23:9*
hand
taken away my r.   *Job 27:2*
(A)(B)(E)(R)
acknowledge you to be r.   *Job 27:5*
(B)(R)
understand what is r. (N)   *Job 32:9*
you are not r. (R)   *Job 33:12*
and perverted that which was *Job 33:27*
r.
twisted that which was r. (B) *Job 33:27*
choose what is r.   *Job 34:4*
(A)(B)(E)(R)(S)
Should I lie against my r.? my *Job 34:6*
Shall even he that hateth r. *Job 34:17*
govern
will not lay upon man more   *Job 34:23*
than r.
Thinkest thou this to be r.   *Job 35:2*
wicked: but giveth r. to the *Job 36:6*
poor
he will disregard no r. (A)   *Job 37:23*
thine own r. hand can save   *Job 40:14*
thee
spoken of me the thing that is *Job 42:7*
r.
spoken of me the thing which *Job 42:8*
is r.
maintained my r. and my cause *Ps 9:4*
satest in the throne judging r. *Ps 9:4*
his case seems r. (A)(B)(R) *Ps 18:17*
The statutes of the Lord are r. *Ps 19:8*
guide humble in what is r.   *Ps 25:9*
(B)(P)
and their r. hand is full of *Ps 26:10*
bribes
For the word of the Lord is r. *Ps 33:4*
awake to my r. (R)   *Ps 35:23*
of thy kingdom is a r. sceptre *Ps 45:6*
thy r. hand did stand the queen *Ps 45:9*
shall help her, and that r. early *Ps 46:5*
and renew a r. spirit within *Ps 51:10*
me
thou hast holden me by my r. *Ps 73:23*
hand
their heart was not r. with him *Ps 78:37*
which his r. hand had   *Ps 78:54*
purchased
sea, and his r. hand in the   *Ps 89:25*
rivers
up the r. hand of his   *Ps 89:42*
adversaries
he led them forth by the r.   *Ps 107:7*
way
and let Satan stand at his r. *Ps 109:6*
hand
stand at the r. hand of the *Ps 109:31*
poor
works are faithful and r. (B) *Ps 111:7*
Lord, that thy judgments are *Ps 119:75*
r.

esteem all thy precepts to   *Ps 119:128*
be r.
Lord is thy shade upon thy r. *Ps 121:5*
hand
let my r. hand forget her   *Ps 137:5*
cunning
the afflicted, and the r. of the *Ps 140:12*
poor
I have led thee in r. paths   *Pr 4:11*
Let thine eyes look r. on, and *Pr 4:25*
let
opening of my lips be r. things *Pr 8:6*
r. to them that find knowledge *Pr 8:9*
passengers go r. on their   *Pr 9:15*
ways
thoughts of the righteous are *Pr 12:5*
r.
way of a fool is r. in his own *Pr 12:15*
eyes
There is a way which seemeth *Pr 14:12*
r.
than great revenues without r. *Pr 16:8*
they love him that speaketh r. *Pr 16:13*
There is a way that seemeth r. *Pr 16:25*
work be pure, and whether it *Pr 20:11*
be r.
but as for the pure, his work is *Pr 21:8*
r.
when thy lips speak r. things *Pr 23:16*
his lips that giveth a r. answer *Pr 24:26*
all travail, and every r. work *Ec 4:4*
wise man's heart is at his r. *Ec 10:2*
hand
And he shall snatch on the r. *Isa 9:20*
hand
to take away the r. from the *Isa 10:2*
poor
turn aside a person who is r. *Isa 29:21*
(B)(R)
Prophesy not unto us r. things *Isa 30:10*
even when the needy speaketh *Isa 32:7*
r.
my r. is passed over (A)(R) *Isa 40:27*
I declare things that are r.   *Isa 45:19*
my r. is with the Lord   *Isa 49:4*
(A)(B)(R)
who declares me to be r. (A) *Isa 50:8*
thee a noble vine, wholly a r. *Jer 2:21*
seed
r. of the needy do they not   *Jer 5:28*
judge
he that getteth riches, and not *Jer 17:11*
by r.
which came out of my lips   *Jer 17:16*
was r.
is evil, and their force is not *Jer 23:10*
r.
r. of redemption is thine to *Jer 32:7*
buy it
for the r. of inheritance is *Jer 32:8*
thine
and had done r. in my sight   *Jer 34:15*
be driven out every man r.   *Jer 49:5*
forth
with his r. hand as an adversary *La 2:4*
To turn aside the r. of a man *La 3:35*
the face of a lion, on the r. *Eze 1:10*
side
them, lie again on thy r. side *Eze 4:6*
the cherubims stood on the r. *Eze 10:3*
side
sister, that dwelleth at thy r. *Eze 16:46*
hand
and do that which is lawful   *Eze 18:5*
and r.
done that which is lawful   *Eze 18:19*
and r.
and do that which is lawful   *Eze 18:21*
and r.
doeth that which is lawful   *Eze 18:27*
and r.
way or other, either on the r. *Eze 21:16*
hand
At his r. hand was the   *Eze 21:22*
divination
until he come whose r. it is *Eze 21:27*
and do that which is lawful   *Eze 33:14*
and r.
done that which is lawful   *Eze 33:16*
and r.
and do that which is lawful   *Eze 33:19*
and r.
arrows to fall out of thy r. *Eze 39:3*
hand
from the r. side of the house *Eze 47:1*
there ran out waters on the r. *Eze 47:2*
side
held up his r. hand and his left *Da 12:7*
for the ways of the Lord are r. *Ho 14:9*

they know not to do r. saith *Am 3:10*
the poor in the gate from their *Am 5:12*
r.
twist everything that is r. (B) *Mic 3:9*
one upon the r. side of the   *Zec 4:3*
bowl
upon the r. side of the   *Zec 4:11*
candlestick
upon his arm and upon his r. *Zec 11:17*
eye
his r. eye shall be utterly   *Zec 11:17*
darkened
shall smite thee on thy r.   *M't 5:39*
cheek
hand know what thy r. hand   *M't 6:3*
doeth
whatsoever is r. I will give *M't 20:4*
and whatsoever is r. that shall *M't 20:7*
ye
may sit the one on thy r. hand *M't 20:21*
but to sit on my r. hand, and *M't 20:23*
on my
shall set the sheep on his r. *M't 25:33*
hand
King say unto them on his r. *M't 25:34*
hand
his head, and a reed in his r. *M't 27:29*
hand
one on the r. hand, and   *M't 27:38*
another on
and clothed, and in his r.   *M'k 5:15*
mind
we may sit, one on thy r.   *M'k 10:37*
hand
But to sit on my r. hand and *M'k 10:40*
on my
standing on the r. side of the *Lu 1:11*
altar
a man whose r. hand was   *Lu 6:6*
withered
Jesus, clothed, and in his r. *Lu 8:35*
mind
unto him, Thou hast answered *Lu 10:28*
r.
yourselves judge ye not what *Lu 12:57*
is r.
high priest, and cut off his r. *Lu 22:50*
ear
one on the r. hand, and the *Lu 23:33*
other
gave her r. to become (E)(N) *Joh 1:12*
my judgment is r. (A)(B)   *Joh 5:30*
I have the r. to (N)   *Joh 10:18*
servant, and cut off his r. ear *Joh 18:10*
the net on the r. side of the *Joh 21:6*
ship
raised to r. hand (P)   *Ac 2:33*
whether it be r. in the sight of *Ac 4:19*
rejoices in the r. (R)   *1Co 13:6*
righteousness on the r. hand *2Co 6:7*
and on
gave the r. hands of fellowship *Ga 2:9*
set him r. again (N)   *Ga 6:1*
set him back on the r. path (P) *Ga 6:1*
parents in the Lord: for this is *Eph 6:1*
r.
whereof they have no r. to   *Heb 13:10*
eat
conduct good and r. (P)   *1Pe 2:12*
revile your r. behavior   *1Pe 3:16*
(A)(R)
Which have forsaken the r.   *2Pe 2:15*
way
he had in his r. hand seven   *Re 1:16*
stars
And he laid his r. hand upon *Re 1:17*
me
which thou sawest in my r.   *Re 1:20*
hand
the seven stars in his r. hand *Re 2:1*
and he set his r. foot upon the *Re 10:2*
sea
to receive a mark in their r. *Re 13:16*
hand
they may have r. to the tree of *Re 22:14*
life

RIGHTEOUS

Noah was a r. man (E)(R)   *Ge 6:9*
thee have I seen r. before me in *Ge 7:1*
upright (B)   *Ge 7:1*
Wilt thou also destroy the r. *Ge 18:23*
with
the good (B)   *Ge 18:23; 18:24-25*
Peradventure there be fifty r. *Ge 18:24*
place for the fifty r. that are *Ge 18:24*
therein
to slay the r. with the wicked *Ge 18:25*

that the *r.* should be as the *Ge 18:25*
wicked
If I find in Sodom fifty *r.* *Ge 18:26*
within the
there shall lack five of the *Ge 18:28*
fifty *r.*
Lord, wilt thou slay also a *r.* *Ge 20:4*
nation
right and just (A) *Ge 20:4;*
       38:26; Job 15:14
blameless innocent (B)(R) *Ge 20:4*
She hath been more *r.* than I *Ge 38:26*
Lord is *r.* and I and my people *Ex 9:27*
right (A)(R) *Ex 9:27*
the innocent and *r.* slay thou *Ex 23:7*
not
guiltless (B) *Ex 23:7*
and perverteth the words of the *Ex 23:8*
r.
Let me die the death of the *r.* *Nu 23:10*
judgments so *r.* as all this law *De 4:8*
upright and just (A) *De 4:8*
judge with *r.* judgment *De 16:18*
(A)(E)(R)
wise, and pervert the words of *De 16:19*
the *r.*
the innocent (B) *De 16:19; 25:1*
then they shall justify the *r.* *De 25:1*
did the *r.* will of Lord (B) *De 33:21*
rehearse the *r.* acts of the Lord *J'g 5:11*
the *r.* acts toward the *J'g 5:11*
inhabitants
all the *r.* acts of the Lord, *1Sa 12:7*
which he
to David, Thou art more *r.* *1Sa 24:17*
than I
upright (A) *1Sa 24:17; Job 4:7*
fairer than I am (B) *1Sa 24:17*
wicked men have slain a *r.* *2Sa 4:11*
person
just man (A) *2Sa 4:11*
a good man (B) *2Sa 4:11*
who fell upon two men more *1Ki 2:32*
r. and
and justifying the *r.* to give *1Ki 8:32*
him
and said to all the people, Ye *2Ki 10:9*
be *r.*
just and innocent (A) *2Ki 10:9*
you are blameless (B) *2Ki 10:9*
and by justifying the *r.* by *2Ch 6:23*
giving
and they said, The Lord is *r.* *2Ch 12:6*
O Lord God of Israel, thou art *Ezr 9:15*
r.
performed thy words; for thou *Ne 9:8*
art *r.*
or where were the *r.* cut off *Job 4:7*
innocent (A) *Job 4:7; 34:5*
mortal man be *r.* (R) *Job 4:17*
though I were *r.* yet would I *Job 9:15*
not
though I am *r.* (E) *Job 9:20*
if I be *r.* yet will I not lift up *Job 10:15*
my
I know I am *r.* (E) *Job 13:18*
of a woman, that he should *Job 15:14*
be *r.*
The *r.* also shall hold on his *Job 17:9*
way
to the Almighty that thou art *r.* *Job 22:3*
The *r.* see it and are glad *Job 22:19*
the *r.* might dispute with him *Job 23:7*
upright person (B)(R) *Job 23:7*
how can man be *r.* (R) *Job 25:4*
because he was *r.* in his own *Job 32:1*
eyes
For Job hath said I am *r.* *Job 34:5*
condemn the *r.* (B)(E)(R) *Job 34:17*
If thou be *r.* what givest thou *Job 35:7*
him
withdraweth not eyes from *Job 36:7*
the *r.*
me that thou mayest be *r.* *Job 40:8*
in the congregation of the *r.* *Ps 1:5*
the Lord knoweth the way of the *Ps 1:6*
r.
For thou Lord wilt bless the *r.* *Ps 5:12*
for the *r.* God trieth the hearts *Ps 7:9*
establish the *r.* (A)(B)(E)(R) *Ps 7:9*
God judgeth the *r.* and God is *Ps 7:11*
be destroyed, what can the *r.* *Ps 11:3*
do
The Lord trieth the *r.*: but the *Ps 11:5*
the *r.* Lord loveth righteousness *Ps 11:7*
God is in the generation of the *Ps 14:5*
r.
Lord are true and *r.* altogether *Ps 19:9*

and contemptuously against *Ps 31:18*
the *r.*
glad in the Lord, and rejoice, *Ps 32:11*
ye *r.*
Rejoice in the Lord, O ye *r.*: for *Ps 33:1*
eyes of the Lord are upon the *Ps 34:15*
r.
The *r.* cry, and the Lord *Ps 34:17*
heareth
Many are the afflictions of the *Ps 34:19*
r.
that hate the *r.* shall be *Ps 34:21*
desolate
be glad, that favour my *r.* *Ps 35:27*
cause
but the Lord upholdeth the *r.* *Ps 37:17*
the *r.* sheweth mercy, and *Ps 37:21*
giveth
yet have I not seen the *r.* *Ps 37:25*
forsaken
The *r.* shall inherit the land *Ps 37:29*
mouth of the *r.* speaketh *Ps 37:30*
wisdom
The wicked watcheth the *r.* *Ps 37:32*
But the salvation of the *r.* is *Ps 37:39*
The *r.* also shall see, and fear *Ps 52:6*
never suffer the *r.* to be *Ps 55:22*
moved.
The *r.* shall rejoice when he *Ps 58:10*
seeth
Verily there is a reward for *Ps 58:11*
the *r.*
The *r.* shall be glad in the Lord *Ps 64:10*
let the *r.* be glad; let them *Ps 68:3*
rejoice
and not be written with the *r.* *Ps 69:28*
In his days shall the *r.* flourish *Ps 72:7*
horns of the *r.* shall be *Ps 75:10*
exalted
The *r.* shall flourish like the *Ps 92:12*
palm
together against the soul of *Ps 94:21*
the *r.*
Light is sown for the *r.* and *Ps 97:11*
Rejoice in the Lord, ye *r.*; and *Ps 97:12*
give
The *r.* shall see it, and rejoice *Ps 107:42*
and full of compassion, and *r.* *Ps 112:4*
the *r.* shall be in everlasting *Ps 112:6*
Gracious is the Lord, and *r.* *Ps 116:5*
is in the tabernacles of the *r.* *Ps 118:15*
Lord, into which the *r.* shall *Ps 118:20*
enter
have learned thy *r.* judgments *Ps 119:7*
thee because of thy *r.* *Ps 119:62*
judgments
that I will keep thy *r.* *Ps 119:106*
judgments
R. art thou, O Lord, and *Ps 119:137*
upright
that thou hast commanded *Ps 119:138*
are *r.*
according to *r.* decree (A) *Ps 119:149*
thy *r.* judgments endureth *Ps 119:160*
for ever
thee because of thy *r.* *Ps 119:164*
judgments
not rest upon the lot of the *r.* *Ps 125:3*
lest the *r.* put forth their *Ps 125:3*
hands
Lord is *r.*; he hath cut asunder *Ps 129:4*
r. shall give thanks unto thy *Ps 140:13*
name
Let the *r.* smite me; it shall be *Ps 141:5*
the *r.* shall compass me about *Ps 142:7*
no man living is *r.* (B)(E)(R) *Ps 143:2*
The Lord is *r.* in all his ways *Ps 145:17*
bowed down: the Lord loveth *Ps 146:8*
the *r.*
layeth up sound wisdom for the *Pr 2:7*
r.
the upright (Ь)(R) *Pr 2:7; 3:32*
men, and keep the paths of the *Pr 2:20*
r.
Lord: but his secret is with the *Pr 3:32*
r.
suffer the soul of the *r.* to *Pr 10:3*
famish
labour of the *r.* tendeth to life *Pr 10:16*
The lips of the *r.* feed many *Pr 10:21*
the desire of the *r.* shall be *Pr 10:24*
granted
the *r.* is an everlasting *Pr 10:25*
foundation
hope of the *r.* shall be gladness *Pr 10:28*
The *r.* shall never be removed *Pr 10:30*
The lips of the *r.* know what is *Pr 10:32*
The *r.* is delivered out of *Pr 11:8*
trouble

When it goeth well with the *r.* *Pr 11:10*
seed of the *r.* shall be *Pr 11:21*
delivered
The desire of the *r.* is only *Pr 11:23*
good
the *r.* shall flourish as a *Pr 11:28*
branch
The fruit of the *r.* is a tree of *Pr 11:30*
life
the *r.* shall be recompensed in *Pr 11:31*
root of the *r.* shall not be *Pr 12:3*
moved
The thoughts of the *r.* are right *Pr 12:5*
but the house of the *r.* shall *Pr 12:7*
stand
but the root of the *r.* yieldeth *Pr 12:12*
fruit
The *r.* is more excellent than *Pr 12:26*
his
The light of the *r.* rejoiceth: but *Pr 13:9*
but to the *r.* good shall be *Pr 13:21*
repayed
The *r.* eateth to the satisfying *Pr 13:25*
but among the *r.* there is favour *Pr 14:9*
the wicked at the gates of the *Pr 14:19*
r.
but the *r.* hath hope in his *Pr 14:32*
death
house of the *r.* is much treasure *Pr 15:6*
the way of the *r.* is made plain *Pr 15:19*
heart of the *r.* studieth to *Pr 15:28*
answer
but he heareth the prayer of *Pr 15:29*
the *r.*
R. lips are the delight of kings *Pr 16:13*
to overthrow the *r.* in judgment *Pr 18:5*
the *r.* runneth into it, and is *Pr 18:10*
safe
wicked shall be a ransom for *Pr 21:18*
the *r.*
but the *r.* giveth and spareth *Pr 21:26*
The father of the *r.* shall *Pr 23:24*
greatly
man, against the dwelling of *Pr 24:15*
the *r.*
saith unto the wicked, Thou *Pr 24:24*
art *r.*
but the *r.* are bold as a lion *Pr 28:1*
Whoso causeth the *r.* to go *Pr 28:10*
astray
when they perish, the *r.* *Pr 28:28*
increase
When the *r.* are in authority *Pr 29:2*
but the *r.* doth sing and rejoice *Pr 29:6*
r. considereth the cause of the *Pr 29:7*
poor
but the *r.* shall see their fall *Pr 29:16*
God shall judge thee *r.* and the *Ec 3:17*
Be not *r.* over much; neither *Ec 7:16*
make
according to the work of the *r.* *Ec 8:14*
that the *r.* and the wise, and *Ec 9:1*
their
there is one even to the *r.* and to *Ec 9:2*
Say ye to the *r.* that it shall be *Isa 3:10*
well
away the righteousness of the *Isa 5:23*
r.
we heard songs, even glory to *Isa 24:16*
the *r.*
r. nation which keepeth the *Isa 26:2*
truth
that we may say, He is *r.* *Isa 26:26*
thrust aside the *r.* (A) *Isa 29:21*
a *r.* and rescuing God *Isa 45:21*
(B)(R)
shall my *r.* servant justify *Isa 53:11*
many
my *r.* servant make many *r.* *Isa 53:11*
(B)(R)
r. perisheth, and no man *Isa 57:1*
layeth
the *r.* is taken away from the *Isa 57:1*
evil
ask of me *r.* judgments *Isa 58:2*
(A)(E)(R)
ask of me *r.* ordinances (B) *Isa 58:2*
Thy people also shall be all *Isa 60:21*
r.
shown herself more *r.* (B)(E) *Jer 3:11*
R. art thou, O Lord, when I *Jer 12:1*
plead
O Lord of hosts, that triest *Jer 20:12*
the *r.*
will raise unto David a *r.* *Jer 23:5*
Branch
Lord is *r.*; for I have rebelled *La 1:18*
that the *r.* sin not, and he doth *Eze 1:21*
not

have made the heart of the *r.*   *Eze 13:22*
sad
they are more *r.* than thou: *Eze 16:52*
yea
the righteousness of the *r.*   *Eze 18:20*
shall be
when the *r.* turneth away   *Eze 18:24*
from his
When a *r.* man turneth away   *Eze 18:26*
from
off from thee the *r.* and the   *Eze 21:3;*
wicked   *21:4*
righteousness of the *r.* shall   *Eze 33:12*
not
neither shall the *r.* be able to   *Eze 33:12*
live
When I shall say to the *r.*   *Eze 33:13*
that he
r. turneth from his   *Eze 33:18*
righteousness
Lord our God is *r.* in all his   *Da 9:14*
works
because they sold the *r.* for   *Am 2:6*
silver
wicked doth compass about   *Hab 1:4*
the *r.*
the man that is more *r.* than   *Hab 1:13*
he
Lord uncompromisingly *r.*   *Zep 3:5*
(A)(B)(E)(R)
he is *r.* and victorious (B)   *Zec 9:9*
between the *r.* and the wicked   *Mal 3:18*
Joseph was a *r.* man (E)   *M't 1:19;*
righteous (S)   *M't 1:19;*
13:49; 27:19, 24; M'k 6:20; Lu 2:25;
15:7; 20:20; 23:50; Ac 10:22
for I am not come to call the   *M't 9:13*
r.
shall the *r.* shine forth as the   *M't 9:43*
sun
wicked from the *r.*   *M't 13:49*
(A)(B)(E)(R)
also outwardly appear *r.* unto   *M't 23:28*
men
and garnish the sepulchres of   *M't 23:29*
the *r.*
all the *r.* blood shed upon the   *M't 23:35*
earth
blood of *r.* Abel unto the   *M't 23:35*
blood of
Then shall the *r.* answer him   *M't 25:37*
but the *r.* into life eternal   *M't 25:46*
that *r.* man (E)(R)   *M't 27:19*
this *r.* man's blood (A)(E)   *M't 27:24*
I came not to call the *r.* but   *M'k 2:17*
sinners
a *r.* and holy man   *M'k 6:20*
(A)(E)(R)
And they were both *r.* before   *Lu 1:6*
God
to the wisdom of the *r.*   *Lu 1:17*
(B)(N)
was *r.* and devout (A)(E)(R)   *Lu 2:25*
I came not to call the *r.* but   *Lu 5:32*
sinners
ninety-nine *r.*   *Lu 15:7*
(A)(B)(E)(N)(P)(R)
in themselves that they were *r.*   *Lu 18:9*
went home made *r.* (B)   *Lu 18:14*
reigned to be *r.* (E)   *Lu 20:20*
a good man and *r.*   *Lu 23:50*
(A)(E)(R)
my judgment is *r.* (E)   *Joh 5:30*
appearance, but judge *r.*   *Joh 7:24*
judgment
O *r.* Father, the world hath   *Joh 17:25*
not
Holy and *R.* One   *Ac 3:14*
(B)(E)(N)(P)(R)
coming of the *R.* One   *Ac 7:52*
(A)(E)(N)(P)
he was a *r.* man (S)   *Ac 11:24*
and revelation of the *r.*   *Ro 2:5*
judgment of
not hearers are *r.* (A)(B)(R)   *Ro 2:13*
There is none *r.*, no, not one   *Ro 3:10*
of one shall many be made *r.*   *Ro 3:19*
be made *r.* in God's sight (B)   *Ro 3:20*
who makes the ungodly *r.* (B)   *Ro 4:5*
made *r.* through faith (B)   *Ro 5:1;*
5:9; 8:30; 1Co 6:11; Ga 2:16
made *r.* and holy (P)   *1Co 1:30*
token of the *r.* judgment of   *2Th 1:5*
God
Seeing it is a *r.* thing with God   *2Th 1:6*
which the Lord, the *r.* judge,   *2Ti 4:8*
shall
he obtained witness that he   *Heb 11:4*
was *r.*

spirits of *r.* men (A)(B)   *Heb 12:23*
made *r.* due to works (B)   *Jas 2:21*
pronounced *r.* due (B)   *Jas 2:24; 2:25*
murdered the *r.* (A)(E)(R)   *Jas 5:6*
committed to *r.* judge (B)   *1Pe 2:23*
the eyes of the Lord are over   *1Pe 3:12*
the *r.*
if the *r.* scarcely be saved,   *1Pe 4:18*
where
delivered *r.* Lot   *2Pe 2:7*
(A)(E)(P)(R)
vexed his *r.* soul from day to   *2Pe 2:8*
day
the Father, Jesus Christ the *r.*   *1Jo 2:1*
If ye know that he is *r.* ye   *1Jo 2:29*
know
righteousness is *r.* even as he is   *1Jo 3:7*
r.
were evil and his brother's *r.*   *1Jo 3:12*
Thou art *r.* O Lord, which art   *Re 16:5*
true and *r.* are thy judgments   *Re 16:7*
For true and *r.* are his   *Re 19:2*
judgments
be filthy still: and he that is *r.*   *Re 22:11*
let him be *r.* still: and he that   *Re 22:11*

RIGHTEOUS MAN, MEN

a little that a *r. man* hath is   *Ps 37:46*
better
the mouth of a *r. man* is a   *Pr 10:11*
well of life
a *r. man* regardeth the life of   *Pr 12:10*
his beast
a *r. man* hateth lying, but   *Pr 13:5*
wicked is loathsome
a *r. man* wisely considereth   *Pr 21:12*
the house
a *r. man* falling down before   *Pr 25:26*
the wicked
when *r. men* do rejoice, there   *Pr 28:12*
is glory
who raised up the *r. man* from   *Isa 41:2*
the east
again, when a *r. man* doth   *Eze 3:20;*
turn   *18:26*
nevertheless, if thou warn the   *Eze 3:21*
r. man
and the *r. men,* they shall   *Eze 23:45*
judge them
receiveth a *r. man* in name of   *M't 10:41*
a *r. man,* shall receive a *r.*
man's reward
many *r. men* have desired to   *M't 13:17*
see those things
saying, Certainly this was a *r.*   *Lu 23:47*
man
scarcely for a *r. man* will one   *Ro 5:7*
die
that the law is not made for a   *1Ti 1:9*
r. man.
the fervent prayer of a *r. man*   *Jas 5:16*
availeth
for that *r. man* dwelling among   *2Pe 2:8*
them

RIGHTEOUSLY

judge *r.* between every man   *De 1:16*
rulers decree *r.* (B)   *2Sa 8:15*
for thou shalt judge the people   *Ps 67:4*
r.
he shall judge the people *r.*   *Ps 96:10*
Open thy mouth, judge *r.* and   *Pr 31:9*
He that walketh *r.* and   *Isa 33:15*
speaketh
O Lord of hosts, that judgest   *Jer 11:20*
r.
holily, *r.,* unblamably (E)(R)   *1Th 2:10*
we should live soberly, *r.* and   *Tit 2:12*
himself to him that judgeth *r.*   *1Pe 2:23*

RIGHTEOUSNESS

r. and justice (S)   *Ge 18:19;*
Ps 89:14; Pr 1:3; 21:3
it shall be our *r.* if we observe   *De 6:25*
to do
it shall be *r.* to thee before   *De 24:13*
Lord
there they shall offer sacrifices   *De 33:19*
of *r.*
executed *r.* of Jehovah   *De 33:21*
(E)(S)
justice and *r.* (S)   *2Sa 8:15;*
1Ch 18:14; 2Ch 9:8; Ps 119:121; Ec 5:8;
Jer 22:15; 23:5; Eze 45:9
to execute justice and *r.* (S)   *1Ki 10:9*
I put on *r.* and it clothed me   *Job 29:14*

and I will ascribe *r.* to my   *Job 36:3*
Maker
in plenteous *r.* (S)   *Job 37:23*
offer sacrifices of *r.* and trust in   *Ps 4:5*
Lord
for the righteous Lord loveth   *Ps 11:7;*
r.   *33:5*
he that worketh *r.* shall never   *Ps 15:2*
be moved
he leadeth me in paths of *r.* for   *Ps 23:3*
name's sake
and *r.* from the God of his   *Ps 24:5*
salvation
I have preached *r.* in the great   *Ps 40:9*
congregation
because of truth, and   *Ps 45:4*
meekness, and *r.*
thou lovest *r.* and hatest   *Ps 45:7;*
wickedness   *Heb 1:9*
thy right hand, O God, is full   *Ps 48:10*
of *r.*
then shalt be pleased with   *Ps 51:19*
sacrifices of *r.*
thou lovest lying, rather than to   *Ps 52:3*
speak *r.*
do ye indeed speak *r.* O   *Ps 58:1*
congregation
he shall judge thy people with   *Ps 72:2*
r. and poor
mountains shall bring peace   *Ps 72:3*
and little hills by *r.*
r. and peace have kissed each   *Ps 85:10*
other
and *r.* shall look down from   *Ps 85:11*
heaven
r. shall go before him, and set   *Ps 85:13*
us in
but judgment shall return unto   *Ps 94:15*
r.
he shall judge the world with   *Ps 96:13;*
r.   *98:9*
r. is the habitation of his   *Ps 97:2*
throne
thou executest *r.* in Jacob   *Ps 99:4;*
103:6
blessed is he that doeth *r.* at   *Ps 106:3*
all times
open to me the gates of *r.* I   *Ps 118:19*
will go into
r. of thy testimonies is   *Ps 119:144*
everlasting
for all thy commandments   *Ps 119:172*
are *r.*
let thy priests be clothed with   *Ps 132:9*
r.
then shalt thou understand *r.*   *Pr 2:9*
yea, durable riches and *r.* are   *Pr 8:18*
with me
I lead in the way of *r.*   *Pr 8:20*
but *r.* delivereth from death   *Pr 10:2;*
11:4
r. of the perfect shall direct his   *Pr 11:5*
way
the *r.* of the upright shall   *Pr 11:6*
deliver them
to him that soweth *r.* shall be   *Pr 11:18*
a reward
as *r.* tendeth to life so he that   *Pr 11:19*
pursueth evil
he that speaketh truth,   *Pr 12:17*
sheweth forth *r.*
in the way of *r.* is life and in   *Pr 12:28*
the pathway
r. keepeth him that is upright   *Pr 13:6*
in the way
r. exalteth a nation, sin is a   *Pr 14:34*
reproach to
he loveth him that followeth   *Pr 15:9*
after *r.*
better is a little with *r.* than   *Pr 16:8*
great revenues
for the throne is established   *Pr 16:12*
by *r.*
is a crown of glory, if found   *Pr 16:31*
in the way of *r.*
he that followeth after *r.* and   *Pr 21:21*
mercy findeth life, *r.* and honour
and the place of *r.* that iniquity   *Ec 3:16*
was there
the place of *r.* (E)   *Ec 3:16*
r. lodged in it, but now   *Isa 1:21*
murderers
the city of *r.*   *Isa 1:26;*
Isa 1:27
her converts with *r.*   *Isa 1:27*
which take away the *r.* of the   *Isa 5:23*
righteous
with justice and *r.*   *Isa 9:7*
(A)(B)(E)(R)(S)

consumption decreed shall overflow with r. — *Isa 10:22*
but with r. shall he judge the poor — *Isa 11:4*
and r. shall be the girdle of his loins — *Isa 11:5*
judging and seeking judgment, and hasting r. — *Isa 16:5*
the inhabitants of the world will learn r. — *Isa 26:9*
let favour be shewed, yet will he not learn r. — *Isa 26:10*
and r. will I lay to the plummet — *Isa 28:17*
and r. shall remain in the fruitful field — *Isa 32:16*
and the work of r. shall be peace, and the effect of r. — *Isa 32:17*
Lord hath filled Zion with judgment and r. — *Isa 33:5*
let skies pour down r. and let r. spring up together — *Isa 45:8*
I the Lord speak r. I declare right things — *Isa 45:19*
in the Lord have I r. — *Isa 45:24*
hearken unto me, ye that are far from r. — *Isa 46:12; 51:17*
ye that follow after r. — *Isa 51:1*
ye that know r. — *Isa 51:7*
their r. is of me, saith the Lord — *Isa 54:17*
yet they seek me as a nation that did r. — *Isa 58:2*
for he put on r. as a breastplate — *Isa 59:17*
will make thy officers peace, thine exact r. — *Isa 60:17*
that they might be called trees of r. — *Isa 61:3*
he hath covered me with the robe of r. — *Isa 61:10*
so Lord will cause r. and praise to spring forth — *Isa 61:11*
until the r. thereof go forth as brightness — *Isa 62:1*
thou meetest him that rejoiceth and worketh r. — *Isa 64:5*
that I am the Lord which exercise r. — *Jer 9:24*
execute ye judgment and r. and deliver — *Jer 22:3*
execute judgment and r. (B) — *Jer 23:5*
this is his name, the Lord our r. — *Jer 23:6; 33:16*
habitation of r. (B)(E)(R) — *Jer 31:23*
at that time will I cause the branch of r. to grow up to David, and he shall execute r. — *Jer 33:15*
the Lord hath brought forth our r. — *Jer 51:10*
deliver their own souls by their r. — *Eze 14:14; 14:20*
the r. of the righteous shall be upon him — *Eze 18:20*
r. of the righteous shall not deliver him — *Eze 33:12*
and break off thy sins by r. — *Da 4:27*
O Lord r. belongeth unto thee, but to us — *Da 9:7*
to bring in everlasting r. — *Da 9:24*
that turn many to r. shall shine as stars — *Da 12:3*
till he come and rain r. upon you — *Ho 10:12*
who leave off r. in the earth — *Am 5:7*
and let r. run down as a mighty stream — *Am 5:24*
ye have turned the fruit of r. into hemlock — *Am 6:12*
that ye may know the r. of the Lord — *Mic 6:5*
all ye meek of earth, seek r. seek meekness — *Zep 2:3*
to you that fear shall the Sun of r. arise — *Mal 4:2*
thus it becometh us to fulfil all r. — *M't 3:15*
blessed are they that hunger and thirst after r. — *M't 5:6*
except your r. exceed the r. of the Scribes — *M't 5:20*
for John came to you in the way of r. — *M't 21:32*
in r. before him all the days of our life — *Lu 1:75*
claim r. in human eyes (A) — *Lu 16:15*
impress fellowmen with r. (N) — *Lu 16:15*

he will reprove the world of sin and of r. — *Joh 16:8*
of r. because I go to my Father, ye see me no more — *Joh 16:10*
he that worketh r. is accepted with him — *Ac 10:35*
thou enemy of all r. wilt thou not cease — *Ac 13:10*
as he reasoned of r. and judgment Felix trembled — *Ac 24:25*
for therein is the r. of God revealed — *Ro 1:17*
if uncircumcision keep the r. of the law — *Ro 2:26*
if our unrighteousness commend the r. of God — *Ro 3:5*
the r. of God, without the law is manifested — *Ro 3:21*
even the r. of God which is by faith of Christ — *Ro 3:22*
to whom God imputeth r. without works — *Ro 4:6*
God reckoneth r. (E)(R) — *Ro 4:6*
a seal of the r. of the faith, — *Ro 4:11*
that r. might be imputed — *Ro 4:11*
reckoned to them (E) — *Ro 4:11*
the promise was through the r. of faith — *Ro 4:13*
they which receive gift of r. shall reign — *Ro 5:17*
so by the r. of one the free gift came on all — *Ro 5:18*
so might grace reign through r. to eternal life — *Ro 5:21*
yield your members instruments of r. to God — *Ro 6:13*
whether of sin to death, or of obedience unto r. — *Ro 6:16*
free from sin, ye became the servants of r. — *Ro 6:18*
so now yield your members servants to r. — *Ro 6:19*
when ye were servants of sin, ye were free from r. — *Ro 6:20*
that the r. of the law might be fulfilled in us — *Ro 8:4*
but the spirit is life because of r. — *Ro 8:10*
Gentiles followed not after r. have attained to r. even the r. of — *Ro 9:30*
Israel which followed after the law of r. hath not attained to the law of r. — *Ro 9:31*
going about to establish their own r. have not submitted to the r. of God — *Ro 10:3*
Moses describeth the r. which is of the law — *Ro 10:5*
the r. which is of faith speaketh on this wise — *Ro 10:6*
for with the heart man believeth unto r. — *Ro 10:10*
kingdom of God not meat and drink, but r. — *Ro 14:17*
in Christ, who of God is made unto us r. — *1Co 1:30*
awake to r. and sin not, for some have not — *1Co 15:34*
much more doth the ministration of r. — *2Co 3:9*
that we might be made the r. of God in him — *2Co 5:21*
by the armour of r. on the right hand and left — *2Co 6:7*
what fellowship hath r. with unrighteousness — *2Co 6:14*
your seed and increase the fruits of your r. — *2Co 9:10*
be transformed as the ministers of r. — *2Co 11:15*
if r. come by law, Christ is dead in vain — *Ga 2:21*
reckoned to him for r. (E)(N)(P)(R) — *Ga 3:6*
verily, r. should have been by the law — *Ga 3:21*
we through the Spirit wait for the hope of r. — *Ga 5:5*
fruit of the Spirit is in all r. and truth — *Eph 5:9*
and having on the breastplate of r. — *Eph 6:14*
being filled with the fruits of r. by Jesus — *Ph'p 1:11*
touching r. which is in the law, blameless — *Ph'p 3:6*
but the r. which is of God by faith — *Ph'p 3:9*

and follow after r. — *1Ti 6:11; 2Ti 2:22*
there is laid up for me a crown of r. — *2Ti 4:8*
not by works of r. which we have done — *Tit 3:5*
a sceptre of r. is sceptre of thy kingdom — *Heb 1:8*
is unskilful in the word of r. he is a babe — *Heb 5:13*
first being by interpretation king of r. — *Heb 7:2*
and became heir of the r. which is by faith — *Heb 11:7*
through faith subdued kingdoms, wrought r. — *Heb 11:33*
afterward it yieldeth peaceable fruit of r. — *Heb 12:11*
wrath of man worketh not r. of God — *Jas 1:20*
the fruit of r. is sown in peace of them — *Jas 3:18*
we being dead to sin should live unto r. — *1Pe 2:24*
obtained like faith through the r. of God — *2Pe 1:1*
spared not, but saved Noe a preacher of r. — *2Pe 2:5*
been better not to have known the way of r. — *2Pe 2:21*
we look for a new earth, wherein dwelleth r. — *2Pe 3:13*
every one that doeth r. is born of God — *1Jo 2:29*
he that doeth r. is righteous, as he is righteous — *1Jo 3:7*
whosoever doth not r. is not of God — *1Jo 3:10*
for the fine linen is the r. of saints — *Re 19:8*

FOR RIGHTEOUSNESS

Abram believed the Lord, and he counted it for r. — *Ge 15:6*
Ps 106:31; Ro 4:3
for thy r. sake bring my soul out of — *Ps 143:11*
he looked for r. but behold a cry — *Isa 5:7*
blessed are they which are persecuted for r. — *M't 5:10*
his faith is counted for r. — *Ro 4:5; Ga 3:6*
reckoned, imputed to him for r. — *Ro 4:9; 4:22; Jas 2:23*
for Christ is the end of the law for r. — *Ro 10:4*
if ye suffer for r. sake, happy are ye — *1Pe 3:14*

HIS RIGHTEOUSNESS

the Lord render to every man his r. — *1Sa 26:23*
to give according to his r. — *1Ki 8:32; 2Ch 6:23*
for he will render unto man his r. — *Job 33:26*
I will praise the Lord according to his r. — *Ps 7:17*
they shall declare his r. to a people be borne — *Ps 22:31*
the heavens shall declare his r. — *Ps 50:6; 97:6*
his r. hath he openly shewed in the sight — *Ps 98:2*
and his r. unto children's children — *Ps 103:17*
and his r. endureth for ever — *Ps 111:3; 112:3, 9*
there is a just man that perisheth in his r. — *Ec 7:15*
the Lord is well pleased for his r. sake — *Isa 42:21*
brought salvation, and his r. sustained him — *Isa 59:16*
again, when a righteous man doth turn from his r. — *Eze 3:20; 18:24, 26*
in his r. that he hath done he shall live — *Eze 18:22*
not be able to live for his r. in the day — *Eze 33:12*
if he trust to his own r. and commit iniquity, his r. he hath done shall not be remembered — *Eze 33:13*
will bring to light, and I shall behold his r. — *Mic 7:9*
but seek the kingdom of God, and his r. — *M't 6:33*

to declare *his* r. for remission Ro 3:25;
of sins 3:26
given to the poor, *his* r. 2Co 9:9
remaineth for ever

IN RIGHTEOUSNESS

in r. shalt thou judge thy Le 19:15
neighbour
as he walked before thee in 1Ki 3:6
truth and *in* r.
and he shall judge the world *in* r. Ps 9:8
as for me, I will behold thy Ps 17:15
face *in* r.
by terrible things *in* r. wilt thou Ps 65:5
answer
all the words of my mouth are *in* Pr 8:8
r.
his throne shall be established Pr 25:5
in r.
God that is holy shall be Isa 5:16
sanctified *in* r.
a king shall reign *in* r. and Isa 32:1
princes
I the Lord have called thee *in* Isa 42:6
r.
I have raised him *in* r. and Isa 45:13
will direct
the word is gone out of my Isa 45:23
mouth *in* r.
mention the God of Israel, but Isa 48:1
not *in* r.
in r. shalt thou be established Isa 54:14
I that speak *in* r. mighty to Isa 63:1
save
thou shalt swear, the Lord Jer 4:2
liveth, *in* r.
I will betroth thee unto me *in* Ho 2:19
r.
sow to yourselves *in* r. reap in Ho 10:12
mercy
I will be their God in truth and Zec 8:8
in r.
that they may offer an offering Mal 3:3
in r.
he will judge the world *in* r. Ac 17:31
he will finish and cut it short Ro 9:28
in r.
which after God is created *in* Eph 4:24
r.
scripture is for instruction *in* 2Ti 3:16
r.
in r. he doth judge and make Re 19:11
war

MY RIGHTEOUSNESS

so *my* r. answer for me in Ge 30:33
time to come
saying, For *my* r. Lord hath De 9:4
brought me
Lord rewarded me according 2Sa 22:2;
to *my* r. 22:25; Ps 18:20, 24
yea, return again, *my* r. is in it Job 6:29
my r. I hold fast, and will not Job 27:6
let it go
that thou saidst, My r. is Job 35:2
more than God's
hear me when I call, O God of Ps 4:1
my r.
judge me, O Lord, according to Ps 7:8
my r.
uphold thee with the right Isa 41:10
hand of *my* r.
I bring near *my* r. Isa 46:13
my r. is near Isa 51:5
and *my* r. shall not be Isa 51:6
abolished
but *my* r. shall be for ever, and Isa 51:8
my salvation
salvation is near to come, *my* r. Isa 56:1
to be revealed
may be found, not having Ph'p 3:9
mine own r.

THY RIGHTEOUSNESS

nor for *thy* r. or uprightness De 9:5; 9:6
make the habitation of *thy* r. Job 8:6
prosperous
and *thy* r. may profit the son Job 35:8
of man
lead me, O Lord, in *thy* r. Ps 5:8
because
in thee I trust, deliver me in *thy* Ps 31:1;
r. 71:2
judge me, O Lord, according Ps 35:24
to *thy* r.

and my tongue shall speak of Ps 35:28;
thy r. 71:24
thy r. is like the great Ps 36:6
mountains
O continue *thy* r. to the Ps 36:10
upright in heart
he shall bring forth *thy* r. as the Ps 37:6
light
I have not hid *thy* r. within my Ps 40:10
heart
and my tongue shall sing Ps 51:14
aloud of *thy* r.
and let them not come into Ps 69:27
thy r.
my mouth shall shew forth *thy* Ps 71:15
r. all day
I will make mention of *thy* r. Ps 71:16
of thine only
thy r. O God, is very high, Ps 71:19
who is like to thee
and give *thy* r. unto the king's Ps 72:1
son
thy r. be known in land of Ps 88:12
forgetfulness
and in *thy* r. shall they be Ps 89:16
exalted
quicken me in *thy* r. Ps 119:40;
word of *thy* r. 119:123
thy r. is an everlasting Ps 119:142
righteousness thy law is
in faithfulness answer me, Ps 143:1
and in *thy* r.
and they shall sing of *thy* r. Ps 145:7
then had *thy* r. been as waves Isa 48:18
of the sea
I will declare *thy* r. and thy Isa 57:12
works
thy r. shall go before thee, Isa 58:8
glory of Lord
and the Gentiles shall see *thy* Isa 62:2
r. and kings
O Lord, according to all *thy* r. Da 9:16

RIGHTEOUSNESS'

for thy r. sake bring my soul Ps 143:11
out
is well pleased for his r. sake Isa 42:21
which are persecuted for r. M't 5:10
sake
But and if ye suffer for r. sake 1Pe 3:14

RIGHTEOUSNESSES

and all our r. are as filthy rags Isa 64:6
all his r. shall not be Eze 33:13
remembered
supplications before thee for Da 9:18
our r.
the r. of the saints (S) Re 19:8

RIGHTFUL

stripped himself of all Ph'p 2:7
privileges and r. dignity (A)(P)

RIGHTLY

he said, Is not he r. named Ge 27:36
Jacob
said unto him, Thou hast r. Lu 7:43
judged
that thou sayest and teachest Lu 20:21
ashamed, r. dividing the word 2Ti 2:15

RIGHTS

her marital r. (B)(R) Ex 21:10
do not violate r. of immigrant De 24:17
or orphan
defend the r. of the poor (B) Pr 23:11
pervert the r. of afflicted Pr 31:5
(B)(R)
maintain the r. of (R) Pr 31:9
your r. are overlooked (B) Isa 40:27
r. of Israel as a nation (A) Eph 2:12

RIGOUR

children of Israel to serve with Ex 1:13
r.
reduced Israelites to severe Ex 1:13
slavery (A)
enslaved the sons of Israel (B) Ex 1:13
they made them serve, was Ex 1:14
with r.
service with harshness and Ex 1:14
severity (A)

forced them by harsh treatment Ex 1:14
(B)
Thou shalt not rule over him Le 25:43
with r.
rule over him with harshness Le 25:43
(A)(R)
lord it over him with severity Le 25:43
(B)
not rule one over another with Le 25:46
r.
rule over another with Le 25:46
harshness (A)(R)
not lord it with severity (B) Le 25:46
other shall not rule with r. Le 25:53
over him
rule over him with harshness Le 25:53
(A)(R)
not severely lord it over him Le 25:53
(B)

RIM

rim (S) Ex 25:11;
25:24, 25; 30:3, 4; 37:2, 11-12, 26-27
under the r. of it (A) Ex 30:4

RIMMON

and Shilhim, and Ain, and R. Jos 15:32
the wilderness unto the rock J'g 20:45
of R.
to the wilderness unto the J'g 20:47
rock R.
abode in the rock R. four J'g 20:47
months
Benjamin that were in the J'g 21:13
rock R.
the sons of R. a Beerothite, of 2Sa 4:2
the sons of R. the Beerothite 2Sa 4:5;
4-9
master goeth into the house of 2Ki 5:18
R.
I bow myself in the house of 2Ki 5:18
R.
bow down myself in the house 2Ki 5:18
of R.
villages were, Etam, and Ain, 1Ch 4:32
R.
R. with her suburbs, Tabor 1Ch 6:77
Geba to R. south of Zec 14:10
Jerusalem

RIMMON-PAREZ

from Rithmah, and pitched at Nu 33:19
R.
And they departed from R. Nu 33:20

RIMS

their naves and their r. (S) 1Ki 7:33
as for their r. (S) Eze 1:18

RING

ring (B)(R) Ge 24:22;
24:30, 47; Job 42:11; Pr 25:12
r. in her nose (S) Ge 24:22; 24:30, 47
Pharaoh took off his r. from Ge 41:42
his
above the head of it unto one Ex 26:24
r.
at the head thereof, to one r. Ex 36:29
the king took his r. from his Es 3:10
hand
and sealed with the king's r. Es 3:12
And the king took off his r. Es 8:2
name, and seal it with the king's Es 8:8
r.
name, and sealed with the king's Es 8:8
r.
and sealed it with the king's r. Es 8:10
r. of gold in a swine's Pr 11:22
(A)(B)(E)(R)
nose r. of gold (A) Pr 25:12
put r. on nostril Eze 16:12
(A)(B)(E)(R)
put a r. on his hand, and Lu 15:22
shoes on
assembly a man with a gold r. Jas 2:2

RINGLEADER

a r. of the sect of the Ac 24:5
Nazarenes

RINGS

shalt cast four r. of gold for it Ex 25:12
25:12, 14, 15, 26, 27

RINGS (cont.)

make their r. of gold for places for	Ex 26:29
four brasen r. in the four corners	Ex 27:4
the staves shall be put into the r.	Ex 27:7
upon the breastplate two r. of gold	Ex 28:23; 28:24, 26-28
two golden r. shalt thou make to it	Ex 30:4
bracelets, and earrings, and r.	Ex 35:22
made their r. of gold to be places	Ex 36:34
And he cast for it four r. of gold, to	Ex 37:3 37:5, 13, 14, 27
he cast four r. for the four ends	Ex 38:5
he put the staves into the r. on	Ex 38:7
two ouches of gold, and two gold r.	Ex 39:6; 39:16, 17, 19, 20, 21
chains, and bracelets, r., earrings	Nu 31:50
to silver r. and pillars of marble	Es 1:6
His hands are as gold r. set	Ca 5:14
The r. and nose jewels	Isa 3:21
the r. (S)	Isa 3:21
As for their r. they were so high	Eze 1:18
and their r. were full of eyes round	Eze 1:18

RINGSTRAKED

he goats that were r. and spotted	Ge 30:35
streaked (A)	Ge 30:35; 39:39, 40, 31:8, 10, 12
striped (B)(R)	Ge 30:35; 39:39, 40; 31:8, 10, 12
brought forth cattle r., speckled	Ge 30:39
the faces of the flocks toward the r.	Ge 30:40
said thus, The r. shall be thy hire	Ge 31:8
then bare all the cattle r.	Ge 31:8
leaped upon the cattle were r.	Ge 31:10
which leap upon the cattle are r.	Ge 31:12

RINNAH

of Shimon were, Amnon, and R.	1Ch 4:20

RINSED

be both scoured, and r. in water	Le 6:28
and hath not r. his hands in water	Le 15:11
vessel of wood shall be r. in water	Le 15:12

RIOT

but rather a r. (A)(B)(N)(R)	M't 27:24
for raising a r. (A)(B)(P)	Lu 23:19
for r. and murder (A)(B)(P)	Lu 23:25
wine, wherein is r. (E)	Eph 5:18
faithful children not accused of r.	Tit 1:6
with them to the same excess of r.	1Pe 4:4
count it pleasure to r. in the day	2Pe 2:13

RIOTERS

with some other r. (P)	M'k 5:7

RIOTING

abounding in r. (B)	Eze 22:5
not in r. and drunkenness, not in	Ro 13:13

RIOTOUS

among r. eaters of flesh	Pr 23:20
is a companion of r. men shameth	Pr 28:7
wasted his substance with r. living	Lu 15:13

RIOTS

without mobs or r. (B)	Ac 24:18
r., mobbings (A)(B)(P)(R)	2Co 6:5

RIP

and r. up their women with child	2Ki 8:12

RIPE

clusters brought forth r. grapes	Ge 40:10
delay to offer the first of thy r. fruits	Ex 22:29
figs, even like the figs that are first r.	Jer 24:2
in the sickle, for the harvest is r.	Joe 3:13
r. for destruction (A)	Ro 9:22
the time was r. (N)	Eph 1:10
for the harvest of the earth is r.	Re 14:15
earth; for her grapes are fully r.	Re 14:18

RIPENING

the sour grape is r. in the flower	Isa 18:5

RIPHATH

sons of Gomer; Ashkenaz and R.	Ge 10:3
sons of Gomer; Ashchenaz, and R.	1Ch 1:6

RIPPED

the women with child he r. up	2Ki 15:16
women with child shall be r. up	Ho 13:16
have r. up the women with child of Gilead	Am 1:13

RISE

if he r. again and walk abroad	Ex 21:19
and a sceptre shall r. out of Israel	Nu 24:17
smite them that r. that they r. not again	De 33:11
they shall r. and go through the land	Jos 18:4
then they said, R. thou, and fall on us	J'g 8:21
thou shalt r. early, and set upon the city	J'g 9:33
that he should r. to lie in wait	1Sa 22:13
and suffered them not to r. against Saul	1Sa 24:7
when child was dead, thou didst r.	2Sa 12:21
all that r. against thee be as Absalom is	2Sa 18:32
upon my right hand r. the youth	Job 30:12
wounded them, they were not able to r.	Ps 18:38
tho' war should r. against me, will be confident	Ps 27:3
they are cast down, shall not be able to r.	Ps 36:12
at midnight I will r. to give thanks to thee	Ps 119:62
into deep pits, that they r. not up again	Ps 140:10
for their calamity shall r. suddenly	Pr 24:22
when the wicked r. a man is hidden	Pr 28:12; 28:28
her children r. up (S)	Pr 31:28
I will r. now and go about the city	Ca 3:2
prepare slaughter, that they do not r.	Isa 14:21
the earth shall fall and not r. again	Isa 24:20
they are deceased, they shall not r.	Isa 26:14
now will I r. saith the Lord	Isa 33:10
they shall lie down together they shall not r.	Isa 43:17
every tongue that shall r. thou shalt condemn	Isa 54:17
then shall thy light r. in obscurity	Isa 58:10
Shall they fall, and not r. (S)	Jer 8:4
drink ye, spue, fall and r. no more	Jer 25:27
Babylon shall not r. from evil I will bring	Jer 51:64
the virgin of Israel shall no more r.	Am 5:2
I will r. against the house of Jeroboam	Am 7:9
he maketh sun to r. on evil and good	M't 5:45
crucify him, and third day he shall r. again	M't 20:19 M'k 9:31; 10:34; Lu 18:33; 24:7
nation shall r. against nation	M't 24:7; M'k 13:8; Lu 21:10
many false prophets shall r.	M't 24:11; M'k 13:22
r. let us be going, behold, he is at hand	M't 26:46
after three days I will r. again	M't 27:63; M'k 8:31
and should sleep, and r. night and day	M'k 4:27
be of good comfort, r. he calleth thee	M'k 10:49
in resurrection, when they r.	M'k 12:23; 12:25
and as touching the dead, that they r.	M'k 12:26
trouble me not, I cannot r. and give	Lu 11:7
though he will not r. because he is his friend	Lu 11:8
when ye see a cloud r. out of the west	Lu 12:54
he said to them, Why sleep ye? r. and pray	Lu 22:46
it behoved Christ to suffer and to r. from	Lu 24:46
Jesus saith, R., take up thy bed and walk	Joh 5:8
Jesus saith, Thy brother shall r. again	Joh 11:23
I know he shall r.	Joh 11:24
he must r. again	Joh 20:9
came a voice R. Peter, kill and eat	Ac 10:13
but r. and stand upon thy feet	Ac 26:16
should be the first that should r. from the dead	Ac 26:23
he that shall r. to reign over Gentiles	Ro 15:12
if so be the dead r. not	1Co 15:15; 15:16, 29, 32
the dead in Christ shall r. first	1Th 4:16
what need that another priest should r.	Heb 7:11
r. and measure the temple of God	Re 11:1

RISE UP

ye shall r. up early and go on your ways	Ge 19:2
let it not displease, that I cannot r. up	Ge 31:35
r. up and stand before Pharaoh	Ex 8:20; 9:13
r. up and get you forth from my people	Ex 12:31
thou shalt r. up before the hoary head	Le 19:32
r. up, Lord, let enemies be scattered	Nu 10:35
if men come to call thee up, r. up and go	Nu 22:20
r. up, Balak, and hear, thou son of Zippor	Nu 23:18
the people shall r. up as a lion	Nu 23:24
now r. up, said I, and get over brook	De 2:13
r. ye up, and pass over the river Arnon	De 2:24
if a man r. up against his neighbour	De 19:11
one witness shall not r. up against a man	De 19:15
if a false witness r. up against any man	De 19:16
the Lord will cause thine enemies that r. up	De 28:7
the generation that shall r. up after you	De 29:22
this people will r. up, and go a whoring	De 31:16
their gods, let them r. up and help you	De 32:38
then ye shall r. up from the ambush	Jos 8:7
should make a great flame r. up	J'g 20:38; 20:40

wherefore, r. up early in   *1Sa 29:10*
morning
and they said, Let us r. up and   *Ne 2:18*
build
and the earth shall r. up   *Job 20:27*
against him
many are they that r. up against   *Ps 3:1*
me
save them from those that r. up   *Ps 17:7*
against them
liftest me above those that r.   *Ps 18:48*
up against me
false witnesses did r. up, they   *Ps 35:11*
laid to my charge
now that he lieth, he shall r. up   *Ps 41:8*
no more
we will tread them under that   *Ps 44:5*
r. up against us
defend me from them that r. up   *Ps 59:1*
against me
the tumult of those that r. up   *Ps 74:23*
against thee
desire of the wicked that r. up   *Ps 92:11*
against me
who will r. up for me against   *Ps 94:16*
the evil-doers
it is vain for you to r. up   *Ps 127:2*
early, to sit up late
grieved with those that r. up   *Ps 139:21*
against thee
her children r. up, and call her   *Pr 31:28*
blessed
if the spirit of the ruler r. up   *Ec 10:4*
against thee
he shall r. *up* at the voice of   *Ec 12:4*
the bird
my beloved said to me, R. *up*   *Ca 2:10*
my love
woe unto them that r. up in   *Isa 5:11*
the morning
I will r. up against them, saith   *Isa 14:22*
the Lord
the Lord shall r. up as in   *Isa 28:21*
mount Perazim
r. up, ye women at ease, hear   *Isa 32:9*
my voice
should r. up every man in his   *Jer 37:10*
tent
behold, waters r. up out of the   *Jer 47:2*
north
gather against her, and r. up   *Jer 49:14*
to battle
against them that r. up against   *Jer 51:1*
me, a wind
from whom I am not able to r.   *La 1:14*
up
it shall r. up wholly as a flood   *Am 8:8;*
                                9:5
even they shall fall, and never   *Am 8:14*
r. up again
let us r. up against Edom in   *Ob 1*
battle
affliction shall not r. up the   *Na 1:9*
second time
shall they not r. up suddenly   *Hab 2:7*
that bite
until the day that I r. up to the   *Zep 3:8*
prey
his hand r. up against his   *Zec 14:13*
neighbour
children r. up against   *M't 10:21;*
parents, put to death   *M'k 13:12*
the men of Nineveh shall r.   *M't 12:41;*
up   *Lu 11:32*
queen of the south shall r. up   *M'k 2:42;*
                               Lu 11:31
and if Satan r. up against   *M'k 3:26*
himself
r. *up*, lo, he that betrayeth   *M'k 14:42*
me is at hand
whether is easier to say, R. up   *Lu 5:23*
and walk
he said, R. up and stand forth in   *Lu 6:8*
the midst
in the name of Jesus r. up and   *Ac 3:6*
walk
I saw a beast r. up out of the   *Re 13:1*
sea

RISEN

The sun was r. upon the earth   *Ge 19:23*
If the sun be r. upon him, there   *Ex 22:3*
ye are r. up in your fathers'   *Nu 32:14*
stead
ye r. up against my father's   *J'g 9:18*
when she was r. up to glean,   *Ru 2:15*
Boaz

Yet a man is r. to pursue   *1Sa 25:29*
thee, and
the whole family is r. against   *2Sa 14:7*
thine
I am r. up in the room of   *1Ki 8:20*
David my
the servant of God was r.   *2Ki 6:15*
early
am r. up in the room of   *2Ch 6:10*
David my
Solomon the son of David, is   *2Ch 13:6*
r. up
Jehoram was r. up to the   *2Ch 21:4*
kingdom
but we are r. and stand upright   *Ps 20:8*
witnesses are r. up against me   *Ps 27:12*
strangers are r. up against me   *Ps 54:3*
the proud are r. against me   *Ps 86:14*
glory of the Lord is r. upon   *Isa 60:1*
thee
Violence is r. up into a rod of   *Eze 7:11*
for the waters were r. waters   *Eze 47:5*
my people is r. up as an enemy   *Mic 2:8*
hath not r. a greater than   *M't 11:11*
John
Baptist; he is r. from the dead   *M't 14:2*
the Son of man be r. again   *M't 17:9*
But after I am r. again, I will   *M't 26:32*
go
the people, He is r. from the   *M't 27:64*
dead
He is not here: for he is r. as   *M't 28:6*
he
his disciples that he is r. from   *M't 28:7*
John the Baptist was r. from   *M'k 6:14*
beheaded: he is r. from the   *M'k 6:16*
dead
Son of man were r. from the   *M'k 9:9*
dead
after that I am r. I will go   *M'k 14:28*
before
he is r.; he is not here: behold   *M'k 16:6*
Jesus was r. early the first   *M'k 16:9*
day of
had seen him after he was r.   *M'k 16:14*
a great prophet is r. up among   *Lu 7:16*
that John was r. from the dead   *Lu 9:7*
of the old prophets was r. again   *Lu 9:8*
one of the old prophets is r.   *Lu 9:19*
again
the master of the house is r.   *Lu 13:25*
up
He is not here, but is r.:   *Lu 24:6*
remember
The Lord is r. indeed, and   *Lu 24:34*
hath
therefore he was r. from the   *Joh 2:22*
dead
after that he was r. from the   *Joh 21:14*
dead
suffered, r. again from the   *Ac 17:3*
dead
died, yea rather, that is r.   *Ro 8:34*
again
of the dead, then is Christ   *1Co 15:13*
not r.
And if Christ be not r. then   *1Co 15:14*
is our
But now is Christ r. from the   *1Co 15:20*
dead
r. with him through the faith   *Col 2:12*
If ye then be r. with Christ,   *Col 3:1*
seek
sun is r. with a burning heat   *Jas 1:11*

RISEST

liest down, and when thou r. up   *De 6:7;*
                                   11:19

RISETH

a man r. against his neighbour   *De 22:26*
r. up and buildeth this city   *Jos 6:26*
Jericho
when the sun r. even a   *2Sa 23:4*
morning
commandeth the sun, and it r.   *Job 9:7*
not
So man lieth down, and r.   *Job 14:12*
not
he r. up, and no man is sure   *Job 24:22*
of life
that r. up against me as   *Job 27:7*
then shall I do when God r.   *Job 31:14*
up
falleth seven times, and r. up   *Pr 24:16*
again

She r. also while it is yet   *Pr 31:15*
night, and
shalt not know from whence   *Isa 47:11*
it r.
Egypt r. up like a flood, and   *Jer 46:8*
his
daughter r. up against her   *Mic 7:6*
mother
He r. from supper, and laid   *Joh 13:4*
aside

RISING

have in the skin of his flesh a   *Le 13:2*
r.
if the r. be white in the skin   *Le 13:10*
there be quick raw flesh in   *Le 13:10*
the r.
place of the boil there be a   *Le 13:19*
white r.
it is a r. of the burning, and   *Le 13:28*
the r. of the sore be white   *Le 13:43*
reddish
for a r. and for a scab, and   *Le 14:56*
east side toward the r. of   *Nu 2:3*
the sun
Jordan toward the r. of the   *Jos 12:1*
sun
god-like form r. from earth   *1Sa 28:13*
(B)(E)(R)
r. up betimes, and sending   *2Ch 36:15*
spears from the r. of the   *Ne 4:21*
morning
my leanness r. up in me   *Job 16:8*
beareth
their work; r. betimes for a   *Job 24:5*
prey
murderer r. with the light   *Job 24:14*
killeth
the earth from the r. of the sun   *Ps 50:1*
From the r. of the sun unto   *Ps 113:3*
r. early in the morning, it   *Pr 27:14*
shall be
against whom there is no r.   *Pr 30:31*
up
from the r. of the sun shall   *Isa 41:25*
he call
may know from the r. of   *Isa 45:6*
the sun
and his glory from the r. of   *Isa 59:19*
the sun
kings to the brightness of thy   *Isa 60:3*
r.
r. up early and speaking, but   *Jer 7:13*
ye
r. up early and sending them   *Jer 7:25*
r. early and protesting, saying   *Jer 11:7*
unto you, r. early and   *Jer 25:3*
speaking
the prophets, r. early and   *Jer 25:4*
sending
both r. up early, and sending   *Jer 26:5*
them
r. up early and sending them   *Jer 29:19*
r. up early and teaching   *Jer 32:33*
them, yet
unto you, r. early and   *Jer 35:14*
speaking
r. up early and sending them   *Jer 35:15*
the prophets r. early and   *Jer 44:4*
sending
sitting down, and their r. up   *La 3:63*
from the r. of the sun even   *Mal 1:11*
unto
r. up a great while before   *M'k 1:35*
day, he
the r. from the dead should   *M'k 9:10*
mean
the sepulchre at the r. of the   *M'k 16:2*
sun
and r. again of many in Israel   *Lu 2:34*
angel r. out of the east (N)   *Re 7:2*

RISKED

r. his life (B)(R)   *J'g 9:17*
r. himself in the theatre   *Ac 19:31*
(B)(P)

RISSAH

from Libnah, and pitched at   *Nu 33:21*
R.
And they journeyed from R.   *Nu 33:22*

RITES

according to all the r. of it   *Nu 9:3*
various r. of cleansing (N)   *Heb 9:10*

RITHMAH

Hazeroth, and pitched in R.	Nu 33:18
And they departed from R.	Nu 33:19

RIVAL

her r. provoked her (A)(B)(R)	1Sa 1:6
rival (B)(R)	Ph'p 1:15; Jas 3:14, 16

RIVALRY

envy, murder, r. (N)	Ro 1:29

RIVER

a r. went out of Eden to water the	Ge 2:10
the name of the second r. is Gihon	Ge 2:13
name of the third r. is Hiddekel	Ge 2:14
And the fourth r. is Euphrates	Ge 2:14
I given this land, the r. of Egypt	Ge 15:18
unto the great r. the r. Euphrates	Ge 15:18
he rose up, and passed over the r.	Ge 31:21
Saul of Rehoboth by the r. reigned	Ge 36:37
and, behold, he stood by the r.	Ge 41:1
came up out of the r.	Ge 41:2
seven kine came up after them out of the r.	Ge 41:3
other kine upon the brink of the r.	Ge 41:3
I stood upon the bank of the r.	Ge 41:17
came up out of the r. seven kine	Ge 41:18
Every son ye shall cast into the r.	Ex 1:22
came down to wash herself at the r.	Ex 2:5
shalt take of the water of the r.	Ex 4:9
water thou takest out of the r.	Ex 4:9
upon the waters which are in the r.	Ex 7:17
the fish that is in the r. shall die	Ex 7:18
and the r. shall stink; and the	Ex 7:18
loathe to drink of the water of the r.	Ex 7:18
smote the waters that were in the r.	Ex 7:20
all the waters that were in the r.	Ex 7:20
And the fish that was in the r. died	Ex 7:21
and the r. stank, and the Egyptians	Ex 7:21
could not drink the water of the r.	Ex 7:21; 7:24
digged round about the r. for water	Ex 7:24
that the Lord had smitten the r.	Ex 7:25
And the r. shall bring forth frogs	Ex 8:3
they may remain in the r. only	Ex 8:9
they shall remain in the r. only	Ex 8:11
rod, wherewith thou smotest the r.	Ex 17:5
and from the desert unto the r.	Ex 23:31
by the r. of the land of the children	Nu 22:5
from Azmon unto the r. of Egypt	Nu 34:5
unto the great r., the r. Euphrates	De 1:7
and pass over the r. Arnon	De 2:24
is by the brink of the r. of Arnon	De 2:36
and from the city that is by the r.	De 2:36
nor unto any place of the r. Jabbok	De 2:37
from the r. of Arnon unto mount	De 3:8
Aroer, which is by the r. Arnon	De 3:12
from Gilead even unto the r. Arnon	De 3:16

the border even unto the r. Jabbok	De 3:16
is by the bank of the r. Arnon	De 4:48
from the r. the r. Euphrates	De 11:24
unto the great r., the r. Euphrates	Jos 1:4
from the r. Arnon unto mount	Jos 12:1
is upon the bank of the r. Arnon	Jos 12:2
and from the middle of the r.	Jos 12:2
even unto the r. Jabbok, which	Jos 12:2
is upon the bank of the r. Arnon	Jos 13:9
city that is in the midst of the r.	Jos 13:9
that is on the bank of the r. Arnon	Jos 13:16
city that is in the midst of the r.	Jos 13:16
and went out unto the r. of Egypt	Jos 15:4
which is on the south side of the r. of Egypt, and the great sea	Jos 15:7
the r. of Egypt, and the great sea	Jos 15:47
westward unto the r. Kanah	Jos 16:8
the r. Kanah, southward of the r.	Jos 17:9
was on the north side of the r.	Jos 17:9
to the r. that is before Jokneam	Jos 19:11
beyond the r. (A)(B)(E)(S)	Jos 24:2
will draw to the r. Kishon Sisera	J'g 4:7
Harosheth unto the r. of Kishon	J'g 4:13
The r. of Kishon swept them away	J'g 5:21
that ancient r. the r. Kishon	J'g 5:21
his border at the r. Euphrates	2Sa 8:3
Syrians that were beyond the r.	2Sa 10:16
city, and will draw it into the r.	2Sa 17:13
lieth in the midst of the r. of Gad	2Sa 24:5
from the r. unto the land of	1Ki 4:21
all the region on this side the r.	1Ki 4:24
over all the kings on this side the r.	1Ki 4:24
of Hamath unto the r. of Egypt	1Ki 8:65
shall scatter them beyond the r.	1Ki 14:15
Aroer, which is by the r. Arnon	2Ki 10:33
and in Habor by the r. of Gozan	2Ki 17:6
and in Habor by the r. of Gozan	2Ki 18:11
king of Assyria to the r. Euphrates	2Ki 23:29
had taken from the r. of Egypt	2Ki 24:7
unto the r. Euphrates all that	2Ki 24:7
Shaul of Rehoboth by the r.	1Ch 1:48
wilderness from the r. Euphrates	1Ch 5:9
and Hara, and to the r. Gozan	1Ch 5:26
his dominion by the r. Euphrates	1Ch 18:3
Syrians that were beyond the r.	1Ch 19:16
of Hamath unto the r. of Egypt	2Ch 7:8
from the r. even unto the land	2Ch 9:26
rest that are on this side the r.	Ezr 4:10
servants the men on this side the r.	Ezr 4:11
have no portion on this side the r.	Ezr 4:16
and unto the rest beyond the r.	Ezr 4:17
over all countries beyond the r.	Ezr 4:20
governor on this side the r.	Ezr 5:3
Apharsachites on this side the r.	Ezr 5:6
Tatnai, governor beyond the r.	Ezr 6:6
Apharsachites beyond the r.	Ezr 6:6
even of the tribute beyond the r.	Ezr 6:8
Tatnai, governor on this side the r.	Ezr 6:13

treasurers which are beyond the r.	Eze 7:21
the people that are beyond the r.	Ezr 7:25
to the r. that runneth to Ahava	Ezr 8:15
a fast there, at the r. of Ahava	Ezr 8:21
we departed from the r. of Ahava	Ezr 8:31
to the governors on this side the r.	Ezr 8:36
to the governors beyond the r.	Ne 2:7, 9
of the governor on this side the r.	Ne 3:7
drinketh up a r. and hasteth not	Job 40:23
drink of the r. of thy pleasures	Ps 36:8
There is a r. the streams whereof	Ps 46:4
enrichest it with the r. of God	Ps 65:9
passed through r. on foot (A)(B)(E)(R)	Ps 66:6
and from the r. unto the ends	Ps 72:8
sea, and her branches unto the r.	Ps 80:11
they ran in the dry places like a r.	Ps 105:41
namely, by them beyond the r.	Isa 7:20
up upon them the waters of the r.	Isa 8:7
shall he shake his hand over the r.	Isa 11:15
the r. shall be wasted and dried up	Isa 19:5
seed of Sihor, the harvest of the r.	Isa 23:3
Pass through thy land as a r.	Isa 23:10
channel of the r. unto the stream	Isa 27:12
then had thy peace been as a r.	Isa 48:18
I will extend peace to her like a r.	Isa 66:12
to drink the waters of the r.	Jer 2:18
spreadeth out her roots by the r.	Jer 17:8
which was by the r. Euphrates	Jer 46:2
the north by the r. Euphrates	Jer 46:6
north country by the r. Euphrates	Jer 46:10
let tears run down like a r. day	La 2:18
the captives by the r. of Chebar	Eze 1:1
of the Chaldeans by the r. Chebar	Eze 1:3
that dwelt by the r. of Chebar, and	Eze 3:15
which I saw by the r. of Chebar	Eze 3:23
that I saw by the r. of Chebar	Eze 10:15
God of Israel by the r. of Chebar	Eze 10:20
faces, I saw by the r. of Chebar	Eze 10:22
My r. is mine own, and I have	Eze 29:3
The r. is mine, and I have made it	Eze 29:9
vision I saw by the r. Chebar	Eze 43:3
was a r. that I could not pass	Eze 47:5
a r. that could not be passed	Eze 47:5
me to return to the brink of the r.	Eze 47:6
bank of the r. were very many trees	Eze 47:7
shall live whither the r. cometh	Eze 47:9
by the r. upon the bank thereof, on	Eze 47:12
in Kadesh, the r. to the great sea	Eze 47:19
and to the r. toward the great sea	Eze 48:28
vision, and I was by the r. of Ulai	Da 8:2
there stood before the r. a ram	Da 8:3
I had seen standing before the	Da 8:6
as I was by the side of the great r.	Da 10:4
on this side of the bank of the r.	Da 12:5
on that side of the bank of the r.	Da 12:5

was upon the waters of the	Da 12:6; 12:7	whose waters are moved as the r.	Jer 46:7	**ROAR**

was upon the waters of the *Da 12:6; 12:7*
r.
unto the r. of the wilderness. *Am 6:14*
from the fortress even to the *Mic 7:12*
r.
from the r. even to the ends of *Zec 9:10*
all the deeps of the r. shall *Zec 10:11*
dry up
baptized of him in the r. of *M'k 1:5*
Jordan
we went out of the city by a *Ac 16:13*
r. side
bound in the great r. *Re 9:14*
Euphrates
water like a r. *Re 12:15*
(B)(E)(P)(R)
vIal upon the great r. *Re 16:12*
Euphrates
shewed me a pure r. of water *Re 22:1*
of life
of it, and on either side of the *Re 22:2*
r.

RIVERS

upon their streams, upon their *Ex 7:19*
r.
over the r. and over the ponds *Ex 8:5*
waters, in the seas, and in the *Le 11:9*
r.
scales in the seas, and in the *Le 11:10*
r.
to Jotbath, a land of r. of *De 10:7*
waters
and Pharpar, r. of Damascus *2Ki 5:12*
up all the r. of besieged *2Ki 19:24*
places
He shall not see the r., the *Job 20:17*
floods
cutteth out r. among the *Job 28:10*
rocks
the rock poured me out r. of *Job 29:6*
oil
a tree planted by the r. of water *Ps 1:3*
flood: thou driedst up mighty *Ps 74:15*
r.
caused waters to run down *Ps 78:16*
like r.
had turned their r. into blood *Ps 78:44*
r. to blood (A)(B)(E)(R) *Ps 78:44*
sea, and his right hand in the *Ps 89:25*
r.
r. clap their hands (A)(B) *Ps 90:8*
He turneth r. into a *Ps 107:33*
wilderness
R. of waters run down *Ps 119:136*
mine
By the r. of Babylon, there *Ps 137:1*
we sat
and r. of waters in the streets *Pr 5:16*
hand of the Lord, as the r. of *Pr 21:1*
water
All the r. run into the sea; yet *Ec 1:7*
the place from whence the r. *Ec 1:7*
come
eyes of doves by the r. of *Ca 5:12*
waters
nor can r. drown it (B) *Ca 8:7*
uttermost part of the r. of *Isa 7:18*
Egypt
which is beyond the r. of *Isa 18:1*
Ethiopia
whose land the r. have spoiled *Isa 18:2; 18:7*
And they shall turn the r. far *Isa 19:6*
away
r. and streams of waters in *Isa 30:25*
as rivers of water in a dry *Isa 32:2*
place
a place of broad r. and *Isa 33:21*
streams
all the r. of the besieged *Isa 37:25*
places
I will open r. in high places *Isa 41:18*
and I will make the r. *Isa 42:15*
islands, and
and through the r. they shall *Isa 43:2*
not
the wilderness, and r. in the *Isa 43:19; 43:20*
desert
Be dry, and I will dry up thy *Isa 44:27*
r.
uncover the thigh, pass over *Isa 47:2*
the r.
the sea, I make the r. a *Isa 50:2*
wilderness
them to walk by the r. of *Jer 31:9*
waters

whose waters are moved as *Jer 46:7*
the r.
his waters are moved like the *Jer 46:8*
r.
runneth down with r. of water *La 3:48*
hills, to the r. and to the *Eze 6:3*
valleys
that lieth in the midst of his r. *Eze 29:3*
will cause the fish of thy r. to *Eze 29:4*
stick
thee up out of the midst of thy *Eze 29:4*
r.
and all the fish of thy r. shall *Eze 29:4*
stick
thee and all the fish of thy r. *Eze 29:5*
am against thee, and against *Eze 29:10*
thy r.
And I will make the r. dry, *Eze 30:12*
and sell
r. running round about his *Eze 31:4*
plants
little r. unto all the trees of the *Eze 31:4*
field
are broken by all the r. of *Eze 31:12*
the land
and thou camest forth with *Eze 32:2*
thy r.
with thy feet, and fouledst *Eze 32:2*
their r.
and the r. shall be full of thee *Eze 32:6*
and cause their r. to run like *Eze 32:14*
oil
the mountains of Israel by *Eze 34:13*
the r.
and in all thy r. shall they *Eze 35:8*
fall that
hills, to the r. and to the *Eze 36:4, 6*
valleys
whithersoever the r. shall *Eze 47:9*
come
for the r. of waters are dried *Joe 1:20*
up
r. of Judah shall flow with *Joe 3:18*
waters
or with ten thousands of r. of *Mic 6:7*
oil
it dry, and drieth up all the r. *Na 1:4*
The gates of the r. shall be *Na 2:6*
opened
No, that was situate among the *Na 3:8*
r.
the Lord displeased against *Hab 3:8*
the r.
was thine anger against the *Hab 3:8*
r.? was
Thou didst cleave the earth *Hab 3:9*
with r.
From beyond the r. of *Zep 3:10*
Ethiopia my
belly shall flow r. of living *Joh 7:38*
water
it fell upon the third part of *Re 8:10*
the r.
poured out his vial upon the r. *Re 16:4*

RIVER'S

laid it in the flags by the r. *Ex 2:3*
brink
maidens walked by the r. side *Ex 2:5*
thou shalt stand by the r. *Ex 7:15*
brink
forth, as gardens by the r. *Nu 24:6*
side

RIZPAH

a concubine, whose name was *2Sa 3:7*
R.
the king took the two sons of *2Sa 21:8*
R.
And R. the daughter of *2Sa 21:10*
Aiah took
told David what R. had *2Sa 21:11*
done

ROAD

r. lead into destructon (B) *Nu 22:32*
Whither have ye made a r. *1Sa 27:10*
to day

ROADS

r. and hedgerows (P) *Lu 14:21*

ROAM

the foxes r. about (B) *La 5:18*

ROAR

Let the sea r. and the *1Ch 16:32*
fulness
waters thereof r. and be *Ps 46:3*
troubled
waters r. and foam (A) *Ps 46:3*
Thine enemies r. in the midst *Ps 74:4*
let the sea r. and the fulness *Ps 96:11*
Let the sea r. and the fulness *Ps 98:7*
The young lions r. after *Ps 104:21*
their prey
lion, they shall r. like young *Isa 5:29*
lions
yea, they shall r. and lay hold *Isa 5:29*
that day they shall r. against *Isa 5:30*
them
a man of war: he shall cry, *Isa 42:13*
yea, r.
We r. all like bears, and *Isa 59:11*
mourn
though they r. yet can they *Jer 5:22*
not
The Lord shall r. from on *Jer 25:30*
high
mightily r. upon his *Jer 25:30*
habitation
the sea when the waves *Jer 31:35*
thereof r.
their voice shall r. like the *Jer 50:42*
sea, and
They shall r. together like *Jer 51:38*
lions
her waves do r. like great *Jer 51:55*
waters
the Lord: he shall r. like a *Ho 11:10*
lion
when he shall r. then the *Ho 11:10*
children
The Lord also shall r. out of *Joe 3:16*
Zion
he said, The Lord will r. from *Am 1:2*
Zion
Will a lion r. in the forest *Am 3:4*
r. of the surging sea (N)(P) *Lu 21:25*

ROARED

a young lion r. against him *J'g 14:5*
r. by reason of the disquietness *Ps 38:8*
divided the sea, whose waves *Isa 51:15*
r.
The young lions r. upon him *Jer 2:15*
r. loudly (R) *Jer 2:15*
The lion hath r. who will not *Am 3:8*
fear

ROARETH

After it a voice r.: he *Job 37:4*
thundereth
mercy; their voice r. like the *Jer 6:23*
sea
a loud voice, as when a lion r. *Re 10:3*

ROARING

The r. of the lion, and the *Job 4:10*
voice of
me, and from the words of my *Ps 22:1*
r.
as a ravening and a r. lion *Ps 22:13*
my bones waxed old through *Ps 32:3*
my r.
king's wrath is as the r. of a *Pr 19:12*
lion
fear of a king is as the r. of *Pr 20:2*
a lion
As a r. lion, and a ranging *Pr 28:15*
bear
Their r. shall be like a lion, *Isa 5:29*
they
shall roar like the r. of the *Isa 5:30*
sea
and the young lion r. on his *Isa 31:4*
prey
thereof, by the noise of his r. *Eze 19:7*
like a r. lion ravening the *Eze 22:25*
prey
princes make her as r. lions *Zep 3:3*
a voice of the r. of young *Zec 11:3*
lions
the sea and the waves r. *Lu 21:25*
devil, as a r. lion, walketh *1Pe 5:8*
about

ROARINGS

r. are poured out like the | Job 3:24
waters
groanings poured out like | Job 3:24
water (A)(B)(E)(R)

ROARS

r. from Jerusalem (B) | Joe 3:16

ROAST

the flesh in that night, r. with | Ex 12:8
fire
at all with water, but r. with | Ex 12:9
fire
And thou shalt r. and eat it in | De 16:7
Give flesh to r. for the priest | 1Sa 2:15
He roasteth r. and is satisfied | Isa 44:16
r. in its branches (B)(N) | M't 13:32

ROASTED

two bushels of r. grain (B) | 1Sa 25:18
And they r. the passover | 2Ch 35:13
with fire
I have r. flesh, and eaten it | Isa 44:19
whom the king of Babylon r. | Jer 29:22
in the

ROASTETH

slothful man r. not that which | Pr 12:27
he
he r. roast, and is satisfied | Isa 44:16

ROB

thy neighbour, neither r. him | Le 19:13
which shall r. you of your | Le 26:22
children
and they r. the threshingfloors | 1Sa 23:1
pass by and r. him (E) | Ps 89:41
R. not the poor, because he is | Pr 22:22
that they may r. the fatherless | Isa 10:2
us, and the lot of them that r. | Isa 17:14
us
and r. those that robbed | Eze 39:10
them, saith
Will a man r. God? Yet ye | Mal 3:8
have
r. his belongings (B) | M't 12:29
do ye r. temples (E)(N)(R) | Ro 2:22
r. you of the prize (E) | Col 2:18

ROBBED

robbed (A) | De 28:29;
J'g 2:14, 16; Jer 21:12; 22:3; Eze 18:18
robbed (B) | De 28:29;
Jer 21:12; Eze 18:18; 23:46; Hab 2:8
robbed (E) | De 28:29;
Jer 21:12; 22:3; Eze 18:18; 23:46
robbed (R) | De 28:29;
Jer 21:12; 22:3; Eze 18:18
they r. all that came along that | J'g 9:25
as a bear r. of her whelps in | 2Sa 17:8
bands of the wicked have r. | Ps 119:61
me
Let a bear r. of her whelps | Pr 17:12
meet a
and have r. their treasures | Isa 10:13
and I
But this is a people r. and | Isa 42:22
spoiled
her treasures; and they shall | Jer 50:37
be r.
pledge, give again that he | Eze 33:15
had r.
rob those that r. them, saith | Eze 39:10
man rob God? Yet ye have r. | Mal 3:8
ye say, Wherein have we r. | Mal 3:8
thee
for ye have r. me, even this | Mal 3:9
whole
let yourself be r. (N) | 1Co 6:8
I r. other churches, taking | 2Co 11:8
wages

ROBBER

r. swalloweth up their | Job 5:5
substance
the r. shall prevail against him | Job 18:9
poverty come as a r. (E) | Pr 6:11;
24:34
poverty come as a r. (R) | Pr 24:34
If he beget a son that is a r. | Eze 18:10

way, the same is a thief and | Joh 10:1
a r.
Barabbas, Now Barabbas | Joh 18:40
was a r.
a robber (B)(R) | 1Co 5:11

ROBBERS

The tabernacles of r. prosper | Job 12:6
for a spoil, and Israel to the | Isa 42:24
r.
become a den of r. in your | Jer 7:11
eyes
for the r. shall enter into it | Eze 7:22
the r. of thy people shall | Da 11:14
exalt
And as troops of r. wait for a | Ho 6:9
and the troop of r. spoileth | Ho 7:1
without
thieves came to thee, if r. by | Ob 5
night
came before me are thieves | Joh 10:8
which are neither r. of | Ac 19:37
churches
greedy and r. (R) | 1Co 5:10
nor r. (B)(R) | 1Co 6:10
in perils of waters, in perils | 2Co 11:26
of r.

ROBBERY

filled with r. (A)(B)(E)(R) | Le 6:2;
Eze 18:7, 12, 16, 18
and become not vain in r.: if | Ps 62:10
The r. of the wicked shall | Pr 21:7
destroy
I hate r. for burnt offering | Isa 61:8
used oppression, and | Eze 22:29
exercised r.
violence and r. in their | Am 3:10
palaces
city! it is all full of lies and r. | Na 3:1
it not r. to be equal with God | Ph'p 2:6

ROBBETH

robs r. (B)(E) | Ps 35:10
Whoso r. his father or his | Pr 28:24
mother

ROBE

took a r. and laid it on (B) | Ge 9:23
and a r. and a broidered coat | Ex 28:4
make the r. of the ephod all of | Ex 28:31
blue
upon the hem of the r. round | Ex 28:34
about
the coat, and the r. of the | Ex 29:5
ephod
the r. of the ephod of woven | Ex 39:22
work
was an hole in the midst of | Ex 39:23
the r.
they made upon the hems of | Ex 39:24
the r.
upon the hem of the r. round | Ex 39:25
round about the hem of | Ex 39:26
the r. to
clothed him with the r. and put | Le 8:7
a beautiful r. (B) | Jos 7:21
the little r. (E)(R) | 1Sa 2:19
Jonathan stripped himself of | 1Sa 18:4
the r.
cut off the skirt of Saul's r. | 1Sa 24:4
privily
see the skirt of thy r. in my | 1Sa 24:11
hand
in that I cut off the skirt of | 1Sa 24:11
thy r.
long r. with sleeves (A)(R) | 2Sa 13:18;
13:19
a new r. (B) | 1Ki 11:29
David was clothed with a r. | 1Ch 15:27
of fine
my judgment was as a r. and | Job 29:14
as with a r. (B) | Ps 104:2
be as r. (B) | Ps 109:19
a rich r. sackcloth | Isa 3:24
(A)(B)(E)(R)(S)
trailing of his r. filled (B) | Ps 6:1
And I will clothe him with | Ps 22:21
thy r.
me with the r. of | Ps 61:10
righteousness
clothes naked with a r. (B) | Eze 18:7
and he laid his r. from him | Jon 3:6
ye pull off the r. with the | Mic 2:8
garment

touched fringe of r. (B) | M't 9:20
not dressed in wedding r. | M't 22:11
(B)
him, and put on him a | M't 27:28
scarlet r.
they took the r. off from | M't 27:31
him, and
clothed in r. of white | M'k 16:15
(A)(B)(E)(N)(P)(R)
Bring forth the best r. and | Lu 15:22
put it
and arrayed him in a | Lu 23:11
gorgeous r.
put a bright r. upon him (B) | Lu 23:11
laid aside his r. (B) | Joh 13:4
and they put on him a purple | Joh 19:2
r.
crown of thorns, and the | Joh 19:5
purple r.
dressed in a r. (A)(B)(P)(R) | Re 1:13
clothed in a r. (A)(B)(R) | Re 19:13;
19:16

ROBED

r. down to the feet (N) | Re 1:13
r. in white robes (B)(N) | Re 7:13
r. in purple (A)(B) | Re 17:4

ROBES

r. of skins (B) | Ge 3:21
robes (B) | Nu 20:26;
20:38; 1Sa 18:4; 2Sa 10:4; Ps 45:8;
Isa 59:17; 61:10
to his royal r. (A) | 1Sa 19:24
for with such r. were the | 2Sa 13:18
king's
his throne, having put on | 1Ki 22:10
their r.
the battle; but put thou on | 1Ki 22:30
thy r.
gold, r., harness (B) | 2Ch 9:24; Re 3:5
on his throne, clothed in | 2Ch 18:9
their r.
the battle; but put thou on | 2Ch 18:29
thy r.
the festival r. (S) | Isa 3:22
thrones, and lay awake their | Eze 26:16
r.
which desire to walk in long | Lu 20:46
r.
clothed in white r. (B) | Re 4:4
white r. were given unto every | Re 6:11
one
clothed with white r. and palms | Re 7:9
these which are arrayed in | Re 7:13
white r.
robed in white r. (B)(N) | Re 7:13
have washed their r. and made | Re 7:14
wash their r. (S) | Re 22:14

ROBS

r., robbeth (B)(E) | Ps 35:10

ROBOAM

Solomon begat R.; and R. | M't 1:7
begat

ROCK

thee there upon the r. in | Ex 17:6
Horeb
and thou shall smite the r. and | Ex 17:6
me, and thou shalt stand | Ex 33:21
upon a r.
I will put thee in a clift of a | Ex 33:22
r. and
ye unto the r. before their | Nu 20:8
eyes
forth to them water out of the | Nu 20:8
r.
congregation together before | Nu 20:10
the r.
we fetch you water out of | Nu 20:10
this r.
with his rod he smote the r. | Nu 20:11
twice
and thou puttest thy nest in | Nu 24:21
a r.
forth water out of the r. of | De 8:15
flint
He is the R. his work is | De 32:4
perfect
him to suck honey out of the | De 32:13
r.
and oil out of the flinty r. | De 32:13
esteemed the R. of his | De 32:15
salvation

Of the _R._ that begat thee thou art | _De 32:18_
except their _R._ and sold them, and | _De 32:30_
For their _r._ is not as our _R._ even | _De 32:31_
gods, their _r._ in whom they trusted | _De 32:37_
from the _r._ and upward | _J'g 1:36_
cakes, and lay them upon this _r._ | _J'g 6:20_
there rose up fire out of the _r._ | _J'g 6:21_
thy God upon the top of this _r._ | _J'g 6:26_
they slew Oreb upon the _r._ Oreb | _J'g 7:25_
offered it upon a _r._ unto the Lord | _J'g 13:19_
dwelt in the top of the _r._ Etam | _J'g 15:8_
went to the top of the _r._ Etam | _J'g 15:11_
and brought him up from the _r._ | _J'g 15:13_
wilderness unto the _r._ of Rimmon | _J'g 20:45;_ _20:47_
and abode in the _r._ Rimmon four | _J'g 20:47_
that were in the _r._ Rimmon | _J'g 21:13_
is there any _r._ like our God | _1Sa 2:2_
was a sharp _r._ on the one side | _1Sa 14:4_
and a sharp _r._ on the other side | _1Sa 14:4_
wherefore he came down into a _r._ | _1Sa 23:25_
and spread it for her upon the _r._ | _2Sa 21:10_
said, The Lord is my _r._ and my | _2Sa 22:2_
The God of my _r._; in him will I | _2Sa 22:3_
and who is a _r._ save our God | _2Sa 22:32_
Lord liveth: and blessed be my _r._ | _2Sa 22:47_
the God of the _r._ of my salvation | _2Sa 22:47_
said, the _R._ of Israel spake to me | _2Sa 23:3_
went down to the _r._ to David, into | _1Ch 11:15_
them unto the top of the _r._ | _2Ch 25:12_
them down from the top of _r._ | _2Ch 25:12_
them out of the _r._ for their thirst | _Ne 9:15_
the _r._ is removed out of his place | _Job 14:18_
the _r._ be removed out of his place | _Job 18:4_
iron pen and lead in the _r._ for ever | _Job 19:24_
embrace the _r._ for want of a shelter | _Job 24:8_
putteth forth his hand upon the _r._ | _Job 28:9_
the _r._ poured me out rivers of oil | _Job 29:6_
wild goats of the _r._ bring forth | _Job 39:1_
dwelleth and abideth on the _r._ | _Job 39:28_
upon the crag of the _r._ and | _Job 39:28_
on the _r._ he dwells (R) | _Job 39:28_
The Lord is my _r._ and my fortress | _Ps 18:2_
Lord? or who is a _r._ save our God | _Ps 18:31_
Lord liveth: and blessed be my _r._ | _Ps 18:46_
Lord is my _R._ (A)(B)(E)(R) | _Ps 19:14;_ _144:1_
me; he shall set me up upon a _r._ | _Ps 27:5_
Unto thee will I cry, O Lord my _r._ | _Ps 28:1_
be thou my strong _r._ for an house | _Ps 31:2_
thou art my _r._ and my fortress | _Ps 31:3_
clay, and set my feet upon a _r._ | _Ps 40:2_
I will say unto God my _r._, Why hast | _Ps 42:9_
lead me to the _r._ that is higher | _Ps 61:2_
He only is my _r._ and my salvation | _Ps 62:2;_ _62:6_
the _r._ of my strength, and my | _Ps 62:7_
thou art my _r._ and my fortress | _Ps 71:3_
brought streams also out of the _r._ | _Ps 78:16_
he smote the _r._ that the waters | _Ps 78:20_

remembered that God was their _r._ | _Ps 78:35_
with honey out of the _r._ should I | _Ps 81:16_
God, and the _r._ of my salvation | _Ps 89:26_
he is my _r._ and there is no | _Ps 92:15_
And my God is the _r._ of my refuge | _Ps 94:22_
noise to the _r._ of our salvation | _Ps 95:1_
He opened the _r._ and the waters | _Ps 105:41_
turned the _r._ into a standing water | _Ps 114:8_
the way of a serpent upon a _r._ | _Pr 30:19_
that are in the clefts of the _r._ | _Ca 2:14_
Enter into the _r._ and hide thee | _Isa 2:10_
stumbling and for a _r._ of offence | _Isa 8:14_
slaughter of Midian at _r._ of Oreb | _Isa 10:26_
mindful of the _r._ of thy strength | _Isa 17:10_
the _r._ of your refuge (R) | _Isa 17:10_
an habitation for himself in a _r._ | _Isa 22:16_
the _R._ of Ages (B)(E)(R) | _Isa 26:4_
shadow of a great _r._ in a weary land | _Isa 32:2_
let the inhabitants of the _r._ sing | _Isa 42:11_
the waters to flow out of the _r._ for | _Isa 48:21_
he clave the _r._ also, and the waters | _Isa 48:21_
unto the _r._ whence ye are hewn | _Isa 51:1_
made their faces harder than a _r._ | _Jer 5:3_
and hide it there in a hole of the _r._ | _Jer 13:4_
snow from the _r._ of the field | _Jer 18:14_
of the valley, and _r._ of the plain | _Jer 21:13_
hammer that breaketh the _r._ | _Jer 23:29_
the cities, and dwell in the _r._ | _Jer 48:28_
that dwellest in the clefts of the _r._ | _Jer 49:16_
her: she set it upon the top of a _r._ | _Eze 24:7_
set her blood upon the top of a _r._ | _Eze 24:8_
and make her like the top of a _r._ | _Eze 26:4_
will I make thee like the top of a _r._ | _Eze 26:14_
Shall horses run upon the _r._ | _Am 6:12_
that dwellest in the clefts of the _r._ | _Ob 3_
which built his house upon a _r._ | _M't 7:24_
not: for it was founded upon a _r._ | _M't 7:25_
upon this _r._ I will build my church | _M't 16:18_
which he had hewn out in the _r._ | _M't 27:60_
sepulchre was hewn out of a _r._ | _M'k 15:46_
and laid the foundation on a _r._ | _Lu 6:48_
it: for it was founded upon a _r._ | _Lu 6:48_
And some fell upon a _r._; and as | _Lu 8:6_
They on the _r._ are they, which | _Lu 8:13_
Cephas, meaning a _r._ (P) | _Joh 1:42_
a stumblingstone and _r._ of offence | _Ro 9:33_
they drank of that spiritual _R._ that | _1Co 10:4_
them: and that _R._ was Christ | _1Co 10:4_
a _r._ of offence, even to them | _1Pe 2:8_

ROCKS

from the top of the _r._ I see him | _Nu 23:9_
caves, and in thickets, and in _r._ | _1Sa 13:6_
men upon the _r._ of the wild goats | _1Sa 24:2_
brake in pieces the _r._ before | _1Ki 19:11_
cutteth out rivers among the _r._ | _Job 28:10_
caves of the earth, and in the _r._ | _Job 30:6_
He clave the _r._ in the wilderness | _Ps 78:15_

goats: and the _r._ for the conies | _Ps 104:18_
make they their houses in the _r._ | _Pr 30:26_
shall go into the holes of the _r._ | _Isa 2:19_
To go into the clefts of the _r._ | _Isa 2:21_
and into the tops of the ragged _r._ | _Isa 2:21_
valleys, and in the holes of the _r._ | _Isa 7:19_
shall be the munitions of _r._ | _Isa 33:16_
valleys under the clifts of the _r._ | _Isa 57:5_
and climb up upon the _r._: every | _Jer 4:29_
hill and out of the holes of the _r._ | _Jer 16:16_
and roll thee down from the _r._ | _Jer 51:25_
the _r._ are thrown down by him | _Na 1:6_
earth did quake, and the _r._ rent | _M't 27:51_
we should have fallen upon _r._ | _Ac 27:29_
hidden _r._ in your feasts (E) | _Jude 12_
and in the _r._ of the mountains | _Re 6:15_
And said to the mountains and _r._ | _Re 6:16_

ROCKY

a _r._ crag (A)(E)(R) | _1Sa 14:4_

ROD

in thine hand? And he said, A _r._ | _Ex 4:2_
it, and it became a _r._ in his hand | _Ex 4:4_
shalt take this _r._ in thine hand | _Ex 4:17_
and Moses took the _r._ of God in his | _Ex 4:20_
Take thy _r._ and cast it before | _Ex 7:9_
and Aaron cast down his _r._ before | _Ex 7:10_
they cast down every man his _r._ | _Ex 7:12_
Aaron's _r._ swallowed up their rods | _Ex 7:12_
_r._ which was turned to a serpent | _Ex 7:15_
smite with the _r._ in mine hand | _Ex 7:17_
Say unto Aaron, Take thy _r._ | _Ex 7:19_
he lifted up the _r._ and smote | _Ex 7:20_
Stretch forth thine hand with thy _r._ | _Ex 8:5_
Stretch out thy _r._ and smite the | _Ex 8:16_
stretched out his hand with his _r._ | _Ex 8:17_
stretched his _r._ toward heaven | _Ex 9:23_
stretched forth his _r._ over the land | _Ex 10:13_
but lift thou up thy _r._ and stretch | _Ex 14:16_
and thy _r._ wherewith thou smotest | _Ex 17:5_
with the _r._ of God in mine hand | _Ex 17:9_
his servant, or his maid, with a _r._ | _Ex 21:20_
of whatsoever passeth under the _r._ | _Le 27:32_
and take of every one of them a _r._ | _Nu 17:2_
thou every man's name upon his _r._ | _Nu 17:2_
Aaron's name upon the _r._ of Levi | _Nu 17:3_
for one _r._ shall be for the head of | _Nu 17:3_
the man's _r._ whom I shall choose | _Nu 17:5_
their princes gave him a _r._ apiece | _Nu 17:6_
_r._ of Aaron was among their rods | _Nu 17:6_
_r._ of Aaron for the house of Levi | _Nu 17:8_
looked, and took every man his _r._ | _Nu 17:9_
Bring Aaron's _r._ again before the | _Nu 17:10_
Take the _r._ and gather thou | _Nu 20:8_
Moses took the _r._ from before the | _Nu 20:9_
with his _r._ he smote the rock twice | _Nu 20:11_
end of the _r._ that was in his hand | _1Sa 14:27_

end of the *r*. that was in   *1Sa 14:43*
mine hand
chasten him with the *r*. of   *2Sa 7:14*
man
Let him take his *r*. away   *Job 9:34*
from me
neither is the *r*. of God upon   *Job 21:9*
them
shalt break them with a *r*. of   *Ps 2:9*
iron
r. and thy staff they comfort   *Ps 23:4*
me
the *r*. of thine inheritance,   *Ps 74:2*
which
their transgression with the *r*.   *Ps 89:32*
the *r*. of thy strength out of   *Ps 110:2*
Zion
the *r*. of the wicked shall not   *Ps 125:3*
rest
a *r*. is for the back of him   *Pr 10:13*
that is
that spareth his *r*. hateth his   *Pr 13:24*
son
mouth of foolish is a *r*. of   *Pr 14:3*
pride
and the *r*. of his anger shall   *Pr 22:8*
fail
r. of correction shall drive it   *Pr 22:15*
far
for if thou beatest him with   *Pr 23:13*
the *r*.
Thou shalt beat him with the   *Ps 23:14*
r.
the ass, and a *r*. for the fool's   *Pr 26:3*
back
The *r*. and reproof give   *Pr 29:15*
wisdom
shoulder, the *r*. of his   *Isa 9:4*
oppressor
the *r*. of mine anger, and the   *Isa 10:5*
staff
r. should shake itself against   *Isa 10:15*
them
he shall smite thee with a *r*.   *Isa 10:24*
and as his *r*. was upon the   *Isa 10:26*
sea, so
forth a *r*. out of the stem of   *Isa 11:1*
Jesse
smite the earth with the *r*. of   *Isa 11:4*
his
r. of him that smote thee is   *Isa 14:29*
broken
a staff, and the cummin with   *Isa 28:27*
a *r*.
beaten down, which smote   *Isa 30:31*
with a *r*.
I said, I see a *r*. of an almond   *Jer 1:11*
tree
Israel is the *r*. of his   *Jer 10:16*
inheritance
staff broken, and the   *Jer 48:17*
beautiful *r*.
Israel is the *r*. of his   *Jer 51:19*
inheritance
seen affliction by the *r*. of his   *La 3:1*
wrath
the *r*. hath blossomed, pride   *Eze 7:10*
is risen up into a *r*. of   *Eze 7:11*
wickedness
is gone out of a *r*. of her   *Eze 19:14*
branches
hath no strong *r*. to be a   *Eze 19:14*
sceptre
cause you to pass under the   *Eze 20:37*
r.
it contemneth the *r*. of my   *Eze 21:10*
son, as
if the sword contemn even   *Eze 21:13*
the *r*.
smite the judge of Israel with   *Mic 5:1*
a *r*.
hear ye the *r*. and who hath   *Mic 6:9*
Feed thy people with thy *r*.   *Mic 7:14*
shall I come unto you with a   *1Co 4:21*
r.
Aaron's *r*. that budded, and   *Heb 9:4*
shall rule them with *r*. of   *Re 2:27*
iron
was given me a reed like unto   *Re 11:1*
a *r*.
to rule all nations with a *r*. of   *Re 12:5*
iron
he shall rule them with a *r*.   *Re 19:15*
of iron

RODE

and they *r*. upon the camels   *Ge 24:61*
had thirty sons that *r*. on   *J'g 10:4*
thirty ass colts

---

that *r*. on threescore and ten   *J'g 12:14*
ass colts
And it was so, as she *r*. on   *1Sa 15:20*
the ass
and arose, and *r*. upon an   *1Sa 25:42*
ass
young men, which *r*. upon   *1Sa 30:17*
camels
Absalom *r*. upon a mule, and   *2Sa 18:9*
he *r*. upon a cherub, and did   *2Sa 22:11*
fly
him the ass: and he *r*.   *1Ki 13:13*
thereon
And Ahab *r*. and went to   *1Ki 18:45*
Jezreel
So Jehu *r*. in a chariot, and   *2Ki 9:16*
went to
I and thou *r*. together after   *2Ki 9:25*
Ahab
me, save the beast that I *r*.   *Ne 2:12*
upon
the posts that *r*. upon mules   *Es 8:14*
he *r*. upon a cherub, and did   *Ps 18:10*
fly

RODS

Jacob took him *r*. of green   *Ge 30:37*
poplar
white appear which was in   *Ge 30:37*
the *r*.
he set the *r*. which he had   *Ge 30:38*
pilled
the flocks conceived before   *Ge 30:39*
the *r*.
Jacob laid the *r*. before the   *Ge 30:41*
eyes of
they might conceive among   *Ge 30:41*
the *r*.
Aaron's rod swallowed up   *Ex 7:12*
their *r*.
house of their fathers, twelve *r*.   *Nu 17:2*
fathers' houses, even twelve *r*.   *Nu 17:6*
rod of Aaron was among   *Nu 17:6*
their *r*.
laid up the *r*. before the Lord   *Nu 17:7*
Moses brought out all the *r*.   *Nu 17:9*
from
strong *r*. for the sceptres of   *Eze 19:11*
them
her strong *r*. were broken   *Eze 19:12*
Thrice was I beaten with *r*.,   *2Co 11:25*
once

ROE

was as light of foot as a wild   *2Sa 2:18*
r.
like a deer in the field (B)   *2Sa 2:18*
as a wild gazelle (R)   *2Sa 2:18*
the loving hind and pleasant *r*.   *Pr 5:19*
loving hind and pleasant doe   *Pr 5:19*
(A)(B)(E)(R)
Deliver thyself as a *r*. from the   *Pr 6:5*
deliver yourself as a captured   *Pr 6:5*
gazelle (B)(R)
beloved is like a *r*. or a young   *Ca 2:9*
hart
like a gazelle (A)(B)(R)   *Ca 2:9;*
        2:17; 8:14
be thou like a *r*. or a young   *Ca 2:17*
hart
thou like to a *r*. or to a young   *Ca 8:14*
hart
And it shall be as the chased   *Isa 13:14*
r.
as a chased gazelle (B)(R)   *Isa 13:14*

ROEBUCK

as of the *r*. and as of the   *De 12:15*
hart
as the gazelle (A)   *De 12:15; 15:22*
of the antelope and of the   *De 12:15;*
deer (B)   *12:22*
the gazelle and the hart (R)   *De 12:15;*
        12:22; 15:22
as the *r*. and the hart is   *De 12:22*
eaten
The hart, and the *r*. and the   *De 14:5*
gazelle and *r*. (S)   *De 14:5*
it alike, as the *r*. and as the   *De 15:22*
hart

ROEBUCKS

harts, and *r*. and fallowdeer   *1Ki 4:23*
gazelles and *r*. (S)   *1Ki 4:23*

ROES

were as swift as the *r*. upon   *1Ch 12:8*
swift as gazelles (A)(R)   *1Ch12:8*
fast as deer (B)   *1Ch 12:8*
by the *r*. and by the hinds of   *Ca 2:7*
by the gazelles (A)(B)(R)   *Ca 2:7;*
        3:5; 4:5; 7:3
by the *r*. and by the hinds of   *Ca 3:5*
like two young *r*. that are   *Ca 4:5;*
twins   *7:3*

ROGELIM

and Barzillai the Gilleadite   *2Sa 17:27*
of R.
the Gileadite came down   *2Sa 19:31*
from R.

ROGUES

dupes of crafty *r*. (N)   *Eph 4:14*

ROHGAH

the sons of Shamer; Ahi, and   *1Ch 7:34*
R.

ROLL

the *r*. of Adam's genealogy (B)   *Ge 5:1*
and till they *r*. the stone from   *Ge 29:8*
R. great stones upon the   *Jos 10:18*
mouth of
r. a great stone unto me this   *1Sa 14:33*
day
in the province of the Medes, a   *Ezr 6:2*
r.
r. of the book (B)(E)(P)(R)   *Ps 40:7;*
        Heb 10:7
Take thee a great *r*. and write   *Isa 8:1*
in
Take thee a *r*. of a book, and   *Jer 36:2*
write
unto him, upon a *r*. of a book   *Jer 36:4*
and read in the *r*. which thou   *Jer 36:6*
hast
Take in thine hand the *r*.   *Jer 36:14*
wherein
Baruch took the *r*. in his   *Jer 36:14*
hand
they laid up the *r*. in the   *Jer 36:20*
chamber
king sent Jehudi to fetch the   *Jer 36:21*
r.
until all the *r*. was consumed   *Jer 36:23*
king that he would not burn   *Jer 36:25*
the *r*.
that the king had burned the   *Jer 36:27*
r.
Take thee again another *r*.   *Jer 36:28*
words that were in the first *r*.   *Jer 36:28*
Thou hast burned this *r*.   *Jer 36:29*
saying
Then took Jeremiah another   *Jer 36:32*
r.
and *r*. thee down from the   *Jer 51:25*
rocks
and, lo, a *r*. of a book was   *Eze 2:9*
therein
eat this *r*. and go speak unto   *Eze 3:1*
and he caused me to eat that   *Eze 3:2*
r.
fill thy bowels with this *r*. that   *Eze 3:3*
of Aphrah *r*. thyself in the   *Mic 1:10*
dust
and looked, and behold, a   *Zec 5:1*
flying *r*.
I see a flying *r*.; the length   *Zec 5:2*
thereof
Who shall *r*. us away the   *M'k 16:3*
stone

ROLLED

they *r*. the stone from the   *Ge 29:3*
well's
r. the stone from the well's   *Ge 29:10*
I *r*. away from the reproach   *Jos 5:9*
of Egypt
they *r*. themselves upon me   *Job 30:14*
noise, and garments *r*. in blood   *Isa 9:5*
the heavens shall be *r*.   *Isa 34:4*
together as
and he *r*. a great stone to   *M't 27:60*
the door
came and *r*. back the stone   *M't 28:2*
from
and *r*. a stone unto the door   *M'k 15:46*
of the

saw that the stone was *r.* away *M'k 16:4*

stone *r.* away from the sepulchre *Lu 24:2*

as a scroll when it is *r.* together *Re 6:14*

ROLLER

to put a *r.* to bind it, to make it *Eze 30:21*

ROLLETH

he that *r.* a stone, it will return *Pr 26:27*

ROLLING

a *r.* thing before the whirlwind *Isa 17:13*

ROLLS

was made in the house of the *r.* *Ezr 6:1*

ROMAMTI-EZER

Giddalti, and *R.,* Joshbekashah *1Ch 25:4*

The four and twentieth to *R.* he *1Ch 25:31*

ROMAN

you to scourge a man that is a *R.* *Ac 22:25*

thou doest: for this man is a *R.* *Ac 22:26*

Tell me, art thou a *R.?* He said *Ac 22:27*

after he knew that he was a *R.* *Ac 22:29*

having understood that he was a *R.* *Ac 23:27*

ROMANS

R. shall come and take away both *Joh 11:48*

neither to observe, being *R.* *Ac 16:21*

us openly uncondemned, being *R.* *Ac 16:37*

when they heard that they were *R.* *Ac 16:38*

not the manner of the *R.* to deliver *Ac 25:16*

Jerusalem into the hands of the *R.* *Ac 28:17*

ROME

and strangers of *R.,* Jews and *Ac 2:10*

all Jews to depart from *R.* *Ac 18:2*

have been there, I must also see *R.* *Ac 19:21*

must thou bear witness also at *R.* *Ac 23:11*

days: and so we went toward *r.* *Ac 28:14*

And when we came to *R.* the *Ac 28:16*

To all that be in *R.* beloved of God *Ro 1:7*

gospel to you that are at *R.* also *Ro 1:15*

when he was in *R.* he sought me *2Ti 1:17*

ROOF

they under the shadow of my *r.* *Ge 19:8*

shalt make a battlement for thy *r.* *De 22:8*

them up to the *r.* of the house *Jos 2:6*

she had laid in order upon the *r.* *Jos 2:6*

she came up unto them upon the *r.* *Jos 2:8*

upon the *r.* about three thousand *J'g 16:27*

upon the *r.* of the king's house *2Sa 11:2*

and from the *r.* he saw a woman *2Sa 11:2*

the watchman went up to the *r.* *2Sa 18:24*

every one upon the *r.* of his house *Ne 8:16*

cleaved to the *r.* of their mouth *Job 29:10*

cleave to the *r.* of my mouth: if I *Ps 137:6*

r. of thy mouth like the best wine *Ca 7:9*

cleaveth to the *r.* of his mouth *La 4:4*

cleave to the *r.* of thy mouth *Eze 3:26*

r. of one little chamber to the *r.* *Eze 40:13*

thou shouldest come under my *r.* *M't 8:8*

uncovered the *r.* where he was *M'k 2:4*

thou shouldest enter under my *r.* *Lu 7:6*

ROOFS

upon whose *r.* they have burned *Jer 19:13*

upon whose *r.* they have offered *Jer 32:29*

ROOM

is there *r.* in thy father's house *Ge 24:23*

straw enough, and *r.* to lodge in *Ge 24:25*

the house, and *r.* for the camels *Ge 24:31*

now the Lord hath made *r.* for us *Ge 26:22*

r. and board (B) *J'g 17:9*

me continually in the *r.* of Joab *2Sa 19:13*

of Jehoiada in his *r.* over the host *1Ki 2:35*

the king put in the *r.* of Abiathar *1Ki 2:35*

him king in the *r.* of his father *1Ki 5:1*

I will set upon thy throne in thy *r.* *1Ki 5:5*

I am risen up in the *r.* of David my *1Ki 8:20*

he killed him, and reigned in his *r.* *2Ki 15:25*

king in the *r.* of Josiah his father *2Ki 23:34*

the inner *r.* (B) *2Ch 4:20; 5:9*

king in the *r.* of his father Amaziah *2Ch 26:1*

r. in distress (R) *Ps 4:1*

thou hast set my feet in a large *r.* *Ps 31:8*

Thou preparedst *r.* before it *Ps 80:9*

A man's gift maketh *r.* for him *Pr 18:16*

the bride out of her *r.* (S) *Joe 2:16*

builds upper *r.* (R) *Am 9:6*

shall not be *r.* enough to receive it *Mal 3:10*

Judaea in the *r.* of his father Herod *M't 2:22*

enter inner *r.* (A)(B)(P)(R) *M't 6:6*

there was no *r.* to receive them *M'k 2:2*

shew you a large upper *r.* furnished *M'k 14:15*

there was no *r.* for them in the *Lu 2:7*

have no *r.* where to bestow my fruits *Lu 12:17*

sit not down in the highest *r.;* *Lu 14:8*

with shame to take the lowest *r.* *Lu 14:9*

go sit down in the lowest *r.* *Lu 14:10*

commanded, and yet there is *r.* *Lu 14:22*

shew you a large upper *r.* furnished *Lu 22:12*

in, they went up into an upper *r.* *Ac 1:13*

Porcius Festus came into Felix *r.* *Ac 24:27*

occupieth the *r.* of the unlearned *1Co 14:16*

ROOMS

r. shalt thou make in the ark *Ge 6:14*

place, and put captains in their *r.* *1Ki 20:24*

unto this day, and dwelt in their *r.* *1Ch 4:41*

love the uppermost *r.* at feasts *M't 23:6*

and the uppermost *r.* at feasts *M'k 12:39*

how they chose out the chief *r.* *Lu 14:7*

synagogues the chief *r.* at feasts *Lu 20:46*

ROOSTER

the *r.* (A)(B) *M't 26:34; 26:74; Joh 13:38*

ROOSTS

birds have their *r.* (B)(N) *M't 8:20*

ROOT

among you a *r.* that beareth gall *De 29:18*

there a *r.* of them against Amalek *J'g 5:14*

r. up Israel out of this good land *1Ki 14:15*

of Judah shall yet again take *r.* *2Ki 19:30*

I have seen the foolish taking *r.* *Job 5:3*

the *r.* thereof wax old in the earth *Job 14:8*

the *r.* of the matter is found in me *Job 19:28*

r. was spread out by the waters *Job 29:19*

and would *r.* out all mine increase *Job 31:12*

and *r.* thee out of the land of *Ps 52:5*

didst cause it to take deep *r.* *Ps 80:9*

r. of the righteous shall not be *Pr 12:3*

r. of the righteous yieldeth fruit *Pr 12:12*

r. up house of proud (E) *Pr 15:25*

so their *r.* shall be as rottenness *Isa 5:24*

that day there shall be a *r.* of Jesse *Isa 11:10*

out of the serpent's *r.* shall come *Isa 14:29*

I will kill thy *r.* with famine, and he *Isa 14:30*

that come of Jacob to take *r.* *Isa 27:6*

house of Judah shall again take *r.* *Isa 37:31*

their stock shall not take *r.* in the *Isa 40:24*

and as a *r.* out of a dry ground *Isa 53:2*

to *r.* out, and to pull down, and to *Jer 1:10*

yea, they have taken *r.:* they grow *Jer 12:2*

for his *r.* was by great waters *Eze 31:7*

their *r.* is dried up, they shall bear *Ho 9:16*

I will *r.* out your Asherim (A)(R) *Mic 5:14*

I will *r.* your shame-images (B) *Mic 5:14*

leave them neither *r.* nor branch *Mal 4:1*

ax is laid unto the *r.* of the trees *M't 3:10*

and because they had no *r.* *M't 13:6*

Yet hath he not *r.* in himself, but *M't 13:21*

ye *r.* up also the wheat with them *M't 13:29*

because it had no *r.* it withered *M'k 4:6*

And have no *r.* in themselves, and *M'k 4:17*

axe is laid unto the *r.* of the trees *Lu 3:9*

these have no *r.* which for a while *Lu 8:13*

Be thou plucked up by the *r.* *Lu 17:6*

as a *r.* sprout (B) *Joh 15:6*

and if the *r.* be holy, so are *Ro 11:16*

of the *r.* and fatness of the olive *Ro 11:17*

bearest not the *r.* but the *r.* thee *Ro 11:18*

There shall be a *r.* of Jesse, and he *Ro 15:12*

love of money is the *r.* of all evil *1Ti 6:10*

lest any *r.* of bitterness springing *Heb 12:15*

the tribe of Juda, the *R.* of David *Re 5:5*

the *r.* and the offspring of David *Re 22:16*

ROOTED

the Lord *r.* them out of their land *De 29:28*

r. out Baal (A) *2Ki 10:28*
His confidence shall be r. *Job 18:14*
out of his
eat; yea, let my offspring be *Job 31:8*
r. out
transgressors shall be r. out of *Pr 2:22*
day, and Ekron shall be r. up *Zep 2:4*
hath not planted, shall be r. *M't 15:13*
up
ye, being r. and grounded in *Eph 3:17*
love
R. and built up in him, and *Col 2:7*
implanted and r. (A) *Jas 1:21*

ROOTS

will I pluck them up by the *2Ch 7:20*
r. out
His r. are wrapped about the *Job 8:17*
heap
His r. shall be dried up *Job 18:16*
beneath
overturneth the mountains by *Job 28:9*
the r.
and juniper r. for their meat *Job 30:4*
a Branch shall grow out of *Isa 11:1*
his r.
spreadeth out her r. by the *Jer 17:8*
river
and the r. thereof were under *Eze 17:6*
him
vine did bend her r. toward *Eze 17:7*
him
shall he not pull up the r. *Eze 17:9*
thereof
to pluck it up by the r. thereof *Eze 17:9*
the stump of his r. in the *Da 4:15*
earth
leave the stump of the r. *Da 4:23*
thereof in
to leave the stump of the tree *Da 4:26*
r.
first horns plucked up by the r. *Da 7:8*
out of a branch of her r. shall *Da 11:7*
one
and cast forth his r. as *Ho 14:5*
Lebanon
from above, and his r. from *Am 2:9*
beneath
the fig tree dried up from the *M'k 11:20*
r.
twice dead, plucked up by the *Jude 12*
r.

ROPE

with a r. (A)(R) *Jos 2:15*
strand of r. (B)(S) *J'g 16:9*
with r. of his own sin (B) *Pr 5:22*
instead of a girdle a r. (S) *Isa 3:24*
and sin as it were with a cart *Isa 5:18*
r.
with r. (A)(R) *Jer 38:6; 38:11-13*

ROPES

two new r. (B)(E)(R) *J'g 15:13; 15:14*
If they bind me fast with *J'g 16:11*
new r.
Delilah therefore took new r. *J'g 16:12*
shall all Israel bring r. to *2Sa 17:13*
that city
on our loins, and r. upon *1Ki 20:31*
our heads
loins, and put r. on their *1Ki 20:32*
heads
soldiers cut off the r. of the *Ac 27:32*
boat

ROSE

r. up against Abel his brother *Ge 4:8*
And the men r. up from *Ge 18:16*
thence
Lot seeing them r. up to meet *Ge 19:1*
them
Abimelech r. early in the *Ge 20:8*
morning
Abraham r. up early in the *Ge 21:14*
morning
then Abimelech r. up, and *Ge 21:32*
Phichol
And Abraham r. up early in *Ge 22:3*
and r. up, and went unto the *Ge 22:3*
place
they r. up and went together *Ge 22:19*
and they r. up in the *Ge 24:54*
morning, and
drink, and r. up, and went *Ge 25:34*
his way

they r. up betimes in the *Ge 26:31*
morning
Jacob r. up early in the *Ge 28:18*
morning
Then Jacob r. up, and set his *Ge 31:17*
sons
he r. up, and passed over the *Ge 31:21*
river
early in the morning Laban *Ge 31:55*
r. up
he r. up that night, and took *Ge 32:22*
his
over Penuel the sun r. upon *Ge 32:31*
him
daughters r. up to comfort *Ge 37:35*
him
and r. up, and went down to *Ge 43:15*
Egypt
And Jacob r. up from *Ge 46:5*
Beer-sheba
neither r. any from his place *Ex 10:23*
And Pharaoh r. up in the *Ex 12:30*
night, he
hast overthrown them that r. *Ex 15:7*
up
and r. up early in the morning *Ex 24:4*
And Moses r. up, and his *Ex 24:13*
minister
And they r. up early on the *Ex 32:6*
morrow
eat and to drink, and r. up to *Ex 32:6*
play
that all the people r. up, and *Ex 33:8*
stood
the people r. up and *Ex 33:10*
worshipped
Moses r. up early in the *Ex 34:4*
morning
And they r. up early in the *Nu 14:40*
morning
And they r. up before Moses, *Nu 16:2*
with
Moses r. up and went unto *Nu 16:25*
Dathan
And Balaam r. up in the *Nu 22:13*
morning
And the princess of Moab *Nu 22:14*
r. up and
And Balaam r. up in the *Nu 22:21*
morning
And Balaam r. up, and went *Nu 24:25*
r. up from among the *Nu 25:7*
congregation
and r. up from Seir unto them *De 33:2*
Joshua r. early in the morning *Jos 3:1*
the waters r. up upon an *Jos 3:16*
heap
Joshua r. early in the morning *Jos 6:12*
they r. early about the *Jos 6:15*
dawning of
Joshua r. up early in the *Jos 7:16;*
morning *8:10*
that they hasted and r. up *Jos 8:14*
early
and there r. up fire out of the *J'g 6:21*
rock
for he r. up early on the *J'g 6:38*
morrow
Gideon r. up early, and *J'g 7:1*
pitched
And Abimelech r. up, and all *J'g 9:34*
and Abimelech r. up, and the *J'g 9:35*
people
he r. up against them, and *J'g 9:43*
smote
morning, that he r. up to *J'g 19:5*
depart
when the man r. up to depart *J'g 19:7;*
19:9
but he r. up and departed, *J'g 19:10*
and came
And her lord r. up in the *J'g 19:27*
morning
the man r. up and gat him *J'g 19:28*
unto his
the men of Gibeah r. against *J'g 20:5*
the children of Israel r. up in *J'g 20:19*
men of Israel r. up out of *J'g 20:33*
their place
the people r. early and built *J'g 21:4*
there
she r. up before one could *Ru 3:14*
know
Hannah r. up after they had *1Sa 1:9*
eaten
they r. up in the morning *1Sa 1:19*
early
when Samuel r. early to *1Sa 15:12*
meet Saul

Samuel r. up and went to *1Sa 16:13*
Ramah
David r. up early in the *1Sa 17:20*
morning
But Saul r. up out of the *1Sa 24:7*
cave and
Then they r. up and went *1Sa 28:25*
away
So David r. up early to *1Sa 29:11*
depart
And Absalom r. up early and *2Sa 15:2*
stood
of all them that r. up *2Sa 18:31*
against thee
them that r. up hast thou *2Sa 22:40*
subdued
above them that r. up *2Sa 22:49*
against me
and r. up and went every *1Ki 1:49*
man his
And the king r. up to meet *1Ki 2:19*
her and
I r. in the morning to give *1Ki 3:21*
my child
r. up to go down to the *1Ki 21:16*
vineyard
they r. up early in *2Ki 3:22*
the morning
r. up and smote the Moabites *2Ki 3:24*
And they r. up in the twilight *2Ki 7:5*
r. by night and smote the *2Ki 8:21*
Edomites
And they r. early in the *2Ch 20:20*
morning
r. up and smote the *2Ch 21:9*
Edomites
leprosy even r. up in his *2Ch 26:19*
forehead
men expressed by name r. *2Ch 28:15*
up
Then Hezekiah the king r. *2Ch 29:20*
early
Then r. up the chief of the *Ezr 1:5*
fathers
Then r. up Zerubbabel the son *Ezr 5:2*
I r. up from my heaviness (S) *Ezr 9:5;*
10:5
Ezra r. up from before the *Ezr 10:6*
house
Then Eliashib the high priest r. *Ne 3:1*
up
And I looked, and r. up, and *Ne 4:14*
said
and r. up early in the morning *Job 1:5*
subdued under me those that *Ps 18:39*
r. up
our side when men r. up *Ps 124:2*
against us
I am the r. of Sharon, and the *Ca 2:1*
lily
I r. up to open to my beloved *Ca 5:5*
rejoice, and blossom as the r. *Isa 35:1*
Then r. up certain of the *Jer 26:17*
elders
lips of those that r. up against *La 3:62*
me
was astonied, and r. up in *Da 3:24*
haste
I r. up, and did the king's *Da 8:27*
business
Jonah r. up to flee unto *Jon 1:3*
Tarshish
when the morning r. the next *Jon 4:7*
day
they r. early and corrupted all *Zep 3:7*
and he r. and followed (S) *M'k 2:12;*
2:14
garment, r. and came to *M'k 10:50*
Jesus
r. up, and thrust him out of *Lu 4:29*
the city
immediately he r. up before *Lu 5:25*
them
he left all, r. up, and followed *Lu 5:28*
him
though one r. from the dead *Lu 16:31*
And when he r. up from *Lu 22:45*
prayer, and
And they r. up the same *Lu 24:33*
hour, and
that she r. up hastily and *Joh 11:31*
went out
Then the high priest r. up, and *Ac 5:17*
all
For before these days r. up *Ac 5:36*
Theudas
After this man r. up Judas of *Ac 5:37*
with him after he r. from the *Ac 10:41*
dead

him, he *r.* up, and came into   *Ac 14:20*
the city
r. up certain of the sect of the   *Ac 15:5*
Peter *r.* up, and said unto   *Ac 15:7*
them
r. up together against them: *Ac 16:22*
and
r. against Paul (B)(E)   *Ac 18:12*
the king *r.* up, and the   *Ac 26:30*
governor
this end Christ both died, and   *Ro 14:9*
r.
to eat and drink, and *r.* up   *1Co 10:7*
to play
and that he *r.* again the third   *1Co 15:4*
day
preached that he *r.* from the   *1Co 15:12*
dead
which died for them and *r.*   *2Co 5:15*
again
that Jesus died and *r.* again,   *1Th 4:14*
even
her smoke *r.* up for ever and   *Re 19:3*
ever

ROSETTES

sockets or *r.* of gold (A)   *Ex 28:11;*
                   28:13, 25

ROSH

and *R.* Muppim, and   *Ge 36:21*
Huppim

ROT

doth make thy thigh to *r.* and   *Nu 5:21*
belly to swell, and thy thigh   *Nu 5:22*
to *r.*
shall swell, and her thigh shall   *Nu 5:27*
r.
the name of the wicked shall *r.*   *Pr 10:7*
chooseth a tree that will not   *Isa 40:20*
r.
tongue *r.* in mouths (R)   *Zec 14:12*

ROTATION

priestly *r.* (B)   *2Ch 5:11*

ROTTED

dirty clothes of old way of   *Eph 4:22*
living which were *r.* (P)
r. and ruined (A)(B)(N)(P)(R)   *Jas 5:2*

ROTTEN

made us a *r.* stench (A)   *Ex 5:21*
he, as a *r.* thing, consumeth,   *Job 13:28*
as a
iron as straw, brass as *r.*   *Job 41:27*
wood
old cast clouts and old *r.*   *Jer 38:11*
rags
old cast clouts and *r.* rags   *Jer 38:12*
under
The seed is *r.* under their   *Joe 1:17*
clods
tree *r.*, fruit *r.* (A)(P)   *M't 12:33*

ROTTENNESS

ashamed is as *r.* in his bones   *Pr 12:4*
flesh: but envy the *r.* of the   *Pr 14:30*
bones
the stench of *r.*   *Isa 3:24*
(A)(B)(E)(R)(S)
so their roots shall be as *r.* and   *Isa 5:24*
and to the house of Judah as   *Ho 5:12*
r.
r. entered into my bones,   *Hab 3:16*
and I
all kinds of *r.* (P)   *M't 23:27*

ROUGH

down the heifer unto a *r.*   *De 21:4*
valley
he stayeth his *r.* wind in the   *Isa 27:8*
day
straight, and the *r.* places   *Isa 40:4*
plain
to come up as the *r.*   *Jer 51:27*
caterpillers
the *r.* goat is the king of   *Da 8:21*
Grecia
wear a *r.* garment to deceive   *Zec 13:4*
the *r.* ways shall be made   *Lu 3:5*
smooth

ROUGHLY

them, and spake *r.* unto them   *Ge 42:7*
spake *r.* to us, and took us   *Ge 42:30*
for spies
what if thy father answer   *1Sa 20:10*
thee *r.*
the king answered the   *1Ki 12:13*
people *r.*
And the king answered   *2Ch 10:13*
them *r.*
but the rich answereth *r.*   *Pr 18:23*

ROUND

flows *r.* all the land (B)(R)   *Ge 2:11;*
                     2:13
compassed the house *r.* old and   *Ge 19:4*
young
there lay a small *r.* thing on   *Ex 16:14*
ground
the inhabitants shall environ us   *Jos 7:9*
r.
going *r.* around   *J'g 11:18*
(A)(B)(E)(R)
the molten sea was *r.* all   *1Ki 7:23*
about
a *r.* compass   *1Ki 7:35*
top of the throne was *r.*   *1Ki 10:19*
was *r.* the city (E)(R)   *2Ki 6:15*
were *r.* about (S)   *Ps 18:5*
strong bulls of Bashan have   *Ps 22:12*
beset me *r.*
goes *r.* and *r.* (B)(R)   *Ec 1:6*
thy navel is like a *r.* goblet   *Ca 7:2*
the Lord will take away their   *Isa 3:18*
r. tires
thine enemies shall compass   *Lu 19:43*
thee *r.*

ROUND *ABOUT*

the terror of God was on   *Ge 35:5*
cities *r.* about
digged *r.* about the river for   *Ex 7:24*
water
in the morning dew lay *r.*   *Ex 16:13*
about the host
thou shalt set bounds to the   *Ex 19:12*
people *r.* about
cause the house to be scraped   *Le 14:41*
r. about
the Levites encamp *r.* about   *Nu 1:50*
tabernacle
Moses set the elders *r.*   *Nu 11:24*
about the tabernacle
all Israel, that were *r.* about   *Nu 16:34*
them fled
company shall lick up all that   *Nu 22:4*
are *r.* about us
gods of the people *r.* about   *De 6:14;*
you   *13:7*
giveth rest from enemies *r.*   *De 12:10;*
about   *25:19; Jos 21:44; 2Ch 15:15*
measure the cities *r.* about him   *De 21:2*
that is slain
and ye shall go *r.* about the   *Jos 6:3*
city once
men beset the house *r.* about   *J'g 19:22;*
                     20:5
for Saul compassed David *r.*   *1Sa 23:26*
about
sent into the land of the   *1Sa 31:9;*
Philistines *r.* about   *1Ch 10:9*
made darkness pavilions *r.*   *2Sa 22:12*
about
Solomon had peace on all   *1Ki 4:24*
sides *r.* about
and his fame was in all   *1Ki 4:31*
nations *r.* about
and the water ran *r.* about   *1Ki 18:35*
the altar
and chariots of fire *r.* about   *2Ki 6:17*
Elisha
they lodged *r.* about the   *1Ch 9:27*
house of God
thine hands have fashioned me   *Job 10:8*
r. about
his archers compass me *r.*   *Job 16:13*
about
his troops encamp *r.* about   *Job 19:12*
my tabernacle
therefore snares are *r.* about   *Job 22:10*
thee
it is turned *r.* about by his   *Job 37:12*
counsels
his teeth are terrible *r.* about   *Job 41:14*
that set themselves against me   *Ps 3:6*
r. about
head be lifted above mine   *Ps 27:6*
enemies *r.* about

angel encampeth *r.* about   *Ps 34:7*
them that fear him
a decision to them   *Ps 44:13; 79:4*
that are *r.* about
walk about Zion, and go *r.*   *Ps 48:12*
about her
make a noise, and go *r.* about   *Ps 59:6;*
the city   *59:14*
let all *r.* about him bring   *Ps 76:11*
presents to him
they came *r.* about me daily   *Ps 88:17*
like water
or like to thy faithfulness *r.*   *Ps 89:8*
about thee
he burneth up his enemies *r.*   *Ps 97:3*
about him
as the mountains are *r.* about   *Ps 125:2*
Jerusalem
children like olive plants *r.*   *Ps 128:3*
about thy table
I will camp against thee *r.*   *Isa 29:3*
about
and it hath set him on fire *r.*   *Isa 42:25*
about
lift up thine eyes *r.* about   *Isa 49:18;*
and behold   *60:4*
a fire, it shall devour all   *Jer 21:14*
things *r.* about it
for fear was *r.* about, saith   *Jer 46:5*
the Lord
camp against Babylon *r.*   *Jer 50:29*
about
in trouble they shall be   *Jer 51:2*
against her *r.* about
the wheels were full of eyes   *Eze 10:12*
r. about
will make places *r.* about my   *Eze 34:26*
hill a blessing
gather yourselves together *r.*   *Joe 3:11*
about
there will sit to judge all the   *Joe 3:12*
heathen *r.* about
an adversary even *r.* about   *Am 3:11*
the land
the depth closed me *r.* about,   *Jon 2:5*
the weed
I will be to her a wall of fire *r.*   *Zec 2:5*
about
he hedged the vineyard *r.*   *M't 21:33*
fear came on all that dwelt *r.*   *Lu 1:65*
about
the glory of the Lord shone *r.*   *Lu 2:9*
about them
shined *r.* about him a light   *Ac 9:3*
from heaven
r. about to Illyricum, I have   *Ro 15:19*
preached
there was a rainbow *r.* about   *Re 4:3*
the throne
r. about the throne were four   *Re 4:4*
and twenty seats
four beasts angels *r.*   *Re 4:6; 5:11*
about the throne

ROUSE

an old lion; who shall *r.* him   *Ge 49:9*
up

ROUT

arrows *r.* them (R)   *Ps 144:6*
come to *r.* them, cast down   *Zec 1:21*
(B)
r. of the kings (N)   *Heb 7:1*

ROUTED

r. the Amalekites (R)   *Ge 14:7*
attacked and *r.* (A)   *Ge 14:15*
routed (S)   *Nu 14:45;*
    Jos 10:10; J'g 4:15; 1Sa 7:10; 2Sa 7:10
r. Sisera (R)   *J'g 4:15*
r. the entire army (B)   *J'g 8:12*
they were *r.* (A)(R)   *J'g 11:33; 20:35*
Lord hath *r.*   *1Sa 4:3; 2Ch 20:22*
r. them (R)   *2Sa 22:15*
were *r.* (B)   *1Ki 8:33*

ROVERS

David against the band of   *1Ch 12:21*
the *r.*
band of raiders (A)(B)(R)   *1Ch 12:21*

ROW

the first *r.* shall be a sardius   *Ex 28:17*
carbuncle: this shall be the   *Ex 28:17*
first *r.*

the second *r.* shall be an emerald   *Ex 28:18*
the third *r.* a ligure, and agate, and   *Ex 28:19*
the fourth *r.* a beryl, and an onyx   *Ex 28:20*
the first *r.* was a sardius, a topaz   *Ex 39:10*
a carbuncle: this was the first *r.*   *Ex 39:10*
second *r.* an emerald, a sapphire   *Ex 39:11*
the third *r.* a ligure, an agate   *Ex 39:12*
the fourth *r.* a beryl, an onyx, and   *Ex 29:13*
set them in two rows, six on a *r.*   *Le 24:6*
put pure frankincense upon each *r.*   *Le 24:7*
stone, and a *r.* of cedar beams.   *1Ki 6:36*
on forty five pillars, fifteen in a *r.*   *1Ki 7:3*
stones, and a *r.* of cedar beams   *1Ki 7:12*
stones, and a *r.* of good timber   *Ezr 6:4*
there was a *r.* of building round   *Eze 46:23*

ROWED

men *r.* hard to bring it to the land   *Jon 1:13*
they had *r.* about five and twenty   *Joh 6:19*

ROWERS

Thy *r.* have brought thee into   *Eze 27:26*

ROWING

And he saw them toiling in *r.*   *M'k 6:48*

ROWS

of stones, even four *r.* of stones   *Ex 28:17*
And they set in it four *r.* of stones   *Ex 39:10*
And thou shalt set them in two *r.*   *Le 24:6*
court with three *r.* of hewed stone   *1Ki 6:36*
upon four *r.* of cedar pillars   *1Ki 7:2*
And there were windows in three *r.*   *1Ki 7:4*
was with three *r.* of hewed stones   *1Ki 7:12*
two *r.* round about upon the one   *1Ki 7:18*
were two hundred in *r.* round about   *1Ki 7:20*
the knops were cast in two *r.* when   *1Ki 7:24*
r. of pomegranates for one network   *1Ki 7:42*
Two *r.* of oxen were cast when it   *2Ch 4:3*
r. of pomegranates on each wreath   *2Ch 4:13*
With three *r.* of great stones   *Ezr 6:4*
are comely with *r.* of jewels   *Ca 1:10*
with boiling places under the *r.*   *Eze 46:23*

ROYAL

fat, and he shall yield *r.* dainties   *Ge 49:20*
great city as one of the *r.* cities   *Jos 10:2*
to his *r.* robes (A)   *1Sa 19:24*
the servant dwell in the *r.* city   *1Sa 27:5*
of Ammon, and took the *r.* city   *2Sa 12:26*
Solomon gave her of his *r.* bounty   *1Ki 10:13*
arose and destroyed all the seed *r.*   *2Ki 11:1*
the son of Elishama the seed *r.*   *2Ki 25:25*
such *r.* majesty as had not been   *1Ch 29:25*
the seed *r.* of the house of Judah   *2Ch 22:10*
r. wine in abundance, according   *Es 1:7*
feast for the women in the *r.* house   *Es 1:9*

before the king with the crown *r.*   *Es 1:11*
go a *r.* commandment from him.   *Es 1:19*
king give her *r.* estate unto another   *Es 1:19*
king Ahasuerus into his house *r.*   *Es 2:16*
he set the *r.* crown upon her head   *Es 2:17*
Esther put on her *r.* apparel   *Es 5:1*
upon his *r.* throne in the *r.* house   *Es 5:1*
Let the *r.* apparel be brought   *Es 6:8*
crown *r.* which is set upon his head   *Es 6:8*
in *r.* apparel of blue and white   *Es 8:15*
r. diadem in the hand of thy God   *Isa 62:3*
the son of Elishama, of the seed *r.*   *Jer 41:1*
spread his *r.* pavilion over them   *Jer 43:10*
together to establish a *r.* statute   *Da 6:7*
Herod, arrayed in *r.* apparel sat   *Ac 12:21*
If ye fulfill the *r.* law according to   *Jas 2:8*
a *r.* priesthood, an holy nation, a   *1Pe 2:9*
receive *r.* authority (B)(E)(N)(P)   *Re 17:12*
exercise of *r.* authority (N)   *Re 17:13*

ROYALTY

acquire *r.* by intrigues (B)   *Da 11:21*

RUBBED

and every shoulder was *r.* raw (S)   *Eze 29:18*

RUBBING

did eat, *r.* them in their hands   *Lu 6:1*

RUBBISH

turn to *r.* heaps (B)   *2Ki 19:25*
heaps of the *r.* which are burned   *Ne 4:2*
is decayed, and there is much *r.*   *Ne 4:10*
body go to the *r.* heap (P)   *M't 5:29; 5:30; 23:33*
regard as waste, consider as *r.* (B)(P)   *Ph'p 3:8*

RUBIES

the price of wisdom is above *r.*   *Job 28:18*
wisdom is above that of pearls (B)(R)   *Job 28:18*
She is more precious than *r.*   *Pr 3:15*
more valuable than jewels (B)(R)   *Pr 3:15; 8:11*
For wisdom is better than *r.*   *Pr 8:11*
There is gold, and a multitude of *r.*   *Pr 20:15*
a multitude of pearls (A)   *Pr 20:15*
a mass of costly stones (B)(R)   *Pr 20:15*
woman? for her price is far above *r.*   *Pr 31:10*
more precious than jewels (B)(R)   *Pr 31:10*
were more ruddy in body than *r.*   *La 4:7*

RUDDER

the sea, and loosed the *r.* bands   *Ac 27:40*

RUDDY

Now he was *r.* and withal of   *1Sa 16:12*
for he was but a youth, and *r.* and   *1Sa 17:42*
My beloved is white and *r.* the   *Ca 5:10*
were more *r.* in body than rubies   *La 4:7*

RUDE

r. and uncultivated state (A)   *Ps 92:6*
not *r.* (N)(R)   *1Co 13:5*
But though I be *r.* in speech, yet   *2Co 11:6*

RUDIMENTARY

r. and elemental teachings (A)   *Col 2:8*

RUDIMENTS

r. of the world (E)   *Ga 4:3*
beggarly *r.* (B)(E)   *Ga 4:9*
after the *r.* of the world, and   *Col 2:8*
rudimentary and elemental teachings (A)   *Col 2:8*
world's elementary principles (B)   *Col 2:8*
elemental spirits of the world (N)(R)   *Col 2:8*
men's idea of nature of the world (P)   *Col 2:8*
be dead from the *r.* of the world   *Col 2:20*
world's crude and elemental notions and teachings of externalism (A)   *Col 2:20*
elementary principles of the world (B)   *Col 2:20*
elemental spirits of the world (N)(R)   *Col 2:20*
principles of this world's life (P)   *Col 2:20*
the *r.* of Christianity (N)   *Heb 6:1*

RUE

for ye tithe mint and *r.* and all   *Lu 11:42*
he will not *r.* it (B)   *Heb 7:21*

RUFUS

the father of Alexander and *R.*   *M'k 15:21*
Salute *R.* chosen in the Lord   *Ro 16:13*

RUHAMAH

Ammi; and to your sisters, *R.*   *Ho 2:1*

RUIN

ye shall go down to *r.* (B)   *De 8:19*
single him out for *r.* (A)(R)   *De 29:21*
kings abandoned to *r.* (B)(R)   *2Ch 34:11*
r. has been decided (B)   *Es 7:7*
the *r.* of my race (B)   *Es 8:6*
r. ready for his stumbling (B)   *Job 18:12*
rejoiced at the *r.* of him (R)   *Job 31:29*
ungodly end in *r.* (B)   *Ps 1:6*
son of mother bring to *r.* (B)   *Ps 50:20*
hast brought his strong holds to *r.*   *Ps 89:40*
the *r.* of the wicked (A)(R)   *Pr 3:25*
poverty of poor is their *r.* (A)(B)(R)   *Pr 10:15; 13:3; 14:28; 18:7*
lack of people is prince's *r.* (A)(B)   *Pr 14:28*
folly brings way to *r.* (R)   *Pr 19:3*
who knoweth the *r.* of them both   *Pr 24:22*
and a flattering mouth worketh *r.*   *Pr 26:28*
and let this *r.* be under thy hand   *Isa 3:6*
thereof; and he brought it to *r.*   *Isa 23:13*
city an heap of a defenced city a *r.*   *Isa 25:2*
lest I *r.* you (B)   *Jer 1:17*
so iniquity shall not be your *r.*   *Eze 18:30*
r., *r.* I will make it (B)(R)   *Eze 21:27*
midst of the seas in day of thy *r.*   *Eze 27:27*
Upon his *r.* shall all the fowls of the   *Eze 31:13*
the day of their *r.* (A)(R)   *Ob 12*
and the *r.* of that house was great   *Lu 6:49*
cause the *r.* of (A)(B)(P)(R)   *Ro 14:15*
do not *r.* work of God (N)   *Ro 14:20*
those on way to *r.* (N)   *1Co 1:18*
the *r.* of the flesh (B)   *1Co 5:5*
not for your *r.* (B)   *2Co 10:6*
he once reviled, set out to *r.* (A)   *Ga 1:23*
penalty of everlasting *r.* (A)   *2Th 1:9*
is the *r.* to those who listen (N)(R)   *2Ti 2:14*

RUINED

you have r. me (A)	Ge 34:30
land not r. (A)(B)	Ge 41:36
being r. by gadflies (B)(R)	Ex 8:24
my life is r. (B)	Job 17:1
r. their vines (B)	Ps 105:33
For Jerusalem is r. and Judah	Isa 3:8
we are r. (E)(R)	Jer 4:13; Mic 2:4
ruined (B)	Jer 4:30; 9:19; Zec 11:2
land r. and laid waste	Jer 9:12
(A)(B)(R)	
and r. cities are become	Eze 36:35
fenced	
that I the Lord build the r.	Eze 36:36
places	
harvest of field is r. (B)	Joe 2:11
r. and laid waste (A)	Mic 2:4; Zec 11:3
Nineveh is r. (B)	Na 3:7
the skins are r. (A)(B)(P)	M't 9:17
whole nation r. (B)	Joh 11:50
weak man is r. (A)(B)	1Co 8:11
r., exploited no one (B)(P)	2Co 7:2
destined to be r. by wear (B)	Col 2:22
its appearance is r. (B)	Jas 1:11
rotted and r.	Jas 5:2
(A)(B)(N)(P)(R)	

RUINING

r. whole families (N)	Tit 1:11

RUINOUS

waste fenced cities into r. heaps	2Ki 19:25
a city, and it shall be a r. heap	Isa 17:1
waste defenced cities into r. heaps	Isa 37:26
introduce r. heresies (B)	2Pe 2:1

RUINS

make cities r. (B)	Le 26:31; 26:33; Isa 51:3; 58:12; Hag 1:9
a heap of r. (R)	Jos 8:28
in the r. (S)	2Ch 34:6
lies in r. (R)	Ne 2:17
foolishness r. his affairs (B)	Pr 19:3
r. without residents (B)	Isa 6:11; 9:9; 12:6; 33:24
faint, and their r. be multiplied	Eze 21:15
gates battered into r. (B)(R)	Eze 24:12
vanished in everlasting r. (R)	Ho 9:6
great house into r. (A)	Am 6:11
and I will raise up his r. and I will	Am 9:11
this house lies in r. (A)(B)(R)	Hag 1:4
no moth r. (B)(P)	Lu 12:33
I will build again the r. thereof	Ac 15:16
r. the temple of God (B)	1Co 3:17

RULE

the greater light to r. the day	Ge 1:16
and the lesser light to r. the night	Ge 1:16
to r. over the day and over the	Ge 1:18
r. over (B)	Ge 1:26
husband, and he shall r. over thee	Ge 3:16
he shall dominate you (B)	Ge 3:16
desire, and thou shalt r. over him	Ge 4:7
you must master it (A)(B)(R)	Ge 4:7
shalt not r. over him with rigour	Le 25:43
neither lord it over him (B)	Le 25:43; 25:46, 53
r. over him with harshness (A)(R)	Le 25:43
r. one over another with rigour	Le 25:46
shall not r. with rigour over him in	Le 25:53
R. thou over us, both thou	J'g 8:22
unto them, I will not r. over you	J'g 8:23
neither shall my son r. over you	J'g 8:23
you: the Lord shall r. over you	J'g 8:23
which bare r. over the people that	1Ki 9:23
officials who supervised (B)	1Ki 9:23

who had charge over the people (R)	1Ki 9:23
captains that had r. over his chariots	1Ki 22:31
may r. my people (R)	2Ch 1:11
fifty, that bare r. over the people	2Ch 8:10
revolted from the r. of Judah (A)(R)	2Ch 21:8
servants bare r. over the people	Ne 5:15
according to the r. (B)	Es 1:8
should bare r. in his own house	Es 1:22
Jews had r. over them that hated	Es 9:1
establish their r. in earth (A)(B)(R)	Job 38:33
r. thou in the midst of thine	Ps 110:2
The sun to r. by day: for his	Ps 136:8
The moon and stars to r. by night	Ps 136:9
By me princes r. and nobles	Pr 8:16
hand of the diligent shall bare r.	Pr 12:24
servant shall have r. over a son	Pr 17:2
a servant to have r. over princes	Pr 19:10
hath no r. over his own spirit	Pr 25:28
but when the wicked beareth r.	Pr 29:2
he have r. over all my labour	Ec 2:19
and babes shall r. over them	Isa 3:4
oppressors, women r. over them	Isa 3:12
they shall r. over their oppressors	Isa 14:2
a fierce king shall r. over them	Isa 19:4
r. this people which is in Jerusalem	Isa 28:14
and princes shall r. in judgment	Isa 32:1
and his arm shall r. for him	Isa 40:10
him, and made him r. over kings	Isa 41:2
r. over them make them to howl	Isa 52:5
thou never barest r. over them	Isa 63:19
priests bare r. by their means	Jer 5:31
the sceptres of them that bare r.	Eze 19:11
no strong rod to be a sceptre to r.	Eze 19:14
poured out, will I r. over you	Eze 20:33
shall no more r. over the nations	Eze 29:15
shall bare r. over all the earth	Da 2:39
known that the heavens do r.	Da 4:26
that shall r. with great dominion	Da 11:3
shall cause them to r. over many	Da 11:39
the heathen should r. over them	Joe 2:17
shall r. my house (A)(R)	Zec 3:7
shall sit and r. upon his throne	Zec 6:13
that shall r. my people Israel	M't 2:6
accounted to r. over the Gentiles	M'k 10:42
the r. I lay down (P)(R)	1Co 7:17
he shall have put down all r. and	1Co 15:24
the r. which God hath distributed	2Co 10:13
you according to our r. abundantly	2Co 10:15
many as walk according to this r.	Ga 6:16
all r. and authority (A)(E)(R)	Eph 1:21
let us walk by the same r. let us	Ph'p 3:16
all r. and authority (A)(B)(P)(R)	Col 2:10
the peace of God r. in your hearts	Col 3:15
know not how to r. his own house	1Ti 3:5
young women r. the house (S)	1Ti 5:14
the elders that r. well be counted	1Ti 5:17
them which have the r. over you	Heb 13:7
Obey them that have r. over you	Heb 13:17

Salute all that have r. over you	Heb 13:24
shall r. them with a rod of iron	Re 2:27
r. all nations with a rod of iron	Re 12:5
he shall r. them with a rod of iron	Re 19:15

RULED

house, that r. over all that he had	Ge 24:2
word shall all my people be r.	Ge 41:40
and r. from Aroer, which is upon	Jos 12:2
in the days when the judges r.	Ru 1:1
which r. over the people that	1Ki 5:16
who r. Moab (A)(R)	1Ch 4:22
that r. throughout the house	1Ch 26:6
which have r. over all countries	Ezr 4:20
that hated them r. over them	Ps 106:41
he that r. the nations in anger, is	Isa 14:6
have r. us (A)(R)	Isa 26:13
Servants have r. over us: there	La 5:8
and with cruelty have ye r. them	Eze 34:4
God r. in the kingdom of men	Da 5:21
our rulers who r. us (R)	Da 9:12
to his dominion which he r.	Da 11:4

RULER

he made him r. over all the land	Ge 41:43
he said to the r. of his house	Ge 43:16
a r. throughout all the land of	Ge 45:8
nor curse the r. of thy people	Ex 22:28
When a r. hath sinned, and	Le 4:22
done	
a man, every one a r. among them	Nu 13:2
Zebul the r. of the city heard	J'g 9:30
no r. in the land (B)	J'g 18:7
appointed thee r. over Israel	1Sa 25:30
me r. over the people of the Lord	2Sa 6:21
the sheep, to be r. over my people	2Sa 7:8
Jairite was a chief r. about David	2Sa 20:26
appointed him to be r. over Israel	1Ki 1:35
made him r. over all the charge	1Ki 11:28
them he made Gedaliah r.	2Ki 25:22
and of him came the chief r.	1Ch 9:11
the r. of the house of God	1Ch 9:11
Phinehas was the r. over them in	1Ch 9:20
shalt be r. over my people Israel	1Ch 11:2
be r. over my people Israel	1Ch 17:7
Shebuel was r. of the treasures	1Ch 26:24
his course was Mikloth also the r.	1Ch 27:4
r. of the Reubenites was Eliezer the	1Ch 27:16
he hath chosen Judah to be the r.	1Ch 28:4
anointed him r. (B)	1Ch 29:22
to be a r. over my people Israel	2Ch 6:5
fail thee a man to be r. in Israel	2Ch 7:18
to be r. among his brethren: for	2Ch 11:22
the r. of the house of Judah, for	2Ch 19:11
the scribe and Maaseiah the r.	2Ch 26:11
which Cononiah the Levite was r.	2Ch 31:12
Azariah the r. of the house of God	2Ch 31:13
r. of the half part of Jerusalem	Ne 3:9
r. of the half part of Jerusalem, he	Ne 3:12
the r. of part of Beth-haccerem	Ne 3:14
Col-hozeh, the r. of part of Mizpah	Ne 3:15
the r. of the half part of Beth-zur	Ne 3:16
the r. of the half part of Keliah	Ne 3:17; 3:18
son of Jeshua, the r. of Mizpah	Ne 3:19

and Hananiah the *r.* of the   *Ne 7:2*
palace
was the *r.* of the house of   *Ne 11:11*
God
r. over the nations (A)(E)   *Ps 22:28*
is little Benjamin with their *r.*   *Ps 68:27*
the *r.* of the people, and let   *Ps 105:20*
him
house, and *r.* of all his   *Ps 105:21*
substance
having no guide, overseer, or *r.*   *Pr 6:7*
When thou sittest to eat with a   *Pr 23:1*
r.
is a wicked *r.* over the poor   *Pr 28:15*
people
If a *r.* hearken to lies, all his   *Pr 29:12*
the spirit of the *r.* rise up   *Ec 10:4*
against
which proceedeth from the *r.*   *Ec 10:5*
be thou our *r.* and let this ruin   *Isa 3:6*
make me not a *r.* of the people   *Isa 3:7*
Send ye the lamb to the *r.* of   *Isa 16:1*
violence in the land, *r.*   *Jer 51:46*
against
there is no king, lord, nor *r.*   *Da 2:10*
hath made thee *r.* over them   *Da 2:38*
all
him *r.* over the whole   *Da 2:48*
province of
be the third *r.* in the kingdom   *Da 5:7;*
                               5:16, 29
unto me that is to be *r.* in   *Mic 5:2*
Israel
things, that have no *r.* over   *Hab 1:14*
them
shall came a *r.* (R)   *M't 2:6*
came a certain *r.* and   *M't 9:18*
worshipped
hath made *r.* over his   *M't 24:45*
household
make him *r.* over all his   *M't 24:47*
goods
make thee *r.* over many   *M't 25:21;*
things   *25:23*
from the *r.* of the   *M'k 5:35*
synagogue's
saith unto the *r.* of the   *M'k 5:36*
synagogue
house of the *r.* of the   *M'k 5:38*
synagogue
and he was a *r.* of the   *Lu 8:41*
synagogue
the *r.* of the synagogue's house   *Lu 8:49*
shall make *r.* over his   *Lu 12:42*
household
make him *r.* over all that he   *Lu 12:44*
hath
the *r.* of the synagogue   *Lu 13:14*
answered
And a certain *r.* asked him,   *Lu 18:18*
saying
bear to *r.* of the feast (E)   *Joh 2:8*
When the *r.* of the feast had   *Joh 2:9*
tasted
named Nicodemus, a *r.* of the   *Joh 3:1*
Jews
made thee a *r.* and a judge   *Ac 7:27*
over us
Who made thee a *r.* and a   *Ac 7:35*
judge
God send to be a *r.* and a   *Ac 7:35*
deliverer
the chief *r.* of the synagogue   *Ac 18:8;*
                               18:17
speak evil of the *r.* of thy   *Ac 23:5*
people
angelic *r.* and authorities   *Eph 3:10*
(A)(B)(N)(P)

RULERS

then make them *r.* over my   *Ge 47:6*
cattle
the *r.* of the congregation   *Ex 16:22*
came
r. of thousands, and *r.* of   *Ex 18:21*
hundreds
r. of fifties, and *r.* of tens   *Ex 18:21*
r. of thousands, *r.* of   *Ex 18:25*
hundreds
r. of fifties, and *r.* of tens   *Ex 18:25*
the *r.* of the congregation   *Ex 34:31*
returned
And the *r.* brought onyx   *Ex 35:27*
stones
and I will make them *r.* over   *De 1:13*
you
that the Philistines are *r.*   *J'g 15:11*
over us
r. decree righteously (B)   *2Sa 8:15*

and David's sons were chief *r.*   *2Sa 8:18*
to Samaria, unto the *r.* of   *2Ki 10:1*
Jezreel
and fetched the *r.* over   *2Ki 11:4*
hundreds
And he took the *r.* over   *2Ki 11:19*
hundreds
to Joab and to their *r.* of the   *1Ch 21:2*
people
David made *r.* over   *1Ch 26:32*
Reubenites
these were the *r.* of the   *1Ch 27:31*
substance
with the *r.* of the king's work   *1Ch 29:6*
and gathered the *r.* of the   *2Ch 29:20*
city, and
Jethiel, *r.* of the house of   *2Ch 35:8*
God
r. hath been chief in this   *Ezr 9:2*
trespass
r. of all the congregation   *Ezr 10:14*
stand
the *r.* knew not whither I   *Ne 2:16*
went
nor to the nobles, nor to the   *Ne 2:16*
r. nor
said unto the nobles, and to   *Ne 4:14*
the *r.*
the *r.* were behind all the   *Ne 4:16*
house of
unto the nobles, and to the *r.*   *Ne 4:19*
I rebuked the nobles, and the *r.*   *Ne 5:7*
hundred and fifty of the Jews   *Ne 5:17*
and *r.*
together the nobles, and the *r.*   *Ne 7:5*
And the *r.* of the people dwelt   *Ne 11:1*
I and the half of the *r.* with   *Ne 12:40*
me
Then contended I with the *r.*   *Ne 13:11*
to the *r.* of every people of   *Es 3:12*
every
deputies and *r.* of the provinces   *Es 8:9*
And all the *r.* of the provinces   *Es 9:3*
and the *r.* take counsel together   *Ps 2:2*
O *r.* of the earth   *Ps 2:10*
(A)(B)(R)
makes *r.* of earth (R)   *Ps 40:23*
word of the Lord, ye *r.* of   *Isa 1:10*
Sodom
wicked, and the sceptre of the   *Isa 14:5*
r.
All thy *r.* are fled together   *Isa 22:3*
prophets and your *r.* the   *Isa 29:10*
seers
abhorreth, to a servant of *r.*   *Isa 49:7*
the *r.* also transgressed against   *Jer 2:8*
me (S)
to be *r.* over the seed of   *Jer 33:26*
Abraham
I break in pieces captains   *Jer 51:23*
and *r.*
all the *r.* thereof, and all the   *Jer 51:28*
land
and her *r.* and her mighty   *Jer 51:57*
men
clothed with blue, captains   *Eze 23:6*
and *r.*
and *r.* clothed most   *Eze 23:12*
gorgeously
captains and *r.* great lords   *Eze 23:23*
r. or nations (A)   *Eze 36:6*
and all the *r.* of the provinces   *Da 3:2*
to
and all the *r.* of the province   *Da 3:3*
were
our *r.* who directed us   *Da 9:12*
(B)(R)
her *r.* with shame do love,   *Ho 4:18*
Give ye
one of the *r.* of the   *M'k 5:22*
synagogue
before *r.* and kings for my   *M'k 13:9*
sake
to *r.* and authorities   *Lu 12:11*
(B)(E)(R)
kings and *r.* for my name's   *Lu 21:12*
sake
priests and the *r.* and the   *Lu 23:13*
people
the *r.* also with them derided   *Lu 23:35*
him
chief priests and our *r.*   *Lu 24:20*
delivered
Do the *r.* know indeed that   *Joh 7:26*
this is
of the *r.* or of the Pharisees   *Joh 7:48*
believed
among the chief *r.* many   *Joh 12:42*
believed
ye did it as did also your *r.*   *Ac 3:17*

their *r.* and elders, and scribes   *Ac 4:5*
Ye *r.* of the people, and elders   *Ac 4:8*
and the *r.* were gathered   *Ac 4:26*
together
the *r.* of the synagogue sent   *Ac 13:15*
unto
dwell at Jerusalem, and their   *Ac 13:27*
r.
also of the Jews with their *r.*   *Ac 14:5*
into the marketplace unto the   *Ac 16:19*
r.
r. commanded they be beaten   *Ac 16:22*
brethren unto the *r.* of the city   *Ac 17:6*
the people and the *r.* of the   *Ac 17:8*
city
r. are not a terror to good   *Ro 13:3*
works
against the *r.* of the darkness   *Eph 6:12*
r. or authorities (A)(B)   *Col 1:16*
r. and authorities (E)   *Tit 3:1*

RULER'S

nor *r.* staff from (E)(R)   *Ge 49:10*
Many seek the *r.* favour: but   *Pr 29:26*
every
when Jesus came into the *r.*   *M't 9:23*
house

RULES

my orders, my *r.* (B)   *Ge 26:6*
r. and laws (B)   *Ex 18:16*
make clean *r.* (B)   *Ex 18:20*
not follow their *r.* (B)   *Le 18:3*
r. over the nations (B)(R)   *Ps 22:28*
break all *r.* of conduct (N)   *Ro 1:28*
why submit to *r.* and   *Col 2:20*
regulations (A)(B)(R)
earlier *r.* are cancelled (N)   *Heb 7:18*
r. for service of God   *Heb 9:1*
(A)(P)(R)
external *r.* and regulations   *Heb 9:10*
(A)(P)

RULEST

r. not thou over all the   *2Ch 20:6*
kingdoms
Thou *r.* the raging of the sea   *Ps 89:9*

RULETH

He that *r.* over men must be   *2Sa 23:3*
just
let them know that God *r.* in   *Ps 59:13*
Jacob
He *r.* by his power for ever;   *Ps 66:7*
his
and his kingdom *r.* over all   *Ps 103:19*
he that *r.* his spirit than he   *Pr 16:32*
that
The rich *r.* over the poor, and   *Pr 22:7*
wherein one man *r.* over another   *Ec 8:9*
the cry of him that *r.* among   *Ec 9:17*
fools
that the most High   *Da 4:17; 4:25, 32*
r. in the
but Judah yet *r.* with God,   *Ho 11:12*
and is
he that *r.* with diligence; he   *Ro 12:8*
that
One that *r.* well his own house   *1Ti 3:4*

RULING

must be just, *r.* in the fear of   *2Sa 23:3*
God
their *r.* tyrants are (B)(R)   *Isa 3:12*
David, and *r.* any more in   *Jer 22:30*
Judah
my *r.* in all churches (B)   *1Co 7:17*
r. their children and their   *1Ti 3:12*
own

RUMAH

the daughter of Padaiah of   *2Ki 23:36*
R.

RUMBLING

at the *r.* of his wheels the   *Jer 47:3*
fathers

RUMOR

sound of a *r.* (A)(R)(S)   *Jer 10:22*

RUMORS

r. from the east (A)   *Da 11:44*
r. of this came (A)   *Ac 11:22*

RUMOUR

and he shall hear a r. and   *2Ki 19:7*
shall
he shall hear a r. and return   *Isa 37:7*
to
I have heard a r. from the   *Jer 49:14*
Lord
fear for the r. that shall be   *Jer 51:46*
heard
a r. shall both come one   *Jer 51:46*
year, and
in another year shall come a   *Jer 51:46*
r. and
mischief and r. shall be upon   *Eze 7:26*
r.
We have heard a r. from the   *Ob 1*
Lord
And this r. of him went forth   *Lu 7:17*

RUMOURS

shall hear of wars and r. of   *M't 24:6;*
wars   *M'k 13:7*

RUMP

take of the ram the fat and   *Ex 29:22*
the r.
fat tail (A)(B)(E)(R)   *Ex 29:22;*
   Le 3:9; 7:3; 8:25; 9:19
the fat thereof and the whole r.   *Le 3:9*
the r. and the fat that covereth   *Le 7:3*
And he took the fat and the r.   *Le 8:25*
the bullock and of the ram   *Le 9:19*
the r.

RUN

whose branches r. over the   *Ge 49:22*
wall
whether his flesh r. with his   *Le 15:3*
issue
or if it r. beyond the time of   *Le 15:25*
her
lest angry fellows r. upon   *J'g 18:25*
thee
some shall r. before his   *1Sa 8:11*
chariots
and r. to the camp to thy   *1Sa 17:17*
brethren
that he might r. to   *1Sa 20:6*
Beth-lehem his
R. find out now the arrows   *1Sa 20:36*
which
and fifty men to r. before him   *2Sa 15:1*
Let me now r. and bear the   *2Sa 18:19*
king
me, I pray thee, also r. after   *2Sa 18:22*
Cushi
Wherefore wilt thou r. my   *2Sa 18:22*
son
But howsoever, said he, let   *2Sa 18:23*
me r.
And he said unto him R.   *2Sa 18:23*
Then
by thee I have r. through a   *2Sa 22:30*
troop
and fifty men to r. before him   *2Sa 15:1*
that I may r. to the man   *2Ki 4:22*
of God
R. now, I pray thee, to   *2Ki 4:26*
meet her
r. after him, and take   *2Ki 5:20*
somewhat
the eyes of the Lord r. to and   *2Ch 16:9*
fro
by thee, I have r. through a   *Ps 18:29*
troop
rejoiceth as a strong man to r.   *Ps 19:5*
as waters which r. continually   *Ps 58:7*
They r. and prepare themselves   *Ps 59:4*
waters to r. down like rivers   *Ps 78:16*
valleys, which r. among the   *Ps 104:10*
hills
r. the way of thy   *Ps 119:32*
commandments
of waters r. down mine   *Ps 119:136*
eyes
For their feet r. to evil, and   *Pr 1:16*
make
All the rivers r. into the sea;   *Ec 1:7*
yet
Draw me, we will r. after thee   *Ca 1:4*

of locusts shall he r. upon   *Isa 33:4*
them
they shall r. and not be weary   *Isa 40:31*
that knew not thee shall r.   *Isa 55:5*
unto thee
Their feet r. to evil, and they   *Isa 59:7*
make
R. to and fro through the   *Jer 5:1*
streets
eyes may r. down with tears   *Jer 9:18;*
   13:17; 14:17
If thou hast r. with the   *Jer 12:5*
footmen
and r. to and fro by the   *Jer 49:3*
hedges
I will suddenly make him r.   *Jer 49:19*
away
I will make them suddenly r.   *Jer 50:44*
away
One post shall r. to meet   *Jer 51:31*
another
let tears r. down like a river   *La 2:18*
day
neither shall thy tears r.   *Eze 24:16*
down
and cause their rivers to r.   *Eze 32:14*
like oil
many shall r. to and fro, and   *Da 12:4*
and as horsemen, so shall they   *Joe 2:4*
r.
They shall r. like mighty men;   *Joe 2:7*
they
They shall r. to and fro in   *Joe 2:9*
the city
they shall r. upon the wall,   *Joe 2:9*
they
let judgment r. down as   *Am 5:24*
waters
Shall horses r. upon the rock   *Am 6:12*
shall r. to and fro to seek the   *Am 8:12*
word
they shall r. like the lightnings   *Na 2:4*
that he may r. that readeth it   *Hab 2:2*
ye r. every man unto his own   *Hag 1:9*
house
R. speak to this young man,   *Zec 2:4*
saying
r. to and fro through the   *Zec 4:10*
whole
did r. to bring his disciples   *M't 28:8*
word
that they which r. in a race   *1Co 9:24*
r. all
prize? So r. that ye may   *1Co 9:24*
obtain
therefore so r. not as   *1Co 9:26*
uncertainly
means I should r. or had r., in   *Ga 2:2*
vain
Ye did r. well; who did hinder   *Ga 5:7*
you
that I have not r. in vain,   *Ph'p 2:16*
neither
let us r. with patience the   *Heb 12:1*
race that
strange that ye r. not with   *1Pe 4:4*
them to

RUNNEST

and when thou r. thou shalt   *Pr 4:12*
not

RUNNETH

to the river that r. to Ahava   *Ezr 8:15*
He r. upon him, even on his   *Job 15:26*
neck
breach, he r. upon me like a   *Job 16:14*
giant
my head with oil; my cup r.   *Ps 23:5*
over
earth: his word r. very   *Ps 147:15*
swiftly
the righteous r. into it, and is   *Pr 18:10*
safe
eye, mine eye r. down with   *La 1:16*
water
Mine eye r. down with rivers   *La 3:48*
of
bottles break, and the wine r.   *M't 9:17*
out
Then she r. and cometh to   *Joh 20:2*
Simon
him that willeth, nor of him   *Ro 9:16*
that r.

RUNNING

in an earthen vessel over r.   *Le 14:5*
water

that was killed over the r.   *Le 14:6*
water
in an earthen vessel over r.   *Le 14:50*
water
the slain bird, and in the r.   *Le 14:51*
water
of the bird, and with the r.   *Le 14:52*
water
hath a r. issue out of his flesh   *Le 15:2*
and bathe his flesh in r. water   *Le 15:13*
is a leper, or hath a r. issue   *Le 22:4*
r. water shall be put thereto   *Nu 19:17*
in a
looked, and behold a man r.   *2Sa 18:24*
the watchman saw another   *2Sa 18:26*
man r.
said, Behold another man r.   *2Sa 18:26*
alone
the r. of the foremost is   *2Sa 18:27*
like
the r. of Ahimaaz the son of   *2Sa 18:27*
Zadok
Naaman saw him r. after   *2Ki 5:21*
him, he
noise of the people r. and   *2Ch 23:12*
praising
r. waters out of thine own   *Pr 5:15*
well
feet that be swift in r. to   *Pr 6:18*
mischief
as the r. to and fro of locusts   *Isa 33:4*
shall
rivers r. round about his   *Eze 31:4*
plants
amazed, and r. to him   *M'k 9:15*
saluted him
that the people came r.   *M'k 9:25*
together
there came one r. and   *M'k 10:17*
kneeled to
and shaken together, and r.   *Lu 6:38*
over
And r. under a certain island   *Ac 27:16*
of many horses r. to battle   *Re 9:9*

RUSH

Can the r. grow up without   *Job 8:11*
mire
Israel head and tail, branch   *Isa 9:14*
and r.
nations shall r. like the   *Isa 17:13*
rushing of
head or tail, branch or r.   *Isa 19:15*
may do

RUSHED

Abimelech r. forward, and   *J'g 9:44*
stood
in wait hasted, and r. upon   *J'g 20:37*
Gibeah
kingdom has been r. (B)   *M't 11:12*
they r. with one accord   *Ac 19:29*
into the

RUSHES

laid it in the r. (A)   *Ex 2:3*
reeds and r. shall wither   *Isa 19:6*
(A)(B)(R)
shall be grass with reeds and   *Isa 35:7*
r.

RUSHETH

as the horse r. into the battle   *Jer 8:6*

RUSHING

the r. serpent (B)   *Job 26:13*
and to the r. of nations, that   *Isa 17:12*
make
of nations, that make a r.   *Isa 17:12*
like the
like the r. of mighty waters   *Isa 17:12*
rush like the r. of many   *Isa 17:13*
waters
like a r. stream (B)(E)(R)   *Isa 59:19*
at the r. of his chariots, and   *Jer 47:3*
behind me a voice of a great   *Eze 3:12*
r.
them, and a noise of a great   *Eze 3:13*
r.
from heaven as of a r. mighty   *Ac 2:2*
wind

RUST

where moth and r. doth   *M't 6:19*
corrupt

neither moth nor *r.* doth corrupt   *M't 6:20*
the *r.* of them shall be a witness   *Jas 5:3*
covered with *r.* (B)   *Jas 5:3*

RUSTED

completely *r.* (A)(E)(N)(R)   *Jas 5:3*
your gold and silver is *r.* (S)   *Jas 5:3*

RUSTLING

sound like *r.* of a serpent (A)   *Jer 46:22*

RUTH

and the name of the other *R.*   *Ru 1:4*
in law; but *R.* clave unto her   *Ru 1:14*
R. said, Intreat me not to leave   *Ru 1:16*
returned, and *R.* the Moabitess   *Ru 1:22*
R. the Moabitess said unto Naomi   *Ru 2:2*
Then said Boaz unto *R.*, Hearest   *Ru 2:8*
R. the Moabitess said, He said unto   *Ru 2:21*
Naomi said unto *R.* her daughter   *Ru 2:22*
answered, I am *R.* thine handmaid   *Ru 3:9*
must buy it also of *R.* the Moabitess   *Ru 4:5*
R. the Moabitess, wife of Mahlon   *Ru 4:10*
Boaz took *R.* and she was his wife   *Ru 4:13*
and Booz begat Obed of *R.*   *M't 1:5*

RUTHLESS

years laid up for the *r.* (R)   *Job 15:20*
r. men seek my life (A)(R)   *Ps 54:3*
the *r.* nations (B)   *Isa 25:3*
the *r.* nations (R)   *Isa 25:3; 25:4-5; 29:5, 20; Jer 15:21*
the *r.* of the nations (B)   *Eze 28:7; 31:12*

S

SABACHTHANI

loud voice, saying, Eli, Eli, lama *s.*   *M't 27:46*
voice, saying, Eloi, Eloi, lama *s.*   *M'k 15:34*

SABAOTH

Except the Lord of *S.* had left us   *Ro 9:29*
Lord of hosts (A)(B)(N)(R)   *Ro 9:29; Jas 5:4*
into the ears of the Lord of *s.*   *Jas 5:4*

SABBATH

rest of the holy *s.* unto the Lord   *Ex 16:23*
for to-day is a *s.* unto the Lord   *Ex 16:25*
on the seventh day, which is the *s.*   *Ex 16:26*
that the Lord hath given you the *s.*   *Ex 16:29*
Remember the *s.* day to keep it holy   *Ex 20:8*
seventh day is the *s.* of the Lord thy   *Ex 20:10*
the Lord blessed the *s.* day   *Ex 20:11*
Ye shall keep the *s.* therefore; for it   *Ex 31:14*
but in the seventh is the *s.* of rest   *Ex 31:15*
whosoever doeth any work in the *s.*   *Ex 31:15*
shall keep the *s.* to observe the *s.*   *Ex 31:16*
an holy day, a *s.* of rest to the Lord   *Ex 35:2*
kindle no fire upon the *s.* day   *Ex 35:3*

It shall be a *s.* of rest unto you and   *Le 16:31*
but the seventh day is the *s.* of rest   *Le 23:3*
s. of the Lord in all your dwellings   *Le 23:3*
morrow after the *s.* the priest shall   *Le 23:11*
you from the morrow after the *s.*   *Le 23:15*
unto the morrow after the seventh *s.*   *Le 23:16*
shall ye have a *s.* a memorial   *Le 23:24*
It shall be unto you a *s.* of rest,   *Le 23:32*
unto even, shall ye celebrate your *s.*   *Le 23:32*
on the first day shall be a *s.*   *Le 23:39*
on the eighth day shall be a *s.*   *Le 23:39*
Every *s.* he shall set it in order   *Le 24:8*
then shall the land keep a *s.* unto   *Le 25:2*
shall be a *s.* of rest unto the land   *Le 25:4*
a *s.* for the Lord: thou shalt neither   *Le 25:4*
s. of the land shall be meat for you   *Le 25:6*
gathered sticks upon the *s.* day   *Nu 15:32*
And on the *s.* day two lambs of the   *Nu 28:9*
is the burnt offering of every *s.*   *Nu 28:10*
Keep the *s.* day to sanctify it, as the   *De 5:12*
seventh day is the *s.* of the Lord   *De 5:14*
commanded thee to keep the *s.* day   *De 5:15*
it is neither new moon, nor *s.*   *2Ki 4:23*
part of you that enter in on the *s.*   *2Ki 11:5*
of all you that go forth on the *s.*   *2Ki 11:7*
men that were to come in on the *s.*   *2Ki 11:9*
them that should go out on the *s.*   *2Ki 11:9*
covert for the *s.* that they had built   *2Ki 16:18*
shewbread, to prepare it every *s.*   *1Ch 9:32*
third part of you entering on the *s.*   *2Ch 23:4*
men that were to come in on the *s.*   *2Ch 23:8*
them that were to go out on the *s.*   *2Ch 23:8*
as she lay desolate she kept *s.*   *2Ch 36:21*
And madest known thy holy *s.*   *Ne 9:14*
ware or any victuals on the *s.* day   *Ne 10:31*
would not buy it of them on the *s.*   *Ne 10:31*
treading wine presses on the *s.*   *Ne 13:15*
brought into Jerusalem on the *s.*   *Ne 13:15*
sold on the *s.* unto the children of   *Ne 13:16*
that ye do, and profane the *s.* day   *Ne 13:17*
more wrath by profaning the *s.*   *Ne 13:18*
began to be dark before the *s.*   *Ne 13:19*
not be opened till after the *s.*   *Ne 13:19*
burden be brought in on the *s.* day   *Ne 13:19*
forth came they no more on the *s.*   *Ne 13:21*
keep the gates, to sanctify the *s.* day   *Ne 13:22*
A Psalm or Son for the *s.* day   *Ps 92 title*
keepeth the *s.* from polluting it   *Isa 56:2; 56:6*
thou turn away thy foot from the *s.*   *Isa 58:13*
and call the *s.* a delight, the holy of   *Isa 58:13*
another, and from one *s.* to another   *Isa 66:23*
and bear no burden on the *s.* day   *Jer 17:21*
burden out of your houses on the *s.*   *Jer 17:22*

hallow the *s.* day, as I commanded   *Jer 17:22*
the gates of this city on the *s.* day   *Jer 17:24*
but hallow the *s.* day, to do no work   *Jer 17:24*
hearken unto me to hallow the *s.*   *Jer 17:27*
gates of Jerusalem on the *s.* day   *Jer 17:27*
but on the *s.* it shall be opened, and   *Eze 46:1*
shall offer unto the Lord in the *s.*   *Eze 46:4*
offerings, as he did on the *s.* day   *Eze 46:12*
and the *s.* that we may set forth   *Am 8:5*
Jesus went on the *s.* day   *M't 12:1*
is not lawful to do upon the *s.* day   *M't 12:2*
how that on the *s.* days the priests   *M't 12:5*
in the temple profane the *s.* and are   *M't 12:5*
of man is Lord even of the *s.* day   *M't 12:8*
Is it lawful to heal on the *s.* days   *M't 12:10*
and if it fall into a pit on the *s.* day   *M't 12:11*
is lawful to do well on the *s.* days   *M't 12:12*
in the winter, neither on the *s.* day   *M't 24:20*
In the end of the *s.* as it began to   *M't 28:1*
s. day he entered the synagogue   *M'k 1:21*
through the corn fields on the *s.*   *M'k 2:23*
on the *s.* that which is not lawful   *M'k 2:24*
The *s.* was made for man, and not   *M'k 2:27*
for man, and not man for the *s.*   *M'k 2:27*
Son of man is Lord also of the *s.*   *M'k 2:28*
he would heal him on the *s.* day   *M'k 3:2*
it lawful to do good on the *s.* days   *M'k 3:4*
And when the *s.* day was come   *M'k 6:2*
that is, the day before the *s.*   *M'k 15:42*
And when the *s.* was past, Mary   *M'k 16:1*
into the synagogue on the *s.* day   *Lu 4:16*
and taught them on the *s.* days   *Lu 4:31*
pass on the second *s.* after the first   *Lu 6:1*
is not lawful to do on the *s.* days   *Lu 6:2*
Son of man is Lord also of the *s.*   *Lu 6:5*
it came to pass also on another *s.*   *Lu 6:6*
whether he would heal on the *s.*   *Lu 6:7*
lawful on the *s.* days to do good   *Lu 6:9*
in one of the synagogues on the *s.*   *Lu 13:10*
that Jesus had healed on the *s.* day   *Lu 13:14*
and be healed, and not on the *s.* day   *Lu 13:14*
of you on the *s.* loose his ox or   *Lu 13:15*
loosed from this bond on the *s.* day   *Lu 13:16*
Pharisees to eat bread on the *s.* day   *Lu 14:1*
Is it lawful to heal on the *s.* day   *Lu 14:3*
straightway pull him out on the *s.*   *Lu 14:5*
the preparation, and the *s.* drew on   *Lu 23:54*
and rested the *s.* day according to   *Lu 23:56*
and on the same day was the *s.* according to   *Joh 5:9*
It is the *s.* day: it is not lawful for   *Joh 5:10*
had done these things on the *s.* day   *Joh 5:16*
he not only had broken the *s.*   *Joh 5:18*

SABBATH (continued)

ye on the *s.* day circumcise a | Joh 7:22
man
on the *s.* day receive | Joh 7:23
circumcision
man every whit whole on the | Joh 7:23
s. day
s. day when Jesus made the | Joh 9:14
clay
because he keepeth not the *s.* | Joh 9:16
day
remain upon the cross on the | Joh 19:31
s. day
(for that *s.* day was an | Joh 19:31
high day
from Jerusalem a *s.* day's | Ac 1:12
journey
into the synagogue on the *s.* | Ac 13:14
day
prophets which are read | Ac 13:27
every *s.*
be preached to them the next | Ac 13:42
s.
next *s.* day came almost the | Ac 13:44
whole
read in the synagogues every | Ac 15:21
s. day
on the *s.* we went out of the | Ac 16:13
city by
three *s.* days reasoned with | Ac 17:2
them
reasoned in the synagogue | Ac 18:4
every *s.*
of the new moon, or of the *s.* | Col 2:16
days
a *s.* day (S) | Col 2:16

SABBATHS

Verily my *s.* ye shall keep: | Ex 31:13
for it
and his father, and keep my *s.* | Le 19:3
Ye shall keep my *s.* and | Le 19:30
reverence
offering; seven *s.* shall be | Le 23:15
complete
Beside the *s.* of the Lord, and | Le 23:38
thou shalt number seven *s.* | Le 25:8
of years
the space of the seven *s.* of | Le 25:8
years
Ye shall keep my *s.* and | Le 26:2
reverence
Them shall the land enjoy her | Le 26:34
s.
shall the land rest, and enjoy | Le 26:34
her *s.*
because it did not rest in | Le 26:35
your *s.*
left of them, and shall enjoy | Le 26:43
her *s.*
sacrifices unto the Lord in | 1Ch 23:31
the *s.*
on the *s.* and on the new | 2Ch 2:4;
moons | 8:13
and the burnt offerings for | 2Ch 31:3
the *s.*
until the land had enjoyed | 2Ch 36:21
her *s.*
of the *s.* of the new moons | Ne 10:33
the new moons and *s.* the | Isa 1:13
calling
unto the eunuchs that keep | Isa 56:4
my *s.*
saw her, and did mock at her *s.* | La 1:7
feasts and *s.* to be forgotten in | La 2:6
Moreover also I gave them | Eze 20:12
my *s.*
and my *s.* they greatly | Eze 20:13
polluted
in my statutes, but polluted | Eze 20:16
my *s.*
And hallow my *s.;* and they | Eze 20:20
shall be
they polluted my *s.:* then I | Eze 20:21
said
statutes, and had polluted | Eze 20:24
my *s.*
things, and hast profaned my | Eze 22:8
s.
and have hid their eyes from | Eze 22:26
my *s.*
same day, and have | Eze 23:38
profaned my *s.*
and they shall hallow my *s.* | Eze 44:24
and in the new moons, and | Eze 45:17
in the *s.*
in the *s.* and in the new | Eze 46:3
moons
her new moons, and her *s.* | Ho 2:11
and all

SABEANS

And the *S.* fell upon them | Job 1:15
and of the *S.* men of stature | Isa 45:14
brought *S.* from the | Eze 23:42
wilderness
and they shall sell them to the | Joe 3:8
S.

SABTA

Seba, and Havilah, and *S.* | 1Ch 1:9

SABTAH

Seba, and Havilah, and *S.* and | Ge 10:7

SABTECHA

Sabta, and Raamah, and *S.* | 1Ch 1:9

SABTECHAH

Sabtah, and Raamah, and *S.* | Ge 10:7

SACAR

Ahiam the son of *S.* the | 1Ch 11:35
Hararite
Joah the third, and *S.* the | 1Ch 26:4
fourth

SACK

every man's money into his *s.* | Ge 42:25
as one of them opened his *s.* | Ge 42:27
to give
restored; and lo, it is even in | Ge 42:28
my *s.*
bundle of money was in his | Ge 42:35
s.
money was in the mouth of | Ge 43:21
his *s.*
down every man his *s.* to the | Ge 44:11
ground
and opened every man his *s.* | Ge 44:11
the cup was found in | Ge 44:12
Benjamin's *s.*
of wood, or raiment, or skin, | Le 11:32
or *s.*
sealed up in a *s.* (B) | Job 14:17

SACKBUT

of the cornet, flute, harp, *s.* | Da 3:5

SACKCLOTH

clothes, put *s.* upon his loins | Ge 37:34
your clothes, and gird you | 2Sa 3:31
with *s.*
Rizpah the daughter of Aiah | 2Sa 21:10
took *s.*
us, I pray thee, put *s.* on | 1Ki 20:31
our loins
So they girded *s.* on their | 1Ki 20:32
loins
clothes, and put *s.* upon his | 1Ki 21:27
flesh
and fasted, and lay in *s.* and | 1Ki 21:27
went
he had *s.* within upon his | 2Ki 6:30
flesh
clothes, and covered himself | 2Ki 19:1
with *s.*
elders of the priests, covered | 2Ki 19:2
with *s.*
of Israel, who were clothed | 1Ch 21:16
in *s.*
clothes, and put on *s.* with | Es 4:1
ashes
into the king's gate clothed with | Es 4:2
s.
and many lay in *s.* and ashes | Es 4:3
and to take away his *s.* from | Es 4:4
him
I have sewed *s.* upon my | Job 16:15
skin, and
thou hast put off my *s.* and | Ps 30:11
girded
they were sick, my clothing | Ps 35:13
was *s.*
I made *s.* also my garment; | Ps 69:11
and I
of a stomacher a girding of *s.* | Isa 3:24
they shall gird themselves with | Isa 15:3
s.
and loose the *s.* from off thy | Isa 20:2
loins
to baldness, and to girding | Isa 22:12
with *s.*
you bare, and gird *s.* upon | Isa 32:11
your loin
and covered himself with *s.* | Isa 37:1
elders of the priests covered | Isa 37:2
with *s.*
and I make *s.* their covering | Isa 50:3
to spread *s.* and ashes under | Isa 58:5
gird you with *s.* lament and | Jer 4:8
howl
gird thee with *s.* and wallow | Jer 6:26
thyself
be cuttings, and upon the | Jer 48:37
loins *s.*
of Rabbah, gird you with *s.;* | Jer 49:3
lament
they have girded themselves | La 2:10
with *s.*
shall also gird themselves | Eze 7:18
with *s.*
bald for thee, and gird them | Eze 27:31
with *s.*
with fasting, and *s.* and ashes | Da 9:3
Lament like a virgin girded | Joe 1:8
with *s.*
come, lie all night in *s.* ye | Joe 1:13
ministers
and I will bring up *s.* upon all | Am 8:10
loins
proclaimed a fast, and put on | Jon 3:5
s.
and covered him with *s.* and | Jon 3:6
sat in
man and beast be covered with | Jon 3:8
s.
repented long ago in *s.* and | M't 11:21
ashes
repented, sitting in *s.* and | Lu 10:13
ashes
the sun became black as *s.* of | Re 6:12
hair
and threescore days, clothed | Re 11:3
in *s.*

SACKCLOTHES

with fasting, and with *s.* and | Nu 9:1

SACKED

s. the whole region (B) | Ge 14:7
Menahem *s.* Tappuah (R) | 2Ki 15:16

SACKS

Joseph commanded to fill | Ge 42:25
their *s.*
to pass as they emptied their | Ge 42:35
s.
fruits in your *s.* (A)(B) | Ge 42:1;
 | 1Sa 9:7
the money in the mouth of | Ge 43:12
your *s.*
money that was returned in | Ge 43:18
our *s.*
that we opened our *s.* and | Ge 43:21
tell who put our money in | Ge 43:22
our *s.*
hath given you treasure in | Ge 43:23
your *s.*
saying, Fill the men's *s.* with | Ge 44:1
food
and took old *s.* upon their | Jos 9:4
asses
bread in our *s.* (R) | 1Sa 9:7
20,000 *s.* of wheat (B) | 1Ki 5:11
a hundred *s.* of wheat (B) | Lu 16:7

SACK'S

for, behold, it was in his *s.* | Ge 42:27
every man's money in his *s.* | Ge 44:1
cup, in the *s.* mouth of the | Ge 44:2
youngest

SACKS'

which we found in our *s.* | Ge 44:8
mouths

SACRED

a *s.* gathering (B) | Ex 12:16
s. trees, totem pole gods (B) | Ex 34:13
the *s.* gifts (B) | Nu 5:10
they are *s.* (B) | Nu 16:37
the *s.* portion (B) | Nu 18:29
the *s.* portion (R) | Nu 26:13
a *s.* meeting (B) | Nu 28:18;
 | 28:25-26; 29:1, 7, 12

have a *s.* meeting (B)	Nu 29:35	of the *s.* of the peace offerings	Le 7:37
burn their *s.* trees (B)	De 12:3	a burnt *s.* for a sweet savour	Le 8:21
are *s.* to the Lord (R)	Jos 6:19	offerings, to *s.* before the Lord	Le 9:4
money of *s.* offerings (B)	2Ki 12:4	beside the burnt *s.* of the	Le 9:17
took *s.* treasures (B)	2Ki 12:18	morning	
violating *s.* things (B)	1Ch 2:7	the ram for a *s.* of peace	Le 9:18
praise his *s.* memory (B)	Ps 30:4	offerings	
their *s.* stones destroy (B)	Ho 10:2	time of evening *s.* (A)(B)(R)	Le 9:21
temple made the gold *s.*	M't 23:17;	offereth a burnt offering or *s.*	Le 17:8
(A)(B)(R)	23:19	if ye offer a *s.* of peace	Le 19:5
a *s.* responsibility (P)	1Co 9:17	offerings	
engaged in *s.* services (A)	Tit 2:3	offereth a *s.* of peace	Le 22:21
		offerings unto	
		ye will offer a *s.* of	Le 22:29

SACREDNESS

maintain *s.* of sabbaths (B)	Eze 44:24

SACRIFICE

Jacob offered *s.* upon the	Ge 31:54	ye shall *s.* one kid of the goats	Le 23:19
mount		year for a *s.* of peace	Le 23:19
we may *s.* to the Lord our	Ex 3:18	offerings	
God		a meat offering, a *s.* and	Le 23:37
and *s.* unto the Lord, our God	Ex 5:3	drink	
Let us go and *s.* to our God	Ex 5:8	they do not offer a *s.* unto	Le 27:11
Let us go and do *s.* to the	Ex 5:17	the Lord	
Lord		the ram for a *s.* of peace	Nu 6:17
go, they may do *s.* unto the Lord	Ex 8:8	offerings	
Go ye, *s.* to your God in the	Ex 8:25	it in the fire which is under	Nu 6:18
land		the *s.*	
we shall *s.* the abomination of	Ex 8:26	*s.* of peace offerings	Nu 7:17;
shall we *s.* the abomination of	Ex 8:26	7:23, 29, 35, 41, 47, 53, 59, 65, 71, 77,	
and *s.* to the Lord our God,	Ex 8:27		83, 88
as he		or a *s.* in performing a vow	Nu 15:3
ye may *s.* to the Lord your	Ex 8:28	with the burnt offering or *s.*	Nu 15:5
God in		or for a *s.* in performing a	Nu 15:8
the people go to *s.* to the Lord	Ex 8:29	vow, or	
we may *s.* unto the Lord our	Ex 10:25	*s.* made by fire unto the	Nu 15:25
God		Lord, and	
It is the *s.* of the Lord's	Ex 12:27	he stood by his burnt *s.*, he,	Nu 23:6
passover		and	
I *s.* to the Lord all that	Ex 13:15	a *s.* made by fire unto the	Nu 28:6
openeth		Lord	
s. thereon thy burnt offerings	Ex 20:24	thou shalt offer it, a *s.* made	Nu 28:8
not offer the blood of my *s.*	Ex 23:18	by fire	
shall the fat of my *s.* remain	Ex 23:18	a *s.* made by fire unto the	Nu 28:13
of the *s.* of their peace	Ex 29:28	Lord	
offerings		ye shall offer a *s.* made by	Nu 28:19
incense thereon, nor burnt *s.*	Ex 30:9	fire for a	
and do *s.* unto their gods, and	Ex 34:15	the meat of the *s.* made by	Nu 28:24
call thee, and thou eat of his	Ex 34:15	fire, of	
s.		a *s.* made by fire unto the	Nu 29:6
the blood of my *s.* with	Ex 34:25	Lord	
leaven		a *s.* made by fire, of a sweet	Nu 29:13;
the *s.* of the feast of the	Ex 34:25		29:36
passover		shalt not *s.* it unto the Lord	De 15:21
offering be a burnt *s.* of the	Le 1:3	thy	
herd		shalt therefore *s.* the passover	De 16:2
to be a burnt *s.* an offering	Le 1:3	Thou mayest not *s.* the	De 16:5
or of the goats, for a burnt *s.*	Le 1:10	passover	
it is a burnt *s.* an offering	Le 1:13	thou shalt *s.* the passover at	De 16:6
if the burnt *s.* for his offering	Le 1:14	even	
it is a burnt *s.* an offering	Le 1:17	shalt not *s.* unto the Lord thy	De 17:1
made by		God	
oblation be a *s.* of peace	Le 3:1	people, from them that offer a	De 18:3
offering		*s.*	
offer of the *s.* of the peace	Le 3:3	whole burnt *s.* upon thine	De 33:10
offering		altar	
it on the altar upon the burnt *s.*	Le 3:5	not for burnt offering, nor	Jos 22:26
offering for a *s.* of peace	Le 3:6	for *s.*	
offering		offer a burnt *s.* with the wood	J'g 6:26
offer of the *s.* of the peace	Le 3:9	a great *s.* unto Dagon their	J'g 16:23
offering		god	
bullock of the *s.* of peace	Le 4:10	to *s.* unto the Lord of hosts in	1Sa 1:3
offerings		offer unto the Lord the yearly	1Sa 1:21
the fat of the *s.* of peace	Le 4:26	*s.*	
offerings		that, when any man offered a	1Sa 2:13
from off the *s.* of peace	Le 4:31	her husband to offer the	1Sa 2:19
offerings		yearly *s.*	
from the *s.* of the peace	Le 4:35	Wherefore kick ye at my *s.*	1Sa 2:29
offerings		and at	
law of the *s.* of peace offerings	Le 7:11	shall not be purged with *s.*	1Sa 3:14
offer with the *s.* of	Le 7:12	nor	
thanksgiving		*s.* of the people to day in the	1Sa 9:12
bread with the *s.* of	Le 7:13	high	
thanksgiving		come, because he doth bless	1Sa 9:13
the flesh of the *s.* of his peace	Le 7:15	the *s.*	
if the *s.* of his offering be a	Le 7:16	to *s.* sacrifices of peace	1Sa 10:8
vow		offerings	
same day that he offereth his	Le 7:16	oxen, to *s.* unto the Lord thy	1Sa 15:15
s.		God	
the remainder of the flesh of	Le 7:17	*s.* unto the Lord thy God in	1Sa 15:21
the *s.*		Gilgal	
flesh of the *s.* of his peace	Le 7:18	to obey is better than *s.* and	1Sa 15:22
offerings		say, I am come to *s.* to the	1Sa 16:2
flesh of *s.* of peace offerings	Le 7:20;	Lord	
	7:21	call Jesse to the *s.* and I will	1Sa 16:3
offereth the *s.* of his peace	Le 7:29	I am come to *s.* unto the Lord	1Sa 16:5
of the *s.* of his peace offerings	Le 7:29	and come with me to the *s.*	1Sa 16:5
		sons, and called them to the	1Sa 16:5
		s.	
		there is a yearly *s.* there for	1Sa 20:6
		all the	

our family hath a *s.* in the	1Sa 20:29
city	
here be oxen for burnt *s.*	2Sa 24:22
king went to Gibeon to *s.*	1Ki 3:4
there	
him, offered *s.* before the	1Ki 8:62
Lord.	
And Solomon offered a *s.* of	1Ki 8:63
peace	
this people go up to do *s.* in	1Ki 12:27
the offering of the evening *s.*	1Ki 18:29
and pour it on the burnt *s.*	1Ki 18:33
of the offering of the	1Ki 18:36
evening *s.*	
fell, and consumed the burnt	1Ki 18:38
s.	
neither burnt offering nor *s.*	2Ki 5:17
I have a great *s.* to do to	2Ki 10:19
Baal	
as yet the people did *s.* and	2Ki 14:4
burnt	
offering, and the king's	2Ki 16:15
burnt *s.*	
and all the blood of the *s.*	2Ki 16:15
nor serve them, nor *s.* to	2Ki 17:35
them	
worship, and to him shall ye	2Ki 17:36
do *s.*	
save only to burn *s.* before	2Ch 2:6
him	
And king Solomon offered a *s.*	2Ch 7:5
of	
place to myself for an	2Ch 7:12
house of *s.*	
to *s.* unto the Lord God of	2Ch 11:16
their	
will I *s.* to them, that they	2Ch 28:23
may	
people did *s.* in the high	2Ch 33:17
places	
we do *s.* unto him since the	Ezr 4:2
days	
I sat astonied until evening	Ezr 9:4
s.	
at the evening *s.* I arose up	Ezr 9:5
will they *s.*? will they make an	Ne 4:2
offerings, and accept thy burnt	Ps 20:3
s.	
S. and offering thou didst not	Ps 40:6
made a covenant with me by *s.*	Ps 50:5
For thou desirest not *s.*; else	Ps 51:16
I will freely *s.* unto thee: I will	Ps 54:6
And let them *s.* the sacrifices	Ps 107:22
offer to thee *s.* of	Ps 116:17
thanksgiving	
bind the *s.* with cords, even	Ps 118:27
unto	
up of my hands as the	Ps 141:2
evening *s.*	
s. of the wicked is an	Pr 15:8
abomination	
acceptable to the Lord than *s.*	Pr 21:3
s. of the wicked is	Pr 21:27
abomination	
hear, than to give the *s.* of	Ec 5:1
fools	
day, and shall do *s.* and	Isa 19:21
oblation	
the Lord hath a *s.* in Bozrah	Isa 34:6
thither wentest thou up to	Isa 57:7
offer *s.*	
that shall bring the *s.* of	Jer 33:11
praise	
offerings, and to do *s.*	Jer 33:18
continually	
the Lord God of hosts hath	Jer 46:10
a *s.* in	
yourselves on every side to	Eze 39:17
my *s.*	
that I do *s.* for you, even a	Eze 39:17
great	
s. upon the mountains of	Eze 39:17
Israel	
s. which I have sacrificed	Eze 39:19
for you	
slew the burnt offering and	Eze 40:42
the *s.*	
offering and the *s.* for the	Eze 44:11
people	
house shall boil the *s.* of the	Eze 46:24
people	
by him the daily *s.* was taken	Da 8:11
away	
daily *s.* by reason of	Da 8:12
transgression	
the vision concerning the daily	Da 8:13
s.	
s. and the oblation to cease	Da 9:27
and shall take away the daily	Da 11:31
s.	

SACRIFICE (cont.)

the daily s. shall be taken — Da 12:11
away
and without a s. and without — Ho 3:4
s. upon the tops of the — Ho 4:13
mountains
whores, and they s. with — Ho 4:14
harlots
For I desired mercy, and not s. Ho 6:6
They s. flesh for the sacrifices Ho 8:13
vanity: they s. bullocks in — Ho 12:11
Gilgal
the men that s. kiss the calves Ho 13:2
a s. of thanksgiving with — Am 4:5
leaven
and offered a s. unto the — Jon 1:16
Lord
will s. unto thee with the voice Jon 2:9
Therefore they s. unto their — Hab 1:16
net
for the Lord hath prepared a s. Zep 1:7
pass in the day of the Lord's — Zep 1:8
s.
they that s. shall come and — Zec 14:21
take
And if ye offer the blind for s. Mal 1:8
is it
I will have mercy, and not s.: M't 9:13
or
I will have mercy, and not s. M't 12:7
ye
every s. shall be salted with M'k 9:49
salt
And to offer a s. according to Lu 2:24
that
and offered s. unto the idol — Ac 7:41
and would have done s. with — Ac 14:13
they had not done s. unto — Ac 14:18
them
a reconciling s. in his blood — Ro 3:25
(B)
ye present your bodies a living Ro 12:1
s.
that are offered in s. unto idols 1Co 8:4
is offered in s. to idols is any 1Co 10:19
thing
the things which the Gentiles 1Co 10:20
s.
they s. to devils, and not to 1Co 10:20
God
This is offered in s. unto — 1Co 10:28
idols, eat
for us an offering and a s. to — Eph 5:2
God
the s. and service of your — Ph'p 2:17
faith
s. acceptable, wellpleasing to Ph'p 4:18
God
to offer up s. first for his — Heb 7:27
own sins
offered himself a s. — Heb 9:14
(A)(B)(P)
to put away sin by the s. of — Heb 9:26
himself
S. and offering thou wouldest Heb 10:5
not
S. and offering and burnt — Heb 10:8
offerings
after he had offered one s. — Heb 10:12
for sins
remaineth no more s. for — Heb 10:26
sins
God a more excellent s. than Heb 11:4
Cain
let us offer the s. of praise — Heb 13:5
to God
an atoning s. for our sins (B) 1Jo 2:2;
4:10

SACRIFICED

s. peace offerings of oxen unto Ex 24:5
it, and have s. thereunto, and Ex 32:8
said
They s. unto devils, not to — De 32:17
God; to
the Lord, and s. peace — Jos 8:31
offerings
and they s. there unto the Lord J'g 2:5
said to the man that s. Give 1Sa 2:15
flesh
s. sacrifices the same day unto 1Sa 6:15
the Lord
and there they s. sacrifices 1Sa 11:15
of peace
six paces, he s. oxen and — 2Sa 6:13
fatlings
Only the people s. in high — 1Ki 3:2
places

only he s. and burnt incense in 1Ki 3:3
high
incense and s. unto their — 1Ki 11:8
gods
the people still s. and burnt — 2Ki 12:3
incense
the people s. and burnt — 2Ki 15:4
incense still
the people s. and burned — 2Ki 15:35
incense
he s. and burnt incense in the 2Ki 16:4
high
which s. for them in the — 2Ki 17:32
houses of
the Jebusite, then he s. there 1Ch 21:28
they s. sacrifices unto the — 1Ch 29:21
Lord, and
s. sheep and oxen, which — 2Ch 5:6
could not
He s. also and burnt incense 2Ch 28:4
in the
he s. unto the gods of — 2Ch 28:23
Damascus
and s. thereon peace — 2Ch 33:16
offerings and
Amon s. unto all the carved 2Ch 33:22
images
graves of them that s. unto — 2Ch 34:4
them
s. their sons and their — Ps 106:37
daughters
they s. unto the idols of — Ps 106:38
Canaan
thou s. unto them to be — Eze 16:20
devoured
sacrifice which I have s. — Eze 39:19
for you
they s. unto Baalim, and — Ho 11:2
burned
Christ our passover is s. for 1Co 5:7
us
to eat things s. unto idols, and Re 2:14
and to eat things s. unto — Re 2:20
idols
thou wert s. and bought (B) — Re 5:9

SACRIFICEDST

which thou s. the first day at De 16:4
even

SACRIFICES

and offered s. unto the God of Ge 46:1
his
give us also s. and burnt — Ex 10:25
offerings
a burnt offering and s. for — Ex 18:12
God
of the s. of your peace — Le 7:32
offerings
off the s. of their peace — Le 7:34
offerings
offer their s. (A) — Le 7:38
of the s. of the Lord made by Le 10:13
fire
out of the s. of peace — Le 10:14
offerings of
children of Israel may bring Le 17:5
their s.
no more offer their s. unto — Le 17:7
devils
over the s. of your peace — Nu 10:10
offerings
the people unto the s. of their Nu 25:2
gods
my bread for my s. made by Nu 28:2
fire
and your s. and your tithes — De 12:6
your burnt offerings, and — De 12:11
your s.
the blood of thy s. shall be De 12:27
poured
Which did eat the fat of — De 32:38
their s. and
they shall offer s. of — De 33:19
righteousness
s. of the Lord of Israel — Jos 13:14
made by fire
with our s. and with our — Jos 22:27
peace
not for burnt offerings, nor Jos 22:28
for s.
for meat offerings, or for s. Jos 22:29
beside
sacrificed s. the same day — 1Sa 6:15
unto the
to sacrifice s. of peace — 1Sa 10:8
offerings

they sacrificed s. of peace — 1Sa 11:15
offerings
elight in burnt offerings — 1Sa 15:22
and s. as
even from Giloh, while he — 2Sa 15:12
offered s.
they went in to offer s. and 2Ki 10:24
burnt
they offered burnt s. and — 1Ch 16:1
peace
to offer all burnt s. unto the 1Ch 23:31
Lord
they sacrificed s. unto the — 1Ch 29:21
Lord
and s. in abundance for all 1Ch 29:21
Israel
the burnt offerings and the s. 2Ch 7:1
people offered s. before the 2Ch 7:4
Lord
every evening burnt s. and — 2Ch 13:11
sweet
bring s. and thank offerings 2Ch 29:31
into
the congregation brought in 2Ch 29:31
s. and
the place where they offered s. Ezr 6:3
they may offer s. of sweet — Ezr 6:10
savours
pleasing s. (A)(R) — Ezr 6:10
that day they offered great s. Ne 12:43
Offer the s. of righteousness Ps 4:5
I offer in his tabernacle s. of Ps 27:6
I will not reprove thee for thy Ps 50:8
s. or
The s. of God are a broken Ps 51:17
spirit
with the s. of righteousness Ps 51:19
unto thee burnt s. of fatlings Ps 66:15
and ate the s. of the dead — Ps 106:28
sacrifice the s. of — Ps 107:22
thanksgiving, and
than an house full of s. with Pr 17:1
strife
the multitude of your s. unto Isa 1:11
me
ye year to year; let them kill Isa 29:1
s.
hast thou honoured me with Isa 43:23
thy s.
thou filled me with the fat of Isa 43:24
thy s.
s. shall be accepted upon mine Isa 56:7
nor your s. sweet unto me — Jer 6:20
your burnt offerings unto your Jer 7:21
s.
concerning burnt offerings or Jer 7:22
s.
bringing burnt offerings, and Jer 17:26
s.
incense, and bringing s. of Jer 17:26
praise
and they offered there their Eze 20:28
s.
tables, whereupon they slew Eze 40:41
their s.
be ashamed because of their s. Ho 4:19
flesh for the s. of mine — Ho 8:13
offerings
their s. shall be unto them as Ho 9:4
and bring your s. every — Am 4:4
morning
ye offered unto me s. and — Am 5:25
offerings
all whole burnt offerings — M'k 12:33
and s.
Pilate had mingled with their Lu 13:1
s.
offered to me slain beasts and Ac 7:42
s.
which eat of the s. — 1Co 10:18
partakers of the
may offer both gifts and s. for Heb 5:1
sins
is ordained to offer gifts and Heb 8:3
s.
were offered both gifts and s. Heb 9:9
that
with better s. than these — Heb 9:23
can never with those s. which Heb 10:1
they
in those s. there is a — Heb 10:3
remembrance
In burnt offerings and s. for Heb 10:6
sin
offering oftentimes the same Heb 10:11
s.
with such s. God is well — Heb 13:16
pleased
to offer up spiritual s. — 1Pe 2:5
acceptable

SACRIFICETH

He that *s.* unto any god, save unto   *Ex 22:20*
him that *s.* and to him that *s.* not   *Ec 9:2*
s. in gardens, and burneth incense   *Isa 65:3*
he that *s.* a lamb, as if he cut off a   *Isa 66:3*
s. unto the Lord a corrupt thing   *Mal 1:14*

SACRIFICIAL

expiating sin by his *s.* death (N)   *Ro 3:25*

SACRIFICING

s. sheep and oxen, that could not   *1Ki 8:5*
s. unto the calves that he had made   *1Ki 12:32*

SACRILEGE

appalling *s.* (A)(R)   *M't 24:15*
idols, dost thou commit *s.*   *Ro 2:22*
do you rob temples (E)(R)   *Ro 2:22*
do you rob their shrines (N)   *Ro 2:22*
honest toward property of heathen temples (P)   *Ro 2:22*

SAD

them, and, behold, they were *s.*   *Ge 40:6*
why is your heart *s.* (R)   *1Sa 1:8*
and her countenance was no more *s.*   *1Sa 1:18*
Why is thy spirit so *s.* that thou   *1Ki 21:5*
been beforetime *s.* in his presence   *Ne 2:1*
Why is thy countenance *s.* seeing   *Ne 2:2*
should not my countenance be *s.*   *Ne 2:3*
s. at heart (B)(R)   *Pr 14:13*
made the heart of the righteous *s.*   *Eze 13:22*
whom I have made *s.;* and   *Eze 13:22*
hypocrites, of a *s.* countenance   *M't 6:16*
went away *s.* (A)   *M't 19:22*
he was *s.* at that saying, and went   *M'k 10:22*
s. and hurt (A)   *M'k 14:19*
s. overwhelmed with grief (A)   *M'k 14:34*
he was very *s.* (B)   *Lu 18:23*
to another, as ye walk, and are *s.*   *Lu 24:17*
s. at heart (N)   *Joh 16:22*
grieved and made *s.* (A)(B)(P)   *2Co 2:2*

SADDENED

went away *s.* (B)   *M'k 10:22*
s. them (P)(R)   *Ac 20:38*
s. over many (B)   *2Co 12:21*

SADDLE

in the camel's *s.* and sat upon it (S)   *Ge 31:34*
what *s.* soever he rideth upon that   *Le 15:9*
I will *s.* me an ass, that I may ride   *2Sa 19:26*
said unto his sons, *S.* me the ass   *1Ki 13:13*
to his sons, saying, *S.* me the ass   *1Ki 13:27*

SADDLED

in the morning, and *s.* his ass   *Ge 22:3; Nu 22:21*
there were with him two asses *s.*   *J'g 19:10*
met him, with a couple of asses *s.*   *2Sa 16:1*
he *s.* his ass, and arose, and gat him   *2Sa 17:23*
And Shimei arose, and *s.* his ass   *1Ki 2:40*
So they *s.* him the ass; and he rode   *1Ki 13:13*

that he *s.* for him the ass, to wit   *1Ki 13:23*
Saddle me the ass. And they *s.* him   *1Ki 13:27*
Then she *s.* an ass and said to her   *2Ki 4:24*

SADDUCEES

saw many of the Pharisees and *S.*   *M't 3:7*
Pharisees also with the *S.* came   *M't 16:1*
leaven of the Pharisees and *S.*   *M't 16:6; 16:11*
doctrine of the Pharisees and *S.*   *M't 16:12*
The same day came to him the *S.*   *M't 22:23*
that he had put the *S.* to silence   *M't 22:34*
Then come unto him the *S.*   *M'k 12:18*
Then came to him certain of the *S.*   *Lu 20:27*
captain of the temple, and the *S.*   *Ac 4:1*
(which is the sect of the *S.*)   *Ac 5:17*
perceived that the one part were *S.*   *Ac 23:6*
between the Pharisees and the *S.*   *Ac 23:7*
S. say that there is no resurrection   *Ac 23:8*

SADLY

Wherefore look ye so *s.* to-day   *Ge 40:7*

SADNESS

s. of heart (R)   *Ne 2:2*
by the *s.* of the countenance the   *Ec 7:3*

SADOC

begat *S.;* and *S.* begat Achim   *M't 1:14*

SAFE

on every side, and ye dwelled *s.*   *1Sa 12:11*
Is the young man Absalom *s.*   *2Sa 18:29; 18:32*
Their houses are *s.* from fear   *Job 21:9*
Hold me up, and I shall be *s.*   *Ps 119:117*
runneth into it, and is *s.*   *Pr 18:10*
his trust in the Lord shall be *s.*   *Pr 29:25*
prey, and shall carry it away *s.*   *Isa 5:29*
and they shall be *s.* in their land   *Eze 34:27*
he hath received him *s.* and sound   *Lu 15:27*
s. and well (A)(B)   *Lu 15:27*
and bring him *s.* unto Felix   *Ac 23:24*
pass, that they escaped all *s.* to land   *Ac 27:44*
is not grievous, but for you it is *s.*   *Ph'p 3:1*

SAFEGUARD

but with me thou shalt be in *s.*   *1Sa 22:23*

SAFELY

the full, and dwell in your land *s.*   *Le 26:5*
And Judah and Israel dwelt *s.* every   *1Ki 4:25*
he led them on *s.* so that they feared   *Ps 78:53*
hearkeneth unto me shall dwell *s.*   *Pr 1:33*
Then shalt thou walk in thy way *s.*   *Pr 3:23*
of her husband doth *s.* trust in her   *Pr 31:11*
He pursued them, and passed *s.*   *Isa 41:3*
be saved, and Israel shall dwell *s.*   *Jer 23:6*
and I will cause them to dwell *s.*   *Jer 32:37*
saved, and Jerusalem shall dwell *s.*   *Jer 33:16*
And they shall dwell *s.* therein, and   *Eze 28:26*

they shall dwell *s.* in the wilderness   *Eze 34:25*
they shall dwell *s.* and none shall   *Eze 34:28*
and they shall dwell *s.* all of them   *Eze 38:8*
them that are at rest, that dwell *s.*   *Eze 38:11*
my people of Israel dwelleth *s.*   *Eze 38:14*
when they dwelt *s.* in their land   *Eze 39:26*
and will make them to lie down *s.*   *Ho 2:18*
but Jerusalem shall be *s.* inhabited   *Zec 14:11*
take him, and lead him away *s.*   *M'k 14:44*
charging the jailor to keep them *s.*   *Ac 16:23*

SAFETY

and ye shall dwell in the land in *s.*   *Le 25:18*
eat your fill, and dwell therein in *s.*   *Le 25:19*
round about, so that ye dwell in *s.*   *De 12:10*
beloved of the Lord shall dwell in *s.*   *De 33:12*
Israel then shall dwell in *s.* alone   *De 33:28*
I was not in *s.* neither had I rest   *Job 3:26*
His children are far from *s.*   *Job 5:4*
which mourn may be exalted to *s.*   *Job 5:11*
and thou shalt take thy rest in *s.*   *Job 11:18*
Though it be given him to be in *s.*   *Job 24:23*
Lord, only makest me dwell in *s.*   *Ps 4:8*
set him in *s.* from him that puffeth   *Ps 12:5*
set him in *s.* he panteth for (E)(R)   *Ps 12:5*
An horse is a vain thing for *s.*   *Ps 33:17*
multitude of counsellors there is *s.*   *Pr 11:14*
day of battle: but *s.* is of the Lord   *Pr 1:31*
multitude of counsellors there in *s.*   *Pr 24:6*
and the needy shall lie down is *s.*   *Isa 14:30*
prison found we shut with all *s.*   *Ac 5:23*
when they shall say, Peace and *s.*   *1Th 5:3*

SAFFRON

Spikenard and *s.;* calamus and   *Ca 4:14*
my nard and *s.* (R)   *Ca 4:14*

SAGACIOUS

set aside the keenness of the *s.* (B)   *1Co 1:19*

SAGES

Pharaoh called the *s.* (B)   *Ex 7:11*
sent prophets and *s.* (B)   *M't 23:24*

SAGGED

he *s.* down in sleep (B)   *Ac 20:9*

SAID

Adam *s.,* This is bone of my bone   *Ge 2:23*
the serpent *s.* hath God *s.* ye shall not eat   *Ge 3:1*
Noah *s.,* Blessed be the Lord God of Shem   *Ge 9:26*
in all that Sarah hath *s.* hearken to her   *Ge 21:12*
And Abraham *s.* unto his young   *Ge 22:5*
the servant had *s.,* It is my master   *Ge 24:65*
the dearth began to come, as Joseph *s.*   *Ge 41:54*
Moses returned to the Lord and *s.*   *Ex 5:22*
Rise up, go, serve the Lord as ye have *s.*   *Ex 12:31*

take your flocks and herds, *Ex 12:32*
as ye have *s.*
so Joshua did as Moses had *Ex 17:10*
s. to him
they carried them out, as *Le 10:5*
Moses had *s.*
hast *s.*, I will give them flesh *Nu 11:21*
to eat
little ones, ye *s.* should be a *Nu 14:31;*
prey *De 1:39*
Balak did as Balaam had *s. Nu 23:30*
and offered
tribe of the sons of Joseph *Nu 36:5*
hath *s.* well
as the God of thy fathers *De 1:21*
hath *s.*
gave Hebron to Caleb as *J'g 1:20*
Moses *s.*
If thou wilt save Israel, as *J'g 6:36;*
thou hast *s.* *6:37*
Tell me, I pray thee, what *1Sa 10:15*
Samuel *s.*
Who is that *s.*, Shall Saul *1Sa 11:12*
reign over us
I have hearkened to you in *1Sa 12:1*
all ye *s.* to me
heard it *s.* (S) *1Sa 13:4; 1Ki 16:16*
David *s.*, I perish by hand of *1Sa 27:1*
Saul
and now, O Lord, do as thou *2Sa 7:25*
hast *s.*
Behold, as thy servant *s.* so *2Sa 13:35*
it is
David, son of Jesse, *s.* and *2Sa 23:1*
the sweet psalmist of Israel
s.
as my lord king hath *s.*, so *1Ki 2:38*
will I do
eyes open toward place thou *1Ki 8:29;*
hast *s.* my name shall be *2Ch 6:20*
there
Jeroboam *s.*, Now shall *1Ki 12:26*
kingdom return
Elijah *s.* to her, go, do as *1Ki 17:13*
thou hast *s.*
one *s.* on this manner, *1Ki 22:20*
another *s.* on that
he died, as man of God had *2Ki 7:17*
s.
Therefore, Lord, do as thou *1Ch 17:23*
hast *s.*
Azariah answered him, *2Ch 31:10*
and *s.*
As thou hast *s.*, so must we *Ezr 10:12*
do
there were that *s.*, We are *Ne 5:2;*
many *5:3*
that he may do as Esther hath *Es 5:5*
s.
I will do to-morrow as the king *Es 5:8*
hath *s.*
For thou hast *s.*, My doctrine *Job 11:4*
is pure
If the men of my tabernacle *Job 31:31*
s. not
when I *s.*, Hitherto shalt *Job 38:11*
thou come
who *s.*, With our tongue will *Ps 12:4*
we prevail
fool *s.* in his heart, There is *Ps 14:1;*
no God *53:1*
my heart, *s.* to thee, Thy face *Ps 27:8*
will I seek
with an impudent face *s.* to *Pr 7:13*
him
thou hast *s.*, I will ascend *Isa 14:13*
into heaven
s., We have made a covenant *Isa 28:15*
with death
ye *s.*, No, for we will flee *Isa 30:16*
upon horses
for thou hast *s.*, None seeth *Isa 47:10*
me
The priests *s.* not, Where is the *Jer 2:8*
Lord
I have heard what the *Jer 23:25*
prophets *s.*
even the prophet Jeremiah *s.*, *Jer 28:6*
Amen
ye *s.* Lord hath raised up *Jer 29:15*
prophets
Declare what thou hast *s.* to *Jer 38:25*
the king, also what king *s.* to thee
of whom we *s.*, Under his *La 4:20*
shadow shall live
I *s.*, Ah, Lord God, wilt thou *Eze 9:8*
destroy
hath not the rebellious house *Eze 12:9*
s. to thee
Tyrus hath *s.* against *Eze 26:2;*
Jerusalem *36:2*

Tyrus, thou hast *s.*, I am of *Eze 27:3*
perfect beauty
because thou hast *s.*, I am a *Eze 28:2*
god, I sit
great dragon *s.*, My river is *Eze 29:3*
mine
Nebuchadnezzar *s.*, Blessed be *Da 3:28*
God of Shadrach
and another saint *s.* to that *Da 8:13*
saint who spake
Jonah *s.*, It is better for me to *Jon 4:8*
die
her who *s.* to me, Where is *Mic 7:10*
the Lord
the city that *s.* in her heart, I *Zep 2:15*
Ye have *s.*, It is vain to serve *Mal 3:14*
God
a voice which *s.*, This is my *M't 17:5;*
beloved Son *Lu 3:22*
Likewise also *s.* all the *M't 26:35*
disciples
Jesus saith unto him, Thou *M't 26:64*
hast *s.*
Sir, we remember that that *M't 27:63*
deceiver *s.*
as he passed by, he *s.* to *M'k 2:14*
Levi, Follow me
the angel *s.* to him, Fear not *Lu 1:13;*
1:30
the scribes *s.*, Master, thou *Lu 20:39*
hast well *s.*
seen angels, who *s.* that he *Lu 24:23*
was alive
found it even so as the *Lu 24:24*
women had *s.*
Make straight the way, as *s.* *Joh 1:23*
Esaias
but *s.* also, that God was his *Joh 5:18*
Father
the scripture hath *s.* out of *Joh 7:38*
his belly flow
These things *s.* Esaias, when *Joh 12:41*
he saw
even as the Father *s.* unto *Joh 12:50*
me, so I speak
then Peter *s.*, Repent, and be *Ac 2:38*
baptized
reported all the chief priests *Ac 4:23*
had *s.*
This is that Moses who *s.* unto *Ac 7:37*
Israel
as certain of your own poets *Ac 17:28*
have *s.*
except law had *s.*, Thou shalt *Ro 7:7*
not covet
as we *s.* before, so say I now *Ga 1:9*
by him that *s.* to him, The *Heb 7:21*
Lord sware
we know him that hath *s.*, *Heb 10:30*
Vengeance
and the four beasts *s.*, Amen *Re 5:14*

ANSWERED AND SAID

and all the people *answered* *Ex 24:3*
and s.
one of the same place *1Sa 10:12*
answered and s.
Satan *answered and s.*, Skin *Job 2:4*
for skin
moreover the Lord *answered* *Job 40:1*
Job and s.
he *answered and s.*, Friend *M't 20:13*
John *answered and s.*, Master, *Lu 9:49*
we saw one

GOD SAID

yea, hath *God s.* ye shall not *Ge 3:1;*
eat *3:3*
circumcised the same day, as *Ge 17:23*
God had s.
whatsoever *God hath s.* unto *Ge 31:16*
thee, do
set an idol in the house of *2Ch 33:7*
which *God s.*
and the nation will I judge, *s.* *Ac 7:7*
God
temple of the living God, as *2Co 6:16*
God hath s.

HE SAID

he *s.*, Escape for thy life, look *Ge 19:17*
s. he not unto me, She is my *Ge 20:5*
sister
if *he s.* thus, speckled shall be *Ge 31:8*
thy wages
he s., Lift up thine eyes and *Ge 31:12*
see, the rams
he s., Let me go, for the day *Ge 32:26*
breaketh

he *s.*, What is thy name? *Ge 32:27*
And *he s.*, Jacob
God, *s. he*, hath made me *Ge 41:51*
forget my toil
so Moses did all that *he* had *Ex 18:24*
s.
no man able to stand before *De 11:25;*
you, as *he* hath *s.* *18:2; 29:13;*
Jos 13:14, 33
the Lord hath kept me alive, *Jos 14:10*
as *he s.*
their angel was abated when *he J'g 8:3*
had *s.* that
if thou hide any thing *he s.* *1Sa 3:17*
to thee
not fail the, *s. he*, a man on *1Ki 2:4*
throne
do as *he* hath *s.* fall upon him, *1Ki 2:31*
and bury him
and *he s.* by all his servants *2Ki 17:23*
build the house, as *he s.* of *1Ch 22:11*
he s. Lord, look on it, and *2Ch 24:22*
to man *he s.*, Behold, fear *Job 28:28*
of the Lord
he hath *s.* in his heart *Ps 10:6;*
11:13
he s. that he would destroy *Ps 106:23*
them
to whom *he s.*, This is rest *Isa 28:12*
The voice said, Cry, *he s.* *Isa 40:6*
What shall I cry
for *he s.*, Surely they are my *Isa 63:8*
people
now the Lord hath done as *Jer 40:3*
he s.
to the others *he s.* in mine *Eze 9:5*
hearing
because *he* hath *s.*, The river *Eze 29:9*
is mine
God repented of the evil *he Jon 3:10*
had *s.*
for *he s.*, I am the Son of *M't 27:43*
he is not here, for he is *M't 28:6*
risen, as *he s.*
came and found as *he s.* *M'k 14:16;*
Lu 22:13
there shall ye see him, as *he M'k 16:7*
s. unto you
Peter said, not knowing what *Lu 9:33*
he s.
when *he s.* these, his *Lu 13:17*
adversaries were
disciples remembered that *he Joh 2:22*
s. this
this *he s.* to prove him, for he *Joh 6:6*
What sayest thou? *He s.*, He *Joh 9:17*
is a prophet
this *he s.* not that he cared for *Joh 12:6*
the poor
he s. signifying what death *Joh 12:33*
he should die
As soon as *he s.* to them, I *Joh 18:6*
am he, they fell
he s., It is finished and *Joh 19:30*
bowed his head
when *he* had so *s.* he shewed *Joh 20:20*
his hands
when *he* had *s.* this, he *Joh 20:22*
breathed on them
when *he* had *s.* this, he fell *Ac 7:60*
asleep
he s., Who art thou, Lord? I *Ac 9:5*
how *he s.*, It is more blessed *Ac 20:35*
to give than to
when *he* had so *s.* there arose *Ac 23:7*
a dissension
he s., My grace is sufficient *2Co 12:9*
to which of the angels *s. he Heb 1:5;*
1:13
then *s. he*, Lo, I come, to do *Heb 10:9*
thy will
for *he* hath *s.*, I will never *Heb 13:5*
leave thee
he that *s.*, Do not commit *Jas 2:11*
adultery
he s., These things are faithful *Re 22:6*

I SAID

Because *I s.*, Lest I die for her *Ge 26:9*
I have *s.*, I will bring you up *Ex 3:17*
out of Egypt
in all things that *I* have *Ex 23:13*
s. be circumspect
I s., I would scatter them into *De 32:26*
corners
that have I given, as *I s.* to *Jos 1:3*
Moses
I s. unto you, I am the Lord *J'g 6:10*
I s. indeed, that thy house *1Sa 2:30*
should walk

Bring the portion of which *I* s., Set it by	*1Sa 9:23*
I s., Thou and Ziba divide the land	*2Sa 19:29*
house of which *I* s., My name shall	*2Ki 23:27*
this is one thing, therefore *I* s. it	*Job 9:22*
then *I* s., I shall die in my nest, multiply	*Job 29:18*
I s., Days should speak, and years teach	*Job 32:7*
in prosperity *I* s., I shall never be moved	*Ps 30:6*
I s., I will take heed to my ways, not to sin	*Ps 39:1*
then s., I, Lo, I come	*Ps 40:7; Heb 10:7*
I s. Lord, be merciful to me, heal my soul	*Ps 41:4*
I have s., Ye are gods, and are children	*Ps 82:6*
when *I* s., My foot slippeth, mercy held me up	*Ps 94:18*
I s., O my God, take me not away	*Ps 102:24*
I s., Thou art my refuge and portion	*Ps 142:5*
I s. in my heart, Go to now	*Ec 2:1; 2:15; 3:17-18*
then s. *I.*, Lord, how long	*Isa 6:11*
I s. not to seed of Jacob, Seek ye me	*Isa 45:19*
I s., Behold me, behold me, to a nation	*Isa 65:1*
I s. when thou wast in thy blood, Live	*Eze 16:6*
this is he of whom *I* s., After me cometh	*Joh 1:30*
Marvel not that *I* s., Ye must be born again	*Joh 3:7*
the same that *I* s. from the beginning	*Joh 8:25*
because *I* s. I am the Son of	*Joh 10:36*
s. *I* not to thee, if thou wouldest believe	*Joh 11:40*
I s. it, that they may believe	*Joh 11:42*
ye have heard how *I* s. I go	*Joh 14:28*
these things *I* s. not at the beginning	*Joh 16:4*
and in secret have *I* s. nothing	*Joh 18:20*
ask them which heard me, what *I* have s.	*Joh 18:21*
I s. Not so, Lord, for nothing common	*Ac 11:8*
I have s. that ye are in our hearts	*2Co 7:3*
I sent, that as *I* s. ye may be ready	*2Co 9:3*

SHE SAID

God, s. *she,* hath appointed me another	*Ge 4:25*
even *she* herself s., He is my brother	*Ge 20:5*
wilt thou go with this man? she s., I will	*Ge 24:58*
then *she* s., A bloody husband thou art	*Ex 4:26*
I have somewhat to say, *she* s., Say on	*1Ki 2:14*
she s. Truth, Lord, yet dogs eat crumbs	*M't 15:27*
she s., No man, Lord; Jesus said to her	*Joh 8:11*
when *she* had so s. she went her way	*Joh 11:28*
when *she* had thus s. she turned herself	*Joh 20:14*
and *she* s., Yea, for so much	*Ac 5:8*

THEY SAID

they s., All that the Lord hath said will we do, and be obedient	*Ex 24:7*
they have well s. all they have spoken	*De 5:28*
s. *they,* he is the son of Jehoshaphat	*2Ch 22:9*
they buried in field, for *they* s., He is a leper	*2Ch 26:23*
they have s., Come, let us cut them off	*Ps 83:4*
neither s. *they,* Where is the Lord	*Jer 2:6*
Believe ye? *they* s. unto him, Yea, Lord	*M't 9:28*
they all s., Let him be crucified	*M't 27:22*

for *they* s. he is beside himself	*M'k 3:21*
Because *they* s., He had an unclean spirit	*M'k 3:30*
amazed, nor s. *they* any thing to any man	*M'k 16:8*
they s., The Lord hath need of him	*Lu 19:34*
Then s. *they,* It is his angel	*Ac 12:15*

SAIDST

Why s. thou, She is my sister? so	*Ge 12:19*
and how s. thou, She is my sister	*Ge 26:9*
the Lord which s. unto me, Return	*Ge 32:9*
thou s. I will surely do thee good	*Ge 32:12*
thou s. unto thy servants, Bring	*Ge 44:21*
thou s. unto thy servants, Except	*Ge 44:23*
s. unto them, I will multiply your	*Ex 32:13*
thy mouth, wherewith thou s.	*J'g 9:38*
and thou s. unto me, The word that	*1Ki 2:42*
that thou s. My righteousness is	*Job 35:2*
For thou s. What advantage will	*Job 35:3*
When thou s. Seek my face; my	*Ps 27:8*
s. I have laid help upon one that is	*Ps 89:19*
thou s. I shall be a lady for ever	*Isa 47:7*
yet s. thou not, There is no hope	*Isa 57:10*
thou s. I will not transgress; when	*Jer 2:20*
thou s. There is no hope: no; for I	*Jer 2:25*
but thou s. I will not hear	*Jer 22:21*
called upon thee: thou s. Fear not	*La 3:57*
Because thou s., Aha, against him	*Eze 25:3*
whom thou s. Give me a king and	*Ho 13:10*
husband: in that s. thou truly	*Joh 4:18*

SAIL

they could not spread the s.	*Isa 33:23*
thou spreadest forth to be thy s.	*Eze 27:7*
as he was about to s. into Syria	*Ac 20:3*
For Paul had determined to s. by	*Ac 20:16*
that we should s. into Italy, they	*Ac 27:1*
to s. by the coasts of Asia; one	*Ac 27:2*
strake s. and so were driven	*Ac 27:17*
thee all them that s. with thee	*Ac 27:24*

SAILED

But as they s. he fell asleep	*Lu 8:23*
and from thence they s. to Cyprus	*Ac 13:4*
thence s. to Antioch, from whence	*Ac 14:26*
took Mark, and s. unto Cyprus	*Ac 15:39*
brethren, and s. thence into Syria	*Ac 18:18*
God will. And he s. from Ephesus	*Ac 18:21*
we s. away from Philippi after	*Ac 20:6*
before to ship, and s. unto Assos	*Ac 20:13*
we s. thence, and came the next	*Ac 20:15*
on the left hand, and s. into Syria	*Ac 21:3*
we s. under Cyprus, because	*Ac 27:4*
we had s. over the sea of Cilicia	*Ac 27:5*
when we had s. slowly many days	*Ac 27:7*
we s. under Crete, over against	*Ac 27:7*
thence, they s. close by Crete	*Ac 27:13*

SAILING

a ship s. over unto Phenicia, we	*Ac 21:2*
a ship of Alexandria s. into Italy	*Ac 27:6*
and when s. was now dangerous	*Ac 27:9*

SAILORS

the s. deemed that they (S)	*Ac 27:27; 27:30*
s. and as many as trade by sea	*Re 18:17*

SAINT

and Aaron the s. of the Lord	*Ps 106:16*
the holy one (A)(B)(R)	*Ps 106:16; Da 8:13*
Then I heard one s. speaking	*Da 8:13*
and another s. said unto that	*Da 8:13*
said unto that certain s. which	*Da 8:13*
Salute every s. in Christ Jesus	*Ph'p 4:21*

SAINTS

came with ten thousands of s.	*De 33:2*
thousands of holy ones (A)(E)(R)	*De 33:2*
all his s. are in thy hand: and	*De 33:3*
those consecrated to him are in your hand (A)(R)	*De 33:3*
He will keep the feet of his s.	*1Sa 2:9*
guard feet of his holy ones (A)(E)	*1Sa 2:9*
guards footsteps of his worshippers (B)	*1Sa 2:9*
guards feet of his faithful ones (R)	*1Sa 2:9*
and let thy s. rejoice in goodness	*2Ch 6:41*
to which of the s. wilt thou turn	*Job 5:1*
to which of the holy angels (A)	*Job 5:1*
to which of the holy ones (B)(E)(R)	*Job 5:1*
he putteth no trust in his s.	*Job 15:15*
puts no trust in his holy ones (A)(B)(E)(R)	*Job 15:15*
But to the s. that are in the earth	*Ps 16:3*
as for the godly in the land (B)	*Ps 16:3*
Sing unto the Lord, O ye s. of his	*Ps 30:4*
O love the Lord, all ye his s.	*Ps 31:23*
love the Lord all ye godly (B)	*Ps 31:23*
O fear the Lord, ye his s.: for	*Ps 34:9*
and forsaketh not his s.; they	*Ps 37:28*
are	
Gather my s. together unto me	*Ps 50:5*
Gather to me all my holy ones (B)	*Ps 50:5*
Gather to me my faithful ones (R)	*Ps 50:5*
name; for it is good before thy s.	*Ps 52:9*
in the presence of thy followers (B)	*Ps 52:9*
in the presence of the godly (R)	*Ps 52:9*
the flesh of thy s. unto the beasts	*Ps 79:2*
the flesh of thy worshippers (B)	*Ps 79:2; 85:8*
peace unto his people, and to his s.	*Ps 85:8*
also in the congregation of the s.	*Ps 89:5*
assembly of the holy ones-the angels (A)	*Ps 89:5*
assembly of the holy ones (B)(R)	*Ps 89:5; 89:7*
be feared in the assembly of the s.	*Ps 89:7*
he preserveth the souls of his s.	*Ps 97:10*
preserve lives of his devoted ones (B)	*Ps 97:10*
of the Lord is the death of his s.	*Ps 116:15*
and let thy s. shout for joy	*Ps 132:9*
and her s. shall shout aloud for joy	*Ps 132:16*

Lord; and thy *s.* shall bless | Ps 145:10
thee
his people, the praise of all | Ps 148:14
his *s.*
the praise for all his godly | Ps 148:14
ones (A)(B)
praise in the congregation of | Ps 149:1
s.
the congregation of the godly | Ps 149:1;
(B) | 149:5, 9
the assembly of the faithful | Ps 149:1;
(R) | 149:5
Let the *s.* be joyful in glory: | Ps 149:5
let
this honour have all his *s.* | Ps 149:9
Praise
and preserveth the way of his *s.* | Pr 2:8
the *s.* of the most High shall | Da 7:18
take
same horn made war with the | Da 7:21
s.
judgment was given to the *s.* | Da 7:22
that the *s.* possessed the | Da 7:22
kingdom
wear out the *s.* of the most | Da 7:25
High
people of the *s.* of the most | Da 7:27
High
God, and is faithful with the | Ho 11:12
s.
with the faithful Holy One | Ho 11:12
(A)
is faithful to the Holy One | Ho 11:12
(B)(E)(R)
shall come, and all the *s.* | Zec 14:5
with thee
all the holy ones | Zec 14:5
(A)(B)(E)(R)
bodies of the *s.* which slept | M't 27:52
arose
many of God's people (N) | M't 27:52
bodies of holy men (P) | M't 27:52
much evil he hath done to thy | Ac 9:13
s. at
also to the *s.* which dwelt at | Ac 9:32
Lydda
he had called the *s.* and | Ac 9:41
widows
many of the *s.* did I shut up | Ac 26:10
in prison
many of the faithful holy | Ac 26:10
ones (A)
many of God's people (N) | Ac 26:10
Rome, beloved of God, called | Ro 1:7
to be *s.*
God's loved ones (B) | Ro 1:7
God's beloved (R) | Ro 1:7
he maketh intercession for the | Ro 8:27
s.
Distributing to the necessity | Ro 12:13
of *s.*
Jerusalem to minister unto | Ro 15:25
the *s.*
the poor *s.* which are at | Ro 15:26
Jerusalem
Jerusalem may be accepted | Ro 15:31
of the *s.*
her in the Lord as becometh *s.* | Ro 16:2
and all the *s.* which are with | Ro 16:15
them
in Christ Jesus, called to be *s.* | 1Co 1:2
the unjust, and not before the | 1Co 6:1
s.
that the *s.* shall judge the | 1Co 6:2
world
of peace, as in all churches | 1Co 14:33
of the *s.*
concerning the collection for | 1Co 16:1
the *s.*
addicted to the ministry | 1Co 16:15
of the *s.*
all the *s.* which are in all | 2Co 1:1
Achaia
fellowship of ministering to | 2Co 8:4
the *s.*
as touching the ministering to | 2Co 9:1
the *s.*
not only supplieth the want | 2Co 9:12
of the *s.*
All the *s.* salute you | 2Co 13:13
to the *s.* which are at | Eph 1:1
Ephesus, and
Lord Jesus, and love unto all | Eph 1:15
the *s.*
the glory of his inheritance | Eph 1:18
in the *s.*
fellowcitizens with the *s.* and | Eph 2:19
of the
who am less than the least of | Eph 3:8
all *s.*

to comprehend with all *s.* | Eph 3:18
what is the
For the perfecting of the *s.* | Eph 4:12
for the
named among you, as | Eph 5:3
becometh *s.*
and supplication for all *s.* | Eph 6:18
to all the *s.* in Christ Jesus | Ph'p 1:1
which are
All the *s.* salute you, chiefly | Ph'p 4:22
they
To the *s.* and faithful | Col 1:2
brethren in
the love which ye have to all | Col 1:4
the *s.*
of the inheritance of the *s.* | Col 1:12
in light
but now is made manifest to | Col 1:26
his *s.*
the coming of Christ with | 1Th 3:13
all his *s.*
with all the holy ones (B) | 1Th 3:13
with all those who are his | 1Th 3:13
own (N)
with all those who belong to | 1Th 3:13
him (P)
he shall come to be glorified | 2Th 1:10
in his *s.*
the Lord Jesus, and toward all | Ph'm 5
s.
the bowels of the *s.* are | Ph'm 7
refreshed by
in that ye have ministered to | Heb 6:10
the *s.*
have the rule over you, and | Heb 13:24
all the *s.*
faith once delivered unto the | Jude 3
s.
cometh with ten thousands of | Jude 14
his *s.*
with his myriads of holy ones | Jude 14
(B)(E)(P)
with his myriads of angels | Jude 14
(N)
came with his holy myriads | Jude 14
(R)
odours, which are the prayers | Re 5:8
of *s.*
offer it with the prayers of all | Re 8:3
s.
came with the prayers of the *s.* | Re 8:4
servants the prophets and to | Re 11:18
the *s.*
unto him to make war with | Re 13:7
the *s.*
the patience and the faith of | Re 13:10
the *s.*
Here is the patience of the *s.* | Re 14:12
true are thy ways, thou King | Re 15:3
of *s.*
shed the blood of *s.* and | Re 16:6
prophets
drunken with the blood of the | Re 17:6
s.
the blood of prophets, and of | Re 18:24
s. and
fine linen is the righteousness | Re 19:8
of *s.*
and compassed the camp of | Re 20:9
the *s.*

SAINTS'

if she have washed the *s.* feet, | 1Ti 5:10
if she

SAITH

the one *s.*, This is my son that | 1Ki 3:23
liveth, and the other *s.*, Nay
thus *s.* Benhadad, Thy silver | 1Ki 20:2
and gold is mine
servant Benhadad *s.*, I pray | 1Ki 20:32
thee, let me live
s. king, put this fellow in | 1Ki 22:27;
prison | 2Ch 18:26
thus *s.* the king, Is it peace | 2Ki 9:18;
| 9:19
thus *s.* the great king, the | 2Ki 18:19
king of Assyria
thus *s.* king, Let not | 2Ki 18:29;
Hezekiah deceive, not able | 18:31;
to deliver you | 2Ch 32:10; Isa 36:14
thus *s.* Hezekiah, This a day | 2Ki 19:3;
of trouble | Isa 37:3
thus *s.* Cyrus, king of | 2Ch 36:23;
Persia | Ezr 1:2
the depth *s.*, the sea *s.*, It is | Job 28:14
not in me

he is gracious to him, and *s.* | Job 33:24
Deliver him
but none *s.*, Where is God my | Job 35:10
maker
the transgression of the wicked | Ps 36:1
s.
that want understanding, | Pr 9:4;
she *s.* to him | 9:16
it is naught, it is naught, *s.* the | Pr 20:14
buyer
slothful man *s.*, There is a | Pr 22:13
lion
that deceiveth, and *s.*, Am not | Pr 26:19
I in sport
who is he that *s.* and it | La 3:37
cometh to pass
not every one that *s.* to me, | M't 7:21
Lord, Lord
say to him, Master *s.* my | M't 26:18
time is at hand
Peter *s.* to him, Thou art the | M'k 8:29
Christ
scripture was fulfilled | M'k 15:28;
which *s.* | Jas 2:23
Lord said, Hear what the | Lu 18:6
unjust judge *s.*
if thou knewest who it is that | Joh 4:10
s. Give
the scripture might be | Joh 19:28
fulfilled, *s.* I thirst
in temples made with hands, | Ac 7:48
as *s.* prophet
thus *s.* the Holy Ghost, so | Ac 21:11
the Jews do
the law *s.*, it *s.* to them that | Ro 3:19
are under
for what *s.* the scripture | Ro 4:3; 10:8
for scripture *s.* to Pharaoh, | Ro 9:17
for this purpose
for scripture *s.* whosoever | Ro 10:11
believeth on him
for Esaias *s.* | Ro 10:16
first Moses *s.* | Ro 10:19
But Esaias *s.* | Ro 11:20
wot ye not what the scripture | Ro 11:2
s. of Elias
but what *s.* the answer of God | Ro 11:4
to him
for while one *s.* I am of Paul, | 1Co 3:4
another
or *s.* not the law the same | 1Co 9:8
also
woman to be under | 1Co 14:34
obedience, as also *s.* law
what *s.* the scripture | Ga 4:30; 1Ti 5:18
as the Holy Ghost *s.* if ye | Heb 3:7
will hear
do ye think the scripture *s.* | Jas 4:5
in vain
let him hear what the Spirit *s.* | Re 2:7;
to the churches | 2:11, 17, 29; 3:6, 13, 22
s. the first and the last | Re 2:8
s. Son of God | Re 2:18
s. the Amen | Re 3:14
yea, *s.*, the Spirit | Re 14:13
she *s.* I sit a queen, and am | Re 18:7
no widow
he *s.*, Surely I come quickly, | Re 22:20
Amen

GOD SAITH

what my *God s.* that I will | 2Ch 18:13
speak
thus *s.* God, Why transgress | 2Ch 24:20
ye commands
to wicked *God s.*, What hast | Ps 50:16
thou to do
thus *s.* God that created | Isa 42:5
heavens
when thou wast refused, *s.* thy | Isa 54:6
God
there is no peace, *s.* my God, | Isa 57:21
to wicked
bring forth and shut the | Isa 66:9
womb *s.* thy God
come to pass in the last days, *s.* | Ac 2:17
God

HE SAITH

go to Joseph, what *he s.* | Ge 41:55
to you, do
all that *he s.* cometh surely | 1Sa 9:6
to pass
let us hear likewise what *he s.* | 2Sa 17:5
when *he s.* to the, Wash and | 2Ki 5:13
be clean

for _he_ s. to the snow, Be thou | Job 37:6
on earth
eat and drink, s. _he_ to thee, | Pr 23:7
his heart
_he_ that s. to wicked, Thou art | Pr 24:24
righteous
nor s. _he,_ For whom do I | Ec 4:8
labour
and _he_ s. to every one that he | Ec 10:3
is a fool
believe those things _he_ s. | M'k 11:23
shall come to pass, he
shall have whatsoever _he_ s.
whatsoever _he_ s. to you, do it | Joh 2:5
what is this _he_ s.? we | Joh 16:18
cannot tell what _he_ s.
and he knoweth that _he_ s. | Joh 19:35
true
_he_ s. to Peter, Feed my | Joh 21:15;
lambs | 21:16
which, s. _he,_ ye have heard of | Ac 1:4
me
they kept the more silence, | Ac 22:2
and _he_ s.
to Israel _he_ s. | Ro 10:21
again _he_ s. | Ro 15:10
for two, s. _he,_ shall be one | 1Co 6:16
flesh
s. _he_ it altogether for our | 1Co 9:10
sakes
_he_ s. I have heard thee in a | 2Co 6:2
time
_he_ s. not, and to seeds, as of | Ga 3:16
many
see, s. _he,_ that thou make all | Heb 8:5
things
in that _he_ s. a new covenant, | Heb 8:13
he made first old

SAKE

I will not curse the ground for | Ge 8:21
man's s.
he entreated Abram well | Ge 12:16
for her s.
he said, I will not do it for | Ge 18:29
forty's s.
not for twenty's s. | Ge 18:31
not for ten's s. | Ge 18:32
they will slay me for my | Ge 20:11
wife's s.
I will multiply thy seed for | Ge 26:24
Abraham's s.
blessed the Egyptian's house | Ge 39:5
for Joseph's s.
Lord had done to Egypt for | Ex 18:8
Israel's s.
let him go free for eye's s. | Ex 21:26
for tooth's s. | Ex 21:27
Moses said, Enviest thou for | Nu 11:29
my s.
while he was zealous for my | Nu 25:11
s. among them
was slain in day of the | Nu 25:18
plague for Peor's s.
not forsake his people for | 1Sa 12:22
name's s.
Saul seeketh to destroy the | 1Sa 23:10
city for my s.
Lord exalted kingdom for | 2Sa 5:12
Israel's s.
for thy word's s. hast done | 2Sa 7:21;
all | 1Ch 17:19
I may shew him kindness for | 2Sa 9:1;
Jonathan's s. | 9:7
deal gently for my s. with | 2Sa 18:5
young man Absalom
stranger cometh out of a far | 1Ki 8:41;
country for thy name's s. | 2Ch 6:32
for David thy father's s. | 1Ki 11:12;
13:32, 34; 15:4; 2Ki 8:19; 19:34; 20:6;
Ps 132:10
for Jerusalem's s. which I | 1Ki 11:13
have chosen
Lord, for thy servant's s. and | 1Ch 17:19
far country for thy great | 2Ch 6:32
name's s.
not consume them for great | Ne 9:31
mercies' s.
entreated for children's s. of | Job 19:17
my body
save me for thy mercies' s. | Ps 6:4;
| 31:16
he leadeth me for his name's s. | Ps 23:3;
| 31:3
remember thou me for thy | Ps 25:7
goodness' s.
for thy name's s. pardon | Ps 25:11
mine iniquity
arise, redeem us for thy | Ps 44:26
mercies' s.

not be confounded for my s. O | Ps 69:6
God
for thy s. I have borne reproach | Ps 69:7
purge away our sins for thy | Ps 79:9
name's s.
he saved them for his name's | Ps 106:8
s.
but do thou for me, for thy | Ps 109:21
name's s.
give glory, for thy mercy and | Ps 115:1
truth's s.
quicken me, for thy name's | Ps 143:11
s. for thy righteousness s.
bring my soul out
for mine own s. and David's | Isa 37:35
Lord is well pleased for his | Isa 42:21
righteousness' s.
for your s. I have sent to | Isa 43:14
Babylon
blotteth out transgressions | Isa 43:25
for my own s.
for Jacob's s. I have even | Isa 45:4
called thee
for my name's s. will I defer | Isa 48:9
mine anger
even for mine own s. will I | Isa 48:11
do it
against thee shall fall for | Isa 54:15
thy s.
for Zion's s. for Jerusalem's s. | Isa 62:1
I will not
return for thy servant's s. the | Isa 63:17
tribes
that cast you out for my | Isa 66:5
name's s. said
O Lord do thou it for thy | Jer 14:7
name's s.
do not abhor us for thy | Jer 14:21
name's s.
but I wrought for my name's | Eze 20:9;
s. that it should not | 14:22; 36:22
wrought with you for my | Eze 20:44
name's s.
shine on thy sanctuary, for | Da 9:17
the Lord's s.
defer not for thine own s. O | Da 9:19
my God
for my s. this great tempest is | Jon 1:12
on you
shall Zion for your s. be | Mic 3:12
plowed as a field
who are persecuted for | M't 5:10
righeousness' s.
shall say evil against you | M't 5:11
falsely for my s.
ye shall be brought before | M't 10:18;
governors and | M'k 13:9; Lu 21:12
kings, for my s.
and ye shall be hated of all | M't 10:22;
men, for my name's s. 24:9; M'k 13:13;
| Lu 21:17
he that loseth his life for | M't 10:39;
my s. shall find it | 16:25; M'k 8:35;
| Lu 9:24
Herod bound John for | M't 14:3;
Herodias' s. | M'k 6:17
nevertheless, for the oath's s. | M't 14:9;
| M'k 6:26
eunuchs for the kingdom of | M't 19:12
heaven's s.
that hath left lands for my | M't 19:29;
name's s. shall | M'k 10:29; Lu 18:29
receive hundred fold
no flesh be saved, but for | M't 24:22;
elect's s. those days be | M'k 13:20
shortened
persecution ariseth for the | M'k 4:17
word's s.
cast out your name for Son of | Lu 6:22
man's s.
the people came not for | Joh 12:9
Jesus' s. only
wilt thou lay down thy life | Joh 13:38
for my s.
else believe me for the very | Joh 14:11
works' s.
these things do to you for | Joh 15:21
my name's s.
things he must suffer for my | Ac 9:16
name's s.
for which hope's s. I am | Ac 26:7
accused of Jews
it was not written for his s. | Ro 4:23
alone
for gospel, they are enemies | Ro 11:28
for your s.
ye must needs be subject for | Ro 13:5
conscience' s.

for Lord's s. strive with me | Ro 15:30
in prayers
we are fools for Christ's s. | 1Co 4:10
and this I do for the | 1Co 9:23
gospel's s.
asking no question for | 1Co 10:25;
conscience' s. | 10:27
offered in sacrifice to idols, | 1Co 10:28
eat not, for his s. and for
conscience' s.
ourselves your servants for | 2Co 4:5
Jesus' s.
we are alway delivered to | 2Co 4:11
death for Jesus' s.
I take pleasure in distresses | 2Co 12:10
for Christ's s.
as God for Christ's s. | Eph 4:32
forgave you
but it is given also to suffer | Ph'p 1:29
for his s.
for his body's s. which is the | Col 1:24
church
for which things' s. wrath of | Col 3:6
God cometh
what manner of men for your | 1Th 1:5
s.
to esteem them highly for | 1Th 5:13
their work's s.
use a little wine, for | 1Ti 5:23
stomach's s.
teaching things for filthy | Tit 1:11
lucre's s.
yet for love's s. I rather | Ph'm 9
beseech thee
submit to every ordinance for | 1Pe 2:13
Lord's s.
but and if ye suffer for | 1Pe 3:14
righteousness' s.
your sins are forgiven for | 1Jo 2:12
name's s.
for the truth's s. that dwelleth in | 2Jo 2
us
because for his name's s. they | 3Jo 7
went forth
and for my name's s. hast | Re 2:3
laboured

THY SAKE

cursed is the ground for _thy_ s. | Ge 3:17
that it may be well with me | Ge 12:13
for _thy_ s.
that the Lord hath blessed me | Ge 30:27
for _thy_ s.
for _thy_ s. are we killed all | Ps 44:22;
day long | Ro 8:36
because for _thy_ s. I have borne | Ps 69:7
reproach
who gather against thee, | Isa 54:15
shall fall for _thy_ s.
for _thy_ s. I have suffered | Jer 15:15
rebuke
I will lay down my life for | Joh 13:37
thy s.

SAKES

I will spare the place for | Ge 18:26
their s.
I will for their s. remember | Le 26:45
the covenant
also the Lord was angry with | De 1:37
me for your s. | 3:26; 4:21
be favourable to them for | J'g 21:22
our s.
it grieveth me much for your | Ru 1:13
s.
he reproved kings for their | 1Ch 16:21;
s. | Ps 105:14
for their s. therefore return | Ps 7:7
thou on high
it went ill with Moses for | Ps 106:32
their s.
for my brethren and | Ps 122:8
companions' s.
so will I do for my servant's | Isa 65:8
s.
I do not this for your s. | Eze 36:22;
| 36:32
but for their s. that shall make | Da 2:30
known
I will rebuke the devourer | Mal 3:11
for your s.
and for their s. which sat | M'k 6:26
with him
I am glad for your s. I was | Joh 11:15
not there
this voice came not for me, | Joh 12:30
but for your s.
and for their s. I sanctify | M'k 17:19
myself

they are beloved for the   *Ro 11:28*
father's *s.*
I have transferred for your *s.*   *1Co 4:6*
or saith he it for our *s.?* for   *1Co 9:10*
our *s.* no doubt
for all things are for your *s.*   *2Co 4:15*
though rich, yet for your *s.*   *2Co 8:9*
became poor
we joy for your *s.* before God   *1Th 3:9*
I endure all things for the   *2Ti 2:10*
elect's *s.*

SALA

of Heber, which was the son   *Lu 3:35*
of S.

SALAH

Arphaxad begat *S.;* and *S.*   *Ge 10:24*
begat
five and thirty years, and   *Ge 11:12*
begat *S.*
Arphaxad lived after he   *Ge 11:13*
begat *S.*
S. lived thirty years, and   *Ge 11:14*
begat
S. lived after he begat Eber   *Ge 11:15*
four

SALAMIS

And when they were at *S.* they   *Ac 13:5*

SALARY

appoint me *s.* (A)   *Ge 30:28*

SALATHIEL

sons of Jeconiah; Assir, *S.* his   *1Ch 3:17*
to Babylon, Jechonias begat   *M't 1:12*
S.
and *S.* begat Zorobabel   *M't 1:12*
which was the son of *S.* which   *Lu 3:27*

SALCAH

in mount Hermon, and in *S.*   *Jos 12:5*
Hermon, and all Bashan   *Jos 13:11*
unto *S.*
in the land of Bashan unto *S.*   *1Ch 5:11*

SALCHAH

all Bashan, unto *S.* and Edrei   *De 3:10*

SALE

count the years of the *s.*   *Le 25:27*
thereof
price of his *s.* shall be   *Le 25:50*
according
cometh of the *s.* of his   *De 18:8*
patrimony

SALEM

Melchizedek king of *S.*   *Ge 14:18*
brought
In *S.* also is his tabernacle,   *Ps 76:2*
and his
For this Melchisedec king of   *Heb 7:1*
S.
after that also King of *S.*   *Heb 7:2*
which is

SALES

Father's house a *s.* shop (B)   *Joh 2:16*

SALIM

was baptizing in Aenon near   *Joh 3:23*
to *S.*

SALIVA

let *s.* run down beard (B)   *1Sa 21:13*

SALLAI

And after him Gabbai, *S.* nine   *Ne 11:8*
Of *S.,* Kallai; of Amok,   *Ne 12:20*
Eber

SALLU

S. the son of Meshullam, the   *1Ch 9:7;*
son   *Ne 11:7*
S. Amok, Hilkiah, Jedaiah   *Ne 12:7*

SALMA

begat *S.* and *S.* begat Boaz   *1Ch 2:11*
S. the father of Beth-lehem   *1Ch 2:51*
The sons of *S.;* Beth-lehem   *1Ch 2:54*

SALMON

Nahshon, and Nahshon begat   *Ru 4:20*
S.
And *S.* begat Boaz and Boaz   *Ru 4:21*
in it, it was white as snow in   *Ps 68:14*
S.
Naasson; and Naasson begat   *M't 1:4*
S.
S. begat Booz of Rachab; and   *M't 1:5*
Booz
of Booz, which was the son of   *Lu 3:32*
S.

SALMONE

under Crete, over against *S.*   *Ac 27:7*

SALOME

the less and of Joses, and *S.*   *M'k 15:40*
Mary the mother of James,   *M'k 16:1*
and *S.*

SALT

s. sea   *Ge 14:3;*
Nu 34:3, 12; De 3:17; Jos 3:16; 12:3;
             15:2, 5; 18:19
she became a pillar of *s.*   *Ge 19:26*
offering season with *s.*   *Le 2:13*
covenant of *s.*   *Le 2:13;*
     Nu 18:19; 2Ch 13:5
land is brimstone and *s.*   *De 29:23;*
                Jer 17:6
the city of *s.*   *Jos 15:62*
sowed the city with *s.*   *J'g 9:45*
the valley of *s.*   *2Sa 8:13;*
2Ki 14:7; 1Ch 18:12; 2Ch 25:11; Ps 60,
                title
wheat, *s.,* wine, and oil,   *Ezr 6:9*
according
s. without prescribing   *Ezr 7:22*
how much
is unsavoury be eaten without   *Job 6:6*
s.
priests shall cast *s.* upon   *Eze 43:24*
them
be healed; they shall be   *Eze 47:11*
given to *s.*
Ye are the *s.* of the earth: *M't 5:13*
but if the
but if the *s.* have lost his   *M't 5:13*
savour
sacrifice shall be salted with   *M'k 9:49*
s.
S. is good: but if the *s.* have   *M'k 9:50*
lost
Have *s.* in yourselves, and   *M'k 9:50*
have
S. is good: but if the *s.*   *Lu 14:34*
have lost
always with grace, seasoned   *Col 4:6*
with *s.*
both yield *s.* water and fresh   *Jas 3:12*

SALTED

not *s.* at all, nor swaddled at   *Eze 16:4*
all
savour, wherewith shall it be   *M't 5:13*
s.
For every one shall be *s.* with   *M'k 9:49*
fire
every sacrifice shall be *s.*   *M'k 9:49*
with salt

SALTNESS

but if the salt have lost his *s.*   *M'k 9:50*

SALTPITS

the breeding of nettles, and *s.*   *Zep 2:9*

SALU

was Zimri, the son of *S.* a   *Nu 25:14*
prince

SALUTATION

what manner of *s.* this should   *Lu 1:29*
be
when Elisabeth heard the *s.* of   *Lu 1:41*
Mary

voice of thy *s.* sounded in   *Lu 1:44*
mine ears
s. of me Paul with mine   *1Co 16:21*
own hand
The *s.* by the hand of me   *Col 4:18*
Paul
The *s.* of Paul with mine   *2Th 3:17*
own hand

SALUTATIONS

salutations (S)   *M't 23:7;*
        Lu 11:43; 20:46
and love *s.* in the   *M'k 12:38*
marketplaces

SALUTE

And they will *s.* thee, and   *1Sa 10:4*
give
to meet him, that he might   *1Sa 13:10*
s. him
of the wilderness to *s.* our   *1Sa 25:14*
master
son unto king David to *s.*   *2Sa 8:10*
him
if thou meet any man, *s.* him   *2Ki 4:29*
not
and if any *s.* thee, answer   *2Ki 4:29*
him not
to *s.* the children of the king   *2Ki 10:13*
And if ye *s.* your brethren   *M't 5:47*
on y
when ye come into an   *M't 10:12*
house, *s.* it
began to *s.* him, Hail, King   *M'k 15:18*
of the
shoes: and *s.* no man by the   *Lu 10:4*
way
came unto Caesarea to *s.*   *Ac 25:13*
Festus
S. my well beloved Epaenetus   *Ro 16:5*
S. Andronicus and Junia, my   *Ro 16:7*
S. Urbane, our helper in   *Ro 16:9*
Christ
S. Apelles approved in Christ   *Ro 16:10*
S. them which are of   *Ro 16:10*
Aristobulus'
S. Herodion my kinsman.   *Ro 16:11*
Greet
S. Tryphena and Tryphosa   *Ro 16:12*
S. the beloved Persis, which   *Ro 16:12*
S. Rufus chosen in the Lord   *Ro 16:13*
S. Asyncritus, Phlegon,   *Ro 16:14*
Hermas
S. Philologus, and Julia,   *Ro 16:15*
Nereus
S. one another with an holy   *Ro 16:16*
kiss
The churches of Christ *s.* you   *Ro 16:16*
and Sosipater, my kinsmen,   *Ro 16:21*
s. you
who wrote this epistle, *s.* you   *Ro 16:22*
in the
The churches of Asia *s.* you   *1Co 16:19*
Aquila and Priscilla *s.* you   *1Co 16:19*
much in
All the saints *s.* you   *2Co 13:13*
S. every saint in Christ Jesus   *Ph'p 4:21*
All the saints *s.* you chiefly   *Ph'p 4:21*
they
S. the brethren in Laodicea   *Col 4:15*
S. Prisca and Aquila, and the   *2Ti 4:19*
All that are with me *s.* thee   *Tit 3:15*
There *s.* thee Epaphras, my   *Ph'm 23*
S. all them that have the   *Heb 13:24*
rule over
all the saints. They of Italy   *Heb 13:24*
s. you
Peace be to thee. Our friends *s.*   *3Jo 14*
thee

SALUTED

house of Micah, and *s.* him   *J'g 18:15*
and came and *s.* his brethren   *1Sa 17:22*
near to the people, he *s.*   *1Sa 30:21*
them
he *s.* him, and said to him,   *2Ki 10:15*
Is thine
amazed, and running to him   *M'k 9:15*
s. him
house of Zacharias, and *s.*   *Lu 1:40*
Elisabeth
and gone up, and *s.* the   *Ac 18:22*
church, he
and *s.* the brethren, and abode   *Ac 21:7*
when he had *s.* them, he   *Ac 21:19*
declared

SALUTETH

and of the whole church, *s.* you	Ro 16:23
the chamberlain of the city *s.* you	Ro 16:23
Aristarchus *s.* you, and Marcus	Col 4:10
Epaphras, who is one of you *s.* you	Col 4:12
church that is at Babylon, *s.* you	1Pe 5:13

SALVATION

see the *s.* of the Lord	Ex 14:13; 2Ch 20:17
lightly esteemed the rock of his *s.*	De 32:15
the Lord wrought *s.* in Israel to-day	1Sa 11:13
Jonathan, who hath wrought this great *s.*	1Sa 14:45
wrought this great deliverance (A)	1Sa 14:45
this great victory for Israel (B)(R)	1Sa 14:45
the Lord wrought a great *s.* for all Israel	1Sa 19:5
worked out a great deliverance (A)(B)	1Sa 19:5
wrought a great victory (E)(R)	1Sa 19:5
he is the tower of *s.* for his king	2Sa 22:51
great deliverance giveth he to his king (E)	2Sa 22:51
great triumphs gives to his king (R)	2Sa 22:51
shew forth from day to day his *s.*	1Ch 16:23
save us, O God of our *s.* and gather us	1Ch 16:35
let thy priests be clothed with *s.*	2Ch 6:41
s. belongeth to the Lord, thy blessing is	Ps 3:8
in *s.* for which he pants (A)	Ps 12:5
O, that the *s.* of Israel were come	Ps 14:7; 53:6
and righteousness from the God of his *s.*	Ps 24:5
my soul shall rejoice in his *s.*	Ps 35:9
the *s.* of the righteous is of the Lord	Ps 37:39
to him will I shew the *s.* of God	Ps 50:23
wilt thou answer us, O God of our *s.*	Ps 65:5
blessed be the God of our *s.*	Ps 68:19
he that is our God, is the God of *s.*	Ps 68:20
working *s.* in the midst of the earth	Ps 74:12
because they trusted not in his *s.*	Ps 78:22
help us, O God of our *s.* for the glory	Ps 79:9
turn us, O God of our *s.* cause anger	Ps 85:4
surely his *s.* is nigh them that fear him	Ps 85:9
make a joyful noise to the rock of our *s.*	Ps 95:1
shew forth his *s.* from day to day	Ps 96:2
holy arm wrought *s.* (A)(E)	Ps 98:1
the Lord hath made known his *s.*	Ps 98:2
ends of the earth have seen the *s.* of God	Ps 98:3
take the cup of *s.* and call on name	Ps 116:13
voice of *s.* is in tabernacles of righteous	Ps 118:15
s. is far from wicked, they seek not thy	Ps 119:155
I will clothe her priests with *s.*	Ps 132:16
it is he that giveth *s.* unto kings	Ps 144:10
he will beautify the meek with *s.*	Ps 149:4
draw water out of the wells of *s.*	Isa 12:3
we will be glad and rejoice in his *s.*	Isa 25:9
s. will God appoint for walls	Isa 26:1
be thou our *s.* in the time of trouble	Isa 33:2

wisdom and knowledge, and strength of *s.*	Isa 33:6
let earth open, let them bring forth *s.*	Isa 45:8
Israel shall be saved with an everlasting *s.*	Isa 45:17
I will place *s.* in Zion for Israel	Isa 46:13
in a day of *s.* have I helped thee	Isa 49:8
the feet of him that publisheth *s.*	Isa 52:7
ends of earth see the *s.* of our God	Isa 52:10
we look for *s.* but it is far from us	Isa 59:11
therefore his arm brought *s.* unto him	Isa 59:16
he put on an helmet of *s.* upon his head	Isa 59:17
shalt call thy walls *s.* thy gates praise	Isa 60:18
he hath clothed me with garments of *s.*	Isa 61:10
the *s.* thereof as a lamp that burneth	Isa 62:1
therefore mine own arm brought *s.* to me	Isa 63:5
in vain is *s.* hoped for, truly in the Lord is the *s.* of Israel	Jer 3:23
quietly wait for the *s.* of the Lord	La 3:26
s. is of the Lord	Jon 2:9
thou didst ride on thy chariots of *s.*	Hab 3:8
thou wentest forth for *s.* of thy people, *s.* with thine anointed	Hab 3:13
thy King, he is just and having *s.* (A)	Zec 9:9
sound of thy *s.* (A)	Lu 1:44
who hath raised up an horn of *s.*	Lu 1:69
to give knowledge of *s.* to his people	Lu 1:77
all flesh shall see the *s.* of God	Lu 3:6
this day is *s.* come to this house	Lu 19:9
what we worship, for *s.* is of Jews	Joh 4:22
neither is there *s.* in any other	Ac 4:12
to you is the word of this *s.* sent	Ac 13:26
shouldest be for *s.* to ends of the earth	Ac 13:47
these men shew to us the way of *s.*	Ac 16:17
the *s.* of God is sent to the Gentiles	Ac 28:28
the gospel is the power of God to *s.*	Ro 1:16
with the mouth confession is made to *s.*	Ro 10:10
through their fall *s.* is come to Gentiles	Ro 11:11
our *s.* nearer than when we believed	Ro 13:11
whether we be comforted, it is for your *s.*	2Co 1:6
in the day of *s.* have I succoured thee: behold now is the day of *s.*	2Co 6:2
godly sorrow worketh repentance to *s.*	2Co 7:10
after ye heard the gospel of your *s.*	Eph 1:13
take the helmet of *s.* and the sword	Eph 6:17
to you an evident token of *s.*	Ph'p 1:28
work out your own *s.* with fear	Ph'p 2:12
and for an helmet the hope of *s.*	1Th 5:8
appointed us to obtain *s.* by our Lord	1Th 5:9
God hath chosen you to *s.*	2Th 2:13
they may obtain the *s.* in Christ	2Ti 2:10
scriptures able to make thee wise to *s.*	2Ti 3:15
the grace of God that bringeth *s.*	Tit 2:11
for them who shall be heirs of *s.*	Heb 1:14
how escape, if we neglect so great *s.*	Heb 2:3
make the captain of *s.* perfect through	Heb 2:10
became the author of eternal *s.*	Heb 5:9
better things, things that accompany *s.*	Heb 6:9

appear the second time without sin to *s.*	Heb 9:28
who are kept through faith unto *s.*	1Pe 1:5
receiving end of your faith, *s.* of your souls	1Pe 1:9
of which *s.* the prophets have inquired	1Pe 1:10
the long-suffering of the Lord is *s.*	2Pe 3:15
to write to you of the common *s.*	Jude 3;
s. to our God	Re 7:10
now is come *s.* and strength	Re 12:10
s. to Lord	Re 19:1

MY SALVATION

Lord is my song, he is become *my s.*	Ex 15:2
he is my shield, the horn of *my s.*	2Sa 22:3
exalted be the rock of *my s.*	2Sa 22:47; Ps 18:46
for this is all *my s.* and all my desire	2Sa 23:5
he also shall be *my s.*	Job 13:16
for thou art the God of *my s.*	Ps 25:5
Lord is my light and *my s.*	Ps 27:1; 62:6; Isa 12:2
leave me not, O God of *my s.*	Ps 27:9; 51:14; 88:1
O Lord *my s.*	Ps 38:22
my soul waits on God from him cometh *my s.*	Ps 62:1
he only is *my s.*	Ps 62:2; 62:6
in God is *my s.*	Ps 62:7
my God, rock of *my s.*	Ps 89:26
I will satisfy him and shew him *my s.*	Ps 91:16
the Lord is become *my s.*	Ps 118:14; 118:21; Isa 12:2
O God, the Lord, the strength of *my s.*	Ps 140:7
behold, God is *my s.* he is become *my s.*	Isa 12:2
my righteousness not far, *my s.* shall not tarry	Isa 46:13
mayest be *my s.* to the end the earth	Isa 49:6
my s. is gone forth	Isa 51:5
my s. shall be for ever the end of the earth	Isa 51:6
and *my s.* from generation to generation	Isa 51:8
my s. is near to come	Isa 56:1
I will wait for the God of *my s.* my God	Mic 7:7
I will joy in the God of *my s.*	Hab 3:18
I know that this shall turn to *my s.*	Ph'p 1:19

THY SALVATION

I have waited for *thy s.*, O Lord	Ge 49:18
mouth enlarged, because I rejoice in *thy s.*	1Sa 2:1
thou hast also given me the shield of *thy s.*	2Sa 22:36; Ps 18:35
I will rejoice in *thy s.*	Ps 9:14
my heart shall rejoice in *thy s.*	Ps 13:5
we will rejoice in *thy s.* and set up banners	Ps 20:5
and in *thy s.* how greatly shall he rejoice	Ps 21:1
his glory is great in *thy s.* honour	Ps 21:5
say unto my soul, I am *thy s.*	Ps 35:3
I have declared thy faithfulness and *thy s.*	Ps 40:10
let such as love *thy s.* say, Lord be	Ps 40:16
restore unto me the joy of *thy s.*	Ps 51:12; 70:4
O God, hear me in the truth of *thy s.*	Ps 69:13
I am poor, let *thy s.* set me up on high	Ps 69:29
my mouth shall shew forth *thy s.*	Ps 71:15
O Lord, grant us *thy s.*	Ps 85:7
remember me, O visit me with *thy s.*	Ps 106:4
let *thy s.* come according to thy word	Ps 119:41
my soul fainteth for *thy s.*	Ps 119:81
mine eyes fail for *thy s.* and for the word	Ps 119:123
Lord, I have hoped for *thy s.* and done	Ps 119:166

I have longed for *thy s.*, O   Ps 119:174
Lord
thou hast forgotten the God   Isa 17:10
of *thy s.*
say to Zion, Behold, *thy s.*   Isa 62:11
cometh
for mine eyes have seen *thy s.*   Lu 2:30

SALVE

anoint thine eyes with eye-*s.*   Re 3:18
s. to put on your eyes   Re 3:18
(A)(B)(P)(R)
ointment for your eyes (N)   Re 3:18
anoint thine eyes with *s.* (S)   Re 3:18

SAMARIA

against high-places which   1Ki 13:32
are in S.
Omri bought the hill *S.* of   1Ki 16:24
Shemer
Ben-hadad besieged S.   1Ki 20:1;
  2Ki 6:24
if dust of *S.* shall suffice for   1Ki 20:10
handfuls
there are men come out of   1Ki 20:17
S.
entrance of the gate of S.   1Ki 22:10;
  2Ch 18:9
one washed the chariot in   1Ki 22:38
the pool of S.
they were in the midst of *S.*   2Ki 6:20
barley for a shekel in the gate   2Ki 7:1;
of S.   7:18
the king of Assyria took S.   2Ki 17:6;
  18:10
delivered *S.* out of mine   2Ki 18:34;
hand   Isa 36:19
stretch over Jerusalem the   2Ki 21:13
line of S.
bones of the prophet that   2Ki 23:18
came out of S.
soldiers fell on the cities   2Ch 25:13
from S.
the noble Asnapper set in the   Ezr 4:10
cities of S.
Sanballat spake before the   Ne 4:2
army of S.
head of Ephraim is *S.* and the   Isa 7:9
head of S.
and the spoil of *S.* shall be   Isa 8:4
taken away
Ephraim and inhabitants of *S.*   Isa 9:9
shall know
is not Hamath as Arpad? *S.* as   Isa 10:9
Damascus
I have seen folly in the   Jer 23:13
prophets of S.
yet plant vines on the   Jer 31:5
mountains of S.
there came certain from   Jer 41:5
Shechem and S.
thine elder sister is S.   Eze 16:46
nor hath *S.* committed half of   Eze 16:51
thy sins
S. is Aholah, and Jerusalem   Eze 23:4
Aholibah
then the wickedness of *S.* was   Ho 7:1
discovered
thy calf, O *S.* hath cast thee   Ho 8:5
off
but the calf of *S.* shall be   Ho 8:6
broken in pieces
the inhabitants of *S.* shall   Ho 10:5
fear for the calves
for *S.* her king is cut off as   Ho 10:7
foam on water
S. shall become desolate,   Ho 13:16
she hath rebelled
assemble yourselves on   Am 3:9
mountains of S.
hear, ye kine of Bashan in   Am 4:1
mountain of S.
woe to them that trust in the   Am 6:1
mountain of S.
they that swear by the sin of   Am 8:14
S. and say
they shall possess the fields of   Ob 19
S.
the word which he saw   Mic 1:1
concerning S.
I will make *S.* as an heap of   Mic 1:6
the field
he passed through the midst   Lu 17:11
of S.
and he must needs go through   Joh 4:4
S.
askest drink of me, who am   Joh 4:9
woman of S.

were scattered through regions   Ac 8:1
of S.
Philip preached Christ to them   Ac 8:5
of S.
apostles heard that *S.* received   Ac 8:14
word

IN SAMARIA

and there was a sore famine   1Ki 18:2
in S.
streets in Damascus, as my   1Ki 20:34
father made *in* S.
to meet Ahab king of Israel   1Ki 21:18
which is *in* S.
now Jehoram began to reign   2Ki 3:1
in S.
would God my lord were   2Ki 5:3
with the prophet *in* S.
and there was a great famine   2Ki 6:25
in S.
Jehu slew all that remained   2Ki 10:17
to Ahab *in* S.
reigned *in* S.   2Ki 13:1;
  13:10; 1Ki 16:29; 22:51
and there remained the grove   2Ki 13:6
also *in* S.
buried *in* S.   2Ki 13:9;
  13:13; 14:16; 1Ki 16:28; 22:37
Jeroboam the son of Joash   2Ki 14:23
reigned *in* S.
Zechariah reigned over   2Ki 15:8;
Israel *in* S.   15:13
Menahem, Pekah, Hoshea   2Ki 15:17;
in S.   15:27; 17:1
for Ahaziah was hid *in* S.   2Ch 22:9
Israel be taken out that dwell   Am 3:12
in S.
be witnesses to me in Judaea   Ac 1:8
and *in* S.
then had the churches rest *in*   Ac 9:31
S.

TO, UNTO SAMARIA

Ahab being displeased came   1Ki 20:43
to S.
so the king died and was   1Ki 22:37
brought *to* S.
Elisha returned from Carmel   2Ki 2:25
to S.
Elisha led them *to* S. open   2Ki 6:19
eyes of these men
Jehu sent letters *to* S.   2Ki 10:1
came *to* S.   2Ki 10:12; 12:17
Jehoash took hostages, and   2Ki 14:14;
returned *to* S.   14:24
Menahem came *to* S. and   2Ki 15:14
smote Shallum
the king of Assyria went up   2Ki 17:5
to S.
Jehoshaphat went down *to* S.   2Ch 18:2
Israel brought the spoil of   2Ch 28:8
Judah *to* S.
as I have done *unto* S. and   Isa 10:11
her idols

SAMARITAN

But a certain *S.* as he   Lu 10:33
journeyed
him thanks: and he was a S.   Lu 17:16
Say we not well that thou art   Joh 8:48
a S.

SAMARITANS

places which the *S.* had   2Ki 17:29
into any city of the *S.* enter   M't 10:5
not
and entered into a village of   Lu 9:52
the S.
Jews have no dealings with the   Joh 4:9
S.
many of the *S.* of that city   Joh 4:39
believed
when the *S.* were come unto   Joh 4:40
him
gospel in many villages of the   Ac 8:25
S.

SAME

saying, This *s.* shall comfort us   Ge 5:29
in our work
the *s.* became mighty men, men   Ge 6:4
of renown
the very *s.* (S)   Ge 7:13;
17:23, 26; Ex 12:17, 41, 51; De 32:48;
Jos 5:11; Eze 40:1; M't 8:13; 1Co 12:11;
  2Co 5:5; 7:11

and Resen, the *s.* is a great   Ge 10:12
city
the *s.* is Zoar,   Ge 14:8
the *s.* is Hebron in the land   Ge 23:2
Mamre: the *s.* is Hebron in   Ge 23:19
let the *s.* be she thou hast   Ge 24:14;
appointed   24:44
the Lord appeared to Isaac   Ge 26:24
the *s.* night
he overtook and spake to   Ge 44:6
them these *s.* words
in the way of Ephrath, the *s.*   Ge 48:7
is Beth-lehem
s. day came they into   Ex 19:1
wilderness
his flowers shall be of the   Ex 25:31;
s.   37:17
knops and branches shall be   Ex 25:36;
of the *s.*   37:22
his horns shall be of the *s.*   Ex 27:2;
  37:25; 38:2
curious girdle of ephod shall   Ex 28:8;
be of *s.*   39:5
that *s.* (S)   Le 23:14; 23:21
cover the *s.* with a covering of   Nu 4:8
s. goodness will we do unto   Nu 10:32
thee
presumptuously, the *s.*   Nu 15:30
reproacheth Lord
the Jebusite, the *s.* is   Jos 15:8
Jerusalem
the *s.* shall go, the *s.* shall not   J'g 7:4
go
the *s.* shall reign over my   1Sa 9:17
people
Zion the *s.* is the city of David   2Sa 5:7
nor turn by the *s.* way thou   1Ki 13:9
camest
in second year eat that   2Ki 19:29;
which springeth of the *s.*   Isa 37:30
Abram, the *s.* is Abraham   1Ch 1:27
confirmed the *s.* to Jacob   1Ch 16:17;
  Ps 105:10
the *s.* may be a priest of   2Ch 13:9
them, no gods
the *s.* is Micaiah the son of   2Ch 18:7
Imla
therefore the name of the *s.*   2Ch 20:26
place
hath not the *s.* Hezekiah   2Ch 32:12
taken away
Shimei and Kelaiah, the *s.*   Ezr 10:23
is Kelita
month Adar, on thirteenth day   Es 9:1
of the *s.*
they that sow wickedness reap   Job 4:8
the *s.*
what ye know, the *s.* do I   Job 13:2
know also
and the tongue of thy dogs in   Ps 68:23
the *s.*
full of mixture, he poureth out   Ps 75:8
of the *s.*
thou art the *s.*, thy years   Ps 102:27
have no end
to the going down of the *s.*   Ps 113:3;
  Mal 1:11
the *s.* as the companion of the   Pr 28:24
destroyer
no man remembered that *s.*   Ec 9:15
poor man.
At the *s.* time spake the Lord   Isa 20:2
so Hananiah the prophet   Jer 28:17
died the *s.* year
the *s.* wicked man shall die   Eze 3:18
in his iniquities
this shall not be the *s.*:   Eze 21:26
exalt him that
prince go out by the way of   Eze 44:3
the *s.*
the *s.* horn made war with the   Da 7:21
saints
a man and his father go in to   Am 2:7
the *s.* maid
the *s.* shall be called great in   M't 5:19
the kingdom
do not even the publicans the   M't 5:46
s.
the *s.* is my brother and   M't 12:50;
sister   M'k 3:35
did the *s.* (S)   M't 20:5; 21:30, 36
stone builders rejected, the   M't 21:42;
s. is become the head   Lu 20:17; 1Pe 2:7
shall endure, *s.* shall be   M't 24:13;
saved   M'k 13:13
that dippeth his hand the *s.*   M't 26:23
shall betray me
that *s.* is he, hold him fast   M't 26:48;
  M'k 14:44

the thieves also cast the s. in | *M't 27:44*
his teeth
lose life, the s. shall save it | *M'k 8:35;*
  | *Lu 9:24*
desire to be first, the s. shall | *M'k 9:35*
be last of all
for sinners also do even the s. | *Lu 6:33*
for with the s. measure that ye | *Lu 6:38*
mete withal
to whom little is forgiven, s. | *Lu 7:47*
loveth little
least among you, the s. shall | *Lu 9:48*
be great
s. was accused that he wasted | *Lu 16:1*
his goods
the s. shall receive greater | *Lu 20:47*
damnation
And the s. day Pilate and | *Lu 23:12*
Herod
the s. had not consented to | *Lu 23:51*
the counsel
the s. was in the beginning | *Joh 1:2*
with God
the s. came for a witness of | *Joh 1:7*
the light
s. is he which baptizeth with | *Joh 1:33*
Holy Ghost
in the s. manner (S) | *Joh 5:19*
the s. is true | *Joh 7:18*
the s. I said to you from the | *Joh 8:25*
beginning
the s. is a thief | *Joh 10:1*
he abode two days still in the | *Joh 11:6*
s. place
being high priest that s. | *Joh 11:49;*
year | *18:13*
the s. shall judge him in the | *Joh 12:48*
last day
abideth in me, s. bringeth | *Joh 15:5*
forth much fruit
s. Jesus shall so come in like | *Ac 1:11*
manner
God made s. Jesus both Lord | *Ac 2:36*
and Christ
the s. dealt subtilly with our | *Ac 7:19*
kindred
s. did God send to be a ruler | *Ac 7:35*
and deliverer
began at the s. scripture and | *Ac 8:35*
preached Jesus
God gave them the s. gift | *Ac 11:17*
(S)
God hath fulfilled the s. to us | *Ac 13:33*
their children
the s. heard Paul speak, who | *Ac 14:9*
beholding him
the s. followed Paul and us, | *Ac 16:17*
and cried
or else let these s. here say, if | *Ac 24:20*
they found
who knowing not only do the | *Ro 1:32*
s
judgest them which do, and | *Ro 2:3*
doest the s.
who hath subjected the s. in | *Ro 8:20*
hope
s. Lord over all is rich to all | *Ro 10:12*
that call
all the members have not the | *Ro 12:4*
s. office
be of the s. mind one | *Ro 12:16;*
toward another | *1Co 1:10; Ph'p 4:2;*
  | *1Pe 4:1*
do good, and thou shalt have | *Ro 13:3*
praise of the s.
I beseech that ye all speak | *1Co 1:10*
the s. thing
or saith not the law the s. also | *1Co 9:8*
did all eat the s. spiritual meat | *1Co 10:3*
the s. drink | *1Co 10:4*
but the s. spirit | *1Co 12:4;*
  | *2Co 4:13; 12:8*
but the s. Lord | *1Co 12:5*
but it is the s. God | *1Co 12:6*
all flesh is not the s. flesh | *1Co 15:39*
but the s. which is made sorry | *2Co 2:2*
by me
I wrote this s. unto you | *2Co 2:3*
lest,when I came
administered to the glory of | *2Co 8:19*
the s. Lord
s. might be ready as a matter | *2Co 9:5*
of bounty
s. was mighty in me to the | *Ga 2:8*
Gentiles
the s. are the children of | *Ga 3:7*
Abraham
he that descended is the s. | *Eph 4:10*
that ascended
s. shall he receive of the Lord | *Eph 6:8*

having the s. conflict ye saw | *Ph'p 1:30*
in me
having s. love, being of one | *Ph'p 2:2*
accord
walk by the s. rule, mind s. | *Ph'p 3:16*
things
and watch in the s. with | *Col 4:2*
thanksgiving
the s. commit thou to faithful | *2Ti 2:2*
men
At the s. time (S) | *Ph'm 22*
art the s. thy years shall not | *Heb 1:12*
fail
he also himself likewise took | *Heb 2:14*
part of the s.
the heirs with him of the s. | *Heb 11:9*
promise
Christ, s. yesterday, to-day, | *Heb 13:8*
and for ever
if any offend not, the s. is a | *Jas 3:2*
perfect man
even so minister the s. one to | *1Pe 4:10*
another
of the s. is he brought in | *2Pe 2:19*
bondage
by the s. word are kept in | *2Pe 3:7*
store, reserved
denies the Son, s. hath not the | *1Jo 2:23*
Father
as the s. anointing teacheth | *1Jo 2:27*
you all things
overcometh the s. shall be | *Re 3:5*
clothed in white

SAMGAR-NEBO

Nergal-sharezer, S., | *Jer 39:3*
Sarsechim

SAMLAH

S. of Masrekah reigned in his | *Ge 36:36*
S. died, and Saul of | *Ge 36:37*
Rehoboth
S. of Masrekah reigned in his | *1Ch 1:47*
S. was dead, Shaul of | *1Ch 1:48*
Rehoboth

SAMOS

and the next day we arrived | *Ac 20:15*
at S.

SAMOTHRACIA

came with a straight course | *Ac 16:11*
to S.

SAMSON

the woman called his name | *J'g 13:24*
S.
S. went to Timnath | *J'g 14:1*
pleased S. well | *J'g 14:7*
S. made there a feast | *J'g 14:10*
S.'s wife wept | *J'g 14:16*
S. caught foxes | *J'g 15:4*
are we come to bind S. | *J'g 15:10*
S. is come hither | *J'g 16:2*
S. lay till midnight | *J'g 16:3*
the Philistines be upon thee, | *J'g 16:9;*
S. | *16:12, 14, 20*
our God hath delivered S. | *J'g 16:23*
into our hand
S. called unto the Lord | *J'g 16:28*
S. took hold | *J'g 16:29*
S. said, Let me die with | *J'g 16:30*
Philistines
the time would fail me to | *Heb 11:32*
tell of S.

SAMUEL

Hannah bare a son, and | *1Sa 1:20*
called him S.
S. ministered before the | *1Sa 2:18*
Lord
S. grew | *1Sa 2:21*
the Lord called S. he | *1Sa 3:4;*
answered | *3:6, 8, 10*
and S. feared to shew Eli the | *1Sa 3:15*
vision
the Lord revealed himself to | *1Sa 3:21*
S. in Shiloh
and the word of S. came to | *1Sa 4:1*
all Israel
S. judged the children of Israel | *1Sa 7:6;*
  | *7:15*
S. cried to the Lord for Israel | *1Sa 7:9*
Lord was against Philistines | *1Sa 7:13*
all days of S.
displeased S. when they | *1Sa 8:6*
said, Give us a king

the people refused to obey | *1Sa 8:19*
the voice of S.
and S. heard all the words of | *1Sa 8:21*
the people
Lord told S. in his ear before | *1Sa 9:15*
Saul came
so Saul did eat with S. that | *1Sa 9:24*
day
S. called Saul to the top of | *1Sa 9:26*
the house
S. took a vial of oil and | *1Sa 10:1*
anointed Saul
we came to S. | *1Sa 10:14*
tell me, I pray thee, what S. | *1Sa 10:15*
said to you
then S. told the manner of | *1Sa 10:25*
the kingdom
whosoever cometh not forth | *1Sa 11:7*
after Saul and S.
the Lord sent S. | *1Sa 12:11*
all the people greatly feared | *1Sa 12:18*
the Lord and S.
he tarried the set time that S. | *1Sa 13:8*
had appointed
it grieved S. | *1Sa 15:11*
as S. turned about to go | *1Sa 15:27*
away S. mantle rent
S. hewed Agag in pieces | *1Sa 15:33*
nevertheless, S. mourned for | *1Sa 15:35*
Saul
Jesse made seven of his sons | *1Sa 16:10*
to pass before S.
S. took the horn of oil and | *1Sa 16:13*
anointed David
David fled and came to S. | *1Sa 19:18*
to Ramah
he said, Where are S. and | *1Sa 19:22*
David
S. died | *1Sa 25:1*
Saul said to the woman, | *1Sa 28:11*
bring me up S.
Saul perceived that it was | *1Sa 28:14*
S. and bowed himself
sons of S. | *1Ch 6:28*
whom David and S., the seer | *1Ch 9:22*
did ordain
according to the word of the | *1Ch 11:3*
Lord by S.
all that S. had dedicated | *1Ch 26:28*
was no passover like that | *2Ch 35:18*
from S.
S. among them that call on his | *Ps 99:6*
name
though Moses and S. stood | *Jer 15:1*
before me
the prophets from S. have | *Ac 3:24*
foretold
gave them judges 450 years | *Ac 13:20*
till S. prophet
the time would fail me to tell | *Heb 11:32*
of S.

SANBALLAT

S. heard of it, it grieved him | *Ne 2:10;*
  | *2:19*
when S. heard we builded he | *Ne 4:1;*
was wroth | *4:7*
S. sent to me | *Ne 6:2*
my God, think upon S. | *Ne 6:5; 6:14*
for Tobiah and S. had hired | *Ne 6:12*
him
the son of Joiada was | *Ne 13:28*
son-in-law to S.

SANCTIFICATION

anoint it for its s. (B) | *Ex 29:36*
righteousness to s. | *Ro 6:19*
(A)(E)(R)
unto s. (E)(R) | *Ro 6:22*
in Christ, who of God is | *1Co 1:30*
made to us s.
our consecration (A) | *1Co 1:30*
holiness (B) | *1Co 1:30*
we are consecrated and made | *1Co 1:30*
free (N)
made righteous and holy (P) | *1Co 1:30*
this is the will of God, even | *1Th 4:3*
your s.
that you should be | *1Th 4:3*
consecrated—separated and set
apart for pure and holy living
(A)
your growing holy, to keep | *1Th 4:3*
yourselves away from lewdness
(B)
that you should be holy (N) | *1Th 4:3*
God's plan is to make you | *1Th 4:3*
holy (P)

should know how to possess his vessel in *s.* — *1Th 4:4*

possess body in consecration and honor (A) — *1Th 4:4*

win his own wife in purity and honor (B) — *1Th 4:4*

learn to gain mastery over his own body, to hallow and to honour it (N) — *1Th 4:4*

learn to control his body, keeping it pure and treating with respect (P) — *1Th 4:4*

take a wife for himself in holiness and honor (R) — *1Th 4:4*

but to *s.* (E) — *1Th 4:7*

through *s.* of the Spirit — *2Th 2:13; 1Pe 1:2*

continue in *s.* (E) — *1Ti 2:15*

SANCTIFIED

God blessed the seventh day and *s.* it — *Ge 2:3*

set it apart and hallowed it (A) — *Ge 2:3*

consecrated (B) — *Ge 2:3; Ex 19:14; Le 8:10, 15*

hallowed it (E)(R) — *Ge 2:3*

Moses *s.* the people — *Ex 19:14*

the tabernacle shall be *s.* by my glory — *Ex 29:43*

s. tabernacle, and all that was therein — *Le 8:10*

s. the altar — *Le 8:15*

s. Aaron and his garments — *Le 8:30*

I will be *s.* in them that come nigh me — *Le 10:3*

hallowed (A)(B) — *Le 10:3*

if he that *s.* it will redeem his house — *Le 27:15*

dedicates (A)(R) — *Le 27:15; 27:19*

and if he that *s.* the field will redeem it — *Le 27:19*

s. the tabernacle, instruments — *Nu 7:1*

consecrated (A)(B)(R) — *Nu 7:1; 8:17; 1Sa 7:1; 16:5*

they set apart (B) — *Nu 7:1*

I *s.* the firstborn of Israel for myself — *Nu 8:17*

because ye *s.* me not in the midst — *De 32:51*

s. Eleazar his son to keep the ark — *1Sa 7:1*

he *s.* Jesse and his sons to the sacrifice — *1Sa 16:5*

though it were *s.* this day in the vessel — *1Sa 21:5*

consecrated (B)(R) — *1Sa 21:5; 1Ch 11:14; 2Ch 7:16*

the priests and Levites *s.* themselves — *1Ch 15:14*

all the priests present were *s.* — *2Ch 5:11*

dedicated themselves (B) — *2Ch 5:11*

I have chosen and *s.* this house — *2Ch 7:16; 7:20*

hallowed this house (E) — *2Ch 7:16*

their brethren, and *s.* themselves — *2Ch 29:15*

they *s.* the house of the Lord in eight days — *2Ch 29:17*

all the vessels have we prepared and *s.* — *2Ch 29:19*

till the other priests had *s.* themselves — *2Ch 29:34*

priests had not *s.* themselves sufficiently — *2Ch 30:3*

his sanctuary which he hath *s.* for ever — *2Ch 30:8*

Levites were ashamed, and *s.* themselves — *2Ch 30:15*

many in the congregation were not *s.* — *2Ch 30:17*

a great number of the priests *s.* themselves — *2Ch 30:24*

in their set office they *s.* themselves — *2Ch 31:18*

set themselves apart (A) — *2Ch 31:18*

faithful in keeping themselves holy (R) — *2Ch 31:18*

they built and *s.* the sheep gate — *Ne 3:1*

consecrated it (A)(R) — *Ne 3:1*

dedicated it (B) — *Ne 3:1*

they *s.* holy things to the Levites, and and Levites *s.* — *Ne 12:47*

children of Aaron set apart what was for Levites (A)(B)(E)(R) — *Ne 12:47*

Job sent and *s.* his sons and his daughters — *Job 1:5*

to purify and hallow them (A) — *Job 1:5*

to dedicate them (B) — *Job 1:5*

holy God shall be *s.* in righteousness — *Isa 5:16*

holy in righteousness (A)(B)(R) — *Isa 5:16*

I have commanded my *s.* ones — *Isa 13:3*

my designated ones (A) — *Isa 13:3*

those dedicated to me (B) — *Isa 13:3*

my consecrated ones (E)(R) — *Isa 13:3*

I *s.* thee, and ordained thee a prophet — *Jer 1:5*

separated and set you apart (A) — *Jer 1:5*

I dedicated you (B) — *Jer 1:5*

I consecrated you (R) — *Jer 1:5*

I will be *s.* in you — *Eze 20:41 30:23*

I will manifest my holiness among you (A)(R) — *Eze 20:41*

when I shall be *s.* in her — *Eze 28:22*

set apart, separated (A) — *Eze 28:22; 28:25*

be *s.* in them in sight of the heathen — *Eze 28:25; 39:27*

it shall be for the priests that are *s.* — *Eze 48:11*

for the consecrated priests (A)(R) — *Eze 48:11*

say ye of him, whom the Father hath *s.* — *Joh 10:36*

Father consecrated, dedicated, set apart (A)(N)(P)(R) — *Joh 10:36*

the Father dedicated (B) — *Joh 10:36*

that they also might be *s.* thro' thy truth — *Joh 17:19*

may be consecrated (B)(N)(R) — *Joh 17:19*

an inheritance among them *s.* — *Ac 20:32; 26:18*

among all God's set-apart ones (A) — *Ac 20:32*

among all those made holy (B) — *Ac 20:32*

among all who are dedicated (N) — *Ac 20:32*

who are consecrated (P) — *Ac 20:32*

being *s.* by the Holy Ghost — *Ro 15:16*

consecrated and made holy (A)(B)(N) — *Ro 15:16*

to them that are *s.* in Christ Jesus — *1Co 1:2*

those consecrated, purified, made holy (A) — *1Co 1:2*

those made holy (B)(P) — *1Co 1:2*

people dedicated to him (N) — *1Co 1:2*

but now ye are *s.* in the name of the Lord — *1Co 6:11*

you were consecrated, set apart, hallowed (A) — *1Co 6:11*

made holy (B) — *1Co 6:11*

been dedicated (N) — *1Co 6:11*

the unbelieving husband is *s.* by the wife — *1Co 7:14*

set apart, separated (A) — *1Co 7:14*

dedicated, consecrated (A)(P)(R) — *1Co 7:14*

it is *s.* by the word of God and prayer — *1Ti 4:5*

consecrated by the Word of God (A)(B)(P)(R) — *1Ti 4:5*

hallowed by God's own word (N) — *1Ti 4:5*

a vessel *s.* for the Master's use — *2Ti 2:21*

a vessel set apart and useful (A)(B) — *2Ti 2:21*

which are valued and dedicated (N) — *2Ti 2:21*

consecrated and useful (R) — *2Ti 2:21*

they who are *s.* are all one — *Heb 2:11*

those being made holy (A) — *Heb 2:11*

those whom he consecrates (N) — *Heb 2:11*

by which will we are *s.* through Jesus — *Heb 10:10*

those who have been made holy (A)(B) — *Heb 10:10*

those who have been consecrated (N) — *Heb 10:10*

he hath perfected forever them that are *s.* — *Heb 10:14*

perfected those consecrated and made holy (A) — *Heb 10:14*

perfected those who are being made holy (B) — *Heb 10:14*

perfected those who are consecrated (N) — *Heb 10:14*

perfected those whom he makes holy (P) — *Heb 10:14*

blood of the covenant wherewith he was *s.* — *Heb 10:29*

blood by which he was consecrated (A)(N) — *Heb 10:29*

blood by which he was made holy (B) — *Heb 10:29*

blood by which he was once made holy (P) — *Heb 10:29*

to them that are *s.* by God — *Jude 1*

to those who are separated, set apart (A) — *Jude 1*

to those who have been chosen (B) — *Jude 1*

SANCTIFIETH

or the temple that *s.* the gold — *M't 23:17*

temple that made the gold sacred (A)(B)(R) — *M't 23:17; 23:19*

both he that *s.* and they who are sanctified — *Heb 2:11*

if blood of bulls *s.* to the purifying of — *Heb 9:13*

SANCTIFY

s. unto me all the firstborn — *Ex 13:2*

Consecrate, set apart (A)(R) — *Ex 13:2*

dedicate to me all the firstborn (B) — *Ex 13:2*

go and *s.* them today and to-morrow — *Ex 19:10*

consecrate them today and tomorrow — *Ex 19:10; 19:22, 23; 28:41; 29:27*

garments to *s.* him (A)(E) — *Ex 28:3*

thou shalt *s.* the altar — *Ex 29:36*

anoint it to consecrate it (A) — *Ex 29:36*

anoint it for its sanctification (B) — *Ex 29:36*

I will *s.* the tabernacle and the altar — *Ex 29:44*

I will consecrate the tent of meeting (R) — *Ex 29:44*

thou shalt *s.* the tabernacle and all its vessels — *Ex 30:29; 40:10-11; Le 8:11*

you shall consecrate them (R) — *Ex 30:29*

ye may know that I am the Lord that doth *s.* you — *Ex 31:13; Le 20:8; 21:8; Eze 20:12*

I am the Lord who consecrates you (B) — *Ex 31:13*

ye shall *s.* yourselves — *Le 11:44; 20:7; Nu 11:18; Jos 3:5; 7:13; 1Sa 16:5*

consecrate yourselves to be holy (A)(R) — *Le 11:44*

Set yourselves apart (B) — *Le 11:44*

I the Lord doth *s.* — *Le 21:15; 21:23; 22:9, 16*

when a man shall *s.* his house — *Le 27:14*

If a man dedicates his house (A)(B)(R) — *Le 27:14*

If a man shall *s.* a field (A)(B)(R) — *Le 27:16*

If a man dedicates a field (A)(B)(R) — *Le 27:16*

only the Lord's firstling, no man shall *s.* it — *Le 27:26*

no man may dedicate it (A)(B)(R) — *Le 27:26*

ye believed me not, to *s.* me — *Nu 20:12; 27:14*

to vindicate my holiness (B) — *Nu 20:12*

keep sabbeth to *s.* it — *De 5:12; Ne 13:22*

Observe sabbath to keep it holy (A)(B)(E)(R) — *De 5:12*

all firstling males thou shalt *s.* — *De 15:19*

firstling males you shall set apart (A) — *De 15:19*

first-born males you shall dedicate (B) — *De 15:19*

firstling males you shall consecrate (R) — *De 15:19*

up *s.* the people, *s.* yourselves — *Jos 7:13*

consecrate people, consecrate yourselves (B) — *Jos 7:13*

s. a solemn assembly (A)(B)(E)(R) — *2Ki 10:20*

s. yourselves — *1Ch 15:12; 2Ch 29:5; 35:6*

consecrate yourselves (B) — *1Ch 15:12*

he should *s.* the most holy things — *1Ch 23:13*

Aaron was set apart to consecrate (B) — *1Ch 23:13*

Levites more upright in heart to *s.* selves — *2Ch 29:34*

for every one was not clean to *s.* — *2Ch 30:17*

s. the Lord of hosts himself — *Isa 8:13*

regard him as Holy *Isa 8:13*
(A)(B)(R)
they shall *s*. the Holy One of *Isa 29:23*
Jacob
they shall revere the Holy *Isa 29:23*
one (A)
they that *s*. themselves in *Isa 66:17*
gardens
Those who connecrate and *Isa 66:17*
cleanse (B)
I will *s*. my great name *Eze 36:23*
I will vindicate the holiness *Eze 36:23*
of my great name and separate
it for (A)
I will vindicate my great *Eze 36:23*
name (B)
the Lord do *s*. Israel *Eze 37:28*
I the Lord do set apart and *Eze 37:28*
consecrate (A)
I will magnify myself, and *s*. *Eze 38:23*
myself
I will demonstrate my *Eze 38:23*
holiness (A)(B)(R)
shall not *s*., people with *Eze 44:19*;
garments 46:20
s. ye a fast *Joe 1:14; 2:15*
s. the congregation *Joe 2:16*
arrange a holy convocation *Joe 2:16*
s. them through the truth *Joh 17:17*
Consecrate them by the *Joh 17:17*
truth (N)
for their sakes I *s*. myself *Joh 17:19*
I consecrate myself *Joh 17:19*
(B)(N)(P)(R)
that he might *s*. the church *Eph 5:26*
cleansing it (N) *Eph 5:26*
the God of peace *s*. you *1Th 5:23*
wholly
make you holy through and *1Th 5:23*
through (B)(N)(P)
that he might *s*. the people *Heb 13:12*
with his blood
purify and consecrate the *Heb 13:12*
people (A)
to consecrate the people *Heb 13:12*
(N)
s. the Lord God in your *1Pe 3:15*
hearts
set Christ apart as holy as *1Pe 3:15*
Lord (A)
revere Christ in your hearts *1Pe 3:15*
as Lord (B)
hold Christ in reverence in *1Pe 3:15*
(N)(R)
concentrate on being devoted *1Pe 3:15*
to Christ (P)

SANCTUARIES

that he profane not my *s*.: for *Le 21:23*
and bring your *s*. unto *Le 26:31*
desolation
strangers are come into the *Jer 51:51*
s. of
Thou hast defiled thy *s*. by *Eze 28:18*
the *s*. of Israel shall be laid *Am 7:9*
waste

SANCTUARY

thou shalt plant them in the *s*. *Ex 15:17*
let them make me a *s*. that I *Ex 25:8*
may dwell
give every one after the *Ex 30:13*
shekel of the *s*.
of cassia 500 shekels after *Ex 30:24*
the shekel of the *s*.
to work all manner of work *Ex 36:1*;
for the *s*. 36:4
not make any more work for *Ex 36:6*
offering of the *s*.
shekels, after the shekel of *Ex 38:24*;
the *s*. *Ex 38:25, 26; Le 5:15; 27:3; 25;*
Nu 3:47, 50; 7:13, 19, 29, 31, 37; 18:16
of 100 talents were cast the *Ex 38:27*
sockets of the *s*.
sprinkle blood before the veil *Le 4:6*
of *s*.
carry your brethren from *Le 10:4*
before the *s*.
nor come into *s*. till her *Le 12:4*
purifying fulfilled
make an atonement for the *Le 16:33*
holy *s*.
ye shall reverence my *s*., I am *Le 19:30;*
the Lord 26:2
neither go out of *s*. nor *Le 21:12*
profane *s*.
males 8600, keeping charge of *Nu 3:28*
the *s*.

Aaron and his sons keeping *Nu 3:38*
charge of the *s*.
wherewith they minister in the *Nu 4:12*
s.
when they have made an end *Nu 4:15*
of covering the *s*.
the service of *s*. belonging unto *Nu 7:9*
them
when children of Israel come *Nu 8:19*
nigh to the *s*.
Kohathites set forward, *Nu 10:21*
bearing the *s*.
with thee shall bear the *Nu 18:1*
iniquity of the *s*.
they shall not come nigh the *Nu 18:3*
vessels of the *s*.
and ye shall keep the charge *Nu 18:5*
of the *s*.
because he hath defiled the *s*. *Nu 19:20*
of the Lord
he set up a great stone by *Jos 24:26*
the *s*.
the inner *s*. (R) *1Ki 6:5; 6:16, 20*
the inner *s*. (S) *1Ki 6:5;*
6:16, 19-23, 31; 7:49; 8:6, 8;
2Ch 3:16; 4:20; 5:7, 9
within the *s*. (A)(B) *1Ki 6:16*
prepared a *s*. (B)(R) *1Ki 6:19; 6:20*
the sanctuary (B)(R) *1Ki 6:21;*
6:22; 7:49; 8:6, 8; 28:2
to oversee the instruments of *1Ch 9:29*
the *s*.
arise, and build ye the *s*. of *1Ch 22:19*
the Lord
divided by lot, for the *1Ch 24:5*
governors of the *s*.
hath chosen to build an *1Ch 28:10*
house for the *s*.
the inner *s*. (A)(R) *2Ch 4:20*
the *s*. of the house (A) *2Ch 5:7*
they have built thee a *s*. *2Ch 20:8*
therein
go out of the *s*. for thou hast *2Ch 26:18*
trespassed
for a sin offering for the *s*. *2 Ch 29:21*
and Judah
but yield yourselves to Lord, *2Ch 30:8*
enter into his *s*.
according to the purification *2Ch 30:19*
of the *s*.
the king of Babylon slew *2Ch 36:17*
men in the *s*.
where are the vessels of the *Ne 10:39*
s.
the Lord send thee help from *Ps 20:2*
the *s*.
to see thee, as I have seen thee *Ps 63:2*
in the *s*.
they have seen thy goings in *Ps 68:24*
the *s*.
till I went into the *s*. of God, *Ps 73:17*
I understood
all that the enemy hath done *Ps 74:3*
wickedly in *s*.
they have cast fire into thy *s*. *Ps 74:7*
they have defiled
thy way, O God, is in the *s*. *Ps 77:13*
who so great
he brought them to the border *Ps 78:54*
of his *s*.
and he built his *s*. like high *Ps 78:69*
palaces
strength and beauty are in his *Ps 96:6*
s.
he hath looked from the *Ps 102:19*
height of his *s*.
Judah was his *s*. Israel his *Ps 114:2*
dominion
lift up your hands in the *s*. *Ps 134:2*
bless the Lord
praise the Lord, praise God *Ps 150:1*
in his *s*.
the Lord of hosts, he shall be *Isa 8:14*
for a *s*.
that he shall come to his *s*. to *Isa 16:12*
pray
I have profaned the princes *Isa 43:28*
of the *s*.
to beautify the place of my *s*. *Isa 60:13*
the courts of my *s*. *Isa 62:9*
(B)(E)(R)
our adversaries have trodden *Isa 63:18*
down thy *s*.
from the beginning is the *Jer 17:12*
place of our *s*.
hath seen the heathen entered *La 1:10*
into her *s*.
the Lord hath abhorred his *s*. *La 2:7*
shall the priest and prophet be *La 2:20*
slain in the *s*.

stones of the *s*. are poured out *La 4:1*
in the street
because thou hast defiled my *Eze 5:11*
s.
yet will I be to them as a *Eze 11:16*
little *s*.
they defiled my *s*. in the *Eze 23:38*
same day
they came the same day into *Eze 23:39*
my *s*. to profane it
between the *s*. and the *Eze 42:20*
profane place
with every going forth of the *Eze 44:5*
s.
and in the day that he *Eze 44:27*
goeth into the *s*.
in it shall be the *s*. and most *Eze 45:3*
holy place
because their waters they *Eze 47:12*
issued out of the *s*.
the *s*. shall be in the midst *Eze 48:8;*
of it 48:10, 21
and the place of his *s*. was *Da 8:11*
cast down
to give the *s*. to be trodden *Da 8:13*
under foot
he said to me, Then shall the *Da 8:14*
s. be cleansed
and cause thy face to shine *Da 9:17*
upon thy *s*.
the people shall destroy the *Da 9:26*
city and the *s*.
they shall pollute the *s*. of *Da 11:31*
strength
it is the king's *s*. (S) *Am 7:13*
it shall be a *s*. (B) *Ob 17*
her priests have polluted the *s*. *Zep 3:4*
profaned the holy *s*. *Mal 2:11*
(A)(B)(R)
slain between altar and *s*. *Lu 11:51*
(A)(P)
a minister of the *s*. and the *Heb 8:2*
true tabernacle
verily the first covenant had a *Heb 9:1*
worldly *s*.
there was a tabernacle, which *Heb 9:2*
is called the *s*.
enter the *s*. (N)(R) *Heb 10:19*
whose blood is brought into *Heb 13:11*
the *s*.

SAND

s. which is upon the sea *Ge 22:17*
shore
make thy seed as the *s*. of *Ge 32:12*
the sea
gathered corn as the *s*. of the *Ge 41:49*
sea
the Egyptian, and hid him in *Ex 2:12*
the *s*.
seas, and of treasures hid in *De 33:19*
the *s*.
as the *s*. that is upon the sea *Jos 11:4*
shore
the *s*. by the sea side for *J'g 7:12*
multitude
as the *s*. which is on the sea *1Sa 13:5*
shore
as the *s*. that is by the sea *2Sa 17:11*
many, as the *s*. which is by *1Ki 4:20*
the sea
as the *s*. that is on the sea *1Ki 4:29*
shore
be heavier than the *s*. of the *Job 6:3*
sea
I shall multiply my days as *Job 29:18*
the *s*.
fowls like as the *s*. of the sea *Ps 78:27*
are more in number than the *Ps 139:18*
s.
stone is heavy, and the *s*. *Pr 27:3*
weighty
people Israel be as the *s*. of *Isa 10:22*
the sea
Thy seed also had been as *Isa 48:19*
the *s*.
descendants like the *s*. *Isa 48:19*
(A)(B)(E)(R)
have placed the *s*. for the *Jer 5:22*
bound of
to me above the *s*. of the seas *Jer 15:8*
neither the *s*. of the sea *Jer 33:22*
measured
Israel shall be as the *s*. of the *Ho 1:10*
sea
shall gather the captivity as *Hab 1:9*
the *s*.
which built his house upon *M't 7:26*
the *s*.

of Israel be as the s. of the   *Ro 9:27*
sea
as the s. which is by the   *Heb 11:12*
sea shore
And I stood upon the s. of the   *Re 13:1*
sea
the number is as the s. of the   *Re 20:8*
sea

SANDAL

thread of a s.-strap (B)   *Ge 14:23*
thread of a s.-thong (R)   *Ge 14:23*
loosen his s. (B)(R)   *De 25:9*
pulled off his s. (A)(B)(R)   *Ru 4:7;*
   4:8
s.-strap not break (B)   *Isa 5:27*
s.-thong be broken (R)   *Isa 5:27*
s. straps not fit to untie (B)   *M'k 1:7*
the string of whose s.   *Joh 1:27*
(A)(B)(R)
your feet s. (B)   *Ex 12:11*

SANDALS

take your s. off (B)   *Ex 3:5*
your s. on your feet (R)   *Ex 12:11*
s. not worn of (A)(B)(R)   *De 29:5*
s. of his feet (A)(R)   *1Ki 2:5*
gave them s. (B)(R)   *2Ch 28:15*
feet in s. (A)(B)(E)(R)   *Ca 7:1*
remove the s. (B)   *Isa 20:2*
s. on your feet (A)(B)   *Eze 24:17;*
   24:23; Am 2:6; 8:6
sandals (A)(B)(R)   *M't 3:11*
10:10; M'k 1:7; Lu 3:16; 10:4; 15:22;
   22:35; Ac 7:33; 13:35
s. not worthy to unloose   *M'k 1:7*
(A)(R)
But be shod with s.; and not   *M'k 6:9*
go with s. on feet   *M'k 6:9*
(A)(B)(N)(P)(R)
Gird thyself, and bind on thy   *Ac 12:8*
s.

SANE

dressed and s. (B)   *M'k 5:15*
words of truth and s.   *Ac 26:25*
thinking (B)
if we are perfectly s. (P)   *2Co 5:13*

SANG

Then s. Moses and the   *Ex 15:1*
children of
Then Israel s. this song,   *Nu 21:17*
Spring up
Then s. Deborah and Barak the   *J'g 5:1*
Is not this David, of whom   *1Sa 29:5*
they s.
the singers s. and the   *2Ch 29:28*
trumpeters
they s. praises with   *2Ch 29:30*
gladness, and
And they s. together by   *Ezr 3:11*
course in
the singers s. loud, with   *Ne 12:42*
Jezrahiah
the morning stars s. together   *Job 38:7*
David, which he s. unto the   *Ps 7 title*
Lord
they his words; they s. his   *Ps 106:12*
praise
prayed, and s. praises unto   *Ac 16:25*
God

SANHEDRIN

the Sanhedrin (A)(B)   *M't 5:22*
the Sanhedrin (A)(B)   *M't 26:59*

SANK

they s. into the bottom as   *Ex 15:5*
stone
s. as lead in the mighty   *Ex 15:10*
waters
s. into his forehead (E)(R)   *1Sa 17:49*
he s. down (A)(R)   *2Ki 9:24;*
he s. down in the mire   *Jer 38:6*
(A)(B)(E)(R)
s. into deep sleep (R)   *Ac 20:9*

SANSANNAH

Ziklag, and Madmannah,   *Jos 15:31*
and S.

SAP

The trees of the Lord are   *Ps 104:16*
full of s.

SAPH

Sibbechai the Hushathite   *2Sa 21:18*
slew S.

SAPHIR

ye away, thou inhabitant of   *Mic 1:11*
S.

SAPPHIRA

named Ananias, with S. his   *Ac 5:1*
wife

SAPPHIRE

were a paved work of a s.   *Ex 24:10*
stone
row shall be a emerald, a s.   *Ex 28:18*
the second row, an emerald,   *Ex 39:11*
a s.
with the precious onyx, or   *Job 28:16*
the s.
rubies, their polishing was of s.   *La 4:7*
as the appearance of a s.   *Eze 1:26*
stone
over them as it were a s.   *Eze 10:1*
stone
and the jasper, the s. the   *Eze 28:13*
emerald
s. blue and sulphur (A)(R)   *Re 9:17*
was jasper; the second, s.; the   *Re 21:19*

SAPPHIRES

stones of it are the place of s.   *Job 28:6*
is as bright ivory overlaid   *Ca 5:14*
with s.
and lay thy foundations with   *Isa 54:11*
s.

SAPS

s. the life (B)   *Le 26:16*

SARA

S. herself received strength   *Heb 11:11*
as S. obeyed Abraham, calling   *1Pe 3:6*
him lord

SARAH

not Sarai, but S. shall her   *Ge 17:15*
name be
S. thy wife shall bear thee a   *Ge 17:19;*
son   *18:14*
where is S.   *Ge 18:9*
it ceased to be with S. after   *Ge 18:11*
manner of women
S. laughed   *Ge 18:12*
wherefore did S. laugh   *Ge 18:13*
Abraham said of S. she is my   *Ge 20:2*
sister
Abimelech restored S.   *Ge 20:14*
because of S.   *Ge 20:18*
the Lord did unto S. as he   *Ge 21:1*
had spoken
the S. should have given   *Ge 21:17*
children suck
in all that S. said to thee,   *Ge 21:12*
hearken to her
years of the life of S. 127   *Ge 23:1*
S. died   *Ge 23:2*
Abraham buried S. his wife   *Ge 23:19*
there was Abraham buried   *Ge 25:10;*
and S.   *49:31*
name of the daughter of   *Nu 26:46*
Asher was S.
look to Abraham and to S.   *Isa 51:2*
that bare you
at this time I will come, S.   *Ro 9:9*
shall have a son
through faith S. received   *Heb 11:11*
strength to conceive
as S. obeyed Abraham, calling   *1Pe 3:6*
him lord

SARAH'S

her into his mother S. tent   *Ge 24:67*
S. handmaid, bare unto   *Ge 25:12*
Abraham
yet the deadness of S. womb   *Ro 4:19*

SARAI

the name of Abram's wife   *Ge 11:29*
was S.
but S. was barren, she had   *Ge 11:30;*
no child   *16:1*
the Lord plagued Pharaoh   *Ge 12:17*
because of S.
when S. dealt hardly with   *Ge 16:6*
Hagar, she fled
she said, I flee from the face   *Ge 16:8*
of my mistress S.
thou shalt not call her name   *Ge 17:15*
S., but Sarah

SARAI'S

he said, Hagar, S. maid,   *Ge 16:8*
whence

SARAPH

S. who had the dominion in   *1Ch 4:22*
Moab

SARDINE

upon like a jasper and a s.   *Re 4:3*
stone

SARDIS

and unto Thyatira, and unto   *Re 1:11*
S.
the angel of the church in S.   *Re 3:1*
write
Thou hast a few names even in   *Re 3:4*
S.

SARDITES

of Sered, the family of the   *Nu 26:26*
S.: of

SARDIUS

the first row shall be a s., a   *Ex 28:17*
topaz
the first row was a s., a   *Ex 39:10*
topaz
thy covering, the s. and the   *Eze 28:13*
diamond
like a jasper and a s. (S)   *Re 4:3*
The fifth, sardonyx; the sixth,   *Re 21:20*
s.

SARDONYX

The fifth, s.; the sixth,   *Re 21:20*
sardius

SAREPTA

save unto S. a city of Sidon   *Le 4:26*

SARGON

S. the king of Assyria sent him   *Isa 20:1*

SARID

of their inheritance was unto   *Jos 19:10*
S.
And turned from S. eastward   *Jos 19:12*

SARON

all that dwelt at Lydda and S.   *Ac 9:35*
saw

SARSECHIM

Nergal-sharezer, Samgar-nebo,   *Jer 39:3*
S.

SARUCH

Which was the son of S.   *Lu 3:35*

SASHES

and the s. (S)   *Isa 3:20*

SAT

Rachel had taken and s. upon   *Ge 31:34*
the images
Tamar covered with a veil, s.   *Ge 38:14*
in open place
firstborn of Pharaoh that s.   *Ex 12:29*
on throne
when we s. by the fleshpots,   *Ex 16:3*
and did eat
on the morrow Moses s. to   *Ex 18:13*
judge the people

they wept and *s.* before the *J'g 20:26*
Lord
how Eli *s.* on a seat by post of *1Sa 1:9*
temple
Eli *s.* on a seat by the *1Sa 4:13*
wayside, watching
as soon as he *s.* on his *1Ki 16:11*
throne, he slew
the children of Belial *s.* *1Ki 21:13*
before Naboth
the two kings *s.* each on his *1Ki 22:10*
throne
but Elisha *s.* in his house, *2Ki 6:32*
and elders *s.* with him
as David *s.* in his house, he *1Ch 17:1*
said
David *s.* before the Lord and *1Ch 17:16*
said, Who am I
they made booths, and *s.* *Ne 8:17*
under them
I chose out their way, and *s.* *Job 29:25*
chief
I have not *s.* with vain persons *Ps 26:4*
in the ways hast thou *s.* for *Jer 3:2*
them
I *s.* not in the assembly of *Jer 15:17*
the mockers, I *s.* alone
now the king *s.* in the *Jer 36:22*
winterhouse
I *s.* where they *s.* and *Eze 3:15*
remained there
as I *s.* in my house, the elders *Eze 8:1*
s. before me
behold, there *s.* women *Eze 8:14*
weeping for Tammuz
the elders came to inquire of *Eze 20:1*
the Lord and *s.*
but Daniel *s.* in the gate of *Da 2:49*
the king
people *s.* in darkness saw *M't 4:16*
light; them that *s.* in shadow
for them which *s.* with him *M't 4:9;*
M'k 6:26
I *s.* daily with you teaching *M't 26:55*
in the temple
Peter *s.* with the servants to *M't 26:58*
see the end
blind Bartimaeus *s.* by the *M'k 10:46;*
wayside begging *Lu 18:35; Joh 9:8*
and he *s.* on the right hand *M'k 16:19*
of God
he that was dead *s.* up, and *Lu 7:15*
began to speak
Mary *s.* at Jesus' feet, and *Lu 10:39*
heard his words
a colt whereon never man *s. Lu 19:30;*
M'k 11:2
Jesus wearied, *s.* thus on the *Joh 4:6*
well
cloven tongues *s.* upon each of *Ac 2:3*
them
he who *s.* for alms at the *Ac 3:10*
beautiful gate
he that *s.* on the throne was *Re 4:3*
like a jasper
on the cloud one *s.* like the *Re 14:14*
Son of man
he that *s.* upon him was *Re 19:11*
called Faithful
to make war against him *Re 19:19*
that *s.* on the horse

SAT *DOWN*

the people *s. down* to eat *Ex 32:6*
and to drink
and they *s. down* at thy feet *De 33:3*
plucked off hair, and *s. down* *Ezr 9:3*
astonied
they *s. down* to examine the *Ezr 10:16*
matter
I *s. down* and mourned certain *Ne 1:4*
days
the king and Haman *s. down* *Es 3:15*
to drink
Job *s. down* among the ashes *Job 2:8*
there we *s. down*, yea, we *Ps 137:1*
wept
I *s. down* under his shadow *Ca 2:3*
with delight
many sinners came and *s.* *M't 9:10*
down with him
he *s. down* with the twelve *M't 26:20;*
Lu 22:14
gave book to the minister, and *Lu 4:20*
s. down
s. down and taught the people *Lu 5:3*
out of the ship

people came, he *s. down* and *Joh 8:2*
taught them
they went into the synagogue *Ac 13:14*
and *s. down*
we *s. down* and spake to the *Ac 16:13*
women
s. down on the right hand of *Heb 1:3;*
God *10:12*

SATAN

S. stood up against Israel and *1Ch 21:1*
and *S.* came also among them *Job 1:6*
Lord said unto *S.* Whence *Job 1:7*
comest
S. answered the Lord, and said *Job 1:7*
the Lord said unto *S.* Hast *Job 1:8*
thou
S. answered the Lord, and said *Job 1:9*
Lord said unto *S.* Behold, all *Job 1:12*
S. went forth from the *Job 1:12*
presence of
and *S.* came also among them *Job 2:1*
Lord said unto *S.* From *Job 2:2*
whence
S. answered the Lord and said *Job 2:2*
the Lord said unto *S.* Hast *Job 2:3*
thou
S. answered the Lord, and *Job 2:4*
said
Lord said unto *S.* Behold, he *Job 2:6*
is in
went *S.* forth from the *Job 2:7*
presence of
and let *S.* stand at his right *Ps 109:6*
hand
S. standing at his right hand to *Zec 3:1*
the Lord said unto *S.* The *Zec 3:2*
Lord
Lord rebuke thee, O *S.*; even *Zec 3:2*
unto him, Get thee hence, *S.* *M't 4:10*
And if *S.* cast out *S.*, he is *M't 12:26*
divided
Get thee behind me, *S.*: thou *M't 16:23*
art
forty days, tempted of *S.*; *M'k 1:13*
and was
parables, How can *S.* cast *M'k 3:23*
out *S.*
S. rise up against himself, *M'k 3:26*
and be
S. cometh immediately, and *M'k 4:15*
taketh
saying, Get thee behind me, *M'k 8:33*
S.
unto him, Get thee behind me, *Lu 4:8*
S.
I beheld *S.* as lightning fall *Lu 10:18*
from
S. also be divided against *Lu 11:18*
himself
of Abraham, whom *S.* hath *Lu 13:16*
bound
Then entered *S.* into Judas *Lu 22:3*
S. hath desired to have you *Lu 22:31*
after the sop *S.* entered into *Joh 13:27*
him
why hath *S.* filled thine heart *Ac 5:3*
to lie
from the power of *S.* unto *Ac 26:18*
God, that
bruise *S.* under your *Ro 16:20*
feet shortly
To deliver such an one unto *S.* *1Co 5:5*
that *S.* tempt you not for your *1Co 7:5*
S. should get an advantage of *2Co 2:11*
us
S. himself is transformed *2Co 11:14*
into an
the messenger of *S.* to buffet *2Co 12:7*
me
and again; but *S.* hindered us *1Th 2:18*
is after the working of *S.* with *2Th 2:9*
all
whom I have delivered unto *S.* *1Ti 1:20*
are already turned aside after *1Ti 5:15*
S.
not, but are the synagogue of *S.* *Re 2:9*
slain among you, where *S.* *Re 2:13*
dwelleth
have not known the depths of *Re 2:24*
S.
make them of the synagogue of *Re 3:9*
S.
serpent, called the Devil, and *Re 12:9*
S.
serpent, which is the Devil, *Re 20:2*
and *S.*

S. shall be loosed out of his *Re 20:7*
prison

SATAN'S

dwellest, even where *S.* seat is *Re 2:13*

SATED

s. with own counsel (B) *Pr 1:31*

SATCHELS

the *s.* (E) *Isa 3:22*

SATEST

s. in the throne judging right *Ps 9:4*
s. upon a stately bed, and a *Eze 23:41*
table

SATIATE

And I will *s.* the soul of the *Jer 31:14*
priests
satisfy fully the life of priests *Jer 31:14*
(A)
feast the soul of the priests *Jer 31:14*
(B)(R)
and it shall be *s.* and made *Jer 46:10*
drunk

SATIATED

I have *s.* the weary soul, and *Jer 31:25*

SATINS

dressed in silks and *s.* (N) *M't 11:8;*
Lu 7:25

SATISFACTION

no *s.* for the life of a *Nu 35:31*
murderer
no *s.* for him that is fled to *Nu 35:32*
the city

SATISFACTORY

had proved *s.* (P) *Heb 8:7*

SATISFIED

my lust shall be *s.* upon them *Ex 15:9*
and ye shall eat, and not be *Le 26:26*
s.
shall come, and shall eat and *De 14:29*
be *s.*
O Naphtali, *s.* with favour *De 33:23*
and was *s.* (S) *Ru 2:14*
God, and are not *s.* with my *Job 19:22*
flesh
offspring shall not be *s.* with *Job 27:14*
bread
had of his flesh we cannot *Job 31:31*
be *s.*
I shall be *s.* when I awake *Ps 17:15*
The meek shall eat and be *s.* *Ps 22:26*
They shall be abundantly *s.* *Ps 36:8*
days of famine, they shall be *Ps 37:19*
s.
meat, and grudge if they be *Ps 59:15*
not *s.*
My soul shall be *s.* as with *Ps 63:5*
marrow
we shall be *s.* with the *Ps 65:4*
goodness of
of the rock should I have *s.* *Ps 81:16*
thee
earth is *s.* with the fruit of *Ps 104:13*
thy
s. them with the bread of *Ps 105:40*
heaven
He that tilleth his land shall be *Pr 12:11*
s.
A man shall be *s.* with good *Pr 12:14*
by the
a good man, shall be *s.* from *Pr 14:14*
himself
A man's belly shall be *s.* with *Pr 18:20*
he that hath it shall abide *s.*; *Pr 19:23*
he
and thou shalt be *s.* with *Pr 20:13*
bread
so the eyes of man are never *Pr 27:20*
s.

Sheol never *s.*   *Pr 27:20*
(A)(B)(E)(R)
are three things that are   *Pr 30:15*
never *s.*
the eye is not *s.* with seeing,   *Ec 1:8*
nor
neither is his eye *s.* with riches *Ec 4:8*
He that loveth silver shall not   *Ec 5:10*
be *s.*
left hand, and they shall not   *Isa 9:20*
be *s.*
flesh; he roasteth roast, and   *Isa 44:16*
is *s.*
travail of his soul, and shall   *Isa 53:11*
be *s.*
suck, and be *s.* with the   *Isa 66:11*
breasts
and my people shall be *s.*   *Jer 31:14*
with my
all that spoil her shall be *s.*   *Jer 50:10*
saith
and his soul shall be *s.* upon   *Jer 50:19*
mount
the Assyrians, to be *s.* with   *La 5:6*
bread
them, and yet couldest not be   *Eze 16:28*
s.
you were not *s.* (R)   *Eze 16:28*
and yet thou wast not *s.*   *Eze 16:29*
herewith
oil, and ye shall be *s.*   *Joe 2:19*
therewith
ye shall eat in plenty, and be   *Joe 2:26*
s.
drink water; but they were not   *Am 4:8*
s.
Thou shalt eat, but not be *s.*   *Mic 6:14*
and is as death, and cannot   *Hab 2:15*
be *s.*
if you are *s.* I am a true (P)   *Ac 16:15*

SATISFIEST

s. the desire of every living   *Ps 145:16*
thing

SATISFIETH

s. thy mouth with good things   *Ps 103:5*
he *s.* the longing soul, and   *Ps 107:9*
filleth
your labour for that which *s.*   *Isa 55:2*
not

SATISFY

s. the desolate and waste   *Job 38:27*
ground
O *s.* us early with thy mercy   *Ps 90:14*
With long life will I *s.* him   *Ps 91:16*
I will *s.* her poor with bread   *Ps 132:15*
let her breasts *s.* thee at all   *Pr 5:19*
times
if he steal to *s.* his soul when *Pr 6:30*
he
hungry, and *s.* the afflicted   *Isa 58:10*
soul
s. thy soul in drought, and   *Isa 58:11*
make
s. full life of priests (A)   *Jer 31:14*
they shall not *s.* their souls   *Eze 7:19*
can a man *s.* these men with   *M'k 8:4*
bread

SATISFYING

eateth to the *s.* of his soul   *Pr 13:25*
s. bodily appetites (N)   *Ro 13:14*
any honour to the *s.* of the   *Col 2:23*
flesh

SATRAPS

delivered to the king's *s.* (S)   *Ezr 8:36*

SATYR

and the *s.* shall cry to his   *Isa 34:14*
fellow
the shaggy wild goat will call   *Isa 34:14*
(A)(B)
the wild goat shall cry (E)   *Isa 34:14*

SATYRS

satyrs (R)   *Le 17:7; 2Ch 11:15*
there, and *s.* shall dance there *Isa 3:21*

wild goats will dance   *Isa 13:21*
(A)(E)
shaggy goats will be skipping   *Isa 13:21*
(B)

SAUL

S. of Rehoboth reigned   *Ge 36:37*
S. died   *Ge 36:38*
Kish had a son, whose name   *1Sa 9:2;*
was *S.*   *14:51*
the Lord told Samuel a day   *1Sa 9:15*
before *S.* came
when Samuel saw *S.*   *1Sa 9:17*
S. drew near to Samuel   *1Sa 9:18*
set it before *S.* So *S.* did   *1Sa 9:24*
eat with Samuel
is *S.* also among the   *1Sa 10:11;*
prophets   *10:12; 19:24*
S. was taken   *1Sa 10:21*
shall *S.* reign over us   *1Sa 11:12*
the Spirit of God came upon   *1Sa 11:6*
S. anger kindled
whosoever cometh not forth   *1Sa 11:7*
after *S.* and Samuel
people went to Gilgal, there   *1Sa 11:15*
they made *S.* king
S. blew the trumpet through   *1Sa 13:3*
all the land
as for *S.* he was yet in Gilgal, *1Sa 13:7*
and all the people
S. went out to meet Samuel   *1Sa 13:10*
S. numbered   *1Sa 13:15*
for *S.* had injured the   *1Sa 14:24*
people, saying
S. built an altar   *1Sa 14:35*
S. asked counsel of God   *1Sa 14:37*
S. went up from following   *1Sa 14:46*
the Philistines
when *S.* saw any strong man   *1Sa 14:52*
he took him
it repenteth me that I have   *1Sa 15:11*
set up *S.*
Samuel turned again after *S.*;   *1Sa 15:31*
S. worshipped
and Samuel came no more   *1Sa 15:35*
to see *S.*
Lord said, How long wilt   *1Sa 16:1*
thou mourn for *S.*
if *S.* hear it   *1Sa 16:2*
the Spirit of the Lord   *1Sa 16:14*
departed from *S.*
the evil Spirit from God was   *1Sa 16:23;*
on *S.*   *18:10; 19:9*
am not I a Philistine, and you   *1Sa 17:8*
servants to *S.*
Jesse went for an old man   *1Sa 17:12*
in the days or *S.*
S. and all Israel were in the   *1Sa 17:19*
valley of Elah
and *S.* armed David with his   *1Sa 17:38*
armour
came out to meet king *S.*   *1Sa 18:6*
S. eyed David from that day   *1Sa 18:9*
and forward
S. afraid of David; Lord   *1Sa 18:12*
departed from *S.*
when *S.* saw that he behaved   *1Sa 18:15;*
very wisely   *18:30*
S. became David's enemy   *1Sa 18:29*
continually
Jonathan spake good of   *1Sa 19:4*
David to *S.* his father
Jonathan brought David to *S.*   *1Sa 19:7*
S. sent messengers to take   *1Sa 19:11;*
David   *18:14-15, 20*
S. cast a javelin   *1Sa 20:33*
David arose and fled that   *1Sa 21:10*
day for fear of *S.*
saying, *S.* hath slain his   *1Sa 21:11;*
thousands   *29:5*
I knew that he would surely   *1Sa 22:22*
tell *S.*
will *S.* come down as   *1Sa 23:11*
thy servant hath heard
shall be king, and that *S.* my   *1Sa 23:17*
father knoweth
S. returned from pursuing   *1Sa 23:28*
after David
David suffered them not to   *1Sa 24:7*
rise against *S.*
David cried after *S.*   *1Sa 24:8*
David sware to *S.*   *1Sa 24:22*
David understood *S.* was   *1Sa 26:4*
come in very deed
and David beheld the place   *1Sa 26:5*
where *S.* lay
behold, *S.* lay sleeping within   *1Sa 26:7*
the trench
S. knew David's voice   *1Sa 26:17*
S. returned   *1Sa 26:25*

I shall perish one day by the   *1Sa 27:1*
hand of *S.*
behold, thou knowest what *S.*   *1Sa 28:9*
hath done
S. sware to her by Lord   *1Sa 28:10*
for thou art *S.*   *1Sa 28:12*
S. fell straightway all along   *1Sa 28:20*
on the earth
is not this David servant of   *1Sa 29:3*
S. king of Israel
Philistines followed hard   *1Sa 31:2;*
upon *S.* and his sons   *1Ch 10:2*
that *S.* and his sons were   *1Sa 31:7;*
dead   *1Ch 10:7*
Jabesh-gilead heard what   *1Sa 31:11;*
the Philistines had done to   *1Ch 10:11*
S. leaned on his spear   *2Sa 1:6*
shield of *S.*   *2Sa 1:21*
ye daughters of Israel, weep   *2Sa 1:24*
over *S.*
be ye valiant, for your master   *2Sa 2:7*
S. is dead
the house of *S.* waxed   *2Sa 3:1*
weaker and weaker
to translate kingdom from   *2Sa 3:10;*
house of *S.* and David   *1Ch 12:23*
one brought tidings saying,   *2Sa 4:10*
S. is dead
in time past, when *S.* was   *2Sa 5:2;*
king   *1Ch 11:2*
mercy shall not depart, as I   *2Sa 7:15*
took it from *S.*
is there yet any left of the   *2Sa 9:1;*
house of *S.*   *9:3*
I will restore thee all the land   *2Sa 9:7*
of *S.* thy father
delivered thee out of the   *2Sa 12:7;*
hand of *S.*   *22:1*
on thee all the blood of the   *2Sa 16:8*
house of *S.*
it is for *S.* and for his bloody *2Sa 21:1*
house
will have no silver nor gold   *2Sa 21:4*
of *S.* nor his house
David took the bones of *S.*   *2Sa 21:12*
from men of Jabesh
in the days of *S.* they made   *1Ch 5:10*
war
so *S.* died for his   *1Ch 10:13*
transgression against the Lord
David kept himself close   *1Ch 12:1*
because of *S.*
we inquired not at it in the   *1Ch 13:3*
days of *S.*
all that Samuel and *S.* had   *1Ch 26:28*
dedicated
Ramah is afraid, Gibeah of   *Isa 10:29*
S. is fled
at a young man's feet whose   *Ac 7:58*
name was *S.*
and *S.* was consenting unto his   *Ac 8:1*
death
as for *S.* he made havoc of the   *Ac 8:3*
church
S., *S.* why persecutest thou me *Ac 9:4;*
                                   22:7; 26:14
and inquire for one called *S.*   *Ac 9:11*
of Tarsus
brother *S.* the Lord hath sent   *Ac 9:17;*
me   *22:13*
but *S.* increased more in   *Ac 9:22*
strength
but their laying await was   *Ac 9:24*
known of *S.*
when *S.* was come to   *Ac 9:26*
Jerusalem, he assayed
Barnabas went to Tarsus to   *Ac 11:25*
seek *S.*
sent relief by the hands of   *Ac 11:30*
Barnabas and *S.*
at Antioch prophets brought   *Ac 31:1*
up with *S.*
Holy Ghost said, Separate me   *Ac 13:2*
Barnabas and *S.*
Sergius Paulus called for   *Ac 13:7*
Barnabas and *S.*
S. set his eyes on him, and   *Ac 13:9*
said, O full of all
God gave unto them *S.* the   *Ac 13:21*
son of Cis

SAUL'S

asses of Kish *S.* father were   *1Sa 9:3*
lost
S. uncle said unto him and   *1Sa 10:14*
S. uncle said, Tell me, I   *1Sa 10:15*
pray thee
the name of *S.* wife was   *1Sa 14:50*
Ahinoam

was Abner, the son of Ner, *1Sa 14:50*
S. uncle
S. servants said unto him, *1Sa 16:15*
Behold
and also in the sight of S. *1Sa 18:5*
servants
and there was a javelin in S. *1Sa 18:10*
hand
S. daughter should have been *1Sa 18:19*
given
Michal S. daughter loved *1Sa 18:20*
David
S. servants spake those *1Sa 18:23*
words in
that Michal S. daughter *1Sa 18:28*
loved him
Jonathan S. son delighted *1Sa 19:2*
much in
he slipped away out of S. *1Sa 19:10*
presence
and Abner sat by S. side *1Sa 20:25*
Then S. anger was kindled *1Sa 20:30*
against
Jonathan S. son arose, and *1Sa 23:16*
went to
and cut off the skirt of S. *1Sa 24:4*
robe
because he had cut off S. *1Sa 24:5*
skirt
the cruse of water from S. *1Sa 26:12*
bolster
and Melchi-shua, S. sons *1Sa 31:2*
But Abner captain of S. host *2Sa 2:8*
Ish-bosheth S. son was forty *2Sa 2:10*
years
thou first bring Michal S. *2Sa 3:13*
daughter
messengers to Ish-bosheth S. *2Sa 3:14*
son
S. son heard that Abner was *2Sa 4:1*
dead
Jonathan, S. son, had a *2Sa 4:4*
son lame
Michal S. daughter looked *2Sa 6:16*
through
the king called to Ziba, S. *2Sa 9:9*
servant
even of S. brethren of *1Ch 12:2*
Benjamin

SAVAGE

but are really s. wolves *M't 7:15*
(N)(P)
s. wolves will (B)(N)(P) *Ac 20:29*
the ignorant s. (P) *Ro 1:14*

SAVE

to s. your life (B) *Ge 45:5*
God sent me before you to s. *Ge 45:7*
to assure continuance on earth *Ge 45:7*
(B)
to preserve a remnant (E)(R) *Ge 45:7*
the Lord goeth with you to s. *De 20:4*
you
to give you victory (B)(R) *De 20:4*
she cried, and there was none *De 22:27*
to s. her
no one to rescue her (B) *De 22:27*
be spoiled, and no man shall *De 28:29*
s. thee
no one to rescue you (B) *De 28:29*
none to help you (R) *De 28:29*
go in might, thou shalt s. *J'g 6:14*
Israel
O my Lord, wherewith shall I *J'g 6:15*
s. Israel
will ye plead for Baal? will ye *J'g 6:31*
s. him
if thou wilt s. Israel by mine *J'g 6:36*
hand
then shall I know that thou *J'g 6:37*
wilt s. Israel
by the 300 men that lapped will *J'g 7:7*
I s. you
anoint him, that he may s. *1Sa 9:16*
my people
he shall deliver my people *1Sa 9:16*
(B)
people shouted God s. the *1Sa 10:24;*
king *2Sa 16:16;*
2Ki 11:12; 2Ch 23:11
long live the king *1Sa 10:24;*
(A)(B)(E)(R) *2Sa 16:16; 2Ki 11:12;*
2Ch 23:11
no restraint, to s. by many, *1Sa 14:6*
or by few
if thou s. not thyself this *1Sa 19:11*
night

Lord said to David, go and s. *1Sa 3:2*
Keliah
by hand of David I will s. *2Sa 3:18*
Israel
rescue my people Israel (B) *2Sa 3:18*
s. me out of every trouble (B) *2Sa 4:9*
afflicted people thou wilt s. *2Sa 22:28;*
Ps 22:28;
afflicted people you will *2Sa 22:28*
deliver (A)(R)
there was none to s. them *2Sa 22:42;*
Ps 18:41
thou mayest s. thine own life *1Ki 1:12*
may preserve your life (B) *1Ki 1:12*
behold, they say, God s. king *1Ki 1:25*
Adonijah
Long live king Adonijah *1Ki 1:25*
(A)(B)(E)(R)
blow trumpet, say, God s. *1Ki 1:34;*
king Solomon *1:39*
Long live king Solomon *1Ki 1:34*
(A)(B)(E)(R)
go to king, peradventure he *1Ki 20:31*
will s. thy life
in the house s. a pot of oil *2Ki 4:2*
I will defend this city to s. *2Ki 19:34;*
it, for my own sake *Isa 37:35*
left him, s. Jehoahaz, the *2Ch 21:17*
would us go into the temple to *Neh 6:11*
s. his life
he is in thine hand, but s. *Job 2:6*
his life
spare his life (A)(B)(E)(R) *Job 2:6*
he shall not s. of that which *Job 20:20*
he desired
and he shall s. the humble *Job 22:29*
person
that thine own right hand *Job 40:14*
can s. thee
s. Lord, let the king hear us *Ps 20:9*
s. thy people, fed them also *Ps 28:9;*
Jer 31:7
he shall s. them, because they *Ps 37:40*
trust in
neither did their own arm s. *Ps 44:3*
them
neither did own arm gain *Ps 44:3*
deliverance (B)
nor did own arm give victory *Ps 44:3*
(R)
s. with thy right hand, and *Ps 60:5;*
hear me *108:6*
God will s. Zion, and will *Ps 69:35*
build Judah
he shall s. the children of the *Ps 72:4*
needy
and he shall s. the souls of *Ps 72:13*
the needy
when God arose to s. the meek *Ps 76:9*
of earth
O my God, s. thy servant that *Ps 86:2*
trusteth in
and s. the son of thine *Ps 86:16*
handmaid
s. him from those that *Ps 109:31*
condemn his soul
s. I beseech thee, send *Ps 118:25*
prosperity
he also will hear their cry, *Ps 145:19*
and s. them
wait on the Lord, and he *Pr 20:22*
shall s. thee
your God will come and s. *Isa 35:4*
you
and pray unto a god that *Isa 45:20*
cannot s.
he cannot answer, nor s. him *Isa 46:7*
out of trouble
let now the astrologers stand *Isa 47:13*
up and s. thee
they shall wander, none shall *Isa 47:15*
s. thee
thus saith the Lord, I will s. *Isa 49:25*
thy children
Lord's hand is not shortened, *Isa 59:1*
that it cannot s.
I that speak in righteousness, *Isa 63:1*
mighty to s.
let them arise, if they can s. *Jer 2:28*
thee
but they shall not s. them at *Jer 11:12*
all in trouble
shouldest be as a mighty man *Jer 14:9*
that cannot s.
for I am with thee to s. *Jer 15:20;*
thee, and to deliver thee *30:11; 42:11;*
46:27
I will s. thee from afar, and *Jer 30:10*
thy seed
s. your lives, be like the heath *Jer 48:6*
in wilderness

to warn the wicked, to s. his *Eze 3:18*
life
therefore will I s. my flock, *Eze 34:22*
and judge
I will s. you *Eze 36:29*
I will s. them *Eze 37:23*
I will s. them by the Lord their *Ho 1:7*
God
where is there any other that *Ho 13:10*
may s. thee
s. them from Sheol (A) *Ho 13:14*
cry to thee of violence, and *Hab 1:2*
thou wilt not s.
he will s., he will rejoice *Zep 3:17*
over thee
I will s. her that halteth, and *Zep 3:19*
gather her
I will s. my people from the *Zec 8:7*
east country
the Lord their God shall s. *Zec 9:16*
them in the day
and I will s. the house of *Zec 10:6*
Joseph
the Lord also shall s. the *Zec 12:7*
tents of Judah first
Jesus, shall s. his people *M't 1:21*
from their sins
whosoever will s. his life *M't 16:25;*
shall lose it *8:35; Lu 9:24; 17:33*
for the Son of man is come *M't 18:11;*
to s. that which was lost *Lu 19:10*
thou that destroyest the *M't 27:40;*
temple, and buildest it in *M'k 15:30*
three days, s. thyself
saved others, himself he *M't 27:42;*
cannot s. *M'k 15:31*
let us see whether Elias will *M't 27:49*
come to s. him
is it lawful to s. life, or to *M'k 3:4;*
kill *Lu 6:9*
is not come to destroy men's *Lu 9:56*
lives, but to s.
who loses it shall s. it (N) *Lu 17:33*
let him s. himself, if he be *Lu 23:35*
Christ
s. thyself *Lu 23:37*
if Christ, s. thyself and us *Lu 23:39*
I came not to judge, but to *Joh 12:47*
s. the world
s. yourselves from this *Ac 2:40*
generation
but the centurion, willing to *Ac 27:43*
s. Paul
if I might s. some of them *Ro 11:14;*
1Co 9:22
by the foolishness of *1Co 1:21*
preaching to s. them
shalt s. thy husband, shalt s. *1Co 7:16*
thy wife
Christ came into the world to *1Ti 1:15*
s. sinners
in doing this thou shalt s. *1Ti 4:16*
thyself and them
he will s. me for (B)(E)(R) *2Ti 4:18*
to him that was able to s. him *Heb 5:7*
from death
he is able also to s. them to *Heb 7:25*
the uttermost
the word, which is able to s. *Jas 1:21*
your souls
and have not works, can faith *Jas 2:14*
s. him
one lawgiver, who is able to s. *Jas 4:12*
and to destroy
the prayer of faith shall s. the *Jas 5:15*
sick
shall s. a soul from death, *Jas 5:20*
and hide sins
others s. with fear, pulling *Jude 23*
them out of fire

SAVE ME

s. me out of hand of the king *2Ki 16:7*
of Syria
arise, O Lord, s. me, O my God *Ps 3:7*
s. me for thy mercies' sake *Ps 6:4;*
31:16; 109:26
s. me from all them that *Ps 7:1*
persecute me
s. me from the lion's mouth *Ps 22:21*
be thou for an house of *Ps 31:2*
defence to s. me
not trust in bow, nor shall my *Ps 44:6*
sword s. me
s. me, O God, by thy name, *Ps 54:1*
and judge me
I will call on God, and the *Ps 55:16*
Lord shall s. me
he shall send from heaven and *Ps 57:3*
s. me

deliver me, and *s. me* from　Ps 59:2
bloody men
s. me, for waters are come in Ps 69:1
unto my soul
incline thine ear unto me, and Ps 71:2
s. me
thou hast given commandment Ps 71:3
to *s. me*
s. me, for I have sought thy Ps 119:94
precepts
I cried unto thee, *s. me*,　Ps 119:146
and I shall keep
and thy right hand shall *s. me* Ps 138:7
Lord was ready to *s. me*, we Isa 38:20
will sing
O Lord, *s. me*, and I shall be Jer 17:14
saved
Peter cried, saying, Lord, *s. M't 14:30
me*
Father, *s. me* from this　Joh 12:27
hour

SAVE US

come up to us quickly, and *s. Jos 10:6
us*
if it be in rebellion, *s. us* not Jos 22:22
this day
the ark may *s. us* from our　1Sa 4:3
enemies
cease not to cry to the Lord,　1Sa 7:8
that he will *s. us*
men of Belial said, How　1Sa 10:27
shall this man *s. us*
if there be no man to *s. us*,　1Sa 11:3
we will come
s. thou *us* out of his hand　2Ki 19:19;
Isa 37:20
s. us, O God of our　1Ch 16:35
salvation
stir up thy strength, and come Ps 80:2
and *s. us*
s. us, O Lord our God, and Ps 106:47
gather us
we have waited for him, he　Isa 25:9
will *s. us*
the Lord is our king, he will Isa 33:22
s. us.
in their trouble they will say, Jer 2:27
s. us
watched for a nation that　La 4:17
could not *s. us*
Asshur shall not *s. us*, we　Ho 14:3
will not ride
they awoke him, saying,　M't 8:25
Lord, *s. us*
even baptism, doth also now 1Pe 3:21
s. us

SAVE, except for

s. what the young men have Ge 14:24
eaten
he knew not aught, *s.* the　Ge 39:6
bread he did eat
s. that which every man must Ex 12:16
eat
he that sacrificeth to any god, Ex 22:20
s. to the Lord
s. Caleb　　　　　　Nu 14:30;
26:65; 32:12; De 1:36
s. when there shall be no poor De 15:4
among you
Israel burned none, *s.* Hazor Jos 11:13
only
that made peace with Israel, Jos 11:19
s. the Hivites
they gave no part to the　Jos 14:4
Levites, *s.* cities
is nothing else, *s.* the sword of J'g 7:14
Gideon
there is none other, *s.* that　1Sa 21:9
here
there escaped none, *s.* 400 1Sa 30:17
young men
s. to every man his wife and 1Sa 30:22
his children
poor man had nothing, *s.*　2Sa 12:3
one ewe lamb
who is God, *s.* the Lord　2Sa 22:32;
Ps 18:31
was no stranger in the house, 1Ki 3:18
s. we two
there was nothing in the ark *s.* 1Ki 8:9
the two tables
s. in the matter of Uriah the 1Ki 15:5
Hittite
fight not, *s.* with the king of 1Ki 22:31
Israel
hath not any thing *s.* a pot of 2Ki 4:2
oil

s. that the high places were　2Ki 15:4
not removed
s. only to burn sacrifice before 2Ch 2:6
him
no son left, *s.* Jehoahaz the 2Ch 21:17
youngest
nor any with me, *s.* the beast Ne 2:12
I rode on
ask a petition *s.* of thee, O　Da 6:7;
king　　　　　　　　6:12
nor knoweth any the Father, M't 11:27
s. Son
not without honour, *s.* in his M't 13:57
own country
they saw no man, *s.* Jesus　M't 17:8;
only　　　　　　　　M'k 9:8
cannot receive, *s.* they to　M't 19:11
whom it is given
and he suffered no man to　M'k 5:37;
follow him, *s.* Peter,　　Lu 8:51
James, and John
s. that he laid his hands upon a M'k 6:5
few sick folk
that they should take nothing M'k 6:8
s. a staff only
sent, *s.* unto Sarepta, a city of Lu 4:26
Sidon
none found that returned, *s.* Lu 17:18
this stranger
none is good, *s.* one, that is Lu 18:19
God
there was no other boat, *s.*　Joh 6:22
that one
hath seen the Father, *s.* he　Joh 6:46
which is of God
he needeth not, *s.* to wash Joh 13:10
his feet
s. that the Holy Ghost　　Ac 20:23
witnesseth
s. to keep themselves from　Ac 21:25
fornication
not to know any thing, *s.*　1Co 2:2
Jesus Christ
s. the spirit of man which is 1Co 2:11
in man
five times received I forty　2Co 11:24
stripes, *s.* one
I saw none, *s.* James, the　Ga 1:19
Lord's brother
God forbid that I should　Ga 6:14
glory, *s.* in the cross
buy or sell, *s.* he that had the Re 13:17
mark

SAVED

they said, Thou hast *s.* our　Ge 47:25
lives
midwives *s.* the men children Ex 1:17;
alive　　　　　　　　1:18
I had slain thee, and *s.* her Nu 22:33
alive
Moses said, Have ye *s.* all Nu 31:15
the women alive
Joshua *s.* Rahab the harlot Jos 6:25
alive
lest Israel say, Mine own hand J'g 7:2
hath *s. me*
if he had *s.* them alive, I　J'g 8:19
would not slay you
they gave them wives which J'g 21:14
they had *s.*
David *s.* the inhabitants of 1Sa 23:5
Keilah
David *s.* neither man nor　1Sa 27:11
woman alive
servants who this day have　2Sa 19:5
s. thy life
the king *s. us*, and now he 2Sa 19:9
is fled for Absalom
s. himself there, not once nor 2Ki 6:10
twice
thou gavest them saviours,　Ne 9:27
who *s.* them
no king is *s.* by multitude of Ps 33:16
an host
but thou hast *s. us* from our Ps 44:7
enemies
nevertheless, he *s.* them for Ps 106:8
his name's sake
he *s.* them from him that　Ps 106:10
hated them
I have declared, and have *s.* Isa 43:12
and shewed
look to me, and be ye *s.* all Isa 45:22
the ends of earth
wash thy heart, that thou　Jer 4:14
mayest be *s.*
the summer is ended, and we Jer 8:20
are not *s.*

disciples saying, Who then　M't 19:25;
can be *s.*　　M'k 10:26; Lu 18:26
no flesh should be *s.*　　M'k 13:20
M't 24:22;
he *s.* others　　　　　　M't 27:42;
M'k 15:31; Lu 23:35
s. them and set them free (N) Lu 1:68
that we should be *s.* from our Lu 1:71
enemies
said, Thy faith hath *s.*　　Lu 7:50;
thee　　　　　　　　18:42
taketh away, lest they should Lu 8:12
believe and be *s.*
Lord, are there few that be *s.* Lu 13:23
that the world, through him, Joh 3:17
might be *s.*
these things I say, that ye　Joh 5:34
might be *s.*
the Lord added such as should Ac 2:47
be *s.*
is no other name whereby we Ac 4:12
must be *s.*
except ye be circumcised, ye Ac 15:1
cannot be *s.*
he said, Sirs, what must I do Ac 16:30
to be *s.*
all hope we should be *s.* was Ac 27:20
taken away
except these abide in ship,　Ac 27:31
ye cannot be *s.*
we are *s.* by hope, hope seen Ro 8:24
is not hope
my prayer for Israel is, that Ro 10:1
they may be *s.*
to *us* who are *s.* it is the　1Co 1:18
power of God
that the spirit may be *s.* in 1Co 5:5
day of the Lord
but the profit of many, that 1Co 10:33
they may be *s.*
by which also ye are *s.* if ye 1Co 15:2
keep in memory
we are sweet savour in them 2Co 2:15
that are *s.*
hath quickened us with　　Eph 2:5
Christ, (by grace are *s.*)
for by grace are ye *s.* through Eph 2:8
faith
to the Gentiles that they might 1Th 2:16
be *s.*
love of the truth, that they 2Th 2:10
might be *s.*
who will have all men to be *s.* 1Ti 2:4
and come
but according to his mercy he Tit 3:5
s. us
wherein eight souls were *s.* by 1Pe 3:20
water
if the righteous scarcely be *s.* 1Pe 4:18
where shall
but *s.* Noah, eighth person, a 2Pe 2:5
preacher
nations *s.* shall walk in the Re 21:24
light of it

GOD, LORD SAVED

Lord *s.* Israel that day　　Ex 14:30;
1Sa 14:23
who is like thee, O people, De 33:29
s. by Lord
ye have rejected your God,　1Sa 10:19
who *s.* you
Lord *s.* them by hand of　2Ki 14:27
Jeroboam
Lord *s.* them by a great　1Ch 11:14
deliverance
thus Lord *s.* Hezekiah from 2Ch 32:22
Sennacherib
Lord *s.* him out of all his　Ps 34:6
troubles
the Lord *s.* them out of their Ps 107:13
distresses
angel of his presence, *s.* them Isa 63:9
in his love
God who hath *s. us* and called 2Ti 1:9
us
how that the Lord, having *s.* the Jude 5
people

SHALL, SHALT BE SAVED

ye *shall* be *s.* from your　Nu 10:9
enemies
I *shall* be *s.* from　　　　2Sa 22:4;
mine enemies　　　　　　Ps 18:3
cause thy face to shine, we Ps 80:3;
shall be *s.*　　　　　　80:7, 19
whoso walketh uprightly *shall* Pr 28:18
be *s.*

in returning and rest *shall* ye *Isa 30:15*
be *s.*
but Israel *shall be s.* in Lord *Isa 45:17*
with salvation
in those is continuance, and *Isa 64:5*
we *shall be s.*
O Lord, save me, and I *shall Jer 17:14*
be *s.*
in his days Judah *shall be s. Jer 23:6;*
33:16
Jacob's trouble, but he *shall be Jer 30:7*
s. out of it
he that endureth to end *M't 10:22;*
shall be s. *24:13;* M'k 13:13
he that believeth *shall be s.* M'k 16:16
by me, if any man enter, he *Joh 10:9*
shall be s.
whosoever shall call on the *Ac 2:21;*
name of the Lord, *shall be s.* Ro 10:13
whereby thou and thy house *Ac 11:14*
shall be s.
we believe that through grace *Ac 15:11*
we *shall be s.*
believe on Lord Jesus, and *Ac 16:31*
thou *shalt be s.*
we *shall be s.* from wrath *Ro 5:9*
through him
being reconciled, we *shall be Ro 5:10*
s. by his life
though Israel be as sand, a *Ro 9:27*
remnant *shall be s.*
shalt believe God raised him, *Ro 10:9*
thou *shalt be s.*
so all Israel *shall be s.* as it *Ro 11:26*
is written
but he himself *shall be s.* yet *1Co 3:15*
so as by fire
shall be s. in childbearing, if *1Ti 2:15*
continue

SAVEST

my Saviour, thou *s.* me from *2Sa 22:3*
violence
how *s.* thou arm that hath no *Job 26:2*
strength
O thou that *s.* by thy right *Ps 17:7*
hand

SAVETH

as the Lord liveth, who *s.* *1Sa 14:39*
Israel
the Lord *s.* not with sword *1Sa 17:47*
and spear
but he *s.* the poor from the *Job 5:15*
sword
my defence is of God, who *s. Ps 7:10*
the upright
now know I that the Lord *s. Ps 20:6*
his anointed
he *s.* such as be of a contrite *Ps 34:18*
spirit
they cry, he *s.* them out of *Ps 107:19*
their distresses

SAVING

mercy thou hast shewed me *Ge 19:19*
in *s.* my life
s. that every one put them off *Ne 4:23*
for washing
with the *s.* strength of his right *Ps 20:6*
hand
he is the *s.* strength of his *Ps 28:8*
anointed
thy *s.* health among all nations *Ps 67:2*
s. the beholding of them with *Ec 5:11*
their eyes
s. that I will not utterly *Am 9:8*
destroy Jacob
s. for the cause of fornication, *M't 5:32*
causeth her
and none was cleansed, *s. Lu 4:27*
Naaman
plotting against *s.* purposes *Ac 13:10*
of God (B)
but of them that believe to *Heb 10:39*
s. of the soul
Noah prepared an ark to the *Heb 11:7*
s. of his house
no man knoweth, *s.* he that *Re 2:17*
receiveth it

SAVIOR

s. from harm (B) *2Sa 22:3*
righteous God and a *S.* (R) *Isa 45:21*

SAVIOUR

raised a *s.* (E) *J'g 3:9*
my high tower, my refuge, my *2Sa 22:3*
s.

and the Lord gave Israel a *s. 2Ki 13:5*
they forgat God their *s.* who *Ps 106:21*
had done
he shall send them a *s.* and a *Isa 19:20*
great one
for I am the Holy One of *Isa 43:3*
Israel thy *S.*
I am the Lord, beside me *Isa 43:11*
there is no *s.*
that hidest thyself, O God of *Isa 45:15*
Israel, the *S.*
a just God and a *S.;* there is *Isa 45:21*
none beside me
all flesh shall know that I am *Isa 49:26*
thy *S.*
thou shalt know that I the *Isa 60:16*
Lord am thy *S.*
they are my people, so he was *Isa 63:8*
their *S.*
the *s.* of Israel in time of *Jer 14:8*
trouble
for there is no *s.* beside me *Ho 13:4*
my spirit hath rejoiced in God *Lu 1:47*
my *S.*
is born this day in the city of *Lu 2:11*
David a *S.*
this is Christ the *S.* of the *Joh 4:42*
world
him hath God exalted to be a *Ac 5:31*
Prince and *S.*
hath God raised to Israel a *Ac 13:23*
S., Jesus
and Christ is the *s.* of the *Eph 5:23*
body
from whence we look for the *Ph'p 3:20*
S.
by the commandment of God *1Ti 1:1*
our *S.*
is acceptable in the sight of *1Ti 2:3*
God our *S.*
we trust in living God, who is *1Ti 4:10*
S. of all men
manifest by the appearing of *2Ti 1:10*
our *S.*
according to the *Tit 1:3*
commandment of God our *S.*
peace from the Lord Jesus *Tit 1:4*
Christ our *S.*
they may adorn the doctrine *Tit 2:10*
of God our *S.*
looking for the glorious *Tit 2:13*
appearing of our *S.*
after the kindness of God our *Tit 3:4*
S. appeared
he shed on us abundantly *Tit 3:6*
through Christ our *S.*
through righteousness of God *2Pe 1:1*
and our *S.*
into everlasting kingdom of *2Pe 1:11*
our Lord and *S.*
knowledge of the Lord and *2Pe 2:20*
S. Jesus
of us the apostles of the Lord *2Pe 3:2*
and *S.*
but grow in the knowledge of *2Pe 3:18*
our *S.* Christ
the Father sent the Son to be *1Jo 4:14*
the *S.*
to the only wise God our *S.* *Jude 25*
be glory

SAVIOURS

thou gavest them *s.* who saved *Ne 9:27*
them
and *s.* shall come up on mount *Ob 21*
Zion

SAVOUR

ye have made our *s.* to be *Ex 5:21*
abhorred
will not smell *s.* of your *Le 26:31*
sweet odours
the ointment to send forth a *Ec 10:1*
stinking *s.*
because of the *s.* of thy good *Ca 1:3*
ointment
his stink and his ill *s.* shall *Joe 2:20*
come up
if the salt has lost his *s.* *M't 5:13;*
Lu 14:34
maketh manifest the *s.* of his *2Co 2:14*
knowledge
the *s.* of death unto death, *s. 2Co 2:16*
of life unto life

SWEET SAVOUR

and the Lord smelled a *sweet Ge 8:21*
s.

it is a *sweet s.* an offering to *Ex 29:18;*
the Lord *Le 1:9, 13, 17; 2:9; 3:5; 8:21;*
Nu 15:14; 18:17; 28:8
for a *sweet s.* an offering to *Ex 29:25;*
the Lord *29:41; Le 2:12; 3:16; 4:31;*
6:15, 21; 8:28; 17:6; 23:13; Nu 15:7,
24; 28:2, 6, 13, 27; 29:2, 6, 8; Eze 16:19
of a *sweet s.* *Le 23:18;*
Nu 28:24; 29:13, 36
to make a *sweet s.* unto the *Nu 15:3*
Lord
for a burnt offering of a *Nu 28:13*
sweet s. to Lord
where they did offer *sweet Eze 6:13*
to their idols
there also they made their *Eze 20:28*
sweet s.
I will accept you with your *Eze 20:41*
sweet s.
for we are to God a *sweet s. 2Co 2:15*
of Christ
a sacrifice to God for a *Eph 5:2*
sweet-smelling *s.*

SWEET SAVOURS

may offer sacrifices of *sweet Ezr 6:10*
s. to God

SAVOUREST

thou *s.* not things of God *M't 16:23;*
M'k 8:33

SAVOURY

make me *s.* meat, such as I *Ge 27:4;*
love *27:7, 14*
Esau had made *s.* meat and *Ge 27:31*
brought it

SAW

the woman *s.* the tree was good *Ge 3:6*
for food
the sons of God *s.* the *Ge 6:2*
daughters of men
Ham *s.* the nakedness of his *Ge 9:22*
father
they *s.* not *Ge 9:23*
Abraham *s.* the place afar *Ge 22:4*
they said, We *s.* the Lord *Ge 26:28*
was with thee
when he *s.* that he prevailed *Ge 32:25*
not against him
for she *s.* that Shelah was *Ge 38:14*
grown, not given
his master *s.* that the Lord was *Ge 39:3*
with him
in that we *s.* the anguish of *Ge 42:21*
his soul
when Joseph *s.* Benjamin *Ge 43:16*
with them
when he *s.* the wagons which *Ge 45:27*
Joseph sent
Issachar *s.* that rest was *Ge 49:15*
good, and land
his brethren *s.* that their *Ge 50:15*
father was dead
Joseph *s.* Ephraim's children *Ge 50:23*
of third generation
when she *s.* that he was *Ex 2:2*
a goodly child
when he *s.* that there was no *Ex 2:12*
man, he slew
they *s.* not one another for *Ex 10:23*
three days
Israel *s.* that great work the *Ex 14:31*
Lord did
and they *s.* the God of Israel *Ex 24:10;*
24:11
all the people *s.* the cloudy *Ex 33:10*
pillar stand
we *s.* the children of Anak *Nu 13:28*
there
ass *s.* the angel of the Lord *Nu 22:23;*
in the way *22:27*
and when Phinehas *s.* it, he *Nu 25:7*
rose up
when they *s.* the land, they *Nu 32:9*
discouraged Israel
ye heard a voice, but *s.* no *De 4:12;*
similitude *4:15*
the great temptations which *De 7:19*
thine eyes *s.*
all that *s.* it said, no such *J'g 19:30*
deed was done
when she *s.* she was stedfastly *Ru 1:18*
minded
they *s.* the ark, and rejoiced *1Sa 6:13*
to see it

when he *s.* that they were no *1Sa 10:14* where
Israel, when they *s.* the man, *1Sa 17:24* fled from him
Saul *s.* that the Lord was *1Sa 18:28* with David
David *s.* a woman washing *2Sa 11:2* herself
s. that the wisdom of God *1Ki 3:28* was in him
when Zimri *s.* that the city *1Ki 16:18* was taken
when Ahab *s.* Elijah he said *1Ki 18:17* to him
when he *s.* that, he arose and *1Ki 19:3* went for his life
Elisha *s.* it, and he *s.* him no *2Ki 2:12* more
s. the water on the other side *2Ki 3:22* as red as blood
when the man of god *s.* her *2Ki 4:25* afar off
Lord opened eyes of the *2Ki 6:17* young man and he *s.*
for he *s.* the oppression of *2Ki 13:4* Israel
Ahaz *s.* an altar that was at *2Ki 16:10* Damascus
they *s.* that the Lord was with *2Ch 15:9* him
and they *s.* one another in *2Ch 25:21* the face
when princes *s.* heaps, they *2Ch 31:8* blessed the Lord
when *s.* these things they were *Ne 6:16* cast down
the princes which *s.* the king's *Es 1:14* face
he *s.* that there was evil *Es 7:7* determined against him
they *s.* that his grief was very *Job 2:13* great
had not been, as infants *Job 3:16* which never *s.* light
eye which *s.* him, shall see *Job 20:9* him no more
the young men *s.* me and hid *Job 29:8* themselves
when the eye *s.* me, it gave *Job 29:11* witness to me
they *s.* it, and so they *Ps 48:5* marvelled
waters *s.* thee, O God, the *Ps 77:16* waters *s.* thee
your fathers proved me, and *s. Ps 95:9* my work
the earth *s.* his lightnings and *Ps 97:4* trembled
sea *s.* it and fled, Jordan was *Ps 114:3* driven back
s. ye him whom my soul loveth *Ca 3:3*
isles *s.* it, and feared, ends of *Isa 41:5* the earth
and her treacherous sister *Jer 3:7* Judah *s.* it
when Zedekiah *s.* them, and *Jer 39:4* men of war
for then we were well, and *s. Jer 44:17* no evil
adversaries *s.* her and did mock *La 1:7* at her
so I went in, and *s.;* behold, *Eze 8:10* every form
then they *s.* every high hill, *Eze 20:28* offered there
as soon as she *s.* them, she *Eze 23:16* doted on them
s. these men on whom fire *Da 3:27* had no power
whereas the king *s.* a watcher *Da 4:23* coming down
the king *s.* part of the hand *Da 5:5* that wrote
when Ephraim *s.* his sickness *Ho 5:13* and Judah *s.* his wound, then went Ephraim
who among you *s.* this house *Hag 2:3* in first glory
the star which they *s.* went *M't 2:9* before them
s. the Spirit of God *M't 3:16;* descending *M'k 1:10*
the blind and dumb both *M't 12:22* spake and *s.*
they *s.* no man, save Jesus *M't 17:8* only
but when the husbandmen *s. M't 21:38* the son
s. a man who had not on *M't 22:11* wedding garment

Lord, when *s.* we thee an *M't 25:37;* hungered *25:44*
when *s.* we thee stranger *M't 25:38*
when *s.* thee sick *M't 25:39*
another maid *s.* him, and *M't 26:71;* said, This was with Jesus *M'k 14:69;* *Lu 22:58*
Judas, when *s.* he was *M't 27:3* condemned, repented
when they *s.* him they *M't 28:17* worshipped him
when Jesus *s.* their faith, he *M'k 2:5* said to sick
spit on his eyes, he asked *M'k 8:23* him, if he *s.* aught
Master, we *s.* one casting *M'k 9:38;* out devils in thy name *Lu 9:49*
when they *s.* what was done, *Lu 8:34* they fled
when the woman *s.* that she *Lu 8:47* was not hid
when they were awake, they *s. Lu 9:32* his glory
his father *s.* him, had *Lu 15:20* compassion on him
one of them, when he *s.* he *Lu 17:15* was healed
they found it even so, but *Lu 24:24* him they *s.* not
ye seek me, not because ye *s. Joh 6:26* miracles
Abraham *s.* my day, and was *Joh 8:56* glad
these things said Esaias, *Joh 12:41* when he *s.* his glory
he that *s.* it bare record, his *Joh 19:35* record is true
disciples were glad when *Joh 20:20* they *s.* the Lord
when they *s.* the boldness of *Ac 4:13* Peter
s. his face as it had been face *Ac 6:15* of an angel
Stephen *s.* glory of God and *Ac 7:55* Jesus standing
when Simon *s.* that Holy *Ac 8:18* Ghost was given
caught Philip, that eunuch *s. Ac 8:39* him no more
when his eyes were opened, he *Ac 9:8* *s.* no man
all at Lydda *s.* him, and *Ac 9:35* turned to the Lord
and when Tabitha *s.* Peter, *Ac 9:40* she sat up
Cornelius *s.* a vision *Ac 10:3*
s. heaven opened *Ac 10:11*
and because he *s.* it pleased *Ac 12:3* the Jews
David *s.* corruption *Ac 13:36*
s. no corruption *Ac 13:37*
masters *s.* the hope of their *Ac 16:19* gain was gone
he *s.* the city wholly given to *Ac 17:16* idolatry
they *s.* indeed the light and *Ac 22:9* were afraid
had looked, and *s.* no harm *Ac 28:6* come to him
when they *s.* that the gospel of *Ga 2:7* the uncircumcision
having the same conflict *Ph'p 1:30* which ye *s.*
your fathers *s.* my works forty *Heb 3:9* years
because they *s.* he was a *Heb 11:23* proper child
who bare record of all things *Re 1:2* he *s.*
great fear fell on them who *s. Re 11:11*
when the dragon *s.* that he *Re 12:13* was cast out
cried, when they *s.* smoke of *Re 18:18* her burning

SAW with LORD, GOD

and *God s.* the light that it was *Ge 1:4* good
God called the dry land earth, *Ge 1:10;* and *God s.* that it was good *1:12, 18, 21, 25, 31*
God s. that the wickedness of *Ge 6:5* man was great
when the *Lord s.* that Leah *Ge 29:31* was hated
when the *Lord s.* that he turned *Ex 3:4* aside
when the *Lord s.* it, he *De 32:19* abhorred

the Lord *s.* the affliction of *2Ki 14:26* Israel
when *Lord s.* they humbled *2Ch 12:7* themselves
the Lord *s.* it, and it *Isa 59:15* displeased him
Lord s. that there was no *Isa 59:16* man, and wondered
God s. their works, that they *Jon 3:10* turned
Lord s. her, he had *Lu 7:13* compassion on her

SAW, a tool

shall *s.* magnify against him *Isa 10:15* that shaketh it

I SAW

such as *I* never *s.* in Egypt *Ge 41:19* for badness
one went out, and *I s.* him *Ge 44:28* not since
when *I s.* among the spoils a *Jos 7:21* garment
when *I s.* that he delivered me *J'g 12:3*
I s. the son of Jesse coming *1Sa 22:9* to Nob
I s. gods ascending out of the *1Sa 28:13* earth
I s. Absalom hanged in an *2Sa 18:10* oak
I s. great tumult, but knew *2Sa 18:29* not what it was
I s. all Israel scattered on *1Ki 22:17* the hills
I s. the Lord on his throne *1Ki 22:19;* *2Ch 18:18*
in those days *s. I* in Judah *Ne 13:15* some trading
when *I s.* my help in the *Job 31:21* gate
when *I s.* the prosperity of the *Ps 73:3* wicked
then *I s.* and considered it *Pr 24:32*
this also *I s.* from the hand of *Ec 2:24* God
so *I s.* the wicked buried, who *Ec 8:10* had gone
among whom *I s.* Jaazaniah *Eze 11:1* son of Azur
therefore I took them away *Eze 16:50* as *I s.* good
then *I s.* that she was defiled, *Eze 23:13* took one way
I s. your fathers as firstripe *Ho 9:10* in fig tree
Ephraim, as *I s.* Tyrus, is *Ho 9:13* planted in pleasant
I s. the Spirit descending upon *Joh 1:32*
when thou wast under the *Joh 1:48* fig tree, *I s.* thee
I s. in the way a light from *Ac 26:13* heaven
but other of the apostles *s. I Ga 1:19*
when *I s.* that they walked *Ga 2:14* not uprightly
when *I s.* him, I fell at his feet *Re 1:17* as dead

SAWS

he put Ammonites under *s. 2Sa 12:31;* *1Ki 7:9; 2Ch 20:3*

SAWED

these were of costly stones, *s. 1Ki 7:9* with saws

SAWEST

what *s.* thou that *Ge 20:10* hast done this thing
thou *s.* it and didst rejoice *1Sa 19:5*
king said, Be not afraid, for *1Sa 28:13* what *s.* thou
Joab said, And, behold, *2Sa 18:11* thou *s.* him
when thou *s.* a thief thou *Ps 50:18* consentedst
thou, O king, *s.* a great image *Da 2:31*
thou *s.* till that a stone was *Da 2:34;* cut out *2:45*
the tree thou *s.* which grew *Da 4:20* and was strong
the ram which thou *s.* having *Da 8:20* two horns
seven stars thou *s.* seven *Re 1:20* candlesticks *s.*
the beast that thou *s.* was, and *Re 17:8* is not

the ten horns which thou s. *Re 17:12;*
are ten kings *19:16*
waters thou s. where whore *Re 17:15*
sitteth are peoples
the woman which thou s. is *Re 17:18*
that great city

SAWN

they were stoned, they were *Heb 11:37*
s. asunder

SAY

s. I pray thee, thou art my *Ge 12:13*
sister
lest thou shouldest s. I have *Ge 14:23*
made Abraham
what ye shall s. to me I will *Ge 34:11;*
give *34:12*
for I heard them s. Let us go *Ge 37:17*
to Dothan
we will s. some evil beast *Ge 37:20*
hath devoured him
I have heard s. that thou *Ge 41:15*
canst interpret it
Judah said, What shall we s. *Ge 44:16*
to my Lord
so shall ye s. to Joseph, *Ge 50:17*
Forgive I pray
thus shall ye s.; I AM hath *Ex 3:14;*
sent me to you *3:15; 19:3; 20:22*
I will teach you what thou *Ex 4:12*
shalt s.
when your children shall s. *Ex 12:26*
unto you
Pharaoh will s. of the children *Ex 14:3*
of Israel
if the servant shall s. I love my *Ex 21:5*
master
and the woman shall s. Amen *Nu 5:22*
that thou shouldest s. to me, *Nu 11:12*
Carry them
that I may know what the *Nu 22:19*
Lord will s.
have I power to all to s. any *Nu 22:38*
thing
s. unto them, Go not up, *De 1:42*
neither fight
hear all that the Lord our *De 5:27*
God shall s.
then thou shalt s. to thy son, *De 6:21*
We were
a people great, of whom thou *De 9:2*
hast heard s.
in the morning thou shalt s. *De 28:67*
and at even s.
so that they will s. in that *De 31:17*
day, Are not
lest they should s. our hand is *De 32:27*
your children may not s. our *Jos 22:27*
children
when they should s. to us *Jos 22:28*
in time to come
and thou shalt hear what they *J'g 7:11*
s.
they said to him, S. now *J'g 12:6*
Shibboleth
she said, How canst thou s. I *J'g 16:15*
love thee
what is this ye s. to me, what *J'g 18:24*
aileth thee
in all they s. unto thee, *1Sa 8:7*
hearken to voice
if they s. thus, come up to us, *1Sa 14:10*
we will go
and he said to him, S. on *1Sa 15:16;*
2Sa 14:12; 1Ki 2:14, 16; Lu 7:40;
Ac 13:15
if he s. thus, thy servant *1Sa 20:7*
shall have peace
therefore thou shalt s. to my *2Sa 7:8;*
servant David, I took *1Ch 7:21*
if he s. I have no delight in *2Sa 15:26*
thee
what you shall s. that will I do *2Sa 21:4*
for you
the Lord God of my lord s. so *1Ki 1:36*
speak I pray thee, for he will *1Ki 2:17*
not s. thee nay
shall s. why hath Lord done *1Ki 9:8;*
thus to this land and house *2Ch 7:21*
of which the Lord did s. *1Ki 13:22*
Eat no bread
let not the king s. so *1Ki 22:8;*
2Ch 18:7
if we s. we will enter into the *2Ki 7:4*
city
so that they shall not s. this *2Ki 9:37*
is Jezebel

that thou s. nothing but *2Ch 18:15*
truth to me
I told them what they should s. *Ezr 8:17*
to Iddo
O our God, what shall we s. *Ezr 9:10*
after this
he takes away, who can *Job 9:12;*
hinder him? will s. to him, *Ec 8:4*
What doest thou
they s. unto God, Depart *Job 21:14*
from us
then shalt thou s. there is *Job 22:29*
lifting up
understand what he would s. *Job 23:5*
to me
destruction and death s. we *Job 28:22*
have heard
whilst you searched out *Job 32:11*
what to s.
if any s. I have sinned, and *Job 33:27*
perverted
teach us what we shall s. *Job 37:19*
unto him
many s. of my soul, there is *Ps 3:2*
no help
that s. who will shew us any *Ps 4:6*
good
not s. we have swallowed him *Ps 35:25*
up
so that a man shall s. there is *Ps 58:11*
a reward
they belch out, for who s. *Ps 59:7*
they, doth hear
yet they s. Lord shall not see, *Ps 94:7*
nor God
nor do they s. blessing of the *Ps 129:8*
Lord
if they s. come, yet us lay wait *Pr 1:11*
for blood
s. not to thy neighbour Go and *Pr 3:28*
come again
who can s. I have made my *Pr 20:9*
heart clean
They have stricken me, shalt *Pr 23:35*
thou s.
s. not, I will do so to him as *Pr 24:29*
he hath done
lest I deny thee, and s. who is *Pr 30:9*
the Lord
s. not thou, what is cause *Ec 7:10*
former days
when thou shalt s. I have no *Ec 12:1*
pleasure
many people shall go and s. *Isa 2:3*
Come ye
s. ye to righteous, shall be *Isa 3:10*
well with him
they s. who seeth us, and *Isa 29:15*
who knoweth us
shall work s. of him that *Isa 29:16*
made it? or thing framed s.
of him that framed it
who s. to the seers, see not, *Isa 30:10*
and to prophets
and the inhabitant shall not *Isa 33:24*
s. I am sick
s. to them that are of fearful *Isa 35:4*
heart, fear not
s. to the cities of Judah, *Isa 40:9*
Behold your God
or let them hear, and s. it is *Isa 43:9*
truth
one shall s. I am the Lord's, *Isa 44:5*
and another
surely shall one s. in Lord *Isa 45:24*
have I righteousness
lest thou shouldest s. my idol *Isa 48:5*
hath done them
lest thou shouldest s. Behold, I *Isa 48:7*
knew them
neither let the eunuch s. I am *Isa 56:3*
a dry tree
why have we fasted s. they, *Isa 58:3*
and thou seest not
thou shalt cry, and he shall s. *Isa 58:9*
Here I am
s. ye to daughter of Zion, *Isa 62:11*
Behold thy
s. not, I am a child, for thou *Jer 1:7*
shalt go
in trouble they will s. Arise *Jer 2:27*
and save us
neither understandest what *Jer 5:15*
they s.
thus shall ye s. them, The *Jer 10:11*
gods shall perish
therefore thou shalt s. this *Jer 14:17*
word to them
report, s. they, and we will *Jer 20:10*
report it

they shall no more s., The *Jer 23:7*
Lord liveth
they shall s. no more fathers *Jer 31:29*
have eaten
do to him even as he shall s. *Jer 39:12*
unto thee
according to all that the *Jer 42:20*
Lord shall s.
s. ye, Stand fast, and prepare *Jer 46:14*
thee
ask her that escapeth, and s. *Jer 48:19*
What is done
s. Babylon is taken, Bel is *Jer 50:2*
confounded
and stamp with thy foot, and *Eze 6:11*
s. Alas
s. I am your sign, like as I *Eze 12:11*
have done
whereas ye s. The Lord saith *Eze 13:7*
it
and s., What is thy mother? a *Eze 19:2*
lioness
S., A sword, a sword is *Eze 21:9*
sharpened
s. The sword is drawn for *Eze 21:28*
the slaughter
wilt thou yet s. before him *Eze 28:9*
that slayeth thee
s. unto him, Take away all *Ho 14:2*
iniquity
nor will we s. to the work of *Ho 14:3*
our hands
Ephraim shall s. What have I *Ho 14:8*
to do with idols
let them s., Spare thy people, *Joe 2:17*
O Lord
let the weak s. I am strong *Joe 3:10*
prophesy ye not, s. they to *Mic 2:6*
them that prophesy
they will s., Is not the Lord *Mic 3:11*
among us
I will watch to see what he *Hab 2:1*
will s. to me
s. unto them, Turn ye unto me *Zec 1:3*
they that sell them, s. I am *Zec 11:5*
rich
yet ye s., Wherein loved us *Mal 1:2;*
2:14, 17; 3:13
think not to s. in yourselves *M't 3:9;*
Lu 3:8
shall s. all manner of evil *M't 5:11*
against you falsely
many will s. to me in that *M't 7:22*
day, Lord, Lord
have ye understood? they s. *M't 13:51*
Yea, Lord
whom do men s. that I the *M't 16:13;*
Son of man am *M'k 8:27; Lu 9:18*
whom s. ye that I am *M't 16:15;*
M'k 8:29; Lu 9:20
if any man s. ought to you, *M't 21:3*
ye shall s.
and s. to him, Hearest thou *M't 21:16*
what these s.
if we s. From heaven, he *M't 21:25*
will
s. to us, Why not believe *M'k 11:31;*
Lu 20:5
if we shall s. Of men *M't 21:26;*
M'k 11:32; Lu 20:6
do not their works, for they *M't 23:3*
s. and do not
and saith, See thou s. nothing *M'k 1:44*
to any man
he wist not what to s. for they *M'k 9:6*
were afraid
Verily I s. unto you, That *M'k 12:43*
this poor widow
ye will surely s. this proverb, *Lu 4:23*
heal thyself
s. in a word, and my servant *Lu 7:7*
shall be healed
Simon, I have somewhat to *Lu 7:40*
s. to thee
go out into the streets of the *Lu 10:10*
same, and s.
s. not ye, There are yet four *Joh 4:35*
months
he speaketh, and they s. *Joh 7:26*
nothing to him
I have many things to s. of *Joh 8:26;*
you *16:12*
s. we not well, that thou hast *Joh 8:48*
a devil
of whom ye s. that he is your *Joh 8:54*
God
s. ye of him the Father hath *Joh 10:36*
sanctified

ye call me Master, ye *s.* *Joh 13:13*
well, for so I am
him shall ye hear in all things *Ac 3:22*
he shall *s.*
they could *s.* nothing against it *Ac 4:14*
we heard him *s.* that Jesus *Ac 6:14*
shall destroy
do therefore this that we *s.* to *Ac 21:23*
thee
who hath something to *s.* *Ac 23:18*
unto thee
or else let these same here *s.* *Ac 24:20*
if found evil
none other things but what *Ac 26:22*
Moses did *s.*
what shall we *s.*? Is God *Ro 3:5*
unrighteous
as some affirm that we *s.* Let us *Ro 3:8*
do evil
what shall we *s.* then, Shall we *Ro 4:1*;
continue in sin *6:1; 7:7; 8:31; 9:14, 30*
shall thing formed *s.* to him *Ro 9:20*
that formed it
no man can *s.* that Jesus is *1Co 12:3*
the Lord
how shall he *s.* Amen at thy *1Co 14:16*
giving thanks
will they not *s.* that ye are *1Co 14:23*
mad
how *s.* some that there is no *1Co 15:12*
resurrection
we, that we *s.* not you, should *2Co 9:4*
be ashamed
for his letters, *s.* they, are *2Co 10:10*
weighty
this we *s.* to you by word of *1Th 4:15*
the Lord
understanding neither what they *1Ti 4:7*
s.
having no evil thing to *s.* of *Tit 2:8*
you
albeit I do not *s.* how thou *Ph'm 19*
owest me
of whom we have many *Heb 5:11*
things to *s.*
as I may so *s.* Levi paid tithes *Heb 7:9*
in Abraham
that is to *s.* not of this *Heb 9:11*
building
for us thro' the veil, that is *Heb 10:20*
to *s.* his flesh
they that *s.* such things *Heb 11:14*
declare plainly
so that we may boldly *s.* Lord *Heb 13:6*
is my helper
let no man *s.* when he is *Jas 1:13*
tempted
go to, now, ye that *s.*, To-day *Jas 4:13*
or to-morrow
for that ye ought to *s.*, If the *Jas 4:15*
Lord will
if we *s.* we have fellowship *1Jo 1:6*
with him
if we *s.* we have no sin, we *1Jo 1:8;*
deceive ourselves *1:10*
if man *s.* I love God, and *1Jo 4:20*
hateth his brother
I do not *s.* that he shall pray *1Jo 5:16*
for it
which *s.* they are apostles, and *Re 2:2*
are not
which *s.* they are Jews, and *Re 2:9;*
are not *3:9*
and the spirit and the bride *Re 22:17*
s., Come

I SAY

his name, what shall *I s.* to *Ex 3:13*
them
I s. unto thee, Let my son go *Ex 4:23*
to serve me
speak all that *I s.* unto thee *Ex 6:29;*
Eze 44:5
what shall *I s.* when Israel *Jos 7:8*
turneth backs
of whom *I s.*, This shall go with *J'g 7:4*
thee
if *I s.* expressly to the lad, *1Sa 20:21*
Behold
did not *I s.*, Do not deceive *2Ki 4:28*
me
behold, *I s.* they are as all *2Ki 7:13*
the multitude
behold, *I s.* how they reward *2Ch 20:11*
us
did *I s.*, Bring unto me, or *Job 6:22*
Give reward
when *I s.*, My bed shall *Job 7:13*
comfort me

if *I s.* I am perfect, it shall *Job 9:20*
prove me perverse
if *I s.* I will forget my *Job 9:27*
complaint, leave off
I will *s.* to God, Do not *Job 10:2*
condemn me
be of courage, wait, *I s.* on *Ps 27:14*
the Lord
if *I s.* I will speak thus, I *Ps 73:15*
should offend
I will *s.* of the Lord, He is my *Ps 91:2*
refuge
I s. more than they that *Ps 130:6*
watch for morning
if *I s.* the darkness shall *Ps 139:11*
cover me
I s. an untimely birth is better *Ec 6:3*
than he
I s. sayest thou, but they are *Isa 36:5*
but vain words
what shall *I s.*? he hath both *Isa 38:15*
spoken to me
I will *s.* to the north, Give up, *Isa 43:6*
and the south
son of man, hear what *I s.* *Eze 2:8*
unto thee
when *I s.* to the wicked *Eze 3:18;*
33:8, 14
I will *s.* the word, and will *Eze 12:25*
perform it
because *I s.* ye are come to *Eze 21:24*
remembrance
when *I s.* to the righteous, he *Eze 33:13*
shall live
I s. unto this man, Go *M't 8:9; Lu 7:8*
I s. not unto thee, Until *M't 18:22*
seven times, but
I s. to thee, Arise *M'k 2:11;*
5:41; Lu 5:24; 7:14
and do not the things which *I* *Lu 6:46*
s.
these things *I s.* that ye might *Joh 5:34*
be saved
if *I s.* the truth, why do ye *Joh 8:46*
not believe me
if *I should s.* I know him *Joh 8:55*
not, shall be a liar
what shall *I s.*? Father save *Joh 12:27*
me from this hour
he gave me commandment, *Joh 12:49*
what *I should s.*
to declare, *I s.* his *Ro 3:26*
righteousness
I s. the truth in Christ, I lie *Ro 9:1*
not
this *I s.* that every one of *1Co 1:12*
you saith
but this *I s.* brethren, the *1Co 7:29*
time is short
s. I. these things as a man? or *1Co 9:8*
saith not the law
I speak as to wise men, *1Co 10:15*
judge ye what *I s.*
what *s. I.* then? that the *1Co 10:19*
idol is any thing
conscience, *I s.* not thy *1Co 10:29*
own, but of others
what shall *I s.* to you? *1Co 11:22*
shall I praise you
now this *I s.* brethren *1Co 15:50;*
2Co 9:6; Ga 3:17; 5:16; Eph 4:17;
Col 2:4
as we said before, so *s. I* now *Ga 1:9*
again
consider what *I s.;* Lord give *2Ti 2:7*
thee understanding
knowing thou wilt do more *Ph'm 21*
than *I s.*
what shall *I* more *s.*? time *Heb 11:32*
would fail me

I SAY UNTO YOU

when *I s. unto you,* Smite *2Sa 13:28*
Amnon
he said, Did *I* not *s.* unto *2Ki 2:18*
you, Go not
I s. unto you, that Solomon in *M't 6:29*
all his glory
I s. unto you, that publicans *M't 21:31*
go before you
what *I s. unto you,* I say *M'k 13:37*
unto all, Watch
I s. not *unto you,* I will pray *Joh 16:26*
the Father
I Paul *s. unto you,* if ye be *Ga 5:2*
circumcised
unto you I s. and to the rest *Re 2:24*
in Thyatira

SAYEST

see, thou *s.* to me, Bring *Ex 33:12*
up this people
I will do whatsoever thou *s.* *Nu 22:17*
unto me
all that thou *s.* unto me, I will *Ru 3:5*
do
and now thou *s.* Go, tell thy *1Ki 18:11;*
lord *18:14*
thou *s.*, I have counsel and *2Ki 18:20;*
strength *Isa 36:5*
thou *s.* Lo, thou hast smitten *2Ch 25:19*
Edom
we will restore, so will we do *Ne 5:12*
as thou *s.*
there are no such things done *Ne 6:8*
as thou *s.*
and thou *s.*, How doth God *Job 22:13*
know
and *s.*, Return, ye children of *Ps 90:3*
men
If thou *s.*, Behold, we knew it *Pr 24:12*
not
why *s.* thou, O Jacob, and *Isa 40:27*
speak, O Israel
that *s.* in thine heart, I am, *Isa 47:8*
and none else
yet thou *s.* because I am *Jer 2:35*
innocent
thou *s.*, Prophesy not against *Am 7:16*
Israel
saying, I know not what *M't 26:70*
thou *s.*
art thou king of Jews? *M't 27:11;*
Jesus said, Thou *s.* *M'k 15:2;*
Lu 23:3; Joh 18:37
Peter denied, neither *M'k 14:68;*
understand what thou *s.* *Lu 22:60*
Master, we know that thou *s.* *Lu 20:21*
rightly
Who art thou? What *s.* thou *Joh 1:22*
of thyself
that such should be stoned, *Joh 8:5*
but what *s.* thou
s. thou, ye shall be made *Joh 8:33;*
free *12:34; 14:9*
they say to blind man, What *Joh 9:17*
s. thou of him
s. thou this of thyself or did *Joh 18:34*
others tell
thou that *s.* a man should not *Ro 2:22*
steal
he understandeth not what *1Co 14:16*
thou *s.*
because thou *s.* I am rich, and *Re 3:17*
increased

SAYING

brethren envied, but his *Ge 37:11*
father observed *s.*
and the *s.* pleased me well *De 1:23*
the *s.* displeased Saul, and he *1Sa 18:8*
said
and the *s.* pleased Absalom *2Sa 17:4*
well
shall we do after his *s.*? if not, *2Sa 7:6*
speak thou
David, according to the *s.* of *2Sa 24:19*
God. went up
and Shimei said, The *s.* is good *1Ki 2:38*
that he might perform his *s.* *1Ki 12:15*
by Ahijah
when Jeroboam heard *s.* of *1Ki 13:4*
the man of God
the *s.* which he cried by the *1Ki 13:32*
Princes
according to the *s.* of the *1Ki 15:29;*
Lord *2Ki 10:17*
according to the *s.* of Elijah *1Ki 17:15;*
2Ki 2:22
according to the *s.* of man *2Ki 5:14;*
of God *8:2*
the *s.* pleased the king and the *Es 1:21*
princes
I will open my dark *s.* upon *Ps 49:4*
the harp
was not this my *s.* when in my *Jon 4:2*
country
were offended after they *M't 15:12*
heard this *s.*
all men cannot receive this *M't 19:11*
s. save they
but when the young man *M't 19:22*
heard this *s.*
he prayed third time, *s.* the *M't 26:44*
same words

this *s.* is commonly reported　*M't 28:15*
among Jews
for this *s.* go thy way, the devil　*M'k 7:29*
is gone
and he spake that *s.* openly　*M'k 8:32*
and they kept that *s.* with　*M'k 9:10*
themselves
they understood not that *s.*　*M'k 9:32;*
　　　　　　　　　　　　　Lu 2:50; 9:45
he was sad at that *s.* and　*M'k 10:22*
went away
s. I am Christ, and shall　*M'k 13:6*
deceive many
she was troubled at his *s.* and　*Lu 1:29*
cast in mind
they made known abroad *s.*　*Lu 2:17*
that was told
and they feared to ask him of　*Lu 9:45*
that *s.*
Master, thus *s.* thou　*Lu 11:45*
reproachest us also
this *s.* was hid from them,　*Lu 18:34*
nor knew they
herein is that *s.* true, One　*Joh 4:37*
soweth
many believed, for the *s.* of　*Joh 4:39*
the woman
now we believe, not because of　*Joh 4:42*
thy *s.*
this is an hard *s.* who can　*Joh 6:60*
hear it
what manner of *s.* is this that　*Joh 7:36*
he said
many, when they heard this　*Joh 7:40*
s. said
I say to you, If a man keep　*Joh 8:51;*
my *s.*　　　　　　　　　　　*8:52*
but I know him and keep his　*Joh 8:55*
s.
that the *s.* of Esaias might　*Joh 12:38*
be fulfilled
if they have kept my *s.* they　*Joh 15:20*
will keep yours
that the *s.* of Jesus might　*Joh 18:9;*
be fulfilled　　　　　　　　*18:32*
when Pilate heard that *s.* he　*Joh 19:8*
was afraid
then went this *s.* abroad　*Joh 21:23*
among brethren
the *s.* pleased the whole　*Ac 6:5*
multitude
then fled Moses at this *s.* into　*Ac 7:29*
Midian
a voice, *s.,* Arise, Peter, slay　*Ac 11:7*
and eat
s. none other things than　*Ac 26:22*
those which
it is briefly comprehended in　*Ro 13:9*
this *s.*
then shall be brought to　*1Co 15:54*
pass the *s.*
this is faithful *s.* that Christ　*1Ti 1:15;*
Jesus came to save sinners　　*4:9;*
　　　　　　　　　　2Ti 2:11; Tit 3:8
this is a true *s.* If a man desire　*1Ti 3:1*
the office

SAYINGS

Moses told these *s.* to the　*Nu 14:39*
people
that when thy *s.* come to　*J'g 13:17*
pass, may do
so David's young men told　*1Sa 25:12*
all those *s.*
Ahijah's *s.* are written in　*2Ch 13:22*
the story
that are written among the　*2Ch 33:19*
s. of the seers
yet their posterity approve　*Ps 49:13*
their *s.*
open in parables, I will utter　*Ps 78:2*
dark *s.* of old
to understand the dark *s.* of　*Pr 1:6*
the wise
hear, O my son, and receive　*Pr 4:10*
my *s.*
my son attend, incline thine　*Pr 4:20*
ear to my *s.*
whoso heareth these *s.*　*M't 7:24;*
　　　　　　　　7:26; Lu 6:47
when Jesus had ended these　*M't 7:28;*
s. the people were astonished　*19:1;*
　　　　　　　　　26:1; Lu 7:1
all these *s.* were noised abroad　*Lu 1:65*
in Judaea
his mother kept all these *s.* in　*Lu 2:51*
her heart
let these sink down into your　*Lu 9:44*
ears

there was a division again　*Joh 10:19*
for these *s.*
he that loveth me not,　*Joh 14:24*
keepeth not my *s.*
spoken in dark *s.* (E)　*Joh 16:25*
with these *s.* scarce restrained　*Ac 14:18*
they people
when heard these *s.* they　*Ac 19:28*
were full of wrath
that thou mightest be justified　*Ro 3:4*
in thy *s.*
he saith to me, These are true　*Re 19:9*
s. of God
he said to me, These *s.* are　*Re 22:6*
faithful and true
blessed is he that keepeth the　*Re 22:7*
s. of this book
and of them who keep the *s.*　*Re 22:9*
of this book
seal not the *s.* of the　*Re 22:10*
prophecy of this book

SCAB

when shall have in skin of his　*Le 13:2*
flesh a *s.*
it is but a *s.*　*Le 13:6*
is *s.* spread much in skin　*Le 13:7-8*
this is the law for a *s.* and　*Le 14:56*
for a bright spot
the Lord will smite thee with a　*De 28:27*
s.
therefore the Lord will smite　*Isa 3:17*
with a *s.*

SCABBARD

O sword, put up thyself into　*Jer 47:6*
thy *s.*

SCABBED

he that is scurvy or *s.* shall　*Le 21:20*
not approach
or scurvy, or *s.* ye shall not　*Le 22:22*
offer to the Lord

SCABBY

s. eruption (S)　*Le 13:30;*
　　　13:31-33, 35, 37, 14:54

SCAFFOLD

Solomon had made a brasen　*2Ch 6:13*
s.

SCALE

I will *s.* the heavens (B)　*Isa 14:13*

SCALES

these that have *s.* eat ye　*Le 11:9;*
　　　　　　　　　　　De 14:9
that have no *s.* ye shall not　*Le 11:10;*
eat　　　　　　　*11:12; De 14:10*
honest *s.* (B)　*Le 19:36*
s. of justice are the Lord's　*Pr 16:11*
(B)
his *s.* are his pride, shut up　*Job 41:15*
together
who weighed the mountains　*Isa 40:12*
in *s.* and hills
I will cause the fish to stick　*Eze 29:4*
to thy *s.*
there fell from his eyes as it　*Ac 9:18*
had been *s.*

SCALETH

a wise man *s.* the city of　*Pr 21:22*
the mighty

SCALL

it is a dry *s.* even a leprosy　*Le 13:30*
on the head
plague of the *s.* be not deeper　*Le 13:31;*
shut up him that hath the　*13:33*
s. seven days
and behold, if the *s.* spread　*Le 13:32;*
not　　　　　　　　　　　*13:34*
he shall be shaven, but the *s.*　*Le 13:33*
shall he not shave
but if the *s.* spread much, he　*Le 13:35;*
is unclean　　　　　　　　　*13:36*
if the *s.* be at a stay, the *s.* is　*Le 13:37*
healed
this is the law of all manner　*Le 14:54*
of leprosy and *s.*

SCALP

hairy *s.* of such an one as　*Ps 68:21*
goeth

SCANDAL

does not carry a *s.* (B)　*Ps 15:3*
at once he feels *s.* (B)　*M't 13:21*
scandal-mongers (N)　*Ro 1:30*
may not be exposed to *s.* (N)　*1Ti 3:7*
who will not talk *s.* (N)　*1Ti 3:11*

SCANDALIZE

does it *s.* you (A)　*Joh 6:61*

SCANDALIZED

though all rest feel *s.,* I　*M't 26:33*
never (B)

SCANT

the *s.* measure that is　*Mic 6:10*
abominable

SCAPEGOAT

Lord, and the other lot for the　*Le 16:8*
s.
the other for Azazel　*Le 16:8;*
(A)(B)(E)(R)　　　*16:10, 26*
on which the lot fell to be the　*Le 16:10*
s.
him go for a *s.* into the　*Le 16:10*
wilderness
goat for the *s.* shall wash his　*Le 16:26*

SCAR

it is the *s.* of the burn　*Le 13:28*
(A)(B)(E)(R)

SCARCE

Jacob was yet *s.* gone out　*Ge 27:30*
from the
s. restrained they the people　*Ac 14:18*
s. were come over against　*Ac 27:7*
Cnidus

SCARCELY

s. for a righteous man will one　*Ro 5:7*
die
if the righteous *s.* be saved,　*1Pe 4:18*
where

SCARCENESS

thou shalt eat bread without *s.*　*De 8:9*

SCARED

s. out of their wits (P)　*M'k 6:50*

SCARFS

spangled face veils and *s.*　*Isa 3:19*
(A)(R)

SCAREST

Then thou *s.* me with dreams　*Job 7:14*

SCARLET

bound upon his hand a *s.*　*Ge 38:28*
thread
had the *s.* thread upon his　*Ge 38:30*
hand
crimson string (B)　*Ge 38:30*
purple, and *s.* and fine linen　*Ex 25:4*
and blue, and purple, and *s.*　*Ex 26:1*
veil of blue, and purple, and　*Ex 26:31*
s.
of blue, and purple, and *s.*　*Ex 26:36*
of blue, and purple, and *s.*　*Ex 27:16*
purple, and *s.* and fine linen　*Ex 28:5*
of blue, and of purple, of *s.*　*Ex 28:6*
　　　　　　　　　　　　　Ex 28:8
blue, and of purple, and　*Ex 28:15;*
of *s.*　　　　　　　　　　*28:33*
And blue, and purple, and *s.*　*Ex 35:6*
found blue, and purple, and *s.*　*Ex 35:23*
of blue, and purple, and　*Ex 35:25*
of *s.*
in blue, and in purple, in *s.*　*Ex 35:35*
and blue, and purple, and *s.*　*Ex 36:8*
veil of blue, and purple, and　*Ex 36:35*
s.
door of blue, and purple, and　*Ex 36:37*
s.
of blue, and purple, and *s.*　*Ex 38:18*
purple, and in *s.* and fine　*Ex 38:23*
linen
of the blue, and purple, and *s.*　*Ex 39:1*
gold, blue, and purple, and *s.*　*Ex 39:2*
in the purple, and in the *s.*　*Ex 39:3*

gold, blue, and purple, and *Ex 39:5;*
s.   *39:8*
of blue, and purple, and s.   *Ex 39:24*
purple, and s. of needlework   *Ex 39:29*
cedar wood, and s. and hyssop   *Le 14:4*
and the cedar wood, and the s.   *Le 14:6*
cedar wood, and s. and   *Le 14:49*
hyssop
and the hyssop, and the s.   *Le 14:51*
with the hyssop, and with the   *Le 14:52*
s.
spread upon them a cloth of s.   *Nu 4:8*
cedarwood, and hyssop, and s.   *Nu 19:6*
shalt bind this line of s.   *Jos 2:18*
thread in
bound the s. line in the   *Jos 2:21*
window
over Saul, who clothed you in   *2Sa 1:24*
s.
household are clothed with s.   *Pr 31:21*
Thy lips are like a thread of s.   *Ca 4:3*
though your sins be as s. they   *Isa 1:18*
they that were brought up in s.   *La 4:5*
shall be clothed with s. and   *Da 5:7*
have
thou shalt be clothed with s.   *Da 5:16*
they clothed Daniel with s.   *Da 5:29*
and put
red, the valiant men are in s.   *Na 2:3*
him, and put on him a s.   *M't 27:28*
robe
water, and s. wool, and   *Heb 9:19*
hyssop
woman sit upon a s. coloured   *Re 17:3*
beast
arrayed in purple and s.   *Re 17:4*
colour
and purple, and silk, and s.   *Re 18:12*
in fine linen, and purple, and   *Re 18:16*
s.

SCATTER

did the Lord s. them abroad   *Ge 11:9*
in Jacob, and s. them in Israel   *Ge 49:7*
I will s. you among the   *Le 26:33*
heathen
and s. thou the fire yonder   *Nu 16:37*
shall s. you among the nations   *De 4:27*
Lord shall s. thee among all   *De 28:64*
people
said, I would s. them into   *De 32:26*
corners
and shall s. them beyond the   *1Ki 14:15*
river
s. you abroad among the   *Ne 1:8*
nations
s. them by thy power; and   *Ps 59:11*
bring
s. thou the people that delight   *Ps 68:30*

and to s. them in the lands   *Ps 106:27*
Cast forth lightning, and s.   *Ps 144:6*
them
the fitches, and s. the   *Isa 28:25*
cummin
and the whirlwind shall s.   *Isa 41:16*
s. them also among the   *Jer 9:16*
heathen
will I s. them as the stubble   *Jer 13:24*
I will s. them as with an east   *Jer 18:17*
wind
that destroy and s. the sheep of   *Jer 23:1*

I will s. into all winds them   *Jer 49:32*

will s. them toward all those   *Jer 49:36*
winds
third part thou shalt s. in the   *Eze 5:2*
wind
remnant will I s. into all   *Eze 5:10*
the winds
and I will s. a third part into   *Eze 5:12*
all the
s. your bones about your   *Eze 6:5*
altars
coals, and s. them over the   *Eze 10:2*
city
I will s. toward every wind   *Eze 12:14*
all that
shall s. them among the   *Eze 12:15*
nations
would s. them among the   *Eze 20:23*
heathen
I will s. thee among the   *Eze 22:15*
heathen
I will s. the Egyptians   *Eze 29:12*
among the
will s. the Egyptians   *Eze 30:23;*
among the   *30:26*

off his leaves, and s. his fruit   *Da 4:14*
he shall s. among them the   *Da 11:24*
prey
to s. the power of the holy   *Da 12:7*
people
came out as a whirlwind to   *Hab 3:14*
s. me
over the land of Judah to s. it   *Zec 1:21*
where you did not s.   *M't 25:24;*
(E)(N)   *25:26*

SCATTERED

we be s. abroad upon the   *Ge 11:4*
face of
So the Lord s. them abroad   *Ge 11:8*
people were s. abroad   *Ex 5:12*
throughout
s. them on the water   *Ex 32:20*
(A)(B)(R)
scattered (S)   *Ex 32:20; 2Ch 34:4*
Lord, and let thine enemies   *Nu 10:35*
be s.
the Lord thy God hath s. thee   *De 30:3*
that they which remained   *1Sa 11:11*
were s.
and the people were s. from   *1Sa 13:8*
him
that the people were s. from   *1Sa 13:11*
me
the battle was there s. over the   *2Sa 18:8*
he sent out arrows, and s.   *2Sa 22:15*
them
I saw all Israel s. upon the   *1Ki 22:17*
hills as
and all his army were s. from   *2Ki 25:5*
him
all Israel s. upon the   *2Ch 18:16*
mountains
is a certain people s. abroad   *Es 3:8*
stout lion's whelps are s.   *Job 4:11*
abroad
brimstone shall be s. upon   *Job 18:15*
his
sulphur s. (A)(B)   *Job 18:15*
sent out his arrows, and s.   *Ps 18:14*
them
and hast s. us among the   *Ps 44:11*
heathen
God hath s. the bones of him   *Ps 53:5*
that
hast cast us off, thou hast s.   *Ps 60:1*
us
God arise, let his enemies be s.   *Ps 68:1*
When the Almighty s. kings   *Ps 68:14*
in it
thou hast s. thine enemies   *Ps 89:10*
the workers of iniquity shall   *Ps 92:9*
be s.
Our bones are s. at the   *Ps 141:7*
grave's
s. of Judah (B)   *Isa 11:12*
to a nation s. and peeled, to a   *Isa 18:2*
present, of a people s. and   *Isa 18:7*
peeled
up of thyself the nations were   *Isa 33:3*
s.
hast s. thy ways to the   *Jer 3:13*
strangers
and all their flocks shall be s.   *Jer 10:21*
Ye have s. my flock, and   *Jer 23:2*
driven
all nations whither I have s.   *Jer 30:11*
thee
He that s. Israel will gather   *Jer 31:10*
him
gathered unto thee should be   *Jer 40:15*
s.
Israel is a s. sheep; the lions   *Jer 50:17*
and all his army was s. from   *Jer 52:8*
him
shall be s. through the   *Eze 6:8*
countries
have s. them among the   *Eze 11:16*
countries
the countries where ye have   *Eze 11:17*
been s.
shall be s. toward all winds   *Eze 17:21*
of the countries wherein ye   *Eze 20:34*
are s.
countries wherein ye have   *Eze 20:41*
been s.
the people among whom   *Eze 28:25*
they are s.
the people whither they were   *Eze 29:13*
s.
And they were s. because   *Eze 34:5*
there is
of the field when they were s.   *Eze 34:5*
was s. upon all the face of the   *Eze 34:6*
earth

he is among his sheep that   *Eze 34:12*
are s.
all places where they have   *Eze 34:12*
been s.
horns, till ye have s. them   *Eze 34:21*
abroad
And I s. them among the   *Eze 36:19*
heathen
s. every man from his   *Eze 46:18*
possession
they have s. among the nations   *Joe 3:2*
people is s. upon the   *Na 3:18*
mountains
the everlasting mountains   *Hab 3:6*
were s.
the horns which have s.   *Zec 1:19;*
Judah   *1:21*
I s. them with a whirlwind   *Zec 7:14*
among
and the sheep shall be s.; and   *Zec 13:7*
I
were s. abroad, as sheep   *M't 9:36*
having
of the flock shall be s.   *M't 26:31*
abroad
shepherd, and the sheep   *M'k 14:27*
shall be s.
s. the proud in the   *Lu 1:51*
imagination of
children of God that were s.   *Joh 11:52*
is now come, that ye shall   *Joh 16:32*
be s.
were s. and brought to nought   *Ac 5:36*
adherents were s.   *Ac 5:37*
(A)(B)(E)(N)(R)
they were all s. abroad   *Ac 8:1*
throughout
they that were s. abroad went   *Ac 8:4*
they which were s. abroad   *Ac 11:19*
word s. and spread (A)   *Ac 13:49*
twelve tribes which are s.   *Jas 1:1*
abroad
strangers s. throughout Pontus   *1Pe 1:1*

SCATTERETH

cloud: he s. his bright cloud   *Job 37:11*
s. the east wind upon the   *Job 38:24*
earth
he s. the hoarfrost like ashes   *Ps 147:16*
There is that s. and yet   *Pr 11:24*
increaseth
s. away all evil with his eyes   *Pr 20:8*
A wise king s. the wicked   *Pr 20:26*
s. abroad the inhabitants   *Isa 24:1*
thereof
gathereth not with me s.   *M't 12:30*
abroad
he that gathereth not with   *Lu 11:23*
me s.
catcheth them, and s. the   *Joh 10:12*
sheep

SCATTERING

s. them (B)   *2Ch 34:4*
as a s. club (B)   *Pr 25:18*
s. and tempest, and   *Isa 30:30*
hailstones
s. them on the road   *M't 21:8*
(B)(E)(P)(R)

SCHEME

s. framed against Jews (A)(B)   *Es 8:3*
s. Haman concocted (B)   *Es 8:5*
Haman's wicked s.   *Es 9:25*
(A)(B)(R)
devise an empty s. (A)(B)   *Ps 2:1*

SCHEMED

they s. together (A)(B)(R)   *Ps 31:13*

SCHEMES

s. of the wily (R)   *Job 5:13*
s. of the wicked (B)   *Job 10:3*
s. to do me wrong (B)(R)   *Job 21:27*
s. they devised (A)(B)(R)   *Ps 10:2*
nor promote their s. (B)   *Ps 140:8*
deviseth wicked s. (B)   *Pr 6:18*
many s. in man's mind (B)   *Pr 19:21*
devised s. (A)(R)   *Jer 11:19*
follow own s. (B)   *Jer 18:12*
devised s. (A)(B)   *Jer 18:18*
s. shall be devised (A)(B)   *Da 11:25*
his s. (B)   *2Co 2:11*

SCHEMING

know all their *s.* (B)	Isa 18:23

SCENT

s. of son as odor of field (A)	Ge 27:27
through the *s.* of water it will bud	Job 14:9
s. of garments (R)(S)	Ca 4:11
s. of breath like apples (A)(R)	Ca 7:8
in him, and his *s.* is not changed	Jer 48:11
s. thereof shall be as the wine	Ho 14:7
the *s.* of Christ (P)	2Co 2:15

SCEPTER

hallowed with *s.* and staves (A)(B)	Nu 21:18
send your mighty *s.* (R)	Ps 110:2

SCEPTRE

s. shall not depart from Judah	Ge 49:10
and a *S.* shall rise out of Israel	Nu 24:17
king shall hold out the golden *s.*	Es 4:11
held out to Esther the golden *s.*	Es 5:2
near, and touched the top of the *s.*	Es 5:2
out the golden *s.* toward Esther	Es 8:4
and ever: the *s.* of thy kingdom	Ps 45:6
of thy kingdom is a right *s.*	Ps 45:6
the wicked, and the *s.* of the rulers	Isa 14:5
she hath no strong rod to be a *s.* to	Eze 19:14
him that holdeth the *s.* from Ashkelon	Am 1:5
that holdeth the *s.* from Ashkelon	Am 1:8
the *s.* of Egypt shall depart away	Zec 10:11
a *s.* of righteousness is the *s.*	Heb 1:8

SCEPTRES

she had strong rods for the *s.* of	Eze 19:11

SCEVA

there were seven sons of one *S.*	Ac 19:14

SCHISM

there should be no *s.* in the body	1Co 12:25
no division or discord (A)(B)(N)(R)	1Co 12:25

SCHOLAR

the great, the teacher as the *s.*	1Ch 25:8
the master and the *s.* out of	Mal 2:12
scholar (B)	1Co 1:20

SCHOOL

daily in the *s.* of one Tyrannus	Ac 19:9

SCHOOLING

without *s.* or skill (B)	Ac 4:13

SCHOOLMASTER

law was our *s.* to bring us unto	Ga 3:24
we are no longer under a *s.*	Ga 3:25

SCIENCE

knowledge, and understanding *s.*	Da 1:4
oppositions of *s.* falsely so called	1Ti 6:20

SCOFF

the impious *s.* at thee (R)	Ps 74:22
s. no more (B)(R)	Isa 28:32
And they shall *s.* at the kings	Hab 1:10
began to sneer, ridicule, *s.* (A)	Lu 16:14

SCOFFED

s. at the Rock (R)	De 32:15

s. at me (A)	J'g 8:15
he *s.* at them (B)	1Sa 25:14
have *s.* and boasted (R)	Zep 2:10
s. at him (B)	M't 27:39
s. at him (E)(N)(R)	Lu 16:14
made sport of, *s.*, spit upon (A)	Lu 18:32; 22:63
s. and ridiculed him (A)	Lu 23:11
rulers *s.* and sneered (A)(E)(P)(R)	Lu 23:35
some *s.* (A)(B)(N)	Ac 17:32
s. at duty to parents (P)	Ro 1:30

SCOFFER

voice of the *s.* and scorner (B)	Ps 44:16
scoffer (S)	Pr 9:7; 9:8; 13:1; 14:6; 15:12; 19:25; 21:11, 24; 22:10; 24:9; Isa 29:20

SCOFFERS

scoffers (S)	Pr 1:22; 19:29; Ho 7:5
do not be *s.* (A)(E)(S)	Isa 28:22
you *s.* and scorners (A)(B)(N)(R)	Ac 13:41
shall come in the last days *s.*	2Pe 3:3
there will be *s.* (A)(B)(R)	Jude 18

SCOFFEST

if thou *s.* (S)	Pr 9:12

SCOFFING

s. and jeering at Jesus (P)	Lu 23:11

SCOFFS

the enemy *s.* (B)(R)	Ps 74:18

SCOLDING

quarrelsome *s.* (A)	Pr 25:24

SCORCH

unto him to *s.* men with fire	Re 16:8

SCORCHED

s. before it comes up (B)	2Ki 19:26
the sun was up, they were *s.*	M't 13:6
when the sun was up, it was *s.*	M'k 4:6
And men were *s.* with great heat	Re 16:9

SCORCHING

s. bases of the hills (B)	De 32:22

SCORN

treated with *s.* (B)	De 32:15
thee, and laughed thee to *s.*	2Ki 19:21
but they laughed them to *s.*	2Ch 30:10
heard it, they laughed us to *s.*	Ne 2:19
s. to lay hands on Mordecai alone	Es 3:6
the just upright man is laughed to *s.*	Job 12:4
My friends *s.* me: but mine eye	Job 16:20
and the innocent laugh them to *s.*	Job 22:19
they that see me laugh me to *s.*	Ps 22:7
the *s.* of all my adversaries (R)	Ps 31:11
the *s.* to the fool (R)	Ps 39:8
a *s.* and a derision to them	Ps 44:13
an object of *s.* (A)(E)(R)	Ps 69:11
a *s.* and derision to them that	Ps 79:4
s. of all his neighbors (B)(R)	Ps 89:41
thee, and laughed thee to *s.*	Isa 37:22
an object of *s.* (B)	Eze 5:15
thou shalt be laughed to *s.*	Eze 23:32
princes shall be a *s.* unto them	Hab 1:10
sleepeth, they laughed him to *s.*	M't 9:24
And they laughed him to *s.*	M'k 5:40
they laughed him to *s.*	Lu 8:53
knowing	
show *s.* or disgust (N)	Ga 4:14
who pour *s.* on religion (N)	Jude 18

SCORNED

s. his birthright (A)	Ge 25:34
he *s.* and despised him (A)	1Sa 17:12
s. the Counsel of Most High (B)	Ps 107:11
utterly *s.* and despised (A)(R)	Ca 8:7

s. made nothing of rest (A)	Lu 18:9
s. nor spurned me (B)	Ga 4:14

SCORNER

voice of the scoffer and *s.* (B)	Ps 44:16
He that reproveth a *s.* getteth to	Pr 9:7
Reprove not a *s.* lest he hate thee	Pr 9:8
but a *s.* heareth not rebuke	Pr 13:1
A *s.* seeketh wisdom, and findeth	Pr 14:6
A *s.* loveth not one that reproveth	Pr 15:12
Smite a *s.* and the simple will	Pr 19:25
wine is a *s.* (B)	Pr 20:1
When the *s.* is punished, the simple	Pr 21:11
Proud and haughty *s.* is his name	Pr 21:24
Cast out the *s.* and contention	Pr 22:10
the *s.* is an abomination to men	Pr 24:9
the *s.* is consumed, and all	Isa 29:20

SCORNERS

the *s.* delight in their scorning	Pr 1:22
Surely he scorneth the *s.*: but he	Pr 3:34
Judgments are prepared for *s.*	Pr 19:29
he stretched out his hand with *s.*	Ho 7:5
you scoffers and *s.* (A)(B)(N)(R)	Ac 13:41

SCORNEST

if thou *s.* thou alone shalt bear	Pr 9:12
as an harlot, in that thou *s.* hire	Eze 16:31

SCORNETH

He *s.* the multitude of the city	Job 39:7
high, she *s.* the horse and his rider	Job 39:18
Surely he *s.* the scorners: but he	Pr 3:34
An ungodly witness *s.* judgment	Pr 19:28

SCORNFUL

nor sitteth in the seat of the *s.*	Ps 1:1
S. men bring a city into a snare	Pr 29:8
the word of the Lord, ye *s.* men	Isa 28:14

SCORNFULLY

would be *s.* refused (B)	Ca 8:7

SCORNING

who drinketh up *s.* like water	Job 34:7
the *s.* of those that are at ease	Ps 123:4
the scorners delight in their *s.*	Pr 1:22

SCORNS

s. to obey mother (A)(B)(R)	Pr 30:17

SCORPION

ask an egg, will he offer him a *s.*	Lu 11:12
torment was as the torment of a *s.*	Re 9:5

SCORPIONS

were fiery serpents, and *s.* and	De 8:15
but I will chastise you with *s.*	1Ki 12:11; 12:14
but I will chastise you with *s.*	2Ch 10:11; 10:14
thee, and thou dost dwell among *s.*	Eze 2:6
power to tread on serpents and *s.*	Lu 10:19
as the *s.* of the earth have power	Re 9:3
And they had tails like unto *s.*	Re 9:10

SCOUNDRELS

worthless *s.* (E)(R)	2Ch 13:7
two *s.*, rascals (B)	1Ki 21:13

SCOUR

s. sea and land (P) M't 23:15

SCOURED

pot, it shall be both s. and Le 6:28
rinsed

SCOURGE

be hid from the s. of the Job 5:21
tongue
If the s. slay suddenly, he will Job 9:23
the Lord of hosts shall stir Isa 10:26
up a s.
overflowing s. shall pass Isa 28:15;
through 28:18
will s. you in their M't 10:17
synagogues
to mock, and to s. and to M't 20:19
crucify
some of them shall ye s. in M't 23:34
your
shall s. him, and shall spit M'k 10:34
upon
they shall s. him, and put him Lu 18:33
he had made a s. of small Joh 2:15
cords
Is it lawful for you to s. a Ac 22:25
man

SCOURGED

the Lord s. Pharaoh (A) Ge 12:17
she shall be s.; they shall not Le 19:20
and when he had s. Jesus, he M't 27:26
when he had s. him, to be M'k 15:15
crucified
therefore took Jesus, and s. Joh 19:1
him

SCOURGERS

to the s. (B) M't 18:34

SCOURGES

s. in your sides, and thorns Jos 23:13
in your

SCOURGETH

s. every son whom he Heb 12:6
receiveth

SCOURGING

that he should be examined Ac 22:24
by s.

SCOURGINGS

trial of cruel mockings and Heb 11:36
s.

SCRABBLED

and s. on the doors of the 1Sa 21:13
gate

SCRAPE

the dust that they s. off Le 14:41
without
a potsherd to s. himself withal Job 2:8
I will also s. her dust from her Eze 26:4

SCRAPED

cause the house to be s. within Le 14:41
and after he hath s. the house Le 14:43

SCRAPS

gathered s. of food under my J'g 1:7
table (S)

SCREAM

let out a loud s. (P) M'k 1:26

SCREECH

the s. owl (S) De 14:16
the s. owl also shall rest there Isa 34:14
the night monster (A)(B)(E) Isa 34:14
the night hag (R) Isa 34:14

SCREEN

a s. for wrongdoing (N) 1Pe 2:16

SCRIBE

priests; and Seraiah was the 2Sa 8:17
s.

And Sheva was s.: and 2Sa 20:25
Zadok and
the king's s. and the high 2Ki 12:10
priest
Shebna the s. and Joah 2Ki 18:18
the son 18:37
Shebna the s. and the elder 2Ki 19:2
the son of Meshullam, the s. 2Ki 22:3
priest said unto Shaphan the 2Ki 22:8
s.
Shaphan the s. shewed the 2Ki 22:10
king
And Shaphan the s. and 2Ki 22:12
Asahiah a
and the principal s. of the 2Ki 25:19
host
the priests; and Shavsha 1Ch 18:16
was s.
Shemaiah son of Nethaneel 1Ch 24:6
the s.
a counsellor, a wise man, 1Ch 27:32
and a s.
kings s. and high priests 2Ch 24:11
officer
Jeiel the s. and Maaseiah the 2Ch 26:11
ruler
Hilkiah said to Shaphan 2Ch 34:15
the s.
Then Shaphan the s. told the 2Ch 34:18
king
and Shaphan the s. and 2Ch 34:20
Asaiah a
Shimshai the s. wrote a Ezr 4:8
letter
the chancellor, and Shimshai Ezr 4:9
the s.
chancellor, and to Shimshai Ezr 4:17
the s.
before Rehum, and Shimshai Ezr 4:23
the s.
a ready s. in the law of Moses Ezr 7:6
gave unto Ezra the priest, the Ezr 7:11
s.
even a s. of the Ezr 7:11
commandments
s. of the law of God of Ezr 7:12;
heaven 7:21
and they spake unto Ezra the s. Ne 8:1
And Ezra the s. stood upon a Ne 8:4
pulpit
and Ezra the priest the s. Ne 8:9
were gathered unto Ezra the Ne 8:13
s.
and of Ezra, the priest, the s. Ne 12:26
of God, and Ezra the s. Ne 12:36
before them
Shelemiah and Zadok the Ne 13:13
s.
Where is the s.? where is the Isa 33:18
Shebna the s. and Joah, Isa 36:3
Asaph's
Shebna the s. and Joah, the Isa 36:22
son of
and Shebna the s. and the Isa 37:2
elders of
Gemariah, son of Shaphan Jer 36:10
the s.
sat there, even Elishama the Jer 36:12
s. and
in the chamber of Elishama Jer 36:20
the s.
to take Baruch the s. and Jer 36:26
Jeremiah
roll, and gave it to Baruch the Jer 36:32
s.
in the house of Jonathan the Jer 37:15
s.
to the house of Jonathan the Jer 39:20
s.
and the principal s. of the Jer 52:25
host, who
And a certain s. came, and M't 8:19
said
every s. which is instructed M't 13:52
unto
the s. said unto him, Well, M'k 12:32
Master
Where is the wise? where is 1Co 1:20
the s.

SCRIBES

sent for s. (B) Ge 41:8; Ex 8:19; 9:11
and Ahiah, the sons of Shisha, 1Ki 4:3
s.
the families of the s. which 1Ch 2:55
dwelt at
and of the Levites there 2Ch 34:13
were s.
Then were the king's s. called Es 3:12
on

Then were the king's s. called at Es 8:9
he it; the pen of the s. is in Jer 8:8
vain
chief priests and s. of the M't 2:4
people
exceed the righteousness of M't 5:20
the s.
having authority, and not as M't 7:29
the s.
behold, certain of the s. said M't 9:3
within
certain of the s. and of the M't 12:38
Pharisees
came to Jesus s. and M't 15:1
Pharisees
the elders and chief priests M't 16:21
and s.
Why then say the s. that M't 17:10
Elias must
the chief priests and unto the M't 20:18
s.
when the chief priests and s. M't 21:15
saw
s. and the Pharisees sit in M't 23:2
Moses'
But woe unto you, s. and M't 23:13;
Pharisees 23:14-15, 23, 25, 27, 29;
 Lu 11:44
prophets, and wise men, and M't 23:34
the chief priests, and the s. M't 26:3
and the
s. and the elders were M't 26:57
assembled
mocking him, with the s. M't 27:41
and elders
had authority, and not as the M'k 1:22
s.
were certain of the s. sitting M'k 2:6
there
the s. and Pharisees saw him M'k 2:16
eat
s. which came down from M'k 3:22
Jerusalem
Pharisees, and certain of the M'k 7:1
the Pharisees and s. asked M'k 7:5
him
and of the chief priests, and M'k 8:31
s.
Why say the s. that Elias M'k 9:11
must first
and the s. questioning with M'k 9:14
them
he asked the s., What M'k 9:16
question ye
the chief priests, and unto M'k 10:33
the s.
And the s. and chief priests M'k 11:18
heard it
the chief priests, and the s. M'k 11:27
and the
and one of the s. came, M'k 12:28
and having
How say the s. that Christ is M'k 12:35
the son
Beware of the s. which love M'k 12:38
to go
chief priests and the s. M'k 14:1
sought how
from the chief priests and M'k 14:43
the s. and
priests and the elders and the M'k 14:53
s.
consultation with the elders M'k 15:1
and s.
said among themselves with M'k 15:31
the s.
s. and Pharisees began to Lu 5:21
reason
their s. and Pharisees Lu 5:30
murmured
the s. and Pharisees watched Lu 6:7
him
the elders and chief priests Lu 9:22
and s.
s. and the Pharisees began to Lu 11:53
urge
Pharisees and s. murmured Lu 15:2
saying
the chief priests and the s. Lu 19:47
and the
priests and the s. came upon Lu 20:1
him
chief priests and s. the Lu 20:19
same hour
certain of the s. answering Lu 20:39
said

SCRIBES (continued)

Beware of the s. which desire | Lu 20:46
to
the chief priests and s. sought | Lu 22:2
how
priests and the s. came | Lu 22:66
together
And the chief priests and s. | Lu 23:10
stood
s. and Pharisees brought unto | Joh 8:3
him
that their rulers, and elders, | Ac 4:5
and s.
the people, and the elders, and | Ac 6:12
the s.
s. that were of the Pharisees' | Ac 23:9
part

SCRIBE'S

king's house, into the s. | Jer 36:12
chamber
it out of Elishama the s. | Jer 36:21
chamber

SCRIP

bag which he had, even in a | 1Sa 17:40
s.
the shepherd's bag | 1Sa 17:40
(B)(E)(R)
Nor s. for your journey, | M't 10:10
neither
provisions bag or a wallet | M't 10:10;
(A) | M'k 6:8; Lu 9:3
a bag (B)(R) | M't 10:10;
| M'k 6:8; Lu 9:3
no wallet (E) | M't 10:10;
| M'k 6:8; Lu 9:3
no pack (N) M't 10:10 M'k 6:8; Lu 9:3
no knapsack (P) | M't 10:10
no s. no bread, no money in | M'k 6:8
neither staves, nor s. neither | Lu 9:3
Carry neither purse, nor s. nor | Lu 10:4;
| 22:35-36
no provisions bag (A) | Lu 10:4;
| 22:35-36
no wallet (B)(E) | Lu 10:4
pack (N) | Lu 10:4
bag (P)(R) | Lu 10:4
sent you without purse, and | Lu 22:35
s. and
bag (B)(R) | Lu 22:35; 22:36
wallet (E)(P) | Lu 22:35; 22:36
pack (N) | Lu 22:35; 22:36
let him take it, and likewise | Lu 22:36
his s.

SCRIPTURE

which is noted in the s. of | Da 10:21
truth
in the writing or book of | Da 10:21
truth (A)
the book of truth (B)(R) | Da 10:21
in the writing of truth (E) | Da 10:21
have ye not read this s.; | M'k 12:10
The stone
the s. was fulfilled, which | M'k 15:28
saith
This day is this s. fulfilled in | Lu 4:21
your
they believed the s. and the | Joh 2:22
word
as the s. hath said, out of his | Joh 7:38
belly
Hath not the s. said, That | Joh 7:42
Christ
came, and the s. cannot be | Joh 10:35
broken
that the s. may be fulfilled, | Joh 13:18
He that
that the s. might be fulfilled | Joh 17:12;
| 19:24, 28
s. should be fulfilled, A bone | Joh 19:36
of him
again another s. saith, They | Joh 19:37
shall
For as yet they knew not the | Joh 20:9
s.
s. must needs have been | Ac 1:16
fulfilled
The place of the s. which he | Ac 8:32
read
began at the same s. and | Ac 8:35
preached
For what saith the s.? | Ro 4:3
Abraham
the s. saith unto Pharaoh, | Ro 9:17
Even for
the s. saith, Whosoever | Ro 10:11
believeth

Wot ye not what the s. saith | Ro 11:2
of Elias
the s. forseeing that God would | Ga 3:8
the s. hath concluded all under | Ga 3:22
sin
Nevertheless what saith the s. | Ga 4:30
the s. saith, Thou shalt not | 1Ti 5:18
muzzle
All s. is given by inspiration | 2Ti 3:16
of God
the royal law according to the | Jas 2:8
s.
And the s. was fulfilled which | Jas 2:23
saith
ye think that the s. saith in | Jas 4:5
vain
Wherefore it is contained in | 1Pe 2:6
the s.
no prophecy of the s. is | 2Pe 1:20
of private

SCRIPTURES

Did ye never read in the s. | M't 21:42
Ye do err, not knowing the | M't 22:29
s. nor
how then shall the s. be | M't 26:54
fulfilled
s. of the prophets might be | M't 26:56
fulfilled
err, because ye know not | M'k 12:24
the s.
me not: but the s. must be | M'k 14:49
fulfilled
expounded unto them in all | Lu 24:27
the s.
and while he opened to us | Lu 24:32
the s.
that they might understand | Lu 24:45
the s.
Search the s.; for in them ye | Joh 5:39
think
reasoned with them out of the | Ac 17:2
s.
and searched the s. daily, | Ac 17:11
whether
eloquent man, and mighty in | Ac 18:24
the s.
shewing by the s. that Jesus | Ac 18:28
was
afore by his prophets in the | Ro 1:2
holy s.
patience and comfort of the s. | Ro 15:4
we
by the s. of the prophets, | Ro 16:26
according
died for our sins according | 1Co 15:3
to the s.
the third day according to | 1Co 15:4
the s.
child thou hast known the | 2Ti 3:15
holy s.
wrest, as they do also the | 2Pe 3:16
other s.

SCROLL

scroll (S) | Ezr 6:2;
Jer 36:2, 4, 6, 14, 20-21, 23, 25, 27-29,
| 32; Eze 2:9; 3:1, 3; Zec 5:1-2
shall be rolled together as a s. | Isa 34:4
in the s. of the book (N) | Heb 10:7
scroll (S) | Re 5:1;
| 5:2-3, 5, 7-9; 10:2, 8-10
And the heaven departed as a | Re 6:14
s.

SCRUPLES

pass judgment on s. | Ro 14:1
(A)(E)(P)
tender s. of weaker men (N) | Ro 15:1
another man's s. (A)(R) | 1Co 10:29

SCRUTINIZED

if we s. ourselves (B) | 1Co 11:31

SCULPTURED

cherubim of s. work (B) | 2Ch 3:10

SCUM

to the pot whose s. is therein | Eze 24:6
and whose s. is not gone out | Eze 24:6
of it
that the s. of it may be | Eze 24:11
consumed

great s. went not forth out | Eze 24:12
of her
her s. shall be in the fire | Eze 24:12
s. of the earth (B)(N)(P) | 1Co 4:13

SCURVY

hath a blemish in his eye, or | Le 21:20
be s.
or maimed, or having a wen, | Le 22:22
or s.

SCYTHIAN

Barbarian, S. bond nor free | Col 3:11

SEA

stretch thine hand over the s. | Ex 14:16;
| 14:27
Lord caused the s. to go | Ex 14:21
back, made the s. dry
thou didst blow, the s. | Ex 15:10
covered them
Lord made the s. and all | Ex 20:11;
that is therein | Ps 95:5; Jon 1:9;
| Ac 4:24; 14:15
the s. gull (A)(B)(R) | Le 11:16
the s-mew (E) | Le 11:16
a wind brought quails from | Nu 11:31
s.
nor is it beyond s. that thou | De 30:13
shouldest go over the s. for
us and bring it
you came unto the s. | Jos 24:6
Egyptians pursued
he brought the s. upon them | Jos 24:7
and covered them
the king had at s. a navy of | 1Ki 10:22
Tarshish
he said, Go up now, look | 1Ki 18:43
toward the s.
he restored the coast to the | 2Ki 14:25
s. of plain
let the s. roar | 1Ch 16:32;
| Ps 96:11; 98:7
cometh a multitude against | 2Ch 20:2
thee beyond s.
thou didst divide the s. went | Ne 9:11;
tho' by the s. | Job 26:12; Ps 74:13; 78:13;
| Jer 31:35
am I a s. | Job 7:12
the measure thereof is | Job 11:9
broader than the s.
as the waters fail from s. | Job 14:11
and flood decays
and the s. saith, It is not | Job 28:14
with me
or who shut up the s. | Job 38:8
he maketh the s. like a pot | Job 41:31
of ointment
he turned the s. into dry land | Ps 66:6
he shall have dominion from s. | Ps 72:8
to s.
but the s. overwhelmed their | Ps 78:53
enemies
she sent out her boughs to s. | Ps 80:11
and branches
so is this great wide s. | Ps 104:25
wherein are things
they that go down to the s. | Ps 107:23
in ships
the s. saw it and fled; O | Ps 114:3;
thou s. | 14:5
when he gave to the s. his | Pr 8:29
decree
as the waters cover the s. | Isa 11:9;
| Hab 2:14
branches are stretched and | Isa 16:8
gone over s.
waters shall fail from the s. | Isa 19:5
and rivers
the merchants of Zidon that | Isa 23:2
pass over s.
be ashamed, O Zion, for the | Isa 23:4
s. hath spoken
he stretched out his hand over | Isa 23:11
the s. he shook
they shall cry aloud from the | Isa 24:14
s.
sing to the Lord, ye that go | Isa 42:10
down to the s.
behold, at my rebuke I dry up | Isa 50:2
the s.
art thou not it which hath | Isa 51:10
dried the s.
but the wicked are like the | Isa 57:20
troubled s.
their voice roareth like s. and | Jer 6:23
they ride

sound like s. roaring (R)   *Jer 6:23*
O vine of Sibmah, thy plants   *Jer 48:32*
are gone over s.
their voice shall roar like the   *Jer 50:42*
s. shall ride
sound of s. roaring (A)(R)   *Jer 50:42*
I will dry up her s. and make   *Jer 51:36*
her springs dry
the s. is come up upon   *Jer 51:42*
Babylon, she is covered
for thy breach is great like the   *La 2:13*
s.
as the s. causeth his waves to   *Eze 26:3*
come
four great beasts came up from   *Da 7:3*
the s.
they shall wander from s. to   *Am 8:12*
s.
what shall we do, that s. may   *Jon 1:11*
be calm
in that day he shall come   *Mic 7:12*
from s. to s.
he rebuketh the s. and maketh   *Na 1:4*
it dry
populous No, whose rampart   *Na 3:8*
was the s.
was thy wrath against s. that   *Hab 3:8*
didst ride
thou didst walk through the   *Hab 3:15*
s. with thy horses
I will shake the heavens,   *Hag 2:6*
earth, and s.
his dominion shall be from s.   *Zec 9:10*
to s.
he shall pass through the s.   *Zec 10:11*
with affliction
then he arose and rebuked   *M't 8:26*
the s.
even winds and s. obey him   *M't 8:27;*
   M'k 4:39, 41
go thou to the s. and cast an   *M't 17:27*
hook
woe to hypocrites, for ye   *M't 23:15*
compass s. and land
distress, the s. and the waves   *Lu 21:25*
roaring
they committed themselves to   *Ac 27:40*
the s.
this man, though he hath   *Ac 28:4*
escaped the s.
all our fathers passed   *1Co 10:1*
through the s.
and before the throne was a s.   *Re 4:6*
of glass
to whom it was given to hurt   *Re 7:2*
the earth and s.
saying, Hurt not the earth nor   *Re 7:3*
the s.
who created the s. and the   *Re 10:6*
things therein
fear God, and worship him   *Re 14:7*
that made the s.
I saw a s. of glass, mingled   *Re 15:2*
with fire
who work the s. for a living   *Re 18:17*
(B)(E)(P)
the s.-captains (N)   *Re 18:17*
and the s. gave up the dead   *Re 20:13*
that were in it
first earth passed, and there   *Re 21:1*
was no more s.

SEA, molten

he made a molten s.   *1Ki 7:23; 2Ch 4:2*
there were knops compassing   *1Ki 7:24*
s. round about
the s. was set above upon   *1Ki 7:25;*
oxen   *2Ch 4:4*
set the s. on right side of the   *1Ki 7:39*
house eastward
Ahaz took down the s. from   *2Ki 16:17*
oxen
the s. did Chaldees break in   *2Ki 25:13;*
pieces   *25:16*
the s. was for the priests to   *2Ch 4:6*
wash in
one s. and twelve oxen under   *2Ch 4:15*
it
saith Lord, concerning the   *Jer 27:19*
pillars and s.

SEA *SHORE*

thy seed as sand which is   *Ge 22:17*
upon s. *shore*
saw the Egyptians dead upon   *Ex 14:30*
s. *shore*
came together as the sand   *Jos 11:4*
upon s. shore

Asher continued on the s.   *J'g 5:17*
shore
the Philistines as sand on the   *1Sa 13:5*
s. *shore*
largeness of heart as sand on   *1Ki 4:29*
s. *shore*
given it a charge against the   *Jer 47:7*
s. *shore*
of one sprang many, as sand   *Heb 11:12*
by s. *shore*

SEA SIDE

turn you, and go by the way of   *De 1:7*
the s. *side*
the Midianites lay as sand by   *J'g 7:12*
the s. *side*
Solomon went to Eloth at the   *2Ch 8:17*
s. *side*
the same day Jesus sat by   *M't 13:1*
the s. *side*
and he went forth again by   *M'k 2:13*
the s. *side*
and he began again to teach   *M'k 4:1*
by the s. *side*
Simon, whose house is by the   *Ac 10:6;*
s. *side*   *10:32*

BY THE SEA

before it shall ye encamp by   *Ex 14:2*
the s.
Egyptians overtook them   *Ex 14:9*
encamping *by the* s.
all Israel be gathered as   *2Sa 17:11*
sand *by the* s.
Judah and Israel as sand *by*   *1Ki 4:20*
the s.
I will convey them *by the* s.   *1Ki 5:9;*
   2Ch 2:16
woe to that land sendeth   *Isa 18:2*
ambassadors *by the* s.
as Carmel *by the* s. so shall   *Jer 46:18*
he come
the multitude was *by the* s. on   *M'k 4:1*
the land
as many as trade *by the* s.   *Re 18:17*
stood afar off

IN, INTO THE SEA

host of Pharaoh that came   *Ex 14:28*
into the s.
horse and rider hath he   *Ex 15:1;*
thrown *into the* s.   *15:21*
Pharaoh's host hath he cast   *Ex 15:4*
into the s.
his horse with horsemen went   *Ex 15:19*
into the s.
thy way is *in the* s. thy path   *Ps 77:19*
in great
I will set his hand also *in*   *Ps 89:25*
the s.
all rivers run *into the* s. yet sea   *Ec 1:7*
not full
he shall slay the dragon that   *Isa 27:1*
is *in the* s.
saith Lord, which maketh a   *Isa 43:16*
way *in the* s.
renowned city that was   *Eze 26:17*
strong *in the* s.
the isles that are *in the* s.   *Eze 26:18*
shall be troubled
waters go *into the* s. being   *Eze 47:8*
brought forth *into the* s. the
waters shall be healed
there was a mighty tempest   *Jon 1:4*
in the s.
mariners cast forth the wares   *Jon 1:5*
into the s.
take me up, and cast me *into*   *Jon 1:12;*
the s.   *1:15*
he will smite her power *into*   *Zec 9:4*
the s.
he shall smite the waves *into*   *Zec 10:11*
the s.
casting a net *into the* s.   *M't 4:18;*
   M'k 1:16
there arose a great tempest *in*   *M't 8:24*
the s.
whole herd of swine ran   *M'k 8:32;*
into the s.   *Mk 5:13*
kingdom of heaven like a   *M't 13:47*
net cast *into the* s.
be thou cast *into the* s.   *M't 21:21;*
   M'k 11:23
and he were cast *into the* s.   *M'k 9:42;*
   Lu 17:2
ye might say, Be thou planted   *Lu 17:6*
in the s.

Peter did cast himself *into*   *Joh 21:7*
the s.
and cast out the wheat *into*   *Ac 27:38*
the s.
they should cast themselves   *Ac 27:43*
first *into the* s.
all baptized in the cloud, and   *1Co 10:2*
in the s.
in perils *in the* s. among   *2Co 11:26*
false brethren
beasts and things *in the* s. is   *Jas 3:7*
tamed
every creature *in the* s. saying,   *Re 5:13*
Blessing
great mountain burning was   *Re 8:8*
cast *into the* s.
and every living soul died *in*   *Re 16:3*
the s.
were made rich all that had   *Re 18:19*
ships *in the* s.
a mighty angel cast a   *Re 18:21*
millstone *into the* s.

OF THE SEA

have dominion over   *Ge 1:26;*
fish *of the* s.   *1:28; Ps 8:8*
the fear of you upon all fishes   *Ge 9:2*
of the s.
and make thy seed as the   *Ge 32:12*
sand *of the* s.
Joseph gathered corn as the   *Ge 41:49*
sand *of the* s.
Zebulun shall dwell at the   *Ge 49:13*
haven *of the* s.
depths congealed in the heart   *Ex 15:8*
of the s.
brought again the waters *of*   *Ex 15:19*
the s. upon them
shall all the fish *of the* s. be   *Nu 11:22*
gathered
and the channels *of the* s.   *2Sa 22:16*
appeared
there ariseth a cloud out *of*   *1Ki 18:44*
the s.
it would be heavier than the   *Job 6:3*
sand *of the* s.
which treadeth upon the waves   *Job 9:8*
of the s.
the fishes *of the* s. shall declare   *Job 12:8*
to thee
behold he coverteth the   *Job 36:30*
bottom *of the* s.
hast thou entered into the   *Job 38:16*
springs *of the* s.
he gathereth the waters *of the*   *Ps 33:7*
s. together
I will bring my people from   *Ps 68:22*
depths *of the* s.
feathered fowls like as the   *Ps 78:27*
sand *of the* s.
thou rulest the raging *of the* s.   *Ps 89:9*
when waves
the Lord is mightier than the   *Ps 93:4*
waves *of the* s.
and dwell in the uttermost   *Ps 139:9*
parts *of the* s.
against them, like the roaring   *Isa 5:30*
of the s.
afterwards afflict her by the   *Isa 9:1*
way *of the* s.
tho Israel be as sand *of the*   *Isa 10:22;*
s. yet a remnant shall return   *Ho 1:10;*
   Ro 9:27
even the strength *of the* s.   *Isa 23:4*
hath spoken
thy righteousness as the   *Isa 48:18*
waves *of the* s.
that hath made the depths *of*   *Isa 51:10*
the s.
abundance *of the* s. shall be   *Isa 60:5*
converted unto thee
he that brought them up out   *Isa 63:11*
of the s.
placed the sand for the bound   *Jer 5:22*
of the s.
neither the sand *of the* s. be   *Jer 33:22*
measured
the princes *of the* s. shall   *Eze 26:16*
come down
Tyrus, O thou situate at the   *Eze 27:3*
entry *of the* s.
the ships *of the* s. were in   *Eze 27:9*
thee to occupy
all the pilots *of the* s. shall   *Eze 27:29*
come down
the fishes *of the* s. shall   *Eze 38:20*
shake at my presence
the fishes *of the* s. shall be   *Ho 4:3*
taken away

that calleth for the waters *of*   *Am 5:8;*
the s.   *9:6*
hid from my sight in the   *Am 9:3*
bottom *of the s.*
thou wilt cast their sins into   *Mic 7:19*
depths *of s.*
and makest men as the fishes   *Hab 1:14*
of the s.
I will consume the fishes *of*   *Zep 1:3*
the s.
by the way *of the s.* beyond   *M't 4:15*
Jordan
better he were drowned in the   *M't 18:6*
depth *of the s.*
he that wavereth is like a wave   *Jas 1:6*
of the s.
raging waves *of the s.* foaming   *Jude 13*
out their
the third part *of the s.* became   *Re 8:8*
blood
woe to the inhabiters of earth   *Re 12:12*
and *of the s.*
I stood and saw a beast rise   *Re 13:1*
up out *of the s.*
the number of whom is as the   *Re 20:8*
sand *of the s.*

ON, UPON THE SEA

of them that are afar off *upon*   *Ps 65:5*
the s.
fainthearted, there is sorrow   *Jer 49:23*
on the s.
walking *on s.*   *M't 14:25;*
walking *on the s.*   *M't 14:25;*
    M'k 6:48; Joh 6:19
disciples saw him walking *on*   *M't 4:26;*
the s.   *M'k 6:49*
that the wind should not blow   *Re 7:1*
on the s.
and he set his right foot *upon*   *Re 10:2*
the s.
the angel which I saw stand   *Re 10:5;*
upon the s.   *10:8*
and I saw them stand *on the s.*   *Re 15:2*
of glass
the second angel poured out   *Re 16:3*
his vial *upon the s.*

SEACOAST

s. belong to Judah (A)(R)   *Zep 2:7*

SEACOASTS

upon the *s.* (S)   *Es 10:1*

SEAFARING

that was inhabited of   *Eze 26:17*
s. men
who live by *s.* (A)   *Re 18:17*

SEA-MONSTER

heads of the *s.* (E)   *Ps 74:13*
sea-monster (S)   *Isa 27:1; 51:9*

SEA-MONSTERS

even the *s.* draw out   *La 4:3*
the breast

SEAL

as a *s.* is engraved (B)   *Ex 28:11;*
   28:21, 36; 29:14, 20
name, and sealed them with   *1Ki 21:8*
his *s.*
Levites, and priests, *s.* unto it   *Ne 9:38*
set their *s.* (S)   *Ne 10:1*
name, and *s.* it with the king's   *Es 8:8*
ring
It is turned as clay to the *s.*   *Job 38:14*
shut up together as with a   *Job 41:15*
close *s.*
Set me as a *s.* upon thine heart   *Ca 8:6*
as a *s.* upon thine arm: for love   *Ca 8:6*
s. the law among my disciples   *Isa 8:16*
subscribe evidences, and *s.*   *Jer 32:44*
them
to *s.* up the vision and   *Da 9:24*
prophecy
confirm the prophetic vision   *Da 9:24*
(B)
shut up the words, and *s.* the   *Da 12:4*
book
hath set to his *s.* that God is   *Joh 3:33*
true
certifies that God is true (B)   *Joh 3:33*

attest that God is true (N)   *Joh 3:33*
acknowledging that God is   *Joh 3:33*
true (P)
s. of the righteousness of the   *Ro 4:11*
faith
righteousness might be   *Ro 4:11*
accredited (B)
the hall-mark of righteousness   *Ro 4:11*
(N)
s. of mine apostleship are ye   *1Co 9:2*
in the
my certificate of apostleship   *1Co 9:2*
(B)
proof of God's call to me (P)   *1Co 9:2*
of God standeth sure, having   *2Ti 2:19*
this *s.*
stands firm with this   *2Ti 2:19*
inscription (N)
with this double inscription   *2Ti 2:19*
(P)
when he had opened the second   *Re 6:3*
s.
when he had opened the third *s.*   *Re 6:5*
when he had opened the fourth   *Re 6:7*
s.
And when he had opened the   *Re 6:9*
fifth *s.*
when he had opened the sixth   *Re 6:12*
s.
east, having the *s.* of the   *Re 7:2*
living God
when he had opened the   *Re 8:1*
seventh *s.*
not the *s.* of God in their   *Re 9:4*
foreheads
s. up those things which the   *Re 10:4*
seven
shut him up, and set a *s.* upon   *Re 20:3*
him
s. not the sayings of the   *Re 22:10*
prophecy

SEALED

and *s.* up among my   *De 32:34*
treasures
name, and *s.* them with his   *1Ki 21:8*
seal
Now those that *s.* were,   *Ne 10:1*
Nehemiah
written, and *s.* with the king's   *Es 3:12*
ring
name, and *s.* with the king's   *Es 8:8*
ring
s. it with the king's ring, and   *Es 8:10*
sent
My transgression is *s.* up in   *Job 14:17*
a bag
s. up in a sack (B)   *Job 14:17*
a spring shut up, a fountain *s.*   *Ca 4:12*
as the words of a book that   *Isa 29:11*
is *s.*
and he saith, I cannot; for it   *Isa 29:11*
is *s.*
subscribed the evidence, and   *Jer 32:10*
s. it
which was *s.* according to   *Jer 32:11*
the law
both which is *s.*, and this   *Jer 32:14*
evidence
the king *s.* it with his own   *Da 6:17*
signet
up and *s.* till the time of the   *Da 12:9*
end
for him hath God the Father   *Joh 6:27*
s.
this, and have *s.* to them this   *Ro 15:28*
fruit
Who hath also *s.* us, and   *2Co 1:22*
given the
s. with that holy Spirit of   *Eph 1:13*
promise
marked with promised Holy   *Eph 1:13*
Spirit (B)
stamped with promised Holy   *Eph 1:13*
Spirit (P)
are *s.* unto the day of   *Eph 4:30*
redemption
marked against day of   *Eph 4:30*
redemption (B)
marked for day of final   *Eph 4:30*
liberation (N)
personal pledge of eventual   *Eph 4:30*
full redemption (P)
the backside, *s.* with seven seals   *Re 5:1*
we have *s.* the servants of our   *Re 7:3*
God
the number of them which were   *Re 7:4*
s.

there were *s.* an hundred and   *Re 7:4*
forty
of Juda were *s.* twelve thousand   *Re 7:5*
Reuben were *s.* twelve thousand   *Re 7:5*
of Gad were *s.* twelve thousand   *Re 7:5*
of Aser were *s.* twelve thousand   *Re 7:6*
Nepthalim were *s.* twelve   *Re 7:6*
thousand
Manasses were *s.* twelve   *Re 7:6*
thousand
of Simeon were *s.* twelve   *Re 7:7*
thousand
of Levi were *s.* twelve thousand   *Re 7:7*
Issachar were *s.* twelve   *Re 7:7*
thousand
Zabulon were *s.* twelve   *Re 7:8*
thousand
Joseph were *s.* twelve thousand   *Re 7:8*
Benjamin were *s.* twelve   *Re 7:8*
thousand

SEALEST

Thou *s.* up the sum, full of   *Eze 28:12*
full measure and pattern of   *Eze 28:12*
exactness (A)
You complete the sum (B)   *Eze 28:12*
you were the signet of   *Eze 28:12*
perfection (R)

SEALETH

riseth not; and *s.* up the stars   *Job 9:7*
locks up the stars (B)   *Job 9:7*
of men, and *s.* their   *Job 33:16*
instruction
affirms the warnings directed   *Job 33:16*
to them (B)
terrifies them with warnings   *Job 33:16*
(R)
He *s.* up the hand of every   *Job 37:7*
man

SEALING

s. the stone, and setting a   *M't 27:66*
watch

SEALS

the backside, sealed with seven   *Re 5:1*
s.
book, and to loose the *s.*   *Re 5:2*
thereof
and to loose the seven *s.* thereof   *Re 5:5*
the book, and to open the *s.*   *Re 5:9*
thereof
when the Lamb opened one of   *Re 6:1*
the *s.*

SEAM

now the coat was without *s.*,   *Joh 19:23*
woven

SEAMAN

s. had knowledge of the sea   *1Ki 9:27*
(S)

SEANCE

tried a medium's *s.* (B)   *1Ch 10:13*

SEARCH

He shall not *s.* whether it be   *Le 27:33*
good
to *s.* out a resting place for   *Nu 10:33*
them
men, that they may *s.* the land   *Nu 13:2*
of
through which we have gone   *Nu 13:32*
to *s.*
which we passed through to *s.*   *Nu 14:7*
it
which Moses sent to *s.* the   *Nu 14:36*
land
the men that went to *s.* the   *Nu 14:38*
land
and they shall *s.* us out the   *De 1:22*
land
to *s.* you out a place to pitch   *De 1:33*
your
shalt thou enquire, and make   *De 13:14*
s.
of Israel to *s.* out the country   *Jos 2:2*
be come to *s.* out all the country   *Jos 2:3*
to spy out the land, and to *s.*   *J'g 18:2*
it

said unto them, Go, *s.* the land | J'g 18:2
that I will *s.* him out throughout | 1Sa 23:23
to *s.* the city, and to spy it out | 2Sa 10:3
and they shall *s.* thine house | 1Ki 20:6
S. and look that there be here | 2Ki 10:23
servants come unto thee for to *s.* | 1Ch 19:3
s. may be made in the book of the | Ezr 4:15
and *s.* hath been made, and it is | Ezr 4:19
be *s.* made in the king's treasure | Ezr 5:17
s. was made in the house of the | Ezr 6:1
thyself to me *s.* of their fathers | Job 8:8
Is it good that he should *s.* you | Job 13:9
walked in the *s.* of the depth | Job 38:16
Shall not God *s.* this out? for he | Ps 44:21
They *s.* out iniquities; they | Ps 64:6
they accomplish a diligent *s.* | Ps 64:6
and my spirit made diligent *s.* | Ps 77:6
sift and *s.* out my path (A) | Ps 139:3
S. me, and know my heart | Ps 139:23
of kings is to *s.* out a matter | Pr 25:2
to *s.* their own glory is not glory | Pr 25:27
to seek and *s.* out by wisdom | Ec 1:13
and to *s.* and to seek out wisdom | Ec 7:25
I have not found it by secret *s.* | Jer 2:34
I the Lord *s.* the heart, I try | Jer 17:10
shall *s.* for me with all your heart | Jer 29:13
Let us *s.* and try our ways | La 3:40
none did *s.* or seek after them | Eze 34:6
did my shepherds *s.* for my flock | Eze 34:8
I. will both *s.* my sheep, and seek | Eze 34:11
end of seven months shall they *s.* | Eze 39:14
will *s.* and take them out thence | Am 9:3
I will *s.* Jerusalem with candles | Zep 1:12
s. diligently for the young child | M't 2:8
S. the scriptures; for in them ye | Joh 5:39
S. and look: for out of Galilee | Joh 7:52

SEARCHED

Laban *s.* all the tent, but found | Ge 31:34
he *s.* but found not the images | Ge 31:35
whereas thou hast *s.* all my stuff | Ge 31:37
he *s.* and began at the eldest | Ge 44:12
s. the land from the wilderness | Nu 13:21
of the land which they had *s.* unto | Nu 13:32
were of them that *s.* the land, rent | Nu 14:6
of the days in which ye *s.* the land | Nu 14:34
the valley of Eshcol, and *s.* it out | De 1:24
Lo this, we have *s.* it, so it is | Job 5:27
it; he prepared it, yea, and *s.* it out | Job 28:27
the cause which I knew not I *s.* out | Job 29:16
whilst ye *s.* out what to say | Job 32:11
the number of his years be *s.* out | Job 36:26
O Lord, thou hast *s.* me, and | Ps 139:1
the foundations of the earth *s.* out | Jer 31:37
through it cannot be *s.*; because | Jer 46:23
I had *s.* for them (S) | Eze 20:6
How are the things of Esau *s.* out | Ob 6
s. the scriptures daily, whether | Ac 17:11
have enquired and *s.* diligently | 1Pe 1:10

SEARCHEST

mine iniquity, and *s.* after my sin | Job 10:6
s. out my path (E)(R) | Ps 139:3
and *s.* for her as for hid treasures | Pr 2:4

SEARCHETH

for the Lord *s.* all hearts | 1Ch 28:9
and *s.* out all perfection: the | Job 28:3
and he *s.* after every green thing | Job 39:8
his neighbour cometh and *s.* him | Pr 18:17
hath understanding *s.* him out | Pr 28:11
And he that *s.* the hearts knoweth | Ro 8:27
for the Spirit *s.* all things, yea, the | 1Co 2:10
he which *s.* the reins and hearts | Re 2:23

SEARCHING

they returned from *s.* of the land | Nu 13:25
Canst thou by *s.* find out God | Job 11:7
s. all the inward parts of the belly | Pr 20:27
s. all innermost parts (A)(E)(R) | Pr 20:27
is no *s.* of his understanding | Isa 40:28
s. with great anxiety (N) | Lu 2:48
S. what, or what manner of time | 1Pe 1:11

SEARCHINGS

there were great *s.* of heart | J'g 5:16

SEARED

conscience *s.* with a hot iron | 1Ti 4:2
branded in their own consciences (E) | 1Ti 4:2
conscience branded with the devil's sign (N) | 1Ti 4:2
consciences dead as seared flesh (P) | 1Ti 4:2

SEAS

of the waters called the *S.*: and | Ge 1:10
and fill the waters in the *s.* | Ge 1:22
and scales in the waters, in the *s.* | Le 11:9
have not fins and scales in the *s.* | Le 11:10
suck of the abundance of the *s.* | De 33:19
the *s.* and all that is therein | Ne 9:6
passeth through the paths of the *s.* | Ps 8:8
For he hath founded it upon the *s.* | Ps 24:2
Which stilleth the noise of the *s.* | Ps 65:7
the *s.* and every thing that moveth | Ps 69:34
earth, in the *s.* and all deep places | Ps 135:6
a noise like the niose of the *s.* | Isa 17:12
to me above the sand of the *s.* | Jer 15:8
borders are in the midst of the *s.* | Eze 27:4
very glorious in the midst of the *s.* | Eze 27:25
broken thee in the midst of the *s.* | Eze 27:26
shall fall into the midst of the *s.* in | Eze 27:27
thy wares went forth out of the *s.* | Eze 27:33
thou shalt be broken by the *s.* in | Eze 27:34
seat of God, in the midst of the *s.* | Eze 28:2
that are slain in the midst of the *s.* | Eze 28:8
and thou art as a whale in the *s.* | Eze 32:2
of his palace between the *s.* in | Da 11:45
the deep, in the midst of the *s.* | Jon 2:3
into a place where two *s.* met | Ac 27:41

SEASON

and they continued a *s.* in ward | Ge 40:4
continued in custody for some time (A)(R) | Ge 40:4
remained in custody for quite a period (B) | Ge 40:4
keep this ordinance in his *s.* from | Ex 13:10
time (A)(B)(R) | Ex 13:10;
 | Nu 9:2-3, 7, 13; 28:2; Jos 24:7;
 | 2Ch 15:3
offering shalt thou *s.* with salt | Le 2:13
I will give you rain in due *s.* | Le 26:4
the passover at his appointed *s.* | Nu 9:2
ye shall keep it in his appointed *s.* | Nu 9:3
of the Lord in his appointed *s.* | Nu 9:7;
 | 9:13
to offer unto me in their due *s.* | Nu 28:2
the rain of your land in his due *s.* | De 11:14
the *s.* that thou camest forth out | De 16:6
the time of your exodus from Egypt (B)(R) | De 16:6
the rain unto thy land in his *s.* | De 28:12
dwelt in the wilderness a long *s.* | Jos 24:7
About this *s.* according to the | 2Ki 4:16
bare a son at that *s.* that Elisha had | 2Ki 4:17
offering, were at that *s.* in | 1Ch 21:29
a long *s.* Israel hath been without | 2Ch 15:3
shock of corn cometh in in his *s.* | Job 5:26
are pierced in me in the night *s.* | Job 30:17
bring forth Mazzaroth in his *s.* | Job 38:32
bringeth forth his fruit in his *s.* | Ps 1:3
in the night *s.* and am not silent | Ps 22:2
give them their meat in due *s.* | Ps 104:27
furnish their timely feed (B) | Ps 104:27
givest them their meat in due *s.* | Ps 145:15
food in their proper time (B) | Ps 145:15
a word spoken in due *s.* how good | Pr 15:23
word spoken at the right moment (A) | Pr 15:23
good is a word at the right time (B) | Pr 15:23
To every thing there is a *s.* and | Ec 3:1
and thy princes eat in due *s.* | Ec 10:17
feast to the proper time (A)(R) | Ec 10:17
know how to speak a word in *s.* to | Isa 50:4
how to speak a timely word (B) | Isa 50:4
know how to sustain with words (E)(R) | Isa 50:4
the former and the latter, in his *s.* | Jer 5:24
not be day and night in their *s.* | Jer 33:20
the shower to come down in his *s.* | Eze 34:26
their lives were prolonged for a *s.* | Da 7:12
and my wine in the *s.* thereof | Ho 2:9
to give them meat in due *s.* | M't 24:45
supplies at the proper time (A)(N)(P)(R) | M't 24:45
provide their sustenance on time (B) | M't 24:45
saltness, wherewith will ye *s.* it | M'k 9:50
the *s.* he sent to the husbandmen | M'k 12:2
which shall be fulfilled in their *s.* | Lu 1:20
fulfilled in appointed and proper time (A) | Lu 1:20
shall come true at the proper time (B)(N)(P) | Lu 1:20
fulfilled in their time (R) | Lu 1:20
he departed from him for a *s.* | Lu 4:13
another more opportune and favorable time (A) | Lu 4:13
left him for a time (B) | Lu 4:13

devil departed, biding his time *Lu 4:13* (N)
withdrew until his next *Lu 4:13* opportunity (P)
departed until an opportune *Lu 4:13* time (R)
them their portion of meat in *Lu 12:42* due *s.*
allowance of food at the *Lu 12:42* appointed time (A)
food allowance at the proper *Lu 12:42* time (B)(N)(P)(R)
were present at that *s.* some *Lu 13:1*
Just at that time (A)(N)(R) *Lu 13:1*
Just at this moment (P) *Lu 13:1*
at the *s.* he sent a servant to *Lu 20:10*
he was desirous to see him of *Lu 23:8* a long *s.*
for a long time *Lu 23:8* (A)(B)(E)(P)
had long been wanting to see *Lu 23:8* him (N)
had long desired to see him *Lu 23:8* (R)
down at a certain *s.* into the *Joh 5:4* pool
at intervals an angel descended *Joh 5:4* (B)
ye were willing for a *s.* to *Joh 5:35* rejoice
blind, not seeing the sun for *Ac 13:11* a *s.*
he himself stayed in Asia for *Ac 19:22* a *s.*
stayed in Asia for a while *Ac 19:22* (A)(B)(E)(P)(R)
stayed some time longer (N) *Ac 19:22*
when I have a convenient *s.* I *Ac 24:25* will
sorry, though it were but for *2Co 7:8* a *s.*
only for a little while (A)(R) *2Co 7:8*
only for a time (N) *2Co 7:8*
for in due *s.* we shall reap, if *Ga 6:9* we
at its proper time (B) *Ga 6:9*
shall in due time reap (N) *Ga 6:9*
Preach when it is and is not *2Ti 4:2* in *s.*
preach whether the *2Ti 4:2* opportunity seems favorable or unfavorable, convenient or inconvenient, welcome or unwelcome (A)
preach when it is and is not *2Ti 4:2* convenient (B)
be instant out of *s.*; reprove *2Ti 4:2* he therefore departed for a *s.* *Ph'm 15* that
enjoy the pleasures of sin *Heb 11:25* for a *s.*
the fleeting enjoyment of a *Heb 11:25* sinful life (A)(R)
enjoying the short-lived *Heb 11:25* pleasures (B)
enjoy the transient pleasures *Heb 11:25* of sin (N)
rejoice, though now for a *s.* if *1Pe 1:6*
though now for a little while *1Pe 1:6* (A)(B)(E)(N)(R)
they should rest yet for a little *Re 6:11* *s.*
a little while longer *Re 6:11* (A)(B)(N)(P)(R)
for a little time (E) *Re 6:11*
that he must be loosed a little *Re 20:3* *s.*
for a short time (A)(E) *Re 20:3*
for a little while (B)(P)(R) *Re 20:3*
for a short while (N) *Re 20:3*

SEASONED

his savour, wherewith shall it *Lu 14:34* be *s.*
be alway with grace, *s.* with *Col 4:6* salt

SEASONS

let them be for signs, and for *Ge 1:14* *s.*
them judge the people at all *Ex 18:22* *s.*
judge the people at all times *Ex 18:22;* (A)(R) *18:26*
regularly administer justice *Ex 18:22* (B)
they judged the people at all *Ex 18:26* *s.*

which ye shall proclaim in *Le 23:4* their *s.*
at their appointed times (B) *Le 23:4*
reins also instruct me in the *Ps 16:7* night *s.*
He appointed the moon for *Ps 104:19* *s.*
the appointed *s.* (R) *Eze 46:11*
he changeth the times and the *Da 2:21* *s.*
render him the fruits in their *M't 21:41* *s.*
for you to know the times or *Ac 1:7* the *s.*
not for you to know dates or *Ac 1:7* times (N)(P)
us rain from heaven, and *Ac 14:17* fruitful *s.*
I have been with you at all *s.* *Ac 20:18*
of the times and the *s.* *1Th 5:1* brethren
Relative to periods and dates *1Th 5:1* (B)
About dates and times (N) *1Th 5:1*

SEAT

shalt make a mercy *s.* of pure *Ex 25:17* gold
in the two ends of the mercy *Ex 25:18* *s.*
even of the mercy *s.* shall ye *Ex 25:19* make the
the mercy *s.* with their wings *Ex 25:20*
toward the mercy *s.* shall the *Ex 25:20* faces
put the mercy *s.* above upon *Ex 25:21* the ark
with thee from above the *Ex 25:22* mercy *s.*
put the mercy *s.* upon the *Ex 26:34* ark of the
before the mercy *s.* that is *Ex 30:6* over the
and the mercy *s.* that is *Ex 31:7* thereupon
staves thereof, with the *Ex 35:12* mercy *s.*
he made the mercy *s.* of pure *Ex 37:6* gold
on the two ends of the mercy *Ex 37:7* *s.*
out of the mercy *s.* made he *Eze 37:8*
with their wings over the *Ex 37:9* mercy *s.*
toward the mercy *s.* (S) *Ex 37:9*
the staves thereof, and the *Ex 39:35* mercy *s.*
and put the mercy *s.* above *Ex 40:20* upon the
within the veil before the *Le 16:2* mercy *s.*
in the cloud upon the mercy *s.* *Le 16:2*
the incense may cover the *Le 16:13* mercy *s.*
finger upon the mercy *s.* *Le 16:14* eastward
and before the mercy *s.* shall *Le 16:14* he
and sprinkle it upon the *Le 16:15* mercy *s.*
and before the mercy *s.* *Le 16:15*
unto him from off the mercy *Nu 7:89* *s.* that
thee. And he arose out of his *J'g 3:20* *s.*
Eli the priest sat upon a *s.* by *1Sa 1:9* a post
lo, Eli sat upon a *s.* by *1Sa 4:13* the wayside
he fell from off the *s.* *1Sa 4:18* backward by
because thy *s.* will be empty *1Sa 20:18*
And the king sat upon his *s.* *1Sa 20:25* as at
times, even upon a *s.* by the *1Sa 20:25* wall
The Tachmonite that sat in *2Sa 23:8* *s.*
s. to be set for the king's *1Ki 2:19* mother
either side on the place of *1Ki 10:19* the *s.*
and of the place of the *1Ch 28:11* mercy *s.*
and set his *s.* above all the *Es 3:1* princes
that I might come even to his *Job 23:3* *s.*
I prepared my *s.* in the street *Job 29:7*

nor sitteth in the *s.* of the *Ps 1:1* scornful
on a *s.* in the high places of the *Pr 9:14*
the *s.* of the image of jealousy *Eze 8:3*
I am a God, I sit in the *s.* of *Eze 28:2* God
cause the *s.* of violence to *Am 6:3* come
set his *s.* on high (B) *Hab 2:9*
and the Pharisees sit in *M't 23:2* Moses'
he was set down on the *M't 27:19* judgment *s.*
the chief *s.* (S) *Lu 14:8*
and sat down in the judgment *Joh 19:13* *s.* in a
and brought him to the *Ac 18:12* judgment *s.*
he drave them from the *Ac 18:16* judgment *s.*
and beat him before the *Ac 18:17* judgment *s.*
next day sitting on the *Ac 25:6* judgment *s.*
Paul, I stand at Cæsar's *Ac 25:10* judgment *s.*
the morrow I sat on the *Ac 25:17* judgment *s.*
before the judgment *s.* of *Ro 14:10;* Christ *2Co 5:10*
dwellest, even where Satan's *s.* *Re 2:13* is
and his *s.* and great authority *Re 13:2*
out his vial upon the *s.* of *Re 16:10* the beast

SEATED

portion of the lawgiver, was *De 33:21* he *s.*
am *s.* on the throne (S) *2Ch 6:10*
when he was *s.* (S) *M't 5:1*
seated (S) *M't 27:19;* *Lu 22:55; Joh 13:12*
who is *s.* on the right hand of *Heb 8:1* God (S)
him that is *s.* (S) *Re 4:9; 4:10*

SEATS

and the *s.* of them that sold *M't 21:12* doves
and the chief *s.* in the *M't 23:6* synagogues
s. of honor (B) *M't 23:6*
and the *s.* of them that sold *M'k 11:15* doves
the chief *s.* in the *M'k 12:39* synagogues, and
put down the mighty from *Lu 1:52* their *s.*
uppermost *s.* in the *Lu 11:43* synagogues
the highest *s.* in the *Lu 20:46* synagogues
draw you before the judgment *Jas 2:6* *s.*
throne were four and twenty *s.* *Re 4:4*
upon the *s.* I saw four and *Re 4:4* twenty
which sat before God on *Re 11:16* their *s.*

SEATWARD

to the mercy *s.* were the faces *Ex 37:9* of the

SEBA

S. and Havilah, and Sabtah *Ge 10:7*
S. and Havilah, and *1Ch 1:9* Sabta, and
of Sheba and *S.* shall offer *Ps 72:10* gifts
ransom, Ethiopia and *S.* for *Isa 43:3* thee

SEBAT

month, which is the month *S.* *Zec 1:7*

SECACAH

Beth-arabah, Middin, and *S.* *Jos 15:61*

SECLUSION

works in *s.* (N) *Joh 7:4*

SECOND

with s. and third stories make   Ge 6:16
the ark
and so commanded he the s.   Ge 32:19
and third
he made him to ride in the   Ge 41:43
s. chariot
the coupling of the s.   Ex 26:4;
       26:5, 10; 36:11-12, 17
the s. row shall be an   Ex 28:18;
emerald   39:11
he shall offer the s. for a burnt   Le 5:10
offering
they shall set forth in the s.   Nu 2:16
rank
the s. lot came forth to   Jos 19:1
Simeon
the s. bullock of seven years   J'g 6:25
old
take s. bullock, and offer; the   J'g 6:26;
s. was offered   6:28
then he sent out a s. on   2Ki 9:19
horseback
with them brethren of the s.   1Ch 15:18
degree
his servants put him in the   2Ch 35:24
s. chariot
silver basons of a s. sort 410,   Ezr 1:10
vessels
to confirm this s. letter of   Es 9:29
Purim
there is one alone, there is not   Ec 4:8
a s.
with the s. child that shall   Ec 4:15
stand up in his stead
the s. face was the face of a   Eze 10:14
man
behold, another beast, a s. like   Da 7:5
to a bear
noise of a cry, an howling   Zep 1:10
from the s.
in the s. chariot were black   Zec 6:2
horses
he came to the s. and said   M't 21:30
likewise
likewise, the s. had her, and   M't 22:26;
the   M'k 12:21; Lu 20:30
s. commandment is like   M't 22:39;
unto it   M'k 12:31
and it came to pass on the s.   Lu 6:1
sabbath
if he shall come in s. watch   Lu 12:38
or the third
the s. came saying, Lord   Lu 19:18
thy pound gained
this is the s. miracle that   Joh 4:54
Jesus did
when they were past the s.   Ac 12:10
ward
as it is written in s. psalm,   Ac 13:33
Thou art my son
first apostles, s. prophets   1Co 12:28
(S)
the s. man is the Lord from   1Co 15:47
heaven
that ye might have a s.   2Co 1:15
benefit
after the first and s.   Tit 3:10
admonition, reject
no place should have been   Heb 8:7
sought for s.
and after the s. veil, the   Heb 9:3
tabernacle
into the s. went the high priest   Heb 9:7
once a year
taketh away first, that   Heb 10:9
he may establish s.
this s. epistle I now write unto   2Pe 3:1
you
shall not be hurt of the s.   Re 2:11;
death   20:6
the s. beast like a calf, the   Re 4:7
third had a face
I heard the s. beast say,   Re 6:3
Come and see
s. angel sounded, and as it were   Re 8:8
a mountain
the s. woe is past, the third   Re 11:14
woe cometh
the s. angel poured out his   Re 16:3
vial on the sea
death and hell, this is the s.   Re 20:14;
death   21:8
the s. foundation of the wall   Re 21:19
was sapphire

SECOND TIME

the angel called to Abraham   Ge 22:15
the s. time

Pharaoh slept, and dreamed   Ge 41:5
the s. time
surely now we had returned   Ge 43:10
this s. time
then it shall be washed the s.   Le 13:58
time
when you blow an alarm the s.   Nu 10:6
time
and circumcise Israel the s.   Jos 5:2
time
I will not smite him the   1Sa 26:8
s. time
Absalom sent to Joab the s.   2Sa 14:29
time
the Lord appeared to Solomon   1Ki 9:2
the s. time
do it the s. time, they did it   1Ki 18:34
the s. time
the angel came again to   1Ki 19:7
Elijah the s. time
Jehu wrote a letter the s. time   2Ki 10:6
they made Solomon king the   1Ch 29:22
s. time
when virgins were gathered   Es 2:19
the s. time
Lord set his hand the s. time   Isa 11:11
to recover
word of Lord came to me the   Jer 1:13;
s. time saying   13:3; 33:1
the word came to Jonah the s.   Jon 3:1
time
affliction shall not rise up the s.   Na 1:9
time
he went again the s. time   M't 26:42
and prayed
and the s. time the cock   M'k 14:72
crew
can he enter the s. time   Joh 3:4
into the womb
Jesus saith to Peter the s.   Joh 21:16
time, Simon
at the s. time Joseph was   Ac 7:13
made known
the voice spake to Peter again   Ac 10:15
the s time
as if I were present the   2Co 13:2
s. time
he shall appear the s. time   Heb 9:28
without sin

SECOND YEAR

they came the s. year to   Ge 47:18
Joseph, and said
in the s. year, the first day of   Ex 40:17
the month
in the s. year after they were   Nu 1:1
come
in first month of s. year, the   Nu 9:1
Lord spake to Moses
in the s. year the cloud was   Nu 10:11
taken up
this a sign, ye shall eat in   2Ki 19:29;
the s. year   Isa 37:30
Ammon paid Jotham the   2Ch 27:5
s. year
in the s. year of their coming   Ezr 3:8
to Jerusalem
it ceased the s. year of Darius   Ezr 4:24
king of Persia
in the s. year of reign of   Da 2:1
Nebuchadnezzar
in s. year of Darius   Hag 1:1;
       1:15; 2:10; Zec 1:7

SECONDARILY

God set s. prophets, thirdly   1Co 12:28
teachers

SECRET

soul, come not thou into their   Ge 49:6
s.
do not share in their plot (B)   Ge 49:6
come not into their council   Ge 49:6
(E)(R)
and be kept s. (S)   Nu 5:13
and putteth it in a s. place   De 27:15
s. things belong unto the Lord   De 29:29
I have a s. errand unto thee   J'g 3:19
after my name, seeing it is s.   J'g 13:18
ask my name, seeing it is   J'g 13:18
wonderful (A)(B)(E)(R)
had emerods in their s. parts   1Sa 5:9
and abide in a s. place, and   1Sa 19:2
hide
that thou wouldest keep me   Job 14:13
s.
conceal me until your wrath   Job 14:13
is past (A)(B)(R)

Hast thou heard the s. of   Job 15:8
God
Did you listen to the council   Job 15:8
of God (B)(R)
is there any s. thing with   Job 15:11
thee
darkness be hid in his s.   Job 20:26
places
s. of God was upon my   Job 29:4
tabernacle
friendship and counsel of   Job 29:4
God (A)
friendship of God lingered in   Job 29:4
my tent (B)(E)(R)
and bind their faces in s.   Job 40:13
in the s. places doth he murder   Ps 10:8
in hiding places he murders   Ps 10:8
(A)(B)(R)
a young lion lurking in s.   Ps 17:12
places
lion lurking in hidden places   Ps 17:12
(A)
lion waiting in ambush   Ps 17:12
(B)(R)
He made darkness his s. place   Ps 18:11
He made darkness his   Ps 18:11
covering (B)(R)
He made darkness his   Ps 18:11
hiding-place (E)
cleanse thou me from s. faults   Ps 19:12
Clear me of hidden,   Ps 19:12
unconscious faults (A)
Clear me from hidden faults   Ps 19:12
(E)(R)
the s. of the Lord is with   Ps 25:14
them
companionship of the Lord is   Ps 25:14
with (B)
friendship of Jehovah is with   Ps 25:14
them (E)
in the s. of his tabernacle shall   Ps 27:5
he
hide them in the s. of thy   Ps 31:20
presence
In the shelter of his presence   Ps 31:20
(B)
In the covert of his presence   Ps 31:20
(E)(R)
Hide me from the s. counsel of   Ps 64:2
from s. counsel of evil-doers   Ps 64:2
(E)
from s. plots of wicked (R)   Ps 64:2
may shoot in s. at the perfect   Ps 64:4
shoot from ambush   Ps 64:4
(A)(B)(R)
thee in the s. place of thunder   Ps 81:7
in the hiding place of thunder   Ps 81:7
(B)
thee, our s. sins in the light of   Ps 90:8
thy
dwelleth in the s. place of the   Ps 91:1
most
in the shelter of the most High   Ps 91:1
(R)
from thee when I was made   Ps 139:15
in s.
but his s. is with the righteous   Pr 3:32
intimate counsel is with the   Pr 3:32
upright (B)
friendship is with the upright   Pr 3:32
(E)
the upright are his confidence   Pr 3:32
(R)
and bread eaten in s. is   Pr 9:17
pleasant
A gift in s. pacifieth anger   Pr 21:14
and discover not a s. to   Pr 25:9
another
better than love that is hidden   Pr 25:5
(A)(E)(R)
better than love concealed (B)   Pr 25:5
better than love that is hidden   Pr 25:5
judgment, with every s. thing   Ec 12:14
into judgment everything   Ec 12:14
hidden (B)(E)
in the s. places of the stairs, let   Ca 2:14
Lord will discover their s.   Isa 3:17
parts
cause them to be stripped   Isa 3:17
naked (A)
hidden riches of s. places, that   Isa 45:3
I have not spoken in s. in   Isa 45:19
a dark
I have not spoken in s. from   Isa 48:16
I have not found it by s.   Jer 2:34
search
did not find it by   Jer 2:34
house-breaking (A)
did not catch them in act of   Jer 2:34
burglary (B)

did not find them breaking in *Jer 2:34*
(E)(R)
weep in *s.* places for your *Jer 13:17*
pride
Can any hide himself in *s.* *Jer 23:24*
places
I have uncovered his *s.* *Jer 49:10*
places, and
uncovered his hiding places *Jer 49:10*
(A)(R)
disclosed his lurking places *Jer 49:10*
(B)
in wait, and as a lion in *s.* *La 3:10*
places
as a lion in hidden places (B) *La 3:10*
as a lion in hiding (R) *La 3:10*
and they shall pollute my *s.* *Eze 7:22*
place
they shall profane my jewel *Eze 7:22*
(B)
shall profane my precious *Eze 7:22*
place (R)
which entereth into their *Eze 21:14*
s. chambers (S)
is no *s.* that they can hide *Eze 28:3*
from
God of heaven concerning this *Da 2:18*
s.
concerning this mystery *Da 2:18;*
(B)(R) *2:19, 27, 47*
s. revealed unto Daniel in a *Da 2:19*
night
revealeth the deep and *s.* things *Da 2:22*
deep and mysterious things *Da 2:22*
(B)(R)
s. which the king hath *Da 2:27*
demanded
this *s.* is not revealed to me *Da 2:30*
for
seeing thou couldest reveal *Da 2:47*
this *s.*
and no *s.* troubleth me, tell me *Da 4:9*
no mystery is any trouble *Da 4:9*
(B)(R)
revealeth his *s.* unto his servants *Am 3:7*
That thine alms may be in *s.* *M't 6:4*
and thy Father which seeth in *M't 6:4*
s.
pray to thy Father which is in *M't 6:6*
s.
thy Father which seeth in *s.; M't 6:6;*
shall *6:18*
but unto thy Father which is *M't 6:18*
in *s.*
things which have been *M't 13:35*
kept *s.*
hidden since foundation of *M't 13:35*
world (A)(B)(E)(P)(R)
behold, he is in the *s.* *M't 24:26*
chambers
in the inner rooms. *M't 24:26*
chambers (E)(N)(P)(R)
neither was any thing kept *s.* *M'k 4:22*
but
s. of God's kingdom *M'k 4:11*
(B)(N)(P)(R)
For nothing is *s.* that shall not *Lu 8:17*
nothing hid that shall not be *Lu 8:17*
disclosed (A)(E)(R)
nothing hidden that shall not *Lu 8:17*
be disclosed (B)(N)(P)
a candle, putteth it in a *s.* *Lu 11:33*
place
puts it in a cellar or crypt *Lu 11:33*
or bushel (A)
puts it in hiding or grain *Lu 11:33*
measure (B)
putteth it in a cellar or *Lu 11:33*
bushel (E)(R)
puts it in a cellar (N) *Lu 11:33*
puts it in a cupboard or *Lu 11:33*
bucket (P)
no man that doeth any thing *Joh 7:4*
in *s.*
does things not observed (B) *Joh 7:4*
in public eye if he works in *Joh 7:4*
seclusion (N)
not openly, but as it were in *Joh 7:10*
s.
and in *s.* have I said *Joh 18:20*
nothing
I have spoken openly to the *Joh 18:20*
world (A)(B)(E)(N)(P)(R)
ignorant of this *s.* (B) *Ro 11:25*
God's *s.* plan (P) *Ro 11:25; 16:25*
was kept *s.* since the world *Ro 16:25*
began
revealing of the *s.* *Ro 16:25*
(B)(N)(P)

kept in silence through times *Ro 16:25*
eternal (E)
God's hidden wisdom, *s.* *1Co 2:7*
purpose (N)
mysterious *s.* wisdom (P) *1Co 2:7*
a *s.* and hidden wisdom (R) *1Co 2:7*
disclose, expose *s.* aims *1Co 4:5*
(A)(P)
see through every *s.* (B) *1Co 13:2*
uttering *s.* matters (B) *1Co 14:2*
I am telling you a *s.* *1Co 15:51*
(B)(P)
renounced *s.* thoughts (A) *2Co 4:2*
known the *s.* of his purpose *Eph 1:9*
(B)
know the *s.* of his plan (P) *Eph 1:9*
the *s.* made known to me *Eph 3:3*
(B)(N)(P)
I understand the *s.* of Christ *Eph 3:4*
(N)
which are done of them in *s.* *Eph 5:12*
the *s.* of the gospel (P) *Eph 6:19*
that mystic *s.* of God (A) *Col 2:2*
grasp God's *s.* (N)(P) *Col 2:2*
the *s.* power of wickedness *2Th 2:7*
(N)
the mystic *s.* of faith (A) *1Ti 3:9*
s. meaning of seven stars *Re 1:20*
(N)(P)
a name with *s.* meaning *Re 17:5*
(N)(P)

SECRETLY

slip away *s.* (A) *Ge 31:20*
didst thou flee away *s.* and *Ge 31:27*
steal
entice thee *s.* saying, Let us go *De 13:6*
he that smiteth his neighbour *De 27:24*
s.
eat them for want of all *De 28:57*
things *s.*
out of Shittim two men to spy *Jos 2:1*
s.
Commune with David *s.* and *1Sa 18:22*
say
Saul *s.* practised mischief *1Sa 23:9*
against
For thou didst it *s.*: but I *2Sa 12:12*
will do
the children of Israel did *s.* *2Ki 17:9*
those
a thing was *s.* brought to me *Job 4:12*
you, if ye do *s.* accept *Job 13:10*
persons
my heart hath been *s.* *Job 31:27*
enticed, or
secretly (S) *Ps 10:8; 11:2; 31:4; 64:5;*
101:5; 142:3; Pr 1:11, 18; M'k 6:32;
Ga 2:4; 2 Pe 2:1
He lieth in wait *s.* as a lion in *Ps 10:9*
his
shalt keep them *s.* in a *Ps 31:20*
pavilion
king asked him *s.* in his *Jer 37:17*
house
the king sware *s.* unto *Jer 38:16*
Jeremiah
spake to Gedaliah in Mizpah *Jer 40:15*
s.
was as to devour the poor *s.* *Hab 3:14*
wav, and called Mary her *Joh 11:28*
sister *s.*
Jesus, but *s.* for fear of the *Joh 19:38*
Jews
s. smuggled in (A) *Ga 2:4*
admission *s.* gained (R) *Jude 4*

SECRETS

hand, and taketh him by the *De 25:11*
by the private parts *De 25:11*
(A)(B)(R)
shew thee the *s.* of wisdom, *Job 11:6*
that
for he knoweth the *s.* of the *Ps 44:21*
heart
A talebearer revealeth *s.*: but *Pr 11:13*
he
talebearer betrays confidence *Pr 11:13*
(B)
about as a talebearer *Pr 20:19*
a God in heaven that *Da 2:28*
revealeth *s.*
who reveals mysteries (B)(R) *Da 2:28*
and he that revealeth *s.* *Da 2:29*
maketh

lord of kings, and a revealer *Da 2:47*
of *s.*
s. of God (N)(P) *M't 13:11*
arrest Jesus by *s.* and deceit *M'k 14:1*
(A)
God shall judge the *s.* of men *Ro 2:16*
speaking spiritual *s.* (P) *1Co 14:2*
the *s.* of his heart made *1Co 14:25*
manifest

SECT

which is the *s.* of the *Ac 5:17*
Sadducees
party of the Sadducees *Ac 5:17*
(A)(B)(N)(P)(R)
up certain of the *s.* of the *Ac 15:5*
Pharisees
the Pharisee party *Ac 15:5*
(B)(N)(P)(R)
ringleader of the *s.* of the *Ac 24:5*
Nazarenes
ringleader of the Nazarene *Ac 24:5*
heresy (B)
the most straitest *s.* of our *Ac 26:5*
religion
strictest group in our religion *Ac 26:5*
(N)
strictest party of our religion *Ac 26:5*
(R)
for as concerning this *s.* we *Ac 28:22*
know
as far as this heresy is *Ac 28:22*
concerned (B)

SECTION

a *s.* of the field (B) *1Ch 11:13; 11:14*
Obijah *s.* of priesthood (P) *Lu 1:5*

SECTIONS

the rear *s.* (S) *1Ki 7:25; 2Ch 4:4*
organized into *s.* (A) *1Ch 23:6*

SECUNDUS

Aristarchus and *S.*; and Gaius *Ac 20:4*

SECURE

the host: for the host was *s.* *J'g 8:11*
of the Zidonians, quiet and *s.* *J'g 18:7*
ye shall come unto a people *J'g 18:10*
s. and
a people that were at quiet *J'g 18:27*
and *s.*
thou shalt be *s.* because *Job 11:18*
there is
and they that provoke God *Job 12:6*
are *s.*
he that hateth suretiship is *s.* *Pr 11:15*
(S)
will persuade him, and *s.* you *M't 28:14*
much work to *s.* the boat (S) *Ac 27:16*

SECURELY

Jericho was *s.* shut up (S) *Jos 6:1*
we will bind thee *s.* (S) *J'g 15:13;*
16:11
seeing he dwelleth *s.* by thee *Pr 3:29*
thou dwellest *s.* (S) *Isa 47:8; Eze 39:6*
pass by *s.* as men averse from *Mic 2:8*
war

SECURITIES

s. for debts (B)(R) *Pr 7:23; 22:26*

SECURITY

I will be *s.* for him (A) *Ge 43:9*
I became *s.* for him (A) *Ge 44:32*
s. for (A) *Pr 6:1; 11:15; 17:18; 20:16; 27:13*
when they had taken *s.* of *Ac 17:9*
Jason
required bail from Jason (B) *Ac 17:9*
bound over Jason (N) *Ac 17:9*
binding them over (P) *Ac 17:9*
the *s.* deposit and guarantee *2Co 1:22*
of promise (A)
Spirit's *s.* deposit (B) *2Co 1:22*

SEDITION

that they have moved *s.* within *Ezr 4:15*
continually revolted (B) *Ezr 4:15*

rebellion and *s.* have been made   *Eze 4:19*
rebellion and revolution made (B)   *Ezr 4:19*
for a certain *s.* made in the city   *Lu 23:19*
for raising a riot (A)(B)(P)   *Lu 23:19*
for certain insurrection (E)(R)   *Lu 23:19*
for *s.* and murder was cast into   *Lu 23:25*
into prison for riot and murder (A)(B)(P)   *Lu 23:25*
for insurrection and murder (E)(N)(R)   *Lu 23:25*
a mover of *s.* among all the Jews   *Ac 24:5*
an agitator, source of disturbance (A)   *Ac 24:5*
a veritable plague, stirring up (B)   *Ac 24:5*
a mover of insurrection (E)   *Ac 24:5*
a fomenter of discord (N)   *Ac 24:5*
a pestilential disturber of peace (P)   *Ac 24:5*
a pestilent fellow, an agitator (R)   *Ac 24:5*

SEDITIONS

emulations, wrath, strife, *s.*   *Ga 5:20*

SEDUCE

s. neighbor's wife (B)   *Eze 18:6*
to *s.* if it were possible, even   *M'k 13:22*
lead astray (A)(B)(E)(R)   *M'k 13:22*
mislead God's chosen (N)   *M'k 13:22*
to deceive (P)   *M'k 13:22*
you, concerning them that *s.* you   *1Jo 2:26*
those who mislead you (B)(N)   *1Jo 2:26*
that would lead you astray (E)(P)   *1Jo 2:26*
who would deceive you (R)   *1Jo 2:26*
to teach and to *s.* my servants to   *Re 2:20*
teaching and leading astray (A)   *Re 2:20*
teaches my servants deceitfully (B)   *Re 2:20*
by her teaching deceives (P)   *Re 2:20*
teaching and beguiling (R)   *Re 2:20*

SEDUCED

Manasseh *s.* them to do more evil   *2Ki 21:9*
Manasseh misled them (B)   *2Ki 21:9*
they have also *s.* of Egypt, even they   *Isa 19:13*
led Egypt astray (A)(B)(E)(R)   *Isa 19:13*
your knowledge *s.* you (B)   *Isa 47:10*
they have *s.* my people, saying   *Eze 13:10*
in cunning *s.* Eve (N)   *2Co 11:3*
spiritually *s.* by demons (P)   *1Ti 4:1*

SEDUCERS

and *s.* shall wax worse and worse   *2Ti 3:13*
impostors will go from bad to worse (A)(B)(E)(R)   *2Ti 3:13*
charlatans will make progress (N)   *2Ti 3:13*
deceitful men will go from bad to worse (P)   *2Ti 3:13*

SEDUCETH

the way of the wicked *s.* them   *Pr 12:26*
wicked leads them astray (A)(B)(R)   *Pr 12:26*
wicked causeth them to err (E)   *Pr 12:26*

SEDUCING

giving heed to *s.* spirits, and   *1Ti 4:1*
deluding spirits (B)   *1Ti 4:1*
subversive doctrines inspired by devils (N)   *1Ti 4:1*
spiritually seduced by teachings of demons (P)   *1Ti 4:1*
deceitful spirits (R)   *1Ti 4:1*

SEDUCTION

mistress of *s.* (B)   *Na 3:4*

SEE

brought to Adam, to *s.* what he would call   *Ge 2:19*
send a dove to *s.* if the waters were abated   *Ge 8:8*
the Lord came down to *s.* the city   *Ge 11:5*
He said unto him, *S.* I have accepted thee   *Ge 19:21*
s. the smell of my son is as the smell of a field   *Ge 27:27*
he said, I *s.* your father's countenance   *Ge 31:5*
Dinah went out to *s.* the daughters of land   *Ge 34:1*
but to *s.* the nakedness of the land   *Ge 42:9; 42:12*
thou saidst, You shall *s.* my face no more   *Ge 44:23*
your eyes *s.* and the eyes of my brother   *Ge 45:12*
he said, *S.* that ye fall not out by the way   *Ge 45:24*
I will go and *s.* Joseph before I die   *Ge 45:28*
I had not thought to *s.* thy face, and lo   *Ge 48:11*
and when ye *s.* them upon the stools   *Ex 1:16*
to *s.* what would be done (S)   *Ex 2:4*
I will turn aside, and *s.* this great sight   *Ex 3:3; 3:4*
s. whether my brethren be yet alive   *Ex 4:18*
s. that thou do those wonders before Pharaoh   *Ex 4:21*
the officers did *s.* they were in evil case   *Ex 5:19*
now shalt thou *s.* what I will do to Pharaoh   *Ex 6:1*
that one cannot be able to *s.* the earth   *Ex 10:5*
take heed to thyself, *s.* my face no more   *Ex 10:28*
hast spoken well, I will *s.* thy face no more   *Ex 10:29*
when I *s.* the blood, I will pass over you   *Ex 12:13*
lest the people repent when they *s.* war   *Ex 13:17*
stand still and *s.* the salvation of the Lord   *Ex 14:13*
s. for the Lord hath given you the sabbath   *Ex 16:29*
they may *s.* the bread wherewith I fed you   *Ex 16:32*
see (S)   *Ex 25:40; 2Ki 10:23*
for there shall no man *s.* me and live   *Ex 33:20*
thou shalt *s.* my back parts   *Ex 33:23*
people shall *s.* the work of the Lord   *Ex 34:10*
and the priest shall *s.* him   *Le 13:10; 13:17*
if a man shall *s.* her nakedness, and she *s.* his   *Le 20:17*
shall not go in to *s.* holy things covered   *Nu 4:20*
shalt *s.* whether my word come to pass   *Nu 11:23*
s. the land what it is, and people that dwell   *Nu 13:18*
nor shall any that provoked me *s.* it   *Nu 14:23*
that thence he might *s.* the utmost part   *Nu 22:41*
for from the top of the rocks I *s.* him   *Nu 23:9*
whence thou mayest *s.* them, thou shalt *s.* but the utmost part of them   *Nu 23:13*
I shall *s.* him, but not now, I shall behold   *Nu 24:17*
and *s.* the land, which I have given to Israel   *Nu 27:12*
I sent your fathers from Kadesh to *s.* land   *Nu 32:8*
none of the men that came out of Egypt shall *s.* the land   *Nu 32:11; De 1:35*
save Caleb, he shall *s.* land will give   *De 1:36*
I pray thee, let me *s.* the good land   *De 3:25*
cause to inherit the land which thou shalt *s.*   *De 3:28*
that he *s.* no unclean thing in thee   *De 23:14*
all people shall *s.* that thou art called by   *De 28:10*

SEE

sight of thine eyes which thou shalt *s.*   *De 28:34; 28:67*
thou shalt *s.* it no more again, and be sold   *De 28:68*
the Lord hath not given you eyes to *s.*   *De 29:4*
when they *s.* the plagues of that land   *De 29:22*
s. I have set before thee life and good   *De 30:15*
he said, I will *s.* what their end will be   *De 32:20*
s. now, I, even I, am he, there is no God with   *De 32:39*
thou shalt *s.* land before thee, but not go   *De 32:52*
I have caused thee to *s.* it with thine eyes   *De 34:4*
they built there a great altar to *s.* to   *Jos 22:10*
Samson turned aside to *s.* the carcase   *J'g 14:8*
s. wherein his great strength lieth   *J'g 16:5*
shall *s.* an enemy in my habitation   *1Sa 2:32*
they saw the ark, and rejoiced to *s.* it   *1Sa 6:13*
now *s.* this great thing the Lord will do   *1Sa 12:16*
ye may *s.* that your wickedness is great   *1Sa 12:17*
number now, and *s.* who is gone from us   *1Sa 14:17*
and *s.* wherein this sin hath been this day   *1Sa 14:38*
Samuel came no more to *s.* Saul   *1Sa 15:35*
that thou mightest *s.* the battle   *1Sa 17:28*
and what I *s.* that I will tell thee   *1Sa 19:3*
Saul sent messengers again to *s.* David   *1Sa 19:15*
let me get away, I pray, and *s.* my brethren   *1Sa 20:29*
then said Achish, You *s.* the man is mad   *1Sa 21:15*
know and *s.* his place, where his haunt is   *1Sa 23:22*
my father *s.* yea, *s.* the skirt of thy robe   *1Sa 24:11*
s. where king's spear is, and cruse of water   *1Sa 26:16*
when thy father cometh to *s.* thee, let Tamar come, that I may *s.* it and eat   *2Sa 13:5*
now therefore, let me *s.* the king's face   *2Sa 14:32*
s. thy matters are good and right   *2Sa 15:3*
that the eyes of my Lord the king may *s.* it   *2Sa 24:3*
s. what answer I shall return him that sent me   *2Sa 24:13*
s. to thy house, David   *1Ki 12:16; 2Ch 10:16*
and Elijah said, *S.* thy son liveth   *1Ki 17:23*
and *s.* how this man seeketh mischief   *1Ki 20:7*
prophet said, Mark and *s.* what thou dost   *1Ki 20:22*
thou shalt *s.* in that day   *1Ki 22:25; 2Ch 18:24*
if thou *s.* when I am taken from thee   *2Ki 2:10*
s. how he seeketh a quarrel against me   *2Ki 5:7*
Lord, I pray, open his eyes that he may *s.*   *2Ki 6:17*
open the eyes of these men that they may *s.*   *2Ki 6:20*
s. how this son of a murderer hath sent to   *2Ki 6:32*
s. it with thine eyes, but not eat   *2Ki 7:2; 7:19*
let us send and *s.*; saying, Go and *s.*   *2Ki 7:13; 7:14*
went down to *s.* Joram   *2Ki 8:29; 9:16; 2Ch 22:6*
the watchman said, I *s.* a company   *2Ki 9:17*
go *s.* now this cursed woman, and bury her   *2Ki 9:34*
come with me, and *s.* my zeal for the Lord   *2Ki 10:16*
open, Lord, thine eyes, and *s.*   *2Ki 19:16; Isa 37:17*

then, he said, What title is *2Ki 23:17*
that that I s.
he said, I did s. all Israel *2Ch 18:16*
scattered
s. the salvation of the Lord *2Ch 20:17*
with you
go, and s. that ye hasten the *2Ch 24:5*
matter
come, let us s. one another *2Ch 25:17*
in the face
was not meet to s. the king's *Ezr 4:14*
dishonour
didst s. affliction of our fathers *Ne 9:9*
in Egypt
to s. if Mordecai's matters *Es 3:4*
would stand
so long as I s. Mordecai the *Es 5:13*
Jew sitting
how can I endure to s. the *Es 8:6*
evil? to s. the destruction
neither let it s. the dawning of *Job 3:9*
the day
mine eye shall no more s. *Job 7:7*
good; my life wind
the eye that hath seen me shall *Job 7:8*
s. me no more
now my days flee away, they *Job 9:25*
s. no good
therefore s. thou mine *Job 10:15*
affliction
as for my hope, who shall s. *Job 17:15*
it
worms destroy, yet in my *Job 19:26*
flesh shall I s.
whom I shall s. for myself, *Job 19:27*
and not another
the eye which saw him shall *Job 20:9*
s. him no more
his eyes shall s. his *Job 21:20*
destruction, shall drink
the righteous s. it, and are *Job 22:19*
glad
why do they that know him *Job 24:1*
not s. his days
the adulterer saith, No eye *Job 24:15*
shall s. me
then did he s. it, and *Job 28:27*
declare it, he prepared it
doth not he s. my ways, and *Job 31:4*
count my steps
shall pray, and he will s. his *Job 33:26*
face with joy
his soul, and his life shall s. *Job 33:28*
the light
look unto the heavens, and s. *Job 35:5*
the clouds
every man may s. it, man *Job 36:25*
may behold it
he hath said, God will never s. *Ps 10:11*
it
God looked to s. if any did *Ps 14:2;*
understand *53:2*
neither wilt suffer thine Holy *Ps 16:10;*
One to s. corruption *Ac 2:27, 31; 13:35*
all they that s. me laugh me to *Ps 22:7*
scorn
believed to s. the goodness of *Ps 27:13*
the Lord
that did s. me without, fled *Ps 31:11*
from me
O taste and s. that the Lord is *Ps 34:8*
good
loveth many days, that he may *Ps 34:12*
s. good
when wicked are cut off, thou *Ps 37:34*
shalt s. it
many shall s. it and trust in the *Ps 40:3*
Lord
if he come to s. me, he *Ps 41:6*
speaketh vanity
he shall go, they shall never *Ps 49:19*
s. light
the righteous also shall s. and *Ps 52:6*
fear and laugh
God shall let me s. my desire *Ps 59:10;*
92:11; 118:7
to s. thy power and glory, as I *Ps 63:2*
have seen
they commune, they say, Who *Ps 64:5*
shall s. them
all that s. them shall flee away *Ps 64:8*
come and s. the works of God, *Ps 66:5*
he is terrible
the humble shall s. this, and *Ps 69:32*
be glad
that they which hate me may *Ps 86:17*
s. it
thou shalt s. the reward of the *Ps 91:8*
wicked
and all the people s. his glory *Ps 97:6*

that I may s. the good of thy *Ps 106:5*
chosen
these s. the works of the Lord *Ps 107:24*
in the deep
righteous shall s. it and *Ps 107:42*
rejoice
till he s. his desire upon his *Ps 112:8*
enemies
the wicked shall s. it and be *Ps 112:10*
grieved
they will be glad when they *Ps 119:74*
s. me
shalt s. the good of Jerusalem *Ps 128:5*
all days
shalt s. thy children's children *Ps 128:6*
thy eyes did s. my substance *Ps 139:16*
yet unperfect
s. if there be any wicked *Ps 139:24*
way in me
lest the Lord s. and it *Pr 24:18*
displease him
but the righteous shall s. their *Pr 29:16*
fall
whereof it may be said, S. *Ec 1:10*
this is new
till I might s. what was good *Ec 2:3*
for sons
men might s. that themselves *Ec 3:18*
are beasts
bring him to s. what shall be *Ec 3:22*
after him
by it there is profit to them *Ec 7:11*
that s. the sun
to s. the business that is done *Ec 8:16*
upon earth
O my dove, let me s. thy *Ca 2:14*
countenance
garden of nuts to s. the fruits, *Ca 6:11;*
and to s. whether the vine *7:12*
flourished
let him hasten his work, that *Isa 5:19*
we may s.
lest they s. with their eyes, *Isa 6:10*
hear with ears
that s. thee shall narrowly *Isa 14:16*
look on thee
they shall s. and be ashamed *Isa 26:11*
for their envy
eyes of the blind shall s. out *Isa 29:18*
of obscurity
but thine eyes shall s. thy *Isa 30:20*
teachers
the eyes of them that s. shall *Isa 32:3*
not be dim
thine eyes shall s. the king *Isa 33:17*
in his beauty
eyes shall s. Jerusalem a *Isa 33:20*
quiet habitation
shall s. the glory of the Lord *Isa 35:2*
and excellency
glory revealed, and all flesh *Isa 40:5*
shall s. it together
that they may s. and know, *Isa 41:20*
and consider
s. all this; kings shall s. and *Isa 48:6;*
arise *49:7*
for they shall s. eye to eye, *Isa 52:8*
when the Lord
the earth shall s. salvation of *Isa 52:10*
our God
what had not been told them *Isa 52:15*
shall they s.
when we shall s. him, there is *Isa 53:2*
no beauty
s. his seed, he shall prolong *Isa 53:10*
his days
s. of travail of his soul, and *Isa 53:11*
be satisfied
then thou shalt s. and flow *Isa 60:5*
together
all that s. them shall *Isa 61:9*
acknowledge them
the Gentiles shall s. thy *Isa 62:2*
righteousness
s. we beseech, we are all thy *Isa 64:9*
people
and they shall come and s. *Isa 66:18*
my glory
I s. a rod; I s. a seething pot *Jer 1:11;*
1:13
send to Kedar, s. if there be *Jer 2:10*
such a thing
know and s. that it is an evil *Jer 2:19*
thing and bitter
s. thy way in the valley what *Jer 2:23*
thou hast done
and s. where thou hast not *Jer 3:2*
been lien with
how long shall I s. the *Jer 4:21*
standard, and hear

s. now and know, and seek in *Jer 5:1*
the broad places
stand ye in the ways and s. *Jer 6:16*
and ask for paths
go to my place, and s. what I *Jer 7:12*
did to it
let me s. thy vengeance on *Jer 11:20;*
them *20:12*
out of the womb to s. labour *Jer 20:18*
and sorrow
he shall die and s. this land *Jer 22:12*
no more
s. whether a man doth travail *Jer 30:6*
with child I s. every man
and shalt s. and shalt read *Jer 51:61*
all these words
s. O Lord, consider, for I *La 1:11*
become vile
s. if there be any sorrow like *La 1:12*
my sorrow
thou shalt s. greater *Eze 8:6;*
abominations *13:15*
that s. vanity; s. visions of *Eze 13:9,*
peace for her *13:16*
that they may s. all thy *Eze 16:37*
nakedness
all flesh shall s. that I the *Eze 20:48*
Lord have kindled it
whiles they s. vanity unto *Eze 21:29*
thee, and divine
Pharaoh shall s. them, and *Eze 32:31*
shall be comforted
but if the watchman s. the *Eze 33:6*
sword come
all the heathen shall s. my *Eze 39:21*
judgment
why should he s. your faces *Da 1:10*
worse liking
I s. four men loose, walking in *Da 3:25*
the fire
old men dream dreams, your *Joe 2:28;*
young men s. visions *Ac 2:17*
pass ye to Calneh and s. go ye *Am 6:2*
to Hamath
might s. what would become of *Jon 4:5*
the man of wisdom shall s. *Mic 6:9*
thy name
then she that is mine enemy *Mic 7:10*
shall s. it
the nations shall s. and be *Mic 7:16*
confounded
I will watch to s. what he will *Hab 2:1*
say to me
to s. what is the breadth thereof *Zec 2:2*
shall s. the plummet in hand *Zec 4:10*
of Zerubbabel
what seest thou? I answered, I *Zec 5:2*
s. a flying roll
lift up your eyes s. what is this that *Zec 5:5*
goeth forth
Ashkelon shall s. it, and fear, *Zec 9:5*
Gaza shall s. it
yea, their children shall s. it, *Zec 10:7*
and be glad
and your eyes shall s. and ye *Mal 1:5*
shall say
blessed pure in heart, they *M't 5:8*
shall s. God
they may s. your good works, *M't 5:16*
and glorify
s. clearly to cast out the *M't 7:5;*
mote out of thy brother's *Lu 6:42*
eye
s. thou tell no man, shew *M't 8:4;*
thyself to the priest *9:30; M'k 1:44;*
Ac 23:22
tell John those things ye do *M't 11:4*
hear and s.
what went you into *M't 11:7;*
wilderness to s. *11:8-9; Lu 7:24-26*
Master, we would s. a sign *M't 12:38*
from thee
seeing, ye shall s. *M't 13:14;*
M'k 4:12 ;Ac 28:26
heart gross, lest at any time *M't 13:15;*
they should s. with their eyes *Ac 28:27*
but blessed are your eyes, *M't 13:16*
for they s.
many desired to s. those *M't 13:17*
things which ye s.
when they saw the blind to *M't 15:31;*
s. *Lu 7:22*
till they s. the Son of man *M't 16:28*
coming
when the king came in to s. *M't 22:11*
the guests
shall hear of wars, s. that ye *M't 24:6*
be not troubled

they shall *s.* the Son of man *M't* 24:30;
coming   *M'k* 13:26; *Lu* 21:27
Peter sat with servants to *s.* *M't* 26:58
the end
they said, *S.* thou that; *s.* *M't* 27:4;
ye to it   27:24
let us *s.* whether Elias will *M't* 27:49
come to save
come *s.* the place where the *M't* 28:6
Lord lay
they go into Galilee, *M't* 28:10
there shall they *s.* me
they went out to *s.* what was *M'k* 5:14
done
he looked to *s.* her that had *M'k* 5:32
done this thing
go and *s.*; I *s.* men as trees *M'k* 6:38;
walking   8:24
let Christ descend that we *M'k* 15:32
may *s.* and believe
let us go to Bethlehem and *s.* *Lu* 2:15
this
and all flesh shall *s.* the *Lu* 3:6
salvation of God
they who enter in may *s.* light *Lu* 8:16;
              11:33
brethren stand without, *Lu* 8:20
desiring to *s.* thee
who is this? and he desired to *Lu* 9:9;
s. him   23:8
not taste of death till *s.* *Lu* 9:27
kingdom of God
bought ground, I must go *Lu* 14:18
and *s.* it
ye shall desire to *s.* one of *Lu* 17:22
the days
s. here, or *s.* there, go not *Lu* 17:23
after them
Zaccheus sought to *s.* Jesus, *Lu* 19:3
who he was
he climbed into a *Lu* 19:4
sycamore tree to *s.* him
will reverence him when they *Lu* 20:13
s. him
it is I myself, handle me and *Lu* 24:39
s.
on whom thou shalt *s.* Spirit *Joh* 1:33
descending
come and *s.* *Joh* 1:39; 11:34; *Re* 6:1,
              3, 5, 7
thou shalt *s.* greater things *Joh* 1:50
than these
s. a man who told me all *Joh* 4:29
things ever I did
if man keeps my sayings, *Joh* 8:51
shall never *s.* death
your father Abraham rejoiced *Joh* 8:56
to *s.* my day
I washed, and do *s.* *Joh* 9:15
they asked then, How then *Joh* 9:19
doth he now *s.*
I was blind, now I *s.* *Joh* 9:25
I came into world, that they *Joh* 9:39
who *s.* not might *s.* and who
s. might be blind
if believe, thou shouldest *s.* *Joh* 11:40
the glory of God
but that they might *s.* *Joh* 12:9
Lazarus also
the Greeks, saying, Sir, we *Joh* 12:21
would *s.* Jesus
ye have sorrow, but I will *s.* *Joh* 16:22
you again
except I *s.* in his hands the *Joh* 20:25
print of nails
and visit our brethren and *s.* *Ac* 15:36
how they do
after I have been there, I *Ac* 19:21
must also *s.* Rome
ye all shall *s.* my face no *Ac* 20:25;
more   20:38
shouldst know his will, and *s.* *Ac* 22:14
that just One
for this cause I called you, to *Ac* 28:20
s. you
for I long to *s.* you, that I may *Ro* 1:11
impart
I *s.* another law in my *Ro* 7:23
members, warring
whom he was not spoken of, *Ro* 15:21
they shall *s.*
for I trust to *s.* you in my *Ro* 15:24
journey
if any man *s.* thee that hast *1Co* 8:10
knowledge
s. that he may be with you *1Co* 16:10
without fear
s. that ye abound in this grace *2Co* 8:7
also

I went up to Jerusalem to *s.* *Ga* 1:18
Peter
to make all men *s.* what is *Eph* 3:9
fellowship
s. that ye walk *Eph* 5:15
circumspectly, not as fools
the wife *s.* that she reverence *Eph* 5:33
her husband
whether I come and *s.* you *Ph'p* 1:27
or be absent
so soon as I *s.* how it will go *Ph'p* 2:23
with me
to *s.* your face with great *1Th* 2:17
desire
desiring greatly to *s.* us as we *1Th* 3:6
also to *s.* you
s. that none render evil for *1Th* 5:15
evil to any man
whom no man hath seen, nor *1Ti* 6:16
can *s.*
greatly desiring to *s.* thee, *2Ti* 1:4
being mindful
s. thou make all according to *Heb* 8:5
the pattern
holiness, without which no *Heb* 12:14
man *s.* the Lord
s. that ye refuse not him *Heb* 12:25
that speaketh
with whom, if he *Heb* 13:23
come shortly, I will *s.* you
s. that ye love one another *1Pe* 1:22
fervently
he that will *s.* good days, let *1Pe* 3:10
him refrain
if any man *s.* his brother sin *1Jo* 5:16
a sin not
but I trust I shall shortly *s.* *3Jo* 14
thee
he cometh, and every eye shall *Re* 1:7
s. him
I turned to *s.* the voice that *Re* 1:12
spake with me
anoint with eye-salve, that *Re* 3:18
thou mayest *s.*
and *s.* thou hurt not the oil and *Re* 6:6
the wine
shall *s.* their dead bodies three *Re* 11:9
days and half
lest he walk naked, and they *Re* 16:15
s. his shame
for she saith, I sit a queen, *Re* 18:7
shall *s.* no sorrow
when they shall *s.* the smoke *Re* 18:9
of her burning
he said to me, *S.* thou do *Re* 19:10;
it not   22:9
and they shall *s.* his face, *Re* 22:4
name in foreheads

SEE *NOT, NOT* SEE

let me *not s.* the death of *Ge* 21:16
the child
when Isaac was old, that he *Ge* 27:1
could *not s.*
man did protest, ye shall *not* *Ge* 43:3;
s. my face   43:5
for we may *not s.* the man's *Ge* 44:26
face except
eyes of Israel were dim, he *Ge* 48:10
could *not s.*
thou canst *not s.* my face and *Ex* 33:20
live
let me *not s.* my *Nu* 11:15
wretchedness
surely they shall *not s.* the *Nu* 14:23
land I sware
utmost part, and shall *not s.* *Nu* 23:13
them all
thou shalt *not s.* thy brother's *De* 22:1
ox go astray
thou shalt *not s.* thy brother's *De* 22:4
ass fall down
Eli, his eyes dim, he could *not* *1Sa* 3:2;
               4:15
not s. my face, except thou *2Sa* 3:13
first bring
the king said, Let *not* *2Sa* 14:24
Absalom *s.* my face
Ahijah could *not s.* his eyes *1Ki* 14:4
set
ye shall *not s.* wind, nor shall *2Ki* 3:17
ye see rain
thine eyes shall *not s.* all *2Ki* 22:20
evil I will bring
lo, he goeth by me, and I *s.* *Job* 9:11
him *not*
he shall *not s.* the rivers of *Job* 20:17
honey and butter

or darkness that thou canst *Job* 22:11
not s.
he hideth himself that I *Job* 23:9
cannot s. him
that which I *s. not* teach thou *Job* 34:32
me
though thou sayest, thou shalt *Job* 35:14
not s. him
men *s. not* the bright light in *Job* 37:21
the clouds
should still live, and *not s.* *Ps* 49:9
corruption
pass away, that they may *not* *Ps* 58:8
s. the sun
let their eyes be darkened, *Ps* 69:23
that they *s. not*
we *s. not* our signs, there is no *Ps* 74:9
more prophet
what man liveth, and shall *Ps* 89:48
not s. death
yet they say, The Lord shall *Ps* 94:7
not s.
he that formed the eye, shall *Ps* 94:9
he *not s.*
eyes have they, but they *s.* *Ps* 115:5;
not   135:16
when thy hand is lifted up, *Isa* 26:11
they will *not s.*
children, which say to the *Isa* 30:10
seers, *S. not*
thou shalt *not s.* a fierce *Isa* 33:19
people, a people
I shall *not s.* the Lord, even *Isa* 38:11
the Lord
they *s. not*, that they may be *Isa* 44:9
ashamed
he hath shut their eyes, that *Isa* 44:18
they *cannot s.*
which have eyes, and *s. not* *Jer* 5:21;
              Eze 12:12
they said, He shall *not s.* our *Jer* 12:4
last end
the prophets say, Ye shall *Jer* 14:13
not s. the sword
like heath, he shall *not s.* *Jer* 17:6
when good cometh
he shall *not s.* when heat *Jer* 17:8
cometh
can any hide, that I shall *not* *Jer* 23:24
s. him
that thou *s. not* the ground *Eze* 12:6;
              12:12
yet shall he *not s.* it, though *Eze* 12:13
he shall die there
hast praised gods of gold, *Da* 5:23
which *s. not*
thou shalt *not s.* evil any *Zep* 3:15
more
because they seeing *s. not* *M't* 13:13
and hear not
ye shall *not s.* me *M't* 23:39;
henceforth   *Lu* 13:35
Jesus said, *S.* ye *not* all *M't* 24:2
these things
having eyes *s.* ye *not*? and *M'k* 8:18
ears, hear not
not s. death, before he had *Lu* 2:26
seen Christ
that seeing, they might *not s.* *Lu* 8:10
and hearing
shall desire to see and ye *Lu* 17:22
shall *not s.* it
he *cannot s.* the kingdom of *Joh* 3:3
God
shall *not s.* life, but wrath *Joh* 3:36
abideth on him
I am come, that they who *s.* *Joh* 9:39
not might see
that they should *not s.* with *Joh* 12:40
their eyes
a little while, and ye shall *Joh* 16:16;
not s. me   16:17, 19
did I *not s.* thee in the *Joh* 18:26
garden with him
when I could *not s.* for the *Ac* 22:11
g'ory
hath given eyes, that they *Ro* 11:8
should *not s.*
let their eyes be darkened, *Ro* 11:10
that they may *not s.*
for I will *not s.* you now by *1Co* 16:7
the way
but we *s. not* yet all things *Heb* 2:8
put under him
was translated, that he should *Heb* 11:5
not s. death
though now ye *s.* him *not*, yet *1Pe* 1:8
believing
he is blind and *cannot s.* afar *2Pe* 1:9
off

WE SEE

we shall *s.* what will become   *Ge 37:20*
of dreams
in thy light shall *we s.* light   *Ps 36:9*
neither shall *we s.* sword or   *Jer 5:12*
famine
go into Egypt, where *we*   *Jer 42:14*
shall *s.* no war
that *we* may *s.* and believe   *M'k 15:32;*
                         Joh 6:30
now we say, *We s.* your sin   *Joh 9:41*
remaineth
but if we hope for that *we s.*   *Ro 8:25*
not
now *we s.* through a glass   *1Co 13:12*
darkly
praying that *we* might *s.* your   *1Th 3:10*
face
but *we s.* Jesus who was made   *Heb 2:9*
a little lower
so *we s.* that they could not   *Heb 3:19*
enter in because
be like him, for *we* shall *s.* him   *1Jo 3:2*
as he is

YE SEE, SEE YE

ye shall *s.* them again no   *Ex 14:13*
more
then *ye* shall *s.* the glory of the   *Ex 16:7*
Lord
when *ye s.* the ark of the   *Jos 3:3*
covenant
s. ye him whom Lord hath   *1Sa 10:24*
chosen
to hissing, as *ye s.* with your   *2Ch 29:8*
eyes
who gave them up to   *2Ch 30:7*
desolation, as *ye s.*
I said, *Ye s.* the distress that   *Ne 2:17*
we are in
ye s. my casting down, and   *Job 6:21*
are afraid
what will *ye s.* in the   *Ca 6:13*
Shulamite
and *s. ye* indeed, but perceive   *Isa 6:9*
not
s. ye, when he lifteth up an   *Isa 18:3*
ensign
hear, ye deaf, look, ye blind,   *Isa 42:18*
that *ye* may *s.*
when *ye s.* your hearts shall   *Isa 66:14*
rejoice
O generation *s. ye* the word of   *Jer 2:31*
the Lord
and *ye* shall *s.* this place no   *Jer 42:18*
more
therefore *ye* shall *s.* no more   *Eze 13:23*
vanity
ye shall *s.* their way and   *Eze 14:22*
their doings
they shall comfort you when   *Eze 14:23*
ye s. their ways
because *ye s.* the thing is gone   *Da 2:8*
from me
many have desired to see   *M't 13:17;*
those things which *ye s.*   *Lu 10:23*
Jesus said, *S. ye* not all   *M't 24:2*
these things
when *ye* shall *s.* all these   *M't 24:33;*
things, know   *M'k 13:29; Lu 21:31*
hereafter shall *ye s.* the Son   *M'k 14:62*
of man sitting   *M't 27:24;*
I am innocent, *s. ye* to it   *M't 27:24;*
                    M'k 15:36
in Galilee there shall *ye s.*   *M't 28:7;*
him   *M'k 16:7*
when *ye s.* a cloud rise out of   *Lu 12:54*
the west
and when *ye s.* the south   *Lu 12:55*
wind blow, ye say
when *ye* shall *s.* Abraham   *Lu 13:28*
and the prophets
when *ye* shall *s.* Jerusalem   *Lu 21:20*
compassed
ye s. and know of yourselves,   *Lu 21:30*
summer is nigh
hath not flesh and bones, as   *Lu 24:39*
ye s. me have
hereafter *ye* shall *s.* heaven   *Joh 1:51*
open
except *ye s.* signs, ye will not   *Joh 4:48*
believe
what if *ye* shall *s.* the Son of   *Joh 6:62*
man ascend
but *ye s.* me; and *ye s.* me   *Joh 14:19;*
no more   *16:10*
a little while *ye* shall *s.* me   *Joh 16:16;*
                   16:17, 19

shed this which *ye* now *s.* and   *Ac 2:33*
hear
made this man strong, whom   *Ac 3:16*
ye s. and know
ye s. and hear, that not alone   *Ac 19:26*
at Ephesus
ye s. this man, about whom   *Ac 25:24*
Jews dealt
for *ye s.* your calling, brethren   *1Co 1:26*
ye s. how large a letter I have   *Ga 6:11*
written
when *ye s.* him again, ye   *Ph'p 2:28*
may rejoice
much more, as *ye s.* day   *Heb 10:25*
approaching
ye s. how that by works man   *Jas 2:24*
is justified
though now *ye s.* him not, yet   *1Pe 1:8*
ye rejoice

SEED

bring forth herbs yielding *s.*   *Ge 1:11;*
                   1:12, 29
give us *s.*; lo, here is *s.* for   *Ge 47:19;*
you   *47:23*
and four parts shall be your   *Ge 47:24*
own for *s.*
the manna was like coriander   *Ex 16:31*
s.
their carcase fall on any   *Le 11:37*
sowing *s.*
but if any water be put upon   *Le 11:38*
the *s.*
shalt not sow thy field with   *Le 19:19*
mingled *s.*
and ye shall sow your *s.* in   *Le 26:16*
vain
thy estimation shall be   *Le 27:16*
according to the *s.* an homer
of barley *s.*
all tithe of the *s.* of land is   *Le 27:30*
the Lord's
it is no place of *s.* or of figs   *Nu 20:5*
or vines
not as Egypt, where thou   *De 11:10*
sowedst *s.*
shalt surely tithe all the   *De 14:22*
increase of thy *s.*
lest the fruit of thy *s.* sown be   *De 22:9*
defiled
thou shalt carry much *s.* into   *De 28:38*
the field
the king will take the tenth of   *1Sa 8:15*
your *s.*
a trench contain two   *1Ki 18:32*
measures of *s.*
will the unicorn bring home   *Job 39:12*
thy *s.*
he that goeth forth bearing   *Ps 126:6*
precious *s.*
in the morning sow thy *s.* and   *Ec 11:6*
evening
the *s.* of an homer shall yield   *Isa 5:10*
an ephah
in the morning make thy *s.*   *Isa 17:11*
to flourish
and by great waters the *s.* of   *Isa 23:3*
Sihor
it may give *s.* to the sower   *Isa 55:10*
nor shall sow *s.* nor plant   *Jer 35:7*
vineyard
neither have we vineyard,   *Jer 35:9*
field, nor *s.*
he took also of the *s.* of the   *Eze 17:5*
land
the *s.* is rotten under their   *Joe 1:17*
clods
treader overtake him that   *Am 9:13*
soweth *s.*
is the *s.* yet in the barn? yea,   *Hag 2:19*
as yet
for the *s.* shall be prosperous,   *Zec 8:12*
the vine
I will corrupt your *s.* and   *Mal 2:3*
spread
which receive *s.* by the   *M't 13:19*
way side
s. in stony places; *s.* among   *M't 13:20;*
thorns   *13:22*
but he that received *s.* into   *M't 13:23*
good ground
a man which sowed good *s.*   *M't 13:24*
in his field
didst not thou sow good *s.*   *M't 13:27*
in thy field
he that soweth good *s.* is the   *M't 13:37*
Son of man
good *s.* are the children of   *M't 13:38*
the kingdom

if a man should cast *s.* into   *M'k 4:26*
the ground
the *s.* should spring and grow   *M'k 4:27*
up
a sower went out to sow his *s.*   *Lu 8:5*
some fell
the parable is this; the *s.* is   *Lu 8:11*
word of God
and to every *s.* his own body   *1Co 15:38*
he that ministereth *s.* to the   *2Co 9:10*
sower
being born again, not of   *1Pe 1:23*
corruptible *s.*
not from perishable *s.* (R)   *1Pe 1:23*
for his *s.* remaineth in him,   *1Jo 3:9*
cannot sin

SEED, for posterity

God hath appointed me   *Ge 4:25*
another *s.*
child (A)   *Ge 4:25; 15:3; Le 12:21*
to keep *s.* alive upon face of   *Ge 7:3*
the earth
Abram said, To me thou hast   *Ge 15:3*
given no *s.*
offspring (A)   *Ge 15:3;*
38:8;   *Le 21:21; 22:4; Ru 4:12;*
1Ch 16:13; Es 6:13; Job 21:8; Ps 21:10;
22:23; 37:28; Isa 1:4; 45:25; 57:3; 61:9;
Jer 23:8; 31:37; 33:22; Eze 20:5; 43:19;
44:22; Da 9:1; Mal 2:15; Joh 7:42;
                   Ro 9:8
offspring (B)   *Ge 15:3;*
38:8;   *Le 22:4; Nu 16:40;*
1Sa 2:20; 2Ki 11:1; 25:25; Ezr 9:2;
Ps 21:10; 37:28; 69:36; 102:28; 106:27;
Ps 11:21; Isa 45:25; 57:3; Jer 7:15;
23:8; Mal 2:15; M'k 12:20; Joh 7:42;
Ac 13:23; Ro 9:8, 29; Ga 3:19; Re 12:17
offspring (R)   *Ge 15:3;*
19:32; 38:8-9; 1Ch 16:13; Job 21:8;
Ps 21:10; Isa 1:4; 45:19, 25; 57:34;
65:23; Jer 7:15; Mal 2:15; Ga 3:19;
                   Re 12:17
we may preserve *s.* of our   *Ge 19:32;*
father   *19:34*
marry her, and raise up *s.* to   *Ge 38:8;*
brother   *M't 22:24; M'k 12:19; Lu 20:28*
family (A)(B)   *Ge 38:8;*
     1Ki 11:14; Eze 43:19; Da 1:3
Onan knew that the *s.* should   *Ge 38:9*
not be his
if a woman have conceived *s.*   *Le 12:2*
and born
that hath a blemish of the *s.*   *Le 21:21*
of Aaron
descendants (B)   *Le 21:21;*
De 1:8; 4:37; 1Sa 24:21; 1Ki 11:39;
1Ch 16:13; Es 9:27-28; Isa 1:4; 14:20;
45:19; 61:9; Jer 31:36; 33:22; Eze 20:5;
                   Ro 4:16
descendants (R)   *Le 21:21;*
Nu 16:40; De 1:8; 4:37; 31:21;
1Ki 11:14, 39; 2Ki 17:20; Es 9:27-28;
Ps 106:27; Isa 14:20; 61:9; Jer 23:8;
      31:36-37; 33:22; Ro 4:16
what man of the *s.* of Aaron   *Le 22:4*
is a leper
then the woman shall conceive   *Nu 5:28*
s.
children (R)   *Nu 5:28;*
Ru 4:12; 1Sa 2:20; Ps 37:28; 69:36;
102:28; M'k 12:20; Ro 9:29
which is not of *s.* of Aaron   *Nu 16:40*
come near
to give it to their *s.* after them   *De 1:8;*
                   11:9
descendants (A)   *De 1:8;*
4:37; 31:21; 1Ki 11:39; 2Ki 11:1; 17:20;
Es 9:27-28; Ps 106:27; Isa 14:20; 45:19;
61:9; 65:23; Ac 13:23; Ro 4:16; Re 12:17
he chose their *s.* after   *De 4:37;*
them   *10:15*
forgotten out of the mouths   *De 31:21*
of their *s.*
children (B)   *De 31:21;*
   2Ki 17:20; Job 21:8; Isa 57:4
s. the Lord shall give of this   *Ru 4:12*
woman
the Lord give thee *s.* of this   *1Sa 2:20*
woman
children (A)   *1Sa 2:20;*
Ps 69:36; 102:28; M'k 12:20; Ro 9:8
that thou wilt not cut off my   *1Sa 24:21*
s. after me
he was of the king's *s.* in   *1Ki 11:14*
Edom
royal descent (A)   *1Ki 11:14*
house (R)   *1Ki 11:14*

will for this afflict the *s.* of *1Ki 11:39*
David
Athaliah destroyed all the *2Ki 11:11;*
s. royal *2Ch 22:10*
family (R) *2Ki 11:11;*
25:25; Eze 43:19; Da 1:3
the Lord rejected all the *s.* *2Ki 17:20*
of Israel
Ishmael of the *s.* royal *2Ki 25:25;*
came *Jer 41:1*
O ye *s.* of Israel his servant *1Ch 16:13*
they could not shew their *s.* *Ezr 2:59;*
Ne 7:61
descent (R) *Ezr 2:59*
the holy *s.* have mingled *Ezr 9:2*
themselves
the *s.* of Israel separated *Ne 9:2*
themselves
Israelites (R) *Ne 9:2*
if Mordecai be of the *s.* of *Es 16:13*
the Jews
race (B) *Es 6:13; Da 9:1*
Jewish people (R) *Es 6:13*
the Jews took upon them and *Es 9:27;*
their *s.* *9:31*
nor memorial of them perish *Es 9:28*
from their *s.*
their *s.* is established in their *Job 21:8*
sight
their *s.* shalt thou destroy *Ps 21:10*
from earth
all ye *s.* of Jacob, glorify *Ps 22:23*
him; and fear him, all ye *s.* of
sons (B)(R) *Ps 22:23*
a *s.* shall serve him, it shall *Ps 22:30*
be counted
posterity (A) *Ps 22:30; Jer 7:15; 31:36*
posterity (B) *Ps 22:30*
posterity (R) *Ps 22:30; Ac 13:23*
but the *s.* of the wicked shall *Ps 37:28*
be cut off
the *s.* also of his servants *Ps 69:36*
shall inherit it
their *s.* shall be established *Ps 102:28*
before thee
to overthrow their *s.* among *Ps 106:27*
the nations
the *s.* of the righteous shall be *Pr 11:21*
delivered
ah, sinful nation, a *s.* of *Isa 1:4*
evildoers
holy *s.* shall be the substance *Isa 6:13*
thereof
s. of evildoers shall never be *Isa 14:20*
renowned
I said not unto *s.* of Jacob, *Isa 45:19*
Seek ye me
in the Lord shall all *s.* of *Isa 45:25*
Israel be justified
the *s.* of the adulterer and the *Isa 57:3*
whore
children of transgression, a *s.* *Isa 57:4*
of falsehood
their *s.* shall be known among *Isa 61:9*
Gentiles; they are the *s.* which
I will bring forth a *s.* out of *Isa 65:9*
Jacob
they are the *s.* of the blessed *Isa 65:23*
of the Lord
I had planted thee wholly a *Jer 2:21*
right *s.*
stock (B) *Jer 2:21*
I will cast out the whole *s.* of *Jer 7:15*
Ephraim
which led the *s.* of the *Jer 23:8*
house of Israel
I will sow with *s.* of man *Jer 31:27*
and *s.* of beast
then of Israel also shall *Jer 31:36*
cease as a nation
I will cast off all the *s.* of *Jer 31:37;*
Israel *33:26*
inhabitants (B) *Jer 31:37*
so will I multiply the *s.* of *Jer 33:22*
David
and hath taken of the king's *Eze 17:13*
s.
I lifted up my hand to the *s.* *Eze 20:5*
of Jacob
give to priests that be of the *Eze 43:19*
s. of Zadok
they shall take maidens of *Eze 44:22*
the *s.* of Israel
bring of the children of the *Da 1:3*
king's *s.*
mingle themselves with the *s.* *Da 2:43*
of men
Darius of the *s.* of the Medes *Da 9:1*
was made king
that he might seek a godly *s.* *Mal 2:15*

the first dying left no *s.* *M'k 12:20;*
12:21-22
that Christ cometh of the *s.* *Joh 7:42*
of David
descended (P)(R) *Joh 7:42*
Ro 1:3; 9:6
of this man's *s.* hath God *Ac 13:23*
raised Jesus
was made of the *s.* of David *Ro 1:3;*
2Ti 2:8
descended (B)(P) *Ro 1:3*
stock (N) *Ro 1:3*
that the promise might be *Ro 4:16*
sure to all his *s.*
posterity (N) *Ro 4:16*
the children of the promise *Ro 9:8*
counted for the *s.*
except the Lord of Sabaoth *Ro 9:29*
had left us a *s.*
it was added, till the *s.* should *Ga 3:19*
come
Sarah received strength to *Heb 11:11*
conceive *s.*
conception (B) *Heb 11:11*
to make war with the *Re 12:17*
remnant of her *s.*

HIS SEED

my covenant with Isaac and *Ge 17:19*
his *s.*
posterity (A) *Ge 17:19*
children (B) *Ge 17:19*
descendants (R) *Ge 17:19;*
48:19; Ex 28:43; Nu 14:24; 25:13;
2Sa 4:8; 22:51; 1Ki 2:33; Ne 9:8;
Ps 112:2; Jer 29:32; 33:26
Jacob came, and all his *s.* *Ge 46:6;*
with him *46:7*
descendants (A) *Ge 46:6;*
Ex 28:43; Nu 14:24; 25:13; 1Ki 2:33;
Ne 9:8; Jer 33:26; Ac 7:5-6
descendants (B) *Ge 46:6;*
48:19; Ex 28:43; Nu 14:24; 25:13;
2Sa 4:8; 1Ki 2:33; Ne 9:8; Jer 33:26
offspring (B) *Ge 46:6;*
Jos 24:3; Isa 53:10; Jer 22:30; 36:31
and his *s.* shall become *Ge 48:19*
a multitude of nations
offspring (A) *Ge 48:19;*
Nu 24:7; Jos 24:3; 2Sa 4:8; 22:51;
Ps 35:13; 37:26; 89:29; 112:2; Isa 53:10;
Jer 22:28, 30; 29:32; 36:31; 49:10
a statute of his *s.* after him *Ex 28:43;*
30:21
that giveth any of his *s.* to *Le 20:2;*
Mo'ech *20:3-4*
offspring (B) *Le 20:2;*
21:15; Nu 24:7; Jos 24:3; 2Sa 22:51;
Ps 25:13; 37:25-26; 112:2; Jer 22:28, 30;
36:31; 49:10; Ac 7:5-6
nor shall ye profane his *s.* *Le 21:15*
among people
children (R) *Le 21:15;*
20:2; Ps 25:13; 37:25-26; Jer 22:28;
49:10
servant Caleb and his *s.* shall *Nu 14:24*
possess it
and his *s.* shall be in many *Nu 24:7*
waters
he shall have it, and his *s.* *Nu 25:13*
after him
I multiplied his *s.* and gave *Jos 24:3*
Isaac
hath avenged thee of Saul and *2Sa 4:8*
his *s.*
shewed mercy to David and *2Sa 22:51;*
his *s.* for evermore *Ps 18:50*
on Joab, and his *s.* for ever, *1Ki 2:33*
upon David and his *s.* peace
made a covenant to give *Ne 9:8*
it to his *s.*
and speaking peace to all his *Es 10:3*
s.
race (A)(B) *Es 10:3*
his *s.* shall inherit the *Ps 25:13*
earth
nor have I seen his *s.* begging *Ps 37:25*
bread
he is merciful, and his *s.* is *Ps 37:26*
blessed
his *s.* also will I make to *Ps 89:29;*
endure *89:36*
his line (R) *Ps 89:29*
his *s.* shall be mighty upon *Ps 112:2*
earth
shall see his *s.* shall prolong *Isa 53:10*
his days
followers (B) *Isa 53:10*
why are they cast out, he and *Jer 22:28*
his *s.*

for no man of his *s.* shall *Jer 22:30*
prosper
and I will punish Shemaiah *Jer 29:32*
and his *s.*
I will not take any of his *s.* *Jer 33:26*
to be rulers
will punish Jehoiachim and *Jer 36:31*
his *s.*
Esau, his *s.* is spoiled, and *Jer 49:10*
he is not
give it to him and his *s.* after *Ac 7:5*
him
posterity (R) *Ac 7:5; 7:6*
that his *s.* should sojourn in a *Ac 7:6*
strange land

THY SEED

put enmity between *thy s.* and *Ge 3:15*
her seed
offspring (A) *Ge 3:15;*
17:12; 21:13; 48:11; 2Sa 7:12; 2Ki 5:27;
Isa 43:5; 44:3; 54:3; 66:22
offspring (B) *Ge 3:15;*
12:7; 15:5; 17:12; 21:13; 22:18; 48:11;
Le 18:21; 21:17; 22:3; Nu 18:19;
De 30:6; Job 5:25; Ps 89:4; Isa 43:5;
44:3; Ga 3:16
to *thy s.* will I give this land *Ge 12:7;*
12:13, 15; 15:18; 17:8; 24:7; 26:3; 28:4;
13; 35:12; 48:4; Ex 33:1; De 34:4
descendants (A) *Ge 12:7;*
13:16; 15:5, 13; 17:7; 22:17; 26:24;
32:12; De 28:46, 59; 30:6, 19; 1Sa 20:42;
Isa 48:19
descendants (R) *Ge 12:7;*
13:16; 15:5, 13; 17:7, 9; 21:12; 22:17-
18; 26:24; 32:12; Ex 32:13; Le 21:17;
22:3; De 28:46; 59; 30:6; 1Sa 20:42;
2Ki 5:27; Job 5:25; Ps 89:4; Isa 44:3;
48:19; 54:3; 66:22; Jer 30:10
I will make *thy s.* as dust *Ge 13:16;*
16:10; 28:14
descendants (B) *Ge 13:16;*
15:13; 17:7, 9; 22:17; 26:24; 32:12;
28:46, 59; 1Sa 20:42; 2Ki 5:27;
Isa 48:19; 54:3
he said to him, So shall *thy s.* *Ge 15:5;*
be *Ro 4:18*
that *thy s.* shall be a stranger *Ge 15:13*
in a land
covenant between me and *thy Ge 17:7;*
s. to be a God to thee and *thy s.* *17:10*
thou and *thy s.* after thee in *Ge 17:9*
their generations
a stranger not of *thy s.* shall *Ge 17:12*
be circumcised
offspring (R) *Ge 17:12;*
21:13; Nu 18:19; Isa 43:5; Ga 3:16
in Isaac shall *thy s.* be *Ge 21:12*
called *Heb 11:18*
posterity (A) *Ge 21:12;*
Nu 18:19; Jer 30:10
make Ishmael a nation, *Ge 21:13*
because he is *thy s.*
thy s. possess the gate of *Ge 22:17;*
enemies *24:60*
in *thy s.* shall all the nations *Ge 22:18;*
of the earth *26:4; 28:14; Ac 3:25*
multiply *thy s.* for Abraham's *Ge 26:24*
sake
I will make *thy s.* as the *Ge 32:12*
sand
God hath shewed me also *thy Ge 48:11*
s.
children (R) *Ge 48:11;*
Le 18:21; Isa 59:21
not any of *thy s.* pass *Le 18:21*
through the fire
children (A) *Le 18:21;*
Job 5:25; Isa 59:21
whosoever of *thy s.* hath any *Le 21:17*
blemish
sons (A) *Le 21:17*
heave offerings I gave thee *Nu 18:19*
and *thy s.*
curses for a sign of *thy s.* for *De 28:46*
ever
Lord will make plagues of *thy De 28:59*
s. wonderful
Lord will circumcise the heart *De 30:6*
of *thy s.*
choose life, that thou and *thy De 30:19*
s. may live
children (B) *De 30:19; Isa 59:21*
the Lord be between my *1Sa 20:42*
seed and *thy s.*
I will set up *thy s.* *2Sa 7:12; 1Ch 17:11*
posterity (A) *2Sa 7:12; Jer 30:10*
son (R) *2Sa 7:12*

leprosy shall cleave to thee   *2Ki 5:27*
and *thy* s.
thou shalt know that *thy* s.   *Job 5:25*
shall be great
thy s. will I establish for ever,   *Ps 89:4*
and build
I will bring *thy* s. from the   *Isa 43:5*
east and gather
I will pour my Spirit upon *thy*   *Isa 44:3*
s. and blessing
thy s. also had been as the   *Isa 48:19*
sand and offspring
and thy s. shall inherit the   *Isa 54:3*
Gentiles
my Spirit shall not depart   *Isa 59:21*
out of the mouth of *thy* s.
nor *thy* seed's s.
thy s. from the land of   *Jer 30:10;*
captivity   *46:27*
and to *thy* s. which is Christ   *Ga 3:16*

YOUR SEED

all this land will I give to   *Ex 32:13*
your s.
whosoever of *your* s. goeth to   *Le 22:3*
holy things
so shall *your* s. and your   *Isa 66:22*
name remain
progeny (B)   *Isa 66:22*

SEEDS

s. and skins (B)(R)   *Nu 6:4*
not sow thy vineyard with   *De 22:9*
divers *s.*
some *s.* fell by the way side   *M't 13:4*
which indeed is the least of   *M't 13:32*
all *s.*
is less than all the *s.* that be   *M'k 4:31*
in the
He saith not, And to *s.* as of   *Ga 3:16*
many

SEED'S

out of the mouth of thy *s.*   *Isa 59:21*
seed
children's (A)(R)   *Isa 59:21*
grandchildren (B)   *Isa 59:21*

SEEDTIME

s. and harvest shall not   *Ge 8:22*
cease

SEEING

what wilt thou give me, s. I   *Ge 15:2*
go childless
s. thou hast not withheld   *Ge 22:12*
thine only son
s. the Lord hath prospered   *Ge 24:56*
my way
wherefore come ye to me, s.   *Ge 26:27*
ye hate me
s. his life is bound up in the   *Ge 44:30*
lad's life
or who maketh the s. or the   *Ex 4:11*
blind
any beast be driven away,   *Ex 22:10*
no man s.
s. all the congregation are   *Nu 16:3*
holy
s. him not, cast it on him   *Nu 35:23*
that he die
why askest thou my name, s.   *J'g 13:18*
it is secret
do me good, s. I have a   *J'g 17:13*
Levite priest
s. women are destroyed out   *J'g 21:16*
of Benjamin
s. the Lord hath testified   *Ru 1:21*
against me
s. I have rejected him from   *1Sa 16:1*
reigning
s. the Lord is departed   *1Sa 28:16*
from thee
given one to sit, mine eyes   *1Ki 1:48*
even s. it
s. there is no wrong in mine   *1Ch 12:17*
hands
s. the root of the matter is   *Job 19:28*
found in me
s. he judgeth those that are   *Job 21:22*
high
s. times are not hidden from   *Job 24:1*
the Almighty
s. thou hatest instruction, and   *Ps 50:17*
castest
s. he dwelleth securely by thee   *Pr 3:29*

the Lord maketh the s. eye   *Pr 20:12*
the eye is not satisfied with s.   *Ec 1:8*
nor ear
I was dismayed at the s. of it   *Isa 21:3*
that shutteth his eyes from s.   *Isa 33:15*
evil
s. many things, but thou   *Isa 42:20*
observest not
s. I have lost my children and   *Isa 49:21*
am desolate
s. the Lord hath given it a   *Jer 47:7*
charge
s. vanity, and divining lies   *Eze 22:28*
to them
s. thou couldst reveal this   *Da 2:47*
secret
in parables, because they s.   *M't 13:13*
see not
s. ye shall see and shall not   *M't 3:14;*
perceive   *M'k 4:12; Ac 28:26*
how shall this be, s. I know   *Lu 1:34*
not a man
s. thou art in the same   *Lu 23:40*
condemnation
he went and washed and came   *Joh 9:7*
s.
he s. this, spake of the   *Ac 2:31*
resurrection
s. Peter and John about to go   *Ac 3:3*
to the temple
s. one of them suffer wrong,   *Ac 7:24*
defended him
the people s. the miracles that   *Ac 8:6*
he did
speechless, hearing a voice, but   *Ac 9:7*
s. no man
be blind, not s. the sun for a   *Ac 13:11*
season
s. he is the Lord of heaven   *Ac 17:24*
and earth
s. he giveth to all life   *Ac 17:25*
and breath
s. it is one God who shall   *Ro 3:30*
justify
s. then that we have such   *2Co 3:12*
hope
s. that ye have put off the old   *Col 3:9*
man
s. it remaineth some must   *Heb 4:6*
enter
s. then that we have a great   *Heb 4:14*
high priest
hard to be uttered, s. ye are   *Heb 5:11*
dull of hearing
s. they crucify the Son of God   *Heb 6:6*
afresh
s. he ever liveth to make   *Heb 7:25*
intercession
he endured as s. him who is   *Heb 11:27*
invisible
s. we are compassed about   *Heb 12:1*
with witnesses
s. ye have purified your souls   *1Pe 1:22*
in obeying
s. and hearing, vexed his   *2Pe 2:8*
righteous soul
s. ye look for such things, be   *2Pe 3:14*
diligent
s. ye know these things   *2Pe 3:17*
before, beware lest

SEEK

Joseph said, I s. my brethren   *Ge 37:16*
s. out a man (S)   *Ge 41:33*
that he may s. occasion   *Ge 43:18*
against us
and s. ye the priesthood also   *Nu 16:10*
Balaam went not to s. for   *Nu 24:1*
enchantments
neither s. after wizards to   *Le 19:31*
be defiled by them
if thou s. him with all thy   *De 4:29*
heart
even to his habitation shall   *De 12:5*
ye s. and come
sheep be with thee till thy   *De 22:2*
brother s. after it
Kish said to Saul his son, Go   *1Sa 9:3*
s. the asses
whither went ye? he said,   *1Sa 10:14*
To s. the asses
to s. out a cunning player   *1Sa 16:16*
on an harp
Saul comes to s. his left   *1Sa 23:15;*
  23:25; 24:2; 26:2
they that s. evil to my Lord,   *1Sa 25:26*
be as Nabal
yet a man is risen to pursue   *1Sa 25:29*
and s. thy soul

for king of Israel is come   *1Sa 26:20*
out to s. a flea
Saul shall despair to s. me   *1Sa 27:1*
any more
s. me a woman that hath a   *1Sa 28:7*
familiar spirit
the Philistines came up to s.   *2Sa 5:17*
David
Shimei went to s. his servants   *1Ki 2:40*
whither my lord hath not   *1Ki 18:10*
sent to s. thee
they s. my life to take it   *1Ki 19:10;*
away   *19:14*
let them go, and s. thy master   *2Ki 2:16*
I will bring you to the man   *2Ki 6:19*
s. the commandments of the   *1Ch 28:8*
Lord
if thou s. him, he will be   *1Ch 28:9;*
found   *2Ch 15:2*
in his sickness he did not s.   *2Ch 16:12*
(B)
hast prepared thine heart to   *2Ch 19:3*
s. God
that prepareth his heart to   *2Ch 30:19*
s. God
to s. his God, he did it   *2Ch 31:21*
with all his heart
Josiah began to s. after the   *2Ch 34:3*
God of David
build, for we s. your God as   *Ezr 4:2*
ye do
Ezra had prepared his heart to   *Ezr 7:10*
s. the law
to s. him right way for us,   *Ezr 8:21*
and our little
name of God is on them for   *Ezr 8:22*
good that s. him
come a man to s. the welfare   *Ne 2:10*
of Israel
I would s. unto God, and unto   *Job 5:8*
God commit
shalt s. me in morning, but I   *Job 7:21*
shall not be
if thou wouldst s. unto God   *Job 8:5*
betimes
his children shall s. to please   *Job 20:10*
the poor
will ye love vanity, and s.   *Ps 4:2*
leasing
thou hast not forsaken them   *Ps 9:10*
that s. thee
s. out his wickedness till   *Ps 10:15*
thou find none
to see if did s. God   *Ps 14:2; 53:2*
this is the generation of them   *Ps 24:6*
that s. him
one thing have I desired, that   *Ps 27:4*
will I s. after
s. ye my face, thy face, Lord,   *Ps 27:8*
will I s.
s. peace, and pursue it   *Ps 34:14;*
  1Pe 3:11
let them be put to shame that   *Ps 35:4*
s. my soul
they that s. my life they that   *Ps 38:12*
s. my hurt
be confounded that s. after   *Ps 40:14;*
my soul   *70:2*
s. your favor with gifts (B)   *Ps 45:12*
and oppressors s. after my soul   *Ps 54:3*
that art my God, early will I   *Ps 63:1*
s. thee
those that s. my soul go into   *Ps 63:9*
the lower parts
let not those that s. thee be   *Ps 69:6*
confounded
and your heart shall live that   *Ps 69:32*
s. God
let all that s. thee rejoice and   *Ps 70:4*
be glad
be covered with   *Ps 71:13*
dishonour that s. my hurt
are brought unto shame that s.   *Ps 71:24*
my hurt
that they may s. thy name, O   *Ps 83:16*
Lord
the young lions s. their meat   *Ps 104:21*
from God
let his children s. their bread   *Ps 109:10*
that s. him with their whole   *Ps 119:2*
heart
I will walk at liberty, for I   *Ps 119:45*
s. thy precepts
I have gone astray as a   *Ps 119:176*
sheep, s.
for the house of God, I will   *Ps 122:9*
s. thy good
they shall s. me, but shall not   *Pr 1:28*
find me

and those that *s.* me early shall *Pr 8:17* find me

vanity tossed to and fro of *Pr 21:6* them that *s.* death

they that go to *s.* mixed *Pr 23:30* wine

when I shall awake, I will *s.* *Pr 23:35* it yet again

bloodthirsty hate upright, *Pr 29:10* just *s.* his soul

many *s.* the ruler's favour, *Pr 29:26* judgment from Lord

I gave my heart to *s.* out by *Ec 1:13* wisdom

I applied mine heart to *s.* out *Ec 7:25* wisdom

tho' a man labour to *s.* it, not *Ec 8:17* able to find it

I will *s.* him whom my soul *Ca 3:2* loveth

thy beloved, that we may *s.* *Ca 6:1* him with thee

learn to do well, *s.* judgment *Isa 1:17*

when say, *s.* unto them that *Isa 8:19* have familiar spirits; should not a people *s.* unto God

be root of Jesse, to it shall *Isa 11:10* the Gentiles *s.*

they shall *s.* to the charmers *Isa 19:3* and wizards

with my spirit within me will *Isa 26:9* I *s.* thee early

s. ye out of the book of the *Isa 34:16* Lord, and read

thou shalt *s.* them, and not *Isa 41:12* find them

when the needy *s.* water, and *Isa 41:17* there is none

I said not to Jacob, *S.* ye *Isa 45:19* me in vain

yet they *s.* me daily, and *Isa 58:2* delight to know

that *s.* her, in her month *Jer 2:24* shall find her

why trimmest thou thy way to *Jer 2:33* *s.* love

thy lovers despise thee, they *Jer 4:30* will *s.* thy life

the men of Anathoth, that *s.* *Jer 11:21* thy life

to fall by them that *s.* their *Jer 19:7;* lives *21:7*

they that *s.* their lives shall *Jer 19:9* straiten them

into hand of them that *s.* *Jer 22:25;* thy life *38:16*

s. the peace of the city, *Jer 29:7* whither carried

ye shall *s.* me, and find me, *Jer 29:13* when ye search me

into hand of them that *s.* their *Jer 34:30;* life *34:21*

I will give Pharaoh to them *Jer 44:30* that *s.* his life

Egyptians to those that *s.* *Jer 46:26* their lives

Elam dismayed before them *Jer 49:37* that *s.* their life

all her people sigh, they *s.* *La 1:11* bread

they shall *s.* peace there shall *Eze 7:25* be none

then shall they *s.* a vision of *Eze 7:26* the prophet

flock was scattered, none did *Eze 34:6* *s.* after them

I will search my sheep, and *Eze 34:11* *s.* them out

as a shepherd so will I *s.* out *Eze 34:12* my sheep

I will *s.* that which was lost *Eze 34:16* and bring again

I set my face unto God, to *s.* *Da 9:3* by prayer

he shall *s.* them, but not find *Ho 2:7* them

saith the Lord, *S.* me, and *Am 5:4* ye shall live

s. him that maketh the seven *Am 5:8* stars and Orion

s. good and not evil, that ye *Am 5:14* may live

to *s.* the word of the Lord, *Am 8:12* and not find it

whence shall I *s.* comforters *Na 3:7* for thee

thou shalt be hid, thou shalt *s.* *Na 3:11* strength

s. ye the Lord, ye meek of the *Zep 2:3* earth

a shepherd shall not *s.* the *Zec 11:16* young one

in that day I will *s.* to destroy *Zec 12:9* all the nations

they should *s.* the law at his *Mal 2:7* mouth

that he might *s.* a godly seed, *Mal 2:15* take heed

Herod will *s.* young child to *M't 2:13* destroy him

after all these things do the *M't 6:32* Gentiles *s.*

s. ye first the kingdom of *M't 6:33;* God *Lu 12:31*

s. and ye shall find, knock *M't 7:7;* *Lu 11:9*

for I know that ye *s.* Jesus *M't 28:5;* *M'k 16:6*

they said to him, All men *s.* *M'k 1:37* for thee

thy mother and thy brethren *M'k 3:32* *s.* for thee

this generation *s.* after a sign *M'k 8:12;* *Lu 11:29*

these things do the nations *s.* *Lu 12:30* after

many, I say unto you, will *s.* *Lu 13:24* to enter in

doth she not *s.* diligently till *Lu 15:8* she find it

whosoever shall *s.* to save his *Lu 17:33* life, shall lose it

the Son of man is come to *s.* *Lu 19:10* and to save

why *s.* ye the living among the *Lu 24:5* dead

Jesus saith unto them, What *Joh 1:38* *s.* ye

ye *s.* me, not because ye saw *Joh 6:26* the miracles

is not this he whom they *s.* to *Joh 7:25* kill

ye shall *s.* me, and shall not *Joh 7:34;* find me *7:36*

ye shall *s.* me, and shall die *Joh 8:21* in your sins

are Abraham's seed but ye *s.* *Joh 8:37;* to kill me *8:40*

ye shall *s.* me, and whither I *Joh 13:33* go cannot come

Jesus said unto them, Whom *Joh 18:4;* *s.* ye *18:7*

if ye *s.* me, let these go their *Joh 18:8* way

Spirit said, Behold, three *Ac 10:19* men *s.* thee

Peter said, Behold I am he *Ac 10:21* whom ye *s.*

Barnabas departed to Tarsus, *Ac 11:25* to *s.* Saul

to them who *s.* for glory and *Ro 2:7* honour

I am left alone, and they *s.* my *Ro 11:3* life

and the Greeks *s.* after *1Co 1:22* wisdom

let no man *s.* his own, but *1Co 10:24* another's wealth

s. that ye may excel to *1Co 14:12* edifying of church

since ye *s.* a proof of Christ *2Co 13:3* speaking

do I persuade, or *s.* to please *Ga 1:10* men

s. ye favor of (S) *Ga 1:10*

if while we *s.* to be justified *Ga 2:17* by Christ

they zealously *s.* you (S) *Ga 4:17*

that you might *s.* them (S) *Ga 4:17*

for all *s.* their own things, *Ph'p 2:21* not Christ's

if risen, *s.* those things which *Col 3:1* are above

he is a rewarder of them that *Heb 11:6* *s.* him

they declare plainly that *Heb 11:14* they *s.* a country

here we have no city, but we *Heb 13:14* *s.* one to come

in those days shall men *s.* *Re 9:6* death, not find it

NOT SEEK, SEEK NOT

the priest shall *not s.* for *Le 13:36* yellow hair

that ye *s. not* after your own *Nu 15:39* heart

thou shalt *not s.* their peace *De 23:6;* *Ezr 9:12*

daughter, shall I *not s.* rest for *Ru 3:1* thee

the wicked will *not s.* after *Ps 10:4* God

the wicked, they *s. not* thy *Ps 119:155* statutes

all thy lovers, they *s.* thee *not* *Jer 30:14*

seekest thou great things? *s.* *Jer 45:5* them *not*

but *s. not* Beth-el, nor enter *Am 5:5* into Gilgal

a shepherd shall *not s.* the *Zec 11:16* young one

s. not what ye shall eat or *Lu 12:29* drink

because *s. not* mine own *Joh 5:30* will, but will

s. not the honour that cometh *Joh 5:44* from God

I *s. not* mine own glory, there *Joh 8:50* is one seeketh

s. not to be loosed, *s. not* a *1Co 7:27* wife

for I *s. not* yours, but you *2Co 12:14*

SEEKEST

asked him, saying, What *s.* *Ge 37:15* thou

shew thee the man whom thou *J'g 4:22* *s.*

the man whom thou *s.* is as *2Sa 17:3* if all

thou *s.* to destroy a city and *2Sa 20:19*

thou *s.* to go to thine own *1Ki 11:22* country

If thou *s.* her as silver, and *Pr 2:4*

s. thou great things for thyself *Jer 45:5*

yet no man said, What *s.* *Joh 4:27* thou

why weepest thou? whom *s.* *Joh 20:15* thou

SEEKETH

Saul my father *s.* to kill thee *1Sa 19:2*

thy father, that he *s.* my life *1Sa 20:1*

for he that *s.* my life *s.* thy *1Sa 22:23* life

that Saul *s.* to come to *1Sa 23:10* Keilah, to

saying, Behold, David *s.* thy *1Sa 24:9* hurt

forth of my bowels, *s.* my *2Sa 16:11* life

and see how this man *s.* *1Ki 20:7* mischief

see how he *s.* a quarrel against *2Ki 5:7* me

From thence she *s.* the prey *Job 39:29*

the righteous, and *s.* to slay *Ps 37:32* him

s. good procureth favour: but *Pr 11:27*

he that *s.* mischief, it shall *Pr 11:27* come

A scorner *s.* wisdom, and *Pr 14:6* findeth

hath understanding, *s.* *Pr 15:14* knowledge

covereth a transgression *s.* love *Pr 17:9*

an evil man *s.* only rebellion *Pr 17:11*

exalteth his gate *s.* *Pr 17:19* destruction

s. and intermeddleth with all *Pr 18:1*

the ear of the wise *s.* *Pr 18:15* knowledge

She *s.* wool, and flax, and *Pr 31:13*

Which yet my soul *s.* but I *Ec 7:28* find

s. unto him a cunning *Isa 40:20* workman

executeth judgment, *s.* the *Jer 5:1* truth

is Zion, whom no man *s.* *Jer 30:17* after

s. not the welfare of this *Jer 38:4* people

wait for him, to the soul that *La 3:25* *s.* him

punishment of him that *s.* *Eze 14:10* unto

As a shepherd *s.* out his flock *Eze 34:12*

receiveth; and he that *s.* *M't 7:8* findeth

evil generation *s.* after a *M't 12:39* sign

wicked generation *s.* after a *M't 16:4* sign

and *s.* that which is gone *M't 18:12* astray

receiveth; and he that *s.* Lu 11:10
findeth
the Father *s.* such to worship Joh 4:23
him
he himself *s.* to be known Joh 7:4
openly
speaketh of himself *s.* his Joh 7:18
own glory
he that *s.* his glory that sent Joh 7:18
him
there is one that *s.* and Joh 8:50
judgeth
there is none that *s.* after God Ro 3:11
not obtained that which he *s.* Ro 11:7
for
itself unseemly, *s.* not her 1Co 13:5
own

SEEKING

s. number of wives 2Ch 11:23
(A)(B)(E)
s. the wealth of his people, and Es 10:3
judging, and *s.* judgment, and Isa 16:5
places, *s.* rest, and findeth M't 12:43
none
a merchant man, *s.* goodly M't 13:45
pearls
him, *s.* of him a sign from M'k 8:11
heaven
back again to Jerusalem, *s.* Lu 2:45
him
walketh through dry places, Lu 11:24
s. rest
and *s.* to catch something out Lu 11:54
of his
three years I come *s.* fruit Lu 13:7
on this
came to Capernaum, *s.* for Joh 6:24
Jesus
s. to turn away the deputy Ac 13:8
from the
s. some to lead him by the Ac 13:11
hand
not *s.* mine own profit, but 1Co 10:33
about, *s.* whom he may devour 1Pe 5:8

SEEM

shall *s.* to him as a deceiver Ge 27:12
It shall not *s.* hard unto thee De 15:18
brother should *s.* vile unto De 25:3
thee
s. evil unto you to serve the Jos 24:15
as it shall *s.* good unto thee 1Sa 24:4
what shall *s.* good unto thee 2Sa 19:37
which shall *s.* good unto thee 2Sa 19:38
if it *s.* good to thee, I will 1Ki 21:2
give
If it *s.* good unto you, and 1Ch 13:2
that it
if it *s.* good to the king, let Ezr 5:17
there be
whatsoever shall *s.* good to Ezr 7:18
thee
let not all the trouble *s.* little Ne 9:32
If it *s.* good unto the king, let Es 5:4
the thing *s.* right before the Es 8:5
king
If it *s.* good unto thee to Jer 40:4
come
but if it *s.* ill unto thee to Jer 40:4
come
they shall *s.* like torches, they Na 2:4
if any man *s.* to be 1Co 11:16
contentious
body, which *s.* to be more 1Co 12:22
feeble
I may not *s.* as if I would 2Co 10:9
terrify
of you should *s.* to come Heb 4:1
short of it
man among you *s.* to be Jas 1:26
religious

SEEMED

he *s.* as one that mocked Ge 19:14
unto
s. unto him but a few days Ge 29:20
all that *s.* good to Israel, and 2Sa 3:19
that *s.* good to the whole 2Sa 3:19
house of
the sun, and it *s.* great unto Ec 9:13
me
as *s.* good to the potter to Jer 18:4
make it
have given it unto whom it *s.* Jer 27:5
meet
for so it *s.* good in thy sight M't 11:26

It *s.* good to me also, having Lu 1:3
had
for so it *s.* good in thy sight Lu 10:21
words *s.* to them as idle Lu 24:11
tales, and
s. good unto us, being Ac 15:25
assembled
For it *s.* good to the Holy Ac 15:28
Ghost
But of these who *s.* to be Ga 2:6
somewhat
s. to be somewhat in conference Ga 2:6
and John, who *s.* to be pillars Ga 2:9

SEEMETH

It *s.* to me there is as it were Le 14:35
S. it but a small thing unto Nu 16:9
you
as it *s.* good and right unto Jos 9:25
thee
us whatsoever *s.* good unto J'g 10:15
thee
unto them what *s.* good unto J'g 19:24
you
Do what *s.* thee good; tarry 1Sa 1:23
until
let him do what *s.* him good 1Sa 3:18
with us all that *s.* good unto 1Sa 11:10
you
Do whatsoever *s.* good unto 1Sa 14:36
thee
Do what *s.* good unto thee 1Sa 14:40
S. it to you a light thing to 1Sa 18:23
be a
Lord do that which *s.* him 2Sa 10:12
good
him do to me as *s.* good 2Sa 15:26
unto him
What *s.* you best I will do 2Sa 18:4
offer up what *s.* good unto 2Sa 24:22
him
with them as it *s.* good to thee Es 3:11
a way which *s.* right unto a Pr 14:12
man
is a way that *s.* right unto a Pr 16:25
man
that is first in his own cause Pr 18:17
s. just
do with me as *s.* good and Jer 26:14
meet
it *s.* good and convenient for Jer 40:4
thee
wheresoever it *s.* convenient Jer 40:5
unto
S. it a small thing unto you to Eze 34:18
have
even that which he *s.* to have Lu 8:18
He *s.* to be a setter forth of Ac 17:18
strange
it *s.* to me unreasonable to Ac 25:27
send a
you *s.* to be wise in this world 1Co 3:18
for the present *s.* to be Heb 12:11
joyous, but

SEEMLY

Delight is not *s.* for a fool Pr 19:10
so honour is not *s.* for a fool Pr 26:1
things which are not *s.* (S) Ro 1:28
but for that which is *s.* (S) 1Co 7:35
is it *s.* that a woman pray 1Co 11:13
(S)

SEEN

were the tops of the mountains Ge 8:5
s.
that the bow shall be *s.* in the Ge 9:14
cloud
I also have *s.* him (S) Ge 16:13
in the mount of the Lord it Ge 22:14
shall be *s.*
God hath *s.* mine affliction Ge 31:42
such locusts as fathers have Ex 10:6
not *s.*
no leavened bread be *s.* Ex 13:7;
De 16:4
back parts, but my face shall Ex 33:23
not be *s.*
neither let any man be *s.* Ex 34:3
through the mount
whether he hath *s.* or known Le 5:1
swearing
that thou, Lord, art *s.* face Nu 14:14
to face
those men which have *s.* my Nu 14:22
glory
nor hath he *s.* perverseness Nu 23:21
in Israel

when thou hast *s.* it, thou Nu 27:13
shalt be
we have *s.* the sons of the De 1:28
Anakims
hast *s.* how the Lord bare thee De 1:31
as a man
thine eyes have *s.* all the Lord De 3:21
hath done
s. what the Lord did because of De 4:3
Baal-peor
lest thou forget the things thine De 4:9
eyes have *s.*
we have *s.* that God doth talk De 5:24
with man
great and terrible things thine De 10:21
eyes have *s.*
have not *s.* the chastisement of De 11:2
the Lord
your eyes have *s.* all the great De 11:7
acts
hands have not shed, nor have De 21:7
our eyes *s.* it
the great temptations thine De 29:3
eyes have *s.*
who said to his mother, I have De 33:9
not *s.* him
eyes have *s.* what I have done Jos 24:7
in Egypt
the elders who had *s.* the great J'g 2:7
works
was there a shield or spear *s.* J'g 5:8
among 40,000
we shall die, because we have J'g 13:22
s. God
we have *s.* land, behold, it is J'g 18:9
very good
there was no such deed done J'g 19:30
nor *s.*
five lords had *s.* it, they 1Sa 6:16
returned
see his place, and who hath 1Sa 23:22
s. him there
behold, this day thine eyes 1Sa 24:10
have *s.* how
go tell the king what thou 2Sa 18:21
hast *s.*
he was *s.* upon the wings of 2Sa 22:11
the wind
all was cedar, there was no 1Ki 6:18
stone *s.*
ends of the staves were not *s.* 1Ki 8:8
in holy place
queen of Sheba had *s.* 1Ki 10:4
Solomon's wisdom
till I came and mine eyes 1Ki 10:7;
had *s.* 2Ch 9:3, 6
no such almug trees were *s.* 1Ki 10:12
unto this day
sons had *s.* what way man 1Ki 13:12
of God went
hast thou *s.* all this great 1Ki 20:13
multitude
what have they *s.*? Hezekiah 2Ki 20:15;
said, All things Isa 39:4
he slew Josiah, when he had 2Ki 23:29
s. him
many that had *s.* the first Ezr 3:12
house, wept
of that which they had *s.* Es 9:26
concerning
eye that hath *s.* me shall see Job 7:8
me no more
his place shall say, I have not Job 8:18
s. thee
oh that I had died, and no Job 10:18
eye had *s.* me
mine eye hath *s.* all this, Job 13:1
mine ear heard
they that have *s.* him shall say, Job 20:7
Where is he
a path which the vulture's eye Job 28:7
hath not *s.*
hast thou *s.* doors of the Job 38:17
shadow of death
or hast thou *s.* the treasures Job 38:22
of hail
thou hast *s.* it, for thou Ps 10:14
beholdest mischief
his flesh is consumed, it Ps 33:21
cannot be *s.*
our eye hath *s.*; this thou Ps 35:21;
hast *s.* 35:22
so have we *s.* in city of the Ps 48:8
Lord of hosts
mine eye hath *s.* his desire Ps 54:7
on enemies
they have *s.* thy goings, O Ps 68:24
God
and the years wherein we Ps 90:15
have *s.* evil

the ends of earth have *s.*   *Ps 98:3*
salvation of God
the prince whom thine eyes   *Pr 25:7*
have *s.*
who hath not *s.* the evil work   *Ec 4:3*
that is
he hath not *s.* the sun, nor   *Ec 6:5*
known any
yea, though I live, yet hath he   *Ec 6:6*
s. no good
for mine eyes have *s.* the Lord   *Isa 6:5*
of hosts
that walked in darkness have *s.*   *Isa 9:2*
a great light
when it is *s.* that Moab is   *Isa 16:12*
weary
thy nakedness covered, thy   *Isa 47:3*
shame shall be
and his giory shall be *s.* upon   *Isa 60:2*
thee
nor hath eye *s.* what he hath   *Isa 64:4*
prepared for
who hath heard, who hath *s.*   *Isa 66:8*
such things
to the isles afar off that have   *Isa 66:19*
not *s.* my glory
then said the Lord, Thou   *Jer 1:12*
hast well *s.*
hast thou *s.* what backsliding   *Jer 3:6*
Israel hath done
thou hast *s.* me, and tried my   *Jer 12:3*
heart
because they have *s.* her   *La 1:8*
nakedness
she hath *s.* heathen entered   *La 1:10*
into her sanctuary
prophets have *s.* vain and   *La 2:14*
foolish things; they have *s.* false
burdens
thy enemies say, We have   *La 2:16*
found, we have *s.* it
O Lord thou hast *s.* my   *La 3:59*
wrong, judge my cause
thou hast *s.* all their   *La 3:60*
vengeance against me
thou hast *s.* what the ancients   *Eze 8:12*
do
then said he, Hast thou *s.*   *Eze 8:15;*
this   *8:17; 47:6*
and have *s.* nothing; they   *Eze 13:3;*
have *s.* vanity   *13:6*
have ye not *s.* a vain vision,   *Eze 13:7*
whereas ye say
Gabriel whom I had *s.* in the   *Da 9:21*
vision
and the Lord shall be *s.*   *Zec 9:14*
over them
and the diviners have *s.* a lie,   *Zec 10:2*
and told
for we have *s.* his star in the   *M't 2:2*
east
do not your alms to be *s.* of   *M't 6:1;*
men   *6:5*
saying, It was never so *s.* in   *M't 9:33*
Israel
those things and have   *M't 13:17;*
not *s.* them   *Lu 10:24*
and ye, when ye had *s.* it,   *M't 21:32*
repented not
all their works they do to be   *M't 23:5*
s. of men
till they have *s.* the kingdom   *M'k 9:1*
of God
they should tell no man what   *M'k 9:9*
things they had *s.*
they heard that he had been   *M'k 16:11*
s. of her
they believed not them   *M'k 16:14*
which had *s.* him
they perceived that he had *s.* a   *Lu 1:22*
vision
praising God for all things they   *Lu 2:20*
had *s.*
not see death before he had *s.*   *Lu 2:26*
Lord's Christ
for mine eyes have *s.* thy   *Lu 2:30*
salvation
saying, We have *s.* strange   *Lu 5:26*
things to-day
told no man the things which   *Lu 9:36*
they had *s.*
for all the mighty works that   *Lu 19:37*
they had *s.*
he hoped to have *s.* some   *Lu 23:8*
miracle done
saying, That they had *s.* a   *Lu 24:23*
vision of angels
and supposed that they had   *Lu 24:37*
s. a spirit
no man hath *s.* God *Joh 1:18; 1Jo 4:12*

verily we testify that we have   *Joh 3:11*
s.
what he hath *s.* and heard that   *Joh 3:32*
he testifieth
the Galileans had *s.* all he did   *Joh 4:45*
at Jerusalem
ye have not at any time *s.* his   *Joh 5:37*
shape
those men, when they had *s.*   *Joh 6:14*
the miracle
not that any man hath *s.* the   *Joh 6:46*
Father
not fifty years old, and hast   *Joh 8:57*
thou *s.* Abraham
the neighbours which before   *Joh 9:8*
had *s.* him
thou hast both *s.* and it is he   *Joh 9:37*
that talketh
had *s.* what Jesus did,   *Joh 11:45*
believed on him
he that hath *s.* me, hath *s.*   *Joh 14:9*
the Father
have *s.* and hated both me   *Joh 15:24*
and my Father
she had *s.* the Lord; have *s.*   *Joh 20:18;*
the Lord   *20:25*
Thomas, because thou hast   *Joh 20:29*
s. hast believed
being *s.* of them forty days   *Ac 1:3;*
                   13:31
we cannot but speak things we   *Ac 4:20*
have *s.*
according to the fashion that   *Ac 7:44*
he had *s.*
he hath *s.* in a vision a man   *Ac 9:12*
named Ananias
declared to them how he had   *Ac 9:27*
s. the Lord
what this vision he had *s.*   *Ac 10:17*
should mean
he shewed us how he had *s.*   *Ac 11:13*
an angel
when he had *s.* the grace of   *Ac 11:23*
God was glad
after he had *s.* vision we   *Ac 16:10*
went to Macedonia
they had *s.* the brethren, they   *Ac 16:40*
comforted them
they had *s.* before with him   *Ac 21:29*
Trophimus
be witness of what thou hast   *Ac 22:15;*
s.   *26:16*
the invisible things of him are   *Ro 1:20*
clearly *s.*
but hope that is *s.* is not   *Ro 8:24*
hope, for what a man
eye hath not *s.* nor ear heard   *1Co 2:9*
have I not *s.* Jesus Christ our   *1Co 9:1*
Lord
he was *s.* of Cephas, then of   *1Co 15:5*
the twelve
after that he was *s.* of above   *1Co 15:6*
500 brethren
s. of James; last of all he   *1Co 15:7;*
was *s.* of me also   *15:8*
look not at things that are *s.*   *2Co 4:18*
but at things which are not *s.*
things ye have heard and *s.* in   *Ph'p 4:9*
me, do
things (A)(P), unseen   *Col 1:16*
and for as many as have not *s.*   *Col 2:1*
my face
intruding into those things he   *Col 2:18*
hath not *s.*
God was manifest in flesh, *s.*   *1Ti 3:16*
of angels
whom no man hath *s.* or can   *1Ti 6:16*
see
faith is the evidence of things   *Heb 11:1*
not *s.*
so that things which are *s.*   *Heb 11:3*
were not made
Noah being warned of God of   *Heb 11:7*
things not *s.*
having *s.* them afar off were   *Heb 11:13*
persuaded
whom having not *s.* ye love, in   *1Pe 1:8*
whom
that which we have *s.* with our   *1Jo 1:1*
eyes
the life was manifested, and   *1Jo 1:2*
we have *s.* it
that which we have *s.* declare   *1Jo 1:3*
we unto you
whosoever sinneth hath not *s.*   *1Jo 3:6*
him nor known
we have *s.* and do testify,   *1Jo 4:14*
Father sent the Son
loveth not his brother whom   *1Jo 4:20*
he hath *s.* how can he love God

whom he hath not *s.*
he that doeth evil hath not *s.*   *3Jo 11*
God
write the things which thou   *Re 1:19*
hast *s.*
there was *s.* in his temple the   *Re 11:19*
ark
when I had heard and *s.* I fell   *Re 22:8*
down to worship

HAVE I SEEN

thee *have I s.* righteous before   *Ge 7:1*
me
now *have I s.* thy people to   *1Ch 29:17*
offer
yet *have I* not *s.* the   *Ps 37:25*
righteous forsaken
all things *have I s.* in days of   *Ec 7:15*
my vanity
all this *have I s.* and applied   *Ec 8:9*
my heart
this wisdom *have I s.* under   *Ec 9:13*
the sun
wherefore *have I s.* them   *Jer 46:5*
dismayed
for now *have I s.* with mine   *Zec 9:8*
eyes

I HAVE SEEN

I have s. all that Laban doth   *Ge 31:12*
to thee
I have s. God face to face,   *Ge 32:30*
and am preserved
for therefore *I have s.* thy   *Ge 33:10;*
face   *46:30*
I have s. the affliction of my   *Ex 3:7*
people
I have also *s.* the oppression   *Ex 3:9;*
                  3:16
Lord said, *I have s.* this   *Ex 32:9;*
people   *De 9:13*
alas, for because *I have s.* an   *J'g 6:22*
angel
I have s. a woman in Timnah,   *J'g 14:2*
get her
I have s. a son of Jesse   *1Sa 16:18*
cunning
I have s. yesterday blood of   *2Ki 9:26*
Naboth
saith Lord, *I have s.* thy tears *2Ki 20:5;*
                  Isa 38:5
even as *I have s.* they that plow *Job 4:8*
iniquity
I have s. the foolish taking   *Job 5:3*
root, but I cursed
hear me, that which *I have*   *Job 15:17*
s. I declare
if *I have s.* any perish for   *Job 31:19*
want of clothing
I have s. the wicked in great   *Ps 37:35*
power
I have s. violence and strife in   *Ps 55:9*
the city
glory, so as *I have s.* thee in   *Ps 63:2*
the sanctuary
I have s. an end of all   *Ps 119:96*
perfection
I have s. all the works under   *Ec 1:14*
the sun
I have s. the travail which   *Ec 3:10*
God hath given
there is a sore evil which *I*   *Ec 5:13*
have s. under sun
behold that which *I have s.* it   *Ec 5:18*
is good to eat
there is an evil which *I have s.*   *Ec 6:1;*
                  10:5
I have s. servants upon horses, *Ec 10:7*
and princes walk
he saith, I am warm, *I have*   *Isa 44:16*
s. the fire
I have s. his ways, and will   *Isa 57:18*
heal him
behold, *I have s.* it saith the   *Jer 7:11*
Lord
I have s. thine adulteries and   *Jer 13:27*
neighings
I have s. folly in prophets of   *Jer 23:13;*
Samaria   *23:14*
I have s. affliction by rod of his *La 3:1*
wrath
make known unto me the   *Da 2:26*
dream *I have s.*
the vision of my dream that I   *Da 4:9;*
have s.   *4:18*
I have s. an horrible thing in   *Ho 6:10*
Israel

I speak that *I* have *s.* with my Father   *Joh 8:38*

I have *s.* the affliction of my people   *Ac 7:34*

YE HAVE SEEN

tell my father of all that *ye have s.*   *Ge 45:13*

the Egyptians whom *ye have s.* to-day   *Ex 14:13*

ye have s. what I did unto the Egyptians   *Ex 19:4*

ye have s. that I have talked with you   *Ex 20:22*

ye have s. all the Lord did in Egypt unto Pharaoh   *De 29:2; Jos 23:3*

ye have s. their abominations and idols   *De 29:17*

what *ye have s.* me do, do as I have done   *J'g 9:48*

have ye s. this man that is come up   *1Sa 17:25*

behold, all *ye* yourselves *have s.* it   *Job 27:12*

ye have s. the breaches of the city   *Isa 22:9*

ye have s. all the evil I have brought   *Jer 44:2*

ye have s. lies, therefore I am against you   *Eze 13:8*

tell John what things *ye have s.*   *Lu 7:22*

ye also *have s.* me, and believe not   *Joh 6:36*

ye do that *ye have s.* with your Father   *Joh 8:38*

henceforth *ye* know him, and *have s.* him   *Joh 14:7*

Jesus shall so come, as *ye have s.* him go   *Ac 1:11*

ye have s. the end of the Lord   *Jas 5:11*

SEER

Come, and let us go to the *s.*   *1Sa 9:9*

Prophet was beforetime called a *S.*   *1Sa 9:9*

and said unto them, Is the *s.* here   *1Sa 9:11*

answered Saul, and said, I am the *s.*   *1Sa 9:19*

Zadok the priest, Art not thou a *s.*   *2Sa 15:27*

unto the prophet Gad, David's *s.*   *2Sa 24:11*

the prophet Gad (A)(B)   *2Sa 24:11*

David and Samuel the *s.* did ordain   *1Ch 9:22*

Lord spake unto Gad, David's *s.*   *1Ch 21:9*

the sons of Heman the king's *s.* in   *1Ch 25:5*

all that Samuel the *s.* and Saul   *1Ch 26:28*

in the book of Samuel the *s.*   *1Ch 29:29*

and in the book of Gad the *s.*   *1Ch 29:29*

and in the visions Iddo the *s.*   *2Ch 9:29*

Iddo the *s.* concerning genealogies   *2Ch 12:15*

Hanani the *s.* came to Asa king   *2Ch 16:7*

Then Asa was wroth with the *s.*   *2Ch 16:10*

of Hanani the *s.* went out to meet   *2Ch 19:2*

of David, and of Gad the king's *s.*   *2Ch 29:25*

of David, and of Asaph the *s.*   *2Ch 29:30*

Heman, and Jeduthun the king's *s.*   *2Ch 35:15*

O thou *s.*, go, flee thee away into   *Am 7:12*

SEERS

all the prophets, and by all the *s.*   *2Ki 17:13*

words of the *s.* that spake to him   *2Ch 33:18*

written among the sayings of the *s.*   *2Ch 33:19*

your rulers, the *s.* hath he covered   *Isa 29:10*

Which say to the *s.*, See not   *Isa 30:10*

Then shall the *s.* be ashamed   *Mic 3:7*

SEER'S

Tell me where the *s.* house is   *1Sa 9:18*

SEEST

For all the land which thou *s.* to   *Ge 13:15*

spake unto her, Thou God *s.* me   *Ge 16:13*

and all that thou *s.* is mine   *Ge 31:43*

day thou *s.* my face thou shalt die   *Ex 10:28*

and when thou *s.* the sun, and   *De 4:19*

offerings in every place thou *s.*   *De 12:13*

and *s.* horses, and chariots, and a   *De 20:1*

s. among the captives a beautiful   *De 21:11*

s. the shadow of the mountains as   *J'g 9:36*

S. thou how Ahab humbleth   *1Ki 21:29*

of flesh? or *s.* thou as man seeth   *Job 10:4*

S. thou a man diligent in his   *Pr 22:29*

S. thou a man wise in his own   *Pr 26:12*

S. thou a man that is hasty in his   *Pr 29:20*

thou *s.* the oppression of the poor   *Ec 5:8*

fasted, say they, and thou *s.* not   *Isa 58:3*

when thou *s.* the naked, that thou   *Isa 58:7*

saying, Jeremiah, what *s.* thou   *Jer 1:11*

second time, saying, What *s.* thou   *Jer 1:13*

S. thou not what they do in   *Jer 7:17*

and *s.* the reins and the heart, let   *Jer 20:12*

unto me, What *s.* thou, Jeremiah   *Jer 24:3*

to pass; and, behold, thou *s.* it   *Jer 32:24*

Son of man, *s.* thou what they do   *Eze 8:6*

declare all that thou *s.* to the house   *Eze 40:4*

as thou *s.* deal with thy servants   *Da 1:13*

said unto me, Amos, what *s.* thou   *Am 7:8*

And he said, Amos, what *s.* thou   *Am 8:2*

And said unto me, What *s.* thou   *Zec 4:2*

he said unto me, What *s.* thou   *Zec 5:2*

s. the multitude thronging thee   *M'k 5:31*

him, *S.* thou these great buildings   *M'k 13:2*

unto Simon, *S.* thou this woman   *Lu 7:44*

him, Thou *s.*, brother, how many   *Ac 21:20*

S. thou how faith wrought with his   *Jas 2:22*

What thou *s.* write in a book   *Re 1:11*

SEETH

here looked after him that *s.* me   *Ge 16:13*

when he *s.* that the lad is not with   *Ge 44:31*

when he *s.* thee, he will be glad in   *Ex 4:14*

he *s.* the blood upon the lintel   *Ex 12:23*

when the priest *s.* it, behold, it be   *Le 13:20*

he *s.* that their power is gone, and   *De 32:36*

him: for the Lord *s.* not as man   *1Sa 16:7*

not as man *s.*; for man looketh   *1Sa 16:7*

this city is pleasant, as my lord *s.*   *2Ki 2:19*

heap, and *s.* the place of stones   *Job 8:17*

of flesh? or seest thou as man *s.*   *Job 10:4*

he *s.* wickedness also; will he not   *Job 11:11*

a covering to him, that he *s.* not   *Job 22:14*

his eye *s.* every precious thing   *Job 28:10*

and *s.* under the whole heaven   *Job 28:24*

of man, and he *s.* all his goings   *Job 34:21*

the ear; but now mine eye *s.* thee   *Job 42:5*

for he *s.* that his day is coming   *Ps 37:13*

he *s.* that wise men die, likewise   *Ps 49:10*

rejoice when he *s.* the vengeance   *Ps 58:10*

neither day nor night *s.* sleep with   *Ec 8:16*

let him declare what he *s.*   *Isa 21:6*

he that looketh upon it *s.* while it   *Isa 28:4*

the dark, and they say, Who *s.* us   *Isa 29:15*

when he *s.* his children, the work   *Isa 29:23*

thou hast said, None *s.* me   *Isa 47:10*

The Lord *s.* us not; the Lord hath   *Eze 8:12*

the earth, and the Lord *s.* not   *Eze 9:9*

vision that he *s.* is for many days   *Eze 12:27*

s. all his father's sins which   *Eze 18:14*

s. the sword come upon the land   *Eze 33:3*

when any *s.* a man's bone, then   *Eze 39:15*

and thy Father which *s.* in secret   *M't 6:4*

thy Father which *s.* in secret shall   *M't 6:6*

which *s.* in secret shall reward thee   *M't 6:18*

the tumult, and them that wept   *M'k 5:38*

s. Abraham afar off, and Lazarus   *Lu 16:23*

John *s.* Jesus coming unto him   *Joh 1:29*

but what he *s.* the Father do   *Joh 5:19*

that every one which *s.* the Son   *Joh 6:40*

means he now *s.* we know not; or   *Joh 9:21*

s. the wolf coming, and leaveth   *Joh 10:12*

he *s.* the light of this world   *Joh 11:9*

that *s.* me *s.* him that sent me   *Joh 12:45*

it *s.* him not, neither knoweth him   *Joh 14:17*

and the world *s.* me no more; but   *Joh 14:19*

s. the stone taken away from   *Joh 20:1*

sepulchre, and *s.* the linen clothes   *Joh 20:6*

s. two angels in white sitting, the   *Joh 20:12*

s. the disciple whom Jesus loved   *Joh 21:20*

for what a man *s.* why doth he   *Ro 8:24*

me above that which he *s.* me to be   *2Co 12:6*

and *s.* his brother have need   *1Jo 3:17*

SEETHE

to-day, and *s.* that ye will *s.*   *Ex 16:23*

boil (A)(E)(R)   *Ex 16:23; 23:19; 29:31; 34:26; De 14:21*

not *s.* a kid in his mother's milk   *Ex 23:19; 29:31; 34:26; De 14:21*

boil (B)   *Ex 23:19; 29:31; 34:26; De 14:21*

and *s.* pottage for the sons of   *2Ki 4:38*

cook pottage (A)   *2Ki 4:38*

boil stew (B)   *2Ki 4:38*

boil pottage (E)(R)   *2Ki 4:38*

let them *s.* the bones of it therein   *Eze 24:5*

boil well (E)   *Eze 24:5*

and take of them, and *s.* therein   *Zec 14:21*

boil their sacrifices (A)(B)(E)(R)   *Zec 14:21*

SEETHING

came while the flesh was in *s.*   *1Sa 2:13*

while flesh was boiling (A)(B)(E)(R)   *1Sa 2:13*

as out of a *s.* pot or caldron   *Job 41:20*

SEETHING

boiling pot (B)(E)(R)   *Job 41:20;*
    Jer 1:13
I see a *s.* pot; and the face   *Jer 1:13*
thereof

SEGUB

thereof in his youngest son *S. 1Ki 16:34*
years old; and she bare him   *1Ch 2:21*
S.
And *S.* begat Jair, who had   *1Ch 2:22*
three

SEINE

collects them in their *s.* (B)   *Hab 1:15*
burn incense to their *s.*   *Hab 1:16*
(B)(R)
like a *s.* (B)   *M't 13:47*

SEIR

to the land of *S.* the country   *Ge 32:3*
of Edom
lead softly, till I come to my   *Ge 33:14*
lord to *S.*
these are sons of *S.*   *Ge 36:20;*
    36:21; 1Ch 1:38
S. shall be a possession for   *Nu 24:18*
enemies
the Amorites destroyed you in *De 1:44*
S.
the Lord came from Sinai and *De 33:2*
rose up from *S.*
Lord, when thou wentest out of *J'g 5:4*
S.
made an end of the   *2Ch 20:23*
inhabitants of *S.*
Amaziah smote of children *2Ch 25:11*
of *S.* 10,000
he brought the gods of the *2Ch 25:14*
children of *S.*
he calleth to me out of *S.,*   *Isa 21:11*
Watchman
because that Moab and *S.* do *Eze 25:8*
say

MOUNT SEIR

and the Horites in their   *Ge 14:6*
mount S.
thus dwelt Esau in *mount S.*   *Ge 36:8;*
    36:9
we compassed *mount S.* many *De 2:1*
days
I have given *mount S.* to Esau *De 2:5;*
    Jos 24:4
of sons of Simeon 500 went *1Ch 4:42*
to *mount S.*
mount S. whom wouldst not *2Ch 20:10*
let invade
the Lord set ambushments *2Ch 20:22*
against *mount S.*
Ammon and Moab stood up *2Ch 20:23*
against *mount S.*
set thy face against *mount Eze 35:2*
S.
say to, behold O *mount S. Eze 35:3*
I am against thee
thus will I make *mount S. Eze 35:7;*
most desolate   *35:15*

SEIRATH

the quarries, and escaped unto *J'g 3:26*
S.

SEIZE

the ambush, and *s.* upon the   *Jos 8:7*
city
that night, let darkness *s.* upon *Job 3:6*
it
Let death *s.* upon them, and *Ps 55:15*
chase and *s.* him (B)(R)   *Ps 71:11*
agony will *s.* them (B)(R)   *Isa 13:8*
shall *s.* them (B)   *Jer 20:5*
and let us *s.* on his   *M't 21:38*
inheritance

SEIZED

to flee, and fear hath *s.* on   *Jer 49:24*
her
they *s.* him (R)   *Ac 24:6*

SEIZING

s. men and women (N)   *Ac 8:3*

SELA

the land from *S.* to the   *Isa 16:1*
wilderness

SELAH

and took *S.* by war, and   *2Ki 14:7*
called the
Selah   *Ps 3:2, 4, 8;*
4:2, 4; 7:5; 9:16, 20; 20:3; 21:2; 24:6,
10; 32:4, 5, 7; 39:5, 11; 44:8; 46:3, 7,
11; 47:4; 48:8; 49:13, 15; 50:6; 52:3, 5;
54:3; 55:7, 19; 57:3, 6; 59:5, 13; 60:4;
61:4; 62:4, 8; 66:4, 7, 15; 67:1, 4; 68:7,
19, 32; 75:3; 76:3, 9; 77:3, 9, 15; 81:7;
82:2; 83:8; 84:4, 8; 85:2; 87:3, 6; 88:7,
10; 89:4, 37, 45, 48; 140:3, 5, 8; 148:6
Selah   *Hab 3:3; 3:9, 13*

SELAH-HAMMAHLEKOTH

therefore they called that   *1Sa 23:28*
place *S.*

SELECT

S. out the best of master's   *2Ki 10:3*
sons (S)

SELECTION

selection (A)   *Ro 9:11;*
    11:5, 28; 1Th 1:4

SELED

sons of Nadab; *S.* and   *1Ch 2:30*
Appaim
but *S.* died without children *1Ch 2:30*

SELEUCIA

the Holy Ghost, departed unto *Ac 13:4*
S.

SELF

suffer no *s.* accusation (B)   *1Sa 25:31*
my lonely *s.* (B)   *Ps 22:20*
my inmost *s.* (B)   *Ps 94:19*
your inner *s.* (A)   *Pr 3:22*
I try the inner *s.* (B)   *Jer 17:10*
lose his true *s.* (N)   *M't 16:26*
grasping *s.*-indulgence   *M't 23:25*
(A)(N)(P)
s.-seeking, *s.*-willed (A)   *Ro 2:8*
governed by *s.* ambition (N)   *Ro 2:8*
in my inmost *s.* (A)(N)(R)   *Ro 7:22*
s.-willed people (A)   *Ro 10:21*
are utterly *s.*-centered (P)   *Ro 16:18*
filled with *s.* importance (N) *1Co 4:18*
lack of *s.* (B)(E)(R)   *1Co 7:5*
if they cannot have *s.* let them *1Co 7:9*
(S)
have *s.*-control (A)(P)(R)   *1Co 7:9*
s.-control (R)   *1Co 9:25*
our inner *s.* being renewed *2Co 4:16*
(A)(B)
s.-control   *Ga 5:23; 2Pe 1:6*
(A)(B)(N)(P)(R)(S)
let us have no *s.*-conceit (R) *Ga 5:26*
not in *s.*-gratification (P)   *1Th 4:5*
neither principles nor *s.*-control *1Ti 1:9*
(R)
power, love, *s.*-discipline (N) *2Ti 1:7*
power, love, *s.*-control (B)(R) *2Ti 1:7*
without *s.* (E)   *2Ti 3:3*
s.-controlled (B)(P)(R)   *Tit 1:8*
to be *s.*-controlled (A)   *Tit 2:5*
be perfectly *s.*-controlled (N) *1Pe 1:13*
keep sound-minded,   *1Pe 4:7*
s.-restrained (A)
be calm, *s.*-controlled (P)   *1Pe 4:7*
be *s.*-controlled (P)   *1Pe 5:8*
daring and *s.*-willed (E)(N)   *2Pe 2:10*

OWN SELF

to whom swarest by thine   *Ex 32:13*
own s.
I can of mine *own s.* do   *Joh 5:30*
nothing
Father, glorify thou me with *Joh 17:5*
thine *own s.*
yea, I judge not mine *own s.*   *1Co 4:3*
thou owest unto me even   *Ph'm 19*
thine *own s.*
who his *own s.* bare our sins *1Pe 2:24*
in his body

SELFISHNESS

nothing through strife, *s.*   *Ph'p 2:3*
(A)(R)

SELFSAME

In the *s.* day entered Noah   *Ge 7:13*
of their foreskin in the *s.* day *Ge 17:23*
in the *s.* day was Abraham *Ge 17:26*
this *s.* day have I brought *Ex 12:17*
your
even the *s.* day it came to *Ex 12:41*
pass
And it came to pass the *s. Ex 12:51*
day
s. day that ye have brought *Le 23:14*
ye shall proclaim on the *s. Le 23:21*
day
spake unto Moses that *s.* day *De 32:48*
and parched corn in the *s. Jos 5:11*
day
the *s.* day the hand of the *Eze 40:1*
Lord
servant was healed in the *s. M't 8:13*
hour
worketh that one and the *s. 1Co 12:11*
Spirit
wrought us for the *s.* thing is *2Co 5:5*
For behold this *s.* thing, that *2Co 7:11*

SELFWILL

their *s.* they digged down a   *Ge 49:6*
wall
insolence (B)   *Ge 49:6*
wantonness (R)   *Ge 49:6*

SELFWILLED

not *s.* not soon angry, not   *Tit 1:7*
given to
Presumptuous are they, *s.,*   *2Pe 2:10*
they

SELL

said, *S.* me this day thy   *Ge 25:31*
birthright
and let us *s.* him to the   *Ge 37:27*
Ishmeelites
s. his daughter to be a   *Ex 21:7*
maidservant
to *s.* her unto a strange   *Ex 21:8*
nation he
then they shall *s.* the live ox *Ex 21:35*
ox, or a sheep, and kill it, or *Ex 22:1*
s. it
thou *s.* ought unto thy   *Ex 25:14*
neighbour
of the fruits he shall *s.* unto *Ex 25:15*
thee
of the fruits doth he *s.* unto *Ex 25:16*
thee
s. a dwelling house in a   *Ex 25:29*
walled city
and *s.* himself unto the   *Ex 25:47*
stranger or
Thou shalt *s.* me meat for   *De 2:28*
money
thou mayest *s.* it unto an   *De 14:21*
alien
shalt not *s.* her at all for   *De 21:14*
money
s. for money or enslave   *De 21:14*
(B)(E)(R)
or *s.* him (E)(R)   *De 24:7*
the Lord shall *s.* Sisera into *J'g 4:9*
did *s.* himself to work   *1Ki 21:25*
wickedness
Go, *s.* the oil, and pay thy debt *2Ki 4:7*
and will ye even *s.* your   *Ne 5:8*
brethren
victuals on the sabbath day *Ne 10:31*
to *s.*
Buy the truth, and *s.* it not;   *Pr 23:23*
also
s. the land into the hand of *Eze 30:12*
And they shall not *s.* of it, *Eze 48:14*
neither
And I will *s.* your sons and   *Joe 3:8*
your
they shall *s.* them to the   *Joe 3:8*
Sabeans
be gone, that we may *s.* corn   *Am 8:5*
yea, and *s.* the refuse of the   *Am 8:6*
wheat
they that *s.* them say, Blessed *Zec 11:5*
be

go and *s.* that thou hast, *M't 19:21*
and give
go ye rather to them that *s.* *M't 25:9*
s. whatsoever thou hast, and *M'k 10:21*
give
S. that ye have and give alms *Lu 12:33*
s. all that thou hast, and *Lu 18:22*
distribute
no sword, let him *s.* his *Lu 22:36*
garment
and buy and *s.* and get gain *Jas 4:13*
that no man might buy or *s.* *Re 13:17*
save

SELLER

as with the buyer, so with the *Isa 24:2*
s.
buyer rejoice, nor the *s.* *Eze 7:12*
mourn
For the *s.* shall not return to *Eze 7:13*
that
named Lydia, a *s.* of purple *Ac 16:14*

SELLERS

merchants and *s.* of all kinds *Ne 13:20*
of

SELLEST

Thou *s.* thy people for nought *Ps 44:12*

SELLETH

that stealeth a man, and *s.* *Ex 21:16*
him
merchandise of him, or *s.* him *De 24:7*
s. a parcel of land, which was *Ru 4:3*
our
upon the head of him that *s.* *Pr 11:26*
it
She maketh fine linen, and *s.* *Pr 31:24*
it
s. nations through her *Na 3:4*
whoredoms
goeth and *s.* all that he hath *M't 13:44*

SELLING

s. him (B) *De 24:7*

SELVEDGE

from the *s.* in the coupling *Ex 26:4;*
36:11

SELVES

also of your own *s.* shall men *Ac 20:30*
rise
but first gave their own *s.* to *2Co 8:5*
the Lord
prove your own *s.* know ye *2Co 13:5*
not your own *s.*
men shall be lovers of their *2Ti 3:2*
own *s.*
not hearers, deceiving your *Jas 1:22*
own *s.*

SEM

which was the son of *S.* which *Lu 3:36*

SEMACHIAH

were strong men, Elihu, and *1Ch 26:7*
S.

SEMEI

which was the son of *S.* which *Lu 3:26*

SEMEN

has emission of *s.* (A)(R) *Le 15:16;*
15:17-18

SENAAH

The children of *S.* three *Ezr 2:35;*
thousand *Ne 7:38*

SENATE

all the *s.* of the children of *Ac 5:21*
Israel

SENATORS

the senators (B) *Ge 50:7*
pleasure; and teach his *s.* *Ps 105:22*
wisdom
teach elders wisdom *Ps 105:22*
(A)(B)(E)(R)

SEND

God shall *s.* his angel before *Ge 24:7;*
thee *24:40*
I pray thee, *s.* me good *Ge 24:12*
speed this day
he said, *S.* me away unto *Ge 24:54;*
my master *24:56*
wilt thou give me a pledge *Ge 38:17*
till thou *s.* it
if thou wilt *s.* our brother *Ge 43:4*
with us
God did *s.* me before you, to *Ge 45:5*
preserve life
s. by hand of him whom thou *Ex 4:13*
wilt *s.*
that he *s.* children of Israel *Ex 7:2*
out of his land
s. therefore now, and gather *Ex 9:19*
thy cattle
that they might *s.* them out *Ex 12:33*
in haste
nor let me know whom thou *Ex 33:12*
wilt *s.*
s. him away by the hand of a *Le 16:21*
fit man
s. thou men to search land, *Nu 13:2*
of every tribe shall ye *s.* a man
of every tribe *s.* a thousand to *Nu 31:4*
the war
we will *s.* men before us to *De 1:22*
search
thy God will *s.* the hornet *De 7:20*
among them
the elders shall *s.* and fetch *De 19:12*
him thence
give her a bill of divorce, and *De 24:1*
s. her out
Lord shall *s.* upon thee *De 28:20*
cursing and
shall serve enemies Lord *De 28:48*
shall *s.* against
let man of God thou didst *s.* *J'g 13:8*
come
s. away the ark of God *1Sa 5:11; 6:8*
tell us wherewith we shall *s.* it *1Sa 6:2*
to
if ye *s.* away the ark of God, *1Sa 6:3*
s. it not
saying, Up, that I may *s.* thee *1Sa 9:26*
away
give us respite, that we may *1Sa 11:3*
s. messengers
the Lord shall *s.* thunder *1Sa 12:17*
and rain
Samuel said to Jesse, *S.* *1Sa 16:11*
and fetch David
Saul sent and said, *S.* me *1Sa 16:19*
David thy son
I saw not the young men *1Sa 25:25*
thou didst *s.*
David saying, *S.* me Uriah *2Sa 11:6*
S. out all men from me (S) *2Sa 13:9*
come hither, that I may *s.* *2Sa 14:32*
thee to king
by them ye shall *s.* unto *2Sa 15:36*
me every thing
now *s.* quickly, and tell *2Sa 17:16*
David
all thou didst *s.* for thy servant *1Ki 20:9*
I will do
he said, not *s.*; he said, *S.* *2Ki 2:16;*
2:17
s. to me to recover a man of *2Ki 5:7*
his leprosy
spy where he is, that I may *s.* *2Ki 6:13*
and fetch
let us *s.* and see *2Ki 7:13*
s. to meet Jehu *2Ki 9:17*
the Lord began to *s.* against *2Ki 15:37*
Judah Rezin
let us *s.* abroad unto our *1Ch 13:2*
brethren
s. me a man cunning to work *2Ch 2:7*
s. me also cedar trees, *2Ch 2:8*
fir trees, algum trees
then hear thou, and *s.* rain *2Ch 6:27*
upon thy land
Ahaz did *s.* to king of *2Ch 28:16*
Assyria to help
Sennacherib did *s.* servants, *2Ch 32:9*
to Hezekiah

s. greetings (S) *Ezr 4:11*
let the king *s.* his pleasure to *Ezr 5:17*
us
that thou wouldest *s.* me unto *Ne 2:5*
Judah
it pleased the king to *s.* me, I *Ne 2:6*
set a time
eat, drink, and *s.* portions *Ne 8:10;*
unto them *8:12*
they *s.* forth their little ones *Job 21:11*
as a flock
canst thou *s.* lightnings, that *Job 38:35*
they may go
s. thee help from the sanctuary *Ps 20:2*
O *s.* out thy light and truth, let *Ps 43:3*
them lead
he shall *s.* from heaven, and *Ps 57:3*
save me; God shall *s.* forth his
thou. O God, didst *s.* a *Ps 68:9*
plentiful rain
he doth *s.* out his voice, a *Ps 68:33*
mighty voice
shall *s.* rod of thy strength *Ps 110:2*
out of Zion
Lord, I beseech thee, *s.* now *Ps 118:25*
prosperity
s. thine hand from above, rid *Ps 144:7*
me
so is the sluggard to them *Pr 10:26*
that *s.* him
words of truth to them that *Pr 22:21*
s. to thee
so is faithful messenger to *Pr 25:13*
them that *s.*
ointment to *s.* forth a stinking *Ec 10:1*
savour
whom shall I *s.?* I said, Here *Isa 6:8*
am I, *s.* me
Lord shall *s.* among his fat *Isa 10:16*
ones leanness
s. ye the lamb to the ruler of *Isa 16:1*
the land
he shall *s.* them a Saviour, a *Isa 19:20*
great one
that *s.* forth thither the feet *Isa 32:20*
of ox and ass
didst *s.* thy messengers far off, *Isa 57:9*
and debase
thou shalt go to all that I shall *Jer 1:7*
s. thee
s. unto Kedar; *s.* for cunning *Jer 2:10;*
women *9:17*
s. the yokes to king of Edom *Jer 27:3*
and Moab
s. to all them of the *Jer 29:31*
captivity, saying
for the which the Lord shall *s.* *Jer 42:5*
thee to us
we will obey the Lord, to *Jer 42:6*
whom we *s.* thee
pray ye the Lord he will *s.* *M't 9:38;*
forth labourers into his harvest *Lu 10:2*
think not that I am come to *M't 10:34*
s. peace
till he *s.* forth judgment *M't 12:20*
unto victory
Son of man shall *s.* forth his *M't 13:41;*
angels *24:31; M'k 13:27*
s. her away, for she crieth *M't 15:23*
after us
straightway he will *s.* them *M't 21:3;*
M'k 11:3
that he might *s.* them to *M'k 3:14;*
preach *6:7*
would not *s.* them away out *M'k 5:10*
of the country
besought him, saying, *S.* us *M'k 5:12*
into the swine
s. Lazarus; *s.* to my father's *Lu 16:24;*
house *16:27*
whom the Father will *s.* in my *Joh 14:26*
name
they have believed that thou *Joh 17:8*
didst *s.* me
he shall *s.* Jesus Christ who *Ac 3:20*
was preached
same God did *s.* to be a ruler *Ac 7:35*
and deliverer
and now *s.* men to Joppa *Ac 10:5;*
10:32; 11:13
disciples determined to *s.* *Ac 11:29*
relief to brethren
to *s.* chosen men of their *Ac 15:22;*
company *15:25*
that he would *s.* for him to *Ac 25:3*
Jerusalem
it seemeth unreasonable to *s.* *Ac 25:27*
a prisoner and

SEND (continued)

I trust in the Lord to *s*.   *Ph'p 2:19;*
Timotheus   *2:23*
I supposed it necessary to *s*.   *Ph'p 2:25*
Epaphroditus
for this cause God shall *s*.   *2Th 2:11*
delusions
when I shall *s*. Artemas unto   *Tit 3:12*
thee
doth fountain *s*. sweet water   *Jas 3:11*
and bitter
write and *s*. it to seven   *Re 1:11*
churches in Asia
and they shall *s*. gifts one to   *Re 11:10*
another

I SEND

behold, I *s*. an angel before   *Ex 23:20*
thee
did I not earnestly *s*. unto   *Nu 22:37*
thee
if there be good, and I *s*.   *1Sa 20:12*
not to thee
know the business   *1Sa 21:2*
whereabout I *s*. thee
if I *s*. pestilence   *2Ch 7:13; Eze 14:19*
voice of the Lord, saying,   *Isa 6:8*
Whom shall I *s*.
cause all, to whom I *s*. thee   *Jer 25:15*
to drink it
I *s*. thee to the children of   *Eze 2:3;*
Israel   *2:4*
when I *s*. my four sore   *Eze 14:21*
judgments
behold, I *s*. you forth as   *M't 10:16*
sheep
I *s*. my messenger before   *M't 11:10;*
thy face to prepare   *M'k 1:2; Lu 7:27*
I *s*. you prophets and wise   *M't 23:34*
men
if I *s*. them away fasting, they   *M'k 8:3*
will faint
I *s*. you forth as lambs among   *Lu 10:3*
wolves
I *s*. the promise of my Father   *Lu 24:49*
upon you
he that receiveth whom I *s*.   *Joh 13:20*
receiveth me
as my Father sent me, even   *Joh 20:21*
so *s*. I you
to be kept till I *s*. him to   *Ac 25:21*
Caesar
from Gentiles, unto whom   *Ac 26:17*
now I *s*. thee

I WILL SEND

I will *s*. and fetch thee from   *Ge 27:45*
thence
come, and I will *s*. thee unto   *Ge 37:13*
them
he said, I will *s*. thee a kid   *Ge 38:17*
from the flock
I will *s*. thee unto Pharaoh   *Ex 3:10;*
  Ac 7:34
I will *s*. swarms of flies upon   *Ex 8:21*
thee
I will *s*. all my plagues upon   *Ex 9:14*
thine heart
I will *s*. my fear; I will *s*.   *Ex 23:27;*
hornets   *23:28*
I will *s*. an angel before thee,   *Ex 33:2*
and drive out
I will *s*. wild beasts among   *Le 26:22*
you
I will *s*. pestilence; I will *s*.   *Le 26:25;*
faintness   *26:36*
I will *s*. grass in thy fields for   *De 11:15*
cattle
I will *s*. the teeth of beasts   *De 32:24*
upon them
I will *s*. thee a man of   *1Sa 9:16*
Benjamin
I will *s*. thee to Jesse the   *1Sa 16:1*
Beth-lehemite
then I will *s*. shew it thee,   *1Sa 20:13*
and send thee away
and I will *s*. rain upon the   *1Ki 18:1*
earth
yet I will *s*. my servants unto   *1Ki 20:6*
thee to-morrow
I will *s*. thee away with this   *1Ki 20:34*
covenant
I will *s*. a blast upon him   *2Ki 19:7;*
  Isa 37:7
I will *s*. him against   *Isa 10:6*
hypocritical nation
I will *s*. those that escape   *Isa 66:19*
unto the nations
behold, I will *s*. serpents   *Jer 8:17*
among you

I will *s*. a sword after them   *Jer 9:16;*
  24:10; 25:16, 27; 29:17; 49:37
I will *s*. for many fishers,   *Jer 16:16*
many hunters
I will *s*. and take the families   *Jer 25:9*
of the north
I will *s*. Nebuchadnezzar my   *Jer 43:10*
servant
behold, I will *s*. unto him   *Jer 48:12*
wanderers
and I will *s*. unto Babylon   *Jer 51:2*
fanners
I will *s*. famine   *Eze 5:16;*
  5:17; 14:13; Am 8:11
I will *s*. mine anger upon thee   *Eze 7:3*
and judge
I will *s*. unto her pestilence   *Eze 28:23*
and blood
I will *s*. you corn, and wine,   *Joe 2:19*
and oil
I will *s*. a curse   *Mal 2:2*
I will *s*. my messenger, and he   *Mal 3:1*
shall prepare
I will *s*. Elijah   *Mal 4:5*
I will not *s*. them away   *M't 15:32*
fasting
I will *s*. them prophets and   *Lu 11:49*
apostles
what shall I do? I will *s*. my   *Lu 20:13*
beloved son
the Comforter whom I will   *Joh 15:26;*
s.   *16:7*
I will *s*. thee far hence to the   *Ac 22:21*
Gentiles
whom you shall approve,   *1Co 16:3*
them I will *s*.

SENDEST

thou *s*. him out free from   *De 15:13*
thee
thou *s*. him away free from   *De 15:18*
thee
whithersoever thou *s*. us, we   *Jos 1:16*
will
thou *s*. to enquire of   *2Ki 1:6*
Baal-zebub
his continuance, and *s*. him   *Job 14:20*
away
Thou *s*. forth thy spirit, they   *Ps 104:30*

SENDETH

hand, and *s*. her out of his   *De 24:3*
house
until the day that the Lord *s*.   *1Ki 17:14*
rain
and *s*. waters upon the fields   *Job 5:10*
he *s*. them out, and they   *Job 12:15*
overturn
He *s*. the springs into the   *Ps 104:10*
valleys
He *s*. forth his   *Ps 147:15*
commandment upon
He *s*. out his word, and   *Ps 147:18*
melteth
s. a message by the hand of a   *Pr 26:6*
fool
my spikenard *s*. forth the   *Ca 1:12*
smell
That *s*. ambassadors by the   *Isa 18:2*
sea
and *s*. rain on the just and on   *M't 5:45*
he *s*. forth two of his   *M'k 11:1;*
disciples   *14:13*
he *s*. an ambassage, and   *Lu 14:32*
desireth
excellent governor Felix *s*.   *Ac 23:26*
greeting

SENDING

this evil in *s*. me away is   *2Sa 13:16*
greater
rising up betimes, and *s*.;   *2Ch 36:15*
because
and of *s*. portions one to   *Es 9:19;*
another   *9:22*
by *s*. evil angels among them   *Ps 78:49*
it shall be for the *s*. forth of   *Isa 7:25*
oxen
daily rising up early and *s*.   *Jer 7:25*
them
prophets, rising early and *s*.   *Jer 25:4;*
them   *29:19; 35:15; 44:4*
both rising up early, and *s*.   *Jer 26:5*
them
in *s*. his ambassadors into   *Eze 17:15*
Egypt
God *s*. his own Son in the   *Ro 8:3*
likeness

SENEH

and the name of the other *S*.   *1Sa 14:4*

SENIR

Bashan unto Baal-hermon   *1Ch 5:23*
and *S*.
thy ship boards of fir trees of   *Eze 27:5*
S.

SENNACHERIB

did *S*. king of Assyria come   *2Ki 18:13*
up
and hear the words of *S*.   *2Ki 19:16*
which
thou hast prayed to me   *2Ki 19:20;*
against *S*.   *Isa 37:21*
So *S*. king of Assyria   *2Ki 19:36;*
departed   *Isa 37:37*
S. king of Assyria came, and   *2Ch 32:1*
Hezekiah saw that *S*. was   *2Ch 32:2*
come
this did *S*. king of Assyria   *2Ch 32:9*
send his
Thus saith *S*. king of   *2Ch 32:10*
Assyria
the hand of *S*. the king of   *2Ch 32:22*
Assyria
that *S*. king of Assyria came   *Isa 36:1*
up
and hear all the words of *S*.   *Isa 37:17*
which

SENSE

of God distinctly, and gave the   *Ne 8:8*
s.
man without *s*. (R)   *Pr 7:7;*
  10:13; 11:12; 12:11; 17:18; 24:30
man without *s*. (A)   *Pr 10:13;*
  11:12; 12:11
lacks good *s*. (B)   *Pr 11:12; 12:11*
without heart and *s*. (A)   *Pr 15:21*
who lacks *s*. (B)(R)   *Pr 15:21*
just don't make *s*. to him (P)   *1Co 2:14*

SENSELESS

s. people (A)(R)   *De 32:6*
s., disreputable brood (R)   *Job 30:8*
s. young man (B)   *Pr 7:7*
s. wood idols (A)(B)(R)   *Ho 4:12*
s. ones (A)   *Lu 11:40*
s. and absurd (A)   *Ac 25:27*
stupid. *s*. controversies (R)   *2Ti 2:23*
refractory, *s*. talkers (B)   *Tit 1:10*

SENSES

have their *s*. exercised to   *Heb 5:14*
discern

SENSIBLE

temperate, *s*. (R)   *1Ti 3:2*
s., fair (B)   *Tit 1:8*
venerable, *s*. (A)(B)   *Tit 2:2*
to be *s*. (B)(P)(R)   *Tit 2:5*

SENSUAL

to *s*. nature (P)   *Ro 8:12*
mortify *s*. appetites (A)   *Col 3:5*
above, but is earthly, *s*.   *Jas 3:15*
devilish
unspiritual (A)(R)   *Jas 3:15*
animalistic (B)   *Jas 3:15*
lower nature (P)   *Jas 3:15*
spend it in *s*. pleasure   *Jas 4:3*
(A)(B)(E)
refrain from *s*. urges (B)   *1Pe 2:11*
who yield to the *s*. (B)   *2Pe 2:10*
s. lusts and debauchery (N)(P)   *2Pe 2:18*
s. having not the Spirit   *Jude 19*
worldly (B)(R)   *Jude 19*
unspiritual (N)   *Jude 19*

SENSUALITY

out of heart proceeds *s*. (P)   *M'k 7:22*
not repented of *s*.   *2Co 12:21*
(A)(B)(N)
work of flesh manifest, *s*. (P)   *Ga 5:19*
abandoned to unbridled *s*.   *Eph 4:19*
(A)(B)(P)
not in *s*. even as the Gentiles   *1Th 4:5*
(S)
meant *s*., lust (P)   *1Pe 4:3*
bent on perverted *s*. (B)   *Jude 7*
clothing polluted by *s*. (B)(N)   *Jude 23*

SENSUOUS

puffed up by *s.* mind (R)   Col 2:18

SENT

they *s.* the coat of many   Ge 37:32
colours
it is a present *s.* to my lord   Ge 32:18
Esau
Judah *s.* the kid by hand of   Ge 38:20
his friend
Tamar *s.* to her father in   Ge 38:25
law, saying
then Pharaoh *s.* and called   Ge 41:14
Joseph
Benjamin Jacob *s.* not with   Ge 42:4
his brethren
it was not you that *s.* me   Ge 45:8
hither, but God
they *s.* a messenger unto   Ge 50:16
Joseph, saying
thou shalt say, I AM hath *s.*   Ex 3:14
me to you
Lord, why is it that thou hast   Ex 5:22
s. me
the names of the men Moses   Nu 13:16;
s.   14:36
Balak the king of Moab hath   Nu 22:10
s. unto me
Balak *s.* yet again princes   Nu 22:15
more honourable
because she hid the   Jos 6:17
messengers we *s.*
forty years old was I when   Jos 14:7
Moses *s.* me
s. to spy   (A)(B)(E)(R)   J'g 1:23
her in pieces and *s.* her through J'g 20:6
Israel
s. into the land of the   1Sa 31:9
Philistines
what answer return him that   2Sa 24:13
s. me
I am *s.* to thee with heavy   1Ki 14:6
tidings
no nation whither my lord   1Ki 18:10
hath not *s.*
the elders did as Jezebel had   1Ki 21:11
s. unto them
return unto the king that *s.*   2Ki 1:6
you, and say
and king of Israel *s.* to the   2Ki 6:10
place the man
thistle *s.* to the cedar in   2Ki 14:9
Lebanon, saying
Urijah built according as   2Ki 16:11
Ahaz had *s.*
my master *s.* me to thy   2Ki 18:27;
master   Isa 36:12
his master *s.* to reproach the   2Ki 19:4
living God
thus saith the Lord, Tell man   2Ki 22:15;
that *s.* you unto me   22:18; 2Ch 34:23
this is the copy of the letter   Ezr 4:11
they *s.*
forasmuch as thou art *s.* of   Ezr 7:14
the king
they *s.* unto me four times after Ne 6:4
this sort
king *s.* and loosed him, the   Ps 105:20
ruler
cruel messenger be *s.* against   Pr 17:11
him
Lord God and his Spirit hath   Isa 48:16
s. me
their nobles have *s.* their little Jer 14:3
ones
I have not *s.* these prophets,   Jer 23:21
yet they ran
because thou hast *s.* letters in Jer 29:25
thy name
thus shall ye say unto the king   Jer 37:7
that *s.* you
whom ye *s.* to present your   Jer 42:9;
supplication   42:20
an ambassador is *s.* unto the   Jer 49:20
heathen
an hand was *s.* unto me, and   Eze 2:9
lo
art not *s.* to a people of a   Eze 3:5
strange speech
unto whom a messenger was   Eze 23:40
s. and lo
ye have *s.* for men to come   Eze 23:40
from far
who had *s.* his angel and   Da 3:28
delivered
then was part of the hand *s.*   Da 5:24
from him
then Ephraim went and *s.* to   Ho 5:13
king Jareb

an ambassador is *s.* among the   Ob 1
heathen
when they had *s.* unto the   Zec 7:2
house of God
receiveth me, receiveth him   M't 10:40;
that *s.* me   M'k 9:37; Lu 9:48;
                                  Joh 13:20
I am not *s.* but unto lost   M't 15:24
sheep of Israel
then *s.* Jesus two disciples,   M't 21:1
saying to them
and stonest them who are *s.*   M't 23:37;
                                  Lu 13:34
Pilate's wife *s.* unto him,   M't 27:19
saying
immediately the king *s.* an   M'k 6:27
executioner
I am Gabriel, and am *s.* to   Lu 1:19
speak to thee
angel Gabriel was *s.* from God   Lu 1:26
unto Nazareth
but unto none of them was   Lu 4:26
Elias *s.* save
John Baptist hath *s.* us unto   Lu 7:20
thee
Jesus *s.* them two and two   Lu 10:1
before his face
he *s.* his servant at   Lu 14:17
supper time to say
they *s.* a message after him,   Lu 19:14
saying
mocked him, and *s.* him   Lu 23:11
again to Pilate
a man *s.* from God, whose   Joh 1:6
name was
John was *s.* to bear witness of Joh 1:8
that light
we may give answer to them   Joh 1:22
that *s.* us
they who were *s.* were of the   Joh 1:24
Pharisees
I said, I am not Christ, but *s.* Joh 3:28
before him
my meat is to do will of him   Joh 4:34
that *s.* me
honoureth not the Father   Joh 5:23
who hath *s.* me
that believeth on him that *s.*   Joh 5:24;
                                  12:44
but will of him who *s.* me   Joh 5:30;
                                  6:38-40
Ye *s.* unto John, and he bare   Joh 5:33
witness to truth
works I do bear witness that   Joh 5:36;
the Father hath *s.* me   5:37; 6:57;
                                  8:16, 18
except the Father which *s.* me   Joh 6:44
draw him
my doctrine is not mine, but   Joh 7:16
his that *s.* me
but he that seeketh his glory   Joh 7:18
that *s.* him
Pharisees and priests *s.*   Joh 7:32
officers to take him
I must work the works of him   Joh 9:4
that *s.* me
wash in Siloam, which is by   Joh 9:7
interpretation S.
say ye of him whom the   Joh 10:36
Father hath *s.*
that they may believe thou   Joh 11:42
hast *s.* me
he that seeth me, seeth him   Joh 12:45
that *s.* me
Father who *s.* me gave me a   Joh 12:49
commandment
nor he that is *s.* greater than   Joh 13:16
he that *s.* him
word is not mine, but   Joh 14:24
Father's who *s.* me
because they know not him   Joh 15:21
that *s.* me
but now I go my way to him   Joh 16:5
that *s.* me
is life eternal, to know Jesus   Joh 17:3
whom thou *s.*
as thou hast *s.* me into the   Joh 17:18
world, so I *s.*
the world may believe that   Joh 17:21
thou hast *s.* me
that the world may know   Joh 17:23
thou hast *s.* me
and these have known that   Joh 17:25
thou hast *s.* me
as my Father hath *s.* me,   Joh 20:21
even so send I you
s. to the prison to have them   Ac 5:21
brought
men that were *s.* had made   Ac 10:17
inquiry

Peter went to the men who   Ac 10:21;
were *s.*   11:11
came I to you as soon as I   Ac 10:29
was *s.* for
I ask for what intent ye have   Ac 10:29
s. for me
s. it to the elders by   Ac 11:30
Barnabas and Saul
so they being *s.* forth by the   Ac 13:4
Holy Ghost
the rulers of the synagogue *s.*   Ac 13:15
to you is the word of this   Ac 13:26
salvation *s.*
we have therefore *s.* Judas   Ac 15:27
and Silas
the magistrates have *s.* to let   Ac 16:36
you go
Paul's friends *s.* unto him,   Ac 19:31
desiring him
salvation of God is *s.* unto   Ac 28:28
the Gentiles
how shall they preach, except   Ro 10:15
they be *s.*
Christ *s.* me not to baptize,   1Co 1:17
but to preach
we have *s.* with him the   2Co 8:18;
brother   8:22
in Thessalonica ye *s.* once   Ph'p 4:16
and again
received things which were *s.*   Ph'p 4:18
from you
spirits *s.* forth to minister for Heb 1:14
them
with the Holy Ghost *s.* from   1Pe 1:12
heaven
or unto governors, as them   1Pe 2:14
that are *s.*
testify that the Father *s.* the   1Jo 4:14
Son
the seven spirits *s.* forth into   Re 5:6
the earth

SENT *AWAY*

Pharaoh *s. away* Abraham   Ge 12:20
and his wife
Abraham *s.* Ishmael and   Ge 21:14
Hagar *away*
they *s. away* Rebekah their   Ge 24:59
sister
Abraham *s.* Keturah's children   Ge 25:6
away
seeing ye hate me and have   Ge 26:27
s. me *away*
as we have *s.* thee *away* in   Ge 26:29
peace, thou art
Isaac *s. away* Jacob to   Ge 28:5
Padan-aram
Isaac had blessed Jacob and *s.*   Ge 28:6
him *away*
I might have *s.* thee *away*   Ge 31:27
with mirth
surely thou hadst *s.* me *away*   Ge 31:42
empty
he *s.* his brethren *away*,   Ge 45:24
they departed
s. her *away*, may not take her De 24:4
again
Rahab *s.* spies *away*, they   Jos 2:21
departed
Joshua *s.* Reubenites and   Jos 22:6;
Gadites *away*   22:7
Jephthah *s.* his daughter   J'g 11:38
away
Samuel *s.* all the people   1Sa 10:25
away
Saul said, Why hast thou *s.*   1Sa 19:17
away my enemy
David *s.* Abner *away*, and he   2Sa 3:21
went
why is it that thou hast *s.*   2Sa 3:24
him *away*
cut garments, and *s.* them   2Sa 10:4;
away   1Ch 19:4
lords of Philistines *s.* David   1Ch 12:19
away
thou hast *s.* widows *away*   Job 22:9
empty
beat him and *s.* him   M'k 12:3;
away   12:4; Lu 20:10-11
and the rich he hath *s.* empty   Lu 1:53
away
but Jesus *s.* him *away*, saying Lu 8:38
laid hands on them, they *s.*   Ac 13:3
them *away*
brethren immediately *s.*   Ac 17:10;
away Paul   17:14

SENT *FORTH*

Noah s. *forth* a raven; s. *forth*   Ge 8:7;
dove   8:10
she hath s. *forth* her maidens,   Pr 9:3
she crieth
Herod s. *forth* and slew all   M't 2:16
the males
these twelve Jesus s. *forth,*   M't 10:5
and commanded
and s. *forth* his servants to   M't 22:3
call them bidden
Herod s. *forth* and laid hold   M'k 6:17
upon John
chief priests and scribes s.   Lu 20:20
forth spies
the brethren s. him *forth* to   Ac 9:30
Tarsus
they s. *forth* Barnabas as far   Ac 11:22
as Antioch

SENT *OUT*

God s. Lot *out* of midst of   Ge 19:29
overthrow
David therefore s. *out* spies   1Sa 26:4
and he s. *out* arrows   2Sa 22:15;
                        Ps 18:14
who hath s. *out* the wild ass   Job 39:5
free
clouds poured out, skies s. *out* Ps 77:17
a sound
she s. *out* her boughs to sea,   Ps 80:11
and branches
whom I have s. *out* of this   Jer 24:5
place to Chaldeans
she hath s. *out* her little   Eze 31:4
rivers to trees
Jacob s. *out* our fathers first   Ac 7:12
Rahab had s. them *out*   Jas 2:25
another way

GOD SENT

God s. me before you to   Ge 45:7
preserve life
the *God* of your fathers hath s.   Ex 3:13
me
the *God* of Jacob hath s. me   Ex 3:15
unto you
God s. evil spirit between   J'g 9:23
Abimelech
God s. an angel unto   1Ch 21:15
Jerusalem
I perceived that *God* had not   Ne 6:12
s. him
for which the Lord their *God*   Jer 43:1
s. him
God hath not s. to thee to   Jer 43:2
say, Go not into Egypt
God hath s. his angel, and hath   Da 6:22
shut
God s. not his Son to   Joh 3:17
condemn world
he whom *God* hath s.   Joh 3:34
speaketh words of God
God hath raised his Son Jesus,   Ac 3:26
s. him
word *God* s. unto the   Ac 10:36
children of ¹Israel
God s. forth his Son made of a   Ga 4:4
woman
God hath s. forth the Spirit of   Ga 4:6
his Son
God s. his only begotten Son   1Jo 4:9
into world
God s. his Son to be a   1Jo 4:10
propitiation for our sins
God s. his angel to shew his   Re 22:6
servants

HE SENT

to his father he s. after this   Ge 45:23
manner
he s. Judah before him unto   Ge 46:28
Joseph
took Zipporah, after he had s.   Ex 18:2
her back
Ammon hearkened not to   J'g 11:28
words he s.
rehearsed words, and he s.   1Sa 17:31
for David
he s. of the spoil unto the   1Sa 30:26
elders of Judah
he s. to meet them   2Sa 10:5; 1Ch 19:5
when he s. again, he would   2Sa 14:29
not come
he s. from above, took me   2Sa 22:17;
                      Ps 18:16

for he s. unto me for my   1Ki 20:7
wives
therefore he s. lions among   2Ki 17:26
them
yet he s. prophets to them   2Ch 24:19
to bring
he s. unto Amaziah a   2Ch 25:15
prophet
he s. and called for his friends   Es 5:10
he s. them meat to the full   Ps 78:25
he s. a man before them,   Ps 105:17
even Joseph
he s. Moses his servant and   Ps 105:26
Aaron
he s. darkness, and made it   Ps 105:28
dark
but he s. leanness into their   Ps 106:15
soul
he s. his word and healed   Ps 107:20
them
he s. redemption unto his   Ps 111:9
people
he s. me to bind up   Isa 61:1;
brokenhearted   Lu 4:18
he s. unto us in Babylon,   Jer 29:28
saying
for the which he hath s. me   Jer 42:21
unto you
from above he s. fire into my   La 1:13
bones
after glory hath he s. me to   Zec 2:8
nations
he s. other servants more   M't 21:36
than first
last of all he s. his son   M't 21:37;
                    M'k 12:4
he s. forth his armies, and   M't 22:7
destroyed
he that s. me to baptize with   Joh 1:33
water
for whom he hath s. him ye   Joh 5:38
believe not
that ye believe on him whom   Joh 6:29
he hath s.
he that s. me is true, ye   Joh 7:28;
know not   8:26
but I know him, and he hath   Joh 7:29
s. me
he that s. me is with me; the   Joh 8:29
Father
neither came I of myself, but   Joh 8:42
he s. me
wherefore he s. for Paul the   Ac 24:26
oftener
he s. and signified by his angel   Re 1:1
to John

I SENT

I have s. to ten my lord   Ge 32:5
I s. this kid, and thou hast   Ge 38:23
not found
this shall be a token that *I*   Ex 3:12
have s. thee
did your fathers when *I* s.   Nu 32:8
I s. Moses also and Aaron   Jos 24:5;
                      Mic 6:4
save Israel have not *I* s. thee   J'g 6:14
I have s. Naaman my servant   2Ki 5:6
to thee
the law which *I* s. to you by   2Ki 17:13
servants
who is deaf, as my   Isa 42:19
messenger that *I* s.
for your sake *I* have s. to   Isa 43:14
Babylon
it shall prosper in the thing   Isa 51:11
whereto *I* s. it
I s. unto you all my servants   Jer 7:25;
the prophets,   26:5; 35:15; 44:4
I s. them not, nor   Jer 14:14;
commanded   14:15; 23:21, 32; 27:15;
                      29:9
I s. him not, he caused you   Jer 29:31
to trust in a lie
surely had *I* s. thee to them   Eze 3:6
would hearken
O Daniel understand; to thee   Da 10:11
am *I* now s.
my great army which *I* s.   Joe 2:25
among you
I have s. among you the   Am 4:10
pestilence
I have s. forth thy prisoners   Zec 9:11
out of pit
and ye shall know that *I* have   Mal 2:4
s. this
I must preach, for therefore   Lu 4:43
am *I* s.

when *I* s. you without purse   Lu 22:35
and scrip
so have *I* s. them into the   Joh 17:18
world
doubting nothing, for *I* have   Ac 10:20
s. them
immediately therefore *I* s.   Ac 10:33
thee, hast well done
for this cause have *I* s. to   1Co 4:17
you Timotheus
yet have *I* s. brethren, lest our   2Co 9:3
boasting
did I make a gain of you by   2Co 12:17
any whom *I* s.
I desired Titus, and with   2Co 12:18
him *I* s. a brother
whom *I* s. for same purpose   Eph 6:22;
                       Col 4:8
I s. him therefore the more   Ph'p 2:28
carefully
for this *I* s. to know your   1Th 3:5
faith
whom I have s. again, receive   Ph'm 12
him

SENTENCE

shall shew thee the s. of   De 17:9
judgment
make clear to you the   De 17:9;
decision (A)(B)(R)   17:10-11
thou shalt do according to   De 17:10
the s.
According to the s. of the   De 17:11
law
from the s. which they shall   De 17:11
shew
pronounced s. upon him   2Ki 25:6
(A)(B)(R)
Let my s. come forth from thy   Ps 17:2
my judgment of vindication   Ps 17:2
(B)
my vindication (R)   Ps 17:2
caused s. to be heard (A)(E)   Ps 76:8
Lord revoked his s. (A)   Ps 106:45;
Am 7:3, 6; 8:14; Jon 3:10; 4:2; Joe 2:13
divine s. is in the lips of the   Pr 16:10
king
divinely directed decisions are   Pr 16:10
(A)
a godly decision is on the lips   Pr 16:10
of (B)
inspired decisions are on the   Pr 16:10
lips of (R)
s. against an evil work is not   Ec 8:11
also will I give s. against them   Jer 4:12
I will speak in judgment   Jer 4:12
against (A)(B)(R)
will I also utter judgments   Jer 4:12
against (E)
passed s. upon (A)(B)(R)   Jer 39:5
there is but one s. (A)(B)(R)   Da 2:9
dismissed s. against you (B)   Zep 3:15
I did not revoke s. (A)   Zec 8:14
s. him to death (A)(B)   M't 20:18
greater condemnation,   M't 23:14
heavier s. (A)
s. of perdition (B)   M't 23:33
Pilate gave s. that it should   Lu 23:24
be
under the same s. (N)(R)   Lu 23:40
to judge and pass s.   Joh 3:17
(A)(E)(N)(P)
does not s. any man (B)   Joh 5:22
he comes under no s. (B)   Joh 5:24
raised to meet s. (A)   Joh 5:29
s. him according to (A)(B)   Joh 18:31
now is this world's s. (B)   Joh 21:21
my s. is, that we trouble not   Ac 15:19
them
request for s. against him   Ac 25:15
(B)(E)(R)
passing s. on another (B)   Ro 2:1
God's s. rests in fairness (B)   Ro 2:2
escape God's s. (B)   Ro 2:3
s. brought condemnation   Ro 5:16
(A)(B)(R)
draw s. on themselves (B)   Ro 13:2
passed s. on (B)   1Co 5:3
Therefore it is my opinion   1Co 15:19
that (A)(P)
It is my judgment that   1Co 15:19
(B)(E)(N)(R)
we had the s. of death in   2Co 1:9
ourselves
fall under a similar s. (B)   1Ti 3:6
dreadful anticipation of s.   Heb 10:27
(B)

passed judgment and *s.* on (A)(B) — *Heb 11:7*

of old *s.* for them (A)(B) — *2Pe 2:3*

authority to pass *s.* (A)(B) — *Re 20:4*

SENTENCED

s. to hell (R) — *M't 23:33*

s. by our law (A)(B) — *Ac 24:6*

s. to death (A)(R) — *1Co 4:9*

SENTENCES

shewing of hard *s.* and dissolving — *Da 5:12*

to clarify riddles, and solve knotty problems (A) — *Da 5:12*

solve riddles, and unravel knots (B) — *Da 5:12*

explain riddles and solve problems (A) — *Da 5:12*

understanding dark *s.* shall stand — *Da 8:23*

understanding dark trickery and craftiness (A) — *Da 8:23*

skilled in intrigues (B) — *Da 8:23*

who understands riddles (R) — *Da 8:23*

SENTENCING

s. the wrongdoer (B) — *1Ki 8:32*

SENTEST

thou *s.* forth thy wrath, which — *Ex 15:7*

unto the land whither thou *s.* us — *Nu 13:27*

messengers which thou *s.* unto me — *Nu 24:12*

the things which thou *s.* to me for — *1Ki 5:8*

SENTINEL

the *s.* went up (B) — *2Sa 18:24; 18:25-27*

the *s.* (B) — *M'k 13:34*

SENUAH

son of *S.* was second over the city — *Ne 11:9*

SEORIM

third to Harim, the fourth to *S.* — *1Ch 24:8*

SEPARATE

s. thyself, I pray thee, from me — *Ge 13:9*

And Jacob did *s.* the lambs — *Ge 30:40*

him that was *s.* from his brethren — *Ge 49:26*

shall ye *s.* the children of Israel — *Le 15:31*

purify the Israelites (B) — *Le 15:31*

s. themselves from the holy things — *Le 22:2*

stay away from the holy things (A) — *Le 22:2*

behave guardedly about sacred things (B) — *Le 22:2*

keep away from the holy things (R) — *Le 22:2*

s. themselves to vow a vow of — *Nu 6:2*

to *s.* themselves unto the Lord — *Nu 6:2*

making the vow of a Nazarite—namely, to live in consecration to the Lord (B)(E)(R) — *Nu 6:2*

He shall *s.* himself from wine — *Nu 6:3*

thou *s.* the Levites from among the — *Nu 8:14*

S. yourselves from among this — *Nu 16:21*

Thou shalt *s.* three cities for thee — *De 19:2; 19:7*

set apart three cities (A)(B)(E)(R) — *De 19:2; 19:7*

s. him unto evil out of all the tribes — *De 29:21*

single him out for ruin (A)(R) — *De 29:21*

set him apart from all (B)(R) — *De 29:21*

the *s.* cities for the children of — *Jos 16:9*

s. them from among all the people — *1Ki 8:53*

set them apart from all people (B) — *1Ki 8:53*

separate (S) — *2Ki 15:5; 2Ch 26:21*

s. yourselves from the people of the — *Ezr 10:11*

s. and set apart (A) — *Jer 1:5*

to *s.* himself thence in the midst — *Jer 37:12*

my name and *s.* it (A) — *Eze 36:23*

was before the *s.* place at the end — *Eze 41:12*

the *s.* place, and the building, with — *Eze 41:13*

and of the *s.* place toward the east — *Eze 41:14*

the *s.* place which was behind it — *Eze 41:15*

that was over against the *s.* place — *Eze 42:1*

the east, over against the *s.* place — *Eze 42:10*

which are before the *s.* place, they — *Eze 42:13*

s. the wicked from among the just (S) — *M't 13:49*

he shall *s.* them one from another — *M't 25:32*

shall *s.* you from their company — *Lu 6:22*

exclude and excommunicate you (A) — *Lu 6:22*

exclude and denounce and defame (B) — *Lu 6:22*

outlaw you and insult you (N) — *Lu 6:22*

turn you out of their company (P) — *Lu 6:22*

exclude you and revile you (R) — *Lu 6:22*

S. me Barnabas and Saul for — *Ac 13:2*

Set me apart Barnabas and Saul (B)(N)(P)(R) — *Ac 13:2*

shall *s.* us from the love of Christ — *Ro 8:35*

able to *s.* us from the love of God — *Ro 8:39*

them, and be ye *s.*, saith the Lord — *2Co 6:17*

in many *s.* revelations (A) — *Heb 1:1*

undefiled, *s.* from sinners — *Heb 7:26*

in a different class from sinners (B) — *Heb 7:26*

These be they who *s.* themselves — *Jude 19*

SEPARATED

they *s.* themselves the one from — *Ge 13:11*

after that Lot was *s.* from him — *Ge 13:14*

two manner of people shall be *s.* — *Ge 25:23*

so shall we be *s.* I and thy people — *Ex 33:16*

have *s.* you from other people — *Le 20:24*

I have *s.* from you as unclean — *Le 20:25*

s. you from other people (S) — *Le 20:26*

God of Israel hath *s.* you from the — *Nu 16:9*

time the Lord *s.* the tribe of Levi — *De 10:8*

when he *s.* the sons of Adam, he — *De 32:8*

him that was *s.* from his brethren — *De 33:16*

s. himself from the Kenites (S) — *J'g 4:11*

horses of fire *s.* them (S) — *2Ki 2:11*

there *s.* themselves unto David — *1Ch 12:8*

and Aaron was *s.* that he should — *1Ch 23:13*

s. to the service of the sons of Asaph — *1Ch 25:1*

Then Amaziah *s.* them, to wit, the — *2Ch 25:10*

s. themselves unto them from — *Ezr 6:21*

Then I *s.* twelve of the chief of the — *Ezr 8:24*

not *s.* themselves from the people of — *Ezr 9:1*

himself *s.* from the congregation of — *Ezr 10:8*

all of them by their names, were *s.* — *Ezr 10:16*

we are *s.* upon the wall, one far — *Ne 4:19*

seed of Israel *s.* themselves from — *Ne 9:2*

all they that had *s.* themselves from — *Ne 10:28*

they *s.* from Israel all the mixed — *Ne 13:3*

cannot be *s.* (A)(B)(R) — *Job 41:17*

desire a man, having *s.* himself — *Pr 18:1*

the poor is *s.* from his neighbour — *Pr 19:4*

Lord hath utterly *s.* me from his — *Isa 56:3*

your iniquities have *s.* between you — *Isa 59:2*

out of their *s.* (B) — *Jer 8:1*

I shall set apart, *s.* (A) — *Eze 28:22; 28:25*

themselves are *s.* with whores — *Ho 4:14*

s. themselves unto that shame — *Ho 9:10*

from them, and *s.* the disciples — *Ac 19:9*

apostle, *s.* unto the gospel of God — *Ro 1:1*

who *s.* me from my mother's womb — *Ga 1:15*

he withdrew and *s.* himself, fearing — *Ga 2:12*

s. and set apart for pure holy living (A) — *1Th 4:3*

those set apart, *s.* (A) — *Jude 1*

SEPARATETH

which he *s.* himself unto the Lord — *Nu 6:5*

that he *s.* himself unto the Lord — *Nu 6:6*

and a whisperer *s.* chief friends — *Pr 16:28*

repeateth a matter *s.* very friends — *Pr 17:9*

alienates a close friend (B)(R) — *Pr 17:9*

which *s.* himself from me, and — *Eze 14:7*

who abandons me (B) — *Eze 14:7*

SEPARATING

s. myself, as I have done these so — *Zec 7:3*

fasting as I have done many years (B) — *Zec 7:3*

SEPARATION

according to the days of the *s.* — *Le 12:2*

be unclean two weeks, as in her *s.* — *Le 12:5*

she lieth upon in her *s.* shall be — *Le 15:20*

many days out of the time of her *s.* — *Le 15:25*

in her period of uncleanness (B) — *Le 15:25*

in the days of her impurity (E)(R) — *Le 15:25*

if it run beyond, the time of her *s.* — *Le 15:25*

shall be as the days of her *s.*: she — *Le 15:25*

be unto her as the bed of her *s.* — *Le 15:26*

as the uncleanness of her *s.* — *Le 15:26*

All the days of his *s.* shall he eat — *Nu 6:4*

entire period of his consecration (B) — *Nu 6:4; 6:12-13, 19, 21*

days of the vow of his *s.* there shall — *Nu 6:5*

the days of his *s.* he is holy unto — *Nu 6:8*

unto the Lord the days of his *s.* — *Nu 6:12*

be lost, because his *s.* was defiled — *Nu 6:12*

when the days of his *s.* are fulfilled — *Nu 6:13*

shave the head of his *s.* at the door — *Nu 6:18*

take the hair of the head of his *s.* — *Nu 6:18*

after the hair of his *s.* is shaven — *Nu 6:19*

his offering unto the Lord for his *s.* — *Nu 6:21*

he must do after the law of his *s.* — *Nu 6:21*

children of Israel for a water of *s.* — *Nu 19:9*

water for impurity (A)(E)(R) — *Nu 19:9; 19:21; 31:23*

water of uncleanness (B)   *Nu 19:9;*
                    19:20, 21; 31:23
the water of *s.* was not   *Nu 19:13*
sprinkled
water of *s.* hath not been   *Nu 19:20*
sprinkled
he that sprinkleth the water   *Nu 19:21*
of *s.*
he that toucheth water of *s.*   *Nu 19:21*
be purified with the water of   *Nu 31:23*
s.
to make a *s.* between the   *Eze 42:20*
sanctuary

SEPHAR

as thou goest unto *S.* a   *Ge 10:30*
mount of

SEPHARAD

the captivity which is in *S.*   *Ob 20*

SEPHARVAIM

and from Hamath, and from   *2Ki 17:24*
S.
and Anammelech, the gods   *2Ki 17:31*
of *S.*
where are the gods of *S.*   *2Ki 18:34*
Hena
the king of the city of *S.* of   *2Ki 19:13*
Hena
Arphad? where are the gods   *Isa 36:19*
of *S.*
and the king of the city of *S.*   *Isa 37:13*
Hena

SEPHARVITES

the *S.* burnt their children in   *2Ki 17:31*
fire

SEPSIS

spread like *s.* (P)   *2Ti 2:17*

SEPULCHRE

shall withhold from thee his *s.*   *Ge 23:6*
tomb (B)   *Ge 23:6;*
De 34:6;   *J'g 8:32;*   *1Sa 10:2;*   *2Sa 2:32;*
4:12;   *17:23;*   *21:14;*   *1Ki 13:22;*   *2Ki 21:26;*
23:17, 30;   *Isa 22:16;*   *M't 27:60-61, 64;*
28:1, 8;   *M'k 15:46;*   *16:2-3, 5, 8;*
Lu 23:53, 55;   *24:1-2, 9, 12, 22, 24;*
Joh 19:41-42;   *20:1-4, 6, 8, 11;*   *Ac 2:29;*
                      7:16; 13:29
but no man knoweth of his *s.*   *De 34:6*
grave (B)   *De 34:6;*
2Sa 2:32;   *4:12;*   *21:14;*   *1Ki 13:22;*
        2Ki 21:26;   *23:17, 30*
and was buried in the *s.* of   *J'g 8:32*
Joash
tomb (B)   *J'g 8:32;*
1Sa 10:2;   *2Sa 17:23;*   *M't 27:60-61, 64;*
28:1, 8;   *M'k 15:46;*   *16:2-3, 5, 8;*
Lu 23:53, 55;   *24:1-2, 9, 12, 22, 24;*
Joh 19:41-42;   *20:2, 4, 6, 11;*   *Ac 2:29;*
                      7:16; 13:29
shalt find two men by   *1Sa 10:2*
Rachel's *s.*
buried him in the *s.* of his   *2Sa 2:32*
father
and buried it in the *s.* of   *2Sa 4:12*
Abner in
was buried in the *s.* of his   *2Sa 17:23*
father
Zelah, in the *s.* of Kish his   *2Sa 21:14*
father
not come unto the *s.* of thy   *1Ki 13:22*
fathers
s. wherein the man of God   *1Ki 13:31*
is buried
grave (A)   *1Ki 13:31;*
        2Ki 13:21; Ro 3:13
him in his *s.* with his fathers   *2Ki 9:28*
cast the man into the *s.* of   *2Ki 13:21*
Elisha
in his *s.* in the garden of   *2Ki 21:26*
Uzza
It is the *s.* of the man of God   *2Ki 23:17*
and buried him in his own *s.*   *2Ki 23:30*
their throat is an open *s.;* they   *Ps 5:9*
cast out of thy *s.* (S)   *Isa 14:19*
thou hast hewed thee out a *s.*   *Isa 22:16*
here
hews him a *s.* (A)(B)(E)   *Isa 22:16*
that heweth him out a *s.* on   *Isa 22:16*
high

Their quiver is as an open *s.*   *Jer 5:16*
a great stone to the door of   *M't 27:60*
the *s.*
tomb (E)   *M't 27:60;*
28:8; M'k 15:46; 16:2-3, 5, 8; Lu 23:53,
55; 24:1-2, 9, 12, 22, 24; Joh 19:41-42;
20:1, 3-4, 6, 8, 11; Ac 2:29; 7:16; 13:29
tomb (N)(P)(R)   *M't 27:60;*
28:8; M'k 15:46; 16:2-3, 8; Lu 23:53;
24:1-2, 9, 22, 24; Joh 19:41-42; 20:1, 3-
  4, 6, 8, 11; Ac 2:29; 7:16; 13:29
Mary, sitting over against   *M't 27:61*
the *s.*
s. be made sure until the   *M't 27:64*
third day
So they went, and made the   *M't 27:66*
s. sure
and the other Mary to see the   *M't 28:1*
s.
they departed quickly from   *M't 28:8*
the *s.*
laid him in a *s.* which was   *M'k 15:46*
hewn
a stone unto the door of the   *M'k 15:46*
s.
they came unto the *s.* at the   *M'k 16:2*
rising
the stone from the door of   *M'k 16:3*
the *s.*
And entering into the *s.* they   *M'k 16:5*
saw
out quickly, and fled from   *M'k 16:8*
the *s.*
and laid it in a *s.* that was   *Lu 23:53*
hewn
beheld the *s.* and how his   *Lu 23:55*
body
morning, they came unto the *s.*   *Lu 24:1*
the stone rolled away from the   *Lu 24:2*
s.
returned from the *s.* and told   *Lu 24:9*
all
arose Peter, and ran unto the   *Lu 24:12*
s.
which were early at the *s.*   *Lu 24:22*
which were with us went to   *Lu 24:24*
the *s.*
in the garden a new *s.*   *Joh 19:41*
wherein
day; for the *s.* was nigh at   *Joh 19:42*
hand
when it was yet dark, unto the   *Joh 20:1*
s.
the stone taken away from   *Joh 20:1*
the *s.*
taken away the Lord out of   *Joh 20:2*
the *s.*
other disciple, and came to   *Joh 20:3*
the *s.*
outrun Peter, and came to   *Joh 20:4*
the *s.*
and went into the *s.* and seeth   *Joh 20:6*
disciple, which came first to   *Joh 20:8*
the *s.*
But Mary stood without at   *Joh 20:11*
the *s.*
stooped down, and looked in   *Joh 20:11*
the *s.*
his *s.* is with us unto this day   *Ac 2:29*
and laid in the *s.* that   *Ac 7:16*
Abraham
from the tree, and laid him   *Ac 13:29*
in a *s.*
Their throat is an open *s.*   *Ro 3:13*

SEPULCHRES

in the choice of our *s.* bury   *Ge 23:6*
thy
in any tomb or grave (A)   *Ge 23:6*
he spied the *s.* that were   *2Ki 23:16*
there in
tombs (A)   *2Ki 23:16;*
2Ch 21:20; 24:25; 28:27; 32:33; 35:24;
          M't 23:27, 29; Lu 11:47
and took the bones out of   *2Ki 23:16*
the *s.* and
And they buried him in his   *2Ch 16:14*
own *s.*
in his own tomb (A)   *2Ch 16:14*
buried him in his own vault   *2Ch 16:14*
(B)
David, but not in the *s.* of   *2Ch 21:20*
the kings
buried him not in the *s.* of   *2Ch 24:25*
the kings
him not into the *s.* of the   *2Ch 28:27*
kings of
in the chiefest of the *s.* of   *2Ch 32:33*
the sons

buried in one of the *s.* of   *2Ch 35:24*
his fathers
the city, the place of my   *Ne 2:3*
fathers' *s.*
unto the city of my fathers' *s.*   *Ne 2:5*
place over against the *s.* of   *Ne 3:16*
David
ye are like unto whited *s.*   *M't 23:27*
which
tombs (B)(N)(P)(R)   *M't 23:27; 23:29*
garnish the *s.* of the   *M't 23:29*
righteous
for ye build the *s.* of the   *Lu 11:47*
prophets
monuments (B)   *Lu 11:47*
killed them, and ye build   *Lu 11:48*
their *s.*

SEQUENCE

in *s.* of his series (B)   *Lu 1:8*

SERAH

and Beriah, and *S.* their   *Ge 46:17;*
sister   *1Ch 7:30*

SERAIAH

priests; and *S.* was the scribe   *2Sa 8:17*
the guard took *S.* the chief   *2Ki 25:18;*
priest   *Jer 52:24*
and *S.* the son of   *2Ki 25:23;*
Tanhumeth   *Jer 40:8*
the son of Kenaz, Othniel,   *1Ch 4:13*
and *S.*
and *S.* begat Joab, the father   *1Ch 4:14*
of
the son of Josibiah, the son   *1Ch 4:35*
of *S.*
begat *S.* and *S.* begat   *1Ch 6:14*
Jehozadak
Jeshua, Nehemiah, *S.*, Reelaiah   *Ezr 2:2*
Ezra the son of *S.* the son of   *Ezr 7:1*
S., Azariah, Jeremiah   *Ne 10:2*
S. the son of Hilkiah, the son   *Ne 11:11*
of
and Jeshua: *S.*, Jeremiah, Ezra   *Ne 12:1*
chief of the fathers: of *S.*   *Ne 12:12*
Meraiah
S. the son of Azriel, and   *Jer 36:26*
Shelemiah
commanded *S.* the son of   *Jer 51:59*
Neriah
And this *S.* was a quiet   *Jer 51:59*
prince
Jeremiah said to *S.*, When   *Jer 51:61*
thou

SERAPHIMS

Above it stood the *s.*: each one   *Isa 6:2*
Then flew one of the *s.* unto   *Isa 6:6*
me

SERED

sons of Zebulun; *S.* and Elon   *Ge 46:14*
of *S.* the family of the   *Nu 26:26*
Sardites

SERENADED

maidens not *s.* (B)   *Ps 78:63*

SERGIUS

S. Paulus, a prudent man;   *Ac 13:7*
who

SERIES

sequence of his *s.* (B)   *Lu 1:8*

SERIOUS

composure may remedy *s.*   *Ec 10:4*
mistakes (B)
make trespass more *s.* (B)   *Ro 5:20*
be *s.*-minded (B)   *1Pe 4:7*

SERIOUSLY

s. upsets brother (P)   *Ro 14:15*

SERJEANTS

the magistrates sent the *s.*   *Ac 16:35*
saying
magistrates sent policemen   *Ac 16:35;*
(A)   *16:38*

magistrates sent their   *Ac 16:35;*
orderlies (B)   *16:38*
magistrates sent their officers *Ac 16:35;*
(N)   *16:38*
magistrates sent constables   *Ac 16:35;*
(P)   *16:38*
magistrates sent police (R)   *Ac 16:35;*
           16:38
the *s.* told these words unto *Ac 16:38*

SERPENT

s. was more subtil than any   *Ge 3:1*
beast
woman said unto the *s.*, We   *Ge 3:2*
may eat
s. said unto the woman, Ye   *Ge 3:4*
shall not
The *s.* beguiled me, and I did *Ge 3:13*
eat
Lord God said unto the *s.*,   *Ge 3:14*
Because
Dan shall be a *s.* by the way *Ge 49:17*
on the ground, and it became   *Ex 4:3*
a *s.*
became a snake (B)   *Ex 4:3;*
         7:9, 10, 15
Pharaoh, and it shall become   *Ex 7:9*
a *s.*
his servants, and it became a *Ex 7:10*
s.
the rod which was turned to a *Ex 7:15*
s.
Make thee a fiery *s.* and set   *Nu 21:8*
it
Moses made a *s.* of brass, and *Nu 21:9*
put
that if a *s.* had bitten any   *Nu 21:9*
man
when he beheld the *s.* of brass, *Nu 21:9*
he
the brasen *s.* that Moses had *2Ki 18:4*
made
hand hath formed the   *Job 26:13*
crooked *s.*
swift *s.* (A)(E)(R)   *Job 26:13;*
          Isa 27:1
poison is like the poison of a *s. Ps 58:4*
s. trample under feet   *Ps 91:13*
(A)(E)(R)(S)
sharpened their tongues like a *Ps 140:3*
s.
At the last it biteth like a *s.* *Pr 23:32*
the way of a *s.* upon a rock; *Pr 30:19*
the way
breaketh an hedge, a *s.* shall   *Ec 10:8*
bite
s. will bite without   *Ec 10:11*
enchantment
his fruit shall be a fiery flying *Isa 14:29*
s.
punish leviathan the piercing   *Isa 27:1*
s.
even leviathan that crooked *s. Isa 27:1*
the coiling *s.* (B)   *Isa 27:1*
lion, the viper and fiery flying *Isa 30:6*
voice thereof shall go like a *s. Jer 46:22*
sound like rustling of a *s.* (A) *Jer 46:22*
hand on the wall, and a *s.* bit *Am 5:19*
him
sea, thence will I command the *Am 9:3*
s.
They shall lick the dust like a *Mic 7:17*
s.
ask a fish, will he give him a *M't 7:10*
fish, will he for a fish give him *Lu 11:11*
a *s.*
And as Moses lifted up the *s. Joh 3:14*
in the
as the *s.* beguiled Eve   *2Co 11:3*
through his
old *s.* called the Devil, and   *Re 12:9*
Satan
half a time, from the face of *Re 12:14*
the *s.*
the *s.* cast out of his mouth *Re 12:15*
water
old *s.* which is the Devil,   *Re 20:2*
and Satan

SERPENTS

man his rod, and they became *Ex 7:12*
s.
the Lord sent fiery *s.* among *Nu 21:6*
that he take away the *s.* from *Nu 21:7*
us

wilderness, wherein were fiery *De 8:15*
s.
with the poison of *s.* of the   *De 32:24*
dust
venom of *s.* (B)(E)(R)(S)   *De 32:33*
thou brakest the heads of the *Ps 74:13*
s. (S)
ye *s.* and all deeps (S)   *Ps 148:7*
I will send *s.* cockatrices,   *Jer 8:17*
among
be ye therefore wise as *s.* and *M't 10:16*
Ye *s.* ye generation of vipers *M't 23:33*
They shall take up *s.*; and if *M'k 16:18*
they
power to tread on *s.* and   *Lu 10:19*
scorpions
tempted, and were destroyed *1Co 10:9*
of *s.*
of *s.* and of things in the sea   *Jas 3:7*
for their tails were like unto *s. Re 9:19*

SERPENT'S

out of the *s.* root shall come *Isa 14:29*
forth
and dust shall be the *s.* meat *Isa 65:25*
you *s.* brood (P)   *M't 3:7*

SERUG

and thirty years, and begat S. *Ge 11:20*
Reu lived after he begat S.   *Ge 11:21*
two
S. lived thirty years, and   *Ge 11:22*
begat
S. lived after he begat Nahor *Ge 11:23*
two
S., Nahor, Terah   *1Ch 1:26*

SERVANT

Canaan, a *s.* of servants shall *Ge 9:25*
he be
and he said, I am Abraham's *Ge 24:34*
s.
Issachar bowed and became *Ge 49:15*
a *s.* to tribute
if he say, I love my *Ex 21:5*
master
his *s.* Joshua (S)   *Ex 24:13*
remember that thou wast a *s. De 5:15*
in Egypt
thou shalt not deliver the *s. De 23:15*
that is escaped
priest's *s.* came and said   *1Sa 2:13*
Samuel said, Bid the *s.* pass *1Sa 9:27*
on before us
let thy handmaid be a *s.* to *1Sa 25:41*
wash the feet
is not this David the *s.* of   *1Sa 29:3*
Saul the king
I am a young man *s.* to an *1Sa 30:13*
Amalekite
of house of Saul, *s.* named   *2Sa 9:2;*
Ziba   *19:17*
Ziba the *s.* of Mephibosheth *2Sa 16:1*
met David
a *s.* girl went (B)   *2Sa 17:17*
when Joab sent the king's *s. 2Sa 18:29*
and me thy *s.*
Jeroboam Solomon's *s.* lift *1Ki 11:26*
up his hand
if thou wilt be a *s.* to this   *1Ki 12:7*
people this day
she said to her *s.*, Drive and *2Ki 4:24*
go forward
the *s.* said   *2Ki 4:43*
(A)(B)(E)(R)(S)
when the *s.* of the man of   *2Ki 6:15*
God was risen
Tobiah the *s.* the Ammonite *Ne 2:10;*
heard   *2:19*
and the *s.* is there free from   *Job 3:19*
his master
as a *s.* earnestly desireth the *Job 7:2*
shadow
wilt thou take Leviathan for a *Job 41:4*
s. for ever
even Joseph, who was sold *Ps 105:17*
for a *s.*
the fool shall be *s.* to the wise *Pr 11:29*
of heart
he that is despised and hath a *Pr 12:9*
s. is better
the king's favour is toward a *Pr 14:35*
wise *s.*
a wise *s.* shall have rule over a *Pr 17:2*
son that
much less for a *s.* to rule over *Pr 19:10*
princes

and the borrower is *s.* to the   *Pr 22:7*
lender
a *s.* will not be corrected with *Pr 29:19*
words
accuse not *s.* to his master,   *Pr 30:10*
lest he curse thee
the earth cannot bear a *s.*   *Pr 30:22*
when he reigneth
as with the *s.* so with his   *Isa 24:2*
master
to a *s.* of rulers; is Israel a *Isa 49:7;*
s.   *Jer 2:14*
O Daniel, *s.* of the living God *Da 6:20*
how can *s.* of my lord talk *Da 10:17*
with my lord
s. honoureth his master, if I be *Mal 1:6*
a master
nor the *s.* above his lord   *M't 10:24*
it is enough for the *s.* to be *M't 10:25*
as his lord
the *s.* fell down and   *M't 18:26*
worshipped him
the lord of that *s.* was   *M't 18:27*
moved with compassion
O thou wicked *s.* I forgave *M't 18:32*
thee all that debt
must be your *s.* (A)(N)(R) *M't 20:26*
among you, let him be   *M't 20:27;*
your *s.*   *23:11; M'k 10:44*
who then is a faithful and   *M't 24:45*
wise *s.* whom lord
blessed is that *s.* whom   *M't 24:46;*
his lord   *Lu 12:43*
but if that evil *s.* shall say *M't 24:48*
          Lu 12:45
the lord of that *s.* shall   *M't 24:50;*
come   *Lu 12:46*
well done good, faithful *s.* *M't 25:21;*
      25:23; Lu 19:17
thou wicked and slothful *s.* *M't 25:26;*
          Lu 19:22
cast the unprofitable *s.* into *M't 25:30*
outer darkness
Peter struck *s.* of high   *M't 26:51;*
priest,   *M'k 14:47; Joh 18:10*
and he sent to the   *M'k 12:2*
husbandmen a *s.*
that *s.* which knew his lord's *Lu 12:47*
will
so that *s.* came and shewed *Lu 14:21*
his lord
which of you having an *s.*   *Lu 17:7*
plowing
doth he thank that *s.*? I trow *Lu 17:9*
not
and at the season he sent a *Lu 20:10;*
s.   *20:11*
whoso committeth sin, is the *Joh 8:34*
s. of sin
the *s.* abideth not in the   *Joh 8:35*
house for ever
the *s.* is not greater than his *Joh 13:16;*
lord   *15:20*
the *s.* knoweth not what his *Joh 15:15*
lord doth
a *s.* and a witness (N)(P)   *Ac 26:16*
Paul a *s.* of Jesus Christ, an   *Ro 1:1*
apostle
he is God's *s.* (A)(P)(R)   *Ro 13:4*
who art thou that judgest   *Ro 14:4*
another man's *s.*
commend Phebe, a *s.* of the   *Ro 16:1*
church
art thou called being a *s*?   *1Co 7:21*
care not
is called, being a *s.* is the   *1Co 7:22*
Lord's freeman
yet have made myself a *s.*   *1Co 9:19*
unto all
I should not be the *s.* of   *Ga 1:10*
Christ
as a child differeth nothing   *Ga 4:1*
from a *s.*
wherefore thou art no more a   *Ga 4:7*
s. but a son
he took upon him the form   *Ph'p 2:7*
of a *s.*
Epaphras, a *s.* of Christ,   *Col 4:12*
saluteth you
s. of Lord must not strive,   *2Ti 2:24*
but be gentle
not now as a *s.* but above a   *Ph'm 16*
s. a brother
Moses was faithful in his   *Heb 3:5*
house as a *s.*
Simon Peter, a *s.* of Jesus   *2Pe 1:1*
Christ
Jude the *s.* of Jesus Christ to   *Jude 1*
sanctified

SERVANT *OF GOD*

as Moses the *s. of God*   1Ch 6:49
commanded
the collection, Moses the *s.*   2Ch 24:9
of God said
God's law, given by Moses   Ne 10:29
the *s. of God*
Daniel *s. of* the living *God*   Da 6:20
written in the law of Moses   Da 9:11
the *s. of God*
Paul, a *s. of God*   Tit 1:1
James a *s. of God*   Jas 1:1
not using liberty, but as the *s.*   1Pe 2:16
of God
sang the song of Moses the *s.*   Re 15:3
of God

HIS SERVANT

and Canaan shall be *his s.*   Ge 9:26;
  9:27
people believed Lord and *his*   Ex 14:31
s. Moses
if a man smite *his s.* and die   Ex 21:20
if he smite the eye of *his s.*   Ex 21:26
that it perish
his s. Joshua departed not   Ex 33:11
out of tabernacle
Joshua said, What saith my   Jos 5:14
Lord to *his s.*
God commanded *his s.* Moses   Jos 9:24
to give
Gideon went down with   J'g 7:11
Phurah *his s.*
the Levite went, having *his s.*   J'g 19:3
with him
when the man rose to depart,   J'g 19:9
he and *his s.*
let not the king sin against   1Sa 19:4
his s.
let not king impute any   1Sa 22:15
thing to *his s.*
the Lord hath kept *his s.*   1Sa 25:39
from evil
why doth my Lord pursue   1Sa 26:18
after *his s.*
let my lord king hear the   1Sa 26:19
words of *his s.*
as my lord hath commanded   2Sa 9:11
his s.
king hath fulfilled the   2Sa 14:22
request of *his s.*
wherefore is my lord come   2Sa 24:21
to *his s.*
swear, that he will not slay   1Ki 1:51
his s.
which he promised by hand   1Ki 8:56
of Moses *his s.*
he maintain the cause of *his*   1Ki 8:59
s.
he spake by hand of *his s.*   1Ki 14:18;
Ahijah   15:29
Elijah came and left *his s.* at   1Ki 19:3
Beer-sheba
word which he spake by *his s.*   2Ki 9:36
Elijah
the word which he spake by   2Ki 14:25
his s. Jonah
Hoshea became *his s.* and   2Ki 17:3
gave presents
and Jehoiakim became *his s.*   2Ki 24:1
three years
O ye seed of Israel *his s.*   1Ch 16:13
spake against *his s.*   2Ch 32:16
Hezekiah
let every one with *his s.* lodge   Ne 4:22
within
Lord hath pleasure in   Ps 35:27
prosperity of *his s.*
O ye seed of Abraham *his s.*   Ps 105:6
he is our God
he sent Moses *his s.* and   Ps 105:26
Aaron his chosen
for he remembered Abraham   Ps 105:42
his s.
gave even an heritage unto   Ps 136:22
Israel *his s.*
that delicately bringeth up *his*   Pr 29:21
s.
that confirmeth the word of   Isa 44:26
his s.
the Lord hath redeemed *his*   Isa 48:20
s. Jacob
Lord formed me from womb   Isa 49:5
to be *his s.*
who that obeyeth the voice of   Isa 50:10
his s.
ye caused every man *his s.* to   Jer 34:16
return

his s. was healed in the same   M't 8:13
hour
he hath holpen *his s.* Israel in   Lu 1:54
mercy
beseeching that he would come   Lu 7:3
and heal *his s.*
and sent *his s.* at supper time   Lu 14:17
to say
signified it by angel unto *his s.*   Re 1:1
John

MY SERVANT

I will multiply thy seed for   Ge 26:24
my s. sake
he with whom it is found   Ge 44:10;
shall be *my s.*   44:17
my s. Moses is not so, who is   Nu 12:7
faithful
why were ye not afraid to   Nu 12:8
speak against *my s.*
but *my s.* Caleb had another   Nu 14:24
spirit
Moses *my s.* is dead, therefore   Jos 1:2
arise
that my son had stirred up   1Sa 22:8
my s.
therefore he shall be *my s.*   1Sa 27:12
for ever
my lord, O king, *my s.*   2Sa 19:26
deceived me
I have therewith sent Naaman   2Ki 5:6
my s.
according to the law *my s.*   2Ki 21:8
Moses commanded
hast thou considered *my s.*   Job 1:8;
  2:3
I called *my s.* and he gave   Job 19:16
me no answer
ye have not spoken right, as   Job 42:7
my s. Job hath
go to *my s.* Job, he shall pray   Job 42:8
for you
like as *my s.* Isaiah hath   Isa 20:3
walked naked
in that day I will call *my s.*   Isa 22:20
Eliakim
but thou, Israel, art *my s.*   Isa 41:8;
fear not   41:9
behold *my s.* whom I uphold,   Isa 42:1
mine elect
who is blind but *my s.* that I   Isa 42:19
sent
ye are witnesses and *my s.* I   Isa 43:10
have chosen
hear, O Jacob, *my s.*; fear   Isa 44:1;
not, O Jacob, *my s.*   44:2
remember those, for thou   Isa 44:21;
art *my s.*   49:3
it is a light thing thou   Isa 49:6
shouldest be *my s.*
behold *my s.* shall deal   Isa 52:13
prudently, be very
Nebuchadnezzar *my s.*   Jer 25:9;
  27:6; 43:10
fear thou not, O *my s.*   Jer 30:10;
Jacob   46:27-28
land I have given *my s.*   Eze 28:25;
Jacob   37:25
I will take thee, O   Hag 2:23
Zerubbabel *my s.*
I will bring forth *my s.* the   Zec 3:8
BRANCH
remember the law of Moses   Mal 4:4
my s.
my s. lieth at home sick of the   M't 8:6
palsy
speak, and *my s.* shall be   M't 8:8;
healed   Lu 7:7
and to *my s.* do this, and he   M't 8:9;
doeth it   Lu 7:8
behold *my s.* whom I have   M't 12:18
chosen
where I am, there shall also   Joh 12:26
my s. be

THY SERVANT

pass not away, I pray thee,   Ge 18:3
from *thy s.*
behold, *thy s.* hath found   Ge 19:19;
grace   Ne 2:5
be she that thou hast   Ge 24:14
appointed for *thy s.*
not worthy of the mercies   Ge 32:10
shewed to *thy s.*
then thou shalt say, They be   Ge 32:18
thy s. Jacob's
the children which God hath   Ge 33:5
given *thy s.*

gray hairs of *thy s.* to the   Ge 44:31
grave
thy s. became surety for the   Ge 44:32
lad to father
nor since thou hast spoken   Ex 4:10
unto *thy s.*
be meat for you, and for *thy s.*   Le 25:6
wherefore hast afflicted *thy s.*   Nu 11:11
begun to shew *thy s.* thy   De 3:24
greatness
through ear, and he shall be   De 15:17
thy s. for ever
go thou down with Phurah *thy*   J'g 7:10
s.
this great deliverance into   J'g 15:18
hand of *thy s.*
speak, Lord, for *thy s.*   1Sa 3:9;
heareth   3:10
thy s. slew both the lion and   1Sa 17:36
the bear
if he say thus, *thy s.* shall   1Sa 20:7
have peace
for *thy s.* knew nothing of   1Sa 22:15
all this
O Lord God, I beseech thee,   1Sa 23:11
tell *thy s.*
surely thou shalt know what   1Sa 28:2
thy s. can do
for thou, Lord God, knowest   2Sa 7:20
thy s.
let it please thee to bless the   2Sa 7:29
house of *thy s.*
Mephibosheth answered,   2Sa 9:6
Behold *thy s.*
king's sons came, as *thy s.*   2Sa 13:35
said, so it is
in death or life, even there   2Sa 15:21
will *thy s.* be
he hath slandered *thy s.* unto   2Sa 19:27
my lord
O Lord, take away the   2Sa 24:10
iniquity of *thy s.*
even me *thy s.*, Zadok the   1Ki 1:26
priest, and *thy s.* Solomon
hath he not called
as my lord the king said, so   1Ki 2:38
will *thy s.* do
and *thy s.* is in the midst of   1Ki 3:8
thy people
give *thy s.* an understanding   1Ki 3:9
heart, to judge
have thou respect to the   1Ki 8:28
prayer of *thy s.*
but I *thy s.* fear the Lord   1Ki 18:12
from my youth
let it be known this day that   1Ki 18:36
I am *thy s.*
thy s. Benhadad saith, I pray   1Ki 20:32
let me live
thy s. was busy he was gone   1Ki 20:40
thy s. my husband is dead,   2Ki 4:1
knowest *thy s.* did fear Lord
the Lord pardon *thy s.* in this   2Ki 5:18
thing
Gehazi said, Thy *s.* went no   2Ki 5:25
whither
but what, is *thy s.* a dog; I   2Ki 8:13;
am *thy s.*   16:7
prosper, I pray thee, *thy s.*   Ne 1:11
this day
moreover, by them is *thy s.*   Ps 19:11
warned
keep back *thy s.* from   Ps 19:13
presumptuous sins
put not *thy s.* away in anger,   Ps 27:9
leave me not
make thy face to shine upon   Ps 31:16
thy s. save me
hide not thy face from *thy s.*   Ps 69:17
in trouble
O my God, save *thy s.* that   Ps 86:2
trusteth in thee
give thy strength unto *thy s.*   Ps 86:16
and save me
thou hast made void the   Ps 89:39
covenant of *thy s.*
truly I am *thy s.*   Ps 116:16;
  119:125; 143:12
lest thou hear *thy s.* curse thee   Ec 7:21
O God, hear the prayer of *thy*   Da 9:17
s.
lettest thou *thy s.* depart in   Lu 2:29
peace

SERVANTS

Canaan, a servant of *s.* shall   Ge 9:25
he be
all his brethren have I given   Ge 27:37
him for *s.*

to me the children of Israel   *Le 25:55*
are s.
shall be bond s. (S)   *De 20:11;*
  Jos 17:13
go meet them, and say, We   *Jos 9:11*
are our s.
that ye be not s. unto the   *1Sa 4:9*
Hebrews
am not I a Philistine, and you   *1Sa 17:8*
s. to Saul
if he kill me, we be your s.,   *1Sa 17:9*
but if I kill him, ye be our s.
but the s. of the king would   *1Sa 22:17*
not put forth
many s. break away from   *1Sa 25:10*
their masters
to wash the feet of the s. of   *1Sa 25:41*
my lord
so the Moabites became   *2Sa 8:2*
David's s.
the Syrians s.; they of Edom   *2Sa 8:6;*
became David's s.   *8:14*
now Ziba had fifteen sons and   *2Sa 9:10*
twenty s.
all in the house of Ziba s. to   *2Sa 9:12*
Mephibosheth
Hanun took David's s. and   *2Sa 10:4;*
shaved the   *1Ch 19:4*
the s. of my Lord are   *2Sa 11:11*
encamped in fields
two of the s. of Shimei ran   *1Ki 2:39*
away
his s. (B)   *1Ki 10:5;*
  Ezr 7:24; Ps 103:21; 104:4; Isa 61:6
the s. of Amon conspired   *2Ki 21:23*
against him
the temple s. (B)(R)   *1Ch 9:2*
but are they not all my lord's   *1Ch 21:3*
s.
of the children of Israel   *2Ch 8:9*
Solomon made no s.
carried to Babylon, where   *2Ch 36:20*
they were s.
the temple s. (R)   *Ezr 2:43;*
2:58; 7:7, 24; 8:17, 20; Ne 3:26; 10:28;
  11:21
we are the s. of the God of   *Ezr 5:11*
heaven
their s. bare rule over the   *Ne 5:15*
people
behold, we are s. this day, s.   *Ne 9:36*
in the land
they have slain the s. with   *Job 1:15;*
the sword   *1:17*
as the eyes of s. look to their   *Ps 123:2*
masters
I got me s. and had s. born in   *Ec 2:7*
my house
I have seen s. upon horses,   *Ec 10:7*
and princes walking as s.
upon the earth
Israel shall possess them for s.   *Isa 14:2*
and handmaids
caused s. to return, and   *Jer 34:11*
brought into subjection for s.
s. have ruled over us, none   *La 5:8*
deliver
ye s. of the most high God,   *Da 3:26*
come forth
upon the s. will I pour out my   *Joe 2:29*
Spirit
behold, they shall be a spoil to   *Zec 2:9*
their s.
then said the king to the s.,   *M't 22:13*
Bind him
the lord of those s. cometh   *M't 25:19*
and reckoneth
the s. did strike Jesus with   *M'k 14:65*
their hands
s. of the gospel (N)   *Lu 1:2*
blessed are those s. found   *Lu 12:37;*
watching   *12:38*
say, are unprofitable s. have   *Lu 17:10*
done our duty
henceforth I call you not s.   *Joh 15:15*
for servant
these men are s. of the most   *Ac 16:17*
high God
to whom ye yield yourselves s.   *Ro 6:16*
to obey
God be thanked, that ye were   *Ro 6:17*
the s. of sin
made free, ye became the s. of   *Ro 6:18*
righteousness
as ye have yielded your   *Ro 6:19*
members s. to sin
s. of sin, ye were free from   *Ro 6:20*
righteousness
being free from sin, and   *Ro 6:22*
become s. to God

s. of Christ (B)(R)   *1Co 4:1*
ye are bought, be not ye the   *1Co 7:23*
s. of men
and ourselves your s. for   *2Co 4:5*
Jesus' sake
s. of God (A)(N)(R)   *2Co 6:4*
s. of righteousness (B)(R)   *2Co 11:15*
s. be obedient to your masters   *Eph 6:5*
according to the flesh *Col 3:22; Tit 2:9;*
  1Pe 2:18
not with eye-service, but as   *Eph 6:6*
the s. of Christ
Paul and Timotheus the s. of   *Ph'p 1:1*
Christ
masters, give your s. what is   *Col 4:1*
just
let as many s. as are under the   *1Ti 6:1*
yoke
not using liberty, but as the s.   *1Pe 2:16*
of God
they themselves are the s. of   *2Pe 2:19*
corruption
till we have sealed the s. of   *Re 7:3*
our God

SERVANTS *OF* GOD

forgive the s. *of* the God of   *Ge 50:17*
thy father
till we have sealed the s. *of* God   *Re 7:3*
in

HIS SERVANTS

Pharaoh made a feast unto   *Ge 40:20*
all *his* s.
Pharaoh made *his* s. flee into   *Ex 9:20*
houses
Pharaoh rose in the night.,   *Ex 12:30*
he and *his* s.
Balaam riding, and *his* two   *Nu 22:22*
s. with him
Lord shall repent himself for   *De 32:36*
his s.
for he will avenge the blood   *De 32:43*
of *his* s.
take the best, and give to *his*   *1Sa 8:14;*
s.   *8:15*
ye will take the tenth, ye shall   *1Sa 8:17*
be *his* s.
Saul spake to all *his* s. to kill   *1Sa 19:1*
David
and all *his* s. were standing   *1Sa 22:6*
about him
his s. came near, and spake   *2Ki 5:13*
unto him
are not *his* s. come to thee to   *1Ch 19:3*
search
nevertheless, they shall be *his*   *2Ch 12:8*
s.
his s. spake yet more   *2Ch 32:16*
against the Lord God
we *his* s. will arise and build   *Ne 2:20*
he put no trust in *his* s. and   *Job 4:18*
angels
the seed also of *his* s. shall   *Ps 69:36*
inherit it
turned their heart, to deal   *Ps 105:25*
subtilly with *his* s.
he will repent himself   *Ps 135:14*
concerning *his* s.
if hearken to lie, all *his* s. are   *Pr 22:12*
wicked
to love the name of the Lord,   *Isa 56:6*
to be *his* s.
the Lord shall call *his* s. by   *Isa 65:15*
another name
hand of the Lord be known   *Isa 66:14*
toward *his* s.
riding in chariots, on horses,   *Jer 22:4*
he and *his* s.
punish him, *his* seed and *his*   *Jer 36:31*
s. for iniquity
if the prince give a gift to   *Eze 46:17*
his s.
and delivered *his* s. that   *Da 3:28*
trusted in him
king who would take   *M't 18:23*
account of *his* s.
he sent *his* s. to the   *M't 21:34*
husbandmen to
called *his* ten s. and delivered   *Lu 19:13*
them
his s. ye are to whom ye obey   *Ro 6:16*
to shew *his* s. thing that must   *Re 1:1;*
come   *22:6*
hath avenged blood of *his* s. at   *Re 19:2*
her hand
praise God, all ye *his* s.   *Re 19:5*
throne be in it, and *his* s. shall   *Re 22:3*
serve him

MY SERVANTS

they are *my* s. whom I   *Le 25:42;*
brought out   *25:55*
I have appointed *my* s. such a   *1Sa 21:2*
place
my s. shall be with thy   *1Ki 5:6;*
servant   *2Ch 2:8*
yet I will send *my* s. unto thee   *1Ki 20:6*
to-morrow
let *my* s. go with thy servants   *1Ki 22:49*
in the ships, but
that I may avenge the blood   *2Ki 9:7*
of *my* s.
the half of *my* s. wrought in   *Ne 4:16*
the work
neither I nor *my* s. put off our   *Ne 4:23*
clothes
I and *my* s. might exact of   *Ne 5:10*
them money, corn
all *my* s. were gathered thither   *Ne 5:16*
to the work
and some of *my* s. set I at   *Ne 13:19*
the gates
mine elect and *my* s. shall   *Isa 65:9*
dwell there
my s. shall eat; *my* s. shall   *Isa 65:13;*
sing for joy   *65:14*
I have even sent to you all *my*   *Jer 7:25;*
s.   *44:4*
if kingdom of world, then   *Joh 18:36*
would *my* s. fight
on *my* s. I will pour out of my   *Ac 2:18*
Spirit
calls herself a prophetess to   *Re 2:20*
seduce *my* s.

THY SERVANTS

we are true men, *thy* s. are   *Ge 42:11*
no spies
God hath found out the   *Ge 44:16*
iniquity of *thy* s.
thy s. are shepherds, both we   *Ge 47:3*
and our fathers
his brethren said, Behold, we   *Ge 50:18*
be *thy* s.
wherefore dealest thou thus   *Ex 5:15*
with *thy* s.
these *thy* s. shall bow down   *Ex 11:8*
themselves to me
remember Abraham and   *Ex 32:13;*
Israel *thy* s.   *De 9:27*
thy s. will do as my lord   *Nu 32:25;*
command   *32:31*
Gibeonites said to Joshua, We   *Jos 9:8*
are *thy* s.
saying, Slack not thy hand   *Jos 10:6*
from *thy* s.
pray for *thy* s. to the Lord   *1Sa 12:19*
thy God
who is so faithful among all   *1Sa 22:14*
thy s. as David
and speak comfortably to *thy*   *2Sa 19:7*
s.
they sent this word, return   *2Sa 19:14*
thou and all *thy* s.
they told Shimei, *Thy* s. be in   *1Ki 2:39*
Gath
my servants shall be with *thy*   *1Ki 5:6;*
s.   *2Ch 2:8*
who keepest covenant and   *1Ki 8:23*
mercy with *thy* s.
hear thou and judge *thy* s.   *1Ki 8:32;*
  2Ch 6:23
happy are these *thy* s.   *1Ki 10:8;*
  2Ch 9:7
they will be *thy* s. for ever   *1Ki 12:7;*
  2Ch 10:7
one said, Be content, and go   *2Ki 6:3*
with *thy* s.
now these are *thy* s. and thy   *Ne 1:10*
people
let thine ear be attentive to   *Ne 1:11*
prayer of *thy* s.
the bodies of *thy* s. have they   *Ps 79:2*
given
by the revenging of the blood   *Ps 79:10*
of *thy* s. shed
remember, Lord, the reproach   *Ps 89:50*
of *thy* s.
let it repent thee concerning   *Ps 90:13*
thy s.
let thy work appear to *thy* s.   *Ps 90:16*
for *thy* s. take pleasure in   *Ps 102:14*
her stones
children of *thy* s. shall   *Ps 102:28*
continue, their seed

they continue this day, for   *Ps 119:91*
all are *thy s.*
by *thy s.* hast thou   *Isa 37:24*
reproached the Lord
prove *thy s.* I beseech thee,   *Da 1:12*
ten days
and as thou seest, deal with   *Da 1:13*
thy s.
grant unto *thy s.* that with all   *Ac 4:29*
boldness

SERVANT'S

but thou hast spoken of thy *s.*   *2Sa 7:19*
house
for Jacob my *s.* sake, and   *Isa 45:4*
Israel mine elect
so will I do for my *s.* sake   *Isa 65:8*

SERVANTS'

s. trade hath been about   *Ge 46:34*
cattle
of Pharaoh, and into his *s.*   *Ex 8:24*
houses
Return, for thy *s.* sake, the   *Isa 63:17*
tribes of
so will I do for my *s.* sake   *Isa 65:8*
that I

SERVE

thy seed shall *s.* them 400   *Ge 15:13*
years
that nation whom they shall   *Ge 15:14*
s. will I judge
and the elder shall *s.* the   *Ge 25:23*
younger
let people *s.* thee, nations   *Ge 27:29*
bow down to thee
by thy sword shalt thou live,   *Ge 27:40*
and *s.* brother
shouldst thou therefore *s.* me   *Ge 29:15*
for nought
I will *s.* thee seven years for   *Ge 29:18*
Rachel
thou shalt *s.* with me seven   *Ge 29:27*
other years
they made Israel to *s.* with   *Ex 1:13*
rigour
ye shall *s.* God upon this   *Ex 3:12*
mountain
I say, Let my son go, that he   *Ex 4:23*
may *s.* me
let my people go, that they   *Ex 7:16*;
may *s.* me   *8:1, 20; 9:1, 13; 10:3*
they may *s.* the Lord their   *Ex 10:7*
God
may *s.* Egyptians, for it   *Ex 14:2*
had been better to *s.* them
not bow down to them, nor *s.*   *Ex 20:5*;
                   De 5:9
an Hebrew servant, six years he   *Ex 21:2*
shall *s.*
bore his ear, and he shall *s.*   *Ex 21:6*
him for ever
to *s.* as priests (R)   *Ex 28:1; 29:44*
to *s.* as priests (B)   *Ex 29:44*
not compel him to *s.* as   *Le 25:39*
bondservant
do not make him *s.*   *Le 25:39*
(B)(E)(R)
he shall *s.* thee unto the year   *Le 25:40*
of jubile
the family of the Gershonites   *Nu 4:24*
to *s.*
bear all made for them, so   *Nu 4:26*
shall they *s.*
from the age of fifty they shall   *Nu 8:25*
s. no more
the tenth to Levi, for their   *Nu 18:21*
service they *s.*
thou shouldest be driven to *s.*   *De 4:19*
them
fear the Lord thy God and *s.*   *De 6:13*;
him   *10:12, 20; 11:13; 13:4;*
Jos 22:5; 24:14-15; 1Sa 7:3; 12:14, 20,
                         24
if brother be sold to thee,   *De 15:12*
and *s.* six years
be tributaries to thee, and   *De 20:11*
shall *s.* thee
therefore shalt thou *s.* thine   *De 28:48*
enemies
choose you this day whom   *Jos 24:15*
you will *s.*
should *s.* Shechem, should *s.*   *J'g 9:28*
Hamor
who is Abimelech, that we   *J'g 9:38*
should *s.* him

do thou as occasion shall *s.*   *1Sa 10:7*
thee
covenant with us, and we will   *1Sa 11:1*
s. thee
but now deliver us, and we   *1Sa 12:10*
will *s.* thee
then shall ye be our servants,   *1Sa 17:9*
and *s.* us
whom should I *s.*? should I   *2Sa 16:19*
not *s.*
people I knew not shall *s.*   *2Sa 22:44*;
me   *Ps 18:43*
make this heavy yoke lighter,   *1Ki 12:4;*
and we will *s.* thee   *2Ch 10:4*
but Jehu shall *s.* Baal much   *2Ki 10:18*
dwell in the land, and *s.* the   *2Ki 25:24;*
king of Babylon   *Jer 27:11-12, 17;*
              28:14; 40:9
and *s.* him with a perfect   *1Ch 28:9*
heart
the Lord hath chosen you to   *2Ch 29:11*
s. him
Josiah made all present to   *2Ch 34:33*
s. the Lord
what Almighty, that we   *Job 21:15*
should *s.* him
if they obey and *s.* him, they   *Job 36:11*
shall spend
will the unicorn be willing to   *Job 39:9*
s. thee
a seed shall *s.* him, and be   *Ps 22:30*
accounted
yea, all kings, all nations   *Ps 72:11*
shall *s.* him
confounded be all they that *s.*   *Ps 97:7*
images
walketh in a perfect way, he   *Ps 101:6*
shall *s.* me
bondage wherein thou wast   *Isa 14:3*
made to *s.*
Egyptians shall *s.* with the   *Isa 19:23*
Assyrians
I have not caused thee to *s.*   *Isa 43:23*
with offering
thou hast made me to *s.* with   *Isa 43:24*
thy sins
join themselves to the Lord to   *Isa 56:6*
s. him
nation that will not *s.* thee   *Isa 60:12*
shall perish
so shall ye *s.* strangers in land   *Jer 5:19*
I will cause thee to *s.* thine   *Jer 17:4*
enemies
these nations shall *s.* king of   *Jer 25:11*
Babylon
many nations shall *s.*   *Jer 25:14;*
themselves   *27:7*
beasts of the field have I given   *Jer 27:6*
to *s.* him
nation that will not *s.* king of   *Jer 27:8;*
Babylon   *27:13*
the prophets that say ye shall   *Jer 27:9;*
not *s.*   *27:14*
strangers no more *s.*   *Jer 30:8*
themselves of him
that none should *s.* himself   *Jer 34:9;*
of them   *34:10*
fear not to *s.* the Chaldeans;   *Jer 40:9*
dwell
as for me, I will *s.* the   *Jer 40:10*
Chaldeans
families of the countries to *s.*   *Eze 20:32*
wood
house of Israel go *s.* every   *Eze 20:39*
one his idols
Israel all of them in the land   *Eze 20:40*
shall *s.* me
his army *s.* against Tyrus   *Eze 29:18*
increase for food to them   *Eze 48:18*
that *s.* the city
that *s.* the city, shall *s.* it   *Eze 48:19*
out of all tribes
our God whom we *s.* is able to   *Da 3:17*
deliver
might not *s.* any, except their   *Da 3:28*
own God
nations, and languages, should   *Da 7:14*
s. him
and all dominions shall *s.* and   *Da 7:27*
obey him
call on Lord, to *s.* him with   *Zep 3:9*
consent
ye have said it is in vain to   *Mal 3:14*
s. God
him only shalt thou *s.*   *M't 4:10;*
                Lu 4:8
no man can *s.* two masters;   *M't 6:24;*
ye cannot *s.* God and mammon *Lu 16:13*
not be served, but *s.*   *M't 20:28*
(B)(N)(P)(R)

that we being delivered,   *Lu 1:74*
might *s.* him
that my sister hath left me   *Lu 10:40*
to *s.* alone
I say, he will come forth and   *Lu 12:37*
s. them
lo, these many years do I *s.*   *Lu 15:29*
thee
will not rather say, Gird   *Lu 17:8*
thyself and *s.* me
and he that is chief, as he   *Lu 22:26*
that doth *s.*
if any man *s.* me, let him   *Joh 12:26*
follow me
we leave word of God, and *s.*   *Ac 6:2*
tables
they come forth and *s.* me in   *Ac 7:7*
this place
stood by me the angel of God   *Ac 27:23*
whom I *s.*
God is my witness, whom I *s.*   *Ro 1:9*
with my spirit in gospel of his
Son
that henceforth we should not   *Ro 6:6*
s. sin
that we should *s.* in newness of   *Ro 7:6*
spirit, not in
so then, with the mind I *s.* the   *Ro 7:25*
law of God
it was said, The elder shall *s.*   *Ro 9:12*
the younger
for they that are such *s.* not   *Ro 16:18*
our Lord
but by love *s.* one another   *Ga 5:13*
receive reward, for ye *s.* the   *Col 3:24*
Lord Christ
ye turned from idols to *s.*   *1Th 1:9*
living God
I thank God whom I *s.* from   *2Ti 1:3*
my fathers
who *s.* to the example of   *Heb 8:5*
heavenly things
purge from dead works to *s.*   *Heb 9:14*
the living God
grace, whereby we may *s.*   *Heb 12:28*
God acceptably
no right to eat, which *s.* the   *Heb 13:10*
tabernacle
they *s.* him day and night in   *Re 7:15*
his temple
of the Lamb, and his servants   *Re 22:3*
shall *s.* him

SERVE *GODS*

not *s.* their *gods*   *Ex 23:24;*
De 6:14; 28:14; Jos 23:7; 2Ki 17:35;
            Jer 25:6 ; 35:15
if thou *s.* their *gods*, it will   *Ex 23:33*
be a snare to thee
there ye shall *s.* *gods* the   *De 4:28;*
work of men's hands, wood   *28:36, 64;*
               Jer 16:13
turn, that they may *s.* other   *De 7:4;*
gods   *31:20*
if thou *s.* other *gods*, and   *De 8:19;*
worship them   *11:16; 30:17; Jos 24:20;*
               2Ch 7:19
how do these nations *s.* their   *De 12:30*
gods
let us go after and *s.* other   *De 13:2;*
gods   *13:6, 13*
turneth away from God to *s.*   *De 29:18*
other *gods*
God forbid we should *s.*   *Jos 24:16*
other *gods*
corrupted themselves to *s.*   *J'g 2:19;*
other *gods*   *Jer 11:10; 13:10*
driven me, saying, Go *s.*   *1Sa 26:19*
other *gods*
provoke me to anger, to *s.*   *Jer 44:3*
other *gods*
they *s.* not thy *gods*, nor   *Da 3:12*
worship image
do ye not *s.* my *gods*; we   *Da 3:14;*
will not *s.* thy *gods*   *3:18*

SERVED

twelve years they *s.*   *Ge 14:4*
Chedorlaomer
Jacob *s.* seven years for   *Ge 29:20;*
Rachel   *29:30*
give me my children for   *Ge 30:26*
whom I *s.* thee
he said, Thou knowest how I   *Ge 30:29*
have *s.* thee
with all my power I have *s.*   *Ge 31:6*
your father
I *s.* thee fourteen years for thy   *Ge 31:41*
two daughters

which *s.* at the door of the tabernacle (S)	Ex 38:8
s. as priests (B)(R)	Nu 3:4
wherein the nations *s.* their gods	De 12:2
hath gone and *s.* other gods	De 17:3;
and	29:26; Jos 23:16
your fathers *s.* other gods	Jos 24:2; 24:15
put away the gods which your fathers *s.*	Jos 24:14
Israel *s.* Lord all the days of	Jos 24:31;
Joshua, and all the elders	J'g 2:7
Israel *s.* Baalim	J'g 2:11; 2:13; 3:7; 10:6, 10
they gave daughters to sons, and *s.* their gods	J'g 3:6
Israel *s.* Chushan-rishathaim eight years	J'g 3:8
so Israel *s.* Eglon king of Moab eighteen years	J'g 3:14
men of Ephraim said, Why hast thou *s.* us thus	J'g 8:1
ye have forsaken me, and *s.* other gods	J'g 10:13
they put away gods, *s.* Lord	J'g 10:16; 1Sa 7:4
the Syrians made peace and *s.* him (A)	2Sa 10:19
s. him (R)	2Sa 13:17; 1Ki 19:21
	Da 7:10; M't 8:15
as I have *s.* in thy father's presence	2Sa 16:19
s. him (B)	1Ki 1:4; Da 7:10
they brought presents and *s.* Solomon	1Ki 4:21
because they *s.* other gods	1Ki 9:9; 2Ch 7:22
Ahab *s.* Baal; Ahaziah *s.* Baal	1Ki 16:31; 22:53
Jehu said, Ahab *s.* Baal a little	2Ki 10:18
Hezekiah *s.* not the king of Assyria	2Ki 18:7
Manasseh *s.* host of heaven	2Ki 21:3; 2Ch 33:3
Amon *s.* idols his father *s.*	2Ki 21:21; 2Ch 33:22
how the men were *s.* And he sent	1Ch 19:5
princes of Judah *s.* groves and idols	2Ch 24:18
they have not *s.* thee in their kingdom	Ne 9:35
and they *s.* their idols, which were	Ps 106:36
that rewardeth thee as thou hast *s.* us	Ps 137:8
the king himself is *s.* by the field	Ec 5:9
as ye have *s.* strange gods in your land	Jer 5:19
before the sun and moon, whom they have *s.*	Jer 8:2
have walked after other gods and *s.* them	Jer 16:11
they worshipped other gods and *s.* them	Jer 22:9
when he hath *s.* thee six years, let him go	Jer 34:14
for the service which he had *s.*	Eze 29:18; 29:20
delivered out of the hand of those that *s.*	Eze 34:27
Israel *s.* for a wife, he kept sheep	Ho 12:12
not be *s.*, but serve (B)(N)(P)(R)	M't 20:28
Anna *s.* God night and day in the temple	Lu 2:37
they made him a supper, and Martha *s.*	Joh 12:2
after David had *s.* his generation	Ac 13:36
who worshipped and *s.* the creature	Ro 1:25
he hath *s.* with me in the gospel	Ph'p 2:22

SERVEDST

thou *s.* not the Lord with gladness	De 28:47

SERVEST

thy God whom thou *s.* will deliver	Da 6:16
is thy God whom thou *s.* able to deliver thee	Da 6:20

SERVETH

under the charge of Merari all that *s.*	Nu 3:36
as a man spareth his son that *s.* him	Mal 3:17
between him that *s.* God, and him that *s.* not	Mal 3:18
whether greater, he that sitteth at meat or he that *s.*? I am as one that *s.*	Lu 22:27
he that in these things *s.* Christ is	Ro 14:18
prophecy *s.* not them that believe not	1Co 14:22
wherefore then *s.* the law	Ga 3:19

SERVICE

for the *s.* that thou shalt serve with me	Ge 29:27
thou knowest the *s.* which I have done	Ge 30:26
in all manner of *s.* in field; all their *s.* they made them serve	Ex 1:14
s. with harshness and severity (A)	Ex 1:14
come to land, ye shall keep this *s.*	Ex 12:25; 13:5
children shall say, What mean you by this *s.*	Ex 12:26
all vessels in all the *s.* thereof be of brass	Ex 27:19
may make the clothes of the *s.*	Ex 31:10; 35:19
people bring more than enough for the *s.*	Ex 36:5
tribe of Levi to do *s.* of tabernacle	Nu 3:7; 3:8
the charge of the Gershonites for the *s.*	Nu 3:26
s. of sanctuary the charge of Kohathites	Nu 3:31; 4:4
Aaron and sons shall appoint them to the *s.*	Nu 4:19
all that enter in to perform the *s.* to do work	Nu 4:23
this is the *s.* of the Gershonites	Nu 4:24; 27:28
the *s.* of the sons of Merari	Nu 4:30; 33:43
that they may do the *s.* of the tabernacle	Nu 7:5
the Levites may execute *s.* of the Lord	Nu 8:11
go in to wait upon *s.* of tabernacle	Nu 8:24
from fifty years shall cease waiting on the *s.*	Nu 8:25
a small thing to bring you to do the *s.*	Nu 16:9
the Levites be joined to thee for all the *s.*	Nu 18:4
the Levites are given as a gift to do the *s.*	Nu 18:6
given all tenth in Israel for their *s.*	Nu 18:21; 18:31
be a witness, that we might do the *s.*	Jos 22:27
make thou the grievous *s.* lighter	1Ki 12:4
whom David set over the *s.*	1Ch 6:31
very able men for the work of *s.*	1Ch 9:13; 26:8
vessels of *s.* (S)	1Ch 9:28
David distributed them in their *s.*	1Ch 24:3
the Levites for all the work of the *s.*	1Ch 28:13
the priests shall be with thee for all the *s.*	1Ch 28:21
who is willing to consecrate his *s.* to Lord	1Ch 29:5
gave for the *s.* of house of God	1Ch 29:7
the courses of the priests to their *s.*	2Ch 8:14
s. of thy father (A)(E)(R)	2Ch 10:4
they may know my *s.* and *s.* of kingdoms	2Ch 12:8
and gave the money to such as did the *s.*	2Ch 24:12
so the *s.* of the house was set in order	2Ch 29:35
appointed every man according to his *s.*	2Ch 31:2
in every work that he began in the *s.*	2Ch 31:21
encouraged them to the *s.* of the Lord	2Ch 35:2

so the *s.* of the Lord was prepared	2Ch 35:10; 35:16
in their courses, for the *s.* of God	Ezr 6:18; 7:19
with the third part of a shekel for *s.*	Ne 10:32
next to them in *s.* (S)	Ne 12:9
causeth herb to grow for the *s.* of man	Ps 104:14
put to bond *s.* (B)	Isa 31:8
that useth neighbour's *s.* without wages	Jer 22:13
caused his army to serve a great *s.*	Eze 29:18
keepers of the charge of house for all the *s.*	Eze 44:14
in connection with *s.* to his god (B)	Da 6:5
they pressed him into *s.* (N)	M'k 15:21
daily *s.* of Abia (A)	Lu 1:5
to take part in divine *s.* (N)	Lu 1:8
who killeth you will think he doth God *s.*	Joh 16:2
to whom pertaineth the *s.* of God	Ro 9:4
sacrifice to God, which is your reasonable *s.*	Ro 12:1
that my *s.* may be accepted of the saints	Ro 15:31
varieties of *s.* (N)(R)	1Co 12:5
part in this *s.* (B)(N)	2Co 8:4
the administration of this *s.* not only	2Co 9:12
s. this fund renders (B)(E)(R)	2Co 9:12
taking wages of them to do you *s.*	2Co 11:8
did *s.* to them who by nature are no gods	Ga 4:8
with good will doing *s.* as to the Lord	Eph 6:7
if I be offered upon *s.* of your faith	Ph'p 2:17
to supply your lack of *s.* toward me	Ph'p 2:30
rather do *s.* because they are beloved	1Ti 6:2
first covenant had ordinances of divine *s.*	Heb 9:1
the priests accomplishing the *s.* of God	Heb 9:6
could not make him that did the *s.* perfect	Heb 9:9
I know thy works, and charity, and *s.*	Re 2:19

SERVILE

ye shall do no *s.* work	Le 23:7; 23:8, 21, 25, 35-36; Nu 28:18, 25-26; 29:1, 12, 35
strenuous labor (B)	Le 23:7
laborious work (R)	Le 23:7

SERVING

that we have let Israel go from *s.* us	Ex 14:5
lookingglasses of the women *s.* (S)	Ex 38:8
worth a double hired servant in *s.* thee	De 15:18
s. as priest (A)	Lu 1:8
Martha was cumbered about much *s.*	Lu 10:40
s. the Lord with all humility of mind	Ac 20:19
our twelve tribes instantly *s.* God day and night	Ac 26:7
not slothful, fervent in spirit, *s.* Lord	Ro 12:11
different ways of *s.* God (P)	1Co 12:6
engaged in sacred *s.* (A)	Tit 2:3
were sometimes foolish, *s.* divers lusts	Tit 3:3

SERVITOR

s. said, Shall I set this before 100 men	2Ki 4:43
servant (A)(B)(E)(R)	2Ki 4:43

SERVITUDE

submit to *s.* (B)	Ge 49:15
ease somewhat grievous *s.* of thy father	2Ch 10:4
service (A)(E)(R)	2Ch 10:4
Judah is gone because of great *s.*	La 1:3

SET

God *s.* stars in firmament of   *Ge 1:17*
heaven
s. apart and hallowed it (A)   *Ge 2:3*
and the Lord *s.* a mark upon   *Ge 4:15*
Cain
door of the ark shalt *s.* in the   *Ge 6:16*
side thereof
I do *s.* my bow in the cloud   *Ge 9:13*
for a token
Abraham *s.* calf before them,   *Ge 18:8*
they did eat
the angels *s.* Lot without the   *Ge 19:16*
city Sodom
there was *s.* meat before him   *Ge 24:33*
to eat
sun was *s.*; a ladder was *s.*   *Ge 28:11;*
upon earth   *28:12*
s. it before my brethren and   *Ge 31:37*
thy brethren
let Pharaoh *s.* him over the   *Ge 41:33*
land of Egypt
I have *s.* thee over all the   *Ge 41:41*
land of Egypt
if I bring him not, and *s.* him   *Ge 43:9*
before thee
Jacob *s.* Ephraim before   *Ge 48:20*
Manasseh
nor did he *s.* his heart to this   *Ex 7:23*
also
s. apart (S)   *Ex 8:22;*
9:4; De 4:41; 10:8; 19:2, 7; 29:21;
  Eze 39:14
consecrate, *s.* apart (A)(R)   *Ex 13:2*
s. apart to Lord all that open *Ex 13:12*
the matrix
s. bounds; *s.* the table   *Ex 19:12;*
without   *19:23; 26:35*
judgments which thou shalt *s.* *Ex 21:1*
before them
I will *s.* thy bounds from the   *Ex 23:31*
Red sea
stones *s.* in ephod   *Ex 25:7;*
  28:11; 35:9, 27
thou shalt *s.* on table shew   *Ex 25:30*
bread before me
two tenons *s.* in order   *Ex 26:17*
against another
knowest people, they are *s.*   *Ex 32:22*
on mischief
the rings *s.*; the lamps *s.* in   *Ex 37:3;*
order   *39:37*
s. in order things that are to   *Ex 40:4*
be *s.* in order
s. altar of gold; *s.* altar of   *Ex 40:5;*
burnt offering   *40:6*
s. laver; *s.* staves; the bread   *Ex 40:7;*
  40:20, 21
s. yourselves apart (B)   *Le 11:44*
every sabbath he shall *s.* it in *Le 24:8*
order before Lord
I will *s.* my tabernacle among *Le 26:11*
you
field *s.* apart for him (B)   *Le 27:21*
camp of Judah, these shall first *Nu 2:9*
s. forth
as the camp is to *s.* forward   *Nu 4:15*
the priest shall *s.* her before   *Nu 5:16*
the Lord
they *s.* apart the tabernacle (B) *Nu 7:1*
thou shalt *s.* the Levites   *Nu 8:13*
before Aaron
s. forward, bearing the   *Nu 10:17*
tabernacle
Lord said. *S.* the fiery serpent *Nu 21:8*
upon a pole
let the Lord *s.* a man over   *Nu 27:16*
the congregation
I have *s.* the land before you   *De 1:8;*
  1:21
as all this law which I *s.*   *De 4:8;*
before your   *4:44*
Lord did not *s.* his love on you, *De 7:7*
because more
I *s.* before you a blessing and *De 11:26*
a curse
to do all the judgments   *De 11:32*
which I *s.* before you
choose to *s.* his name there   *De 14:24;*
  Ne 1:9
males you shall *s.* apart (A)   *De 15:19*
and shalt say, I will *s.* a king *De 17:14*
over me
in any wise shalt *s.* him the   *De 17:15*
Lord shall choose
s. apart cities (A)(B)(E)(R)   *De 19:2;*
  19:7
landmark, which they of old   *De 19:14*
time have *s.*

s. down the basket before the   *De 26:4;*
altar   *26:10*
the Lord thy God will *s.* thee   *De 28:1*
on high
would not *s.* sole of her foot   *De 28:56*
on the ground
s. him apart from all people   *De 29:21*
(B)
I have *s.* before you life and   *De 30:15;*
death   *30:19*
he *s.* bounds of the people   *De 32:8*
by the numbers
s. your hearts unto all the   *De 32:46*
words I testify
did Joshua *s.* up in Gilgal (S) *Jos 4:20*
s. apart for the Lord (B)   *Jos 6:19*
he *s.* them a statute in   *Jos 24:25*
Shechem
till I bring and *s.* my present   *J'g 6:18*
before thee
that lappeth, him shalt thou *s.*   *J'g 7:5*
by himself
and they had but newly *s.* the *J'g 7:19*
watch
Lord *s.* every man's sword   *J'g 7:22*
against his fellow
raiseth up poor out of dust, to *1Sa 2:8*
s. among princes; he hath
s. world
the Philistines *s.* the ark of   *1Sa 5:2*
God by Dagon
and will *s.* them to ear his   *1Sa 8:12*
ground
as for thine asses *s.* not thy   *1Sa 9:20*
mind on them
ye have said, Nay, but *s.*   *1Sa 10:19*
a king over us
the Lord hath *s.* a king over   *1Sa 12:13*
you
Saul and Israel *s.* the battle   *1Sa 17:2;*
in array   *17:8; 2Sa 10:17; 1Ki 20:12;*
  1Ch 19:17
so that his name was much *s.* *1Sa 18:30*
by
behold, as thy life was much   *1Sa 26:24*
s. by this day
they *s.* the ark of God on a   *2Sa 6:3*
new cart
s. Uriah in forefront of the   *2Sa 11:15*
hottest battle
crown *s.* on David head   *2Sa 12:30;*
  1Ch 20:2
yet didst thou *s.* thy servant   *2Sa 19:28*
at thy table
that all Israel *s.* their faces on *1Ki 2:15*
me
a seat to be *s.* for the king's *1Ki 2:19*
mother
son. whom I will *s.* on throne *1Ki 5:5*
shall build
he *s.* the one in Beth-el, the *1Ki 12:29*
other in Dan
Ahijah could not see, for his *1Ki 14:4*
eyes were *s.*
and *s.* Naboth on high   *1Ki 21:9;*
among the people   *21:12*
thou shalt *s.* aside that which *2Ki 4:4*
is full
let us *s.* for him there a bed   *2Ki 4:10*
and a table
according to the *s.* time of   *2Ki 4:17*
life (S)
s. on the great pot, and   *2Ki 4:38*
seethe pottage
what, should I *s.* this before   *2Ki 4:43*
an hundred men
s. bread and water before   *2Ki 6:22*
them to eat and drink
the money that every man is *s.* *2Ki 12:4*
s. house in order, shalt die   *2Ki 20:1;*
  Isa 38:1
porters appointed in their *s.*   *1Ch 9:22*
office
they *s.* the ark in midst of   *1Ch 16:1*
the tent
Joab saw the battle was *s.*   *1Ch 19:10*
against him
in it: and it was *s.* upon   *1Ch 20:2*
David's head
s. your heart to seek the   *1Ch 22:19*
Lord your God
s. apart to consecrate (R)   *1Ch 23:13*
David gave onyx stones and   *1Ch 29:2*
stones to be *s.*
because I *s.* my affection to   *1Ch 29:3*
house of God
and the sea was *s.* above upon *2Ch 4:4*
them
and I am *s.* on the throne of   *2Ch 6:10*
Israel

s. their hearts to seek the   *2Ch 11:16*
Lord
he feared, and *s.* himself to   *2Ch 20:3*
seek the Lord
they *s.* the house of God in   *2Ch 24:13*
his state
service of the house of Lord   *2Ch 29:35*
was *s.* in order
in their *s.* office to give their *2Ch 31:15*
brethren
in their *s.* office they   *2Ch 31:18*
sanctified themselves
they *s.* themselves apart (A) *2Ch 31:18*
s. their seal (S)   *Ne 10:1*
s. apart for Levites   *Ne 12:12*
(A)(B)(E)(R)
I would *s.* my cause before   *Job 23:4*
him (S)
and what should be *s.* on   *Job 36:16*
thy table
Josiah *s.* the priests in their   *Job 35:2*
charges
they *s.* the priests in their   *Ezr 6:18*
divisions
it pleased the king, and I *s.*   *Ne 2:6*
him a time
we *s.* a watch against them day *Ne 4:9*
and night
yieldeth much increase to   *Ne 9:37*
kings *s.* over us
I gathered and *s.* them in   *Ne 13:11*
their place
terrors of God *s.* themselves   *Job 6:4*
against me
thou shouldst *s.* thine heart   *Job 7:17*
upon him
why *s.* me as a mark against   *Job 7:20*
thee
who shall *s.* me a time to   *Job 9:19*
plead
and he hath *s.* darkness in my *Job 19:8*
paths
disdained to *s.* with the dogs *Job 30:1*
of my flock
they *s.* forward my calamity *Job 30:13*
s. thy words in order before   *Job 33:5*
me
if he *s.* his heart upon man, *Job 34:14*
if he gather
break mighty men and *s.*   *Job 34:24*
others in stead
canst thou *s.* dominion   *Job 38:33*
thereof in earth
the kings of the earth *s.*   *Ps 2:2*
themselves
yet have I *s.* my king on my   *Ps 2:6*
holy hill
I will not be afraid if 10,000 *s.* *Ps 3:6*
themselves
Lord hath *s.* apart him that is *Ps 4:3*
godly
who hast *s.* thy glory above the *Ps 8:1*
heavens
his eyes are privily *s.* against *Ps 10:8*
the poor
s. him in safety from him that *Ps 12:5*
puffeth
I have *s.* the Lord always   *Ps 16:8*
before me
in them he *s.* a tabernacle for *Ps 19:4*
the sun
thou hast *s.* my feet in a large *Ps 31:8*
room
brought me up, and *s.* feet   *Ps 40:2*
upon rock
I will *s.* them in order before *Ps 50:21*
thine eyes
they have not *s.* God before   *Ps 54:3*
them
if riches, *s.* not your heart   *Ps 62:10*
upon them
thou didst *s.* them in slippery *Ps 73:18*
places
thou hast *s.* all the borders of *Ps 74:17*
the earth
that they might *s.* their hope *Ps 78:7*
in God
a generation that *s.* not their *Ps 78:8*
heart aright
and shall *s.* us in the way of   *Ps 85:13*
his steps
violent men have not *s.* thee   *Ps 86:14*
before them
thou hast *s.* our iniquities   *Ps 90:8*
before thee
because he *s.* his love upon   *Ps 91:14*
me, I will deliver him and *s.*
him on high
I will *s.* no wicked thing   *Ps 101:3*
before my eyes

hast *s.* bound that they may | *Ps 104:9*
not pass over
s. thou a wicked man over | *Ps 109:6*
him, let Satan
that he may *s.* him with | *Ps 113:8*
princes
Lord answered, and *s.* me in | *Ps 118:5*
large place
there are *s.* thrones of | *Ps 122:5*
judgment, of David
fruit of body will I *s.* upon | *Ps 132:11*
thy throne
the proud have *s.* gins for me | *Ps 140:5*
let my prayer be *s.* forth | *Ps 141:2*
before thee
a watch, O Lord, before my | *Ps 141:3*
mouth
ye have *s.* at nought all my | *Pr 1:25*
counsel
the landmark which thy | *Pr 22:28*
fathers have *s.*
wilt thou *s.* eyes on that which | *Pr 23:5*
is not
he hath *s.* the world in their | *Ec 3:11*
heart
God hath *s.* the one against | *Ec 7:14*
the other
the heart is fully *s.* in them to | *Ec 8:11*
do evil
folly *s.* in great dignity; rich | *Ec 10:6*
sit in low place
he sought out, and *s.* in order | *Ec 12:9*
proverbs
his eyes are as the eyes of | *Ca 5:12*
doves fitly *s.*
his hands are as gold rings *s.* | *Ca 5:14*
with the beryl
his legs are *s.* upon sockets of | *Ca 5:15*
fine gold
thy belly as a heap of wheat *s.* | *Ca 7:2*
with lilies
s. me as a seal upon thine heart | *Ca 8:6*
and instead of well *s.* hair, | *Isa 3:24*
baldness
let us *s.* a king in midst of it | *Isa 7:6*
the Lord will *s.* them in their | *Isa 14:1*
own land
and thou shalt *s.* it with | *Isa 17:10*
strange slips
I will *s.* Egyptians against | *Isa 19:2*
Egyptians
go *s.* a watchman, let him | *Isa 21:6*
declare what
I am *s.* in my ward whole | *Isa 21:8*
nights
shall *s.* themselves in array at | *Isa 22:7*
the gate
be *s.* apart to the Lord (B) | *Isa 23:18*
who would *s.* briers and | *Isa 27:4*
thorns against me
I will *s.* in the desert, the | *Isa 41:19*
fir tree
till he have *s.* judgment in the | *Isa 42:4*
earth
who as I, shall *s.* it in order | *Isa 44:7*
for me
they carry him, and *s.* him in | *Isa 46:7*
his place
on a high mountain hast thou | *Isa 57:7*
s. thy bed
I have *s.* watchmen on thy | *Isa 62:6;*
walls | *Jer 6:17*
I will *s.* a sign among them | *Isa 66:19*
separate and *s.* apart (A) | *Jer 1:5*
see, I have *s.* thee over the | *Jer 1:10*
nations
lay wait, they *s.* a trap, they | *Jer 5:26*
catch men
s. in array, as men for war | *Jer 6:23;*
| *Joe 2:5*
I have *s.* thee for a tower and | *Jer 6:27*
a fortress
the place where I *s.* my name | *Jer 7:12*
at the first
they *s.* their abominations in | *Jer 7:30*
the house
forsaken my law which I *s.* | *Jer 9:13*
before them
I *s.* before you the way of life | *Jer 21:8*
and death
for I will *s.* mine eyes on | *Jer 24:6*
them for good
to walk in my law, which I *s.* | *Jer 26:4*
before you
children's teeth are *s.* on | *Jer 31:29;*
edge | *Eze 18:2*
man that eateth, his teeth | *Jer 31:30*
shall be *s.* on edge
his servant, whom he had *s.* | *Jer 34:16*
at liberty

s. pots of wine before sons of | *Jer 35:5*
Rechabites
women said, Thy friends | *Jer 38:22*
have *s.* thee on
nor walked in statutes I *s.* | *Jer 44:10*
before you
s. me in dark places, as dead of | *La 3:6*
old
he hath *s.* me as a mark for | *La 3:12*
the arrow
I have *s.* it in the midst of the | *Eze 5:5*
nations
therefore have I *s.* it far from | *Eze 7:20*
them
s. a mark on the foreheads of | *Eze 9:4*
men that sigh
for I have *s.* thee for a sign | *Eze 12:6*
unto Israel
thou hast *s.* my oil before | *Eze 16:18;*
thy images | *16:19*
I will take off highest | *Eze 17:22*
branch, I will *s.* it
then nations *s.* against him | *Eze 19:8*
on every side
in thee have they *s.* light by | *Eze 22:7*
father and mother
they humbled her that was *s.* | *Eze 22:10*
apart
king of Babylon *s.* himself | *Eze 24:2*
against Jerusalem
s. on a pot, *s.* it on, and also | *Eze 24:3*
pour water
her blood, she *s.* it upon the | *Eze 24:7;*
top of a rock | *24:8*
when I take them whereon | *Eze 24:25*
they *s.* their minds
I shall *s.* glory in the land of | *Eze 26:20*
the living
they of Persia *s.* forth thy | *Eze 27:10*
comeliness
tho' thou *s.* thy heart as the | *Eze 28:2*
heart of God
art anointed cherub, and I | *Eze 28:14*
have *s.* thee so
I shall *s.* apart, separated | *Eze 28:22;*
(A) | *28:25*
they *s.* her a bed in the | *Eze 32:25*
midst of her slain
I will *s.* my sanctuary in | *Eze 37:26*
midst of them
Lord do *s.* apart and (A) | *Eze 37:28*
I will *s.* my glory among the | *Eze 39:21*
heathen
s. thy heart upon all that I | *Eze 40:4*
shall shew thee
have *s.* keepers of my charge | *Eze 44:8*
in my sanctuary
king thought to *s.* him over the | *Da 6:3*
realm
he *s.* his heart on Daniel to | *Da 6:14*
deliver him
judgment was *s.*, books were | *Da 7:10*
opened
to walk in his laws which he *s.* | *Da 9:10*
before us
thou didst *s.* thine heart to | *Da 10:12*
understand
lest I *s.* her as in day she was | *Ho 2:3*
born
and they *s.* their heart on | *Ho 4:8*
their iniquity
O Judah, he hath *s.* an | *Ho 6:11*
harvest for thee
how shall I *s.* thee as | *Ho 11:8*
Zeboim
be gone, that we may *s.* | *Am 8:5*
forth wheat
I will *s.* mine eyes upon them | *Am 9:4*
for evil, not for
though thou *s.* thy nest among | *Ob 4*
the stars
the gates of thy land shall be | *Na 3:13*
s. open
that he may *s.* his nest on | *Hab 2:9*
high, be delivered
I said, Let them *s.* a fair mitre | *Zec 3:5*
on his head
it shall be *s.* there upon her | *Zec 5:11*
own base
make crowns, and *s.* them on | *Zec 6:11*
head of Joshua
I *s.* all men, every one against | *Zec 8:10*
neighbour
a city *s.* on a hill cannot be | *M't 5:14*
hid
I am come to *s.* a man at | *M't 10:35*
variance
he shall *s.* the sheep on his | *M't 25:33*
right hand

when he was *s.* on | *M't 27:19*
judgment seat, wife
when sun did *s.* they brought | *M'k 1:32*
diseased
a candle, and not to be *s.* on | *M'k 4:21*
a candlestick
must suffer many things, and | *M'k 9:12*
be *s.* at nought
and *s.* an hedge about it, and | *M'k 12:1*
digged
this child is *s.* for the fall and | *Lu 2:34*
rising
to *s.* at liberty them that are | *Lu 4:18*
bruised
for I also am a man *s.* | *Lu 7:8*
under authority
eat such things as are *s.* | *Lu 10:8*
before you
and *s.* him on his own beast | *Lu 10:34*
and brought
friend come, I have nothing to | *Lu 11:6*
s. before you
Herod with men of war, *s.* | *Lu 23:11*
him at nought
there were *s.* six waterpots | *Joh 2:6*
of stone
every man doth *s.* forth good | *Joh 2:10*
wine
he hath *s.* to his seal, that | *Joh 3:33*
God is true
the stone *s.* at nought of you | *Joh 4:11*
builders
Father *s.* apart | *Joh 10:36*
(A)(N)(P)(R)
no not so much as to *s.* his | *Ac 7:5*
foot on
all God's *s.* apart ones (A) | *Ac 10:32*
s. apart Barnabas and Saul | *Ac 13:2*
(B)(N)(P)(R)
then Paul *s.* his eyes on him | *Ac 13:9*
and said
I have *s.* thee to be a light | *Ac 13:47*
to the Gentiles
no man shall *s.* on thee to | *Ac 18:10*
hurt thee
our craft is in danger to be *s.* | *Ac 19:27*
at nought
I *s.* no store by life (N) | *Ac 20:24*
this man might have been *s.* | *Ac 26:32*
at liberty
God *s.* forth to be a | *Ro 3:25*
propitiation
why dost thou *s.* at | *Ro 14:10*
nought thy brother
you were *s.* apart (A) | *1Co 1:11; 7:14*
God hath *s.* forth us the | *1Co 4:9*
apostles last
s. them to judge who are least | *1Co 6:4*
esteemed in church
do ye *s.* (S) | *1Co 6:4*
whatsoever is *s.* before you | *1Co 10:27*
eat
now God hath *s.* the | *1Co 12:18*
members in the body
God hath *s.* some in the | *1Co 12:28*
church
s. hearts on the greatest (P) | *1Co 12:31*
s. your mind to prophecy (B) | *1Co 14:39*
Christ had been evidently *s.* | *Ga 3:1*
forth crucified
when he *s.* him at his own | *Eph 1:20*
right hand
I am *s.* for the defence of | *Ph'p 1:17*
the gospel
s. affection, on things above, | *Col 3:2*
not on earth
separated and *s.* apart for | *1Th 4:3*
pure holy living (A)
vessel *s.* apart and useful | *2Ti 2:21*
(A)(B)
didst *s.* him over work of thy | *Heb 2:7*
hands
to lay hold on the hope *s.* | *Heb 6:18*
before us
who is *s.* on right hand of the | *Heb 8:1;*
throne | *12:2*
let us run the race that is *s.* | *Heb 12:1*
before us
who for joy that was *s.* before | *Heb 12:2*
him, endured
our brother Timothy is *s.* at | *Heb 13:23*
liberty
s. Christ apart as holy (A) | *1Pe 3:15*
those *s.* apart, separated (A) | *Jude 1*
the cities are *s.* forth for an | *Jude 7*
example
I have *s.* before thee an open | *Re 3:8*
door
am *s.* down with my Father | *Re 3:21*
in throne

a throne was *s*. in heaven, one   *Re 4:2*
sat on throne
he shut him up, and *s*. a seal   *Re 20:3*
upon him

SET *DAY*

on a *s. day*, Herod arrayed in   *Ac 12:21*
royal apparel

SET *TIME*

Sarah shall bear to thee at   *Ge 17:21*
this *s. time*
at the *s. time* of which God   *Ge 21:2*
had spoken
the Lord appointed a *s. time*,   *Ex 9:5*
saying
according to *s. time* Samuel   *1Sa 13:8*
appointed
Amasa tarried longer than   *2Sa 20:5*
the *s. time*
that thou wouldest appoint   *Job 14:13*
me a *s. time*
the *s. time* to favour her is   *Ps 102:13*
come

SET *UP*

Jacob took the stone and *s*.   *Ge 28:18;*
it *up* for a pillar   *28:22; 31:45; 35:14*
shalt *s. up* the tabernacle of   *Ex 40:2*
the tent
s. up court, boards, veil   *Ex 40:8;*
   40:18, 21
s. up hanging at door of   *Ex 40:28;*
tabernacle   *40:33*
nor shall ye *s. up* any image of   *Le 26:1*
stone
the tabernacle, Levites shall *s*.   *Nu 1:51*
it *up*
that Moses had fully *s. up* the   *Nu 7:1*
tabernacle
and other did *s*. it *up* against   *Nu 10:21*
they came
that thou shalt *s. up* these   *De 27:2;*
stones   *27:4*
Joshua *s. up* twelve stones in   *Jos 4:9*
Jordan
shall he *s. up* gates of it   *Jos 6:26;*
   1Ki 16:34
children of Dan *s. up*   *J'g 18:30*
graven image
they *s*. them *up* Micah's   *J'g 18:31*
graven image
it repenteth me I have *s. up*   *1Sa 15:11*
Saul
Saul hath *s*. him *up* a place,   *1Sa 15:12*
and gone
to *s. up* throne of David over   *2Sa 3:10*
Israel
I will *s. up* thy seed after   *2Sa 7:12*
thee
to *s. up* his son after him   *1Ki 15:4*
they *s*. them *up* images and   *2Ki 17:10*
groves
s. them *up* an altar in   *1Ch 21:18*
threshing floor
Amaziah *s*. them *up* to be   *2Ch 25:14*
his gods
Manasseh *s. up* groves and   *2Ch 33:19*
images
offered freely to *s. up* God's   *Ezr 2:68*
house
Jews have *s. up* the walls   *Ezr 4:12;*
thereof   *13:16*
the house a great king of   *Ezr 5:11*
Israel, *s. up*
being *s. up*, let him be hanged   *Ezr 6:11*
thereon
a reviving to *s. up* house of   *Ezr 9:9*
God
built sheep gate and *s. up* the   *Ne 3:1;*
doors of it   *3:6, 13-15; 7:1*
though at that time I had not *s. up*   *Ne 6:1*
up the doors
to *s. up* on high those that be   *Job 5:11*
low
hath shaken me and *s*. me *up*   *Job 16:12*
for his mark
the name of God we will *s. up*   *Ps 20:5*
our banners
hide me, and *s*. me *up* upon a   *Ps 27:5*
rock
let thy salvation, O God, *s*.   *Ps 69:29*
me *up* on high
they *s. up* their ensigns for   *Ps 74:4*
signs
thou hast *s. up* right hand of   *Ps 89:42*
adversaries

I was *s. up* from everlasting   *Pr 8:23*
from beginning
Lord shall *s. up* adversaries of   *Isa 9:11*
Rezin
he shall *s. up* an ensign for   *Isa 11:12*
the nations
they *s. up* towers thereof,   *Isa 23:13*
raised palaces
that *s. up* wood of their   *Isa 45:20*
graven image
I will *s. up* my standard to   *Isa 49:22*
people
thou hast *s. up* thy   *Isa 57:8*
remembrance
s. up the standard toward Zion,   *Jer 4:6*
retire
there is none to *s. up* my   *Jer 10:20*
curtains
have ye *s. up* altars to   *Jer 11:13*
shameful thing
and I will *s. up* shepherds over   *Jer 23:4*
them
s. thee *up* waymarks, make   *Jer 31:21*
high heaps
s. up a standard, publish   *Jer 50:2;*
   51:12, 27
s. up the watchmen, prepare   *Jer 51:12*
ambushes
he hath *s. up* horn of thy   *La 2:17*
adversaries
these men have *s. up* their   *Eze 14:3*
idols
deep *s*. him *up* on high with   *Eze 31:4*
her rivers
I will *s. up* one shepherd   *Eze 34:23*
over them
God of heaven shall *s. up* a   *Da 2:44*
kingdom
nor worship the golden image   *Da 3:14*
I have *s. up*
whom he would he *s. up* and   *Da 5:19*
put down
abomination that maketh   *Da 12:11*
desolate *s. up*
they have *s. up* kings but not   *Ho 8:4*
by me
they that work wickedness   *Mal 3:15*
are *s. up*
s. up over his head this   *M't 27:37*
accusation
and *s. up* false witnesses, who   *Ac 6:13*
said
I will build again the ruins,   *Ac 15:16*
and *s*. it *up*

SETH

a son, and called his name *S*.   *Ge 4:25*
to *S*., to him also there was   *Ge 4:26*
born a
his image; and called his name   *Ge 5:3*
S.
of Adam after he had begotten   *Ge 5:4*
S.
S. lived an hundred and five   *Ge 5:6*
years
S. lived after he begat Enos   *Ge 5:7*
eight
And all the days of *S*. were   *Ge 5:8*
nine
Enos, which was the son of *S*.   *Lu 3:38*

SETHUR

of Asher, *S*. the son of   *Nu 13:13*
Michael

SETTER

to be a *s*. forth of strange   *Ac 17:18*
gods

SETTEST

in all that thou *s*. thine hand   *De 23:20;*
to   *28:8, 20*
that thou *s*. a watch over me   *Job 7:12*
s. a print upon the heels of   *Job 13:27*
my feet
thou *s*. a crown of pure gold   *Ps 21:3*
on
and *s*. me before thy face for   *Ps 41:12*
ever

SETTETH

when the tabernacle *s*.   *Nu 1:51*
forward
And when the camp *s*. forward   *Nu 4:5*
is poor, and *s*. his heart upon   *De 24:15*
it

that *s*. light by his father or   *De 27:16*
his
and *s*. me upon my high   *2Sa 22:34;*
places   *Ps 18:33*
He *s*. an end to darkness   *Job 28:3*
he *s*. himself in a way that is   *Ps 36:4*
not
his strength *s*. fast the   *Ps 65:6*
mountains
God *s*. the solitary in families: *Ps 68:6*
he
down one, and *s*. up another   *Ps 75:7*
flame in the mountains on fire   *Ps 83:14*
s. he the poor on high from   *Ps 107:41*
affliction
they lay wait, as he that *s*.   *Jer 5:26*
snares
of Neriah *s*. thee on against   *Jer 43:3*
us
that *s. up* his idols in his   *Eze 14:4;*
heart   *14:7*
removeth kings, and *s. up*   *Da 2:21*
kings
and *s. up* over it the basest of   *Da 4:17*
men
and *s*. him on the pinnacle of   *M't 4:5*
s. it on a candlestick, that   *Lu 8:16*
they
s. on fire the course of nature   *Jas 3:6*

SETTING

In their *s*. of their threshold   *Eze 43:8*
by
sealing the stone, and *s*. a   *M't 27:66*
watch
Now when the sun was *s*. all   *Lu 4:40*
they

SETTINGS

in *s*. of gold (E)(R)(S)   *Ex 28:11;*
   28:13, 25
chains of the *s*. (A)(E)(R)   *Ex 28:14*
thou shalt set in it *s*. of   *Ex 28:17*
stones
in *s*. of gold (A)(E)(R)   *Ex 39:6;*
   39:13
in *s*. of gold filigree (R)   *Ex 39:13*
made two *s*. of gold (R)   *Ex 39:16*
put on two *s*. (A)(E)(R)   *Ex 39:18*

SETTLE

settle (B)   *Ge 20:15*
   34:10, 16; 35:1; Jos 24:13; Job 3:5
I will *s*. him in mine house   *1Ch 17:14*
will *s*. you after your old   *Eze 36:11*
estates
the lower *s*. shall be two   *Eze 43:14*
cubits
the lesser *s*. even to the   *Eze 43:14*
greater
greater *s*. shall be four   *Eze 43:14*
cubits
the *s*. shall be fourteen cubits   *Eze 43:17*
long
and on the four corners of   *Eze 43:20;*
the *s*.   *45:19*
enter and *s*. down (N)   *M't 12:45*
S. it therefore in your hearts,   *Lu 21:14*
not
s. nothing, lead nowhere (B)   *Tit 3:9*
stablish, strengthen, *s*. you   *1Pe 5:10*

SETTLED

there they *s*. (B)(R)   *Ge 11:2*
among whom I have *s*. (A)   *Ge 24:3*
he *s*. down (B)   *Jg 17:8; Isa 23:7*
a *s*. place for thee to abide in   *1Ki 8:13*
he *s*. his countenance   *2Ki 8:11*
stedfastly
s. in tents (B)   *Ps 78:55*
O Lord, thy word is *s*. in   *Ps 119:89*
heaven
Before the mountains were *s*.   *Pr 8:25*
he hath *s*. on his lees, and   *Jer 48:11*
s. on your people (B)   *Da 9:24*
the men that are *s*. on their   *Zep 1:12*
lees
s. plan and foreknowledge   *Ac 2:23*
(A)
be *s*. in regular assembly   *Ac 19:26*
(E)(R)
in the faith grounded and *s*.   *Co. 1:23*

SETTLEMENTS

boundaries of their *s*. (B)   *Ac 17:26*

SETTLEST

thou *s.* the furrows thereof *Ps 65:10*

SEVEN

there came up *s.* well favoured *Ge 41:2*
kine
s. other kine came up *Ge 41:3;*
41:4, 18-20, 26-27
s. ears of corn came up, rank *Ge 41:5*
and good
s. thin ears, and blasted *Ge 41:6;*
41:7, 22-24, 26-27
swallowed *s.* large ears *Ge 41:7*
(B)(E)(R)
the sons of Bilhah, all the *Ge 46:25*
souls were *s.*
priest of Midian had *s.* *Ex 2:16*
daughters
s. sabbaths shall be complete *Le 23:15*
shalt number *s.* sabbaths of *Le 25:8*
years to thee
Balaam said, Build me *s.* *Nu 23:1;*
altars, prepare *s.* oxen, *s.* rams 23:29
he said, I have prepared *s.* *Nu 23:4;*
altars 23:14
s. nations greater and mightier *De 7:1*
than thou
s. weeks thou shalt number to *De 16:9*
thee, begin
Lord cause enemies to flee *De 28:7*
before thee *s.* ways
thou shalt flee *s.* ways *De 28:25*
before them
s. priests bearing *s.* trumpets *Jos 6:4;*
6:6, 8, 13
there remained of Israel *s.* *Jos 18:2*
tribes not received
and they shall divide it into *Jos 18:5;*
s. parts 18:6
described it by cities into *s.* *Jos 18:9*
parts in a book
if they bind me with *s.* green *J'g 16:7*
withs
weavest *s.* locks; shave off *s.* *J'g 16:13;*
locks 16:19
so that the barren hath born *s.* *1Sa 2:5*
the ark was with the Philistines *1Sa 6:1*
s. months
Jesse made *s.* of his sons to *1Sa 16:10*
pass
they fell all *s.* together *2Sa 21:9*
and the sons of Elioenai were *1Ch 3:24*
s.
brethren of house of their *1Ch 5:13*
fathers were *s.*
they brought *s.* bullocks, *s.* *2Ch 29:21*
rams
sent of king and of his *s.* *Ezr 7:14*
counsellors
s. chamberlains served in *Es 1:10*
presence
the *s.* princes which saw the *Es 1:14*
king's face
he gave her *s.* maidens meet to *Es 2:9*
be given her
in *s.* troubles no evil shall *Job 5:19*
touch thee
yea *s.* are an abomination *Pr 6:16*
unto him
wisdom hath hewn out her *s.* *Pr 9:1*
pillars
for there are *s.* abominations *Pr 26:25*
in his heart
give a portion to *s.* also to *Ec 11:2*
eight
in that day *s.* women take hold *Isa 4:1*
of one man
the Lord shall smite it in the *Isa 11:15*
s. streams
she that hath born *s.* *Jer 15:9*
languisheth
s. months shall they be *Eze 39:12*
burying them
after the end of *s.* months *Eze 39:14*
shall they search
they went up unto it by *s.* *Eze 40:22;*
steps 40:26
and the breadth of the door *Eze 41:3*
s. cubits
unto the Messiah, shall be *s.* *Da 9:25*
weeks
we shall raise against him *s.* *Mic 5:5*
shepherds
behold, upon one stone shall *Zec 3:9*
be *s.* eyes

his *s.* lamps thereon, and *s.* *Zec 4:2*
pipes to *s.* lamps
plummet in hand of *Zec 4:10*
Zerubbabel with those *s.*
they said, S. loaves *M't 15:34;*
15:36; M'k 8:5
they took up *s.* baskets full *M't 15:37;*
M'k 8:8
nor the *s.* loaves among four *M't 16:10*
thousand
now there were with us *s.* *M't 22:25;*
brethren *M'k 12:20; Lu 20:29*
in resurrection whose wife *M't 22:28*
shall she be of *s.*
and *s.* had her *M'k 12:22;*
12:23; Lu 20:31, 33
out of whom he cast *s.* devils *M'k 16:9;*
Lu 8:2
when he destroyed *s.* nations *Ac 13:19*
in Canaan
Philip who was one of the *s.* *Ac 21:8*
deacons
John to *s.* churches in Asia *Re 1:4*
write, send it to the *s.* *Re 1:11*
churches in Asia
being turned, I saw *s.* golden *Re 1:12*
candlesticks
in midst of *s.* candlesticks one *Re 1:13*
like Son of man
s. stars are angels of churches, *Re 1:20*
s. candlesticks are the *s.* churches
who walketh in midst of *s.* *Re 2:1*
golden candlesticks
Lamb as slain, having *s.* horns, *Re 5:6*
s. eyes, which are *s.* spirits of
I saw the *s.* angels which stood *Re 8:2*
before God
the *s.* angels prepared *Re 8:6*
themselves to sound
when he cried, *s.* thunders *Re 10:3*
uttered voices
seal up what the *s.* thunders *Re 10:4*
have uttered
great dragon, having *s.* heads, *Re 12:3;*
and *s.* crowns upon heads 13:1; 17:3, 7
I saw *s.* angels having the *s.* *Re 15:1;*
last plagues 15:6
gave to *s.* angels *s.* golden *Re 15:7*
vials full of wrath
no man able to enter into *Re 15:8*
temple, till *s.* plagues of *s.*
angels were fulfilled
I heard a voice, saying to the *Re 16:1*
s. angels
and there came one of the *s.* *Re 17:1;*
angels which had the *s.* 21:9
vials and talked with me
the *s.* heads are *s.* mountains *Re 17:9*
on which
there are *s.* kings, five are *Re 17:10*
fallen, one is, other
the beast is of the *s.* and *Re 17:11*
goeth into perdition

SEVEN *BULLOCKS*

prepare me her *s.* bullocks *Nu 23:29*
on the seventh day *s.* *Nu 29:32*
bullocks, two rams
Levites offered *s.* bullocks *1Ch 15:26*
they brought *s.* bullocks *2Ch 29:21*
take to you now, *s.* bullocks *Job 42:8*
prepare a burnt offering *s.* *Eze 45:23*
bullocks

SEVEN *MEN*

let *s.* men of his sons be *2Sa 21:6*
delivered
than *s.* men that can render a *Pr 26:16*
reason
took *s.* men that were near *Jer 52:25*
the king
look out *s.* men of honest *Ac 6:3*
report full of Holy Ghost

SEVEN *SONS*

thy daughter is better than *s.* *Ru 4:15*
sons
and there were born unto him *Job 1:2*
s. sons
he had also *s.* sons, and *Job 42:13*
three daughters
there were *s.* sons of one *Ac 19:14*
Sceva a Jew

SEVEN *SPIRITS*

then taketh with himself *s.* *M't 12:45;*
other *spirits* more wicked *Lu 11:26*
from *s.* spirits before the *Re 1:4*
throne of God
these saith he that hath the *s.* *Re 3:1*
spirits of God
seven lamps, which are the *s.* *Re 4:5*
spirits of God
seven eyes, which are the *s.* *Re 5:6*
spirits of God

SEVEN *STARS*

seek him that maketh the *s.* *Am 5:8*
stars
had in his right hand *s.* stars *Re 1:16;*
2:1; 3:1
mystery of *s.* stars in my right *Re 1:20*
hand; *s.* stars are angels of

SEVEN *TIMES*

Jacob bowed before Esau *s.* *Ge 33:3*
times
priest sprinkle blood *s.* times *Le 4:6;*
4:17; 8:11; 14:7; 16:14, 19; Nu 19:4
sprinkle oil with fingers *s.* *Le 14:16;*
times 14:27
dip in blood, and sprinkle the *Le 14:51*
house *s.* times
thou shalt number *s.* times *Le 25:8*
seven years
punish you *s.* times more *Le 26:18;*
26:21, 24, 28
he shall compass the city *s.* *Jos 6:4*
times 6:15
said to his servant, Go again, *1Ki 18:43*
s. times
child sneezed *s.* times, and *2Ki 4:35*
opened eyes
Elisha sent, Go wash in *2Ki 5:10;*
Jordan *s.* times 5:14
words are as silver purified *s.* *Ps 12:6*
times
s. times a day do I praise *Ps 119:164*
thee, because
a just man falleth *s.* times, and *Pr 24:16*
riseth
heat furnace *s.* times *Da 3:19*
more than
let *s.* times pass over him *Da 4:16;*
4:23, 25-26
how oft forgive? till *s.* times *M't 18:21*
I say not, till *s.* times, but *M't 18:22*
until seventy times
if brother trespass against thee *Lu 17:4*
s. times a day, and *s.* times a
day turn again

SEVEN *YEARS*

I will serve thee *s.* years for *Ge 29:18*
Rachel
serve *s.* years *Ge 29:30; 29:27, 30*
seven good kine are *s.* years *Ge 41:26*
and seven good ears are *s.* years
seven thin kine are *s.* years, *Ge 41:27*
seven empty ears shall be *s.*
years of famine
there come *s.* years of plenty *Ge 41:29;*
41:34, 47-48
there shall arise *s.* years of *Ge 41:30;*
famine 41:36, 54
the *s.* years of plenteousness *Ge 41:53*
were ended
shalt number seven times *s.* *Le 25:8*
years
Hebron built *s.* years before *Nu 13:22*
Zoan
at end of *s.* years a release *De 15:1;*
31:10
Lord delivered Israel to Midian *J'g 6:1*
s. years
take the second bullock of *s.* *J'g 6:25*
years old
Ibzan of Beth-lehem judged *J'g 12:9*
Israel *s.* years
David was king in Hebron *s.* *2Sa 2:11;*
years 5:5; 1Ki 2:11; 1Ch 29:27
shall *s.* years of famine come *2Sa 24:13*
to thee
Solomon was *s.* years in *1Ki 6:38*
building temple
famine shall come upon land *2Ki 8:1*
s. years
she sojourned with the *2Ki 8:2*
Philistines *s.* years
s. years old was Jehoash *2Ki 11:21;*

when he began to reign　　　2Ch 24:1
at end of *s.* years let ye go　Jer 34:14
every man
shall burn weapons with fire　Eze 39:9
s. years
Anna lived with an husband *s.*　Lu 2:36
years

SEVENFOLD

vengeance be taken on him *s.*　Ge 4:15
If Cain shall be avenged *s.*　Ge 4:24
truly
truly Lamech seventy and *s.*　Ge 4:24
render unto our neighbours *s.*　Ps 79:12
into
if he be found, he shall restore　Pr 6:31
s.
and the light of the sun shall　Isa 30:26
be *s.*

SEVENS

beast thou shalt take to thee by　Ge 7:2
s.
Of fowls also of the air by　Ge 7:3
s. the
assembly at sixes and *s.* (P)　Ac 19:32

SEVENTEEN

Joseph, being *s.* years old　Ge 37:2
in the land of Egypt *s.* years　Ge 47:28
even threescore and *s.* men　J'g 8:14
reigned *s.* years in　1Ki 14:21;
Jerusalem　　　　　2Ch 12:13
Samaria, and reigned *s.* years　2Ki 13:1
s. thousand and two hundred　1Ch 7:11
of Harim, a thousand and *s.*　Ezr 2:39;
　　　　　Ne 7:42
the money, even *s.* shekels of　Jer 32:9

SEVENTEENTH

month, the *s.* day of the　Ge 7:11
month
on the *s.* day of the month　Ge 8:4
Israel in Samaria the *s.* year　1Ki 22:51
the *s.* year of Pekah the son　2Ki 16:1
of
The *s.* to Hezir, the　1Ch 24:15
eighteenth
The *s.* to Joshbekashah, he　1Ch 25:24

SEVENTH

in *s.* he shall go out free for　Ex 21:2
nothing
in the *s.* is the sabbath of rest　Ex 31:15
unto the morrow after *s.*　Le 23:16
sabbath
at the *s.* time when the priests　Jos 6:16
blew
s. lot came out for the tribe　Jos 19:40
of Dan
at the *s.* time there arose a　1Ki 18:44
cloud
David was the *s.* son of Jesse　1Ch 2:15
the *s.* lot came forth to　1Ch 24:10
Hakkoz
Elioenai the *s.* son of　1Ch 26:3
Meshelemiah
Elioenai the *s.* son of　1Ch 26:3
Obed-edom
s. captain for *s.* month was　1Ch 27:10
Helez
second also, and the third,　M't 22:26
to the *s.*
yesterday at *s.* hour fever left　Joh 4:52
him
Enoch the *s.* from Adam　Jude 14
prophesied
and when he had opened the *s.*　Re 8:1
seal
in the days of the voice of the　Re 10:7
s. angel
the *s.* angel sounded, there　Re 11:15
were voices
s. angel poured out his vial　Re 16:17
into the air
the *s.* foundation was　Re 21:20
chrysolite

SEVENTH *MONTH*

ark rested in *s.* month on the　Ge 8:4
mountains
in *s.* month afflict your souls　Le 16:29;
　　　　　23:27; 25:9

in the *s.* month shall ye have　Le 23:24
a sabbath
in *s.* month an holy　Nu 29:1;
convocation　　　　　29:12
Israel assembled at feast of　1Ki 8:2
the *s.* month
in *s.* month Ishmael killed　2Ki 25:25;
Gedaliah, the Jews with him　Jer 41:1
in *s.* month Solomon sent　2Ch 7:10
them away
they finished the heaps in the　2Ch 31:7
s. month
when *s.* month was come, and　Ezr 3:1;
children of Israel in cities　Ne 7:73
from first day of *s.* month　Ezr 3:6
began to offer
on first day of *s.* month Ezra　Ne 8:2
read
in feasts of *s.* month Israel　Ne 8:14
dwell in booths
so Hananiah died in the *s.*　Jer 28:17
month
in the *s.* month shall he do　Eze 45:25
the like
in the *s.* month the word　Hag 2:1
came to Haggai
when ye mourned in fifth and　Zec 7:5
s. month
the fast of the *s.* month shall　Zec 8:19
be to Judah joy

SEVENTH *YEAR*

but the *s.* year thou shalt let　Ex 23:11
it rest
in the *s.* year shall be a　Le 25:4
sabbath of rest
if ye say, What shall we eat　Le 25:20
in the *s.* year
the *s.* year, year of release　De 15:9
in the *s.* year thou shalt let　De 15:12
him go free
in *s.* year Jehoiada sent and　2Ki 11:4;
set the rulers with captains　2Ch 23:1
in *s.* year of Jehu Jehoash　2Ki 12:1
began to reign
in *s.* year of Hoshea king of　2Ki 18:9
Assyria came
went to Jerusalem in *s.* year　Ezr 7:7;
　　　　　7:8
leave *s.* year exaction of　Ne 10:31
every debt
Esther was taken to king in *s.*　Es 2:16
year
people carried away captive　Jer 52:28
in *s.* year
in the *s.* year elders came to　Eze 20:1
inquire

SEVENTY

if Cain, truly Lamech *s.*　Ge 4:24
sevenfold
and Cainan lived *s.* years, and　Ge 5:12
begat
Terah lived *s.* years, and　Ge 11:26
begat Abram
Abram was *s.* five years old,　Ge 12:4
when he
of the loins of Jacob were *s.*　Ex 1:5
souls
come up, thou, and *s.* elders　Ex 24:1;
of Israel　　　　　24:9
the brass of the offering was　Ex 38:29
s. talents
offering one silver bowl of *s.*　Nu 7:13;
shekels 7:19, 25, 31, 37, 43, 49, 55, 61,
　　　　　67, 73, 79, 85
gather unto me *s.* men of　Nu 11:16;
elders　　　　　11:24
he gave of the spirit unto the　Nu 11:25
s. elders
wickedness, in slaying his *s.*　J'g 9:56
brethren
Ahab had *s.* sons in Samaria　2Ki 10:1;
　　　　　10:6
they took king's sons, and　2Ki 10:7
slew *s.* persons
children of Hodaviah *s.* four　Ezr 2:40;
　　　　　Ne 7:43
of sons of Elam, with Jeshaiah　Ezr 8:7
s. males
of the sons of Zabbud, with　Ezr 8:14
them *s.* males
that Tyre shall be forgotten　Isa 23:15
s. years
after end of *s.* years, Lord　Isa 23:17
will visit Tyre
shall serve king of Babylon *s.*　Jer 25:11
years

when *s.* years are　Jer 25:12;
accomplished　　　　　29:10
there stood before them　Eze 8:11
s. men
accomplish *s.* years in　Da 9:2
desolation of Jerusalem
s. weeks are determined upon　Da 9:24
thy people
even those *s.* years did ye fast　Zec 7:5
to me
not till seven times, but until　M't 18:22
s. times
Lord appointed other *s.* also,　Lu 10:1
and sent
s. returned again with joy,　Lu 10:17
saying, Lord
make ready *s.* horsemen (S)　Ac 23:23

SEVENTY-SIX

we were in all *s.* souls (S)　Ac 27:37

SEVER

s. in that day the land of　Ex 8:22
Goshen
shall *s.* between the cattle of　Ex 9:4
Israel
they shall *s.* out men of　Eze 39:14
continual
s. the wicked from among　M't 13:49
the just

SEVERAL

a *s.* tenth deal of flour　Nu 28:13
mingled with
A *s.* tenth deal shalt thou　Nu 28:21
offer for
A *s.* tenth deal unto one　Nu 28:29
lamb
A *s.* tenth deal for one lamb　Nu 29:10
And a *s.* tenth deal to each　Nu 29:15
lamb of
a garment of *s.* colors (S)　2Sa 13:18;
　　　　　13:19
death, and dwelt in a *s.*　2Ki 15:5;
house　　　　　2Ch 26:21
And in every *s.* city he put　2Ch 11:12
shields
in every *s.* city of Judah he　2Ch 28:25
made
suburbs of their cities, in　2Ch 31:19
every *s.*
man according to his *s.*　M't 25:15
ability
every *s.* gate was of one pearl　Re 21:21

SEVERALLY

dividing to every man *s.* as　1Co 2:11
he will

SEVERE

famine was *s.* (B)(R)　Ge 12:10
it will be wholly *s.* (B)　Ge 41:31
the famine was *s.* (S)　Ge 41:56
severe (S)　Ge 41:57;
43; 47:4, 13; De 6:22; 28:59; J'g 20:34;
2Sa 2:17; 1Ki 17:17; 18:2; 2Ki 3:26;
2 Ch 21:19; Ps 71:20; Ec 1:13; Eze 14:21
(A)
reduced Israelites to *s.* slavery　Ex 1:11
(A)
this sickness grew *s.* (B)　2Ch 16:12
a *s.* man (R)　Lu 19:21
more *s.* penalty (N)　Heb 10:29

SEVERED

and have *s.* you from other　Le 20:26
people
s. three cities on this side　De 4:41
Jordan
had *s.* himself from the　J'g 4:11
Kenites
s. from ordinances　Da 9:5
(A)(B)(E)(R)

SEVERELY

severely (S)　1Sa 31:3;
1Ch 10:3; 2Ch 35:23; Ps 44:19; 64:12

SEVERITY

service with harshness and *s.*　Ex 1:14
(A)
lord it over him with *s.* (B)　Le 25:43;
　　　　　25:46

Behold the goodness and *s.* of God   *Ro 11:22*
on them which fell, *s.*; but toward   *Ro 11:22*

SEW

A time to rend, and a time to *s.*   *Ec 3:7*
Woe to the women that *s.* pillows   *Eze 13:18*

SEWAGE

a pipe for *s.* (P)   *Ro 9:21*

SEWED

they *s.* fig leaves together, and   *Ge 3:7*
I have *s.* sackcloth upon my skin   *Job 16:15*

SEWEST

and thou *s.* up mine iniquity   *Job 14:17*

SEWETH

No man *s.* a piece of new cloth   *M'k 2:21*

SEX

not playing with *s.* (P)   *Ro 13:13*

SEXUAL

had *s.* relations (B)   *Nu 5:19*
all *s.* impurity (A)(P)   *Ac 15:20*
gave them up to *s.* impurity (A)   *Ro 1:24*
s. immorality (A)(B)(N)(P)(R)   *1Co 5:1*
s. immorality (A)(R)   *1Co 6:13; 6:18; 7:2*
s. promiscuity (P)   *1Co 6:13*
lack of restraint of *s.* (A)(P)   *1Co 7:5*
s. vice (A)   *1Co 12:21*
immorality, *s.* vice (A)(P)(R)   *Eph 5:3*
no *s.* vice (A)   *Eph 5:5*
abstain, shrink from *s.* vice (A)   *1Th 4:3*
clean from *s.* immorality (P)(R)   *1Th 4:3*
for *s.* perverts (B)(N)   *1Ti 1:10*
gave themselves to *s.* perversity (A)   *Jude 7*
abandoned to *s.* immorality (B)(P)   *Jude 7*

SEXUALLY

the *s.* uncontrolled (P)   *1Ti 1:10*

SHAALABBIN

And *S.*, and Ajalon, and Jethlah   *Jos 19:42*

SHAALBIM

mount Heres in Aijalon, and in *S.*   *J'g 1:35*
son of Dekar, in Makaz, and in *S.*   *1Ki 4:9*

SHAALBONITE

Eliahba the *S.* of the sons of   *2Sa 23:32*
the Baharumite, Elihaba the *S.*   *1Ch 11:33*

SHAAPH

and Pelet, and Ephah. and *S.*   *1Ch 2:47*
She bare also *S.* the father of   *1Ch 2:49*

SHAARAIM

fell down by the way to *S.* even   *1Sa 17:52*
and at Beth-birei, and at *S.*   *1Ch 4:31*

SHAASHGAZ

to the custody of *S.* the king's   *Es 2:14*

SHABBETHAI

and *S.* the Levite helped them   *Ezr 10:15*

S., Hodijah, Maaseiah, Kelita   *Ne 8:7*
And *S.* and Jozabad, of the chief   *Ne 11:16*

SHABBY

in *s.* clothes (A)(R)   *Jas 2:2*

SHABBILY

treat me so *s.* (B)   *Ge 43:6*
dressed *s.* (B)   *Jas 2:2*

SHACHIA

And Jeuz, and *S.* and Mirma   *1Ch 8:10*

SHACKLES

cast their *s.* from us (B)   *Ps 2:3*

SHADE

the *s.* below quake (B)(R)   *Job 26:5*
Lord is thy *s.* upon thy right hand   *Ps 121:5*
for a *s.* in the day (A)(B)(E)(R)   *Isa 4:6*

SHADES

it rouses the *s.* (R)   *Isa 14:9*
they are *s.*, they shall not rise (R)   *Isa 26:14*
her roads to the *s.* (B)(R)   *Pr 2:18*
the *s.* of the dead (A)   *Pr 9:28*

SHADOW

come they under the *s.* of my roof   *Ge 19:8*
come and put your trust in my *s.*   *J'g 9:15*
Thou seest the *s.* of the mountains   *J'g 9:36*
the *s.* return backward ten degrees   *2Ki 20:10*
for the *s.* to go down ten degrees   *2Ki 20:10*
the *s.* return backward ten degrees   *2Ki 20:10*
the *s.* ten degrees backwards   *2Ki 20:11*
our days on the earth are as a *s.*   *1Ch 29:15*
and the *s.* of death stain it; let   *Job 3:5*
servant earnestly desireth the *s.*   *Job 7:2*
our days upon earth are a *s.*   *Job 8:9*
of darkness and the *s.* of death   *Job 10:21*
and of the *s.* of death, without any   *Job 10:22*
bringeth out to light the *s.* of death   *Job 12:22*
is cut down: he fleeth also as a *s.*   *Job 14:2*
on my eyelids is the *s.* of death   *Job 16:16*
and all my members are as a *s.*   *Job 17:7*
is to them even as the *s.* of death   *Job 24:17*
are in the terrors of the *s.* of death   *Job 24:17*
of darkness, and the *s.* of death   *Job 28:3*
is no darkness, nor *s.* of death   *Job 34:22*
seen the doors of the *s.* of death   *Job 38:17*
trees cover him with their *s.*   *Job 40:22*
hide me under the *s.* of thy wings   *Ps 17:8*
the valley of the *s.* of death   *Ps 23:4*
trust under the *s.* of thy wings   *Ps 36:7*
and covered us with the *s.* of death   *Ps 44:19*
in the *s.* of thy wings will I make   *Ps 57:1*
in the *s.* of thy wings will I rejoice   *Ps 63:7*
hills were covered with the *s.*   *Ps 80:10*
abide under the *s.* of the Almighty   *Ps 91:1*
days are like a *s.* that declineth   *Ps 102:11*
in darkness and in the *s.* of death   *Ps 107:10*
out of darkness and the *s.* of death   *Ps 107:14*
I am gone like the *s.* when it   *Ps 109:23*

days are as a *s.* that passeth away   *Ps 144:4*
vain life which he spendeth as a *s.*   *Ec 6:12*
prolong his days, which are as a *s.*   *Ec 8:13*
I sat down under his *s.* with great   *Ca 2:3*
tabernacle for a *s.* in the daytime   *Isa 4:6*
dwell in the land of the *s.* of death   *Isa 9:2*
make thy *s.* as the night in the   *Isa 16:3*
a *s.* from the heat, when the blast   *Isa 25:4*
even the heat with the *s.* of a cloud   *Isa 25:5*
and to trust in the *s.* of Egypt   *Isa 30:2*
the trust in the *s.* of Egypt your   *Isa 30:3*
shelter in *s.* of Egypt (R)   *Isa 30:3*
s. of a great rock in a weary land   *Isa 32:2*
and hatch, and gather under her *s.*   *Isa 34:15*
bring again the *s.* of the degrees   *Isa 38:8*
in the *s.* of his hand hath he hid me   *Isa 49:2*
thee in the *s.* of mine hand   *Isa 51:16*
of drought and of the *s.* of death   *Jer 2:6*
light, he turn it into the *s.* of death   *Jer 13:16*
fled stood under the *s.* of Heshbon   *Jer 48:45*
Under his *s.* we shall live among   *La 4:20*
the *s.* of the branches thereof shall   *Eze 17:23*
under his *s.* dwelt all great nations   *Eze 31:6*
the earth are gone down from his *s.*   *Eze 31:12*
dwelt under his *s.* in the midst of   *Eze 31:17*
beasts of the field had *s.* under it   *Da 4:12*
because the *s.* thereof is good   *Ho 4:13*
dwell under his *s.* shall return   *Ho 14:7*
the *s.* of death into the morning   *Am 5:8*
sat under it in the *s.* till he might   *Jon 4:5*
that it might be a *s.* over his head   *Jon 4:6*
sat in the region and *s.* of death   *M't 4:16*
the air may lodge under the *s.* of it   *M'k 4:32*
in darkness and in the *s.* of death   *Lu 1:79*
the *s.* of Peter passing by might   *Ac 5:15*
I am no *s.* boxer (P)   *1Co 9:26*
Which are a *s.* of things to come   *Col 2:17*
example and *s.* of heavenly things   *Heb 8:5*
s. of heavenly things (B)(E)(N)(R)   *Heb 8:5*
the law having a *s.* of good things   *Heb 10:1*
variableness, either *s.* of turning   *Jas 1:17*
no *s.* of inconsistency (A)(B)(E)(N)(P)(R)   *Jas 1:17*

SHADOWING

Woe to the land *s.* with wings   *Isa 18:1*
with a *s.* shroud, and of an high   *Eze 31:3*
of glory *s.* the mercyseat   *Heb 9:5*

SHADOWS

day break, and the *s.* flee away   *Ca 2:17*
the day break, and the *s.* flee away   *Ca 4:6*
s. of the evening are stretched out   *Jer 6:4*

SHADRACH

and to Hananiah, of *S.*; and to   *Da 1:7*
set *S.*, Meshach, and Abed-nego   *Da 2:49*
of the province of Babylon.   *Da 3:12; S. 3:13-14, 16, 19-20, 22-23, 26, 28-30*

SHADY

He lieth under the *s.* trees — Job 40:21
The *s.* trees cover him with — Job 40:22
their

SHAFT

his *s.* and his branches, his — Ex 25:31
bowls
his *s.* and his branch, his — Ex 37:17
bowls
beaten gold, unto the *s.* thereof — Nu 8:4
getteth up to the water *s.* (S) — 2Sa 5:8
whose spear's *s.* like a — 1Ch 20:5
weaver's beam (S)
me, and made me a polished *s.* — Isa 49:2
made me a polished arrow — Isa 49:2
(A)(B)(R)
strike through with his *s.* — Hab 3:14
(B)(R)
key of *s.* of the abyss — Re 9:1;
(A)(N)(R) — 9:2

SHAGE

the son of *S.* the Hararite — 1Ch 11:34

SHAGGY

s. goats will be skipping (B) — Isa 13:21
the *s.* wild goat (A)(B) — Isa 34:14

SHAHAR

chief Musician upon — Ps 22 Title
Aijeleth *S.*

SHAHARAIM

S. begat children in the — 1Ch 8:8
country

SHAHAZIMAH

coast reacheth to Tabor, and — Jos 19:22
S.

SHAKE

tremble and *s.* (B) — De 2:25
times before, and *s.* myself — J'g 16:20
So God *s.* out every man from — Ne 5:13
which made all my bones to — Job 4:14
s.
s. off his unripe grape as the — Job 15:33
vine
you, and *s.* mine head at you — Job 16:4
shoot out the lip, they *s.* the — Ps 22:7
head
mountains *s.* with the swelling — Ps 46:3
make their loins continually to — Ps 69:23
s.
fruit thereof shall *s.* like — Ps 72:16
Lebanon
ariseth to *s.* terribly the — Isa 2:19;
earth — 2:21
if the rod should *s.* itself — Isa 10:15
against
he shall *s.* his hand against — Isa 10:32
shall he *s.* his hand over — Isa 11:15
the river
s. the hand, that they may go — Isa 13:2
into
I will *s.* the heavens, and the — Isa 13:13
to tremble, that did *s.* — Isa 14:16
kingdoms
the foundations of the earth — Isa 24:18
do *s.*
and Carmel *s.* off their fruits — Isa 33:9
S. thyself from the dust: arise — Isa 52:2
s. the head (A)(B)(E)(R) — Jer 18:16
all my bones *s.*; I am like a — Jer 23:9
s. the fist (B)(R) — La 2:15
thy walls shall *s.* at the noise — Eze 26:10
the isles *s.* at the sound of — Eze 26:15
thy fall
suburbs shall *s.* at the sound — Eze 27:28
their inward parts to *s.* (S) — Eze 29:7
nations to *s.* at the sound of — Eze 31:16
his fall
of the earth, shall *s.* at my — Eze 38:20
presence
s. off his leaves, and scatter — Da 4:14
the heavens and the earth — Joe 3:16
shall *s.*
the earth *s.* (B) — Am 8:8
of the door, that the posts — Am 9:1
may *s.*

while, and I will *s.* the — Hag 2:6
heavens
I will *s.* all nations, and the — Hag 2:7
desire
I will *s.* the heavens and the — Hag 2:21
earth
I will *s.* mine hand upon them — Zec 2:9
or city, *s.* off the dust of your — M't 10:14
feet
for fear of him the keepers — M't 28:4
did *s.*
s. off the dust under your — M'k 6:11
feet for
that house, and could not *s.* it — Lu 6:48
s. off the very dust from your — Lu 9:5
feet
once more I *s.* not the earth — Heb 12:26
only

SHAKED

upon me they *s.* their heads — Ps 109:25

SHAKEN

the sound of a *s.* — Le 26:36
leaf chase them
Israel, as a reed is *s.* in the — 1Ki 14:15
water
of Jerusalem hath *s.* her — 2Ki 19:21
head at
even thus be he *s.* out, and — Ne 5:13
by my neck, and *s.* me to — Job 16:12
pieces
people are *s.* (A)(B)(R) — Job 34:20
the wicked might be *s.* out — Job 38:13
of the hills moved and were *s.* — Ps 18:7
of Jerusalem hath *s.* her — Isa 37:22
head at
the fir trees, shall be — Na 2:3
terribly *s.*
if they be *s.* they shall even — Na 3:12
fall
to see? A reed *s.* with the — M't 11:7
wind
powers of the heavens shall — M't 24:29
be *s.*
that are in heaven shall be — M'k 13:25
s.
measure, pressed down, *s.* — Lu 6:38
together
to see? A reed *s.* with the — Lu 7:24
wind
the powers of heaven shall — Lu 21:26
be *s.*
the place was *s.* where they — Ac 4:31
were
foundations of the prison — Ac 16:26
were *s.*
That ye be not soon *s.* in — 2Th 2:2
mind, or
removing of those things — Heb 12:27
that are *s.*
which cannot be *s.* may — Heb 12:27
remain
when she is *s.* of a mighty — Re 6:13
wind

SHAKETH

s. the earth out of her place — Job 9:6
of the Lord *s.* the wilderness — Ps 29:8
Lord *s.* the wilderness of — Ps 29:8
Kadesh
the breaches thereof; for it *s.* — Ps 60:2
itself against him that *s.* it — Isa 10:15
Lord of hosts, which he *s.* — Isa 19:16
over it
that *s.* his hands from holding — Isa 33:15

SHAKING

he laugheth at the *s.* of a — Job 41:29
spear
a *s.* of the head among the — Ps 44:14
people
left in it, as the *s.* of an olive — Isa 17:6
tree
the *s.* of the hand of the — Isa 19:16
Lord of
shall be as the *s.* of an olive — Isa 24:13
tree
battles of *s.* will be fight with — Isa 30:32
was a noise, and behold a *s.* — Eze 37:7
be a great *s.* in the land of — Eze 38:19
Israel

SHALEM

And Jacob came to *S.* a — Ge 33:18
city of

SHALIM

passed through the land of *S.* — 1Sa 9:4

SHALISHA

passed through the land of *S.* — 1Sa 9:4

SHALLECHETH

westward, with the gate *S.* — 1Ch 26:16

SHALLOWNESS

their *s.* be obvious (B) — 2Ti 3:9

SHALLUM

S. the son of Jabesh — 2Ki 15:10
conspired
S. the son of Jabesh began to — 2Ki 15:13
and smote *S.* the son of — 2Ki 15:14
Jabesh in
And the rest of the acts of *S.* — 2Ki 15:15
the wife of *S.* the son of — 2Ki 22:14
Tikvah
Sisamai, and Sisamai begat — 1Ch 2:40
S.
S. begat Jekamiah, and — 1Ch 2:41
Jekamiah
the third Zedekiah, the fourth — 1Ch 3:15
S.
S. his son, Mibsam his son — 1Ch 4:25
begat Zadok, and Zadok — 1Ch 6:12
begat *S.*
S. begat Hilkiah, and Hilkiah — 1Ch 6:13
Jezer, and *S.* the sons of — 1Ch 7:13
Bilhah
the porters were, *S.* and — 1Ch 9:17
Akkub
their brethren: *S.* was the — 1Ch 9:17
chief
And *S.* the son of Kore, — 1Ch 9:19
the son of
the firstborn of *S.* the — 1Ch 9:31
Korahite
Jehizkiah the son of *S.* and — 2Ch 28:12
Amasa
the wife of *S.* the son of — 2Ch 34:22
Tikvath
the children of *S.* the children — Ezr 2:42
The son of *S.* the son of — Ezr 7:2
Zadok
porters; *S.* and Telem, and — Ezr 10:24
Uri
S., Amariah, and Joseph — Ezr 10:42
repaired *S.* the son of — Ne 3:12
Halohesh
The porters: the children of *S.* — Ne 7:45
saith the Lord touching *S.* — Jer 22:11
the son
Hanamee the son of *S.* — Jer 32:7
thine uncle
chamber of Maaseiah the son — Jer 35:4
of *S.*

SHALLUN

gate of the fountain repaired — Ne 3:15
S.

SHALMAI

the children of *S.* the children — Ezr 2:46
of Hagaba, the children of *S.* — Ne 7:48

SHALMAN

as *S.* spoiled Beth-arbel in — Ho 10:14
the day

SHALMANESER

him came up *S.* king of — 2Ki 17:3
Assyria
that *S.* king of Assyria came — 2Ki 18:9
up

SHAMA

S. and Jehiel the sons of — 1Ch 11:44
Hothan

SHAMBLES

Whatsoever is sold in the *s.* — 1Co 10:25
sold in the meat market — 1Co 10:25
(A)(B)(N)(P)(R)

SHAME

made them naked unto their *Ex 32:25*
s.
Aaron let them get out of *Ex 32:25*
control (A)
Aaron allowed them to cast *Ex 32:25*
off restraint (B)
Aaron had let them break *Ex 32:25*
loose (E)(R)
that might put them to s. in *J'g 18:7*
any
might embarrass them (B) *J'g 18:7*
removes s. from Israel (B) *1Sa 17:26*
s. of mother *1Sa 20:30*
(A)(B)(E)(R)(S)
because his father had done *1Sa 20:34*
him s.
whither shall I cause my s. *2Sa 13:13*
to go
covered with s. (S) *2Sa 19:5*
cut off s. images (B) *2Ki 18:4, 23:14*
remove the s. images (B) *2Ch 17:6;*
19:3; 31:1; 33:3; 34:3, 7
with s. of face to his own *2Ch 32:21*
land
returned in disgrace (B) *2Ch 32:21*
to utter s. (A)(R) *Ezr 9:7*
hate thee shall be clothed *Job 8:22*
with s.
without s. (B) *Job 11:15*
long will ye turn my glory into *Ps 4:2*
s.
not be put to s. (A)(E)(R) *Ps 25:3*
put to s. (A)(B)(E)(R) *Ps 31:1;*
31:17; 69:6
put to s. that seek after my soul *Ps 35:4*
be put to s. (A)(E)(R) *Ps 35:4*
let them be clothed with s. *Ps 35:26*
and put to s. that wish me *Ps 40:14*
evil
for a reward of their s. that *Ps 40:15*
say
hast put them to s. that hated *Ps 44:7*
us
hast cast off, and put us to s. *Ps 44:9*
the s. of my face hath covered *Ps 44:15*
me
thou hast put them to s. *Ps 53:5*
because
put to s. (A)(B)(E)(R) *Ps 69:6;*
71:13
reproach; s. hath covered my *Ps 69:7*
face
confusion has covered my face *Ps 69:7*
(B)
known my reproach, and my *Ps 69:19*
s.
be put to s. and confounded *Ps 70:2*
(A)(B)(E)
for a reward of their s. that *Ps 70:3*
say
never be put to s. (B)(E)(R) *Ps 71:1*
for they are brought unto s. *Ps 71:24*
that
put to everlasting s. (R) *Ps 78:66*
Fill their faces with s.; that *Ps 83:16*
they
let them be put to s. and *Ps 83:17*
perish
thou hast covered him with s. *Ps 89:45*
covered him with disgrace *Ps 89:45*
(B)
put to s. (A)(B)(E)(R) *Ps 97:7; 129:5*
s.
adversaries be clothed with *Ps 109:29*
s.
O Lord, put me not to s. *Ps 119:31*
His enemies will I clothe *Ps 132:18*
with s.
s. shall be the promotion of *Pr 3:35*
fools
a scorner getteth to himself s. *Pr 9:7*
in harvest is a son that *Pr 10:5*
causeth s.
pride cometh, then cometh s. *Pr 11:2*
but a prudent man covereth s. *Pr 12:16*
a prudent man ignores insult *Pr 12:16*
(A)(B)(R)
is loathsome, and cometh to s. *Pr 13:5*
Poverty and s. shall be to him *Pr 13:18*
is against him that causeth s. *Pr 14:35*
have rule over a son that *Pr 17:2*
causeth s.
it, it is folly and s. unto him *Pr 18:13*
a folly and a reproach (B) *Pr 18:13*
mother, is a son that causeth *Pr 19:26*
s.
thy neighbour hath put thee to *Pr 25:8*
s.

he that heareth it put thee to *Pr 25:10*
s.
himself bringeth his mother *Pr 29:15*
to s.
uncovered, to the s. of Egypt *Isa 20:4*
shall be the s. of thy lord's *Isa 22:18*
house
a disgrace of master's palace *Isa 22:18*
(A)(B)
s. images, sun-pillars (B) *Isa 27:9*
strength of Pharaoh be your s. *Isa 30:3*
profit, but a s. and also a *Isa 30:5*
reproach
all come to s. (B)(R) *Isa 30:5*
yea, thy s. shall be seen *Isa 47:3*
not my face from s. and *Isa 50:6*
spitting
from insult and spitting (B) *Isa 50:6*
for thou shalt not be put to s. *Isa 54:4*
shalt forget the s. of thy *Isa 54:4*
youth
For your s. ye shall have *Isa 61:7*
double
thief brought to s. (A) *Jer 2:26*
s. hath devoured the labour of *Jer 3:24*
We lie down in our s. and our *Jer 3:25*
thy face, that thy s. may *Jer 13:26*
appear
nakedness be exposed (B) *Jer 13:26*
days should be consumed *Jer 20:18*
with s.
a perpetual s. which shall not *Jer 23:40*
be
an everlasting reproach *Jer 23:40*
(A)(B)
the s. images (B) *Jer 27:9; Mic 5:14*
The nations have heard of *Jer 46:12*
thy s.
hath Moab turned the back *Jer 48:39*
with s.
s. hath covered our faces: for *Jer 51:51*
and s. shall be upon all faces *Eze 7:18*
bear thine own s. for thy *Eze 16:52*
sins that
confounded also, and bear *Eze 16:52*
thy s.
That thou mayest bear thine *Eze 16:54*
own s.
mouth any more because of *Eze 16:63*
thy s.
yet have they borne their s. *Eze 32:24;*
32:25
and bear their s. with them *Eze 32:30*
that go
put to s. (A)(B)(E)(R) *Eze 32:30*
neither bear the s. of the *Eze 34:29*
heathen
reproach of nations *Eze 34:29;*
(A)(B)(R) *36:6-7*
yet have borne the s. of the *Eze 36:6*
heathen
about you, they shall bear *Eze 36:7*
their s.
bear in thee the s. of the *Eze 36:15*
heathen
reproach of the nations (A) *Eze 36:15*
sneer of the nations (B) *Eze 36:15*
disgrace of the peoples (R) *Eze 36:15*
After that they have borne *Eze 39:26*
their s.
but they shall bear their s. *Eze 44:13*
Misgab is put to s. *Eze 48:1*
(A)(B)(E)(R)
to s. and everlasting contempt *Da 12:2*
will I change their glory into s. *Ho 4:7*
her rulers with s. do love, Give *Ho 4:18*
ye
love s. more than glory (S) *Ho 4:18*
separated themselves that s. *Ho 9:10*
Ephraim shall receive s. and *Ho 10:6*
brother Jacob s. shall cover thee *Ob 10*
of Saphir, having thy s. *Mic 1:11*
naked
them, that they shall not take s. *Mic 2:6*
root out your s. - images (B) *Mic 5:14*
s. shall cover her which said *Mic 7:10*
and the kingdom thy s. *Na 3:5*
hast consulted s. to thy *Hab 2:10*
house by
Thou art filled with s. for *Hab 2:16*
glory
and s. come upon thee (S) *Hab 2:16*
but the unjust knoweth no s. *Zep 3:5*
land where they have been put *Zep 3:19*
to s.
to put her to s. (R) *M't 1:19*
opponents put to s. *Lu 13:17*
(A)(E)(P)(R)
begin with s. to take the *Lu 14:9*
lowest

humiliation, guilty sense of *Lu 14:9*
impropriety (A)
feeling deeply embarrassed (B) *Lu 14:9*
you will look foolish (N) *Lu 14:9*
with considerable *Lu 14:9*
embarrassment (P)
worthy to suffer s. for his *Ac 5:41*
name
worthy to suffer disgrace (B) *Ac 5:41*
worthy to suffer dishonor *Ac 5:41*
(E)(R)
worthy to suffer indignity (N) *Ac 5:41*
worthy to bear humiliation *Ac 5:41*
(P)
hope putteth not to s. (E) *Ro 5:5*
to s. the wise (B)(N)(P)(R) *1Co 1:27*
I write not these things to s. *1Co 4:14*
you
I speak to your s., Is it so *1Co 6:5*
it be a s. for a woman to be *1Co 11:6*
shorn
it is disgraceful for a *1Co 11:6*
woman (A)(B)(N)(P)(R)
have long hair, it is a s. *1Co 11:14*
unto him
of God, and s. them who have *1Co 11:22*
not
s. for women to speak *1Co 14:35*
in church
it is disgraceful *1Co 14:35*
for a woman (A)
it is improper for a woman *1Co 14:35*
(B)
it is a shocking thing for a *1Co 14:35*
woman (N)
something indecorous about *1Co 14:35*
a woman (P)
of God: I speak this to *1Co 15:34*
your s.
through honor and s. (B) *2Co 6:8*
a s. even to speak of those *Eph 5:12*
things
it is a disgrace to mention *Eph 5:12*
(B)
and whose glory is in their *Ph'p 3:19*
s. who
afresh, and put him to an *Heb 6:6*
open s.
exposing him to public *Heb 6:6*
disgrace (B)
making mock of his death *Heb 6:6*
(N)
endured the cross, despising *Heb 12:2*
the s.
the sea, foaming out their own *Jude 13*
s.
foam up their own disgrace *Jude 13*
(B)
s. of thy nakedness do not *Re 3:18*
appear
he walk naked, and they see *Re 16:15*
his s.

SHAMED

Let her take it to her, lest we *Ge 38:23*
be s.
we do not want to be *Ge 38:23*
ridiculed (B)
lest we be laughed at (R) *Ge 38:23*
hast s. this day the faces of *2Sa 19:5*
all thy
Ye have s. the counsel of the *Ps 14:6*
poor
be confounded and s. (B) *Ps 35:4*
s. and disgraced (B)(R) *Ps 71:24*
s. and dismayed (A)(E)(R) *Ps 83:17*

SHAMEFACEDNESS

unto us s. (B) *Da 9:7*
apparel, with s. and sobriety *1Ti 2:9*
adorn themselves modestly, *1Ti 2:9*
appropriately, and sensibly
in seemly apparel (A)
dress modestly and prudently *1Ti 2:9*
(B)
dress modestly and soberly *1Ti 2:9*
(N)
dress modestly and sensibly *1Ti 2:9*
(R)

SHAMEFUL

a s. deed committed (B) *Ge 34:7*
a s. thing (R) *Le 20:17*
make s. charges (A)(R) *De 22:17;*
22:14
done a s. thing (A)(R) *Jos 7:15*
have ye altars to that s. *Jer 11:13*
thing

SHAMEFUL

s. spewing shall be on thy glory	*Hab 2:16*
s. passions (B)(N)	*Ro 1:26*
committing *s.* acts (A)(R)	*Ro 1:27*
slander and *s.* language (A)(B)(E)	*Col 3:8*

SHAMEFULLY

s. sinful (A)	*Pr 11:1; 11:20; 12:22*
acts *s.* and (B)	*Pr 19:26*
that conceived them hath done *s.*	*Ho 2:5*
treated them *s.* (A)(E)(R)(S)	*M't 22:6*
head, and sent him away *s.* handled	*M'k 12:4*
s. treated and spit upon (E)(R)	*Lu 18:32*
beat him also, and entreated him *s.*	*Lu 20:11*
s. treated, laid waste (A)	*Ac 8:3*
to treat them *s.* (E)	*Ac 14:5*
and were *s.* entreated, as ye know	*1Th 2:2*

SHAMELESS

s. persistence and insistence (A)	*Lu 11:8*
living in *s.*, insolent wantonness (A)	*1Pe 4:3*

SHAMELESSLY

vain fellows *s.* uncovereth himself	*2Sa 6:20*

SHAMELESSNESS

very *s.* of request (N)	*Lu 11:8*

SHAMER

the son of Bani, the son of *S.*	*1Ch 6:46*
the sons of *S.; Ahi,* and Rohgah	*1Ch 7:34*

SHAMES

hope never disappoints, deludes, or *s.* (A)(B)	*Ro 5:5*

SHAMETH

of riotous men *s.* his father	*Pr 28:7*

SHAMGAR

him was *S.* the son of Anath	*J'g 3:31*
In the days of *S.* the son of Anath	*J'g 5:6*

SHAMHUTH

fifth month was *S.* the Izrahite	*1Ch 27:8*

SHAMIR

And in the mountains, *S.*	*Jos 15:48*
he dwelt in *S.* in mount Ephraim	*J'g 10:1*
and died, and was buried in *S.*	*J'g 10:2*
Michah: of the sons of Michah; *S.*	*1Ch 24:24*

SHAMMA

and Hod, and *S.* and Shilshah	*1Ch 7:37*

SHAMMAH

and Zerah, *S.* and Mizzah	*Ge 36:13*
duke Zerah, duke *S.*, duke Mizzah	*Ge 36:17*
Then Jesse made *S.* to pass by	*1Sa 16:9*
him Abinadab, and the third *S.*	*1Sa 17:13*
after him was *S.* the son of Agee	*2Sa 23:11*
S. the Harodite, Elika the Harodite	*2Sa 23:25*
S. the Hararite, Ahiam the son of	*2Sa 23:33*
Nahath, Zerah, *S.* and Mizzah	*1Ch 1:37*

SHAMMAI

sons of Onan were *S.* and Jada	*1Ch 2:28*
And the sons of *S.*; Nadab	*1Ch 2:28*
the sons of Jada the brother of *S.*	*1Ch 2:32*
Jorkoam: and Rekem begat *S.*	*1Ch 2:44*
And the son of *S.* was Maon:	*1Ch 2:45*
and she bare Miriam, and *S.*	*1Ch 4:17*

SHAMMOTH

S. the Harorite, Helez the	*1Ch 11:27*

SHAMMUA

of Reuben, *S.* the son of Zaccur	*Nu 13:4*
S. and Shobab, Nathan and	*1Ch 14:4*
and Abda the son of *S.* the son of	*Ne 11:17*
Of Bilgah, *S.*; of Shemaiah	*Ne 12:18*

SHAMMUAH

S. and Shobab, and Nathan	*2Sa 5:14*

SHAMSHERAI

S. and Shehariah, and Athaliah	*1Ch 8:26*

SHAPE

s. of any statue (B)	*De 4:16*
a bodily *s.* like a dove upon him	*Lu 3:22*
bodily form like a dove (A)(E)(N)(R)	*Lu 3:22;*
voice at any time, nor seen his *s.*	*Joh 5:37*
the very *s.* of knowledge (N)	*Ro 2:20*

SHAPED

s. in likeness of his son (N)	*Ro 8:29*

SHAPEN

I was *s.* in iniquity; and in sin	*Ps 51:5*
brought forth in iniquity (A)(E)(R)	*Ps 51:5*
in sinful state I was born (B)	*Ps 51:5*

SHAPES

s. it with chisels (B)	*Isa 44:13*
s. of the locusts were like unto	*Re 9:7*

SHAPETH

s. it with planes (E)	*Isa 44:13*

SHAPHAM

Joel the chief, and *S.* the next	*1Ch 5:12*

SHAPHAN

the king sent *S.* the son of Azaliah	*2Ki 22:3; 22:8-10, 12, 14*
son of Ahikam, the son of *S.* ruler	*2Ki 25:22*
he sent *S.* the son of Azaliah, and	*2Ch 34:8; 34:15-16, 18, 20*
the hand of Ahikam the son of *S.*	*Jer 26:24*
By the hand of Elasah the son of *S.*	*Jer 29:3*
Gemariah the son of *S.* the scribe	*Jer 36:10*
the son of Gemariah, the son of *S.*	*Jer 36:11*
and Gemariah the son of *S.*	*Jer 36:12*
the son of Ahikam the son of *S.*	*Jer 39:14*
the son of Ahikam the son of *S.*	*Jer 40:5*
son of Ahikam the son of *S.* sware	*Jer 40:9*
the son of Ahikam the son of *S.*	*Jer 40:11*
son of Ahikam the son of *S.*	*Jer 41:2*
the son of Ahikam the son of *S.*	*Jer 43:6*
stood Jaazaniah the son of *S.*	*Eze 8:11*

SHAPHAT

of Simeon, *S.* the son of Hori	*Nu 13:5*
son of *S.* of Abel-meholah shalt	*1Ki 19:16*
found Elisha the son of *S.* who was	*1Ki 19:19*
He is Elisha the son of *S.*, which	*2Ki 3:11*
if the head of Elisha the son of *S.*	*2Ki 6:31*
Bariah, and Neariah, and *S.*, six	*1Ch 3:22*
next, and Jaanai, and *S.* in Bashan	*1Ch 5:12*
in the valleys was *S.* the son	*1Ch 27:29*

SHAPHER

and pitched in mount *S.*	*Nu 33:23*
And they removed from mount *S.*	*Nu 33:24*

SHARAI

Machnadebai, Shashai, *S.*	*Ezr 10:40*

SHARAIM

S. and Adithaim, and Gederah	*Jos 15:36*

SHARAR

Ahiam the son of *S.* the Hararite	*2Sa 23:33*

SHARE

to sharpen every man his *s.*	*1Sa 13:20*
let him *s.* with him (A)(B)(N)(P)(R)	*Lu 3:11*
s. the likeness of his son (B)	*Ro 8:29*
can light and darkness *s.* (P)	*2Co 6:14*
share (S)	*Ga 6:6;*
s. his sufferings (A)(B)(N)(P)(R)	*Ph'p 4:14; 1Ti 6:18; Heb 13:16*
	Ph'p 3:10
s. burden of (N)(P)(R)	*Ph'p 4:14*
ready to *s.* (A)(B)(N)	*1Ti 6:18*
first *s.* of crops (B)(P)(R)	*2Ti 2:6*
did not *s.* fate of disobedient (P)	*Heb 11:31*
s. his doom (N)	*Jude 11*

SHARED

s. in his riches (P)	*Joh 1:16*
s. meals with unaffected joy (N)	*Ac 2:46*
no church *s.* with me (S)	*Ph'p 4:15*
s. sufferings of prisoners (N)	*Heb 10:34*

SHARERS

s. together of the promise (N)	*Eph 3:6*
be *s.* with them (A)	*Eph 5:7*
s. in the heavenly calling (B) (B)(R)	*Heb 3:1*
became *s.* with Christ	*Heb 3:14*
s. of the Holy Spirit (A)	*Heb 6:4*
s. of his holiness (A)	*Heb 12:10*
become *s.* of divine nature (A)(B)	*2Pe 1:4*

SHAREZER

and *S.* his son smote him with the	*2Ki 19:37; Isa 37:38*

SHARING

s. meals with simple joy (P)	*Ac 2:46*
s. the blood of Christ (N)(P)	*1Co 10:16*
s. in sufferings (A)(B)(N)(P)(R)	*Ph'p 3:10*
s. as companions (B)	*Ph'p 4:14*
s. the devil's downfall (P)	*1Ti 3:6*
practice *s.* (B)	*1Ti 6:18*
s. faith (A)(B)(P)(R)	*Ph'm 6*

SHARON

and in all the suburbs of *S.*	*1Ch 5:16*
over the herds that fed in *S.* was	*1Ch 27:29*
I am the rose of *S.*, and the lily of	*Ca 2:1*

S. is like a wilderness; and Bashan   *Isa 33:9*
the excellency of Carmel and *S.*   *Isa 35:2*
And *S.* shall be a fold of flocks, and   *Isa 65:10*

SHARONITE

fed in Sharon was Shitrai the *S.*   *1Ch 27:29*

SHARP

Then Zipporah took a *s.* stone   *Ex 4:25*
took a flint knife (A)(B)   *Ex 4:25*
took a flint (E)(R)   *Ex 4:25*
unto Joshua, Make thee *s.* knives   *Jos 5:2*
made knives of flint (A)(E)(R)   *Jos 5:2; 5:3*
make stone knives (B)   *Jos 5:2*
Joshua made him *s.* knives   *Jos 5:3*
was a *s.* rock on the one side   *1Sa 14:4*
a rocky crag (A)(E)(R)   *1Sa 14:4*
and a *s.* rock on the other side   *1Sa 14:4*
S. stones are under him: he   *Job 41:30*
nether part like potsherds (B)   *Job 41:30*
leave threshing-sledge grooves in mire (B)(R)   *Job 41:30*
s. pointed things upon the mire   *Job 41:30*
Thine arrows are *s.* in the heart   *Ps 45:5*
mischiefs; like a *s.* rasor, working   *Ps 52:2*
and their tongue a *s.* sword   *Ps 57:4*
S. arrows of the mighty, with   *Ps 120:4*
S. as a two-edged sword   *Pr 5:4*
maul, and a sword, and a *s.* arrow   *Pr 25:18*
Whose arrows are *s.* and all their   *Isa 5:28*
a new *s.* threshing instrument   *Isa 41:15*
made my mouth like a *s.* sword   *Isa 49:2*
take thee a *s.* knife, take thee   *Eze 5:1*
contention was so *s.* between them   *Ac 15:39*
mouth went a *s.* two-edged sword   *Re 1:16*
hath the *s.* sword with two edges   *Re 2:12*
crown, and in his hand a *s.* sickle   *Re 14:14*
heaven, he also having a *s.* sickle   *Re 14:17*
cry to him that had the *s.* sickle   *Re 14:18*
Thrust in thy *s.* sickle, and gather   *Re 14:18*
out of his mouth goeth a *s.* sword   *Re 19:15*

SHARPEN

to *s.* every man his share and his   *1Sa 13:20*
for the axes, and to *s.* the goads   *1Sa 13:21*
s. his sword (B)   *Ps 7:12*
s. the edge (B)   *Ec 10:10*

SHARPENED

s. his tongue (B)   *Ps 64:3*
They have *s.* their tongues like a   *Ps 140:3*
A sword, a sword is *s.* and also   *Eze 21:9*
It is *s.* to make a sore slaughter   *Eze 21:10*
this sword is *s.* and it is furbished   *Eze 21:11*

SHARPENETH

mine enemy *s.* his eyes upon me   *Job 16:9*
Iron *s.* iron; so a man *s.* the   *Pr 27:17*

SHARPER

the most upright is *s.* than a thorn   *Mic 7:4*
and *s.* than any two-edged sword   *Heb 4:12*

SHARPLY

And they did chide with him *s.*   *J'g 8:1*
spoke *s.* to evil spirit (P)   *M'k 9:25*
they contended *s.* (S)   *Ac 23:9*
fall into *s.* divided groups (N)   *1Co 11:18*
Wherefore rebuke them *s.* that   *Tit 1:13*

SHARPNESS

lest being present I should use *s.*   *2Co 13:10*

SHARUHEN

And Beth-lebaoth, and *S.*   *Jos 19:6*

SHASHAI

Machnadebai, *S.*, Sharai   *Eze 10:40*

SHASHAK

And Ahio, *S.*, and Jeremoth   *1Ch 8:14*
and Penuel, the sons of *S.*   *1Ch 8:25*

SHATTERED

s. them (B)   *J'g 9:43*
chains lay *s.* (B)   *M'k 5:4*

SHAUL

and *S.* the son of a Canaanitish   *Ge 46:10*
S. the son of a Canaanitish woman   *Ex 6:15*
of *S.* the family of the Shaulites   *Nu 26:13*
S. of Rehoboth by the river reigned   *1Ch 1:48*
when *S.* was dead, Baal-hanan the   *1Ch 1:49*
and Jamin, Jarib, Zerah, and *S.*   *1Ch 4:24*
son, Uzziah his son, and *S.* his son   *1Ch 6:24*

SHAULITES

of Shaul, the family of the *S.*   *Nu 26:13*

SHAVE

but the scall shall he not *s.*   *Le 13:33*
s. off all his hair, and wash himself   *Le 14:8*
s. all his hair off his head and   *Le 14:9*
even all his hair he shall *s.* off   *Le 14:9*
s. around your temples (S)   *Le 19:27*
they *s.* off the corner of their beard   *Le 21:5*
shall *s.* his head in the day of   *Nu 6:9*
on the seventh day shall he *s.* it   *Nu 6:9*
shall *s.* the head of his separation   *Nu 6:18*
let them *s.* all their flesh, and   *Nu 8:7*
she shall *s.* her head, and pare   *De 21:12*
to *s.* off the seven locks of his head   *J'g 16:19*
Lord *s.* with a razor that is hired   *Isa 7:20*
Neither shall they *s.* their heads   *Eze 44:20*
them, that they may *s.* their heads   *Ac 21:24*

SHAVED

and he *s.* himself, and changed his   *Ge 41:14*
s. off the one half of their beards   *2Sa 10:4*
s. them, and cut off their garments   *1Ch 19:4*
s. his head, and fell down upon   *Job 1:20*

SHAVEH

and the Emims in *S.* Kiriathaim   *Ge 14:5*
at the valley of *S.*, which is   *Ge 14:17*

SHAVEN

He shall be *s.* but the scall   *Le 13:33*
the hair of his separation is *s.*   *Nu 6:19*
if I be *s.* then my strength will   *J'g 16:17*

hair grow again after he was *s.*   *J'g 16:22*
men, having their beards *s.*   *Jer 41:5*
is even all one as if she were *s.*   *1Co 11:5*
for a woman to be shorn or *s.* let   *1Co 11:6*

SHAVSHA

the priests; and *S.* was scribe   *1Ch 18:16*

SHEAF

and, lo, my *s.* arose, and also stood   *Ge 37:7*
about, and made obeisance to my *s.*   *Ge 37:7*
shall bring a *s.* of the firstfruits   *Le 23:10*
shall wave the *s.* before the Lord   *Le 23:11*
ye wave the *s.* an he lamb without   *Le 23:12*
brought the *s.* of the wave offering   *Le 23:15*
and hast forgot a *s.* in the field   *De 24:19*
take away the *s.* from the hungry   *Job 24:10*
and like a torch of fire in a *s.*   *Zec 12:6*

SHEAL

Jashub, and *S.* and Ramoth   *Ezr 10:29*

SHEALTIEL

and Zerubbabel the son of *S.*   *Ezr 3:2*
began Zerubbabel the son of *S.*   *Ezr 3:8*
rose up Zerubbabel the son of *S.*   *Ezr 5:2*
up with Zerubbabel the son of *S.*   *Ne 12:1*
unto Zerubbabel the son of *S.*   *Hag 1:1*
Then Zerubbabel the son of *S.* and   *Hag 1:12*
spirit of Zerubbabel the son of *S.*   *Hag 1:14*
now to Zerubbabel the son of *S.*   *Hag 2:2*
my servant, the son of *S.* saith   *Hag 2:23*

SHEAR

And Laban went to *s.* his sheep   *Ge 31:19*
up to Timnath to *s.* his sheep   *Ge 38:13*
nor *s.* the firstling of thy sheep   *De 15:19*
that Nabal did *s.* his sheep   *1Sa 25:4*

SHEARER

hopper, stripper, *s.* (B)   *Joe 2:25*
like a lamb dumb before his *s.*   *Ac 8:32*

SHEARERS

I have heard that thou hast *s.*   *1Sa 25:7*
flesh that I have killed for my *s.*   *1Sa 25:11*
as a sheep before her *s.* is dumb   *Isa 53:7*

SHEARIAH

Ishmael, and *S.*, and Obadiah   *1Ch 8:38; 9:44*

SHEARING

he was *s.* his sheep in Carmel   *1Sa 25:2*
at the *s.* house in the way   *2Ki 10:12*
at the pit of the *s.* house, even   *2Ki 10:14*

SHEAR-JASHUB

meet Ahaz, thou, and *S.* thy son   *Isa 7:3*

SHEARS

branches with pruning *s.* (B)   *Isa 18:5*

SHEATH

and drew it out of his *s.* thereof   *1Sa 17:51*

upon his loins in the s.   2Sa 20:8
thereof
put his sword again into the   1Ch 21:27
s.
forth my sword out of his s.   Eze 21:3
my sword go forth out of his   Eze 21:4
s.
drew forth my sword out of   Eze 21:5
his s.
cause it to return into his   Eze 21:30
s.? I will
Put up thy sword into the s.   Joh 18:11

SHEAVES

we were binding s. in the   Ge 37:7
fields
behold, your s. stood round   Ge 37:7
about
after the reapers among the s.   Ru 2:7
Let her glean even among the   Ru 2:15
s.
bringing in s. and lading   Ne 13:15
asses
rejoicing, bringing his s. with   Ps 126:6
him
nor he that bindeth s. his   Ps 129:7
bosom
a cart is pressed that is full   Am 2:13
of s.
gather them as the s. into the   Mic 4:12
floor

SHEBA

sons of Raamah; S. and   Ge 10:7
Dedan
And Obal, and Abimael, and   Ge 10:28
S.
And Jokshan begat S. and   Ge 25:3
Dedan
inheritance Beer-sheba, and S.   Jos 19:2
man of Belial, whose name   2Sa 20:1;
was S.   20:2, 6-7, 10, 13, 21-22
queen of S. heard of the fame   1Ki 10:1
queen of S. had seen all   1Ki 10:4
Solomon's
queen of S. gave to king   1Ki 10:10
Solomon
unto the queen of S. all her   1Ki 10:13
desire
sons of Raamah; S. and   1Ch 1:9
Dedan
And Ebal, and Abimael, and   1Ch 1:22
S.
sons of Jokshan; S. and   1Ch 1:32
Dedan
Meshullam; and S., and Jorai   1Ch 5:13
queen of S. heard of the   2Ch 9:1
fame of
queen of S. had seen the   2Ch 9:3
wisdom
spice as the queen of S. gave   2Ch 9:9
king
to the queen of S. all her   2Ch 9:12
desire
companies of S. waited   Job 6:19
for them
kings of S. and Seba shall   Ps 72:10
offer
shall be given of the gold of   Ps 72:15
S.
all they from S. shall come: Isa 60:6
they
there to me incense from S.   Jer 6:20
the merchants of S., Asshur   Eze 27:23
Raamah
the merchants of S., Asshur   Eze 27:23
S. and Dedan, and the   Eze 38:13
merchants
men of S. (S)   Joe 3:8

SHEBAH

And he called it S.:   Ge 26:33
therefore the

SHEBAM

Elealeh, and S. and Nebo, and   Nu 32:3

SHEBANIAH

And S. and Jehoshaphat   1Ch 15:24
Kadmiel, S., Bunni, Sherebiah   Ne 9:4
Hodiah, S., and Pethahiah,   Ne 9:5
said
Hattush, S., Malluch   Ne 10:4
their brethren, S., Hodijah,   Ne 10:10
Kelita

Zaccur, Sherebiah, S.   Ne 10:12
Melicu, Jonathan; of S.,   Ne 12:14
Joseph

SHEBARIM

from before the gate even   Jos 7:5
unto S.

SHEBER

Caleb's concubine, bare S.   1Ch 2:48

SHEBNA

S. the scribe, and Joah the   2Ki 18:18
son of
S. and Joah, unto   2Ki 18:26
Rab-shakeh
S. the scribe, and Joah the   2Ki 18:37
son of
the household, and S. the   2Ki 19:2
scribe
unto this treasurer, even unto   Isa 22:15
S.
over the house, and S. the   Isa 36:3
scribe
Then said Eliakim and S.   Isa 36:11
S. the scribe and Joah, the   Isa 36:22
son of
S. the scribe, and the elders of   Isa 37:2

SHEBUEL

of Gershom, S. was the   1Ch 23:16
chief
Uzziel, S., and Jerimoth   1Ch 25:4
And S. the son of Gershom,   1Ch 26:24
the son

SHECANIAH

ninth to Jeshuah, the tenth   1Ch 24:11
to S.
and Shemaiah, Amariah,   2Ch 31:15
and S.

SHECHANIAH

sons of Obadiah, the sons of   1Ch 3:21
S.
the sons of S.; Shemaiah   1Ch 3:22
Of the sons of S. of the sons   Ezr 8:3
Of the sons of S.; the son of   Ezr 8:5
And S. the son of Jehiel, one   Ezr 10:2
also Shemaiah the son of S.   Ne 3:29
son in law of S. the son of   Ne 6:18
Arah
S., Rehum, Meremoth   Ne 12:3

SHECHEM

Jacob came to Shalem a city   Ge 33:18
of S.
S. lay with Dinah   Ge 34:2
they slew   Ge 34:26
Jacob hid them under an oak   Ge 35:4
that was by S.
went to feed their father's   Ge 37:12
flock in S.
Joseph came from the vale of   Ge 37:14
Hebron to S.
of S. the family of the   Nu 26:31
Shechemites
there was a lot for the children   Jos 17:2
of S.
S. in mount Ephraim   Jos 20:7;
  21:21; 1Ch 6:67
Joshua gathered all the tribes   Jos 24:1
of Israel to S.
and the bones of Joseph   Jos 24:32
buried they in S.
Gideon's concubine in S. bare   J'g 8:31
a son
Abimelech the son of Jerubbaal   J'g 9:1
went to S.
Jotham cried, Hearken to me,   J'g 9:7
ye men of S.
let fire come out from the men   J'g 9:20
of S.
who is S.   J'g 9:28
Gaal and brethren come to S.   J'g 9:31
thrust out, that they should   J'g 9:41
not dwell in S.
the evil of the men of S. did   J'g 9:57
God render
Rehoboam went to S.   1Ki 12:1;
  2Ch 10:1
Jeroboam built S. in mount   1Ki 12:25
Ephraim

the sons of Shemida, Ahian,   1Ch 7:19
and S.
I will rejoice, I will divide S.   Ps 60:6;
  108:7
that there came certain from   Jer 41:5
S.

SHECHEMITES

of Shechem, the family of   Nu 26:31
the S.

SHECHEM'S

the children of Hamor, S.   Ge 33:19
father
and took Dinah out of S.   Ge 34:26
house

SHED

by man shall his blood be s.:   Ge 9:6
for
S. no blood, but cast him   Ge 37:22
into
die, there shall no blood be s.   Ex 22:2
for him
him, there shall be blood s.   Ex 22:3
for him
he hath s. blood: and that man   Le 17:4
be cleansed of the blood that   Nu 35:33
is s.
but by the blood of him that   Nu 35:33
s. it
That innocent blood be not   De 19:10
s. in
Our hands have not s. this   De 21:7
blood
thee from coming to s.   1Sa 25:26
blood
thou hast s. blood causeless,   1Sa 25:31
me this day from coming to   1Sa 25:33
s. blood
s. out his bowels to the   2Sa 20:10
ground
and s. the blood of war in   1Ki 2:5
peace
the innocent blood, which   1Ki 2:31
Joab s.
Manasseh s. innocent blood   2Ki 21:16
for the innocent blood that   2Ki 24:4
he s.
Thou hast s. blood   1Ch 22:8
abundantly, and
thou hast s. much blood   1Ch 22:8
upon the
a man of war, and hast s.   1Ch 28:3
blood
Their blood have they s. like   Ps 79:3
water
blood of thy servants which is   Ps 79:10
s.
s. innocent blood, even the   Ps 106:38
blood
to evil, and make haste to s.   Pr 1:16
blood
and hands that s. innocent   Pr 6:17
blood
make haste to s. innocent   Isa 59:7
blood
s. not innocent blood in this   Jer 7:6
place
s. innocent blood in this place   Jer 22:3
and for to s. innocent blood   Jer 22:17
s. the blood of the just in   La 4:13
the midst
wedlock and s. blood are   Eze 16:38
judged
in thy blood that thou hast s.   Eze 22:4
in thee to their power to s.   Eze 22:6
blood
are men that carry tales to s.   Eze 22:9
blood
have taken gifts to s.   Eze 22:12
blood
ravening the prey, to s.   Eze 22:27
blood, and
manner of women that s.   Eze 23:45
blood
toward your idols, and s.   Eze 33:25
blood
hast s. the blood of the   Eze 35:5
children
that they had s. upon the   Eze 36:18
land
s. innocent blood in their land   Joe 3:19
righteous blood s. upon the   M't 23:35
earth
s. for many for the   M't 26:28
remission of sins

testament, which is *s.* for M'k 14:24
many
which was *s.* from the Lu 11:50
foundation
in my blood, which is *s.* for Lu 22:20
you
he hath *s.* forth this, which ye Ac 2:33
now
blood of thy martyr Stephen Ac 22:20
was *s.*
Their feet are swift to *s.* blood Ro 3:15
the love of God is *s.* abroad in Ro 5:5
our
s. on us abundantly through Tit 3:6
Jesus
For they have *s.* the blood of Re 16:6
saints

SHEDDER

son that is a robber, a *s.* of Eze 18:10
blood

SHEDDETH

Whoso *s.* man's bood, by man Ge 9:6
The city *s.* blood in the midst Eze 22:3
of it

SHEDDING

oak *s.* withering leaves (B) Isa 1:30
s. innocent blood (S) Jer 22:17
and without *s.* of blood is no Heb 9:29

SHEDEUR

of Reuben; Elizur the son of S. Nu 1:5
Reuben shall be Elizur the son Nu 2:10
of S.
the fourth day Elizur the son Nu 7:30
of S.
the offering of Elizur the son Nu 7:35
of S.
his host was Elizur the son Nu 10:18
of S.

SHEEP

Abel a keeper of *s.*, Cain tiller Ge 4:2
of ground
Rachel his daughter cometh Ge 29:6;
with the *s.* 29:9
the hand of the Lord is upon the Ex 9:3
s.
ye shall take it out from the *s.* Ex 12:5
or the goats
thou shalt sacrifice thereon Ex 20:24
thy *s.* and oxen
if a man steal a *s.* and kill it Ex 22:1;
or sell it 22:4, 9
if a man give to his Ex 22:10
neighbour a *s.* to keep
likewise do with the firstling Ex 22:30;
of *s.* 34:19
if his offering be of the *s.* or Le 1:10
goats
shall eat no manner of fat of *s.* Le 7:23
or of goats
ye shall offer a male of the *s.* Le 22:19;
or goats 22:21
no man shall sanctify the Le 27:26
firstling of a *s.*
the firstling of *s.* thou shalt Nu 18:17
not redeem
build ye cities and folds for Nu 32:24;
your *s.* 32:36
he will bless the flocks of thy De 7:13
s.
thou shalt not sacrifice *s.* De 17:1
wherein is blemish
the priest's due from them De 18:3;
that offer *s.* 18:4
thou shalt not see thy De 22:1
brother's *s.* go astray
blessed shall be the flocks of De 28:4
thy *s.*
cursed shall be the flocks of De 28:18;
thy *s.* 31:51
that he might eat butter of De 32:14
kine, milk of *s.*
they destroyed at Jericho ox Jos 6:21
and *s.*
Joshua took Achan's *s.* and Jos 7:24
tent, and all he had
the Midianites left neither *s.* J'g 6:4
nor oxen
the king will take the tenth of 1Sa 8:17
your *s.*
the people flew upon the spoil 1Sa 14:32
and took *s.*

bring hither every man his ox 1Sa 14:34
and his *s.*
slay both ox and *s.* 1Sa 15:3
Saul spread the *s.* 1Sa 15:9
what meaneth this bleating 1Sa 15:14
of *s.* in my ears
the people took of the spoil 1Sa 15:21
s. and oxen
the youngest, behold, he 1Sa 16:11
keepeth the *s.*
send me David thy son, who 1Sa 16:19
is with the *s.*
David returned to feed his 1Sa 17:15
father's *s.*
he rose early and left the *s.* 1Sa 17:20
with a keeper
David said, Thy servant kept 1Sa 17:34
his father's *s.*
Nabal had 3000 *s.* he 1Sa 25:2
was shearing his *s.*
Abigail hasted, and took five 1Sa 25:18
s. ready dressed
David took away the *s.*, the 1Sa 27:9
oxen, and asses
I took thee from following the 2Sa 7:8
s.
Barzillai brought David 2Sa 17:29
butter and *s.*
David said, I have sinned, 2Sa 24:17;
but these *s.*, what have 1Ch 21:17
they done
Adonijah hath slain oxen, 1Ki 1:19;
and fat cattle and *s.* 1:25
Solomon's provision for one 1Ki 4:23
day hundred *s.*
all the congregation sacrificing 1Ki 8:5
s. and oxen
Solomon offered *s.* 1Ki 8:63;
2Ch 5:6; 7:5
is it a time to receive *s.* and 2Ki 5:26
oxen
they took from Hagarites 1Ch 5:21
250,000 *s.*
they brought oxen and 1Ch 12:40
s. abundantly
Asa carried from the 2Ch 14:15
Ethiopians *s.*
and they offered of the spoil 2Ch 15:11
7000 *s.*
Ahab killed *s.* and oxen for 2Ch 18:2
Jehoshaphat
the consecrated things 2Ch 29:33
were 3000 *s.*
Hezekiah the king did give 2Ch 30:24
7000 *s.* and the princes gave
to the congregation 10,000 *s.*
they brought in the tithes of 2Ch 31:6
oxen and *s.*
for Nehemiah daily one ox, Ne 5:18
six choice *s.*
his substance also was 7000 *s.*, Job 1:3
3000 camels
the fire is fallen, and hath Job 1:16
burnt up the *s.*
if he were not warmed with Job 31:20
fleece of my *s.*
for he had 14,000 *s.* and Job 42:12
6000 camels
for thou hast given him all *s.* Ps 8:7
and oxen
thou hast given us like *s.* for Ps 44:11
meat
like *s.* are laid in the grave, Ps 49:14
death feed
why doth thine anger smoke Ps 74:1
against thy *s.*
but made his own people go Ps 78:52
forth like *s.*
so we thy people and *s.* of Ps 79:13
thy pasture
and we are the *s.* of his hand Ps 95:7;
100:3
I have gone astray like a Ps 119:176
lost *s.*
that our *s.* may bring forth Ps 144:13
thousands
thy teeth are like a flock of *s.* Ca 4:2;
6:6
in that day a man shall Isa 7:21
nourish two *s.*
behold, joy and gladness, Isa 22:13
and killing of *s.*
brought me the *s.* (S) Isa 43:23
all we like *s.* are gone astray Isa 53:6
pull them out like *s.* for the Jer 12:3
slaughter
woe be unto the pastors that Jer 23:1
scatter the *s.*
my people hath been lost *s.*: Jer 50:6
their shepherds

Israel is a scattered *s.*: lions Jer 50:17
have driven him
my *s.* wander through the Eze 34:6
mountains
will search my *s.* and seek Eze 34:11;
them out 34:12
Israel served, and for a wife Ho 12:12
he kept *s.*
the flocks of *s.* are made Joe 1:18
desolate
as a young lion among the Mic 5:8
flocks of *s.*
smite the shepherd and *s.* Zec 13:7;
shall be scattered M't 26:31; M'k 14:27
go rather to the lost *s.* of the M't 10:6
house of Israel
if one *s.* fall into a pit on M't 12:11
the sabbath
how much then is man M't 12:12
better than a *s.*
I am not sent but unto the M't 15:24
lost *s.* of Israel
if a man have 100 *s.* and M't 18:12
one be gone
he rejoiceth more of that *s.* M't 18:13;
Lu 15:4, 6
as a shepherd divideth his *s.* M't 25:32
from goats
he shall set *s.* on his right M't 25:33
hand, but goats
he found in the temple those Joh 2:14
that sold *s.*
he drove them out of the Joh 2:15
temple, and the *s.*
that entereth by door is Joh 10:2
shepherd of the *s.*
the *s.* hear his voice Joh 10:3
the *s.* follow him Joh 10:4; 10:27
then said Jesus, Verily I am Joh 10:7
the door of the *s.*
were robbers, but the *s.* did Joh 10:8
not hear them
the good Shepherd giveth his Joh 10:11
life for his *s.*
an hireling leaveth the *s.* Joh 10:12;
and fleeth 10:13
good Shepherd, I know my Joh 10:14;
s. 10:16
the Father, and I lay down Joh 10:15
my life for the *s.*
other *s.* have I which are Joh 10:16
not
because ye are not of my *s.* Joh 10:26
I said unto you
He saith unto Peter, Feed Joh 21:16;
my *s.* 21:17
Lord Jesus, that great Heb 13:20
Shepherd of *s.*
none buyeth *s.*, horses, slaves, Re 18:13
and souls

SHEEP *GATE*

Eliashib and brethren built the Ne 3:1
s. gate
between going up of the Ne 3:32
corner to the *s.* gate
they went on to the *s.* gate, Ne 12:39
and they stood

SHEEP *MARKET*

at Jerusalem by the *s.* market Joh 5:2
a pool, called Bethesda

AS SHEEP

be not *as s.* which have no Nu 27:17
shepherd
all Israel scattered on hills, 1Ki 22:17;
as s. that have no shepherd 2Ch 18:16
killed all day long, we are Ps 44:22;
counted *as s.* for the slaughter Ro 8:36
it shall be *as s.* that no man Isa 13:14
taketh up
as a s. before his shearers is Isa 53:7
dumb
I will put them together *as s.* Mic 2:12
of Bozra
and were scattered *as* M't 9:36;
s. having no shepherd M'k 6:34
I send you forth *as s.* in M't 10:16
midst of wolves
he was led *as a s.* to the Ac 8:32
slaughter
ye were *as s.* going astray, 1Pe 2:25
but returned

SHEEPCOTE

I took thee from the s.   2Sa 7:8;
                             1Ch 17:7

SHEEPCOTES

Saul came to the s. after   1Sa 24:3
David

SHEEPFOLD

he that entereth not the s. by   Joh 10:1
the door

SHEEPFOLDS

we will build s. for our cattle   Nu 32:16
why abodest thou among the   J'g 5:16
s.
s. for flock (A)(B)   2Ch 32:28
have lien among the s. (S)   Ps 68:13
he chose David, took him   Ps 78:70
from the s.

SHEEPMASTER

Mesha king of Moab was a   2Ki 3:4
s.

SHEEP'S

which come to you in s.   M't 7:15
clothing

SHEEPSHEARERS

went unto his s. to   Ge 38:12
Timnath
Absalom had s. in   2Sa 13:23
Baal-hazor
Behold now, thy servant   2Sa 13:24
hath s.

SHEEPSKINS

they wandered about in s.   Heb 11:37

SHEER

struck them as s. imagination   Lu 24:11
(P)
s. nonsense to Gentiles (P)   1Co 1:23

SHEET

great s. knit at the four   Ac 10:11
corners
a sheet (A)(B)(N)(P)(R)   Ac 10:11;
                             10:16; 11:5
as it had been a great s. let   Ac 11:5
down

SHEETS

will give you thirty s. and   J'g 14:12
thirty
then shall ye give me thirty s.   J'g 14:13

SHEHARIAH

Shamsherai, and S. and   1Ch 8:26
Athaliah

SHEKEL

golden earring of half a s.   Ge 24:22
weight
a quarter ounce ring (B)   Ge 24:22
half a s. after the s. of the   Ex 30:13;
sanctuary   30:15, 24; 38:24-26
Le 5:15; 27:3, 25; Nu 7:13, 19, 25, 31,
37, 43, 47, 49-50, 55, 61, 67, 73, 79, 85-
                             86; 18:16
a s. is twenty gerahs   Ex 30:13; Le 27:25
half a shekel   Ex 30:13
half a dollar (B)   Ex 30:13
half a s.   Ex 30:15
poor no less than fifty cents   Ex 30:15
(B)
five hundred shekels   Ex 30:24
the fourth part of a s. of silver   1Sa 9:8
I have a silver quarter (B)   1Sa 9:8
of fine flour be sold for a s.   2Ki 7:1
sold for a dollar (B)   2Ki 7:1; 7:16, 18
and two measures of barley for   2Ki 7:1
a s.
of fine flour was sold for a   2Ki 7:16
s. and

and two measures of barley   2Ki 7:16
for a s.
Two measures of barley for a   2Ki 7:18
s.
and a measure of fine flour for   2Ki 7:18
a s.
you will find a s.   M't 17:27
(A)(E)(R)

SHEKELS

my lord, the land is worth   Ge 23:15;
400 s.   23:16
land is worth 250 dollars (B)   Ge 23:15
two bracelets for her hands   Ge 24:22
of ten s. weight
two five ounce golden   Ge 24:22
bracelets (B)
he shall give her master   Ex 21:32
thirty s.
250 dollars worth of pure   Ex 21:32
myrrh (B)
of pure myrrh 500 s. of sweet   Ex 30:23
cinnamon, 250 s. of
sweet calamus, 250 s.
the estimation by s.   Le 5:15;
                   27:3-6, 7, 16
one spoon of ten s. of gold   Nu 7:14;
full of incense   7:20, 26, 32, 38, 44,
                50, 56, 62, 68, 74, 80
pan of about four ounces   Nu 7:14;
(B)   7:20, 26, 32, 38, 44, 50, 56, 62,
                      68, 74, 80
they shall amerce him in 100   De 22:19
s.
fine him one hundred dollars   De 22:19
(B)
man shall give to the damsel's   De 22:29
father fifty s.
must pay fifty dollars (B)   De 22:29
when I saw in the spoils 200   Jos 7:21
s. of silver
with 200 dollars (B)   Jos 7:21
weight of golden earrings was   J'g 8:26
1700 s.
was equal to about 17,000   J'g 8:26
dollars (B)
the 1100 s. I took it   J'g 17:2
1,100 pieces of silver (B)   J'g 17:2
restored the s.   J'g 17:3
I will give thee ten s. of   J'g 17:10
silver by the year
ten pieces of silver (B)   J'g 17:10
Absalom weighed his hair,   2Sa 14:26
200 s.
weighed over three pounds   2Sa 14:26
(B)
I would have given thee ten   2Sa 18:11
s. and a girdle
ten pieces of silver (B)   2Sa 18:11
David bought oxen for fifty s.   2Sa 24:24
of Araunah
fifty silver dollars (B)   2Sa 24:24
six hundred s. of gold to one   1Ki 10:16
target
6000 dollars worth of gold   1Ki 10:16
(B)
exacted of each man fifty s.   2Ki 15:20
of silver
so David gave to Ornan 600   1Ch 21:25
s.
the area 6,000 dollars worth   1Ch 21:25
of gold (B)
former governor had taken   Ne 5:15
forty s. by year
worth a thousand s. of silver   Isa 7:23
(S)
I bought the field for   Jer 32:9
seventeen s. of silver
meat shall be by weight   Eze 4:10
twenty s. a day
weighed an ample half pound   Eze 4:10
(B)

SHELAH

a son; and called his name S.   Ge 38:5
house till S. my son be grown   Ge 38:11
for she saw that S. was   Ge 38:14
grown
that I gave her not to S. my   Ge 38:26
son
of Judah; Er, and Onan, and   Ge 46:12
S.
of S. the family of the   Nu 26:20
Shelanites
Arphaxad begat S. and S.   1Ch 1:18
begat
Shem. Arphaxad, S.   1Ch 1:24
of Judah; Er, and Onan, and   1Ch 2:3
S.

The sons of S. the son of   1Ch 4:21
Judah

SHELANITES

S., the family of the   Nu 26:20
Shelanites

SHELAMIAH

And the lot eastward fell to   1Ch 26:14
S.
And S. and Nathan, and   Ezr 10:39
Adaiah
Azareel, and S. Shemariah   Ezr 10:41
repaired Hananiah the son of   Ne 3:30
S.
over the treasuries, S. the   Ne 13:13
priest
the son of S. the son of Cushi   Jer 36:14
Azriel, and S. the son of   Jer 36:26
Abdeel, to
the king sent Jehucal the   Jer 37:3
son of S.
name was Irijah, the son of   Jer 37:13
S.
and Jucal the son of S. and   Jer 38:1
Pashur

SHELEPH

Joktan begat Almodad, and   Ge 10:26;
S.   1Ch 1:20

SHELESH

and Imna, and S. and Amal   1Ch 7:35

SHELOMI

of Asher, Ahihud the son of   Nu 34:27
S.

SHELOMITH

his mother's name was S. the   Le 24:11
and Hananiah, and S. their   1Ch 3:19
sister
S. and Haziel, and Haran,   1Ch 23:9
three
Of the sons of Izhar; S.   1Ch 23:18
their chief
and Zichri his son, and S.   1Ch 26:25
his son
Which S. and his brethren   1Ch 26:26
were
thing, it was under the hand   1Ch 26:28
of S.
Abijah, and Attai, and Ziza,   2Ch 11:20
and S.
And of the son of S.; and son   Ezr 8:10

SHELOMOTH

S.: of the sons of S.; Jahath   1Ch 24:22

SHELTER

come to s. in (B)   Ru 2:12
embrace the rock for want of   Job 24:8
a s.
in the s. of his presence (B)   Ps 31:20
thou hast been a s. for me   Ps 61:3
the s. of your wing   Ps 61:4
(A)(R)(S)
in the s. of Most High (R)   Ps 91:1
Most High your s. (B)   Ps 91:9
a s. hiding place (A)   Isa 16:4
s. in shadow of Egypt (R)   Isa 30:3
his s. as a lion (A)   Jer 25:38
shall be their s.   Re 7:15
(A)(E)(P)(R)

SHELUMIEL

S. the son of Zurishaddai   Nu 1:6
shall be S. the son of   Nu 2:12
Zurishaddai
fifth day S. the son of   Nu 7:36
Zurishaddai
of S. the son of Zurishaddai   Nu 7:41
was S. the son of   Nu 10:19
Zurishaddai

SHEM

Noah begat S., Ham, and   Ge 5:32
Japheth
Noah begat three sons, S., Ham   Ge 6:10
same day entered Noah, and   Ge 7:13
S.

that went forth of the ark were S.	Ge 9:18
S. and Japheth took a garment	Ge 9:23
Blessed be the Lord God of S.	Ge 9:26
he shall dwell in the tents of S.	Ge 9:27
the sons of Noah; S., Ham	Ge 10:1
Unto S. also, the father of all the	Ge 10:21
children of S.; Elam, and Ashur	Ge 10:22
the sons of S. after their families	Ge 10:31
These are the generations of S.	Ge 11:10
S. was an hundred years old	Ge 11:10
S. lived after he begat Arphaxad	Ge 11:11
Noah, S., Ham, and Japheth	1Ch 1:4
The sons of S.; Elam, and Asshur	1Ch 1:17
S., Arphaxad, Shelah	1Ch 1:24

SHEMA

Amam, and S. and Moladah	Jos 15:26
and Tappuah, and Rekem, and S.	1Ch 2:43
And S. begat Raham, the father of	1Ch 2:44
Bela the son of Azaz, the son of S.	1Ch 5:8
Beriah also, and S. who were	1Ch 8:13
him stood Mattithiah, and S.	Ne 8:4

SHEMAAH

the sons of S. the Gebeathite	1Ch 12:3

SHEMAIAH

word of God came unto S.	1Ki 12:22
And the sons of Shechaniah; S.	1Ch 3:22
and the sons of S.; Hattush	1Ch 3:22
the son of Shimri, the son of S.	1Ch 4:37
S. his son, Gog his son, Shimei his	1Ch 5:4
S. the son of Hasshub, the son of	1Ch 9:14
And Obadiah the son of S. the son	1Ch 9:16
S. the chief, and his brethren two	1Ch 15:8
S. and Eliel, and Amminadab	1Ch 15:11
And S. the son of Nethaneel	1Ch 24:6
S. the firstborn, Jehozabad	1Ch 26:4
Also unto S. his son were sons	1Ch 26:6
The sons of S.; Othni, and Rephael	1Ch 26:7
the word of the Lord came to S.	2Ch 11:2
came S. the prophet to Rehoboam	2Ch 12:5
the word of the Lord came to S.	2Ch 12:7
they not written in the book of S.	2Ch 12:15
with them he sent Levites, even S.	2Ch 17:8
sons of Jeduthun; S. and Uzziel	2Ch 29:14
and S., Amariah, and Shecaniah	2Ch 31:15
also, and S. and Nethaneel, his	2Ch 35:9
are these, Eliphelet, Jeiel, and S.	Ezr 8:13
sent I for Eliezer, for Ariel, for S.	Ezr 10:16
and Elijah, and S. and Jehiel, and	Ezr 10:21
Ishijah, Malchiah, S., Shimeon	Ezr 10:31
After him repaired also S. the son	Ne 3:29
I came unto the house of S.	Ne 6:10
Bilgai, S.; these were the priests	Ne 10:8
the Levites: S. the son of Hashub	Ne 11:15
S. and Joiarib, Jedaiah	Ne 12:6
Shammua; of S., Jehonathan	Ne 13:18
Benjamin, and S. and Jeremiah	Ne 13:34
the son of S., the son of Mattaniah	Ne 13:35

And his brethren, S., and Azarael	Ne 13:36
And Maaseiah, and S. and Eleazar	Ne 13:42
the son of S. of Kirjath-jearim	Jer 26:20
Thus shalt thou also speak to	Jer 29:24
Thus saith the Lord concerning S.	Jer 29:31
that S. hath prophesied unto you	Jer 29:31
I will punish S. the Nehelamite	Jer 29:32
and Delaiah the son of S.	Jer 36:12

SHEMARIAH

Bealiah, and S. and Shephatiah	1Ch 12:5
Jeush, and S. and Zaham	2Ch 11:19
Benjamin, Malluch, and S.	Ezr 10:32
Azareel, and Shelemiah, S.	Ezr 10:41

SHEMEBER

S. king of Zeboiim, and the king	Ge 14:2

SHEMER

bought the hill Samaria of S.	1Ki 16:24
after the name of S., owner of the	1Ki 16:24

SHEMIDA

S. the family of the Shemidaites	Nu 26:32
Hepher, and for the children of S.	Jos 17:2

SHEMIDAH

And the sons of S. were, Ahian	1Ch 7:19

SHEMIDAITES

of Shemida, the family of the S.	Nu 26:32

SHEMINITH

with harps on the S. to excel	1Ch 15:21
Musician on Neginoth upon S.	Ps 6 title
To the chief Musician upon S.	Ps 12 title

SHEMIRAMOTH

and Jaaziel, and S. and Jehiel	1Ch 15:18
and Aziel, and S. and Jehiel, and	1Ch 15:20
to him Zachariah, Jeiel, and S.	1Ch 16:5
Asahel, and S. and Jehonathan	2Ch 17:8

SHEMUEL

Simeon, S. the son of Ammihud	Nu 34:20
the son of Joel, the son of S.	1Ch 6:33
S. heads of their father's house	1Ch 7:2

SHEN

and set it between Mizpeh and S.	1Sa 7:12

SHENAZAR

also, and Pedaiah, and S.	1Ch 3:18

SHENIR

and the Amorites call it S.	De 3:9
from the top of S. and Hermon	Ca 4:8

SHEOL

sheol (S)	Ge 37:35;

42:38;   44:29,   31;   Nu 16:30,   33;
De 32:22;   1Sa 2:6;   2Sa 22:6;   1Ki 2:6,   9;
Job 7:9;   11:8;   14:13;   17:13,   16;   21:13;
24:19;   26:6;   Ps 6:5;   9:17;   16:10;   18:5;
30:3;   31:17;   49:14,   15;   55:15;   86:13;
88:3;   89:48;   116:3;   139:8;   141:7;

Pr 1:12;   5:5;   7:27;   9:18;   15:11,   24;
23:14;   27:20;   30:16;   Ec 9:10;   Ca 8:6;
Isa 5:14;   14:9,   11,   15;   28:15,   18;
38:10,   18;   57:9;   Eze 31:15,   16,   17;   32:21,
27;   Ho 13:14;   Am 9:2;   Jon 2:2;   Hab 2:5

go down alive into S. (A)(E)(R)	Nu 16:30
in the lowest S. (A)(E)(R)	De 32:22
the cords of S. were (A)(E)(R)	2Sa 22:6
deeper than S. (A)(B)(E)(R)	Job 11:8
S. and Abaddon (A)(B)(E)(R)	Job 15:11; 27:20
if I look to S. (A)(E)(R)	Job 17:13
go down into S. (A)(B)(E)(R)	Job 17:16
S. naked before God (A)(B)(E)(R)	Job 26:6
wicked turned into S. (A)(B)(E)(R)	Ps 9:17
the cords of S. (B)(E)(R)	Ps 18:5
go down alive into S. (A)(B)(E)(R)	Ps 55:15
terrors of S. had hold (A)(E)(R)	Ps 116:3
if I make my bed in S. (A)(E)(R)	Ps 139:8
her steps take hold of S. (A)(E)(R)	Pr 5:5
house the way to S. (A)(B)(E)(R)	Pr 7:27
in the depths of S. (A)(B)(E)(R)	Pr 9:18
S. before the Lord (A)(E)(R)	Pr 15:11
deliver his life from S. (A)(B)(E)(R)	Pr 23:14
S. never satisfied (A)(B)(E)(R)	Pr 27:20
S. has enlarged herself (A)(E)(R)	Isa 5:14
S. is stirred up (A)(E)(R)	Isa 14:9
brought down to S. (A)(B)(E)(R)	Isa 14:15
agreement with S. (A)(B)(E)(R)	Isa 28:15; 28:18
debased to S. (A)(B)(E)(R)	Isa 57:9
cast down to S. (A)(B)(E)(R)	Eze 31:16
shall go down to S. (A)(E)(R)	Eze 31:17
out of the midst of S. (A)(E)(R)	Eze 32:21
are gone down to S. (A)(B)(E)(R)	Eze 32:27
save them from S. (A)	Ho 13:14
dig into S. (A)(B)(E)(R)	Am 9:2
innermost part of S. (B)	Jon 1:17
out of the belly of S. (A)(B)(E)(R)	Jon 2:2
appetite large as S. (A)(E)(R)	Jon 2:5

SHEPHAM

border from Hazar-enan to S.	Nu 34:10
shall go down from S. to Riblah	Nu 34:11

SHEPHATIAH

and the fifth, S. the son of Abital	2Sa 3:4
The fifth, S. of Abital: the sixth	1Ch 3:3
and Meshullam the son of S.	1Ch 9:8
Shemariah, and S. the Haruphite	1Ch 12:5
Simeonites, S. the son of Maachah	1Ch 27:16
and Azariah, and Michael, and S.	2Ch 21:2
The children of S. three hundred	Ezr 2:4
The children of S. the children of	Ezr 2:57
And of the sons of S.; Zebadiah the	Ezr 8:8
The children of S., three hundred	Ne 7:9
The children of S., the children	Ne 7:59
the son of S. the son of Mahalaleel	Ne 11:4
Then S. the son of Mattan	Jer 38:1

SHEPHELAH

Shephelah (S)	De 9:4;

11:3 ;   Jos 9:1;   10:40;   11:2,   16;   12:8;

15:33; J'g 1:9; 1Ki 10:27; 1Ch 27:28;
2Ch 1:15; 9:27; 26:10; 28:18; Jer 32:44;
33:13; Ob 19; Zec 7:7
the S., foothills (B)(R) 1Ki 10:27

SHEPHERD

every s. is an abomination Ge 46:34
(from thence is the s. the Ge 49:24
stone of
be not as sheep which have Nu 27:17
no s.
hills, as sheep that have not 1Ki 22:17
a s.
as sheep that have no s. 2Ch 18:16
The Lord is my s.; I shall not Ps 23:1
want
Give ear, O S. of Israel thou Ps 80:1
that
which are given from one s. Ec 12:11
He shall feed his flock like a Isa 40:11
s.
That saith of Cyrus, He is my Isa 44:28
of the sea with the s. of his Isa 63:11
flock
escape being a s. (A)(E)(S) Jer 17:16
and keep him, as a s. doth Jer 31:10
his flock
as a s. putteth on his Jer 43:12
garment
and who is that s. that will Jer 49:19;
stand 50:44
in pieces, the s. and his Jer 51:23
flock
scattered, because there is no Eze 34:5
s.
because there was no s. Eze 34:8
neither did
As a s. seeketh out his flock Eze 34:12
in the
And I will set up one s. over Eze 34:23
them
feed them, and he shall Eze 34:23
be their s.
and they all shall have one s.: Eze 37:24
they
As the s. taketh out of the Am 3:12
mouth of
troubled, because there was Zec 10:2
no s.
yet the instruments of a Zec 11:15
foolish s.
lo, I will raise up a S. in the Zec 11:16
land
Woe to the idol s. Zec 11:17
that leaveth the
Awake, O sword, against my Zec 13:7
s.
smite, the s. and the sheep Zec 13:7
shall be
abroad, as sheep having no s. M't 9:36
as a s. divideth his sheep M't 25:32
from the
I will smite the s. and the M't 26:31
sheep of
they were as sheep not M'k 6:34
having a s.
I will smite the s. and the M'k 14:27
sheep
in by the door is the s. of the Joh 10:2
sheep
I am the good s. the good s. Joh 10:11
giveth
that is an hireling, and not Joh 10:12
the s.
I am the good s. and know Joh 10:14
my
there shall be one fold, and Joh 10:16
one s.
Jesus, that great s. of the Heb 13:20
sheep
returned unto the S. and 1Pe 2:25
Bishop of
And when the chief S. shall 1Pe 5:4
appear

SHEPHERDED

by a prophet he was s. (B) Ho 12:13

SHEPHERDS

the men are s. for their trade Ge 46:32
Thy servants are s. both we Ge 47:3
And the s. came and drove Ex 2:17
them
us out of the hand of the Ex 2:19
s. and
now thy s. which were with 1Sa 25:7
us, we

neither shall the s. make Isa 13:20
their fold
when a multitude of s. is Isa 31:4
called forth
they are s. that cannot Isa 56:11
understand
s. have transgressed Jer 2:8;
(A)(B)(E)(R) 3:15; 10:21; 12:10;
  22:22; 23:1-2
I will give you s. (S) Jer 3:15
The s. with their flocks shall Jer 6:3
come
the s. have become brutish Jer 10:21
(S)
Many s. have destroyed my Jer 12:10
vineyard (S)
wind shall eat up all my s. Jer 22:22
(S)
the s. that destroy and scatter Jer 23:1
(S)
against the s. that feed my Jer 23:2
people (S)
And I will set up s. over them Jer 23:4
which
Howl, ye s. and cry; and Jer 25:34
wallow
And the s. shall have no way Jer 25:35
to flee
A voice of the cry of the s. Jer 25:36
an habitation of s. causing Jer 33:12
their
their s. have caused them to go Jer 50:6
prophesy against the s. of Eze 34:2
Israel
saith the Lord God unto the Eze 34:2
s.; Woe
Woe be to the s. of Israel that Eze 34:2
should not the s. feed the Eze 34:2
flocks
ye s. hear the word of the Eze 34:7
Lord
did my s. search for my flock Eze 34:8
but the s. fed themselves, and Eze 34:8
fed
O ye s. hear the word of the Eze 34:9
Lord
Behold, I am against the s.: Eze 34:10
and I
neither shall the s. feed Eze 34:10
themselves
habitations of the s. shall Am 1:2
mourn
shall we raise against him Mic 5:5
seven s.
Thy s. slumber, O king of Na 3:18
Assyria
be dwellings and cottages for Zep 2:6
s. and
anger was kindled against the Zec 10:3
s.
is a voice of the howling of Zec 11:3
the s.
and their own s. pity them Zec 11:5
not
Three s. also I cut off in one Zec 11:8
month
country s. abiding in the field Lu 2:8
the s. said one to another, Let Lu 2:15
us
which were told them by the s. Lu 2:18
And the s. returned, glorifying Lu 2:20
as s. of the church (N)(P) Ac 20:28

SHEPHERD'S

put them in a s. bag which 1Sa 17:40
he had
the s. bag (B)(E)(R) 1Sa 17:40
is removed from me as a s. Isa 38:12
tent

SHEPHERDS'

feed thy kids beside the s. tents Ca 1:8

SHEPHI

and Ebal, S. and Onam 1Ch 1:40

SHEPHO

and Ebal, S. and Onam Ge 36:23

SHEPHUPHAN

And Gera, and S. and Huram 1Ch 8:5

SHERAH

his daughter was S. who built 1Ch 7:24

SHERD

be found in the bursting of it Isa 30:14
a s.

SHERDS

thou shalt break the s. Eze 23:34
thereof

SHEREBIAH

and S. with his sons and his Ezr 8:18
S. Hashabiah, and ten of Ezr 8:24
their
and Bani, and S., Jamin, Akkub Ne 8:7
Bunni, S., Bani, and Chenani Ne 9:4
Bani, Hashabniah, S., Hodijah Ne 9:5
Zaccur, S., Shebaniah Ne 10:12
Binnui, Kadmiel, S., Judah Ne 12:8
Hashabiah, S., and Jeshua the Ne 12:24
son

SHERESH

the name of his brother was 1Ch 7:16
S.

SHEREZER

S. and Regem-melech, and Zec 7:2
their

SHERIFFS

the s. and all the rulers of the Da 3:2

SHESHACH

king of S. shall drink Jer 25:26
after them
How is S. taken! and how is Jer 51:41

SHESHAI

S. and Talmai, the children Nu 13:22
sons of Anak, S. and Jos 15:14
Ahiman, and
and they slew S. and Ahiman J'g 1:10

SHESHAN

And the sons of Ishi; S. 1Ch 2:31
And the children of S.; Ahlai 1Ch 2:31
S. had no sons, but daughters 1Ch 2:34
And S. had a servant, an 1Ch 2:34
Egyptian
S. gave his daughter to Jarha 1Ch 2:35
his

SHESHBAZZAR

and numbered them unto S. Ezr 1:8
All these did S. bring up with Ezr 1:11
them
unto one, whose name was Ezr 5:14
S. whom
Then came the same S. and Ezr 5:16
laid

SHETH

and destroy all the children of Nu 24:17
S.
Adam, S., Enosh 1Ch 1:1

SHETHAR

Carshena, S., Admatha, Es 1:14
Tarshish

SHETHAR-BOZNAI

and S. and their companions Ezr 5:3
and S. and his companions the Ezr 5:6
S., and your companions the Ezr 6:6
S. their companions, Ezr 6:13
according

SHEVA

And S. with scribe: and 2Sa 20:25
Zadok and
S. the father of Machbenah 1Ch 2:49

SHEW

Pharaoh shall speak, s. miracle Ex 7:9
I raised thee up for to s. in Ex 9:16
my power

that I might *s.* my signs before *Ex 10:1* him
and thou shalt *s.* thy son in *Ex 13:8* that day
see salvation Lord will *s.* to *Ex 14:13* you to-day
shalt *s.* way they must walk *Ex 18:20; De 1:33*
made it according to all that I *Ex 25:9 s.* thee
s. me now thy way *Ex 33:13*
s. me thy glory *Ex 33:18*
I stood to *s.* you the word of the *De 5:5* Lord
make no covenant, nor *s.* *De 7:2* mercy unto them
that the Lord may *s.* thee *De 13:17* mercy
shall *s.* thee sentence of *De 17:9* judgment
thou shalt do as they shall *s. De 17:10;* thee *17:11*
not regard old, nor *s.* favour *De 28:50* to young
ask thy father, and he will *s. De 32:7* thee
Lord sware he would not *s.* the *Jos 5:6* land
spies said, *S.* us entrance into *J'g 1:24* the city, and we will *s.* thee mercy
then *s.* me a sign that thou *J'g 6:17* talkest with me
Samuel feared to *s.* Eli the *1Sa 3:15* vision
s. the manner of the king *1Sa 8:9* that shall reign
man of God peradventure can *s. 1Sa 9:6* us our way
stand, that I may *s.* thee the *1Sa 9:27* word of God
I will come and *s.* thee *1Sa 10:8* what thou shalt do
come up to us, and we will *s. 1Sa 14:12* you a thing
my father will do nothing, he *1Sa 20:2* will *s.* it me
if I then send not unto thee, *1Sa 20:12* and *s.* it thee
they knew when he fled, and *1Sa 22:17* did not *s.* it
ask thy young men, and they *1Sa 25:8* will *s.* thee
he will *s.* me, both it and his *2Sa 15:25* habitation
if he will *s.* himself a worthy *1Ki 1:52* man
be thou strong therefore, and *1Ki 2:2 s.* thyself a man
came to Elijah, go *s.* thyself *1Ki 18:1;* to Ahab *18:2*
will ye not *s.* me which of us *2Ki 6:11* is for king
to *s.* himself strong in behalf *2Ch 16:9* of them
could not *s.* fathers' house, *Ezr 2:59;* whether they were of Israel *Ne 7:61*
the pillar of fire to *s.* them *Ne 9:19* light
to *s.* the people and princes *Es 1:11* her beauty
Mordecai charged her not to *s. Es 2:10* her kindred
gave him a copy of the writing *Es 4:8* to *s.* Esther
s. me wherefore thou *Job 10:2* contendest with me
he would *s.* thee the secrets *Job 11:6* of wisdom
I was afraid, durst not *s.* you *Job 32:6* my opinion
if a messenger to *s.* to man *Job 33:23* his uprightness
many will say, Who will *s.* us *Ps 4:6* any good
that I may *s.* forth all thy praise *Ps 9:14* in gates
s. me the path of life, in thy *Ps 16:11* presence
s. me thy ways, O Lord, teach *Ps 25:4* me
the Lord will *s.* them his *Ps 25:14* covenant
every man walketh in a vain *s. Ps 39:6* and my mouth shall *s.* forth thy praise *Ps 51:15*
my mouth *s.* forth thy *Ps 71:15* righteousness
we thy people will *s.* forth *Ps 79:13* thy praise

s. us mercy, grant us thy *Ps 85:7* salvation
s. me a token of good, that *Ps 86:17* they may see it
wilt thou *s.* wonders to the *Ps 88:10* dead
to *s.* that Lord is upright, he *Ps 92:15* is my rock
O God whom vengeance *Ps 94:1* belongeth *s.* thyself
who can *s.* forth all his *Ps 106:2* praise
a man must *s.* himself *Pr 18:24* friendly
the *s.* of their countenance *Isa 3:9* doth witness
he that formed them will *s. Isa 27:11* no favour
the Lord shall *s.* lighting *Isa 30:30* down of his arm
bring them forth and *s.* us *Isa 41:22* what shall happen let them *s.* former things
s. the things that are to come *Isa 41:23* hereafter
who among them can *s.* us *Isa 43:9* former things
people I formed shall *s.* forth *Isa 43:21* my praise
things that are coming, let *Isa 44:7* them *s.* to them
remember this, and *s.* *Isa 46:8* yourselves men
say to them in darkness, *S. Isa 49:9* yourselves
s. my people their *Isa 58:1* transgression and sins
they shall *s.* forth the praises *Isa 60:6* of the Lord
thou shalt *s.* them all these *Jer 16:10* words
into a land, where I will not *Jer 16:13 s.* you favour
thy God may *s.* us the way we *Jer 42:3* may walk
to *s.* the king of Babylon his *Jer 51:31* city is taken
thou shalt *s.* her all her *Eze 22:2* abominations
for with their mouth they *s. Eze 33:31* much love
wilt thou not *s.* us what *Eze 37:18* thou meanest
set thine heart upon all that I *Eze 40:4* shall *s.* thee
son of man, *s.* to house of *Eze 43:10* Israel
s. them the form of the *Eze 43:11* house and fashion
the sorcerers for to *s.* king his *Da 2:2* dreams
and we will *s.* the *Da 2:4;* interpretation *2:7*
if ye *s.* the dream and *Da 2:6* interpretaion
not a man that can *s.* the *Da 2:10* king's matter
he would *s.* the king the *Da 2:16* interpretation
secret cannot wise men *s.* to *Da 2:27* the king
thought good to *s.* signs and *Da 4:2* wonders
whosoever shall *s.* me *Da 5:7* the interpretation
command came, and I am *Da 9:23* come to *s.* thee
why dost thou *s.* me iniquity *Hab 1:3*
go thy way, *s.* thyself to the *M't 8:4* priest *M'k 1:44; Lu 5:14; 17:14*
go and *s.* John these things ye *M't 11:4* do hear
he shall *s.* judgment to the *M't 12:18* Gentiles
he is risen, therefore mighty *M't 14:2;* works do *s.* forth themselves *M'k 6:14* in him
the Pharisees desired he *M't 16:1* would *s.* a sign
s. me the tribute money *M't 22:19; Lu 20:24*
came to *s.* him the buildings *M't 24:1* of the temple
arise false Christs, and shall *M't 24:24; s.* great signs and wonders *M'k 13:22*
s. you a large upper room *M'k 14:15;* furnished, there make ready *Lu 22:12*
I am sent to *s.* thee these glad *Lu 1:19* tidings

s. how great things God hath *Lu 8:39* done to thee
and for a *s.* make long *Lu 20:47* prayers
he will *s.* him greater works *Joh 5:20* than these
if thou do these things *s.* *Joh 7:4* thyself to world
if any knew where he was *Joh 11:57* they should *s.* it
s. us the Father and it *Joh 14:8;* sufficeth us *14:9*
and he will *s.* you things to *Joh 16:13* come
he shall receive of mine, *Joh 16:14;* and *s.* it to you *16:15*
but I shall *s.* you plainly of *Joh 16:25* the Father
Lord *s.* whether of these thou *Ac 1:24* hast chosen
and come into the land which I *Ac 7:3* shall *s.* thee
he said, Go *s.* these things to *Ac 12:17* James
men who *s.* to us the way of *Ac 16:17* salvation
Felix willing to *s.* the Jews a *Ac 24:27* pleasure
that he should *s.* light to the *Ac 26:23* people
who *s.* the work of the law *Ro 2:15* written
I have raised thee, that I *Ro 9:17* might *s.* my power
what if God, willing to *s.* his *Ro 9:22* wrath, endured
ye do *s.* the Lord's death *1Co 11:26* till he come
yet *s.* I to you a more *1Co 12:31* excellent way
I *s.* you mystery, we shall *1Co 15:51* not all sleep
s. ye to them the proof of *2Co 8:24* your love
as many as desire to make a *Ga 6:12* fair *s.* in flesh
that he might *s.* the exceeding *Eph 2:7* riches
spoiled powers, made *s.* of *Col 2:15* them openly
things have *s.* of wisdom in *Col 2:23* will worship
for they themselves *s.* of us *1Th 1:9* what manner
that Christ might *s.* all *1Ti 1:16* long-suffering
let them learn first to *s.* piety *1Ti 5:4* at home
which in his times he shall *s. 1Ti 6:15* who is the
study to *s.* thyself approved *2Ti 2:15* to God
that every one of you *s.* the *Heb 6:11* same diligence
God willing to *s.* to the heirs *Heb 6:17* of promise
s. me thy faith without thy *Jas 2:18* works
let him *s.* his works out of *Jas 3:13* good conversation
ye should *s.* forth the praises *1Pe 2:9* of him
and *s.* unto you that eternal *1Joh 1:2* life
he sent his angel to *s.* his *Re 1:1;* servants *22:6*

I WILL SHEW

get thee unto a land that *I will Ge 12:1 s.* thee
I will s. mercy on whom I *Ex 33:19 will s.* mercy
I will s. thee man whom thou *J'g 4:22* seekest
I will s. thee what thou shalt *1Sa 16:3* do
to do thee evil, then *I will s. 1Sa 20:13* it thee
I will surely *s.* myself to *1Ki 18:15* Ahab
I will s. you what Syrians *2Ki 7:12* have done
I will s. thee that which I *Job 15:17* have seen
I also *will s.* mine opinion *Job 32:10; 32:17; 36:2*
I will s. forth thy marvelous *Ps 9:1* works
I will s. the salvation of God *Ps 50:23; 91:16*

I will *s.* them the back, and   Jer 18:17
not face
I will *s.* thee great and mighty   Jer 33:3
things
I will *s.* mercies unto you   Jer 42:12
I will *s.* the king   Da 2:24
the interpretation
I will *s.* thee what is noted   Da 10:21
in script
and now I will *s.* thee the   Da 11:2
truth
I will *s.* wonders in heaven   Joe 2:30;
   Ac 2:19
I will *s.* to him marvelous   Mic 7:15
things
I will *s.* the nations thy   Na 3:5
nakedness
angel said, I will *s.* thee what   Zec 1:9
these be
I will *s.* you to whom he is   Lu 6:47
like
I will *s.* him how great things   Ac 9:16
he must suffer
I will *s.* thee my faith by my   Jas 2:18
works
I will *s.* thee things which must   Re 4:1
be
I will *s.* thee the judgment of   Re 17:1
the whore
I will *s.* thee the bride the   Re 21:9
Lamb's wife

SHEWBREAD

shalt set upon the table *s.*   Ex 25:30
and all his vessels, and the *s.*   Ex 35:13
the vessels thereof, and the *s.*   Ex 39:36
upon the table of *s.* they shall   Nu 4:7
spread
was no bread there but the *s.*   1Sa 21:6
of gold, whereupon the *s.* was   1Ki 7:48
were over the *s.* to prepare it   1Ch 9:32
Both for the *s.* and for the   1Ch 23:29
fine
he gave gold for the tables   1Ch 28:16
of *s.*
incense, and for the continual   2Ch 2:4
s.
tables whereon the *s.* was set   2Ch 4:19
the *s.* also set they in order   2Ch 13:11
and the *s.* table, with all the   2Ch 29:18
vessels
For the *s.* and the   Ne 10:33
continual
eat the *s.* which was not   M't 12:4
lawful
eat the *s.* which is not lawful   M'k 2:26
and did take and eat the *s.* and   Lu 6:4
and the table, and the *s.*   Heb 9:2

SHEWED

a white spot, and it be *s.* to   Le 13:19;
priest   13:49
and *s.* them the fruit of the   Nu 13:26
land
which Moses *s.* in the sight of   De 34:12
Israel
and when he *s.* them the   J'g 1:25
entrance
s. Sisera, that Barak was gone   J'g 4:12
up to Tabor
the woman made haste, and   J'g 13:10
s. her husband
come up, for he hath *s.* me all   J'g 16:18
his heart
it hath been *s.* me all that   Ru 2:11
thou hast done
came and *s.* it to the men of   1Sa 11:9
Jabesh
Jonathan *s.* him all those   1Sa 19:7
things
Abiathar *s.* David that Saul   1Sa 22:21
had slain priests
Saul said to David, Thou   1Sa 24:18
hast *s.* this day how thou hast
dealt well with me
messenger *s.* David all Joab   2Sa 11:22
had sent
thou hast not *s.* it to thy   1Ki 1:27
servant
Omri, and his might that he   1Ki 16:27;
s.   22:45
where fell it? he *s.* him the   2Ki 6:6
place
took an oath, and *s.* them the   2Ki 11:4
king's son
Hezekiah hearkened to   2Ki 20:13;
them, and *s.* them all the house   Isa 39:2
of his precious things

there is nothing I have not   2Ki 20:15;
s. them   Isa 39:4
when he *s.* riches of his glorious   Es 1:4
kingdom
Esther had not *s.* her people   Es 2:10;
nor kindred   2:20
for they had *s.* him the people   Es 3:6
of Mordecai
to afflicted pity should be *s.*   Job 6:14
from his friend
until I have *s.* thy strength to   Ps 71:18
this generation
they *s.* his signs among   Ps 105:27;
them   Ac 7:36
poured my complaint, I *s.*   Ps 142:2
before him my
his wickedness shall be *s.*   Pr 26:26
before congregation
labour, wherein I have *s.*   Ec 2:19
myself wise
who *s.* to him the way of   Isa 40:14
understanding
they *s.* no difference between   Eze 22:26
clean
and *s.* to chief priests all   M't 28:11
things done
devil *s.* him all kingdoms of the   Lu 4:5
world
the disciples of John *s.* him   Lu 7:18
these things
and he said, He that *s.* mercy   Lu 10:37
on him
that servant came and *s.* his   Lu 14:21
lord these things
that the dead are raised,   Lu 20:37
Moses *s.* at bush
many good works have I *s.*   Joh 10:32
you
he *s.* unto them his hands   Joh 20:20;
and his side
Jesus *s.* himself again to   Joh 21:1;
disciples   21:14; Ac 1:3
on whom this miracle of   Ac 4:22
healing was *s.*
Moses *s.* himself to them as   Ac 7:26
they strove
after he had *s.* wonders and   Ac 7:36
signs
which *s.* before of the coming   Ac 7:52
of the just One
he *s.* how he had seen an   Ac 11:13
angel in his house
many that believed confessed,   Ac 19:18
s. their deeds
but have *s.* and have taught   Ac 20:20
you publicly
I have *s.* you all things, how   Ac 20:35
so labouring
tell no man thou hast *s.* these   Ac 23:22
things to me
but first Paul *s.* to them of   Ac 26:20
Damascus
the barbarous people *s.* no   Ac 28:2
little kindness
none of brethren *s.* or spake   Ac 28:21
any harm of thee
eat not, for his sake that *s.*   1Co 10:28
it
love which we have *s.* toward   Heb 6:10
his name
shall have judgment that *s.* no   Jas 2:13
mercy
angel *s.* me the great city   Re 21:10
Jerusalem
he *s.* me a pure river of water   Re 22:1
of life
I fell down to worship the   Re 22:8
angel who *s.* me

GOD, LORD SHEWED
(expressed or implied)

thy mercy *s.* to me in saving   Ge 19:19
my life
that thou hast *s.* kindness to   Ge 24:14
my master
not worthy of the least of the   Ge 32:10
mercies *s.*
the Lord *s.* Joseph mercy,   Ge 39:21
and gave favour
God *s.* Pharaoh what he is   Ge 41:25
about to do
forasmuch as God hath *s.*   Ge 41:39
thee all this
and lo, God hath *s.* me also   Ge 48:11
thy seed
he cried, and the Lord *s.* him   Ex 15:25
a tree
look thou make them after   Ex 25:40;
to the pattern the Lord had *s.*   Nu 8:4;
   27:8; Heb 8:5

that the mind of the Lord   Le 24:12
might be *s.*
to the pattern the Lord had *s.*   Nu 8:4
Moses
all signs I have *s.* among   Nu 14:11;
them   De 6:22
and upon earth he *s.* thee his   De 4:36
great fire
behold, the Lord our God *s.*   De 5:24
us his glory
the Lord *s.* him all the land of   De 34:1
Gilead
nor would he have *s.* all these   J'g 13:23
things
Solomon said, Thou hast *s.* to   1Ki 3:6;
thy servant David my   2Ch 1:8
father great mercy
Lord hath *s.* me, he shall   2Ki 8:10
surely die
the Lord hath *s.* me that thou   2Ki 8:13
shalt be king
for goodness the Lord had *s.*   2Ch 7:10
David
grace hath been *s.* from Lord   Ezr 9:8
our God
he hath *s.* me his marvellous   Ps 31:21
kindness
thou hast *s.* thy people hard   Ps 60:3
things
thou hast *s.* me great and   Ps 71:20
sore troubles
they forgat his wonders he   Ps 78:11
had *s.* them
his righteousness hath *s.* in   Ps 98:2
sight of heathen
he *s.* his people the power of   Ps 111:6
his works
God is the Lord who hath *s.*   Ps 118:27
us light
let favour be *s.* to wicked,   Isa 26:10
yet not learn
I have *s.* when there was no   Isa 43:12
strange god
I *s.* them; I did them   Isa 48:3
suddenly, and it came to pass
before it came to pass I *s.* it   Isa 48:5
thee
the Lord *s.* me two baskets of   Jer 24:1
figs
this is the word that the Lord   Jer 38:21
hath *s.* me
all things that the Lord hath   Eze 11:25
s. me
gave statutes and *s.* them my   Eze 20:11
judgments
thus had the Lord *s.* me   Am 7:1;
   7:4, 7; 8:1
he hath *s.* thee, O man, what   Mic 6:8
is good
and the Lord *s.* me four   Zec 1:20
carpenters
he *s.* me Joshua standing   Zec 3:1
before angel of Lord
he hath *s.* strength with his   Lu 1:51
arm
heard how Lord had *s.* great   Lu 1:58
mercy on her
but those things which God   Ac 3:18
before had *s.*
God *s.* I should not call any   Ac 10:28
man common
God raised him the third day   Ac 10:40
and *s.* him
is manifest, for God hath *s.* it   Ro 1:19
to them
even as our Lord Jesus hath   2Pe 1:14
s. me

SHEWEDST

And *s.* signs and wonders   Ne 9:10
upon
it; then thou *s.* me their   Jer 11:18
doings

SHEWEST

s. mercy unto thy servants,   2Ch 6:14
that walk
thou *s.* thyself marvellous   Job 10:16
upon me
Thou *s.* lovingkindness unto   Jer 32:18
What sign *s.* thou unto us,   Joh 2:18
seeing
What sign *s.* thou then, that   Joh 6:30
we

SHEWETH

about to do he *s.* unto   Ge 41:28
Pharaoh

and whatsoever he *s.* me I   Nu 23:3
will tell
is none that *s.* me that my   1Sa 22:8
son
or *s.* unto me that my son   1Sa 22:8
hath
and *s.* mercy to his   2Sa 22:51
anointed, unto
Then he *s.* them their work   Job 36:9
The noise thereof *s.*   Job 36:33
concerning it
and *s.* mercy to his anointed   Ps 18:50
the firmament *s.* his   Ps 19:1
handywork
night unto night *s.* knowledge   Ps 19:2
righteous *s.* mercy, and giveth   Ps 37:21
A good man *s.* favour, and   Ps 112:5
lendeth
He *s.* his word unto Jacob   Ps 147:19
He that speaketh truth *s.*   Pr 12:17
forth
tender grass *s.* itself and   Pr 27:25
herbs
there is none that *s.*, yea,   Isa 41:26
there is
and *s.* him all the kingdoms of   M't 4:8
the world
s. him all things that himself   Joh 5:20
doeth
runneth, but of God that *s.*   Ro 9:16
mercy
he that *s.* mercy, with   Ro 12:8
cheerfulness

SHEWING

s. mercy unto thousands of   Ex 20:6;
them   De 5:10
s. to the generation to come   Ps 78:4
s. himself through the lattice   Ca 2:9
iniquities by *s.* mercy to the   Da 4:27
poor
s. of hard sentences, and   Da 5:12
dissolving
till the day of his *s.* unto Israel   Lu 1:80
preaching and *s.* the glad   Lu 8:1
tidings
s. the coats and garments   Ac 9:39
which
s. by the scriptures that Jesus   Ac 18:28
was Christ
of God, *s.* himself that he is   2Th 2:4
God
s. thyself a pattern of good   Tit 2:7
works
in 'doctrine *s.* uncorruptness,   Tit 2:7
gravity
but *s.* all good fidelity; that   Tit 2:10
gentle, *s.* all meekness unto all   Tit 3:2
men

SHIBBOLETH

said they unto him, Say now *S.*   J'g 1:6

SHIBMAH

names being changed, and *S.*   Nu 32:38

SHICRON

and the border was drawn to   Jos 15:11
S.

SHIELD

Fear not, Abram: I am thy   Ge 15:1
s. and
by the Lord, the *s.* of thy help   De 33:29
was there a *s.* or spear seen   J'g 5:8
among
one bearing a *s.* went before   1Sa 17:7
him
man that bare the *s.* went   1Sa 17:41
before
and with a spear, and with a   1Sa 17:45
s.
s. of the mighty is vilely cast   2Sa 1:21
away
the *s.* of Saul, as though he   2Sa 1:21
had not
he is my *s.* and the horn   2Sa 22:3
of my
a *s.* to all (B)(E)(R)   2Sa 22:31;
   1Ch 5:18; Ps 18:2; 35:2; 91:4; Pr 2:7
shield (S)   2Sa 22:31;
   1Ch 5:18; Ps 18:2, 30; Pr 2:7
given me the *s.* of thy   2Sa 22:36
salvation

gold went into each *s.*   1Ki 10:16
(A)(R)
three pound of gold went to   1Ki 10:17
one *s.*
nor come before it with *s.*   2Ki 19:32
nor cast
that could handle *s.* and   1Ch 12:8
buckler
The children of Judah that   1Ch 12:24
bare *s.*
with *s.* and spear thirty and   1Ch 12:34
seven
gold to each *s.* (A)(B)(R)   2Ch 9:15
shekels of gold went to one *s.*   2Ch 9:16
him armed men with bow   2Ch 17:17
and *s.*
that could handle spear and *s.*   2Ch 25:5
a thick ornamental *s.*   Job 15:26
(A)(B)(R)(S)
the glittering spear and the   Job 39:23
s.
But thou, O Lord, art a *s.* for   Ps 3:3
me
thou compass him as with a *s.*   Ps 5:12
given me the *s.* of thy   Ps 18:35
salvation
The Lord is my strength and   Ps 28:7
my *s.*
the Lord: he is our help and   Ps 33:20
our *s.*
Take hold of *s.* and buckler   Ps 35:2
bring them down, O Lord our   Ps 59:11
s.
he the arrows of the bow, the   Ps 76:3
s.
Behold, O God our *s.* and look   Ps 84:9
For the Lord God is a sun   Ps 84:11
and *s.*
his truth shall be thy *s.* and   Ps 91:4
he is their help and   Ps 115:9;
their *s.*   115:10, 11
art my hiding place and my *s.*   Ps 119:114
my *s.* and he in whom I trust   Ps 144:2
he is a *s.* unto them that put   Pr 30:5
their trust
arise, ye princes, and anoint   Isa 21:5
the *s.*
and Kir uncovered the *s.*   Isa 22:6
Order ye the buckler and *s.*   Jer 46:3
the Libyans, that handle the *s.*   Jer 46:9
buckler and *s.* and helmet   Eze 23:24
round
hanged the *s.* and helmet in   Eze 27:10
thee
all of them with *s.* and   Eze 38:5
helmet
s. of his mighty men is made   Na 2:3
red
taking the *s.* of faith,   Eph 6:16
wherewith

SHIELDS

David took the *s.* of gold that   2Sa 8:7
200 *s.* of gold (A)(R)   1Ki 10:16
three hundred *s.* of beaten   1Ki 10:17
gold
took away all the *s.* of gold   1Ki 14:26
which
made in their stead brazen *s.*   1Ki 14:27
give king David's spears and   2Ki 11:10
s.
David took the *s.* of gold that   1Ch 18:7
were
200 *s.* of bucklers   2Ch 9:15
(A)(B)(E)(R)
three hundred *s.* made of   2Ch 9:16
beaten
every several city he puts *s.*   2Ch 11:12
he carried away also the *s.* of   2Ch 12:9
gold
king Rehoboam made *s.* of   2Ch 12:10
brass
that bare *s.* and drew bows,   2Ch 14:8
two
spears, and bucklers, and *s.*   2Ch 23:9
them throughout all the host   2Ch 26:14
s.
and darts and *s.* in   2Ch 32:5
abundance
and for *s.* and for all manner   2Ch 32:27
the spears, the *s.* and the bows   Ne 4:16
the *s.* of the earth belong unto   Ps 47:9
God
bucklers, all *s.* of mighty men   Ca 4:4
a thousand *s.* (B)   Ca 4:4
nor come before it with *s.*   Isa 37:33

bright the arrows; gather the   Jer 51:11
s.
hanged their *s.* upon thy   Eze 27:11
walls
company with bucklers and *s.*   Eze 38:4
both the *s.* and the bucklers   Eze 39:9
all bearing *s.* (B)   2Co 14:8

SHIGGAION

S. of David, which he sang   Ps 7 title
unto

SHIGIONOTH

Habakkuk the prophet upon *S.*   Hab 3:1

SHIHON

And Haphraim, and *S.* and   Jos 19:9

SHIHOR

from *S.* of Egypt even unto   1Ch 13:5

SHIHOR-LIBNATH

to Carmel westward, and to   Jos 19:26
S.

SHILHI

was Azubah the daughter   1Ki 22:42;
of *S.*   2Ch 20:31

SHILHIM

Lebaoth, and *S.* and Ain   Jos 15:32

SHILLEM

and Guni, and Jezer, and *S.*   Ge 46:24
of *S.* the family of the   Nu 26:49
Shillemites

SHILLEMITES

of Shillem, the family of the   Nu 26:49
S.

SHILLING

agreed on a *S.* a day (E)   M't 20:2;
   20:9-10, 13
a measure of wheat for a *S.*   Re 6:6
(E)

SHILLINGS

a hundred *S.* (E)   M't 18:28
two hundred *S.* (E)   M'k 6:37; Joh 6:7

SHILOAH

people refuseth the waters of *S.*   Isa 8:6

SHILOH

between his feet, until *S.*   Ge 49:10
come
of Israel assembled together at   Jos 18:1
S.
lots for you before the Lord   Jos 18:8
in *S.*
again to Joshua to the host at   Jos 18:9
S.
Joshua cast lots for them in   Jos 18:10
S.
an inheritance by lot in *S.*   Jos 19:51
before
spake unto them at *S.* in the   Jos 21:2
land
the children of Israel out of   Jos 22:9
S.
together at *S.* to go up to   Jos 22:12
war
that the house of God was in   J'g 18:31
S.
brought them unto the camp   J'g 21:12
to *S.*
is a feast of the Lord in *S.*   J'g 21:19
yearly
daughters of *S.* come out to   J'g 21:21
dance
his wife of the daughters of   J'g 21:21
S.
sacrifice unto the Lord in *S.*   1Sa 1:3
rose up after they had eaten in   1Sa 1:9
S.

unto the house of the Lord in *1Sa 1:24*
S.
they did in S. unto all the *1Sa 2:14*
Israelites
the Lord appeared again in S. *1Sa 3:21*
revealed himself to Samuel in *1Sa 3:21*
S.
the covenant of the Lord out *1Sa 4:3*
of S.
So the people sent to S. that *1Sa 4:4*
came to S. the same day with *1Sa 4:12*
his
the Lord's priest in S. *1Sa 14:3*
wearing an
concerning the house of Eli *1Ki 2:27*
in S.
and get thee to S.: behold *1Ki 14:2*
there is
did so, and arose, and went *1Ki 14:4*
to S.
he forsook the tabernacle of S. *Ps 78:60*
unto my place which was in S. *Jer 7:12*
your fathers, as I have done to *Jer 7:14*
S.
will I make this house like S. *Jer 26:6*
This house shall be like S. and *Jer 26:9*
certain from Shechem, from S. *Jer 41:5*

SHILONI

son of Zechariah, the son of S. *Ne 11:5*

SHILONITE

the S. found him in the way *1Ki 11:29*
the Lord spake by Ahijah *1Ki 12:15*
the S.
spake by his servant Ahijah *1Ki 15:29*
the S.
in the prophecy of Ahijah *2Ch 9:29*
the S.
spake by the hand of *2Ch 10:15*
Ahijah the S.

SHILONITES

And of the S.; Asiah the *1Ch 9:5*
firstborn

SHILSHAH

Shamma, and S., and Ithran *1Ch 7:37*

SHIMEA

S. and Shobab, and Nathan *1Ch 3:5*
S. his son, Haggiah his son, *1Ch 6:30*
Asaiah
son of Berachiah, the son of *1Ch 6:39*
S.
Jonathan the son of S. *1Ch 20:7*
David's

SHIMEAH

the son of S. David's brother *2Sa 13:3;*
13:32
Jonathan the son of S. the *2Sa 21:21*
And Mikloth begat S. And *1Ch 8:32*
these

SHIMEAM

And Mikloth begat S. And *1Ch 9:38*

SHIMEATH

For Jozachar the son of S. *2Ki 12:21*
the son of S. an *2Ch 24:26*
Ammonitess, and

SHIMEATHITES

the Tirathites, the S. and *1Ch 2:55*

SHIMEI

by their families; Libni, and S. *Nu 3:18*
whose name was S. the son *2Sa 16:5*
And thus said S. when he *2Sa 16:7*
cursed
S. went along on the hill's *2Sa 16:13*
side over
S. the son of Gera, a *2Sa 19:16*
Benjamite
S. the son of Gera fell down *2Sa 19:18*
before
Shall not S. be put to death *2Sa 19:21*
for this

the king said unto S. Thou *2Sa 19:23*
shalt
Nathan the prophet, and S. *1Ki 1:8*
hast with thee S. the son of *1Ki 2:8*
Gera
And the king sent and called *1Ki 2:36*
for S.
S. said unto the king, The *1Ki 2:38*
saying
S. dwelt in Jerusalem many *1Ki 2:38*
days
two of the servants of S. ran *1Ki 2:39*
away
And they told S. saying, *1Ki 2:39*
Behold
And S. arose, and saddled his *1Ki 2:40*
ass
S. went, and brought his *1Ki 2:40*
servants
was told Solomon that S. had *1Ki 2:41*
gone
And the king sent and called *1Ki 2:42*
for S.
The king said moreover to S. *1Ki 2:44*
Thou
S. the son of Elah, in *1Ki 4:18*
Benjamin
Pedaiah were, Zerubbabel, *1Ch 3:19*
and S.
son, Zacchur his son, S. his *1Ch 4:26*
And S. had sixteen sons and *1Ch 4:27*
six
his son, Gog his son, S. his *1Ch 5:4*
son
sons of Gershom; Libni, and *1Ch 6:17*
S.
Libni his son, S. his son, *1Ch 6:29*
Uzza his
the son of Zimmah, the son *1Ch 6:42*
of S.
Gershonites were, Laadan, *1Ch 23:7*
and S.
The sons of S. Shelomith *1Ch 23:9*
And the sons of S. were *1Ch 23:10*
Jahath
These four were the sons of *1Ch 23:10*
S.
The tenth to S. he, his sons *1Ch 25:17*
over the vineyards was S. *1Ch 27:27*
the sons of Heman, Jehiel, *2Ch 29:14*
and S.
and S. his brother was the *2Ch 31:12*
next
the hand of Cononiah and *2Ch 31:13*
S. his
of the Levites; Jozabad, and *Ezr 10:23*
S.
Jeremai, Manasseh, and S. *Ezr 10:33*
And Bani, and Binnui, S. *Ezr 10:38*
the son of Jair, the son of S. *Es 2:5*
the family of S. a part, and *Zec 12:13*
their

SHIMEON

Ishijah, Malchiah, *Ezr 10:31*
Shemaiah, S.

SHIMHI

and Shimrath, the sons of S. *1Ch 8:21*

SHIMI

S. according to their families *Ex 6:17*

SHIMITES

Libnites, and the family of *Nu 3:21*
the S.

SHIMMA

the second, and S. the third *1Ch 2:13*

SHIMON

the sons of S. were, Amnon *1Ch 4:20*

SHIMRATH

and S. the sons of Shimhi *1Ch 8:21*

SHIMRI

the son of Jedaiah, the son *1Ch 4:27*
of S.
Jediael the son of S. and *1Ch 11:45*
Joha his
sons of Elizaphan; S. and *2Ch 29:13*
Jeiel

SHIMRITH

and Jehozabad the son of S. *2Ch 24:26*

SHIMROM

and Puah, Jashub, and S. four *1Ch 7:1*

SHIMRON

and Phuvah, and Job, and S. *Ge 46:13*
of S. the family of the *Nu 26:24*
Shimronites
and to the king of S. and to *Jos 11:1*
Kattath, and Nahallal, and *Jos 19:15*
S. and

SHIMRONITES

of Shimron, the family of the *Nu 26:24*
S.

SHIMRON-MERON

The king of S. one; the king *Jos 12:20*

SHIMSHAI

S. the scribe wrote a letter *Ezr 4:8*
and S. the scribe, and the rest *Ezr 4:9*
to S. the scribe, and to the *Ezr 4:17*
rest of
S. the scribe, and their *Ezr 4:23*
companions

SHIN

s. armour of bronze (S) *1Sa 17:6*

SHINAB

S. king of Admah, and *Ge 14:2*
Shemeber

SHINAR

and Calneh, in the land of S. *Ge 10:10*
found a plain in the land of S. *Ge 11:2*
in the days of Amraphel king *Ge 14:1*
of S.
Amraphel king of S. and *Ge 14:9*
Arioch
and from S. and from Hamath *Isa 11:11*
land of S. to the house of his *Da 1:2*
god
build it an house in the land *Zec 5:11*
of S.

SHINE

Lord make his face s. upon *Nu 6:25*
thee
neither let the light s. upon it *Job 3:4*
s. upon the counsel of the *Job 10:3*
wicked
thou shalt s. forth, thou shalt *Job 11:17*
be
the spark of his fire shall not *Job 18:5*
s.
the light shall s. upon thy *Job 22:28*
ways
commandeth it not to s. by *Job 36:32*
the cloud
caused the light of his cloud *Job 37:15*
to s.
By his neesings a light doth *Job 41:18*
s.
He maketh a path to s. after *Job 41:32*
him
thy face to s. upon thy *Ps 31:16*
servant
and cause his face to s. upon *Ps 67:1*
us
between the cherubims, s. *Ps 80:1*
forth
and cause thy face to s.; and *Ps 80:3;*
we *80:7, 19*
oil to make his face to s. *Ps 104:15*
thy face to s. upon thy *Ps 119:135*
servant
man's wisdom maketh his face *Ec 8:1*
to s.
shall not cause her light to s. *Isa 13:10*
Arise, s.; for thy light is come *Isa 60:1*
They are waxen fat, they s.: *Jer 5:28*
yea
thy face to s. upon thy *Da 9:17*
sanctuary
they that be wise shall s. as the *Da 12:3*

Let your light so *s.* before men	*M't 5:16*
Then shall the righteous *s.* forth	*M't 13:43*
his face did *s.* as the sun, and his	*M't 17:2*
image of God, should *s.* unto them	*2Co 4:4*
who commanded the light to *s.*	*2Co 4:6*
among whom ye *s.* as lights in darkness	*Ph'p 2:15*
light of a candle shall *s.* no more	*Re 18:23*
neither of the moon, to *s.* in it	*Re 21:23*

SHINED

he *s.* forth from mount Paran	*De 33:2*
When his candle *s.* upon my head	*Job 29:3*
If I beheld the sun when it *s.*	*Job 31:26*
perfection of beauty, God hath *s.*	*Ps 50:2*
upon them hath the light *s.*	*Isa 9:2*
and the earth *s.* with his glory	*Eze 43:2*
s. round about him, a light from	*Ac 9:3*
him, and a light *s.* in the prison	*Ac 12:7*
of darkness, hath *s.* in our hearts	*2Co 4:6*

SHINETH

even to the moon, and it *s.* not	*Job 25:5*
but the night *s.* as the day	*Ps 139:12*
s. more and more unto the perfect	*Pr 4:18*
east, and *s.* even unto the west	*M't 24:27*
s. unto the other part under	*Lu 17:24*
And the light *s.* in darkness	*Joh 1:5*
unto a light that *s.* in a dark place	*2Pe 1:19*
is past, and the true light now *s.*	*1Jo 2:8*
was as the sun *s.* in his strength	*Re 1:16*

SHINING

of the earth by clear *s.* after rain	*2Sa 23:4*
path of the just is as the *s.* light	*Pr 4:18*
the *s.* of a flaming fire by night	*Isa 4:5*
s.-gleam, son of morning (B)	*Isa 14:12*
the stars shall withdraw their *s.*	*Joe 2:10; 3:15*
at the *s.* of thy glittering spear	*Hab 3:11*
And his raiment became *s.*	*M'k 9:3*
bright *s.* of a candle doth give thee	*Lu 11:36*
men stood by them in *s.* garments	*Lu 24:4*
He was a burning and a *s.* light	*Joh 5:35*
s. round about me and them	*Ac 26:13*

SHIP

way of a *s.* in the midst of the sea	*Pr 30:19*
oars, neither shall gallant *s.* pass	*Isa 33:21*
made all thy *s.* boards of fir trees	*Eze 27:5*
he found a *s.* going to Tarshish	*Jon 1:3*
that the *s.* was like to be broken	*Jon 1:4*
the wares that were in the *s.* into	*Jon 1:5*
gone down into the sides of the *s.*	*Jon 1:5*
in a *s.* with Zebedee their father	*M't 4:21*
they immediately left the *s.*	*M't 4:22*
when he was entered into a *s.* his	*M't 8:23*
the *s.* was covered with the waves	*M't 8:24*
he entered into a *s.* and passed	*M't 9:1*

so that he went into a *s.* and sat	*M't 13:2*
he departed thence by *s.* into	*M't 14:13*
his disciples to get into a *s.*	*M't 14:22*
s. was now in the midst of the sea	*M't 14:24*
Peter was come down out of the *s.*	*M't 14:29*
when they were come into the *s.*	*M't 14:32*
they that were in the *s.* came and	*M't 14:33*
took *s.* and came into the coasts	*M't 15:39*
were in the *s.* mending their nets	*M'k 1:19*
left their father Zebedee in the *s.*	*M'k 1:20*
that a small *s.* should wait on him	*M'k 3:9*
so that he entered into a *s.*	*M'k 4:1*
took him even as he was in the *s.*	*M'k 4:36*
and the waves beat into the *s.* so	*M'k 4:37*
he was in the hinder part of the *s.*	*M'k 4:38*
when he was come out of the *s.*	*M'k 5:18*
And when he was come into the *s.*	*M'k 5:18*
again by *s.* unto the other side	*M'k 5:21*
into a desert place by *s.* privately	*M'k 6:32*
his disciples to get into the *s.*	*M'k 6:45*
the *s.* was in the midst of the sea	*M'k 6:47*
he went up unto them into the *s.*	*M'k 6:51*
when they were come out of the *s.*	*M'k 6:54*
straightway he entered into a *s.*	*M'k 8:10*
and entering into the *s.* again	*M'k 8:13*
had they in the *s.* with them more	*M'k 8:14*
and taught the people out of the *s.*	*Lu 5:3*
which were in the other *s.* that	*Lu 5:7*
that he went into a *s.* with his	*Lu 8:22*
and he went up into the *s.* and	*Lu 8:37*
entered into a *s.* and went over	*Joh 6:17*
sea, and drawing nigh unto the *s.*	*Joh 6:19*
willingly received him into the *s.*	*Joh 6:21*
and immediately the *s.* was at	*Joh 6:21*
and entered into a *s.* immediately	*Joh 21:3*
the net on the right side of the *s.*	*Joh 21:6*
other disciples came in a little *s.*	*Joh 21:8*
we went before to *s.* and sailed	*Ac 20:13*
they accompanied him unto the *s.*	*Ac 20:38*
And finding a *s.* sailing over	*Ac 21:2*
the *s.* was to unlade her burden	*Ac 21:3*
leave one of another, we took *s.*	*Ac 21:6*
entering into a *s.* of Adramyttium	*Ac 27:2*
centurion found a *s.* of Alexandria	*Ac 27:2*
not only of the lading and *s.*	*Ac 27:10*
the master and the owner of the *s.*	*Ac 27:11*
And when the *s.* was caught	*Ac 27:15*
used helps, undergirding the *s.*	*Ac 27:17*
the next day they lightened the *s.*	*Ac 27:18*
own hands the tackling of the *s.*	*Ac 27:19*
man's life among you, but of the *s.*	*Ac 27:22*
were about to flee out of the *s.*	*Ac 27:30*
Except these abide in the *s.*	*Ac 27:31*
were in all in the *s.* two hundred	*Ac 27:37*
they lightened the *s.* and cast out	*Ac 27:38*
it were possible, to thrust in the *s.*	*Ac 27:39*
seas met, they ran the *s.* aground	*Ac 27:41*

some on broken pieces of the *s.*	*Ac 27:44*
we departed in a *s.* of Alexandria	*Ac 28:11*

SHIPHI

and Ziza the son of *S.* the son of	*1Ch 4:37*

SHIPHMITE

wine cellars was Zabdi the *S.*	*1Ch 27:27*

SHIPHRAH

which the name of the one was *S.*	*Ex 1:15*

SHIPHTAN

Ephraim, Kemuel the son of *S.*	*Nu 34:24*

SHIPMASTER

So the *s.* came to him, and	*Jon 1:6*
the captain came to him (A)(B)(R)	*Jon 1:6*
every *s.* and all the company (A)	*Re 18:17*
ship captains (A)	*Re 18:17*
Every helmsman (B)	*Re 18:17*
the sea-captains (N)	*Re 18:17*

SHIPMEN

s. that had knowledge of the	*1Ki 9:27*
s. deemed that they drew near to	*Ac 27:27*
the *s.* were about to flee out of the	*Ac 27:30*

SHIPPING

they also took *s.* and came to	*Joh 6:24*

SHIPS

and he shall be for an haven of *s.*	*Ge 49:13*
s. shall come from the coast	*Nu 24:24*
bring thee into Egypt again with *s.*	*De 28:68*
and why did Dan remain in *s.*	*J'g 5:17*
made a navy of *s.* in Ezion-geber	*1Ki 9:26*
Jehoshaphat made *s.* of Tharshish	*1Ki 22:48*
the *s.* were broken at Ezion-geber	*1Ki 22:48*
go with thy servants in the *s.*	*1Ki 22:49*
him by the hands of his servants...	*2Ch 8:18*
the king's *s.* went to Tarshish	*2Ch 9:21*
the *s.* of Tarshish bringing gold	*2Ch 9:21*
him to make *s.* to go to Tarshish	*2Ch 20:36*
they made the *s.* in Ezion-geber	*2Ch 20:36*
the *s.* were broken, that they	*2Ch 20:37*
are passed away as the swift *s.*	*Job 9:26*
Thou breakest the *s.* of Tarshish	*Ps 48:7*
There go the *s.*: there is that	*Ps 104:26*
They that go down to the sea in *s.*	*Ps 107:23*
She is like the merchants' *s.*	*Pr 31:14*
And upon all the *s.* of Tarshish	*Isa 2:16*
Howl, ye *s.* of Tarshish; for it	*Isa 23:1*
Howl, ye *s.* of Tarshish: for your	*Isa 23:14*
Chaldeans, whose cry is in the *s.*	*Isa 43:14*
for me, and the *s.* of Tarshish first	*Isa 60:9*
s. of the sea with their mariners	*Eze 27:9*
The *s.* of Tarshish did sing of thee	*Eze 27:25*
shall come down from their *s.*	*Eze 27:29*
messengers go forth from me in *s.*	*Eze 30:9*
s. of Chittim shall come against	*Da 11:30*

with horsemen, and with many *s.*   *Da 11:40*

were also with him other little *s.*   *M'k 4:36*

saw two *s.* standing by the lake   *Lu 5:2*

And he entered into one of the *s.*   *Lu 5:3*

they came, and filled both the *s.*   *Lu 5:7*

they had brought their *s.* to land   *Lu 5:11*

Behold also the *s.* which though   *Jas 3:4*

third part of the *s.* were destroyed   *Re 8:9*

all the company in *s.* and sailors   *Re 18:17*

made rich all that had *s.* in the sea   *Re 18:19*

SHIPWRECK

thrice I suffered *s.* a night and a   *2Co 11:25*

concerning faith have made *s.*   *1Ti 1:19*

SHIRT

his *s.* (P)   *Joh 19:2*

SHISHA

and Ahiah, the sons of *S.* scribes   *1Ki 4:3*

SHISHAK

into Egypt, unto *S.* king of Egypt   *1Ki 11:40*

S. king of Egypt came up against   *1Ki 14:25;* *2Ch 12:2*

together to Jerusalem because of *S.*   *2Ch 12:5*

I also left you in the hand of *S.*   *2Ch 12:5*

upon Jerusalem by the hand of *S.*   *2Ch 12:7*

S. king of Egypt came up against   *2Ch 12:9*

SHITRAI

in Sharon was *S.* the Sharonite   *1Ch 27:29*

SHITTAH

cedar, the *s.* tree, and the myrtle   *Isa 41:19*

SHITTIM

and badgers' skins, and *s.* wood   *Ex 25:5*

they shall make an ark of *s.* wood   *Ex 25:10*

thou shalt make staves of *s.* wood   *Ex 25:13*

shalt also make a table of *s.* wood   *Ex 25:23*

shalt make the staves of *s.* wood   *Ex 25:28*

boards for the tabernacle of *s.* wood   *Ex 26:15*

thou shalt make bars of *s.* wood   *Ex 26:26*

hang it upon four pillars of *s.* wood   *Ex 26:32*

the hanging five pillars of *s.* wood   *Ex 26:37*

thou shalt make an altar of *s.* wood   *Ex 27:1*

for the altar, staves of *s.* wood   *Ex 27:6*

of *s.* wood shalt thou make it   *Ex 30:1*

shalt make the staves of *s.* wood   *Ex 30:5*

and badgers' skins, and *s.* wood   *Ex 35:7*

with whom was found *s.* wood for   *Ex 35:24*

for the tabernacle of *s.* wood   *Ex 36:20*

And he made bars of *s.* wood; five   *Ex 36:31*

thereunto four pillars of *s.* wood   *Ex 36:36*

Bezaleel made the ark of *s.* wood   *Ex 37:1*

and he made staves of *s.* wood   *Ex 37:4*

and he made the table of *s.* wood   *Ex 37:10*

And he made the staves of *s.* wood   *Ex 37:15*

made the incense altar of *s.* wood   *Ex 37:25*

And he made the staves of *s.* wood   *Ex 37:28*

altar of burnt offering of *s.* wood   *Ex 38:1*

And he made the staves of *s.* wood   *Ex 38:6*

And I made an ark of *s.* wood, and   *De 10:3*

SHITTIM, a place

And Israel abode in *S.* and   *Nu 25:1*

son of Nun sent out of *S.* two men   *Jos 2:1*

they removed from *S.* and came   *Jos 3:1*

and shall water the valley of *S.*   *Joe 3:18*

answered him from *S.* unto Gilgal   *Mic 6:5*

SHIVERS

potter shall they be broken to *s.*   *Re 2:27*

SHIZA

Adina the son of *S.* the Reubenite   *1Ch 11:42*

SHOA

all the Chaldeans, Pekod, and *S.*   *Eze 23:23*

SHOAL

they struck a *s.* (P)(R)   *Ac 23:41*

SHOBAH

Shammuah, and *S.* and Nathan   *2Sa 5:14*

sons are these; Jesher, and *S.*   *1Ch 2:18*

Shimea, and *S.* and Nathan   *1Ch 3:5*

and *S.* Nathan, and Solomon   *1Ch 14:4*

SHOBACH

and *S.* the captain of the host of   *2Sa 10:16*

smote *S.* the captain of their host   *2Sa 10:18*

SHOBAI

the children of *S.*, in all an   *Ezr 2:42*

of Hatita, the children of *S.* an   *Ne 7:45*

SHOBAL

Lotan, and *S.* and Zibeon   *Ge 36:20*

And the children of *S.* were these   *Ge 36:23*

duke Lotan, duke of *S.*, duke Zibeon   *Ge 36:29*

the sons of Seir, and Lotan, and *S.*   *1Ch 1:38*

The sons of *S.*; Alion, and   *1Ch 1:40*

S. the father of Kirjath-jearim   *1Ch 2:50;* *2:52*

and Carmi, and Hur, and *S.*   *1Ch 4:1*

And Reaiah the son of *S.* begat   *1Ch 4:2*

SHOBEK

Hallohesh, Pileha, *S.*   *Ne 10:24*

SHOBI

S. the son of Nahash of Rabbah   *2Sa 17:27*

SHOCHO

and *S.* with the villages thereof   *2Ch 28:18*

SHOCHOH

and were gathered together at *S.*   *1Sa 17:1*

pitched between *S.* and Azekah   *1Sa 17:1*

SHOCK

s. of corn cometh in in his season   *Job 5:26*

s. of grain (A)(B)(E)(R)   *Job 5:26*

does it *s.* you (A)(N)   *Joh 6:61*

SHOCKED

you have *s.* me (B)   *Ge 34:30*

queen deeply *s.* (B)   *Es 4:4*

were *s.* at hearing you (B)   *M't 15:12*

s. and distressed (P)   *M'k 14:19*

s. by dissolute habits (N)   *2Pe 2:7*

SHOCKING

it is a *s.* thing (N)   *1Co 14:35*

SHOCKS

and burnt up both the *s.* and also   *J'g 15:5*

SHOCO

Beth-zur, and *S.*, and Adullam   *2Ch 11:7*

SHOD

arrayed them, and *s.* them   *2Ch 28:15*

gave them sandals (B)(R)   *2Ch 28:15*

and *s.* thee with badgers' skin   *Eze 16:10*

But be *s.* with sandals; and not   *M'k 6:9*

go with sandals on their feet (A)   *M'k 6:9*

but wear sandals (B)(N)(P)(R)   *M'k 6:9*

your feet *s.* with the preparation   *Eph 6:15*

gospel of peace bound under feet (B)   *Eph 6:15*

shoes be the gospel of peace (N)   *Eph 6:15*

gospel of peace firmly on your feet (P)   *Eph 6:15*

SHOE

thread of a *s.*-lace (A)   *Ge 14:23*

and loose his *s.* from off his foot   *De 25:9*

loosen his sandal from his foot (B)(R)   *De 25:9*

of him that hath his *s.* loosed   *De 25:10*

s. is not waxen old upon thy foot   *De 29:5*

sandals have not worn off (A)(B)(R)   *De 29:5*

Loose thy *s.* from off thy foot; for   *Jos 5:15*

a man plucked off his *s.* and gave   *Ru 4:7*

pulled off his sandal (A)(B)(R)   *Ru 4:7;* *4:8*

it for thee. So he drew off his *s.*   *Ru 4:8*

over Edom will I cast out my *s.*   *Ps 60:8;* *108:9*

and put off thy *s.* from thy foot   *Isa 20:2*

remove the sandals (B)   *Isa 20:2*

SHOELATCHET

from a thread even to a *s.*   *Ge 14:23*

thread or a shoelace (A)   *Ge 14:23*

thread or sandal-strap (B)   *Ge 14:23*

thread or sandal-thong (R)   *Ge 14:23*

SHOES

put off thy *s.* from off thy feet   *Ex 3:5*

take your sandals off (B)   *Ex 3:5*

your *s.* on your feet, and your staff   *Ex 12:11*

your feet sandaled (B)   *Ex 12:11*

your sandals on your feet (R)   *Ex 12:11*

Thy *s.* shall be iron and brass   *De 33:25*

your castles and strongholds of iron (A)   *De 33:25*

your bolts be iron and bronze (B)   *De 33:25*

Thy bars be iron and brass (E)(R)   *De 33:25*

old *s.* and clouted upon their feet   *Jos 9:5*

the sandals on their feet (B)(R)   Jos 9:5; 9:13
and patched s. (S)   Jos 9:5
our s. are become old by reason of   Jos 9:13
and in his s. that were on his feet   1Ki 2:5
on sandals of his feet (A)(R)   1Ki 2:5
How beautiful are thy feet with s.   Ca 7:1
feet in sandals (A)(B)(E)(R)   Ca 7:1
the latchet of their s. be broken   Isa 5:27
his sandal-strap does not break (B)   Isa 5:27
not a sandal-thong broken (R)   Isa 5:27
and put on thy s. upon thy feet   Eze 24:17
sandals on your feet (A)(B)   Eze 24:17; 24:23; Am 2:6; 8:6
heads. and your s. upon your feet   Eze 24:23
and the poor for a pair s.   Am 2:6
and the needy for a pair of s.   Am 8:6
whose s. I am not worthy to bear   M't 3:11
sandals (A)(B)(R)   M't 3:11; 10:10; M'k 1:7; Lu 3:16; 10:4; 15:22; 22:35; Ac 7:33; 13:25
neither two coats, neither s.   M't 10:10
the latchet of whose s. I am not   M'k 1:7; Lu 3:16
neither purse, nor scrip, nor s.   Lu 10:4
on his hand, and s. on his feet   Lu 15:22
without purse, and scrip, and s.   Lu 22:35
Put off thy s. from thy feet: for the   Ac 7:33
s. of his feet I am not worthy to   Ac 13:25

SHOE'S

s. latchet I am not worthy to   Joh 1:27
the string of whose sandal (A)(B)(R)   Joh 1:27

SHOHAM

Beno, and S. and Zaccur   1Ch 24:27

SHOMER

and Jehozabad the son of S. his   2Ki 12:21
And Heber begat Japhlet, and S.   1Ch 7:32

SHONE

wist not that the skin of his face s.   Ex 34:29
behold, the skin of his face s.; and   Ex 34:30
that the skin of Moses' face s.: and   Ex 34:35
and the sun s. upon the water, and   2Ki 3:22
and the glory of the Lord s. round   Lu 2:9
shone (S)   Ac 9:3; 12:7; 2Co 4:6
s. from heaven a great light round   Ac 22:6
the day s. not for a third part of it   Re 8:12

SHOOK

took hold of it; for the oxen s.   2Sa 6:6
Then the earth s. and trembled   2Sa 22:8
foundations of heaven moved and s.   2Sa 22:8
Also I s. my lap, and said, So God   Ne 5:13
Then the earth s. and trembled   Ps 18:7
The earth s. the heavens also   Ps 68:8
world: the earth trembled and s.   Ps 77:18
they s. their heads (S)   Ps 109:25
over the sea, he s. the kingdoms   Isa 23:11
s. off the dust of their feet against   Ac 13:51
he s. his raiment, and said unto   Ac 18:6

he s. off the beast into the fire, and   Ac 28:5
Whose voice then s. the earth: but   Heb 12:26

SHOOT

the middle bar to s. through thereof   Ex 36:33
s. three arrows on the side   1Sa 20:20
find out now the arrows which I s.   1Sa 20:36
that they would s. from the wall   2Sa 11:20
Then Elisha said, S. And he shot   2Ki 13:17
into this city, nor s. an arrow there   2Ki 19:32
and sword, and to s. with bow   1Ch 5:18
s. arrows and great stones withal   2Ch 26:15
privily s. at the upright in heart   Ps 11:2
they s. out the lip, they shake   Ps 22:7
he bendeth his bow to s. his arrows   Ps 58:7
bend their bows to s. their arrows   Ps 64:3
may s. in secret at the perfect   Ps 64:4
suddenly do they s. at him, and   Ps 64:4
God shall s. at them with an arrow   Ps 64:7
s. out thine arrows, and destroy   Ps 144:6
into this city, nor s. an arrow there   Isa 37:33
bow, s. at her, spare no arrows   Jer 50:14
s. up their top among the thick   Eze 31:14
ye shall s. forth your branches, and   Eze 36:8
When they now s. forth, ye see   Lu 21:30

SHOOTERS

s. shot from off the wall upon thy   2Sa 11:24

SHOOTETH

his branch s. forth in his garden   Job 8:16
In measure, when it s. forth, thou   Isa 27:8
s. out great branches; so that   M'k 4:32

SHOOTING

left in hurling stones and s. arrows   1Ch 12:2
of the s. up of the latter growth   Am 7:1

SHOOTS

his s. go forth (A)(B)(E)(R)   Job 8:16; 14:7
s. with pruning hooks (R)   Isa 18:5
turn into bastard s. (B)   Jer 2:21
his s. shall (A)(B)   Ho 14:6
s. became soft (A)(N)   M't 24:32

SHOP

market place, a sales shop (A)   Joh 2:16
Father s. house a sales s. (B)   Joh 2:16

SHOPHACH

and S. the captain of the host of   1Ch 19:16
Killed S. the captain of the host   1Ch 19:18

SHOPHAN

S. and Jaazer, and Jogbehah   Nu 32:35

SHORE

the sand which is upon the sea s.   Ge 22:17
the Egyptians dead upon the sea s.   Ex 14:30
that is upon the sea s. in multitude   Jos 11:4
was from the s. of the salt sea   Jos 15:2

Asher continued on the sea s.   J'g 5:17
as the sand which is on the sea s.   1Sa 13:5
as the sand that is on the sea s.   1Ki 4:29
on the s. of the Red sea, in Ashkelon, and against the sea s.   1Ki 9:26; Jer 47:7
whole multitude stood on the s.   M't 13:2
when it was full, they drew to s.   M't 13:48
of Gennesaret, and drew to the s.   M'k 6:53
now come, Jesus stood on the s.   Joh 21:4
and we kneeled down on the s.   Ac 21:5
discovered a certain creek with a s.   Ac 27:39
to the wind, and made toward s.   Ac 27:40
as the sand which is by the sea s.   Heb 11:12

SHORELINE

and the s. of the children (S)   Jos 15:12

SHORN

a flock of sheep that are even s.   Ca 4:2
residents s. of his strength (B)(R)   Isa 37:27
having s. his head in Cenchrea   Ac 18:18
cut his hair short (A)(B)(N)(P)(R)   Ac 18:18
be not covered, let her also be s.   1Co 11:6
she should cut her hair (A)(B)(N)(R)   1Co 11:6
have her hair cropped (P)   1Co 11:6
it be a shame for a woman to be s.   1Co 11:6

SHORT

Is the Lord's hand waxed s.   Nu 11:23
days the Lord began to cut Israel s.   2Ki 10:32
the light is s. because of darkness   Job 17:12
the triumphing of the wicked is s.   Job 20:5
Remember how s. my time is   Ps 89:47
and come s. of the glory of God   Ro 3:23
and cut it s. in righteousness   Ro 9:28
a s. work will the Lord make   Ro 9:28
this I say, brethren, the time is s.   1Co 7:29
being taken from you for a s. time   1Th 2:17
not s. tempered (N)   Tit 1:7
of you should seem to come s. of it   Heb 4:1
knoweth that he hath but a s. time   Re 12:2
he must continue a s. space   Re 17:10

SHORTAGE

she from her s. (B)   Lu 21:4

SHORTCOMINGS

forgive s. (A)   M'k 11:25; 11:26

SHORTENED

steps of his strength shall be s. (S)   Job 18:7
The days of his youth hast thou s.   Ps 89:45
strength in the way; he s. my days   Ps 102:23
the years of the wicked shall be s.   Pr 10:27
Is my hand s. at all, that it cannot   Isa 50:2
Behold, the Lord's hand is not s.   Isa 59:1
is the spirit of the Lord s. (S)   Mic 2:7
except those days should be s.   M't 24:22
elect's sake those days shall be s.   M't 24:22

that the Lord had *s.* those days   *M'k 13:20*

he hath chosen, he hath *s.* the days   *M'k 13:20*

SHORTER

the bed is *s.* than that a man can   *Isa 28:20*

Now the upper chambers were *s.*   *Eze 42:5*

SHORTLY

and God will *s.* bring it to pass   *Ge 41:32*

s. he brought again from Babylon   *Jer 27:16*

I *s.* pour out my fury upon thee   *Eze 7:8*

himself depart *s.* thither   *Ac 25:4*

bruise Satan under your feet *s.*   *Ro 16:20*

I will come to you *s.* if the Lord   *1Co 4:19*

to send Timotheus *s.* unto you   *Ph'p 2:19*

that I also myself shall come *s.*   *Ph'p 2:24*

thee, hoping to come unto thee *s.*   *1Ti 3:14*

thy diligence to come *s.* unto me   *2Ti 4:9*

with whom, if he come *s.* I will see   *Heb 13:23*

that *s.* I must put off this my   *2Pe 1:14*

But I trust I shall *s.* see thee, and   *3Jo 14*

which must *s.* come to pass   *Re 1:1*

things which must *s.* be done   *Re 22:6*

SHOSHANNIM

To the chief Musician upon *S.*   *Ps 45 title; 69 title*

SHOSHANNIM-EDUTH

To the chief Musician upon *S.*   *Ps 80 title*

SHOT

budded, and her blossoms *s.* forth   *Ge 40:10*

and *s.* at him, and hated him   *Ge 49:23*

archers *s.* at him (B)(R)   *Ge 49:23*

surely be stoned, or *s.* through   *Ex 19:13*

We have *s.* at them; Heshbon is   *Nu 21:30*

thereof, as though I *s.* at a mark   *1Sa 20:20*

ran, he *s.* an arrow beyond him   *1Sa 20:36*

the arrow which Jonathan had *s.*   *1Sa 20:37*

And the shooters *s.* from off the wall   *2Sa 11:24*

s. Jehoram between arms (B)(R)   *2Ki 9:24*

Then Elisha said, Shoot, And he *s.*   *2Ki 13:17*

And the archers *s.* at king Josiah   *2Ch 35:23*

and he *s.* out lightnings, and   *Ps 18:14*

tongue is as an arrow *s.* out; it   *Jer 9:8*

forth branches, and *s.* forth sprigs   *Eze 17:6*

s. forth her branches toward him   *Eze 17:7*

multitude of waters he *s.* forth   *Eze 31:5*

he hath *s.* up his top among   *Eze 31:10*

SHOULD

is not good that the man *s.* be alone   *Ge 2:18*

Cain, lest any finding him *s.* kill him   *Ge 4:15*

that the righteous *s.* be as the wicked   *Ge 18:25*

that Sarah *s.* have given children suck   *Ge 21:7*

it be your mind that I *s.* bury my dead   *Ge 23:8*

men of the place *s.* kill me for Rebekah   *Ge 26:7*

why *s.* I be deprived also of you both   *Ge 27:45*

is it time that the cattle *s.* be gathered   *Ge 29:7*

than that I *s.* to give her to another man   *Ge 29:19*

s. conceive when they came to drink   *Ge 30:38*

and if men *s.* overdrive them one day   *Ge 33:13*

S. he deal with our sister as with an   *Ge 34:31*

Onan knew that the seed *s.* not be his   *Ge 38:9*

that he *s.* give seed to his brother   *Ge 38:9*

that they *s.* put me into the dungeon   *Ge 40:15*

heard that they *s.* eat bread there   *Ge 43:25*

God forbid that thy servants *s.* do   *Ge 44:7*

how then *s.* we steal out of thy lord's   *Ge 44:8*

he said, God forbid that I *s.* do so   *Ge 44:17*

for if he *s.* leave his father, his father   *Ge 44:22*

for why *s.* we die in thy presence? for   *Ge 47:15*

that Pharaoh *s.* have the fifth part   *Ge 47:26*

Who am I, that I *s.* go unto Pharaoh   *Ex 3:11*

and that I *s.* bring forth the children   *Ex 3:11*

I *s.* obey his voice to let Israel go   *Ex 5:2*

than that we *s.* die in the wilderness   *Ex 14:12*

him; for he *s.* make full restitution   *Ex 22:3*

Wherefore *s.* the Egyptians speak   *Ex 32:12*

hath commanded, that ye *s.* do them   *Ex 35:1*

that they *s.* be stones for a memorial   *Ex 39:7*

about the hole, that it *s.* not rend   *Ex 39:23*

things which *s.* not be done   *Le 4:13; 4:22*

the Lord commanded that ye *s.* do   *Le 9:6*

ye *s.* indeed have eaten it in the holy   *Le 10:18*

s. it have been accepted in the sight   *Le 10:19*

unclean with them, that he *s.* be defiled   *Le 11:43*

from other people, that ye *s.* be mine   *Le 20:26*

s. bring forth him that had cursed   *Le 24:23*

that ye *s.* not be their bondmen   *Le 26:13*

beasts, which *s.* be the Lord's firstling   *Le 27:26*

that they *s.* bear upon their shoulders   *Nu 7:9*

Israel, that they *s.* keep the passover   *Nu 9:4*

Whence *s.* I have flesh to give unto all   *Nu 11:13*

s. she not be ashamed seven days   *Nu 12:14*

wives and our children *s.* be a prey   *Nu 14:3*

little ones, which ye said *s.* be a prey   *Nu 14:31*

not declared what *s.* be done to him   *Nu 15:34*

that we and our cattle *s.* die there   *Nu 20:4*

God is not a man, that he *s.* lie; neither   *Nu 23:19*

the son of man, that he *s.* repent   *Nu 23:19*

Why *s.* the name of our father be done   *Nu 27:4*

that they *s.* not go into the land which   *Nu 32:9*

Because he *s.* have remained in the city   *Nu 35:28*

he *s.* come again to dwell in the land   *Nu 35:32*

that time all the things which ye *s.* do   *De 1:18*

to shew you by what way ye *s.* go, and   *De 1:33*

little ones, which ye said *s.* be a prey   *De 1:39*

that ye *s.* do so in the land whither ye   *De 4:5*

and sware that I *s.* not go over Jordan   *De 4:21*

that I *s.* not go in unto that good land   *De 4:21*

which *s.* kill his neighbour unawares   *De 4:42*

Now therefore why *s.* we die   *De 5:25*

to the end that he *s.* multiply horses   *De 17:16*

so *s.* ye sin against the Lord your God   *De 20:18*

if he *s.* exceed, and beat him above   *De 25:3*

then thy brother *s.* seem vile unto thee   *De 25:3*

Lest there *s.* be among you a man, or   *De 29:18*

lest there *s.* be among you a root that   *De 29:18*

adversaries *s.* behave themselves   *De 32:27*

and lest they *s.* say, Our hand is high   *De 32:27*

How *s.* one chase a thousand, and two   *De 32:30*

that they *s.* take his carcase down   *Jos 8:29*

that they *s.* bless the people of Israel   *Jos 8:33*

day, in the place which he *s.* choose   *Jos 9:27*

they *s.* come against Israel in battle   *Jos 11:20*

s. so say to us or to our generations   *Jos 22:28*

that we *s.* rebel against the Lord   *Jos 22:29*

God forbid that we *s.* forsake the Lord   *Jos 24:16*

that we *s.* give bread unto thine army   *J'g 8:6*

that we *s.* give bread unto thy men   *J'g 8:15*

S. I leave my fatness, wherewith by   *J'g 9:9*

S. I forsake my sweetness, and my   *J'g 9:11*

S. I leave my wine, which cheereth   *J'g 9:13*

who is Shechem, that we *s.* serve him   *J'g 9:28*

of Shechem: for why *s.* we serve him   *J'g 9:28*

is Abimelech, that we *s.* serve him   *J'g 9:38*

that they *s.* not dwell in Shechem   *J'g 9:41*

they *s.* make a great flame with smoke   *J'g 20:38*

s. be to day one tribe lacking in Israel   *J'g 21:3*

them at this time, that ye *s.* be guilty   *J'g 21:22*

If I *s.* say, I have hope   *Ru 1:12*

if I *s.* have an husband also to night   *Ru 1:12*

also to night, and *s.* also bear sons   *Ru 1:12*

thy father *s.* walk before me for ever   *1Sa 2:30*

me, that I *s.* not reign over them   *1Sa 8:7*

shew us our way that we *s.*   *1Sa 9:6*

further. if the man *s.* yet come thither   *1Sa 10:22*

for then *s.* ye go after vain things   *1Sa 12:21*

forbid that I *s.* sin against the Lord   *1Sa 12:23*

which *s.* have been utterly destroyed   *1Sa 15:21*

for he is not a man, that he *s.* repent   *1Sa 15:29*

he *s.* defy the armies of the living God   *1Sa 17:26*

that I *s.* be son in law to the king   *1Sa 18:18*

daughter *s.* have been given to David   *1Sa 18:19*

his servants, that they *s.* kill David   *1Sa 19:1*

me, Let me go; why *s.* I kill thee   *1Sa 19:17*

s. my father hide this thing from me   *1Sa 20:2*

s. not fail to sit with the king at meat   *1Sa 20:5*

that he *s.* rise against me, to   *1Sa 22:13*
lie in
The Lord forbid that I *s.* do   *1Sa 24:6*
this thing
forbid that I *s.* stretch forth   *1Sa 26:11*
mine hand
that I *s.* speedily escape into   *1Sa 27:1*
the land
s. thy servant dwell in the   *1Sa 27:5*
royal city
Lest they *s.* tell on us, saying,   *1Sa 27:11*
So did
for wherewith *s.* he reconcile   *1Sa 29:4*
himself
s. it not be with the heads of   *1Sa 29:4*
these men
s. I smite thee to the ground   *2Sa 2:22*
how then *s.* I hold up my face   *2Sa 2:22*
to Joab
now he is dead, wherefore *s.*   *2Sa 12:23*
I fast
unto him, Why *s.* he go with   *2Sa 13:26*
thee
s. I this day make thee go up   *2Sa 15:20*
and down
Why *s.* this dead dog curse   *2Sa 16:9*
my lord
And again, whom *s.* I serve   *2Sa 16:19*
s. I not serve in presence   *2Sa 16:19*
of his son
Though I *s.* receive a   *2Sa 18:12*
thousand shekels
I *s.* have wrought falsehood   *2Sa 18:13*
against
that the king *s.* take it to his   *2Sa 19:19*
heart
ye *s.* this day be adversaries   *2Sa 19:22*
unto me
that I *s.* go up with the king   *2Sa 19:34*
s. thy servant be yet a   *2Sa 19:35*
burden unto
why *s.* the king recompense   *2Sa 19:36*
it me
advice *s.* not be first had in   *2Sa 19:43*
bringing
me, that I *s.* swallow up or   *2Sa 20:20*
destroy
we *s.* be destroyed from   *2Sa 21:5*
remaining in
far from me, O Lord, that I   *2Sa 23:17*
s. do this
who *s.* sit on the throne of   *1Ki 1:27*
my lord
of David drew nigh that he *s.*   *1Ki 2:1*
die
set their faces on me, that I *s.*   *1Ki 2:15*
reign
beams *s.* not be fastened in   *1Ki 6:6*
the walls
the good way wherein they *s.*   *1Ki 8:36*
walk
that he *s.* not go after other   *1Ki 11:10*
gods
me that I *s.* be king over this   *1Ki 14:2*
people
I *s.* give the inheritance of   *1Ki 21:3*
my fathers
son that *s.* have reigned in   *2Ki 3:27*
his stead
s. I set this before an hundred   *2Ki 4:43*
men
what *s.* I wait for the Lord   *2Ki 6:33*
any longer
the Lord *s.* make windows in   *2Ki 7:19*
heaven
a dog, that he *s.* do this great   *2Ki 8:13*
thing
them that *s.* go out on the   *2Ki 11:9*
sabbath
that they *s.* be the Lord's   *2Ki 11:17*
people
them, that they *s.* not do   *2Ki 17:15*
like them
taught them how they *s.*   *2Ki 17:28*
fear the Lord
s. deliver Jerusalem out of   *2Ki 18:35*
mine hand
s. become a desolation and   *2Ki 22:19*
a curse
they *s.* bring them in and out   *1Ch 9:28*
by tale
forbid it me, that I *s.* do   *1Ch 11:19*
this thing
for those that *s.* make a   *1Ch 16:42*
sound
on thy people, that they *s.*   *1Ch 21:17*
be plagued
David *s.* go up, and set up   *1Ch 21:18*
an altar

he *s.* sanctify the most holy   *1Ch 23:13*
things
s. keep the charge of the   *1Ch 23:32*
tabernacle
who *s.* prophesy with harps   *1Ch 25:1*
that we *s.* be able to offer   *1Ch 29:14*
so willingly
am I then, that I *s.* build him   *2Ch 2:6*
an house
they *s.* burn after the manner   *2Ch 4:20*
before
the good way, wherein they   *2Ch 6:27*
s. walk
Lord God of Israel *s.* be put   *2Ch 15:13*
to death
that *s.* praise the beauty of   *2Ch 20:21*
holiness
kings, that they *s.* be the   *2Ch 23:16*
Lord's people
was unclean in any thing *s.*   *2Ch 23:19*
enter in
that they *s.* not go with him   *2Ch 25:13*
to battle
that ye *s.* minister unto him,   *2Ch 29:11*
and burn
sin offering *s.* be made for   *2Ch 29:24*
all Israel
they *s.* come to the house of   *2Ch 30:1*
the Lord
that they *s.* come to keep the   *2Ch 30:5*
passover
Why *s.* the kings of Assyria   *2Ch 32:4*
come, and
your God *s.* be able to   *2Ch 32:14*
deliver you
they *s.* not eat of the most   *Ezr 2:63*
holy things
why *s.* damage grow to the   *Ezr 4:22*
hurt of the
s. there be wrath against the   *Ezr 7:23*
realm
told them what they *s.* say   *Ezr 8:17*
unto Iddo
that *s.* bring unto us ministers   *Ezr 8:17*
S. we break thy   *Ezr 9:14*
commandments
there *s.* be no remnant nor   *Ezr 9:14*
escaping
that they *s.* do according to   *Ezr 10:5*
this word
they *s.* gather themselves   *Ezr 10:7*
together
all his substance *s.* be   *Ezr 10:8*
forfeited, and
why *s.* not my countenance be   *Ne 2:3*
sad
they *s.* do according to this   *Ne 5:12*
promise
why *s.* the work cease, whilst I   *Ne 6:3*
leave
And I said, *S.* such a man as I   *Ne 6:11*
flee
that I *s.* be afraid, and do so,   *Ne 6:13*
and sin
they *s.* not eat of the most holy   *Ne 7:65*
things
children of Israel *s.* dwell in   *Ne 8:14*
booths
s. publish and proclaim in all   *Ne 8:15*
their
light in the way wherein they   *Ne 9:12*
s. go
that they *s.* go in to possess the   *Ne 9:15*
land
light, and the way wherein   *Ne 9:19*
they *s.* go
fathers, that they *s.* go in to   *Ne 9:23*
possess it
s. bring the firstfruits of our   *Ne 10:37*
dough
a certain portion *s.* be for   *Ne 11:23*
the singers
s. not come into the   *Ne 13:1*
congregation of
Balaam against them, that he   *Ne 13:2*
s. curse
I commanded that the gates   *Ne 13:19*
s. be shut
s. not be opened till after the   *Ne 13:19*
sabbath
there *s.* no burden be   *Ne 13:19*
brought in on
that they *s.* cleanse   *Ne 13:22*
themselves, and
that they *s.* come and keep   *Ne 13:22*
the gates
they *s.* do to every man's   *Es 1:8*
pleasure
that every man *s.* bear rule in   *Es 1:8;*
his own   *1:22*

that it *s.* be published   *Es 1:22*
according to
charged her that she *s.* not   *Es 2:10*
shew it
Esther did, and what *s.*   *Es 2:11*
become of her
that they *s.* be ready against   *Es 3:14*
that day
her that she *s.* go in unto the   *Es 4:8*
king
the Jews *s.* be ready against   *Es 8:13*
that day
they *s.* keep the fourteenth day   *Es 9:21*
they *s.* make them days of   *Es 9:22*
feasting
s. return upon his own head   *Es 9:25*
his sons *s.* be hanged on the   *Es 9:25*
gallows
so as it *s.* not fail, that they   *Es 9:27*
would keep
these days *s.* be remembered   *Es 9:28*
and kept
days of Purim *s.* not fail from   *Es 9:28*
among
me? or why the breasts that I   *Job 3:12*
s. suck
now *s.* I have lain still and   *Job 3:13*
been quiet
still and been quiet, I *s.* have   *Job 3:13*
slept
Then *s.* I yet have comfort: *Job 6:10*
yea, I
What is my strength, that I *s.*   *Job 6:11*
hope
is mine end, that I *s.* prolong   *Job 6:11*
my life
pity *s.* be shewed from his   *Job 6:14*
friend
yet thy latter end *s.* greatly   *Job 8:7*
increase
but how *s.* man be just with   *Job 9:2*
God
a man, as I am, not I *s.*   *Job 9:32*
answer him
we *s.* come together in   *Job 9:32*
judgment
I *s.* have been as though I   *Job 10:19*
had not
I *s.* have been carried from   *Job 10:19*
the womb
S. not the multitude of words   *Job 11:2*
be answered
and *s.* a man full of talk be   *Job 11:2*
justified
S. thy lies make men hold   *Job 11:3*
their peace
your peace! and it *s.* be your   *Job 13:5*
wisdom
It is good that the *s.* search   *Job 13:9*
you out
S. a wise man utter vain   *Job 15:2*
knowledge
S. he reason with unprofitable   *Job 15:3*
talk
What is man, that he *s.* be   *Job 15:14*
clean? and
of a woman, that he *s.* be   *Job 15:14*
righteous
of my lips *s.* assuage your   *Job 16:5*
grief
But ye *s.* say, Why persecute   *Job 19:28*
we him
so, why *s.* not my spirit be   *Job 21:4*
troubled
is the Almighty, that we *s.*   *Job 21:15*
serve him
what profit *s.* we have, if we   *Job 21:15*
pray unto
so *s.* I be delivered for ever   *Job 23:7*
from my
God forbid that I *s.* justify   *Job 27:5*
you: till I
why then *s.* I think upon a   *Job 31:1*
maid
I *s.* have denied the God that   *Job 31:28*
is above
I said, Days *s.* speak, and   *Job 32:7*
multitude of years *s.* teach   *Job 32:7*
wisdom
Lest ye *s.* say, We have   *Job 32:13*
found out
S. I lie against my right? my   *Job 34:6*
wound
that he *s.* delight himself with   *Job 34:9*
God
it from God that he is *s.* do   *Job 34:10*
wickedness
Almighty, that he *s.* commit   *Job 34:10*
iniquity

he s. enter into judgment with God | Job 34:23
S. it be according to thy mind? he will | Job 34:33
and that which s. be set on thy table | Job 36:16
be set on thy table s. be full of fatness. | Job 36:16
prevented me, that I s. repay him | Job 41:11
Though an host s. encamp against me | Ps 27:3
though war s. rise against me, in this | Ps 27:3
alive, that I s. not go down to the pit | Ps 30:3
lest otherwise they s. rejoice over me | Ps 38:16
Wherefore s. I fear in the days of evil | Ps 49:5
That he s. still live for ever, and not | Ps 49:9
which s. have been for their welfare | Ps 69:22
I s. offend against the generation of | Ps 73:15
s. make them known to their children | Ps 78:5
even the children which s. be born | Ps 78:6
who s. arise and declare them to their | Ps 78:6
Wherefore s. the heathen say, Where | Ps 79:10
I s. soon have subdued their enemies | Ps 81:14
haters of the Lord s. have submitted | Ps 81:15
their time s. have endured for ever | Ps 81:15
s. have fed them also with the finest | Ps 81:16
of the rock s. I have satisfied thee | Ps 81:16
that they s. not enter into my rest | Ps 95:11
that it s. not be removed for ever | Ps 104:5
his wrath, lest he s. destroy them | Ps 106:23
Wherefore s. the heathen say, Where | Ps 115:2
I s. have perished in mine affliction | Ps 119:92
If I s. count them, they are more in | Ps 139:18
to know the way wherein I s. walk | Ps 143:8
waters s. not pass his commandment | Pr 8:29
Train up a child in the way he s. go | Pr 22:6
s. he take away thy bed from under | Pr 22:27
which they s. do under the heaven all | Ec 2:3
I s. leave it unto the man that shall | Ec 2:18
a man, than that he s. eat and drink | Ec 2:24
that he s. make his soul enjoy good | Ec 2:24
also that every man s. eat and drink | Ec 3:13
doeth it, that men s. fear before him | Ec 3:14
a man s. rejoice in his own works | Ec 3:22
wherefore s. God be angry at thy voice | Ec 5:6
that man s. find nothing after him | Ec 7:14
why s. I be as one that turneth aside | Ca 1:7
when I s. find thee without, I would | Ca 8:1
kiss thee; yea, I s. not be despised | Ca 8:1
His left hand s. be under my head | Ca 8:3
and his right hand s. embrace me | Ca 8:3
Why s. ye be stricken any more | Isa 1:5
remnant, we s. have been as Sodom | Isa 1:9
we s. have been like unto Gomorrah | Isa 1:9
he looked that it s. bring forth grapes | Isa 5:2

I looked that it s. bring forth grapes | Isa 5:4
I s. not walk in the way of this people | Isa 8:11
s. not a people seek unto their God | Isa 8:19
if the rod s. shake itself against them | Isa 10:15
or as if the staff s. lift up itself, as if it | Isa 10:15
Lord s. deliver Jerusalem out of my | Isa 36:20
it with nails, that it s. not be moved | Isa 41:7
for how s. my name be polluted? and I | Isa 48:11
his name s. not have been cut off nor | Isa 48:19
she s. not have compassion on the son | Isa 49:15
that I s. know how to speak a word in | Isa 50:4
and that he s. not die in the pit, nor | Isa 51:14
in the pit, nor that his bread s. fail | Isa 51:14
is no beauty that we s. desire him | Isa 53:2
waters of Noah s. no more go over the | Isa 54:9
offering, S. I receive comfort in these | Isa 57:6
for the spirit s. fail before me, and the | Isa 57:16
wilderness, that they s. not stumble | Isa 63:13
thy sons and thy daughters s. eat: | Jer 5:17
my days s. be consumed with shame | Jer 20:18
s. have turned them from their evil | Jer 23:22
name, and s. ye be utterly unpunished | Jer 25:29
that they s. not give him into the hand | Jer 26:24
I s. drive you out, and ye s. perish | Jer 27:10
wherefore s. this city be laid waste | Jer 27:17
that ye s. be officers in the house of | Jer 29:26
I s. remove it from before my face | Jer 32:31
they s. do this abomination, to cause | Jer 32:35
and that there s. not be day and night | Jer 33:20
that he s. not have a son to reign upon | Jer 33:21
they s. be no more a nation before | Jer 33:24
That every man s. let his manservant | Jer 34:9
that none s. serve himself of them | Jer 34:9
that every one s. let his manservant | Jer 34:10
that none s. serve themselves of them | Jer 34:10
yet s. they rise up every man in his | Jer 37:10
s. commit Jeremiah into the court | Jer 37:21
they s. give him daily a piece of bread | Jer 37:21
Shaphan, that he s. carry him home | Jer 39:14
wherefore s. he slay thee, that all the | Jer 40:15
are gathered unto thee s. be scattered | Jer 40:15
they s. return into the land of Judah | Jer 44:14
king of Babylon s. come, and smite the | Jer 46:13
Babylon s. mount up to heaven | Jer 51:53
and though she s. fortify the height | Jer 51:53
a'l the evil that s. come upon Babylon | Jer 51:60
they s. not enter thy congregation | La 1:10
comforter that s. relieve my soul is far | La 1:16
his adversaries s. be round about him | La 1:17
It is good that a man s. both hope and | La 3:26

than our prayer s. not pass through | La 3:44
enemy s. have entered into the gates | La 4:12
that I s. go far off from my sanctuary | Eze 8:6
bread, to slay the souls that s. not die | Eze 13:19
to save the souls alive that s. not live | Eze 13:19
he s. not return from his wicked way | Eze 13:22
s. I be enquired of at all by them | Eze 14:5
they s. deliver but their own souls by | Eze 14:14
any pleasure that the wicked s. die | Eze 18:23
not that he s. return from his ways | Eze 18:23
his voice s. no more be heard upon the | Eze 19:9
that it s. not be polluted before the | Eze 20:9; 20:14
it s. not be polluted in the sight of the | Eze 20:22
judgments whereby they s. not live | Eze 20:25
s. we then make mirth? it contemneth | Eze 21:10
s. make up the hedge and stand in | Eze 22:30
for the land, that I s. not destroy it | Eze 22:30
top of a rock, that it s. not be covered | Eze 24:8
away in them, how s. we then live | Eze 33:10
s. not the shepherds feed the flocks | Eze 34:2
he s. bring certain of the children of | Da 1:3
why s. he see your faces worse liking | Da 1:10
meat, and the wine that they s. drink | Da 1:16
the king had said he s. bring them in | Da 1:18
forth that the wise men s. be slain | Da 2:13
Daniel and his fellows s. not perish | Da 2:18
bed, what s. come to pass hereafter | Da 2:29
they s. offer an oblation and sweet | Da 2:46
s. be cast into the midst of a burning | Da 3:11
they s. heat the furnace one seven | Da 3:19
that they s. read this writing | Da 5:15
s. be the third ruler in the kingdom | Da 5:29
which s. be over the whole kingdom | Da 6:1
and the king s. have no damage | Da 6:2
they s. take Daniel up out of the den | Da 6:23
nations, and languages, s. serve him | Da 7:14
Lord; what then s. a king do to us | Ho 10:3
in my desire that I s. chastise them | Ho 10:10
he s. not stay long in the place of the | Ho 13:13
that the heathen s. rule over them | Joe 2:17
s. they say among the people, Where | Joe 2:17
s. not I spare Nineveh, that great city | Jon 4:11
that I s. make thee a desolation. and | Mic 6:16
so their dwelling s. not be cut off | Zep 3:7
time that the Lord's house s. be built | Hag 1:2
saying, S. I weep in the fifth month | Zec 7:3
S. ye not hear the words which | Zec 7:7
their ears, that they s. not hear | Zec 7:11
lest they s. hear the law, and | Zec 7:12
s. it also be marvellous in mine eyes | Zec 8:6
s. I accept this of your hand? saith the | Mal 1:13

the priest's lips s. keep knowledge	Mal 2:7
and they s. seek the law at his mouth	Mal 2:7
of them where Christ s. be born	M't 2:4
that they s. not return to Herod	M't 2:12
that one of thy members s. perish	M't 5:29
thy whole body s. be cast into hell	M't 5:29
that one of thy members s. perish	M't 5:30
thy whole body s. be cast into hell	M't 5:30
ye would that men s. do to you	M't 7:12
Art thou he that s. come or do we	M't 11:3
that they s. not make him known	M't 12:16
any time they s. see with their eyes	M't 13:15
and s. understand with their heart	M't 13:15
s. be converted, and I s. heal them	M't 13:15
Whence s. we have so much bread in	M't 15:33
that ye s. beware of the leaven of the	M't 16:11
s. tell no man that he was Jesus the	M't 16:20
lest we s. offend them, go thou to the	M't 17:27
that one of these little ones s. perish	M't 18:14
into prison, till he s. pay the debt	M't 18:30
he s. pay all that was due unto him	M't 18:34
he s. put his hands on them, and pray	M't 19:13
that they s. have received more	M't 20:10
because they s. hold their peace	M't 20:31
except those days s. be shortened	M't 24:22
there s. no flesh be saved: but for the	M't 24:22
coming I s. have received mine own	M't 25:27
Though I s. die with thee, yet will	M't 26:35
multitude that they s. ask Barabbas	M't 27:20
a small ship s. wait on him because of	M'k 3:9
multitude, lest they s. throng him	M'k 3:9
that they s. not make him known	M'k 3:12
twelve, that they s. be with him	M'k 3:14
at any time they s. be converted	M'k 4:12
and their sins s. be forgiven them	M'k 4:12
secret, but that it s. come abroad	M'k 4:22
a man s. cast seed into the ground	M'k 4:26
And s. sleep, and rise night and day	M't 4:27
and the seed s. spring and grow up	M'k 4:27
them straitly that no man s. know it	M'k 5:43
that something s. be given her to eat	M'k 5:43
they s. take nothing for their journey	M'k 6:8
and preached that men s. repent	M'k 6:12
them that they s. tell no man	M'k 7:36
them that they s. tell no man of him	M'k 8:30
s. tell no man what things they had	M'k 9:9
the rising from the dead s. mean	M'k 9:10
disciples that they s. cast him out	M'k 9:18
would not that any man s. know it	M'k 9:30
themselves, who s. be the greatest	M'k 9:34

to him, that he s. touch them: and	M'k 10:13
what things s. happen unto him	M'k 10:32
What would ye that I s. do for you	M'k 10:36
him that he s. hold his peace	M'k 10:48
What wilt thou that I s. do unto thee	M'k 10:51
that any man s. carry any vessel	M'k 11:16
that his brother s. take his wife, and	M'k 12:19
those days, no flesh s. be saved	M'k 13:20
If I s. die with thee, I will not	M'k 14:31
that he s. rather release Barabbas	M'k 15:11
upon them, what every man s. take	M'k 15:24
what manner of salutation this s. be	Lu 1:29
mother of my Lord s. come to me	Lu 1:43
time came that she s. be delivered	Lu 1:57
we s. be saved from our enemies, and	Lu 1:71
that all the world s. be taxed	Lu 2:1
accomplished that she s. be delivered	Lu 2:6
that he s. not see death, before he had	Lu 2:26
him, that he s. not depart from them	Lu 4:42
that they s. come and help them	Lu 5:7
as ye would that men s. do to you	Lu 6:31
was worthy for whom he s. do this	Lu 7:4
Art thou he that s. come? or look	Lu 7:19; 7:20
lest they s. believe and be saved	Lu 8:12
they s. tell no man what was done	Lu 8:56
except we s. go and buy meat for all	Lu 9:13
he s. accomplish at Jerusalem	Lu 9:31
them, which of them s. be greatest	Lu 9:46
was come that he s. be received up	Lu 9:51
It was meet that we s. make merry	Lu 15:32
he s. offend one of these little ones	Lu 17:2
planted in the sea; and it s. obey	Lu 17:6
when the kingdom of God s. come	Lu 17:20
him, that he s. hold his peace; but he	Lu 18:39
of God s. immediately appear	Lu 19:11
would not that I s. reign over them,	Lu 19:27
if these s. hold their peace, the stones	Lu 19:40
s. give him of the fruits of the vineyard	Lu 20:10
which s. feign themselves just men	Lu 20:20
his brother s. take his wife, and raise	Lu 20:28
them it was that s. do this thing	Lu 22:23
of them s. be accounted the greatest	Lu 22:24
that it s. be as they required	Lu 23:24
holden that they s. not know him	Lu 24:16
he which s. have redeemed Israel	Lu 24:21
remission of sins s. be preached in his	Lu 24:47
that he s. be made manifest to Israel	Joh 1:31
needed not that any s. testify of man	Joh 2:25
believeth in him s. not perish	Joh 3:15; 3:16
light, lest his deeds s. be reproved	Joh 3:20
That all men s. honour the Son, even	Joh 5:23
prophet that s. come into the world	Joh 6:14

he hath given me I s. lose nothing	Joh 6:39
s. raise it up again at the last day	Joh 6:39
believed not, and who s. betray him	Joh 6:64
for it was that s. betray him	Joh 6:71
the law of Moses s. not be broken	Joh 7:23
that believe on him s. receive	Joh 7:39
us, that such s. be stoned	Joh 8:5
ye s. have known my Father also	Joh 8:19
and if I s. say, I know him not, I	Joh 8:55
of God s. be made manifest in him	Joh 9:3
he s. be put out of the synagogue	Joh 9:22
If ye were blind, ye s. have no sin	Joh 9:41
of God, which s. come into the world	Joh 11:27
even this man s. not have died	Joh 11:37
that one man s. die for the people	Joh 11:50
that Jesus s. die for that nation	Joh 11:51
he s. gather together in one the	Joh 11:52
he s. shew it, that they might take	Joh 11:57
Simon's son, which s. betray him	Joh 12:4
that the Son of man s. be glorified	Joh 12:23
signifying what death he s. die	Joh 12:33
that they s. not see with their eyes	Joh 12:40
and be converted, and I s. heal them	Joh 12:40
they s. be put out of the synagogue	Joh 12:42
on me s. not abide in darkness	Joh 12:46
what I s. say, and what I s. speak	Joh 12:49
hour was come that he s. depart out	Joh 13:1
For he knew who s. betray him	Joh 13:11
that ye s. do as I have done to you	Joh 13:15
that he s. ask who it s. be of whom	Joh 13:24
that he s. give something to the poor	Joh 13:29
me, ye s. have known my Father also	Joh 14:7
that he s. go and bring forth fruit	Joh 15:16
fruit, and that your fruit s. remain	Joh 15:16
unto you, that ye s. not be offended	Joh 16:1
needest not that any man s. ask thee	Joh 16:30
s. give eternal life to as many as thou	Joh 17:2
all things that s. come upon him	Joh 18:4
that one man s. die for the people	Joh 18:14
judgment hall, lest they s. be defiled	Joh 18:28
signifying what death he s. die	Joh 18:32
I s. not be delivered to the Jews	Joh 18:36
that I s. bear witness unto the truth	Joh 18:37
that I s. release unto you one at the	Joh 18:39
bodies s. not remain upon the cross on	Joh 19:31
done, that the scripture s. be fulfilled	Joh 19:36
by what death he s. glorify God	Joh 21:19
brethren, that that disciple s. not die	Joh 21:23
which, if they s. be written every one	Joh 21:25
contain the books that s. be written	Joh 21:25
they s. not depart from Jerusalem	Ac 1:4

not possible that he s. be *Ac 2:24*
holden of
right hand, that I s. not be *Ac 2:25*
moved
the church daily from as s. be *Ac 2:47*
saved
his prophets, that Christ s. *Ac 3:18*
suffer
people, lest they s. have been *Ac 5:26*
stoned
you that ye s. not teach in this *Ac 5:28*
name
they s. not speak in name *Ac 5:40*
of Jesus
that we s. leave the word of *Ac 6:2*
God, and
his seed s. sojourn in a strange *Ac 7:6*
land
that they s. bring them into *Ac 7:6*
bondage
he s. make it according to the *Ac 7:44*
fashion
can I, except some man s. *Ac 8:31*
guide me
vision which he hath seen s. *Ac 10:17*
mean
that I s. not call any man *Ac 10:28*
common
water, that these s. not be *Ac 10:47*
baptized
that he s. go as far as *Ac 11:22*
Antioch
s. be great dearth *Ac 11:28*
throughout all
commanded they s. be put *Ac 12:19*
to death
desired they Pilate that he s. *Ac 13:28*
be slain
word of God s. first have been *Ac 13:46*
spoken
that ye s. turn from these *Ac 14:15*
vanities
s. go up to Jerusalem unto the *Ac 15:2*
apostles
Gentiles by my mouth s. hear *Ac 15:7*
the word
That they s. seek the Lord, if *Ac 17:27*
haply
reason would that I s. bear *Ac 18:14*
with you
people, that they s. believe on *Ac 19:4*
him
on him which s. come after *Ac 19:4*
him, that
great goddess Diana s. be *Ac 19:27*
despised
her magnificence s. be *Ac 19:27*
destroyed
that they s. see his face no *Ac 20:38*
more
that he s. not go up to *Ac 21:4*
Jerusalem
an old disciple, with whom *Ac 21:16*
we s. lodge
an offering s. be offered for *Ac 21:26*
every one
earth: for it is not fit that he *Ac 22:22*
s. live
that he s. be examined by *Ac 22:24*
scourging
him which s. have examined *Ac 22:29*
him
Paul s. have been pulled in *Ac 23:10*
pieces of
and s. have been killed of *Ac 23:27*
them
he s. forbid none of his *Ac 24:23*
acquaintance
that money s. have been *Ac 24:26*
given him of
that Paul s. be kept at *Ac 25:4*
Caesarea, and
s. it be thought a thing *Ac 26:8*
incredible
with you, that God s. raise the *Ac 26:8*
dead
that they s. repent and turn to *Ac 26:20*
God
prophets and Moses say s. *Ac 26:22*
come
That Christ s. suffer, and *Ac 26:23*
that he
suffer, and that he s. be the *Ac 26:23*
first that
be the first that s. risen from *Ac 26:23*
the dead
s. shew light unto the people *Ac 26:23*
determined that we s. sail into *Ac 27:1*
Italy

lest they s. fall into the *Ac 27:17*
quicksands
all hope that we s. be saved *Ac 27:20*
was then
ye s. have hearkened unto *Ac 27:21*
me, and
lest we s. have fallen upon *Ac 27:29*
rocks
lest any of them s. swim out *Ac 27:42*
s. cast themselves first into *Ac 27:43*
the sea
looked when he s. have *Ac 28:6*
swollen
lest they s. see with their *Ac 28:27*
eyes, and
with their heart, and s. be *Ac 28:27*
converted
be converted, and I s. heal *Ac 28:27*
them
that preachest a man s. not *Ro 2:21*
steal
sayest a man s. not commit *Ro 2:22*
adultery
that he s. be the heir of the *Ro 4:13*
world
so we also s. walk in newness *Ro 6:4*
of life
that henceforth we s. not serve *Ro 6:6*
sin
that ye s. obey it in the lusts *Ro 6:12*
thereof
that ye s. be married to *Ro 7:4*
another
that we s. bring forth fruit *Ro 7:4*
unto God
that we s. serve in newness of *Ro 7:6*
spirit
know not what we s. pray for *Ro 8:26*
as we
eyes that they s. not see, and *Ro 11:8*
ears
and ears that they s. not *Ro 11:8*
hear; unto
Have they stumbled that they *Ro 11:11*
s. fall
that ye s. be ignorant of this *Ro 11:25*
mystery
ye s. be wise in your own *Ro 11:25*
conceits
I s. be the minister of Jesus *Ro 15:16*
Christ to
lest I s. build upon another *Ro 15:20*
man's
s. say that I had baptized in *1Co 1:15*
mine own
the cross of Christ s. be *1Co 1:17*
made of none
That no flesh s. glory in his *1Co 1:29*
presence
your faith s. not stand in the *1Co 2:5*
wisdom
small thing that I s. be judged *1Co 4:3*
of you
that one s. have his father's *1Co 5:1*
wife
he that ploweth s. plow in *1Co 9:10*
hope
in hope s. be partaker of his *1Co 9:10*
hope
lest we s. hinder the gospel *1Co 9:12*
of Christ
preach the gospel s. live of *1Co 9:14*
the gospel
things that it s. be so done *1Co 9:15*
unto me
any man s. make my glorying *1Co 9:15*
void
to others, I myself s. be a *1Co 9:27*
castaway
I would not that ye s. be *1Co 10:1*
ignorant
intent we s. not lust after evil *1Co 10:6*
things
that ye s. have fellowship *1Co 10:20*
with devils
judge ourselves, we s. not be *1Co 11:31*
judged
s. not be condemned with *1Co 11:32*
the world
there s. be no schism in the *1Co 12:25*
body
s. have the same care one *1Co 12:25*
for another
that we s. not trust in *2Co 1:9*
ourselves, but
that with me there s. be yea *2Co 1:17*
yea, and
I s. have sorrow from them of *2Co 2:3*
whom I

not that ye s. be grieved, *2Co 2:4*
but that ye
Lest Satan s. get an *2Co 2:11*
advantage of us
the image of God, s. shine *2Co 4:4*
unto them
s. not henceforth live unto *2Co 5:15*
themselves
no man s. blame us in this *2Co 8:20*
abundance
lest our boasting of you s. be *2Co 9:3*
in vain
s. be ashamed in this same *2Co 9:4*
confident
though I s. boast somewhat *2Co 10:8*
more of
destruction, I s. not be *2Co 10:8*
ashamed
so your minds s. be *2Co 11:3*
corrupted from
lest any man s. think of me *2Co 12:6*
above
lest I s. be exalted above *2Co 12:7*
measure
me, lest I s. be exalted above *2Co 12:7*
measure
evil; not that we s. appear *2Co 13:7*
approved
that ye s. do that which is *2Co 13:7*
honest
lest being present I s. use *2Co 13:10*
sharpness
men, I s. not be the servant of *Ga 1:10*
Christ
lest by any means I s. run, *Ga 2:2*
or had run
that we s. go unto the *Ga 2:9*
heathen, and
would that we s. remember *Ga 2:10*
the poor
that ye s. not obey the truth, *Ga 3:1*
before
it s. make the promise of *Ga 3:17*
none effect
the seed s. come to whom the *Ga 3:19*
promise
verily righteousness s. have *Ga 3:21*
been by
the faith which s. afterwards *Ga 3:23*
be
you that ye s. not obey the *Ga 5:7*
truth
s. suffer persecution for the *Ga 6:12*
cross of
God forbid that I s. glory, *Ga 6:14*
save in the
s. be holy and without blame *Eph 1:4*
before
s. be to the praise of his *Eph 1:12*
glory, who
Not of works, lest any man s. *Eph 2:9*
boast
ordained that we s. walk in *Eph 2:10*
them
That the Gentiles s. be *Eph 3:6*
fellowheirs
I s. preach among the *Eph 3:8*
Gentiles the
it s. be holy and without *Eph 5:27*
blemish
But I would ye s. understand *Ph'p 1:12*
the name of Jesus every knee *Ph'p 2:10*
s. bow
every tongue s. confess that *Ph'p 2:11*
Jesus
lest I s. have sorrow upon *Ph'p 2:27*
sorrow
that in him s. all fulness dwell *Col 1:19*
lest any man s. beguile you *Col 2:4*
with
That no man s. be moved by *1Th 3:3*
these
that we s. suffer tribulation *1Th 3:4*
that ye s. abstain from *1Th 4:3*
fornication
one of you s. know how to *1Th 4:4*
possess his
that day s. overtake you as a *1Th 5:4*
thief
or sleep, we s. live together *1Th 5:10*
with him
delusion, that they s. believe a *2Th 2:11*
lie
any would not work, neither *2Th 3:10*
s. he eat
them which s. hereafter *1Ti 1:16*
believe
we s. live soberly, righteously *Tit 2:12*
we s. be made heirs according *Tit 3:7*

that thy benefit s. not be as it | Ph'm 14
were
lest at any time we s. let | Heb 2:1
them slip
he by the grace of God s. | Heb 2:9
taste death
whom sware he that they s. | Heb 3:18
not enter
any of you s. seem to come | Heb 4:1
short of it
was there that another priest | Heb 7:11
s. rise
were on earth, he s. not be | Heb 8:4
a priest
then s. no place have been | Heb 8:7
sought for
of things in the heaven s. be | Heb 9:23
purified
Nor yet that he s. offer | Heb 9:25
himself often
purged s. have no more | Heb 10:2
conscience
of bulls and of goats s. take | Heb 10:4
away sins
translated that he s. not see | Heb 11:5
death
a place which he s. after | Heb 11:8
receive
destroyed the firstborn s. | Heb 11:28
touch them
without us s. not be made | Heb 11:40
perfect
that the word s. not be | Heb 12:19
spoken to them
that we s. be a kind of | Jas 1:18
firstfruits of his
of the grace that s. come | 1Pe 1:10
unto you
Christ, and the glory that s. | 1Pe 1:11
follow
that ye s. shew forth the | 1Pe 2:9
praises of
example, that ye s. follow | 1Pe 2:21
his steps
to sins, s. live unto | 1Pe 2:24
righteousness
called, that ye s. inherit the | 1Pe 3:9
blessing
That he no longer s. live the | 1Pe 4:2
rest of
those that after s. live ungodly | 2Pe 2:6
not willing that any s. perish, | 2Pe 3:9
but
but that all s. come to | 2Pe 3:9
repentance
that we s. be called the sons | 1Jo 3:1
of God
beginning, that we s. love one | 1Jo 3:11
another
we s. believe on the name of | 1Jo 3:23
his Son
ye have heard that it s. come | 1Jo 4:3
from the beginning, ye s. walk in | 2Jo 6
it
ye s. earnestly contend for the | Jude 3
faith
they told you there s. be | Jude 18
mockers
s. walk after their own | Jude 18
ungodly lusts
earth, and that they s. kill one | Re 6:4
another
they s. rest yet for a little | Re 6:11
season
that s. be killed as they were | Re 6:11
be killed as they were, s. be | Re 6:11
fulfilled
the wind s. not blown on the | Re 7:1
earth. nor
that he s. offer it, with the | Re 8:3
prayers of
that they s. not hurt the grass | Re 9:4
it was given that they s. not kill | Re 9:5
them
that they s. be tormented five | Re 9:5
months
that they s. not worship devils | Re 9:20
that there s. to time no longer | Re 10:6
the mystery of God s. be | Re 10:7
finished, as
that they s. be judged, and | Re 11:18
that thou
they s. feed her there a | Re 12:6
thousand two
they s. make an image to the | Re 13:14
beast
the image of the beast s. | Re 13:15
both speak
the image of the beast s. be | Re 13:15
killed

that she s. be arrayed in fine | Re 19:8
linen
that with it he s. smite the | Re 19:15
nations
that he s. deceive the nations | Re 20:3
no more
till the thousand years s. be | Re 20:3
fulfilled

SHOULDER

putting the bread on | Ge 21:14;
Hagar's s. |
Rebekah with pitcher upon | Ge 24:15;
s. | 24:45
and let down her pitcher | Ge 24:46
from her s.
Issachar bowed his s. to | Ge 49:15
bear, became servant
the ephod shall have two s. | Ex 28:7
pieces
put the ends of the chains on | Ex 28:25
the s. pieces
sanctify the s. of the | Ex 29:27
heave-offering
they made s. pieces for it to | Ex 39:4
couple it
priest take sodden s. | Nu 6:19; De 18:3
take ye every man a stone | Jos 4:5
upon his s.
Abimelech laid a bow on his | J'g 9:48
s.
and the cook took up the s. | 1Sa 9:24
withdrew the s. and hardened | Ne 9:29
their neck
surely I would take it on | Job 31:36
my s. bind it
I removed his s. from the | Ps 81:6
burden
thou hast broken the staff of | Isa 9:4
his s.
and the government shall be | Isa 9:6
upon his s.
his burden shall be taken | Isa 10:27
from off thy s.
the key of David will lay | Isa 22:22
upon his s.
they bear him upon the s. | Isa 45:7
they carry him
I bare it on my s. in their | Eze 12:7
sight
prince shall bear upon his s. | Eze 12:12
in the twilight
gather the pieces even the | Eze 24:4
thigh and s.
thou didst break and rend all | Eze 29:7
their s.
and every s. was peeled | Ex 29:18
ye have thrust with side and | Eze 34:21
with s.
but they refused and pulled | Zec 7:11
away the s.
when found it lays it on his s. | Lu 15:5
rejoicing

SHOULDER BLADE

then let mine arm fall from | Job 31:22
my s. blade

HEAVE SHOULDER

the heave s. have I taken | Le 7:34;
 | Nu 6:20
the heave s. shall ye eat in | Le 10:14
a clean place
heave s. and wave breast | Le 10:15
shall they bring

RIGHT SHOULDER

thou shalt take of the ram | Ex 29:22
the right s.
the right s. shall ye give unto | Le 7:32
the priest
offereth, shall have the right s. | Le 7:33
for his part
Moses took the fat and the | Le 8:25
right s.
put them on the fat, and upon | Le 8:26
the right s.
the right s. waved in thine | Le 9:21;
 | Nu 18:18

SHOULDERPIECES

It shall have the two s. thereof | Ex 28:7
on the s. of the ephod before | Ex 28:25
They made s. for it, to couple | Ex 39:4
and put them on the s. of the | Ex 39:18
ephod

SHOULDERS

and laid it upon both their | Ge 9:23
s. and
up in their clothes upon | Ex 12:34
their s.
stones upon the s. of the | Ex 28:12
ephod
upon his two s. for | Ex 28:12
a memorial
he put them on the s. of the | Ex 39:7
ephod
that they should bear upon their | Nu 7:9
s.
and he shall dwell between | De 33:12
his s.
put them upon his s. and | J'g 16:3
carried
from his s. and upward he was | 1Sa 9:2
the people from his s. and | 1Sa 10:23
upward
a target of brass between his | 1Sa 17:6
s.
bare the ark of God upon | 1Ch 15:15
their s.
shall not be a burden upon | 2Ch 35:3
your s.
fly upon the s. of the | Isa 11:14
Philistines
burden depart from off their | Isa 14:25
s.
riches upon the s. of young | Isa 30:6
asses
shall be carried upon their s. | Isa 49:22
sight shalt thou bear it upon | Eze 12:6
thy s.
borne, and lay them on men's | M't 23:4
s.
hath found it, he layeth it on | Lu 15:5
his s.

SHOULDEST

commanded thee that thou s. | Ge 3:11
not eat
lest thou s. say, I have made | Ge 14:23
Abram
thou s. have brought | Ge 26:10
guiltiness upon
s. thou therefore serve me | Ge 29:15
for nought
that thou s. say unto me, | Nu 11:12
Carry them
s. be driven to worship them | De 4:19
thou s. keep all his | De 26:18
commandments
That thou s. enter into | De 29:12
covenant
It is not in heaven, that thou | De 30:12
s. say
is it beyond the sea, that | De 30:13
thou s. say
people Israel, and s. thou | J'g 11:23
possess it
that thou s. take knowledge of | Ru 2:10
me
why s. thou bring me to thy | 1Sa 20:8
father
thou s. look upon such a dead | 2Sa 9:8
dog
that thou s. tell them who | 1Ki 1:20
shall sit
told me that thou s. surely | 2Ki 8:14
recover
Thou s. have smitten five or | 2Ki 13:19
six
for why s. thou meddle to | 2Ki 14:10
thy hurt
that thou s. fall, even thou | 2Ki 14:10
thou s. be to lay waste | 2Ki 19:25
fenced cities
s. be ruler over my people | 1Ch 17:7
Israel
S. thou help the ungodly, and | 2Ch 19:2
love
forbear; why s. thou be | 2Ch 25:16
smitten
why s. thou meddle to thine | 2Ch 25:19
hurt
that thou s. fall, even thou | 2Ch 25:19
is man, that thou s. magnify | Job 7:17
him
thou s. set thine heart upon | Job 7:17
him
that thou s. visit him every | Job 7:18
morning
it good unto thee that thou s. | Job 10:3
oppress
thou s. despise the work of | Job 10:3
thine

thou *s.* take it to the bound *Job 38:20*
thereof
thou *s.* know the paths to *Job 38:20*
the house
s. take my covenant in thy *Ps 50:16*
mouth
If thou, Lord, *s.* *Ps 130:3*
mark iniquities, O
Lest thou *s.* ponder the path of *Pr 5:6*
life
than that thou *s.* be put lower *Pr 25:7*
in the
thou *s.* bray a fool in a *Pr 27:22*
mortar among
Better is it that thou *s.* not vow *Ec 5:5*
than that thou *s.* vow and not *Ec 5:5*
pay
wise: why *s.* thou destroy *Ec 7:16*
thyself
why *s.* thou die before thy *Ec 7:17*
time
is good that thou *s.* take hold *Ec 7:18*
of this
that thou *s.* be to lay waste *Isa 37:26*
defenced
lest thou *s.* say, Mine idol hath *Isa 48:5*
done
lest thou *s.* say, Behold, I *Isa 48:7*
knew them
thee by the way that thou *s.* *Isa 48:17*
light thing that thou *s.* be my *Isa 49:6*
servant
s. be afraid of a man that *Isa 51:12*
shall die
why *s.* thou be as a stranger *Jer 14:8*
in the
Why *s.* thou be as a man *Jer 14:9*
astonied
that thou *s.* put him in *Jer 29:26*
prison, and in
s. make thy nest as high as *Jer 49:16*
the eagle
thou *s.* not have looked on the *Ob 12*
day of
neither *s.* thou have rejoiced *Ob 12*
over
neither *s.* thou have spoken *Ob 12*
proudly
Thou *s.* not have entered into *Ob 13*
thou *s.* not have looked on their *Ob 13*
s. thou have stood in the *Ob 14*
crossway
neither *s.* thou have delivered *Ob 14*
that thou *s.* come under my *M't 8:8*
roof
S. not thou also have had *M't 18:33*
compassion
thou *s.* do for us *M'k 10:35*
whatsoever we shall
that thou *s.* enter under my roof *Lu 7:6*
believe thou *s.* see the glory *Joh 11:40*
of God
thou *s.* take them out of the *Joh 17:15*
world
thou thou *s.* keep them from *Joh 17:15*
the evil
that thou *s.* be for salvation *Ac 13:47*
unto the
that thou *s.* know his will, *Ac 22:14*
and see
and *s.* hear the voice of his *Ac 22:14*
mouth
that thou *s.* set in order the *Tit 1:5*
things
that thou *s.* receive him for *Ph'm 15*
ever
thou *s.* give reward unto thy *Re 11:18*
servants
s. destroy them which destroy *Re 11:18*

SHOUT

voice of them that *s.* for *Ex 32:18*
mastery
the *s.* of a king is among *Nu 23:21*
them
the trumpet, all the people *Jos 6:5*
shall *s.*
with a great *s.;* and the wall of *Jos 6:5*
shall not *s.* nor make any *Jos 6:10*
noise
day I bid you *s.;* then shall *Jos 6:10*
ye *s.*
Joshua said unto the people *Jos 6:16*
S.
the people shouted with a *Jos 6:20*
great *s.*
all Israel shouted with a great *1Sa 4:5*
s.
Philistines heard the noise of *1Sa 4:6*
the *s.*

noise of this great *s.* in the *1Sa 4:6*
camp
Then the men of Judah gave *2Ch 15:15*
a *s.*
the people shouted with a *Ezr 3:11*
great *s.*
not discern the noise of the *s.* *Ezr 3:13*
of joy
the people shouted with a *Ezr 3:13*
loud *s.*
let them ever *s.* for joy, *Ps 5:11*
because
s. for joy, all ye that are *Ps 32:11*
upright in
Let them *s.* for joy, and be *Ps 35:27*
glad
s. unto God with the voice of *Ps 47:1*
God is gone up with a *s.* the *Ps 47:5*
Lord
they *s.* for joy, they also sing *Ps 65:13*
and let thy saints *s.* for joy *Ps 132:9*
her saints shall *s.* aloud for *Ps 132:16*
joy
Cry out and *s.* thou inhabitant *Isa 12:6*
s. from the top of the *Isa 42:11*
mountains
s. ye lower parts of the earth *Isa 44:23*
the *s.* of battle (B) *Jer 4:19*
he shall give a *s.* as they that *Jer 25:30*
tread
s. among the chief of *Jer 31:7*
the nations
S. against her round about: *Jer 50:15*
she
they shall lift up a *s.* against *Jer 51:14*
thee
when I cry and *s.* he shutteth *La 3:8*
out
s., O Israel; be glad and *Zep 3:14*
rejoice
Zion: *s.,* O daughter of *Zec 9:9*
Jerusalem
s. from the housetops (N) *M't 10:27*
And the people gave a *s.* *Ac 12:22*
descend from heaven with *1Th 4:16*
a *s.*
s. of the archangel (A)(P) *1Th 4:16*
s. of a great crowd (A) *Re 19:1*
s. of a vast throng (A) *Re 19:6*

SHOUTED

the noise of the people as *Ex 32:17*
they *s.*
when all the people saw, they *Le 9:24*
s.
people *s.* when the priests *Jos 6:20*
blew
the people *s.* with a great *Jos 6:20*
shout
Lehi, the Philistines *s.* *J'g 15:14*
against him
all Israel *s.* with a great shout, *1Sa 4:5*
so
the people *s.* and said, God *1Sa 10:24*
save the
to the fight, and *s.* for the *1Sa 17:20*
battle
of Israel and of Judah arose *1Sa 17:52*
and *s.*
as the men of Judah *s.* it *2Ch 13:15*
came to
all the people *s.* with a great *Ezr 3:11*
shout
voice; and many *s.* aloud for *Ezr 3:12*
joy
for the people *s.* with a loud *Ezr 3:13*
shout
and all the sons of God *s.* for *Job 38:7*
joy

SHOUTETH

man that *s.* by reason of wine *Ps 78:65*

SHOUTING

up the ark of the Lord with *2Sa 6:15*
s.
up the ark of the Lord *1Ch 15:28*
with *s.*
with a loud voice, and with *2Ch 15:14*
s. and
thunder of the captains, and *Job 39:25*
the *s.*
when the wicked perish, there *Pr 11:10*
is *s.*
for the *s.* for thy summer *Isa 16:9*
fruits
singing, neither shall there be *Isa 16:10*
s.

made their vintage *s.* to *Isa 16:10*
cease
morning, and the *s.* at *Jer 20:16*
noontide
none shall tread with *s.* *Jer 48:33*
their *s.* shall be no *s.* *Jer 48:33*
to lift up the voice with *s.* *Eze 21:22*
thereof, with *s.* in the day of *Am 1:14*
battle
Moab shall die with tumult, *Am 2:2*
with *s.*

SHOUTINGS

full of *s.* (S) *Isa 22:2*
joyful *s.* upon the mountains *Eze 7:7*
(S)
the headstone thereof with *s.* *Zec 4:7*

SHOVEL

s. among thy weapons (S) *De 23:13*
hath been winnowed with the *Isa 30:24*
s.
his *s.* in his hand (N) *M't 3:12*

SHOVELS

and his *s.* and his basons, and *Ex 27:3*
his
pots, and the *s.* and the *Ex 38:3*
basons
the fleshhooks, and the *s.* and *Nu 4:14*
Hiram made the lavers, and *1Ki 7:40*
the *s.*
pots, and the *s.* and the *1Ki 7:45*
basons
pots, and the *s.* and the *2Ki 25:14*
snuffers
Huram made the pots, and *2Ch 4:11*
the *s.*
The pots also, and the *s.* and *2Ch 4:16*
shovels (A)(B)(E) *Isa 3:22*
The caldrons also, and the *s.* *Jer 52:18*

SHOW

not *s.* partially (S) *De 16:9*
s. ourselves to them (B)(R) *1Sa 14:8*
make a *s.* of religion (N) *M't 6:1*
to *s.* our ready mind (S) *2Co 8:19*
by his noble living *s.* (A) *Jas 3:13*
s. by good life (E) *Jas 3:13*

SHOWER

there shall be an overflowing *Eze 13:11*
s.
and there shall be an *Eze 13:13*
overflowing *s.*
I will cause the *s.* to come *Eze 34:26*
down in
ye say, There cometh a *s.;* *Lu 12:54*
and so

SHOWERS

and as the *s.* upon the grass *De 32:2*
wet with the *s.* of the *Job 24:8*
mountains
thou makest it soft with *s.:* *Ps 65:10*
thou
grass; as *s.* that water the *Ps 72:6*
earth
the *s.* have been withholden *Jer 3:3*
rain? or can the heavens give *Jer 14:22*
s.
there shall be *s.* of blessing *Eze 34:26*
the Lord, as the *s.* upon the *Mic 5:7*
grass
clouds, and give them *s.* of *Zec 10:1*
rain

SHOWING

s. and proving by (A)(B)(E) *Ac 18:2*

SHOWN

thou hast *s.* care (S) *2Ki 4:13*

SHRANK

eat not of the sinew which *s.* *Ge 32:32*
Jacob's thigh in the sinew *Ge 32:32*
that *s.*

SHRED

s. them into the pot of *2Ki 4:39*
pottage

SHREWD

a *s.* person (R)   2Sa 13:3

SHREWDLY

deal *s.* with them (A)(B)(R)   Ex 1:10
acting *s.* and prudently   Lu 16:8
(A)(B)

SHRINE

both it and its *s.* (B)   2Sa 15:25
the innermost *s.* (P)(R)   Heb 6:19

SHRINES

I looked at your *s.* (P)   Ac 17:23
which made silver *s.* for   Ac 19:24
Diana

SHRINK

foreigners *s.* in despair (B)   2Sa 22:46
abstain, *s.* from sexual vice   1Th 4:3
(A)

SHROUD

and with a shadowing *s.* and   Eze 31:3

SHRUB

like the *s.* in the desert (S)   Jer 17:6;
                                          48:6

SHRUBS

cast the child under one of   Ge 21:15
the *s.*

SHRUNK

members overgrown or *s.* (B)   Le 22:23

SHUA

daughter of *S.* the Canaanitess   1Ch 2:3
and Hotham, and *S.* their   1Ch 7:32
sister

SHUAH

and Midian, and Ishbak, and   Ge 25:2
S.
Canaanite, whose name was *S.*   Ge 38:2
daughter of *S.* Judah's wife   Ge 38:12
died
and Midian, and Ishbak, and   1Ch 1:32
S.
the brother of *S.* begat Mehir   1Ch 4:11

SHUAL

to Ophrah, unto the land of   1Sa 13:17
S.
and Harnepher, and *S.* and   1Ch 7:36
Beri

SHUBAEL

Of the sons of Amram; *S.*   1Ch 24:20
thirteenth to *S.* he, his   1Ch 25:20
sons, and

SHUDDER

you will *s.* (R)   Isa 32:10
demons believe and *s.*   Jas 2:19
(B)(P)(R)

SHUDDERED

the depths *s.* (A)(B)   Ps 77:16;
                                          Isa 32:11

SHUHAM

S. the family of the   Nu 26:42
Shuhamites

SHUHAMITES

of Shuham, the family of the   Nu 26:42
S.
the families of the *S.*   Nu 26:43
according

SHUHITE

the Temanites, and Bildad the   Job 2:11
S.
Then answered Bildad the *S.*   Job 8:1;
and   18:1; 25:1
the Temanite and Bildad the   Job 42:9
S.

SHULAMITE

Return, return, O *S.*; return   Ca 6:13
What will ye see in the *S.*   Ca 6:13

SHUMATHITES

the Puhites, and the *S.* and   1Ch 2:53

SHUN

But *s.* profane and vain   2Ti 2:16
babblings

SHUNAMMITE

and found Abishag a *S.* and   1Ki 1:3
Abishag the *S.* ministered   1Ki 1:15
he gave me Abishag the *S.* to   1Ki 2:17
wife
Abishag the *S.* be given to   1Ki 2:21
Adonijah
ask Abishag the *S.* for   1Ki 2:22
Adonijah
to Gehazi his servant, Call   2Ki 4:12
this *S.*
servant; Behold, yonder is   2Ki 4:25
that *S.*
called Gehazi, and said, Call   2Ki 4:36
this *S.*

SHUNEM

Jezreel, and Chesulloth, and   Jos 19:18
S.
and came and pitched in *S.*   1Sa 28:4
on a day, that Elisha passed to   2Ki 4:8
S.

SHUNI

and Haggi, *S.* and Ezbon, Eri   Ge 46:16
of *S.* the family of the   Nu 26:15
Shunites

SHUNITES

of Shuni, the family of the *S.*   Nu 26:15

SHUNNED

feared God and *s.* evil (S)   Job 1:1
feareth God and *s.* evil (S)   Job 1:8;
                                          2:3
I have not *s.* to declare unto   Ac 20:27
you

SHUPHAM

S. the family of the   Nu 26:39
Shuphamites

SHUPHAMITES

Of Shupham, the family of   Nu 26:39
the *S.*

SHUPPIM

S. also, and Huppim, the   1Ch 7:12
children
to wife the sister of Huppim   1Ch 7:15
and *S.*
To *S.* and Hosah the lot   1Ch 26:16
came forth

SHUR

by the fountain in the way to   Ge 16:7
S.
dwelled between Kadesh and   Ge 20:1
S.
they dwelt from Havilah   Ge 25:18
unto *S.*
went out into the wilderness   Ex 15:22
of *S.*
Havilah until thou comest to   1Sa 15:7
S.
as thou goest to *S.* even unto   1Sa 27:8

SHUSHAN

year, as I was in *S.* the palace   Ne 1:1
throne which was in *S.* the   Es 1:2
palace
the people that were present in   Es 1:5
S.
all the fair young virgins unto *S.*   Es 2:3
in *S.* the palace was a certain   Es 2:5
Jew
were gathered together unto *S.*   Es 2:8
decree was given in *S.* the   Es 3:15
palace
but the city *S.* was perplexed   Es 3:15
of the decree that was given at   Es 4:8
S.
all the Jews that are present in   Es 4:16
S.
decree was given at *S.* the   Es 8:14
palace
the city of *S.* rejoiced and was   Es 8:15
glad
in *S.* the palace the Jews slew   Es 9:6
the number of those slain in   Es 9:11
S.
destroyed five hundred men in   Es 9:12
S.
granted to the Jews which are   Es 9:13
in *S.*
and the decree was given at *S.*   Es 9:14
the Jews that were in *S.*   Es 9:15
gathered
and slew three hundred men at   Es 9:15
S.
the Jews that were at *S.*   Es 9:18
assembled
saw, that I was at *S.* in the   Da 8:2
palace

SHUSHAN-EDUTH

To the chief Musician upon   Ps 60 title
S.

SHUT

went in of all flesh, the Lord,   Ge 7:16
s. him in
the wilderness hath *s.* them in   Ex 14:3
let her be *s.* out from camp   Nu 12:14
seven days
Miriam was *s.* out from the   Nu 12:15
camp seven days
nor *s.* thy hand from thy poor   De 15:7
brother
they *s.* the gate of Jericho   Jos 2:7
they *s.* the tower to them, and   J'g 9:51
gat them up
for he is *s.* in, by entering   1Sa 23:7
into a town
I commanded gates to be *s.*   Ne 13:19
till after sabbath
let not the pit *s.* her mouth   Ps 69:15
upon me
s. their eyes, lest they see with   Isa 6:10
their eyes
key of David, so he shall   Isa 22:22
open and none shall *s.* he shall
s. and none shall open
for he hath *s.* their eyes, they   Isa 44:18
cannot see
to open before him, and gates   Isa 45:1
shall not be *s.*
the kings shall *s.* their mouths   Isa 52:15
at him
thy gates shall not be *s.* day   Isa 60:11
nor night
shall I *s.* the womb, saith thy   Isa 66:9
God
Spirit said, Go *s.* thyself   Eze 3:24
within thine house
gate which looketh toward   Eze 44:1
the east was *s.*
this gate be *s.* it shall not be   Eze 44:2
opened, God hath entered in by it
therefore, it shall be *s.*
the gate shall be *s.* the six   Eze 46:1
working-days
the gate shall not be *s.* till the   Eze 46:2
evening
after his going forth, one   Eze 46:12
shall *s.* the gate
my God hath *s.* the lions'   Da 6:22
mouths
the prison truly found we *s.* in   Ac 5:23
safety
these have power to *s.*   Re 11:6
heaven that it rain not
gates shall not be *s.* by day,   Re 21:25
no night there

SHUT *UP*

priest *s.* him *up* that hath plague seven days	Le 13:4; 13:5, 21, 26, 31, 33, 50, 54
the priest shall not *s.* him *up,* he is unclean	Le 13:11
the priest shall *s. up* the house seven days	Le 14:38
he that goeth in while the house is *s. up*	Le 14:46
wrath he kindled, and he *s. up* heaven	De 11:17
except their rock the Lord had *s.* them *up*	De 32:30
when he seeth there is none *s. up* nor left	De 32:36
now when Jericho was straitly *s. up*	Jos 6:1
the Lord had *s. up* Hannah's womb	1Sa 1:5
because the Lord had *s. up* her womb	1Sa 1:6
hid them and *s. up* their calves at home	1Sa 6:10
concubines were *s. up* to day of their death	1Sa 20:3
when heaven is *s. up*	1Ki 8:35; 2Ch 6:26; 7:13
cut off from Jeroboam him that is *s. up*	1Ki 14:10; 21:21; 2Ki 9:8
there was not any *s. up* nor left	2Ki 14:26
therefore the king of Assyria *s.* him *up*	2Ki 17:4
Ahaz *s. up* doors of house	2Ch 28:24; 29:7
the house of Shemaiah who was *s. up*	Ne 6:10
because it *s.* not *up* my mother's womb	Job 3:10
if he cut off, and *s. up,* who can hinder him	Job 11:10
or who hath *s. up* the sea with doors	Job 38:8
his scales are *s. up* together as a seal	Job 41:15
hast not *s.* me *up* into hand of the enemy	Ps 31:8
hath he in anger *s. up* his tender mercies	Ps 77:9
I am *s. up* and I cannot come forth	Ps 88:8
a spring *s. up,* a fountain sealed	Ca 4:12
every house is *s. up,* no man can come in	Isa 24:10
they shall be *s. up* in the prison, and be visited	Isa 24:22
the cities of the south shall be *s. up*	Jer 13:19
his word was as fire *s. up* in my bones	Jer 20:9
the prophet was *s. up* by Zedekiah	Jer 32:2; 32:3
word of Lord came, while he was *s. up*	Jer 33:1; 39:15
I am *s. up,* I cannot go to the Lord's house	Jer 36:5
s. up the vision	Da 8:26
s. up the words	Da 12:4
ye *s. up* kingdom of heaven against men	M't 23:13
added this, that he *s. up* John in prison	Lu 3:20
when the heaven was *s. up* three years	Lu 4:25
many saints did I *s. up* in prison	Ac 26:10
s. up all under sin (E)	Ga 3:22
s. up to the faith that should be revealed	Ga 3:23
s. up the devil and set a seal upon him	Re 20:3

SHUTHALHITES

Shuthelah, the family of the *S.*	Nu 26:35

SHUTHELAH

of *S.* the family of Shuthalhites	Nu 26:35
And these are the sons of *S.*	Nu 26:36
sons of Ephraim; *S.* and Bered	1Ch 7:20
And Zabad his son, and *S.* his son	1Ch 7:21

SHUTTETH

he *s. up* a man, and there can be	Job 12:14
He *s.* his eyes to devise froward	Pr 16:30
that *s.* his lips is esteemed a man	Pr 17:28
and *s.* his eyes from seeing evil	Isa 33:15
and shout, he *s.* out my prayer	La 3:8
s. up his bowels of compassion	1Jo 3:17
he that openeth, and no man *s.*	Re 3:7
and *s.* and no man openeth	Re 3:7

SHUTTING

about the time of *s.* of the gate	Jos 2:5

SHUTTLE

days are swifter than a weaver's *s.*	Job 7:6

SIA

children of *S.* the children of	Ne 7:47

SIAHA

children of *S.* the chilren of	Ezr 2:44

SIBBECAI

S. the Hushathite, Ilaithe, Ahohite	1Ch 11:29
was *S.* the Hushathite, of the sons	1Ch 27:11

SIBBECHAI

S. the Hushathite slew Saph	2Sa 21:18
S. the Hushathite slew Sippai	1Ch 20:4

SIBBOLETH

and he said *S.:* for he could not	J'g 12:6

SIBMAH

S. and Zareth-shahar in the	Jos 13:19
languish, and the vine of *S.*	Isa 16:8
weeping of Jazer the vine of *S.*	Isa 16:9
O vine of *S.* I will weep for thee	Jer 48:32

SIBRAIM

S. which is between the border	Eze 47:16

SICHEM

the land unto the place of *S.*	Ge 12:6

SICK

Joseph, Behold, thy father is *s.*	Ge 48:1
of her that is *s.* of her flowers	Le 15:33
to take David, she said, He is *s.*	1Sa 19:14
because three days agone I fell *s.*	1Sa 30:13
bare unto David, and it was very *s.*	2Sa 12:15
that he fell *s.* for his sister Tamar	2Sa 13:2
on thy bed, and make thyself *s.*	2Sa 13:5
lay down, and made himself *s.*	2Sa 13:6
Abijah the son of Jeroboam fell *s.*	1Ki 14:1
of thee for her son; for he is *s.*	1Ki 14:5
the mistress of the house, fell *s.*	1Ki 17:17
that was in Samaria, and was *s.*	2Ki 1:2
the king of Syria was *s.;* and it	2Ki 8:7
Ahab in Jezreel because he was *s.*	2Ki 8:29
Elisha was fallen *s.* of his sickness	2Ki 13:14
days was Hezekiah *s.* unto death	2Ki 20:1

heard that Hezekiah had been *s.*	2Ki 20:12
Ahab at Jezreel, because he was *s.*	2Ch 22:6
left him very *s.* (E)	2Ch 24:25
days Hezekiah was *s.* to the death	2Ch 32:24
sad, seeing thou art not *s.*	Ne 2:2
when they were *s.* my clothing	Ps 35:13
Hope deferred maketh the heart *s.*	Pr 13:12
shalt thou say, and I was not *s.*	Pr 23:35
me with apples: for I am *s.* of love	Ca 2:5
that ye tell him, I am *s.* of love	Ca 5:8
the whole head is *s.* and the whole	Isa 1:5
inhabitant shall not say, I am *s.*	Isa 33:24
days was Hezekiah *s.* unto death	Isa 38:1
king of Judah, when he had been *s.*	Isa 38:9
he had heard that he had been *s.*	Isa 39:1
them that are *s.* with famine	Jer 14:18
heart mortally *s.* (A)	Jer 17:9
have ye healed that which was *s.*	Eze 34:4
nor healed the *s.* (A)(B)(R)	Eze 34:4
will strengthen that which was *s.*	Eze 34:16
fainted, and was *s.* certain days	Da 8:27
king the princes have made him *s.*	Ho 7:5
will I make thee *s.* in smiting thee	Mic 6:13
if ye offer the lame and *s.* is it not	Mal 1:8
was torn, and the lame, and the *s.*	Mal 1:13
brought unto him all *s.* people	M't 4:24
servant at home *s.* of the palsy	M't 8:6
wife's mother laid *s.* of a fever	M't 8:14
and healed all that were *s.*	M't 8:16
brought a man *s.* of the palsy	M't 9:2
faith said unto the *s.* of the palsy	M't 9:2
(then saith he to the *s.* of the palsy	M't 9:6
physician, but they that are *s.*	M't 9:12
Heal the *s.* cleanse the lepers	M't 10:8
toward them, and he healed their *s.*	M't 14:14
all that were *s.* (A)(E)(R)	M't 14:35
I was *s.* and ye visited me: I was	M't 25:36
when saw we thee *s.* or in prison	M't 25:39
s. and in prison, and ye visited me	M't 25:43
naked, or *s.* or in prison, and did	M't 25:44
Simon's wife's mother lay *s.*	M'k 1:30
he healed many that were *s.*	M'k 1:34
him bringing one *s.* of the palsy	M'k 2:3
bed wherein the *s.* of the palsy lay	M'k 2:4
he said unto the *s.* of the palsy, Son	M'k 2:5
it easier to say to the *s.* of the palsy	M'k 2:9
sins, (he saith to the *s.* of the palsy	M'k 2:10
physician, but they that are *s.*	M'k 2:17
laid his hands upon a few *s.* folks	M'k 6:5
anointed with oil many that were *s.*	M'k 6:13
in beds those that were *s.*	M'k 6:55
they laid the *s.* in the streets	M'k 6:55
they shall lay hands on the *s.* and	M'k 16:18
all they that had any *s.* with divers	Lu 4:40
(he said unto the *s.* of the palsy	Lu 5:24
physician; but they that are *s.*	Lu 5:31
him, was *s.* and ready to die	Lu 7:2
the servant whole that had been *s.*	Lu 7:10

kingdom of God, and to heal | Lu 9:2
the s.
And heal the s. that are therein | Lu 10:9
whose son was s. at | Joh 4:46
Capernaum
performed on the s. | Joh 6:2
(A)(B)(E)(N)(P)
Now a certain man was s. | Joh 11:1
named
hair, whose brother Lazarus | Joh 11:2
was s.
behold, he whom thou lovest | Joh 11:3
is s.
had heard therefore that he | Joh 11:6
was s.
they brought forth the s. into | Ac 5:15
bringing s. folks, and them | Ac 5:16
which
years, and was s. of the palsy | Ac 9:33
days, that she was s. and died | Ac 9:37
brought unto the s. | Ac 19:12
handkerchiefs
father of Publius lay s. of a | Ac 28:8
fever and
ye had heard that he had | Ph'p 2:26
been s.
indeed he was s. nigh unto | Ph'p 2:27
death
Trophimus have I left at | 2Ti 4:20
Miletum s.
Is my s. among you? let him | Jas 5:14
call
prayer of faith shall save the | Jas 5:15
s.

SICKENING

a s. dread (B) | Isa 7:16
in day of sorrow, s. (A) | Isa 17:11

SICKLE

beginnest to put the s. to the | De 16:9
corn
not move a s. unto thy | De 23:25
neighbour's
his axe and his s. (S) | 1Sa 13:20
that handleth the s. in the | Jer 50:16
time of
Put ye in the s. for the | Joe 3:13
harvest is
immediately he putteth in the | M'k 4:29
s.
crown, and in his hand a | Re 14:14
sharp s.
cloud, Thrust in thy s. and | Re 14:15
reap
cloud thrust in his s. on the | Re 14:16
earth
heaven, he also having a | Re 14:17
sharp s.
cry to him that had the | Re 14:18
sharp s.
Thrust in thy sharp s. and | Re 14:18
gather
angel thrust in his s. into the | Re 14:19
earth

SICKLES

had a file for the s. (S) | 1Sa 13:21

SICKLY

many are weak and s. | 1Co 11:30
among you
another horse, s. pale (N) | Re 6:8
a horse s. green in color (P) | Re 6:8

SICKNESS

I will take s. away from the | Ex 23:25
midst
lie with a woman having her | Le 20:18
s.
will take away from thee all s. | De 7:15
Also every s. and every | De 28:61
plague
every s. and | De 28:61
affliction (A)(B)(R)
plague, whatsoever s. there be | 1Ki 8:37
his s. was so sore, that there | 1Ki 17:17
recover from this s. (E)(R) | 2Ki 1:2;
| 8:8
Now Elisha was fallen sick | 2Ki 13:14
of his s.
sore or whatsoever s. there be | 2Ch 6:28
in his s. he did not seek (B) | 2Ch 16:12
shalt have great s. by | 2Ch 21:15
disease of

bowels fall out by reason of | 2Ch 21:15
the s.
bowels fell out by reason of | 2Ch 21:19
his s.
because of s. (B) | 2Ch 21:19
wilt make all his bed in his s. | Ps 41:3
spirit will endure s. (B)(R) | Pr 18:14
sorrow and wrath with his s. | Ec 5:17
sick, and was recovered of his | Isa 38:9
s.
he will cut me off with | Isa 38:12
pining s.
acquainted with s. (A)(B) | Isa 53:3
borne s., weakness (A) | Isa 53:4
When Ephraim saw his s. and | Ho 5:13
healing all manner of s. and | M't 4:23
healing every s. and every | M't 9:35
disease
to heal all manner of s. and | M't 10:1
This s. is not unto death, but | Joh 11:4

SICKNESSES

sore s. and of long | De 28:59
continuance
s. which the Lord hath laid | De 29:22
upon
borne our s. (B) | Isa 53:4
our infirmities, and bare our | M't 8:17
s.
to have power to heal s. and | M'k 3:15
cured of s. (A)(E) | Lu 7:21

SIDDIM

joined together in the vale of | Ge 14:3
S.
battle with them in the vale of | Ge 14:8
S.
the vale of S. was full of | Ge 14:10
slimepits

SIDE

door of the ark shall set in the | Ge 6:16
s. thereof
her maidens walked along by | Ex 2:5
river s.
the west s. of the desert (S) | Ex 3:1
shalt strike blood on the two | Ex 12:7;
s. posts | 12:22
he seeth blood on lintel and | Ex 12:23
s. posts
Aaron and Hur stayed up | Ex 17:12
Moses' hands, one on one
s. other on other s.
who is on the Lord's s. let | Ex 32:26
him come
go in
every man his sword by his s. | Ex 32:27
shall kill it on s. of altar | Le 1:11
northward
blood be wrung out at the s. | Le 1:15
of altar
blood of sin-offering sprinkled | Le 5:9
on s. of altar
wall on this s. and a wall on | Nu 22:24
that s.
spread as gardens by the | Nu 24:6
river's s.
we will not inherit on yonder | Nu 32:19
s. Jordan
ask from one s. of heaven to | De 4:32
the other
put the book of the law in s. | De 31:26
of the ark
on the s. belonging to (S) | Jos 22:11
a Levite sojourning on s. of | J'g 19:1;
Ephraim | 19:18
fell backward by the s. of the | 1Sa 4:18
gate
put mice in a coffer by s. of | 1Sa 6:8
the ark
I will shoot three arrows on | 1Sa 20:20
the s. thereof
king sat, and Abner sat by | 1Sa 20:25
Saul's s.
thrust his sword into his | 2Sa 2:16
fellow's s.
king's sons came by way of | 2Sa 13:34
the hill s.
Shimei went along on the | 2Sa 16:13
hill's s. against
to the one s. and to the other | 2Ki 2:8;
(S) | 2:14
Jehu said, Who is on my s.? | 2Ki 9:32
who
thine are we, David, and on | 1Ch 12:18
thy s.
having Judah and Benjamin | 2Ch 11:12
on his s.

every one had his sword | Ne 4:18
girded by his s.
and destruction shall be | Job 18:12
ready at his s.
thousand shall fall at thy s. ten | Ps 91:7
thousand
the Lord is on my s., I will | Ps 118:6
not fear
if it had not been Lord on | Ps 124:1;
our s. | 124:2
on the s. of their oppressors | Ec 4:1
was power
thy daughters shall be nursed | Isa 60:4
as thy s.
not turn from one s. to | Eze 4:8
another
the number of days thou shalt | Eze 4:9
lie upon thy s.
with a writer's inkhorn by his s. | Eze 9:2;
| 9:3, 11
I will open the s. of Moab | Eze 25:9
from the cities
ye have thrust with s. and | Eze 34:21
shoulder
by the s. of (S) | Eze 42:7
it raised up itself on one s. | Da 7:5
three ribs
she shall not stand on his s. | Da 11:17
nor be
the two thieves, on either s. | Joh 19:18
one of soldiers with a spear | Joh 19:34
pierced his s.
he shewed unto them his | Joh 20:20
hands and his s.
except I thrust hand into s., | Joh 20:25
I will not believe
reach thy hand, and thrust it | Joh 20:27
into my s.
angel smote Peter on the s. | Ac 12:7
raised him up
on the sabbath we went out | Ac 16:13
by a river s.
on either s. of river was the | Re 22:2
tree of life

EVERY SIDE

from tabernacle of Abiram | Nu 16:27
on *every s.*
blow ye the trumpets on *every* | J'g 7:18
delivered them from enemies | J'g 8:34;
on *every s.* | 1Sa 12:11
Saul fought against enemies | 1Sa 14:47
every s.
wars which were about him on | 1Ki 5:3
every s.
the Lord hath given me rest on | 1Ki 5:4
every s.
hath he not given you rest | 1Ch 22:18
on *every s.*
he hath given us rest on | 2Ch 14:7
every s.
thus the Lord guided them | 2Ch 32:22
on *every s.*
put hedge about all he hath | Job 1:10
on *every s.*
terror shall make him afraid | Job 18:11
on *every s.*
he hath destroyed me on | Job 19:10
every s.
the wicked walk on *every s.* | Ps 12:8
while
fear on *every s.* while they | Ps 31:13
took counsel
and the little hills rejoice on | Ps 65:12
every s.
thou shalt comfort me on | Ps 71:21
every s.
fear is on *every s.* | Jer 6:25;
| 20:10; 49:29
that they may come to thee | Eze 16:33
on *every s.*
the nations set against him | Eze 19:8
on *every s.*
I will bring them against | Eze 23:22
thee on *every s.*
judged by the sword upon | Eze 28:23
her on *every s.*
they have swallowed you up | Eze 36:3
on *every s.*
saith Lord, I will gather | Eze 37:21
them on *every s.*
gather yourselves to my | Eze 39:17
sacrifice on *every s.*
enemies shall keep thee in | Lu 19:43
on *every s.*
we are troubled on *every s.* | 2Co 4:8;
| 7:5

FARTHER SIDE

Jesus came by the *farther s.* M'k 10:1
of Jordan

ON THIS SIDE

one cherub on this s. other on   Ex 37:8
that side
brought quails a day's   Nu 11:31
journey on this s.
a wall being on this s. and on   Nu 22:24
that side
inheritance on this s. Jordan   Nu 32:19;
32:32; 34:15
three cities of refuge on this   Nu 35:14
s. Jordan
some on this s. of Ai, and   Jos 8:22
some on
Israel and judges stood on   Jos 8:33
this s. the ark
if I say, The arrows are on   1Sa 20:21
this s.
Saul went on this s. of the   1Sa 23:26
mountain
shalt have no portion on this   Ezr 4:16
s. the river
governor on this s. the river   Ezr 5:3;
5:6; 6:13; 8:36
to throne of the governor on   Ne 3:7
this s. river
every one had two wings, on   Eze 1:23
this s.
were two tables on this s.   Eze 40:39
and two on that
four tables on this s. four   Eze 40:41
tables on that side
on bank of river on this   Eze 47:12
s. shall grow trees
there stood other two, the one   Da 12:5
on this s.
that stealeth be cut off as on   Zec 5:3
this s. every one that sweareth,
on that side

ON OTHER SIDE

your fathers dwelt on   Jos 24:2
other s. the flood
I and Jonathan will be on   1Sa 14:40
the other s.
saw water on other s. as red   2Ki 3:22
as blood
twelve lions stood on one   2Ch 9:19
and other s.
on the day that thou stoodest   Ob 11
on the other s.
found him on the other s. of   Joh 6:25
the sea

RIGHT SIDE

door for middle chamber was   1Ki 6:8
on right s.
put five bases on right s.   1Ki 7:39
of house, set sea on right s.
of house
five candlesticks on the   1Ki 7:49
right s.
placed five [tables] on   2Ch 4:8
right s.
set sea on the right s.   2Ch 4:10
had the face of a lion on the   Eze 1:10
right s.
lie again on thy right s. and   Eze 4:6
shalt bear
from under right s. of house   Eze 47:1;
ran waters   41:2
olive-trees, one on right s. the   Zec 4:3;
bowl   4:11
saw young man on right s. of   M'k 16:5
sepulchre
angel standing on right s. of   Lu 1:11
the altar
cast the net on the right s. of   Joh 21:6
the ship

SIDES

the tables were written on   Ex 32:15
both s.
shall be thorns in your s.   Nu 33:55;
J'g 2:3
they shall be scourges in your   Jos 23:13
s.
a prey of needle-work on both   J'g 5:30
s.
David and his men in s. of   1Sa 24:3
the cave

Solomon had peace on all s.   1Ki 4:24
round
beautiful is Zion on s. of the   Ps 48:2
north
wife as a fruitful vine by s. of   Ps 128:3
house
I will sit also on the s. of   Isa 14:13
the north
thou shalt be brought down   Isa 14:15
to s. of the pit
be borne upon her s. and   Isa 66:12
dandled
great nation raised from s. of   Jer 6:22
earth
maketh her nest in the s. of   Jer 48:28
the holes
I will bring their calamity   Jer 49:32
from all s.
they went upon their four s.   Eze 1:17;
10:11
whose graves are set in the s.   Eze 32:23
of the pit
for these are his s. east and   Eze 48:1
west
say unto him that is by s. of   Am 6:10
the house
Jonah was gone down to s. of   Jon 1:5
the ship

SIDON

And Canaan begat S. his   Ge 10:15
firstborn
of the Canaanites was from   Ge 10:19
S.
had been done in Tyre and   M't 11:21
S.
be more tolerable for Tyre   M't 11:22
and S.
into the coasts of Tyre and   M't 15:21
S.
and they about Tyre and S. a   M'k 3:8
great
into the borders of Tyre and   M'k 7:24
S.
from the coasts of Tyre and   M'k 7:31
S.
save unto Sarepta, a city of S.   Lu 4:26
from the sea coast of Tyre   Lu 6:17
and S.
had been done in Tyre and S.   Lu 10:13
be more tolerable for Tyre   Lu 10:14
and S.
displeased with them of   Ac 12:20
Tyre and S.
And the next day we touched   Ac 27:3
at S.

SIDONIANS

Which Hermon the S. call   De 3:9
Sirion
and Mearah that is beside the   Jos 13:4
S.
and all the S., them will I   Jos 13:6
drive out
and all the Canaanites, and the   J'g 3:3
S.
skill to hew timber like unto   1Ki 5:6
the S.

SIEGE

down to employ them in   De 20:19
the s.
in the s. and in the straitness   De 28:53
he hath nothing left in the s.   De 28:55
secretly in the s. and   De 28:57
straitness
and all Israel laid s. to   1Ki 15:27
Gibbethon
but he himself laid s. against   2Ch 32:9
Lachish
ye abide in the s. in   2Ch 32:10
Jerusalem
and will lay s. against thee   Isa 29:3
with a
s. mound (S)   Jer 6:6; Eze 21:22; 26:8
eat the flesh of his friend in   Jer 19:9
the s.
s. mounds (S)   Jer 32:24;
33:4; Eze 17:17
And lay s. against it, and build   Eze 4:2
and thou shalt lay s. against it   Eze 4:3
face toward the s. of Jerusalem   Eze 4:7
thou hast ended the days of   Eze 4:8
thy s.
when the days of the s.   Eze 5:2
are fulfilled
troops: he hath laid s.   Mic 5:1
against us

Draw thee waters for the s.,   Na 3:14
fortify
shall be in the s. both against   Zec 12:2
Judah

SIEVE

the nations with the s. of   Isa 30:28
vanity
nations, like as corn is sifted   Am 9:9
in a s.

SIFT

s. and search out my path   Ps 139:3
(A)
to s. the nations with the   Isa 30:28
I will s. the house of Israel   Am 9:9
among
you, that he may s. you as   Lu 22:31
wheat

SIFTED

nations, like as corn is s. in a   Am 9:9
sieve

SIGH

the people s. (E)   Pr 29:2
all the merryhearted do s.   Isa 24:7
priests s. her virgins are   La 1:4
afflicted
All her people s., they seek   La 1:11
bread
They have heard that I s.:   La 1:21
there is
upon the foreheads of the men   Eze 9:4
that s.
S. therefore, thou son of   Eze 21:6
man, with
with bitterness s. before their   Eze 21:6
eyes
s. within ourselves (B)   Ro 8:23;
2Co 5:2; 5:4

SIGHED

children of Israel s. by reason   Ex 2:23
deeply moved and s.   Jer 11:33
(A)(N)(R)
And looking up to heaven,   M'k 7:34
he s.
he s. deeply in his spirit, and   M'k 8:12
saith
s. Cyprus   Ac 21:3
(A)(B)(E)(N)(P)(R)

SIGHEST

say unto thee, Wherefore s.   Eze 21:7
thou

SIGHETH

yea, she s. and turneth   La 1:8
backward

SIGHING

For my s. cometh before I   Job 3:24
eat
of the poor, for the s. of the   Ps 12:5
needy
with grief, and my years with   Ps 31:10
s.
my s. is not hid (A)(B)(R)   Ps 38:9
the s. of the prisoner come   Ps 79:11
before
the sound of my s. (B)   Ps 102:5
the s. thereof have I made to   Isa 21:2
cease
and sorrow and s. shall flee   Isa 35:10
away
fainted in my s. and I find no   Jer 45:3
rest
s. in throes in unison (B)   Ro 8:22

SIGHS

for my s. are many, and my   La 1:22
heart
s. too deep for words (B)(R)   Ro 8:26

SIGHT

every tree that is pleasant to   Ge 2:9
the s.
I will now turn and see this   Ex 3:3
great s.

s. of glory of Lord was like	Ex 24:17
devouring fire	
the plague in s. be deeper,	Le 13:3;
	13:20, 25, 30
in s. be not deeper than the	Le 13:4;
skin	13:31-32, 34
if the plague in s. be lower	Le 14:37
than the wall	
we saw giants, we were in	Nu 13:33
our own s. as grasshoppers,	
so we were in their s.	
before congregation and give	Nu 27:19
him charge in their s.	
shalt be mad for s. of thine	De 28:34;
eyes	28:67
God shall drive them from	Jos 23:5
out of your s.	
which did those great signs	Jos 24:17
in our s.	
stupid in your s.	(A)(B)(R) Job 13:3
why are we reputed vile in	Job 18:3
your s.	
me for a stranger, I am an	Job 19:15
alien in their s.	
their seed is established in	Job 21:8
their s. with them	
he striketh them in the	Job 34:26
open s. of others	
shall not one be cast down at	Job 41:9
the s. of him	
be known among the heathen	Ps 79:10
in our s.	
better is s. of the eyes than	Ec 6:9
wandering	
them that are prudent in their	Isa 5:21
own s.	
he shall not judge after the s.	Isa 11:3
of his eyes	
I will render evil done in	Jer 51:24
Zion in your s.	
thou shalt bake it with dung	Eze 4:12
in their s.	
prepare, and remove by day	Eze 12:3
in their s.	
dig thou thro' the wall in	Eze 12:5
their s. and carry out	
in whose s. I made myself	Eze 20:9
known to them	
heathen in whose s. I	Eze 20:14;
brought them out	20:22
shall loathe yourselves in	Eze 20:43;
your own s.	36:31
shall be as a false divination	Eze 21:23
in their s.	
shew the forms thereof, and	Eze 43:11
write in their s.	
s. thereof to end of all the	Da 4:11;
earth	4:20
put away her whoredoms out	Ho 2:2
of her s.	
blind receive s.	M't 11:5; 20:34; Lu 7:21
preach recovering of s. to the	Lu 4:18
blind	
that came to that s. smote	Lu 23:48
their breasts	
they knew him, he vanished	Lu 24:31
out of their s.	
I went and washed, and I	Joh 9:11
received s.	
a cloud received him out of	Ac 1:9
their s.	
when Moses saw it, he	Ac 7:31
wondered at the s.	
was three days without s. nor	Ac 9:9
eat nor drink	
received s. forthwith, arose,	Ac 9:18
was baptized	
for we walk by faith, not by s.	2Co 5:7
so terrible was the s. that	Heb 12:21
Moses	

SIGHT *OF GOD*

find good understanding in the	Pr 3:4
s. of God	
is abomination in the s. of	Lu 16:15
God	
whether right in s. of God to	Ac 4:19
hearken	
thy heart is not right in the	Ac 8:21
of God	
alms had in remembrance in	Ac 10:31
s. of God	
in the s. of God speak we in	2Co 2:17
Christ	
to everyman's conscience in	2Co 4:2
the s. of God	
care for you in s. of God	2Co 7:12
might appear	
no man justified by law in s.	Ga 3:11
of God	

remembering work of faith in	1Th 1:3
s. of God	
this is good and acceptable in	1Ti 2:3
s. of God	
I give thee charge in the s. of	1Ti 6:13
God	
which is in s. of God of great	1Pe 3:4
price	

HIS SIGHT

if do that which is right in	Ex 15:26
his s.	
if the plague in his s. be at a	Le 13:5
stay	
but if the scall be in his s. at	Le 13:37
a stay	
one shall burn the heifer in his	Nu 19:5
s.	
he brought thee out in his s.	De 4:37
out of Egypt	
angel of Lord departed out of	J'g 6:21
his s.	
why despised Lord, to do evil	2Sa 12:9
in his s.	
so Tamar went and made	2Sa 13:8
cakes in his s.	
remove them out of his s.	2Ki 17:18;
	17:20, 23; 24:3
the Lord do what is good	1Ch 19:13
in his s.	
the heavens are not clean in	Job 15:15
his s.	
yea, the stars are not pure in	Job 25:5
his s.	
judgments are far above out of	Ps 10:5
his s.	
precious shall their blood be	Ps 72:14
in his s.	
God giveth to a man that is	Ec 2:26
good in his s.	
be not hasty to go out of his s.	Ec 8:3
stand not	
will raise us, and we shall live	Ho 6:2
in his s.	
Bartimaeus immediately	M'k 10:52;
received his s. and followed	Lu 18:43
Jesus	
asked how he had received	Joh 9:15;
his s.	9:18
a vision that he might receive	Ac 9:12
his s.	
by law shall no flesh	Ro 3:20
be justified in his s.	
thro' death to present you	Col 1:22
holy in his s.	
every creature is manifest in	Heb 4:13
his s.	
working what is well	Heb 13:21
pleasing in his s.	
do things that are pleasing in	1Jo 3:22
his s.	

IN THE SIGHT

thing was grievous in	Ge 21:11
Abraham's s.	
there is not ought left in the	Ge 47:18
s. of my lord	
did the signs in the s. of the	Ex 4:30
people	
he smote the waters in the s.	Ex 7:20
of Pharaoh	
Moses sprinkled the ashes in	Ex 9:8
the s. of Pharaoh	
Moses great in the s. of	Ex 11:3
Pharaoh's servants	
Moses did so in the s. of	Ex 17:6
elders of Israel	
the Lord will come down in	Ex 19:11
the s. of people	
fire by night in the s. of	Ex 40:38
Israel all journeys	
shall be cut off in the s. of	Le 20:17
their people	
out of Egypt in the s. of the	Le 26:45
heathen	
Ithamar ministered in the s. of	Nu 3:4
Aaron	
Aaron and Eleazar went in	Nu 20:27
the s. of congregation	
brought Midianitish woman in	Nu 25:6
the s. of Moses	
went with high hand in the s.	Nu 33:3
of Egyptians	
for this is your wisdom in the s.	De 4:6
of nations	
Moses said to Joshua in the s.	De 31:7
of all Israel	
terror Moses shewed in the s.	De 34:12
of all Israel	

to magnify thee in the s. of	Jos 3:7;
Israel	4:14
said, in the s. of Israel,	Jos 10:12
Sun, stand still	
David accepted in the s. of	1Sa 18:5
the people	
lie with thy wives in the s.	2Sa 12:11
of this sun	
in the s. of all Israel keep	1Ch 28:8
commandments	
Lord magnified Solomon in	1Ch 29:25
the s. of Israel	
Hezekiah magnified in s. of	2Ch 32:23
nations	
shewed mercy in the s. of	Ezr 9:9
kings of Persia	
grant him mercy in the s. of	Ne 1:11
this man	
opened the book in the s. of all	Ne 8:5
the people	
marvellous things did he in s. of	Ps 78:12
of fathers	
he openly shewed in the s. of	Ps 98:2
the heathen	
in vain net is spread in the s.	Pr 1:17
of any bird	
tender and beloved in the s. of	Pr 4:3
my mother	
and walk in the s. of thine	Ec 11:9
eyes	
break the bottle in the s. of	Jer 19:10
the men	
I gave evidence in the s. of	Jer 32:12
Hanameel	
hid stones in the s. of the men	Jer 43:9
of Judah	
execute judgments in the s. of	Eze 5:8
the nations	
Jerusalem a reproach in s. of	Eze 5:14
all that pass	
judgment on thee in the s. of	Eze 16:41
many women	
name not be polluted in s.	Eze 20:22
of the heathen	
I will bring thee to ashes in	Eze 28:18
the s. of all	
be sanctified in s. of	Eze 28:25;
heathen	39:27
lay desolate in the s. of all	Eze 36:34
them that pass	
I will discover lewdness in	Ho 2:10
s. of her lovers	
gave him wisdom in the s. of	Ac 7:10
Pharaoh	
provide things honest in s. of	Ro 12:17
all men	
maketh fire come down in s.	Re 13:13
of men	
miracles he had power to do	Re 13:14
in s. of beast	

MINE, MY SIGHT

that I may bury my dead out	Ge 23:4;
of my s.	23:8
thou hast found grace in my	Ex 33:12;
s.	33:17
thy coming in is good in my	1Sa 29:6
s.	
I know that thou art good in	1Sa 29:9
my s.	
and will be base in mine	2Sa 6:22
own s.	
let Tamar come, and dress	2Sa 13:5
the meat in my s.	
come, and make me a couple	2Sa 13:6
of cakes in my s.	
not fail thee a man in my s.	1Ki 8:25;
	2Ch 6:16
this house, I have hallowed	1Ki 9:7;
will I cast out of my s.	2Ch 7:20
if thou wilt do that is right	1Ki 11:38
in my s.	
have done that which was	2Ki 21:11
evil in my s.	
I will remove Judah also out	2Ki 23:27
of my s.	
thou hast shed much blood	1Ch 22:8
in my s.	
that tell lies, shall not tarry	Ps 101:7
in my s.	
since thou wast precious in	Isa 43:4
my s.	
will put away abominations out	Jer 4:1
of my s.	
cast you out of my s. as your	Jer 7:15
brethren	
children of Judah have done	Jer 7:30
evil in my s.	
cast them out of my s. and let	Jer 15:1
them go	

if it do evil in *my s.* that it   Jer 18:10
obey not
turned, and had done right   Jer 34:15
in *my s.*
he went in *my s.* to fill his   Eze 10:2
hand
mounted up from the earth   Eze 10:19
in *my s.*
be hid from *my s.* in bottom of   Am 9:3
the sea
that I might receive *my s.*   M'k 10:51;
     Lu 18:41

THINE, THY SIGHT

thy servant hath found grace   Ge 19:19
in *thy s.*
God said, Let it not be   Ge 21:12
grievous in *thy s.*
if I have found grace in *thy*   Ge 33:10;
s.   47:29; Ex 33:13, 16; 34:9; J'g 6:17
shall not rule with rigour in   Le 25:53
thy s.
when thou wast little in   1Sa 15:17
thine own s.
have cut off thine enemies out   2Sa 7:9
of *thy s.*
this was yet a small thing in   2Sa 7:19
thy s.
knoweth I have found grace   2Sa 14:22
in *thy s.*
let my life be precious in *thy*   2Ki 1:13;
s.   1:14
done what was good in *thy*   2Ki 20:3;
s.   Isa 38:3
the foolish shall not stand in   Ps 5:5
thy s.
arise, Lord, let heathen be   Ps 9:19
judged in *thy s.*
meditations of heart be   Ps 19:14
acceptable in *thy s.*
I have sinned, and done this   Ps 51:4
evil in *thy s.*
who may stand in *thy s.* when   Ps 76:7
thou art angry
thousand years in *thy s.* are as   Ps 90:4
yesterday
for in *thy s.* shall no man be   Ps 143:2
justified
so have we been in *thy s.* O   Isa 26:17
Lord
neither blot out their sin   Jer 18:23
from *thy s.*
then I said, I am cast out of   Jon 2:4
thy s.
it seemed good in *thy s.*   M't 11:26;
     Lu 10:21
sinned against heaven and in   Lu 15:21
thy s.
Jesus said unto him, Receive   Lu 18:42
thy s.
sent me that thou mightest   Ac 9:17
receive *thy s.*
stood and said, Receive *thy s.*   Ac 22:13

SIGHTED

when we had s. Cyprus (S)   Ac 21:3

SIGHTS

fearful s. and great signs shall   Lu 21:11

SIGN

a s. (B)   Ge 9:12; 9:17;
  17:11; Ex 13:16; Ps 86:17; 2Th 3:17
a s. (R)   Ge 9:12;
9:13, 17; 17:11; Ex 3:12; Nu 17:10;
  Jos 2:12; Ps 86:17; M'k 14:44
it shall be a s. of the   Ge 17:11;
covenant (S)   Nu 17:10; M'k 14:44
sign (A)   Ex 3:12;
Nu 17:10; Jos 2:12; Ps 86:17; Ph'p 1:28
hearken to the voice of the first   Ex 4:8
s.
will believe the voice of the   Ex 4:8
latter s.
people: to morrow shall this s.   Ex 8:23
for a s. unto thee upon thine   Ex 13:9
hand
s. on forehead (B)   Ex 13:16
for it is a s. between me and   Ex 31:13
you
a s. between me and the   Ex 31:17
children of
they shall be a s. unto the   Nu 16:38
children
fifty men: and they became a   Nu 26:10
s.

bind them for a s. upon thine   De 6:8
hand
bind them as a token (B)   De 6:8;
     11:18
s. and deeds he performed   De 11:3
(A)(B)(E)(R)
bind them for a s. upon your   De 11:18
hand
and giveth thee a s. or a   De 13:1
wonder
the s. or the wonder come to   De 13:2
pass
they shall be upon thee for a   De 28:46
s. and
s. and great wonders   De 29:3
(A)(B)(E)(R)
That this may be a s. among   Jos 4:6
you
This shall be a symbol (B)   Jos 4:6
me a s. that thou talkest with   J'g 6:17
there was an appointed s.   J'g 20:38
between
the appointed signal   J'g 20:38
(A)(B)(R)
this shall be a s. unto thee   1Sa 2:34
hand: and this shall be a s.   1Sa 14:10
unto us
he gave a s. the same day,   1Ki 13:3
saying
the s. which the Lord hath   1Ki 13:3
spoken
according to the s. which the   1Ki 13:5
man of
And this shall be a s. unto   2Ki 19:29
thee, Ye
What shall be the s. that the   2Ki 20:8
Lord
This s. shalt thou have of the   2Ki 20:9
Lord
unto him, and he gave him   2Ch 32:24
a s.
Ask thee a s. of the Lord thy   Isa 7:11
God
the Lord himself shall give   Isa 7:14
you a s.
it shall be for a s. and for a   Isa 19:20
witness
s. and wonder upon Egypt and   Isa 20:3
upon
this shall be a s. unto thee,   Isa 37:30
Ye shall
this shall be a s. unto thee   Isa 38:7
from the
What is the s. that I shall go   Isa 38:22
up to
for an everlasting s. that   Isa 55:13
shall not be
I will set a s. among them,   Isa 66:19
and I
up a s. of fire in Beth-haccerem   Jer 6:1
and s. deeds (A)(B)(R)(S)   Jer 32:44
And this shall be a s. unto   Jer 44:29
you
shall be a s. to the house of   Eze 4:3
Israel
for a s. unto the house of   Eze 12:6
Israel
I am making you a symbol   Eze 12:6;
(B)   12:11
Say, I am your s.: like as I   Eze 12:11
will make him a s. and a   Eze 14:8
proverb
to be a s. between me and   Eze 20:12
them
shall be a s. between me and   Eze 20:20
you
Thus Ezekiel is unto you a s.   Eze 24:24
and thou shalt be a s. unto   Eze 24:27
them
then shall he set up a s. by it,   Eze 39:15
till
and s. the writing, that it be   Da 6:8
not
are a s. or omen (A)   Zec 3:8
we would see a s. from thee   M't 12:38
see a token of proof (B)   M't 12:38
generation seeketh after a s.   M't 12:39
and there shall no s. be   M't 12:39
given to it
but the s. of the prophet   M't 12:39
Jonas
would shew them a s. from   M't 16:1
heaven
generation seeketh after a s.   M't 16:4
and there no s. be given   M't 16:4
unto it
but the s. of the prophet   M't 16:4
Jonas
what shall be the s. of thy   M't 24:3
coming

appear the s. of the Son of   M't 24:30
man in
that betrayed him gave them   M't 26:48
a s.
had given them a signal   M't 26:48
(B)
seeking of him a s. from   M'k 8:11
heaven
doth this generation seek   M'k 8:12
after a s.
no s. be given unto this   M'k 8:12
generation
what shall be the s. when all   M'k 13:4
these
given them a s. (P)   M'k 14:44
And this shall be a s. unto   Lu 2:12
you; Ye
this is a token for you (B)   Lu 2:12
and for a s. which shall be   Lu 2:34
spoken
sought of him a s. from   Lu 11:16
heaven.
an evil generation: they seek   Lu 11:29
a s.
and there shall no s. be given   Lu 11:29
but the s. of Jonas the   Lu 11:29
prophet
Jonas was a s. unto the   Lu 11:30
Ninevites
what s. will there be when   Lu 21:7
these
first of his s.   Joh 2:11
(A)(B)(E)(N)(P)(R)
him, What s. shewest thou   Joh 2:18
unto us
seeing his s.   Joh 2:23
(A)(B)(E)(N)(P)(R)
second s. Jesus did   Joh 4:54
(A)(B)(E)(N)(P)(R)
because you saw his s.   Joh 6:26
(B)(E)(N)(P)(R)
What s. shewest thou then,   Joh 6:30
that we
signs (B)(E)(P)(R)   Joh 7:31
9:16; 11:47; 12:37; Ac 2:22; 6:8; 8:6, 13;
     15:12
John wrought no s.   Joh 10:41
(B)(E)(N)(P)(R)
a notable s. (B)(R)   Ac 4:16; 4:22
whose s. was Castor and   Ac 28:11
Pollux
as its figurehead   Ac 28:11
(A)(B)(P)(R)
he received the s. of   Ro 4:11
circumcision
the mark of   Ro 4:11
circumcision (A)(B)
as the hall-mark of   Ro 4:11
righteousness (N)
For the Jews require a s.   1Co 1:22
and the
Wherefore tongues are for a   1Co 14:22
s.
I saw another s. in heaven,   Re 15:1
great
another wonder (A)   Re 15:1
another portent (B)(N)(R)   Re 15:1

SIGNAL

the appointed s. (A)(B)(R)   Jos 20:38
I will raise my s. (B)(R)   Isa 49:22
set up a s. (A)(B)   Jer 50:2
had given them a s. (B)   M't 26:48
given them a s. (A)(B)(N)   M'k 14:44

SIGNALS

see the war s. (B)   Jer 4:21

SIGNATURE

likeness and s. (B)   M't 22:20

SIGNED

s. the deed (A)(B)(R)(S)   Jer 32:10;
     32:12
king Darius s. the writing and   Da 6:9
Daniel knew that the writing   Da 6:10
was s.
Hast thou not s. a decree, that   Da 6:12
nor the decree that thou hast   Da 6:13
s. but

SIGNET

Thy s. and thy bracelets, and   Ge 38:18
the s. and bracelets, and staff   Ge 38:25
stone, like the engravings of   Ex 28:11
a s.

as a seal is engraved (B)   Ex 28:11;
                                28:21, 36; 29:14, 20
names, like the engravings of   Ex 28:21
a s.
upon it, like the engravings of Ex 28:36
a s.
names, like the engravings of a Ex 39:14
s.
like to the engravings of a s.   Ex 39:30
were the s. upon my right   Jer 22:24
hand
the king sealed it with his   Da 6:17
own s.
and with the s. of his lords: Da 6:17
that the
Lord, and will make thee as   Hag 2:23
a s.

SIGNETS

of gold, graven, as s. are   Ex 39:6
graven

SIGNIFICATION

and none of them is without 1Co 14:10
s.
none without meaning   1Co 14:10
(A)(B)(R)
nothing is altogether   1Co 14:10
soundless (N)
each has a distinct meaning   1Co 14:10
(P)

SIGNIFIED

s. by the spirit that   Ac 11:28
there should be
prophecied through the   Ac 11:28
Spirit (A)
revealed through the Spirit   Ac 11:28
(B)
inspired to predict (N)   Ac 11:28
foretold by the Spirit (P)(R)   Ac 11:28
s. it by his angel unto his   Re 1:1
servant
sent and communicated it (A)   Re 1:1
sent the communication to (B)   Re 1:1
made it known by sending   Re 1:1
(P)(R)

SIGNIFIETH

s. the removing of those   Heb 12:27
things
indicates the final removal   Heb 12:27
(A)(B)(R)
means their removal   Heb 12:27
(N)(P)

SIGNIFY

to s. the accomplishment of   Ac 21:26
to give notice   Ac 21:26
(A)(N)(P)(R)
to announce the completion   Ac 21:26
(B)
declaring the fulfillment (E)   Ac 21:26
the council s. to the chief   Ac 23:15
captain
to give notice (A)(R)   Ac 23:15
send word to (B)   Ac 23:15
to apply to (N)   Ac 23:15
make it plain (P)   Ac 23:15
to s. the crimes laid   Ac 25:27
state the accusations (A)   Ac 25:27
indicating the charges (N)   Ac 25:27
indicate the charges (R)   Ac 25:27
of Christ which was in them   1Pe 1:11
did s.
indicated when it predicted   1Pe 1:11
did point unto (E)(B)(N)   1Pe 1:11
was indicated by the Spirit   1Pe 1:11
(R)

SIGNIFYING

said, s. what death he   Joh 12:33
should die
to indicate the kind of death   Joh 12:33
(N)
to show the kind of death   Joh 12:33
(P)(R)
spake s. what death he should   Joh 18:32
die
to show what manner of   Joh 18:32
death (A)
indicating the nature of his   Joh 18:32
death (B)
indicated the manner of   Joh 18:32
death (N)

to show what death he was   Joh 18:32
to die (R)
s. by what death he should   Joh 21:19
glorify
to indicate what kind of   Joh 21:19
death (A)(B)(N)
to show the kind of death   Joh 21:19
(P)(R)
The Holy Ghost this s.   Heb 9:8
that the
the Holy Spirit points out that Heb 9:8
(A)
The Holy Spirit evidences that   Heb 9:8
(B)
the Holy Spirit means us to   Heb 9:8
understand (P)
the Holy Spirit indicates that   Heb 9:8
(R)

SIGNS

let them be for s. and for   Ge 1:14
seasons
let them be for markers of   Ge 1:14
seasons (B)
will not believe also these two s.   Ex 4:9
believe these two evidences (B) Ex 4:9
hand, wherewith thou shalt do   Ex 4:17
s.
all the s. which he had   Ex 4:28
commanded
did the s. in the sight of the   Ex 4:30
people
my s. and my wonders in the   Ex 7:3
land of
might shew these my s. before   Ex 10:1
him
work these my wonders (B)   Ex 10:1
and my s. which I have done   Ex 10:2
among
for all the s. which I have   Nu 14:11
shewed
all the miracles (B)   Nu 14:11
by s. and by wonders, and by   De 4:34
war
the Lord shewed s. and   De 6:22
wonders
by portents and marvels (B)   De 6:22
and the s. and the wonders   De 7:19
and with s. and with wonders   De 26:8
the s. and those great miracles De 29:3
In all the s. and the wonders,   De 34:11
which
which did those great s. in   Jos 24:17
our sight
performed these great   Jos 24:17
miracles (B)
when these s. are come unto   1Sa 10:7
thee
all those s. came to pass that   1Sa 10:9
day
sun, moon and s. of the   2Ki 23:5
Zodiac (B)
s. and wonders upon Pharaoh   Ne 9:10
afraid of nature's s.   Ps 65:8
(A)(B)(R)
signs (S)   Ps 65:8; 86:17; 135:9
they set up their ensigns for s. Ps 74:4
We see not our s.: there is no   Ps 74:9
more
we see not our symbols   Ps 74:9
(A)(B)
How he had wrought his s. in   Ps 78:43
Egypt
shewed his s. among them   Ps 105:27
sent s. and wonders   Ps 135:9
(A)(B)(R)
are for s. and for wonders in   Isa 8:18
Israel
s. and portents (B)(R)   Isa 8:18;
                                  Joe 2:30
who frustrates s. (A)   Isa 44:25
not dismayed at the s. of   Jer 10:2
heaven
hast set s. and wonders in the   Jer 32:20
land
out of the land of Egypt   Jer 32:21
with s. and
I thought it good to shew the   Da 4:2
s. and
How great are his s.! and how   Da 4:3
and he worketh s. and   Da 6:27
wonders in
ye not discern the s. of the   M't 16:3
times
shall shew great s. and   M't 24:24
wonders
and shall shew s. and   M'k 13:22
wonders, to
And these s. shall follow   M'k 16:17
them that

and confirming the word   M'k 16:20
with s.
s. were made unto them (S)   Lu 1:22
they made s. to his father,   Lu 1:62
how he
not coming with s. (A)(R)   Lu 17:20
s. shall there be from heaven   Lu 21:11
And there shall be s. in the   Lu 21:25
sun
Except ye see s. and wonders,   Joh 4:48
ye
signs (N)   Joh 7:31; 9:16; 11:47; 12:37
signs (A)   Joh 11:47; Ac 2:22; 6:8
many other s. truly did Jesus   Joh 20:30
in the
above. and s. in the earth   Ac 2:19
beneath
by miracles and wonders and   Ac 2:22
s.
wonders and s. were done by   Ac 2:43
that s. and wonders may be   Ac 4:30
done by
were many s. and wonders   Ac 5:12
wrought
did great s. (N)(P)   Ac 6:8;
                                15:12; Ro 12:19
shewed wonders and s. in the   Ac 7:36
land
miracles and s. which were   Ac 8:13
done
granted s. and wonders to be   Ac 14:3
done
Through mighty s. and   Ro 15:19
wonders, by
Truly the s. of an apostle   2Co 12:12
in s. and wonders, and   2Co 12:12
mighty
of Satan with all power and s.   2Th 2:9
witness, both with s. and   Heb 2:4
wonders
s. and wonders   Heb 2:4
(A)(B)(E)(R)
doeth great s. (E)(R)   Re 13:13
because of his s.   Re 13:14
(A)(E)(P)(R)
that perform s. (A)(E)(R)   Re 16:14
wrought the s. (E)(R)   Re 19:20

SIHON

Israel sent messengers unto   Nu 21:21
S.
S. would not suffer Israel to   Nu 21:23
pass
but S. gathered all his people   Nu 21:23
For Heshbon was the city of   Nu 21:26
S. the
city of S. be built   Nu 21:27
and prepared
a flame from the city of S.:   Nu 21:28
it hath
into captivity unto S. king of   Nu 21:29
him as thou didst unto S. king   Nu 21:34
kingdom of S. king of the   Nu 32:33
Amorites
After he had slain S. the king   De 1:4
into thine hand S. the Amorite   De 2:24
wilderness of Kedemoth unto   De 2:26
S.
S. king of Heshbon would not   De 2:30
let us
have begun to give S. and   De 2:31
his land
Then S. came out aginst us   De 2:32
as thou didst unto S. king of   De 3:2
as we did unto S. king of   De 3:6
Heshbon
land of S. king of the   De 4:46
Amorites
this place, S. the king of   De 29:7
Heshbon
shall do unto them as he did   De 31:4
to S.
the other side Jordan, S. and   Jos 2:10
Og
to S. king of Heshbon, and to   Jos 9:10
Og
S. king of the Amorites, who   Jos 12:2
dwelt
the border of S. king of   Jos 12:5
Heshbon
cities of S. king of the   Jos 13:10
Amorites
all the kingdom of S. king of   Jos 13:21
which were dukes of S.   Jos 13:21
dwelling
kingdom of S. king of   Jos 13:27
Heshbon
Israel sent messengers unto   J'g 11:19
S.

But *S.* trusted not Israel to   *J'g 11:20*
pass
S. gathered all his people   *J'g 11:20*
together
Lord God of Israel delivered   *J'g 11:21*
S. and
country of *S.* king of the   *1Ki 4:19*
Amorites
So they possessed the land of   *Ne 9:22*
S.
S. king of the Amorites, and   *Ps 135:11*
Og
S. king of the Amorites: for   *Ps 136:19*
and a flame from the midst   *Jer 48:45*
of *S.*

SIHOR

From *S.* which is before   *Jos 13:3*
Egypt
And by great waters the seed   *Isa 23:3*
of *S.*
Egypt to drink the water of *S.*   *Jer 2:18*

SILAS

Barsabas, *S.* chief   *Ac 15:22*
men among
have sent therefore Judas and   *Ac 15:27*
S.
Judas and *S.* being prophets   *Ac 15:32*
it pleased *S.* to abide   *Ac 15:34*
there still
And Paul chose *S.* and   *Ac 15:40*
departed
they caught Paul and *S.*   *Ac 16:19*
and drew
at midnight Paul and *S.*   *Ac 16:25*
prayed
and fell down before Paul   *Ac 16:29*
and *S.*
and consorted with Paul and   *Ac 17:4*
S.
sent away Paul and *S.* by   *Ac 17:10*
night
but *S.* and Timotheus abode   *Ac 17:14*
there
receiving a commandment   *Ac 17:15*
unto *S.*
when *S.* and Timotheus were   *Ac 18:5*
come

SILENCE

thee, O king: who said, Keep   *J'g 3:19*
s.
there was *s.* and I heard a   *Job 4:16*
voice
waited, and kept *s.* at my   *Job 29:21*
counsel
that I kept *s.* and went not   *Job 31:34*
out of
not keep *s.* (A)(B)(E)(R)   *Job 41:12*
Let the lying lips be put to *s*   *Ps 31:18*
When I kept *s.* my bones   *Ps 32:3*
waxed
keep not *s.*: O Lord, be not   *Ps 35:22*
far
I was dumb with *s.* I held my   *Ps 39:2*
shall come, and shall not keep   *Ps 50:3*
s.
hast thou done, and I kept *s.*   *Ps 50:21*
Keep not thou *s.* O God: hold   *Ps 83:1*
my soul had almost dwelt in *s.*   *Ps 94:17*
neither any that go down   *Ps 115:17*
into *s.*
a time to keep *s.* and a time to   *Ec 3:7*
is laid waste, and brought to   *Isa 15:1*
s.
Keep *s.* before me, O islands   *Isa 41:1*
mention of the Lord, keep not   *Isa 62:6*
s.
I will not keep *s.* but will   *Isa 65:6*
the Lord our God hath put us   *Jer 8:14*
to *s.*
sit upon the ground, and keep   *La 2:10*
s.
He sitteth alone and keepeth   *La 3:28*
s.
Therefore the prudent shall   *Am 5:13*
keep *s.*
shall cast them forth with *s.*   *Am 8:3*
temple: let all the earth keep   *Hab 2:20*
s.
he had put the Sadducees to   *M't 22:34*
s.
Then all the multitude kept *s.*   *Ac 15:12*
when there was made a great   *Ac 21:40*
s.
to them, they kept the more *s.*   *Ac 22:2*

kept in *s.* through times   *Ro 16:25*
eternal (E)
let him keep *s.* in the   *1Co 14:28*
church
Let your women keep *s.* in   *1Co 14:34*
with all
Let the woman learn in *s.*   *1Ti 2:11*
over the man, but to be in *s.*   *1Ti 2:12*
put to *s.* the ignorance of   *1Pe 2:15*
foolish
there was *s.* in heaven about   *Re 8:1*

SILENCED

s. the Jews (N)   *Ac 9:22*

SILENT

mouth no longer *s.* (A)   *1Sa 2:1*
the wicked shall be *s.* in   *1Sa 2:9*
darkness
in the night season, and am   *Ps 22:2*
not *s.*
O Lord my rock; be not *s.* to   *Ps 28:1*
me
lest, if thou be *s.* to me, I   *Ps 28:1*
become
sing praise to thee, and not   *Ps 30:12*
be *s.*
and let them be *s.* in the   *Ps 31:17*
grave
man of understanding   *Pr 11:12*
remains *s.* (B)
fool when *s.* is wise (B)(R)   *Pr 17:28*
I was *s.*, restraining myself   *Isa 42:14*
(B)(E)
Sit thou *s.* and get thee into   *Isa 47:5*
cities and let us be *s.* there   *Jer 8:14*
Be *s.* O all flesh, before the   *Zec 2:13*
Lord

SILK

her clothing is *s.* and purple   *Pr 31:22*
clothing is fine linen   *Pr 31:22*
(A)(B)(E)(R)
linen, and I covered thee   *Eze 16:10*
with *s.*
raiment was of fine linen,   *Eze 16:13*
and *s.*
and purple, and *s.* and scarlet   *Re 18:12*

SILKS

dressed in *s.* and satins (N)   *M't 11:8;*
  Lu 7:25

SILLA

Millo, which goeth down to   *2Ki 12:20*
S.

SILLINESS

conversation not be nastiness,   *Eph 5:4*
s., flippancy (P)

SILLY

man, and envy slayeth the *s.*   *Job 5:2*
one
indignation slay the simple   *Job 5:2*
(A)(B)(R)
Ephraim also is like a *s.* dove   *Ho 7:11*
their *s.* minds further (P)   *Ro 1:21*
no filthiness, nor *s.* talk (R)   *Eph 5:4*
avoid *s.* myths (A)(R)   *1Ti 4:7*
led captive *s.* women laden   *2Ti 3:6*
with
weak-natured women (B)   *2Ti 3:6*
miserable women (N)   *2Ti 3:6*
weak women (R)   *2Ti 3:6*

SILOAH

the wall of the pool of *S.* by   *Ne 3:15*

SILOAM

upon whom the tower in *S.*   *Lu 13:4*
fell
him, Go, wash in the pool of   *Joh 9:7*
S.
said unto me, Go to the pool   *Joh 9:11*
of *S.*

SILVANUS

even by me and *S.* and   *2Co 1:19*
Timotheus

Paul, and *S.* and Timotheus,   *1Th 1:1;*
unto   *2Th 1:1*
By *S.* a faithful brother unto   *1Pe 5:12*
you

SILVER

was very rich in cattle, in *s.*   *Ge 13:2*
thy brother a thousand pieces   *Ge 20:16*
of *s.*
worth four hundred shekels of   *Ge 23:15*
s.
Abraham weighed to Ephron   *Ge 23:16*
the *s.*
four hundred shekels of *s.*   *Ge 23:16*
current
given him flocks, and herds,   *Ge 24:35*
and *s.*
servants brought forth jewels   *Ge 24:53*
of *s.*
Ishmeelites for twenty pieces   *Ge 37:28*
of *s.*
the *s.* cup, in the sack's mouth   *Ge 44:2*
we steal out of thy lord's house   *Ge 44:8*
s. or
he gave three hundred pieces   *Ge 45:22*
of *s.*
in her house, jewels of *s.* and   *Ex 3:22*
of her neighbour, jewels of *s.*   *Ex 11:2*
of the Egyptians jewels of *s.*   *Ex 12:35*
shall not make with me gods   *Ex 20:23*
of *s.*
their master thirty shekels of   *Ex 21:32*
s.
of them: gold, and *s.* and   *Ex 25:3*
brass
forty sockets of *s.* under the   *Ex 26:19*
twenty
And their forty sockets of *s.*;   *Ex 26:21*
two
boards, and their sockets of   *Ex 26:25*
s.
gold, upon the four sockets of   *Ex 26:32*
s.
pillars and their fillets shall   *Ex 27:10*
be of *s.*
the pillars and their fillets of   *Ex 27:11*
s.
the court shall be filleted   *Ex 27:17*
with *s.*
their hooks shall be of *s.* and   *Ex 27:17*
their
to work in gold, and in *s.* and   *Ex 31:4*
the Lord; gold, and *s.* and   *Ex 35:5*
brass
offer an offering of *s.* and   *Ex 35:24*
brass
to work in gold, and in *s.*   *Ex 35:32*
and in
forty sockets of *s.* he made   *Ex 36:24*
under
And their forty sockets of *s.*;   *Ex 36:26*
two
sockets were sixteen sockets   *Ex 36:30*
of *s.*
he cast for them four sockets   *Ex 36:36*
of *s.*
pillars and their fillets were   *Ex 38:10*
of *s.*
pillars and their fillets of   *Ex 38:11;*
s.   *38:12*
the pillars and their fillets of   *Ex 38:17*
overlaying of their chapiters   *Ex 38:17*
of *s.*
of the court were filleted with   *Ex 38:17*
their hooks of *s.* and the   *Ex 38:19*
overlaying
their chapiters and their   *Ex 38:19*
fillets of *s.*
the *s.* of them that were   *Ex 38:25*
numbered
the hundred talents of *s.* were   *Ex 38:27*
cast
with thy estimation by shekels   *Le 5:15*
of *s.*
estimation shall be fifty   *Le 27:3*
shekels of *s.*
be of the male five shekels of   *Le 27:6*
s.
for the female three shekels   *Le 27:6*
of *s.*
be valued at fifty shekels of *s.*   *Le 27:16*
his offering was one *s.*   *Nu 7:13;*
charger *7:19, 25, 31, 37, 43, 49, 55, 61,*
  67, 73, 79
one *s.* bowl of seventy shekels   *Nu 7:13*
7:19, 25, 31, 37, 43, 49, 55, 61, 67, 73,
  79

charges of *s.* twelve *s.* bowls Nu 7:84
Each charger of *s.* weighing Nu 7:85
Make thee two trumpets of *s.* Nu 10:2
give me his house full of *s.* Nu 22:18;
and gold 24:13
Only the gold, and the *s.* the Nu 31:22
brass
thou shalt not desire the *s.* or De 7:25
gold
thy *s.* and thy gold is De 8:13
multiplied
multiply to himself *s.* and De 17:17
gold
him in an hundred shekels of De 22:19
s.
damsel's father fifty shekels De 22:29
of *s.*
idols, wood and stone, *s.* and De 29:17
gold
But all the *s.* and gold, and Jos 6:19
vessels
only the *s.* and the gold, and Jos 6:24
and two hundred shekels of *s.* Jos 7:21
midst of my tent, and the *s.* Jos 7:21
under it
hid in his tent, and the *s.* Jos 7:22
under it
and the *s.* and the garment Jos 7:24
with *s.* and with gold, and Jos 22:8
with
for an hundred pieces of *s.* Jos 24:32
him threescore and ten pieces of J'g 9:4
s.
of us eleven hundred pieces of J'g 16:5
s.
The eleven hundred shekels of J'g 17:2
s.
mine ears, behold, the *s.* is J'g 17:2
with me
the eleven hundred shekels of J'g 17:3
s.
dedicated the *s.* unto the Lord J'g 17:3
took two hundred shekels of *s.* J'g 17:4
and I will give thee ten shekels J'g 17:10
of *s.*
and crouch to him for a piece 1Sa 2:36
of *s.*
the fourth part of a shekel of 1Sa 9:8
s.
s. and gold that he had 2Sa 8:11
dedicated
have given thee ten shekels 2Sa 18:11
of *s.*
receive a thousand shekels of 2Sa 18:12
s. in
We will have no *s.* nor gold of 2Sa 21:4
Saul
and the oxen for fifty shekels 2Sa 24:24
of *s.*
even the *s.* and the gold, and 1Ki 7:51
were of pure gold; none 1Ki 10:21
were of *s.*
bringing gold, and *s.*, ivory 1Ki 10:22
s. to be in Jerusalem as 1Ki 10:27
stones
for six hundred shekels of *s.* 1Ki 10:29
into the house of the Lord, 1Ki 15:15
s. and
Asa took all the *s.* and the 1Ki 15:18
gold
unto thee a present of *s.* and 1Ki 15:19
gold
Thy *s.* and thy gold is mine; 1Ki 20:3
thy
Thou shalt deliver me thy 1Ki 20:5
s. and
and for my *s.* and for my 1Ki 20:7
gold
or else thou shalt pay a 1Ki 20:39
talent of *s.*
give them, I pray thee, a 2Ki 5:22
talent of *s.*
was sold for fourscore pieces 2Ki 6:25
of *s.*
of dove's dung for five pieces 2Ki 6:25
of *s.*
and carried thence *s.* and gold 2Ki 7:8
any vessels of gold, or 2Ki 12:13
vessels of *s.*
And he took all the gold and 2Ki 14:14
s. and
of each man fifty shekels of 2Ki 15:20
s. to
Ahaz took the *s.* and gold 2Ki 16:8
that was
Judah three hundred talents 2Ki 18:14
of *s.*
Hezekiah gave him all the *s.* 2Ki 18:15
the *s.* and the gold, and the 2Ki 20:13
spices

may sum the *s.* which is 2Ki 22:4
brought
tribute of an hundred talents 2Ki 23:33
of *s.*
Jehoiakim gave the *s.* and 2Ki 23:35
the gold
he exacted the *s.* and the 2Ki 23:35
gold of the
were of gold, in gold, and of 2Ki 25:15
s. in *s.*
s. and the gold that he 1Ch 18:11
brought
Of the gold, the *s.* and the 1Ch 22:16
brass
of all manner of service; *s.* 1Ch 28:14
for all instruments of *s.* by 1Ch 28:14
weight
for the candlesticks of *s.* by 1Ch 28:15
weight
and likewise *s.* for the tables 1Ch 28:16
of *s.*
for every bason; and 1Ch 28:17
likewise *s.*
by weight for every bason 1Ch 28:17
of *s.*
of gold, and the *s.* for things 1Ch 29:2
of *s.*
own proper good, of gold 1Ch 29:3
and *s.*
of gold, and the *s.* for things 1Ch 29:5
of *s.*
and of *s.* ten thousand 1Ch 29:7
talents, and
made *s.* and gold as 2Ch 1:15
plenteous
for six hundred shekels of *s.* 2Ch 1:17
cunning to work in gold, and 2Ch 2:7
in *s.*
skilful to work in gold, and in 2Ch 2:14
s.
and the *s.* and the gold, and 2Ch 5:1
all the
brought gold and *s.* to 2Ch 9:14
Solomon
were of pure gold: none were 2Ch 9:20
of *s.*
bringing gold, and *s.* ivory 2Ch 9:21
vessels of *s.* and vessels of 2Ch 9:24
gold
made *s.* in Jerusalem as 2Ch 9:27
stones
dedicated *s.* and gold, and 2Ch 15:18
vessels
Asa brought out *s.* and gold 2Ch 16:2
out of
behold, I have sent thee *s.* 2Ch 16:3
and gold
brought presents, and 2Ch 17:11
tribute *s.*
father gave them great gifts 2Ch 21:3
of *s.*
spoons, and vessels of gold 2Ch 24:14
and *s.*
And he took all the gold 2Ch 25:24
and the *s.*
he made himself treasuries 2Ch 32:27
for *s.*
men of his place help him with Ezr 1:4
s.
of gold, a thousand chargers Ezr 1:9
of *s.*
s. basons of a second sort Ezr 1:10
four
All the vessels of gold and of Ezr 1:11
s.
and five thousand pound of Ezr 2:69
s.
And to carry the *s.* and gold, Ezr 7:15
which
all the *s.* and gold that thou Ezr 7:16
canst
with the rest of the *s.* and Ezr 7:18
the gold
And weighed unto them the *s.* Ezr 8:25
the *s.* and the gold are a Ezr 8:28
freewill
the weight of the *s.* and the Ezr 8:30
gold
was the *s.* and the gold Ezr 8:33
weighed
and wine, beside forty shekels Ne 5:15
of *s.*
and two hundred pound of *s.* Ne 7:71
gold, and two thousand pound Ne 7:72
of *s.*
to *s.* rings and pillars of marble Es 1:6
the beds were of gold and *s.* Es 1:6
s. is given to thee, the people Es 3:11
who filled their houses with *s.* Job 3:15

and thou shalt have plenty Job 22:25
of *s.*
Though he heap up *s.* as the Job 27:16
dust
and the innocent shall divide Job 27:17
the *s.*
Surely there is a vein for the Job 28:1
s.
s. be weighed for the price Job 28:15
as *s.* tried in a furnace of Ps 12:6
earth
thou hast tried us, as *s.* is Ps 66:10
tried
the wings of a dove covered Ps 68:13
with *s.*
submit himself with pieces of Ps 68:30
s.
He brought them forth also Ps 105:37
with *s.*
Their idols are *s.* and gold, Ps 115:4
the work
me than thousands of gold Ps 119:72
and *s.*
idols of the heathen are *s.* Ps 135:15
and gold
If thou seekest her as *s.* and Pr 2:4
is better than the merchandise Pr 3:14
of *s.*
Receive my instruction, and Pr 8:10
not *s.*
and my revenue than choice *s.* Pr 8:19
tongue of the just is as choice Pr 10:20
s.
rather to be chosen than *s.* Pr 16:16
fining pot is for *s.* and the Pr 17:3
furnace
and loving favour rather than Pr 22:1
s. and
Take away the dross from the Pr 25:4
s.
like apples of gold in pictures Pr 25:11
of *s.*
a potsherd covered with *s.* Pr 26:23
dross
fining pot for *s.* and the Pr 27:21
furnace
I gathered me also *s.* and gold Ec 2:8
He that loveth *s.* shall not be Ec 5:10
shall not be satisfied with *s.* Ec 5:10
Or ever the *s.* cord be loosed, Ec 12:6
or the
borders of gold with studs of *s.* Ca 1:11
He made the pillars thereof of Ca 3:10
s.
will build upon her a palace of Ca 8:9
s.
was to bring a thousand Ca 8:11
pieces of *s.*
Thy *s.* is become dross, thy Isa 1:22
wine
Their land also is full of *s.* Isa 2:7
and gold
day a man shall cast his idols Isa 2:20
of *s.*
a thousand *s.* shekels Isa 7:23
(A)(R)(S)
Medes which shall not Isa 13:17
regard *s.*
covering of thy graven Isa 30:22
images of *s.*
man shall cast away his idols Isa 31:7
the *s.* and the gold, and the Isa 39:2
spices
with gold, and casteth *s.* Isa 40:19
chains
and weigh *s.* in the balance Isa 46:6
I have refined thee, but not Isa 48:10
with *s.*
their *s.* and their gold with Isa 60:9
them
and for iron I will bring *s.* Isa 60:17
and for
Reprobate *s.* shall men call Jer 6:30
them
They deck it with *s.* and with Jer 10:4
S. spread into plates is Jer 10:9
brought
even seventeen shekels of *s.* Jer 32:9
gold, and that which was of Jer 52:19
s. in *s.*
shall cast their *s.* in the Eze 7:19
streets,
their *s.* and their gold shall Eze 7:19
not be
wast thou decked with gold Eze 16:13
and *s.*

fair jewels of my gold and of *Eze 16:17*
my *s.*
they are even the dross of *s.* *Eze 22:18*
they gather *s.* and brass, and *Eze 22:20*
iron
As *s.* is melted in the midst *Eze 22:22*
with *s.* iron, tin, and lead, *Eze 27:12*
they
gold and *s.* into thy treasures *Eze 28:4*
to carry away *s.* and gold, to *Eze 38:13*
gold, his breast and his arms *Da 2:32*
of *s.*
clay, the brass, the *s.* and the *Da 2:35*
gold
brass, the clay, the *s.* and the *Da 2:45*
gold
praised the gods of gold, and *Da 5:4*
of *s.*
thou hast praised the gods of *Da 5:23*
s.
shall he honour with gold, *Da 11:38*
and *s.*
the treasures of gold and of *s.* *Da 11:43*
and multiplied her *s.* and gold *Ho 2:8*
her to me for fifteen pieces of *Ho 3:2*
s.
of their *s.* and their gold have *Ho 8:4*
they
pleasant places for their *s.* *Ho 9:6*
nettles
them molten images of their *Ho 13:2*
s. and
ye have taken my *s.* and my *Joe 3:5*
gold
they sold the righteous for *s.* *Am 2:6*
That we may buy the poor for *Am 8:6*
s.
Take ye the spoil of *s.*, take the *Na 2:9*
it is laid over with gold and *Hab 2:19*
s. and
all they that bear *s.* are cut off *Zep 1:11*
Neither their *s.* nor their gold *Zep 1:18*
shall
s. is mine, and the gold is *Hag 2:8*
mine
Then take *s.* and gold, and *Zec 6:11*
make
heaped up *s.* as the dust, and *Zec 9:3*
fine
for my price thirty pieces of *Zec 11:12*
s.
I took the thirty pieces of *s.* *Zec 11:13*
and will refine them as *s.* is *Zec 13:9*
refined
together, gold, and *s.* and *Zec 14:14*
apparel
sit as a refiner and purifier of *Mal 3:3*
s.
and purge them as gold, and *Mal 3:3*
s.
neither gold, nor *s.* nor brass *M't 10:9*
in
with him for thirty pieces of *M't 26:15*
s.
the thirty pieces of *s.* to the *M't 27:3*
chief
he cast down the pieces of *s.* *M't 27:5*
in the
the chief priests took the *s.* *M't 27:6*
pieces
took the thirty pieces of *s.* *M't 27:9*
the price
what woman having ten *Lu 15:8*
pieces *s.*
said, *S.* and gold have I none; *Ac 3:6*
but
the Godhead is like unto *Ac 17:29*
gold, or *s.*
found it fifty thousand pieces *Ac 19:19*
of *s.*
which make *s.* shrines for *Ac 19:24*
Diana
I have coveted no man's *s.* or *Ac 20:33*
gold
this foundation gold, *s.* *1Co 3:12*
precious
not only vessels of gold and *2Ti 2:20*
of *s.*
Your gold and *s.* is cankered *Jas 5:3*
corruptible things, as *s.* and *1Pe 1:18*
gold
devils, and idols of gold, and *Re 9:20*
s. and
The merchandise of gold, and *Re 18:12*
s.

TALENTS OF SILVER

bought hill Samaria for two *1Ki 16:24*
talents of s.

Naaman took with him ten *2Ki 5:5*
talents of s.
and bound two *talents of s.* *2Ki 5:23*
into two bags
Menahem gave Pul 1000 *2Ki 15:19*
talents of s.
Hanun sent 1000 *talents of s.* *1Ch 19:6*
I prepared a thousand *1Ch 22:14*
thousand *talents of s.*
and seven thousand *talents of* *1Ch 29:4*
refined *s.*
hired mighty men for 100 *2Ch 25:6*
talents of s.
Ammon gave Jotham 100 *2Ch 27:5*
talents of s.
condemned land in 100 *2Ch 36:3*
talents of s.
I decree it be done to 100 *Ezr 7:22*
talents of s.
weighed to their hand 650 *Ezr 8:26*
talents of s.
I will pay ten thousand *talents* *Es 3:9*
of s.

VESSELS OF SILVER

all the *s. vessels* weighed 2400 *Nu 7:85*
shekels
Joram brought with him *2Sa 8:10*
vessels of s.
every man his present, *1Ki 10:25*
vessels of s.
there were not made *vessels* *2Ki 12:13*
of s.
and with him all manner of *1Ch 18:10;*
vessels of s., gold and brass *2Ch 24:14*
strengthened their hands with *Ezr 1:6*
vessels of s.
vessels of gold and *s.* of the *Ezr 5:14*
house of God, which
Nebuchadnezzar took
let the golden and *s.* vessels be *Ezr 6:5*
restored
I weighed *s. vessels* an *Ezr 8:26*
hundred talents
commanded to bring golden *Da 5:2*
and *s. vessels*
carry with their precious *Da 11:8*
vessels of s. and gold

SILVERLINGS

a thousand vines at a *Isa 7:23*
thousand *s.*
a thousand silver shekels *Isa 7:23*
(A)(R)
a thousand dollars (B) *Isa 7:23*

SILVERSMITH

gave them to the *s.* (S) *J'g 17:4*
certain man named *Ac 19:24*
Demetrius, a *s.*

SIMEON

Leah bare a son and called *Ge 29:33*
his name *S.*
S. and Levi took each man *Ge 34:25*
his sword
S. son of Leah *Ge 35:23*
Joseph took from them *S.* *Ge 42:24*
S. is not *Ge 42:36*
and he brought *S.* out unto *Ge 43:23*
them
the sons of *S.* *Ge 46:10;*
Ex 6:15; Nu 1:22; 26:12; 1Ch 4:24, 42;
                                        12:25
as Reuben and *S.* they shall be *Ge 48:5*
mine
S. and Levi are brethren, *Ge 49:5*
they slew a man
S. son of Israel *Ex 1:2*
prince of the *S.* was Shelumiel *Nu 1:6;*
                                        2:12; 7:36
(*S.*, Levi stand to bless *De 27:12*
the second lot came forth to *Jos 19:1*
S. had their inheritance within *Jos 19:9*
Judah
S. went with Judah *J'g 1:3; 1:17*
the strangers out of *S.* fell to *2Ch 15:9*
Asa
so did Josiah in the cities of *2Ch 34:6*
S. to Naphtali
S. have a portion *Eze 48:24*
one gate of *S.* *Eze 48:33*
a man in Jerusalem, whose *Lu 2:25*
name was *S.*
S. blessed Joseph and Mary, *Lu 2:34*
and said to Mary

Levi, which was the son of *S.* *Lu 3:30*
at Antioch, *S.* that was called *Ac 13:1*
Niger
S. hath declared how God did *Ac 15:14*
visit Gentiles

TRIBE OF SIMEON

of the *tribe of S.* numbered *Nu 1:23*
59,300
the *tribe of S.* shall pitch by *Nu 2:12*
Reuben
over the host of the *tribe of* *Nu 10:19*
S. Shelumiel
of the *tribe of S.*, Shaphat to *Nu 13:5*
spy the land
of *tribe of S.*, Shemuel to *Nu 34:20*
divide the land
second lot came out for the *Jos 19:1*
tribe of S.
this is the inheritance of the *Jos 19:8*
tribe of S.
Levites had out of *tribe of S.* *Jos 21:4;*
                              21:9; 1Ch 6:65
of the *tribe of S.* were sealed *Re 7:7*
12,000

SIMEONITES

of a chief house among the *Nu 25:14*
S.
These are the families of the *Nu 26:14*
S.
of the *S.*, Shephatiah the son *1Ch 27:16*

SIMILITUDE

the *s.* of the Lord shall he *Nu 12:8*
behold
behold the form of the Lord *Nu 12:8*
(A)(B)(R)
the form of Jehovah he shall *Nu 12:8*
behold (E)
voice of the words, but saw *De 4:12*
no *s.*
but saw no form *De 4:12;*
(A)(B)(E)(R)   *4:15*
ye saw no manner of *s.* on the *De 4:15*
day
the *s.* of any figure, the *De 4:16*
likeness of
under it was the *s.* of oxen, *2Ch 4:3*
which
figures of oxen (A)(B) *2Ch 4:3*
the likeness of oxen (E) *2Ch 4:3*
figures of gourds (R) *2Ch 4:3*
their glory into the *s.* of an *Ps 106:20*
ox
for the image of a calf *Ps 106:20*
(A)(B)(R)
the likeness of an ox (E) *Ps 106:20*
polished after the *s.* of a *Ps 144:12*
palace
like pillars of a palace (A) *Ps 144:12*
like sculptured corner pillars *Ps 144:12*
(B)(R)
s. of the sons of men *Da 10:16*
touched my
likeness of the sons of men *Da 10:16*
(A)(E)(R)
resembling a human form *Da 10:16*
(B)
the *s.* of Adam's transgression *Ro 5:14*
the *s.* of Melchisedec there *Heb 7:15*
ariseth
likeness of Melchizedek *Heb 7:15*
(A)(E)(R)
who resembles Melchizedek *Heb 7:15*
(B)
are made after the *s.* of God *Jas 3:9*
made in God's likeness *Jas 3:9*
(A)(B)(E)(N)(P)(R)

SIMILITUDES

and used *s.* by the ministry of *Ho 12:10*

SIMON

S. the Canaanite *M't 10:4; M'k 3:18*
his brethren James, Joses *S.* *M't 13:55;*
                                        M'k 6:3
Jesus said, Blessed art thou, *M't 16:17*
S. Bar-jona
what thinkest thou, *S.*? of *M't 17:25*
whom do kings
in the house of *S.* the leper *M't 26:6;*
                                        M'k 14:3
a man of Cyrene, *S.* by *M't 27:32;*

name to bear the cross *M'k 15:21;*
Lu 23:26
they entered into house of S. *M'k 1:29;*
Lu 4:38
S. sleepest thou? couldest *M'k 14:37*
not thou watch
he said unto S., Launch out into *Lu 5:4*
the deep
James and John who were *Lu 5:10*
partners with S.
and S. called Zelotes *Lu 6:15; Ac 1:13*
S, I have somewhat to say *Lu 7:40*
unto thee
S., S. Satan hath desired to *Lu 22:31*
have you
the Lord is risen, and hath *Lu 24:34*
appeared to S.
he first findeth his own *Joh 1:41*
brother S.
Jesus said, Thou art S. the *Joh 1:42*
son of Jona
Judas Iscariot the son of S. *Joh 6:71*
12:4; 13:2, 26
S. son of Jonas, lovest thou *Joh 21:15;*
me *21:16, 17*
a man S. who before time used *Ac 8:9*
sorcery
then S. himself believed also, *Ac 8:13;*
when baptized *8:18, 24*
Peter tarried many days at *Ac 9:43;*
Joppa with one S. a tanner *10:5, 6, 18,*
32
call for S. whose surname is *Ac 11:13*
Peter
S. Peter, a servant and an *2Pe 1:1*
apostle

SIMON'S

But S. wife's mother lay sick *M'k 1:30*
and entered into S. house. And *Lu 4:38*
S. wife's mother was taken *Lu 4:38*
with a
into one of the ships, which was *Lu 5:3*
S.
disciples, Judas Iscariot, S. *Joh 12:4*
son
the heart of Judas Iscariot, S. *Joh 13:2*
son
had made enquiry for S. *Ac 10:17*
house

SIMPLE

Lord is sure, making wise the *Ps 19:7*
s.
The Lord preserveth the s.: I *Ps 116:6*
Lord takes care of the *Ps 116:6*
helpless (B)
giveth understanding unto *Ps 119:130*
the s.
To give subtilty to the s. to the *Pr 1:4*
give insight to the s. *Pr 1:4*
(A)(B)(E)(R)
How long, ye s. ones, will ye *Pr 1:22*
love
the turning away of the s. shall *Pr 1:32*
And beheld among the s. ones *Pr 7:7*
O ye s. understand wisdom: and *Pr 8:5*
Whoso is s. let him turn in *Pr 9:4*
hither
she is s. and knoweth nothing *Pr 9:13*
Whoso is s. let him turn in *Pr 9:16*
hither
The s. believeth every word *Pr 14:15*
s. inherit folly: but the *Pr 14:18*
prudent
a scorner, and the s. will *Pr 19:25*
beware
is punished, the s. is made *Pr 21:11*
wise
the s. pass on, and are *Pr 22:3;*
punished *27:12*
that erreth, and for him that *Eze 45:20*
is s.
revealing to the s. (N) *M't 11:25*
sharing meals with s. joy (P) *Ac 2:46*
the simple (N) *Ro 1:14*
deceive the hearts of the s. *Ro 16:18*
the unsuspecting and *Ro 16:18*
simple-minded (A)
the unsuspecting (B) *Ro 16:18*
the innocent (E)(N) *Ro 16:18*
the simple-hearted (P) *Ro 16:18*
the simple-minded (R) *Ro 16:18*
is good, and s. concerning *Ro 16:19*
evil
good, innocent and guileless *Ro 16:19*
as to evil (A)

goodness and innocent to evil *Ro 16:19*
(B)
experts in goodness, *Ro 16:19*
simpletons in evil (N)
to simplehearted to see *Ro 16:19*
through them (P)
guileless as to what is evil *Ro 16:19*
(R)

SIMPLICITY

and they went in their s. and *2Sa 15:11*
they accompanied him *2Sa 15:11*
innocently (B)
ye simple ones, will ye love s. *Pr 1:22*
that giveth, let him do it with *Ro 12:8*
s.
with genuine cheerfulness *Ro 12:8*
joyful eagerness (A)(B)(E)(N)(R)
who feels sympathy act *Ro 12:8*
cheerfully (P)
that in s. and godly sincerity *2Co 1:12*
from the s. that is in Christ *2Co 11:3*
from wholehearted, sincere *2Co 11:3*
and pure devotion (A)
from single-hearted devotion *2Co 11:3*
(N)(P)
from sincere and true *2Co 11:3*
devotion (R)
in s. of purpose (A) *Col 3:22*

SIMPLEMINDEDNESS

s. of the gospel message (P) *1Co 1:21*

SIMPLETON

simpleton (B) *Lu 12:20; 1Co 15:36*

SIMPLETONS

simpletons (B) *Lu 11:40; 24:25*
s. in evil (N) *Ro 16:18*
not like s. (N) *Eph 5:15*

SIMRI

Hosah had sons; S. the *1Ch 26:10*
chief

SIN

if thou doest not well s. lieth at *Ge 4:7*
door
what is my s. (A) *Ge 31:36*
how can I do this wickedness *Ge 39:9*
and s. against God
Reuben said, Do not s. *Ge 42:22*
against the child
his fear may be before you, *Ex 20:20*
that s. not
not dwell, lest they make thee *Ex 23:33*
s. against me
forgiving iniquity, *Ex 34:7*
transgression, and s.
if a soul shall s. thro' ignorance *Le 4:2*
against commandments
if priest s. according to s. of *Le 4:3*
people, bring for his s. a young
bullock for a s. offering
if congregation s. *Le 4:13*
when s. is known, *Le 4:14*
congregation shall offer
a young bullock for the s.
if any one of the common *Le 4:27*
people s. thro' ignorance
if a soul s. and hear the voice *Le 5:1*
of swearing
if a soul commit a trespass *Le 5:15;*
and s. thro' ignorance *5:17; Nu 15:27*
in the holy things
if a soul s. and lie unto his *Le 6:2*
neighbour
the priest that offereth it for *Le 6:26;*
s. *9:15*
and not suffer s. upon thy *Le 19:17*
neighbour for his s. which he
hath done, and
the s. which he hath done, *Le 19:22*
shall be forgiven
when a man or woman shall *Nu 5:6*
commit s.
be innocent of any s. (B) *Nu 5:15;*
14:19; 23:21; Jos 22:17
I beseech thee lay not the s. *Nu 12:11*
upon us
shall one s. wilt thou be *Nu 16:22*
wroth with all
it is a purification for s. *Nu 19:9*
our father died in his own s. *Nu 27:3*
had no sons

cry to Lord and it be s. to *De 15:9;*
thee *24:15*
one witness shall not rise up *De 19:15*
for any s.
so should you s. against Lord *De 20:18*
your God
if man have committed s. *De 21:22*
worthy of death
there is in damsel no s. *De 22:26*
worthy of death
Lord shall require it, and it *De 23:21*
would s. in thee
if thou forbear to vow, it *De 23:22*
shall be no s.
thou shalt not cause the land *De 24:4*
to s. Lord give
every man shall be put to *De 24:16;*
death for his own s. *2Ki 14:6; 2Ch 25:4*
if one man s. against *1Sa 2:25*
another; if a man s. against
the Lord, who shall entreat
God forbid I should s. in *1Sa 12:23*
ceasing to pray
behold, the people s. against *1Sa 14:33*
the Lord
slay them, and s. not in *1Sa 14:34*
eating with the blood
let not the king s. against his *1Sa 19:4*
servant
why wilt thou s. against *1Sa 19:5*
innocent blood
forgive the s. of thy people *1Ki 8:34*
Israel
forgive s. of thy servants *1Ki 8:36;*
2Ch 6:25-27
if they s. against thee *1Ki 8:46;*
2Ch 6:36
and this thing became a s. *1Ki 12:30;*
13:34
for rebellion is as s. of *1Ki 15:23*
witchcraft
s. money was the priest's *2Ki 12:16*
Manasseh made Judah to s. *2Ki 21:11*
with idols
if a man s. against his *2Ch 6:22*
neighbour
s. of the nations (B) *Ezr 6:21*
that I should be afraid, and *Ne 6:13*
do so, and s.
did not Solomon s. by these *Ne 13:26*
things
in all this did not Job s. with *Job 2:10*
his lips
thou shalt visit thy habitation *Job 5:24*
and not s.
if I s. thou markest me, not *Job 10:14*
acquit
his bones are full of s. of his *Job 20:11*
youth
neither have I suffered my *Job 31:30*
mouth to s.
stand in awe, and s. not, *Ps 4:4*
commune
blessed is he whose s. is *Ps 32:1*
covered
I will take heed that I s. not *Ps 39:1*
with my tongue
and in s. did my mother *Ps 51:5*
conceive me
for s. of their mouth let them *Ps 59:12*
be taken
and let his prayer become s. *Ps 109:7*
let not the s. of his mother *Ps 109:14*
be blotted out
that I might not s. against *Ps 119:11*
thee
the fruit of the wicked *Pr 10:16*
tendeth to s.
in multitude of words there *Pr 10:19*
wanteth not s.
fools make a mock at s. *Pr 14:9*
but s. is a reproach to any *Pr 14:34*
people
and the plowing of the wicked *Pr 21:4*
is s.
the thought of foolishness is s. *Pr 24:9*
suffer not thy mouth to cause *Ec 5:6*
thy flesh to s.
woe to them draw s. as with *Isa 5:18*
cart-rope
and cover, that they may add *Isa 30:1*
s. to s.
his idols which your hands *Isa 31:7*
have made for s.
thou shalt make his soul an *Isa 53:10*
offering for s.
he bare s. of many, and *Isa 53:12*
made intercession
children of s., disloyal brood *Isa 57:4*
(B)

s. of Judah written with a pen *Jer 17:1*
of iron
I will give high place for a *s.* *Jer 17:3*
do this abomination to cause *Jer 32:35*
Judah to *s.*
though their land was filled *Jer 51:5*
with *s.*
than the punishment of the *s.* *La 4:6*
of Sodom
that righteous *s.* not, and he *Eze 3:21*
doth not *s.*
they eat up *s.* of my people *Ho 4:8*
because Ephraim hath made *Ho 8:11*
many altars to *s.*, altars
shall be unto him to *s.*
the *s.* of Israel shall be *Ho 10:8*
destroyed
shall find no iniquity in me *Ho 12:8*
that were *s.*
fell in *s.* through Baal (B) *Ho 13:1*
and now they *s.* more and *Ho 13:2*
more and made
they that swear by the *s.* of *Am 8:14*
Samaria
she is the beginning of *s.* to *Mic 1:13*
Zion
give fruit of my body for *s.* of *Mic 6:7*
my soul
there shall be a fountain *Zec 13:1*
opened for *s.*
if eye causes you to *s.* (R) *M't 5:29;*
5:30
all manner of *s.* shall be *M't 12:31*
forgiven to men
cause one to stumble and *s.* *M't 18:6*
(A)(E)(R)
Lord, how oft shall my *M't 18:21*
brother *s.*
which taketh away the *s.* of *Joh 1:29*
the world
s. no more, lest worse thing *Joh 5:14*
come to thee
he that is without *s.* among *Joh 8:7*
you, let him cast
neither do I condemn thee, *s.* *Joh 8:11*
no more
whoso committeth *s.* is the *Joh 8:34*
servant of *s.*
who did *s.*, this man or his *Joh 9:2*
parents
if ye were blind, he should *Joh 9:41*
have no *s.*
if I had not come, they had *Joh 15:22;*
not had *s.* 15:24
Comforter, he will reprove *Joh 16:8*
the world of *s.*
of *s.* because they believe not *Joh 16:9*
on me
he that delivered me hath *Joh 19:11*
the greater *s.*
Lord, lay not this *s.* to their *Ac 7:60*
charge
proved Jews and Gentiles all *Ro 3:9*
under *s.*
for by the law is the *Ro 3:20*
knowledge of *s.*
blessed are they whose *s.* is *Ro 4:7*
covered
s. entered into the world, and *Ro 5:12*
death by *s.*
for till the law *s.* was in the *Ro 5:13*
world
where *s.* abounded, grace *Ro 5:20*
much more abound
that as *s.* reigned unto death, *Ro 5:21*
even so grace
what shall we say? shall we *Ro 6:1*
continue in *s.*
how shall we that are dead to *Ro 6:2*
s. live therein
that body of *s.* might be *Ro 6:6*
destroyed that henceforth we
should not serve *s.*
for he that is dead is freed *Ro 6:7*
from *s.*
for in that he died, he died to *Ro 6:10*
s. once
reckon ye yourselves to be *Ro 6:11*
dead indeed unto *s.*
let not *s.* therefore reign in *Ro 6:12*
your mortal body
nor yield your members as *Ro 6:13*
instruments to *s.*
for *s.* shall not have dominion *Ro 6:14*
over you
shall we *s.* because we are not *Ro 6:15*
under law
his servants ye are, whether of *Ro 6:16*
s. unto death

God be thanked, ye were the *Ro 6:17*
servants of *s.*
being then made free from *s.* *Ro 6:18;*
6:22
for when ye were the servants *Ro 6:20*
of *s.* ye were
for wages of *s.* is death, but *Ro 6:23*
the gift of God
is law *s*? God forbid, I had not *Ro 7:7*
known *s.*
s. taking occasion wrought in *Ro 7:8*
me all manner of
concupiscence: without law *s.*
was dead
commandment came, *s.* revived, *Ro 7:9*
and I died
for *s.* by the commandment *Ro 7:11*
slew me
but *s.* that it might appear, *s.* *Ro 7:13*
that *s.* by the commandment
become exceeding sinful
law is spiritual, but I am *Ro 7:14*
carnal, sold under *s.*
no more I, but *s.* that *Ro 7:17;*
dwelleth in me 7:20
and bringing me into captivity *Ro 7:23*
to law of *s.*
but with the flesh, the law of *s.* *Ro 7:25*
and for *s.* condemned *s.* in the *Ro 8:3*
flesh
if Christ be in you, body is *Ro 8:10*
dead because of *s.*
for whatsoever is not of *Ro 14:23*
faith, is *s.*
every *s.* a man doth is *1Co 6:18*
without body
when ye *s.* against brethren *1Co 8:12*
and wound their conscience,
ye *s.* against Christ
awake to righteousness, and *1Co 15:34*
s. not
sting of death is *s.*; *1Co 15:56*
strength of *s.* is law
made him to be *s.* for us, who *2Co 5:21*
knew no *s.*
is therefore Christ the minister *Ga 2:17*
of *s.*
the scripture hath concluded *Ga 3:22*
all under *s.*
be detected in some *s.* (P) *Ga 6:1*
be ye angry, and *s.* not, let *Eph 4:26*
not the sun
that man of *s.* be revealed *2Th 2:3*
them that *s.* rebuke before all *1Ti 5:20*
be hardened thro' the *Heb 3:13*
deceitfulness of *s.*
was tempted like as we are, *Heb 4:15*
yet without *s.*
but once hath he appeared to *Heb 9:26*
put away *s.*
he shall appear without *s.* to *Heb 9:28*
salvation
in sacrifices for *s.* thou hast *Heb 10:6*
had no pleasure
offering for *s.* thou wouldst *Heb 10:8*
not, nor pleasure
where remission, is no more *Heb 10:18*
offering for *s.*
if we *s.* wilfully after *Heb 10:26*
knowledge of truth
than to enjoy pleasures of *s.* *Heb 11:25*
for a season
let us lay aside *s.* that doth *Heb 12:1*
easily beset us
ye have not yet resisted, *Heb 12:4*
striving against *s.*
the bodies of those beasts *Heb 13:11*
for *s.* are burnt
when lust hath conceived, it *Jas 1:15*
brings *s.*; and *s.* when
finished, brings death
if ye have respect to persons, *Jas 2:9*
ye commit *s.*
knoweth, and doth not good, *Jas 4:17*
to him it is *s.*
if you *s.* (E) *1Pe 2:20*
who did no *s.* nor was guile *1Pe 2:22*
found
that suffered in flesh hath *1Pe 4:1*
ceased from *s.*
having eyes that cannot cease *2Pe 2:14*
from *s.*
blood of Christ cleanseth us *1Jo 1:7*
from all *s.*
if we say we have no *s.* we *1Jo 1:8*
deceive ourselves
I write unto you that ye *s.* not, *1Jo 2:1*
and if any man *s.* we have an
advocate

whoso committeth *s.* *1Jo 3:4*
transgresseth law, for *s.* is
transgression of law
he was manifested, and in him *1Jo 3:5*
is no *s.*
he that committeth *s.* is of the *1Jo 3:8*
devil
whosoever is born of God doth *1Jo 3:9*
not commit *s.*
he cannot *s.* because he is *1Jo 3:9*
born of God
if man see brother *s.* a *s.* *1Jo 5:16*
which is not to death, there
is a *s.* unto death
all unrighteousness is *s.* and *1Jo 5:17*
there is a *s.* not unto death

GREAT SIN

brought on me and my *Ge 20:9*
kingdom great *s.*
that hast brought this great *s.* *Ex 32:21*
on them
Moses said, Ye have sinned a *Ex 32:30*
great *s.*
oh, this people have sinned a *Ex 32:31*
great *s.*
s. of the young men was very *1Sa 2:17*
great
Jeroboam made them sin a *2Ki 17:21*
great *s.*

HIS SIN

bring for *his s.* he sinned a *Le 4:3*
young bullock
or if *his s.* come to his *Le 4:23;*
knowledge 4:28
priest make atonement for *his* *Le 4:26;*
s. and it shall be forgiven 4:35; 5:6, 10;
13
he shall bring a kid of the *Le 4:28*
goats for *his s.*
he shall bring his trespass *Le 5:6*
offering for *his s.*
Nadab walked in the way of *1Ki 15:26*
his s.
Baasha walked in way of *1Ki 15:34*
Jeroboam and *his s.*
[Zimri] walked in *his s.* *1Ki 16:19*
[Omri] walked in *his s.* *1Ki 16:26*
beside *his s.* wherewith *2Ki 21:16*
made Judah
acts of Manasseh, and *his s.* *2Ki 21:17*
that he sinned
all *his s.* before he *2Ch 33:19*
was humbled
for he addeth rebellion to *Job 34:37*
his s.
this is all the fruit to take *Isa 27:9*
away *his s.*
he shall die in *his s.* *Eze 3:20; 18:24*
if he turn from *his s.* and do *Eze 33:14*
right
iniquity is bound up, *his s.* is *Ho 13:12*
hid
truly I am full to declare to *Mic 3:8*
Israel *his s.*

MY SIN

what is *my s.* that thou hast *Ge 31:36*
pursued me
therefore forgive *my s.* only *Ex 10:17*
this once
I pray thee, pardon *my s.* *1Sa 15:25*
turn with me
what is *my s.* before thy *1Sa 20:1*
father to seek my life
come to call *my s.* to *1Ki 17:18*
remembrance
that thou searchest after *my* *Job 10:6*
s.
make me to know *Job 13:23*
transgression and *my s.*
dost thou not watch over *my* *Job 14:16*
s.
what profit if I be cleansed *Job 35:3*
from *my s.*
I acknowledge *my s.* and *Ps 32:5*
thou forgavest the iniquity
of *my s.*
nor rest in my bones because *Ps 38:3*
of *my s.*
mine iniquity, for I will be *Ps 38:18*
sorry for *my s.*
wash me throughly, cleanse me *Ps 51:2*
from *my s.*
my s. is ever before me *Ps 51:3*
not for *my s.* O Lord *Ps 59:3*

who can say, I am pure from | *Pr 20:9*
my *s.*
and whilst I was confessing | *Da 9:20*
my *s.*

OUR SIN

pardon our iniquity and *our s.* | *Ex 34:9*
what is *our s.* we have | *Jer 16:1*
committed

THEIR SIN

Lord said, Because *their s.* is | *Ge 18:20*
very grievous
forgive, I pray thee, *their s.* | *Ge 50:17;*
| *2Ch 7:14*
yet now, if thou wilt forgive | *Ex 32:32*
their s.
in the day when I visit, I will | *Ex 32:34*
visit *their s.*
they shall confess *their s.* they | *Nu 5:7*
have done
look not unto stubbornness, | *De 9:27*
nor *their s.*
if they turn from *their s.* | *1Ki 8:35;*
| *2Ch 6:26*
let not *their s.* be blotted out | *Ne 4:5*
from thee
forgiven, thou hast covered all | *Ps 85:2*
their s.
they declare *their s.* as Sodom, | *Isa 3:9*
hide it not
I will recompense *their s.* | *Jer 16:18*
double
neither blot out *their s.* from | *Jer 18:23*
thy sight
and I will remember *their s.* | *Jer 31:34*
no more
that I may forgive their | *Jer 36:3*
iniquity and *their s.*
now they have no cloak for | *Joh 15:22*
their s.

THY SIN

the Lord also hath put away | *2Sa 12:13*
thy s.
thine iniquity is taken away, | *Isa 6:7*
thy s. is purged

YOUR SIN

I shall make atonement for | *Ex 32:30*
your s.
be sure *your s.* will find you | *Nu 32:23*
out
I took *your s.* the calf which ye | *De 9:21*
had made
ye say we see, therefore *your* | *Joh 9:41*
s. remaineth

SIN, place

came unto the wilderness of *S.* | *Ex 16:1*
journeyed from the wilderness | *Ex 17:1*
of *S.*
encamped in the wilderness | *Nu 33:11*
of *S.*
journey out of the wilderness | *Nu 33:12*
of *S.*
And I will pour my fury | *Eze 30:15*
upon *S*
S. shall have great pain, and | *Eze 30:16*

SINA

him in the wilderness of Mount | *Ac 7:30*
S.
which spake to him in the | *Ac 7:38*
mount *S.*

SINAI

which is between Elim and *S.* | *Ex 16:1*
came they into the wilderness | *Ex 19:1*
of *S.*
were come to the desert of *S.* | *Ex 19:2*
of all the people upon mount | *Ex 19:11*
S.
And mount *S.* was altogether | *Ex 19:18*
Lord came down upon mount | *Ex 19:20*
S.
cannot come up to mount *S.* | *Ex 19:23*
of the Lord abode upon | *Ex 24:16*
mount *S.*
him upon mount *S.* two | *Ex 31:18*
tables
up in the morning unto mount | *Ex 34:2*
S.

and went up unto mount *S.* as | *Ex 34:4*
Moses came down from | *Ex 34:29*
mount *S.*
had spoken with him in | *Ex 34:32*
mount *S.*
commanded Moses in mount | *Le 7:38*
S. in
the Lord, in the wilderness of | *Le 7:38*
S.
spake unto Moses in mount *S.* | *Le 25:1*
children of Israel in mount *S.* | *Le 26:46*
the children of Israel in | *Le 27:34*
mount *S.*
unto Moses in the wilderness | *Nu 1:1*
of *S.*
them in the wilderness of *S.* | *Nu 1:19*
spake with Moses in mount *S.* | *Nu 3:1*
the Lord, in the wilderness of | *Nu 3:4*
S.
unto Moses in the wilderness | *Nu 3:14;*
of *S.* | *9:1*
at even in the wilderness of *S.* | *Nu 9:5*
journeys out of wilderness | *Nu 10:12*
of *S.*
of Israel in the wilderness of | *Nu 26:64*
S.
which was ordained in mount | *Nu 28:6*
S.
and pitched in the wilderness | *Nu 33:15*
of *S.*
removed from the desert of | *Nu 33:16*
S.
The Lord came from *S.* and | *De 33:2*
rose
even that *S.* from before the | *J'g 5:5*
Lord
camest down also upon mount | *Ne 9:13*
S.
even *S.* itself was moved, at | *Ps 68:8*
the Lord is among them, as | *Ps 68:17*
in *S.*
the one from the mount *S.* | *Ga 4:24*
which
this Agar is mount *S.* in | *Ga 4:25*
Arabia

SINCE

Lord hath blessed thee *s.* my | *Ge 30:30*
coming
in pieces; and I saw him not | *Ge 44:28*
s.
let me die, *s.* I have seen thy | *Ge 46:30*
face
nor *s.* thou hast spoken unto | *Ex 4:10*
thy
s. I came to Pharaoh to speak | *Ex 5:23*
in
in Egypt *s.* the foundation | *Ex 9:18*
thereof
all the land of Egypt *s.* it | *Ex 9:24*
became a
s. the day that they were upon | *Ex 10:6*
hast ridden ever *s.* I was | *Nu 22:30*
thine
s. the day that God created | *De 4:32*
man
a prophet *s.* in Israel like | *De 34:10*
unto
s. I have shewed you kindness | *Jos 2:12*
s. the Lord spake this word | *Jos 14:10*
unto
law *s.* the death of thine | *Ru 2:11*
husband
works which they have done *s.* | *1Sa 8:8*
hath it been kept for thee *s.* | *1Sa 9:24*
I said
about these three days, *s.* I | *1Sa 21:5*
came out
him *s.* he fell unto me unto | *1Sa 29:3*
this day
s. the day of thy coming unto | *1Sa 29:6*
me unto
s. the time that I brought up | *2Sa 7:6*
the
as *s.* the time that I | *2Sa 7:11*
commanded
S. the day that I brought forth | *1Ki 8:16*
my
field *s.* the day that she left the | *2Ki 8:6*
land
s. the day their fathers came | *2Ki 21:15*
forth
s. the day that I brought up | *1Ch 17:5*
Israel
s. the time that I commanded | *1Ch 17:10*
judges
S. the day that I brought forth | *2Ch 6:5*
my
s. the time of Solomon the | *2Ch 30:26*
son of

S. the people began to bring | *2Ch 31:10*
unto him *s.* the days of | *Ezr 4:2*
Esar-haddon
s. that time even until now | *Ezr 5:16*
hath
s. the days of our fathers have | *Ezr 9:7*
we been
s. the days of Jeshua the son | *Ne 8:17*
of Nun
s. the time of the kings of | *Ne 9:32*
Assyria
s. man was placed upon earth | *Job 20:4*
commanded the morning *s.* | *Job 38:12*
thy days
S. thou art laid down, no | *Isa 14:8*
feller is
spoken concerning Moab *s.* | *Isa 16:13*
that time
S. thou wast precious in my | *Isa 43:4*
sight
me *s.* I appointed the ancient | *Isa 44:7*
people
s. the beginning of the world | *Isa 64:4*
men
S. the day that your fathers | *Jer 7:25*
came
s. they return not from their | *Jer 15:7*
ways
For *s.* I spake, I cried out, | *Jer 20:8*
I cried
s. ye say, The burden of the | *Jer 23:38*
Lord
for *s.* I spake against him, I | *Jer 31:20*
do
s. we left off to burn incense | *Jer 44:18*
for *s.* thou spakest of him, | *Jer 48:27*
thou
s. thou hast not hated bood | *Eze 35:6*
(S)
as never was *s.* there was a | *Da 12:1*
nation
S. those days were, when one | *Hag 2:16*
came
not *s.* the beginning of the | *M't 24:21*
world to
How long is it ago *s.* this | *M'k 9:21*
came
have been *s.* the world began | *Lu 1:70*
but this woman *s.* the time I | *Lu 7:45*
came
s. that time the kingdom of | *Lu 16:16*
God is
third day *s.* these things were | *Lu 24:21*
done
S. the world began was it not | *Joh 9:32*
holy prophets *s.* the world | *Ac 3:21*
began
the Holy Ghost *s.* ye believed | *Ac 19:2*
but twelve days *s.* I went up | *Ac 24:11*
to
was kept secret *s.* the world | *Ro 16:25*
began
For *s.* by man came death, | *1Co 15:21*
by man
S. ye seek a proof of Christ | *2Co 13:3*
S. we heard of your faith in | *Col 1:4*
Christ
also in you, *s.* the day ye | *Col 1:6*
heard of it
s. the day we heard it, do not | *Col 1:9*
cease
of the oath, which was *s.* the | *Heb 7:28*
law
s. the foundation of the | *Heb 9:26*
world
s. the fathers fell asleep, all | *2Pe 3:4*
such as was not *s.* men were | *Re 16:18*

SINCERE

you are *s.* (A)(B) | *M't 22:16; M'k 12:4*
let love be *s.* a real thing | *Ro 12:9*
(A)(B)
ye may be *s.* and without | *Ph'p 1:10*
offence
be untainted, pure, unerring, | *Ph'p 1:10*
blameless (A)
be unsullied and blameless | *Ph'p 1:10*
(B)
be flawless and without | *Ph'p 1:10*
blame (N)
be pure and blameless (R) | *Ph'p 1:10*
straightforward and *s.* (N) | *Jas 3:17*
desire the *s.* milk of the word, | *1Pe 2:2*
that
the pure spiritual milk | *1Pe 2:2*
(A)(E)(R)
unadulterated, | *1Pe 2:2*
thought-nourishing milk (B)
unadulterated pure spiritual | *1Pe 2:2*
milk (P)

SINCERELY

if ye have done truly and s. in   J'g 9:16
If ye then have dealt truly and   J'g 9:19
s.
teach way of God s. (B)   Lu 20:21
preach Christ of contention,   Ph'p 1:16
not s.

SINCERITY

and serve him in s. and in   Jos 24:14
truth
love in all s. (N)   Ro 12:9
with the unleavened bread of   1Co 5:8
s.
with unfermented batches of   1Co 5:8
purity and truth (B)
with unleavened bread of   1Co 5:8
unadulterated truth (P)
that in simplicity and godly s.   2Co 1:12
but as of s. but as of God, in   2Co 2:17
but from the purest motives   2Co 2:17
(B)
and to prove the s. of your   2Co 8:8
love
test the genuineness of your   2Co 8:8
love (B)(R)
putting your love to the test   2Co 8:8
(N)
prove the reality of your love   2Co 8:8
(P)
love our Lord Jesus Christ in   Eph 6:24
s.
love with undying and   Eph 6:24
incorruptible love (A)
never diminishing love (B)   Eph 6:24
love with a love incorruptible   Eph 6:24
(E)
love with unfailing love (P)   Eph 6:24
love with love undying (R)   Eph 6:24
shewing uncorruptness, gravity   Tit 2:7
regard for truth and purity of   Tit 2:7
motive (A)
teaching what is unadulterated   Tit 2:7
and dignified (B)
show integrity and high   Tit 2:7
principle (N)

SINEW

eat not of the s. which shrank   Ge 32:32
the hip-muscle (B)   Ge 32:32
Jacob's thigh in the s. that   Ge 32:32
shrank
and thy neck is an iron s. and   Isa 48:4
thy

SINEWS

hast fenced me with bones   Job 10:11
and s.
season: and my s. take no rest   Job 30:17
s. of his belly (A)   Job 40:16
the s. of his stones are   Job 40:17
wrapped
health to nerves and s. (A)   Pr 3:8
And I will lay s. upon you   Eze 37:6
s. and the flesh came up upon   Eze 37:8
held together with ligaments   Col 2:19
and s. (B)

SINFUL

an increase of s. men, to   Nu 32:14
augment
shamefully s. (A)   Pr 11:1; 11:20; 12:22
Ah s. nation, a people laden   Isa 1:4
their s. apostasies (B)   Eze 37:23
Lord God are upon the s.   Am 9:8
kingdom
this adulterous and s.   M'k 8:38
generation
from me; for I am a s. man, O   Lu 5:8
Lord
delivered into the hands of s.   Lu 24:7
men
the sinful (P)   Ro 4:5
s. impulses (S)   Ro 7:5
sin might become exceeding   Ro 7:13
s.
own Son in the likeness of s.   Ro 8:3
flesh
the impious and s.   1Pe 4:18;
(B)(E)(N)   Jude 4

SINFULNESS

all deception of s. (N)   2Th 2:10
make s. their choice (N)   2Th 2:12

SING

s. to the Lord   Ex 15:21;
1Ch 16:23; Ps 30:4; 95:1; 96:1, 2; 98:1;
      147:7; 149:1; Isa 12:5
but the noise of them that s.   Ex 32:18
do I hear
spring up, O well, s. ye unto   Nu 21:17
did they not s. one to   1Sa 21:11
another
s. unto him, s. psalms unto   1Ch 16:9
him
then shall the trees of the   1Ch 16:33
wood s. out
to s. in the house of the Lord   1Ch 25:6
(S)
when they began to s. and   2Ch 20:22
praise
Hezekiah commanded the   2Ch 29:30
Levites to s.
I cause the widow's heart to   Job 29:13
s. for joy
so will we s. and praise thy   Ps 21:13
power
praise the Lord, s. to him with   Ps 33:2
the psaltery
s. unto him a new song   Ps 33:3;
      Isa 42:10
my tongue s. of thy   Ps 51:14;
righteousness   145:7
the valleys shout for joy, they   Ps 65:13
also s.
s. forth the honour of his   Ps 66:2
name, make praise
the earth s. to thee, they shall   Ps 66:4
s. to thy name
let the nations be glad and s.   Ps 67:4
for joy
s. to God, ye kingdoms of the   Ps 68:32
earth
to thee will I s. with the   Ps 71:22;
harp   98:5
s. aloud unto God our   Ps 81:1
strength, make noise
the fowls which s. among the   Ps 104:12
branches
s. to him, s. psalms unto him,   Ps 105:2
talk ye
saying, S. us one of the songs   Ps 137:3
of Zion
how shall we s. Lord's song   Ps 137:4
in a strange land
yea, they shall s. in the ways of   Ps 138:5
the Lord
let the saints s. aloud upon   Ps 149:5
their beds
but the righteous doth s. and   Pr 29:6
rejoice
after seventy years shall Tyre   Isa 23:15
s. as harlot
they shall s. for the majesty of   Isa 24:14
the Lord
awake and s. ye that dwell in   Isa 26:19
dust
in that day s. ye to her,   Isa 27:2
vineyard of red wine
then shall the tongue of the   Isa 35:6
dumb s.
therefore we will s. my songs   Isa 38:20
all days
let the inhabitants of the   Isa 42:11
rock s.
s. O ye heavens, for Lord   Isa 44:23;
hath done it   49:13
with the voice together shall   Isa 52:8
they s.
s. to the Lord, ye waste places   Isa 52:9
of Jerusalem
s. O barren, thou that didst   Isa 54:1
not bear
behold, my servants shall s.   Isa 65:14
for joy of heart
s. with gladness for Jacob, and   Jer 31:7
shout
they shall come and s. in the   Jer 31:12
height of Zion
all that is therein shall s. for   Jer 51:48
Babylon
the ships of Tarshish did s. of   Eze 27:25
thee
she shall s. as in the days of   Ho 2:15
youth
s. idle songs to the sound   Am 6:5
(A)(E)(R)
their voice shall s. in the   Zep 2:14
windows
s. O daughter of Zion   Zep 3:14;
      Zec 2:10
s. thankfully in hearts (N)(R)   Col 3:16

is any merry? let him s.   Jas 5:13
psalms
they s. song of Moses and of   Re 15:3
the Lamb

I WILL SING

I will s. to the Lord   Ex 15:1;
      J'g 5:3; Ps 13:6
my heart is fixed, O God, I   Ps 57:7
will s.
I will s. unto thee among the   Ps 57:9
nations
I will s. of thy power, of thy   Ps 59:16;
mercy   89:1
unto thee, O my strength, will   Ps 59:17
I s. for God is
I will s. of mercy and   Ps 101:1
judgment, O Lord
I will s. to the Lord as   Ps 104:33
long as I live
I will s. a new song unto   Ps 144:9
thee, O God
now will I s. to my   Isa 5:1
well-beloved a song
for this cause will I s. to thy   Ro 15:9
name
I will s. with spirit, and I   1Co 14:15
will s. with understanding

SINGED

nor was an hair of their head s.   Da 3:27

SINGER

Heman a s. the son of Joel   1Ch 6:33
To the chief s. on my   Hab 3:19
stringed

SINGERS

harps also and psalteries for   1Ki 10:12
s.
these are the s. chief of the   1Ch 9:33
fathers
the s. with instruments of   1Ch 15:16
music
So the s. Heman, Asaph   1Ch 15:19
that bare the ark and the s.   1Ch 15:27
the master of the song with   1Ch 15:27
the s.
the Levites which were the s.   2Ch 5:12
the trumpeters and s. were as   2Ch 5:13
one
and harps and psalteries for   2Ch 9:11
s.
he appointed s. unto the   2Ch 20:21
Lord, and
the s. with instruments of   2Ch 23:13
musick
and the s. sang, and the   2Ch 29:28
trumpets
And the s. the sons of Asaph   2Ch 35:15
The s.: the children of Asaph   Ezr 2:41
people, and the s. and the   Ezr 2:70
porters
priests, and the Levites, and   Ezr 7:7
the s.
Levites, s. porters, Nethinims   Ezr 7:24
Of the s. also; Eliashib: and   Ezr 10:24
and the s. and the Levites were   Ne 7:1
The s.: the children of Asaph   Ne 7:44
Levites, and the porters, and   Ne 7:73
the s.
the Levites, the porters, the   Ne 10:28
s.
minister, the porters, and   Ne 10:39
the s.
the s. were over the business   Ne 11:22
of the
certain portion should be for   Ne 11:23
the s.
And the sons of the s.   Ne 12:28
gathered
s. had builded them villages   Ne 12:29
round
the s. sang loud, with   Ne 12:42
Jezrahiah
both the s. and the porters   Ne 12:45
kept
of old they were chief of the   Ne 12:46
s.
gave the portions of the s.   Ne 12:47
and the
be given to the Levites, and   Ne 13:5
the s.
the Levites, and the s. that   Ne 13:10
did the
The s. went before, the   Ps 68:25
players on

As well the *s.* as the players on   Ps 87:7
I gat me men *s.* and women *s.*   Ec 2:8
the chambers of the *s.* in the   Eze 40:44
inner

SINGETH

so is he that *s.* songs to an   Pr 25:20
heavy

SINGING

cities of Israel, *s.* and   1Sa 18:6
dancing
the voice of *s.* men and *s.*   2Sa 19:35
women
of the congregation with *s.*   1Ch 6:32
until
with *s.* and with harps, and   1Ch 13:8
Moses, with rejoicing and   2Ch 23:18
with *s.*
s. with loud instruments   2Ch 30:21
unto the
all the *s.* men and the *s.*   2Ch 35:25
women
two hundred *s.* men and *s.*   Ezr 2:65
women
and five *s.* men and *s.* women   Ne 7:67
with thanksgivings, and with   Ne 12:27
s.
come before his presence   Ps 100:2
with *s.*
laughter, and our tongue with   Ps 126:2
s.
time of the *s.* of birds is come   Ca 2:12
is quiet: they break forth into   Isa 14:7
s.
the vineyards there shall be   Isa 16:10
no *s.*
and rejoice even with joy and   Isa 35:2
s.
break forth into *s.* ye   Isa 44:23
mountains
with a voice of *s.* declare ye,   Isa 48:20
tell
break forth into *s.*, O   Isa 49:13
mountains
return, and come with *s.*   Isa 51:11
unto Zion
break forth into *s.* and cry   Isa 54:1
also
shall break forth before you   Isa 55:12
into *s.*
love, he will joy over thee   Zep 3:17
with *s.*
s. and making melody in   Eph 5:19
your
s. with grace in your hearts   Col 3:16
to the

SINGLE

s. him out for ruin (A)(R)   De 29:21
if therefore thine eye be *s.*   M't 6:22
thy
if your eye is sound   M't 6:22;
(A)(B)(N)(P)(R)   Lu 11:34
therefore when thine eye is   Lu 11:34
s. thy
the *s.* (B)   1Co 7:8; 7:11, 32
the *s.* (A)   1Co 7:11
s.-mindedly (N)   Eph 6:5

SINGLENESS

with gladness and *s.* of heart   Ac 2:46
with united purpose (A)(B)   Ac 2:46
shared meals with unaffected   Ac 2:46
joy (N)
sharing meals with simple joy   Ac 2:46
(P)
partook with glad and   Ac 2:46
generous hearts (R)
in *s.* of your heart, as unto   Eph 6:5
Christ
with reverence, awe, unmixed   Eph 6:5
motives (B)
single-mindedly (N)   Eph 6:5
sincerely with a proper sense   Eph 6:5
of respect and responsibility (P)
but in *s.* of heart, fearing   Col 3:22
God
in simplicity of purpose (A)   Col 3:22
with unmixed motives (B)   Col 3:22
with single-mindedness (N)   Col 3:22
as a sincere expression (P)   Col 3:22

SINGULAR

when a man shall make a *s.*   Le 27:2
vow

a special vow (A)(R)   Le 27:2
sets apart a vowed offering (B)   Le 27:2
accomplish a vow (E)   Le 27:2

SINIM

and these from the land of *S.*   Isa 49:12
from the land of Syene   Isa 49:12
(B)(R)

SINITE

Hivite, and the Arkite, and   Ge 10:17;
the *S.*   1Ch 1:15

SINK

I *s.* in deep mire, where there   Ps 69:2
is
out of the mire, and let me   Ps 69:14
not *s.*
Thus shall Babylon *s.* and   Jer 51:64
shall
beginning to *s.* he cried,   M't 14:30
saying
the ships, so that they began to   Lu 5:7
s.
sayings *s.* down into your ears   Lu 9:44

SINKING

s. in his forehead (A)   1Sa 17:49
we are *s.* (N)   M't 8:25

SINKS

her house *s.* down to death   Pr 2:18
(A)(B)(R)
ceiling, roof *s.* (B)(E)(R)   Ec 10:18

SINNED

wherein have I *s.* (E)(R)   Ge 20:9
Pharaoh *s.* yet more, hardened   Ex 9:34
his heart
Moses said, Ye have *s.* a   Ex 32:30;
great sin   32:31
whosoever hath *s.*, him will   Ex 32:33
I blot out
bring for the sin he hath *s.* a   Le 4:3
bullock
when the sin the congregation   Le 4:14
have *s.*
when ruler *s.*   Le 4:22
if sin, wherein *s.*, come to   Le 4:23
his knowledge
one of common people *s.*   Le 4:28
he shall confess he hath *s.* in   Le 5:5
that thing
for sin which he hath *s.* shall   Le 5:6
bring a female
priest shall make atonement   Le 5:10;
for the sin he hath *s.*   11:13; Nu 6:11
and shall be
because, he hath *s.* shall restore   Le 6:4
what he took
lay not sin on us wherein we   Nu 12:11
have *s.*
behold, ye have *s.* against the   Nu 32:23
Lord
I looked, and behold ye had *s.*   De 9:16
against Lord
your sins which ye *s.* in   De 9:18
doing wickedly
Israel hath *s.* and   Jos 7:11
transgressed my covenant
wherefore I have not *s.*   J'g 11:27
against thee
know that I have not *s.*   1Sa 24:11
against thee
they have *s.* against thee,   1Ki 8:33;
and shall turn again   8:35; 2Ch 6:24, 26
forgive thy people that *s.*   1Ki 8:50;
  2Ch 6:39
s. against you (A)   1Ki 8:50
sins of Jeroboam which he   1Ki 15:30;
s.   16:13, 19
what have I *s.* that thou   1Ki 18:9
wouldst deliver
Israel had *s.* against Lord   2Ki 17:7
their God
the sin that Manasseh had *s.*   2Ki 21:17
is written
you have *s.* (B)   Ezr 10:10
but *s.* against thy judgments   Ne 9:29
Job said, It may be that my   Job 1:5
sons have *s.*
in all this Job *s.* not, nor   Job 1:22
charged God foolishly

if children have *s.* against him   Job 8:4
and have cast
so doth the grave those who   Job 24:19
have *s.*
they *s.* yet more against him   Ps 78:17;
  78:32
thy first father hath *s.* and   Isa 43:27
thy teachers
because thou sayest, I have not   Jer 2:35
s.
their iniquity, whereby they   Jer 33:8
have *s.* against me
what have I *s.* (A)(E)   Jer 37:18
because ye have *s.* and not   Jer 40:3;
obeyed   44:23
because they have *s.* against   Jer 50:7;
the Lord   Zep 1:17
for Babylon hath *s.* against   Jer 50:14
the Lord
Jerusalem hath grievously *s.* is   La 1:8
removed
our father have *s.* and are not,   La 5:7
we have borne
fathers have *s.* against me (B)   Eze 2:3
in sin he hath *s.* in them   Eze 18:24
shall he
have filled with violence,   Eze 28:16
and thou hast *s.*
of their dwelling places   Eze 37:23
wherein they *s.*
as they increased so they *s.*   Ho 4:7
against me
O Israel thou hast *s.* from   Ho 10:9
days of Gibeah
and thou hast *s.* against thy   Hab 2:10
soul
neither this man *s.* nor his   Joh 9:3
parents
neither have I *s.* (E)   Ac 25:8
as many as have *s.* without   Ro 2:12
law; as have *s.* in law, shall
be judged by
for all have *s.* and come   Ro 3:23;
short   5:12
death reigned even over them   Ro 5:14
that had not *s.*
not as it was by one that *s.* so   Ro 5:16
is the gift
thou marry, thou hast not   1Co 7:28
s. and if a virgin marry she
hath not *s.*
I shall bewail many that   2Co 12:21
have *s.*
I write to them which   2Co 13:2
heretofore have *s.*
was it not with them that   Heb 3:17
had *s.*
for if God spared not the   2Pe 2:4
angels that *s.*
if we say we have not *s.* we   1Jo 1:10
deceive ourselves

I HAVE SINNED

Pharaoh said, *I have s.* this   Ex 9:27;
time   10:16
Balaam said to angel of   Nu 22:34
Lord, *I have s.*
indeed *I have s.* against Lord   Jos 7:20
God of Israel
Saul said, *I have s.*   1Sa 15:24;
  15:30; 26:21
David said, *I have s.* against   2Sa 12:13;
the Lord   24:10, 17; 1Ch 21:8. 17
thy servant doth know that *I*   2Sa 19:20
have s.
I have s.   Job 7:20
if any say *I have s.*   Job 33:17
heal my soul, for *I have s.*   Ps 41:4
against thee
against thee, thee only have I   Ps 51:4
s. done this evil
I have s. against him, till he   Mic 7:9
plead my cause
Judas said, *I have s.* in   M't 27:4
betraying innocent
the prodigal said, Father, *I*   Lu 15:18;
have s.   15:21

WE HAVE SINNED

lay not sin on us, wherein   Nu 12:11
we have s.
we will go up, for *we have*   Nu 14:40;
s.   De 1:41
we have s. we have spoken   Nu 21:7
against the Lord
we have s. because we have   J'g 10:10;
forsaken God and   1Sa 12:10

we have s.: do to us what   J'g 10:15
seemeth good to thee
they fasted that day, and said,   1Sa 7:6
We have s.
we have s. and have done   1Ki 8:47
perversely
we have s. (B)   1Ki 8:47
saying, *We have s.* we have   2Ch 6:37
done amiss
and confess the sins which *we*   Ne 1:6
have s.
we have s. with our fathers,   Ps 106:6
we have
the Lord, he against whom   Isa 42:24
we have s.
behold thou art wroth, for *we*   Isa 64:5
have s.
we lie down in our shame, for   Jer 3:25
we have s.
hath given us water of gall,   Jer 8:14
for *we have s.*
for our backslidings are many,   Jer 14:7
we have s.
acknowledge our wickedness,   Jer 14:20
for *we have s.*
crown is fallen, woe to us that   La 5:16
we have s.
we have s. and have committed   Da 9:5
iniquity
to us belongeth confusion,   Da 9:8
because *we have s.*
O Lord, *we have s.* we have   Da 9:15
done wickedly

SINNER

much more the wicked and   Pr 11:31
the *s.*
wickedness overthroweth the *s.*   Pr 13:6
the wealth of the *s.* is laid up   Pr 13:22
but to the *s.* he giveth travail   Ec 2:26
but the *s.* shall be taken by   Ec 7:26
her
Though a *s.* do evil an   Ec 8:12
hundred
as is the good, so is the *s.*;   Ec 9:2
and he
but one *s.* destroyeth much   Ec 9:18
good
the *s.* being an hundred years   Isa 65:20
old
woman in the city, which was   Lu 7:37
a *s.*
that toucheth him: for she is a   Lu 7:39
s.
heaven over one *s.* that   Lu 15:7
repenteth
of God over one *s.* that   Lu 15:10
repenteth
saying, God be merciful to   Lu 18:13
me a *s.*
to be guest with a man that   Lu 19:7
is a *s.*
man that is a *s.* do such   Joh 9:16
miracles
we know that this man is a *s.*   Joh 9:24
Whether he be a *s.* or no, I   Joh 9:25
know not
why yet am I also judged as a   Ro 3:7
s.
converteth the *s.* from the   Jas 5:20
error of
shall the ungodly and the *s.*   1Pe 4:18
appear

SINNERS

men of Sodom were wicked   Ge 13:13
and *s.*
The censers of these *s.*   Nu 16:38
against
destroy the *s.* the Amalekites   1Sa 15:18
nor standeth in the way of *s.*   Ps 1:1
nor *s.* in the congregation of   Ps 1:5
therefore will he teach *s.* in   Ps 25:8
the way
Gather not my soul with *s.* nor   Ps 26:9
s. shall be converted unto thee   Ps 51:13
when *s.* spring as grass (B)   Ps 92:7;
   94:3; 104:35
s. be consumed out of the   Ps 104:35
earth
if *s.* entice thee, consent thou   Pr 1:10
not
Evil pursueth *s.* but to the   Pr 13:21
Let not thine heart envy *s.*   Pr 23:17
but be
of the transgressors and of the   Isa 1:28
s.
and he shall destroy the *s.*   Isa 13:9
thereof

The *s.* in Zion are afraid;   Isa 33:14
fearfulness
All the *s.* of my people shall   Am 9:10
die by
many publicans and *s.* came   M't 9:10
your Master with publicans   M't 9:11
and *s.*
the righteous, but *s.* to   M't 9:13
repentance
a friend of publicans and *s.*   M't 11:19
is betrayed into the hands of   M't 26:45
s.
publicans and *s.* sat also   M'k 2:15
together
saw him eat with publicans   M'k 2:16
and *s.*
and drinketh with publicans   M'k 2:16
and *s.*
the righteous, but *s.* to   M'k 2:17
repentance
is betrayed into the hands   M'k 14:41
of *s.*
eat and drink with publicans   Lu 5:30
and *s.*
the righteous, but *s.* to   Lu 5:32
repentance
for *s.* also love those that   Lu 6:32
love them
ye? for *s.* also do even the   Lu 6:33
same
s. also lend to *s.* to receive   Lu 6:34
as much
a friend of publicans and *s.*   Lu 7:34
were *s.* above all the   Lu 13:2
Galilaeans
were *s.* above all men that   Lu 13:4
dwelt in
publicans and *s.* for to hear   Lu 15:1
him
This man receiveth *s.* and   Lu 15:2
eateth
we know that God heareth   Joh 9:31
not *s.*
while we were yet *s.* Christ   Ro 5:8
died for
disobedience many were made   Ro 5:19
s.
by nature, and not *s.* of the   Ga 2:15
Gentiles
we ourselves also are found *s.*   Ga 2:17
for the ungodly and for *s.* for   1Ti 1:9
unholy
Jesus came into the world to   1Ti 1:15
save *s.*
undefiled, separate from *s.*   Heb 7:26
contradiction of *s.* against   Heb 12:3
himself
Cleanse your hands, ye *s.*; and   Jas 4:8
ungodly *s.* have spoken   Jude 15
against him

SINNEST

If thou *s.* what doest thou   Job 35:6
against

SINNETH

for the soul that *s.* ignorantly   Nu 15:28
s. by ignorance before the   Nu 15:28
Lord
for him that *s.* through   Nu 15:29
ignorance
for any sin, in any sin that   De 19:15
he *s.*
for there is no man that *s.*   1Ki 8:46
not
for there is no man which *s.*   2Ch 6:36
not
s. against me wrongeth his   Pr 8:36
own
He that despiseth his   Pr 14:21
neighbour *s.*
and he that hasteth with his   Pr 19:2
feet *s.*
whoso provoketh him to anger   Pr 20:2
earth, that doeth good, and *s.*   Ec 7:20
not
when the land *s.* against me   Eze 14:13
by
mine: the soul that *s.* it shall   Eze 18:4
die
The soul that *s.* it shall die   Eze 18:20
righteousness in the day that   Eze 33:12
he *s.*
fornication *s.* against his own   1Co 6:18
body
let him do what he will, he *s.*   1Co 7:36
not

he that is such is subverted,   Tit 3:11
and *s.*
Whosoever abideth in him   1Jo 3:6
s. not
whosoever *s.* hath not seen him   1Jo 3:6
for the devil *s.* from the   1Jo 3:8
beginning
whosoever is born of God *s.*   1Jo 5:18
not

SINNING

for I also withheld thee from   Ge 20:6
s.
these that a man doeth, *s.*   Le 6:3
therein

SINS

s. of the fathers (B)   Ex 20:5
if a person *s.* (B)   Le 6:2
s. against neighbor (A)(E)(R)   1Ki 8:31
shall give Israel up, because   1Ki 14:16
of *s.* of
Abijam walked in the *s.* of   1Ki 15:3
Rehoboam
smote Nadab because of the   1Ki 15:30
s. of Jeroboam
for all the *s.* of Baasha, and   1Ki 16:13
the *s.* of Elah
for his *s.* which Zimri   1Ki 16:19
sinned in doing evil
a light thing to walk in the   1Ki 16:31
s. of Jeroboam
Jehoram cleaved to *s.* of   2Ki 3:3
Jeroboam
from *s.* of Jeroboam Jehu   2Ki 10:29
departed not
Israel departed not from *s.* of   2Ki 13:6
Jeroboam
Joash, Jeroboam departed   2Ki 13:11;
not from *s.*   14:24
Zachariah, Menahem   2Ki 15:9;
departed not from *s.*   15:18
Pekahiah, Pekah departed   2Ki 15:24;
not from *s.*   15:28
Israel walked in all the *s.* of   2Ki 17:22
Jeroboam
to remove Judah for the *s.* of   2Ki 24:3
Manasseh
are there not even with you   2Ch 28:10
s.
and confess the *s.* of the   Ne 1:6
children of Israel
how many are mine   Job 13:23
iniquities and *s.*
cleanse from secret *s.* (B)   Ps 19:12
keep servant from   Ps 19:13
presumptuous *s.*
remember not the *s.* of my   Ps 25:7
youth
shall be holden with the cords   Pr 5:22
of his *s.*
hatred stirreth up strifes, love   Pr 10:12
covereth all *s.*
he that covereth his *s.* shall   Pr 28:13
not prosper
she hath received double for   Isa 40:2
all her *s.*
but thou hast made me to   Isa 43:24
serve with thy *s.*
I blot out and will not   Isa 43:25
remember thy *s.*
I have blotted out as a cloud   Isa 44:22
thy *s.*
substance will I give to spoil   Jer 15:13
for all thy *s.*
because thy *s.* were   Jer 30:14;
increased   30:15
s. of Judah sought for, and   Jer 50:20
not be found
a man for the punishment of   La 3:39
his *s.*
for the *s.* of her prophets and   La 4:13
her priests
O daughter of Edom, he will   La 4:22
discover thy *s.*
nor hath Samaria committed   Eze 16:51
half thy *s.*
bear thou thine own shame   Eze 16:52
for thy *s.*
if he beget son that seeth all   Eze 18:14
his father's *s.*
if the wicked will turn from   Eze 18:21
all his *s.*
and he shall bear the *s.* of   Eze 23:49
your idols
none of his *s.* shall be   Eze 33:16
mentioned to him
break off thy *s.* by   Da 4:27
righteousness

seventy weeks are determined | Da 9:24
to make an end of s.
for the s. of the house of | Mic 1:5
Israel
in making thee desolate | Mic 6:3
because of thy s.
shed for many for the | M't 26:28
remission of s.
John did preach baptism of | M'k 1:4;
repentance for remission of s. | Lu 3:3
forgive s. (P) | M'k 11:26; Col 2:13
if your brother s. | Lu 17:3;
(A)(B)(E)(R) | 17:4
that remission of s. should be | Lu 24:37
preached
thou wast altogether born in | Joh 9:34
s.
whosoever s. ye remit, | Joh 20:23
whose s. ye retain
repent and be baptized for | Ac 2:38
remission of s.
to give repentance and | Ac 5:31
remission of s.
whoso believeth, shall receive | Ac 10:43
remission of s.
wash away thy s., calling on | Ac 22:16
name of
for the remission of s. that | Ro 3:25
are past
delivered for our s. (P) | Ro 4:25
the motions of s. did work in | Ro 7:5
our members
not counting their s. (A)(P) | 2Co 5:19
hath quickened, who were | Eph 2:1;
dead in s. | 2:5
dead in s. and wickedness | Eph 2:1
(N)
in putting off the body of s. | Col 2:11
of the flesh
forgiven all s. (N) | Col 2:13
nor be partakers of other | 1Ti 5:22
men's s.
some men's s. open | 1Ti 5:24
beforehand, going
who lead captive silly women | 2Ti 3:6
laden with s.
to make reconciliation for s. | Heb 2:17
of people
that he may offer gifts and | Heb 5:1
sacrifices for s.
for people, so also for | Heb 5:3
himself, to offer for s.
first for his own s., then for | Heb 7:27
the people's
Christ was once offered to | Heb 9:28
bear s.
should have had no more | Heb 10:2
conscience of s.
there is a remembrance | Heb 10:3
again made of s.
not possible that blood of | Heb 10:4
bulls take away s.
the same sacrifices can | Heb 10:11
never take away s.
after he had offered one | Heb 10:12
sacrifice for s.
there remaineth no | Heb 10:26
more sacrifice for s.
confess your s. | Jas 5:12
(B)(E)(N)(P)(R)
save soul, and hide multitude | Jas 5:20
of s.
being dead to s. should live | 1Pe 2:24
to righteousness
for Christ also hath once | 1Pe 3:18
suffered for s.
for charity shall cover the | 1Pe 4:8
multitude of s.
forgotten he was purged from | 2Pe 1:9
old s.
but also for s. of the whole | 1Jo 2:2
world
that ye be not partakers of | Re 18:4
her s.
for her s. have reached unto | Re 18:5
heaven

MY SINS

hide thy face from my s. and | Ps 51:9
out
O God my s. are not hid from | Ps 69:5
thee
thou hast cast my s. behind | Isa 38:17
thy back

OUR SINS

we have added to all our s. | 1Sa 12:19
this evil

ye intend to add more to | 2Ch 28:13
our s.
the kings set over us because | Ne 9:37
of our s.
purge away our s. for thy | Ps 79:9
name's
our secret s. in light of thy | Ps 90:8
countenance
hath not dealt with us | Ps 103:10
according to our s.
for our s. testify against us | Isa 59:12
if our s. be upon us, we pine | Eze 33:10
away
because of our s. thy people | Da 9:16
Christ died for our s. | 1Co 15:3
according to
gave himself for our s. to | Ga 1:4
deliver us
had himself purged our s. sat | Heb 1:3
down
his own self bare our s. in his | 1Pe 2:24
body
if we confess our s. he is | 1Jo 1:9
faithful and just to forgive us
our s. and to
he is the propitiation for our | 1Jo 2:2;
s. | 4:10
he was manifested to take | 1Jo 3:5
away our s.
washed us from our s. in his | Re 1:5
blood

THEIR SINS

because of transgressions in | Le 16:16
their s.
shall confess over the live | Le 16:21
goat all their s.
to make atonement for their | Le 16:34
s. once a year
lest ye be consumed in all | Nu 16:26
their s.
they provoked him with | 1Ki 14:22
their s.
to provoke me to anger with | 1Ki 16:2
their s.
Israel stood and confessed their | Ne 9:2
s.
shew the house of Jacob their | Isa 58:1
s.
and visit their s. | Jer 14:10;
| Ho 8:13; 9:9
cast all their s. into the depth | Mic 7:19
of the sea
he shall save his people from | M't 1:21
their s.
were baptized, confessing their | M't 3:6;
s. | M'k 1:5
and their s. should be | M'k 4:12
forgiven them
of salvation by the remission | Lu 1:77
of their s.
when I shall take away their | Ro 11:27
s.
to fill up their s. alway | 1Th 2:16
for I will be merciful to their | Heb 8:12
s.
their s. I will remember no | Heb 10:17
more

YOUR SINS

that ye may be clean from all | Le 16:30
your s.
punish yet seven times for | Le 26:18;
your s. | 26:24, 28
bring plagues on you | Le 26:21
according to your s.
nor drink water, because of | De 9:18
your s.
an holy God, will not forgive | Jos 24:19
your s.
tho' your s. be as scarlet, be | Isa 1:18
as snow
and your s. have hid his face | Isa 59:2
from you
your s. have withholden good | Jer 5:25
things
in all your doings your s. | Eze 21:24
for I know your transgressions | Am 5:12
and mighty s.
ye shall seek me, and die | Joh 8:21;
in your s. | 8:24
repent, that your s. may be | Ac 3:19
blotted out
if Christ be not raised, ye | 1Co 15:17
are in your s.
you being dead in your s. | Col 2:13
hath he quickened

because your s. are forgiven | 1Jo 2:12
you

SION

unto mount S. which is | De 4:48
Hermon
waiteth for thee, O God, in S. | Ps 65:1
Tell ye the daughter of S., | M't 21:5
Behold
Fear not, daughter of S.; | Joh 12:15
behold
I lay in S. a stumblingstone | Ro 9:33
shall come out of S. the | Ro 11:26
Deliverer
But ye are come unto | Heb 12:22
mount S.
I lay in S. a chief corner stone | 1Pe 2:6
lo, a Lamb stood on the | Re 14:1
mount S.

SIPHMOTH

and to them which were in S. | 1Sa 30:28

SIPPAI

Sibbechai the Hushathite | 1Ch 20:4
slew S.

SIR

O s. we came indeed down at | Ge 43:20
S. didst not thou sow good | M't 13:27
seed in
and said, I go s.; and went | M't 21:30
not
S. we remember that that | M't 27:63
deceiver
S. thou hast nothing to draw | Joh 4:11
with
S. give me this water, that I | Joh 4:15
thirst
S. I perceive thou art a | Joh 4:19
prophet
S. come down ere my child | Joh 4:49
die
S. I have no man, when the | Joh 5:7
water
saying S. we would see Jesus | Joh 12:21
S. if thou have borne him | Joh 20:15
hence
I said unto him, S. thou | Re 7:14
knowest

SIRAH

him again from the well of S. | 2Sa 3:26

SIRION

Heron the Sidonians call S. | De 3:9
Lebanon and S. like a | Ps 29:6
unicorn

SIRS

S. ye are brethren; why do ye | Ac 7:26
saying S. why do ye these | Ac 14:15
things
S. what must I do to be | Ac 16:30
saved
S. ye know that by this craft | Ac 19:25
S. I perceive that this voyage | Ac 27:10
will
S. ye should have hearkened | Ac 27:21
unto

SISAMAI

Eleasah begat S. and S. begat | 1Ch 2:40

SISERA

the captain of whose host was | J'g 4:2
S.
S. the captain of Jabin's army | J'g 4:7
the Lord shall sell S. into the | J'g 4:9
hand
And they shewed S. that | J'g 4:12
Barak the
And S. gathered together all | J'g 4:13
his
Lord hath delivered S. into | J'g 4:14
thine
And the Lord discomfited S. | J'g 4:15
that S. lighted down off his | J'g 4:15
chariot
host of S. fell upon the edge | J'g 4:16
of the
S. fled away on his feet to the | J'g 4:17
tent

SISERA (continued)

And Jael went out to meet S. — J'g 4:18
as Barak pursued S. Jael came — J'g 4:22
out
S. lay dead, and the nail was — J'g 4:22
in his
in their courses fought against — J'g 5:20
S.
and with the hammer she — J'g 5:26
smote S.
The mother of S. looked out — J'g 5:28
at a
to S. a prey of divers colours — J'g 5:30
he sold them into the hand of — 1Sa 12:9
S.
the children of S. the children — Ezr 2:53;
Ne 7:55
as to S. as to Jabin, at the — Ps 83:9
brook

SISTER

they sent away Rebekah their — Ge 24:59
s.
art our s. be mother of — Ge 24:60
thousands
Rachel envied her s. and said — Ge 30:1
to Jacob
he had defiled Dinah their s. — Ge 34:13;
34:27
cannot give s. to one — Ge 34:14
uncircumcised
should he deal with our s. as — Ge 34:31
an harlot
his s. stood afar off to wit what — Ex 2:4
Amram took his father's s. to — Ex 6:20
wife
Miriam s. of Aaron took a — Ex 15:20
timbrel in hand
not uncover the nakedness of — Le 18:9
thy s.
she is thy s. — Le 18:11
not nakedness of father's s. — Le 18:12
nakedness of thy mother's s. — Le 18:13
not take a wife to her s. — Le 18:18
if a man take his s. and see — Le 20:17
nakedness
nor nakedness of thy father's — Le 20:19
s. mother's s.
for his s. a virgin, may he be — Le 21:3
defiled
a Nazarite shall not be defiled — Nu 6:7
for his s.
cursed be he that lieth with — De 27:22
his s.
is not her younger s. fairer — J'g 15:2
than she
Absalom had a fair s. named — 2Sa 13:1
Tamar
Amnon fell sick for his s. — 2Sa 13:2
Tamar
I love Tamar, my brother — 2Sa 13:4
Absalom's s.
because he had forced his s. — 2Sa 13:22;
Tamar — 13:32
Jehosheba s. of Ahaziah took — 2Ki 11:2;
Joash hid him — 2Ch 22:11
we have a little s. what shall we — Ca 8:8
do for our s. in the day
and her treacherous s. Judah — Jer 3:7
saw it
her s. feared not — Jer 3:8
her s. hath not turned — Jer 3:10
shalt not lament for him, — Jer 22:18
saying, Ah, my s.
thou art the s. of thy sisters — Eze 16:45
who loatheth
thy elder s. is Samaria, thy — Eze 16:46
younger s. Sodom
Sodom thy s. hath not done — Eze 16:48
as thou hast done
this was the iniquity of thy — Eze 16:49
s. Sodom, pride
for thy s. Sodom was not — Eze 16:56
mentioned in the day
another in thee hath — Eze 22:11
humbled his s.
Aholah the elder, and — Eze 23:4
Aholibah her s.
and when her s. Aholibah — Eze 23:11
saw this
like as my mind was — Eze 23:18
alienated from her s.
thou hast walked in the way — Eze 23:31
of thy s.
with the cup of thy s. — Eze 23:33
Samaria
for s. that hath no husband — Eze 44:25
they may defile
same is my brother, s. and — M't 12:50
mother

she had a s. called Mary — Lu 10:39;
Joh 11:1, 5
therefore his s. sent unto him, — Joh 11:3
saying, Lord
there stood by the cross his — Joh 19:25
mother's s.
I commend to you Phebe our — Ro 16:1
s. a servant
a brother or a s. is not under — 1Co 7:15
bondage
have we not power to lead — 1Co 9:5
about a s. a wife
if a brother of s. be naked — Jas 2:15
and destitute
the children of thy elect s. greet — 2Jo 13
thee

SISTER IN LAW

thy s. in law is gone back to — Ru 1:15
her people, return thou
after thy s. in law

MY SISTER

say, I pray thee, thou art my — Ge 12:13
s.
why saidst thou, She is my s. — Ge 12:19;
20:2, 5, 12; 26:7,9
I have wrestled with my s. — Ge 30:8
and prevailed
say to him, Let my s. Tamar — 2Sa 13:5;
come — 13:6
Amnon said to her, Come lie — 2Sa 13:11
with me, my s.
Absalom said, Hold now thy — 2Sa 13:20
peace, my s.
I have said to the worm, — Job 17:14
Thou art my s.
say to wisdom, Thou art my s. — Pr 7:4
and call
hast ravished my heart, my s. — Ca 4:9
my spouse
how fair is thy love, my s. — Ca 4:10
my spouse
a garden inclosed is my s. my — Ca 4:12
spouse, a spring
I am come into my garden my — Ca 5:1
s. my spouse
open to me, my s. my love, my — Ca 5:2
undefiled
same is my brother, my s. — M'k 3:35
and mother
dost thou not care that my s. — Lu 10:40
left me

SISTERS

and my brethren, and my s. — Jos 2:13
and all
Whose s. were Zeruiah, and — 1Ch 2:16
Abigail
called for their three s. to eat — Job 1:4
and to
him all his brethren, and all — Job 42:11
his s.
thou art the sister of thy s. — Eze 16:45
which
hast justified thy s. in all thine — Eze 16:51
Thou also, which hast — Eze 16:52
judged thy s.
in that thou hast justified — Eze 16:52
thy s.
thy s. Sodom and her — Eze 16:55
daughters
when thou shalt receive thy — Eze 16:61
s. thine
Ammi; and to your s. — Ho 2:1
Ruhamah
And his s. are they not all — M't 13:56
with us
forsaken houses or brethren, — M't 19:29
or s.
and are not his s. here with — M'k 6:3
us
hath left house, or brethren, — M'k 10:29
or s.
houses, and brethren, and s. — M'k 10:30
and
and children, and brethren, — Lu 14:26
and s.
Therefore his s. sent unto — Joh 11:3
him
the younger as s. with all — 1Ti 5:2
purity

SISTER'S

and bracelets upon his s. — Ge 24:30
hands

heard the tidings of Jacob — Ge 29:13
his s. son
he hath uncovered his s. — Le 20:17
nakedness
whose s. name was Maachah — 1Ch 7:15
shalt drink of thy s. cup deep — Eze 23:32
when Paul's s. son heard of — Ac 23:16
and Marcus, s. son to — Col 4:10
Barnabas

SIT

shall brethren go to war and — Nu 32:6
ye s. here
speak ye that s. in judgment — J'g 5:10
and walk
s. still, my daughter, till thou — Ru 3:18
know
ho, such a one, turn aside, s. — Ru 4:1;
down here — 4:2
and made them s. in the — 1Sa 9:22
chiefest place
we will not s. down till he — 1Sa 16:11
come hither
I should not fail to s. with the — 1Sa 20:5
king
behold, the king doth s. in — 2Sa 19:8
the gate
Solomon shall s. on my — 1Ki 1:13;
throne — 1:17
who hath given one to s. on — 1Ki 1:48;
my throne — 3:6
there shall not fail thee a — 1Ki 8:25
man to s. on the throne of — 2Ch 6:16;
Israel — Jer 33:17
why s. we here till we die — 2Ki 7:3; 7:4
thy sons shall s. on the — 2Ki 10:30;
throne — 15:12
sent me to men who s. on — 2Ki 18:27;
wall — Isa 36:12
and will not s. with the wicked — Ps 26:5
they that s. in the gate speak — Ps 69:12
against me
such as s. in darkness and — Ps 107:10
shadow of death
said to my Lord, S. thou at — Ps 110:1
my right hand
princes also did s. and speak — Ps 119:23
against me
it is vain for you to rise early — Ps 127:2
and s. up late
their children shall s. upon — Ps 132:12
thy throne
folly in dignity, and rich s. in — Ec 10:6
low place
being desolate, shall s. on the — Isa 3:26
ground
I will s. upon mount of the — Isa 14:13
congregation
he shall s. upon the throne in — Isa 16:5
truth
I have cried, their strength is — Isa 30:7
to s. still
bring them that s. in darkness — Isa 42:7
out of prison
s. in the dust, s. on the — Isa 47:1;
ground — 52:2
s. thou silent, get thee into — Isa 47:5
darkness, O daughter
thou that sayest, I shall not s. — Isa 47:8
as a widow
there shall not be a fire to s. — Isa 47:14
before it
why do we s. still? assemble — Jer 8:14
yourselves
I will fill them that s. on — Jer 13:13
David's throne
s. down now — Jer 13:18; 36:15
he shall have none to s. upon — Jer 36:30
the throne
and s. in thirst — Jer 48:18
how doth city s. solitary was — La 1:1
full of people
elders of Zion s. on ground — La 2:10
and keep silence
they shall s. upon the ground — Eze 26:16
because thou hast said, I s. in — Eze 28:2
seat of God
and they s. before thee as my — Eze 33:31
people
prince shall s. in it to eat — Eze 44:3
bread before Lord
I beheld till the ancient of days — Da 7:9
did s.
but the judgment shall s. they — Da 7:26
shall take away
there will I s. to judge the — Joe 3:12
heathen
they shall s. every man under — Mic 4:4
his vine

when I *s.* in darkness, Lord	*Mic 7:8*
shall be a light	
thou and thy fellows that *s.*	*Zec 3:8*
before me	
he shall *s.* and rule upon his	*Zec 6:13*
throne	
he shall *s.* as a refiner and	*Mal 3:3*
purifier of silver	
many shall *s.* down with	*M't 8:11*
Abraham	
when Son *s.* on throne of	*M't 19:28;*
glory, ye *s.* on twelve thrones	*25:31;*
	Lu 22:30
my two sons may *s.* one on	*M't 20:21*
thy right hand	
but to *s.* on my right hand	*M't 20:23*
	M'k 10:37, 40
s. thou on my right hand	*M't 22:44;*
till	*M'k 12:36; Lu 20:42; Hab 1:13*
the scribes and Pharisees *s.* in	*M't 23:2*
Moses' seat	
s. ye here while I pray	*M't 26:36;*
yonder	*M'k 14:32*
make them *s.* by fifties in a	*Lu 9:14*
company	
make them to *s.* down, and	*Lu 12:37*
will serve them	
and shall *s.* down in the	*Lu 13:29*
kingdom of God	
when bidden *s.* not down in	*Lu 14:8*
highest room	
take thy bill *s.* down quickly,	*Lu 16:6*
and write fifty	
will say to him, Go and *s.*	*Lu 17:7*
down to meat	
Jesus said, Make the men *s.*	*Joh 6:10*
down	
would raise up Christ to *s.* on	*Ac 2:30*
his throne	
that he would come up and *s.*	*Ac 8:31*
with him	
to see thee *s.* at meat in the	*1Co 8:10*
idol's temple	
hath made us *s.* in heavenly	*Eph 2:6*
places	
and say, *S.* thou here in a good	*Jas 2:3*
place	
s. down to supper with him (N)	*Re 3:20*
will I grant to *s.* with me in	*Re 3:21*
my throne	
I saw a woman *s.* on	*Re 17:3*
scarlet coloured beast	
for she saith in her heart, I *s.*	*Re 18:7*
a queen	
of them that *s.* on them	*Re 19:18*

SITES

and the *s.* wherein he built	*2Ch 33:19*
(S)	

SITH

s. thou hast not hated blood	*Eze 35:6*

SITNAH

and he called the name of it	*Ge 26:21*
S.	

SITTEST

why *s.* thou thyself alone,	*Ex 18:14*
and all	
them when thou *s.* in thine	*De 6:7;*
house	*11:19*
Thou *s.* and speakest against	*Ps 50:20*
thy	
When thou *s.* to eat with a	*Pr 23:1*
ruler	
that *s.* upon the throne of	*Jer 22:2*
David	
s. thou to judge me after the	*Ac 23:3*
law	

SITTETH

Pharaoh that *s.* upon his	*Ex 11:5*
throne	
every thing, whereon he *s.*	*Le 15:4*
shall be	
he that *s.* on any thing	*Le 15:6*
whereon he	
every thing also that she *s.*	*Le 15:20*
upon	
bed, or on any thing	*Le 15:23*
whereon she *s.*	
and whatsoever she *s.* upon	*Le 15:26*
shall be	
when he *s.* upon the throne	*De 17:18*
of his	

s. above the cherubim (E)	*1Sa 4:4*
Solomon *s.* on the throne of	*1Ki 1:46*
the Jew, that *s.* at the king's	*Es 6:10*
gate	
nor *s.* in the seat of the scornful	*Ps 1:1*
that *s.* in the heavens shall	*Ps 2:4*
laugh	
He *s.* in the lurking places of	*Ps 10:8*
The Lord *s.* upon the flood	*Ps 29:10*
yea, the Lord *s.* King for ever	*Ps 29:10*
s. upon the throne of his	*Ps 47:8*
holiness	
he *s.* between the cherubims;	*Ps 99:1*
let	
For she *s.* at the door of her	*Pr 9:14*
house	
that *s.* in the throne of	*Pr 20:8*
judgment	
when he *s.* among the elders	*Pr 31:23*
of the	
While the king *s.* at his table	*Ca 1:12*
to him that *s.* in judgment	*Isa 28:6*
that *s.* upon the circle of the	*Isa 40:22*
earth	
As the partridge *s.* on eggs	*Jer 17:11*
that *s.* upon the throne of	*Jer 29:16*
David	
He *s.* alone and keepeth	*La 3:28*
silence	
all the earth *s.* still, and is at	*Zec 1:11*
rest	
that *s.* in the midst of the	*Zec 5:7*
ephah	
of God, and by him that *s.*	*M't 23:22*
thereon	
s. not down first, and	*Lu 14:28*
counteth	
s. not down first, and	*Lu 14:31*
consulteth	
is greater, he that *s.* at meat,	*Lu 22:27*
or he	
is not he that *s.* at meat? but	*Lu 22:27*
I am	
be revealed to another that *s.*	*1Co 14:30*
by	
Christ *s.* on the right hand of	*Col 3:1*
God	
he as God *s.* in the temple of	*2Th 2:4*
God	
unto him that *s.* upon the	*Re 5:13*
throne	
face of him that *s.* on the	*Re 6:16*
throne	
our God which *s.* upon the	*Re 7:10*
throne	
he that *s.* on the throne shall	*Re 7:15*
dwell	
whore that *s.* upon many	*Re 17:1*
waters	
mountains, on which the	*Re 17:9*
woman *s.*	
where the whore *s.* are	*Re 17:15*
peoples	

SITTING

s. among sons of Heth	*Ge 23:10*
(B)(E)(R)	
and the dam *s.* upon the	*De 22:6*
young, or	
and he was *s.* in a summer	*J'g 3:20*
parlour	
table, and the *s.* of his	*1Ki 10:5*
servants	
and found him *s.* under an	*1Ki 13:14*
oak	
I saw the Lord *s.* on his	*1Ki 22:19*
throne, and	
of the prophets were *s.* before	*2Ki 4:38*
him	
the captains of the host were	*2Ki 9:5*
s.	
table, and the *s.* of his	*2Ch 9:4*
servants	
stays on each side of the *s.*	*2Ch 9:18*
place	
I saw the Lord *s.* upon	*2Ch 18:18*
his throne	
unto me, (the queen also *s.* by	*Ne 2:6*
him	
Mordecai *s.* at the king's	*Es 5:13*
gate	
s. among army (B)	*Job 9:25*
saw also the Lord *s.* upon a	*Isa 6:1*
throne	
princes *s.* upon the throne of	*Jer 17:25*
David	
kings *s.* upon the throne of	*Jer 22:4*
David	
s. upon the throne of David	*Jer 22:30*
then *s.* in the gate of Benjamin	*Jer 38:7*

Behold their *s.* down, and	*La 3:63*
s. at the receipt of custom	*M't 9:9*
unto children *s.* in the	*M't 11:16*
markets	
two blind men *s.* by the	*M't 20:30*
way side	
thee, meek, and *s.* upon an	*M't 21:5*
ass	
Son of man *s.* on the right	*M't 26:64*
hand	
s. down they watched him	*M't 27:36*
there	
Mary, *s.* over against the	*M't 27:61*
sepulchre	
were certain of the scribes *s.*	*M'k 2:6*
there	
Alphaeus *s.* at the receipt of	*M'k 2:14*
custom	
had the legion *s.* and clothed	*M'k 5:15*
Son of man *s.* on the right	*M'k 14:62*
hand of	
a young man *s.* on the right	*M'k 16:5*
side	
s. in the midst of the doctors	*Lu 2:46*
and doctors of the law *s.* by	*Lu 5:17*
Levi, *s.* at the receipt of	*Lu 5:27*
custom	
unto children *s.* in the market	*Lu 7:32*
place	
s. at the feet of Jesus, clothed	*Lu 8:35*
repented *s.* in sackcloth and	*Lu 10:13*
ashes	
and the changers of money *s.*	*Joh 2:14*
them that were *s.* down (S)	*Joh 6:11*
King cometh, *s.* on an ass's	*Joh 12:15*
colt	
And seeth two angels, in	*Joh 20:12*
white *s.*	
all the house where they were *s.*	*Ac 2:2*
s. in his chariot read Esaias	*Ac 8:28*
next day *s.* on the judgment	*Ac 25:6*
seat	
s. at the table (S)	*1Co 8:10*
I saw four and twenty elders *s.*	*Re 4:4*

SITUATE

one was *s.* northward over	*1Sa 14:5*
against	
that art *s.* at the entry of the	*Eze 27:3*
sea	
No, that was *s.* among the	*Na 3:8*
rivers	

SITUATED

situated (S)   *1Sa 14:5; Eze 27:3; Na 3:8*

SITUATION

the *s.* of this city is pleasant	*2Ki 2:19*
Beautiful for *s.* the joy of the	*Ps 48:2*
a sorry *s.* (B)	*Ec 4:8*
explain *s.* (P)	*Ac 11:4*

SIVAN

third month, that is, the month	*Es 8:9*
S.	

SIX

s. cakes on a row on the pure	*Le 24:6*
table	
s. covered wagons, and twelve	*Nu 7:3*
oxen	
man of great stature had on	*2Sa 21:20;*
every hand *s.* fingers, every	*1Ch 20:6*
foot *s.* toes	
Shimei had sixteen sons and	*1Ch 4:27*
s. daughters	
eastward were *s.* Levites,	*1Ch 26:17*
northward four	
burnt offering that the prince	*Eze 46:4*
shall offer shall be *s.* lambs	
in day of new moon shall be	*Eze 46:6*
s. lambs	

SIX BOARDS

westward thou shalt make *s.*	*Ex 26:22*
boards	
for the sides of tabernacle he	*Ex 36:27*
made *s.* boards	

SIX BRETHREN

moreover these *s.* brethren	*Ac 11:12*
accompanied	

SIX CITIES

there shall be *s. cities* for refuge   Nu 35:6; 35:13, 15

SIX CUBITS

Goliath's height was *s. cubits* and a span   1Sa 17:4
middle chamber was *s. cubits* broad   1Ki 6:6
a measuring reed of *s. cubits* long   Eze 40:5
the little chambers were *s. cubits* on this side   Eze 40:12
measured posts *s. cubits* broad on one side   Eze 41:1
door *s. cubits*; wall of the house *s. cubits*   Eze 41:3; 41:5
foundations were a full reed of *s. great cubits*   Eze 41:8
the breadth of the image of gold *s. cubits*   Da 3:1

SIX CURTAINS

couple *s. curtains* by themselves   Ex 26:9; 36:16

SIX MEASURES

Boaz gave Ruth of barley *s. measures*   Ru 3:15
she said, These *s. measures* of barley gave he me   Ru 3:17

SIX MEN

s. men came from way of the higher gate   Eze 9:2

SIX MONTHS

David was king in Hebron, seven years, *s. months*   2Sa 2:11; 5:5; 1Ch 3:4
s. months Joab remained in Edom   1Ki 11:16
Zachariah reigned *s. months* over Israel   2Ki 15:8
purifying *s. months* with oil of myrrh, and *s. months* with sweet odours   Es 2:12
heaven was shut up three years and *s. months*   Lu 4:25; Jas 5:17
Paul continued at Corinth a year *s. months*   Ac 18:11

SIX NAMES

s. names on one stone, and the other *s. names*   Ex 28:10

SIX PACES

when Levites gone *s. paces* he sacrificed   2Sa 6:13

SIX SHEEP

prepared for me daily *s. choice sheep*   Ne 5:18

SIX SONS

will dwell with me, I have born *s. sons*   Ge 30:20
and the *sons* of Shechaniah *s.*   1Ch 3:22
and Azel had *s. sons*, whose names are   1Ch 8:38; 9:44

SIX STEPS

the throne had *s. steps*, top round   1Ki 10:19
twelve lions on the *s. steps*   1Ki 10:20; 2Ch 9:18

SIX THINGS

these *s. things* doth the Lord hate   Pr 6:16

SIX TIMES

shouldst have smitten five or *s. times*   2Ki 13:19

SIX TROUBLES

shall deliver thee in *s. troubles*, in seven   Job 5:19

SIX WATERPOTS

there were set there *s. waterpots* of stone   Joh 2:6

SIX WINGS

stood the seraphims, each one had *s. wings*   Isa 6:2
four beasts had each *s. wings* about him   Re 4:8

SIX YEARS

I served thee *s. years* for thy cattle   Ge 31:41
s. years he shall serve, and in seventh he shall go out free   Ex 21:2; De 15:12; Jer 34:14
s. years thou shalt sow thy land and gather   Ex 23:10
s. years thou shalt prune thy vineyard   Le 25:3
double hired servant in serving *s. years*   De 15:18
and Jephthah judged Israel *s. years*   J'g 12:7
Omri reigned *s. years* in Tirzah   1Ki 16:23
Joash was hid in the house of the Lord *s. years*   2Ki 11:3; 2Ch 22:12

SIXSCORE

to the king *s. talents* of gold   1Ki 9:14
more than *s. thousand*   Jon 4:11

SIXES

assembly at *s.* and sevens (P)   Ac 19:32

SIXTEEN

she bare unto Jacob, even *s.*   Ge 46:18
sockets of silver, *s. sockets*   Ex 26:25
their sockets were *s. sockets* of   Ex 36:30
s. thousand and five hundred   Nu 26:22
the persons were *s. thousand*   Nu 31:40
And *s. thousand* persons   Nu 31:46
s. thousand seven hundred   Nu 31:52
s. cities with their villages   Jos 15:41; 19:22
Samaria and reigned, *s. years*   2Ki 13:10
which was *s. years* old, and   2Ki 14:21
S. years old was he when he reigned *s. years* in Jerusalem   2Ki 15:2; 2Ki 15:33; 16:2; 2Ch 27:1, 8; 28:1
Shimei had *s. sons* and six   1Ch 4:27
of Eleazar there were *s. chief*   1Ch 24:4
two sons, and *s. daughters*   2Ch 13:21
Uzziah, who was *s. years* old   2Ch 26:1
S. years old was Uzziah when   2Ch 26:3
threescore and *s. souls*   Ac 27:37

SIXTEENTH

to Bilgah, the *s.* to Immer   1Ch 24:14
The *s.* to Hananiah, he, his   1Ch 25:23
in the *s. day* of the first month   2Ch 29:17

SIXTH

and the morning were the *s. day*   Ge 1:31
again, and bare Jacob the *s. son*   Ge 30:19
on the *s. day* they shall prepare one *s.*   Ex 16:5
on the *s. day* they gathered twice   Ex 16:22
on the *s. day* the bread of two days   Ex 16:29
shalt double the *s. curtain* in   Ex 26:9
blessing upon you in the *s. year*   Le 25:21
On the *s. day* Eliasaph the son of   Nu 7:42
on the *s. day* eight bullocks, two   Nu 29:29
The *s. lot* came out to the children   Jos 19:32
the *s.* Ithream, by Eglah David's   2Sa 3:5
In the twenty and *s. year* of Asa   1Ki 16:8
even in the *s. year* of Hezekiah   2Ki 18:10
Ozem the *s.*, David the seventh   1Ch 2:15
s. Ithream by Eglah his wife   1Ch 3:3
Attai the *s.* Eliel the seventh   1Ch 12:11
to Malchijah, the *s.* to Mijamin   1Ch 24:9
The *s.* to Bukkiah, he, his sons   1Ch 25:13
Elam the fifth, Jehohanan the *s.*   1Ch 26:3
Ammiel the *s.*, Issachar the   1Ch 26:5
The *s.* captain for the *s. month* was   1Ch 27:9
was in the *s. year* of the reign of   Ezr 6:15
and Hanun the *s. son* of Zalaph   Ne 3:30
by measure, the *s. part* of an hin   Eze 4:11
pass in the *s. year*, in the *s. month*   Eze 8:1
and leave but the *s. part* of thee   Eze 39:2
offer: the *s. part* of an ephah of an   Eze 45:13
give the *s. part* of an ephah of an   Eze 45:13
the *s. part* of an ephah, and   Eze 46:14
of Darius the king, in the *s. month*   Hag 1:1
and twentieth day of the *s. month*   Hag 1:15
out about the *s.* and ninth hour   M'k 20:5
the *s. hour* there was darkness   M't 27:45
when the *s. hour* was come, there   M'k 15:33
the *s. month* the angel Gabriel was   Lu 1:26
this is the *s. month* with her, who   Lu 1:36
it was about the *s. hour*, and   Lu 23:44
well: and it was about the *s. hour*   Joh 4:6
passover, and about the *s. hour*   Joh 19:14
housetop to pray about the *s. hour*   Ac 10:9
when he had opened the *s. seal*   Re 6:12
the *s. angel* sounded, and I heard a   Re 9:13
Saying to the *s. angel* which had   Re 9:14
And the *s. angel* poured out his vial   Re 16:12
The fifth, sardonyx; the *s.* sardius   Re 21:20

SIXTY

Mahalaleel lived *s.* and five years   Ge 5:15
Jared lived an hundred *s.* and two   Ge 5:18
Jared and nine hundred *s.* and two   Ge 5:20
And Enoch lived *s.* and five years   Ge 5:21
of Enoch were three hundred *s.* and   Ge 5:23
Methuselah were nine hundred *s.*   Ge 5:27
from twenty years old even unto *s.*   Le 27:3
if it be from *s. years* old and above   Le 27:7
the rams *s.* and he goats *s.*   Nu 7:88
the lambs of the first year *s.*   Nu 7:88
Adonikam, six hundred *s.* and six   Ezr 2:13
some an hundredfold, some *s.*   M't 13:23
some thirty, and some *s.* and   M'k 4:8
some thirtyfold, some *s.* and   M'k 4:20
widow under *s. years* of age (S)   1Ti 5:9

SIXTYFOLD

some *s.* some thirtyfold   M't 13:8

SIZE

the curtains were all of one *s.*   Ex 36:9
the eleven curtains were of one *s.*   Ex 36:15
were of one measure and one *s.*   1Ki 6:25

casting, one measure, and one *1Ki 7:37*
s.
for all manner of measure   *1Ch 23:29*
s.

SKIES

waters, and thick clouds of the *s.*	*2Sa 22:12; Ps 18:11*
breath *s.* are cleared (A)(B)	*Job 26:13*
out water; and *s.* sent out a sound	*Ps 77:17*
let the *s.* pour down righteousness	*Isa 45:8*
and is lifted up even to the *s.*	*Jer 51:9*

SKILFUL

s. hunter (E)(R)(S)	*Ge 25:27*
of *s.* work (S)	*Ex 26:1;*
26:31; 28:6, 15; 35:33, 35; 36:8, 35;	*38:23; 39:38*
skilful (B)(E)	*Ex 28:15; 38:23; 39:8*
to design *s.* (S)	*Ex 31:4*
s. in playing (B)(E)(R)(S)	*1Sa 16:16*
and *s.* in war, were four and forty	*1Ch 5:18*
about the song, because he was *s.*	*1Ch 15:22*
all manner of *s.* men (S)	*1Ch 22:15*
brethren instructed in songs were *s.* (S)	*1Ch 25:7*
every willing *s.* man, for any (S)	*1Ch 28:21*
send me a man *s.* to work	*2Ch 2:7; 2:13-14*
s. to work in gold, and in silver, by	*2Ch 2:14*
invented by *s.* men (S)	*2Ch 26:15*
were *s.* with instruments of music (S)	*2Ch 34:12*
casting spell *s.* (B)	*Ps 58:5*
walks in *s.* wisdom (A)	*Pr 28:26*
work of a *s.* workman (S)	*Ca 7:1*
expert craftsman and *s.*	*Isa 3:3*
enchanter (A)(B)(E)(R)(S) *s.* craftsman (A)(R)(B)(E)(R)(S)	*Isa 40:20*
s. women (A)(B)(E)(R)(S)	*Jer 9:17*
s. men (A)(B)(E)(R)	*Jer 10:9*
of brutish men, and *s.* to destroy	*Eze 21:31*
favoured, and *s.* in all wisdom	*Da 1:4*
such as are *s.* of lamentation	*Am 5:16*
the *s.* enchanter (A)(E)	*Ac 3:3*

SKILFULLY

cherubims *s.* embroidered (A)(B)(R)	*Ex 26:1*
plays *s.* on lyre (A)	*1Sa 16:16*
plays *s.* (A)(E)(R)	*1Sa 16:18*
song; play *s.* with a loud noise	*Ps 32:3*

SKILFULNESS

them by the *s.* of his hands	*Ps 78:72*

SKILL

endowed with *s.* (A)(B)	*Ex 28:3; 31:3, 6; 35:26, 31; 36:2*
can *s.* to hew timber like unto	*1Ki 5:6*
and *s.* to work in brass (S)	*1Ki 7:14*
s. to grave with the cunning men	*2Ch 2:7*
thy servants can *s.* to cut timber	*2Ch 2:8*
could *s.* of instruments of musick	*2Ch 34:12*
will acquire *s.* (R)	*Pr 1:5*
nor yet favour to men of *s.*	*Ec 9:11*
by understanding and *s.* (A)(B)(E)(R)	*Jer 10:12*
and *s.* in all learning and wisdom	*Da 1:17*
to give thee *s.* and understanding	*Da 9:22*
without schooling or *s.* (B)	*Ac 4:13*
if I lack *s.* in rhetoric (B)	*2Co 11:6*

SKILLED

all the *s.* artisans (B)	*Ex 36:4*
s. in intrigues (B)	*Da 8:23*
a *s.* architect (B)(R)	*1Co 3:10*

SKIN

to a *s.* of water (B)(R)	*Ge 21:14*
only, it is his raiment for his *s.*	*Ex 22:27*

the flesh of the bullock, and his *s.*	*Ex 29:14*
wist not that the *s.* of his face shone	*Ex 34:29*
behold, the *s.* of his face shone	*Ex 34:30*
that the *s.* of Moses' face shone	*Ex 34:35*
And the *s.* of the bullock, and all	*Le 4:11*
himself the *s.* of the burnt offering	*Le 7:8*
vessel of wood, or raiment, or *s.* or	*Le 11:32*
the *s.* of his flesh	*Le 13:2; 13:3, 11, 39, 42*
in sight be not deeper than the *s.*	*Le 13:4; 13:25, 30-32, 34*
and the plague spread not in the *s.*	*Le 13:5; 13:6-7, 22, 27-28, 34-36*
if the rising be white in the *s.*	*Le 13:10*
leprosy break out abroad in the *s.*	*Le 13:12*
leprosy cover all the *s.* of him	*Le 13:12*
in the *s.* thereof, was a boil,	*Le 13:18*
it be in sight lower than the *s.* and	*Le 13:20*
and if it be not lower than the *s.*	*Le 13:21*
s. whereof there is a hot burning	*Le 13:24*
it be no lower than the other *s.*	*Le 13:26*
in the *s.* of their flesh bright spots	*Le 13:38*
spot that groweth in the *s.*: he is	*Le 13:39*
in a *s.* or in any thing made of *s.*	*Le 13:48*
reddish in the garment, or in the *s.*	*Le 13:49*
in the woof, or in any thing of *s.*	*Le 13:49; 13:53, 57*
the warp, or in the woof, or in a *s.*	*Le 13:51*
or in any work that is made of *s.*	*Le 13:51*
or any thing of *s.* wherein the	*Le 13:52*
out of the garment, or out of the *s.*	*Le 13:56*
or whatsoever thing of *s.* it be	*Le 13:58*
And every garment, and every *s.*	*Le 15:17*
burn he heifer in his sight; her *s.*	*Nu 19:5*
opened a *s.* of water (A)(R)	*J'g 4:19*
s. of wine (A)(B)(R)	*1Sa 1:24; 10:3; 16:20; 2Sa 16:1*
S. for *s.* yea, all that a man	*Job 2:4*
my *s.* is broken, and become	*Job 7:5*
hast clothed me with *s.* and flesh	*Job 10:11*
have sewed sackcloth upon my *s.*	*Job 16:15*
shall devour the strength of his *s.*	*Job 18:13*
My bones cleave to my *s.*	*Job 19:20*
and I am escaped with the *s.* of my	*Job 19:20*
though after my *s.* worms destroy	*Job 19:26*
My *s.* is black upon me, and	*Job 30:30*
thou fill his *s.* with barbed irons	*Job 41:7*
my bones cleave to my *s.*	*Ps 102:5*
Can the Ethiopian change his *s.*	*Jer 13:23*
flesh and my *s.* hath he made old	*La 3:4*
their *s.* cleaveth to their bones	*La 4:8*
Our *s.* was black like an oven	*La 5:10*
and shod thee with badgers' *s.*	*Eze 16:10*
upon you, and cover you with *s.*	*Eze 37:6*
and the *s.* covered them above: but	*Eze 37:8*
pluck off their *s.* from off them	*Mic 3:2*
and flay their *s.* from off them; and	*Mic 3:3*
strip *s.* off of them (A)(B)	*Mic 3:3*
a girdle of a *s.* about his loins	*M'k 1:6*

SKINNING

Levites did the *s.* (A)(B)	*2Ch 35:11*

SKINS

did the Lord God make coats of *s.*	*Ge 3:21*
she put the *s.* of the kids of	*Ge 27:16*
rams' *s.* dyed red, and badgers' *s.*	*Ex 25:5; 35:7*
for the tent of rams' *s.* dyed red	*Ex 26:14*
and a covering above of badgers' *s.*	*Ex 26:14*
and red *s.* of rams, and badgers' *s.*	*Ex 35:23*
for the tent of rams' *s.* dyed red	*Ex 36:19*
and a covering of badgers' *s.* above	*Ex 36:19*
the covering of rams' *s.* dyed red	*Ex 39:34*
the covering of badgers' *s.* and the	*Ex 39:34*
warp or woof, or any thing of *s.*	*Le 13:59*
they shall burn in the fire their *s.*	*Le 16:27*
thereon the covering of badgers' *s.*	*Nu 4:6*
same with a covering of badgers' *s.*	*Nu 4:8*
within a covering of badgers' *s.*	*Nu 4:10; 4:11*
it with a covering of badgers' *s.*	*Nu 4:11*
them with a covering of badgers' *s.*	*Nu 4:12*
upon it a covering of badgers' *s.*	*Nu 4:14*
covering of the badgers' *s.* that is	*Nu 4:25*
seeds and *s.* (B)(R)	*Nu 6:4*
all that is made of *s.* and all work	*Nu 31:20*
two *s.* of wine (A)(B)(R)	*1Sa 25:18*
the *s.* are ruined (A)(B)(N)(P)(R)	*M't 9:17*

SKIP

them also to *s.* like a calf	*Ps 29:6*

SKIPPED

The mountains *s.* like rams	*Ps 114:4*
mountains, that ye *s.* like rams	*Ps 114:6*

SKIPPEDST

spakest of him, thou *s.* for joy	*Jer 48:27*

SKIPPING

the mountains, *s.* upon the hills	*Ca 2:8*
shaggy goats will be *s.* (B)	*Isa 13:21*

SKIRT

wife, nor discover his father's *s.*	*De 22:30*
he uncovereth his father's *s.*	*De 27:20*
spread therefore thy *s.* over thine	*Ru 3:9*
laid hold upon the *s.* of his mantle	*1Sa 15:27*
cut off the *s.* of Saul's robe privily	*1Sa 24:4*
because he had cut off Saul's *s.*	*1Sa 24:5*
see the *s.* of thy robe in my hand	*1Sa 24:11*
in that I cut off the *s.* of thy robe	*1Sa 24:11*
and I spread my *s.* over thee	*Eze 16:8*
holy flesh in the *s.* of his garment	*Hag 2:12*
and with his *s.* do touch bread, or	*Hag 2:12*
hold of the *s.* of him that is a Jew	*Zec 8:23*

SKIRTS

down to the *s.* of his garments	*Ps 133:2*
upon the edge of his garments	*Ps 133:2*
on the collar of his robe (R)	*Ps 133:2*
Also in thy *s.* is found the blood of	*Jer 2:34*
iniquity are thy *s.* discovered	*Jer 13:22*

I discover thy *s*. upon thy face — Jer 13:26

Her filthiness is in her *s*.; she — La 1:9

number, and bind them in thy *s*. — Eze 5:3

will discover thy *s*. upon the face — Na 3:5

SKULL

head, and all to break his *s*. — J'g 9:53

found no more of her than the *s*. — 2Ki 9:35

that is to say, a place of a *s*. — M't 27:33

being interpreted, The place of a *s*. — M'k 15:22

into a place called the place of a *s*. — Joh 19:17

SKY

and in his excellency on the *s*. — De 33:26

thou with him spread out the *s*. — Job 37:18

be fair weather: for the *s*. is red — M't 6:2

day: for the *s*. is red and lowering — M't 16:3

ye can discern the face of the *s*. — M't 16:3; Lu 12:56

so many as the stars of the *s*. in — Heb 11:12

SLACK

not be *s*. to him that hateth him — De 7:10

thy God, thou shalt not *s*. to pay it — De 23:21

S. not thy hand from thy servants — Jos 10:6

How long are ye *s*. to go to possess — Jos 18:3

s. not thy riding for me, except I — 2Ki 4:24

poor that dealeth with a *s*. hand — Pr 10:4

Zion, Let not thine hands be *s*. — Zep 3:16

The Lord is not *s*. concerning his — 2Pe 3:9

not grow *s*. (P) — Heb 6:12

because of *s*. hands (B) — Ec 10:18

SLACKED

the law is *s*. and judgment doth — Hab 1:4

SLACKING

never *s*. in interest (B) — Ro 12:11

SLACKNESS

promise, as some men count *s*. — 2Pe 3:9

SLAIN

I have *s*. a man to my wounding — Ge 4:23

sons of Jacob came upon the *s*. — Ge 34:27

them in the blood of the *s*. bird — Le 14:51

shall be *s*. before your enemies — Le 26:17

flocks of the herds be *s*. for — Nu 11:22

hath *s*. them in the wilderness — Nu 14:16

one that is *s*. with a sword in — Nu 19:16

a bone, or one *s*. or one dead, or a — Nu 19:18

surely now also I had *s*. thee — Nu 22:33

and drink the blood of the *s*. — Nu 23:24

name of the Israelite that was *s*. — Nu 25:14

was *s*. with the Midianitish woman — Nu 25:14

Midianitish woman that was *s*. was — Nu 25:15

was *s*. in the day of the plague for — Nu 25:18

the rest of them that were *s*. — Nu 31:8

and whoever hath touched any *s*. — Nu 31:19

he had *s*. Sihon the king of the — De 1:4

be found *s*. in the land which — De 21:1

it be not known who hath *s*. him — De 21:1

are round about him that is *s*. — De 21:2

city which is next unto the *s*. man — De 21:3

that are next unto the *s*. man shall — De 21:6

Thine ox shall be *s*. before thine — De 28:31

with the blood of the *s*. and of the — De 32:42

deliver them up all *s*. before Israel — Jos 11:6

among them that were *s*. by them — Jos 13:22

and have *s*. his sons, threescore — J'g 9:18

an ass have I *s*. a thousand men — J'g 15:16

husband of the woman that was *s*. — J'g 20:4

night, and thought to have *s*. me — J'g 20:5

Hophni and Phinehas, were *s*. — 1Sa 4:11

Saul hath *s*. his thousands — 1Sa 18:7; 21:11

the Lord liveth, he shall not be *s*. — 1Sa 19:6

to-morrow thou shalt be *s*. — 1Sa 19:11

Wherefore shall he be *s*. — 1Sa 20:32

Saul had *s*. the Lord's priests — 1Sa 22:21

and fell down *s*. in mount Gilboa — 1Sa 31:1; 1Ch 10:1

the Philistines came to strip the *s*. — 1Sa 31:8; 1Ch 10:8

I have *s*. the Lord's anointed — 2Sa 1:16

The beauty of Israel is *s*. upon thy — 2Sa 1:19

From the blood of the *s*. from the — 2Sa 1:22

thou wast *s*. in thine high places — 2Sa 1:25

were *s*. (R) — 2Sa 2:31; 2Ki 3:23

he had *s*. their brother Asahel — 2Sa 3:30

men have *s*. a righteous person in — 2Sa 4:11

and hast *s*. him with the sword of — 2Sa 12:9

Absalom hath *s*. all the king's — 2Sa 13:30

s. all the young men the king's — 2Sa 13:32

people of Israel were *s*. before — 2Sa 18:7

Philistines had *s*. Saul in Gilboa — 2Sa 21:12

sword, thought to have *s*. David — 2Sa 21:16

s. oxen and fat cattle and sheep — 1Ki 1:19; 1:25

s. the Canaanites that dwelt in — 1Ki 9:16

host was gone up to bury the *s*. — 1Ki 11:15

which hath torn him, and *s*. him — 1Ki 13:26

and hath also *s*. the king to be *s*. (A) — 1Ki 16:16; 1Ki 18:9

how he had *s*. all the prophets — 1Ki 19:1

s. thy prophets with the sword — 1Ki 19:10; 19:14

the kings are surely *s*. and they — 2Ki 3:23

have attacked and *s*. (B) — 2Ki 3:23

the king's sons which were *s*. — 2Ki 11:2

from Athaliah, so that he was not *s*. — 2Ki 11:2

within the ranges, let him be *s*. — 2Ki 11:8

Let her not be *s*. in the house of the — 2Ki 11:15

king's house: and there was she *s*. — 2Ki 11:16

his servants which had *s*. the king — 2Ki 14:5

there fell down many *s*. because — 1Ch 5:22

hundred *s*. by him at one time — 1Ch 11:11

fell down *s*. of Israel five hundred — 2Ch 13:17

also hast *s*. thy brethren of thy — 2Ch 21:13

to the camp had *s*. all the eldest — 2Ch 22:1

and when they had *s*. him, they — 2Ch 22:9

among the king's sons that were *s*. — 2Ch 22:11

her, let him be *s*. with the sword — 2Ch 23:14

they had *s*. Athaliah with the sword — 2Ch 23:21

and ye have *s*. them in a rage — 2Ch 28:9

my people, to be destroyed, to be *s*. — Es 7:4

of those that were *s*. in Shushan — Es 9:11

The Jews have *s*. and destroyed — Es 9:12

s. the servants with the edge — Job 1:15; 1:17

and where the *s*. are there is she — Job 39:30

ye shall be *s*. all of you: as a — Ps 62:3

like the *s*. that lie in the grave — Ps 88:5

Rahab in pieces as one that is *s*. — Ps 89:10

strong men have been *s*. by her — Pr 7:26

without, I shall be *s*. in the streets — Pr 22:13

and those that are ready to be *s*. — Pr 24:11

and they shall fall under the *s*. — Isa 10:4

as the raiment of those that are *s*. — Isa 14:19

thy land, and *s*. thy people — Isa 14:20

s. men are not *s*. with the sword — Isa 22:2

and shall no more cover her *s*. — Isa 26:21

he *s*. according to the slaughter of — Isa 27:7

of them that are *s*. by him — Isa 27:7

Their *s*. also shall be cast out — Isa 34:3

the *s*. of the Lord shall be many — Isa 66:16

the *s*. of the daughter of my people — Jer 9:1

then behold the *s*. with the sword — Jer 14:18

young men be *s*. by the sword in — Jer 18:21

s. of the Lord shall be at that day — Jer 25:33

whom I have *s*. in mine anger — Jer 33:5

day after he had *s*. Gedaliah — Jer 41:4

he had *s*. because of Gedaliah — Jer 41:9

filled it with them that were *s*. — Jer 41:9

s. Gedaliah the son of Ahikam — Jer 41:16

son of Nethaniah had *s*. Gedaliah — Jer 41:18

the *s*. shall fall in the land of — Jer 51:4

her *s*. shall fall in the midst of her — Jer 51:47

hath caused the *s*. of Israel to fall — Jer 51:49

shall fall the *s*. of all the earth — Jer 51:49

the priest and the prophet be *s*. in — La 2:20

s. them in the day of thine anger — La 2:21

thou hast *s*. thou hast not pitied — La 3:43

They that be *s*. with the sword are — La 4:9

than they that be *s*. with hunger — La 4:9

down your *s*. men before your idols — Eze 6:4

the *s*. shall fall in the midst of you — Eze 6:7

when their *s*. men shall be among — Eze 6:13

house, and fill the courts with the *s*. — Eze 9:7

have multiplied your *s*. in this city — Eze 11:6

filled the streets thereof with the *s*. — Eze 11:6

Your *s*. whom ye have laid in — Eze 11:7

That thou hast *s*. my children, and — Eze 16:21

the third time, the sword of the *s*. — Eze 21:14

sword of the great men that are *s*. — Eze 21:14

upon the necks of them that are *s*. — Eze 21:29

when they had *s*. their children to — Eze 23:39

the field shall be *s*. by the sword — Eze 26:6

are *s*. in the midst of the seas — Eze 28:8

when the *s*. shall fall in Egypt — Eze 30:4

Egypt, and fill the land with the *s*. — Eze 30:11

them that be *s*. with the sword — Eze 31:17; 31:18; 32:20, 28, 30, 32

lie uncircumcised, *s*. by the sword — Eze 32:21; 32:25-26

all of them *s*. fallen by the sword — Eze 32:22; 32:23-24

set her a bed in the midst of   *Eze 32:25*
the s.
put in the midst of them   *Eze 32:25*
that be s.
by them that were s. by the   *Eze 32:29*
sword
which are gone down with   *Eze 32:30*
the s.
Pharaoh and all his army s.   *Eze 32:31*
by the
fill his mountains with his s.   *Eze 35:8*
men
they fall that are s. with the   *Eze 35:8*
sword
breathe upon these s. that   *Eze 37:9*
they
that the wise men should be s.   *Da 2:13*
Daniel and his fellows to be s.   *Da 2:13*
was the king of the   *Da 5:30*
Chaldeans s.
I beheld even till the beast was   *Da 7:11*
s.
and many shall fall down s.   *Da 11:26*
s. them by the words of my   *Ho 6:5*
mouth
young men have I s. with the   *Am 4:10*
sword
and there is a multitude of s.   *Na 3:3*
also, ye shall be s. by my   *Zep 2:12*
sword
be s. and be raised the third   *Lu 9:22*
day
s. between altar and   *Lu 11:51*
sanctuary (A)(P)
wicked hands have crucified   *Ac 2:23*
and s.
who was s.; and all, as many   *Ac 5:36*
as
have ye offered to me s.   *Ac 7:42*
beasts and
they have s. them which   *Ac 7:52*
shewed
they Pilate that he should be   *Ac 13:28*
s.
eat nothing until we have s.   *Ac 23:14*
Paul
cross, having s. the enmity   *Eph 2:16*
thereby
were s. with the sword   *Heb 11:37*
martyr, who was s. among you   *Re 2:13*
stood a Lamb as it had been s.   *Re 5:6*
thou wast s. and hast redeemed   *Re 5:9*
Worthy is the Lamb that was   *Re 5:12*
s. to
that were s. for the word of   *Re 6:9*
God
were s. of men seven   *Re 11:13*
thousand
the Lamb s. from the   *Re 13:8*
foundation
of all that were s. upon the   *Re 18:24*
earth
remnant were s. with the   *Re 19:21*
sword of

SLANDER

by bringing up a s. upon the   *Nu 14:36*
land
starting a whispering   *Nu 14:36*
campaign (B)
bringing an evil report   *Nu 14:36*
(E)(R)
not s. with tongue   *Ps 15:3*
(A)(B)(E)(R)
For I have heard the s. of   *Ps 31:13*
many
and he that uttereth a s. is a   *Pr 10:18*
fool
s. and detest all you (P)   *Lu 6:22*
s. and shameful language   *Col 3:8*
(A)(B)(E)
lest he be involved in s.   *1Ti 3:7*
(A)(B)
opponent occasion for s. (N)   *1Ti 5:14*
abuse, insults, s.   *1Ti 6:4*
(A)(B)(P)(R)
s. base suspicions (N)(R)   *1Ti 6:5*

SLANDERED

hath s. thy servant unto my   *2Sa 19:27*
lord
being s. we bless (B)   *1Co 4:12*

SLANDERER

s. is no better (A)   *Ec 10:11*
a s. or drunkard (N)   *1Co 5:11*

SLANDERERS

slanderers (A)(B)   *Ps 35:15*
slanderers (A)(B)(R)   *Ro 1:30*

SLANDEREST

s. thine own mother's son   *Ps 50:20*
son of your mother you bring   *Ps 50:20*
to ruin (B)

SLANDERETH

Whoso privily s. his   *Ps 101:5*
neighbour

SLANDERING

opponent incentive for s. (B)   *1Ti 5:14*

SLANDEROUS

s. speech (B)   *Isa 58:9*

SLANDEROUSLY

(as we be s. reported, and as   *Ro 3:8*
some

SLANDERS

save me from s. (B)   *Ps 57:3*
revolters, walking with s.   *Jer 6:28*
going about as talebearers   *Jer 6:28*
(B)
every neighbour will walk with   *Jer 9:4*
s.
every neighbor goes about   *Jer 9:4*
gossiping (B)
s., foul talk (A)(R)   *Col 3:8*

SLANDERERS

must their wives be grave, not   *1Ti 3:11*
s.
not gossipers (A)   *1Ti 3:11*
not given to slandering (B)   *1Ti 3:11*
who will not talk scandal (N)   *1Ti 3:11*

SLANG

and took thence a stone,   *1Sa 17:49*
and s. it

SLAPPED

some s. him (A)(B)(P)(R)   *M't 26:67*

SLASHES

he s. open my (A)(R)   *Job 16:13*

SLAUGHTER

from the s. of Chedorlaomer   *Ge 14:17*
slaying of Chedor-laomer (A)   *Ge 14:17*
the defeat of Chedor-laomer   *Ge 14:17*
(B)(R)
s. an animal (S)   *Ge 43:16*
one shall s. her (A)(B)(R)   *Nu 19:3*
and slew them with a great   *Jos 10:10*
s. at
defeat to them at Gibeon   *Jos 10:10*
(B)
slaying them with a very   *Jos 10:20*
great s.
the vineyards, with a very   *J'g 11:33*
great s.
with heavy casualties (B)   *Jg 11:33*
them hip and thigh with a   *J'g 15:8*
great s.
and there was a very great s.   *1Sa 4:10*
Israel was defeated (B)(R)   *1Sa 4:10*
there hath been also a great   *1Sa 4:17*
s.
people have suffered a   *1Sa 4:17*
disastrous defeat (B)
many of the people with a   *1Sa 6:19*
great s.
s. many people (A)(R)   *1Sa 6:19*
And that first s. which   *1Sa 14:14*
Jonathan
not been now a much   *1Sa 14:30*
greater s.
David returned from the s.   *1Sa 17:57*
of the
David returned from killing   *1Sa 17:57*
Goliath (A)
David returned from slaying   *1Sa 17:57*
the Philistine (B)

David was returned from the   *1Sa 18:6*
s. of
David returned from killing   *1Sa 18:6*
the Philistine (A)
David's slaying the Philistine   *1Sa 18:6*
(B)(R)
and slew them with a great s.   *1Sa 19:8*
defeating them with heavy   *1Sa 19:8;*
losses (B)   *23:5*
and smote them with a great   *1Sa 23:5*
s.
David was returned from the   *2Sa 1:1*
s. of
s. among the people that   *2Sa 17:9*
follow
there was there a great s.   *2Sa 18:7*
that day
slew the Syrians with a great   *1Ki 20:21*
s.
people slew them with a   *2Ch 13:17*
great s.
come from the s. of the   *2Ch 25:14*
Edomites
who smote him with a great   *2Ch 28:5*
s.
who defeated him (A)(B)(R)   *2Ch 28:5*
who smote him (E)   *2Ch 28:5*
the sword, and s. and destruction   *Es 9:5*
we are counted as sheep for   *Ps 44:22*
the s.
as an ox goeth to the s. or as   *Pr 7:22*
according to the s. of Midian   *Isa 10:26*
Prepare s. for his children   *Isa 14:21*
for the
according to the s. of them   *Isa 27:7*
that
of waters in the day of the   *Isa 30:25*
great s.
he hath delivered them to the   *Isa 34:2*
s.
a great s. in the land of   *Isa 34:6*
Idumea
he is brought as a lamb to the   *Isa 53:7*
s.
and ye shall all bow down to   *Isa 65:12*
the s.
of Hinnom, but the valley of   *Jer 7:32;*
s.   *19:6*
or an ox that is brought to   *Jer 11:19*
the s.
pull them out like sheep for   *Jer 12:3*
the s.
and prepare them for the day   *Jer 12:3*
of s.
for the days of your s. and   *Jer 25:34*
of your
young men are gone to the   *Jer 48:15*
s.
let them go down to the s.:   *Jer 50:27*
woe
them down like lambs to the   *Jer 51:40*
s.
every man a s. weapon in his   *Eze 9:2*
hand
It is sharpened to make a   *Eze 21:10*
sore s.
bright, it is wrapped up for   *Eze 21:15*
the s.
to open the mouth in the s.   *Eze 21:22*
is drawn: for the s. it is   *Eze 21:28*
furbished
when the s. is made in the   *Eze 26:15*
midst
revolters are profound to make   *Ho 5:2*
s.
mount of Esau may be cut off by   *Ob 9*
s.
my God; Feed the flock of   *Zec 11:4*
the s.
And I will feed the flock of s.   *Zec 11:7*
even
s. them in my presence   *Lu 19:27*
(A)(N)
He was led as a sheep to the   *Ac 8:32*
s.
s. against the disciples of the   *Ac 9:1*
Lord
threatening and murderous   *Ac 9:1*
desire (A)
breathing out threats and   *Ac 9:1*
murder (B)(R)
breathing murderous threats   *Ac 9:1*
(N)(P)
are accounted as sheep for the   *Ro 8:36*
returning from the s. of the   *Heb 7:1*
kings
returned from the defeat of   *Heb 7:1*
the kings (B)(P)

returning from the rout of the *Heb 7:1*
kings (N)
your hearts, as in a day of *s.* *Jas 5:5*

SLAUGHTERED

s. chosen men (B) *Ps 78:31*

SLAVE

slave (S) *Ge 44:33;*
De 15:15; 16:12; 24:18, 22; Re 6:15
strikes eye of a *s.* (R) *Ex 21:26*
buy a *s.* (R) *Le 22:11*
Israel a servant? is he a *Jer 2:14*
homeborn *s.*
you contemptible *s.* (B) *M't 18:32*
must be your *s.* (P) *M't 20:26*
not be a *s.* mastered *1Co 6:12*
(A)(B)(P)
consenting to be a *s.* by *Ph'p 2:7*
nature (P)

SLAVEHOLDER'S

his *s.* rod (B) *Isa 9:4*

SLAVERY

reduced Israelites to severe *s.* *Ex 1:11*
(A)
downed by cruel *s.* (B) *Ex 6:9*

SLAVES

slaves (S) *Ge 43:18;*
44:9; Le 25:42, 44; De 6:21; 28:68;
Jos 9:23; 1Ki 9:22; 2Ki 4:1; 2Ch 28:10;
Ezr 9:9; Es 7:4
make *s.* (S) *Jer 25:14*
s. of depravity (A) *2Pe 2:19*
chariots, and *s.* and souls of *Re 18:13*
men

SLAY

one that findeth me shall *s.* me *Ge 4:14*
will kill me (A)(B) *Ge 4:14*
s. the righteous with the *Ge 18:25*
wicked
thou *s.* also a righteous nation *Ge 20:4*
they will *s.* me for my wife's *Ge 20:11*
sake
will kill me (B)(R) *Ge 20:11*
and took the knife to *s.* his *Ge 22:10*
son
then will I *s.* my brother *Ge 27:41*
Jacob
I will kill my brother *Ge 27:41*
(A)(B)(R)
together against me, and *s.* *Ge 34:30*
me
conspired against him to *s.* *Ge 37:18*
him
conspired to kill him *Ge 37:18;*
(A)(B)(R) *37:20*
let us *s.* him, and cast him *Ge 37:20*
into
What profit is it if we *s.* our *Ge 37:26*
brother
S. my two sons, if I bring *Ge 42:37*
him not
Bring these men home, and *s.* *Ge 43:16*
kill an animal (A) *Ge 43:16*
see to the butchering (B) *Ge 43:16*
this thing he sought to *s.* *Ex 2:15*
Moses
took steps to kill Moses *Ex 2:15*
(B)(R)
I will *s.* thy son, even thy *Ex 4:23*
firstborn
I am about to kill your *Ex 4:23*
firstborn (B)
put a sword in their hand to *s.* *Ex 5:21*
us
handing them a sword to kill *Ex 5:21*
us (B)(R)
s. the Egyptians (A)(R) *Ex 12:23*
his neighbour, to *s.* him with *Ex 21:14*
guile
kills him with design (B)(R) *Ex 21:14*
innocent and righteous *s.* thou *Ex 23:7*
not
condemn to death the *Ex 23:7*
righteous (A)
do not execute the innocent *Ex 23:7*
(B)
And thou shalt *s.* the ram, and *Ex 29:16*
kill the ram (A) *Ex 29:16*
Slaughter the ram (B)(R) *Ex 29:16*

out, to *s.* them in the *Ex 32:12*
mountains
to kill them in the mountains *Ex 32:12*
(B)
s. every man his brother, and *Ex 32:27*
s. the sin offering in the place *Le 4:29*
of
kill it in the place (A)(E)(R) *Le 4:29*
butcher the sin offering at the *Le 4:29*
place (B)
s. it for a sin offering in the *Le 4:33*
place
kill it in the place (A)(E)(R) *Le 4:33*
he shall *s.* the lamb in the *Le 14:13*
place
he shall kill the lamb *Le 14:13*
(A)(B)(E)(R)
death: and ye shall *s.* the *Le 20:15*
beast
kill the animal (B)(R) *Le 20:15*
one shall *s.* her before his *Nu 19:3*
face
one shall slaughter her *Nu 19:3*
(A)(B)(R)
S. ye every one his men that *Nu 25:5*
were
execute those men (B) *Nu 25:5*
himself shall *s.* the murderer *Nu 35:19*
execute the murderer (B) *Nu 35:19*
put the murderer to death *Nu 35:19*
(R)
he meeteth him, he shall *s.* *Nu 35:19*
him
of blood shall *s.* the *Nu 35:21*
murderer
shall surely be put to death *Nu 35:21*
(A)(E)(R)
shall certainly be executed *Nu 35:21*
(B)
out to *s.* them in the *De 9:28*
wilderness
the way is long, and *s.* him *De 19:6*
he shall smite him mortally *De 19:6*
(B)(E)(R)
reward to *s.* an innocent *De 27:25*
person
bribe to murder (B) *De 27:25*
children of Israel *s.* with the *Jos 13:22*
sword
Israelites killed with the *Jos 13:22*
sword (A)(R)
saved them alive, I would not *J'g 8:19*
s. you
I would not kill you (B) *J'g 8:19*
his firstborn, Up, and *s.* them *J'g 8:20*
stand up and kill them (B) *J'g 8:20*
Draw thy sword, and *s.* me *J'g 9:54*
because the Lord would *s.* *1Sa 2:25*
them
ark, to us, to *s.* us and our *1Sa 5:10*
people
to kill us and our people (B) *1Sa 5:10;*
5:11
that it *s.* us not, and our *1Sa 5:11*
people
sheep and *s.* them here, and *1Sa 14:34*
eat
but *s.* both man and woman *1Sa 15:3*
I will *s.* you (B) *1Sa 17:46*
blood, to *s.* David without a *1Sa 19:5*
cause
him, and to *s.* him in the *1Sa 19:11*
morning
kill him in the morning *1Sa 19:11*
(A)(B)(R)
to me in the bed, that I may *1Sa 19:15*
s. him
that I may dispatch him (B) *1Sa 19:15*
that I may kill him (R) *1Sa 19:15*
be in me iniquity, *s.* me *1Sa 20:8*
thyself
kill me yourself (A) *1Sa 20:8*
you yourself dispatch me (B) *1Sa 20:8*
determined of his father to *1Sa 20:33*
s. David
determined to kill David *1Sa 20:33*
(A)(B)
to put David to death *1Sa 20:33*
(E)(R)
Turn, and *s.* the priests of *1Sa 22:17*
the Lord
execute the Lord's priests *1Sa 22:17*
(B)
kill the priests of the Lord *1Sa 22:17*
(R)
Stand upon me, and *s.* me *2Sa 1:9*
stand and kill me (B) *2Sa 1:9*
it was not of the king to *s.* *2Sa 3:37*
Abner

Saul sought to *s.* them in his *2Sa 21:2*
zeal
tried to destroy them (B) *2Sa 21:2*
not *s.* his servant with the *1Ki 1:51*
sword
not kill his servant (B) *1Ki 1:51*
the living child, and in no *1Ki 3:26;*
wise *s.* it *3:27*
do not kill him (B) *1Ki 3:26; 3:27*
did Baasha *s.* him, and *1Ki 15:28*
reigned in
Baasha killed him (B)(R) *1Ki 15:28*
to remembrance, and to *s.* *1Ki 17:18*
my son
to kill my son (B) *1Ki 17:18*
cause the death of my son (R) *1Ki 17:18*
into the hand of Ahab, to *s.* *1Ki 18:9*
me
to be slain (A) *1Ki 18:9*
to kill him (B)(R) *1Ki 18:9*
he cannot find thee, he shall *1Ki 18:12*
s. me
he will kill me (A)(B)(R) *1Ki 18:12;*
18:14
Elijah is here: and he shall *1Ki 18:14*
s. me
the sword of Hazael shall *1Ki 19:17*
Jehu *s.*
will kill (B) *1Ki 19:17*
the sword of Jehu shall *1Ki 19:17*
Elisha *s.*
from me, a lion shall *s.* thee *1Ki 20:36*
a lion will kill you (B)(R) *1Ki 20:36*
young men will thou *s.* with *2Ki 8:12*
young men you will kill (B) *2Ki 8:12*
the captains, Go in, and *s.* *2Ki 10:25*
them
enter and kill them (B) *2Ki 10:25*
s. them, because they know *2Ki 17:26*
not
they are killing them *2Ki 17:26*
(A)(R)
killed some of them (B) *2Ki 17:26*
utterly to *s.* and destroy them *2Ch 20:23*
to destroy and *2Ch 20:23*
annihilate them (B)
destroying them utterly (R) *2Ch 20:23*
S. her not in the house of the *2Ch 23:14*
Lord
and *s.* them, and cause the *Ne 4:11*
work to
for they will come to *s.* thee *Ne 6:10*
they are coming to kill you *Ne 6:10*
(A)(B)(R)
the night will they come to *s.* *Ne 6:10*
thee
to *s.* and to cause to perish, all *Es 8:11*
If the scourge *s.* suddenly, he *Job 9:23*
will
Though he *s.* me, yet will I *Job 13:15*
trust
the viper's tongue shall *s.* *Job 20:16*
him
Evil shall *s.* the wicked: and *Ps 34:21*
they
and to *s.* such as be of *Ps 37:14*
upright
righteous, and seeketh to *s.* *Ps 37:32*
him
seeks to put him to death *Ps 37:32*
(A)(B)
S. them not, lest my people *Ps 59:11*
forget
s. the widow and the stranger *Ps 94:6*
they kill the widow (B) *Ps 94:6*
might even *s.* the broken in *Ps 109:16*
heart
Surely thou wilt *s.* the *Ps 139:19*
wicked
away of the simple shall *s.* *Pr 1:32*
them
of his lips shall he *s.* the *Isa 11:4*
wicked
and he shall *s.* thy remnant *Isa 14:30*
he shall *s.* the dragon that is *Isa 27:1*
in the
for the Lord God shall *s.* *Isa 65:15*
thee, and
lion out of the forest shall *s.* *Jer 5:6*
them
sword to *s.* and the dogs to *Jer 15:3*
tear
their counsel against me to *s.* *Jer 18:23*
me
and shall *s.* them with the *Jer 20:4*
sword
he shall *s.* them before your *Jer 29:21*
eyes
son of Nethaniah to *s.* thee *Jer 40:14*

and I will s. Ishmael the son *Jer 40:15* of
wherefore should he s. thee, *Jer 40:15* that
that said unto Ishmael, S. us *Jer 41:8* not
S. all her bullocks; let them *Jer 50:27* go
S. utterly old and young, both *Eze 9:6*
to s. the souls that should *Eze 13:19* not die
they shall s. their sons and *Eze 23:47* their
s. with the sword thy *Eze 26:8* daughters in
he shall s. thy people by the *Eze 26:11* sword
to s. thereon the burnt *Eze 40:39* offering
they shall s. the burnt offering *Eze 44:11*
was gone forth to s. the wise *Da 2:14* men
a dry land, and s. her with *Ho 2:3* thirst
all its princes I will kill (B) *Ho 2:3*
I s. even the beloved fruit of *Ho 9:16* their
will s. all the princes thereof *Am 2:3* with
s. the last of them with the *Am 9:1* sword
the sword, and it shall s. them *Am 9:4*
spare continually to s. the *Hab 1:17* nations
Whose possessors s. them, *Zec 11:5* and hold
and some of them they shall *Lu 11:49* s. and
they will put to death (A) *Lu 11:49*
they will kill *Lu 11:49* (B)(E)(N)(P)(R)
hither, and s. them before *Lu 19:27* me
slaughter them in my presence *Lu 19:27* (A)(N)
execute them in my presence *Lu 19:27* (B)(P)
Jesus, and sought to s. him *Joh 5:16*
sought to kill him (A) *Joh 5:16*
heart, and took counsel to s. *Ac 5:33* them
to kill his disciples *Ac 5:33* (A)(P)(R)
determined to destroy them *Ac 5:33* (B)
wanted to put them to death *Ac 5:33* (N)
but they went about to s. him *Ac 9:29*
they undertook to murder him *Ac 9:29* (B)(N)
seeking to kill him (E)(R) *Ac 9:29*
made several attempts on his *Ac 9:29* life (P)
unto me, Arise, Peter; s. and *Ac 11:7* eat
kill and eat *Ac 11:7* (A)(B)(E)(N)(P)(R)
s. with the breast (A)(E)(R) *2Th 2:8*
year, for to s. the third part of *Re 9:15* men
to destroy one third of men *Re 9:15* (A)
kill one third of men *Re 9:15* (B)(E)(N)(P)(R)

SLAYER

that the s. may flee thither *Nu 35:11*
between the s. and the *Nu 35:24* revenger
congregation shall deliver the *Nu 35:25* s.
But if the s. shall at any *Nu 35:26* time come
the revenger of blood kill the *Nu 35:27* s.
s. shall return into the land *Nu 35:28* of his
That the s. might flee thither *De 4:42*
that every s. may flee thither *De 19:3*
this is the case of the s. which *De 19:4*
avenger of the blood pursue *De 19:6* the s.
That the s. that killeth any *Jos 20:3* person
they shall not deliver the s. up *Jos 20:5* into
then shall the s. return, and *Jos 20:6* come

city of refuge for s. *Jos 21:13;*
    21:21, 27, 32, 38
to give it into the hand of *Eze 21:11* the s.

SLAYETH

him, Therefore whosoever s. *Ge 4:15* Cain
his neighbour, and s. him *De 22:26*
man, and envy s. the silly one *Job 5:2*
before him that s. thee, I am *Eze 28:9* God
in the hand of him that s. *Eze 28:9* thee

SLAYING

s. of Chedorlaomer (A) *Ge 14:17*
end of s. all the inhabitants *Jos 8:24* of Ai
had made an end of s. them *Jos 10:20* with
father, in s. his seventy *J'g 9:56* brethren
from s. the Philistine (B) *1Sa 17:57;*   *18:6*
thought of s. David (S) *2Sa 21:16*
whom I sojourn, by s. her *1Ki 17:20* son
s. the Moabites (A) *2Ki 3:24*
s. oxen, and killing sheep, *Isa 22:13* eating
s. the children in the valleys *Isa 57:5*
to pass, while they were s. *Eze 9:8* them

SLAYS

that s. him (A)(B)(R) *De 27:24*

SLEDGE

like a heavy s. hammer (A) *Pr 25:18*
with a threshing s. (B)(R) *Isa 28:27;*   *14:15*

SLEDGES

with iron s. (A)(R) *Am 1:3*

SLEDS

iron threshing s. (B) *Am 1:3*

SLEEKER

mouth s. than butter (B) *Ps 55:21*

SLEEP

a deep s. to fall upon Adam *Ge 2:21*
down, a deep s. fell upon *Ge 15:12* Abram
and lay down in that place to *Ge 28:11* s.
and Jacob awake out of his *Ge 28:16* s.
and my s. departed from *Ge 31:40* mine eyes
for his skin: wherein shall he *Ex 22:27* s.
poor, shall not s. with *De 24:12* his pledge
that he may s. in his own *De 24:13* raiment
thou shalt s. with thy fathers *De 31:16*
in a deep s. (B)(E) *J'g 4:21*
And he awaked out of s. and *J'g 16:14* went
she made him s. upon her *J'g 16:19* knees
he awoke out of his s. and *J'g 16:20* said
was, and Samuel was laid *1Sa 3:3* down to s.
a deep s. from the Lord was *1Sa 26:12* fallen
and thou shalt s. with thy *2Sa 7:12* fathers
the king shall s. with his *1Ki 1:21* fathers
that night could not the king *Es 6:1* s.
when deep s. falleth on men *Job 4:13*
for now shall I s. in the dust *Job 7:21*
awake, nor be raised out of *Job 14:12* their s.

when deep s. falleth upon *Job 33:15* men, in
both lay me down in peace, and *Ps 4:8* s.
God: lighten mine eyes, lest I *Ps 13:3* s.
lest I s. the s. of death *Ps 13:3*
spoiled, they have slept their s. *Ps 76:5*
and horse is cast into a dead *Ps 76:6* s.
the Lord awaked as one out *Ps 78:65* of s.
as with a flood: they are as a *Ps 90:5* s.
Israel shall neither slumber *Ps 121:4* nor s.
for so he giveth his beloved s. *Ps 127:2*
I will not give s. to mine *Ps 132:4* eyes, or
down, and thy s. shall be sweet *Pr 3:24*
For they s. not, except they *Pr 4:16* have
and their s. is taken away, *Pr 4:16* unless
Give not s. to thine eyes, nor *Pr 6:4*
How long wilt thou s. O *Pr 6:9* sluggard
when wilt thou arise out of thy *Pr 6:9* s.
Yet a little s. a little *Pr 6:10;* slumber, a *24:33*
a little folding of the hands to *Pr 6:10;* s. *24:33*
Slothfulness casteth into a *Pr 19:15* deep s.
Love not s. lest thou come to *Pr 20:13*
s. of a labouring man is sweet *Ec 5:12*
of the rich will not suffer him *Ec 5:12* to s.
nor night seeth s. with his eyes *Ec 8:16*
I s. but my heart waketh: it is *Ca 5:2*
none shall slumber nor s.; *Isa 5:27* neither
out upon you the spirit of *Isa 29:10* deep s.
and my s. was sweet unto me *Jer 31:26*
that they may rejoice, and s. *Jer 51:39*
a perpetual s. and not wake *Jer 51:39;*   *51:57*
mighty men: and they shall s. *Jer 51:57*
wilderness, and s. in the *Eze 34:25* woods
and his s. brake from him *Da 2:1*
him: and his s. went from him *Da 6:18*
I was in a deep s. on my *Da 8:18;* face *10:9*
many of them that s. in the *Da 12:2* dust
man that is wakened out of *Zec 4:1* his s.
Joseph being raised from s. *M't 1:24* did as
S. on now, and take your *M't 26:45;* rest *M'k 14:41*
And should s. and rise night *M'k 4:27*
were with him were heavy *Lu 9:32* with s.
Why s. ye? Rise and pray, lest *Lu 22:46* ye
that I may awake him out of *Joh 11:11* s.
Lord, if he s. he shall do *Joh 11:12* well
had spoken of taking of rest *Joh 11:13* in s.
fell on s. and was laid unto *Ac 13:36* his
of the prison awaking out of *Ac 16:27* his s.
being fallen into a deep s. *Ac 20:9*
he sunk down with s. and fell *Ac 20:9*
he sagged down in s. (B)(R) *Ac 20:9*
it is high time to awake out *Ro 13:11* of s.
sickly among you, and many *1Co 11:30* s.
We shall not all s. but we *1Co 15:51* shall all
so them also which s. in *1Th 4:14* Jesus
let us not s. as do others: but *1Th 5:6*
For they that s. s. in the night *1Th 5:7*
for us, that, whether we *1Th 5:10* wake or s.

SLEEPER

What meanest thou, O s.? *Jon 1:6* arise

SLEEPEST

why s. thou, O Lord? arise,   *Ps 44:23*
cast
when thou s. it shall keep thee   *Pr 6:22*
saith unto Peter, Simon, s.   *M'k 14:37*
thou
Awake thou that s. and arise   *Eph 5:14*
from

SLEEPETH

peradventure he s. and must   *1Ki 18:27*
be
s. in harvest is a son that   *Pr 10:5*
causeth
wait: their baker s. all the night   *Ho 7:6*
for the maid is not dead, but   *M't 9:24*
s.
the damsel is not dead, but s.   *M'k 5:39*
weep not; she is not dead, but   *Lu 8:52*
s.
unto them, Our friend   *Joh 11:11*
Lazarus s.

SLEEPING

Saul lay s. within the trench   *1Sa 26:7*
s. lying down, loving to   *Isa 56:10*
slumber
coming suddenly he find you   *M'k 13:36*
s.
he cometh, and findeth them   *M'k 14:37*
s.
he found them s. for sorrow   *Lu 22:45*
Peter was s. between two   *Ac 12:6*
soldiers

SLEET

with s. their sycamores (B)   *Ps 78:47*

SLEIGHT

by the s. of men, and cunning   *Eph 4:14*

SLEPT

to fall upon Adam, and he s.   *Ge 2:21*
And he s. and dreamed the   *Ge 41:5*
second
Uriah s. at the door of the   *2Sa 11:9*
king's
David s. with his fathers, and   *1Ki 2:10*
while thine handmaid s. and   *1Ki 3:20*
laid
that David s. with his fathers   *1Ki 11:21*
And Solomon s. with his   *1Ki 11:43*
fathers
he s. with his fathers, and   *1Ki 14:20*
Nadab
And Rehoboam s. with his   *1Ki 14:31;*
fathers   *2Ch 12:16*
And Abijam s. with his   *1Ki 15:8*
fathers, and
Asa s. with his fathers and   *1Ki 15:24*
So Baasha s. with his   *1Ki 16:6*
fathers, and
So Omri s. with his   *1Ki 16:28*
fathers, and
he lay and s. under a juniper   *1Ki 19:5*
tree
So Ahab s. with his fathers   *1Ki 22:40*
Jehoshaphat s. with his   *1Ki 22:50;*
fathers   *2Ch 21:1*
And Joram s. with his   *2Ki 8:24*
fathers, and
And Jehu s. with his fathers   *2Ki 10:35*
And Jehoahaz s. with his   *2Ki 13:9*
fathers
And Joash s. with his   *2Ki 13:13*
fathers and
And Jehoash s. with his   *2Ki 14:16*
fathers
that the king s. with his   *2Ki 14:22;*
fathers   *2Ch 26:2*
And Jeroboam s. with his   *2Ki 14:29*
fathers
So Azariah s. with his   *2Ki 15:7*
fathers; and
And Menahem s. with his   *2Ki 15:22*
fathers
Jotham s. with his fathers   *2Ki 15:38;*
    2Ch 27:9
Ahaz s. with his fathers, and   *2Ki 16:20;*
    2Ch 28:27
And Hezekiah s. with his   *2Ki 20:21;*
fathers   *2Ch 32:33*
And Manasseh s. with his   *2Ki 21:18;*
fathers   *2Ch 33:20*

So Jehoiakim s. with his   *2Ki 24:6*
fathers
Solomon s. with his fathers   *2Ch 9:31*
So Abijah s. with his   *2Ch 14:1*
fathers, and
Asa s. with his fathers, and   *2Ch 16:13*
died in
So Uzziah s. with his   *2Ch 26:23*
fathers, and
and been quiet, I should have   *Job 3:13*
s.
I laid me down and s.; I   *Ps 3:5*
awaked
spoiled, they have s. their sleep *Ps 76:5*
But while men s. his enemy   *M't 13:25*
came
tarried, they all slumbered   *M't 25:5*
and s.
bodies of the saints which s.   *M't 27:52*
arose
and stole him away while we   *M't 28:13*
s.
the firstfruits of them that s. *1Co 15:20*

SLEW

slew (A)   *Ex 12:27;*
12:29; Nu 3:13; 21:35; Jos 7:5; 10:10;
11:17; 1Sa 6:19; 2Sa 14:7; 2Ki 8:21;
    19:35
slew (R)   *Ex 12:27;*
Nu 3:13; 8:17; 21:24, 35; Jos 7:5;
10:10; J'g 9:43; 2Ki 15:25; 19:35;
    Ps 78:31; Isa 37:36, 38
the Lord s. all the firstborn in *Ex 13:15*
Egypt
s. bullock and took the blood   *Le 8:15;*
    8:23
Aaron s. the calf of sin   *Le 9:8;*
offering   *9:15*
s. burnt offering, presented the *Le 9:12*
blood
slew (B)   *Nu 8:17; 21:35*
they s. all the males of   *Nu 31:7*
Midian
s. kings of Midian, Balaam   *Nu 31:8*
also they s.
they turned and s. the men of   *Jos 8:21*
Ai
delivered Gibeonites, they s.   *Jos 9:26*
them not
Joshua s. five kings and   *Jos 10:26*
hanged them
they s. of them in Bezek 10,000 *J'g 1:4*
men
s. Sheshai; s. Canaanites   *J'g 1:10; 1:17*
they s. of Moab 10,000 men,   *J'g 3:29*
all lusty
Shamgar s. of the Philistines   *J'g 3:31*
600 men
they s. Oreb and Zeeb the two   *J'g 7:25*
princes
s. men of Penuel; s. Zebah,   *J'g 8:17;*
Zalmunna   *8:21*
what manner of men whom ye   *J'g 8:18*
s.
Abimelech s. his brethren   *J'g 9:5*
seventy persons on one stone
Samson s. thirty men of   *J'g 14:19*
Ashkelon
with the jawbone Samson s.   *J'g 15:15*
1000 men
delivered our enemy, who s.   *J'g 16:24*
many of us
dead, he s. at his death were   *J'g 16:30*
more
Elkanah and Hannah s. a   *1Sa 1:25*
bullock
the Philistines s. of Israel   *1Sa 4:2*
4000 men
Israel s. Ammonites until   *1Sa 11:11*
heat of day
his armour-bearer s. after   *1Sa 14:13*
him
people, s. oxen and calves   *1Sa 14:32*
on ground
every man brought his ox   *1Sa 14:34*
and s. them there
thy servant s. both the lion   *1Sa 17:36*
and the bear
put his life in his hand, and   *1Sa 19:5*
s. Philistine
Doeg s. 85 persons that did   *1Sa 22:18*
wear an ephod
of whom they sang, Saul s.   *1Sa 29:5*
thousands
the Amalekites s. not any   *1Sa 30:2*
great or small
the Philistines s. Jonathan   *1Sa 31:2*
and Abindab

Joab and Abishai his brother   *2Sa 3:30*
s. Abner
David s. them and cut off   *2Sa 4:12*
their hands
David s. of the Syrians 22,000   *2Sa 8:5*
men
David s. men of 700   *2Sa 10:18*
chariots of Syrians
for Saul, because he s. the   *2Sa 21:1*
Gibeonites
s. two lion-like men, s. lion   *2Sa 23:20;*
in midst of a pit   *1Ch 11:22*
he s. an Egyptian, a goodly   *2Sa 23:21;*
man   *1Ch 11:23*
did to Abner and Amasa,   *1Ki 2:5*
whom he s.
Zimri on the throne s. all   *1Ki 16:11*
house of Baasha
what I did when Jezebel s.   *1Ki 18:13*
prophets of Lord
took them, and Elijah s.   *1Ki 18:40*
prophets of Baal
had Zimri peace, who s. his   *2Ki 9:31*
master
behold, I s. him, but who s.   *2Ki 10:9*
all these
he s. all that remained to   *2Ki 10:17*
Ahab in Samaria
the people s. Mattan the   *2Ki 11:18*
priest of Baal
they s. Athaliah   *2Ki 11:20*
    2Ch 23:15, 17
Amaziah s. servants *2Ki 14:5; 2Ch 25:3*
but their children he s. not   *2Ki 14:6;*
    2Ch 25:4
he s. of Edom in valley of   *2Ki 14:7;*
salt   *1Ch 18:12*
king of Assyria took   *2Ki 16:9*
Damascus and s. Rezin
the Lord sent lions which s.   *2Ki 17:25*
some of them
servants of Amon conspired   *2Ki 21:23*
and s. him
people of the land s. them   *2Ki 21:24;*
    2Ch 33:25
Josiah s. all the priests of   *2Ki 23:20*
the high places
s. sons of Zedekiah   *2Ki 25:7;*
    Jer 39:6; 52:10
whom men of Gath in that   *1Ch 7:21*
land s.
Jehoram s. all his brethren   *2Ch 21:4*
with sword
Jehu found, and s. the   *2Ch 22:8*
princes of Judah
Pekah s. in Judah in one day *2Ch 28:6*
120,000
they s. thy prophets which   *Ne 9:26*
testified
the Jews s. of their foes 75,000 *Es 9:16*
wrath of God s. the fattest of *Ps 78:31*
them
when he s. them, then they   *Ps 78:34*
sought him
turned waters into blood,   *Ps 105:29*
and s. their fish
s. great kings; s. famous   *Ps 135:10;*
kings   *136:18*
he that killeth an ox is as if   *Isa 66:3*
he s. a man
because he s. me not from   *Jer 20:17*
the womb
Ishmael s. all the Jews with   *Jer 41:3*
him
s. them not among their   *Jer 41:8*
brethren
s. all that were pleasant to the *La 2:4*
eye
fire s. the men that took up   *Da 3:22*
Shadrach
whom he would be s. he kept   *Da 5:19*
alive
Herod sent, and s. all the   *M't 2:16*
children
the remnant took his servants *M't 22:6*
and s. them
whom ye s. between the   *M't 23:35*
temple and altar
on whom tower in Siloam fell *Lu 13:4*
and s.
raised Jesus, whom s. and   *Ac 5:30*
hanged on tree
Jesus whom they s. and   *Ac 10:39*
hanged on a tree
for sin by the commandment   *Ro 7:11*
s. me
not as Cain who s. his   *1Jo 3:12*
brother

SLEW *HIM*

Cain rose up against Abel and　*Ge 4:8*
s. him
Er was wicked, and the Lord　*Ge 38:7*
s. him
thing displeased Lord, and he　*Ge 38:10*
s. him
men say not of me, a woman　*J'g 9:54*
s. him
they took and *s. him* at　*J'g 12:6*
passages of Jordan
I caught him by beard and　*1Sa 17:35*
s. him
David smote the Philistine　*1Sa 17:50*
and *s. him*
so I stood upon him and *s.*　*2Sa 1:10*
him
they smote Ish-bosheth and　*2Sa 4:7*
him
I took hold of him, and *s.*　*2Sa 4:10*
him in Ziklag
young men compassed　*2Sa 18:15*
Absalom and *s. him*
Jonathan the son of　*2Sa 21:21*
Shimeah *s. him*
went down and *s. him* with　*2Sa 23:21*
own spear
Benaiah fell upon Joab and *s.*　*1Ki 2:34*
him
lion met him by the way,　*1Ki 13:24;*
and *s. him*　　　　　　　　　*20:36*
I conspired against my　*2Ki 9:10*
master and *s. him*
Amaziah fled, but they sent　*2Ki 14:19;*
after him and *s. him*　　*2Ch 25:27*
Shallum conspired against　*2Ki 15:10*
him and *s. him*
Menahem smote Shallum,　*2Ki 15:14*
and *s. him*
Hoshea conspired against　*2Ki 15:30*
Pekah and *s. him*
Pharaoh-necho *s. him* at　*2Ki 23:29*
Megiddo
inquired not of Lord:　*1Ch 10:14*
therefore *s.* he *him*
hid Joash, so that Athaliah　*2Ch 22:11*
s. him not
his own servants *s. him* on　*2Ch 24:25*
his bed
they that came forth of his　*2Ch 32:21*
own bowels *s. him*
his servants *s. him* in his　*2Ch 33:24*
own house
fetched Urijah to Jehoiakim　*Jer 26:23*
who *s. him*
Ishmael *s. him* whom king　*Jer 41:2*
made governor
they cast him out of　*M't 21:39*
vineyard and *s. him*
I kept the raiment of them　*Ac 22:20*
that *s. him*

SLEWEST

whom thou *s.* in the valley　*1Sa 21:9*
of Elah

SLIDDEN

this people of Jerusalem *s.*　*Jer 8:5*
back
turned away with perpetual　*Jer 8:5*
turning away (A)
turned away in perpetual　*Jer 8:5*
backsliding (B)(R)

SLIDE

their foot shall *s.* in due time　*De 32:35*
when their foot shall slip　*De 32:35*
(B)(R)
the Lord; therefore I shall not　*Ps 26:1*
s.
his heart; none of his steps　*Ps 37:31*
shall *s.*
his steps shall not waver (B)　*Ps 37:31*
his steps do not slip (R)　*Ps 37:31*

SLIDETH

s. back as a backsliding heifer　*Ho 4:16*
Israel has behaved stubbornly　*Ho 4:16*
(A)(E)
Israel is stubborn (B)(R)　*Ho 4:16*

SLIGHT

do not *s.* grace (B)　*Ga 2:21*
the slighter does not *s.* (B)　*1Th 4:8*

SLIGHTER

the *s.* does not slight (B)　*1Th 4:8*

SLIGHTLY

of the daughter of my people　*Jer 6:14;*
s.　　　　　　　　　　　　　*8:11*

SLIGHTS

s., pays no attention to (A)　*Lu 10:16*

SLIME

stone, and *s.* had they for　*Ge 11:3*
morter
asphalt for mortar (B)　*Ge 11:3*
bitumen for mortar (R)　*Ge 11:3*
daubed it with *s.* and with　*Ex 2:3*
pitch
daubing it with bitumen and　*Ex 2:3*
pitch (A)(R)
daubed it with asphalt and　*Ex 2:3*
pitch (B)

SLIMEPITS

the vale of Siddim was full　*Ge 14:10*
of *s.*
slime or bitumen pits (A)　*Ge 14:10*
full of tar pits (B)　*Ge 14:10*
full of bitumen pits (R)　*Ge 14:10*

SLING

could *s.* stones at an hair　*J'g 20:16*
breadth
and his *s.* as in his hand:　*1Sa 17:40*
and he
with a *s.* and with a stone　*1Sa 17:50*
enemies, them shall he *s.*　*1Sa 25:29*
out, as
as out of the middle of a *s.*　*1Sa 25:29*
As he that bindeth a stone in　*Pr 26:8*
a *s.*
s. out the inhabitants of the　*Jer 10:18*
land
devour, and subdue with *s.*　*Zec 9:15*
stones

SLINGERS

the *s.* went about it, and　*2Ki 3:25*
smote it

SLINGS

and bows, and *s.* to cast　*2Ch 26:14*
stones

SLINGSTONES

s. are turned with him into　*Job 41:28*

SLIP

when their foot shall *s.*　*De 32:35*
(B)(R)
me; so that my feet did not　*2Sa 22:37*
s.
He that is ready to *s.* with　*Job 12:5*
his feet
thy paths, that my footsteps *s.*　*Ps 17:5*
not
under me, that my feet did　*Ps 18:36*
not
his steps do not *s.* (R)　*Ps 27:31*
we all make many a *s.*, who　*Ps 113:2*
makes no *s.* (B)
at any time we should let　*Heb 2:1*
them *s.*

SLIPPED

he *s.* away out of Saul's　*1Sa 19:10*
presence
gone; my steps had well nigh *s.*　*Ps 73:2*
s. on his clothes (P)　*Joh 21:7*
s. in (R)　*Ga 2:4*

SLIPPERY

Let their way be dark and *s.*　*Ps 35:6*
thou didst set them in *s.*　*Ps 73:18*
places
way shall be unto them as *s.*　*Jer 23:12*
ways
heart *s.* (B)　*Heb 10:2*

SLIPPETH

and the head *s.* from the helve　*De 19:5*
when my foot *s.* they magnify　*Ps 38:16*
When I said, My foot *s.*; thy　*Ps 94:18*
mercy

SLIPS

and shalt set it with strange　*Isa 17:10*
s.
s. in one point (B)　*Jas 2:10*

SLOPES

the *s.* of Pisgah (S)　　　　*De 3:17;*
　　　　　　　4:49; Jos 12:3; 13:20
the *s.* of Pisgah (B)(E)(R)　*De 4:49*
the *s.* (A)(E)(R)　*Jos 10:40; 12:8*

SLOTHFUL

be not *s.* to go, and to enter　*J'g 18:9*
to
Do not be slow (A)(R)　*J'g 18:9*
Do not delay (B)　*J'g 18:9*
but the *s.* shall be under　*Pr 12:24*
tribute
the slack hand (B)　*Pr 12:24*
The *s.* man roasteth not that　*Pr 12:27*
which
way of the *s.* man is as an　*Pr 15:19*
hedge
The way of the sluggard　*Pr 15:19*
(A)(B)(E)(R)
He also that is *s.* in his work　*Pr 18:9*
is
loose and slack in his work　*Pr 18:9*
(A)
he who is slack in his work　*Ps 18:9*
(B)(E)(R)
A *s.* man hideth his hand in　*Ps 19:24*
his
the sluggard buries his hand　*Ps 19:24*
(A)(B)(E)(R)
The desire of the *s.* killeth　*Pr 21:25*
him
desire of the sluggard slays　*Pr 21:25*
him (B)(E)(R)
The *s.* man saith, There is a　*Pr 22:13;*
lion　　　　　　　　　　　　　*26:13*
The sluggard says　*Pr 22:13;*
(A)(B)(E)(R)　　　　　　　　　*26:13*
I went by the field of the *s.*,　*Pr 24:30*
and by
went by the field of the lazy　*Pr 24:30*
man (A)(B)
the field of the sluggard　*Pr 24:30*
(E)(R)
hinges, so doth the *s.* upon　*Pr 26:14*
his bed
the lazy man upon his bed　*Pr 26:14*
(A)
the sluggard upon his bed　*Pr 26:14*
(B)(E)(R)
s. hideth his hand in his　*Pr 26:15*
bosom
the sluggard buries his hand　*Pr 26:15*
(B)(E)(R)
Thou wicked and *s.* servant　*M't 25:26*
wicked lazy, and idle　*M't 25:26*
servant (A)
Despicable and lazy slave　*M't 25:26*
(B)
You lazy rascal (N)　*M't 25:26*
You're a wicked, lazy　*M't 25:26*
servant (P)
Not *s.* in business; fervent in　*Ro 12:11*
spirit
Never lag in zeal, in earnest　*Ro 12:11*
endeavor (A)
never slacking in interest (B)　*Ro 12:11*
With unflagging energy (N)　*Ro 12:11*
Never flag in zeal (R)　*Ro 12:11*
That ye be not *s.* but　*Heb 6:12*
followers of
not disinterested or spiritual　*Heb 6:12*
sluggards (A)(B)
not sluggish (E)(R)　*Heb 6:12*
not to become lazy (N)　*Heb 6:12*
not grow slack (P)　*Heb 6:12*

SLOTHFULNESS

S. casteth into a deep sleep　*Pr 19:15*
Laziness makes one sleep　*Pr 19:15*
heavily (B)
By much *s.* the building　*Ec 10:18*
decayeth

through idleness the house leaks (A)   *Ec 10:18*
because of slack hands the house leaks (B)   *Ec 10:18*
through indolence the house leaks (R)   *Ec 10:18*

SLOUGH

plunge me into a *s.* (B)   *Job 9:31*

SLOW

s. of speech, and of a *s.* tongue   *Ex 4:10*
s. to anger, and of great kindness   *Ne 9:17; Joe 2:13; Jon 4:2*
s. to anger, and plenteous in mercy   *Ps 103:8*
s. to anger, and of great mercy   *Ps 145:8*
He that is *s.* to wrath is of great   *Pr 14:29*
that is *s.* to anger appeaseth strife   *Pr 15:18*
He that is *s.* to anger is better than   *Pr 16:32*
The Lord is *s.* to anger, and great   *Na 1:3*
O fools, and *s.* of heart to believe   *Lu 24:25*
alway liars, evil beasts, *s.* bellies   *Tit 1:12*
to hear, *s.* to speak, *s.* to wrath   *Jas 1:19*
s., as some men suppose (N)   *2Pe 3:9*

SLOWLY

when we had sailed *s.* many days   *Ac 27:7*

SLOWNESS

some people's conceptions of *s.* (A)   *2Pe 3:9*

SLUGGARD

Go to the ant, thou *s.*; consider   *Pr 6:6*
How long wilt thou sleep, O *s.*   *Pr 6:9*
so is the *s.* to them that send him   *Pr 10:26*
The soul of the *s.* desireth, and   *Pr 13:4*
the way of the *s.* (A)(B)(E)(R)   *Pr 15:19*
the *s.* buries his hand (A)(B)(E)(R)   *Pr 19:24*
The *s.* will not plow by reason of   *Pr 20:4*
the *s.* slays him (B)(E)(R)   *Pr 21:25*
the *s.* says (A)(B)(E)(R)   *Pr 22:13; 26:13*
the field of the *s.* (E)(R)   *Pr 24:30*
the *s.* buries his hand (B)(E)(R)   *Pr 26:15*
The *s.* is wiser in his own conceit   *Pr 26:16*

SLUGGARDS

not spiritual *s.* (A)(B)   *Heb 6:12*

SLUGGISH

not *s.*, but followers (E)(R)   *Heb 6:12*

SLUICES

that make *s.* and ponds for fish   *Isa 19:10*
those who build dams will be grieved (A)   *Isa 19:10*

SLUMBER

he that keepeth thee will not *s.*   *Ps 121:3*
Israel shall neither *s.* nor sleep   *Ps 121:4*
to my eyes, or *s.* to mine eyelids   *Ps 132:4*
thine eyes, nor *s.* to thine eyelids   *Pr 6:4*
Yet a little sleep, a little *s.* a   *Pr 6:10; 24:33*
none shall *s.* nor sleep; neither   *Isa 5:27*
sleeping, lying down, loving to *s.*   *Isa 56:10*
Thy shepherds *s.* O king of   *Na 3:18*
hath given them the spirit of *s.*   *Ro 11:8*

SLUMBERED

tarried, they all *s.* and slept   *M't 25:5*

SLUMBERETH

not, and their damnation *s.* not   *2Pe 2:3*

SLUMBERINGS

upon men, in *s.* upon the bed   *Job 33:15*

SLUMPED

he *s.* in his chariot (B)   *2Ki 9:24*

SMALL

with blindness, both *s.* and great   *Ge 19:11*
a *s.* matter that thou hast taken   *Ge 30:15*
shall become *s.* dust in all the land   *Ex 9:9*
wilderness, lay a *s.* round thing   *Ex 16:14*
as *s.* as the hoar frost on the ground   *Ex 16:14*
every *s.* matter they shall judge   *Ex 18:22*
s. matter they judged themselves   *Ex 18:26*
thou shalt beat some of it very *s.*   *Ex 30:36*
full of sweet incense beaten *s.*   *Le 16:12*
it but a *s.* thing unto you, that   *Nu 16:9*
s. thing that thou hast brought us   *Nu 16:13*
and took the *s.* towns thereof   *Nu 32:41*
hear the *s.* as well as the great   *De 1:17*
stamped it, and ground it very *s.*   *De 9:21*
even until it was as *s.* as dust   *De 9:21*
divers weights, a great and a *s.*   *De 25:13*
divers measures, a great and a *s.*   *De 25:14*
as the *s.* rain upon the tender herb   *De 32:2*
men of the city, both *s.* and great   *1Sa 5:9*
will do nothing either great or *s.*   *1Sa 20:2*
slew not any, either great or *s.*   *1Sa 30:2*
to them, neither *s.* nor great   *1Sa 30:19*
this was yet a *s.* thing in thy sight   *2Sa 7:19*
be not one *s.* stone found there   *2Sa 17:13*
I beat them as *s.* as the dust of the   *2Sa 22:43*
I desire one *s.* petition of thee   *1Ki 2:20*
and after the fire a still *s.* voice   *1Ki 19:12*
Fight neither with *s.* nor great   *1Ki 22:31*
the place is too *s.* (S)   *2Ki 6:1*
their inhabitants were of *s.* power   *2Ki 19:26*
all the people, both *s.* and great   *2Ki 23:2*
and stamped it *s.* to powder   *2Ki 23:6; 23:15*
all the people both *s.* and great   *2Ki 25:26*
this was a *s.* thing in thine eyes   *1Ch 17:17*
ward, as well the *s.* as the great   *1Ch 25:8*
lots, as well as the *s.* as the great   *1Ch 26:13*
put to death, whether *s.* or great, save   *2Ch 15:13*
Fight ye not with *s.* or great, save   *2Ch 18:30*
came with a *s.* company of men   *2Ch 24:24*
as well to the great as to the *s.*   *2Ch 31:15*
and all the people, great and *s.*   *2Ch 34:30*
thousand and six hundred *s.* cattle   *2Ch 35:8*

offerings five thousand *s.* cattle   *2Ch 35:9*
of the house of God, great and *s.*   *2Ch 36:18*
both unto great and *s.* seven days   *Es 1:5*
honour, both to great and *s.*   *Es 1:20*
The *s.* and great are there   *Job 3:19*
Though thy beginning was *s.*, yet   *Job 8:7*
consolations of God *s.* with thee   *Job 15:11*
he maketh *s.* the drops of water   *Job 36:27*
likewise to the *s.* rain, and to   *Job 37:6*
did I beat them *s.* as the dust before   *Ps 18:42*
both *s.* and great beasts   *Ps 104:25*
fear the Lord, both *s.* and great   *Ps 115:13*
I am *s.* and despised: yet do not   *Ps 119:141*
day of adversity, thy strength is *s.*   *Pr 24:10*
possessions of great and *s.* cattle   *Ec 2:7*
left unto us a very *s.* remnant   *Isa 1:9*
Is it a *s.* thing for you to weary men   *Isa 7:13*
the remnant shall be very *s.*   *Isa 16:14*
all vessels of *s.* quantity from   *Isa 22:24*
thy strangers shall be like as *s.* dust   *Isa 29:5*
their inhabitants were of *s.* power   *Isa 37:27*
counted as the *s.* dust of the balance   *Isa 40:15*
the mountains, and beat them *s.*   *Isa 41:15*
me the *s.* cattle of thy burnt offerings   *Isa 43:23*
For a *s.* moment have I forsaken   *Isa 54:7*
and a *s.* one a strong nation   *Isa 60:22*
Both the great and the *s.* shall die   *Jer 16:6*
them, and they shall not be *s.*   *Jer 30:19*
Yet a *s.* number that escape   *Jer 44:28*
I will make thee *s.* among   *Jer 49:15*
of thy whoredoms a *s.* matter   *Eze 16:20*
Seemeth it a *s.* thing unto you   *Eze 34:18*
become strong with a *s.* people   *Da 11:23*
shall Jacob arise? for he is *s.*   *Am 7:2; 7:5*
forth wheat, making the ephah *s.*   *Am 8:5*
made thee *s.* among the heathen   *Ob 2*
hath despised the day of *s.* things   *Zec 4:10*
that a *s.* ship should wait on him   *M'k 3:9*
And they had a few *s.* fishes   *M'k 8:7*
he had made a scourge of *s.* cords   *Joh 2:15*
five barley loaves, two *s.* fishes   *Joh 6:9*
was no *s.* stir among the soldiers   *Ac 12:18*
no *s.* dissension and disputation   *Ac 15:2*
arose no *s.* stir about that way   *Ac 19:23*
no *s.* gain unto the craftsman   *Ac 19:24*
witnessing both to *s.* and great   *Ac 26:22*
and no *s.* tempest lay on us   *Ac 27:20*
with me it is a very *s.* thing that   *1Co 4:3*
turned about with a very *s.* helm   *Jas 3:4*
that fear thy name, *s.* and great   *Re 11:18*
both *s.* and great, rich and poor   *Re 13:16*
that fear him, both *s.* and great   *Re 19:5*
free and bond, both *s.* and great   *Re 19:18*
And I saw the dead, *s.* and great   *Re 20:12*

SMALLEST

of the *s.* of the tribes of Israel   *1Sa 9:21*
unworthy to judge the *s.* matters   *1Co 6:2*

SMART

for a stranger shall *s.* for it　Pr 11:15
certain calamity comes to　Pr 11:15
him that (B)

SMASH

s. all stone altars (R)　　　Nu 33:52

SMELL

he smelled the *s.* of his　　Ge 27:27
raiment
s. of my sons is as the *s.* of a　Ge 27:27
field
make like unto that, to *s.*　Ex 30:38
thereto
Whoever makes any like　Ex 30:38
perfume (A)(R)
Whoever prepares the like　Ex 30:38
fragrance (B)
I will not *s.* the savour of　Le 26:31
your sweet
see, nor hear, nor eat, nor *s.*　De 4:28
All thy garments *s.* of myrrh　Ps 45:8
noses have they, but they *s.*　Ps 115:6
not
my spikenard sendeth forth　Ca 1:12
the *s.*
fragrance　(A)(B)(E)(R)　　　Ca 1:12;
　　　　　　　　　　　　　　2:13; 4:10
the tender grape give a good *s.*　Ca 2:13
and the *s.* of thine ointments　Ca 4:10
than
the *s.* of thy garments is like　Ca 4:11
odor of garments, odor of　Ca 4:11
Lebanon (A)
fragrance of garments (B)　Ca 4:11
scent of garments (R)　　Ca 4:11
garments is like the *s.* of　Ca 4:11
Lebanon
and the *s.* of thy nose like　Ca 7:8
apples
scent of your breath like apples　Ca 7:8
(A)(R)
fragrance of your breath like　Ca 7:8
apples (B)
The mandrakes give a *s.* and　Ca 7:13
mandrakes give forth　　　Ca 7:13
fragrance (A)(B)(E)(R)
instead of sweet *s.* there shall　Isa 3:24
be
instead of sweet odor (A)　Isa 3:24
instead of sweet spices (E)　Isa 3:24
instead of perfume (R)　　Isa 3:24
nor the *s.* of fire had passed　Da 3:27
on
olive tree, and his *s.* as　　Ho 14:6
Lebanon
his fragrance like Lebanon　Ho 14:6
(A)(B)(R)
not *s.* in your solemn　　　Am 5:21
assemblies
an odour of a sweet *s.*, a　Ph'p 4:18
sacrifice
fragrant odor of an offering　Ph'p 4:18
(A)
a fragrant perfume (B)　　Ph'p 4:18
a fragrant offering (N)(R)　Ph'p 4:18
a lovely fragrance (P)　　Ph'p 4:18

SMELLED

And the Lord *s.* a sweet　　Ge 8:21
savour
Lord discerned the pleasing　Ge 8:21
fragrance (B)
and he *s.* the smell of his　Ge 27:27
raiment
scent of my son is as odor of　Ge 27:27
field (A)

SMELLETH

and he *s.* the battle afar off　Job 39:25
scenting the battle from afar　Job 39:25
(B)

SMELLING

river became foul *s.* (A)(B)(E)　Ex 7:18
my fingers with sweet *s.* myrrh　Ca 5:5
lilies, dropping sweet *s.* myrrh　Ca 5:13
lilies dropping liquid myrrh　Ca 5:13
(A)(B)(E)(R)
were hearing, where were　1Co 12:17
the *s.*

SMELTED

brass is *s.* out of stone (S)　Job 28:2

SMILED

If I *s.* on them (S)　　　　Job 29:24

SMIRCHES

anything that *s.* soul and body　2Co 7:1
(P)

SMITE

neither will I again *s.* any　Ge 8:21
more
never again curse the ground　Ge 8:21
(A)(B)(E)(R)
come to the one company,　Ge 32:8
and *s.* it
destroy it (B)(R)　　　　　Ge 32:8
him, lest he will come and *s.*　Ge 32:11
me
slay me (B)(R)　　　　　　Ge 32:11
s. Egypt with all my wonders　Ex 3:20
strike (B)　　　Ex 3:20; 7:17; 12:12, 23
I will *s.* with the rod that is in　Ex 7:17
mine
I will *s.* all thy borders with　Ex 8:2
frogs
afflict your country with frogs　Ex 8:2
(B)
plague your country with frogs　Ex 8:2
(R)
and *s.* the dust of the land,　Ex 8:16
that it
strike the dust (A)(B)(R)　Ex 8:16
I may *s.* thee and thy people　Ex 9:15
with
struck you (A)(R)　　　　Ex 9:15
stricken you (B)　　　　　Ex 9:15
smitten thee (E)　　　　　Ex 9:15
will *s.* all the firstborn in the　Ex 12:2
land
you, when I *s.* the land of　Ex 12:13
Egypt
pass through to *s.* the　　　Ex 12:23
Egyptians
slay the Egyptians (A)(R)　Ex 12:23
come in unto your houses to　Ex 12:23
s. you
thou shalt *s.* the rock, and　Ex 17:6
there
strike the rock (A)(B)(R)　Ex 17:6
and one *s.* another with a　Ex 21:18
stone
one strikes another (A)(R)　Ex 21:18;
　　　　　　　　　　　　　　　21:20
one hits the other (B)　　Ex 21:18;
　　　　　　　　　　　　　　　21:26
And if a man *s.* his servant,　Ex 21:20
or his
if a man *s.* the eye of his　Ex 21:26
servant
strikes the eye of a slave (R)　Ex 21:26
he *s.* out his manservant's　Ex 21:27
tooth
knocks out his teeth　　　Ex 21:27
(A)(B)(R)
I will *s.* them with the　　Nu 14:12
pestilence
I will destroy them with a　Nu 14:12
plague (B)
I will strike them with　　Nu 14:12
pestilence (R)
that we may *s.* them, and that　Nu 22:6
I may
be able to defeat them　　Nu 22:6
(A)(B)(R)
and shall *s.* the corners of　Nu 24:17
Moab
crush the corners of Moab　Nu 24:17
(A)(B)(R)
Vex the Midianites, and *s.*　Nu 25:17
them
attack them (A)　　　　　Nu 25:17;
　　　　　　　　　　　35:17-18, 21
if he *s.* him with an　　　Nu 35:16
instrument of
he struck him down (A)(R)　Nu 35:16
one hits another (B)　　　Nu 35:16
if he *s.* him with throwing a　Nu 35:17
stone
if he strikes him (B)　　　Nu 35:17;
　　　　　　　　　　　　35:18, 21
if he *s.* him with an hand　Nu 35:18
weapon
Or in enmity *s.* him with his　Nu 35:21
hand

thou shalt *s.* them, and utterly　De 7:2
Thou shalt surely *s.* the　De 13:15
inhabitants
and *s.* him mortally that he　De 19:11
die, and
thou shalt *s.* every male　De 20:13
thereof
shall *s.* thee with a　　　De 28:22
consumption
s. thee with the botch of　De 28:27
Egypt
Lord shall *s.* thee with　　De 28:28
madness
The Lord shall *s.* thee in the　De 28:35
knees
s. through the loins of them　De 33:11
that
thousand men go up and *s.* Ai　Jos 7:3
go up and attack Ai (A)(R)　Jos 7:3
strike at Ai (B)　　　　　Jos 7:3
help me, that we may *s.*　　Jos 10:4
Gibeon
and *s.* the hindmost of them　Jos 10:19
fall upon their rear (A)(R)　Jos 10:19
Lord and the children of　Jos 12:6
Israel *s.*
defeated (A)(B)(R)　　Jos 12:6; 13:12
these did Moses *s.* and cast　Jos 13:12
them
shalt *s.* the Midianites as one　J'g 6:16
man
destroy (B)　　　　　　　J'g 6:16
and they began to *s.* of the　J'g 20:31
people
kill (B)　　　J'g 20:31; 20:39; 1Sa 20:33
Benjamin began to *s.* and kill　J'g 20:39
of the
saving, Go and *s.* the　　J'g 21:10
inhabitants of
execute the inhabitants (B)　J'g 21:10
Now go and *s.* Amalek, and　1Sa 15:3
utterly
strike (A)　　　　　　　1Sa 15:3;
2Sa 2:22; 13:28; 17:2; 18:11; 1Ki 20:35,
37; 2Ki 13:19; 2Ch 21:14; Pr 19:25;
Isa 11:4; 58:4; Jer 21:6; Eze 5:2; 21:12,
14, 17; 39:3; Mic 5:1; Zec 10:11;
M't 5:39; M'k 14:27; Lu 22:49; Ac 23:2,
　　　　　　　　　　　　　　　　　3
I will *s.* thee, and take thine　1Sa 17:46
head
I will slay you (B)　　　　1Sa 17:46
strike (R)　　　　　　　1Sa 17:46;
26:8; 2Sa 13:28; 17:2; 18:11; 20:35, 37;
2Ki 6:18; 9:7; 13:18, 19; Ps 141:5;
Pr 19:25; Eze 5:2; 39:3; Mic 5:1;
Zec 12:4; 13:7; M't 5:39; 26:31;
M'k 14:27; Lu 22:49 Ac 23:2; 2Co 11:20;
　　　　　　　　　　　　　　　Re 11:6
I will *s.* David even to the　1Sa 18:11
wall with
pin David to the wall　　　1Sa 18:11
(A)(B)(R)
Saul sought to *s.* David even　1Sa 19:10
to the
Saul cast a javelin at him to　1Sa 20:33
s. him
Shall I go and *s.* these　　1Sa 23:2
Philistines
defeat the Philistines (B)　1Sa 23:2
attack these Philistines (R)　1Sa 23:2
Go, and *s.* the Philistines,　1Sa 23:2
and save
therefore let me *s.* him, I　1Sa 26:8
pray thee
nail him to the ground (B)　1Sa 26:8
and I will not *s.* him the　1Sa 26:8
second time
Lord liveth the Lord shall *s.*　1Sa 26:10
him
should I *s.* thee to the ground　2Sa 2:22
strike (A)　　　　　　　2Sa 2:22;
13:28; 17:2; 18:11; 1Ki 20:35, 37;
2Ki 9:7; 13:18-19; Pr 19:25; Eze 5:2;
6:11; M't 5:39; 26:31; M'k 14:27;
　　　　Lu 22:49; Ac 23:2-3; 2Co 1:20
to *s.* the host of the　　　2Sa 5:24
Philistines
when I say unto you, S.　　2Sa 13:28
Amnon
and *s.* the city with the edge　2Sa 15:14
of the
cut down (B)　　　2Sa 15:14; 2Ki 6:21-22
flee; and I will *s.* the king　2Sa 17:2
only
thou not *s.* him there to the　2Sa 18:11
ground
the Lord shall *s.* Israel as a　1Ki 14:15
reed
beat Israel (B)　　　　　1Ki 14:15

word of the Lord, *S*. me, I *1Ki 20:35*
pray thee
And the man refused to *s*. *1Ki 20:35*
him
man, and said, *S*. me, I pray *1Ki 20:37*
thee
And ye shall *s*. every fenced *2Ki 3:19*
city
conquer every city (R) *2Ki 3:19*
S. this people, I pray thee, *2Ki 6:18*
with
smite (A) *2Ki 6:18;*
Ps 78:20; Isa 30:31; 41:7
inflict this people (B) *2Ki 6:18*
shall I *s*. them? shall I *s*. *2Ki 6:21*
them
slay (A)(R) *2Ki 6:21; 6:22*
answered, Thou shalt not *s*. *2Ki 6:22*
them
thou *s*. those whom thou hast *2Ki 6:22*
taken
thou shalt *s*. the house of *2Ki 9:7*
Ahab thy
overthrow the house of Ahab *2Ki 9:7*
(B)
and said, *S*. him also in the *2Ki 9:27*
chariot
shoot him (B)(R) *2Sa 9:27*
thou shalt *s*. the Syrians in *2Sa 13:17*
Aphek
king of Israel, *S*. upon the *2Sa 13:18*
ground
now thou shalt *s*. Syria but *2Sa 13:19*
thrice
to *s*. the host of the *1Ch 14:15*
Philistines
plague will the Lord *s*. thy *2Ch 21:14*
people
s. them not able (E) *Ps 18:38*
The sun shall not *s*. thee by *Ps 121:6*
day
Let the righteous *s*. me; it *Ps 141:5*
shall be
S. a scorner, and the simple *Pr 19:25*
will
Lord will *s*. with a scab the *Isa 3:17*
crown
he shall *s*. thee with a rod *Isa 10:24*
he shall *s*. the earth with the *Isa 11:4*
rod of
and shall *s*. it in the seven *Isa 11:15*
streams
And the Lord shall *s*. Egypt: *Isa 19:22*
he
he shall *s*. and heal it: and *Isa 19:22*
they
s. upon the breasts (S) *Isa 32:12*
shall the heat nor sun *s*. *Isa 49:10*
them
plague them (B) *Isa 49:10*
and to *s*. with the fist of *Isa 58:4*
wickedness
and let us *s*. him with the *Jer 18:18*
tongue
devise schemes against (B) *Jer 18:18*
make plots against (R) *Jer 18:18*
And I will *s*. the inhabitants *Jer 21:6*
of this
he shall *s*. them with the edge *Jer 21:7*
of the
he shall *s*. the land of Egypt *Jer 43:11*
come and *s*. the land of *Jer 46:13*
Egypt
which Nebuchadrezzar shall *Jer 49:28*
s.
part, and *s*. about it with a *Eze 5:2*
knife
S. with thine hand, and *Eze 6:11*
stamp with
clap hands (R) *Eze 6:11; 21:17*
after him through the city, and *Eze 9:5*
s.
s. therefore upon thy thigh *Eze 21:12*
and *s*. thine hands together *Eze 21:14*
I will also *s*. mine hands *Eze 21:17*
together
when I shall *s*. all them that *Eze 32:15*
dwell
And I will *s*. thy bow out of *Eze 39:3*
thy left
s. their images (E) *Ho 10:2*
I will *s*. the winter house *Am 3:15*
with the
cut off (B) *Am 3:15*
and he will *s*. the great house *Am 6:11*
with
S. the lintel of the door, that *Am 9:1*
s. the judge of Israel with a *Mic 5:1*
rod

the knees *s*. together, and *Na 2:10*
much
and he will *s*. her power in the *Zec 9:4*
sea
and shall *s*. the waves in the *Zec 10:11*
sea
they shall *s*. the land, and out *Zec 11:6*
of
crush the earth (R) *Zec 11:6*
s. every horse with *Zec 12:4*
astonishment
s. every horse of the people *Zec 12:4*
with
s. the shepherd, and the sheep *Zec 13:7*
shall
the Lord will *s*. all the *Zec 14:12*
people that
the Lord will *s*. the heathen *Zec 14:18*
that
come and *s*. the earth with a *Mal 4:6*
curse
shall *s*. thee on thy right *M't 5:39*
cheek
begin to *s*. his fellowservants *M't 24:49*
begin to beat (A)(R) *Mt 24:49*
I will *s*. the shepherd, and *M't 26:31;*
M'k 14:27
Lord, shall we *s*. with the *Lu 22:49*
sword
by him to *s*. him on the mouth *Ac 23:2*
God shall *s*. thee, thou whited *Ac 23:3*
wall
if a man *s*. you on the face *2Co 11:20*
to *s*. the earth with all plagues *Re 11:6*
scourge (B) *Re 11:6*
with it he should *s*. the *Re 19:15*
nations

SMITERS

s., slanderers, revilers (A) *Ps 35:15*
I gave my back to the *s*. and *Isa 50:6*
my

SMITEST

Wherefore *s*. thou thy fellow *Ex 2:13*
evil: but if well, why *s*. *Joh 18:23*
thou me

SMITETH

He that *s*. a man, so that he *Ex 21:12*
die
Whoever strikes a man *Ex 21:12;*
(A)(R) *Lu 6:29*
if a man hits another (B) *Ex 21:12*
he that *s*. his father, or his *Ex 21:15*
mother
Whoever strikes his father *Ex 21:15*
(B)
out of the hand of him that *De 25:11*
s. him
beating (A)(B)(R) *De 25:11*
he that *s*. his neighbour *De 27:24*
secretly
slays (A)(B)(R) *De 27:24*
He that *s*. Kirjath-sepher *Jos 15:16;*
J'g 1:12
attacks (B) *Jos 15:16; J'g 1:12*
attacks (R) *J'g 1:12*
and *s*. the Jebusites, and the *2Sa 5:8*
lame
strike down (B) *2Sa 5:8; 1Ch 11:6*
Whosoever *s*. the Jebusites *1Ch 11:6*
first
he *s*. through the proud *Job 26:12*
turneth not unto him that *s*. *Isa 9:13*
them
giveth his cheek to him that *s*. *La 3:30*
him
know that I am the Lord that *Eze 7:9*
s.
him that *s*. thee on the one *Lu 6:29*
cheek
hits you on the cheek (B) *Lu 6:29*

SMITH

no *s*. found throughout all *1Sa 13:19*
the
metal worker (A) *1Sa 13:19*
blacksmith (B) *1Sa 13:19*
The *s*. with the tongs both *Isa 44:12*
the ironsmith (A)(B) *Isa 44:12*
worker with an iron tool (B) *Isa 44:12*
created the *s*. that bloweth *Isa 54:16*

SMITHS

and all the craftsmen and *s*. *2Ki 24:14*
craftsmen and *s*. a thousand *2Ki 24:16*

with the carpenters and *s*. *Jer 24:1*
from
and the carpenters, and the *s*. *Jer 29:2*
were

SMITING

he spied an Egyptian *s*. an *Ex 2:11*
Hebrew
beating (A)(B) *Ex 2:11*
he returned from *s*. of the *2Sa 8:13*
Syrians
he slew (A) *2Sa 8:13*
striking down (B) *2Sa 8:13*
him,, so that in *s*. he *1Ki 20:37*
wounded him
striking (A)(B) *1Ki 20:37*
they went forward *s*. the *2Ki 3:24*
Moabites
slaving Moabites (A) *2Ki 3:24*
struck down (B) *2Ki 3:24*
smote those *s*. him (B) *Isa 27:7*
will I make thee sick in *s*. *Mic 6:13*
thee

SMITTEN

that the Lord had *s*. the river *Ex 7:25*
stroke (B) *Ex 7:25*
struck (B) *Ex 7:25;*
22:2; Nu 14:42; 22:28, 32; 33:4;
2Sa 11:15; 2Ki 2:14; 13:19; 1Ch 18:10;
10; Job 16:10; Ac 23:3; Re 8:12
And the flax and the barley *Ex 9:31*
was *s*.
beaten (B) *Ex 9:31;*
22:2; De 1:42; J'g 20:36; 1Sa 4:2; 13:4;
1Ch 18:10; 2Ch 20:22; 25:19
ruined (R) *Ex 9:31; 9:32*
the wheat and the rie were not *Ex 9:32*
s.
ruined (B) *Ex 9:32*
breaking up, and be *s*. that he *Ex 22:2*
die
struck (A) *Ex 22:2;*
Nu 14:42; 22:32; 33:4; De 28:25;
2Ki 2:14; 13:19; Job 16:10; Ps 3:7;
Eze 22:13; Ac 23:3
ye be not *s*. before your *Nu 14:42*
enemies
decimated before enemies *Nu 14:42*
(B)
thou hast *s*. me these three *Nu 22:28*
times
strike (A) *Nu 22:28*
hit me (B) *Nu 22:28*
thou *s*. thine ass these three *Nu 22:32*
times
struck (B) *Nu 22:32;*
33:4; 2Sa 2:31; 11:15; 2Ki 2:14; 13:19;
2Ch 26:20; Ps 3:7
which the Lord had *s*. among *Nu 33:4*
them
lest ye be *s*. before your *De 1:42*
enemies
defeated (B) *De 1:42;*
28:7, 25; 1Sa 4:2, 10; 13:4; 2Sa 8:9-10;
10:15; 1Ki 8:33; 2Ch 28:17; Jer 37:10
thee to be *s*. before thy face: *De 28:7*
they
defeated (A) *De 28:7;*
J'g 20:36; 1Sa 7:10; 13:4; 2Sa 8:9-10;
10:15, 19; 1Ch 18:9, 10; Jer 37:10
thee to be *s*. before thine *De 28:25*
enemies
defeat (B) *De 28:25;*
1Sa 4:3, 10; 7:10; 2Sa 8:10; 10:15;
2Ki 14:10
s. it with the edge of the sword *J'g 1:8*
smote (A)(R) *J'g 1:8; Am 4:9*
attack (B) *J'g 1:8; 20:39; 2Ch 28:17*
They are *s*. down before us *J'g 20:32*
as at
routed (A)(R) *J'g 20:32*
killed (B) *J'g 20:32; 2Ch 25:16*
of Benjamin saw that they *J'g 20:36*
were *s*.
Surely they are *s*. down *J'g 20:39*
before us
falling before us (B) *J'g 20:39*
Israel was *s*. before the *1Sa 4:2*
Philistines
Wherefore hath the Lord *s*. us *1Sa 4:3*
routed (R) *1Sa 4:3; 2Ch 20:22*
Philistines fought, and Israel *1Sa 4:10*
was *s*.
died not were *s*. with the *1Sa 5:12*
emerods
stricken (A)(R) *1Sa 5:12;*
Jer 2:30; Ho 6:1

plagued (B)   1Sa 5:12
the Lord had s. many of the   1Sa 6:19
people
slaughter (A)(R)   1Sa 6:19
slew   1Sa 6:19
and they were s. before Israel   1Sa 7:10
that Saul had s. a garrison of   1Sa 13:4
s. Ziklag, and burned it with   1Sa 30:1
fire
struck down (A)   1Sa 30:1;
       2Sa 11:15; 1Ki 8:33
servants of David s. of   2Sa 2:31
Benjamin
slain (R)   2Sa 2:31; 2Ki 3:23
that David had s. all the host   2Sa 8:9
of
overcome (B)   2Sa 8:9; 1Ch 18:9
against Hadadezer and s.   2Sa 8:10
him
that they were s. before   2Sa 10:15;
Israel   10:19
ye from him, that he may be   2Sa 11:15
s.
When thy people Israel be s.   1Ki 8:33
down
routed (B)   1Ki 8:33
he had s. every male in   1Ki 11:15
Edom
slew every male (A)   1Ki 11:15
cut down or off (B)(R)   1Ki 11:15
when he also had s. the   2Ki 2:14
waters
and they have s. one another: 2Ki 3:23
now
attacked and slain (B)   2Ki 3:23
shouldest have s. five or six   2Ki 13:19
times
s. Syria till thou hadst   2Ki 13:19
consumed it
Thou hast indeed s. Edom   2Ki 14:10
how David had s. all the host   1Ch 18:9
of
against Hadarezer, and s.   1Ch 18:10
him
against Judah; and they   2Ch 20:22
were s.
forbear; why shouldest thou   2Ch 25:16
be s.
put to death (A)(R)   2Ch 25:16
Lo, thou hast s. the   2Ch 25:19
Edomites
out, because the Lord had s.   2Ch 26:20
him
Edomites had come and s.   2Ch 28:17
Judah
they have s. me upon the   Job 16:10
cheek
s. all mine enemies upon the   Ps 3:7
cheek
smote (R)   Ps 3:7
persecute him whom thou   Ps 69:26
hast s.
My heart is s. and withered   Ps 102:4
like
crushed (B)(R)   Ps 102:4; 143:3
he hath s. my life down to   Ps 143:3
trampled my life to the   Ps 143:3
ground (B)(R)
against them, and hath s.   Isa 5:25
them
and the gate is s. with   Isa 24:12
destruction
gates battered to ruins   Isa 24:12
(B)(R)
Hath he s. him as he smote   Isa 27:7
those
stricken, s. of God, and   Isa 53:4
afflicted
In vain have I s. your children   Jer 2:30
stricken (B)   Jer 2:30
why hast thou s. us, and   Jer 14:19
there is no
ye had s. the whole army of   Jer 37:10
smite (B)   Jer 37:10
have s. mine hand at thy   Eze 22:13
dishonest
strike (B)(R)   Eze 22:13
unto me, saying, The city is   Eze 33:21
s.
city is fallen (R)   Eze 33:21
year after that the city was s.   Eze 40:1
in
he hath s. and he will bind us   Ho 6:1
up
Ephraim is s. their root is   Ho 9:16
dried
I have s. you with blasting and   Am 4:9
me to be s. contrary to the   Ac 23:3
law

the third part of the sun was   Re 8:12
s.
blight fell on the sun (B)   Re 8:12

SMOKE

the s. of the country went up   Ge 19:28
as
went up as the s. of a   Ge 19:28
furnace
Sinai was altogether on a s.   Ex 19:18
fire: and the s. thereof   Ex 19:18
ascended
ascended as the s. of a   Ex 19:18
furnace
jealousy shall s. against that   De 29:20
man
the s. of the city ascended up   Jos 8:20
to
and that the s. of the city   Jos 8:21
ascended
great flame with s. rise up   J'g 20:38
out of
up out of the city with a pillar   J'g 20:40
of s.
went up a s. out of his   2Sa 22:9;
nostrils, and   Ps 18:8
Out of his nostrils goeth s.   Job 41:20
as out
into s. shall they consume   Ps 37:20
away
As s. is driven away, so drive   Ps 68:2
them
thine anger s. against the   Ps 74:1
sheep
my days are consumed like s.   Ps 102:3
toucheth the hills, and they   Ps 104:32
s.
am become like a bottle in   Ps 119:83
the s.
the mountains, and they shall   Ps 144:5
s.
to the teeth, and as s. to the   Pr 10:26
eyes
of the wilderness like pillars of   Ca 3:6
s.
assemblies, a cloud and s. by   Isa 4:5
day
and the house was filled with s.   Isa 6:4
mount up like the lifting up   Isa 9:18
of s.
there shall come from the   Isa 14:31
north a s.
the s. thereof shall go up for   Isa 34:10
ever
heavens shall vanish away like   Isa 51:6
s.
These are a s. in my nose a   Isa 65:5
fire that
and as the s. out of the   Ho 13:3
chimney
blood, and fire, and pillars of   Joe 2:30
s.
I will burn her chariots in the   Na 2:13
s.
blood, and fire, and vapour of   Ac 2:19
s.
flood, fire, drifting, s. (N)   Ac 2:19
like a puff of s. (P)   Jas 4:14
And the s. of the incense, which   Re 8:4
And there arose a s. out of the   Re 9:2
pit
as the s. of a great furnace: Re 9:2
and the
was darkened by reason of the   Re 9:2
s.
there came out of the s. locusts   Re 9:3
issued fire and s. and   Re 9:17
brimstone
killed, by the fire, and by the   Re 9:18
s.
by s. and sulphur   Re 9:18
(A)(B)(N)(P)(R)
the s. of their torment   Re 14:11
ascendeth
filled with s. from the glory   Re 15:8
of God
they shall see the s. of her   Re 18:9
burning
when they saw the s. of her   Re 18:18
burning
And her s. rose up for ever   Re 19:3
and ever

SMOKING

behold, a s. furnace, and a   Ge 15:17
burning
the trumpet, and the   Ex 20:18
mountain s.

the two tails of these s.   Isa 7:4
firebrands
the s. flax shall he not   Isa 42:3;
quench   M't 12:20

SMOOTH

a hairy man, and I am a s.   Ge 27:11
man
hands, and upon the s. of his   Ge 27:16
neck
chose him five s. stones out   1Sa 17:40
of the
people tall and s. (B)(E)(R)   Isa 18:2;
       18:7
speak unto us s. things,   Isa 30:10
prophesy
Among the s. stones of the   Isa 57:6
stream
the rough ways shall be made s.   Lu 3:5
s. and specious words (N)   Ro 16:18

SMOOTHER

of his mouth were s. than   Ps 55:21
butter
His mouth is sleeker than   Ps 55:21
butter (B)
and her mouth is s. than oil   Pr 5:3

SMOOTHETH

and he that s. with the   Isa 41:7
hammer
polishes with the hammer (B)   Isa 41:7

SMOTE

and s. the Rephaims in   Ge 14:5
Ashteroth
attacked and subdued (A)   Ge 14:5
conquered (B)   Ge 14:5;
Nu 32:4; De 2:33; 4:46; Jos 10:40;
       1Sa 30:17
subdued (R)   Ge 14:5; 14:7
s. all the country of the   Ge 14:7
Amalekites
sacked the whole Amalekite   Ge 14:7
region (B)
routed the Amalekites (R)   Ge 14:7
by night, and s. them, and   Ge 14:15
pursued
attacked and routed (A)   Ge 14:15
defeated (B)   Ge 14:15;
36:35; De 3:3; 29:7; Jos 10:26; 11:8;
12:1, 7; 13:21; J'g 3:13; 11:21; 12:4;
1Sa 14:48; 2Sa 8:3; 2Ki 10:32; 18:8;
1Ch 1:46; 18:3; 2Ch 13:15; 28:5; Jer 46:2
s. the men that were at the   Ge 19:11
door of
struck (A)   Ge 19:11;
Nu 22:23, 25, 27; J'g 7:13; 1Sa 6:9;
17:49-50; 19:10; 2Sa 14:6; 18:15; 20:10;
1Ki 22:24; 2Ki 2:8; 14; 13:18; 15:10;
Ca 5:7; Jer 41:2; Da 8:7; M't 26:68;
       M'k 14:47
struck (B)   Ge 19:11;
Ex 7:20; 8:17; 9:25; 12:29; Nu 11:33;
20:11; 22:27; J'g 15:8; 1Sa 6:9; 15:7;
17:35, 50; 2Sa 1:15; 4:6; 5:20, 25; 8:2;
10:18; 11:21; 14:6-7; 18:15; 20:10; 23:10;
1Ki 16:10; 22:24, 34; 2Ki 2:8, 14; 3:24;
13:18; 15:5; 1Ch 4:41, 43; 13:10; 14:11,
16; 18:2; 21:7; 2Ch 14:12; 18:23; 21:9,
18; 25:11; Job 1:19; 2:7; Ps 78:20;
Ca 5:7; Da 2:35; Jon 4:7; M't 26:68;
M'k 14:47; Lu 18:13; 22:50, 64;
       Joh 18:10
struck (R)   Ge 19:11;
Ex 7:20; 8:17; 9:25; Nu 20:11; 22:23, 25,
27; 24:10; J'g 5:26; 7:13; 1Sa 6:9, 19;
14:31; 17:49-50; 19:10; 2Sa 14:6-7;
18:15; 20:10; 23:10; 1Ki 1:27; 16:10;
22:24, 34; 2Ki 2:8, 14; 12:21; 13:18;
15:14, 30; 1Ch 18:2-3; 2Ch 18:23, 33;
Job 1:19; Jer 41:2; Da 8:7; M't 26:5,
68; M'k 14:47; Lu 22:50, 64; Joh 18:10;
       Ac 12:7
who s. Midian in the field of   Ge 36:35
Moab
defeated   Ge 36:35
Nu 14:45; De 2:33; 4:46; 29:7;
Jos 10:40; 12:1, 7; 13:21; J'g 3:13;
11:21; 20:35; 1Sa 13:3; 15:7; 2Sa 5:20;
8:1-3; 2Ki 10:32; 1Ch 1:46; 14:11;
18:1; 2Ch 13:15; 14:12; 28:5, 23; Jer 46:2
s. the waters that were in the   Ex 7:20
river
his rod and s. the dust of the   Ex 8:17
earth

the hail s. throughout the land Ex 9:25
of
the hail s. every herb of the Ex 9:25
field
Egypt, when he s. the Ex 12:27
Egyptians
slew (A) Ex 12:27;
12:29; Nu 3:13; 21:35; Jos 7:5; 10:10;
11:17; 1Sa 6:19; 2Sa 14:7; 2Ki 8:21;
19:35
smiting (B) Ex 12:27
slew (R) Ex 12:27;
Nu 3:13; 8:17; 21:24 35; Jos 7:5; 10:10;
J'g 9:43; 2Ki 15:25; 19:35; Ps 78:31;
Isa 37:36, 38
the Lord s. all the firstborn Ex 12:29
in
that I s. all the firstborn in Nu 3:13
the land
killed (B) Nu 3:13;
Jos 7:5; 20:5; 1Ki 15:27, 29; 2Ki 10:25;
12:21; 15:10; 19:35; 25:25; 2Ch 25:13;
Ps 105:36
that I s. every firstborn in Nu 8:17
the land
slew (B) Nu 8:17;
21:35; Jos 11:10; 1Sa 6:19; Isa 37:38;
Jer 41:2
Lord s. the people with a Nu 11:33
very great
and s. them, and discomfited Nu 14:45
them
attack (B) Nu 14:45; Jos 11:8;
2Sa 21:17; 2Ki 3:25; 2Ch 14:15; 28:23
s. them and beat them (E) Nu 14:45
with his rod he s. the rock Nu 20:11
twice
Israel s. him with the edge Nu 21:24
of the
cut down, cut off (B) Nu 21:24;
De 25:18; 2Ki 15:14, 25, 30; 25:21;
M't 26:51
So they s. him, and his sons Nu 21:35
Balaam s. the ass, to turn Nu 22:23
her into
hit (B) Nu 22:23;
1Sa 17:49; 19:10; 2Ch 18:33
the wall; and he s. her again Nu 22:25
strike (B) Nu 22:25; Isa 41:7; Da 2:34
and he s. the ass with a staff Nu 22:27
and he s. his hands together Nu 24:10
striking (B) Nu 24:10;
2Sa 24:17; Ne 13:25
the country which the Lord s. Nu 32:4
we s. him and his sons, and De 2:33
all his
we s. him until none was left to De 3:3
him
Moses and the children of De 4:46
Israel s.
the way, and s. the hindmost De 25:18
of thee
cut off (A)(R) De 25:18; M't 26:51
us in battle, and we s. them De 29:7
men of Ai s. of them about Jos 7:5
thirty
killed (A) Jos 7:5;
20:5; 2Sa 11:21; 1Ki 15:29; 25:25; 2Ch 25:13
and s. them in the going down Jos 7:5
they s. them, so that they Jos 8:22
let none
unto Ai, and s. it with the Jos 8:24
edge of
the children of Israel s. them Jos 9:18
not
slay (A) Jos 9:18;
kill (R) Jos 9:18; 20:5;
2Sa 11:21; 1Ki 15:29; 25:25; 2Ch 25:13
and s. them to Azekah, and Jos 10:10
unto
afterward Joshua s. them, Jos 10:26
and slew
and s. it with the edge of Jos 10:28;
the sword 10:30, 32, 35, 37
and Joshua s. him and his Jos 10:33
people
s. them with the edge of the Jos 10:39
sword
Joshua s. the country of the Jos 10:40
hills
s. them from Kadesh-barnea Jos 10:41
even
overcame (B) Jos 10:41;
2Sa 8:1; 18:1; 20:1
who s. them, and chased them Jos 11:8
unto
s. them, until they left them Jos 11:8
none
s. the king thereof with the Jos 11:10
sword

s. all the souls that were Jos 11:11
therein
destroyed (B) Jos 11:11;
J'g 1:25; 1Ki 20:21; 2Ki 8:21; 15:16
utterly destroying (R) Jos 11:11
s. them with the edge of the Jos 11:12
sword
ravaged (B) Jos 11:12; 19:47
every man they s. with the Jos 11:14
edge of
massacred (B) Jos 11:14
their kings he took, and s. Jos 11:17
them
put them to death (B) Jos 11:17
land, which the children of Jos 12:1
Israel s.
Joshua and the children of Jos 12:7
Israel s.
whom Moses s. with the Jos 13:21
princes of
and s. it with the edge of the Jos 19:47
sword
he s. his neighbour Jos 20:5
unwittingly
they s. the city with the edge J'g 1:25
of the
and Amalek, and went and s. J'g 3:13
Israel
and s. the nail into his temples J'g 4:21
drove (A)(B)(R) J'g 4:21
with the hammer she s. Sisera J'g 5:26
she s. off his head, when she J'g 5:26
had
unto a tent, and s. it that it J'g 7:13
fell
Gideon went up and s. the J'g 8:11
host
attack (R) J'g 8:11;
2Sa 21:17; 2Ki 3:24; Jon 4:7
rose up against them and s. J'g 9:43
them
shattered (B) J'g 9:43
hand of Israel, and they s. J'g 11:21
them
And he s. them from Aroer, J'g 11:33
even
routed (B) J'g 11:33; 20:35
and the men of Gilead s. J'g 12:4
Ephraim
s. them hip and thigh with a J'g 15:8
great
s. them with the edge of J'g 18:27;
the sword 20:48
Lord s. Benjamin before J'g 20:35
Israel
overcame (A) J'g 20:35
s. all the city with the edge J'g 20:37
of the
are the Gods that s. the 1Sa 4:8
Egyptians
s. them with emerods, even 1Sa 5:6
Ashdod
punished (B) 1Sa 5:6
afflicted (R) 1Sa 5:6; 5:9; Job 2:7
s. the men of the city, both 1Sa 5:9
small
afflicted (A) 1Sa 5:9
that it is not his hand that s. 1Sa 6:9
us
he s. the men of 1Sa 6:19
Beth-shemesh
pursued the Philistines, and s. 1Sa 7:11
them
beat (B) 1Sa 7:11;
14:31; Ps 78:66; Jer 20:2
s. the garrison of the 1Sa 13:3
Philistines
overpowered (B) 1Sa 13:3; 2Ch 16:4
And they s. the Philistines 1Sa 14:31
that day
an host, and s. the 1Sa 14:48
Amalekites, and
And Saul s. the Amalekites 1Sa 15:7
from
I went out after him, and s. 1Sa 17:35
him
caught him by his beard, 1Sa 17:35
and s. him
and s. the Philistine in his 1Sa 17:49
forehead
with a stone, and s. the 1Sa 17:50
Philistine
and he s. the javelin into the 1Sa 19:10
wall
s. he with the edge of the 1Sa 22:19
sword
and s. them with a great 1Sa 23:5
slaughter
afflicted (B) 1Sa 23:5
the Lord s. Nabal, that he 1Sa 25:38
died

David s. the land, and left 1Sa 27:9
neither
David s. them from the 1Sa 30:17
twilight
him. And he s. him that he 2Sa 1:15
died
and s. him there under the 2Sa 3:27
fifth rib
stabbed (B) 2Sa 3:27; 4:7
and they s. him under the fifth 2Sa 4:6
rib
and they s. him and slew him 2Sa 4:7
and David s. them there, and 2Sa 5:20
said
s. the Philistines from Geba 2Sa 5:25
until
that David s. the Philistines 2Sa 8:1
he s. Moab, and measured 2Sa 8:2
them
David s. also Hadadezer, the 2Sa 8:3
son
s. Shobach captain of their 2Sa 10:18
host
wounded (R) 2Sa 10:18; 2Ch 22:5
Who s. Abimelech the son 2Sa 11:21
of
the one s. the other, and 2Sa 14:6
slew him
Deliver him that s. his 2Sa 14:7
brother, that
and s. Absalom and slew 2Sa 18:15
him
he s. him therewith in the 2Sa 20:10
fifth rib
and s. the Philistine, and 2Sa 21:17
killed him
s. the Philistines until his 2Sa 23:10
hand was
David's heart s. him after 2Sa 24:10
that he
conscience accused him (B) 2Sa 24:10
he saw the angel that s. the 2Sa 24:17
people
smiting (A) 2Sa 24:17
the cities of Israel, and s. 1Ki 15:20
Ijon, and
captured (B) 1Ki 15:20
conquered (R) 1Ki 15:20;
2Ki 3:25; 2Ch 16:4
and Baasha s. him at 1Ki 15:27
Gibbethon
he s. all the house of 1Ki 15:29
Jeroboam
Zimri went in and s. him, 1Ki 16:10
and killed
s. the horses and chariots, 1Ki 20:21
and slew
captured (R) 1Ki 20:21
near, and s. Micaiah on the 1Ki 22:24
cheek
s. the king of Israel between 1Ki 22:34
his mantle and s. the waters 2Ki 2:8
the mantle and s. the 2Ki 2:14
waters
rose up and s. the Moabites 2Ki 3:24
the slingers went about it, 2Ki 3:25
and s. it
s. them with blindness 2Ki 6:18
according
smite (A) 2Ki 6:18;
Ps 78:20; Isa 30:31; 41:7
strike (R) 2Ki 6:18; Isa 41:7; Ac 7:24
rose by night, and s. the 2Ki 8:21
Edomites
and s. Jehoram between his 2Ki 9:24
arms
shot (B)(R) 2Ki 9:24
s. them with the edge of the 2Ki 10:25
sword
Hazael s. them in all the 2Ki 10:32
coasts of
his servants, s. him, and he 2Ki 12:21
died
And he s. thrice, and stayed 2Ki 13:18
And the Lord s. the king, so 2Ki 15:5
that he
s. him before the people, 2Ki 15:10
and slew
and s. Shallum the son of 2Ki 15:14
Jabesh in
Then Menahem s. Tiphsah, 2Ki 15:16
and all
sacked (R) 2Ki 15:16
not to him, therefore he s. it 2Ki 15:16
against him, and s. him in 2Ki 15:25
Samaria
attacked (A) 2Ki 15:25
s. him, and slew him, and 2Ki 15:30
reigned

s. the Philistines, even unto Gaza	2Ki 18:8
s. in the camp of the Assyrians an	2Ki 19:35
And the king of Babylon s. them	2Ki 25:21
ten men with him, and s. Gedaliah	2Ki 25:25
which s. Midian in the field of Moab	1Ch 1:46
s. their tents, and the habitations	1Ch 4:41
destroyed (A)(R)	1Ch 4:41; 4:43
they s. the rest of the Amalekites	1Ch 4:43
kindled against Uzza, and he s. him	1Ch 13:10
and David s. them there	1Ch 14:11
s. the hosts of the Philistines from	1Ch 14:16
that David s. the Philistines	1Ch 18:1
And he s. Moab; and the Moabites	1Ch 18:2
David s. Hadarezer king of Zobah	1Ch 18:3
Joab s. Rabbah and destroyed it	1Ch 20:1
this thing; therefore he s. Israel	1Ch 21:7
God s. Jeroboam and all Israel	2Ch 13:15
Lord s. the Ethiopians before Asa	2Ch 14:12
they s. all the cities round about	2Ch 14:14
overthrew (B)	2Ch 14:14
They s. also the tents of cattle	2Ch 14:15
and they s. Ijon, and Dan	2Ch 16:4
and s. Micaiah upon the cheek	2Ch 18:23
s. the king of Israel between up by night, and s. the Edomites	2Ch 18:33 2Ch 21:9
the Lord s. him in his bowels with	2Ch 21:18
and the Syrians s. Joram	2Ch 22:5
wounded (A)(B)	2Ch 22:5
and s. of the children of Seir ten	2Ch 25:11
and s. three thousand of them, and	2Ch 25:13
who s. him with a great slaughter	2Ch 28:5
who s. him (E)	2Ch 28:5
gods of Damascus, which s. him	2Ch 28:23
s. certain of them, and plucked off	Ne 13:25
beat (A)	Ne 13:25; Jer 20:2
beat (R)	Ne 13:25; Ca 5:7; Jer 20:2; Lu 18:13; 23:48
the Jews s. all their enemies with	Es 9:5
s. the four corners of the house	Job 1:19
s. Job with sore boils from the	Job 2:7
and s. of Edom in the valley the	Ps 60 title
he s. the rock, that the waters	Ps 78:20
s. down the chosen men of Israel	Ps 78:31
slaughtered (B)	Ps 78:31
And s. all the firstborn in Egypt	Ps 78:51
And he s. his enemies in the hinder	Ps 78:66
He s. their vines also and their fig	Ps 105:33
ruined (A)	Ps 105:33
He s. also all the firstborn in their	Ps 105:36
Who s. the firstborn of Egypt, both	Ps 135:8
Who s. great nations, and slew	Ps 135:10
him that s. Egypt in their firstborn	Ps 136:10
To him which s. great kings	Ps 136:17
me, they s. me, they wounded me	Ca 5:7
again stay upon him that s. them	Isa 10:20
He who s. the people in wrath with	Isa 14:6
rod of him that s. thee is broken	Isa 14:29
Hath he smitten him, as he s.	Isa 27:7
s. those smiting him (B)	Isa 27:7

beaten down, which s. with a rod	Isa 30:31
smites (B)	Isa 30:31
and s. in the camp of the Assyrians	Isa 37:36
his sons s. him with the sword	Isa 37:38
the hammer him that s. the anvil	Isa 41:7
for in my wrath I s. thee, but in my	Isa 60:10
Pashur s. Jeremiah the prophet	Jer 20:2
was instructed, I s. upon my thigh	Jer 31:19
s. Gedaliah the son of Ahikam	Jer 41:2
Nebuchadrezzar king of Babylon s.	Jer 46:2
before that Pharaoh s. Gaza	Jer 47:1
And the king of Babylon s. them	Jer 52:27
s. the image upon his feet that were	Da 2:34
the stone that s. the image became	Da 2:35
his knees s. one against another	Da 5:6
knocked (A)(R)	Da 5:6
and s. the ram, and brake his two	Da 8:7
butted (B)	Da 8:7
and it s. the gourd that it withered	Jon 4:7
I s. you with blasting and with	Hag 2:17
the high priest's, and s. off his ear	M't 26:51
thou Christ, Who is he that s. thee	M't 26:68
and s. a servant of the high priest	M'k 14:47
s. upon his breast, saying, God be	Lu 18:13
striking (A)	Lu 18:13; Ac 7:24
s. the servant of the high priest	Lu 22:50
Prophesy, who is it that s. thee	Lu 22:64
s. their breasts, and returned	Lu 23:48
beating (A)(B)	Lu 23:48
and s. the high priest's servant	Joh 18:10
oppressed, and s. the Egyptian	Ac 7:24
slaying (B)	Ac 7:24
he s. Peter on the side, and raised	Ac 12:7
touching (B)	Ac 12:7

SMOTE HIM

then shall he that s. him be quit	Ex 21:19
he that struck him shall be clear (A)(R)	Ex 21:19
one who hit shall be unpunished (B)	Ex 21:19
he that s. him shall surely die	Nu 35:21
one who did the striking be executed (B)	Nu 35:21
struck the blow shall be put to death (R)	Nu 35:21
afterwards David's heart s. him	1Sa 24:5
s. him under the fifth rib	2Sa 2:23; 3:27; 4:6
gave him a back-thrust in abdomen (B)	2Sa 2:23
God s. him for his error	2Sa 6:7; 1Ch 13:10
God struck him on the spot (B)	2Sa 6:7
man s. him, so that he wounded him	1Ki 20:37
the man struck him (A)(B)(R)	1Ki 20:37
his sons s. him with sword	2Ki 19:37; Isa 37:38
his sons killed him (A)	2Ki 19:37
his sons cut him down (B)	2Ki 19:37
his sons slew him with the sword (R)	2Ki 19:37
Syria s. him, king of Israel s. him	2Ch 28:5
Syria defeated him (A)(B)(R)	2Ch 28:5
as he smote those who s. him	Isa 27:7
smote those who were smiting him (B)	Isa 27:7
for iniquity of covetousness I s. him	Isa 57:17

princes wroth with Jeremiah and s. him	Jer 37:15
princes enraged beat him (A)(B)(R)	Jer 37:15
others s. him with palms of hands	M't 26:67
some slapped him (A)(B)(P)(R)	M't 26:67
others struck him (N)	M't 26:67
took a reed and s. him on the head	M't 27:30; M'k 15:19; Lu 22:63; Joh 19:3
struck him on his head (A)(B)(R)	M't 27:30
beat him on the head (N)	M't 27:30
hit him on the head (P)	M't 27:30
angel of the Lord s. him	Ac 12:23
angel of the Lord struck him (B)(N)(P)	Ac 12:23

SMOTEST

rod, wherewith thou s. the river	Ex 17:5

SMUGGLED

secretly s. in (A)	Ga 2:4

SMUT

from the s. of this world (B)	Jas 1:27

SMYRNA

unto S. and unto Pergamos	Re 1:11
unto the angel of the church in S.	Re 2:8

SNAIL

and the lizard, and the s. and the	Le 11:30
As a s. which melteth, let every	Ps 58:8

SNAKE

become a s. (B)	Ex 4:3; 7:10, 15
treat on a s. (B)	Ps 91:13

SNAPPED

s. his chains (P)	Mk 5:4

SNAPS

a strand of rope s. (B)	J'g 16:9

SNARE

shall this man be a s. unto us	Ex 10:7
threaten our ruin (B)	Ex 10:7
it will surely be a s. unto thee	Ex 23:33
it be for a s. in the midst of thee	Ex 34:12
for that will be a s. unto thee	De 7:16
their gods shall be as a s. unto you	J'g 2:3
thing became a s. unto Gideon	J'g 8:27
that she may be a s. to him	1Sa 18:21
then layest thou a s. for my life	1Sa 28:9
feet, and he walketh upon a s.	Job 18:8
s. is laid for him in the ground	Job 18:10
Let their table become a s. before	Ps 69:22
thee from the s. of the fowler, and	Ps 91:3
rescues from the hunter's trap (B)	Ps 91:3
idols: which were a s. unto them	Ps 106:36
became seductive bait to them (B)	Ps 106:36
The wicked have laid a s. for me	Ps 119:110
bird out of the s. of the fowlers	Ps 124:7
s. is broken, and we are escaped	Ps 124:7
The proud have hid a s. for me	Ps 140:5
have they privily laid a s. for me	Ps 142:3
concealed a trap for me (B)(R)	Ps 142:3
as a bird hasteth to the s. and	Pr 7:23
and his lips are the s. of his soul	Pr 18:7

SNARE

It is a *s.* to the man who devoureth — *Pr 20:25*
his ways, and get a *s.* to thy soul — *Pr 22:25*
of an evil man there is a *s.* — *Pr 29:6*
Scornful men bring a city into a *s.* — *Pr 29:8*
The fear of man bringeth a *s.* — *Pr 29:25*
birds that are caught in the *s.* — *Ec 9:12*
and for a *s.* to the inhabitants of — *Isa 8:14*
for a trap and a *s.* (A)(B)(R) — *Isa 8:14*
the pit, and the *s.* are upon thee — *Isa 24:17*
of the pit shall be taken in the *s.* — *Isa 24:18*
lay a *s.* for him that reproveth in — *Isa 29:21*
the pit, and the *s.* shall be upon — *Jer 48:43*
a trap before me (B) — *Jer 48:43; 48:44*
of the pit shall be taken in the *s.* — *Jer 48:44*
I have laid a *s.* for thee, and thou — *Jer 50:24*
Fear and a *s.* is come upon us — *La 3:47*
and he shall be taken in my *s.* — *Eze 12:13*
him, and he shall be taken in my *s.* — *Eze 17:20*
ye have been a *s.* on Mizpah — *Ho 5:1*
the prophet is a *s.* of a fowler in all — *Ho 9:8*
a bird fall in a *s.* upon the earth — *Am 3:5*
shall one take up a *s.* from the — *Am 3:5*
Satan, you are a *s.* to me (B) — *M't 16:23*
suddenly as a *s.* (E)(R) — *Lu 21:34*
as a *s.* shall it come on all them — *Lu 21:35*
Let their table be made a *s.* — *Ro 11:9*
not that I may cast a *s.* upon you — *1Co 7:35*
reproach and the *s.* of the devil — *1Ti 3:7*
rich fall into temptation and a *s.* — *1Ti 6:9*
themselves out of the *s.* of the devil — *2Ti 2:26*

SNARED

unto thee, lest thou be *s.* therein — *De 7:25*
thou be not *s.* by following them — *De 12:30*
ensnared in following them (A)(E)(R) — *De 12:30*
be lured into imitating them (B) — *De 12:30*
wicked is *s.* in the work of his own — *Ps 9:16*
s. with the words of thy mouth — *Pr 6:2*
wicked is *s.* by the transgression — *Pr 12:13*
ensnared by transgression (B)(R) — *Pr 12:13*
the sons of men *s.* man evil time — *Ec 9:12*
trapped in a disastrous time (B) — *Ec 9:12*
be broken, and be *s.* and be taken — *Isa 8:15; 28:13*
be broken, trapped, and taken (B) — *Isa 8:15*
they are all of them *s.* in holes — *Isa 42:22*
entrapped in holes (B) — *Isa 42:22*
trapped in holes (R) — *Isa 42:22*

SNARES

shall be *s.* and traps unto you — *Jos 23:13*
the *s.* of death prevented me — *2Sa 22:6*
Therefore *s.* are round about thee — *Job 22:10*
eyes: his nose pierceth through a *s.* — *Job 40:24*
Upon the wicked he shall rain *s.* — *Ps 11:6*
the *s.* of death prevented me — *Ps 18:5*
seek after my life lay *s.* for me — *Ps 38:12*
they commune of laying *s.* privily — *Ps 64:5*
the *s.* of death (R) — *Ps 116:3*
me from the *s.* which they have — *Ps 141:9*

keep me from the trap laid *s.* for evil-doers (A)(B)(R) — *Ps 141:9*
life, to depart from the *s.* of death — *Pr 13:14; 14:27*
violence of wicked *s.* them (B) — *Pr 21:7*
Thorns and *s.* are in the way of — *Pr 22:5*
whose heart is *s.* and nets, and — *Ec 7:26*
lay wait, as he that setteth *s.* — *Jer 5:26*
they set a trap (A)(E)(R) — *Jer 5:26*
they act like a trap (B) — *Jer 5:26*
to take me, and hid *s.* for my feet — *Jer 18:22*
taken in their *s.* (A) — *La 4:20*

SNATCH

s. them away from camp (B) — *De 2:15*
And he shall *s.* on the right hand — *Isa 9:20*
no man able to *s.* (A)(B)(E)(N)(P)(R) — *Joh 10:28*

SNATCHED

s. the spear out (A)(B)(R) — *2Sa 23:21*
s. him from his property (A) — *Job 8:18*

SNATCHES

s. away his goods (A) — *Ps 35:10*

SNEAK

s. into homes (B) — *2Ti 3:6*

SNEAKED

people *s.* in (B) — *Jude 4*

SNEER

began to *s.*, ridicule, scoff (A)(P) — *Lu 16:14*

SNEERED

s. at him (B) — *Lu 16:14*
rulers scoffed and *s.* (A)(B) — *Lu 23:35*

SNEERING

s. and jeering (B) — *Isa 57:4*
s. of the nations (B) — *Eze 36:6*

SNEERINGLY

others said *s.* (B) — *Ac 2:13*

SNEERS

he sniffs and *s.* at them (A)(B) — *Ps 10:5*

SNEEZED

and the child *s.* seven times — *2Ki 4:35*

SNEEZINGS

his *s.* flash (A)(B)(E)(R)(S) — *Job 41:18*

SNIFF

you *s.* at it (A)(B)(R) — *Mal 1:13*

SNIFFED

ye have *s.* at it (S) — *Mal 1:13*

SNIFFS

he *s.* and sneers at them (A)(B) — *Ps 10:5*

SNOBBERY

you must not show *s.* (N)(P) — *Jas 2:1*
if you show *s.* (N) — *Jas 2:9*

SNORTING

The *s.* of his horses was heard — *Jer 8:16*

SNOUT

As a jewel of gold in a swine's *s.* — *Pr 11:22*

SNOW

behold, his hand was leprous as *s.* — *Ex 4:6*
became leprous, white as *s.* — *Nu 12:10*
in the midst of a pit in time of *s.* — *2Sa 23:20*
his presence a leper as white as *s.* — *2Ki 5:27*
the ice, and wherein the *s.* is hid — *Job 6:16*
If I wash myself with *s.* water, and — *Job 9:30*
and heat consume the *s.* waters — *Job 24:19*
For he saith to the *s.* Be thou on — *Job 37:6*
entered into the treasures of the *s.* — *Job 38:22*
me, and I shall be whiter than *s.* — *Ps 51:7*
in it, it was white as *s.* in Salmon — *Ps 68:14*
He giveth *s.* like wool: he — *Ps 147:16*
Fire, and hail; *s.* and vapours — *Ps 148:8*
As the cold of *s.* in the time of — *Pr 25:13*
As *s.* in summer, and as rain in — *Pr 26:1*
She is not afraid of the *s.* for her — *Pr 31:21*
scarlet, they shall be as white as *s.* — *Isa 1:18*
down, and the *s.* from heaven, and — *Isa 55:10*
Will a man leave the *s.* of Lebanon — *Jer 18:14*
Her Nazarites were purer than *s.* — *La 4:7*
whose garment was white as *s.* — *Da 7:9*
and his raiment white as *s.* — *M't 28:3*
shining, exceeding white as *s.* — *M'k 9:3*
were white like wool, as white as *s.* — *Re 1:14*

SNOWY

slew a lion in a pit in a *s.* day — *1Ch 11:22*

SNUFFDISHES

the *s.* thereof, shall be of pure — *Ex 25:38*
snuffers and ash trays (A)(B)(R) — *Ex 25:38; 37:23; Nu 4:9*
his snuffers, and his *s.* of pure gold — *Ex 37:23*
lamps, and his tongs, and his *s.* — *Nu 4:9*

SNUFFED

my days are *s.* out (A) — *Job 17:1*
they *s.* up the winds like dragons — *Jer 14:6*
they pant for air like jackals (A)(B)(E)(R) — *Jer 14:6*
ye have *s.* at it, saith the Lord of — *Mal 1:13*
you have sniffed at it (A)(B) — *Mal 1:13*
you sniff at me (R) — *Mal 1:13*

SNUFFERS

s. and ash trays (A)(B)(R) — *Ex 25:38; 37:23; Nu 4:9*
made his seven lamps, and his *s.* — *Ex 37:23*
snuffers (A)(B)(R) — *Nu 4:9*
the bowls, and the *s.* and the *s.* — *1Ki 7:50*
of the Lord bowls of silver, *s.* — *2Ki 12:13*
pots, and the shovels, and the *s.* — *2Ki 25:14*
the snuffers (A) — *2Ch 4:21*
And the *s.* and the basons — *2Ch 4:22*
and the *s.* and the bowls — *Jer 52:18*

SNUFFETH

s. up the wind at her pleasure — *Jer 2:24*
in her heat snuffing at the wind (A)(R) — *Jer 2:24*

SO

so Abraham departed as Lord *Ge 12:4*
had spoken
as the stars, *so* shall thy seed *Ge 15:5;*
be   *Ro 4:18*
Rebekah said, If it be *so*, *Ge 25:22*
why am I thus
old, and his eyes were dim, *Ge 27:1*
so that he
thou hast now done foolishly *Ge 31:28*
in *so* doing
if it must be *so* now do this, *Ge 43:11*
take fruits
Moses spake *so* to children of *Ex 6:9*
Israel
the magicians did *so* with their *Ex 8:7*
And they did *so:* for Aaron *Ex 8:17*
stretched
the magicians did *so* with *Ex 8:18*
their
so there were lice upon man, *Ex 8:18*
and upon
Moses said, It is not meet *so* *Ex 8:26*
to do
let Lord be *so* with you, as I *Ex 10:10*
will let you go
And the children of Israel *Ex 16:17*
did *so*
after the pattern, even *so* shall *Ex 25:9*
ye make it
that thou hast brought *so* *Ex 32:21*
great a sin
as the Lord commanded, *so* *Ex 39:43*
had they done it
as sin offering, *so* is trespass *Le 7:7*
offering
for *so* I am commanded *Le 8:35; 10:13*
as he hath done, *so* shall be *Le 24:19;*
done   *24:20*
bear all that is made, *so* shall *Nu 4:26*
they serve
And Aaron did *so* *Nu 8:3*
as ye are, *so* shall the stranger *Nu 15:15*
be before Lord
was I ever wont to do *so* *Nu 22:30*
unto thee
so the plague was stayed *Nu 25:8;*
   Ps 106:30
So these things shall be for *Nu 35:29*
a statute of
so shall the Lord do to all the *De 7:19*
nations
as nations Lord destroyeth, *so* *De 8:20*
shall ye perish
so thou shalt put evil away *De 17:7;*
from you   *19:19; 21:21; 22:21-22, 24*
as when man riseth, even *so* *De 22:26*
is this matter
So the Lord alone did lead *De 32:12*
him, and
and as thy days, *so* shalt thy *De 33:25*
strength be
So the sun stood still in the *Jos 10:13*
midst of
as strength then, even *so* is *Jos 14:11*
strength now
as I have done, *so* God hath *J'g 1:7*
requited me
so let all thine enemies *J'g 5:31*
perish, O Lord
they answered, As thou art, *J'g 8:18*
so were they
for as the man is, *so* is his *J'g 8:21*
strength
as they did to me, *so* have I *J'g 15:11*
done to them
wherefore then speakest thou *1Sa 9:21*
so to me
so shall it be done unto his *1Sa 11:7*
oxen
so shall thy mother be *1Sa 15:33*
childless among women
Saul said, Why hast thou *1Sa 19:17*
deceived me *so*
as his name is, *so* is he, Nabal *1Sa 25:25*
is his name
so shall his part be that *1Sa 30:24*
tarrieth by the stuff
so shalt thou say to my *2Sa 7:8*
servant David
as thy servants said, *so* it is *2Sa 13:35*
so let him curse, Wherefore *2Sa 16:10*
hast thou done *so*
then say, Why hast thou *1Ki 1:6*
done *so*
so shall I be saved from my *2Sa 22:4;*
enemies   *Ps 18:3*
so the Lord was entreated *2Sa 24:25*
for the land

even *so* will I certainly do *1Ki 1:30*
this day
the Lord God of my lord the *1Ki 1:36*
king say *so* too
God do *so* to me, and more *1Ki 2:23*
also, if
the king said, So shall thy *1Ki 20:40*
judgment be
Why is thy spirit *so* sad, that *1Ki 21:5*
thou
he said, Let not king say *so* *1Ki 22:8;*
   2Ch 18:7
prophesied *so* saying, Go *1Ki 22:12*
up to
So he called her. And when *2Ki 4:36*
she was
so it fell to him, people *2Ki 7:20*
trode on him
a saviour, *so* that they went *2Ki 13:5*
out from
all this vision, *so* did *1Ch 17:15*
Nathan speak
so be established, *so* shall *2Ch 20:20*
ye prosper
so kill passover and sanctify *2Ch 35:6*
yourselves
and *so* thou shalt endamage *Ezr 4:13*
the
so it ceased to the second *Ezr 4:24*
year of Darius
so I prayed; So God shake out *Ne 2:4;*
   5:13
to that day had not children *Ne 8:17*
of Israel done *so*
so didst thou get thee a name, *Ne 9:10*
as it is this day
and so will I go in unto the *Es 4:16*
king
so it is, hear it; and if it *Job 5:27;*
were *so*   *21:4*
I know it is *so* of truth, but *Job 9:2*
how should man
and if it were *so* why should *Job 21:4*
not my
so should I be delivered for *Job 23:7*
ever from my judge
in *so* doing, my maker *Job 32:22*
would take me away
so will we sing and praise thy *Ps 21:13*
power
let them not say, *so* would we *Ps 35:25*
have it
do good, *so* shalt thou dwell in *Ps 37:3*
the land
so panteth my soul after thee, *Ps 42:1*
O God
so shall the King desire thy *Ps 45:11*
beauty
as we heard, *so* have we seen *Ps 48:8*
in city
so is thy praise to the ends of *Ps 48:10*
the earth
to see thy glory, *so* as seen *Ps 63:2*
thee in sanctuary
As smoke is driven away, *so* *Ps 68:2*
drive them
so foolish was I, and *Ps 73:22*
ignorant, as a beast
so he fed them; *so* we thy *Ps 78:72;*
people   *79:15*
so will not we go back from *Ps 80:18*
thee, quicken
so I gave them up; *so* is thy *Ps 81:12;*
wrath   *90:11*
so the Lord pitieth them *Ps 103:13*
that fear him
flower of the field, *so* he *Ps 103:15*
flourisheth
so let it come, *so* let it be *Ps 109:17*
far from him
so is every one that trusteth *Ps 115:8;*
in them   *135:18*
the oppression of man; *so* *Ps 119:134*
will I keep
he hath not dealt *so* with *Ps 147:20*
any nation
so find favour and good *Pr 3:4*
understanding
so shall they be life to thy soul, *Pr 3:22*
grace to neck
so shall thy poverty come *Pr 6:11;*
   24:34
as the whirlwind, *so* is the *Pr 10:25*
wicked no more
as he thinketh in his heart, *so* *Pr 23:7*
is he
as the one dieth, *so* dieth the *Ec 3:19*
other
in all points as came, *so* *Ec 5:16*
shall he go

as is the good, *so* is sinner; he *Ec 9:2*
that sweareth
even *so* thou knowest not the *Ec 11:5*
so their root shall be as *Isa 5:24*
rottenness
as I have thought, *so* shall it *Isa 14:24*
come
for *so* Lord said to me, I will *Isa 18:4*
take my rest
as with the people, *so* with *Isa 24:2*
the priest
so have we been in thy sight, *Isa 26:17*
O Lord
so shall the multitude of all *Isa 29:8*
the
as birds flying, *so* will the *Isa 31:5*
Lord
so is Pharaoh king of Egypt *Isa 36:6*
to all trust in him
if *so* be thou shalt be able to *Isa 47:12*
profit; if *so* thou mayest prevail
as a lamb, *so* he openeth not *Isa 53:7*
his mouth
so shall thy sons; *so* shall *Isa 62:5*
God rejoice over thee
they are my people, *so* he was *Isa 63:8*
their Saviour
so will I comfort you, ye shall *Isa 66:13*
be comforted
so shall your seed and name *Isa 66:22*
remain
and my people love to have it *Jer 5:31*
so
will distress them, that they *Jer 10:18*
may find it *so*
so shall be my people, I your *Jer 11:4;*
God   *Eze 37:23*
so will I break this people *Jer 19:11*
and city
let us go, *so* we dwell at *Jer 35:11*
Jerusalem
obey the Lord, *so* shall it be *Jer 38:20*
well
so he dwelt among the *Jer 39:14*
people
so shall be with all men *Jer 42:17*
that set faces
so shall Moab be a derision *Jer 48:39*
mouth in dust, if *so* be there *La 3:29*
may be hope
So the spirit lifted me up, *Eze 3:14*
and took me
as I have done, *so* shall be *Eze 12:11*
done to them
as is the mother, *so* is the *Eze 16:44*
daughter
repent, *so* iniquity shall not *Eze 18:30*
be your ruin
so that she hath no strong *Eze 19:14*
rod to be a
so that in all your doings *Eze 21:24*
your sins do
cherub that covereth, I have *Eze 28:14*
set thee *so*
so thou shalt do *so* shall ye *Eze 45:20*
reconcile house
if it be *so*, our God is able to *Da 3:17*
deliver us
So he told me, and made me *Da 7:16*
know the
shalt abide for me, *so* will I be *Ho 3:3*
for thee
so were they filled; *so* shall *Ho 13:6*
they run
so the Lord of hosts shall be *Am 5:14;*
with you   *Joe 2:24*
if *so* be that God will think *Jon 1:6*
upon us
so their dwelling not be cut off *Zep 3:7*
so my Spirit remaineth *Hag 2:5*
among you
so is this people, *so* is this *Hag 2:14*
nation before me
to our doings, *so* hath he dealt *Zec 1:6*
with us
So I answered and spake to *Zec 4:4*
the angel
so will I save you *Zec 8:13*
so shall be plague of horse *Zec 14:15*
Suffer it to be *so* now, it *M't 3:15*
becometh
so persecuted they prophets *M't 5:12*
before you
let your light *so* shine; shall *M't 5:16;*
teach men *so*   *5:19*
if God *so* clothe the grass of *M't 6:30*
the field
as thou hast believed, *so* be it *M't 8:13*
done unto thee

marvelled, saying it was never *M't 9:33*
so seen in Israel
even *so*, Father for *so* it   *M't 11:26;*
seemed   *Lu 10:21*
so shall Son of man be   *M't 12:40;*
     Lu 11:30; 17:24
if the case of man be *so*   *M't 19:10*
with his wife
when cometh shall find *so*   *M't 24:46;*
doing   *Lu 12:43*
So they went, and made the   *M't 27:66*
are ye *so* without   *M'k 7:18*
understanding also
but *so* shall it not be among *M'k 10:43*
you
if *so* (S)   *Lu 5:36; 2Co 11:16*
if he come in watch and find *Lu 12:38*
them *so*
so it is; found it *so* as   *Lu 12:54;*
women said   *24:24*
God *so* loved the world that *Joh 3:16*
he gave his
even as the Father said to *Joh 12:50*
me, *so* I speak
ye say well, for *so* I am; *so* *Joh 13:13;*
I do   *14:31*
ye bear much fruit, *so* shall *Joh 15:8*
be my disciples
as Father hath loved me, *so* *Joh 15:9*
have I loved you
so have I also sent them   *Joh 17:18;*
into world   *17:20-21*
Answerest thou the high   *Joh 18:22*
priest *so*
this Jesus shall *so* come in like *Ac 1:11*
manner
he hath *so* fulfilled; are these *Ac 3:18;*
things *so*   *7:1*
as a lamb dumb, *so* opened *Ac 8:32*
not mouth
for *so* hath the Lord   *Ac 13:47*
commanded us
so spake, that a great   *Ac 14:1*
multitude believed
so were churches established *Ac 16:5*
in faith
so mightily grew word of   *Ac 19:20*
God
so had appointed, minding to *Ac 20:13*
go a-foot
so worship I the God of my *Ac 24:14*
fathers
so came to pass they escaped *Ac 27:44*
to land
not as the offence, *so* also is *Ro 5:15*
free gift
so they that are in flesh cannot *Ro 8:8*
please God
so then it is not of him that *Ro 9:16*
willeth nor
so all Israel shall be saved, *Ro 11:26*
as it is written
so doing shalt heap coals of *Ro 12:20*
fire on his head
so every one shall give   *Ro 14:12*
account to God
he shall be saved yet *so* as   *1Co 3:15*
by fire
let man *so* account of us, as *1Co 4:1*
ministers of
concerning him that hath *so* *1Co 5:3*
done this deed
is it *so* that there is not wise *1Co 6:5*
man
so let him walk, *so* ordain I *1Co 7:17*
in all churches
I say that it is good for a   *1Co 7:26*
man *so* to be
she is happier if she *so* abide *1Co 7:40*
when ye sin *so* against the *1Co 8:12*
brethren
even *so* hath Lord ordained *1Co 9:14*
to live by gospel
so run; *so* let him eat that *1Co 9:24;*
bread   *9:26; 11:28*
all members, are one body, *1Co 12:12*
so also is Christ
so we preach, and *so* ye *1Co 15:11*
believed
as he is Christ's, *so* are we *2Co 10:7*
Christ's
so will I keep from being   *2Co 11:9*
burdensome
Hebrews? *so* am I;   *2Co 11:22*
Israelites? *so* am I
but be it *so*. I did not   *2Co 12:16*
burden you
as then persecuted, even *so* it *Ga 4:29*
is now

bear burdens, and *so* fulfil the   *Ga 6:2*
law of Christ
of twain, one new man, *so*   *Eph 2:15*
making peace
brethren, mark them which *Ph'p 3:17*
walk *so*
my brethren, *so* stand fast in *Ph'p 4:1*
the Lord
as ye receive Christ, *so* walk in *Col 2:6*
him
even *so* we speak, not as   *1Th 2:4*
pleasing men
and *so* shall we ever be with *1Th 4:17*
the Lord
so I sware in my wrath, shall *Heb 3:11*
not enter
as I may *so* say, Levi paid   *Heb 7:9*
tithes in Abraham
so be ye holy; *so* is the will *1Pe 1:15;*
of God   *2:15*
it is better, if the will of God *1Pe 3:17*
be *so*, to suffer
you; and *so* doth Marcus my *1Pe 5:13*
son
he ought himself *so* to walk *1Jo 2:6*
as he walked
God *so* loved us, we ought to *1Jo 4:11*
love one another
because as he is, *so* are we in *1Jo 4:17*
this world
even *so* amen; even *so* come, *Re 1:7;*
Lord Jesus   *22:20*
So he carried me away in the *Re 17:3*
spirit

SO BE IT

Rahab said, According to   *Jos 2:21*
your words, *so be it*
I answered and said, *So be it,* *Jer 11:5*
O Lord

SO THAT

so that all that hear will laugh *Ge 21:6*
with me
so that I come again to my   *Ge 28:21*
father's house
so that land of Egypt and   *Ge 47:13*
Canaan fainted
so that he would not let   *Ex 10:20;*
Israel go   *11:10*
he that smiteth a man, *so*   *Ex 21:12*
that he die
so that thou shalt be mad   *De 28:34*
for sight of eyes
so that they could not longer *J'g 2:14*
stand
shouted, *so that* the earth rang *1Sa 4:5*
again
so that his name was much *1Sa 18:30*
set by
so that thy child, take heed *1Ki 8:25;*
   2Ch 6:16
spread it on his face, *so that* *2Ki 8:15*
he died
so that they shall not say,   *2Ki 9:37*
This is Jezebel
so that after him was none *2Ki 18:5*
like him of kings
so that there should be no *Ezr 9:14*
remnant
so that this man was greatest *Job 1:3*
in the east
set as a mark, *so that* I am a *Job 7:20*
burden to
so that I am not able to look *Ps 40:12*
up
so that a man shall say,   *Ps 58:11*
There is a reward
he led them safely, *so that* *Ps 78:53*
they feared not
so that it went ill with   *Ps 106:32*
Moses for their sakes
so that he wanteth nothing for *Ec 6:2*
his soul
so that thou didst not lay *Isa 47:7*
things to heart
been forsaken, *so that* no *Isa 60:15*
men went thro' thee
so that I will not take any of *Jer 33:26*
his seed
so that the Lord could no *Jer 44:22*
longer bear
so that in all your doings *Eze 21:24*
sins appear
so that all the trees in Eden *Eze 31:9*
envied him
so that no beast might stand *Da 8:4*
before him

so that no man did lift up his *Zec 1:21*
head
Jesus answered not, *so that* *M'k 15:5*
Pilate marvelled
so that they which would *Lu 16:26*
pass to you
so that they are without   *Ro 1:20*
excuse
so that from Jerusalem I   *Ro 15:19*
preached gospel
so that contrariwise ye should *2Co 2:7*
forgive
so that I rejoiced the more   *2Co 7:7*
so that ye cannot do the   *Ga 5:17*
things ye would
so that ye were ensamples to *1Th 1:7*
all that believed
so that we may boldly say, *Heb 13:6*
Lord is my helper

NOT SO

do *not so* wickedly; oh *not*   *Ge 19:7;*
so, my Lord   *19:13*
it must *not* be *so* done in our *Ge 29:26*
country
not so my father, this is the *Ge 48:18*
firstborn
not so go ye that are men   *Ex 10:11*
and serve Lord
servant Moses is *not so* who *Nu 12:7*
is faithful
obeying the Lord, but they did *J'g 2:17*
not so
is it *not so*; it is *not so*   *J'g 14:15;*
   1Sa 20:2
the matter is *not so*, but a *2Sa 20:21*
man lifted up
altho my house be *not so*   *2Sa 23:5*
with God, yet
not fear him, but it is *not so* *Job 9:35*
with me
if it be *not so*, who will   *Job 24:25*
make me a liar
but now because it is *not so* *Job 35:15*
he hath visited
ungodly are *not so*, but are like *Ps 1:4*
the chaff
the heart of the foolish doeth *Pr 15:7*
not so
meaneth *not so*, nor heart *Isa 10:7*
think so
the pride of Moab, but his *Isa 16:6*
lies shall *not* be *so*
not be *so*, his lies shall *not so* *Jer 48:30*
effect it
but from the beginning it was *M't 19:8*
not so
it shall *not* be *so* among you *M't 20:26*
not so, lest there be not   *M't 25:9*
enough for us
not so, but he shall be called *Lu 1:60*
John
exercise lordship over them, *Lu 22:26*
shall *not* be *so*
if it were *not so*, I would *Joh 14:2*
have told you
but Peter said, *Not so*,   *Ac 10:14;*
Lord   *11:8*
not only *so* but we glory in *Ro 5:3*
tribulations
not only *so*, but we also joy in *Ro 5:11*
God
but ye have *not so* learned *Eph 4:20*
Christ
these things ought *not so* to *Jas 3:10*
be

WAS SO, SO WAS

and it *was so*   *Ge 1:7;*
   1:9, 11, 15, 24, 30
as he interpreted to us, so it *Ge 41:13*
was
so it *was* always, cloud *Nu 9:16*
covered it by
so It *was* when cloud was on *Nu 9:20*
tabernacle
so it *was* when cloud abode *Nu 9:21*
from even
dew be on the fleece only, and *J'g 6:38*
it *was* so
it *was* so that all who saw it *J'g 19:30*
said, No such deed
when men of Ashdod saw that *1Sa 5:7*
it *was* so
it *was* so that when he turned *1Sa 10:9*
from Samuel
it *was* so from that day *1Sa 30:25*
forward made a statute

it *was so* when any came to king	2Sa 15:2
it *was so* that when any man came nigh	2Sa 15:5
so was all the counsel of Ahithophel	2Sa 16:23
so was it charged me by word of Lord	1Ki 13:9
so it was that Israel had sinned	2Ki 17:7
so was Israel carried away to Assyria	2Ki 17:23
so was the commandment of Lord	2Ch 29:25
and *so it was* that while they were there	Lu 2:6
Jesus, who *was so* named of the angel	Lu 2:21
and *so was* also James and John astonished	Lu 5:10
Rhoda constantly affirmed it *was so*	Ac 12:15

SO, a person

messengers to *S.* king of Egypt	2Ki 17:4

SOAKED

their land shall be *s.* with blood	Isa 34:7
land shall be glutted with blood (B)	Isa 34:7
land shall be drunken with blood (E)	Isa 34:7

SOAP

take much *s.* (A)(B)(E)(R)	Jer 2:22; Mal 3:2

SOBER

or whether we be *s.*, it is for your	2Co 5:13
if we are in our right mind (A)(N)(R)	2Co 5:13
if we are thoughtful (B)	2Co 5:13
if we are perfectly sane (P)	2Co 5:13
others: but let us watch and be *s.*	1Th 5:6
let us be on guard and composed (B)	1Th 5:6
keep awake, with our wits about us (P)	1Th 5:6
But let us, who are of the day, be *s.*	1Th 5:8
husband of one wife, vigilant, *s.*	1Ti 3:2
circumspect, temperate (A)	1Ti 3:2
temperate, discreet (B)	1Ti 3:2
temperate, sensible (R)	1Ti 3:2
wives be grave not slanderers, *s.*	1Ti 3:11
a lover of good men, *s.*, just	Tit 1:8
sensible, fair (B)	Tit 1:8
right-minded (N)	Tit 1:8
fair-minded (P)	Tit 1:8
master of himself, upright (R)	Tit 1:8
That the aged men be *s.* grave	Tit 2:2
venerable, sensible (A)(B)	Tit 2:2
temperate, serious (P)(R)	Tit 2:2
teach the young women to be *s.*	Tit 2:4
likewise exhort to be *s.* minded	Tit 2:6
to behave prudently (A)(B)	Tit 2:6
to be temperate in all things (N)	Tit 2:6
to control themselves (R)	Tit 2:6
be *s.* and hope to the end for	1Pe 1:13
be perfectly composed (B)	1Pe 1:13
be perfectly self-controlled (N)	1Pe 1:13
be ye therefore *s.* and watch unto	1Pe 4:7
keep sound-minded and self-restrained (A)	1Pe 4:7
be serious-minded (B)	1Pe 4:7
be calm, self-controlled (P)	1Pe 4:7
Be *s.* be vigilant; because your	1Pe 5:8
Be well-balanced-temperate, sober-minded (A)	1Pe 5:8
Be composed; Be on guard (B)	1Pe 5:8
Awake! be on the alert (N)	1Pe 5:8
Be self-controlled (P)	1Pe 5:8

SOBERLY

but to think *s.* according as	Ro 12:3
but to think in a humble way (B)	Ro 12:3

we should live *s.*, righteously	Tit 2:12
to live dscreet (A)(B)	Tit 2:12
to live a life of temperance (N)	Tit 2:12
to live responsible lives (P)	Tit 2:12

SOBER-MINDED

sober-minded (S)	1Th 5:6; 1Ti 3:2; 3:11; Tit 1:8; 2:2, 4; 1Pe 4:7
to be *s.* (E)	Tit 2:5
be well-balanced temperate, *s.* (A)	1Pe 5:8

SOBERNESS

forth the words of truth and *s.*	Ac 26:25
uttering straight sound truth (A)	Ac 26:25
words of truth and sane thinking (B)	Ac 26:25

SOBRIETY

with shamefacedness and *s.*	1Ti 2:9
and charity and holiness with *s.*	1Ti 2:15

SOCHO

and Heber the father of *S.*	1Ch 4:18

SOCHOH

to him pertained *S.* and all	1Ki 4:10

SOCKET

hundred talents, a talent for a *s.*	Ex 38:27

SOCKETS

forty *s.* of silver under the	Ex 26:19;
twenty	26:21; 36:24, 26
two *s.* under one board for	Ex 26:19;
his two	26:21, 25; 36:24, 26 ,30
be of gold, upon the four *s.*	Ex 26:32;
of silver	27:16; 36:36; 38:19
shall cast five *s.* of brass	Ex 26:37;
for them	36:38
their twenty *s.* shall be of brass	Ex 27:10; 27:11; 38:10-11
their pillars ten, and their *s.* ten	Ex 27:10; 38:12
pillars three, and their *s.*	Ex 27:14;
three	27:15; 38:14-15
be of silver, and their *s.* of brass	Ex 27:17; 38:17
twined linen, and their *s.* of brass	Ex 27:18
set in *s.* or rosettes of gold (A)(B)	Ex 28:11; 28:13, 25
chains of the *s.* (B)	Ex 28:14
his bars, his pillars, and his *s.*	Ex 35:11
his pillars, and their *s.* and silver	Ex 35:17
and their *s.* were sixteen *s.* of silver	Ex 36:30
were cast the *s.* of the sanctuary	Ex 38:27
sanctuary, and the *s.* of the veil	Ex 38:27
hundred *s.* of the hundred talents	Ex 38:27
s. to the door of the tabernacle	Ex 38:30
And the *s.* of the court round about	Ex 38:31
and the *s.* of the court gate, and all	Ex 38:31
his bars, and his pillars, and his *s.*	Ex 39:33
of the court, his pillars, and his *s.*	Ex 39:40
fastened his *s.*, and set up the boards	Ex 40:18
the pillars thereof, and the *s.* thereof	Nu 3:36; 3:37
their *s.* and their pins, and their	Nu 3:37; 4:32
of marble, set upon *s.* of fine gold	Ca 5:15

SOCIETY

habits of lawless *s.* (N)	2Pe 2:7

SOCOH

and Adullam *S.*, and Azekah	Jos 15:35
Shamir, and Jattir, and *S.*	Jos 15:48

SOD

and Jacob *s.* pottage: and Esau	Ge 25:29
Jacob was boiling pottage (A)(B)(E)(R)	Ge 25:29
other holy offerings *s.* they in pots	2Ch 35:13
cooked the holy offerings (A)	2Ch 35:13
boiled in pots (B)(E)(R)	2Ch 35:13

SODA

as vinegar upon *s.* (S)	Pr 25:20

SODDEN

it raw, nor *s.* at all with water	Ex 12:9
boiled (A)(E)(R)	Ex 12:9; Le 6:28; Nu 6:19; 1Sa 2:15; La 4:10
cooked (B)	Ex 12:9; Le 6:28
the earthen vessel wherein it is *s.*	Le 6:28
and if it be *s.* in a brasen pot	Le 6:28
priest shall take the *s.* shoulder	Nu 6:19
boiled (B)	Nu 6:19; 1Sa 2:15; La 4:10
he will not have *s.* flesh of thee	1Sa 2:15
women have *s.* their own children	La 4:10

SODI

Zebulun, Gaddiel the son of *S.*	Nu 13:10

SODOM

before Lord destroyed *S.* and Gomorrah	Ge 13:10
the men of *S.* were wicked exceedingly	Ge 13:13
they took all the goods of *S.* and Gomorrah	Ge 14:11
they took Lot who dwelt in *S.* and his goods	Ge 14:12
the king of *S.* went out to meet Abram	Ge 14:17
Lord said, Because the cry of *S.* is great	Ge 18:20
if I find in *S.* fifty righteous, I will spare	Ge 18:26
Lord rained upon *S.* fire out of heaven	Ge 19:24
like the overthrow of *S.* and Gomorrah	De 29:23; Isa 13:19; Jer 49:18; 50:40
their vine is of the vine of *S.* and Gomorrah	De 32:32
we should have been as *S.* like Gomorrah	Isa 1:9
hear the word of the Lord, ye rulers of *S.*	Isa 1:10
and they shall declare their sin as *S.*	Isa 3:9
they are all of them unto me as *S.*	Jer 23:14
greater than the punishment of sin of *S.*	La 4:6
thy younger sister is *S.*	Eze 16:46; 16:48-49, 55
when I bring again the captivity of *S.*	Eze 16:53
overthrown you, as God overthrew *S.*	Am 4:11
as I live, surely Moab shall be as *S.*	Zep 2:9
it shall be more tolerable for the land of *S.*	M't 10:15; 11:24; M'k 6:11; Lu 10:12
the same day that Lot went out of *S.*	Lu 17:29
had left us a seed, we had been as *S.*	Ro 9:29
turning cities of *S.* and Gomorrah into ashes	2Pe 2:6
even as *S.* and Gomorrah and cities about them	Jude 7
great city spiritually called *S.* and Egypt	Re 11:8

SODOMA

We had been as *S.* and been made   *Ro 9:29*

SODOMITE

nor a *s.* of the sons of Israel   *De 23:17*

SODOMITES

there were also *s.* in the land   *1Ki 14:24*
took away the *s.* out of the land   *1Ki 15:12*
And the remnant of the *s.* which   *1Ki 22:46*
he brake down the houses of the *s.*   *2Ki 23:7*

SOEVER

what saddles *s.* he rideth upon that   *Le 15:9*
man *s.* there be of the house of Israel   *Le 17:3*
What man *s.* of the seed of Aaron is a   *Le 22:4*
What thing *s.* I command you   *De 12:32*
that what thing *s.* thou shalt hear out   *2Sa 15:35*
unto the people, how many *s.* they be   *2Sa 24:3*
What prayer and supplication *s.*   *1Ki 8:38*
what prayer or what supplication *s.*   *2Ch 6:29*
And what cause *s.* shall come to you   *2Ch 19:10*
blasphemies wherewith *s.* they   *M'k 3:28*
what place *s.* ye enter into an   *M'k 6:10*
What things *s.* ye desire, when   *M'k 11:24*
for what things *s.* he doeth, these   *Joh 5:19*
Whose *s.* sins ye remit, they are   *Joh 20:23*
whose *s.* sins ye retain, they   *Joh 20:23*
that what things *s.* the law saith   *Ro 3:19*

SOFT

For God maketh my heart *s.*   *Job 23:16*
made my heart faint, timid, broken (A)   *Job 23:16*
made my heart faint (B)(E)(R)   *Job 23:16*
will he speak *s.* words unto thee   *Job 41:3*
will he use friendly words (B)   *Job 41:3*
thou makest it *s.* with showers   *Ps 65:10*
A *s.* answer turneth away wrath   *Pr 15:1*
A pleasant answer turns away wrath (B)   *Pr 15:1*
and a *s.* tongue breaketh the bone   *Pr 25:15*
A man clothed in *s.* raiment   *M't 11:8*
A man dressed in silks and satins (N)   *M't 11:8*
A man dressed in fine clothes (P)   *Lu 7:25*
behold they that wear *s.* clothing   *M't 11:8*
A man clothed in *s.* raiment   *Lu 7:25*
A man elegantly dressed (B)   *Lu 7:25*

SOFTENED

s. with oil (A)(B)(R)   *Isa 1:6*

SOFTER

his words were *s.* than oil, yet   *Ps 55:21*

SOFTLY

I will lead on *s.* according as   *Ge 33:14*
lead on slowly (A)(B)(R)   *Ge 33:14*
lead on gently (E)   *Ge 33:14*
and went *s.* unto him, and smote   *J'g 4:21*
came *s.* and uncovered his feet   *Ru 3:7*
Quietly she moved near (B)   *Ru 3:7*
and lay in sackcloth, and went *s.*   *1Ki 21:27*

went quietly (A)   *1Ki 21:27*
went about sadly (B)   *1Ki 21:27*
went about dejectedly (R)   *1Ki 21:27*
the waters of Shiloah that go *s.*   *Isa 8:6*
that go gently (A)(B)(R)   *Isa 8:6*
I shall go *s.* all my years in   *Isa 38:15*
And when the south wind blew *s.*   *Ac 27:13*
we answer *s.* (A)   *1Co 4:13*

SOIL

vinedressers and *s.*-tillers (A)   *2Ki 25:12*
he loved the *s.* (B)(R)   *2Ch 26:10*
It was planted in a good *s.* by   *Eze 17:8*
tillers of the *s.* (R)   *Joe 1:11*
s. yielded its produce (B)   *Jas 5:18*

SOILED

s. garments (B)   *Zec 3:3; 3:4*
s. their clothes (A)(B)(R)   *Re 3:4*

SOJOURN

went down into Egypt to *s.* there   *Ge 12:10*
to live temporarily (A)   *Ge 12:10; 19:9; 26:3; Le 17:8, 10; 19:33; Jer 42:15; 43:2; Eze 20:38*
to stay a while (B)   *Ge 12:10*
This one fellow came in to *s.*   *Ge 19:9*
came here as an immigrant (B)   *Ge 19:9*
S. in this land, and I will be with   *Ge 26:3*
For to *s.* in the land are we come   *Ge 47:4*
to live temporarily (B)   *Ge 47:4*
when a stranger shall *s.* with thee   *Ex 12:48*
an alien live among you (B)   *Ex 12:48; Le 17:8, 10; 19:33, 25:45; Nu 15:14*
the strangers which *s.* among you   *Le 17:8; 17:10, 13*
And if a stranger *s.* with thee in   *Le 19:33*
or of the strangers that *s.* in Israel   *Le 20:2*
every stranger who resides in Israel (B)   *Le 20:2*
the strangers that do *s.* among you   *Le 25:45*
if a stranger shall *s.* among you   *Nu 9:14*
If a stranger resides among you (B)   *Nu 9:14*
And if a stranger *s.* with you, or   *Nu 15:14*
to *s.* where he could find a place   *J'g 17:8*
he settled down (B)   *J'g 17:8*
I go to *s.* where I may find a place   *J'g 17:9*
went to *s.* in the country of Moab   *Ru 1:1*
to live for a while (B)   *Ru 1:1*
evil upon the widow with whom I *s.*   *1Ki 17:20*
with whom I am staying (B)   *1Ki 17:20*
and *s.* wheresoever thou canst   *2Ki 8:1*
Woe is me, that I *s.* in Mesech, that   *Ps 120:5*
I lodge near Mesech (B)   *Ps 120:5*
feet shall carry her afar off to *s.*   *Isa 23:7*
carry her off to settle (A)   *Isa 23:7*
to settle far away (B)   *Isa 23:7*
aforetime into Egypt to *s.* there   *Isa 52:4*
enter into Egypt, and go to *s.* there   *Jer 42:15*
faces to go into Egypt to *s.* there   *Jer 42:17*
to live there (B)   *Jer 42:17; 42:22; 44:12*
whither ye desire to go and to *s.*   *Jer 42:22*
say, Go not into Egypt to *s.* there   *Jer 43:2*
the land of Egypt to *s.* there   *Jer 44:12; 44:14, 28*
They shall no more *s.* there   *La 4:15*
not tarry longer here (A)   *La 4:15*
out of the country where they *s.*   *Eze 20:38*

where they stay (B)   *Eze 20:38*
to the strangers that *s.* among you   *Eze 47:22*
strangers who reside among you (A)   *Eze 47:22*
immigrants who permanently reside (B)   *Eze 47:22*
should *s.* in a strange land   *Ac 7:6*
alien in a foreign land (B)(N)   *Ac 7:6*

SOJOURNED

Kadesh and Shur, and *s.* in Gerar   *Ge 20:1*
lived temporarily in Gerar (A)   *Ge 20:1*
lived for a time in Gerar (B)   *Ge 20:1*
to the land wherein thou hast *s.*   *Ge 21:23*
you are an immigrant (B)   *Ge 21:23*
And Abraham *s.* in the Philistines   *Ge 21:34*
lived as a stranger (B)   *Ge 21:34*
I have *s.* with Laban, and stayed   *Ge 32:4*
where Abraham and Isaac *s.*   *Ge 35:27*
had pilgrimaged (B)   *Ge 35:27*
gates out of all Israel, where he *s.*   *De 18:6*
a temporary resident (A)   *De 18:6; Heb 11:9*
temporarily been residing (B)   *De 18:6*
Egypt, and *s.* there with a few   *De 26:5*
who was a Levite, and he *s.* there   *J'g 17:7*
lived there (B)   *J'g 17:7*
and he *s.* in Gibeah; but the men   *J'g 19:16*
living in Gibeah (B)   *J'g 19:16*
and *s.* in the land of the Philistines   *2Ki 8:2*
stayed in the land of the Philistines (B)   *2Ki 8:2*
and Jacob *s.* in the land of Ham   *Ps 105:23*
a migrant in the land of Ham (B)   *Ps 105:23*
s. in Egypt (E)   *Ac 13:17*
faith he *s.* in the land of promise   *Heb 11:9*
he lived around in (B)   *Heb 11:9*

SOJOURNER

sojourner (S)   *Ge 15:13; 17:8; 28:4; 37:1; Ex 12:19; 23:12; Le 17:15; 19:10; 23:22; 24:16, 22; Nu 9:14; 15:14, 30; De 1:16; 10:18-19; 14:21; 26:11-13; 27:19; 28:43; 29:11; 31:12; Jos 8:33; 2Sa 1:13; Job 31:32; Ps 119:19; Jer 7:6; 14:8; 22:3; Eze 22:7, 29; Zec 7:10; Mal 3:5; Ac 7:29*
I am a stranger and a *s.* with you   *Ge 23:4*
a stranger and immigrant (B)   *Ge 23:4*
sojourner (A)   *Ge 28:4; Ex 20:10; Le 24:22; Jos 8:33; Jer 14:8*
a *s.* of the priest, or an hired   *Le 22:10*
though he be a stranger, or a *s.*   *Le 25:35*
temporary resident (A)   *Le 25:35; 25:40; Nu 35:15; Ps 39:12*
foreigner (B)   *Le 25:35; 35:15*
But as an hired servant, and as a *s.*   *Le 25:40*
a temporary resident (B)   *Le 25:40*
a *s.* or stranger wax rich by thee   *Le 25:47*
sell himself unto the stranger or *s.*   *Le 25:47*
and for the *s.* among them   *Nu 35:15*
wrest justice of *s.* (E)   *De 24:17*
justice due a *s.* (E)(R)   *De 27:19*
and a *s.* as all my fathers were   *Ps 39:12*

SOJOURNERS

dwell as *s.* (R)   *Ex 6:4*
sojourners (S)   *Ex 22:21; 23:9; Le 19:34; 22:18; De 10:19; 24:14; Jos 8:35; 1Ch 16:19; 22:2; 2Ch 2:17; 15:9; 30:25; Ps 105:12; 146:9; Isa 5:17; 14:1; Jer 35:7; Ac 2:10; 13:17; 1Pe 1:1; 2:11*
ye are strangers and *s.* with me   *Le 25:23*
temporary residents (A)   *Le 25:23*
lodgers and tenants (B)   *Le 25:23*

and were *s.* there until this day   *2Sa 4:3*
residents up to this day (B)   *2Sa 4:3*
are strangers before thee,   *1Ch 29:15*
and *s.*
mere tenants, temporary   *1Ch 29:15*
residents (B)
Lord watches over *s.* (R)   *Ps 146:9*
strangers and *s.* (E)(R)(S)   *Eph 2:19*
s., exiles (A)   *1Pe 2:11*

SOJOURNETH

of her that *s.* in her house,   *Ex 3:22*
jewels
her that resideth in her house   *Ex 3:22*
(A)
lodger in her house (B)   *Ex 3:22*
unto the stranger that *s.*   *Ex 12:49*
among
stranger who lives among   *Ex 12:49;*
you   (B)   *Le 16:29;   17:12;   18:26;*
  Nu 15:15-16, 26, 29; 19:10; Jos 20:9
or a stranger that *s.* among   *Le 16:29*
you
dwells temporarily among   *Le 16:29;*
you   (A)   *17:12; Nu 15:26*
any stranger that *s.* among   *Le 17:12*
you eat
nor any stranger that *s.* among   *Le 18:26*
you
for thy stranger that *s.* with   *Le 25:6*
thee
temporary resident (A)   *Le 25:6;*
  Nu 15:15
for the stranger that *s.*   *Nu 15:15;*
with you   *15:16*
the stranger that *s.* among   *Nu 15:26;*
them   *15:29; 19:10; Jos 20:9*
remaineth in any place where   *Ezr 1:4*
he *s.*
or of the stranger that *s.* in   *Eze 14:7*
Israel
alien resident (B)   *Eze 14:7*
that in what tribe the   *Eze 47:23*
stranger *s.*
the foreigner resides (A)   *Eze 47:23*
the immigrant homes (B)   *Eze 47:23*

SOJOURNING

years of my *s.* (R)   *Ge 47:9*
the *s.* of the children of   *Ex 12:40*
Israel
Israelites dwelt in Egypt (A)   *Ex 12:40*
Israelites stay in Egypt (B)   *Ex 12:40*
a certain Levite *s.* on the side   *J'g 19:1*
of
living temporarily in Ephraim   *J'g 19:1*
(A)
living as an outsider in   *J'g 19:1*
Ephraim (B)
the time of your *s.* here in   *1Pe 1:17*
fear
time of your temporary   *1Pe 1:17*
residence (A)
during your pilgrimage (B)   *1Pe 1:17*

SOJOURNINGS

land of their *s.* (E)   *Ex 6:4*

SOLACE

let us *s.* ourselves with loves   *Pr 7:18*
console and delight ourselves   *Pr 7:18*
(A)
delight ourselves with love   *Pr 7:18*
(B)(R)

SOLD

he *s.* his birthright unto   *Ge 25:33*
Jacob
for he hath *s.* us, and hath   *Ge 31:15*
quite
and *s.* Joseph to the   *Ge 37:28*
Ishmeelites
Midianites *s.* him into Egypt   *Ge 37:36*
and *s.* unto the Egyptians   *Ge 41:56*
he it was that *s.* to all the   *Ge 42:6*
people
brother, whom ye *s.* into   *Ge 45:4*
Egypt
yourselves, that ye *s.* me   *Ge 45:5*
hither
Egyptians *s.* every man his   *Ge 47:20*
field
wherefore they *s.* not their   *Ge 47:22*
lands

then he shall be *s.* for his theft   *Ex 22:3*
The land shall not be *s.* for   *Le 25:23*
ever
hath *s.* away of his   *Le 25:25*
possession
redeem that which his   *Le 25:25*
brother *s.*
unto the man to whom he *s.*   *Le 25:27*
it
that which is *s.* shall remain   *Le 25:28*
in
within a whole year after it is   *Le 25:29*
s.
then the house that was *s.*   *Le 25:33*
and the
of their cities may not be *s.*   *Le 25:34*
waxen poor, and be *s.* unto   *Le 25:39*
thee
they shall not be *s.* as   *Le 25:42*
bondmen
After he is *s.* he may be   *Le 25:48*
redeemed
from the year that he was *s.*   *Le 25:50*
to him
he have *s.* the field to another   *Le 27:20*
man
be *s.* according to thy   *Le 27:27*
estimation
possession, shall be *s.* or   *Le 27:28*
redeemed
Hebrew woman, be *s.* unto   *De 15:12*
thee
ye shall be *s.* unto your   *De 28:68*
enemies
except their Rock had *s.*   *De 32:30*
them, and
he *s.* them into the hands of   *J'g 2:14*
their
and he *s.* them into the hand of   *J'g 3:8*
Lord *s.* them into the hand of   *J'g 4:2*
Jabin
and he *s.* them into the hands   *J'g 10:7*
of the
he *s.* them into the hand of   *1Sa 12:9*
Sisera
hast *s.* thyself to work evil in   *1Ki 21:20*
ass's head was *s.* for   *2Ki 6:25*
fourscore pieces
of fine flour be *s.* for a shekel   *2Ki 7:1*
of fine flour was *s.* for a   *2Ki 7:16*
shekel
and *s.* themselves to do evil   *2Ki 17:17*
in the
which were *s.* unto the heathen   *Ne 5:8*
or shall they be *s.* unto us   *Ne 5:8*
in the day wherein they *s.*   *Ne 13:15*
victuals
s. on the sabbath unto the   *Ne 13:16*
children
For we are *s.* I and my people   *Es 7:4*
if we had been *s.* for bondmen   *Es 7:4*
Joseph, who was *s.* for a   *Ps 105:17*
servant
creditors is it to whom I have   *Isa 50:1*
s. you
iniquities have ye *s.*   *Isa 50:1*
yourselves
Ye have *s.* yourselves for   *Isa 52:3*
nought
which hath been *s.* unto thee   *Jer 34:14*
money; our wood is *s.* unto us   *La 5:4*
shall not return to that which   *Eze 7:13*
is *s.*
s. a girl for wine, that they   *Joe 3:3*
might
have ye *s.* unto the Grecians   *Joe 3:6*
the place whither ye have *s.*   *Joe 3:7*
them
they *s.* the righteous for silver   *Am 2:6*
not two sparrows *s.* for a   *M't 10:29*
farthing
went and *s.* all that he had   *M't 13:46*
his lord commanded him to   *M't 18:25*
be *s.*
that *s.* and bought in the   *M't 21:12*
temple
the seats of them that *s.*   *M't 21:12*
doves
ointment might have been *s.*   *M't 26:9*
for
that *s.* and bought in the   *M'k 11:15*
temple
and the seats of them that   *M'k 11:15*
s. doves
s. for more than three   *M'k 14:5*
hundred
five sparrows *s.* for two   *Lu 12:6*
farthings
they bought, they *s.*, they   *Lu 17:28*
planted

to cast out them that *s.*   *Lu 19:45*
therein and
in the temple those that *s.*   *Joh 2:14*
oxen, and
said unto them that *s.* doves,   *Joh 2:16*
Take
this ointment *s.* for three   *Joh 12:5*
hundred
And *s.* their possessions and   *Ac 2:45*
goods
of lands or houses *s.* them   *Ac 4:34*
prices of the things that were   *Ac 4:34*
s.
Having land, *s.* it, and   *Ac 4:37*
brought the
Sapphira his wife, *s.* a   *Ac 5:1*
possession
and after it was *s.* was it not in   *Ac 5:4*
whether ye *s.* the land for so   *Ac 5:8*
much
with envy, *s.* Joseph into   *Ac 7:9*
Egypt
but I am carnal, *s.* under sin   *Ro 7:14*
Whatsoever is *s.* in the   *1Co 10:25*
shambles
morsel of meat *s.* his   *Heb 12:16*
birthright

SOLDERING

saying of the *s.*   *Isa 41:7*
(A)(B)(E)(R)

SOLDIER

made four parts to every *s.*   *Joh 19:23*
a part
a devout *s.* of them that   *Ac 10:7*
waited on
by himself with a *s.* that kept   *Ac 28:16*
him
as a good *s.* of Jesus Christ   *2Ti 2:3*
who hath chosen him to be a   *2Ti 2:4*
s.

SOLDIERS

soldiers (B)   *Nu 31:21;*
31:28, 32, 49, 53; Jos 5:4, 6; 8:1; 11:7;
2Ki 25:4, 19; Jer 38:4; 41:3, 16; Eze
              27:10; 39:20
fathers, were bands of *s.* for   *1Ch 7:4*
war
were units of the army for   *1Ch 7:4*
war (A)(R)
came military fighting units   *1Ch 7:4*
(B)
were bands of hosts for war   *1Ch 7:4*
(E)
thousand and two hundred *s.*   *1Ch 7:11*
able and fit for service in   *1Ch 7:11*
war (A)(R)
on active duty for war (B)   *1Ch 7:11*
able to go forth in the host   *1Ch 7:11*
for war (E)
the *s.* of the army which   *2Ch 25:13*
Amaziah
the men of the troops (B)   *2Ch 25:13*
the men of the army   *2Ch 25:13*
(E)(R)
to require of the king a band   *Ezr 8:22*
of *s.*
ashamed to ask for troops   *Ezr 8:22*
(B)
the armed *s.* of Moab cry   *Isa 15:4*
out
the soldiers (A)(R)   *Jer 38:4; 41:3, 16*
the soldiers (A)   *Eze 39:20*
authority, having *s.* under me   *M't 8:9*
have servants under me (B)   *M't 8:9*
the *s.* of the governor took   *M't 27:27*
Jesus
unto him the whole band of   *M't 27:27*
s.
they gave large money unto   *M't 28:12*
the *s.*
the *s.* led him away into the   *M'k 15:16*
hall
the *s.* likewise demanded of   *Lu 3:14*
him
authority, having under me *s.*   *Lu 7:8*
Herod joined his *s.* (N)(R)   *Lu 23:11*
the *s.* also mocked him,   *Lu 23:36*
coming to
the *s.* platted a crown of   *Joh 19:2*
thorns
s. when they had crucified   *Joh 19:23*
Jesus
These things therefore the *s.*   *Joh 19:24*
did

Then came the *s.* and brake   Joh 19:32
one of the *s.* with a spear   Joh 19:34
pierced
him to four quarternions of *s.*   Ac 12:4
Peter was sleeping between   Ac 12:6
two *s.*
was no small stir among the   Ac 12:18
s.
Who immediately took *s.* and   Ac 21:32
saw the chief captain and the   Ac 21:32
s.
that he was borne of the *s.*   Ac 21:35
for the
commanded the *s.* to go   Ac 23:10
down, and
Make ready two hundred *s.*   Ac 23:23
to go to
the *s.* as it was commanded   Ac 23:31
them
said to the centurion and to   Ac 27:31
the *s.*
Then the *s.* cut off the ropes   Ac 27:32
of the

SOLDIERS'

And the *s.* counsel was to kill   Ac 27:42

SOLE

no rest for the *s.* of her foot   Ge 8:9
from the *s.* of thy foot   De 28:35
unto the top
to set the *s.* of her foot upon   De 28:56
shall the *s.* of thy foot have   De 28:65
rest
the *s.* of your foot shall tread   Jos 1:3
upon
from the *s.* of his foot even   2Sa 14:25
to the
with the *s.* of my feet have I   2Ki 19:24
dried
the *s.* of his foot unto his   Job 2:7
crown
s. of the foot even unto the   Isa 1:6
head
with the *s.* of my feet have I   Isa 37:25
dried
s. of their feet was like the *s.*   Eze 1:7
of a

SOLEMN

it is a *s.* assembly; and ye   Le 23:36
shall
it is a festive gathering (B)   Le 23:36
gladness, and in your *s.* days   Nu 10:10
in your *s.* feasts, to make a   Nu 15:3
sweet
day ye shall have a *s.*   Nu 29:35
assembly
have a sacred meeting (B)   Nu 29:35
seventh day shall be a *s.*   De 16:8
assembly
thou keep a *s.* feast unto the   De 16:15
Lord
Proclaim a *s.* assembly for   2Ki 10:20
Baal
on the *s.* feasts of the Lord   2Ch 2:4
your
set occasions (B)   2Ch 2:4
appointed feasts (R)   2Ch 2:4
day they made a *s.* assembly   2Ch 7:9
new moons, and on the *s.*   2Ch 8:13
feasts
set feasts (B)   2Ch 8:13
the three annual feasts (R)   2Ch 8:13
the eighth day was a *s.*   Ne 8:18
assembly
closing festival (B)   Ne 8:18
appointed, on our *s.* feast day   Ps 81:3
upon the harp with a *s.* sound   Ps 92:3
it is iniquity, even the *s.*   Isa 1:13
meeting
because none come to the *s.*   La 1:4
feasts
Lord hath caused the *s.* feasts   La 2:6
Lord, as in the day of a *s.* feast   La 2:7
called as in a *s.* day my   La 2:22
terrors
of Jerusalem in her *s.* feasts   Eze 36:38
appointed feasts   Eze 36:38;
(B)(E)(R)   Eze 46:9
before the Lord in the *s.*   Eze 46:9
feasts
her sabbaths, and all her *s.*   Ho 2:11
feasts
What will ye do in the *s.* day   Ho 9:5
the great assembly day (B)   Ho 9:5
the day of appointed festival   Ho 9:5
(R)

as in the days of the *s.* feast   Ho 12:9
the days of the harvest   Ho 12:9
festival (B)
the days of the appointed   Ho 12:9
feast (R)
ye a fast, call a *s.* assembly   Joe 1:14
sanctify a fast, call a *s.*   Joe 2:15
assembly
not smell in your *s.*   Am 5:21
assemblies
keep thy *s.* feasts, perform thy   Na 1:15
are sorrowful for the *s.*   Zep 3:18
assembly
even the dung of your *s.* feasts   Mal 2:3
bear *s.* testimony (A)(B)   Ac 10:42

SOLEMNITIES

Look upon Zion, the city of   Isa 33:20
our *s.*
the city of our festivals (B)   Isa 33:20
the city of our appointed   Isa 33:20
feasts (R)
in all *s.* of the house of   Eze 45:17
Israel
all the appointed feasts   Eze 45:17
(A)(B)(E)(R)
in the *s.* the meat offering   Eze 46:11
shall be
the appointed festivals (B)   Eze 46:11
the appointed seasons (R)   Eze 46:11

SOLEMNITY

in the *s.* of the year of   De 31:10
release
at the set time of year of   De 31:10
release (A)(E)(R)
the night when a holy *s.* is   Isa 30:29
kept
when a holy feast is kept   Isa 30:29
(A)(E)(R)
the night consecrated to   Isa 30:29
feasting (B)

SOLEMNLY

The man did *s.* protest unto   Ge 43:3
us
warned us sternly (B)   Ge 43:3
he had *s.* sworn (S)   Ex 13:19
howbeit yet protest *s.* unto   1Sa 8:9
them

SOLES

s. of your feet shall tread   De 11:24
shall be
the *s.* of the feet of the   Jos 3:13
priests that
s. of the priests' feet were   Jos 4:18
lifted
put them under the *s.* of his   1Ki 5:3
feet
down at the *s.* of thy feet   Isa 60:14
and the place of the *s.* of my   Eze 43:7
feet
be ashes under the *s.* of your   Mal 4:3
feet

SOLID

not of *s.* food (S)   Heb 5:12; 5:14

SOLITARILY

which dwell *s.* in the wood   Mic 7:14
who live alone in the forest   Mic 7:14
(B)

SOLITARY

Lo, let that night be *s.* let no   Job 3:7
let the night be barren   Job 3:7
(B)(E)(R)
For want and famine they   Job 30:3
were *s.*
gaunt with want and famine   Job 30:3
(A)(E)
Exhausted with want and   Job 30:3
hunger (B)
God setteth the *s.* in families   Ps 68:6
God makes the lonely to live   Ps 68:6
(B)
God gives the desolate a home   Ps 68:6
(R)
in the wilderness in a *s.* way   Ps 107:4
s. place shall be glad for them   Isa 35:1
wilderness and dry land   Isa 35:1
(A)(B)(E)(R)

How doth the city sit *s.* that   La 1:1
was
How sits she all alone (B)   La 1:1
How lonely sits the city (R)   La 1:1
out, and departed into a *s.*   M'k 1:35
place
went out to a deserted place   M'k 1:35
(A)(E)(P)
went out to a lonely spot   M'k 1:35
(B)(N)(R)

SOLOMON

there was born to David in   2Sa 5:14;
Jerusalem *S.*   1Ch 3:5; 14:4
called his name *S.* and   2Sa 12:24
God loved him
S. his brother he called not   1Ki 1:10;
    1:19, 26
S. thy son shall reign   1Ki 1:13;
after me   1:17, 30
I, and my son *S.* shall be   1Ki 1:21
counted offenders
God save king *S.*   1Ki 1:34
Lord been with David even so   1Ki 1:37
be with *S.*
made *S.* king   1Ki 1:39; 1:43
God make the name of *S.*   1Ki 1:47
better than thine
let *S.* swear to me that he   1Ki 1:51
will not slay me
David charged *S.* his son;   1Ki 2:1;
king *S.* sware   2:23
the kingdom was established   1Ki 2:46
in the hand of *S.*
S. made affinity with Pharaoh   1Ki 3:1
king of Egypt
S. loved Lord   1Ki 3:3
Lord appeared to *S.*   1Ki 3:5;
    9:2; 2Ch 1:7; 7:12
S. had asked this thing   1Ki 3:10
God gave *S.* wisdom   1Ki 4:29;
exceeding much   5:12
came to hear the wisdom of   1Ki 4:34;
S. from all kings   M't 12:42;
    Lu 11:31
Hiram king of Tyre sent his   1Ki 5:1
servants to *S.*
king *S.* raised a levy out of   1Ki 5:13
all Israel
so *S.* built the house and   1Ki 6:14;
finished it   2Ch 7:11; Ac 7:47
so was ended all the work   1Ki 7:51
that *S.* made
S. assembled the elders of   1Ki 8:1;
Israel   2Ch 5:2
S. spread forth his hands to   1Ki 8:22
heaven
when *S.* made an end of   1Ki 8:54;
praying   2Ch 7:1
S. held a feast; *S.* made a   1Ki 8:65;
navy of ships   9:26
when queen of Sheba heard   1Ki 10:1;
of fame of *S.* came to   2Ch 9:1
prove him
all the earth sought to *S.*   1Ki 10:24;
    2Ch 9:23
but king *S.* loved many   1Ki 11:1
strange women
S. clave to these in love;   1Ki 11:2;
when *S.* was old   11:4
S. went after Ashtoreth and   1Ki 11:5
after Milcom
S. did evil   1Ki 11:6
S. built for Chemosh and   1Ki 11:7
Molech
the Lord was angry with *S.*   1Ki 11:9
Hadad the Edomite, an   1Ki 11:14
adversary to *S.*
S. built Millo   1Ki 11:27
S. made Jeroboam ruler   1Ki 11:28
over house of Joseph
S. sought therefore to kill   1Ki 11:40
Jeroboam
S. slept with his fathers, and   1Ki 11:43
was buried
Jeroboam fled from the   1Ki 12:2
presence of *S.*
shields of gold which *S.*   1Ki 14:26;
made   2Ch 12:9
Lord said to David and to *S.*   2Ki 21:7;
I will put my name for ever   2Ch 33:7
S. my son is young and   1Ch 22:5
tender
for his name shall be *S.*; to   1Ch 22:9;
help *S.*   22:17
S. thy son, he shall build my   1Ch 28:6
house

thou *S.* my son, know the   *1Ch 28:9*
God of thy fathers
David gave to *S.* the pattern *1Ch 28:11*
of the house
S. my son, whom God alone *1Ch 29:1*
hath chosen
give to *S.* my son a perfect *1Ch 29:19*
heart to keep
S. sat on the throne of the *1Ch 29:23*
Lord as king
the Lord magnified *S.*,   *1Ch 29:25*
exceedingly before Israel
S. numbered all the strangers *2Ch 2:17*
in Israel
are the things wherein *S.* was *2Ch 3:3*
instructed
since time of *S.* not such *2Ch 30:26*
joy in Jerusalem
according to the   *Ne 12:45*
commandment of *S.*
did not king *S.* sin by these *Ne 13:26*
things
the proverbs of *S.*   *Pr 1:1;*
            10:1; 25:1
I am black, but comely, as the *Ca 1:5*
curtains of *S.*
behold king *S.*   *Ca 3:11*
S. had a vineyard at   *Ca 8:11*
Baal-harmon
S. must have a thousand *Ca 8:12*
the sea *S.* made was carried *Jer 52:20*
away
David begat *S*; *S.* begat *M't 1:6;*
Roboam   *1:7*
S. in all his glory, not   *M't 6:29;*
arrayed   *Lu 12:27*
a greater than *S.* is here *M't 12:42;*
             Lu 11:31

SOLOMON'S

And *S.* provision for one day *1Ki 4:22*
was
all that came unto king *S.* *1Ki 4:27*
table
S. wisdom excelled the *1Ki 4:30*
wisdom of
Beside the chief of *S.* officers *1Ki 5:16*
which
S. builders, and Hiram's *1Ki 5:18*
builders
fourth year of *S.* reign over *1Ki 6:1*
Israel
S. desire which he was *1Ki 9:1*
pleased to
present unto his daughter, *S.* *1Ki 9:16*
wife
the officers that were over *S.* *1Ki 9:23*
work
of Sheba had seen all *S.* *1Ki 10:4*
wisdom
all king *S.* drinking vessels *1Ki 10:21*
were
S. servant, whose mother's *1Ki 11:26*
name
S. son was Rehoboam, Abia *1Ch 3:10*
his son
all that came into *S.* heart to *2Ch 7:11*
make
were the chief of king *S.* *2Ch 8:10*
officers
The children of *S.* servants *Ezr 2:55*
and the children of *S.*   *Ezr 2:58;*
servants   *Ne 7:57, 60; 11:3*
The song of songs, which is *S.* *Ca 1:1*
Behold his bed, which is *S.* *Ca 3:7*
walked in the temple in *S.* *Joh 10:23*
porch
them in the porch that is *Ac 3:11*
called *S.*
all with one accord in *S.* *Ac 5:12*
porch

SOLVE

give explanations, *s.* problems *Da 5:16*
(B)

SOME

Lot said, Lest *s.* evil take *Ge 19:19*
me and I die
to the field, and take me *s.* *Ge 27:3*
venison
Let me leave with thee *s.* of *Ge 33:15*
the folk
slay him, and cast him into *Ge 37:20*
s. pit and say, *S.* evil
beast hath devored him
took *s.* of brethren and *Ge 47:2*
presented to Pharaoh

and they gathered *s.* more, *s.* *Ex 16:17*
less
but *s.* of them left of it till *Ex 16:20*
the morning
s. went out on seventh day to *Ex 16:27*
gather
put *s.* of blood on horns of *Le 4:7;*
altar   *4:18*
priest shall dip his finger in *s.* *Le 4:17*
of blood
the priest shall take *s.* of the *Le 14:25*
blood of
Arad took *s.* of them   *Nu 21:1*
prisoners
put *s.* of thine honour upon *Nu 27:20*
him
he hath found *s.* uncleanness *De 24:1*
in her
let fall *s.* of handfuls for her *Ru 2:16*
s. bade me kill thee, but *1Sa 24:10*
spared me
hid in *s.* pit, or in *s.* other *2Sa 17:9*
place
in him is found *s.* good *1Ki 14:13*
thing
did eat and left *s.* (S)   *2Ki 4:44*
s. mischief will come upon us *2Ki 7:9*
but I will grant *s.* deliverance *2Ch 12:7*
Asa oppressed *s.* of people *2Ch 16:10*
same time
s. had wives by whom they *Ezr 10:44*
had children
s. said, We have mortgaged *Ne 5:3*
our lands
saw I *s.* treading wine *Ne 13:15*
presses on Sabbath
and *s.* of my servants set I at *Ne 13:19*
the gates
s. remove landmarks, take *Job 24:2*
away flocks
s. trust in chariots, *s.* in horses *Ps 20:7*
I looked for *s.* to take pity, *Ps 69:20*
was none
sleep taken away, unless cause *Pr 4:16*
s. fall
they not leave *s.* gleaning *Jer 49:9*
grapes
it cast down *s.* of the host *Da 8:10*
and stars
s. of them of understanding *Da 11:35*
shall fall
s. to everlasting life, and *s.* *Da 12:2*
to shame
overthrown *s.* as God   *Am 4:11*
overthrew Sodom
would they not leave *s.* grapes *Ob 5*
s. fell by way side   *M't 13:4;*
           M'k 4:4; Lu 8:5
s. fell on stony places, not *M't 13:5;*
much earth   *M'k 4:5*
s. fell among thorns   *M't 13:7;*
          M'k 4:7; Lu 8:7
s. say thou art John the *M't 16:14;*
Baptist, *s.* Elias *M'k 8:28; Lu 9:19*
there be *s.* standing here *M't 16:28;*
who shall not taste of   *M'k 9:1;*
death till   *Lu 9:19*
s. enunchs which were so *M't 19:12*
born, *s.* made
s. kill and crucify, *s.* shall *M't 23:34*
scourge
they worshipped him, but *s.* *M't 28:17*
doubted
for *s.* have come from far (S) *M'k 8:3*
s. fell upon a rock, and   *Lu 8:6*
withered away
s. of you shall cause to be *Lu 21:16*
put to death
there are *s.* of you that *Joh 6:64*
believe not
shadow of Peter overshadow *s.* *Ac 5:15*
of them
giving out that himself was *s.* *Ac 8:9*
great one
how can I except *s.* man *Ac 8:31*
should guide me
seeking *s.* to lead him by the *Ac 13:11*
hand
s. of them believed; hear *s.* *Ac 17:4;*
new thing   *17:21*
s. mocked   *Ac 17:32*
when *s.* were hardened (S) *Ac 19:9*
s. cried one thing, *s.* another *Ac 19:32;*
           21:34
I pray take *s.* meat   *Ac 27:34*
s. on boards, *s.* on broken *Ac 27:44*
pieces of ship
s. believed and *s.* believed *Ac 28:24*
not

that I may impart to you *s.* *Ro 1:11*
spiritual gift
that I might have *s.* fruit *Ro 1:13*
among you also
for what if *s.* did not believe *Ro 3:3*
as *s.* affirm that we say, let us *Ro 3:8*
do evil that
for a good man *s.* would even *Ro 5:7*
dare to die
if by any means I might save *Ro 11:14*
s. of them
and if *s.* of the branches be *Ro 11:17*
broken off
s. are puffed up as though *1Co 4:18*
not come
such were *s.* of you, but ye *1Co 6:11*
are washed
for *s.* with conscience of the *1Co 8:7*
idol eat it
that I might by all means *1Co 9:22*
save *s.*
neither be idolaters as were *1Co 10:7*
s. of them
commit fornication, as *s.* *1Co 10:8*
of them committed
as *s.* tempted Christ and were *1Co 10:9*
destroyed
nor murmur ye as *s.* of them *1Co 10:10*
murmured
and God hath set *s.* in the *1Co 12:28*
church
greater part remain, *s.* *1Co 15:6*
fallen asleep
how say *s.* that there is no *1Co 15:12*
resurrection
for *s.* have not the knowledge *1Co 15:34*
of God
I think to be bold against *2Co 10:2*
s. who think
for we dare not compare *2Co 10:12*
ourselves with *s.*
but there be *s.* that trouble you *Ga 1:7*
he gave *s.* prophets, *s.* *Eph 4:11*
evangelists
s. indeed preach Christ even *Ph'p 1:15*
of envy
there are *s.* among you walk *2Th 3:11*
disorderly
charge *s.* that they teach no *1Ti 1:3*
other doctrine
from which *s.* having swerved, *1Ti 1:6*
have turned
s. having put away, have *1Ti 1:19*
made shipwreck
in latter times *s.* shall depart *1Ti 4:1*
from faith
s. are already turned aside *1Ti 5:15*
after Satan
s. men's sins open   *1Ti 5:24*
beforehand, *s.* men follow
good works of *s.* are manifest *1Ti 5:25*
beforehand
while *s.* coveted after, they *1Ti 6:10*
have erred
and overthrew the faith of *s.* *2Ti 2:18*
s. vessels to honour and *s.* to *2Ti 2:20*
dishonour
for every house is builded by *Heb 3:4*
s. man
for *s.* when they heard, did *Heb 3:16*
provoke
it remaineth, that *s.* must *Heb 4:6*
enter therein
not forsaking as the manner *Heb 10:25*
of *s.* is
having provided *s.* better *Heb 11:40*
thing for us
for thereby *s.* entertained *Heb 13:2*
angels unawares
Lord is not slack, as *s.* count *2Pe 3:9*
slackness
which are *s.* things hard to be *2Pe 3:16*
understood
s. have compassion, making a *Jude 22*
difference
devil shall cast *s.* of you into *Re 2:10*
prison

SOMEBODY

Jesus said, *S.* hath touched me *Lu 8:46*
Theudas, boasting himself to *Ac 5:36*
be *s.*

SOMEHOW

Lest *s.* if they of Macedonia *2Co 9:4*
(S)

SOMETHING

we will show you s. (S)   1Sa 14:12
S. hath befallen him, he is   1Sa 20:26
not
that s. should be given her to   M'k 5:43
eat
to catch s. out of his mouth   Lu 11:54
that he should give s. to the   Joh 13:29
poor
expecting to receive s. of   Ac 3:5
them
s. more perfectly concerning   Ac 23:15
him
thee, who hath s. to say unto   Ac 23:18
thee
a man think himself to be s.   Ga 6:3
when

SOMETIME

you, that were s. alienated   Col 1:21
and
Which s. were disobedient,   1Pe 3:20
when

SOMETIMES

ye who s. were far off are   Eph 2:13
made
For ye were s. darkness, but   Eph 5:8
now
we ourselves also were s.   Tit 3:3
foolish

SOMEWHAT

they have done s. against any   Le 4:13
of the
done s. through ignorance   Le 4:22
against
while he doeth s. against any   Le 4:27
of the
behold, if the plague be s.   Le 13:6
dark
bright spot, white, and s.   Le 13:19
reddish
than the skin, but be s. dark   Le 13:21
bright spot, s. reddish, or   Le 13:24
white
the other skin, but be s. dark   Le 13:26
not in the skin, but it be s.   Le 13:28
dark
be s. dark after the washing   Le 13:56
of it
I have s. to say unto thee   1Ki 2:14
run after him, and take s. of   2Ki 5:20
him
ease thou s. the grievous   2Ch 10:4
servitude
Ease s. the yoke that thy   2Ch 10:9
father did
but make thou it s. lighter   2Ch 10:10
for us
Simon, I have s. to say unto   Lu 7:40
thee
enquire s. of him more   Ac 23:20
perfectly
had, I might have s. to write   Ac 25:26
I be s. filled with your   Ro 15:24
company
that ye may have s. to   2Co 5:12
answer them
boast s. more of our   2Co 10:8
authority
But of these who seemed to be   Ga 2:6
s.
who seemed to be s. in   Ga 2:6
conference
that this man have s. also to   Heb 8:3
offer
Nevertheless I have s. against   Re 2:4
thee

SON

I will give thee a s. of   Ge 17:16;
Sarah   17:19; 18:10, 14
Sarah bare Abraham a s. in   Ge 21:2;
his old age   21:7
cast out this bondwoman   Ge 21:10
and her s.
Sarah my master's wife bare   Ge 24:36
a s.
Lord hath appointed for my   Ge 24:44
master's s.
he hath therefore given me   Ge 29:33
this s. also
God hath heard me, and   Ge 30:6
given me a s.

the Lord shall add to me   Ge 30:24
another s.
fear not, thou shalt have this   Ge 35:17
s. also
because he was the s. of his   Ge 37:3
old age
if it be a s. then ye shall kill   Ex 1:16
him
every s. that is born cast into   Ex 1:22
river
the child grew, and he became   Ex 2:10
her s.
Zipporah cut off the foreskin   Ex 4:25
of her s.
whether gored a s. or a   Ex 21:31
daughter
s. of thy handmaid may be   Ex 23:12
refreshed
that s. that is priest in stead   Ex 29:30
put them
the days of her purifying for a   Le 12:6
s.
the s. of an Israelitish woman   Le 24:10
strove in
the Israelitish woman's s.   Le 24:11
blasphemed
his uncle, or uncle's s. may   Le 25:49
redeem
hearken unto me thou s. of   Nu 23:18
Zippor
because he hath no s.; if die   Nu 27:4;
and have no s.   27:8
if s. of thy mother entice thee   De 13:6
secretly
not make the s. of the   De 21:16;
beloved, firstborn, before   21:17
the s. of the hated
if man have a stubborn and   De 21:18
rebellious s.
this our s. is stubborn and   De 21:20
rebellious
eye shall be evil towards her   De 28:56
s.
in his youngest s. set up gates   Jos 6:26
of it
border went by valley of s. of   Jos 15:8
Hinnom
lead captive, thou s. of   J'g 5:12
Abinoam
made the s. of his   J'g 9:18
maidservant king
Gaal said, Is not he the s. of   J'g 9:28
Jerubbaal
for thou art the s. of a strange   J'g 11:2
woman
besides her he had neither s.   J'g 11:34
nor daughter
thou shalt conceive and bear   J'g 13:3;
a s.   13:5, 7
the woman bare a s. and   J'g 13:24
called him Samson
Ruth bare s.; s. born to   Ru 4:13;
Naomi   4:17
Hannah gave s. suck until   1Sa 1:23
weaned
women said, Fear not, thou   1Sa 4:20
hast born a s.
Kish had s. whose name was   1Sa 9:2
Saul
what is this that is come to   1Sa 10:11
s. of Kish
seen the s. of Jesse that is   1Sa 16:18
cunning
whose s. is this; whose s.   1Sa 17:55;
art thou   17:58
wherefore cometh not the   1Sa 20:27
s. of Jesse
thou s. of the perverse   1Sa 20:30
rebellious woman
as long as the s. of Jesse   1Sa 20:31
liveth on ground
will s. of Jesse give you fields,   1Sa 22:7
vineyards
Doeg said, I saw s. of Jesse   1Sa 22:9
coming to Nob
Saul said, Hear now, thou s.   1Sa 22:12
of Ahitub
who is s. of Jesse; he is such   1Sa 25:10;
s. of Bel   25:17
he said, I am the s. of a   2Sa 1:13
stranger
Jonathan hath yet s. who is   2Sa 9:3
lame on feet
given master's s. all that   2Sa 9:9
pertained to Saul
master's s. may have   2Sa 9:10
food; master's s. shall eat at
my table
I will shew kindness to the   2Sa 10:2
s. of Nahash

the s. born to thee (B)   2Sa 12:14
king said, And where is thy   2Sa 16:3
master's s.
not put forth my hand against   2Sa 18:12
the king's s.
I have no s. to keep my name   2Sa 18:18
in remembrance
shall bear no tidings, because   2Sa 18:20
king's s. is dead
nor have we inheritance in   2Sa 20:1
the s. of Jesse
hast given him a s. to sit on   1Ki 3:6
throne
for her bowels yearned upon   1Ki 3:26
her s.
given David a wise s. over   1Ki 5:7
people
Hiram a widow's s. of tribe of   1Ki 7:14
Naphtali
no inheritance in s. of Jesse   1Ki 12:16;
  2Ch 10:16
Abijah the s. of Jeroboam fell   1Ki 14:1
sick
she cometh to ask a thing of   1Ki 14:5
thee for her s.
s. of the mistress of the house   1Ki 17:17
fell sick
brought evil on the widow, by   1Ki 17:20
slaying her s.
carry him to Joash king's s.   1Ki 22:26;
  2Ch 18:25
Jehoram reigned, he had   2Ki 1:17
she said to her s., Bring me   2Ki 4:6
yet a vessel
about this season thou shalt   2Ki 4:16
embrace a s.
and the woman bare a s. at   2Ki 4:17
that season
did I desire s.; took up her   2Ki 4:28;
s.   4:37
give s. to eat him, and she hath   2Ki 6:29
hid her s.
see ye how this s. of a   2Ki 6:32
murderer hath sent
the woman whose s. he had   2Ki 8:1
restored to life
this is her s. whom Elisha   2Ki 8:5
restored to life
Athaliah saw her s. was   2Ki 11:1;
dead   2Ch 22:10
Jehoiada shewed them the   2Ki 11:4
king's s.
brought the king's s. and put   2Ki 11:12
crown
and on thy side, thou s. of   1Ch 12:18
Jesse
and he also was the s. of the   1Ch 20:6
giant
a s. be born to thee, a man of   1Ch 22:9
rest
there was never a s. left him   2Ch 21:17
him, because he is s.   2Ch 22:9
of Jehoshaphat
he said Behold, the king's s.   2Ch 23:3
shall reign
Zabdiel their overseer, s.   Ne 11:14
of great
he shall neither have s. nor   Job 18:19
nephew
kiss the S. lest he be angry,   Ps 2:12
and perish
thou slanderest thine own   Ps 50:20
mother's s.
and thy righteousness unto   Ps 72:1
the king's s.
the s. thou hast raised (B)   Ps 80:15
and save the s. of thine   Ps 86:16
handmaid
nor shall the s. of wickedness   Ps 89:22
afflict him
I am the s. of thine   Ps 116:16
handmaid
as a father s. in whom he   Pr 3:12
delighteth
I was my father's s. only   Pr 4:3
beloved of my mother
a wise s. maketh a glad father   Pr 10:1;
  15:20
gathereth in summer is wise   Pr 10:5;
sleepeth in harvest, s.   17:2; 19:26
causeth shame
a wise s. heareth his father's   Pr 13:1
instruction
foolish s. is a grief to his   Pr 17:25
father
foolish s. is the calamity of   Pr 19:13
his father
whoso keepeth the law, is a   Pr 28:7
wise s.

the *s.* of my womb *s.* of my | Pr 31:2
vows
he begetteth a *s.* nothing in his | Ec 5:14
hand
blessed land, when king is *s.* | Ec 10:17
of nobles
not afraid of anger of *s.* of | Isa 7:4
Remaliah
let us set a king in it, even the | Isa 7:6
s. of Tabeal
the head of Samaria is | Isa 7:9
Remaliah's *s.*
a virgin shall conceive and | Isa 7:14
bear a *s.*
unto us a child is born, a *s.* is | Isa 9:6
given
how art fallen, O Lucifer, *s.* | Isa 14:12
of morning
I will cut off from Babylon *s.* | Isa 14:22
and nephew
s. or son's *s.* (A)(B)(E) | Isa 14:22
I am *s.* of the wise, the *s.* of | Isa 19:11
ancient kings
not have compassion on the | Isa 49:15
s. of her womb
neither let the *s.* of the | Isa 56:3
stranger speak
make thee mourning, as for | Jer 6:26
an only *s.*
a *s.* born (A)(B)(R) | Jer 20:15
not have a *s.* to reign on his | Jer 33:21
throne
shall deliver neither *s.* nor | Eze 14:20
daughter
soul of the *s.* is mine, soul | Eze 18:4
that sins die
if he beget *s.* that is a | Eze 18:10
robber, shedder of
a *s.* seeth father's sins and | Eze 18:14
doeth not
why not *s.* bear iniquity of | Eze 18:19
father when *s.* hath done
what is lawful
s. not bear iniquity of | Eze 18:20
father nor father of *s.*
for *s.* or daughter they may | Eze 44:25
defile them.
took Gomer, which bare him | Ho 1:3;
s. | 7:8
he is an unwise *s.* for he | Ho 13:13
should not stay
I was no prophet, nor | Am 7:14
prophet's *s.*
I will make it as mourning of | Am 8:10
an only *s.*
for the *s.* dishonoureth the | Mic 7:6
father
s. honoureth his father, a | Mal 1:6
servant his
she shall bring forth a *s.* | M't 1:21;
| Lu 1:31
conceive and bear a *s.* (B) | M't 1:23
Jesus said, S. be of good | M't 9:2;
cheer | M'k 2:5
loveth *s.* or daughter more | M't 10:37
than me
no man knoweth *s.* but | M't 11:27;
Father, nor Father, save *s.* | Lu 10:22
and he to whom *s.*
the carpenter's *s.* | M't 13:55;
| M'k 6:3; Lu 4:22
thou art Christ the S. of | M't 16:16;
the living God | Joh 6:69
s. go work to-day in my | M't 21:28
vineyard
but when husbandmen saw | M't 21:38
the *s.* they said
what think ye of Christ? | M't 22:42
whose *s.* is he
a *s.* of perdition (B) | M't 23:15
a *s.* of hell (E) | M't 23:15
thou *s.* of the most high God | M'k 5:7
having yet one *s.* his | M'k 12:6
well-beloved
father shall betray the *s.* | M'k 13:12
children rise
that hour knoweth not the | M'k 13:32
s. but Father
art thou the Christ, the *s.* of | M'k 14:61
the blessed
Elisabeth bear thee *s.* name | Lu 1:13
John
he shall be called the *s.* of the | Lu 1:32
Highest
Elisabeth conceived a *s.*; | Lu 1:36;
brought forth *s.* | 1:57
s. why hast thou dealt with us | Lu 2:48
Jesus being, as was supposed, | Lu 3:23
s. of Joseph, who was *s.* of Heli

dead man carried out, only *s.* | Lu 7:12
of mother
if *s.* of peace be there, your | Lu 10:6
peace rest
if a *s.* shall ask bread of any | Lu 11:11
of you
the father shall be divided | Lu 12:53
against the *s.*
the younger *s.* gathered all | Lu 15:13
together
s. thou art ever with me, all | Lu 15:31
is thine
s. remember, that thou in thy | Lu 16:25
lifetime
forasmuch as he also is the *s.* | Lu 19:9
of Abraham
only begotten *s.* in bosom of | Joh 1:18
Father
found Jesus of Nazareth *s.* of | Joh 1:45
Joseph
the Father loveth the *s.* given | Joh 3:35;
| 5:20
that believeth on the *s.* that | Joh 3:36
believeth not *s.*
a certain nobleman whose *s.* | Joh 4:46
was sick
s. can do nothing of himself, | Joh 5:19
what things seeth Father do,
doth *s.* likewise
even so the *s.* quickeneth | Joh 5:21
whom he will
but hath committed all | Joh 5:22
judgment to the *s.*
all men honour *s.* he that | Joh 5:23
honoureth not *s.* honoureth
not the Father
so hath he given to *s.* to have | Joh 5:26
life in himself
every one who seeth *s.* and | Joh 6:40
believeth on him
they said, Is not this Jesus | Joh 6:42
the *s.* of Joseph
but *s.* abideth for ever | Joh 8:35
if *s.* therefore shall make you | Joh 8:36
free, shall be free
is this your *s.* | Joh 9:19
his parents said, We know | Joh 9:20
that this is the *s.*
that the Father may be | Joh 14:13
glorified in the *s.*
none of them is lost but the | Joh 17:12
s. of perdition
Simon *s.* of Jonas, lovest thou | Joh 21:15
me more
Barnabas, *s.* of consolation, a | Ac 4:36
Levite
took him up, and nourished | Ac 7:21
for her own *s.*
I have found David the *s.* of | Ac 13:22
Jesse
I am Pharisee, the *s.* of a | Ac 23:6
Pharisee
Paul's sister's *s.* heard of | Ac 23:16
lying in wait
share the likeness of his *s.* | Ro 8:29
(B)(N)
at this time Sarah shall have a | Ro 9:9
s.
then shall *s.* also himself be | 1Co 15:28
subject
no more servant but *s.* and if | Ga 4:7
s. then an heir
cast out bondwoman and *s.* | Ga 4:30
for *s.* of bondwoman not be
heir with *s.*
as a *s.* with father, he served | Ph'p 2:22
in gospel
the S. of his love (A)(B)(E) | Col 1:13
and Marcus sister's *s.* to | Col 4:10
Barnabas
that man of sin the *s.* of | 2Th 2:3
perdition
charge I commit to thee *s.* | 1Ti 1:18
Timothy
I will be a father and he | Heb 1:5
shall be a *s.*
but to the *s.* he saith, Thy | Heb 1:8
throne is for ever
but Christ is a *s.* over his own | Heb 3:6
house
tho' he were a *s.* yet learned | Heb 5:8
he obedience
but the word of the oath | Heb 7:28
maketh the *s.*
refused to be called *s.* of | Heb 11:24
Pharaoh's daughter
and scourgeth every *s.* whom | Heb 12:6
he receiveth
for what *s.* is he whom | Heb 12:7
father chasteneth not

following way of Balaam, *s.* | 2Pe 2:15
of Bozor
is antichrist that denieth | 1Jo 2:22
Father and S.
whosoever denieth S. hath | 1Jo 2:23
not Father, but he that
acknowledgeth S.
shall continue in the S. and | 1Jo 2:24
in Father
Father sent S. to be Saviour | 1Jo 4:14
of world
he that hath S. hath life; he | 1Jo 5:12
that hath not S. of God hath
not life
from Jesus Christ S. of the | 2Jo 3
Father
he that abideth hath both Father | 2Jo 9
and S.

SON *IN LAW*

hast thou here any besides | Ge 19:12
s. in law
Samson the *s. in law* of the | J'g 15:6
Timnite
damsel's father said unto his | J'g 19:5
s. in law
I should be *s. in law* to king | 1Sa 18:18;
| 18:23
Saul said, Thou shalt this | 1Sa 18:21
day be my *s. in law*
now therefore be the king's | 1Sa 18:22
s. in law
it pleased David well to be | 1Sa 18:26
king's *s. in law*
that he might be the king's | 1Sa 18:27
s. in law
who is so faithful as the | 1Sa 22:14
king's *s. in law*
Jehoram was *s. in law* of | 2Ki 8:27
house of Ahab
Tobiah was *s. in law* to | Ne 6:18
Shechaniah
was *s. in law* to Sanballat the | Ne 13:28
Horonite

SON *OF DAVID*

Jesus Christ, the *s. of David* | M't 1:1
Joseph, thou *s. of David* | M't 1:20
Thou *s. of David*, have mercy | M't 9:27;
on us | 20:30-31
Is not this the *s. of David* | M't 12:23
on me, O Lord, thou *s. of* | M't 15:22;
David | Lu 18:38-39
Hosanna to the *s. of David* | Mt 21:9;
| 21:15
They say unto him, The *s.* | M't 22:42
of David
Jesus, thou *s. of David*, | M'k 10:47;
have mercy | 10:48
that Christ is the *s. of* | M'k 12:35
David
which was the *s. of David* | Lu 3:31
they say that Christ is | Lu 20:41
David's *s.*

SON *OF GOD*

form of fourth is like *s. of* | Da 3:25
God
if thou be *s. of God*, | M't 4:3;
command stones be made bread | Lu 4:3, 9
Jesus thou *s. of G.?* art thou | M't 8:29;
come to torment us | Lu 8:28
saying, Of a truth thou art | M't 14:33
the *s. of God*
tell us whether be Christ the | M't 26:63
s. of God
for he said, I am the *s. of* | M't 27:43
God
truly this was the *s. of God* | M't 27:54;
| M'k 15:39
the gospel of Jesus Christ the | M'k 1:1
s. of God
saying, Thou art the *s. of* | M'k 3:11;
God | Joh 1:49
that holy thing be called *s. of* | Lu 1:35
God
was son of Adam, which was | Lu 3:38
s. of God
devils came out crying, Thou | Lu 4:41;
art Christ the *s. of God* | Joh 6:69; 11:27
they said, Art thou then the | Lu 22:70
s. of God
I bare record, that this is *s.* | Joh 1:34
of God
not believed in only begotten | Joh 3:18
s. of God

dead shall hear voice of the s. Joh 5:25
of God
he said, Dost thou believe on Joh 9:35
s. of God
because I said, I am the s. Joh 10:36
of God
that the s. of God might be Joh 11:4
glorified thereby
because he made himself the Joh 19:7
s. of God
believe Jesus is Christ, the s. Joh 20:31
I believe Jesus Christ is s. of Ac 8:37
God
preached Christ, that he is the Ac 9:20
s. of God
declared to be s. of God with Ro 1:4
power
for the s. of God was not 2Co 1:19
yea and nay
I live by the faith of the s. of Ga 2:20
God
come in unity of knowledge Eph 4:13
of s. of God
a great high priest, Jesus the Heb 4:14
s. of God
they crucify to themselves s. Heb 6:6
of God afresh
made life to s. of God abideth Heb 7:3
a priest
hath trodden under foot the Heb 10:29
s. of God
this purpose s. of God was 1Jo 3:8
manifested
whoso shall confess Jesus is 1Jo 4:15
the s. of God
he that believeth Jesus is the s. 1Jo 5:5
of God
he that believeth on s. of God 1Jo 5:10
hath witness
that ye may believe on name 1Jo 5:13
of s. of God
and we know that the s. of 1Jo 5:20
God is come
write these things, saith the s. Re 2:18
of God

SON *OF MAN*

s. of man, stand upon thy feet Eze 2:1
s. of man, I send thee to Eze 2:3
children of Israel
thou, s. of man, be not afraid Eze 2:6
of them
thou s. of man, hear what I say Eze 2:8
unto thee
s. of man, eat this roll Eze 3:1
s. of man, cause thy belly to eat Eze 3:3
s. of man, go get thee to the Eze 3:4
house of Israel
s. of man, all words that I Eze 3:10
speak receive
s. of man, I have made thee Eze 3:17
a watchman
s. of man, they shall put bands Eze 3:25
upon thee
s. of man, take thee a tile before Eze 4:1
thee
s. of man, I will break staff of Eze 4:16
bread in Jerusalem
thou s. of man, take thee a Eze 5:1
sharp knife
s. of man, set thy face towards Eze 6:2
mountains
thou s. of man, thus saith the Eze 7:2
Lord God
s. of man, lift up thine eyes Eze 8:5
toward north
he said, S. of man, seest thou Eze 8:6
what they do
he said, S. of man, dig now in Eze 8:8
the wall
s. of man, hast thou seen what Eze 8:12
ancients do
hast thou seen this O s. of Eze 8:15;
man 8:17
s. of man, these are the men Eze 11:2
that devise
prophesy against them O s. of Eze 11:4
man
s. of man, thy brethren are Eze 11:15
they unto whom
s. of man, thou dwellest in Eze 12:2
rebellious house
therefore thou s. of man, Eze 12:3
prepare thee stuff
s. of man, hath not the house Eze 12:9
of Israel said
s. of man, eat thy bread with Eze 12:18
quaking

s. of man, what is that Eze 12:22
proverb that ye have
s. of man, they of house of Eze 12:27
Israel say
s. of man, prophesy against Eze 13:2
the prophets
thou s. of man, set face Eze 13:17
against people
s. of man, these men have Eze 14:3
set up their idols
s. of man, when the land Eze 14:13
sinneth against me
s. of man, what is vine tree Eze 15:2
more than any tree
s. of man, cause Jerusalem Eze 16:2
know her abomination
s. of man, put forth a riddle Eze 17:2
and speak
s. of man, speak to the elders Eze 20:3
of Israel
s. of man, wilt thou judge Eze 20:4
them
therefore s. of man, speak to Eze 20:27
house of Israel
s. of man, set thy face Eze 20:46
toward the south
s. of man, set thy face toward Eze 21:2
Jerusalem
sigh thou s. of man, with Eze 21:6
bitterness
s. of man prophesy and say, Eze 21:9;
A sword, a sword 21:28
cry and howl, s. of man for Eze 21:12
it shall be on people
s. of man, prophesy and Eze 21:14
smite thine hands
also thou s. of man, appoint Eze 21:19
thee two ways
thou s. of man, wilt thou Eze 22:2
judge the city
s. of man, house of Israel Eze 22:18
is become dross
s. of man, say to her, Thou Eze 22:24
art the land that
s. of man there were two Eze 23:2
women of one
s. of man judge Aholah Eze 23:36
and Aholibah
s. of man, write the name of Eze 24:2
the day
s. of man, I take away the Eze 24:16
desire of thine eyes
s. of man, shall it not be in Eze 24:25
the day when
s. of man, set thy face Eze 25:2
against Ammonites
s. of man, because that Tyrus Eze 26:2
hath said
s. of man, take up a Eze 27:2;
lamentation 28:12
s. of man, say unto the prince Eze 28:2
of Tyrus
s. of man set thy face Eze 28:21
against Zidon
s. of man, set thy face Eze 29:2
against Pharaoh
s. of man, Nebuchadrezzar Eze 29:18
caused his army
s. of man, prophesy, Thus Eze 30:2
saith Lord
s. of man, I have broken the Eze 30:21
arm of Pharaoh
s. of man, speak to Pharaoh Eze 31:2
king of Egypt
s. of man, take up Eze 32:2
lamentation for Pharaoh
s. of man, wail for the Eze 32:18
multitude of Egypt
s. of man, speak to children Eze 33:2
of thy people
thou, O s. of man I have set Eze 33:7
thee a watchman
O s. of man, speak to house Eze 33:10
of Israel
s. of man, say to children of Eze 33:12
Israel
s. of man, they that inhabit Eze 33:24
those wastes
s. of man, thy people still Eze 33:30
are talking
s. of man, prophesy against Eze 34:2
the shepherds
s. of man, set thy face Eze 35:2
against mount Seir
s. of man, prophesy to the Eze 36:1
mountains
s. of man, when the house Eze 36:17
of Israel dwelt
he said, S. of man, can these Eze 37:3
bones live

prophesy, s. of man, and say Eze 37:9
to wind
s. of man, these bones are Eze 37:11
house of Israel
s. of man, take thee one Eze 37:16
stick, and write on it
s. of man, set thy face Eze 38:2
against Gog
s. of man, prophesy and say Eze 38:14
unto Gog
s. of man, prophesy against Eze 39:1
Gog and say
s. of man thus saith the Eze 39:17;
Lord 43:18
s. of man, behold with thine Eze 40:4
eyes
s. of man, the place of my Eze 43:7
throne
s. of man, shew house to Eze 43:10
house of Israel
s. of man, mark well, behold Eze 44:5
with eyes
s. of man, hast thou seen this Eze 47:6
S. of man hath power on M't 9:6;
earth M'k 2:10; Lu 5:24
S. of man come eating and M't 11:19;
drinking Lu 7:34
S. of man is Lord of the M't 12:8;
sabbath M'k 2:28; Lu 6:5
speak a word against the S. M't 12:32;
of man Lu 12:10
S. of man three days in heart M't 12:40
of earth
soweth good seed is the S. M't 13:37
of man
S. of man shall send forth M't 13:41
angels
men say that I the S. of M't 16:13
man am
S. of man shall come in his M't 16:27;
glory 16:28; 19:28; 24:30; 25:31;
M'k 13:26; Lu 21:27
until the S. of man be risen M't 17:9;
M'k 9:9
S. of man suffer of them M't 17:12;
M'k 8:31; Lu 9:22
S. of man shall be betrayed M't 17:22;
into 20:18; 26:2, 24, 45; M'k 14:21, 41
S. of man is come to save M't 18:11;
Lu 19:10
S. of man come not to M't 20:28;
be ministered unto M'k 10:45
also the coming of the S. of M't 24:27;
man be 24:37, 39, 44; 25:13
sign of the S. of man in M't 24:30
heaven
S. of man goeth as it is M't 26:24;
written M'k 9:12; 14:21; Lu 22:22
S. of man sitting on the M't 26:64;
right hand M'k 14:62; Lu 22:69
shall the S. of man be Mk 8:38;
ashamed Lu 9:26
S. of man shall be delivered M'k 9:31;
10:33; Lu 9:44; 24:7
S. of man is as a man M'k 13:34
taking a
as evil for the S. of man's Lu 6:22
sake
S. of man came not to destroy Lu 9:56
S. of man hath not where to Lu 9:58
lay
S. of man shall be to this Lu 11:30
generation
shall the S. of man also Lu 12:8
confess
S. of man cometh at an hour Lu 12:40
when
see one of the days of the S. Lu 17:22;
of man 17:26
also the S. of man be in his Lu 17:24;
day 17:30
when S. of man cometh he Lu 18:8
find faith
prophets concerning the S. of Lu 18:31
man
and to stand before the S. of Lu 21:36
man
betrayest thou S. of man Lu 22:48
with kiss
angels descending upon the S. Joh 1:51
of man
the S. of man which is in Joh 3:13
heaven
so must the S. of man be Joh 3:14
lifted up
because he is the S. of man Joh 5:27
which the S. of man shall Joh 6:27
give unto
eat the flesh of the S. of man Joh 6:53
see the S. of man ascend up Joh 6:62

when ye have lifted up the *S.*   Joh 8:28
of man
lifted up? Who is this *S. of*   Joh 12:34
man
S. of man standing on right   Ac 7:56
hand of
the *s. of man*, that thou   Heb 2:6
visitest
one like the *S. of man*   Re 1:13
one sat like unto the *S. of*   Re 14:14
man

HIS SON

called city after name of *his s.*   Ge 4:17
Enoch
Noah knew what *his* younger   Ge 9:24
s. had done
thing was very grievous   Ge 21:11
because of *his s.*
Abraham took the knife to   Ge 22:10
slay *his s.*
offered him for burnt offerings   Ge 22:13
instead of *his s.*
take master's brother's   Ge 24:48
daughter to *his s.*
sent from Isaac *his s.* while he   Ge 25:6
yet lived
after the death of Abram,   Ge 25:11
God blessed *his s.*
Shechem *his s.* came to gate   Ge 34:20
of their city
they slew Hamor and   Ge 34:26
Shechem *his s.*
Jacob mourned for *his s.*   Ge 37:34
many days
if he hath betrothed her to *his*   Ex 21:9
s.
consecrate, even every man   Ex 32:29
upon *his s.*
but for *his s.* he may be   Le 21:2
defiled
and put them on Eleazar *his*   Nu 20:26;
s.   20:28
God bare thee, as a man doth   De 1:31
bear *his s.*
thy daughter thou shalt not   De 7:3
give to *his s.*
as man chasteneth *his s.* so   De 8:5
Lord chasteneth
not maketh *his s.* to pass   De 18:10
thro' fire
David mourned for *his s.*   2Sa 13:37
every day
should I not serve in   2Sa 16:19
presence of *his s.*
how the king was grieved for   2Sa 19:2
his s.
to *his s.* will I give one tribe   1Ki 11:36
give him a lamp, to set up *his*   1Ki 15:4
s. after him
for all the sins of Elah *his s.*   1Ki 16:13
they sinned
his eldest *s.* should have   2Ki 3:27
reigned
Ahaz made *his s.* to pass   2Ki 16:3
thro' the fire
Manasseh made *his s.* pass   2Ki 21:6
through fire
of Lord said to David and   2Ki 21:7;
Solomon *his s.* will I put   2Ch 33:7
my name
no man make *his s.* pass   2Ki 23:10
through fire
thus Joash the king slew *his*   2Ch 24:22
s.
he that spareth his rod,   Pr 13:24
hateth *his s.*
shall have him become *his s.*   Pr 29:21
at length
all nations serve *his s.* and *his*   Jer 27:7
son's *s.*
thou *his s.* O Belshazzar hast   Da 5:22
not humbled
spare them, as a man spareth   Mal 3:17
his s.
what man, whom if *his s.* ask   M't 7:9
bread
last of all he sent unto them   M't 21:37
his s.
a king who made a marriage   M't 22:2
for *his s.*
how is he *his s.*   M't 22:45;
   M'k 12:37; Lu 20:44
that he gave *his* only begotten   Joh 3:16
S.
God sent not *his S.* to   Joh 3:17
condemn the world
ground Jacob gave to *his s.*   Joh 4:5
Joseph

that he would come down   Joh 4:47
and heal *his s.*
God hath glorified *his S.* Jesus   Ac 3:13
God raised up *his S.* Jesus sent   Ac 3:26
him
whom I serve in the gospel of   Ro 1:9
his S.
were reconciled to God by   Ro 5:10
death of *his S.*
God sending *his* own *S.* in   Ro 8:3
likeness of flesh
to be conformed to the image   Ro 8:29
of *his S.*
he that spared not *his* own *S.*   Ro 8:32
but delivered
called to fellowship of *his S.*   1Co 1:9
Jesus
it pleased God to reveal *his S.*   Ga 1:16
in me
God sent forth *his S.* made of a   Ga 4:4
woman
God sent the spirit of *his S.*   Ga 4:6
into your hearts
translated us into kingdom of   Col 1:13
his dear *S.*
and to wait for *his S.* from   1Th 1:10
heaven
God in last days hath spoken   Heb 1:2
to us by *his S.*
Abraham offered up *his*   Heb 11:17
only begotten *s.*
when had offered Isaac *his s.*   Jas 2:21
on altar
our fellowship is with Father   1Jo 1:3
and *his S.* Jesus
blood of Jesus *his S.* cleanseth   1Jo 1:7
from sin
that we believe on the name   1Jo 3:23
of *his S.* Jesus
God sent *his* only begotten *S.*   1Jo 4:9
into world
sent *his S.* to be propitiation   1Jo 4:10
for our sins
the witness, which he hath   1Jo 5:9
testified of *his S.*
believeth not record God gave   1Jo 5:10
of *his S.*
this life is in *his S.*; we are   1Jo 5:11;
in *his S.*   5:20

MY SON

Ishmael shall not be heir   Ge 21:10
with *my s.*
swear thou wilt not deal   Ge 21:23
falsely with *my s.*
my father, and he said, Here   Ge 22:7
am I, *my s.*
my s. God will provide   Ge 22:8
himself a lamb
not take wife to *my s.* of   Ge 24:3;
Canaanites   24:37
go to kindred, take wife to   Ge 24:4
my s.   24:7, 38
thou bring not *my s.* thither   Ge 24:6;
again   24:8
therefore, *my s.* obey my voice   Ge 27:8;
   27:43
upon me be thy curse, *my s.*   Ge 27:13
he said, Here am I, who art   Ge 27:18
thou, *my s.*
whether thou be *my* very *s.*   Ge 27:21;
Esau   27:24
smell of *my s.* is as smell of   Ge 27:27
a field
what shall I do now unto   Ge 27:37
thee, *my s.*
soul of *my s.* longeth for your   Ge 34:8
daughter
I will go into the grave to   Ge 37:35
my s. mourning
remain, till Shelah *my s.* be   Ge 38:11
grown
because I gave her not to   Ge 38:26
Shelah *my s.*
my s. shall not go down with   Ge 42:38
you
he said, God be gracious to   Ge 43:29
thee, *my s.*
it is enough, Joseph *my s.* is   Ge 45:28
yet alive
Jacob said, I know it, *my s.*   Ge 48:19
I know it
from the prey, *my s.* thou art   Ge 49:9
Israel is *my s.* even my   Ex 4:22
firstborn
let *my s.* go, that he may serve   Ex 4:23
me

my s. give glory to the God of   Jos 7:19
Israel
neither shall *my s.* rule over   J'g 8:23
you
mother said, Blessed be thou   J'g 17:2
of the Lord *my s.*
dedicated for *my s.* to make a   J'g 17:3
graven image
I called not *my s.* lie down   1Sa 3:6
again
and he said, What is there   1Sa 4:16
done, *my s.*
sorroweth, what shall I do   1Sa 10:2
for *my s.*
though it be Jonathan *my s.*   1Sa 14:39
he shall die
I and Jonathan *my s.* will be   1Sa 14:40
on other side
cast lots between me and   1Sa 14:42
Jonathan *my s.*
my s. made league with son   1Sa 22:8
of Jesse. *my s.* stirred up servant
is this thy voice, *my s.*   1Sa 24:16;
David   26:17
I have sinned, return, *my s.*   1Sa 26:21
David
Saul said, Blessed be thou,   1Sa 26:25
my s. David
I will be his father, he shall   2Sa 7:14
be *my s.*
king said, *my s.* let us not all   2Sa 13:25
now go
not suffer revengers, lest   2Sa 14:11
they destroy *my s.*
destroy me and *my s.* out of   2Sa 14:16
the inheritance
my s. who came forth of my   2Sa 16:11
bowels
wherefore wilt thou run, *my*   2Sa 18:22
s.
O *my s.* Absalom, *my s.* my   2Sa 18:33;
s.   19:4
I and *my s.* be counted   1Ki 1:21
offenders
arose and took *my s.* from   1Ki 3:20
beside me
it was not *my s.* which I did   1Ki 3:21
bear
woman said, Nay, but the   1Ki 3:22
living is *my s.*
thy son is the dead, and my   1Ki 3:23
s. is the living
that I may dress it for me   1Ki 17:12
and *my s.*
said, Art thou come to me to   1Ki 17:18
slay *my s.*
we will eat *my s.* to-morrow   2Ki 6:28
so we boiled *my s.* and did   2Ki 6:29
eat him, give thy son
give thy daughter to *my s.*   2Ki 14:9;
   2Ch 25:18
and he shall be *my s.*   1Ch 17:13; 22:10
now, *my s.* Lord will be with   1Ch 22:11
thee, and prosper
I have chosen him to be *my*   1Ch 28:6
s. will be his father
Solomon, *my s.* know God of   1Ch 28:9
thy father
Solomon *my s.* whom God   1Ch 29:1
alone hath chosen
give to Solomon *my s.* a   1Ch 29:19
perfect heart to keep
Lord said to me, Thou art *my s.*   Ps 2:7;
this day have I begotten thee   Ac 13:33;
   Heb 1:5; 5:5
my s. despise not chastening,   Pr 3:11;
nor be weary of correction   Heb 12:5
do this now, *my s.* and deliver   Pr 6:3
thyself
my s. give me thine heart,   Pr 23:26
observe my ways
my s. fear thou the Lord and   Pr 24:21
the king
my s. be wise, and make my   Pr 27:11
heart glad
what, *my s.* and what, the son   Pr 31:2
of my vows
further, by these *my s.* be   Ec 12:12
admonished
is Ephraim *my* dear *s.*? is   Jer 31:20
pleasant child
it contemneth rod of *my s.*   Eze 21:10
as every tree
I called *my s.* out of Egypt   Ho 11:1;
   M't 2:15
voice saying, This is *my*   M't 3:17;
beloved *S.*   17:5
Lord, have mercy on *my s.*   M't 17:15
he is lunatic

they will reverence *my s.*   M't 21:37; M'k 12:6

Master, I have brought to thee *my s.*   M'k 9:17

Master, I beseech thee, look upon *my s.*   Lu 9:38

for this *my s.* was dead and is alive again   Lu 15:24

to Timothy *my own s.* in the faith   1Ti 1:2

my s. be strong in grace that is in   2Ti 2:1

to Titus *mine own s.* after common faith   Tit 1:4

I beseech thee for *my s.* Onesimus   Ph'm 10

I will be his God, he shall be *my s.*   Re 21:7

THY SON

take now *thy s.* thine only son Isaac   Ge 22:2

not withheld *thy s.* thine only son   Ge 22:12; 22:16

needs bring *thy s.* again to the land   Ge 24:51

he said, I am *thy s.* firstborn Esau   Ge 27:32

behold, *thy s.* Joseph cometh unto thee   Ge 48:2

I will slay *thy s.* even thy firstborn   Ex 4:23

tell in the ears of *thy s.* and son's son   Ex 10:2

thou shalt shew *thy s.* in that day   Ex 13:8

when *thy s.* asketh thee   Ex 13:14; De 6:20

not do work, thou, nor *thy s.*   Ex 20:10; De 5:14

then thou shalt say unto *thy s.*   De 6:21

nor his daughter shalt take unto *thy s.*   De 7:3

will turn away *thy s.* from following me   De 7:4

eat them thou and *thy s.*   De 12:18; 16:11, 14

if *thy s.* entice thee secretly, saying   De 13:6

bring out *thy s.* that he may die   J'g 6:30

rule over us, thou, *thy s.* and thy son's son   J'g 8:22

Saul said, Send me David *thy s.*   1Sa 16:19

give to thy servants, and to *thy s.* David   1Sa 25:8

there shall not one hair of *thy s.* fall   2Sa 14:11

save thy life and life of *thy s.*   1Ki 1:12

thy s. Solomon reign after me   1Ki 1:13; 1:17, 30

dead is *thy s.*; *thy s.* is the dead   1Ki 3:22; 3:23

thy s. whom I will set upon thy throne   1Ki 5:5

I will rend it out of the hand of *thy s.*   1Ki 11:12

I will give one tribe to *thy s.* for David's   1Ki 11:13

and after make for thee and for *thy s.*   1Ki 17:13

give me *thy s.*; Elisha said, See, *thy s.* liveth   1Ki 17:19; 17:23

when she came, he said, Take up *thy s.*   2Ki 4:36

give *thy s.* that we may eat him to-day   2Ki 6:28; 6:29

saying, I am thy servant, and *thy s.*   2Ki 16:7

Solomon *thy s.* build my house, I have chosen him to be my son   1Ch 28:6; 2Ch 6:9

chasten *thy s.* while there is hope   Pr 19:18

correct *thy s.* and he shall give thee rest   Pr 29:17

Jesus said, Bring *thy s.* hither   Lu 9:41

no more worthy to be called *thy s.*   Lu 15:19; 15:21

as soon as this *thy s.* was come who devoured   Lu 15:30

go thy way, *thy s.* liveth   Joh 4:50; 4:51, 53

glorify *thy s.* that *thy s.* may glorify thee   Joh 17:1

saith to mother, Woman, behold *thy s.*   Joh 19:26

SONG

of Israel this *s.* unto the Lord   Ex 15:1

Moses sang this hymn (B)   Ex 15:1

The Lord is my strength and *s.*   Ex 15:2

Israel sang this *s.*, Spring up   Nu 21:17

therefore write ye this *s.* for you   De 31:19

that this *s.* may be a witness for me   De 31:19

this *s.* shall testify against them as   De 31:21

Moses therefore wrote this *s.*   De 31:22

of Israel the words of this *s.*   De 31:30

and spake all the words of this *s.* in   De 32:44

Deborah: awake, awake, utter a *s.*   J'g 5:12

unto the Lord the words of this *s.*   2Sa 22:1

David set over the service of *s.*   1Ch 6:31

chief of the Levites, was for *s.*   1Ch 15:22

he instructed about the *s.* because   1Ch 15:22

Chenaniah the master of the *s.* with   1Ch 15:27

the hands of their father for *s.* in   1Ch 25:6

s. of the Lord began also with the   2Ch 29:27

And now am I their *s.* I am   Job 30:9

In the titles of   Ps 18, 30, 45-46, 48, 65-68, 75-76, 83, 87-88, 92, 108, 120-134

and with my *s.* will I praise him   Ps 28:7

Sing unto him a new *s.*; play   Ps 33:3

he hath put a new *s.* in my mouth   Ps 40:3

in the night his *s.* shall be with me   Ps 42:8

and I was the *s.* of the drunkards   Ps 69:12

praise the name of God with a *s.*   Ps 69:30

I call to remembrance my *s.* in   Ps 77:6

praised in a wedding *s.* (A)(E)(R)   Ps 78:63

O sing unto the Lord a new *s.*; for   Ps 96:1; 98:1

The Lord is my strength and *s.*   Ps 118:14

captive required of us a *s.*   Ps 137:3

How shall we sing the Lord's *s.* in a   Ps 137:4

I will sing a new *s.* unto thee   Ps 144:9

Sing unto the Lord a new *s.*   Ps 149:1; Isa 42:10

for a man to hear the *s.* of fools   Ec 7:5

The *s.* of songs, which is Solomon's   Ca 1:1

will sing to my wellbeloved a *s.*   Isa 5:1

Jehovah is my strength and my *s.*   Isa 12:2

shall not drink wine with a *s.*   Isa 24:9

this *s.* be sung in the land of Judah   Isa 26:1

Ye shall have a *s.* as in the night   Isa 30:29

whose *s.* is in ships (S)   Isa 43:14

my people; and their *s.* all the day   La 3:14

art unto them as a very lovely *s.*   Eze 33:32

And they sung a new *s.* saying   Re 5:9

And they sung as it were a new *s.*   Re 14:3

no man could learn that *s.* but   Re 14:3

And they sing the *s.* of Moses   Re 15:3

and the *s.* of the Lamb, saying   Re 15:3

SONGS

thee away with mirth, and with *s.*   Ge 31:27

and his *s.* were a thousand and five   1Ki 4:32

instructed in the *s.* of the Lord   1Ch 25:7

s. of praise and thanksgiving unto   Ne 12:46

maker, who giveth *s.* in the night   Job 35:10

me about with *s.* of deliverance   Ps 32:7

Thy statutes have been my *s.* in   Ps 119:54

Sing us one of the *s.* of Zion   Ps 137:3

he that singeth *s.* to an heavy heart   Pr 25:20

The song of *s.* which is Solomon's   Ca 1:1

make sweet melody, sing many *s.*   Isa 23:16

part of the earth have we heard *s.*   Isa 24:16

to Zion with *s.* and everlasting   Isa 35:10

we will sing my *s.* to the stringed   Isa 38:20

cause the noise of thy *s.* to cease   Eze 26:13

away from me the noise of thy *s.*   Am 5:23

sing idle *s.* to the sound (A)(E)(R)   Am 6:5

And the *s.* of the temple shall be   Am 8:3

and all your *s.* into lamentation   Am 8:10

psalms and hymns and spiritual *s.*   Eph 5:19; Col 3:16

SONS

s. of Noah entered into the ark   Ge 7:13

s. of Noah went forth of ark   Ge 9:18

these are the three *s.* of Noah   Ge 9:19

to them were *s.* born after the flood   Ge 10:1

Lot went out and spake to his *s.* in law   Ge 19:14

sitting among *s.* of Heth (B)(E)(R)   Ge 23:10

in the presence of the *s.* of Babylon   Ge 23:11; Isa 39:7

let thy mother's *s.* bow down to thee   Ge 27:29

s. of Jacob came upon slain and spoiled   Ge 34:27

the lad was with the *s.* of Bilhah   Ge 37:2

the *s.* of Israel came to buy corn   Ge 42:5

we are one man's *s.* we are   Ge 42:11; 42:32

s. of Israel carried Jacob in wagons   Ge 46:5

break off earrings in ears of *s.*   Ex 32:2

ye shall eat the flesh of your *s.*   Le 26:29

take too much on you, *s.* of Levi   Nu 16:7

stood in door of tents their wives and *s.*   Nu 16:27

father died in his own sin, and had no *s.*   Nu 27:3

if they be married to *s.* of other tribes   Nu 36:3

nor a sodomite of the *s.* of Israel   De 23:17

their *s.*, nor *s.* for (B)   De 24:16

Thou shalt beget *s.* and daughters   De 28:41

when he separated the *s.* of   De 32:8

Caleb drove three *s.* of Anak   Jos 15:14; J'g 1:20

the *s.* of a king (A)(B)(R)   J'g 8:18

there were the *s.* of my mother   J'g 8:19

Gideon had seventy *s.*; Jair had thirty   J'g 8:30; 10:4

Abdon had forty *s.* and thirty nephews   J'g 12:14

certain *s.* of Belial beset house round   J'g 19:22

are there yet any *s.* in my womb   Ru 1:11

am not I better to thee than ten *s.*   1Sa 1:8

s. of Eli were *s.* of Belial   1Sa 2:12

take your *s.* and appoint them for   1Sa 8:11

were three *s.* of Zeruiah there   2Sa 2:18

these men *s.* of Zeruiah be too hard   2Sa 3:39

Mephibosheth eat as one of king's *s.*   2Sa 9:11

Absalom invited all the king's *s.*   2Sa 13:23

Absalom hath slain all the king's *s.*   2Sa 13:30

what to do with you *s.* of Zeruiah   2Sa 16:10; 19:22

but s. of Belial shall be as   2Sa 23:6
thorns
he called all the king's s.   1Ki 1:9;
       19:25
but shew kindness to s. of   1Ki 2:7
Barzillai
for he was wiser than the s.   1Ki 4:31
of Mahol
a certain man of the s. of   1Ki 20:35
the prophets
set two men, s. of Belial,   1Ki 21:10
before him
shut door upon her and upon   2Ki 4:5
her s.
look out the meetest of your   2Ki 10:3
master's s.
brought the heads of the   2Ki 10:8
king's s.
stole him from the king's   2Ki 11:2;
       2Ch 22:11
slew s. of Zedekiah   2Ki 25:7;
       Jer 39:6; 52:10
sons (S)   1Ch 2:30;
2:31-32; M't 5:9, 45; 8:12; 9:15; 12:27;
13:38; 17:25; 23:31; M'k 2:19; Lu 5:34;
6:35; 16:8; 20:34, 36; Joh 4:12; 12:36;
Ac 3:25; Ro 9:26; Ga 3:7, 26; Eph 1:5;
    2:2 5:6 Col 3:6 1Th 5:5 Heb 12:5
birthright given to s. of   1Ch 5:1
Joseph
Hashabiah of the s. of   1Ch 9:14
Merari
Ornan and his four s. with   1Ch 21:20
him hid
of Mahli came Eleazar, who   1Ch 24:28
had no s.
among s. of my fathers, he   1Ch 28:4
liked me
the Lord said of the s. of   2Ch 23:3
David
for blood of s. of Jehoiada   2Ch 24:25
one of the s. of Joiada was   Ne 13:28
son in law
the ten s. of Haman slew they   Es 9:10
let Haman's ten s. be hanged   Es 9:13;
on gallows   9:14
s. of pride (A)(B)(E)(R)   Job 41:34
who among s. of mighty can   Ps 89:6
be likened
our s. may be as plants   Ps 144:12
grown up
as apple tree so is my beloved   Ca 2:3
among s.
there is none to guide her   Isa 51:18
among all s.
s. of stranger join themselves   Isa 56:6
to Lord
draw near hither, ye s. of the   Isa 57:3
sorceress
s. of the stranger shall build   Isa 60:10
walls
s. of them that afflicted thee   Isa 60:14
shall come
the s. of the alien shall be   Isa 61:5
your plowmen
s. of the stranger shall not   Isa 62:8
drink thy wine
the fathers and s. shall fall   Jer 6:21
upon them
even fathers and s. together   Jer 13:14
will I dash
they built the high places to   Jer 19:5
burn their s.
take wives, beget s. take wives   Jer 29:6
for your s.
s. of base men (E)   Jer 30:8
I set before s. of Rechabites   Jer 35:5
pots full of wine
ye shall drink no wine, ye, nor   Jer 35:6
your s. for ever
hath Israel no s.? hath he no   Jer 49:1
heir
precious s. of Zion, comparable   La 4:2
to gold
fathers shall eat their s. s.   Eze 5:10
their fathers
when ye make s. pass   Eze 20:31
through fire
caused their s. to pass   Eze 23:37
through fire
ye are the s. of the living God   Ho 1:10
I raised up of your s. for   Am 2:11
prophets
he shall purify s. of Levi, and   Mal 3:3
purge them
therefore ye s. of Jacob are   Mal 3:6
not consumed
s. of God   M't 5:9
(A)(B)(E)(N)(P)(R)

s. of the kingdom   M't 8:12
(A)(B)(E)(R)
s. of the bridechamber (E)   M't 9:15
s. of the kingdom   M't 13:38
(E)(P)(R)
s. of those who murdered   M't 23:31
(B)(E)(N)(P)(R)
Boanerges, which is, the s. of   M'k 3:17
thunder
s. of the highest   Lu 6:35
(A)(B)(E)(N)(R)
by whom do your s. cast   Lu 11:19
them out
s. of light (A)(B)(E)(R)   Lu 16:8
s. of light   Joh 12:36;
(A)(B)(E)(P)(R)   1Th 5:5
s. of age, world (B)(E)(R)   Joh 20:34
s. of the prophets (E)(P)(R)   Ac 3:25
Spirit that makes us s.   Ro 8:15
(N)(R)
wait for God to make us s. (N)   Ro 8:23
they were made s. (N)   Ro 9:4
but as my beloved s. I warn   1Co 4:14
you
that we might receive the   Ga 4:5
adoption of s.
might attain status of s. (N)   Ga 4:5
because ye are s. God hath   Ga 4:6
sent forth Spirit
accepted us as s. (N)   Eph 1:5
destined us to be s. (R)   Eph 1:5
bring many s. to glory to   Heb 2:10
make captain
Jacob blessed both s. of   Heb 11:21
Joseph and worshipped
if chastened, God dealeth   Heb 12:7
with you as with s.
if not chastened, then are ye   Heb 12:8
bastards, and not s.

SONS OF GOD

s. of God saw the daughters of   Ge 6:2
men
the s. of God came in to the   Ge 6:4
daughters of men
s. of God came to present   Job 1:6;
themselves   2:1
when all the s. of God   Job 38:7
shouted for joy
said, Ye are s. of the living   Ho 1:10
God
gave them power to become   Joh 1:12
s. of God
led by Spirit of God, are s. of   Ro 8:14
God
waiteth for the manifestation   Ro 8:19
of s. of God
that ye may be harmless, s.   Ph'p 2:15
of God
that we should be called the s.   1Jo 3:1
of God
now are we the s. of God   1Jo 3:2

SONS OF THE PROPHETS

man of the s. of the   1Ki 20:35
prophets said
s. of the prophets that were at   2Ki 2:3
Bethel
s. of the prophets that were at   2Ki 2:5
Jericho
fifty men of the s. of the   2Ki 2:7
prophets
when the s. of the prophets   2Ki 2:15
which
one of wives of the s. of the   2Ki 4:1
prophets
as s. of the prophets were   2Ki 4:38
sitting
see the pottage for the s. of   2Ki 4:38
the prophets
young men of the s. of the   2Ki 5:22
prophets
the s. of the prophets said to   2Ki 6:1
Elisha

HIS SONS

Noah went into ark and his s.   Ge 7:7
Noah went forth, and his s.   Ge 8:18
God blessed Noah and his s.   Ge 9:1
and said
his s. Isaac and Ishmael   Ge 25:9
buried him
he gave them into the hands   Ge 30:35
of his s.
his s. Esau and Jacob buried   Ge 35:29
him
had made an end of   Ge 49:33
commanding his s.

his s. did unto him as he   Ge 50:12
commanded
his s. carried him into the   Ge 50:13
land of Canaan
Jethro came with his s. and   Ex 18:5
wife
take Aaron and his s. to   Ex 28:1
minister to me
thou shalt put the garments   Ex 28:41;
on his s.   29:8
put blood on tip of right ear   Ex 29:20
of his s.
thou shalt sprinkle the blood   Ex 29:21
upon his s.
sanctify that which is for his   Ex 29:27;
s.   Le 8:30
priest of his s. that is anointed   Le 6:22
shall
they smote Og and his s. and   Nu 21:35
people
they smote Sihon, his s. and   De 2:33
people
Lord hath chosen him and his   De 18:5
s. to minister
when he maketh his s. to   De 21:16
inherit
slain his s. seventy persons on   J'g 9:18
one stone
the Levite was to him as one   J'g 17:11
of his s.
he and his s. were priests to   Jg 18:30
tribe of Dan
now Eli heard all that his s.   1Sa 2:22
did
because his s. made   1Sa 3:13
themselves vile
Samuel when old made his s.   1Sa 8:1
judges
his s. walked not in his ways,   1Sa 8:3
but turned
I have provided me a king   1Sa 16:1
among his s.
people grieved, every man for   1Sa 30:6
his s.
Philistines followed hard   1Sa 31:2;
upon Saul and his s.   1Ch 10:2
let seven men of his s. be   2Sa 21:6
delivered to us
his s. came and told him all   1Ki 13:11
works
his s. had seen what way   1Ki 13:12
man of God went
I have seen blood of Naboth   2Ki 9:26
and his s.
his s. smote him with sword   2Ki 19:37;
       Isa 37:38
Jeroboam and his s. had   2Ch 11:14
cast them off
to him and his s. by a   2Ch 13:5
covenant of salt
to give a light to him, and   2Ch 21:7
his s. for ever
carried away his s. save   2Ch 21:17
youngest of his s.
were servants to him and   2Ch 36:20
his s.
pray for life of the king and   Ezr 6:10
his s.
that he and his s. be hanged   Es 9:25
on gallows
his s. went and feasted in their   Job 1:4
houses
his s. come to honour, he   Job 14:21
knoweth it not
or canst thou guide Arcturus   Job 38:32
with his s.
after this, Job saw his s. and   Job 42:16
his sons' sons
Jonadab commanded his s.   Jer 35:14
not to drink wine
if prince give a gift to any   Eze 46:16
of his s.
his s. shall be stirred up and   Da 11:10

MY SONS

Joseph said, They are my s.   Ge 48:9
my s. for it is no good report   1Sa 2:24
I hear
Samuel said, Behold, my s.   1Sa 12:2
are with you
of all my s. he hath chosen   1Ch 28:5
Solomon
Hezekiah said, My s. be not   2Ch 29:11
negligent
Job said, It may be my s. have   Job 1:5
sinned
ask me of things to come   Isa 45:11
concerning my s.
but as my beloved s. I warn   1Co 4:14
you

THY SONS

come into ark, thou and *thy*   *Ge 6:18*
s.
go forth of ark, thou, thy   *Ge 8:16*
wife, and *thy* s.
ordinance to thee and *thy* s.   *Ex 12:24;*
  Nu 18:8
firstborn of *thy* s. shalt thou   *Ex 22:29*
give to me
make *thy* s. go a whoring   *Ex 34:16*
after their gods
all firstborn of *thy* s. shalt   *Ex 34:20*
redeem
do not drink wine, nor *thy* s.   *Le 10:9*
with thee
thou and *thy* s. shall bear the   *Nu 18:1*
iniquity
but thou and *thy* s. with thee   *Nu 18:2*
shall minister
thou and *thy* s. shall keep   *Nu 18:7*
your priests' office
shall be most holy for thee   *Nu 18:9*
and for *thy* s.
I have given them to thee   *Le 18:11*
and to *thy* s.
but teach them *thy* s. and thy   *De 4:9*
son's sons
and honourest *thy* s. above   *1Sa 2:29*
me
thou art old, and *thy* s. walk   *1Sa 8:5*
not in thy ways
to-morrow thou and *thy* s.   *1Sa 28:19*
be with thee
shalt shut door upon thee and   *2Sa 4:4*
thy s.
thou and *thy* s. shall till land   *2Sa 9:10*
thy s. shall sit on throne of   *2Ki 15:12;*
Israel to fourth generation   *1Ch 17:11*
thy s. shall be eunuchs in   *2Ki 20:18;*
Babylon   *Isa 39:7*
they shall bring *thy* s. in   *Isa 49:22*
their arms
thy s. have fainted, they lie at   *Isa 51:20*
head of
they come, *thy* s. shall come   *Isa 60:4;*
from far   *60:9*
as young man marrieth virgin,   *Isa 62:5*
so *thy* s.
thy s. and daughters taken   *Jer 48:46*
captives
and raised up *thy* s. O Zion,   *Zec 9:13*
against *thy* s.

TWO SONS

to Eber were born *two* s.   *Ge 10:25;*
  1Ch 1:19
unto Joseph were born *two* s.   *Ge 41:50*
slay my *two* s.   *Ge 42:37*
my wife bare me *two* s.   *Ge 44:27*
took with him his *two* s.   *Ge 48:1*
thy *two* s., Ephraim and   *Ge 48:5*
Manasseh
her *two* s.; of which the name   *Ex 18:3;*
of   *18:6*
he, and his wife, and *two* s.   *Ru 1:1;*
  1:2-3, 5
And the *two* s. of Eli   *1Sa 1:3;*
  2:34; 4:4, 11, 17
thy handmaid had *two* s.   *2Sa 14:6*
peace, and your *two* s. with   *2Sa 15:27*
you
have there with them their   *2Sa 15:36*
two s.
king took the *two* s. of   *2Sa 21:8*
Rizpah
come to take unto him my *two*   *2Ki 4:1*
Grant that my *two* s. may   *M't 20:21*
sit
A certain man had *two* s.   *M't 21:28;*
  Lu 15:11
Peter and the *two* s. of   *M't 26:37*
Zebedee
of Madian, where he begat   *Ac 7:29*
two s.
Abraham had *two* s.   *Ga 4:22*

SON'S

Lot the son of Haran his s.   *Ge 11:31*
son
Abram called his s. name   *Ge 16:15*
with my son, nor with my s.   *Ge 21:23*
son
let her be thy master's s.   *Ge 24:51*
wife, as
me, and I will eat of my s.   *Ge 27:25*
venison

---

arise, and eat of his s.   *Ge 27:31*
venison
Give me of thy s. mandrakes   *Ge 30:14*
take away my s. mandrakes   *Ge 30:15*
also
thee to night for thy s.   *Ge 30:15*
mandrakes
hired thee with thy s.   *Ge 30:16*
mandrakes
now whether it be thy s. coat   *Ge 37:32*
or no
knew it, and said, It is my s.   *Ge 37:33*
coat
ears of thy son, and of thy s.   *Ex 10:2*
son
The nakedness of thy s.   *Le 18:10*
daughter
she is thy s. wife; thou shalt   *Le 18:15*
not
shalt thou take her s.   *Le 18:17*
daughter
thou, and thy son, and thy s.   *De 6:2*
son
and thy son, and thy s. son   *J'g 8:22*
also
the kingdom out of his s.   *1Ki 11:35*
hand
in his s. days will I bring   *1Ki 21:29*
the evil
his name, and what is his s.   *Pr 30:4*
name
him, and his son, and his s.   *Jer 27:7*
son

SONS'

wife, and thy s. wives with   *Ge 6:18*
thee
his wife, and his s. wives with   *Ge 7:7;*
him   *8:18*
sons, and thy s. wives with   *Ge 8:16*
thee
His sons, and his s. sons with   *Ge 46:7*
him
his daughters, and his s.   *Ge 46:7*
daughters
besides Jacob's s. wives, all   *Ge 46:26*
the
sons, and his s. garments   *Ex 29:21*
with him
it shall be Aaron's and his s.   *Ex 29:28*
by a
of Aaron shall be his s. after   *Ex 29:29*
him
and his s. garments to   *Ex 39:41*
minister in
shall be Aaron's and his s.   *Le 2:3;*
  2:10
breast shall be Aaron's and his   *Le 7:31*
s.
hands, and upon his s. hands   *Le 8:27*
and upon his s. garments with   *Le 8:30*
him
sons, and his s. garments with   *Le 8:30*
him
it is thy due, and thy s. due   *Le 10:13*
for they be thy due, and thy   *Le 10:14*
s. due
shall be thine, and thy s. with   *Le 10:15*
thee
And it shall be Aaron's and   *Le 24:9*
his s.
them thy sons, and thy s. sons   *De 4:9*
and s. sons, an hundred and   *1Ch 8:40*
fifty
his s. sons even four   *Job 42:16*
generations
inheritance thereof shall be   *Eze 46:16*
his s.
but his inheritance shall be   *Eze 46:17*
his s.

SONSHIP

Spirit of s. (B)   *Ro 8:15*
the right of s. (B)   *Ro 8:23*
theirs is the s. (B)(R)   *Ro 9:4*
predestined us for s. (B)   *Eph 1:5*

SOON

as s. as he had left   *Ge 18:33*
communing
as s. as Isaac had made an   *Ge 27:30*
end of
As s. as the morning was   *Ge 44:3*
light, the
How is it that ye are come so   *Ex 2:18*
As s. as I am gone out of the   *Ex 9:29*
city, I

---

as s. as he came nigh unto   *Ex 32:19*
the camp
ye shall s. utterly perish from   *De 4:26*
off
as s. as they which pursued   *Jos 2:7*
after
And as s. as we had heard   *Jos 2:11*
these
as s. as the soles of the feet   *Jos 3:13*
of the
as s. as he had stretched out   *Jos 8:19*
his hand
and as s. as the sun was   *Jos 8:29*
down, Joshua
to pass, as s. as Gideon was   *J'g 8:33*
dead
as s. as the sun is up, thou   *J'g 9:33*
shalt rise
As s. as ye be come into the   *1Sa 9:13*
city, ye
that as s. as he had made an   *1Sa 13:10*
end of
And as s. as the lad was   *1Sa 20:41*
gone, David
and as s. as ye be up early   *1Sa 29:10*
in the
And as s. as David had made   *2Sa 6:18*
an end
as s. as he had made an end   *2Sa 13:36*
of
As s. as ye hear the sound   *2Sa 15:10*
of the
as s. as they hear, they shall   *2Sa 22:45*
be
as s. as he sat on his throne,   *1Ki 16:11*
that he
pass, as s. as I am gone up   *1Ki 18:12*
from thee
as s. as thou art departed   *1Ki 20:36*
from me
as s. as he was departed   *1Ki 20:36*
from him
Now as s. as this letter   *2Ki 10:2*
cometh to you
as s. as he had made an end   *2Ki 10:25*
of offering
as s. as the kingdom was   *2Ki 14:5*
confirmed
as s. as the commandment   *2Ch 31:5*
came
my maker would s. take me   *Job 32:22*
away
s. as they hear of me, they   *Ps 18:44*
shall obey
shall s. be cut down like the   *Ps 37:2*
grass
go astray as s. as they be born   *Ps 58:3*
Ethiopia shall s. stretch out   *Ps 68:31*
her
s. have subdued their enemies   *Ps 81:14*
for it is s. cut off, and we fly   *Ps 90:10*
away
They s. forgat his works;   *Ps 106:13*
they
that is s. angry dealeth   *Pr 14:17*
foolishly
s. has Zion travailed, she   *Isa 66:8*
brought
s. as she saw them with her   *Eze 23:16*
eyes
for they are s. to come (S)   *Eze 36:8*
How s. is the fig tree   *M't 21:20*
withered
And as s. as he had spoken   *M'k 1:42*
As s. as Jesus heard the   *Mk 5:36*
word that
and as s. as ye be entered into   *M'k 11:2*
it, ye
And as s. as he was come,   *M'k 14:45*
he goeth
s. as the days of his   *Lu 1:23*
ministration
as s. as the voice of thy   *Lu 1:44*
salutation
s. as it was sprung up, it   *Lu 8:6*
withered
as s. as this thy son, was   *Lu 15:30*
come
And as s. as it was day, the   *Lu 22:66*
elders
And as s. as he knew that he   *Lu 23:7*
belonged
as s. as she heard that Jesus   *Joh 11:20*
was
As s. as she heard that, she   *Joh 11:29*
arose
but as s. as she is delivered   *Joh 16:21*
of the
As s. then as he had said   *Joh 18:6*
unto

As *s.* then as they were come | Joh 21:9
to
gainsaying, as *s.* as I was | Ac 10:29
sent for
as *s.* as it was day, there was | Ac 12:18
no
ye are so *s.* removed from him | Ga 1:6
so *s.* as I shall see how it | Ph'p 2:23
will go
That ye be not *s.* shaken in | 2Th 2:2
mind
not *s.* angry, not given to wine | Tit 1:7
as *s.* as I had eaten it, my | Re 10:10
belly
for to devour her child as *s.* | Re 12:4
as it

SOONER

I may be restored to you | Heb 13:19
the *s.*
sun is no *s.* risen with a | Jas 1:11
burning heat

SOOTHE

would *s.* my sufferings (A) | Job 16:5

SOOTHED

my sorrow is *s.* (A)(B) | Job 16:6

SOOTHSAYER

Balaam also the son of Beor, | Jos 13:22
the *s.*
Balaam the diviner (B) | Jos 13:22

SOOTHSAYERS

and are *s.* like the Philistines | Isa 2:6
confounds omens of *s.* (B) | Isa 44:25
the *s.* shew unto the king | Da 2:27
the Chaldeans, and the *s.* | Da 4:7;
| 5:7
astrologers, Chaldeans, and *s.* | Da 5:11
and thou shalt have no more | Mic 5:12
s.

SOOTHSAYING

her masters much gain by *s.* | Ac 16:16
fortunetelling (A)(B)(N)(P) | Ac 16:16

SOP

He it is, to whom I shall | Joh 13:26
give a *s.*
when he had dipped the *s.* | Joh 13:26
he gave
after the *s.* Satan entered | Joh 13:27
into him
He then having received the | Joh 13:30
s.

SOPATER

accompanied him into Asia | Ac 20:4
S. of

SOPE

and take thee much *s.* yet | Jer 2:22
thine
soap (A)(B)(E)(R) | Jer 2:22; Mal 3:2
refiner's fire, and like fullers' | Mal 3:2
s.

SOPHERETH

of Sotai, the children of *S.* | Ezr 2:55;
| Ne 7:57

SOPHISTRIES

we demolish *s.* (N) | 2Co 10:5

SORCERER

called the wise men and the *s.* | Ex 7:11
magicians (B) | Ex 7:11
or a *s.* (A)(E)(R) | De 18:10
nor to your *s.* which speak | Jer 27:9
unto
and the *s.* and the Chaldeans | Da 2:2
be a swift witness against the | Mal 3:5
s.
they found a certain *s.* a false | Ac 13:6
a Jewish magician (B)(P)(R) | Ac 13:6;
| 13:8

But Elymas the *s.* (for so is | Ac 13:8
his
and whoremongers, and *s.* | Re 21:8
the practicers of magic (A)(B) | Re 21:8;
| 22:15
For without are dogs, and *s.* | Re 22:15

SORCERESS

suffer not a *s.* to live | Ex 22:18
(B)(E)(R)
near hither, ye sons of the *s.* | Isa 57:3

SORCERIES

her *s.* are many (R) | 2Ki 9:22
for the multitude of thy *s.* | Isa 47:9
and with the multitude of | Isa 47:12
thy *s.*
your many enchantments (B) | Isa 47:12
will cut off *s.* (B)(R) | Mic 5:12
he had bewitched them with *s.* | Ac 8:11
with his skill of magic arts | Ac 8:11
(A)(B)
with his magic (N)(R) | Ac 8:11
by his magical practices (P) | Ac 8:11
of their murders, nor of their | Re 9:21
s.
their magic arts (N) | Re 9:21
by thy *s.* were all nations | Re 18:23
deceived
by your magic spells (A)(B) | Re 18:23

SORCERY

a woman who practices *s.* | Ex 22:18
(A)
fees of *s.* in hand (B) | Nu 22:7
and used *s.* (A)(B)(E)(R)(S) | 2Ch 33:6;
| Ga 5:20
beforetime in the same city | Ac 8:9
used *s.*
practiced magic arts | Ac 8:9
(A)(B)(R), *s.*
Idolatry, *s.*, hatred (S) | Ga 5:20

SORDID

for *s.* gain (N) | Tit 1:11
all that is *s.* (N) | Jas 1:21

SORE

famine was *s.* (E) | Ge 12:10
And they pressed *s.* upon the | Ge 19:9
man
ears: and the men were *s.* | Ge 20:8
afraid
thou *s.* longedst after thy | Ge 31:30
father's
when they were *s.* that two | Ge 34:25
the famine waxed *s.* in the | Ge 41:56
land of
the famine was so *s.* in all | Ge 41:57
lands
And the famine was *s.* in the | Ge 43:1
land
famine is *s.* in the land of | Ge 47:4
Canaan
the famine was very *s.* so | Ge 47:13
that the
a great and very *s.* | Ge 50:10
lamentation
them; and they were *s.* afraid | Ex 14:10
bald forehead, a white | Le 13:42
reddish *s.*
rising of the *s.* be white | Le 13:43
reddish
Moab was *s.* afraid of the | Nu 22:3
people
signs and wonders, great and | De 6:22
s.
a *s.* botch that cannot be | De 28:35
healed
and *s.* sicknesses, and of long | De 28:59
we were *s.* afraid of our lives | Jos 9:24
so that Israel was *s.* distressed | J'g 10:9
her, because she lay *s.* upon | J'g 14:17
him
And he was *s.* athirst, and | J'g 15:18
called
all Israel, and the battle was | J'g 20:34
s.
up their voices, and wept *s.* | J'g 21:2
adversary also provoked her *s.* | 1Sa 1:6
prayed unto the Lord, and | 1Sa 1:10
wept *s.*
his hand is *s.* upon us, and | 1Sa 5:7
upon

was *s.* war against the | 1Sa 14:52
Philistines
fled from him, and were *s.* | 1Sa 17:24
afraid
was *s.* afraid of Achish the | 1Sa 21:12
king of
Saul answered, I am *s.* | 1Sa 28:15
distressed
on the earth, and was *s.* | 1Sa 28:20
afraid
and saw that he was *s.* | 1Sa 28:21
troubled
the battle went *s.* against Saul | 1Sa 31:3
he was *s.* wounded of the | 1Sa 31:3
archers
would not; for he was *s.* | 1Sa 31:4
afraid
there was a very *s.* battle that | 2Sa 2:17
day
and all his servants wept | 2Sa 13:36
very *s.*
and his sickness was so *s.* | 1Ki 17:17
that
there was a *s.* famine in | 1Ki 18:2
Samaria
that the battle was too *s.* for | 2Ki 3:26
him
king of Syria was *s.* troubled | 2Ki 6:11
for this
thy sight. And Hezekiah wept | 2Ki 20:3
s.
the battle went *s.* against | 1Ch 10:3
Saul
would not; for he was *s.* | 1Ch 10:4
afraid
whatsoever *s.* or whatsoever | 2Ch 6:28
one shall know his own *s.* | 2Ch 6:29
and his
so he died of *s.* diseases | 2Ch 21:19
and transgressed *s.* against | 2Ch 28:19
the Lord
me away; for I am *s.* | 2Ch 35:23
wounded
for the people wept very *s.* | Ezr 10:1
of heart. Then I was very *s.* | Ne 2:2
afraid
it grieved me *s.*: therefore I | Ne 13:8
cast
smote Job with *s.* boils from | Job 2:7
For he maketh *s.* and bindeth | Job 5:18
up
and vex them in his *s.* | Ps 2:5
displeasure
My soul is also *s.* vexed: but | Ps 6:3
thou
enemies be ashamed and *s.* | Ps 6:10
vexed
in me, and thy hand presseth | Ps 38:2
me *s.*
I am feeble and *s.* broken: I | Ps 38:8
friends stand aloof from my | Ps 38:11
s.
s. broken us in the place of | Ps 44:19
dragons
My heart is *s.* pained within | Ps 55:4
me: and
shewed me great and *s.* | Ps 71:20
troubles
my *s.* ran in the night, and | Ps 77:2
ceased
Thou hast thrust *s.* at me | Ps 118:13
that I might
The Lord hath chastened me | Ps 118:18
s.
this *s.* travail hath God given | Ec 1:13
to
is also vanity, yea, it is a *s.* | Ec 4:8
travail
a *s.* evil which I have seen | Ec 5:13
under
this also is a *s.* evil, that in all | Ec 5:16
his *s.* and great and strong | Isa 27:1
sword
sight. And Hezekiah wept *s.* | Isa 38:3
like bears, and mourn *s.* like | Isa 59:11
doves
Be not wroth very *s.* O Lord | Isa 64:9
thy peace, and afflict us very | Isa 64:12
s.
and mine eye shall weep *s.* | Jer 13:17
and run
but weep *s.* for him that | Jer 22:10
goeth away
mother shall be *s.* | Jer 50:12
confounded
the famine was *s.* in the city | Jer 52:6
She weepeth *s.* in the night, and | La 1:2
her
Mine enemies chased me *s.* | La 3:52
like a

I send my four s. judgments   *Eze 14:21*
upon
sharpened to make a s.   *Eze 21:10*
slaughter
and their kings shall be s.   *Eze 27:35*
afraid
was s. displeased with himself   *Da 6:14*
you, even with a s.   *Mic 2:10*
destruction
s. displeased with your fathers   *Zec 1:2*
very s. displeased with the   *Zec 1:15*
heathen
on their face, and were s.   *M't 17:6*
afraid
for he is lunatick, and s.   *M't 17:15*
vexed
of David; they were s.   *M't 21:15*
displeased
to say; for they were s. afraid   *M'k 9:6*
the spirit cried, and rent him   *M'k 9:26*
s.
began to be s. amazed, and   *M'k 14:33*
to be
them: and they were s. afraid   *Lu 2:9*
s. troubled because (E)   *Ac 4:2*
Paul, being s. troubled (E)   *Ac 16:18*
they all wept s. and fell on   *Ac 20:37*
Paul's
s. distressed by filthy (E)(R)   *2Pe 2:7*
fell a noisome and grievous s.,   *Re 16:2*
upon

SOREK

loved a woman in the valley   *J'g 16:4*
of S.

SORELY

The archers have s. grieved   *Ge 49:23*
him
they be s. pained at the report   *Isa 23:5*
of Tyre
been s. displeased with thy   *Zec 1:2*
fathers (S)
Paul, s. annoyed (A)(B)   *Ac 16:18*
became s. displeased   *Heb 3:10*
(B)(E)(P)

SORER

Of how much s. punishment   *Heb 10:29*
worse (sterner, heavier)   *Heb 10:29*
punishment (A)(B)(R)
more severe a penalty (N)   *Heb 10:29*
more dreadful punishment   *Heb 10:29*
(P)

SORES

break out in open s. (B)(R)   *Ex 9:9*
having infected s. (B)   *Le 22:22*
and bruises, and putrifying s.   *Isa 1:6*
fresh and bleeding stripes (A)   *Isa 1:6*
welts and raw wounds (B)   *Isa 1:6*
fresh stripes (E)   *Isa 1:6*
bruises, s. and bleeding wounds   *Isa 1:6*
(R)
was laid at his gate, full of s.   *Lu 16:20*
the dogs came and licked his   *Lu 16:21*
s.
foul and evil s. (N)(R)   *Re 16:2*
because of their pains and   *Re 16:11*
their s.
their sufferings and s. (B)   *Re 16:11*

SORREL

red horses, s., and white (S)   *Zec 1:8*

SORROW

said, I will greatly multiply   *Ge 3:16*
thy s.
greatly multiply grief and   *Ge 3:16*
suffering in pregnancy and the
pangs of child-bearing; with
spasms of distress you shall
bring forth (A)
greatly increase pregnancy   *Ge 3:16*
troubles; you shall suffer
birth-pangs (B)
greatly multiply pain and   *Ge 3:16*
conception; in pain thou
shalt bring forth children (E)
greatly multiply pain in   *Ge 3:16;*
childbearing; in pain you   *Ps 38:17;*
shall bring forth (R)   *Jer 14:3;*
  Jer 30:15; 51:29; 2Co 2:3
in s. shalt thou bring forth   *Ge 3:16*
in s. shalt thou eat of it all   *Ge 3:17*

in toil eat of it all days of life   *Ge 3:17*
(B)(E)(R)
my gray hairs with s. to the   *Ge 42:38;*
grave   *44:29*
grief (A)   *Ge 42:38;*
  Job 17:7; Isa 50:11; Lu 22:45; Joh 16:21;
  Ro 9:2; 2Co 7:10
our father with s. to the   *Ge 44:31*
grave
s. take hold on the   *Ex 15:14*
inhabitants
pangs (A)(E)(R)   *Ex 15:14*
anguish (B)   *Ex 15:14*
the eyes, and cause s. of   *Le 26:16*
heart
life pine away (A)(E)(R)   *Le 26:16*
saps the life (B)   *Le 26:16*
failing of eyes, and s. of   *De 28:65*
mind
fainting of mind (A)   *De 28:65*
a languishing spirit (B)(R)   *De 28:65*
pining of soul (E)   *De 28:65*
Because I bare him with s.   *1Ch 4:9*
pain (A)(B)(R)   *1Ch 4:9; Jer 30:15*
not to my s. (E)   *1Ch 4:10*
affliction and s. (A)(R)   *1Ch 6:29*
own plagues and s. (E)   *1Ch 6:29*
this is nothing else but s. of   *Ne 2:2*
heart
sadness of heart (R)   *Ne 2:2*
turned unto them from s. to   *Es 9:22*
joy
womb, nor hid s. from mine   *Job 3:10*
eyes
trouble (B)(E)   *Job 3:10*
yea, I would harden myself in   *Job 6:10*
s.
my s. is soothed (A)(B)   *Job 16:6*
eye also is dim by reason of   *Job 17:7*
s.
grief (R)   *Job 17:7; Jer 8:18; 2Co 7:10*
s. is turned into joy before   *Job 41:22*
him
terror (A)(E)(R)   *Job 41:22*
soul, having s. in my heart   *Ps 13:2*
daily
life spent with s.   *Ps 31:10*
(A)(B)(E)(R)
my s. is continually before   *Ps 38:17*
from good; and my s. was   *Ps 39:2*
stirred
distress (A)(B)(R)   *Ps 39:2; Isa 5:30*
mischief and s. are in the   *Ps 55:10*
midst
trouble (R)   *Ps 55:10; 90:10*
tell of s. of wounded (E)   *Ps 69:26*
because of s. (B)(R)   *Ps 88:9*
yet is their strength labour   *Ps 90:10*
and s.
grief (B)   *Ps 90:10;*
116:3; Pr 15:13; 17:21; Ec 5:17; 11:10;
  Joh 16:20, 22; Ph'p 2:27; Re 21:4
oppression, affliction, and s.   *Ps 107:39*
upon me: I found trouble   *Ps 116:3*
and s.
anguish (R)   *Ps 116:3*
winketh with the eye causeth s.   *Pr 10:10*
heartache (B)   *Pr 10:10*
trouble (R)   *Pr 10:10*
rich, and he addeth no s.   *Pr 10:22*
with it
but by s. of the heart the   *Pr 15:13*
spirit is
begetteth a fool doeth it to his   *Pr 17:21*
s.
Who hath woe? who hath s.   *Pr 23:29*
knowledge increaseth s.   *Ec 1:18*
distress (B)   *Ec 1:18; Isa 5:30; Ro 9:2*
s. and wrath with his sickness   *Ec 5:17*
grief (R)   *Ec 5:17*
S. is better than laughter   *Ec 7:3*
Therefore remove s. from thy   *Ec 11:10*
heart
the land, behold darkness and   *Isa 5:30*
s.
distress (R)   *Isa 5:30*
shall give thee rest from thy s.   *Isa 14:3*
suffering (B)   *Isa 14:3; La 1:18*
day of grief and of desperate   *Isa 17:11*
s.
in day of s., sickening (A)   *Isa 17:11*
pain (B)   *Isa 17:11; Jer 30:15*
there shall be heaviness and s.   *Isa 29:2*
mourning (B)   *Isa 29:2*
and s. and sighing shall flee   *Isa 35:10*
away
mine hand; ye shall lie down   *Isa 50:11*
in s.
torment (B)(R)   *Isa 50:11*

s. and mourning shall flee   *Isa 51:11*
away
but ye shall cry for s. of   *Isa 65:14*
heart, and
anguish of spirit (R)   *Isa 65:14*
I would comfort myself   *Jer 8:18*
against s.
of the womb to see labour   *Jer 20:18*
and s.
s. is incurable for the   *Jer 30:15*
multitude
pain (E)   *Jer 30:15; 51:29*
they shall not s. any more at   *Jer 31:12*
all
pine away (B)   *Jer 31:12*
languish (R)   *Jer 31:12*
make them rejoice from their   *Jer 31:13*
s.
Lord hath added grief to my   *Jer 45:3*
s.
there is s. on the sea; it   *Jer 49:23*
trouble and anxiety (A)   *Jer 49:23*
troubled (B)   *Jer 49:23*
And the land shall tremble   *Jer 51:29*
and s.
writhes in anguish (B)   *Jer 51:29*
if there be any s. like unto my   *La 1:12*
s.
you, all people, and behold my   *La 1:18*
s.
suffering (R)   *La 1:18*
Give them s. of heart, thy   *La 3:65*
curse
hardness of heart (A)   *La 3:65*
dullness of heart (B)   *La 3:65*
be filled with drunkenness   *Eze 23:33*
and s.
great s. shall be upon   *Eze 30:4;*
Ethiopia (A)   *30:9*
they shall s. a little for the   *Ho 8:10*
burden
I felt s. for the people (N)   *M't 15:32*
he found them sleeping for s.   *Lu 22:45*
grief (N)   *Lu 22:45; Ro 9:2*
unto you, s. hath filled your   *Joh 16:6*
heart
distressed (P)   *Joh 16:6*
but your s. shall be turned   *Joh 16:20*
into joy
plunged into grief (N)   *Joh 16:20;*
  16:21
pain (P)   *Joh 16:20*
when she is in travail hath s.   *Joh 16:21*
And ye now therefore have   *Joh 16:22*
s.
sad at heart (N)   *Joh 16:22*
and continual s. in my heart   *Ro 9:2*
depressed (P)   *Ro 9:2*
s. from them of whom I ought   *2Co 2:3*
to
made miserable (N)   *2Co 2:3*
great s., deep distress (A)   *2Co 2:4*
be swallowed up with   *2Co 2:7*
overmuch s.
despair (N)   *2Co 2:7*
For godly s. worketh   *2Co 7:10*
repentance
the s. of the world worketh   *2Co 7:10*
death
s. over many (A)   *2Co 12:21*
also, lest I should have s.   *Ph'p 2:27*
upon s.
that ye s. not, even as others   *1Th 4:13*
which
grieve (A)(B)(N)(P)(R)   *1Th 4:13*
have bitter s. (P)   *Re 1:7*
so much torment and s. give   *Re 18:7*
her
mourning (E)(R)   *Re 18:7; 21:4*
mete out grief and torment   *Re 18:7*
(N)
torment (R)   *Re 18:7*
am no widow, and shall see   *Re 18:7*
no s.
neither s. nor crying, neither   *Re 21:4*
shall
mourning (R)   *Re 21:4*

SORROWED

sorry, but that ye s. to   *2Co 7:9*
repentance
thing, that ye s. after a godly   *2Co 7:11*
sort

SORROWETH

s. for you, saying, What shall   *1Sa 10:2*
I

SORROWFUL

lord, I am a woman of a s.   1Sa 1:15
spirit
deeply grieved (B)   1Sa 1:15
sorely troubled (R)   1Sa 1:15
refused to touch are as my s.   Job 6:7
meat
diseased meat (A)   Job 6:7
loathsome (B)(E)(R)   Job 6:7
But I am poor and s.: let thy   Ps 69:29
pain (B)(R)   Ps 69:29
Even in laughter the heart is   Pr 14:13
s.
sad (B)(R)   Pr 14:13
I have replenished every s.   Jer 31:25
soul
weary (B)(R)   Jer 31:25
are s. for the solemn   Zep 3:18
assembly
grieve (A)   Zep 3:18
also shall see it, and be very s.   Zec 9:5
sore pained (E)   Zec 9:5
that saying, he went away   M't 19:22
s.: for
sad (grieved in much   M't 19:22
distress) for (A)
heavy heart (N)   M't 19:22
turned away crestfallen (P)   M't 19:22
they were exceeding s. and   M't 26:22
began
greatly distressed (B)   M't 26:22;
   26:37; Lu 18:23
in great distress (N)(P)   M't 26:22
and began to be s. and very   M't 26:37
heavy
grief and distress of mind   M't 26:37
(A)
anguish and dismay (N)   M't 26:37
terrible distress and misery   M't 26:37
(P)
My soul is exceeding s. even   M't 26:38
unto
mortally grieved (B)   M't 26:38
break with grief (N)   M't 26:38
heart nearly breaking (P)   M't 26:38
went away s. (E)(R)   M'k 10:22
And they began to be s.   M'k 14:19
and to say
sad and hurt (A)   M'k 14:19
disturbed (B)   M'k 14:19
dismayed (N)   M'k 14:19
shocked and distressed (P)   M'k 14:19
My soul is exceeding s. unto   M'k 14:34
death
sad-overwhelmed with grief   M'k 14:34
(A)
horror and dismay (N)   M'k 14:34
heart nearly breaking (P)   M'k 14:34
when he heard this, he was   Lu 18:23
very s.
sad (B)   Lu 18:23
his heart sank (N)   Lu 18:23
greatly distressed (P)   Lu 18:23
when Jesus saw he was very   Lu 18:24
s.
ye shall be s. but your   Joh 16:20
sorrow
be weeping and moaning   Joh 16:20
(B)
be greatly distressed (P)   Joh 16:20
As s. yet always rejoicing   2Co 6:10
As grieved and mourning   2Co 6:10
(A)
that it may be the less s.   Ph'p 2:28
less disquieted (A)   Ph'p 2:28

SORROWING

father and I sought thee s.   Lu 2:48
distressed and tormented (A)   Lu 2:48
searching with great anxiety   Lu 2:48
(N)
very wearied (P)   Lu 2:48
S. most of all for the words   Ac 20:38
distressed and sorrowful (A)   Ac 20:38
grieved especially over (B)   Ac 20:38
distressed them (N)   Ac 20:38
saddened them (P)(R)   Ac 20:38

SORROWS

taskmasters; for I know their   Ex 3:7
s.
sufferings (R)   Ex 3:7; Job 9:28
s. of hell compassed me   2Sa 22:6
about
cords of Sheol (A)(B)(E)(R)   2Sa 22:6
I am afraid of all my s. I know   Job 9:28
God distributeth s. in his   Job 21:17
anger

young ones they cast out   Job 39:3
their s.
pains (A)(E)(R)   Job 39:3
Their s. shall be multiplied   Ps 16:4
that
The s. of death compassed   Ps 18:4;
me   116:3
cords or bands of death (A)   Ps 18:4
snares of death (A)   Ps 18:5
cords of Sheol (B)(E)(R)   Ps 18:5
Many s. shall be to the   Ps 32:10
wicked: but
pangs (R)   Ps 32:10;
   Jer 13:21; Ho 13:13; 1Ti 6:10
cords of death (B)(E)   Ps 116:3
snares of death (R)   Ps 116:3
sit up late, to eat the bread of   Ps 127:2
s.
bread of toil (A)(B)(E)(R)   Ps 127:2
all his days are s. and his   Ec 2:23
travail
pains (B)   Ec 2:23
and s. shall take hold of them   Isa 13:8
pains and agonies seize them   Isa 13:8
(B)
agony will seize them (R)   Isa 13:8
a man of s. and acquainted   Isa 53:3
with
man of sufferings (B)   Isa 53:3
our griefs, and carried our s.   Isa 53:4
shall not s. take thee, as a   Jer 13:21
woman
pangs (A)(B)   Jer 13:21
anguish and s. have taken   Jer 49:24
her, as
panic seized her (R)   Jer 49:24
vision my s. are turned upon   Da 10:16
me
agonies (B)   Da 10:16
pains (R)   Da 10:16
The s. of a travailing woman   Ho 13:13
shall
pains (A)   Ho 13:13
All these are the beginning of   M't 24:8
s.
beginning of early pains of   M't 24:8;
birth pangs-of intolerable   M'k 13:8
anguish (A)
early pains of childbirth   M't 24:8;
   M'k 13:8
beginning of travail (E)   M't 24:8;
   M'k 13:8
birth pangs of a new age   M't 24:8;
begin (N)   M'k 13:8
beginning of birth pangs (P)   M't 24:8;
   M'k 13:8
beginning of sufferings (R)   M't 24:8;
these are the beginning of s.   M'k 13:8
themselves through with many   1Ti 6:10
s.
many acute (mental) pangs (A)   1Ti 6:10
thorny griefs (N)   1Ti 6:10
agonies of mind (P)   1Ti 6:10

SORRY

Lord was s. he made man (R)   Ge 6:6
I am s. I have made (R)   Ge 6:7
is none of you that is s. for   1Sa 22:8
me
sympathy (B)   1Sa 22:8
neither be ye s.; for the joy of   Ne 8:10
grieved and depressed (A)   Ne 8:10
do not grieve (B)(E)(R)   Ne 8:10
iniquity; I will be s. for my   Ps 38:18
sin
anxious (B)   Ps 38:18
a s. situation (B)   Ec 4:8
thee; who shall be s. for thee   Isa 51:19
bemoan (E)   Isa 51:19
condole (R)   Isa 51:19
And the king was s.:   M't 14:9
nevertheless
distressed (B)   M't 14:9; 17:23; 18:31
deeply distressed (N)   M't 14:9;
   18:31; M'k 6:26
aghast at (P)   M't 14:9; M'k 6:26
again. And they were   M't 17:23
exceeding s.
deeply and exceedingly   M't 17:23
grieved and distressed (A)   M't 17:23
filled with grief (N)   M't 17:23
greatly distressed (P)(R)   M't 18:31
what was done, they were   M't 18:31
very s.
greatly distressed (A)   M't 18:31
horrified (P)   M't 18:31
And the king was exceeding   M'k 6:26
s.
For if I make you s. who is   2Co 2:2
he

grieved and made sad   2Co 2:2
(A)(B)(P)
pain (R)   2Co 2:2
the same which is made s. by   2Co 2:2
me
though I made you s. with a   2Co 7:8
letter
the same epistle hath made   2Co 7:8
you s.
grieved (A)(B)(P)   2Co 7:8
rejoice, not that ye were made   2Co 7:9
s.
pained (A)   2Co 7:9
grieved (B)(R)   2Co 7:9
were made s. after a godly   2Co 7:9
manner

SORT

two of every s. shalt thou   Ge 6:19
bring into
kind (B)   Ge 6:19; 6:20; 7:14
two of every s. shall come   Ge 6:20
unto thee
his kind, every bird of every s.   Ge 7:14
kind (A)   Ge 7:14
save the poorest s. of the   2Ki 24:14
people
were divided by lot, one s.   1Ch 24:5
with another
group (A)(B)   1Ch 24:5
able to offer so willingly   1Ch 29:14
after this s.
long time in such s. as it was   2Ch 30:5
written
as prescribed (A)(B)   2Ch 30:5
silver basons of a second s.   Ezr 1:10
four
to Artaxerxes the king in this s.   Ezr 4:8
unto me four times after this s.   Ne 6:4
men of the common s. were   Eze 23:42
brought
unto the ravenous birds of   Eze 39:4
every s.
of every s. of your oblations,   Eze 44:30
shall
kinds (A)   Eze 44:30
children which are of your s.   Da 1:10
God that can deliver after this   Da 3:29
s.
this way (A)(R)   Da 3:29
this manner (B)   Da 3:29
certain lewd fellows of the   Ac 17:5
baser s.
more boldly unto you in   Ro 15:15
some s.
every man's work of what s.   1Co 3:13
it is
that ye sorrowed after a   2Co 7:11
godly s.
For of this s. are they which   2Ti 3:6
creep
same s. of disobedience (R)   Heb 4:11
on their journey after a godly s.   3Jo 6

SORTS

all s. of choice gifts (B)   Ge 24:10
shalt not wear a garment of   De 22:11
divers s.
mingled stuff (A)   De 22:11
in ten days store of all s. of   Ne 5:18
wine
He sent divers s. of flies   Ps 78:45
among them
spake and there came divers   Ps 105:31
s. of flies
musical instruments, and that   Ec 2:8
of all s.
thy merchants in all s. of   Eze 27:24
things
clothed with all s. of armour   Eze 38:4
all s. of trials (B)   Jas 1:2

SOSIPATER

and S. my kinsmen, salute   Ro 16:21
you

SOSTHENES

Greeks took S. the chief ruler   Ac 18:17
will of God, and S. our   1Co 1:1
brother

SOTAI

the children of S. the children   Ezr 2:55;
of   Ne 7:57

SOTTISH

they are s. children, and they	Jer 4:22
stupid, thick-headed children	Jer 4:22
(A)	
foolish, stupid, experts in evil	Jer 4:22
(B)(R)	

SOUGHT

and he s. where to weep; and	Ge 43:30
this thing, he s. to slay Moses	Ex 2:15
the men are dead which s. thy	Ex 4:19
life	
Lord met him, and s. to kill	Ex 4:24
him	
every one which s. the Lord	Ex 33:7
went	
Moses diligently s. the goat of	Le 10:16
his enemy, neither s. his	Nu 35:23
harm	
he hath s. to thrust thee	De 13:10
away from	
the pursuers s. them	Jos 2:22
throughout	
that he s. an occasion against	J'g 14:4
the Danites s. them an	J'g 18:1
inheritance	
by which Jonathan s. to go	1Sa 14:4
over	
Saul s. to smite David even	1Sa 19:10
to the	
and he s. no more again for	1Sa 27:4
him	
Ye s. for David in times past	2Sa 3:17
to be	
Saul thine enemy, which s. thy	2Sa 4:8
life	
they had s. and could not	2Sa 17:20
find them	
and Saul s. to slay them in	2Sa 21:2
his zeal	
Let there be s. for my lord the	1Ki 1:2
king	
So they s. for a fair damsel	1Ki 1:3
And all the earth s. to	1Ki 10:24
Solomon	
Solomon s. to kill Jeroboam	1Ki 11:40
s. three days, but found him	2Ki 2:17
not	
the reign of David they were	2Ki 26:31
s. for	
and the congregation s. unto it	2Ch 1:5
earth s. the presence of	2Ch 9:23
Solomon	
he s. many wives (S)	2Ch 11:23
we have s. the Lord our God	2Ch 14:7
his disease he s. not to the	2Ch 16:12
Lord	
David, and s. not unto	2Ch 17:3
Baalim	
s. to the Lord God of his	2Ch 17:4
father	
he s. Ahaziah: and they	2Ch 22:9
caught	
who s. the Lord with all his	2Ch 22:9
heart	
s. after the gods of the	2Ch 25:15
people	
they s. after the gods of	2Ch 25:20
Edom	
he s. God in the days of	2Ch 26:5
Zechariah	
as long as he s. the Lord,	2Ch 26:5
God made	
These s. their register among	Ezr 2:62;
	Ne 7:64
they s. the Levites out of all	Ne 12:27
their	
fair young virgins s. for the	Es 2:2
king	
s. to lay hand on king	Es 2:21;
Ahasuerus	6:2
Haman s. to destroy all the	Es 3:6
Jews	
lay hand on such as s. their	Es 9:2
hurt	
I s. the Lord, and he heard me	Ps 34:4
day of my trouble I s. the	Ps 77:2
Lord	
violent men have s. after my	Ps 86:14
soul	
s. out of all that have	Ps 111:2
pleasure	
my whole heart have I s.	Ps 119:10
thee	
save me; for I have s. thy	Ps 119:94
precepts	
I s. in mine heart to give myself	Ec 2:3
they have s. out many	Ec 7:29
inventions	

and s. out, and set in order	Ec 12:9
many	
s. to find out acceptable	Ec 12:10
words	
called, S. out, A city not	Isa 62:12
forsaken	
I am s. of them that asked	Isa 65:1
not for	
am found of them that s. me	Isa 65:1
not	
in, for my people that have	Isa 65:10
s. me	
whom they have s. and whom	Jer 8:2
they	
brutish, and have not s. the	Jer 10:21
Lord	
the king s. to put him to	Jer 26:21
death	
his enemy, and that s. his life	Jer 44:30
iniquity of Israel shall be s.	Jer 50:20
for	
while they s. their meat to	La 1:19
relieve	
And I s. for a man among	Eze 22:30
them	
though thou be s. for, yet	Eze 26:21
shalt	
neither have ye s. that which	Eze 34:4
was	
they s. Daniel and his fellows	Da 2:13
and my lords s. unto me: and	Da 4:36
I was	
to find occasion against	Da 6:4
Daniel	
the vision, and s. for the	Da 8:15
meaning	
how are his hidden things s. up	Ob 6
those that have not s. the Lord	Zep 1:6
and s. to go that they might	Zec 6:7
walk	
which s. the young child's life	M't 2:20
when they s. to lay hands on	M't 21:46
him	
he s. opportunity to betray	M't 26:16
him	
s. false witness against	M't 26:59
Jesus, to	
and s. how they might	M'k 11:18
destroy him	
And they s. to lay hold on	M'k 12:12
him, but	
scribes s. how they might	M'k 14:1
take him	
he s. how he might	M'k 14:11
conveniently	
council s. for witness	M'k 14:55
against Jesus	
and I have s. thee sorrowing	Lu 2:48
unto them, How is it that ye	Lu 2:49
s. me	
and they s. means to bring	Lu 5:18
him in	
whole multitude s. to touch	Lu 6:19
him	
him, s. of him a sign from	Lu 11:16
heaven	
and he came and s. fruit	Lu 13:6
thereon	
And he s. to see Jesus who he	Lu 19:3
was	
of the people s. to destroy	Lu 19:47
him	
same hour s. to lay hands on	Lu 20:19
him	
scribes s. how they might kill	Lu 22:2
him	
s. opportunity to betray him	Lu 22:6
unto	
persecute Jesus, and s. to slay	Joh 5:16
him	
the Jews s. the more to kill	Joh 5:18
him	
because the Jews s. to kill him	Joh 7:1
Then the Jews s. him at the	Joh 7:11
feast	
Then they s. to take him: but	Joh 7:30
they s. again to take him:	Joh 10:39
but he	
the Jews of late s. to stone	Joh 11:8
thee	
Then s. they for Jesus, and	Joh 11:56
spake	
thenceforth Pilate s. to	Joh 19:12
release him	
And when Herod had s. for	Ac 12:19
him	
s. to bring them out to the	Ac 17:5
people	
Because they s. it not by faith	Ro 9:32

I was found of them that s.	Ro 10:20
me not	
it is good to be zealously s.	Ga 4:18
(S)	
Nor of men s. we glory, neither	1Th 2:6
of	
he s. me out very diligently	2Ti 1:17
then should no place have	Heb 8:7
been s.	
though he s. it carefully with	Heb 12:17
tears	

SOUGHT *HIM*

when s. him he could not be	1Sa 10:21
found	
the Lord hath s. him a man	1Sa 13:14
to be captain	
Saul s. him everyday, God	1Sa 23:14
delivered	
we s. him not after the due	1Ch 15:13
order	
have s. him, he hath given us	2Ch 14:7
rest	
when they s. him, he was	2Ch 15:4
found of them	
for they s. him with their	2Ch 15:15
whole desire	
I s. him, but he could not be	Ps 37:36
found	
when he slew them, then they	Ps 78:34
s. him	
on my bed I s. him; I s. him	Ca 3:1;
but I found him not	3:2; 5:6
they s. him among their	Lu 2:44
kinsfolk	
the people s. him, and came	Lu 4:42
unto him	

SOUL

God breathed and man became	Ge 2:7
a living s.	
man became a living being	Ge 2:7
(A)(R)	
the s. of my son longeth for	Ge 34:8
your daughter	
affections centered upon (B)	Ge 34:8
as her s. was in departing,	Ge 35:18
for she died	
if a s. shall sin through	Le 4:2
ignorance	
person (B)	Le 4:2;
5:1, 4, 17; 6:2; 22:11; 23:30; Nu 9:13;	
Pr 19:15; Ro 13:1	
any one (E)(R)	Le 4:2;
5:1, 2, 4, 17; 6:2	
if a s. sin, and hear the voice	Le 5:1
of swearing	
if s. touch any unclean thing	Le 5:2
if a s. swear; if a s. commit a	Le 5:4;
trespass	5:15
if a s. sin and commit any of	Le 5:17
these things	
if a s. lie	Le 6:2
it is blood maketh an	Le 17:11
atonement for the s.	
no s. of you shall eat blood	Le 17:12
if the priest buy any s. with	Le 22:11
his money	
slave (R)	Le 22:11
whatsoever s. doth any work	Le 23:30
in that day	
person (R)	Le 23:30; Nu 9:13; Ro 13:1
or if your s. abhor my	Le 26:15
judgments	
makes s. pine away	Le 26:16
(A)(E)(R)	
because their s. abhorred my	Le 26:43
statutes	
my s. spurn them (A)(R)	Le 26:44
even the same s. shall be cut	Nu 9:13
off	
s. of the people was much	Nu 21:4
discouraged	
spirit (B)	Nu 21:4
every bond she hath bound	Nu 30:4;
her s. shall stand	30:5-13
herself (R)	Nu 30:4;
30:5-13	
one s. of five hundred for the	Nu 31:28
Lord	
and to serve him with all	De 11:13
your s.	
all heart and entire being	De 11:13;
(A)	11:18; 13:3
ye shall lay up these my	De 11:18
words in your s.	
love the Lord your God with	De 13:3;
all your s.	Jos 22:5; 1Ki 2:4
pining of s. (E)	De 28:65

s. of Jonathan was knit to *s.*   *1Sa 18:1* of David

s. of my lord bound up in   *1Sa 25:29* bundle of life

life (A)   *1Sa 25:29;* *Job 12:10; 24:12; Ps 34:22; 49:8; 72:14;* *74:19; 94:21; 107:5; Pr 25:13; Jer 4:10;* *20:13; 31:12, 14; La 2:12; Jon 2:5*

life (B)   *1Sa 25:29;* *Job 12:10; Ps 34:22; 49:8; 72:14; 94:21;* *Pr 22:23; Jer 4:10; 20:13; 31:12; La 2:12*

s. of all the people was   *1Sa 30:6* grieved

the blind that are hated of   *2Sa 5:8* David's *s.*

the *s.* of David longed to go   *2Sa 13:39* to Absalom

spirit (A)(R)   *2Sa 13:39* heart (B)   *2Sa 13:39*

so return to thee with all   *1Ki 8:48* their *s.*

mind and heart (A)   *1Ki 8:48;* *1Ch 22:19*

heart (B)   *1Ki 8:48*

let this child's *s.* come into   *1Ki 17:21* him again

life (B)   *1Ki 17:21;* *Job 12:10; Ps 49:8;   74:19;   94:21;* *Jer 20:13; Jon 2:5*

let her alone for her *s.* is   *2Ki 4:27* vexed

to keep commandments with   *2Ki 23:3* all their *s.*

now set your *s.* to seek the   *1Ch 22:19* Lord

minds and hearts (B)(R)   *1Ch 22:19;* *2Ch 6:38*

if they return to thee with all   *2Ch 6:38* their *s.*

to seek the Lord God with   *2Ch 15:12* all their *s.*

why is life given to the bitter   *Job 3:20* in *s.*

in whose hand is *s.* of every   *Job 12:10* living

if your *s.* were in my soul's   *Job 16:4* stead

and the *s.* of the wounded   *Job 24:12* crieth out

law of Lord is perfect   *Ps 19:7* converting the *s.*

whole person (A)   *Ps 19:7* test my *s.* and attitude (B)   *Ps 26:2* deliver their *s.* from death   *Ps 33:19* and keep alive

the Lord redeemeth the *s.* of   *Ps 34:22* his servants

the redemption of their *s.* is   *Ps 49:8* precious

he shall redeem their *s.* from   *Ps 72:14* deceit

my *s.* was grieved (S)   *Ps 73:21* O deliver not the *s.* of thy   *Ps 74:19* turtledove

he spared not their *s.* from   *Ps 78:50* death

rejoice the *s.* of thy servant, O   *Ps 86:4* Lord

they gather against the *s.* of   *Ps 94:21* the righteous

but he sent leanness into   *Ps 106:15* their *s.*

hungry and thirsty their *s.*   *Ps 107:5* fainted in them

he satisfieth longing *s.* and   *Ps 107:9* filleth hungry *s.*

their *s.* abhorreth all manner   *Ps 107:18* of meat

their *s.* is melted because of   *Ps 107:26* trouble

their courage melts away   *Ps 107:26* (A)

not suffer *s.* of righteous to   *Pr 10:3* famish

liberal *s.* shall be made fat   *Pr 11:25* that watereth

person (A)   *Pr 11:25;* *19:15; Jer 31:25; Ro 13:1*

s. of transgressors shall eat   *Pr 13:2* violence

s. of the sluggard desireth and   *Pr 13:4* hath not

the desire accomplished is   *Pr 13:19* sweet to the *s.*

pleasant words are sweet to   *Pr 16:24* the *s.*

mind (A)   *Pr 16:24* *s.* be without knowledge it is   *Pr 19:2* not good

and an idle *s.* shall suffer   *Pr 19:15* hunger

the *s.* of the wicked desireth   *Pr 21:10* evil

Lord will spoil *s.* of those   *Pr 22:23* that spoiled them

my *s.* will rejoice (R)   *Pr 23:16* for he refresheth the *s.* of his   *Pr 25:13* masters

spirit (R)   *Pr 25:13* as cold waters to thirsty *s.* so   *Pr 25:25* is good news

full *s.* loatheth an honeycomb;   *Pr 27:7* but to hungry *s.* every bitter thing is sweet

woe to their *s.* they have   *Isa 3:9* rewarded evil

s. moans like a lyre (R)   *Isa 16:11* to make empty the *s.* of the   *Isa 32:6* hungry

let your *s.* delight itself in   *Isa 55:2* fatness

come unto me, hear, and   *Isa 55:3* your *s.* shall live

and if thou satisfy the   *Isa 58:10* afflicted *s.*

their *s.* delighteth in their   *Isa 66:3* abominations

whereas the sword reacheth to   *Jer 4:10* the *s.*

he hath delivered the *s.* of   *Jer 20:13* the poor

their *s.* shall be as a watered   *Jer 31:12* garden

I will satiate the *s.* of the   *Jer 31:14* priests

I have satiated the weary *s.*   *Jer 31:25* and I have replenished every sorrowful *s.*

as the Lord liveth, that made   *Jer 38:16* us this *s.*

lives (A)   *Jer 38:16* hath given for meat to relieve   *La 1:11* the *s.*

when their *s.* was poured out   *La 2:12* into bosom

the Lord is good to the *s.* that   *La 3:25* seeketh him

as *s.* of father, so *s.* of son   *Eze 18:4;* is mine, the *s.* that sinneth,   *18:20* it shall die

what your *s.* pitieth shall fall   *Eze 24:21* by sword

their *s.* shall not come into   *Ho 9:4* house of Lord

waters compassed me about   *Jon 2:5* even to the *s.*

not able to kill *s.* fear him   *M't 10:28* that can destroy both *s.* and body in hell

to love him with all the   *M'k 12:33* heart and *s.*

fear came on every *s.* many   *Ac 2:43* wonders done

every *s.* which will not hear   *Ac 3:23* that prophet

multitude that believed of one   *Ac 4:32* heart and *s.*

anguish on every *s.* that doeth   *Ro 2:9* evil

human being (R)   *Ro 2:9* let every *s.* be subject to   *Ro 13:1* higher powers

person (N)   *Ro 13:1* that your *s.* and body be   *1Th 5:23* preserved

word of God piercing to   *Heb 4:12* dividing of *s.*

the breath of life (A)   *Heb 4:12* life and spirit (N)   *Heb 4:12* which hope we have as an   *Heb 6:19* anchor of *s.*

but of them that believe to   *Heb 10:39* saving of *s.*

shall save a *s.* from death and   *Jas 5:20* hide

fleshly lusts which war against   *1Pe 2:11* the *s.*

Lot vexed his righteous *s.*   *2Pe 2:8* day to day

heart (N)   *2Pe 2:8* and every living *s.* died in the   *Re 16:3* sea

living thing (A)(N)(P)(R)   *Re 16:3* living creature (B)   *Re 16:3*

HIS SOUL

his s. clave to Dinah Jacob's   *Ge 34:3* daughter

guilty, when we saw anguish   *Ge 42:21* of *his s.*

shall give a ransom for *his s.*   *Ex 30:12* himself (A)   *Ex 30:12;* *Nu 30:2; Ps 24:4; 25:13; 89:48; Pr 6:30;* *18:7; 22:5; Ec 2:24; Isa 44:20*

his life (B)   *Ex 30:12;* *Pr 16:17;   29:10;   Isa 53:11;   Jer 51:6;* *Eze 18:27;   33:5;   M't 16:26*

himself (B)   *Ex 30:12;* *Job 14:22   Ps 25:13;   49:18;   Pr 18:7;* *Isa 53:10*

swear an oath to bind *his s.*   *Nu 30:2* to Lord

himself (B)   *Nu 30:2; Pr 6:2* *his s.* grieved for misery of   *J'g 10:16* Israel

heart (A)   *J'g 10:16* she urged him, so that *his s.*   *J'g 16:16* was vexed

no king like Josiah who   *2Ki 23:25;* turned to Lord with all *his s.*   *2Ch 34:31*

and *his s.* within him shall   *Job 14:22* mourn

another dieth in the   *Job 21:25* bitterness of *his s.*

what *his s.* desireth, even   *Job 23:13* that he doeth

hypocrite, when God taketh   *Job 27:8* away *his s.*

life (A)   *Job 27:8;* *33:28; Ps 11:5; 109:13; Pr 16:17; 23:14;* *29:10;   Ec 6:3;   Isa 53:12;   Jer 51:6;* *Eze 18:27; 33:5; M't 16:26*

his life (B)   *Job 27:8;* *31:30;   33:20;   Pr 16:17;   23:14;   29:10;* *Jer 51:6;   Eze 18:27;   33:5;   M't 16:26*

neither sin, by wishing a   *Job 31:30* curse to *his s.*

he keepeth back *his s.* from   *Job 33:18* the pit

and *his s.* abhorreth dainty   *Job 33:20* meat

yea. *his s.* draweth near unto   *Job 33:22* the grave

he will deliver *his s.* from   *Job 33:28;* the pit   *33:30*

wicked loveth violence, *his s.*   *Ps 11:5* hateth

who hath not lifted up *his s.*   *Ps 24:4* to vanity

his s. shall dwell at ease   *Ps 25:13* though while he lived he   *Ps 49:18* blessed *his s.*

shall he deliver *his s.* from   *Ps 89:48* the grave

to save from those that   *Ps 109:31* condemn *his s.*

if he steal to satisfy *his s.*   *Pr 6:30* when hungry

his appetite (R)   *Pr 6:30;* *13:25; Job 6:7*

righteous eateth to satisfying   *Pr 13:25* of *his s.*

he that keepeth his way,   *Pr 16:17* preserveth *his s.*

a fool's lips are the snare of   *Pr 18:7* *his s.*

whoso keepeth his mouth,   *Pr 21:23* keepeth *his s.*

doth keep *his s.* shall be far   *Pr 22:5* from them

and shalt deliver *his s.* from   *Pr 23:14* hell

hate the upright, but the just   *Pr 29:10* seek *his s.*

that he should make *his s.*   *Ec 2:24* enjoy good

so that he wanteth nothing for   *Ec 6:2* *his s.*

and *his s.* be not filled with   *Ec 6:3* good

he awaketh and *his s.* is   *Isa 29:8* empty; he is faint and *his s.* hath appetite

that he cannot deliver *his s.*   *Isa 44:20* nor say

shalt make *his s.* an offering   *Isa 53:10* for sin

him (A)   *Isa 53:10* see of travail of *his s.* and be   *Isa 53:11* satisfied

because he poured out *his s.*   *Isa 53:12* unto death

his s. be satisfied on mount   *Jer 50:19* Ephraim

flee and deliver every man his   *Jer 51:6;* *s.*   *51:45*

doeth what is right, he shall   *Eze 18:27* save *his s.*

he that taketh warning, shall   *Eze 33:5*
deliver *his s.*
his s. that is lifted up, is not   *Hab 2:4*
upright
if gain whole world, lose   *M't 16:26;*
his own *s.* what give in   *M'k 8:37*
exchange for *s.*
true self (N)   *M't 16:26*
his s. was not left in hell nor   *Ac 2:31*
flesh did

MY SOUL

my s. shall live because of   *Ge 12:3*
thee
my life (A)   *Ge 12:13;*
19:20; 1Sa 24:11; 26:21; 2Sa 4:9;
Job 10:1; 27:2; 30:16; Ps 6:4; 7:2, 5;
23:3; 30:3; 31:7; 34:2; 35:4, 7; 40:14;
42:6; 54:34; 55:18; 56:6, 13; 57:4; 59:3;
63:9; 69:1; 70:2; 86:2, 14; 88:3; 109:20;
116:8; 119:25, 28, 109; 120:6; 141:8;
142:4, 7; 143:11; Isa 38:17; Jer 12:7;
18:20
my life (B)   *Ge 12:13;*
19:20; 1Sa 24:11; 26:21; Job 9:21;
Ps 26:9; 54:4; 86:4, 14; 109:20; 119:109;
141:8; 143:11; Jer 18:20
my life (R)   *Ge 12:13;*
19:20; 1Sa 24:11; 26:21; 2Sa 4:9;
Job 9:21; 10:1; Ps 6:3; 7:5; 25:20; 26:9;
35:4, 7, 17; 40:14; 54:3-4; 56:6; 59:3;
63:9; 70:2; 86:2, 14; 109:20; 119:109;
143:3; Isa 38:17; Jer 18:20
let me escape, and *my s.*   *Ge 19:20*
shall live
that *my s.* may bless thee   *Ge 27:4;*
before I die   *27:25*
my s. come not into their secret *Ge 49:6*
my s. shall not abhor you   *Le 26:11;*
26:30
my s. hast trodden down   *J'g 5:21*
strength
have poured out *my s.* before *1Sa 1:15*
Lord
yet thou huntest *my s.* to   *1Sa 24:11*
take it
because *my s.* was precious   *1Sa 26:21*
in thine eyes
David answered, As Lord   *2Sa 4:9;*
liveth, who hath redeemed   *1Ki 1:29*
my s.
me (B)   *2Sa 4:9; Ps 3:2; 120:2; 142:4*
things *my s.* refused, are as my *Job 6:7*
meat
my s. chooseth strangling and *Job 7:15*
death
perfect, yet would I not know *Job 9:21*
my s.
my s. is weary of life, speak *Job 10:1*
bitterness of *my s.*
how long will ye vex *my s.* *Job 19:2*
with words
me (A)   *Job 19:2;*
Ps 3:2; 11:1; 13:2; 16:10; 25:20; 26:9;
35:3; 49:15; 66:16; 69:18; 88:14;
119:175; 120:2
me (R)   *Job 19:2;*
Ps 11:1; 16:10; 41:4; 88:14; 119:175;
120:2; 141:8; 143:11
and the Almighty, who hath *Job 27:2*
vexed *my s.*
they pursue *my s.* as the   *Job 30:15*
wind
and now *my s.* is poured out *Job 30:16*
upon me
was not *my s.* grieved for   *Job 30:25*
the poor
my heart (A)   *Job 30:25*
who say of *my s.*, There is no   *Ps 3:2*
help in God
my s. is sore vexed   *Ps 6:3*
my inner self (A)   *Ps 6:3,*
31:9; 41:9; 42:2, 5; 63:1; 138:3; 139:14
deliver *my s.*   *Ps 6:4,*
17:13; 22:20; 116:4; 120:2
lest he tear *my s.* like a lion,   *Ps 7:2*
rending it
let the enemy persecute *my s.*   *Ps 7:5*
and take it
how say ye to *my s.*, Flee as a   *Ps 11:1*
bird to
how long shall I take counsel *Ps 13:2*
in *my s.*
wilt not leave *my s.* in hell *Ps 16:10;*
  Ac 2:27
he restoreth *my s.*; I lift *my s. Ps 23:3;*
  25:1
keep *my s.* and deliver me, I *Ps 25:20*
trust in

gather not *my s.* with sinners   *Ps 26:9*
thou hast brought up *my s.*   *Ps 30:3*
from the grave
thou hast known *my s.* in   *Ps 31:7*
adversities
my s. and my belly are   *Ps 31:9*
consumed
my s. shall make her boast in *Ps 34:2*
the Lord
say unto *my s.*, I am thy   *Ps 35:3*
salvation
let them be put to shame that *Ps 35:4*
seek after *my s.*
without cause they have digged *Ps 35:7*
a pit for *my s.*
and *my s.* shall be joyful in the *Ps 35:9*
Lord
they rewarded me to the   *Ps 35:12*
spoiling of *my s.*
as for me, I humbled *my s.*   *Ps 35:13*
with fasting
myself (R)   *Ps 35:13; Eze 4:14*
rescue *my s.* from their   *Ps 35:17*
destructions
myself (A)   *Ps 35:17;*
42:4; 69:10; 86:4; 119:129; Ec 4:8
be confounded that seek after *Ps 40:14*
my s.
heal *my s.* for I have sinned *Ps 41:4*
against thee
as the heart, so panteth *my s. Ps 42:1*
after thee
my s. thirsteth for the living *Ps 42:2;*
God   *143:6*
when I remember, I pour out *Ps 42:4*
my s. in me
why cast down, O *my s.*   *Ps 42:5;*
  42:11; 43:5
O my God, *my s.* is cast down *Ps 42:6*
within me
God will redeem *my s.* from *Ps 49:15*
the grave
and oppressors seek after *my Ps 54:3*
s.*
the Lord is with them that   *Ps 54:4*
uphold *my s.*
he hath delivered *my s.* in   *Ps 55:18*
peace
mark my steps, when they wait *Ps 56:6*
for *my s.*
for thou hast delivered *my s. Ps 56:13*
from death
be merciful, for *my s.* trusteth *Ps 57:1*
in thee
my s. among lions; *my s. Ps 57:4;*
bowed down   *57:6*
for lo they lie in wait for *my s. Ps 59:3*
truly *my s.* waiteth upon God *Ps 62:1*
my s. wait thou only upon *Ps 62:5*
God, my expectation
my s. thirsteth for thee in a *Ps 63:1*
dry land
my s. shall be satisfied as with *Ps 63:5*
marrow
my whole being (A)   *Ps 63:5; 63:8*
my s. followeth hard after thee *Ps 63:8*
those that seek *my s.* to   *Ps 63:9*
destroy it shall
declare what God hath done *Ps 66:16*
for *my s.*
for the waters are come in   *Ps 69:1*
unto *my s.*
I wept and chastened *my s. Ps 69:10*
with fasting
myself (B)   *Ps 69:10; Ec 4:8*
draw nigh to *my s.* and   *Ps 69:18*
redeem it
confounded that seek after *my Ps 70:2;*
s.   *71:13*
my s. rejoice which thou hast *Ps 71:23*
redeemed
my inner being (A)   *Ps 71:23*
my sore ran, *my s.* refused to *Ps 77:2*
be comforted
my s. longeth for the courts of *Ps 84:2*
the Lord
preserve *my s.*   *Ps 86:2*
to thee do I lift up *my s.*   *Ps 86:4;*
  143:8
delivereth *my s.*   *Ps 86:13*
assemblies of violent men   *Ps 86:14*
sought after *my s.*
my s. full of troubles, my life *Ps 88:3*
draweth
Lord why casteth thou off *my Ps 88:14*
s.*
my s. had almost dwelt in   *Ps 94:17*
silence
thoughts within comforts   *Ps 94:19*
delight *my s.*

my inmost self (B)   *Ps 94:19*
bless Lord, O *my s.*   *Ps 103:1;*
103:2, 22; 104:1, 35
reward of them that speak *Ps 109:20*
against *my s.*
return unto thy rest, O *my s. Ps 116:7*
for thou hast delivered *my s. Ps 116:8*
from death
my s. breaketh for the   *Ps 119:20*
longing it hath
my heart (B)   *Ps 119:20*
my s. cleaveth to the dust, *Ps 119:25*
quicken thou me
my s. melteth for heaviness, *Ps 119:28*
strengthen me
my s. fainteth for salvation, *Ps 119:81*
but I hope
my s. is continually in my *Ps 119:109*
hand
therefore doth *my s.* keep *Ps 119:129*
them
my s. hath kept thy   *Ps 119:167*
testimonies
let *my s.* live, and it shall *Ps 119:175*
praise thee
deliver *my s.* O Lord, from *Ps 120:2*
lying lips
my s. dwelt with him that   *Ps 120:6*
hateth peace
I wait for the Lord, *my s.*   *Ps 130:5;*
doth wait   *130:6*
my s. is even as a weaned *Ps 131:2*
child
and strengthen me with   *Ps 138:3*
strength in *my s.*
and that *my s.* knoweth   *Ps 139:14*
right well
in thee is my trust, leave not *Ps 141:8*
my s. destitute
refuge failed me, no man   *Ps 142:4*
cared for *my s.*
bring *my s.* out of prison,   *Ps 142:7*
that I may praise
for the enemy hath   *Ps 143:3*
persecuted *my s.*
Lord, bring *my s.* out of   *Ps 143:11*
trouble
praise the Lord, praise the *Ps 146:1*
Lord, O *my s.*
for whom do I bereave *my s.* of *Ec 4:8*
good
which yet *my s.* seekest, but I *Ec 7:28*
find not
my heart (B)   *Ec 7:28*
O thou whom *my s.* loveth   *Ca 1:7;*
  3:1-4
my s. failed when he spake, I *Ca 5:6*
sought him
my s. like chariots of   *Ca 6:12*
Ammin-adib
new moons and feasts *my s. Isa 1:14*
hateth
with *my s.* have I desired thee *Isa 26:9*
in the night
thou hast in love to *my s. Isa 38:17*
delivered it
mine elect, in whom *my s. Isa 42:1*
delighteth
my s. shall be joyful in my *Isa 61:10*
God
hast heard, O *my s.* sound of *Jer 4:19*
trumpet
my s. is wearied because of *Jer 4:31*
murderers
shall not *my s.* be avenged   *Jer 5:9;*
  5:29; 9:9
be instructed, lest *my s.* depart *Jer 6:8*
from thee
beloved of *my s.* into hand of *Jer 12:7*
her enemies
my s. weep in secret places *Jer 13:17*
for your pride
for they have digged a pit   *Jer 18:20*
for *my s.*
I will rejoice over them with *Jer 32:41*
my whole s.
my whole heart, whole being *Jer 32:41*
(A)
comforter that should relieve *La 1:16*
my s.
thou hast removed *my s.* far *La 3:17*
off from
my s. hath them still in   *La 3:20*
remembrance
Lord is my portion, saith *my La 3:24*
s. will I hope
my living being (A)   *La 3:24*
thou hast pleaded the causes *La 3:58*
of *my s.*
my s. hath not been polluted *Eze 4:14*

when *my s.* fainted within me, *Jon 2:7* I

fruit of my body for the sin of *Mic 6:7* *my s.*

my s. desired the first ripe *Mic 7:1* fruit

heart **(B)** *Mic 7:1*

three shepherds I cut off, *my Zec 11:8* *s.* loathed

my beloved, in whom *my s.* is *M't 12:18* is well pleased

my s. is exceeding sorrowful *M't 26:38;* *M'k 14:34*

my s. doth magnify the Lord *Lu 1:46*

I will say to *my s.,* Soul, eat, *Lu 12:19* drink

is *my s.* troubled, and what *Joh 12:27* shall I say

I call God for a record upon *2Co 1:23* *my s.*

my s. shall have no pleasure *Heb 10:38* in him

OUR SOUL

our s. is dried away, nothing *Nu 11:6* but manna

our strength **(R)** *Nu 11:6*

no bread, *our s.* loatheth this *Nu 21:5* light bread

our s. waiteth for Lord, he is *Ps 32:20* our help

our inner selves **(A)** *Ps 33:20*

for *our s.* is bowed down to *Ps 44:25* the dust

our lives **(A)** *Ps 44:25*

bless our God, who holdeth *our Ps 66:9 s.* in life

our s. is exceedingly filled with *Ps 123:4* scorning

our life **(A)** *Ps 123:4*

the stream had gone over *Ps 124:4;* *our s.* *124:5*

our s. is escaped as a bird *Ps 124:7* out of the snare

the desire of *our s.* is to thy *Isa 26:8* name

OWN SOUL

if a friend is as thine *own s. De 13:6* entice thee

our life **(A)** *De 13:6;* *1Sa 18:1; Pr 6:32; 19:8, 16; 20:2; 29:24;* *M't 16:26*

David, he loved him as his *1Sa 18:1* *own s.* *18:3; 20:17*

none can keep alive his *own Ps 22:29 s.*

himself **(A)** *Ps 22:29; Pr 8:36; 11:17;* *15:32*

himself **(R)** *Ps 22:29;* *Pr 6:32; 8:36; 11:17; 15:32; 19:8*

he that doeth it destroyeth his *Pr 6:32* *own s.*

himself **(B)** *Pr 6:32;* *11:17; 15:32; 29:24*

but he that sinneth, wrongeth *Pr 8:36* his *own s.*

merciful man doeth good to *Pr 11:17* his *own s.*

he that refuseth instruction *Pr 15:32* despiseth his *own s.*

he that getteth wisdom, loveth *Pr 19:8* his *own s.*

own life **(B)** *Pr 19:8; 20:2; M't 16:26*

he that keepeth *Pr 19:16* commandments keepeth his *own s.*

his life **(R)** *Pr 19:16;* *20:2; 29:24; M't 16:26*

provoketh king, sinneth *Pr 20:2* against his *own s.*

whoso is partner with thief, *Pr 29:24* hateth *own s.*

gain whole world and *M't 16:26;* lose *own s.* *M'k 8:36*

his true self **(N)** *M't 16:26*

sword shall pierce thro' thy *Lu 2:35* *own s.* also

the heart **(N)** *Lu 2:35*

THAT SOUL

not circumcised, *that s.* shall *Ge 17:14;* be cut off *Ex 31:14; Le 7:20-21, 25, 27;* *19:8; Nu 15:30*

that person **(B)** *Ge 17:14;* *Ex 12:15, 19; Le 17:10; 22:3; 23:30;* *Nu 15:31*

whoso eateth leavened *Ex 12:15;* bread, *that s.* shall be cut off *12:19;* *Nu 19:13, 20*

that person **(A)** *Ex 12:15;* *Le 17:10; Nu 15:31*

that person **(R)** *Ex 12:15;* *12:19; Le 17:10; 22:3; 23:30; Nu 15:31*

I will set my face against *Le 17:10;* *that s.* *20:6*

that s. shall be cut off from *Le 22:3* my presence

that s. will I destroy from his *Le 23:30* people

that s. shall utterly be cut off *Nu 15:31*

THY SOUL

eat, that *thy s.* may bless me *Ge 27:19;* *27:31*

take heed, and keep *thy s. De 4:9* diligently

your life **(A)** *De 4:9;* *6:5; 1Sa 25:29; Ps 121:7; Pr 24:14;* *Isa 58:10; Hab 2:10*

your life **(B)** *De 4:9;* *1Sa 25:29; Hab 2:10*

shalt find him, if seek him *De 4:29* with all *thy s.*

love the Lord thy God with all *De 6:5;* *thy s.* *30:6*

to serve the Lord thy God *De 10:12* with all *thy s.*

your heart and entire being *De 10:12;* **(A)** *26:16; 30:2, 10*

whatsoever *thy s.* lusteth *De 12:15;* after *14:26*

do with all *thy s.:* obey with *De 26:16;* all *thy s.* *30:2*

obey his voice with all thy *De 30:2* heart and *thy s.*

if thou turn unto the Lord *De 30:10* with all *thy s.*

take as much as *thy s. 1Sa 2:16* desireth

whatsoever *thy s.* desireth, I *1Sa 20:4* will do

come according to all the *1Sa 23:20* desire of *thy s.*

heart's desire **(R)** *1Sa 23:20*

a man is risen to pursue and *1Sa 25:29* seek *thy s.*

your life **(R)** *1Sa 25:29;* *Ps 121:7; Jer 38:17; Eze 3:19; Hab 2:10*

reign according all *thy s. 1Ki 11:37* desireth

the Lord shall preserve *thy s. Ps 121:7*

when knowledge is pleasant to *Pr 2:10* *thy s.*

your heart **(A)** *Pr 2:10; 29:17*

your heart **(R)** *Pr 2:10;* *19:18; 29:17; M't 22:37*

be life to *thy s.* and grace to *Pr 3:22* thy neck

your inner self **(A)** *Pr 3:22*

and let not *thy s.* spare for *Pr 19:18* his crying

your heart **(B)** *Pr 19:18*

learn his ways, and get a *Pr 22:25* snare to *thy s.*

yourself **(R)** *Pr 22:25; Isa 58:10*

he that keepeth *thy s.* doth *Pr 24:12* not he know

so knowledge of wisdom be *Pr 24:14*

yea, he shall give delight to *Pr 29:17* *thy s.*

which have said to *thy s., Isa 51:23* Bow down

if thou draw out *thy s.* to the *Isa 58:10* hungry

the Lord shall satisfy *thy s. Isa 58:11* in drought

your desire **(R)** *Isa 58:11*

hath *thy s.* loathed Zion *Jer 14:19*

go forth then, *thy s.* shall *Jer 38:17;* live *38:20*

thou hast delivered *thy s. Eze 3:19;* *3:21; 33:9*

yourself **(A)** *Eze 3:19*

and thou hast sinned against *Hab 2:10* *thy s.*

love Lord with all thy heart *M't 22:37;* and with all *thy s. M'k 12:30; Lu 10:27*

this night *thy s.* be required *Lu 12:20* of thee

your life **(R)** *Lu 12:20*

mayest prosper, even as *thy s. 3Jo 2* prospereth

fruits *thy s.* lusted after are *Re 18:14* departed

SOULS

and the *s.* that they had gotten *Ge 12:5*

persons **(A)** *Ge 12:5;* *46:18, 22, 25-27; Ex 1:5; 12:4; Jer 2:34;* *Eze 13:19; Ac 7:14; 15:24*

personnel **(B)** *Ge 12:5*

persons **(R)** *Ge 12:5;* *46:18, 22, 25-27; Ex 1:5; 12:4; Le 18:29;* *Jos 10:28, 32, 35, 37, 39; Ac 27:37;* *1Pe 3:20*

the *s.* of his sons and his *Ge 46:15* daughters

persons **(A)** *Ge 46:15;* *46:18, 26; Le 18:29; Eze 13:19*

bare unto Jacob, even sixteen *Ge 46:18* *s.*

to Jacob: all the *s.* were *Ge 46:22* fourteen

unto Jacob: all the *s.* were *Ge 46:25* seven

All the *s.* that came with *Ge 46:26* Jacob

all the *s.* were threescore and *Ge 46:26* six

born him in Egypt, were two *Ge 46:27* *s.*

all the *s.* of the house of *Ge 46:27* Jacob

all the *s.* that came out of the *Ex 1:5* loins

the loins of Jacob were seventy *Ex 1:5* *s.*

according to the number of *Ex 12:4* the *s.*

make an atonement for your *Ex 30:15;* *s.* *30:16*

yourselves **(A)** *Ex 30:15;* *Le 16:29; 31; 20:25; 23:27, 32; 29:7;* *Jer 44:7*

yourselves **(R)** *Ex 30:15;* *Le 16:29, 31; 20:25; 23:27, 32; Nu 29:7;* *Jer 44:7*

ye shall afflict your *s.* and do *Le 16:29* no

humble yourselves **(B)** *Le 16:29;* *20:25; 23:27; Nu 29:7*

ye shall afflict your *s.* by a *Le 16:31* statute

to make an atonement for *Le 17:11* your *s.*

the *s.* that commit them shall *Le 18:29* be

make your *s.* abominable by *Le 20:25* beast

ye shall afflict your *s.* and *Le 23:27* offer an

of rest, and ye shall afflict *Le 23:32* your *s.*

these sinners against their *Nu 16:38* own *s.*

themselves **(A)** *Nu 16:38*

lives **(B)** *Nu 16:38;* *Ps 97:10; Eze 13:18; 14:14; 1Th 1:8*

lives **(R)** *Nu 16:38;* *1Sa 25:29; Ps 72:18; 97:10; Pr 14:25;* *Eze 14:14, 20; 22:25, 27; Lu 21:19*

ye shall not afflict your *s.:* ye *Nu 29:7*

they have bound their *s.* shall *Nu 30:9*

herself **(A)(B)(R)** *Nu 30:9*

to make an atonement for *Nu 31:50* our *s.*

ourselves **(A)** *Nu 31:50; Jer 26:19*

and all the *s.* that were *Jos 10:28;* therein *10:30, 35, 37, 39*

inhabitants **(B)** *Jos 10:28;* *10:32, 35, 37, 39*

smote all the *s.* that were *Jos 11:11* therein

all your hearts and in all *Jos 23:14* your *s.*

the *s.* of thine enemies, them *1Sa 25:29* shall

and shall save the *s.* of the *Ps 72:13* needy

lives **(A)** *Ps 72:13;* *97:10; Pr 11:30; 14:25; La 1:19;* *1Th 2:8*

Eze 13:18, 20; 14:14, 20; 22:25, 27;

preserveth the *s.* of his saints *Ps 97:10*

life; and he that winneth *s.* is *Pr 11:30* wise

A true witness delivereth *s.: Pr 14:25* but a

and the *s.* which I have *Isa 57:16* made

the blood of the *s.* of the poor *Jer 2:34*

and ye shall find rest for your *Jer 6:16* *s.*

procure great evil against our *s.*   *Jer 26:19*
ourselves (B)(R)   *Jer 26:19*
ye this great evil against your *s.*   *Jer 44:7*
sought their meat to relieve their *s.*   *La 1:19*
themselves (B)   *La 1:19; Eze 14:20*
strength (R)   *La 1:19*
they shall not satisfy their *s.*   *Eze 7:19*
their animal cravings (A)   *Eze 7:19*
head of every stature to hunt *s.*   *Eze 13:18*
Will ye hunt the *s.* of my people   *Eze 13:18*
will ye save the *s.* alive that come   *Eze 13:18*
to slay the *s.* that should not die   *Eze 13:19*
to save the *s.* alive that should not   *Eze 13:19*
there hunt the *s.* to make them fly   *Eze 13:20*
your arms, and will let the *s.* go   *Eze 13:20*
s. that ye hunt to make them fly   *Eze 13:20*
they should deliver but their own *s.*   *Eze 14:14*
they shall but deliver their own *s.*   *Eze 14:20*
Behold, all *s.* are mine; as the soul   *Eze 18:4*
they have devoured *s.*: they have   *Eze 22:25*
to shed blood, and to destroy *s.* to   *Eze 22:27*
ye shall find rest unto your *s.*   *M't 11:29*
your patience possess ye your *s.*   *Lu 21:19*
your true life (N)   *Lu 21:19*
unto them about three thousand *s.*   *Ac 2:41*
kindred, threescore and fifteen *s.*   *Ac 7:14*
persons (N)   *Ac 7:14*
people (P)   *Ac 7:14*
Confirming the *s.* of the disciples   *Ac 14:22*
with words, subverting your *s.*   *Ac 15:24*
minds (B)(N)(R)   *Ac 15:24*
hundred threescore and sixteen *s.*   *Ac 27:37*
of God only, but also our own *s.*   *1Th 2:8*
for they watch for your *s.* as they   *Heb 13:17*
yourselves (P)   *Heb 13:17*
word, which is able to save your *s.*   *Jas 1:21*
faith, even the salvation of your *s.*   *1Pe 1:9*
have purified your *s.* in obeying the   *1Pe 1:22*
hearts (A)   *1Pe 1:22*
Shepherd and Bishop of your *s.*   *1Pe 2:25*
is, eight *s.* were saved by water   *1Pe 3:20*
commit the keeping of their *s.* to   *1Pe 4:19*
from sin; beguiling unstable *s.*   *2Pe 2:14*
doubting *s.* need pity (N)   *Jude 22*
under the altar the *s.* of them that   *Re 6:9*
chariots, and slaves, and *s.* of men   *Re 18:13*
the *s.* of them that were beheaded   *Re 20:4*

SOUL'S

if your soul were in my *s.* stead   *Job 16:4*

SOUND

and his *s.* shall be heard when he   *Ex 28:38*
trumpet of the jubile to *s.* on   *Le 25:9*
the trumpet *s.* throughout all your   *Le 25:9*
the *s.* of a shaken leaf shall chase   *Le 26:36*
blow, but ye shall not *s.* an alarm   *Na 10:7*
when ye hear the *s.* of the trumpet   *Jos 6:5*

people heard the *s.* of the trumpet   *Jos 6:20*
David of *s.* judgment (B)   *1Sa 16:18*
the *s.* of a going in the tops of the   *2Sa 5:24*
and with the *s.* of the trumpet   *2Sa 6:15*
as ye hear the *s.* of the trumpet   *2Sa 15:10*
the earth rent with the *s.* of them   *1Ki 1:40*
Joab heard the *s.* of the trumpet   *1Ki 1:41*
when Ahijah heard the *s.* of her feet   *1Ki 14:6*
there is a *s.* of abundance of rain   *1Ki 18:41*
s. of his master's feet behind him   *2Ki 6:32*
hear a *s.* of going in the tops of the   *1Ch 14:15*
to *s.* with cymbals of brass   *1Ch 15:19*
and with *s.* of the cornet, and with   *1Ch 15:28*
but Asaph made a *s.* with cymbals   *1Ch 16:5*
for those that should make a *s.*   *1Ch 16:42*
s. aloud (S)   *1Ch 16:42*
one *s.* to be heard in praising   *2Ch 5:13*
ye hear the *s.* of the trumpet   *Ne 4:20*
A dreadful *s.* is in his ears   *Job 15:21*
and rejoice at the *s.* of the organ   *Job 21:12*
s. of their words (B)(R)   *Job 33:8*
the *s.* that goeth out of his mouth   *Job 37:2*
he that it is the *s.* of the trumpet   *Job 39:24*
s. of their cry (A)(R)   *Ps 5:2*
the Lord with the *s.* of a trumpet   *Ps 47:5*
s. of his praise (B)(R)   *Ps 66:8*
out water; the skies sent out a *s.*   *Ps 77:17*
the people that know the joyful *s.*   *Ps 89:15*
recognize the festal call (B)(R)   *Ps 89:15*
upon the harp with a solemn *s.*   *Ps 92:3*
With trumpets and *s.* of cornet   *Ps 98:6*
s. of my sighing (B)   *Ps 102:5*
s. of his word (B)   *Ps 103:20*
s. of thy thunder (B)   *Ps 104:7*
Let my heart be *s.* in thy statutes   *Ps 119:80*
heart be healthy in thy statutes (B)   *Ps 119:80*
heart be perfect in thy statutes (E)   *Ps 119:80*
heart be blameless in thy statutes (R)   *Ps 119:80*
with him the *s.* of the trumpet   *Ps 150:3*
He layeth up *s.* wisdom for   *Pr 2:7*
keep *s.* wisdom and discretion   *Pr 3:21*
Counsel is mine, and *s.* wisdom   *Pr 8:14*
A *s.* heart is the life of the flesh   *Pr 14:30*
calm, undisturbed mind and heart are the life and   *Pr 14:30*
health of the body (A)   *Pr 14:30*
relaxed mind makes physical health (B)   *Pr 14:30*
tranquil heart is life of the flesh (E)(R)   *Pr 14:30*
when the *s.* of the grinding is low   *Ec 12:4*
s. of one calling (B)   *Isa 6:8*
my bowels shall *s.* like an harp for   *Isa 16:11*
s. of your cry (A)(B)(R)   *Isa 30:19*
s. of weeping (A)(R)   *Isa 65:19*
the *s.* of the trumpet, the alarm of   *Jer 4:19*
and hear the *s.* of the trumpet   *Jer 4:21*
Hearken to the *s.* of the trumpet   *Jer 6:17*
s. like sea roaring (R)   *Jer 6:23*
trembled at the *s.* of the neighing   *Jer 8:16*
s. of wailing (A)(B)(R)   *Jer 9:19*
a *s.* of a rumor (S)   *Jer 10:22*
s. of the millstones, and the light   *Jer 25:10*
nor hear the *s.* of the trumpet   *Jer 42:14*
s. like rustling of a serpent (A)   *Jer 46:22*
s. of a cry (A)   *Jer 48:3*

mine heart shall *s.* for Moab like   *Jer 48:36*
mine heart shall *s.* like pipes for   *Jer 48:36*
A *s.* of battle is in the land, and of   *Jer 50:22*
s. of sea roaring (A)(R)   *Jer 50:42*
A *s.* of a cry cometh from Babylon   *Jer 51:54*
s. of a great earthquake (B)   *Eze 3:12*
the *s.* of the cherubims' wings was   *Eze 10:5*
s. of a careless crowd (A)(R)   *Eze 23:43*
the *s.* of thy harps shall be no more   *Eze 26:13*
the isles shake at the *s.* of thy fall   *Eze 26:15*
shake at the *s.* of the cry of thy   *Eze 27:28*
nations to shake at the *s.* of his fall   *Eze 31:16*
whosoever heareth the *s.* of   *Eze 33:4*
He heard the *s.* of the trumpet, and   *Eze 33:5*
s. like many waters (R)   *Eze 43:2*
ye hear the *s.* of the cornet, flute   *Da 3:5*
people heard the *s.* of the cornet   *Da 3:7*
that shall hear the *s.* of the cornet   *Da 3:10*
ye hear the *s.* of the cornet, flute   *Da 3:15*
s. of great words (A)(R)   *Da 7:11*
s. of his words (A)(B)(R)   *Da 10:6; 10:9*
s. an alarm in my holy mountain   *Joe 2:1*
and with the *s.* of the trumpet   *Am 2:2*
That chant to the *s.* of the viol, and   *Am 6:5*
sing idle songs to the *s.* (A)(E)(R)   *Am 6:5*
quivered at the *s.* (A)(B)(R)   *Hab 3:16*
do not *s.* a trumpet before thee   *M't 6:2*
if your eye is *s.* (A)(B)(N)(P)(R)   *M't 6:2; Lu 11:34*
do not announce it with a flourish of trumpets (N)   *M't 6:2*
hire a trumpeter (P)   *M't 6:2*
angels with a great *s.* of a trumpet   *M't 24:31*
hand restored *s.* as the other (S)   *M'k 3:5*
s. of your salvation (A)   *Lu 1:44*
if thine eye be *s.* (S)   *Lu 11:34*
he hath received him safe and *s.*   *Lu 15:27*
safe and well (A)(B)   *Lu 15:27*
thou hearest the *s.* thereof, but   *Joh 3:8*
there came a *s.* from heaven as   *Ac 2:2*
uttering straight *s.* truth (A)   *Ac 26:25*
their *s.* went into all the earth   *Ro 10:18*
their voice has gone out (A)(B)(R)   *Ro 10:18*
even things without life giving *s.*   *1Co 14:7*
give distinct notes (A)   *1Co 14:7*
produce distinct tones (B)(R)   *1Co 14:7*
if the trumpet give an uncertain *s.* (A)(B)   *1Co 14:8*
gives an uncertain call (A)(B)   *1Co 14:8*
gives an uncertain voice (E)   *1Co 14:8*
trumpet call not clear (N)(P)   *1Co 14:8*
the trumpet shall *s.* and the dead   *1Co 15:52*
that is contrary to *s.* doctrine   *1Ti 1:10*
wholesome teaching (A)(B)(N)(P)   *1Ti 1:10*
keep you *s.* in spirit (N)   *1Th 5:23*
and of love and of a *s.* mind   *2Ti 1:7*
well-balanced mind (A)   *2Ti 1:7*
self-control (B)(R)   *2Ti 1:7*
discipline (E)(N)   *2Ti 1:7*
Hold fast the form of *s.* words   *1Ti 1:13*
wholesome teachings (B)   *1Ti 1:13*
an outline of *s.* teaching (N)   *1Ti 1:13*
they will not endure *s.* doctrine   *1Ti 4:3*
wholesome instruction (B)   *1Ti 4:3*
he may be able by *s.* doctrine both   *Tit 1:9*
wholesome teaching (B)   *Tit 1:9*
true doctrine (N)   *Tit 1:9*

that they may be *s.* in the faith   *Tit 1:13*
things which become *s.*   *Tit 2:1*
doctrine
wholesome doctrine (B)(N)   *Tit 2:1*
s. in faith, in charity, in   *Tit 2:2*
patience
S. speech, that cannot be   *Tit 2:8*
wholesome, unobjectionable   *Tit 2:8*
message (B)
wholesome speech (N)   *Tit 2:8*
speech unaffected and logical   *Tit 2:8*
(P)
And the *s.* of a trumpet   *Heb 12:19*
blast of a trumpet   *Heb 12:19*
(A)(N)(P)
keep *s.*-minded, self-restrained   *1Pe 4:7*
(A)
his voice as the *s.* of many   *Re 1:15*
waters
angels prepared themselves to   *Re 8:6*
s.
ready to blow them   *Re 8:6*
(B)(N)(P)(R)
the three angels, which are yet   *Re 8:13*
to *s.*
and the *s.* of their wings was   *Re 9:9*
as the
as the *s.* of chariots of many   *Re 9:9*
horses
noise made by the wings   *Re 9:9*
(A)(P)(R)
the drone of their wings (B)   *Re 9:9*
angel, when he shall begin to   *Re 10:7*
s.
at the point of blowing (B)   *Re 10:7*
announced by the trumpet   *Re 10:7*
blast (P)
s. of great waterfall (P)   *Re 14:2*
s. of a millstone shall be   *Re 18:22*
heard no
s. of harpests (A)(P)(R)   *Re 18:22*

SOUNDED

when the voice of the trumpet   *Ex 19:19*
s.
when I have *s.* my father   *1Sa 20:12*
priests *s.* trumpets before   *2Ch 7:6*
them
blew trumpets (A)(B)   *2Ch 7:6; 13:14*
the priests *s.* with the   *2Ch 13:14*
trumpets
blew trumpets (R)   *2Ch 13:14*
rejoiced, and *s.* with   *2Ch 23:13*
trumpets
blowing trumpets (A)(R)   *2Ch 23:13*
sang, and the trumpeters *s.*   *2Ch 29:28*
he that *s.* the trumpet was   *Ne 4:18*
by me
of thy salutation *s.* in mine   *Lu 1:44*
ears
greeting reached my ears (B)   *Lu 1:44*
voice of salutation came into   *Lu 1:44*
mine ears (E)
heard my greeting (N)   *Lu 1:44*
voice of greeting came to my   *Lu 1:44*
ears (R)
s. and found it twenty fathoms   *Ac 27:28*
they *s.* again, and found it   *Ac 27:28*
fifteen
you *s.* out the word of the   *1Th 1:8*
Lord
resounded forth (A)   *1Th 1:8*
message go out from you (B)   *1Th 1:8*
word of the Lord rang out   *1Th 1:8*
(N)
sounding board from which   *1Th 1:8*
word of Lord (P)
The first angel *s.* and there   *Re 8:7*
blew his trumpet   *Re 8:7;*
(A)(N)(P)(R)   *8:8, 10, 12; 9:1, 13; 11:15*
blew his trumpet (R)   *Re 8:7;*
  8:8, 10, 12; 9:13; 11:15
the second angel *s.* and as it   *Re 8:8*
were
the third angel *s.* and there   *Re 8:10*
fell a
the fourth angel *s.* and the   *Re 8:12*
third
the fifth angel *s.* and I saw a   *Re 9:1*
star
the sixth angel *s.* and I heard   *Re 9:13*
And the seventh angel *s.*; and   *Re 11:15*
s. like rushing water (N)   *Re 14:2*

SOUNDETH

when the trumpet *s.* long,   *Ex 19:13*
they shall
at the lengthy blast of ram's   *Ex 19:13*
horn (B)

SOUNDING

harps and cymbals, *s.* by   *1Ch 15:16*
lifting
twenty priests *s.* with   *2Ch 5:12*
trumpets
with *s.* trumpets to cry   *2Ch 13:12*
alarm
him upon the high *s.*   *Ps 150:5*
cymbals
the *s.* of thy bowels and of   *Isa 63:15*
not the *s.* again of the   *Eze 7:7*
mountains
I am become as *s.* brass, or a   *1Co 13:1*

SOUNDNESS

no *s.* in my flesh because of   *Ps 38:3*
thine
and there is no *s.* in my flesh   *Ps 38:7*
unto the head there is no *s.* in   *Isa 1:6*
him hath given him this   *Ac 3:16*
perfect *s.*
gave him this perfect health   *Ac 3:16*
(B)(R)
made him completely well (N)   *Ac 3:16*
gave him perfect health and   *Ac 3:16*
strength (P)

SOUNDS

my inner being *s.* like harp   *Isa 16:11*
(A)
they give a distinction in the   *1Co 14:7*
s.

SOUR

and the *s.* grape is ripening   *Isa 18:5*
flower becomes a ripening   *Isa 18:5*
grape (A)(R)
bud is becoming a ripening   *Isa 18:5*
grape (B)
The fathers have eaten a *s.*   *Jer 31:29*
grape
every man that eateth the *s.*   *Jer 31:30*
grape
The fathers have eaten *s.*   *Eze 18:2*
grapes
Their drink is *s.*: they have   *Ho 4:18*

SOURCE

a *s.* of disturbance (A)   *Ac 24:5*

SOUTH

Abram journeyed towards the   *Ge 12:9*
s.
Abram went up into *s.*   *Ge 13:1;*
went from *s.*   *13:3*
thou shalt spread abroad to   *Ge 28:14*
north and *s.*
on side of tabernacle toward   *Ex 26:35*
the *s.*
Amalekites dwell in land of   *Nu 13:29*
the *s.*
O Naphtali, possess thou   *De 33:23*
west and *s.*
Joshua smote the country of   *Jos 10:40*
the *s.*
Judah shall abide in their   *Jos 18:5*
coast on the *s.*
to fight against the Canaanites   *J'g 1:9*
in the *s.*
David arose out of a place   *1Sa 20:41*
toward *s.*
against *s.* of Judah, *s.* of   *1Sa 27:10*
Jerahmeelites
Amalekites had invaded the   *1Sa 30:1;*
s.   *30:14*
they went out to the *s.* of   *2Sa 24:7*
Judah
three looking towards *s.*   *1Ki 7:25;*
  2Ch 4:4
the porters were toward the   *1Ch 9:24*
s.
Philistines invaded the *s.* of   *2Ch 28:18*
Judah
which maketh the chambers of   *Job 9:9*
the *s.*
out of the *s.* cometh the   *Job 37:9*
whirlwind
and stretch her wings   *Job 39:26*
toward the *s.*
promotion cometh not from   *Ps 75:6*
east nor *s.*
the north and *s.* thou hast   *Ps 89:12*
created them

and gathered them from the   *Ps 107:3*
north and *s.*
turn our captivity as streams   *Ps 126:4*
in the *s.*
the wind goeth toward the *s.*   *Ec 1:6*
if tree falleth toward the *s.* or   *Ec 11:3*
north
as whirlwinds in the *s.* pass   *Isa 21:1*
through
the burden of the beasts of   *Isa 30:6*
the *s.*
and I will say to the *s.*, Keep   *Isa 43:6*
not back
the cities of the *s.* shall be   *Jer 13:19*
shut up
from the *s.* bringing burnt   *Jer 17:26*
offerings
men shall buy fields in cities   *Jer 32:44*
of the *s.*
in cities of the *s.* shall the   *Jer 33:13*
flocks pass
set face toward *s.*, drop thy   *Eze 20:46*
word toward *s.*, prophesy
against *s.* field
say to forest of *s.* from *s.* to   *Eze 20:47*
north, be burned
sword against all flesh from *s.*   *Eze 21:4*
to north
by which we as the frame of   *Eze 40:2*
a city on *s.*
after that he brought me   *Eze 40:24*
toward the *s.*
and their prospect was   *Eze 40:44*
toward the *s.*
and another door was   *Eze 41:11*
toward the *s.*
go out by way of *s.* gate; and   *Eze 46:9*
he that entereth by way of *s.*
a little horn waxed great   *Da 8:9*
toward the *s.*
and the king of the *s.* shall be   *Da 11:5*
strong
king's daughter of the *s.* shall   *Da 11:6*
come to north
king of the *s.* shall come into   *Da 11:9*
his kingdom
king of the *s.* shall be moved   *Da 11:11*
with choler
and the arms of the *s.* shall   *Da 11:15*
not withstand
and the king of the *s.* shall   *Da 11:25*
be stirred up
he shall return, and come   *Da 11:29*
toward the *s.*
the king of the *s.* shall push   *Da 11:40*
at him
they of *s.* shall possess the   *Ob 19*
mount of Esau
the captivity shall possess the   *Ob 20*
cities of the *s.*
when men inhabited the *s.* and   *Zec 7:7*
God shall go with the   *Zec 9:14*
whirlwinds of the *s.*
half of the mountain remove   *Zec 14:4*
toward the *s.*
queen of *s.* shall rise in   *M't 12:42*
judgment
come from *s.* to sit down   *Lu 13:29*
with Abraham
saying, Arise, and go toward   *Ac 8:26*
the *s.*
on the *s.* three gates, on the   *Re 21:13*
west three

SOUTH *BORDER*

s. border outmost coast of   *Nu 34:3*
salt sea
the *s. border* of Judah from   *Jos 15:2*
the shore

SOUTH *COUNTRY*

Abraham sojourned toward   *Ge 20:1*
the *s. country*
for Isaac dwelt in the   *Ge 24:62*
the *s. country*
Joshua took all the   *Jos 11:16;*
s. country   *12:8*
grisled go forth toward the   *Zec 6:6*
s. country

SOUTH *FIELD*

prophesy against the forest   *Eze 20:46*
of the *s. field*

SOUTH *LAND*

thou hast given me *s. land*   *Jos 15:19;*
  J'g 1:15

SOUTH *QUARTER*

s. quarter from Zin by coast of Edom	Nu 34:3
s. quarter from end of Kirjath-jearim	Jos 18:15

SOUTH *RAMOTH*

to them which were in s. Ramoth	1Sa 30:27

SOUTH *SIDE*

twenty boards on the s. side	Ex 26:18; 36:23
on s. side shall be standard of Reuben	Nu 2:10
camps which lie on the s. side go forward	Nu 10:6
he measured the s. side 500 reeds	Eze 42:18
the waters came at the s. side of the altar	Eze 47:1
the s. side 4500 measures	Eze 48:16; 48:33

SOUTH *WEST*

Phenice lying towards the s. west	Ac 27:12

SOUTH *WIND*

he quieteth the earth by the s. wind	Job 37:17
by his power he brought in the s. wind	Ps 78:26
come, thou s. wind, blow on my garden	Ca 4:16
when see s. wind blow there will be heat	Lu 12:55
and when the s. wind blew softly	Ac 27:13

SOUTHWARD

s. and eastward, and westward	Ge 13:14
twenty boards for the south side s.	Ex 26:18
south side s. there shall be hangings	Ex 27:9
twenty boards for the southside s.	Ex 36:23
on the southside s. the hangings	Ex 38:9
the south side of the tabernacle s.	Ex 40:24
on the side of the tabernacle s.	Nu 3:29
Get you up this way s. and go up	Nu 13:17
northward, and s. and eastward	De 3:27
the wilderness of Zin s., was	Jos 15:1
sea, from the bay that looketh s.	Jos 15:2
Judah toward the coast of Edom s.	Jos 15:21
unto the river Kanah, s. of the river	Jos 17:9
S. it was Ephraim's, and northward	Jos 17:10
side of Luz, which is Beth-el, s.	Jos 18:13
compassed the corner of the sea s.	Jos 18:14
hill that lieth before Beth-horon s.	Jos 18:14
the other s. over against Gibeah	1Sa 14:5
To Obed-edom s.; and to his sons	1Ch 26:15
northward four a day, s. four a day	1Ch 26:17
the south side s. from Tamar	Eze 47:19
sea. And this is the south side s.	Eze 47:19
border of Gad, at the south side s.	Eze 48:28
westward, and northward, and s.	Da 8:4

SOVEREIGN

s. over all mankind (N)	Joh 17:2
purpose of s. will (P)	Eph 1:11
blessed, only S. (A)(B)(R)	1Ti 6:15

SOVEREIGNTIES

thrones, s., authorities and powers (N)	Col 1:16

SOW

for you, and ye shall s. the land	Ge 47:23
six years thou shalt s. thy land	Ex 23:10
shalt not s. thy field with mingled	Le 19:19
Six years thou shalt s. thy field	Le 25:3
thou shalt neither s. thy field, nor	Le 25:4
ye shall not s. neither reap	Le 25:11
we shall not s. nor gather in our	Le 25:20
And ye shall s. the eighth year	Le 25:22
and ye shall s. your seed in vain	Le 26:16
not s. thy vineyard with divers	De 22:9
in the third year s. ye, and reap	2Ki 19:29
plow iniquity, and s. wickedness	Job 4:8
Then let me s. and let another eat	Job 31:8
s. the fields, and plant vineyards	Ps 107:37
that s. in tears shall reap in joy	Ps 126:5
observeth the wind shall not s.	Ec 11:4
In the morning, s. thy seed, and in	Ec 11:6
the plowman plow all day to s.	Isa 28:24
seed, that thou shalt s. the ground	Isa 30:23
Blessed are ye that s. beside	Isa 32:20
in the third year s. ye, and reap	Isa 37:30
ground, and s. not among thorns	Jer 4:3
that I will s. the house of Israel	Jer 31:27
shall ye build house, nor s.	Jer 35:7
I will s. her unto me in the earth	Ho 2:23
S. to yourselves in righteousness	Ho 10:12
Thou shalt s. but thou shalt not	Mic 6:15
I will s. them among the people	Zec 10:9
the fowls of the air: for they s. not	M't 6:26
a sower went forth to s.	M't 13:3
Sir, didst thou not s. good seed in	M't 13:27
there went out a sower to s.	M'k 4:3
A sower went out to s. his seed	Lu 8:5
for they neither s. nor reap; which	Lu 12:24
reapest that thou didst not s.	Lu 19:21
down, and reaping that I did not s.	Lu 19:22
the s. that was washed to her	2Pe 2:22

SOWED

Then Isaac s. in that land	Ge 26:12
down the city, and s. it with salt	J'g 9:45
when he s. some seeds fell by	M't 13:4
unto a man which s. good seed in	M't 13:24
came and s. tares among the wheat	M't 13:25
which a man took, and s. in his field	M't 13:31
The enemy that s. them is the devil	M't 13:39
knewest that I reap where I s. not	M't 25:26
as he s. some fell by the way side	M'k 4:4; Lu 8:5

SOWEDST

where thou s. thy seed, and	De 11:10

SOWER

that it may give seed to the s.	Isa 55:10
Cut off the s. from Babylon	Jer 50:16

Behold, a s. went forth to sow	M't 13:3
Hear ye the parable of the sower	M't 13:18
Behold, there went out a s. to sow	M'k 4:3
The s. soweth the word	M'k 4:14
A s. went out to sow his seed	Lu 8:5
he that ministereth seed to the s.	2Co 9:10

SOWEST

which thou s. is not quickened	2Co 15:36
And that which thou s.	1Co 15:37
thou s. not that body that shall be	1Co 15:37

SOWETH

continually; he s. discord	Pr 6:14
that s. discord among brethren	Pr 6:19
but to him that s. righteousness	Pr 11:18
A froward man s. strife: and	Pr 16:28
He that s. iniquity shall reap	Pr 22:8
treader of grapes him that s. seed	Am 9:13
He that s. the good seed is the Son	M't 13:37
The sower s. the word	M'k 4:14
that both he that s. and he	Joh 4:36
true, One s. and another reapeth	Joh 4:37
He which s. sparingly shall reap	2Co 9:6
he which s. bountifully shall reap	2Co 9:6
whatsoever a man s. that shall he	Ga 6:7
For he that s. to his flesh shall	Ga 6:8
but he that s. to the Spirit shall	Ga 6:8

SOWING

their carcase fall upon any s. seed	Le 11:37
shall reach unto the s. time	Le 26:5

SOWN

which thou hast s. in the field	Ex 23:16
any sowing seed which is to be s.	Le 11:37
which is neither eared nor s.	De 21:4
fruit of thy seed which thou hast s.	De 22:9
and burning, that it is not s.	De 29:23
And so it was when Israel had s.	J'g 6:3
Light is s. for the righteous	Ps 97:11
every thing s. by the brooks	Isa 19:7
yea, they shall not be s.: yea	Isa 40:24
things that are s. in it to spring	Isa 61:11
in a land that was not s.	Jer 2:2
They have s. wheat, but shall reap	Jer 12:13
you, and ye shall be tilled and s.	Eze 36:9
For they have s. the wind, and	Ho 8:7
that no more of thy name be s.	Na 1:14
Ye have s. much, and bring in	Hag 1:6
that which was s. in his heart	M't 13:19
reaping where thou hast not s.	M't 25:24
the way side, where the word is s.	M'k 4:15
the word that was s. in their hearts	M'k 4:15
which are s. on stony ground; who	M'k 4:16
they which are s. among thorns	M'k 4:18
they which are s. on good ground	M'k 4:20
when it is s. in the earth, is less	M'k 4:31
But when it is s. it groweth up, and	M'k 4:32
have s. unto you spiritual things	1Co 9:11
It is s. in corruption; it is raised in	1Co 15:42
It is s. in dishonour; it is raised in	1Co 15:43
it is s. in weakness; it is raised in	1Co 15:43

It is *s*. a natural body; it is   *1Co 15:44*
raised
multiply your seed *s*. and   *2Co 9:10*
increase
message *s*. in hearts (P)   *Jas 1:21*
fruit of righteousness is *s*. in   *Jas 3:18*
peace

SPACE

abode with him the *s*. of a   *Ge 29:14*
month
put a *s*. betwixt drove and   *Ge 32:16*
drove
the *s*. of the seven sabbaths of   *Le 25:8*
within the *s*. of a full year   *Le 25:30*
And the *s*. in which we came   *De 2:14*
shall be a *s*. between you and   *Jos 3:4*
a great *s*. being between   *1Sa 26:13*
them
a little *s*. grace hath been   *Ezr 9:8*
shewed
within the *s*. of two full   *Jer 28:11*
years
s. also before the little   *Eze 40:12*
chambers
the *s*. was one cubit on that   *Eze 40:12*
side
And about the *s*. of one hour   *Lu 22:59*
it was about the *s*. of three   *Ac 5:7*
hours
to put the apostles forth a   *Ac 5:34*
little *s*.
by the *s*. of forty years in the   *Ac 7:42*
the *s*. of four hundred and   *Ac 13:20*
fifty years
of Benjamin, but the *s*. of   *Ac 13:21*
forty years
after they had tarried there a   *Ac 15:33*
s.
boldly for the *s*. of three   *Ac 19:8*
months
continued by the *s*. of two   *Ac 19:10*
years
about the *s*. of two hours   *Ac 19:34*
cried out
the *s*. of three years I ceased   *Ac 20:31*
the *s*. of three years and six   *Jas 5:17*
months
And I gave her *s*. to repent of   *Re 2:21*
her
in heaven about the *s*. of half   *Re 8:1*
an hour
s. of a thousand and six   *Re 14:20*
hundred
cometh, he must continue a   *Re 17:10*
short *s*.

SPACIOUS

to a *s*. place (R)   *Ps 66:12*

SPADE

a paddle or *s*. (A)(B)   *Nu 35:18*

SPAIN

I take my journey into *S*. I   *Ro 15:24*
fruit, I will come by you into   *Ro 15:28*
S.

ANGEL SPAKE

the *angel* of God *s*. unto me   *Ge 31:11*
in a dream
the *angel* of the Lord *s*. these   *J'g 2:4*
words
an *angel s*. unto me by the   *1Ki 13:18*
word
an *angel s*. to him   *Joh 12:29*
the *angel* which *s*. to him   *Ac 7:38*
the *angel* of the Lord *s*. unto   *Ac 8:26*
Philip
the *angel* which *s*. to   *Ac 10:7*
Cornelius

GOD SPAKE

God s. unto Noah   *Ge 8:15; 9:8*
God s. unto me and sware   *Ge 24:7*
the *God* of your father *s*.   *Ge 31:29*
unto me
in the place where *God s*.   *Ge 35:15*
with him
God s. unto Israel in visions   *Ge 46:2*
God s. unto Moses   *Ex 6:2; Joh 9:29*
God s. all these words, saying   *Ex 20:1*
in the bush *God s*. to him   *M'k 12:26*
God s. on this wise   *Ac 7:6*

LORD SPAKE

the *Lord* that *s*. unto Hagar   *Ge 16:13*
the *Lord s*.   *Ex 6:10;*
6:28, 29; 8:1, 5; 13:1; 14:1; 16:11; 25:1;
30:11, 17, 22; 31:1, 12; 33:11; 40:1;
Le 4:1; 5:14; 6:1, 8, 19, 24; 7:22, 28;
8:1; 10:3; 12:1; 14:1; 16:1; 17:1; 18:1;
19:1; 20:1; 21:16; 22:1, 17, 26, 23:1; 9,
23, 26, 33; 24:1, 13; 25:1; 27:1; Nu 1:1;
3:1, 5, 11, 14, 44; 4:21; 5:1, 4, 5, 11;
6:1, 22; 7:4; 8:1, 5, 23; 9:1, 9; 10:1;
12:4; 13:1; 15:1, 17, 37; 16:20, 23, 36,
44; 17:1; 18:25; 20:7; 25:10, 16; 26:52;
28:1; 31:1, 25; 33:50; 34:1, 16;
35:1, 9; De 1:6; 2:1, 2, 17; 4:12, 15;
5:22; 9:10, 13; 10:4; 32:48; Jos 1:1; 4:1,
8, 15; 14:10, 12; 20:1, 2; 23:14;
24:27; J'g 2:4; 1Sa 16:4; 1Ki 5:5; 12:15;
13:26; 17:16; 2Ki 10:10, 17; 15:12;
21:9; 1Ch 21:9; 2Ch 33:10; Isa 7:10; 8:5;
11; 20:2; Jer 30:4; 50:1; Jon 2:10;
  Mal 3:16; Ac 18:9
the *Lord s*. unto Moses and   *Ex 6:13;*
Aaron 7:8, 19; 12:1; 16:9; Le 11:1; 13:1,
33; 15:1; Nu 2:1; 4:1, 17; 14:26; 19:1;
  20:12, 23
The *Lord s*. unto Aaron   *Le 10:8;*
  Nu 18:8, 20
whereof the *Lord s*. unto   *Nu 21:16*
Moses
the *Lord s*. unto Moses and   *Nu 26:1*
Eleazar
the word that the *Lord s*.   *Jer 46:13*

HE (God) SPAKE

hath done to him, as *he s*.   *1Sa 28:17*
by me
he s. by   *1Ki 14:18;*
15:29; 16:34; 22:38; 2Ki 9:36; 10:10;
14:25; 24:2; 2Ch 10:15; Ps 33:9; 99:7;
105:31, 34; Jer 37:2; 51:12; Eze 2:2;
10:2; Zec 1:21; 3:4; 4:6; 6:8; Lu 1:55,
  70; Ac 2:31; Heb 4:4

HE (Christ) SPAKE

he s.   *M't 9:18;*
17:5, 13; 21:45; 26:47; M'k 3:9; 5:35;
8:32; 14:43; Lu 8:49; 9:11, 31, 34; 11:27,
37; 14:3; 22:47; 24:6; Joh 2:21; 6:71;
7:39; 8:27, 30; 10:6; 13:22, 24, 28;
  18:32; 21:19
he s. a parable in parables   *M't 13:3;*
13:33, 34; 22:1; M'k 4:33, 34; Lu 5:36;
6:39; 8:4; 12:16; 13:6; 15:3; 18:1, 9;
  19:11; 21:29; Joh 10:6

I (God) SPAKE

when *I s*. ye did not hear   *Isa 65:12;*
  66:4
I s. unto you   *Jer 7:13; 22:21; 36:2*

JESUS SPAKE

Jesus s. unto them   *M't 14:27; 28:18*
Then *s. Jesus* again   *Joh 8:12*
these words *s. Jesus*   *Joh 8:20;*
  12:36; 17:1
Jesus s. of his death   *Joh 11:13*

(Men) SPAKE

chief captain *s*. unto   *Ge 21:22*
Abraham
Isaac *s*. unto Abraham his   *Ge 22:7*
father
s. unto the sons of Heth   *Ge 23:3*
saying
he *s*. unto Ephron in the   *Ge 23:13*
audience
Thus *s*. the man unto me;   *Ge 24:30*
that he
when Isaac *s*. to Esau his son   *Ge 27:5*
Rebekah *s*. unto Jacob her son   *Ge 27:6*
And while he yet *s*. with them   *Ge 29:9*
and *s*. kindly unto the damsel   *Ge 34:3*
And Shechem *s*. unto his   *Ge 34:4*
father
as she *s*. to Joseph day by   *Ge 39:10*
day
house, and *s*. unto them,   *Ge 39:14*
saying
And she *s*. unto him   *Ge 39:17*
according to
of his wife, which she *s*. unto   *Ge 39:19*
him
s. the chief butler unto   *Ge 41:9*
Pharaoh

them, and *s*. roughly unto   *Ge 42:7*
them
That is it that I *s*. unto you,   *Ge 42:14*
saying
S. I not unto you, saying, Do   *Ge 42:22*
not
he *s*. unto them by an   *Ge 42:23*
interpreter
lord of the land *s*. roughly to   *Ge 42:30*
us
Reuben *s*. unto his father,   *Ge 42:37*
saying
And Judah *s*. unto him,   *Ge 43:3*
saying, The
well, the old man of whom   *Ge 43:27*
ye *s*.
brother, of whom ye *s*. unto   *Ge 43:29*
me
and he *s*. unto them these   *Ge 44:6*
same
Pharaoh *s*. unto Joseph,   *Ge 47:5*
saying, Thy
it that their fathers *s*. unto   *Ge 49:28*
them
were past, Joseph *s*. unto the   *Ge 50:4*
house
And Joseph wept when they   *Ge 50:17*
s. unto
them, and *s*. kindly unto   *Ge 50:21*
them
s. to the Hebrew midwives   *Ex 1:15*
Aaron *s*. all the words which   *Ex 4:30*
and they *s*. to the people,   *Ex 5:10*
saying
Moses *s*. to the children of   *Ex 6:9;*
Israel 34:34; 35:4; Le 24:23; Nu 9:4;
16:26; 17:6; 30:1, 3; De 1:1, 3, 9, 43;
  4:45; 31:1, 30; 32:44
Aaron *s*. unto the   *Ex 16:10*
congregation
Moses *s*. unto Aaron   *Le 1:12*
Miriam and Aaron *s*. against   *Nu 12:1*
Moses
children of Israel *s*. unto   *Nu 17:12;*
Moses   *20:3*
the people *s*. against God   *Nu 21:5*
And the people *s*. against God   *Nu 21:5*
and *s*. unto him the words of   *Nu 22:7*
Balak
S. I not also to thy   *Nu 24:12*
messengers
Moses *s*. to the Lord   *Nu 27:15; Ex 6:12*
Reuben came and *s*. unto   *Nu 32:2*
Moses
children of Reuben *s*. unto   *Nu 32:25*
Moses
to pass whereof he *s*. unto   *De 13:2*
thee
the Levites *s*. unto all Israel,   *De 27:9*
saying
by the way whereof I *s*. unto   *De 28:68*
thee
the tribe of Manasseh, *s*.   *Jos 1:12*
Joshua
Joshua *s*. unto the priests,   *Jos 3:6*
saying
of Israel, as Moses *s*. unto   *Jos 4:12*
them
And he *s*. unto the children of   *Jos 4:21*
Israel
and *s*. unto them, saying, Go   *Jos 7:2*
up and
inhabitants of our country *s*.   *Jos 9:11*
to us
them, and he *s*. unto them,   *Jos 9:22*
saying
Then *s*. Joshua to the Lord   *Jos 10:12*
children of Joseph *s*. unto   *Jos 17:14*
Joshua
Joshua *s*. unto the house of   *Jos 17:17*
Joseph
they *s*. unto them at Shiloh in   *Jos 21:2*
he *s*. unto them, saying, Return   *Jos 22:8*
and they *s*. with them,   *Jos 22:15*
saying,
and the children of   *Jos 22:30*
Manasseh *s*.
Penuel, and *s*. unto them   *J'g 8:8*
likewise
he *s*. also unto the men of   *J'g 8:9*
Penuel
his mother's brethren *s*. of him   *J'g 9:3*
there
Gaal *s*. again and said, See   *Jg 9:37*
there
And they *s*. unto him, saying,   *J'g 15:13*
No
and *s*. to the master of the   *J'g 19:22*
house
kinsman of whom Boaz *s*. came   *Ru 4:1*

Now Hannah, she s. in her heart	1Sa 1:13	I s. unto Naboth the Jezreelite, and	1Ki 21:6	s. the priests, and the prophets unto	Jer 26:11
And Samuel s. unto all the house of	1Sa 7:3	of Jezebel also s. the Lord	1Ki 21:23	s. Jeremiah unto all the princes	Jer 26:12
went to enquire of God, thus he s.	1Sa 9:9	gone to call Micaiah s. unto him	1Ki 22:13	s. to all the assembly of the people	Jer 26:17
the man whom I s. to thee of! this	1Sa 9:17	he s. unto him, Thou man of God	2Ki 1:9	s. to all the people of Judah, saying	Jer 26:18
the kingdom, whereof Samuel s. he	1Sa 10:16	to the saying of Elisha which he s.	2Ki 2:22	I s. also to Zedekiah king of Judah	Jer 27:12
s. according to the same words	1Sa 17:23	s. unto him, and said, My father, if	2Ki 5:13	Also I s. to the priests and to	Jer 27:16
David s. to the men that stood by	1Sa 17:26	who s. when the king came down	2Ki 7:17	s. unto me in the house of the Lord	Jer 28:1
heard when he s. unto the men	1Sa 17:28	Then s. Elisha unto the woman	2Ki 8:1	And Hananiah s. in the presence of	Jer 28:11
and s. after the same manner	1Sa 17:30	Thus and thus s. he to me, saying	2Ki 9:12	for since I s. against him, I	Jer 31:20
words were heard which David s.	1Sa 17:31	they s. to the king of Assyria	2Ki 17:26	Jeremiah the prophet s. all	Jer 34:6
Saul's servants s. those words in the	1Sa 18:23	in the Jews' language and s.	2Ki 18:28	the king's house, and s. to the king	Jer 38:8
saying, On this manner s. David	1Sa 18:24	heardest what I s. against this place	2Ki 22:19	the son of Kareah s. to	Jer 40:15
And Saul s. to Jonathan his son, and	1Sa 19:1	And he s. kindly to him, and set his	2Ki 25:28	s. Azariah the son of Hoshaiah, and	Jer 43:2
And Jonathan s. good of David unto	1Sa 19:4	David s. to the chief of the Levites	1Ch 15:16	that Jeremiah the prophet s.	Jer 45:1
Saul s. not any thing that day: for	1Sa 20:26	s. I a word to any of the judges of	1Ch 17:6	And s. kindly unto him, and set his	Jer 52:32
s. to Nabal according to all those	1Sa 25:9	which he s. in the name of the Lord	1Ch 21:19	and I heard a voice of one that s.	Eze 1:28
they s. unto her, saying, David sent	1Sa 25:40	Then Solomon s. unto all Israel, to	2Ch 1:2	I s. unto them of the captivity	Eze 11:25
and the woman s. to Saul, saying	1Sa 28:12	that which he s. with his mouth	2Ch 6:4	So I s. unto the people in	Eze 24:18
for the people s. of stoning him	1Sa 30:6	all Israel came and s. to Rehoboam	2Ch 10:3	And the king s. unto Ashpenaz	Da 1:3
And Abner also s. in the ears of	2Sa 3:19	they s. unto him, saying, If thou	2Ch 10:7	Then s. the Chaldeans to the king	Da 2:4
s. saying, Behold, we are thy bone	2Sa 5:1	brought up with him s. unto him	2Ch 10:10	They s. and said to the king	Da 3:9
which s. unto David, saying, Except	2Sa 5:6	answer the people that s. unto thee	2Ch 10:10	Nebuchadnezzar s. and said	Da 3:14
s. I a word with any of the tribes	2Sa 7:7	that went to call Micaiah s. to him	2Ch 18:12	therefore he s. and commanded	Da 3:19
child was yet alive, we s. unto him	2Sa 12:18	one s. saying after this manner	2Ch 18:19	rose up in haste, and s. and	Da 3:24
And Absalom s. unto his brother	2Sa 13:22	Hezekiah s. comfortably unto all	2Ch 30:22	s. and said, Shadrach, Meschach	Da 3:26
the woman of Tekoah s. to the king	2Sa 14:4	s. comfortably to them, saying	2Ch 32:6	Then Nebuchadnezzar s. and	Da 3:28
Absalom s. unto him, saying	2Sa 17:6	his servants s. yet more against the	2Ch 32:16	The king s. and said, Belteshazzar	Da 4:19
Then she s. saying, They were won	2Sa 20:18	s. against the God of Jerusalem	2Ch 32:19	The king s. and said, Is not	Da 4:30
David s. unto the Lord the words	2Sa 22:1	he s. unto him, and he gave him a	2Ch 32:24	king s. and said to the wise men	Da 5:7
David s. unto the Lord when he saw	2Sa 24:17	words of the seers that s. to him in	2Ch 33:18	and the queen s. and said, O king	Da 5:10
Nathan s. unto Bath-sheba	1Ki 1:11	and they s. to her to that effect	2Ch 34:22	the king s. and said unto Daniel	Da 5:13
while he yet s. behold, Jonathan	1Ki 1:42	the singing women s. of Josiah in	2Ch 35:25	and s. before the king concerning	Da 6:12
word which he s. concerning me	1Ki 2:4	he s. before his brethren and	Ne 4:2	the king s. and said unto Daniel	Da 6:16
he s. concerning the house of Eli in	1Ki 2:27	and they s. unto Ezra the scribe	Ne 8:1	and the king s. and said to Daniel	Da 6:20
son. Thus they s. before the king	1Ki 3:22	their children s. half in the speech	Ne 13:24	Daniel s. and said, I saw in my	Da 7:2
Then s. the woman whose the living	1Ki 3:26	pass, when they s. daily unto	Es 3:4	the great words which the horn s.	Da 7:11
he s. three thousand proverbs	1Ki 4:32	again Esther s. unto Hatach	Es 4:10	a mouth that s. very great things	Da 7:20
he s. also of beasts, and of fowl, and	1Ki 4:33	And Esther s. yet again before	Es 8:3	unto that certain saint which s.	Da 8:13
he s. of trees, from the cedar tree	1Ki 4:33	and none s. a word unto him: for	Job 2:13	which s. in thy name to our kings	Da 9:6
which I s. unto David thy father	1Ki 6:12	And Job s. and said	Job 3:2	which he s. against us, and against	Da 9:12
Then s. Solomon, The Lord said	1Ki 8:12	I arose, and they s. against	Job 19:18	then I opened my mouth, and s.	Da 10:16
s. with his mouth unto David	1Ki 8:15	After my words they s. not again	Job 29:22	in Beth-el, and there he s. with us	Ho 12:4
hath performed his word that he s.	1Ki 8:20	(for they s. not, but stood still, and	Job 32:16	When Ephraim s. trembling	Ho 13:1
Israel came, and s. unto Rehoboam	1Ki 12:3	Elihu s. moreover, and said	Job 35:1	And she s. out with a loud voice	Lu 1:42
they s. unto him, saying, If thou	1Ki 12:7	who s. unto the Lord the words	Ps 18 title	and his tongue loosed, and he s.	Lu 1:64
grown up with him s. unto him	1Ki 12:10	burned: then s. I with my tongue	Ps 39:3	s. of him to all them that looked	Lu 2:38
unto this people that s. unto thee	1Ki 12:10	Yea, they s. against God: they said	Ps 78:19	the saying which he s. unto	Lu 2:50
s. to them after the counsel of the	1Ki 12:14	so that he s. unadvisedly with his	Ps 106:33	amazed, and s. among themselves	Lu 4:36
he s. to his sons, saying, Saddle me	1Ki 13:27	the man s. unto Ithiel, even	Pr 30:1	he s. within himself, saying, This	Lu 7:39
him, that he s. to his sons, saying	1Ki 13:31	My beloved s. and said unto me	Ca 2:10	devil was gone out, the dumb s.	Lu 11:14
God, and s. unto the king of Israel	1Ki 20:28	gone; my soul failed when he s.	Ca 5:6	And s. unto him, saying, Tell us	Lu 20:2
Ahab s. unto Naboth, saying, Give	1Ki 21:2	and heard, but they s. not aright	Jer 8:6	And as some s. of the temple	Lu 21:5
		them, neither s. unto them	Jer 14:14	while he yet s. the cock crew	Lu 22:60
		which I commanded not, nor s. it	Jer 19:5	blasphemously s. they against him	Lu 22:65
		For since I s. I cried out, I cried	Jer 20:8	And as they thus s. Jesus himself	Lu 24:36
		the prophet s. unto all the people of	Jer 25:2	are the words, which I s. unto you	Lu 24:44
				This was he of whom I s.	Joh 1:15
				He that	
				Never man s. like this man	Joh 1:46

things that John s. of this man | Joh 10:41
might be fulfilled, which he s. | Joh 12:38
he saw his glory, and s. of him | Joh 12:41
might be fulfilled, which he s. | Joh 18:9
and s. unto her that kept the door | Joh 18:16
I s. openly to the world; I ever | Joh 18:20
David s. before concerning Judas | Ac 1:16
And as they s. unto the people | Ac 4:1
s. the word of God with boldness | Ac 4:31
wisdom and spirit by which he s. | Ac 6:10
unto those things which Philip s. | Ac 8:6
s. boldly in the name of the Lord | Ac 9:29
voice s. unto him again the second | Ac 10:15
while Peter yet s. these words | Ac 10:44
s. unto the Grecians, preaching the | Ac 11:20
s. against those things which were | Ac 13:45
and so s. that a great multitude | Ac 14:1
s. unto the women which resorted | Ac 16:13
s. unto him the word of the Lord | Ac 16:32
s. and taught diligently the things | Ac 18:25
and s. with tongues, and prophesied | Ac 19:6
s. boldly for the space of three | Ac 19:8
but s. evil of that way before | Ac 19:9
of all for the words which he s. | Ac 20:38
he s. unto them in the Hebrew | Ac 21:40
he s. in the Hebrew tongue to them | Ac 22:2
heard not the voice of him that s. | Ac 22:9
And as he thus s. for himself | Ac 26:24
But when the Jews s. against it | Ac 28:19
shewed or s. any harm of thee | Ac 28:21
When I was a child, I s. as a child | 1Co 13:11
I would that ye all s. with tongues | 1Co 14:5
as we s. all things to you in truth | 2Co 7:14
Where is then the blessedness ye s. | Ga 4:15
s. in time past unto the fathers | Heb 1:1
of which tribe Moses s. nothing | Heb 7:14
refused him that s. on earth, who | Heb 12:25
men of God s. as they were moved | 2Pe 1:21
And I turned to see the voice that s. | Re 1:12
from heaven s. unto me again the | Re 10:8
like a lamb, and he s. as a dragon | Re 13:11

SPIRIT SPAKE

The Spirit of the Lord s. by me | 2Sa 23:2

SPAKEST

the man that s. unto the woman | J'g 13:11
cursedst, and s. of also in mine ears | J'g 17:2
thy words which thou s. unto me | 1Sa 28:21
thou s. also with thy mouth | 1Ki 8:24
thou s. unto thy servant David my | 1Ki 8:26
as thou s. by the hand of Moses thy | 1Ki 8:53
s. with thy mouth, and hast fulfilled | 2Ch 6:15
and s. with them from heaven | Ne 9:13
Then thou s. in vision to thy holy | Ps 89:19
for since thou s. of him, thou | Jer 48:27

SPAN

a s. shall be the length thereof | Ex 28:16
nine inches square (B) | Ex 28:16; 39:9
a s. shall be the breadth thereof | Ex 28:16
a s. was the length thereof, and a | Ex 39:9
and a s. the breadth thereof, being | Ex 39:9
whose height was six cubits and a s. | 1Sa 17:4
and meted out heaven with the s. | Isa 40:12
fruit, and children of a s. long | La 2:20
thereof round about shall be a s. | Eze 43:13
nine inches high (B) | Eze 43:13

SPANGLED

s. face veils and scarfs (A)(R) | Isa 3:19

SPANGLES

cheeks of jeweled s. (B) | Ca 1:10

SPANNED

right hand hath s. the heavens | Isa 48:13
hath spread out the heavens (A)(B)(E)(R) | Isa 48:13

SPARE

also destroy and not s. the place | Ge 18:24
will s. all the place for their sakes | Ge 18:26
eye pity him, neither shalt thou s. | De 13:8
The Lord will not s. him, but then | De 29:20
that they have, and s. them not | Isa 15:3
defend and s. it (B) | 2Ki 19:24
did not s. young men | 2Ch 36:17
s. me according to the greatness | Ne 13:22
s. my life (A)(B)(E)(R) | Job 2:6
let him not s.; for I have not | Job 6:10
my reins asunder, and doth not s. | Job 16:13
Though he s. it, and forsake it not | Job 20:13
shall cast upon him, and not s. | Job 27:22
me, and s. not to spit in my face | Job 30:10
O s. me, that I may recover | Ps 39:13
He shall s. the poor and needy | Ps 72:13
will not s. in the day of vengeance | Pr 6:34
let not thy soul s. for his crying | Pr 19:18
fire, no man shall s. his brother | Isa 9:19
their eye shall not s. children | Isa 13:18
broken in pieces; he shall not s. | Isa 30:14
s. not, lengthen thy cords, and | Isa 54:2
Cry aloud, s. not, lift up thy voice | Isa 58:1
I will not pity, nor s. nor have | Jer 13:14
he shall not s. them, neither have | Jer 21:7
bow, shoot at her, s. no arrows | Jer 50:14
s. ye not her young men; destroy | Jer 51:3
neither shall mine eye s. | Eze 5:11
mine eye shall not s. thee | Eze 7:4
And mine eye shall not s. | Eze 7:9
mine eyes shall not s. neither | Eze 8:18
let not your eye s. neither have ye | Eze 9:5
mine eye shall not s. neither will I | Eze 9:10
I will not go back, neither will I s. | Eze 24:14
S. thy people, O Lord, and give not | Joe 2:17
should not I s. Nineveh, that great | Jon 4:11

and not s. continually to slay | Hab 1:17
I will s. them, as a man spareth | Mal 3:17
have bread enough and to s. | Lu 15:17
take heed lest he also s. not thee | Ro 11:21
trouble in the flesh: but I s. you | 1Co 7:28
to s. you I came not as yet unto | 2Co 1:23
that, if I come again, I will not s. | 2Co 13:2

SPARED

my life is s. (A) | Ge 32:30
But Saul and the people s. Agag | 1Sa 15:9
people s. the best of the sheep and | 1Sa 15:15
but mine eye s. thee; and I said | 1Sa 24:10
he s. to take of his own flock | 2Sa 12:4
But the king s. Mephibosheth | 2Sa 21:7
my master hath s. Naaman this | 2Ki 5:20
he s. not their soul from death | Ps 78:50
mine eye s. them from destroying | Eze 20:17
He that s. not his own Son, but | Ro 8:32
if God s. not the natural branches | Ro 11:21
if God s. not the angels that sinned | 2Pe 2:4
And s. not the old world, but saved | 2Pe 2:5

SPARETH

He that s. his rod hateth his son | Pr 13:24
that hath knowledge s. his words | Pr 17:27
but the righteous giveth and s. not | Pr 21:26
man s. his own son that serveth | Mal 3:17

SPARING

wolves enter not s. the flock | Ac 20:29

SPARINGLY

which soweth s. shall reap also s. | 2Co 9:6

SPARK

the s. of his fire shall not shine | Job 18:5
the flame of his fire (A)(R) | Job 18:5
the glow of his fire (B) | Job 18:5
as tow, and the maker of it as a s. | Isa 1:31

SPARKLE

eyes had no s. (B) | Ge 29:17

SPARKLED

s. like the colour of burnished | Eze 1:7

SPARKS

trouble, as the s. fly upward | Job 5:7
lamps, and s. of fire leap out | Job 41:19
compass yourselves about with s. | Isa 50:11
and in the s. that ye have kindled | Isa 50:11

SPARROW

Yea, the s. hath found an house | Ps 84:3
am as a s. alone upon the house | Ps 102:7

SPARROWS

Are not two s. sold for a farthing | M't 10:29
ye are of more value than many s. | M't 10:31
not five s. sold for two farthings | Lu 12:6
ye are of more value than many s. | Lu 12:7

SPASMS

with *s.* of distress you will (A)   *Ge 3:16*

SPAT

spat (S)   *M't 26:67; 27:30; M'k 7:33*
he *s.* on the ground, and made *Joh 9:6*

SPATTERED

blood was *s.* (B)   *Le 6:27*

SPEAK

I have taken on me to *s.* to God   *Ge 18:27; 18:31*
we cannot *s.* onto thee bad or good   *Ge 24:50*
take heed *s.* not to Jacob good or bad   *Ge 31:24*
thus shall ye *s.* to my lord Esau   *Ge 32:4; 32:19*
speak (S)   *Ge 34:6; 1Sa 18:22; Ps 64:5*
what shall we say? what shall we *s.*   *Ge 44:16*
Aaron. I know that he can *s.* well   *Ex 4:14*
since I came to *s.* to Pharaoh in thy name   *Ex 5:23*
the *s.* (S)   *Ex 9:32; Isa 28:25*
s. thou with us, and we will hear   *Ex 20:19*
not *s.* in a cause to decline after many   *Ex 23:2*
I will meet you, to *s.* there to thee   *Ex 29:42*
wherefore should Egyptians *s.* and say   *Ex 32:12*
until he went in to *s.* with the Lord   *Ex 34:35*
were not afraid to *s.* against Moses   *Nu 12:8*
who have heard the fame of thee will *s.*   *Nu 14:15*
s. ye to the rock before their eyes   *Nu 20:8*
why they that *s.* in proverbs say, Come   *Nu 21:27*
bring word, as the Lord shall *s.* to me   *Nu 22:8*
the word I *s.* to thee, that thou shalt *s.*   *Nu 22:35*
return to Balak, and thus thou shalt *s.*   *Nu 23:5*
must I not take heed to *s.* that which Lord   *Nu 23:12*
the daughters of Zelophehad *s.* right   *Nu 27:7*
s. no more to me of this matter   *De 3:26*
s. thou to us all that Lord shall *s.* to thee   *De 5:27*
words which he shall *s.* in my name   *De 18:19*
who shall presume to *s.* a word in my name   *De 18:20*
and thou shalt *s.* and say before the Lord   *De 26:5*
your children *s.* to our children   *Jos 22:24*
s. ye that ride on white asses   *J'g 5:10*
take advice, and *s.* your minds   *J'g 19:30*
s. Lord for thy servant heareth   *1Sa 3:9; 3:10*
son of Belial that man cannot *s.* to   *1Sa 25:17*
and Abner went also to *s.* to David   *2Sa 3:19*
Joab took him aside to *s.* with him quietly   *2Sa 3:27*
according to this vision so did Nathan *s.* to David   *2Sa 7:17*
shall we do after his saying? if not *s.* thou   *2Sa 17:6*
why *s.* ye not one word of bringing back   *2Sa 19:10*
come near hither than I may *s.* with thee   *2Sa 20:16*
they were wont to *s.* in old time, saying   *2Sa 20:18*
she went to *s.* to him for Adonijah   *1Ki 2:19*
wilt *s.* good words to them   *1Ki 12:7; 10:7*
saying, Thus shalt thou *s.* to this people   *1Ki 12:10*
s. that which is good   *1Ki 22:13; 2Ch 18:12*

spirit from me to *s.* to the   *1Ki 22:24; 2Ch 18:23*
s. in Syrian language   *2Ki 18:26; Isa 36:11*
my master sent me to thy   *2Ki 18:27;*
master to *s.* these words   *Isa 36:12*
what can David *s.* more to thee   *1Ch 17:18*
wrote letters to *s.* against God   *2Ch 32:17*
could not *s.* in the Jews' language   *Ne 13:24*
and to-morrow *s.* thou to the king   *Es 5:14*
to *s.* to the king to hang Mordecai   *Es 6:4*
how long wilt thou *s.* these things   *Job 8:2*
but oh that God would *s.* against thee   *Job 11:5*
or *s.* to the earth and it shall teach thee   *Job 12:8*
will ye *s.* wickedly for God and talk   *Job 13:7*
or let me *s.* and answer thou me   *Job 13:22*
mark and afterwards we will *s.*   *Job 18:2*
my lips not *s.* wickedness nor deceit   *Job 27:4*
I said days should *s.* and teach wisdom   *Job 32:7*
s. for I desire to justify thee   *Job 33:32*
therefore *s.* what thou knowest   *Job 34:33*
shew I have yet to *s.* on God's behalf   *Job 36:2*
if a man *s.* he shall be swallowed up   *Job 37:20*
will he *s.* soft words unto thee   *Job 41:3*
then shall he *s.* to them in his wrath   *Ps 2:5*
thou shalt destroy them that *s.* leasing   *Ps 5:6*
s. vanity they *s.* with a double heart   *Ps 12:2*
with their mouth they *s.* proudly   *Ps 17:10*
which *s.* peace to their neighbours   *Ps 28:3*
in his temple every one *s.* of his glory   *Ps 29:9*
which *s.* grievous things proudly   *Ps 31:18*
they *s.* not peace but devise deceitful   *Ps 35:20*
my tongue shall *s.* of thy righteousness   *Ps 35:28*
they *s.* mischievous things all day long   *Ps 38:12*
if I would declare and *s.* of them   *Ps 40:5*
enemies *s.* evil of me when shall he die   *Ps 41:5*
my mouth *s.* of wisdom and meditation   *Ps 49:3*
lovest lying rather than to *s.* righteousness   *Ps 52:3*
and for cursing and lying which they *s.*   *Ps 59:12*
mouth of them that *s.* lies shall be stopped   *Ps 63:11*
they that sit in the gate *s.* against me   *Ps 69:12*
for mine enemies *s.* against me   *Ps 71:10*
are corrupt they *s.* wickedly *s.* loftily   *Ps 73:8*
lift not your horn *s.* not with a stiff neck   *Ps 75:5*
I will hear what the Lord will *s.* peace to his people   *Ps 85:8*
how long shall they utter and *s.* hard things   *Ps 94:4*
let this be the reward of them that *s.* evil   *Ps 109:20*
they have mouths but they *s.* not   *Ps 115:5; 135:16*
princes also did sit and *s.* against me   *Ps 119:23*
my tongue shall *s.* of thy word   *Ps 119:172*
they shall *s.* with the enemies in the gate   *Ps 127:5*
for they *s.* against thee wickedly   *Ps 139:20*
men shall *s.* of might of thy terrible acts   *Ps 145:6*

they shall *s.* of the glory of thy kingdom   *Ps 145:11*
my mouth shall *s.* the praise of the Lord   *Ps 145:21*
my mouth shall *s.* truth   *Pr 8:7*
s. not in the ears of a fool   *Pr 23:9*
my reins rejoice, when lips *s.* right things   *Pr 23:16*
a time to be silent, and a time to *s.*   *Ec 3:7*
causing lips that are asleep to *s.*   *Ca 7:9*
s. word, it shall not stand, God is with us   *Isa 8:10*
if they *s.* not according to this word   *Isa 8:20*
all they shall *s.* and say unto thee   *Isa 14:10*
five cities in Egypt *s.* language of Canaan   *Isa 19:18*
with another tongue he *s.* to people   *Isa 28:11*
and thou shalt *s.* out of the ground   *Isa 29:4*
who say, *s.* unto us smooth things   *Isa 30:10*
tongue of the stammerers shall *s.* plainly   *Isa 32:4*
for the vile person will *s.* villainy   *Isa 32:6*
s. ye comfortably to Jerusalem cry to her   *Isa 40:2*
let them come near, then let them *s.*   *Isa 41:1*
that I should know how to *s.* in season   *Isa 50:4*
they shall know that I am he that doth *s.*   *Isa 52:6*
neither let the son of a stranger *s.* saying   *Isa 56:3*
trust in vanity, and *s.* lies, conceive mischief   *Isa 59:4*
whatsoever I command thee, shalt *s.*   *Jer 1:7*
s. to them all that I command thee   *Jer 1:17*
saith the Lord, because ye *s.* this word   *Jer 5:14*
thou shalt *s.* all these words to them   *Jer 7:27*
they will not *s.* the truth, taught to *s.* lies   *Jer 9:5*
idols are upright as palm tree, they *s.* not   *Jer 10:5*
believe not, tho' they *s.* fair words   *Jer 12:6*
therefore thou shalt *s.* this word to them   *Jer 13:12*
at what instant I *s.* about a nation   *Jer 18:7; 18:9*
I stood before thee to *s.* good for them   *Jer 18:20*
I will not *s.* any more in his name   *Jer 20:9*
they *s.* a vision of their own heart   *Jer 23:16*
hath my word, let him *s.* word faithfully   *Jer 23:28*
s. all the words I commanded thee to *s.*   *Jer 26:2; 26:8*
the Lord hath sent me to *s.* these words   *Jer 26:15*
thus shalt thou also *s.* to Shemaiah   *Jer 29:24*
and shall *s.* with him mouth to mouth   *Jer 32:4*
he shall *s.* with thee mouth to mouth   *Jer 34:3*
and thou shalt *s.* my words to them   *Eze 2:7*
all my words that I *s.* receive in heart   *Eze 3:10*
and *s.* (A)(B)(E)(R)   *Eze 4:9*
they say doth he not *s.* parables   *Eze 20:49*
and thou shalt *s.* and be no more dumb   *Eze 24:27*
strong among the mighty shall *s.* to him   *Eze 32:21*
if dost not *s.* to warn wicked from his way   *Eze 33:8*
thus ye *s.*   *Eze 33:10*
and *s.* one to another   *Eze 33:30*
when the children of thy people shall *s.*   *Eze 37:18*
ye have prepared corrupt words to *s.*   *Da 2:9*
s. any thing amiss against the God of Shadrach   *Da 3:29*

he shall *s.* great words against   *Da 7:25*
most High
and I said, Let my lord *s.*   *Da 10:19*
shall *s.* lies at one table, but   *Da 11:27*
not prosper
but at the end it shall *s.* and   *Hab 2:3*
not lie
s. every man the truth   *Zec 8:16;*
    Eph 4:25
only *s.* word, my servant be   *M't 8:8*
healed
how or what ye shall *s.*   *M't 10:19;*
    M'k 13:11
for it is not ye that *s.*   *M't 10:20;*
    M'k 13:11
what I tell in darkness, that   *M't 10:27*
s. ye in light
how can ye being evil *s.*   *M't 12:34*
good things
every idle word men shall *s.*   *M't 12:36*
give account
mother stood without,   *M't 12:46*
desiring to *s.* with
why doth this man thus *s.*   *M'k 2:7*
blasphemies
do a miracle, that lightly *s.*   *M'k 9:39*
evil of me
what shall be given in that   *M'k 13:11*
hour, *s.* ye
I know not this man of   *M'k 14:71*
whom ye *s.*
in my name they shall *s.*   *M'k 16:17*
with new tongues
I am sent to *s.* to thee and to   *Lu 1:19*
shew
not able to *s.* till these shall be   *Lu 1:20*
performed
when he came out, he could   *Lu 1:22*
not *s.* to them
he rebuking them, suffered   *Lu 4:41*
them not to *s.*
woe to you, when all men   *Lu 6:26*
shall *s.* well of you
to provoke him to *s.* of many   *Lu 11:53*
things
whosoever shall *s.* a word   *Lu 12:10*
against the Son of man
s. to my brother, that he   *Lu 12:13*
divide inheritance
we *s.* that we do know, and   *Joh 3:11*
testify
he is of age, ask him, he shall   *Joh 9:21*
s. for himself
he shall not *s.* of himself,   *Joh 16:13*
that shall he *s.*
I shall no more *s.* to you in   *Joh 16:25*
proverbs
are not all these which *s.*   *Ac 2:7*
Galileans
we hear them *s.* in tongues   *Ac 2:11*
works of God
let me freely *s.* to you of   *Ac 2:29*
David
that they *s.* to no man in this   *Ac 4:17*
name
commanded not to *s.* at all   *Ac 4:18*
we cannot but *s.*   *Ac 4:20*
with all boldness they may *s.*   *Ac 4:29*
thy word
go, stand and *s.* in temple to   *Ac 5:20*
the people
commanded that they should   *Ac 5:40*
not *s.*
we heard him *s.* blasphemous   *Ac 6:11*
words
man ceaseth not to *s.*   *Ac 6:13*
blasphemous words
when he cometh shall *s.* unto   *Ac 10:32*
thee
as I began to *s.*   *Ac 11:15*
same heard Paul *s.*   *Ac 14:9*
s. the word in Asia   *Ac 16:6*
(B)(E)(R)
be not afraid, but *s.* hold not   *Ac 18:9*
thy peace
I beseech thee suffer me to *s.*   *Ac 21:39*
to people
shalt not *s.* evil of ruler of thy   *Ac 23:5*
Paul, thou art permitted to *s.*   *Ac 26:1*
for thyself
I *s.* forth words of truth and   *Ac 26:25*
soberness
I will not dare to *s.* of any   *Ro 15:18*
of those things
that all *s.* same thing and no   *1Co 1:10*
divisions
which things we *s.* not in   *1Co 2:13*
man's wisdom
I could not *s.* as to spiritual   *1Co 3:1*
but carnal

do all *s.* with tongues   *1Co 12:30*
with other lips will I *s.*   *1Co 14:21*
If all *s.* with tongues   *1Co 14:23*
let him *s.* to himself and to   *1Co 14:28*
God
let prophets *s.* two or three,   *1Co 14:29*
the other judge
it is a shame for women to *s.*   *1Co 14:35*
in church
and forbid not to *s.* with   *1Co 14:39*
tongues
in the sight of God *s.* we in   *2Co 2:17*
Christ
we also believe and therefore   *2Co 4:13*
s.
we *s.* before God in Christ,   *2Co 12:19*
for edifying
it is a shame to *s.* of those   *Eph 5:12*
things done
i may make manifest, as I   *Col 4:4*
ought to *s.*
so that we need not to *s.* any   *1Th 1:8*
thing
even so we *s.* not as pleasing   *1Th 2:4*
men but God
forbidding us to *s.* to the   *1Th 2:16*
s. things that become sound   *Tit 2:1*
doctrine
these things *s.* and exhort, and   *Tit 2:15*
rebuke
put them in mind to *s.* evil   *Tit 3:2*
of no man
the world to come, whereof we   *Heb 2:5*
s.
tho' we thus *s.*   *Heb 6:9*
of which we cannot *s.*   *Heb 9:5*
brethren, let every man be   *Jas 1:19*
slow to *s.*
so *s.* as they that shall be   *Jas 2:12*
judged
s. not evil one of another,   *Jas 4:11*
brethren
they *s.* against you as   *1Pe 2:12*
evil-doers
let him refrain his lips that *s.*   *1Pe 3:10*
no guile
whereas they *s.* evil of you,   *1Pe 3:16*
as of evil-doers
let him *s.* as the oracles of   *1Pe 4:11*
God
are not afraid to *s.* evil of   *2Pe 2:10*
dignities
s. evil of things that they   *2Pe 2:12*
understand not
when they *s.* great swelling   *2Pe 2:18*
words of vanity
are of world, therefore *s.* they   *1Jo 4:5*
of world
these filthy dreamers *s.* evil of   *Jude 8*
dignities
these *s.* evil of things they   *Jude 10*
know not
not known depths of Satan, as   *Re 2:24*
they *s.*
the image of the beast should   *Re 13:15*
both *s.*

I SPEAK

that the people may hear when   *Ex 19:9*
I *s.*
but if thou shalt obey and do   *Ex 23:22*
all that I *s.*
God putteth in my mouth   *Nu 22:38*
that shall I *s.*
hear judgments which I *s.*   *De 5:1*
in your ears
I *s.* not with children who   *De 11:2*
have not known
what the Lord saith, that will   *1Ki 22:14*
I *s.*
if I *s.* of strength, lo, he is   *Job 9:19*
strong
then would I *s.* and not fear   *Job 9:35*
him
surely I would *s.* to the   *Job 13:3*
Almighty
hold peace, let me alone,   *Job 13:13*
that I may *s.*
I also could *s.* as ye do, I   *Job 16:4*
could heap words
though I *s.* my grief is not   *Job 16:6*
assuaged
shall it be told him that I *s.*   *Job 37:20*
I *s.* of things which I have   *Ps 45:1*
made
I am so troubled that I cannot   *Ps 77:4*
s.
but when I *s.* they are for   *Ps 120:7*
war

I the Lord *s.* righteousness, I   *Isa 45:19*
declare
I that *s.* in righteousness,   *Isa 63:1*
mighty to save
ah, Lord, I cannot *s.* for I am   *Jer 1:6*
a child
to whom shall I *s.* and give   *Jer 6:10*
warning
hear this word that I *s.* in   *Jer 28:7*
thine ears
obey the voice of the Lord   *Jer 38:20*
which I *s.*
when I *s.* I will open mouth   *Eze 3:27*
O Daniel, understand words   *Da 10:11*
that I *s.*
therefore *s.* I to them in   *M't 13:13*
parables
Jesus saith, I that *s.* to thee   *Joh 4:26*
am he
the words that I *s.* to you,   *Joh 6:63*
they are spirit
whether it be of God or   *Joh 7:17*
whether I *s.* of myself
I *s.* to world those things I   *Joh 8:26*
heard of him
as my Father taught me, I *s.*   *Joh 8:28*
these things
I *s.* that which I have seen   *Joh 8:38*
with my Father
he gave commandment, what   *Joh 12:49*
I should *s.*
when I *s.* as the Father said   *Joh 12:50*
to me, so I *s.*
I *s.* not of all, I know whom   *Joh 13:18*
I have chosen
the words that I *s.* I *s.* not   *Joh 14:10*
of myself
these things I *s.* in the world   *Joh 17:13*
may I *s.* to thee   *Ac 21:37*
I also *s.* freely   *Ac 26:26*
is God unrighteous? I *s.* as a   *Ro 3:5*
man
I *s.* after the manner of men   *Ro 6:19;*
    Ga 3:15
for I *s.* to them that know the   *Ro 7:1*
law
I *s.* to you Gentiles, I am   *Ro 11:13*
apostle of
I *s.* to your shame   *1Co 6:5; 15:34*
I *s.* this by permission, not of   *1Co 7:6*
commandment
but to the rest *s.* I, not the   *1Co 7:12*
Lord
and this I *s.* for your own   *1Co 7:35*
profit
I *s.* as to wise men, judge   *1Co 10:15*
ye what I say
though I *s.* with tongues of   *1Co 13:1*
men and angels
except I shall *s.* to you by   *1Co 14:6*
revelation
I *s.* with tongues more than   *1Co 14:18*
you all
I had rather *s.* five words   *1Co 14:19*
with understanding
I *s.* as to my children, be   *2Co 6:13*
enlarged
I *s.* not this to condemn you,   *2Co 7:3*
for I have said
that which I *s.* I *s.* it not   *2Co 11:17*
after the Lord
I *s.* as concerning reproach,   *2Co 11:21*
I *s.* foolishly
are they ministers? I *s.* as a   *2Co 11:23*
fool, I am more
but I *s.* concerning Christ   *Eph 5:32*
and church
that therein I may *s.* boldly,   *Eph 6:20*
as I ought to *s.*
not that I *s.* in respect of   *Ph'p 4:11*
want
I *s.* the truth in Christ I lie not   *1Ti 2:7*

I WILL, WILL I SPEAK

let not Lord be angry, and I   *Ge 18:30;*
will *s.*   *18:32*
and I *will s.* to him in a   *Nu 12:6*
dream
with him *will I s.* mouth to   *Nu 12:8*
mouth apparently
what Lord saith that *will I*   *Nu 24:13;*
s.   *1Ki 22:14; 2Ch 18:13*
give ear, O ye heavens, and I   *De 32:1*
will s.
Gideon said, I *will s.* but this   *J'g 6:39*
once
thy handmaid said, I *will s.*   *2Sa 14:15*
to king
well, I *will s.* for thee to the   *1Ki 2:18*
king

I will s. in the anguish of my   *Job 7:11*
spirit
I will s. in the bitterness of   *Job 10:1*
my soul
I will s. that I may be   *Job 32:20*
refreshed
mark well, hold thy peace,   *Job 33:31*
and *I will s.*
hear, I beseech thee, and *I*   *Job 42:4*
will s.
hear, O my people, and *I will*   *Ps 50:7*
s.
if I say, *I will s.* thus, I   *Ps 73:15*
should offend
I will s. of thy testimonies   *Ps 119:46*
before kings
I will s. of the honour of thy   *Ps 145:5*
majesty
hear, for *I will s.* of excellent   *Pr 8:6*
things
I will get me to great men, and   *Jer 5:5*
I will s.
stand on thy feet, and *I will*   *Eze 2:1*
s. to thee
I will s. and word I speak   *Eze 12:25*
shall come to pass
I will allure her, and *s.*   *Ho 2:14*
comfortably to her
with other lips *will I s.* to   *1Co 14:21*
this people

SPEAKER

not an evil *s.* be established   *Ps 140:11*
a gifted *s.* (P)   *Isa 18:24*
because he was the chief *s.*   *Ac 14:12*
I may be no *s.* (N)(P)   *2Co 11:6*

SPEAKEST

wherefore then *s.* thou so to   *1Sa 9:21*
me
him, Why *s.* thou any more   *2Sa 19:29*
of thy
words thou *s.* in thy   *2Ki 6:12*
bedchamber
Thou *s.* as one of the foolish   *Job 2:10*
women
sittest and *s.* against thy   *Ps 50:20*
brother
mightest be justified when thou   *Ps 51:4*
s.
Why sayest thou, O Jacob,   *Isa 40:27*
and *s.*
for thou *s.* falsely of   *Jer 40:16*
Ishmael
unto Jeremiah, Thou *s.* falsely   *Jer 43:2*
from his
nor *s.* to warn the wicked from   *Eze 3:18*
his
thou *s.* lies in the name of   *Zec 13:3*
the Lord
Why *s.* unto them in parables   *M't 13:10*
Lord, *s.* thou this parable   *Lu 12:41*
unto us
unto him, Lo, now *s.* thou   *Joh 16:29*
plainly
thou plainly, and *s.* no   *Joh 16:29*
proverb
unto him, *S.* thou not unto   *Joh 19:10*
me
new doctrine, whereof thou *s.*   *Ac 17:19*

SPEAKETH

it is my mouth that *s.* unto   *Ge 45:12*
you
to face, as a man *s.* unto his   *Ex 33:11*
friend
All that the Lord *s.* that I   *Nu 23:26*
must do
When a prophet *s.* in the   *De 18:22*
name of
said, Thus *s.* Ben-hadad,   *1Ki 20:5*
saying
as one of the foolish women   *Job 2:10*
s.
He that *s.* flattery to his   *Job 17:5*
friends
God *s.* once, yea twice, yet   *Job 33:14*
man
the tongue that *s.* proud things   *Ps 12:3*
and *s.* the truth in his heart   *Ps 15:2*
mouth of the righteous *s.*   *Ps 37:30*
wisdom
if he come to see me, he *s.*   *Ps 41:6*
vanity
Whose mouth *s.* vanity, and   *Ps 144:8*
children, whose mouth *s.*   *Ps 144:11*
vanity
the man that *s.* froward things   *Pr 2:12*
he *s.* with his feet, he teacheth   *Pr 6:13*

A false witness that *s.* lies, and   *Pr 6:19*
he
mouth of the wicked *s.*   *Pr 10:32*
frowardness
He that *s.* truth showeth forth   *Pr 12:17*
s. like the piercings of a   *Pr 12:18*
sword
but a deceitful witness *s.* lies   *Pr 14:25*
and they love him that *s.*   *Pr 16:13*
right
he that *s.* lies shall not escape   *Pr 19:5*
and he that *s.* lies shall perish   *Pr 19:9*
man that heareth *s.*   *Pr 21:28*
constantly
When he *s.* fair, believe him   *Pr 26:25*
not
and every mouth *s.* folly   *Isa 9:17*
words, even when the needy *s.*   *Isa 32:7*
right
righteously, and *s.* uprightly   *Isa 33:15*
as an arrow shot out; it *s.*   *Jer 9:8*
deceit
one *s.* peaceably to his   *Jer 9:8*
neighbour
word which the Lord *s.* unto   *Jer 10:1*
you
Thus *s.* the Lord of hosts   *Jer 28:2;*
God   *29:25*
Thus *s.* the Lord God of   *Jer 30:2*
Israel
of the Almighty God when he   *Eze 10:5*
s.
they abhor him that *s.*   *Am 5:10*
uprightly
Thus *s.* the Lord of hosts,   *Hag 1:2;*
saying   *Zec 6:12; 7:9*
of your Father which *s.* in   *M't 10:20*
you
whosoever *s.* a word against   *M't 12:32*
whosoever *s.* against the Holy   *M't 12:32*
out of the heart the mouth *s.*   *M't 12:34*
Who is this which *s.*   *Lu 5:21*
blasphemies
of the heart his mouth *s.*   *Lu 6:45*
earth is earthly, and *s.* of the   *Joh 3:31*
earth
God hath sent *s.* the words of   *Joh 3:34*
God
He that *s.* of himself seeketh   *Joh 7:18*
his
But lo, he *s.* boldly, and they   *Joh 7:26*
say
When he *s.* a lie, he *s.* of his   *Joh 8:44*
own
himself a king *s.* against   *Joh 19:12*
Caesar
For David *s.* concerning him,   *Ac 2:25*
I
thee, of whom *s.* the prophet   *Ac 8:34*
this
which is of faith *s.* on this   *Ro 10:6*
wise
he that *s.* is an unknown   *1Co 14:2*
tongue
s. not unto men, but unto   *1Co 14:2*
God: for
in the spirit he *s.* mysteries   *1Co 14:2*
he that prophesieth *s.* unto   *1Co 14:3*
men
s. in an unknown tongue   *1Co 14:4*
edifieth
than he that *s.* with tongues   *1Co 14:5*
be unto him that *s.* a   *1Co 14:11*
barbarian
and he that *s.* shall be a   *1Co14:11*
barbarian
let him that *s.* in an   *1Co 14:13*
unknown
the Spirit *s.* expressly, that in   *1Ti 4:1*
and by it he being dead yet   *Heb 11:4*
s.
which *s.* unto you as unto   *Heb 12:5*
children
that *s.* better things than   *Heb 12:24*
that of
See that ye refuse not him   *Heb 12:25*
that *s.*
away from him that *s.* from   *Heb 12:25*
heaven
He that *s.* evil of his brother   *Jas 4:11*
s. evil of the law, and judgeth   *Jas 4:11*
mouth *s.* great swelling words   *Jude 16*

SPEAKING

to pass, before he had done *s.*   *Ge 24:15*
before I had done *s.* in mine   *Ge 24:45*
heart
when he had made an end of   *Ex 31:18*
s. (S)

till Moses had done *s.* with   *Ex 34:33*
them
heard the voice of one *s.* unto   *Nu 7:89*
him
made an end of *s.* all these   *Nu 16:31*
words
God *s.* out of the midst of the   *De 4:33;*
fire   *5:26*
s. of them when thou sittest   *De 11:19*
made an end of *s.* unto the   *De 20:9*
people
Moses made an end of *s.* all   *De 32:45*
these
when he had made an end of   *J'g 15:17*
with her, then she left *s.* unto   *Ru 1:18*
her
out of grief have I been *s.*   *1Sa 1:16*
(S)
had made an end of *s.* unto   *1Sa 18:1*
Saul
an end of *s.* these words   *1Sa 24:16*
unto Saul
soon as he had made an end   *2Sa 13:36*
of *s.*
the prophet *s.* from the   *2Ch 36:12*
mouth of
people, and *s.* peace to all his   *Es 10:3*
seed
While he was yet *s.* there   *Job 1:16;*
  1:17-18
who can withhold himself   *Job 4:2*
from *s.*
answered no more: they left   *Job 32:15*
off *s.*
evil, and thy lips from *s.* guile   *Ps 34:13*
as soon as they be born, *s.* lies   *Ps 58:3*
forth of the finger, and *s.*   *Isa 58:9*
vanity
s. wickedly (E)(R)   *Isa 58:9*
pleasure, nor *s.* thine own   *Isa 58:13*
words
s. oppression and revolt,   *Isa 59:13*
conceiving
while they are yet *s.* I will   *Isa 65:24*
hear
rising up early and *s.* but ye   *Jer 7:13*
heard
rising early and *s.*; but ye   *Jer 25:3*
have
heard Jeremiah *s.* these words   *Jer 26:7*
in
Jeremiah had made an end of   *Jer 26:8*
s. all
unto you, rising early and *s.*   *Jer 35:14*
people, in *s.* such words unto   *Jer 38:4*
them
So they left off *s.* with him;   *Jer 38:27*
for the
had made an end of *s.* unto   *Jer 43:1*
all the
I heard him *s.* unto me out   *Eze 43:6*
of the
man, and a mouth *s.* great   *Da 7:8*
things
Then I heard one saint *s.* and   *Da 8:13*
Now as he was *s.* with me, I   *Da 8:18*
was in
And whiles I was *s.* and   *Da 9:20*
praying
while I was *s.* in prayer, even   *Da 9:21*
shall be heard for their much   *M't 6:7*
s.
Now when he had left *s.* he   *Lu 5:4*
said
s. of the things pertaining to   *Ac 1:3*
s. unto Moses, that he should   *Ac 7:44*
s. the word (E)(R)   *Ac 11:19*
who, *s.* to them persuaded   *Ac 13:43*
them
abode thy *s.* boldly in the Lord   *Ac 14:3*
s. God's message (N)   *Ac 16:6*
s. perverse things, to draw   *Ac 20:30*
away
I heard a voice *s.* unto me   *Ac 26:14*
that no man *s.* by the Spirit   *1Co 12:3*
of God
I come unto you *s.* with   *1Co 14:6*
tongues
ye seek a proof of Christ *s.*   *2Co 13:3*
in me
s. the truth in love, may   *Eph 4:15*
grow up
and evil *s.* be put away from   *Eph 4:31*
you
S. to yourselves in psalms   *Eph 5:19*
S. lies in hypocrisy; having   *1Ti 4:2*
their
s. things which they ought not   *1Ti 5:13*

same excess of riot, *s.* evil of you   *1Pe 4:4*
the dumb ass *s.* with man's voice   *2Pe 2:16*
epistles, *s.* in them of these things   *2Pe 3:16*
him a mouth *s.* great things   *Re 13:5*

SPEAKINGS

and envies, and all evil *s.*   *1Pe 2:1*

SPEAR

Stretch out the *s.* that is in thy   *Jos 8:18*
Joshua stretched out the *s.* that   *Jos 8:18*
wherewith he stretched out the *s.*   *Jos 8:26*
a shield or *s.* seen among forty   *J'g 5:8*
neither sword nor *s.* found in the   *1Sa 13:22*
staff of his *s.* was like a weaver's   *1Sa 17:7*
to me with a sword, and with a *s.*   *1Sa 17:45*
Lord saveth not with sword and *s.*   *1Sa 17:47*
here under thine hand *s.* or sword   *1Sa 21:8*
having his *s.* in his hand, and   *1Sa 22:6*
his *s.* stuck in the ground at his   *1Sa 26:7*
with the *s.* even to the earth   *1Sa 26:8*
now in the *s.* that is at his bolster   *1Sa 26:11*
So David took this *s.* and the cruse   *1Sa 26:12*
now see where the king's *s.* is and   *1Sa 26:16*
and said, Behold the king's *s.*   *1Sa 26:22*
behold, Saul leaned upon his *s.*   *2Sa 1:6*
end of the *s.* smote him under the   *2Sa 2:23*
that the *s.* came out behind him   *2Sa 2:23*
s. weighed three hundred shekels   *2Sa 21:16*
of whose *s.* was like a weaver's   *2Sa 21:19*
with iron and the staff of a *s.:* and   *2Sa 23:7*
lift up his *s.* against eight hundred   *2Sa 23:8*
lift up his *s.* against three hundred   *2Sa 23:18*
the Egyptian had a *s.* in his hand   *2Sa 23:21*
the *s.* out of the Egyptian's hand   *2Sa 23:21*
hand, and slew him with his own *s.*   *2Sa 23:21*
up his *s.* against three hundred   *1Ch 11:11; 11:20*
was a *s.* like a weaver's beam; and   *1Ch 11:23*
the *s.* out of the Egyptian's hand   *1Ch 11:23*
hand, and slew him with his own *s.*   *1Ch 11:23*
of Judah that bare shield and *s.*   *1Ch 12:24*
them with shield and *s.* thirty and   *1Ch 12:34*
whose *s.* staff was like a weaver's   *1Ch 20:5*
that could handle *s.* and shield   *2Ch 25:5*
the glittering *s.* and the shield   *Job 39:23*
the *s.* the dart, nor the habergeon   *Job 41:26*
he laugheth at the shaking of a *s.*   *Job 41:29*
Draw out also the *s.* and stop   *Ps 35:3*
bow, and cutteth the *s.* in sunder   *Ps 46:9*
They shall lay hold on bow and *s.*   *Jer 6:23*
hold the bow and the *s.* (B)(E)(R)   *Jer 50:42*
bright sword and the glittering *s.*   *Na 3:3*
at the shining of thy glittering *s.*   *Hab 3:11*

soldiers with a *s.* pierced his side   *Joh 19:34*
thrust through with a *s.* (S)   *Heb 12:20*

SPEARMEN

Rebuke the company of *s.* the   *Ps 68:30*
s. two hundred, at the third hour   *Ac 23:23*

SPEARS

Hebrews make them swords or *s.*   *1Sa 13:19*
give king David's *s.* and shields   *2Ki 11:10*
several city he put shields and *s.*   *2Ch 11:12*
of men that bare targets and *s.*   *2Ch 14:8*
to the captains of hundreds *s.*   *2Ch 23:9*
all the host shields, and *s.*   *2Ch 26:14*
their swords, their *s.* and their   *Ne 4:13*
half of them held both the *s.*   *Ne 4:16*
half of them held the *s.* from   *Ne 4:21*
irons? or his head with fish *s.*   *Job 41:7*
whose teeth are *s.* and arrows   *Ps 57:4*
and their *s.* into pruninghooks   *Isa 2:4*
furbish the *s.* and put on the   *Jer 46:4*
and the handstaves, and the *s.*   *Eze 39:9*
and your pruninghooks into *s.*   *Joe 3:10*
and their *s.* into pruninghooks   *Mic 4:3*

SPEAR'S

his *s.* head weighed six hundred   *1Sa 17:7*
whose *s.* shaft like a weaver's beam (S)   *1Ch 20:5*

SPECIAL

a *s.* vow (A)(R)(S)   *Le 27:2*
to be a *s.* people unto himself   *De 7:6*
my *s.* possession (B)(E)(R)   *Mal 3:17*
God wrought *s.* miracles   *Ac 19:11*

SPECIALLY

S. the day that thou stoodest before   *De 4:10*
and *s.* before thee, O king Agrippa   *Ac 25:26*
of all men, *s.* of those that believe   *1Ti 4:10*
and *s.* for those of his own house   *1Ti 5:8*
s. they of the circumcision   *Tit 1:10*
servant, a brother beloved *s.* to me   *Ph'm 16*

SPECIFICALLY

God's spirit *s.* tells (P)   *1Ti 4:1*

SPECIOUS

smooth and *s.* words (N)   *Ro 16:18*

SPECKLED

thence all the *s.* and spotted cattle   *Ge 30:32*
not *s.* and spotted among the goats   *Ge 30:33*
she goats that were *s.* and spotted   *Ge 30:35*
cattle ringstraked, *s.* and spotted   *Ge 30:39*
said thus, The *s.* shall be thy wages   *Ge 31:8*
wages; then all the cattle bare *s.*   *Ge 31:8*
were ringstraked, *s.* and grisled   *Ge 31:10*
are ringstraked, *s.* and grisled   *Ge 31:12*
heritage is unto me as a *s.* bird   *Jer 12:9*
there red horses, *s.* and white   *Zec 1:8*

SPECTACLE

we are made a *s.* unto the world   *1Co 4:9*
an exhibition to the universe (B)   *1Co 4:9*

SPECULATIONS

endulged in useless *s.* (B)   *Ro 1:21*
by delusive *s.* (N)   *Col 2:8*
useless *s.* (A)(N)(P)(R)   *1Ti 1:4*
ignorant *s.* (N)   *2Ti 2:23*
steer clear of foolish *s.* (N)(P)   *Tit 3:9*

SPED

Have they not *s.?* have they not   *J'g 5:30*

SPEECH

of Lamech, hearken unto my *s.*   *Ge 4:23*
was of one language, and of one *s.*   *Ge 11:1*
of one accent and mode of expression (A)   *Ge 11:1*
and the same words (B)   *Ge 11:1*
and few words (R)   *Ge 11:1*
not understand one another's *s.*   *Ge 11:7*
confuse their *s.* (B)   *Ge 11:7*
but I am slow of *s.* and of a slow   *Ex 4:10*
Balaam took up figurative *s.* (A)   *Nu 23:7*
give occasions of *s.* against her   *De 22:14*
charges her with shameful things and gives her an evil reputation (A)   *De 22:14*
brings damaging charges against her, giving her a bad name (B)   *De 22:14*
lay shameful things to her charge, and bring an evil name upon her (E)   *De 22:14*
charges her with shameful conduct, and brings an evil name upon her (R)   *De 22:14*
given occasions of *s.* against her   *De 22:17*
made shameful charges against her (A)   *De 22:17*
bring a shameful name upon her (B)   *De 22:17*
lay shameful things to her charge (E)   *De 22:17*
made shameful charges against her (R)   *De 22:17*
whose *s.* thou wilt (B)   *De 28:49*
my *s.* shall distil as the dew   *De 32:2*
To fetch about this form of *s.* hath   *2Sa 14:20*
in order to change the course of matters (A)   *2Sa 14:20*
to place the matter in a different light (B)   *2Sa 14:20*
to change the face of the matter (E)   *2Sa 14:20*
to change to course of affairs (R)   *2Sa 14:20*
s. of all Israel is come to the king   *2Sa 19:11*
the word of all Israel has come (A)(R)   *2Sa 19:11*
the invitations of all Israel have come (B)   *2Sa 19:11*
s. pleased the Lord, that Solomon   *1Ki 3:10*
with a loud voice in the Jews' *s.*   *2Ch 32:18*
in the Jewish language (A)(B)(E)(R)   *2Ch 32:18*
spake half in the *s.* of Ashdod   *Ne 13:24*
into the Ashdod tongue (B)   *Ne 13:24*
the language of Ashdod (R)   *Ne 13:24*
removeth away the *s.* of the trusty   *Job 12:20*
Hear diligently my *s.* and my   *Job 13:17*
Hear diligently my *s.* and let this be   *Job 21:2*
and make my *s.* nothing worth   *Job 24:25*
disqualify my statement (B)   *Job 24:25*
nothing in what I say (R)   *Job 24:25*
and my *s.* dropped upon them   *Job 29:22*
we cannot order our *s.* by reason of   *Job 37:19*
thine ear to me, and hear my *s.*   *Ps 17:6*
Day unto day uttereth *s.* and night   *Ps 19:2*
There is no *s.* nor language where   *Ps 19:3*
no *s.,* nor spoken word (A)   *Ps 19:3*

s. of one whom I know not | Ps 81:5
(A)(B)
a people of alien s. (B) | Ps 114:1
With her much fair s. she | Pr 7:21
caused
her justifying and enticing | Pr 7:21
argument (A)
with the flattery of her lips | Pr 7:21
(B)
Excellent s. becometh not a | Pr 17:7
fool
of scarlet, and thy s. is comely | Ca 4:3
their s. and doings (A)(R) | Isa 3:8
my voice; hearken, and hear | Isa 28:23
my s.
listen to my words (A)(B) | Isa 28:23
thy s. shall be low out of the | Isa 29:4
dust
words will whisper (B) | Isa 29:4
thy s. shall whisper out of the | Isa 29:4
dust
daughters; give ear unto my s. | Isa 32:9
a people of a deeper s. than | Isa 33:19
thou
slanderous s. (B) | Isa 58:9
use this s. in the land of | Jer 31:23
Judah
the voice of s. as the noise of | Eze 1:24
not sent to a people of a | Eze 3:5
strange s.
people of a foreign tongue (B) | Eze 3:5
to many a people of a strange | Eze 3:6
s. and
O Lord, I have heard thy s. | Hab 3:2
let s. be yea, yea; nay, nay | M't 5:37
(E)
them; for thy s. bewrayeth | M't 26:73
thee
your accent shows you up | M't 26:73
(A)(B)(N)(P)(R)
and had an impediment in | M'k 7:32
his s.
and thy s. agreeth thereto | M'k 14:70
Why do ye not understand | Joh 8:43
my s.
my message (A)(B) | Joh 8:43
my language (N) | Joh 8:43
my words (P) | Joh 8:43
using figures of s. (N)(R) | Joh 16:25
our own native s. (B) | Ac 2:8
made a s. to them (P) | Ac 12:21
saying in the s. of Lycaonia | Ac 14:11
continued his s. until midnight | Ac 20:7
kept on with his message | Ac 20:7
(A)(B)
with excellency of s. or of | 1Co 2:1
wisdom
lofty words of eloquence or | 1Co 2:1
human philosophy (A)
with no distinction of | 1Co 2:1
eloquence (B)
without display of fine words | 1Co 2:1
(N)
my s. and my preaching was | 1Co 2:4
not
my language and my message | 1Co 2:4
(A)
my message and my preaching | 1Co 2:4
(B)
not the s. of them that are | 1Co 4:19
puffed up
talk of these puffed up | 1Co 4:19
arrogant spirits (A)(R)
words of these conceited | 1Co 4:19
persons (B)(P)
the word of them that are | 1Co 4:19
puffed up (E)
ecstatic s. (N) | 1Co 14:1
hope, we use great plainness | 2Co 3:12
of s.
we speak very freely, openly, | 2Co 3:12
fearlessly (A)
we speak quite unreservedly | 2Co 3:12
(B)
we speak out boldly (N) | 2Co 3:12
we are quite frank and open | 2Co 3:12
(P)
we are very bold (R) | 2Co 3:12
Great is my boldness of s. | 2Co 7:4
toward
I am perfectly frank with you | 2Co 7:4
(N)
I talk to you with utter | 2Co 7:4
frankness (P)
is weak, and his s. | 2Co 10:10
contemptible
as a speaker he is beneath | 2Co 10:10
contempt (N)(P)
But though I be rude in s. | 2Co 11:6
yet not

if I am unskilled in speaking | 2Co 11:6
(A)(R)
if I lack skill in rhetoric (B) | 2Co 11:6
I may be no speaker (N) | 2Co 11:6
perhaps I am not a polished | 2Co 11:6
speaker (P)
no foul s. whatever (B)(E) | Eph 4:29
Let your s. be always with | Col 4:6
grace
in speech (A)(B)(N)(P)(R) | 1Ti 4:12
Sound s. that cannot be | Tit 2:8
condemned
your instruction be sound, fit, | Tit 2:8
wise, wholesome, vigorous,
irrefutable, and above censure (A)
a wholesome, unobjectionable | Tit 2:8
message that will shame
the opponent (B)

SPEECHES

apparently, and not in dark s. | Nu 12:8
I speak in person, plainly, not | Nu 12:8
obscurely (B)
and the s. of one that is | Job 6:26
desperate
utterances of a desperate man | Job 6:26
(B)
s. wherewith he can do no | Job 15:3
good
will I answer him with your | Job 32:14
s.
Job, I pray thee, hear my s. | Job 33:1
confuse their s. (B) | Ps 55:9
fair s. deceive the hearts of | Ro 16:18
by means of ingratiating | Ro 16:18
words and flattery (B)
with smooth and specious | Ro 16:18
words (N)
with plausible and attractive | Ro 16:18
arguments (P)
by fair and flattering words | Ro 16:18
(R)
hard s. which ungodly sinners | Jude 15
have

SPEECHLESS

wedding garment? And he | M't 22:12
was s.
unto them, and remained s. | Lu 1:22
which journeyed with him | Ac 9:7
stood s.

SPEED

send me good s. this day and | Ge 24:12
shew
cause me to meet with good | Ge 24:12
success (A)(R)
prosper me, I pray, this day | Ge 24:12
(B)
the lad, Make s. haste, stay | 1Sa 20:38
not
Be quick! Hurry! Don't | 1Sa 20:38
delay! (B)
Hurry, make haste, stay not | 1Sa 20:38
(R)
make s. to depart, lest he | 2Sa 15:14
overtake
Make haste to depart (A) | 2Sa 15:14
Hurry and leave (B) | 2Sa 15:14
go in haste (R) | 2Sa 15:14
Rehoboam made s. to get | 1Ki 12:18;
him up to | 2Ch 10:18
Rehoboam hastened to go | 2Ch 10:18
up (A)
Rehoboam hurriedly | 2Ch 10:18
mounted (B)
Rehoboam made haste to | 2Ch 10:18
mount (R)
a decree; let it be done with | Ezr 6:12
s.
Let him make s. and hasten | Isa 5:19
his
they shall come with s. swiftly | Isa 5:26
for to come to him with all s. | Ac 17:15
house, neither bid him God s. | 2Jo 10
nor extend him your greeting | 2Jo 10
(B)(E)
do not welcome or give | 2Jo 10
greeting (N)(R)
For he that biddeth him God s. | 2Jo 11
who bids him welcome (B) | 2Jo 11
he that giveth him greeting | 2Jo 11
(E)(N)(R)

SPEEDILY

they s. took down every man | Ge 44:11
his

quickly every man lowered | Ge 44:11
his sack (A)(R)
hurriedly each of them | Ge 44:11
lowered (B)
they hasted and took down | Ge 44:11
sacks (E)
I should s. escape unto the | 1Sa 27:1
land of
the wilderness, but s. pass | 2Sa 17:16
over
divided them s. among all | 2Ch 35:13
the people
the king had sent, so they did | Ezr 6:13
s.
accordingly with all diligence | Ezr 6:13
(B)
thou mayest buy s. with this | Ezr 7:17
money
shall require of you, it be | Ezr 7:21
done s.
judgment be executed s. upon | Ezr 7:26
him
and he s. gave her her things | Es 2:9
readily supplied the cosmetics | Es 2:9
(B)
quickly supplied her with | Es 2:9
ointments (R)
thine ear to me; deliver me s. | Ps 31:2
for I am in trouble; hear me | Ps 69:17
s.
thy tender mercies s. prevent | Ps 79:8
us
in the day when I call answer | Ps 102:2
me s.
answer me readily (B) | Ps 102:2
Hear me s. O Lord: my spirit | Ps 143:7
answer me quickly (B) | Ps 143:7
make haste to answer me (R) | Ps 143:7
an evil work is not executed s. | Ec 8:11
thine health shall spring forth | Isa 58:8
s.
s. will I return your | Joe 3:4
recompence
us go s. to pray before the | Zec 8:21
Lord
that he will avenge them s. | Lu 18:8
will do justice in short order | Lu 18:8
(B)
will vindicate them soon | Lu 18:8
enough (N)
not delay in seeing justice | Lu 18:8
done (P)

SPEEDY

a s. riddance of all them that | Zep 1:18
dwell

SPELLS

casting s. so cunningly (A)(B) | Ps 58:5
had been using magic s. (N) | Ac 19:18
frequent s. of illness (P) | 1Ti 5:23
by your magic s. (A)(B) | Re 18:23

SPELT

and millet and s. (S) | Eze 4:9

SPEND

s. the night (A) | Ge 19:2
s. the night (R) | Ge 19:2; J'g 19:6, 10
I will s. mine arrows upon | De 32:23
them
They s. their days in wealth | Job 21:13
shall s. their days in | Job 36:11
prosperity
we s. our years as a tale that | Ps 90:9
is told
do ye s. money for that which | Isa 55:2
he would not s. the time in | Ac 20:16
Asia
I will very gladly s. and be | 2Co 12:15
spent
s. it in sensual pleasure | Jas 4:3
(A)(B)(E)

SPENDEST

whatsoever thou s. more | Lu 10:35
when I

SPENDETH

wise; but a foolish man s. it | Pr 21:20
up
with harlots s. his substance | Pr 29:3
vain life which he s. as a | Ec 6:12
shadow

SPENDTHRIFT

a s. and a drunkard (B)   De 21:20

SPENT

And the water was s. in the bottle   Ge 21:15
my lord how that our money is s.   Ge 47:18
your strength shall be s. in vain   Le 26:20
were by Jebus, the day was far s.   J'g 19:11
for the bread is s. in our vessels   1Sa 9:7
shuttle, and are s. without hope   Job 7:6
For my life is s. with grief   Ps 31:10
life s. with sorrow (A)(B)(E)(R)   Ps 31:10
utterly s. and crashed (R)   Ps 38:8
I have s. my strength for nought   Isa 49:4
all the bread in the city were s.   Jer 37:21
had s. all that she had, and   M'k 5:26
when the day was now far s. his   M'k 6:35
which had s. all her living upon   Lu 8:43
when he had s. all, there arose a   Lu 15:14
evening, and the day is far s.   Lu 24:29
there s. their time in nothing else   Ac 17:21
after he had s. some time there   Ac 18:23
Now when much time was s.   Ac 27:9
The night is far s. the day is   Ro 13:12
gladly spend and be s. for you   2Co 12:15

SPERM

an emission of s. (B)   Le 15:16; 15:17-18
not from perishable s. (N)   1Pe 1:23

SPEWING

shameful s. shall be on thy glory   Hab 2:16

SPHERE

abandoned their proper s. (P)   Jude 6

SPICE

s. and oil for the light, and   Ex 35:28
of the traffick of the s. merchants   1Ki 10:15
there any such s. as the queen   2Ch 9:9
gathered my myrrh with my s.   Ca 5:1
consume the flesh, and s. it well   Eze 24:10

SPICED

cause thee to drink of s. wine   Ca 8:2

SPICERY

bearing s. and balm and myrrh   Ge 37:25

SPICES

s. and myrrh, nuts, and almonds   Ge 43:11
s. for anointing oil, and for sweet   Ex 25:6
also unto thee principal s. of pure   Ex 30:23
Take unto thee sweet s. stacte   Ex 30:34
sweet s. with pure frankincense   Ex 30:34
s. for anointing oil, and for   Ex 35:8
and the pure incense of sweet s.   Ex 37:29
with camels that bare s. and   1Ki 10:2
of gold, and of s. very great store   1Ki 10:10
no more such abundance of s. as   1Ki 10:10
garments, and armour, and s. and   1Ki 10:25
gold, and the s. and the precious   2Ki 20:13
and the frankincense, and the s.   1Ch 9:29

priests made the ointment of the s.   1Ch 9:30
and camels that bare s. and gold in   2Ch 9:1
of gold, and of s. great abundance   2Ch 9:9
raiment, harness, and s. horses   2Ch 9:24
sweet odours and divers kinds of s.   2Ch 16:14
a bed filled with sweet s. (B)(R)   2Ch 16:14
precious stones, and for s.   2Ch 32:27
with sweet s. and perfumes (A)(R)   Es 2:12
smell of thine ointments than all s.   Ca 4:10
and aloes, with all the chief s.   Ca 4:14
that the s. thereof may flow out   Ca 4:16
His cheeks are as a bed of s.   Ca 5:13
into his garden, to the beds of s.   Ca 6:2
hart upon the mountains of s.   Ca 8:14
and the gold, and the s. and   Isa 39:2
burnings of s. and perfumes   Jer 34:5
in thy fairs with chief of all   Eze 27:22
and Salome, had bought sweet s.   M'k 16:1
and prepared s. and oinments   Lu 23:56
bringing the s. which they had   Lu 24:1
wound it in linen clothes with the s.   Joh 19:40

SPIDER

The s. taketh hold with her hands   Pr 30:28

SPIDER'S

and whose trust shall be a s. web   Job 8:14
eggs, and weave the s. web   Isa 59:5

SPIED

And he s. an Egyptian smiting   Ex 2:11
men that had s. out the country   Jos 6:22
he s. the company of Jehu as he   2Ki 9:17
that, behold, they s. a band of men   2Ki 13:21
he s. the sepulchres that were there   2Ki 23:16
abominations that were s. in   2Ki 23:24

SPIES

and said unto them, Ye are s.   Ge 42:9
true men, thy servants are no   Ge 42:11
spake unto you, saying, Ye are s.   Ge 42:14
the life of Pharaoh surely ye are s.   Ge 42:16
and took us for s. of the country   Ge 42:30
We are true men; we are no s.   Ge 42:31
I know that ye are no s. but that   Ge 42:34
Israel came by the way of the s.   Nu 21:1
young men that were s. went in   Jos 6:23
the s. saw a man come forth out of   J'g 1:24
David therefore sent out s.   1Sa 26:4
Absalom sent s. throughout all   2Sa 15:10
watched him, and sent forth s.   Lu 20:20
when she had received the s. with   Heb 11:31

SPIKE

with a hook or s. (A)(E)(R)   Job 41:2

SPIKENARD

my s. sendeth forth the smell   Ca 1:12
my nard gave forth fragrance (R)   Ca 1:12
pleasant fruits; camphire, with s.   Ca 4:13
henna and nard (R)   Ca 4:13

S. and saffron; calamus and nard and saffron (R)   Ca 4:14 / Ca 4:14
box of ointment of s. very   M'k 14:3
alabaster jar of pure nard (A)(E)(N)(R)   M'k 14:3
alabaster jar of pure nard perfume (B)   M'k 14:3
Mary a pound of ointment of s.   Joh 12:3
pound of ointment of pure liquid nard (A)(E)(R)   Joh 12:3
pound of costly perfume of purest nard (B)(N)   Joh 12:3
pound of expensive perfume (P)   Joh 12:3

SPIKES

driven like s. (B)   Ec 12:11
pick off s. of grain (A)   M't 12:1
picked some of the s. (A)(B)   Lu 6:1

SPILLED

that he s. it on the ground, lest   Ge 38:9
the bottles, and the wine is s.   M'k 2:22
will burst the bottles, and be s.   Lu 5:37

SPILT

and are as water s. on the ground   2Sa 14:14

SPIN

that were wise hearted did s.   Ex 35:25
they toil not, neither do they s.   M't 6:28
grow: they toil not, they s. not   Lu 12:27

SPINDLE

She layeth her hands to the s.   Pr 31:19

SPIRIT

Pharaoh's s. was troubled in the morning   Ge 41:8
the s. of Jacob their father revived   Ge 45:27
hearkened not to Moses for anguish of s.   Ex 6:9
every one whom his s. made willing   Ex 35:21
I will take of s. that is on thee   Nu 11:17; 11:25
s. rested upon them and they prophesied   Nu 11:26
that the Lord would put his s. upon them   Nu 11:29
Caleb had another s. with him   Nu 14:24
s. of the people (B)   Nu 21:4
take Joshua, a man in whom is the s.   Nu 27:18
for the Lord thy God hardened his s.   De 2:30
a languishing s. (B)(R)   De 28:65
nor was there s. in them any more   Jos 5:1
when he had drunk his s. came again   Jos 15:19
when he had eaten his s. came to him   1Sa 30:12
the s. of David (A)(R)   2Sa 13:39
there was no s. in her   1Ki 10:5; 2Ch 9:4
Jezebel his wife said, Why is thy s. so sad   1Ki 21:5
there came forth a s.   1Ki 22:21; 2Ch 18:20
let a double portion of s. be on me   2Ki 2:9
they said, s. of Elijah doth rest on Elisha   2Ki 2:15
put a s. in him (A)(B)(E)(R)   2Ki 19:7
the Lord stirred up the s. of Pul   1Ch 5:26
then the s. came upon Amassai, and said   1Ch 12:18
the pattern of all that he had by the s.   1Ch 28:12
against Jehoram s. of Philistines   2Ch 21:16
with them whose s. God raised to go   Ezr 1:5
testifiedst by the s. in thy prophets   Ne 9:30

then a *s.* passed before my   *Job 4:15*
face
s. of every mortal (B)   *Job 12:10*
that thou turnest thy *s.*   *Job 15:13*
against God
my *s.* is broken (A)(R)   *Job 17:1*
my *s.* is consumed (E)   *Job 17:1*
s. of my understanding   *Job 20:3*
causeth me to answer
and whose *s.* came from thee   *Job 26:4*
by his *s.* he garnished the   *Job 26:13*
heavens
is a *s.* in man, inspiration of   *Job 32:8*
Almighty
the *s.* within me   *Job 32:18*
constraineth me
if he gather to himself his *s.*   *Job 34:14*
and breath
and in whose *s.* there is no   *Ps 32:2*
guile
clean heart, renew a right *s.*   *Ps 51:10*
within me
and uphold me with thy free   *Ps 51:12*
s.
he shall cut off the *s.* of   *Ps 76:12*
princes
my *s.* faints (R)   *Ps 77:3*
and whose *s.* was not stedfast   *Ps 78:8*
with God
thou sendest forth thy *s.*   *Ps 104:30*
they are created
provoked his *s.* so he spake   *Ps 106:33*
unadvisedly
whither shall I go from thy *s.*   *Ps 139:7*
s. is good, lead me to land   *Ps 143:10*
of uprightness
he that is hasty of *s.* exalteth   *Pr 14:29*
folly
but perverseness therein is a   *Pr 15:4*
breach in the *s.*
and an haughty *s.* goeth   *Pr 16:18*
before a fall
that ruleth *s.* better than he   *Pr 16:32*
that taketh city
the *s.* of a man will sustain   *Pr 18:14*
his infirmity
s. will endure sickness (B)(R)   *Pr 18:14*
the *s.* of man is the candle of   *Pr 20:27*
the Lord
refreshes the *s.* (R)   *Pr 25:13*
that hath no rule over his *s.*   *Pr 25:28*
is like a city
who knoweth *s.* of man, *s.* of   *Ec 3:21*
beast
be not hasty in thy *s.* to be   *Ec 7:9*
angry
no man hath power over *s.* to   *Ec 8:8*
retain the *s.*
if the *s.* of the ruler rise   *Ec 10:4*
against thee
thou knowest not what is the   *Ec 11:5*
way of the *s.*
and the *s.* shall return to God   *Ec 12:7*
who gave it
the *s.* of Egypt shall fail in   *Isa 19:3*
midst
as a *s.* of one dead (B)   *Isa 29:4*
Lord poured on you the *s.* of   *Isa 29:10*
deep sleep
they that erred in *s.* come to   *Isa 29:24*
understanding
and their horses flesh and not   *Isa 31:3*
s.
till *s.* be poured upon us   *Isa 32:15*
from on high
and his *s.* it hath gathered   *Isa 34:16*
them
he that giveth *s.* to them that   *Isa 42:5*
walk therein
the Lord God and his *s.* hath   *Isa 48:16*
sent me
as a woman forsaken and   *Isa 54:6*
grieved in *s.*
a penitent *s.* (A)   *Isa 57:15*
s. fail before me and souls I   *Isa 57:16*
have made
the *s.* of Lord God is on me   *Isa 61:1;*
  Lu 4:18
the garment of praise for the   *Isa 61:3*
s. of heaviness
anguish of *s.* (R)   *Isa 65:14*
arouse *s.* of destroyer (B)(R)   *Jer 51:1*
Lord raised the *s.* of king of   *Jer 51:11*
Medes
whither *s.* was to go, they   *Eze 1:12;*
went   *1:20*
for the *s.* was in the wheels   *Eze 1:21;*
  10:17
s. entered into me when he   *Eze 2:2;*
spake to me   *3:24*

then the *s.* took me up and I   *Eze 3:12;*
heard   *11:24*
so *s.* lifted me up, and took   *Eze 3:14;*
me away, and I   *8:30; 11:1*
went in heat of my *s.*
woe to prophets that follow   *Eze 13:3*
their own *s.*
s. shall faint, all knees be   *Eze 21:7*
weak as water
Nebuchadnezzar's *s.* was   *Da 2:1*
troubled
in whom is *s.* of holy gods,   *Da 4:8;*
before him I told the   *9:18; 5:11, 14*
dream
an excellent *s.* were found in   *Da 5:12;*
Daniel   *6:3*
man who has the *s.* is mad   *Ho 9:7*
(E)(R)
if man walking in *s.* and   *Mic 2:11*
falsehood
Lord stirred up the *s.* of   *Hag 1:14*
Zerubbabel
hath sent in his *s.* by former   *Zec 7:12*
prophets
and formeth *s.* of man within   *Zec 12:1*
him
yet had he residue of *s.*   *Mal 2:15;*
therefore take heed to your *s.*   *2:16*
Spirit (for Ghost) (S)   *M't 1:18;*
1:20; 3:11; 12:31, 32; 27:50; 28:19;
M'k 1:8; 3:29; 12:36; 13:11; 15:37, 39;
Lu 1:15, 35, 41, 67; 2:25, 26; 3:16, 22;
4:1; 12:10, 12; 23:46; Joh 1:33; 7:39;
14:26; 19:30; 20:22; Ac 1:2, 5, 8, 16;
2:4, 33, 38; 4:8; 31; 5:3, 32; 6:3; 5; 7:51,
55; 8:15, 17, 18, 19; 9:17, 31; 10:44, 45,
47; 11:15, 16; 24; 13:2, 4, 9, 52; 15:8,
28; 16:6; 19:2, 6; 20:23, 28; 21:11;
1Co 2:13; 6:19; 12:3; 2Co 6:6; 13:14;
1Th 1:5, 6; 2Ti 1:14; Tit 3:5; Heb 2:4;
3:7; 6:4; 9:8; 10:15; 1Pe 1:12; 2Pe 1:21;
1Jo 5:7 Jude 20
Jesus was led up of the *s.*   *M't 4:1;*
  Lu 4:1
troubled, saying, It is a *s.*   *M't 14:26;*
  M'k 6:49
how doth David in *s.* call him   *M't 22:43*
Lord
the *s.* indeed is willing   *M't 26:41;*
  M'k 14:38
S. descending on him   *M'k 1:10;*
  Joh 1:32
the *s.* driveth him into the   *M'k 1:12*
wilderness
and he sighed deeply in his *s.*   *M'k 8:12*
and saith
s. tare him   *M'k 9:20*
s. cried and rent him   *M'k 9:26*
go before him in the *s.* of Elias   *Lu 1:17*
the child waxed strong in *s.*   *Lu 1:80;*
  2:40
and he came by the *S.* into the   *Lu 2:27*
temple
Jesus returned in power of *S.*   *Lu 4:14*
into Galilee
her *s.* came again, and she   *Lu 8:55*
arose
know not what manner of *s.*   *Lu 9:55*
ye are of
in that hour Jesus rejoiced in   *Lu 10:21*
s. and
Jesus rejoiced in the *S.* (S)   *Lu 10:21*
a woman who had a *s.* of   *Lu 13:11*
infirmity
they supposed that they had   *Lu 24:37*
seen a *s.*
for a *s.* hath not flesh and   *Lu 24:39*
bones as I have
on whom thou see *S.*   *Joh 1:33*
descending
God giveth not the *S.* by   *Joh 3:34*
measure to him
worship the Father in *S.* and   *Joh 4:23*
in truth
God is a *S.* they must   *Joh 4:24*
worship him in *s.*
the *s.* that quickeneth; words   *Joh 6:63*
that I speak unto you are *s.* and
this spake he of *S.*   *Joh 7:39*
he groaned in *s.*   *Joh 11:33*
he was troubled in *s.* and   *Joh 13:21*
testified
they spake as *S.* gave them   *Ac 2:4*
utterance
and they were not able to   *Ac 6:10*
resist the *s.*
the *S.* said to Philip, Go near   *Ac 8:29*
and join
the *S.* said unto Peter   *Ac 10:19; 11:12*

Agabus signified by *S.* should   *Ac 11:28*
be dearth
they assayed, but the *S.*   *Ac 16:7*
suffered them not
his *s.* was stirred within him   *Ac 17:16*
when he saw
Paul pressed in *s.*   *Ac 18:5*
being fervent in *s.*   *Ac 18:25*
now I go bound in the *s.* to   *Ac 20:22*
Jerusalem
the disciples said to Saul   *Ac 21:4*
through the *S.*
Sadducees say that there is no   *Ac 23:8*
angel nor *s.*
but if a *s.* or an angel   *Ac 23:9*
hath spoken to him
Son of God according to *s.* of   *Ro 1:4*
holiness
circumcision is that of heart   *Ro 2:29*
in the *s.*
who walk not after flesh, but   *Ro 8:1;*
after *S.*   *8:4*
the law of the *S.* of life hath   *Ro 8:2*
made me free
they that are after the *S.* the   *Ro 8:5*
things of the *S.*
the mind of the Holy *S.*   *Ro 8:6*
(A)(R)
ye are not in the flesh but *S.* if   *Ro 8:9*
so be that *S.*
but the *S.* is life because of   *Ro 8:10*
righteousness
if *S.* of him that raised Jesus   *Ro 8:11*
from dead, quicken your
mortal bodies by his *S.*
but if ye thro' the *S.* mortify   *Ro 8:13*
deeds of body
S. of sonship (B)   *Ro 8:15*
S. that makes us sons (N)(R)   *Ro 8:15*
the *S.* itself witness with our *s.*   *Ro 8:16*
but ourselves who have   *Ro 8:23*
firstfruits of the *S.*
S. also helpeth our infirmities;   *Ro 8:26*
S. maketh intercession for
us with groanings
he knoweth what is the mind   *Ro 8:27*
of the *S.*
fervent in *S.*   *Ro 12:11*
for the love of the *S.*   *Ro 15:30*
but in demonstration of *S.* and   *1Co 2:4*
of power
God hath revealed them unto   *1Co 2:10*
us by his *S.* for the *S.*
searcheth all things
save the *s.* of a man which is   *1Co 2:11*
in him
not *s.* of world, but *s.* of   *1Co 2:12*
God
as absent in body, but present   *1Co 5:3*
in *s.*
s. may be saved in day of   *1Co 5:5*
Lord Jesus
he that is joined to the Lord   *1Co 6:17*
is one *s.*
glorify God in your body and   *1Co 6:20*
in your *s.*
that she may be holy both in   *1Co 7:34*
body and *s.*
diversities of gifts, but same   *1Co 12:4;*
S.   *12:8, 9*
to one is given by the *S.* the   *1Co 12:8*
word of wisdom
But all these worketh that   *1Co 12:11*
selfsame *S.*
by one *S.* are we all baptized   *1Co 12:13*
into one body; have been
made to drink into one *S.*
howbeit in the *s.* he speaketh   *1Co 14:2*
mysteries
I will sing with *s.*   *1Co 14:15*
bless with the *s.*   *1Co 14:16*
the last Adam was made a   *1Co 15:45*
quickening *s.*
ministers of new testament,   *2Co 3:6*
not of letter but of *s.* letter
killeth, but *s.* giveth life
how shall not ministration of   *2Co 3:8*
s. be rather glorious
the Lord is that *S.* where the   *2Co 3:17*
S. of Lord is
we having the same *s.* of faith,   *2Co 4:13*
we believe
cleanse from all filthiness of   *2Co 7:1*
the flesh and *s.*
because his *s.* was refreshed   *2Co 7:13*
by you all
another *s.* which ye have not   *2Co 11:4*
received
walked we not in same *s.*   *2Co 12:18*
same steps

received *s.* by the works of the *Ga 3:2*
law
are ye so foolish, having begun *Ga 3:3*
in the *S.*
he therefore that ministereth to *Ga 3:5*
you the *S.*
might receive promise of the *Ga 3:14*
S. thro' faith
God hath sent forth the *S.* of *Ga 4:6*
his son
we thro' *S.* wait for hope of *Ga 5:5*
righteousness
walk in the *S.* *Ga 5:16*
flesh lusteth against *S.* and *S.* *Ga 5:17*
against flesh, and these are
if ye be led of the *S.* *Ga 5:18*
if we live in the *S.* let us walk *Ga 5:25*
in the *S.*
soweth to *S.* shall of *S.* reap life *Ga 6:8*
everlasting
grace of our Lord be with *Ga 6:18;*
your *s.* *Ph'm 25*
the *s.* that now worketh in the *Eph 2:2*
children
we have access by one *S.* to *Eph 2:18*
the Father
for an habitation of God *Eph 2:22*
through the *S.*
as now revealed to his *Eph 3:5*
apostles by *S.*
strengthened by his *S.* in *Eph 3:16*
inner man
to keep unity of the *S.* in the *Eph 4:3*
bond of peace
there is one body, and one *S.* *Eph 4:4*
as ye are called
and be renewed in the *s.* of *Eph 4:23*
your mind
be not drunk with wine, but *Eph 5:18*
be filled with *S.*
take sword of the *S.* which is *Eph 6:17*
word of God
praying always with all *Eph 6:18*
prayer in the *S.*
the supply of the *S.* of Jesus *Ph'p 1:19*
Christ
that ye stand fast in one *s.* *Ph'p 1:27*
with one mind
if there be any fellowship of *Ph'p 2:1*
the *S.* if bowels
the circumcision, which *Ph'p 3:3*
worship God in the *s.*
who declared to us your love *Col 1:8*
in the *S.*
tho' absent in flesh, yet am I *Col 2:5*
with you in *s.*
quench not *S.* despise not *1Th 5:19*
prophesying
your *s.* soul, and body, be *1Th 5:23*
preserved blameless
be troubled neither by *s.* nor *2Th 2:2*
word
Lord shall consume with the *s.* *2Th 2:8*
of his mouth
chosen you thro' *2Th 2:13*
sanctification of *S.* and belief
God manifest, justified in *S.* *1Ti 3:16*
the *S.* speaketh expressly in *1Ti 4:1*
latter times
be thou an example in *s.* in *1Ti 4:12*
faith, in purity
the Lord Jesus Christ be with *2Ti 4:22*
thy *s.*
to the dividing asunder of *Heb 4:12*
soul and *s.*
life and *s.* (N) *Heb 4:12*
who thro' the eternal *S.* *Heb 9:14*
offered himself
as the body without the *s.* is *Jas 2:26*
dead
the *s.* that dwelleth in us *Jas 4:5*
lusteth to envy
thro' sanctification of *S.* to *1Pe 1:2*
obedience
purified in obeying truth *1Pe 1:22*
thro' the *S.*
even the ornament of a meek *1Pe 3:4*
and quiet *s.*
put to death in flesh, *1Pe 3:18*
quickened by *S.*
but live according to God in *1Pe 4:6*
the *s.*
by the *S.* which he hath given *1Jo 3:24*
us
believe not every *s.* but try *1Jo 4:1*
spirits
every *s.* that confesseth Jesus *1Jo 4:2*
Christ is come

every *s.* that confesseth not *1Jo 4:3*
that Jesus Christ is come
dwell in him, because he hath *1Jo 4:13*
given us of his *S.*
it is the *S.* that beareth *1Jo 5:6*
witness, *S.* is truth
witness in earth, the *s.*, water, *1Jo 5:8*
and blood
these be sensual, not having *Jude 19*
the *S.*
I was in the *S.* on the Lord's *Re 1:10*
day
hear what *S.* saith to churches *Re 2:7;*
2:11, 17, 29; 3:6, 13, 22
immediately I was in the *s.* and *Re 4:2*
the *s.* of life from God *Re 11:11*
entered into them
blessed are the dead, yea, *Re 14:13*
saith the *S.*
so he carried me away in the *Re 17:3;*
s. *21:10*
and the *S.* and the bride say, *Re 22:17*
Come

SPIRIT *OF ADOPTION*

but ye have received the *S.* of *Ro 8:15*
adoption

SPIRIT *OF ANTICHRIST*

that is that *s.* of antichrist ye *1Jo 4:3*
heard

SPIRIT *OF BONDAGE*

ye have not reecived the *s.* of *Ro 8:15*
bondage

SPIRIT *OF BURNING*

blood of Jerusalem by the *s.* of *Isa 4:4*
burning

SPIRIT *OF CHRIST*

if any man have not the *S.* of *Ro 8:9*
Christ
what *S.* of Christ in them did *1Pe 1:11*
signify

SPIRIT *OF COUNSEL*

the *s.* of counsel shall rest *Isa 11:2*
upon him

SPIRIT *OF DIVINATION*

a damsel possessed with *s.* of *Ac 16:16*
divination

SPIRIT *OF ERROR*

hereby know we the *s.* of truth *1Jo 4:6*
and error

SPIRIT *OF FEAR*

God hath not given us the *s.* *2Ti 1:7*
of fear

SPIRIT *OF GOD*

s. of God moved on face of *Ge 1:2*
waters
a man in whom the *s.* of *Ge 41:38*
God is
filled Bezaleel with *s.* of God *Ex 31:3;*
35:31
the *s.* of God came on Balaam *Nu 24:2*
s. of God came on Saul *1Sa 10:10;*
11:6; 19:23
s. of God came on *1Sa 19:20*
messengers of Saul
the *s.* of God came upon *2Ch 15:1*
Azariah
and the *s.* of God is in my *Job 27:3*
nostrils
s. of God made me, breath of *Job 33:4*
Almighty
in vision by *s.* of God into *Eze 11:24*
Chaldea
saw *S.* of God descending *M't 3:16*
like a dove
if I cast out devils by the *S.* *M't 12:28*
of God
if the *S.* of God dwell in you *Ro 8:9*
for as many as are led by the *Ro 8:14*
S. of God
mighty signs by power of *S.* *Ro 15:19*
of God

knoweth no man, but the *S.* *1Co 2:11*
of God
receiveth not the things of *1Co 2:14*
the *S.* of God
and that the *S.* of God *1Co 3:16*
dwelleth in you
ye are sanctified by the *S.* of *1Co 6:11*
our God
I think also that I have the *S.* *1Co 7:40*
of God
no man speaking by *S.* of *1Co 12:3*
God, calleth
written with the *S.* of the living *2Co 3:3*
God
and grieve not the holy *S.* of *Eph 4:30*
God
for the *s.* of God resteth on *1Pe 4:14*
you
hereby know ye the *S.* of God *1Jo 4:2*

SPIRIT *OF GLORY*

for the *s.* of glory resteth on *1Pe 4:14*
you

SPIRIT *OF GRACE*

pour on house of David *s.* *Zec 12:10*
of grace
hath done despite to the *S.* *Heb 10:29*
of grace

SPIRIT *OF JEALOUSY*

s. of jealousy come upon him *Nu 5:14;*
5:30

SPIRIT *OF JUDGMENT*

purged blood of Jerusalem by *Isa 4:4*
s. of judgment
Lord be for a *s.* of judgment *Isa 28:6*

SPIRIT *OF KNOWLEDGE*

s. of knowledge shall rest upon *Isa 11:2*
him

SPIRIT *OF MEEKNESS*

shall I come in the *s.* of *1Co 4:21*
meekness
restore such an one in *s.* of *Ga 6:1*
meekness

SPIRIT *OF PROMISE*

sealed with that holy *S.* of *Eph 1:13*
promise

SPIRIT *OF PROPHECY*

testimony of Jesus is *s.* of *Re 19:10*
prophecy

SPIRIT *OF SLUMBER*

God hath given them *s.* of *Ro 11:8*
slumber

SPIRIT *OF TRUTH*

S. of truth world cannot *Joh 14:17*
receive
even the *S.* of truth which *Joh 15:26*
proceedeth
when *S.* of truth is come, *Joh 16:13*
will guide you
hereby know we *s.* of truth *1Jo 4:6*
and error

SPIRIT *OF UNDERSTANDING*

s. of understanding shall rest *Isa 11:2*
upon him

SPIRIT *OF WHOREDOMS*

s. of whoredoms caused them *Ho 4:12*
to err
s. of whoredoms is in the *Ho 5:4*
midst of them

SPIRIT *OF WISDOM*

whom I have filled with *s.* of *Ex 28:3*
wisdom
Joshua was full of the *s.* of *De 34:9*
wisdom

the *s. of wisdom* shall rest   Isa 11:2
upon him
God may give to you *s. of*   Eph 1:17
wisdom

BORN OF THE SPIRIT

except that man be *born of the*   Joh 3:5
S. he cannot
that which is *born of the S.* is   Joh 3:6
spirit
so is every one that is *born of*   Joh 3:8
the S.
persecuted him that was *born*   Ga 4:29
after the S.

BROKEN SPIRIT

the sacrifices of God are a   Ps 51:17
broken s.
by sorrow of the heart, the *s.*   Pr 15:13
is *broken*
but a *broken s.* drieth the   Pr 17:22
bones

DUMB SPIRIT

I brought my son, who hath   M'k 9:17
a *dumb s.*
thou *dumb s.* I charge thee,   M'k 9:25
come out of him

EARNEST OF THE SPIRIT

who hath given us the   2Co 1:22;
earnest of the S.   5:5

FAITHFUL SPIRIT

he that is of *faithful s.*   Pr 11:13
concealeth matter

FOUL SPIRIT

he rebuked the *foul s.* saying   M'k 9:25
to him
Babylon is become hold of   Re 18:2
every *foul s.*

FRUIT OF THE SPIRIT

the *fruit of the S.* is love, joy,   Ga 5:22
peace
for the *fruit of the S.* is in all   Eph 5:9
goodness

GOOD SPIRIT

gavest thy *good s.* to instruct   Ne 9:20
them
thy *s.* is *good*, lead me into   Ps 143:10
land

HUMBLE SPIRIT

better it is to be of an   Pr 16:19
humble s.
but honour shall uphold the   Pr 29:23
humble in s.
with him also that is of an   Isa 57:15
humble s.

MY SPIRIT

my s. shall not always strive   Ge 6:3
with man
the poison whereof drinketh   Job 6:4
up *my s.*
I will speak in the anguish of   Job 7:11
my s.
and thy visitation hath   Job 10:12
preserved *my s.*
if so, why should not *my s.* be   Job 21:4
troubled
into thine hand I commit *my*   Ps 31:5
s.
my s. was overwhelmed   Ps 77:3
and *my s.* made diligent search   Ps 77:6
when *my s.* was overwhelmed   Ps 142:3
in me
therefore is *my s.*   Ps 143:4
overwhelmed in me
hear me speedily, O Lord, *my*   Ps 143:7
s. faileth
I will pour out *my s.* unto you   Pr 1:23
with *my s.* will I seek thee   Isa 26:9
early
cover with covering, but not   Isa 30:1
of *my s.*

in all these things is the life   Isa 38:16
of *my s.*
I have put *my s.* upon him   Isa 42:1
I will pour *my s.* upon thy   Isa 44:3
seed
my s. that is upon thee shall   Isa 59:21
not depart
and I went in the heat of *my*   Eze 3:14
s.
and I will put *my s.* within   Eze 36:27;
you   37:14
poured out *my s.* on house of   Eze 39:29
Israel
my s. was troubled   Da 2:3
grieve in *my s.*   Da 7:15
pour out *my s.* upon all flesh   Joe 2:28;
    2:29; Ac 2:17, 18
so *my s.* remaineth among   Hag 2:5
you
not by might, nor by power,   Zec 4:6
but by *my s.*
have quieted *my s.* in north   Zec 6:8
country
I will put *my s.* upon him   M't 12:18
my s. rejoiced in God my   Lu 1:47
Saviour
Father, into thy hands I   Lu 23:46
commend *my s.*
Stephen said, Lord Jesus,   Ac 7:59
receive *my s.*
I serve with *my s.* in the gospel   Ro 1:9
when gathered together and   1Co 5:4
my s.
my s. prayeth, but my   1Co 14:14
understanding is
for they have refreshed *my*   1Co 16:18
s. and yours
I had no rest in *my s.*   2Co 2:13

NEW SPIRIT

will put a *new s.* within you   Eze 11:19;
    36:26
make you a new heart and a   Eze 18:31
new s.

NEWNESS OF SPIRIT

we should serve in *newness of*   Ro 7:6
s.

PATIENT SPIRIT

patient in *s.* is better than   Ec 7:8
proud

PERVERSE SPIRIT

Lord hath mingled a *perverse*   Isa 19:14
s.

POOR SPIRIT

blessed are the *poor* in *s.*   M't 5:3

SORROWFUL SPIRIT

I am a woman of a *sorrowful*   1Sa 1:15
s.

UNCLEAN SPIRIT

cause *unclean s.* to pass out of   Zec 13:2
land
when *unclean s.* is gone out   M't 12:43;
of man, he walketh thro'   Lu 11:24
in synagogue a man with an   M'k 1:23
unclean s.
and when the *unclean s.* had   M'k 1:26
torn him
because they said, He hath an   M'k 3:30
unclean s.
there met him a man with an   M'k 5:2
unclean s.
come out, thou *unclean s.*   M'k 5:8;
    Lu 8:29
whose young daughter had   M'k 7:25
an *unclean s.*
Jesus rebuked *unclean s.* and   Lu 9:42
healed

WOUNDED SPIRIT

but a *wounded s.* who can   Pr 18:14
bear

SPIRITS

Regard not that have familiar   Le 19:31
s.

do not turn to mediums   Le 19:31
(B)(R)
turneth after such as have   Le 20:6
familiar *s.*
who turns *s.* and wizards (B)   Le 20:6
if a person turns to mediums   Le 20:6
(R)
God, the God of the *s.* of all   Nu 16:22
flesh
Lord, the God of the *s.* of all   Nu 27:16
flesh
who knows the dispositions   Nu 27:16
of all mankind (R)
or a consulter with familiar   De 18:11
s.
a medium (A)(B)(R)   De 18:11
were in high *s.* (B)   J'g 16:25
put away those that had   1Sa 28:3
familiar *s.*
Saul had put away mediums   1Sa 28:3
(A)(B)(R)
cut off those that have   1Sa 28:9
familiar *s.*
Saul has cut off mediums   1Sa 28:9
(A)(B)(R)
dealt with familiar *s.* and   2Ki 21:6
wizards
he dealt with mediums   2Ki 21:6
(A)(R)
he provided necromancers   2Ki 21:6
(B)
Moreover workers with   2Ki 23:24
familiar *s.*
Josiah put away mediums   2Ki 23:24
(A)(R)
Josiah exterminated the   2Ki 23:24
necromancers (B)
Who maketh his angels *s.*; his   Ps 104:4
Who makes winds his   Ps 104:4
messengers (A)(E)(R)
the *s.* of the dead (A)   Pr 2:18
eyes; but the Lord weigheth   Pr 16:2
the *s.*
abide in congregation of *s.* (A)   Pr 21:16
Seek them that have familiar   Isa 8:19
s.
consult for direction of   Isa 8:19
mediums (A)(R)
Consult the necromancers (B)   Isa 8:19
and to them that have   Isa 19:3
familiar *s.*
fortunetellers (B)   Isa 19:3
the mediums (R)   Isa 19:3
are the four *s.* of the heavens   Zec 6:5
These are the four winds of   Zec 6:5
heaven (B)(E)
These are going forth to the   Zec 6:5
four winds (R)
he cast out the *s.* with his   M't 8:16
word
gave them power against   M't 10:1
unclean *s.*
seven other *s.* more wicked   M't 12:45
commandeth he even the   M'k 1:27
unclean *s.*
unclean *s.* when they saw   M'k 3:11
him, fell
And the unclean *s.* went out   M'k 5:13
gave them power over unclean   M'k 6:7
s.
he commandeth the unclean *s.*   Lu 4:36
that were vexed with unclean   Lu 6:18
s.
and plagues, and of evil *s.*   Lu 7:21
which had been healed of evil   Lu 8:2
s.
that the *s.* are subject unto   Lu 10:20
you
s. submit (B)(N)   Lu 10:20
seven other *s.* more wicked   Lu 11:26
which were vexed with   Ac 5:16
unclean *s.*
unclean *s.* crying with loud   Ac 8:7
voice
and the evil *s.* went out of   Ac 19:12
them
call over them which had evil   Ac 19:13
s.
these arrogant *s.* (A)(R)   1Co 4:19
to another discerning of *s.* to   1Co 12:10
s. of the prophets are   1Co 14:32
subject to the
elemental *s.* of world (N)(R)   Ga 2:20
beggarly *s.* (N)(R)   Ga 4:9
giving heed to seducing *s.* and   1Ti 4:1
Who maketh his angels *s.* and   Heb 1:7
his
Who makes his angels winds   Heb 1:7
(A)(E)(N)(P)(R)

Are they not all ministering *s.* sent	*Heb 1:14*
in subjection unto the Father of *s.*	*Heb 12:9*
to the *s.* of just men made perfect	*Heb 12:23*
and preached unto the *s.* in prison	*1Pe 3:19*
try the *s.* whether they are of God	*1Jo 4:1*
the seven *S.* which are before his	*Re 1:4*
he that hath the seven *S.* of God	*Re 3:1*
which are the seven *S.* of God	*Re 4:5*
which are the seven *S.* of God sent	*Re 5:6*
three unclean *s.* like frogs come out	*Re 16:13*
they are the *s.* of devils, working	*Re 16:14*

SPIRIT'S

S., security deposit (B)	*2Co 1:22*

SPIRITUAL

mixed her *s.* wine (A)	*Pr 9:2; 9:5*
is a fool, the *s.* man is mad	*Ho 9:7*
the man who is inspired is mad (A)	*Ho 9:7*
the man who has the spirit is mad (E)(R)	*Ho 9:7*
may impart unto you some *s.* gift	*Ro 1:11*
no *s.* wisdom (P)	*Ro 2:20*
For we know that the law is *s.*: but	*Ro 7:14*
s.-mindedness means life and peace (B)	*Ro 8:6*
made partakers of their *s.* things	*Ro 15:27*
s. endowment of Christian grace (A)	*1Co 1:7*
comparing *s.* things with *s.*	*1Co 2:13*
estimated from *s.* standpoint (B)	*1Co 2:14*
But he that is *s.* judgeth all things	*1Co 2:15*
not speak unto you as unto *s.*	*1Co 3:1*
if we have sown unto you *s.* things	*1Co 9:11*
And did all eat the same *s.* meat	*1Co 10:3*
And did all drink the same *s.* drink	*1Co 10:4*
drank of that *s.* Rock that followed	*1Co 10:4*
Now concerning *s.* gifts, brethren, I	*1Co 12:1*
after charity, and desire *s.* gifts	*1Co 14:1*
speaking *s.* secrets (P)	*1Co 14:2*
as ye are zealous of *s.* gifts, seek	*1Co 14:12*
himself to be a prophet, or *s.*	*1Co 14:37*
a prophet or inspired (B)(N)	*1Co 14:37*
a spiritually-minded man (P)	*1Co 14:37*
natural body; it is raised a *s.* body	*1Co 15:44*
natural body and there is a *s.* body	*1Co 15:44*
that was not first which is *s.* but	*1Co 15:46*
and afterward that which is *s.*	*1Co 15:46*
fight on a *s.* level (P)	*2Co 10:3*
help your *s.* life (P)	*2Co 12:19*
ye which are *s.* restore such an one	*Ga 6:1*
blessed us with all *s.* blessings in	*Eph 1:3*
s. dwelling of God (N)	*Eph 2:22*
in psalms and hymns and *s.* songs	*Eph 5:19*
against *s.* wickedness in high	*Eph 6:12*
all wisdom and *s.* understanding	*Col 1:9*
in psalms and hymns and *s.* songs	*Col 3:16*
s. illumination (A)	*1Ti 6:20*
not *s.* sluggards (A)(B)	*Heb 6:12*
stones, are built up a *s.* house	*1Pe 2:5*
priesthood, to offer up *s.* sacrifices	*1Pe 2:5*
suffering *s.* agonies (P)	*2Pe 2:8*

SPIRITUALLY

but to be *s.* minded is life and	*Ro 8:6*
the mind of the Holy Spirit (A)(R)	*Ro 8:6*
spiritual-mindedness means life and peace (B)	*Ro 8:6*
keeping *s.* aglow (B)(R)	*Ro 12:11*
strengthen, build up *s.* (A)(B)	*Ro 15:2*
the *s.* mature (A)(P)	*1Co 2:6*
because they are *s.* discerned	*1Co 2:14*
a *s.*-minded man (P)	*1Co 14:37*
you were *s.* dead (P)	*Eph 2:1*
who are *s.* mature (A)(B)(N)(R)	*Ph'p 3:15*
s. seduced by demons (P)	*1Ti 4:1*
which *s.* is called Sodom and Egypt	*Re 11:8*

SPIT

he that hath the issue *s.* upon him	*Le 15:8*
her father had but *s.* in her face	*Nu 12:14*
and *s.* in his face, and shall answer	*De 25:9*
as one before whom men *s.* (S)	*Job 17:6*
me, and spare not to *s.* in my face	*Job 30:10*
Then did they *s.* in his face	*M't 26:67*
And they *s.* upon him, and took the	*M't 27:30*
and he *s.* and touched his tongue	*M'k 7:33*
when he had *s.* on his eyes, and put	*M'k 8:23*
and shall *s.* upon him, and shall	*M'k 10:34*
And some began to *s.* on him, and to	*M'k 14:65*
did *s.* upon him, and bowing their	*M'k 15:19*
made sport of, scoffed, *s.* upon (A)	*Lu 18:32; 22:63*

SPITE

in *s.* of the injunction (B)	*Es 4:16*
thou beholdest mischief and *s.* to	*Ps 10:14*
you note trouble, grief, and vexation (A)	*Ps 10:14*
take note of trouble and grief (B)	*Ps 10:14*
note trouble and vexation (R)	*Ps 10:14*

SPITEFULLY

servants, and entreated them *s.*	*M't 22:6*
treated them shamefully (A)(E)(R)	*M't 22:6*
ill-treated and killed them (B)	*M't 22:6*
attacked them brutally (N)	*M't 22:6*
treated them disgracefully (P)	*M't 22:6*
shall be mocked, and *s.* entreated	*Lu 18:32*
insulted and spit upon (A)	*Lu 18:32*
insulted and spat upon (B)(P)	*Lu 18:32*
shamefully treated and spit upon (E)(R)	*Lu 18:32*
maltreated and spat upon (N)	*Lu 18:32*

SPITTED

spitefully entreated, and *s.* on	*Lu 18:32*

SPITTING

hid not my face from shame and *s.*	*Isa 50:6*

SPITTLE

let his *s.* fall down upon his beard	*1Sa 21:13*
drooled on his beard (A)	*1Sa 21:13*
let his saliva run down on his beard (B)	*1Sa 21:13*
alone till I swallow down my *s.*	*Job 7:19*
ground, and made clay of the *s.*	*Joh 9:6*
made clay with his saliva (A)(B)	*Joh 9:6*

SPLATTERED

blood was *s.* on (A)	*2Ki 9:33*

SPLENDID

shall be excellent and *s.* (S)	*Isa 4:2*
the *s.* power (P)	*2Co 4:7*

SPLENDOR

it was perfect through my *s.* (S)	*Eze 16:14*
they set forth thy *s.* (S)	*Eze 27:10*
called you to *s.* and might (N)	*2Pe 1:3*

SPLIT

s. the wood (A)	*Ge 22:3*
the ground *s.* open (A)(B)(R)	*Nu 16:31*
s. open a hollow (A)(R)	*J'g 15:19*
s. the wood (A)(B)(R)	*1Sa 6:14*
the earth *s.* with the sound (S)	*1Ki 1:40*
the veils were *s.* (S)	*M't 27:51*
s. up into small groups (P)	*1Co 11:18*

SPLITTETH

he that *s.* wood shall be endangered (S)	*Ec 10:9*

SPLITS

s. and flashes lightning (A)(B)	*Ps 29:7*
keep an eye on those who cause *s.* (B)	*Ro 16:17*

SPOIL

and at night he shall divide the *s.*	*Ge 49:27*
loot (B)	*Ge 49:27; De 3:7; Jos 8:2; 1Sa 14:32; 15:19; 20:26; 30:26; 2Ch 25:13; 28:14, 15; Es 9:10; Isa 33:23; Na 2:9; Zep 2:9*
and ye all shall *s.* the Egyptians	*Ex 3:22*
strip (A)(B)	*Ex 3:22; Isa 11:14; 17:14*
despoil (R)	*Ex 3:22; Pr 22:23; Isa 11:14; 17:14*
will overtake, I will divide the *s.*	*Ex 15:9*
plunder (A)	*Ex 15:9; 1Sa 14:36; 30:16, 22; 2Sa 3:22; 12:30; 2Ki 21:14; 1Ch 20:2; 2Ch 14:13; 15:11; 20:25; 24:23; Ezr 9:7; Es 3:13; Ps 44:10; 89:41; 109:11; Pr 16:19; Isa 3:14; 11:14; 33:4; Jer 50:10; Eze 7:21; 26:12; Da 11:33; Zec 2:9; 14:1; M'k 3:27*
and took the *s.* of all their cattle	*Nu 31:9*
booty (A)	*Nu 31:9; 31:53; De 2:35; 2Ch 14:13*
booty (B)	*Nu 31:9; 31:11, 12, 53; De 2:35; 20:14; J'g 4:30; 1Sa 30:19; 2Sa 8:12; 23:10; 2Ch 14:14; 28:8; Ps 68:12; Isa 9:3; 10:6; Eze 25:7; 38:12*
prey (E)	*Nu 31:9; Job 29:17; Jer 20:5; Zep 2:9*
And they took all the *s.* and all the	*Nu 31:11*
and the *s.* unto Moses, and Eleazer	*Nu 31:12*
(For the men of war had taken *s.*	*Nu 31:53*
booty (E)(R)	*Nu 31:53; 2Ch 14:13*
the *s.* of the cities which we took	*De 2:35*
the cattle, and the *s.* of the cities	*De 3:7*
thou shalt gather all the *s.* of it into	*De 13:16*
and all the *s.* thereof every whit	*De 13:16*
all the *s.* thereof, shalt thou take	*De 20:14*
shalt eat the *s.* of thine enemies	*De 20:14*
only the *s.* thereof, and the cattle	*Jos 8:2*
s. of that city Israel took for a prey	*Jos 8:27*
the *s.* of these cities, and the cattle	*Jos 11:14*
divide the *s.* of your enemies	*Jos 22:8*
the necks of them that take the *s.*	*J'g 5:30*
spoil (S)	*J'g 5:30; 8:24, 25; Es 3:13; 9:15*

men of them, and took their   J'g 14:19
s.
had eaten freely to day of the   1Sa 14:30
s. of
And the people flew upon   1Sa 14:32
the s.
and s. them until the   1Sa 14:36
morning light
plunder (A)   1Sa 14:36;
15:19;   2Ch 14:14;   28:8;   Ps 109:11;
Pr 1:13;   Jer 20:5;   Da 11:33;   Ho 13:15;
   Hab 2:8;   Zec 2:9;   M't 12:29;   M'k 3:27
but didst fly upon the s. and   1Sa 15:19
didst
But the people took of the s.   1Sa 15:21
sheep
because of all the great s.   1Sa 30:16
that they
neither s. nor any thing that   1Sa 30:19
they
cattle, and said, This is   1Sa 30:20
David's s.
prize (B)   1Sa 30:20
will not give them ought of   1Sa 30:22
the s.
of the s. unto the elders of   1Sa 30:26
Judah
a present for you of the s.   1Sa 30:26
of the
and brought in a great s. with   2Sa 3:22
them
and of the s. of Hadadezer,   2Sa 8:12
son of
he brought forth the s. of   2Sa 12:30
the city
returned after him only to s.   2Sa 23:10
strip the slain   2Sa 23:10
now therefore, Moab, to the   2Ki 3:23
s.
prey and a s. to all their   2Ki 21:14
enemies
he brought also exceeding   1Ch 20:2
much s.
they carried away very   2Ch 14:13
much s.
was exceeding much s. in   2Ch 14:14
them
plunder (R)   2Ch 14:14;
Es 3:13; 8:11; 9:10; Ps 109:11; Isa 11:14;
Jer 20:5;   50:10;   Da 11:33;   Na 2:9;
Hab 2:8; Zep 2:9; Zec 2:9; M't 12:29;
     M'k 3:27
of the s. which they had   2Ch 15:11
brought
came to take away the s. of   2Ch 20:25
them
three days in gathering of   2Ch 20:25
the s.
sent all the s. of them unto   2Ch 24:23
the king
thousand of them, and took   2Ch 25:13
much s.
took also away much s. from   2Ch 28:8
them
and brought the s. to   2Ch 28:8
Samaria
the s. before the princes and   2Ch 28:14
with the s. clothed all that   2Ch 28:15
to a s. and to confusion of   Ezr 9:7
face, as
plunder (E)   Ezr 9:7;
    Eze 39:10; Hab 2:8
to take the s. of them for a   Es 3:13;
prey   8:11
take over their property (B)   Es 8:11
on the s. laid they not their   Es 9:10
hand
and plucked the s. out of his   Job 29:17
teeth
prey (A)   Job 29:17; Jer 50:10; Zep 2:9
prey (B)   Job 29:17
prey (R)   Job 29:17; Col 2:8
which hate us s. for   Ps 44:10
themselves
that tarried at home divided   Ps 68:12
the s.
All that pass by the way s.   Ps 89:41
him
rob (E)   Ps 89:41
despoil (R)   Ps 89:41;
    Isa 17:14; Eze 39:10
and let the strangers s. his   Ps 109:11
labour
word, as one that findeth   Ps 119:162
great s.
finds great beauty (B)   Ps 119:162
we shall fill our houses with s.   Pr 1:13
than to divide the s. with the   Pr 16:19
proud

and s. the soul of those that   Pr 22:23
spoiled
righteous; s. not his resting   Pr 24:15
place
do no violence to his home   Pr 24:15
(B)(R)
destroy (E)   Pr 24:15;
    Isa 33:1; Jer 5:6; 49:28
so that he shall have no need   Pr 31:11
of s.
never lack profit, gain   Pr 31:11
(B)(E)(R)
the little foxes, that s. the   Ca 2:15
vines
the s. of the poor is in your   Isa 3:14
houses
the s. of Samaria shall be   Isa 8:4
taken
men rejoice when they divide   Isa 9:3
the s.
to take the s. and to take the   Isa 10:6
prey
they shall s. them of the east   Isa 11:14
is the portion of them that s.   Isa 17:14
us
pillage (B)   Isa 17:14; Eze 26:5
when thou shalt cease to s.   Isa 33:1
thou
devastate (B)   Isa 33:1
destroy (R)   Isa 33:1;
Jer 5:6; 49:28; Eze 25:7; Ho 10:2
your s. shall be gathered like   Isa 33:4
is the prey of a great s.   Isa 33:23
divided
for a s. and none saith,   Isa 42:22
Restore
Who gave Jacob for a s. and   Isa 42:24
divide the s. with the strong   Isa 53:12
wolf of the evenings shall s.   Jer 5:6
them
destroy (A)   Jer 5:6;
    47:4; 49:28; Ho 10:2
destroy (B)   Jer 5:6; 47:4; Ho 10:2
violence and s. is heard in her   Jer 6:7
destruction (A)(B)(E)(R)   Jer 6:7;
    20:8; Hab 2:17
thy treasures will I give to   Jer 15:13
the s.
and all thy treasures to the s.   Jer 17:3
which shall s. them, and take   Jer 20:5
them
seize them (B)   Jer 20:5
cried out, I cried violence and   Jer 20:8
and they that s. thee shall be   Jer 30:16
a
shall be a s. and all that prey   Jer 30:16
cometh to s. all the Philistines   Jer 47:4
destroying (R)   Jer 47:4
for the Lord will s. the   Jer 47:4
Philistines
to Kedar, and s. the men of   Jer 49:28
the east
despoil (B)   Jer 49:28; Eze 39:10
the multitude of their cattle   Jer 49:32
a s.
and Chaldea shall be a s.:   Jer 50:10
all that
prey (E)   Jer 50:10; Eze 7:21
all that s. her shall be   Jer 50:10
satisfied
to the wicked of the earth for   Eze 7:21
a s.
they s. it, so that it be   Eze 14:15
desolate
ravage (A)(B)(E)(R)   Eze 14:15
will deliver thee for a s. to   Eze 25:7
it shall become a s. to the   Eze 26:5
nations
they shall make a s. of thy   Eze 26:12
riches
and take her s. and take her   Eze 29:19
prey
they shall s. the pomp of   Eze 32:12
Egypt
bring to nothing (A)   Eze 32:12
bring to naught (E)   Eze 32:12
To take a s. and to take a   Eze 38:12
prey
thee, Art thou come to take   Eze 38:13
a s.
cattle and goods, to take a   Eze 38:13
great s.
they shall s. those that   Eze 39:10
spoiled
despoil (A)   Eze 39:10
remove violence and s. and   Eze 45:9
oppression (R)   Eze 45:9
among them the prey and s.   Da 11:24
prey, s., substance (E)   Da 11:24

by captivity, and by s. many   Da 11:33
days
altars he shall s. their images   Ho 10:2
smite (E)   Ho 10:2
he shall s. the treasure of all   Ho 13:15
strip his treasury (R)   Ho 13:15
the s. of silver, take the s. of   Na 2:9
gold
of the people shall s. thee   Hab 2:8
rob (B)   Hab 2:8; M't 12:29
and the s. of beasts, which   Hab 2:17
made
destruction (E)   Hab 2:17
residue of my people shall s.   Zep 2:9
them
shall be a s. to their servants   Zec 2:9
thy s. shall be divided in the   Zec 14:1
midst
moth and rust s. them (P)   M't 6:19
man's house, and s. his   M't 12:29
goods
carry off his goods (A)   M't 12:29
ransack his house (N)(P)   M't 12:29;
    M'k 3:27
man? and then he will s. his   M't 12:29
house
man's house, and s. his   M'k 3:27
goods
ransack his household (A)   M'k 3:27
man; and then he will s. his   M'k 3:27
house
Beware lest any man s. you   Col 2:8
carrying you captive (B)   Col 2:8
captured (N)   Col 2:8
nothing can destroy, s. (N)   1Pe 1:4

SPOILED

came upon the slain, and s.   Ge 34:27
the city
plundered (A)   Ge 34:27;
1Sa 14:48; 17:53; 2Ki 7:16; 2Ch 14:14;
Isa 13:16;   42:22;   Jer 9:19;   10:20;
plundered (B)   Ge 34:27;
    Am 3:11; Hab 2:8; Zec 2:8;
J'g 2:14,   16;   1Sa 17:53;   2Ki 7:16;
2Ch 14:14;   Isa 13:16;   42:22;   Am 3:11;
    Zec 2:8
plundered (E)   Ge 34:27;
1Sa 17:53;   2Ki 7:16;   Isa 42:22;
Jer 39:10; Am 3:11; Hab 2:8; Zec 2:8
plundered (R)   Ge 34:27;
J'g 2:14, 16; 1Sa 14:48; 17:53; 2Ki 7:16;
2Ch 14:14;   Isa 13:16;   42:22;   Am 3:11;
    Hab 2:8
s. even all that was in the   Ge 34:29
house
looted (B)   Ge 34:29; Isa 13:16; 24:3
prey (E)   Ge 34:29; Jer 2:14
captured (R)   Ge 34:29
And they s. the Egyptians   Ex 12:36
stripped (A)   Ex 12:36;
    Job 12:17; Ps 76:5
took a heavy payment from   Ex 12:36
Egypt (B)
despoiled (E)   Ex 12:36;
J'g 2:14,   16;   1Sa 14:48;   2Ch 14:14;
    Pr 22:23; Col 2:15
despoiled (R)   Ex 12:36; Zec 11:3
be only oppressed and s. ever-   De 28:29
more
robbed (A)   De 28:29;
J'g 2:14, 16; Jer 21:12; 22:3; Eze 18:18
robbed (B)   De 28:29;
Jer 21:12; Eze 18:18; 23:46; Hab 2:8
robbed (E)   De 28:29;
Jer 21:12; 22:3; Eze 18:18; 23:46
robbed (R)   De 28:29;
    Jer 21:12; 22:3; Eze 18:18
the hands of spoilers that s.   J'g 2:14
them
of the hand of those that s.   J'g 2:16
them
of the hands of them that s.   1Sa 14:48
them
plunderers (B)   1Sa 14:48
Philistines, and they s. their   1Sa 17:53
tents
out, and s. the tents of the   2Ki 7:16
Syrians
and they s. all the cities: 2Ch 14:14
for there
He leadeth counsellors away   Job 12:17
s.
barefoot (B)   Job 12:17; 12:19
stripped (E)   Job 12:17; 12:19
stripped (R)   Job 12:17; 12:19; Ps 76:5
He leadeth princes away s.   Job 12:19
The stouthearted are s. they   Ps 76:5
have
have their loot taken (B)   Ps 76:5

the soul of those that *s.* them   Pr 22:23
despoil (R)   Pr 22:23;
     Isa 24:3; Eze 39:10
their houses shall be *s.* and   Isa 13:16
   their
rifled (E)   Isa 13:16
whose land the rivers have *s.*   Isa 18:2
divide (A)(B)(E)(R)   Isa 18:2; 18:7
whose land the rivers have *s.*   Isa 18:7
   to the
be utterly emptied, and utterly   Isa 24:3
   s.
pillaged (A)   Isa 24:3
laid waste (E)   Isa 24:3;
     Jer 4:20; 25:36; 48:1, 15, 20; 49:3
that spoilest, and thou wast   Isa 33:1
   not *s.*
destroyed (A)   Isa 33:1; Jer 4:13; 49:10
devastated (B)   Isa 33:1; Zec 11:3
destroyed (E)   Isa 33:1;
Jer 10:20; 49:10; Ho 10:14; Zec 11:2, 3
destroyed (R)   Isa 33:1;
     Jer 4:20; 10:20; 49:10; Ho 10:14
cease to spoil, thou shalt be *s.*   Isa 33:1
But this is a people robbed   Isa 42:22
   and *s.*
he a homeborn slave? why is   Jer 2:14
   he *s.*
a captive and a prey (A)   Jer 2:14
a victim (B)   Jer 2:14
prey (R)   Jer 2:14
Woe unto us! for we are *s.*   Jer 4:13
ruined (A)   Jer 4:13; Mic 2:4
ruined (R)   Jer 4:13; 9:19; Mic 2:4
is cried; for the whole land is   Jer 4:20
   s.
laid waste (A)   Jer 4:20;
     48:1; 49:3; Zec 11:2
laid waste (B)   Jer 4:20;
     25:36; 48:1, 20; 49:3
suddenly are my tents *s.* and   Jer 4:20
   my
when thou art *s.* what wilt   Jer 4:30
   thou do
made desolate (A)   Jer 4:30
ruined (B)   Jer 4:30; 9:19; Zec 11:2
desolate (E)   Jer 4:30; 9:19
heard out of Zion, How are   Jer 9:19
   we *s.*
My tabernacle is *s.* and all   Jer 10:20
   my
destroyed (B)   Jer 10:20
deliver him that is *s.* out of   Jer 21:12
deliver the *s.* out of the hand   Jer 22:3
for the Lord hath *s.* their   Jer 25:36
   pasture
despoiling (R)   Jer 25:36
Woe unto Nebo! for it is *s.*   Jer 48:1
laid waste (B)   Jer 48:1; 48:20; 49:3
Moab is *s.* and gone up out   Jer 48:15
   of her
made desolate (A)   Jer 48:15; 48:20
tell ye it in Arnon, that   Jer 48:20
   Moab is *s.*
Howl, O Heshbon, for Ai is *s.*   Jer 49:3
his seed is *s.* and his   Jer 49:10
   brethren, and
Because the Lord hath *s.*   Jer 51:55
   Babylon
devastating Babylon (B)   Jer 51:55
laying Babylon waste (R)   Jer 51:55
hath *s.* none by violence hath   Eze 18:7
   wronged (A)   Eze 18:7, 12
hath *s.* by violence, hath not   Eze 18:12
   robbery (B)   Eze 18:12
s. his brother by violence,   Eze 18:18
   and did
give them to be removed   Eze 23:46
   and *s.*
they shall spoil those that *s.*   Eze 39:10
   them
despoiled (A)(B)   Eze 39:10
and all thy fortresses shall be   Ho 10:14
   s.
wasted and destroyed (A)   Ho 10:14
destroyed (B)   Ho 10:14
as Shalman *s.* Beth-arbel in   Ho 10:14
thee, and thy palaces shall be   Am 3:11
   s.
strengtheneth the *s.* against the   Am 5:9
destruction (A)(E)(R)   Am 5:9
that the *s.* shall come against   Am 5:9
and say, We be utterly *s.:* he   Mic 2:4
   hath
ruined and laid waste (A)   Mic 2:4
thou hast *s.* many nations, all   Hab 2:8
me unto the nations which *s.*   Zec 2:8
   you
fallen; because the mighty are   Zec 11:2
   s.

for their glory is *s.:* a voice of   Zec 11:3
ruined (A)   Zec 11:3
lions: for the pride of Jordan   Zec 11:3
   is *s.*
having *s.*   Col 2:15
   principalities powers
disarming princes and   Col 2:15
   authorities (B)
discarded cosmic powers (N)   Col 2:15
exposed them, shattered,   Col 2:15
   empty, and defeated (P)
disarmed principalities and   Col 2:15
   powers (R)

SPOILER

to them from the face of the   Isa 16:4
   s.
destroyer (A)(E)(R)   Isa 16:4;
   21:2; Jer 6:26; 15:8; 48:18, 32; 51:56
devastator, pillager (B)   Isa 16:4
the *s.* ceaseth, the oppressors   Isa 16:4
   are
treacherously, and the *s.*   Isa 21:2
   spoileth
destroyer (B)   Isa 21:2; Jer 6:26
the *s.* shall suddenly come   Jer 6:26
   upon us
of the young men a *s.* at   Jer 15:8
   noonday
devastation (B)   Jer 15:8; 51:56
the *s.* shall come upon every   Jer 48:8
   city
s. of Moab shall come upon   Jer 48:18
   thee
s. is fallen upon thy summer   Jer 48:32
   fruits
Because the *s.* is come upon   Jer 51:56
   her

SPOILERS

the hands of *s.* that spoiled   J'g 2:14
   them
plunderers (A)(B)(R)   J'g 2:14
the *s.* that came out of the   1Sa 13:17
   camp of the
raiders (A)(B)(R)   1Sa 13:17; 14:15
and the *s.* they also   1Sa 14:15
   trembled, and
them into the hand of *s.*   2Ki 17:20
plunderers (B)   2Ki 17:20
s. are come upon all high   Jer 12:12
   places
destroyers (E)(R)   Jer 12:12; 51:48, 53
the *s.* shall come unto her   Jer 51:48
   from the
yet from me shall a *s.* come   Jer 51:53
   unto her

SPOILEST

Woe to thee that *s.* and thou   Isa 33:1
   wast
destroyer (A)(R)   Isa 33:1
devastator (B)   Isa 33:1
destroyest (E)   Isa 33:1

SPOILETH

the needy from him that *s.*   Pr 35:10
   him
who snatches away his goods   Ps 35:10
   (A)
robs robbeth (B)(E)   Ps 35:10
despoils (R)   Ps 35:10
treacherously and the spoiler   Isa 21:2
   s.
destroys (A)(E)   Isa 21:2; Na 3:16
demolishes (B)   Isa 21:2
plunders (R)   Isa 21:2
the troop of robbers *s.*   Ho 7:1
   without
ravage and raid (A)   Ho 7:1
raid (B)(R)   Ho 7:1
ravageth (E)   Ho 7:1
the cankerworm *s.* and fleeth   Na 3:16
   away

SPOILING

s. prospects (B)   Ex 5:21
evil for good to the *s.* of my   Ps 35:12
   soul
to my personal bereavement   Ps 35:12
   (A)(B)(E)
my soul is forlorn (R)   Ps 35:12
because of the *s.* of the   Isa 22:4
   daughter
destruction (A)(E)(R)   Isa 22:4;
     Jer 48:3; Hab 1:3

devastation (B)   Isa 22:4
s. and great destruction   Jer 48:3
for *s.* and violence are before   Hab 1:3
   me
oppression (B)   Hab 1:3
everything *s.* it (P)   M't 13:41
took joyfully the *s.* of your   Heb 10:34
   goods
plundering (A)(B)(R)   Heb 10:34
seizure of possessions (N)   Heb 10:34
goods were confiscated (P)   Heb 10:34

SPOILS

among the *s.* a goodly   Jos 7:21
   Babylonish
Out of the *s.* won in battles   1Ch 26:27
plunder (B)   1Ch 26:27; Lu 11:22
together with the *s.* of their   Isa 25:11
   hands
he trusted, and divideth his *s.*   Lu 11:22
plunder (A)(N)   Lu 11:22
Abraham gave the tenth of   Heb 7:4
   the *s.*
first fruits (B)   Heb 7:4

SPOILT

the skins are *s.* (N)   M't 9:17

SPOKE

spoke (S)   Ge 23:8;
     34:8, 20; 42:24; 43:19; Ec 1:16
the women *s.* as they played   1Sa 18:7
   (S)
Jesus *s.* first to him (S)   M't 17:25
s. sharply to evil spirit (P)   M'k 9:25
s. boldly, persuading (A)   Ac 19:8

SPOKEN

Lord bring what he hath *s.*   Ge 18:19
   of him
as ye have *s.* in mine ears, so   Nu 14:28
   will I do
we have *s.* against the Lord   Nu 21:7
   and thee
hath he *s.* and shall he not   Nu 23:19
   make it good
I have heard words they have   De 5:28
   s. they have well said all they
   have *s.*
because he hath *s.* to turn you   De 13:5
   away from Lord
they have well *s.* that which   De 18:17
   they have *s.*
the Lord hath done all he   1Sa 25:30
   hath *s.*
unless thou hadst *s.* people   2Sa 2:27
   had gone
turn from ought my lord the   2Sa 14:19
   king hath *s.*
Ahithophel hath *s.* after this   2Sa 17:6
   manner
if Adonijah have not *s.* this   1Ki 2:23
   word
what counsel give ye, that we   1Ki 12:9;
may answer this people who   2Ch 10:9
   have *s.*
and all the people said, It is   1Ki 18:24
   well *s.*
wouldst thou be *s.* for to the   2Ki 4:13
   king
my tongue hath *s.* in my   Job 33:2
   mouth
Job hath *s.* without   Job 34:35
   knowledge and wisdom
ye have not *s.* of me as my   Job 42:7;
   servant Job   42:8
no speech, nor *s.* word (A)   Ps 19:3
my mouth hath *s.* when in   Ps 66:14
   trouble
glorious things *s.* of thee, city   Ps 87:3
   of God
they have *s.* against me with   Ps 109:2
   a lying tongue
word *s.* in due season, how   Pr 15:23
   good
a word fitly *s.* is like apples   Pr 25:11
   of gold
take no heed to all words that   Ec 7:21
   are *s.*
in the day when she shall be *s.*   Ca 8:8
for the sea hath *s.*   Isa 23:4
he hath *s.*   Isa 38:15
hands are defiled, your lips   Isa 59:3
   have *s.* lies
he hath *s.* to us in the name   Jer 26:16
   of the Lord
and have *s.* lying words in   Jer 29:23
   my name

considerest what this people | Jer 33:24
have s.
ye and your wives have s. | Jer 44:25
with mouths
have ye not s. a lying | Eze 13:7
divination
because ye have s. vanity, and | Eze 13:8
seen lies
king Nebuchadnezzar, to thee | Da 4:31
it is s.
yet they have s. lies against | Ho 7:13
me
they have s. words, swearing | Ho 10:4
falsely
Lord be with you, as ye have | Am 5:14
s.
nor shouldst thou have s. | Ob 12
proudly
the inhabitants thereof have | Mic 6:12
s. lies
the idols have s. vanity and | Zec 10:2
diviners
what have we s. so much | Mal 3:13
against thee
high priest saying, He hath s. | M't 26:65
blasphemy
shall be s. of for a memorial | M'k 14:9
of her
marvelled at things s. of him | Lu 2:33
and for a sign which shall be | Lu 2:34
s. against
what s. in darkness, what s. in | Lu 12:3
ear
nor knew they the things | Lu 18:34
which were s.
if I had not come and s. to | Joh 15:22
them
as many have s. foretold these | Ac 3:24
days
none of things ye have s. | Ac 8:24
come on me
lest that come on you s. in the | Ac 13:40
prophets
the word should first have | Ac 13:46
been s. to you
Lydia attended to things that | Ac 16:14
were s.
seeing these things cannot be | Ac 19:36
s. against
but if a spirit or angel hath s. | Ac 23:9
to him
more than those things s. by | Ac 27:11
Paul
when had s. took bread and | Ac 27:35
gave thanks
we know every where it is s. | Ac 28:22
against
your faith is s. of thro' whole | Ro 1:8
world
according to that which was s. | Ro 4:18
so seed be
let not then your good be | Ro 14:16
evil s. of
to whom he was not s. of | Ro 15:21
they shall see
why am I evil s. of that for | 1Co 10:30
which
how shall it be known what | 1Co 14:9
is s.
hath in last days s. to us by | Heb 1:2
his Son
for if the word s. by angels | Heb 2:2
was stedfast
for a testimony of things to | Heb 3:5
be s. after
would not afterward s. of | Heb 4:8
another day
he of whom these things are | Heb 7:13
s. pertaineth
of things which we have s. | Heb 8:1
this is the sum
intreated the word not be s. | Heb 12:19
any more
who have s. unto you the | Heb 13:7
word of God
on their part he is evil s. of | 1Pe 4:14
the way of truth shall be evil | 2Pe 2:2
s. of
may be mindful of words which | 2Pe 3:2
were s.
ungodly sinners have s. against | Jude 15
him
remember the words which | Jude 17
were s. before

SPOKEN with *GOD*

at set time of which God had | Ge 21:2
s. to him
an holy people to thy God as | De 26:19
he hath s.

God hath s. in his holiness | Ps 60:6;
| 108:7
God hath s. once, twice have | Ps 62:11
I heard
that which was s. to you by | M't 22:31
God
which God hath s. by his holy | Ac 3:21
prophets

SPOKEN with *PROPHET*

prophet hath s. it | De 18:22
presumptuously
if prophet be deceived when | Eze 14:9
he hath s.
was s. by Jeremy the prophet | M't 2:17;
| 27:9
that it might be fulfilled which | M't 2:23
was s. by the prophet | M't 13:35; 27:35
this is he that was s. of by the | M't 3:3
prophet Esaias
that it might be fulfilled | M't 4:14;
which was s. by the | 8:17; 12:17; 21:4
prophet
the abomination of | M't 24:15;
desolation s. of by Daniel | M'k 13:14
the prophet
to believe all that the | Lu 24:25
prophets have s.
this was s. of by the prophet | Ac 2:16
Joel
take, my brethren, prophets | Jas 5:10
who have s.

I HAVE, HAVE I SPOKEN

I have done which I have s. | Ge 28:15
to thee
this is the thing I have s. to | Ge 41:28
Pharaoh
all this land I have s. of will | Ex 32:13
I give
lead people to the place of | Ex 32:34
which I have s.
out of my grief have I s. | 1Sa 1:16
hitherto
perform against Eli all things | 1Sa 3:12
which I have s.
as touching the matter | 1Sa 20:23
which I have s.
and after that I have s. mock | Job 21:3
on
once have I s. but I will not | Job 40:5
answer
I believed, therefore have I | Ps 116:10;
s. | 2Co 4:13
I have not s. in secret | Isa 45:19; 48:16
I have s. it, I will also bring | Isa 46:11
it to pass
I, even I, have s. I have | Isa 48:15
called him
I have s. it, I have proposed it | Jer 4:28
I have not s. to them yet | Jer 23:21
they prophesied
I have s. to you rising early, | Jer 25:3;
and speak | 35:14
write thee all words I have s. | Jer 30:2;
| 36:2
I have s. but they have not | Jer 35:17
heard
word which I have s. shall | Eze 12:28
be done
ye say, Lord saith it, albeit I | Eze 13:7
have not s.
for I have s. it, saith the | Eze 26:5;
Lord | 28:10
in the fire of my jealousy | Eze 36:5;
have I s. | 33:6
art he of whom I have s. in | Eze 38:17
old time
for in jealousy and fire of | Eze 38:19
my wrath have I s.
it is come, this is the day | Eze 39:8
whereof I have s.
I have also s. by the prophets | Ho 12:10
word that I have s. shall | Joh 12:48
judge him
for I have not s. of myself | Joh 12:49
but the Father
these things have I s. | Joh 14:25;
| 15:11; 16:1, 25, 33
are clean thro' word I have s. | Joh 15:3
to you
if I have s. evil, bear witness | Joh 18:23
of the evil

HAD SPOKEN

according to the word Joseph | Ge 44:2
had s.

and Balak did as Balaam had | Nu 23:2
s.
told father words he had s. | 1Ki 13:11
to king
Naboth the Jezreelite had s. | 1Ki 21:4
to him
according to word which | 2Ki 1:17
Elijah had s.
it came to pass as the man of | 2Ki 7:18
God had s.
because we had s. unto the | Ezr 8:22
king
I told also king's words that | Ne 2:18
he had s.
Mordecai, who had s. good for | Es 7:9
the king
now Elihu had waited till Job | Job 32:4
had s.
Baruch wrote words Lord had | Jer 36:4
s. by Jeremiah
and when he had s. this | Da 10:11
word to me
when he had s. such words, I | Da 10:15
became dumb
when he had s. unto me, I | Da 10:19
was strengthened
as soon as he had s. the | M'k 1:42
leprosy departed
they knew he had s. the | M'k 12:12;
parable against them | Lu 20:19
when he had thus s. | Lu 19:28;
24:40; Joh 9:6; 18:22; Ac 19:41; 20:36;
| 26:30
man believed word Jesus had | Joh 4:50
s.
they thought he had s. of | Joh 11:13
taking rest
when he had s. this he saith | Joh 21:19
Follow me
Barnabas declared he had s. | Ac 9:27
unto
departed after Paul had s. | Ac 28:25
one word
Moses had s. every precept | Heb 9:19

THOU HAST SPOKEN

this city for the which thou | Ge 19:21
hast s.
nor since thou hast s. to thy | Ex 4:10
servant
Moses said, Thou hast s. well, | Ex 10:29
not see
I will do this thing that thou | Ex 33:17
hast s.
power of Lord be great, as | Nu 14:17
thou hast s.
the thing which thou hast s. is | De 1:14
good
thou hast s. friendly to | Ru 2:13
handmaid
maidservants which thou | 2Sa 6:22
hast s. of
thou hast s. of thy servant's | 2Sa 7:19;
house for a great | 7:25; 1Ch 17:7, 23
while
Hezekiah to Isaiah, good is | 2Ki 20:19;
the word of Lord which | Isa 39:8
thou hast s.
let nothing fail of all that thou | Es 6:10
hast s.
surely thou hast s. in my | Job 33:8
hearing
thou hast s. and done evil | Jer 3:5
things
that which thou hast s. is | Jer 32:24
come to pass
as for the word that thou | Jer 44:16
hast s. unto us
O Lord, thou hast s. against | Jer 51:62
this place
I have heard blasphemies | Eze 35:12
thou hast s.

SPOKES

their felloes, and their s. | 1Ki 7:33
were all

SPOKESMAN

he shall be thy s. unto the | Ex 4:16
people
as a mouthpiece (A) | Ex 4:16
he shall be as a mouth to you | Ex 4:16
(R)
he was the s. (N) | Ac 14:12
s. in every town (N) | Ac 15:21
a s., one Tertullus (R) | Ac 24:1

SPOON

One *s.* of ten shekels of gold, *Nu 7:14*
full
bowl (A) *Nu 7:14;*
7:20, 26, 32, 38, 44, 50, 56, 62, 68, 74,
80
pan (B) *Nu 7:14;*
7:20, 26, 32, 38, 44, 50, 56, 62, 68, 74, 80
dish (R) *Nu 7:14;*
7:20, 26, 32, 38, 44, 50, 56, 62, 68, 74,
80
One *s.* of gold of ten shekels, *Nu 7:20*
full of
One golden *s.* of ten shekels *Nu 7:26;*
7:32, 38, 44, 50, 56, 62, 68, 74, 80

SPOONS

the dishes thereof, and *s.* *Ex 25:29*
thereof
bowls (A) *Ex 25:29;*
37:16; Nu 4:7; 7:84, 86
bowls (B) *Ex 25:29;*
37:16; 2Ki 25:14; 2Ch 24:14
the table, his dishes and his *Ex 37:16*
s.
thereon the dishes, and the *s.* *Nu 4:7*
silver bowls, twelve *s.* of gold *Nu 7:84*
pans (B) *Nu 7:84; 7:86; 1Ki 7:50*
dishes (E) *Nu 7:84;*
7:86; 2Ki 25:14; 2Ch 4:23; 24:14;
Jer 52:18-19
The golden *s.* were twelve, full *Nu 7:86*
the gold of the *s.* was an *Nu 7:86*
hundred
and the *s.* and the censers of *1Ki 7:50*
pure
the snuffers, and the *s.* and *2Ki 25:14*
dishes (A) *2Ki 25:14; 2Ch 4:22*
bowls (A) *2Ki 25:14; Jer 52:19*
and the *s.* and the censers, of *2Ch 4:22*
pure
s. and vessels of gold and *2Ch 24:14*
silver
the bowls, and the *s.* and all *Jer 52:18*
the candlesticks, and the *s.* *Jer 52:19*

SPORT

made *s.* of me (R) *Nu 22:29*
Samson, that he may make *J'g 16:25*
us *s.*
amuse us (B) *J'g 16:25*
house; and he made them *s.* *J'g 16:25*
that beheld while Samson *J'g 16:27*
made *s.*
It is as *s.* to a fool to do *Pr 10:23*
mischief
neighbour, and saith, Am I *Pr 26:19*
in *s.*
joking (A)(B) *Pr 26:19*
Against whom do ye *s.* *Isa 57:4*
yourselves
sneering, jeering (B) *Isa 57:4*
made *s.* of him (A) *M't 27:29*
made *s.* of him (A) *M't 27:41*
made *s.* of, scoffed, spit *Lu 18:32;*
upon (A) *22:63*
made *s.* of him (B) *Lu 22:63*

SPORTING

Isaac was *s.* with Rebekah *Ge 26:8*
caressing Rebekah his wife *Ge 26:8*
(A)(B)
Isaac fondling Rebekah (R) *Ge 26:8*
s. themselves with their own *2Pe 2:13*
revelling in their deception *2Pe 2:13*
(A)(R)
stuff themselves at your tables *2Pe 2:13*
(B)
an ugly blot on your *2Pe 2:13*
company (N)
playing tricks at your table *2Pe 2:13*
(P)

SPOT

flesh a rising, a scab, or bright *Le 13:2*
s.
If the bright *s.* be white in the *Le 13:4*
skin
be a white rising, or a bright *Le 13:19*
s.
But if the bright *s.* stay in his *Le 13:23*
place
that burneth have a white *Le 13:24*
bright *s.*
the hair in the bright *s.* be *Le 13:25*
turned

be no white hair in the bright *Le 13:26*
s.
And if the bright *s.* stay in *Le 13:28*
his place
it is a freckled *s.* that *Le 13:39*
groweth in
a leprous *s.* (S) *Le 13:55*
and for a scab, and for a *Le 14:56*
bright *s.*
bring thee a red heifer *Nu 19:2*
without *s.*
without blemish (B) *Nu 19:2*
without defect, no blemish *Nu 19:2*
(R)
lambs of the first year without *Nu 28:3*
s.
flawless yearlings (B) *Nu 28:3;*
28:9, 11; 29:17
without blemish (B) *Nu 28:3;*
28:9, 11; 29:17; Heb 9:14
without blemish (R) *Nu 28:3;*
28:9, 11; 29:17; Job 11:15; Heb 9:14;
1Pe 1:19
lambs of the first year *Nu 28:9;*
without *s.* 29:17, 26
their *s.* is not of his children *De 32:5*
that is their blemish (A) *De 32:5*
it is not their blemish (B) *De 32:5*
because of their blemish (R) *De 32:5*
thou lift up thy face without *Job 11:15*
s.
without stain of sin (A) *Job 11:15*
without shame (B) *Job 11:15*
my love; there is no *s.* in *Ca 4:7*
thee
there is no flaw in you (A)(R) *Ca 4:7*
there is blemish in you (B) *Ca 4:7*
not having *s.* or wrinkle, or *Eph 5:27*
keep this commandment *1Ti 6:14*
without *s.*
unsullied flawless, *1Ti 6:14*
irreproachable (A)
stainless and irreproachable *1Ti 6:14*
(B)
irreproachably and without *1Ti 6:14*
fault (N)
unstained and free from *1Ti 6:14*
reproach (R)
offered himself without *s.* to *Heb 9:14*
God
offered himself an *Heb 9:14*
unblemished sacrifice (A)
offered himself a flawless *Heb 9:14*
sacrifice (B)
offered himself without *Heb 9:14*
blemish (E)(N)(R)
offered himself as a perfect *Heb 9:14*
sacrifice (P)
without blemish and without *1Pe 1:19*
s.
flawless and spotless (B) *1Pe 1:19*
without mark or blemish (N) *1Pe 1:19*
unblemished and unstained *1Pe 1:19*
(P)
found of him in peace, *2Pe 3:14*
without *s.*
spotless and blameless (B) *2Pe 3:14*
unblemished and above *2Pe 3:14*
reproach (N)
clean and blameless (P) *2Pe 3:14*

SPOTLESS

be kept in *s.* integrity (P) *1Th 5:23*
flawless and *s.* (B) *1Pe 1:19*
s. and blameless (B) *2Pe 3:14*
they are *s.* (R) *Re 14:5*

SPOTLESSLY

s. holy before God (B) *1Th 3:13*

SPOTS

bright *s.* even white bright *s.* *Le 13:38*
if the bright *s.* in the skin of *Le 13:39*
their
his skin, or the leopard his *s.* *Jer 3:23*
S. they are and blemishes *2Pe 2:13*
they are blots and blemishes *2Pe 2:13*
(A)(B)(R)
an ugly blot on your *2Pe 2:13*
company (N)
These are *s.* in your feasts of *Jude 12*
charity
are hidden reefs in your feasts *Jude 12*
(A)
are stains in your love feasts *Jude 12*
(B)

are hidden rocks in your love *Jude 12*
feasts (E)
a blot on your love feasts (N) *Jude 12*
a menace to good fellowship *Jude 12*
(P)
are blemishes on your love *Jude 12*
feasts (R)

SPOTTED

all the speckled and *s.* cattle *Ge 30:32*
s. and speckled among the *Ge 30:32*
goats
is not speckled and *s.* among *Ge 30:33*
goats that were ringstraked *Ge 30:35*
and *s.*
goats that were speckled and *Ge 30:35*
and *s.*
ringstraked, speckled, and *s.* *Ge 30:39*
streaked, speckled, *s.* (A)(S) *Ge 31:10*
even the garment *s.* by the *Jude 23*
flesh
polluted by sensuality (B) *Jude 23*
contaminated with sensuality *Jude 23*
(N)
garments their deeds have *Jude 23*
fouled (P)

SPOUSE

with me from Lebanon, my *s.* *Ca 4:8*
my bride (A)(B)(E)(R) *Ca 4:8;*
4:9-12; 5:1
my heart, my sister, my *s.*; *Ca 4:9*
fair is thy love, my sister, my *Ca 4:10*
s.
Thy lips, O my *s.*, drop as the *Ca 4:11*
garden inclosed is my sister, *Ca 4:12*
my *s.*
into my garden, my sister, my *Ca 5:1*
s.

SPOUSES

and your *s.* shall commit *Ho 4:13*
adultery
daughters commit adultery *Ho 4:13;*
(A)(B)(E)(R) 4:14
your *s.* when they commit *Ho 4:14*
adultery

SPOUTS

golden tubes or *s.* (A)(B)(E) *Zec 4:12*

SPRANG

and immediately it *s.* up, *M'k 4:5*
because
yield fruit that *s.* up and *M'k 4:8*
increased
and the thorns *s.* up with it *Lu 8:7*
fell on good ground, and *s.* up *Lu 8:8*
s. up and walked *Ac 14:10*
(B)(N)(P)(R)
he called for a light, and *s.* in *Ac 16:29*
that our Lord *s.* out of Juda *Heb 7:14*
Therefore *s.* there even of *Heb 11:12*
one, and

SPREAD

field where Jacob had *s.* his *Ge 33:19;*
tent 35:21
plague *s.* not in the skin *Le 13:5;*
13:6, 23, 28
and behold, if the scall *s.* not *Le 13:32;*
13:34
but if the scall *s.* much in *Le 13:36*
the skin
if the plague be *s.* in a *Le 13:51;*
garment 14:39, 44
if the plague be not *s.* *Le 13:53;*
13:55; 14:48
on table *s.* cloth of blue *Nu 4:7; 4:11*
s. a scarlet cloth *Nu 4:8*
s. a purple cloth *Nu 4:13*
s. on it covering of badgers *Nu 4:14*
skins
s. the cloth before the elders *De 22:17*
of city
they *s.* a garment, and cast in *J'g 8:25*
earrings
then the Philistines *s.* *J'g 15:9*
themselves in Lehi
Philistines *s.* themselves in *2Sa 5:18;*
valley of Rephaim 5:22; 1Ch 14:9, 13
s. Absalom a tent on top of *2Sa 16:22*
the house
woman *s.* a covering on *2Sa 17:19*
well's mouth

Rizpah s. sackcloth for her on rock   2Sa 21:10

s. gold on cherubims and palm trees   1Ki 6:32

he arose, with his hands s. up to heaven   1Ki 8:54

Hazael s. a thick cloth on his face   2Ki 8:15

s. letter before the Lord   2Ki 19:14; Isa 37:14

he s. a cloud for a covering   Ps 105:39

they have s. a net by the wayside   Ps 140:5

surely in vain net is s. in sight of fowler   Pr 1:17

worm is s. under thee, worms cover thee   Isa 14:11

they that s. nets on the waters shall languish   Isa 19:8

they could not s. the sail, lame take the prey   Isa 33:23

s. out heavens (A)(B)(E)(R)   Isa 48:12

and to s. sackcloth and ashes under him   Isa 58:5

and they shall s. them before the sun   Jer 8:2

silver s. into plates is brought from Tarshish   Jer 10:9

he hath s. net for my feet, turned me back   La 1:13

and he s. the roll before me   Eze 2:10

my net also will I s. upon him   Eze 12:13; 17:20

thou shalt be a place to s. nets upon   Eze 26:14

because ye have been a net s. upon Tabor   Ho 5:1

when they shall go, I will s. my net on them   Ho 7:12

his branches shall s. his beauty as olivetree   Ho 14:6

as the morning s. upon the mountains   Joe 2:2

their horsemen shall s. themselves   Hab 1:8

behold, I will s. dung upon your faces   Mal 2:3

multitude s. their garments in the way   M't 21:8; M'k 11:8; Lu 19:36

spread (S)   M't 21:8; 25:24, 26; M'k 11:8

and to s. abroad (S)   M'k 1:45

s. the good news (N)   M'k 5:20

(for his name was s. abroad:)   M'k 6:14

that it s. no further among people   Ac 4:17

word s. far and wide (A)(N)(P)(R)   Ac 13:49

s. like sepsis (P)   2Ti 2:17

s. tabernacle over and shelter them with presence (A)(E)   Re 7:15

SPREAD ABROAD

families of Caaanites s. abroad   Ge 10:18

thou shalt s. abroad to the west and east   Ge 28:14

I will s. abroad hands to Lord   Ex 9:29

Moses s. abroad his hands to the Lord   Ex 9:33

s. abroad the tent over tabernacle   Ex 40:19

but if the scab s. much abroad   Le 13:7; 22:27

they s. abroad the quails round the camp   Nu 11:32

they were s. abroad on the earth   1Sa 30:16

stamp and s. abroad mine enemies   2Sa 22:43

Philistines s. themselves abroad   1Ch 14:13

Uzziah's name s. abroad   2Ch 26:8; 26:15

my cities thro' prosperity be s. abroad   Zec 1:17

I have s. you abroad as the four winds   Zec 2:6

s. abroad fame   M't 9:31; M'k 1:28; 6:14

faith to God-ward is s. abroad   1Th 1:8

SPREAD FORTH

as valleys are they s. forth as gardens   Nu 24:6

cherubims s. forth their two wings   1Ki 8:7

Solomon s. forth hands   1Ki 8:22; 2Ch 6:12-13

s. forth hands towards this house   1Ki 8:38; 2Ch 6:29

when ye s. forth your hands, I will   Isa 1:15

s. forth hands, as he that swimmeth   Isa 25:11

thus saith God, he that s. forth the earth   Isa 42:5

they shall be a place to s. forth nets   Eze 47:10

SPREAD OVER

s. over it a cloth wholly of blue   Nu 4:6

s. thy skirt over thine handmaid   Ru 3:9

the veil that is s. over all nations   Isa 25:7

s. his royal pavilion over them   Jer 43:10

he shall s. his wings over Moab   Jer 48:40

he shall s. his wings over Bozrah   Jer 49:22

I s. my skirt over thee and covered   Eze 16:8

then the nations s. their net over him   Eze 19:8

SPREAD OUT

cherubims s. out wings   Ex 37:9; 1Ch 28:18

I s. out my hands to the Lord my God   Ezr 9:5

my root was s. out by the waters   Job 29:19

hast thou with him s. out the sky   Job 37:18

s. out my hands to rebellious people   Isa 65:2

the adversary hath s. out his hand   La 1:10

I will s. out my net over thee   Eze 32:3

SPREADEST

which thou s. forth to be thy sail   Eze 27:7

SPREADETH

the scab s. in the skin, then   Le 13:8

As an eagle s. abroad her wings   Le 32:11

Which alone s. out the heavens   Job 9:8

throne, and s. his cloud upon it   Job 26:9

Behold, he s. his light upon it   Job 36:30

he s. sharp pointed things upon   Job 41:30

his neighbour s. a net for his feet   Pr 29:5

that swimmeth s. forth his hands   Isa 25:11

the goldsmith s. it over with gold   Isa 40:19

s. them out as a tent to dwell   Isa 40:22

s. abroad the earth by myself   Isa 44:24

that s. her hands, saying, Woe   Jer 4:31

that s. out her roots by the river   Jer 17:8

Zion s. forth her hands, and   La 1:17

SPREADING

thing of skin; it is a s. plague   Le 13:57

s. himself like a green bay tree   Ps 37:35

became a s. vine of low stature   Eze 17:6

be a place for the s. of nets in the   Eze 26:5

SPREADINGS

understand the s. of the clouds   Job 36:29

SPREADS

s. tent over them (B)   Re 7:15

SPRIGS

cut off the s. with pruning hooks   Isa 18:5

branches with pruning shears (B)   Isa 18:5

shoots with pruning hooks (R)   Isa 18:5

forth branches, and shot forth s.   Eze 17:6

shot forth leafy twigs (A)   Eze 17:6

put forth foliage (B)(R)   Eze 17:6

SPRING

a s. of water (A)(B)(R)   Ge 16:7

a s., cistern, reservoir (A)(R)   Le 11:36

sang this song, S. up, O well   Nu 21:17

and depths that s. out of valleys   De 8:7

springs and lakes s. up (B)   De 8:7

when the day began to s. they let   J'g 19:25

the dawn began to break (A)(R)   J'g 19:25

at daybreak they let her go (B)   J'g 19:25

at the dawning of the day (E)   J'g 19:25

to pass about the s. of the day   1Sa 9:26

and about dawn (A)(B)(R)   1Sa 9:26

forth unto the s. of the waters   2Ki 2:21

neither doth trouble s. out of   Job 5:6

bud of the tender herb to s. forth   Job 38:27

Truth shall s. out of the earth   Ps 85:11

Truth sprouts from the earth (B)   Ps 85:11

When the wicked s. as the grass   Ps 92:7

fountain, and a corrupt s.   Pr 25:26

a s. shut up, a fountain sealed   Ca 4:12

before they s. forth I tell you   Isa 42:9

now it shall s. forth; shall ye   Isa 43:19

they shall s. up as among the grass   Isa 44:4

let righteousness s. up together   Isa 45:8

thine health shall s. forth speedily   Isa 58:8

like a s. of water, whose waters   Isa 58:11

that are sown in it to s. forth   Isa 61:11

and praise to s. forth before all the   Isa 61:11

wither in all the leaves of her s.   Eze 17:9

and his s. shall become dry, Ho 13:15 and

pastures of the wilderness do s.   Joe 2:22

and the seed should s. and grow   M'k 4:27

s. of water welling up (A)(N)(P)(R)   Joh 4:14

s. of action is love (P)   2Co 5:14

SPRINGETH

the hyssop that s. out of the wall   1Ki 4:33

year that which s. of the same   2Ki 19:29; Isa 37:30

thus judgment s. up as hemlock   Ho 10:4

SPRINGING

and found there a well of s. water   Ge 26:19

as tender grass s. out of the earth   2Sa 23:4

thou blessest the s. thereof   Ps 65:10

of water s. up into everlasting life   Joh 4:14

spring of water welling up (A)(N)(P)(R)   Joh 4:14

water that bubbles up for eternal life (B)   Joh 4:14

lest any root of bitterness s. up   Heb 12:15

SPRINGS

discovered hot s. (A)(B)(E)(R)   Ge 36:24

the plain, under the s. of Pisgah   De 4:49

the slopes of Pisgah (B)(E)(R)   De 4:49

s. and lakes spring up (A)(B)(E)(R)   De 8:7

and of the s. and all their kings   Jos 10:40

the slopes (A)(E)(R)   Jos 10:40; 12:8

the foothills (B)   Jos 10:40; 12:8

and in the s. and in the wilderness	Jos 12:8
land: give me also s. of water	Jos 15:19
her the upper s. and the nether s.	Jos 15:19
land: give me also s. of water	J'g 1:15
her the upper s. and the nether s.	J'g 1:15
all the s. (B)(R)	1Ki 18:5
the waters of the s. (B)(R)	2Ch 32:3; 32:4
entered into the s. of the sea	Job 38:16
fountains of the sea (B)	Job 38:16
cleave s. and brooks (R)	Ps 74:15
be there: all my s. are in thee	Ps 87:7
All my fountains are in thee (B)(E)	Ps 87:7
He sendeth the s. into the valleys	Ps 104:10
the s. of water (B)(R)	Ps 107:33; 107:35
your s. be dispersed (B)(E)(R)	Pr 5:16
there were no s. (B)(R)	Pr 8:24
and the thirsty land s. of water	Isa 35:7
and the dry land s. of water	Isa 41:18
s. of water shall he guide them	Isa 49:10
up her sea, and make her s. dry	Jer 51:36
s. of living waters (A)(B)(N)(P)(R)	Re 7:17
s. of water (A)(B)(N)(P)	Re 8:10; 14:7; 16:4

SPRINKLE

let Moses s. it toward the heaven	Ex 9:8
let Moses toss it to the sky (B)	Ex 9:8
throw them toward heaven (R)	Ex 9:8
and s. it round about the altar	Ex 29:16
throw it against the altar (A)(R)	Ex 29:16
blood upon the altar round	Ex 29:20
dash the rest of the blood against (A)	Ex 29:20
s. it upon Aaron, and upon his	Ex 29:21
s. the blood round about upon	Le 1:5
dash (A)	Le 1:5; 1:11; 7:2; 17:6; 2Ki 16:15
throw (R)	Le 1:5; 1:11; 3:2, 8, 13; 2Ki 16:15
s. his blood round about upon	Le 1:11
shall s. the blood upon the altar	Le 3:2
throw (A)	Le 3:2; 3:8, 13
s. the blood thereof round about	Le 3:8
s. the blood thereof upon the altar	Le 3:13
s. of the blood seven times before	Le 4:6
s. it seven times before the Lord	Le 4:17
s. of the blood of the sin offering	Le 5:9
he s. round about upon the altar	Le 7:2
thrown (R)	Le 7:2
s. upon him that is to be cleansed	Le 14:7
shall s. of the oil with his finger	Le 14:16
shall s. with his right finger some	Le 14:27
water, and s. the house seven times	Le 14:51
and s. it with his finger upon	Le 16:14
he s. of the blood with his finger	Le 16:14
and s. it upon the mercy seat	Le 16:15
he shall s. of the blood upon it	Le 16:19
priest shall s. the blood upon	Le 17:6
S. water of purifying upon them	Nu 8:7
shalt s. their blood upon the altar	Nu 18:17
s. of her blood directly before the	Nu 19:4
s. it upon the tent, and upon all the	Nu 19:18
the clean person shall s. upon the	Nu 19:19
and s. upon it all the blood of	2Ki 16:15
So shall he s. many nations	Isa 52:15
startle many nations (A)(R)	Isa 52:15
will I s. clean water upon you, and	Eze 36:25

thereon, and to s. blood thereon	Eze 43:18
throwing (R)	Eze 43:18

SPRINKLED

Moses s. it up toward heaven	Ex 9:10
threw (A)	Ex 9:10; 2Ch 20:16
tossed (B)	Ex 9:10
threw (R)	Ex 9:10; 24:6, 8; Le 8:19; 9:12, 18; 2Ki 16:13; 2Ch 29:22; 30:16
half of the blood he s. on the altar	Ex 24:6
dashed (A)	Ex 24:6; Le 8:19, 24; 9:12, 18; 2Ki 16:13; 2Ch 29:22
the blood, and s. it on the people	Ex 24:8
when there is s. of the blood	Le 6:27
spattered (B)	Le 6:27
whereon it was s. in the holy place	Le 6:27
he s. upon the altar seven times	Le 8:11
and Moses s. the blood upon	Le 8:19; 8:24
s. it upon Aaron, and upon his	Le 8:30
he s. round about upon the altar	Le 9:12
which he s. upon the altar round	Le 9:18
water of separation was not s. upon	Nu 19:13
thrown (R)	Nu 19:13; 19:20
water hath not been s. upon him	Nu 19:20
of her blood was s. on the wall	2Ki 9:33
splattered (A)	2Ki 9:33
bespattered (B)	2Ki 9:33
spattered (R)	2Ki 9:33
s. the blood of his peace offerings	2Ki 16:13
the blood, and s. it on the altar	2Ch 29:22
they s. the blood upon the altar	2Ch 29:22
the priests s. the blood, which they	2Ch 30:16
the priests s. the blood from their	2Ch 35:11
s. dust upon their heads toward	Job 2:12
cast dust upon their heads (A)	Job 2:12
blood be s. upon my garments	Isa 63:3
and s. both the book, and all	Heb 9:19
s. with blood both the tabernacle	Heb 9:21
hearts s. from an evil conscience	Heb 10:22

SPRINKLETH

be the priest's that s. the blood	Le 7:14
dash (A)	Le 7:14
throws (R)	Le 7:14
he that s. the water of separation	Nu 19:21

SPRINKLING

ashes of an heifer s. the unclean	Heb 9:13
the passover, and the s. of blood	Heb 11:28
to the blood of s. that speaketh	Heb 12:24
and s. of the blood of Jesus Christ	1Pe 1:2

SPROUT

be cut down, that it will s. again	Job 14:7

SPROUTED

earth s. vegetation (P)	Jas 5:18

SPROUTS

truth s. from earth (B)	Ps 85:11

SPRUNG

the east wind s. up after them	Ge 41:6
the east wind, s. up after them	Ge 41:23
a leprosy s. up in his bald head	Le 13:42

and shadow of death light is s. up	M't 4:16
and forthwith they s. up, because	M't 13:5
the thorns s. up, and choked them	M't 13:7
But when the blade was s. up, and	M't 13:26
soon as it was s. up, it withered	Lu 8:6

SPUE

That the land s. not you out also	Le 18:28
throw you out (B)	Le 18:28
vomit (E)	Le 18:28
vomited (R)	Le 18:28
to dwell therein, s. you not out	Le 20:22
vomit (A)	Le 20:22; Jer 25:27
throw you up (B)	Le 20:22
vomit (R)	Le 20:22; Jer 25:27
be drunken, and s. and fall	Jer 25:27
vomit (R)	Jer 25:27
I will s. thee out of my mouth	Re 3:16
spit you out (N)(R)	Re 3:16

SPUED

as it s. out the nations that were	Le 18:28

SPUN

brought that which they had s.	Ex 35:25
them up in wisdom s. goats' hair	Ex 35:26
tales artfully s. (N)	2Pe 1:16

SPUNGE

a s. and filled it with vinegar	M't 27:48
ran and filled a s. full of vinegar	M'k 15:36
and they filled a s. with vinegar	Joh 19:29

SPUR

pierce his jaw with a s. (B)	Job 41:2

SPURN

my soul s. them (A)(R)	Le 26:44
wicked s. God (B)	Ps 10:13
does not s. evil (R)	Ps 36:4
do not s. us (R)	Jer 14:21
s. justice (B)	Mic 3:9
tales artfully s. (N)	1Pe 1:16

SPURNED

have s. the Lord (B)	Nu 11:20
he s. them (A)(B)(R)	De 32:19
s. the covenant (B)	Ps 89:39
s. the counsel of the most High (A)(R)	Ps 107:11
scorned nor s. me (B)	Ga 4:14

SPY

Moses sent to s. out the land	Nu 13:16
Moses sent them to s. out the land	Nu 13:17
And Moses sent to s. out Jaazer	Nu 21:32
of Shittim two men to s. secretly	Jos 2:1
Joshua sent to s. out Jericho	Jos 6:25
Moses sent to s. out the land (S)	Jos 14:7
sent to s. (A)(B)(E)(R)(S)	J'g 1:23
to s. out the land, and to search it	J'g 18:2
went to s. out the country of Laish	J'g 18:14
men that went to s. out the land	J'g 18:17
to search the city, and to s. it out	2Sa 10:3
Go and s. where he is, that I may	2Ki 6:13
overthrow, and to s. out the land	1Ch 19:3
came in privily to s. out our liberty	Ga 2:4

SQUABBLING

squabbling (P)	1Co 3:3
jealousy and s. (P)	1Co 3:3

SQUANDERED

s. his goods (B)(N)(P)(R)   Lu 15:13

SQUANDERING

s. livelihood (B)   Lu 15:30
s. his possessions (A)(N)   Lu 16:1

SQUARE

spend night in the s. (A)   Ge 19:2
all the doors and posts were s.   1Ki 7:5
s. in the four squares thereof   Eze 43:16
hundred in breadth, s. round   Eze 45:2
about

SQUARED

The posts of the temple   Eze 41:21
were s.

SQUARES

square in the four s. thereof   Eze 43:16
and fourteen broad in the   Eze 43:17
four s.

SQUEEZE

s. into its own mold (P)   Ro 12:2

STABBED

s. him under (B)   2Sa 3:27; 4:7

STABBERS

s.- in-the-back (P)   Ro 1:30

STABILITY

shall be the s. of thy times   Isa 33:6
lose your own s. (B)   1Pe 3:17

STABLE

the world also shall be s.   1Ch 16:30
that it
the s. clean (B)   Pr 14:4
will make Rabbah a s. for   Eze 25:5
camels

STABLISH

I will s. the throne of his   2Sa 7:13
kingdom
and I will s. his throne for   1Ch 17:12
ever
to s. his dominion by the   1Ch 18:3
river
There will I s. the throne of   2Ch 7:18
thy
To s. this among them, that   Es 9:21
S. thy word unto thy servant   Ps 119:38
to s. you according to my   Ro 16:25
gospel
To the end he may s. your   1Th 3:13
hearts
and s. you in every good   2Th 2:17
word and
who shall s. you, and keep   2Th 3:3
you
Be ye also patient; s. your   Jas 5:8
hearts
make you perfect, s.,   1Pe 5:10
strengthen

STABLISHED

the Lord s. the kingdom in   2Ch 17:5
his
the world also is s. that it   Ps 93:1
cannot
He hath also s. them for ever   Ps 148:6
and s. in the faith, as ye have   Col 2:7
been

STABLISHETH

blood, and s. a city by   Hab 2:12
iniquity
he which s. us with you in   2Co 1:21
Christ

STACHYS

in Christ, and S. my beloved   Ro 16:9

STACKS

in thorns, so that the s. of   Ex 22:6
corn

STACTE

Take unto thee sweet spices,   Ex 30:34
s.

STAFF

for with my s. I passed over   Ge 32:10
and thy s. that is in thine   Ge 38:18
hand
the signet, and bracelets, and   Ge 38:25
s.
was leader's s. from (A)(B)   Ge 49:10
was ruler's s. from (E)(R)   Ge 49:10
feet, and your s. in your   Ex 12:11
hand
and walk abroad upon his s.   Ex 21:19
have broken the s. of your   Le 26:26
bread
bare it between two upon a   Nu 13:23
s.
and he smote the ass with a   Nu 22:27
s.
put forth the end of the s.   J'g 6:21
that was
And the s. of his spear was   1Sa 17:7
like a
And he took his s. in his   1Sa 17:40
hand, and
is a leper, or that leaneth on   2Sa 3:29
a s.
the s. of whose spear was   2Sa 21:19
like a
with iron and the s. of a   2Sa 23:7
spear
but he went down to him   2Sa 23:21
with a s.
and take my s. in thine hand   2Ki 4:29
lay my s. upon the face of   2Ki 4:29
the child
and laid the s. upon the face   2Ki 4:31
of the
thou trustest upon the s. of   2Ki 18:21
he went down to him with a   1Ch 11:23
spear s. was like a weaver's   1Ch 20:5
beam
rod and thy s. they comfort me   Ps 23:4
he brake the whole s. of   Ps 105:16
bread
from Judah the stay, and the s.   Isa 3:1
the s. of his shoulder, the rod   Isa 9:4
stick for the shoulder (B)   Isa 9:4
and the s. in their hand is   Isa 10:15
mine
or as if the s. should lift up   Isa 10:15
itself
the cane lift him (B)   Isa 10:15
and shall lift up his s.   Isa 10:24
against thee
hath broken the s. of the   Le 14:5
wicked
the fitches are beaten out   Le 28:27
with a s.
where the grounded s. shall   Isa 30:32
pass
Lo, thou trustest in the s. of   Isa 36:6
How is the strong s. broken   Jer 48:17
I will break the s. of bread in   Eze 4:16
and will break your s. of   Eze 5:16
bread
and will break the s. of the   Eze 14:13
bread
they have been a s. of reed to   Eze 29:6
and their s. declareth unto   Ho 4:12
them
every man with his s. in his   Zec 8:4
hand
And I took my s. even   Zec 11:10
Beauty
the stick (B)   Zec 11:10; 11:14
Then I cut asunder mine   Zec 11:14
other s.
nor take s.   M't 10:10
(A)(B)(P)(R)(S)
for their journey, save a s.   M'k 6:8
only
leaning upon the top of his   Heb 11:21
s.

STAFFS

took two s. (A)(R)   Zec 11:7

STAGES

these are the s. of (R)   Nu 33:1

STAGGER

them to s. like a drunken   Job 12:25
man
fro, and s. like a drunken   Ps 107:27
man
they s. but not with strong   Isa 29:9
drink

STAGGERED

He s. not at the promise of   Re 4:20
God

STAGGERETH

as a drunken man s. in his   Isa 19:14
vomit

STAGGERING

wine of s. (E)   Ps 60:3

STAIN

and the shadow of death s. it   Job 3:5
without s. of sin (A)   Job 11:15
to s. the pride of all glory,   Isa 23:9
and to
and I will s. all my raiment   Isa 63:3

STAINING

s. the whole body (R)   Jas 3:6

STAINLESS

s., irreproachable (B)   1Ti 6:14

STAINS

s. in your love feasts (B)   Jude 12

STAIRS

with winding s. into the   1Ki 6:8
middle
it under him on the top of   2Ki 9:13
the s.
the s. that go down from the   Ne 3:15
city
up upon the s. of the Levites   Ne 9:4
up by the s. of the city of   Ne 12:37
David
rock, in the secret places of   Ca 2:14
the s.
east, and went up the s.   Eze 40:6
thereof
his s. shall look toward the   Eze 43:17
east
and when he came upon the   Ac 21:35
s.
Paul stood on the s. and   Ac 21:40
beckoned

STAKES

not one of the s. thereof   Isa 33:20
shall ever
thy cords, and strengthen thy   Isa 54:2
s.

STALK

ears of corn came up upon   Ge 41:5
one s.
seven ears came up in one s.   Ge 41:22
full
reap the whirlwind: it hath no   Ho 8:7
s.

STALKS

and hid them with the s. of   Jos 2:6
flax

STALL

calves out of the midst of the   Am 6:4
s.
and grow up as calves of the   Mal 4:2
s.
loose his ox or his ass from   Lu 13:15
the s.

STALLED

than a *s.* ox and hatred therewith	Pr 15:17

STALLS

had forty thousand *s.* of horses	1Ki 4:26
had four thousand *s.* for horses	2Ch 9:25
and *s.* for all manner of beasts, and	2Ch 32:28
s. for the flocks (B)	2Ch 32:28
there shall be no herd in the *s.*	Hab 3:17

STAMMERERS

s. shall be ready to speak plainly	Isa 32:4

STAMMERING

with *s.* lips and another tongue	Isa 28:11
of a *s.* tongue, that thou canst not	Isa 33:19

STAMP

I did *s.* them as the mire of	2Sa 22:43
crushed them as mire (A)(E)	2Sa 22:43
like mud I trample them (B)	2Sa 22:43
thine hand, and *s.* with thy foot	Eze 6:11
s. of his being (N)(R)	Heb 1:3

STAMPED

and burnt it with fire, and *s.* it	De 9:21
crushed it, grinding it small (A)(B)(R)	De 9:21
s. it small to powder and cast	2Ki 23:6
beat it to dust (A)(E)(R)	2Ki 23:6
ground it to dust (B)	2Ki 23:6
s. it small to powder, and cast burned	2Ki 23:6
beating them to dust (A)(E)(R)	2Ki 23:15
Asa cut down her idol, and *s.* it	2Ch 15:16
crushed it (A)(R)	2Ch 15:16
smashing it (B)	2Ch 11:16
and *s.* with the feet, and rejoiced	Eze 25:6
s. the residue with the feet of it	Da 7:7
crushed and trampled (A)	Da 7:7; 7:19
and *s.* the residue with his feet	Da 7:19
trampling what remained (B)	Da 7:19
to the ground, and *s.* upon him	Da 8:7
trampled on him (A)(B)(R)	Da 8:7
to the ground, and *s.* upon them	Da 8:10
trampled on them (A)(B)(E)(R)	Da 8:10
s. with promised Holy Spirit (P)	Eph 1:13

STAMPING

noise of the *s.* of the hoofs of his	Jer 47:3

STANCHED

immediately her issue of blood *s.*	Lu 8:44
her flow of blood ceased (A)(R)	Lu 8:44
her hemorrhage was over (B)(N)(P)	Lu 8:44

STAND

people saw cloudy pillar *s.* at door	Ex 33:10
priest estimate it, so shall it *s.*	Le 27:14; 27:17
then all her vows shall *s.*	Nu 30:4; 30:5, 7, 11
her vows or bond shall not *s.*	Nu 30:12
God hath chosen him to *s.* to minister	De 18:5
if he *s.* to it and say, I like not to take her	De 25:8
he shall *s.* at entering gate of city	Jos 20:4

now *s.* and see this great thing	1Sa 12:16
I will go out and *s.* before my father	1Sa 19:3
priests could not *s.* to minister, because of cloud	1Ki 8:11;
Elijah said, As Lord liveth, before whom I *s.*	1Ki 17:1; 18:15; 2Ki 3:14; 5:16
I thought he will come out and *s.*	2Ki 5:11
two kings stood not, how shall we *s.*	2Ki 10:4
David saw the angel of the Lord *s.*	1Ch 21:16
to *s.* every morning to praise Lord	1Ch 23:30
he caused all present to *s.* to it	2Ch 34:32
let all the rulers of congregation *s.*	Ezr 10:14
to see if Mordecai's matters would *s.*	Es 3:4
gather themselves, and *s.* for their life	Es 8:11
he shall lean on his house, it shall not *s.*	Job 8:15
that he shall *s.* at the latter day on earth	Job 19:25
take thy *s.* (S)	Job 33:5
it is turned, and they *s.* as a garment	Job 38:14
and my kinsman *s.* afar off	Ps 38:11
on right hand did *s.* queen in gold of Ophir	Ps 45:9
and he made the waters to *s.* as an heap	Ps 78:13
and let Satan *s.* at his right hand	Ps 109:6
he shall *s.* at the right hand of the poor	Ps 109:31
our feet *s.* within thy gates, O Jerusalem	Ps 122:2
if mark iniquities, O Lord, who shall *s.*	Ps 130:3
but the house of the righteous shall *s.*	Pr 12:7
nevertheless counsel of the Lord shall *s.*	Pr 19:21
and *s.* not in place of great men	Pr 25:6
s. not in an evil thing	Ec 8:3
thus saith God, It shall not *s.*	Isa 7:7; 8:10
a root of Jesse, shall *s.* for an ensign	Isa 11:10
and as I have purposed, so it shall *s.*	Isa 14:24
my lord, I *s.* continually on watchtower	Isa 21:8
and your agreement with hell shall not *s.*	Isa 28:18
and by liberal things shall he *s.*	Isa 32:8
but the word of our God shall *s.* for ever	Isa 40:8
counsel shall *s.* and I will do all my pleasure	Isa 46:10
s. now with thine enchantments and sorceries	Isa 47:12
strangers shall *s.* and feed your flocks	Isa 61:5
s. ye in the ways and see, ask for old paths	Jer 6:16
know whose word shall *s.* mine or theirs	Jer 44:28
did not *s.* because day was come on them	Jer 46:21
but by keeping of his covenant it might *s.*	Eze 17:14
thou madest their loins to be at a *s.*	Eze 29:7
and the kingdom shall *s.* for ever	Da 2:44
king of the north shall not *s.* nor his arm	Da 11:6
but the king of the south shall not *s.*	Da 11:25
nor shall he *s.* that handleth the bow	Am 2:15
he shall *s.* and feed in strength of the Lord	Mic 5:4
S., *s.* shall they cry, none shall look back	Na 2:8
and who shall *s.* when he appeareth	Mal 3:2
a house or kingdom divided shall not *s.*	M't 12:25; 12:26; M'k 3:24-25; Lu 11:18
and when ye *s.* praying, forgive	M'k 11:25

detest all you *s.* for (P)	Lu 6:22
why *s.* ye gazing up into heaven	Ac 1:11
go *s.* and speak in the temple	Ac 5:20
I *s.* and am judged for hope of promise	Ac 25:6
Paul said, I *s.* at Caesar's judgment seat	Ac 25:10
have access into grace wherein we *s.*	Ro 5:2
purpose of God according to election might *s.*	Ro 9:11
for God is able to make him *s.*	Ro 14:4
I declare the gospel wherein ye *s.*	1Co 15:1
and why *s.* we in jeopardy every hour	1Co 15:30
helpers of your joy, for by faith ye *s.*	2Co 1:24
you *s.* for it (B)	2Co 11:20
to withstand and having done all to *s.*	Eph 6:13
s. having your loins girt about with truth	Eph 6:14
this is true grace of God wherein ye *s.*	1Pe 5:12
behold, I *s.* at the door and knock	Re 3:20
great day is come, who shall be able to *s.*	Re 6:17
merchants *s.* afar off for fear of her torments	Re 18:15

STAND *ABROAD*

s. abroad man, shall bring the pledge	De 24:11

STAND *AGAINST*

nor *s.* against blood of thy neighbour	Le 19:16
every vow of a widow shall *s.* against her	Nu 30:9
my words shall *s.* against you for evil	Jer 44:29
may be able to *s.* against wiles of devil	Eph 6:11

STAND *ALOOF*

my lovers and my friends *s.* aloof	Ps 38:11

STAND *BACK*

s. back this fellow came in to sojourn	Ge 19:9

STAND *BEFORE*

rise early *s.* before Pharaoh	Ex 8:20; 9:13
magicians could not *s.* before Moses	Ex 9:11
I will *s.* before thee on the rock in Horeb	Ex 17:6
nor any woman *s.* before a beast	Le 18:23
have no power to *s.* before your enemies	Le 26:37; Jos 7:12, 13; J'g 2:14
to *s.* before the congregation to minister	Nu 16:9
he shall *s.* before Eleazar the priest	Nu 27:21
till he *s.* before congregation	Nu 35:12; Jos 20:6
no man be able to *s.* before thee	De 7:24; 11:25; Jos 1:5; 10:8; 23:9
who can *s.* before the children of Arnak	De 9:2
tribe of Levi *s.* before the Lord to minister	De 10:8; 2Ch 29:11; Eze 44:11, 15
both the men shall *s.* before the Lord	De 19:17
s. this day all of you *before* the Lord	De 29:10
who is able to *s.* before holy Lord God	1Sa 6:20
let David, I pray thee, *s.* *before* me	1Sa 16:22
let a young virgin *s.* before the king	1Ki 1:2
happy are servants who *s.* *before* thee and hear thy wisdom	1Ki 10:8; 2Ch 9:7
go, and *s.* on the mount *before* the Lord	1Ki 19:11

we *s. before* this house in thy 2Ch 20:9
presence
we cannot *s. before* thee   Ezr 9:15
because of this
who then is able to *s. before*   Job 41:10
me
cast forth ice, who can *s.*   Ps 147:17
before his cold
man diligent in business shall   Pr 22:29
s. before kings, not *s. before*
mean men
but who is able to   Pr 27:4
s. before envy
come and *s. before* me in this   Jer 7:10
house
if thou return, thou shalt *s.*   Jer 15:19
before me
Jonadab shall not want a   Jer 35:19
man to *s. before* me
who is that shepherd that   Jer 49:19;
will *s. before* me   50:44
at the end they might *s. before* Da 1:5
king
so that no beast might *s.*   Da 8:4
before him
no power in the ram, to *s.*   Da 8:7
before him
none shall *s. before* him, he   Da 11:16
shall stand
who can *s. before* his   Na 1:6
indignation
worthy to *s. before* the Son   Lu 21:36
of man
all *s. before* judgment seat of   Ro 14:10
Christ
dead small and great *s.*   Re 20:12
before God

STAND BY

behold, I *s. by* the well of   Ge 24:43
water
and thou shalt *s. by* the river's Ex 7:15
brink
and thou shalt *s. by* the   Ex 17:15
river's brink
and all the people *s. by* thee   Ex 18:14
unto even
s. by thy burnt offering, and I   Nu 23:3
will go
while they *s. by* let them shut   Ne 7:3
the doors
s. by thyself, I am holier than   Isa 65:5
s. by the way and ask, What   Jer 48:19
is done
prince shall *s. by* the post of   Eze 46:2
the gate
places to walk among these   Zec 3:7
that *s. by*
two anointed ones that *s. by*   Zec 4:14
the Lord
because of the people which   Joh 11:42
s. by

STAND FAST

my covenant shall *s. fast* with   Ps 89:28
him
all his commandments *s. fast*   Ps 111:8
for ever
say ye, *S. fast* and prepare   Jer 46:14
thee
watch ye, *s. fast* in faith, be   1Co 16:13
strong
s. fast therefore in liberty   Ga 5:1
Christ made us
s. fast in one spirit   Ph'p 1:27
s. fast in Lord   Ph'p 4:1
for now we live, if ye *s. fast*   1Th 3:8
in Lord
s. fast, and hold traditions   2Th 2:15
taught

STAND FORTH

get up, and *s. forth* with your   Jer 46:4
helmets
saith to man, *S. forth*   M'k 3:3; Lu 6:8

STAND HERE

I *s. here* by the well of water   Ge 24:13
s. here by thy burnt offering   Nu 23:15
but as for thee, *s.* thou *here* by De 5:31
me
king said, Turn aside, and *S.*   2Sa 18:30
here
why *s.* ye *here* all day idle   M't 20:6
some *s. here* who shall not   M'k 9:1
taste death
by him doth this man *s. here*   Ac 4:10
whole

STAND IN

s. in the door of the tent, and   J'g 4:20
say
s. in holy place according to   2Ch 35:5
divisions
ungodly shall not *s. in* judgment Ps 1:5
s. in awe, sin not, commune   Ps 4:4
with your heart
foolish shall not *s. in* thy sight, Ps 5:5
thou hatest
and who shall *s. in* his holy   Ps 24:3
place
let all inhabitants of world *s.*   Ps 33:8
in awe
who may *s. in* thy sight when   Ps 76:7
angry
hast not made him to *s. in*   Ps 89:43
the battle
who by night *s. in* house of   Ps 134:1;
Lord   135:2
s. in gate of Lord's house and   Jer 7:2
proclaim
the wild asses did *s. in* the   Jer 14:6
high places
s. in the gate of children of   Jer 17:19
people
s. in the court of Lord's house   Jer 26:2
and speak
have not gone up to *s. in*   Eze 13:5
battle
that should *s. in* gap before   Eze 22:30
me
in controversy they shall *s.*   Eze 44:24
in judgment
as had ability to *s. in* king's   Da 1:4
palace
and he shall *s. in* the   Da 11:16
glorious land
shall *s. in* thy lot at the end   Da 12:13
of days
feet *s. in* that day on Mount   Zec 14:4
of Olives
when ye see abomination *s. in* M't 24:15
holy place
I am Gabriel, that *s. in*   Lu 1:19
presence of God
faith should not *s. in* wisdom   1Co 2:5
of men
to change my voice, for I *s. in* Ga 4:20
doubt of you

STAND ON

to-morrow I will *s. on* top of   Ex 17:9
the hill
if the head of Elisha shall   2Ki 6:31
s. on him
she shall not *s. on* his side   Da 11:17
nor be for him
arms shall *s. on* his part,   Da 11:31
pollute the sanctuary
s. on sea of glass, having the   Re 15:2
harps of God

STAND OUT

their eyes *s. out* with fatness   Ps 73:7

STAND PERFECT

s. perfect and complete in   Col 4:12
will of God

STAND STILL

Moses said *s. still*   Ex 14:13;
and see salvation of God   2Ch 20:17
s. still, hear what Lord will   Nu 9:8
command
that bear ark *s. still* in Jordan Jos 3:8
sun *s. still* upon Gibeon, and   Jos 10:12
moon in
s. still a while, that I may   1Sa 9:27
shew
now *s. still* that I may reason   1Sa 12:7
with you
then we will *s. still* in our   1Sa 14:9
place
s. still and consider works of   Job 37:14
God
have escaped sword *s.* not   Jer 51:50
still
eunuch commanded chariot   Ac 8:38
to *s. still*

STAND STRONG

hast made mountain to *s.*   Ps 30:7
strong

STAND THERE

that they may *s. there* with   Nu 11:16
thee
Levites who *s. there* before   De 18:7
Lord
and say to the poor, *S.* thou   Jas 2:3
there

STAND TOGETHER

let us *s. together*, who is mine Isa 50:8
adversary

STAND UP

s. up and bless God for ever   Ne 9:5
I *s. up*, and thou regardest   Job 30:20
me not
set thy words in order before   Job 33:5
me, *s. up*
take hold of shield, *s. up* for   Ps 35:2
my help
who will *s. up* for me against   Ps 94:16
workers
with child that shall *s. up* in   Ec 4:15
his stead
the groves and images shall   Isa 27:9
not *s. up*
let them *s. up* yet they shall   Isa 44:11
fear
let the monthly   Isa 47:13
prognosticators *s. up*
when I call to them, they *s.*   Isa 48:13
up together
awake, awake, *s. up* O   Isa 51:17
Jerusalem
nor their trees *s. up* in their   Eze 31:14
height
four kingdoms *s. up* out of   Da 8:22
nation
a king of fierce countenance   Da 8:23
shall *s. up*
he shall *s. up* against prince   Da 8:25
of princes
there shall *s. up* three kings in Da 11:2
Persia
a mighty king shall *s. up* and   Da 11:3;
rule   11:4
out of a branch of her roots   Da 11:7
shall one *s. up*
many shall *s. up* against king   Da 11:14
of the south
then shall *s. up* in his estate   Da 11:20
a raiser of taxes
and in his estate shall *s. up* a   Da 11:21
vile person
and at that time shall Michael Da 12:1
s. up
Peter said, *S. up*; I myself   Ac 10:26
also am a man

STAND UPON

Lord said, Thou shalt *s. upon* Ex 33:21
a rock
these shall *s. upon* mount   De 27:12
Gerizim
these shall *s. upon* mount   De 27:13
Ebal to curse
and they shall *s. upon* an   Jos 3:13
heap
Saul said, *S. upon* me, slay me 2Sa 1:9
s. upon the mount before   1Ki 19:11
the Lord
son of man, *s. upon* thy feet   Eze 2:1;
   Ac 26:16
the pilots of the sea shall *s.*   Eze 27:29
upon the land
ye *s. upon* sword, ye work   Eze 33:26
abominations
fishes shall *s. upon* it from   Eze 47:10
En-gedi to
and made *s. upon* the feet as   Da 7:4
a man
I will *s. upon* my watch, set   Hab 2:1
me on
flesh consume, while *s. upon*   Zec 14:12
feet
angel I saw *s. upon* sea, lifted Re 10:5
up hand

STAND UPRIGHT

but we are risen and *s. upright* Ps 20:8
Daniel, understand words, *s.*   Da 10:11
upright
said to cripple, *S. upright* on   Ac 14:10
feet

STAND *WITH*

names of men that shall *s.* with   Nu 1:5
you

STAND *WITHOUT*

and we are not able to *s.*   Ezr 10:13
without
s. without desiring to speak   M't 12:47;
                                   Lu 8:20
ye begin to *s. without* and to   Lu 13:25
knock

STANDARD

and every man by his own *s.*   Nu 1:52
of Israel shall pitch by his own   Nu 2:2
s.
they of the *s.* of the camp of   Nu 2:3
Judah
be the *s.* of the camp of   Nu 2:10
Reuben
be the *s.* of the camp of   Nu 2:18
Ephraim
The *s.* of the camp of Dan   Nu 2:25
shall be
went the *s.* of the camp of   Nu 10:14
Judah
And the *s.* of the camp of   Nu 10:18
Reuben
the *s.* of the camp of   Nu 10:22
Ephraim
And the *s.* of the camp of   Nu 10:25
Dan
and set up my *s.* to the   Isa 49:22
people
I will raise high my signal   Isa 49:22
(B)(R)
set up my ensign (E)   Isa 49:22
Spirit of the Lord shall lift   Isa 59:19
up a *s.*
stones; lift up a *s.* for the   Isa 62:10
people
lift up a banner (B)   Isa 62:10
lift up an ensign for the   Isa 62:10
peoples (E)(R)
Set up the *s.* toward Zion: Jer 4:6
retire
How long shall I see the *s.*   Jer 4:21
how long must I see the flag   Jer 4:21
(A)
see the war signals (B)   Jer 4:21
and publish, and set up a *s*   Jer 50:2
set up a signal (A)   Jer 50:2
set up a banner (R)   Jer 50:2
Set *s.* upon the walls of   Jer 51:12
Babylon
Set ye up a *s.* in the land,   Jer 51:27
blow the

STANDARDBEARER

shall be as when a *s.* fainteth   Isa 10:18
as a sick man wasting away   Isa 10:18
(B)(R)

STANDARDS

every man in his place by   Nu 2:17
their *s.*
shall go hindmost with their *s.*   Nu 2:31
so they pitched by their *s.* and   Nu 2:34
you judge by human *s.*   Joh 8:16
(B)(P)
you judge by worldly *s.* (N)   Joh 8:16
s. of teaching (A)(B)(R)   Ro 6:17
fall below your *s.* (N)   1Co 6:7

STANDEST

wherefore *s.* thou without?   Ge 24:31
for I
the place whereon thou is   Ex 3:5;
holy   Jos 5:15
Why *s.* thou afar off, O Lord?   Ps 10:1
why
for the place where thou is   Ac 7:33
holy
broken off, and thou *s.* by   Ro 11:20
faith

STANDETH

and that thy cloud *s.* over   Nu 14:14
them
son of Nun, which *s.* before   De 1:38
thee
that *s.* to minister there   De 17:12
before the

him that *s.* here with us this   De 29:15
day
pillars hereupon the house   J'g 16:26
s.
Behold, Haman *s.* in the court   Es 6:5
gallows *s.* in the house of   Es 7:9
Haman
nor *s.* in the way of sinners, nor   Ps 1:1
My foot *s.* in an even place;   Ps 26:12
in the
The counsel of the Lord *s.*   Ps 33:11
for ever
God *s.* in the congregation of   Ps 82:1
but my heart *s.* in awe of   Ps 119:161
thy word
She *s.* in the top of high places,   Pr 8:2
by
he *s.* behind our wall, he looketh   Ca 2:9
The Lord *s.* up to plead   Isa 3:13
and *s.* to judge the people   Isa 3:13
and set him in his place, and   Isa 46:7
he *s.*
backward and justice *s.* afar   Isa 59:14
off
prince which *s.* for the children   Da 12:1
broken, nor feed that that *s.*   Zec 11:16
still
but there *s.* one among you   Joh 1:26
which *s.* and heareth him   Joh 3:29
to his own master he *s.* or   Ro 14:4
falleth
he that *s.* stedfast in his   1Co 7:37
heart
I will eat no flesh while the   1Co 8:13
world *s.*
let him that thinketh he *s.*   1Co 10:12
take
the foundation of God *s.* sure   2Ti 2:19
every priest *s.* daily   Heb 10:11
ministering
behold, the judge *s.* before the   Jas 5:9
door
the angel which *s.* upon the   Re 10:8
sea and

STANDING

stacks of corn, or the *s.* corn   Ex 22:6
tabernacle of shittim wood *s.*   Ex 26:15
tabernacle of shittim wood, *s.*   Ex 36:20
neither rear you up a *s.* image   Le 26:1
angel of the Lord *s.* in the   Nu 22:23;
way   22:31
When thou comest into the *s.*   De 23:25
corn
sickle unto thy neighbour's *s.*   De 23:25
corn
into the *s.* corn of the   J'g 15:5
Philistines
the shocks, and also the *s.*   J'g 15:5
corn
Samuel *s.* as appointed over   1Sa 19:20
them
his servants were *s.* about   1Sa 22:6
him
and the lion *s.* by the   1Ki 13:25
carcase
ass and the lion *s.* by the   1Ki 13:28
carcase
and all the host of heaven *s.*   1Ki 22:19
by him
place, and two lions *s.* by the   2Ch 9:18
stays
the host of heaven *s.* on his   2Ch 18:18
right
Esther the queen *s.* in the court   Es 5:2
deep mire, where there is no   Ps 69:2
s.
the wilderness into a *s.* water   Ps 107:35
turned the rock into a *s.*   Ps 114:8
water
I had seen *s.* before the river   Da 8:6
I saw the Lord *s.* upon the   Am 9:1
altar
he shall receive of you his *s.*   Mic 1:11
thy *s.* images out of the   Mic 5:13
midst of
the high priest *s.* before the   Zec 3:1
angel
Satan *s.* at his right hand to   Zec 3:1
resist
from *s.* before the Lord of all   Zec 6:5
to pray *s.* in the synagogues   M't 6:5
There be some *s.* here,   M't 16:28
which shall
others *s.* idle in the   M't 20:3
marketplace
went out, and found others *s.*   M't 20:6
idle
and *s.* without, sent unto him   M'k 3:31

desolation *s.* where it   M'k 13:14
ought not
s. on the right side of the altar   Lu 1:11
And saw two ships *s.* by the   Lu 5:2
lake
there be some *s.* here, which   Lu 9:27
shall
publican, *s.* afar off, would   Lu 18:13
not lift
and the woman *s.* in the midst   Joh 8:9
disciple *s.* by, whom he   Joh 19:26
loved
herself back, and saw Jesus   Joh 20:14
s.
Peter, *s.* up with the eleven,   Ac 2:14
lifted
the man which was healed *s.*   Ac 4:14
with
keepers *s.* without before the   Ac 5:23
doors
put in prison are *s.* in the   Ac 5:25
temple
Jesus *s.* on the right hand of   Ac 7:55
God
Son of man *s.* on the right   Ac 7:56
hand of
I also was *s.* by, and   Ac 22:20
consenting
voice, that I cried *s.* among   Ac 24:21
them
the first tabernacle was yet *s.*   Heb 9:8
earth *s.* out of the water and   2Pe 3:5
four angels *s.* on the four   Re 7:1
corners
two candlesticks *s.* before the   Re 11:4
God
S. afar off for fear of her   Re 18:10
torment
And I saw an angel *s.* in the   Re 19:17
sun

STANDPOINT

estimated from spiritual *s.* (B)   1Co 2:14

STANDS

Lord *s.* up to hold court   Isa 3:13
(A)(B)(E)(R)

STANDSTILL

plague at a *s.* (A)   Le 13:5; 13:37
kept *s.* there (S)   2Sa 20:12
will purchase a good *s.* (S)   1Ti 3:13

STANK

and the river *s.* and the   Ex 7:21
Egyptians
the river became foul smelling   Ex 7:21
(A)
the Nile stunk (B)   Ex 7:21
the river became foul (E)(R)   Ex 7:21
upon heaps: and the land *s.*   Ex 8:14
the land reeked (B)   Ex 8:14
morning, and it bred worms,   Ex 16:20
and *s.*
grew wormy and rancid (B)   Ex 16:20
bred worms and became foul   Ex 16:20
(E)(R)
saw that they *s.* before   2Sa 10:6
David, the
made themselves obnoxious   2Sa 10:6
and disgusting to (A)
how seriously they   2Sa 10:6
antagonized David (B)
they were become odious to   2Sa 10:6
David (E)(R)

STAR

shall come a *S.* out of Jacob   Nu 24:17
your images, the *s.* of your   Am 5:26
god
for we have seen his *s.* in the   M't 2:2
east
what time the *s.* appeared   M't 2:7
the *s.* which they saw in the   M't 2:9
east
When they saw the *s.* they   M't 2:10
rejoiced
and the *s.* of your god   Ac 7:43
Remphan
for one *s.* differeth from   1Co 15:41
another
differeth from another *s.* in   1Co 15:41
glory
the day *s.* arise in your hearts   2Pe 1:19
And I will give him the   Re 2:28
morning *s.*

there fell a great *s.* from heaven   *Re 8:10*
name of the *s.* is called Wormwood   *Re 8:11*
I saw a *s.* fall from heaven unto the   *Re 9:1*
and the bright and morning *s.*   *Re 22:16*

STARE

bones: they look and *s.* upon me   *Ps 22:17*

STARGAZERS

now the astrologers, the *s.*   *Isa 47:13*

STARS

the night: he made the *s.* also   *Ge 1:16*
now toward heaven, and tell the *s.*   *Ge 15:5*
thy seed as the *s.* of the heaven   *Ge 22:17*
seed to multiply as the *s.* of heaven   *Ge 26:4*
eleven *s.* made obeisance to me   *Ge 37:9*
your seed as the *s.* of heaven   *Ex 32:13*
as the *s.* of heaven for multitude   *De 1:10*
the sun, and the moon, and the *s.*   *De 4:19*
made these as the *s.* of heaven   *De 10:22*
ye were as the *s.* of heaven   *De 28:62*
the *s.* in their courses fought   *J'g 5:20*
Israel like to the *s.* of the heavens   *1Ch 27:23*
the morning till the *s.* appeared   *Ne 4:21*
thou as the *s.* of heaven, and   *Ne 9:23*
Let the *s.* of the twilight be dark   *Job 3:9*
it riseth not; and sealeth up the *s.*   *Job 9:7*
and behold the height of the *s.* how   *Job 22:12*
yea, the *s.* are not pure in his sight   *Job 25:5*
When the morning *s.* sang together   *Job 38:7*
the moon and the *s.* which thou   *Ps 8:3*
The moon and *s.* to rule by night   *Ps 136:9*
He telleth the number of the *s.*   *Ps 147:4*
moon: praise him, all ye *s.* of light   *Ps 148:3*
moon, or the *s.* be not darkened   *Ec 12:2*
For the *s.* of heaven and the   *Isa 13:10*
will exalt my throne above the *s.*   *Isa 14:13*
and of the *s.* for a light by night   *Jer 31:35*
and make the *s.* thereof dark   *Eze 32:7*
host and of the *s.* to the ground   *Da 8:10*
as the *s.* for ever and ever   *Da 12:3*
the *s.* shall withdraw their shining   *Joe 2:10; 3:15*
Seek him that maketh the seven *s.*   *Am 5:8*
made cluster of stars called Pleiades (A)   *Am 5:8*
who makes Pleiades (B)(E)(R)   *Am 5:8*
thou set thy nest among the *s.*   *Ob 4*
merchants above the *s.* of heaven   *Na 3:16*
and the *s.* shall fall from heaven   *M't 24:29*
And the *s.* of heaven shall fall, and   *M'k 13:25*
sun, and in the moon, and in the *s.*   *Lu 21:25*
sun nor *s.* in many days appeared   *Ac 27:20*
moon, and another glory of the *s.*   *1Co 15:41*
as the *s.* of the sky in multitude   *Heb 11:12*
wandering *s.* to whom is reserved   *Jude 13*
he had in his right hand seven *s.*   *Re 1:16*
The mystery of the seven *s.* which   *Re 1:20*
seven *s.* are the angels of the seven   *Re 1:20*

he that holdeth the seven *s.* in his   *Re 2:1*
Spirits of God, and the seven *s.*   *Re 3:1*
the *s.* of heaven fell unto the earth   *Re 6:13*
moon, and the third part of the *s.*   *Re 8:12*
upon her head a crown of twelve *s.*   *Re 12:1*
the third part of the *s.* of heaven   *Re 12:4*

STARTLE

s. many nations (A)(R)   *Isa 52:15*

STARTLED

that the man was *s.* (S)   *Ru 3:8*

STARVE

he will *s.* on the spot (B)   *Jer 38:9*

STARVING

kill all of us by *s.* (B)   *Ex 16:3*
I am *s.* (B)(N)   *Lu 15:17*

STATE

The man asked us straitly of our *s.*   *Ge 43:7*
they set the house of God in his *s.*   *2Ch 24:13*
set up house of God according to its design (A)   *2Ch 24:13*
restored house of God to its proper condition (B)(R)   *2Ch 24:13*
according to the *s.* of the king   *Es 1:7*
according to liberality of the king (A)   *Es 1:7*
in keeping with the king's generosity (B)   *Es 1:7*
according to the bounty of the king (E)(R)   *Es 1:7*
according to the *s.* of the king   *Es 2:18*
gifts in keeping with generosity of the king (A)   *Es 2:18*
awarded donations with regal liberality (B)   *Es 2:18*
according to the bounty of the king (E)   *Es 2:18*
gave gifts with royal liberality (R)   *Es 2:18*
at his best *s.* is altogether vanity   *Ps 39:5*
to know the *s.* of thy flocks   *Pr 27:23*
the *s.* thereof shall be prolonged   *Pr 28:2*
and from thy *s.* shall he pull thee   *Isa 22:19*
from your station be pulled down (A)(E)(R)   *Isa 22:19*
pull you down from your position (B)   *Isa 22:19*
the last *s.* of that man is worse than   *M't 12:45*
last condition of that man becomes worse (A)(B)   *M't 12:45*
the man's plight is worse (N)   *M't 12:45*
in a terrible *s.* (P)   *M't 15:22; 17:15*
the last *s.* of that man is worse than   *Lu 11:26*
comfort, when I know your *s.*   *Ph'p 2:19*
will naturally care for your *s.*   *Ph'p 2:20*
citizens of a new *s.* (A)   *Ph'p 3:20*
in whatsoever *s.* I am, therewith   *Ph'p 4:11*
my *s.* shall Tychicus declare   *Col 4:7*
he might know of your *s.* (S)   *Col 4:8*

STATELY

that are *s.* in their going (S)   *Pr 30:29*
satest upon a *s.* bed, and a table   *Eze 23:41*

STATES

first *s.* his case seems right (A)(B)(R)   *Pr 18:17*

STATION

set in my *s.* (A)   *Isa 21:8*
And I will drive thee from thy *s.*   *Isa 22:19*
pull you down from your position (B)   *Isa 22:19*

STATIONED

he *s.* in the chariot cities (S)   *2Ch 9:25*

STATUE

erect a *s.* (B)(P)   *Re 13:14;*
    13:15; 14:9, 11; 15:2; 16:2; 19:20; 20:4
s. of the beast (A)   *Re 13:15;*
    14:9; 15:2; 19:20; 20:4

STATURE

we saw in it are men of a great *s.*   *Nu 13:32*
or on the height of his *s.*; because   *1Sa 16:7*
where was a man of great *s.* that   *2Sa 21:20*
an Egyptian, a man of great *s.*   *1Ch 11:23*
Gath, where was a man of great *s.*   *1Ch 20:6*
his *s.* like Lebanon (B)   *Ca 5:15*
This thy *s.* is like to a palm tree   *Ca 7:7*
high ones of *s.* shall be hewn down   *Isa 10:33*
and of the Sabeans, men of *s.*   *Isa 45:14*
the head of every *s.* to hunt souls   *Eze 13:18*
became a spreading vine of low *s.*   *Eze 17:6*
her *s.* was exalted among the thick   *Eze 19:11*
shadowing shroud of an high *s.*   *Eze 31:3*
can add one cubit unto his *s.*   *M't 6:27*
Jesus increased in wisdom and *s.*   *Lu 2:52*
thought can add to his *s.* one cubit   *Lu 12:25*
press, because he was little of *s.*   *Lu 19:3*
unto the measure of the *s.* of   *Eph 4:13*

STATUS

might attain *s.* of sons (N)   *Ga 4:5*

STATUTE

Joseph made it a *s.* (E)(R)   *Ge 47:26*
there he made for them a *s.*   *Ex 15:25*
it shall be a *s.* for ever   *Ex 27:21;*
    28:43; 29:28; 30:21; Le 6:18, 22; 7:34,
    36; 10:9 15; 16:29, 31, 34; 17:7; 23:14,
    21, 41; 24:3; Nu 18:11, 19, 23; 19:10
an everlasting institution (B)   *Ex 27:21*
shall be a *s.* for ever   *Ex 28:43*
a perpetual ordinance (B)   *Ex 28:43;*
    Le 3:17; 10:15; 16:29, 31, 34; 23:14, 41;
    Da 6:7
by a *s.* for ever   *Ex 29:28*
a perpetual obligation (B)   *Ex 29:28*
it shall be a *s.* for ever   *Le 6:18*
an everlasting decree (B)   *Le 6:18*
It shall be a *s.* for ever   *Le 24:3*
an everlasting regulation (B)   *Le 24:3;*
    Nu 19:21
the *s.* of the passover one *s.*   *Nu 9:14*
(S)
shall be a perpetual *s.*   *Nu 19:21;*
    Le 3:17; 24:9
children of Israel a *s.* of judgment   *Nu 27:11*
things shall be for a *s.* of judgment   *Nu 35:29*
shape of any *s.* (B)   *De 4:16*
set them a *s.* and an ordinance in   *Jos 24:25*
he made it a *s.* and an ordinance   *1Sa 30:25*
defined for Jacob a *s.* (B)(E)(R)   *1Ch 16:17*
For this was a *s.* for Israel   *Ps 81:4*
the *s.* he gave them (A)(E)(R)   *Ps 99:7*
confirmed to Jacob by a *s.* (E)(R)   *Ps 105:10*
together to establish a royal *s.*   *Da 6:7*
no decree nor *s.* which the king   *Da 6:15*

STATUTES

I do make them know *s.* of God   *Ex 18:16*
rules and laws (B)   *Ex 18:16*

teach them *s*. (E)(R)	Ex 18:20	changed *my s*. more than	Eze 5:6
that ye may teach Israel all	Le 10:11	nations	
the *s*.		Lord because ye have not	Eze 5:7
ordinances (B)	Le 10:11	walked in *my s*.	
walk in their *s*. (A)(E)(R)	Le 18:3	they may walk in *my s*. and	Eze 11:20
keep my *s*. (S)	Le 18:4	do them	
all the *s*. of the (A)(E)(R)	Nu 9:12	when the sun hath kept all	Eze 18:19
there are *s*. Lord commanded	Nu 30:16	*my s*.	
regulations (B)	Nu 30:16; 2Ch 33:8	and I will cause you to walk	Eze 36:27
which shall hear all these *s*.	De 4:6	in *my s*.	
laws (B)	De 4:6	*my s*. did take hold of your	Zec 1:6
the Lord commanded to do all	De 6:24	fathers	
these *s*.		my decrees (B)	Zec 1:6
requirements (B)	De 6:24		
thou shalt observe and do	De 16:12		
these *s*.		**THY STATUTES**	
that he may learn to keep	De 17:19	give him a perfect heart to	1Ch 29:19
these *s*. to do		keep *my s*.	
walking in *s*. of David his	1Ki 3:3	teach me *thy s*.	Ps 119:12;
father			119:26, 33, 64, 68, 124, 135
walked in *s*. of the heathen	2Ki 17:8; 17:19	I will delight myself in *thy s*.	Ps 119:16
customs of the heathen	2Ki 17:8	but thy servant did meditate	Ps 119:23
(A)(B)		in *thy s*.	
neither do they after their *s*.	2Ki 17:34	and I will meditate in *thy s*.	Ps 119:48
or ordinances		*thy s*. been my songs in my	Ps 119:54
they follow *s*. (B)	2Ki 17:34;	pilgrimage	
	2Ki 17:37	I have been afflicted, that I	Ps 119:71
the *s*. he wrote, ye shall		might learn *thy s*.	
observe to do		let my heart be sound in *thy*	Ps 119:80
that they take heed to do the	2Ch 33:8	*s*.	
s.		I am like a bottle, I do not	Ps 119:83
thou commandest them *s*. and	Ne 9:14	forget *thy s*.	
laws		I inclined my heart to	Ps 119:112
s. of Lord are right, rejoicing	Ps 19:8	perform *thy s*. alway	
heart		I will have respect to *thy s*.	Ps 119:117
the precepts of the Lord	Ps 19:8	continually	
(A)(B)		trodden down them that err	Ps 119:118
injunctions and *s*. he gave (B)	Ps 99:7	from *thy s*.	
disregarded the *s*.	Isa 24:5	for the wicked seek not *thy*	Ps 119:155
(A)(B)(E)(R)		*s*.	
I gave them *s*. that were not	Eze 20:25	praise, when thou hast	Ps 119:171
good		taught *thy s*.	
if the wicked walk in the *s*.	Eze 33:15		
of life		**STAVES**	
s. of Omri are kept and	Mic 6:16	make *s*. of shittim-wood and	Ex 25:13;
works of Ahab		overlay with gold	25:28; 27:6; 30:5;
turned away from my *s*.	Mal 3:7		37:4
(B)(R)		poles (A)(B)(R)	Ex 25:13;
			25:14; 37:15; 40:20; Nu 4:6; 1Ch 15:15
HIS STATUTES		put *s*. into rings	Ex 25:14;
if thou wilt keep all *his s*.	Ex 15:26;		25:15; 27:7; 37:5; 38:7
	De 6:17; 10:13; 11:1	made *s*. of shittim-wood	Ex 37:15;
injunctions (B)	Ex 15:26		37:28; 38:5
shalt do *his s*. which I	De 27:10	set *s*. on ark and put	Ex 40:20
command		mercy seat	
if thou wilt not observe to do	De 28:15	they shall put in *s*. thereof	Nu 4:6;
his s.			4:8, 11, 14
his s. I did not depart from	2Sa 22:23	nobles of the people digged	Nu 21:18
them		with their *s*.	
let your hearts be perfect to	1Ki 8:61	hallowed with scepter and *s*.	Nu 21:18
walk in *his s*.		(A)(B)(E)	
they rejected *his s*. and his	2Ki 17:15	am I a dog, that comest to	1Sa 17:43
covenant		me with *s*.	
made a covenant to keep *his*	2Ki 23:3;	sticks (A)(B)(R)	1Sa 17:43
s.	2Ch 34:31	he took three *s*. and thrust	2Sa 18:14
to Ezra even a scribe of *his s*.	Ezr 7:11	them (S)	
to Israel		the Levites bare the ark	1Ch 15:15
I did not put away *his s*. from	Ps 18:22	with *s*.	
me		thou didst strike through	Hab 3:14
that they might observe *his*	Ps 105:45	with his *s*.	
s. and laws		arrows (A)	Hab 3:14
nor walked in his law, nor in	Jer 44:23	shafts (B)(R)	Hab 3:14
his s.		I took two *s*. I fed the flock	Zec 11:7
		staffs (A)(R)	Zec 11:7
MY STATUTES		sticks (B)	Zec 11:7
Abraham kept *my s*. and	Ge 26:5	nor take two coats nor *s*.	M't 10:10;
laws			Lu 9:3
my orders, my rules (B)	Ge 26:5	staff (A)(B)(P)(R)	M't 10:10
Ye shall therefore keep	Le 18:5;	stick (N)	M't 10:10
my s.	18:26; 19:19	Judas and a great multitude	M't 26:47;
my ordinances (B)	Le 18:5; 25:18	with *s*. from chief priests	M'k 14:43
ye shall do *my s*.	Le 25:18	clubs (A)(B)	M't 26:47; 26:55
if ye walk in *my s*.	Le 26:3	cudgels (N)	M't 26:47; 26:55
if ye despise *my s*.	Le 26:15	we come as against thief	M't 26:55;
they abhorred *my s*.	Le 26:43	with swords and *s*.	M'k 14:48; Lu 22:52
if thou wilt keep *my s*. as	1Ki 3:14		
David did		**STAY**	
will not keep *my s*.	1Ki 9:6	to *s*. awhile (B)	Ge 12:10
hast not kept *my s*.	1Ki 11:11	stay (B)	Ge 19:12;
he kept *my s*.	1Ki 11:34	27:44; 20:27; Le 14:8; Nu 22:19;	
keep *my s*.	2Ki 17:13	J'g 6:18; 19:6, 9, 10; 1Sa 1:23; 14:9;	
if ye turn and forsake *my s*.	2Ch 7:19	2Sa 10:5; 11:12; 24:2, 4, 6; Ps 101:7;	
my laws (B)	2Ch 7:19	M't 26:38; M'k 14:34; Lu 24:29;	
what hast thou to do to	Ps 50:16	Joh 4:40; Ac 10:48; 28:14; 1Co 16:7	
declare *my s*.		neither *s*. thou in all the	Ge 19:17
if they break *my s*. keep not	Ps 89:31	plain	
commandments		stay (B)	Ge 27:44;
neither have they walked in	Jer 44:10	J'g 6:18; 2Sa 19:7; 2Ki 14:10; Lu 24:29,	
my s.		49; Joh 4:40; Ac 18:20; 28:14; 1Co 16:8	

stay (B)	Ex 2:21;
J'g 17:10; 1Ki 17:9; Ps 15:1	
let you go, and ye shall *s*. no	Ex 9:28
longer	
the plague in his sight be at a	Le 13:5
s.	
at a standstill (A)	Le 13:5; 13:37
arrested (B)	Le 13:5
checked (R)	Le 13:5; 13:37
if the bright spot *s*. in his	Le 13:23
place	
does not spread (A)	Le 13:23
remain (B)	Le 13:23
if the scall be in his sight at	Le 13:37
a *s*.	
inactive (B)	Le 13:37
stay (A)	Le 14:8;
J'g 19:6, 10; 2Ki 14:10; 1Ch 19:5;	
M't 26:38; Joh 21:22, 23; Ac 10:48;	
	28:14
s. away from holy things (A)	Le 22:2
And *s*. ye not, but pursue	Jos 10:19
after you	
stand (B)	Jos 10:19
would ye *s*. for them from	Ru 1:13
having	
wait (B)	Ru 1:13; 1Sa 15:16
S. and I will tell thee what	1Sa 15:16
stop (R)	1Sa 15:16
the lad, Make speed, haste, *s*.	1Sa 20:38
not	
delay (B)	1Sa 20:38
calamity: but the Lord was	2Sa 22:19
my *s*.	
support (B)	2Sa 22:19;
	Ps 18:18; Isa 3:1
It is enough: *s*. now thine	2Sa 24:16
hand	
relaxed (B)	2Sa 24:16; 1Ch 21:15
It is enough, *s*. now thine	1Ch 21:15
hand	
will not *s*. them when his	Job 37:4
voice	
restrains not (A)(B)(E)(R)	Job 37:4
who can *s*. the bottles of	Job 38:37
heaven	
overturn (B)	Job 38:37
pour out (E)	Job 38:37
til the waterskins of the	Job 38:37
heavens (R)	
calamity: but the Lord was	Ps 18:18
my *s*.	
flee to the pit; let no man *s*.	Pr 28:17
him	
stop (A)	Pr 28:17; Isa 29:9
help (B)(R)	Pr 28:17
S. me with flagons, comfort me	Ca 2:5
Sustain (A)(B)(R)	Ca 2:5
from Judah the *s*.; and the staff	Isa 3:1
the staff, the whole *s*. of bread	Isa 3:1
bread, and the whole *s*. of	Isa 3:1
water	
no more *s*. upon him that	Isa 10:20
smote	
lean upon (A)(B)(E)(R)	Isa 10:20
shall *s*. upon the Lord, the	Isa 10:20
Holy	
are the *s*. of the tribes	Isa 19:13
thereof	
cornerstones (A)(B)(E)(R)	Isa 19:13
S. yourselves and wonder;	Isa 29:9
cry	
confuse (B)	Isa 29:9;
tarry (E)	Isa 29:9; Ho 13:13
stupify (R)	Isa 29:9
and perverseness, and *s*.	Isa 30:12
thereon	
rely on (A)(B)(E)(R)	Isa 30:12;
	31:1; 50:10
s. on horses, and trust in	Isa 31:1
chariots	
and *s*. upon the God of	Isa 48:2
Israel	
depend on (A)(B)	Isa 48:2
of the Lord, and *s*. upon his	Isa 50:10
God	
toward Zion: retire *s*. not	Jer 4:6
do not remain (B)	Jer 4:6
with forbearing, and I could	Jer 20:9
not *s*.	
cannot contain it longer (A)	Jer 20:9
cannot continue (B)	Jer 20:9
none can *s*. his hand, or	Da 4:35
say unto	
he should not *s*. long in the	Ho 13:13
place	
stay (P)	M't 26:38;
M'k 14:34; Lu 24:29, 49; Joh 4:40;	
21:22; Ac 10:48; 18:20; 28:14; 1Co 16:8	

stay (N)   *Lu 24:29;*
24:49; Joh 4:40; Ac 10:48; 18:20; 28:14
s. with you forever (B)   *Joh 14:16*

STAYED

And he s. yet other seven days   *Ge 8:10;*
                                  8:12
with Laban, and s. there until   *Ge 32:4*
now
your flocks, and your herds   *Ex 10:24*
be s.
leave behind (A)(R)   *Ex 10:24*
Aaron and Hur s. up his   *Ex 17:12*
hands
held up (A)(B)(R)   *Ex 17:12*
and the plague was s.   *Nu 16:48; 16:50*
checked (B)   *Nu 16:48; Ps 106:30*
stopped (R)   *Nu 16:48*
plague was s. from the   *Nu 25:8*
children of
came to a stop (B)   *Nu 25:8*
I s. in the mount, according   *De 10:10*
to the
the sun stood still, and the   *Jos 10:13*
moon s.
stood still (B)   *Jos 10:13*
And when thou hast s. three   *1Sa 20:19*
days
David s. his servants with   *1Sa 24:7*
these
checked (A)   *1Sa 24:7*
restrained (B)   *1Sa 24:7;*
 2Sa 24:21; 1Ch 21:22; Eze 31:15
persuaded (R)   *1Sa 24:7*
those that were left behind s.   *1Sa 30:9*
and Ahimaaz s. by En-rogel   *2Sa 17:17*
s. faithfully with (A)   *2Sa 20:2*
plague may be s. from the   *2Sa 24:21*
people
and the plague was s. from   *2Sa 24:25*
Israel
the king was s. up in his   *1Ki 22:35*
chariot
not a vessel more. And the oil   *2Ki 4:6*
s.
stopped (A)(R)   *2Ki 4:6; 13:18*
ceased flowing (B)   *2Ki 4:6*
s. in the land (B)   *2Ki 8:2*
And he smote thrice, and s.   *2Ki 13:18*
stopped (B)   *2Ki 13:18*
back, and s. not there in the   *2Ki 15:20*
land
plague may be s. from the   *1Ch 21:22*
people
averted (A)(R)   *1Ch 21:22*
king s. himself up in his   *2Ch 18:34*
chariot
here shall thy proud waves   *Job 38:11*
be s.
and so the plague was s.   *Ps 106:30*
peace, whose mind is s. on   *Isa 26:3*
thee
moment, and no hands s. on   *La 4:6*
her
and the great waters were s.   *Eze 31:15*
the heaven over you is s.   *Hag 1:10*
from dew
and the earth is s. from her   *Hag 1:10*
fruit
withheld (B)(R)   *Hag 1:10*
s. him, that he should not   *Lu 4:42*
depart
keep him from leaving (B)   *Lu 4:42*
prevent him from leaving (P)   *Lu 4:42*
he himself s. in Asia for a   *Ac 19:22*
season

STAYETH

he s. his rough wind in the   *Isa 27:8*
day of

STAYS

there were s. on either side   *1Ki 10:19*
arm rests (A)(R)   *1Ki 10:19*
arms (B)   *1Ki 10:19*
and two lions stood beside   *1Ki 10:19*
the s.
s. on each side of the sitting   *2Ch 9:18*
place
arms (A)(B)   *2Ch 9:18*
arm rests (R)   *2Ch 9:18*
and two lions standing by the   *2Ch 9:18*
s.

STEAD

burnt offering in the s. of his   *Ge 22:13*
son

instead (A)(B)(R)   *Ge 22:13*
Am I in God's s. who hath   *Ge 30:2*
withheld
place (B)   *Ge 30:2;*
36:35, 36; Le 6:22; Nu 32:14; Jos 5:7;
1Ki 1:30, 35; 11:43; 14:31; 15:8, 24, 28;
16:6, 10; 22:40, 50; 2Ki 1:17; 3:27; 8:24;
10:35; 12:21; 13:9, 24; 14:16, 29; 15:7,
10, 14, 22, 30, 38; 16:20; 19:37; 20:21;
21:18, 24, 26; 23:30; 24:6, 17; 2Ch 1:8;
12:16; 14:1; 17:1; 21:1; 22:1; 24:27;
27:9; 28:27; 32:33; 3320, 25; 36:1, 8;
          Job 16:4; 34:24; Pr 11:8
died, and Jobad reigned   *Ge 36:33*
in his s.
the Husham reigned in his   *Ge 36:34*
s.
succeeded (B)   *Ge 36:34;*
      36:38; De 10:6; 1Ch 1:44, 50
died, and Hadad reigned in   *Ge 36:35*
his s.
and Samlah reigned in his s.   *Ge 36:36*
succeeded (A)   *Ge 36:36*
died, and Saul reigned in   *Ge 36:37*
his s.
Baal-hanan reigned in his s.   *Ge 36:38*
died, and Hadar reigned in   *Ge 36:39*
his s.
And that son that is priest in   *Ex 29:30*
his s.
succeeds (B)   *Ex 29:30; 2Sa 10:1*
place (R)   *Ex 29:30;*
 Le 16:32; 2Sa 16:8; Job 16:4; 34:24
his sons that is anointed in his   *Le 6:22*
s.
succeed (R)   *Le 6:22*
the priest's office in his   *Le 16:32*
father's s.
ye are risen up in your   *Nu 32:14*
father's s.
before them, and dwelt in   *De 2:12*
their s.
and dwelt in their s. even unto   *De 2:22*
this
them, and dwelt in their s.   *De 2:23*
in the priest's office in his s.   *De 10:6*
whom he raised up in their s.   *Jos 5:7*
Hanun his son reigned in his   *2Sa 10:1*
s.
Saul, in whose s. thou hast   *2Sa 16:8*
reigned
sha1l sit upon my throne in   *1Ki 1:30*
my s.
for he shall be king in my s.   *1Ki 1:35*
stead (S)   *1Ki 1:35;*
   5:1, 5; 8:20; 19:16; 2Ki 15:25;
             23:34; 2Ch 6:10
Rehoboam his son reigned   *1Ki 11:43*
in his s.
Rehoboam made in their s.   *1Ki 14:27*
brasen
Abijam his son reigned in   *1Ki 14:31*
his s.
and Asa his son reigned in   *1Ki 15:8*
his s.
Jehoshaphat reigned in his   *1Ki 15:24*
s.
Baasha reigned in his s.   *1Ki 15:28*
and Elah his son reigned in   *1Ki 16:6*
his s.
And Zimri reigned in   *1Ki 16:10*
his s.
Ahaziah his son reigned in   *1Ki 22:40*
his s.
Jehoram his son reigned in   *1Ki 22:50*
his s.
And Jehoram reigned in his   *2Ki 1:17*
s. in
that should have reigned in   *2Ki 3:27*
his s.
died: and Hazael reigned in   *2Ki 8:15*
his s.
Ahaziah his son reigned in   *2Ki 8:24*
his s.
Jehoahaz his son reigned in   *2Ki 10:35*
his s.
Amaziah his son reigned in   *2Ki 12:21*
his s.
and Joash his son reigned in   *2Ki 13:9*
his s.
Ben-hadad his son reigned   *2Ki 13:24*
in his s.
Jeroboam his son reigned in   *2Ki 14:16*
his s.
Zachariah his son reigned in   *2Ki 14:29*
his s.
Jotham his son reigned in his   *2Ki 15:7*
s.
And Shallum reigned in his   *2Ki 15:10*
s.

Menahem reigned in his s.   *2Ki 15:14*
Pekahiah his son reigned in   *2Ki 15:22*
s.
And Hoshea reigned in his   *2Ki 15:30*
s.
and Ahaz his son reigned in   *2Ki 15:38*
his s.
Hezekiah his son reigned in   *2Ki 16:20*
his s.
Esar-haddon reigned in his   *2Ki 19:37*
s.
Manasseh his son reigned in   *2Ki 20:21*
his s.
and Amon his son reigned in   *2Ki 21:18*
his s.
made Josiah his son king in   *2Ki 21:24*
his s.
Josiah his son reigned in his   *2Ki 21:26*
s.
made him king in his   *2Ki 23:30*
father's s.
Jehoiachin his son reigned   *2Ki 24:6*
in his s.
his father's brother king in   *2Ki 24:17*
his s.
dead, Jacob reigned in his   *1Ch 1:44*
s.
dead, Husham reigned in his   *1Ch 1:45*
s.
dead, Hadad reigned in his   *1Ch 1:46*
s.
dead, Samlah reigned in his   *1Ch 1:47*
s.
dead, Shaul reigned in his s.   *1Ch 1:48*
Baal-hanan reigned in his s.   *1Ch 1:49*
was dead, Hadad reigned in   *1Ch 1:50*
his s.
dwelt in their s. (S)   *1Ch 4:41*
died, and his son reigned in   *1Ch 19:1*
his s.
and hast made me to reign in   *2Ch 1:8*
his s.
and Abijah his son reigned   *2Ch 12:16*
in his s.
and Asa his son reigned in   *2Ch 14:1*
his s.
Jehoshaphat reigned in his   *2Ch 17:1*
s.
Jehoram his son reigned in   *2Ch 21:1*
his s.
made Ahaziah king in his s.   *2Ch 22:1*
Amaziah his son reigned in   *2Ch 24:27*
his s.
And Ahaz his son reigned in   *2Ch 27:9*
his s.
Hezekiah his son reigned in   *2Ch 28:27*
his s.
Manasseh his son reigned in   *2Ch 32:33*
his s.
and Amon his son reigned   *2Ch 33:20*
in his s.
made Josiah his son king in   *2Ch 33:25*
his s.
Jehoahaz, king in his   *2Ch 36:1*
father's s.
Jehoiachin his son reigned in   *2Ch 36:8*
his s.
if your soul were in my soul's   *Job 16:4*
s. I
according to thy wish in   *Job 33:6*
God's s.
number, and set others in   *Job 34:24*
their s.
and the wicked cometh in   *Pr 11:8*
instead (R)   *Pr 11:8; Jer 29:26*
Esar-haddon reigned in his   *Isa 37:38*
s.
thee priest in the s. of   *Jer 29:26*
Jehoiada
we pray you in Christ's s. be   *2Co 5:20*
ye
Christ's sake (B)   *2Co 5:20*
in Christ's name (N)   *2Co 5:20*
in behalf of Christ (R)   *2Co 5:20*
in thy s. he might have   *Ph'm 13*
ministered

STEADILY

s. the waters moved back (B)   *Ge 8:3*

STEADS

dwelt in their s. until the   *1Ch 5:22*
captivity
dwelt in their territory until   *1Ch 5:22*
(A)
dwelt in their place until (B)   *1Ch 5:22*
settled in enemies' former   *1Ch 5:22*
territory (R)

STEADY

his hands were s. until the Ex 17:12
going

STEAL

secretly, and s. away from Ge 31:27
me
cheat me, and did not tell me Ge 31:27
(A)(B)
should we s. out of thy lord's Ge 44:8
house
Thou shalt not s. Ex 20:15
If a man shall s. an ox, or a Ex 22:1
sheep
Ye shall not s. neither deal Le 19:11
falsely
Neither shalt thou s. De 5:19
as people being ashamed s. 2Sa 19:3
away
if he s. to satisfy his soul when Pr 6:30
he
or lest I be poor, and s. and Pr 30:9
take
Will ye s. murder, and commit Jer 7:9
that s. my words every one Jer 23:30
from his
thieves break through and s. M't 6:19
thieves do not break through M't 6:20
nor s.
s. his property (P) M't 12:29
Thou shalt not s. Thou shalt M't 19:18
not
come by night, and s. him M't 27:64
away
Do not kill, Do not s. Do M'k 10:19;
not bear Lu 18:20
The thief cometh not, but Joh 10:10
for to s.
a man should not s. dost thou Ro 2:21
s.
shalt not kill, Thou shalt not Ro 13:9
s.
Let him that stole s. no Eph 4:28
more: but
not s. by taking things of Tit 2:10
small value (A)

STEALETH

he that s. a man, and selleth Ex 21:16
him
tempest s. him away in the Job 27:20
night
for every one that s. shall be Zec 5:3
cut off

STEALING

If a man be found s. De 24:7
any of his
and lying, and killing, and s. Ho 4:2

STEALS

he s. (B) Eze 18:12

STEALTH

them by s. that day into the 2Sa 19:3
city
arrest Jesus by s. (B) M't 26:4
arrest him by s. (R) M'k 14:11

STEALTHILY

skirt of Saul's robe s. (S) 1Sa 24:4
crept in s. (A) Jude 4

STEDFAST

s. love (R) Ge 32:10;
   2Ch 6:42; Ps 106:7; 119:41; Jer 16:5
remained s. toward (S) 2Sa 20:2
yea, thou shalt be s. and Job 11:15
shalt not
shown his s. love (R) Ps 31:21
whose spirit was not s. with Ps 78:8
God
neither were they s. in his Ps 78:37
covenant
my heart is s. (R) Isa 57:7
is the living God, and s. for Da 6:26
ever
keep you s. (P) 1Co 1:8
he that standeth s. in his 1Co 7:37
heart

resolved in his heart (A) 1Co 7:37
firmly established in his heart 1Co 7:37
(B)
his mind stand firm (R) 1Co 7:37
my beloved brethren, be ye 1Co 15:58
s.
And our hope of you is s. 2Co 1:7
knowing
if the word spoken by angels Heb 2:2
was s.
word was authentic and Heb 2:2
proved sure (A)
message declared by angels Heb 2:2
was valid (B)
word spoken by angels had Heb 2:2
such force (N)
message given through angels Heb 2:2
proved authentic (P)
message spoken by angels held Heb 2:2
to be true (R)
of our confidence s. unto the Heb 3:14
end
firm and unshaken to the Heb 3:14
end (A)
hold first confidence firm to Heb 3:14
the end (B)(E)(N)
steadily maintain until the Heb 3:14
end (P)
maintain firmly until the end Heb 3:14
(R)
anchor of the soul, both sure Heb 6:19
and s.
anchor the soul safely and Heb 6:19
securely (R)
blessed who are s. Jas 5:11
(A)(B)(E)(P)(R)
Whom resist s. in the faith 1Pe 5:9
be firm in the faith 1Pe 5:9
(A)(B)(N)(P)(R)

STEDFASTLY

followed s. (R) 2Sa 20:2
she was s. minded to go with Ru 1:18
her
he settled his countenance s. 2Ki 8:11
stared steadily at him (A) 2Ki 8:11
fixed his gaze and stared at 2Ki 8:11
him (B)
s. set his face to go to Lu 9:51
Jerusalem
they looked s. toward heaven Ac 1:10
gazing intently into heaven Ac 1:10
(A)(B)
they continued s. in the Ac 2:42
apostles
looking s. on him, saw his Ac 6:15
face as
gazed intently at Stephen Ac 6:15
(A)(B)
looked up s. into heaven, and Ac 7:55
saw
gazed into heaven (A)(B) Ac 7:55
Paul speak: who s. beholding Ac 14:9
him
gazing intently at him (A)(B) Ac 14:9
could not s. behold the face of 2Co 3:7
to look steadily at (A) 2Co 3:7
could not s. look to the end 2Co 3:13
of that

STEDFASTNESS

and the s. of your faith in Col 2:5
Christ
firmness of your faith (B)(R) Col 2:5
firm front your faith confronts Col 2:5
(N)
the wicked, fall from your 2Pe 3:17
own s.
lose your own stability (B) 2Pe 3:17
do not lose your own safe 2Pe 3:17
foothold (N)
lose your own proper 2Pe 3:17
foothold (P)
slip from your own moorings 2Pe 3:17
(R)

STEEL

bow of a s. is broken by 2Sa 22:35
mine arms
bend a bow of bronze 2Sa 22:35
(A)(B)(R)
bend a bow of brass (E) 2Sa 22:35
and the bow of s. shall Job 20:24
strike him
a bronze arrow will strike Job 20:24
him (B)
the bow or brass will strike Job 20:24
(E)

the bronze bow shall pierce Job 20:24
him (R)
bow of s. is broken by mine Ps 18:34
arms
my arms bend a bow of Ps 18:34
bronze (A)(B)
my arms bend a bow of brass Ps 18:34
(E)(R)
the northern iron and the s. Jer 15:12
north iron and the bronze Jer 15:12
(A)(B)
iron from the north and Jer 15:12
brass (E)

STEEP

s. places shall fall, and every Eze 38:20
wall
that are poured down a s. Mic 1:4
place
ran violently down a s. place M't 8:32
into
herd ran violently down a s. M'k 5:13;
place Lu 8:33

STEER

s. clear of unchristian 2Ti 2:16
babblings (P)
s. clear of foolish speculations Tit 3:9
(N)(P)

STEERSMAN

where s. willeth (B)(E) Jas 3:4

STEM

forth a rod out of the s. of Isa 11:1
Jesse
stock of Jesse (A)(E) Isa 11:1
stump of Jesse (B)(R) Isa 11:1

STENCH

made us a rotten s. (A) Ex 5:21
the s. of rottenness (A) Isa 3:24
s. of dead bodies Isa 34:3;
(A)(B)(E)(R)(S) Joe 2:20; Am 4:10
there will be a s. (N) Joh 11:39

STEP

is but a s. between me and 1Sa 20:3
death
If my s. hath turned out of Job 31:7
the way

STEPHANAS

baptized also the household 1Co 1:16
of S.
brethren, (ye know the 1Co 16:15
house of S.
I am glad of the coming of 1Co 16:17
S. and

STEPHEN

they chose S. a man full of Ac 6:5
faith
And S. full of faith and power, Ac 6:8
did
and of Asia, disputing with S. Ac 6:9
they stoned S. calling upon Ac 7:59
God
devout men carried S. to his Ac 8:2
burial
the persecution that arose Ac 11:19
about S.
blood of thy martyr S. was Ac 22:20
shed

STEPPE

a dry land and a s. (B) Jer 51:43

STEPPED

the troubling of the water s. in Joh 5:4

STEPPETH

coming, another s. down Joh 5:7
before

STEPS

thou go up by *s.* unto mine altar — Ex 20:26
ark advanced six *s.* (B) — 2Sa 6:13
hast enlarged my *s.* under me — 2Sa 22:37
The throne had six *s.* and the top — 1Ki 10:19
and on the other upon the six *s.* — 1Ki 10:20
gone down on *s.* of Ahaz (B) — 2Ki 20:11
And there were six *s.* to the throne — 2Ch 9:18
and on the other upon the six *s.* — 2Ch 9:19
For now thou numberest my *s.* — Job 14:16
s. of his strength shall be straitened — Job 18:7
My foot hath held his *s.* his way — Job 23:11
When I washed my *s.* with butter — Job 29:6
see my ways, and count all my *s.* — Job 31:4
unto him the number of my *s.* — Job 31:37
have now compassed us in our *s.* — Ps 17:11
hast enlarged my *s.* under me — Ps 18:36
The *s.* of a good man are ordered — Ps 37:23
his heart; none of his *s.* shall slide — Ps 37:31
have our *s.* declined from thy way — Ps 44:18
they mark my *s.* when they wait — Ps 56:6
have prepared a net for my *s.* — Ps 57:6
gone; my *s.* had well nigh slipped — Ps 73:2
shall set us in the way of his *s.* — Ps 85:13
Order my *s.* in thy word: and let — Ps 119:133
thy *s.* shall not be straitened — Pr 4:12
to death; her *s.* take hold on hell — Pr 5:5
way: but the Lord directeth his *s.* — Pr 16:9
the poor, and the *s.* of the needy — Isa 26:6
man that walketh to direct his *s.* — Jer 10:23
They hunt our *s.* that we cannot — La 4:18
went up its *s.* (S) — Eze 40:6
they went up unto it by seven *s.* — Eze 40:22
there were seven *s.* to go up to it — Eze 40:26
going up to it had eight *s.* — Eze 40:31; 40:34, 37
he brought me by the *s.* whereby — Eze 40:49
the Ethiopians shall be at his *s.* — Da 11:43
walk in the *s.* of that faith of — Ro 4:12
spirit? walked we not in the same *s.* — 2Co 12:18
that ye should follow his *s.* — 1Pe 2:21

STERILE

dead *s.* principles (P) — Ga 4:9

STERN

a *s.* vision is told me (R) — Isa 21:2
the *s.* (S) — M'k 4:38;
a *s.* man (A) — Ac 19:21
cast four anchors out of the *s.* — Ac 27:29
                                    Ac 27:41

STEW

boil *s.* for sons of (B) — 2Ki 4:38

STEWARD

the *s.* of my house is this — Ge 15:2
to the *s.* of Joseph's house — Ge 43:19
commanded the *s.* of his house — Ge 44:1
far off, Joseph said unto his *s.* — Ge 44:4
Arza *s.* of his house in Tirzah — 1Ki 16:9
s. of his house (B) — 1Ki 18:3
of the vineyard saith unto his *s.* — M't 20:8

the wife of Chuza Herod's *s.* — Lu 8:3
then is that faithful and wise *s.* — Lu 12:42
a certain rich man, which had a *s.* — Lu 16:1
for thou mayest be no longer *s.* — Lu 16:2
Then the *s.* said within himself — Lu 16:3
the lord commended the unjust *s.* — Lu 16:8
take it to *s.* of the feast (N)(R) — Joh 2:8
must be blameless, as the *s.* of God — Tit 1:7

STEWARDS

the *s.* over all the substance — 1Ch 28:1
and *s.* of the mysteries of God — 1Co 4:1
Moreover it is required in *s.* — 1Co 4:2
under guardians and *s.* (E) — Ga 4:2
s. of the manifold grace of God — 1Pe 4:10

STEWARDSHIP

give an account of thy *s.*; for thou — Lu 16:2
lord taketh away from me the *s.* — Lu 16:3
when I am put out of the *s.* they — Lu 16:4
a *s.* entrusted to me (E) — 1Co 9:17
s. of God's grace (A)(R) — Eph 3:2
the divine *s.* (A) — Col 1:25

STICK

And he cut down a *s.* and cast it — 2Ki 6:6
bones that were not seen *s.* out — Job 33:21
they *s.* together, that they cannot — Job 41:17
For thine arrows *s.* fast in me — Ps 38:2
s. for the shoulder (A) — Isa 9:4
is withered, it is become like a *s.* — La 4:8
the fish of thy rivers to *s.* unto thy — Eze 29:4
the fish of thy rivers shall *s.* unto — Eze 29:4
thou son of man, take thee one *s.* — Eze 37:16
then take another *s.* and write upon — Eze 37:16
For Joseph, the *s.* of Ephraim, and — Eze 37:16
them one to another into one *s.* — Eze 37:17
Behold, I will take the *s.* of Joseph — Eze 37:19
with him, even with the *s.* of Judah — Eze 37:19
and make them one *s.* and — Eze 37:19
the *s.* (B) — Zec 11:10; 11:14

STICKETH

is a friend that *s.* closer than — Pr 18:24

STICKS

they found a man that gathered *s.* — Nu 15:32
they that found him gathering *s.* — Nu 15:33
come to me with *s.* (A)(B)(R) — 1Sa 17:43
woman was there gathering of *s.* — 1Ki 17:10
behold, I am gathering two *s.* that — 1Ki 17:12
the *s.* whereon thou writest shall — Eze 37:20
took two *s.* (B) — Zec 11:7
Paul had gathered a bundle of *s.* — Ac 28:3

STIFF

thy rebellion, and thy *s.* neck — De 31:27
your rebellion and stubbornness (A) — De 31:27
how rebellious and stubborn you are (B) — De 31:27
on high: speak not with a *s.* neck — Ps 75:5
speak with insolent neck (B)(R) — Ps 75:5

but made their neck *s.* that they — Jer 17:23
stiffened their neck (A)(B)(R)(S) — Jer 17:23

STIFFENED

but he *s.* his neck, and hardened — 2Ch 36:13
s. their neck (B)(R)(S) — Jer 17:3

STIFFHEARTED

are impudent children and *s.* — Eze 2:4
impudent and hard of heart (A) — Eze 2:4
impudent and stubborn (B)(R) — Eze 2:4

STIFFNECKED

and, behold, it is a *s.* people — Ex 32:9
thee; for thou art a *s.* people — Ex 33:3
Ye are a *s.* people; I will come — Ex 33:5
among us; for it is a *s.* people — Ex 34:9
for thou art a *s.* people — De 9:6
hard and stubborn people (A) — De 9:6; 9:13
a stubborn people (B) — De 9:6; 9:13
and, behold, it is a *s.* people — De 9:13
your heart, and be no more *s.* — De 10:16
no longer stubborn and hardened (A) — De 10:16
no longer stubborn (B) — De 10:16
be ye not *s.* as your fathers — 2Ch 30:8
Ye *s.* and uncircumcised in heart — Ac 7:51

STIGMA

to take away our *s.* (B) — Isa 4:1
he considered the *s.* (N) — Heb 11:26
bearing the *s.* (N) — Heb 13:13

STILL

going on *s.* toward the south — Ge 12:9
but they were *s.* ill favoured, as at — Ge 41:21
and wilt hold them *s.* — Ex 9:2
not stand *s.* and see the salvation — Ex 14:13
arm they shall be as *s.* as a stone — Ex 15:16
thou shalt let it rest and lie *s.* — Ex 23:11
And if it appear *s.* in the garment — Le 13:57
them, Stand *s.* and I will hear what — Nu 9:8
that went to search the land, lived *s.* — Nu 14:38
Jordan, ye shall stand *s.* in Jordan — Jos 3:8
Sun, stand thou *s.* upon Gibeon — Jos 10:12
And the sun stood *s.* and the moon — Jos 10:13
So the sun stood *s.* in the midst of — Jos 10:13
cities that stood *s.* in their strength — Jos 11:13
Balaam; therefore he blessed you *s.* — Jos 24:10
it is very good: and are ye *s.* — J'g 18:9
Then said she, Sit *s.* my daughter — Ru 3:18
but stand thou *s.* a while, that I may — 1Sa 9:27
Now therefore stand *s.* that I may — 1Sa 12:7
But if ye shall *s.* do wickedly, ye shall — 1Sa 12:25
then we will stand *s.* in our place — 1Sa 14:9
great things, and also shalt *s.* prevail — 1Sa 26:25
Asahel fell down and died stood *s.* — 2Sa 2:23
and all the people stood *s.* — 2Sa 2:28
But David tarried *s.* at Jerusa'em — 2Sa 11:1
good for me to have been there *s.* — 2Sa 14:32
came forth, and cursed *s.* as he came — 2Sa 16:5
And he turned aside, and stood *s.* — 2Sa 18:30
saw that all the people stood *s.* — 2Sa 20:12

every one that came by him | *2Sa 20:12*
stood *s.*
and after the fire a *s.* small | *1Ki 19:12*
voice
Gilead is ours, and we be *s.* | *1Ki 22:3*
And it came to pass, as they | *2Ki 2:11*
s. went
and if we sit *s.* here, we die | *2Ki 7:4*
also
the people *s.* sacrificed and | *2Ki 12:3*
burnt
burnt incense *s.* on the high | *2Ki 15:4*
places
and burned incense *s.* in the | *2Ki 15:35*
high
stand ye *s.* and see the | *2Ch 20:17*
salvation of
no power to keep *s.* the | *2Ch 22:9*
kingdom
did sacrifice *s.* in the high | *2Ch 33:17*
places
they stood *s.* in the prison | *Ne 12:39*
gate
s. he holdeth fast his integrity | *Job 2:3*
Dost thou *s.* retain thine | *Job 2:9*
integrity
For now should I have lain *s.* | *Job 3:13*
It stood *s.* but I could not | *Job 4:16*
discern
but keep it *s.* within his | *Job 20:13*
mouth
they spake not, but stood *s.* | *Job 32:16*
stand *s.* and consider the | *Job 37:14*
wondrous
heart upon your bed, and be *s.* | *Ps 4:4*
thou mightest *s.* the enemy and | *Ps 8:2*
leadeth me beside the *s.* waters | *Ps 23:2*
Be *s.* and know that I am | *Ps 46:10*
God: I
That he should *s.* live for ever | *Ps 49:9*
one as goeth on *s.* in his | *Ps 68:21*
trespasses
the earth feared, and was *s.* | *Ps 76:8*
For all this they sinned *s.* and | *Ps 78:32*
thy peace, and be not *s.* O | *Ps 83:1*
they will be *s.* praising thee | *Ps 84:4*
They shall *s.* bring forth fruit | *Ps 92:14*
in old
so that the waves thereof are | *Ps 107:29*
s.
when I awake, I am *s.* with | *Ps 139:18*
thee
he *s.* taught the people | *Ec 12:9*
knowledge
but his hand is stretched | *Isa 5:25;*
out *s.* | *9:12; 9:17, 21; 10:4*
Be *s.* ye inhabitants of the isle | *Isa 23:2*
this, Their strength is to sit *s.* | *Isa 30:7*
I have been *s.* and refrained | *Isa 42:14*
Why do we sit *s.*? assemble | *Jer 8:14*
They say *s.* unto them that | *Jer 23:17*
despise me
I let remain *s.* in their own | *Jer 27:11*
land
I do earnestly remember | *Jer 31:20*
him, *s.*
If ye will *s.* abide in this | *Jer 42:10*
land, then
into thy scabbard, rest, and be | *Jer 47:6*
s.
the sword, go away, stand | *Jer 51:50*
not *s.*
soul hath them *s.* in | *La 3:20*
remembrance
thy people *s.* are talking | *Eze 33:30*
against thee
a winding about *s.* upward to | *Eze 41:7*
the side
about the house went *s.* | *Eze 41:7*
upward
breadth of the house was *s.* | *Eze 41:7*
upward
The sun and moon stood *s.* | *Hab 3:11*
all the earth sitteth *s.* and is | *Zec 1:11*
nor feed that that standeth | *Zec 11:16*
s.
Jesus stood *s.* and called | *M't 20:32*
them
said unto the sea, Peace, be | *M'k 4:39*
s.
Jesus stood *s.* and | *M'k 10:49*
commanded
and they that bare him stood | *Lu 7:14*
s.
unto them, he abode *s.* in | *Joh 7:9*
Galilee
abode two days *s.* in the | *Joh 11:6*
same place
him: but Mary sat *s.* in the | *Joh 11:20*
house

commanded the chariot to | *Ac 8:38*
stand *s.*
it pleased Silas to abide there | *Ac 15:34*
s.
Silas and Timotheus abode | *Ac 17:14*
there *s.*
also, if they abide not *s.* in | *Ro 11:23*
unbelief
thee to abide *s.* at Ephesus, | *1Ti 1:3*
when
is unjust, let him be unjust *s.* | *Re 22:11*
which is filthy, let him be | *Re 22:11*
filthy *s.*
righteous, let him be | *Re 22:11*
righteous *s.*
he that is holy, let him be | *Re 22:11*
holy *s.*

STILLED

Caleb *s.* the people before | *Nu 13:30*
Moses
So the Levites *s.* all the people | *Ne 8:11*

STILLEST

waves thereof arise, thou *s.* | *Ps 89:9*
them

STILLETH

Which *s.* the noise of the seas | *Ps 65:7*

STIMULATE

revive and *s.* me (A)(B)(R) | *Ps 119:25*
they *s.* and encourage (N) | *1Co 14:3*
s. one another to love (B) | *Heb 10:24*

STIMULATED

your enthusiasm *s.* the | *2Co 9:2*
majority (A)(P)

STING

O death, where is thy *s.*? O | *1Co 15:55*
grave
the *s.* of death is sin; and | *1Co 15:56*

STINGETH

a serpent, and *s.* like an | *Pr 23:32*
adder

STINGING

s. serpents (B) | *Nu 21:6; 21:8*

STINGS

and there were *s.* in their tails | *Re 9:10*

STINK

have troubled me to make | *Ge 34:30*
me to *s.*
making me infamous (A) | *Ge 34:30*
making me odious | *Ge 34:30*
(B)(E)(R)
shall die, and the river shall *s.* | *Ex 7:18*
river shall become foul | *Ex 7:18*
smelling (A)(B)(E)
river will have such an odor | *Ex 7:18*
(R)
it did not *s.* neither was there | *Ex 16:24*
any
did not become foul | *Ex 16:24*
(A)(B)(E)
neither rancid or wormy (R) | *Ex 16:24*
My wounds *s.* and are corrupt | *Ps 38:5*
wounds loathsome and corrupt | *Ps 38:5*
(A)(E)
wounds grow foul and fester | *Ps 38:5*
(B)
wounds repulsive and festering | *Ps 38:5*
(P)
of sweet smell there shall | *Isa 3:24*
be *s.*
instead of sweet odor of | *Isa 3:24*
spices there shall be the
stench of rottenness (A)
instead of perfume rottenness | *Isa 3:24*
(B)(E)(R)
their *s.* shall come up out of | *Isa 34:3*
their
stench of dead bodies shall | *Isa 34:3*
arise (A)(B)(E)(R)
his *s.* shall come up, and his | *Joe 2:20*
ill

its stench shall come up | *Joe 2:20*
(A)(B)(E)(R)
made the *s.* of your camps to | *Am 4:10*
come
the stench of your camp | *Am 4:10*
come up (A)(B)(E)(R)

STINKETH

their fish, *s.* because there is | *Isa 50:2*
no
him, Lord, by this time he *s.* | *Joh 11:39*
throws off an offensive odor | *Joh 11:39*
(A)
there will be an odor | *Joh 11:39*
(B)(R)
the body decayeth (E) | *Joh 11:39*
there will be a stench (N) | *Joh 11:39*
he will be decaying (P) | *Joh 11:39*

STINKING

to send forth *a s.* savour: so | *Ec 10:1*
send forth a vile odor (A) | *Ec 10:1*
send forth an evil odor | *Ec 10:1*
(B)(E)
putrefy the perfumer's | *Ec 10:1*
ointment (R)

STIR

a great lion: who shall *s.* him | *Nu 24:9*
up
trying to *s.* up trouble (B) | *2Ki 5:7*
way *s.* up trouble (B) | *2Ki 14:10*
the innocent shall *s.* up | *Job 17:8*
himself
is so fierce that dare *s.* him | *Job 41:10*
up
S. up thyself, and awake | *Ps 35:23*
to my
and did not *s.* up all his wrath | *Ps 78:38*
and Manasseh *s.* up thy | *Ps 80:2*
strength
but grievous words *s.* up anger | *Pr 15:1*
ye *s.* not up, nor awake my | *Ca 2:7*
love
ye *s.* not up, nor awake my | *Ca 3:5*
love
ye *s.* not up, nor awake my | *Ca 8:4*
love
Lord of hosts shall *s.* up a | *Isa 10:26*
scourge
I will *s.* up the Medes | *Isa 13:17*
against them
he shall *s.* up jealousy like a | *Isa 42:13*
man
shall *s.* up all against the | *Da 11:2*
realm of
And he shall *s.* up his power | *Da 11:25*
no small *s.* among the | *Ac 12:18*
soldiers
there arose no small *s.* about | *Ac 19:23*
to *s.* Israel to emulation | *Ro 11:11;*
(N) | *11:14*
s. up to imitate (A) | *Ro 11:14*
that thou *s.* up the gift of God | *2Ti 1:6*
to *s.* you up by putting you in | *2Pe 1:13*
I *s.* up your pure minds by | *2Pe 3:1*
way of

STIRRED

every one whose heart *s.* him | *Ex 35:21*
up
women whose heart *s.* them | *Ex 35:26*
up in
one whose heart *s.* him up to | *Ex 36:2*
come
son hath *s.* up my servant | *1Sa 22:8*
against
Lord have *s.* thee up against | *1Sa 26:19*
me
the Lord *s.* up an adversary | *1Ki 11:14*
unto
God *s.* him up another | *1Ki 11:23*
adversary
whom Jezebel his wife *s.* up | *1Ki 21:25*
the God of Israel *s.* up the | *1Ch 5:26*
spirit
the Lord *s.* up against | *2Ch 21:16*
Jehoram the
Lord *s.* up the spirit of | *2Ch 36:22;*
Cyrus king | *Ezr 1:1*
good; and my sorrow was *s.* | *Ps 39:2*
Sheol is *s.* up (A)(B)(E)(R) | *Isa 14:9*
But his sons shall be *s.* up | *Da 11:10*
then shall he return, and be | *Da 11:10*
s. up.
king of the south shall be *s.* | *Da 11:25*
up to

And the Lord *s.* up the spirit   *Hag 1:14*
of
s. up the people (S)   *M'k 15:11*
s. the water (B)(P)   *Joh 5:4*
And they *s.* up the people, and   *Ac 6:12*
the Jews *s.* up the devout and   *Ac 13:50*
Jews *s.* up the Gentiles, and   *Ac 14:2*
thither also, and *s.* up the   *Ac 17:13*
people
his spirit was *s.* in him, when   *Ac 17:16*
s. up all the people, and laid   *Ac 21:27*
your zeal has *s.* up a number   *2Co 9:2*
(B)(E)(R)

STIRRETH

As an eagle *s.* up her nest   *De 32:11*
Hatred *s.* up strifes: but love   *Pr 10:12*
A wrathful man *s.* up strife   *Pr 15:18*
is of a proud heart *s.* up strife   *Pr 28:25*
An angry man *s.* up strife,   *Pr 29:22*
and a
it *s.* up the dead for thee,   *Isa 14:9*
even all
that *s.* up himself, to take   *Isa 64:7*
hold of
He *s.* up the people, teaching   *Lu 23:5*

STIRS

Thou that art full of *s.* a   *Isa 22:2*

STOCK

to the *s.* of the stranger's   *Le 25:47*
family
the *s.* thereof die in the   *Job 14:8*
ground
its stump die in the ground   *Job 14:8*
(B)(R)
the *s.* which thy right hand   *Ps 80:15*
(R)
their *s.* shall not take root in   *Isa 40:24*
their stem taken root (B)   *Isa 40:24*
shall I fall down to the *s.* of   *Isa 44:19*
a tree
worship a block of wood   *Isa 44:19*
(A)(B)
cast myself down to a log of   *Isa 44:19*
wood (A)
Saying to a *s.* Thou art my   *Jer 2:27*
father
say to a tree, You are my   *Jer 2:27*
father (A)(B)
say to a piece of wood, You   *Jer 2:27*
are my (R)
the *s.* is a doctrine of vanities   *Jer 10:8*
instruction of idols is but   *Jer 10:8*
wood (A)(B)
instruction of idols in wooden   *Jer 10:8*
(R)
children of the *s.* of   *Ac 13:26*
Abraham, and
race, family, people   *Ac 13:26;*
(A)(B)(R)   *Ph'p 3:5*
the eighth day, of the *s.* of   *Ph'p 3:5*
Israel

STOCKINGS

bound in their coats, and *s.* (S)   *Da 3:21*

STOCKS

puttest my feet also in the *s.*   *Job 18:27*
He putteth my feet in the *s.*   *Job 33:11*
a fool to the correction of the   *Pr 7:22*
s.
adultery with stones and with   *Jer 3:9*
s.
adultery with idols of stones   *Jer 3:9*
and trees (A)(B)
put him in the *s.* that were in   *Jer 20:2*
forth Jeremiah out of the *s.*   *Jer 20:3*
put him in prison, and in the   *Jer 29:26*
s.
My people ask counsel at their   *Ho 4:12*
s.
ask counsel of senseless wood   *Ho 4:12*
idols (A)(B)(R)
and made their feet fast in   *Ac 16:24*
the *s.*

STOICS

and of the *S.* encountered   *Ac 17:18*
him

STOLE

Jacob *s.* away unawares to   *Ge 31:20*
Laban

Absalom *s.* the hearts of the   *2Sa 15:6*
men
s. him from among the king's   *2Ki 11:2;*
sons   *2Ch 22:11*
and *s.* him away while we   *M't 28:13*
slept
Let him that *s.* steal no   *Eph 4:28*
more; but

STOLEN

that shall be counted *s.* with   *Ge 30:33*
me
Rachel had *s.* the images that   *Ge 31:19*
were
thou hast *s.* away unawares   *Ge 31:26*
to me
wherefore hast thou *s.* my   *Ge 31:30*
gods
knew not that Rachel had *s.*   *Ge 31:32*
them
whether *s.* by day, or *s.* by   *Ge 31:39*
night
I was *s.* away out of the land   *Ge 40:15*
and it be *s.* out of the man's   *Ex 22:7*
house
if it be *s.* from him, he shall   *Ex 22:12*
make
have also *s.* and dissembled   *Jos 7:11*
also
the men of Judah *s.* thee   *2Sa 19:41*
away
had *s.* them from the street   *2Sa 21:12*
of
S. waters are sweet, and bread   *Pr 9:17*
not have *s.* till they have enough   *Ob 5*

STOMACH

go into thy *s.* (B)   *Nu 5:22*
cheeks and *s.* (B)(R)(S)   *De 18:3*
turns in own *s.* (A)(B)(R)   *Job 20:14*
ejects from his *s.* (B)   *Job 20:15*
whose *s.* thou dost fill (B)   *Ps 17:14*
the *s.* of the wicked (A)(B)   *Pr 13:25*
a man's *s.* is filled (B)   *Pr 18:20*
filled his *s.* (B)   *Jer 51:34*
fill your *s.* (A)(B)(R)(S)   *Eze 3:3;*
  7:19
passed into the *s.*   *M't 15:17*
(B)(N)(P)(R)(S)
get his *s.* fil'ed (B)   *Lu 15:16*
meats for the *s.*   *1Co 6:13*
(A)(B)(P)(R)
god is their *s.* (A)(B)   *Ph'p 3:19*
embitter your *s.*   *Re 10:9*
(A)(B)(N)(R)

STOMACHER

of a *s.* a girding of sackcloth   *Isa 3:24*
instead of a rich robe,   *Isa 3:24*
sackcloth (A)(B)(E)(R)

STOMACHS

neither fill their *s.* (S)   *Eze 7:19*

STOMACH'S

a little wine for thy *s.* sake   *1Ti 5:23*

STONE

brick for *s.* and slime for   *Ge 11:3*
mortar
Jacob set up *s.* for a pillar   *Ge 28:18;*
  28:22; 31:45
they rolled *s.* from the well's   *Ge 29:3;*
mouth   *29:8, 10*
Jacob set up a pillar of *s.*   *Ge 35:14*
in the place
from thence is the shepherd,   *Ge 49:24*
s. of Israel
Zipporah took a sharp *s.* and   *Ex 4:25*
cut off
shall we sacrifice, and will   *Ex 8:26*
they not *s.* us
they sank into the bottom as a   *Ex 15:5*
s.
by greatness of arm they   *Ex 15:16*
shall be as still as *s.*
they be almost ready to *s.* me   *Ex 17:4*
and they took a *s.* and put it   *Ex 17:12*
under him
if thou wilt make me an altar   *Ex 20:25*
of *s.*
and if one smite another with   *Ex 21:18*
a *s.*

six names on one *s.* six on   *Ex 28:10*
other *s.*
with the work of an engraver   *Ex 28:11*
in *s.*
people of land *s.* him with   *Le 20:2*
stones
they shall *s.* the wizards with   *Le 20:27*
stones
congregation *s.* him that   *Le 24:14;*
cursed   *24:16, 23*
congregation *s.* them with   *Nu 14:10*
stones
they shall *s.* the   *Nu 15:35;*
sabbath-breaker   *15:36*
nor shall ye set up any image   *Nu 26:1*
of *s.*
smash all *s.* altars (R)(S)   *Nu 33:52*
if he smite him with   *Nu 35:17;*
throwing a *s.*   *35:23*
shalt *s.* with stones   *De 13:10*
s. idolaters   *De 17:5*
s. rebellious son   *De 21:21*
s. her that playeth the whore   *De 22:21*
s. adulterers with stones, that   *De 22:24*
they die
take ye up every man of you *s.*   *Jos 4:5*
the border went up to the *s.*   *Jos 15:6*
of Bohan
the border descended to the   *Jos 18:17*
s. of Bohan
this *s.* shall be a witness   *Jos 24:27*
unto us
he slew seventy persons on one   *J'g 9:5;*
s.   *9:18*
which *s.* remaineth unto this   *1Sa 6:18*
day
Samuel set up a *s.* and called   *1Sa 7:12*
it Eben-ezer
David took from bag a *s.*   *1Sa 17:49*
and slang it, and the *s.*
sunk into Philistine's forehead
David prevailed over the   *1Sa 17:50*
Philistine with a *s.*
and thou shalt remain by   *1Sa 20:19*
the *s.* Ezel
Nabal's heart died in him,   *1Sa 25:37*
he became as a *s.*
till there be not one small *s.*   *2Sa 17:13*
found there
house was built of *s.* made   *1Ki 6:7*
ready
all was cedar, there was no *s.*   *1Ki 6:18*
seen
carry Naboth out, *s.* him   *1Ki 21:10*
that he die
on good land cast every man   *2Ki 3:25*
his *s.*
there are with thee hewers   *1Ch 22:15*
of *s.*
skilful to work in gold   *2Ch 2:14*
silver and *s.*
threwest as a *s.* into mighty   *Ne 9:11*
waters
and brass is molten out of   *Job 28:2*
the *s.*
waters are hid as with a *s.*,   *Job 38:30*
deep is frozen
his heart is as firm as a *s.* as   *Job 41:24*
hard as
angels bear thee up lest dash   *Ps 91:12;*
foot against a *s.*   *M'k 4:6; Lu 4:11*
s. builders refused is   *Ps 118:22;*
become head *s.* of corner   *M't 21:42;*
  M'k 12:10
as he that bindeth a *s.* in a   *Pr 26:8*
sling, so is he
he that rolleth *s.* it will return   *Pr 26:27*
upon him
a *s.* is heavy, a fool's wrath is   *Pr 27:3*
heavier
and to a *s.* thou hast brought   *Jer 2:27*
me forth
shall not take of thee a *s.* for   *Jer 51:26*
a corner nor a *s.* for foundations
they have cast a *s.* upon me   *La 3:53*
they shall *s.* thee with stones   *Eze 16:40*
company shall *s.* them with   *Eze 23:47*
stones
a *s.* was cut out of the   *Da 2:34;*
mountain   *2:45*
a *s.* was laid upon the mouth   *Da 6:17*
of the den
for the *s.* shall cry out of the   *Hab 2:11*
wall
woe to him that saith to   *Hab 2:19*
dumb *s.*, Arise
before *s.* was laid upon a *s.*   *Hag 2:15*
in temple
the *s.* that I laid before   *Zec 3:9*
Joshua: upon one *s.* shall be

he shall bring forth the head s. *Zec 4:7*
thereof
they made their hearts as *Zec 7:12*
adamant s.
if ask bread will he give s. *M't 7:9;*
Lu 11:11
whosoever shall fall on this *M't 21:44;*
s. shall be broken; on *Lu 20:18*
whomsoever it shall fall
there shall not be left one s. *M't 24:2;*
upon another *M'k 13:2; Lu 19:44; 21:6*
sealing the s. *M't 27:66*
angel rolled back s. *M't 28:2*
command this s. that it be made *Lu 4:3*
bread
if we say, Of men the people *Lu 20:6*
will s. us
s. which builders rejected is *Lu 20:17;*
become head of *Ac 4:11; 1Pe 2:7*
corner
found s. rolled away *Lu 24:2;*
M'k 16:4; Joh 20:1
Cephas, which is by *Joh 1:42*
interpretation, A s.
there were set there six *Joh 2:6*
waterpots of s.
that is without sin let him *Joh 8:7*
first cast s. at her
Jews took up stones again to *Joh 10:31*
s. him
for which of those good *Joh 10:32*
works do ye s. me
saying, For a good work we *Joh 10:33*
s. thee not
Master, the Jews of late *Joh 11:8*
sought to s. thee
it was a cave and a s. lay *Joh 11:38*
upon it
take ye away s. *Joh 11:39*
they took away the s. *Joh 11:41*
there was an assault made to *Ac 14:5*
s. them
that the Godhead is like to s. *Ac 17:29*
graven
hail fell every s. the weight of *Re 16:21*
a talent
angel took up s. like a great *Re 18:21*
millstone

STONE with WOOD

may be blood in vessels of *Ex 7:19*
wood and s.
there serve gods the work of *De 4:28;*
men's hands, wood and s. *28:36, 64;*
29:17; 2Ki 19:18; Isa 37:19; Eze 20:32
praised the gods of gold, wood *Da 5:4;*
s. *5:23*
should not worship idols of *Re 9:20*
wood, s.

STONE OF ZOHELETH

Adonijah slew sheep by s. of *1Ki 1:9*
Zoheleth

BURDENSOME STONE

I will make Jerusalem a *Zec 12:3*
burdensome s.

HEWN STONE

thou shalt not build altar of *Ex 20:25*
hewn s.
to builders and masons to *2Ki 22:6;*
buy and hewn s. to repair *2Ch 34:11*
the house
he hath enclosed my ways with *La 3:9*
hewn s.
the four tables were of hewn *Eze 40:42*
s.
have built houses of hewn s. *Am 5:11*
but not
laid it in sepulchre that was *Lu 23:53*
hewn in s.

LIVING STONE

to whom coming as to living s. *1Pe 2:4*
chosen of God

PRECIOUS STONE

a gift is a precious s. to him *Pr 17:8*
that hath it

I lay in Zion a precious *Isa 28:16;*
corner s. *1Pe 2:6*
every precious s. was thy *Eze 28:13*
covering
she was decked with gold and *Re 17:4*
precious s.
her light was like to a s. *Re 21:11*
most precious

TABLES OF STONE

I will give thee tables of s. *Ex 24:12;*
31:18
Lord said, Hew thee two *Ex 34:1;*
tables of s. *De 10:1*
he hewed two tables of s. *Ex 34:4;*
De 10:3
he wrote on the two tables of *De 4:13;*
s. *5:22*
when I was gone up to receive *De 9:9*
tables of s.
the Lord delivered to me two *De 9:10*
tables of s.
the Lord gave me the two *De 9:11*
tables of s.
nothing in ark save two tables *1Ki 8:9;*
of s. *De 10:1*
not in tables of s. but in *2Co 3:3*
fleshly tables of heart

TRIED STONE

I lay in Zion a stone, a tried *Isa 28:16*
s.

WHITE STONE

I will give him a white s. and *Re 2:17*

STONED

but he shall surely be s. or *Ex 19:13*
shot
then the ox shall be surely s. *Ex 21:28*
the ox shall be s. and his *Ex 21:29*
owner
of silver, and the ox shall be *Ex 21:32*
s.
s. him with stones, and he *Nu 15:36*
died
And all Israel s. him with *Jos 7:25*
stones
after they had s. them with *Jos 7:25*
stones
and all Israel s. him with *1Ki 12:18*
stones
s. him with stones, that he *1Ki 21:13*
died
saying, Naboth is s. and is *1Ki 21:14*
dead
Jezebel heard that Naboth *1Ki 21:15*
was s.
children of Israel s. him *2Ch 10:18*
and s. him with stones at *2Ch 24:21*
and killed another, and s. *M't 21:35*
another
commanded us, that such be *Joh 8:5*
s.
lest they should have been s. *Ac 5:26*
him out of the city, and s. him *Ac 7:58*
they s. Stephen, calling upon *Ac 7:59*
God
having s. Paul, drew him out *Ac 14:19*
once was I s. thrice I *2Co 11:25*
suffered
They were s. they were *Heb 11:37*
sawn
it shall be s. or thrust *Heb 12:20*
through

STONES

Jacob said to his brethren, *Ge 31:46*
Gather s.
shalt engrave the two s. *Ex 28:11;*
28:12
set in it settings of s. even *Ex 28:17*
four rows of s.
the s. shall be with the names *Ex 28:21*
of Israel
that they should be s. for a *Ex 39:7*
memorial
command that they take *Le 14:40*
away s.
shall put other s. in the place *Le 14:42*
of those s.

break down the house, the s. *Le 14:45*
or hath his s. broken, shall *Le 21:20*
not offer
a land whose s. are iron *De 8:9*
that is wounded in the s. shall *De 23:1*
not enter
ye shall set up these s. in *De 27:4*
mount Ebal
build altar of s. *De 27:5*
write on s. words *De 27:8*
and take you hence twelve s. *Jos 4:3;*
4:9
saying, What mean you by *Jos 4:6;*
these s. *4:21*
took twelve s. out of midst of *Jos 4:8*
Jordan
those twelve s. did Joshua *Jos 4:20*
pitch in Gilgal
he wrote on the s. a copy of *Jos 8:32*
the law
every one could sling s. at an *J'g 20:16*
hair
David chose him five smooth *1Sa 17:40*
s.
Shimei cast s. at David *2Sa 16:6; 16:13*
prepared timber and s. to *1Ki 5:18*
build
s. of eight cubits, and s. of *1Ki 7:10*
ten cubits
made silver in Jerusalem as *1Ki 10:27;*
s. *2Ch 1:15; 9:27*
took away s. of Ramah *1Ki 15:22;*
2Ch 16:6
Elijah took twelve s. *1Ki 18:31*
according to
with s. he built an altar in *1Ki 18:32*
name of Lord
mar every good piece of land *2Ki 3:19*
with s.
only Kir-haraseth left they *2Ki 3:25*
the s. thereof
and put it upon a pavement *2Ki 16:17*
of s.
in hurling of s. and arrows *1Ch 12:2*
Uzziah prepared slings to *2Ch 26:14*
cast s.
will they revive s. out of heaps *Ne 4:2*
shalt be in league with s. of *Job 5:23*
field
is my strength the strength of *Job 6:12*
s.
roots are wrapped, and seeth *Job 8:17*
place of s.
waters wear the s. thou *Job 14:19*
washest away
the gold of Ophir as the s. *Job 22:24*
of the brooks
the s. of it are the place of *Job 28:6*
sapphires
sinews of his s. are wrapped *Job 40:17*
together
servants take pleasure in her *Ps 102:14*
s.
dasheth the little ones against *Ps 137:9*
the s.
a moss of costly s. (B)(R) *Pr 20:15*
time to cast away s. a time to *Ec 3:5*
gather s.
whoso removeth s. shall be *Ec 10:9*
hurt therewith
fenced it and gathered out s. *Isa 5:2*
thereof
that go down to the s. of the *Isa 14:19*
pit
he maketh the s. of the altar *Isa 27:9*
as chalk s.
I will lay thy s. with fair *Isa 54:11*
colours
I will make the borders of *Isa 54:12*
pleasant s.
among the smooth s. of the *Isa 57:6*
stream
bring for s. iron *Isa 60:17*
gather out the s. *Isa 62:10*
committed adultery with s. and *Jer 3:9*
stocks
and I will set his throne on *Jer 43:10*
these s.
s. of the sanctuary are poured *La 4:1*
out
they shall lay thy s. in the *Eze 26:12*
water
hast walked in midst of s. of *Eze 28:14*
fire
I will destroy thee from *Eze 28:16*
midst of the s. of fire
their sacred s. destroy (B) *Ho 10:2*
I will pour down the s. into *Mic 1:6*
the valley

shall consume it with the *s.* thereof — *Zec 5:4*

for they shall be as a *s.* of a crown lifted up — *Zec 9:16*

of these *s.* to raise up children — *M't 3:9; Lu 3:8*

command that these *s.* be made bread — *M't 4:3*

crying, and cutting himself with *s.* — *M'k 5:5*

at him they cast *s.* and wounded him — *M'k 12:4*

Master, see what manner of *s.* are here — *M'k 13:1*

the *s.* would immediately cry out — *Lu 19:40*

they took up *s.* to cast at him — *Joh 8:59; 10:31*

if ministration engraven in *s.* was glorious — *2Co 3:7*

as lively *s.* are built up spiritual house — *1Pe 2:5*

STONES *OF DARKNESS*

he searcheth out the *s.* of darkness — *Job 28:3*

STONES *OF EMPTINESS*

he shall stretch out upon it *s.* of emptiness — *Isa 34:11*

CORNER STONES

that our daughters may be as corner *s.* — *Ps 144:12*

GLISTERING STONES

I have prepared glistering *s.* for house — *1Ch 29:2*

GRAVEL STONES

he hath broken my teeth with gravel *s.* — *La 3:16*

HEAP OF STONES

raised a great heap of *s.* on Achan — *Jos 7:26*

raise a great heap of *s.* on the king of Ai — *Jos 8:29*

they laid a heap of *s.* on Absalom — *2Sa 18:17*

HEWED STONES

they brought hewed *s.* to lay foundation — *1Ki 5:17*

according to the measures of hewed *s.* — *1Ki 7:9; 7:11*

HEWN STONES

bricks fallen, but we will build with hewn *s.* — *Isa 9:10*

MARBLE STONES

I have prepared marble *s.* in abundance — *1Ch 29:2*

PRECIOUS STONES

was a talent of gold with precious *s.* — *2Sa 12:30*

queen of Sheba came with precious *s.* — *1Ki 10:2*

navy of Hiram brought precious *s.* — *1Ki 10:11; 2Ch 9:10*

I prepared all manner of precious *s.* — *1Ch 29:2*

whom precious *s.* were found — *1Ch 29:8*

garnished house with precious *s.* — *2Ch 3:6*

made treasuries for precious *s.* — *2Ch 32:27*

they occupied in thy fairs with precious *s.* — *Eze 27:22*

god shall he honour. with precious *s.* — *Da 11:38*

if any man build on this foundation precious *s.* — *1Co 3:12*

for no man buyeth precious *s.* any more — *Re 18:12*

great city decked with gold and precious *s.* — *Re 18:16*

foundations garnished with precious *s.* — *Re 21:19*

WHOLE STONES

build the altar of whole *s.* — *De 27:6; Jos 8:31*

WROUGHT STONES

he set masons to hew wrought *s.* — *1Ch 22:2*

STONE'S

from them about a *s.* cast — *Lu 22:41*

STONESQUARERS

builders did hew them, and the *s.* — *1Ki 5:18*

STONEST

s. them which are sent unto thee — *M't 23:37*

s. them that are sent unto thee — *Lu 13:34*

STONING

for the people spake of *s.* him — *1Sa 30:6*

STONY

are overthrown in *s.* places — *Ps 141:6*

take the *s.* heart out of their flesh — *Eze 11:19*

away the *s.* heart out of your flesh — *Eze 36:26*

Some fell upon *s.* places, where — *M't 13:5*

received the seed into *s.* places — *M't 13:20*

And some fell on *s.* ground, where — *M'k 4:5*

which are sown on *s.* ground — *M'k 4:16*

STOOD

but Abraham *s.* yet before the Lord — *Ge 18:22*

the pillar of cloud *s.* behind them — *Ex 14:19*

he *s.* between the dead and the living — *Nu 16:48*

came near and *s.* under the mountain — *De 4:11*

I *s.* between the Lord and you — *De 5:5*

waters *s.* and rose up on an heap — *Jos 3:16*

take twelve stones where the priest's feet *s.* — *Jos 4:3; 4:9*

Joash said to all that *s.* against him — *J'g 6:31*

two middle pillars on which the house *s.* — *J'g 16:29*

Lord *s.* and called, Samuel, Samuel — *1Sa 3:10*

when he *s.* among people, he was higher — *1Sa 10:23*

Goliath *s.* and cried to the armies of Israel — *1Sa 17:8*

Saul said to the servants that *s.* about him — *1Sa 22:7*

the king said to footmen that *s.* about him — *1Sa 22:17*

all congregation of Israel *s.* — *1Ki 8:14; 2Ch 6:3; 7:6*

Solomon *s.* and blessed all the congregation — *1Ki 8:55*

sons of prophets *s.* to view afar off — *2Ki 2:7*

and all the people *s.* to the covenant — *2Ki 23:3*

and on the brasen scaffold Solomon *s.* — *2Ch 6:13*

s. at their posts (S) — *2Ch 7:6*

they *s.* and confessed their sins — *Ne 9:2*

the other Jews *s.* for their lives — *Es 9:16*

he commanded and it *s.* fast — *Ps 33:9*

above it *s.* seraphims each had six — *Isa 6:2*

they *s.* not because Lord did drive — *Jer 46:15*

they *s.* under the shadow of Heshbon — *Jer 48:45*

and when those *s.* these *s.* — *Eze 1:21; 10:17*

when they *s.* they let down their wings — *Eze 1:24*

and there was a voice when they *s.* — *Eze 1:25*

was stunned, *s.* aghast (B) — *Da 4:19*

Gabriel came near where I *s.* — *Da 8:17*

when he had spoken I *s.* trembling — *Da 10:11*

I *s.* to confirm and to strengthen him — *Da 11:1*

I looked and behold, there *s.* other two — *Da 12:5*

he *s.* and measured the earth — *Hab 3:6*

he *s.* among the myrtle trees — *Zec 1:8; 1:10-11*

his mother and brethren *s.* without — *M't 12:46*

he that had the withered hand *s.* forth — *Lu 6:8*

Pharisee *s.* and prayed thus with himself — *Lu 18:11*

Simon Peter *s.* and warmed himself — *Joh 18:25*

Mary *s.* without at sepulchre weeping — *Joh 20:11*

lame man leaping up *s.* and walked — *Ac 3:8*

men which journeyed with him *s.* speechless — *Ac 9:7*

there *s.* a man of Macedonia and prayed — *Ac 16:9*

but Paul *s.* forth in the midst of them — *Ac 27:21*

s. against us (A)(B)(N)(R) — *Col 2:14*

s. only in meats, and drinks — *Heb 9:10*

STOOD *ABOVE*

behold, the Lord *s.* above the ladder — *Ge 28:13*

Zechariah *s.* above the people — *2Ch 24:20*

the waters *s.* above the mountains — *Ps 104:6*

STOOD *AFAR*

his sister *s.* afar off to wit what — *Ex 2:4*

people removed and *s.* afar off — *Ex 20:18; 20:21*

ten that were lepers, who *s.* afar off — *Lu 17:12*

all his acquaintance *s.* afar off beholding — *Lu 23:49*

as many as trade by sea *s.* afar off — *Re 18:17*

STOOD *AT*

they *s.* at nether part of the mount — *Ex 19:17*

they *s.* every man at his tent door — *Ex 33:8*

cloudy pillar *s.* at door of tabernacle — *Ex 33:9*

Naaman *s.* at door of house of Elisha — *2Ki 5:9*

singers *s.* at the east end of altar — *2Ch 5:12*

king *s.* at his pillar, at the entering in — *2Ch 23:13*

cherubims *s.* at door of the east gate — *Eze 10:19*

the king *s.* at the parting of the way — *Eze 21:21*

woman *s.* at his feet weeping — *Lu 7:38*

but Peter *s.* at the door without — *Joh 18:16*

another angel came and *s.* at the altar — *Re 8:3*

STOOD *BEFORE*

to the place where he *s.* before Lord — *Ge 19:27*

down to Egypt, and *s.* before Joseph — *Ge 43:15*

took ashes and *s.* before Pharaoh — *Ex 9:10*

the congregation *s.* before the Lord — *Le 9:5*

daughters of Zelophehad *s.* before Moses — *Nu 27:2*

until he *s.* before the congregation — *Jos 20:9*

Phinehas *s.* before ark in those days — *J'g 20:28*

David came and *s.* before Saul — *1Sa 16:21*

Bath-sheba *s.* before king David — *1Ki 1:28*

Solomon *s.* before the ark of the covenant — *1Ki 3:15*

two women that were harlots *s.* before him — *1Ki 3:16*

Solomon *s.* before the altar — *1Ki 8:22; 2Ch 6:12*

old men that *s. before* Solomon 1Ki 12:6; 2Ch 10:6
young men that *s. before* him 1Ki 12:8; 2Ch 10:8
spirit *s. before* the Lord 1Ki 22:21; 2Ch 18:20
the Shunammite *s. before* Elisha 2Ki 4:12
Naaman returned and *s. before* Elisha 2Ki 5:15
Gehazi went in and *s. before* his master 2Ki 5:25
Hazael came and *s. before* Elisha 2Ki 8:9
behold, two kings *s.* not *before* him 2Ki 10:4
so Esther arose, and *s. before* the king Es 8:4
Moses is chosen *s. before* him Ps 106:23
though Moses and Samuel *s. before* me Jer 15:1
I *s. before* thee to speak good for them Jer 18:20
there *s. before* them seventy men Eze 8:11
they *s. before* the king Da 1:19; 2:2
O king, this great image, *s. before* thee Da 2:31
they *s. before* the image Nebuchadnezzar set Da 3:3
ten thousand times ten thousand *s. before* him Da 7:10
there *s. before* the river a ram Da 8:3
s. before me as the appearance of a man Da 8:15
now Joshua *s. before* the angel Zec 3:3
and he spake to those that *s. before* him Zec 3:4
and Jesus *s. before* the governor M't 27:11
behold, three men *s. before* the gate Ac 10:17
a man *s. before* me in bright clothing Ac 10:30
she told how Peter *s. before* the gate Ac 12:14
let these say, while I *s. before* the council Ac 24:20
I saw multitude *s. before* the throne Re 7:9
I saw the seven angels which *s. before* God Re 8:2
and the dragon *s. before* the woman Re 12:4

STOOD BESIDE

Absalom *s. beside* the way of the gate 2Sa 15:2
and two lions *s. beside* the stays 1Ki 10:19
the princes which *s. beside* the king Jer 36:21
the six men *s. beside* the brasen altar Eze 9:2
then he went in and *s. beside* the wheels Eze 10:6

STOOD BY

he looked, and lo, three men *s. by* him Ge 18:2
behold, he *s. by* the camels at the well Ge 24:30
Pharaoh dreamed, and, lo, he *s. by* the river Ge 41:1
not refrain himself before all that *s. by* him Ge 45:1
Moses sat, and the people *s. by* Moses Ex 18:13
Balak *s. by* his burnt sacrifice Nu 23:6; 23:17
all that *s. by* him went out from him J'g 3:19
the men *s. by* the entering of the gate J'g 18:16
the woman that *s. by* thee, praying 1Sa 1:26
servants *s. by* with clothes rent 2Sa 13:31
Jeroboam *s. by* the altar to burn 1Ki 13:1
ass *s. by* it, the lion also *s. by* the carcase 1Ki 13:24
and they two *s. by* Jordan 2Ki 2:7; 2:13
behold, the king *s. by* a pillar 2Ki 11:14; 23:3
they *s. by* conduit of upper pool 2Ki 18:17; Isa 36:2

the angel *s. by* the threshing floor 1Ch 21:15
then the women that *s. by* answered Jer 44:15
and the man *s. by* me and said Eze 43:6
I came near to one of them that *s. by* Da 7:16
and the angel of the Lord *s. by* Zec 3:5
one of them that *s. by* drew a sword M'k 14:47
some that *s. by* when they heard M'k 15:35
s. by the lake of Gennesaret Lu 5:1
he said to them that *s. by,* Take from him Lu 19:24
two men *s. by* them in shining garments Lu 24:4
an officer that *s. by* struck Jesus Joh 18:22
there *s. by* the cross of Jesus his mother Joh 19:25
two men *s. by* them in white apparel Ac 1:10
and all the widows *s. by* him weeping Ac 9:39
Paul said to the centurion that *s. by* Ac 22:25
commanded them that *s. by* to smite him Ac 23:2
that *s. by* said, Revilest the high priest Ac 23:4
the night following the Lord *s. by* him Ac 23:11
there *s. by* me the angel of God Ac 27:23

STOOD IN

Moses and Aaron, who *s. in* the way Ex 5:20
then Moses *s. in* the gate of the camp Ex 32:26
Lord *s. in* the door of the tabernacle Nu 12:5
laid incense thereon, and *s. in* the door Nu 16:18
Dathan and Abiram *s. in* door of tents Nu 16:27
the angel of the Lord *s. in* the way Nu 22:22; 22:24
angel went further and *s. in* narrow place Nu 22:26
the priests *s. in* midst of Jordan Jos 3:17; 4:10
Jotham *s. in* the top of mount Gerizim J'g 9:7
Gaal *s. in* the entering of the gate of the city J'g 9:35
Abimelech; priests *s. in* the entering J'g 9:44; 18:17
he *s. in* the midst of the ground 2Sa 23:12
and he *s. in* entering in of the cave 1Ki 19:13
they gathered, and *s. in* the border 2Ki 3:21
the Shunammite *s. in* the door 2Ki 4:15
and they *s. in* their place 2Ch 30:16; 35:10
king *s. in* his place, and made a covenant 2Ch 34:31
and all the people *s. in* their place Ne 8:7
Esther *s. in* the inner court of house Es 5:1
Jeremiah *s. in* court of Lord's house Jer 19:14
for who hath *s. in* counsel of the Lord Jer 23:18
but if they had *s. in* my counsel and caused Jer 23:22
Jaazaniah *s. in* the midst of them Eze 8:11
nor shouldest *s. in* cross-way to cut off Ob 14
Jesus *s. in* midst of them Lu 24:36; Joh 20:19, 26
Paul *s. in* the midst of Mars' hill Ac 17:22
in the midst of the elders *s. a* lamb Re 5:6

STOOD ON

Philistines *s. on* mountain on one side, Israel *s. on* a mountain on other side 1Sa 17:3

then David *s. on* the top of an hill 1Sa 26:13
Benjamin *s. on* the top of an hill 2Sa 2:25
Asaph, who *s. on* his right hand 1Ch 6:39
the sons of Merari *s. on* the left hand 1Ch 6:44
the cherubims *s. on* their feet 2Ch 3:13
the cherubims *s. on* the right side Eze 10:3
the whole multitude *s. on* the shore M't 13:2
when morning, Jesus *s. on* the shore Joh 21:4
Paul *s. on* stairs and beckoned to people Ac 21:40
and lo, a lamb *s. on* the mount Sion Re 14:1

STOOD OVER

the pillar of cloud *s. over* the door De 31:15
glory of Lord *s. over* the threshold Eze 10:4
glory of the Lord *s. over* cherubims Eze 10:18
star *s. over* where young child was M't 2:9
he *s. over* her and rebuked the fever Lu 4:39

STOOD ROUND

behold, your sheaves *s. round* about Ge 37:7
as the disciples *s. round* about him Ac 14:20
Jews *s. round* about Paul, and laid complaints Ac 25:7
all the angels *s. round* about the throne Re 7:11

STOOD STILL

sun *s. still,* and the moon stayed Jos 10:13
as for cities that *s. still* in their strength Jos 11:13
as many as came to the place *s. still* 2Sa 2:23
Joab blew a trumpet and all people *s. still* 2Sa 2:28
when the man saw that all people *s. still* 2Sa 20:12
and they *s. still* in the prison gate Ne 12:39
a spirit *s. still* but I could not discern Job 4:16
for they spake not, but *s. still* Job 32:16
sun and moon *s. still* in their habitation Hab 3:11
and Jesus *s. still* and called them M't 20:32
Jesus *s. still* and commanded him Mk 10:49
and they that bare him *s. still* Lu 7:14

STOOD THERE

Lord descended and *s.* with him *there* Ex 34:5
ark came into the field and *s. there* 1Sa 6:14
twelve lions *s. there* 1Ki 10:20; 2Ch 9:19
behold, the glory of the Lord *s. there* Eze 3:23
from the days of Gibeah *there* they *s.* Ho 10:9
some of them that *s. there* M't 27:47; M'k 11:5
the servants and officers *s. there* Joh 18:18

STOOD UP

Abraham *s. up* from before his dead Ge 23:3
Abraham *s. up* and bowed himself to people Ge 23:7
out Moses *s. up* and helped them Ex 2:17
people *s. up* all that day and night Nu 11:32
Satan *s. up* against Israel and provoked 1Ch 21:1

then David the king *s. up* upon his feet   1Ch 28:2

Abijah *s. up* and said, Hear me   2Ch 13:4

the Levites *s. up* to praise the Lord God   2Ch 20:19

Ammon and Moab *s. up* against mount Seir   2Ch 20:23

s. up against them that came from war   2Ch 28:12

not eat holy things till *s. up*   Ezr 2:63; Ne 7:65

priest with Urim and Thummim

when he opened the book people *s. up*   Ne 8:5

they *s. up* in their place and read the law   Ne 9:3

then *s. up* upon the stairs, of the Levites   Ne 9:4

Haman saw that Mordecai *s.* not *up*   Es 5:9

Haman *s. up* to make request for his life   Es 7:7

spirit passed, the hair of my flesh *s. up.*   Job 4:15

young men saw me, and aged arose and *s. up*   Job 29:8

I *s. up* and cried in the congregation   Job 30:28

then *s. up* Phinehas and executed judgment   Ps 106:30

they lived, and *s. up* upon their feet   Eze 37:10

broken, whereas four *s. up* for it   Da 8:22

Jesus *s. up* to read in the synagogue   Lu 4:16

a certain lawyer *s. up* and tempted him   Lu 10:25

in those days Peter *s. up* and said   Ac 1:15

kings of the earth *s. up* against the Lord   Ac 4:26

then *s. up* one Gamaliel, a doctor of law   Ac 5:34

Agabus *s. up,* and signified by the spirit   Ac 11:28

Paul *s. up,* and beckoning with his hand   Ac 13:16

against whom when the accusers *s. up*   Ac 25:18

STOOD *UPON*

I *s. upon* the bank of the river   Ge 41:17

David ran and *s. upon* the Philistine   1Sa 17:51

so I *s. upon* Saul, and slew him   2Sa 1:10

sea *s. upon* twelve oxen   1Ki 7:25; 2Ch 4:4

he revived, and *s. upon* his feet   2Ki 13:21

Ezra the scribe *s. upon* a pulpit of wood   Ne 8:4

glory of the Lord *s. upon* the mount   Eze 11:23

Lord *s. upon* a wall made by a line   Am 7:7

the two prophets *s. upon* their feet   Re 11:11

I *s. upon* the sand of the sea, and saw   Re 13:1

STOOD *WITH*

there *s. with* him no man, while Joseph   Ge 45:1

every man *s. with* his weapons in hand   2Ki 11:11

the Levites *s. with* instruments   2Ch 29:26

then Joshua *s. with* his sons and brethren   Ezr 3:9

he *s. with* his right hand as an adversary   La 2:4

they saw the two men that *s.* with him   Lu 9:32

Judas who also betrayed *s.* with them   Joh 18:5

Peter *s. with* them, and warmed himself   Joh 18:18

no man *s. with* me   2Ti 4:16

Lord *s. with* me   2Ti 4:17

STOODEST

I knew not that thou *s.* in the way   Nu 22:34

day that thou *s.* before the Lord   De 4:10

day that thou *s.* on the other side   Ob 11

STOOL

there a bed, and a table, and the *s.*   2Ki 4:10

STOOLS

women, and see them upon the *s.*   Ex 1:16

birthstools (A)(B)(E)(R)   Ex 1:16

STOOP

proud helpers do *s.* under him   Job 9:13

in the heart of man maketh it *s.*   Pr 12:25

They *s.* they bow down together   Isa 46:2

I am not worthy to *s.* down   M'k 1:7

STOOPED

he *s.* down, he couched as a lion   Ge 49:9

David *s.* with his face to the earth   1Sa 24:8

he *s.* with his face to the ground   1Sa 28:14

old man, or him that *s.* for age   2Ch 36:17

But Jesus *s.* down, and with his   Joh 8:6

again he *s.* down, and wrote on the   Joh 8:8

she *s.* down, and looked into   Joh 20:11

STOOPETH

Bel boweth down, Nebo *s.* their   Isa 46:1

STOOPING

and *s.* down, he beheld the linen   Lu 24:12

he *s.* down, and looking in, saw   Joh 20:5

STOP

down, that the rain *s.* thee not   1Ki 18:44

s. all wells of water, and mar every   2Ki 3:19

to *s.* the waters of the fountains   2Ch 32:3

and *s.* the way against them that   Ps 35:3

and all iniquity shall *s.* her mouth   Ps 107:42

and it shall *s.* the noses of the   Eze 39:11

s. here (N)   M't 26:38; M'k 14:34

no man shall *s.* me of this boasting   2Co 11:10

STOPPED

the windows of heaven were *s.*   Ge 8:2

the Philistines had *s.* them   Ge 26:15

for the Philistines had *s.* them after   Ge 26:18

or his flesh be *s.* from his issue, it   Le 15:3

and they *s.* all the wells of water   2Ki 3:25

smote thrice and *s.* (S)   2Ki 13:18

he *s.* building Ramah (S)   2Ch 16:5

who *s.* all the fountains, and   2Ch 32:4

s. the upper watercourse of Gihon   2Ch 32:30

that the breaches began to be *s.*   Ne 4:7

of them that speak lies shall be *s.*   Ps 63:11

that the passages are *s.* and   Jer 51:32

s. their ears, that they should not   Zec 7:11

s. their ears, and ran upon him   Ac 7:57

that every mouth may be *s.* and all   Ro 3:19

Whose mouths must be *s.* who   Tit 1:11

promises, *s.* the mouths of lions   Heb 11:33

STOPPETH

hope, and iniquity *s.* her mouth   Job 5:16

like the deaf adder that *s.* her ear   Ps 58:4

Whoso *s.* his ears at the cry of the   Pr 21:13

that *s.* his ears from hearing of blood   Isa 33:15

STORAGE

storage (S)   Ge 41:36; 1Ki 9:19; 2Ch 8:4, 6; 11:11; 16:4; 17:12

chambers for the *s.* (S)   Ne 12:44

STORE

of herds, and great *s.* of servants   Ge 26:14

a great supply (A)   Ge 26:14

a great household (B)(E)   Ge 26:14

that food shall be for *s.* to the land   Ge 41:36

s. cities (B)(E)(R)   Ex 1:11

fruits come in ye shall eat of the old *s.*   Le 25:22

And ye shall eat old *s.* and bring   Le 26:10

shall be thy basket and thy *s.*   De 28:5

kneadingtrough (A)(B)(E)(R)   De 28:5

Is not this laid up in *s.* with me   De 32:34

the cities of *s.* that Solomon had   1Ki 9:19

and of spices very great *s.*   1Ki 10:10

which thy fathers have laid up in *s.*   2Ki 20:17

all this *s.* that we have prepared   1Ch 29:16

all the *s.* cities, which he built   2Ch 8:4

all the *s.* cities that Solomon had   2Ch 8:6

s. of victual, and of oil and wine   2Ch 11:11

and all the *s.* cities of Naphtali   2Ch 16:4

in Judah castles, and cities of *s.*   2Ch 17:12

that which is left is this great *s.*   2Ch 31:10

in ten days *s.* of all sorts of wine   Ne 5:18

be full, affording all manner of *s.*   Ps 144:13

which thy fathers have laid up in *s.*   Isa 39:6

who *s. up* violence and robbery in   Am 3:10

for there is none end of the *s.*   Na 2:9

s. my crops (B)(N)(R)   Lu 12:17

s. my grain, goods (A)(B)(E)(N)(P)(R)   Lu 12:18

of his full *s.* received (N)   Joh 1:16

every one of you lay by him in *s.*   1Co 16:2

Laying up in *s.* for themselves   1Ti 6:19

laying good foundation for future (A)(B)(N)(R)   1Ti 6:19

by the same word are kept in *s.*   2Pe 3:7

STOREHOUSE

the *s.* of Asuppim (S)   1Ch 26:15; 26:17

I made in the *s.* (S)   Ne 13:12; 13:13

Bring ye all the tithes into the *s.*   Mal 3:10

which neither have *s.* nor barn   Lu 12:24

STOREHOUSES

And Joseph opened all the *s.*   Ge 41:56

the blessing upon thee in thy *s.*   De 28:8

over the *s.* in the fields, in   1Ch 27:25

S. also for the increase of corn   2Ch 32:28

the *s.* of the gates (S)   Ne 12:25

heap: he layeth up the depth in *s.*   Ps 33:7

the utmost border, open her *s.*   Jer 50:26

STORES

we have *s.* in the field (S)   Jer 41:8

STORIES

second, and third s. shalt thou   Ge 6:16
make it
lower, second, and third decks   Ge 6:16
(B)(R)
galleries round about on   Eze 41:16
their three s.
was gallery against gallery in   Eze 42:3
three s.
For they were in three s. but   Eze 42:6
had not
that buildeth his s. in the   Am 9:6
heaven
builds his upper chambers   Am 9:6
(A)(B)
buildeth his chambers in the   Am 9:6
heavens (E)
builds his upper room in the   Am 9:6
heavens (R)
cleverly devised s., fables,   1Pe 1:16
myths (A)(B)(R)

STORK

the s., the heron after her   Le 11:19
kind
And the s. and the heron   De 14:18
after her
as for the s., the fir trees are   Ps 104:17
her
the s. in the heaven knoweth   Jer 8:7
her
had wings like the wings of a   Zec 5:9
s.

STORM

chaff that the s. carried   Job 21:18
away
as a s. hurleth him out of   Job 27:21
his place
my escape from the windy s.   Ps 55:8
storm (A)   Ps 55:8;
    M't 8:24; Ac 27:18; Heb 12:18
and make them afraid with   Ps 83:15
thy s.
He maketh the s. a calm, so   Ps 107:29
for a covert from s. and from   Isa 4:6
rain
a refuge from the s. a shadow   Isa 25:4
from
blast is as a s. against the   Isa 25:4
wall
tempest of hail and a   Isa 28:2
destroying s.
great noise, with s. and   Isa 29:6
tempest
shalt ascend and come like a   Eze 38:9
s.
in the whirlwind and in the s.   Na 1:3
storm (P)(R)   M't 8:24; Ac 27:18
kingdom taken by s. (P)   M't 11:12
there will be a s. today (P)   M't 16:3
there arose a great s. of   M'k 4:37
wind, and
there came down a s. of wind   Lu 8:23

STORMY

raiseth the s. wind, which   Ps 107:25
lifteth
vapours; s. wind fulfilling his   Ps 148:8
word
fall; and a s. wind shall rend   Eze 13:11
it
even rend it with a s. wind   Eze 13:13
in my
it will be a s. day (A)(R)   M't 16:3

STORY

in the s. of the prophet of   2Ch 13:22
Iddo
in the s. of the book of the   2Ch 24:27
kings
cleverly written up s. (P)   1Pe 1:16

STOUT

the s. lion's whelps are   Job 4:11
scattered
punish the fruit of the s.   Isa 10:12
heart of
arrogant boasting of (B)   Isa 10:12
arrogant heart of (R)   Isa 10:12
look was more s. than his   Da 7:20
fellows
look was greater (A)(B)   Da 7:20
that seemed stronger than (R)   Da 7:20
words have been s. against   Mal 3:13
me

STOUTHEARTED

The s. are spoiled, they have   Ps 76:5
Hearken unto me, ye s. that   Isa 46:12

STOUTNESS

say in the pride and s. of heart   Isa 9:9

STRAGGLERS

all s. in your rear (A)   De 25:18

STRAIGHT

ascend up every man s. before   Jos 6:5
him
the city, every man s. before   Jos 6:20
him
the kine took the s. way to   1Sa 6:12
brought it s. down to the   2Ch 32:30
west side
make thy way s. before my face   Ps 5:8
let thine eyelids look s. before   Pr 4:25
thee
keep way s. (A)(B)(R)   Pr 11:5
is crooked cannot be made s.   Ec 1:15
for who can make that s.   Ec 7:13
which he
make s. in the desert a   Isa 40:3
highway
the crooked shall be made s.   Isa 40:4
before them, and crooked   Isa 42:16
things s.
and make the crooked places   Isa 45:2
s.
by the river of waters in a s.   Jer 31:9
way
their feet were s. feet; and the   Eze 1:7
sole
they went every one s. forward   Eze 1:9;
    1:12
the firmament were their   Eze 1:23
wings s.
they went every one s.   Eze 10:22
forward
of the Lord, make his paths s.   M't 3:3
way of the Lord, make his   M'k 1:3;
paths s.   Lu 3:4
and the crooked shall be made   Lu 3:5
s.
and immediately she was   Lu 13:13
made s.
Make s. the way of the Lord   Joh 1:23
into the street which is called   Ac 9:11
S.
falsifying s. ways of the Lord   Ac 13:10
(N)(B)
with a s. course to   Ac 16:11
Samothracia
came with a s. course unto   Ac 21:1
Coos
uttering s. sound truth (A)   Ac 26:25
And make s. paths for your   Heb 12:13
feet

STRAIGHTEN

s. yourselves out (P)   2Co 13:11

STRAIGHTENED

pressed down, not s. (E)   1Co 4:8

STRAIGHTFORWARD

s. and sincere (N)   Jas 3:17

STRAIGHTWAY

into the city, ye shall s. find   1Sa 9:13
him
Saul fell s. all along on the   1Sa 28:20
earth
He goeth after her s. as an ox   Pr 7:22
s. there remained no strength   Da 10:17
in
went up s. out of the water   M't 3:16
they s. left their nets, and   M't 4:20
followed
s. Jesus constrained his   M't 14:22
disciples
But s. Jesus spake unto them   M't 14:27
s. ye shall find an ass tied, and   M't 21:2
of them; and s. he will send   M't 21:3
them
ability; and s. took his   M't 25:15
journey
And s. one of them ran, and   M't 27:48
took a

And s. coming up out of the   M'k 1:10
water
And s. they forsook their   M'k 1:18
nets, and
And s. he called them: and   M'k 1:20
they
s. on the sabbath day he   M'k 1:21
entered
and s. they tell him of her   M'k 1:30
(S)
s. many were gathered   M'k 2:2
together
s. took counsel with the   M'k 3:6
Herodians
s. the fountain of her blood   M'k 5:29
was
s. the damsel arose, and   M'k 5:42
walked
And she came in s. with   M'k 6:25
haste unto
And s. he constrained his   M'k 6:45
disciples
out of the ship, s. they knew   M'k 6:54
him
And s. his oars were opened   M'k 7:35
s. he entered into a ship with   M'k 8:10
his
s. all the people, when they   M'k 9:15
beheld
he saw him, s. the spirit tare   M'k 9:20
him
s. the father of the child   M'k 9:24
cried out
and s. he will send him   M'k 11:3
hither
he was come, he goeth s.   M'k 14:45
to him
s. in the morning the chief   M'k 15:1
priests
drink cold wine s. desireth   Lu 5:39
new
came again, and she arose s.   Lu 8:55
s. ye say, There cometh a   Lu 12:54
shower
not s. pull him out on the   Lu 14:5
sabbath
himself, and shall s. glorify   Joh 13:32
him
Then fell she down s. at his   Ac 5:10
feet
And s. he preached Christ in   Ac 9:20
was baptized, he and all his   Ac 16:33
s.
Then s. they departed from   Ac 22:29
him
man, I sent s. to thee, and   Ac 23:30
gave
s. forgetteth what manner of   Jas 1:24
man

STRAIN

s. with which he toils (R)   Ec 2:22
blind guides, which s. at a   M't 23:24
gnat
s. the patience of God (P)   Ac 15:10

STRAINED

Jacob's thigh was s. (E)   Ge 32:25

STRAIT

Israel saw that they were in a   1Sa 13:6
s.
said unto Gad, I am in a   2Sa 24:14
great s.
dwell with thee is too s. for us   2Ki 6:1
said unto Gad, I am in a   1Ch 21:13
great s.
remove thee out of the s.   Job 36:16
into a
ears, The place is too s. for   Isa 49:20
me
Enter ye in at the s. gate: for   M't 7:13
wide
s. is the gate, and narrow   M't 7:14
is the
Strive to enter in at the s.   Lu 13:24
gate
For I am in a s. betwixt two   Ph'p 1:23

STRAITEN

that seek their lives, shall s.   Jer 19:9
them

STRAITENED

steps of his strength shall be   Job 18:7
s.

the breadth of the waters is / s. — *Job 37:10*
goest, thy steps shall not be s. — *Pr 4:12*
the building was s. more than — *Eze 42:6*
Jacob, is the spirit of the Lord — *Mic 2:7* / s.
am I s. till it be / accomplished — *Lu 12:50*
Ye are not s. in us, but ye — *2Co 6:12*
but ye are s. in your own / bowels — *2Co 6:12*

STRAITENETH
the nations, and s. them / again — *Job 12:23*

STRAITEST
that after the most s. sect of / our — *Ac 26:5*

STRAITLY
The man asked us s. of our / state — *Ge 43:7*
had s. sworn the children of / Israel — *Ex 13:19*
Jericho was s. shut up because — *Jos 6:1*
Thy father s. charged the / people — *1Sa 14:28*
Jesus s. charged them, saying, / See — *M't 9:30*
he s. charged him, and forth / with — *M'k 1:43*
And he s. charged them that / they — *M'k 3:12*
he charged them s. that no / man — *M'k 5:43*
he s. charged them, and / commanded — *Lu 9:21*
let us s. threaten them, that / they — *Ac 4:17*
Did not we s. command you / that ye — *Ac 5:28*

STRAITNESS
in the siege, and in the s. — *De 28:53;* / *De 28:55*
things secretly in the siege / and s. — *De 28:57*
broad place, where there is / no s. — *Job 36:16*
of his friend in the siege and / s. — *Jer 19:9*

STRAITS
of his sufficiency he shall be / in s. — *Job 20:22*
overtook her between the s. — *La 1:3*

STRAKE
s. sail, and so were driven — *Ac 27:17*
lowered the gear / (A)(B)(E)(R) — *Ac 27:17*
lowered the mainsail (N) — *Ac 27:17*
shortened the sail (P) — *Ac 27:17*

STRAKES
and pilled white s. in them / (A)(B)(E) — *Ge 30:37*
peeled white streaks in them / (R) — *Ge 30:37*
peeled white stripes in them — *Ge 30:37*
walls of the house with / hollow s. — *Le 14:37*
with depressed spots in them / (A) — *Le 14:37*
in greenish or reddish / cavities (B) — *Le 14:37*
with hollow streaks (E) — *Le 14:37*
spots (R) — *Le 14:37*

STRAND
a s. of rope snaps (B)(S) — *J'g 16:9*

STRANDS
with woven s. (B) — *Ps 118:27*

STRANGE
Put away the s. gods, among / you — *Ge 35:2*

foreign gods (B) — *Ge 35:2;* / *35:4; Jos 24:20; J'g 10:16; 1Sa 7:3;* / *2Ch 33:15; Jer 5:19*
foreign gods (E) — *Ge 35:2;* / *35:4; Jos 24:20, 23; J'g 10:16; 1Sa 7:3;* / *2Ch 33:15*
gave unto Jacob all the s. gods — *Ge 35:4*
but made himself s. unto them — *Ge 42:7*
treated them like strangers — *Ge 42:7*
I have been a stranger in a s. / land — *Ex 2:22*
foreign land (B) — *Ex 2:22;* / *18:3; Ps 137:4; Heb 11:9*
foreign land (E) — *Ex 2:22;* / *18:3; Ps 137:4*
foreign land (R) — *Ex 2:22; 18:3*
I have been an alien in a s. / land — *Ex 18:3*
to sell her unto a s. nation he / shall — *Ex 21:8*
foreign people (A)(B)(E) — *Ex 21:8*
outsiders (R) — *Ex 21:8*
Ye shall offer no s. incense — *Ex 30:9*
unholy incense (A)(B) — *Ex 30:9*
and offered s. fire before the / Lord — *Le 10:1*
unholy fire (B) — *Le 10:1;* / *Nu 3:4; 26:61*
they offered s. fire before the / Lord — *Nu 3:4*
improper fire (R) — *Nu 3:4; 26:61*
they offered s. fire before the / Lord — *Nu 26:61*
s. gods (A) — *De 31:16; Jer 5:19*
and there was no s. god with / him — *De 32:12*
foreign gods (A) — *De 32:12;* / *Jos 24:23; J'g 10:16; 1Sa 7:3; 2Ch 33:15;* / *Da 11:39; Mal 2:11*
foreign god (B)(E) — *De 32:12;* / *Da 11:39; Mal 2:11*
him to jealousy with s. gods — *De 32:16*
the Lord, and serve s. gods, — *Jos 24:20*
the s. gods which are among / you — *Jos 24:23*
put away the s. gods from / among — *J'g 10:16*
thou art the son of a s. woman — *J'g 11:2*
then put away the s. gods and — *1Sa 7:3*
Solomon loved many s. / women — *1Ki 11:1*
foreign women (A) — *1Ki 11:1; Ne 13:27*
foreign women (B) — *1Ki 11:1;* / *Ezr 10:2, 10, 17-18, 44; Ne 13:27*
foreign women (E) — *1Ki 11:1;* / *Ezr 10:2, 10, 14, 17-18; Ne 13:27;* / *Pr 23:27; 27:13*
foreign women (R) — *1Ki 11:1;* / *Ezr 10:2, 10-11, 14, 17-18, 44; Ne 13:27*
likewise did he for all his s. / wives — *1Ki 11:8*
foreign wives (A) — *1Ki 11:8;* / *Ezr 10:2, 10, 14, 17, 44*
foreign wives (B) — *1Ki 11:8;* / *Ezr 10:11, 14*
foreign wives (E) — *1Ki 11:8; Ezr 10:44*
foreign wives (R) — *1Ki 11:8*
have digged and drunk s. / waters — *2Ki 19:24*
foreign waters (A)(B) — *2Ki 19:24*
away the altars of the s. gods — *2Ch 14:3*
foreign altars / (A)(B)(E)(R) — *2Ch 14:3*
he took away the s. gods, / and the — *2Ch 33:15*
foreign gods (R) — *2Ch 33:15; Jer 5:19*
have taken s. wives of the / people — *Ezr 10:2*
and have taken s. wives to / increase — *Ezr 10:10*
of the land, and from the s. / wives — *Ezr 10:11*
all them which have taken s. / wives — *Ezr 10:14*
all the men that had taken s. / wives — *Ezr 10:17*
found that had taken s. / wives — *Ezr 10:18*
All these had taken s. wives — *Ezr 10:44*
s. women caused him to sin / (A) — *Ne 13:26*
transgress in marrying s. / wives — *Ne 13:27*
that ye make yourselves s. to / me — *Job 19:3*
My breath is s. to my wife — *Job 19:17*
repulsive (A)(B) — *Job 19:17*
a s. punishment to the workers — *Job 31:3*

stretched out hands to a s. / god — *Ps 44:20*
There shall no s. god be in / thee — *Ps 81:9*
shalt thou worship any s. god — *Ps 81:9*
Jacob from a people of s. / language — *Ps 114:1*
alien speech (R) — *Ps 114:1*
sing the Lord's song in a s. / land — *Ps 137:4*
from the hand of s. children — *Ps 144:7*
hostile alien tribes (A) — *Ps 144:7*
aliens (B)(E) — *Ps 144:7*
alien's children (R) — *Ps 144:7*
me from the hand of s. / children — *Ps 144:11*
deliver thee from the s. woman — *Pr 2:16*
alien women (A) — *Pr 2:16*
loose women (B) — *Pr 2:16;* / *5:3 20; 7:5; 22:14*
loose women (R) — *Pr 2:16; 5:3, 20*
the lips of a s. woman drop as — *Pr 5:3*
loose woman (A) — *Pr 5:3;* / *5:20; 6:24; 7:5; 22:14; 23:27, 33*
son, be ravished with a s. / woman — *Pr 5:20*
bosom of a s. woman (E) — *Pr 5:20; 7:5*
of the tongue of a s. woman — *Pr 6:24*
adventuress (A) — *Pr 6:24; 23:27*
foreigner's tongue (E) — *Pr 6:24*
keep thee from the s. woman — *Pr 7:5*
a pledge of him for a s. / woman — *Pr 20:16*
stranger (A) — *Pr 20:16; 27:13*
foreigners (B) — *Pr 20:16; 27:13*
foreigners (E)(R) — *Pr 20:16*
way of man is froward and s. — *Pr 21:8*
mouth of s. woman is a deep / pit — *Pr 22:14*
and a s. woman is a narrow / pit — *Pr 23:27*
alien women (R) — *Pr 23:27; 27:13*
Thine eyes shall behold s. / women — *Pr 23:33*
a pledge of him for a s. / woman — *Pr 27:13*
and shalt set it with s. slips — *Isa 17:10*
alien god (B) — *Isa 17:10*
he may do his work, his s. / work — *Isa 28:21*
alien work (B) — *Isa 28:21*
bring to pass his act, his s. / act — *Isa 28:21*
there was no s. god among / you — *Isa 43:12*
the degenerate plant of a s. / vine — *Jer 2:21*
wild vine (A)(B) — *Jer 2:21*
foreign vine (E) — *Jer 2:21*
alien vine (R) — *Jer 2:21*
and served s. gods in your / land — *Jer 5:19*
images, and with s. vanities — *Jer 8:19*
foreign idols (A)(B)(R) — *Jer 8:19*
foreign vanities (E) — *Jer 8:19*
not sent to a people of a s. / speech — *Eze 3:5*
Not to many people of a s. — *Eze 3:6*
foreign tongue (R) — *Eze 3:6*
most strong holds with a s. / god — *Da 11:39*
they have begotten s. children — *Ho 5:7*
alien children (A)(B) — *Ho 5:7*
they were counted as a s. / thing — *Ho 8:12*
as are clothed with s. apparel — *Zep 1:8*
foreign apparel (A)(E)(R) — *Zep 1:8*
foreign attire (B) — *Zep 1:8*
married the daughter of a s. / god — *Mal 2:11*
We have seen s. things to day — *Lu 5:26*
seed should sojourn in a s. land — *Ac 7:6*
foreign land (N)(P)(R) — *Ac 7:6*
to be a setter forth of s. gods — *Ac 17:18*
foreign deities (A)(N) — *Ac 17:18*
foreign divinities (B) — *Ac 17:18*
certain s. things to our ears — *Ac 17:20*
I persecuted them unto s. / cities — *Ac 26:11*
foreign cities / (A)(B)(E)(N)(R) — *Ac 26:11*
distant cities (P) — *Ac 26:11*
land of promise, as in a s. / country — *Heb 11:9*
foreign country (R) — *Heb 11:9*
about with divers and s. / doctrines — *Heb 13:9*
alien teachings (A) — *Heb 13:9*
outlandish teachings (N) — *Heb 13:9*
peculiar teachings (P) — *Heb 13:9*

think it *s.* ye run not with them   *1Pe 4:4*
very queer (A)(P)   *1Pe 4:4*
surprised (B)(R)   *1Pe 4:4; 4:12*
cannot understand it (N)   *1Pe 4:4*
think it not *s.* concerning the   *1Pe 4:12*
fiery
some *s.* thing happened   *1Pe 4:12*
unto you
bewildered, something   *1Pe 4:12*
extraordinary (N)
unduly alarmed (P)   *1Pe 4:12*
and going after *s.* flesh, are set   *Jude 7*

STRANGELY

should behave themselves *s.*   *De 32:27*
lest enemies misconstrue it   *De 32:27*
(A)(R)
lest adversaries judge amiss   *De 32:27*
(B)(E)

STRANGER

be a *s.* in a land that is not   *Ge 15:13*
theirs
sojourner (B)   *Ge 15:13;*
Ex 2:22; 12:19; 20:10; Le 17:15; 19:10;
24:16, 22; 25:6; Nu 9:14; 15:30;
De 5:14; 10:18, 19, 29; 16:11; 23:7;
24:17, 19; 26:11, 12, 13; 27:19; 28:43;
29:11; 31:12; Jos 8:33; 2Sa 1:13;
Job 31:32; Ps 39:12; 94:6; 119:19;
Eze 22:7, 29; Zec 7:10; Mal 3:5
sojourner (E)   *Ge 15:13;*
23:4; Ex 12:19; 22:21; 23:9; 12;
Le 19:10; 24:16, 22; De 1:16; 10:18, 19;
14:21, 29; 16:11; 23:7, 20; 24:17, 19;
26:11, 12, 13; 27:19; 28:43; 29:11; 31:12;
Jos 8:33; 2Sa 1:16; Job 31:32; Ps 94:6;
119:19; Jer 7:6; 14:8; 22:3; Eze 22:7, 29;
Zec 7:10; Mal 3:5; Ac 7:29
sojourner (R)   *Ge 15:13;*
Ex 2:22; 12:19; 20:10; Le 17:15; 19:10;
22:10; 25:6; De 5:14; 10:18, 19; 14:29;
16:11; 23:7; 24:17, 19; 26:11, 12, 13;
27:19; 28:43; 29:11; 31:12; Jos 8:33;
2Sa 1:13; Job 31:32; Ps 39:12; 94:6;
119:19; Eze 22:7, 29; Zec 7:10; Mal 3:5
the land wherein thou art a *s.*   *Ge 17:8*
bought with money of any *s.*   *Ge 17:12*
foreigner (A)   *Ge 17:12;*
17:27; Eze 12:43; De 17:15; 23:20;
29:22; J'g 19:12; Ru 2:10; 2Sa 1:13;
15:19; Isa 56:6; Eze 44:9; 47:23
foreigner (E)   *Ge 17:12;*
17:27; Ex 12:43; De 14:21; 17:15; 23:20;
29:22; J'g 19:12; Ru 2:10; 2Sa 15:19;
1Ki 8:41, 43; 2Ch 6:32, 33; Isa 56:3, 6;
62:8; Eze 44:9; Lu 17:18
foreigner (E)   *Ge 17:12;*
17:27; Ex 12:43; De 17:15; 29:22;
J'g 19:12; Ru 2:10; 2Sa 15:19; 8:41, 43;
2Ch 6:32, 33; Pr 2:16; Isa 56:3, 6; 62:8;
Eze 44:9
foreigner (R)   *Ge 17:12;*
17:27; Ex 12:43; De 14:21; 17:15; 23:20;
29:22; J'g 19:12; Ru 2:10; 2Sa 15:19;
1Ki 8:41, 43; 2Ch 6:32, 33; Pr 20:16;
Isa 56:3-6; 62:8; Eze 44:9; Lu 17:18
bought with money of the *s.*   *Ge 17:27*
lived as a *s.* (B)   *Ge 21:34*
I am a *s.* and a sojourner   *Ge 23:4*
with you
the land wherein thou art a *s.*   *Ge 28:4*
sojourner (A)   *Ge 28:4;*
Ex 20:10; Le 24:22; Jos 8:33; Jer 14:8
land wherein his father was a   *Ge 37:1*
s.
I have been a *s.* in a strange   *Ex 2:22*
land
foreign land (E)   *Ex 2:22*
whether he be a *s.* or born in   *Ex 12:19*
There shall no *s.* eat thereof   *Ex 12:43*
when a *s.* shall sojourn with   *Ex 12:48*
thee
the *s.* that sojourneth among   *Ex 12:49*
you
nor thy *s.* that is within thy   *Ex 20:10*
gates
Thou shalt neither vex a *s.*   *Ex 22:21*
nor
Also thou shalt not oppress a   *Ex 23:9*
s.
for ye know the heart of a *s.*   *Ex 23:9*
seeing
son of thy handmaid, and the   *Ex 23:12*
s.
alien (A)   *Ex 23:12; Isa 62:8*
alien (B)   *Ex 23:12;*

De 1:16; Job 19:15; Jer 7:6; 22:3;
  Eze 47:23
alien (R)   *Ex 23:12;*
De 1:16; Job 19:15; Pr 5:10; 22:3;
  Eze 47:23
but a *s.* shall not eat thereof   *Ex 29:33*
putteth any of it upon a *s.*   *Ex 30:33*
a *s.* that sojourneth among   *Le 16:29*
you
any *s.* that sojourneth among   *Le 17:12*
you
be one of your own country,   *Le 17:15*
or a *s.*
any *s.* that sojourneth among   *Le 18:26*
you
shalt leave them for the poor   *Le 19:10*
and *s.*
if a *s.* sojourn with thee in   *Le 19:33*
your land
But the *s.* that dwelleth with   *Le 19:34*
you
There shall no *s.* eat of the   *Le 22:10*
holy
daughter married unto a *s.*   *Le 22:12*
but there shall no *s.* eat   *Le 22:13*
thereof
them unto the poor, and the *s.*   *Le 23:22*
as well the *s.* as he that is   *Le 24:16*
born in
as well for the *s.* as for one   *Le 24:22*
of your
thy *s.* that sojourneth with   *Le 25:6*
thee
though he be a *s.* or a   *Le 25:35*
sojourner
sojourner or *s.* wax rich by   *Le 25:47*
thee
and sell himself unto the *s.* or   *Le 25:47*
s. that cometh nigh shall be   *Nu 1:51;*
put   *Nu 3:10; 3:38*
if a *s.* shall sojourn among   *Nu 9:14*
you
for the *s.* and for him that   *Nu 9:14*
was born
And if a *s.* sojourn with you   *Nu 15:14*
for the *s.* that sojourneth   *Nu 15:15*
with you
so shall the *s.* be before the   *Nu 15:15*
Lord
for the *s.* that sojourneth   *Nu 15:16*
with you
the *s.* that sojourneth   *Nu 15:26;*
among them   *15:29*
he be born in the land, or a   *Nu 15:30*
s.
no *s.* which is not of the   *Nu 16:40*
seed
a *s.* shall not come nigh unto   *Nu 18:4*
you
the *s.* that cometh nigh shall   *Nu 18:7*
be put
s. that sojourneth among   *Nu 19:10*
them
children of Israel, and for   *Nu 35:15*
the *s.*
brother, and the *s.* that is with   *De 1:16*
him
nor thy *s.* that is within thy   *De 5:14*
gates
and loveth the *s.* in giving   *De 10:18*
him food
Love ye therefore the *s.:* for   *De 10:19*
ye
shalt give it unto the *s.* that   *De 14:21*
is in thy
and the *s.* and the fatherless   *De 14:29;*
  16:14
the *s.* and the fatherless, and   *De 16:11*
mayest not set a *s.* over thee   *De 17:15*
because thou wast a *s.* in his   *De 23:7*
land
Unto a *s.* thou mayest lend   *De 23:20*
not pervert the judgment of   *De 24:17*
the *s.*
it shall be for the *s.*   *De 24:19;*
  24:20-21
not marry without unto a *s.*   *De 25:5*
and the *s.* that is among you   *De 26:11*
s. the fatherless, and the   *De 26:12*
widow
unto the *s.* to the fatherless   *De 26:13*
perverteth the judgment of   *De 27:19*
the *s.*
The *s.* that is within thee shall   *De 28:43*
yet
and thy *s.* that is in thy camp   *De 29:11*
far
the *s.* that shall come from a   *De 29:22*
and thy *s.* that is within thy   *De 31:12*
gates

as well the *s.* as he that was   *Jos 8:33*
born
for the *s.* that sojourneth   *Jos 20:9*
among
aside hither into the city of a   *J'g 19:12*
s.
knowledge of me, seeing I am   *Ru 2:10*
a *s.*
answered, I am the son of a   *2Sa 1:13*
s.
thou art a *s.* and also an exile   *2Sa 15:19*
was no *s.* with us in the   *1Ki 3:18*
house
Moreover concerning a *s.*   *1Ki 8:41*
that is
all that the *s.* calleth to thee   *1Ki 8:43*
for
Moreover concerning the *s.*   *2Ch 6:32*
which
to all that the *s.* calleth to   *2Ch 6:33*
thee for
and no *s.* passed among   *Job 15:19*
them
and my maids, count me for   *Job 19:15*
a *s.*
The *s.* did not lodge in the   *Job 31:32*
street
I am a *s.* with thee, and a   *Ps 39:12*
sojourner
I am a *s.* unto my brethren   *Ps 69:8*
They slay the widow and the   *Ps 94:6*
s.
I am a *s.* in the earth: hide   *Ps 119:19*
not thy
from the *s.* which flattereth   *Pr 2:16*
with
alien woman (A)   *Pr 2:16*
adventuress (B)(R)   *Pr 2:16; 5:20; 7:5*
thy labours be in the house of   *Pr 5:10*
a *s.*
and embrace the bosom of a *s.*   *Pr 5:20*
strange woman (E)   *Pr 5:20; 7:5*
hast stricken thy hand with a *s.*   *Pr 6:1*
from the *s.* which flattereth with   *Pr 7:5*
loose woman (A)   *Pr 7:5*
that is surety for a *s.* shall   *Pr 11:15*
smart
a *s.* doth not intermeddle   *Pr 14:10*
with his
his garment that is surety for   *Pr 20:16*
a *s.*
a *s.* and not thine own lips   *Pr 27:2*
his garment that is surety for   *Pr 27:13*
a *s.*
eat thereof, but a *s.* eateth it   *Ec 6:2*
Neither let the son of the *s.*   *Isa 56:3*
that
also the sons of the *s.* that join   *Isa 56:6*
the sons of the *s.* shall not   *Isa 62:8*
drink
If ye oppress not the *s.,* the   *Jer 7:6*
the transient and the alien (A)   *Jer 7:6*
thou be as a *s.* in the land   *Jer 14:8*
no wrong, do no violence to   *Jer 22:3;*
the *s.* that sojourneth in   *Eze 14:7*
Israel
dealt by oppression with the   *Eze 22:7*
s.
have oppressed the *s.*   *Eze 22:29*
wrongfully
s. uncircumcised in heart   *Eze 44:9*
of any *s.* that is among the   *Eze 44:9*
in what tribe the *s.*   *Eze 47:23*
sojourneth
in the day that he became a *s.*   *Ob 12*
widow, nor the father.ess, the   *Zec 7:10*
s.
turn aside the *s.* from his right   *Mal 3:5*
I was a *s.* and ye took me in   *M't 25:35*
When saw we thee a *s.* and   *M't 25:38*
took
I was a *s.* and ye took me   *M't 25:43*
not in
or a *s.* or naked, or sick, or   *M't 25:44*
to give glory to God, save   *Lu 17:18*
this *s.*
alien (A)   *Lu 17:18*
foreigner (N)   *Lu 17:18*
Art thou only a *s.* in   *Lu 24:18*
Jerusalem
a visitor (B)(R)   *Lu 24:18*
And a *s.* will they not follow   *Joh 10:5*
was a *s.* in the land of   *Ac 7:29*
Madian
an exile and an alien (A)   *Ac 7:29*
an exile (B)(P)(R)   *Ac 7:29*

STRANGERS

Are we not counted of him *s.*   *Ge 31:15*
outsiders (B)   *Ge 31:15; Ps 18:44*

foreigners (E) *Ge 31:15;*
2Sa 22:45, 46; Ne 9:2; 13:30; Ps 18:44,
45; Isa 2:6; 60:10; Eze 44:7
foreigners (R) *Ge 31:15;*
2Sa 22:45, 46; Ne 9:2; Isa 2:6; Eze 7:21;
11:9; 28:10; 30:12; 31:12; 44:7; Ac 17:21
and the land wherein they *Ge 36:7*
were *s.*
immigrants (B) *Ge 36:7;*
De 10:19; 24:14; Ps 46:9; Eze 47:22
pilgrimage, wherein they were *Ex 6:4*
s.
sojourners (R) *Ex 6:4;*
Le 22:18; De 10:19; 24:14; Jos 8:35;
1Ch 16:19; 30:25; Ps 18:44, 45; 105:12;
146:9; Isa 60:10
for ye were *s.* in the land of *Ex 22:21*
Egypt
aliens (B) *Ex 22:21;*
23:9; 1Ch 22:3; 2Ch 2:17; Ps 5:10;
Isa 14:1; 61:5; Eze 28:7; 30:12; 44:7;
Joe 3:17
sojourners (E) *Ex 22:21;*
23:9; Le 22:18; De 10:19; 24:14;
Jos 8:35; 1Ch 16:19; 22:2; 2Ch 2:17;
30:25; Ps 105:12; 146:9; Isa 14:1;
Ac 2:10; 1Pe 1:1; 2:11
ye were *s.* in the land of Egypt *Ex 23:9*
s. which sojourn among you *Le 17:8;*
17:10, 13
for ye were *s.* in the land of *Le 19:34*
Egypt
of the *s.* that sojourn in Israel *Le 20:2*
foreigners (B) *Le 20:2;*
22:18; Jos 8:35; 2Sa 22:46; Ne 9:2;
13:30; Ps 18:45; Isa 1:7; 2:6; 5:17; 25:2,
5; Eze 28:10; Ho 8:7; Ac 17:21
house of Israel, or of the *s.* *Le 22:18*
in Israel
foreigners (A) *Le 22:18;*
2Sa 22:45, 46; Ne 9:2; Ps 18:44, 45;
Isa 14:1; 60:10; 61:5; Eze 11:9; 47:22
ye are *s.* and sojourners with *Le 25:23*
me
lodgers and tenants (B) *Le 25:23*
the *s.* that do sojourn among *Le 25:45*
you
ye were *s.* in the land of *De 10:19*
Egypt
thy *s.* that are in thy land *De 24:14*
within
after the gods of the *s.* of the *De 31:16*
land
strange gods (A) *De 31:16; Jer 5:19*
s. that were conversant among *Jos 8:35*
S. shall submit themselves *2Sa 22:45*
S. shall fade away, and they *2Sa 22:46*
but few, even a few, and *s.* *1Ch 16:19*
in it
pilgrims (B) *1Ch 16:19; 1Pe 1:1*
to gather together the *s.* that *1Ch 22:2*
aliens (R) *1Ch 22:2;*
2Ch 2:17; Isa 1:7; 14:1; 25:2, 5; 61:5;
Jer 51:51; Eze 47:22; Ho 7:9; 8:7
For we are *s.* before thee *1Ch 29:15*
tenants (B) *1Ch 29:15*
Solomon numbered all the *s.* *2Ch 2:17*
aliens (A) *2Ch 2:17*
the *s.* with them out of *2Ch 15:9*
Ephraim
the *s.* that came out of the *2Ch 30:25*
land of
sojourners (A) *2Ch 30:25*
foreign residents (B) *2Ch 30:25*
Israel separated from all *s.* *Ne 9:2*
Thus cleansed I them from *Ne 13:30*
all *s.*
s. shall submit themselves *Ps 18:44*
The *s.* shall fade away, and *Ps 18:45*
For *s.* are risen up against me *Ps 54:3*
insolent men (A) *Ps 54:3*
yea, very few and *s.* in it *Ps 105:12*
and let the *s.* spoil his *Ps 109:11*
labour
The Lord preserveth the *s.;* *Ps 146:9*
he
Lest *s.* be filled with thy wealth *Pr 5:10*
land, *s.* devour it in your *Isa 1:7*
presence
it is desolate, as overthrown by *Isa 1:7*
s.
themselves in the children of *s.* *Isa 2:6*
aliens (A) *Isa 2:6; 25:2, 5; Eze 44:7*
places of the fat ones shall *s.* *Isa 5:17*
eat
sojourners and aliens (A) *Isa 5:17*
wanderers (E) *Isa 5:17*
the *s.* shall be joined with *Isa 14:1*
them
a palace of *s.* to be no city; it *Isa 25:2*

shalt bring down the noise of *Isa 25:5*
s. as
multitude of thy *s.* be *Isa 29:5*
like dust
foes (E)(R) *Isa 29:5*
sons of *s.* shall build up thy *Isa 60:10*
walls
s. shall stand and feed your *Isa 61:5*
flocks
for I have loved *s.* and after *Jer 2:25*
them
hast scattered thy ways to the *Jer 3:13*
s.
so shall ye serve *s.* in a land *Jer 5:19*
s. shall no more serve *Jer 30:8*
themselves
days in the land where ye be *Jer 35:7*
s.
temporary residents (A) *Jer 35:7*
s. are come into the *Jer 51:51*
sanctuaries
Our inheritance is turned to *s.* *La 5:2*
into the hands of the *s.* for a *Eze 7:21*
prey
and deliver you into the *Eze 11:9*
hands of *s.*
taketh *s.* instead of her *Eze 16:32*
husband
therefore I will bring *s.* upon *Eze 28:7*
thee
uncircumcised by the hand *Eze 28:10*
of *s.*
that is therein, by the hand *Eze 30:12*
of *s.*
And *s.* the terrible of the *Eze 31:12*
nations
brought into my sanctuary *s.* *Eze 44:7*
to the *s.* that sojourn among *Eze 47:22*
you
s. who reside (A) *Eze 47:22*
S. have devoured his strength *Ho 7:9*
it yield, the *s.* shall swallow it *Ho 8:7*
up
shall no *s.* pass through her *Joe 3:17*
any
s. carried away captive his *Ob 11*
forces
of their own children, or of *M't 17:25*
aliens (N) *M't 17:25; Eph 2:19*
Peter saith unto him, Of *s.* *M't 17:26*
Jesus
the potter's field, to bury *s.* in *M't 27:7*
foreigners (N)(P) *M't 27:7*
for they know not the voice *Joh 10:5*
of *s.*
s. of Rome, Jews and *Ac 2:10*
proselytes
visitors (B)(N)(P)(R) *Ac 2:10*
dwelt as *s.* in land of Egypt *Ac 13:17*
s. which were there spent their *Ac 17:21*
foreign residents (A)(N) *Ac 17:21*
foreign visitors (P) *Ac 17:21*
s. from the covenants of *Eph 2:12*
promise
ye are no more *s.* and *Eph 2:19*
foreigners
outsiders, exiles, migrants, *Eph 2:19*
aliens (A)
s. and immigrants (B) *Eph 2:19*
outsiders or aliens (P) *Eph 2:19*
up children, if she have lodged *1Ti 5:10*
s.
s. to all good (N) *2Ti 3:3*
confessed that they were *s.* *Heb 11:13*
exiles and foreigners (P) *Heb 11:13*
Be not forgetful to entertain *Heb 13:2*
s.
to the *s.* scattered throughout *1Pe 1:1*
exiles (A)(P)(R) *1Pe 1:1*
I beseech you as *s.* and *1Pe 2:11*
pilgrims
aliens and exiles (A) *1Pe 2:11*
aliens (N) *1Pe 2:11*
doest to the brethren, and to *s.* *3Jo 5*

STRANGER'S

Neither from a *s.* hand shall *Le 22:25*
foreigner (A)(B)(E)(R) *Le 22:25*
or to the stock of the *s.* *Le 25:47*
family
the offspring of a foreign *Le 25:47*
race (B)

STRANGERS'

thine own, and not *s.* with thee *Pr 5:17*

STRANGLED

whelps, and *s.* for his *Na 2:12*
lionesses
fornication, and from things *Ac 15:20*
s.
and from blood and from *Ac 15:29*
things *s.*
and from *s.* and from *Ac 21:25*
fornication

STRANGLING

So that my soul chooseth *s.* *Job 7:15*

STRATAGEM

they proceeded with *s.* (B) *Jos 9:4*
arrest Jesus by *s.* (A) *M't 26:4*

STRATEGIES

s. and deceits of the devil *Eph 6:11*
(A)

STRAW

We have both *s.* and *Ge 24:25*
provender
s. and provender for the *Ge 24:32*
camels
give the people *s.* to make brick *Ex 5:7*
go and gather *s.* for themselves *Ex 5:7*
Pharaoh, I will not give you *s.* *Ex 5:10*
get you *s.* where ye can find it; *Ex 5:11*
yet
to gather stubble instead of *s.* *Ex 5:12*
daily tasks as when there was *s.* *Ex 5:13*
is no *s.* given unto thy *Ex 5:16*
servants
for there shall no *s.* be given *Ex 5:18*
you
Yet there is both *s.* and *J'g 19:19*
provender
Barley also and *s.* for the *1Ki 4:28*
horses
He esteemeth iron as *s.* and *Job 41:27*
brass
and the lion shall eat *s.* like *Isa 11:7*
the ox
even as *s.* is trodden down *Isa 25:10*
for the
lion shall eat *s.* like the *Isa 65:25*
bullock

STRAWED

powder, and *s.* it upon the *Ex 32:20*
water
scattered them on the water *Ex 32:20*
(A)(B)(R)
the trees, and *s.* them in the *M't 21:8*
way
scattering them on the road *M't 21:8*
(A)
spread clothes on the road *M't 21:8*
(B)(E)(P)(R)
carpeted the road with *M't 21:8;*
cloaks (N) *M'k 11:8*
gathering where thou hast *M't 25:24*
not *s.*
where you had not *M't 25:24;*
winnowed (A)(B)(R) *25:26*
where you did not scatter *Mt 25:24;*
(E)(N) *25:26*
and gather where I have not *M't 25:26*
s.
the trees and *s.* them in the *M'k 11:8*
way
spread garments on the road *M'k 11:8*
(A)(B)(E)(R)

STREAKED

streaked (A) *M'k 30:35;*
30:39, 40; 31:8, 10, 12
s., speckled, spotted (A) *M'k 31:10*

STREAKS

peeled white *s.* *Ge 30:37;*
(A)(B)(E)(R) *30:38*

STREAM

at the *s.* of the brooks that *Nu 21:15*
goeth
as the *s.* of brooks they pass *Job 6:15*
away
poured out as a *s.* (A) *Job 22:16*

us, the s. had gone over our soul	Ps 124:4
of the river unto the s. of Egypt	Isa 27:12
his breath, as an overflowing s.	Isa 30:28
like a s. of brimstone, doth kindle	Isa 30:33
Among the smooth stones of the s.	Isa 57:6
like a rushing s. (B)(E)(R)	Isa 59:19
of the Gentiles like a flowing s.	Isa 66:12
be an overflowing s. (A)(E)	Jer 47:2
A fiery s. issued and came forth	Da 7:10
and righteousness as a mighty s.	Am 5:24
the s. beat vehemently upon that	Lu 6:48
against which the s. did beat	Lu 6:49
swallowed up s. of water (A)(B)(E)(N)(P)(R)	Re 12:16

STREAMS

the waters of Egypt, upon their s.	Ex 7:19
thine hand with thy rod over the s.	Ex 8:5
s. stood like a wall (B)	Ex 15:8
rivers and flowing s. (A)(B)(E)(R)	Job 20:17; 28:11
s. of ungodliness (A)(B)	Ps 18:4
the s. whereof shall make glad	Ps 46:4
He brought s. also out of the rock	Ps 78:16
gushed out, and the s. overflowed	Ps 78:20
their s., that they could not drink (S)	Ps 78:44
cleave fountains and s. (A)	Ps 74:15
O Lord, as the s. in the south	Ps 126:4
waters, and s. from Lebanon	Ca 4:15
and shall smite it in the seven s.	Isa 11:15
rivers and s. of waters in the day	Isa 30:25
us a place of broad rivers and s.	Isa 33:21
the s. thereof shall be turned into	Isa 34:9
break out, and s. in the desert	Isa 35:6
s. upon dry ground (B)(E)(R)	Isa 44:3

STREET

we will abide in the s. all night	Ge 19:2
of it into the midst of the s. thereof	De 13:16
the doors of thy house into the s.	Jos 2:19
he sat him down in a s. of the city	J'g 19:15
wayfaring man in the s. of the city	J'g 19:17
upon me; only lodge not in the s.	J'g 19:20
them from the s. of Beth-shan	2Sa 21:12
stamp them as the mire of the s.	2Sa 22:43
them together into the east s.	2Ch 29:4
him in the s. of the gate of the city	2Ch 32:6
sat in the s. of the house of God	Ezr 10:9
s. that was before the water gate	Ne 8:1; 8:3
and in the s. of the water gate, and	Ne 8:16
in the s. of the gate of Ephraim	Ne 8:16
to Mordecai unto the s. of the city	Es 4:6
horseback through the s. of the	Es 6:9; 6:11
shall have no name in the s.	Job 18:17
when I prepared my seat in the s.	Job 29:7
stranger did not lodge in the s.	Job 31:32
through the s. near her corner	Pr 7:8
his voice to be heard in the s.	Isa 42:2
as the s. to them that went over	Isa 51:23
truth is fallen in the s. and equity	Isa 59:14

piece of bread out of the bakers' s.	Jer 37:21
for hunger in the top of every s.	La 2:19
poured out in the top of every s.	La 4:1
thee an high place in every s.	Eze 16:24
makest thine high place in every s.	Eze 16:31
the s. shall be built again, and	Da 9:25
the s. which is called Straight	Ac 9:11
out, and passed on through one s.	Ac 12:10
dead bodies shall lie in the s.	Re 11:8
the s. of the city was pure gold	Re 21:21
In the midst of the s. of it	Re 22:2

STREETS

publish it not in the s. of Askelon	2Sa 1:20
shalt make s. for thee in Damascus	1Ki 20:34
cast them out as the dirt in the s.	Ps 18:42
and guile depart not from her s.	Ps 55:11
and ten thousands in our s.	Ps 144:13
there be no complaining in our s.	Ps 144:14
she uttereth her voice in the s.	Pr 1:20
abroad, and rivers of waters in	Pr 5:16
Now is she without, now in the s.	Pr 7:12
without, I shall be slain in the s.	Pr 22:13
a lion in the way; a lion is in the s.	Pr 26:13
the doors shall be shut in the s.	Ec 12:4
and the mourners go about the s.	Ec 12:5
now, and go about the city in the s.	Ca 3:2
were torn in the midst of the s.	Isa 5:25
them down like the mire of the s.	Isa 10:6
In their s. they shall gird themselves	Isa 15:3
in their s. every one shall howl	Isa 15:3
is a crying for wine in the s.	Isa 24:11
they lie at the head of all the s. as	Isa 51:20
and fro through the s. of Jerusalem	Jer 5:1
of Judah and in the s. of Jerusalem	Jer 7:17
from the s. of Jerusalem, the voice	Jer 7:34
and the young men from the	Jer 9:21
Judah, and in the s. of Jerusalem	Jer 11:6
the number of the s. of Jerusalem	Jer 11:13
be cast out in the s. of Jerusalem	Jer 14:16
Judah and in the s. of Jerusalem	Jer 33:10
of Judah and in the s. of Jerusalem	Jer 44:6
Judah, and in the s. of	Jer 44:9; 44:17, 21
of Moab, and in the s. thereof	Jer 48:38
her young men shall fall in her s.	Jer 49:26
shall her young men fall in the s.	Jer 50:30
that are thrust through in her s.	Jer 51:4
and the sucklings swoon in the s.	La 2:11
swooned as the wounded in the s.	La 2:12
the old lie on the ground in the s.	La 2:21
delicately are desolate in the s.	La 4:5
they are not known in the s.	La 4:8
wandered as blind men in the s.	La 4:14
steps, that we cannot go in our s.	La 4:18
shall cast their silver in the s.	Eze 7:19
filled the s. thereof with the slain	Eze 11:6

shall he tread down all thy s.	Eze 26:11
pestilence, and blood into her s.	Eze 28:23
Wailing shall be in all the s.	Am 5:16
trodden down as the mire of the s.	Mic 7:10
The chariots shall rage in the s.	Na 2:4
dashed in pieces at top of the s.	Na 3:10
I made their s. waste, that none	Zep 3:6
and old women dwell in the s.	Zec 8:4
s. of the city shall be full of boys	Zec 8:5
and girls playing in the s. thereof	Zec 8:5
and fine gold as the mire of the s.	Zec 9:3
in the mire of the s. in the battle	Zec 10:5
in the synagogues and in the s.	M't 6:2
and in the corners of the s.	M't 6:5
any man hear his voice in the s.	M't 12:19
they laid the sick in the s.	M'k 6:56
go your ways out into the s.	Lu 10:10
and thou hast taught in our s.	Lu 13:26
Go out quickly into the s. and lanes	Lu 14:21
great s. and small s. (A)	Lu 14:21
s. and alleys of the city (B)(N)	Lu 14:21
brought forth the sick into the s.	Ac 5:15

STRENGTH

ground not henceforth yield her s.	Ge 4:12
not yield its full produce (B)	Ge 4:12
by s. the Lord brought you out	Ex 13:3; 14:16
by a mighty hand (B)	Ex 13:3
my s. is dried up (R)	Nu 11:6
he hath the s. of an unicorn	Nu 23:22; 24:8
the horns of a wild ox (R)	Nu 23:22
O my soul, thou hast trodden down s.	J'g 5:21
woman of s. (A)	Ru 3:11
they that stumbled are girt with s.	1Sa 2:4
for by s. shall no man prevail	1Sa 2:9
power (B)	1Sa 2:9; 2:10; 1Ch 16:27; 2Ch 13:20; Ps 68:34; Isa 25:4; Eze 30:18; 1Co 15:5; Re 12:10; 17:13
might (R)	1Sa 2:9; Job 12:13; Ec 9:16; Da 2:37
give s. unto his king, and exalt	1Sa 2:10
horn	
the s. of Israel will not lie, nor repent	1Sa 15:29
the glory of Israel (R)	1Sa 15:29
eat, that thou mayest have s. in going on	1Sa 28:22
thou hast girded me with s. to battle	2Sa 22:40; Ps 18:22, 39
I have counsel and s. for war	2Ki 18:20; Isa 36:5
there is no s. to bring forth	2Ki 19:3; Isa 37:3
men of s. of mind and spirit (A)	1Ch 5:24
s. and gladness are in his place	1Ch 16:27
give to Lord glory and s.	1Ch 16:28; Ps 29:1; 96:7
might (B)	1Ch 16:28; Ne 12:13; Ps 20:6; 68:34
their sons, and brethren, able men for s.	1Ch 26:8
in thine hand it is to give s. unto all	1Ch 29:12
neither did Jeroboam recover s. again	2Ch 13:20
power (B)	2Ch 13:20; Ps 68:34; 1Co 15:16; Heb 11:11; Re 3:8; 5:12; 12:10; 17:13
s. of the bearers of burdens is decayed	Ne 4:10
s. failing (R)	Ne 4:10
if I speak of s. he is strong	Job 9:19
with him is wisdom and s.	Job 12:13; 2:16
might (R)	Job 12:13; 38:19; Pr 8:14; 24:15
he weakeneth the s. of the mighty	Job 12:21

defiled my *s.* in the dust (S)   *Job 16:15*
it shall devour the *s.* of his   *Job 18:13*
skin
no, but he would put *s.* in me   *Job 23:6*
whereto might *s.* of their   *Job 30:2*
hands profit me
he will not esteem all the   *Job 36:19*
forces of *s.*
hast thou given the horse *s.*   *Job 39:19*
his mighty *s.*   *Job 41:12*
(A)(B)(E)(R)
in his neck remaineth *s.*   *Job 41:22*
out of mouth of babes hast   *Ps 8:2*
ordained *s.*
founded a bulwark (R)
with the saving *s.* of his right   *Ps 20:6*
hand
Lord is *s.* of my life, of whom   *Ps 27:1*
be afraid
stronghold (B)   *Ps 27:1;*
                               52:7; Joe 3:16
stronghold (E)   *Ps 27:1;*
   Isa 23:4; 25:4; Eze 30:15; Joe 3:16
and he is the saving *s.* of his   *Ps 28:8*
anointed
defense (B)   *Ps 28:8; 60:7*
the Lord will give *s.* to his   *Ps 29:11*
people
my *s.* is dried up   *Ps 32:4*
the mighty is not delivered by   *Ps 33:16*
much *s.*
spare me, that I may recover   *Ps 39:13*
s. before I go
God is our refuge and *s.* a   *Ps 46:1;*
help   *81:1*
fortress (B)   *Ps 46:1*
Ephraim is the *s.* of mine   *Ps 60:7;*
head   *108:8*
Ephraim is my defense (E)   *Ps 60:7*
Ephraim is my helmet (R)   *Ps 60:7*
ascribe ye *s.* unto God, his *s.*   *Ps 68:34*
is in clouds
God is he that giveth *s.* and   *Ps 68:35*
power
but God is the *s.* of my heart   *Ps 73:26*
and portion
sing aloud unto God our *s.*   *Ps 81:1*
make a noise
blessed is the man whose *s.* is   *Ps 84:5*
in thee
go from *s.* to *s.* every one in   *Ps 84:7*
Zion
and if by reason of *s.* they be   *Ps 90:10*
fourscore
the Lord is clothed with   *Ps 93:1*
majesty and *s.*
the *s.* of the hills is his also   *Ps 95:4*
heights of the hills (E)   *Ps 95:4*
s. and beauty are in his   *Ps 96:6*
sanctuary
the king's *s.* also loveth   *Ps 99:4*
judgment
strengthenedst me with *s.* in   *Ps 138:3*
my soul
God the Lord, the *s.* of my   *Ps 140:7*
salvation
my strong deliverer (R)   *Ps 140:7*
I have *s.*   *Pr 8:14*
way of Lord is *s.*   *Pr 10:29*
a wife of *s.* (B)   *Pr 12:4; 31:10*
but much increase is by the *s.*   *Pr 14:4*
of ox
a wise man casteth down the   *Pr 21:22*
s. thereof
a man of knowledge increaseth   *Pr 24:5*
s.
she girdeth her loins with *s.*   *Pr 31:17*
s. and honour are her   *Pr 31:25*
clothing, she shall rejoice
then said I, Wisdom is better   *Ec 9:16*
than *s.*
if iron be blunt, then must   *Ec 10:10*
put to more *s.*
princes eat for *s.* and not for   *Ec 10:17*
drunkenness
men of *s.* to mingle strong   *Isa 5:22*
drink
by the *s.* of my hand I have   *Isa 10:13*
done it
sea hath spoken, even the *s.*   *Isa 23:4*
of the sea
stronghold (E)   *Isa 23:4;*
   25:4; Eze 30:15; Joe 3:16
thou hast been a *s.* to the poor,   *Isa 25:4*
a *s.* to the needy in his distress
in the Lord JEHOVAH is   *Isa 26:4*
everlasting *s.*
the Rock of Ages (B)   *Isa 26:4*
the everlasting rock (E)(R)   *Isa 26:4*

for *s.* to them that turn the   *Isa 28:6*
battle to gate
the *s.* of Pharaoh shall be   *Isa 30:3*
your shame
wisdom be stability and *s.* of   *Isa 33:6*
salvation
residents shorn of *s.* (B)(R)   *Isa 37:27*
O Jerusalem, lift up thy voice   *Isa 40:9*
with *s.*
to them that have no might,   *Isa 40:29*
he increaseth *s.*
he hath poured on him the *s.*   *Isa 42:25*
of battle
he worketh it with the *s.* of   *Isa 44:12*
his arms
in the Lord have I   *Isa 45:24*
righteousness and *s.*
awake, put on *s.* O arm of   *Isa 51:9*
Lord
I will deliver all *s.* of this city   *Jer 20:5*
she should fortify the height   *Jer 51:53*
of her *s.*
they are gone without *s.* before   *La 1:6*
pursuer
pour my fury on sin, *s.* of   *Eze 30:15*
Egypt
pomp of her *s.* shall cease   *Eze 30:18;*
in her   *33:28*
power (E)   *Eze 30:18;*
1Co 15:56; Heb 11:11; Re 3:8; 5:8;
   12:10; 17:13
God hath given thee power, *s.*   *Da 2:37*
glory
but there shall be in it of the   *Da 2:41*
s. of the iron
firmness of iron (B)(R)   *Da 2:41*
neither shall there be any *s.*   *Da 11:15*
to withstand
to enter with the *s.* of his   *Da 11:17*
whole kingdom
they shall pollute the   *Da 11:31*
sanctuary of *s.*
Lord the *s.* of the children of   *Joe 3:16*
Israel
have we not taken horns by   *Am 6:13*
our own *s.*
Ethiopia and Egypt were her *s.*   *Na 3:9*
also shalt seek *s.* because of   *Na 3:11*
the enemy
I will destroy *s.* of kingdoms   *Hag 2:22*
of
he hath shewed *s.* with his   *Lu 1:51*
arm
might (N)   *Lu 1:51*
s. to escape (N)(R)   *Lu 21:36*
his feet and ankle bones   *Ac 3:7*
received *s.*
bringing new *s.* (N)   *Ac 15:41*
when yet without *s.* Christ died   *Ro 5:6*
powerless (N)   *Ro 5:6*
their coming to full *s.* (N)   *Ro 11:12*
sting is sin, the *s.* of sin is   *1Co 15:56*
the law
gains its power from the law   *1Co 15:56*
(N)
pressed out of measure, above   *2Co 1:8*
s.
Sara herself received *s.* to   *Heb 11:11*
conceive seed
received potency for   *Heb 11:11*
conception (B)
gained physical vitality (P)   *Heb 11:11*
thou hast a little *s.* hast kept   *Re 3:8*
my word
little power (P)   *Re 3:8*
worthy is Lamb to receive *s.*   *Re 5:12*
and honour
saying, Now is come   *Re 12:10*
salvation and *s.*
shall give their power and *s.*   *Re 17:13*
to beast
exercise of royal authority   *Re 17:13*
(N)
hand over their power and   *Re 17:13*
authority (P)

HIS STRENGTH

and the sea returned to *his s.*   *Ex 14:27*
he is the beginning of *his s.*   *De 21:17*
rise thou, for as man is, so is   *J'g 8:21*
his s.
power (B)   *J'g 8:21; Ps 68:34*
entice him, see wherein *his*   *J'g 16:5*
great *s.* lieth
his s. not known   *J'g 16:9*
his s. went   *J'g 16:19*
Jehu drew a bow with *his* full   *2Ki 9:24*
s.
seek the Lord and *his s.*   *1Ch 16:11;*
   Ps 105:4

might (B)   *1Ch 16:11*
the steps of *his s.* shall be   *Job 18:7*
straitened
his s. shall be hunger-bitten   *Job 18:12*
first born of death shall   *Job 18:13*
devour *his s.*
dieth in *his* full *s.* being   *Job 21:23*
wholly at ease
he saith to the great rain of   *Job 37:6*
his s.
wilt thou trust him because   *Job 39:11*
his s. is great
rejoiceth in *his s.*   *Job 39:21*
his s. in his loins   *Job 40:16*
nor deliver any by *his* great *s.*   *Ps 33:17*
power (E)   *Ps 33:17*
might (R)   *Ps 33:17*
this man made not God *his s.*   *Ps 52:7*
because of *his s.* will I wait   *Ps 59:9*
upon thee
who by *his s.* setteth fast the   *Ps 65:6*
mountains
might (B)   *Ps 65:6; Isa 63:1*
ascribe strength to God, *his s.*   *Ps 68:34*
is in the clouds
power (R)   *Ps 68:34; 78:61*
shewing to the generation to   *Ps 78:4*
come *his s.*
delivered *his s.* into captivity   *Ps 78:61*
he is hungry and *his s.*   *Isa 44:12*
faileth
the Lord hath sworn by the   *Isa 62:8*
arm of *his s.*
travelling in the greatness of   *Isa 63:1*
his s.
by *his s.* stir up all against   *Da 11:2*
Grecia
wealth (B)   *Da 11:2*
riches (E)   *Da 11:2*
strangers devoured *his s.*   *Ho 7:9*
by *his s.* he had power with   *Ho 12:3*
God
countenance as the sun in *his*   *Re 1:16*
s.

IN STRENGTH

his bow abode in *s.*   *Ge 49:24*
went *in s.* of that meat forty   *1Ki 19:8*
days
he is wise in heart, and   *Job 9:4;*
mighty *in s.*   *36:5*
I will go in the *s.* of the Lord   *Ps 71:16*
bless Lord, ye angels that   *Ps 103:20*
excel *in s.*
he delighteth not *in* the *s.* of   *Ps 147:10*
an horse
strengthen themselves *in s.* of   *Isa 30:2*
Pharaoh
he shall feed *in* the *s.* of the   *Mic 5:4*
Lord
but Saul increased the more *in*   *Ac 9:22*
s.

MY STRENGTH

Reuben the beginning of *my s.*   *Ge 49:3*
Lord is *my s.*   *Ex 15:2;*
2Sa 22:33; Ps 18:2; 28:7; 118:14;
   Isa 12:2
as *my s.* then, even so *my s.*   *Jos 14:11*
now
if I be shaven, *my s.* will go   *J'g 16:17*
what is *my s.* that I should   *Job 6:11*
hope
is *my s.* of stones? or is my   *Job 6:12*
flesh of brass
I will love thee, O Lord *my s.*   *Ps 18:1*
Lord *my s.*   *Ps 19:14; 22:19*
my Rock (A)(B)(E)(R)   *Ps 19:14;*
   144:1
my s. is dried up   *Ps 22:15*
pull me out of net thou art   *Ps 31:4*
my s.
stronghold (B)   *Ps 31:4; 43:2; 59:17*
stronghold (E)   *Ps 31:4*
my refuge (R)   *Ps 31:4; 43:2*
my s. faileth because of my   *Ps 31:10;*
iniquity   *38:10; 71:9*
art God of *my s.* why go I   *Ps 43:2*
mourning
to thee O *my s.* will I sing   *Ps 59:17*
rock of *my s.*   *Ps 62:7*
he weakened *my s.*   *Ps 102:23*
blessed be Lord *my s.* who   *Ps 144:1*
teacheth
let him take hold of *my s.*   *Isa 27:5*
my protection (B)(R)   *Isa 27:5*
I have spent *my s.* for nought   *Isa 49:4*
my God shall be *my s.*   *Isa 49:5*

Lord *my s.*	*Jer 16:19*
he made *my s.* to fall	*La 1:14*
my s. and hope is perished	*La 3:18*
God is *my s.*	*Hab 3:19*
shall be *my s.* in Lord of hosts	*Zec 12:5*
my s. is made perfect in weakness	*2Co 12:9*
my power (E)(N)(P)(R)	*2Co 12:9*

THEIR STRENGTH

as for cities that stood still in *their s.*	*Jos 11:13*
he is *their s.* in the time of trouble	*Ps 37:39*
their stronghold (A)(E)	*Ps 37:39*
their fortress (B)	*Ps 37:39; 73:4*
their refuge (R)	*Ps 37:39*
no bands in their death *their s.* is firm	*Ps 73:4*
he smote the chief of *their s.*	*Ps 78:51; 105:36*
for thou art the glory of *their s.*	*Ps 89:17*
yet is *their s.* labour and sorrow	*Ps 90:10*
the glory of young men is *their s.*	*Pr 20:29*
I cried, *Their s.* is to sit still	*Isa 30:7*
that wait on Lord shall renew *their s.*	*Isa 40:31*
and let the people renew *their s.*	*Isa 41:1*
I will bring down *their s.* to the earth	*Isa 63:6*
their lifeblood (A)(B)(E)(R)	*Isa 63:6*
when I take from them *their s.*	*Eze 24:25*
their stronghold (B)(R)	*Eze 24:25*
the fig tree and vine do yield *their s.*	*Joe 2:22*

THY STRENGTH

thou hast guided them in *thy s.*	*Ex 15:13*
thy might (B)	*Ex 15:13*
as thy days, so shall *thy s.* be	*De 33:25*
tell me wherein *thy s.* lieth	*J'g 16:6; 16:15*
thou and ark of *thy s.*	*2Ch 6:41; Ps 132:8*
thy might (R)	*2Ch 6:41; Ps 54:1; 71:18; 74:13; 77:14; 80:2; Isa 63:15*
the king shall joy in *thy s.* O Lord	*Ps 21:1*
be exalted, O Lord, in *thine* own *s.*	*Ps 21:13*
judge me by *thy s.*	*Ps 54:1*
thy power (B)	*Ps 54:1; 71:18; 74:13; 77:14*
thy might (E)	*Ps 54:1; 80:2*
thy God hath commanded *thy s.*	*Ps 68:28*
until I have shewed *thy s.* to this	*Ps 71:18*
thou didst divide the sea by *thy s.*	*Ps 74:13*
your might (A)	*Ps 74:13; 80:2*
hast declared *thy s.* among the people	*Ps 77:14*
your power (A)	*Ps 77:14*
stir up *thy s.* and come and save us	*Ps 80:2*
turn to me, give *thy s.* to thy servant	*Ps 86:16*
Lord shall send rod of *thy s.* out of Zion	*Ps 110:2*
your mighty scepter (R)	*Ps 110:2*
if faint in day of adversity, *thy s.* small	*Pr 24:10*
give not *thy s.* unto women	*Pr 31:3*
not been mindful of rock of *thy s.*	*Isa 17:10*
your protection (B)	*Isa 17:10*
rock of thy refuge (R)	*Isa 17:10*
awake, awake, put on *thy s.* O Zion	*Isa 52:1*
where is thy zeal and *thy s.*	*Isa 63:15*
he shall bring down *thy s.* from thee	*Am 3:11*
your defenses (A)(R)	*Am 3:11*
your strongholds (B)	*Am 3:11*
love the Lord with all thy heart and with all *thy s.*	*M'k 12:30; 12:33; Lu 10:27*

YOUR STRENGTH

and *your s.* shall be spent in vain	*Le 26:20*
for the joy of the Lord is *your s.*	*Ne 8:10*
howl, ye ships, *your s.* is laid waste	*Isa 23:14*
your stronghold (B)(E)(R)	*Isa 23:14*
in quietness and confidence will be *your s.*	*Isa 30:15*
my sanctuary, excellency of *your s.*	*Eze 24:21*
your power (E)(R)	*Eze 24:21*

STRENGTHEN

encourage him, and *s.* him	*De 3:28*
s. me I pray thee, only this once	*J'g 16:28*
S. thine heart (S)	*J'g 19:5, 8*
Go, *s.* thyself, and mark, and see	*1Ki 20:22*
to *s.* their hands in the work of the	*Ezr 6:22*
therefore, O God, *s.* my hands	*Ne 6:9*
I would *s.* you with my mouth	*Job 16:5*
sanctuary, and *s.* thee out of Zion	*Ps 20:2*
and he shall *s.* thine heart	*Ps 27:14*
courage, and he shall *s.* your heart	*Ps 31:24*
Lord will *s.* him upon the bed of	*Ps 41:3*
s. O God, that which thou hast	*Ps 68:28*
mine arm also shall *s.* him	*Ps 89:21*
s. me according unto thy word	*Ps 119:28*
robe, and *s.* him with thy girdle	*Isa 22:21*
to *s.* the strength of Pharaoh	*Isa 30:2*
they could not well *s.* their mast	*Isa 33:23*
S. ye the weak hands and confirm	*Isa 35:3*
I will *s.* thee; I will help thee	*Isa 41:10*
thy cords, and *s.* thy stakes	*Isa 54:2*
they *s.* also the hands of evildoers	*Jer 23:14*
s. himself in the iniquity of his life	*Eze 7:13*
s. the hand of the poor and needy	*Eze 16:49*
s. the arms of the king of Babylon	*Eze 30:24; 30:25*
and will *s.* that which was sick	*Eze 34:16*
I, stood to confirm and to *s.* him	*Da 11:1*
support and *s.* (B)	*Da 11:1*
the strong shall not *s.* his force	*Am 2:14*
I will *s.* the house of Judah	*Zec 10:6*
I will *s.* them in the Lord	*Zec 10:12*
art converted, *s.* thy brethren	*Lu 22:32*
to encourage and *s.* (N)(P)	*Ac 14:32*
s., build up spiritually (A)(B)	*Ro 15:2*
perfect, stablish, *s.*, settle you	*1Pe 5:10*
and *s.* the things which remain	*Re 3:2*

STRENGTHENED

Israel *s.* himself, and sat upon	*Ge 48:2*
Lord *s.* Eglon the king of Moab	*J'g 3:12*
shall thine hands be *s.* to go down	*J'g 7:11*
the wood, and *s.* his hand in God	*1Sa 23:16*
Therefore now let your hands be *s.*	*2Sa 2:7*
s. themselves in his kingdom	*1Ch 11:10*
Solomon was *s.* in his kingdom	*2Ch 1:1*
So they *s.* the kingdom of Judah	*2Ch 11:17*
the kingdom, and had *s.* himself	*2Ch 12:1*
So king Rehoboam *s.* himself in	*2Ch 12:13*
s. themselves against Rehoboam	*2Ch 13:7*
and *s.* himself against Israel	*2Ch 17:1*

s. himself, and slew all his brethren	*2Ch 21:4*
seventh year Jehoiada *s.* himself	*2Ch 23:1*
house of God in his state, and *s.* it	*2Ch 24:13*
Amaziah *s.* himself, and led forth	*2Ch 25:11*
for he *s.* himself exceedingly	*2Ch 26:8*
and distressed him, but *s.* him not	*2Ch 28:20*
Also he *s.* himself, and built up all	*2Ch 32:5*
s. their hands with vessels of silver	*Ezr 1:6*
I was *s.* as the hand of the Lord my	*Ezr 7:28*
s. their hands for this good work	*Ne 2:18*
and thou hast *s.* the weak hands	*Job 4:3*
and thou hast *s.* the feeble knees	*Job 4:4*
and *s.* himself in his wickedness	*Ps 52:7*
he hath *s.* the bars of thy gates	*Ps 147:13*
he *s.* the fountains of the deep	*Pr 8:28*
and *s.* the hands of the wicked	*Eze 13:22*
The diseased have ye not *s.* neither	*Eze 34:4*
appearance of a man, and he *s.* me	*Da 10:18*
he had spoken unto me, I was *s.*	*Da 10:19*
my lord speak; for thou hast *s.* me	*Da 10:19*
and he that *s.* her in these times	*Da 11:6*
but he shall not be *s.* by it	*Da 11:12*
I have bound and *s.* their arms	*Ho 7:15*
he had received meat, he was *s.*	*Ac 9:19*
s. them (A)(B)(R)	*Ac 14:32*
s. the churches (B)(P)(R)	*Ac 15:41*
to be *s.* with might by his spirit	*Eph 3:16*
S. with all might according to his	*Col 1:11*
s. one another (P)	*1Th 5:11*
Lord stood with me, and *s.* me	*2Ti 4:17*

STRENGTHENEDST

s. me with strength in my soul	*Ps 138:3*

STRENGTHENETH

s. himself against the Almighty	*Job 15:25*
and bread which *s.* man's heart	*Ps 104:15*
with strength, and *s.* her arms	*Pr 31:17*
Wisdom *s.* the wise more than ten	*Ec 7:19*
the oak, which he *s.* for himself	*Isa 44:14*
s. the spoiled against the strong	*Am 5:9*
things through Christ which *s.* me	*Ph'p 4:13*

STRENGTHENING

an angel from heaven, *s.* him	*Lu 22:43*
in order, *s.* all the disciples	*Ac 18:23*

STRENUOUS

s. work (B)	*Le 23:7*

STRESS

s. of provocation (B)	*1Sa 1:16*
will come times of *s.* (R)	*2Ti 3:1*

STRETCH

s. out of my hand, and smite	*Ex 3:20*
I *s.* forth mine hand upon Egypt	*Ex 7:5*
s. out thine hand upon the waters	*Ex 7:19*
S. forth thine hand with thy rod	*Ex 8:5*
S. out thy rod, and smite the dust	*Ex 8:16*

For now I will *s.* out my hand, that | Ex 9:15
S. thine hand toward heaven | Ex 9:22
S. out thine hand over Egypt | Ex 10:12
S. out thine hand toward heaven | Ex 10:21
and *s.* out thine hand over the sea | Ex 14:16
S. out thine hand over the sea, that | Ex 14:26
cherubims *s.* forth their wings | Ex 25:20
S. out the spear that is in thy | Jos 8:18
to *s.* forth mine hand against him | 1Sa 24:6
s. forth his hand against the Lord's | 1Sa 26:9
s. mine hand against the Lord's | 1Sa 26:11; 26:23
not afraid to *s.* forth thine hand | 2Sa 1:14
I will *s.* over Jerusalem the line | 2Ki 21:13
s. out thine hands toward him | Job 11:13
not *s.* out his hand to the grave | Job 30:24
s. her wings toward the south | Job 39:26
Ethiopia shall soon *s.* out her | Ps 68:31
s. thine hand against the wrath | Ps 138:7
I *s.* forth my hands unto thee | Ps 143:6
than that a man can *s.* himself | Isa 28:20
the Lord shall *s.* out his hand | Isa 31:3
s. out upon it the lihe of confusion | Isa 34:11
and let them *s.* forth the curtains | Isa 54:2
s. my hand upon the inhabitants | Jer 6:12
none to *s.* forth my tent any more | Jer 10:20
will I *s.* out my hand against thee | Jer 15:6
I will *s.* out mine hand upon thee | Jer 51:25
So will I *s.* out my hand upon them | Eze 6:14
and I will *s.* out my hand upon him | Eze 14:9
then will I *s.* out mine hand upon it | Eze 14:13
I will *s.* out mine hand upon thee | Eze 25:7
also *s.* out mine hand upon Edom | Eze 25:13
s. mine hand upon the Philistines | Eze 25:16
s. it out upon the land of Egypt | Eze 30:25
I will *s.* out mine hand against thee | Eze 35:3
He shall *s.* forth his hand also | Da 11:42
s. themselves upon their couches | Am 6:4
also *s.* out mine hand upon Judah | Zep 1:4
s. out his hand against the north | Zep 2:13
he to the man *S.* forth thine hand | M't 12:13
unto the man, *S.* forth thine hand | M'k 3:5
unto the man, *S.* forth thy hand | Lu 6:10
old, thou shalt *s.* forth thy hands | Joh 21:18
we *s.* not ourselves beyond our | 2Co 10:14

STRETCHED

And Abraham *s.* forth his hand | Ge 22:10
And Israel *s.* out his right hand | Ge 48:14
will redeem you with a *s.* out arm | Ex 6:6
Aaron *s.* his hand over the waters | Ex 8:6
Aaron *s.* out his hand with his rod | Ex 8:17
Moses *s.* his rod toward heaven | Ex 9:23
Moses *s.* forth his rod over Egypt | Ex 10:13

Moses *s.* his hand toward heaven | Ex 10:22
Moses *s.* out his hand over the sea | Ex 14:21
Moses *s.* forth his hand over the sea | Ex 14:27
a mighty hand, and by a *s.* out arm | De 4:34
a mighty hand and by a *s.* out arm | De 5:15
mighty hand, and the *s.* out arm | De 7:19
mighty power and by thy *s.* out arm | De 9:29
mighty hand, and his *s.* out arm | De 11:2
Joshua *s.* out the spear that he had | Jos 8:18
as soon as he had *s.* out his hand | Jos 8:19
back, wherewith he *s.* out the spear | Jos 8:26
when the angel *s.* out his hand | 2Sa 24:16
s. the wings of the cherubims | 1Ki 6:27
hand, and of thy *s.* out arm | 1Ki 8:42
he *s.* himself upon the child three | 1Ki 17:21
and he *s.* himself upon the child | 2Ki 4:34
went up, and *s.* himself upon him | 2Ki 4:35
with great power and a *s.* out arm | 2Ki 17:36
sword *s.* out over Jerusalem | 1Ch 21:16
mighty hand, and thy *s.* out arm | 2Ch 6:32
or who hath *s.* the line upon it | Job 38:5
s. our hands to a strange god | Ps 44:20
I have *s.* out my hands unto thee | Ps 88:9
To him that *s.* out the earth above | Ps 136:6
strong hand, and a *s.* out arm | Ps 136:12
I have *s.* out my hand, and no man | Pr 1:24
and walk with *s.* forth necks | Isa 3:16
s. forth his hand against them | Isa 5:25
away, but his hand is *s.* out still | Isa 5:25
but his hand is *s.* out still | Isa 9:12; 9:17, 21
away, but his hand is *s.* out still | Isa 10:4
hand *s.* out upon all the | Isa 14:26
his hand is *s.* out, and who shall | Isa 14:27
her branches are *s.* out, they are | Isa 16:8
He *s.* out his hand over the sea | Isa 23:11
the heavens, and *s.* them out | Isa 42:5
my hands, have *s.* out the heavens | Isa 45:12
that hath *s.* forth the heavens, and | Isa 51:13
shadows of the evening are *s.* out | Jer 6:4
s. out the heavens by his discretion | Jer 10:12
by thy great power and *s.* out arm | Jer 32:17
strong hand, and with a *s.* out arm | Jer 32:31
and hath *s.* out the heaven by his | Jer 51:15
he hath *s.* out a line, he hath not | La 2:8
and their wings were *s.* upward | Eze 1:11
s. forth over their heads above | Eze 1:22
And one cherub *s.* forth his hand | Eze 10:7
I have *s.* out my hand over thee | Eze 16:27
and with a *s.* out arm, and with fury | Eze 20:33
mighty hand, and with a *s.* out arm | Eze 20:34
he *s.* out his hand with scorners | Ho 7:1
he *s.* out his hand with scorners | Ho 7:5
and the banquet of them that *s.* | Am 6:7
shall be *s.* forth upon Jerusalem. | Zec 1:16

he *s.* it forth; and it was restored | M't 12:13
And he *s.* forth his hand toward his | M't 12:49
Jesus *s.* forth his hand, and his sword | M't 14:31
s. out his hand, and drew his sword | M't 26:51
And he *s.* it out; and his hand was | M'k 3:5
ye *s.* forth no hands against me | Lu 22:53
Herod the king *s.* forth his hands | Ac 12:1
Then Paul *s.* forth the hand | Ac 26:1
I have *s.* forth my hands unto a | Ro 10:21
s. and broken on wheel (B) | Heb 11:35

STRETCHEDST

Thou *s.* out thy right hand, the (P) | Ex 15:12

STRETCHEST

s. my stride (B) | 2Sa 22:27
s. out the heavens like a curtain | Ps 104:2

STRETCHETH

for the deep that *s.* out (S) | De 33:13
he *s.* out his hand against God | Job 15:25
He *s.* out the north over the empty | Job 26:7
She *s.* out her hand to the poor | Pr 31:20
s. out the heavens as a curtain | Isa 40:22
The carpenter *s.* out his rule he | Isa 44:13
that *s.* forth the heavens alone | Isa 44:24
Lord, which *s.* forth the heavens | Zec 12:1

STRETCHING

the *s.* out of his wings shall fill | Isa 8:8
By *s.* forth thine hand to heal | Ac 4:30

STREWED

s. it (A)(E)(R) | 2Ch 34:4

STRICKEN

Sarah were old and well *s.* in age | Ge 18:11
well advanced in years (A) | Ge 18:11; 24:1; Jos 23:1, 2; 1Ki 1:1; Lu 1:7, 18
well advanced in years (B) | Ge 18:11; 1Ki 1:1
advanced in age (R) | Ge 18:11; 24:1; Jos 13:1; 23:1, 2; 1Ki 1:1; Lu 1:7, 18
Abraham was old, and well *s.* in age | Ge 24:1
Now Joshua was old, and *s.* in years | Jos 13:1
gone far in years (A) | Jos 13:1
Thou art old and *s.* in years | Jos 13:1
that Joshua waxed old and *s.* in age | Jos 23:1
unto them, I am old and *s.* in age | Jos 23:2
and *s.* through his temples | J'g 5:26
stricken (A)(R) | 1Sa 5:12; Jer 2:30; Ho 6:1
king David was old and *s.* in years | 1Ki 1:1
s. within me (R) | Ps 109:22
hast *s.* thy hand with a stranger | Pr 6:1
given your pledge to (A)(R) | Pr 6:1
They have *s.* me, shalt thou say | Pr 23:35
Why should ye be *s.* any more | Isa 1:5
smitten (R) | Isa 1:5
shall ye mourn; surely they are *s.* | Isa 16:7
yet we did esteem him *s.* smitten | Isa 53:4
regarded him as *s.* (A)(B) | Isa 53:4
transgression of my people he *s.* | Isa 53:8
thou hast *s.* them, but they | Jer 5:3
s. through for want of the fruits of | La 4:9

was *s*. dumb (E)   *Da 4:19*
both were now well *s*. in years   *Lu 1:7*
getting up in years (B)   *Lu 1:7*
well on in years (N)   *Lu 1:7; 1:18*
getting on in years (P)   *Lu 1:7; 1:18*
man, and my wife well *s*. in   *Lu 1:18*
years

STRICTEST

after the most *s*. sect I lived   *Ac 26:5*
(S)

STRICTLY

strictly (S)   *1Sa 14:28;*
M't 9:30; M'k 1:43; 3:12; 5:43; Lu 9:21;
Ac 5:28

STRIDE

stretchest my *s*. (B)   *2Sa 22:27*

STRIDING

s. triumphantly (A)   *Isa 63:1*

STRIFE

was a *s*. between the herdmen   *Ge 13:7*
conflict (B)   *Ge 13:7; J'g 12:2*
said unto Lot, Let there be   *Ge 13:8*
no *s*.
disputing (B)   *Ge 13:8*
of Zin, in the *s*. of the   *Nu 27:14*
congregation
rebelled against (B)   *Nu 27:14*
and your burden, and your *s*.   *De 1:12*
I and my people were at great   *J'g 12:2*
s.
had a great feud (R)   *J'g 12:2*
the people were at *s*.   *2Sa 19:9*
throughout
people were blaming each   *2Sa 19:9*
other (B)
a pavilion from the *s*. of   *Ps 31:20*
tongues
have seen violence and *s*. in   *Ps 55:9*
the city
us a *s*. unto our neighbours   *Ps 80:6*
contention (B) *Ps 80:6; Pr 22:10; 26:20*
angered him at the waters   *Ps 106:32*
of *s*.
A wrathful man stirreth up *s*.   *Pr 15:18*
contention (B)   *Pr 15:18*
that is slow to anger   *Pr 15:18*
appeaseth *s*.
A froward man soweth *s*.:   *Pr 16:28*
and a
an house full of sacrifices   *Pr 17:1*
with *s*.
The beginning of *s*. is as   *Pr 17:14*
when one
loveth transgression that   *Pr 17:19*
loveth *s*.
honour for a man to cease   *Pr 20:3*
from *s*.
yea, *s*. and reproach shall   *Pr 22:10*
cease
meddleth with *s*. belonging   *Pr 26:17*
vexed himself with *s*. (E)   *Pr 26:17*
is no talebearer, he *s*. ceaseth   *Pr 26:20*
is a contentious man to   *Pr 26:21*
kindle *s*.
is of a proud heart stirreth   *Pr 28:25*
up *s*.
An angry man stirreth up *s*.   *Pr 29:22*
and a
forcing of wrath bringeth forth   *Pr 30:33*
s.
ye fast for *s*. and debate   *Isa 58:4*
quarrel and fight (R)   *Isa 58:4*
a man of *s*. and a man of   *Jer 15:10*
contention
even to the waters of *s*. in   *Eze 47:19*
Kadesh
unto the waters of *s*. in   *Eze 48:28*
Kadesh
and there are that raise up *s*.   *Hab 1:3*
there was also a *s*. among   *Lu 22:24*
them
controversy (B)   *Lu 22:24*
dispute (N)(P)(R)   *Lu 22:24*
s. more violent (A)   *Ac 23:10*
murder *s*. (A)(E)(R)(S)   *Ro 1:29*
wantonness, not in *s*. and   *Ro 13:13*
envying
quarrels (N)   *Ro 13:13*
quarreling (P)(R)   *Ro 13:13*
you envying, and *s*. and   *1Co 3:3*
divisions

quarreling (B)   *1Co 3:3*
squabbling (P)   *1Co 3:3*
emulations, wrath, *s*., seditions *Ga 5:20*
dissension (R)   *Ga 5:20; 1Ti 6:4*
quarrels (N)   *Ga 5:20*
quarreling (P)   *Ga 5:20*
wrath, *s*., seditions (S)   *Ga 5:20*
preach Christ even of envy   *Ph'p 1:15*
and *s*.
rivalry (B)   *Ph'p 1:15; Jas 3:14, 16*
jealous and quarrelsome   *Ph'p 1:15*
spirit (N)
preaching Christ out of   *Ph'p 1:15*
jealousy (P)
rivalry (R)   *Ph'p 1:15*
Let nothing be done through   *Ph'p 2:3*
s.
nothing through *s*., selfishness   *Ph'p 2:3*
(A)(R)
whereof cometh envy, *s*.,   *1Ti 6:4*
railings
oath is to them an end of   *Heb 6:16*
all *s*.
dispute (B)(N)(R)   *Heb 6:16*
envying and *s*. in your hearts   *Jas 3:14*
For where envying and *s*. is,   *Jas 3:16*
there

STRIFES

Hatred stirreth up *s*.; but   *Pr 10:12*
love
contentions (A)(B)   *Pr 10:12*
envyings, wraths, *s*.,   *2Co 12:20*
backbitings
about questions and *s*. of   *1Ti 6:4*
words
war of words (B)   *1Ti 6:4*
quarreling (N)(P)   *1Ti 6:4*
disputes about words (R)   *1Ti 6:4*
knowing that they do gender   *2Ti 2:23*
s.
quarrels (B)(N)(R)   *2Ti 2:23*

STRIKE

s. Egypt (B)   *Ex 3:20; 7:17; 12:12, 23*
s. the dust (A)(B)(R)   *Ex 8:16*
and *s*. it on the two side posts   *Ex 12:7*
s. the lintel and the two side   *Ex 12:22*
posts
s. the rock (A)(B)(R)   *Ex 17:6*
s. with pestilence (R)   *Nu 14:12*
strike (B)   *Nu 22:25;*
Isa 41:7; Da 2:34
and shall *s*. off the heifer's   *De 21:4*
neck
s. at Ai (B)   *Jos 7:3*
strike (A)   *1Sa 15:3;*
2Sa 2:22; 13:28; 17:2; 18:11; 1Ki 20:35,
37; 2Ki 13:19; 2Ch 21:14; Pr 19:25;
Isa 11:4; 58:4; Jer 21:6; Eze 5:2; 21:12,
14, 17; 39:3; Mic 5:1; Zec 10:11;
M't 5:39; M'k 14:27; Lu 22:49; Ac 23:2-
3
strike (R)   *1Sa 17:46;*
26:8; 2Sa 13:28; 17:2; 18:11; 20:35, 37;
2Ki 13:19; 9:7; 13:18, 19; Ps 141:5;
Pr 19:25; Eze 5:2; 39:3; Mic 5:1;
Zec 12:4; 13:7; M't 5:39; 26:31;
M'k 14:27; Lu 22:49; Ac 23:2;
2Co 11:20; Re 11:6
strike (A)   *2Sa 2:22;*
13:28; 17:2; 18:11; 1Ki 20:35, 37;
2Ki 9:7; 13:18, 19; Pr 19:25; Zec 9:4;
6:11; M't 5:39; 26:31; M'k 14:27;
Lu 22:49; Ac 23:2-3; 2Co 11:20
s. down (B)   *2Sa 5:8; 1Ch 11:6*
and *s*. his hand over the place   *1Ch 11:6*
strike (R)   *2Ki 6:18; Isa 41:7; Ac 7:24*
is he that will *s*. hands with   *Job 17:3*
me
give security to me (A)(B)   *Job 17:3*
bow of steel shall *s*. him   *Job 20:24*
through
pierce him through (B)(R)   *Job 20:24;*
Hab 3:14
God shall *s*. the head (B)(E)   *Ps 68:21*
The Lord shall *s*. through   *Ps 110:5*
kings
shatter kings (A)(B)(R)   *Ps 110:5*
Till a dart *s*. through his liver; *Pr 7:23*
as
who are securities for debts   *Pr 7:23*
(B)(R)
good nor to *s*. princes for   *Pr 17:26*
equity
flog noble men (B)(R)   *Pr 17:26*
Be not one of them that *s*.   *Pr 22:26*
hands

who are securities for debts   *Pr 22:26*
(B)(R)
didst *s*. through with his   *Hab 3:14*
staves
s. through with his shafts   *Hab 3:14*
(B)(R)
did *s*. him with the palms of   *M'k 14:65*
their

STRIKER

Not given to wine, no *s*. not   *1Ti 3:3*
greedy
not combative, but gentle (A)   *1Ti 3:3*
not a fist fighter (B)   *1Ti 3:3*
not a brawler (N)   *1Ti 3:3*
not violent, but gentle (P)(R)   *1Ti 3:3*
not given to wine, no *s*., not   *Tit 1:7*
given to
not be quick tempered (A)(R)   *Tit 1:7*
not hot tempered (B)(P)   *Tit 1:7*
not short tempered (N)   *Tit 1:7*

STRIKES

whoever *s*. a man (A)(R)   *Ex 21:12;*
Lu 6:29
whoever *s*. his father (B)   *Ex 21:15*
s. eye of a slave (R)   *Ex 21:26*
if he *s*. him (B)   *Nu 35:17; 5:18, 21*

STRIKETH

He *s*. them as wicked men   *Job 34:26*
in the
void of understanding *s*.   *Pr 17:18*
hands
surety for another (A)(B)(R)   *Pr 17:18*
a scorpion, when he *s*. a man   *Re 9:5*

STRIKING

striking (B)   *Nu 24:10;*
2Sa 24:17; Ne 13:25
one did the *s*. shall (B)   *Nu 35:21*
returned from *s*. down (B)   *2Sa 8:13*
s. he wounded him (A)(B)   *1Ki 20:37*
s. breast (A)   *Lu 18:13; Ac 7:24*

STRING

a crimson *s*. (B)   *Ge 38:30*
ready their arrow upon the *s*.   *Ps 11:2*
the *s*. of his tongue was   *M'k 7:35*
loosed

STRINGED

praise him with *s*. instruments   *Ps 150:4*
my songs to the *s*. instrument   *Isa 38:20*
chief singer on my *s*.   *Hab 3:19*
instruments

STRINGS

arrows upon thy *s*. against   *Ps 21:12*
and an instrument of ten *s*.   *Ps 33:2*
Upon an instrument of ten *s*.   *Ps 92:3*
and an instrument of ten *s*.   *Ps 144:9*
will I
s. of jewels (A)(E)(R)   *Ca 1:10*

STRIP

strip (A)(B)   *Ex 3:2; Isa 11:14; 17:14*
s. Aaron of his garments,   *Nu 20:26*
and put
the Philistines came to *s*. the   *1Ch 10:8*
slain
s. the slain (R)   *2Sa 23:10*
did Hezekiah *s*. off the gold   *2Ki 18:16*
(S)
the Philistines came to *s*. the   *1Ch 10:8*
slain
s. off outer garment   *Job 41:13*
(A)(E)(R)
cause them to *s*. naked (A)   *Isa 3:17*
s. you, and make you bare   *Isa 32:11*
s. off skirts   *Jer 13:26*
shall *s*. thee also of thy   *Eze 16:39*
clothes
shall also *s*. thee out of thy   *Eze 23:26*
clothes
Lest I *s*. her naked, and set her   *Ho 2:3*
as
s. his treasury (R)   *Ho 13:15*
s. the skin off of them (A)(B)   *Mic 3:2*
makes her cheerless, *s*. her   *Re 17:16*
(A)

STRIPE

wound for wound, s. for s.   Ex 21:25

STRIPED

striped (B)(R)(S)   Ge 30:35;
      30:39-40; 31:9-10
s., speckled, mottled (B)(R)   Ge 31:10

STRIPES

peeled white s. in (R)   Ge 30:37
Forty s. he may give him, and   De 25:3
him above these with many s.   De 25:3
with the s. of the children of   2Sa 7:14
men
rod, and their iniquity with s.   Ps 89:32
than an hundred s. into a   Pr 17:10
fool
and s. for the back of fools   Pr 19:29
so do s. the inward parts   Pr 20:30
fresh and bleeding s. (A)(E)   Isa 1:6
and with his s. we are   Isa 53:5
healed
will, shall be beaten with   Lu 12:47
many s.
commit things worthy of s.   Lu 12:48
shall
shall be beaten with few s.   Lu 12:48
For
they had laid many s. upon   Ac 16:23
them
of the night, and washed   Ac 16:33
their s.
In s. in imprisonments in   2Co 6:5
tumults
in s. above measure, in   2Co 11:23
prisons
times received I forty s.   2Co 11:24
save one
by whose s. ye were healed   1Pe 2:24

STRIPLING

Enquire whose son this s. is   1Sa 17:56

STRIPPED

stripped (A)   Ex 12:36;
      Job 12:17; Ps 76:5
children of Israel s. themselves   Ex 33:6
Moses s. Aaron of his   Nu 20:28
garments
he was s. for work   Jos 21:7
(A)(B)(N)(R)
Jonathan s. himself of the   1Sa 18:4
robe
And he s. off his clothes   1Sa 19:24
also, and
s. off his clothes (B)(R)   1Sa 19:24
off his head and s. off his   1Sa 31:9
armour
when they had s. him, they   1Ch 10:9
took
which they s. off for   2Ch 20:25
themselves
stripped (E)(R)   Job 12:17; 2:19
He hath s. me of my glory   Job 19:9
and s. the naked of their   Job 22:6
clothing
s. of coat of mail (B)   Job 41:13
to be s. naked (A)   Isa 3:17
scattered and s. (S)   Isa 18:2; 18:7
he s. the covering of Judah   Isa 22:8
(S)
and howl, I will go s. and   Mic 1:8
naked
And they s. him, and put on   M't 27:28
him
which s. him of his raiment   Lu 10:30
s. himself of all privileges and   Ph'p 2:7
rightful dignity (A)(P)

STRIPPER

hopper, s., shearer (B)   Joe 2:25

STRIPPETH

the Lord s. the forests (S)   Ps 29:9

STRIPS

s. bare the forest   Ps 29:9
(A)(B)(E)(R)

STRIPT

they s. Joseph out of his   Ge 37:23
coat, his

STRIVE

My spirit shall not s. with   Ge 6:3
man
not forever remain in man (B)   Ge 6:3
shall not abide in man forever   Ge 6:3
(R)
did s. with Isaac's herdmen   Ge 26:20
quarreled (A)(R)   Ge 26:20
disputed with (B)   Ge 26:20
the people did s. (S)   Ex 17:2
if men s. together, and one   Ex 21:18
smite
quarrel (A)   Ex 21:28; Pr 25:8
quarrel (B)   Ex 21:18; 21:22; 2Ti 2:24
contend (E)   Ex 21:18
If men, s. and hurt a woman   Ex 21:22
contend (A)   Ex 21:22
s. for justice (B)(R)   De 16:20
men s. together one with   De 25:11
another
are fighting (B)   De 25:11
fight with each other (R)   De 25:11
whom thou didst s. at the   De 33:8
waters
contended (A)   De 33:8;
      Ps 35:1; Pr 3:30
contending with (B)   De 33:8
will you s. for Baal (B)   J'g 6:31
did he ever s. against Israel,   J'g 11:25
or did
Why dost thou s. against   Job 33:13
him? for
accused him (B)   Job 33:13
contend (R)   Job 33:13;
      Ps 35:1; Pr 3:30; Ho 4:4
Lord, with them that s. with   Ps 35:1
me
contend (B)   Ps 35:1
s. with those who s.   Ps 35:1
(A)(B)(R)
S. not with a man without   Pr 3:30
cause
Go not forth hastily to s. lest   Pr 25:8
thou
they that s. with thee shall   Isa 41:11
perish
the potsherd s. with the   Isa 45:9
potsherds
no man s. nor reprove another   Ho 4:4
enter a complaint (B)   Ho 4:4
are as they s. with the   Ho 4:4
priest
He shall not s. nor cry;   M't 12:19
neither
quarrel (B)   M't 12:19
not wrangle (R)   M't 12:19
S. to enter in at the strait   Lu 13:24
gate
struggle to get in (N)   Lu 13:24
do your utmost to get in (P)   Lu 13:24
ye s. together with me in   Ro 15:30
your
unite with me (A)   Ro 15:30
agonize with me in prayer   Ro 15:30
(B)
be my allies in the fight (N)   Ro 15:30
stand behind me in earnest   Ro 15:30
prayer (P)
if a man also s. for masteries   2Ti 2:5
competes (B)(R)   2Ti 2:5
contend (E)   2Ti 2:5
not crowned, except he s.   2Ti 2:5
lawfully
s. not about words to no   2Ti 2:14
profit
avoid petty controversy over   2Ti 2:14
words (A)
indulge in no war of words   2Ti 2:14
(B)
stop disputing over mere   2Ti 2:14
words (N)(R)
not fight wordy battles (P)   2Ti 2:14
servant of the Lord must not   2Ti 2:24
s.
must not be quarrelsome   2Ti 2:24
(A)(N)(R)

STRIVED

so have I s. to preach the   Ro 15:20
gospel
my ambition has been to   Ro 15:20
preach (A)(N)(P)(R)
I endeavored to preach (B)   Ro 15:20
making it my aim to preach   Ro 15:20
(E)

STRIVEN

thou hast s. against the Lord   Jer 50:24
struggled and contended   Jer 50:24
against (A)
you provoked the Lord (B)   Jer 50:24

STRIVETH

unto him that s. with his   Isa 45:9
Maker
every man that s. for the   1Co 9:25
mastery

STRIVING

s. of Israel (E)(S)   Ex 17:7
s. of his heart (E)   Ec 2:22
s. after wind (B)   Ec 6:9
one mind s. together for the   Ph'p 1:27
faith
s. according to his working   Col 1:29
wrestling with the energy (B)   Col 1:29
toiling strenuously with all   Col 1:29
the energy (N)
s. earnestly (A)(E)   Col 4:12
resisted unto blood s. against   Heb 12:4
sin
struggled and fought   Heb 12:4
agonizingly against (A)
struggling against sin   Heb 12:4
(B)(N)(R)
fight against sin (P)   Heb 12:4

STRIVINGS

delivered me from the s. of   2Sa 22:44
my
delivered me from the s. of   Ps 18:43
contentions, and s. about the   Tit 3:9
law

STROKE

between s. and s. being   De 17:8
matters
his hand fetcheth a s. with the   De 19:5
axe
controversy and every s. be   De 21:5
tried
enemies with the s. of the   Es 9:5
sword
s. is heavier than my   Job 23:2
groaning
he take thee away with his s.   Job 36:18
Remove thy s. away from me   Ps 39:10
the people with a continual   Isa 14:6
s.
and healeth the s. of their   Isa 30:26
wound
the desire of thine eyes with   Eze 24:16
a s.

STROKES

and his mouth calleth for s.   Pr 18:6
s. reach innermost parts   Pr 20:30
(A)(B)(E)(R)

STROLLING

s. Jews, exercises (P)(R)   Ac 19:13

STRONG

Issachar is a s. ass, couching   Ge 49:14
down
the arms of his hands were   Ge 49:24
made s.
mourned with a s.   Ge 50:10
lamentation (S)
with a s. hand let them go   Ex 6:1; 13:9
Lord turned a mighty s. west   Ex 10:19
wind
Lord caused sea go back   Ex 14:21
by s. east wind
Edom came against him with   Nu 20:20
s. hand
border of the children of   Nu 21:24
Ammon was s.
Balaam said, S. is thy   Nu 24:21
dwellingplace
the s. wine to be poured out   Nu 28:7
to the Lord
there was not one city too s.   De 2:36
for us
a nation s. of face shall not   De 28:50
regard
as yet I am as s. as I was   Jos 14:11
day

when Israel were waxen *s.*	*Jos 17:13;* *J'g 1:28*	Lord bringeth waters, *s.* and many	*Isa 8:7*	the child grew and waxed *s.*	*Lu 1:80;* *2:40*	

Lord hath driven out great   *Jos 23:9*
nations and *s.*
but there was a *s.* tower   *J'g 9:51*
within the city
out of the *s.* came forth   *J'g 14:14*
sweetness
Micah saw that they were   *J'g 18:26*
too *s.* for him
when Saul saw any *s.* man,   *1Sa 14:52*
he took
Abner made himself *s.* for   *2Sa 3:6*
house of Saul
make thy battle more *s.*   *2Sa 11:25*
against the city
conspiracy was *s.* the people   *2Sa 15:12*
increased
he delivered me from my *s.*   *2Sa 22:18;*
enemy, they were too *s.*   *Ps 18:17*
for me
shall hear of thy name and *s.*   *1Ki 8:42*
hand
a great and *s.* wind rent the   *1Ki 19:11*
mountains
he made the cities exceeding   *2Ch 11:12*
s.
so they made Rehoboam *s.*   *2Ch 11:17*
three years
eyes run to shew himself *s.* in   *2Ch 16:9*
behalf of
when Uzziah was *s.* he was   *2Ch 26:16*
lifted up
thou hast redeemed by thy *s.*   *Ne 1:10*
hand
and they took *s.* cities and a   *Ne 9:25*
fat land
words of thy mouth be like a *s.*   *Job 8:2*
wind
if I speak of strength, lo, he   *Job 9:19*
is *s.*
with thy *s.* hand thou   *Job 30:21*
opposest thyself
hast thou spread out the sky   *Job 37:18*
that is *s.*
bones are as *s.* pieces of   *Job 40:18*
brass like bars
rejoiceth as a *s.* man to run a   *Ps 19:5*
race
Lord *s.* and mighty in battle   *Ps 24:8*
thou hast made my mountain   *Ps 30:7*
to stand *s.*
be thou my *s.* rock, and house   *Ps 31:2*
to save me
he hath shewed me his   *Ps 31:21*
kindness in a *s.* city
the poor from him that is too   *Ps 35:10*
s. for him
mine enemies are lively and   *Ps 38:19*
they are *s.*
who will bring me into *s.* city   *Ps 60:9;*
   108:10
thou hast been a *s.* tower from   *Ps 61:3*
the enemy
be my *s.* habitation   *Ps 71:3*
art my *s.* refuge   *Ps 71:7*
branch thou madest *s.* for   *Ps 80:15;*
thyself   *80:17*
s. arm of children of Lot (R)   *Ps 83:8*
Lord, who is a *s.* Lord like   *Ps 89:8*
unto thee
s. is thy hand, and high is   *Ps 89:13*
thy right hand
with *s.* hand and stretched   *Ps 136:12;*
out arm brought them out   *Jer 32:21*
many *s.* men have been slain   *Pr 7:26*
by her
rich man's wealth is his *s.*   *Pr 10:15;*
city   *18:11*
woman retains honour, and *s.*   *Pr 11:16*
men retain
in the fear of the Lord is a *s.*   *Pr 14:26*
tower
the name of the Lord is a *s.*   *Pr 18:10*
tower
a brother is harder to be won   *Pr 18:19*
than a *s.* city
a reward in the bosom   *Pr 21:14*
pacifieth *s.* wrath
wise man is *s.*   *Pr 24:5*
ants are a people not *s.*   *Pr 30:25*
I saw that the battle is not to   *Ec 9:11*
the *s.*
when the *s.* men shall bow   *Ec 12:3*
themselves
set me as a seal, love is *s.* as   *Ca 8:6*
death
s. shall be as tow, maker as a   *Isa 1:31*
spark

Lord spake thus to me with a   *Isa 8:11*
s. hand
his *s.* cities shall be as a   *Isa 17:9*
forsaken bough
therefore shall the *s.* people   *Isa 25:3*
glorify thee
shall this song be sung, we   *Isa 26:1*
have a *s.* city
with his *s.* sword shall punish   *Isa 27:1*
Leviathan
the Lord hath a mighty and *s.*   *Isa 28:2*
one
not mockers, lest your bands   *Isa 28:22*
be made *s.*
that trust in horsemen,   *Isa 31:1*
because they are *s.*
the Lord will come with a *s.*   *Isa 40:10*
hand
for that he is *s.* in power,   *Isa 40:26*
not one faileth
bring forth your *s.* reasons   *Isa 41:21*
he shall divide the spoil with   *Isa 53:12*
s.
a small one shall become a *s.*   *Isa 60:22*
I will fight against you with   *Jer 21:5*
a *s.* arm
we are mighty, *s.* men for   *Jer 48:14*
war
how is the *s.* staff broken   *Jer 48:17*
he shall come against   *Jer 49:19*
habitation of the *s.*
their Redeemer is *s.* the Lord   *Jer 50:34*
of hosts
shall come up unto   *Jer 50:44*
habitation of *s.*
make the watch *s.* set up the   *Jer 51:12*
watchmen
I made thy face *s.*, thy   *Eze 3:8*
forehead *s.*
the hand of the Lord was *s.*   *Eze 3:14*
upon me
I will make the pomp of the   *Eze 7:24*
s. to cease
had *s.* rods for sceptres of   *Eze 19:11*
them that rule
her *s.* rods were broken and   *Eze 19:12*
withered
she hath no *s.* rod to be a   *Eze 19:14*
sceptre to rule
s. garrisons shall go down to   *Eze 26:11*
ground
renowned city which wast *s.*   *Eze 26:17*
in the sea
to bind it, to make it *s.* to   *Eze 30:21*
hold sword
I will break the *s.* arms of   *Eze 30:22*
Pharaoh
s. shall speak to him out of   *Eze 32:21*
midst of hell
but I will destroy the fat and   *Eze 34:16*
the *s.*
the tree grew and was *s.*   *Da 4:11; 4:20*
it is thou. O king, art grown *s.*   *Da 4:22*
the fourth beast terrible, *s.*   *Da 7:7*
exceedingly
when he was *s.* the great horn   *Da 8:8*
was broken
he shall become *s.* with a   *Da 11:23*
small people
s. box of their silver (B)   *Ho 9:6*
nation is come up on my   *Joe 1:6;*
land, *s.*   *2:2*
as noise of *s.* people set in   *Joe 2:5*
battle array
for he is *s.* that executeth his   *Joe 2:11*
word
let the weak say, I am *s.*   *Joe 3:10*
the Amorite was *s.* as the   *Am 2:9*
oaks
and the *s.* shall not strengthen   *Am 2:14*
his force
that strengtheneth the spoiled   *Am 5:9*
against the *s.*
he shall rebuke *s.* nations afar   *Mic 4:3*
off
make her that was cast far   *Mic 4:7*
off, *s.* nations
hear. ye *s.* foundations of the   *Mic 6:2*
earth
make thy loins *s.*, fortify thy   *Na 2:1*
power
s. nations shall come to seek   *Na 8:22*
the Lord
how can one enter *s.* man's   *M't 12:29;*
house except he bind *s.* man   *M'k 3:27*
felt a *s.* wind (A)   *M't 14:30*

when a *s.* man armed   *Lu 11:21*
keepeth palace
thro' faith hath made this   *Ac 3:16*
man *s.*
was *s.* in faith, giving glory to   *Ro 4:20*
God
we *s.* ought to bear infirmities   *Ro 15:1*
of weak
we are weak, but ye are *s.*   *1Co 4:10*
for when I am weak, then   *2Co 12:10*
am I *s.*
when we are weak, and ye   *2Co 13:9*
are *s.*
God shall send them *s.*   *2Th 2:11*
delusion
had offered up prayers with *s.*   *Heb 5:7*
crying
have need of milk and not *s.*   *Heb 5:12*
meat
s. meat belongs to them of   *Heb 5:14*
full age
have a *s.* consolation who   *Heb 6:18*
have fled
who out of weakness were   *Heb 11:34*
made *s.*
ye are *s.* word of God   *1Jo 2:14*
abideth in
I saw a *s.* angel proclaim with   *Re 5:2*
loud voice
he cried with a *s.* voice,   *Re 18:2*
Babylon is fallen
for *s.* is the Lord God who   *Re 18:8*
judgeth her

STRONG HOLD, HOLDS

whether in tents or in *s.*   *Nu 13:19*
holds
Israel made them caves and *s.*   *J'g 6:2*
holds
David abode in *s.* holds   *1Sa 23:14*
doth not David hide himself   *1Sa 23:19*
in *s.* holds
and David dwelt in *s.* holds   *1Sa 23:29*
at En-gedi
David took the *s.* hold of Zion   *2Sa 5:7*
and came to the *s.* hold of   *2Sa 24:7*
Tyre
their *s.* holds wilt thou set on   *2Ki 8:12*
fire
Rehoboam fortified the *s.*   *2Ch 11:11*
holds
hast brought his *s.* holds to   *Ps 89:40*
ruin
to destroy the *s.* holds   *Isa 23:11*
thereof
pass over to his *s.* holds for   *Isa 31:9*
fear
the spoiler shall destroy thy   *Jer 48:18*
s. holds
Kerioth is taken, the *s.* holds   *Jer 48:41*
are surprised
he hath thrown down *s.* holds   *La 2:2*
the Lord hath destroyed his *s.*   *La 2:5*
holds
forecast devices against the   *Da 11:24*
s. holds
thus shall he do in the most   *Da 11:39*
s. holds
the *s.* hold of the daughter of   *Mic 4:8*
Zion
Lord is a *s.* hold in the day of   *Na 1:7*
trouble
all thy *s.* holds shall be like   *Na 3:12*
fig trees
draw waters for siege, fortify   *Na 3:14*
s. hold
they shall deride every *s.*   *Hab 1:10*
hold
Tyrus did build herself a *s.*   *Zec 9:3*
hold
turn ye to *s.* hold, prisoners   *Zec 9:12*
of hope
mighty to pulling down of *s.*   *2Co 10:4*
holds

STRONG ONES

that poor may fall by his *s.*   *Ps 10:10*
ones
at sound of the neighing of   *Jer 8:16*
his *s.* ones

BE STRONG

see whether they *be s.* or   *Nu 13:18*
weak
the people *be s.* that dwell in   *Nu 13:28*
the land

keep commandments, that ye   *De 11:8*
may *be s.*
drive out Canaanites, though   *Jos 17:18*
they *be s.*
be s. and quit yourselves like   *1Sa 4:9*
men
the hands of all with thee   *2Sa 16:21*
shall *be s.*
be thou *s.* and shew thyself a   *1Ki 2:2*
man
if Syrians *be* too *s.* for me,   *1Ch 19:12*
if Ammon *be* too *s.* for thee   *2Sa 10:11*
Lord hath chosen thee, *be s.*   *1Ch 28:10*
and do it
be s. your work shall be   *2Ch 15:7*
rewarded
if thou wilt go, do it, *be s.*   *2Ch 25:8*
for the battle
ye may *be s.* and eat good of   *Ezr 9:12*
land
that our oxen may *be s.* to   *Ps 144:14*
labour
say to them of a fearful heart,   *Isa 35:4*
Be s.
can thy hands *be s.* in days   *Eze 22:14*
I deal
the fourth kingdom shall *be s.*   *Da 2:40*
as iron
kingdom *be* partly *s.* partly   *Da 2:42*
broken
he said, peace be to thee, *be*   *Da 10:19*
s. yea, *be s.*
king of the south shall *be s.*   *Da 11:5*
and he shall *be s.* above him
but people that know their   *Da 11:32*
God shall *be s.*
be s. O Zerubbabel, *be s.* O   *Hag 2:4*
Joshua, *be s.* all ye people of
land, and work
let hands *be s.* ye that hear   *Zec 8:9*
fear not but let your hands *be*   *Zec 8:13*
s.
stand fast in faith, *be s.*   *1Co 16:13*
finally, brethren, *be s.* in the   *Eph 6:10*
Lord
my son, *be s.* in grace in   *2Ti 2:1*
Christ

STRONGER

shall be *s.* than the other   *Ge 25:23*
people
the *s.* cattle did conceive   *Ge 30:41*
were Laban's, and the *s.*   *Ge 30:42*
Jacob's
people; for they are *s.* than   *Nu 13:31*
we
honey? and what is *s.* than a   *J'g 14:18*
lion
eagles, they were *s.* than lions   *2Sa 1:23*
but David waxed *s.* and the   *2Sa 3:1*
but, being *s.* than she,   *2Sa 13:14*
forced her
therefore they were *s.* than   *1Ki 20:23*
we
surely we shall be *s.* than   *1Ki 20:23;*
they   *20:25*
that hath clean hands shall   *Job 17:9*
be *s.*
made them *s.* than their   *Ps 105:24*
enemies
persecutors; for they are *s.*   *Ps 142:6*
than I
thou art *s.* than I, and hast   *Jer 20:7*
hand of him that was *s.* than   *Jer 31:11*
he
when a *s.* than he shall come   *Lu 11:22*
upon
the weakness of God is *s.*   *1Co 1:25*
than men
to jealousy? are we *s.* than   *1Co 10:22*
he

STRONGEST

A lion which is *s.* among   *Pr 30:30*
beasts
the *s.* fortresses (S)   *Da 11:39*

STRONGLY

the foundations thereof be *s.*   *Ezr 6:3*
laid
I *s.* appealed (B)   *1Co 16:12*

STRONGHOLD

stronghold (S)   *J'g 9:46;*
1Sa 22:4, 5; 24:22; 2Sa 5:17; 23:14;
1Ch 11:16; 12:8, 16; Isa 29:7

my *s.* (A)   *2Sa 22:3*
my *s.* (R)   *2Sa 22:3; Ps 18:2; 144:2*
s. of king's house (A)   *1Ki 16:18*
in Shushan the *s.* (B)   *Es 1:5;*
  3:15; 9:6, 12; Da 8:2
David took the *s.* of Zion (S)   *1Ch 11:5;*
  11:7
stronghold (B)   *Ps 27:1; 52:7; Joe 3:16*
stronghold (R)   *Ps 27:1;*
  Isa 23:4; 25:4; Eze 30:15; Joe 3:16
you are my *s.* (B)(E)   *Ps 31:4;*
  43:2; 59:17
he is their *s.* (A)(E)   *Ps 37:39*
my lofty *s.* (B)   *Ps 144:2*
stronghold (E)   *Isa 23:4;*
  25:4; Eze 30:15; Joe 3:16
your *s.* laid waste   *Isa 23:14*
(B)(E)(R)
her and her *s.* (A)(E)(R)   *Isa 29:7*
put them in a *s.* (B)   *Eze 19:9*
take their *s.* (B)(R)   *Eze 24:25*

STRONGHOLDS

castles and *s.* of iron (A)   *De 33:25*
strongholds (S)   *Isa 33:16;*
  Jer 51:30; Eze 19:9
bring down your *s.* (B)   *Am 3:11*

STROVE

Esek; because they *s.* with   *Ge 26:20*
him
quarreled (A)   *Ge 26:20;*
  26:21; 2Sa 14:6
disputed with (B)   *Ge 26:20*
contended with (E)   *Ge 26:20*
another well, and *s.* for that   *Ge 26:21*
also
dispute (B)   *Ge 26:21; 26:22*
another well; for that they   *Ge 26:22*
s. not
quarrel (A)(R)   *Ge 26:22*
men of the Hebrews *s.*   *Ex 2:13*
together
quarreling and fighting (A)   *Ex 2:13;*
  Ac 7:26
quarreling (B)   *Ex 2:13*
struggling together (R)   *Ex 2:13*
s. with masses (E)   *Ex 17:2*
of Israel *s.* together in the   *Le 24:10*
camp
quarreled (B)   *Le 24:10*
people *s.* with Moses (E)(S)   *Nu 20:3*
children of Israel *s.* with the   *Nu 20:13*
Lord
contended (A)(B)(R)   *Nu 20:13; 26:9*
who *s.* against Moses and   *Nu 26:9*
against
when they *s.* against the Lord   *Nu 26:9*
they two *s.* together in the   *2Sa 14:6*
field
fought (B)   *2Sa 14:6*
when he *s.* with   *Ps 60 title*
Aram-naharaim
four winds of the heaven *s.*   *Da 7:2*
upon
stirring up the great sea   *Da 7:2*
(A)(B)(R)
brake forth upon the great sea   *Da 7:2*
(E)
Jews *s.* among themselves   *Joh 6:52*
contended (A)   *Joh 6:52*
wrangled (B)   *Joh 6:52*
dispute (E)   *Joh 6:52*
disputed (R)   *Joh 6:52*
he shewed himself as they *s.*   *Ac 7:26*
fighting (B)   *Ac 7:26*
quarrel, quarreling (E)(R)   *Ac 7:26*
the Pharisees' part arose, and   *Ac 23:9*
s.
contended (R)   *Ac 23:9*
s. to make them blaspheme   *Ac 26:11*
(E)

STROWED

s. it upon the graves of them   *2Ch 34:4*
that
strewed it (A)(E)(R)   *2Ch 34:4*
scattering them (B)   *2Ch 34:4*

STRUCK

the Lord *s.* Pharaoh (R)   *Ge 12:17*
struck (A)   *Ge 19:11;*
Nu 22:23, 25, 27; J'g 7:13; 1Sa 6:9;
17:49, 50; 19:10; 2Sa 14:6; 18:15; 20:10;
1Ki 22:24; 2Ki 2:8, 14; 13:18; 15:10;
Ca 5:7; Jer 41:2; Da 8:7; M't 26:68;
  M'k 14:47

struck (B)   *Ge 19:11;*
Ex 7:20; 8:17; 9:25; 12:29; Nu 11:33;
20:11; 22:27; J'g 15:8; 1Sa 6:9; 15:7;
17:25, 50; 2Sa 1:15; 4:6; 5:20, 25; 8:2;
10:18; 11:21; 14:6, 7; 18:15; 20:10;
23:10; 1Ki 16:10; 22:24, 34; 2Ki 2:8, 14;
3:24; 13:18; 15:5; 1Ch 4:41, 43; 13:10;
14:11, 16; 18:2; 21:7; 2Ch 14:12; 18:23;
21:9, 18; 25:11; Job 1:19; 2:7; Ps 78:20;
Ca 5:7; Da 2:35; Jon 4:7; M't 26:68;
  M'k 14:47; Lu 18:13; 22:50, 64;
  Joh 18:10
struck (R)   *Ge 19:11;*
Ex 7:20; 8:17; 9:25; Nu 20:11; 22:23,
25, 27; 24:10; J'g 5:26; 7:13; 1Sa 6:9,
19; 14:31; 17:49, 50; 19:10; 2Sa 14:6, 7;
18:15; 20:10; 23:10; 1Ki 15:27; 16:10;
22:24, 34; 2Ki 2:8, 14; 12:21; 13:18;
15:14, 30; 1Ch 18:2, 3; 2Ch 18:23, 33;
Job 1:19; Jer 41:2; Da 8:7; M't 26:5,
  68; M'k 14:47; Lu 22:50, 64; Joh 18:10;
  Ac 12:7
struck (R)   *Ex 7:25;*
22:2; Nu 14:42; 22:28, 32; 33:4;
2Sa 11:15; 2Ki 2:14; 13:19; 1Ch 18:9,
  10; Job 16:10; Ac 23:3; Re 8:12
he that *s.* him (A)(R)   *Ex 21:19*
struck (A)   *Ex 22:2;*
Nu 14:42; 22:32; 33:4; De 28:25;
2Ki 2:14; 13:19; Job 16:10; Ps 3:7;
  Eze 22:13; Ac 23:3
struck (B)   *Nu 22:32;*
33:4; 2Sa 2:31; 11:15; 2Ki 2:14; 13:19;
  2Ch 26:20; Ps 3:7
be *s.* down (A)(R)   *Nu 35:16;*
  35:17, 18, 21
And he *s.* it into the pan, or   *1Sa 2:14*
kettle
s. down (A)   *1Sa 30:1;*
  2Sa 11:15; 1Ki 8:33
the Lord *s.* the child that   *2Sa 12:15*
Uriah's
the ground, and *s.* him not   *2Sa 20:10*
again
s. to the sword (B)   *2Sa 23:10*
the man *s.* him (A)(B)(R)   *1Ki 20:37*
s. down the Moabites (B)   *2Ki 3:24*
and the Lord *s.* him, and he   *2Ch 13:20*
cried
s. cheek insolently   *Job 16:10*
(A)(B)(R)
thou hast *s.* thy hand to a   *Pr 6:1*
stranger (S)
s. a servant of the high   *M't 26:51*
priest's
others *s.* him (N)   *M't 26:67*
s. him on the head   *M't 27:30*
(A)(B)(R)
him, they *s.* him on the face   *Lu 22:64*
s. them as sheer imagination   *Lu 24:11*
(P)
s. Jesus with the palm of his   *Joh 18:22*
angel of Lord *s.* him   *Ac 12:23*
(B)(N)(P)
they *s.* sail (S)   *Ac 27:17*

STRUCTURE

a *s.* like a city (S)   *Eze 40:2*

STRUGGLED

children *s.* together within   *Ge 25:22*
her
my servants would have *s.*   *Joh 18:36*
(B)

STRUGGLES

toil and *s.* (A)(P)   *1Th 2:9*

STRUT

the godless *s.* around (A)   *Ps 12:8*

STUBBLE

to gather *s.* instead of straw   *Ex 5:12*
wrath, which consumed them   *Ex 15:7*
as *s.*
and wilt thou pursue the dry   *Job 13:25*
s.
They are as *s.* before the   *Job 21:18*
wind
slingstones are turned into   *Job 41:28*
s.
Darts are counted as *s.*: he   *Job 41:29*
wheel; as the *s.* before the   *Ps 83:13*
wind
as the fire devoureth the *s.*   *Isa 5:24*
chaff, ye shall bring forth *s.*   *Isa 33:11*

shall take them away as s.   Isa 40:24
sword, and as driven s. to his   Isa 41:2
bow
Behold, they shall be as s.;   Isa 47:14
the fire
scatter them as the s. that   Jer 13:24
passeth
flame of fire that devoureth the   Joe 2:5
s.
flame and the house of Esau for   Ob 18
s.
they shall be devoured as s.   Na 1:10
all that do wickedly, shall be   Mal 4:1
s.
precious stones, wood, hay, s.   1Co 3:12

STUBBORN

hard and s. people (A)(B)   De 9:6;
       9:13
no longer s. (A)(B)   De 10:16
man have a s. and rebellious   De 21:18
soul
This our son is s. and   De 21:20
rebellious
I walk in my s. way (B)   De 29:19
rebellious and s. (B)   De 31:37
doings, nor from their s. way   J'g 2:19
a s. and rebellious generation   Ps 78:8
(She is loud and s.; her feet   Pr 7:11
abide
s. in heart (S)   Isa 46:12
like a s. heifer (A)(B)(E)(R)   Ho 4:16
grow s. as in rebellion   Heb 3:15
(B)(R)

STUBBORNLY

s. follows own heart (R)   Jer 23:17
Israel has behaved s. (A)(E)   Ho 4:16

STUBBORNNESS

look not unto the s. of this   De 9:27
people
rebellion and s. (A)   De 31:37
and s. is as iniquity and   1Sa 15:23
idolatry
walks after s. of mind   Jer 23:17
(A)(B)(E)

STUCK

his spear s. in the ground at   1Sa 26:7
his
I have s. unto thy   Ps 119:31
testimonies
the forepart s. fast, and   Ac 27:41
remained

STUDIES

s. day and night (B)   Ps 1:2

STUDIETH

of the righteous s. to answer   Pr 15:28
For their heart s. destruction   Pr 24:2

STUDS

borders of gold with s. of   Ca 1:11
silver

STUDY

much s. is a weariness of the   Ec 12:12
flesh
that ye s. to be quiet, and to   1Th 4:11
do
S. to show thyself approved   2Ti 2:15
unto God

STUFF

thou hast searched all my s.   Ge 31:37
my household goods (A)(B)   Ge 31:37
goods (R)   Ge 31:37; 45:20; Ex 22:7
thou found of all thy   Ge 31:37
household s.
Also regard not your s.; for   Ge 45:20
goods (A)   Ge 45:20; Ex 22:7
furniture (B)   Ge 45:20
his neighbour money or s. to   Ex 22:7
keep
articles (B)   Ex 22:7
s. they had was sufficient for   Ex 36:7
all
material (B)   Ex 36:7
garment of mingled s. (A)   De 22:11

put it even among their own   Jos 7:11
s.
baggage (A)   Jos 7:11;
   1Sa 10:22; 25:13; 30:24; Eze 12:4, 7
belongings (B)   Jos 7:11
he hath hid himself among   1Sa 10:22
the s.
baggage (B)   1Sa 10:22; 30:24
baggage (E)   1Sa 10:22;
   25:13; 30:24
baggage (R)   1Sa 10:22;
   25:13; 30:24; Eze 12:3, 4, 7
and two hundred abode by   1Sa 25:13
the s.
supplies (B)   1Sa 25:13
his part be that tarrieth by   1Sa 30:24
the s.
forth all the household s. of   Ne 13:8
Tobiah
house furnishings (A)   Ne 13:8
personal items (B)   Ne 13:8
household furniture (R)   Ne 13:8
prepare thee s. for removing   Eze 12:3
belongings (A)   Eze 12:3; Lu 17:31
necessary equiment (B)   Eze 12:3
shalt thou bring forth thy s.   Eze 12:4
by day
belongings (B)   Eze 12:4;
   12:7; Lu 17:31
in their sight, as s. for   Eze 12:4
removing
I brought forth my s. by day   Eze 12:7
as s. for captivity, and in the   Eze 12:7
even
longing to s. himself (B)(P)   Lu 15:16
housetop, and his s. in the   Lu 17:31
house
goods (E)(P)(R)   Lu 17:31
belongings (N)   Lu 17:31
s. themselves at your tables   2Pe 2:13
(B)

STULTIFY

refuse to s. grace (P)   Ga 2:21

STUMBLE

in many things we all s. (E)   Ps 113:2
no one can make them s.   Ps 119:165
(R)
safely, and thy foot shall not   Pr 3:23
s.
thou runnest, thou shalt not s.   Pr 4:12
they know not at what they s.   Pr 4:19
shall be weary nor s. among   Isa 5:27
them
And many among them shall   Isa 8:15
s.
err in vision, they s. in   Isa 28:7
judgment
we s. at noon day as in the   Isa 59:10
night
wilderness, that they should   Isa 63:13
not s.
feet s. upon the dark   Jer 13:16
mountains
caused them to s. sin in their   Jer 18:15
ways
therefore my persecutors   Jer 20:11
shall s.
way, wherein they shall not s.   Jer 31:9
shall s. and fall toward the   Jer 46:6
north
the most proud shall s. and   Jer 50:32
fall
shall s. and fall, and not be   Da 11:19
found
they shall s. in their walk: they   Na 2:5
corpses; they s. upon their   Na 3:3
corpses
have caused many to s. at the   Mal 2:8
law
if eye causes you to s. (E)   M't 5:29
he is caused to s. (A)   M't 13:21
lest we cause them to s. (E)   M't 17:37
cause one to s. and sin   M't 18:6
(A)(E)
many shall s. (E)   M't 24:10
though are offended and s.   M't 26:33
(A)
doth this cause you to s. (E)   Joh 6:61
not be caused to s. (E)   Joh 16:1
makes him s. or offends   Ro 14:21
(A)(B)(R)
if eating causes brother to s.   1Co 8:13
(B)(E)
cause none to s. (B)(E)(P)   1Co 10:32
made to s. and fall   2Co 11:29
(A)(E)(N)

not stumbling or causing   Ph'p 1:10
others to s. (A)
in many things we all s. (S)   Jas 3:2
even to them which s. at the   1Pe 2:8
word
a rock to s. over (B)(N)   1Pe 2:8

STUMBLED

that s. are girded with strength   1Sa 2:4
to hold the ark; for the oxen   1Ch 13:9
s.
eat up my flesh, they s. and fell   Ps 27:2
none among tribes s. (R)   Ps 105:37
man hath s. against the   Jer 46:12
mighty
they s. at that stumblingstone   Ro 9:32
Have they s. that they should   Ro 11:11
fall

STUMBLES

s. in one point (E)   Jas 2:10

STUMBLETH

thine heart be glad when he s.   Pr 24:17
man walk in the day, he s.   Joh 11:9
not
if a man walk in the night,   Joh 11:10
he s.
anything whereby thy brother   Ro 14:21
s.
whereby your brother s. (E)   Ro 14:21

STUMBLING

my s., limping (A)(B)(R)   Ps 35:15
no occasion of s. (E)   Ps 119:165
for a stone of s. and for a   Isa 8:14
rock of
take up the s. block out of   Isa 57:14
the way
no occasion of s. (E)   M't 11:6
gather all things that cause s.   M't 13:41
(E)
an occasion of s. (B)   M't 18:6
if a man is a cause of s. (N)   M't 18:6
find in me an occasion of s.   M't 26:31
(B)
their s. (A)   Ro 11:12
not s. or causing others to   Ph'p 1:10
stumble (A)
And a stone of s. and a rock   1Pe 2:8
there is none occasion of s. in   1Jo 2:10
him
keep you from s. (A)(B)(E)   Jude 24

STUMBLINGBLOCK

deaf, nor put a s. before the   Le 19:14
blind
put obstruction before them   Le 19:14;
(B)   Isa 57:14
no s. is in their path (B)   Ps 119:165
s. out of the way   Isa 57:14
obstruction (R)   Isa 57:14
iniquity, and I lay a s. before   Eze 3:20
him
because it is the s. of their   Eze 7:19
iniquity
put the s. of their iniquity   Eze 14:3
before
set temptations to sin (B)   Eze 14:3;
   14:7
putteth the s. of his iniquity   Eze 14:4;
   14:7
does not find me a s. (N)   M't 11:6
Satan, you are a s. (E)(N)   M't 16:23
is this a s. (A)   Joh 6:61
made a snare, and a trap, and   Ro 11:9
a s.
a pitfall (A)(R)   Ro 11:9
no man put a s. or an   Ro 14:13
occasion to
unto the Jews a s. and unto   1Co 1:23
an obstacle to the Jews (B)   1Co 1:23
become a s. to them that are   1Co 8:9
weak
hindrance (A)(B)   1Co 8:9
a pitfall to the weak (N)   1Co 8:9
ceased to be a s. (A)(E)(R)   Ga 5:11
to cast a s. before the children   Re 2:14
put a temptation before (N)   Re 2:14

STUMBLINGBLOCKS

I will lay s. before this people   Jer 6:21
sea, and the s. with the wicked   Zep 1:3
gather all s. (B)   M't 13:14

STUMBLINGSTONE

For they stumbled at that *s.*   *Ro 9:32*
I lay in Zion a *s.* and rock of   *Ro 9:33*

STUMP

only the *s.* of Dagon was left   *1Sa 5:4*
to him
leave the *s.* of his roots in the   *Da 4:15*
yet leave the *s.* of the roots   *Da 4:23*
thereof
to leave the *s.* of the tree   *Da 4:26*
roots

STUNG

they were *s.* to the heart (A)   *Ac 2:37*

STUNNED

like a man *s.* (A)   *Jer 14:9*
was *s.*, stood aghast (B)   *Da 4:19*
were *s.* and bewildered (A)   *M't 8:27*

STUPID

s. man (A)(B)(R)   *Job 11:12*
s. in your sight (A)(B)(R)   *Job 13:3*
its *s.* die in the ground   *Job 14:8*
(B)(R)
fool and the *s.* (A)(R)   *Ps 49:10*
stupid (S)   *Ps 49:10;*
92:6; 94:8; Pr 12:1; 30:2; Isa 19:11;
     Jer 10:8, 14, 21; 51:17
s. and indiscriminating   *Pr 12:1*
(A)(R)
too *s.* to be a man (B)(R)   *Pr 30:2*
give *s.* counsel (R)   *Isa 19:11*
s. thick-headed   *Jer 4:22*
(A)(B)(R)(S)
irrational and *s.* (A)   *Jer 10:8*
both *s.* and foolish (B)(R)   *Jer 10:8;*
     10:14
their *s.* minds were dark (B)   *Ro 1:21*
no coarse, *s.*, flippant talk   *Eph 5:4*
(N)
s., senseless controversies   *2Ti 12:23*
(R)
steer clear of *s.* arguments (P)   *Tit 3:9*

STUPIDITY

world's cleverness is *s.* (P)   *1Co 3:19*

STUPIFIED

gaze *s.* and aghast (A)(R)   *Isa 13:8*
s. with conceit (A)   *1Ti 6:4*

STUPIFY

s. yourselves and be in a   *Isa 29:9*
stupor (R)

STUPOR

stupify yourselves and be in a   *Isa 29:9*
s. (R)

STYLISHLY

s. dressed (B)   *Lu 7:25*

SUAH

S. and Harnepher, and   *1Ch 7:36*
Shual

SUBDUE

and replenish the earth, and *s.*   *Ge 1:28*
to *s.* him (A)   *J'g 16:5; 16:6*
Moreover I will *s.* thine   *1Ch 17:10*
enemies
He shall *s.* the people under us   *Ps 47:3*
let us *s.* them (B)(R)   *Ps 74:8*
holden, to *s.* nations before   *Isa 45:1*
him
first, and he shall *s.* three   *Da 7:24*
kings
he will *s.* our iniquities; and   *Mic 7:19*
thou
devour, and *s.* with sling   *Zec 9:15*
stones
to *s.* all things unto   *Ph'p 3:21*
himself
subject everything to himself   *Ph'p 3:21*
(A)(B)(E)(N)(R)
makes him the master of   *Ph'p 3:21*
everything (P)

SUBDUED

s. Rephaims (A)(R)   *Ge 14:5*
the land be *s.* before the   *Nu 32:22*
Lord
and the land shall be *s.*   *Nu 32:29*
before you
war with thee, until it be *s.*   *De 20:20*
And the land was *s.* before   *Jos 18:1*
them
So Moab was *s.* that day   *J'g 3:30*
under the
So God *s.* on that day Jabin   *J'g 4:23*
was Midian *s.* before the   *J'g 8:28*
children
the children of Ammon were   *J'g 11:33*
s.
So the Philistines were *s.* and   *1Sa 7:13*
they
smote the Philistines, and *s.*   *2Sa 8:1*
them
of all nations which he *s.*   *2Sa 8:11*
against me hast thou *s.* under   *2Sa 22:40*
me
smote the Philistines, and *s.*   *1Ch 18:1*
them
of the giant; and they were *s.*   *1Ch 20:4*
and the land is *s.* before the   *1Ch 22:18*
Lord
children of Israel were *s.*   *2Ch 13:18*
(S)
thou hast *s.* under me those   *Ps 18:39*
that
should soon have *s.* their   *Ps 81:14*
enemies
to be *s.* and abolished   *1Co 15:26*
(A)(B)(E)(N)
all things shall be *s.* unto   *1Co 15:28*
him
Who through faith *s.*   *Heb 11:33*
kingdoms
overcame kingdoms (B)   *Heb 11:33*
conquered kingdoms (R)   *Heb 11:33*

SUBDUEDST

and thou *s.* before them the   *Ne 9:24*

SUBDUETH

me, and *s.* the people under   *Ps 18:47*
me
trust; who *s.* my people under   *Ps 144:2*
me
in pieces and *s.* all things: *Da 2:40*
and as
beats all things down (B)   *Da 2:40*
breaks to pieces and shatters   *Da 2:40*
all things (R)

SUBJECT

s. to forced labor (S)   *J'g 1:30*
Nazareth, and was *s.* unto   *Lu 2:51*
them
obedient unto them   *Lu 2:51*
(A)(P)(R)
submit himself (B)   *Lu 2:51*
continued under their   *Lu 2:51*
authority (N)
devils are *s.* unto us through   *Lu 10:17*
thy
obey (P)   *Lu 10:17; Ro 13:1, 5*
not, that the spirits are *s.*   *Lu 10:20*
unto you
submit (B)(N)   *Lu 10:20*
for it is not *s.* to the law of   *Ro 8:7*
God
submit itself to God's law   *Ro 8:7*
(A)(R)
submissive (B)   *Ro 8:7;*
     Eph 5:24; 1Pe 2:18
the creature was made *s.* to   *Ro 8:20*
vanity
brought under bondage (B)   *Ro 8:20*
made the victim of   *Ro 8:20*
frustration (N)
every soul be *s.* unto the   *Ro 13:1*
higher
render obedience (B)   *Ro 13:1*
submit (N)   *Ro 13:1; 13:5*
Wherefore ye must needs be *s.*   *Ro 13:5*
not
the prophets are *s.* to the   *1Co 14:32*
prophets
in subjection to (B)   *1Co 14:32*
the Son also himself be *s.*   *1Co 15:28*
unto him
as the church is *s.* unto   *Eph 5:24*
Christ

s. to himself   *Ph'p 3:2*
(A)(B)(E)(N)(R)
the world, are ye *s.* to   *Col 2:20*
ordinances
in mind to be *s.* to   *Tit 3:1*
principalities
submissive to (A)(N)(R)   *Tit 3:1;*
     1Pe 2:18
all their lifetime *s.* to   *Heb 2:15*
bondage
servitude (N)   *Heb 2:15*
Elias a man *s.* to like   *Jas 5:17*
passions
Servants, be *s.* to your   *1Pe 2:18*
masters
submission (N)   *1Pe 2:18; 3:22*
submit (P)   *1Pe 2:18*
powers being made *s.* unto   *1Pe 3:22*
him
subservient to (A)(P)   *1Pe 3:22*
all of you be *s.* one to another   *1Pe 5:5*

SUBJECTED

who hath *s.* the same in hope   *Ro 8:20*

SUBJECTION

brought into *s.* under their   *Ps 106:42*
hand
brought them into *s.* for   *Jer 34:11*
servants
to return, and brought them   *Jer 34:16*
into *s.*
my body, and bring it into *s.*   *1Co 9:27*
your professed *s.* unto the   *2Co 9:13*
gospel
To whom we gave place by *s.*   *Ga 2:5*
no
woman learn in silence with   *1Ti 2:11*
all *s.*
submissiveness (A)(B)   *1Ti 2:11*
submission (N)(R)   *1Ti 2:11*
his children in *s.* with all   *1Ti 3:4*
gravity
submissive (B)   *1Ti 3:4; 1Pe 3:1, 5*
not put in *s.* the world to   *Heb 2:5*
come
Thou hast put all things in *s.*   *Heb 2:8*
under
in that he put all in *s.* under   *Heb 2:8*
him
rather be in *s.* unto the   *Heb 12:9*
Father of
be in *s.* to your own husbands   *1Pe 3:1*
submissive (R)   *1Pe 3:1; 3:5*
in *s.* unto their own husbands   *1Pe 3:5*
submission (N)   *1Pe 3:5*
submissive (P)   *1Pe 3:5*

SUBJECTS

s. of forced labor (S)   *J'g 1:30; 1:33*
ye purpose of *s.* Judah (S)   *2Ch 28:10*

SUBMISSION

decline *s.* to me (B)   *Ex 10:3*
women learn in *s.* (N)(R)   *1Ti 2:11*

SUBMISSIVE

children *s.* (R)   *1Ti 3:4*

SUBMIT

and *s.* thyself under her hands   *Ge 16:9*
Strangers shall *s.* themselves   *2Sa 22:45*
unto
strangers shall *s.* themselves   *Ps 18:44*
unto
shall thine enemies *s.*   *Ps 66:3*
themselves
s. himself with pieces of silver   *Ps 68:30*
spirits *s.* (B)(N)   *Lu 10:20*
s. itself to God's law (A)(R)   *Ro 8:7*
That ye *s.* yourselves unto   *1Co 16:16*
such
Wives, *s.* yourselves unto   *Eph 5:22;*
     Col 3:18
rule over you, and *s.*   *Heb 13:17*
yourselves
S. yourselves therefore to God   *Jas 4:7*
S. yourselves to every   *1Pe 2:13*
ordinance
s. yourselves unto the elder   *1Pe 5:5*

SUBMITTED

s. themselves unto Solomon	1Ch 29:24
should have s. themselves	Ps 81:15
have not s. themselves unto	Ro 10:3

SUBMITTING

S. yourselves one to another in	Eph 5:21

SUBORNED

Then they s. men, which said	Ac 6:11
instigated and instructed men (A)	Ac 6:11
secretly instigated men (B)(R)	Ac 6:11
they bribed men (P)	Ac 6:11

SUBSCRIBE

s. with his hand unto the Lord	Isa 44:5
write (tattoo) on the hand (A)(B)	Isa 44:5
inscribed on the hand (R)	Isa 44:5
and s. evidences, and seal them	Jer 32:44
sign deeds (A)(B)(R)	Jer 32:44

SUBSCRIBED

I s. the evidence, and sealed it	Jer 32:10
signed the deed (A)	Jer 32:10; 32:12
witnesses that s. the book of	Jer 32:12

SUBSERVIENT

made s. to (A)(P)	1Pe 3:22

SUBSIDED

the water s. (S)	Ge 8:1

SUBSTANCE

living s. that I have made will I	Ge 7:4
living thing (B)(E)(R)	Ge 7:4; 7:23; De 11:6
And every living s. was destroyed	Ge 7:23
living thing (A)	Ge 7:23; De 11:6
all their s. that they had gathered	Ge 12:5
possessions (A)	Ge 12:5; 13:6; 15:14; 34:23; 36:6; Jos 14:4; 2Ch 21:17; 32:29; 35:7; Ezr 8:21; Job 1:10; Pr 12:27; 28:8; Ob 13; Heb 10:34
possessions (B)	Ge 12:5; 13:6; 15:14; 2Ch 21:17; 31:3; 32:29; 35:7; Job 1:10; Ps 105:21
possessions (R)	Ge 12:5; 13:6; 15:14; 2Ch 21:17; 31:3; 32:29; 35:7; Job 1:10; Ps 105:21
for their s. was great, so that they	Ge 13:6
shall they come out with great s.	Ge 15:14
all his s. (E)	Ge 31:18
shall not their cattle and their s.	Ge 34:23
property (B)	Ge 34:23; 36:6; 1Ch 27:31; 28:1; Ezr 10:8; Lu 15:13; Heb 10:34
property (R)	Ge 34:23; 36:6; 1Ch 27:31; 28:1; Ezr 10:8; Lu 15:13; Heb 10:34
all his s. which he had got in	Ge 36:6
possessions (E)	Ge 36:6
s. that was in their possession	De 11:6
Bless, Lord, his s. and accept	De 33:11
for their cattle and for their s.	Jos 14:4
rulers of the s. which was king	1Ch 27:31
the stewards over all the s. and	1Ch 28:1
away all the s. that was found in	2Ch 21:17
portion of his s. for the burnt	2Ch 31:3
personal contribution (A)	2Ch 31:3
God had given him s. very much	2Ch 32:29
these were of the king's s.	2Ch 35:7
for our little ones, and for all our s.	Ezr 8:21
goods (B)(R)	Ezr 8:21; Pr 1:13; 6:31; Ob 13
elders, all his s. should be forfeited	Ezr 10:8
property (A)	Ezr 10:8
His s. also was seven thousand	Job 1:3
and his s. is increased in the land	Job 1:10
the robber swalloweth up their s.	Job 5:5
wealth (B)	Job 5:5; 6:22; 15:29; Pr 8:21; 12:27; 28:8; Ca 8:7; Jer 15:13; 17:3; Ho 12:8; Mic 4:13
wealth (R)	Job 5:5; 6:22; 15:29; Pr 8:21; 12:27; 28:8; Ca 8:7; Jer 15:13; 17:3; Ho 12:8; Mic 4:13
Give a reward for me of your s.	Job 6:22
wealth (A)	Job 6:22; 15:29; 20:18; Ps 17:14; Jer 17:3; Ho 12:8
rich, neither shall his s. continue	Job 15:29
according to his s. shall the	Job 20:18
Whereas our s. is not cut down	Job 22:20
upon it, and dissolvest my s.	Job 30:22
leave the rest of their s. to their	Ps 17:14
his house, and ruler of all his s.	Ps 105:21
My s. was not hid from thee	Ps 139:15
my frame not hid from you (A)(E)(R)	Ps 139:15
Thine eyes did see my s. yet	Ps 139:16
We shall find all precious s. we	Pr 1:13
goods (A)	Pr 1:13; Ca 8:1
Honour the Lord with thy s.	Pr 3:9
capital and sufficiency (A)	Pr 3:9
he shall give all the s. of his house	Pr 6:31
those that love me to inherit s.	Pr 8:21
riches (A)	Pr 8:21
casteth away the s. of the wicked	Pr 10:3
the s. of a diligent man is precious	Pr 12:27
and unjust gain increaseth his s.	Pr 28:8
with harlots spendeth his s.	Pr 29:3
give all the s. of his house for love	Ca 8:7
as an oak, whose s. is in them	Isa 6:13
stump (B)(R)	Isa 6:13
stock (A)	Isa 6:13
the holy seed shall be the s. thereof	Isa 6:13
Thy s. and thy treasures will	Jer 15:13
I will give thy s. and all thy	Jer 17:3
much s. and equipment (A)(E)	Da 11:13
prey, spoil, s. (E)	Da 11:24
return with great s. (E)(R)	Da 11:28
rich, I have found me out s.	Ho 12:8
wealth (E)	Ho 12:8
laid hands on their s. in the day	Ob 13
their s. unto the Lord of the whole	Mic 4:13
treasure (A)	Mic 4:13
ministered unto him of their s.	Lu 8:3
property and personal belongings (A)	Lu 8:3
means (B)(R)	Lu 8:3
resources (N)(P)	Lu 8:3
portion of s. (E)	Lu 15:12
wasted his s. with riotous living	Lu 15:13
fortune (A)	Lu 15:13
property (N)(P)	Lu 15:13
a better and an enduring s.	Heb 10:34
possessions (N)	Heb 10:34
goods (P)	Heb 10:34
faith is the s. of things hoped	Heb 11:1
assurance (A)(B)(E)(R)	Heb 11:1
full confidence (P)	Heb 11:1

SUBTIL

the serpent was more s. than	Ge 3:1
the serpent, wiliest of all field animals (B)	Ge 3:1
and Jonadab was a very s. man	2Sa 13:3
a very crafty man (A)(B)	2Sa 13:3
a shrewd person (R)	2Sa 13:3
attire of an harlot, and s. of heart	Pr 7:10
cunning of heart (A)	Pr 7:10
wily of heart (B)(E)	Pr 7:10
a crafty mind (R)	Pr 7:10

SUBTILLY

told me that he dealeth very s.	1Sa 23:22
deals very craftily (A)	1Sa 23:22
very cunning (B)	1Sa 23:22
behaves very shrewdly (R)	1Sa 23:22
to deal s. with his servants	Ps 105:25
deal very craftily (A)(B)	Ps 105:25
deal deceitfully (R)	Ps 105:25
The same dealt s. with our kindred	Ac 7:19
dealt treacherously (A)	Ac 7:19
dealt craftily (B)(E)	Ac 7:19
made a crafty attack (N)	Ac 7:19
cleverly victimized our race (P)	Ac 7:19
defrauded our race (R)	Ac 7:19

SUBTILTY

The brother came with s. and	Ge 27:35
came with crafty cunning (A)	Ge 27:35
came with guile (B)(E)	Ge 27:35
came with pretence (R)	Ge 27:35
But Jehu did it in s. to the intent	2Ki 10:19
did it with trickery (A)	2Ki 10:19
did it with cunning (B)	2Ki 10:19
did this deceitfully (R)	2Ki 10:19
To give s. to the simple, to the	Pr 1:4
give prudence to the simple (A)(B)(E)	Pr 1:4
give insight to the simple (R)	Pr 1:4
that they might take Jesus by s.	M't 26:4
arrest Jesus by stratagem (A)	M't 26:4
arrest Jesus by stealth (B)	M't 26:4
have Jesus arrested by some trick (N)(P)	M't 26:4
to arrest Jesus underhandedly (R)	M't 26:4
take him with s. (B)	M'k 14:11
O full of all s. and all mischief	Ac 13:10
master of every form of deception and recklessness, unscrupulousness and wickedness (A)	Ac 13:10
full of all deceit and villainy (B)(R)	Ac 13:10
full of all guile and villainy (E)	Ac 13:10
you utter imposter and charlatan (N)	Ac 13:10
you monster of trickery and evil (P)	Ac 13:10
beguiled Eve through his s.	2Co 11:3
beguiled Eve through his cunning (A)(B)(R)	2Co 11:3
beguiled Eve by his craftiness (E)	2Co 11:3
in his cunning seduced Eve (N)	2Co 11:3

SUBTLETIES

s. and contradictions in knowledge (A)	1Ti 6:20

SUBURBAN

the s. lands (S)	2Ch 11:14

SUBURBS

field of the s. of their cities may	Le 25:34
unto the Levites s. for the cities	Nu 35:2
and the s. of them shall be for their	Nu 35:3
the s. of the cities, which ye shall	Nu 35:4
shall be to them the s. of the cities	Nu 35:5
them shall ye give with their s.	Nu 35:7
suburbs (B)	Jos 13:32; 13:28; 15:32, 36, 41, 44-47, 51, 54, 57, 59, 60, 62; 16:9; 18:24; 19:6-8, 15-16, 22, 23, 30, 31, 38, 39, 48; 21:12; 2Ch 28:18
their s. for their cattle and for their	Jos 14:4
with the s. thereof for our cattle	Jos 21:2
the Lord, these cities and their s.	Jos 21:3
Levites these cities with their s.	Jos 21:8
with the s. thereof round about it	Jos 21:11

SUBURBS (cont.)

with her s.   Jos 21:13; 21:14-18,
21-25, 27-32, 34-39; 1Ch 6:57-60, 67-81
with their s.   Jos 21:19;
21:26, 33; Jos 21:41, 42; 1Ch 6:57, 64;
                                        13:2
chamberlain, which was in   2Ki 23:11
the s.
towns, and in all the s. of   1Ch 5:16
Sharon
and the s. thereof round   1Ch 6:55
about it
left their s. and   2Ch 11:14
their possession
in the fields of the s. of   2Ch 31:19
their cities
The s. shall shake at the   Eze 27:28
sound of
round about for the s. thereof Eze 45:2
for the city, for dwelling,   Eze 48:15
and for s.
the s. of the city shall be   Eze 48:17
toward

SUBVERSION

a charge of s. (N)   Lu 23:14

SUBVERSIVE

s. doctrines inspired by devils   1Ti 4:1
(N)

SUBVERT

To s. a man in his cause, the La 3:36
Lord
to refuse a man justice (B)   La 3:36
who s. whole houses, teaching Tit 1:11
upset whole houses (B)(P)   Tit 1:11
overthrow whole houses (E)   Tit 1:11
ruining whole families (N)   Tit 1:11
upsetting whole families (R)   Tit 1:11

SUBVERTED

s. me with guile (R)   Ps 119:78
Knowing that he that is such   Tit 3:11
is s.
is perverted and corrupted   Tit 3:11
(A)
such a person is distorted (B) Tit 3:11
such a one is perverted   Tit 3:11
(E)(R)
has a distorted mind (N)   Tit 3:11
he is a moral twist (P)   Tit 3:11

SUBVERTING

s. our nation (N)   Lu 23:2
you with words, s. your souls Ac 15:24
unsettling their minds and   Ac 15:24
throwing you into confusion (A)
troubled you, unsettled your   Ac 15:24
minds (B)(R)
disturbed you, unsettled your Ac 15:24
minds (N)
caused deep distress,   Ac 15:24
unsettled your minds (P)
profit but to the s. of the   2Ti 2:14
hearers
upsets and undermines the   2Ti 2:14
faith (A)(P)
completely upsets the listeners 2Ti 2:14
(B)
is the ruin to those who listen 2Ti 2:14
(N)(R)

SUBVERTS

s. cause of the right (R)   Ex 23:8
s. cause of innocent (B)   De 16:19
foolishness s. his way (A)(E) Pr 19:3

SUCCEED

made all to flourish and s.   Ge 39:3
(A)
it will not s. (A)(R)   Nu 14:41
shall s. in the name of his   De 25:6
brother
you will s. (B)(R)   1Sa 26:25
s. in everything (B)   1Ki 2:3
made him s. in every venture   2Ki 18:7
(B)
you cannot s. (R)   2Ch 13:12
entice him, and also s.   2Ch 18:21
(A)(B)(E)
you will s. (B)(R)   2Ch 20:20
you cannot s. (B)   2Ch 24:20
wisdom helps s. (A)(R)   Ec 10:10
you will be able to s. (R)   Isa 47:12
cause of orphan s. (B)   Jer 5:28

SUCCEEDED

but the children of Esau s.   De 2:12
them
they s. them, and dwelt in   De 2:21;
their   2:22
whatever it did it s. (B)   Da 8:12

SUCCEEDEST

and thou s. them, and   De 12:29;
dwellest in   19:1

SUCCESS

meet with good s. (A)(R)   Ge 24:12
gave him s. (B)   Ge 39:23
and then thou shalt have good Jos 1:8
s.
David had s. (B)(R)   1Sa 18:5;
                                18:14, 15
asked about s. of fighting (B) 2Sa 11:7

SUCCESSFUL

the trip s. (B)   Ge 24:40
made my journey s. (B)   Ge 24:56
his heart and was s. (B)   2Ch 31:21;
                                        32:30

SUCCOTH

Jacob journeyed to S. and   Ge 33:17
built
the name of the place is   Ge 33:17
called S.
journeyed from Rameses to   Ex 12:37
S.
they took their journey from   Ex 13:20
S.
from Rameses, and pitched in   Nu 33:5
S.
they departed from S. and   Nu 33:6
pitched
Beth-nimrah, and S. and   Jos 13:27
Zaphon
men of S. Give, I pray you,   J'g 8:5
loaves
And the princes of S. said, Are J'g 8:6
as the men of S. had answered J'g 8:8
him
a young man of the men of S.   J'g 8:14
he described the princes of S. J'g 8:14
And he came unto the men of   J'g 8:15
S.
with them he taught the men   J'g 8:16
of S.
ground between S. and   1Ki 7:46
Zarthan
ground between S. and   2Ch 4:17
Zeredathah
and mete out the valley of S. Ps 60:6;
                                        108:7

SUCCOTH-BENOTH

And the men of Babylon   2Ki 17:30
made S.

SUCCOUR

Syrians of Damascus came to   2Sa 8:5
s.
that thou s. us out of the city 2Sa 18:3
is able to s. them that are   Heb 2:18
tempted
able to bring aid to those   Heb 2:18
tempted (B)
able to help those in test   Heb 2:18
(N)(P)(R)

SUCCOURED

Abishai the son of Zeruiah   2Sa 21:17
s. him
the day of salvation have I s. 2Co 6:2

SUCCOURER

for she hath been a s. of   Ro 16:2
many
been a helper of many   Ro 16:2
(A)(E)(R)
been an assistant of many (B) Ro 16:2
has been a friend to many   Ro 16:2
(N)
been a great assistance to   Ro 16:2
many (P)

SUCH

Jabal was father of s. as dwell Ge 4:20
in tents
Jubal was father of s. as   Ge 4:21
handle the harp
make me savoury meat, s. as   Ge 27:4
I love
meat for thy father, s. as he Ge 27:9
loveth
savoury meat, s. as his father Ge 27:14
loved
Jacob take wife, s. as these   Ge 27:46
speckled and spotted, s. shall Ge 30:32
be my hire
s. as I never saw in Egypt   Ge 41:19
for badness
wot ye not that s. a man as I Ge 44:15
can divine
s. hail as hath not been in   Ex 9:18;
Egypt   9:24
hail s. as there was none like Ex 9:24
it in
were no s. locusts as they, nor Ex 10:14
shall be s.
great cry, s. as there was none Ex 11:6
like it
shalt provide able men s. as   Ex 18:21
fear God
s. as have not been done in   Ex 34:10
all earth
meat on which s. water   Le 11:34
cometh be unclean, all drink
in very s. vessel
two pigeons s. as able to get Le 14:22;
                                14:30, 31
soul turneth after s. I will cut Le 20:6
off
soul hath touched any s. be   Le 22:6
unclean
giveth of s. to the Lord, shall Le 27:9
be holy
instead of s. as open every   Nu 8:16
womb
whether there hath been any s. De 4:32
thing
that there were s. an heart in De 5:29
them to fear
shall do no more any s.   De 13:11;
wickedness   19:20
that s. abomination is   De 13:14;
wrought   17:4
s. time as thou beginnest to   De 16:9
put sickle
at least s. as before knew   J'g 3:2
nothing
no s. deed done or seen to   J'g 19:30
this day
hath not been s. a thing   1Sa 4:7
heretofore
he is s. a son of Belial, a   1Sa 25:17
man cannot
should look on s. a dead dog   2Sa 9:8
as I
with s. robes were virgins   2Sa 13:18
apparalled
wherefore hast thou thought   2Sa 14:13
s. a thing
that s. as be faint may drink 2Sa 16:2
why recompense me with s.   2Sa 19:36
reward
came no more s. abundance of   1Ki 10:10
spices
came no s. almug-trees   1Ki 10:12;
                                 2Ch 9:11
beware thou pass not s. a   2Ki 6:9
place
if Lord make windows, s. a   2Ki 7:19
thing be
am bringing s. evil on   2Ki 21:12
Jerusalem and Judah
surely there was not holden   2Ki 23:22
s. a passover
s. as went forth to battle   1Ch 12:33;
                                        12:36
Lord bestowed s. royal   1Ch 29:25
majesty
s. as none of the kings have   2Ch 1:12
nor was any s. spice as the   2Ch 9:9
queen gave
there was none s.   2Ch 9:11
(algum trees)
s. as set their hearts to seek 2Ch 11:16
the Lord
people rejoiced, and s.   2Ch 23:13
taught to sing
gave it to s. as did work of   2Ch 24:12
the house
not done it of a long time in 2Ch 30:5
s. sort

peace, and at *s.* a time　Ezr 4:10;
　　　　　　　　　　4:11, 17; 7:12
all *s.* as had separated　Ezr 6:21
themselves
all *s.* as know the laws of　Ezr 7:25
thy God
hath put *s.* a thing in the　Ezr 7:27
king's heart
and of *s.* as lay in wait by the　Ezr 8:31
way
and hast given us *s.*　Ezr 9:13
deliverance as this
put away wives, and *s.* are born Ezr 10:3
of them
I said, Should *s.* a man as I　Ne 6:11
flee
except *s.* to whom the king　Es 4:11
hold out
art come to the kingdom for *s.*　Es 4:14
a time
to lay hand on *s.* as sought　Es 9:2
their hurt
upon all *s.* as joined　Es 9:27
themselves to them
lettest *s.* words go out of thy Job 15:13
mouth
surely *s.* are dwellings of the Job 18:21
wicked
to *s.* as keep his covenant　Ps 25:10;
　　　　　　　　　　103:18
s. as breathe out cruelty risen Ps 27:12
up
to slay *s.* as be of upright　Ps 37:14
conversation
s. as be blessed of him shall　Ps 37:22
inherit earth
respecteth not proud nor *s.*　Ps 40:4
turn to lies
let *s.* as love thy salvation　Ps 40:16;
say　　　　　　　　　　70:4
hands against *s.* as be at　Ps 55:20
peace with him
God is good to *s.* as are of a　Ps 73:1
clean heart
s. as sit in darkness, and　Ps 107:10
shadow of
as for *s.* as turn aside to　Ps 125:5
crooked ways
s. knowledge is too wonderful Ps 139:6
for me
happy is that people in *s.* a　Ps 144:15
case
s. as are upright are his　Pr 11:20
delight
s. as keep the law contend　Pr 28:4
with them
in cause of *s.* appointed to　Pr 31:8
destruction
the tears of *s.* as were oppressed Ec 4:1
dimness not be *s.* as was in her Isa 9:1
vexation
s. as are escaped of house of　Isa 10:20
Jacob
s. is our expectation, whether Isa 20:6
we flee
eat this year *s.* as groweth of Isa 37:30
itself
is it *s.* a fast that I have　Isa 58:5
chosen
who hath heard *s.* thing? who Isa 66:8
hath seen *s.*
consider if there be *s.* a thing Jer 2:10
my soul be avenged on *s.* a　Jer 5:9;
nation　　　　　　　　5:29; 9:9
s. as are for death; *s.* for　Jer 15:2;
sword *s.* for famine, *s.*　　43:11
for captivity
I will deliver *s.* as are left in Jer 21:7
this city
in speaking *s.* words unto　Jer 38:4
them
none shall return, but *s.* as　Jer 44:14
escape
s. as had ability in them to　Da 1:4
stand
when he had spoken *s.* words Da 10:15
to me
s. as do wickedly shall he　Da 11:32
corrupt
be a time of trouble, *s.* as　Da 12:1
never was
they shall call *s.* as are skilful Am 5:16
to wailing
in anger and fury *s.* they　Mic 5:15
have not heard
s. as are clothed with strange Zep 1:8
apparel
glorified God who had given *s.* M't 9:8
power to men

who shall receive one *s.* little　M't 18:5;
child in my name,　　　　M'k 9:37
receiveth me
suffer children to come to　M't 19:14;
me, of, *s.* is kingdom of God M'k 10:14;
　　　　　　　　　　Lu 18:16
then be great tribulation, *s.*　M't 24:21;
as was not since beginning　M'k 13:19
of world
in *s.* an hour as think not　M't 24:44
Son cometh
go into the city to *s.* a man　M't 26:18
and say
sown among thorns, *s.* to　M'k 4:18
hear word
sown in good ground, are *s.*　M'k 4:20
as hear word
with many *s.* parables spake M'k 4:33
he to them
the Father seeketh *s.* to　Joh 4:23
worship him
Moses commanded *s.* should　Joh 8:5
be stoned
can man that is a sinner do *s.* Joh 9:16
miracles
Lord added daily *s.* as　Ac 2:47
should be saved
s. as I have give I thee, rise up Ac 3:6
and walk
to whom we gave no *s.*　Ac 15:24
commandment
having received *s.* a charge　Ac 16:24
thrust them
for I will be no judge of *s.*　Ac 18:15
matters
concluded, that they observe　Ac 21:25
no *s.* thing
away with *s.* a fellow from　Ac 22:22
earth
I doubted of *s.* manner of　Ac 25:20
questions
were almost and altogether *s.* Ac 26:29
as I am
they that are *s.* serve not　Ro 16:18
our Lord
s. fornication not so much　1Co 5:1
named
s. were some of you, but ye　1Co 6:11
are washed
brother or sister not under　1Co 7:15
bondage in *s.* cases
s. shall have trouble in flesh,　1Co 7:28
but I spare you
no temptation, but *s.* as is　1Co 10:13
common
seem to be contentious, we　1Co 11:16
have no *s.* custom
s. are they that are earthy,　1Co 15:48
s. are they that
submit yourselves to *s.* and　1Co 16:16
every one
therefore acknowledge ye　1Co 16:18
them that are *s.*
sufficient to *s.* a man is this　2Co 2:6
punishment
s. trust have we through　2Co 3:4
Christ
seeing then that we have *s.*　2Co 3:12
hope
let *s.* one think, *s.* as we are 2Co 10:11
in word by letters, *s.* will
we be when present
s. are false apostles,　2Co 11:13
deceitful workers
I fear, I shall not find you　2Co 12:20
s. as I would; that I be found
to you *s.* as ye would not
meekness against *s.* there is　Ga 5:23
no law
not spot or wrinkle, or any *s.* Eph 5:27
thing
receive him, and hold *s.* in　Ph'p 2:29
reputation
the Lord is the avenger of all 1Th 4:6
s.
now them that are *s.* we　2Th 3:12
command
corrupt men, from *s.* withdraw 1Ti 6:5
traitors, heady, from *s.* turn　2Ti 3:5
away
he that is *s.* is subverted and Tit 3:11
sinneth
are become *s.* as have need　Heb 5:12
of milk
s. an high priest became us,　Heb 7:26
who is holy
have *s.* an high priest set on　Heb 8:1
right hand
that endured *s.* contradiction Heb 12:3
of sinners

for with *s.* sacrifices God is　Heb 13:16
well pleased
to morrow we will go into *s.* Jas 4:13
a city
in your boastings, all *s.*　Jas 4:16
rejoicing is evil
when there came *s.* a voice to 2Pe 1:17
him
we therefore ought to receive *s.*　3Jo 8
to be
s. as are in the sea heard I　Re 5:13
saying
s. as not since men were on　Re 16:18
earth
on *s.* the second death hath no Re 20:6
power

SUCH *AN ONE*

can we find *s. an one* as this Ge 41:38
is
ho, *s. an one,* turn aside, sit　Ru 4:1
down
open thine eyes on *s. an one*　Job 14:3
thoughtest I was *s. a one* as Ps 50:21
thyself
hairy scalp of *s. a one* as　Ps 68:21
goeth on in
to deliver *s. an one* unto　1Co 5:5
Satan
if a drunkard, with *s. an one* 1Co 5:11
no not to eat
s. a one be swallowed up with 2Co 2:7
sorrow
let *s. an one* think this, that 2Co 10:11
such as we
s. an one caught up to the　2Co 12:2
third heaven
of *s. an one* will I glory, yet 2Co 12:5
not of myself
restore *s. an one* in spirit of　Ga 6:1
meekness
being *s. an one* as Paul the　Ph'm 9
aged

SUCH *AND SUCH*

appointed servants to *s. and*　1Sa 21:2
s. place
would have given *s. and s.*　2Sa 12:8
things
in *s. and s.* a place be my　2Ki 6:8
camp

SUCH *LIKE*

considereth, and doeth not *s.* Eze 18:14
like
drunkenness, revellings, and *s.* Ga 5:21
like

SUCH *THINGS*

they lent *s. things* as　Ex 12:36
required
and *s. things* have befallen　Le 10:19
me
that do *s. things* are an　De 25:16
abomination
nor have told us *s. things* as J'g 13:23
these
Eli said, Why do ye *s. things* 1Sa 2:23
eat *s. things* as grow of　2Ki 19:29
themselves
captain took *s. things* as　2Ki 25:15
were of gold
are no *s. things* done as thou Ne 6:8
sayest
with *s. things* as belonged to　Es 2:9
her
who knoweth not *s. things* as Job 12:3
these
Job said, I have heard many Job 16:2
s. things
and many *s. things* are with Job 23:14
him
now who hath heard *s.*　Jer 18:13
things
shall he escape that doth *s.* Eze 17:15
things
no king that asked *s. things* Da 2:10
many other *s. like things* ye M'k 7:8;
do　　　　　　　　　　7:13
be not troubled, *s. things*　M'k 13:7
must needs be
who is this of whom I hear *s.* Lu 9:9
things
eating *s. things* as they give Lu 10:7;
　　　　　　　　　　10:8
give alms of *s. things* as ye Lu 11:41
have

sinners, because they suffered   *Lu 13:2*
s. things
that the people murmured s.   *Joh 7:32*
things
brought no accusation of s.   *Ac 25:18*
things
laded us with s. things as   *Ac 28:10*
necessary
commit s. things are worthy   *Ro 1:32*
of death
judgment against them who   *Ro 2:2*
commit s. things
that judgest them which do s.   *Ro 2:3*
things
do s. things shall not inherit   *Ga 5:21*
kingdom
they that say s. things   *Heb 11:14*
declare
be content with s. things as ye   *Heb 13:5*
have
seeing that ye look for s.   *2Pe 3:14*
things

SUCHATHITES

the Shimeathites, and S.   *1Ch 2:55*

SUCK

should have given children s.   *Ge 21:7*
nurse (A) *Ge 21:7; 1Ki 3:21; Isa 66:11*
him to s. honey out of the   *De 32:13*
rock
s. of the abundance of the   *De 33:19*
seas
gave her son s. until she   *1Sa 1:23*
weaned
nursed (A)   *1Sa 1:23;*
     Isa 66:12; Lu 23:29
in the morning to give my   *1Ki 3:21*
child s.
why the breasts that I should   *Job 3:12*
s.
He shall s. the poison of   *Job 20:16*
asps
Her young ones also s. up   *Job 39:30*
blood
also s. the milk of the   *Isa 60:16*
Gentiles
and shalt s. the breast of   *Isa 60:16*
kings
That ye may s. and be   *Isa 66:11*
satisfied
then shall ye s. ye shall be   *Isa 66:12*
borne
they give s. to their young ones   *La 4:3*
shalt even drink it and s. it   *Eze 23:34*
out
and those that s. the breasts   *Joe 2:16*
and to them that give s. in   *M't 24:19*
those
who have nursing babes   *M't 24:19;*
(A)   *M'k 13:17; Lu 21:23*
to them that give s. in those *M'k 13:17;*
days   *Lu 21:23*
and the paps which never   *Lu 23:29*
gave s.

SUCKED

that s. the breasts of my   *Ca 8:1*
mother
nursed from breast of my   *Ca 8:1*
mother (A)
and the paps which thou hast *Lu 11:27*
s.

SUCKERS

his s. and shoats shall (A)   *Ho 14:6*

SUCKING

nursing father beareth the s.   *Nu 11:12*
child
Samuel took a s. lamb, and   *1Sa 7:9*
offered
the s. child shall play on the   *Isa 11:8*
hole
Can a woman forget her s.   *Isa 49:15*
child
The tongue of the s. child   *La 4:4*
cleaveth

SUCKLING

the s. also with the man of   *De 33:25*
gray
infant and s. ox and sheep,   *1Sa 15:3*
camel
you man and woman, child   *Jer 44:7*
and s.

SUCKLINGS

men and women, children   *1Sa 22:19*
and s.
Out of the mouth of babes and *Ps 8:2*
s.
and the s. swoon in the streets *La 2:11*
Out of the mouth of babes   *M't 21:16*
and s.

SUDDEN

thee and s. fear troubleth   *Job 22:10*
thee
Be not afraid of s. fear,   *Pr 3:25*
neither of
then s. destruction cometh   *1Th 5:3*
upon

SUDDENLY

if any man die very s. by him   *Nu 6:9*
And the Lord spake s. unto   *Nu 12:4*
Moses
if he thrust him s. without   *Nu 35:22*
enmity
against you, and destroy thee s. *De 7:4*
therefore came unto them s.   *Jos 10:9*
them by the waters of Merom *Jos 11:7*
s.
lest he overtake us s. and   *2Sa 15:14*
bring
people: for the thing was   *2Ch 29:36*
done s.
root: but s. I cursed his   *Job 5:3*
habitation
If the scourge slay s. he will   *Job 9:23*
laugh
them return and be ashamed s. *Ps 6:10*
s. do they shoot at him, and   *Ps 64:4*
fear
arrow; s. shall they be   *Ps 64:7*
wounded
shall his calamity come s.   *Pr 6:15*
s. shall he be broken without   *Pr 6:15*
For their calamity shall rise s. *Pr 22:22*
shall s. be destroyed, and that *Pr 29:1*
time, when it falleth s.   *Ec 9:12*
them
yea, it shall be at an instant s. *Isa 29:5*
breaking cometh s. at an   *Isa 30:13*
instant
desolation shall come upon   *Isa 47:11*
thee s.
them; I did them s. and they *Isa 48:3*
came
s. are my tents spoiled, and   *Jer 4:20*
my
the spoiler shall s. come upon *Jer 6:26*
us
I have caused him to fall   *Jer 15:8*
upon it s.
shalt bring a troop s. upon   *Jer 18:22*
them
s. make him run away from   *Jer 49:19*
her
make them s. run away from *Jer 50:44*
her
Babylon is s. fallen and   *Jer 51:8*
destroyed
Shall they not rise up s. that *Hab 2:7*
shall
seek, shall s. come to his   *Mal 3:1*
temple
s. when they had looked   *M'k 9:8*
round
coming s. he find you   *M'k 13:36*
sleeping
And s. there was with the   *Lu 2:13*
angel a
taketh him, and he s. crieth   *Lu 9:39*
s. there came a sound from   *Ac 2:2*
heaven
s. there shined round about   *Ac 9:3*
him a
s. there was a great   *Ac 16:26*
earthquake
s. there shone from heaven a *Ac 22:6*
great
swollen, or fallen down dead *Ac 28:6*
s.
Lay hands s. on no man,   *1Ti 5:22*
neither

SUE

If any man will s. thee at law *M't 5:40*

SUED

s. for peace (N)   *Ac 12:20*

SUFFER

will not s. the destroyer to   *Ex 12:23*
come
not allow (A)   *Ex 12:23;*
22:18;   Le 2:13;   Nu 21:23;   Jos 10:19;
J'g 1:34;   15:1;   Job 9:18;   1Ki 15:17;
Ps 55:22; 89:33; 121:3; Pr 10:3; Ec 5:6;
     Eze 44:20; M't 23:13; M'k 7:12;
             Ac 13:35; Re 11:9
not allow (B)   *Ex 12:23;*
Ps 16:10;   55:22;   121:3;   Ec 5:6;
M'k 11:16; Ac 13:35; 1Ti 2:12; Re 11:9
not allow (R)   *Ex 12:23;*
Nu 21:23; J'g 1:34; 15:1; M'k 11:16
Thou shalt not s. a witch to *Ex 22:18*
live
not allow (B)   *Ex 22:18;*
Job 21:3;   M't 3:15;   19:14;   23:13;
M'k 7:12; 10:14; Lu 9:59; 18:16; 22:51
not permit (R)   *Ex 22:18;*
1Ki 15:17;   Ps 55:22;   M't 23:13;
            M'k 7:12; 1Ti 2:12
shalt thou s. the salt to be   *Le 2:13*
lacking
not let (R)   *Le 2:13;*
Jos 10:19; Job 9:18; Ps 121:3; Pr 10:3;
             Ec 5:6, 13
neighbour not s. sin upon   *Le 19:17*
him
Or s. them to bear the   *Le 22:16*
iniquity of
Sihon would not s. Israel to *Nu 21:23*
pass
s. them not to enter into   *Jos 10:19*
their cities
do not let (B)   *Jos 10:19*
would not s. them to come   *J'g 1:34*
down to
father would not s. him to go *J'g 15:1*
refused to let (B)   *J'g 15:1*
S. me that I may feel the   *J'g 16:26*
pillars
allow (A)   *J'g 16:26;*
Job 21:3;   M't 19:14;   M'k 10:14;
     Lu 18:16; Ac 21:39; 1Ti 2:12
let (B)   *J'g 16:26;*
Job 9:18; Pr 10:3; Ec 5:12; Eze 44:20;
             Ac 21:39
let (R)   *J'g 16:26;*
Ps 16:10;   Eze 44:20;   M't 3:15;   8:21;
19:14; M'k 10:14; Lu 8:32; 9:59; 18:16;
  Ac 2:27;   23:35;   1Co 10:13;   Re 11:9
s. no self-accusation (B)   *1Sa 25:31*
not s. the revengers of blood *2Sa 14:11*
that he might not s. any to   *1Ki 15:17*
go out
not for the king's profit to s. *Es 3:8*
them
to tolerate (A)   *Es 3:8; Ps 101:5*
tolerate (B)   *Es 3:8;*
       Ps 101:5; 2Co 11:19
tolerate (R)   *Es 3:8*
will not s. me to take my   *Job 9:18*
breath
bear with (B)   *Job 21:3;*
36:2;   M't 17:17;   M'k 9:19;   Lu 9:41;
     2Co 11:19, 20; Heb 13:22
tread their winepresses, and *Job 24:11*
s. thirst
S. me a little, and I will shew *Job 36:2*
thee
bear with (B)   *Job 36:2;*
       Ps 88:15; Pr 19:19
consider my trouble which I s. *Ps 9:13*
wilt thou s. thine Holy One *Ps 16:10*
to see
young lions do lack, and s.   *Ps 34:10*
hunger
he shall never s. the righteous *Ps 55:22*
I s. thy terrors I am   *Ps 88:15*
distracted
from him, nor s. my   *Ps 89:33*
faithfulness
and a proud heart will not I *Ps 101:5*
s.
not endure (R)   *Ps 101:5*
will not s. thy foot to be   *Ps 121:3*
moved
will not s. the righteous to   *Pr 10:3*
famish
an idle soul shall s. hunger   *Pr 19:15*
great wrath shall s.   *Pr 19:19*
punishment
S. not thy mouth to cause thy *Ec 5:6*
flesh
the rich will not s. him to   *Ec 5:12*
sleep
heads, nor s. their locks to   *Eze 44:20*
grow long

said unto him, S. it to be so M't 3:15
now
permit it (A) M't 3:15;
M'k 11:16; Lu 9:59
let (N) M't 3:15;
8:21; 19:14; M'k 10:14; Lu 8:32; 9:59,
18:16; 22:51; Ac 2:27; 13:35
let (P) M't 3:15;
8:21; 19:14; M'k 10:14; Lu 9:59; 18:16;
Ac 21:39
s. me first to go and bury my M't 8:21
let (A) M't 8:21; Ac 2:27; 1Co 10:13
M't 8:21;
permit (B)
Ac 2:27; 1Co 10:13
s. us to go away into the herd M't 8:31
s. many things of the elders M't 16:21
also the Son of man s. of M't 17:12
them
with you? how long shall I s. M't 17:17
you
put up with (B) M't 17:17; M'k 9:19
endure (N) M't 17:17;
M'k 9:19; Lu 9:41
put up with (P) M't 17:17;
M'k 9:19; Lu 9:41
S. little children, and forbid M't 19:14
them
neither s. ye them that are M't 23:13
entering
allow (P) M't 23:13; Lu 8:32
ye s. him no more to do M'k 7:12
ought for
no longer permitted (N) M'k 7:12
Son of man must s. many M'k 8:31
things
man, that he must s. many M'k 9:12
things
with you? how long shall I s. M'k 9:19
you
bear with (A) M'k 9:19;
Lu 9:41; 2Co 11:19; Heb 13:22
S. the little children to come M'k 10:14
unto
would not s. that any man M'k 11:16
should
not allow (N) M'k 11:16; 1Co 10:13
would s. them to enter into Lu 8:32
them
give permission (B) Lu 8:32
Son of man must s. many Lu 9:22
things
shall I be with you, and s. you Lu 9:41
endure (B) Lu 9:41
Lord, s. me first to go and Lu 9:59
bury my
But first must he s. many Lu 17:25
things
S. little children to come Lu 18:16
unto me
this passover with you before Lu 22:15
I s.
answered and said, S. ye thus Lu 22:51
far
and thus it behoved Christ to Lu 24:46
s.
wilt thou s. thine Holy One to Ac 2:27
see
prophets, that Christ should s. Ac 3:18
counted worthy to s. shame Ac 5:41
for his
seeing one of them s. wrong, Ac 7:24
he
him how great things he must Ac 9:16
s.
shalt not s. thine Holy One Ac 13:35
to see
s. me to speak unto the Ac 21:39
people
That Christ should s. and Ac 26:23
that he
if so be that we s. with him, Ro 8:17
that
shall be burned, he shall s. 1Co 3:15
loss
bless; being persecuted, we s. 1Co 4:12
it
rather s. yourselves to be 1Co 6:7
defrauded
but s. all things, lest we 1Co 9:12
should
will not s. you to be 1Co 10:13
tempted above
allow (P) 1Co 10:13; 1Ti 2:12; Re 11:9
whether one member s. all 1Co 12:26
all the members s. with it; 1Co 12:26
or one
same sufferings which we also 2Co 1:6
s.

For ye s. fools gladly, seeing 2Co 11:19
ye
put up with it (N) 2Co 11:19
bear with (N) 2Co 11:19; Heb 13:22
For ye s. if a man bring 2Co 11:20
you into
endure it (A) 2Co 11:20
stand for it (B) 2Co 11:20
put up with it (N) 2Co 11:20
why do I yet s. persecution? Ga 5:11
then
should s. persecution for the Ga 6:12
cross
on him, but also to s. for his Ph'p 1:29
sake
both to abound and to s. need Ph'p 4:12
before that we should s. 1Th 3:4
tribulation
kingdom of God, for which ye 2Th 1:5
also s.
I s. not a woman to teach, 1Ti 2:12
nor to
permit (N) 1Ti 2:12
we both labour and s. 1Ti 4:10
reproach
which cause I also s. these 2Ti 1:12
things
Wherein I s. trouble, as an evil 2Ti 2:9
doer
If we s. we shall also reign 2Ti 2:12
with
Christ Jesus shall s. 2Ti 3:12
persecution
did sympathize and s. long Heb 10:34
(A)(B)(P)
Choosing rather to s. Heb 11:25
affliction
and them which s. adversity, Heb 13:3
as
those who s. (P) Heb 13:3
s. the word of exhortation Heb 13:22
when we do well, and s. for it, 1Pe 2:20
ye
if ye s. for righteousness' 1Pe 3:14
sake
that ye s. for well doing, than 1Pe 3:17
for
if censured and s. abuse (A) 1Pe 4:14
let none of you s. as 1Pe 4:15
a murderer, or
if any man s. as a Christian, 1Pe 4:16
let him
let them that s. according to 1Pe 4:19
of those things which thou Re 2:10
shalt s.
not s. their dead bodies to be Re 11:9
put in
refuse (N) Re 11:9

SUFFERED

s. I thee not to touch her Ge 20:6
give occasion to touch her (A) Ge 20:6
restrained (B) Ge 20:6; 1Sa 24:7
Ge 20:6;
let (R)
De 8:3; Job 31:30; M't 3:15; 24:43;
Ac 19:30
but God s. him not to hurt me Ge 31:7
allow (A) Ge 31:7;
2Sa 21:10; M'k 1:34
permitted (B) Ge 31:7;
De 18:14; J'g 3:28; M't 19:8; M'k 5:37;
10:4; Lu 8:32; 12:39
permit (R) Ge 31:7; 31:28
not s. me to kiss my sons Ge 31:28
and my
permit (A) Ge 31:28;
M'k 5:19; Lu 4:41; Ac 16:7; 19:30
and s. thee to hunger, and fed De 8:3
thee
allowed (A) De 8:3;
1Ch 16:21; Ps 105:14; M't 24:43;
M'k 10:4
thy God hath not s. thee so De 18:14
to do
allowed (R) De 18:14;
J'g 3:28; 1Ch 16:21; Ps 105:14
Moab and s. not a man to J'g 3:28
pass over
permitted (A) J'g 3:28;
M't 16:8; M'k 8:51; Lu 12:39; Ac 14:16;
28:16
and s. them not to rise 1Sa 24:7
against Saul
let Job (A) 1Sa 24:7; 31:30
permit (R) 1Sa 24:7
and s. neither the birds of the 2Sa 21:10
air
let (B) 2Sa 21:10; Ac 14:16

allow (R) 2Sa 21:10
He s. no man to do them 1Ch 16:21
wrong
granted (B) 1Ch 16:21
Neither have I s. my mouth Job 31:30
to sin
He s. no man to do them Ps 105:14
wrong
allowed (B) Ps 105:14;
M't 24:43; Lu 8:51; Ac 28:16
that for thy sake I have s. Jer 15:15
rebuke
all righteousness. Then he s. M't 3:15
him M't 3:15; Lu 4:41
let (N) M't 3:15;
24:43; M'k 1:34; Lu 8:32; 12:39;
Ac 19:30
let (P) M't 3:15; Lu 8:32; 12:39
s. you to put away your wives M't 19:8
permission (N) M't 19:8
allowed (P) M't 19:8;
24:43; M'k 5:37; Ac 14:16
allowed (R) M't 19:8;
M'k 5:37; 10:4; Ac 14:16; 28:16
have s. his house to be M't 24:43
broken up
for I have s. many things M't 27:19
this day
and s. not the devils to speak M'k 1:34
permit (B) M'k 1:34; Ac 16:7; 19:30
allow (P) M'k 1:34
Lu 4:41; 8:51; Ac 16:7; 19:30
permit (R) M'k 1:34
Howbeit Jesus s. him not, M'k 5:19
but saith
allow (N) M'k 5:19; Ac 16:7
refused (R) M'k 5:19
s. many things of many M'k 5:26
physicians
And he s. no man to follow M'k 5:37
him M'k 5:37;
allowed (N)
Lu 8:51; Ac 14:16; 28:16
s. to write a bill of M'k 10:4
divorcement
permitted (N) M'k 10:4
rebuking s. them not to speak Lu 4:41
forbade (N) Lu 4:41
rebuked (R) Lu 4:41
enter into them. And he s. Lu 8:32
them
gave leave (R) Lu 8:32
he s. no man to go in, save Lu 8:51
Peter
permitted (R) Lu 8:51
s. his house to be broken Lu 12:39
through
because they s. such things Lu 13:2
not Christ to have s. these Lu 24:26
things
s. he their manners in the Ac 13:18
endured (A) Ac 13:18
bore (N)(P)(R) Ac 13:18
s. all nations to walk in their Ac 14:16
own
but the Spirit s. them not Ac 16:7
allow (N) Ac 16:7
that Christ must needs have s. Ac 17:3
people, the disciples s. him Ac 19:30
not
Paul was s. to dwell by Ac 28:16
himself
permission (P) Ac 28:16
nor for his cause that s. 2Co 7:12
wrong, but
was I stoned, thrice I s. 2Co 11:25
shipwreck
Have ye s. so many things in Ga 3:4
vain
I have s. the loss of all things Ph'p 3:8
even after that we had s. 1Th 2:2
before
s. like things of your 1Th 2:14
countrymen
he himself hath s. being Heb 2:18
tempted
he obedience by the Heb 5:8
things he s.
were not s. to continue by Heb 7:23
reason
For then must he often have Heb 9:26
s.
considered abuse s. (R) Heb 11:26
his own blood, s. without Heb 13:12
the gate
because Christ also s. for us 1Pe 2:21
when he s. he threatened not 1Pe 2:23
Christ also hath once s. for 1Pe 3:18
sins

as Christ hath *s.* for us in the　*1Pe 4:1*
flesh
for he that hath *s.* in the flesh　*1Pe 4:1*
hath
after that ye have *s.* a while,　*1Pe 5:10*
make

SUFFEREST

thou *s.* that woman Jezebel　*Re 2:20*
tolerate (A)(B)(N)(P)(R)　*Re 2:20*

SUFFERETH

and *s.* not our feet to be　*Ps 66:9*
moved
allowed (A)　*Ps 66:9*
allow (B)　*Ps 66:9; 107:38; Ac 28:4*
let our feet slip (R)　*Ps 66:9*
and *s.* not their cattle to　*Ps 107:38*
decrease
allows (A)　*Ps 107:38*
the kingdom of heaven *s.*　*M't 11:12*
violence
endured (A)　*M't 11:12*
sea, yet vengeance *s.* not to　*Ac 28:4*
live
permitted (A)　*Ac 28:4*
allowed (R)　*Ac 28:4*
Charity *s.* long, and is kind　*1Co 13:4*
endures (A)(B)　*1Co 13:4*

SUFFERING

s. in pregnancy (A)　*Ge 3:16*
s. was very great (B)(R)　*Job 2:13*
tested by *s.* (B)　*Job 36:21*
in time of their *s.* (A)(R)　*Ne 9:27*
behold my *s.* (R)　*La 1:18*
rest from *s.* (B)　*Isa 14:3; La 1:18*
s. tortures of Hades (B)　*Lu 16:23*
after his *s.* (B)(P)　*Ac 1:3*
s. from evil spirits (P)　*Ac 5:16*
the wind not *s.* us, we sailed　*Ac 27:7*
under
wind did not permit (A)　*Ac 27:7*
wind did not allow (R)　*Ac 27:7*
our *s.* on your behalf　*Eph 3:13*
(A)(N)(R)
with grave *s.* (N)　*1Th 1:6*
than the angels for the *s.* of　*Heb 2:9*
death
for an example of *s.* affliction　*Jas 5:10*
example of *s.* (E)(P)(R)　*Jas 5:10*
God endure grief, *s.*　*1Pe 2:19*
wrongfully
pain of unjust *s.* (B)　*1Pe 2:19*
s. spiritual agonies (P)　*2Pe 2:8*
s. wrong as the hire of　*2Pe 2:13*
wrong-doing (E)(N)(R)
s. the vengeance of eternal fire　*Jude 7*

SUFFERINGS

I know their *s.* (R)　*Ex 3:7; Job 9:28*
would soothe my *s.* (A)　*Job 16:5*
man of *s.* (B)　*Isa 53:3*
beginning of *s.* (R)　*M't 24:8; M'k 13:8*
such great *s.* as (B)　*M't 24:21*
rejoice in *s.* (A)(B)(N)(P)(R)　*Ro 5:3*
I reckon that the *s.* of this　*Ro 8:18*
present
as the *s.* of Christ abound in　*2Co 1:5*
us
enduring of the same *s.* which　*2Co 1:6*
we
that as ye are partakers of the　*2Co 1:7*
s.
and the fellowship of his *s.*　*Ph'p 3:10*
share his *s.*　*Ph'p 3:10*
(A)(B)(N)(P)(R)
Who now rejoice in my *s.* for　*Col 1:24*
you
their salvation perfect　*Heb 2:10*
through *s.*
shared *s.* of prisoners (N)　*Heb 10:34*
testified beforehand the *s.* of　*1Pe 1:11*
Christ
as ye are partakers of　*1Pe 4:13*
Christ's *s.*
and a witness of the *s.* of　*1Pe 5:1*
Christ
share in *s.* (N)　*Re 1:9*
their *s.* and sores (B)　*Re 16:11*

SUFFERS

wicked man *s.* torment (A)　*Job 15:20*
s. terribly (A)(R)　*M't 17:15*
outer man *s.* decay　*2Co 4:16*
(B)(N)(P)

SUFFICE

herds be slain for them, to *s.*　*Nu 11:22*
them
gathered for them to *s.* them　*Nu 11:22*
Lord said unto me, Let it *s.*　*De 3:26*
thee
dust of Samaria *s.* for　*1Ki 20:10*
handfuls
it *s.* you of all your　*Eze 44:6*
abominations
Let it *s.* you, O princes of　*Eze 45:9*
Israel
the time past of our life may *s.*　*1Pe 4:3*
us

SUFFICED

and yet so they *s.* them not　*J'g 21:14*
corn, and she did eat, and　*Ru 2:14*
was *s.*
she had reserved after she was　*Ru 2:18*
s.

SUFFICETH

shew us the Father, and it *s.*　*Joh 14:8*
us

SUFFICIENCY

In the fulness of his *s.* he　*Job 20:22*
shall be
of ourselves; but our *s.* is of　*2Co 3:5*
God
always having all *s.* in all　*2Co 9:8*
things

SUFFICIENT

stuff they had was *s.* for all　*Ex 36:7*
surely lend him *s.* for his need　*De 15:8*
meet the need amply (B)　*De 15:8*
let his hands be *s.* for him　*De 33:7*
eat so much as is *s.* for thee,　*Pr 25:16*
lest
And Lebanon is not *s.* to　*Isa 40:16*
burn, nor
the beasts thereof *s.* for a　*Isa 40:16*
burnt
s. unto the day is the evil　*M't 6:34*
thereof
cost, whether he have *s.* to　*Lu 14:28*
finish it
pennyworth of bread is not *s.*　*Joh 6:7*
for
s. to such is this punishment　*2Co 2:6*
And who is *s.* for these　*2Co 2:16*
things
Not that we are *s.* of　*2Co 3:5*
ourselves to
unto me, My grace is *s.* for　*2Co 12:9*
thee

SUFFICIENTLY

had not sanctified themselves　*2Ch 30:3*
s.
eat *s.* and for durable clothing　*Isa 23:18*

SUGGESTIONS

s. of wicked are deceptive (B)　*Pr 12:5*
observing the *s.* (B)　*1Co 11:2*
let it be as God's *s.* (B)　*1Pe 4:11*

SUIT

a *s.* of apparel, and thy　*J'g 17:10*
victuals
the little *s.* (B)　*1Sa 2:19*
that every man which has any　*2Sa 15:4*
s.
many shall make *s.* unto　*Job 11:19*
thee

SUITABLE

s. for the necks of them (S)　*J'g 5:30*
seven maidens which were *s.*　*Es 2:9*
(S)
if it is *s.* I will go (S)　*1Co 16:4*

SUITS

changes of new *s.* (B)　*Ge 45:22*
take money and *s.* (B)　*2Ki 5:26*
The changeable *s.* of apparel　*Isa 3:22*

SUKKIIMS

the Lubims, the *S.* and the　*2Ch 12:3*

SULLEN

Ahab came into his house *s.*　*1Ki 21:4*
(S)

SULLIED

s. my holy name (B)　*Eze 48:8*

SULPHUR

rained *s.* (B)　*Ge 19:24; Ps 11:6*
s. scattered (A)(B)　*Job 18:15*
sapphire blue and *s.* (A)(R)　*Re 9:17*
s. yellow (B)(N)　*Re 9:17*
by smoke and *s.*　*Re 9:18*
(A)(B)(N)(P)(R)
burns with *s.* (B)(P)　*Re 19:20*
burns with *s.* flames (N)　*Re 19:20;*
　　　　　　　　　　　　　　21:8
burns with fire and *s.* (B)(P)　*Re 21:8*

SULTRY

a *s.* east wind (A)(B)(E)(R)　*Jon 4:8*

SUM

be laid on him a *s.* of money　*Ex 21:30*
takest the *s.* of the children　*Ex 30:12*
This is the *s.* of the　*Ex 38:21*
tabernacle
Take ye the *s.* of the　*Nu 1:2*
congregation
Levi, neither take the *s.* of　*Nu 1:49*
them
Take the *s.* of the sons of　*Nu 4:2*
Kohath
Take the *s.* of the sons of　*Nu 4:22*
Gershon
Take the *s.* of all the　*Nu 26:2*
congregation
Take the *s.* of the people　*Nu 26:4*
Take the *s.* of the prey that　*Nu 31:26*
have taken the *s.* of the men　*Nu 31:49*
of war
the *s.* of the number of the　*2Sa 24:9*
people
that he may *s.* the silver　*2Ki 22:4*
which is
the *s.* of the number of the　*1Ch 21:5*
people
the *s.* of the money that Haman　*Es 4:7*
God! how great is the *s.* of　*Ps 139:17*
them
to *s.* up the whole matter　*Ec 12:13*
(B)
Thou sealest up the *s.* full of　*Eze 28:12*
and told the *s.* of the matters　*Da 7:1*
Abraham bought for a *s.* of　*Ac 7:16*
money
a great *s.* obtained I this　*Ac 22:28*
freedom
we have spoken this is the *s.*　*Heb 8:1*

SUMMED

s. up in a (A)(E)(N)(P)(R)　*Ro 13:9*

SUMMER

cold and heat, and *s.* and　*Ge 8:22*
winter
and he was sitting in a *s.*　*J'g 3:20*
parlour
covereth his feet in his *s.*　*J'g 3:24*
chamber
and an hundred of *s.* fruits,　*2Sa 16:1*
and a
s. fruit for the young men to　*2Sa 16:2*
eat
is turned into the drought of *s.*　*Ps 32:4*
thou hast made *s.* and winter　*Ps 74:17*
Provideth her meat in the *s.*　*Pr 6:8*
that gathereth in *s.* is a wise　*Pr 10:5*
son
As snow in *s.* and as rain in　*Pr 26:1*
they prepare their meat in the　*Pr 30:25*
s.
for the shouting for thy *s.*　*Isa 16:9*
fruits
and the fowls shall *s.* upon　*Isa 18:6*
them
as the hasty fruit before the *s.*　*Isa 28:4*
The harvest is past, the *s.* is　*Jer 8:20*
ended
gather ye wine, and *s.* fruits　*Jer 40:10*
gathered wine and *s.* fruits　*Jer 40:12*
very
spoiler is fallen upon thy *s.*　*Jer 48:32*
fruits

the chaff of the *s.* threshingfloors — Da 2:35

winter house with the *s.* house — Am 3:15

me: and behold a basket of *s.* fruit — Am 8:1

And I said, A basket of *s.* fruit — Am 8:2

they have gathered the *s.* fruits — Mic 7:1

sea: in *s.* and in winter shall it be — Zec 14:8

leaves, ye know that *s.* is nigh — M't 24:32; M'k 13:28

selves that *s.* is now nigh at hand — Lu 21:30

SUMMIT

s. of the temple (B) — M't 4:9

SUMMON

who will *s.* me (A)(E)(R) — Job 9:19

the king commanded to *s.* (E) — Da 2:2

SUMPTUOUS

things which were dainty and *s.* (S) — Re 18:14

SUMPTUOUSLY

fine linen, and fared *s.* every day — Lu 16:19

made merry in splendor every day (A) — Lu 16:19

enjoyed luxurious living every day (B) — Lu 16:19

feasted in magnificence every day (N) — Lu 16:19

lead a life of daily luxury (P) — Lu 16:19

SUN

And when the *s.* was going down — Ge 15:12

The *s.* was risen upon the earth — Ge 19:23

all night, because the *s.* was set — Ge 28:11

as he passed over Penuel the *s.* rose — Ge 32:31

the *s.* and the moon and the eleven — Ge 37:9

when the *s.* waxed hot, it melted — Ex 16:21

until the going down of the *s.* — Ex 17:12

If the *s.* be risen upon him, there — Ex 22:3

unto him by that the *s.* goeth down — Ex 22:26

And when the *s.* is down, he shall be — Le 22:7

toward the rising of the *s.* shall they — Nu 2:3

up before the Lord against the *s.* — Nu 25:4

and when thou seest the *s.* — De 4:19

the way where the *s.* goeth down — De 11:30

at the going down of the *s.* at — De 16:6

either the *s.* or moon, or any of the — De 17:3

when the *s.* is down, he shall come — De 23:11

again when the *s.* goeth down — De 24:13

neither shall the *s.* go down upon it — De 24:15

fruits brought forth by the *s.* — De 33:14

sea toward the going down of the *s.* — Jos 1:4

and as soon as the *s.* was down — Jos 8:29

S. stand thou still upon Gibeon — Jos 10:12

And the *s.* stood still, and the moon — Jos 10:13

s. stood still in the midst of heaven — Jos 10:13

the time of the going down of the *s.* — Jos 10:27

Jordan toward the rising of the *s.* — Jos 12:1

as the *s.* when he goeth forth in his — J'g 5:31

from battle before the *s.* was up — J'g 8:13

as soon as the *s.* is up, thou shalt — J'g 9:33

day before the *s.* went down — J'g 14:18

and the *s.* went down upon them — J'g 19:14

by that time the *s.* be hot, ye shall — 1Sa 11:9

the *s.* went down when they were — 2Sa 2:24

or ought else, till the *s.* be down — 2Sa 3:35

with thy wives in the sight of this *s.* — 2Sa 12:11

before all Israel, and before the *s.* — 2Sa 12:12

of the morning, when the *s.* riseth — 2Sa 23:4

host about the going down of the *s.* — 1Ki 22:36

and the *s.* shone upon the water — 2Ki 3:22

burned incense unto Baal, to the *s.* — 2Ki 23:5

s., moon and constellations (A)(R) — 2Ki 23:5

s., moon and signs of the Zodiac (B) — 2Ki 23:5

kings of Judah had given to the *s.* — 2Ki 23:11

and burned the chariots of the *s.* — 2Ki 23:11

time of the *s.* going down he died — 2Ch 18:34

be opened until the *s.* be hot — Ne 7:3

He is green before the *s.* and his — Job 8:16

Which commandeth the *s.* and it — Job 9:7

I went mourning without the *s.* — Job 30:28

If I beheld the *s.* when it shined — Job 31:26

hath he set a tabernacle for the *s.* — Ps 19:4

the earth from the rising of the *s.* — Ps 50:1

that they may not see the *s.* — Ps 58:8

as long as the *s.* and moon endure — Ps 72:5

be continued as long as the *s.* — Ps 72:17

hast prepared the light and the *s.* — Ps 74:16

For the Lord God is a *s.* and shield — Ps 84:11

and his throne as the *s.* before me — Ps 89:36

the *s.* knoweth his going down — Ps 104:19

The *s.* ariseth, they gather — Ps 104:22

From the rising of the *s.* unto — Ps 113:3

The *s.* shall not smite thee by day — Ps 121:6

The *s.* to rule by day: for his mercy — Ps 136:8

Praise ye him, *s.* and moon: praise — Ps 148:3

labour he taketh under the *s.* — Ec 1:3

The *s.* also ariseth, and the *s.* goeth — Ec 1:5

there is no new thing under the *s.* — Ec 1:9

works that are done under the *s.* — Ec 1:14

and there was no profit under the *s.* — Ec 2:11

work that is wrought under the *s.* — Ec 2:17

labour I had taken under the *s.* — Ec 2:18

shewed myself wise under the *s.* — Ec 2:19

labour which I took under the *s.* — Ec 2:20

he hath laboured under the *s.* — Ec 2:22

under the *s.* the place of judgment — Ec 3:16

the oppressions done under the *s.* — Ec 4:1

evil work that is done under the *s.* — Ec 4:3

and I saw vanity under the *s.* — Ec 4:7

the living which walk under the *s.* — Ec 4:15

sore evil I have seen under the *s.* — Ec 5:13

labour that he taketh under the *s.* — Ec 5:18

evil which I have seen under the *s.* — Ec 6:1

Moreover he hath not seen the *s.* — Ec 6:5

shall be after him under the *s.* — Ec 6:12

is profit to them that see the *s.* — Ec 7:11

work that is done under the *s.* — Ec 8:9

hath no better thing under the *s.* — Ec 8:15

which God giveth him under the *s.* — Ec 8:15

the work that is done under the *s.* — Ec 8:17

things that are done under the *s.* — Ec 9:3

any thing that is done under the *s.* — Ec 9:6

he hath given thee under the *s.* — Ec 9:9

labour thou takest under the *s.* — Ec 9:9

I returned, and saw under the *s.* — Ec 9:11

wisdom have I seen under the *s.* — Ec 9:13

evil which I have seen under the *s.* — Ec 10:5

it is for the eyes to behold the *s.* — Ec 11:7

While the *s.* or the light, or — Ec 12:2

because the *s.* hath looked upon me — Ca 1:6

fair as the moon, clear as the *s.* — Ca 6:10

s. shall be darkened in his going — Isa 13:10

confounded, and the *s.* ashamed — Isa 24:23

Asherim and *s.*-images (A)(E) — Isa 27:9

shame images, *s.*-pillars (B) — Isa 27:9

moon shall be as the light of the *s.* — Isa 30:26

light of the *s.* shall be sevenfold — Isa 30:26

is gone down in the *s.* dial of Ahaz — Isa 38:8

So the *s.* returned ten degrees — Isa 38:8

from the rising of the *s.* shall — Isa 41:25

may know from the rising of the *s.* — Isa 45:6

shall the heat nor *s.* smite them — Isa 49:10

his glory from the rising of the *s.* — Isa 59:19

The *s.* shall be no more thy light by — Isa 60:19

Thy *s.* shall no more go down — Isa 60:20

they shall spread them before the *s.* — Jer 8:2

her *s.* is gone down while it was yet — Jer 15:9

giveth the *s.* for a light by day — Jer 31:35

your *s.*-pillars be broken (A) — Eze 6:4

s.-images be broken (E) — Eze 6:4

s.-images hewn down (A)(B)(E) — Eze 6:6

they worshipped the *s.* toward the — Eze 8:16

I will cover the *s.* with a cloud, and — Eze 32:7

laboured till going down of the *s.* — Da 6:14

the *s.* and the moon shall be dark — Joe 2:10

s. shall be turned into darkness — Joe 2:31

s. and the moon shall be darkened — Joe 3:15

cause the *s.* to go down at noon — Am 8:9

came to pass, when the *s.* did arise — Jon 4:8

the *s.* beat upon the head of Jonah — Jon 4:8

and the *s.* shall go down over — Mic 3:6

when the *s.* ariseth they flee away — Na 3:17

The *s.* and moon stood still in their — Hab 3:11

from the rising of the *s.* even unto — Mal 1:11

the *S.* of righteousness arise with — Mal 4:2

for he maketh his *s.* to rise on the — M't 5:45

And when the *s.* was up, they were — M't 13:6

the righteous shine forth as the *s.* — M't 13:43

his face did shine as the *s.* and his — M't 17:2

days shall the *s.* be darkened — *M't 24:29*
when the *s.* did set, they brought — *M'k 1:32*
But when the *s.* was up, it was — *M'k 4:6*
the *s.* shall be darkened, and the — *M'k 13:24*
the sepulchre at the rising of the *s.* — *M'k 16:2*
Now when the *s.* was setting, all they — *Lu 4:40*
And there shall be signs in the *s.* — *Lu 21:25*
And the *s.* was darkened, and — *Lu 23:45*
s. shall be turned into darkness — *Ac 2:20*
blind, not seeing the *s.* for a season — *Ac 13:11*
above the brightness of the *s.* — *Ac 26:13*
when neither *s.* nor stars in many — *Ac 27:20*
There is one glory of the *s.* and — *1Co 15:41*
not the *s.* go down upon your wrath — *Eph 4:26*
For the *s.* is no sooner risen with a — *Jas 1:11*
as the *s.* shineth in his strength — *Re 1:16*
the *s.* became black as sackcloth of — *Re 6:12*
neither shall the *s.* light on them — *Re 7:16*
the third part of the *s.* was smitten — *Re 8:12*
the *s.* and the air were darkened by — *Re 9:2*
and his face was as it were the *s.* — *Re 10:1*
a woman clothed with the *s.* — *Re 12:1*
poured out his vial upon the *s.* — *Re 16:8*
I saw an angel standing in the *s.* — *Re 19:17*
And the city had no need of the *s.* — *Re 21:23*
no candle, neither light of the *s.* — *Re 22:5*

SUNDER

bow, and cutteth the spear in *s.* — *Ps 46:9*
death, and break their bands in *s.* — *Ps 107:14*
of brass, and cut the bars of iron in *s.* — *Ps 107:16*
as chalkstones that are beaten in *s.* — *Isa 27:9*
and cut in *s.* the bars of iron — *Isa 45:2*
thee, and will burst thy bonds in *s.* — *Na 1:13*
he is not aware, and will cut him in *s.* — *Lu 12:46*

SUNDERED

together, that they cannot be *s.* — *Job 41:17*
cannot be separated (A)(B)(R) — *Job 41:17*

SUNDRY

at *s.* times and in divers manners — *Heb 1:1*
in many separate revelations (A) — *Heb 1:1*
at various times (B) — *Heb 1:1*
God of old time (E) — *Heb 1:1*
in former times God spoke (N) — *Heb 1:1*
in many and various ways (R) — *Heb 1:1*

SUNG

In that day shall this song be *s.* in — *Isa 26:1*
when they had *s.* an hymn, they — *M't 26:30; M'k 14:26*
s. with a lovely feeling (B) — *Col 3:16*
they *s.* a new song, saying, Thou — *Re 5:9*
s. as it were a new song before the — *Re 14:3*

SUNK

the stone *s.* into his forehead — *1Sa 17:49*

sinking in his forehead (A) — *1Sa 17:49*
drilled into his forehead (B) — *1Sa 17:49*
sank into his forehead (E)(R) — *1Sa 17:49*
and he *s.* down in his chariot — *2Ki 9:24*
sank down (A) — *2Ki 9:24; Jer 38:6*
he slumped in his chariot (B) — *2Ki 9:24*
He sank down in his chariot (R) — *2Ki 9:24*
heathen are *s.* down in the pit — *Ps 9:15*
mire: so Jeremiah *s.* in the mire — *Jer 38:6*
he sank down in the mire (A)(B)(E)(R) — *Jer 38:6*
thy feet are *s.* in the mire, and they — *Jer 38:22*
Her gates are *s.* into the ground — *La 2:9*
preaching, he *s.* down with sleep — *Ac 20:9*
completely overcome by sleep (A)(N)(P) — *Ac 20:9*
he sagged down in his sleep (B) — *Ac 20:9*
being borne down in his sleep (E) — *Ac 20:9*
sank into deep sleep (R) — *Ac 20:9*

SUNRISE

toward the *s.* (R) — *Nu 21:11; 34:15; Jos 19:12*
on the *s.* side (A)(R) — *Jos 1:15*
regions of the *s.* (B) — *Isa 24:15*

SUNRISING

is before Moab, toward the *s.* — *Nu 21:11*
on the eastern border (B) — *Nu 21:11; 34:15*
toward the sunrise (R) — *Nu 21:11; 34:15*
Jericho eastward, toward the *s.* — *Nu 34:15*
side Jordan toward the *s.* — *De 4:41; 4:47*
to the east (A)(B)(R) — *De 4:41; 4:47*
this side Jordan toward the *s.* — *Jos 1:15*
on the sunrise side (A)(R) — *Jos 1:15*
eastward (B) — *Jos 1:15; 13:5*
and all Lebanon, toward the *s.* — *Jos 13:5*
toward the east (A)(B)(R) — *Jos 13:5; 19:34; J'g 20:43*
Sarid eastward toward the *s.* — *Jos 19:12*
And turneth toward the *s.* to — *Jos 19:27*
upon Jordan toward the *s.* — *Jos 19:34*
against Gibeah toward the *s.* — *J'g 20:43*

SUP

faces shall *s.* up as the east wind — *Hab 1:9*
Make ready wherewith I may — *Lu 17:8*
get my supper ready (A)(B)(N)(P)(R) — *Lu 17:8*
in to him, and will *s.* with him — *Re 3:20*
eat with him (A)(R) — *Re 3:20*
dine with him (B)(P) — *Re 3:20*
sit down to supper with him (N) — *Re 3:20*

SUPER

grace *s.* abounded (A) — *Ro 5:20*

SUPERFLUITY

filthiness and *s.* of naughtiness — *Jas 1:21*
rampant out growth of wickedness (A) — *Jas 1:21*
outgrowth of evil (B) — *Jas 1:21*
overflowing of wickedness (E) — *Jas 1:21*
malice that hurries excess (N) — *Jas 1:21*
rank growth of wickedness (R) — *Jas 1:21*

SUPERFLUOUS

hath a flat nose, or any thing *s.* — *Le 21:18*
or a limb too long (A)(B)(R) — *Le 21:18*
anything *s.* or lacking in his parts — *Le 22:23*
some part too long or too short (A)(R) — *Le 22:23*
members overgrown or shrunk (B) — *Le 22:23*
it is *s.* for me to write to you — *2Co 9:1*

SUPERHUMAN

s. powers (B) — *Ro 8:38*

SUPERINTENDENT

made him a *s.* (B) — *Ge 39:1*

SUPERIOR

s. to wisdom of (B) — *1Ki 4:30*
who makes you *s.* (A) — *1Co 4:7*
regard others as better, *s.* (A)(B) — *Ph'p 2:3*
a *s.* covenant (N) — *Heb 7:22; 9:18*

SUPERLATIVE

s. apostles (N)(R) — *2Co 11:5*

SUPERSCRIPTION

whose likeness and title are these (A) — *M't 22:20*
likeness and signature (B) — *M't 22:20*
whose inscription (N)(P)(R) — *M't 22:20*
them, Whose is this image and *s.* — *M'k 12:16*
whose image and inscription (B)(N)(P)(R) — *M'k 12:16*
the *s.* of his accusation was written — *M'k 15:26*
inscription (A)(B)(N)(R) — *M'k 15:26*
Whose image and *s.* hath it — *Lu 20:24*
inscription (A)(B)(N)(P)(R) — *Lu 20:24*
And a *s.* also was written over him — *Lu 23:38*
inscription (A)(B)(N)(R) — *Lu 23:38*

SUPERSTITION

against him of their own *s.* — *Ac 25:19*

SUPERSTITIOUS

that in all things ye are too *s.* — *Ac 17:22*

SUPERVISED

officials who *s.* (B) — *1Ki 9:23*

SUPERVISOR

made him a *s.* (A) — *Ge 39:4; 39:5*

SUPERVISORS

over to the *s.* (B) — *2Ch 34:17*
railings, evil *s.* (S) — *1Ti 6:4*
slander, base *s.* (N)(R) — *1Ti 6:5*

SUPPED

he took the cup, when he had *s.* — *1Co 11:25*

SUPPER

birthday made a *s.* to his lords — *M'k 6:21*
banquet (A)(N) — *M'k 6:21*
banquet (B) — *M'k 6:21; Re 19:9, 17*
banquet (R) — *M'k 6:21; Lu 14:12, 16, 17, 24*
When thou makest a dinner or a *s.* — *Lu 14:12*
dinner (N) — *Lu 14:12; 14:16, 17*
A certain man made a great *s.* and — *Lu 14:16*
sent his servant at *s.* time to — *Lu 14:17*
say to
were bidden shall taste of my *s.* — *Lu 14:24*
banquet (N) — *Lu 14:24*
Likewise also the cup after *s.* — *Lu 22:20*
There they made him a *s.*; and — *Joh 12:2*
s. being ended, the devil having — *Joh 13:2*
He riseth from *s.* and laid aside — *Joh 13:4*
also leaned on his breast at *s.* and — *Joh 21:20*
this is not to eat the Lord's *s.* — *1Co 11:20*
one taketh before other his own *s.* — *1Co 11:21*
sit down to *s.* with him (N) — *Re 3:20*

SUPPER

wedding s. of the Lamb (N)	Re 14:9
unto the marriage s. of the Lamb	Re 19:9
unto the s. of the great God	Re 19:17

SUPPLANT

for every brother will utterly s.	Jer 9:4

SUPPLANTED

for he hath s. me these two times	Ge 27:36
he has over-reached me (B)	Ge 27:36

SUPPLANTER

brother is a s. (A)(B)(R)	Jer 9:4

SUPPLE

thou washed in water to s. thee	Eze 16:4
to cleanse you (A)(B)(E)(R)	Eze 16:4

SUPPLIANTS

the rivers of Ethiopia my s.	Zep 3:10
those who pray to me (A)	Zep 3:10
bring my supplicants (B)	Zep 3:10
bring my s. (B)	Zep 3:16

SUPPLICATION

I have not made s. unto the Lord	1Sa 13:12
prayed (B)	1Sa 13:12; 1Ki 8:59
entreated (E)(R)	1Sa 13:12
prayer of thy servant, and to his s.	1Ki 8:28
And hearken thou to the s. of thy	1Ki 8:30
prayer (A)	1Ki 8:30
make s. unto thee in this house	1Ki 8:33
beseeching (A)	1Ki 8:33
implore (B)	1Ki 8:33; 8:47
prayer and s. soever be made by	1Ki 8:38
in heaven their prayer and their s.	1Ki 8:45
and make s. unto thee in the land	1Ki 8:47
their prayer and their s. in heaven	1Ki 8:49
be open unto the s. of thy servant	1Ki 8:52
and unto the s. of thy people Israel	1Ki 8:52
all this prayer and s. unto the Lord	1Ki 8:54
I have made s. before the Lord	1Ki 8:59
have heard thy prayer and thy s.	1Ki 9:3
prayer of thy servant, and to his s.	2Ch 6:19
make s. before thee in this house	2Ch 6:24
what s. soever shall be made	2Ch 6:29
heavens their prayer and their s.	2Ch 6:35
and heard his s. and brought him	2Ch 33:13
entreated (B)	2Ch 33:13; Ho 12:4
the king to make s. unto him	Es 4:8
beg for mercy and to plead (B)	Es 4:8
and make thy s. to the Almighty	Job 8:5
implore mercy (B)	Job 8:5
but I would make s. to my judge	Job 9:15
appeal for mercy (A)	Job 9:15
plead for mercy (B)	Job 9:15
make s. to the children (S)	Job 19:17
The Lord hath heard my s.; the	Ps 6:9
pleading (B)	Ps 6:9
and unto the Lord I made s.	Ps 30:8
and hide not thyself from my s.	Ps 55:1
petition (B)	Ps 55:1; 119:170
Let my s. come before thee:	Ps 119:170
unto the Lord did I make my s.	Ps 142:1
they shall make s. unto thee	Isa 45:14
plead with (B)	Isa 45:14
present their s. before the Lord	Jer 36:7

let my s. I pray thee, be accepted	Jer 37:20
my plea (B)	Jer 37:20; 38:26
I presented my s. before the king	Jer 38:26
my humble plea (A)	Jer 38:26
our s. be accepted before thee	Jer 42:2
me to present your s. before him	Jer 42:9
present your request (B)	Jer 42:9
and making s. before his God	Da 6:11
making humble petition (B)	Da 6:11
presenting my s. before the Lord	Da 9:20
he wept, and made s. unto him	Ho 12:4
sought his favor (A)	Ho 12:4
with one accord in prayer and s.	Ac 1:14
Spirit to meet our s. (A)	Ro 8:26
with all prayer and s. in the Spirit	Eph 6:18
perseverance and s. for all saints	Eph 6:18
entreaty, interceding (A)(N)	Eph 6:18
entreaty, appeal (B)	Eph 6:18
by prayer and s. with thanksgiving	Ph'p 4:6
petition (A)(N)	Ph'p 4:6
pleading (B)	Ph'p 4:6
s. of righteous (E)	Jas 5:16

SUPPLICATIONS

s. for the land (R)	2Sa 21:14
unto the s. of thy servant	2Ch 6:21
requests (A)	2Ch 6:21
their prayer and their s. and	2Ch 6:39
Will he make many s. unto thee	Job 41:3
pleading (B)	Job 41:3
Hear the voice of my s. when I cry	Ps 28:2
he hath heard the voice of my s.	Ps 28:6
heardest the voice of my s. when I	Ps 31:22
and attend to the voice of my s.	Ps 86:6
cry of entreaty (B)	Ps 86:6
he hath heard my voice and my s.	Ps 116:1
be attentive to the voice of my s.	Ps 130:2
hear the voice of my s. O Lord	Ps 140:6
prayer, O Lord, give ear to my s.	Ps 143:1
heed their s. (R)	Isa 19:22
weeping and s. of the children	Jer 3:21
pleading (A)	Jer 3:21
and with s. will I lead them	Jer 31:9
Lord God, to seek by prayer and s.	Da 9:3
prayer of thy servant, and his s.	Da 9:17
for we do not present our s. before	Da 9:18
petitions (B)	Da 9:18; 9:23; 1Ti 2:1; 5:5; Heb 5:7
At the beginning of thy s. the	Da 9:23
prayers (A)	Da 9:23
the spirit of grace and of s.	Zec 12:10
that, first of all, s., prayers	1Ti 2:1
petitions (A)	1Ti 2:1
petitions (N)	1Ti 2:1; Heb 5:7
continueth in s. and prayers night	1Ti 5:5
he had offered up prayers and s.	Heb 5:7

SUPPLIED

s. his father (A)	Ge 47:12
lacking on your part they have s.	1Co 16:17
which came from Macedonia s.	2Co 11:9

SUPPLIES

food s. (S)	Ge 14:11; Ex 12:39; Le 25:37; Jos 1:11; J'g 20:10; 1Ki 4:7, 27; 11:18; 2Ch 11:11
army and abundant s. (R)	Da 11:13
s. you with Spirit (A)(E)(R)	1Co 3:5

SUPPLIETH

not only s. the want of the saints	2Co 9:12
by that which every joint s.	Eph 4:16

SUPPLY

a great s. (A)	Ge 26:14
woman to s. thee (B)	1Ki 17:9
abundance be a s. for their want	2Co 8:14
also may be a s. for your want	2Co 8:14
the s. of the Spirit of Jesus Christ	Ph'p 1:19
to s. your lack of service toward	Ph'p 2:30
But my God shall s. all your need	Ph'p 4:19

SUPPORT

will s. you (R)	Ge 45:11
unable to s. himself (B)	Le 25:35
s. your words (B)	1Ki 1:14
s. for himself (B)	2Ki 15:19
s. to children of Lot (B)	Ps 83:8
s. and strengthen (B)	Da 11:1
deserves his s. (A)(B)	M't 10:10
labouring ye ought to s. the weak	Ac 20:35
s. the weak, be patient toward all	1Th 5:14

SUPPORTED

s. his father (B)	Ge 47:12
right hand s. me (R)	Ps 18:35
s. them out of (B)	Lu 8:3

SUPPORTS

under laver were s. (S)	1Ki 7:30; 7:34

SUPPOSE

s. there be fifty (A)(R)	Ge 18:24; 18:29-32; 31:31
suppose (S)	Ge 18:24; 18:28-32; 24:5, 39; Jos 9:7
s. he hate us (B)	Ge 50:15
not my lord s. that they have slain	2Sa 13:32
I s. that he, to whom he forgave	Lu 7:43
S. ye that I am come to give peace	Lu 12:51
S. ye that these Galilæans were	Lu 13:2
I s. that even the world itself	Joh 21:25
these are not drunken, as ye s.	Ac 2:15
I s. therefore that this is good for	1Co 7:26
I s. I was not a whit behind	2Co 11:5
much sorer punishment, s. ye	Heb 10:29
a faithful brother as I s.	1Pe 5:12
slow, as some men s. (N)	2Pe 3:9

SUPPOSED

s. that they should have received	M't 20:10
sea, they s. it had been a spirit	M'k 6:49
s. to rule Gentiles (B)(R)	M'k 10:32
being (as was s.) the son of Joseph	Lu 3:23
and s. that they had seen a spirit	Lu 24:37
For he s. his brethren would	Ac 7:25
whom they s. Paul had brought	Ac 21:29
accusation of such things as I s.	Ac 25:18
I s. it necessary to send to you	Ph'p 2:25

SUPPOSING

they, s. him in the company	Lu 2:44
She, s. him to be the gardener	Joh 20:15
out of the city, s. he had been dead	Ac 14:19
s. that the prisoners had been fled	Ac 16:27
s. that they had obtained their	Ac 27:13
s. to add affliction to my bonds	Ph'p 1:16
truth, s. that gain is godliness	1Ti 6:5

SUPREME

whether it be to the king, as *1Pe 2:13*
s.

SUPPRESS

s. and mistreat him (A)   *Ge 19:33*

SUPPRESSED

not fail nor be s. (B)   *Isa 42:4*

SUR

part shall be at the gate of S. *2Ki 11:6*

SURE

borders round about, were   *Ge 23:17*
made s.
were made s. unto Abraham   *Ge 23:20*
for a
I am s. the king of Egypt will *Ex 3:19*
not
and be s. your sin will find   *Nu 32:23*
you out
be s. that thou eat not the   *De 12:23*
blood
and I will build him a s.   *1Sa 2:35*
house
be s. evil is determined by   *1Sa 20:7*
him
certainly make my lord a s.   *1Sa 25:28*
house
I was s. that he could not live *2Sa 1:10*
ordered in all things, and s.   *2Sa 23:5*
and build thee a s. house, as   *1Ki 11:38*
I built
we make a s. covenant, and   *Ne 9:38*
write
riseth up, and no man is s.   *Job 24:22*
of life
the testimony of the Lord is s. *Ps 19:7*
Thy testimonies are very s.   *Ps 93:5*
all his commandments are s.   *Ps 111:7*
thyself, and make s. thy friend *Pr 6:3*
and he that hateth suretyship   *Pr 11:15*
is s.
righteousness shall be a s.   *Pr 11:18*
reward
fasten him as a nail in a s.   *Isa 22:23*
place
nail that is fastened in the s. *Isa 22:25*
place
corner stone, a s. foundation   *Isa 28:16*
and in s. dwellings, and in   *Isa 32:18*
quiet
given him; his waters shall   *Isa 33:16*
be s.
you, even the s. mercies of   *Isa 55:3*
David
and the interpretation thereof *Da 2:45*
s.
thy kingdom shall be s. unto   *Da 4:26*
thee
sepulchre be made s. until   *M't 27:64*
the third
your way, make it as s. as   *M't 27:65*
ye can
went, and made the   *M't 27:66*
sepulchre s.
be ye s. of this, that the   *Lu 10:11*
kingdom
are s. that thou art that   *Joh 6:69*
Christ
Now are we s. that thou   *Joh 16:30*
knowest
give you the s. mercies of   *Ac 13:34*
David
we are s. that the judgment of *Ro 2:2*
God
might be s. to all the seed   *Ro 4:16*
And I am s. that, when I   *Ro 15:29*
come
I am s. (P)(R)   *Ph'p 1:6*
the foundation of God   *2Ti 2:19*
standeth s.
of the soul, both s. and   *Heb 6:19*
stedfast
make your calling and   *2Pe 1:10*
election s.
also a more s. word of   *2Pe 1:19*
prophecy

SURELY

in day thou eatest thereof   *Ge 2:17*
shalt s. die

serpent said to woman, Ye   *Ge 3:4*
shall not s. die
s. your blood of your lives will *Ge 9:5*
I require
Abraham shall s. become a   *Ge 18:18*
great nation
if thou restore her not, thou   *Ge 20:7*
shalt s. die
s. the fear of God is not in   *Ge 20:11*
this place
Jacob said, S. Lord is in this *Ge 28:16*
place
I will s. give the tenth unto   *Ge 28:22*
thee
Laban said, S. thou art my   *Ge 29:14*
bone and flesh
s. the Lord looked upon my   *Ge 29:32*
affliction
come in unto me, s. I have   *Ge 30:16*
hired thee
s. thou hadst sent me away   *Ge 31:42*
now empty
and thou saidst, I will s. do   *Ge 32:12*
thee good
s. ye are spies   *Ge 42:16*
s. now we had returned this   *Ge 43:10*
second time
s. he is torn   *Ge 44:28*
I will also s. bring thee up   *Ge 46:4*
again
God will s. visit you   *Ge 50:24;*
                          50:25; Ex 13:19
Moses said, S. this thing is   *Ex 2:14*
known
I have s. seen affliction of   *Ex 3:7;*
Israel   *3:16*
s. a bloody husband art thou   *Ex 4:25*
to me
he shall s. thrust you out   *Ex 11:1*
hence
thou wilt s. wear away, thou   *Ex 18:18*
he shall s. be stoned, or shot *Ex 19:13*
through
if he die, he shall be s.   *Ex 21:20;*
punished   *21:22*
if an ox gore, the ox shall be *Ex 21:28*
s. stoned
shall s. pay ox for ox, dead   *Ex 21:36*
shall be his
that kindleth fire shall s. make *Ex 22:6*
restitution
if it be hurt or die, he shall s. *Ex 22:14*
make it good
if lie with her s. endow her   *Ex 22:16*
to be his wife
if they cry at all to me, I will *Ex 22:23*
s. hear
thou shalt s. bring it back to   *Ex 23:4*
him again
if thou see, thou shalt s. help *Ex 23:5*
him
if serve their gods, will s.   *Ex 22:33;*
besnare   *1Ki 11:2*
anointing s. be an everlasting *Ex 40:15*
priesthood
surely (S)   *Le 19:17;*
                De 17:15; 21:23; 22:7
s. it floweth with milk and   *Nu 13:27*
honey
s. they shall not see land   *Nu 14:23*
which I sware
I will s. do it to all this evil *Nu 14:35*
congregation
firstborn of man shalt thou   *Nu 18:15*
s. redeem
s. I had slain thee, and saved *Nu 22:33*
her alive
s. there is no enchantment   *Nu 23:23*
against Jacob
Lord had said, They shall   *Nu 26:65*
s. die in wilderness
shalt s. give them a possession *Nu 27:7*
of inheritance
s. none from twenty years   *Nu 32:11;*
old and upward, shall see land *De 1:35*
s. this great nation is a wise *De 4:6*
people
I testify that ye shall s. perish *De 8:19;*
                                30:18
but thou shalt s. kill the   *De 13:9*
idolater
s. smite the inhabitants of   *De 13:15*
that city
s. lend him sufficient for his *De 15:8*
need
s. give poor brother not to be *De 15:10*
grieved
s. rejoice in the feast of   *De 16:15*
tabernacles

shalt s. help him to lift them *De 22:4*
up again
the Lord will s. require thy   *De 23:21*
vow of thee
and I will s. hide my face in   *De 31:18*
that day
s. the land shall be thine   *Jos 14:9*
inheritance
they said, S. he covereth his   *J'g 3:24*
feet
Deborah said, I will s. go with *J'g 4:9*
thee
Lord said to Gideon, S. I will *J'g 6:16*
be with thee
cometh forth to meet me, s.   *J'g 11:31*
be Lord's
bind, but s. we will not kill   *J'g 15:13*
thee
s. they are smitten down   *J'g 20:39*
before us
all that he saith cometh s. to *1Sa 9:6*
pass
s. the bitterness of death is   *1Sa 15:32*
past
they said, s. to defy Israel is *1Sa 17:25*
he come
for Saul thought, s. he is not *1Sa 20:26*
clean
I knew it that Doeg would s.   *1Sa 22:22*
tell Saul
I know well that thou shalt   *1Sa 24:20*
s. be king
s. in vain have I kept all   *1Sa 25:21*
this fellow
s. there had not been left to   *1Sa 25:34*
Nabal any
s. shalt know what thy   *1Sa 28:2*
servant can do
s. as Lord liveth, thou hast   *1Sa 29:6*
been upright
pursue, for thou shalt s.   *1Sa 30:8*
overtake them
s. the people had gone up   *2Sa 2:27*
every one
s. shew thee kindness for   *2Sa 9:7*
Jonathan's sake
he said, S. the men prevailed   *2Sa 11:23*
against us
s. where the king shall be,   *2Sa 15:21*
there will I be
I will s. go forth with you   *2Sa 18:2*
myself also
she spake, they shall s. ask   *2Sa 20:18*
counsel
but I will s. buy it of thee at *2Sa 24:24*
a price
I have s. built thee an house   *1Ki 8:13*
I will s. rend the kingdom   *1Ki 11:11*
from thee
saying against altar shall s.   *1Ki 13:32*
come to pass
I will s. shew myself unto   *1Ki 18:15*
him to-day
s. we shall be stronger than   *1Ki 20:23;*
they   *20:25*
they said, S. it is the king   *1Ki 22:32*
of Israel
s. were it not I regard   *2Ki 3:14*
Jehoshaphat
this is blood, the kings are s. *2Ki 3:23*
slain
I thought, he will s. come out *2Ki 5:11*
to me
he told me thou shouldest s.   *2Ki 8:14*
recover
s. I have seen the blood of   *2Ki 9:26*
Naboth
Lord will s. deliver us   *2Ki 18:30;*
                                Isa 36:15
s. not holden such a   *2Ki 23:22*
passover
s. at command of Lord came   *2Ki 24:3*
this on Judah
not prevail, but shalt s. fall *Es 6:13*
before him
if pure and upright, s. would   *Job 8:6*
awake
s. I would speak to the   *Job 13:3*
Almighty
will s. reprove if ye accept   *Job 13:10*
persons
s. mountain falling cometh   *Job 14:18*
to nought
s. such are the dwellings of   *Job 18:21*
wicked
s. not feel quietness in his   *Job 20:20*
belly
s. there is a vein for the silver *Job 28:1*
s. take it upon my shoulder   *Job 31:36*

s. thou hast spoken in mine *Job 33:8* hearing
s. God will not do wickedly *Job 34:12*
s. God will not hear vanity *Job 35:13*
s. in floods they shall not come *Ps 32:6* nigh
s. every man walketh in vain *Ps 39:6* shew
beauty consumes, s. every *Ps 39:11* man is vanity
s. didst set them in slippery *Ps 73:18* places
s. the wrath of man shall *Ps 76:10* praise thee
s. I will remember thy *Ps 77:11* wonders of old
s. salvation is nigh them that *Ps 85:9* fear him
s. shall deliver from snare of *Ps 91:3* fowler
s. he shall not be moved for *Ps 112:6* ever
s. have behaved and quieted *Ps 131:2* myself
s. I will not come into my *Ps 132:3* house
s. thou wilt slay the wicked, *Ps 139:19* O God
s. righteous give thanks to *Ps 140:13* thy name
s. in vain net is spread in sight *Pr 1:17* of bird
s. scorneth scorners, giveth *Pr 3:34* grace to
s. for thy neighbor *Pr 6:1;* (A)(B)(E)(R) *6:3*
he that walketh uprightly, *Pr 10:9* walketh s.
s. in presence of neighbor *Pr 17:18;* (A)(B)(E)(R) *27:14*
giveth to rich, shall s. come *Pr 22:16* to want
s. is an end *Pr 23:18*
s. I am brutish *Pr 30:2*
s. churning of milk bringeth *Pr 30:33* forth butter
s. this is also vanity and *Ec 4:16* vexation
s. oppression maketh a wise *Ec 7:7* man mad
s. be well with them that fear *Ec 8:12* God
s. serpent will bite without *Ec 10:11* enchantment
not believe, s. not be *Isa 7:9* established
s. as I thought so shall it *Isa 14:24* come to pass
Kir-haresheth shall mourn, s. *Isa 16:7* are stricken
s. the princes of Zoan are *Isa 19:11* fools
s. this iniquity shall not be *Isa 22:14* purged
behold, the Lord will s. cover *Isa 22:17* thee
will s. violently turn and toss *Isa 22:18* thee like ball
s. your turning of things *Isa 29:16* upside down
the grass withereth, s. the *Isa 40:7* people is grass
s. God is in thee, and there *Isa 45:14* is none else
s. in the Lord have I *Isa 45:24* righteousness
yet s. my judgment is with the *Isa 49:4* Lord
s. borne our griefs, and *Isa 53:4* carried our sorrows
they shall s. gather together, *Isa 54:15* but not
s. the isles shall wait for me *Isa 60:9*
s. no more give thy corn to *Isa 62:8* enemies
s. they are my people, children *Isa 63:8* not lie
thou sayest, s. his anger shall *Jer 2:35* turn
s. as a wife treacherously *Jer 3:20* departeth from
s. thou hast greatly deceived *Jer 4:10* this people
s. swear falsely *Jer 5:2*
s. these are poor *Jer 5:4*
I will s. consume them, saith *Jer 8:13* the Lord
s. our fathers have inherited *Jer 16:19* lies, vanity
yet s. I will make thee a *Jer 22:6* wilderness

s. be ashamed for thy *Jer 22:22* wickedness
s. saith Lord, so will I give *Jer 24:8* Zedekiah
s. bring innocent blood on *Jer 26:15* yourselves
s. heard Ephraim bemoaning *Jer 31:18* himself
s. after that I was turned, I *Jer 31:19* repented
therefore I will s. have mercy *Jer 31:20* on him
but thou shalt s. be taken and *Jer 34:3* delivered
we will s. tell the king of all *Jer 36:16* these words
the Chaldeans shall s. depart *Jer 37:9* from us
city shall s. be given to king *Jer 38:3* of Babylon's army
I will s. deliver thee, thou *Jer 39:18* shalt not fall
we will s. perform our vows *Jer 44:25*
my words s. stand against *Jer 44:29* you for evil
s. as Carmel by the sea, so *Jer 46:18* shall he come
not go unpunished, but s. *Jer 49:12* drink it
s. least of flock shall draw *Jer 49:20;* them *50:45*
saying, S. I will fill thee with *Jer 51:14* men
Lord God of recompences, *Jer 51:56* shall s. requite
he shall s. live, because he is *Eze 3:21;* warned *18:9, 17, 19, 21, 28; 33:13, 15,* *16*
s. because thou hast defiled *Eze 5:11* my sanctuary
s. in the place where the *Eze 17:16* king dwelleth
s. with a mighty hand will I *Eze 20:33* rule
he shall s. deal with him *Eze 31:11*
s. they in wastes fall by *Eze 33:27* sword
s. because my flock became a *Eze 34:8* prey
s. in fire of jealousy have I *Eze 36:5* spoken
s. the heathen, they shall *Eze 36:7* bear their shame
s. in that day shall be a *Eze 38:19* great shaking
made known that which shall *Ho 5:9*
s. they are vanity, they *Ho 12:11* sacrifice bullocks
s. Lord will do nothing, but he *Am 3:7* reveals
Gilgal shall s. go into captivity *Am 5:5*
Israel shall s. be led away *Am 7:11;* captive *7:17*
s. I will never forget any of *Am 8:7* their works
I will s. assemble, O Jacob, I *Mic 2:12* will s. gather remnant of Israel
it will s. come, it will not *Hab 2:3* tarry
as I live s. Moab shall be as *Zep 2:9* Sodom
s. thou wilt fear me, and *Zep 3:7* receive
s. thou art one of them *M't 26:73;* *M'k 14:70*
things most s. believed among *Lu 1:1* us
will s. say this proverb, *Lu 4:23* Physician
have known s. that I came *Joh 17:8* out from thee
saying, S. blessing I will *Heb 6:14* bless thee
S. I come quickly, even so *Re 22:20* come Lord Jesus

SURELY BE PUT TO DEATH

toucheth this man, s. be put *Ge 26:11* to death
toucheth mount, s. be put to *Ex 19:12* death
he that killeth a man, s. be *Ex 21:12* put to death
he that smiteth his father s. *Ex 21:15* be put to death
he that stealeth a man, s. be *Ex 21:16* put to death
that curseth his father shall *Ex 21:17;* s. be put to death *Le 20:9*

whosoever lieth with a beast *Ex 22:19;* shall s. be put to death *Le 20:15-16*
defileth the sabbath s. be put *Ex 31:14;* to death *31:15*
giveth seed to Molech s. be *Le 20:2* put to death
adulterer and adulteress s. be *Le 20:10* put to death
lieth with father's wife both *Le 20:11* s. be put to death
lie with his daughter in law *Le 20:12* both s. be put to death
if a man lie with mankind, *Le 20:13* both s. be put to death
he that blasphemeth, s. be *Le 24:16* put to death
he that killeth any man, *Le 24:17;* shall s. be put to death *24:18, 21, 31;* *Nu 35:16-17*
not be redeemed, but shall s. *Le 27:9* be put to death
who came not up, shall s. be *J'g 21:5* put to death
wilt thou not s. put me to *Jer 38:15* death

SURETIES

or of them that are s. for *Pr 22:26* debts
surety (A)(R) *Pr 22:26*

SURETY

Know of a s. that thy seed *Ge 15:13* shall be
know positively (A) *Ge 15:13*
know with certainty (B) *Ge 15:13*
Shall I of a s. bear a child, *Ge 18:13* which
Shall I really bear a child *Ge 18:13* (A)
could I possibly bear a child *Ge 18:13* (B)
Shall I indeed bear a child *Ge 18:13* (R)
said, Behold, of a s. she is thy *Ge 26:9* wife
she is certainly your wife (A) *Ge 26:9*
she is really your wife (B) *Ge 26:9*
I will be s. for him: of my *Ge 43:9* hand
I will be a security for him *Ge 43:9* (A)
I will stand guaranty for him *Ge 43:9* (B)
servant became s. for the lad *Ge 44:32* unto
became security for (A) *Ge 44:32*
went guaranty for (B) *Ge 44:32*
down now, put me in a s. *Job 17:3*
security for (A) *Job 17:3;* *Pr 6:1; 11:15; 17:18; 20:16; 27:13*
Be s. for thy servant for *Ps 119:122* good: let
My son, if thou be s. for thy *Pr 6:1* friend
He that is s. for a stranger *Pr 11:15* shall
he that hateth s. *Pr 11:15* (A)(B)(E)(R)
becometh s. in the presence *Pr 17:18* of his
garment that is s. for a *Pr 20:16;* stranger *27:13*
Now I know of a s. that the *Ac 12:11* Lord
Now I really know (A) *Ac 12:11*
Now I know for certain *Ac 12:11* (B)(P)
Now I know of a truth (E) *Ac 12:11*
Now I know it is true (N) *Ac 12:11*
Now I am sure (R) *Ac 12:11*
made a s. of a better *Heb 7:22* testament

SURETYSHIP

it: and he that hateth s. is *Pr 11:15* sure
surety (A)(B)(E)(R) *Pr 11:15*

SURFEITING

hearts be overcharged with s. *Lu 21:34*
with giddiness, headache, *Lu 21:34*
nausea of self-indulgence (A)
with dissipation *Lu 21:34*
(B)(N)(P)(R)

SURGE

roar and s. of the sea (N)   *Lu 21:25*

SURGING

before me as the s. of waters   *2Sa 5:20*
(S)
roar of the s. sea (P)   *Lu 21:25*

SURMISINGS

cometh envy, strife, railings,   *1Ti 6:4*
evil s.
base suspicions (A)(N)(R)   *1Ti 6:4*
bad suspicions (B)   *1Ti 6:4*

SURNAME

s. himself by the name of   *Isa 44:5*
Israel
whose s. was Thaddaeus   *M't 10:3*
for one Simon, whose s. is   *Ac 10:5*
Peter
hither Simon, whose s. is   *Ac 10:32*
Peter
call for Simon, whose s. is   *Ac 11:13*
Peter
of John, whose s. was Mark   *Ac 12:12*
them John, whose s. was   *Ac 12:25;*
Mark   *15:37*

SURNAMED

I have s. thee, though thou   *Isa 45:4*
hast
And Simon he s. Peter   *M'k 3:16*
he s. them Boanerges, which   *M'k 3:17*
Satan into Judas s. Iscariot   *Lu 22:3*
Barsabas, who was s. Justus   *Ac 1:23*
by the apostles was s.   *Ac 4:36*
Barnabas
whether Simon, which was s.   *Ac 10:18*
Peter
Judas s. Barsabas, and Silas,   *Ac 15:22*
chief

SURPASSED

s. wisdom of the east (R)   *1Ki 4:30*

SURPLUS

a s. of prosperity (A)   *De 28:11*

SUPREME

the s. court (P)   *M't 5:22*
in all things alone s. (N)   *Col 1:8*
faith reached s. expression   *Jas 2:22*
(B)

SURPRISE

to the governor's great s.   *M't 27:14*
(B)
noticed with s. (N)(P)   *Lu 11:38*

SURPRISED

fearfulness hath s. the   *Isa 33:14*
hypocrites
like a man s. (B)   *Jer 14:9*
taken, and the strong holds   *Jer 48:41*
are s.
is the praise of the whole   *Jer 51:41*
earth s.
s. at staying so long (N)   *Lu 1:21*
which s. them all (B)   *Lu 1:63*
do not feel s. (B)   *Joh 3:7*
s. to find him talking   *Joh 4:27*
(B)(N)(P)
Be not s. at this (A)(B)   *Joh 5:26*
Jews were s. (B)   *Joh 7:15*
Why so s. at this   *Ac 3:12*
(A)(B)(N)(P)
I am s. and (A)   *Ga 1:6*
Do not be s. (A)(B)(N)(P)   *1Jo 3:13*

SURREPTITIOUSLY

s. entered the church (P)   *Jude 4*

SURROUND

shall s. us and cut off (S)   *Jos 7:9*
s. with good will (A)(B)   *Ps 5:12*
surround (A)(B)(R)   *Ps 17:9;*
   32:7; 49:5; 142:7
they s. me (A)(B)(R)   *Ps 88:17*
s. and gird (A)   *Isa 50:11*
surround you (A)(R)   *Lu 19:43*

SURROUNDS

wicked s. the righteous   *Hab 1:4*
(A)(R)

SURROUNDED

s. the house (A)(B)(R)   *Ge 19:4*
they s. him (A)(B)(R)   *J'g 16:2*
s. and struck Absalom   *2Sa 18:15*
(A)(R)
s. the city (A)(B)(R)   *2Ki 6:14*
who had s. him (R)   *2Ki 8:21*
they s. us (A)(B)(R)   *Ps 17:11*
bulls have s. me (A)(B)   *Ps 22:12*
evils s. me (B)   *Ps 40:12*
all nations s. me (R)   *Ps 118:10*
s. me with bitterness (A)(B)   *La 3:5*
s. by armies (A)(B)(P)(R)   *Lu 21:20*
s. by a great cloud   *Heb 12:1*
(A)(P)(R)
s. the encampment (B)(R)   *Re 20:9*

SURROUNDING

s. him (A)   *1Sa 23:26*
s., hemming in (P)   *Lu 19:43*

SUSANCHITES

the S., the Dehavites, and the   *Ezr 4:9*

SUSANNA

wife of Herod's steward, and   *Lu 8:3*
S.

SUSI

of Mannasseh, Gaddi the son   *Nu 13:11*
of S.

SUSTAIN

a widow woman there to s.   *1Ki 17:9*
thee
provide for (A)   *1Ki 17:9*
supply (B)   *1Ki 17:9*
feed (R)   *1Ki 17:9*
Yea, forty years didst thou s.   *Ne 9:21*
them
upon the Lord, and he shall   *Ps 55:22*
s. thee
spirit of a man will s. his   *Pr 18:14*
infirmity
endure (B)(R)   *Pr 18:14*

SUSTAINED

with corn and wine have I s.   *Ge 27:37*
him
I awaked; for the Lord s. me   *Ps 3:5*
and his righteousness, it s.   *Isa 59:16*
him

SUSTENANCE

left no s. for Israel, neither   *J'g 6:4*
sheep
nourishment (A)   *J'g 6:4*
nothing edible (B)   *J'g 6:4*
he had provided the king of   *2Sa 19:32*
s.
food (A)(R)   *2Sa 19:32*
provisions (B)   *2Sa 19:32*
and our fathers found no s.   *Ac 7:11*
nourishment (B)   *Ac 7:11*
food (R)   *Ac 7:11*

SURVIVE

no human being s.   *M't 24:22*
(A)(B)(N)(P)(R)

SURVIVES

s. this test (A)(B)(P)(R)   *1Co 3:14*

SURVIVING

the s. Rephaim (B)   *De 3:11;*
   Jos 12:4; 13:12

SURVIVORS

the s. of Amorites (B)   *2Sa 21:2;*
   2Ki 19:30
the few s. (B)   *Isa 1:9; 10:20*
your s. be devoured (R)   *Eze 23:25*

SUSPENSE

your life in s. (B)   *De 28:66*
in s., waiting (A)(B)   *Lu 3:15*
excited, worried, in s. (A)   *Lu 12:29*

SUSPENDED

he was s. between earth and   *2Sa 18:9*
heaven (S)

SUSPICIONS

base s. (A)(B)(N)(R)   *1Ti 6:4*

SUSTAIN

s. and provide for you (A)   *Ge 45:11*
let no man s. him (S)   *Pr 28:17*
S. me with flagons   *Ca 2:5*
(A)(B)(E)(R)(S)
s. you to the end (R)   *1Co 1:8*

SUSTAINED

he s. Israel (B)   *Lu 1:54*
she was to be s. (N)   *Re 12:14*

SUSTAINS

right hand s. me (B)   *Ps 18:35*
s. universe by his almighty   *Heb 1:3*
word (B)

SUSTENANCE

suit of apparel and s. (S)   *J'g 17:10*

SWADDLED

those I have s. and brought   *La 2:22*
up
nursed (A)   *La 2:22*
fondled (B)   *La 2:22*
dandled (E)(R)   *La 2:22*
wast not salted at all, nor s.   *Eze 16:4*
at all

SWADDLING

and wrapped him in s. clothes   *Lu 2:7*
find the babe wrapped in s.   *Lu 2:12*
clothes

SWADDLINGBAND

and thick darkness a s. for it   *Job 38:9*

SWALLOW

open her mouth, and s. them   *Nu 16:30*
up
said, Lest the earth s. us up   *Nu 16:34*
also
why wilt thou s. up the   *2Sa 20:19*
inheritance
me, that I should s. up or   *2Sa 20:20*
destroy
me alone till I s. down my   *Job 7:19*
spittle
he restore, and shall not s. it   *Job 20:18*
down
Lord shall s. them up in his   *Ps 21:9*
wrath
O God: for man would s. me   *Ps 56:1*
up
Mine enemies would daily s.   *Ps 56:2*
me up
reproach of him that would s.   *Ps 57:3*
me
neither let the deep s. me up   *Ps 69:15*
house, and the s. a nest for   *Ps 84:3*
herself
us s. them up alive as the   *Pr 1:12*
grave
by wandering, as the s. by   *Pr 26:2*
flying
the lips of a fool will s. up   *Ec 10:12*
himself
He will s. up death in victory   *Isa 25:8*
Like a crane or a s. so did I   *Isa 38:14*
like a s. I clamor (B)   *Isa 38:14*
s. observe the time of their   *Jer 8:7*
coming
yield, the strangers shall s. it   *Ho 8:7*
up
this, O ye that s. up the needy   *Am 8:4*
drink, and they shall s. down   *Ob 16*
a great fish to s. up Jonah   *Jon 1:17*
strain at a gnat, and s. a   *M't 23:24*
camel
S. up widow's houses (A)   *M't 23:14*

SWALLOWED

s. seven large ears (B)(E)(R)   *Ge 41:7*
but Aaron's rod s. up their   *Ex 7:12*
rods
thy right hand, the earth s.   *Ex 15:12*
them
and s. them up, and their   *Nu 16:32*
houses
and s. them up together with   *Nu 26:10*
Korah
s. them up, and their   *De 11:6*
households
lest the king be s. up, and   *2Sa 17:16*
all the
sea: therefore my words are s.   *Job 6:3*
up
He hath s. down riches, and   *Job 20:15*
he
man speak, surely he shall   *Job 37:20*
be s. up
them not say, We have s. him   *Ps 35:25*
up
The earth opened and s. up   *Ps 106:17*
Dathan
Then they had s. us up quick,   *Ps 124:3*
when
they are s. up of wine, they   *Isa 28:7*
are out
that s. thee up shall be far   *Isa 49:19*
away
he hath s. me up like a   *Jer 51:34*
dragon, he
mouth that which he hath s.   *Jer 51:44*
up
Lord hath s. up all the   *La 2:2*
habitations
as an enemy: he hath s. up   *La 2:5*
Israel
he hath s. up all her palaces   *La 2:5*
We have s. her up: certainly   *La 2:16*
this is
and s. you up on every side   *Eze 36:3*
Israel is s. up: now shall they   *Ho 8:8*
be
written, Death is s. up in   *1Co 15:54*
victory
be s. up with overmuch   *2Co 2:7*
sorrow
that mortality might be s. up   *2Co 5:4*
of life
s. up the flood which the   *Re 12:16*
dragon

SWALLOWETH

the robber s. up their   *Job 5:5*
substance
He s. the ground with   *Job 39:24*
fierceness

SWALLOWS

s. iniquity (A)(B)(E)   *Pr 19:28*
wicked s. up the man   *Hab 1:13*
(B)(E)(R)

SWAMPS

s. and marshes (A)(R)   *Eze 47:11*

SWAN

And the s. and the pelican   *Le 11:18*
the marsh hen (B)   *Le 11:18*
the water hen (R)   *Le 11:18*
owl, and the great owl, and   *De 14:16*
the s.
the water hen (B)(R)   *De 14:16*

SWARE

because there they s. both of   *Ge 21:31*
them
made an oath (B)   *Ge 21:31;*
   24:7; De 4:31; 1Sa 19:6; 2Ch 15:14
me, and that s. unto me,   *Ge 24:7*
saying
s. to him concerning that   *Ge 24:9*
matter
me this day; and he s.   *Ge 25:33*
him
oath which I s. unto Abraham   *Ge 26:3*
thy
the morning, and s. one to   *Ge 26:31*
another
took oaths (A)   *Ge 26:31*
Jacob s. by the fear of his   *Ge 31:53*
father

unto me. And he s. unto him   *Ge 47:31*
the land which he s. to   *Ge 50:24*
Abraham
he s. unto thy fathers to give   *Ex 13:5*
thee
he s. unto thee and to thy   *Ex 13:11*
fathers
the land which I s. unto   *Ex 33:1*
Abraham
the land which he s. unto   *Nu 14:16*
them
land which I s. unto their   *Nu 14:23*
fathers
promised by oath (B)   *Nu 14:23;*
32:11; De 6:18, 23; 7:13; 8:1; 31:21;
   J'g 2:1
I s. to make you dwell   *Nu 14:30*
therein
kindled the same time, and   *Nu 32:10*
he s.
the land which I s. unto   *Nu 32:11*
Abraham
land which the Lord s. unto   *De 1:8*
your
your words, and was wroth,   *De 1:34*
and s.
land, which I s. to give unto   *De 1:35*
your
the host, as the Lord s. unto   *De 2:14*
them
had sworn (A)   *De 2:14*
s. that I should not go over   *De 4:21*
Jordan
covenant which he s. unto   *De 4:31*
them
land which he s. unto thy   *De 6:10*
fathers
which the Lord s. unto thy   *De 6:18*
fathers
land which he s. unto our   *De 6:23*
fathers
which he s. unto thy fathers   *De 7:12*
land which he s. unto thy   *De 7:13*
fathers
The Lord s. unto your fathers   *De 8:1*
his covenant which he s. unto   *De 8:18*
thy
which the Lord s. unto thy   *De 9:5*
fathers
which I s. unto their fathers   *De 10:11*
to give
the Lord s. unto your fathers   *De 11:9;*
   11:21
which the Lord s. unto your   *De 26:3*
fathers
which the Lord s. unto thy   *De 28:11;*
fathers   *30:20*
land which I s. unto their   *De 31:20*
them into the land which I s.   *De 31:21*
into the land which I s. unto   *De 31:23*
them
the land which I s. unto   *De 34:4*
Abraham
which I s. unto their fathers to   *Jos 1:6*
give
I vowed (B)   *Jos 1:6; 5:6; Ps 95:11*
the Lord s. that he would not   *Jos 5:6*
show
land, which the Lord s. unto   *Jos 5:6*
their
all that she hath, as ye s. unto   *Jos 6:22*
her
pledged (B)   *Jos 6:22*
princes of the congregation s.   *Jos 9:15*
unto
sware by oath (B)   *Jos 9:15;*
   9:20; Lu 1:73
of the oath which we s. unto   *Jos 9:20*
them
And Moses s. on that day,   *Jos 14:9*
saying
said under oath (B)   *Jos 14:9*
he s. to give unto their   *Jos 21:43*
fathers
to all that he s. unto their   *Jos 21:44*
fathers
land which I s. unto your   *J'g 2:1*
fathers
and Saul s. As the Lord   *1Sa 19:6*
liveth, he
And David s. moreover, and   *1Sa 20:3*
said
asserted with an oath (B)   *1Sa 20:3*
And David s. unto Saul.   *1Sa 24:22*
And Saul
gave his oath (A)   *1Sa 24:22; 2Sa 19:23*
Saul s. to her by the Lord,   *1Sa 28:10*
saying
while it was yet day, David s.   *2Sa 3:35*

took an oath (A)   *2Sa 3:35;*
   1Ki 1:29; 2Ch 15:14; Ezr 10:5
not die. And the king s.   *2Sa 19:23*
unto him
confirmed it with an oath   *2Sa 19:23*
(B)
Then the men of David s.   *2Sa 21:17*
unto him
the king s. and said, As the   *1Ki 1:29*
Lord
Even as I s. unto thee by the   *1Ki 1:30*
Lord
and I s. to him by the Lord,   *1Ki 2:8*
saying
Then King Solomon s. by the   *1Ki 2:23*
Lord
Gedaliah s. to them, and to   *2Ki 25:24*
their
s. unto the Lord with a loud   *2Ch 15:14*
voice
according to this word. And   *Ezr 10:5*
they s.
Unto whom I s. in my wrath   *Ps 95:11*
that
he s. unto the Lord, and   *Ps 132:2*
vowed
So Zedekiah the king s.   *Jer 38:16*
secretly
son of Shaphan s. unto them   *Jer 40:9*
and to
I s. unto thee, and entered   *Eze 16:8*
into a
plighted my troth (A)(B)   *Eze 16:8*
and s. by him that liveth for   *Da 12:7*
ever
he s. unto her, Whatsoever   *M'k 6:23*
thou
put himself under oath (A)   *M'k 6:23*
vowed (R)   *M'k 6:23*
The oath which he s. to our   *Lu 1:73*
father
sealed by oath (A)   *Lu 1:73*
So I s. in my wrath, They   *Heb 3:11*
shall not
vowed (N)   *Heb 3:11; 3:18*
to whom s. he that they   *Heb 3:18*
should not
swear (A)   *Heb 3:18*
by no greater, he s. by   *Heb 6:13*
himself
The Lord s. and will not   *Heb 7:21*
repent
has sworn (A)(N)   *Heb 7:21*
s. by him that liveth for ever   *Re 10:6*

SWAREST

to whom thou s. by thine   *Ex 32:13*
own self
swore (A)   *Ex 32:13;*
   Nu 11:12; De 26:15; 1Ki 1:17; Ps 89:49
swear (B)   *Ex 32:13*
promised (R)   *Ex 32:13*
the land which thou s. unto   *Nu 11:12*
their
promised (B)   *Nu 11:12; De 26:15*
sweat (R)   *Nu 11:12;*
   De 26:15; Ps 89:49
as thou s. unto our fathers, a   *De 26:15*
land
thou s. by the Lord thy God   *1Ki 1:17*
unto
swore (B)(R)   *1Ki 1:17*
thou s. unto David in thy   *Ps 89:49*
truth
pledge (B)   *Ps 89:49*

SWARM

there came a grievous s. of   *Ex 8:24*
flies
by reason of the s. of flies   *Ex 8:24*
was a s. of bees and honey in   *J'g 14:8*

SWARMS

I will send s. of flies upon thee   *Ex 8:21*
Egyptians shall be full of s. of   *Ex 8:21*
flies
that no s. of flies shall be   *Ex 8:22*
there
that the s. of flies may depart   *Ex 8:29*
from
and he removed the s. of   *Ex 8:31*
flies from

SWEAR

therefore s. unto me here by   *Ge 21:23*
God

And Abraham said, I will s. | Ge 21:24
I will make thee s. by the | Ge 24:3
Lord, the
And my master made me s., | Ge 24:37
saying
And Jacob said, S. to me this | Ge 25:33
day
And he said, S. unto me. | Ge 47:31
And he
My father made me s. saying, | Ge 50:5
Lo
according as he made thee s. | Ge 50:6
I did s. to give it to Abraham | Ex 6:8
Or if a soul s. pronouncing | Le 5:4
with
ye shall not s. by my name | Le 19:12
falsely
thou didst s. to thy fathers | Nu 11:12
(S)
or s. an oath to bind his soul | Nu 30:2
him, and shalt s. by his name | De 6:13
thou cleave, and s. by his | De 10:20
name
s. unto me by the Lord, since | Jos 2:12
I
oath which thou hast made us | Jos 2:17
s.
oath which thou hast made us | Jos 2:20
to s.
nor cause to s. by them, | Jos 23:7
neither
said unto them, S. unto me, | J'g 15:12
that
Jonathan caused David to s. | 1Sa 20:17
again
S. now unto me by the | 1Sa 24:21
Lord
S. unto me by God, that | 1Sa 30:15
thou wilt
for I s. by the Lord, if thou | 2Sa 19:7
go not
O king, s. unto thine | 1Ki 1:13
handmaid
Let king Solomon s. unto me | 1Ki 1:51
I not make thee to s. by the | 1Ki 2:42
Lord
laid upon him to cause him | 1Ki 8:31
to s.
be laid upon him to make | 2Ch 6:22
him s.
who had made him s. by | 2Ch 36:13
God
to s. that they should do | Ezr 10:5
according
and made them s. by God, | Ne 13:25
saying
In that day shall he s. saying, I | Isa 3:7
and s. to the Lord of hosts; | Isa 19:18
one
shall bow, every tongue shall | Isa 45:23
s.
which s. by the name of the | Isa 48:1
Lord
earth shall s. by the God of | Isa 65:16
truth
And thou shalt s., The Lord | Jer 4:2
liveth
Lord liveth; surely they s. | Jer 5:2
falsely
commit adultery, and s. falsely | Jer 7:9
to s. by my name, The Lord | Jer 12:16
liveth
taught my people to s. by | Jer 12:16
Baal
I s. by myself, saith the Lord, | Jer 22:5
that
thou didst s. to their fathers | Jer 33:22
to give
Beth-aven, nor s. The Lord | Ho 4:15
liveth
They that s. by the sin of | Am 8:14
Samaria
worship and that s. by the | Zep 1:5
Lord
and that s. by Malcham | Zep 1:5
S. not at all; neither by | M't 5:34
heaven
Neither shalt thou s. by thy | M't 5:36
head
Whosoever shall s. by the | M't 23:16
temple
shall s. by the gold of the | M't 23:16
temple
Whosoever shall s. by the | M't 23:18
altar, it
therefore shall s. by the altar | M't 23:20
And whoso shall s. by the | M't 23:21
temple
And he that shall s. by | M't 23:22
heaven

to s. by (A) | M't 26:63
Then began he to curse and | M't 26:74
to s.
But he began to curse and | M'k 14:71
to s.
because he could s. by no | Heb 6:13
greater
For men verily s. by the | Heb 6:16
greater
all things, my brethren, s. not | Jas 5:12

SWEARERS

and against false s. and | Mal 3:5
against

SWEARETH

lieth concerning it, and s. | Le 6:3
falsely
He that s. to his own hurt, and | Ps 15:4
one that s. by him shall glory | Ps 63:11
he that s. as he that feareth an | Ec 9:2
he that s. in the earth shall | Isa 65:16
swear
every one that s. shall be cut | Zec 5:3
off as
of him that s. falsely by my | Zec 5:4
name
whosoever s. by the gift | M't 23:18
that is
s. by it, and by all things | M't 23:20
thereon
s. by it, and by him that | M't 23:21
dwelleth
by heaven, s. by the throne | M't 23:22
of God

SWEARING

soul sin, and hear the voice of | Le 5:1
s.
sworn to testify (A) | Le 5:1
voice of adjuration (E) | Le 5:1
public adjuration (R) | Le 5:1
because of s. the land | Jer 23:10
mourneth
the curse of God (A)(B)(R) | Jer 23:10
By s. and lying, and killing | Ho 4:2
s. falsely in making a | Ho 10:4
covenant
false oaths (B) | Ho 10:4
empty oaths (R) | Ho 10:4

SWEAT

In the s. of thy face shalt thou | Ge 3:19
eat
with any thing that causeth | Eze 44:18
s.
his s. was as it were great | Lu 22:44
drops of

SWEEP

shall s. them away (A)(E)(R) | Pr 21:7
and I will s. it with the | Isa 14:23
besom of
hail shall s. away the refuge | Isa 28:17
of lies
light a candle, and s. the | Lu 15:8
house

SWEEPING

is like a s. rain that leaveth no | Pr 28:3
like a cloudburst (B) | Pr 28:3
is a beating rain (R) | Pr 28:3

SWEET

And the Lord smelled a s. | Ge 8:21
savour
pleasing (A)(B) | Ge 8:21
pleasing odor (R) | Ge 8:21;
29:18, 25, 41; Le 1:9; 2:2, 9, 12; 3:5, 16;
4:31; 6:15, 21, 28; 17:6; 23:13, 18;
26:31; Nu 15:3, 7, 10, 14, 24; 18:17
waters, the waters were made | Ex 15:25
enjoyable (B) | Ex 15:25
anointing oil, and for s. | Ex 25:6
incense
perfumed (B) | Ex 25:6;
30:7; 31:11; 35:15, 28; 39:38
incense (R) | Ex 25:6;
30:7; 31:11; 35:8, 15, 28; 37:29; 39:38;
30:27; Le 4:7; Nu 4:16
it is a s. savour, an offering | Ex 29:18
made

an acceptable odor (B) | Ex 29:18
for a s. savour before the | Ex 29:25
Lord
acceptable fragrance (B) | Ex 29:25;
29:41
for a s. savour, an offering | Ex 29:41
made
burn thereon s. incense every | Ex 30:7
and of s. cinnamon half so | Ex 30:23
much
fragrant cinnamon (B) | Ex 30:23;
37:29; 40:27; Le 16:12; Nu 4:16;
2Ch 2:4
of s. calamus two hundred | Ex 30:23
and fifty
Take unto thee s. spices, | Ex 30:34
stacte
s. spices with pure | Ex 30:34
frankincense
and s. incense for the holy | Ex 31:11
place
anointing oil for the s. | Ex 35:8
incense
anointing oil, and the s. | Ex 35:15
incense
anointing oil, and for the s. | Ex 35:28
incense
and the pure incense of s. | Ex 37:29
spices
anointing oil, and the s. | Ex 39:38
And he burnt s. incense | Ex 40:27
thereon
of a s. savour unto the Lord | Le 1:9;
1:13, 17
pleasing fragrance (B) | Le 1:9;
2:9, 12; 3:5; 17:6; 23:13, 18; Nu 15:3, 7,
10, 14, 24; 18:17; 28:2, 6, 8, 13, 24 27:
9:2, 6, 8, 13, 36
by fire, of a s. savour to the | Le 2:2
Lord
agreeable fragrance (B) | Le 2:2;
3:16; 4:31; 6:15, 21; 8:28
by fire, of a s. savour unto | Le 2:9
the Lord
burnt on the altar for a s. | Le 2:12
savour
by fire, of a s. savour unto | Le 3:5
the Lord
made by fire for a s. savour | Le 3:16
the horns of the altar of s. | Le 4:7
incense
for a s. savour unto the Lord | Le 4:31
it upon the altar for a s. | Le 6:15
savour
offer for a s. savour unto the | Le 6:21
Lord
a burnt sacrifice for a s. | Le 8:21
savour
were consecrations for a s. | Le 8:28
savour
his hands full of s. incense | Le 16:12
beaten
fat for a s. savour unto the | Le 17:6
Lord.
fire unto the Lord for a s. | Le 23:13
savour
by fire, of s. savour unto the | Le 23:18
Lord
smell the savour of your s. | Le 26:31
odours
pleasant odors (B) | Le 26:31
for the light, and the s. | Nu 4:16
incense
to make a s. savour unto the | Nu 15:3
Lord
wine, for a s. savour unto the | Nu 15:7
Lord
fire, of a s. savour unto the | Nu 15:10;
15:13
by fire, of a s. savour unto | Nu 15:14
the Lord
for a s. savour unto the Lord | Nu 15:24
fire, for a s. savour unto the | Nu 18:17
Lord
by fire, for a s. savour unto | Nu 28:2
me
in mount Sinai for a s. savour | Nu 28:6
by fire, of a s. savour unto the | Nu 28:8
Lord
for a burnt offering of a s. | Nu 28:13
savour
fire, of a s. savour unto the | Nu 28:24
Lord
for a s. savour unto the | Nu 28:27;
29:2
for a s. savour, a sacrifice | Nu 29:6
made by
unto the Lord for a s. savour | Nu 29:8

fire, of a s. savour unto the | Nu 29:13;
Lord | 29:36
and the s. psalmist of Israel | 2Sa 23:1
and to burn before him s. | 2Ch 2:4
incense
burnt sacrifices and s. | 2Ch 13:11
incense
in the bed filled with s. | 2Ch 16:14
odours
s. savours unto the God of | Ezr 6:10
heaven
pleasing sacrifices (A)(R) | Ezr 6:10
well-pleasing (B) | Ezr 6:10
way, eat the fat, and drink the | Ne 8:10
s.
and six months with s. odours | Es 2:12
wickedness be s. in his | Job 20:12
mouth
The clods of the valley shall | Job 21:33
be s.
bind the s. influences of | Job 38:31
Pleiades
the chains of Pleiades | Job 38:31
(A)(R)
bonds of Pleiades (B) | Job 38:31
We took s. counsel together | Ps 55:14
My meditation of him shall | Ps 104:34
be s.
pleasing (R) | Ps 104:34
How s. are thy words unto | Ps 119:103
my
hear my words: for they are | Ps 141:6
s.
lie down, and thy sleep shall | Pr 3:24
be s.
Stolen waters are s. and bread | Pr 9:17
desire accomplished is s. to | Pr 13:19
as an honeycomb, s. to the | Pr 16:24
soul
Bread of deceit is s. to a | Pr 20:17
man, but
vomit up, and lose thy s. | Pr 23:8
words
compliments (B) | Pr 23:8
the honeycomb, which is s. to | Pr 24:13
thy
hungry soul every bitter thing | Pr 27:7
is s.
The sleep of a labouring man | Ec 5:12
is s.
Truly the light is s. and a | Ec 11:7
pleasant
and his fruit was s. to my taste | Ca 2:3
s. is thy voice, and thy | Ca 2:14
countenance
fingers with s. smelling myrrh | Ca 5:5
as a bed of spices, as s. | Ca 5:13
flowers
lilies, dropping s. smelling | Ca 5:13
myrrh
His mouth is most s.: yea, he | Ca 5:16
is
instead of s. smell shall be | Isa 3:24
stink
put bitter for s. and s. for | Isa 5:20
bitter
make s. melody, sing many | Isa 23:16
songs
hast bought me no s. cane | Isa 43:24
with money
their own blood, as with s. | Isa 49:26
wine
the s. cane from a far country | Jer 6:20
nor your sacrifices s. unto me | Jer 6:20
and my sleep was s. unto me | Jer 31:26
offer s. savour to all their | Eze 6:13
idols
set it before them for a s. | Eze 16:19
savour
there also they made their s. | Eze 20:28
savour
soothing odors (R) | Eze 20:28
will accept you with your s. | Eze 20:41
savour
pleasant (B) | Eze 20:41
an oblation and s. odours | Da 2:46
unto him
soothing odors (B) | Da 2:46
the mountains shall drop s. | Am 9:13
wine
and s. wine, but shalt not | Mic 6:15
drink
and Salome, had bought s. | M'k 16:1
spices
aromatics (B) | M'k 16:1
aromatic oils (N) | M'k 16:1
are unto God a s. savour of | 2Co 2:15
Christ
Christ's fragrance (B) | 2Co 2:15

scent of Christ (P) | 2Co 2:15
the aroma of Christ (R) | 2Co 2:15
an odour of a s. smell, a | Ph'p 4:18
sacrifice
fragrant perfume (B) | Ph'p 4:18
fragrant offering (N)(R) | Ph'p 4:18
lovely fragrance (P) | Ph'p 4:18
same place s. water and bitter | Jas 3:11
it shall be in thy mouth s. as | Re 10:9
honey
and it was in my mouth s. as | Re 10:10
honey

SWEETER

What is s. than honey? and | J'g 14:18
s. than honey and the | Ps 19:10
honeycomb
yea, s. than honey to my | Ps 119:103
mouth

SWEETLY

the worm shall feed s. on | Job 24:20
him
that goeth down s. causing the | Ca 7:9

SWEETNESS

Should I forsake my s. and | J'g 9:11
my
and out of the strong came | J'g 14:14
forth s.
s. of the lips increaseth | Pr 16:21
learning
winsome speech increases | Pr 16:21
learning (A)
pleasant speech increases | Pr 16:21
persuasiveness (B)
so doth the s. of a man's | Pr 27:9
friend by
was in my mouth as honey for | Eze 3:3
s.

SWEETSMELLING

a sacrifice to God for a s. | Eph 5:2
savour
sweet fragrance (A) | Eph 5:2
fragrant offering (B) | Eph 5:2
fragrant odor (R) | Eph 5:2

SWELL

thigh to rot, and thy belly to | Nu 5:21
s.
to make thy belly to s. and | Nu 5:22
thy
and her belly shall s. and her | Nu 5:27
thigh
neither did thy foot s. these | De 8:4
forty
s. with pride (B) | 2Co 12:7

SWELLED

waxed not old, and their feet | Ne 9:21
s. not

SWELLING

swelling (S) | Le 13:2;
| 13:10, 19, 28, 43; 14:56
the mountains shake with the | Ps 46:3
s.
s. out in a high wall, whose | Isa 30:13
wall, bulging out (A)(B)(R) | Isa 30:13
wilt thou do in the s. of | Jer 12:5
Jordan
jungle of the Jordan (B)(R) | Jer 12:5;
| 49:19; 50:44
up like a lion from the s. of | Jer 49:19;
Jordan | 50:44
speak great s. words of vanity | 2Pe 2:18
mouth speaketh great s. words | Jude 16

SWELLINGS

backbitings, whisperings, s. | 2Co 12:20

SWEPT

The river of Kishon s. them | J'g 5:21
away
s. away by his wind (B) | Job 15:30
Why are thy valiant men s. | Jer 46:15
away
broken and s. away | Da 11:22
(A)(B)(P)

findeth it empty, s. and | M't 12:44
garnished
he findeth it s. and garnished | Lu 11:25
s. off their feet (N) | Ac 8:9

SWERVE

not s. from testimonies | Ps 119:157
(A)(E)(R)

SWERVED

never s. aside (B) | Job 23:11
From which some having s. | 1Ti 1:6
have

SWIFT

of the earth, as s. as the | De 28:49
eagle flieth
were as s. as the roses upon | 1Ch 12:8
are passed away as the s. | Job 9:26
ships
He is s. as the waters; their | Job 24:18
s. serpent (A)(E)(R) | Job 26:13;
| Isa 27:1
feet be s. in running to | Ps 6:18
mischief
that the race is not to the s. | Ec 9:11
nor
Go, ye s. messengers, to a | Isa 18:2
nation
the Lord rideth upon a s. | Isa 19:1
cloud
flee; and, We will ride upon | Isa 30:16
the s.
shall they that pursue you be | Isa 30:16
s.
upon mules, and upon s. | Isa 66:20
beasts
thou art a s. dromedary | Jer 2:23
traversing
Let not the s. flee away, nor | Jer 46:6
the flight shall perish from | Am 2:14
the s.
and he that is s. of foot shall | Am 2:15
not
bind the chariot to the s. | Mic 1:13
beast
I will be a s. witness against | Mal 3:5
Their feet are s. to shed blood | Ro 3:15
let every man be s. to hear, | Jas 1:19
slow
upon themselves s. destruction | 2Pe 2:1

SWIFTER

they were s. than eagles, they | 2Sa 1:23
My days are s. than a weaver's | Job 7:6
Now my days are s. than a | Job 9:25
post
his horses are s. than eagles | Jer 4:13
persecutors are s. than the | La 4:19
eagles
horses are s. than the | Hab 1:8
leopards

SWIFTLY

earth: his word runneth very | Ps 147:15
s.
they shall come with speed s. | Isa 5:26
and s. executing justice (S) | Isa 16:5
being caused to fly s. touched | Da 9:21
me
s. and speedily will I return | Joe 3:4
your

SWIM

it in thither; and the iron did | 2Ki 6:6
s.
all the night make I my bed to | Ps 6:6
s.
spreadeth forth his hands to | Isa 25:11
s.
waters were risen, waters to | Eze 47:5
s. in
lest any of them should s. out | Ac 27:42
they which could s. should | Ac 27:43
cast

SWIMMEST

thy blood the land wherein | Eze 32:6
thou s.

SWIMMETH

that s. spreadeth forth his | Isa 25:11
hands

SWINDLER

a swindler (A)(N)(P)   1Co 5:11

SWINDLERS

grabbers and s. (N)   1Co 5:10; 6:10
or swindlers (N)(P)   1Co 6:10

SWINE

the s. though he divide the   Le 11:7
hoof
the s. because it divideth the   De 14:8
hoof
neither cast ye pearls before   M't 7:6
s.
them an herd of many s.   M't 8:30
feeding
us to go away into the herd   M't 8:31
of s.
out, they went into the herd   M't 8:32
of s.
whole herd of s. ran violently   M't 8:32
down
a great herd of s. feeding   M'k 5:11
Send us into the s. that we   M'k 5:12
may
went out, and entered into   M'k 5:13
the s.
they that fed the s. fled, and   M'k 5:14
told
the devil, and also   M'k 5:16
concerning the s.
an herd of many s. feeding on   Lu 8:32
of the man, and entered into   Lu 8:33
the s.
he sent him into his fields to   Lu 15:15
feed s.
with the husks that the s. did   Lu 15:16
eat

SWINE'S

As a jewel of gold in a s.   Pr 11:22
snout, so
which eat s. flesh, and broth   Isa 65:4
oblation, as if he offered s.   Isa 66:3
blood
tree in the midst, eating s.   Isa 66:17
flesh

SWINGETH

his hand s. a stroke (S)   De 19:5

SWOLLEN

red, s. with weeping   Job 16:16
(A)(B)(E)(R)
looked when he should have s.   Ac 28:6

SWOON

the sucklings s. in the streets   La 2:11
faint (A)(R)   La 2:11; 2:12

SWOONED

when they s. as the wounded   La 2:12

SWORD

placed cherubims, and flaming   Ge 3:24
s.
each man his s. and came on   Ge 34:25
the city
put a s. in their hands to slay   Ex 5:21
us
put every man his s. by his   Ex 32:27
side
nor the s. go through your   Le 26:6
land
I will bring a s. upon you   Le 26:25;
     Eze 5:17; 6:3; 14:17; 29:8; 33:2
I will draw out a s. after you   Le 26:33
they shall fall as it were   Le 26:37
before a s.
angel's s. drawn in his hand   Nu 22:23;
                                      22:31
I would there were a s. in   Nu 22:29
mine hand
the s. without, and terror   De 32:25
within
and who is the s. of thy   De 33:29
excellency
stood with s. drawn in his   Jos 5:13
hand
not with thy s. nor with thy   Jos 24:12
bow

this is nothing save the s. of   J'g 7:14
Gideon
s. of the Lord, and of Gideon   J'g 7:18;
                                      7:20
Lord set every man's s.   J'g 7:22;
against his fellow   1Sa 14:20
there fell 120,000 men that   J'g 8:10
drew s.
youth drew not his s. for he   J'g 8:20
feared
he said, Draw thy s. and slay   J'g 9:54
me
four hundred thousand that   J'g 20:2;
drew s.   20:27
twenty six thousand men that   J'g 20:15
drew s.
eighteen thousand men; all   J'g 20:25
drew the s.
Israel destroyed 25,100 men   J'g 20:35
that drew s.
all that fell were 25,000 that   J'g 20:46
drew the s.
neither s. nor spear was   1Sa 13:22
found
as thy s. made women   1Sa 15:33
childless, so
David girded his s. on   1Sa 17:39;
armour   25:13
there was no s. in the hand   1Sa 17:50
of David
David ran and took his s.   1Sa 17:51
and slew him
even to his s. and bow and   1Sa 18:4
girdle
is there not here a spear or s.   1Sa 21:8
the s. of Goliath is here   1Sa 21:9
wrapped in a cloth
and he gave him the s. of   1Sa 22:10
Goliath
thou hast given him bread,   1Sa 22:13
and a s.
David said, Gird on every   1Sa 25:13
man his s. and they girded
on every man his s.
draw thy s. and thrust me   1Sa 31:4
through therewith; Saul took
a s. and fell upon it
armour-bearer fell also upon   1Sa 31:5
his s. and died
the s. of Saul returned not   2Sa 1:22
empty
thrust his s. in his fellow's   2Sa 2:16
side
Abner said, Shall the s.   2Sa 2:26
devour for ever
not fail one that falleth on   2Sa 3:29
the s.
s. devoureth one as well as   2Sa 11:25
another
s. shall never depart from   2Sa 12:10
thy house
the wood devoured more than   2Sa 18:8
the s.
Amasa took no heed to s.   2Sa 20:10
in his hand
and his hand clave unto   2Sa 23:10
the s.
in Israel 800,000 men that   2Sa 24:9
drew the s.
bring me a s. and they   1Ki 3:24
brought a s.
him that escapeth the s. of   1Ki 19:17
Hazael
men able to bear buckler and   1Ch 5:18
s.
draw thy s. and thrust me   1Ch 10:4
through therewith; so Saul took
a s. and fell upon it
his armour-bearer fell   1Ch 10:5
likewise on the s.
an hundred thousand men   1Ch 21:5
that drew s. and Judah was
470,000 that drew s.
while the s. of thine enemies   1Ch 21:12
overtake, or else three days
the s. of the Lord
the angel having a s. drawn   1Ch 21:16
in his hand
and he put up his s. again   1Ch 21:27
into the sheath
he was afraid, because of   1Ch 21:30
the s. of the angel
as when s. or judgment   2Ch 20:9
cometh
we and our kings are delivered   Ezr 9:7
to s.
every one had s. girded by his   Ne 4:18
side
Jews smote their enemies with   Es 9:5
the s.

in war to deliver from power   Job 5:20
of the s.
and he is waited for of the   Job 15:22
s.
be ye afraid of the s. for   Job 19:29
wrath bringeth the punishment
of the s.
the glittering s. cometh out   Job 20:25
of his gall
if children be multiplied,   Job 27:14
it is for the s.
can make his s. to approach   Job 40:19
unto him
s. of him that layeth at him   Job 41:26
cannot
if he turn not he will whet his   Ps 7:12
s.
deliver from wicked, which is   Ps 17:13
thy s.
the wicked have drawn out   Ps 37:14
the s.
their s. shall enter into their   Ps 37:15
own heart
gird thy s. on thy thigh, with   Ps 45:3
thy glory
and their tongue a sharp s.   Ps 57:4
who whet their tongue like a s.   Ps 64:3
there brake he the shield and   Ps 76:3
the s.
he gave his people over unto   Ps 78:62
the s.
and a two-edged s. in their   Ps 149:6
hand
her end is sharp as a two-edged   Pr 5:4
s.
that speaketh like the   Pr 12:18
piercings of a s.
a man that beareth false   Pr 25:18
witness is a s.
every man hath s. upon his   Ca 3:8
thigh
nation not lift up s. against   Isa 2:4
nation
s. not of a mean man shall   Isa 31:8
devour him
the s. of the Lord is filled   Isa 34:6
with blood
he gave them as the dust to   Isa 41:2
his s.
he hath made my mouth like   Isa 49:2
a sharp s.
the famine and the s. are   Isa 51:19
come to thee
therefore will I number you   Isa 65:12
to the s.
by his s. will Lord plead   Isa 66:16
with all flesh
your own s. devoured your   Jer 2:30
prophets
whereas the s. reacheth unto   Jer 4:10
the soul
neither shall we see s. nor   Jer 5:12;
famine   14:13
for the s. of the enemy is on   Jer 6:25
every side
I will send a s. after them till   Jer 9:16;
I have consumed them   24:10; 25:27;
                            29:17; 49:37
for the s. of the Lord shall   Jer 12:12
devour
prophets say, Ye shall not see   Jer 14:13
the s.
s. and famine shall not be in   Jer 14:15
this land
be cast in streets because of   Jer 14:16
the s.
such as are for the s. to the s.   Jer 15:2;
                                      43:11
I will appoint the s. to slay   Jer 15:3
residue of them will I deliver   Jer 15:9
to the s.
pour out their blood by force   Jer 18:21
of s.
they shall be mad because of   Jer 25:16
the s.
for I will call for a s.   Jer 25:29;
                                   Eze 38:21
he will give them that are   Jer 25:31
wicked to the s.
the people left of the s. found   Jer 31:2
grace
the city is given because of   Jer 32:24
the s.
I proclaim a liberty for you   Jer 34:17
to the s.
the s. ye feared shall   Jer 42:16
overtake you then
yet a small number which   Jer 44:28
escape the s.

the *s.* shall devour and be   *Jer 46:10;* satiate   *46:14*
O thou *s.* of the Lord, how   *Jer 47:6* long
O madmen, the *s.* shall pursue *Jer 48:2* thee
cursed that keepeth back his   *Jer 48:10* *s.* from blood
for fear of the oppressing *s.*   *Jer 50:16* they shall
a *s.* is on the Chaldeans,   *Jer 50:35* saith the Lord
s. is on liars, a *s.* is on   *Jer 50:36* mighty men
s. is on horses, a *s.* on   *Jer 50:37* treasures
ye that have escaped the *s.*   *Jer 51:50* go away
we gat bread by peril because *La 5:9* of *s.*
I will draw out a *s.* after   *Eze 5:2;* them   *5:12*
smite about it with a *s.* (S)   *Eze 5:2*
and I will bring the *s.* upon *Eze 5:17;* thee   *6:3*
ye may have some that shall   *Eze 6:8* escape the *s.*
the *s.* is without, the   *Eze 7:15* pestilence within
have feared the *s.*, I will bring *Eze 11:8* a *s.*
if I bring a *s.* and say, S.   *Eze 14:17* go through
I send my four sore   *Eze 14:21* judgments, the *s.*
prophesy a *s.*, a *s.* is   *Eze 21:9;* sharpened   *21:11*
terrors, by reason of the *s.*   *Eze 21:12* on my people
what if the *s.* contemn even *Eze 21:13* the rod
let their *s.* be doubled, the *s. Eze 21:14* of great men slain, it is the *s.* of great men
set the point of the *s.*   *Eze 21:15* against the gates
appoint two ways, that the   *Eze 21:19* *s.* may come
appoint a way, that *s.* may   *Eze 21:20* come
the *s.* the *s.* is drawn for the *Eze 21:28* slaughter
and the *s.* shall come upon   *Eze 30:4* Egypt
to make it strong to hold   *Eze 30:21* the *s.*
cause the *s.* to fall out of his *Eze 30:22* hand
s. of the king of Babylon   *Eze 32:11* shall come
if he seeth the *s.* come on the *Eze 33:3* land
if the *s.* come and take him   *Eze 33:4;* away   *33:6*
if the watchmen see the *s.*   *Eze 33:6* come, if the *s.* come and take any person
ye stand upon your *s.* and ye *Eze 33:26* defile
thou hast shed blood by the   *Eze 35:5* force of the *s.*
and I will break the bow and *Ho 2:18* the *s.*
and the *s.* shall abide on   *Ho 11:6* his cities
thence will I command the *s.*   *Am 9:4* nation not lift up *s.* against   *Mic 4:3* nation
thou deliverest, will I give up *Mic 6:14* to the *s.*
the *s.* shall devour the young *Na 2:13* lions
the horsemen lifteth up both   *Na 3:3* the bright *s.*
there the *s.* shall cut thee off   *Na 3:15* made thee as *s.* of a mighty *Zec 9:13* man
the *s.* shall be upon his arm *Zec 11:17*
awake, O *s.* against my   *Zec 13:7* shepherd
I came not to send peace,   *M't 10:34* but a *s.*
one of them drew his *s.* and *M't 26:51;* struck a servant   *M'k 14:47;* put up again thy *s.*   *M't 26:52;*   *Joh 18:11*
a *s.* shall pierce through   *Lu 2:35* own soul
he that hath no *s.* let him   *Lu 22:36* buy one

he drew his *s.* and would   *Ac 16:27* have killed
s. separate us from love of   *Ro 8:35* Christ
for he beareth not the *s.* in   *Ro 13:4* vain
s. of spirit which is the word *Eph 6:17* of God
and sharper than any   *Heb 4:12* two-edged *s.*
out of his mouth went a   *Re 1:16* two-edged *s.*
which hath the sharp *s.* with   *Re 2:12* two edges
and there was given to him a   *Re 6:4* great *s.*
out of his mouth goeth a   *Re 19:15;* sharp *s.*   *19:21*

BY THE SWORD

by the *s.* thou shalt live   *Ge 27:40*
shall fall before you *by the s.*   *Le 26:7;*   *26:8*
because they were fallen *by*   *2Sa 1:12* the *s.*
our fathers have fallen *by the 2Ch 29:9 s.*
and his life from perishing *Job 33:18 by the s.*
they obey not, they perish   *Job 36:12* *by the s.*
they got not the land *by their Ps 43:3 s.*
their priests fell *by the s.*   *Ps 78:64*
their young men shall die *by Jer 11:22; the s.*   *18:21; La 2:21*
but I will consume them *by Jer 14:12 the s.*
by s. and famine shall those *Jer 14:15* prophets be consumed
shall be consumed *by the s.*   *Jer 16:4;*   *44:12, 18, 27*
I will cause them to fall *by the Jer 19:7 s.*
abideth, shall die *by the s.*   *Jer 21:9;*   *38:2; 42:17, 22*
why will ye die *by the s.* by   *Jer 27:13* famine
this city shall be delivered *by Jer 32:36 the s.*
houses which are thrown   *Jer 33:4* down *by the s.*
O Zedekiah, thou shalt not   *Jer 34:4* die *by the s.*
as I have punished Jerusalem *Jer 44:13 by the s.*
daughters shall be slain *by*   *Eze 26:6* the *s.*
he shall slay thy people *by*   *Eze 26:11* the *s.*
wounded shall be judged in   *Eze 28:23* her *by the s.*
lie with them that be slain   *Eze 31:18;* *by the s.*   *32:20-22, 25, 30; 33:27*
trespassed, so they fell *by*   *Eze 39:23* the *s.*
I will not save them by bow   *Ho 1:7* nor *by s.*
Jeroboam shall die *by the s.*   *Am 7:11*
sinners of my people shall die *Am 9:10 by the s.*
every one *by the s.* of his   *Hag 2:22* brother
had the wound *by a s.* and   *Re 13:14* did live

FROM THE SWORD

delivered me *from the s.* of   *Ex 18:4* Pharaoh
they shall flee as fleeing *from Le 26:36 a s.*
him that escapeth *from the s.* *1Ki 19:17* of Jehu
that escaped *from the s.*   *2Ch 36:20* carried he
but he saveth the poor *from*   *Job 5:15* the *s.*
neither turneth he back *from Job 39:22 the s.*
deliver my soul *from the s.*   *Ps 22:20*
who delivereth David *from*   *Ps 144:10* the *s.*
for they fled *from the drawn Isa 21:15 s.*
but he shall flee *from the s.*   *Isa 31:8*
such as left *from the s.* from   *Jer 21:7* famine
let us go *from the oppressing Jer 46:16 s.*

I'll leave a few men of them   *Eze 12:16* *from the s.*
the land that is brought   *Eze 38:8* back *from the s.*

MY SWORD

I took from Amorite with   *Ge 48:22* *my s.*
I will draw *my s.* my hand   *Ex 15:9* destroy
and if I whet *my* glittering *s. De 32:41*
and *my s.* shall devour flesh *De 32:42*
neither brought *my s.* nor   *1Sa 21:8* weapons
neither shall *my s.* save me   *Ps 44:6*
my s. shall be bathed in   *Isa 34:5* heaven
I will draw *my s.* out of his   *Eze 21:3* sheath
therefore *my s.* shall go out   *Eze 21:4* of his sheath
Lord have drawn *my s.* out   *Eze 21:5* of his sheath
I have put *my s.* in his   *Eze 30:24;* hand   *30:25*
be afraid, when I shall   *Eze 32:10* brandish *my s.*
Ethiopians shall be slain by   *Zep 2:12* *my s.*

WITH THE SWORD

daughters as captives taken   *Ge 31:26* *with the s.*
lest he fall on us *with the s.*   *Ex 5:3*
I will kill you *with the s.*   *Ex 22:24*
whoso toucheth one slain   *Nu 19:16* *with the s.*
lest I come out against thee   *Nu 20:18* *with the s.*
Balaam also they slew *with*   *Nu 31:8* the *s.*
Lord shall smite thee *with*   *De 28:22* the *s.*
whom Israel slew *with the s.* *Jos 10:11;*   *13:22*
he smote the king of Hazor *Jos 11:10 with the s.*
thou comest to me *with a s.*   *1Sa 17:45*
the Lord saveth not *with s.*   *1Sa 17:47* and spear
thou hast killed Uriah   *2Sa 12:9* *with the s.*
with a s. fastened upon his   *2Sa 20:8* loins
shbi-benob being girded   *2Sa 21:16* *with a s.*
not slay his servant *with*   *1Ki 1:51* the *s.*
I will not put thee to death   *1Ki 2:8* *with the s.*
better than he, and slew them *1Ki 2:32 with the s.*
had slain all the prophets   *1Ki 19:1* *with the s.*
and slain thy prophets *with 1Ki 19:10;* the *s.*   *19:14*
young men slay *with the s.*   *2Ki 8:12*
have Athaliah forth, and   *2Ki 11:15;* him that followeth her,   *2Ch 23:14* kill *with the s.*
they slew Athaliah *with the 2Ki 11:20;* *s.*   *2Ch 23:21*
smote Sennacherib king of   *2Ki 19:37;* Assyria *with the s. 2Ch 32:21; Isa 37:38*
and slew all his brethren *with 2Ch 21:4* the *s.*
who slew their young men   *2Ch 36:17*
as *with a s.* in my bones   *Ps 42:10* enemies reproach
rebel, ye shall be devoured   *Isa 1:20* *with the s.*
that are slain, thrust through *Isa 14:19 with a s.*
thy slain men are not slain   *Isa 22:2* *with the s.*
Lord *with his* strong *s.* shall   *Isa 27:1* punish
shall impoverish thy cities   *Jer 5:17* *with the s.*
then behold the slain *with*   *Jer 14:18* the *s.*
and he shall slay Judah *with Jer 20:4* the *s.*
who slew Urijah *with the s. Jer 26:23* and cast
that nation will I punish *with Jer 27:8* the *s.*

I will persecute them *with the s.*	Jer 29:18	
smote Gedaliah *with the s.* and slew him	Jer 41:2	
they that be slain *with the s.* are better	La 4:9	
he that is in field shall die *with the s.*	Eze 7:15	
the Assyrians slew her *with the s.*	Eze 23:10	
shall slay the daughters of Tyrus *with the s.*	Eze 26:8	
they went down to hell with *them that be slain with the s.*	Eze 31:17; 32:28, 32; 35:8	
he did pursue his brother *with the s.*	Am 1:11	
your young men have I slain *with the s.*	Am 4:10	
rise against house of Jeroboam *with the s.*	Am 7:9	
I will slay the last of them *with the s.*	Am 9:1	
waste the land of Assyria *with the s.*	Mic 5:6	
that take the sword shall perish *with the s.*	M't 26:52	
Lord, shall we smite *with the s.*	Lu 22:49	
Herod killed James *with the s.*	Ac 12:2	
were tempted, were slain *with the s.*	Heb 11:37	
I will fight against them *with the s.*	Re 2:16	
power to kill *with s.* and with hunger	Re 6:8	
that killeth *with the s.* must be killed *with the s.*	Re 13:10	
the remnant were slain *with the s.*	Re 19:21	

SWORDS

Lest the Hebrews make them *s.*	1Sa 13:19
cut themselves with *s.* (S)	1Ki 18:28
seven hundred men that drew *s.*	2Ki 3:26
after their families with their *s.*	Ne 4:13
than oil, yet were they drawn *s.*	Ps 55:21
their mouths: *s.* are in their lips	Ps 59:7
a generation, whose teeth are as *s.*	Pr 30:14
all hold *s.* being expert in war	Ca 3:8
shall beat their *s.* into plowshares	Isa 2:4
For they fled from the *s.*	Isa 21:15
thrust thee through with their *s.*	Eze 16:40
and dispatch them with their *s.*	Eze 23:47
draw their *s.* against the beauty of	Eze 28:7
shall draw their *s.* against Egypt	Eze 30:11
By the *s.* of the mighty will I cause	Eze 32:12
have laid their *s.* under their heads	Eze 32:27
and shields, all of them handling *s.*	Eze 38:4
Beat your plowshares into *s.*	Joe 3:10
shall beat their *s.* into plowshares	Mic 4:3
with him a great multitude with *s.*	M't 26:47
come out as against a thief with *s.*	M't 26:55
with him a great multitude, with *s.*	M'r 14:43
come out, as against a thief, with *s.*	M'r 14:48
Lord, behold, here are two *s.*	Lu 22:38
come out, as against a thief, with *s.*	Lu 22:52

SWORE

you *s.* (A)	Ex 32:13; Nu 11:12; De 26:15; 1Ki 1:17; Ps 89:49

SWORN

By myself have I *s.*, saith the Lord	Ge 22:16

straitly *s.* the children of Israel	Ex 13:19
had demanded an oath (B)	Ex 13:19
Lord hath *s.* that the	Ex 17:16
s. to testify (A)	Le 5:1
about which he hath *s.* falsely	Le 6:5
the Lord had *s.* (A)	De 2:14
keep the oath which he hath *s.*	De 7:8
thee, as he hath *s.* unto thy fathers	De 13:17
as he hath *s.* unto thy fathers	De 19:8
himself, as he hath *s.* unto thee	De 28:9
and as he hath *s.* unto thy fathers	De 29:13
Lord hath *s.* unto their fathers to	De 31:7
the princes had *s.* unto them	Jos 9:18
We have *s.* unto them by the Lord	Jos 9:19
and as the Lord had *s.* unto them	J'g 2:15
the men of Israel had *s.* in Mizpeh	J'g 21:1
seeing we have *s.* by the Lord that	J'g 21:7
for the children of Israel have *s.*	J'g 21:18
I have *s.* unto the house of Eli	1Sa 3:14
we have *s.* both of us in the name of	1Sa 20:42
as the Lord hath *s.* to David, even	2Sa 3:9
children of Israel had *s.* unto them	2Sa 21:2
for they had *s.* with all their heart	2Ch 15:15
many in Judah *s.* unto him	Ne 6:18
which thou hadst *s.* to give them	Ne 9:15
unto vanity, nor *s.* deceitfully	Ps 24:4
I have *s.* unto David my servant	Ps 89:3
Once have I *s.* by my holiness that	Ps 89:35
mad against me are *s.* against me	Ps 102:8
Lord hath *s.* and will not repent	Ps 110:4
I have *s.* and I will perform it	Ps 119:106
Lord hath *s.* in truth unto David	Ps 132:11
The Lord of hosts hath *s.* saying	Isa 14:24
I have *s.* by myself, the word is	Isa 45:23
I have *s.* that the waters of Noah	Isa 54:9
so have I *s.* that I would not be	Isa 54:9
Lord hath *s.* by his right hand, and	Isa 62:8
and *s.* by them that are no gods	Jer 5:7
the oath which I have *s.* unto your	Jer 11:5
I have *s.* by my great name, saith	Jer 44:26
I have *s.*, by myself, saith the Lord	Jer 49:13
Lord of hosts hath *s.* by himself	Jer 51:14
sight, to them that have *s.* oaths	Eze 21:23
Lord God hath *s.* by his holiness	Am 4:2
The Lord God hath *s.* by himself	Am 6:8
hath *s.* by the excellency of Jacob	Am 8:7
which thou hast *s.* unto our father	Mic 7:20
God had *s.* with an oath to him	Ac 2:30
which God had *s.* to Abraham, the	Ac 7:17
As I have *s.* in my wrath, if they	Heb 4:3

SYCAMINE

ye might say unto the *s.* tree, Be	Lu 17:6
mulberry tree (A)(B)	Lu 17:6
sycamore-tree (N)	Lu 17:6
fig-tree (P)	Lu 17:6

SYCAMORE

the *s.* tree (N)	Lu 17:6

SYCHAR

city of Samaria, which is called *s.*	Joh 4:5

SYCHEM

And were carried over into *S.*	Ac 7:16
sons of Emmor the father of *S.*	Ac 7:16

SYCOMORE

as the *s.* trees that are in the vale	1Ki 10:27
s. trees that were in the low plains	1Ch 27:28
mulberry trees (B)	1Ch 27:28
cedar trees made he as the *s.* trees	2Ch 1:15; 9:27
hail, and their *s.* trees with frost	Ps 78:47
herdman, and a gatherer of *s.* fruit	Am 7:14
climbed up into a *s.* tree to see	Lu 19:4

SYCOMORES

the *s.* are cut down, but we will	Isa 9:10

SYENE

from the land of *S.* (B)(R)	Isa 49:12
from the tower of *S.* even unto	Eze 29:10
from the tower of *S.* shall they fall	Eze 30:6

SYMBOL

this shall be a *s.* (B)	Jos 4:6
making you a *s.* (B)	Eze 12:6; 12:11
a *s.* of current time (B)	Heb 9:9
s. of the reality (N)	Heb 9:24

SYMBOLIC

s. of present time (N)	Heb 9:9
a *s.* title inscribed (B)	Re 17:5

SYMBOLS

we see not our *s.* (A)(B)	Ps 74:9

SYMPATHETIC

deeply *s.* (B)	M'k 1:41
s. with one (A)(B)(R)	1Pe 3:8

SYMPATHETICALLY

deal *s.* with ignorant (P)	Heb 5:2

SYMPATHIES

deep felt *s.* (B)	Ph'p 2:1
deep *s.* (B)	1Jo 3:17

SYMPATHIZE

to *s.* with him (B)	Job 2:11
did *s.* and suffer long (A)(B)(P)	Heb 10:34

SYMPATHY

no sympathy (B)	1Sa 22:8
having *s.* with (B)	1Sa 23:21
I looked for *s.* (B)	Ps 69:20
granted favor and *s.* (B)	Da 1:9
pity, *s.*, deeply moved (A)	M't 15:32
had *s.* for (A)(R)	M'k 5:19
felt *s.* for her (B)	Lu 7:13
moved with pity, *s.* (A)(B)(N)(P)	Lu 10:33
passionate *s.* (A)(P)(R)	Ph'p 2:1
true love and *s.* (P)	1Pe 3:8

SYNAGOGUE

thence, he went into their *s.*	M't 12:9
country, he taught them in their *s.*	M't 13:54

sabbath day he entered into *M'k 1:21*
the *s.*
in their *s.* a man with an *M'k 1:23*
unclean
when they were come out of *M'k 1:29*
the *s.*
And he entered again into the *M'k 3:1*
s.
cometh one of the rulers of *M'k 5:22*
the *s.*
unto the ruler of the *s.*, Be *M'k 5:36*
not
to the house of the ruler of *M'k 5:38*
the *s.*
come, he began to teach in *M'k 6:2*
the *s.*
he went into the *s.* on the *Lu 4:16*
sabbath
eyes of all them that were in *Lu 4:20*
the *s.*
And all they in the *s.* when *Lu 4:28*
they
in the *s.* there was a man, *Lu 4:33*
which
he arose out of the *s.* and *Lu 4:38*
entered
he entered into the *s.* and *Lu 6:6*
taught
nation, and he hath built us a *Lu 7:5*
s.
and he was a ruler of the *s.* *Lu 8:41*
the ruler of the *s.* answered *Lu 8:14*
with
These things said he in the *s.* *Joh 6:59*
he should be put out of the *s.* *Joh 9:22*
lest they should be put out of *Joh 12:42*
the *s.*
I ever taught in the *s.* and *Joh 18:20*
in the
Then there arose certain of the *Ac 6:9*
s.
is called the *s.* of the Libertines *Ac 6:9*
and went into the *s.* on the *Ac 13:14*
sabbath
the rulers of the *s.* sent unto *Ac 13:15*
them
the Jews were gone out of *Ac 13:42*
the *s.*
both together into the *s.* of the *Ac 14:1*
where was a *s.* of the Jews *Ac 17:1*
thither went into the *s.* of the *Ac 17:10*
Jews
disputed he in the *s.* with the *Ac 17:17*
Jews
reasoned in the *s.* every *Ac 18:4*
sabbath
whose house joined hard to *Ac 18:7*
the *s.*
Crispus, the chief ruler of the *Ac 18:8*
s.
Sosthenes, the chief ruler of *Ac 18:17*
the *s.*
but he himself entered into *Ac 18:19*
the *s.*
he began to speak boldly in *Ac 18:26*
the *s.*
And he went into the *s.* and *Ac 19:8*
spake
and beat in every *s.* them *Ac 22:19*
I punished them oft in every *Ac 26:11*
s.
and are not, but are the *s.* of *Re 2:9*
Satan
I will make them of the *s.* of *Re 3:9*
Satan

SYNAGOGUES

have burned up all the *s.* of *Ps 74:8*
God
teaching in their *s.* and *M't 4:23*
preaching
as the hypocrites do in the *s.* *M't 6:2*
they love to pray standing in *M't 6:5*
the *s.*
teaching in their *s.* and *M't 9:35*
preaching
they will scourge you in *M't 10:17*
their *s.*
feasts, and the chief seats in *M't 23:6*
the *s.*
of them shall ye scourge in *M't 23:34*
your *s.*
he preached in their *s.* *M'k 1:39*
throughout
And the chief seats in the *s.* *M'k 12:39*
and in the *s.* ye shall be *M'k 13:9*
beaten
And he taught in their *s.* being *Lu 4:15*

he preached in the *s.* of *Lu 4:44*
Galilee
love the uppermost seats in *Lu 11:43*
the *s.*
when they bring you unto the *Lu 12:11*
s.
he was teaching in one of the *Lu 13:10*
s.
and the highest seats in the *s.* *Lu 20:46*
delivering you up to the *s.* *Lu 21:12*
and into
They shall put you out of the *Joh 16:2*
s.
him letters to Damascus to *Ac 9:2*
the *s.*
he preached Christ in the *s.* *Ac 9:20*
that
preached the word of God in *Ac 13:5*
the *s.*
being read in the *s.* every *Ac 15:21*
sabbath
neither in the *s.* nor in the *Ac 24:12*
city

SYNAGOGUE'S

came from the ruler of the *s.* *M'k 5:35*
house
one from the ruler of the *s.* *Lu 8:49*
house

SYNTYCHE

I beseech Euodias, and *Ph'p 4:2*
beseech *S.*

SYRACUSE

landing at *S.* we tarried *Ac 28:12*
there

SYRIA

and the gods of *S.* and the *J'g 10:6*
gods of
put garrisons in *S.* of *2Sa 8:6*
Damascus
Of *S.* and of Moab, and of *2Sa 8:12*
vow while I abode at Geshur *2Sa 15:8*
in *S.*
Hittites, and for the kings of *1Ki 10:29*
S.
Israel, and reigned over *S.* *1Ki 11:25*
the son of Hezion, king of *1Ki 15:18*
S. that
anoint Hazael to be king *1Ki 19:15*
over *S.*
Ben-hadad the king of *S.* *1Ki 20:1*
gathered
the king of *S.* escaped on an *1Ki 20:20*
horse
king of *S.* will come up *1Ki 20:22*
against thee
servants of the king of *S.* *1Ki 20:23*
said unto
without war between *S.* and *1Ki 22:1*
Israel
not out of the hand of the *1Ki 22:3*
king of *S.*
king of *S.* commanded his *1Ki 22:31*
thirty
captain of the host of the king *2Ki 5:1*
of *S.*
Lord had given deliverance *2Ki 5:1*
unto *S.*
the king of *S.* said, Go to, go, *2Ki 5:5*
and I
king of *S.* warred against *2Ki 6:8*
Israel
the heart of the king of *S.* *2Ki 6:11*
was sore
the bands of *S.* came no *2Ki 6:23*
more into
Ben-hadad king of *S.* *2Ki 6:24*
gathered all
uttermost part of the camp of *2Ki 7:5*
S.
Ben-hadad the king of *S.* was *2Ki 8:7*
sick
Ben-hadad king of *S.* hath sent *2Ki 8:9*
me
that thou shalt be king over *2Ki 8:13*
S.
the war against Hazael king *2Ki 8:28*
of *S.*
he fought against Hazael king *2Ki 8:29*
of *S.*
Israel, because of Hazael *2Ki 9:14*
king of *S.*
he fought with Hazael king *2Ki 9:15*
of *S.*

Then Hazael king of *S.* went *2Ki 12:17*
up, and
and sent it to Hazael king *2Ki 12:18*
of *S.*
into the hand of Hazael king *2Ki 13:3*
of *S.*
the king of *S.* oppressed them *2Ki 13:4*
the king of *S.* had *2Ki 13:7*
destroyed them
the arrow of deliverance *2Ki 13:17*
from *S.*
then hadst thou smitten *S.* *2Ki 13:19*
till thou
now thou shalt smite *S.* but *2Ki 13:19*
thrice
Hazael king of *S.* oppressed *2Ki 13:22*
Israel
So Hazael king of *S.* died: *2Ki 13:24*
and
against Judah Rezin the *2Ki 15:37*
king of *S.*
Then Rezin king of *S.* and *2Ki 16:5*
Pekah
Rezin king of *S.* recovered *2Ki 16:6*
Elath
recovered Elath to *S.* and *2Ki 16:6*
drave the
me out of the hand of the *2Ki 16:7*
king of *S.*
for the kings of *S.* by their *2Ch 1:17*
means
and sent to Ben-hadad king *2Ch 16:2*
of *S.*
thou hast relied on the king *2Ch 16:7*
of *S.*
king of *S.* escaped out of *2Ch 16:7*
thine hand
With these thou shalt push *2Ch 18:10*
S. until
the king of *S.* had *2Ch 18:30*
commanded the
from beyond the sea on his *2Ch 20:2*
side *S.*
to war against Hazael king *2Ch 22:5*
of *S.*
he fought with Hazael king *2Ch 22:6*
of *S.*
the host of *S.* came up *2Ch 24:23*
against him
him into the hand of the *2Ch 28:5*
king of *S.*
gods of the kings of *S.* help *2Ch 28:23*
them
Rezin the king of *S.* and Pekah *Isa 7:1*
S. is confederate with Ephraim *Isa 7:2*
for the fierce anger of Rezin *Isa 7:4*
with *S.*
Because *S.*, Ephraim, and *Isa 7:5*
the son
For the head of *S.* is *Isa 7:8*
Damascus, and
Damascus, and the remnant *Isa 17:3*
of *S.*
thy reproach of the *Eze 16:57*
daughters of *S.*
S. was thy merchant by *Eze 27:16*
reason of
Jacob fled into the country *Ho 12:12*
of *S.*
people of *S.* shall go into *Am 1:5*
captivity
his fame went throughout all *M't 4:24*
S.
when Cyrenius was governor of *Lu 2:2*
S.
of the Gentiles in Antioch *Ac 15:23*
and *S.*
he went through *S.* and *Ac 15:41*
Cilicia
brethren, and sailed thence *Ac 18:18*
into *S.*
as he was about to sail into *S.* *Ac 20:3*
he
sailed into *S.* and landed at *Ac 21:3*
Tyre
I came into the regions of *S.* *Ga 1:21*

SYRIACK

the Chaldeans to the king in *S.* *Da 2:4*

SYRIA-DAMASCUS

David put garrisons in *S.* *1Ch 18:6*

SYRIA-MAACHAH

and out of *S.* and out of *1Ch 19:6*
Zobah

SYRIAN

of Bethuel the S. of Padan-aram	Ge 25:20
the sister to Laban the S.	Ge 25:20
unto Laban, son of Bethuel the S.	Ge 28:5
away unawares to Laban the S.	Ge 31:20
And God came to Laban the S. in a	Ge 31:24
A S. ready to perish was my father	De 26:5
master hath spared Naaman this S.	2Ki 5:20
to thy servants in the S. language	2Ki 18:26
letter was written in the S. tongue	Ezr 4:7
and interpreted in the S. tongue	Ezr 4:7
thy servant in the S. language	Isa 36:11
cleansed, saving Naaman the S.	Lu 4:27

SYRIANS

S. of Damascus came to succour	2Sa 8:5
David slew of the S. two and twenty	2Sa 8:5
the S. became servants to David	2Sa 8:6
from smiting of the S. in the valley	2Sa 8:13
and hired the S. of Beth-rehob	2Sa 10:6
and the S. of Zoba, twenty thousand	2Sa 10:6
the S. of Zoba, and of Rehob, and	2Sa 10:8
put them in array against the S.	2Sa 10:9
If the S. be too strong for me, then	2Sa 10:11
him, unto the battle against the S.	2Sa 10:13
of Ammon saw that the S. were fled	2Sa 10:14
the S. saw that they were smitten	2Sa 10:15
the S. that were beyond the river	2Sa 10:16
S. set themselves in array against	2Sa 10:17
And the S. fled before Israel; and	2Sa 10:18
of seven hundred chariots of the S.	2Sa 10:18
the S. feared to help the children of	2Sa 10:19
S. fled; and Israel pursued them	1Ki 20:20
slew the S. with a great slaughter	1Ki 20:21
that Ben-hadad numbered the S.	1Ki 20:26
kids; but the S. filled the country	1Ki 20:27
Because the S. have said, The Lord	1Ki 20:28
the children of Israel slew of the S.	1Ki 20:29
With these shalt thou push the S.	1Ki 22:11
up in his chariot against the S.	1Ki 22:35
the S. had gone out by companies	2Ki 5:2
for thither the S. are come down	2Ki 6:9
let us fall unto the host of the S.	2Ki 7:4
to go unto the camp of the S.	2Ki 7:5
made host of the S. to hear a noise	2Ki 7:6
We came to the camp of the S. and	2Ki 7:10
you what the S. have done to us	2Ki 7:12
the king sent after the host of the S.	2Ki 7:14
which the S. had cast away in their	2Ki 7:15
out, and spoiled the tents of the S.	2Ki 7:16
and the S. wounded Joram	2Ki 8:28
wounds which the S. had given him	2Ki 8:29; 9:15
out from under the hand of the S.	2Ki 13:5
for thou shalt smite the S. in Aphek	2Ki 13:17
and the S. came to Elath, and dwelt	2Ki 16:6
bands of the S. and bands of the	2Ki 24:2
the S. of Damascus came to help	1Ch 18:5
David slew of the S. two and twenty	1Ch 18:5
and the S. became David's servants	1Ch 18:6
and put them in array against the S.	1Ch 19:10
If the S. be too strong for me, then	1Ch 19:12
nigh before the S. unto the battle	1Ch 19:14
Ammon saw that the S. were fled	1Ch 19:15
the S. saw that they were put to the	1Ch 19:16
the S. that were beyond the river	1Ch 19:16
the battle in array against the S.	1Ch 19:17
But the S. fled before Israel	1Ch 19:18
David slew of the S. seven thousand	1Ch 19:18
the S. help the children of Ammon	1Ch 19:19
in his chariot against the S. until	2Ch 18:34
and the S. smote Joram	2Ch 22:5
army of the S. came with a small	2Ch 24:24
The S. before, and the Philistines	Isa 9:12
and for fear of the army of the S.	Jer 35:11
from Caphtor, and the S. from Kir	Am 9:7

SYROPHENICIAN

The woman was a Greek, a S. by	M'k 7:26

T

TAANACH

The king of T. one; the king of	Jos 12:21
the inhabitants of T. and her towns	Jos 17:11
nor T. and her towns, nor the	J'g 1:27
fought the kings of Canaan in T.	J'g 5:19
to him pertained T. and Megiddo	1Ki 4:12
T. and her towns, Megiddo and her	1Ch 7:29

TAANATH-SHILOH

went about eastward unto T.	Jos 16:6

TABBAOTH

of Hasupha, the children of T.	Ezr 2:43
of Hashupha, the children of T.	Ne 7:46

TABBATH

border of Abel-meholah, unto T.	J'g 7:22

TABEAL

the midst of it, even the son of T.	Isa 7:6

TABEEL

wrote Bishlam, Mithredath, T.	Ezr 4:7

TABERAH

called the name of the place T.	Nu 11:3
And at T. and at Massah, and at	De 9:22

TABERING

of doves, t. upon their breasts	Na 2:7
beating upon their breasts (A)(B)(E)(R)	Na 2:7

TABERNACLE

pattern of the t.	Ex 25:9
curtains for the t.	Ex 26:1; 26:7, 9, 12-13; Nu 4:25
it shall be one t.	Ex 26:8; 36:13
boards for the t.	Ex 26:15; 26:17-18, 26-27; 36:20, 22-23, 31-32; Nu 3:36
north side of the t.	Ex 26:20; 40:22; Nu 3:35
west side of the t.	Ex 26:22; 36:27
corners of the t.	Ex 26:23; 36:28
setting up of the t.	Ex 26:30; 39:7; 40:17-18, 21-22, 24, 28-29, 33; Nu 1:51; 7:1; 10:21; Jos 18:1
south side of the t.	Ex 26:35; 40:24; Nu 3:29
court of the t.	Ex 27:9; Le 6:16, 28; Nu 3:26
vessels of the t.	Ex 27:19; 38:40; 1Ki 8:4
t. of the congregation	Ex 27:21; 28:43; 29:4, 10, 11, 30, 32, 42; 30:16, 18, 20, 36; 31:7; 33:7, 8, 9, 11; 35:21; 38:30; 40:12; Le 1:1; 3:8, 13; 4:5, 7, 14, 16, 18; 6:30; 9:5, 23; 10:7, 9; 12:6; 14:11, 23; 15:14, 29; 16:7, 16, 17, 20, 23, 33; 17:4, 5, 6, 9; 24:3; Nu 1:1, 50; 2:2, 17; 3:7, 8, 25, 38; 4:3, 4, 15, 25, 28, 30, 31, 33, 35, 37, 39, 41, 43, 47; 7:89; 8:9, 19, 22, 24, 26; 10:3, 11; 11:16; 12:4; 14:10; 16:42, 43, 50; 17:4; 18:4; 19:4; 20:6; 25:6; 27:2; 31:54; De 31:14; Jos 18:1; 19:51; 1Ki 8:4; 1Ch 6:32; 9:21; 23:32; 2Ch 1:3, 6, 13; 5:5
the door of the t.	Ex 29:4; 29:11, 32, 42; 33:9; 35:15; 36:17; 38:8; 40:12; Le 1:3, 5; 3:2; 4:4, 7, 18; 8:3, 4; 8:31, 35; 10:7; 12:6; 14:11, 23; 15:14, 29; 16:7; 17:4, 5, 6, 9; 19:21; Nu 4:25; 6:10, 13, 18; 10:3; 12:5; 16:18; 20:6; 25:6; 27:2; Jos 19:51; 1Sa 2:22; 1Ch 9:21
t. sanctified	Ex 29:43; 29:44
service of the t.	Ex 30:16; Nu 3:7; 4:31, 33, 35, 37, 41; 7:5, 15, 22, 24; 16:9; 18:4, 6, 21-23, 31
anoint the t.	Ex 30:26; 40:9; Le 8:10
testimony of the t.	Ex 30:36
furniture of the t.	Ex 31:7
cloud over the t.	Ex 33:9; 33:10; Nu 9:15, 17-20, 22; 12:10; De 31:15
tent of the t.	Ex 35:11; 36:14; 38:32; 40:2, 6, 19, 29; Nu 3:25; 2Sa 7:6
pins of the t.	Ex 35:18; 38:20-21
work of the t.	Ex 35:21; 36:8; Nu 4:23, 30, 35, 39, 43
bars of the t.	Ex 36:32
hanging for the t. door	Ex 36:37; 39:38; 40:5, 28
sum of the t.	Ex 38:21
t. of the testimony	Ex 38:21; Nu 1:50, 53
t. brought to Moses	Ex 39:33
glory fills the t.	Ex 40:34; 40:35, 36, 38
not go out of the door of the t.	Le 8:33
defile my t.	Le 15:31
atonement for the t.	Le 16:33
my t. among Israel	Le 24:3; 26:11
t. set forward	Nu 1:51
floor of the t.	Nu 5:17
t. taken down	Nu 10:11; 10:17
t. of the Lord	Nu 16:9; 17:13; 19:13; 31:30, 47; 1Ki 2:28-30; 1Ch 16:39; 21:29; 2Ch 1:5
t. of witness	Nu 17:4; 17:7-8; 18:2; 2Ch 24:6; Ac 7:43
the Lord's t.	Jos 22:19
the t. that David pitched	2Sa 6:17
took horn of oil out of the t.	1Ki 1:39
Joab fled into the t.	1Ki 2:28-30; 2:29
the t. of the house of God	1Ch 6:48
the gates of the t.	1Ch 9:19
the house of the t.	1Ch 9:23
gone from one t. to another	1Ch 17:5
no more carry the t.	1Ch 23:26

know that thy *t.* shall be in peace   Job 5:24

The light shall be dark in his *t.* and   Job 18:6

confidence be rooted out of his *t.*   Job 18:14

It shall dwell in his *t.* because it is   Job 18:15

me, and encamp round about my *t.*   Job 19:12

go ill with him that is left in his *t.*   Job 20:26

the secret of God was upon my *t.*   Job 29:4

If the men of my *t.* said not, Oh   Job 31:31

the clouds, or the noise of his *t.*   Job 36:29

Lord, who shall abide in thy *t.*   Ps 15:1

In them hath he set a *t.* for the sun   Ps 19:4

In the secret of his *t.* shall he hide   Ps 27:5

will I offer in his *t.* sacrifices of joy   Ps 27:6

I will abide in thy *t.* for ever: I will   Ps 61:4

In Salem also is his *t.* and his   Ps 76:2

So that he forsook the *t.* of Shiloh   Ps 78:60

he refused the *t.* of Joseph   Ps 78:67

not come unto the *t.* of my house   Ps 132:3

the *t.* of the upright shall flourish   Pr 14:11

a *t.* for a shadow in the daytime   Isa 4:6

upon it in truth in the *t.* of David   Isa 16:5

a *t.* that shall not be taken down   Isa 33:20

My *t.* is spoiled, and all my cords   Jer 10:20

in the *t.* of the daughter of Zion   La 2:4

he hath violently taken away his *t.*   La 2:6

My *t.* also shall be with them   Eze 37:27

which was the breadth of the *t.*   Eze 41:1

the *t.* of your Moloch and Chiun   Am 5:26

day will I raise up the *t.* of David   Am 9:11

ye took up the *t.* of Moloch   Ac 7:43

to find a *t.* for the God of Jacob   Ac 7:46

will build again the *t.* of David   Ac 15:16

our earthly house of this *t.*   2Co 5:1

For we that are in this *t.* do groan   2Co 5:4

and of the true *t.* which the Lord   Heb 8:2

when he was about to make the *t.*   Heb 8:5

For there was a *t.* made; the first   Heb 9:2

t. which is called the Holiest of all   Heb 9:3

priests went always into the first *t.*   Heb 9:6

as the first *t.* was yet standing   Heb 9:8

by a greater and more perfect *t.*   Heb 9:11

he sprinkled with blood both the *t.*   Heb 9:21

no right to eat which serve the *t.*   Heb 13:10

as long as I am in this *t.* to stir   2Pe 1:13

shortly I must put off this my *t.*   2Pe 1:14

spread *t.* over them (A)(E)   Re 7:15

to blaspheme his name and his *t.*   Re 13:6

temple of the *t.* of the testimony   Re 15:5

the *t.* of God is with men, and he   Re 21:3

TABERNACLED

t. his tent of flesh (A)   Joh 1:14

TABERNACLES

be the feast of *t.* for seven days   Le 23:34

tents, O Jacob, and thy *t.* O Israel   Nu 24:5

observe the feast of *t.* seven days   De 16:13

feast of weeks, and in the feast of *t.*   De 16:16

the year of release, in the feast of *t.*   De 31:10

feast of weeks, and in the feast of *t.*   2Ch 8:13

They kept also the feast of *t.* as it is   Ezr 3:4

let not wickedness dwell in thy *t.*   Job 11:14

The *t.* of robbers prosper, and they   Job 12:6

fire shall consume the *t.* of bribery   Job 15:34

put away iniquity far from thy *t.*   Job 22:23

me unto thy holy hill, and to thy *t.*   Ps 43:3

place of the *t.* of the most High   Ps 46:4

of their strength in the *t.* of Ham   Ps 78:51

t. of Edom, and the Ishmaelites   Ps 83:6

How amiable are thy *t.*, O Lord of   Ps 84:1

is in the *t.* of the righteous   Ps 118:15

We will go into his *t.*: we will   Ps 132:7

he shall plant the *t.* of his palace   Da 11:45

them: thorns shall be in their *t.*   Ho 9:6

will yet make thee to dwell in *t.*   Ho 12:9

of hosts, and to keep the feast of *t.*   Zec 14:16

not up to keep the feast of *t.*   Zec 14:18; 14:19

the scholar, out of the *t.* of Jacob   Mal 2:12

let us make here three *t.* one   M't 17:4

let us make three *t.* one for thee   M'k 9:5

the Jews' feast of *t.* was at hand   Lu 9:33 Joh 7:2

dwelling in *t.* with Isaac, Jacob   Heb 11:9

TABITHA

a certain disciple named *T.*   Ac 9:36

him to the body said, *T.*, arise   Ac 9:40

TABLE

also make a *t.* of shittim wood   Ex 25:23

places of the staves to bear the *t.*   Ex 25:27

that the *t.* may be borne with them   Ex 25:28

thou shalt set upon the *t.* shewbread   Ex 25:30

thou shalt set the *t.* without the veil   Ex 26:35

the candlestick over against the *t.*   Ex 26:35

shalt put the *t.* on the north side   Ex 26:35

And the *t.* and all his vessels   Ex 30:27

And the *t.* and his furniture   Ex 31:8

The *t.* and his staves, and all his   Ex 35:13

And he made the *t.* of shittim wood   Ex 37:10

places for the staves to bear the *t.*   Ex 37:14

them with gold, to bear the *t.*   Ex 37:15

the vessels which were upon the *t.*   Ex 37:16

The *t.* and all the vessels thereof   Ex 39:36

And thou shalt bring in the *t.*   Ex 40:4

And he put the *t.* in the tent of the   Ex 40:22

over against the *t.* on the side   Ex 40:24

upon the pure *t.* before the Lord   Le 24:6

charge shall be the ark, and the *t.*   Nu 3:31

upon the *t.* of shewbread they shall   Nu 4:7

gathered their meat under my *t.*   J'g 1:7

sit with the king at the *t.* (S)   1Sa 20:5; 20:27

he cometh not unto the king's *t.*   1Sa 20:29

Jonathan arose from the *t.* in fierce   1Sa 20:34

and thou shalt eat bread at my *t.*   2Sa 9:7

son shall eat bread alway at my *t.*   2Sa 9:10

he shall eat at my *t.* as one   2Sa 9:11

did eat continually at the king's *t.*   2Sa 9:13

them that did eat at thine own *t.*   2Sa 19:28

them be of those that eat at thy *t.*   1Ki 2:7

that came unto king Solomon's *t.*   1Ki 4:27

the altar of gold, and the *t.* of gold   1Ki 7:48

the meat of his *t.* and the sitting   1Ki 10:5

it came to pass, as they sat at the *t.*   1Ki 13:20

hundred, which eat at Jezebel's *t.*   1Ki 18:19

us set for him there a bed, and a *t.*   2Ki 4:10

tables of shewbread, for every *t.*   1Ch 28:16

the meat of his *t.* and the sitting   2Ch 9:4

set they in order upon the pure *t.*   2Ch 13:11

and the shewbread *t.* with all the   2Ch 29:18

there were at my *t.* an hundred and   Ne 5:17

that which should be set on thy *t.*   Job 36:16

Thou preparest a *t.* before me   Ps 23:5

Let their *t.* become a snare before   Ps 69:22

God furnish a *t.* in the wilderness   Ps 78:19

like olive plants round about thy *t.*   Ps 128:3

them upon the *t.* of thine heart   Pr 3:3

write them upon the *t.* of thine heart   Pr 7:3

she hath also furnished her *t.*   Pr 9:2

While the king sitteth at his *t.*   Ca 1:12

Prepare the *t.* watch in the   Isa 21:5

Now go, write it before them in a *t.*   Isa 30:8

that prepare a *t.* for that troop   Isa 65:11

graven upon the *t.* of their heart   Jer 17:1

bed, and a *t.* prepared before it   Eze 23:41

Thus ye shall be filled at my *t.* with   Eze 39:20

This is the *t.* that is before the Lord   Eze 41:22

and they shall come near to my *t.*   Eze 44:16

and they shall speak lies at one *t.*   Da 11:27

The *t.* of the Lord is contemptible   Mal 1:7

say, The *t.* of the Lord is polluted   Mal 1:12

which fall from their masters' *t.*   M't 15:27

yet the dogs under the *t.* eat of the   M'k 7:28

And he asked for a writing *t.*   Lu 1:63

which fell from the rich man's *t.*   Lu 16:21

betrayeth me is with me on the *t.*   Lu 22:21

ye may eat and drink at my *t.* in my   Lu 22:30

carry to the *t.* manager (A)(B)   Joh 2:8

of them that sat at the *t.* with him   Joh 12:2

Now no man at the *t.* knew for what   Joh 13:28

saith, Let their *t.* be made a snare   Ro 11:9

sitting at the *t.* (S)   1Co 9:10

cannot be partakers of the Lord's *t.*   1Co 10:21

and of the *t.* of devils   1Co 10:21

and the *t.* and the shewbread   Heb 9:2

TABLES

and I will give thee *t.* of stone   Ex 24:12
two *t.* of testimony, *t.* of stone   Ex 31:18
two *t.* of the testimony were in his   Ex 32:15
t. were written on both their sides   Ex 32:15
And the *t.* were the work of God   Ex 32:16
writing of God, graven upon the *t.*   Ex 32:16
and he cast the *t.* out of his hands   Ex 32:19
two *t.* of stone like unto the first   Ex 34:1
I will write upon these *t.* the words   Ex 34:1
in the first *t.* which thou brakest   Ex 34:1
two *t.* of stone like unto the first   Ex 34:4
took in his hand the two *t.* of stone   Ex 34:4
wrote upon the *t.* the words of the   Ex 34:28
two *t.* of testimony in Moses' hand   Ex 34:29
he wrote them upon two *t.* of stone   De 4:13
he wrote them in two *t.* of stone   De 5:22
the mount to receive the *t.* of stone   De 9:9
t. of the covenant which the Lord   De 9:9
delivered unto me two *t.* of stone   De 9:10
Lord gave me the two *t.* of stone   De 9:11
stone, even the *t.* of the covenant   De 9:11
two *t.* of the covenant were in my   De 9:15
I took the two *t.* and cast them out   De 9:17
I will write on the *t.* the words that   De 10:2
in the first *t.* which thou brakest   De 10:2
two *t.* of stone like unto the first   De 10:3
having the two *t.* in mine hand   De 10:3
he wrote on the *t.* according to the   De 10:4
and put the *t.* in the ark which I had   De 10:5
in the ark save the two *t.* of stone   1Ki 8:9
gave gold for the *t.* of shewbread   1Ch 28:16
likewise silver for the *t.* of silver   1Ch 28:16
He made also ten *t.* and placed   2Ch 4:8
t. whereon the shewbread was set   2Ch 4:19
nothing in the ark save the two *t.*   2Ch 5:10
For all *t.* are full of vomit and   Isa 28:8
in the porch of the gate were two *t.*   Eze 40:39
this side, and two *t.* on that side   Eze 40:39
entry of the north gate, were two *t.*   Eze 40:40
the porch of the gate, were two *t.*   Eze 40:40
Four *t.* were on this side, and four   Eze 40:41
and four *t.* on that side, by the side   Eze 40:41
eight *t.* whereupon they slew their   Eze 40:41
four *t.* were of hewn stone for the   Eze 40:42
and upon the *t.* was the flesh of the   Eze 40:43
vision, and make it plain upon it.   Hab 2:2
the *t.* of the moneychangers   M't 21:12
and pots, brasen vessels, and of *t.*   M'k 7:4
the *t.* of the moneychangers   M'k 11:15
money, and overthrew the *t.*   Joh 2:15
leave the word of God and serve *t.*   Ac 6:2

living God; not in *t.* of stone   2Co 3:3
but in fleshy *t.* of the heart   2Co 3:3
budded, and the *t.* of the covenant   Heb 9:4

TABLET

tablet (S)   Isa 30:9; Jer 17:1; Lu 1:63
get a clay *t.* (B)   Eze 4:1
t. of human hearts (A)(B)(R)   2Co 3:3

TABLETS

and earrings, and rings, and *t.* all   Ex 35:22
necklaces (A)(B)   Ex 35:22
armlets or necklaces (E)(R)   Ex 35:22
bracelets, rings, earrings, and *t.*   Nu 31:50
neck ornaments (A)   Nu 31:50
necklaces (B)   Nu 31:50
armlets or necklaces (E)(R)   Nu 31:50
headbands, and the *t.* and   Isa 3:20
perfume boxes (A)(B)(E)(R)   Isa 3:20

TABOR

And the coast reacheth to *T.*, and   Jos 19:22
Go and draw toward mount *T.*   J'g 4:6
Barak was gone up to mount *T.*   J'g 4:12
Barak went down from mount *T.*   J'g 4:14
men were they whom ye slew at *T.*   J'g 8:18
thou shalt come to the plain of *T.*   1Sa 10:3
her suburbs, *T.* with her suburbs   1Ch 6:77
T. and Hermon shall rejoice in thy   Ps 89:12
as *T.* is among the mountains, and   Jer 46:18
Mizpah, and a net spread upon *T.*   Ho 5:1

TABRET

with songs, with *t.* and with harp   Ge 31:27
tambourine (A)(B)   Ge 31:27; 1Sa 10:5; Isa 5:12
tambourine (R)   Ge 31:27
and a *t.* and a pipe, and a harp   1Sa 10:5
and aforetime I was as a *t.*   Job 17:6
a byword (A)(B)(E)(R)   Job 17:6
the *t.* and pipe, and wine, are   Isa 5:12
timbrel (R)   Isa 5:12

TABRETS

to meet king Saul, with *t.*   1Sa 18:6
timbrels (A)   1Sa 18:6; Isa 24:8; 30:32; Jer 31:4
tambourines (B)   1Sa 18:6
timbrels (E)   1Sa 18:6
The mirth of *t.* ceaseth, the noise   Isa 24:8
timbrels (B)   Isa 24:8; 30:32
him, it shall be with *t.* and harps   Isa 30:32
shalt again be adorned with thy *t.*   Jer 31:4
the workmanship of thy *t.* and of   Eze 28:13

TABRIMON

them to Ben-hadad son of *T.*   1Ki 15:18

TACHES

thou shalt make fifty *t.* of gold   Ex 26:6
clasps (A)(B)(E)   Ex 26:6; 26:11, 33; 36:13, 18; 39:33
clasps (R)   Ex 26:6; 26:11, 33; 36:13, 18
the curtains together with the *t.*   Ex 26:6
thou shalt make fifty *t.* of brass   Ex 26:11
and put the *t.* into the loops   Ex 26:11
shalt hang up the veil under the *t.*   Ex 26:33
his covering, his *t.* and his boards   Ex 35:11

hooks (A)(R)   Ex 35:11
clasps (B)(E)   Ex 35:11
And he made fifty *t.* of gold   Ex 36:13
one unto another with the *t.*: so   Ex 36:13
made fifty *t.* of brass to couple the   Ex 36:18
all his furniture, his *t.* his boards   Ex 39:33
hooks (R)   Ex 39:33

TACHMONITE

The *T.* that sat in the seat, chief   2Sa 23:8

TACKLE

cast out the *t.* (S)   Ac 27:19

TACKLING

our own hands the *t.* of the ship   Ac 27:19

TACKLINGS

Thy *t.* are loosed; they could not   Isa 33:23

TACT

answer with wisdom and *t.* (B)   Da 2:14

TADMOR

Baalath, and *T.* in the wilderness   1Ki 9:18
he built *T.* in the wilderness   2Ch 8:4

TAHAN

T. the family of the Tahanites   Nu 26:35
and Telah his son, and *T.* his son   1Ch 7:25

TAHANITES

of Tahan, the family of the *T.*   Nu 26:35

TAHAPANES

the children of Noph and *T.* have   Jer 2:16

TAHATH

Makheloth, and encamped at *T.*   Nu 33:26
they departed from *T.* and pitched   Nu 33:27
T. his son, Uriel his son, Uzziah   1Ch 6:24
The son of *T.* the son of Assir   1Ch 6:37
Bered his son, and *T.* his son   1Ch 7:20
Eladah his son, and *T.* his son   1Ch 7:20

TAHPANHES

Lord: thus came they even to *T.*   Jer 43:7
of the Lord unto Jeremiah in *T.*   Jer 43:8
the entry of Pharaoh's house in *T.*   Jer 43:9
which dwell at Migdol, and at *T.*   Jer 44:1
and publish in Noph and in *T.*   Jer 46:14

TAHPENES

wife the sister of *T.* the queen   1Ki 11:19
sister of *T.* bare him Genubath   1Ki 11:20
T. weaned in Pharaoh's house   1Ki 11:20

TAHREA

and Melech, and *T.* and Ahaz   1Ch 9:41

TAHTIM-HODSHI

to Gilead, and to the land of *T.*   2Sa 24:6

TAIL

thine hand, and take it by the *t.*	*Ex 4:4*
fat *t.* (A)(B)(E)(R)	*Ex 29:22;*
	Le 3:9; 7:3; 8:25; 9:19
thee the head, and not the *t.*	*De 28:13*
the head, and thou shalt be	*De 28:44*
the *t.*	
turned *t.* to *t.* and put a	*J'g 15:4*
firebrand	
He moveth his *t.* like a	*Job 40:17*
cedar, the	
cut off from Israel head and *t.*	*Isa 9:14*
that teacheth lies, he is the *t.*	*Isa 9:15*
which the head or *t.* branch	*Isa 19:15*
his *t.* drew the third part of	*Re 12:4*

TAILS

in the midst between two *t.*	*J'g 15:4*
two *t.* of these smoking	*Isa 7:4*
firebrands	
they had *t.* like unto scorpions	*Re 9:10*
and there were stings in their	*Re 9:10*
t.	
is in their mouth, and in their	*Re 9:19*
t.	
their *t.* were like unto serpents	*Re 9:19*

TAINTED

t. with blood (B)	*Isa 59:3*
use money, *t.* as it is (P)	*Lu 16:9*
t. the whole body (B)	*Jas 3:6*

TAKE

if thou *t.* the left hand I will	*Ge 13:9*
go	
give me the persons, *t.* goods	*Ge 14:21*
to thyself	
arise, *t.* thy wife and two	*Ge 19:15*
daughters	
t. now thy son, thine only son	*Ge 22:2*
Isaac	
not *t.* a wife to my son of	*Ge 24:3;*
	24:37
to *t.* my master's brother's	*Ge 24:48*
daughter	
what is thine with me, *t.* it	*Ge 31:32*
if *t.* other wives besides my	*Ge 31:50*
daughters	
and *t.* our daughters unto you	*Ge 34:9*
and we will *t.* your daughters	*Ge 34:16*
to us	
let her *t.* it lest we be	*Ge 38:23*
shamed	
I will *t.* you to me for a people	*Ex 6:7*
thereof must we *t.* to serve	*Ex 10:26*
the Lord	
and thy rod *t.* in thine hand,	*Ex 17:5*
and go	
not *t.* the name of the Lord	*Ex 20:7;*
in vain, not hold guiltless	*De 5:11*
t. him from mine altar, he	*Ex 21:14*
may die	
thou shalt *t.* no gift	*Ex 23:8;*
	De 16:19
pardon and *t.* us for thine	*Ex 34:9*
inheritance	
lest thou *t.* their daughters	*Ex 34:16;*
	De 7:3
neither *t.* her son's daughter	*Le 18:17*
neither shalt thou *t.* a wife to	*Le 18:18*
her sister	
if a man *t.* a wife, and her	*Le 20:14*
mother	
priests not *t.* wife that is a	*Le 21:7;*
whore, nor *t.* a woman	*Eze 44:22*
put away	
he shall *t.* a wife in her	*Le 21:13*
virginity	
t. thou no usury of him, or	*Le 25:36*
increase	
t. them as an inheritance for	*Le 25:46*
children	
t. the Levites from among	*Nu 8:6*
Israel	
I will *t.* of the spirit that is	*Nu 11:17*
on thee	
ye *t.* too much upon you	*Nu 16:3; 16:7*
t. no satisfaction for the life	*Nu 35:31;*
	35:32
t. ye wise men, and	*De 1:13*
understanding	
t. him a nation, from the	*De 4:34*
midst of nation	
then thou shalt *t.* an awl,	*De 15:17*
and thrust	
the elders of that city shall *t.*	*De 22:18*
that man	

a man shall not *t.* his father's	*De 22:30*
wife	
may not *t.* her again to be his	*De 24:4*
wife	
no man shall *t.* a millstone to	*De 24:6*
pledge	
nor *t.* a widow's raiment to	*De 24:17*
pledge	
if he say, I like not to *t.* her	*De 25:8*
when ye *t.* of the accursed	*Jos 6:18*
thing	
family the Lord shall *t.* the	*Jos 7:14*
household the Lord shall *t.*	
t. his carcase down from the	*Jos 8:29*
tree	
their land did Joshua *t.* at	*Jos 10:42*
one time	
they shall *t.* him into the city	*Jos 20:4*
to them	
then *t.* ye possession among	*Jos 22:19*
us	
for the necks of them that *t.*	*J'g 5:30*
spoil	
goest to *t.* a wife of	*J'g 14:3*
uncircumcised	
have ye called us to *t.* that	*J'g 14:15*
we have	
consider, *t.* advice, speak	*J'g 19:30*
your minds	
thou shouldest *t.* knowledge of	*Ru 2:10*
me	
then *t.* as much as thy soul	*1Sa 2:16*
desireth, and if not I will *t.* it	
he will *t.* your sons for	*1Sa 8:11*
himself	
will *t.* daughters	*1Sa 8:13*
t. your fields	*1Sa 8:14*
t. tenth of seed	*1Sa 8:15*
t. menservants	*1Sa 8:16*
how thy brethren fare, and	*1Sa 17:18*
t. their pledge	
and *t.* thine head from thee	*1Sa 17:46*
Saul sent messengers to *t.*	*1Sa 19:14;*
David	*19:20*
if thou wilt *t.* that, *t.* it, there	*1Sa 21:9*
is	
yet thou huntest my soul to	*1Sa 24:11*
t. it	
shall I then *t.* my bread	*1Sa 25:11*
t. now the spear that is at	*1Sa 26:11*
his bolster	
he spared to *t.* of his own	*2Sa 12:4*
flock	
I will *t.* thy wives before	*2Sa 12:11*
thine eyes	
t. it, lest I *t.* the city, and it	*2Sa 12:28*
be called	
let me go over, and *t.* off his	*2Sa 16:9*
head	
king should *t.* it to heart	*2Sa 19:19;*
	13:33
Mephibosheth said, Yea, let	*2Sa 19:30*
him *t.* all	
he said to Jeroboam, T. ten	*1Ki 11:31*
pieces	
I will not *t.* the whole	*1Ki 11:34*
kingdom	
t. ten loaves	*1Ki 14:3*
t. prophets of Baal	*1Ki 18:40*
come for war or peace, *t.*	*1Ki 20:18*
them alive	
arise, *t.* possession of the	*1Ki 21:15;*
vineyard	*21:16*
t. Micaiah, carry him back	*1Ki 22:26;*
	2Ch 18:25
the creditor is come to *t.* my	*2Ki 4:1*
sons	
t. my staff	*2Ki 4:29*
t. a blessing	*2Ki 5:15*
urged him to *t.* it	*2Ki 5:16*
I will *t.*	*2Ki 5:20*
t. two talents	*2Ki 5:23*
t. a present	*2Ki 8:8*
t. this box of oil in thine	*2Ki 9:1;*
hand	*9:3*
t. him into the chamber (S)	*2Ki 9:2*
t. ye the heads of your	*2Ki 10:6*
master's sons	
t. them alive	*2Ki 10:14*
let the priests *t.* it	*2Ki 12:5*
Elisha said, T. bow and	*2Ki 13:15;*
arrows	*13:18*
t. one of the priests (S)	*2Ki 17:27*
yet *t.* root downward	*2Ki 19:30;*
	Isa 37:31
I will not *t.* that which is	*1Ch 21:24*
thine	
T. me away for I am	*2Ch 35:23*
wounded (S)	
those did Cyrus *t.*	*Ezr 5:14*

t. vessels	*Ezr 5:15*
not *t.* their daughters	*Ezr 9:12;*
	Ne 10:30; 13:25
and to *t.* the spoil of them for	*Es 3:13*
a prey	
t. apparel, and do so to	*Es 6:10*
Mordecai	
he knoweth the way that I *t.*	*Job 23:10*
they *t.* the widow's ox for a	*Job 24:3*
pledge	
and they *t.* a pledge of the	*Job 24:9*
poor	
and my sinews *t.* no rest	*Job 30:17*
I would *t.* it upon my	*Job 31:36*
shoulder	
wilt thou *t.* him for a servant	*Job 41:4*
for ever	
therefore *t.* to you now seven	*Job 42:8*
bullocks	
rulers *t.* counsel against the	*Ps 2:2*
Lord	
let enemy persecute my soul,	*Ps 7:5*
and *t.* it	
I will *t.* no bullock out of thy	*Ps 50:9*
house	
shouldest *t.* my covenant in	*Ps 50:16*
thy mouth	
and *t.* not thy Holy Spirit	*Ps 51:11*
from me	
t. him, for there is none to	*Ps 71:11*
deliver him	
t. a psalm	*Ps 81:2*
t. the houses of God	*Ps 83:12*
my kindness will I not utterly	*Ps 89:33*
t. from him	
and let another *t.* his office	*Ps 109:8*
I will *t.* the cup of salvation	*Ps 116:13*
and call	
t. not the word of truth	*Ps 119:43*
utterly out	
if I *t.* the wings of the	*Ps 139:9*
morning	
and thine enemies *t.* thy	*Ps 139:20*
name in vain	
own iniquities shall *t.* the	*Pr 5:22*
wicked	
neither let her *t.* thee with her	*Pr 6:25*
eyelids	
can man *t.* fire in bosom, not	*Pr 6:27*
be burned	
let us *t.* our fill of love till the	*Pr 7:18*
morning	
t. garment that is surety for	*Pr 20:16;*
stranger, *t.* pledge for a	*27:13*
strange woman	
t. the name of my God in vain	*Pr 30:9*
shall *t.* nothing of his labour	*Ec 5:15*
to *t.* his portion and rejoice in	*Ec 5:19*
his labour	
t. us the foxes, the little foxes	*Ca 2:15*
cause them of Jacob to *t.* root	*Isa 27:6*
from time it goeth, it shall *t.*	*Isa 28:19*
you	
not a sherd *t.* fire from the	*Isa 30:14*
hearth	
prey is divided, the lame *t.*	*Isa 33:23*
prey	
their stock shall not *t.* root	*Isa 40:24*
in the earth	
he will *t.* thereof and warm	*Isa 44:15*
himself	
t. the millstones, and grind	*Isa 47:2*
meal	
I will *t.* vengeance, I will not	*Isa 47:3*
meet as	
vanity shall *t.* them, wind	*Isa 57:13*
carry them	
they *t.* delight in approaching	*Isa 58:2*
to God	
I will *t.* of them for priests	*Isa 66:21*
and Levites	
t. thee much soap	*Jer 2:22*
t. one of a city	*Jer 3:14*
t. the girdle that thou hast	*Jer 13:4;*
got	*13:6*
sorrows *t.* thee as a woman	*Jer 13:21*
in travail	
t. forth the precious from the	*Jer 15:19*
vile	
not *t.* thee a wife in this place	*Jer 16:2*
for they have digged a pit to	*Jer 18:22*
t. me	
t. of ancients of people of	*Jer 19:1*
priests	
we shall *t.* our revenge on	*Jer 20:10*
him	
I will *t.* all the families of	*Jer 25:9*
the north	
I will *t.* from them the voice	*Jer 25:10*
of mirth	

if they refuse to *t.* cup at thine hand — Jer 25:28

t. wives, and beget sons and daughters — Jer 29:6

they are come to the city to *t.* it — Jer 32:24

buy field for money, *t.* witnesses — Jer 32:25; 32:44

Nebuchadrezzar king of Babylon shall *t.* it — Jer 32:28

t. Jeremiah, and look well to him — Jer 39:12

go up into Gilead, and *t.* balm — Jer 46:11; 51:8

t. vengeance on her; as she hath done — Jer 50:15

not *t.* of thee a stone for a corner — Jer 51:26

I will *t.* vengeance for thee — Jer 51:36

what thing shall I *t.* to witness — La 2:13

t. a tile — Eze 4:1

t. an iron pan — Eze 4:3

t. wheat, barley, and beans — Eze 4:9

t. a sharp knife, *t.* a rasor, *t.* balances — Eze 5:1

t. fire from between the wheels — Eze 10:6

I will *t.* stony heart out of their flesh — Eze 11:19

that I may *t.* the house of Israel — Eze 14:5

will men *t.* a pin of it to hang vessel — Eze 15:3

remove the diadem, *t.* off the crown — Eze 21:26

shalt *t.* thine inheritance in thyself — Eze 22:16

t. the choice of flock, and burn bones — Eze 24:5

cause fury to come up to *t.* vengeance — Eze 24:8

when I *t.* from them their strength — Eze 24:25

t. a multitude, *t.* her spoil, *t.* her prey — Eze 29:19

if people of land *t.* a man of their coasts — Eze 33:2

I will *t.* you from among the heathen — Eze 36:24

t. thee one stick, *t.* another stick, write — Eze 37:16

I will *t.* the stick of Joseph, and will put — Eze 37:19

to *t.* a spoil and to *t.* a prey — Eze 38:12

thou come to *t.* prey, to *t.* a great spoil — Eze 38:13

prince not *t.* the people's inheritance — Eze 46:18

but the saints shall *t.* the kingdom — Da 7:18

king shall *t.* the most fenced cities — Da 11:15

he shall turn to isles, shall *t.* many — Da 11:18

go *t.* unto thee a wife of whoredoms — Ho 1:2

I was as they that *t.* off the yoke — Ho 11:4

t. with you words, and turn to Lord — Ho 14:2

ye *t.* from him burdens of wheat — Am 5:11

they afflict the just, they *t.* a bribe — Am 5:12

thence shall mine hand *t.* them — Am 9:2; 9:3

t. I beseech thee, my life from me — Jon 4:3

covet fields and *t.* them by violence — Mic 2:2

not prophesy, that they shall not *t.* shame — Mic 2:6

Lord will *t.* vengeance on adversaries — Na 1:2

t. spoil of silver, *t.* the spoil of gold — Na 2:9

for they shall heap dust and *t.* it — Hab 1:10

build the house, I will *t.* pleasure in it — Hag 1:8

will I *t.* thee, O Zerubbabel my servant — Hag 2:23

t. of them of the captivity — Zec 6:10

t. instruments of a foolish shepherd — Zec 11:15

fear not to *t.* Mary thy wife — M't 1:20

t. the young child and its mother — M't 2:13

t. no thought for your life — M't 6:25; 6:28, 31, 34; 10:19; M'k 13:11; Lu 12:11,

the violent *t.* the kingdom by force — M't 11:12; 11:22, 26

t. my yoke upon you, and learn of me — M't 11:29

not meet to *t.* children's bread — M't 15:26; M'k 7:27

they had forgotten to *t.* bread — M't 16:5; M'k 8:14

of whom kings of the earth *t.* custom — M't 17:25

then *t.* with thee one or two more — M't 18:16

t. that thine is and go thy way — M't 20:14

him on housetop not come down to *t.* any thing — M't 24:17; M'k 13:15

t. therefore the talent from him, give it — M't 25:28

that they might *t.* Jesus — M't 26:4;

Jesus took bread and said, *T.* eat, this is my body — M't 26:26; M'k 14:22; 1Co 11:24

sleep on now, and *t.* your rest — M't 26:45; M'k 14:41

they that *t.* the sword perish by sword — M't 26:52

with swords and staves to *t.* me — M't 26:55; M'k 14:48

t. nothing for their journey — M'k 6:8; Lu 9:3

his brother *t.* his wife — M'k 12:19; Lu 20:28

casting lots what every man should *t.* — M'k 15:24

whether Elias will come to *t.* him down — M'k 15:36

David did *t.* and eat shewbread — Lu 6:4

forbid him not to *t.* thy coat also — Lu 6:29

t. care of him — Lu 10:35

soul, *t.* thine ease — Lu 12:19

begin with shame to *t.* the lowest room — Lu 14:9

t. thy bill — Lu 16:6; 16:7

t. this and divide it — Lu 22:17

t. from him the pound, and give it — Lu 19:24

he that hath a purse, let him *t.* it — Lu 22:36

Jesus said, *T.* these things hence — Joh 2:16

that every one of them may *t.* a little — Joh 6:7

that they would come and *t.* him by force — Joh 6:15

they sought to *t.* him — Joh 7:30; 7:32, 39; 11:57

lay down my life that I might *t.* it again — Joh 10:17; 10:18

he shall *t.* of mine, and shew it unto you — Joh 16:15

thou shouldest *t.* them out of the world — Joh 17:15

t. ye him, and judge him according to — Joh 18:31

Pilate saith, *T.* ye him, and crucify him — Joh 19:6

his bishopric let another *t.* — Ac 1:20

Herod proceeded further to *t.* Peter — Ac 12:3

to *t.* out of them a people for his name — Ac 15:14

Barnabas determined to *t.* John — Ac 15:37

Paul thought not good to *t.* him — Ac 15:38

sailed to Assos, intending to *t.* in Paul — Ac 20:13

wherefore I *t.* you to record this day — Ac 20:26

them *t.* and purify thyself with them — Ac 21:24

Paul besought them to *t.* meat — Ac 27:33; 27:34

why do you not rather *t.* wrong — 1Co 6:7

shall I then *t.* the members of Christ — 1Co 6:15

doth God *t.* care for oxen — 1Co 9:9

t. upon us the ministering to saints — 2Co 8:4

for ye suffer, if a man *t.* of you — 2Co 11:20

therefore I *t.* pleasure in infirmities — 2Co 12:10

t. the whole armour of God — Eph 6:13

t. the helmet of salvation — Eph 6:17

how shall he *t.* care of the church — 1Ti 3:5

t. Mark, and bring him with thee — 2Ti 4:11

commandment to *t.* tithes of people — Heb 7:5

t. my brethren, prophets, as an example — Jas 5:10

if ye *t.* it patiently, it is acceptable — 1Pe 2:20

hold fast, that no man *t.* thy crown — Re 3:11

art worthy to *t.* the book, and to open — Re 5:9

power given him to *t.* peace from earth — Re 6:4

t. the little book — Re 10:8

t. it and eat it — Re 10:9

let him *t.* the water of life freely — Re 22:17

TAKE *AWAY*

wouldest *t. away* my son's mandrakes — Ge 30:15

and ye will *t.* Benjamin *away* — Ge 42:36

t. this child *away*, and nurse it — Ex 2:9

that he may *t. away* the frogs from me — Ex 8:8

he may *t. away* from me this death — Ex 10:17

I will *t.* sickness *away* — Ex 23:25; De 7:15

I will *t. away* mine hand, thou shalt see — Ex 33:23

it shall he *t. away* — Le 3:4; 3:10, 15; 4:9; 7:4

t. away all the fat thereof — Le 4:31; 4:35

command that they *t. away* the stones — Le 14:40

shalt *t. away* ashes from the altar — Nu 4:13

t. away their murmurings — Nu 17:10

pray he may *t. away* serpents from us — Nu 21:7

until ye *t. away* the accursed thing — Jos 7:13

shall I not *t.* you *away* from earth — 2Sa 4:11

except thou *t. away* blind and lame — 2Sa 5:6

t. away the iniquity of thy servant — 2Sa 24:10

mayest *t. away* innocent blood — 1Ki 2:31

t. away remnant of house of Jeroboam — 1Ki 14:10

t. away posterity of — 1Ki 16:3; 21:21

it is enough now, *t. away* my life — 1Ki 19:4

they seek my life, to *t.* it *away* — 1Ki 19:10; 19:14

what is pleasant, my servants *t. away* — 1Ki 20:6

t. kings *away* put captains in their rooms — 1Ki 20:24

Lord will *t. away* thy master — 2Ki 2:3; 2:5

he hath sent to *t. away* mine head — 2Ki 6:32

till I come and *t.* you *away* — 2Ki 18:32; Isa 36:16

I will not *t. away* my mercy — 1Ch 17:13

sent to *t. away* sackcloth from him — Es 4:4

dost thou not *t. away* mine iniquity — Job 7:21

let him *t. away* from me his rod — Job 9:34

they violently *t. away* flocks — Job 24:2

they *t. away* the sheaf from the hungry — Job 24:10

in doing, my maker would soon *t.* me *away* — Job 32:22

beware, lest he *t.* thee *away* with stroke — Job 36:18

they devised to *t. away* my life — Ps 31:13

he shall *t.* thee *away* and pluck thee — Ps 52:5

he shall *t.* them *away* as a whirlwind — Ps 58:9

t. me not *away* in midst of days — Ps 102:24

why should he *t. away* thy bed — Pr 22:27

t. away the dross from the   Pr 25:4
silver
t. away the wicked from   Pr 25:5
before the king
and I will *t. away* all thy tin   Isa 1:25
t. away stay and staff   Isa 3:1
t. away bravery   Isa 3:18
to *t. away* reproach   Isa 4:1
t. away hedge   Isa 5:5
t. away the righteousness of   Isa 5:23
the righteous
to *t. away* the right from the   Isa 10:2
poor
the rebuke of his people shall   Isa 25:8
he *t. away*
this is all the fruit, to *t. away*   Isa 27:9
his sin
and of thy sons shall they *t.*   Isa 39:7
away
the whirlwind shall *t. them*   Isa 40:24
away
if thou *t. away* from the midst   Isa 58:9
of thee
t. away the foreskins of your   Jer 4:4
heart
destroy and *t. away* her   Jer 5:10
battlements
t. me not *away* in thy   Jer 15:15
longsuffering
shall *t. away* the detestable   Eze 11:18
things
they shall *t. away* thy nose   Eze 23:25
and thine ears
t. away fair jewels   Eze 23:26
t. away labour   Eze 23:29
behold, I *t. away* the desire   Eze 24:16
of thine eyes
if sword come and *t. him*   Eze 33:4;
away   33:6
I will *t. away* the stony   Eze 36:26
heart out of
t. away your exactions from   Eze 45:9
my people
they shall *t. away* his   Da 7:26
dominion
they shall *t. away* the daily   Da 11:31
sacrifice
but I will utterly *t. them away*   Ho 1:6
t. away my corn in time   Ho 2:9
thereof
for I will *t. away* the names   Ho 2:17
of Baalim
whoredom, wine, *t. away* the   Ho 4:11
heart
I will *t. away* and none shall   Ho 5:14
rescue
say unto him, *T. away* all   Ho 14:2
iniquity
that he will *t. you away* with   Am 4:2
hooks
t. away from me the noise of   Am 5:23
thy viols
they covet houses, and *t. them*   Mic 2:2
away
I will *t. away* out of midst of   Zep 3:11
thee
t. away filthy garments from   Zec 3:4
him
I will *t. away* his blood out of   Zec 9:7
his mouth
one shall *t. you away* with   Mal 2:3
dung
t. away coat, let him have   M't 5:40
t. away and cast him into   M't 22:13
outer darkness
Father, *t. away* this cup   M'k 14:36
from me
to *t. away* my reproach among   Lu 1:25
men
let him not come down to *t.*   Lu 17:31
it *away*
Jesus said, *T. away* the stone   Joh 11:39
Romans shall *t. away* our   Joh 11:48
place
when I shall *t. away* their   Ro 11:27
sins
that blood of bulls should *t.*   Heb 10:4
away sins
he was manifested to *t. away*   1Jo 3:5
our sins
if any man *t. away* from   Re 22:19
words of the book, God shall
t. away his part out of book

TAKE *HEED*

t. heed thou speak not to   Ge 31:24;
Jacob   31:29
t. heed to thyself   Ex 10:28;
34:12; De 4:9; 12:13, 19, 30; 1Sa 19:2;
1Ti 4:16

t. heed to yourselves   Ex 19:12;
De 2:4; 4:15, 23; 11:16; Jos 23:11;
Jer 17:21
must I not *t. heed* to speak   Nu 23:12
that which
t. heed in the plague of   De 24:8
leprosy
t. heed and hearken, O Israel,   De 27:9
this day
t. diligent *heed* to do   Jos 22:5
commandment
if thy children *t. heed* to their   1Ki 2:4;
way   8:25; 2Ch 6:16
t. heed for Lord hath   1Ch 28:10
chosen thee
t. heed what ye do, ye judge   2Ch 19:6
not for men
let fear of Lord be on you, *t.*   2Ch 19:7
heed
so they will *t. heed* to do   2Ch 33:8;
  Ezr 4:22
t. heed regard not iniquity   Job 36:21
I said, I will *t. heed* to my   Ps 39:1
ways
t. no *heed* to all words spoken   Ec 7:21
say unto him, *T. heed* and be   Isa 7:4
quiet
t. ye *heed* every one of his   Jer 9:4
neighbour
left off to *t. heed* to the Lord   Ho 4:10
therefore *t. heed* to your   Mal 2:15;
spirit   2:16
t. heed, do not alms before   M't 6:1
men
t. heed of leaven of   M't 16:6;
Pharisees   M'k 8:15
t. heed that ye despise not   M't 18:10
one of these
t. heed no man deceive you   M't 24:4;
  M'k 13:5
he said, *T. heed* what you   M'k 4:24
hear
t. heed to yourselves   M'k 13:9;
Lu 17:3; 21:34; Ac 5:35; 20:28
t. heed I have foretold you   M'k 13:23
t. heed watch, pray   M'k 13:33
t. heed therefore how ye hear   Lu 8:18
t. heed light in thee be not   Lu 11:35
darkness
t. heed and beware of   Lu 12:15
covetousness
he said, *T. heed* that ye be   Lu 21:8
not deceived
saying, *T. heed* what thou   Ac 22:26
doest
t. heed lest he also spare not   Ro 11:21
thee
let every man *t. heed* how he   1Co 3:10
buildeth
t. heed lest this liberty of   1Co 8:9
yours become
let him that standeth *t. heed*   1Co 10:12
lest he fall
t. heed be not consumed one   Ga 5:15
of another
t. heed to the ministry   Col 4:17
received
t. heed of an evil heart of   Heb 3:12
unbelief
whereunto ye do well to *t.*   2Pe 1:19
heed

TAKE HOLD

sorrow *t. hold* on the   Ex 15:14
inhabitants
trembling shall *t. hold* upon   Ex 15:15
them
that the loops may *t. hold* one   Ex 26:5
of another
if mine hand *t. hold* of   De 32:41
judgment
terrors *t. hold* on him as   Job 27:20
waters
judgment and justice *t. hold*   Job 36:17
on thee
it might *t. hold* on ends of   Job 38:13
earth
t. hold of shield and buckler   Ps 35:2
let thy wrathful anger *t. hold*   Ps 69:24
of them
nor *t. hold* of the paths of life   Pr 2:19
t. hold of instruction, let her   Pr 4:13
not go
her feet go down, her steps *t.*   Pr 5:5
hold on hell
it is good thou *t. hold* of this   Ec 7:18
I will *t. hold* of the boughs   Ca 7:8
thereof
when a man *t. hold* of his   Isa 3:6
brother

seven women shall *t. hold* of   Isa 4:1
one man
pangs and sorrows *t. hold* of   Isa 13:8
them
let him *t. hold* of my strength   Isa 27:5
to eunuchs that *t. hold* of my   Isa 56:4
covenant
stirreth up himself to *t. hold*   Isa 64:7
of the
thou shalt *t. hold* but not   Mic 6:14
deliver
did they not *t. hold* of your   Zec 1:6
fathers
ten men *t. hold* of him that is   Zec 8:23
a Jew
that they might *t. hold* of his   Lu 20:20
words
they could not *t. hold* of his   Lu 20:26
words

TAKE *UP*

t. up fifth part of land of   Ge 41:34
Egypt
the priest shall *t. up* the ashes   Le 6:10
t. up censers out of the   Nu 16:37
burning
t. up the ark of the covenant   Jos 3:6;
  6:6
t. up every man a stone out of   Jos 4:5
Jordan
when the Lord would *t. up*   2Ki 2:1
Elijah
t. up thy son   2Ki 4:36
t. up the iron   2Ki 6:7
t. up cast him into portion of   2Ki 9:25
field
we *t. up* corn that we may eat   Ne 5:2
nor *t. up* their names into my   Ps 16:4
lips
then the Lord will *t. me up*   Ps 27:10
that thou shalt *t. up* this   Isa 14:4
proverb
t. up stumblingblock out of   Isa 57:14
way
t. up a lamentation on high   Jer 7:29
places
for the mountains will *t. up*   Jer 9:10
weeping
t. up wailing   Jer 9:18
t. up Jeremiah   Jer 38:10
t. up a lamentation for the   Eze 19:1
princes
t. up a lamentation for   Eze 26:17;
Tyrus   27:2, 32
t. up a lamentation upon   Eze 28:12
king of Tyrus
t. up a lamentation for   Eze 32:2
Pharaoh
one *t. up* a snare from the   Am 3:5
earth
hear this word which I *t. up*   Am 5:1
against you
and a man's uncle shall *t.*   Am 6:10
him *up*
t. me up and cast me into the   Jon 1:12
sea
in that day shall one *t. up* a   Mic 2:4
parable
they *t. up* all of them with   Hab 1:15
the angle
shall not all these *t. up* a   Hab 2:6
parable against him
Jesus saith, Arise, *t. up* thy   M't 9:6;
bed M'k 2:9, 11; Lu 5:24; Joh 5:8, 11,
  12
let him *t. up* his cross and   M't 16:24;
follow me   M'k 8:34; 10:21; Lu 9:23
and *t. up* the fish that first   M't 17:27
cometh up
they shall *t. up* serpents   M'k 16:18

TAKEN

rib which Lord God had *t.*   Ge 2:22
from man
called woman, because she   Ge 2:23
was *t.* out of man
for out of that ground wast   Ge 3:19;
thou *t.*   3:23
vengeance shall be *t.* on him   Ge 4:15
sevenfold
the woman was *t.* into   Ge 12:15
Pharaoh's house
so I might have *t.* her to me   Ge 12:19
to wife
Abram heard that his brother   Ge 14:14
was *t.*
I have *t.* upon me to speak   Ge 18:27
to the Lord

the woman which thou hast *t. Ge 20:3*
is a wife
who, where is he that hath *t. Ge 27:33*
venison
the riches God hath *t.* from *Ge 31:16*
our father
Rachel had *t.* the images, *Ge 31:34*
and put them
staves shall not be *t.* from the *Ex 25:15*
rings
heave shoulder have I *t.* of *Le 7:34*
Israel
I have *t.* the Levites for the *Nu 3:12;*
firstborn of Israel *8:16, 18; 18:6*
neither she be *t.* with the *Nu 5:13*
manner
and the tabernacle was *t. Nu 10:17*
down
I have not *t.* one ass from *Nu 16:15*
them
we have *t.* the sum of the *Nu 31:49*
men of war
their inheritance be *t.* from *Nu 36:3*
the lot
Lord hath *t.* you out of iron *De 4:20*
furnace
betrothed a wife, and hath not *De 20:7*
t. her
when a man hath *t.* a wife, *De 24:1*
and married
when man hath *t.* new wife, *De 24:5*
he shall be free and cheer
up his wife he hath *t.*
they have *t.* of the accursed *Jos 7:11*
thing
he that is *t.* shall be burnt *Jos 7:15*
with fire
and the tribe of Judah was *t. Jos 7:16*
Zabdi was *t. Jos 7:17*
Achan was *t. Jos 7:18*
as the Lord hath *t.* vengeance *J'g 11:36*
he told not he had *t.* the *J'g 14:9*
honey
because he had *t.* his wife, *J'g 15:6*
and given
1100 shekels that were *t.* from *J'g 17:2*
thee
the ark of God was *t. 1Sa 4:11;*
4:17, 19, 21, 22
the cities which the *1Sa 7:14*
Philistines had *t.*
Saul was *t. 1Sa 10:21*
whose ox have I *t. 1Sa 12:3*
nor hast *t.* ought of any man *1Sa 12:4*
and Saul and Jonathan were *1Sa 14:41*
t.
Saul said, Cast lots, and *1Sa 14:42*
Jonathan was *t.*
David's two wives were *t. 1Sa 30:5*
captives
nothing lacking they had *t. 1Sa 30:19*
to them
hast *t.* his wife to be thy *2Sa 12:9;*
wife *12:10*
I have *t.* the city of waters *2Sa 12:27*
behold, thou art *t.* in thy *2Sa 16:8*
mischief
because they cannot be *t. 2Sa 23:6*
with hands
when Zimri saw the city was *1Ki 16:18*
t.
hast thou killed and also *t. 1Ki 21:19*
possession
if thou see me when I am *t. 2Ki 2:10*
from thee
ninth year of Hosea, *2Ki 18:10*
Samaria was *t.*
one principal household *1Ch 24:6*
being *t.* for Eleazar, and
one *t.* for Ithamar
deliver the captives you *2Ch 28:11*
have *t.*
king had *t.* counsel to keep *2Ch 30:2*
the passover
they have *t.* of their daughters *Ezr 9:2*
we have *t.* strange wives *Ezr 10:2;*
10:14, 17, 18
all these had *t.* strange wives *Ezr 10:44*
had *t.* of them bread and wine *Ne 5:15*
who had *t.* Esther for his *Es 2:15*
daughter
so Esther was *t.* to king *Es 2:16*
Ahasuerus
king took off ring he had *t. Es 8:2*
from Haman
he hath also *t.* me by my *Job 16:12*
neck
he hath *t.* the crown from *Job 19:9*
mine head

thou hast *t.* a pledge from thy *Job 22:6*
brother
they are *t.* out of the way, *Job 24:24*
as all other
iron is *t.* out of earth, brass *Job 28:2*
is molten
in net they hid is their own *Ps 9:15*
foot *t.*
let them be *t.* in devices they *Ps 10:2*
have
let them even be *t.* in their *Ps 59:12*
pride
t. crafty counsel against thy *Ps 83:3*
people
thy testimonies have I *t.* as *Ps 119:111*
an heritage
Lord shall keep thy foot from *Pr 3:26*
being *t.*
thou art *t.* with words of thy *Pr 6:2*
mouth
he hath *t.* a bag of money with *Pr 7:20*
him
transgressors be *t.* in their own *Pr 11:6*
I hated my labour which I had *Ec 2:18*
t.
nothing put to it, nor any *Ec 3:14*
thing *t.* from it
but the sinner shall be *t.* by *Ec 7:26*
her
as the fishes that are *t.* in an *Ec 9:12*
evil net
have *t.* evil counsel against *Isa 7:5*
thee
many be broken, and snared, *Isa 8:15*
and *t.*
trapped and *t.* (B) *Isa 8:15*
who hath *t.* counsel against *Isa 23:8*
Tyre
shall be *t.* in the snare *Isa 24:18;*
Jer 48:44
they might be broken, *Isa 28:13*
snared, and *t.*
tabernacle that shall not be *Isa 33:20*
t. down
thou whom I have *t.* from *Isa 41:9*
ends of earth
shall the prey be *t.* from *Isa 49:24*
the mighty
I have *t.* the cup of *Isa 51:22*
trembling
he was *t.* from prison and *Isa 53:8*
judgment
husband with the wife shall be *Jer 6:11*
t.
the wise men are ashamed, *Jer 8:9*
dismayed, and *t.*
thou hast planted, they have *t. Jer 12:2*
root
but thou shalt surely be *t. Jer 34:3;*
38:23
till the day that Jerusalem *Jer 38:28*
was *t.*
when they had *t.* him, they *Jer 39:5*
brought him
when he had *t.* him, being *Jer 40:1*
bound
dwell in your cities, that ye *Jer 40:10*
have *t.*
Kiriathaim is *t. Jer 48:1*
thou shalt be *t. Jer 48:7*
joy and gladness is *t.* from *Jer 48:33*
plentiful field
Kirioth is *t. Jer 48:41*
sons are *t.* captives *Jer 48:46*
hear counsel he hath *t. Jer 49:20*
against Edom
anguish and sorrows have *t. Jer 49:24*
Damascus
Nebuchadnezzar hath *t. Jer 49:30*
counsel against
publish and say, Babylon is *t. Jer 50:2;*
50:24; 51:31
the anointed of the Lord was *La 4:20*
t.
prince of Israel be *t.* in my *Eze 12:13*
snare
shall wood be *t.* thereof to *Eze 15:3*
do any work
thou hast also *t.* thy fair *Eze 16:17*
iewels of gold
thou hast *t.* thy sons and thy *Eze 16:20*
daughters
is come, and hath *t.* the king *Eze 17:12*
thereof
t. of the king's seed, hath *t. Eze 17:13*
an oath of him
and he shall be *t.* in my *Eze 17:20*
snare
not upon usury, neither hath *Eze 18:8*
t. increase

hath given upon usury, hath *Eze 18:13*
t. increase
that hath *t.* off his hand *Eze 18:17*
from the poor
heard of him, *t.* in their pit *Eze 19:4;*
19:8
call to remembrance, they *Eze 21:23*
may be *t.*
in thee have they *t.* gifts, *Eze 22:12*
hast *t.* usury
t. vengeance with a *Eze 25:15*
despiteful heart
vessels, which their father had *t. Da 5:2;*
5:3
ye have *t.* my silver and gold *Joe 3:5*
will cry out, if ye have *t. Am 3:4;*
nothing *3:5*
so shall Israel be *t.* that dwell *Am 3:12*
in Samaria
have we not *t.* horns by our *Am 6:13*
strength
the city shall be *t.* and houses *Zec 14:2*
rifled
the bridegroom shall be *t. M't 9:15*
from them
it is because we have *t.* no *M't 16:7*
bread
kingdom of God shall be *t. M't 21:43*
from you
one shall be *t. M't 24:40;*
Lu 17:34-36
had *t.* counsel, they gave *M't 28:12*
large money
from him *t.* even that which *M'k 4:25*
he hath
when he had *t.* five loaves *M'k 6:41*
looked up
when he had *t.* him in his *M'k 9:36*
arms, he said
we toiled all night, have *t. Lu 5:5*
nothing
at the draught of fishes which *Lu 5:9*
they had *t.*
if I have *t.* any thing from any *Lu 19:8*
man
some of them would have *t. Joh 7:44*
him
brought a woman *t.* in *Joh 8:3;*
adultery *8:4*
ye have *t.* and crucified *Ac 2:23*
for his life is *t.* from the earth *Ac 8:33*
this man was *t.* of the Jews *Ac 23:27*
continued fasting having *t. Ac 27:33*
nothing
not as tho' word hath *t.* none *Ro 9:6*
effect
there hath no temptation *t. 1Co 10:13*
you
being *t.* from you for a short *1Th 2:17*
time
will let, until he be *t.* out of *2Th 2:7*
the way
let not a widow be *t.* into the *1Ti 5:9*
number
who are *t.* captive by him at *2Ti 2:26*
his will
every high priest *t.* from *Heb 5:1*
among men
made to be *t.* and destroyed, *2Pe 2:12*
speak evil
when he had *t.* the book, the *Re 5:8*
beasts
thou hast *t.* to thee thy great *Re 11:17*
power
and the blast was *t.* and with *Re 19:20*
him

TAKEN *AWAY*

well Abimlech's servants had *Ge 21:25*
t. away
Jacob hath *t. away* thy *Ge 27:35*
blessing
behold now he hath *t. away* *Ge 27:36*
my blessing
God hath *t. away* my *Ge 30:23*
reproach
Jacob hath *t. away* all that is *Ge 31:1*
our father's
God hath *t. away* the cattle of *Ge 31:9*
your father
hast thou *t.* us *away* to die in *Ex 14:11*
wilderness
as fat is *t. away* from *Le 4:31;*
sacrifice *4:35*
trespass in a thing *t. away* by *Le 6:2*
violence
after that he hath *t. away* the *Le 14:43*
stones

nor *t.* away ought for unclean use	De 26:14	
thine ass shall be violently *t.* away from	De 28:31	
ye have *t.* away my gods which I made	J'g 18:24	
in the day when it was *t.* away	1Sa 21:6	
high places were not *t.* away	1Ki 22:13; 2Ki 12:3; 14:4; 2Ch 15:17; 20:33	
ask before I be *t.* away from thee	2Ki 2:9	
whose altars Hezekiah hath *t.* away	2Ki 18:22; 2Ch 32:12; Isa 36:7	
in that thou hast *t.* away groves	2Ch 19:3	
Lord gave, and Lord hath *t.* away	Job 1:21	
violently *t.* away an house he built not	Job 20:19	
as God liveth who hath *t.* away my judgment	Job 27:2	
God hath *t.* away my judgment	Job 34:5	
mighty shall be *t.* away without hand	Job 34:20	
thou hast *t.* away all thy wrath	Ps 85:3	
sleep is *t.* away unless they cause	Pr 4:16	
iniquity is *t.* away, thy sin purged	Isa 6:7	
spoil of Samaria shall be *t.* away	Isa 8:4	
burden shall be *t.* away from shoulder	Isa 10:27	
gladness is *t.* away	Isa 16:10	
Damascus is *t.* away	Isa 17:1	
captives of mighty shall be *t.* away	Isa 49:25	
that my people is *t.* away for nought	Isa 52:5	
merciful are *t.* away, righteous is *t.* away	Isa 57:1	
iniquities like wind have *t.* us away	Isa 64:6	
I have *t.* away peace from people	Jer 16:5	
hath violently *t.* away his tabernacle	La 2:6	
he is *t.* away in his iniquity	Eze 33:6	
they had their dominion *t.* away	Da 7:12	
by him the daily sacrifice was *t.* away	Da 8:11; 12:11	
fishes of the sea also shall be *t.* away	Ho 4:3	
and I have *t.* away your horses	Am 4:10	
ye have *t.* away my glory for ever	Mic 2:9	
Lord hath *t.* away thy judgments	Zep 3:15	
from him shall be *t.* away	M't 13:12; 25:29; Lu 8:18; 19:26	
even that he hath		
bridegroom shall be *t.* away	M'k 2:20; Lu 5:35	
that good part shall not be *t.* away	Lu 10:42	
ye *t.* away the key of knowledge	Lu 11:52	
that they might be *t.* away	Joh 19:31	
seeth stone *t.* away from sepulchre	Joh 20:1	
t. away the Lord	Joh 20:2	
t. away my Lord	Joh 20:13	
in humiliation judgment was *t.* away	Ac 8:33	
all hope we should be saved was *t.* away	Ac 27:20	
he that hath done this, might be *t.* away	1Co 5:2	
the veil shall be *t.* away	2Co 3:16	

TAKEN *HOLD*

have *t.* hold upon other gods	1Ki 9:9	
days of affliction have *t.* hold on me	Job 30:16	
mine iniquities have *t.* hold on me	Ps 40:12	
trouble, anguish have *t.* hold on me	Ps 119:143	
pangs have *t.* hold on me, as a woman	Isa 21:3	
anguish hath *t.* hold on us, and pain	Jer 6:24	

TAKEN *UP*

cloud was *t.* up from tabernacle	Ex 40:36	
cloud not *t.* up till it was *t.* up	Ex 40:37	
when the cloud was *t.* up	Nu 9:17; 9:21	
when it was *t.* up they journeyed	Nu 9:22; 10:11	
Absalom was *t.* up between heaven	2Sa 18:9	
have *t.* up their lodging at Geba	Isa 10:29	
shall be *t.* up a curse by Judah	Jer 29:22	
ye are *t.* up in the lips of talkers	Eze 36:3	
so Daniel was *t.* up out of the den	Da 6:23	
there was *t.* up of the fragments	Lu 9:17	
till the day in which he was *t.* up	Ac 1:2	
while they beheld, he was *t.* up	Ac 1:9	
this same Jesus which is *t.* up	Ac 1:11	
unto that same day he was *t.* up	Ac 1:22	
Eutychus fell down, was *t.* up dead	Ac 20:9	
had *t.* up boat	Ac 27:17	
had *t.* up the anchors	Ac 27:40	

TAKER

as with the *t.* of usury, so with the	Isa 24:2	

TAKEST

the water which thou *t.* out of	Ex 4:9	
thou *t.* the sum of the children	Ex 30:12	
the journey that thou *t.* shall not be	J'g 4:9	
if thou *t.* heed to fulfil the statutes	1Ch 22:13	
thou *t.* away their breath, they die	Ps 104:29	
labour thou *t.* under the sun	Ec 9:9	
our soul, and thou *t.* no knowledge	Isa 58:3	
t. up that thou layedst not down	Lu 19:21	

TAKETH

guiltless that *t.* his name in vain	Ex 20:7; De 5:11	
not persons, nor *t.* reward	De 10:17	
for he *t.* a man's life to pledge	De 24:6	
hand, and *t.* him by the secrets	De 25:11	
that *t.* reward to slay an innocent	De 27:25	
t. them, beareth them on her wings	De 32:11	
tribe which the Lord *t.* shall come	Jos 7:14	
smiteth Kirjath-sepher, and *t.* it	Jos 15:16; J'g 1:12	
t. away the reproach from Israel	1Sa 17:26	
as a man *t.* away dung, till it be	1Ki 14:10	
and *t.* it even out of the thorns	Job 5:5	
He *t.* the wise in their craftiness	Job 5:13	
he *t.* away, who can hinder him	Job 9:12	
t. away the understanding of the	Job 12:20	
He *t.* away the heart of the chief	Job 12:24	
and trembling *t.* hold on my flesh	Job 21:6	
gained, when God *t.* away his soul	Job 27:8	
He *t.* it with his eyes: his nose	Job 40:24	
nor *t.* up a reproach against his	Ps 15:3	
nor *t.* reward against the innocent	Ps 15:5	
Lord *t.* my part with them that help	Ps 118:7	
that *t.* and dasheth thy little ones	Ps 137:9	
is man, that thou *t.* knowledge of him	Ps 144:3	
t. not pleasure in the legs of a man	Ps 147:10	
Lord *t.* pleasure in them that fear	Ps 147:11	
the Lord *t.* pleasure in his people	Ps 149:4	
which *t.* away the life of the owners	Pr 1:19	
his spirit than he that *t.* a city	Pr 16:32	
man *t.* a gift out of the bosom	Pr 17:23	
As he that *t.* away a garment	Pr 25:20	
like one that *t.* a dog by the ears	Pr 26:17	
The spider *t.* hold with her hands	Pr 30:28	
labour which he *t.* under the sun	Ec 1:3	
yea, his heart *t.* not rest in the night	Ec 2:23	
his labour that he *t.* under the sun	Ec 5:18	
and as a sheep that no man *t.* up	Isa 13:14	
he *t.* up the isles as a very little	Isa 40:15	
and *t.* the cypress and the oak	Isa 44:14	
there any that *t.* her by the hand	Isa 51:18	
polluting it *t.* hold of my covenant	Isa 56:6	
which *t.* strangers instead of her	Eze 16:32	
of the trumpet, and *t.* not warning	Eze 33:4	
that *t.* warning shall deliver his soul	Eze 33:5	
t. out of the mouth of the lion	Am 3:12	
devil *t.* him up into the holy city	M't 4:5	
devil *t.* him up into an exceeding	M't 4:8	
in to fill it up *t.* from the garment	M't 9:16	
And he that *t.* not his cross	M't 10:38	
t. with himself seven other spirits	M't 12:45	
after six days Jesus *t.* Peter, James	M't 17:1	
that filled it up *t.* away from the old	M'k 2:21	
and *t.* away the word that was sown	M'k 4:15	
he *t.* the father and the mother of	M'k 5:40	
six days Jesus *t.* with him Peter	M'k 9:2	
wheresoever he *t.* him, he teareth	M'k 9:18	
he *t.* with him Peter and James and	M'k 14:33	
him that *t.* away thy cloke forbid	Lu 6:29	
of him that *t.* away thy goods ask	Lu 6:30	
t. away the word out of their hearts	Lu 8:12	
lo, a spirit *t.* him, and he suddenly	Lu 9:39	
he *t.* from him all his armour	Lu 11:22	
and *t.* to him seven other spirits	Lu 11:26	
t. away from me the stewardship	Lu 16:3	
which *t.* away the sin of the world	Joh 1:29	
No man *t.* it from me, but I lay it	Joh 10:18	
me that beareth not fruit he *t.* away	Joh 15:2	
and your joy no man *t.* from you	Joh 16:22	
and *t.* bread, and giveth them	Joh 21:13	
unrighteous who *t.* vengeance	Ro 3:5	
t. the wise in their own craftiness	1Co 3:19	
t. before other his own supper	1Co 11:21	
no man *t.* this honour unto himself	Heb 5:4	
He *t.* away the first, that he may	Heb 10:9	

TAKING

respect of persons, nor *t.* of *2Ch 19:7*
gifts
I have seen the foolish *t.* root *Job 5:3*
by *t.* heed thereto according *Ps 119:9*
to thy
At the noise of the *t.* of *Jer 50:46*
Babylon the
the house of Judah by *t.* *Eze 25:12*
vengeance
also to go, *t.* them by their *Ho 11:3*
arms
Which of you by *t.* thought *M't 6:27*
can
of man is as a man *t.* a far *M'k 13:34*
journey
t. him up into an high *Lu 4:5*
mountain
And which of you with *t.* *Lu 12:25*
thought
man, *t.* up that I laid not *Lu 19:22*
down
he had spoken of *t.* of rest *Joh 11:13*
in sleep
But sin, *t.* occasion by the *Ro 7:8*
For sin, *t.* occasion by the *Ro 7:11*
t. my leave of them, I went *2Co 2:13*
from
other churches, *t.* wages of *2Co 11:8*
them
Above all, *t.* the shield of *Eph 6:16*
faith
t. vengeance on them that *2Th 1:8*
know
flock *t.* the oversight thereof, *1Pe 5:2*
not
forth, *t.* nothing of the Gentiles *3Jo 7*

TALE

And the *t.* of the bricks, which *Ex 5:8*
the fixed number of bricks *Ex 5:8;*
(A)(B)(E)(R) *5:18*
yet shall ye deliver the *t.* of *Ex 5:18*
bricks
they gave them in full *t.* to *1Sa 18:27*
the king
the full number *1Sa 18:27*
(A)(B)(E)(R)
bring them in and out by *t.* *1Ch 9:28*
required to count them *1Ch 9:28*
(A)(E)(R)
by number they both brought *1Ch 9:28*
(B)
spend our years as a *t.* that is *Ps 90:9*
told
spend our years as a sighing *Ps 90:9*
(B)
spend years to an end as a *Ps 90:9*
sigh (E)(R)

TALEBEARER

down as a *t.* among thy *Le 19:16*
people
A *t.* revealeth secrets: but he *Pr 11:13*
The words of a *t.* are as *Pr 18:8*
wounds
about as a *t.* revealeth secrets *Pr 20:19*
there is no *t.* the strife *Pr 26:20*
ceaseth
The words of a *t.* are as *Pr 26:22*
wounds

TALEBEARERS

going about as *t.* (B) *Jer 6:28*

TALENT

Of a *t.* of pure gold shall he *Ex 25:39*
make
Of a *t.* of pure gold made he *Ex 37:24*
it. and
hundred talents, a *t.* for a *Ex 38:27*
socket
a *t.* of gold with the *2Sa 12:30*
precious stones
Or else thou shalt pay a *t.* *1Ki 20:39*
of silver
give them, I pray thee, a *t.* of *2Ki 5:22*
silver
talents of silver, and a *t.* of *2Ki 23:33*
gold
and found it to weigh a *t.* of *1Ch 20:2*
gold
talents of silver and a *t.* of *2Ch 36:3*
gold

there was lifted up a *t.* of lead *Zec 5:7*
he which had received the *M't 25:24*
one *t.*
went and hid thy *t.* in the *M't 25:25*
earth
Take therefore the *t.* from *M't 25:28*
him, and
stone about the weight of a *t.* *Re 16:21*

TALENTS

offering, was twenty and nine *Ex 38:24*
t.
the silver was an hundred *t.* *Ex 38:25*
of the hundred *t.* of silver *Ex 38:27*
were cast
hundred sockets of the *Ex 38:27*
hundred *t.*
brass of the offering was *Ex 38:29*
seventy *t.*
sent to the king sixscore *t.* of *1Ki 9:14*
gold
gold, four hundred and *1Ki 9:28*
twenty *t.*
an hundred and twenty *t.* of *1Ki 10:10*
gold
threescore and six *t.* of gold *1Ki 10:14*
of Shemer for two *t.* of *1Ki 16:24*
silver
and took with him ten *t.* of *2Ki 5:5*
silver
said, Be content, take two *t.* *2Ki 5:23*
bound two *t.* of silver in two *2Ki 5:23*
bags
gave Pul a thousand *t.* of *2Ki 15:19*
silver
unto Hezekiah three *2Ki 18:14*
hundred *t.*
of silver and thirty *t.* of gold *2Ki 18:14*
tribute of an hundred *t.* of *2Ki 23:33*
silver
Ammon sent a thousand *t.* of *1Ch 19:6*
silver
an hundred thousand *t.* of *1Ch 22:14*
gold
a thousand thousand *t.* of *1Ch 22:14*
silver
Even three thousand *t.* of *1Ch 29:4*
gold, of
seven thousand *t.* of refined *1Ch 29:4*
silver
of gold five thousand *t.* and *1Ch 29:7*
ten
and of silver ten thousand *t.* *1Ch 29:7*
and of brass eighteen *1Ch 29:7*
thousand *t.*
one hundred thousand *t.* of *1Ch 29:7*
iron
gold, amounting to six *2Ch 3:8*
hundred *t.*
four hundred and fifty *t.* of *2Ch 8:18*
gold
an hundred and twenty *t.* of *2Ch 9:9*
gold
and threescore and six *t.* of *2Ch 9:13*
gold
Israel for an hundred *t.* of *2Ch 25:6*
silver
the hundred *t.* which I have *2Ch 25:9*
given
same year an hundred *t.* of *2Ch 27:5*
silver
the land in an hundred *t.* of *2Ch 36:3*
silver
Unto an hundred *t.* of silver *Ezr 7:22*
six hundred and fifty *t.* of *Ezr 8:26*
silver
and silver vessels an hundred *Ezr 8:26*
and of gold an hundred *t.* *Ezr 8:26*
I will pay ten thousand *t.* of *Es 3:9*
silver
which owed him ten *M't 18:24*
thousand *t.*
And unto one he gave five *t.* *M't 25:15*
and to
he that had received the five *M't 25:16*
t. went
same, and made them other *M't 25:16*
five *t.*
And so he that had received *M't 25:20*
five *t.*
came and brought other five *M't 25:20*
t.
thou deliveredst unto me five *M't 25:20*
t.
gained beside them five *t.* *M't 25:20*
more
He also that had received *M't 25:22*
two *t.*

thou deliveredst unto me *M't 25:22*
two *t.*
gained two other *t.* beside *M't 25:22*
them
give it unto him which hath *M't 25:28*
ten *t.*

TALES

men that carry *t.* to shed *Eze 22:9*
blood
words seemed to them as idle *Lu 24:11*
t.
unholy and old-womanish *t.* *1Ti 4:7*
(B)
Jewish fairy *t.* (P) *Tit 1:14*
t. artfully spun (N) *2Pe 1:16*

TALITHA

hand, and said unto her, T. *M'k 5:41*
cumi

TALK

come down, and *t.* with thee *Nu 11:17*
there
this day that God doth *t.* with *De 5:24*
man
t. of them when thou sittest in *De 6:7*
thine
T. no more so exceeding *1Sa 2:3*
proudly
I will *t.* with my father (S) *1Sa 19:3*
and *t.* not in the Jews' *2Ki 18:26*
language
t. ye of all his wondrous *1Ch 16:9*
works
should a man full of *t.* be *Job 11:2*
justified
man full of *t.* be free from *Job 11:2*
guilt (A)
God? and *t.* deceitfully for *Job 13:7*
him
he reason with unprofitable *t.* *Job 15:3*
they *t.* to the grief of those *Ps 69:26*
whom
also shall *t.* of thy *Ps 71:24*
righteousness
all thy work, and *t.* of thy *Ps 77:12*
doings
t. ye of all his wondrous *Ps 105:2*
works
so shall I *t.* of thy wondrous *Ps 119:27*
works
thy kingdom, and *t.* of thy *Ps 145:11*
power
thou awakest, it shall *t.* with *Pr 6:22*
thee
but the *t.* of the lips tendeth *Pr 14:23*
only
and their lips *t.* of mischief *Pr 24:2*
the end of his *t.* is *Ec 10:13*
mischievous
t. with thee of thy judgments *Jer 12:1*
plain, and I will there *t.* with *Eze 3:22*
thee
the servant *t.* with this my *Da 10:17*
lord
they might entangle him in *M't 22:15*
his *t.*
Hereafter I will not *t.* much *Joh 14:30*
with
no evil *t.* come out (R) *Eph 4:29*
turned off into empty *t.* *1Ti 1:6*
(B)(E)
all empty *t.* (A) *2Ti 2:16*

TALKED

And Cain *t.* with Abel his *Ge 4:8*
brother
on his face: and God *t.* with *Ge 17:3*
him
in the place where he *t.* with *Ge 35:13;*
him *35:14*
after that his brethren *t.* with *Ge 45:15*
him
that I have *t.* with you from *Ex 20:22*
heaven
and the Lord *t.* with Moses *Ex 33:9*
his face shone while he *t.* *Ex 34:29*
with him
unto him: and Moses *t.* with *Ex 24:31*
them
The Lord *t.* with you face to *De 5:4*
face
talked (S) *J'g 9:1;*
1Sa 9:25; 25:39; 1Ki 10:2; 2Ki 22:14;
2Ch 9:1; Zec 1:14

went down, and *t.* with the　*J'g 14:7*
woman
pass, while Saul *t.* unto the　*1Sa 14:19*
priest
And as he *t.* with them,　*1Sa 17:23*
behold
lo, while she yet *t.* with the　*1Ki 1:22*
king
to pass, as they still went on,　*2Ki 2:11*
and *t.*
And while he yet *t.* with　*2Ki 6:33*
them
the king *t.* with Gehazi the　*2Ki 8:4*
servant
as he *t.* with him, that the　*2Ch 25:16*
king said
princes hear I have *t.* with　*Jer 38:25*
thee
informed me, and *t.* with me　*Da 9:22*
And the angel that *t.* with me　*Zec 1:9*
said
answered the angel that *t.*　*Zec 1:13*
with me
said unto the angel that *t.*　*Zec 1:19;*
with me　　　　　　　　　　*6:4*
angel that *t.* with me went　*Zec 2:3;*
forth　　　　　　　　　　　*5:5*
angel that *t.* with me came　*Zec 4:1*
again
spake to the angel that *t.* with　*Zec 4:4*
me
the angel that *t.* with me　*Zec 4:5*
answered
said I to the angel that *t.*　*Zec 5:10*
with me
While he yet *t.* to the　*M't 12:46*
people
And immediately *t.* with　*M'k 6:50*
them
there *t.* with him two men,　*Lu 9:30*
which
they *t.* together of all these　*Lu 24:14*
things
while he *t.* with us by the　*Lu 24:32*
way
marvelled, he *t.* with the　*Joh 4:27*
woman
as he *t.* with him, he went in　*Ac 10:27*
and *t.* a long while, even till　*Ac 20:11*
break
aside, they *t.* between　*Ac 26:31*
themselves
t. with me, saying unto me,　*Re 17:1*
Come
t. with me, saying, Come　*Re 21:9*
hither
that *t.* with me had a golden　*Ro 21:15*
reed

TALKER

amateur *t.* trying (B)　*Ac 17:18*

TALKERS

ye are taken up in the lips of　*Eze 36:3*
t.
unruly and vain *t.* and　*Tit 1:10*
deceivers

TALKEST

me a sign that thou *t.* with me　*J'g 6:17*
while thou *t.* there with the　*1Ki 1:14*
king
thou? or, Why *t.* thou with　*Joh 4:27*
her

TALKETH

and his tongue *t.* of judgment　*Ps 37:30*
him, and it is he that *t.* with　*Joh 9:37*
thee

TALKING

And he left off *t.* with him　*Ge 17:22*
he ceased *t.* with Abraham　*Ge 18:33*
(S)
either he is *t.* or he is　*1Ki 18:27*
pursuing
while they were yet *t.* with him　*Es 6:14*
The princes refrained *t.* and　*Job 29:9*
laid
people still are *t.* against　*Eze 33:30*
thee
them Moses and Elias *t.* with　*M't 17:3*
him
Moses: and they were *t.* with　*M'k 9:4*
Jesus
nor foolish *t.*, nor jesting　*Eph 5:4*
it were of a trumpet *t.* with me　*Re 4:1*

TALL

a people great, and many, and　*De 2:10;*
t.　　　　　　　　　　　　*2:21*
A people great and *t.* the　*De 9:2*
children
will cut down the *t.* cedar　*2Ki 19:23*
trees
man five cubits *t.* (S)　*1Ch 11:23*
a people *t.*, a people dreaded　*Isa 18:2*
(B)
I will cut down the *t.* cedars　*Isa 37:24*
thereon

TALLER

people is greater and *t.* than　*De 1:28*
we
t. than any of the people (S)　*1Sa 9:2;*
　　　　　　　　　　　　　　10:23

TALMAI

where Ahiman, Sheshai, and　*Nu 13:22*
T.
Sheshai, and Ahiman, and *T.*　*Jos 15:14*
slew Sheshai, and Ahiman,　*J'g 1:10*
and *T.*
the daughter of *T.* king of　*2Sa 3:3;*
Geshur　　　　　　　　　　*1Ch 3:2*
But Absalom fled, and went　*2Sa 13:37*
to *T.*

TALMON

Shallum, and Akkub, and *T.*　*1Ch 9:17*
children of Ater, the children　*Ezr 2:42;*
of *T.*
the porters, Akkub, *T.* and　*Ne 7:45*
Meshullam, *T.* Akkub, were　*Ne 11:19*
porters　　　　　　　　　　*Ne 12:25*

TAMAH

of Sisera, the children of *T.*　*Ne 7:55*

TAMAR

his firstborn, whose name was　*Ge 38:6*
T.
Judah to *T.* his daughter in　*Ge 38:11*
law
T. went and dwelt in her　*Ge 38:11*
father's
And it was told *T.* saying,　*Ge 38:13*
Behold
T. thy daughter in law hath　*Ge 38:24*
played
Pharez, whom *T.* bare unto　*Ru 4:12*
Judah
a fair sister, whose name　*2Sa 13:1*
was *T.*
that he fell sick for his sister　*2Sa 13:2*
T.
I love *T.* my brother　*2Sa 13:4*
Absalom's
let my sister *T.* come, and　*2Sa 13:5*
give me
let *T.* my sister come, and　*2Sa 13:6*
make me
David sent home to *T.*　*2Sa 13:7*
saying, Go
So *T.* went to her brother　*2Sa 13:8*
Amnon's
And Amnon said unto *T.*,　*2Sa 13:10*
Bring the
T. took the cakes which she　*2Sa 13:10*
had
T. put ashes on her head,　*2Sa 13:19*
and rent
So *T.* remained desolate in　*2Sa 13:20*
her
because he had forced his　*2Sa 13:22*
sister *T.*
the day that he forced his　*2Sa 13:32*
sister *T.*
one daughter, whose name　*2Sa 14:27*
was *T.*
T. his daughter in law bare　*1Ch 2:4*
him
the concubines, and *T.* their　*1Ch 3:9*
sister
from *T.* even to the waters　*Eze 47:19*
of strife
from *T.* unto the waters of　*Eze 48:28*
strife in

TAMARISK

planted a *t.* tree　*Ge 21:33*
(A)(B)(E)(R)

TAMBOURINE

tambourine (A)(B)(R)　*Ge 31:27;*
　　　　　　　　　1Sa 10:5; Isa 5:12
a tambourine (B)(R)　*Ex 15:20;*
　　　　　　　　　　　Job 21:12
a tambourine (B)　*Ps 149:3*
a tambourine (A)　*Ps 150:4*

TAMBOURINES

tambourines (A)　*Ex 15:20;*
　2Sa 6:5; 1Ch 13:8; Ps 68:25
tambourines (B)　*1Sa 18:6*
tambourines (R)　*2Sa 6:5; 1Ch 13:8*

TAME

neither could any man *t.* him　*M'k 5:4*
But the tongue can no man *t.*　*Jas 3:8*

TAMED

and of things in the sea, is *t.*　*Jas 3:7*
and hath been *t.* of mankind　*Jas 3:7*

TAMMUZ

there sat women weeping for　*Eze 8:14*
T.

TAMPER

t. with God's word (R)　*2Co 4:2*

TANACH

Manasseh, *T.* with her　*Jos 21:25*
suburbs

TANHUMETH

the son of *T.* the　*2Ki 25:23*
Netophathite
Kareah, and Seraiah the son　*Jer 40:8*
of *T.*

TANNER

days in Joppa with one Simon　*Ac 9:43*
a *t.*
He lodgeth with one Simon a　*Ac 10:6*
t.
in the house of one Simon a　*Ac 10:32*
t. by the

TAPESTRY

decked my bed with coverings　*Pr 7:16*
of *t.*
She maketh herself coverings　*Pr 31:22*
of *t.*

TAPHATH

T., daughter of Solomon to　*1Ki 4:11*
wife

TAPPUAH

The king of *T.* one; the king　*Jos 12:17*
and En-gannim, *T.* and　*Jos 15:34*
Enam
from *T.* westward unto the　*Jos 16:8*
river
Now Manasseh had the land　*Jos 17:8*
of *T.*
but *T.* on the border of　*Jos 17:8*
Manasseh
the sons of Hebron; Korah,　*1Ch 2:43*
and *T.*

TAR

full of *t.* pits (B)　*Ge 14:10*

TARAH

from Tahath, and pitched at　*Nu 33:27*
they removed from *T.* and　*Nu 33:28*
pitched

TARALAH

And Rekem, and Irpeel, and　*Jos 18:27*
T.

TARDY

How long are ye *t.* to possess　*Jos 18:3*
(S)

TARE

king arose, and *t.* his garments	2Sa 13:31
t. forty and two children of them	2Ki 2:24
him, straightway the spirit *t.* him	M'k 9:20
devil threw him down, and *t.* him	Lu 9:42

TAREA

and Melech, and *T.* and Ahaz	1Ch 8:35

TARES

and sowed *t.* among the wheat	M't 13:25
sowed darnel (A)	M't 13:25; 13:26-27, 30, 36, 38, 40
sowed darnel (B)	M't 13:25; 13:29
fruit then appeared the *t.* also	M't 13:26
field? from whence then hath it *t.*	M't 13:27
Nay: lest while ye gather up the *t.*	M't 13:29
wild wheat (A)	M't 13:29
Gather ye together first the *t.*	M't 13:30
weeds (B)	M't 13:30; 13:36, 38, 40
us the parable of the *t.* of the field	M't 13:36
the *t.* are the children of the wicked	M't 13:38
the *t.* are gathered and burned in the	M't 13:40

TARGET

t. of brass between his shoulders	1Sa 17:6
bronze javelin across his shoulders (A)(B)(E)(R)	1Sa 17:6
shekels of gold went to one *t.*	1Ki 10:16
600 shekels of gold for each shield (A)(R)	1Ki 10:16
each buckler, 6000 dollars of gold (B)(E)	1Ki 10:16
of beaten gold went to one *t.*	2Ch 9:15
600 shekels of gold to each shield (A)(B)(R)	2Ch 9:15
600 shekels of gold for each buckler (E)	2Ch 9:15

TARGETS

two hundred *t.* of beaten gold	1Ki 10:16; 2Ch 9:15
200 shields of gold (A)(R)	1Ki 10:16
200 bucklers of gold (B)(E)	1Ki 10:16
200 shields or bucklers (A)(B)(E)(R)	2Ch 9:15
had an army of men that bare *t.*	2Ch 14:8
bore bucklers (A)(E)(R)	2Ch 14:8
bearing shields (B)	2Ch 14:8

TARNISHED

gold and silver are *t.* (P)	Jas 5:3

TARPELITES

the Apharsathchites, the *T.*	Ezr 4:9

TARRIED

were with him, and *t.* all night	Ge 24:54
certain place, and *t.* there all night	Ge 28:11
bread, and *t.* all night in the mount	Ge 31:54
cloud *t.* long upon the tabernacle	Nu 9:19
the cloud *t.* upon the tabernacle	Nu 9:22
they *t.* till they were ashamed	J'g 3:25
And Ehud escaped while they *t.*	J'g 3:26
And they *t.* until afternoon	J'g 19:8
that she *t.* a little in the house	Ru 2:7
he *t.* seven days according to	1Sa 13:8
Saul *t.* in the uttermost part	1Sa 14:2
But David *t.* still at Jerusalem	2Sa 11:1
and *t.* in a place that was far off	2Sa 15:17

to Jerusalem: and they *t.* there	2Sa 15:29
but he *t.* longer than the set time	2Sa 20:5
again to him, (for he *t.* at Jericho	2Ki 2:18
Rabbah. But David *t.* at Jerusalem	1Ch 20:1
and she that *t.* at home divided the	Ps 68:12
While the bridegroom *t.* they all	M't 25:5
that he *t.* so long in the temple	Lu 1:21
child Jesus *t.* behind in Jerusalem	Lu 2:43
and there he *t.* with them	Joh 3:22
he *t.* many days in Joppa with one	Ac 9:43
after they had *t.* there a space	Ac 15:33
Paul after this *t.* there yet a good	Ac 18:18
These going before *t.* at Troas	Ac 20:5
at Samos, and *t.* at Trogyllium	Ac 20:15
disciples, we *t.* there seven days	Ac 21:4
And as we *t.* there many days	Ac 21:10
he had *t.* among them more than	Ac 25:6
the fourteenth day that ye have *t.*	Ac 27:33
at Syracuse, we *t.* there three days	Ac 28:12

TARRIEST

And now why *t.* thou? arise, and be	Ac 22:16

TARRIETH

his part be that *t.* by the stuff	1Sa 30:24
upon the grass, that *t.* not for man	Mic 5:7

TARRY

t. all night, and wash your feet	Ge 19:2
spend the night (A)	Ge 19:2
stay (B)	Ge 19:2; 27:44; 30:27; Le 14:8; Nu 22:19; J'g 6:18; 19:6, 9-10; 1Sa 1:23; 14:9; 2Sa 10:5; 11:12; 2Ki 2:2, 4, 6; Ps 101:7; M't 26:38; M'k 14:34; Lu 24:29; Joh 4:40; Ac 10:48; 28:14; 1Co 16:7
spend the night (R)	Ge 19:2; J'g 19:6, 10
And *t.* with him a few days, until	Ge 27:44
linger and dwell for a while (A)	Ge 27:44
stay (R)	Ge 27:44; J'g 6:18; 2Sa 19:7; 2Ki 14:10; Lu 24:29, 49; Joh 4:40; Ac 18:20; 28:14; 1Co 16:8
I have found favour in thine eyes *t.*	Ge 30:27
Egypt: come down unto me, *t.* not	Ge 45:9
delay (A)(B)	Ge 45:9; Ex 12:39; Heb 10:37
out of Egypt, and could not *t.*	Ex 12:39
T. ye here for us, until we	Ex 24:14
wait (B)	Ex 24:14; 2Ki 7:9; Hab 2:3; 1Co 11:33
t. abroad out of his tent seven days	Le 14:8
stay (A)	Le 14:8; J'g 19:6, 10; 2Ki 14:10; 1Ch 19:5; M't 26:38; Joh 21:22-23; Ac 10:48; 28:14
t. ye also here this night, that I may	Nu 22:19
why *t.* the wheels of his chariots	J'g 5:28
I will *t.* until thou come again	J'g 6:18
wait (A)	J'g 6:18; Ru 1:13; 1Sa 10:8; 14:9; 15:28; 2Ki 7:9; 1Co 11:33
and *t.* all night, and let thine	J'g 19:6
evening, I pray you *t.* all night	J'g 19:9
But the man would not *t.* that night	J'g 19:10

t. for them till they were grown	Ru 1:13
wait (B)	Ru 1:13; 1Sa 10:8; Lu 24:49
wait (R)	Ru 1:13; 1Sa 1:23; 10:8; 14:9; 2Ki 7:9; Hab 2:3; 1Co 11:33
T. this night, and it shall be in the	Ru 3:13
remain (A)	Ru 3:13; 1Sa 1:23; 2Sa 11:12; 19:7; M'k 14:34; Lu 24:49; Joh 4:40; Ac 18:20; 1Co 16:7-8
Remain (B)	Ru 3:13; Joh 21:22; Ac 18:20; 1Co 16:8
Remain (R)	Ru 3:13; 2Sa 10:5; 11:12; 15:28; 1Ch 19:5; M't 26:38; M'k 14:34; Joh 21:22; Ac 10:48
t. until thou have weaned him	1Sa 1:23
seven days shalt thou *t.* till I come	1Sa 10:8
T. until we come to you; then we	1Sa 14:9
T. at Jericho until your beards be	2Sa 10:5; 1Ch 19:5
T. here to day also, and to morrow	2Sa 11:12
t. in the plain of the wilderness	2Sa 15:28
Moab, I may not *t.* thus with thee	2Sa 18:14
there will not *t.* one with thee this	2Sa 19:7
unto Elisha, *T.* here, I pray thee	2Ki 2:2
him, Elisha, *t.* here, I pray thee	2Ki 2:4
unto him, *T.* I pray thee, here	2Ki 2:6
if we *t.* till the morning light, some	2Ki 7:9
open the door, and flee, and *t.* not	2Ki 9:3
glory of this, and *t.* at home; for	2Ki 14:10
he that telleth lies shall not *t.* in	Ps 101:7
dwell (A)	Ps 101:7
They that *t.* long at the wine; they	Pr 23:30
off, and my salvation shall not *t.*	Isa 46:13
that turneth aside to *t.* for a night	Jer 14:8
not lie: though it *t.* wait for it	Hab 2:3
it will surely come, it will not *t.*	Hab 2:3
lag (B)	Hab 2:3
t. ye here, and watch with me	M't 26:38
abide (E)	M't 26:38; M'k 14:34; Lu 24:29; Joh 4:49; Ac 18:20
stop here (N)	M't 26:38; M'k 14:34
stay (P)	M't 26:38; M'k 14:34; Lu 24:29. 49; Joh 4:40; 21:22; Ac 10:48; 18:20; 28:14; 1Co 16:8
unto death: *t.* ye here, and watch	M'k 14:34
And he went in to *t.* with them	Lu 24:29
stay (N)	Lu 24:29; 24:49; Joh 4:40; Ac 10:48; 18:20; 28:14
but *t.* ye in the city of Jerusalem	Lu 24:49
him that he would *t.* with	Joh 4:40
If I will that he *t.* till I come	Joh 21:22; 21:23
wait (N)	Joh 21:22; 1Co 11:33
prayed they him to *t.* certain days	Ac 10:48
they desired him to *t.* longer time	Ac 18:20
desired to *t.* with them seven days	Ac 28:14
together to eat, *t.* one for another	1Co 11:33
wait (E)(P)	1Co 11:33
I trust to *t.* a while with you	1Co 16:7
will *t.* at Ephesus until Pentecost	1Co 16:8
remain (N)	1Co 16:8
But if I *t.* long, that thou mayest	1Ti 3:15
if I am detained (A)	1Ti 3:15
delayed (N)(R)	1Ti 3:15
delay (P)	1Ti 3:15
come will come, and will not *t.*	Heb 10:37
delay (P)	Heb 10:37

TARRYING

deliverer: make no *t.* O my God   *Ps 40:17*
delay not (B)
my deliverer; O Lord, make no *t.*   *Ps 40:17*
    Ps 70:5

TARSHISH

sons of Javan: Elishah, and T.   *Ge 10:4; 1Ch 1:7*
For the king's ships went to T.   *2Ch 9:21*
came the ships of T. bringing gold   *2Ch 9:21*
him to make ships to go to T.   *2Ch 20:36*
they were not able to go to T.   *2Ch 20:37*
Admatha, T., Meres, Marsena   *Es 1:14*
Thou breakest the ships of T.   *Ps 48:7*
The kings of T. and of the isles   *Ps 72:10*
And upon all the ships of T.   *Isa 2:16*
Howl, ye ships of T.: for it is laid   *Isa 23:1*
Pass ye over to T.; howl, ye   *Isa 23:6*
land, as a river, O daughter of T.   *Isa 23:10*
Howl, ye ships of T.: for your   *Isa 23:14*
for me, and the ships of T. first   *Isa 60:9*
them unto the nations, to T., Pul   *Isa 66:19*
into plates is brought from T.   *Jer 10:9*
T. was thy merchant by reason of   *Eze 27:12*
The ships of T. did sing of thee   *Eze 27:25*
Dedan, and the merchants of T.   *Eze 38:13*
But Jonah rose up to flee unto T.   *Jon 1:3*
and he found a ship going to T.   *Jon 1:3*
unto it, to go with them unto T.   *Jon 1:3*
Therefore I fled before unto T.   *Jon 4:2*

TARSUS

Judas for one called Saul, of T.   *Ac 9:11*
Cæsarea, and sent him forth to T.   *Ac 9:30*
Then departed Barnabas to T.   *Ac 11:25*
I am a man which am a Jew of T.   *Ac 21:39*
man which am a Jew, born in T.   *Ac 22:3*

TARTAK

the Avites made Nibhaz and T.   *2Ki 17:31*

TARTAN

And the king of Assyria sent T.   *2Ki 18:17*
year that T. came unto Ashdod   *Isa 20:1*

TARTARUS

to black dungeons of T. (B)   *2Pe 2:4*

TASK

fulfilled your *t.* in making brick   *Ex 5:14*
from your bricks of your daily *t.*   *Ex 5:19*

TASKMASTERS

they did set over them *t.*   *Ex 1:11*
gang foremen (B)   *Ex 1:11*
their cry by reason of their *t.*   *Ex 3:7*
slave drivers (B)   *Ex 3:7; 5:10, 13-14*
And Pharaoh commanded the *t.*   *Ex 5:6*
foremen (B)   *Ex 5:6*
And the *t.* of the people went out   *Ex 5:10*
And the *t.* hasted them, saying   *Ex 5:13*
Pharaoh's *t.* had set over them   *Ex 5:14*
righteousness your *t.* (A)(R)   *Isa 60:17*

TASKMASTER'S

hear *t.* voice (A)(B)(E)(R)   *Job 3:18*

TASKS

Fulfil your works, your daily *t.*   *Ex 5:13*

TASKWORK

taskwork (E)   *Ge 49:15; Jos 16:10; 17:13; J'g 1:28; 2Sa 20:24; 1Ki 4:6; 12:18; 2Ch 10:18; Pr 12:24*
forced labor (R)   *Ge 49:15; Jos 16:10; 17:13; J'g 1:28; 2Sa 20:24; 1Ki 4:6; 12:18; 2Ch 10:18; Pr 12:24*
become subject to *t.* (E)   *Isa 31:8*

TASSALS

tassals (B)(R)   *Nu 15:38; 15:39; De 22:12*
their law reminding *t.* (B)   *M't 23:5*

TASTE

t. of it was like wafers, made with   *Ex 16:31*
the *t.* of it was as the *t.* of fresh oil   *Nu 11:8*
I did but *t.* a little honey with the   *1Sa 14:43*
to me, and more also, if I *t.* bread   *2Sa 3:35*
t. what I eat or what I drink   *2Sa 19:35*
there any *t.* in the white of an egg   *Job 6:6*
my *t.* discern perverse things   *Job 6:30*
and the mouth *t.* his meat   *Job 12:11*
O *t.* and see that the Lord is good   *Ps 34:8*
teach me good *t.* (B)   *Ps 119:66*
sweet are thy words unto my *t.*   *Ps 119:103*
beautiful woman who neglects good *t.* (B)   *Pr 11:22*
honeycomb, which is sweet to thy *t.*   *Pr 24:13*
and his fruit was sweet to my *t.*   *Ca 2:3*
therefore his *t.* remained in him   *Jer 48:11*
beast, herd nor flock, *t.* any thing   *Jon 3:7*
here, which shall not *t.* of death   *M't 16:28; M'k 9:1; Lu 9:27*
were bidden shall *t.* of my supper   *Lu 14:24*
saying, he shall never *t.* of death   *Joh 8:52*
(Touch not; *t.* not; handle not   *Col 2:21*
should *t.* death for every man   *Heb 2:9*

TASTED

So none of the people *t.* any food   *1Sa 14:24*
because I *t.* a little of this honey   *1Sa 14:29*
Belshazzar, whiles he *t.* the wine   *Da 5:2*
had *t.* thereof, he would not drink   *M't 27:34*
t. the water that was made wine   *Joh 2:9*
and have *t.* of the heavenly gift, and   *Heb 6:4*
And have *t.* the good word of God   *Heb 6:5*
ye have *t.* that the Lord is gracious   *1Pe 2:3*

TASTELESS

can the *t.* be eaten (R)   *Job 6:6*

TASTETH

words, as the mouth *t.* meat   *Job 34:3*

TATNAI

T., governor on this side the   *Ezr 5:3; 5:6*
T., governor beyond the river   *Ezr 6:3*
T., governor on this side the river   *Ezr 6:13*

TATTLERS

idle, but *t.* also and busybodies   *1Ti 5:13*

TATTOO

nor *t.* any marks upon you (S)   *Le 19:28*

TAUGHT

I have *t.* you statutes and   *De 4:5*
day, and *t.* it the children of Israel   *De 31:22*
them he *t.* the men of Succoth   *J'g 8:16*
t. them how they should fear   *2Ki 17:28*
thou hast *t.* me the good way   *2Ch 6:27*
they *t.* in Judah, and had the book   *2Ch 17:9*
cities of Judah, and *t.* the people   *2Ch 17:9*
and such as *t.* to sing praise   *2Ch 23:13*
t. the good knowledge of the Lord   *2Ch 30:22*
unto the Levites that *t.* all Israel   *2Ch 35:3*
and the Levites that *t.* the people   *Ne 8:9*
thou hast *t.* me from my youth   *Ps 71:17*
judgments: for thou hast *t.* me   *Ps 119:102*
when thou hast *t.* me thy statutes   *Ps 119:171*
He *t.* me also, and said unto me   *Pr 4:4*
I have *t.* thee in the way of wisdom   *Pr 4:11*
prophecy that his mother *t.* him   *Pr 31:1*
he still *t.* the people knowledge   *Ec 12:9*
fear toward me is *t.* by the precept   *Isa 29:13*
being his counsellor hath *t.* him   *Isa 40:13*
t. him in the path of judgment   *Isa 40:14*
and *t.* him knowledge, and shewed   *Isa 40:14*
children shall be *t.* of the Lord   *Isa 54:13*
hast thou also *t.* the wicked ones   *Jer 2:33*
have *t.* their tongue to speak lies   *Jer 9:5*
Baalim, which their fathers *t.*   *Jer 9:14*
them *t.* my people to swear by Baal   *Jer 12:16*
thou hast *t.* them to be captains   *Jer 13:21*
hast *t.* rebellion against the Lord   *Jer 28:16*
hath *t.* rebellion against the Lord   *Jer 29:32*
though I *t.* them, rising up early   *Jer 32:33*
be *t.* not to do after your   *Eze 23:48*
Ephraim is as an heifer, that is *t.*   *Ho 10:11*
I *t.* Ephraim also to go, taking   *Ho 11:3*
t. me to keep cattle from my youth   *Zec 13:5*
he opened his mouth, and *t.* them   *M't 5:2*
he *t.* them as one having   *M't 7:29*
he *t.* them in their synagogue   *M't 13:54*
the money, and did as they were *t.*   *M't 28:15*
entered into the synagogue, and *t.*   *M'k 1:21*
for he *t.* them as one that had   *M'k 1:22*
resorted unto him, and he *t.* them   *M'k 2:13*
he *t.* them many things by parables   *M'k 4:2*
they had done, and what they had *t.*   *M'k 6:30*
For he *t.* his disciples, and said unto   *M'k 9:31*
as he was wont, he *t.* them again   *M'k 10:1*
he *t.* saying unto them, Is it not   *M'k 11:17*

and said, while he *t.* in the   *M'k 12:35*
temple
And he *t.* in their synagogues,   *Lu 4:15*
being
t. them on the sabbath days   *Lu 4:31*
and *t.* the people out of the   *Lu 5:3*
ship
entered into the synagogue and   *Lu 6:6*
t.
pray, as John also *t.* his   *Lu 11:1*
disciples
and thou hast *t.* in our   *Lu 13:26*
streets
And he *t.* daily in the temple   *Lu 19:47*
as he *t.* the people in the   *Lu 20:1*
temple
And they shall be all *t.* of   *Joh 6:45*
God
synagogue, as he *t.* in   *Joh 6:59*
Capernaum
went up into the temple, and   *Joh 7:14*
t.
cried Jesus in the temple as   *Joh 7:28*
he *t.*
and he sat down, and *t.* them   *Joh 8:2*
treasury, as he *t.* in the   *Joh 8:20*
temple
as my Father hath *t.* me, I   *Joh 9:28*
speak
I ever *t.* in the synagogue,   *Joh 18:20*
and in
grieved that they *t.* the people   *Ac 4:2*
temple early in the morning,   *Ac 5:21*
and *t.*
the church, and *t.* much   *Ac 11:26*
people
to that city, and had *t.* many   *Ac 14:21*
down from Judæa *t.* the   *Ac 15:1*
brethren
t. diligently the things of the   *Ac 18:25*
Lord
you, and have *t.* you   *Ac 20:20*
publicly
t. according to the perfect   *Ac 22:3*
manner
it of man, neither was I *t.* it   *Ga 1:12*
Let him that is *t.* in the word   *Ga 6:6*
heard him, and been *t.* by   *Eph 4:21*
him
in the faith, as ye have been *t.*   *Col 2:7*
are *t.* of God to love one   *1Th 4:9*
another
traditions which ye have   *2Th 2:15*
been *t.*
faithful word as he hath been *t.*   *Tit 1:9*
no lie, and even as it hath *t.*   *1Jo 2:27*
you
t. Balac to cast a   *Re 2:14*
stumblingblock

TAUNT

Elijah began to *t.* them (B)   *1Ki 18:27*
turn their *t.* upon own (A)(R)   *Ne 4:4*
in order to *t.* me (R)   *Ne 6:13*
the *t.* of the simpleton (B)   *Ps 39:8*
a *t.* of our neighbors   *Ps 44:13*
(A)(B)(R)
a *t.* to our neighbors (R)   *Ps 79:4*
my enemies *t.* me (R)   *Ps 102:8*
an answer to those who *t.*   *Ps 119:42*
me (R)
take up this *t.* (R)   *Isa 14:4*
and a proverb, a *t.* and a   *Jer 24:9*
curse
So it shall be a reproach and   *Eze 5:15*
a *t.*
an object of scorn (B)   *Eze 5:15*
take up a *t.* song (R)   *Mic 2:4*
take up a *t.* song (A)(B)(R)   *Hab 2:6*

TAUNTED

t. me (B)(E)(R)   *J'g 8:15*
the enemies have *t.*   *Ps 89:51*
(A)(B)(R)
have *t.* my people (R)   *M'k 15:32;*
they *t.* him (N)   *Lu 23:39*

TAUNTER

words of the *t.* (A)(R)   *Ps 44:16*

TAUNTING

take up this *t.* parable   *Isa 14:4*
(A)(E)
and a *t.* proverb against him   *Hab 2:6*

TAUNTS

no more *t.* (B)   *1Sa 2:3*
an enemy who *t.* me (R)   *Ps 55:12*
t. with which they have (R)   *Ps 79:12*

TAVERNS

far as Appii forum, The   *Ac 28:15*
three *t.*

TAX

the *t.* of Moses (A)(E)(R)   *2Ch 24:9*
not pay *t.* (B)   *Ezr 4:13; 4:20; 7:24*
to pay king's *t.*   *Ne 5:4*
(A)(B)(R)(S)
t. collectors, gatherers   *M't 5:45*
(A)(B)(N)(P)(R)
t. collector's office   *M't 9:9;*
(A)(B)(N)(R)   *M'k 2:14; Lu 5:27*
t. collectors (A)(B)(P)(R)   *M't 10:3;*
   18:17; Lu 5:27; 18:10-11, 13
collectors of temple *t.*   *M't 17:24*
(A)(B)(N)(P)
pay the *t.* (R)   *M't 17:25;*
   22:17, 19; M'k 12:14; Ro 13:6
pay *t.* or toll (N)(P)   *M't 17:25;*
   22:17, 19; Lu 20:22; 23:2; Ro 13:6-7
pay *t.* and toll (N)   *Ro 13:6*

TAXATION

of every one according to   *2Ki 23:35*
his *t.* to

TAXED

he *t.* the land to give the   *2Ki 23:35*
money
that all the world should be *t.*   *Lu 2:1*
all went to be *t.* every one   *Lu 2:3*
into his
be *t.* with Mary his espoused   *Lu 2:5*
wife

TAXES

not have to pay *t.* (B)   *Ezr 7:24*
a raiser of *t.* in the glory of   *Da 11:20*
pay *t.* (B)   *M't 17:24;*
   22:17; M'k 12:14; Lu 23:2; Ro 13:6-7
their rates and *t.* (P)   *M't 17:25*
for this reason pay *t.*   *Ro 13:6*
(A)(P)(R)

TAXING

And this *t.* was first made   *Lu 2:2*
when
Judas of Galilee in the days   *Ac 5:37*
of the *t.*

TEACH

I will *t.* you what ye shall do   *Ex 4:15*
convey to him the message   *Ex 4:15*
(A)
God, put in his heart that he   *Ex 35:34*
may *t.*
instruct (B)   *Ex 35:34;*
   J'g 13:8; 1Sa 12:23; Ps 25:8, 12; 105:22
that ye may *t.* Israel all   *Le 10:11*
statutes
to *t.* when it is unclean and   *Le 14:57*
when clean
hearken to judgments which I   *De 4:1*
t. you
and that they may *t.* their   *De 4:10*
children
Lord commanded me to *t.*   *De 4:14;*
you   *6:1*
t. you not to do after their   *De 20:18*
abominations
to all that priests the Levites   *De 24:8*
shall *t.* you
write and *t.* children of Israel   *De 31:19*
this song
they shall *t.* Jacob thy   *De 33:10*
judgments
t. us what we shall do to the   *J'g 13:8*
child
t. you the good and right   *1Sa 12:23*
way
bade them *t.* the use of the   *2Sa 1:18*
bow
taught (B)(R)   *2Sa 1:18*
to *t.* in the cities of Judah   *2Ch 17:7*
to *t.* in Israel statutes and   *Ezr 7:10*
judgments

shall any *t.* God knowledge   *Job 21:22*
I will *t.* you by the hand of   *Job 27:11*
God
multitude of years should *t.*   *Job 32:7*
wisdom
t. us what we shall say unto   *Job 37:19*
him
he will *t.* sinners in the way   *Ps 25:8*
the meek will he guide and *t.*   *Ps 25:9*
his way
that feareth Lord shall he *t.*   *Ps 25:12*
in the way
I will *t.* you the fear of the   *Ps 34:11*
Lord
then will I *t.* transgressors thy   *Ps 51:13*
ways
so *t.* us to number our days   *Ps 90:12*
that we may
to bind princes, *t.* his   *Ps 105:22*
senators wisdom
t. me good taste (B)   *Ps 119:66*
a just man, and he will   *Pr 9:9*
increase in
he will *t.* us of his ways   *Isa 2:3;*
   Mic 4:2
whom shall he *t.* knowledge   *Isa 28:9*
his God doth instruct and *t.*   *Isa 28:26*
him discretion
t. your daughters wailing and   *Jer 9:20*
t. no more every man his   *Jer 31:34;*
neighbour for all shall   *Heb 8:11*
know Lord
t. my people the difference   *Eze 44:23*
between
whom they might *t.* learning   *Da 1:4*
of Chaldeans
priests thereof *t.* for hire and   *Mic 3:11*
prophets
saith to the dumb stone,   *Hab 2:19*
Arise, it shall *t.*
shall *t.* men so   *M't 5:19*
shall *t.* men so; *t.* all nations   *M't 5:19;*
   28:19
t. all nations   *M't 28:19*
Lord, *t.* us to pray, as John   *Lu 11:1*
taught his
the Holy Ghost shall *t.* you   *Lu 12:12*
what to say
t. the Gentiles   *Joh 7:35*
dost thou *t.* us   *Joh 9:34*
the Holy Ghost shall *t.* you   *Joh 14:26*
all things
all that Jesus began to do and   *Ac 1:1*
t.
to speak nor *t.* in name of   *Ac 4:18;*
Jesus   *5:28*
they ceased not to *t.* and   *Ac 5:42*
preach Jesus
t. customs which are not   *Ac 16:21*
lawful for us
t. distorted things (B)   *Ac 20:30*
as I *t.* every where in every   *1Co 4:17*
church
I *t.* in all congregations (N)   *1Co 7:17*
doth not even nature itself   *1Co 11:14*
t. you
that by my voice I might *t.*   *1Co 14:19*
others
charge some they *t.* no other   *1Ti 1:3*
doctrine
but I suffer not a woman to *t.*   *1Ti 2:12*
nor usurp
a bishop must be apt to *t.*   *1Ti 3:2;*
   2Ti 2:24
these things command and *t.*   *1Ti 4:11*
these things *t.* and exhort   *1Ti 6:2*
if any man *t.* otherwise, he is   *1Ti 6:3*
proud
faithful men who shall be able   *2Ti 2:2*
to *t.*
that they *t.* young women to   *Tit 2:4*
be sober
train (A)(B)(R)   *Tit 2:4*
ye have need that one *t.* you   *Heb 5:12*
again
need not that any man *t.* you   *1Jo 2:27*
thou sufferest that woman   *Re 2:20*
Jezebel to *t.*

TEACH *ME*

t. me and I will hold my   *Job 6:24*
tongue
that which I see not, *t.* thou   *Job 34:32*
me
t. me thy paths   *Ps 25:4*
lead me and *t.* me   *Ps 25:5*
t. me thy way, O Lord and   *Ps 27:11;*
lead me   *86:11*

t. me thy statutes   *Ps 119:12;*
     119:26, 33, 64, 68, 124, 135
t. me judgments   *Ps 119:66; 119:108*
t. me to do thy will, thou art   *Ps 143:10*
my God

TEACH *THEE*

I will *t. thee* what thou shalt   *Ex 4:12*
say
sentence which they shall *t.*   *De 17:11*
thee
thy fathers, shall not they *t.*   *Job 8:10*
thee
ask the beasts, and they shall   *Job 12:7*
t. thee
or speak to the earth, and it   *Job 12:8*
shall *t. thee*
hold thy peace, I shall *t.*   *Job 33:33*
thee wisdom
I will *t. thee* in way thou shalt   *Ps 32:8*
go
thy right hand *t. thee* terrible   *Ps 45:4*
things

TEACH *THEM*

shalt *t. them* ordinances and   *Ex 18:20*
laws
I have written that thou   *Ex 24:12*
mayest *t. them*
t. them thy sons, and sons' sons   *De 4:9*
judgments which thou shalt *t.*   *De 5:31*
them
t. them diligently to children   *De 6:7;*
                          11:9
Israel might know to *t. them*   *J'g 3:2*
war
thou *t. them* the good way   *1Ki 8:36*
where
let him *t. them* the manner   *2Ki 17:27*
of the God
t. ye *them* that know them   *Ezr 7:25*
not
keep my testimony I shall *t.*   *Ps 132:12*
them
whosoever shall do and *t.*   *M't 5:19*
them
he began to *t. them* many   *M'k 6:34*
things
to *t. them* the son of man   *M'k 8:31*
must suffer

TEACHER

as the great, the *t.* as the   *1Ch 25:8*
scholar
master (B)   *1Ch 25:8*
the molten image, and a *t.* of   *Hab 2:18*
lies
instructor (B)   *Hab 2:18*
teacher (S)   *M't 10:24;*
     10:25; Lu 3:12; 6:40; Joh 3:10
Rabbi, translated *t.*   *Joh 1:38*
(A)(B)(N)(R)
that thou art a *t.* come from   *Joh 3:2*
God
t. of the law   *Ac 5:34*
(A)(B)(N)(P)(R)(S)
a *t.* of babes, which hast the   *Ro 2:20*
form
a *t.* of the Gentiles in faith   *1Ti 2:7*
an apostle, and a *t.* of the   *2Ti 1:11*
Gentiles

TEACHERS

understanding than all my *t.*   *Ps 119:99*
have not obeyed the voice of   *Pr 5:13*
my *t.*
not thy *t.* be removed into a   *Isa 30:20*
corner
but thine eyes shall see thy *t.*   *Isa 30:20*
t. have transgressed against   *Isa 43:27*
me
t. of the message (P)   *Lu 1:2*
sitting among *t.*   *Lu 2:46*
(A)(B)(E)(N)(P)(R)(S)
t. of the law   *Lu 5:17*
(A)(B)(N)(R)(S)
at Antioch certain prophets   *Ac 13:1*
and *t.*
10,000 *t.* in Christ (A)(P)   *1Co 4:15*
secondarily prophets, thirdly   *1Co 12:28*
t.
are all prophets? are all *t.*   *1Co 12:29*
and some, pastors, and *t.*   *Eph 4:11*
Desiring to be *t.* of the law   *1Ti 1:7*
shall they heap to themselves *t.*   *2Ti 4:3*
to much wine, *t.* of good things *Tit 2:3*

---

when for the time ye ought   *Heb 5:12*
to be *t.*
be not many *t.* (S)   *Jas 3:1*
there shall be false *t.* among   *2Pe 2:1*
you

TEACHES

God *t.* him aright (R)   *Isa 28:26*

TEACHEST

Lord, and *t.* him out of thy   *Ps 94:12*
law
true, and *t.* the way of God   *M't 22:16*
in truth
men, but *t.* the way of God   *M'k 12:14*
in truth
know that thou sayest and *t.*   *Lu 20:21*
rightly
of any, but *t.* the way of God   *Lu 20:21*
truly
that thou *t.* all the Jews   *Ac 21:21*
which are
Thou therefore which *t.*   *Ro 2:21*
another
t. thou not thyself? thou that *Ro 2:21*

TEACHETH

He *t.* my hands to war; so   *2Sa 22:35*
that a
Who *t.* us more than the   *Job 35:11*
beasts of
by his power: who *t.* like   *Job 36:22*
him
He *t.* my hands to war, so   *Ps 18:34*
that a
he that *t.* man knowledge,   *Ps 94:10*
shall not
which *t.* my hands to war,   *Ps 144:1*
and my
his feet, he *t.* with his fingers   *Pr 6:13*
The heart of the wise *t.* his   *Pr 16:23*
mouth
prophet that *t.* lies, he is the   *Isa 9:15*
tail
thy God which *t.* thee to   *Isa 48:17*
profit
man, that *t.* all men every   *Ac 21:28*
where
or he that *t.* on teaching   *Ro 12:7*
the words which man's   *1Co 2:13*
wisdom *t.*
but which the Holy Ghost *t.*   *1Co 2:13*
unto him that *t.* in all good   *Ga 6:6*
things
as the same anointing *t.* you   *1Jo 2:27*

TEACHING

without a *t.* priest, and   *2Ch 15:3*
without
to my *t.* incline (A)   *Ps 78:1*
t. of thy mother (A)(B)(R)   *Pr 1:8*
forget not my *t.* (A)(B)(R)   *Pr 3:1;*
                           4:2
the *t.* of light (B)(R)   *Pr 6:23*
t. of the wise (A)(B)(R)   *Pr 13:14*
t. is on her tongue (B)   *Pr 31:26*
to the *t.* of our God (B)(R)   *Isa 1:10*
not hearkened to my words,   *Jer 6:19;*
my *t.* (B)   *16:11; 26:4*
them, rising up early and *t.*   *Jer 32:33*
them
all Galilee, *t.* in their   *M't 4:23*
synagogues
and villages, *t.* in their   *M't 9:35*
synagogues
t. for doctrines the   *M't 15:9;*
commandments   *M'k 7:7*
people came unto him as he   *M't 21:23*
was *t.*
sat daily with you *t.* in the   *M't 26:55*
temple
T. them to observe all   *M't 28:20*
things
he went round about the   *M'k 6:6*
villages, *t.*
was daily with you *t.* in the   *M'k 14:49*
temple *t.*
pass on a certain day, as he   *Lu 5:17*
was *t.*
he was *t.* in one of the   *Lu 13:10*
synagogues
through the cities and   *Lu 13:22*
villages, *t.*
day time he was *t.* in the   *Lu 21:37*
temples
the people, *t.* throughout all   *Lu 23:5*
Jewry

---

exasperated at their *t.* (N)(R)   *Ac 4:2*
in the temple, and *t.* the   *Ac 5:25*
people
t. and preaching the word of   *Ac 15:35*
t. the word of God among   *Ac 18:11*
them
t. those things which concern   *Ac 28:31*
standard of *t.*   *Ro 6:17*
(A)(B)(N)(P)(R)
or he that teacheth, on *t.*   *Ro 12:7*
bring them up in Christian *t.*   *Eph 6:4*
(P)
and *t.* every man in all   *Col 1:28*
wisdom
t. and admonishing one   *Col 3:16*
another
wholesome *t.* (A)(B)(N)(P)   *1Ti 1:10*
pattern of wholesome *t.*   *2Ti 1:13*
(A)(B)(E)(N)(R)
profitable for *t.*   *2Ti 3:16*
(B)(E)(N)(P)(R)
t. things which they ought   *Tit 1:11*
not, for
T. us that, denying   *Tit 2:12*
ungodliness

TEACHINGS

wholesome *t.* (B)   *2Ti 1:13*
alien *t.* (A)   *Heb 13:9*
strange *t.* (B)(R)   *Heb 13:9*
outlandish *t.* (N)   *Heb 13:9*
peculiar *t.* (P)   *Heb 13:9*

TEAR

t. down altars (B)(E)   *Ex 34:13*
tear (S)   *Le 10:6*
  13:56; 21:10; 2Sa 3:31; 1Ki 11:11-13,
  31; 2Ch 34:27; Ec 3:7; Eze 29:7;
  Ho 13:8; Joe 2:13; M'k 2:21; Lu 5:36;
                            Joh 19:24
I will *t.* your flesh with the   *J'g 8:7*
thorns
Lest he *t.* my soul like a lion   *Ps 7:2*
they did *t.* me, and ceased   *Ps 35:15*
not
lest I *t.* you in pieces, and   *Ps 50:22*
there be
sword to slay, and the dogs to   *Jer 15:3*
t.
shall men *t.* themselves for   *Jer 16:7*
them
and I will *t.* them from your   *Eze 13:20*
arms
Your kerchiefs also will I *t.*   *Eze 13:21*
t. your own breasts   *Eze 23:34*
(A)(B)(E)(R)
I, even I, will *t.* and go away: *Ho 5:14*
I will
lion: the wild beast shall *t.*   *Ho 13:8*
them
and his anger did *t.*   *Am 1:11*
perpetually
t. the skin off (R)   *Mic 3:2*
The lion did *t.* in pieces   *Na 2:12*
enough for
the fat, and *t.* their claws in   *Zec 11:16*
pieces
t. it out and fling away   *M't 5:29*
(N)
t. down calculations (B)   *2Co 10:5*

TEARETH

t. the arm with the crown of   *De 33:20*
He *t.* me in his wrath, who   *Job 16:9*
hateth
He *t.* himself in his anger: *Job 18:4*
shall
both treadeth down, and *t.* in   *Mic 5:8*
pieces
he taketh him, he *t.* him: *M'k 9:18*
and
and it *t.* him that he foameth *Lu 9:39*
again

TEARING

a *t.* wolf (B)   *Ge 49:27*

TEARS

thy prayer, I have seen thy *t.* *2Ki 20:5*
besought him with *t.* to put   *Es 8:3*
away
mine eye poureth out *t.* unto   *Job 16:20*
God
to swim; I water my couch with   *Ps 6:6*
t.

my cry; hold not thy peace at   *Ps 39:12*
my *t.*
My *t.* have been my meat day   *Ps 42:3*
put thou my *t.* into thy bottle: *Ps 56:8*
are
feedest them with the bread of   *Ps 80:5*
t.
them *t.* to drink in great   *Ps 80:5*
measure
mine eyes from *t.* and my   *Ps 116:8*
feet from
They that sow in *t.* shall reap   *Ps 126:5*
in joy
foolish one *t.* it down   *Pr 14:1*
(A)(B)(R)
t. down house of proud   *Pr 15:29*
(A)(B)(R)
the *t.* of such as were oppressed   *Ec 4:1*
I will water thee with my *t.* O   *Isa 16:9*
Lord God will wipe away *t.*   *Isa 25:8*
from off
heard thy prayer, I have seen   *Isa 38:5*
thy *t.*
and mine eyes a fountain of *t.*   *Jer 9:1*
that our eyes may run down   *Jer 9:18*
with *t.*
weep sore, and run down   *Jer 13:17*
with *t.*
Let mine eyes run down with   *Jer 14:17*
t.
weeping, and thine eyes from   *Jer 31:16*
night, and her *t.* are on her   *La 1:2*
cheeks
Mine eyes do fail with *t.* my   *La 2:11*
let *t.* run down like a river   *La 2:18*
day and
weep, neither shall thy *t.* run   *Eze 24:16*
down
covering, altar of the Lord   *Mal 2:13*
with *t.*
and said with *t.* Lord, I   *M'k 9:24*
believe
and began to wash his feet   *Lu 7:38*
with *t.*
she hath washed my feet with   *Lu 7:44*
t.
humility of mind, and with   *Ac 20:19*
many *t.*
every one night and day   *Ac 20:31*
with *t.*
I wrote unto you with many   *2Co 2:4*
t.; not
to see thee, being mindful of   *2Ti 1:4*
thy *t.*
with strong crying and *t.* unto   *Heb 5:7*
him
he sought it carefully with   *Heb 12:17*
t.
and God shall wipe away all *t.*   *Re 7:17;*
  21:4

TEASING

son of Hagar *t.* (B)   *Ge 21:9*

TEATS

They shall lament for the *t.*   *Isa 32:12*
beat your breasts   *Isa 32:12*
(A)(B)(E)(R)
bruised the *t.* of their   *Eze 23:3*
virginity
bosoms pressed - breasts   *Eze 23:3*
handled (A)(R)
bosom pressed-nipples   *Eze 23:3*
stroked (B)
breasts pressed - bosom   *Eze 23:3*
handled (E)
in bruising thy *t.* by the   *Eze 23:21*
Egyptians
handled bosom - girlish   *Eze 23:21*
breasts (A)(E)
handled breasts - girlish   *Eze 23:21*
bosom (B)
handled bosom - pressed   *Eze 23:21*
breasts (R)

TEBAH

was Reumah, she bare also   *Ge 22:24*
T.

TEBALIAH

Hilkiah the second, *T.* the   *1Ch 26:11*
third

TEBETH

month, which is the month *T.*   *Es 2:16*

TEDIOUS

that I be not further *t.* unto   *Ac 24:4*
thee

TEEMED

minds *t.* with inventions (P)   *Ro 1:30*

TEETH

wine, and his *t.* white with   *Ge 49:12*
milk
the flesh was yet between   *Nu 11:33*
their *t.*
also send the *t.* of beasts   *De 32:24*
upon them
a fleshhook of three *t.* in his   *1Sa 2:13*
hand
lions, and the *t.* of the young   *Job 4:10*
lions
do I take my flesh in my *t.*   *Job 13:14*
and put
he gnasheth upon me with   *Job 16:9*
his *t.*
I am escaped with the skin   *Job 19:20*
of my *t.*
and plucked the spoil out of   *Job 29:17*
his *t.*
his *t.* are terrible round   *Job 41:14*
about
hast broken the *t.* of the   *Ps 3:7*
ungodly
they gnashed upon me with   *Ps 35:16*
their *t.*
and gnasheth upon him   *Ps 37:12*
with his *t.*
whose *t.* are spears and arrows   *Ps 57:4*
Break their *t.* O God, in their   *Ps 58:6*
break out the great *t.* of the   *Ps 58:6*
young
he shall gnash with his *t.*   *Ps 112:10*
not given us as a prey to   *Ps 124:6*
their *t.*
As vinegar to the *t.* and as   *Pr 10:26*
smoke
generation, whose *t.* are as   *Pr 30:14*
swords
their jaw *t.* as knives, to   *Pr 30:14*
devour
Thy *t.* are like a flock of   *Ca 4:2*
sheep
Thy *t.* are as a flock of sheep   *Ca 6:6*
which
threshing instrument having   *Isa 41:15*
t.
the children's *t.* are set on   *Jer 31:29;*
edge   *Eze 18:2*
grape, his *t.* shall be set on   *Jer 31:30*
edge
thee: they hiss and gnash   *La 2:16*
the *t.*
broken my *t.* with gravel   *La 3:16*
stones
mouth of it between the *t.* of it   *Da 7:5*
it had great iron *t.:* it   *Da 7:7*
devoured
whose *t.* were of iron, and his   *Da 7:19*
nails
whose *t.* are the *t.* of a lion   *Joe 1:6*
hath the cheek *t.* of a great   *Joe 1:6*
lion
have given you cleanness of *t.*   *Am 4:6*
people err, that bite with their   *Mic 3:5*
t.
abominations from between   *Zec 9:7*
his *t.*
be weeping and gnashing of   *M't 8:12;*
t.   *22:13; 24:51; 25:30; Lu 13:28*
be wailing and gnashing of   *M't 13:42;*
t.   *13:50*
with him, cast the same in   *M't 27:44*
his *t.*
foameth, and gnasheth with   *M'k 9:18*
his *t.*
they gnashed on him with   *Ac 7:54*
their *t.*
and their *t.* were as of lions   *Re 9:8*
were as the *t.* of lions   *Re 9:8*

TEETOTALERS

be willing to be *t.* (P)   *Ro 14:21*

TEHAPHNEHES

At *T.,* the day shall be   *Eze 30:18*
darkened

TEHINNAH

and *T.* the father of   *1Ch 4:12*
Ir-nahash

TEIL

as a *t.* tree, and as an oak,   *Isa 6:13*
whose
terebinth tree (A)(B)(E)(R)   *Isa 6:13*

TEKEL

Mene, Mene, *T.*   *Da 5:25*
Upharsin
T.; Thou art weighed in the   *Da 5:27*

TEKOA

bare him Ashur the father of   *1Ch 2:24*
T.
Ashur the father of *T.* had   *1Ch 4:5*
two
even Beth-lehem, and Etam,   *2Ch 11:6*
and *T.*
went forth into the   *2Ch 20:20*
wilderness of *T.*
and blow the trumpet in *T.* and   *Jer 6:1*
who was among the herdmen   *Am 1:1*
of *T.*

TEKOAH

And Joab sent to *T.,* and   *2Sa 14:2*
fetched
woman of *T.* spake to the   *2Sa 14:4*
king
woman of *T.* said unto the   *2Sa 14:9*
king

TEKOITE

Ira the son of Ikkesh the *T.*   *2Sa 23:26;*
  1Ch 11:28
was Ira the son of Ikkesh   *1Ch 27:9*
the *T.*

TEKOITES

next unto them the *T.* repaired   *Ne 3:5*
the *T.* repaired another piece   *Ne 3:27*

TEL-ABIB

to them of the captivity at *T.*   *Eze 3:15*

TELAH

T. his son, and Tahan his   *1Ch 7:25*
son

TELAIM

and numbered them in *T.*   *1Sa 15:4*

TELASSAR

children of Eden which were   *Isa 37:12*
in *T.*

TELEM

Ziph, and *T.* and Bealoth   *Jos 15:24*
porters; Shallum, and *T.*   *Ezr 10:24*

TEL-HARESHA

Tel-melah, *T.* Cherub, Addon   *Ne 7:61*

TEL-HARSA

Tel-melah, *T.,* Cherub,   *Ezr 2:59*
Addan

TELL

t. the stars if thou be able to   *Ge 15:5*
number
and I have sent to *t.* my Lord   *Ge 32:5*
to find grace
as to *t.* the man whither ye   *Ge 43:6*
had a brother
we cannot *t.* who put our   *Ge 43:22*
money in our sacks
t. my father of all my glory   *Ge 45:13*
in Egypt
mayest *t.* in the ears of thy   *Ex 10:2*
son
t. the priest, saying, It   *Le 14:35*
seemeth to me

they will *t.* it to the inhabitants	*Nu 14:14*
I will *t.* you (A)(R)	*Nu 24:14; Ru 4:4*
I thought to *t.* thee (S)	*Ru 4:4*
Samuel feared to *t.* Eli (S)	*1Sa 3:15*
t. us wherewith we shall send it to his	*1Sa 6:2*
give to the man of God, to *t.* us our way	*1Sa 9:8*
as the soul liveth, O king, I cannot *t.*	*1Sa 17:55*
I knew that he would surely *t.* Saul	*1Sa 22:22*
O God of Israel, I beseech thee *t.* thy servant	*1Sa 23:11*
lest they should *t.* on us, saying, So did David	*1Sa 27:11*
t. it not in Gath, publish it not in	*2Sa 1:20*
go *t.* my servant David	*2Sa 7:5; 1Ch 17:4*
feared to *t.* him that the child was dead	*2Sa 12:18*
while the child was alive, I said, Who can *t.*	*2Sa 12:22*
thou shalt *t.* to Zadok and Abiathar	*2Sa 15:35*
go *t.* the king what thou hast seen	*2Sa 18:21*
that thou shouldest *t.* who shall reign	*1Ki 1:20*
go *t.* thy lord, Elijah is here	*1Ki 18:8; 11:14*
when I come and *t.* Ahab, he will slay me	*1Ki 18:12*
t. my lord the king, all thou didst send	*1Ki 20:9*
t. him, let not him that girdeth on his harness	*1Ki 20:11*
that we may *t.* the king's household	*2Ki 7:9*
and they said, It is false; *t.* us now	*2Ki 9:12*
let none escape to go to *t.* it in Jezreel	*2Ki 9:15*
t. the man that sent you	*2Ki 22:15; 2Ch 34:23*
I may *t.* all my bones, they stare on me	*Ps 22:17*
publish and *t.* of all thy wondrous works	*Ps 26:7*
go round about her, *t.* the towers thereof	*Ps 48:12*
that ye may *t.* the generation following	*Ps 48:13*
what his son's name, if thou canst *t.*	*Pr 30:4*
who can *t.* what shall be after	*Ec 6:12; 10:14*
for who can *t.* him when it shall be	*Ec 8:7*
that which hath wings shall *t.* the matter	*Ec 10:20*
t. him that I am sick of love	*Ca 5:8*
go and *t.* this people	*Isa 6:9*
t. this	*Isa 48:20*
t. such as are for death, to death	*Jer 15:2*
by their dreams which they *t.*	*Jer 23:27; 28:32*
we will *t.* the king of all these words	*Jer 36:16*
t. us now how thou didst write these words	*Jer 36:17*
t. in Arnon, that Moab is spoiled	*Jer 48:20*
wilt thou not *t.* us what things are	*Eze 24:19*
O king, *t.* thy servants the dream	*Da 2:4; 7:9*
we will *t.* the king the interpretation	*Da 2:36*
t. ye your children, let your children *t.*	*Joe 1:3*
who can *t.* if God will turn and repent	*Jon 3:9*
see thou *t.* no man	*M't 8:4; M'k 8:26, 30; 9:9; Lu 5:14; 8:56; Ac 23:22*
charged his disciples that they should *t.* no man	*M't 16:20; M'k 7:36; Lu 9:21*
t. the vision to no man, until Son of man	*M't 17:9*
t. him his fault	*M't 18:15*
t. it unto the church	*M't 18:17*
t. ye the daughter of Sion, thy king	*M't 21:5*
t. us when shall these things be	*M't 24:3; M'k 13:4*
t. us, whether thou be the Christ the Son of God	*M't 26:63; Lu 22:67; Joh 10:24*
go and *t.* his disciples that he is risen	*M't 28:7*
as they went to *t.* his disciples	*M't 28:9; M'k 16:7*
demand anon they *t.* him of her	*M'k 1:30*
t. how great things Lord hath done	*M'k 5:19*
we cannot *t.*	*M'k 11:33; M't 21:27; Lu 20:7*
t. John what things ye have seen	*Lu 7:22*
go ye, *t.* that fox, I cast out devils	*Lu 13:32*
but canst not *t.* whence it cometh	*Joh 3:8*
when he is come, he will *t.* us all things	*Joh 4:25*
cannot *t.* whence I come, whither I go	*Joh 8:14*
a little while? we cannot *t.* he saith	*Joh 16:18*
or did others *t.* it thee of me	*Joh 18:34*
who shall *t.* you the same things	*Ac 15:27*
but either to *t.* or hear some new thing	*Ac 17:21*
he hath a certain thing to *t.* him	*Ac 23:17*
whether out of body I cannot *t.*	*2Co 12:2; 12:3*
for time would fail to *t.* of Gideon	*Heb 11:32*

TELL ME

why didst not *t.* me she was wife	*Ge 12:18*
nor didst thou *t.* me nor heard I of it	*Ge 21:26*
t. me whose daughter art thou	*Ge 24:23*
t. me, and if not, *t.* me that I may turn	*Ge 24:49*
t. me what shall thy wages	*Ge 29:15*
steal away from me, didst not *t.* me	*Ge 31:27*
t. me thy name	*Ge 32:29*
t. me where they feed	*Ge 37:16*
t. me what thou hast done, hide it not	*Jos 7:19*
t. me wherein thy great strength lieth	*J'g 16:6*
if thou wilt not redeem it, *t.* me	*Ru 4:4*
t. me where the seer's house	*1Sa 9:18*
t. me what Samuel said to you	*1Sa 10:15*
Saul said, T. me what thou hast done	*1Sa 14:43*
David said to Jonathan, Who shall *t.* me	*1Sa 20:10*
how went the matter, *t.* me	*2Sa 1:4*
why art thou lean, wilt thou not *t.* me	*2Sa 13:4*
t. me nothing but the truth	*1Ki 22:16*
what shall I do for thee, *t.* me	*2Ki 4:2*
t. me great things Elisha hath done	*2Ki 8:4*
let men of understanding *t.* me	*Job 34:34*
t. me O thou whom my soul loveth	*Ca 1:7*
ask one thing, which if you *t.* me	*M't 21:24*
t. me which of them will love most	*Lu 7:42*
t. me where thou hast laid him	*Joh 20:15*
t. me whether ye sold land for so much	*Ac 5:8*
t. me art thou a Roman? he said, Yea	*Ac 22:27*
what is that thou hast to *t.* me	*Ac 23:19*
t. me, ye that desire to be under law	*Ga 4:21*

TELL THEE

on one of mountains I will *t.* thee of	*Ge 22:2*
dwell in the land which I will *t.* thee of	*Ge 26:2*

this is word we did *t.* thee in Egypt	*Ex 14:12*
what he sheweth me, I will *t.* thee	*Nu 23:3*
judgment which they shall *t.* thee	*De 17:11*
ask thy elders, and they will *t.* thee	*De 32:7*
I have not told it and shall I *t.* it thee	*J'g 14:16*
he will *t.* thee what thou shalt do	*Ru 3:4*
I will *t.* thee all that is in thine heart	*1Sa 9:19*
I will *t.* thee what Lord hath said to me	*1Sa 15:16*
and what I see, that I will *t.* thee	*1Sa 19:3*
if I knew, then would not I *t.* it thee	*1Sa 20:9*
t. thee what shall become of child	*1Ki 14:3*
did I not *t.* thee that he would prophesy no good thing	*1Ki 22:18; 2Ch 18:17*
I *t.* thee that Lord will build thee	*1Ch 17:10*
I escaped alone to *t.* thee	*Job 1:15; 1:16, 17, 19*
shall not thy fathers teach and *t.* thee	*Job 8:10*
ask fowls of air, they shall *t.* thee	*Job 12:7*
if I were hungry I would not *t.* thee	*Ps 50:12*
let thy wise men *t.* thee now	*Isa 19:12*
proclaim words that I shall *t.* thee	*Jer 19:2*
I *t.* thee, thou shalt not depart thence	*Lu 12:59*
I *t.* thee, cock shall not crow twice till	*Lu 22:34*
t. thee thou oughtest to do	*Ac 10:6; 10:11, 14*
t. thee the mystery of the woman	*Re 17:7*

I TELL YOU, TELL I YOU

I may *t.* you what shall befall you	*Ge 49:1*
t. you what I will do to my vineyard	*Isa 5:5*
before they spring forth, I *t.* you of them	*Isa 42:9*
what I *t.* you in darkness, that speak	*M't 10:27*
neither *t.* I you by what authority I do these things	*M't 21:27; M'k 11:33; Lu 20:8*
t. you by what authority I do	*M'k 11:29*
but I *t.* you of a truth	*Lu 4:25; 9:27*
I *t.* you that many prophets and kings	*Lu 10:24*
I *t.* you, nay, but rather division	*Lu 12:51*
I *t.* you nay, but except ye repent	*Lu 13:3; 13:5*
I *t.* you I know you not whence you are	*Lu 13:27*
I *t.* you there shall be two in one bed	*Lu 17:34*
I *t.* you he will avenge them speedily	*Lu 18:8*
I *t.* you this man went to house justified	*Lu 18:14*
I *t.* you if these should hold their peace	*Lu 19:40*
he said, If I *t.* you ye will not believe	*Lu 22:67*
how believe if I *t.* you of heavenly	*Joh 3:12*
because I *t.* you the truth	*Joh 8:45; Ga 4:16*
I *t.* you before it come, that when it	*Joh 13:19*
I *t.* you the truth, it is expedient for you	*Joh 16:7*
which I *t.* you before, as I have told	*Ga 5:21*
of whom I now *t.* you even weeping	*Ph'p 3:18*

TELLER

medium or fortune *t.* (B)	*Le 20:27*

TELLEST

Thou *t*. my wanderings: put thou   *Ps 56:8*

TELLETH

Also the Lord *t*. thee that he   *2Sa 7:11*
t. the king of Israel the words that   *2Ki 6:12*
when he goeth abroad, he *t*. it   *Ps 41:6*
he that *t*. lies shall not tarry in my   *Ps 101:7*
He *t*. the number of the stars; he   *Ps 147:4*
the hands of him that *t*. them   *Jer 33:13*
Philip cometh and *t*. Andrew; and   *Joh 12:22*

TELLING

Gideon heard the *t*. of the dream   *J'g 7:15*
an end of *t*. the matters of the war   *2Sa 11:19*
as he was *t*. the king how he   *2Ki 8:5*
t. the mesage (B)   *Ac 11:19*

TEL-MELAH

were they which went up from T.   *Ezr 2:59*
they which went up also from T.   *Ne 7:61*

TEMA

Hadar, and T., Jetur, Naphish   *Ge 25:15*
and Dumah, Massa, Hadad, and T.   *1Ch 1:30*
The troops of T. looked, the   *Job 6:19*
inhabitants of T. brought water   *Isa 21:14*
Dedan, and T., and Buz, and all   *Jer 25:23*

TEMAN

And the sons of Eliphaz were T.   *Ge 36:11*
duke T., duke Omar, duke Zepho   *Ge 36:15*
Duke Kenaz, duke T., duke Mibzar   *Ge 36:42*
The sons of Eliphaz: T., and Omar   *1Ch 1:36*
Duke Kenaz, duke T., duke Mibzar   *1Ch 1:53*
Is wisdom no more in T.? is counsel   *Jer 49:7*
against the inhabitants of T.   *Jer 49:20*
I will make it desolate from T.   *Eze 25:13*
But I will send a fire upon T., which   *Am 1:12*
And thy mighty men, O T. shall be   *Ob 9*
God came from T., and the Holy   *Hab 3:3*

TEMANI

Husham of the land of T. reigned   *Ge 36:34*

TEMANITE

Eliphaz the T., and Bildad   *Job 2:11*
Eliphaz the T. answered and said   *Job 4:1*
Then answered Eliphaz the T.   *Job 15:1*
Eliphaz the T. answered and said   *Job 22:1*
the Lord said to Eliphaz the T. My   *Job 42:7*
So Eliphaz the T. and Bildad   *Job 42:9*

TEMANITES

Husham of the land of the T.   *1Ch 1:45*

TEMENI

Hepher, and T., and Haahashtari   *1Ch 4:6*

TEMPER

Haman's *t*. grew (B)   *Es 5:9*
hin of oil, to *t*. with the fine flour   *Eze 46:14*

TEMPERANCE

as he reasoned of righteousness, *t*.   *Ac 24:25*
control of passions (A)(B)   *Ac 24:25*
self-control (E)(N)(P)(R)   *Ac 24:25; Ga 5:23*
Meekness, *t*.: against such there is   *Ga 5:23*
self-control (A)(B)   *Ga 5:23; 2Pe 1:6*
And to knowledge *t*.; and to   *2Pe 1:6*
and to *t*. patience: and to patience   *2Pe 1:6*

TEMPERATE

for the mastery is *t*. in all things   *1Co 9:25*
self-control (R)   *1Co 9:25*
circumspect, *t*. (A)(B)(R)(S)   *1Ti 3:2*
of good men, sober, just, holy *t*.   *Tit 1:8*
self-controlled (B)(P)(R)   *Tit 1:8*
the aged men be sober, grave, *t*.   *Tit 2:2*
t., serious (P)(R)   *Tit 2:2*
to be *t*. (N)   *Tit 2:5*
be *t*. in all things (N)   *Tit 2:6*
live a life of *t*. (N)   *Tit 2:12*
be well-balanced, *t*. (A)   *1Pe 5:8*

TEMPERED

cakes unleavened *t*. with oil   *Ex 29:2*
mixed (A)(B)(R)   *Ex 29:2*
mingled (E)   *Ex 29:2*
t. together, pure and holy   *Ex 30:35*
mixed (A)   *Ex 30:35*
blended (R)   *Ex 30:35*
but God hath *t*. the body together   *1Co 12:24*
adjusted (A)(R)   *1Co 12:24*
constituted (B)   *1Co 12:24*
combined (N)   *1Co 12:24*
harmonized (P)   *1Co 12:24*
not quick *t*. (A)(B)(N)(R)   *Tit 1:7*

TEMPEST

For he breaketh me with a *t*.   *Job 9:17*
t. stealeth him away in the night   *Job 27:20*
windstorm (A)   *Job 27:20*
whirlwind (B)   *Job 27:20*
and brimstone, and an horrible *t*.   *Ps 11:6*
scorching wind (A)(B)   *Ps 11:6*
burning wind (E)   *Ps 11:6*
from the windy storm and *t*.   *Ps 55:8*
storm (A)   *Ps 55:8*
   M't 8:24; Ac 27:18; Heb 12:18
So persecute them with thy *t*.   *Ps 83:15*
wind (A)   *Ps 83:15*
strong one, which as a *t*. of hail   *Isa 28:2*
and great noise, with storm and *t*.   *Isa 29:6*
scattering, and *t*. and hailstones   *Isa 30:30*
the wind, and a covert from the *t*.   *Isa 32:2*
O thou afflicted, tossed with *t*. and   *Isa 54:11*
destructive *t*. from Almighty (A)   *Joe 1:15*
a *t*. in the day of the whirlwind   *Am 1:14*
there was a mighty *t*. in the sea   *Jon 1:4*
my sake this great *t*. is upon you   *Jon 1:12*
there arose a great *t*. in the sea   *M't 8:24*
storm (R)   *M't 8:24; Ac 27:18; 2Pe 2:17*
storm (P)   *M't 8:24; Ac 27:18*
being exceedingly tossed with a *t*.   *Ac 27:18*
storm (E)   *Ac 27:18; 2Pe 2:17*
and no small *t*. lay on us, all hope   *Ac 27:20*
storm (N)   *Ac 27:20; 2Pe 2:17*
blackness, and darkness, and *t*.   *Heb 12:18*

whirlwind (N)   *Heb 12:18*
rushing wind (P)   *Heb 12:18*
clouds that are carried with a *t*.   *2Pe 2:17*
whirlwind driven fogs (B)   *2Pe 2:17*
whirling storm clouds (P)   *2Pe 2:17*

TEMPESTUOUS

it shall be very *t*. round about him   *Ps 50:3*
for the sea wrought, and was *t*.   *Jon 1:11*
wrought, and was *t*. against them   *Jon 1:13*
there arose against it a *t*. wind   *Ac 27:14*

TEMPLE

Eli sat on seat by post of the *t*.   *1Sa 1:9*
he did hear my voice out of his *t*.   *2Sa 22:7; Ps 18:6*
the *t*. before it was forty cubits long   *1Ki 6:17*
the *t*. servants (B)(R)   *1Ch 9:2*
when Josiah had prepared the *t*.   *2Ch 35:20*
and put the vessels in his *t*. at Babylon   *2Ch 36:7*
the *t*. attendants (B)   *Ezr 2:43; 2:58; 7:7, 24; 8:17, 20; Ne 3:26; 10:28; 11:21*
that they builded the *t*. unto the Lord   *Ezr 4:1*
vessels took out of *t*. brought to *t*.   *Ezr 5:14; 6:5*
hid in the *t*. shut doors of the *t*.   *Ne 6:10*
beauty of Lord and to inquire his *t*.   *Ps 27:4*
in his *t*. doth every one speak of his glory   *Ps 29:9*
we have thought of thy loving kindness, O God, in the midst of thy *t*.   *Ps 48:9*
because of thy *t*. at Jerusalem kings   *Ps 68:29*
lifted up, and his train filled the *t*.   *Isa 6:1*
to the *t*. thy foundation shall be laid   *Isa 44:28*
a voice from the *t*. a voice of the Lord   *Isa 66:6*
declare vengeance of his *t*.   *Jer 50:28; 51:11*
afterward he brought me to the *t*.   *Eze 41:1*
golden vessels taken out of the *t*.   *Da 5:2; 5:3*
songs of *t*. shall be howlings that day   *Am 8:3*
let your hands be strong, that the *t*. might be built   *Zec 8:9*
Lord shall come suddenly to his *t*.   *Mal 3:1*
set him on a pinnacle of *t*.   *M't 4:5; Lu 4:9*
turret of the *t*. (A)   *M't 4:5*
in this place is one greater than the *t*.   *M't 1:6*
collectors of *t*. tax (A)(B)(N)(P)   *M't 17:24*
blind guides, whosoever shall swear by the *t*. or by the gold of the *t*.   *M't 23:16; 17:21*
whom ye slew between *t*. and the altar   *M't 23:35*
to shew him buildings of *t*.   *M't 24:1; Lu 21:5*
I am able to destroy the *t*. of God   *M't 26:61*
thou that destroyest the *t*.   *M't 27:40; M'k 15:29*
behold the veil of the *t*. was rent in twain   *M't 27:51; M'k 15:38; Lu 23:45*
should carry any vessel thro' the *t*.   *M'k 11:16*
I will destroy this *t*. made with hands   *M'k 14:58*
Anna a widow departed not from the *t*.   *Lu 2:37*
he drove them all out of the *t*.   *Joh 2:15*
destroy this *t*.   *Joh 2:19*
forty and six years was this *t*. in building   *Joh 2:20*
spake of *t*. of his body   *Joh 2:21*
whom they laid daily at the gate of the *t*. to ask alms   *Ac 3:2; 3:10*

t. of goddess Diana should be despised	*Ac 19:27*
took Paul and drew him out of the *t.*	*Ac 21:30*
who also hath gone about to profane the *t.*	*Ac 24:6*
neither against the *t.* nor against Caesar	*Ac 25:8*
know ye not ye are the *t.* of God	*1Co 3:16*
if any man defile *t.* of God, shall God destroy, for *t.* of God is holy, which *t.* ye are	*1Co 3:17*
your body is the *t.* of the Holy Ghost	*1Co 6:19*
see these sit at meat in an idol's *t.*	*1Co 8:10*
they who minister live of things of *t.*	*1Co 9:13*
what agreement hath *t.* of God with idols? for ye are *t.* of living God	*2Co 6:16*
and serve him day and night in his *t.*	*Re 7:15*
saying, Rise and measure the *t.* of God	*Re 11:1*
t. of God opened in heaven, and ark of testament was seen in his *t.*	*Re 11:19*
another angel came out of the *t.*	*Re 14:15; 14:17*
the *t.* of the tabernacle was opened	*Re 15:5*
and the seven angels came out of the *t.*	*Re 15:6*
t. filled with smoke from glory of God	*Re 15:8*
I heard a great voice out of *t.*	*Re 16:1; 16:17*
I saw no *t.* therein, for Lord God Almighty and Lamb are *t.*	*Re 21:22*

IN, *INTO* THE TEMPLE

king David's spears were *in* *t.*	*2Ki 11:10*
executed the priest's office *in* the *t.*	*1Ch 6:10*
fastened his head *in the t.* of Dagon	*1Ch 10:10*
he set ten candlesticks *in the t.*	*2Ch 4:7; 4:8*
go carry these vessels *into* the *t.*	*Ezr 5:15*
would go *into the t.* to save his life	*Ne 6:11*
priests *in the t.* profane the sabbath	*M't 12:5*
went *into the t.* cast out	*M't 21:12*
them that sold *in the t.*	*M'k 11:15; Lu 19:45*
blind and lame came to him *in the t.*	*M't 21:14*
children crying *in the t.* saying, Hosanna	*M't 21:15*
I sat daily teaching *in the t.*	*M't 26:55; Lu 21:37*
he cast down the pieces of silver *in the t.*	*M't 27:5*
I was daily teaching *in the t.*	*M'k 14:49; Lu 22:53*
marvelled that he tarried so long *in the t.*	*Lu 1:21*
they perceived that he had seen a vision *in the t.*	*Lu 1:22*
and he came by the spirit *into the t.*	*Lu 2:27*
found him *in the t.* sitting in midst	*Lu 2:46*
two men went up *into the t.* to pray	*Lu 18:10*
were continually *in the t.* praising God	*Lu 24:53*
continuing with one accord *in the t.*	*Ac 2:46*
Peter and John went up together *into the t.*	*Ac 3:1*
about to go *into the t.*	*Ac 3:3*
speak *in the t.*	*Ac 5:20*
men are standing *in the t.* and teaching	*Ac 5:25*
Paul entered *into the t.*	*Ac 21:26*
saw him *in the t.*	*Ac 21:27*
brought Greeks also *into the t.*	*Ac 21:28; 21:29*
while I prayed *in the t.* I was in a trance	*Ac 22:17*
they neither found me *in the t.* disputing	*Ac 24:12*
certain Jews found me	*Ac 24:18*

purified *in the t.*	
for these causes the Jews caught me *in the t.*	*Ac 26:21*
that he as God sitteth *in the t.* of God	*2Th 2:4*
him will I make pillar *in the t.* of God	*Re 3:12*
and no man was able to enter *into the t.*	*Re 15:8*

TEMPLES

and smote the nail into his *t.*	*J'g 4:21*
lay dead, and the nail was in his *t.*	*J'g 4:22*
pierced and stricken through his *t.*	*J'g 5:26*
t. are like a piece of a pomegranate	*Ca 4:3*
a piece of a pomegranate are thy *t.*	*Ca 6:7*
his Maker, and buildeth *t.*	*Ho 8:14*
have carried into your *t.* my goodly	*Joe 3:5*
dwelleth not in *t.* made with hands	*Ac 7:48; 17:24*
are neither robbers of *t.* (S)	*Ac 19:37*
do you rob *t.* (E)(P)(R)	*Ro 2:22*

TEMPORAL

the things which are seen are *t.*	*2Co 4:18*

TEMPORARILY

to live *t.* (A)	*Ge 12:10; 19:9; 26:3; Le 17:8, 10; 19:33; Jer 42:15; 43:2; Eze 20:38*
lived *t.* in Gerar (A)	*Ge 20:1*
to live *t.* (B)	*Ge 47:4*
they lived *t.* (B)	*Ex 6:4*
dwells *t.* (A)	*Le 16:29; 17:12; Nu 15:26*
t. been residing (B)	*De 18:6*
living *t.* in (A)	*J'g 19:1*

TEMPORARY

land of *t.* residence (A)	*Ex 6:4*
a *t.* resident (A)	*Le 25:6; Job 31:32; Ps 39:12; Zec 7:10*
t. residents (A)	*Le 25:23*
t. resident (A)	*Le 25:35; 25:40; Nu 35:15; Ps 39:12*
a *t.* resident (B)	*Le 25:35*
a *t.* resident (A)	*De 18:6 Heb 11:9*
mere tenants, *t.* residents	*1Ch 29:15*
t. residents (A)	*Jer 35:7*
t. residents, exiles (A)	*Heb 11:13*
your *t.* residence (A)	*1Pe 1:17*
as strangers, *t.* residents	*1Pe 2:11*

TEMPT

things, that God did *t.* Abraham	*Ge 22:1*
me? wherefore do ye *t.* the Lord	*Ex 17:2*
put God to the test (B)	*Ex 17:2; De 6:16; Isa 7:12; Mal 3:15; M't 4:7; M'k 12:15; Lu 4:12; Ac 5:9*
put the Lord to proof (R)	*Ex 17:2*
Ye shall not *t.* the Lord your God	*De 6:16*
put God to the test (R)	*De 6:16; Isa 7:12; Mal 3:15; M't 22:18; M'k 12:15; 1Co 10:9*
not ask, neither will I *t.* the Lord	*Isa 7:12*
that *t.* God are even delivered	*Mal 3:15*
test (A)	*Mal 3:15; M't 4:7; M'k 12:15; Lu 4:12*
trial of the Lord (E)	*M't 4:7; 22:18; M'k 12:15; Lu 4:12; Ac 15:10; 1Co 10:9*
put God to the test (N)	*M't 4:7; Lu 4:12; Ac 5:9; 1Co 10:9*
said, Why *t.* ye me, ye hypocrites	*M't 22:18*
put me to the test (A)	*M't 22:18*
why do you try me (B)	*M't 22:18*
catch me out (N)	*M't 22:18; M'k 12:15*
Why do you try me (P)	*M't 22:18; M'k 12:15*
said unto them, Why ye me	*M'k 12:15*
shall not *t.* the Lord thy God	*Lu 4:12*

and said unto them, Why *t.* ye me	*Lu 20:23*
to *t.* the Spirit of the Lord	*Ac 5:9*
trying the Lord's Spirit (A)	*Ac 5:9*
try the Spirit of the Lord (E)	*Ac 5:9*
put Spirit of the Lord to such a test (P)	*Ac 5:9*
Now therefore why *t.* ye God, to	*Ac 15:10*
why be a trial to God (A)(B)(R)	*Ac 15:10; 1Co 10:9*
provoke God (N)	*Ac 15:10*
strain the patience of God (P)	*Ac 15:10*
t. you not for your incontinence	*1Co 7:5*
Neither let us *t.* Christ, as some of	*1Co 10:9*

TEMPTATION

in the day of *t.* in the wilderness	*Ps 95:8*
in the day of Massah (E)(R)	*Ps 95:8*
lead us not into *t.* but deliver	*M't 6:13*
test (N)	*M't 6:13; 26:41; M'k 14:38; Lu 11:4; 1Co 10:13*
and pray, that ye enter not into *t.*	*M't 26:41*
ye and pray, lest ye enter into *t.*	*M'k 14:38*
when the devil had ended all the *t.*	*Lu 4:13*
believe, and in time of *t.* fall away	*Lu 8:13*
in time of trial fall away (B)	*Lu 8:13*
in time testing fall away (N)	*Lu 8:13; 22:40*
lead us not into *t.*; but deliver	*Lu 11:4*
Pray that ye enter not into *t.*	*Lu 22:40*
rise and pray, lest ye enter into *t.*	*Lu 22:46*
There hath no *t.* taken you but such	*1Co 10:13*
no trial beyond what man can bear (N)	*1Co 10:13; Jas 1:12*
with the *t.* make a way to escape	*1Co 10:13*
And my *t.* which was in my flesh ye	*Ga 4:14*
a trial (A)(B)(P)(R)	*Ga 4:14; Re 3:10*
will be rich fall into *t.* and a snare	*1Ti 6:9*
one of the world's traps (P)	*1Ti 6:9*
in the day of *t.* in the wilderness	*Heb 3:8*
day of testing (A)(N)(R)	*Heb 3:8*
the time of the desert ordeal (B)	*Heb 3:8*
the day of trial (E)	*Heb 3:8*
is the man that endureth *t.*	*Jas 1:12*
who endureth trial (R)	*Jas 1:12*
put a *t.* before (N)	*Re 2:14*
will keep thee from the hour of *t.*	*Re 3:10*
the hour of trial (E)(P)(R)	*Re 3:10*
the ordeal that is to come (N)	*Re 3:10*

TEMPTATIONS

by *t.*, by signs, by wonders	*De 4:34*
by trials (A)(R)	*De 4:34; 7:19; 29:3; Lu 22:28; Ac 20:19*
by tests (B)	*De 4:34*
by trials (E)	*De 4:34; 7:19; 29:3; Ac 20:19; 1Pe 1:6*
tests (B)	*De 7:19; 29:3*
The great *t.* which thine eyes have	*De 29:3*
set to sin (B)	*Eze 14:3; 14:7*
woe to the world for *t.* to sin (A)(R)	*M't 18:7*
have continued with me in my *t.*	*Lu 22:28*
trials (B)	*Lu 22:28; Ac 20:19; Jas 1:2; 1Pe 1:6*
trials (N)	*Lu 22:28; Ac 20:19; Jas 1:2; 1Pe 1:6; 2Pe 2:9*
and *t.*, which befell me by the lying	*Ac 20:19*
all joy when ye fall into divers *t.*	*Jas 1:2*
trials (R)	*Jas 1:2; 1Pe 1:6; 2Pe 2:9*
manifold (E)	*Jas 1:2*
in heaviness through manifold *t.*	*1Pe 1:6*
how to deliver the godly out of *t.*	*2Pe 2:9*

TEMPTED

because they *t.* the Lord,   *Ex 17:7*
saying
tested (A)   *Nu 14:22; Ps 95:9; Heb 3:9*
your God, as ye *t.* him in   *De 6:16*
Massah
they *t.* God in their heart by   *Ps 78:18*
asking
they turned back, and *t.* God   *Ps 78:41*
they *t.* and provoked the   *Ps 78:56*
most high
When your fathers *t.* me,   *Ps 95:9*
proved me
wilderness, and *t.* God in   *Ps 106:14*
the desert
put God to the test (R)   *Ps 106:14;*
    Heb 3:9
wilderness to be *t.* of the   *M't 4:1*
devil
wilderness forty days, *t.* of   *M'k 1:13*
Satan
Being forty days *t.* of the devil   *Lu 4:2*
lawyer stood up, and *t.* him   *Lu 10:25*
as some of them also *t.* and   *1Co 10:9*
were
became a trial (A)   *1Co 10:9*
put Lord to the test (N)   *1Co 10:9*
not suffer you to be *t.* above   *1Co 10:13*
that ye
allow to be tested (N)   *1Co 10:13;*
    Ga 6:1
thyself, lest thou also be *t.*   *Ga 6:1*
means the tempter have *t.* you   *1Th 3:5*
he himself hath suffered   *Heb 2:18*
being *t.*
is able to succour them that   *Heb 2:18*
are *t.*
when your fathers *t.* me,   *Heb 3:9*
proved
tried me (A)   *Heb 3:9*
tested (N)   *Heb 3:9; 4:15*
was in all points *t.* like as   *Heb 4:15*
we are
they were sawn asunder   *Heb 11:37*
were *t.*
say when he is *t.,* I am *t.* of   *Jas 1:13*
God
for God cannot be *t.* with   *Jas 1:13*
evil
every man is *t.* when he is   *Jas 1:14*
drawn

TEMPTER

And when the *t.* came to him,   *M't 4:3*
he
means the *t.* have tempted you   *1Th 3:5*

TEMPTETH

with evil, neither *t.* he any   *Jas 1:13*
man

TEMPTING

are *t.* morsels (B)   *Pr 18:8*
and *t.* desired him that he   *M't 16:1*
would
trying him (E)   *M't 16:1;*
19:3; 22:35; M'k 8:11; 10:2; Lu 11:16;
    Joh 8:6
to test him (N)   *M't 16:1;*
19:3; 22:35; M'k 8:11; 10:2; Lu 11:16
to test him (P)   *M't 16:1;*
    Lu 11:6; Joh 8:6
came unto him, *t.* him and   *M't 19:3*
saying
put him to the test (A)   *M't 19:3;*
22:35; M'k 8:11; 10:2; Lu 11:16;
    Joh 8:6
to test him (B)   *M't 19:3;*
22:35; M'k 8:11; Lu 11:16
asked him a question, *t.* him   *M't 22:35*
of him a sign from heaven, *t.*   *M'k 8:11*
him
a man to put away his wife?   *M'k 10:2*
t. him
others *t.* him, sought of him   *Lu 11:16*
a sign
This they said, *t.* him, that   *Joh 8:6*
they

TEN

Abraham dwelt *t.* years in   *Ge 16:3*
Canaan
peradventure *t.* shall be   *Ge 18:32*
found there

the servant took *t.* camels of   *Ge 24:10*
his masters
took bracelets for her hands   *Ge 24:22*
of *t.* shekels
Jacob took *t.* bulls and *t.*   *Ge 32:15*
foals for Esau
Joseph's *t.* brethren went to   *Ge 42:3*
buy corn
Joseph sent *t.* asses and *t.*   *Ge 45:23*
she asses
make a tabernacle with *t.*   *Ex 26:1*
curtains
their pillars *t.* and their   *Ex 27:12*
sockets *t.*
wrote *t.* commandments   *Ex 34:28;*
    De 4:13; 10:4
t. women shall bake your   *Le 26:26*
bread
for the female *t.* shekels *Le 27:5; 27:7*
one spoon of *t.* shekels *Nu 7:14; 20:26*
he that gathered least   *Nu 11:32*
gathered *t.* homers
and on the fourth day *t.*   *Nu 29:23*
bullocks
there fell *t.* portions to   *Jos 17:5*
Manasseh
Kohath had by lot out of   *Jos 21:5;*
Ephraim, Manasseh, and   *1Ch 6:61*
Dan, *t.* cities
Israel sent with Phinehas *t.*   *Jos 22:14*
princes
Gideon took *t.* men of his   *J'g 6:27*
servants
Elon a Zebulonite judged   *J'g 12:11*
Israel *t.* years
I will give thee *t.* shekels of   *J'g 17:10*
silver
we will take *t.* men of an   *J'g 20:10*
hundred
they dwelt in Moab about *t.*   *Ru 1:4*
years
Boaz took *t.* men of the elders   *Ru 4:2*
of the city,
am not I better to thee than *t.*   *1Sa 1:8*
sons
take these *t.* loaves, and run *1Sa 17:17*
to the camp
carry these *t.* cheeses to the *1Sa 17:18*
captain
David sent out *t.* young men   *1Sa 25:5*
to Nabal
David left *t.* concubines to   *2Sa 15:16*
keep
and I would have given thee   *2Sa 18:11*
t. shekels
t. young men smote   *2Sa 18:15*
Absalom, and slew
they said, We have *t.* parts   *2Sa 19:43*
in the king
king took his *t.* concubines,   *2Sa 20:3*
and put
t. fat oxen in one day for   *1Ki 4:23*
Solomon
t. knots in a cubit compassing   *1Ki 7:24*
the sea
and he made *t.* bases of   *1Ki 7:27;*
brass   *7:37*
he made *t.* lavers of brass   *1Ki 7:38;*
    7:43; 2Ch 4:6
take thee *t.* pieces, I will   *1Ki 11:31;*
give *t.* tribes   *11:35*
take with thee *t.* loaves to   *1Ki 14:3*
Ahijah
Naaman took *t.* talents, *t.*   *2Ki 5:5*
changes
leave but fifty horsemen and   *2Ki 13:7*
t. chariots
Menahem reigned *t.* years in *2Ki 15:17*
Samaria
Ishmael came, and *t.* men *2Ki 25:25;*
with him, and smote *Jer 41:1, 2*
Gedaliah
made *t.* candlesticks   *2Ch 4:7*
t. tables   *2Ch 4:8*
and *t.* of their brethren with   *Ezr 8:24*
them
bring one of *t.* to dwell at   *Ne 11:1*
Jerusalem
the *t.* sons of Haman slew   *Es 9:10;*
they   *9:12*
and let Haman's *t.* sons be   *Es 9:13;*
hanged   *9:14*
instrument of *t.* strings   *Ps 33:2;*
    92:3; 144:9
more than *t.* mighty men in   *Ec 7:19*
the city
t. acres of vineyard yield one   *Isa 5:10*
bath
an homer of *t.* baths; *t.*   *Eze 45:14*
baths an homer

the fourth beast had *t.* horns   *Da 7:7;*
    7:20, 24
shall leave *t.* to the house of   *Am 5:3*
Israel
if *t.* men remain in one house   *Am 6:9*
shall die
of twenty measures, there   *Hag 2:16*
were but *t.*
the breadth of the roll is *t.*   *Zec 5:2*
cubits
t. men take hold of him that   *Zec 8:23*
is a Jew
and when the *t.* heard it   *M't 20:24;*
    M'k 10:41
the kingdom shall be likened   *M't 25:1*
to *t.* virgins
give it to him that hath *t.*   *M't 25:28*
talents
woman having *t.* pieces of   *Lu 15:8*
silver
there met him *t.* men that   *Lu 17:12*
were lepers
Jesus said, Were there not *t.*   *Lu 17:17*
cleansed
and delivered them *t.* pounds,   *Lu 19:13*
and said
Lord, thy pound hath gained   *Lu 19:16*
t. pounds
well, have thou authority   *Lu 19:17*
over *t.* cities
and give it to him that hath   *Lu 19:24*
t. pounds
they said, Lord hath *t.*   *Lu 19:25*
pounds
t. thousand of angels (B)   *Heb 12:22*
dragon having *t.* horns   *Re 12:3;*
    13:1; 17:3
woman and beast of seven   *Re 17:7*
heads and *t.* horns
the *t.* horns thou sawest are   *Re 17:12*
the *t.* kings
t. horns thou sawest shall   *Re 17:16*
hate the whore

TEN *TIMES*

hath changed my wages *t.*   *Ge 31:7;*
times   *31:41*
have tempted me now these   *Nu 14:22*
t. times
when Jews came, they said   *Ne 4:12*
unto us, *t. times*
these *t. times* have ye   *Job 19:3*
reproached me
he found them *t. times*   *Da 1:20*
better

TENANT

let it out to *t.* farmers (S)   *M't 21:33*

TENANTS

loggers and *t.* (B)   *Le 25:23*
mere *t.,* temporary residents *1Ch 29:15*
(B)
tenants (A)(R)   *M't 21:33;*
21:34, 38, 40, 41; M'k 12:2; 9
tenants (N)   *M't 21:34;*
21:88, 40, 41; M'k 12:2, 9
tenants   *M'k 12:1;*
12:2, 7, 9; Lu 20:9, 10, 14, 16

TEND

the diligent *t.* only to   *Pr 21:5*
plenteousness

TENDED

t. with care (B)   *De 32:10*

TENDENCIES

over to perverted *t.* (B)   *Ro 1:28*

TENDER

and fetched a calf *t.* and good   *Ge 18:7*
Leah was *t.* eyed; but Rachel   *Ge 29:17*
eyes weak, and dull looking   *Ge 29:17*
(A)
eyes had no sparkle (B)   *Ge 29:17*
eyes were weak (R)   *Ge 29:17*
knoweth that the children are   *Ge 33:13*
t.
children were frail (B)(R)   *Ge 33:13*
that the man that is *t.* among   *De 28:54*
you
most refined man (B)   *De 28:54*

The t. and delicate woman among | De 28:56
as the small rain upon the t. herb | De 32:2
rain upon the green herb (B) | De 32:2
t. grass springing out of the earth | 2Sa 23:4
Because thine heart was t. | 2Ki 22:19
thine heart was penitent (B)(R) | 2Ki 22:19
Solomon my son is young and t. | 1Ch 22:5
young and inexperienced | 1Ch 22:5;
Solomon, is yet young and t. | 1Ch 29:1
Because thine heart was t. | 2Ch 34:27
heart was receptive (B) | 2Ch 34:27
heart was penitent (R) | 2Ch 34:27
t. branch thereof will not cease | Job 14:7
the bud of the t. herb to spring forth | Job 38:27
Remember, O Lord, thy t. mercies | Ps 25:6
Withhold not thou thy t. mercies from | Ps 40:11
unto the multitude of thy t. mercies | Ps 51:1
to the multitude of thy t. mercies | Ps 69:16
he in anger shut up his t. mercies | Ps 77:9
let thy t. mercies speedily prevent us | Ps 79:8
with lovingkindness and t. mercies | Ps 103:4
Let thy t. mercies come unto me, that | Ps 119:77
Great are thy t. mercies, O Lord | Ps 119:156
his t. mercies are over all his works | Ps 145:9
t. and only beloved in the sight of | Pr 4:3
the t. mercies of the wicked are cruel | Pr 12:10
and the t. grass sheweth itself, and | Pr 27:25
with the t. grape give a good smell | Ca 2:13
vines blossom, bloom (B)(R) | Ca 2:13; 2:15, 7:12
vines: for our vines have t. grapes | Ca 2:15
whether the t. grape appear | Ca 7:12
thou shalt no more be called t. | Isa 47:1
called dainty and delicate (A) | Isa 47:1
grow up before him as a t. plant | Isa 53:2
the top of his young twigs a t. one | Eze 17:22
Daniel into favour, and t. love | Da 1:9
favor, compassion and lovingkindness (A) | Da 1:9
favor and sympathy (B) | Da 1:9
favor and compassion (R) | Da 1:9
brass in the t. grass of the field | Da 4:15; 4:23
herbage of the earth (B) | Da 4:15; 4:23
any compassion grows warm and t. (R) | Ho 11:8
When his branch is yet t. | M't 24:32
When her branch is yet t. | M'k 13:28
Through the t. mercy of our God | Lu 1:78
t. mercies (S) | Ph'p 1:8; 2:1; Col 3:12
is very pitiful, and of t. mercy | Jas 5:11

TENDERHEARTED

Rehoboam was young and t. | 2Ch 13:7
irresolute and inexperienced (A) | 2Ch 13:7
immature and fainthearted (B) | 2Ch 13:7
young and irresolute (R) | 2Ch 13:7
the hands of a t. woman (S) | La 4:10
t. forgiving one another, even as | Eph 4:32
t. pity and mercy (A) | Col 3:12

TENDERLY

speak t. (S) | Isa 40:2; Ho 2:14
rear them t. in training (A) | Eph 6:4

TENDERNESS

ground for delicateness and t. | De 28:56
moved with pity, t. (A) | Lu 15:20
t. of heart (B) | Col 3:12

TENDETH

The labour of the righteous t. to life | Pr 10:16
As righteousness t. to life; so he that | Pr 11:19
more than is meet, but it t. to poverty | Pr 11:24
the talk of the lips t. only to penury | Pr 14:23
The fear of the Lord t. to life: and he | Pr 19:23

TENONS

Two t. shall there be in one board | Ex 26:17
under one board for his two t. | Ex 26:19
under another board for his two t. | Ex 26:19
One board had two t. equally | Ex 36:22
under one board for his two t. | Ex 36:24
under another board for his two t. | Ex 36:24

TENOR

according to the t. of these words | Ge 43:7
for after the t. of these words I have | Ex 34:27

TENS

rulers of fifties, and rulers of t. | Ex 18:21; 18:25
over fifties, and captains over t. | De 1:15

TEN'S

I will not destroy it for t. sake | Ge 18:32

TENSION

t. between (P) | Ac 23:7
as the t. mounted (P) | Ac 23:10

TENT

and he was uncovered within his t. | Ge 9:21
pitched his t. having Beth-el on the | Ge 12:8
place where his t. had been at | Ge 13:3
and pitched his t. toward Sodom | Ge 13:12
Then Abram removed his t. | Ge 13:18
he sat in the t. door in the heat of | Ge 18:1
he ran to meet them from the t. door | Ge 18:2
Abraham hastened into the t. unto | Ge 18:6
wife? And he said, Behold, in the t. | Ge 18:9
And Sarah heard it in the t. door | Ge 18:10
her into his mother Sarah's t. | Ge 24:67
pitched his t. in the valley of Gerar | Ge 26:17
the Lord, and pitched his t. there | Ge 26:25
Now Jacob had pitched his t. in the | Ge 31:25
into Jacob's t. and into Leah's t. | Ge 31:33
Then went he out of Leah's t. | Ge 31:33
and entered into Rachel's t. | Ge 31:33
And Laban searched all the t. but | Ge 31:34
and pitched his t. before the city | Ge 33:18
a field, where he had spread his t. | Ge 33:19
and spread his t. beyond the tower of | Ge 35:21
welfare and they came into the t. | Ex 18:7
couple the t. together, that it may be | Ex 26:11
remaineth of the curtains of the t. | Ex 26:12
in the length of the curtains of the t. | Ex 26:13
a covering for the t. of rams' skins | Ex 26:14
an hanging for the door of the t. | Ex 26:36
and stood every man at his t. door | Ex 33:8
worshipped, every man in his t. door | Ex 33:10
The tabernacle, his t. and his | Ex 35:11
made curtains of goats' hair for the t. | Ex 36:14
of brass to couple the t. together | Ex 36:18
a covering for the t. of rams' skins | Ex 36:19
the t. of the congregation finished | Ex 39:32
the tabernacle unto Moses, the t. and | Ex 39:33
for the t. of the congregation | Ex 39:40
of the t. of the congregation | Ex 40:6
between the t. of the congregation | Ex 40:7
abroad the t. over the tabernacle | Ex 40:19
and put the covering of the t. above | Ex 40:19
table in the t. of the congregation | Ex 40:22
candlestick in t. of congregation | Ex 40:24
altar of the t. of the congregation | Ex 40:26
of the t. of the congregation | Ex 40:29
between the t. of the congregation | Ex 40:30
went into the t. of the congregation | Ex 40:32
covered the t. of the congregation | Ex 40:34
enter into the t. of the congregation | Ex 40:35
tarry abroad out of his t. seven days | Le 14:8
shall be the tabernacle, and the t. | Nu 3:25
namely, the t. of the testimony | Nu 9:15
every man in the door of his t. | Nu 11:10
t. of meeting (A)(B) | Nu 12:4; 14:10; 17:4; De 31:14; 1Ki 8:4
is the law, when a man dieth in a t. | Nu 19:14
into the t. and all that is in the t. | Nu 19:14
the water, and sprinkle it upon the t. | Nu 19:18
after the man of Israel into the t. | Nu 25:8
in the earth in the midst of my t. | Jos 7:21
they ran unto the t.; and, behold | Jos 7:22
it was hid in his t. and the silver | Jos 7:22
took them out of the midst of the t. | Jos 7:23
and his t. and all that he had | Jos 7:24
his t. unto the plain of Zaanaim | J'g 4:11
Sisera fled away on his feet to the t. | J'g 4:17
he had turned in unto her into the t. | J'g 4:18
Stand in the door of the t. and it | J'g 4:20
Heber's wife took a nail of the t. | J'g 4:21
took a t. pin (A)(E) | J'g 4:21; 4:22; 5:26
And when he came into her t. behold | J'g 4:22
shall she be above women in the t. | J'g 5:24
rest of Israel every man unto his t. | J'g 7:8
host of Midian, and came into a t. | J'g 7:13
overturned it, that the t. lay along | J'g 7:13
We will not any of us go to his t. | J'g 20:8

and they fled every man into *1Sa 4:10*
his *t.*
people he sent every man to *1Sa 13:2*
his *t.*
but he put his armour in his *1Sa 17:54*
t.
walked in a *t.* and in a *2Sa 7:6*
tabernacle
So they spread Absalom a *t.* *2Sa 16:22*
upon
all Israel fled every one to *2Sa 18:17*
his *t.*
Israel had fled every man to *2Sa 19:8*
his *t.*
from the city, every man to *2Sa 20:22*
his *t.*
they went into one *t.* and did *2Ki 7:8*
eat
again, and entered into *2Ki 7:8*
another *t.*
ark of God, and pitched for *1Ch 15:1*
it a *t.*
and set it in the midst of *1Ch 16:1*
the *t.* that
but have gone from *t.* to *t.* *1Ch 17:5*
had pitched a *t.* for it at *2Ch 1:4*
Jerusalem
and they fled every man to *2Ch 25:22*
his *t.*
tent (S) *Job 18:6;*
18:14, 15; 19:12; 20:26; 29:4; 31:31
the *t.* which he placed among *Ps 78:60*
men
shall the Arabian pitch *t.* *Isa 13:20*
there
from me as a shepherd's *t.* *Isa 38:12*
them out as a *t.* to dwell in *Isa 40:22*
Enlarge the place of thy *t.* *Isa 54:2*
and let
none to stretch forth my *t.* *Jer 10:20*
any more
they rise up every man in his *Jer 37:10*
t.

TENTED

t. among us (B) *Joh 1:14*

TENTH

continually until the *t.* month *Ge 8:5;*
2Ki 25:1; 1Ch 27:13; Ezr 10:16; Es 2:16;
Jer 39:1; 52:4; Eze 24:1; 29:1; 33:21
the *t.* (the tithe) *Ge 28:22;*
Le 27:32; Nu 18:21, 26; 1Sa 8:15, 17;
Heb 7:2, 4
the *t.* day of the month *Ex 12:3;*
Le 16:29; 23:27; 25:9; Nu 29:7; Jos 4:19;
2Ki 25:1; Jer 52:4, 12; Eze 20:1; 24:1;
40:1
the *t.* part of an ephah *Ex 16:36;*
Le 5:11; 6:20; Nu 5:15; 28:5
a *t.* deal of flour *Ex 29:40;*
Le 14:21; Nu 15:4; 28:13, 29; 29:4, 10,
15
three *t.* deals of fine flour *Le 14:10;*
Nu 15:9; 28:12, 20, 28; 29:3, 9, 14
two *t.* deals of fine flour *Le 23:13;*
23:17; 24:5; Nu 15:6; 28:9, 12, 20, 28;
29:3, 9, 14
On the *t.* day Ahiezer the son *Nu 7:66*
even to the *t.* generation *De 23:2; 23:3*
Jeremiah the *t.* *1Ch 12:13*
the *t.* to *1Ch 24:11; 25:17*
But yet in it shall be the *t.* *Isa 6:13*
the *t.* year of Zedekiah *Jer 32:1*
contain the *t.* part of an *Eze 45:11*
homer
the *t.* part of a bath *Eze 45:14*
the fast of the *t.* *Zec 8:19*
it was about the *t.* hour *Joh 1:39*
the *t.* part of the city fell *Re 11:13*
the *t.*, a chrysoprasus *Re 21:20*

TENTHS

and *t.* to dwell in other cities *Ne 11:1*
(S)

TENTMAKERS

by their occupation they were *Ac 18:3*
t.
by trade *t.* (E)(N)P)(R) *Ac 18:3*

TENTS

the father of such as dwell in *Ge 4:20*
t.
and he shall dwell in the *t.* of *Ge 9:27*
Shem

Abram, had flocks, and herds, *Ge 13:5*
and *t.*
was a plain man, dwelling in *Ge 25:27*
t.
and into the two *Ge 31:33*
maidservants' *t.*
man for them which are in *Ex 16:16*
his *t.*
children of Israel shall pitch *Nu 1:52*
their *t.*
the children of Israel pitched *Nu 9:17*
their *t.*
tabernacle they rested in their *Nu 9:18*
of the Lord they abode in *Nu 9:20*
their *t.*
children of Israel abode in *Nu 9:22*
their *t.*
of the Lord they rested in the *Nu 9:23*
t.
whether in *t.* or in strong *Nu 13:19*
holds
from the *t.* of these wicked *Nu 16:26*
men
out, and stood in the door of *Nu 16:27*
their *t.*
saw Israel abiding in his *t.* *Nu 24:2*
according
How goodly are thy *t.*, O *Nu 24:5*
Jacob
And ye murmured in your *t.* *De 1:27*
you out a place to pitch your *De 1:33*
t. in
to them, Get you into your *t.* *De 5:30*
again
their households, and their *t.* *De 11:6*
in the morning, and go unto *De 16:7*
thy *t.*
going out; and Issachar, in *De 33:18*
thy *t.*
the people removed from their *Jos 3:14*
t.
return ye, and get you unto *Jos 22:4*
your *t.*
away: and they went unto *Jos 22:6*
their *t.*
sent them away also unto *Jos 22:7*
their *t.*
with much riches unto your *Jos 22:8*
t. and
came up with their cattle *J'g 6:5*
and their *t.*
by the way of them that dwelt *J'g 8:11*
in *t.*
Philistines, and spoiled *1Sa 17:53*
their *t.*
Israel, and Judah, abide in *2Sa 11:11*
t.
every man to his *t.* O Israel *2Sa 20:1*
went unto their *t.* joyful and *1Ki 8:66*
glad
to your *t.* O Israel: now see *1Ki 12:16*
to thine
So Israel departed unto their *1Ki 12:16*
t.
left their *t.* and their horses *2Ki 7:7*
asses tied, and the *t.* as they *2Ki 7:10*
were
and spoiled the *t.* of the *2Ki 7:16*
Syrians
and the people fled into their *2Ki 8:21*
children of Israel dwelt in *2Ki 13:5*
their *t.*
and they fled every man to *2Ki 14:12*
their *t.*
smote their *t.* and the *1Ch 4:41*
habitations
they dwelt in their *t.* *1Ch 5:10*
throughout all
he sent the people away into *2Ch 7:10*
their *t.*
every man to your *t.* O *2Ch 10:16*
Israel:
So all Israel went to their *t.* *2Ch 10:16*
They smote also the *t.* of *2Ch 14:15*
cattle, and
in the gates of the *t.* of the *2Ch 31:2*
Lord
there abode we in *t.* three *Ezr 8:15*
days
tents (S) *Job 11:14;*
12:6; 15:34; 22:23; Heb 11:9
and let none dwell in their *t.* *Ps 69:25*
tribes of Israel to dwell in *Ps 78:55*
their *t.*
than to dwell in the *t.* of *Ps 84:10*
wickedness
But murmured in their *t.* *Ps 106:25*

that I dwell in the *t.* of *Ps 120:5*
Kedar
as the *t.* of Kedar, as the *Ca 1:5*
curtains of
thy kids beside the shepherds' *t.* *Ca 1:8*
suddenly are my *t.* spoiled, *Jer 4:20*
and my
they shall pitch their *t.* against *Jer 6:3*
her
again the captivity of Jacob's *Jer 30:18*
t.
but all your days ye shall *Jer 35:7*
dwell in *t.*
But we have dwelt in *t.* *Jer 35:10*
and have
Their *t.* and their flocks *Jer 49:29*
shall they
I saw the *t.* of Cushan in *Hab 3:7*
affliction
also shall save the *t.* of Judah *Zec 12:7*
first
the beasts that shall be in *Zec 14:15*
these *t.*

TERAH

and twenty years, and begat *Ge 11:24*
T.
and Nahor lived after he *Ge 11:25*
begat *T.*
T. lived seventy years, *Ge 11:26*
and begat
these are the generations of *Ge 11:27*
T.
T. begat Abram, Nahor, and *Ge 11:27*
Haran
Haran died before his father *Ge 11:28*
T. in
T. took Abram his son, and *Ge 11:31*
Lot
days of *T.* were two hundred *Ge 11:32*
five years: and *T.* died in *Ge 11:32*
Haran
even *T.* the father of *Jos 24:2*
Abraham
Serug, Nahor, *T.* *1Ch 1:26*

TERAPHIM

stole *t.* that were (E) *Ge 31:19*
and made an ephod, and *t.* *J'g 17:5*
is in these houses an ephod, *J'g 18:14*
and *t.*
image, and the ephod, and *J'g 18:17*
the *t.*
carved image, the ephod, *J'g 18:18*
and the *t.*
and he took the ephod, and *J'g 18:20*
the *t.*
the *t.*, household gods *2Ki 23:24*
(A)(B)(E)(R)
consults the *t.* *Eze 21:21*
(A)(B)(E)(R)
without an ephod, and without *Ho 3:4*
t.

TEREBINTH

buried beneath the *t.* tree (B) *Ge 35:4*
t. tree (A)(B)(E)(R) *Isa 6:13*

TERESH

chamberlains, Bigthan and *T.* *Es 2:21*
had told of Bigthana and *T.* *Es 6:2*

TERMED

Thou shalt no more be *t.* *Isa 62:4*
Forsaken
thy land any more be *t.* *Isa 62:4*
Desolate

TERMINATION

the *t.* of it shall be (S) *Nu 34:5;*
34:9

TERMS

containing *t.* and conditions *Jer 32:11*
(A)(R)

TERRACES

king made of the algum trees *2Ch 9:11*
t.

TERRESTRIAL

also celestial bodies, and *1Co 15:40*
bodies *t.*

and the glory of the *t.* is   1Co 15:40
another
earthy bodies   1Co 15:40
(A)(B)(E)(P)

TERRIBLE

for it is a *t.* thing that I will   Ex 34:10
do
work of the Lord inspires   Ex 34:10
awe (B)
all that great and *t.* wilderness   De 1:19
is among you, a mighty God   De 7:21
and *t.*
through great and *t.*   De 8:15
wilderness
a great God, a mighty and a   De 10:17
t.
for thee these great and *t.*   De 10:21
things
of an angel of God, very *t.*   J'g 13:6
to be greatly and reverently   J'g 13:6
feared (A)
angel of God, very awe   J'g 13:6
inspiring (B)
to do for you great things,   2Sa 7:23
and *t.*
of heaven, the great and *t.* God   Ne 1:5
great and awful God (B)   Ne 1:5
the Lord, which is great and *t.*   Ne 4:14
great and dreadful (B)   Ne 4:14
great, the mighty, and the *t.*   Ne 9:32
God
the north: with God is *t.*   Job 37:22
majesty
the glory of his nostrils is *t.*   Job 39:20
face? his teeth are *t.* round   Job 41:14
about
hand shall teach thee *t.* things   Ps 45:4
do tremendous things (A)   Ps 45:4
awe-inspiring deeds (B)   Ps 45:4;
   65:5; 66:3; 68:35; 99:3; 106:22; 145:6
teach dreadful deeds (R)   Ps 45:4
For the Lord most high is *t.*;   Ps 47:2
he is
awe-inspiring God (B)   Ps 47:2
By *t.* things in righteousness   Ps 65:5
wilt
fearful and glorious things (A)   Ps 65:5
God, How *t.* art thou in thy   Ps 66:3
works
awesome and fearfully glorious   Ps 66:3
(A)
he is *t.* in his doing toward the   Ps 66:5
He is awesome (B)   Ps 66:5
O God, thou art *t.* out of thy   Ps 68:35
holy
he is *t.* to the kings of the   Ps 76:12
earth
who is dreadful to kings (B)   Ps 76:12
them praise thy great and *t.*   Ps 99:3
name
awesome and reverence   Ps 99:3
inspiring (A)
Ham, and *t.* things by the   Ps 106:22
Red sea
dreadful and awesome things   Ps 106:22
(A)
t. is his name (R)   Ps 111:9
speak of the might of thy *t.*   Ps 145:6
acts
t. as an army with banners   Ca 6:4
captivating as an army (B)   Ca 6:4;
   6:10
and *t.* as an army with   Ca 6:10
banners
lay low the haughtiness of   Isa 13:11
the *t.*
lay low the boasting of the   Isa 13:11
violent (B)
the pride of the arrogant (R)   Isa 13:11
to a people *t.* from their   Isa 18:2
beginning
a people dreaded (B)   Isa 18:2; 18:7
a people feared (B)   Isa 18:2; 18:7
to a people *t.* from their   Isa 18:7
beginning
from the desert, from a *t.*   Isa 21:1
land
the city of the *t.* nations shall   Isa 25:3
fear
ruthless nations (B)   Isa 25:3
ruthless nations (R)   Isa 25:3;
   25:4, 5; 29:5, 20; Jer 15:21
the blast of the *t.* ones is as a   Isa 25:4
storm
the tyrants (B)   Isa 25:4;
   25:5; 29:20; 49:25; 64:3; Jer 15:21
ruthless ones like a rainstorm   Isa 25:4;
(A)   25:5

the branch of the *t.* ones   Isa 25:5
shall be
multitude of the *t.* ones shall   Isa 29:5
be as
For the *t.* one is brought to   Isa 29:20
nought
the prey of the *t.* shall be   Isa 49:25
delivered
prey of the tyrant (R)   Isa 49:25
When thou didst *t.* things   Isa 64:3
which we
thee out of the hand of the *t.*   Jer 15:21
Lord is with me as a mighty   Jer 20:11
t. one
a fear-inspiring warrior (B)   Jer 20:11
an oven because of the *t.*   La 5:10
famine
burning head of famine   La 5:10
(A)(R)
fever heat of famine (B)   La 5:10
was as the colour of the *t.*   Eze 1:22
crystal
as transplanted crystal (B)   Eze 1:22
upon thee, the *t.* of the   Eze 28:7
nations
ruthless of the nations (B)   Eze 28:7;
   37:12
with him, the *t.* of the   Eze 30:11
nations
most violent of nations (B)   Eze 30:11
the *t.* of the nations, have   Eze 31:12
cut him
the *t.* of the nations, all of   Eze 32:12
them
thee; and the form thereof   Da 2:31
was *t.*
the appearance was   Da 2:31
frightening (R)
a fourth beast, dreadful and *t.*   Da 7:7
day of the Lord is great   Joe 2:11
very *t.*
the great and the *t.* day of   Joe 2:31
the Lord
They are *t.* and dreadful: Hab 1:7
their
The Lord will be *t.* unto them   Zep 2:11
my name is *t.* among the   Mal 1:14
heathen (S)
the great and *t.* day of the   Mal 4:5
Lord (S)
in *t.* distress (R)   M't 8:6
in a *t.* state (P)   M't 15:22; 17:15
t. distress, and misery (P)   M't 26:37
so *t.* was the sight, that   Heb 12:21
Moses
was so dreadful (B)   Heb 12:21

TERRIBLENESS

and with great *t.* and   De 26:8
with signs
great awesome power (A)   De 26:8
awe-inspiring terror (B)   De 26:8
thee a name of greatness   1Ch 17:21
and *t.*
Thy *t.* hath deceived thee,   Jer 49:16
and the

TERRIBLY

he ariseth to shake *t.* the   Isa 2:19;
earth   2:21
she came down *t.* (S)   La 1:9
and the fir trees shall be *t.*   Na 2:3
shaken
suffers *t.* (A)(R)   M't 17:15

TERRIFIED

they were *t.* at his presence   Ge 45:3
neither be ye *t.* because of   De 20:3
them
be not alarmed or *t.* (B)   De 20:3
t. him (B)   1Sa 16:14; Ps 83:17; 90:7
he was *t.* (R)   1Sa 28:21; Job 23:15
not dismayed or *t.*   Job 39:22
(A)(B)(R)
ashamed and *t.* (B)   Ps 83:17
I am *t.* (B)   Isa 21:3
they were *t.* (R)(N)   M't 6:50
they were *t.* (A)(P)   M't 14:26
absolutely (P)   M'k 6:5
do not be *t.* (A)(B)(R)   M'k 16:6
of wars and commotions, be   Lu 21:9
not *t.*
tumults, be not *t.* (E)(R)   Lu 21:9
But they were *t.* and   Lu 24:37
affrighted

in nothing *t.* by your   Ph'p 1:28
adversaries
the remnant were *t.* (S)   Re 11:13

TERRIFIES

t. them with warnings (R)   Job 33:16

TERRIFIEST

dreams, and *t.* me through   Job 7:14
visions

TERRIFY

to *t.* them (A)(R)   2Ch 32:18
let the blackness of the day *t.*   Job 3:5
it
from me, and let not his fear   Job 9:34
t. me
the contempt of families *t.*   Job 31:34
me
t. them in his fury (R)   Ps 2:5
come to *t.* them (E)(R)(S)   Zec 1:21
seems as if I would *t.* you by   2Co 10:9
letters

TERRIFYING

never demand by *t.* (A)   Lu 3:14

TERRITORY

all this *t.* (B)   Ge 26:3
locusts within your *t.* (B)   Ex 10:4
your *t.* (A)(R)   De 11:24
enlarge your *t.* (A)   De 19:8
pass through his *t.* (A)   J'g 11:20
his own *t.* (B)   1Sa 6:9
t. of Israel (A)(R)   1Sa 7:13
limits of their *t.* (N)   Ac 17:26

TERROR

the *t.* of God was upon the   Ge 35:5
cities
I will even appoint over you   Le 26:16
t.
The sword without, and *t.*   De 32:25
within
the great *t.* which Moses   De 34:12
shewed
and that your *t.* is fallen upon   Jos 2:9
us
terror (A)   2Ch 29:8;
   Ps 77:33; Isa 17:14; 65:23
seized with *t.* (A)   Job 18:20
destruction from God was a   Job 31:23
t. to
my *t.* shall not make thee   Job 33:7
afraid
t. turned into joy   Job 41:22
(A)(E)(R)
their years in *t.* (E)(R)   Ps 78:33
not be afraid for the *t.* by   Ps 91:5
night
hosts, shall lop the bough   Isa 10:33
with *t.*
of Judah shall be a *t.* unto   Isa 19:17
Egypt
he with *t.* (A)(B)(E)(R)   Isa 28:19
Thine heart shall meditate *t.*   Isa 33:18
and from *t.*; for it shall not   Isa 54:14
come
health, but behold *t.* (A)   Jer 8:15;
   14:19
Be not a *t.* unto me; thou   Jer 17:17
art my
I will make thee a *t.* to thyself   Jer 20:4
an execration, a *t.* (B)(R)   Jer 29:18
strong hand, and with great   Jer 32:21
t.
a derision, a *t.* to all   Jer 48:39
(B)(R)
are palsied with *t.* (A)(R)   Eze 7:27
which cause their *t.* to be on   Eze 26:17
I will make thee a *t.* and   Eze 26:21
thou
thou shalt be a *t.* and never   Eze 27:36;
shalt   28:19
which caused *t.* in the land   Eze 32:23
of
which caused their *t.* in the   Eze 32:24
land of
their *t.* was caused in the   Eze 32:25
land of
they caused their *t.* in the   Eze 32:26
land of
the *t.* of the mighty in the   Eze 32:27
land of

with their *t.* they are ashamed of | *Eze 32:30*
I have caused my *t.* in the land of | *Eze 32:32*
horse with *t.* (A)(E)(R)(S) | *Zec 12:4*
cried out in *t.* (B)(N) | *M't 14:26*
struck with *t.* (A) | *M'k 14:33*
struck with *t.* (A)(B) | *M'k 16:5*
rulers are not a *t.* to good works | *Ro 13:3*
Knowing the *t.* of the Lord, we | *2Co 5:11*
not afraid with any *t.* (S) | *1Pe 3:6*
be not afraid of their *t.* neither be | *1Pe 3:14*
filled with dread and *t.* (A)(N)(P)(R) | *Re 11:13*
t. of her torture (B) | *Re 18:15*

TERRORIZE

to frighten, *t.* (R) | *2Ch 32:18*
come to *t.* them (A) | *Zec 1:21*

TERRORS

stretched out arm, and by great *t.* | *De 4:34*
t. of God do set themselves in | *Job 6:4*
T. shall make him afraid on every | *Job 18:11*
t. shall bring him to the king of | *Job 18:14*
out of his gall: *t.* are upon him | *Job 20:25*
in the *t.* of the shadow of death | *Job 24:17*
T. take hold on him as waters, a | *Job 27:20*
T. are turned upon me: they | *Job 30:15*
the *t.* of death are fallen upon me | *Ps 55:4*
they are utterly consumed with *t.* | *Ps 73:19*
while I suffer thy *t.* I am distracted | *Ps 88:15*
over me: thy *t.* have cut me off | *Ps 88:16*
t. of Sheol (A)(B)(E)(R) | *Ps 116:3*
it suddenly, and *t.* upon the city | *Jer 15:8*
a solemn day my *t.* round about | *La 2:22*
t. by reason of the sword shall be | *Eze 21:12*

TERTIUS

I *T.*, who wrote this epistle | *Ro 16:22*

TERTULLUS

with a certain orator named *T.* | *Ac 24:1*
T. began to accuse him, saying | *Ac 24:2*

TEST

test (S) | *Ge 22:1;*
Ex 17:2; Nu 14:22; De 6:16; J'g 7:4;
2Ch 32:31; Job 7:18; 12:11; Ps 11:4;
26:2; Isa 7:12; Jer 6:27; 9:7; 17:10;
La 3:40; Da 11:35; Zec 13:9; M't 4:7;
22:18; M'k 12:15; Lu 4:12; 20:23;
Ac 5:9; 15:10; 1Co 3:13; 10:9; 1Pe 4:12;
1Jo 4:1
test (S) | *Ex 16:4;*
20:20; De 8:16; 33:8; J'g 2:22; 3:1, 4;
1Ki 10:1; 2Ch 9:1; Ec 2:1; Da 1:12;
Mal 3:10; Joh 6:6
put God to the *t.* (B) | *Ex 17:2;*
De 8:16; Isa 7:12; Mal 3:15; M't 4:7;
M'k 12:15; Lu 4:12; Ac 5:9
put God to the *t.* (R) | *De 6:16;*
Isa 7:12; Mal 3:15; M't 22:18;
M'k 12:15; 1Co 10:9
test (A) | *J'g 7:4;*
Pr 11:4; Jer 9:7; La 3:40; 1Pe 4:12
test (B) | *J'g 7:4;*
2Ch 32:31; Job 12:11; Ps 11:4; 26:2;
139:23; Jer 6:27; 17:10; La 3:40;
Zec 13:9; 1Co 3:13; 1Pe 4:12; 1Jo 4:1;
Re 3:10
test (R) | *J'g 7:4;*
Job 7:18; Ps 11:4; Jer 9:7; La 3:40;
Zec 13:9; 1Co 3:13; 1Jo 4:1
dost *t.* the heart (B) | *1Ch 29:17*
put God to the *t.* (R) | *Ps 106:14;*
| *Heb 3:9*
God might *t.* them (S) | *Ec 3:18*

t. them as gold is tested | *Zec 13:9;*
(A)(B) | *Re 2:10*
t. God (A) | *Mal 3:15;*
| *M't 4:7; M'k 12:15; Lu 4:12*
put God to the *t.* (N) | *M't 4:7;*
| *Lu 4:12; Ac 5:8; 1Co 10:9*
into a *t.* (N) | *M't 6:13; 26:41;*
M'k 14:38; Lu 11:4; 22:46; 1Co 10:13
to *t.* him (N)(R) | *M't 16:1;*
19:3; 22:35; M'k 8:11; 10:2; Lu 11:16
to *t.* him (P) | *M't 16:1;*
| *Lu 11:16; Joh 8:6*
put him to the *t.* (A) | *M't 19:3;*
22:35; M'k 8:11; 10:2; Lu 11:16;
| *Joh 8:6*
to *t.* him (B) | *M't 19:3;*
22:35; M'k 8:11; Lu 11:16
put me to the *t.* (A) | *M't 22:18*
here lies the *t.* (N) | *Joh 3:19*
put Spirit of the Lord to the *t.* | *Ac 5:9*
(P)
put Lord to the *t.* (N) | *1Co 10:9*
when stood the *t.* | *Jas 1:12*
(A)(B)(E)(N)(R)
fiery ordeal to *t.* you | *1Pe 4:12*
(A)(B)(P)
t. the spirits (N)(P) | *1Jo 4:1*
put them to the *t.* (B)(P) | *Re 2:2*
to *t.* its inhabitants (N)(P) | *Re 3:10*

TESTAMENT

For this is my blood of the new *t.* | *M't 26:28*
blood of the new covenant | *M't 26:28;*
(A)(R) | *M'k 14:24; 1Co 11:25*
my covenanted blood (B) | *M't 26:28;*
M'k 14:24; Lu 22:20; 1Co 11:25; 9:20
the blood of the covenant | *M't 26:28;*
(E) | *M'k 14:24; 1Co 11:25; Heb 9:20*
the blood of the new | *M't 26:28;*
agreement (P) | *M'k 14:24; Lu 22:20;*
| *1Co 11:25; Heb 9:20*
This is my blood of the new | *M'k 14:24*
t.
This cup is the new *t.* in my | *Lu 22:20;*
blood | *1Co 11:25*
us able ministers of the new *t.* | *2Co 3:6*
ministers of the new covenant | *2Co 3:6*
(A)(B)(E)(N)(R)
administrators of the new | *2Co 3:6*
agreement (P)
away in the reading of the | *2Co 3:14*
old *t.*
read from the old covenant | *2Co 3:14*
(A)(E)(N)
Jesus made a surety of a | *Heb 7:22*
better *t.*
better and stronger | *Heb 7:22;*
agreement (A) | *9:15, 20*
surety of a better covenant | *Heb 7:22*
(B)(E)(R)
a superior covenant (N) | *Heb 7:22;*
| *9:18*
guarantee of a better | *Heb 7:22*
agreement (P)
he is the mediator of the | *Heb 9:15*
new *t.*
mediator of a better | *Heb 9:15*
covenant (B)(E)(R)
that were under the first *t.* | *Heb 9:15*
transgressions of the first | *Heb 9:15*
agreement (B)(P)
For where a *t.* is there must | *Heb 9:16*
also of
For a *t.* is of force after men | *Heb 9:17*
Where upon neither the first | *Heb 9:18*
t. was
first covenant inaugurated by | *Heb 9:18*
blood (N)(E)(R)
the first agreement (P) | *Heb 9:18*
This is the blood of the *t.* | *Heb 9:20*
seen in his temple the ark of | *Re 11:19*
his *t.*
the ark of his covenant | *Re 11:19*
(A)(B)(E)(N)(R)
the ark of his agreement (P) | *Re 11:19*

TESTATOR

necessity be the death | *Heb 9:16*
of the *t.*
strength at all while the *t.* | *Heb 9:17*
liveth

TESTED

God *t.* Abraham (A)(B)(R) | *Ge 22:1*
tested (S) | *Ge 42:15;*
42:16; Ex 15:25; 1Sa 17:39; Ps 66:10;
81:7; 95:9; Da 1:14

tested (S) | *Ex 17:7;*
Job 23:10; 34:36; Ps 12:6; 17:3; 66:10;
78:18, 41, 56; 105:19; 106:14; Jer 12:3;
Da 12:10; Zec 13:9; M'k 1:13; 4:2;
Lu 10:25; 1Co 10:9; Heb 3:9; 11:17, 37
t. me (B)(R) | *De 6:16;*
| *Ps 78:18, 41, 56; 95:9*
when he has *t.* me (B) | *Job 23:10*
thou hast *t.* us (B)(R) | *Ps 66:10*
word of Lord *t.* him (R) | *Ps 105:19*
a *t.* stone (A)(B)(R) | *Isa 28:16*
test them as gold is *t.* | *Zec 13:9;*
(A)(B) | *Re 2:10*
Abraham was *t.* | *Heb 11:17*
(A)(B)(N)(P)(R)
t. by fire (A)(B)(R) | *1Pe 1:7*
have *t.* them (A)(R) | *Re 2:2*
you will be *t.* (B)(R) | *Re 2:10*
by fire *t.* gold (B) | *Re 3:10*

TESTETH

your God *t.* you (S) | *De 13:3*
testeth (S) | *1Ch 29:17;*
Job 34:3; Ps 7:9; 11:5; Pr 17:3;
Jer 11:20; 20:12; 1Th 2:4

TESTICLES

wounded in his *t.* (A)(B)(R) | *De 23:1*

TESTIFIED

and it hath been *t.* to his | *Ex 21:29*
owner
the owner has been warned | *Ex 21:29*
(A)(R)
the owner has been cautioned | *Ex 21:29*
(B)
hath *t.* falsely against his | *De 19:18*
brother
accused his brother falsely | *De 19:18*
(A)(B)(R)
seeing the Lord hath *t.* against | *Ru 1:21*
me
Lord has witnessed against me | *Ru 1:21*
(B)
The Lord has afflicted me (R) | *Ru 1:21*
for thy mouth hath *t.* against | *2Sa 1:16*
thee
Yet the Lord *t.* against | *2Ki 17:13*
Israel, and
Lord has warned Israel | *2Ki 17:13;*
(A)(B)(R) | *17:15; Ne 9:26; 13:15, 21*
his testimonies which he *t.* | *2Ki 17:15*
against
Lord; and they *t.* against | *2Ch 24:19*
them
bore witness among them | *2Ch 24:19*
slew thy prophets which *t.* | *Ne 9:26*
against
Prophets warned them (B) | *Ne 9:26*
and I *t.* against them in the | *Ne 13:15*
day
those I rebuked (B) | *Ne 13:15*
Then I *t.* against them, and | *Ne 13:21*
said
I warned them (B) | *Ne 13:21*
the saying of the woman, | *Joh 4:39*
which *t.*
on account of woman's | *Joh 4:39*
testimony (B)(N)(P)(R)
For Jesus himself *t.* that a | *Joh 4:44*
prophet
Jesus Himself declared | *Joh 4:44*
(A)(N)
he was troubled in spirit, | *Joh 13:21*
and *t.*
Jesus exclaimed in deep | *Joh 13:21*
agitation (N)
they had *t.* and preached the | *Ac 8:25*
word
The apostles had borne | *Ac 8:25*
testimony (A)
explained the kingdom of God | *Ac 8:25*
(B)
giving their own testimony | *Ac 8:25*
(N)
had given clear witness (P) | *Ac 8:25*
t. to the Jews that Jesus was | *Ac 18:5*
affirming before the Jews (N) | *Ac 18:5*
as thou hast *t.* of me in | *Ac 23:11*
Jerusalem
borne faithful testimony | *Ac 23:11*
(A)(B)(P)
affirmed the truth (N) | *Ac 23:11*
and *t.* the kingdom of God | *Ac 28:23*
explained to them kingdom | *Ac 28:23*
of God (B)(P)

we have *t.* of God that he | 1Co 15:15
raised
we bore witness (N) | 1Co 15:15
given our solemn testimony | 1Co 15:15
(P)
also have forewarned you and | 1Th 4:6
t.
ransom for all, to be *t.* in due | 1Ti 2:6
time
attested to at the right and | 1Ti 2:6
proper time (A)(B)
stands for all time a witness | 1Ti 2:6
(P)
testimony borne at the right | 1Ti 2:6
time (R)
But one in a certain place *t.* | Heb 2:6
it *t.* beforehand the sufferings | 1Pe 1:11
of
predicted the sufferings of | 1Pe 1:11
Christ (A)(B)(R)
foretold the sufferings of | 1Pe 1:11
Christ (N)(P)
God which he hath *t.* of his | 1Jo 5:9
Son
witness which he has borne | 1Jo 5:9
(A)(N)
testimony of God and his son | 1Jo 5:9
(P)(R)
and *t.* of the truth that is in | 3Jo 3
thee
gave testimony of your fidelity | 3Jo 3
(B)

TESTIFIEDST

And *t.* against them that thou | Ne 9:29
reproved and warned them | Ne 9:29;
(A)(B)(R) | 9:30
t. against them by thy spirit | Ne 9:30
in thy

TESTIFIETH

the pride of Israel, *t.* to his | Ho 7:10
face
hath seen and heard, that he | Joh 3:32
t.
he bears testimony (A)(P) | Joh 3:32
disciple which *t.* of these | Joh 21:24
things
who is bearing witness | Joh 21:24
(A)(R)
who attests what he has | Joh 21:24
written (N)
giving his testimony to (P) | Joh 21:24
For he *t.*, Thou art a priest | Heb 7:17
for ever
it is witnessed of him | Heb 7:17
(A)(B)(R)
here is his testimony (N) | Heb 7:17;
 | Re 22:20
the witness of him is (P) | Heb 7:17
He which *t.* these things saith | Re 22:20
he who affirms this (B) | Re 22:20
he who is witness (P) | Re 22:20

TESTIFY

sworn to *t.* (A) | Le 5:1
one witness shall not *t.* | Nu 35:30
against
I *t.* against you this day that | De 8:19
ye
I warn you (B)(R) | De 8:19
to *t.* against him that which | De 19:16
is
to accuse him (R) | De 19:16
this song shall *t.* against | De 31:21
them as
song shall be a witness | De 31:21
(A)(R)
song a living reminder to (B) | De 31:21
words which I *t.* among you | De 32:46
this
I admonish you this day (B) | De 32:46
I enjoin you this day (R) | De 32:46
thou didst *t.* against them | Ne 9:34
thy warnings did extend to | Ne 9:34
(B)
yea, thine own lips *t.* against | Job 15:6
thee
witness against you (B) | Job 15:6
Israel, and I will *t.* against | Ps 50:7
my people, and I will *t.* unto | Ps 81:8
thee
I will admonish you (A)(R) | Ps 81:8
thee, and our sins *t.* against | Isa 59:12
us
sins witness against you (B) | Isa 59:12
though our iniquities *t.* aginst | Jer 14:7
us

pride of Israel doth *t.* to his | Ho 5:5
face
and *t.* in the house of Jacob, | Am 3:13
saith
bear witness (A) | Am 3:13;
 | 1Jo 4:14; Re 22:16
bear witness to the house of | Am 3:13
Jacob (B)
I wearied thee? *t.* | Mic 6:3
against me
to *t.* before them (N) | M't 10:18;
 | M'k 13:9; Lu 21:13
that he may *t.* unto them, | Lu 16:28
lest
he may give testimony (A) | Lu 16:28
let him strongly warn | Lu 16:28
(B)(N)(P)(R)
not that any should *t.* of | Joh 2:25
man
that he may witness (A)(R) | Joh 2:25
one's evidence about people | Joh 2:25
(B)
know, and *t.* that we have | Joh 3:11
seen
bear witness to what we have | Joh 3:11
seen (R)
and they are which *t.* of | Joh 5:39
me
they are the testimonies of | Joh 5:39
me (B)(N)
they bear witness of me (R) | Joh 5:39
me it hateth, because I *t.* of it | Joh 7:7
I denounce it (A) | Joh 7:7
from the Father he shall *t.* | Joh 15:26
of me
other words did he *t.* and | Ac 2:40
exhort
charged earnestly and warned | Ac 2:40
(B)
he pressed his case (N) | Ac 2:40
to *t.* that it is he which was | Ac 10:42
to bear solemn testimony | Ac 10:42
(A)(B)
affirm that he is the one (N) | Ac 10:42
to *t.* the gospel of the grace | Ac 20:24
of God
to attest the good news (A) | Ac 20:24
to bear witness to the gospel | Ac 20:24
(B)
bear testimony to the gospel | Ac 20:24
(N)
I *t.* unto you (S) | Ac 20:26
if they would *t.* that after the | Ac 26:5
willing to bear witness (B) | Ac 26:5
For I *t.* again to every man | Ga 5:3
that is
I assure every person (B) | Ga 5:3
t. in the Lord, that ye | Eph 4:17
henceforth
I enter my testimony (B) | Eph 4:17
and do *t.* that the Father sent | 1Jo 4:14
we bear witness (B) | 1Jo 4:14
we attest the Father sent the | 1Jo 4:14
Son (N)
sent mine angel to *t.* unto | Re 22:16
you
sent angel to witness (B) | Re 22:16
t. unto every man that | Re 22:18
heareth
I warn every man | Re 22:18
(A)(B)(N)(R)
I bear solemn witness (N) | Re 22:18

TESTIFYING

T. both to the Jews, and also | Ac 20:21
I bore witness (A)(B) | Ac 20:21
was righteous, God *t.* of his | Heb 11:4
gifts
acknowledge his gifts (B) | Heb 11:4
and *t.* that this is the true | 1Pe 5:12
grace
to declare this is the true | 1Pe 5:12
grace (A)
adding my testimony that (B) | 1Pe 5:12

TESTIMONIAL

be a living *t.* to (P) | Tit 2:10

TESTIMONIES

These are the *t.* and the | De 4:45
statutes
his *t.* and his statutes, which | De 6:17
he
What mean the *t.* and the | De 6:20
statutes
his judgments, and his *t.* as it | 1Ki 2:3

his *t.* which he testified | 2Ki 17:15
keep his commandments and | 2Ki 23:3
his *t.*
keep thy commandments, | 1Ch 29:19
thy *t.*
keep his commandments, | 2Ch 34:31
and his *t.*
thy commandments, and thy *t.* | Ne 9:34
as keep his covenant and his | Ps 25:10
t.
high God, and kept not his *t.* | Ps 78:56
Thy *t.* are very sure; holiness | Ps 93:5
they kept his *t.* and the | Ps 99:7
ordinance
Blessed are they that keep his | Ps 119:2
t.
have rejoiced in the way of | Ps 119:14
thy *t.*
contempt; for I have kept | Ps 119:22
thy *t.*
Thy *t.* also are my delight | Ps 119:24
and my
I have stuck unto thy *t.*: O | Ps 119:31
Lord
Incline my heart unto thy *t.* | Ps 119:36
I will speak of thy *t.* also | Ps 119:46
before
and turned my feet unto thy | Ps 119:59
t.
and those that have known | Ps 119:79
thy *t.*
me: but I will consider thy | Ps 119:95
t.
for thy *t.* are my meditation | Ps 119:99
Thy *t.* have taken as an | Ps 119:111
heritage
dross: therefore I love thy | Ps 119:119
t.
that I may know thy *t.* | Ps 119:125
Thy *t.* are wonderful; | Ps 119:129
therefore
Thy *t.* that thou hast | Ps 119:138
commanded
The righteousness of thy *t.* | Ps 119:144
save me, and I shall keep | Ps 119:146
thy *t.*
Concerning thy *t.* I have | Ps 119:152
known of
yet do I not decline from | Ps 119:157
thy *t.*
My soul hath kept thy *t.*; | Ps 119:167
and I
I have kept thy precepts | Ps 119:168
and thy *t.*
nor in his statutes, nor in his | Jer 44:23
t.
they are the *t.* (B)(N) | Joh 5:39

TESTIMONY

before the *T.* | Ex 16:34;
 | 27:21; 30:36; Nu 17:4, 10
thwarts just man's *t.* (B) | Ex 23:8
the ark of the *t.* | Ex 25:16;
 | 25:22; 26:33, 34; 30:6, 26; 31:7; 39:35;
 | 40:3, 5, 21; Nu 4:5; 7:89; Jos 4:16
in the ark thou shalt put the | Ex 25:21;
t. | 40:20
the mercy seat that is over | Ex 30:6;
the *t.* | Le 16:13
two tables of *t.*, tables of | Ex 31:18;
stone | 32:15; 34:29
the tabernacle of the *t.* | Ex 38:21;
 | Nu 1:50, 53; 10:11; Re 15:5
Without the veil of the *t.* | Le 24:3
the tent of the *t.* | Nu 9:15
and this was a *t.* in Israel | Ru 4:7
upon him, and gave him the | 2Ki 11:12
t.
him the crown and gave | 2Ch 23:11
him the *t.*
accept their *t.* (R) | Job 21:29
the *t.* of the Lord is sure, | Ps 19:7
making
he established a *t.* in Jacob | Ps 78:5
he ordained in Joseph for a *t.* | Ps 81:5
so shall I keep the *t.* of thy | Ps 119:88
mouth
unto the *t.* of Israel, to give | Ps 112:4
thanks
and my *t.* that I shall | Ps 132:12
teach them
Bind up the *t.* seal the law | Isa 8:16
among
To the law and to the *t.*: if | Isa 8:20
they
commanded, for a *t.* unto | M't 8:4
them
Moses prescribed (B) | M't 8:4;
 | M'k 1:44; Lu 5:14

as evidence (P)   M't 8:4
for a proof (R)   M't 8:4;
    M'k 1:44; Lu 5:14
a t. against them and the   M't 10:18
Gentiles
to testify before them (N)   M't 10:18;
    M'k 13:9; Lu 21:13
to give witness (P)   M't 10:18;
    M'k 13:9; Lu 21:13; Re 12:11, 17
commanded, for a t. unto   M'k 1:44
them
as proof to the people (A)   M'k 1:44
which Moses prescribed (P)   M'k 1:44;
    Lu 5:14
your feet for a t. against   M'k 6:11
them
for a witness against them   M'k 6:11
(B)
as a protest against them   M'k 6:11;
(P)   Lu 9:5
for my sake, for a t. against   M'k 13:9
them
commanded, for a t. unto   Lu 5:14
them
your feet for a t. against them   Lu 9:5
he may give t. (A)   Lu 16:28
And it shall turn to you for a   Lu 21:13
t.
and no man receiveth his t.   Joh 3:32
he bears t. (A)(P)(R)   Joh 3:32
He that hath received his t.   Joh 3:33
hath
on account of woman's t.   Joh 4:39
(B)(N)(P)(R)
t. valid (A)   Joh 5:31; 5:32; 8:13, 17
t. is reliable (B)   Joh 5:31
But I receive not t. from   Joh 5:34
man: but
I receive not human witness   Joh 5:34
(A)
he bore witness (B)   Joh 5:34; Re 6:9
law that the t. of two men is   Joh 8:17
true
the evidence of two persons   Joh 8:17
(B)
and we know that his t.   Joh 21:24
is true
giving his t. to (P)   Joh 21:24
apostles had borne t. (A)   Ac 8:25
bear solemn t. (A)(B)   Ac 10:42
to whom also he gave t. and   Ac 13:22
said
he bore witness (A)   Ac 13:22
which gave t. unto the word   Ac 14:3
of his
witnessed to the message (B)   Ac 14:3
confirmed the message (N)   Ac 14:3
bear t. to the gospel (N)   Ac 20:24
not receive thy t. concerning   Ac 22:18
borne faithful t. (A)(B)(P)   Ac 23:11
Even as the t. of Christ was   1Co 1:6
the witnessing (A)   1Co 1:6; 2Th 1:10
our witnessing of Christ (B)   1Co 1:6;
    2Th 1:10
evidence of the truth (N)   1Co 1:6
declaring unto you for the t.   1Co 2:1
of God
given solemn t. (P)   1Co 15:15
is this, the t. of our   2Co 1:12
conscience
witness of our conscience   2Co 1:12
(B)
I enter my t. (B)   Eph 4:17
our t. among you was   2Th 1:10
believed
ashamed of the t. of our   2Ti 1:8
Lord
bearing witness of our Lord   2Ti 1:8
(B)
This t. is true (S)   Tit 1:13
a t. of those things which   Heb 3:5
were to be
bearing witness (B)(N)   Heb 3:5
here is his t. (N)   Heb 7:17; Re 22:20
had this t. that he pleased   Heb 11:5
God
adding my t. that (B)   1Pe 5:12
t. of God of his Son (P)(R)   1Jo 5:9
God, and of the t. of Jesus   Re 1:2
Christ
God, and for the t. of Jesus   Re 1:9
Christ
God, and for the t. which they   Re 6:9
held
for the witness they had borne   Re 6:9
(R)
they shall have finished their t.   Re 11:7
Lamb, and by the word of   Re 12:11
their t.

God, and have the t. of Jesus   Re 12:17
Christ
blood of those who bore t.   Re 17:6
(N)
brethren that have the t. of   Re 19:10
Jesus
t. of Jesus is the spirit of   Re 19:10
prohecy
holding fast their witness (P)   Re 19:10

TESTING

testing (S)   M't 16:1;
  19:3; 22:35; M'k 8:11; 10:2; Lu 4:13;
    8:13; 11:16; Joh 8:6; Jas 1:3
in time of t. fall away (N)   Lu 8:13;
    22:40
day of t. (A)(N)(R)   Heb 3:8

TESTS

who t. the righteous   Ps 11:5
(A)(B)(R)
who t. the heart (A)(B)   Jer 11:20
who t. the righteous (B)   Jer 20:12
who t. our hearts (A)(B)(R)   1Th 2:4
t. of mockings (B)(P)(R)   Heb 1:36

TETRARCH

Herod the t. heard of the   M't 14:1
fame of
and Herod being t. of Galilee   Lu 3:1
his brother Philip t. of Ituraea   Lu 3:1
and Lysanias the t. of Abilene   Lu 3:1
Herod the t. being reproved by   Lu 3:19
Herod the t. heard of all that   Lu 9:7
was
been brought up with Herod   Ac 13:1
the t.

THADDAEUS

Labbæus, whose surname   M't 10:3
was T.
the son of Alphæus, and T.   M'k 3:18

THAHASH

Gaham, and T. and Maachah   Ge 22:24

THAMAH

of Sisera, the children of T.   Ezr 2:53

THAMAR

begat Phares and Zara of T.   M't 1:3

THAN

more subtle t. any beast of the   Ge 3:1
field
My punishment is greater t. I   Ge 4:13
can bear
we deal worse with thee, t.   Ge 19:9
with them
shall be stronger t. the other   Ge 25:23
people
us; for thou art much   Ge 26:16
mightier t. we
t. that I should give her to   Ge 29:19
another
and he loved also Rachel   Ge 29:30
more t. Leah
more honourable t. all the   Ge 34:19
house of
riches were more t. that they   Ge 36:7
might
loved Joseph more t. all his   Ge 37:3
children
their father loved him more t.   Ge 37:4
all his
She hath been more   Ge 38:26
righteous t. I
none greater in this house t. I   Ge 39:9
in the throne will I be   Ge 41:40
greater t. thou
younger brother shall be   Ge 48:19
greater t. he
of Israel are more and mightier   Ex 1:9
t. we
t. that we should die in the   Ex 14:12
wilderness
that the Lord is greater t. all   Ex 18:11
gods
poor shall not give less t.   Ex 30:15
half a shekel

much more t. enough for the   Ex 36:5
service
sight be deeper t. the skin of   Le 13:3
his flesh
and in sight be not deeper t.   Le 13:4
the skin
if it be not lower t. the skin,   Le 13:21
and be
it be in sight deeper t. the   Le 13:25
skin
and it be no lower t. the   Le 13:26
other skin
be in sight deeper t. the skin   Le 13:30
it be not in sight deeper t.   Le 13:31
the skin
be not in sight deeper t. the   Le 13:32
skin
nor be in sight deeper t. the   Le 13:34
skin
which in sight are lower t.   Le 14:37
the wall
But if he be poorer t. thy   Le 27:8
estimation
which are more t. the Levites   Nu 3:46
a greater nation and   Nu 14:12
mightier t. they
more, and more honorable t.   Nu 22:15
they
and his king shall be higher   Nu 24:7
t. Agag
The people is greater and   De 1:28
taller t. we
thee greater and mightier t.   De 4:38
thou art
nations greater and mightier t.   De 7:1
thou
ye were more in number t. any   De 7:7
people
heart, These nations are more   De 7:17
t. I
nations greater and mighter t.   De 9:1
thyself
a nation mightier and greater   De 9:14
t. they
nations and mightier t.   De 11:23
yourselves
and a people more t. thou, be   De 20:1
not
and because it was greater t.   Jos 10:2
Ai
t. they whom the children of   Jos 10:11
Israel
themselves more t. their   J'g 2:19
fathers
better t. the vintage of Abiezer   J'g 8:2
art thou any thing better t.   J'g 11:25
Balak
went down, What is sweeter t.   J'g 14:18
t. honey
and what is stronger t. a   J'g 14:18
lion? And he
is not her younger sister fairer   J'g 15:2
t. she
be more blameless t. the   J'g 15:3
Philistines
more t. they which he slew   J'g 16:30
in his life
the latter end t. at the   Ru 3:10
beginning
howbeit there is a kinsman   Ru 3:12
nearer t. I
which is better to thee t.   Ru 4:15
seven sons
am not I better to thee t.   1Sa 1:8
ten sons
of Israel a goodlier person t.   1Sa 9:2
he
he was higher t. any of the   1Sa 9:2;
people   10:23
Behold, to obey is better t.   1Sa 15:22
sacrifice
and to hearken t. the fat of   1Sa 15:22
rams
of thine, that is better t.   1Sa 15:28
thou
wisely t. all the servants of   1Sa 18:30
Saul
to David, Thou art more   1Sa 24:17
righteous t. I
me t. that I should speedily   1Sa 27:1
escape
divided: they were swifter t.   2Sa 1:23
eagles
eagles, they were stronger t.   2Sa 1:23
lions
And I will yet be more vile   2Sa 6:22
t. thus, and
but, being stronger t. she,   2Sa 13:14
forced her

he hated her was greater *t*. 2Sa 13:15
the love
greater *t*. the other that thou 2Sa 13:16
didst
is better *t*. the counsel of 2Sa 17:14
Ahithophel
more people that day *t*. the 2Sa 18:8
sword
worse unto the *t*. all the evil 2Sa 19:7
that
have also more right in 2Sa 19:43
David *t*. ye
fiercer *t*. the words of the 2Sa 19:43
men of Israel
he tarried longer *t*. the set 2Sa 20:5
time
do us more harm *t*. did 2Sa 20:6
Absalom
was more honourable *t*. the 2Sa 23:23
thirty
greater *t*. the throne of my 1Ki 1:37
lord king
name of Solomon better *t*. 1Ki 1:47
thy name
make his throne greater *t*. thy 1Ki 1:47
throne
men more righteous and 1Ki 2:32
better *t*. he
For he was wiser *t*. all men 1Ki 4:31
t. Ethan the Ezrahite, and 1Ki 4:31
Heman
shall be thicker *t*. my 1Ki 12:10
father's loins
did worse *t*. all that were 1Ki 16:25
before him
to anger *t*. all the kings of 1Ki 16:33
Israel that
life; for I am not better *t*. my 1Ki 19:4
fathers
therefore they were stronger 1Ki 20:23
t. we
we shall be stronger *t*. they 1Ki 20:23;
20:25
give thee for it a better 1Ki 21:2
vineyard *t*. it
better *t*. all the waters of 2Ki 5:12
Israel
us are more *t*. they that be 2Ki 6:16
with them
no more of her *t*. the skull 2Ki 9:35
to do more evil *t*. did the 2Ki 21:9
nations
was more honorable *t*. his 1Ch 4:9
brethren
he was more honourable *t*. 1Ch 11:21
the two
Eleazar *t*. of the sons of 1Ch 24:4
Ithamar
shall be thicker *t*. my 2Ch 10:10
father's loins
more *t*. they could carry 2Ch 20:25
away: and
house, which were better *t*. 2Ch 21:13
thyself
is able to give thee much 2Ch 25:9
more *t*. this
to sanctify themselves *t*. the 2Ch 29:34
priests
passover otherwise, *t*. it was 2Ch 30:18
written
for there be more with us *t*. 2Ch 32:7
with him
and to do worse *t*. the 2Ch 33:9
heathen
punished us less *t*. our Ezr 9:13
iniquities
unto another that is better *t*. Es 1:19
she
favour in his sight more *t*. all Es 2:17
the king's house, more *t*. Es 4:13
all the Jews
delight to do honour more *t*. to Es 6:6
myself
dig for it more *t*. for hid Job 3:21
treasures
Shall mortal man be more Job 4:17
just *t*. God
shall a man be more pure *t*. Job 4:17
his maker
be heavier *t*. the sand of the Job 6:3
sea
My days are swifter *t*. a Job 7:6
weaver's
strangling, and death rather *t*. Job 7:15
my life
Now my days are swifter *t*. a Job 9:25
post
God exacteth of thee less *t*. Job 11:6
thine
thereof is longer *t*. the earth Job 11:9

the earth, and broader *t*. the Job 11:9
sea
age shall be clearer *t*. the Job 11:17
noonday
aged men, much elder *t*. thy Job 15:10
father
stroke is heavier *t*. my Job 23:2
groaning
his mouth more *t*. my Job 23:12
necessary food
are younger *t*. I have me in Job 30:1
derision
men: they are viler *t*. the Job 30:8
earth
he justified himself rather *t*. Job 32:2
God
spoken, because they were Job 32:4
elder *t*. he
thee, that God is greater *t*. Job 33:12
man
His flesh shall be fresher *t*. Job 33:25
a child's
regardeth the rich more *t*. Job 34:19
poor
will not lay upon man more Job 34:23
t. right
My righteousness is more *t*. Job 35:2
God's
the clouds which are higher *t*. Job 35:5
Who teacheth us more *t*. the Job 35:11
beasts of
and maketh us wiser *t*. the Job 35:11
fowls of
hast thou chosen rather *t*. Job 36:21
affliction
latter end of Job more *t*. his Job 42:12
beginning
more *t*. in the time that their Ps 4:7
corn and
made him a little lower *t*. the Ps 8:5
angels
are they *t*. gold, yea, *t*. Ps 19:10
much fine gold
sweeter also *t*. honey and Ps 19:10
honeycomb
is better *t*. the riches of many Ps 37:16
wicked
they are more *t*. can be Ps 40:5
numbered
are more *t*. the hairs of mine Ps 40:12
head
Thou art fairer *t*. the children Ps 45:2
of men
wash me, and I shall be whiter Ps 51:7
t. snow
Thou lovest evil more *t*. good Ps 52:3
lying rather *t*. to speak Ps 52:3
righteousness
of his mouth were smoother Ps 55:21
t. butter
his words were softer *t*. oil, Ps 55:21
yet were
lead me to the rock that is Ps 61:2
higher *t*. I
they are altogether lighter *t*. Ps 62:9
vanity
the lovingkindness is better *t*. Ps 63:3
life
are more *t*. the hairs of mine Ps 69:4
head
please the Lord better *t*. an Ps 69:31
ox or
they have more *t*. heart could Ps 73:7
wish
excellent *t*. the mountains of Ps 76:4
prey
in thy courts is better *t*. a Ps 84:10
thousand
t. to dwell in the tents of Ps 84:10
wickedness
Zion more *t*. all the dwellings Ps 87:2
of Jacob
higher *t*. the kings of the Ps 89:27
earth
mightier *t*. the noise of many Ps 93:4
waters
yea, *t*. the mighty waves of the Ps 93:4
sea
made them stronger *t*. their Ps 105:24
enemies
trust Lord *t*. to put Ps 118:8
confidence in man
Lord *t*. to put confidence in Ps 118:9
princes
unto me *t*. thousands of gold Ps 119:72
hast made me wiser *t*. mine Ps 119:98
enemies
understanding *t*. all my Ps 119:99
teachers

I understand more *t*. the Ps 119:100
ancients
yea, sweeter *t*. honey to my Ps 119:103
mouth
Lord more *t*. they that watch Ps 130:6
for the
I say, more *t*. they that watch Ps 130:6
for the
they are more in number *t*. Ps 139:18
the sand
persecutors: for they are Ps 142:6
stronger *t*. I
it is better *t*. the merchandise Pr 3:14
of silver
silver, and the gain thereof *t*. Pr 3:14
fine gold
She is more precious *t*. rubies: Pr 3:15
and all
and her mouth is smoother *t*. Pr 5:3
oil
and knowledge rather *t*. choice Pr 8:10
gold
For wisdom is better *t*. rubies; Pr 8:11
and all
is better *t*. gold, yea *t*. fine Pr 8:19
gold
is that withholdeth more *t*. is Pr 11:24
meet
is better *t*. he that honoureth Pr 12:9
himself
is more excellent *t*. his Pr 12:26
neighbour
t. great treasure and trouble Pr 15:16
therewith
is *t*. a stalled ox and hatred Pr 15:17
therewith
t. great revenues without right Pr 16:8
much better is it to get Pr 16:16
wisdom *t*. gold
rather to be chosen *t*. silver Pr 16:16
t. to divide the spoil with Pr 16:19
the proud
his spirit *t*. he that taketh a Pr 16:32
city
t. an house full of sacrifices Pr 17:1
wise man *t*. an hundred Pr 17:10
stripes into a
meet a man, rather *t*. a fool Pr 17:12
in his folly
is harder to be won *t*. a Pr 18:19
strong city
friend that sticketh closer *t*. a Pr 18:24
brother
t. he that is perverse in his Pr 19:1
lips, and is
and a poor man is better *t*. Pr 19:22
a liar
acceptable to the Lord *t*. Pr 21:3
sacrifice
t. with a brawling woman in a Pr 21:9
wide
t. with a contentious and an Pr 21:19
angry
is rather to be chosen *t*. great Pr 22:1
riches
loving favour rather *t*. silver Pr 22:1
and gold
t. that thou shouldest be put Pr 25:7
lower in
t. with a brawling woman Pr 25:24
and in a
there is more hope of a fool Pr 26:12
t. of him
is wiser in his own conceit *t*. Pr 26:16
seven men
a fool's wrath is heavier *t*. Pr 27:3
them both
Open rebuke is better *t*. Pr 27:5
secret love
that is near *t*. a brother far Pr 27:10
off
t. he that is perverse in his Pr 28:6
ways
favour *t*. he that flattereth Pr 28:23
with the
there is more hope of a fool Pr 29:20
t. of him
Surely I am more brutish *t*. Pr 30:2
any man
wisdom *t*. all they that have Ec 1:16
been
increased more *t*. all that were Ec 2:9
before
wise more *t*. of the fool for Ec 2:16
ever
a man, *t*. that he should eat Ec 2:24
and drink
else can hasten hereunto, more Ec 2:25
t. I

t. that a man should rejoice in *Ec 3:22* his own
t. the living which are yet alive *Ec 4:2*
Yea, better is he *t.* both they, *Ec 4:3* which
t. both the hands full with *Ec 4:6* travail
Two are better *t.* one: because *Ec 4:9* they
wise child *t.* an old and *Ec 4:13* foolish king
to hear, *t.* to give the sacrifice *Ec 5:1* of fools
t. that thou shouldest vow and *Ec 5:5* not pay
for he that is higher *t.* the *Ec 5:8* highest
and there be higher *t.* they *Ec 5:8*
that an untimely birth is better *Ec 6:3* *t.* he
this hath more rest *t.* the other *Ec 6:5*
hath the wise more *t.* the fool *Ec 6:8*
sight of the eyes *t.* the *Ec 6:9* wandering
with him that is mightier *t.* he *Ec 6:10*
A good name is better *t.* *Ec 7:1* precious
day of death *t.* the day of one's *Ec 7:1* birth
t. to go to the house of feasting *Ec 7:2*
Sorrow is better *t.* laughter: for *Ec 7:3* by
t. for a man to hear the song of *Ec 7:5* fools
is the end of a thing *t.* the *Ec 7:8* beginning
in spirit is better *t.* the proud *Ec 7:8* in spirit
the former days were better *t.* *Ec 7:10* these
the wise more *t.* mighty men *Ec 7:19* which
I find more bitter *t.* death the *Ec 7:26* woman
thing under the sun *t.* to eat *Ec 8:15*
living dog is better *t.* a dead *Ec 9:4* lion
said I, Wisdom is better *t.* *Ec 9:16* strength
more *t.* the cry of him that *Ec 9:17* ruleth
Wisdom is better *t.* weapons *Ec 9:18* of war
mouth: for thy love is better *t.* *Ca 1:2* wine
will remember thy love more *t.* *Ca 1:4* mine
how much better is thy love *t.* *Ca 4:10* wine
smell of thine ointments *t.* all *Ca 4:10* spices
thy beloved more *t.* another *Ca 5:9* beloved
a man more precious *t.* fine *Isa 13:12* gold
a man *t.* the golden wedge of *Isa 13:12* Ophir
is shorter *t.* that a man can *Isa 28:20* stretch
narrower *t.* that he can wrap *Isa 28:20* himself
deeper speech *t.* thou canst *Isa 33:19* perceive
to him less *t.* nothing, and *Isa 40:17* vanity
visage was so marred more *Isa 52:14* *t.* any man
and his form more *t.* the *Isa 52:14* sons of men
t. the children of the married *Isa 54:1* wife
as the heavens are higher *t.* *Isa 55:9* the earth
so are my ways higher *t.* your *Isa 55:9* ways
and my thoughts *t.* your *Isa 55:9* thoughts
better *t.* of sons and of *Isa 56:5* daughters
hast discovered thyself to *Isa 57:8* another *t.* me
near to me; for I am holier *t.* *Isa 65:5* thou
herself more *t.* treacherous *Jer 3:11* Judah
his horses are swifter *t.* eagles *Jer 4:13*
have made their faces harder *t.* *Jer 5:3* a rock
neck: they did worse *t.* their *Jer 7:26* fathers

death shall be chosen rather *t.* *Jer 8:3* life by
ye have done worse *t.* your *Jer 16:12* fathers
thou art stronger *t.* I and *Jer 20:7* hast
hand of him that was *Jer 31:11* stronger *t.* he
they are more *t.* the *Jer 46:23* grasshoppers, and
greater *t.* the punishment of the *La 4:6* sin of
Her Nazarites were purer *t.* *La 4:7* snow, they
they were whiter *t.* milk, they *La 4:7* were
were more ruddy in body *t.* *La 4:7* rubies
Their visage is blacker *t.* a *La 4:8* coal; they
t. they that be slain with *La 4:9* hunger
are swifter *t.* the eagles of the *La 4:19* heaven
As an adamant harder *t.* flint *Eze 3:9* have I
wickedness more *t.* the nations *Eze 5:6*
statutes more *t.* the countries *Eze 5:6* that
multipled more *t.* the nations *Eze 5:7* that
more desolate *t.* the *Eze 6:14* wilderness
see greater abominations *t.* *Eze 8:15* these
What is the vine tree more *t.* *Eze 15:2* any tree
or *t.* a branch which is *Eze 15:2* among the
wast corrupted more *t.* they *Eze 16:47* in all thy
thine abominations more *t.* *Eze 16:51* they
committed more abominable *Eze 16:52* *t.* they
they are more righteous *t.* *Eze 16:52* thou: yea
corrupt in her inordinate *Eze 23:11* love *t.* she
more *t.* her sister in her *Eze 23:11* whoredoms
thou art wiser *t.* Daniel: there *Eze 28:3* is no
for the galleries were higher *Eze 42:5* *t.* these
t. the lower, and *Eze 42:5*
t. the middlemost of the *Eze 42:5* building
straitened more *t.* the lowest *Eze 42:6*
faces worse liking *t.* the *Da 1:10* children
fatter in flesh *t.* all the *Da 1:15* children
better *t.* all the magicians and *Da 1:20*
that I have more *t.* any living *Da 2:30*
seven times more *t.* it was *Da 3:19* wont
was more stout *t.* his fellows *Da 7:20*
one was higher *t.* the other *Da 8:3*
fourth shall be far richer *t.* *Da 11:2* they all
more years *t.* the king of the *Da 11:8* north
multitude greater *t.* the *Da 11:13* former
then was it better with me *t.* *Ho 2:7* now
of God more *t.* burnt offerings *Ho 6:6*
be they better *t.* these *Am 6:2* kingdoms
or their border greater *t.* your *Am 6:2* border
for it is better for me to die *t.* *Jon 4:3* to live
said, It is better for me to die *Jon 4:8* *t.* to live
are more *t.* sixscore thousand *Jon 4:11* persons
upright is sharper *t.* a thorn *Mic 7:4* hedge
Art thou better *t.* populous No, *Na 3:8* that
horses also are swifter *t.* the *Hab 1:8* leopards
are more fierce *t.* the evening *Hab 1:8* wolves
art of purer eyes *t.* to behold *Hab 1:13* evil, and
the man that is more *Hab 1:13* righteous *t.* he

shall be greater *t.* of the *Hag 2:9* former
that cometh after me is *M't 3:11* mightier *t.* I
is more *t.* these cometh of *M't 5:37* evil
only, what do ye more *t.* *M't 5:47* others
Is not the life more *t.* meat, *M't 6:25* and the
meat, and the body *t.* raiment *M't 6:25*
them. Are ye not much better *M't 6:26* *t.* they
day of judgment, *t.* for that *M't 10:15* city
are of more value *t.* many *M't 10:31* sparrows
loveth father or mother *M't 10:37* more *t.* me
loveth son or daughter more *M't 10:37* *t.* me
unto you, and more *t.* a *M't 11:9* prophet
hath not risen a greater *t.* *M't 11:11* John the
the kingdom of heaven is *M't 11:11* greater *t.* he
at the day of judgment, *t.* *M't 11:22* for you
in the day of judgment, *t.* *M't 11:24* for thee
place is one geater *t.* the *M't 12:6* temple
much then is a man better *t.* *M't 12:12* a sheep
behold, a greater *t.* Jonas is *M't 12:41* here
behold, a greater *t.* Solomon *M't 12:42* is here
other spirits more wicked *t.* *M't 12:45* himself
state of that man is worse *t.* *M't 12:45* the first
t. having two hands or two *M't 18:8* feet
t. having two eyes to be cast *M't 18:9*
t. of the ninety and nine *M't 18:13* which
t. for a rich man to enter *M't 19:24* into the
sent other servants more *t.* *M't 21:36* the first
more the child of hell *t.* *M't 23:15* yourselves
more *t.* twelve legions of *M't 26:53* angels
last error shall be worse *t.* *M't 27:64* the first
cometh one mightier *t.* I after *M'k 1:7* me
is less *t.* all the seeds that be *M'k 4:31* in the
and becometh greater *t.* all *M'k 4:32* herbs
day of judgment, *t.* for that *M'k 6:11* city
ship with them more *t.* one *M'k 8:14* loaf
t. having two hands to go *M'k 9:43* into hell
t. having two feet to be cast *M'k 9:45* into
t. having two eyes to be cast *M'k 9:47* into
t. for a rich man to enter *M'k 10:25* into the
other commandment greater *M'k 12:31* *t.* these
is more *t.* all whole burnt *M'k 12:33* offerings
t. all they which have cast *M'k 12:43* into the
for more *t.* three hundred *M'k 14:5* pence
no more *t.* that which is *Lu 3:13* appointed
one mightier *t.* I cometh, the *Lu 3:16* latchet
you, and much more *t.* a *Lu 7:26* prophet
a greater prophet *t.* John the *Lu 7:28* Baptist
in the kingdom of God is *Lu 7:28* greater *t.* he
day for Sodom, *t.* for that *Lu 10:12* city
Sidon at the judgment, *t.* for *Lu 10:14* you
a stronger *t.* he shall come *Lu 11:22* upon him

other spirits more wicked *t.*   *Lu 11:26*
himself
of that man is worse *t.* the   *Lu 11:26*
first
behold, a greater *t.* Solomon   *Lu 11:31*
is here
behold, a greater *t.* Jonas is   *Lu 11:32*
here
ye are of more value *t.* many   *Lu 12:7*
sparrows
The life is more *t.* meat   *Lu 12:23*
and the body is more *t.*   *Lu 12:23*
raiment
much more are ye better *t.*   *Lu 12:24*
the fowls
a more honourable man *t.*   *Lu 14:8*
thou be
more *t.* over ninety and nine   *Lu 15:7*
just
wiser *t.* the children of light   *Lu 16:8*
t. one tittle of the law to fail   *Lu 16:17*
t. that he should offend one of   *Lu 17:2*
house justified rather *t.* the   *Lu 18:14*
other
t. for a rich man to enter   *Lu 18:25*
into the
widow hath cast in more *t.*   *Lu 21:3*
they all
thou shalt see greater things   *Joh 1:50*
t. these
loved darkness rather *t.* light   *Joh 3:19*
and baptized more disciples   *Joh 4:1*
t. John
Art thou greater *t.* our father   *Joh 4:12*
Jacob
shew him greater works *t.*   *Joh 5:20*
these, that
I have greater witness *t.* that   *Joh 5:36*
of John
he do more miracles *t.* these   *Joh 7:31*
thou greater *t.* our father   *Joh 8:53*
Abraham
which gave them me, is   *Joh 10:29*
greater *t.* all
of men more *t.* the praise   *Joh 12:43*
of God
The servant is not greater *t.*   *Joh 13:16*
his lord
is sent greater *t.* he that sent   *Joh 13:16*
him
and greater works *t.* these   *Joh 14:12*
shall he do
Father: for my Father is   *Joh 14:28*
greater *t.* I
Greater love hath no man *t.*   *Joh 15:13*
this, that
The servant is not greater *t.*   *Joh 15:20*
his lord
Jonas, lovest thou me more   *Joh 21:15*
t. these
unto you more *t.* unto God,   *Ac 4:19*
judge
ought to obey God rather *t.*   *Ac 5:29*
men
you no greater burden *t.*   *Ac 15:28*
these
These were more noble *t.*   *Ac 17:11*
those in
is more blessed to give *t.* to   *Ac 20:35*
receive
more *t.* forty which had   *Ac 23:13*
made this
for him of them more *t.* forty   *Ac 23:21*
men
among them more *t.* ten days   *Ac 25:6*
saying none other things *t.*   *Ac 26:22*
those
t. those things which were   *Ac 27:11*
spoken
the creature more *t.* the   *Ro 1:25*
Creator
are we better *t.* they? No, in no   *Ro 3:9*
wise
more *t.* conquerors through   *Ro 8:37*
him
more highly *t.* he ought to   *Ro 12:3*
think
nearer *t.* when we believed   *Ro 13:11*
foolishness of God is wiser *t.*   *1Co 1:25*
men
weakness of God is stronger   *1Co 1:25*
t. men
can no man lay *t.* that is   *1Co 3:11*
laid
for it is better to marry *t.* to   *1Co 7:9*
burn
t. that any man should make   *1Co 9:15*
my
to jealousy? are we stronger   *1Co 10:22*
t. he

t. he that speaketh with   *1Co 14:5*
tongues
speak with tongues more *t.*   *1Co 14:18*
ye all
t. ten thousand words in an   *1Co 14:19*
laboured more abundantly *t.*   *1Co 15:10*
they all
t. what ye read or   *2Co 1:13*
acknowledge
t. that which we have preached   *Ga 1:8*
you *t.* that ye have received   *Ga 1:9*
more children *t.* she which   *Ga 4:27*
hath a
who am less *t.* the least of all   *Eph 3:8*
saints
esteem other better *t.*   *Ph'p 2:3*
themselves
rather *t.* godly edifying which   *1Ti 1:4*
the faith, and is worse *t.* an   *1Ti 5:8*
infidel
pleasures more *t.* lovers of   *2Ti 3:4*
God
thou wilt also do more *t.* I   *Ph'm 21*
say
Being made so much better *t.*   *Heb 1:4*
angels
a more excellent name *t.* they   *Heb 1:4*
him a little lower *t.* the angels   *Heb 2:7*
was made a little lower *t.* the   *Heb 2:9*
angels
worthy of more glory *t.* Moses   *Heb 3:3*
house hath more honour *t.* the   *Heb 3:3*
house
sharper *t.* any two-edged   *Heb 4:12*
sword
and made higher *t.* the   *Heb 7:26*
heavens
with better sacrifices *t.* these   *Heb 9:23*
a more excellent sacrifice *t.*   *Heb 11:4*
Cain
t. to enjoy the pleasures of   *Heb 11:25*
sin
greater riches *t.* the   *Heb 11:26*
treasures in
better things *t.* that of Abel   *Heb 12:24*
more precious *t.* of gold that   *1Pe 1:7*
perisheth
for well doing, *t.* for evil   *1Pe 3:17*
doing
worse with them *t.* the   *2Pe 2:20*
beginning
t. after they have known it,   *2Pe 2:21*
to
God is greater *t.* our heart   *1Jo 3:20*
in you, *t.* he that is in the   *1Jo 4:4*
world
no greater joy *t.* to hear that my   *3Jo 4*
and the last to be more *t.* the   *Re 2:19*
first

THANK

to *t.* and praise the Lord   *1Ch 16:4*
God of
first this psalm to *t.* the Lord   *1Ch 16:7*
morning to *t.* and praise the   *1Ch 23:30*
our God, we *t.* thee, and   *1Ch 29:13*
praise thy
t. offerings into the house   *2Ch 29:31*
of the
brought sacrifices and *t.*   *2Ch 29:31*
offerings
peace offerings and *t.*   *2Ch 33:16*
offerings
I *t.* thee, and praise thee, O   *Da 2:23*
thou
and said, I *t.* thee, O   *M't 11:25*
Father, Lord
which love you, what *t.* have   *Lu 6:32*
ye
do good to you, what *t.* have   *Lu 6:33*
ye
ye hope to receive, what *t.*   *Lu 6:34*
have ye
and said, I *t.* thee, O Father,   *Lu 10:21*
Lord
he *t.* that servant because   *Lu 17:9*
God, I *t.* thee, that I am not   *Lu 18:11*
as
I *t.* thee that thou hast   *Joh 11:41*
heard me
I *t.* my God through Jesus   *Ro 1:8*
Christ
I *t.* God through Jesus Christ   *Ro 7:25*
our
I *t.* my God always on your   *1Co 1:4*
behalf
I *t.* God that I baptized none   *1Co 1:14*
of you

I *t.* my God, I speak with   *1Co 14:18*
tongues
t. my God upon every   *Ph'p 1:3*
remembrance
this cause also *t.* we God   *1Th 2:13*
without
We are bound to *t.* God   *2Th 1:3*
always for
And I *t.* Christ Jesus our   *1Ti 1:12*
Lord
I *t.* God, whom I serve from   *2Ti 1:3*
my
I *t.* my God, making mention   *Ph'm 4*
of

THANKED

bowed himself, and *t.* the   *2Sa 14:22*
king
saw, he *t.* God, and took   *Ac 28:15*
courage
But, God be *t.* that ye were   *Ro 6:17*

THANKFUL

be *t.* unto him, and bless his   *Ps 100:4*
name
him not as God, neither were   *Ro 1:21*
t.
called in one body; and be   *Col 3:15*
ye *t.*

THANKFULNESS

most noble Felix, with all *t.*   *Ac 24:3*

THANKING

heard in praising and *t.* the   *2Ch 5:13*
Lord

THANKS

I give *t.* this day (A)   *De 26:3*
Therefore I will give *t.* unto   *2Sa 22:50*
thee
Give *t.* unto the Lord, call   *1Ch 16:8*
upon his
O give *t.* unto the Lord; for   *1Ch 16:34*
he is
we may give *t.* to thy holy   *1Ch 16:35*
name
by name, to give *t.* to the   *1Ch 16:41*
Lord
to give *t.* and to praise the   *1Ch 25:3*
Lord
to minister, and to give *t.*   *2Ch 31:2*
and to
and giving *t.* unto the Lord   *Ezr 3:11*
to praise and to give *t.*   *Ne 12:24*
according
companies of them that   *Ne 12:31;*
gave *t.*   *12:40*
other company of them that   *Ne 12:38*
gave *t.*
in the grave who shall give thee   *Ps 6:5*
t.
will I give *t.* unto thee, O   *Ps 18:49*
Lord
give *t.* at the remembrance of   *Ps 30:4*
his
I will give *t.* unto thee for   *Ps 30:12*
ever
the *t.* in the great   *Ps 35:18*
congregation
Unto thee, O God, do we give   *Ps 75:1*
t.
unto thee do we give *t.:* for   *Ps 75:1*
that
we thy people give thee *t.*   *Ps 79:13*
for ever
good thing to give *t.* unto the   *Ps 92:1*
Lord
give *t.* at the remembrance of   *Ps 97:12*
his
O give *t.* unto the Lord; call   *Ps 105:1*
upon
O give *t.* unto the Lord; for   *Ps 106:1;*
he is   *107:1; 118:1, 29; 136:1*
to give *t.* unto thy holy   *Ps 106:47*
name, and
At midnight I will rise to   *Ps 119:62*
give *t.*
give *t.* unto the name of the   *Ps 122:4*
Lord
O give *t.* unto the God of   *Ps 136:2*
gods: for
O give *t.* to the Lord of   *Ps 136:3*
lords; for
O give *t.* unto the God of   *Ps 136:26*
heaven

the righteous shall give *t.*   *Ps 140:13*
unto thy
prayed, and gave *t.* before his   *Da 6:10*
God
and gave *t.* and brake them   *M't 15:36*
And he took the cup, and   *M't 26:27*
gave *t.*
took the seven loaves, and   *M'k 8:6*
gave *t.*
when he had given *t.* he   *M'k 14:23*
gave it to
gave *t.* likewise unto the Lord   *Lu 2:38*
his face at his feet, giving   *Lu 17:16*
him *t.*
And he took the cup, and   *Lu 22:17*
gave *t.*
And he took bread, and gave   *Lu 22:19*
t.
when he had given *t.* he   *Joh 6:11*
distributed
after that the Lord had given   *Joh 6:23*
t.
gave *t.* to God in presence of   *Ac 27:35*
them
to the Lord, for he giveth God   *Ro 14:6*
t.
he eateth not, and giveth God   *Ro 14:6*
t.
unto whom not only I give *t.*   *Ro 16:4*
of for that for which I give   *1Co 10:30*
t.
when he had given *t.* he   *1Co 11:24*
brake it
say Amen at thy giving of *t.*   *1Co 14:16*
thou verily givest *t.* well,   *1Co 14:17*
but the
But *t.* be to God, which   *1Co 15:57*
giveth us
t. may be given by many on   *2Co 1:11*
our
Now *t.* be unto God, which   *2Co 2:14*
always
But *t.* be to God. which put   *2Co 8:16*
T. be unto God for his   *2Co 9:15*
unspeakable
Cease not to give *t.* for you   *Eph 1:16*
convenient: but rather giving   *Eph 5:4*
of *t.*
Giving *t.* always for all   *Eph 5:20*
things
We give *t.* to God and the   *Col 1:3*
Father
Giving *t.* unto the Father,   *Col 1:12*
which
giving *t.* to God and the   *Col 3:17*
Father by
We give *t.* to God always for   *1Th 1:2*
you
For what *t.* can we render to   *1Th 3:9*
God
In every thing give *t.*: for this   *1Th 5:18*
is
are bound to give *t.* alway to   *2Th 2:13*
God
intercessions, and giving of *t.*   *1Ti 2:1*
let us give *t.* to God (N)   *Heb 12:28*
of our lips giving *t.* to his   *Heb 13:15*
name
t. to him that sat on the   *Re 4:9*
throne
We give thee *t.* O Lord God   *Re 11:17*

THANKSGIVING

If he offer it for a *t.* then he   *Le 7:12*
shall
with the sacrifice of *t.*   *Le 7:12*
unleavened
bread with the sacrifice of *t.*   *Le 7:13*
of his
his peace offerings for *t.* shall   *Le 7:15*
be
offer a sacrifice of *t.* unto the   *Le 22:29*
Lord
principal to begin the *t.* in   *Ne 11:17*
prayer
Mattaniah, which was over   *Ne 12:8*
the *t.*
songs of praise and *t.* unto   *Ne 12:46*
God
may publish with the voice of   *Ps 26:7*
t.
Offer unto God *t.*, and pay   *Ps 50:14*
thy vows
song, and will magnify him   *Ps 69:30*
with *t.*
us come before his presence   *Ps 95:2*
with *t.*
Enter into his gates with *t.*   *Ps 100:4*

them sacrifice the sacrifices   *Ps 107:22*
of *t.*
I will offer to thee the   *Ps 116:17*
sacrifice of *t.*
Sing unto the Lord with *t.*   *Ps 147:7*
gladness shall be found   *Isa 51:3*
therein, *t.*
out of them shall proceed *t.*   *Jer 30:19*
offer a sacrifice of *t.* with   *Am 4:5*
leaven
unto thee with the voice of *t.*   *Jon 2:9*
through the *t.* of many   *2Co 4:15*
redound to
which causeth through us *t.*   *2Co 9:11*
to God
by prayer, and supplication   *Ph'p 4:6*
with *t.*
taught, abounding therein with   *Col 2:7*
t.
and watch in the same with *t.*   *Col 4:2*
to be received with *t.* of them   *1Ti 4:3*
which
be refused, if it be received   *1Ti 4:4*
with *t.*
and wisdom, and *t.* and   *Re 7:12*
honour

THANKSGIVINGS

both with *t.* and with singing   *Ne 12:27*
also by many *t.* unto God   *2Co 9:12*

THANKWORTHY

this is *t.* if a man for   *1Pe 2:19*
conscience

THARA

which was the son of *T.*   *Lu 3:34*

THARSHISH

the king had at sea a navy   *1Ki 10:22*
of *T.*
in three years came the navy   *1Ki 10:22*
of *T.*
Jehoshaphat made ships of   *1Ki 22:48*
T. to
Zethan, and *T.* and   *1Ch 7:10*
Ahishahar

THAT

t. is it which compasseth the   *Ge 2:11*
land
what Adam called, *t.* was the   *Ge 2:19*
name
t. be far from thee, to slay   *Ge 18:25*
righteous
t. shall be accounted stolen   *Ge 30:33*
with me
would *t.* we had died (S)   *Ex 16:3*
whosoever shall make like to   *Ex 30:38*
when Moses heard *t.* he was   *Le 10:20*
content
for all *t.* I will not cast them   *Le 26:44*
away
besides *t. t.* his hands shall   *Nu 6:21*
get
the word which I say, *t.* shalt   *Nu 22:20*
thou do
Lord saith *t.* will I speak   *Nu 24:13;*
  1Ki 22:14
anger abated, when he had said   *J'g 8:3*
t.
do according to *t.* which   *J'g 11:36*
proceeded
t. which is left, set it before   *1Sa 9:24*
Goliath's sword, if thou wilt   *1Sa 21:9*
take *t.*
for *t.* thou hast done to me   *1Sa 24:19*
this day
with *t.* which the Lord hath   *1Sa 30:23*
given us
if *t.* had been too little, I   *2Sa 12:8*
would
in *t.* thou lovest thine   *2Sa 19:6*
enemies and hatest
offer of *t.* which doth cost   *2Sa 24:24*
me nothing
according to *t.* which was   *2Ki 14:6;*
written in the law of Moses   *2Ch 35:26*
t. whch thou hast prayed to   *2Ki 19:20*
me
t. which thou hast promised   *2Ch 6:15;*
  6:16
t. which they have need of be   *Ezr 6:9*
given

t. do after the will of your   *Ezr 7:18*
God
t. which I was afraid of is   *Job 3:25*
come
t. which I have seen I will   *Job 15:17*
declare
he shall not save of *t.* which   *Job 20:20*
he desired
what his soul desireth even   *Job 23:13*
t. he doeth
t. which I see not, teach   *Job 34:32*
thou me
t. will I seek after, *t.* I may   *Ps 27:4*
dwell
I restored *t.* which I took not   *Ps 69:4*
away
when I wept, *t.* was to my   *Ps 69:10*
reproach
thing *t.* hath been, it is *t.* which   *Ec 1:9*
be; *t.* which is done, is *t.* which
t. which is wanting cannot be   *Ec 1:15*
numbered
see what was *t.* good for sons   *Ec 2:3*
of men
what profit in *t.* wherein he   *Ec 3:9*
laboureth
and God requireth *t.* which is   *Ec 3:15*
past
when vowest, pay *t.* thou hast   *Ec 5:4*
vowed
knowest not whether this or *t.*   *Ec 11:6*
prosper
t. which I have heard of the   *Isa 21:10*
Lord
for *t.* which had not been   *Isa 52:15*
told them shall they see, *t.*
they had not heard
t. Manasseh did in Jerusalem   *Jer 15:4*
t. which I built, *t.* which I   *Jer 45:4*
planted
t. Daniel regardeth not thee,   *Da 6:13*
O king
for *t. t.* is determined shall   *Da 11:36*
be done
t. t. dieth, let it die, *t.* is to   *Zec 11:9*
be cut off
for *t.* which is conceived in   *M't 1:20*
her is of
woman made whole from *t.*   *M't 9:22;*
hour   *15:28*
for Sodom than for *t.* city   *M't 10:15;*
  M'k 6:11
taken away *t.* he hath   *M't 13:12;*
  25:29; M'k 4:25
t. shall ye receive   *M't 20:7*
t. they should hold her peace   *M't 20:31*
(S)
t. observe and do   *M't 23:3*
what is *t.* to us? see thou to   *M't 27:4*
t.
t. which cometh out, *t.*   *M'k 7:20*
defileth man
what shall be given in *t.*   *M'k 13:11*
hour, *t.* speak
all will I give, for *t.* is delivered   *Lu 4:6*
to me
shall be taken, even *t.* he   *Lu 8:18*
seemeth to have
he *t.* made *t.* which is   *Lu 11:40*
without make *t.* which is
within also
not faithful in *t.* which is   *Lu 16:12*
another man's
t. which is highly esteemed   *Lu 16:15*
among men
have done *t.* which was our   *Lu 17:10*
duty
wondering as *t.* which was   *Lu 24:12*
come to pass
he was not *t.* light   *Joh 1:8*
t. was the light   *Joh 1:9*
t. born of flesh, *t.* born of the   *Joh 3:6*
Spirit
speak *t.* we know, testify *t.*   *Joh 3:11*
we have seen
is not thy husband, in *t.*   *Joh 4:18*
saidst thou truly
herein is *t.* saying true, one   *Joh 4:37*
soweth another
what man is *t.* which said to   *Joh 5:12*
thee, Take up
labour for *t.* meat which   *Joh 6:27*
endureth
Moses gave you not *t.* bread   *Joh 6:32*
from heaven
I am *t.* bread of life   *Joh 6:48*
this is *t.* bread   *Joh 6:58*
I speak *t.* I have seen with   *Joh 8:38*
my father; ye do *t.* which ye
have seen with

t. do quickly	Joh 13:27
t. will I do	Joh 14:13
what he shall hear, *t.* shall he speak	Joh 16:13
what is *t.* to thee, follow thou me	Joh 21:22; 21:24
went abroad, *t. t.* disciple should not die	Joh 21:23
this is *t.* spoken by prophet Joel	Ac 2:16
all glorified God for *t.* which was done	Ac 4:21
when they heard *t.* they lifted up	Ac 4:24; 5:21, 33
this is *t.* Moses which said unto Israel	Ac 7:37
t. word you know, which was published	Ac 10:37
because *t.* which may be known	Ro 1:19
according to *t.* which was spoken	Ro 4:18
in *t.* he died, in *t.* he liveth	Ro 6:10
t. being dead we were held, *t.* we	Ro 7:6
was then *t.* which is good made death	Ro 7:13
t. I do; I allow not; *t.* I would not, *t.* do I	Ro 7:15; 7:19
put away from you *t.* wicked	1Co 5:13
nay, you defraud, and *t.* your brethren	1Co 6:8
t. spiritual rock, and *t.* rock was Christ	1Co 10:4
spoken of, for *t.* for which I give thanks	1Co 10:30
t. which also I delivered unto you	1Co 11:23
eat of *t.* bread, and drink of *t.* cup	1Co 11:28
t. which is perfect, *t.* which is in part	1Co 13:10
and yet for all *t.* they will not hear me	1Co 14:21
t. which thou sowest thou sowest not *t.* body that shall be	1Co 15:37
t. was not first which is spiritual, but *t.*	1Co 15:46
if *t.* done away was glorious	2Co 3:11
accepted according to *t.* a man hath	2Co 8:12
what I do, *t.* I will do, *t.* I may	2Co 11:12
what man soweth *t.* shall he reap	Ga 6:7
t. I may apprehend *t.* for which	Ph'p 3:12
might perfect *t.* which is lacking	1Th 3:10
prove all things, hold fast *t.*	1Th 5:21
life *t.* now is, and of *t.* which	1Ti 4:8
keep *t.* which is committed to thy	1Ti 6:20
if he oweth put *t.* on mine account	Ph'm 18
and was heard in *t.* he feared	Heb 5:7
which entereth into *t.* within the veil	Heb 6:19
could not endure *t.* commanded	Heb 12:20
for *t.* is unprofitable for you	Heb 13:17
if Lord will, we shall do this or *t.*	Jas 4:15
who is he *t.* will harm you,	1Pe 3:13;
if ye be followers of *t.*	3Jo 1
t. which was from the beginning	1Jo 1:1
t. which we have seen and heard	1Jo 1:3; 2:24
let *t.* abide in you which ye have heard	1Jo 2:24
t. which ye have, hold fast	Re 2:25

THEATRE

rushed with one accord into the *t.*	Ac 19:29
not adventure himself into the *t.*	Ac 19:31

THEBEZ

Then went Abimelech to *T.*	J'g 9:50
encamped against *T.,* and took it	J'g 9:50
from the wall, that he died in *T.*	2Sa 11:21

THEE

t. have I seen righteous before me	Ge 7:1
and I will multiply *t.* exceedingly	Ge 17:2
that in blessing I will bless *t.*	Ge 22:17
field gave I *t.* and cave gave I *t.*	Ge 23:11
kept back any thing from me but *t.*	Ge 39:9
the stranger shall get above *t.*	De 28:43
they have not rejected *t.* but me	1Sa 8:7
the arrows are beyond *t.*	1Sa 20:22; 20:37
the king charged *t.* and Abishai	2Sa 18:12
they have not set *t.* before them	Ps 86:14
cause enemy to entreat *t.* well	Jer 15:11
I will recompense *t.* according to	Eze 7:9
I will leave *t.* and all fish of rivers	Eze 29:5
when saw *t.* an hundred, and fed *t.*	M't 25:37
when saw *t.* a stranger	M't 25:38
saw *t.* sick	M't 25:39
he that bade *t.* and him come	Lu 14:9
the root *t.*	Ro 11:18
lest he spare not *t.*	Ro 11:21

ABOUT THEE

dig *about t.* and take thy rest	Job 11:18
shut thy doors *about t.* hide thyself	Isa 26:20
sword devour round *about t.*	Jer 46:14; Eze 5:12
bring fear from those that be *about t.*	Jer 49:5
among nations round *about t.*	Eze 5:14
astonishment to nations round *about t.*	Eze 5:15
enemies shall cast a trench *about t.*	Lu 19:43
Cast garment *about t.* and follow	Ac 12:8

AFTER THEE

to thy seed *after t.*	Ge 17:7; 17:8, 9, 10; 35:12; 48:4
with thy children *after t.*	De 4:40; 12:25, 28
after t. Benjamin among thy people	J'g 5:14
I will set up thy seed *after t.*	2Sa 7:12
I also will come in *after t.*	1Ki 1:14
nor *after t.* arise like thee	1Ki 3:12; 2Ch 1:12
so panteth my soul *after t.* O God	Ps 42:1
my soul followeth hard *after t.*	Ps 63:8
soul thirsteth *after t.* as thirsty land	Ps 143:6
draw me, we will run *after t.*	Ca 1:4
they shall come *after t.* in chains	Isa 45:14
they have called a multitude *after t.*	Jer 12:6
after t. shall rise another kingdom	Da 2:39
cry at Beth-aven, *after t.* O Benjamin	Ho 5:8

AGAINST THEE

overthrown them that rose *against t.*	Ex 15:7
lest beast of field multiply *against t.*	Ex 23:29
we have sinned, for we have spoken *against t.*	Nu 21:7
the anger of the Lord be kindled *against t.*	De 6:15
he cry to the Lord *against t.*	De 15:9; 24:15
because they hired Balaam *against t.* to curse	De 23:4
come out *against t.* one way, and flee	De 28:7
enemies the Lord send *against t.*	De 28:48; 28:49
that it may be there for a witness *against t.*	De 31:26

Behold, they fortify this city *against t.*	J'g 9:31
we have sinned *against t.*	J'g 10:10; Ne 1:6; Jer 14:7, 20
I have not sinned *against t.*	J'g 11:27; 1Sa 24:11
because he hath not sinned *against t.*	1Sa 19:4
for thy mouth hath testified *against t.*	2Sa 1:16
behold, I will raise up evil *against t.*	2Sa 12:11
avenged of all that rose *against t.*	2Sa 18:31; 18:32
because they have sinned *against t.*	1Ki 8:33; 8:35; 2Ch 6:24, 26
if sin *against t.* and repent	1Ki 8:46; 2Ch 6:36
forgive people that have sinned *against t.* and all transgressions	1Ki 8:50; 2Ch 6:39
king of Syria come up *against t.*	1Ki 20:22
he is come out to fight *against t.*	2Ki 19:9
let not man prevail *against t.*	2Ch 14:11
the Lord hath spoken evil *against t.*	2Ch 18:22
there cometh a great multitude *against t.*	2Ch 20:2
I come not *against t.* this day	2Ch 35:21
we have dealt very corruptly *against t.*	Ne 1:7
nevertheless they rebelled *against t.*	Ne 9:26
why hast thou set me as a mark *against t.*	Job 7:20
but, oh that God would open his lips *against t.*	Job 11:5
yea, thine own lips testify *against t.*	Job 15:6
my wrath is kindled *against t.*	Job 42:7
cast them out, they rebelled *against t.*	Ps 5:10
for they intended evil *against t.*	Ps 21:11
heal my soul, for I have sinned *against t.*	Ps 41:4
hear, O Israel, and I will testify *against t.*	Ps 50:7
against t. have I sinned, and done evil	Ps 51:4
that rise up *against t.*	Ps 74:23; 139:21; Ec 10:4
thy word I hid, that I might not sin *against t.*	Ps 119:11
for they speak *against t.* wickedly	Ps 139:20
have taken evil counsel *against t.* saying	Isa 7:5
Assyrian shall lift up his staff *against t.*	Isa 10:24
they shall fight *against t.* but shall not prevail *against t.*	Jer 1:19; 15:20
I am *against t.*	Jer 21:13; 50:31; 51:25; Eze 5:8; 21:3; 26:3; 28:22; 29:3, 10; 35:3; 38:3; 39:1; Na 2:13; 3:5
thy enemies opened their mouth *against t.*	La 2:16
thy people still are talking *against t.*	Eze 33:30
saying, Amos hath conspired *against t.*	Am 7:10
what have we spoken so much *against t.*	Mal 3:13
that thy brother hath aught *against t.*	M't 5:23
if thy brother trespass *against t.*	M't 18:15; Lu 17:3-4
which these witness *against t.*	M't 26:62; M'k 14:60; 15:4
nevertheless, I have somewhat *against t.*	Re 2:4
I have a few things *against t.*	Re 2:14; 2:20

AT THEE

shaken her head *at t.*	2Ki 19:21; Isa 37:22
the fir trees rejoice *at t.*	Isa 14:8
astonish, *at t.*	Isa 52:14; Eze 26:16; 27:35; 28:19
all that pass clap their hands *at t.*	La 2:15

the merchants shall hiss *at t.*   Eze 27:36
I will make many people   Eze 32:10
amazed *at t.*

BEFORE THEE

is not the whole land *before t.*   Ge 13:9
O that Ishmael might live   Ge 17:18
before t.
my land is *before t.*   Ge 20:15; 47:6
Lord God of heaven send his   Ge 24:7;
angel *before t.*   Ex 23:20, 23; 32:34;
  33:2
Rebekah is *before t.* take her   Ge 24:51
I cannot rise up *before t.*   Ge 31:35
I will go *before t.*   Ge 33:12
set him *before t.*   Ge 43:9
I will stand *before t.* there   Ex 17:6
I will send my fear *before t.*   Ex 23:27
and destroy
I will send hornets *before t.*   Ex 23:28;
which shall drive out the   23:29, 30, 31;
Canaanite *before t.*   34:11; De 4:38;
  9:4, 5; 18:12
make all my goodness pass   Ex 33:19
before t. and proclaim name of
Lord *before t.*
I will cast out *before t.*   Ex 34:24;
  De 6:19; 7:1; 9:4
let them that hate thee flee   Nu 10:35
before t.
no man able to stand before   De 7:24;
t.   Jos 1:5; 10:8
they shall flee *before t.* seven   De 28:7
ways
I have set *before t.* this day   De 30:15
life
Joshua, he shall go over   De 31:3;
before t.   31:8
yet thou shalt see the land   De 32:52
before t.
they shall put incense *before*   De 33:10
t.
is not the Lord gone out   J'g 4:14
before t.
bring forth, and set it before   J'g 6:18;
t.   1Sa 9:24
let me set a morsel of bread   1Sa 28:22
before t.
then shall the Lord go out   2Sa 5:24
before t.
I took from Saul, whom I   2Sa 7:15
put away *before t.*
be established *before t.*   2Sa 7:16;
  7:26; 1Ch 17:24
walk *before t.*   1Ki 3:6
none like *before t.*   1Ki 3:12
thy servants that walk *before*   1Ki 8:23;
t.   2Ch 6:14
stand continually *before t.*   1Ki 10:8;
  2Ch 9:7
done evil above all *before t.*   1Ki 14:9
how I have walked *before t.*   2Ki 20:3;
  Isa 38:3
God is gone forth *before t.*   1Ch 14:15
as I took it from him that   1Ch 17:13
was *before t.*
we are *before t.* in trespasses,   Ezr 9:15
we cannot stand *before t.*
let not their sin be blotted out   Ne 4:5
before t.
and foundest his heart faithful   Ne 9:8
before t.
let not all the trouble seem   Ne 9:32
little *before t.*
all my desire is *before t.*   Ps 38:9
mine age is as nothing *before*   Ps 39:5
t.
mine adversaries are all   Ps 69:19
before t.
so foolish was I, I was as a   Ps 73:22
beast *before t.*
let sighing of the prisoner   Ps 79:11
come *before t.*
let my prayer come *before t.*   Ps 88:2;
incline   141:2
thou hast set our iniquities   Ps 90:8
before t.
my ways *before t.*   Ps 119:168
cry come *before t.*   Ps 119:169
consider diligently what is   Pr 23:1
before t.
they joy *before t.* as men when   Isa 9:3
they
I will go *before t.*   Isa 45:2
thy righteousness shall go   Isa 58:8
before t.
came out of my lips, was   Jer 17:16
right *before t.*

I stood *before t.* to turn   Jer 18:20
away thy wrath
prophets that have been   Jer 28:8
before t. of old
all the land is *before t.*   Jer 40:4
let all wickedness come *before*   La 1:22
t.
they sit *before t.* as my   Eze 33:31
people
before t. O king, have I done   Da 6:22
no hurt
I sent *before t.* Moses, Aaron   Mic 6:4
thou and thy fellows that sit   Zec 3:8
before t.
do not sound a trumpet   M't 6:2
before t.
my messenger; which shall   M't 11:10;
prepare thy way *before t.*   M'k 1:2;
  Lu 7:27
father, I have sinned *before t.*   Lu 15:18
to say *before t.* what   Ac 23:30
they had against him
ought to have been here   Ac 24:19
before t. to object
especially *before t.* O king   Ac 25:26
Agrippa
I have set *before t.* an open   Re 3:8
door

BEHIND THEE

escape for life, look not   Ge 19:17
behind t.
Amalek smote the feeble   De 25:18
behind t.
seeing thou castest my words   Ps 50:17
behind t.
thine ears shall hear a word   Isa 30:21
behind t.

BESIDE THEE

there is none to redeem it   Ru 4:4
beside t.
none *beside t.*   1Sa 2:2;
  2Sa 7:22; 1Ch 17:20
none on earth I desire *beside*   Ps 73:25
t.
other lords *beside t.* had   Isa 26:13
dominion
neither hath the eye seen   Isa 64:4
beside t.

BETWEEN THEE

put enmity *between t.* and the   Ge 3:15
woman
make my covenant *between*   Ge 17:2;
me and *t.*   17:7
let it be for a witness   Ge 31:44;
between me and *t.*   48:50
Lord watch *between* me and   Ge 31:49
t. when absent
Lord be *between t.* and me   1Sa 20:23;
  20:42
set it for a wall of iron *between*   Eze 4:3
t. and city
Lord hath been witness   Mal 2:14
between t.
tell his fault *between t.* and   M't 18:15
him alone

BY THEE

people stand *by t.* from   Ex 18:14
morning
I am woman that stood *by t.*   1Sa 1:26
praying
portion of which I said to   1Sa 9:23
thee, Set it *by t.*
by t. I ran thro' a troop   2Sa 22:30;
  Ps 18:29
by t. have I been holpen   Ps 71:6
when hast it *by t.*   Pr 3:28
dwell securely *by t.*   Pr 3:29
by t. make mention of thy   Isa 26:13
name
when I passed *by t.* saw thee   Eze 16:6;
  16:8
seeing that *by t.* we enjoy   Ac 24:2
quietness
bowels of the saints are   Ph'm 7
refreshed *by t.*

CONCERNING THEE

thing the Lord said *concerning*   Jos 14:6
t. and me
good that he hath spoken   1Sa 25:30
concerning t.

king said, I will give charge   2Sa 14:8
concerning t.
Lord hath spoken evil   1Ki 22:23
concerning t.
Lord hath given   Na 1:14
commandment *concerning t.*
give his angels charge   M't 4:6
concerning t.
neither received we letters   Ac 28:21
concerning t.

FOR THEE

food *for t.*   Ge 6:21
shall pray *for t.*   Ge 20:7
as *for t.* and thy servants, I   Ex 9:30
know
sabbath shall be meat *for t.*   Le 25:6
be most holy *for t.* and thy   Nu 18:9
sons
as *for t.* stand by me   De 5:31;
  18:14; 2Sa 13:13
I will try them *for t.* there   J'g 7:4
till we shall have made ready   J'g 13:15
a kid *for t.*
better *for t.* to be a priest to   J'g 18:19
one man
seek rest *for t.*   Ru 3:1
buy it *for t.*   Ru 4:8
to this time been kept *for t.*   1Sa 9:24
what thy soul desireth, I   1Sa 20:4
will do it *for t.*
I am distressed *for t.*   2Sa 1:26
Jonathan
if Syrians be too strong *for*   2Sa 10:11
t. help me
would God I had died *for t.*   2Sa 18:33
Absalom
what thou requirest, that I   2Sa 19:38
will do *for t.*
I will speak *for t.* unto the   1Ki 2:18
king
after make *for t.* and for thy   1Ki 17:13
son
make streets *for t.* in   1Ki 20:34
Damascus
ask what I shall do *for t.*   2Ki 2:9; 4:2
say now, what is to be done   2Ki 4:13
for t.
and as *for t.*   2Ch 7:17;
  Da 2:29; Zec 9:11
if upright, he would awake *for*   Job 8:6
t.
shall the earth be forsaken   Job 18:4
for t.
my soul thirsteth *for t.* my   Ps 63:1
flesh
praise waiteth *for t.* O God, in   Ps 65:1
Sion
it is time *for t.*, O Lord, to   Ps 119:126
work
fruits I have laid up *for t.*   Ca 7:13
beloved
hell from beneath is moved   Isa 14:9
for t.
Lord, we have waited *for t.*   Isa 26:8;
  33:2
I gave Ethiopia and Seba *for*   Isa 43:3
t.
I loved thee, therefore I give   Isa 43:4
men *for t.*
for my praise will I refrain   Isa 48:9
for t.
come, who shall be sorry *for*   Isa 51:19
t.
there is nothing too hard *for*   Jer 32:17
t.
so shall they burn odours *for*   Jer 34:5
t.
weep *for t.*   Jer 48:32
I laid snare *for t.*   Jer 50:24
therefore will I take   Jer 51:36
vengeance *for t.*
what shall I take to witness   La 2:13
for t.
prophets have seen *for t.* false   La 2:14
burdens
it watcheth *for t.* it is come   Eze 7:6
their king shall be horribly   Eze 32:10
afraid *for t.*
not be for another, so will I be   Ho 3:3
for t.
also, O Judah, he hath set a   Ho 6:11
harvest *for t.*
whence shall I seek comfort *for*   Na 3:7
t.
for it is profitable *for t.*   M't 5:29;
  5:30
be more tolerable for Sodom   M't 11:24
than *for t.*

not lawful *for t.* to have her *M't 14:4;*
M'k 6:18
one *for t.,* one for Moses *M't 17:4;*
M'k 9:5; Lu 9:33
better *for t.* to enter into life *M't 18:8;*
M'k 9:43, 45
they said all men seek *for t.* *M'k 1:37*
thy mother and brethren seek *M'k 3:32*
for t.
how great things the Lord *M'k 5:19*
hath done *for t.*
I have prayed *for t.* that thy *Lu 22:32*
faith
the master is come, and *Joh 11:28*
calleth *for t.*
hard *for t.* to kick against *Ac 9:5;*
pricks *26:14*
to send *for t.* into his house *Ac 10:22*
and to hear
have a convenient season, I *Ac 24:25*
will call *for t.*
he said, My grace is sufficient *2Co 12:9*
for t.

FROM THEE

that be far *from t.* to slay *Ge 18:25*
righteous
until brother's anger turn *Ge 27:45*
away *from t.*
withheld *from t.* the fruit of *Ge 30:2*
the womb
Moses said, I go out *from t.* *Ex 8:29*
now put off thy ornaments *Ex 33:5*
from t.
if the place be too far *from* *De 12:21;*
t. *14:24*
let him go free *from t.* *De 15:12;*
5:13, 18
not go *from t.* *De 15:16*
cities far *from t.* *De 20:15*
not hidden *from t.* neither is *De 30:11*
it far off
the shekels that were taken *J'g 17:2*
from t.
Eli said, put away thy wine *f.* *1Sa 1:14*
t.
hath rent the kingdom *from* *1Sa 15:28;*
t. *1Ki 11:11*
I will take thine head *from* *1Sa 17:46*
t.
far be it *from t.* *1Sa 20:9; M't 16:22*
he will not withhold me *2Sa 13:13*
from t.
what I do, before I be taken *2Ki 2:9*
from t.
sons that shall issue *from t.* *2Ki 20:18;*
Isa 39:7
Jews which came up *from t.* *Ezr 4:12*
to us
no thought can be withholden *Job 42:2*
from t.
and my groaning is not hid *Ps 38:9*
from t.
O God, my sins are not hid *Ps 69:5*
from t.
they that are far *from t.* shall *Ps 73:27*
perish
so wilt not we go back *from* *Ps 80:18*
t.
yea, the darkness hideth not *Ps 139:12*
from t.
my substance was not hid *Ps 139:15*
from t.
in a little wrath I hid my face *Isa 54:8*
from t.
but my kindness shall not *Isa 54:10*
depart *from t.*
be instructed, lest my soul *Jer 6:8*
depart *from t.*
I will cut off *from t.* the *Eze 21:3;*
righteous *21:4*
those that be far *from t.* shall *Eze 22:5*
mock thee
take away *from t.* the desire *Eze 24:16*
of eyes
no secret they can hide *from* *Eze 28:3*
t.
they are gone into captivity *Mic 1:16*
from t.
I have caused thine iniquity to *Zec 3:4*
pass *from t.*
pluck out and cast *from t.* *M't 5:29;*
5:30; 18:8, 9
known that I came out *from* *Joh 17:8*
t.
looking for a promise *from t.* *Ac 23:21*

IN THEE

in t. all families be blessed *Ge 12:3;*
28:14
in t. shall Israel bless, saying *Ge 48:20*
raised thee up, to shew *in t.* *Ex 9:16*
power
that he see no unclean thing *De 23:14*
in t.
be sin *in t.* *De 23:21*
no sin *in t.* *De 23:22*
the king hath delight *in t.* *1Sa 18:22*
evil hath not been found *in* *1Sa 25:28*
t. *29:6*
if he say, I have no delight *2Sa 15:26*
in t.
there are good things found *2Ch 19:3*
in t.
be joyful *in t.* *Ps 5:11*
rejoice *in t.* *Ps 9:2;*
40:16; 70:4; 85:6; Ca 1:4
put their trust *in t.* *Ps 9:10*
16:1; 17:7; 25:2, 20; 55:23
our fathers trusted *in t.* they *Ps 22:4*
trusted
I trusted *in t.* *Ps 31:14*
hope *in t.* *Ps 33:22; 38:15; 39:7*
trust *in t.* *Ps 56:3;*
57:1; 84:12; 86:2; 141:8; 143:8
there shall no strange god be *Ps 81:9*
in t.
blessed is man whose *Ps 84:5*
strength is *in t.*
all my springs are *in t.* *Ps 87:7*
thou art all fair, there is no *Ca 4:7*
spot *in t.*
keep him because he trusteth *Isa 26:3*
in t.
surely God is *in t.* *Isa 45:14*
Hephzibah, for Lord *Isa 62:4*
delighteth *in t.*
that my fear is not *in t.* *Jer 2:19*
do *in t.* what I have not done *Eze 5:9*
I will execute judgments *in t.* *Eze 5:10;*
5:15
the contrary is *in t.* from *Eze 16:34*
other women
kindle a fire *in t.* it shall *Eze 20:47*
devour
were *in t.* to their power to *Eze 22:6*
shed blood
in t. they set light by father *Eze 22:7*
or mother
in t. are men that carry tales *Eze 22:9*
to shed
in t. have they taken gifts to *Eze 22:12*
shed blood
set their palaces *in t.,* *Eze 25:4*
dwellings *in t.*
thy wise men that were *in t.* *Eze 27:8;*
28:9
perfect, till iniquity was *Eze 28:15*
found *in t.*
when I shall be sanctified *in* *Eze 38:16*
t., O God
spirit of holy gods *in t.* *Da 4:9;*
4:18; 5:14
in t. the fatherless findeth *Ho 14:3*
mercy
transgressions of Israel *Mic 1:13*
found *in t.*
why dost thou cry? is there no *Mic 4:9*
king *in t.*
if the light that is *in t.* be *M't 6:23*
darkness
mighty works been done *in* *M't 11:23*
t.
my beloved Son, *in t.* I am *Lu 3:22*
pleased
light which is *in t.* be not *Lu 11:35*
darkness
not leave *in t.* one stone *Lu 19:44*
upon another
thou, Father, art in me, and *Joh 17:21*
I *in t.*
that I might shew my power *Ro 9:17*
in t.
in t. shall all nations be blessed *Ga 3:8*
neglect not the gift that is *in* *1Ti 4:14*
t.
unfeigned faith *in t.* first in *2Ti 1:5*
Lois and Eunice, and am
persuaded *in t.*
stir up the gift of God which *2Ti 1:6*
is *in t.*
brethren testified of truth that *3Jo 3*
is *in t.*
shall be heard no more at all *Re 18:22*
in t.

a candle shall shine no more *Re 18:23*
at all *in t.*

INTO THEE

no more come *into t.* *Isa 52:1*
uncircumcised

OF THEE

I will make *of t.* a great *Ge 12:2;*
nation *17:6; 35:11; 46:3; 48:4; Ex 32:10*
my soul shall live because of *Ge 12:13*
t.
I have heard say *of t.* that *Ge 41:15*
thou canst
which have heard the fame *Nu 14:15*
of t.
begin to put dread *of t.* and *De 2:25*
fear *of t.* and be in anguish
because *of t.*
what doth Lord require *De 10:12;*
of t. *Mic 6:8*
he that did take knowledge *of* *Ru 2:19*
t.
commune with my father *of t.* *1Sa 19:3*
the Lord avenge me *of t.* *1Sa 24:12*
but one thing I will require *2Sa 3:13*
of t.
I will surely buy it *of t.* at a *2Sa 24:24*
price
now I ask one petition *of t.* *1Ki 2:16;*
2:20
Lord said, Forasmuch as *1Ki 11:11*
this is done *of t.*
build the house as he said *1Ch 22:11*
of t.
both riches and honour *1Ch 29:12*
come *of t.*
all things come *of t.* of *1Ch 29:14*
thine have we
God exacteth *of t.* less than *Job 11:6*
thine
for I will demand *of t.* *Job 38:3;*
40:7; 42:4
heard *of t.* by the hearing of *Job 42:5*
the ear
my praise shall be *of t.* *Ps 22:25; 71:6*
glorious things are spoken *of t.* *Ps 87:3*
lest he be weary *of t.* and *Pr 25:17*
hate thee
two things have I required *of* *Pr 30:7*
t.
they that shall be *of t.* shall *Isa 58:12*
build
none stirreth up himself to *Isa 64:7*
take hold *of t.*
I will not make a full end *Jer 30:11;*
of t. *46:28*
thus saith Lord *of t.* Thou *Jer 34:4*
shalt not die
not take *of t.* a stone for a *Jer 51:26*
corner
cut off man and beast out *of* *Eze 29:8*
t.
the rivers shall be full *of t.* *Eze 32:6*
made known what we desired *Da 2:23*
of t.
ask a petition, save *of t.* O *Da 6:7;*
king *6:12*
I will surely assemble all *of* *Mic 2:12*
t.
yet out *of t.* shall come forth *Mic 5:2*
the ruler
and they shall fear because *Mic 7:17*
of t.
one come out *of t.* a wicked *Na 1:11*
counsellor
who are *of t.* to whom the *Zep 3:18*
reproach
for out *of t.* shall come a *M't 2:6*
governor
saying, I have need to be *M't 3:14*
baptized *of t.*
and from him that would *M't 5:42*
borrow *of t.*
no man eat fruit *of t.* *M'k 11:14*
hereafter
holy thing which shall be born *Lu 1:35*
of t.
give to every man that asketh *Lu 6:30*
of t.
this night thy soul shall be *Lu 12:20*
required *of t.*
he said, How is it that I hear *Lu 16:2*
this *of t.*
whatsoever thou hast given *Joh 17:7*
me are *of t.*
send for thee to hear words *Ac 10:22*
of t.

neither shewed nor spake   *Ac 28:21*
any harm *of t.*
we desire to hear *of t.* what   *Ac 28:22*
thou thinkest
say to hand, I have no need   *1Co 12:21*
of t.
let me have joy *of t.* in the   *Ph'm 20*
Lord

OFF THEE

Pharaoh lift up thy head   *Ge 40:19*
from *off t.* and birds eat flesh
from *off t.*
now will I break his yoke   *Na 1:13*
from *off t.*

ON, UPON THEE

my wrong be *upon t.*   *Ge 16:5*
this breach *upon t.*   *Ge 38:29*
put none of these diseases   *Ex 15:26*
upon t.
nor linen or woollen come   *Le 19:19*
upon t.
the Lord make his face shine   *Nu 6:25*
upon t.
the Lord lift up his   *Nu 6:26*
countenance *upon t.*
I will take of the spirit   *Nu 11:17*
which is *upon t.*
all these things are come   *De 4:30;*
upon t.   *30:1*
the Lord may have   *De 13:17;*
compassion *upon t.*   *30:3*
so blood be *upon t.*   *De 19:10*
blessings come *on t.*   *De 28:2*
all these curses shall come   *De 28:15;*
upon t.   *20:45*
the Philistines be *upon t.*   *J'g 16:9;*
                   16:14, 20
is it not *upon t.* and thy   *1Sa 9:20*
father's house
but mine hand shall not be   *1Sa 24:12;*
upon t.   *24:13*
the eyes of all Israel are   *1Ki 1:20*
upon t.
O altar, *upon t.* shall he offer   *1Ki 13:2*
priests, and men's bones
shall be burnt *upon t.*
I will bring evil *upon t.* and   *1Ki 21:21*
take
shut door *upon t.* and pour   *2Ki 4:4*
help us, O Lord, we rest   *2Ch 14:11*
upon t.
therefore is wrath *upon t.*   *2Ch 19:2*
from the Lord
know not what to do, but   *2Ch 20:12*
our eyes *upon t.*
now it is come *upon t.* and   *Job 4:5*
thou faintest
I have called *upon t.*   *Ps 17:6;*
    31:17; 86:5, 7; 88:9; La 3:57
I was cast *upon t.*   *Ps 22:10*
wait *upon t.*   *Ps 25:3; 5:21; 59:9*
meditate *on t.*   *Ps 63:6*
these wait *upon t.*   *Ps 104:27; 145:15*
return, that we may look *upon*   *Ca 6:13*
t.
I will turn my hand *upon t.*   *Isa 1:25*
and purge
fear, and pit, and snare are   *Isa 24:17*
upon t.
keep him, whose mind is   *Isa 26:3*
stayed *upon t.*
they shall come *upon t.* in   *Isa 47:9*
their perfection
evil and desolation come   *Isa 47:11;*
upon t.   *47:13*
bind them *on t.* as a bride   *Isa 49:18*
doth
with kindness have mercy *on*   *Isa 54:8;*
t.   *54:10*
my spirit *upon t.* shall not   *Isa 59:21*
depart
the glory of the Lord is risen   *Isa 60:1;*
upon t.   *60:2*
therefore we will wait *upon*   *Jer 14:22*
t.
who shall have pity *upon t.*   *Jer 15:5*
all that prey *upon t.* give   *Jer 30:16*
for a prey
they shall put bands *upon t.*   *Eze 3:25;*
                   4:8
I will bring the sword *upon*   *Eze 5:17;*
t.   *29:8*
when they leaned *upon t.*   *Eze 29:7*
thou brakest
had compassion, as I had   *M't 18:33*
pity *upon t.*

let no fruit grow *on t.*   *M't 21:19*
henceforward
the Holy Ghost shall come   *Lu 1:35*
upon t.
the days shall come *upon t.*   *Lu 19:43*
the hand of the Lord is *upon*   *Ac 13:11*
t.
no man shall set *on t.* to hurt   *Ac 18:10*
thee
I beat them that believe *on t.*   *Ac 22:19*
prophecies which went before   *1Ti 1:18*
on t.
I will come *on t.* as a thief, not   *Re 3:3*
know what hour I will come
upon t.

OVER THEE

husband, and he shall rule   *Ge 3:16*
over t.
but they shall not reign *over t.*   *De 15:6*
shalt in any wise set king   *De 17:15;*
over t.: thou mayest not set a   *28:36*
stranger *over t.*
Lord will again rejoice *over t.*   *De 30:9*
give angels charge *over t.*   *Ps 91:11;*
                   Lu 4:10
so shall thy God rejoice *over*   *Isa 62:5*
t.
hast taught them to be chief   *Jer 13:21*
over t.
caused enemy to rejoice *over*   *La 2:17*
t.
I spread my skirt *over t.*   *Eze 16:8*
I will spread out my net *over*   *Eze 32:3*
t.
seven times shall pass *over t.*   *Da 4:25;*
                   4:32
all that hear clap hands *over*   *Na 3:19*
t.
rejoice *over t.* he will joy   *Zep 3:17*
over t.

THROUGH THEE

through t. will we push down   *Ps 44:5*
enemies

TO, UNTO THEE

unto t. be his desire, thou shalt   *Ge 4:7*
rule
to t. will I give it   *Ge 13:15;*
   13:17; 17:8; 26:3; 28:4, 13; 35:12
I will certainly return *unto t.*   *Ge 18:10*
he is *to t.* a covering of the   *Ge 20:16*
eyes
let people and nations bow   *Ge 27:29*
down *to t.*
done that which I have   *Ge 28:15*
spoken *to t.* of
I will surely give the tenth of   *Ge 28:22*
all *unto t.*
better I give her *to t.* than to   *Ge 29:19*
another
I have seen all that Laban   *Ge 31:12*
doth *unto t.*
whatsoever God hath said   *Ge 31:16*
unto t. do
discern what is with me, and   *Ge 31:32*
take *to t.*
that which was torn I   *Ge 31:39*
brought not *unto t.*
that I will not pass over this   *Ge 31:52*
heap *to t.*
I pray thee, let me come in   *Ge 38:16*
unto t.
if I bring him not *to t.*   *Ge 42:37;*
             43:9; 44:32
money we brought again *unto*   *Ge 44:8*
t.
forgive, I pray, for they did   *Ge 50:17*
unto t. evil
and this shall be a token *unto*   *Ex 3:12*
t.
he shall be *to t.* instead of a   *Ex 4:16*
mouth
it shall be *unto t.* for a sign   *Ex 13:9;*
      2Ki 19:29; Isa 38:7
a great matter they shall   *Ex 18:22*
bring *unto t.*
take *unto t.* Aaron thy brother   *Ex 28:1*
take thou also *unto t.*   *Ex 30:23*
principal spices
that I may know what to do   *Ex 33:5*
unto t.
be holy *unto t.* for I am holy   *Le 21:8*
that they bring *unto t.* pure oil   *Le 24:2*
olive
the Lord be gracious *unto t.*   *Nu 6:25*
whether my word come to   *Nu 11:23*
pass *unto t.*

that tribe of Levi be joined   *Nu 18:2;*
unto t.   *18:4*
it is a covenant of salt *unto*   *Nu 18:19*
t.
Balaam, lo, I am come *unto*   *Nu 22:38*
t.
unto t. it was shewed that   *De 4:35*
thou
not take gold of their gods   *De 7:25*
cry to Lord and it be sin   *De 15:9;*
unto t.   *24:15*
Lord will raise up *unto t.* a   *De 18:15*
prophet
raise them up a prophet like   *De 18:18*
unto t.
let the dam go, and take   *De 22:7*
young *to t.*
servant escaped from his   *De 23:15*
master *unto t.*
who is like *unto t.*   *De 33:29;*
   1Sa 26:15; Ps 35:10; 71:19
as to Moses, so will we   *Jos 1:17*
hearken *unto t.*
bring father's household home   *Jos 2:18*
unto t.
I say *unto t.* this shall not go   *J'g 7:4*
now therefore I will restore it   *J'g 17:3*
unto t.
if he perform *unto t.* the part   *Ru 3:13*
be *unto t.* a restorer of life,   *Ru 4:15*
daughter in law better *to t.*
than seven sons
am not I better *to t.* than ten   *1Sa 1:8*
sons
in all that they say *unto t.*   *1Sa 8:7*
so do they *unto t.*   *1Sa 8:8*
the man I speak *to t.* of shall   *1Sa 9:17*
reign
and then we will come out *to*   *1Sa 11:3*
t.
anoint him whom I name   *1Sa 16:3*
unto t.
I come *to t.* in the name of   *1Sa 17:45*
the Lord
there is peace *to t.*   *1Sa 20:21*
peace be *to t.*   *1Sa 25:6*
bring him up whom I name   *1Sa 28:8*
unto t.
there shall no punishment   *1Sa 28:10*
happen *to t.*
to bring about all Israel *unto*   *2Sa 3:12*
t.
child that is born *unto t.*   *2Sa 12:14*
shall die
I will bring back all the   *2Sa 17:3*
people *unto t.*
that will be worse *unto t.*   *2Sa 19:7*
than all the evil
his head be thrown *to t.*   *2Sa 20:21*
over the wall
I will give thanks *unto t.*   *2Sa 22:50;*
   Ps 18:49; 30:12; 75:1; 119:62
choose one that I may do it   *2Sa 24:12*
unto t.
neither any arise like *unto t.*   *1Ki 3:12*
hearken in all that they call   *1Ki 8:52*
for *unto t.*
and I will give ten tribes   *1Ki 11:31*
unto t.
be with thee, and give Israel   *1Ki 11:38*
unto t.
I am sent *to t.* with heavy   *1Ki 14:6*
tidings
go back, what have I done   *1Ki 19:20*
to t.
send my servants *unto t.*   *1Ki 20:6*
tomorrow
give inheritance of my fathers   *1Ki 21:3*
unto t.
went the spirit from me to   *1Ki 22:24*
speak *unto t.*
if thou see me, it shall be so   *2Ki 2:10*
unto t.
when this letter is come   *2Ki 5:6*
unto t.
leprosy of Naaman cleave   *2Ki 5:27*
unto t.
take it up *to t.*   *2Ki 6:7*
what said Elisha *to t.*   *2Ki 8:14*
he said, I have an errand *to t.*   *2Ki 9:5*
O captain
wherefore came this mad   *2Ki 9:11*
fellow *to t.*
whence came they *unto t.*   *2Ki 20:14;*
               Isa 39:3
peace be *unto t.* and thine   *1Ch 12:18*
helpers
unto t. will I give land   *1Ch 16:18;*
               Ps 105:11

it appertaineth not *unto t.*   2Ch 26:18
Uzziah
arise, for this matter   Ezr 10:4
belongeth *unto t.*
testified against them to turn   Ne 9:26
them *to t.*
silver is given *to t.* the people   Es 3:11
also
sinned, what shall I do *unto*   Job 7:20
t.
unto me, for *unto t.* will I pray   Ps 5:2;
5:3
the poor committeth himself   Ps 10:14
unto t.
my goodness extendeth not *to*   Ps 16:2
t.
they cried *unto t.* and were   Ps 22:5
delivered
unto t. do I lift up my soul   Ps 25:1;
86:4; 143:8
my heart said *unto t.,* Thy face   Ps 27:8
will I seek
unto t. will I cry   Ps 28:1;
28:2; 30:8; 31:22; 56:9; 61:2; 86:3;
88:13; 130:1; 141:1
may sing praise *to t.*   Ps 30:12;
56:12; 59:17; 66:4; 71:22, 23
I acknowledged my sin *unto*   Ps 32:5
t.
also *unto t.* O Lord,   Ps 62:12
belongeth mercy
and *unto t.* shall be the vow be   Ps 65:1
performed
hearest prayer, *unto t.* shall all   Ps 65:2
flesh come
prayer *unto t.* in an   Ps 69:13
acceptable time
among the gods there is none   Ps 86:8
like *unto t.*
Lord who is a strong Lord   Ps 89:8
like *unto t.*
unto t. O Lord, will I sing   Ps 101:1;
108:3; 138:1; 144:9; Heb 2:12
hear my prayer, let my cry   Ps 102:1
come *unto t.*
what shall be given *unto t.*   Ps 120:3
false tongue
unto t. will I lift up eyes   Ps 123:1;
141:8
darkness and light are alike   Ps 139:12
to t.
made known *to t.,* even *to t.*   Pr 22:19
eat and drink, saith he *to t.*   Pr 23:7
but his heart
better it be said *unto t.,* Come   Pr 25:7
up hither
all they shall speak and say   Isa 14:10
unto t.
will be gracious *unto t.* at   Isa 30:19
thy cry
hath my master sent me *to t.*   Isa 36:12
to speak
but these two things shall   Isa 47:9
come *to t.*
thus shall they be *unto t.*   Isa 47:15
with whom
these gather together and   Isa 49:18
come *unto t.*
these two things are come   Isa 51:19
unto t.
nations that knew not thee   Isa 55:5
run *unto t.*
neither moon give light *unto*   Isa 60:19
t. the Lord shall be
unto t. an everlasting light
we will come no more *unto*   Jer 2:31
we come *unto t.* for thou art   Jer 3:22
our God
forasmuch as there is none   Jer 10:6
like *unto t.*
not fear, for *to t.* doth it   Jer 10:7
appertain
for *unto t.* have I revealed   Jer 11:20;
my cause   20:12
let them return *unto t.* but   Jer 15:19
return not
man-child born *unto t.*   Jer 20:15
making glad
I spake *unto t.* in thy   Jer 22:21
prosperity
I have done these things   Jer 30:15
unto t.
I speak *unto t.* so it shall be   Jer 38:20
well *unto t.*
if thou come; I will look well   Jer 40:4
unto t.
as for the word, we will not   Jer 44:16
hearken *unto t.*
but thy life will I give *unto t.*   Jer 45:5
for a prey

for was not Israel a derision   Jer 48:27
unto t.
what thing shall I liken *to t.,*   La 2:13
what shall I equal *to t.*
the cup also shall pass through   La 4:21
unto t.
turn us *unto t.* we shall be   La 5:21
turned
they would have hearkened   Eze 3:6
unto t.
house of Israel would not   Eze 3:7
hearken *unto t.*
pitied thee, to do any of   Eze 16:5
these *unto t.*
I said *unto t.* when thou wast   Eze 16:6
in blood
reward, and no reward is   Eze 16:34
given *unto t.*
establish *unto t.* an   Eze 16:60
everlasting covenant
I will give them *unto t.* for   Eze 16:61
daughters
thy kingdom shall be sure   Da 4:26
unto t.
to t. it is spoken, the kingdom   Da 4:31
is departed
Lord, righteousness belongeth   Da 9:7
unto t.
Ephraim, what shall I do *unto*   Ho 6:4
t.
to t. will I cry   Joe 1:19
beasts cry *unto t.*   Joe 1:20
will I do *unto t.* I will do   Am 4:12
unto t.
they said, What shall we do   Jon 1:11
unto t.
prayer came in *unto t.* into   Jon 2:7
temple
I will prophesy *unto t.* of   Mic 2:11
wine
unto t. shall it come   Mic 4:8
what have I done *unto t.*   Mic 6:3
he shall come *to t.* even from   Mic 7:12
Assyria
I even cry out *unto t.* of   Hab 1:2
violence
cup of Lord's hand be   Hab 2:16
turned *unto t.*
Lord of hosts hath sent me   Zec 2:11
unto t.
thy king cometh *unto t.*   Zec 9:9;
M't 21:5
hast believed, so be it done   M't 8:13
unto t.
flesh and blood not revealed   M't 16:17
it *unto t.*
I say also *unto t.* that thou   M't 16:18
art Peter
give *unto t.* the keys of the   M't 16:19
kingdom
this shall not be *unto t.*   M't 16:22
let him be *unto t.* as an   M't 18:17
heathen
I say not *unto t.* till seven   M't 18:22
times
I will give this last even as   M't 20:14
unto t.
stonest them sent *unto t.*   M't 23:37;
Lu 13:34
in prison, and did not   M't 25:44
minister *unto t.*
I say *unto t.* arise   M'k 5:41;
Lu 5:24; 7:14
what wilt thou do *unto t.*   M'k 10:51;
Lu 18:41
I am sent to speak *unto t.*   Lu 1:19
not myself worthy to come   Lu 7:7
unto t.
I have some what to say   Lu 7:40
unto t.
how great things God hath   Lu 8:39
done *unto t.*
I that speak *unto t.* am he   Joh 4:26
sin no more, lest worse thing   Joh 5:14
come *unto t.*
what did he *to t.*   Joh 9:26
said I not *unto t.*   Joh 11:40
these are in world, and I   Joh 17:11
am come *to t.*
we would not have delivered   Joh 18:30
him *unto t.*
he that delivered me *unto t.*   Joh 19:11
hath greater sin
what is that *to t.?* follow   Joh 21:22;
me   21:23
Jesus that appeared *unto t.*   Ac 9:17
sent me
when he cometh, shall speak   Ac 10:32
unto t.

immediately therefore I sent   Ac 10:33
to t.
said to captain, May I speak   Ac 21:37
unto t.
have appeared *unto t.* for   Ac 26:16
this purpose
for this cause will I confess *to*   Ro 15:9
t.
that good thing committed   2Ti 1:14
unto t.
but now profitable *to t.* and   Ph'm 11
me
brother to me, but how much   Ph'm 16
more *to t.*
hast taken *to t.* thy great   Re 11:17
power

TOWARDS THEE

works have been good   1Sa 19:4
towards t.
I would not look *towards t.*   2Ki 3:14
thou hast tried mine heart   Jer 12:3
towards t.
so will I make my fury   Eze 16:42
towards t.
when I am pacified *towards*   Eze 16:63
t.
towards t. goodness, if thou   Ro 11:22
continue

UNDER THEE

earth that is *under t.* shall be   De 28:23
iron
arrows whereby people fall   Ps 45:5
under t.
why take thy bed from *under t.*   Pr 22:27
worm is spread *under t.* cover   Isa 14:11
thee
that eat thy bread laid a wound   Ob 7
under t.

WITH THEE

with *t.* will I establish my   Ge 6:18
covenant
my covenant *with t.*   Ge 17:4;
Ex 34:27; De 29:12
now shall we deal worse *with t.*   Ge 19:9
God is *with t.* in all thou   Ge 21:22
doest
the Lord will send his angel   Ge 24:40
with t.
I will be *with t.*   Ge 26:3
I am *with t.*   Ge 26:24;
28:15; 31:3; 46:4; Ex 3:12; 31:23
Jos 1:5; 3:7; 1Ki 11:38; Isa 43:2
saw that the Lord was *with t.*   Ge 26:28
hearken, and God shall be   Ex 18:19
with t.
there I will meet *with t.*   Ex 25:22;
30:6, 36
my presence shall go *with t.*   Ex 33:14;
De 31:6, 8; J'g 6:16
wages not abide *with t.* all   Le 19:13
night
if no man hath lien *with t.*   Nu 5:19
man hath lien *with t.* beside   Nu 5:20
husband
what men are these *with t.*   Nu 22:9
Lord thy God hath been *with t.*   De 2:7
that it may go well *with t.*   De 4:40;
5:16; 6:3, 18; 12:25, 28; 19:13; 22:7
not go because he is well   De 15:16
with t.
Lord thy God is *with t.*   De 20:1;
Jos 1:9; J'g 6:12; 2Sa 7:3
against the city that maketh   De 20:20
war *with t.*
he shall dwell *with t.* even   De 23:16
among you
and she said, I will surely go   J'g 4:9
with t.
the people that are *with t.* are   J'g 7:2
too many
go *with t.*   J'g 7:4
peace be *with t.*   J'g 19:20
that it may be well *with t.*   Ru 3:1
for God is *with t.*   1Sa 10:7; Lu 1:28
I am *with t.* according to   1Sa 14:7
thine heart
Lord be *with t.*   1Sa 17:37;
20:13; 1Ch 22:11, 16
why art thou alone, and no   1Sa 21:1
man *with t.*
I will deliver Israel *with t.*   1Sa 28:19
to Philistines
found, so long as I have been   1Sa 29:8
with t.

behold my hand shall be *with*	2Sa 3:12
t.	
I was *with t.*	2Sa 7:9; 1Ch 17:8
Amnon *with t.*	2Sa 13:20
king said, Why should he go	2Sa 13:26
with t.	
Lord thy God be *with t.*	2Sa 14:17;
	1Ch 28:20
return thou, mercy and truth	2Sa 15:20
be *with t.*	
said Joab, I may not tarry	2Sa 18:14
there will not tarry one *with*	2Sa 19:7
t.	
hast *with t.* Shimei who cursed	1Ki 2:8
me	
walked in uprightness of heart	1Ki 3:6
with t.	
then will I perform my word	1Ki 6:12
with t.	
I will not go in *with t.*	1Ki 13:8; 13:16
what have I to do *with t.*	1Ki 17:18;
2Ki 3:13; 2Ch 35:21; *M'k* 5:7; *Lu* 8:28;	
	Joh 2:4
it is well *with t.*	2Ki 4:26
went heart *with t.*	2Ki 5:26
thou and Judah *with t.*	2Ki 14:10;
	2Ch 25:19
Lord, it is nothing *with t.*	2Ch 14:11
to help	
we will be *with t.*	2Ch 18:3; Ezr 10:4
let not the army of Israel go	2Ch 25:7
with t.	
the beasts shall be at peace	Job 5:23
with t.	
I know that this is *with t.*	Job 10:13
bringest me into judgment	Job 14:3
with t.	
number of his months are	Job 14:5
with t.	
are consolations of God	Job 15:11
small *with t.*	
is there any secret thing	Job 15:11
with t.	
he that is perfect in	Job 36:4
knowledge *with t.*	
behemoth, which I made	Job 40:15
with t.	
neither shall evil dwell *with t.*	Ps 5:4
for *with t.* is the fountain of	Ps 36:9
life	
I am a stranger *with t.*	Ps 39:12
I am continually *with t.*	Ps 73:23
iniquity have fellowship *with*	Ps 94:20
t.	
Lord hath dealt bountifully	Ps 116:7
with t.	
it shall be well *with t.*	Ps 128:2
but there is forgiveness *with*	Ps 130:4
t.	
when I awake, I am still	Ps 139:18
with t.	
hide my commandments	Pr 2:1
with t.	
be thine own, not strangers	Pr 5:17
with t.	
talk *with t.*	Pr 6:22
heart is not *with t.*	Pr 23:7
that we may seek him *with t.*	Ca 6:1
let mine outcasts dwell *with t.*	Isa 16:4
Moab	
I am *with t.*	Isa 41:10;
43:5; Jer 1:8, 19; 15:20; 30:11; 46:28;	
	Ac 18:10
they that strive *with t.*	Isa 41:11;
perish	41:12
contend with him that	Isa 49:25
contendeth *with t.*	
sworn that I would not be	Isa 54:9
wroth *with t.*	
plead *with t.*	Jer 2:35
when I plead *with t.*	Jer 12:1
speak *with t.* mouth to	Jer 34:3
mouth	
with t. will I break in pieces	Jer 51:20
nations	
with t. will I break in pieces	Jer 51:21
horse and rider	
with t. will I break in pieces	Jer 51:22
old and young	
with t. will I break shepherd	Jer 51:23
and husbandman	
though briars and thorns be	Eze 2:6
with t.	
go into plain, I will talk *with*	Eze 3:22
t.	
I entered into a covenant	Eze 16:8
with t.	
I will even deal *with t.*	Eze 16:59

I will establish my covenant	Eze 16:62
with t.	
in the days that I shall deal	Eze 22:14
with t.	
they occupied *with t.* in	Eze 27:21
lambs	
I will fill the beasts of earth	Eze 32:4
with t.	
bands and many people	Eze 38:6;
with t.	9:15; 39:4
the prophet shall fall *with t.*	Ho 4:5
shall say, Is there yet any	Am 6:10
with t.	
the men that were at peace *with*	Ob 7
t.	
come, and all the saints *with*	Zec 14:5
t.	
will he be pleased *with t.*	Mal 1:8
they cried out, What have we	M't 8:29;
to do with *t.*	M'k 1:24; Lu 4:34
stand without, desiring to	M't 12:47
speak *with t.*	
then take *with t.* one or two	M't 18:16
more	
Peter said, Tho' I should	M't 26:35;
die *with t.*	M'k 14:31
I am ready to go *with t.* into	Lu 22:33
prison	
he that was *with t.* beyond	Joh 3:26
Jordan	
seen him, and he talketh *with*	Joh 9:37
t.	
with the glory which I had	Joh 17:5
with t.	
They say unto him, We also	Joh 21:3
go *with t.*	
Peter said, Thy money perish	Ac 8:20
with t.	
honour father that it may be	Eph 6:3
well *with t.*	
grace be *with t.*	1Ti 6:21
bring *with t.*	2Ti 4:11; 4:13

WITHIN THEE

stranger *within t.* shall get	De 28:43
above	
I will now say, peace be	Ps 122:8
within t.	
he hath blessed thy children	Ps 147:13
within t.	
pleasant, if keep them *within*	Pr 22:18
t.	
thy vain thoughts lodge *within*	Jer 4:14
t.	
they shall lay thy children	Lu 19:44
within t.	

WITHOUT THEE

without t. shall no man lift	Ge 41:44
up hand	

THEE-WARD

his works have been to *t.*	1Sa 19:4
very good	

THEFT

then he shall be sold for his *t.*	Ex 22:3
If the *t.* be certainly found in	Ex 22:4
his	

THEFTS

fornications, *t.*, false witness	M't 15:19
T., covetousness, wickedness	M'k 7:22
of their fornication, nor of	Re 9:21
their *t.*	

THEIRS

a stranger in a land that is	Ge 15:13
not *t.*	
and every beast of *t.* be	Ge 34:23
ours	
was five times so much as	Ge 43:34
any of *t.*	
the priest's office shall be *t.*	Ex 29:9
for a	
for *t.* is thine own nakedness	Le 18:10
and touch nothing of *t.* lest	Nu 16:26
ye be	
from the fire: every oblation	Nu 18:9
of *t.*	
every meat offering of *t.* and	Nu 18:9
every	
and every sin offering of *t.*	Nu 18:9
every trespass offering of *t.*	Nu 18:9
which	
Levi, had: for *t.* was the	Jos 21:10
first lot	

the Kohathites: for *t.* was	1Ch 6:54
the lot	
I pray thee, be like one of *t.*	2Ch 18:12
whose words shall stand,	Jer 44:28
mine, or *t.*	
of their multitude, nor of any	Eze 7:11
of *t.*	
dedicated thing in Israel	Eze 44:29
shall be *t.*	
the dwelling places that are	Hab 1:6
not *t.*	
for *t.* is the kingdom of	M't 5:3;
heaven	5:10
Christ our Lord, both *t.* and	1Co 1:2
ours	
manifest unto men, as *t.* also	2Ti 3:9

THELASAR

of Eden which were in T.	2Ki 19:12

THEM

male and female created he *t.*	Ge 1:27
your little ones, *t.* will I	Nu 14:31
bring	
t. will the Lord bring upon	De 28:61
thee	
t. that honour me, I will	1Sa 2:30
honour	
t. shall he sling out, as out	1Sa 25:29
of a sling	
t. they told also to their	1Ki 13:11
father	
t. that burned incense unto	2Ki 23:5
Baal	
t. hath the Lord chosen to	1Ch 15:2
carry	
t. did Solomon make to pay	2Ch 8:8
tribute	
to terrify *t.* (A)(R)	2Ch 32:18
to demoralize *t.* (B)	2Ch 32:18
let *t.* shout for joy, let *t.* that	Ps 5:11
love	
nor let *t.* wink with eye that	Ps 35:19
hate me	
let *t.* also that hate him flee	Ps 68:1
before him	
even *t.* that contended with	Isa 41:12
thee	
t. will I bring to my holy	Isa 56:7
mountain	
Thou shalt also take of *t.* (S)	Eze 5:3
from *t.* shall a fire come forth	Eze 5:4
(S)	
they cast *t.* into the den of	Da 6:24
lions	
t. that worship the host of	Zep 1:5
heaven	
take away *t.* that rejoice in	Zep 3:11
thy pride	
gather out *t.* which do	M't 13:41
iniquity	
let *t.* which be in Judæa	M't 24:16;
flee into mountains	M'k 13:14; Lu 21:21
they told it, neither believed	M'k 16:13
they *t.*	
to set at liberty *t.* that are	Lu 4:18
bruised	
t. that were entering in ye	Lu 11:52
hindered	
cast out *t.* that sold and *t.*	Lu 19:45
that bought	
found eleven, and *t.* that	Lu 24:33
were with *t.*	
other sheep I have, *t.* also	Joh 10:16
must bring	
my sentence is, we trouble	Ac 15:19
not *t.*	
t. take and purify thyself	Ac 21:24
with *t.*	
that I beat *t.* that believed on	Ac 22:19
thee	
moreover, *t.* he also called, *t.*	Ro 8:30
he also justified, and *t.* he	
also glorified	
provoke to emulation *t.*	Ro 11:14
which are my flesh	
to judge *t.* also that are	1Co 5:12
without	
but *t.* that are without God	1Co 5:13
judgeth	
acknowledge ye *t.* that are	1Co 16:18
such	
even so *t.* also that sleep in	1Th 4:14
Jesus	
now *t.* that are such, we	2Th 3:12
command	
save thyself and *t.* that hear	1Ti 4:16
thee	

t. that sin rebuke before all,   *1Ti 5:20*
that
instructing those that oppose   *2Ti 2:25*
t. (S)
perfected *t.* that are   *Heb 10:14*
sanctified
remember *t.* that are in   *Heb 13:3*
bonds
let *t.* that suffer according to   *1Pe 4:19*
will
to torture *t.* (B)(P)(R)   *Re 9:5*
thus I saw horses and *t.* that   *Re 9:17*
sat on *t.*
and measure *t.* that worship   *Re 11:1*
therein
to blaspheme *t.* that dwell in   *Re 13:6*
heaven
beast was taken, *t.* that   *Re 19:20*
worshipped

ABOVE THEM

they dealt proudly, he was   *Ex 18:11*
above t.
of them that were over and   *Nu 3:49*
above t.
lifted *above t.* that rose   *2Sa 22:49*
against me
images *above t.* he cut down   *2Ch 34:4*

ABOUT THEM

terror was on cities round   *Ge 35:5*
about t.
that all the city was moved   *Ru 1:19*
about t.
after heathen that were   *2Ki 17:15*
about t.
make *about t.* walls and   *2Ch 14:7*
towers
all *about t.* strengthened their   *Ezr 1:6*
hands
were full of eyes round *about*   *Eze 1:18*
t.
all that despise round   *Eze 28:26*
about t.
he saw a great multitude   *M'k 9:14*
about t.
fear came on all that dwelt   *Lu 1:65*
about t.
the glory of the Lord shone   *Lu 2:9*
round *about t.*
and the cities *about t.* in like   *Jude 7*
manner

AFTER THEM

seven other kine *after t.*   *Ge 41:3; 19:27*
seven ears withered sprung   *Ge 41:23*
up *after t.*
arise *after t.* seven years of   *Ge 41:30*
famine
issue which thou begettest   *Ge 48:6*
after t.
neither *after t.* shall be such   *Ex 10:14*
locusts
follow *after t.* and I will be   *Ex 14:4*
honoured
that turneth to go a whoring   *Le 20:6*
after t.
give to them and their seed   *De 1:8*
after t.
he chose their seed *after t.*   *De 4:37;*
       10:15
pursue *after t.* quickly   *Jos 2:5*
men pursued *after t.*   *Jos 2:7;*
    8:16; J'g 8:12; 20:45
arose another generation *after*   *J'g 2:10*
t.
field that they reap, go *after t.*   *Ru 2:9*
lords of the Philistines went   *1Sa 6:12*
after t.
followed hard *after t.* in   *1Sa 14:22*
battle
upon children left *after t.*   *1Ki 9:21;*
did Solomon levy tribute   *2Ch 8:8*
they went *after t.* to Jordan   *2Ki 7:15*
Jehu departed not from   *2Ki 10:29*
after t.
go not *after t.*   *1Ch 14:14*
I *after t.*   *Ne 12:38*
they cried *after t.* as after a   *Job 30:5*
thief
I loved strangers, and *after t.*   *Jer 2:25*
will I
I will send a sword *after t.*   *Jer 9:16;*
    49:37; Eze 5:2, 12; 12:14
king of Sheshach drink *after*   *Jer 25:26*
t.
recompensest iniquity of   *Jer 32:18*
fathers into bosom of their

children *after t.*
for the good of their children   *Jer 32:39*
after t.
the Chaldeans' army pursued   *Jer 39:5*
after t.
waste and utterly destroy   *Jer 50:21*
after t.
when they shall look *after t.*   *Eze 29:16*
scattered, none did seek *after*   *Eze 34:6*
t.
another king shall rise *after t.*   *Da 7:24*
the white horses go forth *after*   *Zec 6:6*
t.
thus the land was desolate   *Zec 7:14*
after t.
see here, see there, go not   *Lu 17:23;*
after t.   *21:8*
to draw away disciples *after*   *Ac 20:30*
t.

AGAINST THEM

he divided himself *against t.*   *Ge 14:15*
wrath wax hot *against t.*   *Ex 32:10;*
   Nu 12:9; De 2:15; 31:17; J'g 2:15
Korah gathered congregation   *Nu 16:19*
against t.
Og king of Bashan went out   *Nu 21:33*
against t.
destroy trees by an axe   *De 20:19*
against t.
thou shalt go out one way   *De 28:25*
against t.
this song shall testify   *De 31:21*
against t.
call heaven and earth to   *De 31:28*
record *against t.*
other issued out of city   *Jos 8:22*
against t.
did not intend to go *against*   *Jos 22:33*
t. in battle
did he ever strive or fight   *J'g 11:25*
against t.
he moved David *against t.* to   *2Sa 24:1*
number
testimonies he testified   *2Ki 17:15*
against t.
children of Gad dwelt over   *1Ch 5:11*
against t.
helped *against t.* for they   *1Ch 5:20*
cried to God
to-morrow go down *against*   *2Ch 20:16;*
t.   *20:17*
prophets testified *against t.*   *2Ch 24:19;*
     Ne 9:26, 29, 30, 34
stood up *against t.* that came   *2Ch 28:12*
from war
hired counsellors *against t.*   *Ezr 4:5*
his wrath is *against t.* that   *Ezr 8:22*
forsake him
set a watch *against t.* day and   *Ne 4:9*
night
I set a great assembly *against t.*   *Ne 5:7*
kneweth they dealt proudly   *Ne 9:10*
against t.
brethren were over *against t.*   *Ne 12:9*
in watches
hired Balaam *against t.*   *Ne 13:2*
testified *against t.*   *Ne 13:15; 13:21*
savest from those that rise up   *Ps 17:7*
against t.
the face of the Lord is   *Ps 34:16;*
against t. that do evil   *1Pe 3:12*
countenance doth witness   *Isa 3:9*
against t.
stretched forth his hand   *Isa 5:25*
against t.
I will stir up the Medes   *Isa 13:17*
against t.
rise up *against t.*   *Isa 14:22*
fought *against t.*   *Isa 63:10*
I will utter my judgments   *Jer 1:16*
against t.
given sentence *against t.*   *Jer 4:12*
I am *against t.*   *Jer 23:32*
prophesy *against t.*   *Jer 25:30;*
   Eze 6:2; 13:17; 25:2
evil he pronounced *against t.*   *Jer 26:19;*
     35:17; 36:31
he sent fire, and it prevaileth   *La 1:13*
against t.
I will set my face *against t.*   *Eze 15:7*
to accomplish my anger   *Eze 20:8*
against t.
used out of thy hatred   *Eze 35:11*
against t.
that I would bring thee   *Eze 38:17*
against t.
the same horn prevailed   *Da 7:21*
against t.

mine anger is kindled *against t.*   *Ho 8:5*
the people shall be gathered   *Ho 10:10*
against t.
for a testimony *against t.*   *M't 10:18;*
   M'k 6:11; 13:9; Lu 9:5
spoken parable *against t.*   *M'k 12:12;*
       Lu 20:19
shook off the dust of their   *Ac 13:51*
feet *against t.*
the multitude rose up   *Ac 16:22*
together *against t.*
in whom evil spirit was,   *Ac 19:16*
prevailed *against t.*
gave voice *against t.*   *Ac 26:10*
being mad *against t.*   *Ac 26:11*
judgment of God is *against t.*   *Ro 2:2*
that commit
love your wives, be not bitter   *Col 3:19*
against t.
bring not railing accusation   *2Pe 2:11*
against t.
the beast shall make war   *Re 11:7*
against t.

AMONG, AMONGST THEM

knowest any man of activity   *Ge 47:6*
among t.
bring children of Israel from   *Ex 7:5*
among t.
tell my signs which I have   *Ex 10:2*
done *amongst t.*
that I may dwell *among t.*   *Ex 25:8;*
    29:46; Ps 68:18
that there be no plague   *Ex 30:12*
among t.
defile my tabernacle that is   *Le 15:31*
among t.
Levites not numbered *among t.*   *Nu 1:47*
fire of the Lord burnt *among*   *Nu 11:1;*
t.   *11:3*
mixt multitude *among t.* fell a   *Nu 11:4*
lusting
the Lord is *among t.*   *Nu 16:3; Ps 68:17*
Aaron have no part *among t.*   *Nu 18:20;*
       Jos 14:3
the shout of a king is *among*   *Nu 23:21*
t.
Lord will send the hornet   *De 7:20*
among t.
stranger, as he that was born   *Jos 8:33*
among t.
strangers that were conversant   *Jos 8:35*
among t.
understood that they dwelt   *Jos 9:16*
among t.
give him place that he may   *Jos 20:4*
dwell *among t.*
according to that which I did   *Jos 24:5*
amongst t.
the Canaanites dwelt *among t.*   *J'g 1:30*
put away strange gods from   *J'g 10:16*
among t.
when he wrought *among t.*   *1Sa 6:6;*
       Ne 9:17
made them sit in chiefest   *1Sa 9:22*
place *among t.*
prophets met him, and he   *1Sa 10:10*
prophesied *among t.*
set thy servant *among t.* that   *2Sa 19:28*
did eat
the Lord sent lions *among t.*   *2Ki 17:25*
Levi and Benjamin not   *1Ch 21:6*
counted *among t.*
found mighty men *among t.*   *1Ch 26:31*
found *among t.* abundance   *2Ch 20:25*
of spoil
clothed all that were naked   *2Ch 28:15*
among t.
were *among t.* 200 singing   *Ezr 2:65*
men
come in the midst *among*   *Ne 4:11*
t. and slay
wrote to establish the Purim   *Es 9:21*
among t.
and Satan came also *among t.*   *Job 1:6;*
       2:1
and no stranger passed   *Job 15:19*
among t.
part garments *among t.* cast   *Ps 22:18;*
lots on my vesture *M't 27:35; Joh 19:24*
let death seize them,   *Ps 55:15*
wickedness is *among t.*
I lie *among t.* that are set on   *Ps 57:4*
fire
among t. were damsels playing   *Ps 68:25*
timbrels
he sent divers sorts of flies   *Ps 78:45*
among t.

sending evil angels *among t.*   Ps 78:49
Samuel *among t.* that call upon   Ps 99:6
his name
they shewed his signs *among*   Ps 105:27
t.
brought out Israel from   Ps 136:11
among t.
none is barren *among t.*   Ca 4:2; 6:6
none be weary or stumble   Isa 5:27
among t.
many *among t.* stumble and   Isa 8:15
fall
I beheld, there was no man   Isa 41:28
among t.
who *among t.* can declared this,   Isa 43:9
shew things
which *among t.* declared   Isa 48:14
these things
I will set a sign *among t.*   Isa 66:19
shall fall *among t.* that fall   Jer 6:15;
  8:12
know, O congregation, what is   Jer 6:18
among t.
pluck out house of Judah   Jer 12:14
from *among t.*
send famine and pestilence   Jer 24:10
among t.
because of sword I will send   Jer 25:16
among t.
remained but wounded men   Jer 37:10
among t.
ten men found *among t.* said,   Jer 41:8
Slay us not
Jerusalem as menstruous   La 1:17
woman *among t.*
hath been a prophet *among t.*   Eze 2:5;
  33:33
remained there *among t.*   Eze 3:15
seven days
thou shalt not go out *among t.*   Eze 3:25
one man *among t.* had writer's   Eze 9:2
inkhorn
concerneth all Israel that   Eze 12:10
are *among t.*
the prince that is *among t.*   Eze 12:12
shall bear
am profaned *among t.*   Eze 22:26
I sought a man *among t.*   Eze 22:30
they know that a prophet   Eze 33:33
been *among t.*
my servant David a prince   Eze 34:24
among t.
I will make myself known   Eze 35:11
among t.
among t. none like Daniel   Da 1:19
came up *among t.* another little   Da 7:8
horn
scatter *among t.* the prey and   Da 11:24
spoil
none *among t.* that calleth to   Ho 7:7
me
that is feeble *among t.* be as   Zec 12:8
David
tumult from the Lord be   Zec 14:13
among t.
among t. that are born of   M't 11:11
women
the two fishes divided he   M'k 6:41
among t.
there arose a reasoning *among*   Lu 9:46
t.
there was also a strife *among*   Lu 22:24
t.
Peter sat down *among t.* in   Lu 22:55
the hall
there was a division *among t.*   Joh 9:16
if I had not done *among t.*   Joh 15:24
works
nor any *among t.* that lacked   Ac 4:34
so Paul departed from   Ac 17:33
among t.
continued, teaching word of   Ac 18:11
God *among t.*
inheritance *among t.* that are   Ac 20:32;
sanctified   26:18
wild olive tree grafted in   Ro 11:17
among t.
speak wisdom *among t.* that   1Co 2:6
are perfect
come out from *among t.*   2Co 6:17
and be separate
that righteous man dwelling   2Pe 2:8
among t.
who loveth pre-eminence *among*   3Jo 9
t.
to convince all ungodly *among*   Jude 15
t.
sitteth on throne shall dwell   Re 7:15
among t.

AT THEM

we have shot *at t.*   Nu 21:30
thou shalt not be affrighted *at*   De 7:21
t.
all his enemies, he puffeth *at t.*   Ps 10:5
thou, O Lord, shalt laugh *at t.*   Ps 59:8
God shall shoot *at t.* with an   Ps 64:7
arrow
for the heathen are dismayed   Jer 10:2
at t.

BEFORE THEM

set it *before t.*   Ge 18:8
passed over *before t.*   Ge 33:3
before t. there were no such   Ex 10:14
locusts
Lord went *before t.* by day   Ex 13:21;
  Nu 14:14
judgments which thou shalt set   Ex 21:1
before t.
the ark of the Lord went   Nu 10:33
before t.
to go out and in *before t.*   Nu 27:17;
  1Sa 18:16
destroyed them from *before t.*   De 2:12;
  2:21, 22; 1Ch 5:25; Ne 9:24
thou shalt flee seven ways   De 28:25
before t.
armed men went *before t.*   Jos 6:1
and the land was subdued   Jos 18:1
before t.
stood not a man of enemies   Jos 21:44
before t.
Ehud *before t.*   J'g 3:27
take *before t.* waters   J'g 7:24
with tabret, pipe and harp,   1Sa 10:5
before t.
and Shobach went *before t.*   2Sa 10:16;
  1Ch 19:16
when in Gibeon, Amasa went   2Sa 20:8
before t.
give compassion *before t.*   1Ki 8:50;
  2Ch 30:9
prophets prophesied *before t.*   1Ki 22:10;
  2Ch 18:9
so that the Moabites fled   2Ki 3:24
before t.
Gehazi passed on *before t.*   2Ki 4:31
set it *before t.*   2Ki 4:44
set bread and water *before t.*   2Ki 6:22
whom the Lord carried   2Ki 17:11
away *before t.*
priest sounded trumpets   2Ch 7:6
before t.
and Ezra the scribe *before t.*   Ne 12:36
I'll pay my vows *before t.*   Ps 22:25
they have not set God *before t.*   Ps 54:3;
  86:14
he cast out the heathen   Ps 78:55
before t.
sent a man *before t.* even   Ps 105:17
Joseph
no end of all that have been   Ec 4:16
before t.
love or hatred by all that is   Ec 9:1
before t.
now go write it *before t.* in a   Isa 30:8
table
I will make darkness light   Isa 42:16
before t.
led them, dividing water   Isa 63:12
before t.
not dismayed, lest I confound   Jer 1:17
thee *before t.*
forsaken my law which I set   Jer 9:13
before t.
I charged Baruch *before t.*   Jer 32:13
saying
no more be a nation *before t.*   Jer 33:24
dismayed *before t.* that seek   Jer 49:37
their life
there stood *before t.* seventy   Eze 8:11
men
set mine oil and incense   Eze 16:18;
before t.   16:19
I will set judgment *before t.*   Eze 23:24
they shall judge
when I brandish my sword   Eze 32:10
before t.
stand *before t.* to minister to   Eze 44:11
them
fire devoureth *before t.* and the   Joe 2:3
land is as the garden *before t.*
earth squake *before t.* the sun   Joe 2:10
be dark
I destroyed the Amorite   Am 2:9
before t.

the breaker is come up   Mic 2:13
before t. king pass *before t.*
David as angel of the Lord   Zec 12:8
before t.
star which they saw went   M't 2:9
before t.
she danced *before t.*   M't 14:6
was transfigured *before t.*   M't 17:2;
  M'k 9:2
he denied *before t.*   M't 26:70
gave disciples to set *before t.*   M'k 6:41;
  8:6-7
Jesus went *before t.* they   M'k 10:32
were amazed
Judas went *before t.*   Lu 22:47
he did eat *before t.*   Lu 24:43
Shepherd goeth *before t.* sheep   Joh 10:4
follow
he had done many miracles   Joh 12:37
before t.
set meat *before t.*   Ac 16:34
set Paul *before t.*   Ac 22:30
said to Peter *before t.* all, If   Ga 2:14
thou being

BEHIND THEM

pillar removed and stood   Ex 14:19
behind t.
when men of Ai looked   Jos 8:20
behind t.
the Benjamites looked *behind*   J'g 20:40
t.
but fetch a compass *behind t.*   2Sa 5:23
an ambushment to come   2Ch 13:13
about *behind t.*
behind t. a flame, *behind t.* a   Joe 2:3
wilderness

BESIDE THEM

and the asses were feeding   Job 1:14
beside t.
wheels turned not from   Eze 10:16;
beside t.   10:19; 11:22
gained *beside t.* five talents   M't 25:20;
  25:22

BETWEEN THEM

an oath of Lord *between t.*   Ex 22:11
and bells of gold *between t.*   Ex 28:33
round about
now there was a valley   Jos 8:11
between t. and Ai
a valley *between t.* and the   1Sa 17:3
Philistines
David stood, a great space   1Sa 26:13
being *between t.*
because of the Lord's oath   2Sa 21:7
between t.
they divided the land *between*   1Ki 18:6
t.
that no air can come   Job 41:16
between t.
counsel of peace *between t.*   Zec 6:13
contention was so sharp   Ac 15:39
between t.

BY THEM

after wizards to be defiled *by*   Le 19:31
t.
cause to swear *by t.* nor serve   Jos 23:7
Lord left, to prove Israel *by t.*   J'g 3:1;
  3:4
by t. ye shall send to me   2Sa 15:36
the work was perfected *by t.*   2Ch 24:13
for *by t.* judgeth he the   Job 36:31
people
by t. is thy servant warned   Ps 19:11
namely *by t.* beyond the river   Isa 7:20
have sworn *by t.* that are no   Jer 5:7
gods
creatures went, wheels went   Eze 1:19
by t.
should I be enquired at of all   Eze 14:3
by t.
because *by t.* their portion is   Hab 1:16
fat
it was said *by t.* of old   M't 5:21;
  27:33
cometh, and would have   M'k 6:48
passed *by t.*
two men stood *by t.* in white   Lu 24:4;
  Ac 1:10
a notable miracle has been   Ac 4:16
done *by t.*

what wonders God had wrought *by t.* — *Ac 15:12*

who doeth those things live *by* *Ro 10:5* *t.*

I will provoke you to jealousy *by t.* — *Ro 10:19*

by t. of the house of Chloe — *1Co 1:11*

by t. mightest war a good warfare — *1Ti 1:18*

confirmed to us *by t.* which heard him — *Heb 2:3*

which are now reported to you *by t.* — *1Pe 1:12*

CONCERNING THEM

concerning t. Moses commanded Eleazar — *Nu 32:28*

Samson said *concerning t.,* I shall be blameless — *J'g 15:3*

the king's commandment *concerning t.* — *Ne 11:23*

to be ignorant *concerning t.* which sleep — *1Th 4:13*

have written *concerning t.* that seduce you — *1Jo 2:26*

FOR THEM

it shall be for food for thee and *for t.* — *Ge 6:21*

land, behold, it is large enough *for t.* — *Ge 34:21*

they set on bread *for t.* by themselves — *Ge 43:32*

let us flee, the Lord fighteth *for t.* — *Ex 14:25*

priest make an atonement *for t.* — *Le 4:20; 9:7; 10:17; Nu 8:21; 16:46*

one law *for t.* the priest shall have — *Le 7:7*

to search out a resting place *for t.* — *Nu 10:33*

herds be slain *for t.,* fishes gathered *for t.* — *Nu 11:22*

fail with longing *for t.* all day — *De 28:32*

from right hand went fiery law *for t.* — *De 33:2*

Joshua cast lots *for t.* in Shiloh — *Jos 18:10*

part of Judah was too much *for t.* — *Jos 19:9*

coast of Dan went out too little *for t.* — *Jos 19:47*

how shall we do for wives *for t.* — *J'g 21:16*

there must be an inheritance *for t.* — *J'g 21:17*

would ye tarry *for t.* till they — *Ru 1:13*

but Hezekiah prayed *for t.* — *2Ch 30:18*

go enquire of the Lord *for t.* — *2Ch 34:21*

God keepeth mercy *for t.* that love — *Ne 1:5*

we take up corn *for t.* that we may eat — *Ne 5:2*

brought water *for t.* out of the rock — *Ne 9:15*

come to the banquet I prepare *for t.* — *Es 5:8*

the companies of Sheba waited *for t.* — *Job 6:19*

what can the Almighty do *for t.* — *Job 22:17*

wilderness yieldeth food *for t.* — *Job 24:5*

thou hast laid up *for t.* that fear thee, *for t.* that trust in thee — *Ps 31:19*

to the place that hast founded *for t.* — *Ps 104:8*

he remembered *for t.* his covenant — *Ps 106:45*

Lord hath done great things *for t.* — *Ps 126:2*

till the Assyrian founded it *for t.* — *Isa 23:13*

her merchandise be *for t.* that dwell — *Isa 23:18*

he hath cast the lot *for t.* — *Isa 34:17*

solitary places shall be glad *for t.* — *Isa 35:1*

in the ways hast thou sat *for t.* — *Jer 3:2*

neither lift up cry nor prayer *for t.* — *Jer 7:16*

nor shall men lament *for t.* — *Jer 16:6*

neither shall men tear themselves *for t.* — *Jer 16:7*

stood before thee to speak good *for t.* — *Jer 18:20*

thou shalt make *for t.* yokes of iron — *Jer 28:13*

neither shall be wailing *for t.* — *Eze 7:11*

as *for t.* whose heart walketh after — *Eze 11:21*

cause them to pass thro' fire *for t.* — *Eze 16:21*

to bring into a land I had espied *for t.* — *Eze 20:6*

that my flock may not be meat *for t.* — *Eze 34:10*

I will raise up *for t.* a plant of renown — *Eze 34:29*

I will yet be enquired of to do it *for t.* — *Eze 36:37*

one lamb to make reconciliation *for t.* — *Eze 45:15*

his inheritance shall be his son's *for t.* — *Eze 46:17*

for t. even for the priests shall be — *Eze 48:10*

no place was found *for t.* — *Da 2:35; Re 20:11*

make a covenant *for t.* with beasts — *Ho 2:18*

I will hiss *for t.* and gather them — *Zec 10:8*

Lebanon place shall not be found *for t.* — *Zec 10:10*

pray *for t.* which despitefully use you, and persecute you — *M't 5:44; Lu 6:28*

not lawful *for t.* that were with him — *M't 12:4*

it shall be done *for t.* of my Father — *M't 18:19*

how hard *for t.* that trust in riches — *M'k 10:24*

there was no room *for t.* in the inn — *Lu 2:7*

is not sufficient *for t.* that every one — *Joh 6:7*

I pray *for t.* not for the world — *Joh 17:9; 17:20*

Peter and John prayed *for t.* — *Ac 8:15*

Cornelius waited *for t.* and called friends — *Ac 10:24*

while Paul waited *for t.* at Athens — *Joh 17:16*

things God hath prepared *for t.* — *1Co 2:9*

it is good *for t.* if they abide even as I — *1Co 7:8*

prophesying serveth *for t.* that believe — *1Co 14:21*

live unto him which died *for t.* — *2Co 5:15*

what great conflict I have *for t.* — *Col 2:1*

hath a great zeal *for t.* in Laodicea — *Col 4:13*

spirits sent forth to minister *for t.* — *Heb 1:14*

ever liveth to make intercession *for t.* — *Heb 7:25*

for he hath prepared *for t.* a city — *Heb 11:16*

been better *for t.* not to known — *2Pe 2:21*

give life *for t.* that sin not to death — *1Jo 5:16*

FROM THEM

nothing will be restrained *from t.* — *Ge 11:6*

took *from t.* Simeon and bound him — *Ge 42:24*

I have not taken one ass *from t.* — *Nu 16:15*

tithes which I have given you *from t.* — *Nu 18:26*

from t. that have many give many; but *from t.* that have few give few — *Nu 35:8*

sheep astray, hide thyself *from t.* — *De 22:1; 22:4*

hide my face *from t.* — *De 31:17; 32:20; Eze 7:22; Mic 3:4*

bring their calves home *from t.* — *1Sa 6:7*

go not after them, turn away *from t.* — *1Ch 14:14*

they turned *from t.* and destroyed — *2Ch 20:10*

deliver me *from t.* that persecute me — *Ps 31:15*

defend me *from t.* that rise up against me — *Ps 59:1*

no good thing will he withhold *from t.* — *Ps 84:11*

withhold not good *from t.* to whom — *Pr 3:27*

that keep his soul shall be far *from t.* — *Pr 22:5*

what eyes desired I kept not *from t.* — *Ec 2:10*

was but a little that I passed *from t.* — *Ca 3:4*

things I have given shall pass *from t.* — *Jer 8:13*

leave my people and go *from t.* — *Jer 9:2*

I stood to turn away wrath *from t.* — *Jer 18:20*

I will take *from t.* the voice of mirth — *Jer 25:10*

not turn away *from t.* to do them good — *Jer 32:40*

therefore I have set it far *from t.* — *Eze 7:20*

and her mind was alienated *from t.* — *Eze 23:17*

day when I take *from t.* strength — *Eze 24:25*

therefore hid I my face *from t.* — *Eze 39:23; 39:24*

neither hide my face *from t.* — *Eze 39:29*

he hath withdrawn himself *from t.* — *Ho 5:6*

as they called, so they went *from t.* — *Ho 11:2*

pull off robe with garment *from t.* — *Mic 2:8*

the bridegroom shall be taken *from t.* — *M't 9:15; M'k 2:20; Lu 5:35*

left the cloth, and fled *from t.* naked — *M'k 14:52*

understood not, it was hid *from t.* — *Lu 9:45; 18:34*

parted *from t.* and carried to heaven — *Lu 24:51*

departed, and did hide himself *from t.* — *Joh 12:36*

not obey, but thrust him *from t.* — *Ac 7:39*

that I may be delivered *from* — *Ro 15:31* *t.*

I should have sorrow *from t.* — *2Co 2:3*

I may cut off occasion *from t.* — *2Co 11:12*

whose descent is not counted *from t.* — *Heb 7:6*

clean escaped *from t.* in error — *2Pe 2:18*

desire to die, and death flee *from t.* — *Re 9:6*

IN THEM

Lord made heaven and earth the sea, and all that in *t.* is — *Ex 20:11; Ac 4:24*

to be anointed and be consecrated in *t.* — *Ex 29:29*

I will be sanctified in *t.* that come — *Le 10:3*

he shall live in *t.* — *Le 18:5; Ne 9:29; Eze 20:11, 13, 21; Ga 3:12*

strove, and he was sanctified in *t.* — *Nu 20:13*

that there were such heart in *t.* — *De 5:29*

nor is there any understanding in *t.* — *De 32:28*

nor was there spirit in *t.* any more — *Jos 5:1*

cities ye built not, and ye dwell in *t.* — *Jos 24:13*

may I not wash in *t.* and be clean — *2Ki 5:12*

doth not excellency in *t.* go away — *Job 4:21*

in *t.* he set a tabernacle for the sun — *Ps 19:4*

hungry, thirsty, their soul fainted in *t.* — *Ps 107:5*

so is every one that trusts in *t.* — *Ps 115:8; 135:18*

Lord taketh pleasure in *t.* that fear — *Ps 147:11*

nothing froward or perverse in *t.* — *Pr 8:8*

I know there is no good in *t.* — *Ec 3:12*

their heart is fully set in *t.* to do evil — *Ec 8:11*

thou shalt say I have no pleasure in *t.* — *Ec 12:1*

teil and oak, whose substance is in *t.* — *Isa 6:13*

it is because there is no light in *t.* — *Isa 8:20*

and thou shalt not prosper *in*   Jer 2:37
t.
word not *in t.*   Jer 5:13
wisdom is *in t.*   Jer 8:9
cannot do evil, nor is it *in t.*   Jer 10:5
to do good
and there is no breath *in t.*   Jer 10:14;
  51:17
build houses, and dwell *in t.*   Jer 29:5;
  29:28
statutes they have not walked   Eze 5:6
in t.
when I have accomplished my   Eze 5:13
fury *in t.*
spirit of the living creature   Eze 10:17
was *in t.*
trespass and sin, *in t.* shall   Eze 18:24;
he die   18:26
when I shall be sanctified   Eze 28:25
in t.
pine away *in t.*   Eze 33:10
no breath *in t.*   Eze 37:8
his wives and concubines   Da 5:3;
drank *in t.*   5:23
right and the just shall walk   Ho 14:9
in t.
built houses, but shall not   Am 5:11
dwell *in t.*
they shall kindle *in t.* and   Ob 18
devour them
that doeth evil, he delighteth   Mal 2:17
in t.
in t. is fulfilled prophecy of   M't 13:14
Esaias
in t. therefore come and be   Lu 13:14
healed
in t. ye think ye have eternal   Joh 5:39
life
thine are mine, and I am   Joh 17:10
glorified *in t.*
I *in t.,* thou in me   Joh 17:23
be *in t.,* I *in t.*   Joh 17:26
may be known of God, is   Ro 1:19
manifest *in t.*
but have pleasure *in t.* that do   Ro 1:32
them
in t. that are saved, *in t.* that   2Co 2:15
perish
I will dwell *in t.* and walk *in*   2Co 6:16
t.
God ordained we should   Eph 2:10
walk *in t.*
alienated through ignorance   Eph 4:18
that is *in t.*
ye walked, when ye lived   Col 3:7
in t.
all deceivableness *in t.* that   2Th 2:10
perish
continue *in t.* for in doing   1Ti 4:16
this
not being mixed with faith *in*   Heb 4:2
t.
spirit of Christ which was *in*   1Pe 1:11
t.
speaking *in t.* of these things   2Pe 3:16
all that are *in t.* heard I   Re 5:13
rejoice, ye heavens, ye that   Re 12:12
dwell *in t.*
for *in t.* is filled up the wrath   Re 15:1
of God
delivered up the dead *in t.*   Re 20:13
in t. names of twelve apostles   Re 21:14

INTO THEM

breath came *into t.* and they   Eze 37:10
lived
that we may enter *into t.*   M'k 5:12;
  Lu 8:32
spirit of life from God   Re 11:11
entered *into t.*

OF THEM

eyes *of t.* both were opened   Ge 3:7
cry *of t.* is waxen great   Ge 9:13
before God
generation *of t.* that hate me   Ex 20:5;
  De 5:9
thousands *of t.* that love me   Ex 20:6;
  De 5:10
of t. that do any work and   Ex 35:35
devise
if a soul shall do against any *of*   Le 4:2
t.
not eat *of t.*   Le 11:4
mayest eat *of t.*   Le 11:22; De 20:19
nor make an offering by fire   Le 22:22
of t.

of t. buy bondmen and   Le 25:44;
bondmaids   25:45
land also shall be left *of t.*   Le 26:43
those that were numbered   Nu 1:21;
of t.   1:23, 25; 2:4, 13; 3:22, 34
took money *of t.* that were   Nu 3:49
over
take it *of t.*   Nu 7:5
were *of t.* written   Nu 11:26
nor any *of t.* that provoked   Nu 14:23
me see
fled at cry *of t.*   Nu 16:34
not a man *of t.*   Nu 26:64
that those which ye let   Nu 33:55
remain *of t.*
neither be afraid *of t.*   De 1:29;
  7:18; 20:1, 3; Jos 11:6; Ne 4:14
ye shall buy meat *of t.* buy   De 2:6
water *of t.*
loins *of t.* that rise, and *of*   De 33:11
t. that hate
not a man *of t.* stand before   Jos 10:8
of t. shall I be had in honour   2Sa 6:22
slew them, nor left he any   2Ki 10:14
of t.
they cried, he was entreated   1Ch 5:20
of t.
all *of t.* were expressed by   Ezr 8:20
name
would not buy it *of t.* on   Ne 10:31
sabbath
are low, he perceiveth it not   Job 14:21
of t.
in keeping *of t.* is great   Ps 19:11
reward
make ready arrows against   Ps 21:12
face *of t.*
this is generation *of t.* that   Ps 24:6
seek him
the Lord delivered him out *of*   Ps 34:19
t. all
none *of t.* that trust in him   Ps 34:22
be desolate
if I would speak *of t.* they are   Ps 40:5
more
of t. that art afar off upon the   Ps 65:5
sea
in whose heart are the ways *of*   Ps 84:5
t.
all *of t.* wax old like a   Ps 102:26
garment
tossed to and fro *of t.* that   Pr 21:6
seek death
that feareth God shall come   Ec 7:18
forth *of t.*
they that are led *of t.* are   Isa 9:16
destroyed
this is the portion *of t.* that   Isa 17:14
spoil us
he shall be intreated *of t.*   Isa 19:22
and heal
Hezekiah was glad *of t.* and   Isa 39:2
shewed
that when I asked *of t.* could   Isa 41:28
answer
before they spring forth I tell   Isa 42:9
of t.
they are all *of t.* snared in   Isa 42:22
holes
that make an image, are *of t.*   Isa 44:9
vanity
sought *of t.* that asked not   Isa 65:1;
for me, found *of t.* that   Ro 10:20
sought me not
I will send those that escape   Isa 66:19
of t.
I will take *of t.* for priests   Isa 66:21
and Levites
because *of t.* that dwell in far   Jer 8:19
country
be not afraid *of t.*   Jer 10:5;
  Eze 2:6; Lu 12:4
they are all *of t.* unto me as   Jer 23:14
Sodom
great kings shall serve   Jer 25:14
themselves *of t.*
of t. shall be taken up a   Jer 29:22
curse
out *of t.* shall proceed   Jer 30:19
thanksgiving
none should serve himself *of*   Jer 34:9;
t.   34:10
none *of t.* shall remain   Jer 42:17;
  Eze 7:11
all *of t.* mourning for iniquity   Eze 7:16
all *of t.* in the land shall   Eze 20:40
serve me
all *of t.* desirable young men   Eze 23:6;
  12:23

in dyed attire, all *of t.*   Eze 23:15
princes to look
all *of t.* clothed with all sorts   Eze 38:4
of armour
gates all *of t.* dwelling   Eze 38:11
without walls
say *of t.,* Let men kiss the   Ho 13:2
calves
cut in head *of t.* he that fleeth   Am 9:1
of t.
pluck off their skin from *off*   Mic 3:2;
t.   3:3
land desolate because *of t.*   Mic 7:13
goodly price I was prized at   Zec 11:13
of t.
whether *of t.* twain did   M't 21:31
the will
they perceived that he spake   M't 21:45
of t.
whose wife shall she be *of*   M'k 12:23;
t.   Lu 20:33
of t. he chose twelve named   Lu 6:13
apostles
which *of t.* will love him most   Lu 7:42
which *of t.* should be greatest   Lu 9:46;
  22:24
which *of t.* that should do   Lu 22:23
this thing
another said, Thou art also   Lu 22:58
of t.
then inquired he *of t.* the   Joh 4:52
hour when
may remember that I told   Joh 16:4
you *of t.*
of t. thou gavest me, have I   Joh 18:9
lost none
take out *of t.* a people for   Ac 15:14
his name
there lie in wait *of t.* forty   Ac 23:21
men
fall *of t.* be riches of world,   Ro 11:12
diminishing *of t.* riches of
Gentiles
if the casting away *of t.* be   Ro 11:15
the reconciling
out *of t.* all Lord delivered   2Ti 3:11
me
not *of t.* who draw back,   Heb 10:39
but *of t.*
is sown in peace *of t.* that   Jas 3:18
make peace
of t. which keep the sayings of   Re 22:9
this

ON, UPON THEM

Rachel had taken images and   Ge 31:34
sat *upon t.*
Jacob said, let my name be   Ge 48:16
named *on t.*
my lust shall be satisfied *upon*   Ex 15:9
t.
lest the Lord break forth   Ex 19:22;
upon t.   19:24
hast brought so great a sin   Ex 32:21
upon t.
I will visit their sin *upon t.*   Ex 32:34
their blood shall be *upon t.*   Le 20:11;
  20:12-13, 16, 27
upon t. left will I send   Le 26:36
faintness
I will put of the spirit *upon*   Nu 11:17;
t.   11:29
earth closed *upon t.* and they   Nu 16:33
perished
eye shall have no pity *upon t.*   De 7:16
not desire silver or gold that   De 7:25
is *on t.*
on t. was written all Lord   De 9:10
spake
not lift up any iron tool *upon*   De 27:5
t.
I will heap mischiefs *upon t.*   De 32:23
things that come *upon t.*   De 32:35
make haste
Lord cast down great stones   Jos 10:11
upon t.
upon t. came the curse of   J'g 9:57
Jotham
till the blood gushed out   1Ki 18:28
upon t.
if able to set riders *upon t.*   2Ki 18:23;
  Isa 36:8
he burnt men's bones *upon*   2Ki 23:20
t.
because the charge was   1Ch 9:27
upon t.
they laid their hands *on t.*   2Ch 29:23;
  Ac 6:6; 8:17; 13:3
that wrath of Lord came   2Ch 32:26
not *upon t.*

Lord brought *upon* t. king | 2Ch 33:11
of Assyria
brought *upon* t. king of the | 2Ch 36:17
Chaldees
fear was *upon* t. because of the | Ezr 3:3
people
for the fear of the Jews fell | Es 8:17
upon t.
the fear of Mordecai fell *upon* | Es 9:3
t.
Jews took *upon* t. to keep days | Es 9:27
of Purim
much less *on* t. that dwell in | Job 4:19
houses
neither is the rod of God | Job 21:9
upon t.
eye of Lord *upon* t. that fear | Ps 33:18
him
fear took hold *upon* t. and | Ps 48:6
pain as of
if riches increase, set not | Ps 62:10
heart *upon* t.
pour out thine indignation | Ps 69:24
upon t.
rained down manna *upon* t. | Ps 78:24
to eat
he rained flesh also *upon* t. as | Ps 78:27
dust
he cast *upon* t. the fierceness | Ps 78:49
of his anger
bring *upon* t. their own | Ps 94:23
iniquity
mercy everlasting *upon* t. | Ps 103:17
that fear
the plague brake in *upon* t. | Ps 106:29
shall I see my desire *upon* t. | Ps 118:7
that
upon t. hath the light shined | Isa 9:2
when thy chastening was | Isa 26:16
upon t.
them will not have mercy *on* | Isa 27:11
t.
he that hath mercy *on* t. | Isa 49:10
shall lead
evil shall come *upon* t. saith | Jer 2:3
the Lord
I will bring *upon* t. | Jer 11:8;
     11:11; 23:12; 36:31; 49:37
return, and have compassion | Jer 12:15
on t.
set mine eyes *upon* t. for good | Jer 24:6;
     32:42
return, for I will have mercy | Jer 33:26
upon t.
day of their calamity was | Jer 46:21
come *upon* t.
doted *upon* t. | Eze 23:16
flesh came *upon* t. | Eze 37:8
no wool come *upon* t. while | Eze 44:17
they minister
nor the smell of fire passed | Da 3:27
on t.
pour out my wrath *upon* t. like | Ho 5:10
water
I will spread my net *upon* t. | Ho 7:12
I will set my eyes *upon* t. for | Am 9:4
evil
wherefore lookest thou *upon* t. | Hab 1:13
that deal
bring again, for I have mercy | Zec 10:6
upon t.
who will not come up *upon* | Zec 14:17
t.
should put hands *upon* t. | M't 19:13;
     M'k 10:10
his mercy is *on* t. that | Lu 1:50
fear him
the angel of the Lord came | Lu 2:9
upon t.
when he said this, he | Joh 20:22
breathed *on* t.
as they spake, Sadducees came | Ac 4:1
upon t.
laid hands *on* t. | Ac 4:3
grace was *upon* t. | Ac 4:33
great fear came *on* all t. that | Ac 5:5
heard
Holy Ghost fell *on* t. as on | Ac 11:15;
us | 19:6
took *upon* t. to call over | Ac 19:13
them which
man leaped *on* **t.** and | Ac 19:16
overcame them
four men which have a vow | Ac 21:23
on t.
on t. which fell, severity; but | Ro 11:22
to thee
peace *on* t. and mercy, on | Ga 6:16
Israel

wrath is come *upon* t. to the | 1Th 2:16
uttermost
sudden destruction cometh | 1Th 5:3
upon t.
taking vengeance *on* t. that | 2Th 1:8
know not
and *on* t. that are out of the | Heb 5:2
way
avenge our blood *on* t. that | Re 6:10
dwell
nor sun light *on* t. nor any | Re 7:16
heat
great fear fell *upon* t. which | Re 11:11
saw
and *upon* t. which worshipped | Re 16:2
his image

OVER THEM

they did set *over* t. | Ex 1:11
taskmasters
Pharaoh's taskmasters set | Ex 5:14
over t.
place such *over* t. to be | Ex 18:21
rulers
were *over* t. that were | Nu 7:2
numbered
heard that thy cloud standeth | Nu 14:14
over t.
trees went to anoint a king | J'g 9:8
over t.
people made Jephthah | J'g 11:11
captain *over* t.
rejected me that I should not | 1Sa 8:7
reign *over* t.
manner of king that shall reign | 1Sa 8:9
over t.
Samuel standing as | 1Sa 19:20
appointed *over* t.
David became a captain *over* | 1Sa 22:2
t.
Judah have anointed me king | 2Sa 2:7
over t.
Phinehas was the ruler *over* | 1Ch 9:20
t.
over t. that did the work | 1Ch 27:26
was Ezri
he hath made thee king *over* | 2Ch 2:11;
t. | 9:8
so that they had dominion | Ne 9:28
over t.
enemies hoped to have power | Es 9:1
over t.
upright shall have dominion | Ps 49:14
over t.
they that hated them ruled | Ps 106:41
over t.
a wise king bringeth wheel | Pr 20:26
over t.
babes rule *over* t. | Isa 3:4
women rule *over* t. | Isa 3:12
a fierce king rule *over* t. | Isa 19:4
they that rule *over* t. make | Isa 52:5
them howl
I will appoint *over* t. four | Jer 15:3
kinds
set shepherds *over* t. which | Jer 23:4
shall feed
as I have watched *over* t. to | Jer 31:28
pluck up, so will I watch
over t. to build
I will rejoice *over* t. to do | Jer 32:41
them good
watch *over* t. for evil, not for | Jer 44:27
good
appeared *over* t. as a | Eze 10:1
sapphire stone
glory of God of Israel *over* | Eze 10:19;
     11:22
I will set up one shepherd | Eze 34:23
over t.
David my servant shall be | Eze 37:24
king *over* t.
hath made thee ruler *over* t. | Da 2:38
all
the heathen should rule *over* | Joe 2:17
t.
the day shall be dark *over* t. | Mic 3:6
Lord shall reign *over* t. in | Mic 4:7
mount Zion
creeping things no ruler *over* | Hab 1:14
t.
the Lord shall be seen *over* t. | Zec 9:14
princes of Gentiles exercise | M't 20:25;
dominion *over* t. | M'k 10:42; Lu 22:25
the men that walk *over* t. are | Lu 11:44
not aware
who would, not that I should | Lu 19:27
reign *over* t.

to call *over* t. that had evil | Ac 19:13
spirits
even *over* t. that had not | Ro 5:14
sinned after
a shew of them, triumphing | Col 2:15
over t. in it
they had a king *over* t. whose | Re 9:11
name is
earth shall rejoice *over* t. and | Re 11:10
make merry

THROUGH THEM

that *thro'* t. I may prove | J'g 2:22
Israel
burned up, so none can pass | Jer 9:10
thro' t.

TO, UNTO THEM

come, and I will send thee | Ge 37:13
unto t.
strange *unto* t. spake roughly | Ge 42:7
unto t.
give provision, thus did | Ge 42:25
Joseph *unto* t.
Joseph spoke kindly *unto* t. | Ge 50:21
God had respect *unto* t. | Ex 2:25;
     2Ki 13:23
say *unto* t. | Ex 3:13
darkness *to* t. | Ex 14:20
waters were a wall *to* t. on | Ex 14:22
the right
not bow down thyself *to* t. | Ex 20:5;
nor serve them | Jos 23:7; 2Ki 17:35
be a statute for ever *to* t. | Ex 30:21;
     Le 17:7
I have given it *unto* t. for | Le 6:17
portion
thus do *unto* t. | Nu 4:19
did they *unto* t. | Nu 8:22
swallow up all that appertain | Nu 16:30
unto t.
do to you, as I thought to do | Nu 33:56
unto t.
to t. ye shall add forty two | Nu 35:6
cities
Lord sware to give *unto* t. | De 1:8; 31:23
what nation hath God so nigh | De 4:7
unto t.
do *unto* t. | Jos 9:20
did he *unto* t. | Jos 9:26
they bowed themselves *unto* t. | J'g 2:17
do *to* t. as thou shalt find | J'g 9:33
occasion
as they did, so have I done | J'g 15:11
unto t.
there was nothing lacking *to* | 1Sa 30:19
t.
sent spoil *to* t. | 1Sa 30:27;
     30:28-31
fed them, but went not in | 2Sa 20:3
unto t.
if thou wilt speak good | 1Ki 12:7
word *to* t.
the messenger came *to* t. | 2Ki 9:18;
     9:20
let the priests take it *to* t. | 2Ki 12:5
every man
opening thereof pertained *to* | 1Ch 9:27
t.
and spake comfortably *to* t. | 2Ch 32:6
tribute and custom paid *unto* | Ezr 4:20
t.
such as separated themselves | Ezr 6:21
unto t.
restore *to* t. their lands, | Ne 5:11
houses
month turned *unto* t. from | Es 9:22
sorrow
yet God layeth not folly *to* t. | Job 24:12
morning is *to* t. as shadow | Job 24:17
of death
render *to* t. their desert | Ps 28:4
there is no want *to* t. that | Ps 34:9
fear him
because thou hadst a favour | Ps 44:3
unto t.
do *unto* t. as to the Midianites | Ps 83:9
they that make them are like | Ps 115:8;
unto t. | 135:18
do good *to* t. that are upright | Ps 125:4
in heart
a buckler *to* t. that walk | Pr 2:7
uprightly
a tree of life *to* t. that lay | Pr 3:18
hold on her
they are right *to* t. that find | Pr 8:9
knowledge

so is the sluggard *to t.* that send him   Pr 10:26

mercy and truth be *to t.* that devise   Pr 14:22

so is faithful messenger *to t.* that send   Pr 25:13

shield *unto t.* that put their trust in him   Pr 30:5

wisdom gives life *to t.* that have it   Ec 7:12

seek *to t.* that have familiar spirits   Isa 19:3

word was *unto t.* precept upon precept   Isa 28:13

to t. that have no might he increaseth   Isa 40:29

hath given spirit *to t.* that walk therein   Isa 42:5

things will I do *unto t.* and not forsake   Isa 42:16

to t. that are in darkness   Isa 49:9; M't 4:16; Lu 1:79

to t. will I give in my house a place   Isa 56:5

to t. hast thou poured a drink offering   Isa 57:6

to t. that turn from transgression   Isa 59:20

everlasting joy shall be *unto t.*   Isa 61:7

thus shall it be done *unto t.*   Jer 5:13

word of the Lord is *unto t.* a reproach   Jer 6:10

let them return, but return not *unto t.*   Jer 15:19

repent of the evil I thought to do *unto t.*   Jer 18:8

brake covenant, tho' I was husband *unto t.*   Jer 31:32

do *unto t.* as thou hast done to me   La 1:22

the Lord is good *unto t.* that wait for him   La 3:25

give them sorrow of heart, thy curse *unto t.*   La 3:65

I do send thee *unto t.*   Eze 2:4

had I sent thee *unto t.* they had   Eze 3:6

thou shalt not be *to t.* a reprover   Eze 3:26

yet will I be *to t.* as a little sanctuary   Eze 11:16

as I have done, so shall it be done *unto t.*   Eze 12:11

I made myself known *unto t.*   Eze 20:9

thou art *unto t.* as a lovely song   Eze 33:32

it shall be *to t.* a renown   Eze 39:13

they ministered *unto t.* before idols   Eze 44:12

oblation be *unto t.* a thing most holy   Eze 48:12

be for food *unto t.* that serve the city   Eze 48:18

the dream be *to t.* that hate thee   Da 4:19

that the princes might give account *unto t.*   Da 6:2

and keeping mercy *to t.* that love him   Da 9:4

many shall cleave *to t.* with flatteries   Da 11:34

and their staff declareth *unto t.*   Ho 4:12

destruction *unto t.* because they   Ho 7:13

I was *to t.* as they that take off the yoke   Ho 11:4

say they *to t.* that prophesy, they shall not prophesy *to t.*   Mic 2:6

be not like *unto t.*   M't 6:8

do ye even so *to t.*   M't 7:12

he spake *unto t.* of John the Baptist   M't 17:13

other servants did *unto t.* likewise   M't 21:36

go ye rather *to t.* that sell, and buy   M't 25:9

to t. that are without in parables   M'k 4:11

be given *to t.* for whom it is prepared   M'k 10:40

he went down, and was subject *unto t.*   Lu 2:51

men do to you, do ye also *to t.*   Lu 6:31

if ye do good *to t.* that do good to you   Lu 6:33

---

if lend *to t.* of whom hope to receive   Lu 6:34

give the Holy Spirit *to t.* that ask him   Lu 11:13

he may testify *unto t.* lest they come   Lu 16:28

what shall Lord of vineyard do *unto t.*   Lu 20:15

Jesus turning *unto t.* said, weep not for me   Lu 23:28

their words seemed *unto t.* as idle tales   Lu 24:11

expounded *unto t.* in all scripture   Lu 24:27

to t. gave he power to become sons of God, even *to t.* that believe   Joh 1:12

give an answer *to t.* that sent us   Joh 1:22

Jesus did not commit himself *unto t.*   Joh 2:24

that he spake *to t.* of the Father   Joh 8:27

sins ye remit, they are remitted *unto t.*   Joh 20:23

who was guide *to t.* that took Jesus   Ac 1:16

appeared *unto t.* cloven tongues, as of fire   Ac 2:3

were added *unto t.* about 3,000 souls   Ac 2:41

of the rest durst no man join *to t.*   Ac 5:13

whom God hath given *to t.* that obey him   Ac 5:32

that they had not done sacrifice *unto t.*   Ac 14:18

called us to preach the gospel *unto t.*   Ac 16:10

my necessities, and *to t.* that were with me   Ac 20:34

no man may deliver me *unto t.*   Ac 25:11

is manifest, for God shewed it *unto t.*   Ro 1:19

to t. by patient continuance in well-doing   Ro 2:7

work together for good *to t.* that love God   Ro 8:28

made manifest *unto t.* that asked not after   Ro 10:20

unto t. that are sanctified in Christ   1Co 1:2

unto t. that are called, both Jews and   1Co 1:24

my answer *to t.* that do examine me, is   1Co 9:3

it is not permitted *unto t.* to speak   1Co 14:34

if gospel hid, it is hid *to t.* that are lost   2Co 4:3

to t. which were apostles before me   Ga 1:17

unto t. who are of the household of faith   Ga 6:10

preached peace *to t.* that were nigh   Eph 2:17

is *to t.* an evident token of perdition   Ph'p 1:28

tribulation *to t.* that trouble you   2Th 1:6

meditate, give thyself wholly *to t.*   1Ti 4:15

unto all *t.* that love his appearing   2Ti 4:8

that nothing be wanting *unto t.*   Tit 3:13

but le *to t.* that believed not   Heb 3:18

to us gospel preached as well *as unto t.*   Heb 4:2

I will be *to t.* a God, they to me a people   Heb 8:10

yieldeth *unto t.* that are exercised   Heb 12:11

word not be spoken *to t.* any more   Heb 12:19

Lord promised *to t.* that love him   Jas 1:12; 2:5

gospel preached *to t.* that are dead   1Pe 4:6

to t. that obtained like precious faith   2Pe 1:1

happened *unto t.* according to proverb   2Pe 2:22

unto t. was given power as scorpions   Re 9:3

to t. it was given not kill them   Re 9:5

they sat, and judgment was given *unto t.*   Re 20:4

TOWARD THEM

great his mercy *toward t.* that fear   Ps 103:11

Jesus was moved with compassion *toward t.* and healed   M't 14:14; M'k 6:34

walk in wisdom *toward t.* without   Col 4:5

honestly *toward t.* that are without   1Th 4:12

UNDER THEM

ground clave that was *under t.*   Nu 16:31

and the cloud is not rent *under t.*   Job 26:8

WITH THEM

deal worse with thee than *with t.*   Ge 19:9

Hamor communed *with t.* saying   Ge 34:8

when Joseph saw Benjamin *with t.*   Ge 43:16

established my covenant *with t.*   Ex 6:4

make no covenant *with t.*   Ex 23:32; De 7:2

that are left pine away *with t.*   Le 26:39

to break my covenant *with t.*   Le 26:44

not go *with t.*   Nu 22:12

arise, go *with t.*   Nu 22:20

not inherit *with t.* on yonder side   Nu 32:19

take heed, meddle not *with t.*   De 2:5; 2:19

fear me, that it might be well *with t.*   De 5:29

neither make marriages *with t.*   De 7:3; Jos 23:12

deal *with t.* destroy their altars   De 7:5

keepeth covenant *with t.* that love him   De 7:9

Joshua made peace *with t.*   Jos 9:15; 9:16

they went, the Lord was *with t.*   J'g 1:22

do *with t.* what seemeth good to you   J'g 19:24

and thou shalt prophesy *with t.*   1Sa 10:6

get down, lest I destroy you *with t.*   1Sa 15:6

would not, nor did he eat *with t.*   2Sa 12:17

they have there *with t.* their two sons   2Sa 15:36

thou be angry *with t.*   1Ki 8:46; 2Ch 6:36

are more than they that be *with t.*   2Ki 6:16

with t. that go out on the sabbath, and came to Jehoiada   2Ki 11:9; 2Ch 23:8

there was no reckoning made *with t.*   2Ki 22:7

their brethren were to come *with t.*   1Ch 9:25

and *with t.* 120 priests sounding   2Ch 5:12

with many, or *with t.* that have no power   2Ch 14:11

with t. Levites, and *with t.* Elishama   2Ch 17:8

the book of the law of the Lord *with t.*   2Ch 17:9

he was *with t.* hid in the house of God   2Ch 22:12

with t. were the prophets of God   Ezr 5:2

thou spakest *with t.* from heaven   Ne 9:13

that they might do *with t.* as they would   Ne 9:24

I contended *with t.* and cursed them   Ne 13:25

to do *with t.* as it seemeth good   Es 3:11

seed is established in their sight *with t.*   Job 21:8

their memorial is perished *with t.*   Ps 9:6

secret of Lord is *with t.* that fear him   Ps 25:14

plead my cause *with t.* that strive   Ps 35:1

I went *with t.* to the house of God   Ps 42:4

Lord is *with t.* that uphold | Ps 54:4;
my soul | 118:7
counted *with t.* that go down | Ps 88:4
into pit
for *with t.* thou hast | Ps 119:93
quickened me
my son, walk not thou in way | Pr 1:15
with t.
evil men, neither desire to be | Pr 24:1
with t.
such as keep law contend *with* | Pr 28:4
t.
it shall be well *with t.* that | Ec 8:12
fear God
the stranger shall be joined | Isa 14:1
with t.
thou shalt not be joined *with* | Isa 14:20
t. in burial
the unicorns shall come down | Isa 34:7
with t.
enlarged bed made a | Isa 57:8
covenant *with t.*
this is my covenant *with t.* | Isa 59:21
bring their silver and gold | Isa 60:9
with t.
make an everlasting covenant | Isa 61:8
with t.
blessed of Lord, and | Isa 65:23
offspring *with t.*
deal thus *with t.* in time of | Jer 18:23
anger
if the word of the Lord be | Jer 27:18
with t.
I will gather *with t.* the blind | Jer 31:8
and lame
make an everlasting covenant | Jer 32:40
with t.
madest images of men, | Eze 16:17;
didst commit whoredoms *with t.* | 16:28;
| 23:7, 43
bring down *with t.* that go | Eze 26:20
down to pit
with t. that go down to pit | Eze 31:14;
| 32:18, 24-25, 29
make *with t.* covenant of | Eze 34:25;
peace | 37:26
Lord their God am *with* | Eze 34:30;
t. | Zec 10:5
my tabernacle shall be *with* | Eze 37:27
t.
Judah also shall fall *with t.* | Ho 5:5
can children fast as long as | M't 9:15;
bridegroom is *with t.* M'k 2:19; Lu 5:34
lest ye root up wheat *with t.* | M't 13:29
would not have been | M't 23:30
partakers *with t.*
took lamps, and took no oil | M't 25:3
with t.
they preached, the Lord | M'k 16:20
working *with t.*
eateth *with t.* | Lu 15:2
tho' he hear *with t.* | Lu 18:7
found eleven and them that | Lu 24:33
were *with t.*
while was *with t.* in the | Joh 17:12
world, I kept
Judas which betrayed him | Joh 18:5
stood *with t.*
Thomas not *with t.* when | Joh 20:24
Jesus came
was *with t.* coming in and | Ac 9:28
going out
Dorcas made while she was | Ac 9:39
with t.
go *with t.* | Ac 10:20
eat *with t.* | Ac 11:3
spirit bade me go *with t.* | Ac 11:12
nothing doubting
the hand of the Lord was | Ac 11:21
with t.
took *with t.* John surnamed | Ac 12:25
Mark
rehearsed all God had done | Ac 14:27;
with t. | 15:4
Paul thought not good to | Ac 15:38
take him *with t.*
knee'ed down and prayed | Ac 20:36
with t. all
at charges *with t.* that they | Ac 21:24
may shave
and *with t.* partakest of the | Ro 11:17
root
rejoice *with t.* that do | Ro 12:15
rejoice, weep *with t.* that weep
be not ye therefore partakers | Eph 5:7
with t.
grace be *with t.* that love | Eph 6:24
our Lord
be caught up together *with t.* | 1Th 4:17

peace be *with t.* that call on | 2Ti 2:22
Lord
was it not *with t.* that had | Heb 3:17
sinned
finding fault *with t.* he saith | Heb 8:8
the covenant I will make | Heb 10:16
with t.
harlot Rahab perished | Heb 11:31
not *with t.*
them that are in bonds, as | Heb 13:3
bound *with t.*
ye husbands, dwell *with t.* | 1Pe 3:7
according
that ye run not *with t.* to the | 1Pe 4:4
same excess
latter end is worse *with t.* | 2Pe 2:20
than beginning
had heads, and *with t.* they do | Re 9:19
hurt
tabernacle with men will dwell | Re 21:3
with t.

WITHOUT THEM

while she lieth desolate | Le 26:43
without t.

THEMSELVES

together, and made *t.* aprons | Ge 3:7
hid *t.* from the presence of the | Ge 3:8
Lord
they separated *t.* the one | Ge 13:11
from the
that they wearied *t.* to find | Ge 19:11
the door
set seven ewe lambs of the | Ge 21:28
flock by *t.*
ewe lambs which thou hast | Ge 21:29
set by *t.*
and he put his own flocks by | Ge 30:40
t.
of his servants, every drove | Ge 32:16
by *t.*
their children, and they | Ge 33:6
bowed *t.*
children came near, and | Ge 33:7
bowed *t.*
near and Rachel, and they | Ge 33:7
bowed *t.*
they shall gather *t.* together | Ge 34:30
against
and bowed down *t.* before | Ge 42:6
him with
and bowed *t.* to him to the | Ge 43:26
earth
him by himself, and for them | Ge 43:32
by *t.*
which did eat with him, by *t.* | Ge 43:32
let them go and gather straw | Ex 5:7
for *t.*
and bow down *t.* unto me, | Ex 11:8
saying
they prepared for *t.* any | Ex 12:39
victual
every small matter they | Ex 18:26
judged *t.*
sanctify *t.* lest the Lord break | Ex 19:22
forth
thou shalt couple five | Ex 26:9
curtains by *t.*
and six curtains by *t.* and shalt | Ex 26:9
the people gathered *t.* together | Ex 32:1
unto
the land of Egypt, have | Ex 32:7
corrupted *t.*
sons of Levi gathered *t.* | Ex 32:26
together unto
of Israel stripped *t.* of their | Ex 33:6
ornaments
And he coupled five curtains | Ex 36:16
by *t.*
and six curtains by *t.* | Ex 36:16
they shall both bathe *t.* in | Le 15:18
water, and
that they separate *t.* from the | Le 22:2
holy
shall separate *t.* to vow a vow | Nu 6:2
of a
Nazarite, to separate *t.* unto | Nu 6:2
the Lord
clothes, and so make *t.* clean | Nu 8:7
shall assemble *t.* to thee | Nu 10:3
at the door
of Israel, shall gather *t.* | Nu 10:4
unto thee
them all abroad for *t.* round | Nu 11:32
about
gathered *t.* together against | Nu 16:3;
Moses | 20:2

gathered *t.* together against | Nu 27:3
the Lord
that are left, and hide *t.* | De 7:20
from thee
forth out of Egypt have | De 9:12
corrupted *t.*
and presented *t.* in the | De 31:14
tabernacle of
they shall have eaten and | De 31:20
filled *t.*
They have corrupted *t.* their | De 32:5
spot is
adversaries behave *t.* | De 32:27
strangely
city Israel took for a prey | Jos 8:27
unto *t.*
That they gathered *t.* together, | Jos 9:2
to
king of Eglon, gathered *t.* | Jos 10:5
together.
had avenged *t.* upon their | Jos 10:13
enemies
fled, and hid *t.* in a cave at | Jos 10:16
Makkedah
of Israel took for a prey | Jos 11:14
unto *t.*
children of Israel gathered *t.* | Jos 22:12
together
and they presented *t.* before | Jos 24:1
God
about them, and bowed *t.* | J'g 2:12
unto them
other gods, and bowed *t.* unto | J'g 2:17
them
corrupted *t.* more than their | J'g 2:19
fathers
when the people willingly | J'g 5:2
offered *t.*
offered *t.* willingly among the | J'g 5:9
people
lest Israel vaunt *t.* against me, | J'g 7:2
saying
gathered *t.* together out of | J'g 7:23
Naphtali
men of Ephraim gathered *t.* | J'g 7:24
together
of Israel assembled *t.* | J'g 10:17
together
men of Ephraim gathered *t.* | J'g 12:1
together
in Juda, and spread *t.* in Lehi | J'g 15:9
presented *t.* in the assembly of | J'g 20:2
of Benjamin gathered *t.* | J'g 20:14
together out
men of Israel put *t.* in array | J'g 20:20
to fight
the men of Israel encouraged | J'g 20:22
t.
where they put *t.* in array the | J'g 20:22
first
and put *t.* in array against | J'g 20:30
Gibeah
and put *t.* in array at | J'g 20:33
Baal-tamar
and the liers in wait drew | J'g 20:37
t. along
were full have hired out *t.* for | 1Sa 2:5
bread
because his sons made *t.* vile | 1Sa 3:13
the Philistines put *t.* in array | 1Sa 4:2
against
elders of Israel gathered *t.* | 1Sa 8:4
together
Philistines gathered *t.* | 1Sa 13:5
together to
then the people did hide *t.* | 1Sa 13:6
in caves
Philistines gathered *t.* | 1Sa 13:11
together at
discovered *t.* unto the | 1Sa 14:11
garrison of the
out of the holes where they | 1Sa 14:11
had hid *t.*
that were with him | 1Sa 14:20
assembled *t.*
which had hid *t.* in mount | 1Sa 14:22
Ephraim
threw *t.* on the loot (B) | 1Sa 14:32
have kept *t.* at least from | 1Sa 21:4
women
discontented, gathered *t.* unto | 1Sa 22:2
him
the Philistines gathered *t.* | 1Sa 28:4
together
of Benjamin gathered *t.* | 2Sa 2:25
together
and spread *t.* in the valley of | 2Sa 5:18,
| 5:22
and Maacah, were by *t.* in | 2Sa 10:8
the field

Israel, they gathered *t.* together   *2Sa 10:15*

the Syrians set *t.* in array against   *2Sa 10:17*

came weary, and refreshed *t.* there   *2Sa 16:14*

Strangers shall submit *t.* unto me   *2Sa 22:45*

all the men of Israel assembled *t.*   *1Ki 8:2*

they shall bethink *t.* in the land   *1Ki 8:47*

let them choose one bullock for *t.*   *1Ki 18:23*

and cut *t.* after their manner   *1Ki 18:28*

they set *t.* in array against the city   *1Ki 20:12*

bowed *t.* to the ground before him   *2Ki 2:15*

out of the camp to hide *t.* in the field   *2Ki 7:12*

of Judah, and made a king over *t.*   *2Ki 8:20*

sold *t.* to do evil in the sight of the   *2Ki 17:17*

eat this year such things as grow of *t.*   *2Ki 19:29*

Then all Israel gathered *t.* to David   *1Ch 11:1*

who strengthened *t.* with him in his   *1Ch 11:10*

they set *t.* in the midst of that parcel   *1Ch 11:14*

Gadites there separated *t.* unto David   *1Ch 12:8*

that they may gather *t.* unto us   *1Ch 13:2*

spread *t.* in the valley of Rephaim   *1Ch 14:9*

spread *t.* abroad in the valley   *1Ch 14:13*

sanctified *t.* to bring up the ark of the   *1Ch 15:14*

that they had made *t.* odious to David   *1Ch 19:6*

gathered *t.* together from their cities   *1Ch 19:7*

were come were by *t.* in the field   *1Ch 19:9*

they set *t.* in array against the children   *1Ch 19:11*

and his four sons with him hid *t.*   *1Ch 21:20*

submitted *t.* unto Solomon the king   *1Ch 29:24*

spread *t.* forth twenty cubits   *2Ch 3:13*

all the men of Israel assembled *t.*   *2Ch 5:3*

Yet if they bethink *t.* in the land   *2Ch 6:37*

bowed *t.* with their faces to   *2Ch 7:3*

shall humble *t.* and pray, and seek   *2Ch 7:14*

Israel and the king humbled *t.*   *2Ch 12:6*

the Lord saw that they humbled *t.*   *2Ch 12:7*

They have humbled *t.;* therefore   *2Ch 13:7*

strengthened *t.* against Rehoboam   *2Ch 13:7*

that they could not recover *t.*   *2Ch 14:13*

gathered *t.* together at Jerusalem   *2Ch 15:10*

And Judah gathered *t.* together, to   *2Ch 20:4*

jewels, which they stripped off for *t.*   *2Ch 20:25*

assembled *t.* in the valley of Berachah   *2Ch 20:26*

of Judah. and made *t.* a king   *2Ch 21:8*

their brethren, and sanctified *t.*   *2Ch 29:15*

that were present with him bowed *t.*   *2Ch 29:29*

the other priests had sanctified *t.*   *2Ch 29:34*

more upright in heart to sanctify *t.*   *2Ch 29:34*

had not sanctified *t.* sufficiently   *2Ch 30:3*

had the people gathered *t.* together   *2Ch 30:3*

Manasseh and of Zebulun humbled *t.*   *2Ch 30:11*

were ashamed, and sanctified *t.*   *2Ch 30:15*

and Zebulun, had not cleansed *t.*   *2Ch 30:18*

great number of priests sanctified *t.*   *2Ch 30:24*

for in their set office they sanctified *t.*   *2Ch 31:18*

rested *t.* upon the words of Hezekiah   *2Ch 32:8*

afterward they made ready for *t.*   *2Ch 35:14*

the Levites prepared for *t.*   *2Ch 35:14*

people gathered *t.* together as one   *Ezr 3:1*

brethren the priests, and for *t.*   *Ezr 6:20*

such as had separated *t.* unto them   *Ezr 6:21*

have not separated *t.* from the people   *Ezr 9:1*

taken of their daughters for *t.*   *Ezr 9:2*

mingled *t.* with the people of those   *Ezr 9:2*

that they should gather *t.* together   *Ezr 10:7*

gathered *t.* together unto Jerusalem   *Ezr 10:9*

feeble Jews? will they fortify *t.*   *Ne 4:2*

people gathered *t.* together as one   *Ne 8:1*

and made *t.* booths, every one   *Ne 8:16*

Israel separated *t.* from all strangers   *Ne 9:2*

and delighted *t.* in thy great goodness   *Ne 9:25*

that had separated *t.* from the people   *Ne 10:28*

that willingly offered *t.* to dwell at   *Ne 11:2*

of the singers gathered *t.* together   *Ne 12:28*

the priests and the Levites purified *t.*   *Ne 12:30*

Levites, that they should cleanse *t.*   *Ne 13:22*

in every city to gather *t.* together   *Es 8:11*

that day to avenge *t.* on their enemies   *Es 8:13*

Jews gathered *t.* together in their   *Es 9:2*

gathered *t.* together on the fourteenth   *Es 9:15*

king's provinces gathered *t.* together   *Es 9:16*

upon all such as joined *t.* unto them   *Es 9:27*

had decreed for *t.* and for their   *Es 9:31*

came to present *t.* before the Lord   *Job 1:6; 2:1*

which built desolate places for *t.*   *Job 3:14*

terrors of God do set *t.* in array   *Job 6:4*

have gathered *t.* together against me   *Job 16:10*

the poor of the earth hide *t.* together   *Job 24:4*

had marked for *t.* in the daytime   *Job 24:16*

The young man saw me, and hid *t.*   *Job 29:8*

the desolation they rolled *t.* upon me   *Job 30:14*

the workers of iniquity may hide *t.*   *Job 34:22*

they are firm in *t.:* they cannot be   *Job 41:23*

by reason of breakings they purify *t.*   *Job 41:25*

The kings of the earth set *t.* and the   *Ps 2:2*

have set *t.* against me round about   *Ps 3:6*

nations may know *t.* to be but men   *Ps 9:20*

strangers shall submit *t.* unto me   *Ps 18:44*

rejoiced, and gathered *t.* together   *Ps 35:15*

gathered *t.* together against me   *Ps 35:15*

dishonour that magnify *t.* against me   *Ps 35:26*

delight *t.* in the abundance of peace   *Ps 37:11*

slippeth, they magnify *t.* against me   *Ps 38:16*

and they which hate us spoil for *t.*   *Ps 44:10*

boast *t.* in the multitude of their   *Ps 49:6*

They gathered *t.* together, they hide   *Ps 56:6*

they hide *t.* they mark my steps   *Ps 56:6*

the midst whereof they are fallen *t.*   *Ps 57:6*

They run and prepared *t.* without my   *Ps 59:4*

They encourage *t.* in an evil matter   *Ps 64:5*

their own tongue to fall upon *t.*   *Ps 64:8*

thine enemies submit *t.* unto thee   *Ps 66:3*

nations: let not the rebellious exalt *t.*   *Ps 66:7*

and our enemies laugh among *t.*   *Ps 80:6*

should have submitted *t.* unto him   *Ps 81:15*

all the workers of iniquity boast *t.*   *Ps 94:4*

They gather *t.* together against the   *Ps 94:21*

graven images, that boast *t.* of idols   *Ps 97:7*

sun ariseth, they gather *t.* together   *Ps 104:22*

They joined *t.* also unto Baal-peor   *Ps 106:28*

cover *t.* with their own confusion   *Ps 109:29*

his wicked device; lest they exalt *t.*   *Ps 140:8*

for riches certainly make *t.* wings   *Pr 23:5*

When the wicked rise, men hide *t.*   *Pr 28:28*

might see that they *t.* are beasts   *Ec 3:18*

of rain, they empty *t.* upon the earth   *Ec 11:3*

and the strong men shall bow *t.* and   *Ec 12:3*

please *t.* in the children of strangers   *Isa 2:6*

they have rewarded evil unto *t.*   *Isa 3:9*

they shall be hungry, they shall fret *t.*   *Isa 8:21*

inhabitants of Gebim gather *t.* to flee   *Isa 10:31*

they shall gird *t.* with sackcloth   *Isa 15:3*

and the horsemen shall set *t.* in array   *Isa 22:7*

strengthen *t.* in the strength of   *Isa 30:2*

but *t.* are gone into captivity   *Isa 46:2*

deliver *t.* from the power of   *Isa 47:14*

For they call *t.* of the holy city, and   *Isa 48:2*

and stay *t.* upon the God of Israel   *Isa 48:2*

all these gather *t.* together   *Isa 49:18*

that join *t.* to the Lord, to serve him   *Isa 56:6*

sha'l they cover *t.* with their works   *Isa 59:6*

all they gather *t.* together, they come   *Isa 60:4*

bow *t.* down at the soles of thy feet   *Isa 60:14*

They that sanctify *t.* and purify   *Isa 66:17*

and purify *t.* in the gardens behind   *Isa 66:17*

that seek her will not weary *t.*   *Jer 2:24*

and the nations shall bless *t.* in him   *Jer 4:2*

assembled *t.* by troops in the harlot's   *Jer 5:7*

and though the waves thereof toss *t.*   *Jer 5:22*

do they not provoke *t.* to the   *Jer 7:19*

and weary *t.* to commit iniquity   *Jer 9:5*

done against *t.* to provoke me   *Jer 11:17*

they have put *t.* to pain, but shall not   *Jer 12:13*

shall men lament for them, nor cut *t.*   *Jer 16:6*

nor make *t.* bald for them   *Jer 16:6*

Neither shall men tear *t.* for them in   *Jer 16:7*

great kings shall serve *t.* of them also   *Jer 25:14*

and great kings shall serve *t.* of him   *Jer 27:7*

shall no more serve *t.* of him   *Jer 30:8*

And their nobles shall be of *Jer 30:21*
t. and
none should serve *t.* of them *Jer 34:10*
any
their clothes rent, and having *Jer 41:5*
cut *t.*
they shall take to *t.* their *Jer 49:29*
curtains
shall set *t.* in array against *Jer 50:9*
they have girded *t.* with *La 2:10*
sackcloth
they have polluted *t.* with *La 4:14*
blood, so
and they shall loathe *t.* for the *Eze 6:9*
evils
They shall also gird *t.* with *Eze 7:18*
sackcloth
lifted up, these lifted up *t.* *Eze 10:17*
also
of Chebar, their appearances *Eze 10:22*
and *t.*
but they only shall be *Eze 14:18*
delivered *t.*
they shall clothe *t.* with *Eze 26:16*
trembling
they shall wallow *t.* in the *Eze 27:30*
ashes
shall make *t.* utterly bald for *Eze 27:31*
thee
by the waters exalt *t.* for *Eze 31:14*
their height
shepherds of Israel that do *Eze 34:2*
feed *t.*
the shepherds fed *t.* and fed *Eze 34:8*
not my
the shepherds feed *t.* any *Eze 34:10*
more
hand of those that served *t.* *Eze 34:27*
of them
defile *t.* any more with their *Eze 37:23*
idols
it; and they shall consecrate *Eze 43:26*
t.
gird *t.* with any thing that *Eze 44:18*
causeth
come at no dead person to *Eze 44:25*
defile *t.*
had no husband, they may *Eze 44:25*
defile *t.*
ministers of the house, have *Eze 45:5*
for *t.*
shall mingle *t.* with the seed of *Da 2:43*
men
upon them, so that they fled *Da 10:7*
to hide *t.*
end of years they shall join *t.* *Da 11:6*
together
shall exalt *t.* to establish the *Da 11:14*
vision
together, and appoint *t.* one *Ho 1:11*
head
for *t.* are separated with *Ho 4:14*
whores
they assemble *t.* for corn and *Ho 7:14*
wine
They have deeply corrupted *t.* *Ho 9:9*
as in
and separated *t.* unto that *Ho 9:10*
shame
they shall bind *t.* in their *Ho 10:10*
furrows
And they lay *t.* down upon *Am 2:8*
clothes
and stretch *t.* upon their *Am 6:4*
couches
invent to *t.* instruments of *Am 6:5*
anoint *t.* with the chief *Am 6:6*
ointments
that stretched *t.* shall be *Am 6:7*
removed
they hide *t.* in the top of *Am 9:3*
Carmel
have behaved *t.* ill in their *Mic 3:4*
doings
and their dignity shall *Hab 1:7*
proceed of *t.*
and their horsemen shall *Hab 1:8*
spread *t.*
and magnified *t.* against their *Zep 2:8*
border
magnified *t.* against the *Zep 2:10*
people of
pipes empty the golden oil *Zec 4:12*
out of *t.*
slay them, and hold *t.* not *Zec 11:5*
guilty: and
burden *t.* with it shall be cut *Zec 12:3*
in pieces
do not magnify *t.* against *Zec 12:7*
Judah

of the scribes said within *t.* *M't 9:3*
works do shew forth *t.* in him *M't 14:2*
the villages, and buy *t.* *M't 14:15*
victuals
they reasoned among *t.* *M't 16:7*
saying
made *t.* eunuchs for the *M't 19:12*
kingdom
And they reasoned with *t.* *M't 21:25*
saying
they said among *t.*, This is *M't 21:38*
the
but they *t.* will not move *M't 23:4*
them with
they questioned among *t.* *M'k 1:27*
saying
that they so reasoned with *t.* *M'k 2:8*
have no root in *t.* and so *M'k 4:17*
endure
mighty works do shew forth *M'k 6:14*
t. in him
apostles gathered *t.* together *M'k 6:30*
unto
into the villages, and buy *t.* *M'k 6:36*
bread
they were sore amazed in *t.* *M'k 6:51*
beyond
they reasoned among *t.* *M'k 8:16*
saying
into an high mountain apart *M'k 9:2*
by *t.*
any more, save Jesus only *M'k 9:8*
with *t.*
they kept that saying with *t.* *M'k 9:10*
way they had disputed *M'k 9:34*
among *t.*
saying among *t.*, Who then *M'k 10:26*
can be
they reasoned with *t.* *M'k 11:31*
saying, If we
those husbandmen said *M'k 12:7*
among *t.*
some that had indignation *M'k 14:4*
within *t.*
priests mocking said among *M'k 15:31*
t.
they said among *t.*, Who shall *M'k 16:3*
roll
all amazed, and spake among *Lu 4:36*
t.
the counsel of God against *t.* *Lu 7:30*
with him began to say within *Lu 7:49*
t.
unto certain which trusted in *Lu 18:9*
t.
they reasoned with *t.* saying, *Lu 20:5*
If we
they reasoned among *t.* *Lu 20:14*
saying
which should feign *t.* just *Lu 20:20*
men
they began to enquire among *Lu 22:23*
t.
they were at enmity between *Lu 23:12*
t.
beheld the linen clothes laid *Lu 24:12*
by *t.*
Jews therefore strove among *Joh 6:52*
t.
Then said the Jews among *t.* *Joh 7:35*
before the passover, to *Joh 11:55*
purify *t.*
spake among *t.* as they *Joh 11:56*
stood in
Pharisees therefore said *Joh 12:19*
among *t.*
said some of his disciples *Joh 16:17*
among *t.*
might have my joy fulfilled *Joh 17:13*
in *t.*
it was cold: and they *Joh 18:18*
warmed *t.*
they *t.* went not into the *Joh 18:28*
judgment
They said, therefore among *Joh 19:24*
t., Let
the council, they conferred *Ac 4:15*
among *t.*
of men, about four hundred, *Ac 5:36*
joined *t.*
they assembled *t.* with the *Ac 11:26*
church
and Silas, being prophets *Ac 15:32*
also *t.*
let them come *t.* and fetch us *Ac 16:37*
out
when they opposed *t.* and *Ac 18:6*
blasphemed
keep *t.* from things offered to *Ac 21:25*
idols

and bound *t.* under a curse *Ac 23:12*
which have bound *t.* with an *Ac 23:21*
oath
which they *t.* also allow, that *Ac 24:15*
gone aside, they talked *Ac 26:31*
between *t.*
they committed *t.* unto the *Ac 27:40*
sea, and
swim should cast *t.* first into *Ac 27:43*
the sea
they said among *t.* No doubt *Ac 28:4*
And when they agreed not *Ac 28:25*
among *t.*
had great reasoning among *t.* *Ac 28:29*
Professing *t.* to be wise, they *Ro 1:22*
became
their own bodies between *t.* *Ro 1:24*
receiving in *t.* that *Ro 1:27*
recompence of
not the law, are a law unto *t.* *Ro 2:14*
submitted *t.* unto the *Ro 10:3*
righteousness
resist shall receive to *t.* *Ro 13:2*
damnation
nor abusers of *t.* with *1Co 6:9*
mankind
have addicted *t.* to the *1Co 16:15*
ministry
should not henceforth live *2Co 5:15*
unto *t.*
their power they were willing *2Co 8:3*
of *t.*
with some that commend *t.* *2Co 10:12*
but they measuring *t.* by *t.* *2Co 10:12*
and comparing *t.* among *t.* *2Co 10:12*
transforming *t.* into the *2Co 11:13*
apostles of
neither they *t.* who are *Ga 6:13*
circumcised
given *t.* over unto *Eph 4:19*
lasciviousness
let each esteem other better *Ph'p 2:3*
than *t.*
for they *t.* shew of us what *1Th 1:9*
manner
for them that defile *t.* with *1Ti 1:10*
mankind
that women adorn *t.* in modest *1Ti 2:9*
well purchase to *t.* a good *1Ti 3:13*
degree
pierced *t.* through with many *1Ti 6:10*
Laying up for *t.* a good *1Ti 6:19*
foundation
instructing those that oppose *2Ti 2:25*
t.
recover *t.* out of the snare of *2Ti 2:26*
the devil
lusts shall they heap to *t.* *2Ti 4:3*
teachers
One of *t.* even a prophet of *Tit 1:12*
their
they crucify to *t.* the Son of *Heb 6:6*
God
the heavenly things *t.* with *Heb 9:23*
better
that not unto *t.* but unto us *1Pe 1:12*
adorned *t.* being in subjection *1Pe 3:5*
unto
and bring upon *t.* swift *2Pe 2:1*
destruction
t. are the servants of *2Pe 2:19*
corruption
manner, giving *t.* over to *Jude 7*
fornication
in those things they corrupt *Jude 10*
t.
with you, feeding *t.* without *Jude 12*
fear
These be they who separate *t.* *Jude 19*
hid *t.* in the dens and in the *Re 6:15*
rocks
trumpets prepared *t.* to sound *Re 8:6*

THEN

thereof, *t.* your eyes shall be *Ge 3:5*
opened
t. began men to call upon the *Ge 4:26*
name
T. he put forth his hand, and *Ge 8:9*
took her
the Canaanite was *t.* in the *Ge 12:6*
land
the Perizzite dwelled *t.* in the *Ge 13:7*
land
the left hand, *t.* I will go to *Ge 13:9*
the right
the right hand, *t.* I will go to *Ge 13:9*
the left

T. Lot chose him all the plain of	Ge 13:11	T. they speedily took down every man	Ge 44:11	T. went up Moses, and Aaron, Nadab	Ex 24:9
t. shall thy seed also be numbered	Ge 13:16	T. they rent their clothes, and laded	Ge 44:13	T. shalt thou take the anointing oil	Ex 29:7
T. Abram removed his tent	Ge 13:18	T. Judah came near unto him, and	Ge 44:18	T. shalt thou kill the ram, and take of	Ex 29:20
T. Abraham fell upon his face, and	Ge 17:17	brother be with us, t. will we go down	Ge 44:26	t. thou shalt burn the remainder with	Ex 29:34
T. Sarah denied, saying, I laughed	Ge 18:15	t. I shall bear the blame to my father	Ge 44:32	t. shall they give every man a ransom	Ex 30:12
t. I will spare all the place for their	Ge 18:26	T. Joseph could not refrain himself	Ge 45:1	t. I cast it into the fire, and there came	Ex 32:24
arose; t. the angels hastened Lot	Ge 19:15	T. Joseph came and told Pharaoh, and	Ge 47:1	T. Moses stood in the gate of	Ex 32:26
T. the Lord rained upon Sodom and	Ge 19:24	t. make them rulers over my cattle	Ge 47:6	T. wrought Bezaleel and Aholiab, and	Ex 36:1
T. Abimelech called Abraham	Ge 20:9	T. Joseph said unto the people	Ge 47:23	T. a cloud covered the tent of	Ex 40:34
t. Abimlech rose up, and Phichol the	Ge 21:32	father's bed; t. defiledst thou it	Ge 49:4	t. they journeyed not till the day that	Ex 40:37
T. on the third day Abraham lifted up	Ge 22:4	stools; if it be a son, t. ye shall kill him	Ex 1:16	t. he shall bring his offering of	Le 1:14
t. thou shalt be clear from this my	Ge 24:8	but if it be a daughter, t. she shall live	Ex 1:16	t. shall he offer it before the Lord	Le 3:7
T. shalt thou be clear from this my	Ge 24:41	T. said his sister to Pharaoh's	Ex 2:7	t. he shall offer it before the Lord	Le 3:12
T. Laban and Bethuel answered and	Ge 24:50	T. Zipporah took a sharp stone, and	Ex 4:25	t. let him bring for his sin, which he	Le 4:3
T. again Abraham took a wife, and	Ge 25:1	t. she said, A bloody husband thou	Ex 4:26	t. the congregation shall offer a young	Le 4:14
T. Abraham gave up the ghost, and	Ge 25:8	t. they bowed their heads	Ex 4:31	t. he shall bring his offering, a kid of	Le 4:28
T. Jacob gave Esau bread	Ge 25:34	T. the officers of the children of Israel	Ex 5:15	utter it, t. he shall bear his iniquity	Le 5:1
T. Isaac sowed in that land	Ge 26:12	T. the Lord said unto Moses, Now	Ex 6:1	knoweth of it, t. he shall be guilty	Le 5:3
T. Abimelech went to him from Gerar	Ge 26:26	how t. shall Pharaoh hear me, who am	Ex 6:12	t. he shall be guilty in one of these	Le 5:4
hand; t. will I slay my brother Jacob	Ge 27:41	t. thou shalt say unto Aaron, Take thy	Ex 7:9	t. he shall bring for his trespass, which	Le 5:7
t. I will send, and fetch thee from	Ge 27:45	T. Pharaoh also called the wise men	Ex 7:11	t. he that sinned shall bring	Le 5:11
T. went Esau unto Ishmael, and took	Ge 28:9	T. Pharaoh called for Moses	Ex 8:8	T. shall he bring it to the priest, and	Le 5:12
in peace; t. shall the Lord be my God	Ge 28:21	T. the magicians said unto Pharaoh	Ex 8:19	t. he shall bring for his trespass unto	Le 5:15
T. Jacob went on his journey	Ge 29:1	T. the Lord said unto Moses, Go in	Ex 9:1	t. it shall be, because he hath sinned	Le 6:4
well's mouth; t. we water the sheep	Ge 29:8	T. Pharaoh called for Moses	Ex 10:16	t. he shall offer with the sacrifice of	Le 7:12
wherefore t. hast thou beguiled me	Ge 29:25	T. Moses called for all the elders of	Ex 12:21	T. Moses said unto Aaron, This is it	Le 10:3
T. Rachel said to Leah, Give me	Ge 30:14	him, t. shall he eat thereof	Ex 12:44	t. she shall be unclean seven days	Le 12:2
wages; t. all the cattle bare speckled	Ge 31:8	t. let him come near and keep it	Ex 12:48	shall t. continue in the blood of her	Le 12:4
t. bare all the cattle ringstraked	Ge 31:8	redeem it, t. thou shalt break his neck	Ex 13:13; 34:20	t. she shall be unclean two weeks	Le 12:5
now t. whatsoever God hath said unto	Ge 31:16	T. sang Moses and the children of	Ex 15:1	t. she shall bring two turtles, or two	Le 12:8
T. Jacob rose up, and set his sons and	Ge 31:17	T. the dukes of Edom shall be	Ex 15:15	t. he shall be brought unto Aaron the	Le 13:2
T. Laban overtook Jacob, Now Jacob	Ge 31:25	T. said the Lord unto Moses, Behold	Ex 16:4	t. the priest shall shut him up that	Le 13:4; 13:31
T. went he out of Leah's tent, and	Ge 31:33	t. ye shall know that the Lord hath	Ex 16:6	t. the priest shall shut him up seven	Le 13:5; 13:21, 26
T. Jacob offered sacrifice upon the	Ge 31:54	t. ye shall see the glory of the Lord	Ex 16:7	t. the priest shall pronounce him	Le 13:8; 13:17, 22, 27, 30, 34
T. Jacob was greatly afraid	Ge 32:7	T. came Amalek, and fought with	Ex 17:8	t. he shall be brought unto the priest	Le 13:9
t. the other company which is left	Ge 32:8	T. Jethro, Moses' father in law	Ex 18:2	T. the priest shall consider	Le 13:13
T. thou shalt say, They be thy servant	Ge 32:18	t. thou shalt be able to endure, and all	Ex 18:23	T. the priest shall look upon it; and	Le 13:25; 13:43
T. the handmaidens came near, they	Ge 33:6	t. ye shall be a pecular treasure unto	Ex 19:5	T. the priest shall see the plague	Le 13:30
t. receive my present at my hand	Ge 33:10	t. his wife shall go out with him	Ex 21:3	T. the priest shall look on him: and	Le 13:36
T. we give our daughters unto you	Ge 34:16	T. his master shall bring him unto	Ex 21:6	T. the priest shall look: and, behold	Le 13:39
t. will we take our daughter, and we	Ge 34:17	t. shall he let her be redeemed	Ex 21:8	t. the priest shall command that they	Le 13:54
T. Jacob said unto his household	Ge 35:2	t. shall she go out free without money	Ex 21:11	t. he shall rend it out of the garment	Le 13:56
T. there passed by Midianites	Ge 37:28	t. I will appoint thee a place whither	Ex 21:13	t. it shall be washed the second time	Le 13:58
T. said Judah to Tamar his daughter	Ge 38:11	t. shall he that smote him be quit	Ex 21:19	T. shall the priest command to take	Le 14:4
T. he asked the men of that place	Ge 38:21	follow, t. thou shalt give life for life	Ex 21:23	t. he shall take one lamb for a trespass	Le 14:21
how t. can I do this great wickedness	Ge 39:9	t. the ox shall be surely stoned, and	Ex 21:28	T. the priest shall command that they	Le 14:36; 14:40
T. spake the chief butler unto Pharaoh	Ge 41:9	t. he shall give for the ransom of his	Ex 21:30	T. the priest shall go out of the house	Le 14:38
T. Pharaoh sent and called Joseph	Ge 41:14	t. they shall sell the live ox, and divide	Ex 21:35	T. the priest shall come and look, and	Le 14:44
T. Joseph commanded to fill their	Ge 42:25	t. he shall be sold for his theft	Ex 22:3	t. the priest shall pronounce the house	Le 14:48
t. shall I know that ye are no spies	Ge 42:34	t. the master of the house shall be	Ex 22:8	t. he shall wash his clothes, and bathe	Le 15:8
t. shall ye bring down my gray hairs	Ge 42:38	T. shall an oath of the Lord be	Ex 22:11	t. he shall number to himself seven	Le 15:13
thee, t. let me bear the blame for ever	Ge 43:9	pieces, t. let him bring it for witness	Ex 22:13		
t. should we steal out of thy lord's	Ge 44:8	t. I will be an enemy unto thine	Ex 23:22		

t. he shall wash all his flesh in water   Le 15:16

t. she shall number to herself seven   Le 15:28

T. shall he kill the goat of the sin   Le 16:15

until the even: *t.* shall he be clean   Le 17:15

his flesh; *t.* he shall bear his iniquity   Le 17:16

t. ye shall count the fruit thereof as   Le 19:23

T. I will set my face against that man   Le 20:5

t. he shall put the fifth part thereof   Le 22:14

t. it shall be seven days under the dam   Le 22:27

t. ye shall bring a sheaf of   Le 23:10

T. ye shall sacrifice one kid of the   Le 23:19

t. shall the land keep a sabbath unto   Le 25:2

T. shalt thou cause the trumpet of the   Le 25:9

T. I will command my blessing upon   Le 25:21

t. shall he redeem that which his   Le 25:25

T. let him count the years of the sale   Le 25:27

t. that which is sold shall remain in   Le 25:28

t. he may redeem it within a whole   Le 25:29

t. the house that is in the walled city   Le 25:30

t. the house that was sold, and the city   Le 25:33

with thee; *t.* thou shalt relieve him   Le 25:35

t. shall he depart from thee, both he   Le 25:41

t. he shall count with him   Le 25:52

t. he shall go out in the year of jubile   Le 25:54

T. I will give you rain in due season   Le 26:4

t. I will punish you seven times more   Le 26:18

T. will I also walk contrary unto you   Le 26:24

T. I will walk contrary unto you also   Le 26:28

T. shall the land enjoy sabbaths   Le 26:34

t. shall the land rest, and enjoy her   Le 26:34

if *t.* their uncircumcised hearts be   Le 26:41

they *t.* accept of the punishment of   Le 26:41

T. will I remember my covenant with   Le 26:42

t. thy estimation shall be thirty   Le 27:4

t. thy estimation shall be of the   Le 27:5; 27:6

t. thy estimation shall be fifteen   Le 27:7

t. he shall present himself before the   Le 27:8

t. it and the exchange thereof shall be   Le 27:10

t. he shall present the beast before the   Le 27:11

t. he shall add a fifty part thereof unto   Le 27:13

t. the priest shall estimate it, whether   Le 27:14

t. he shall add the fifth part of the   Le 27:15; 27:19

t. thy estimation shall be according to   Le 27:18

t. the priest shall reckon unto him the   Le 27:18; 27:23

t. he shall redeem it according to   Le 27:27

t. it shall be sold according to thy   Le 27:27

t. both it and the change thereof shall   Le 27:33

T. the tribe of Zebulun: and Eliab the   Nu 2:7

T. the tribe of Gad: and the captain of   Nu 2:14

T. the tabernacle of the congregation   Nu 2:17

T. the tribe of Benjamin: and the   Nu 2:22

T. the tribe of Naphtali; and   Nu 2:29

t. they shall confess their sin which   Nu 5:7

T. shall the man bring his wife unto   Nu 5:15

T. the priest shall charge the woman   Nu 5:21

T. the priest shall take the jealousy   Nu 5:25

t. it shall come to pass, that, if she be   Nu 5:27

t. she shall be free, and shall conceive   Nu 5:28

T. shall the man be guiltless from   Nu 5:31

t. he shall shave his head in the day of   Nu 6:9

t. he heard the voice of one speaking   Nu 7:89

T. let him take a young bullock with   Nu 8:8

t. after that the children of Israel   Nu 9:17

t. the children of Israel kept   Nu 9:19

in the morning, *t.* they journeyed   Nu 9:21

t. the princes, which are heads of   Nu 10:4

t. the camps that lie on the east parts   Nu 10:5

t. the camps that lie on the south side   Nu 10:6

t. ye shall blow an alarm with   Nu 10:9

T. Moses heard the people weep   Nu 11:10

wherefore *t.* were ye not afraid to speak   Nu 12:8

T. Moses and Aaron fell on their faces   Nu 14:5

in us, *t.* he will bring us into this land   Nu 14:8

T. the Egyptians shall hear it   Nu 14:13

t. the nations which have heard the   Nu 14:15

T. the Amalekites came down, and the   Nu 14:45

T. shall he that offereth his offering   Nu 15:4

T. shall he bring with a bullock a   Nu 15:9

T. it shall be, that, when ye eat of the   Nu 15:19

T. it shall be, if ought be committed   Nu 15:24

t. he shall bring a she goat of the first   Nu 15:27

wherefore *t.* lift ye up yourselves   Nu 16:3

all men; *t.* the Lord hath not sent me   Nu 16:29

t. ye shall understand that these men   Nu 16:30

t. ye shall offer up an heave offering of   Nu 18:26

t. it shall be counted unto the Levites   Nu 18:30

T. the priest shall wash his clothes   Nu 19:7

t. the seventh day he shall not be   Nu 19:12

T. came the children of Israel, even   Nu 20:1

drink of thy water, *t.* I will pay for it   Nu 20:19

t. he fought against Israel, and took   Nu 21:1

T. I will utterly destroy their cities   Nu 21:2

T. Israel sang this song, Spring up   Nu 21:17

T. the Lord opened the eyes of   Nu 22:31

T. came the daughters of Zelophehad   Nu 27:1

t. ye shall cause his inheritance to   Nu 27:8

t. ye shall give inheritance unto   Nu 27:9; 27:10-11

t. all her vows shall sound, and every   Nu 30:4

t. her vows shall stand, and her bonds   Nu 30:7

t. he shall make her vow which she   Nu 30:8

t. all her vows shall stand, and every   Nu 30:11

t. whatsoever proceedeth out of her   Nu 30:12

t. he establisheth all her vows, or all   Nu 30:14

them; *t.* he shall bear her iniquity   Nu 30:15

t. afterward ye shall return, and be   Nu 32:22

t. ye shall give them the land of Gilead   Nu 32:29

T. ye shall drive out all the inhabitants   Nu 33:52

t. it shall come to pass, that those   Nu 33:55

T. your south quarter shall be from   Nu 34:3

T. ye shall appoint you cities to be   Nu 35:11

T. the congregation shall judge   Nu 35:24

t. shall their inheritance be taken from   Nu 36:3

t. shall their inheritance be put unto   Nu 36:4

T. I said unto you, Dread not, neither   De 1:29

T. ye answered and said unto me, We   De 1:41

T. we turned, and took our journey   De 2:1

T. Sihon came out against us, he and   De 2:32

T. we turned, and went up the way to   De 3:1

t. shall ye return every man unto his   De 3:20

T. Moses severed three cities   De 4:41

Lord our God any more, *t.* we shall die   De 5:25

T. beware lest thou forget the Lord   De 6:12

T. thou shalt say unto thy son, We   De 6:21

T. thou shalt bless the Lord thy God   De 8:10

T. thine heart be lifted up, and thou   De 8:14

t. I abode in the mount forty days and   De 9:9

t. ye rebelled against commandment   De 9:23

t. the Lord's wrath be kindled against   De 11:17

T. will the Lord drive out all these   De 11:23

T. there shall be a place which the   De 12:11

t. thou shalt kill of thy herd and of thy   De 12:21

T. shalt thou enquire, and make   De 13:14

T. shalt thou turn it into money, and   De 14:25

t. in the seventh year thou shalt let   De 15:12

T. thou shalt take an aul, and thrust   De 15:17

T. shalt thou bring forth that man or   De 17:5

t. shalt thou arise, and get thee up   De 17:8

T. he shall minister in the name of the   De 18:7

t. shalt thou add three cities more for   De 19:9

T. the elders of his city shall send and   De 19:12

T. both the men, between whom the   De 19:17

T. shall ye do unto him, as he had   De 19:19

against it, *t.* proclaim peace unto it   De 20:10

t. it shall be, that all the people that is   De 20:11

against thee, *t.* thou shall besiege it   De 20:12

T. thy elders and thy judges shall   De 21:2

T. thou shalt bring her home to thine   De 21:12

t. thou shalt let her go whither she   De 21:14

T. it shall be, when he maketh his   De 21:16

t. shall his father and his mother lay   De 21:19

t. thou shalt bring it unto thine own   De 22:2

t. thou shalt make a battlement for   De 22:8

T. shall the father of the damsel, and   De 22:15

T. they shall bring out the damsel to	De 22:21	And *t.* the coast turneth westward to	Jos 19:34	*T.* Jephthah went with the elders of	J'g 11:11
t. they shall both of them die, both the	De 22:22	*t.* they shall not deliver the slayer up	Jos 20:5	*T.* Israel sent messengers unto the	J'g 11:17
T. ye shall bring them both out unto	De 22:24	*t.* shall the slayer return, and come	Jos 20:6	*T.* they went along through	J'g 11:18
t. the man only that lay with her shall	De 22:25	*T.* came near the heads of the fathers	Jos 21:1	*T.* the Spirit of the Lord came upon	J'g 11:29
T. the man that lay with her shall	De 22:29	*T.* Joshua called the Reubenites	Jos 22:1	*T.* it shall be, that whatsoever	J'g 11:31
t. keep thee from every wicked thing	De 23:9	unto their tents, *t.* he blessed them	Jos 22:7	*t.* are ye come up unto me this day	J'g 12:3
t. shall he go abroad out of the camp	De 23:10	*t.* pass ye over unto the land of the	Jos 22:19	*T.* Jephthah gathered together all the	J'g 12:4
vineyard, *t.* thou mayest eat grapes	De 23:24	*T.* the children of Reuben and the	Jos 22:21	*T.* said they unto him, Say now	J'g 12:6
t. thou mayest pluck the ears with	De 23:25	*t.* shall the anger of the Lord be	Jos 23:16	*T.* they took him, and slew him at the	J'g 12:6
t. let him write her a bill of or selleth him; *t.* that the thief shall die	De 24:1 De 24:7	*T.* Balak the son of Zippor, king of	Jos 24:9	*T.* died Jephthah the Gileadite, and	J'g 12:7
t. they shall justify the righteous, and	De 25:1	*t.* he will turn and do you hurt, and	Jos 24:20	*T.* died Ibzan, and was buried at	J'g 12:10
t. thy brother should seem vile unto	De 25:3	judges, *t.* the Lord was with the judge	J'g 2:18	*T.* the woman came and told her	J'g 13:6
t. let his brother's wife go up to the	De 25:7	*T.* Ehud went forth through the porch	J'g 3:23	*T.* Manoah intreated the Lord	J'g 13:8
T. the elders of his city shall call him	De 25:8	If thou wilt go with me, *t.* I will go	J'g 4:8	*T.* Manoah knew that he was	J'g 13:21
t. shall his brother's wife come unto	De 25:9	wilt not go with me, *t.* I will not go	J'g 4:8	*T.* his father and his mother said	J'g 14:3
T. thou shalt cut off her hand, thine	De 25:12	*T.* Jael Heber's wife took a nail of the	J'g 4:21	*T.* went Samson down, and his	J'g 14:5
T. thou shalt say before the Lord thy	De 26:13	*T.* sang Deborah and Barak the son	J'g 5:1	*T.* I will give you thirty sheets and	J'g 14:12
T. the Lord will make thy plagues	De 28:59	new gods; *t.* was war in the gates	J'g 5:8	*t.* shall ye give me thirty sheets and	J'g 14:13
but *t.* the anger of the Lord and his	De 29:20	*t.* shall the people of the Lord go down	J'g 5:11	*T.* the Philistines said, Who hath	J'g 15:6
T. men may say, Because they have	De 29:25	*T.* he made him that remaineth	J'g 5:13	*T.* the Philistines went up, and	J'g 15:9
That *t.* the Lord thy God will turn thy	De 30:3	*t.* fought the kings of Canaan	J'g 5:19	*T.* three thousand men of Judah went	J'g 15:11
T. my anger shall be kindled against	De 31:17	*T.* were the horsehoofs broken	J'g 5:22	*T.* went Samson to Gaza, and saw	J'g 16:1
t. will they turn unto other gods, and	De 31:20	with us, why *t.* is all this befallen us	J'g 6:13	*t.* shall I be weak, and be as another	J'g 16:7
t. he forsook God which made him	De 32:15	*t.* shew me a sign that thou talkest	J'g 6:17	*T.* the lords of the Philistines brought	J'g 16:8
Israel *t.* shall dwell in safety alone	De 33:28	*T.* the angel of the Lord put forth the	J'g 6:21	*t.* shall I be weak, and be as another	J'g 16:11
and *t.* thou shalt have good success		*T.* the angel of the Lord departed out	J'g 6:21	*t.* my strength will go from me	J'g 16:17
for *t.* shalt thou make thy way	Jos 1:8	*T.* Gideon built an altar there unto	J'g 6:24	*T.* the lords of the Philistines came up	J'g 16:18
T. Joshua commanded the officers of	Jos 1:10	*T.* Gideon took ten men of his	J'g 6:27	*T.* the lords of the Philistines	J'g 16:23
t. ye shall return unto the land of your	Jos 1:15	*T.* the men of the city said unto Joash	J'g 6:30	*T.* his brethren and all the houses of	J'g 16:31
T. she let them down by a cord	Jos 2:15	*T.* all the Midianites, and the	J'g 6:33	*T.* said Micah, Now know I that the	J'g 17:13
t. we will be quit of thine oath which	Jos 2:20	*t.* shall I know that thou wilt save	J'g 6:37	*T.* the five men departed, and came	J'g 18:7
t. ye shall remove from your place	Jos 3:3	*T.* Jerubbaal, who is Gideon, and all	J'g 7:1	*T.* answered the five men that went	J'g 18:14
T. Joshua called the twelve men	Jos 4:4	*T.* went he down with Phurah his	J'g 7:11	*T.* said the priest unto them, What do	J'g 18:18
T. ye shall answer them, That	Jos 4:7	*t.* blow ye the trumpets also on every	J'g 7:18	*T.* came the woman in the dawning of	J'g 19:26
T. ye shall let your children know	Jos 4:22	*T.* all the men of Ephraim gathered	J'g 7:24	*T.* the man took her up upon an ass	J'g 19:28
day I bid you shout; *t.* shall ye shout	Jos 6:10	*T.* their anger was abated toward	J'g 8:3	*T.* all the children of Israel went out	J'g 20:1
t. I coveted them, and took them; and	Jos 7:21	*t.* I will tear your flesh with the thorns	J'g 8:7	*T.* said the children of Israel, Tell us	J'g 20:3
T. ye shall rise up from the ambush	Jos 8:7	*T.* said he unto Zebah and Zalmunna	J'g 8:18	*T.* all the children of Israel, and all	J'g 20:26
t. they turned again, and slew the men	Jos 8:21	*T.* Zebah and Zalmunna said, Rise	J'g 8:21	*T.* the elders of the congregation said	J'g 21:16
T. Joshua built an altar unto	Jos 8:30	*T.* the men of Israel said unto	J'g 8:22	*T.* they said, Behold, there is a feast	J'g 21:19
T. spake Joshua to the Lord in the	Jos 10:12	*T.* said the trees unto the vine, Come	J'g 9:12	*t.* come ye out of the vineyards	J'g 21:21
T. said Joshua, Open the mouth of the	Jos 10:22	*T.* said all the trees unto the bramble	J'g 9:14	*T.* she arose with her daughters in	Ru 1:6
T. Joshua passed from Makkedah	Jos 10:29	you, *t.* come and put your trust in my	J'g 9:15	*T.* she kissed them: and they lifted	Ru 1:9
T. Horam king of Gezer came up	Jos 10:33	If ye *t.* have dealt truly and sincerely	J'g 9:19	her, *t.* she left speaking unto her	Ru 1:18
T. the children of Judah came unto	Jos 14:6	*t.* rejoice ye in Abimelech, and let	J'g 9:19	why *t.* call ye me Naomi, seeing the	Ru 1:21
as my strength was *t.* even so is	Jos 14:11	*T.* God sent an evil spirit between	J'g 9:23	*T.* said Boaz unto his servant that	Ru 2:5
t. I shall be able to drive them out	Jos 14:12	*T.* would I remove Abimelech	J'g 9:29	*T.* said Boaz unto Ruth, Hearest thou	Ru 2:8
This *t.* was the lot of the tribe of the	Jos 15:1	*t.* mayest thou do to them as thou	J'g 9:33	*T.* she fell on her face, and bowed	Ru 2:10
t. get thee up to the wood country, and	Jos 17:15	*T.* said Zebul unto him, Where is now	J'g 9:38	*T.* she said, Let me find favour in thy	Ru 2:13
t. goeth out to Daberath, and goeth up	Jos 19:12	*T.* went Abimelech to Thebez	J'g 9:50	*T.* Naomi her mother in law said unto	Ru 3:1
t. the coast turneth to Ramah, and to	Jos 19:29	*T.* he called hastily unto the young	J'g 9:54	*t.* will I do the part of a kinsman to	Ru 3:13
		T. the children of Ammon were	J'g 10:17	*T.* said she, Sit still, my daughter	Ru 3:18
		T. Jephthah fled from his brethren	J'g 11:3	*T.* went Boaz up to the gate, and sat	Ru 4:1

redeem it, *t.* tell me, that I may *Ru 4:4* know

T. said Boaz, What day thou *Ru 4:5* buyest

T. said Elkanah her husband *1Sa 1:8* to her

t. I will give him unto the *1Sa 1:11* Lord all the

T. Eli answered and said, Go *1Sa 1:17* in peace

be weaned, and *t.* I will bring *1Sa 1:22* him

t. take as much as thy soul *1Sa 2:16* desireth

t. he would answer him, Nay *1Sa 2:16*

T. Samuel answered, Speak; *1Sa 3:10* for thy

T. Eli called Samuel, and said *1Sa 3:16*

t. ye shall be healed, and it *1Sa 6:3* shall be

T. said they, What shall be the *1Sa 6:4*

t. do ye harden your hearts, as *1Sa 6:6*

t. he hath done us this great *1Sa 6:9* evil

t. we shall know that it is not *1Sa 6:9* his

t. put away the strange gods *1Sa 7:3*

T. the children of Israel did *1Sa 7:4* put away

T. Samuel took a stone, and *1Sa 7:12* set it

T. all the elders of Israel *1Sa 8:4* gathered

t. they passed through the land *1Sa 9:4* of

T. said Saul to his servant, But *1Sa 9:7*

T. said Saul to his servant, *1Sa 9:10* Well said

T. Saul drew near to Samuel *1Sa 9:18* in the

wherefore *t.* speakest thou so *1Sa 9:21* to me

T. Samuel took a vial of oil *1Sa 10:1*

t. thou shalt find two men by *1Sa 10:2* Rachel's

T. shalt thou go on forward *1Sa 10:3* from

t. the people said one to *1Sa 10:11* another

T. Samuel told the people *1Sa 10:25* the manner

T. Nahash the Ammonite *1Sa 11:1* came up

t. if there be no man to save *1Sa 11:3* us, we

T. came the messengers to *1Sa 11:4* Gibeah of

T. said Samuel to the *1Sa 11:14* people, Come

t. the Lord sent Moses and *1Sa 12:8* Aaron

t. shall both ye and also the *1Sa 12:14* king that

t. shall the hand of the Lord *1Sa 12:15* be

t. should ye go after vain *1Sa 12:21* things

t. the people did hide *1Sa 13:6* themselves in

T. said Jonathan, Behold, we *1Sa 14:8* will

Come up unto us; *t.* we will *1Sa 14:10* go up

T. said Saul unto the people *1Sa 14:17* that were

T. answered one of the *1Sa 14:28* people, and

T. said Jonathan, My father *1Sa 14:29* hath

T. they told Saul, saying, *1Sa 14:33* Behold, the

T. said the priest, Let us *1Sa 14:36* draw near

T. said he unto all Israel, Be *1Sa 14:40* ye on

T. Saul said to Jonathan, *1Sa 14:43* Tell me

T. Saul went up from *1Sa 14:46* following the

T. came the word of the *1Sa 15:10* Lord unto

What meaneth *t.* this *1Sa 15:14* bleating of

T. Samuel said unto Saul, *1Sa 15:16* Stay, and

Wherefore *t.* didst thou not *1Sa 15:19* obey the

T. he said, I have sinned: *1Sa 15:30* yet honour

T. said Samuel, Bring ye *1Sa 15:32* hither to

T. Samuel went to Ramah; *1Sa 15:34* and Saul

T. Jesse called Abindab, and *1Sa 16:8* made

T. Jesse made Shammah to *1Sa 16:9* pass by

T. Samuel took the horn of *1Sa 16:13* oil, and

T. answered one of the *1Sa 16:18* servants, and

kill me, *t.* will we be your *1Sa 17:9* servants

t. shall ye be our servants, *1Sa 17:9* and serve

T. said David to the *1Sa 17:45* Philistine, Thou

T. Jonathan and David made *1Sa 18:3*

T. the princes of the *1Sa 18:30* Philistines went

wherefore *t.* wilt thou sin *1Sa 19:5* against

T. went he also to Ramah, *1Sa 19:22* and came

T. said Jonathan unto David *1Sa 20:4*

t. say, David earnestly asked *1Sa 20:6* leave of

t. be sure that evil is *1Sa 20:7* determined by

upon thee, *t.* would not I tell *1Sa 20:9* it thee

T. said David to Jonathan, *1Sa 20:10* Who

I *t.* send not unto thee, and *1Sa 20:12* shew it

t. I will shew it thee, and *1Sa 20:13* send thee

T. Jonathan said to David, *1Sa 20:18* To

t. thou shalt go down *1Sa 20:19* quickly, and

t. come thou: for there is *1Sa 20:21* peace to

T. Saul's anger was kindled *1Sa 20:30* against

T. came David to Nob to *1Sa 21:1* Ahimelech

T. said Achish unto his *1Sa 21:14* servants, Lo

wherefore *t.* have ye brought *1Sa 21:14* him to

T. David departed, and came *1Sa 22:5* into the

T. Saul said unto his servants *1Sa 22:7* that

T. answered Doeg the *1Sa 22:9* Edomite

T. the king sent to call *1Sa 22:11* Ahimelech the

T. Ahimelech answered the *1Sa 22:14* king, and

I *t.* begin to enquire of God *1Sa 22:15* for

T. they told David, saying, *1Sa 23:1* Behold

how much more *t.* if we *1Sa 23:3* come to

T. David enquired of the *1Sa 23:4* Lord yet

T. said David, O Lord God *1Sa 23:10* of Israel

T. said David, Will the men *1Sa 23:12* of Keilah

T. David and his men, *1Sa 23:13* which were

T. came up the Ziphites to *1Sa 23:19* Saul to

T. Saul took three thousand *1Sa 24:2* chosen

T. David arose, and cut off *1Sa 24:4* the skirt

Shall I *t.* take my bread, and *1Sa 25:11*

T. Abigail made haste, and *1Sa 25:18* took two

my lord, *t.* remember thine *1Sa 25:31* handmaid

T. Saul arose, and went down *1Sa 26:2* to the

T. answered David and said *1Sa 26:6* to

T. said Abishai to David, *1Sa 26:8* God hath

T. David went over to the *1Sa 26:13* other side

T. Abner answered and said, *1Sa 26:14* Who art

wherefore *t.* hast thou not *1Sa 26:15* kept thy

T. said Saul, I have sinned: *1Sa 26:21* return

T. Saul said to David, *1Sa 26:25* Blessed be

T. Adhish gave him Ziklag *1Sa 27:6* that day

T. said Saul unto his *1Sa 28:7* servants, Seek

wherefore *t.* layest thou a *1Sa 28:9* snare for

T. said the woman, Whom *1Sa 28:11* shall I

T. said Samuel, Wherefore *1Sa 28:16*

Wherefore *t.* dost thou ask *1Sa 28:16* of me

T. Saul fell straightway all *1Sa 28:20* along on

T. they rose up, and went *1Sa 28:25* away that

T. said the princes of the *1Sa 29:3* Philistines

T. Achish called David, and *1Sa 29:6* said unto

T. David and the people that *1Sa 30:4* were

T. answered all the wicked *1Sa 30:22* men and

T. said David, Ye shall not *1Sa 30:23* do so, my

T. said Saul unto his *1Sa 31:4* armourbearer

T. David took hold on his *2Sa 1:11* clothes

T. there arose and went over *2Sa 2:15*

T. Abner looked behind him *2Sa 2:20*

how *t.* should I hold up my *2Sa 2:22* face to

T. Abner called to Joab, and *2Sa 2:26* said

how long shall it be *t.* ere *2Sa 2:26* thou bid the

surely *t.* in the morning the *2Sa 2:27* people

T. was Abner very wroth for *2Sa 3:8*

T. said Abner unto him, Go, *2Sa 3:16* return

Now *t.* do it: for the Lord *2Sa 3:18* hath

T. Joab came to the king, *2Sa 3:24* and said

T. came all the tribes of Israel *2Sa 5:1* to

that *t.* thou shalt bestir *2Sa 5:24* thyself

t. shall the Lord go out *2Sa 5:24* before thee

T. David returned to bless *2Sa 6:20* his

T. went king David in, and *2Sa 7:18* sat before

T. David put garrisons in *2Sa 8:6* Syria of

T. Toi sent Joram his son *2Sa 8:10* unto king

T. king David sent, and *2Sa 9:5* fetched him

T. the king called to Ziba, *2Sa 9:9* Saul's

T. said Ziba unto the king, *2Sa 9:11* According

T. said David, I will shew *2Sa 10:2* kindness

your beards be grown, and *t.* *2Sa 10:5* return

strong for me, *t.* thou shalt *2Sa 10:11* help me

for thee, *t.* I will come and *2Sa 10:11* help thee

t. fled, they also before *2Sa 10:14* Abishai, and

why *t.* didst thou not go *2Sa 11:10* down unto

shall I *t.* go into mine *2Sa 11:11* house, to eat

T. Joab sent and told David *2Sa 11:18* all the

t. say thou, Thy servant *2Sa 11:21* Uriah the

T. David said unto the *2Sa 11:25* messenger

how will he *t.* vex himself, *2Sa 12:18* if we tell

T. David arose from the *2Sa 12:20* earth, and

t. he came to his own house *2Sa 12:20*

T. said his servants unto *2Sa 12:21* him, What

T. David sent home to *2Sa 13:7* Tamar, saying

T. Amnon hated her   *2Sa 13:15*
exceedingly; so
T. he called his servant that   *2Sa 13:17*
T. his servant brought her   *2Sa 13:18*
out, and
T. said Absalom, If not, I   *2Sa 13:26*
pray thee
Smite Amnon; *t.* kill him,   *2Sa 13:28*
fear not
T. all the king's sons arose   *2Sa 13:29*
T. the king arose, and tare   *2Sa 13:31*
his
T. said she, I pray thee, let   *2Sa 14:11*
the king
T. the woman said, Let   *2Sa 14:12*
thine
Wherefore *t.* hast thou   *2Sa 14:13*
thought
T. thine handmaid said, The   *2Sa 14:17*
word of
T. the king answered and   *2Sa 14:18*
said unto
T. Joab arose, and came to   *2Sa 14:31*
Absalom
t. Absalom called unto him,   *2Sa 15:2*
the Lord
to Jerusalem, *t.* I will serve   *2Sa 15:8*
the Lord
t. ye shall say, Absalom   *2Sa 15:10*
reigneth in
T. said the king to Ittai the   *2Sa 15:19*
Gittite
t. thou shall be a burden   *2Sa 15:33*
unto me
t. mayest thou for me defeat   *2Sa 15:34*
T. said the king to Ziba,   *2Sa 16:4*
Behold
T. said Abishai the son of   *2Sa 16:9*
Zeruiah
Who shall *t.* say, Wherefore   *2Sa 16:10*
hast thou
T. said Absalom to   *2Sa 16:20*
Ahithophel,
t. shall the hands of all that   *2Sa 16:21*
are with
T. said Absalom, Call now   *2Sa 17:5*
Hushai the
t. shall all Israel bring   *2Sa 17:13*
ropes to that
T. said Hushai unto Zadok   *2Sa 17:15*
and to
T. David arose, and all the   *2Sa 17:22*
people that
T. David came to   *2Sa 17:24*
Mahanaim. And
T. said Joab, I may not   *2Sa 18:14*
tarry thus
T. said Ahimaaz the son of   *2Sa 18:19;*
Zadok   *18:22*
T. said Joab to Cushi, Go   *2Sa 18:21*
tell the
T. Ahimaaz ran by the way   *2Sa 18:23*
of the
this day, *t.* it had pleased   *2Sa 19:6*
thee well
T. the king arose, and sat in   *2Sa 19:8*
the gate
wherefore *t.* are ye the last   *2Sa 19:12*
to bring
wherefore *t.* should thy   *2Sa 19:35*
servant be
T. the king went on to   *2Sa 19:40*
Gilgal, and
wherefore *t.* be ye angry for   *2Sa 19:42*
this
why *t.* did ye despise us,   *2Sa 19:43*
that our
T. said the king to Amasa,   *2Sa 20:4*
Assemble
T. cried a wise woman out   *2Sa 20:16*
of the
T. she said unto him, Hear   *2Sa 20:17*
the words
T. she spake, saying, They   *2Sa 20:18*
were wont
T. the woman went unto all   *2Sa 20:22*
T. there was a famine in the   *2Sa 21:1*
days of
T. the men of David sware   *2Sa 21:17*
unto
T. Sibbechai the Hushathite   *2Sa 21:18*
slew
T. the earth shook and   *2Sa 22:8*
trembled
T. did I beat them as small   *2Sa 22:43*
as the
And David was *t.* in an   *2Sa 23:14*
hold, and
the Philistines was *t.* in   *2Sa 23:14*
Beth-lehem

T. they came to Gilead, and   *2Sa 24:6*
to the
T. Adonijah the son of   *1Ki 1:5*
Haggith
throne? why *t.* doth Adonijah   *1Ki 1:13*
reign
T. king David answered and   *1Ki 1:28*
said
T. Bath-sheba bowed with   *1Ki 1:31*
her face to
T. ye shall come up after   *1Ki 1:35*
him, that he
T. sat Solomon upon the   *1Ki 2:12*
throne of
T. she said, I desire one   *1Ki 2:20*
small petition
T. king Solomon sware by   *1Ki 2:23*
the Lord
T. tidings came to Joab: for   *1Ki 2:28*
Joab had
T. Solomon sent Benaiah the   *1Ki 2:29*
son of
Why *t.* hast thou not kept the   *1Ki 2:43*
oath of
did walk, *t.* I will lengthen   *1Ki 3:14*
thy days
T. came there two women   *1Ki 3:16*
T. said the king, The one   *1Ki 3:23*
saith, This
T. spake the woman whose   *1Ki 3:26*
the living
T. the king answered and   *1Ki 3:27*
said, Give
t. he built chambers against   *1Ki 6:10*
all the
t. will I perform my word   *1Ki 6:12*
with thee
T. he made a porch for the   *1Ki 7:7*
throne
T. made he ten lavers of   *1Ki 7:38*
brass: one
T. Solomon assembled the   *1Ki 8:1*
elders
T. spake Solomon, The Lord   *1Ki 8:12*
said
T. hear thou in heaven, and   *1Ki 8:32*
do, and
T. hear thou in heaven, and   *1Ki 8:34;*
          8:36
T. hear thou in heaven thy   *1Ki 8:39*
T. hear thou in heaven their   *1Ki 8:45*
prayer
T. hear thou their prayer and   *1Ki 8:49*
their
T. I will establish the throne   *1Ki 9:5*
of thy
T. will I cut off Israel out of   *1Ki 9:7*
the land
that *t.* king Solomon gave   *1Ki 9:11*
Hiram
built for her: *t.* did he build   *1Ki 9:24*
Millo
T. did Solomon build an high   *1Ki 11:7*
place
T. Pharaoh said unto him,   *1Ki 11:22*
But what
for three days, *t.* come again   *1Ki 12:5*
to me
t. they will be thy servants   *1Ki 12:7*
for ever
T. king Rehoboam sent   *1Ki 12:18*
Adoram who
T. Jeroboam built Shechem   *1Ki 12:25*
in mount
t. shall the heart of this   *1Ki 12:27*
people turn
T. he said unto him, Come   *1Ki 13:15*
home with
t. bury me in the sepulchre   *1Ki 13:31*
wherein
T. Asa took all the silver   *1Ki 15:18*
and the gold
T. king Asa made a   *1Ki 15:22*
proclamation
T. the word of the Lord came   *1Ki 16:1*
to Jehu
T. were the people of Israel   *1Ki 16:21*
follow him: but if Baal, *t.*   *1Ki 18:21*
follow him
T. said Elijah unto the   *1Ki 18:22*
people, I, even
T. the fire of the Lord fell   *1Ki 18:38*
T. Jezebel sent a messenger   *1Ki 19:2*
unto
behold, *t.* an angel touched   *1Ki 19:5*
him, and
my mother, and *t.* I will   *1Ki 19:20*
follow thee
T. he arose, and went after   *1Ki 19:21*
Elijah

T. the king of Israel called all   *1Ki 20:7*
T. he said, Who shall order   *1Ki 20:14*
T. he numbered the young   *1Ki 20:15*
men of the
T. he said, Go ye, bring him   *1Ki 20:33*
T. Ben-hadad came forth to   *1Ki 20:33*
him; and
T. said Ahab, I will send   *1Ki 20:34*
thee away
T. said he unto him,   *1Ki 20:36*
Because thou
T. he found another man,   *1Ki 20:37*
and said
t. shall thy life be for his   *1Ki 20:39*
life, or else
t. carry him out, and stone   *1Ki 21:10*
him, that
T. they carried him forth   *1Ki 21:13*
out of the
T. they sent to Jezebel,   *1Ki 21:14*
saying
T. the king of Israel gathered   *1Ki 22:6*
T. the king of Israel called   *1Ki 22:9*
There was *t.* no king in   *1Ki 22:47*
Edom: a
T. said Ahaziah the son of   *1Ki 22:49*
Ahab
T. Moab rebelled against   *2Ki 1:1*
Israel after
T. the king sent unto him a   *2Ki 1:9*
captain of
let fire come down from   *2Ki 1:10*
heaven
T. he took his eldest son that   *2Ki 3:27*
should
T. he said, Go, borrow the   *2Ki 4:3*
vessels
T. she came and told the man   *2Ki 4:7*
of God
he said, What *t.* is to be done   *2Ki 4:14*
for her
sat on her knees till noon,   *2Ki 4:20*
and *t.* died
T. she saddled an ass, and   *2Ki 4:24*
said to her
T. she said, Did I desire a   *2Ki 4:28*
son of my
T. he said to Gehazi, Gird up   *2Ki 4:29*
thy
T. he returned, and walked   *2Ki 4:35*
in the
T. she went in, and fell at his   *2Ki 4:37*
feet
But he said, *T.* bring meal   *2Ki 4:41*
how much rather *t.* when he   *2Ki 5:13*
saith to
T. went he down, and dipped   *2Ki 5:14*
himself
Shall there not *t.* I pray thee,   *2Ki 5:17*
be
T. the king of Syria warred   *2Ki 6:8*
against
T. he said, God do so and   *2Ki 6:31*
more also to
T. Elisha said, Hear ye the   *2Ki 7:1*
word of
T. a lord on whose hand the   *2Ki 7:2*
king
t. the famine is in the city,   *2Ki 7:4*
and we
T. they said one to another,   *2Ki 7:9*
We do
T. spake Elisha unto the   *2Ki 8:1*
woman
Jehoshaphat being *t.* king of   *2Ki 8:16*
Judah
T. Libnah revolted at the   *2Ki 8:22*
same
T. take the box of oil, and   *2Ki 9:3*
pour it on
T. open the door, and flee,   *2Ki 9:3*
and tarry
T. Jehu came forth to the   *2Ki 9:11*
servants of
T. they hasted, and took   *2Ki 9:13*
every man
t. let none go forth nor   *2Ki 9:15*
escape out of
T. he sent out a second on   *2Ki 9:19*
horseback
T. said Jehu to Bidkar his   *2Ki 9:25*
captain
before him: how *t.* shall we   *2Ki 10:4*
stand
T. he wrote a letter the   *2Ki 10:6*
second time
T. king Jehoash called for   *2Ki 12:7*
Jehoiada

T. Hazael king of Syria went up   2Ki 12:17
T. Elisha said, Shoot. And he shot   2Ki 13:17
t. hadst thou smitten Syria till thou   2Ki 13:19
T. Amaziah sent messengers   2Ki 14:8
T. Menahem smote Tiphsah   2Ki 15:16
T. Rezin king of Syria, and Pekah   2Ki 16:5
T. the king of Assyria came up   2Ki 17:5
T. the king of Assyria commanded   2Ki 17:27
T. one of the priests whom they had   2Ki 18:24
How t. wilt thou turn away the face of   2Ki 18:24
T. said Eliakim the son of Hilkiah   2Ki 18:26
T. Rab-shakeh stood and cried with a   2Ki 18:28
t. eat ye every man of his own vine   2Ki 18:31
T. came Eliakim the son of Hilkiah   2Ki 18:37
T. Isaiah the son of Amoz sent to   2Ki 19:20
T. he turned his face to the wall, and   2Ki 20:2
T. came Isaiah the prophet unto king   2Ki 20:14
T. said Hezekiah unto Isaiah, Good is   2Ki 20:19
T. he said, What title is that that I see   2Ki 23:17
t. he turned and rebelled against him   2Ki 24:1
t. Kedar, and Adbeel, and Mibsam   1Ch 1:29
t. Abiah Hezron's wife bare him   1Ch 2:24
t. they waited on their office according   1Ch 6:32
And his firstborn son Abdon, t. Zur   1Ch 9:36
T. said Saul to his armourbearer   1Ch 10:4
t. they forsook their cities, and fled   1Ch 10:7
T. all Israel gathered themselves to   1Ch 11:1
And David was t. in the hold, and   1Ch 11:16
garrison was t. at Beth-lehem   1Ch 11:16
The chief was Ahiezer, t. Joash, the   1Ch 12:3
T. the spirit came upon Amasai, who   1Ch 12:18
T. David received them, and made   1Ch 12:18
T. David said, God hath broken in   1Ch 14:11
that t. thou shalt go out to battle   1Ch 14:15
T. David said, None ought to carry   1Ch 15:2
T. on that day David delivered first   1Ch 16:7
T. shall the trees of the wood sing   1Ch 16:33
T. Nathan said unto David, Do all   1Ch 17:2
T. David put garrisons in   1Ch 18:6
T. there went certain, and told David   1Ch 19:5
your beards be grown, and t. return   1Ch 19:5
strong for me, t. thou shalt help me   1Ch 19:12
strong for thee, t. I will help thee   1Ch 19:12
city. T. Joab came to Jerusalem   1Ch 19:15
why t. doth my lord require this   1Ch 21:3
T. David and the elders of Israel, who   1Ch 21:16
T. the angel of the Lord commanded   1Ch 21:18
T. David said to Ornan, Grant me the   1Ch 21:22
the Jebusite, t. he sacrificed there   1Ch 21:28
T. David said, This is the house of   1Ch 22:1
T. he called for Solomon his son, and   1Ch 22:6

T. shalt thou prosper, if thou   1Ch 22:13
T. for Zechariah his son, a wise   1Ch 26:14
T. David the king stood up upon his   1Ch 28:2
T. David gave to Solomon his son the   1Ch 28:11
And who t. is willing to consecrate his   1Ch 29:5
T. the chief of the fathers and princes   1Ch 29:6
T. the people rejoiced, for that they   1Ch 29:9
T. Solomon sat on the throne of the   1Ch 29:23
T. Solomon spake unto all Israel, to   2Ch 1:2
T. Solomon came from his journey to   2Ch 1:13
who am I t. that I should build him a   2Ch 2:6
T. Huram the king of Tyre answered   2Ch 2:11
T. Solomon began to build the house   2Ch 3:1
T. Solomon assembled the elders   2Ch 5:2
and did not t. wait by course   2Ch 5:11
t. the house was filled with a cloud   2Ch 5:13
T. said Solomon, The Lord hath   2Ch 6:1
Now t. O Lord God of Israel, let thy   2Ch 6:17
T. hear thou from heaven, and do   2Ch 6:23
T. hear thou from the heavens, and   2Ch 6:25
T. hear thou from heaven, and forgive   2Ch 6:27
T. what prayer or what supplication   2Ch 6:29
T. hear thou from heaven thy   2Ch 6:30
T. hear thou from the heavens, even   2Ch 6:33; 6:39
T. hear thou from the heavens their   2Ch 6:35
T. the king and all the people offered   2Ch 7:4
t. will I hear from heaven, and will   2Ch 7:14
T. will I stablish the throne of thy   2Ch 7:18
T. will I pluck them up by the roots   2Ch 7:20
T. Solomon offered burnt offerings   2Ch 8:12
T. went Solomon to Ezion-geber   2Ch 8:17
T. king Rehoboam sent Hadoram that   2Ch 10:18
T. came Shemaiah the prophet to   2Ch 12:5
T. the men of Judah gave a   2Ch 13:15
T. Asa went out against him   2Ch 14:10
T. Asa brought out silver and gold   2Ch 16:2
T. Asa the king took all Judah; and   2Ch 16:6
T. Asa was wroth with the seer, and   2Ch 16:10
T. he said, I did see all Israel   2Ch 18:16
T. there came out a spirit, and stood   2Ch 18:20
T. Zedekiah that son of Chenaanah   2Ch 18:23
T. the king of Israel said, Take ye   2Ch 18:25
t. hath not the Lord spoken by me   2Ch 18:27
T. there came some that told   2Ch 20:2
affliction, t. thou wilt hear and help   2Ch 20:9
T. upon Jahaziel the son of   2Ch 20:14
T. they returned, every man of Judah   2Ch 20:27
T. Eliezer the son of Dodavah of   2Ch 20:37
T. Jehoram went forth with his   2Ch 21:9
T. they brought out the king's son   2Ch 23:11
T. Athaliah rent her clothes, and said   2Ch 23:13
T. Jehoiada the priest brought out   2Ch 23:14

T. all the people went to the house of   2Ch 23:17
T. the king hearkened unto them   2Ch 24:17
T. Amaziah separated them, to wit   2Ch 25:10
T. the prophet forbare, and said, I   2Ch 25:16
T. Amaziah king of Judah took   2Ch 25:17
T. all the people of Judah took   2Ch 26:1
T. Uzziah was wroth, and had a   2Ch 26:19
T. certain of the heads of the children   2Ch 28:12
brethren: t. they returned to Samaria   2Ch 28:15
T. the Levites arose, Mahath the son   2Ch 29:12
T. they went in to Hezekiah the king   2Ch 29:18
T. Hezekiah the king rose early, and   2Ch 29:20
T. Hezekiah answered and said, Now   2Ch 29:31
T. they killed the passover on the   2Ch 30:15
T. the priests the Levites arose and   2Ch 30:27
T. all the children of Israel returned   2Ch 31:1
T. Hezekiah questioned with   2Ch 31:9
T. Hezekiah commanded to prepare   2Ch 31:11
T. they cried with a loud voice in the   2Ch 32:18
T. Manasseh knew that the Lord he   2Ch 33:13
T. Shaphan the scribe told the king   2Ch 34:18
T. the king sent and gathered   2Ch 34:29
T. the people of the land took   2Ch 36:1
T. rose up the chief of the fathers of   Ezr 1:5
T. stood up Jeshua the son of   Ezr 3:2
T. stood Jeshua with his sons and his   Ezr 3:9
T. they came to Zerubbabel, and to   Ezr 4:2
T. the people of the land weakened   Ezr 4:4
T. wrote Rehum the chancellor   Ezr 4:9
t. will they not pay toll, tribute, and   Ezr 4:13
T. sent the king an answer unto   Ezr 4:17
T. ceased the work of the house of   Ezr 4:24
T. the prophets, Haggai the prophet   Ezr 5:1
T. rose up Zerubbabel the son of   Ezr 5:2
T. said we unto them after this   Ezr 5:4
t. they returned answer by letter   Ezr 5:5
T. asked we those elders, and said   Ezr 5:9
T. came the same Sheshbazzar, and   Ezr 5:16
T. Darius the king made a decree   Ezr 6:1
T. Tatnai, governor on this side the   Ezr 6:13
T. sent I for Eliezer, for Ariel, for   Ezr 8:16
T. I proclaimed a fast there, at the   Ezr 8:21
T. I separated twelve of the chief of   Ezr 8:24
T. we departed from the river   Ezr 8:31
T. were assembled unto me every one   Ezr 9:4
T. arose Ezra, and made the chief   Ezr 10:5
T. Ezra rose up from before   Ezr 10:6
T. all the men of Judah and   Ezr 10:9
T. all the congregation answered and   Ezr 10:12
of heart. T. I was very sore afraid   Ne 2:2
T. the king said unto me, For what   Ne 2:4
T. I came to the governors beyond the   Ne 2:9
T. I went on to the gate of   Ne 2:14
T. went I up in the night by   Ne 2:15
T. said I unto them, Ye see   Ne 2:17

T. I told them of the hand of *Ne 2:18*
my God
T. answered I them, and said *Ne 2:20*
unto
T. Eliashib the high priest rose *Ne 3:1*
up
to be stopped, *t.* they were *Ne 4:7*
very wroth
T. I consulted with myself, and *Ne 5:7*
T. held they their peace, and *Ne 5:8*
found
T. said they, We will restore *Ne 5:12*
them and
T. I called the priests, and *Ne 5:12*
took an
T. sent Sanballat his servant *Ne 6:5*
unto me
T. I sent unto him, saying, *Ne 6:8*
There are
T. he said unto them, Go your *Ne 8:10*
way
T. stood up upon the stairs, of *Ne 9:4*
T. the Levites, Jeshua, and *Ne 9:5*
Kadmiel
T. I brought up the princes *Ne 12:31*
of Judah
T. I commanded, and they *Ne 13:9*
cleansed
T. contented I with the *Ne 13:11*
rulers, and
T. brought all Judah the tithe *Ne 13:12*
of the
T. I contended with the *Ne 13:17*
nobles of
T. I testified against them, *Ne 13:21*
and said
Shall we *t.* hearken unto you *Ne 13:27*
to do all
T. the king said to the wise *Es 1:13*
men
T. said the king's servants that *Es 2:2*
T. thus came every maiden *Es 2:13*
unto
T. the king made a great feast *Es 2:18*
unto
t. Mordecai sat in the king's *Es 2:19*
gate
T. the king's servants, which *Es 3:3*
were in
reverence, *t.* was Haman full of *Es 3:5*
wrath
T. were the king's scribes *Es 3:12*
called on
T. was the queen exceedingly *Es 4:4*
grieved
T. called Esther for Hatach, *Es 4:5*
one of the
T. Mordecai commanded to *Es 4:13*
answer
t. shall there enlargement and *Es 4:14*
T. Esther bade them return *Es 4:15*
Mordecai
T. said the king unto her. What *Es 5:3*
wilt
T. the king said, Cause Haman *Es 5:5*
T. answered Esther, and said, *Es 5:7*
My
T. went Haman forth that day *Es 5:9*
joyful
T. said Zeresh his wife and all *Es 5:14*
his
t. go thou in merrily with the *Es 5:14*
king
T. said the king's servants that *Es 6:3*
T. the king said to Haman, *Es 6:10*
Make
T. took Haman the apparel *Es 6:11*
and the
T. said his wise men and *Es 6:13*
Zeresh his
T. Esther the queen answered *Es 7:3*
T. the king Ahasuerus said *Es 7:5*
T. Haman was afraid before the *Es 7:6*
king
T. the king returned out of the *Es 7:8*
palace
T. said the king, Will he force *Es 7:8*
T. the king said, Hang him *Es 7:9*
thereon
T. was the king's wrath *Es 7:10*
pacified
T. the king held out the golden *Es 8:4*
T. the king Ahasuerus said unto *Es 8:7*
T. were the king's scribes called *Es 8:9*
T. said Esther, If it please the *Es 9:13*
king
T. Esther the queen, the *Es 9:29*
daughter of
T. Satan answered the Lord *Job 1:7;*
1:9

T. Job arose, and rent his *Job 1:20*
mantle, and
T. said his wife unto him, *Job 2:9*
Dost thou
have slept: *t.* had I been at *Job 3:13*
rest
T. Eliphaz the Temanite *Job 4:1*
answered
T. a spirit passed before my *Job 4:15*
face; the
T. should I yet have comfort; *Job 6:10*
yea, I
T. thou scarest me with *Job 7:14*
dreams, and
T. answered Bildad the *Job 8:1*
Shuhite, and
t. it shall deny him, saying, I *Job 8:18*
have not
T. Job answered and said *Job 9:1*
If I be wicked, why *t.* labour *Job 9:29*
I in vain
T. would I speak, and not *Job 9:35*
fear him
If I sin, *t.* thou markest me, *Job 10:14*
and thou
Wherefore *t.* hast thou *Job 10:18*
brought me
cease *t.* and let me alone, *Job 10:20*
that I may
T. answered Zophar the *Job 11:1;*
Naamathite *11:1*
or gather together, *t.* who *Job 11:10*
can hinder
also: will he not *t.* consider *Job 11:11*
T. shalt thou lift up thy *Job 11:15*
face
t. will I not hide myself *Job 13:20*
from thee
T. call thou, and I will *Job 13:22*
answer: or let
T. answered Eliphaz the *Job 15:1*
Temanite
T. Job answered and said *Job 16:1*
t. I shall go the way whence *Job 16:22*
I shall
T. answered Bildad the *Job 18:1;*
Shuhite, and *25:1*
T. Job answered and said *Job 19:1*
How *t.* comfort ye me in *Job 21:34*
vain, seeing
T. Eliphaz the Temanite *Job 22:1*
answered
T. shalt thou lay up gold as *Job 22:24*
dust, and
For *t.* shalt thou have thy *Job 22:26*
delight
t. thou shalt say, There is *Job 22:29*
lifting up
T. Job answered and said *Job 23:1*
How *t.* can man be justified *Job 25:4*
with God
it; why *t.* are ye thus *Job 27:12*
altogether vain
Whence *t.* cometh wisdom? *Job 28:20*
and where
T. did he see it, and declare *Job 28:27*
it; he
the ear heard me, *t.* it *Job 29:11*
blessed me
T. I said, I shall die in my *Job 29:18*
nest. and I
looked for good, *t.* evil *Job 30:26*
came unto me
why *t.* should I think upon a *Job 31:1*
maid
T. let me sow, and let *Job 31:8*
another eat
T. let my wife grind unto *Job 31:10*
another, and
What *t.* shall I do when God *Job 31:14*
riseth up
T. let mine arm fall from *Job 31:32*
my shoulder
T. was kindled the wrath of *Job 32:2*
Elihu the
three men, *t.* his wrath was *Job 32:5*
kindled
T. he openeth the ears of *Job 33:16*
men, and
T. he is gracious unto him, *Job 33:24*
and saith
quietness who *t.* can make *Job 34:29*
trouble
hideth his face, who *t.* can *Job 34:29*
behold him
T. he sheweth them their *Job 36:9*
work, and
t. a great ransom cannot *Job 36:18*
deliver thee

T. the beasts go into dens *Job 37:8*
T. the Lord answered Job out *Job 38:1*
of the
thou it, because thou wast *t.* *Job 38:21*
born
T. Job answered the Lord, *Job 40:3;*
and said *42:1*
T. answered the Lord unto *Job 40:6*
Job out of
T. will I also confess unto *Job 40:14*
thee that
up: who *t.* is able to stand *Job 41:10*
before me
T. came there unto him all *Job 42:11*
his
T. shall he speak unto them in *Ps 2:5*
his
T. the earth shook and *Ps 18:7*
trembled; the
T. the channels of waters *Ps 18:15*
were seen
T. did I beat them small *Ps 18:42*
as the dust
t. shall I be upright, and I *Ps 19:13*
shall be
forsake me, *t.* the Lord will *Ps 27:10*
take me
burned: *t.* spake I with my *Ps 39:3*
tongue
T. said I, Lo, I come: in the *Ps 40:7*
volume
T. will I go unto the altar of *Ps 43:4*
God
a thief, *t.* thou consentedst *Ps 50:18*
with him
T. will I teach transgressors *Ps 51:13*
thy ways
T. shalt thou be pleased with *Ps 51:19*
t. shall they offer bullocks *Ps 51:19*
upon
for *t.* would I fly away, and be *Ps 55:6*
at rest
Lo, *t.* would I wander far off *Ps 55:7*
me; *t.* I could have borne it *Ps 55:12*
t. I would have hid myself *Ps 55:12*
from him
t. shall mine enemies turn back *Ps 56:9*
T. shall the earth yield her *Ps 67:6*
increase
t. I restored that which I took *Ps 69:4*
not
of God; *t.* understood I their *Ps 73:17*
end
he slew them, *t.* they sought *Ps 78:34*
him
T. the Lord awaked as one *Ps 78:65*
out of
Why hast thou *t.* broken *Ps 80:12*
down her
T. thou spakest in vision to *Ps 89:19*
thy
T. will I visit their *Ps 89:32*
transgression
t. shall all the trees of the *Ps 96:12*
wood
T. believed they his words; *Ps 106:12*
they sang
T. stood up Phinehas, and *Ps 106:30*
executed
T. they cried unto the Lord *Ps 107:6;*
in *107:13*
T. they cry unto the Lord in *Ps 107:19;*
107:28
T. are they glad because *Ps 107:30*
they be quiet
T. called I upon the name of *Ps 116:4*
the Lord
T. shall I not be ashamed, *Ps 119:6*
when I
I should *t.* have perished in *Ps 119:92*
mine
T. they had swallowed us up *Ps 124:3*
quick
T. the waters had *Ps 124:4*
overwhelmed us
T. the proud waters had gone *Ps 124:5*
over
T. was our mouth filled with *Ps 126:2*
t. said they among the *Ps 126:2*
heathen
within me, *t.* thou knewest *Ps 142:3*
my path
T. shall they call upon me, but *Pr 1:28*
T. shalt thou understand the *Pr 2:5*
fear
T. shalt thou understand *Pr 2:9*
T. shalt thou walk in thy way *Pr 3:23*
safely
T. I was by him, as one *Pr 8:30*
brought up

When pride cometh, *t.* cometh shame   *Pr 11:2*
how much more *t.* the hearts of the   *Pr 15:11*
cometh, *t.* cometh also contempt   *Pr 18:3*
he is gone his way, *t.* he boastest   *Pr 20:14*
how can a man *t.* understand his own   *Pr 20:24*
found it, *t.* there shall be a reward,   *Pr 24:14*
T. I saw, and considered it well: I   *Pr 24:32*
T. I looked on all the works that my   *Ec 2:11*
T. I saw that wisdom excelleth folly   *Ec 2:13*
T. said I in my heart, As it happeneth   *Ec 2:15*
to me; and why was I *t.* more wise   *Ec 2:15*
T. I said in my heart, that this also is   *Ec 2:15*
T. I returned, and I saw vanity under   *Ec 4:7*
if two lie together, *t.* they have heat   *Ec 4:11*
T. I commended mirth, because a man   *Ec 8:15*
T. I beheld all the work of God, that a   *Ec 8:17*
T. said I, Wisdom is better than   *Ec 9:16*
edge, *t.* must he put to more strength   *Ec 10:10*
T. shall the dust return to the earth   *Ec 12:7*
t. was I in his eyes as one that found   *Ca 8:10*
T. shall the lambs feed after their   *Isa 5:17*
T. said I, Woe is me! for I am undone   *Isa 6:5*
T. flew one of the seraphims unto me   *Isa 6:6*
T. said I, Here am I: send me   *Isa 6:8*
T. said I, Lord, how long? And he   *Isa 6:11*
T. said the Lord unto Isaiah, Go forth   *Isa 7:3*
T. said the Lord to me, Call his name   *Isa 8:3*
t. shall his yoke depart from off them   *Isa 14:25*
shall one *t.* answer the messengers of   *Isa 14:32*
T. the moon shall be confounded, and   *Isa 24:23*
t. ye shall be trodden down by it   *Isa 28:18*
T. shall he give the rain of thy seed   *Isa 30:23*
T. shall the Assyrian fall with   *Isa 31:8*
T. judgment shall dwell in   *Isa 32:16*
t. is the prey of a great spoil   *Isa 33:23*
T. the eyes of the blind shall be   *Isa 35:5*
T. shall the lame man leap as   *Isa 35:6*
T. came forth unto him Eliakim   *Isa 36:3*
How *t.* wilt thou turn away the face of   *Isa 36:9*
T. said Eliakim and Shebna and Joah   *Isa 36:11*
T. Rabshakeh stood, and cried with a   *Isa 36:13*
T. came Eliakim, the son of Hilkiah   *Isa 36:22*
T. Isaiah the son of Amoz sent unto   *Isa 37:21*
T. the angel of the Lord went forth   *Isa 37:36*
T. Hezekiah turned his face toward   *Isa 38:2*
T. came the word of the Lord to   *Isa 38:4*
T. came Isaiah the prophet unto king   *Isa 39:3*
T. said he, What have they seen in   *Isa 39:4*
T. said Isaiah to Hezekiah, Hear the   *Isa 39:5*
T. said Hezekiah to Isaiah, Good is   *Isa 39:8*
To whom *t.* will ye liken God? or what   *Isa 40:18*
To whom *t.* will he liken me, or shall I   *Isa 40:25*

them come near; *t.* let them speak   *Isa 41:1*
T. shall it be for a man to burn: for he   *Isa 44:15*
t. had thy peace been as a river, and   *Isa 48:18*
T. I said, I have laboured in vain, I   *Isa 49:4*
T. shalt thou say in thine heart, Who   *Isa 49:21*
T. shall thy light break forth as   *Isa 58:8*
T. shalt thou call, and the Lord   *Isa 58:9*
t. shall thy light rise in obscurity   *Isa 58:10*
T. shalt thou delight thyself in the   *Isa 58:14*
T. thou shalt see, and flow together   *Isa 60:5*
T. he remembered the days of old   *Isa 63:11*
t. shall ye suck, ye shall be borne   *Isa 66:12*
T. the word of the Lord came   *Jer 1:4;*
unto   *18:5; 28:12; 29:30; 32:26; 35:12;*
  36:27; 37:6; 43:8; Eze 20:2; 33:23
T. said I, Ah, Lord God!   *Jer 1:6;*
behold, I   *14:13*
T. the Lord put forth his hand   *Jer 1:9*
T. said the Lord unto me,   *Jer 1:12*
Thou hast
T. the Lord said unto me, Out   *Jer 1:14*
of the
how *t.* art thou turned into   *Jer 2:21*
of my sight, *t.* shalt thou not   *Jer 4:1*
remove
T. said I, Ah, Lord God! surely thou   *Jer 4:10*
to the full, they *t.* committed adultery   *Jer 5:7*
T. shalt thou answer them, Like as ye   *Jer 5:19*
T. will I cause you to dwell in this   *Jer 7:7*
T. will I cause to cease from the cities   *Jer 7:34*
Why *t.* is this people of Jerusalem   *Jer 8:5*
why *t.* is not the health of   *Jer 8:22*
T. answered I, and said, So be it. O   *Jer 11:5*
T. the Lord said unto me, Proclaim all   *Jer 11:6*
T. shall the cities of Judah   *Jer 11:12*
thou doest evil, *t.* thou rejoicest   *Jer 11:15*
t. thou shewedst me their doings   *Jer 11:18*
t. how canst thou contend with horses   *Jer 12:5*
t. how wilt thou do in the swelling of   *Jer 12:5*
t. shall they be built in the midst of my   *Jer 12:16*
T. I went to Euphrates, and digged   *Jer 13:7*
T. the word of the Lord came unto   *Jer 13:8*
T. shalt thou say unto them,   *Jer 13:13;*
Thus   *25:28*
t. may ye also do good, that are   *Jer 13:23*
T. said the Lord unto me, Pray not   *Jer 14:11*
T. the Lord said unto me, The   *Jer 14:14*
t. behold the slain with the sword   *Jer 14:18*
t. behold them that are sick with   *Jer 14:18*
T. said the Lord unto me, Though   *Jer 15:1*
t. thou shalt tell them, Thus saith   *Jer 15:2*
thou return, *t.* will I bring thee again   *Jer 15:19*
T. shalt thou say unto them, Because   *Jer 16:11*
T. shall there enter into the gates of   *Jer 17:25*
t. will I kindle a fire in the gates   *Jer 17:27*
T. I went down to the potter's house   *Jer 18:3*
t. I will repent of the good, wherewith   *Jer 18:10*
T. said they, Come, and let us devise   *Jer 18:18*

T. shalt thou break the bottle in the   *Jer 19:10*
T. came Jeremiah from Tophet   *Jer 19:14*
T. Pashur smote Jeremiah the   *Jer 20:2*
T. said Jeremiah unto him, The Lord   *Jer 20:3*
T. I said, I will not mention of him   *Jer 20:9*
T. said Jeremiah unto them, Thus   *Jer 21:3*
t. shall there enter in by the gates of   *Jer 22:4*
T. they shall answer, Because they   *Jer 22:9*
justice, and *t.* it was well with him   *Jer 22:15*
and needy; *t.* it was well with him   *Jer 22:16*
surely *t.* shalt thou be ashamed and   *Jer 22:22*
t. they should have turned them from   *Jer 23:22*
thou shalt *t.* say unto them, What   *Jer 23:33*
T. said the Lord unto me, What seest   *Jer 24:3*
T. took I the cup at the Lord's hand   *Jer 25:17*
T. will I make this house like   *Jer 26:6*
Shiloh
t. they came up from the king's house   *Jer 26:10*
T. spake the priests and the prophets   *Jer 26:11*
T. spake Jeremiah unto all   *Jer 26:12*
T. said the princes and all the people   *Jer 26:16*
T. rose up certain of the elders of the   *Jer 26:17*
t. many nations and great kings shall   *Jer 27:7*
t. will I bring them up, and restore   *Jer 27:22*
T. the prophet Jeremiah said unto the   *Jer 28:5*
t. shall the prophet be known, that the   *Jer 28:9*
T. Hananiah the prophet took the   *Jer 28:10*
T. said the prophet Jeremiah unto   *Jer 28:15*
T. shall ye call upon me, and ye shall   *Jer 29:12*
T. shall the virgin rejoice in   *Jer 31:13*
t. the seed of Israel also shall   *Jer 31:36*
cease
For *t.* the king of Babylon's army   *Jer 32:2*
T. I knew that this was the word of   *Jer 32:8*
T. may also my covenant be broken   *Jer 33:21*
t. will I cast away the seed of   *Jer 33:26*
T. Jeremiah the prophet spake   *Jer 34:6*
all
more, *t.* they obeyed, and let them go   *Jer 34:10*
T. I took Jaazaniah the son of   *Jer 35:3*
T. Jeremiah called Baruch the son of   *Jer 36:4*
t. read Baruch in the book the words   *Jer 36:10*
T. he went down into the king's house   *Jer 36:12*
T. Michaiah declared unto them all   *Jer 36:13*
T. Baruch answered them, He   *Jer 36:18*
T. said the princes unto Baruch, Go   *Jer 36:19*
T. took Jeremiah another roll, and   *Jer 36:32*
T. Pharaoh's army was come forth out   *Jer 37:5*
T. Jeremiah went forth out of   *Jer 37:12*
T. said Jeremiah, It is false; I fall not   *Jer 37:14*
T. Zedekiah the king sent, and took   *Jer 37:17; 38:14*
T. Zedekiah the king commanded   *Jer 37:21*
T. Shephatiah son of Mattan   *Jer 38:1*
T. Zedekiah the king said, Behold, he   *Jer 38:5*
T. took they Jeremiah, and cast him   *Jer 38:6*

king *t.* sitting in the gate of Benjamin	*Jer 38:7*
T. the king commanded Ebed-melech	*Jer 38:10*
T. Jeremiah said unto Zedekiah, If I	*Jer 38:15*
T. said Jeremiah unto Zedekiah, Thus	*Jer 38:17*
t. thy soul shall live, and this city shall	*Jer 38:17*
t. shall this city be given into the hand	*Jer 38:18*
T. said Zedekiah unto Jeremiah, Let	*Jer 38:24*
T. thou shalt say unto them, I	*Jer 38:26*
T. came all the princes unto Jeremiah	*Jer 38:27*
t. they fled, and went forth out of the	*Jer 39:4*
T. the king of Babylon slew the sons	*Jer 39:6*
T. Nebuzar-adan the captain of the	*Jer 39:9; 52:15*
T. went Jeremiah unto Gedaliah	*Jer 40:6*
T. they came to Gedaliah to Mizpah	*Jer 40:8*
T. Johanan the son of Kareah spake	*Jer 40:15*
T. arose Ishmael the son of Nethaniah	*Jer 41:2*
T. Ishmael carried away captive all	*Jer 41:10*
T. they took all the men, and went to	*Jer 41:12*
that were with him, *t.* they were glad	*Jer 41:13*
t. took Johanan the son of Kareah	*Jer 41:16*
T. all the captains of the forces, and	*Jer 42:1*
T. Jeremiah the prophet said unto	*Jer 42:4*
T. they said to Jeremiah, The Lord	*Jer 42:5*
T. called he Johanan the son of	*Jer 42:8*
abide in this land, *t.* will I build you	*Jer 42:10*
T. it shall come to pass, that	*Jer 42:16*
T. spake Azariah the son of Hoshaiah	*Jer 43:2*
T. all the men which knew that their	*Jer 44:15*
t. had we plenty of victuals, and were	*Jer 44:17*
T. Jeremiah said unto all the people	*Jer 44:20*
t. the men shall cry, and all	*Jer 47:2*
why *t.* doth their king inherit Gad	*Jer 49:1*
t. shall Israel be heir unto them that	*Jer 49:2*
T. the heaven and the earth, and all	*Jer 51:48*
T. shalt thou say, O Lord, thou hast	*Jer 51:62*
T. the city was broken up, and all	*Jer 52:7*
T. they took the king, and carried	*Jer 52:9*
T. he put out the eyes of Zedekiah	*Jer 52:11*
mine head; *t.* I said, I am cut off	*La 3:54*
T. did I eat it; and it was in my	*Eze 3:3*
T. the spirit took me up, and I heard	*Eze 3:12*
T. I came to them of the captivity at	*Eze 3:15*
T. I arose, and went forth into	*Eze 3:23*
T. the spirit entered into me, and set	*Eze 3:24*
T. said I, Ah Lord God! behold, my	*Eze 4:14*
T. he said unto me, Lo, I have given	*Eze 4:15*
t. take thee balances to weigh	*Eze 5:1*
T. take of them again, and cast them	*Eze 5:4*
T. shall ye know that I am the Lord	*Eze 6:13*
t. shall they seek a vision of	*Eze 7:26*
T. I beheld, and lo a likeness as the	*Eze 8:2*
T. said he unto me, Son of man	*Eze 8:5; 8:8, 12*
T. he brought me to the door of the	*Eze 8:14*
T. said he unto me, Hast thou seen	*Eze 8:15; 8:17*
T. they began at the ancient men	*Eze 9:6*
T. said he unto me, The iniquity of	*Eze 9:9*
T. I looked, and, behold, in	*Eze 10:1*
T. the glory of the Lord went up from	*Eze 10:4*
t. he went in, and stood beside the	*Eze 10:6*
T. the glory of the Lord departed from	*Eze 10:18*
T. said he unto me, Son of man, these	*Eze 11:2*
T. fell I down upon my face, and cried	*Eze 11:13*
T. did the cherubims lift up their	*Eze 11:22*
T. I spake unto them of the captivity	*Eze 11:25*
T. shalt thou bring forth thy stuff by	*Eze 12:4*
T. came certain of the elders of Israel	*Eze 14:1*
t. will I stretch out mine hand upon it	*Eze 14:13*
T. washed I thee with water; yea, I	*Eze 16:9*
t. will I bring again the captivity of	*Eze 16:53*
t. thou and thy daughters shall return	*Eze 16:55*
T. thou shalt remember thy ways, and	*Eze 16:61*
shall he *t.* live? he shall not live: he	*Eze 18:13*
t. she took another of her whelps, and	*Eze 19:5*
T. the nations set against him	*Eze 19:8*
T. said I unto them, Cast ye away	*Eze 20:7*
t. I said, I will pour out my fury upon	*Eze 20:8*
t. I said, I would pour out my fury	*Eze 20:13; 20:21*
t. they saw every high hill, and all the	*Eze 20:28*
T. I said unto them, What is the high	*Eze 20:29*
T. said I, Ah Lord God! they say of	*Eze 20:49*
Seeing *t.* that I will cut off from thee	*Eze 21:4*
glitter: should we *t.* make mirth	*Eze 21:10*
T. say thou, Thus saith the Lord	*Eze 22:3*
T. I saw that she was defiled	*Eze 23:13*
t. my mind was alienated from her	*Eze 23:18*
t. they came the same day into my	*Eze 23:39*
T. said I unto her that was old in	*Eze 23:43*
T. set it empty upon the coals thereof	*Eze 24:11*
T. I answered them, The word of the	*Eze 24:20*
T. all the princes of the sea shall come	*Eze 26:16*
t. shall they dwell in their land that I	*Eze 28:25*
T. will I leave thee upon the land	*Eze 32:4*
T. will I make their waters deep	*Eze 32:14*
T. shall they know that I am the Lord	*Eze 33:15; 33:29*
T. whosoever heareth the sound of the	*Eze 33:4*
away in them, how should we *t.* live	*Eze 33:10*
t. shall they know that a prophet hath	*Eze 33:33*
T. will I sprinkle clean water upon	*Eze 36:25*
T. shall ye remember your own evil	*Eze 36:31*
T. the heathen that are left round	*Eze 36:36*
T. said he unto me, Prophesy unto	*Eze 37:9*
T. he said unto me, Son of man, these	*Eze 37:11*
t. shall ye know that I the Lord have	*Eze 37:14*
t. take another stick, and write upon	*Eze 37:16*
t. shall he set up a sign by it, till he	*Eze 39:15*
t. shall they know that I am the Lord	*Eze 39:28*
T. came he unto the gate which looketh	*Eze 40:6*
T. measured he the porch of the gate	*Eze 40:9*
He measured *t.* the gate from the roof	*Eze 40:13*
T. brought he me into the outward	*Eze 40:17*
T. he measured the breadth from the	*Eze 40:19*
T. went he inward, and measured the	*Eze 41:3*
T. he brought me forth into the utter	*Eze 42:1; 46:21*
T. said he unto me, The north	*Eze 42:13*
t. shall they not go out of the holy	*Eze 42:14*
T. he brought me back the way of the	*Eze 44:1*
T. said the Lord unto me; This gate	*Eze 44:2*
T. brought he me the way of	*Eze 44:4*
t. he shall go forth; but the gate shall	*Eze 46:2*
one shall *t.* open him the gate that	*Eze 46:12*
t. he shall go forth: and after his	*Eze 46:12*
t. it shall be his to the year of liberty	*Eze 46:17*
T. said he unto me, This is the place	*Eze 46:20*
T. said he unto me, These are the	*Eze 46:24*
T. brought me out of the way of	*Eze 47:2*
T. he brought me, and caused me to	*Eze 47:6*
T. said he unto me, These waters	*Eze 47:8*
t. shall ye make me endanger my	*Da 1:10*
T. said Daniel to Melzar, whom the	*Da 1:11*
T. let our countenances be looked	*Da 1:13*
t. the prince of the eunuchs brought	*Da 1:18*
T. the king commanded to call	*Da 2:2*
T. spake the Chaldeans to the king	*Da 2:4*
T. Daniel answered with counsel	*Da 2:14*
T. Arioch made the thing known to	*Da 2:15*
T. Daniel went in, and desired of the	*Da 2:16*
T. Daniel went to his house	*Da 2:17*
T. was the secret revealed unto	*Da 2:19*
T. Daniel blessed the God of heaven	*Da 2:19*
T. Arioch brought in Daniel before	*Da 2:25*
T. was the iron, the clay, the brass	*Da 2:35*
T. the king Nebuchadnezzar fell	*Da 2:46*
T. the king made Daniel a great	*Da 2:48*
T. Daniel requested of the king, and	*Da 2:49*
T. Nebuchadnezzar the king sent to	*Da 3:2*
T. the princes, the governors	*Da 3:3*
T. an herald cried aloud, To you	*Da 3:4*
T. Nebuchadnezzar in his rage	*Da 3:13*
T. they brought these men before	*Da 3:13*
T. was Nebuchadnezzar full of fury	*Da 3:19*
T. these men were bound in their	*Da 3:21*
T. Nebuchadnezzar the king was	*Da 3:24*
T. Nebuchadnezzar came near	*Da 3:26*
T. Shadrach, Meshach, and	*Da 3:26*
T. Nebuchadnezzar spake, and said	*Da 3:28*
t. the king promoted Shadrach	*Da 3:30*

T. came in the magicians, the *Da 4:7*
T. Daniel, whose name was *Da 4:19*
T. they brought the golden *Da 5:3*
vessels
T. the king's countenance was *Da 5:6*
T. came in all the king's wise *Da 5:8*
men
T. was king Belshazzar greatly *Da 5:9*
T. was Daniel brought in *Da 5:13*
before the
T. Daniel answered and said *Da 5:17*
before
T. was the part of the hand *Da 5:24*
sent
T. commanded Belshazzar, *Da 5:29*
and they
T. this Daniel was preferred *Da 6:3*
above
T. the presidents and princes *Da 6:4;*
                                        6:6
T. said these men, We shall not *Da 6:5*
find
T. these men assembled, and *Da 6:11*
found
T. they came near, and spake *Da 6:12*
before
T. answered they and said *Da 6:13*
before
T. the king, when he heard *Da 6:14*
these
T. these men assembled unto *Da 6:15*
T. the king commanded, and *Da 6:16*
they
T. the king went to his palace *Da 6:18*
T. the king arose very early in *Da 6:19*
T. said Daniel unto the king, *Da 6:21*
O king
T. was the king exceeding *Da 6:23*
glad for
T. king Darius wrote unto all *Da 6:25*
people
t. he wrote the dream, and told *Da 7:1*
I beheld *t*. because of the voice *Da 7:11*
of
T. I would know of the truth *Da 7:19*
of the
T. I lifted up mine eyes, and *Da 8:3*
saw
T. I heard one saint speaking *Da 8:13*
t. shall the sanctuary be *Da 8:14*
cleansed
t. behold, there stood before *Da 8:15*
me as
T. I lifted up mine eyes, and *Da 10:5*
looked
t. was I in a deep sleep on my *Da 10:9*
face
T. said he unto me, Fear *Da 10:12*
not, Daniel
t. I opened my mouth, and *Da 10:16*
spake, and
T. there came again and *Da 10:18*
touched me
T. said he, Knowest thou *Da 10:20*
wherefore I
t. shall he return, and be *Da 11:10*
stirred up
T. he shall turn his face *Da 11:19*
toward the
T. shall stand up in his *Da 11:20*
estate a
T. shall he return into his *Da 11:28*
land with
T. I Daniel looked, and, *Da 12:5*
behold, there
T. said I, O my Lord, what *Da 12:8*
shall be the
T. said God, Call his name *Ho 1:9*
Lo-ammi
T. shall the children of Judah *Ho 1:11*
t. shall she say, I will go and *Ho 2:7*
return to
t. was it better with me than *Ho 2:7*
now
T. said the Lord unto me, Go *Ho 3:1*
yet
t. went Ephraim to the *Ho 5:13*
Assyrian
T. shall we know, if we follow *Ho 6:3*
on
t. the iniquity of Ephraim was *Ho 7:1*
Lord, what *t*. should a king *Ho 10:3*
do to us
Israel was a child, *t*. I loved *Ho 11:1*
him, and
t. the children shall tremble *Ho 11:10*
from the
T. will the Lord be jealous *Joe 2:18*
for his
Be glad *t*. ye children of Zion *Joe 2:23*

t. shall Jerusalem be holy, and *Joe 3:17*
there
t. go down to Gath of the *Am 6:2*
Philistines
T. shall he say, Hold thy *Am 6:10*
tongue: for
t. I said, O Lord God, forgive *Am 7:2*
T. said I, O Lord God, cease, I *Am 7:5*
T. said the Lord, Behold, I will *Am 7:8*
set a
T. Amaziah the priest of *Am 7:10*
Beth-el sent
T. answered Amos, and said *Am 7:14*
T. said the Lord unto me, The *Am 8:2*
end is
T. the mariners were afraid, *Jon 1:5*
and cried
T. said they unto him, Tell us, *Jon 1:8*
we
T. were the men exceedingly *Jon 1:10*
afraid
T. said they unto him, What *Jon 1:11*
shall we
T. the men feared the Lord *Jon 1:16*
T. Jonah prayed unto the Lord *Jon 2:1*
his
T. I said, I am cast out of thy *Jon 2:4*
sight
T. said the Lord, Doest thou *Jon 4:4*
well to
T. said the Lord, thou hast *Jon 4:10*
had pity
T. shall they cry unto the *Mic 3:4*
Lord
T. shall the seers be ashamed *Mic 3:7*
t. the remnant of his brethren *Mic 5:3*
shall
t. shall we raise against him *Mic 5:5*
seven
T. she that is mine enemy *Mic 7:10*
shall see
T. shall his mind change, *Hab 1:11*
and he
t. will I turn to the people a *Zep 3:9*
pure
t. I will take away out of the *Zep 3:11*
midst
T. came the word of the Lord *Hag 1:3*
by
T. Zerubbabel the son of *Hag 1:12*
Shealtiel
T. spake Haggai the Lord's *Hag 1:13*
T. said Haggai, If one that is *Hag 2:13*
T. answered Haggai, and *Hag 2:14*
said, So is
T. said I, O my Lord, what *Zec 1:9*
are these
T. the angel of the Lord *Zec 1:12*
answered
T. lifted I up mine eyes, and *Zec 1:18*
saw, and
T. said I, What come these to *Zec 1:21*
do
T. said I, Whither goest thou *Zec 2:2*
t. thou shalt also judge my *Zec 3:7*
house
T. the angel that talked with *Zec 4:5*
me
T. he answered and spake unto *Zec 4:6*
me
T. answered I, and said unto *Zec 4:11*
him
T. said he, These are the two *Zec 4:14*
T. I turned, and lifted up mine *Zec 5:1*
eyes
T. said he unto me, This is the *Zec 5:3*
curse
T. the angel that talked with *Zec 5:5*
me went
T. lifted I up mine eyes, and *Zec 5:9*
looked
T. said I to the angel that *Zec 5:10*
talked with
T. I answered and said unto *Zec 6:4*
T. cried he upon me, and *Zec 6:8*
spake unto
T. take silver and gold, and *Zec 6:11*
make
T. came the word of the Lord *Zec 7:4*
of hosts
T. said I, I will not feed you: *Zec 11:9*
that that
T. I cut asunder mine other *Zec 11:14*
staff, even
t. his father and his mother *Zec 13:3*
that begat
T. he shall answer, Those *Zec 13:6*
with which
T. shall the Lord go forth, *Zec 14:3*
and fight

if *t*. I be a father, where is *Mal 1:6*
mine
T. shall the offering of Judah *Mal 3:4*
T. they that feared the Lord *Mal 3:16*
spake
T. shall ye return, and *Mal 3:18*
discern
T. Joseph her husband, a just *M't 1:19*
T. Joseph being raised from *M't 1:24*
sleep
T. Herod, when he had privily *M't 2:7*
T. Herod when he saw that *M't 2:16*
he was
T. was fulfilled that which *M't 2:17*
was
T. went out to him Jerusalem *M't 3:5*
T. cometh Jesus from Galilee *M't 3:13*
to
righteousness. *T*, he suffered *M't 3:15*
him
T. was Jesus led up of the *M't 4:1*
spirit
T. the devil taketh him up *M't 4:5*
into the
T. saith Jesus unto him, Get *M't 4:10*
thee
T. the devil leaveth him and *M't 4:11*
and *t*. come and offer thy gift *M't 5:24*
t. shalt thou see clearly to cast *M't 7:5*
out
If ye *t*. being evil, know how *M't 7:11*
to
t. will I profess unto them, I *M't 7:23*
never
T. he arose, and rebuked the *M't 8:26*
winds
t. saith he to the sick of the *M't 9:6*
palsy
T. came to him the disciples *M't 9:14*
of
from them, and *t*. shall they *M't 9:15*
fast
T. touched he their eyes, *M't 9:29*
saying
T. saith he unto his disciples *M't 9:37*
T. began he to upbraid the *M't 11:20*
cities
How much *t*. is a man *M't 12:12*
better than
T. saith he to the man, *M't 12:13*
Stretch
T. the Pharisees went *M't 12:14*
out
T. was brought unto him *M't 12:22*
one
how shall *t*. his kingdom *M't 12:26*
stand
t. the kingdom of God is *M't 12:28*
come
and *t*. he will spoil his house *M't 12:29*
T. certain of the scribes and *M't 12:38*
of the
T. he saith, I will return *M't 12:44*
into my
T. goeth he, and taketh with *M't 12:45*
T. one said unto him, *M't 12:47*
Behold, thy
t. cometh the wicked one *M't 13:19*
fruit, *t*. appeared the tares *M't 13:26*
also
from whence *t*. hath it tares *M't 13:27*
Wilt thou *t*. that we go and *M't 13:28*
gather
T. Jesus sent the multitude *M't 13:36*
away
T. shall the righteous shine *M't 13:43*
forth
T. said he unto them, *M't 13:52*
Therefore
Whence *t*. hath this man all *M't 13:56*
these
T. they that were in the ship *M't 14:33*
came
T. came to Jesus scribes and *M't 15:1*
T. came his disciples, and *M't 15:12*
said unto
T. answered Peter and said *M't 15:15*
unto
T. Jesus went thence, and *M't 15:21*
T. came she and worshipped *M't 15:25*
him
T. Jesus answered and said *M't 15:28*
unto
T. Jesus called his disciples *M't 15:32*
unto
T. Jesus said unto them, Take *M't 16:6*
T. understood they how that *M't 16:12*
he
T. charged he his disciples *M't 16:20*
that

T. Peter took him, and began to	M't 16:22
T. said Jesus unto his disciples	M't 16:24
and t. he shall reward every man	M't 16:27
T. answered Peter, and said unto	M't 17:4
Why t. say the scribes that Elias	M't 17:10
T. the disciples understood that	M't 17:13
T. Jesus answered and said, O	M't 17:17
T. came the disciples to Jesus	M't 17:19
unto him, T. are the children free	M't 17:26
t. take with thee one or two more	M't 18:16
T. came Peter to him, and said	M't 18:21
T. the lord of that servant was	M't 18:27
T. the Lord, after that he had	M't 18:32
did Moses t. command to give a	M't 19:7
T. were brought unto him little	M't 19:13
T. said Jesus unto his disciples	M't 19:23
saying, Who t. can be saved	M't 19:25
T. answered Peter and said unto	M't 19:27
T. came to him the mother of	M't 20:20
Olives, t. sent Jesus two disciples	M't 21:1
us, Why did ye not t. believe him	M't 21:25
T. saith he to his servants	M't 22:8
T. said the king to the servants	M't 22:13
T. went the Pharisees, and took	M't 22:15
T. saith he unto them, Render	M't 22:21
T. one of them, which was a	M't 22:35
How t. doth David in spirit call	M't 22:43
If David t. call him Lord, how is he	M't 22:45
T. spake Jesus to the multitude	M't 23:1
Fill ye up t. the measure of your	M't 23:32
T. shall they deliver you up to be	M't 24:9
t. shall many be offended, and shall	M't 24:10
nations; and t. shall the end come	M't 24:14
T. let them which be in Judæa flee	M't 24:16
t. shall be great tribulation, such as	M't 24:21
T. if any man shall say unto you	M't 24:23
t. shall appear the sign of the Son	M't 24:30
t. shall all the tribes of the earth	M't 24:30
T. shall two be in the field; the one	M't 24:40
t. is a faithful and wise servant	M't 24:45
T. shall the kingdom of heaven be	M't 25:1
T. all those virgins arose, and	M't 25:7
T. he that had received the five	M't 25:16
T. he which had received the one	M't 25:24
t. at my coming I should have received	M't 25:27
t. shall he sit upon the throne of	M't 25:31
T. shall the King say unto them on	M't 25:34
T. shall the righteous answer him	M't 25:37
T. shall he say also unto them on	M't 25:41
T. shall they also answer him	M't 25:44
T. shall he answer them, saying	M't 25:45

T. assembled together the chief	M't 26:3
T. one of the twelve, called Judas	M't 26:14
T. Judas, which betrayed him	M't 26:25
T. saith Jesus unto them, All ye	M't 26:31
T. cometh Jesus with them unto a	M't 26:36
T. saith he unto them, My soul is	M't 26:38
T. cometh he to his disciples, and	M't 26:45
T. came they, and laid hands on	M't 26:50
T. said Jesus unto him, Put up	M't 26:52
But how t. shall the scriptures be	M't 26:54
T. all the disciples forsook him	M't 26:56
T. the high priest rent his clothes	M't 26:65; M'k 14:63
T. did they spit in his face	M't 26:67
T., began he to curse and to swear	M't 26:74
T. Judas, which had betrayed him	M't 27:3
T. was fulfilled that which was	M't 27:9
T. said Pilate unto him, Hearest	M't 27:13
And they had t. a notable prisoner	M't 27:16
what shall I do t. with Jesus	M't 27:22
T. answered all the people	M't 27:25
T. released he Barabbas unto	M't 27:26
T. the soldiers of the governor took	M't 27:27
T. were there two thieves crucified	M't 27:38
T. Pilate commanded the body to	M't 27:58
T. said Jesus unto them, Be not	M't 28:10
T. the eleven disciples went away	M't 28:16
and t. shall they fast in those days	M'k 2:20
man; and t. he will spoil his house	M'k 3:27
There came t. his brethren and his	M'k 3:31
and how t. will ye know all parables	M'k 4:13
first the blade, t. the ear, after	M'k 4:28
T. came together unto him the	M'k 7:1
T. the Pharisees and scribes	M'k 7:5
so t. they are no more twain	M'k 10:8
T. Jesus beholding him loved	M'k 10:21
themselves, Who t. can be saved	M'k 10:26
T. Peter began to say unto him	M'k 10:28
say, Why t. did ye not believe him	M'k 11:31
T. come unto him the Sadducees	M'k 12:18
him Lord; and whence is he t. his son	M'k 12:37
t. let them that be in Judaea flee to	M'k 13:14
t. if any man shall say to you, Lo	M'k 13:21
t. shall they see the Son of man	M'k 13:26
And t. shall he send his angels, and	M'k 13:27
What will ye t. that I shall do unto	M'k 15:12
T. Pilate said unto them, Why	M'k 15:14
So t. after the Lord had spoken	M'k 16:19
T. said Mary unto the angel, How	Lu 1:34
T. took he him up in his arms	Lu 2:28
T. said he to the multitude that	Lu 3:7
him, saying, What shall we do t.	Lu 3:10
T. came also publicans to be	Lu 3:12
and t. shall they fast in those days	Lu 5:35
t. both the new maketh a rent	Lu 5:36
T. said Jesus unto them, I will	Lu 6:9

t. shalt thou see clearly to pull out	Lu 6:42
T. Jesus went with them. And	Lu 7:6
T. Jesus answering said unto	Lu 7:22
Whereunto t. shall I liken the men	Lu 7:31
t. cometh the devil, and taketh	Lu 8:12
T. came to him his mother	Lu 8:19
T. he arose, and rebuked the wind	Lu 8:24
T. went the devils out of the man	Lu 8:33
T. they went out to see what was	Lu 8:35
T. the multitude of the country	Lu 8:37
T. he called his twelve disciples	Lu 9:1
t. came the twelve, and said unto	Lu 9:12
T. he took the five loaves and	Lu 9:16
T. there arose a reasoning among	Lu 9:46
T. said Jesus unto him, Go	Lu 10:37
If ye t. being evil, know how to give	Lu 11:13
T. goeth he, and taketh to him	Lu 11:26
T. answered one of the lawyers	Lu 11:45
t. whose shall those things be	Lu 12:20
If ye t. be not able to do that thing	Lu 12:26
If t. God so clothe the grass, which	Lu 12:28
T. Peter said unto him, Lord	Lu 12:41
Who t. is that faithful and wise	Lu 12:42
T. said he unto the dresser of his	Lu 13:7
t. after that thou shall cut it down	Lu 13:9
The Lord t. answered him	Lu 13:15
T. said he, Unto what is the	Lu 13:18
T. said one unto him, Lord are	Lu 13:23
T. shall ye begin to say, We have	Lu 13:26
t. shalt thou have worship in	Lu 14:10
T. said he also to him that bade	Lu 14:12
T. said he unto him, A certain	Lu 14:16
t. the master of the house being	Lu 14:21
T. draw near all the publicans	Lu 15:1
T. the steward said within himself	Lu 16:3
T. said he to another, And how	Lu 16:7
T. he said, I pray thee, therefore	Lu 16:27
T. said he unto the disciples, It is	Lu 17:1
heard it said, Who t. can be saved	Lu 18:26
T. Peter said, Lo, we have left all	Lu 18:28
T. he took unto him the twelve	Lu 18:31
t. he commanded these servants to	Lu 19:15
T. came the first, saying, Lord	Lu 19:16
Wherefore t. gavest not thou my	Lu 19:23
say, Why t. believe ye him not	Lu 20:5
T. began he to speak to the people	Lu 20:9
T. said the lord of the vineyard	Lu 20:13
What is this t. that is written	Lu 20:17
T. came to him certain of the	Lu 20:27
T. certain of the scribes answering	Lu 20:39
calleth Lord, how is he t. his son	Lu 20:44
T. in the audience of all the	Lu 20:45
T. said he unto them, Nation shall	Lu 21:10
t. know that the desolation thereof is	Lu 21:20
T. let them which are in Judaea	Lu 21:21
t. shall they see the Son of man	Lu 21:27
t. look up, and lift up your heads	Lu 21:28
T. entered Satan into Judas	Lu 22:3
T. came the day of unleavened	Lu 22:7

T. said he unto them, But now	*Lu* 22:36
T. Jesus said unto chief priests	*Lu* 22:52
T. took they him, and led him	*Lu* 22:54
T. said they all, Art thou all, Art thou *t*. the Son of God	*Lu* 22:70 *Lu* 22:70
T. said Pilate to the chief priests	*Lu* 23:4
T. he questioned him in many	*Lu* 23:9
T. shall they begin to say to	*Lu* 23:30
T. said Jesus, Father, forgive	*Lu* 23:34
T. arose Peter, and ran unto	*Lu* 24:12
T. he said unto them, O fools, and	*Lu* 24:25
T. opened he their understanding	*Lu* 24:45
him, What *t*.?Art thou Elias	*Joh* 1:21
T. said they unto him, Who art	*Joh* 1:22
Why baptizest thou *t*. if thou be	*Joh* 1:25
T. Jesus turned, and saw them	*Joh* 1:38
well drunk, *t*. that which is worse	*Joh* 2:10
T. answered the Jews and said	*Joh* 2:18
T. said the Jews, Forty and six	*Joh* 2:20
T. there arose a question between	*Joh* 3:25
T. cometh he to a city of Samaria	*Joh* 4:5
T. saith the woman of Samaria	*Joh* 4:9
from whence *t*. hast thou that	*Joh* 4:11
The woman *t*. left her waterpot	*Joh* 4:28
T. they went out of the city	*Joh* 4:30
four months, and *t*. cometh harvest	*Joh* 4:35
T. when he was come into Galilee	*Joh* 4:45
T. said Jesus unto him, Except ye	*Joh* 4:48
T. enquired he of them the hour	*Joh* 4:52
whosoever *t*. first after troubling	*Joh* 5:4
T. asked they him, What man is	*Joh* 5:12
T. answered Jesus and said unto	*Joh* 5:19
When Jesus *t*. lifted up his eyes	*Joh* 6:5
T. those men, when they had seen	*Joh* 6:14
T. they willingly received him into	*Joh* 6:21
T. said they unto him, What shall	*Joh* 6:28
What sign shewest thou *t*. that we	*Joh* 6:30
T. Jesus said unto them, Verily	*Joh* 6:32; 6:53
T. said they unto him, Lord	*Joh* 6:34
The Jews *t*. murmured at him	*Joh* 6:41
how is it *t*. that he saith, I came	*Joh* 6:42
T. said Jesus unto the twelve, Will	*Joh* 6:67
T. Simon Peter answered him	*Joh* 6:68
T. Jesus said unto them, My time	*Joh* 7:6
t. went he also up unto the feast	*Joh* 7:10
T. the Jews sought him at the	*Joh* 7:11
T. said some of them of Jerusalem	*Joh* 7:25
T. cried Jesus in the temple as he	*Joh* 7:28
T. they sought to take him: but not	*Joh* 7:30
T. said Jesus unto them, Yet	*Joh* 7:33
and *t*. I go unto him that sent me	*Joh* 7:33
T. said the Jews among	*Joh* 7:35
T. came the officers to the chief	*Joh* 7:45
T. answered them the Pharisees	*Joh* 7:47
T. spake Jesus again unto them	*Joh* 8:12
T. said they unto him, Where is	*Joh* 8:19
T. said Jesus again unto them, I	*Joh* 8:21
T. said the Jews, Will he kill	*Joh* 8:22
T. said they unto him, Who art	*Joh* 8:25
T. said Jesus unto them, When ye	*Joh* 8:28
t. shall ye know that I am he	*Joh* 8:28
T. said Jesus to those Jews which	*Joh* 8:31
t. are ye my disciples indeed	*Joh* 8:31
T. said they to him, We be not	*Joh* 8:41
T. answered the Jews, and said	*Joh* 8:48
T. said the Jews unto him, Now	*Joh* 8:52
T. said the Jews unto him, Thou	*Joh* 8:57
T. took they up stones to cast	*Joh* 8:59
T. said they unto him, Where is he	*Joh* 9:12
T. again the Pharisees also asked	*Joh* 9:15
born blind? how *t*. doth he now see	*Joh* 9:19
T. again called they the man that	*Joh* 9:24
T. said they to him again, What	*Joh* 9:26
T. they reviled him, and said	*Joh* 9:28
T. said Jesus unto them again	*Joh* 10:7
T. came the Jews round about him	*Joh* 10:24
T. the Jews took up stones again	*Joh* 10:31
T. after that saith he to his	*Joh* 11:7
T. said his disciples, Lord, if he	*Joh* 11:12
T. said Jesus unto them plainly	*Joh* 11:14
T. said Thomas, which is called	*Joh* 11:16
T. when Jesus came, he found that	*Joh* 11:17
T. Martha, as soon as she heard	*Joh* 11:20
T. said Martha unto Jesus, Lord	*Joh* 11:21
The Jews *t*. which were with her	*Joh* 11:31
T. when Mary was come where	*Joh* 11:32
T. said the Jews, Behold how he	*Joh* 11:36
T. they took away the stone from	*Joh* 11:41
T. many of the Jews which came	*Joh* 11:45
T. gathered the chief priests	*Joh* 11:47
T. from that day forth they took	*Joh* 11:53
T. sought they for Jesus, and	*Joh* 11:56
T. Jesus six days before the	*Joh* 12:1
T. took Mary a pound of ointment	*Joh* 12:3
T. saith one of his disciples, Judas	*Joh* 12:4
T. said Jesus, Let her alone	*Joh* 12:7
t. remembered they that these	*Joh* 12:16
T. came there a voice from	*Joh* 12:28
T. Jesus said unto them. Yet	*Joh* 12:35
T. cometh he to Simon Peter	*Joh* 13:6
If I *t*. your Lord and Master have	*Joh* 13:14
T. the disciples looked one on	*Joh* 13:22
He *t*. lying on Jesus' breast saith	*Joh* 13:25
T. said Jesus unto him, That thou	*Joh* 13:27
He *t*. having received the sop went	*Joh* 13:30
and how sayest thou *t*., Shew us the	*Joh* 14:9
T. said some of his disciples	*Joh* 16:17
Judas *t*. having received a band of	*Joh* 18:3
As soon *t*. as he had said unto them	*Joh* 18:6
T. asked he them again, whom	*Joh* 18:7
T. Simon Peter having a sword	*Joh* 18:10
T. said Jesus unto Peter, Put up	*Joh* 18:11
T. the band and the captain	*Joh* 18:12
T. went out that other disciple	*Joh* 18:16
T. saith the damsel that kept	*Joh* 18:17
The high priest *t*. asked Jesus of	*Joh* 18:19
Peter *t*. denied again: and	*Joh* 18:27
T. led they Jesus from Caiaphas	*Joh* 18:28
Pilate *t*. went out unto them, and	*Joh* 18:29
T. said Pilate unto them, Take ye	*Joh* 18:31
T. Pilate entered into the judgment	*Joh* 18:33
world, *t*. would my servants fight	*Joh* 18:36
said unto him, Art thou a king *t*.	*Joh* 18:37
T. cried they all again, saying	*Joh* 18:40
T. Pilate therefore took Jesus	*Joh* 19:1
T. came Jesus forth, wearing	*Joh* 19:5
T. saith Pilate unto him, Speakest	*Joh* 19:10
T. delivered he him therefore	*Joh* 19:16
This title *t*. read many of the Jews	*Joh* 19:20
T. said the chief priests of	*Joh* 19:21
T. the soldiers, when they had	*Joh* 19:23
T. saith he to the disciples	*Joh* 19:27
T. came the soldiers, and brake	*Joh* 19:32
T. took they the body of Jesus	*Joh* 19:40
T. she runneth, and cometh to	*Joh* 20:2
T. cometh Simon Peter following	*Joh* 20:6
T. went in also that other disciple	*Joh* 20:8
T. the disciples went away again	*Joh* 20:10
T. the same day at evening, being	*Joh* 20:19
T. were the disciples glad, when	*Joh* 20:20
T. said Jesus to them again, Peace	*Joh* 20:21
t. came Jesus, the doors being shut	*Joh* 20:26
T. saith he to Thomas, Reach	*Joh* 20:27
T. Jesus saith unto them	*Joh* 21:5
soon *t*. as they were come to land	*Joh* 21:9
Jesus *t*. cometh, and taketh bread	*Joh* 21:13
T. Peter, turning about, seeth the	*Joh* 21:20
T. went this saying abroad among	*Joh* 21:23
T. returned they unto Jerusalem	*Ac* 1:12
T. Peter said unto them, Repent	*Ac* 2:38
T. they that gladly received his	*Ac* 2:41
T. Peter said, Silver and gold have	*Ac* 3:6
T. Peter, filled with the Holy	*Ac* 4:8
T. Peter said unto her, How is it	*Ac* 5:9
T. fell she down straightway at his	*Ac* 5:10
T. the high priest rose up, and all	*Ac* 5:17
T. came one and told them, saying	*Ac* 5:25
T. went the captain with the	*Ac* 5:26
T. Peter and the other apostles	*Ac* 5:29
T. stood there up one in council	*Ac* 5:34
T. the twelve called the multitude	*Ac* 6:2
T. there arose certain of the	*Ac* 6:9
T. they suborned men, which said	*Ac* 6:11
T. said the high priest, Are these	*Ac* 7:1
T. came he out of the land of	*Ac* 7:4
T. sent Joseph, and called his	*Ac* 7:14
T. fled Moses at this saying	*Ac* 7:29
T. Moses trembled, and durst not	*Ac* 7:32
T. said the Lord to him, Put off thy	*Ac* 7:33
T. God turned, and gave them up	*Ac* 7:42

T. they cried out with a loud   Ac 7:57
voice
T. Philip went down to the city   Ac 8:5
of
T. Simon himself believed   Ac 8:13
also
T. laid they their hands on   Ac 8:17
them
T. answered Simon, and said   Ac 8:24
T. the Spirit said unto Philip,   Ac 8:29
Go
T. Philip opened his mouth   Ac 8:35
T. Ananias answered, Lord, I   Ac 9:13
have
T. was Saul certain days with   Ac 9:19
T. the disciples took him by   Ac 9:25
night
T. had the churches rest   Ac 9:31
T. Peter arose and went with   Ac 9:39
T. Peter went down to the   Ac 10:21
men
T. called he them in, and   Ac 10:23
lodged
T. Peter opened his mouth   Ac 10:34
magnify God. *T.* answered   Ac 10:46
Peter
T. prayed they him to tarry   Ac 10:48
T. remembered I the word   Ac 11:16
of the
Forasmuch *t.* as God gave   Ac 11:17
them
T. hath God also to the   Ac 11:18
Gentiles
T. tidings of these things   Ac 11:22
came
T. departed Barnabas to   Ac 11:25
Tarsus
T. the disciples, every man   Ac 11:29
T. were the days of   Ac 12:3
unleavened
even so *T.* said they, It is   Ac 12:15
his
T. Saul, who also is called   Ac 13:9
Paul
T. the deputy, when he saw   Ac 13:12
what
T. Paul stood up and   Ac 13:16
beckoning
T. Paul and Barnabas waxed   Ac 13:46
bold
T. the priest of Jupiter,   Ac 14:13
which was
T. all the multitude kept   Ac 15:12
silence
T. pleased it the apostles   Ac 15:22
T. came he to Derbe and   Ac 16:1
Lystra
T. he called for a light, and   Ac 16:29
t. immediately the brethren   Ac 17:14
sent
T. certain philosophers of the   Ac 17:18
T. Paul stood in the midst of   Ac 17:22
Mars
Forasmuch *t.* as we are the   Ac 17:29
T. spake the Lord to Paul in   Ac 18:9
T. all the Greeks took   Ac 18:17
Sosthenes
and *t.* took his leave of the   Ac 18:18
brethren
Unto what *t.* were ye baptized   Ac 19:3
T. said Paul, John verily   Ac 19:4
baptized
T. certain of the vagabond   Ac 19:13
Jews
Seeing *t.* that these things   Ac 19:36
cannot
T. Paul answered, What   Ac 21:13
mean ye
T. Paul took the men, and the   Ac 21:26
T. the chief captain came   Ac 21:33
near
and *t.* lifted up their voices,   Ac 22:22
and said
T. the chief captain came   Ac 22:27
T. straightway they departed   Ac 22:29
from
T. said Paul unto him, God   Ac 23:3
shall
T. said Paul, I wist not,   Ac 23:5
brethren
T. Paul called one   Ac 23:17
cf centurions
T. the chief captain took   Ac 23:19
him by
captain *t.* let the young man   Ac 23:22
depart
t. came I with an army,   Ac 23:27
and rescued
T. the soldiers, as it was   Ac 23:31

T. Paul, after that   Ac 24:10
governor had
T. the high priest and the   Ac 25:2
chief of
T. said Paul, I stand at   Ac 25:10
Cæsar's
T. Festus, when he had   Ac 25:12
conferred
T. Agrippa said, Festus, I   Ac 25:22
would
T. Agrippa said unto Paul,   Ac 26:1
Thou
T. Paul stretched forth the   Ac 26:1
hand
of Judaea, and *t.* to the   Ac 26:20
Gentiles
T. Agrippa said unto Paul   Ac 26:28
T. said Agrippa unto Festus,   Ac 26:32
This
be saved was *t.* taken away   Ac 27:20
T. fearing lest we should   Ac 27:29
have
T. the soldiers cut off the   Ac 27:32
ropes of
T. were they all of good   Ac 27:36
cheer, and
t. they knew that the island   Ac 28:1
was
What advantage *t.* hath the Jew   Ro 3:1
for *t.* how shall God judge the   Ro 3:6
world
What *t.*? are we better than   Ro 3:9
they
Where is boasting *t.*? It is   Ro 3:27
Do we *t.* make void the law   Ro 3:31
through
What shall we say *t.* that   Ro 4:1
Abraham
Cometh this blessedness *t.* upon   Ro 4:9
How was it *t.* reckoned? when   Ro 4:10
he
Much more *t.* being now   Ro 5:9
justified
What shall we say *t.*? Shall we   Ro 6:1
What *t.*? shall we sin, because   Ro 6:15
Being *t.* made free from sin,   Ro 6:18
ye
fruit had ye *t.* in those things   Ro 6:21
So *t.* if, while her husband   Ro 7:3
liveth
What shall we say *t.*? Is the   Ro 7:7
law
t. that which is good made   Ro 7:13
death
If *t.* I do that which I would   Ro 7:16
not, I
t. it is no more I that do it,   Ro 7:17
but sin
I find *t.* a law, that, when I   Ro 7:21
would
t. with the mind I myself   Ro 7:25
serve the
So *t.* they that are in flesh   Ro 8:8
cannot
if children, *t.* heirs; heirs of   Ro 8:17
God
t. do we with patience wait   Ro 8:25
for it
What shall we *t.* say to these   Ro 8:31
What shall we say *t.*? Is there   Ro 9:14
So *t.* it is not of him that   Ro 9:16
willeth
Thou wilt say *t.* unto me,   Ro 9:19
Why
What shall we say *t.*? That   Ro 9:30
t. shall they call on him in   Ro 10:14
whom
So *t.* faith cometh by hearing   Ro 10:17
I say *t.* Hath God cast away   Ro 11:1
his
Even so *t.* at this present time   Ro 11:5
also
if by grace, *t.* is it no more of   Ro 11:6
works
it be of works, *t.* is it no more   Ro 11:6
grace
What *t.*? Israel hath not   Ro 11:7
obtained
I say *t.* Have they stumbled   Ro 11:11
that
Thou wilt say *t.* The   Ro 11:19
branches
Having *t.* gifts differing   Ro 12:6
according
thou *t.* not be afraid of the   Ro 13:3
power
So *t.* every one of us shall   Ro 14:12
give an
Let not *t.* your good be evil   Ro 14:16
spoken

We *t.* that are strong ought to   Ro 15:1
bear
Who *t.* is Paul, and who is   1Co 3:5
So *t.* neither is he that   1Co 3:7
planteth any
t. shall every man have praise   1Co 4:5
of
t. must ye needs go out of   1Co 5:10
the world
If *t.* ye have judgments of   1Co 6:4
things
I *t.* take the members of   1Co 6:15
Christ
t. he that giveth her in   1Co 7:38
marriage
What is my reward *t.*? Verily   1Co 9:18
What say I *t.*? that the idol   1Co 10:19
is
t. gifts of healings, helps   1Co 12:28
t. that which is in part shall   1Co 13:10
be
a glass, darkly; but *t.* face   1Co 13:12
to face
t. shall I know even as also   1Co 13:12
I am
What is it *t.*? I will pray   1Co 14:15
with the
How is it *t.* brethren? when   1Co 14:26
seen of Cephas, *t.* of the   1Co 15:5
twelve
seen of James; *t.* of all the   1Co 15:7
apostles
of the dead, *t.* is Christ not   1Co 15:13
risen
not risen, *t.* is our preaching   1Co 15:14
vain
rise not, *t.* is not Christ   1Co 15:16
raised
T. they also which are fallen   1Co 15:18
T. cometh the end, when he   1Co 15:24
shall
t. shall the Son also himself   1Co 15:28
be
why are they *t.* baptized for   1Co 15:29
the dead
t. shall be brought to pass   1Co 15:54
who is he *t.* that maketh me   2Co 2:2
glad
Seeing *t.* that we have such   2Co 3:12
hope
So *t.* death worketh in us,   2Co 4:12
but life
if one died for all, *t.* were all   2Co 5:14
dead
Now *t.* we are ambassadors   2Co 5:20
for Christ
We *t.* as workers together   2Co 6:1
with
am weak, *t.* am I strong   2Co 12:10
T. after three years I went up   Ga 1:18
to
T. fourteen years after I went   Ga 2:1
up
the law, *t.* Christ is dead in   Ga 2:21
vain
So *t.* they which be of faith are   Ga 3:9
Wherefore *t.* serveth the law   Ga 3:19
law *t.* against the promises of   Ga 3:21
God
Christ's, *t.* are ye Abraham's   Ga 3:29
seed
t. an heir of God through   Ga 4:7
Christ
Howbeit *t.* when ye knew not   Ga 4:8
Where is *t.* the blessedness ye   Ga 4:15
But as *t.* he that was born   Ga 4:29
after
So *t.* brethren, we are not   Ga 4:31
t. is the offense of the cross   Ga 5:11
ceased
This I say *t.*, Walk in the   Ga 5:16
Spirit
t. shall he have rejoicing in   Ga 6:4
See *t.* that ye walk   Eph 5:15
circumspectly
What *t.*? notwithstanding,   Ph'p 1:18
every
If ye *t.* be risen with Christ,   Col 3:1
seek
t. shall ye also appear with   Col 3:4
him in
t. we beseech you, brethren   1Th 4:1
T. we which are alive and   1Th 4:17
remain
t. sudden destruction cometh   1Th 5:3
upon
t. shall that Wicked be   2Th 2:8
revealed

For Adam was first formed, t. *1Ti 2:13*
Eve
A bishop t. must be blameless *1Ti 3:2*
t. let them use the office of a *1Ti 3:10*
Forasmuch t. as the children *Heb 2:14*
are
t. would he not afterward *Heb 4:8*
have
Seeing t. that we have a *Heb 4:14*
great
own sins, and t. for the *Heb 7:27*
people's
t. should no place have been *Heb 8:7*
sought
T. verily the first covenant *Heb 9:1*
had
a figure for the time t. present *Heb 9:9*
For t. must he often have *Heb 9:26*
suffered
For t. would they not have *Heb 10:2*
ceased
T. said I, Lo, I come (in the *Heb 10:7*
T. said he, Lo, I come to do *Heb 10:9*
thy
t. are ye bastards, and not *Heb 12:8*
sons
Whose voice t. shook the *Heb 12:26*
earth
T. when lust hath conceived, *Jas 1:15*
it
Are ye not t. partial in *Jas 2:4*
yourselves
Ye see t. how that by works a *Jas 2:24*
above is first pure, t. *Jas 3:17*
peaceable
a little time, and t. vanisheth *Jas 4:14*
away
Forasmuch t. as Christ hath *1Pe 4:1*
Whereby the world that t. was *2Pe 3:6*
Seeing t. that all these things *2Pe 3:11*
This t. is the message which *1Jo 1:5*
we
t. have we confidence toward *1Jo 3:21*
God
So t. because thou art *Re 3:16*
lukewarm
T. saith he unto me, See thou *Re 22:9*
do

THENCE

from t. it was parted, and *Ge 2:10*
became
Lord scattered them abroad *Ge 11:8*
from t.
t. did the Lord scatter them *Ge 11:9*
abroad
removed from t. unto a *Ge 12:8*
mountain
And the men rose up from t. *Ge 18:16*
the men turned their faces *Ge 18:22*
from t.
And Abraham journeyed from *Ge 20:1*
t.
take a wife unto my son from *Ge 24:7*
And Isaac departed t. and *Ge 26:17*
pitched
he removed from t. and *Ge 26:22*
digged
he went up from t. to *Ge 26:23*
Beer-sheba
fetch me from t. two good *Ge 27:9*
kids of
I will send, and fetch thee *Ge 27:45*
from t.
take thee a wife from t. of the *Ge 28:2*
to take him a wife from t. *Ge 28:6*
removing from t. all the *Ge 30:32*
speckled
thither, and buy for us from t. *Ge 42:2*
asses with the corn, and *Ge 42:26*
departed t.
(from t. is the shepherd, the *Ge 49:24*
stone
cut down from t. a branch *Nu 13:23*
with one
children of Israel cut down *Nu 13:24*
from t.
From t. they removed, and *Nu 21:12;*
                              21:13
And from t. they went to *Nu 21:16*
Beer: that
t. he might see the utmost *Nu 22:41*
part of
all: and curse me them from *Nu 23:13*
t.
mayest curse me them from *Nu 23:27*
t.
But if from t. thou shalt seek *De 4:29*

thy God brought thee out t. *De 5:15*
through
he brought us out from t. that *De 6:23*
he
From t. they journeyed unto *De 10:7*
his city shall send and fetch *De 19:12*
him t.
thine house, if any man fall *De 22:8*
from t.
Lord thy God redeemed thee *De 24:18*
t.
from t. will the Lord thy God *De 30:4*
thee, and from t. will he *De 30:4*
fetch thee
and bring out t. the woman, *Jos 6:22*
and all
From t. it passed toward *Jos 15:4*
Azmon
And Caleb drove t. the three *Jos 15:14*
sons
he went up t. to the *Jos 15:15*
inhabitants
went over from t. toward *Jos 18:13*
Luz
border was drawn t. and *Jos 18:14*
compassed
And from t. passeth on *Jos 19:13*
along on
and goeth out from t. to *Jos 19:34*
Hukkok
And from t. he went against *J'g 1:11*
expelled t. the three sons of *J'g 1:20*
Anak
he went up t. to Penuel, and *J'g 8:8*
spake
there went from t. of the *J'g 18:11*
family of
passed t. unto mount *J'g 18:13*
Ephraim
from t. am I: and I went to *J'g 19:18*
children of Israel departed t. *J'g 21:24*
went out from t. every man *J'g 21:24*
to his
might bring from t. the ark of *1Sa 4:4*
shalt thou go on forward *1Sa 10:3*
from t.
And they ran and fetched *1Sa 10:23*
him t.
took t. a stone, and slang it *1Sa 17:49*
David therefore departed t. *1Sa 22:1*
David went t. to Mizpeh of *1Sa 22:3*
Moab
And David went up from t. *1Sa 23:29*
bring up from t. the ark of *2Sa 6:2*
God
fetched t. a wise woman, and *2Sa 14:2*
said
t. came out a man of the *2Sa 16:5*
family of
he brought up from t. the *2Sa 21:13*
bones of
they are come up from t. *1Ki 1:45*
rejoicing
and go not forth t. any *1Ki 2:36*
whither
to Ophir, and fetched from t. *1Ki 9:28*
gold
and went out from t. and *1Ki 12:25*
built
So he departed t. and found *1Ki 19:19*
Elisha
shall not be from t. any *2Ki 2:21*
more death
he went up from t. unto *2Ki 2:23*
Beth-el
he went from t. to mount *2Ki 2:25*
Carmel
and from t. he returned to *2Ki 2:25*
Samaria
and take t. every man a beam *2Ki 6:2*
and carried t. silver, and gold *2Ki 7:8*
carried t. also, and went and *2Ki 7:8*
hid it
when he was departed t. he *2Ki 10:15*
lighted
priests whom ye brought *2Ki 17:27*
from t.
whom they carried away *2Ki 17:33*
from t.
brake them down from t. *2Ki 23:12*
and cast
he carried out t. all the *2Ki 24:13*
treasures
to bring up t. the ark of God *1Ch 13:6*
and took t. four hundred and *2Ch 8:18*
fifty
they thrust him out from t., *2Ch 26:20*
yea
beyond the river, be ye far *Ezr 6:6*
from t.

yet will I gather them from *Ne 1:9*
t. and
From t. she seeketh the *Job 39:29*
prey, and
depart ye, go ye out from t. *Isa 52:11*
be no more t. an infant of *Isa 65:20*
days
one that goeth out t. shall be *Jer 5:6*
torn
and take the girdle from t. *Jer 13:6*
hand, yet would I pluck *Jer 22:24*
thee t.
cause to cease from t. man *Jer 36:29*
and beast
separate himself t. in the *Jer 37:12*
midst of
took t. old cast clouts and *Jer 38:11*
old rotten
he shall go forth from t. in *Jer 43:12*
peace
I will bring thee down from *Jer 49:16*
t. saith
will destroy from t. the king *Jer 49:38*
her: from t. she shall be *Jer 50:9*
taken
all the abominations thereof *Eze 11:18*
from t.
give her her vineyards from t. *Ho 2:15*
from t. go ye to Hamath the *Am 6:2*
great
hell, t. shall mine hand take *Am 9:2*
them
to heaven, t. will I bring them *Am 9:2*
down
I will search and take them *Am 9:3*
out t.
t. will I command the serpent *Am 9:3*
t. will I command the sword, *Am 9:4*
and it
t. will I bring thee down, saith *Ob 4*
going on from t. he saw other *M't 4:21*
two
by no means come out t. till *M't 5:26*
as Jesus passed forth from t. *M't 9:9*
he saw
when Jesus departed t. two *M't 9:27*
blind
worthy: and there abide till *M't 10:11*
ye go t.
he departed t. to teach and to *M't 11:1*
preach
when he was departed t. he *M't 12:9*
went
knew it, withdrew himself *M't 12:15*
from t.
these parables he departed t. *M't 13:53*
he departed t. by ship into a *M't 14:13*
desert
Jesus went t. and departed *M't 15:21*
Jesus departed from t. and *M't 15:29*
came
his hands on them, and *M't 19:15*
departed t.
when he had gone a little *M'k 1:19*
farther t.
he went out from t. and came *M'k 6:1*
into
when ye depart t. shake off *M'k 6:11*
from t. he arose, and went *M'k 7:24*
into the
they departed t. and passed *M'k 9:30*
And he arose from t. and *M'k 10:1*
cometh
into, there abide, and t. depart *Lu 9:4*
thou shalt not depart t. till *Lu 12:59*
thou
pass to us, that would come *Lu 16:26*
from t.
Now after two days he *Joh 4:43*
departed t.
went t. unto a country near *Joh 11:54*
to the
from t. when his father was *Ac 7:4*
dead
and from t. they sailed to *Ac 13:4*
Cyprus
And t. sailed to Antioch, *Ac 14:26*
from
from t. to Philippi, which is *Ac 16:12*
the chief
he departed t. and entered *Ac 18:7*
into a
sailed t. into Syria, and with *Ac 18:18*
him
And we sailed t. and came *Ac 20:15*
Rhodes, and from t. unto *Ac 21:1*
Patara

when we had launched from *t.*   *Ac 27:4* we

more part advised to depart   *Ac 27:12* *t.* also

loosing *t.* they sailed close by   *Ac 27:13* Crete

And from *t.* we fetched a   *Ac 28:13* compass

And from *t.* when the   *Ac 28:15* brethren

them, I went from *t.* into   *2Co 2:13* Macedonia

THENCEFORTH

and *t.* it shall be accepted for   *Le 22:27* an

the sight of all nations from   *2Ch 32:23* *t.*

it is *t.* good for nothing, but   *M't 5:13* to be

t. Pilate sought to release   *Joh 19:12*

THEOPHILUS

thee in order, most excellent *T.*   *Lu 1:3* treatise have I made, O *T.* of   *Ac 1:1* all

THERE

Let *t.* be light: and *t.* was light   *Ge 1:3* Let *t.* be a firmament in the   *Ge 1:6* midst

said, Let *t.* be lights in the   *Ge 1:14* firmament

upon the earth, Wherein *t.* is   *Ge 1:30* life

t. was not a man to till the   *Ge 2:5* ground

But *t.* went up a mist from the   *Ge 2:6* earth

t. he put the man whom he had   *Ge 2:8* land of Havilah, where *t.* is   *Ge 2:11* gold

t. is bdellium and the onyx   *Ge 2:12* stone

Adam *t.* was not found an   *Ge 2:20* help meet

to Seth, to him also *t.* was   *Ge 4:26* born a son

T. were giants in the earth in   *Ge 6:4* *T.* went in two and two unto   *Ge 7:9* Noah

shall *t.* any more be a flood to   *Ge 9:11* destroy

land of Shinar; and they dwelt   *Ge 11:2* *t.*

and *t.* confound their language   *Ge 11:7* there (S)   *Ge 11:8;* *11:9; 12:8; 18:16, 22; 19:20, 22; 20:1; 24:6, 24:7; 26:17, 22-23; 27:9, 45; 28:2, 6; 29:3; 30:32; 39:1; 42:2; 26; 49:24; Ex 20:26; Nu 13:23-24; 21:12-13, 16; 22:13, 27, 41; 35:6, 11, 15; De 1:37-39; 4:29; 6:23; 10:7; 12:5-6, 11; 19:3-4, 12; 24:18; 30:4; 32:52; 34:4; J'g 8:27; 18:3, 15, 17; 19:15; 21:10; 1Sa 2:14; 4:4; 5:8; 9:6; 10:3, 5, 10, 22-23; 19:23; 22:1, 3; 23:29; 30:7; 2Sa 2:2; 4:6; 6:2; 14:2; 16:5; 21:13; 1Ki 1:45; 6:7; 9:28; 12:25; 19:9, 19; 2Ki 2:21, 23, 25; 4:8, 10-11; 5:25; 6:2, 6, 9, 14; 7:8; 9:2; 10:15; 17:27, 33, 23:12; 24:13; 1Ch 13:6; 2Ch 1:6; 8:18; 26:20; Ne 1:9; 4:20; 5:16; 13:9; Job 1:21; Isa 7:24-25; 52:11; 55:10; 57:7; Jer 13:6; 22:24; 49:16; Eze 1:20; 11:18; 40:1, 3; 47:9; Ho 2:15; Joe 3:11; Am 6:2; 9:2-4; Ob 4; Zep 2:7; M't 2:4, 21; 5:26; 9:9, 27; 10:11; 11:1; 12:9, 15; 13:53; 14:13; 15:21, 29; 19:15*

Lord did *t.* confound the   *Ge 11:9* language

they came unto Haran, and   *Ge 11:31* dwelt *t.*

t. builded he an altar unto the   *Ge 12:7* Lord

t. he builded an altar unto the   *Ge 12:8* Lord

And *t.* was a famine in the   *Ge 12:10;* land   *26:1*

down into Egypt to sojourn   *Ge 12:10* *t.*

which he had made *t.* at the   *Ge 13:4* first

t. was a strife between the   *Ge 13:7* herdmen

said unto Lot, Let *t.* be no   *Ge 13:8* strife

built *t.* an altar unto the   *Ge 13:18* Lord

And *t.* went out the king of   *Ge 14:8* Sodom

and Gomorrah fled, and fell   *Ge 14:10* *t.*

And *t.* came one that had   *Ge 14:13* escaped

t. be fifty righteous within   *Ge 18:24* the city

t. shall lack five of the fifty   *Ge 18:28* righteous

If I find *t.* forty and five, I   *Ge 18:28* will

t. shall be forty found *t.*   *Ge 18:29* *t.* shall thirty be found *t.*   *Ge 18:30* I will not do it, if I find   *Ge 18:30* thirty *t.*

t. shall be twenty found *t.*   *Ge 18:31* Peradventure ten shall be   *Ge 18:32* found *t.*

t. came two angels to Sodom   *Ge 19:1* at even

is old, and *t.* is not a man in   *Ge 19:31* the earth

t. they sware both of them   *Ge 21:31* called *t.* on the name of the   *Ge 21:33* Lord

and offer him *t.* for a burnt   *Ge 22:2* offering

Abraham built an altar *t.* and   *Ge 22:9* laid

it of me, and I will bury my   *Ge 23:13* dead *t.*

is *t.* room in thy father's   *Ge 24:23* house for

t. was set meat before him to   *Ge 24:33* eat

t. was Abraham buried, and   *Ge 25:10* Sarah

behold, *t.* were twins in her   *Ge 25:24* womb

when he had been *t.* a long   *Ge 26:8* time

in the valley of Gerar, and   *Ge 26:17* dwelt *t.*

found *t.* a well of springing   *Ge 26:19* water

he builded an altar *t.* and   *Ge 26:25* called

the Lord, and pitched his   *Ge 26:25* tent *t.*

and *t.* Isaac's servants digged   *Ge 26:25* a well

said, Let *t.* be now an oath   *Ge 26:28* betwixt

place, and tarried *t.* all night   *Ge 28:11* *t.* were three flocks of sheep   *Ge 29:2* lying

Is *t.* yet any portion or   *Ge 31:14* inheritance

and they did eat *t.* upon the   *Ge 31:46* heap

with Laban, and stayed *t.*   *Ge 32:4* until now

And he lodged *t.* that same   *Ge 32:13* night

and *t.* wrestled a man with   *Ge 32:24* him until

my name? And he blessed   *Ge 32:29* him *t.*

And he erected *t.* an altar   *Ge 33:20* Arise, go up to Beth-el, and   *Ge 35:1* dwell *t.*

and make *t.* an altar unto God   *Ge 35:1* I will make *t.* an altar unto   *Ge 35:3* God

he built *t.* an altar, and called   *Ge 35:7* because *t.* God appeared unto   *Ge 35:7* him

t. was but a little way to   *Ge 35:16* come to

before *t.* reigned any king   *Ge 36:31* over the

pit was empty, *t.* was no   *Ge 37:24* water in it

t. passed by Midianites   *Ge 37:28* merchantmen

And Judah saw *t.* a daughter   *Ge 38:2* of a

said, *T.* was no harlot in this   *Ge 38:21* place

that *t.* was no harlot in this   *Ge 38:22* place

T. is none greater in this   *Ge 39:9* house than I

and *t.* was none of the men   *Ge 39:11* of the

of the men of the house *t.*   *Ge 39:11* within

and he was *t.* in the prison   *Ge 39:20* whatsoever they did *t.* he was   *Ge 39:22* a dream, and *t.* is no   *Ge 40:8* interpreter

t. was of all manner of   *Ge 40:17* bakemeats

t. came up out of the river   *Ge 41:2* seven well

t. was none that could   *Ge 41:8* interpret them

And *t.* was with us a young   *Ge 41:12* man

was *t.* with us a young man,   *Ge 41:12* an

and *t.* is none that can   *Ge 41:15* interpret it

t. came up out of the river   *Ge 41:18* seven kine

t. was none that could   *Ge 41:24* declare it to me

t. come seven years of great   *Ge 41:29* plenty

t. shall arise after them seven   *Ge 41:30* years of

t. is none so discreet and   *Ge 41:39* wise as thou

in all the land of Egypt *t.* was   *Ge 41:54* bread

Jacob saw that *t.* was corn in   *Ge 42:1* Egypt

I have heard that *t.* is corn in   *Ge 42:2* Egypt

proved, whether *t.* be any   *Ge 42:16* truth in you

heart that they should eat   *Ge 43:25* bread *t.*

into his chamber, and wept *t.*   *Ge 43:30* to Joseph's house: for he was   *Ge 44:14* yet *t.*

And *t.* stood no man with   *Ge 45:1* him, while

and yet *t.* are five years, in the   *Ge 45:6* which *t.* shall neither be earing   *Ge 45:6* nor

And *t.* will I nourish thee;   *Ge 45:11* for yet

for yet *t.* are five years of   *Ge 45:11* famine

will *t.* make of thee a great   *Ge 46:3* nation

t. was no bread in all the   *Ge 47:13* land; for

t. is not ought left in the   *Ge 47:18* sight of my

yet *t.* was but a little way to   *Ge 48:7* come

and I buried her *t.* in the way   *Ge 48:7* of

T. they buried Abraham and   *Ge 49:31* Sarah

t. they buried Isaac and   *Ge 49:31* Rebekah

his wife; and *t.* I buried   *Ge 49:31* Leah

of Canaan, *t.* shalt thou bury   *Ge 50:5* me

t. went up with him both   *Ge 50:9* chariots

t. they mourned with a great   *Ge 50:10* *t.* arose up a new king over   *Ex 1:8* Egypt

when *t.* falleth out any war,   *Ex 1:10* they join

t. went a man of the house of   *Ex 2:1* Levi

and when he saw that *t.* was   *Ex 2:12* no man

t. more work be laid upon the   *Ex 5:9* men

daily tasks, as when *t.* was   *Ex 5:13* straw

T. is no straw given unto thy   *Ex 5:16* for *t.* shall no straw be   *Ex 5:18* given you

that *t.* may be blood   *Ex 7:19* throughout all

t. was blood throughout all   *Ex 7:21* the land

t. is none like unto the Lord   *Ex 8:10* our God

when Pharaoh saw that *t.* was   *Ex 8:15* respite

so *t.* were lice upon man, and   *Ex 8:18* upon

that no swarms of flies shall   *Ex 8:22* be *t.*

t. came a grievous swarm of   *Ex 8:24* flies into

from his people; *t.* remained   *Ex 8:31* not one

t. shall be a very grievous murrain *Ex 9:3*

t. shall nothing die of all that is the *Ex 9:4*

t. was not one of the cattle of *Ex 9:7*

that *t.* is none like me in all the earth *Ex 9:14*

that *t.* may be hail in all the land of *Ex 9:22*

So *t.* was hail, and fire mingled with *Ex 9:24*

such as *t.* was none like it in all the *Ex 9:24*

children of Israel were, was *t.* no hail *Ex 9:26*

t. be no more mighty thunderings and *Ex 9:28*

neither shall *t.* be any more hail *Ex 9:29*

t. were no such locusts as they *Ex 10:14*

t. remained not any green thing in *Ex 10:15*

t. remained not one locust in all the *Ex 10:19*

that *t.* may be darkness over the land *Ex 10:21*

t. was a thick darkness in all the land *Ex 10:22*

t. shall not an hoof be left behind: for *Ex 10:26*

t. shall be a great cry throughout all *Ex 11:6*

such as *t.* was none like it, nor shall *Ex 11:6*

day *t.* shall be an holy convocation *Ex 12:16*

Seven days shall *t.* be no leaven found *Ex 12:19*

and *t.* was a great cry in Egypt *Ex 12:30*

cry in Egypt; for *t.* was not a house *Ex 12:30*

house where *t.* was not one dead *Ex 12:30*

T. shall no stranger eat thereof *Ex 12:43*

t. shall no leavened bread be eaten *Ex 13:3*

t. shall no leavened bread be seen with *Ex 13:7*

neither shall *t.* be leaven seen with *Ex 13:7*

Because *t.* were no graves in Egypt *Ex 14:11*

t. remained not so much as one of *Ex 14:28*

t. he made for them a statute *Ex 15:25*

ordinance, and *t.* be proved them *Ex 15:25*

they encamped *t.* by the waters *Ex 15:27*

wilderness *t.* lay a small round thing *Ex 16:14*

neither was *t.* any worm therein *Ex 16:24*

is the sabbath, in it *t.* shall be none *Ex 16:26*

that *t.* went out some of the people on *Ex 16:27*

t. was no water for the people to drink *Ex 17:1*

the people thirsted *t.* for water *Ex 17:3*

I will stand before thee *t.* upon the *Ex 17:6*

t. shall come water out of it, that the *Ex 17:6*

t. Israel camped before the mount *Ex 19:2*

T. shall not an hand touch it, but he *Ex 19:13*

that *t.* were thunders and lightnings *Ex 19:16*

If *t.* be laid on him a sum of money *Ex 21:30*

die, *t.* shall no blood be shed for him *Ex 22:2*

T. shall nothing cast their young, nor *Ex 23:26*

and *t.* was under his feet as it were a *Ex 24:10*

to me into the mount, and be *t.* *Ex 24:12*

t. shall be a knop under two branches *Ex 25:35*

Two tenons shall *t.* be in one board *Ex 26:17*

side *t.* shall be twenty boards *Ex 26:20*

t. shall be hangings for the court of *Ex 27:9*

t. shall be hangings of an hundred *Ex 27:11*

t. shall be an hole in the top of it *Ex 28:32*

meet you, to speak *t.* unto thee *Ex 29:42*

t. I will meet with the children of *Ex 29:43*

that *t.* be no plague among them *Ex 30:12*

of each shall *t.* be a like weight *Ex 30:34*

T. is a noise of war in the camp *Ex 32:17*

into the fire, and *t.* came out this calf *Ex 32:24*

fell of the people that day about *Ex 32:28*

for *t.* shall no man see me, and live *Ex 33:20*

Lord said, Behold, *t.* is a place by me *Ex 33:21*

present thyself *t.* to me in the top *Ex 34:2*

in the cloud, and stood with *Ex 34:5*

he was *t.* with the Lord forty days *Ex 34:28*

day *t.* shall be to you an holy day *Ex 35:2*

And *t.* were eight boards; and their *Ex 36:30*

t. was an hole in the midst of the robe *Ex 39:23*

put water *t.* to wash withal *Ex 40:30*

when *t.* is sprinkled of the blood *Le 6:27*

t. is one law for them: the priest that *Le 7:7*

t. eat it with the bread that is in *Le 8:31*

t. came a fire out from before the Lord *Le 9:24*

t. went out fire from the Lord *Le 10:2*

pit, wherein *t.* is plenty of water *Le 11:36*

t. be quick raw flesh in the rising *Le 13:10*

place of the boil *t.* be a white rising *Le 13:19*

behold, *t.* be no white hairs therein *Le 13:21*

Or if *t.* be any flesh, in the skin whereof *t.* is a hot burning *Le 13:24*

t. be no white hair in the bright spot *Le 13:26*

skin; and *t.* be in it a yellow thin hair *Le 13:30*

skin; and that *t.* is no black hair in it *Le 13:31*

not, and *t.* be in it no yellow hair *Le 13:32*

t. is black hair grown up therein *Le 13:37*

if *t.* be in the bald head, or bald *Le 13:42*

t. is as it were a plague in the house *Le 14:35*

t. shall be no man in the tabernacle *Le 16:17*

place, and shall leave them *t.* *Le 16:23*

What man soever *t.* be of the house of *Le 17:3*

man *t.* be of the house of Israel *Le 17:8; 17:10*

man *t.* be of the children of Israel *Le 17:13*

that *t.* be no wickedness among you *Le 20:14*

T. shall none be defiled for the dead *Le 21:1*

T. shall no stranger eat of the holy *Le 22:10*

but *t.* shall no stranger eat thereof *Le 22:13*

t. shall be no blemish therein *Le 22:21*

seventh month *t.* shall be a day of *Le 23:27*

If *t.* be yet many years behind *Le 25:51*

t. remain but few years unto the year *Le 25:52*

you *t.* shall be a man of every tribe *Nu 1:4*

t. be no wrath upon the congregation *Nu 1:53*

and *t.* be no witness against her *Nu 5:13*

t. shall no rasor come upon his *Nu 6:5*

t. be no plague among the children of *Nu 8:19*

t. were certain men, who were defiled *Nu 9:6*

at even *t.* was upon the tabernacle as *Nu 9:15*

t. the children of Israel pitched *Nu 9:17*

t. is nothing at all, beside this manna *Nu 11:6*

that they may stand *t.* with thee *Nu 11:16*

come down, and talk with thee *t.* *Nu 11:17*

But *t.* remained two of the men in the *Nu 11:26*

t. ran a young man, and told Moses *Nu 11:27*

t. went forth a wind from the Lord *Nu 11:31*

because *t.* they buried the people *Nu 11:34*

If *t.* be a prophet among you, I the *Nu 12:6*

whether *t.* be wood therein, or not *Nu 13:20*

we saw the children of Anak *t.* *Nu 13:28*

t. we saw the giants, the sons of *Nu 13:33*

be consumed, and *t.* they shall die *Nu 14:35*

the Canaanites are *t.* before you *Nu 14:43*

And *t.* came out a fire from the Lord *Nu 16:35*

for *t.* is wrath gone out from the Lord *Nu 16:46*

that *t.* be no wrath any more upon *Nu 18:5*

and upon the persons that were *t.* *Nu 19:18*

Miriam died *t.* and was buried *t.* *Nu 20:1*

t. was no water for the congregation *Nu 20:2*

we and our cattle should die *t.* *Nu 20:4*

neither is *t.* any water to drink *Nu 20:5*

unto his people, and shall die *t.* *Nu 20:26*

and Aaron died *t.* in the top of the *Nu 20:28*

the wilderness? for *t.* is no bread *Nu 21:5*

neither is *t.* any water *Nu 21:5*

For *t.* is a fire gone out of Heshbon *Nu 21:28*

out the Amorites that were *t.* *Nu 21:32*

until *t.* was none left him alive *Nu 21:35*

t. is a people come out from Egypt *Nu 22:5; 22:11*

I would *t.* were a sword in mine hand *Nu 22:29*

t. is no enchantment against Jacob *Nu 23:23*

is *t.* any divination against Israel *Nu 23:23*

t. shall come a Star out of Jacob, and a *Nu 24:17*

t. was no inheritance given them *Nu 26:62*

among these *t.* was not a man of them *Nu 26:64*

And *t.* was not left a man of them *Nu 26:65*

t. were delivered out of the thousands *Nu 31:5*

t. was a plague among the *Nu 31:16*

and *t.* lacketh not one man of us *Nu 31:49*

shall be *t.* in the cities of Gilead *Nu 32:26*

ten palm trees; and they pitched *t.* *Nu 33:9*

and died *t.* in the fortieth year *Nu 33:38*

t. shall be six cities for refuge *Nu 35:6*

T. are eleven days' journey from *De 1:2*

seen the sons of the Anakims *De 1:28*

t. shall not one of these men of this *De 1:35*

unto the days that ye abode *t.* *De 1:46*

t. was not one city too strong for us *De 2:36*

t. was not a city which we took not *De 3:4*

what God is *t.* in heaven or in earth — De 3:24

For what nation is *t.* so great, who — De 4:7

what nation is *t.* so great, that hath — De 4:8

t. ye shall serve gods, the work of — De 4:28

whether *t.* hath been any such thing — De 4:32

he is God; *t.* is none else beside him — De 4:35

the earth beneath: *t.* is none else — De 4:39

For who is *t.* of all flesh, that hath — De 5:26

O that *t.* were such a heart in them — De 5:29

t. shall not be male nor female barren — De 7:14

t. shall no man be able to stand before — De 7:24; 11:25

and drought, where *t.* was no water — De 8:15

t. they be, as the Lord commanded — De 10:5

t. Aaron died, and *t.* he was buried — De 10:6

that *t.* be no rain, and that the land — De 11:17

all your tribes to put his name *t.* — De 12:5

t. ye shall eat before the Lord your — De 12:7

t. shall be a place which the Lord — De 12:11

to cause his name to dwell *t.* — De 12:11

t. thou shalt offer thy burnt — De 12:14

t. thou shalt do all that I — De 12:14

God hath chosen to put his name *t.* — De 12:21

If *t.* arise among you a prophet, or a — De 13:1

thy God hath given thee to dwell *t.* — De 13:12

t. shall cleave nought of the cursed — De 13:17

shall choose to place his name *t.* — De 14:23

God shall choose to set his name *t.* — De 14:24

shalt eat *t.* before the Lord thy God — De 14:26

when *t.* shall be no poor among you — De 15:4

If *t.* be among you a poor man of one — De 15:7

t. be not a thought in thy wicked — De 15:9

And if *t.* be any blemish therein, as if — De 15:21

shall choose to place his name *t.* — De 16:2

t. shall be no leavened bread seen — De 16:4

neither shall *t.* any thing of the flesh — De 16:4

t. thou shalt sacrifice the passover — De 16:6

hath chosen to place his name *t.* — De 16:11

If *t.* be found among you, within — De 17:2

If *t.* arise a matter too hard for thee in — De 17:3

to minister *t.* before the Lord — De 17:12

do, which stand *t.* before the Lord — De 18:7

T. shall not be found among you any — De 18:10

man is *t.* that hath built a new house — De 20:5

man is *t.* that hath betrothed a wife — De 20:7

What man is *t.* that is fearful — De 20:8

the heifer's neck *t.* in the valley — De 21:4

t. is in the damsel no sin worthy of — De 22:26

cried, and *t.* was none to save her — De 22:27

t. be among you any man, that is not — De 23:10

T. shall be no whore of the daughters — De 23:17

If *t.* be a controversy between men — De 25:1

shall choose to place his name *t.* — De 26:2

Egypt, and sojourned *t.* with a few — De 26:5

t. a nation, great, mighty, and — De 26:5

t. shalt thou build an altar unto the — De 27:5

peace offerings, and shalt eat *t.* — De 27:5

and *t.* shall be no might in thine hand — De 28:32

t. shalt thou serve other gods — De 28:36; 28:64

shall give thee *t.* a trembling heart — De 28:65

t. ye shall be sold unto your enemies — De 28:68

Lest *t.* should be among you man, or — De 29:18

lest *t.* should be among you a root that — De 29:18

it may be *t.* for a witness against — De 31:26

and *t.* was no strange god with him — De 32:12

is *t.* any understanding in them — De 32:28

is gone and *t.* is none shut up, or left — De 32:36

I, am he, and *t.* is no god with me — De 32:39

neither is *t.* any that can deliver out — De 32:39

t. they shall offer sacrifices of — De 33:19

t. in a portion of the lawgiver, was — De 33:21

T. is none like unto the God of — De 33:26

the servant of the Lord died *t.* in — De 34:5

t. arose not a prophet since in Israel — De 34:10

T. shall not any man be able to stand — Jos 1:5

house, named Rahab, and lodged *t.* — Jos 2:1

t. came men in hither to night of the — Jos 2:2

T. came men unto me, but I wist not — Jos 2:4

neither did *t.* remain, more courage — Jos 2:11

and hide yourselves *t.* three days — Jos 2:16

mountain, and abode *t.* three days — Jos 2:22

lodged *t.* before they passed over — Jos 3:1

Yet *t.* shall be a space between you — Jos 3:4

lodged, and laid them down *t.* — Jos 4:8

stood: and they are *t.* unto this day — Jos 4:9

neither was *t.* spirit in them any more — Jos 5:1

t. stood a man over against him with — Jos 5:13

So *t.* went up thither of the people — Jos 7:4

T. is an accursed thing in the midst — Jos 7:13

t. was a valley between them and Ai — Jos 8:11

wist not that *t.* were liers in ambush — Jos 8:14

t. was not a man left in Ai or Beth-el — Jos 8:17

And he wrote *t.* upon the stones — Jos 8:32

T. was not a word of all that Moses — Jos 8:35

and *t.* shall none of you be freed — Jos 9:23

t. shall not a man of them stand before — Jos 10:8

And *t.* was no day like that before it — Jos 10:14

t. was not any left to breathe: and he — Jos 11:11

T. was not a city that made peace — Jos 11:19

T. was none of the Anakims left in — Jos 11:22

in Gath, and in Ashdod, *t.* remained — Jos 11:22

t. remaineth yet very much land to be — Jos 13:1

day how the Anakims were *t.* — Jos 14:12

T. was also a lot for the tribe of — Jos 17:1

T. was also a lot for the rest of the — Jos 17:2

And *t.* fell ten portions to Manasseh — Jos 17:5

cut down for thyself *t.* in the land — Jos 17:15

tabernacle of the congregation *t.* — Jos 18:1

t. remained among the children of — Jos 18:2

t. Joshua divided the land unto the — Jos 18:10

t. stood not a man of all their enemies — Jos 21:44

T. failed not ought of any good thing — Jos 21:45

tribe of Manasseh built *t.* an altar — Jos 22:10

t. was a plague in the congregation of — Jos 22:17

and set it up *t.* under an oak — Jos 24:26

him to Jerusalem, and *t.* he died — J'g 1:7

they sacrificed *t.* unto the Lord — J'g 2:5

t. arose another generation after them — J'g 2:10

of valour; and *t.* escaped not a man — J'g 3:29

the sword; and *t.* was not a man left — J'g 4:16

t. was peace between Jabin the king — J'g 4:17

of thee, and say, Is *t.* any man here — J'g 4:20

was *t.* a shield or spear seen among — J'g 5:8

t. shall they rehearse the righteous — J'g 5:11

Out of Ephraim was *t.* a root of them — J'g 5:14

t. were great thoughts of heart — J'g 5:15

t. were great searchings of heart — J'g 5:16

he bowed, *t.* he fell down dead — J'g 5:27

t. came an angel of the Lord, and sat — J'g 6:11

t. rose up fire out of the rock — J'g 6:21

Then Gideon built an altar *t.* unto — J'g 6:24

and upon all the ground let *t.* be dew — J'g 6:39

only, and *t.* was dew on all the ground — J'g 6:40

t. returned of the people twenty — J'g 7:3

and *t.* remained ten thousand — J'g 7:3

and I will try them for thee *t.* — J'g 7:4

t. was a man that told a dream unto — J'g 7:13

t. fell an hundred and twenty — J'g 8:10

and went to Beer, and dwelt *t.* — J'g 9:21

t. come people down from the top — J'g 9:36

t. come people down by the middle — J'g 9:37

t. was a strong tower within the city — J'g 9:51

t. arose to defend Israel Tola the son — J'g 10:1

t. were gathered vain men to Jephthah — J'g 11:3

t. fell at that time of the Ephraimites — J'g 12:6

t. was a certain man of Zorah, of the — J'g 13:2

t. never a woman among the daughters — J'g 14:3

t. was a swarm of bees and honey in — J'g 14:8

and Samson made *t.* a feast — J'g 14:10

the jaw, and *t.* came water thereout — J'g 15:19

to Gaza, and saw *t.* an harlot — J'g 16:1

t. were men lying in wait, abiding — J'g 16:9

t. were liers in wait abiding in the — J'g 16:12

T. hath not come a rasor upon mine — J'g 16:17

lords of the Philistines were *t.* — J'g 16:27

t. were upon the roof about three — J'g 16:27

And *t.* was a man of mount Ephraim — J'g 17:1

In those days *t.* was no king in Israel — J'g 17:6; 18:1

And *t.* was a man out of — J'g 17:7

was a Levite, and he sojourned t.	J'g 17:7
house of Micah, they lodged t.	J'g 18:2
t. was no magistrate in the land, that	J'g 18:7
where t. is no want of any thing	J'g 18:10
t. went from thence of the family	J'g 18:11
that t. is in these houses an ephod	J'g 18:14
t. was no deliverer, because it was far	J'g 18:28
days, when t. was no king in Israel	J'g 19:1
t. was a certain Levite sojourning on	J'g 19:1
and was t. four whole months	J'g 19:2
did eat and drink, and lodged t.	J'g 19:4
him: therefore he lodged t. again	J'g 19:7
t. were with him two asses saddled	J'g 19:10
for t. was no man that took them into	J'g 19:15
t. came an old man from his work	J'g 19:16
t. is no man that receiveth me to	J'g 19:18
t. is both straw and provender for our	J'g 19:19
and t. is bread and wine also for me	J'g 19:19
servants: t. is no want of any thing	J'g 19:19
T. was no such deed done, nor seen	J'g 19:30
t. were seven hundred chosen men	J'g 20:16
wept, and sat t. before the Lord	J'g 20:26
ark of the covenant of God was t.	J'g 20:27
t. came against Gibeah ten thousand	J'g 20:34
Now t. was an appointed sign between	J'g 20:38
t. fell of Benjamin eighteen thousand	J'g 20:44
T. shall not any give his daughter	J'g 21:1
and abode t. till even before God	J'g 21:2
t. should be to day one tribe lacking	J'g 21:3
rose early, and built t. an altar	J'g 21:4
Who is t. among all the tribes of Israel	J'g 21:5
T. is one tribe cut off from Israel this	J'g 21:6
what one is t. of the tribes of Israel	J'g 21:8
t. came none to the camp from	J'g 21:8
t. were none of the inhabitants of	J'g 21:9
inhabitants of Jabesh-gilead t.	J'g 21:9
T. must be an inheritance for them	J'g 21:17
t. is a feast of the Lord in Shiloh	J'g 21:19
In those days t. was no king in Israel	J'g 21:25
that t. was a famine in the land	Ru 1:1
country of Moab, and continued t.	Ru 1:2
they dwelled t. about ten years	Ru 1:4
are t. yet any more sons in my womb	Ru 1:11
will I die, and t. will I be buried	Ru 1:17
t. is a kinsman, nearer than I	Ru 3:12
to the gate, and sat him down t.	Ru 4:1
for t. is none to redeem it beside thee	Ru 4:4
saying, T. is a son born to Naomi	Ru 4:17
Now t. was a certain man of	1Sa 1:1
the priests of the Lord, were t.	1Sa 1:3
t. shall no rasor come upon his head	1Sa 1:11
the Lord, and t. abide for ever	1Sa 1:22
And he worshipped the Lord t.	1Sa 1:28
T. is none holy as the Lord	1Sa 2:2

for t. is none beside thee	1Sa 2:2
neither is t. any rock like our God	1Sa 2:2
And t. came a man of God unto Eli	1Sa 2:27
t. shall not be an old man in thine	1Sa 2:31; 2:32
in those days; t. was no open vision	1Sa 3:1
were t. with the ark of the covenant	1Sa 4:4
for t. hath not been such a thing	1Sa 4:7
and t. was a very great slaughter	1Sa 4:10
for t. fell of Israel thirty thousand	1Sa 4:10
t. ran a man of Benjamin out of the	1Sa 4:12
And he said, What is t. done, my son	1Sa 4:16
and t. hath been also a great slaughter	1Sa 4:17
t. was a deadly destruction throughout	1Sa 5:11
the hand of God was very heavy at	1Sa 5:11
kine, on which t. hath come no yoke	1Sa 6:7
the cart came and stood t.	1Sa 6:14
where t. was a great stone	1Sa 6:14
and said t., We have sinned against	1Sa 7:6
t. was peace between Israel and the	1Sa 7:14
to Ramah; for t. was his house	1Sa 7:17
and t. he judged Israel; and	1Sa 7:17
t. he built an altar unto the Lord	1Sa 7:17
Now t. was a man of Benjamin, whose	1Sa 9:1
t. was not among the children of Israel	1Sa 9:2
land of Shalim, and t. they were not	1Sa 9:4
now, t. is in this city a man of God	1Sa 9:6
t. is not a present to bring to the man	1Sa 9:7
t. is a sacrifice of the people to day	1Sa 9:12
and t. shall meet thee three men	1Sa 10:3
t. is none like him among all	1Sa 10:24
and t. went with him a band of men	1Sa 10:26
and then, if t. be no man to save us	1Sa 11:3
T. shall not a man be put to death	1Sa 11:13
Gilgal, and renew the kingdom t.	1Sa 11:14
t. they made Saul king before the	1Sa 11:15
t. they sacrificed sacrifices of peace	1Sa 11:15
t. Saul and all the men of Israel	1Sa 11:15
t. was no smith found throughout all	1Sa 13:19
that t. was neither sword nor spear	1Sa 13:22
with Jonathan his son was t. found	1Sa 13:22
t. was a sharp rock on the one side	1Sa 14:4
for t. is no restraint to the Lord to	1Sa 14:6
And t. was trembling in the host, in	1Sa 14:15
and his armourbearer were not t.	1Sa 14:17
and t. was a very great discomfiture	1Sa 14:20
and t. was honey upon the ground	1Sa 14:25
for had t. not been now a much	1Sa 14:30
him that night, and slew them t.	1Sa 14:34
But t. was not a man among all the	1Sa 14:39
t. shall not one hair of his head fall to	1Sa 14:45
t. was sore war against the Philistines	1Sa 14:52
said, T. remaineth yet the youngest	1Sa 16:11

and t. was a valley between them	1Sa 17:3
And t. went out a champion out of the	1Sa 17:4
behold, t. came up the champion	1Sa 17:23
have I now done? Is t. not a cause	1Sa 17:29
father's sheep, and t. came a lion	1Sa 17:34
may know that t. is a God in Israel	1Sa 17:46
t. was no sword in the hand of David	1Sa 17:50
and t. was a javelin in Saul's hand	1Sa 18:10
t. was war again: and David went out	1Sa 19:8
in, behold, t. was an image in the bed	1Sa 19:16
t. is but a step between me and death	1Sa 20:3
his city: for t. is a yearly sacrifice	1Sa 20:6
sacrifice t. for all the family	1Sa 20:6
if t. be in me iniquity, slay me thyself	1Sa 20:8
behold, if t. be good toward David	1Sa 20:12
come thou: for t. is peace to thee	1Sa 20:21
he hath commanded me to be t.	1Sa 20:29
in mine hand, or what t. is present	1Sa 21:3
T. is no common bread under mine	1Sa 21:4
mine hand, but t. is hallowed bread	1Sa 21:4
hallowed bread: for t. was no bread	1Sa 21:6
was no bread t. but the shewbread	1Sa 21:6
of the servants of Saul was t. that day	1Sa 21:7
is t. not here under thine hand spear	1Sa 21:8
it: for t. is no other save that here	1Sa 21:9
And David said, T. is none like that	1Sa 21:9
t. were with him about four hundred	1Sa 22:2
t. is none that sheweth me that my	1Sa 22:8
and t. is none of you that is sorry	1Sa 22:8
when Doeg the Edomite was t.	1Sa 22:22
haunt is, and who hath seen him t.	1Sa 23:22
But t. came a messenger unto Saul	1Sa 23:27
and see that t. is neither evil nor	1Sa 24:11
And t. was a man in Maon, whose	1Sa 25:2
neither was t. ought missing unto	1Sa 25:7
t. be many servants now a days that	1Sa 25:10
t. went up after David about four	1Sa 25:13
surely t. had not been left unto Nabal	1Sa 25:34
t. came one of the people in to destroy	1Sa 26:15
t. is nothing better for me than that I	1Sa 27:1
the country, that I may dwell t.	1Sa 27:5
t. is a woman that hath a familiar	1Sa 28:7
t. shall no punishment happen to thee	1Sa 28:10
and t. was no strength in him; for he	1Sa 28:20
and t. escaped not a man of them, save	1Sa 30:17
and t. was nothing lacking to them	1Sa 30:19
came to Jabesh, and burnt them t.	1Sa 31:12
mountains of Gilboa, let t. be no dew	2Sa 1:21
neither let t. be rain, upon you, nor	2Sa 1:21
t. the shield of the mighty is vilely	2Sa 1:21

t. they anointed David king over the — 2Sa 2:4

t. arose and went over by number — 2Sa 2:15

And *t.* was a very sore battle that day — 2Sa 2:17

And *t.* were three sons of Zeruiah — 2Sa 2:18

were three sons of Zeruiah *t.* — 2Sa 2:18

and he fell down *t.* and died in the — 2Sa 2:23

t. lacked of David's servants nineteen — 2Sa 2:30

t. was long war between the house of — 2Sa 3:1

while *t.* was war between the house of — 2Sa 3:6

smote him *t.* under the fifth rib — 2Sa 3:27

let *t.* not fail from the house of Joab — 2Sa 3:29

Know ye not that *t.* is a prince and a — 2Sa 3:38

were sojourners *t.* until this day — 2Sa 4:3

t. were yet sons and daughters born to — 2Sa 5:13

David smote them *t.* and said, The — 2Sa 5:20

t. they left their images, and David — 2Sa 5:21

and God smote him *t.* for his error — 2Sa 6:7

and *t.* he died by the ark of God — 2Sa 6:7

O Lord God: for *t.* is none like thee — 2Sa 7:22

neither is *t.* any God beside thee — 2Sa 7:22

Is *t.* yet any that is left of the house of — 2Sa 9:1

t. was of the house of Saul a servant — 2Sa 9:2

Is *t.* not yet any of the house of Saul — 2Sa 9:3

captain of their host, who died *t.* — 2Sa 10:18

t. followed him a mess of meat from — 2Sa 11:8

t. fell some of the people of — 2Sa 11:17

T. were two men in one city; the one — 2Sa 12:1

t. came a traveller unto the rich man — 2Sa 12:4

And she said unto him, *T.* is no cause — 2Sa 13:16

sons, and *t.* is not one of them left — 2Sa 13:30

t. came much people by the way of the — 2Sa 13:34

to Geshur, and was *t.* three years — 2Sa 13:38

t. was none to part them, but the one — 2Sa 14:6

t. shall not one hair of thy son fall to — 2Sa 14:11

t. was none to be so much praised as — 2Sa 14:25

crown of his head *t.* was no blemish — 2Sa 14:25

unto Absalom *t.* were born three sons — 2Sa 14:27

he hath barley *t*; go and set it on — 2Sa 14:30

good for me to have been *t.* still — 2Sa 14:32

if *t.* be any iniquity in me, let him kill — 2Sa 14:32

t. is no man deputed of the king to — 2Sa 15:3

t. came a messenger to David, saying — 2Sa 15:13

even *t.* also will thy servant be — 2Sa 15:21

until *t.* come word from you to certify — 2Sa 15:28

to Jerusalem: and they tarried *t.* — 2Sa 15:29

hast thou not *t.* with thee Zadok — 2Sa 15:35

have *t.* with them their two sons — 2Sa 15:36

weary, and refreshed themselves *t.* — 2Sa 16:14

T. is a slaughter among the people — 2Sa 17:9

t. shall not be left so much as one — 2Sa 17:12

until *t.* be not one small stone found — 2Sa 17:13

be not one small stone found — 2Sa 17:13

by the morning light *t.* lacked not one — 2Sa 17:22

was *t.* a great slaughter that day — 2Sa 18:7

the battle was *t.* scattered over the — 2Sa 18:8

and why didst thou not smite him *t.* — 2Sa 18:11

for *t.* is no matter hid from the king — 2Sa 18:13

he be alone, *t.* is tidings in his mouth — 2Sa 18:25

t. will not tarry one with thee this — 2Sa 19:7

t. were a thousand men of Benjamin — 2Sa 19:17

And *t.* went over a ferry boat to carry — 2Sa 19:18

shall *t.* any man be put to death this — 2Sa 19:22

t. happened to be a man of Belial — 2Sa 20:1

happened to be *t.* a man of Belial — 2Sa 20:1

And *t.* went out after him Joab's men — 2Sa 20:7

t. was a famine in the days of David — 2Sa 21:1

t. was again a battle with — 2Sa 21:18

t. was again a battle in Gob with the — 2Sa 21:19

And *t.* was yet a battle in Gath, where — 2Sa 21:20

T. went up a smoke out of his nostrils — 2Sa 22:9

They looked, but *t.* was none to save — 2Sa 22:42

defied the Philistines that were *t.* — 2Sa 23:9

and *t.* were in Israel eight hundred — 2Sa 24:9

or that *t.* be three days' pestilence in — 2Sa 24:13

t. died of the people from Dan even to — 2Sa 24:15

David built *t.* an altar unto the — 2Sa 24:25

Let *t.* be sought for my lord the king a — 1Ki 1:2

thou yet talkest *t.* with the king — 1Ki 1:14

anoint him *t.* king over Israel — 1Ki 1:34

t. shall not an hair of him fall to the — 1Ki 1:52

t. shall not fail thee (said he) a man on — 1Ki 2:4

shall *t.* be peace for ever from the — 1Ki 2:33

house in Jerusalem, and dwell *t.* — 1Ki 2:36

t. was no house built unto the name — 1Ki 3:2

king went to Gibeon to sacrifice *t.* — 1Ki 3:4

that *t.* was none like thee before thee — 1Ki 3:12

t. shall not be any among the kings — 1Ki 3:13

t. was no stranger with us in — 1Ki 3:18

And *t.* came of all people to hear the — 1Ki 4:34

that *t.* is neither adversary nor evil — 1Ki 5:4

for thou knowest that *t.* is not among — 1Ki 5:6

cause them to be discharged *t.* — 1Ki 5:9

t. was peace between Hiram — 1Ki 5:12

t. was neither hammer nor axe nor — 1Ki 6:7

all was cedar; *t.* was no stone seen — 1Ki 6:18

to set *t.* the ark of the covenant of — 1Ki 6:19

And *t.* were windows in three rows — 1Ki 7:4

brim of it round about *t.* were knops — 1Ki 7:24

upon the ledges *t.* was a base above — 1Ki 7:29

t. were four undersetters to the four — 1Ki 7:34

top of the base was *t.* a round compass — 1Ki 7:35

and *t.* they are unto this day — 1Ki 8:8

T. was nothing in the ark save the — 1Ki 8:9

which Moses put *t.* at Horeb — 1Ki 8:9

I have set *t.* a place for the ark — 1Ki 8:21

t. is no God like thee, in heaven above — 1Ki 8:23

T. shall not fail thee a man in my — 1Ki 8:25

hast said, My name shall be *t.* — 1Ki 8:29

heaven is shut up, and *t.* is no rain — 1Ki 8:35

If *t.* be in the land famine — 1Ki 8:37

If *t.* be pestilence, blasting, mildew — 1Ki 8:37

locust, or if *t.* be caterpillar — 1Ki 8:37

plague, whatsoever sickness *t.* be — 1Ki 8:37

(for *t.* is no man that sinneth not) — 1Ki 8:46

t. hath not failed one word of all his — 1Ki 8:56

Lord is God, and that *t.* is none else — 1Ki 8:60

for *t.* he offered burnt offerings — 1Ki 8:64

built, to put my name *t.* for ever — 1Ki 9:3

mine heart shall be *t.* perpetually — 1Ki 9:3

T. shall not fail thee a man upon the — 1Ki 9:5

t. was not any thing hid from the king — 1Ki 10:3

the Lord; *t.* was no more spirit in her — 1Ki 10:5

t. came no more such abundance of — 1Ki 10:12

t. came no such almug trees, nor were — 1Ki 10:12

t. were stays on either side on the — 1Ki 10:19

And twelve lions stood *t.* on the — 1Ki 10:20

t. was not the like made in any — 1Ki 10:20

six months did Joab remain *t.* — 1Ki 11:16

have chosen me to put my name *t.* — 1Ki 11:36

t. was none that followed the house of — 1Ki 12:20

t. came a man of God out of Judah by — 1Ki 13:1

t. dwelt an old prophet in Beth-el — 1Ki 13:11

eat no bread nor drink water *t.* — 1Ki 13:17

t. is Ahijah the prophet, which told — 1Ki 14:2

in him *t.* is found some good thing — 1Ki 14:13

tribes of Israel, to put his name *t.* — 1Ki 14:21

t. were also Sodomites in the land — 1Ki 14:24

t. was war between Rehoboam and — 1Ki 14:30; 15:6

t. was war between Abijam — 1Ki 15:7

t. was war between Asa and Baasha — 1Ki 15:16; 15:32

T. is a league between me and thee — 1Ki 15:19

t. shall not be dew nor rain these — 1Ki 17:1

the ravens to feed thee *t.* — 1Ki 17:4

because *t.* had been no rain — 1Ki 17:7

belongeth to Zidon, and dwell *t.* — 1Ki 17:9

a widow woman *t.* to sustain thee — 1Ki 17:9

the widow woman was *t.* gathering — 1Ki 17:10

sore, that *t.* was no breath left in him — 1Ki 17:17

And *t.* was a sore famine in Samaria — 1Ki 18:2

t. is no nation or kingdom whither my — 1Ki 18:10

when they said, He is not *t.* he took — 1Ki 18:10

But *t.* was no voice, nor any that — 1Ki 18:26

that *t.* was neither voice, nor any to — 1Ki 18:29

brook Kishon, and slew them *t.* — 1Ki 18:40

for *t.* is a sound of abundance of rain — 1Ki 18:41

and looked, and said, *T.* is nothing — 1Ki 18:43

t. ariseth a little cloud out of the sea — 1Ki 18:44

and wind, and *t.* was a great 1Ki 18:45
rain
to Judah, and left his servant 1Ki 19:3
t.
t. was a cake baken on the 1Ki 19:6
coals
thither unto a cave, and 1Ki 19:9
lodged *t.*
behold, *t.* came a voice unto 1Ki 19:13
him, and
t. were thirty and two kings 1Ki 20:1
with him
t. came a prophet unto 1Ki 20:13
Ahab king of
T. are men come out of 1Ki 20:17
Samaria
t. came a man of God, and 1Ki 20:28
spake unto
t. a wall fell upon twenty 1Ki 20:30
and seven
as thy servant was busy here 1Ki 20:40
and *t.*
t. came in two men, 1Ki 21:13
children of
t. was none like unto Ahab, 1Ki 21:25
which did
Is *t.* not here a prophet of 1Ki 22:7
the Lord
T. is yet one man, Micaiah 1Ki 22:8
the son of
t. came forth a spirit, and 1Ki 22:21
stood before
t. went a proclamation 1Ki 22:36
throughout
T. was then no king in 1Ki 22:47
Edom: a
it not because *t.* is not a God 2Ki 1:3;
in Israel 1:6
T. came a man up to meet us, 2Ki 1:6
and said
t. came down fire from 2Ki 1:10
heaven, and
Behold, *t.* came fire down 2Ki 1:14
from heaven
t. is no God in Israel to 2Ki 1:16
enquire of
t. appeared a chariot of fire 2Ki 2:11
t. be with thy servants fifty 2Ki 2:16
strong
the waters, and cast the salt 2Ki 2:21
in *t.*
t. shall not be from thence 2Ki 2:21
any more
t. came forth little children 2Ki 2:23
out of the
t. came forth two she bears 2Ki 2:24
out of the
t. was no water for the host, 2Ki 3:9
and for
Is *t.* not here a prophet of 2Ki 3:11
the Lord
t. came water by the way of 2Ki 3:20
Edom, and
t. was great indignation 2Ki 3:27
against Israel
t. cried a certain woman of 2Ki 4:1
the wives
said unto her, T. is not a 2Ki 4:6
vessel more
and let us set for him *t.* a 2Ki 4:10
bed, and
into the chamber, and lay *t.* 2Ki 4:11
but *t.* was neither voice, nor 2Ki 4:31
hearing
t. was a dearth in the land; 2Ki 4:38
and the
thou man of God, *t.* is death 2Ki 4:40
in the pot
eat. And *t.* was no harm in 2Ki 4:41
the pot
t. came a man from 2Ki 4:42
Baal-shalisha, and
know that *t.* is a prophet in 2Ki 5:8
Israel
now I know that *t.* is no God 2Ki 5:15
in all the
Shall *t.* not then, I pray thee, 2Ki 5:17
be given
house of Rimmon to worship 2Ki 5:18
t.
t. be come to me from mount 2Ki 5:22
Ephraim
let us make us a place *t.* 2Ki 6:2
where
and saved himself *t.* not once 2Ki 6:10
nor
t. was a great famine in 2Ki 6:25
Samaria
t. cried a woman unto him, 2Ki 6:26
saying

And *t.* were four leprous men 2Ki 7:3
at the
enter into the city we shall 2Ki 7:4
die *t.*
camp of Syria, behold, *t.* was 2Ki 7:5
no man
of Syria, behold was no man 2Ki 7:5
t.
Syrians, and, behold, *t.* was 2Ki 7:10
no man
was no man *t.*; neither voice 2Ki 7:10
of
out *t.* Jehu the son of 2Ki 9:2
Jehoshaphat
and *t.* shall be none to bury 2Ki 9:10
her
went to Jezreel; for Joram 2Ki 9:16
lay *t.*
t. stood a watchman on the 2Ki 9:17
tower
t. went one on horseback to 2Ki 9:18
meet him
and said to Ahaziah, T. is 2Ki 9:23
treachery
he fled to Megiddo, and died 2Ki 9:27
t.
t. looked out to him two or 2Ki 9:32
three
t. are with you chariots and 2Ki 10:2
horses
t. came a messenger, and 2Ki 10:8
told him
now that *t.* shall fall unto 2Ki 10:10
the earth
t. was not a man left that 2Ki 10:21
came not
and look that *t.* be here with 2Ki 10:23
you none
king's house: and *t.* was she 2Ki 11:16
slain
they saw that *t.* was much 2Ki 12:10
money they
Howbeit *t.* were not made 2Ki 12:13
for the house
t. remained the grove also in 2Ki 13:6
Samaria
t. passed by a wild beast that 2Ki 14:9
was in
him to Lachish, and slew 2Ki 14:19
him *t.*
t. was not any shut up, nor 2Ki 14:26
any left
and stayed not *t.* in the land 2Ki 15:20
to Elath, and dwelt *t.* to this 2Ki 16:6
day
t. burnt incense in all 2Ki 17:11
the high
t. was none left but the tribe 2Ki 17:18
of Judah
the beginning of their 2Ki 17:25
dwelling *t.*
and let them go and dwell *t.* 2Ki 17:27
t. came out to them Eliakim 2Ki 18:18
the son
and *t.* is not strength to bring 2Ki 19:3
forth
this city, nor shoot an 2Ki 19:32
arrow *t.*
t. was nothing in his house, 2Ki 20:13
nor in all
t. is nothing among my 2Ki 20:15
treasures that
t. was no reckoning made 2Ki 22:7
with them
spied the sepulchres that 2Ki 23:16
were *t.*
upon the high places that 2Ki 23:20
were *t.*
t. was not holden such a 2Ki 23:22
passover
like unto him was *t.* no king 2Ki 23:25
before
neither after him arose *t.* 2Ki 23:25
any like him
which I said, My name 2Ki 23:27
shall be *t.*
and he came to Egypt, and 2Ki 23:34
died *t.*
t. was no bread for the 2Ki 25:3
people of the
t. came to Gedaliah to 2Ki 25:23
Mizpah
t. he reigned seven years and 1Ch 3:4
six
t. they dwelt with the king 1Ch 4:23
for his
for they of Ham had dwelt 1Ch 4:40
t. of old
the habitations that were 1Ch 4:41
found *t.*

in their rooms: because *t.* 1Ch 4:41
was pasture
was pasture *t.* for their flocks 1Ch 4:41
escaped, and dwelt *t.* unto 1Ch 4:43
this day
For *t.* fell down many slain, 1Ch 5:22
because
t. the Philistines were 1Ch 11:13
gathered
of the Gadites *t.* separated 1Ch 12:8
themselves
t. came of the children of 1Ch 12:16
Benjamin
seeing *t.* is no wrong in 1Ch 12:17
mine hands
t. fell some of Manasseh to 1Ch 12:19
David
to Ziklag, *t.* fell to him of 1Ch 12:20
Manasseh
day by day *t.* came to 1Ch 12:22
David to help
t. they were with David 1Ch 12:39
three
abundantly; for *t.* was joy 1Ch 12:40
in Israel
ark: and *t.* he died before 1Ch 13:10
God
and David smote them *t.* 1Ch 14:11
when they had left their 1Ch 14:12
gods *t.*
So he left *t.* before the ark 1Ch 16:37
of the
O Lord, *t.* is none like thee, 1Ch 17:20
neither is
neither is *t.* any God beside 1Ch 17:20
thee
Then *t.* went certain, and 1Ch 19:5
told David
gold, and *t.* were precious 1Ch 20:2
stones in it
that *t.* arose war at Gezer 1Ch 20:4
with the
t. was war again with the 1Ch 20:5
Philistines
And yet again *t.* was war at 1Ch 20:6
Gath
and *t.* fell of Israel seventy 1Ch 21:14
thousand
David built *t.* an altar unto 1Ch 21:26
the Jebusite, then he 1Ch 21:28
sacrificed *t.*
Moreover *t.* are workmen 1Ch 22:15
with thee in
brass, and the iron, *t.* is no 1Ch 22:16
number
t. were more chief men 1Ch 24:4
found of the
t. were sixteen chief men of 1Ch 24:4
the house
t. were found among them 1Ch 26:31
mighty
t. fell wrath for it against 1Ch 27:24
Israel
t. shall be with thee for all 1Ch 28:21
manner of
as a shadow, and *t.* is 1Ch 29:15
none abiding
for *t.* was the tabernacle of 2Ch 1:3
neither shall *t.* any after thee 2Ch 1:12
have
And *t.* it is unto this day 2Ch 5:9
T. was nothing in the ark 2Ch 5:10
save the
that my name might be *t.* 2Ch 6:5; 6:6
t. is no God like thee in the 2Ch 6:14
heaven
T. shall not fail thee a man 2Ch 6:16
in my
thou wouldest put thy name 2Ch 6:20
t.
heaven is shut up, and *t.* is 2Ch 6:26
no rain
If *t.* be dearth in the land 2Ch 6:28
if *t.* be pestilence, if *t.* be 2Ch 6:28
blasting
sore, or whatsoever sickness 2Ch 6:28
t. be
for *t.* is no man which 2Ch 6:36
sinneth not
t. he offered burnt offerings 2Ch 7:7
If I shut up heaven that *t.* 2Ch 7:13
be no rain
that my name may be *t.* for 2Ch 7:16
ever
mine heart shall be *t.* 2Ch 7:16
perpetually
T. shall not fail thee a man 2Ch 7:18
to be ruler
the children of Israel to dwell 2Ch 8:2
t.

and *t.* was nothing hid from Solomon   *2Ch 9:2*

Lord; *t.* was no more spirit in her   *2Ch 9:4*

neither was *t.* any such spice as the   *2Ch 9:9*

t. were none such seen before in the   *2Ch 9:11*

And *t.* were six steps to the throne   *2Ch 9:18*

twelve lions stood *t.* on the one   *2Ch 9:19*

T. was not the like made in any   *2Ch 9:19*

tribes of Israel, to put his name *t.*   *2Ch 12:13*

t. were wars between Rehoboam and   *2Ch 12:15*

And *t.* was war between Abijah and   *2Ch 13:2*

t. are gathered unto him vain men   *2Ch 13:7*

t. are with you golden calves, which   *2Ch 13:8*

t. fell down slain of Israel five hundred   *2Ch 13:17*

t. came out against them Zerah the   *2Ch 14:9*

t. was exceeding much spoil in them   *2Ch 14:14*

t. was no peace to him that went out   *2Ch 15:5*

t. was no more war unto the five and   *2Ch 15:19*

T. is a league between me and thee   *2Ch 16:3*

as *t.* was between my father and thy   *2Ch 16:3*

Is *t.* not here a prophet of the Lord   *2Ch 18:6*

T. is yet one man, by whom we may   *2Ch 18:7*

Then *t.* came out a spirit, and stood   *2Ch 18:20*

t. are good things found in thee   *2Ch 19:3*

for *t.* is no iniquity with the Lord our   *2Ch 19:7*

t. came some that told Jehoshaphat   *2Ch 20:2*

T. cometh a great multitude against   *2Ch 20:2*

and in thine hand is *t.* not power and   *2Ch 20:6*

t. they blessed the Lord: therefore   *2Ch 20:26*

t. came a writing to him from Elijah   *2Ch 21:12*

so that *t.* was never a son left him   *2Ch 21:17*

king's house, they slew her *t.*   *2Ch 23:15*

they saw that *t.* was much money   *2Ch 24:11*

t. came a man of God to him, saying   *2Ch 25:7*

t. passed by a wild beast that was in   *2Ch 25:18*

after him, and slew him *t.*   *2Ch 25:27*

But a prophet of the Lord was *t.*   *2Ch 28:9*

but are *t.* not with you, even with you   *2Ch 28:10*

and *t.* is fierce wrath against Israel   *2Ch 28:13*

villages thereof: and they dwelt *t.*   *2Ch 28:18*

And *t.* assembled at Jerusalem much   *2Ch 30:13*

t. were many in the congregation that   *2Ch 30:17*

So *t.* was great joy in Jerusalem: for   *2Ch 30:26*

Israel *t.* was not the like in Jerusalem   *2Ch 30:26*

So *t.* was gathered much people   *2Ch 32:4*

for *t.* be more with us than with him   *2Ch 32:7*

Who was *t.* among all the gods of   *2Ch 32:14*

bowels slew him *t.* with the sword   *2Ch 32:21*

therefore *t.* was wrath upon him, and   *2Ch 32:25*

and of the Levites *t.* were scribes, and   *2Ch 34:13*

And *t.* was no passover like to that   *2Ch 35:18*

his people, till *t.* was no remedy   *2Ch 36:16*

Who is *t.* among you of all his people   *2Ch 36:23; Ezr 1:3*

till *t.* stood up a priest with Urim and   *Ezr 2:63*

of whom *t.* were seven thousand three   *Ezr 2:65*

and *t.* were among them two hundred   *Ezr 2:65*

T. have been mighty kings also over   *Ezr 4:20*

let *t.* be search made in the king's   *Ezr 5:17*

house, which is *t.* at Babylon   *Ezr 5:17*

And *t.* was found at Achmetha, in the   *Ezr 6:2*

hath caused his name to dwell *t.*   *Ezr 6:12*

t. went up some of the children of   *Ezr 7:7*

should *t.* be wrath against the realm   *Ezr 7:23*

t. abode we in tents three days   *Ezr 8:15*

found *t.* none of the sons of Levi   *Ezr 8:15*

Then I proclaimed a fast *t.* at   *Ezr 8:21*

all Israel *t.* present, had offered   *Ezr 8:25*

and abode *t.* three days   *Ezr 8:32*

t. should be no remnant nor escaping   *Ezr 9:14*

t. assembled unto him out of Israel a   *Ezr 10:1*

t. is hope in Israel concerning this   *Ezr 10:2*

among the sons of the priests *t.* were   *Ezr 10:18*

are left of the captivity *t.* in the   *Ne 1:3*

though *t.* were of you cast out unto   *Ne 1:9*

I have chosen to set my name *t.*   *Ne 1:9*

t. was come a man to seek the welfare   *Ne 2:10*

Jerusalem, and was *t.* three days   *Ne 2:11*

neither was *t.* any beast with me   *Ne 2:12*

t. was no place for the beast that was   *Ne 2:14*

t. is much rubbish; so that we are not   *Ne 4:10*

t. was a great story cry of the people and   *Ne 5:1*

t. were that said, We, our sons   *Ne 5:2*

Some also *t.* were that said, We have   *Ne 5:3*

T. were also that said, We have   *Ne 5:4*

t. were at my table an hundred and   *Ne 5:17*

that *t.* was no breach left therein   *Ne 6:1*

T. is a king in Judah: and now shall   *Ne 6:7*

T. are no such things done as thou   *Ne 6:8*

and who is *t.* that, being as I am   *Ne 6:11*

t. were many in Judah sworn unto   *Ne 6:18*

till *t.* stood up a priest with Urim and   *Ne 7:65*

of whom *t.* were seven thousand three   *Ne 7:67*

so. And *t.* was very great gladness   *Ne 8:17*

of old *t.* were chief of the singers   *Ne 12:46*

T. dwelt men of Tyre also therein   *Ne 13:16*

t. should no burden be brought in on   *Ne 13:19*

many nations was *t.* no king like him   *Ne 13:26*

Thus shall *t.* arise too much contempt   *Es 1:18*

t. go a royal commandment from him   *Es 1:19*

Let *t.* be fair young virgins sought for   *Es 2:2*

in the palace *t.* was a certain Jew   *Es 2:5*

T. is a certain people scattered   *Es 3:8*

t. was written according to all that   *Es 3:12*

t. was great mourning among   *Es 4:3*

t. is one law of his to put him to death   *Es 4:11*

enlargement and deliverance arise   *Es 4:14*

unto him, *T.* is nothing done for him   *Es 6:3*

he saw that *t.* was evil determined   *Es 7:7*

T. was a man in the land of Uz   *Job 1:1*

t. were born unto him seven sons and   *Job 1:2*

t. was a day when the sons of God   *Job 1:6*

that *t.* is none like him in the earth   *Job 1:8; 2:3*

t. was a day when his sons and his   *Job 1:13*

And *t.* came a messenger unto Job   *Job 1:14*

speaking, *t.* came also another   *Job 1:16; 1:17-18*

t. came a great wind from the   *Job 1:19*

Again *t.* was a day when the sons of   *Job 2:1*

was said, *T.* is a man child conceived   *Job 3:3*

T. the wicked cease from   *Job 3:17*

and *t.* the weary be at rest   *Job 3:17*

T. the prisoners rest together; they   *Job 3:18*

The small and great are *t.*   *Job 3:19*

t. was silence, and I heard a voice   *Job 4:16*

if *t.* be any that will answer thee   *Job 5:1*

gate, neither is *t.* any to deliver them   *Job 5:4*

in seven *t.* shall no evil touch thee   *Job 5:19*

is *t.* any taste in the white of an egg   *Job 6:6*

is *t.* iniquity in my tongue? cannot   *Job 6:30*

Is *t.* not an apointed time to man   *Job 7:1*

Neither is *t.* any daysman betwixt us   *Job 9:33*

t. is none that can deliver out   *Job 10:7*

thou shalt be secure, because   *Job 11:18*

t. is hope

up a man, and *t.* can be no opening   *Job 12:14*

in a wilderness where *t.* is no way   *Job 12:24*

For *t.* is hope of a tree, if it be cut   *Job 14:7*

is *t.* any secret thing with thee   *Job 15:11*

Are *t.* not mockers with me? and doth   *Job 17:2*

I cry aloud, but *t.* is no judgment   *Job 19:7*

that ye may know *t.* is a judgment   *Job 19:29*

T. shall none of his meat be left   *Job 20:21*

him, as *t.* are innumerable before him   *Job 21:33*

your answers *t.* remaineth falsehood   *Job 21:34*

then thou shalt say, *T.* is lifting up   *Job 22:29*

T. the righteous might dispute   *Job 23:7*

Behold, I go forward, but he is not *t.*   *Job 23:8*

Is *t.* any number of his armies   *Job 25:3*

Surely *t.* is a vein for the silver, and a   *Job 28:1*

T. is a path which no fowl knoweth   *Job 28:7*

I waited for light, *t.* came darkness   *Job 30:26*

what portion of God is *t.* from above   *Job 31:2*

Elihu saw that *t.* was no answer in   *Job 32:5*

But *t.* is a spirit in man; and   *Job 32:8*

t. was none of you that convinced Job   *Job 32:12*

innocent; neither is *t.* iniquity in me   *Job 33:9*

If *t.* be a messenger with him, an   *Job 33:23*

T. is no darkness, nor shadow of   *Job 34:22*

T. they cry, but none giveth   *Job 35:12*

broad place, where *t.* is no straitness   *Job 36:16*

Because *t.* is wrath, beware lest he   *Job 36:18*

the wilderness, wherein *t.* is no man   *Job 38:26*

and where the slain are, *t.* is she   *Job 39:30*

Upon earth *t.* is not his like, who is   *Job 41:33*

Then came *t.* unto him all his   *Job 42:11*

Many *t.* be which say of my soul   *Ps 3:2*

T. is no help for him in God   *Ps 3:2*

T. be many that say, Who will shew   *Ps 4:6*

t. is no faithfulness in their mouth   *Ps 5:9*

For in death *t.* is no remembrance of   *Ps 6:5*

it in pieces, while *t.* is none to deliver   *Ps 7:2*

if *t.* be iniquity in my hands   *Ps 7:3*

hath said in his heart, *T.* is no God   *Ps 14:1; 53:1*

works, *t.* is none that doeth good   *Ps 14:1*

if *t.* were any that did understand   *Ps 14:2*

t. is none that doeth good, no, not one   *Ps 14:3; 53:3*

T. were they in great fear: for   *Ps 14:5*

hand *t.* are pleasures for evermore   *Ps 16:11*

T. went up a smoke out of his nostrils   *Ps 18:8*

cried, but *t.* was none to save them   *Ps 18:41*

T. is no speech nor language, where   *Ps 19:3*

t. is nothing hid from the heat thereof   *Ps 19:6*

in keeping of them *t.* is great reward   *Ps 19:11*

trouble is near; for *t.* is none to help   *Ps 22:11*

What profit is *t.* in my blood, when I   *Ps 30:9*

and in whose spirit *t.* is no guile   *Ps 32:2*

T. is no king saved by the multitude   *Ps 33:16*

for *t.* is no want to them that fear him   *Ps 34:9*

t. is no fear of God before his eyes   *Ps 36:1*

T. are the workers of iniquity   *Ps 36:12*

T. is no soundness in my flesh   *Ps 38:3; 38:7*

neither is *t.* any rest in my bones   *Ps 38:3*

the daughter of Tyre shall be *t.*   *Ps 45:12*

T. is a river, the streams whereof   *Ps 46:4*

Fear took hold upon them *t.*   *Ps 48:6*

in pieces, and *t.* be none to deliver   *Ps 50:22*

iniquity: *t.* is none that doeth good   *Ps 53:1*

if *t.* were any that did understand   *Ps 53:2*

T. were they in great fear, where   *Ps 53:5*

against me: for *t.* were many with me   *Ps 55:18*

Verily *t.* is a reward for the righteous   *Ps 58:11*

on foot: *t.* did we rejoice in him   *Ps 66:6*

T. is little Benjamin with their   *Ps 68:27*

in deep mire, where *t.* is no standing   *Ps 69:2*

some to take pity, but *t.* was none   *Ps 69:20*

that they may dwell *t.* and have it in   *Ps 69:35*

him; for *t.* is none to deliver him   *Ps 71:11*

T. shall be an handful of corn in the   *Ps 72:16*

For *t.* are no bands in their death   *Ps 73:4*

and is *t.* knowledge in the most High   *Ps 73:11*

t. is none upon earth that I desire   *Ps 73:25*

our signs: *t.* is no more any prophet   *Ps 74:9*

neither is *t.* among us any that   *Ps 74:9*

in the hand of the Lord *t.* is a cup   *Ps 75:8*

T. brake he the arrows of the bow   *Ps 76:3*

and *t.* was none to bury them   *Ps 79:3*

T. shall no strange god be in thee   *Ps 81:9*

Among the gods *t.* is none like unto   *Ps 86:8*

are *t.* any works like unto thy works   *Ps 86:8*

Ethiopia; this man was born *t.*   *Ps 87:4*

people, that this man was born *t.*   *Ps 87:6*

the players on instruments shall be *t.*   *Ps 87:7*

T. shall no evil befall thee, neither   *Ps 91:10*

and *t.* is no unrighteousness in him   *Ps 92:15*

T. go the ships   *Ps 104:26*

t. is that leviathan, whom thou   *Ps 104:26*

spake, and *t.* came divers sorts of flies   *Ps 105:31*

t. was not one feeble person among   *Ps 105:37*

enemies; *t.* was not one of them left   *Ps 106:11*

fell down, and *t.* was none to help   *Ps 107:12*

t. he maketh the hungry to dwell   *Ps 107:36*

in the wilderness, where *t.* is no way   *Ps 107:40*

Let *t.* be none to extend mercy unto   *Ps 109:12*

let *t.* be any to favour his fatherless   *Ps 109:12*

t. ariseth light in the darkness   *Ps 112:4*

For *t.* are set thrones of judgment   *Ps 122:5*

But *t.* is forgiveness with thee, that   *Ps 130:4*

for with the Lord *t.* is mercy, and with   *Ps 130:7*

T. will I make the horn of David   *Ps 132:17*

for *t.* the Lord commanded   *Ps 133:3*

neither is *t.* any breath in their   *Ps 135:17*

rivers of Babylon, *t.* we sat down   *Ps 137:1*

For *t.* they that carried us away   *Ps 137:3*

For *t.* is not a word in my tongue, but   *Ps 139:4*

ascend up into heaven, thou art *t.*   *Ps 139:8*

my bed in hell, behold, thou art *t.*   *Ps 139:8*

Even *t.* shall thy hand lead me   *Ps 139:10*

when as yet *t.* was none of them   *Ps 139:16*

see if *t.* be any wicked way in me, and   *Ps 139:24*

t. was no man that would know me   *Ps 142:4*

that *t.* be no breaking in, nor going   *Ps 144:14*

t. be no complaining in our streets   *Ps 144:14*

the son of man, in whom *t.* is no help   *Ps 146:3*

t. met him a woman with the attire of   *Pr 7:10*

t. is nothing froward or perverse in   *Pr 8:8*

t. were no depths, I was brought forth   *Pr 8:24*

t. were no fountains abounding with   *Pr 8:24*

prepared the heavens, I was *t.*   *Pr 8:27*

he knoweth not that the dead are *t.*   *Pr 9:18*

In the multitude of words *t.* wanteth   *Pr 10:19*

when the wicked perish, *t.* is shouting   *Pr 11:10*

multitude of counsellors, *t.* is safety   *Pr 11:14*

T. is that scattereth, and yet   *Pr 11:24*

t. is that withholdeth more than is   *Pr 11:24*

T. is that speaketh like the piercings   *Pr 12:18*

T. shall no evil happen to the just   *Pr 12:21*

in the pathway thereof *t.* is no death   *Pr 12:28*

T. is that maketh himself rich, yet   *Pr 13:7*

T. is that maketh himself poor, yet   *Pr 13:7*

t. is that is destroyed for want of   *Pr 13:23*

but among the righteous *t.* is favour   *Pr 14:9*

T. is a way which seemeth right unto   *Pr 14:12; 16:25*

In all labour *t.* is profit: but the talk   *Pr 14:23*

and in his lips *t.* is as a burning fire   *Pr 16:27*

is *t.* a price in the hand of a fool to   *Pr 17:16*

t. is a friend that sticketh closer than a   *Pr 18:24*

Chasten thy son while *t.* is   *Pr 19:18*

T. are many devices in a man's heart   *Pr 19:21*

T. is gold, and a multitude of rubies   *Pr 20:15*

T. is treasure to be desired and oil in   *Pr 21:20*

T. is no wisdom nor understanding   *Pr 21:30*

The slothful man saith, *T.* is a lion   *Pr 22:13*

For surely *t.* is an end: and thine   *Pr 23:18*

in multitude of counsellors *t.* is safety   *Pr 24:6*

found it, then *t.* shall be a reward   *Pr 24:14*

t. shall be no reward to the evil man   *Pr 24:20*

and *t.* shall come forth a vessel for the   *Pr 25:4*

t. is more hope of a fool than of him   *Pr 26:12*

man saith, *T.* is a lion in the way   *Pr 26:13*

no wood is, *t.* the fire goeth out: so   *Pr 26:20*

t. is no talebearer, the strife ceaseth   *Pr 26:20*

t. are seven abominations in his heart   *Pr 26:25*

men do rejoice, *t.* is great glory   *Pr 28:12*

of an evil man *t.* is a snare   *Pr 29:6*

he rage or laugh, *t.* is no rest   *Pr 29:9*

Where *t.* is no vision, the people   *Pr 29:18*

t. is more hope of a fool than of him   *Pr 29:20*

T. is a generation that curseth their   *Pr 30:11*

T. is a generation that are pure in   *Pr 30:12*

T. is a generation, O how lofty are   *Pr 30:13*

T. is a generation, whose teeth are as   *Pr 30:14*

T. are three things that are never   *Pr 30:15*

T. be three things which are too   *Pr 30:18*

T. be four things which are little upon   *Pr 30:24*

T. be three things which go well, yea   *Pr 30:29*

king, against whom *t.* is no rising up   *Pr 30:31*

t. is no new thing under the sun   *Ec 1:9*

Is *t.* any thing whereof it may be said   *Ec 1:10*

T. is no remembrance of former   *Ec 1:11*

neither shall *t.* be any remembrance   *Ec 1:11*

and *t.* was no profit under the sun   *Ec 2:11*

t. is no remembrance of the wise   *Ec 2:16*

t. is a man whose labour is in wisdom   *Ec 2:21*

T. is nothing better for a man, than   *Ec 2:24*

To every thing *t.* is a season, and a   *Ec 3:1*

I know that *t.* is no good in them, but   *Ec 3:12*

judgment, that wickedness was *t.*   *Ec 3:16*

righteousness, that iniquity was *t*. — Ec 3:16
is a time *t*. for every purpose — Ec 3:17
I perceive that *t*. is nothing better — Ec 3:22
side of their oppressors *t*. was power — Ec 4:1
is one alone, and *t*. is not a second — Ec 4:8
is *t*. no end of all his labour; neither — Ec 4:8
T. is no end of all the people, even of — Ec 4:16
words *t*. are also divers vanities — Ec 5:7
regardeth; and *t*. be higher than they — Ec 5:8
what good is *t*. to the owners thereof — Ec 5:11
T. is a sore evil which I have seen — Ec 5:13
a son, and *t*. is nothing in his hand — Ec 5:14
T. is an evil which I have seen under — Ec 6:1
t. be many things that increase vanity — Ec 6:11
by it *t*. is profit to them that see the — Ec 7:11
t. is just man that perisheth in his — Ec 7:15
t. is a wicked man that prolongeth his — Ec 7:15
For *t*. is not a just man upon earth — Ec 7:20
the word of a king is, *t*. is power — Ec 8:4
to every purpose *t*. is time — Ec 8:6
T. is no man that hath power over — Ec 8:8
and *t*. is no discharge in that war — Ec 8:8
t. is a time wherein one man ruleth — Ec 8:9
T. is a vanity which is done upon the — Ec 8:14
that *t*. be just men, unto whom it — Ec 8:14
again. *t*. be wicked men, to whom it — Ec 8:14
t. is that neither day nor night seeth — Ec 8:16
t. is one event to the righteous — Ec 9:2
the sun, that *t*. is one event unto all — Ec 9:3
is joined to all the living *t*. is hope — Ec 9:4
for *t*. is no work, nor device, nor — Ec 9:10
T. was a little city, and few men — Ec 9:14
and *t*. came a great king against it — Ec 9:14
t. was found in it a poor wise man — Ec 9:15
T. is an evil which I have seen under — Ec 10:5
the tree falleth, *t*. it shall be — Ec 11:3
of making many books *t*. is no end — Ec 12:12
whereon *t*. hang a thousand bucklers — Ca 4:4
all fair, my love; *t*. is no spot in thee — Ca 4:7
t. is not one barren among them — Ca 6:6
T. are threescore queens, and — Ca 6:8
bud forth: *t*. will I give thee my loves — Ca 7:12
t. thy mother brought thee forth — Ca 8:5
t. she brought thee forth that bare — Ca 8:5
unto the head *t*. is no soundness in it — Isa 1:6
is *t*. any end of their treasures — Isa 2:7
neither is *t*. any end of their chariots — Isa 2:7
instead of sweet smell *t*. shall be stink — Isa 3:24
t. shall be a tabernacle for a shadow — Isa 4:6
but *t*. shall come up briers and thorns — Isa 5:6
lay field to field, till *t*. be no place — Isa 5:8
t. be a great forsaking in the midst — Isa 6:12
where *t*. were a thousand vines at a — Isa 7:23

t. shall not come thither the fear of — Isa 7:25
it is because *t*. is no light in them — Isa 8:20
and peace *t*. shall be no end — Isa 9:7
t. was none that moved the wing — Isa 10:14
t. shall come forth a rod out of the — Isa 11:1
in that day *t*. shall be a root of Jesse — Isa 11:10
t. shall be an highway for the remnant — Isa 11:16
shall the Arabian pitch tent *t*. — Isa 13:20
the shepherds make their fold *t*. — Isa 13:20
beasts of the desert shall lie *t*. — Isa 13:21
creatures; and owls shall dwell *t*. — Isa 13:21
and satyrs shall dance *t*. — Isa 13:21
t. shall come from the north a smoke — Isa 14:31
the grass faileth, *t*. is no green thing — Isa 15:6
in the vineyards *t*. shall be no singing — Isa 16:10
neither shall *t*. be shouting — Isa 16:10
Israel: and *t*. shall be desolation — Isa 17:9
shall *t*. be any work for Egypt, which — Isa 19:15
In that day shall *t*. be an altar to the — Isa 19:19
In that day shall *t*. be a highway out — Isa 19:23
a large country: *t*. shalt thou die — Isa 22:18
t. the chariots of thy glory shall be — Isa 22:18
laid waste, so that *t*. is no house — Isa 23:1
of Tarshish: *t*. is no more strength — Isa 23:10
t. also shalt thou have no rest — Isa 23:12
T. is a crying for wine in the streets — Isa 24:11
t. shall be as the shaking of an olive — Isa 24:13
wilderness: *t*. shall the calf feed — Isa 27:10
t. shall he lie down, and consume — Isa 27:10
filthiness, so that *t*. is no place clean — Isa 28:8
line; here a little, and *t*. a little — Isa 28:10; 28:13
and *t*. shall be heaviness and sorrow — Isa 29:2
so that *t*. shall not be found in the — Isa 30:14
t. shall be upon every high mountain — Isa 30:25
t. shall be a bridle in the jaws of the — Isa 30:28
But *t*. the glorious Lord will be — Isa 33:21
the kingdom, but none shall be *t*. — Isa 34:12
the screech owl also shall rest *t*. — Isa 34:14
T. shall the great owl make her — Isa 34:15
t. shall the vultures also be — Isa 34:15
And an highway shall be *t*. and a — Isa 35:8
No lion shall be *t*. nor any — Isa 35:9
up thereon, it shall not be found *t*. — Isa 35:9
but the redeemed shall walk *t*. — Isa 35:9
and *t*. is not strength to bring forth — Isa 37:3
this city, nor shoot an arrow *t*. — Isa 37:33
t. was nothing in his house, nor in all — Isa 39:2
t. is nothing among my treasures that — Isa 39:4
t. shall be peace and truth in my days — Isa 39:8
t. is no searching of his understanding — Isa 40:28
and needy seek water, and *t*. is none — Isa 41:17
yea, *t*. is none that sheweth — Isa 41:26
yea, *t*. is none that declareth — Isa 41:26

t. is none that heareth your words — Isa 41:26
For I beheld, and *t*. was no man; even — Isa 41:28
among them, and *t*. was no counsellor — Isa 41:28
before me *t*. was no God formed — Isa 43:10
formed, neither shall *t*. be after me — Isa 43:10
Lord; and beside me *t*. is no saviour — Isa 43:11
t. was no strange god among you — Isa 43:12
t. is none that can deliver out of my — Isa 43:13
the last; and beside me *t*. is no God — Isa 44:6
my witnesses. Is *t*. a God beside me — Isa 44:8
Yea, *t*. is no God; I know not any — Isa 44:8
neither is *t*. knowledge nor — Isa 44:19
say, Is *t*. not a lie in my right hand — Isa 44:20
I am the Lord, and *t*. is none else — Isa 45:5
t. is no God beside me: I girded thee — Isa 45:5
the west, that *t*. is none beside me — Isa 45:6; 45:18
I am the Lord, and *t*. is none else — Isa 45:6
thee; and *t*. is none else, *t*. is no God — Isa 45:14
and *t*. is no God else beside me; a just — Isa 45:21
and a Saviour; *t*. is none beside me — Isa 45:21
for I am God, and *t*. is none else — Isa 45:22; 46:9
I am God, and *t*. is none like me — Isa 46:9
t. is no throne, O daughter of the — Isa 47:1
t. shall not be a coal to warm at, nor — Isa 47:14
from the time that it was, *t*. am I — Isa 48:16
T. is no peace, saith the Lord, unto — Isa 48:22
when I came, was *t*. no man — Isa 50:2
when I called, was *t*. none to answer — Isa 50:2
t. is no water, and dieth for thirst — Isa 50:2
T. is none to guide her among all the — Isa 51:18
neither is *t*. any that taketh her by the — Isa 51:18
for henceforth *t*. shall no more come — Isa 52:1
aforetime into Egypt to sojourn *t*. — Isa 52:4
t. is no beauty that we should desire — Isa 53:2
yet saidst thou not, *T*. is no hope — Isa 57:10
T. is no peace, saith my God, to the — Isa 57:21
and *t*. is no judgment in their goings — Isa 59:8
we look for judgment, but *t*. is none — Isa 59:11
him that *t*. was no judgment — Isa 59:15
and he saw that *t*. was no man, and — Isa 59:15
wondered that *t*. was no intercessor — Isa 59:16
and of the people, *t*. was none with me — Isa 63:3
And I looked, and *t*. was none to help — Isa 63:5
and I wondered that *t*. was none to — Isa 63:5
t. is none that calleth upon thy name — Isa 64:7
it, and my servants shall dwell *t*. — Isa 65:9
T. shall be no more thence an infant — Isa 65:20
diligently, and see if *t*. be such a thing — Jer 2:10
T. is no hope: no; for I have loved — Jer 2:25
and *t*. hath been no latter rain — Jer 3:3
tree, and *t*. hath played the harlot — Jer 3:6
I beheld, and, lo, *t*. was no man, and — Jer 4:25

if *t.* be any that executeth judgment   *Jer 5:1*

Peace, peace; when *t.* is no peace   *Jer 6:14; 8:11*

purpose cometh *t.* to me incense from   *Jer 6:20*

house, and proclaim *t.* this word   *Jer 7:2*

bury in Tophet, till *t.* be no place   *Jer 7:32*

t. shall be no grapes on the vine, nor   *Jer 8:13*

cities, and let us be silent *t.*   *Jer 8:14*

Is *t.* no balm in Gilead; is *t.* no   *Jer 8:22*

is no physician *t.*? why then is   *Jer 8:22*

as *t.* is none like unto thee, O Lord   *Jer 10:6*

kingdoms, *t.* is none like unto thee   *Jer 10:7*

t. is a multitude of waters in   *Jer 10:13*

falsehood, and *t.* is no breath in them   *Jer 10:14*

t. is none to stretch forth my tent any   *Jer 10:20*

t. shall be no remnant of them: for I   *Jer 11:23*

and hide it *t.* in a hole of the rock   *Jer 13:4*

which I commanded thee to hide *t.*   *Jer 13:6*

for *t.* was no rain in the earth, the   *Jer 14:4*

and forsook it, because *t.* was no grass   *Jer 14:5*

eyes did fail, because *t.* was no grass   *Jer 14:6*

smitten us, and *t.* is no healing for us   *Jer 14:19*

looked for peace, and *t.* is no good   *Jer 14:19*

Are *t.* any among the vanities of the   *Jer 14:22*

t. shall ye serve other gods day   *Jer 16:13*

and things wherein *t.* is no profit   *Jer 16:19*

t. enter into the gates of this city kings   *Jer 17:25*

t. I will cause thee to hear my   *Jer 18:2*

And they said, *T.* is no hope: but we   *Jer 18:12*

proclaim *t.* the words that I shall   *Jer 19:2*

in Tophet, till *t.* be no place to bury   *Jer 19:11*

to Babylon, and *t.* thou shalt die   *Jer 20:6*

and shalt be buried *t.* thou, and all   *Jer 20:6*

of Judah, and speak *t.* this word   *Jer 22:1*

then shall *t.* enter in by the gates of   *Jer 22:4*

were not born; and *t.* shall ye die   *Jer 22:26*

And *t.* was also a man that prophesied   *Jer 26:20*

t. shall they be until the day that   *Jer 27:22*

that ye may be increased *t.*   *Jer 29:6*

T. is none to plead thy cause, that   *Jer 30:13*

For *t.* shall be a day, that the   *Jer 31:6*

t. is hope in thine end, saith the Lord   *Jer 31:17*

t. shall dwell in Judah itself, and in   *Jer 31:24*

t. shall he be until I visit him   *Jer 32:5*

and *t.* is nothing too hard for thee   *Jer 32:17*

flesh: is *t.* any thing too hard for me   *Jer 32:27*

Again *t.* shall be heard in this place   *Jer 33:10*

that *t.* should not be day and night in   *Jer 33:20*

the princes sat *t.* even Elishama   *Jer 36:12*

t. was a fire on the hearth burning   *Jer 36:22*

t. were added besides unto them many   *Jer 36:32*

t. remained but wounded men among   *Jer 37:10*

a captain of the ward was *t.*   *Jer 37:13*

had remained *t.* many days   *Jer 37:16*

said, Is *t.* any word from the Lord   *Jer 37:17*

And Jeremiah said, *T.* is: for, said he   *Jer 37:17*

Jonathan the scribe, lest I die *t.*   *Jer 37:20*

in the dungeon *t.* was no water, but   *Jer 38:6*

for *t.* is no more bread in the city   *Jer 38:9*

to Jonathan's house, to die *t.*   *Jer 38:26*

he was *t.* when Jerusalem was taken   *Jer 38:28*

t. they did eat bread together in   *Jer 41:1*

the Chaldeans that were found *t.*   *Jer 41:3*

That *t.* came certain from Shechem   *Jer 41:5*

of bread; and *t.* will we dwell   *Jer 42:14*

into Egypt, and go to sojourn *t.*   *Jer 42:15*

shall overtake you *t.* in the land of   *Jer 42:16*

follow close after you *t.* in Egypt   *Jer 42:16*

in Egypt; and *t.* ye shall die   *Jer 42:16*

faces to go into Egypt to sojourn *t.*   *Jer 42:17*

Go not into Egypt to sojourn *t.*   *Jer 43:2*

the land of Egypt to sojourn *t.*   *Jer 44:12; 44:14, 28*

have a desire to return to dwell *t.*   *Jer 44:14*

the famine, until *t.* be an end of them   *Jer 44:27*

They did cry *t.* Pharaoh king of   *Jer 46:17*

sea shore? *t.* hath he appointed it   *Jer 47:7*

T. shall be no more praise of Moab   *Jer 48:2*

T. shall be lamentation generally   *Jer 48:38*

the Lord, no man shall abide *t.*   *Jer 49:18*

t. is sorrow on the sea; it cannot be   *Jer 49:23*

for ever: *t.* shall no man abide   *Jer 49:33*

shall no man abide *t.* nor any   *Jer 49:33*

and *t.* shall be no nation whither   *Jer 49:36*

out of the north *t.* cometh up a nation   *Jer 50:3*

be sought for, and *t.* shall be none   *Jer 50:20*

beasts of the islands shall dwell *t.*   *Jer 50:39*

so shall no man abide *t.* neither   *Jer 50:40*

voice, *t.* is a multitude of waters in   *Jer 51:16*

falsehood, and *t.* is no breath in them   *Jer 51:17*

so that *t.* was no bread for the people   *Jer 52:6*

t. were ninety and six pomegranates   *Jer 52:23*

t. was a continual diet given him of   *Jer 52:34*

see if *t.* be any sorrow like unto my   *La 1:12*

hands, and *t.* is none to comfort her   *La 1:17*

bereaveth, at home *t.* is as death   *La 1:20*

that I sigh: *t.* is none to comfort me   *La 1:21*

in the dust; if so be *t.* may be hope   *La 3:29*

They shall no more sojourn *t.*   *La 4:15*

t. is none that doth deliver us out of   *La 5:8*

hand of the Lord was *t.* upon him   *Eze 1:3*

And *t.* was a voice from the firmament   *Eze 1:25*

t. hath been a prophet among them   *Eze 2:5*

t. was written therein lamentations   *Eze 2:10*

sat, and remained *t.* astonished   *Eze 3:15*

hand of the Lord was *t.* upon me   *Eze 3:22*

plain, and I will *t.* talk with thee   *Eze 3:22*

the glory of the Lord stood *t.* as   *Eze 3:23*

neither came *t.* abominable flesh into   *Eze 4:14*

neither shall *t.* be wailing for them   *Eze 7:11*

shall seek peace, and *t.* shall be none   *Eze 7:25*

hand of the Lord fell *t.* upon me   *Eze 8:1*

glory of the God of Israel was *t.*   *Eze 8:4*

And *t.* stood before them seventy men   *Eze 8:11*

t. sat women weeping for Tammuz   *Eze 8:14*

t. appeared over them as it were a   *Eze 10:1*

t. appeared in the cherubims the form   *Eze 10:8*

not see it, though he shall die *t.*   *Eze 12:13*

t. shall be no more any vain vision nor   *Eze 12:24*

T. shall none of my words be prolonged   *Eze 12:28*

saying, Peace; and *t.* was no peace   *Eze 13:10*

t. shall be an overflowing shower; and   *Eze 13:11; 13:13*

and *t.* is no peace, saith the Lord God   *Eze 13:16*

wherewith ye *t.* hunt the souls to   *Eze 13:20*

T. was also another great eagle with   *Eze 17:7*

plead with him *t.* for his trespass   *Eze 17:20*

and they offered *t.* their sacrifices   *Eze 20:28*

t. they presented the provocation   *Eze 20:28*

t. they made their sweet savour   *Eze 20:28*

poured out *t.* their drink offerings   *Eze 20:28*

t. will I plead with you face to face   *Eze 20:35*

t. shall all the house of Israel, all of   *Eze 20:40*

serve me: *t.* will I accept them   *Eze 20:40*

and *t.* will I require your offerings   *Eze 20:40*

t. shall ye remember your ways   *Eze 20:43*

and I will leave you *t.* and melt you   *Eze 22:20*

T. is a conspiracy of her prophets in   *Eze 22:25*

t. were two women, the daughters of   *Eze 23:2*

t. were their breasts pressed   *Eze 23:3*

t. they bruised the teats of their   *Eze 23:3*

t. is no secret that they can hide from   *Eze 28:3*

t. shall be no more a pricking brier   *Eze 28:24*

they shall be *t.* a base kingdom   *Eze 29:14*

t. shall be no more a prince of the land   *Eze 30:13*

shall break *t.* the yokes of Egypt   *Eze 30:18*

Asshur is *t.* and all her company   *Eze 32:22*

T. is Elam and all her multitude   *Eze 32:24*

T. is Meshech, Tubal, and all her   *Eze 32:26*

T. is Edom, her kings, and all her   *Eze 32:29*

T. be the princes of the north, all   *Eze 32:30*

scattered, because *t.* is no shepherd   *Eze 34:5*

because *t.* was no shepherd, neither   *Eze 34:8*

t. shall they lie in a good fold, and   *Eze 34:14*

season; *t.* shall be showers of blessing   *Eze 34:26*

whereas the Lord was *t.*   *Eze 35:10*

t. were very many in the open valley   *Eze 37:2*

t. was a noise, and behold a shaking   *Eze 37:7*

but *t.* was no breath in them   *Eze 37:8*

in that day *t.* shall be a great shaking   *Eze 38:19*

give unto Gog a place *t.* of graves — Eze 39:11
t. shall they bury Gog and all his — Eze 39:11
have left none of them any more *t.* — Eze 39:28
t. was a man, whose appearance — Eze 40:3
t. were narrow windows to the little — Eze 40:16
court, and, lo, *t.* were chambers — Eze 40:17
t. were windows in it and in the arches — Eze 40:25; 40:29
And *t.* were seven steps to go up to it — Eze 40:26
t. was a gate in the inner court toward — Eze 40:27
t. were windows therein and in the — Eze 40:33
t. were pillars by the posts, one in this — Eze 40:49
t. was an enlarging, and a winding — Eze 41:7
t. were made on them, on the doors of — Eze 41:25
t. were thick planks upon the face of — Eze 41:25
t. were narrow windows and palm — Eze 41:26
t. shall they lay the most holy — Eze 42:13
t. they shall lay their garments — Eze 42:14
this *t.* shall be for the sanctuary five — Eze 45:2
t. was a place on the two sides — Eze 46:19
corner of the court *t.* was a court — Eze 46:21
of the court *t.* were courts joined — Eze 46:22
t. was a row of building round about — Eze 46:23
t. ran out waters on the right side — Eze 47:2
t. shall be a very great multitude of — Eze 47:9
t. shall ye give him his inheritance — Eze 47:23
that day shall be, The Lord is *t.* — Eze 48:35
the dream, *t.* is but one decree for you — Da 2:9
T. is not a man upon the earth that — Da 2:10
t. is no king, lord, nor ruler, that — Da 2:10
t. is none other that can shew it before — Da 2:11
t. is a God in heaven that revealeth — Da 2:28
t. shall be in it of the strength of the — Da 2:41
T. are certain Jews whom thou hast — Da 3:12
t. is no other God that can deliver — Da 3:29
mouth, *t.* fell a voice from heaven — Da 4:31
T. is a man in thy kingdom, in whom — Da 5:11
neither was *t.* any error or fault found — Da 6:4
t. came up among them another little — Da 7:8
before whom *t.* were three of — Da 7:8
And *t.* was given him dominion, and — Da 7:14
t. stood before the river a ram which — Da 8:3
neither was *t.* any that could deliver — Da 8:4
t. was no power in the ram to stand — Da 8:7
t. was none that could deliver the ram — Da 8:7
t. stood before me as the appearance — Da 8:15
and *t.* remained no strength in me — Da 10:8; 10:17
I remained *t.* with the kings of — Da 10:13
in me, neither is *t.* breath left in me — Da 10:17
t. came again and touched me one — Da 10:18
t. is none that holdeth with me in these — Da 10:21

t. shall stand up yet three kings in — Da 11:2
in those times *t.* shall many stand up — Da 11:14
neither shall *t.* be any strength to — Da 11:15
t. shall be a time of trouble, such as — Da 12:1
such as never was since *t.* was a nation — Da 12:1
t. stood other two, the one on this side — Da 12:5
t. shall be a thousand two hundred and — Da 12:11
people, *t.* it shall be said unto them — Ho 1:10
she shall sing *t.* as in the days of — Ho 2:15
because *t.* is no truth, nor mercy — Ho 4:1
And *t.* shall be, like people, like priest — Ho 4:9
t. have they dealt treacherously — Ho 6:7
t. is the whoredom of Ephraim — Ho 6:10
t. is none among them that calleth — Ho 7:7
gray hairs are here and *t.* upon him — Ho 7:9
them, that *t.* shall not be a man left — Ho 9:12
in Gilgal: for *t.* I hated them — Ho 9:15
the days of Gibeah: *t.* they stood — Ho 10:9
in Beth-el, and *t.* he spake with us — Ho 12:4
Is *t.* iniquity in Gilead? surely they — Ho 12:11
but me: for *t.* is no saviour beside me — Ho 13:4
t. will I devour them like a lion — Ho 13:8
t. hath not been ever the like, neither — Joe 2:2
plead with them *t.* for my people — Joe 3:2
t. will I sit to judge all the heathen — Joe 3:12
t. shall no strangers pass through her — Joe 3:17
shall *t.* be evil in a city, and the Lord — Am 3:6
An adversary *t.* shall be even round — Am 3:11
when *t.* were yet three months to the — Am 4:7
her land; *t.* is none to raise her up — Am 5:2
and *t.* be none to quench it in Beth-el — Am 5:6
if *t.* remain ten men in one house — Am 6:9
of the house, Is *t.* yet any with thee — Am 6:10
rock? will one plow *t.* with oxen — Am 6:12
and *t.* eat bread, and prophesy *t.* — Am 7:12
t. shall be many dead bodies in every — Am 8:3
thee: *t.* is none understanding in him — Ob 7
deliverance, and *t.* shall be holiness — Ob 17
and *t.* shall not be any remaining of — Ob 18
t. was a mighty tempest in the sea — Jon 1:4
and *t.* made him a booth, and sat — Jon 4:5
their lips: for *t.* is no answer of God — Mic 3:7
is *t.* no king in thee? is thy counseller — Mic 4:9
to Babylon; *t.* shalt thou be delivered — Mic 4:10
t. the Lord shall redeem thee from — Mic 4:10
Are *t.* yet the treasures of wickedness — Mic 6:10
of the vintage: *t.* is no cluster to eat — Mic 7:1
and *t.* is none upright among men — Mic 7:2
T. is one come out of thee, that — Na 1:11
for *t.* is none end of the store and glory — Na 2:9
t. is a multitude of slain, and a great — Na 3:3

and *t.* is none end of their corpses — Na 3:3
T. shall the fire devour thee — Na 3:15
T. is no healing of thy bruise — Na 3:19
and *t.* are that raise up strife — Hab 1:3
t. is no breath at all in the midst of it — Hab 2:19
and *t.* was the hiding of his power — Hab 3:4
and *t.* shall be no herd in the stalls — Hab 3:17
t. shall be the noise of a cry from the — Zep 1:10
mighty man shall cry *t.* bitterly — Zep 1:14
thee, that *t.* shall be no inhabitant — Zep 2:5
heart, I am, and *t.* is none beside me — Zep 2:15
are destroyed, so that *t.* is no man — Zep 3:6
is no man, that *t.* is none inhabitant — Zep 3:6
ye clothe you, but *t.* is none warm — Hag 1:6
that which they offer *t.* is unclean — Hag 2:14
of twenty measures, *t.* were but ten — Hag 2:16
out of the press, *t.* were but twenty — Hag 2:16
and behind him were *t.* red horses — Zec 1:8
behold, *t.* was lifted up a talent of lead — Zec 5:7
and, behold, *t.* came out two women — Zec 5:9
and set *t.* upon her own base — Zec 5:11
behold, *t.* came four chariots out from — Zec 6:1
T. shall yet old men and old women — Zec 8:4
these days *t.* was no hire for man — Zec 8:10
neither was *t.* any peace to him that — Zec 8:10
to pass, that *t.* shall come people — Zec 8:20
troubled, because *t.* was no shepherd — Zec 10:2
T. is a voice of the howling of the — Zec 11:3
that day shall *t.* be a great mourning — Zec 12:11
that day *t.* shall be a fountain opened — Zec 13:1
and *t.* shall be a very great valley — Zec 14:4
that day *t.* shall be one Lord, and his — Zec 14:9
t. shall be no more utter destruction — Zec 14:11
t. shall be the plague, wherewith the — Zec 14:18
that day shall *t.* be upon the bells of — Zec 14:20
in that day *t.* shall be no more the — Zec 14:21
is *t.* even among you that would shut — Mal 1:10
that *t.* may be meat in mine house — Mal 3:10
t. shall not be room enough to receive — Mal 3:10
t. came wise men from the east to — M't 2:1
be thou *t.* until I bring thee word — M't 2:13
And was *t.* until the death of Herod — M't 2:15
In Rama was *t.* a voice heard — M't 2:18
t. followed him great multitudes of — M't 4:25
t. rememberest that thy brother — M't 5:23
Leave *t.* thy gift before the altar — M't 5:24
is, *t.* will your heart be also — M't 6:21
Or what man is *t.* of you, whom if his — M't 7:9
and many *t.* be which go in thereat — M't 7:13
unto life, and few *t.* be that find it — M't 7:14
t. came a leper and worshipped him — M't 8:2
t. came unto him a centurion — M't 8:5
t. shall be weeping and gnashing — M't 8:12; 22:13; 24:51; 25:30; Lu 13:28

t. arose a great tempest in the sea	*M't 8:24*	*t.* shall ye see him: lo, I have told	*M't 28:7*	and *t.* shall meet you a man bearing a	*M'k 14:13*
and the sea: and *t.* was a great calm	*M't 8:26*	Galilee, and *t.* shall they see me	*M't 28:10*	prepared: *t.* make ready for us	*M'k 14:15*
t. met him two possessed with devils	*M't 8:28*	*t.* went out unto him all the land of	*M'k 1:5*	*t.* followed him a certain young man	*M'k 14:51*
And *t.* was a good way off from them	*M't 8:30*	T. cometh one mightier than I after	*M'k 1:7*	*t.* arose certain, and bare false witness	*M'k 14:57*
t. came a certain ruler, and worshipped	*M't 9:18*	*t.* came a voice from heaven, saying	*M'k 1:11*	*t.* cometh one of the maids of the high	*M'k 14:66*
and *t.* abide till ye go thence	*M't 10:11*	*t.* in the wilderness forty days	*M'k 1:13*	And *t.* was one named Barabbas	*M'k 15:7*
t. is nothing covered, that shall not be	*M't 10:26*	*t.* was in their synagogue a man with	*M'k 1:23*	*t.* was darkness over the whole land	*M'k 15:33*
t. hath not risen a greater than John	*M't 11:11*	into a solitary place, and *t.* prayed	*M'k 1:35*	T. were also women looking on afar	*M'k 15:40*
t. was a man which had his hand	*M't 12:10*	towns, that I may preach *t.* also	*M'k 1:38*	*t.* shall ye see him, as he said unto	*M'k 16:7*
What man shall *t.* be among you, that	*M't 12:11*	*t.* came a leper to him, beseeching	*M'k 1:40*	T. was in the days of Herod, the king	*Lu 1:5*
t. shall no sign be given to it, but the	*M't 12:39*	that *t.* was no room to receive them	*M'k 2:2*	*t.* appeared unto him an angel of the	*Lu 1:11*
and they enter in and dwell *t.*	*M't 12:45*	*t.* were certain of the scribes sitting	*M'k 2:6*	and of his kingdom *t.* shall be no end	*Lu 1:33*
t. shall be wailing and gnashing	*M't 13:42; 13:50*	scribes sitting *t.* and reasoning	*M'k 2:6*	*t.* shall be a performance of those	*Lu 1:45*
he did not many mighty works	*M't 13:58*	for *t.* were many, and they followed	*M'k 2:15*	T. is none of thy kindred that is	*Lu 1:61*
evening was come, he was *t.* alone	*M't 14:23*	a man *t.* which had a withered	*M'k 3:1*	that *t.* went out a decree from Cæsar	*Lu 2:1*
up into a mountain, and sat down *t.*	*M't 15:29*	T. came then his brethren and his	*M'k 3:31*	while they were *t.* the days were	*Lu 2:6*
and *t.* shall no sign be given unto it	*M't 16:4*	*t.* was gathered unto him a great	*M'k 4:1*	*t.* was no room for them in the inn	*Lu 2:7*
T. be some standing here, which shall	*M't 16:28*	Behold, *t.* went out a sower to sow	*M'k 4:3*	*t.* were in the same country shepherds	*Lu 2:8*
t. appeared unto them Moses	*M't 17:3*	For *t.* is nothing hid, which shall not	*M'k 4:22*	And suddenly *t.* was with the angel a	*Lu 2:13*
t. came to him a certain man, kneeling	*M't 17:14*	*t.* were also with him other little	*M'k 4:36*	*t.* was a man in Jerusalem, whose	*Lu 2:25*
name, *t.* am I in the midst of them	*M't 18:20*	*t.* arose a great storm of wind, and the	*M'k 4:37*	And *t.* was one Anna, a prophetess, the	*Lu 2:36*
him; and he healed them *t.*	*M't 19:2*	wind ceased, and *t.* was a great calm	*M'k 4:39*	*t.* went out a fame of him through all	*Lu 4:14*
For *t.* are some eunuchs, which were	*M't 19:12*	*t.* met him out of the tombs a man	*M'k 5:2*	*t.* was delivered unto him the book	*Lu 4:17*
t. be eunuchs, which have made	*M't 19:12*	was *t.* nigh unto the mountains	*M'k 5:11*	And in the synagogue *t.* was a man	*Lu 4:33*
were *t.* brought unto him children	*M't 19:13*	*t.* cometh one of the rulers of	*M'k 5:22*	much the more went *t.* a fame abroad	*Lu 5:15*
t. is none good but one, that is, God	*M't 19:17; M'k 10:18*	*t.* came from the ruler of the	*M'k 5:35*	that *t.* were Pharisees and doctors of	*Lu 5:17*
into Bethany; and he lodged *t.*	*M't 21:17*	he could *t.* do no mighty work	*M'k 6:5*	*t.* was a great company of publicans	*Lu 5:29*
T. was a certain householder, which	*M't 21:33*	*t.* abide till ye depart that place	*M'k 6:10*	*t.* was a man whose right hand	*Lu 6:6*
saw *t.* a man which had not on a	*M't 22:11*	for *t.* were many coming and going	*M'k 6:31*	for *t.* went virtue out of him	*Lu 6:19*
which say that *t.* is no resurrection	*M't 22:23*	And many other things *t.* be, which	*M'k 7:4*	behold, *t.* was a dead man carried out	*Lu 7:12*
Now *t.* were with us seven brethren	*M't 22:25*	T. is nothing from without a man	*M'k 7:15*	And *t.* came a fear on all: and they	*Lu 7:16*
T. shall not be left here one stone	*M't 24:2*	*t.* shall no sign be given unto this	*M'k 8:12*	*t.* is not a greater prophet than	*Lu 7:28*
t. shall be famines, and pestilences	*M't 24:7*	That *t.* be some of them that stand	*M'k 9:1*	T. was a certain creditor which had	*Lu 7:41*
shortened, *t.* should no flesh be saved	*M't 24:22*	*t.* appeared unto them Elias with	*M'k 9:4*	*t.* came down a storm of wind on the	*Lu 8:23*
unto you, Lo, here is Christ, or *t.*	*M't 24:23*	*t.* was a cloud that overshadowed	*M'k 9:7*	and they ceased, and *t.* was a calm	*Lu 8:24*
t. shall arise false Christs, and false	*M't 24:24*	for *t.* is no man which shall do a	*M'k 9:39*	*t.* met him out of the city a certain	*Lu 8:27*
is, *t.* will the eagles be gathered	*M't 24:28*	*t.* came one running, and kneeled to	*M'k 10:17*	And *t.* was an herd of many swine	*Lu 8:32*
at midnight *t.* was a cry made	*M't 25:6*	T. is no man that hath left house	*M'k 10:29*	behold, *t.* came a man named Jairus	*Lu 8:41*
lest *t.* be not enough for us and you	*M't 25:9*	certain of them that stood *t.*	*M'k 11:5*	*t.* cometh one from the ruler of the	*Lu 8:49*
earth: lo, *t.* thou hast that is thine	*M't 25:25*	*t.* come to him the chief priests	*M'k 11:27*	house ye enter into, *t.* abide	*Lu 9:4*
lest *t.* be an uproar among the people	*M't 26:5*	which say *t.* is no resurrection; and	*M'k 12:18*	*t.* was taken up of fragments	*Lu 9:17*
T. came unto him a woman having	*M't 26:7*	*t.* were seven brethren: and the first	*M'k 12:20*	of a truth, *t.* be some standing here	*Lu 9:27*
t. shall also this, that this woman	*M't 26:13*	T. is none other commandment	*M'k 12:31*	behold, *t.* talked with him two men	*Lu 9:30*
and said unto them that were *t.*	*M't 26:71*	hast said the truth: for *t.* is one God	*M'k 12:32*	While he thus spake, *t.* came a cloud	*Lu 9:34*
sitting down they watched him *t.*	*M't 27:36*	one God; and *t.* is none other but he	*M'k 12:32*	And *t.* came a voice out of the cloud	*Lu 9:35*
were *t.* two thieves crucified with him	*M't 27:38*	And *t.* came a certain poor widow	*M'k 12:42*	*t.* arose a reasoning among them	*Lu 9:46*
from the sixth hour *t.* was darkness	*M't 27:45*	*t.* shall not be left one stone	*M'k 13:2*	And if the son of peace be *t.* your	*Lu 10:6*
Some of them that stood *t.* when	*M't 27:47*	and *t.* shall be earthquakes in divers	*M'k 13:8*	by chance *t.* came down a certain	*Lu 10:31*
many women were *t.* beholding	*M't 27:55*	and *t.* shall be famines and troubles	*M'k 13:8*	they enter in, and dwell *t.*	*Lu 11:26*
t. came a rich man of Arimathæa	*M't 27:57*	here is Christ; or, lo he is *t.*	*M'k 13:21*	and *t.* shall no sign be given it, but	*Lu 11:29*
t. was Mary Magdalene, and	*M't 27:61*	day, lest *t.* be an uproar of the people	*M'k 14:2*	when *t.* were gathered together	*Lu 12:1*
behold, *t.* was a great earthquake	*M't 28:2*	*t.* came a woman having an alabaster	*M'k 14:3*	For *t.* is nothing covered, that shall	*Lu 12:2*
		And *t.* were some that had indignation	*M'k 14:4*	*t.* will I bestow all my fruits	*Lu 12:18*

treasure is, *t*. will your heart be	*Lu 12:34*
t. shall be five in one house divided	*Lu 12:52*
T. cometh a shower; and so it is	*Lu 12:54*
T. will be heat; and it cometh to pass	*Lu 12:55*
T. were present at that season	*Lu 13:1*
some	
t. was a woman which had a spirit of	*Lu 13:11*
T. are six days in which men ought	*Lu 13:14*
him, Lord, are *t*. few that be saved	*Lu 13:23*
behold, *t*. are last which shall be first	*Lu 13:30*
and *t*. are first which shall be last	*Lu 13:30*
The same day *t*. came certain of the	*Lu 13:31*
t. was a certain man before him	*Lu 14:2*
hast commanded, and yet *t*. is room	*Lu 14:22*
t. went great multitudes with him	*Lu 14:25*
t. is joy in the presence of the angels	*Lu 15:10*
and *t*. wasted his substance with	*Lu 15:13*
t. arose a mighty famine in that land	*Lu 15:14*
T. was a certain rich man, which had	*Lu 16:1*
T. was a certain rich man, which was	*Lu 16:19*
t. was a beggar named Lazarus	*Lu 16:20*
between us and you *t*. is a great gulf	*Lu 16:26*
t. met him ten men that were lepers	*Lu 17:12*
Were *t*. not ten cleansed? but where	*Lu 17:17*
T. are not found that returned to give	*Lu 17:18*
shall they say, Lo here! or, lo *t*.	*Lu 17:21*
shall say to you, See here; or, see *t*.	*Lu 17:23*
night *t*. shall be two men in one bed	*Lu 17:34*
T. was in a city a judge, which feared	*Lu 18:2*
And *t*. was a widow in that city; and	*Lu 18:3*
T. is no man that hath left house, or	*Lu 18:29*
behold, *t*. was a man named Zacchæus	*Lu 19:2*
which deny that *t*. is any resurrection	*Lu 20:27*
T. were therefore seven brethren: and	*Lu 20:29*
t. shall not be left one stone upon	*Lu 21:6*
what sign will *t*. be when these things	*Lu 21:7*
great signs shall *t*. be from heaven	*Lu 21:11*
t. shall not an hair of your head perish	*Lu 21:18*
t. shall be great distress in the land	*Lu 21:23*
t. shall be signs in the sun, and in the	*Lu 21:25*
into the city, *t*. shall a man meet you	*Lu 22:10*
room furnished: *t*. make ready	*Lu 22:12*
t. was also a strife among them	*Lu 22:24*
t. appeared an angel unto him from	*Lu 22:43*
t. followed him a great company of	*Lu 23:27*
t. were also two other, malefactors	*Lu 23:32*
Calvary, *t*. they crucified him	*Lu 23:33*
t. was a darkness over all the earth	*Lu 23:44*
behold, *t*. was a man named Joseph	*Lu 23:50*
things which are come to pass *t*.	*Lu 24:18*
T. was a man sent from God, whose	*Joh 1:6*

t. standeth one among you, whom ye	*Joh 1:26*
Can *t*. any good thing come out of	*Joh 1:46*
the third day *t*. was a marriage in Cana	*Joh 2:1*
and the mother of Jesus was *t*.	*Joh 2:1*
set *t*. six waterpots of stone	*Joh 2:6*
they continued *t*. not many days	*Joh 2:12*
T. was a man of the Pharisees, named	*Joh 3:1*
and *t*. he tarried with them	*Joh 3:22*
to Salim, because *t*. was much water	*Joh 3:23*
because was much water *t*.	*Joh 3:23*
Then *t*. arose a question between some	*Joh 3:25*
Now Jacob's well was *t*. Jesus	*Joh 4:6*
T. cometh a woman of Samaria to	*Joh 4:7*
T. are yet four months, and then	*Joh 4:35*
them: and he abode *t*. two days	*Joh 4:40*
And *t*. was a certain nobleman, whose	*Joh 4:46*
After this *t*. was a feast of the Jews	*Joh 5:1*
Now *t*. is at Jerusalem by the sheep	*Joh 5:2*
And a certain man was *t*. which	*Joh 5:5*
T. is another that beareth witness of	*Joh 5:32*
t. is one that accuseth you, even Moses	*Joh 5:45*
and *t*. he sat with his disciples	*Joh 6:3*
T. is a lad here, which hath five	*Joh 6:9*
Now *t*. was much grass in the place	*Joh 6:10*
saw that *t*. was none other boat	*Joh 6:22*
t. came other boats from Tiberias	*Joh 6:23*
therefore saw that Jesus was not *t*.	*Joh 6:24*
But *t*. are some of you that believe not	*Joh 6:64*
t. is no man that doeth any thing in	*Joh 7:4*
t. was much murmuring among the	*Joh 7:12*
So *t*. was a division among the people	*Joh 7:43*
the truth, because *t*. is no truth in him	*Joh 8:44*
t. is one that seeketh and judgeth	*Joh 8:50*
And *t*. was a division among them	*Joh 9:16*
t. shall be one fold, and one shepherd	*Joh 10:16*
T. was a division therefore again	*Joh 10:19*
at first baptized; and *t*. he abode	*Joh 10:40*
And many believed on him *t*.	*Joh 10:42*
Are *t*. not twelve hours in the day	*Joh 11:9*
stumbleth, because *t*. is no light in him	*Joh 11:10*
for your sakes that I was not *t*.	*Joh 11:15*
She goeth unto the grave to weep *t*.	*Joh 11:31*
and *t*. continued with his disciples	*Joh 11:54*
T. they made him a supper	*Joh 12:2*
Jews therefore knew that he was *t*.	*Joh 12:9*
t. were certain Greeks among them	*Joh 12:20*
I am, *t*. shall also my servant be	*Joh 12:26*
Then came *t*. a voice from heaven	*Joh 12:28*
t. was leaning on Jesus' bosom one of	*Joh 13:23*
that where I am, *t*. ye may be also	*Joh 14:3*
And the servants, and officers stood *t*.	*Joh 18:18*
Now *t*. stood by the cross of Jesus his	*Joh 19:25*
Now *t*. was set a vessel full of vinegar	*Joh 19:29*

and forthwith came *t*. out blood and	*Joh 19:34*
t. came also Nicodemus, which at the	*Joh 19:39*
where he was crucified *t*. was a garden	*Joh 19:41*
T. laid they Jesus therefore	*Joh 19:42*
T. were together Simon Peter	*Joh 21:2*
they saw a fire of coals *t*. and fish	*Joh 21:9*
and for all *t*. were so many, yet was	*Joh 21:11*
t. are also many other things which	*Joh 21:25*
And suddenly *t*. came a sound from	*Ac 2:2*
And *t*. appeared unto them cloven	*Ac 2:3*
t. were dwelling at Jerusalem Jews	*Ac 2:5*
t. were added unto them about three	*Ac 2:41*
Neither is *t*. salvation in any other	*Ac 4:12*
t. is none other name under heaven	*Ac 4:12*
Neither was *t*. any among them that	*Ac 4:34*
T. came also a multitude out of the	*Ac 5:16*
Then stood *t*. up one in the council	*Ac 5:34*
t. arose a murmuring of the Grecians	*Ac 6:1*
t. arose certain of the synagogue	*Ac 6:9*
t. came a dearth over all the land of	*Ac 7:11*
Jacob heard that *t*. was corn in Egypt	*Ac 7:12*
t. appeared to him in the wilderness	*Ac 7:30*
at that time *t*. was a great persecution	*Ac 8:1*
And *t*. was great joy in that city	*Ac 8:8*
But *t*. was a certain man, called Simon	*Ac 8:9*
suddenly *t*. shined round about him a	*Ac 9:3*
t. was a certain disciple at Damascus	*Ac 9:10*
t. fell from his eyes as it had been	*Ac 9:18*
t. he found a certain man named	*Ac 9:33*
Now *t*. was at Joppa a certain disciple	*Ac 9:36*
had heard that Peter was *t*.	*Ac 9:38*
T. was a certain man in Cæsarea	*Ac 10:1*
t. came a voice to him, Rise, Peter	*Ac 10:13*
surnamed Peter, were lodged *t*.	*Ac 10:18*
immediately *t*. were three men already	*Ac 11:11*
And *t*. stood up one of them named	*Ac 11:28*
spirit that *t*. should be great dearth	*Ac 11:28*
t. was no small stir among the soldiers	*Ac 12:18*
from Judæa to Cæsarea, and *t*. abode	*Ac 12:19*
Now *t*. were in the church that was at	*Ac 13:1*
immediately *t*. fell on him a mist and a	*Ac 13:11*
t. cometh one after me, whose shoes	*Ac 13:25*
And when *t*. was an assault made both	*Ac 14:5*
And *t*. they preached the gospel	*Ac 14:7*
And *t*. sat a certain man at Lystra	*Ac 14:8*
t. came thither certain Jews from	*Ac 14:19*
t. they abode long time with	*Ac 14:28*
t. rose up certain of the sect	*Ac 15:5*
And when *t*. had been much disputing	*Ac 15:7*
And after they had tarried *t*. a space	*Ac 15:33*
it pleased Silas to abide *t*. still	*Ac 15:34*
a certain disciple was *t*. named	*Ac 16:1*
T. stood a man of Macedonia	*Ac 16:9*

come into my house, and abide t. — Ac 16:15
suddenly t. was a great earthquake — Ac 16:26
that t. is another king, one Jesus — Ac 17:7
Silas and Timotheus abode t. still — Ac 17:14
and strangers which were t. — Ac 17:21
And he continued t. a year and six — Ac 18:11
Paul after this tarried t. yet a good — Ac 18:18
came to Ephesus, and left them t. — Ac 18:19
after he had spent some time t. he — Ac 18:23
heard whether t. be any Holy Ghost — Ac 19:2
t. were seven sons of one Sceva, a — Ac 19:14
After I have been t. I must also — Ac 19:21
same time t. arose no small stir about — Ac 19:23
what man is t. that knoweth not how — Ac 19:35
the law is open, and t. are deputies — Ac 19:38
this day's uproar, t. being no cause — Ac 19:40
t. abode three months. And when the — Ac 20:3
And t. accompanied him into Asia — Ac 20:4
And t. were many lights in the upper — Ac 20:8
t. sat in a window a certain young — Ac 20:9
Assos, t. intending to take in Paul — Ac 20:13
things that shall befall me t. — Ac 20:22
for t. the ship was to unlade her — Ac 21:3
disiples, we tarried t. seven days — Ac 21:4
And as we tarried t. many days — Ac 21:10
t. came down from Judæa a certain — Ac 21:10
T. went with us also certain of the — Ac 21:16
thousands of Jews t. are which believe — Ac 21:20
when t. was made a great silence, he — Ac 21:40
were t. bound unto Jerusalem — Ac 22:5
t. shone from heaven a great light — Ac 22:6
t. it shall be told thee of all things — Ac 22:10
report of all the Jews which dwelt t. — Ac 22:12
he had so said, t. arose a dissension — Ac 23:7
say that t. is no resurrection — Ac 23:8
t. arose a great cry: and the scribes — Ac 23:9
when t. arose a great dissension, the — Ac 23:10
for t. lie in wait for him of them more — Ac 23:21
that t. are yet but twelve days since — Ac 24:11
t. shall be a resurrection of the dead — Ac 24:15
man, if t. be any wickedness in him — Ac 25:5
t. be judged of these things before — Ac 25:9
if t. be none of these things whereof — Ac 25:11
when they had been t. many days — Ac 25:14
T. is a certain man left in bonds by — Ac 25:14
and t. be judged of these matters — Ac 25:20
And t. the centurion found a ship — Ac 27:6
attain to Phenice, and t. to winter — Ac 27:12
after t. arose against it a tempestuous — Ac 27:14
t. shall be no loss of any man's life — Ac 27:22
For t. stood by me this night the angel — Ac 27:23
for t. shall not an hair fall from the — Ac 27:34

the fire, t. came a viper out of the heat — Ac 28:3
at Syracuse, we tarried t. three days — Ac 28:12
t. was no cause of death in me — Ac 28:18
t. came many to him into his lodging — Ac 28:23
t. is no respect of persons with God — Ro 2:11
or what profit is t. of circumcision — Ro 3:1
T. is none righteous, no, not one — Ro 3:10
T. is none that understandeth — Ro 3:11
t. is none that seeketh after God — Ro 3:11
t. is none that doeth good, no, not one — Ro 3:12
T. is no fear of God before their eyes — Ro 3:18
t. shall no flesh be justified in his — Ro 3:20
that believe: for t. is no difference — Ro 3:22
where no law is, t. is no transgression — Ro 4:15
sin is not imputed when t. is no law — Ro 5:13
T. is therefore now no condemnation — Ro 8:1
Is t. unrighteousness with God? God — Ro 9:14
t. shall they be called the children — Ro 9:26
t. is no difference between the Jew — Ro 10:12
present time also, t. is a remnant — Ro 11:5
T. shall come out of Sion the — Ro 11:26
For t. is no power but of God: the — Ro 13:1
if t. be any other commandment, it is — Ro 13:9
that is nothing unclean of itself — Ro 14:14
saith, T. shall be a root of Jesse — Ro 15:12
and that t. be no divisions among you — 1Co 1:10
that t. are contentions among you — 1Co 1:11
for whereas t. is among you envying — 1Co 3:3
reported that t. is fornication — 1Co 5:1
that t. is not a wise man among you — 1Co 6:5
It is utterly a fault among you — 1Co 7:34
T. is difference also between a wife — 1Co 7:34
and that t. is none other God but one — 1Co 8:4
For though t. be that are called gods — 1Co 8:5
(as t. be gods many, and lords many — 1Co 8:5
But to us t. is but one God, the Father — 1Co 8:6
t. is not in every man that knowledge — 1Co 8:7
T. hath no temptation taken you but — 1Co 10:13
I hear that t. be divisions among you — 1Co 11:18
t. must be also heresies among you — 1Co 11:19
t. are diversities of gifts, but the same — 1Co 12:4
t. are differences of administrations — 1Co 12:5
t. are diversities of operations, but it — 1Co 12:6
t. should be no schism in the body — 1Co 12:25
but whether t. be prophecies, they — 1Co 13:8
whether t. be tongues, they shall — 1Co 13:8
whether t. be knowledge, it shall — 1Co 13:8
T. are, it may be, so many kinds of — 1Co 14:10
t. come in those that are unlearned — 1Co 14:23
t. come in one that believeth not — 1Co 14:24
But if t. be no interpreter, let him — 1Co 14:28
among you that t. is no resurrection — 1Co 15:12

if t. be no resurrection of the dead — 1Co 15:13
but t. is one kind of flesh of men — 1Co 15:39
T. are also celestial bodies — 1Co 15:40
T. is one glory of the sun — 1Co 15:41
T. is a natural body — 1Co 15:44
and t. is a spiritual body — 1Co 15:44
that t. be no gatherings when I come — 1Co 16:2
unto me, and t. are many adversaries — 1Co 16:9
that with me, t. should be yea yea, and — 2Co 1:17
Spirit of the Lord is, t. is liberty — 2Co 3:17
that as t. was a readiness to will — 2Co 8:11
so t. may be a performance also out of — 2Co 8:11
For if t. be first a willing mind, it is — 2Co 8:12
for your want: that t. may be equality — 2Co 8:14
t. was given to me a thorn in the flesh — 2Co 12:7
lest t. be debates, envyings, wraths — 2Co 12:20
but t. be some that trouble you, and — Ga 1:7
for if t. had been a law given which — Ga 3:21
T. is neither Jew nor Greek — Ga 3:28
t. is neither bond nor free — Ga 3:28
t. is neither male nor female: for ye — Ga 3:28
temperance: against such t. is no law — Ga 5:23
T. is one body, and one Spirit, even as — Eph 4:4
neither is t. respect of persons with — Eph 6:9
If t. be therefore any consolation in — Ph'p 2:1
if t. be any virtue, if t. be any praise — Ph'p 4:8
Where t. is neither Greek nor Jew — Col 3:11
done: and t. is no respect of persons — Col 3:25
except t. come a falling away first — 2Th 2:3
t. are some which walk among you — 2Th 3:11
if t. be any other thing that is contrary — 1Ti 1:10
For t. is one God, and one mediator — 1Ti 2:5
t. are not only vessels of gold and of — 2Ti 2:20
t. is laid up for me a crown of — 2Ti 4:8
t. are many unruly and vain talkers — Tit 1:10
for I have determined t. to winter — Tit 3:12
T. salute thee Epaphras, my — Ph'm 23
lest t. be in any of you an evil heart of — Heb 3:12
T. remaineth therefore a rest to the — Heb 4:9
Neither is t. any creature that is not — Heb 4:13
t. he receiveth them, of whom it is — Heb 7:8
what further need was t. that another — Heb 7:11
t. is made of necessity a change also — Heb 7:12
of Melchisedec t. ariseth another — Heb 7:15
For t. is verily a disannulling of the — Heb 7:18
t. are priests that offer gifts according — Heb 8:4
For t. was a tabernacle made — Heb 9:2
t. must also of necessity be the death — Heb 9:16
in those sacrifices t. is a remembrance — Heb 10:3
these is, t. is no more offering for sin — Heb 10:18
t. remaineth no more sacrifice for sins — Heb 10:26
sprang t. even of one, and he as good — Heb 11:12
Lest t. be any fornicator, or profane — Heb 12:16
t. come unto your assembly a man — Jas 2:2

t. come in also a poor man in | *Jas 2:2*
vile
and say to the poor, Stand | *Jas 2:3*
thou *t.*
Thou believest that *t.* is one | *Jas 2:19*
God
t. is confusion and every evil | *Jas 3:16*
work
T. is one lawgiver, who is | *Jas 4:12*
able to save
such a city, and continue *t.* a | *Jas 4:13*
year
t. came such a voice to him | *2Pe 1:17*
from the
t. were false prophets also | *2Pe 2:1*
among the
t. shall be false teachers | *2Pe 2:1*
among you
t. shall come in the last days | *2Pe 3:3*
scoffers
t. is none occasion of | *1Jo 2:10*
stumbling in
even now are *t.* many | *1Jo 2:18*
antichrists
T. is no fear in love; but | *1Jo 4:18*
perfect love
t. are three that bear record in | *1Jo 5:7*
heaven
t. are three that bear witness | *1Jo 5:8*
in earth
T. is a sin unto death: I do | *1Jo 5:16*
not say
is sin: and *t.* is a sin not unto | *1Jo 5:17*
death
t. come any unto you, and | *2Jo 10*
bring not
t. are certain men crept in | *Jude 4*
unawares
t. should be mockers in the | *Jude 18*
last time
thou hast *t.* them that hold the | *Re 2:14*
t. was a rainbow round about | *Re 4:3*
t. were seven lamps of fire | *Re 4:5*
burning
before the throne *t.* was a sea | *Re 4:6*
of glass
t. went out another horse that | *Re 6:4*
was
t. was given unto him a great | *Re 6:4*
sword
and, lo, *t.* was a great | *Re 6:12*
earthquake
t. were sealed an hundred and | *Re 7:4*
forty
t. was silence in heaven about | *Re 8:1*
t. was given unto him much | *Re 8:3*
incense
and *t.* were voices, and | *Re 8:5*
thunderings
t. followed hail and fire | *Re 8:7*
mingled with
and *t.* fell a great star from | *Re 8:10*
heaven
and *t.* arose a smoke out of the | *Re 9:2*
pit
t. came out of the smoke | *Re 9:3*
locusts upon
and *t.* were stings in their tails | *Re 9:10*
t. come two woes more | *Re 9:12*
hereafter
that *t.* should be time no | *Re 10:6*
longer
t. was given me a reed like | *Re 11:1*
unto a rod
same hour was *t.* a great | *Re 11:13*
earthquake
t. were great voices in | *Re 11:15*
heaven, saying
t. was seen in his temple the | *Re 11:19*
ark of
and *t.* were lightnings, and | *Re 11:19*
voices
t. appeared a great wonder in | *Re 12:1*
heaven
t. appeared another wonder in | *Re 12:3*
heaven
should feed her *t.* a thousand | *Re 12:6*
two
t. was war in heaven: Michael | *Re 12:7*
and his
And *t.* was given unto him a | *Re 13:5*
mouth
And *t.* followed another angel, | *Re 14:8*
saying
t. fell a noisome and grievous | *Re 16:2*
sore
t. came a great voice out of | *Re 16:17*
the temple
And *t.* were voices, and | *Re 16:18*
thunders

t. was a great earthquake, | *Re 16:18*
such as
t. fell upon men a great hail | *Re 16:21*
out of
t. came one of the seven | *Re 17:1*
angels which
t. are seven kings: five are | *Re 17:10*
fallen
and *t.* was found no place | *Re 20:11*
for them
passed away; and *t.* was no | *Re 21:1*
more sea
t. shall be no more death, | *Re 21:4*
neither
neither shall *t.* be any more | *Re 21:4*
pain
t. came unto me one of the | *Re 21:9*
seven
at all by day: for *t.* shall be | *Re 21:25*
no night
shall be no night *t.* | *Re 21:25*
t. shall in no wise enter into | *Re 21:27*
it any
of the river, was *t.* the tree of | *Re 22:2*
life
And *t.* shall be no more curse: | *Re 22:3*
but the
shall be no night *t.*; and they | *Re 22:5*

THEREABOUT

they were much perplexed *t.* | *Lu 24:4*

THEREAFTER

it is *t.* good for nothing (S) | *M't 5:13*

THEREAT

wash their hands and their | *Ex 30:19*
feet
washed their hands and their | *Ex 40:31*
feet *t.*
many there be which go in *t.* | *M't 7:13*

THEREBY

t. shall I know that thou hast | *Ge 24:14*
shewed
them, that ye should be | *Le 11:43*
defiled *t.*
peace: *t.* good shall come | *Job 22:21*
unto thee
whosoever is deceived *t.* is not | *Pr 20:1*
wise
cleaveth wood shall be | *Ec 10:9*
endangered *t.*
oars, neither shall gallant | *Isa 33:21*
ship pass *t.*
that passeth *t.* shall be | *Jer 18:16;*
astonished | *19:8*
doth any son of man pass *t.* | *Jer 51:43*
wall in their sight, and carry | *Eze 12:5*
out *t.*
dig through the wall to carry | *Eze 12:12*
out *t.*
he shall not fall *t.* in the day | *Eze 33:12*
that he
iniquity, he shall even die *t.* | *Eze 33:18*
is lawful and right, he shall | *Eze 33:19*
live *t.*
And Hamath also shall border | *Zec 9:2*
t.
of God might be glorified *t.* | *Joh 11:4*
having slain the enmity *t.* | *Eph 2:16*
them which are exercised *t.* | *Heb 12:11*
you, and *t.* many be defiled | *Heb 12:15*
t. some have entertained | *Heb 13:2*
angels
the word, that ye may grow *t.* | *1Pe 2:2*

THEREFORE

T. shall a man leave father | *Ge 2:24*
T. the Lord God sent him | *Ge 3:23*
forth from
T. whosoever slayeth Cain | *Ge 4:15*
T. is the name of it called | *Ge 11:9*
T. it shall come to pass, | *Ge 12:12*
when the
t. behold thy wife, take her, | *Ge 12:19*
and go
Thou shalt keep my covenant | *Ge 17:9*
t. thou
for *t.* are ye come to your | *Ge 18:5*
T. Sarah laughed within | *Ge 18:12*
herself
t. came they under the | *Ge 19:8*
T. the name of the city was | *Ge 19:22*
t. suffered I thee not to touch | *Ge 20:6*

t. restore the man his wife; | *Ge 20:7*
for he
T. Abimelech rose early in the | *Ge 20:8*
Now *t.* sware unto me here | *Ge 21:23*
by God
me and thee? bury *t.* thy | *Ge 23:15*
dead
t. she took a veil, and | *Ge 24:65*
covered herself
t. was his name called Edom | *Ge 25:30*
t. is the name of the city is | *Ge 26:33*
t. take, I pray thee, thy | *Ge 27:3*
weapons
Now *t.* my son, obey my voice | *Ge 27:8;*
| *27:43*
T. God give thee of the dew | *Ge 27:28*
of heaven
shouldest thou *t.* serve me | *Ge 29:15*
for nought
now *t.* my husband will love | *Ge 29:32*
me
he hath *t.* given me this son | *Ge 29:33*
also
t. was his name called Levi | *Ge 29:34*
t. she called his name Judah | *Ge 29:35*
t. called she his name Dan | *Ge 30:6*
T. he shall lie with thee to | *Ge 30:15*
night
t. come thou, let us make a | *Ge 31:44*
covenant
T. was the name of it called | *Ge 31:48*
T. the children of | *Ge 32:32*
Israel eat
for *t.* I have seen thy face, as | *Ge 33:10*
t. the name of the place is | *Ge 33:17*
t. let them dwell in the land | *Ge 34:21*
Come now *t.* and let us slay | *Ge 37:20*
him
thee; *t.* his name was called | *Ge 38:29*
Pharez
t. let Pharaoh look out a | *Ge 41:33*
man discreet
t. is this distress come upon | *Ge 42:21*
t. behold, his blood is | *Ge 42:22*
required
Now *t.* when I come to thy | *Ge 44:30*
servant my
t. I pray thee, let thy servant | *Ge 44:33*
abide
Now *t.* be not grieved, nor | *Ge 45:5*
angry with
t. we pray thee, let thy | *Ge 47:4*
servants dwell
t. let me go up, I pray thee, | *Ge 50:5*
and bury
Now *t.* fear ye not: I will | *Ge 50:21*
nourish you
T. they did set over them | *Ex 1:11*
taskmasters
T. God dealt well with the | *Ex 1:20*
midwives
Now *t.* behold, the cry of the | *Ex 3:9*
children
Come now *t.* and I will send | *Ex 3:10*
thee
Now *t.* go, and I will be with | *Ex 4:12*
thy
t. they cry, saying, Let us go | *Ex 5:8*
t. ye say, Let us go and do | *Ex 5:17*
Go *t.* now, and work; for | *Ex 5:18*
there shall
Send *t.* now, and gather thy | *Ex 9:19*
cattle
Now *t.* forgive, I pray thee, | *Ex 10:17*
my sin
t. shall ye observe this day in | *Ex 12:17*
your
Thou shalt *t.* keep this | *Ex 13:10*
ordinance in
t. I sacrifice to the Lord all | *Ex 13:15*
t. the name of it was called | *Ex 15:23*
t. he giveth you on the sixth | *Ex 16:29*
Now *t.* if ye will obey my | *Ex 19:5*
voice
Ye shall keep the sabbath *t.*; | *Ex 31:14*
for it is
t. let me alone, that my | *Ex 32:10*
wrath may
T. now go, lead the people | *Ex 32:34*
unto the
t. now put off thy ornaments | *Ex 33:5*
from
Now *t.* I pray thee, if I have | *Ex 33:13*
found
T. shall ye abide at the door | *Le 8:35*
Aaron *t.* went unto the altar | *Le 9:8*
ye shall *t.* sanctify yourselves, | *Le 11:44*
and ye

God: ye shall *t.* be holy, for I *Le 11:45* am holy
He shall *t.* burn that garment *Le 13:52*
t. shall he wash his flesh in *Le 16:4* water
T. I said unto the children of *Le 17:12*
t. I said unto the children of *Le 17:14* Israel
Ye shall *t.* keep my statutes, *Le 18:5* and my
t. I do visit the iniquity *Le 18:25* thereof upon
Ye shall *t.* keep my statutes *Le 18:26* and my
T. shall ye keep mine *Le 18:30* ordinance, that
T. every one that eateth it *Le 19:8* shall bear
T. shall ye observe all my *Le 19:37* statutes
Sanctify yourselves *t.* and be *Le 20:7* ye holy
Ye shall *t.* keep all my *Le 20:22* statutes, and
these things, and *t.* I *Le 20:23* abhorred them
Ye shall *t.* put difference *Le 20:25* between
they do offer: *t.* they shall be *Le 21:6* holy
Thou shalt sanctify him *t.*: for *Le 21:8* he
They shall *t.* keep mine *Le 22:9* ordinance
for it, and die *t.* if they *Le 22:9* profane it
T. shall ye keep my *Le 22:31* commandments
Ye shall not *t.* oppress one *Le 25:17* another
Israel: *t.* the Levites shall be *Nu 3:12* mine
t. the Lord will give you *Nu 11:18* flesh, and ye
t. he hath slain them in the *Nu 14:16* Lord, *t.* the Lord will not be *Nu 14:43* with you
before the Lord, *t.* they are *Nu 16:38* hallowed
T. thou and thy sons with *Nu 18:7* thee shall
t. I have said unto them *Nu 18:24*
T. thou shalt say unto them, *Nu 18:30* When ye
t. ye shall not bring this *Nu 20:12*
T. the people came to Moses *Nu 21:7*
He sent messengers *t.* unto *Nu 22:5* Balaam
Come now *t.* I pray thee, *Nu 22:6* curse me
come *t.* I pray thee, curse me *Nu 22:17* this
Now *t.* I pray you, tarry ye *Nu 22:19* also here
now *t.* if I displease thee, I *Nu 22:34* will get
T. now flee thou to thy *Nu 24:11* place: I
come *t.* and I will advertise *Nu 24:14* thee
Give unto us *t.* a possession *Nu 27:4* among
t. kill every male among the *Nu 31:17* little
t. brought an oblation for *Nu 31:50* the Lord
Defile not *t.* the land which *Nu 35:34* ye shall
take ye good heed unto *De 2:4* yourselves *t.*
Now *t.* hearken, O Israel, unto *De 4:1*
Keep *t.* and do them: for this *De 4:6* is your
Take ye *t.* good heed unto *De 4:15* yourselves
t. he chose their seed after *De 4:37* them, and
Know *t.* this day, and *De 4:39* consider it in
Thou shalt keep *t.* his statutes *De 4:40*
t. the Lord commanded *De 5:15*
t. why should we die? for this *De 5:25* great
Ye shall observe to do *t.* as *De 5:32* the Lord
Hear *t.* O Israel, and observe *De 6:3* to do it
Know *t.* that the Lord thy God, *De 7:9* he is
shalt *t.* keep commandments *De 7:11*

T. thou shalt keep the *De 8:6*
Understand *t.* this day, that the *De 9:3* Lord
Understand *t.* that the Lord thy *De 9:6* God
I prayed *t.* unto the Lord, *De 9:26* and said
Circumcise *t.* the foreskin of *De 10:16* your
Love ye *t.* the stranger; for *De 10:19* ye were
T. thou shalt love the Lord *De 11:1* thy God
T. shall ye keep all the *De 11:8*
T. shall ye lay up these my *De 11:18* words in
hoof; *t.* they are unclean unto *De 14:7* you
t. I command thee, saying *De 15:11*
t. I command thee this thing *De 15:15* to
Thou shalt *t.* sacrifice the *De 16:2* passover
hands, *t.* thou shalt surely *De 16:15* rejoice
T. shall they have no *De 18:2* inheritance
before thee; *t.* shall thy camp *De 23:14* be holy
t. I command thee to do *De 24:18; 24:22*
T. it shall be, when the Lord *De 25:19* thy God
thou shalt *t.* keep and do *De 26:16* them with
T. it shall be when ye be gone *De 27:4* over
shalt *t.* obey the voice of the *De 27:10* Lord
T. shalt thou serve thine *De 28:48* enemies
Keep *t.* the words of this *De 29:9* covenant
t. choose life, that both thou *De 30:19* and thy
Now *t.* write ye this song for *De 31:19* you, and
Moses *t.* wrote this song the *De 31:22* same
now *t.* arise, go over this *Jos 1:2* Jordan
Now *t.* I pray you, swear *Jos 2:12* unto me by
Now *t.* take ye twelve men *Jos 3:12* out of the
Joshua *t.* commanded the *Jos 4:17* priests
T. the children of Israel could *Jos 7:12* not
In the morning *t.* ye shall be *Jos 7:14* brought
the first; *t.* we will flee before *Jos 8:6* them
Joshua *t.* sent them forth: and *Jos 8:9* they
now *t.* make ye a league with *Jos 9:6* us
t. now make ye a league with *Jos 9:11* us
Israel: now *t.* we may not *Jos 9:19* touch them
Now *t.* ye are cursed, and *Jos 9:23* there shall
t. we were sore afraid of our *Jos 9:24* lives
T. the five kings of the *Jos 10:5* Amorites, the
Joshua *t.* came unto them *Jos 10:9* suddenly
t. divide this land for an *Jos 13:7* inheritance
t. they gave no part unto the *Jos 14:4* Levites
Now *t.* give me this *Jos 14:12* mountain, whereof
Hebron *t.* became the *Jos 14:14* inheritance of
of war, *t.* he had Gilead and *Jos 17:1* Bashan
T. according to the *Jos 17:4* commandment of
shall *t.* describe the land into *Jos 18:6* seven
t. the children of Simeon had *Jos 19:9* their
t. the children of Dan went *Jos 19:47* up to
t. now return ye, and get you *Jos 22:4* unto

T. we said, Let us now *Jos 22:26* prepare to
T. said we, that it shall be, *Jos 22:28* when they
Be ye *t.* very courageous to *Jos 23:6* keep and
Take good heed *t.* unto your *Jos 23:11* selves
T. it shall come to pass, that *Jos 23:15* as all
t. he blessed you still: so I *Jos 24:10* delivered
Now *t.* fear the Lord, and *Jos 24:14* serve him in
t. will we also serve the *Jos 24:18* Lord: for he
t. put away, said he, the *Jos 24:23* strange gods
it shall be *t.* a witness unto *Jos 24:27* you, lest
T. the Lord left those nations *J'g 2:23*
T. the anger of the Lord was *J'g 3:8* hot
t. they took a key, and opened *J'g 3:25* them
T. on that day he called him *J'g 6:32*
t. go to, proclaim in the ears of *J'g 7:3*
T. when the Lord hath *J'g 8:7* delivered
Now *t.* if ye have done truly *J'g 9:16*
Now *t.* up by night, thou and *J'g 9:32*
T. we turn again to thee now *J'g 11:8*
t. restore those lands again *J'g 11:13* peaceably
why *t.* did ye not recover *J'g 11:26* them within
t. beware, I pray thee, and *J'g 13:4* drink not
now *t.* get her for me to wife *J'g 14:2*
her: *t.* I gave her to thy *J'g 15:2* companion
Delilah *t.* took new ropes, *J'g 16:12* and bound
now *t.* I will restore it unto *J'g 17:3* thee
now *t.* consider what ye have *J'g 18:14* to do
urged him: *t.* he lodged there *J'g 19:7* again
Now *t.* deliver us the men *J'g 20:13*
T. they turned their backs *J'g 20:42* before the
T. they commanded the *J'g 21:20* children of
Wash thyself *t.* and anoint *Ru 3:3* thee, and
spread, *t.* thy skirt over thine *Ru 3:9*
T. the kinsman said unto Boaz, *Ru 4:8* Buy
her; *t.* she wept, and did not *1Sa 1:7* eat
t. Eli thought she had been *1Sa 1:13* drunken
T. also I have lent him to the *1Sa 1:28* Lord
t. Eli said unto Samuel, Go, *1Sa 3:9* lie down
t. I have sworn unto the *1Sa 3:14* house of Eli
T. neither the priests of *1Sa 5:5*
They sent *t.* and gathered all *1Sa 5:8*
T. they sent the ark of God *1Sa 5:10* to Ekron
Now *t.* make a new cart, and *1Sa 6:7* take two
Now *t.* hearken unto their *1Sa 8:9* voice
Now *t.* get you up; for about *1Sa 9:13* this time
T. it became a proverb, Is *1Sa 10:12*
t. present yourselves before *1Sa 10:19* the Lord
T. they enquired of the *1Sa 10:22* Lord further
T. the men of Jabesh said, To *1Sa 11:10*
Now *t.* stand still, that I may *1Sa 12:7* reason
Now *t.* behold the king *1Sa 12:13* whom ye have
Now *t.* stand and see this *1Sa 12:16* great
T. said I, The Philistines *1Sa 13:12* will come
I forced myself *t.* and *1Sa 13:12* offered a burnt
T. Saul said unto the Lord *1Sa 14:41* God of
now *t.* hearken thou unto the *1Sa 15:1* voice of

Now *t*. I pray thee, pardon my sin	*1Sa 15:25*	*t*. now it is better that thou succour us	*2Sa 18:3*	now *t*. come, that we may go and tell	*2Ki 7:9*
T. David ran, and stood upon the	*1Sa 17:51*	Now *t*. arise, go forth, and speak	*2Sa 19:7*	*t*. are they gone out of the camp to	*2Ki 7:12*
T. Saul removed him from him, and	*1Sa 18:13*	*t*. why speak ye not a word of bringing	*2Sa 19:10*	They took *t*. two chariot horses; and	*2Ki 7:14*
thee: now *t*. be the king's son in law	*1Sa 18:22*	*t*. behold, I am come the first this day	*2Sa 19:20*	Now *t*. take and cast him into the plat	*2Ki 9:26*
now *t*. I pray thee, take heed to	*1Sa 19:2*	*T*. the king said unto Shimei, Thou	*2Sa 19:23*	Now *t*. call unto me all the prophets of	*2Ki 10:19*
T. thou shalt deal kindly with thy	*1Sa 20:8*	God: do *t*. what is good in thine eyes	*2Sa 19:27*	now *t*. receive no more money of your	*2Ki 12:7*
T. he cometh not unto the	*1Sa 20:29*	What right *t*. have I yet to cry any	*2Sa 19:28*	*T*. Jehoash king of Israel went up	*2Ki 14:11*
Now *t*. what is under thine hand? give	*1Sa 21:3*	*T*. the Lord hath recompensed me	*2Sa 22:25*	they opened not to him, *t*. he smote it	*2Ki 15:16*
David *t*. departed thence, and escaped	*1Sa 22:1*	*T*. I will give thanks unto	*2Sa 22:50*	*t*. the king of Assyria shut him up, and	*2Ki 17:4*
T. David enquired of the Lord	*1Sa 23:2*	of their lives? *t*. he would not drink it	*2Sa 23:17*	*T*. the Lord was very angry with	*2Ki 17:18*
Now *t*., O king, come down according	*1Sa 23:20*	of three? *t*. he was their captain	*2Sa 23:19*	*t*. the Lord sent lions among them	*2Ki 17:25*
See *t*. and take knowledge of all the	*1Sa 23:23*	now *t*. come, let me, I pray thee, give	*1Ki 1:12*	*t*. he hath sent lions among them, and	*2Ki 17:26*
t. they called that place	*1Sa 23:28*	be thou strong *t*. and show thyself a	*1Ki 2:2*	Now *t*. I pray thee give pledges to my	*2Ki 18:23*
The Lord *t*. be judge, and judge	*1Sa 24:15*	Do *t*. according to thy wisdom, and let	*1Ki 2:6*	stone: *t*. they have destroyed them	*2Ki 19:18*
Swear now *t*. unto me by the Lord	*1Sa 24:21*	Now *t*. hold him not guiltless	*1Ki 2:9*	Now *t*. O Lord our God, I beseech thee	*2Ki 19:19*
t. know and consider what thou wilt	*1Sa 25:17*	Bath-sheba *t*. went unto king	*1Ki 2:19*	*T*. their inhabitants were of small	*2Ki 19:26*
Now *t*. my lord, as the Lord liveth	*1Sa 25:26*	Now *t*. as the Lord liveth, which hath	*1Ki 2:24*	*t*. I will put my hook in thy nose, and	*2Ki 19:28*
David *t*. sent out spies, and	*1Sa 26:4*	Their blood shall *t*. return upon the	*1Ki 2:33*	*T*. thus saith the Lord concerning	*2Ki 19:32*
now *t*. let me smite him, I pray thee	*1Sa 26:8*	*t*. the Lord shall return thy wickedness	*1Ki 2:44*	*T*. thus saith the Lord God of	*2Ki 21:12*
Now *t*. I pray thee, let my lord the	*1Sa 26:19*	Give *t*. thy servant an understanding	*1Ki 3:9*	*t*. my wrath shall be kindled against	*2Ki 22:17*
Now *t*. let not my blood fall to the	*1Sa 26:20*	Now *t*. command thou that they hew	*1Ki 5:6*	Behold *t*. I will gather thee unto	*2Ki 22:20*
him; *t*. he shall be my servant for ever	*1Sa 27:12*	*T*. now, Lord God of Israel, keep	*1Ki 8:25*	*t*. he slew him, and turned	*1Ch 10:14*
T. will I make thee keeper of mine	*1Sa 28:2*	your heart *t*. be perfect with the Lord	*1Ki 8:61*	*T*. came all the elders of Israel to the	*1Ch 11:3*
t. I have called thee, that thou mayest	*1Sa 28:15*	*t*. hath the Lord brought upon	*1Ki 9:9*	*t*. they called it the city of	*1Ch 11:7*
t. hath the Lord done this	*1Sa 28:18*	*t*. made he thee king, to do judgment	*1Ki 10:9*	brought it. *T*. he would not drink it	*1Ch 11:19*
Now *t*. I pray thee, hearken thou also	*1Sa 28:22*	Solomon sought *t*. to kill Jeroboam	*1Ki 11:40*	*t*. they called the name of	*1Ch 14:11*
T. Saul took a sword, and fell upon it	*1Sa 31:4*	now *t*. make thou the grievous service	*1Ki 12:4*	*T*. David inquired again of God; and	*1Ch 14:14*
T. now let your hands be	*2Sa 2:7*	*t*. king Rehoboam made speed to get	*1Ki 12:18*	David *t*. did as God commanded him	*1Ch 14:16*
shall I not *t*. now require his blood	*2Sa 4:11*	They hearkened *t*. to the word of the	*1Ki 12:24*	*t*. thus shalt thou say unto my servant	*1Ch 17:7*
T. he called the name of that	*2Sa 5:20*	*t*. the Lord hath delivered him unto	*1Ki 13:26*	*T*. now, Lord, let the thing that thou	*1Ch 17:23*
Israel: *t*. will I play before the Lord	*2Sa 6:21*	*T*. behold, I will bring evil upon	*1Ki 14:10*	*t*. thy servant hath found in	*1Ch 17:25*
T. Michal the daughter of Saul had	*2Sa 6:23*	Arise thou *t*. get thee to thine own	*1Ki 14:12*	Now *t*. let it please thee to bless the	*1Ch 17:27*
Now *t*. so shalt thou say unto my	*2Sa 7:8*	Now *t*. send, and gather to me all	*1Ki 18:19*	with this thing; *t*. he smote Israel	*1Ch 21:7*
t. hath thy servant found in his heart	*2Sa 7:27*	Let them *t*. give us two bullocks; and	*1Ki 18:23*	*t*. advise thyself what word I shall	*1Ch 21:12*
T. now let it please thee to bless the	*2Sa 7:29*	*t*. they were stronger than we	*1Ki 20:23*	I will *t*. now make preparation for it	*1Ch 22:5*
Thou *t*. and thy sons, and thy	*2Sa 9:10*	*t*. will I deliver all this great multitude	*1Ki 20:28*	Arise *t*. and be doing, and the Lord be	*1Ch 22:16*
Now *t*. the sword shall never depart	*2Sa 12:10*	*t*. thy life shall go for his life, and thy	*1Ki 20:42*	arise *t*. and build ye the sanctuary	*1Ch 22:19*
David *t*. besought God for the child	*2Sa 12:16*	Hear thou *t*. the word of the Lord	*1Ki 22:19*	*t*. they were in one reckoning	*1Ch 23:11*
t. David said unto his servants, Is the	*2Sa 12:19*	Now *t*. behold, the Lord hath put a	*1Ki 22:23*	*t*. Eleazar and Ithamar executed the	*1Ch 24:2*
Now *t*. gather the rest of the people	*2Sa 12:28*	Now *t*. thus saith the Lord, Thou	*2Ki 1:4*	*t*. in the sight of all Israel the	*1Ch 28:8*
Now *t*. I pray thee, speak unto the	*2Sa 13:13*	*t*. thou shalt not come down from	*2Ki 1:6*	Now *t*. our God, we thank thee, and	*1Ch 29:13*
t. let not my lord the king take the	*2Sa 13:33*	*t*. let my life now be precious in thy	*2Ki 1:14*	Send me now *t*. a man cunning to	*2Ch 2:7*
t. that I am come to speak of this	*2Sa 14:15*	*t*. thou shalt not come down off that	*2Ki 1:16*	Now *t*. the wheat, and the barley, the	*2Ch 2:15*
t. the Lord thy God will be with thee	*2Sa 14:17*	they sent *t*. fifty men; and they	*2Ki 2:17*	The Lord *t*. hath performed his word	*2Ch 6:10*
t. bring the young man Absalom	*2Sa 14:21*	another: now *t*. Moab, to the spoil	*2Ki 3:23*	Now *t*. O Lord God of Israel, keep	*2Ch 6:16*
was heavy on him, *t*. he polled it	*2Sa 14:26*	He went in *t*. and shut the door upon	*2Ki 4:33*	Have respect *t*. to the prayer of thy	*2Ch 6:19*
T. Absalom sent for Joab, to have	*2Sa 14:29*	now *t*. I pray thee, take a blessing of	*2Ki 5:15*	Hearken *t*. unto the supplications of	*2Ch 6:21*
T. he said unto his servants, See	*2Sa 14:30*	leprosy *t*. of Naaman shall cleave unto	*2Ki 5:27*	Now *t*. arise, O Lord God, into thy	*2Ch 6:41*
now *t*. let me see the king's face; and	*2Sa 14:32*	*T*. said he, Take it up to thee. And he	*2Ki 6:7*	*t*. hath he brought all this	*2Ch 7:22*
Zadok *t*. and Abiathar carried the ark	*2Sa 15:29*	*T*. the heart of the king of Syria was	*2Ki 6:11*	*t*. made he thee king over them, to do	*2Ch 9:8*
t. it shall be, that what thing soever	*2Sa 15:35*	*T*. sent he thither horses, and	*2Ki 6:14*	now *t*. ease thou somewhat	*2Ch 10:4*
T. I counsel that all Israel be	*2Sa 17:11*	Now *t*. come, and let us fall unto the	*2Ki 7:4*	*t*. have I also left you in the hand of	*2Ch 12:5*
Now *t*. send quickly, and tell David	*2Sa 17:16*				

t. I will not destroy them, but I will — *2Ch 12:7*
T. he saith unto Judah, Let us build — *2Ch 14:7*
Be ye strong *t.* and let not your hands — *2Ch 15:7*
t. is the host of the king of — *2Ch 16:7*
t. henceforth thou shalt have wars — *2Ch 16:9*
T. the Lord stablished the kingdom in — *2Ch 17:5*
T. the king of Israel gathered — *2Ch 18:5*
let thy word *t.* I pray thee, be like one — *2Ch 18:12*
them return *t.* every man to his house — *2Ch 18:16*
T. hear the word of the Lord — *2Ch 18:18*
Now *t.* behold, the Lord hath put a — *2Ch 18:22*
T. they compassed about him to fight — *2Ch 18:31*
t. he said to his chariot man, Turn — *2Ch 18:33*
t. is wrath come upon thee from — *2Ch 19:2*
t. the name of the same place — *2Ch 20:26*
Now hear me *t.* and deliver — *2Ch 28:11*
t. will I sacrifice to them, that they — *2Ch 28:23*
who *t.* gave them up to desolation, as — *2Ch 30:7*
t. the Levites had the charge of the — *2Ch 30:17*
Now *t.* let not Hezekiah deceive you — *2Ch 32:15*
t. there was wrath upon him, and — *2Ch 32:25*
t. my wrath shall be poured out upon — *2Ch 32:25*
t. the Levites prepared for themselves — *2Ch 35:14*
His servants *t.* took him out of that — *2Ch 35:24*
T. he brought upon them the king of — *2Ch 36:17*
t. were they, as polluted, put from the — *Ezr 2:62*
t. have we sent and certified — *Ezr 4:14*
Now *t.* if it seem good to the king, let — *Ezr 5:17*
Now *t.* Tatnai, governor beyond the — *Ezr 6:6*
t. give not your daughters unto their — *Ezr 9:12*
t. let us make a covenant with our God — *Ezr 10:3*
Now *t.* make confession unto the Lord — *Ezr 10:11*
t. we his servants will arise and build — *Ne 2:20*
T. set I in the lower places behind the — *Ne 4:13*
In what place *t.* ye hear the sound of — *Ne 4:20*
t. we take up corn for them, that we — *Ne 5:2*
Come now *t.* and let us take counsel — *Ne 6:7*
Now *t.* O God, strengthen my hands — *Ne 6:9*
T. was he hired, that I should be — *Ne 6:13*
t. were they, as polluted, put from the — *Ne 7:64*
T. thou deliveredst them into — *Ne 9:27*
t. leftest thou them in the hand of — *Ne 9:28*
t. gavest thou them into the hand of — *Ne 9:30*
Now *t.* our God, the great, the mighty — *Ne 9:32*
t. I cast forth all the household stuff — *Ne 13:8*
Horonite: *t.* I chased him from me — *Ne 13:28*
t. was the king very wroth, and his — *Es 1:12*
t. they were both hanged on a tree — *Es 2:23*
t. it is not for the king's profit to suffer — *Es 3:8*
T. the Jews of the villages — *Es 9:19*
T. for all the words of this — *Es 9:26*
t. despise not thou the chastening of — *Job 5:17*
t. my words are swallowed up — *Job 6:3*
Now *t.* be content, look upon me; for — *Job 6:28*

T. I will not refrain my mouth; I — *Job 7:11*
This is one thing, *t.* I said it — *Job 9:22*
confusion; *t.* see thou mine affliction — *Job 10:15*
Know *t.* that God exacteth of thee less — *Job 11:6*
t. shalt thou not exalt them — *Job 17:4*
T. do my thoughts cause me to — *Job 20:2*
t. shall no man look for his — *Job 20:21*
T. they say unto God, Depart from — *Job 21:14*
T. snares are round about — *Job 22:10*
T. am I troubled at his — *Job 23:15*
T. I said, Hearken to me; I also — *Job 32:10*
T. hearken unto me, ye men of — *Job 34:10*
T. he knoweth their works, and he — *Job 34:25*
and not I: *t.* speak what thou knowest — *Job 34:33*
is before him; *t.* trust thou in him — *Job 35:14*
T. doth Job open his mouth in vain — *Job 35:16*
Men do *t.* fear him: he respecteth — *Job 37:24*
t. have I uttered that I understood — *Job 42:3*
T. take unto you now seven bullocks — *Job 42:8*
T. the ungodly shall not — *Ps 1:5*
Be wise now *t.* O ye kings: be — *Ps 2:10*
for their sakes *t.* return thou on high — *Ps 7:7*
T. my heart is glad, and my glory — *Ps 16:9*
T. hath the Lord recompensed me — *Ps 18:24*
T. will I give thanks unto — *Ps 18:49*
T. shalt thou make them turn their — *Ps 21:12*
t. will he teach sinners in the — *Ps 25:8*
also in the Lord; *t.* I shall not slide — *Ps 26:1*
t. will I offer in his tabernacle — *Ps 27:6*
t. my heart greatly rejoiceth — *Ps 28:7*
t. for thy name's sake lead me — *Ps 31:3*
t. the children of men put their trust — *Ps 36:7*
of mine head: *t.* my heart faileth me — *Ps 40:12*
t. will I remember thee from — *Ps 42:6*
t. God hath blessed thee — *Ps 45:2*
t. God, thy God, hath anointed — *Ps 45:7*
t. shall the people praise thee — *Ps 45:17*
T. will not we fear, though the — *Ps 46:2*
have no changes, *t.* they fear not God — *Ps 55:19*
Thou *t.* O Lord God of hosts, the God — *Ps 59:5*
t. in the shadow of thy wings will I — *Ps 63:7*
T. pride compasseth them about as a — *Ps 73:6*
t. his people return hither — *Ps 73:10*
T. the Lord heard this, and was — *Ps 78:21*
T. their days did he consume in — *Ps 78:33*
his love upon me, *t.* will I deliver him — *Ps 91:14*
T. he said that he would destroy them — *Ps 106:23*
T. he lifted up his hand against them — *Ps 106:26*
T. was the wrath of the Lord kindled — *Ps 106:40*
T. he brought down their heart with — *Ps 107:12*
t. shall he lift up the head — *Ps 110:7*
t. will I call upon him as long as I live — *Ps 116:2*
I believed, *t.* have I spoken: I was — *Ps 116:10*
t. shall I see my desire upon them that — *Ps 118:7*
t. I hate every false way — *Ps 119:104*
dross: *t.* I love thy testimonies — *Ps 119:119*
T. I love thy commandments — *Ps 119:127*
T. I esteem all thy precepts — *Ps 119:128*
t. doth my soul keep them — *Ps 119:129*
is very pure: *t.* thy servant loveth it — *Ps 119:140*
depart from me *t.* ye bloody men — *Ps 139:19*

T. is my spirit overwhelmed within — *Ps 143:4*
T. shall they eat of the fruit of their — *Pr 1:31*
is the principal thing; *t.* get wisdom — *Pr 4:7*
Hear me now *t.* O ye children — *Pr 5:7*
T. shall his calamity come — *Pr 6:15*
t. he will not spare in the day of — *Pr 6:34*
T. came I forth to meet thee — *Pr 7:15*
Hearken unto me now *t.* O ye — *Pr 7:24*
Now *t.* hearken unto me, O ye — *Pr 8:32*
t. a cruel messenger shall be sent — *Pr 17:11*
t. leave off contention, before it be — *Pr 17:14*
t. shall he beg in harvest, and have — *Pr 20:4*
t. meddle not with him that flattereth — *Pr 20:19*
thee with mirth, *t.* enjoy pleasure — *Ec 2:1*
T. I hated life; because the work that — *Ec 2:17*
T. I went about to cause my heart to — *Ec 2:20*
earth: *t.* let thy words be few — *Ec 5:2*
t. the misery of man is great upon — *Ec 8:6*
t. the heart of the sons of men — *Ec 8:11*
T. remove sorrow from thy heart — *Ec 11:10*
t. do the virgins love thee — *Ca 1:3*
T. saith the Lord, the Lord of hosts — *Isa 1:24*
T. thou hast forsaken thy people — *Isa 2:6*
humbleth himself: *t.* forgive them not — *Isa 2:9*
T. the Lord will smite with a scab the — *Isa 3:17*
T. my people are gone into — *Isa 5:13*
T. hell hath enlarged herself — *Isa 5:14*
T. as the fire devoureth the stubble — *Isa 5:24*
T. is the anger of the Lord — *Isa 5:25*
T. the Lord himself shall give you — *Isa 7:14*
Now *t.* behold, the Lord bringeth — *Isa 8:7*
T. the Lord shall set up the — *Isa 9:11*
T. the Lord will cut off from Israel — *Isa 9:14*
T. the Lord shall have no joy — *Isa 9:17*
T. shall the Lord, the Lord of hosts — *Isa 10:16*
T. thus saith the Lord God of hosts — *Isa 10:24*
T. with joy shall ye draw water out of — *Isa 12:3*
T. shall all hands be faint — *Isa 13:7*
T. I will shake the heavens — *Isa 13:13*
t. the armed soldiers of Moab — *Isa 15:4*
T. the abundance they have — *Isa 15:7*
T. shall Moab howl for Moab, every — *Isa 16:7*
T. I will bewail with the — *Isa 16:9*
t. shalt thou plant pleasant — *Isa 17:10*
t. are my loins filled with — *Isa 21:3*
T. said I, Look away from me — *Isa 22:4*
t. hath the curse devoured — *Isa 24:6*
t. the inhabitants of the earth — *Isa 24:6*
T. shall the strong people — *Isa 25:3*
t. hast thou visited and destroyed — *Isa 26:14*
t. shall the iniquity of Jacob be — *Isa 27:9*
t. he that made them will not — *Isa 27:11*
T. thus saith the Lord God, Behold — *Isa 28:16*
Now *t.* be ye not mockers, lest your — *Isa 28:22*
T., behold, I will proceed to do a — *Isa 29:14*
T. thus saith the Lord, who — *Isa 29:22*
T. shall the strength of Pharaoh be — *Isa 30:3*
t. have I cried concerning this — *Isa 30:7*
T. this iniquity shall be to you as a — *Isa 30:13*
upon horses; *t.* shall ye flee — *Isa 30:16*
t. shall they that pursue you be — *Isa 30:16*
t. will the Lord wait, that he may — *Isa 30:18*
unto you, and *t.* will he be exalted — *Isa 30:18*
Now *t.* give pledges, I pray thee, to — *Isa 36:8*

stone: *t.* they have destroyed   Isa 37:19
them
Now *t.* O Lord our God,   Isa 37:20
save us from
t. their inhabitants were of   Isa 37:27
small
t. will I put my hook in thy   Isa 37:29
nose, and
T. thus saith the Lord   Isa 37:33
concerning
t. we will sing my songs to   Isa 38:20
the stringed
T. he hath poured upon him   Isa 42:25
the fury
t. will I give men for thee,   Isa 43:4
and people
t. ye are my witnesses, saith   Isa 43:12
the Lord
T. I have profaned the   Isa 43:28
princes of the
T. hear now this, thou that   Isa 47:8
art given
T. shall evil come upon thee;   Isa 47:11
thou
t. shall I not be confounded   Isa 50:7
t. have I set my face like a   Isa 50:7
T. the redeemed of the Lord   Isa 51:11
shall
T. hear now this, thou   Isa 51:21
afflicted
Now *t.* what have I here,   Isa 52:5
saith the
T. my people shall know my   Isa 52:6
t. they shall know in that day   Isa 52:6
that I
T. will I divide him a   Isa 53:12
portion with
t. thou wast not grieved   Isa 57:10
T. is judgment far from us   Isa 59:9
t. his arm brought salvation   Isa 59:16
unto
T. thy gates shall be open   Isa 60:11
continually
t. in their land they shall   Isa 61:7
possess
t. mine own arm brought   Isa 63:5
salvation
t. he was turned to be their   Isa 63:10
enemy
t. will I measure their former   Isa 65:7
work
T. will I number you to the   Isa 65:12
sword
T. thus saith the Lord God   Isa 65:13
Thou *t.* gird up thy loins, and   Jer 1:17
arise
know *t.* and see that it is an   Jer 2:19
evil thing
t. hast thou also taught the   Jer 2:33
wicked
T. the showers have been   Jer 3:3
withholden
T. I said, Surely these are   Jer 5:4
poor; they
t. they are become great, and   Jer 5:27
T. I am full of the fury of the   Jer 6:11
Lord; I
t. they shall fall among them   Jer 6:15
that
T. hear, ye nations, and   Jer 6:18
know, O
T. thus saith the Lord,   Jer 6:21;
Behold, I   11:11; 28:16; 29:32; 51:36
T. will I do unto this house,   Jer 7:14
which is
T. pray not thou for this   Jer 7:16
people
T. thus saith the Lord God   Jer 7:20
T. thou shalt speak all these   Jer 7:27
words
T. behold, the days come,   Jer 7:32
saith
T. will I give their wives unto   Jer 8:10
t. shall they fall among them   Jer 8:12
that
T. thus saith the Lord of hosts   Jer 9:7;
  9:15
t. they shall not prosper, and   Jer 10:21
t. I will bring upon them all   Jer 11:8
the words
T. pray not thou for this   Jer 11:14
people
T. thus saith the Lord of the   Jer 11:21
men
T. thus saith the Lord of   Jer 11:22;
hosts   23:15; 25:8; 35:19; 44:11; 50:18
against me: *t.* have I hated it   Jer 12:8
T. thou shalt speak unto   Jer 13:12
them this

T. will I scatter them as the   Jer 13:24
stubble
T. will I discover thy skirts   Jer 13:26
upon thy
t. the Lord doth not accept   Jer 14:10
them
T. thus saith the Lord   Jer 14:15
concerning
T. thou shalt say this word   Jer 14:17
unto
t. we will wait upon thee: Jer 14:22
for thou
t. will I stretch out my hand   Jer 15:6
against
T. thus saith the Lord, If   Jer 15:19
thou
T. will I cast you out of this   Jer 16:13
land into
T. behold, the days come,   Jer 16:14;
saith   19:6; 23:7
T. behold, I will this once   Jer 16:21
cause
Now *t.* go to, speak to the   Jer 18:11
men of
T. thus saith the Lord; Ask   Jer 18:13
ye
t. deliver up their children   Jer 18:21
to the
t. my persecutors shall   Jer 20:11
T. thus saith the Lord   Jer 22:18
concerning
T. thus saith the Lord God of   Jer 23:2
T. behold, I am against the   Jer 23:30
t. they shall not profit this   Jer 23:32
people at
T. thus saith the Lord;   Jer 23:38
Because
T. behold, I, even I, will   Jer 23:39
utterly
T. thou shalt say unto them,   Jer 25:27
Thus
T. prophesy thou against   Jer 25:30
them all
T. now amend your ways   Jer 26:13
and your
T. hearken not ye to your   Jer 27:9
prophet
T. hearken not unto the   Jer 27:14
words of the
Hear ye *t.* the word of the   Jer 29:20
Lord, all ye
Now *t.* why hast thou not   Jer 29:27
reproved
t. he sent unto us in Babylon   Jer 29:28
T. fear thou not, O my   Jer 30:10
servant Jacob
T. all they that devour thee   Jer 30:16
shall
t. with lovingkindness have I   Jer 31:3
T. they shall come and sing   Jer 31:12
in the
t. my bowels are troubled for   Jer 31:20
t. thou hast caused all this   Jer 32:23
evil to
T. thus saith the Lord   Jer 32:28
And now *t.* thus saith the   Jer 32:36
Lord, the
T. the word of the Lord   Jer 34:12
came to
T. thus saith the Lord; Ye   Jer 34:17
have
T. thus saith the Lord God   Jer 35:17
of hosts
t. go thou, and read in the   Jer 36:6
roll, which
T. all the princes sent Jehudi   Jer 36:14
the son
T. thus saith the Lord of   Jer 36:30
T. hear now, I pray thee, O   Jer 37:20
my lord
T. the princes said unto the   Jer 38:4
king, We
voice, *t.* this thing is come   Jer 40:3
upon you
now *t.* hear the word of the   Jer 42:15
Lord
t. know certainly that ye   Jer 42:22
shall die
T. now thus saith the Lord,   Jer 44:7
the God
t. is your land a desolation,   Jer 44:22
and an
t. this evil is happened unto   Jer 44:23
T. hear ye the word of the   Jer 44:26
Lord
t. his taste remained in him   Jer 48:11
T. behold, the days come,   Jer 48:12;
saith   49:2
T. will I howl for Moab, and   Jer 48:31
T. mine heart shall sound for   Jer 48:36

T. hear the counsel of the   Jer 49:20
Lord
T. her young men shall fall   Jer 49:26
in her
T. shall her young men fall   Jer 50:30
in the
T. the wild beasts of the   Jer 50:39
desert
T. hear ye the counsel of the   Jer 50:45
Lord
wine; *t.* the nations are mad   Jer 51:7
T. behold, the days come,   Jer 51:47
that I
sinned; *t.* she is removed   La 1:8
end; *t.* she came down   La 1:9
wonderfully
t. he made the rampart and the   La 2:8
wall
to my mind, *t.* have I hope   La 3:21
my soul; *t.* will I hope in him   La 3:24
t. hear the word at my   Eze 3:17
mouth, and
T. thou shalt set thy face   Eze 4:7
toward the
T. thus saith the Lord God   Eze 5:7;
  5:8; 21:24; 22:19; 23:35; 25:13, 16;
  26:3; 28:6; 29:8; 29:19; 30:22; 31:10;
  34:20; 39:25
T. the fathers shall eat the   Eze 5:10
sons in
t. will I also diminish thee;   Eze 5:11
neither
t. have I set it far from them   Eze 7:20
T. will I also deal in fury: Eze 8:18
mine eye
T. prophesy against them   Eze 11:4
T. thus saith the Lord God;   Eze 11:7
Your
T. say, Thus saith the Lord   Eze 11:16;
God   11:17
T. thou son of man, prepare   Eze 12:3
thee
Tell them *t.*, Thus saith the   Eze 12:23
Lord
T. say unto them, Thus   Eze 12:28
saith the
t. thus saith the Lord God   Eze 13:8
t. behold, I am against you,   Eze 13:8
saith
T. thus saith the Lord God;   Eze 13:13
I will
T. ye shall see no more   Eze 13:23
vanity
T. speak unto them, and say   Eze 14:4
unto
T. say unto the house of   Eze 14:6
Israel
T. thus saith the Lord God;   Eze 15:6
As
t. I have stretched out my   Eze 16:27
hand
given unto thee, *t.* thou art   Eze 16:34
contrary
t. I will gather all thy lovers,   Eze 16:37
with
t. I also will recompense thy   Eze 16:43
way upon
t. I took them away as I   Eze 16:50
saw good
T. thus saith the Lord God;   Eze 17:19
As I
T. I will judge you, O house   Eze 18:30
of
T. son of man, speak unto   Eze 20:27
t. shall my sword go forth   Eze 21:4
out of his
Sigh *t.* thou son of man, with   Eze 21:6
my people: smite *t.* upon   Eze 21:12
thy thigh
Thou *t.* son of man,   Eze 21:14
prophesy, and
t. have I made thee a   Eze 22:4
reproach
t. I have smitten mine hand   Eze 22:13
at thy
t. I will gather you into the   Eze 22:19
midst
T. have I poured out mine   Eze 22:31
indignation
T. O Aholibah, thus saith   Eze 23:22
t. will I give her cup into   Eze 23:31
thine hand
t. bear thou also thy   Eze 23:35
lewdness and thy
T. thus saith the Lord God;   Eze 24:9
Woe
t. I will deliver thee to the   Eze 25:4
men of

t. I will stretch out mine hand   Eze 25:7

T. behold, I will open the side of   Eze 25:9

t. I will bring strangers upon thee   Eze 28:7

t. I will cast thee as profane out of   Eze 28:16

t. will I bring forth a fire from the   Eze 28:18

t. I am against thee, and against   Eze 29:10

T. his height was exalted above   Eze 31:5

I have *t.* delivered him into the hand   Eze 31:11

I will *t.* spread out my net over thee   Eze 32:3

t. thou shalt hear the word at my   Eze 33:7

T. O thou son of man, speak unto the   Eze 33:10

T. thou son of man, say unto the   Eze 33:12

T. ye shepherds, hear the word of   Eze 34:7; 34:9

T. will I save my flock, and they shall   Eze 34:22

T. as I live, saith the Lord God   Eze 35:6; 35:11

T. prophesy and say, Thus saith   Eze 36:3

T. ye mountains of Israel, hear   Eze 36:4

T. thus saith the Lord God: Surely   Eze 36:5

Prophesy *t.* concerning the land of   Eze 36:6

T. thus saith the Lord God; I have   Eze 36:7

T. thou shalt devour men no more   Eze 36:14

T. say unto the house of Israel   Eze 36:22

T. prophesy and say unto them   Eze 37:12

T. son of man, prophesy and say   Eze 38:14

T. thou son of man, prophesy   Eze 39:1

t. hid I my face from them, and gave   Eze 39:23

t. the breadth of the house   Eze 41:7

t. the building was straitened   Eze 42:6

hath entered in by it, *t.* it   Eze 44:2

shall be shut

t. have I lifted up mine hand   Eze 44:12

t. he requested of the prince of the   Da 1:8

Azariah: *t.* stood they before the king   Da 1:19

t. shew me the dream, and the   Da 2:6

t. tell me the dream, and I shall   Da 2:9

t. there is no king, lord   Da 2:10

T. Daniel went in unto   Da 2:24

T. at that time, when all   Da 3:7

t. he spake, and commanded that they   Da 3:19

T. because the king's   Da 3:22

T. I make a decree, That every   Da 3:29

T. made I a decree to bring in all the   Da 4:6

T. the he goat waxed very great: and   Da 8:8

t. the curse is poured upon us, and the   Da 9:11

T. hath the Lord watched upon the   Da 9:14

Now *t.* O our God, hear the prayer of   Da 9:17

t. understand the matter, and consider   Da 9:23

Know *t.* and understand, that from the   Da 9:25

T. I was left alone, and saw this great   Da 10:8

t. he shall be grieved, and return, and   Da 11:30

t. he shall go forth with great fury to   Da 11:44

let her *t.* put away her whoredoms out   Ho 2:2

T. behold, I will hedge up thy   Ho 2:6

T. will I return, and take away my   Ho 2:9

T. behold, I will allure her   Ho 2:14

T. shall the land mourn, and   Ho 4:3

T. shalt thou fall in the day, and the   Ho 4:5

t. will I change their glory into   Ho 4:7

shame

t. your daughters commit   Ho 4:13

t. the people that doth not understand   Ho 4:14

t. shall Israel and Ephraim fall   Ho 5:5

t. I will pour out my wrath upon them   Ho 5:10

T. will I be unto Ephraim as a moth   Ho 5:12

T. have I hewed them by the   Ho 6:5

workman made it; *t.* it is not God   Ho 8:6

t. he will remember their iniquity, he   Ho 9:9

T. shall a tumult arise among thy   Ho 10:14

T. turn thou to thy God: keep   Ho 12:6

mercy

t. shall he leave his blood upon him   Ho 12:14

T. they shall be as the morning   Ho 13:3

t. have they forgotten me   Ho 13:6

T. I will be unto them as a lion: as a   Ho 13:7

T. also now, saith the Lord, turn   Joe 2:12

T. the flight shall perish from   Am 2:14

t. I will punish you for all   Am 3:2

T. thus saith the Lord God; An   Am 3:11

T. thus will I do unto thee, O   Am 4:12

Forasmuch *t.* as your treading is   Am 5:11

T. the prudent shall keep silence   Am 5:13

T. the Lord, the God of hosts, the   Am 5:16

T. will I cause you to go into captivity   Am 5:27

T. now shall they go captive   Am 6:7

t. will I deliver up the city with all   Am 6:8

Now *t.* hear thou the word of the Lord   Am 7:16

T. thus saith the Lord; Thy wife   Am 7:17

T. I fled unto Tarshish   Jon 4:2

T. now, O Lord, take, I beseech thee   Jon 4:3

T. I will make Samaria as an heap of   Mic 1:6

T. I will wail and howl, I will go   Mic 1:8

t. shalt thou give presents to   Mic 1:14

T. thus saith the Lord; Behold   Mic 2:3

T. thou shalt have none that shall   Mic 2:5

T. night shall be unto you, that ye   Mic 3:6

T. shall Zion for your sake be   Mic 3:12

T. will he give them up, until   Mic 5:3

T. also will I make thee sick in   Mic 6:13

t. ye shall bear the reproach of my   Mic 6:16

T. I will look unto the Lord; I will   Mic 7:7

T. the law is slacked, and   Hab 1:4

righteous: *t.* wrong judgment   Hab 1:4

t. they rejoice and are glad   Hab 1:15

T. they sacrifice unto their net   Hab 1:16

Shall they *t.* empty their net   Zep 1:13

T. their goods shall become a booty   Zep 1:13

T. as I live, saith the Lord of   Zep 2:9

T. wait ye upon me, saith the Lord   Zep 3:8

Now *t.* thus saith the Lord of hosts   Hag 1:5

T. the heaven over you is   Hag 1:10

T. say thou unto them, Thus saith the   Zec 1:3

T. thus saith the Lord; I am   Zec 1:16

t. came a great wrath from the Lord   Zec 7:12

T. it is come to pass, that as he cried   Zec 7:13

feasts, *t.* love the truth and peace   Zec 8:19

t. they went their way as a   Zec 10:2

T. have I also made you contemptible   Mal 2:9

T. take heed to your spirit, and let   Mal 2:15

t. take heed to your spirit, that ye deal   Mal 2:16

t. ye sons of Jacob are not consumed   Mal 3:6

Bring forth *t.* fruits meet for   M't 3:8

t. every tree which bringeth not   M't 3:10

Whosoever *t.* shall break one of   M't 5:19

T. if thou bring thy gift to   M't 5:23

Be ye *t.* perfect, even as your Father   M't 5:48

T. when thou doest thine alms, do   M't 6:2

Be not ye *t.* like unto them: for   M't 6:8

After this manner *t.* pray ye: Our   M't 6:9

if *t.* thine eye be single, thy whole   M't 6:22

If *t.* the light that in thee be   M't 6:23

T. I say unto you, Take no   M't 6:25

T. take no thought, saying, What   M't 6:31

Take *t.* no thought for the morrow   M't 6:34

T. all things whatsoever ye would   M't 7:12

T. whosoever heareth these sayings   M't 7:24

Pray ye *t.* the Lord of the harvest   M't 9:38; Lu 10:2

be ye *t.* wise as serpents   M't 10:16

Fear them not *t.*: for there is   M't 10:26

Fear ye not *t.* ye are of more value   M't 10:31

Whosoever *t.* shall confess me before   M't 10:32

t. they shall be your judges   M't 12:27

T. speak I to them in parables   M't 13:13

Hear ye *t.* the parable of the sower   M't 13:18

As *t.* the tares are gathered   M't 13:40

T. every scribe which is   M't 13:52

t. mighty works do shew forth   M't 14:2

Whosoever *t.* shall humble himself   M't 18:4

T. is the kingdom of heaven   M't 18:23

The servant *t.* fell down   M't 18:26

What *t.* God hath joined together   M't 19:6; M'k 10:9

thee: what shall we have *t.*   M't 19:27

When the lord *t.* of the vineyard   M't 21:40

T. say I unto you, The   M't 21:43

Go ye *t.* into the highways   M't 22:9

Tell us *t.* What thinkest thou? Is it   M't 22:17

Render *t.* unto Caesar the things   M't 22:21; Lu 20:25

T. in the resurrection whose wife   M't 22:28

t. whatsoever they bid you observe   M't 23:3

t. ye shall receive the greater   M't 23:14

Whoso *t.* shall swear by the altar   M't 23:20

ye *t.* shall see the abomination   M't 24:15

Watch *t.*: for ye know not what   M't 24:42

T. be ye also ready: for in   M't 24:44

Watch *t.* for ye know neither the   M't 25:13

Thou oughtest *t.* to have put   M't 25:27

Take *t.* the talent from him   M't 25:28

t. when they were gathered   M't 27:17

Command *t.* that the sepulchre be   M't 27:64

Go ye *t.* and teach all nations   M't 28:19

there also: for *t.* came I forth   M'k 1:38

T. the Son of man is Lord also of   M'k 2:28

t. mighty works do shew forth   M'k 6:14

T. Herodias had a quarrel against   M'k 6:19

Whosoever *t.* shall be ashamed of   M'k 8:38

T. I say unto you, What   M'k 11:24

Having yet *t.* one son, his   M'k 12:6

What shall *t.* the Lord of the   M'k 12:9

In the resurrecton *t.* when they   M'k 12:23

Do ye not *t.* err, because ye   M'k 12:24

the living; ye *t.* do greatly err	M'k 12:27	If the Son *t.* shall make you free, ye	Joh 8:36	*T.* they that were scattered abroad	Ac 8:4
David *t.* himself calleth him Lord	M'k 12:37	ye *t.* hear them not, because	Joh 8:47	Repent *t.* of this thy wickedness	Ac 8:22
Watch ye *t.*: for ye know not when	M'k 13:37	He went his way *t.* and washed	Joh 9:7	Arise *t.* and get thee down, and go	Ac 10:20
t. also that holy thing which shall	Lu 1:35	The neighbours *t.* and they which	Joh 9:8	*T.* came I unto you without	Ac 10:29
Bring forth *t.* fruits worthy of	Lu 3:8	*T.* said they unto him, How were	Joh 9:10	I ask *t.* for what intent ye have	Ac 10:29
every tree *t.* which bringeth not	Lu 3:9	*T.* said some of the Pharisees, This	Joh 9:16	Send *t.* to Joppa, and call hither	Ac 10:32
If thou *t.* wilt worship me, all	Lu 4:7	*T.* said his parents, He is of	Joh 9:23	Immediately *t.* I sent to thee	Ac 10:33
cities also; for *t.* am I sent	Lu 4:43	We see; *t.* your sin remaineth	Joh 9:41	*t.* are we all here present before	Ac 10:33
Be ye *t.* merciful, as your Father	Lu 6:36	*T.* doth my Father love me	Joh 10:17	Peter *t.* was kept in prison	Ac 12:5
Tell me *t.* which of them will love	Lu 7:42	was a division *t.* again among the	Joh 10:19	Be it known unto you *t.* men	Ac 13:38
Take heed *t.* how ye hear: for	Lu 8:18	*T.* they sought again to take him	Joh 10:39	Beware *t.* lest that come upon you	Ac 13:40
T. said he unto them, The harvest	Lu 10:2	*T.* his sisters sent unto him	Joh 11:3	Long time *t.* abode they speaking	Ac 14:3
alone? bid her *t.* that she help me	Lu 10:40	he had heard *t.* that he was sick	Joh 11:6	When *t.* Paul and Barnabas had no	Ac 15:2
t. shall they be your judges	Lu 11:19	When Jesus *t.* saw her weeping	Joh 11:33	Now *t.* why tempt ye God, to put a	Ac 15:10
t. when thine eye is single, thy	Lu 11:34	Jesus *t.* again groaning in himself	Joh 11:38	We have sent *t.* Judas and Silas	Ac 15:27
Take heed *t.* that the light which is	Lu 11:35	Jesus *t.* walked no more openly	Joh 11:54	*T.* loosing from Troas, we came	Ac 16:11
If thy whole body *t.* be full of light	Lu 11:36	the Jews *t.* knew that he was there	Joh 12:9	go: now *t.* depart, and go in peace	Ac 16:36
T. also said the wisdom of God, I	Lu 11:49	people *t.* that was with him when	Joh 12:17	*T.* many of them believed; also of	Ac 17:12
T. whatsoever ye have spoken	Lu 12:3	The Pharisees *t.* said among	Joh 12:19	*T.* disputed he in the synagogue	Ac 17:17
Fear not *t.*: ye are of more value	Lu 12:7	The same came *t.* to Philip	Joh 12:21	know *t.* what these things mean	Ac 17:20
T. I say unto you. Take no	Lu 12:22	The people *t.* that stood by	Joh 12:29	Whom *t.* ye ignorantly worship	Ac 17:23
Be ye *t.* ready also: for the Son of	Lu 12:40	*T.* they could not believe	Joh 12:39	Some *t.* cried one thing, and some	Ac 19:32
in them *t.* come and be healed, and	Lu 13:14	I speak *t.* even as the Father	Joh 12:50	When he *t.* was come up again	Ac 20:11
a wife, and *t.* I cannot come	Lu 14:20	*t.* said he, Ye are not all clean	Joh 13:11	Take heed *t.* unto yourselves, and to	Ac 20:28
t. came his father out, and	Lu 15:28	Simon Peter *t.* beckoned to him	Joh 13:24	*T.* watch, and remember, that by	Ac 20:31
If *t.* ye have not been faithful in	Lu 16:11	*T.* when he was gone out, Jesus	Joh 13:31	What is it *t.*? the multitude must	Ac 21:22
I pray thee, *t.* father, that thou	Lu 16:27	world, *t.* the world hateth you	Joh 15:19	Do *t.* this that we say to thee: We	Ac 21:23
He said *t.*, A certain nobleman	Lu 19:12	*t.* said I, that he shall take of	Joh 16:15	Now *t.* ye with the council signify	Ac 23:15
What *t.* shall the lord of the	Lu 20:15	They said *t.* What is this that he	Joh 16:18	Let them *t.* said he, which among	Ac 25:5
There were *t.* seven brethren	Lu 20:29	And ye now *t.* have sorrow: but I	Joh 16:22	*T.* when they were come hither	Ac 25:17
T. in the resurrection whose wife	Lu 20:33	Jesus *t.* knowing all things that	Joh 18:4	Having *t.* obtained help of God, I	Ac 26:22
David *t.* calleth him Lord, how is he	Lu 20:44	if *t.* ye seek me, let these go their	Joh 18:8	For this cause *t.* have I called for	Ac 28:20
near: go ye not *t.* after them	Lu 21:8	They said *t.* unto him, Art not thou	Joh 18:25	Be it known *t.* unto you, that	Ac 28:28
Settle it *t.* in your hearts, not to	Lu 21:14	The Jews *t.* said unto him, It is not	Joh 18:31	*T.* thou art inexcusable, O man	Ro 2:1
Watch ye *t.* and pray always, that	Lu 21:36	Pilate *t.* said unto him, Art thou a	Joh 18:37	Thou *t.* which teachest another	Ro 2:21
I will *t.* chastise him, and release	Lu 23:16	will ye *t.* that I release unto you	Joh 18:39	*T.* if the uncircumcision keep	Ro 2:26
Pilate *t.* willing to release Jesus	Lu 23:20	Then Pilate *t.* took Jesus	Joh 19:1	*T.* by the deeds of the law there	Ro 3:20
I will *t.* chastise him, and let him	Lu 23:22	Pilate *t.* went forth again, and	Joh 19:4	*T.* we conclude that a man is	Ro 3:28
t. am I come baptizing with	Joh 1:31	the chief priests *t.* and officers saw	Joh 19:6	*T.* it is of faith, that it might	Ro 4:16
When *t.* he was risen from the	Joh 2:22	When Pilate *t.* heard that	Joh 19:8; 19:13	*t.* it was imputed to him for	Ro 4:22
voice: this my joy *t.* is fulfilled	Joh 3:29	*t.* he that delivered me unto	Joh 19:11	*T.* being justified by faith, we	Ro 5:1
When *t.* the Lord knew how	Joh 4:1	Then delivered he him *t.* unto them	Joh 19:16	*T.* as by the offence of one	Ro 5:18
Jesus *t.* being wearied with his	Joh 4:6	They said *t.* among themselves, Let	Joh 19:24	*T.* we are buried with him by	Ro 6:4
T. said the disciples one to	Joh 4:33	These things *t.* the soldiers did	Joh 19:24	Let not sin *t.* reign in your mortal	Ro 6:12
Jews *t.* said unto him that was	Joh 5:10	When Jesus *t.* saw his mother, and	Joh 19:26	There is *t.* now no condemnation	Ro 8:1
And *t.* did the Jews persecute	Joh 5:16	When Jesus *t.* had received	Joh 19:30	*T.* brethren, we are debtors	Ro 8:12
T. the Jews sought the more to	Joh 5:18	The Jews *t.* because it was	Joh 19:31	*T.* hath he mercy on whom he	Ro 9:18
T. they gathered them together	Joh 6:13	He came *t.* and took the body of	Joh 19:38	Behold *t.* the goodness of God	Ro 11:22
When Jesus *t.* perceived that they	Joh 6:15	There laid they Jesus *t.* because of	Joh 19:42	I beseech you *t.* brethren, by	Ro 12:1
when the people *t.* saw that Jesus	Joh 6:24	Peter *t.* went forth, and that other	Joh 20:3	*T.* if thine enemy hunger, feed	Ro 12:20
They said *t.* unto him, What sign	Joh 6:30	other disciples *t.* said unto him	Joh 20:25	Whosoever *t.* resisteth the power	Ro 13:2
Jesus *t.* answered and said unto	Joh 6:43	They cast *t.* and now they were not	Joh 21:6	Render *t.* to all their dues	Ro 13:7
Every man *t.* that hath heard	Joh 6:45	*T.* that disciple whom Jesus loved	Joh 21:7	*t.* love is the fulfilling of the law	Ro 13:10
Jews *t.* strove among themselves	Joh 6:52	When they *t.* were come together	Ac 1:6	us *t.* cast off the works of darkness	Ro 13:12
Many *t.* of his disciples, when they	Joh 6:60	*T.* did my heart rejoice, and	Ac 2:26	whether we live *t.* or die, we are	Ro 14:8
T. said I unto you, that no	Joh 6:65	*T.* being a prophet, and knowing	Ac 2:30	Let us not *t.* judge one another any	Ro 14:13
His brethren *t.* said unto him	Joh 7:3	*T.* being by the right hand of God	Ac 2:33	Let us *t.* follow after the things	Ro 14:19
Moses *t.* gave unto you	Joh 7:22	*T.* let all the house of Israel know	Ac 2:36	*t.* whereof I may glory through	Ro 15:17
Many of the people *t.* when they	Joh 7:40	Repent ye *t.* and be converted	Ac 3:19		
The Pharisees *t.* said unto him	Joh 8:13				
I said *t.* unto you, that ye shall die	Joh 8:24				

When *t.* I have performed this	Ro 15:28
I am glad *t.* on your behalf: but yet	Ro 16:19
T. let no man glory in men	1Co 3:21
T. judge nothing before the time	1Co 4:5
Purge out *t.* the old leaven	1Co 5:7
T. let us keep the feast, not with	1Co 5:8
T. put away from among yourselves	1Co 5:13
Now *t.* there is utterly a fault	1Co 6:7
t. glorify God in your body, and in	1Co 6:20
I say *t.* to the unmarried and	1Co 7:8
I suppose *t.* that this is good for	1Co 7:26
As concerning *t.* the eating of those	1Co 8:4
I *t.* so run, not as uncertainly; so	1Co 9:26
Whether *t.* ye eat, or drink	1Co 10:31
ye come together *t.* into one place	1Co 11:20
is it *t.* not of the body	1Co 12:15; 12:16
T. if I know not the meaning of	1Co 14:11
If *t.* the whole church be come	1Co 14:23
T. whether it were I or they, so we	1Co 15:11
T. my beloved brethren, be ye	1Co 15:58
Let no man *t.* despise him	1Co 16:11
t. acknowledge ye them that are	1Co 16:18
When I *t.* was thus minded, did I	2Co 1:17
T. seeing we have this	2Co 4:1
I believed, and *t.* have I spoken	2Co 4:13
we also believe, and *t.* speak	2Co 4:13
T. we are always confident	2Co 5:6
Knowing *t.* the terror of the Lord	2Co 5:11
T. if any man be in Christ, he is a	2Co 5:17
Having *t.* these promises, dearly	2Co 7:1
T. we were comforted in your	2Co 7:13
I rejoice *t.* that I have confidence in	2Co 7:16
T. as ye abound in every thing	2Co 8:7
Now *t.* perform the doing of it	2Co 8:11
T. I thought it necessary to exhort	2Co 9:5
T. it is no great thing if his	2Co 11:15
gladly *t.* will I rather glory in my	2Co 12:9
T. I take pleasure in infirmities	2Co 12:10
T. I write these things being	2Co 13:10
is *t.* Christ the minister of sin	Ga 2:17
He *t.* that ministereth to you	Ga 3:5
Know ye *t.* that they which are of	Ga 3:7
Am I *t.* become your enemy	Ga 4:16
Stand fast *t.* in the liberty	Ga 5:1
As we have *t.* opportunity	Ga 6:10
Now *t.* ye are no more strangers	Eph 2:19
I *t.* the prisoner of the Lord	Eph 4:1
This I say *t.* and testify in	Eph 4:17
Be ye *t.* followers of God, as dear	Eph 5:1
Be not ye *t.* partakers with them	Eph 5:7
T. as the church is subject unto	Eph 5:24
Stand *t.* having your loins girt	Eph 6:14
If there be *t.* any consolation in	Ph'p 2:1
Him *t.* I hope to send presently	Ph'p 2:23
I sent him *t.* the more carefully	Ph'p 2:28
Receive him *t.* in the Lord with all	Ph'p 2:29
Let us *t.* as many as be perfect	Ph'p 3:15
T. my brethren dearly beloved	Ph'p 4:1
As ye have *t.* received Christ	Col 2:6
Let no man *t.* judge you in meat	Col 2:16

Mortify *t.* your members which are	Col 3:5
Put on *t.* as the elect of God, holy	Col 3:12
T. brethren, we were	1Th 3:7
He *t.* that despiseth, despiseth not	1Th 4:8
T. let us not sleep, as do	1Th 5:6
T. brethren, stand fast, and	2Th 2:15
exhort *t.* that, first of all	1Ti 2:1
I will *t.* that men pray every where	1Ti 2:8
t. we both labour and suffer	1Ti 4:10
t. that the younger women marry	1Ti 5:14
Be not thou *t.* ashamed of the	2Ti 1:8
Thou *t.* my son, be strong in	2Ti 2:1
Thou *t.* endure hardness, as a good	2Ti 2:3
T. I endure all things for the elect's	2Ti 2:10
If a man *t.* purge himself from	2Ti 2:21
I charge thee *t.* before God	2Ti 4:1
thou *t.* receive him, that is, mine own	Ph'm 12
he *t.* departed for a season	Ph'm 15
If thou count me *t.* a partner	Ph'm 17
t. God, even thy God, hath	Heb 1:9
T. we ought to give the more	Heb 2:1
Let us *t.* fear, lest, a promise	Heb 4:1
Seeing *t.* it remaineth that some	Heb 4:6
remaineth *t.* a rest unto the people	Heb 4:9
labour *t.* to enter into that rest	Heb 4:11
Let us *t.* come boldly unto	Heb 4:16
T. leaving the principles of	Heb 6:1
If *t.* perfection were by the	Heb 7:11
It was *t.* necessary that the	Heb 9:23
Having *t.* brethren, boldness	Heb 10:19
Cast not away *t.* your confidence	Heb 10:35
t. sprang there even of one	Heb 11:12
Let us go forth *t.* unto him without	Heb 13:13
By him *t.* let us offer the sacrifice	Heb 13:15
whosoever *t.* will be a friend of	Jas 4:4
Submit yourselves *t.* to God	Jas 4:7
T. to him that knoweth to do good	Jas 4:17
Be patient *t.* brethren, unto the	Jas 5:7
Unto you *t.* which believe he is	1Pe 2:7
be ye *t.* sober, and watch unto	1Pe 4:7
Humble yourselves *t.* under the	1Pe 5:6
Ye *t.* beloved, seeing ye know	2Pe 3:17
Let that *t.* abide in you, which ye	1Jo 2:24
t. the world knoweth us not	1Jo 3:1
t. speak they of the world, and	1Jo 4:5
We *t.* ought to receive such, that	3Jo 8
I will *t.* put you in remembrance	Jude 5
Remember *t.* from whence thou	Re 2:5
Remember *t.* how thou hast	Re 3:3
If *t.* thou shalt not watch, I will	Re 3:3
chasten: be zealous *t.* and repent	Re 3:19
T. are they before the throne	Re 7:15
T. rejoice, ye heavens, and ye	Re 12:12
T. shall her plagues come in one	Re 18:8

THEREFROM

ye turn not aside *t.* to the right hand	Jos 23:6
made Israel to sin; he departed not *t.*	2Ki 3:3; 13:2

THEREIN

in the earth, and multiply *t.*	Ge 9:7
for the fifty righteous that are *t.*	Ge 18:24
and the cave that is *t.* I give it thee	Ge 23:11
field, and the cave was *t.* and all	Ge 23:17
And the field, and the cave that is *t.*	Ge 23:20
be before you; dwell and trade ye *t.*	Ge 34:10
and get you possessions *t.*	Ge 34:10

dwell in the land, and trade *t.*	Ge 34:21
they had possessions *t.* and grew	Ge 47:27
of the cave that is *t.* was	Ge 49:32
and with pitch, and put the child *t.*	Ex 2:3
the men, that they may labour *t.*	Ex 5:9
stink, neither was there any worm *t.*	Ex 16:24
and put an omer full of manna *t.*	Ex 16:33
cover it, and an ox or an ass fall *t.*	Ex 21:33
his sons' after him, to be anointed *t.*	Ex 29:29
altar, and thou shalt put water *t.*	Ex 30:18
for whosoever doeth any work *t.* that	Ex 31:14
doeth work *t.* shall be put to death	Ex 35:2
put *t.* the ark of the testimony	Ex 40:3
the altar, and shall put water *t.*	Ex 40:7
the tabernacle, and all that is *t.*	Ex 40:9
these that a man doeth, sinning *t.*	Le 6:3
that he hath done in trespassing *t.*	Le 6:7
the tabernacle and all that was *t.*	Le 8:10
them his censer, and put fire *t.*	Le 10:1
and, behold, there be no white hairs *t.*	Le 13:21
that there is black hair grown up *t.*	Le 13:37
and keep mine ordinances, to walk *t.*	Le 18:4
and that ye defile not yourselves *t.*	Le 18:30
land, whither I bring you to dwell *t.*	Le 20:22
accepted; there shall be no blemish *t.*	Le 22:21
convocation; ye shall do no work *t.*	Le 23:3
ye shall do no servile work *t.*	Le 23:7; 23:8, 21, 25, 35-36; 29:35
eat your fill, and dwell *t.* in safety	Le 25:19
your enemies which dwell *t.* shall be	Le 26:32
all the tabernacle, and of all that *t.* is	Nu 4:16
and the people that dwelleth *t.*	Nu 13:18
fat or lean, whether there be wood *t.*	Nu 13:20
which I sware to make you dwell *t.*	Nu 14:30
And put fire *t.* and put incense in	Nu 16:7
and put fire *t.* from off the altar	Nu 16:46
shall do no manner of servile work *t.*	Nu 28:18
your souls: ye shall not do any work *t.*	Nu 29:7
the son of Manasseh; and he dwelt *t.*	Nu 32:40
inhabitants of the land, and dwell *t.*	Nu 33:53
be cleansed of the blood that is shed *t.*	Nu 35:33
The Emims dwelt *t.* in times past, a	De 2:10
of giants: giants dwelt *t.* in old time	De 2:20
it unto thee, lest thou be snared *t.*	De 7:25
hast built goodly houses, and dwelt *t.*	De 8:12
God, the earth also, with all that *t.* is	De 10:14
and ye shall possess it, and dwell *t.*	De 11:31
destroying it utterly, and all that is *t.*	De 13:15
And if there be any blemish *t.* as if it	De 15:21
thy God: thou shalt do no work *t.*	De 16:8
and shalt possess it, and shalt dwell *t.*	De 17:14
he shall read *t.* all the days of his life	De 17:19

the people that is found *t.*   De 20:11
shall be
and possessest it, and dwellest De 26:1
t.
an house, and thou shalt not De 28:30
dwell *t.*
nor beareth, nor any grass De 29:23
groweth *t.*
thou shalt meditate *t.* day and Jos 1:8
night
do according to all that is Jos 1:8
written *t.*
even it, and all that are *t.* to Jos 6:17
the Lord
the city with fire, and all that Jos 6:24
was *t.*
them, and all the souls that Jos 10:28
were *t.*
sword, and all the souls that Jos 10:30;
were *t.*   10:32
souls that were *t.* he utterly Jos 10:35
destroyed
thereof, and all the souls that Jos 10:37
were *t.*
utterly, and all the souls Jos 10:37
that were *t.*
destroyed all the souls that Jos 10:39
were *t.*
they smote all the souls that Jos 11:11
were *t.*
and dwelt *t.* and called Jos 19:47
Leshem, Dan
and he built the city, and Jos 19:50
dwelt *t.*
and they possessed it, and Jos 21:43
dwelt *t.*
keep the way of the Lord to J'g 2:22
walk *t.*
did cast *t.* every man the J'g 8:25
earrings
and slew the people that was J'g 9:45
t. and
and upon all the people that J'g 16:30
were *t.*
and saw the people that were J'g 18:7
t.
And they built a city, and J'g 18:28
dwelt *t.*
the women captives, that 1Sa 30:2
were *t.*
brought forth the people that 2Sa 12:31
were *t.*
house, that my name might 1Ki 8:16
be *t.*
they went to Damascus, and 1Ki 11:24
dwelt *t.*
in mount Ephraim, and 1Ki 12:25
dwelt *t.*
me a new cruse, and put salt 2Ki 2:20
t.
put *t.* all the money that was 2Ki 12:9
brought
who made Israel sin, but 2Ki 13:6
walked *t.*
who made Israel sin: but he 2Ki 13:11
walked *t.*
smote Tiphsah, and all that 2Ki 15:16
were *t.*
the women *t.* that were with 2Ki 15:16
child he
let the fields rejoice, and all 1Ch 16:32
that is *t.*
I may build an altar *t.* unto 1Ch 21:22
the Lord
cedars to build him an house 2Ch 2:3
to dwell *t.*
the two tables which Moses 2Ch 5:10
put *t.* at
And they dwelt *t.* and have 2Ch 20:8
built thee
built thee a sanctuary *t.* for 2Ch 20:8
thy name
and sedition have been made Ezr 4:19
t.
and *t.* was a record thus Ezr 6:2
written
and that there was no breach Ne 6:1
left *t.*
but the people were few *t.* and Ne 7:4
up at the first, and found Ne 7:5
written *t.*
And he read *t.* before the street Ne 8:3
earth, and all things that are *t.* Ne 9:6
the seas, and all that is *t.* and Ne 9:6
thou
and *t.* was found written, that Ne 13:1
There dwelt men of Tyre also Ne 13:16
t. which
be solitary, let no joyful voice Job 3:7
come *t.*

be, and he shall not rejoice Job 20:18
the world, and they that dwell Ps 24:1;
    98:7
the land, and dwell *t.* for ever Ps 37:29
Thy congregation hath dwelt Ps 68:10
t.: thou
seas, and every thing that Ps 69:34
moveth *t.*
they that love his name shall Ps 69:36
dwell *t.*
Let the field be joyful, and all Ps 96:12
that is *t.*
the world, and they that dwell Ps 98:7
t.
whom thou hast made to Ps 104:26
play *t.*
the wickedness of them that Ps 107:34
dwell *t.*
out of all them that have Ps 111:2
pleasure *t.*
thy commandments; for *t.* Ps 119:35
do I delight
and earth, the sea, and all Ps 146:6
that *t.* is
but perverseness *t.* is a breach Pr 15:4
in the
abhorred of the Lord shall Pr 22:14
fall *t.*
Whoso diggeth a pit shall fall Pr 26:27
t.
yet to a man that hath not Ec 2:21
laboured *t.*
of it, and also made a Isa 5:2
winepress *t.*
it, and let us make a breach *t.* Isa 7:6
for us
and they that dwell *t.* are Isa 24:6
desolate
the people that dwell *t.* shall Isa 33:24
be
the earth hear, and all that is Isa 34:1
t.
to generation shall they dwell Isa 34:17
t.
men, though fools, shall not Isa 35:8
err *t.*
upon it, and spirit to them Isa 42:5
that walk *t.*
down to the sea, and all that Isa 42:10
is *t.*
mountains, O forest, and Isa 44:23
every tree *t.*
joy and gladness shall be Isa 51:3
found *t.*
and they that dwell *t.* shall die Isa 51:6
in like
whosoever goeth *t.* shall not Isa 59:8
know
foresaken, and not a man Jer 4:29
dwell *t.*
where is the good way, and Jer 6:16
walk *t.*
But they said, We will not Jer 6:16
walk *t.*
in it; the city, and those that Jer 8:16
dwell *t.*
obeyed my voice, neither Jer 9:13
walked *t.*
the wickedness of them that Jer 12:4
dwell *t.*
the sabbath day, to do no Jer 17:24
work *t.*
they shall be driven on, and Jer 23:12
fall *t.*
Lord; and they shall till it, Jer 27:11
and dwell *t.*
write *t.* all the words that I Jer 36:2
have
Why hast thou written *t.* Jer 36:29
saying
who wrote *t.* from the mouth Jer 36:32
of
a desolation, and no man Jer 44:2
dwelleth *t.*
overflow the land, and all that Jer 47:2
is *t.*
the city, and them that dwell Jer 47:2
t.
desolate, without any to dwell Jer 48:9
t.
land desolate, and none shall Jer 50:3
dwell *t.*
dwell there, and the owls Jer 50:39
shall dwell *t.*
neither shall any son of man Jer 50:40
dwell *t.*
all that is *t.* shall sing for Jer 51:48
Babylon

me; and, lo, a roll of a book Eze 2:9
was *t.*
there was written *t.* Eze 2:10
lamentations
and of their detestable things Eze 7:20
t.
may be desolate from all that Eze 12:19
is *t.*
the violence of all them that Eze 12:19
dwell *t.*
t. shall be left a remnant that Eze 14:22
shall be
south to the north shall be Eze 20:47
burned *t.*
let them seethe the bones of Eze 24:5
it *t.*
to the pot whose scum is *t.* Eze 24:6
and whose
And they shall dwell safely Eze 28:26
t. and
the land waste, and all that Eze 30:12
is *t.*
I shall smite all them that Eze 32:15
dwell *t.*
and they shall dwell *t.* even Eze 37:25
they
and there were windows *t.* Eze 40:33
and in the
When the priests enter *t.* Eze 42:14
then shall
and for all that shall be Eze 44:14
done *t.*
and his concubines, might Da 5:2
drink *t.*
one that dwelleth *t.* shall Ho 4:3
languish
but the transgressors shall fall Ho 14:9
t.
up the city with all that is *t.* Am 6:8
and every one mourn that Am 8:8
dwelleth *t.*
melt, and all that dwell *t.* shall Am 9:5
mourn
hearken, O earth, and all that Mic 1:2
t. is
desolate because of them that Mic 7:13
dwell *t.*
yea. the world, and all that Na 1:5
dwell *t.*
of the city, and of all that Hab 2:8;
dwell *t.*   2:17
the maker of his work Hab 2:18
trusteth *t.*
the multitude of men and Zec 2:4
cattle *t.*
black horses which are *t.* go Zec 6:6
forth into
two parts *t.* shall be cut off Zec 13:8
and die
and die; but the third shall be Zec 13:8
left *t.*
come and take of them, and Zec 14:21
seethe *t.*
by it, and by him that M't 23:21
dwelleth *t.*
child, he shall not enter *t.* M'k 10:15
down into the house, M'k 13:15
neither enter *t.*
And heal the sick that are *t.* Lu 10:9
child shall in no wise enter *t.* Lu 18:17
to cast out them that sold *t.* Lu 19:45
the bag, and bare what was Joh 12:6
put *t.*
and let no man dwell *t.* Ac 1:20
sea, and all things that are *t.* Ac 14:15
made the world and all Ac 17:24
things *t.*
sailing into Italy; and he put Ac 27:6
us *t.*
t. is the righteousness of God Ro 1:17
dead to sin, live any longer *t.* Ro 6:2
he is called, *t.* abide with 1Co 7:24
God
that *t.* I may speak boldly, Eph 6:20
as I
and I *t.* do rejoice, yea. Ph'p 1:18
and will
abounding *t.* thanksgiving Col 2:7
that some must enter *t.* Heb 4:6
not, neither hadst pleasure *t.* Heb 10:8
that have been occupied *t.* Heb 13:9
law of liberty, and continueth Jas 1:25
t.
they are again entangled *t.* 2Pe 2:20
the works that are *t.* shall be 2Pe 3:10
things which are written *t.* Re 1:3
and the things that *t.* are Re 10:6
altar, and them that worship *t.* Re 11:1

earth and them which dwell   *Re 13:12*
t.
And I saw no temple *t.*: for   *Re 21:22*

THEREINTO

are in the countries enter *t.*   *Lu 21:21*

THEREOF

thou eatest *t.* thou shalt surely   *Ge 2:17*
die
living creature, that was the   *Ge 2:19*
name *t.*
ribs, and closed up the flesh   *Ge 2:21*
instead *t.*
doth know that in the day ye   *Ge 3:5*
eat *t.*
she took of the fruit *t.* and did   *Ge 3:6*
eat
firstlings of his flock and of   *Ge 4:4*
the fat *t.*
of the ark shalt thou set in the   *Ge 6:16*
side *t.*
with the life *t.* which is the   *Ge 9:4*
blood *t.*
the clusters *t.* brought forth   *Ge 40:10*
ripe
and said, This is the   *Ge 40:18*
interpretation *t.*
of Egypt, and all the wise men   *Ge 41:8*
t.
the fame *t.* was heard in   *Ge 45:16*
Pharaoh's
of Egypt even to the other   *Ge 47:21*
end *t.*
which I will do in the midst *t.*   *Ex 3:20*
ye shall not diminish ought *t.*   *Ex 5:8*
been in Egypt since the   *Ex 9:18*
foundation *t.*
t. must we take to serve the   *Ex 10:26*
Lord our
his legs, and with the   *Ex 12:9*
purtenance *t.*
there shall no stranger eat *t.*   *Ex 12:43*
circumcised him, then shall   *Ex 12:44*
he eat *t.*
and an hired servant shall   *Ex 12:45*
not eat *t.*
neither shall ye break a bone   *Ex 12:46*
t.
no uncircumcised person   *Ex 12:48*
shall eat *t.*
of Israel called the name   *Ex 16:31*
t. Manna
the smoke *t.* ascended as the   *Ex 19:18*
smoke of
and the owner of it shall   *Ex 22:11*
accept *t.* and
make restituton unto the   *Ex 22:12*
owner *t.*
or die, the owner *t.* being not   *Ex 22:14*
with it
if the owner *t.* be with it, he   *Ex 22:15*
shall not
land, and shalt gather in the   *Ex 23:10*
fruits *t.*
the pattern of all the   *Ex 25:9*
instruments *t.*
and a half shall be the length   *Ex 25:10*
t.
and a cubit and a half the   *Ex 25:10*
breadth *t.*
and a cubit and a half the   *Ex 25:10*
height *t.*
it, and put them in the four   *Ex 25:12*
corners *t.*
and a half shall be the length   *Ex 25:17*
t.
and a cubit and a half the   *Ex 25:17*
breadth *t.*
the cherubims on the two   *Ex 25:19*
ends *t.*
two cubits shall be the   *Ex 25:23*
length *t.*
and a cubit the breadth *t.*   *Ex 25:23*
and a cubit and a half the   *Ex 25:23*
heighth *t.*
make a golden crown to the   *Ex 25:25*
border *t.*
corners that are on the four   *Ex 25:26*
feet *t.*
shalt make the dishes *t.* and   *Ex 25:29*
spoons *t.*
and covers *t.* and bowls *t.* to   *Ex 25:29*
cover
thou shalt make the seven   *Ex 25:37*
lamps *t.*
and they shall light the lamps   *Ex 25:37*
t. that

the tongs *t.* and the   *Ex 25:38*
snuffdishes *t.*
to the fashion *t.* which was   *Ex 26:30*
shewed
and the height *t.* shall be three   *Ex 27:1*
cubits
horns of it upon the four   *Ex 27:2*
corners *t.*
vessels *t.* thou shalt make of   *Ex 27:3*
brass
four brasen rings in four   *Ex 27:4*
corners *t.*
the twenty pillars *t.* and their   *Ex 27:10*
twenty
of the tabernacle in all the   *Ex 27:19*
service *t.*
and all the pins *t.* and all the   *Ex 27:19*
pins of
It shall have the two   *Ex 28:7*
shoulderpieces *t.*
joined at the two edges *t.*; and   *Ex 28:7*
so it
of the same, according to the   *Ex 28:8*
work *t.*
doubled; a span shall be the   *Ex 28:16*
length *t.*
and a span shall be the   *Ex 28:16*
breadth *t.*
of the breastplate in the   *Ex 28:26*
border *t.*
underneath, toward the   *Ex 28:27*
forepart *t.*
over against the other   *Ex 28:27*
coupling *t.*
bind the breastplate by the   *Ex 28:28*
rings *t.*
hole in the top of it, in the   *Ex 28:32*
midst *t.*
of scarlet, round about the   *Ex 28:33*
hem *t.*
but a stranger shall not eat *t.*   *Ex 29:33*
because
according to the drink   *Ex 29:41*
offering *t.* for a
A cubit shall be the length *t.*   *Ex 30:2*
a cubit the breadth *t.*:   *Ex 30:2*
foursquare
and two cubits shall be the   *Ex 30:2*
height *t.*
the horns *t.* shall be of the   *Ex 30:2*
same
overlay it with pure gold, the   *Ex 30:3*
top *t.*
and the sides *t.* round about   *Ex 30:3*
and the horns *t.*; and thou   *Ex 30:3*
shalt make
the crown of it, by the two   *Ex 30:4*
corners *t.*
according to the composition   *Ex 30:37*
t.
The ark, and the staves *t.*   *Ex 35:12*
with the
coupled together at the head   *Ex 36:29*
t. to one
two cubits and a half was the   *Ex 37:6*
length *t.*
one cubit and a half the   *Ex 37:6*
breadth *t.*
he the cherubims on the two   *Ex 37:8*
ends *t.*
wood: five cubits was the   *Ex 37:10*
length *t.*
and a cubit the breadth *t.*   *Ex 37:10*
and a cubit
and a cubit and a half the   *Ex 37:10*
height *t.*
made a crown of gold for the   *Ex 37:12*
border *t.*
four corners that were   *Ex 37:13*
in four feet *t.*
six branches going out of the   *Ex 37:18*
sides *t.*
the candlestick out of the one   *Ex 37:18*
side *t.*
candlestick out of the other   *Ex 37:18*
side *t.*
gold made he it, and all the   *Ex 37:24*
vessels *t.*
height of it; horns *t.* were of   *Ex 37:25*
the same
top of it, and the sides *t.*   *Ex 37:26*
round about
rings of gold for it under the   *Ex 37:27*
crown *t.*
corners of it, upon the two   *Ex 37:27*
sides *t.*
wood: five cubits was the   *Ex 38:1*
length *t.*
and five cubits the breadth *t.*;   *Ex 38:1*
it was

and three cubits the height *t.*   *Ex 38:1*
he made the horns *t.* on the   *Ex 38:2*
four
the horns *t.* were of the same: *Ex 38:2*
and he
all the vessels *t.* made he of   *Ex 38:3*
brass
of network under the compass   *Ex 38:4*
t.
of the same, according to the   *Ex 39:5*
work *t.*
double: a span was the length   *Ex 39:9*
t.
a span the breadth *t.* being   *Ex 39:9*
doubled
it, over against the other   *Ex 39:20*
coupling *t.*
ark of the testimony, and the   *Ex 39:35*
staves *t.*
The table, and all the vessels   *Ex 39:36*
t. and
pure candlestick, with the   *Ex 39:37*
lamps *t.*
be set in order, and all the   *Ex 39:37*
vessels *t.*
the candlestick, and light the   *Ex 40:4*
lamps *t.*
shalt hallow it, and all the   *Ex 40:9*
vessels *t.*
his sockets, and set up the   *Ex 40:18*
boards *t.*
and put in the bars *t.* and   *Ex 40:18*
reared up
the blood *t.* shall be wrung out   *Le 1:15*
at the
he shall cleave it with the   *Le 1:17*
wings *t.*
of the flour *t.* and of the oil *t.*   *Le 2:2*
with all the frankincense *t.*; and   *Le 2:2*
from the meat offering a   *Le 2:9*
memorial *t.*
beaten corn *t.* and part of the   *Le 2:16*
oil *t.*
with all the frankincense *t.*; it   *Le 2:16*
is an
Aaron's sons shall sprinkle the   *Le 3:8*
blood *t.*
the fat *t.* and the whole rump, it   *Le 3:9*
shall
Aaron shall sprinkle the blood   *Le 3:13*
t. upon
And he shall offer *t.* his   *Le 3:14*
offering, even
the priest shall take of the   *Le 4:30*
blood *t.*
and shall pour out all the   *Le 4:30*
blood *t.* at
he shall take away all the fat   *Le 4:31*
t. as the
and shall pour out all the   *Le 4:34*
blood *t.* at
he shall take away all the fat   *Le 4:35*
t. as the
his handful of it, even a   *Le 5:12*
memorial *t.*
of the meat offering, and of   *Le 6:15*
the oil *t.*
remainder *t.* shall Aaron and   *Le 6:16*
his sons
it in the morning, and half *t.*   *Le 6:20*
at night
shall touch the flesh *t.* shall be   *Le 6:27*
holy
when there is sprinkled of the   *Le 6:27*
blood *t.*
males among the priests shall   *Le 6:29*
eat *t.*
the blood *t.* shall he sprinkle   *Le 7:2*
round
And he shall offer of it all the   *Le 7:3*
fat *t.*
male among the priests shall eat   *Le 7:6*
the flesh, all that is clean shall   *Le 7:19*
eat *t.*
he sprinkled *t.* upon the altar   *Le 8:11*
seven
him, with the pieces *t.* and the   *Le 9:13*
head
took a handful *t.* and burnt it   *Le 9:17*
upon
he that toucheth the carcase   *Le 11:39*
t. shall
and the hair *t.* be not turned   *Le 13:4*
white
which, even in the skin *t.* was   *Le 13:18*
a boil
skin, and the hair *t.* be   *Le 13:20*
turned white

and the timber *t.* and all the morter	Le 14:45
he shall even pour out the blood *t.*	Le 17:13
the blood of it is for the life *t.*	Le 17:14
for the life of all flesh is the blood *t.*	Le 17:14
I do visit the iniquity *t.* upon it	Le 18:25
count the fruit *t.* as uncircumcised	Le 19:23
all the fruit *t.* shall be holy to praise	Le 19:24
fifth year shall ye eat of the fruit *t.*	Le 19:25
it may yield unto you the increase *t.*	Le 19:25
but there shall no stranger eat *t.*	Le 22:13
he shall put the fifth part *t.* unto it	Le 22:14
neither shall ye make any offering *t.*	Le 22:24
and shall reap the harvest *t.* then ye	Le 23:10
And the meat offering *t.* shall be two	Le 23:13
drink offering *t.* shall be of wine	Le 23:13
fine flour, and bake twelve cakes *t.*	Le 24:5
vineyard, and gather in the fruit *t.*	Le 25:3
land, shall all the increase *t.* be meat	Le 25:7
all the land unto all the inhabitants *t.*	Le 25:10
eat the increase *t.* out of the field	Le 25:12
years thou shalt increase the price *t.*	Le 25:16
let him count the years of the sale *t.*	Le 25:27
it and the exchange *t.* shall be holy	Le 27:10
add a fifth part *t.* unto thy estimation	Le 27:13
shall be according to the seed *t.*	Le 27:16
the possession *t.* shall be the priest's	Le 27:21
he shall add thereto the fifth part *t.*	Le 27:31
it and the change *t.* shall be holy	Le 27:33
testimony, and over all the vessels *t.*	Nu 1:50
the tabernacle, and all the vessels *t.*	Nu 1:50
and those that were numbered *t.*	Nu 2:6; 2:8, 11
the covering *t.* and the hanging for	Nu 3:25
the cords of it for all the service *t.*	Nu 3:26
the hanging, and all the service *t.*	Nu 3:31
and the bars *t.* and the pillars *t.*	Nu 3:36
the sockets *t.* and all the vessels *t.*	Nu 3:36
of blue, and shall put in the staves *t.*	Nu 4:6
snuffdishes, and all the oil vessels *t.*	Nu 4:9
they shall put it and all the vessels *t.*	Nu 4:10
skins, and shall put to the staves *t.*	Nu 4:11
shall put upon it all the vessels *t.*	Nu 4:14
in the sanctuary, and in the vessels *t.*	Nu 4:16
of the tabernacle, and the bars *t.*	Nu 4:31
and the pillars *t.* and sockets *t.*	Nu 4:31
his trespass with the principal *t.*	Nu 5:7
add unto it the fifth part *t.* and give	Nu 5:7
of the offering, even the memorial *t.*	Nu 5:26
sanctified it, and all instruments *t.*	Nu 7:1
both the altar and all the vessels *t.*	Nu 7:1
he lighted the lamps *t.* over against	Nu 8:3

unto the shaft *t.* unto the flowers *t.*	Nu 8:4
shall cease waiting upon the service *t.*	Nu 8:25
and according to all the ceremonies *t.*	Nu 9:3
and according to the manner *t.*, so	Nu 9:14
the colour *t.* as the colour of bdellium	Nu 11:7
land that eateth up the inhabitants *t.*	Nu 13:32
shall give *t.* the Lord's heave offering	Nu 18:28
offering of the Lord, of all the best *t.*	Nu 18:29
even the hallowed part *t.* out of it	Nu 18:29
ye have heaved the best *t.* from it	Nu 18:30
in Heshbon, and in all the villages *t.*	Nu 21:25
Jaazer, and they took the villages *t.*	Nu 21:32
shall the possession *t.* be divided	Nu 26:56
drink offering *t.* shall be the fourth	Nu 28:7
and as the drink offering *t.* thou shalt	Nu 28:8
with oil, and the drink offering *t.*	Nu 29:19
and the meat offering *t.* and their	Nu 29:19
with the cities *t.* in the coasts, even	Nu 32:33
went and took the small towns *t.*	Nu 32:41
and took Kenath and the villages *t.*	Nu 32:42
the land of Canaan with the coasts *t.*	Nu 34:2
and the going forth *t.* shall be from	Nu 34:4
shall be your land with the coasts *t.*	Nu 34:12
nine cubits was the length *t.*	De 3:11
half mount Gilead, and the cities *t.*	De 3:12
plain also, and Jordan, and the coast *t.*	De 3:17
and I cast the dust *t.* into the brook	De 9:21
the unclean and the clean may eat *t.*	De 12:15
all that is therein, and the cattle *t.*	De 13:15
of it into the midst of the street *t.*	De 13:16
city, and all the spoil *t.* every whit	De 13:16
Only thou shalt not eat the blood *t.*	De 15:23
smite every male *t.* with the edge of	De 20:13
is in the city, even all the spoil *t.*	De 20:14
thou shalt not destroy the trees *t.* by	De 20:19
I have not eaten *t.* in my mourning	De 26:14
neither have I taken away ought *t.* for	De 26:14
use, nor given ought *t.* for the dead	De 26:14
and shalt not gather the grapes *t.*	De 28:30
thine eyes, and thou shalt not eat *t.*	De 28:31
that the whole land *t.* is brimstone	De 29:23
things of the earth and fulness *t.*	De 33:16
thine hand Jericho, and the king *t.*	Jos 6:2
he shall lay the foundation *t.* in his	Jos 6:26
come according to the families *t.*	Jos 7:14
only the spoil *t.* and the cattle *t.*	Jos 8:2
and Hivite, and the Jebusite, heard *t.*	Jos 9:1
Ai, and all the men *t.* were mighty	Jos 10:2
and the king *t.* he utterly destroyed	Jos 10:28
the king *t.* unto the hand of Israel	Jos 10:30

but did unto the king *t.* as he did unto	Jos 10:30
and the king *t.* and all the cities *t.*	Jos 10:37; 10:39
so he did to Debir, and to the king *t.*	Jos 10:39
and smote the king *t.* with the sword	Jos 11:10
Reuben was Jordan, and the border *t.*	Jos 13:23
families, the cities and the villages *t.*	Jos 13:23
and the goings out *t.* were at En-rogel	Jos 15:7
was to the great sea, and the coast *t.*	Jos 15:12
and the great sea, and the border *t.*	Jos 15:47
and the goings out *t.* are at the sea	Jos 16:3
and the goings out *t.* were at the sea	Jos 16:8
and the goings out *t.* were at	Jos 18:12; 18:14
by the coasts *t.* round about	Jos 18:20
outgoings *t.* are in the valley of	Jos 19:14
the outgoings *t.* are at the sea from	Jos 19:29
and the outgoings *t.* were at Jordan	Jos 19:33
in, with the suburbs *t.* for our cattle	Jos 21:2
with the suburbs *t.* round about it	Jos 21:11
fields of the city, and the villages *t.*	Jos 21:12
unto the other half *t.* gave Joshua	Jos 22:7
you, and not one thing hath failed *t.*	Jos 23:14
Judah took Gaza with the coast *t.*	J'g 1:18
and Askelon with the coast *t.*	J'g 1:18
and Ekron with the coast *t.*	J'g 1:18
a city, and called the name *t.* Luz	J'g 1:26
which is the name *t.* unto this day	J'g 1:26
least such as before knew nothing *t.*	J'g 3:2
curse ye bitterly the inhabitants *t.*	J'g 5:23
the dream, and the interpretation *t.*	J'g 7:15
princes of Succoth, and the elders *t.*	J'g 8:14
And Gideon made an ephod *t.*	J'g 8:27
he took *t.* in his hands, and went on	J'g 14:9
he called the name *t.* En-hakkore	J'g 15:19
who made *t.* a graven image and a	J'g 17:4
even Ashdod and the coasts *t.*	1Sa 5:6
offering, in a coffer by the side *t.*	1Sa 6:8
the coasts *t.* did Israel deliver out of	1Sa 7:14
sword, and drew it out of the sheath *t.*	1Sa 17:51
I will shoot three arrows on the side *t.*	1Sa 20:20
it, and did bake unleavened bread *t.*	1Sa 28:24
upon his loins in the sheath *t.*	2Sa 20:8
my father David not knowing *t.* to	1Ki 2:32
in no wise slay it: she is the mother *t.*	1Ki 3:27
the length *t.* was threescore cubits	1Ki 6:2
and the breadth *t.* twenty cubits	1Ki 6:2
and the height *t.* thirty cubits	1Ki 6:2
twenty cubits was the length *t.*	1Ki 6:3
and ten cubits was the breadth *t.*	1Ki 6:3
and twenty cubits in the height *t.* and	1Ki 6:20
finished throughout all the parts *t.*	1Ki 6:38
the length was an hundred cubits	1Ki 7:2
and the breadth *t.* fifty cubits	1Ki 7:2
and the height *t.* thirty cubits	1Ki 7:2
pillars; the length *t.* was fifty cubits	1Ki 7:6
and the breadth *t.* thirty cubits: and	1Ki 7:6

pillar, and called the name t. *1Ki 7:21*
Jachin
pillar, and called the name t. *1Ki 7:21*
Boaz
brim t. was wrought like the *1Ki 7:26*
brim of a
base, and four cubits the *1Ki 7:27*
breadth t.
the four corners t. had *1Ki 7:30*
undersetters
the mouth t. was round after *1Ki 7:31*
the work
on the top of the base the *1Ki 7:35*
ledges t.
and the borders t. were of the *1Ki 7:35*
same
For on the plates of the *1Ki 7:36*
ledges t. and
and on the borders t. he *1Ki 7:36*
graved
covered the ark and the staves *1Ki 8:7*
t.
him back from the way *1Ki 13:26*
heard t.
when Baasha heard t. that *1Ki 15:21*
he left off
stones of Ramah, and the *1Ki 15:22*
timber t.
he laid the foundation t. in *1Ki 16:34*
Abiram his
and set up the gates t. in his *1Ki 16:34*
youngest
but make me t. a little cake *1Ki 17:13*
first
chariot of Israel, and the *2Ki 2:12*
horsemen t.
in Kir-haraseth left they the *2Ki 3:25*
stones t.
gathered t. wild gourds his *2Ki 4:39*
lap full
in the pot. And they could *2Ki 4:40*
not eat t.
and full ears of corn in the *2Ki 4:42*
husk t.
They shall eat, and shall *2Ki 4:43*
leave t.
them, and they did eat, and *2Ki 4:44*
left t.
thine eyes, but shalt not eat t. *2Ki 7:2;*
7:19
chariot of Israel, and the *2Ki 13:14*
horsemen t.
therein. and the coasts t. *2Ki 15:16*
from Tirzah
according to all the *2Ki 16:10*
workmanship t.
Samaria, and dwelt in the *2Ki 17:24*
cities t.
unto Gaza, and the borders t. *2Ki 18:8*
from
will cut down the tall cedar *2Ki 19:23*
trees t.
and the choice fir trees t.: *2Ki 19:23*
and I will
plant vineyards, and eat the *2Ki 19:29*
fruits t.
place. and upon the *2Ki 22:16;*
inhabitants t. *2Ch 34:24*
place. and against the *2Ki 22:19;*
inhabitants t. *2Ch 34:27*
and cast the powder t. upon *2Ki 23:6*
the graves
the towns t. even threescore *1Ch 2:23*
cities
and the suburbs t. round *1Ch 6:55*
about it
and the villages t. they gave *1Ch 6:56*
to Caleb
Beth-el and the towns t. and *1Ch 7:28*
eastward
westward Gezer, with the *1Ch 7:28*
towns t.
Sechem also and the towns *1Ch 7:28*
t.
unto Gaza and the towns t. *1Ch 7:28*
built Ono, and Lod, with the *1Ch 8:12*
towns t.
opening t. every morning *1Ch 9:27*
pertained to
Let the sea roar, and the *1Ch 16:32*
fulness t.
up his sword again into the *1Ch 21:27*
sheath t.
nor any vessels of it for the *1Ch 23:26*
service t.
the houses t. and of the *1Ch 28:11*
treasuries t.
and of the upper chambers t. *1Ch 28:11*
and of the inner parlours t. *1Ch 28:11*

candlestick, and for the *1Ch 28:15*
lamps t.
candlestick, and also for the *1Ch 28:15*
lamps t.
the beams, the posts, and the *2Ch 3:7*
walls t.
and the doors t. with gold *2Ch 3:7*
and the breadth t. twenty *2Ch 3:8*
of brass, twenty cubits the *2Ch 4:1*
length t.
and twenty cubits the *2Ch 4:1*
breadth t.
and ten cubits the height t. *2Ch 4:1*
compass, and five cubits the *2Ch 4:2*
height t.
inner doors t. for the most *2Ch 4:22*
holy place
covered the ark and the staves *2Ch 5:8*
t.
candlestick of gold with the *2Ch 13:11*
lamps t.
from him, Beth-el with the *2Ch 13:19*
towns t.
and Jeshanah with the *2Ch 13:19*
towns t.
and Ephrain with the towns *2Ch 13:19*
t.
stones of Ramah, and the *2Ch 16:6*
timber t.
and Shocho with the villages *2Ch 28:18*
t.
and Timnah with the villages *2Ch 28:18*
t.
Gimzo also and the villages *2Ch 28:18*
t: they
burnt offering, with all *2Ch 29:18*
the vessels t.
table with all the vessels t. *2Ch 29:18*
things and the establishment *2Ch 32:1*
t.
and burnt all the places t. *2Ch 36:19*
with fire
and destroyed all the goodly *2Ch 36:19*
vessels t.
and have set up the walls t. *Ezr 4:12*
builded again, and the walls *Ezr 4:16*
t. set up
let the foundations t. be *Ezr 6:3*
strongly laid
the height t. threescore cubits *Ezr 6:3*
and the breadth t. threescore *Ezr 6:3*
cubits
to repair the desolations t. and *Ezr 9:9*
elders of every city, and the *Ezr 10:14*
judges t.
and the gates t. are burned *Ne 1:3;*
with fire *2:17*
the gates t. are consumed *Ne 2:3*
with fire
the gates t. were consumed *Ne 2:13*
with fire
the beams t. and set up the *Ne 3:3;*
doors t. *3:6*
the locks t. and the bars t. *Ne 3:3;*
3:6, 13-15
they built it, and set up the *Ne 3:13*
doors t.
he built it, and set up the *Ne 3:14*
doors t.
and covered it, and set up the *Ne 3:15*
doors t.
was joined together unto the *Ne 4:6*
half t.
that when all our enemies *Ne 6:16*
heard t.
to eat the fruit t. and the *Ne 9:36*
good t.
at Kirjath-arba, and the *Ne 11:25*
villages t.
and at Dibon, and in the *Ne 11:25*
villages t.
at Jekabzeel, and in the *Ne 11:25*
villages t.
at Beer-sheba and in the *Ne 11:27*
villages t.
and at Mekonah and in the *Ne 11:28*
villages t.
at Lachish, and the fields t. *Ne 11:30*
at Azekah, and in the *Ne 11:30*
villages t.
house of my God, and for *Ne 13:14*
the offices t.
province according to the *Es 1:22;*
writing t. *3:12; 8:9*
Esther certified the king t. in *Es 2:22*
on the three and twentieth day *Es 8:9*
t.
together on the thirteenth day *Es 9:18*
t.

and on the fourteenth t.; and *Es 9:18*
the stars of the twilight t. be *Job 3:9*
dark
to me, and mine ear received *Job 4:12*
a little t.
but I could not discern the *Job 4:16*
form t.
her place, and the pillars t. *Job 9:6*
trembled
he covereth the faces of the *Job 9:24*
judges t.
The measure t. is longer than *Job 11:9*
the tender branch t. will not *Job 14:7*
cease
the root t. wax old in the *Job 14:8*
earth
and the stock t. die in the *Job 14:8*
ground
he prolong the perfection t. *Job 15:29*
upon
take away the flocks, and *Job 24:2*
feed t.
the light; they knew not the *Job 24:13*
ways t.
nor abide in the paths t. *Job 24:13*
the waters, and the *Job 26:5*
inhabitants t.
Man knoweth not the price *Job 28:13*
t. neither
shall silver be weighed for *Job 28:15*
the price t.
heard the fame t. with our *Job 28:22*
ears
God understandeth the way *Job 28:23*
t.
and he knoweth the place t. *Job 28:23*
and the fatherless hath not *Job 31:17*
eaten t.
and the furrows likewise t. *Job 31:38*
complain
If I have eaten the friuts t. *Job 31:39*
without
the owners t. to lose their *Job 31:39*
life
down rain according to the *Job 36:27*
vapour t.
The noise t. sheweth *Job 36:33*
concerning it
Who hath laid the measures *Job 38:5*
t. if
are the foundations t. *Job 38:6*
fastened
or who laid the corner stone *Job 38:6*
t.
I made the cloud the garment *Job 38:9*
t.
as for darkness, where is the *Job 38:19*
place t.
thou shouldest take it to the *Job 38:20*
bound t.
know the paths to the house *Job 38:20*
t.
thou set the dominion t. in *Job 38:33*
the earth
there is nothing hid from the *Ps 19:6*
heat t.
earth is the Lord's, and the *Ps 24:1*
fulness t.
the humble shall hear t. and be *Ps 34:2*
glad
Though the waters t. roar and *Ps 46:3*
mountains shake with the *Ps 46:3*
swelling t.
go round about her: tell the *Ps 48:12*
towers t.
of the sun unto the going *Ps 50:1*
down t.
the world is mine, and the *Ps 50:12*
fulness t.
they go about it upon the *Ps 55:10*
walls t.
Wickedness is in the midst t.: *Ps 55:11*
deceit
heal the breaches t.; for *Ps 60:2*
it shaketh
waterest the ridges t. *Ps 65:10*
thou settlest the furrows t. *Ps 65:10*
thou blessest the springing t. *Ps 65:10*
days; for I know not the *Ps 71:15*
numbers t.
the fruit t. shall shake like *Ps 72:16*
Lebanon
they break down the carved *Ps 74:6*
work t. at
all the inhabitants t. are *Ps 75:3*
dissolved
but the dregs t. all the wicked *Ps 75:8*
of the

the boughs t. were like the goodly	Ps 80:10
when the waves t. arise, thou stillest	Ps 89:9
for the world and the fulness t. thou	Ps 89:11
let the sea roar, and the fulness t.	Ps 96:11; 98:7
Let the multitude of isles be glad t.	Ps 97:1
in her stones, and favour the dust t.	Ps 102:14
and the place t. shall know it no more	Ps 103:16
wind, which lifeth up the waves t.	Ps 107:25
a calm, so that the waves t. are still	Ps 107:29
harps upon the willows in the midst t.	Ps 137:2
it, rase it, even to the foundation t.	Ps 137:7
taketh away the life of the owners t.	Pr 1:19
silver, and the gain t. than fine gold	Pr 3:14
in the pathway t. there is no death	Pr 12:28
but the end t. are the ways of death	Pr 14:12; 16:25
the whole disposing t. is of the Lord	Pr 16:33
they that love it shall eat the fruit t.	Pr 18:21
but the end t. shall not be blessed	Pr 20:21
down the strength of the confidence t.	Pr 21:22
and nettles had covered the face t.	Pr 24:31
the stone wall t. was broken down	Pr 24:31
know not what to do in the end t.	Pr 25:8
the fig tree shall eat the fruit t.	Pr 27:18
of a land many are the princes t.	Pr 28:2
knowledge the state t. shall be	Pr 28:2
what good is there to the owners t.	Ec 5:11
riches kept for the owners t. to their	Ec 5:13
and hath given him power to eat t.	Ec 5:19
God giveth him not power to eat t.	Ec 6:2
end of a thing than the beginning t.	Ec 7:8
spikenard sendeth forth the smell t.	Ca 1:12
He made the pillars t. of silver	Ca 3:10
the bottom t. of gold, the covering of	Ca 3:10
midst t. being paved with love	Ca 3:10
that the spices t. may flow out	Ca 4:16
tree, I will take hold of the boughs t.	Ca 7:8
the coals t. are coals of fire	Ca 8:6
every one for the fruit t. was to bring	Ca 8:11
and those that keep the fruit t. two	Ca 8:12
of his people, and the princes	Isa 3:14
blood of Jerusalem from the midst t.	Isa 4:4
it, and gathered out the stones t.	Isa 5:2
I will take away the hedge t.	Isa 5:5
and break down the wall t. and	Isa 5:5
light is darkened in the heavens t.	Isa 5:30
holy seed shall be the substance t.	Isa 6:13
shall destroy the sinners t. out of it	Isa 13:9
of heaven and the constellations t.	Isa 13:10
wilderness, and destroyed the cities t.	Isa 14:17
of Moab; the howling t. unto Eglaim	Isa 15:8
and the howling t. unto Beer-elim	Isa 15:8
broken down the principal plants t.	Isa 16:8
in the outmost fruitful branches t.	Isa 17:6

of Egypt shall fail in the midst t.	Isa 19:3
and I will destroy the counsel t.	Isa 19:3
shall be broken in the purposes t.	Isa 19:10
they that are the stay of the tribes t.	Isa 19:13
a perverse spirit in the midst t.	Isa 19:14
caused Egypt to err in every work t.	Isa 19:14
one that maketh mention t. shall	Isa 19:17
a pillar at the border t. to the Lord	Isa 19:19
all the sighing t. have I made to cease	Isa 21:2
have not looked unto the maker t.	Isa 22:11
city to destroy the strong holds t.	Isa 23:11
wilderness: they set up the towers t.	Isa 23:13
they raised up the palaces t.; and he	Isa 23:13
scattereth abroad the inhabitants t.	Isa 24:1
is defiled under the inhabitants t.	Isa 24:5
transgression t. shall be heavy upon	Isa 24:20
down, and consume the branches t.	Isa 27:10
when the boughs t. are withered	Isa 27:11
When he hath made plain the face t.	Isa 28:25
his anger, and the burden t. is heavy	Isa 30:27
the pile t. is fire and much wood	Isa 30:33
for mount Zion, and for the hill t.	Isa 31:4
not one of the stakes t. shall ever be	Isa 33:20
shall any of the cords t. be broken	Isa 33:20
streams t. shall be turned into pitch	Isa 34:9
and the dust t. into brimstone	Isa 34:9
land t. shall become burning pitch	Isa 34:9
the smoke t. shall go up for ever	Isa 34:10
call the nobles t. to the kingdom	Isa 34:12
and brambles in the fortresses t.	Isa 34:13
and I will cut down the tall cedars t.	Isa 37:24
and the choice fir trees t.: and I will	Isa 37:24
plant vineyards, and eat the fruit t.	Isa 37:30
and all the godliness t. is as the flower	Isa 40:6
beasts t. sufficient for a burnt offering	Isa 40:16
inhabitants t. are as grasshoppers	Isa 40:22
called thee from the chief men t. and	Isa 41:9
the isles, and the inhabitants t.	Isa 42:10
wilderness and the cities t. lift up	Isa 42:11
for he will take t. and warm himself	Isa 44:15
He burneth part t. in the fire; with	Isa 44:16
with part t. he eateth flesh	Isa 44:16
And the residue t. he maketh a god	Isa 44:17
I have baked bread upon the coals t.	Isa 44:19
I make the residue t. an abomination	Isa 44:19
I will raise up the decayed places t.	Isa 44:26
of thy bowels like the gravel t.	Isa 48:19
the righteousness t. go forth as	Isa 62:1
and the salvation t. as a lamp that	Isa 62:1
and the face t. is toward the north	Jer 1:13
against all the walls t. round about	Jer 1:15

the princes t. against the priests t.	Jer 1:18
to eat the fruit t. and the goodness t.	Jer 2:7
and all the cities t. were broken down	Jer 4:26
know, and seek in the broad places t.	Jer 5:1
though the waves t. toss themselves	Jer 5:22
and what will ye do in the end t.	Jer 5:31
We have heard the fame t.: our hands	Jer 6:24
us destroy the tree with the fruit t.	Jer 11:19
mourneth, and the gates t. languish	Jer 14:2
the saviour t. in time of trouble, why	Jer 14:8
then will I kindle a fire in the gates t.	Jer 17:27
and hiss because of all the plagues t.	Jer 19:8
the Lord, and to the inhabitants t.	Jer 19:12
of this city, and all the labours t.	Jer 20:5
and all the precious things t.	Jer 20:5
I will kindle a fire in the forest t. and	Jer 21:14
and the inhabitants t. as Gomorrah	Jer 23:14
and against the inhabitants t.	Jer 25:9
and the kings t. and the princes t. to	Jer 25:18
this city, and upon the inhabitants t.	Jer 26:15
in the peace t. shall ye have peace	Jer 29:7
shall remain after the manner t.	Jer 30:18
the land of Judah and in the cities t.	Jer 31:23
itself, and in all the cities t. together	Jer 31:24
the sea when the waves t. roar	Jer 31:35
Thus saith the Lord the maker t.	Jer 33:2
and in all the cities t. shall be a	Jer 33:12
Jerusalem, against all the cities t.	Jer 34:1
twain, and passed between the parts t.	Jer 34:18
destroy the city and the inhabitants t.	Jer 46:8
voice t. shall go like a serpent; for	Jer 46:22
the cities t. shall be desolate, without	Jer 48:9
of Moab, and in the streets t.	Jer 48:38
the cities t. shall be perpetual wastes	Jer 49:13
and shall hiss at all the plagues t.	Jer 49:17
Gomorrah and the neighbour cities t.	Jer 49:18; 50:40
the noise t. was heard in the Red sea	Jer 49:21
bring their calamity from all sides t.	Jer 49:32
it round about; let none t. escape	Jer 50:29
the captains t. and all the rulers t.	Jer 51:28
with the multitude of the waves t.	Jer 51:42
and the thickness t. was four fingers	Jer 52:21
polluted the kingdom and the princes t.	La 2:2
it hath devoured the foundations t.	La 4:11
and out of the midst t. as the colour of	Eze 1:4
out of the midst t. came the likeness	Eze 1:5
in one vessel, and make thee bread t.	Eze 4:9
and ninety days shalt thou eat t.	Eze 4:9
shalt also take t. a few in number	Eze 5:3
for t. shall a fire come forth into all the	Eze 5:4
for wrath is upon all the multitude t.	Eze 7:12

is touching the whole multitude *t.* — Eze 7:13

my wrath is upon all the multitude *t.* — Eze 7:14

that be done in the midst *t.* — Eze 9:4

and took *t.* and put it into the hands — Eze 10:7

have filled the streets *t.* with the slain — Eze 11:6

I will bring you out of the midst *t.* — Eze 11:9

shall ye be the flesh in the midst *t.* — Eze 11:11

take away all the detestable things *t.* — Eze 11:18

all the abominations *t.* from thence — Eze 11:18

the foundation *t.* shall be discovered — Eze 13:14

ye shall be consumed in the midst *t.* — Eze 13:14

and will break the staff of the bread *t.* — Eze 14:13

Shall wood be taken *t.* to do any work — Eze 15:3

him, and the roots *t.* were under him — Eze 17:6

shall he not pull up the roots *t.* — Eze 17:9

and cut off the fruit *t.* that it wither — Eze 17:9

people to pluck it up by the roots *t.* — Eze 17:9

taken the king *t.* and the princes *t.* — Eze 17:12

in the shadow of the branches *t.* shall — Eze 17:23

land was desolate, and the fulness *t.* — Eze 19:7

the name *t.* is called Bamah unto this — Eze 20:29

and ye shall be melted in the midst *t.* — Eze 22:21

so shall ye be melted in the midst *t.* — Eze 22:22

of her prophets in the midst *t.* — Eze 22:25

made her many widows in the midst *t.* — Eze 22:25

Her princes in the midst *t.* are like — Eze 22:27

and thou shalt break the sherds *t.* and — Eze 23:34

Gather the pieces *t.* into it, even every — Eze 24:4

Then set it empty upon the coals *t.* — Eze 24:11

wise men *t.* were in thee thy calkers — Eze 27:9

and I restrained the floods *t.* — Eze 31:15

heaven, and make the stars *t.* dark — Eze 32:7

all the multitude *t.* shall be destroyed — Eze 32:12

I will destroy also all the beasts *t.* — Eze 32:13

Tarshish, with all the young lions *t.* — Eze 38:13

the east, and went up the stairs *t.* — Eze 40:6

and the posts *t.* two cubits — Eze 40:9

the length *t.* and the breadth *t.* — Eze 40:20

little chambers *t.* were three on this — Eze 40:21

the posts *t.* and the arches *t.* were after — Eze 40:21

the length *t.* was fifty cubits — Eze 40:21

and the arches *t.* were before them — Eze 40:22; 40:26

measured the posts *t.* and the arches *t.* — Eze 40:24

in it and in the arches *t.* round about — Eze 40:25; 40:33, 33

on that side, upon the posts *t.* — Eze 40:26

the little chambers *t.* and the posts *t.* — Eze 40:29; 40:33, 36

and the arches *t.* according to these — Eze 40:29

arches *t.* were toward the utter court — Eze 40:31

and palm trees were upon the posts *t.* — Eze 40:31; 40:34, 37

and the arches *t.* were according to — Eze 40:33

the arches *t.* were toward the outward — Eze 40:34

and the arches *t.* and the windows — Eze 40:36

posts *t.* were toward the utter court — Eze 40:37

the entries *t.* were by the posts of the — Eze 40:38

and he measured the length *t.* forty — Eze 41:2

he measured the length *t.* twenty — Eze 41:4

about, and the length *t.* — Eze 41:12

ninety cubits and the building, with the walls *t.* — Eze 41:13

and the galleries *t.* on the one side and — Eze 41:15

high, and the length *t.* two cubits — Eze 41:22

and the corners *t.* and the length *t.* — Eze 41:22

and the walls *t.* were of wood — Eze 41:22

chambers, the length *t.* was fifty cubits — Eze 42:7

form of the house, and the fashion *t.* — Eze 43:11

and the goings out *t.* — Eze 43:11

and the comings in *t.* — Eze 43:11

and all the forms *t.* — Eze 43:11

and all the ordinances *t.* — Eze 43:11

and all the laws *t.*: and write it in — Eze 43:11

that they may keep the whole form *t.* — Eze 43:11

and all the ordinances *t.* and do them — Eze 43:11

the whole limit *t.* round about shall — Eze 43:12

the breadth a cubit, and the border *t.* — Eze 43:13

by the edge *t.* round about shall be a — Eze 43:13

broad, square in the four squares *t.* — Eze 43:16

fourteen broad in the four squares *t.* — Eze 43:17

the bottom *t.* shall be a cubit about — Eze 43:17

And thou shalt take of the blood *t.* and — Eze 43:20

house of the Lord, and all the laws *t.* — Eze 44:5

of the house, for all the service *t.* — Eze 44:14

This shall be holy in all the borders *t.* — Eze 45:1

cubits round about for the suburbs *t.* — Eze 45:2

measure *t.* shall be after the homer — Eze 45:11

and he shall go forth by the way *t.* — Eze 46:8

the inheritance *t.* shall be his sons — Eze 46:16

But the miry places *t.* and the marishes *t.* shall not be healed — Eze 47:11

And by the river upon the bank *t.* — Eze 47:12

neither shall the fruit *t.* be consumed — Eze 47:12

and the fruit *t.* shall be for meat — Eze 47:12

and the leaf *t.* for medicine — Eze 47:12

sanctuary shall be in the midst *t.* — Eze 48:10; 48:21

and the city shall be in the midst *t.* — Eze 48:15

And these shall be the measures *t.* — Eze 48:16

and the increase *t.* shall be for food — Eze 48:18

at the end *t.* they might stand before — Da 1:5

the dream, with the interpretation *t.* — Da 2:5

the dream, and the interpretation *t.* — Da 2:6

ye can shew me the interpretation *t.* — Da 2:9

I have seen, and the interpretation *t.* — Da 2:26

thee: and the form *t.* was terrible — Da 2:31

and we will tell the interpretation *t.* — Da 2:36

certain, and the interpretation *t.* sure — Da 2:45

cubits, and the breadth *t.* six cubits — Da 3:1

known unto me the interpretation *t.* — Da 4:7

I have seen, and the interpretation *t.* — Da 4:9

the earth, and the height *t.* was great — Da 4:10

and the height *t.* reached unto heaven — Da 4:11

the sight *t.* to the end of all the earth — Da 4:11

The leaves *t.* were fair, and — Da 4:12

and the friut *t.* much, and in it was — Da 4:12

of the heaven dwelt in the boughs *t.* — Da 4:12

declare the interpretation *t.* — Da 4:18

or the interpretation *t.* trouble thee — Da 4:19

the interpretation *t.* to thine enemies — Da 4:19

and the sight *t.* to all the earth — Da 4:20

and the fruit *t.* much, and in it was — Da 4:21

yet leave the stump of the roots *t.* in — Da 4:23

and shew me the interpretation *t.* — Da 5:7

known to the king the interpretation *t.* — Da 5:8

known unto me the interpretation *t.* — Da 5:15; 5:16

I beheld till the wings *t.* were plucked — Da 7:4

and the end *t.* shall be with a flood — Da 9:26

and take away my corn in the time *t.* — Ho 2:9

and my wine in the season *t.* — Ho 2:9

elms, because the shadow *t.* is good — Ho 4:13

and it shall devour the palaces *t.* — Ho 8:14

all that eat *t.* shall be polluted — Ho 9:4

and the priests *t.* that rejoiced on it — Ho 10:5

for the people *t.* shall mourn over it — Ho 10:5

for the glory *t.* because it is, departed — Ho 10:5

the scent *t.* shall be as the wine — Ho 14:7

away; the branches *t.* are made white — Joe 1:7

not turn away the punishment *t.* — Am 1:3; 1:6, 9, 11, 13; 2:1, 2, 4, 6

which shall devour the palaces *t.* — Am 1:7; 1:10, 14

will cut off the judge from the midst *t.* — Am 2:3

will slay all the princes *t.* with him — Am 2:3

the great tumults in the midst *t.* — Am 3:9

and the oppressed in the midst *t.* — Am 3:9

son, and the end *t.* as a bitter day — Am 8:10

is fallen, and close up the breaches *t.* — Am 9:11

plant vineyards, and drink the wine *t.* — Am 9:14

so he paid the fare *t.* and went down — Jon 1:3

pour down the stones *t.* into the valley — Mic 1:6

and I will discover the foundations *t.* — Mic 1:6

the graven images *t.* shall be beaten — Mic 1:7

and all the hires *t.* shall be burned — Mic 1:7

and all the idols *t.* will I lay desolate — Mic 1:7

The heads *t.* judge for reward — Mic 3:11

and the priests *t.* teach for hire — Mic 3:11

and the prophets *t.* divine for money — Mic 3:11

the land of Nimrod in the entrances *t.* — Mic 5:6

For the rich men *t.* are full of violence — Mic 6:12

the inhabitants *t.* have spoken lies — Mic 6:12

and the inhabitants *t.* an hissing — Mic 6:16

will make an utter end of the place *t.* — Na 1:8

they shall make haste to the wall *t.* — Na 2:5

that the maker *t.* hath graven it — *Hab 2:18*

vineyards, but not drink the wine *t.* — *Zep 1:13*

The just Lord is in the midst *t.* — *Zep 3:5*

to see what is the breadth *t.* — *Zec 2:2*

and what is the length *t.* — *Zec 2:2*

I will engrave the graving *t.* — *Zec 3:9*

lamps, which are upon, the top *t.* — *Zec 4:2*

and the other upon the left side *t.* — *Zec 4:3*

forth the headstone *t.* with shoutings — *Zec 4:7*

candlestick and upon the left side *t.* — *Zec 4:11*

roll; the length *t.* is twenty cubits — *Zec 5:2*

and the breadth *t.* ten cubits — *Zec 5:2*

it with the timber *t.* and the stones *t.* — *Zec 5:4*

weight of lead upon the mouth *t.* — *Zec 5:8*

and the cities *t.* round about her, when — *Zec 7:7*

boys and girls playing in the streets *t.* — *Zec 8:5*

and Damascus shall be the rest *t.* — *Zec 9:1*

of Olives shall cleave in the midst *t.* — *Zec 14:4*

and the fruit *t.* even his meat, is — *Mal 1:12*

in Bethlehem, and in all the coasts *t.* — *M't 2:16*

sufficient unto the day is the evil *t.* — *M't 6:34*

they shall give account *t.* in — *M't 12:36*

come and lodge in the branches *t.* — *M't 13:32*

for joy *t.* goeth and selleth all that he — *M't 13:44*

and when the people had heard *t.* they — *M't 14:13*

a nation bringing forth the fruits *t.* — *M't 21:43*

But when the king heard *t.* he was — *M't 22:7*

and when he had tasted *t.* he would — *M't 27:34*

But when Herod heard *t.* said, It is — *M'k 6:16*

owners *t.* said unto them, Why loose — *Lu 19:33*

know that the desolation *t.* is nigh — *Lu 21:20*

I will not any more eat *t.* until — *Lu 22:16*

thou hearest the sound *t.* but canst — *Joh 3:8*

the well, and drank *t.* himself — *Joh 4:12*

a man may eat *t.* and not die — *Joh 6:50*

of it. that the works *t.* are evil — *Joh 7:7*

I will build again the ruins *t.* and I — *Ac 15:16*

that ye should obey it in the lusts *t.* — *Ro 6:12*

for the flesh, to fulfil the lusts *t.* — *Ro 13:14*

and eateth not of the fruit *t.* — *1Co 9:7*

that I might be partaker *t.* with you — *1Co 9:23*

earth is the Lord's and the fulness *t.* — *1Co 10:26; 10:28*

godliness, but denying the power *t.* — *2Ti 3:5*

weakness and unprofitableness *t.* — *Heb 7:18*

the grass, and the flower *t.* falleth — *Jas 1:11*

and the flower *t.* falleth away — *1Pe 1:24*

is among you, taking the oversight *t.* — *1Pe 5:2*

world passeth away, and the lust *t.* — *1Jo 2:17*

the book, and to loose the seals *t.* — *Re 5:2*

book, and to loose the seven seals *t.* — *Re 5:5*

the book, and to open the seals *t.* — *Re 5:9*

water *t.* was dried up, that the way — *Re 16:12*

for the plague *t.* was exceeding great — *Re 16:21*

city, and the gates *t.* and the wall *t.* — *Re 21:15*

he measured the wall *t.* an hundred — *Re 21:17*

lighten it, and the Lamb is the light *t.* — *Re 21:23*

THEREON

and he poured a drink offering *t.* — *Ge 35:14*

and he poured oil *t.* — *Ge 35:14*

and put it under him, and he sat *t.* — *Ex 17:12*

shalt sacrifice *t.* thy burnt offerings — *Ex 20:24*

thy nakedness be not discovered *t.* — *Ex 20:26*

Aaron shall burn *t.* sweet incense — *Ex 30:7*

Ye shall offer no strange incense *t.* — *Ex 30:9*

shall ye pour drink offering *t.* — *Ex 30:9*

And he burnt sweet incense *t.* — *Ex 40:27*

because the cloud abode *t.* and the — *Ex 40:35*

oil upon it, and put frankincense *t.* — *Le 2:1*

part it in pieces, and pour oil *t.* — *Le 2:6*

put oil upon it, lay frankincense *t.* — *Le 2:15*

shall he put any frankincense *t.* — *Le 5:11*

he shall burn *t.* the fat of the peace — *Le 6:12*

put fire therein, and put incense *t.* — *Le 10:1*

and any part of their carcase fall *t.* — *Le 11:38*

put *t.* the covering of badgers' skins — *Nu 4:6*

put *t.* the dishes, and the spoons — *Nu 4:7*

and the continual bread shall be *t.* — *Nu 4:7*

altar, and spread a purple cloth *t.* — *Nu 4:13*

oil upon it, nor put frankincense *t.* — *Nu 5:15*

upon the tabernacle, remaining *t.* — *Nu 9:22*

put fire in them, and laid incense *t.* — *Nu 16:18*

thou shalt offer burnt offerings *t.* — *De 27:6*

and raise *t.* a great heap of stones — *Jos 8:29*

they offered *t.* burnt offerings unto — *Jos 8:31*

or if to offer *t.* burnt offering — *Jos 22:23*

or if to offer peace offerings *t.* let — *Jos 22:23*

mouth, spread ground corn *t.* — *2Sa 17:19*

saddle me an ass, that I may ride *t.* — *2Sa 19:26*

carved *t.* cherubims and palm trees — *1Ki 6:35*

him the ass; and he rode *t.* — *1Ki 13:13*

to the altar, and offered *t.* — *2Ki 16:12*

the God of our fathers look *t.* and — *1Ch 12:17*

their shoulders with the staves *t.* — *1Ch 15:15*

and set *t.* palm trees and chains — *2Ch 3:5*

linen, and wrought cherubims *t.* — *2Ch 3:14*

and sacrificed *t.* peace offerings and — *2Ch 33:16*

to offer burnt offerings *t.* as it is — *Ezr 3:2*

they offered burnt offerings *t.* unto — *Ezr 3:3*

being set up, let him be hanged *t.* — *Ezr 6:11*

that Mordecai may be hanged *t.* — *Es 5:14*

Then the king said, Hang him *t.* — *Es 7:9*

and perverseness, and stay *t.* — *Isa 30:12*

nor any ravenous beast shall go up *t.* — *Isa 35:9*

a pin of it to hang any vessel *t.* — *Eze 15:3*

to slay *t.* the burnt offering and the — *Eze 40:39*

make it, to offer burnt offerings *t.* — *Eze 43:18*

and to sprinkle blood *t.* — *Eze 43:18*

and his seven lamps *t.* and seven — *Zec 4:2*

clothes, and they set him *t.* — *M't 21:7*

found nothing *t.* but leaves — *M't 21:19*

by it, and by all things *t.* — *M't 23:20*

God, and by him that sitteth *t.* — *M't 23:22*

he might find anything *t.* — *M'k 11:13*

And when he thought *t.* he wept — *M'k 14:72*

he came and sought fruit *t.* — *Lu 13:6*

upon the colt, and they set Jesus *t.* — *Lu 19:35*

had found a young ass, sat *t.* — *Joh 12:14*

coals there, and fish laid *t.* — *Joh 21:9*

foundation, and another buildeth *t.* — *1Co 3:10*

to open the book, neither to look *t.* — *Re 5:3*

to read the book, neither to look *t.* — *Re 5:4*

was given to him that sat *t.* — *Re 6:4*

and names written *t.* which are the — *Re 21:12*

THEREOUT

he shall take *t.* his handful of — *De 2:2*

in the jaw, and there came water *t.* — *J'g 15:19*

THERETO

make *t.* a crown of gold round about — *Ex 25:24*

shalt do *t.* according to the meat — *Ex 29:41*

shall make like unto that, to smell *t.* — *Ex 30:38*

and shall add the fifth part *t.* — *Le 5:16*

and shall add the fifth part more *t.* — *Le 6:5*

stand before a beast to lie down *t.* — *Le 18:23*

unto any beast, and lie down *t.* — *Le 20:16*

and shall add a fifth part of it *t.* — *Le 27:27*

shall add *t.* the fifth part thereof — *Le 27:31*

vessels thereof, and all that serveth *t.* — *Nu 3:36*

running water shall be put *t.* in a — *Nu 19:17*

thou shalt not add *t.* nor diminish — *De 12:32*

king of Edom would not hearken *t.* — *J'g 11:17*

prepared; and thou mayest add *t.* — *1Ch 22:14*

your yoke heavy, and I will add *t.* — *2Ch 10:14*

fornication, and compelled Judah *t.* — *2Ch 21:11*

taking heed *t.* according to thy word — *Ps 119:9*

a graven image, and falleth down *t.* — *Isa 44:15*

a Galilaean, and thy speech agreeth *t.* — *M'k 14:70*

no man disanulleth, or addeth *t.* — *Ga 3:15*

THEREUNTO

worshipped it, and have sacrificed *t.* — *Ex 32:8*

he made *t.* four pillars of shittim — *Ex 36:36*

made *t.* a crown of gold round about — *Ex 37:11*

he made *t.* a border of an handbreadth — *Ex 37:12*

and unto all the places nigh *t.* in the — *De 1:7*

and watching *t.* with all — *Eph 6:18*

that we are appointed *t.* — *1Th 3:3*

make the comers *t.* perfect — *Heb 10:1*

knowing that ye are *t.* called — *1Pe 3:9*

THEREUPON

and the mercy seat that is *t.* — *Ex 31:7*

colours, and playedst the harlot *t.* — *Eze 16:16*

the house of Judah; they shall feed *t.* — *Zep 2:7*

man take heed now he buildeth *t.* — *1Co 3:10*

work abide which he hath built *t.* — *1Co 3:14*

THEREWITH

corn, or the field, be   *Ex 22:6*
consumed *t.*
the tabernacle of the   *Ex 30:26*
congregation *t.*
t. he made the sockets to the   *Ex 38:30*
door
that maketh atonement *t.* shall   *Le 7:7*
have it
of the ephod, and bound it   *Le 8:7*
unto him *t.*
goeth from him, and is   *Le 15:32*
defiled *t.*
lie with any beast to defile   *Le 18:23*
thyself *t.*
he shall not eat to defile   *Le 22:8*
himself *t.*
shalt thou eat unleavened   *De 16:3*
bread *t.*
thou shalt dig *t.* and shalt   *De 23:13*
turn back
took it, and slew a thousand   *J'g 15:15*
men *t.*
took new ropes, and bound   *J'g 16:12*
him *t.*
any bribe to blind mine eyes   *1Sa 12:3*
t.
and slew him, and cut off   *1Sa 17:51*
his head *t.*
thy sword, and thrust me   *1Sa 31:4*
through *t.*
so he smote him *t.* in the   *2Sa 20:10*
fifth rib, **and**
I have *t.* sent Naaman my   *2Ki 5:6*
servant to
and repaired *t.* the house of   *2Ki 12:14*
the Lord
thy sword, and thrust me   *1Ch 10:4*
through *t.*
which I made, said David, to   *1Ch 23:5*
praise *t.*
and he built *t.* Geba and   *2Ch 16:6*
Mizpah
than great treasure and   *Pr 15:16*
trouble *t.*
love is, than a stalled ox and   *Pr 15:17*
hatred *t.*
is a dry morsel, and quietness   *Pr 17:1*
t.
thee, lest thou be filled *t.* and   *Pr 25:16*
vomit it
to the sons of man to be   *Ec 1:13*
exercised *t.*
pools of water, to water *t.* the   *Ec 2:6*
wood
removeth stones shall be hurt   *Ec 10:9*
t.
itself against him that   *Isa 10:15*
heweth *t.*
thou shalt prepare thy bread   *Eze 4:15*
t.
and oil, and ye shall be   *Joe 2:19*
satisfied *t.*
whatsoever state I am, *t.* to   *Ph'p 4:11*
be content
and raiment let us be *t.*   *1Ti 6:8*
content
T. bless we God, even the   *Jas 3:9*
t. curse we men, which are   *Jas 3:9*
not content *t.* neither doth   *3Jo 10*

THESE

T. are the generations of the   *Ge 2:4*
T. are the generations of Noah   *Ge 6:9*
T. are three sons of Noah;   *Ge 9:19*
and of
t. are the generations of the   *Ge 10:1*
sons
By *t.* were the isles of the   *Ge 10:5*
Gentiles
T. are the sons of Ham, after   *Ge 10:20*
their
all *t.* were the sons of Joktan   *Ge 10:29*
T. are the sons of Shem,   *Ge 10:31*
after their
T. are the families of the   *Ge 10:32*
sons of
by *t.* were the nations   *Ge 10:32*
divided in
T. are the generations of   *Ge 11:10*
Shem
t. are the generations of   *Ge 11:27*
Terah
That *t.* made war with Bera   *Ge 14:2*
king
All *t.* were joined together in   *Ge 14:3*
t. were confederate with   *Ge 14:13*
Abram

After *t.* things the word of the   *Ge 15:1*
he took unto him all *t.* and   *Ge 15:10*
divided
only unto *t.* men do nothing   *Ge 19:8*
and told all *t.* things in their   *Ge 20:8*
ears
after *t.* things, that God did   *Ge 22:1*
tempt
pass after *t.* things, that it   *Ge 22:20*
was told
t. eight Milcah did bear to   *Ge 22:23*
Nahor
t. were the years of the life of   *Ge 23:1*
Sarah
told, her mother's house *t.*   *Ge 24:28*
things
All *t.* were the children of   *Ge 25:4*
Keturah
And *t.* are the days of the   *Ge 25:7*
years of
Now *t.* are the generations of   *Ge 25:12*
And *t.* are the names of the   *Ge 25:13*
sons of
T. are the sons of Ishmael   *Ge 25:16*
t. are their names, by their   *Ge 25:16*
towns
And *t.* are the years of the   *Ge 26:17*
life of
And *t.* are the generations of   *Ge 25:19*
Isaac
thy seed, I will give all *t.*   *Ge 26:3*
countries
give unto thy seed all *t.*   *Ge 26:4*
countries
hath supplanted me *t.* two   *Ge 27:36*
times
t. words of Esau her elder   *Ge 27:42*
son
as *t.* which are of the   *Ge 27:46*
daughters
And he told Laban all *t.*   *Ge 29:13*
things
T. daughters are my   *Ge 31:43*
daughters
and *t.* children are my   *Ge 31:43*
children
and *t.* cattle are my cattle,   *Ge 31:43*
and all that
I do this day unto *t.* my   *Ge 31:43*
daughter
thou? and whose are *t.*   *Ge 32:17*
before thee
T. are to find grace in the   *Ge 33:8*
sight of my
T. men are peaceable with us   *Ge 34:21*
t. are the sons of Jacob,   *Ge 35:26*
which were
Now *t.* are the generations of   *Ge 36:1;*
Esau   *36:9*
t. are the sons of Esau, which   *Ge 36:5*
were
T. are the names of Esau's   *Ge 36:10*
sons
t. were the sons of Adah   *Ge 36:12*
Esau's
t. are the sons of Reuel;   *Ge 36:13*
Nahath
t. were the sons of   *Ge 36:13*
Bashemath
t. were the sons of   *Ge 36:14*
Aholibamah, the
T. were the dukes of the sons   *Ge 36:15*
of
t. are the dukes that came of   *Ge 36:16*
of Edom; *t.* were the sons of   *Ge 36:16*
Adah
t. are the sons of Reuel   *Ge 36:17*
Esau's son
t. are the dukes that came of   *Ge 36:17*
Reuel
t. are the sons of Bashemath   *Ge 36:17*
Esau's
t. are the sons of   *Ge 36:18*
Aholibamah
t. were the dukes that came   *Ge 36:18*
of
T. are the sons of Esau, who   *Ge 36:19*
is
Edom, and *t.* are their   *Ge 36:19*
dukes
T. are the sons of Seir the   *Ge 36:20*
Horite
t. are the dukes of the   *Ge 36:21*
Horites, the
And the children of Shobal   *Ge 36:23*
were *t.*
t. are the children of Zibeon   *Ge 36:24*
And the children of Anah   *Ge 36:25*
were *t.*

And *t.* are the children of   *Ge 36:26*
Dishon
The children of Ezer are *t.*;   *Ge 36:27*
Bilhan
The children of Dishan are   *Ge 36:28*
t.: Uz
T. are the dukes that came   *Ge 36:29*
of the
t. are the dukes that came of   *Ge 36:30*
Hori
t. are the kings that reigned   *Ge 36:31*
in the
t. are the names of the dukes   *Ge 36:40*
that
t. be the dukes of Edom,   *Ge 36:43*
according
T. are the generations of   *Ge 37:2*
Jacob
man, whose *t.* are, am I with   *Ge 38:25*
child
whose are *t.* the signet, and   *Ge 38:25*
it came to pass that *t.* things,   *Ge 39:7;*
that   *40:1; 48:1*
unto him according to *t.*   *Ge 39:17*
words
away: all *t.* things are   *Ge 42:36*
against me
according to the tenor of *t.*   *Ge 43:7*
words
Bring *t.* men home, and slay   *Ge 43:16*
for *t.* men shall dine with me   *Ge 43:16*
at noon
he spake unto them *t.* same   *Ge 44:6*
words
Wherefore saith my lord *t.*   *Ge 44:7*
words
t. two years hath the famine   *Ge 45:6*
been
t. are the names of the   *Ge 46:8*
children of
T. be the sons of Leah, which   *Ge 46:15*
she
T. are the sons of Zilpah,   *Ge 46:18*
whom
t. she bare unto Jacob, even   *Ge 46:18*
T. are the sons of Rachel,   *Ge 46:22*
which
T. are the sons of Bilhah,   *Ge 46:25*
which
and she bare *t.* unto Jacob;   *Ge 46:25*
all the
Joseph's sons, and said, Who   *Ge 48:8*
are *t.*
All *t.* are the twelve tribes of   *Ge 49:28*
Israel
t. are the names of the children   *Ex 1:1*
of
will not believe also *t.* two   *Ex 4:9*
signs
T. be the heads of their   *Ex 6:14*
father's
Carmi: *t.* be the families of   *Ex 6:14*
Reuben
t. are the families of Simeon   *Ex 6:15*
t. are the names of the sons of   *Ex 6:16*
Levi
t. are the families of Levi   *Ex 6:19*
according
t. are the families of the   *Ex 6:24*
Korhites
t. are the heads of the   *Ex 6:25*
Levites
T. are that Aaron and Moses,   *Ex 6:26*
to
t. are they which spake to   *Ex 6:27*
t. are that Moses and Aaron   *Ex 6:27*
might shew *t.* my signs before   *Ex 10:1*
him
all *t.* thy servants shall come   *Ex 11:8*
down
Moses and Aaron did all *t.*   *Ex 11:10*
wonders
them, but it gave light by   *Ex 14:20*
night to *t.*
will put none of *t.* diseases   *Ex 15:26*
upon thee
T. are the words which thou   *Ex 19:6*
shalt
laid before their faces all *t.*   *Ex 19:7*
words
And God spake all *t.* words,   *Ex 20:1*
saying
Now *t.* are the judgments   *Ex 21:1*
which
if he do not *t.* three unto her,   *Ex 21:11*
then
with you concerning all *t.*   *Ex 24:8*
words
shall he make it, with all *t.*   *Ex 25:39*
vessels

t. are the garments which they shall — Ex 28:4

t. sweet spices with frankincense — Ex 30:34

T. be thy gods, O Israel, which — Ex 32:4; 32:8

the people heard *t.* evil tidings, they — Ex 33:4

I will write upon *t.* tables the words — Ex 34:1

unto Moses, Write thou *t.* words — Ex 34:27

for after the tenor of *t.* words I have — Ex 34:27

T. are the words which the Lord — Ex 35:1

is made of *t.* things unto the Lord — Le 2:8

then he shall be guilty in one of *t.* — Le 5:4; 5:5

sin that he hath sinned in one of *t.* — Le 5:13

commit any of *t.* things which are — Le 5:17

any of all *t.* that a man doeth, sinning — Le 6:3

T. are the beasts which ye shall — Le 11:2

t. shall ye not eat of them that — Le 11:4

T. shall ye eat of all that are in — Le 11:9

t. are they which ye shall have in — Le 11:13

Yet *t.* may ye eat of every — Le 11:21

Even *t.* of them ye may eat — Le 11:22

And for *t.* ye shall be unclean — Le 11:24

T. also shall be unclean unto you — Le 11:29

T. are unclean to you among all — Le 11:31

t. are holy garments; therefore — Le 16:4

ye yourselves in any of *t.* things — Le 18:24

for in all *t.* the nations are defiled — Le 18:24

not commit any of *t.* abominations — Le 18:26

all *t.* abominations have the men — Le 18:27

commit any of *t.* abominations — Le 18:29

any one of *t.* abominable customs — Le 18:30

for they committed all *t.* things — Le 20:23

or an harlot, *t.* shall he not take — Le 21:14

ye shall not offer *t.* unto the Lord — Le 22:22

the bread of your God of any of *t.* — Le 22:25

convocations, even *t.* are my feasts — Le 23:2

T. are the feasts of the Lord — Le 23:4; 23:37

he be not redeemed in *t.* years, then — Le 25:54

will not do all *t.* commandments — Le 26:14

not be reformed by me by *t.* things — Le 26:23

T. are the statutes and judgments — Le 26:46

T. are the commandments, which — Le 27:34

t. are the names of the men that — Nu 1:5

T. were the renowned of the — Nu 1:16

And Moses and Aaron took *t.* men — Nu 1:17

T. are those that were numbered — Nu 1:44

their armies. T. shall first set forth — Nu 2:9

T. are those which were numbered — Nu 2:32

T. also are the generations of — Nu 3:1

t. are the names of the sons of — Nu 3:2; 3:3, 18

t. were the sons of Levi by their — Nu 3:17

T. are the families of the Levites — Nu 3:20; 26:58

t. are the famlies cf Gershonites — Nu 3:21

t. are the famlies of Kohathites — Nu 3:27

t. are the families of Merari — Nu 3:33

t. shall pitch on the side of the — Nu 3:35

T. things are the burden of — Nu 4:15

T. were they that were numbered — Nu 4:37

T. are they that were numbered of — Nu 4:41; 26:57

T. be those that were numbered of — Nu 4:45

priest shall write *t.* curses in a book — Nu 5:23

t. were their names: of the tribe of — Nu 13:4

T. are the names of the men which — Nu 13:16

tempted me now *t.* ten times — Nu 14:22

Moses told *t.* sayings unto all — Nu 14:39

shall do *t.* things after this manner — Nu 15:13

not observed all *t.* commandments — Nu 15:22

thou put out the eyes of *t.* men — Nu 16:14

from the tents of *t.* wicked men — Nu 16:26

hath sent me to do all *t.* works — Nu 16:28

If *t.* men die the common death of — Nu 16:29

that *t.* men have provoked the Lord — Nu 16:30

and end of speaking all *t.* words — Nu 16:31

censers of *t.* sinners against their — Nu 16:38

And Israel took all *t.* cities — Nu 21:25

said, What men are *t.* with thee — Nu 22:9

hast smitten me *t.* three times — Nu 22:28

smitten thine ass *t.* three times — Nu 22:32

and turned from me *t.* three times — Nu 22:33

blessed them *t.* three times — Nu 24:10

T. are the families of the — Nu 26:7; 26:14, 18, 27

T. are the families of Judah — Nu 26:22

T. are the families of Issachar — Nu 26:25

T. are the sons of Gilead: of Jeezer — Nu 26:30

T. are the families of Manasseh — Nu 26:34

T.are the sons of Ephraim after — Nu 26:35

And *t.* are the sons of Shuthelah — Nu 26:36

T. are the families of the sons of — Nu 26:37; 26:47

T. are the sons of Joseph — Nu 26:37

T. are the sons of Benjamin after — Nu 26:41

T. are the sons of Dan after their — Nu 26:42

T. are the families of Dan — Nu 26:42

T. are the families of Naphtali — Nu 26:50

T. were the numbered of the — Nu 26:51

Unto *t.* the land shall be divided for — Nu 26:53

T. are they that were numbered by — Nu 26:63

But among *t.* there was not a man — Nu 26:64

t. are the names of his daughters — Nu 27:1

offer *t.* beside the burnt offering — Nu 28:23

T. things ye shall do unto the Lord — Nu 29:39

T. are the statutes, which the Lord — Nu 30:16

t. caused the children of Israel — Nu 31:16

T. are the journeys of the children — Nu 33:1

t. are their journeys according to — Nu 33:2

T. are the names of the men which — Nu 34:17

And the names of the men are *t.* — Nu 34:19

t. are they whom the Lord — Nu 34:29

t. cities which ye shall give six cities — Nu 35:13

T. six cities shall be a refuge blood according to *t.* — Nu 35:15

judgments — Nu 35:24

So *t.* things shall be for a statute of — Nu 35:29

t. are the commandments and the — Nu 36:13

T. be the words which Moses spake — De 1:1

shall not one of *t.* men of this evil — De 1:35

t. forty years the Lord thy God — De 2:7

t. cities were fenced with high — De 3:5

God hath done unto *t.* two kings — De 3:21

which shall hear all *t.* statutes — De 4:6

all *t.* things are come upon thee — De 4:30

fleeing unto one of *t.* cities he might — De 4:42

T. are the testimonies, and the — De 4:45

T. words the Lord spake unto all — De 5:22

Now *t.* are the commandments — De 6:1

And *t.* words, which I command thee — De 6:6

commanded us to do all *t.* statutes — De 6:24

to do all *t.* commandments before — De 6:25

if ye hearken to *t.* judgments — De 7:12

heart, T. nations are more than I — De 7:17

thy God led thee *t.* forty years — De 8:2

did thy foot swell, *t.* forty years — De 8:4

for the wickedness of *t.* nations — De 9:4; 9:5

for thee *t.* great and terrible things — De 10:21

ye lay up *t.* my words in your heart — De 11:18

keep all *t.* commandments which — De 11:22

the Lord drive out all *t.* nations — De 11:23

T. are the statutes and judgments — De 12:1

near all *t.* words which I command — De 12:28

How did *t.* nations serve their gods — De 12:30

T. are the beasts which ye shall — De 14:4

t. ye shall not eat of them that — De 14:7

T. ye shall eat of all that are in — De 14:9

t. are they of which ye shall not eat — De 14:12

to do all *t.* commandments which — De 15:5

shalt observe and do *t.* statutes — De 16:12

the words of this law and *t.* statutes — De 17:19

that do *t.* things are an abomination — De 18:12

because of *t.* abominations — De 18:12

For *t.* nations, which thou shalt — De 18:14

keep all *t.* commandments to do — De 19:9

cities more for thee, beside *t.* three — De 19:9

die, and fleeth into one of *t.* cities — De 19:11

not of the cities of *t.* nations — De 20:15

But of the cities of *t.* people, which — De 20:16

t. are the tokens of my daughter's — De 22:17

even both *t.* are abomination unto — De 23:18

beat him above *t.* with many stripes — De 25:3

commanded thee to do *t.* statutes — De 26:16

that ye shall set up *t.* stones, which I — De 27:4

T. shall stand upon mount Gerizim — De 27:12

t. shall stand upon mount Ebal to — De 27:13

all *t.* blessings shall come on thee — De 28:2

all *t.* curses shall come upon thee — De 28:15; 28:45

among *t.* nations shalt thou find no — De 28:65

T. are the words of the covenant — De 29:1

and serve the gods of *t.* nations — De 29:18

all *t.* things are come upon thee — De 30:1

all *t.* curses upon thine enemies — De 30:7

and spake *t.* words unto all Israel — De 31:1

destroy *t.* nations from before thee — De 31:3

Are not *t.* evils come upon us	De 31:17
I may speak *t.* words in their ears	De 31:28
an end of speaking all *t.* words	De 32:45
And as soon as we heard *t.* things	Jos 2:11
saying, What mean ye by *t.* stones	Jos 4:6
t. stones shall be for a memorial	Jos 4:7
come, saying, What mean *t.* stones	Jos 4:21
t. bottles of wine, which we filled	Jos 9:13
t. our garments and our shoes are	Jos 9:13
But *t.* five kings fled, and hid	Jos 10:16
your feet upon the necks of *t.* kings	Jos 10:24
t. kings and their land did Joshua	Jos 10:42
where all *t.* kings were met together	Jos 11:5
And all the spoil of *t.* cities, and the	Jos 11:14
Now *t.* are the kings of the land	Jos 12:1
t. are the kings of the country which	Jos 12:7
t. did Moses smite, and cast them out	Jos 13:12
T. are the countries which Moses	Jos 13:32
And *t.* are the countries which the	Jos 14:1
as he said, *t.* forty and five years	Jos 14:10
t. were the male children of	Jos 17:2
t. are the names of his daughters	Jos 17:3
t. cities of Ephraim are among	Jos 17:9
the villages round about *t.* cities	Jos 19:8
t. cities with their villages	Jos 19:16; 19:31, 48
T. are the inheritances, which	Jos 19:51
T. were the cities appointed for all	Jos 20:9
the Lord, *t.* cities and their suburbs	Jos 21:3
unto the Levites *t.* cities with their	Jos 21:8
t. cities which are here mentioned	Jos 21:9
T. cities were every one with their	Jos 21:42
about them: thus were all *t.* cities	Jos 21:42
not left your brethren *t.* many days	Jos 22:3
done unto all *t.* nations because of	Jos 23:3
you by lot *t.* nations that remain	Jos 23:4
That ye come not among *t.* nations	Jos 23:7
t. that remain among you; neither	Jos 23:7
unto the remnant of *t.* nations	Jos 23:12
even *t.* that remain among you, and	Jos 23:12
no more drive out any of *t.* nations	Jos 23:13
Joshua wrote *t.* words in the book	Jos 24:26
And it came to pass after *t.* things	Jos 24:29
the angel of the Lord spake *t.* words	J'g 2:4
Now *t.* are the nations which	J'g 3:1
all the men of Shechem all *t.* words	J'g 9:3
he have shewed us all *t.* things	J'g 13:23
have told us such things as *t.*	J'g 13:23
hast mocked me *t.* three times	J'g 16:15
that there is in *t.* houses an ephod	J'g 18:14
And *t.* went into Micah's house, and	J'g 18:18
draw near to one of *t.* places to lodge	J'g 19:13
sword: all *t.* were men of war	J'g 20:17
men: all *t.* drew the sword	J'g 20:25
hundred men: all *t.* drew the sword	J'g 20:35
men: all *t.* were men of valour	J'g 20:44; 20:46
T. six measures of barley gave he	Ru 3:17
t. are the generations of Pharez	Ru 4:18
out of the hand of *t.* mighty Gods	1Sa 4:8
t. are the Gods that smote the	1Sa 4:8
t. are the golden emerods which	1Sa 6:17
when *t.* signs are come unto thee	1Sa 10:7
the garrison of *t.* uncircumcised	1Sa 14:6
Behold, we will pass over unto *t.* men	1Sa 14:8
names of his two daughters were *t.*	1Sa 14:49
Jesse, The Lord hath not chosen *t.*	1Sa 16:10
t. ten loaves, and run to the camp	1Sa 17:17
And carry *t.* ten cheeses unto the	1Sa 17:18
said unto Saul, I cannot go with *t.*	1Sa 17:39
his servants told David *t.* words	1Sa 18:26
been kept from us about *t.* three days	1Sa 21:5
David laid up *t.* words in his heart	1Sa 21:12
shall I go and smite *t.* Philistines	1Sa 23:2
stayed his servants with *t.* words	1Sa 24:7
made an end of speaking *t.* words	1Sa 24:16
his wife had told him *t.* things, that	1Sa 25:37
What do *t.* Hebrews here	1Sa 29:3
been with me *t.* days, or *t.* years	1Sa 29:3
not be with the heads of *t.* men	1Sa 29:4
t. uncircumcised come and thrust	1Sa 31:4
T. were born to David in Hebron	2Sa 3:5
t. men the sons of Zeruiah be too	2Sa 3:39
t. be the names of those that were	2Sa 5:14
According to all *t.* words, and	2Sa 7:17
hast thou done all *t.* great things	2Sa 7:21
king David heard of all *t.* things	2Sa 13:21
he put all *t.* words in the mouth of	2Sa 14:19
unto Ziba, What meanest thou by *t.*	2Sa 16:2
T. four were born to the giant in	2Sa 21:22
Now *t.* be the last words of David	2Sa 23:1
T. be the names of the mighty men	2Sa 23:8
T. things did *t.* three mighty men	2Sa 23:17
T. things did Benaiah the son of	2Sa 23:22
but *t.* sheep, what have they	2Sa 24:17
All *t.* things did Araunah, as a king	2Sa 24:23
t. were the princes which he had	1Ki 4:2
And *t.* are their names: The son of	1Ki 4:8
All *t.* were of costly stones, according	1Ki 7:9
all *t.* vessels, which Hiram made	1Ki 7:45
And let *t.* my words, wherewith I	1Ki 8:59
What cities are *t.* which thou hast	1Ki 9:13
T. were the chief of the officers that	1Ki 9:23
happy are *t.* thy servants, which	1Ki 10:8
abundance of spices as *t.* which	1Ki 10:10
Solomon clave unto *t.* in love	1Ki 11:2
shall not be dew nor rain *t.* years	1Ki 17:1
and it came to pass after *t.* things	1Ki 17:17
have done all *t.* things at thy word	1Ki 18:36
So *t.* young men of the princes of	1Ki 20:19
And it came to pass after *t.* things	1Ki 21:1
With *t.* shalt thou push the Syrians	1Ki 22:11
the Lord said, *T.* have no master	1Ki 22:17
the mouth of all *t.* thy prophets	1Ki 22:23
to meet you, and told you *t.* words	2Ki 1:7
and the life of *t.* fifty thy servants	2Ki 1:13
the Lord, I have healed *t.* waters	2Ki 2:21
called *t.* three kings together	2Ki 3:10; 3:13
Lord, open the eyes of *t.* men, that	2Ki 6:20
And when *t.* lepers came to the	2Ki 7:8
and slew him: but who slew all *t.*	2Ki 10:9
So *t.* nations feared the Lord, and	2Ki 17:41
and to thee, to speak *t.* words	2Ki 18:27
said unto him, What said *t.* men	2Ki 20:14
of Judah hath done *t.* abominations	2Ki 21:11
proclaimed, who proclaimed *t.* words	2Ki 23:16
and proclaimed *t.* things that thou	2Ki 23:17
the brass of all *t.* vessels was without	2Ki 25:16
like unto *t.* had the second pillar	2Ki 25:17
captain of the guard took *t.*	2Ki 25:20
All *t.* were the son of Joktan	1Ch 1:23
T. are their generations: The	1Ch 1:29
T. are the sons of Ishmael	1Ch 1:31
All *t.* are the sons of Keturah	1Ch 1:33
t. are the kings that reigned in the	1Ch 1:43
'ram. *T.* are the dukes of Edom	1Ch 1:54
T. are the sons of Israel; Reuben	1Ch 2:1
her sons are *t.*; Jesher, and Shobab	1Ch 2:18
t. belonged to the sons of Machir	1Ch 2:23
Zaza. *T.* were the sons of Jerahmeel	1Ch 2:33
T. were the sons of Caleb the son of	1Ch 2:50
T. are the Kenites that came of	1Ch 2:55
Now *t.* were the sons of David	1Ch 3:1
T. six were born unto him in Hebron	1Ch 3:4
And *t.* were born unto him in	1Ch 3:5
T. were all the sons of David, beside	1Ch 3:9
T. are the families of the	1Ch 4:2
And *t.* were of the father of Etam	1Ch 4:3
T. are the sons of Hur, the	1Ch 4:4
T. were the sons of Naarah	1Ch 4:6
Ir-nahash. *T.* are the men of Rechab	1Ch 4:12
And *t.* are the sons of Bithiah	1Ch 4:18
And *t.* are ancient things	1Ch 4:22
T. were the potters, and those	1Ch 4:23
T. were their cities unto the reign	1Ch 4:31
T. were their habitations	1Ch 4:33
T. mentioned by their names were	1Ch 4:38
t. written by name came in the days	1Ch 4:41
T. are the children of Abihail	1Ch 5:14
t. were reckoned by genealogies in	1Ch 5:17
t. were the heads of the house of	1Ch 5:24
And *t.* be the names of the sons of	1Ch 6:17
t. are the families of the Levites	1Ch 6:19
t. are they whom David set over the	1Ch 6:31
t. are they that waited with their	1Ch 6:33

t. are the sons of Aaron: Eleazar his — 1Ch 6:50
Now *t.* are their dwelling places — 1Ch 6:54
to the Levites *t.* cities with their — 1Ch 6:64
t. cities, which are called by their — 1Ch 6:65
All *t.* are the sons of Becher — 1Ch 7:8
All *t.* the sons of Jediael, by — 1Ch 7:11
T. were the sons of Gilead, the son — 1Ch 7:17
In *t.* dwelt the children of Joseph — 1Ch 7:29
T. are the children of Japhlet — 1Ch 7:33
All *t.* were the children of Asher — 1Ch 7:40
And *t.* are the heads of Ehud — 1Ch 8:6
t. are the heads of the fathers — 1Ch 8:6
T. were his sons, heads of — 1Ch 8:10
T. were heads of the fathers by — 1Ch 8:28
chief men. *T.* dwelt in Jerusalem — 1Ch 8:28
t. also dwelt with their brethren — 1Ch 8:32
sons, whose names are *t.* Azrikam — 1Ch 8:38
Hanan. All *t.* were the sons of Azel — 1Ch 8:38
fifty. All *t.* are the sons of Benjamin — 1Ch 8:40
t. men were chief of the fathers in — 1Ch 9:9
t. which were chosen to be porters in — 1Ch 9:22
T. were reckoned by their — 1Ch 9:22
t. Levites, the four chief porters — 1Ch 9:26
And *t.* are the singers, chief of the — 1Ch 9:33
T. chief fathers of the Levites were — 1Ch 9:34
generations: *t.* dwelt at Jerusalem — 1Ch 9:34
had six sons, whose names are *t.* — 1Ch 9:44
Hanan: *t.* were the sons of Azel — 1Ch 9:44
lest *t.* uncircumcised come — 1Ch 10:4
T. also are the chief of the mighty — 1Ch 11:10
shall I drink the blood of *t.* men that — 1Ch 11:19
things did *t.* three mightiest — 1Ch 11:19
T. things did Benaiah the son of — 1Ch 11:24
t. are they that came to David to — 1Ch 12:1
T. were of the sons of Gad, captains — 1Ch 12:14
T. are they that went over — 1Ch 12:15
t. are the numbers of the bands — 1Ch 12:23
t. men of war, that could keep rank — 1Ch 12:38
Now *t.* are the names of his children — 1Ch 14:4
According to all *t.* words — 1Ch 17:15
in making known all *t.* great things — 1Ch 17:19
that he brought from all *t.* nations — 1Ch 18:11
T. were born unto the giant in — 1Ch 20:8
but as for *t.* sheep, what have they — 1Ch 21:17
T. were the chief of the fathers of — 1Ch 23:9
T. four were the sons of Shimei — 1Ch 23:10
T. were the sons of Levi after the — 1Ch 23:24
t. are the divisions of the sons of — 1Ch 24:1
T. were the orderings of them in — 1Ch 24:19
the rest of the sons of Levi were *t.* — 1Ch 24:20
T. were the sons of the Levites — 1Ch 24:30
T. likewise cast lots over against — 1Ch 24:31
All *t.* were the sons of Heman — 1Ch 25:5
All *t.* were under the hands of their — 1Ch 25:6
All *t.* of the sons of Obed-edom — 1Ch 26:8
Among *t.* were the divisions of the — 1Ch 26:12

T. are the divisions of the porters — 1Ch 26:19
T. were the princes of the tribes of — 1Ch 27:22
t. were the rulers of the substance — 1Ch 27:31
I have willingly offered all *t.* things — 1Ch 29:17
and to do all *t.* things, and to build — 1Ch 29:19
t. are the things wherein Solomon — 2Ch 3:3
The wings of *t.* cherubims spread — 2Ch 3:13
Solomon made all *t.* vessels in great — 2Ch 4:18
t. did the priests and Levites bring — 2Ch 5:5
t. were the chief of king Solomon's — 2Ch 8:10
men, and happy are *t.* thy servants — 2Ch 9:7
Let us build *t.* cities, and make — 2Ch 14:7
all *t.* were mighty men of valour — 2Ch 14:8
when Asa heard *t.* words, and the — 2Ch 15:8
And *t.* are the numbers of them — 2Ch 17:14
T. waited on the king, beside those — 2Ch 17:19
With *t.* thou shalt push Syria until — 2Ch 18:10
the Lord said, *T.* have no master — 2Ch 18:16
in the mouth of *t.* thy prophets — 2Ch 18:22
all *t.* were the sons of Jehoshaphat — 2Ch 21:2
t. are they that conspired against — 2Ch 24:26
t. were for a burnt offering to the — 2Ch 29:32
After *t.* things, and the — 2Ch 32:1
t. were of the king's substance — 2Ch 35:7
princes; all *t.* he brought to Babylon — 2Ch 36:18
t. did Sheshbazzar bring up with them — Ezr 1:11
t. are the children of the province — Ezr 2:1
T. were they which went up from — Ezr 2:59
T. sought their register among — Ezr 2:62
to cause *t.* men to cease — Ezr 4:21
house, and to make up *t.* walls — Ezr 5:9
that was builded *t.* many years ago — Ezr 5:11
Take *t.* vessels, go, carry them into — Ezr 5:15
ye shall do to the elders of *t.* Jews — Ezr 6:8
expences be given unto *t.* men — Ezr 6:8
Now after *t.* things, in the reign of — Ezr 7:1
T. are now the chief of their fathers — Ezr 8:1
whose names are *t.* Eliphelet, Jeiel — Ezr 8:13
Now when *t.* were done, the princes — Ezr 9:1
with the people of *t.* abominations — Ezr 9:14
All *t.* had taken strange wives: and — Ezr 10:44
came to pass, when I heard *t.* words — Ne 1:4
Now *t.* are thy servants and thy — Ne 1:10
and said, What do *t.* feeble Jews — Ne 4:2
when I heard their cry and *t.* words — Ne 5:6
be their king, according to *t.* words — Ne 6:6
to the king according to *t.* words — Ne 6:7
according to *t.* their works — Ne 6:14
heathen about us saw *t.* things — Ne 6:16
T. are the children of the province — Ne 7:6
t. were they which went up also from — Ne 7:61
T. sought their register among — Ne 7:64
Shemaiah: *t.* were the priests — Ne 10:8
t. are the chief of the province that — Ne 11:3

t. are the sons of Benjamin; Sallu — Ne 11:7
t. are the priests and the Levites — Ne 12:1
T. were the chief of the priests and — Ne 12:7
T. were in the days of Joiakim the — Ne 12:26
king of Israel sin by *t.* things — Ne 13:26
And when *t.* days were expired — Es 1:5
After *t.* things, when the wrath of — Es 2:1
After *t.* things did king Ahasuerus — Es 3:1
in unto the king *t.* thirty days — Es 4:11
And Mordecai wrote *t.* things — Es 9:20
Wherefore they called *t.* days Purim — Es 9:26
that they would keep *t.* two days — Es 9:27
that *t.* days should be remembered — Es 9:28
and that *t.* days of Purim should not — Es 9:28
To confirm *t.* days of Purim in their — Es 9:31
confirmed *t.* matters of Purim — Es 9:32
How long wilt thou speak *t.* things — Job 8:2
And *t.* things hast thou hid in thine — Job 10:13
who knoweth not such things as *t.* — Job 12:3
knoweth not in all *t.* that the hand — Job 12:9
T. ten times have ye reproached — Job 19:3
Lo, *t.* are parts of his ways — Job 26:14
t. three men ceased to answer Job — Job 32:1
answer in the mouth of *t.* three men — Job 32:5
t. things worketh God oftentimes — Job 33:29
Lord had spoken *t.* words unto Job — Job 42:7
He that doeth *t.* things shall never — Ps 15:5
When I remember *t.* things, I pour — Ps 42:4
T. things hast thou done, and I — Ps 50:21
refuge, until *t.* calamities be overpast — Ps 57:1
t. are the ungodly, who prosper in — Ps 73:12
T. wait all upon thee; that thou — Ps 104:27
T. see the works of the Lord, and — Ps 107:24
is wise, and will observe *t.* things — Ps 107:43
T. six things doth the Lord hate — Pr 6:16
T. things also belong to the wise — Pr 24:23
T. are also proverbs of Solomon — Pr 25:1
the former days were better than *t.* — Ec 7:10
that for all *t.* things God will bring — Ec 11:9
by *t.* my son, be admonished — Ec 12:12
two tails of *t.* smoking firebrands — Isa 7:4
no one of *t.* shall fail, none shall — Isa 34:16
and to thee to speak *t.* words — Isa 36:12
they among all the gods of *t.* lands — Isa 36:20
O Lord, by *t.* things men live — Isa 38:16
in all *t.* things is the life of my spirit — Isa 38:16
said unto him, What said *t.* men — Isa 39:3
behold who hath created *t.* things — Isa 40:26
T. things will I do unto them — Isa 42:16
Remember *t.* O Jacob and Israel — Isa 44:21
evil: I the Lord do all *t.* things — Isa 45:7
didst not lay *t.* things to thy heart — Isa 47:7
But *t.* two things shall come to thee — Isa 47:9
save thee from *t.* things that shall — Isa 47:13
them hath declared *t.* things — Isa 48:14
Behold, *t.* shall come from far: and — Isa 49:12

t. from the north and from the west *Isa 49:12*

west; and t. from the land of Sinim *Isa 49:12*

all t. gather themselves together, and *Isa 49:18*

Who hath begotten me t. seeing I *Isa 49:21*

fro? and who hath brought up t. *Isa 49:21*

left alone; t. where had they been *Isa 49:21*

T. two things are come unto thee *Isa 51:19*

Should I receive comfort in t. *Isa 57:6*

Who are t. that fly as a cloud *Isa 60:8*

thou refrain thyself for t. things *Isa 64:12*

T. are a smoke in my nose, a fire *Isa 65:5*

it by secret search, but upon all t. *Jer 2:34*

said after she had done all t. things *Jer 3:7*

Go and proclaim t. words toward *Jer 3:12*

have procured t. things unto thee *Jer 4:18*

I said, Surely t. are poor; they are *Jer 5:4*

t. have altogether broken the yoke *Jer 5:5*

Shall I not visit for t. things? saith *Jer 5:9; 5:29*

Lord our God all t. things unto us *Jer 5:19*

have turned away t. things *Jer 5:25*

that enter in at t. gates to worship *Jer 7:2*

The temple of the Lord, are t. *Jer 7:4*

delivered to do all t. abominations *Jer 7:10*

because ye have done all t. works *Jer 7:13*

shalt speak all t. words unto them *Jer 7:27*

Shall I not visit them for t. things *Jer 9:9*

for in t. things I delight, saith *Jer 9:24*

for all t. nations are uncircumcised *Jer 9:26*

earth, and from under t. heavens *Jer 10:11*

Proclaim all t. words in the cities of *Jer 11:6*

Wherefore come t. things upon me *Jer 13:22*

for thou hast made all t. things *Jer 14:22*

shalt shew this people all t. words *Jer 16:10*

Jerusalem, that enter in by t. gates *Jer 17:20*

that Jeremiah prophesied t. things *Jer 20:1*

thy people that enter in by t. gates *Jer 22:2*

if ye will not hear t. words, I swear *Jer 22:5*

I have not sent t. prophets, yet thev *Jer 23:21*

Like t. good figs, so will I *Jer 24:5*

against all t. nations round about *Jer 25:9*

t. nations shall serve the king of *Jer 25:11*

thou against them all t. words *Jer 25:30*

heard Jeremiah speaking t. words in *Jer 26:7*

the princes of Judah heard t. things *Jer 26:10*

to speak all t. words in your ears *Jer 26:15*

now have I given all t. lands into the *Jer 27:6*

of Judah according to all t. words *Jer 27:12*

iron upon the neck of all t. nations *Jer 28:14*

Now t. are the words of the letter *Jer 29:1*

t. are the words that the Lord spake *Jer 30:4*

I have done t. things unto thee *Jer 30:15*

of Israel, turn again to t. thy cities *Jer 31:21*

Take t. evidences, this evidence of *Jer 32:14*

spake all t. words unto Zedekiah *Jer 34:6*

t. defenced cities remained of *Jer 34:7*

surely tell the king of all t. words *Jer 36:16*

thou write all t. words at his mouth *Jer 36:17*

He pronounced all t. words unto me *Jer 36:18*

his servants that heard all t. words *Jer 36:24*

t. men have done evil in all that they *Jer 38:9*

Put now t. old cast clouts and rotten *Jer 38:12*

hand of t. men that seek thy life *Jer 38:16*

Let no man know of t. words, and *Jer 38:24*

told them according to all t. words *Jer 38:27*

sent him to them, even all t. words *Jer 43:1*

set his throne upon t. stones that I *Jer 43:10*

when he had written t. words *Jer 45:1*

all t. words that are written against *Jer 51:60*

shalt see, and shalt read all t. words *Jer 51:61*

the brass of all t. vessels was without *Jer 52:20*

the pomegranates were like unto t. *Jer 52:22*

For t. things I weep; mine eye, mine *La 1:16*

for t. pine away, stricken through *La 4:9*

for t. things our eyes are dim *La 5:17*

When those went, t. went; and when *Eze 1:21*

when those stood, t. stood; and when *Eze 1:21*

see greater abominations than t. *Eze 8:15*

When they stood, t. stood; and when *Eze 10:17*

were lifted up, t. lifted up themselves *Eze 10:17*

t. are the men that devise mischief *Eze 11:2*

t. men have set up their idols in *Eze 14:3*

Through t. three men, Noah, Daniel *Eze 14:14*

Though t. three men were in it *Eze 14:16; 14:18*

to do any of t. unto thee, to have *Eze 16:5*

t. hast thou sacrificed unto them to *Eze 16:20*

seeing thou doest all t. things, the *Eze 16:30*

but hast fretted me in all t. things *Eze 16:43*

know ye not what t. things mean *Eze 17:12*

and hath done all t. things, he shall *Eze 17:18*

doeth the like to any one of t. things *Eze 18:10*

he hath done all t. abominations *Eze 18:13*

T. discovered her nakedness *Eze 23:10*

I will do t. things unto thee *Eze 23:30*

not tell us what t. things are to us *Eze 24:19*

goats: in t. were they thy merchants *Eze 27:21*

T. were thy merchants in all sorts *Eze 27:24*

t. cities shall go into captivity *Eze 30:17*

T. two nations and t. two countries *Eze 35:10*

T. are the people of the Lord, and *Eze 36:20*

me, Son of man, can t. bones live *Eze 37:3*

Prophesy upon t. bones, and say *Eze 37:4*

saith the Lord God unto t. bones *Eze 37:5*

breathe upon t. slain, that they may *Eze 37:9*

man, t. bones are the whole house of *Eze 37:11*

shew us what thou meanest by t. *Eze 37:18*

thereof according to t. measures *Eze 40:24; 40:29*

south gate according to t. measures *Eze 40:28*

the gate according to t. measures *Eze 40:32*

were according to t. measures *Eze 40:33*

it according to t. measures *Eze 40:35*

t. are the sons of Zadok among the *Eze 40:46*

the galleries were higher than t. *Eze 42:5*

under t. chambers was the entry *Eze 42:9*

t. are the measures of the altar after *Eze 43:13*

T. are the ordinances of the altar in *Eze 43:18*

when t. days are expired, it shall *Eze 43:27*

t. four corners were of one measure *Eze 46:22*

T. are the places of them that boil *Eze 46:24*

T. waters issue out toward the east *Eze 47:8*

because t. waters shall come thither *Eze 47:9*

Now t. are the names of the tribes *Eze 48:1*

for t. are his sides east and west *Eze 48:1*

t. shall be the measures thereof *Eze 48:16*

and t. are their portions, saith the *Eze 48:29*

t. are the goings out of the city on *Eze 48:30*

among t. were of the children of *Da 1:6*

As for t. four children, God gave *Da 1:17*

of thy head upon thy bed, are t. *Da 2:28*

as iron that breaketh all t. shall it *Da 2:40*

in the days of t. kings shall *Da 2:44*

and consume all t. kingdoms *Da 2:44*

t. men, O king, have not regarded *Da 3:12*

they brought t. men before the king *Da 3:13*

t. men were bound in their coats *Da 3:21*

t. three men, Shadrach, Meshach *Da 3:23*

saw t. men, upon whose bodies the *Da 3:27*

And over t. three presidents; of *Da 6:2*

Then said t. men, We shall not find *Da 6:5*

Then t. presidents and princes *Da 6:6*

Then t. men assembled, and found *Da 6:11*

when he heard t. words, was sore *Da 6:14*

t. men assembled unto the king *Da 6:15*

T. great beasts, which are four, are *Da 7:17*

that holdeth with me in t. things *Da 10:21*

he that strengthened her in t. times *Da 11:6*

both t. kings' hearts shall be to do *Da 11:27*

t. shall escape out of his hand, even *Da 11:41*

shall it be to the end of t. wonders *Da 12:6*

all t. things shall be finished *Da 12:7*

what shall be the end of t. things *Da 12:8*

T. are my rewards that my lovers *Ho 2:12*

and he shall understand t. things *Ho 14:9*

be they better than t. kingdoms *Am 6:2*

Lord straitened? are t. his doings *Mic 2:7*

shall not all t. take up a parable *Hab 2:6*

by a dead body touch any of t. *Hag 2:13*

Then said I, O my lord, what are t. *Zec 1:9*

unto me, I will shew thee what t. be *Zec 1:9*

T. are they whom the Lord hath   *Zec 1:10*

had indignation *t.* threescore   *Zec 1:12*

that talked with me, What be *t.*   *Zec 1:19*

T. are the horns which have   *Zec 1:19*

Then said I, What come *t.* to do   *Zec 1:21*

saying, *T.* are the horns which have   *Zec 1:21*

but *t.* are come to fray them, to cast   *Zec 1:21*

to walk among *t.* that stand by   *Zec 3:7*

me, saying, What are *t.* my lord   *Zec 4:4*

me, Knowest thou now what *t.* be   *Zec 4:5; 4:13*

What are *t.* two olive trees upon the   *Zec 4:11*

What be *t.* two olive branches which   *Zec 4:12*

T. are the two anointed ones, that   *Zec 4:14*

me, Whither do *t.* bear the ephah   *Zec 5:10*

with me, What are *t.* my lord   *Zec 6:4*

T. are the four spirits of the   *Zec 6:5*

t. that go toward the north country   *Zec 6:8*

as I have done *t.* so many years   *Zec 7:3*

remnant of this people in *t.* days   *Zec 8:6*

ye that hear in *t.* days *t.* words by   *Zec 8:9*

before *t.* days there was no hire   *Zec 8:10*

this people to possess all *t.* things   *Zec 8:12*

have I thought in *t.* days to do well   *Zec 8:15*

T. are the things that ye shall do   *Zec 8:16*

for all *t.* are things that I hate   *Zec 8:17*

What are *t.* wounds in thine hands   *Zec 13:6*

the beasts that shall be in *t.* tents   *Zec 14:15*

But while he thought on *t.* things   *M't 1:20*

Herod the king had heard *t.* things   *M't 2:3*

God is able of *t.* stones to raise up   *M't 3:9*

command that *t.* stones be made   *M't 4:3*

him, All *t.* things will I give thee   *M't 4:9*

one of *t.* least commandments   *M't 5:19*

whatsoever is more than *t.* cometh   *M't 5:37*

glory was not arrayed like one of *t.*   *M't 6:29*

all *t.* things do the Gentiles seek   *M't 6:32*

that ye have need of all *t.* things   *M't 6:32*

t. things shall be added unto you   *M't 6:33*

whosoever heareth *t.* sayings of   *M't 7:24*

every one that heareth *t.* sayings of   *M't 7:26*

when Jesus had ended *t.* sayings   *M't 7:28*

While he spake *t.* things unto them   *M't 9:18*

names of the twelve apostles are *t.*   *M't 10:2*

T. twelve Jesus sent forth, and   *M't 10:5*

unto one of *t.* little ones a cup of   *M't 10:42*

hast hid *t.* things from the wise   *M't 11:25*

All *t.* things spake Jesus unto the   *M't 13:34*

Have ye understood all *t.* things   *M't 13:51*

when Jesus finished *t.* parables   *M't 13:53*

this wisdom, and *t.* mighty works   *M't 13:54*

then hath this man all *t.* things   *M't 13:56*

T. are the things which defile a   *M't 15:20*

shall offend one of *t.* little ones   *M't 18:6*

ye despise not one of *t.* little ones   *M't 18:10*

one of *t.* little ones should perish   *M't 18:14*

when Jesus had finished *t.* sayings   *M't 19:1*

All *t.* things have I kept from my   *M't 19:20*

T. last have wrought but one   *M't 20:12*

Grant that *t.* my two sons may sit   *M't 20:21*

unto him, Hearest thou what *t.* say   *M't 21:16*

authority doest thou *t.* things   *M't 21:23*

by what authority I do *t.* things   *M't 21:24; 21:27*

had heard *t.* words, they marvelled   *M't 22:2*

On *t.* two commandments hang all   *M't 22:40*

t. ought ye to have done, and not   *M't 23:23*

All *t.* things shall come upon this   *M't 23:36*

unto them, See ye not all *t.* things   *M't 24:2*

Tell us, when shall *t.* things be   *M't 24:3; M'k 13:4*

for all *t.* things must come to pass   *M't 24:6*

All *t.* are the beginning of sorrows   *M't 24:8*

ye, when ye shall see all *t.* things   *M't 24:33*

pass, till all *t.* things be fulfilled   *M't 24:34*

one of the least of *t.* my brethren   *M't 25:40*

ye did it not to one of the least of *t.*   *M't 25:45*

t. shall go away into everlasting   *M't 25:46*

Jesus had finished all *t.* sayings   *M't 26:1*

what is it which *t.* witness against   *M't 26:62*

reason ye *t.* things in your hearts   *M'k 2:8*

all *t.* things are done in parables   *M'k 4:11*

And *t.* are they by the way side   *M'k 4:15*

t. are they likewise which are sown   *M'k 4:16*

t. are they which are sown among   *M'k 4:18*

t. are they which are sown on good   *M'k 4:20*

whence hath this man *t.* things   *M'k 6:2*

t. evil things come from   *M'k 7:23*

can a man satisfy *t.* men with   *M'k 8:4*

offend one of *t.* little ones   *M'k 9:42*

t. have I observed from my youth   *M'k 10:20*

what authority doest thou *t.* things   *M'k 11:28*

thee this authority to do *t.* things   *M'k 11:28*

by what authority I do *t.* things   *M'k 11:29; 11:33*

commandment greater than *t.*   *M'k 12:31*

t. shall receive greater damnation   *M'k 12:40*

Seest thou *t.* great buildings   *M'k 13:2*

when all *t.* things shall be fulfilled   *M'k 13:4*

t. are the beginnings of sorrows   *M'k 13:8*

ye shall see *t.* things come to pass   *M'k 13:29*

not pass, till all *t.* things be done   *M'k 13:30*

what it is which *t.* witness against   *M'k 14:60*

t. signs shall follow them that   *M'k 16:17*

and to shew thee *t.* glad tidings   *Lu 1:19*

that *t.* things shall be performed   *Lu 1:20*

all *t.* sayings were noised abroad   *Lu 1:65*

But Mary kept all *t.* things   *Lu 2:19*

his mother kept all *t.* sayings in   *Lu 2:51*

God is able of *t.* stones to raise up   *Lu 3:8*

when they heard *t.* things, were   *Lu 4:28*

And after *t.* things he went forth   *Lu 5:27*

When Jesus heard *t.* things, he   *Lu 7:9*

John shewed him of all *t.* things   *Lu 7:18*

And when he had said *t.* things   *Lu 8:8*

have no root, which for *t.*   *Lu 8:13*

are *t.* which hear the word of God   *Lu 8:21*

an eight days after *t.* sayings   *Lu 9:28*

Let *t.* sayings sink down into your   *Lu 9:44*

After *t.* things the Lord appointed   *Lu 10:1*

hast hid *t.* things from the wise   *Lu 10:21*

Which now of *t.* three, thinkest   *Lu 10:36*

as he spake *t.* things a certain   *Lu 11:27*

t. ought ye to have done, and not   *Lu 11:42*

as he said *t.* things unto them, the   *Lu 11:53*

was not arrayed like one of *t.*   *Lu 12:27*

all *t.* things do the nations of   *Lu 12:30*

that ye have need of *t.* things   *Lu 12:30*

t. things shall be added unto you   *Lu 12:31*

Suppose ye that *t.* Galilaeans were   *Lu 13:2*

t. three years I come seeking fruit   *Lu 13:7*

hath bound, lo, *t.* eighteen years   *Lu 13:16*

when he had said *t.* things, all his   *Lu 13:17*

not answer him again to *t.* things   *Lu 14:6*

sat at meat with him heard *t.* things   *Lu 14:15*

came, and shewed his lord *t.* things   *Lu 14:21*

and asked what *t.* things meant   *Lu 15:26*

Lo, *t.* many years do I serve thee   *Lu 15:29*

Pharisees heard all *t.* things   *Lu 16:14*

should offend one of *t.* little ones   *Lu 17:2*

All *t.* have I kept from my youth   *Lu 18:21*

Now when Jesus heard *t.* things   *Lu 18:22*

they understood none of *t.* things   *Lu 18:34*

And as they heard *t.* things   *Lu 19:11*

he commanded *t.* servants to be   *Lu 19:15*

that, if *t.* should hold their peace   *Lu 19:40*

authority doest thou *t.* things   *Lu 20:2*

by what authority I do *t.* things   *Lu 20:8*

come and destroy *t.* husbandmen   *Lu 20:16*

all *t.* have of their abundance cast   *Lu 21:4*

As for *t.* things which ye behold   *Lu 21:6*

Master, but when shall *t.* things be   *Lu 21:7*

when *t.* things shall come to pass   *Lu 21:7*

t. things must first come to pass   *Lu 21:9*

But before all *t.* they shall lay   *Lu 21:12*

For *t.* be the days of vengeance   *Lu 21:22*

when *t.* things begin to come to   *Lu 21:28*

when ye see *t.* things come to pass   *Lu 21:31*

worthy to escape all *t.* things   *Lu 21:36*

if they do *t.* things in a green tree   *Lu 23:31*

stood afar off, beholding *t.* things   *Lu 23:49*

told all *t.* things unto the eleven   *Lu 24:9*

told *t.* things unto the ·   *Lu 24:10*
apostles
they talked together of all *t.*   *Lu 24:14*
things
of communications are *t.* that   *Lu 24:17*
ye
are come to pass there in *t.*   *Lu 24:18*
days
day since *t.* things were done   *Lu 24:21*
Christ to have suffered *t.*   *Lu 24:26*
things
T. are the words which I   *Lu 24:44*
spake
And ye are witnesses of *t.*   *Lu 24:48*
things
T. things were done in   *Joh 1:28*
Bethabara
shalt see greater things than   *Joh 1:50*
t.
sold doves. Take *t.* things   *Joh 2:16*
hence
seeing that thou doest *t.*   *Joh 2:18*
things
for no man can do *t.* miracles   *Joh 3:2*
that
unto him, How can *t.* things   *Joh 3:9*
be
Israel, and knowest not *t.*   *Joh 3:10*
things
After *t.* things came Jesus   *Joh 3:22*
and his
In *t.* lay a great multitude of   *Joh 5:3*
had done *t.* things on the   *Joh 5:16*
sabbath
t. also doeth the Son likewise   *Joh 5:19*
shew him greater works than   *Joh 5:20*
t.
t. things I say, that we might   *Joh 5:34*
be
After *t.* things Jesus went over   *Joh 6:1*
we buy bread, that *t.* may eat   *Joh 6:5*
T. things said he in the   *Joh 6:59*
synagogue
t. things Jesus walked in   *Joh 7:1*
Galilee
If thou do *t.* things, shew   *Joh 7:4*
thyself to
When he had said *t.* words   *Joh 7:9*
unto
will he do more miracles   *Joh 7:31*
than *t.*
T. words spake Jesus in the   *Joh 8:20*
hath taught me, I speak *t.*   *Joh 8:28*
things
As he spake *t.* words, many   *Joh 8:30*
T. words spake his parents   *Joh 9:22*
were with him heard *t.* words   *Joh 9:40*
among the Jews for *t.*   *Joh 10:19*
sayings
T. are not the words of him   *Joh 10:21*
that
T. things said he and after   *Joh 11:11*
that he
T. things understood not his   *Joh 12:16*
that *t.* things were written of   *Joh 12:16*
him
they had done *t.* things unto   *Joh 12:16*
him
T. things spake Jesus, and   *Joh 12:36*
T. things said Esaias, when   *Joh 12:41*
he saw
If ye know *t.* things, happy   *Joh 13:17*
are ye
greater works than *t.* shall   *Joh 14:12*
he do
T. things have I spoken unto   *Joh 14:25;*
you   *15:11; 16:1, 25, 33*
T. things I command you,   *Joh 15:17*
that ye
all *t.* things will they do   *Joh 15:21*
unto you
And *t.* things will they do   *Joh 16:3*
unto you
t. things have I told you, that   *Joh 16:4*
when
t. things I said not unto   *Joh 16:4*
you at the
I have said *t.* things unto you   *Joh 16:6*
T. words spake Jesus, and   *Joh 17:1*
lifted up
but *t.* are in the world, and   *Joh 17:11*
I come
and *t.* things I speak in the   *Joh 17:13*
world
Neither pray I for *t.* alone,   *Joh 17:20*
but for
t. have known that thou hast   *Joh 17:25*
sent
When Jesus had spoken *t.*   *Joh 18:1*
words

ye seek me, let *t.* go their way   *Joh 18:8*
T. things therefore the   *Joh 19:24*
soldiers
For *t.* things were done, that   *Joh 19:36*
he had spoken *t.* things unto   *Joh 20:18*
her
But *t.* are written, that ye   *Joh 20:31*
might
After *t.* things Jesus shewed   *Joh 21:1*
lovest thou me more than *t.*   *Joh 21:15*
which testifieth of *t.* things   *Joh 21:24*
and wrote *t.* things: and we   *Joh 21:24*
know
And when he had spoken *t.*   *Ac 1:9*
things
T. all continued with one   *Ac 1:14*
accord
t. men which have   *Ac 1:21*
companied
whether of *t.* two thou hast   *Ac 1:24*
chosen
not all *t.* which speak Galileans   *Ac 2:7*
said, *T.* men are full of new   *Ac 2:13*
wine
For *t.* are not drunken, as ye   *Ac 2:15*
Ye men of Israel, hear *t.*   *Ac 2:22*
words
have likewise foretold of *t.*   *Ac 3:24*
days
What shall we do to *t.* men   *Ac 4:16*
And Ananias hearing *t.* words   *Ac 5:5*
fell
on all them that heard *t.* things   *Ac 5:5*
upon as many as heard *t.*   *Ac 5:11*
things
the chief priests heard *t.*   *Ac 5:24*
things
we are his witnesses of *t.*   *Ac 5:32*
things
intend to do as touching *t.*   *Ac 5:35*
men
before *t.* days rose up Theudas   *Ac 5:36*
Refrain from *t.* men, and let   *Ac 5:38*
them
the high priest, Are *t.* things so   *Ac 7:1*
not my hand made all *t.* things   *Ac 7:50*
they heard *t.* things, they were   *Ac 7:54*
cut
that none of *t.* things which ye   *Ac 8:24*
have
when he had declared all *t.*   *Ac 10:8*
things
While Peter yet spake *t.*   *Ac 10:44*
words
that *t.* should not be baptized   *Ac 10:47*
t. six brethren   *Ac 11:12*
accompanied me
When they heard *t.* things,   *Ac 11:18*
they
Then tidings of *t.* things came   *Ac 11:22*
unto
in *t.* days came prophets from   *Ac 11:27*
Go shew *t.* things unto James   *Ac 12:17*
Gentiles besought that *t.*   *Ac 13:42*
words
saying, Sirs, why do ye *t.*   *Ac 14:15*
things
turn from *t.* vanities unto the   *Ac 14:15*
t. sayings scarce restrained   *Ac 14:18*
they
the Lord, who doeth all *t.*   *Ac 15:17*
things
burden than *t.* necessary   *Ac 15:28*
things
T. men are the servants of the   *Ac 16:7*
most
T. men, being Jews, do   *Ac 16:20*
exceeding
serieants told *t.* words unto   *Ac 16:38*
T. have turned the world   *Ac 17:6*
upside
t. all do contrary to the   *Ac 17:7*
decrees of
the city, when they heard *t.*   *Ac 17:8*
things
T. were more noble than   *Ac 17:11*
those in
know what *t.* things mean   *Ac 17:20*
After *t.* things Paul departed   *Ac 18:1*
from
After *t.* things were ended,   *Ac 19:21*
Paul
And when they heard *t.*   *Ac 19:28*
sayings
that *t.* things cannot be   *Ac 19:36*
spoken
For ye have brought hither *t.*   *Ac 19:37*
men
T. going before tarried for us   *Ac 20:5*
But none of *t.* things move me   *Ac 20:24*

t. hands have ministered unto   *Ac 20:34*
my
And when we heard *t.* things,   *Ac 21:12*
both
before *t.* days madest an   *Ac 21:38*
uproar.
thou hast shewed *t.* things   *Ac 23:22*
to me
take knowledge of all *t.* things   *Ac 24:8*
saying that *t.* things were so   *Ac 24:9*
Or else let *t.* same here say,   *Ac 24:20*
if they
And when Felix heard *t.*   *Ac 24:22*
things
be judged of *t.* things before   *Ac 25:9*
me
if there be none of *t.* things   *Ac 25:11*
whereof *t.* accuse me, no man   *Ac 25:11*
may
and there be judged of *t.*   *Ac 25:20*
matters
of *t.* things which thou hast   *Ac 26:16*
seen
For *t.* causes the Jews caught   *Ac 26:21*
me
For the king knoweth of *t.*   *Ac 26:26*
things
that none of *t.* things are   *Ac 26:26*
hidden
such as I am, except *t.* bonds   *Ac 26:29*
Except *t.* abide in the ship, ye   *Ac 27:31*
And when he had said *t.*   *Ac 28:29*
words
t. having not the law, are a   *Ro 2:14*
law
What shall we then say to *t.*   *Ro 8:31*
things
in all *t.* things we are more   *Ro 8:37*
than
t. are not the children of God   *Ro 9:8*
how much more shall *t.* which   *Ro 11:24*
be
so have *t.* also now not   *Ro 11:31*
believed
he that in *t.* things serveth   *Ro 14:18*
Christ
having no more place in *t.*   *Ro 15:23*
parts
having a great desire *t.* many   *Ro 15:23*
years
And *t.* things brethren, I have   *1Co 4:6*
I write not *t.* things to shame   *1Co 4:14*
you
Say I *t.* things as a man? or   *1Co 9:8*
saith
But I have used none of *t.*   *1Co 9:15*
things
neither have I written *t.*   *1Co 9:15*
things
Now *t.* things were our   *1Co 10:6*
examples
Now all *t.* things happened   *1Co 10:11*
unto
carried away unto *t.* dumb   *1Co 12:2*
idols
But all *t.* worked that one   *1Co 12:11*
and the
upon *t.* we bestow more   *1Co 12:23*
abundant
faith, hope, charity, *t.*   *1Co 13:13*
three
but the greater of *t.* is   *1Co 13:13*
charity
And who is sufficient for *t.*   *2Co 2:16*
things
Having therefore *t.* promises   *2Co 7:1*
I write *t.* things being absent   *2Co 13:10*
But of *t.* who seemed to be   *Ga 2:6*
for *t.* are the two covenants,   *Ga 4:24*
one
t. are contrary the one to the   *Ga 5:17*
of the flesh are manifest,   *Ga 5:19*
which *t.*
of *t.* things cometh the wrath   *Eph 5:6*
of
be any praise, think on *t.*   *Ph'p 4:8*
things
T. things have indeed a show   *Col 2:23*
(S)
put off all *t.*; anger, wrath,   *Col 3:8*
malice
above all *t.* things put on   *Col 3:14*
charity
T. only are my fellowworkers   *Col 4:11*
unto
should be moved by *t.*   *1Th 3:3*
afflictions
comfort one another with *t.*   *1Th 4:18*
words

yet with you, I told you *t.*   *2Th 2:5*
things
And let *t.* also first be proved   *1Ti 3:10*
T. things write I unto thee   *1Ti 3:14*
in remembrance of *t.* things   *1Ti 4:6*
T. things command and teach   *1Ti 4:11*
Meditate upon *t.* things; give   *1Ti 4:15*
And *t.* things give in charge   *1Ti 5:7*
that thou observe *t.* things   *1Ti 5:21*
without
T. things teach and exhort   *1Ti 6:2*
thou, O man of God, flee *t.*   *1Ti 6:11*
things
which cause I also suffer *t.*   *2Ti 1:12*
things
Of *t.* things put them in   *2Ti 2:14*
therefore purge himself from   *2Ti 2:21*
t.
so do *t.* also resist the truth   *2Ti 3:8*
T. things speak, and exhort   *Tit 2:15*
t. things I will that thou affirm   *Tit 3:8*
T. things are good and   *Tit 3:8*
profitable
in *t.* last days spoken unto us   *Heb 1:2*
by
he of whom *t.* things are   *Heb 7:13*
spoken
t. things were thus ordained   *Heb 9:6*
should be purified with *t.*   *Heb 9:23*
with better sacrifices than *t.*   *Heb 9:23*
Now where remission of *t.*   *Heb 10:18*
T. all died in faith, not   *Heb 11:13*
having
And *t.* all, having obtained   *Heb 11:39*
a good
t. things ought not so to be   *Jas 3:10*
manifest in *t.* last times for   *1Pe 1:20*
you
that by *t.* ye might be partakers   *2Pe 1:4*
For if *t.* things be in you, and   *2Pe 1:8*
he that lacketh *t.* things is blind   *2Pe 1:9*
for if ye do *t.* things, ye shall   *2Pe 1:10*
never
in remembrance of *t.* things   *2Pe 1:12*
t. things always in   *2Pe 1:15*
remembrance
But *t.* as natural brute beasts   *2Pe 2:12*
T. are wells without water,   *2Pe 2:17*
clouds
all *t.* things shall be dissolved   *2Pe 3:11*
speaking in them of *t.* things   *2Pe 3:16*
seeing ye know *t.* things before   *2Pe 3:17*
And *t.* things write we unto   *1Jo 1:4*
you
t. things write I unto you, that   *1Jo 2:1*
ye
T. things have I written unto   *1Jo 2:26;*
you   *5:13*
Holy Ghost; and *t.* three are   *1Jo 5:7*
one
blood: and *t.* three agree in   *1Jo 5:8*
one
Likewise also *t.* filthy dreamers   *Jude 8*
But *t.* speak evil of those   *Jude 10*
things
T. are spots in your feasts of   *Jude 12*
prophesied of *t.* saying,   *Jude 14*
Behold
T. are murmurers, complainers   *Jude 16*
T. be they who separate   *Jude 19*
T. things saith he that holdeth   *Re 2:1*
T. things saith the first and the   *Re 2:8*
T. things saith he which hath   *Re 2:12;*
the   *3:1*
T. things saith the Son of God   *Re 2:18*
T. things saith he that is holy   *Re 3:7*
T. things saith the Amen, the   *Re 3:14*
after I saw four angels   *Re 7:1*
What are *t.* which are arrayed   *Re 7:13*
in
T. are they which came out of   *Re 7:14*
By *t.* three was the third part   *Re 9:18*
of
were not killed by *t.* plagues   *Re 9:20*
yet
T. are the two olive trees, and   *Re 11:4*
T. have power to shut heaven   *Re 11:6*
t. two prophets tormented   *Re 11:10*
them
T. are they which were not   *Re 14:4*
defiled
T. are they which follow the   *Re 14:4*
Lamb
T. were redeemed from among   *Re 14:4*
which hath power over *t.*   *Re 16:9*
plagues
T. have one mind, and shall   *Re 17:13*
give
T. shall make war with the   *Re 17:14*
Lamb

t. shall hate the whore, and   *Re 17:16*
shall
after *t.* things I saw another   *Re 18:1*
angel
The merchants of *t.* things,   *Re 18:15*
which
after *t.* things I heard a great   *Re 19:1*
T. are the true sayings of God   *Re 19:9*
T. both were cast alive into a   *Re 19:20*
lake
for *t.* words are true and   *Re 21:5*
faithful
T. sayings are faithful and   *Re 22:6*
true
I John saw *t.* things, and   *Re 22:8*
heard
angel which shewed me *t.*   *Re 22:8*
things
angel to testify unto you *t.*   *Re 22:16*
things
any man shall add unto *t.*   *Re 22:18*
things
He which testifieth *t.* things   *Re 22:20*
saith

THESSALONIANS

and of the *T.*, Aristarchus and   *Ac 20:4*
unto the church of the *T.*   *1Th 1:1*
which
unto the church of the *T.* in   *2Th 1:1*
God

THESSALONICA

they came to *T.* there was a   *Ac 17:1*
were more noble than those   *Ac 17:11*
in *T.*
the Jews of *T.* had   *Ac 17:13*
knowledge
Aristarchus a Macedonian of   *Ac 27:2*
T.
For even in *T.* ye sent once   *Ph'p 4:16*
and
world, and is departed into *T.*   *2Ti 4:10*

THEUDAS

For before these days rose up   *Ac 5:36*
T.

THEY

of thee a nation mightier   *Nu 14:12*
than *t.*
t. and all theirs went down   *Nu 16:33*
into the pit
not come nigh that *t.* nor you   *Nu 18:3*
also die
sent more, and more   *Nu 22:15*
honourable than *t.*
surely we shall be stronger   *1Ki 20:23;*
than *t.*   *20:25*
are more than *t.* that be with   *2Ki 6:16*
them
until *t.* fall out (S)   *2Ch 21:15*
t. that hate me, *t.* that would   *Ps 69:4*
destroy
regardeth, and there be higher   *Ec 5:8*
than *t.*
t. together shall be against   *Isa 9:21*
Judah
but *t.* also have erred through   *Isa 28:7*
wine
therefore *t.* that pursue you   *Isa 30:16*
be swift
t. are thy lot, to them thou   *Isa 57:6*
hast offered
t. that be of thee shall build   *Isa 58:12*
the old
so, *t.* their kings and priests   *Jer 2:26*
ashamed
whom neither *t.* nor their   *Jer 9:16;*
fathers have known   *19:4; 44:3*
t. whose judgment was not to   *Jer 49:12*
drink of cup
t. and their fathers have   *Eze 2:3*
transgressed
wast corrupted more than *t.*   *Eze 16:47*
in ways
multiplied abominations   *Eze 16:51;*
more than *t.*   *16:52*
they shall know that *t.* are   *Eze 34:30*
my people
what David did when   *M't 12:3;*
hungred, *t.* that were   *M'k 2:25; Lu 6:3*
with him
receive this, save *t.* to whom   *M't 19:11*
it is given
t. that are great exercise   *M't 20:25*
authority upon

t. that are whole have no   *M'k 2:17;*
need   *Lu 5:31*
t. that had eaten were about   *M'k 8:9*
4000
how hardly shall *t.* which   *M'k 10:23*
have riches
t. that went before and *t.* that   *M'k 11:9*
followed
t. that were sent, returning to   *Lu 7:10*
house
t. on the rock are *t.* which   *Lu 8:13*
receive word
ye are *t.* which continued with   *Lu 22:28*
me
for *t.* also went unto the feast   *Joh 4:45*
dead shall hear, *t.* that hear   *Joh 5:25*
shall live
t. that have done good, *t.* that   *Joh 5:29*
have done evil
scriptures, and *t.* are *t.* which   *Joh 5:39*
testify of me
two fishes, but what are *t.*   *Joh 6:9*
amongst many
that *t.* which see not might   *Joh 9:39*
see, and that *t.* which see
might be made blind
t. are not of the world, even   *Joh 17:16*
as I am not
that *t.* all may be one, as   *Joh 17:21*
thou art in me
that *t.* may be made perfect   *Joh 17:23*
in one
Father, that *t.* whom thou   *Joh 17:24*
hast given me be with me,
t. may behold my glory
t. went not in, lest *t.* should   *Joh 18:28*
be defiled
t. of circumcision contended   *Ac 11:2*
with him
now *t.* that were scattered   *Ac 11:19*
abroad on persecution
t. at Jerusalem, because *t.*   *Ac 13:27*
knew him not
through grace be saved, even   *Ac 15:11*
as *t.*
we and *t.* of that place   *Ac 21:12*
besought him
are we better than *t.*? no, in no   *Ro 3:9*
wise
for if *t.* which are the law   *Ro 4:14*
be heirs
t. that are in the flesh cannot   *Ro 8:8*
please God
not only *t.* but ourselves also   *Ro 8:23*
groan
t. which are children of flesh   *Ro 9:8*
t. also, if *t.* abide not still in   *Ro 11:23*
unbelief
t. that are such serve not our   *Ro 16:18*
Lord
t. that have wives, as tho'   *1Co 7:29*
had none
t. that weep, *t.* that rejoice,   *1Co 7:30*
that buy
t. that use this world, as not   *1Co 7:31*
abusing it
that *t.* who run in a race run   *1Co 9:24*
all
that *t.* which are approved   *1Co 11:19*
may be
whether it were I or *t.* so we   *1Co 15:11*
preach
then *t.* which are fallen   *1Co 15:18*
asleep in Christ
afterwards *t.* that are   *1Co 15:23;*
Christ's   *Ga 5:24*
as is earthy, such are *t.* that   *1Co 15:48*
are earthly
t. who seemed somewhat added   *Ga 2:6*
nothing
t. gave the right hand of   *Ga 2:9*
fellowship to me
know ye, that *t.* which are of   *Ga 3:7;*
faith   *3:9*
I would *t.* were cut off that   *Ga 5:12*
trouble you
t. who do such things not   *Ga 5:21*
inherit kingdom
nor *t.* who are circumcised   *Ga 6:13*
keep law
t. shew of us what entering in   *1Th 1:9*
we had
for *t.* that sleep, *t.* that be   *1Th 5:7*
drunken
t. that used the office of a   *1Ti 3:13*
deacon
t. who labour in the word and   *1Ti 5:17*
doctrine
and *t.* that are otherwise   *1Ti 5:25*
cannot be hid

t. that will be rich fall into temptation — 1Ti 6:9
of this sort are *t.* which creep into — 2Ti 3:6
that *t.* which have believed in God — Tit 3:8
obtained more excellent name than *t.* — Heb 1:4
seeing *t.* to whom it was first preached — Heb 4:6
that *t.* without as should not be perfect — Heb 11:40
they watch, as *t.* that must give account — Heb 13:17
salute all saints, *t.* of Italy salute you — Heb 13:24
as *t.* that shall be judged by the law — Jas 2:12
they went out that *t.* might be made manifest, that *t.* were not — 1Jo 2:19
t. are of the world, they speak of the world — 1Jo 4:5
these be *t.* who separate themselves sensual — Jude 19
t. who pierced him, kindreds shall wail — Re 1:7
for *t.* are worthy — Re 3:4; 6:6
whence came *t.* — Re 7:13
t. who came out of great tribulation — Re 7:14
for *t.* are virgins, these are *t.* which follow the Lamb — Re 14:4
here are *t.* that keep the commandments — Re 14:12
but *t.* that are written in Lamb's book — Re 21:27

THICK

there was a *t.* darkness in all the — Ex 10:22
Lo, I come unto thee in a *t.* cloud — Ex 19:9
and a *t.* cloud upon the mount — Ex 19:16
Moses drew near unto the *t.* darkness — Ex 20:21
and the boughs of *t.* trees — Le 23:40
darkness, clouds, and *t.* darkness — De 4:11
the cloud, and of the *t.* darkness — De 5:22
art waxen fat, thou art grown *t.* — De 32:15
under the *t.* boughs of a great oak — 2Sa 18:9
waters, and *t.* clouds of the skies — 2Sa 22:12
and the *t.* beam were before them — 1Ki 7:6
And it was an hand breadth *t.* — 1Ki 7:26
he would dwell in the *t.* darkness — 1Ki 8:12
he took a *t.* cloth, and dipped it in — 2Ki 8:15
he would dwell in the *t.* darkness — 2Ch 6:1
and branches of *t.* trees, to make — Ne 8:15
upon the *t.* bosses of his bucklers — Job 15:26
T. clouds are a covering to him — Job 22:14
up the waters in his *t.* clouds — Job 26:8
by watering he weareth the *t.* cloud — Job 37:11
t. darkness a swaddlingband for it — Job 38:9
dark waters and *t.* clouds of — Ps 18:11
before him his *t.* clouds passed — Ps 18:12
lifted up axes upon the *t.* trees — Ps 74:5
blotted out, as a *t.* cloud, thy — Isa 44:22
stupid, *t.*-headed (A) — Jer 4:22
green tree, and under every *t.* oak — Eze 6:13
and a *t.* cloud of incense went up — Eze 8:11
was exalted among the *t.* branches — Eze 19:11
high hill, and all the *t.* trees — Eze 20:28
his top was among the *t.* boughs — Eze 31:3
up his top among the *t.* boughs — Eze 31:10
up their top among the *t.* boughs — Eze 31:14
of the building was five cubits *t.* — Eze 41:12

t. planks upon the face of the house, and *t.* planks — Eze 41:25 / Eze 41:26
day of clouds, and of *t.* darkness — Joe 2:2
that ladeth himself with *t.* clay — Hab 2:6
a day of clouds and *t.* darkness — Zep 1:15
the people were gathered *t.* together — Lu 11:29

THICKER

finger shall be *t.* than my father's — 1Ki 12:10; 2Ch 10:10

THICKET

a ram caught in a *t.* by his horns — Ge 22:13
walk in the *t.* (B) — Job 38:40
The lion is come up from his *t.* — Jer 4:7

THICKETS

hide themselves in caves, and in *t.* — 1Sa 13:6
shall kindle in the *t.* of the forests — Isa 9:18
it ignites the *t.* (B) — Isa 9:18
shall cut down the *t.* of the forest — Isa 10:34
t. of Arabian desert (B) — Isa 21:13
they shall go into the *t.* and climb — Jer 4:29

THICKNESS

the *t.* of it was an handbreadth — 2Ch 4:5
and the *t.* thereof was four fingers — Jer 52:21
The *t.* of the wall, which was for — Eze 41:9
chambers were in the *t.* of the wall — Eze 42:10

THIEF

If a *t.* be found breaking up — Ex 22:2
if a *t.* be found, let him pay double — Ex 22:7
If the *t.* be not found, then — Ex 22:8
selleth him; then that *t.* shall die — De 24:7
needy, and in the night is as a *t.* — Job 24:14
they cried after them as after a *t.* — Job 30:5
When thou sawest a *t.* then thou — Ps 50:18
Men do not despise a *t.* if he steal — Pr 6:30
Whoso is partner with a *t.* hateth — Pr 29:24
As the *t.* is ashamed when he is — Jer 2:26
the *t.* cometh in, and the troop of — Ho 7:1
enter in at the windows like a *t.* — Joe 2:9
shall enter into the house of the *t.* — Zec 5:4
in what watch the *t.* would come — M't 24:43
Are ye come out as against a *t.* — M't 26:55; M'k 14:48
where no *t.* approacheth, neither — Lu 12:33
what hour the *t.* would come — Lu 12:39
Be ye come out, as against a *t.* — Lu 22:52
way, the same is a *t.* and a robber — Joh 10:1
The *t.* cometh not, but for to steal — Joh 10:10
but because he was a *t.* and had the — Joh 12:6
a thief (P) — 1Co 5:11
Lord so cometh as a *t.* in the night — 1Th 5:2
day should overtake you as a *t.* — 1Th 5:4
you suffer as a murderer, or as a *t.* — 1Pe 4:15
Lord will come as a *t.* in the night — 2Pe 3:10
watch, I will come on thee as a *t.* — Re 3:3
Behold, I come as a *t.* — Re 16:15

THIEVES

rebellious, and companions of *t.* — Isa 1:23
unto thee? was he found *t.* — Jer 48:27
if *t.* by night, they will destroy till — Jer 49:9
If *t.* come to thee, if robbers by — Ob 5
where *t.* break through and steal — M't 6:19
where *t.* do not break through nor — M't 6:20
but ye have made it a den of *t.* — M't 21:13; M'k 11:17; Lu 19:46
there two *t.* crucified with him — M't 27:38
The *t.* also, which were crucified — M't 27:44
And with him they crucify two *t.* — M'k 15:27
to Jericho, and fell among *t.* — Lu 10:30
unto him that fell among the *t.* — Lu 10:36
t., cheats (B) — Lu 18:11
that ever came before me are *t.* — Joh 10:8
cheats as *t.* (P) — 1Co 5:10
Nor *t.* nor covetous, nor drunkards — 1Co 6:10

THIGH

pray thee, thy hand under my *t.* — Ge 24:2
his hand under the *t.* of Abraham — Ge 24:9
he touched the hollow of his *t.* — Ge 32:25
hollow of Jacob's *t.* was out of joint — Ge 32:25
him, and he halted upon his *t.* — Ge 32:31
which is upon the hollow of the *t.* — Ge 32:32
touched the hollow of Jacob's *t.* in — Ge 32:32
I pray thee, thy hand under my *t.* — Ge 47:29
the Lord doth make thy *t.* to rot — Nu 5:21
thy belly to swell, and thy *t.* to rot — Nu 5:22
shall swell, and her *t.* shall rot — Nu 5:27
under his raiment upon his right *t.* — J'g 3:16
took the dagger from his right *t.* — J'g 3:21
And he smote them hip and *t.* with — J'g 15:8
Gird thy sword upon thy *t.* O most — Ps 45:3
man hath his sword upon his *t.* — Ca 3:8
bare the leg, uncover the *t.* — Isa 47:2
instructed, I smote upon my *t.* — Jer 31:19
smite therefore upon thy *t.* — Eze 21:12
good piece, the *t.* and the shoulder — Eze 24:4
and on his *t.* a name written — Re 19:16

THIGHS

the loins even unto the *t.* they — Ex 28:42
thicker than my father's *t.* (S) — 2Ch 10:10
the joints of thy *t.* are like jewels — Ca 7:1
silver, his belly and his *t.* of brass — Da 2:32

THIMNATHAH

And Elon, and *T.,* and Ekron — Jos 19:43

THIN

seven *t.* ears and blasted with the — Ge 41:6
And the seven *t.* ears devoured the — Ge 41:7
behold, seven ears, withered, *t.* — Ge 41:23
the *t.* ears, devoured the seven good — Ge 41:24
the seven *t.* and ill favoured kine — Ge 49:27
they did beat the gold into *t.* plates — Ex 39:3
and there be in it a yellow *t.* hair — Le 13:30

certain additions made of *t.* work   *1Ki 7:29*

the glory of Jacob shall be made *t.*   *Isa 17:4*

THINE

Lift up now *t.* eyes, and look from   *Ge 13:14*

delivered *t.* enemies into thy hand   *Ge 14:20*

that I will not take any thing that is *t.*   *Ge 14:23*

him, saying, This shall not be *t.* heir   *Ge 15:4*

out of *t.* own bowels shall be *t.* heir   *Ge 15:4*

surely die, thou, and all that are *t.*   *Ge 20:7*

up the lad, and hold him in *t.* hand   *Ge 21:18*

Take now thy son, *t.* only son Isaac   *Ge 22:2*

Lay not *t.* hand upon the lad, neither   *Ge 22:12*

withheld thy son, *t.* only son from me   *Ge 22:12*

hast not withheld thy son, *t.* only son   *Ge 22:16*

if I have found favour in *t.* eyes, tarry   *Ge 30:27*

he said, Lift up now *t.* eyes, and see   *Ge 31:12*

discern thou what is *t.* with me   *Ge 31:32*

and thy staff that is in *t.* hand   *Ge 38:18*

days shall Pharaoh lift up *t.* head   *Ge 40:13*

not *t.* anger burn against thy servant   *Ge 44:18*

shall put his hand upon *t.* eyes   *Ge 46:4*

Wherefore shall we die before *t.* eyes   *Ge 47:19*

thou begettest after them, shall be *t.*   *Ge 48:6*

shall be in the neck of *t.* enemies   *Ge 49:8*

Put forth *t.* hand, and take it by the   *Ex 4:4*

him, Put now *t.* hand into thy bosom   *Ex 4:6*

Put *t.* hand into thy bosom again   *Ex 4:7*

And thou shalt take this rod in *t.* hand   *Ex 4:17*

Pharaoh, which I have put in *t.* hand   *Ex 4:21*

but the fault is in *t.* own people   *Ex 5:16*

to a serpent shalt thou take in *t.* hand   *Ex 7:15*

stretch out *t.* hand upon the waters of   *Ex 7:19*

shall go up and come into *t.* house   *Ex 8:3*

and upon thy people, and into *t.* ovens   *Ex 8:3*

Stretch forth *t.* hand with thy rod over   *Ex 8:5*

send all my plagues upon *t.* heart   *Ex 9:14*

Stretch forth *t.* hand toward heaven   *Ex 9:22*

Stretch out *t.* hand over the land of   *Ex 10:12*

Stretch out *t.* hand toward heaven   *Ex 10:21*

be for a sign unto thee upon *t.* hand   *Ex 13:9*

and for a memorial between *t.* eyes   *Ex 13:9*

it shall be for a token upon *t.* hand   *Ex 13:16*

and for frontlets between *t.* eyes   *Ex 13:16*

and stretch out *t.* hand over the sea   *Ex 14:16; 14:26*

in the greatness of *t.* excellency thou   *Ex 15:7*

by the greatness of *t.* arm they shall   *Ex 15:16*

them in the mountain of *t.* inheritance   *Ex 15:17*

thou smotest the river, take in *t.* hand   *Ex 17:5*

offerings, thy sheep, and *t.* oxen   *Ex 20:24*

Likewise shalt thou do with *t.* oxen   *Ex 22:30*

put not *t.* hand with the wicked to be   *Ex 23:1*

meet *t.* enemy's ox or his ass going   *Ex 23:4*

that *t.* ox and *t.* ass may rest, and the   *Ex 23:12*

I will be an enemy unto *t.* enemies   *Ex 23:22*

and an adversary unto *t.* adversaries   *Ex 23:22*

I will make all *t.* enemies turn their   *Ex 23:27*

to whom thou swarest by *t.* own self   *Ex 32:13*

our sin, and take us for *t.* inheritance   *Ex 34:9*

all *t.* offerings thou shalt offer salt   *Le 2:13*

it shall be *t.* and thy sons with thee   *Le 10:15*

for theirs is *t.* own nakedness   *Le 18:10*

approach to his wife; she is *t.* aunt   *Le 18:14*

shalt not hate thy brother in *t.* heart   *Le 19:17*

he shall give *t.* estimation in that day   *Le 27:23*

redeem it according to *t.* estimation   *Le 27:27*

have lain with thee beside *t.* husband   *Nu 5:20*

Lord, and let *t.* enemies be scattered   *Nu 10:35*

shall be *t.* of the most holy things   *Nu 18:9*

And this is *t.*; the heave offering of   *Nu 18:11*

shall bring unto the Lord, shall be *t.*   *Nu 18:13*

every one that is clean in *t.* house   *Nu 18:13*

thing devoted in Israel shall be *t.*   *Nu 18:14*

it be of men or beasts shall be *t.*   *Nu 18:15*

redeem, according to *t.* estimation   *Nu 18:16*

And the flesh of them shall be *t.*   *Nu 18:18*

breast and as the right shoulder are *t.*   *Nu 18:18*

I am thy part and *t.* inheritance   *Nu 18:20*

Am not I *t.* ass upon which thou hast   *Nu 22:30*

ridden ever since I was *t.* unto this   *Nu 22:30*

thou smitten *t.* ass these three times   *Nu 22:32*

is the spirit, and lay *t.* upon him   *Nu 27:18*

shalt put some of *t.* honour upon him   *Nu 27:20*

I have given into *t.* hand Sihon the   *De 2:24*

T. eyes have seen all that the Lord   *De 3:21*

Pisgah, and lift up *t.* eyes westward   *De 3:27*

eastward, and behold it with *t.* eyes   *De 3:27*

the things which *t.* eyes have seen   *De 4:9*

lest thou lift up *t.* eyes unto heaven   *De 4:19*

consider it in *t.* heart that the Lord   *De 4:39*

not *t.* ox, nor *t.* ass, nor any of thy   *De 5:14*

the Lord thy God with all *t.* heart   *De 6:5*

thee this day, shall be in *t.* heart   *De 6:6*

of them when thou sittest in *t.* house   *De 6:7*

bind them for a sign upon *t.* hand   *De 6:8*

shall be as frontlets between *t.* eyes   *De 6:8*

To cast out all *t.* enemies from before   *De 6:19*

and thy wine, and *t.* oil, the increase   *De 7:13*

t. eye shall have no pity upon them   *De 7:16*

say in *t.* heart, These nations are   *De 7:17*

great temptations which *t.* eyes saw   *De 7:19*

shall deliver their kings into *t.* hand   *De 7:24*

bring an abomination into *t.* house   *De 7:26*

thee, to know what was in *t.* heart   *De 8:2*

Thou shalt also consider in *t.* heart   *De 8:5*

Then *t.* heart be lifted up, and thou   *De 8:14*

And thou say in *t.* heart, My power   *De 8:17*

Speak not thou in *t.* heart, after that   *De 9:4*

or for the uprightness of *t.* heart, dost   *De 9:5*

are thy people and *t.* inheritance   *De 9:29*

things, which *t.* eyes have seen   *De 10:21*

in thy corn, and thy wine, and *t.* oil   *De 11:14*

when thou sittest in *t.* house   *De 11:19*

them upon the door posts of *t.* house   *De 11:20*

offerings, or heave offering of *t.* hand   *De 12:17*

in all that thou puttest *t.* hands unto   *De 12:18*

thy friend, which is as *t.* own soul   *De 13:6*

neither shall *t.* eye pity him, neither   *De 13:8*

t. hand shall be first upon him to   *De 13:9*

of thy corn, of thy wine, and of *t.* oil   *De 14:23*

and bind up the money in *t.* hand   *De 14:25*

shalt rejoice, thou, and *t.* household   *De 14:26*

bring forth all the tithe of *t.* increase   *De 14:28*

bless thee in all the work of *t.* hand   *De 14:29*

but that which is *t.* with thy brother   *De 15:3*

with thy brother *t.* hand shall release   *De 15:3*

thee, thou shalt not harden *t.* heart   *De 15:7*

nor shut *t.* hand from thy poor brother   *De 15:7*

thou shalt open *t.* hand wide unto   *De 15:8*

t. eye be evil against thy poor brother   *De 15:9*

t. heart shall not be grieved when thou   *De 15:10*

in all that thou puttest *t.* hand unto   *De 15:10*

open *t.* hand wide unto thy brother   *De 15:11*

because he loveth thee and *t.* house   *De 15:16*

tribute of a freewill offering of *t.* hand   *De 16:10*

God shall bless thee in all *t.* increase   *De 16:15*

and in all the works of *t.* hands   *De 16:15*

of thy wine, and of *t.* oil, and the first   *De 18:4*

say in *t.* heart, How shall we know the   *De 18:21*

T. eye shall not pity him, but *t.* thou   *De 19:13*

of old time have set in *t.* inheritance   *De 19:14*

t. eye shall not pity; but life shall go   *De 19:21*

goest out to battle against *t.* enemies   *De 20:1*

thy God hath delivered it into *t.* hands   *De 20:13*

thou shalt eat the spoil of *t.* enemies   *De 20:14*

goest forth to war against *t.* enemies   *De 21:10*

God hath delivered them into *t.* hands   *De 21:10*

thou shalt bring her home to *t.* house   *De 21:12*

shall remain in *t.* house, and bewail   *De 21:13*

thou shalt bring it unto *t.* own house   *De 22:2*

thou bring not blood upon *t.* house   *De 22:8*

host goeth forth against *t.*   *De* 23:9
enemies
and to give up *t.* enemies   *De* 23:14
before thee
thee in all that thou settest   *De* 23:20
t. hand to
eat grapes thy fill at *t.*   *De* 23:24
own pleasure
mayest pluck the ears with *t.*   *De* 23:25
hand
cuttest down *t.* harvest in thy   *De* 24:19
field
bless thee in all the work of   *De* 24:19
t. hands
When thou beatest *t.* olive   *De* 24:20
tree, thou
off her hand, *t.* eye shall not   *De* 25:12
pity her
have in *t.* house divers   *De* 25:14
measures
given thee rest from all *t.*   *De* 25:19
enemies
shall take the basket out of *t.*   *De* 26:4
hand
given unto thee, and unto *t.*   *De* 26:11
house
all the tithes of *t.* increase   *De* 26:12
the third
keep and do them with all *t.*   *De* 26:16
heart
The Lord shall cause *t.*   *De* 28:7
enemies that
in all that thou settest *t.* hand   *De* 28:8;
unto   28:20
and to bless all the work of   *De* 28:12
t. hand
thee to be smitten before *t.*   *De* 28:25
enemies
T. ox shall be slain before *t.*   *De* 28:31
eyes, and
t. ass shall be violently taken   *De* 28:31
away
sheep shall be given unto *t.*   *De* 28:31
enemies
t. eyes shall look, and fail   *De* 28:32
with
there shall be no might in *t.*   *De* 28:32
hand
shalt be mad for the sight of   *De* 28:34
t. eyes
oil; for *t.* olive shall cast his   *De* 28:40
fruit
shalt thou serve *t.* enemies   *De* 28:48
which
thou shalt eat the fruit of *t.*   *De* 28:53
own body
t. enemies shall distress thee   *De* 28:53;
  28:55
t. enemy shall distress thee   *De* 28:57
in thy
fear of *t.* heart wherewith   *De* 28:67
thou shalt
for the sight of *t.* eyes which   *De* 28:67
thou
temptations which *t.* eyes have   *De* 29:3
seen
with all *t.* heart, and with all   *De* 30:2
thy soul
If any of *t.* be driven out unto   *De* 30:4
the
thy God will circumcise *t.*   *De* 30:6
heart
the Lord thy God with all   *De* 30:6;
t. heart   30:10
put all these curses upon *t.*   *De* 30:7
enemies
plenteous in every work of *t.*   *De* 30:9
hand
But if *t.* heart turn away, so   *De* 30:17
that thou
whole burnt sacrifice upon *t.*   *De* 33:10
altar
t. enemies shall be found   *De* 33:29
liars unto
caused thee to see it with *t.*   *De* 34:4
eyes
thee, which are entered into *t.*   *Jos* 2:3
house
We will be blameless of this *t.*   *Jos* 2:17
oath
then we will be quit of *t.*   *Jos* 2:20
oath which
I have given into *t.* hand   *Jos* 6:2
Jericho
canst not stand before *t.*   *Jos* 7:13
enemies
Ai; for I will give it into *t.*   *Jos* 8:18
hand

And now, behold, we are in   *Jos* 9:25
t. hand
I have delivered them into *t.*   *Jos* 10:8
hand
have trodden shall be *t.*   *Jos* 14:9
inheritance
But the mountain shall be *t.;*   *Jos* 17:18
for it is
and the outgoings of it shall   *Jos* 17:18
be *t.*
and I will deliver him into *t.*   *J'g* 4:7
hand
thou takest shall not be for *t.*   *J'g* 4:9
honour
hath delivered Sisera into *t.*   *J'g* 4:14
hand
So let all *t.* enemies perish, O   *J'g* 5:31
Lord
Let not *t.* anger be hot against   *J'g* 6:39
me
deliver the Midianites into *t.*   *J'g* 7:7
hand
for I have delivered it into *t.*   *J'g* 7:9
hand
shall *t.* hands be strengthened   *J'g* 7:11
Zebah and Zalmunna now in *t.*   *J'g* 8:6;
hand   8:15
we should give bread unto *t.*   *J'g* 8:6
army
to Abimelech, Increase *t.*   *J'g* 9:29
army, and
vengeance for thee of *t.*   *J'g* 11:36
enemies
burn *t.* house upon thee with   *J'g* 12:1
fire
thee, when *t.* heart is not   *J'g* 16:15
with me
lay *t.* hand upon thy mouth,   *J'g* 18:19
and go
Comfort *t.* heart with a   *J'g* 19:5
morsel of
all night, and let *t.* heart be   *J'g* 19:6
merry
said, Comfort *t.* heart, I pray   *J'g* 19:8
thee
here, that *t.* heart may be   *J'g* 19:9
merry
forth the man that came into   *J'g* 19:22
t. house
I will deliver them into *t.*   *J'g* 20:28
hand
Let *t.* eyes be on the field that   *Ru* 2:9
they do
Why have I found grace in *t.*   *Ru* 2:10
eyes
in law since the death of *t.*   *Ru* 2:11
husband
spoken friendly unto *t.*   *Ru* 2:13
handmaid
not like unto one of *t.*   *Ru* 2:13
handmaidens
answered, I am Ruth *t.*   *Ru* 3:9
handmaid
therefore thy skirt over *t.*   *Ru* 3:9
handmaid
that is come into *t.* house like   *Ru* 4:11
Rachel
thy life, and a nourisher of *t.*   *Ru* 4:15
old age
look on the affliction of *t.*   *1Sa* 1:11
handmaid
me, and not forget *t.*   *1Sa* 1:11
handmaid
wilt give unto *t.* handmaid   *1Sa* 1:11
a man
Count not *t.* handmaid for a   *1Sa* 1:16
daughter
Let *t.* handmaid find grace in   *1Sa* 1:18
thy
days come, that I will cut off   *1Sa* 2:31
t. arm
shall not be an old man in *t.*   *1Sa* 2:31
house
not be an old man in *t.* house   *1Sa* 2:32
for ever
the man of *t.* whom I shall   *1Sa* 2:33
not cut
consume *t.* eyes and to grieve   *1Sa* 2:33
t. heart
all the increase of *t.* house   *1Sa* 2:33
shall die
every one that is left in *t.*   *1Sa* 2:36
house shall
and will tell thee all that is in   *1Sa* 9:19
t. heart
for *t.* asses that were lost   *1Sa* 9:20
three days
unto him, Do all that is in *t.*   *1Sa* 14:7
heart

unto the priest, Withdraw *t.*   *1Sa* 14:19
hand
When thou wast little in *t.*   *1Sa* 15:17
own sight
and hath given it to a   *1Sa* 15:28
neighbour of *t.*
fill *t.* horn with oil, and go, I   *1Sa* 16:1
will send
pride, and the naughtiness   *1Sa* 17:28
of *t.* heart
thee, and take *t.* head from   *1Sa* 17:46
thee
that I have found grace in *t.*   *1Sa* 20:3
eyes
if I have found favour in *t.*   *1Sa* 20:29
eyes, let
the son of Jesse to *t.* own   *1Sa* 20:30
confusion
Now therefore what is under   *1Sa* 21:3
t. hand
is there not here under *t.* hand   *1Sa* 21:8
spear
bidding, and is honourable in   *1Sa* 22:14
t. house
deliver the Philistines into *t.*   *1Sa* 23:4
hand
I will deliver *t.* enemy into *t.*   *1Sa* 24:4
hand
this day *t.* eyes have seen   *1Sa* 24:10
how that the
cause, and deliver me out of   *1Sa* 24:15
t. hand
Lord had delivered me into *t.*   *1Sa* 24:18
hand
Israel shall be established in   *1Sa* 24:20
t. hand
both to thee, and peace be to   *1Sa* 25:6
t. house
the young men find favour in   *1Sa* 25:8
t. eyes
whatsoever cometh to *t.* hand   *1Sa* 25:8
unto
and let *t.* handmaid, I pray   *1Sa* 25:24
thee
speak in *t.* audience, and   *1Sa* 25:24
hear the
and hear the words of *t.*   *1Sa* 25:24
handmaid
I *t.* handmaid saw not the   *1Sa* 25:25
young men
avenging thyself with *t.* own   *1Sa* 25:26
hand
now let *t.* enemies, and they   *1Sa* 25:26
that
now this blessing which *t.*   *1Sa* 25:27
handmaid
forgive the trespass of *t.*   *1Sa* 25:28
handmaid
and the souls of *t.* enemies   *1Sa* 25:29
them shall
my lord, then remember *t.*   *1Sa* 25:31
handmaid
unto her, Go up in peace to   *1Sa* 25:35
t. house
let *t.* handmaid be a servant   *1Sa* 25:41
to wash
hath delivered *t.* enemy into *t.*   *1Sa* 26:8
hand
my soul was precious in *t.*   *1Sa* 26:21
eyes this
If I have now found grace in   *1Sa* 27:5
t. eyes
from thee, and is become *t.*   *1Sa* 28:16
enemy
hath rent the kingdom out of   *1Sa* 28:17
t. hand
t. handmaid hath obeyed thy   *1Sa* 28:21
voice
also unto the voice of *t.*   *1Sa* 28:22
handmaid
not afraid to stretch forth *t.*   *2Sa* 1:14
hand to
thou wast slain in *t.* high   *2Sa* 1:25
places
reign over all that *t.* heart   *2Sa* 3:21
desireth
Ish-bosheth the son of Saul *t.*   *2Sa* 4:8
enemy
deliver the Philistines into *t.*   *2Sa* 5:19
hand
the king, Go do all that is in   *2Sa* 7:3
t. heart
have cut off all *t.* enemies out   *2Sa* 7:9
of thy
thee to rest from all *t.*   *2Sa* 7:11
enemies
t. house and thy kingdom   *2Sa* 7:16
shall be
according to *t.* own heart,   *2Sa* 7:21
hast thou

didst thou not go down unto t. house	2Sa 11:10
shall never depart from t. house	2Sa 12:10
evil against thee out of t. own house	2Sa 12:11
I will take thy wives before t. eyes	2Sa 12:11
chamber, that I may eat of t. hand	2Sa 13:10
family is risen against t. handmaid	2Sa 14:7
Go to t. house, and I will give charge	2Sa 14:8
Let t. handmaid, I pray thee, speak	2Sa 14:12
Then t. handmaid said, The word of	2Sa 14:17
words in the mouth of t. handmaid	2Sa 14:19
t. are all that pertained unto	2Sa 16:4
thou go to battle in t. own person	2Sa 17:11
In that thou lovest t. enemies	2Sa 19:6
do therefore what is good in t. eyes	2Sa 19:27
them that did eat at t. own table	2Sa 19:28
him, Hear the words of t. handmaid	2Sa 20:17
t. eyes are upon the haughty	2Sa 22:28
flee three months before t. enemies	2Sa 24:13
people. It is enough: stay now t. hand	2Sa 24:16
let t. hand, I pray thee, be against me	2Sa 24:17
that thou mayest save t. own life, and	1Ki 1:12
O king, swear unto t. handmaid	1Ki 1:13
by the Lord thy God unto t. handmaid	1Ki 1:17
said unto him, Go to t. house	1Ki 1:53
thee to Anathoth, unto t. own fields	1Ki 2:26
thy blood shall be upon t. own head	1Ki 2:37
wickedness which t. heart is privy to	1Ki 2:44
thy wickedness upon t. own head	1Ki 2:44
nor hast asked the life of t. enemies	1Ki 3:11
beside me, while t. handmaid slept	1Ki 3:20
it be neither mine nor t. but divide it	1Ki 3:26
it was in t. heart to build an house	1Ki 8:18
thou didst well that it was in t. heart	1Ki 8:18
and hast fulfilled it with t. hand	1Ki 8:24
That t. eyes may be open toward this	1Ki 8:29
the oath come before t. altar in this	1Ki 8:31
they be thy people, and t. inheritance	1Ki 8:51
That t. eyes may be open unto the	1Ki 8:52
of the earth, to be t. inheritance	1Ki 8:53
thou seekest to go to t. own country	1Ki 11:22
now see to t. own house, David	1Ki 12:16
If thou wilt give me half t. house, I	1Ki 13:8
Bring him back with thee unto t. house	1Ki 13:18
therefore, get thee to t. own house	1Ki 14:12
thee, a morsel of bread in t. hand	1Ki 17:11
thrown down t. altas, and slain thy	1Ki 19:10; 19:14
thy saying, I am t. and all that I have	1Ki 20:4
they shall search t. house, and the	1Ki 20:6
that whatsoever is pleasant in t. eyes	1Ki 20:6
I will deliver it into t. hand this day	1Ki 20:13
all this great multiude into t. hand	1Ki 20:28
eat bread, and let t. heart be merry	1Ki 21:7
shall dogs lick thy blood, even t.	1Ki 21:19
And will make t. house like the house	1Ki 21:22
Turn t. hand, and carry me out of the	1Ki 22:34
T. handmaid hath not any thing in	2Ki 4:2
of God, do not lie unto t. handmaid	2Ki 4:16
and take my staff in t. hand, and go	2Ki 4:29
thou shalt see it with t. eyes, but	2Ki 7:2; 7:19
Arise, and go thou and t. household	2Ki 8:1
Take a present in t. hand, and go	2Ki 8:8
and take this box of oil in t. hand	2Ki 9:1
do thou that which is good in t. eyes	2Ki 10:5
Is t. heart right, as my heart is with	2Ki 10:15
of Israel, Put t. hand upon the bow	2Ki 13:16
and t. heart hath lifted thee up	2Ki 14:10
Lord, bow down t. ear, and hear	2Ki 19:16
open, Lord, t. eyes, and see: and hear	2Ki 19:16
voice, and lifted up t. eyes on high	2Ki 19:22
Set t. house in order; for thou shalt	2Ki 20:1
said, What have they seen in t. house	2Ki 20:15
days come, that all that is in t. house	2Ki 20:17
Because t. heart was tender, and thou	2Ki 22:19
t. eyes shall not see all the evil which	2Ki 22:20
and that t. hand might be with me	1Ch 4:10
T. are we, David, and on thy side	1Ch 12:18
unto thee, and peace be to t. helpers	1Ch 12:18
for I will deliver them into t. hand	1Ch 14:10
unto David, Do all that is in t. heart	1Ch 17:2
cut off all t. enemies from before thee	1Ch 17:8
Moreover I will subdue all t. enemies	1Ch 17:10
was a small thing in t. eyes, O God	1Ch 17:17
according to t. own heart, hast thou	1Ch 17:19
Israel didst thou make t. own people	1Ch 17:22
sword of t. enemies overtaketh thee	1Ch 21:12
It is enough, stay now t. hand	1Ch 21:15
let t. hand, I pray thee, O Lord my	1Ch 21:17
not take that which is t. for the Lord	1Ch 21:24
T. O Lord, is the greatness, and the	1Ch 29:11
is in the heaven and in the earth is t.	1Ch 29:11
t. is the kingdom, O Lord, and thou	1Ch 29:11
and in t. hand is power and might	1Ch 29:12
and in t. hand it is to make great, and	1Ch 29:12
and of t. own have we given thee	1Ch 29:14
build thee an house for t. holy name	1Ch 29:16
cometh of t. hand, and is all t. own	1Ch 29:16
Because this was in t. heart, and thou	2Ch 1:11
or honour, nor the life of t. enemies	2Ch 1:11
as it was in t. heart to build an house	2Ch 6:8
didst well that it was in t. heart	2Ch 6:8
and hast fulfilled it with t. hand, as it	2Ch 6:15
That t. eyes may be open upon this	2Ch 6:20
the oath come before t. altar in this	2Ch 6:22
Now, my God, let t. eyes be open	2Ch 6:40
let t. ears be attent unto the prayer	2Ch 6:40
turn not away the face of t. anointed	2Ch 6:42
I heard in mine own land of t. acts	2Ch 9:5
and now, David, see to t. own house	2Ch 10:16
king of Syria escaped out of t. hand	2Ch 16:7
Lord, he delivered them into t. hand	2Ch 16:8
Turn t. hand, that thou mayest carry	2Ch 18:33
hast prepared t. heart to seek God	2Ch 19:3
in t. hand is there not power	2Ch 20:6
their own people out of t. hand	2Ch 25:15
and t. heart lifteth thee up to boast	2Ch 25:19
why shouldest thou meddle to t. hurt	2Ch 25:19
neither shall it be for t. honour from	2Ch 26:18
Because t. heart was tender, and thou	2Ch 34:27
neither shall t. eyes see all the evil	2Ch 34:28
law of thy God which is in t. hand	Ezr 7:14
wisdom of thy God, that is in t. hand	Ezr 7:25
Let t. ear now be attentive, and	Ne 1:6
and t. eyes open, that thou mayest	Ne 1:6
let now t. ear be attentive to the prayer	Ne 1:11
thou feignest them out of t. own heart	Ne 6:8
But put forth t. hand now, and touch	Job 1:11; 2:5
upon himself put not forth t. hand	Job 1:12
he is in t. hand; but save his life	Job 2:6
Dost thou still retain t. integrity	Job 2:9
t. offspring as the grass of the earth	Job 5:25
t. eyes are upon me, and I am not	Job 7:8
thou shouldest set t. heart upon him	Job 7:17
shouldest despise the work of t. hands	Job 10:3
none that can deliver out of t. hand	Job 10:7
T. hands have made me and	Job 10:8
these things hast thou hid in t. heart	Job 10:13
increasest t. indignation upon me	Job 10:17
is pure, and I am clean in t. eyes	Job 11:4
of the less than t. iniquity deserveth	Job 11:6
If thou prepare t. heart, and stretch	Job 11:13
and stretch out t. hands toward him	Job 11:13
If iniquity be in t. hand, put it far	Job 11:14
And t. age shall be clearer than the	Job 11:17
Withdraw t. hand far from me: and	Job 13:21
thy face, and holdest me for t. enemy	Job 13:24
thou open t. eyes upon such an one	Job 14:3
have a desire to the work of t. hands	Job 14:15
For thy mouth uttereth t. iniquity	Job 15:5
T. own mouth condemneth thee, and	Job 15:6
yea, t. own lips testify against thee	Job 15:6
Why doth t. heart carry thee away	Job 15:12
great? and t. iniquities infinite	Job 22:5
and lay up his words in t. heart	Job 22:22

delivered by the pureness of *t.* hands — *Job 22:30*

him? or what receiveth he of *t.* hand — *Job 35:7*

that *t.* own right hand can save thee — *Job 40:14*

Lay *t.* hand upon him, remember — *Job 41:8*

thee the heathen for *t.* inheritance — *Ps 2:8*

O Lord, rebuke me not in *t.* anger — *Ps 6:1*

Arise, O Lord, in *t.* anger, lift up — *Ps 7:6*

strength because of *t.* enemies — *Ps 8:2*

O God, lift up *t.* hand: forget not the — *Ps 10:12*

heart, thou wilt cause *t.* ear to hear — *Ps 10:17*

wilt thou suffer *t.* Holy One to see — *Ps 16:10*

let *t.* eyes behold the things that are — *Ps 17:2*

incline *t.* ear unto me, and hear my — *Ps 17:6*

Grant thee according to *t.* own heart — *Ps 20:4*

T. hand shall find out all *t.* enemies — *Ps 21:8*

as a fiery oven in the time of *t.* anger — *Ps 21:9*

make ready *t.* arrows upon thy strings — *Ps 21:12*

thou exalted, Lord, in *t.* own strength — *Ps 21:13*

so will I compass *t.* altar, O Lord — *Ps 26:6*

the place where *t.* honour dwelleth — *Ps 26:8*

and he shall strengthen *t.* heart — *Ps 27:14*

thy people, and bless *t.* inheritance — *Ps 28:9*

Bow down *t.* ear to me; deliver me — *Ps 31:2*

Into *t.* hand I commit my spirit: thou — *Ps 31:5*

haste, I am cut off from before *t.* eyes — *Ps 31:32*

he shall give thee the desire of *t.* heart — *Ps 37:4*

For *t.* arrows stick fast in me, and thy — *Ps 38:2*

in my flesh because of *t.* anger — *Ps 38:3*

I am consumed by the blow of *t.* hand — *Ps 39:10*

t. arm, the light of thy countenance — *Ps 44:3*

T. arrows are sharp in the heart of the — *Ps 45:5*

and consider, and incline *t.* ear — *Ps 45:10*

forget also *t.* own people, and thy — *Ps 45:10*

thou slanderest *t.* own mother's son — *Ps 50:20*

and set them in order before *t.* eyes — *Ps 50:21*

shall they offer bullocks upon *t.* altar — *Ps 51:19*

in *t.* anger cast down the people — *Ps 56:7*

shall *t.* enemies submit themselves — *Ps 66:3*

thou didst confirm *t.* inheritance — *Ps 68:9*

he dipped in the blood of *t.* enemies — *Ps 68:23*

the zeal of *t.* house hath eaten me up — *Ps 69:9*

Pour out *t.* indignation upon them — *Ps 69:24*

incline *t.* ear unto me, and save me — *Ps 71:2*

of thy righteousness, even of *t.* only — *Ps 71:16*

why doth *t.* anger smoke against the — *Ps 74:1*

rod of *t.* inheritance, which thou hast — *Ps 74:2*

T. enemies roar in the midst of thy — *Ps 74:4*

The day is *t.* the night also is *t.:* thou — *Ps 74:10*

Arise, O God, plead *t.* own cause — *Ps 74:22*

Forget not the voice of *t.* enemies: the — *Ps 74:23*

has with *t.* arm redeemed thy people — *Ps 77:15*

a sound: *t.* arrows also went abroad — *Ps 77:17*

heathen are come into *t.* inheritance — *Ps 79:1*

For, lo, *t.* enemies make a tumult — *Ps 83:2*

she may lay her young, even *t.* altars — *Ps 84:3*

and look upon the face of *t.* anointed — *Ps 84:9*

thyself from the fierceness of *t.* anger — *Ps 85:3*

and cause *t.* anger toward us to cease — *Ps 85:4*

wilt thou draw out *t.* anger to all — *Ps 85:5*

Bow down *t.* ear, O Lord, hear me: for — *Ps 86:1*

and save the son of *t.* handmaid — *Ps 86:16*

before thee; incline *t.* ear into my cry — *Ps 88:2*

hast scattered *t.* enemies with thy — *Ps 89:10*

the heavens are *t.* the earth also is *t.* — *Ps 89:11*

thou hast been wroth with *t.* anointed — *Ps 89:38*

Wherewith *t.* enemies reproached — *Ps 89:51*

reproached the footsteps of *t.* anointed — *Ps 89:51*

For we are consumed by *t.* anger, and — *Ps 90:7*

Who knoweth the power of *t.* anger — *Ps 90:11*

Only with *t.* eyes shalt thou behold — *Ps 91:8*

For, lo, *t.* enemies, O Lord, for, lo — *Ps 92:9*

t. enemies shall perish; all the — *Ps 92:9*

holiness becometh *t.* house, O Lord — *Ps 93:5*

people, O Lord, and afflict *t.* heritage — *Ps 94:5*

am in trouble; incline *t.* ear unto me — *Ps 102:2*

Because of *t.* indignation and thy — *Ps 102:10*

Who forgiveth all *t.* iniquities; who — *Ps 103:3*

thou openest *t.* hand, they are filled — *Ps 104:28*

that I may glory with *t.* inheritance — *Ps 106:5*

until I make *t.* enemies thy footstool — *Ps 110:1*

rule thou in the midst of *t.* enemies — *Ps 110:2*

servant, and the son of *t.* handmaid — *Ps 116:16*

this day according to *t.* ordinances — *Ps 119:91*

I am *t.* save me; for I have sought — *Ps 119:94*

Let *t.* hand help me; for I have chosen — *Ps 119:173*

thou shalt eat the labour of *t.* hands — *Ps 128:2*

a fruitful vine by the side of *t.* house — *Ps 128:3*

let *t.* ears be attentive to the voice of — *Ps 130:2*

turn not away the face of *t.* anointed — *Ps 132:10*

thou shalt stretch forth *t.* hand against — *Ps 138:7*

forsake not the works of *t.* own hands — *Ps 138:8*

and before, and laid *t.* hand upon me — *Ps 139:5*

T. eyes did see my substance — *Ps 139:16*

and *t.* enemies take thy name in vain — *Ps 139:20*

shoot out *t.* arrows, and destroy them — *Ps 144:6*

Send *t.* hand from above; rid me, and — *Ps 144:7*

Thou openest *t.* hand, and satisfiest — *Ps 145:16*

that thou incline *t.* ear unto wisdom — *Pr 2:2*

and apply *t.* heart to understanding — *Pr 2:2*

When wisdom entereth into *t.* — *Pr 2:10*

let *t.* heart keep my commandments — *Pr 3:1*

write them upon the table of *t.* heart — *Pr 3:3*

Trust in the Lord with all *t.* heart — *Pr 3:5*

lean not unto *t.* own understanding — *Pr 3:5*

Be not wise in *t.* own eyes: fear — *Pr 3:7*

with the firstfruits of all *t.* increase — *Pr 3:9*

son, let not them depart from *t.* eyes — *Pr 3:21*

it is in the power of *t.* hand to do it — *Pr 3:27*

unto me, Let *t.* heart retain my words — *Pr 4:4*

give to *t.* head an ornament of grace — *Pr 4:9*

words; incline *t.* ear unto my sayings — *Pr 4:20*

Let them not depart from *t.* eyes — *Pr 4:21*

keep them in the midst of *t.* heart — *Pr 4:21*

Let *t.* eyes look right on, and let — *Pr 4:25*

let *t.* eyelids look straight before thee — *Pr 4:25*

and bow *t.* ear to my understanding — *Pr 5:1*

Lest thou give *t.* honour unto others — *Pr 5:9*

Drink waters out of *t.* own cistern, and — *Pr 5:15*

and running waters out of *t.* own well — *Pr 5:15*

Let them be only *t.* own, and not — *Pr 5:17*

Give not sleep to *t.* eyes, nor slumber — *Pr 6:4*

eyes, nor slumber to *t.* eyelids — *Pr 6:4*

Bind them continually upon *t.* heart — *Pr 6:21*

Lust not after her beauty in *t.* heart — *Pr 6:25*

live; and my law as the apple of *t.* eye — *Pr 7:2*

write them upon the table of *t.* heart — *Pr 7:3*

Let not *t.* heart decline to her ways, go — *Pr 7:25*

open *t.* eyes, and thou shalt be satisfied — *Pr 20:13*

Bow down *t.* ear, and hear the words — *Pr 22:17*

and apply *t.* heart unto my knowledge — *Pr 22:17*

to be rich: cease from *t.* own wisdom — *Pr 23:4*

thou set *t.* eyes upon that which is not — *Pr 23:5*

Apply *t.* heart unto instruction, and — *Pr 23:12*

and *t.* ears to the words of knowledge — *Pr 23:12*

if *t.* heart be wise, my heart shall — *Pr 23:15*

Let not *t.* heart envy sinners; but be — *Pr 23:17*

and *t.* expectation shall not be cut off — *Pr 23:18*

be wise, and guide *t.* heart in the way — *Pr 23:19*

My son, give me *t.* heart, and let — *Pr 23:26*

heart, and let *t.* eyes observe my ways — *Pr 23:26*

T. eyes shall behold strange women — *Pr 23:33*

t. heart shall utter perverse things — *Pr 23:33*

Rejoice not when *t.* enemy falleth, and — *Pr 24:17*

let not *t.* heart be glad when he — *Pr 24:17*

field; and afterwards build *t.* house — *Pr 24:27*

of the prince whom *t.* eyes have seen — *Pr 25:7*

shame, and *t.* infamy turn not away — *Pr 25:10*

If *t.* enemy be hungry, give him bread — *Pr 25:21*

praise thee, and not *t.* own mouth — *Pr 27:2*

a stranger, and not *t.* own lips — *Pr 27:2*

T. own friend, and thy father's friend — *Pr 27:10*

evil, lay hand upon thy mouth — *Pr 30:32*

not *t.* heart be hasty to utter any thing — *Ec 5:2*

and destroy the work of t. hands	Ec 5:6
also from this withdraw not t. hand	Ec 7:18
oftentimes also t. own heart knoweth	Ec 7:22
in the evening withhold not t. hand	Ec 11:6
and walk in the ways of t. heart, and	Ec 11:9
and in the sight of t. eyes: but know	Ec 11:9
ravished my heart with one of t. eyes	Ca 4:9
smell of t. ointments than all spices	Ca 4:10
turn away t. eyes from me, for they	Ca 6:5
t. eyes like the fishpools in Heshbon	Ca 7:4
T. head upon thee is like Carmel, and	Ca 7:5
and the hair of t. head like purple	Ca 7:5
Set me as a seal upon t. heart, as a seal	Ca 8:6
as a seal upon t. arm; for love is	Ca 8:6
t. iniquity is taken away, and thy sin	Isa 6:7
t. anger is turned away, and thou	Isa 12:1
For thou hast said in t. heart, I will	Isa 14:13
fire of t. enemies shall devour them	Isa 26:11
but t. eyes shall see thy teachers	Isa 30:20
t. ears shall hear a word behind thee	Isa 30:21
T. eyes shall see the king in beauty	Isa 33:17
T. heart shall meditate terror. Where	Isa 33:18
t. eyes shall see Jerusalem a quiet	Isa 33:20
Incline t. ear, O Lord, and hear; open	Isa 37:17
hear; open t. eyes, O Lord, and see	Isa 37:17
thy voice, and lifted up t. eyes on high	Isa 37:23
Set t. house in order: for thou shalt	Isa 38:1
he, What have they seen in t. house	Isa 39:4
days come, that all that is in t. house	Isa 39:6
will hold t. hand, and will keep thee	Isa 42:6
hast wearied me with t. iniquities	Isa 43:24
and my blessing upon t. offspring	Isa 44:3
over unto thee, and they shall be t.	Isa 45:14
and given them into t. hand	Isa 47:6
that sayest in t. heart, I am, and none	Isa 47:8
great abundance of t. enchantments	Isa 47:9
and thou hast said in t. heart, I am	Isa 47:10
Stand now with t. enchantments, and	Isa 47:12
that time that t. ear was not opened	Isa 48:8
Lift up t. eyes round about	Isa 49:18
the other, shall say again in t. ears	Isa 49:20
Then shalt thou say in t. heart, Who	Isa 49:21
have taken out of t. hand the cup of	Isa 51:22
forth the curtains of t. habitations	Isa 54:2
For thy Maker is t. husband	Isa 54:5
thou hast found the life of t. hand	Isa 57:10
thou hide not thyself from t. own flesh	Isa 58:7
t. health shall spring forth speedily	Isa 58:8
honour him, not doing t. own ways	Isa 58:13
nor finding t. own pleasure	Isa 58:13
pleasure, nor speaking t. own words	Isa 58:13
Lift up t. eyes round about, and see	Isa 60:4
t. heart shall fear, and be enlarged	Isa 60:5
peace, and t. exactors righteousness	Isa 60:17
the Lord shall be t. everlasting light	Isa 60:20
thy corn to be meat for t. enemies	Isa 62:8
Wherefore art thou red in t. apparel	Isa 63:2
sake, the tribes of t. inheritance	Isa 63:17
We art t.: thou never barest rule	Isa 63:19
thy name known to t. adversaries	Isa 64:2
of thy youth, the love of t. espousals	Jer 2:2
T. own wickedness shall correct thee	Jer 2:19
yet t. iniquity is marked before me	Jer 2:22
from him, and t. hands upon t. head	Jer 2:37
Lift up t. eyes unto the high places	Jer 3:2
Only acknowledge t. iniquity	Jer 3:13
put away t. abominations out of my	Jer 4:1
wash t. heart from wickedness	Jer 4:14
because it reacheth unto t. heart	Jer 4:18
Lord, are not t. eyes upon the truth	Jer 5:3
shall eat up t. harvest, and thy bread	Jer 5:17
shall eat up thy flocks and t. herds	Jer 5:17
turn back t. hand as a grapegatherer	Jer 6:9
Cut off t. hair, O Jerusalem, and cast	Jer 7:29
T. habitation is in the midst of	Jer 9:6
not in t. anger, lest thou bring me to	Jer 10:24
And if thou say in t. heart, Wherefore	Jer 13:22
For the greatness of t. iniquity are thy	Jer 13:22
I have seen t. adulteries, and thy	Jer 13:27
and t. abominations on the hills in	Jer 13:27
to pass with t. enemies into a land	Jer 15:14
discontinue from t. heritage that I	Jer 17:4
I will cause thee to serve t. enemies in	Jer 17:4
thus with them in the time of t. anger	Jer 18:23
enemies, and t. eyes shall behold it	Jer 20:4
Pashur, and all that dwell in t. house	Jer 20:6
But t. eyes and t. heart are not but for	Jer 22:17
refuse to take the cup at t. hand to	Jer 25:28
now this word that I speak in t. ears	Jer 28:7
one. for the multitude of t. iniquity	Jer 30:14
Why criest thou for t. affliction? thy	Jer 30:15
for the multitude of t. iniquity	Jer 30:15
all t. adversaries, every one of them	Jer 30:16
from weeping, and t. eyes from tears	Jer 31:16
And there is hope in t. end, saith	Jer 31:17
set t. heart toward the highway, even	Jer 31:21
Hanameel the son of Shallum t. uncle	Jer 32:7
the right of redemption is t. to buy it	Jer 32:7
for the right of inheritance is t. and	Jer 32:8
the redemption is t.; buy it for thyself	Jer 32:8
for t. eyes are open upon all the ways	Jer 32:19
t. eyes shall behold the eyes of	Jer 34:3
Take in t. hand the roll wherein thou	Jer 36:14
rotten rags under t. armholes under	Jer 38:12
fire; and thou shalt live, and t. house	Jer 38:17
the chains which were upon t. hand	Jer 40:4
few of many, as t. eyes do behold us	Jer 42:2
Take great stones in t. hand	Jer 43:9
and the pride of t. heart, O thou that	Jer 49:16
abundant in treasures, t. end is come	Jer 51:13
they have not discovered t. iniquity	La 2:14
t. enemies have opened their mouth	La 2:16
caused t. enemy to rejoice over thee	La 2:17
set up the horn of t. adversaries	La 2:17
rest; let not the apple of t. eye cease	La 2:18
pour out t. heart like water before	La 2:19
hast slain them in the day of t. anger	La 2:21
hide not t. ear at my breathing, at my	La 3:56
The punishment of t. iniquity is	La 4:22
he will visit t. iniquity, O daughter of	La 4:22
speak unto thee receive in t. heart	Eze 3:10
heart, and hear with t. ears	Eze 3:10
his blood will I require at t. hand	Eze 3:18; 3:20
me, Go, shut thyself within t. house	Eze 3:24
and t. arm shall be uncovered	Eze 4:7
and cause it to pass upon t. head and	Eze 5:1
like, because of all t. abominations	Eze 5:9
and with all t. abominations, therefore	Eze 5:11
Smite with t. hand, and stamp with	Eze 6:11
upon thee all t. abominations	Eze 7:3
t. abominations shall be in the midst	Eze 7:4
thee for all t. abominations	Eze 7:8
thy ways and t. abominations that are	Eze 7:9
lift up t. eyes now the way toward the	Eze 8:5
fill t. hands with coals of fire between	Eze 10:2
saw thee polluted in t. own blood, I	Eze 16:6
are fashioned, and t. hair is grown	Eze 16:7
thy forehead, and earrings in t. ears	Eze 16:12
and a beautiful crown upon t. head	Eze 16:12
But thou didst trust in t. own beauty	Eze 16:15
t. abominations and thy whoredoms	Eze 16:22
and have diminished t. ordinary food	Eze 16:27
How weak is t. heart, saith the Lord	Eze 16:30
buildest t. eminent place in the head	Eze 16:31
makest t. high place in every street	Eze 16:31
shall throw down t. eminent place	Eze 16:39
they shall burn t. houses with fire, and	Eze 16:41
will recompense thy way upon t. head	Eze 16:43
lewdness above all t. abominations	Eze 16:43
t. elder sister is Samaria she and her	Eze 16:46
multiplied t. abominations more than	Eze 16:51
thy sisters in all t. abominations	Eze 16:51
bear t. own shame for thy sins that	Eze 16:52
That thou mayest bear t. own shame	Eze 16:54
thy lewdness and t. abominations	Eze 16:58

thy sisters, *t*. elder and thy *Eze 16:61*
younger
prophesy, and smite *t*. hands *Eze 21:14*
together
and hast defiled thyself in *t*. *Eze 22:4*
idols
Can *t*. heart endure, or can *Eze 22:14*
can *t*. hands be strong, in *Eze 22:14*
the days
shalt take *t*. inheritance in *Eze 22:16*
thyself
shall take away thy nose and *Eze 23:25*
t. ears
shalt not lift up *t*. eyes unto *Eze 23:27*
them
will I give her cup into *t*. *Eze 23:31*
hand
thereof, and pluck off *t*. own *Eze 23:34*
breasts
the desire of *t*. eyes with a *Eze 24:16*
stroke
bind the tire of *t*. head upon *Eze 24:17*
thee
to cause thee to hear it with *Eze 24:26*
t. ears
Because thou hast clapped *t*. *Eze 25:6*
hands
of Bashan have they made *t*. *Eze 27:6*
oars
of Lud and of Phut were in *Eze 27:10*
t. army
The men of Arvad with *t*. *Eze 27:11*
army were
isles were the merchandise *Eze 27:15*
of *t*. hand
Because *t*. heart is lifted up, *Eze 28:2*
and thou
thou set *t*. heart as the heart *Eze 28:2*
of God
thy wisdom and with *t*. *Eze 28:4*
understanding
t. heart is lifted up because *Eze 28:5*
of thy
hast set *t*. heart as the heart *Eze 28:6*
of God
T. heart was lifted up *Eze 28:17*
because of thy
by the multitude of *t*. *Eze 28:18*
iniquities, by
but his blood will I require at *Eze 33:8*
t. hand
I will even do according to *Eze 35:11*
t. anger
according to *t*. envy which *Eze 35:11*
thou hast
and they shall become one *Eze 37:17*
in *t*. hand
shall be in *t*. hand before *Eze 37:20*
their eyes
will bring thee forth, and all *Eze 38:4*
t. army
turn *t*. hand upon the *Eze 38:12*
desolate places
t. arrows to fall out of thy *Eze 39:3*
right hand
me, Son of man, behold with *Eze 40:4*
t. eyes
eyes, and hear with *t*. ears *Eze 40:4*
set *t*. heart upon all that I *Eze 40:4*
shall shew
mark well, and behold with *Eze 44:5*
t. eyes
hear with *t*. ears all that I *Eze 44:5*
say unto
cause the blessing to rest in *Eze 44:30*
t. house
the heaven hath he given into *Da 2:38*
t. hand
and he will deliver us out of *t*. *Da 3:17*
hand
interpretation thereof to *t*. *Da 4:19*
enemies
t. iniquities by shewing mercy *Da 4:27*
to the
hast not humbled *t*. heart, *Da 5:22*
though
t. anger and thy fury be *Da 9:16*
turned away
O my God, incline *t*. ear, and *Da 9:18*
hear
open *t*. eyes, and behold our *Da 9:18*
defer not, for *t*. own sake, O *Da 9:19*
my God
thou didst set *t*. heart to *Da 10:12*
understand
mad, for the multitude of *Ho 9:7*
t. iniquity
thyself; but in me is *t*. help *Ho 13:9*
for thou hast fallen by *t*. *Ho 14:1*
iniquity

and give not *t*. heritage to *Joe 2:17*
reproach
the pride of *t*. heart hath *Ob 3*
deceived
reward shall return upon *t*. own *Ob 15*
head
What is *t*. occupation? and *Jon 1:8*
whence
came in unto thee, into *t*. holy *Jon 2:7*
temple
thee from the hand of *t*. *Mic 4:10*
enemies
of Zion: for I will make *t*. *Mic 4:13*
horn iron
T. hand shall be lifted up *Mic 5:9*
upon
shall be lifted up upon *t*. *Mic 5:9*
adversaries
and all *t*. enemies shall be cut *Mic 5:9*
off
will cut off witchcrafts out of *Mic 5:12*
t. hand
more worship the work of *t*. *Mic 5:13*
hands
the flock of *t*. heritage, which *Mic 7:14*
dwell
be set wide open unto *t*. *Na 3:13*
enemies
was *t*. anger against the *Hab 3:8*
rivers? was
that thou didst ride upon *t*. *Hab 3:8*
at the light of *t*. arrows they *Hab 3:11*
went
even for salvation with *t*. *Hab 3:13*
anointed
walk through the sea with *Hab 3:15*
t. horses
judgments, he hath cast out *t*. *Zep 3:15*
enemy
and to Zion, Let not *t*. hands *Zep 3:16*
be slack
I have caused *t*. iniquity to *Zec 3:4*
pass from
Lift up now *t*. eyes, and see *Zec 5:5*
what is
What are these wounds in *t*. *Zec 13:6*
hands
Agree with *t*. adversary *M't 5:25*
quickly
perform unto the Lord *t*. *M't 5:33*
oaths
thy neighbour, and hate *t*. *M't 5:43*
enemy
Therefore when thou doest *t*. *M't 6:2*
alms
That *t*. alms may be in secret *M't 6:4*
t. is the kingdom, and the *M't 6:13*
power
when thou fastest, anoint *t*. *M't 6:17*
head
if therefore *t*. eye be single, *M't 6:22*
thy
But if *t*. eye be evil, thy *M't 6:23*
whole body
not the beam that is in *t*. own *M't 7:3*
eye
me pull out the mote out of *t*. *M't 7:4*
eye
behold, a beam is in *t*. own *M't 7:4*
eye
cast out the beam out of *t*. *M't 7:5*
own eye
up thy bed, and go unto *t*. *M't 9:6*
house
to the man, Stretch forth *t*. *M't 12:13*
hand
if *t*. eye offend thee, pluck it *M't 18:9*
out
Take that *t*. is, and go thy *M't 20:14*
way: I
Is *t*. eye evil, because I am *M't 20:15*
good
till I make *t*. enemies thy *M't 22:44*
footstool
lo, there thou hast that is *t*. *M't 25:25*
bed, and go thy way into *t*. *M'k 2:11*
house
the man, Stretch forth *t*. hand *M'k 3:5*
if *t*. eye offend thee, pluck it *M'k 9:47*
out
till I make *t*. enemies thy *M'k 12:36*
footstool
wilt worship me, all shall be *t*. *Lu 4:7*
up thy couch, and go into *t*. *Lu 5:24*
house
Pharisees; but *t*. eat and drink *Lu 5:33*
not the beam that is in *t*. own *Lu 6:41*
eye

pull out the mote that is in *t*. *Lu 6:42*
eye
not the beam that is in *t*. own *Lu 6:42*
eye
out first the beam out of *t*. *Lu 6:42*
own eye
I entered into *t*. house, thou *Lu 7:44*
gavest
Return to *t*. own house, and *Lu 8:39*
shew
therefore when *t*. eye is *Lu 11:34*
single, thy
but when *t*. eye is evil, thy *Lu 11:34*
body also
take *t*. ease, eat, drink, and *Lu 12:19*
be merry
When thou goest with *t*. *Lu 12:58*
adversary
thou art loosed from *t*. *Lu 13:12*
infirmity
with me, and all that I have *Lu 15:31*
is *t*.
Out of *t*. own mouth will I *Lu 19:22*
judge
but now they are hid from *t*. *Lu 19:42*
eyes
that *t*. enemies shall cast a *Lu 19:43*
trench
I make *t*. enemies thy *Lu 20:43*
footstool
not my will, but *t*. be done *Lu 22:42*
zeal of *t*. house hath eaten *Joh 2:17*
me up
where are those *t*. accusers *Joh 8:10*
unto him, How were *t*. eyes *Joh 9:10*
opened
of him, that he hath opened *Joh 9:17*
t. eyes
he to thee? how opened he *t*. *Joh 9:26*
eyes
glorify thou me with *t*. own *Joh 17:5*
self
t. they were, and thou gavest *Joh 17:6*
them
thou hast given me; for they *Joh 17:9*
are *t*.
And all mine are *t*. and *Joh 17:10*
and *t*. are mine; and I am *Joh 17:10*
keep through *t*. own name *Joh 17:11*
those
T. own nation and the chief *Joh 18:35*
wilt thou suffer *t*. Holy One to *Ac 2:27*
see
By stretching forth *t*. hand to *Ac 4:30*
heal
Satan filled *t*. heart to lie to the *Ac 5:3*
it remained, was it not *t*. own *Ac 5:4*
was it not in *t*. own power *Ac 5:4*
conceived this thing in *t*. heart *Ac 5:4*
the thought of *t*. heart may be *Ac 8:22*
If thou believest with all *t*. *Ac 8:37*
heart
t. alms are come up for a *Ac 10:4*
memorial
t. alms are had in *Ac 10:31*
remembrance
shalt not suffer *t*. Holy One *Ac 13:35*
to see
when *t*. accusers are also *Ac 23:35*
come
Say not in *t*. heart, Who shall *Ro 10:6*
shalt believe in *t*. heart that *Ro 10:9*
God
and digged down *t*. altars *Ro 11:3*
Therefore if *t*. enemy hunger, *Ro 12:20*
feed
I say, not *t*. own, but of the *1Co 10:29*
other
sake and *t*. often infirmities *1Ti 5:23*
unto me even *t*. own self *Ph'm 19*
besides
heavens are the works of *t*. *Heb 1:10*
hands
I make *t*. enemies thy *Heb 1:13*
footstool
and anoint *t*. eyes with *Re 3:18*
eyesalve

THING

every creeping *t*. *Ge 1:24;*
6:7; 7:14, 21; 8:17, 19; Le 11:41, 43, 44;
De 18:19
every *t*. that creepeth *Ge 1:25;*
1:26, 30; 6:20; 7:8; De 4:18
every living *t*. *Ge 1:28;*
6:19; 8:1, 17; Le 11:10; 20:25
every *t*. that is in the earth *Ge 6:17*
died
every living *t*. (S) *Ge 7:4; 7:23*

smite any more every *t.* living   *Ge 8:21*
every moving *t.*   *Ge 9:3; 9:8*
will not take any *t.* that is   *Ge 14:23*
thine
hide from Abraham that *t.*   *Ge 18:17*
which I do
cannot do any *t.* till thou be   *Ge 19:22*
come
the *t.* was very grievous to   *Ge 21:11*
Abraham
neither do thou any *t.* unto   *Ge 22:12*
him: for
the *t.* proceedeth from the   *Ge 24:50*
Lord
which *t.* ought not to be done   *Ge 34:7;*
  2Sa 13:12
the young men deferred not   *Ge 34:19*
to do this *t.*
the *t.* he did displeased the   *Ge 38:10;*
Lord   *2Sa 11:27*
because the *t.* is established   *Ge 41:32*
by God
remained not any green *t.* in   *Ex 10:15*
the trees
the *t.* which the Lord   *Ex 16:16;*
commanded *16:32; 35:4; Le 8:5, 6;*
  Nu 22:1; 36:6
in the *t.* wherein they dealt   *Ex 18:11*
proudly he was
the *t.* thou doest is not good   *Ex 18:17*
for any manner of lost *t.*   *Ex 22:9*
which another
if it be an hired *t.* it came   *Ex 22:15*
for his hire
a terrible *t.* that I will do   *Ex 34:10*
with thee
a *t.* most holy of your offerings   *Le 2:3;*
  2:10
the *t.* be hid from the eyes of   *Le 4:13*
assembly
trespass in a *t.* taken away by   *Le 6:2*
violence
the *t.* deceitfully gotten, or the   *Le 6:4*
lost *t.*
every flying creeping *t.*   *Le 11:21*
she shall touch no hallowed *t.*   *Le 12:4*
nor come
it is a wicked *t.* they shall be   *Le 20:17*
cut off
but if Lord make a new *t.*   *Nu 16:30*
earth open
the *t.* which thou hast spoken   *De 1:14*
is good
what *t.* soever I command   *De 12:32*
you, observe
if it be truth, and the *t.*   *De 13:14;*
certain   *17:4*
if the *t.* follow not, nor come   *De 18:22*
to pass
it is not a vain *t.* for you, it   *De 32:47*
is your life
keep yourselves from the   *Jos 6:18*
accursed *t.*
the accursed *t.* *Jos 7:11; 7:13, 15; 22:20*
the *t.* pleased the children of   *Jos 22:33*
Israel
which *t.* became a snare to   *J'g 8:27*
Gideon
do not do this vile *t.* (R)   *J'g 19:23*
unto this man do not so vile   *J'g 19:24*
a *t.*
till he have finished the *t.* to   *Ru 3:18*
day
I will do a *t.* in Israel at   *1Sa 3:11*
which
what is the *t.* that the Lord   *1Sa 3:17*
hath said to thee
there hath not been such a *t.*   *1Sa 4:7*
heretofore
the *t.* displeased Samuel, when   *1Sa 8:6*
they said
come up to us, we will shew   *1Sa 14:12*
you a *t.*
they told Saul, and the *t.*   *1Sa 18:20*
pleased him
let not my lord take the *t.* to   *2Sa 13:33*
heart
wherefore hast thou thought   *2Sa 14:13*
such a *t.*
hide not the *t.* that I shall   *2Sa 14:18*
ask thee
what *t.* thou shalt hear, tell   *2Sa 15:35*
to Zadok
she spread corn, the *t.* was   *2Sa 17:19*
not known
wife of Jeroboam cometh to   *1Ki 14:5*
ask *t.*
Elijah said, Thou hast asked a   *2Ki 2:10*
hard *t.*

make windows in heaven,   *2Ki 7:19*
might such *t.* be
have this sign, that the Lord   *2Ki 20:9*
will do the *t.*
t. was right in the eyes of the   *1Ch 13:4*
people
let the *t.* thou hast spoken   *1Ch 17:23*
be established
for the *t.* was done suddenly   *2Ch 29:36*
the *t.* pleased the king and   *2Ch 30:4*
congregation
hath put such a *t.* in the   *Ezr 7:27*
king's heart
the *t.* pleased the king, and   *Es 2:4*
he did so
the *t.* was known to Mordecai,   *Es 2:22*
who told it
the *t.* pleased Haman, he   *Es 5:14*
caused gallows
and if the *t.* seem right before   *Es 8:5*
the king
the *t.* I greatly feared is come   *Job 3:25*
upon me
now a *t.* was secretly brought   *Job 4:12*
to me
O that God would grant me   *Job 6:8*
the *t.* I long for
he as a rotten *t.* consumeth,   *Job 13:28*
as a garment
who can bring a clean *t.* out   *Job 14:4*
of an unclean
decree a *t.* it shall be   *Job 22:28*
established
he performeth the *t.* is   *Job 23:14*
appointed for me
how hast thou plentifully declared   *Job 26:3*
the *t.* as it is
not spoken of me the *t.* that   *Job 42:7;*
is right   *42:8*
why do the people imagine a   *Ps 2:1*
vain *t.*
an horse is a vain *t.* for   *Ps 33:17*
safety
because I follow the *t.* that   *Ps 38:20*
good is
nor alter the *t.* that is gone   *Ps 89:34*
out of my lips
I will set no wicked *t.* before   *Ps 101:3*
mine eyes
wisdom is the principal *t.*   *Pr 4:7*
therefore get
for it is a pleasant *t.* if thou   *Pr 22:18*
keep them
it is the glory of God to   *Pr 25:2*
conceal a *t.*
the *t.* that hath been, it shall be,   *Ec 1:9*
there is no new *t.* under the sun
better is the end of a *t.* than   *Ec 7:8*
the beginning
and who knoweth the   *Ec 8:1*
interpretation of a *t.*
a man hath no better *t.* than   *Ec 8:15*
to eat and drink
a pleasant *t.* it is for eyes to   *Ec 11:7*
behold the sun
is it a small *t.* for you to   *Isa 7:13*
weary men
there is no green *t.*   *Isa 15:6*
a rolling *t.*   *Isa 17:13*
the *t.* framed say of him that   *Isa 29:16*
framed it
that turn aside the just for a   *Isa 29:21*
t. of nought
he taketh up the isles as a   *Isa 40:15*
very little *t.*
and they shall be as a *t.* of   *Isa 41:12*
nought
I will do a new *t.* it shall   *Isa 43:19*
spring forth
it shall prosper in the *t.*   *Isa 55:11*
whereto I sent it
who hath heard such a *t.* who   *Isa 66:8*
hath seen
consider, and see if there be   *Jer 2:10*
such a *t.*
a horrible *t.* is committed in   *Jer 5:30*
the land
ye set up altars to that   *Jer 11:13*
shameful *t.* to Baal
they prophesy unto you a *t.*   *Jer 14:14*
of nought
the virgin of Israel hath done   *Jer 18:13*
a horrible *t.*
I have seen in the prophets a   *Jer 23:14*
horrible *t.*
Lord hath created a new *t.*   *Jer 31:22*
in the earth
I will ask thee a *t.* hide   *Jer 38:14*
nothing from me

that God may shew us the *t.*   *Jer 42:3*
that we may do
that whatsoever *t.* the Lord   *Jer 42:4*
shall answer you
we will do what *t.* goeth out   *Jer 44:17*
of our mouth
what *t.* shall I take to witness   *La 2:13*
for thee? what *t.* shall I liken
to thee
if deceived when he hath   *Eze 14:9*
spoken a *t.*
but as if it were a very little   *Eze 16:47*
t.
the king said, The *t.* is gone   *Da 2:5;*
from me   *2:8*
it is a rare *t.* that the king   *Da 2:11*
requireth
Arioch made the *t.* known to   *Da 2:15*
Daniel
Daniel made the *t.* known to   *Da 2:17*
Hananiah
same hour was the *t.* fulfilled   *Da 4:33*
on Nebuchadnezzar
could not shew the   *Da 5:15*
interpretation of the *t.*
this is the interpretation of the   *Da 5:26*
t.
the *t.* is true, according to the   *Da 6:12*
law
a *t.* revealed to Daniel, the *t.*   *Da 10:1*
was true, he understood the *t.*
I have seen an horrible *t.* in   *Ho 6:10*
Israel
but they were counted as a   *Ho 8:12*
strange *t.*
ye which rejoice in a *t.* of   *Am 6:13*
nought
and sacrificeth to the Lord a   *Mal 1:14*
corrupt *t.*
no living *t.* survive (N)   *M't 24:22*
what *t.* is this? what new   *M'k 1:27*
doctrine is this
how or what *t.* ye shall   *Lu 12:11*
answer
sin no more, lest a worse *t.*   *Joh 5:14*
come to thee
the man said, Herein is a   *Joh 9:30*
marvellous *t.*
it is unlawful *t.* for a Jew   *Ac 10:28*
but either to tell or hear   *Ac 17:21*
some new *t.*
have written, that they   *Ac 21:25*
observe no such *t.*
for he hath a certain *t.* to tell   *Ac 23:17*
him
Except it be for this one *t.*   *Ac 24:21*
(S)
of whom I have no certain *t.*   *Ac 25:26*
to write
why should it be thought a *t.*   *Ac 26:8*
incredible
which *t.* I also did in   *Ac 26:10*
Jerusalem
shall *t.* formed say to him   *Ro 9:20*
that formed it
I beseech that ye all speak   *1Co 1:10*
the same *t.*
with me it is a very small *t.*   *1Co 4:3*
that I be judged
some eat it as a *t.* offered unto   *1Co 8:7*
an idol
hath wrought the self-same *t.*   *2Co 5:5*
is God
this self-same *t.* that ye   *2Co 7:11*
sorrowed after
nevertheless, let us mind the   *Ph'p 3:16*
same *t.*
seeing it is a righteous *t.* with   *2Th 1:6*
God
the blood of the covenant   *Heb 10:29*
an unholy *t.*
fearful *t.* to fall into hands   *Heb 10:31*
of living God
as though some strange *t.*   *1Pe 4:12*
happened
which *t.* is true in him, and in   *1Jo 2:8*
you
doctrine of Nicolaitans, which   *Re 2:15*
t. I hate
every living *t.* (A)(N)(P)(R)   *Re 16:3*

ANY THING

I will not take any *t.* that is   *Ge 14:23*
thine
is any *t.* too hard for the   *Ge 18:14*
Lord
cannot do any *t.* till thou   *Ge 19:22*
come thither

neither do thou *any t.* unto the lad   Ge 22:12

Jacob said, Thou shalt not give me *any t.*   Ge 30:31

neither hath he kept back *any*   Ge 39:9
t. from me

he looked not to *any t.* under his hand   Ge 39:23

not make unto thee any   Ex 20:4;
likeness of *any t.*   De 4:18, 23, 25; 5:8

nor *any t.* that is thy   Ex 20:17;
neighbour's   De 5:21

forgiven him for *any t.* he hath done   Le 6:7

any t. made of skin   Le 13:48;
  13:49, 52, 53, 57, 59

that sitteth on *any t.* whereon he sat   Le 15:6;
  15:23

who toucheth *any t.* that was under him   Le 15:10;
  15:22

ye shall not eat *any t.* with the blood   Le 19:26

that hath *any t.* superfluous   Le 21:18;
  21:22, 23

go thro' without doing *any t.* else   Nu 20:19

have I now any power at all to say *any t.*   Nu 22:38

cast upon him *any t.* without laying wait   Nu 35:22

if there hath been *any.* such *t.* as this   De 4:32

thou shalt not lack *any t.* in the land   De 8:9

thou shalt not eat *any* abominable *t.*   De 14:3

not eat *any t.* that dieth of itself   De 14:21

nor shall there *any t.* of flesh remain   De 16:4

usury of *any t.* that is lent upon usury   De 23:19

when thou dost lend thy brother *any t.*   De 24:10

their children who have not known *any t.*   De 31:13

failed not ought of *any t.* spoken   Jos 21:45

art thou *any t.* better than Balak   J'g 11:25

might put them to shame in *any t.*   J'g 18:7

where there is no want of *any t.*   J'g 18:10;
  19:19

God do so if thou hide *any t.*   1Sa 3:17

but Saul spake not *any t.* that day   1Sa 20:26

lad knew not *any t.* only Jonathan   1Sa 20:39

let no man know *any t.* of the business   1Sa 21:2

let not king impute *any t.* to his servant   1Sa 22:15

not hurt, neither missed we *any t.*   1Sa 22:15

there was not lacking *any t.* had taken   1Sa 30:19

he thought it hard to do *any t.* to her   2Sa 13:2

went in simplicity, knew not *any t.*   2Sa 15:11

was not *any t.* hid from the king   1Ki 10:3

turned not aside from *any t.* commanded   1Ki 15:5

whether *any t.* would come from him   1Ki 20:33

hath not *any t.* save a pot of oil   2Ki 4:2

whosoever hath dedicated *any t.*   1Ch 26:28

silver was not *any t.* accounted of   2Ch 9:20

none unclean in *any t.* should enter in   2Ch 23:19

is there *any* secret *t.* with thee   Job 15:11

if thou hast *any t.* to say, answer me   Job 33:32

that seek Lord shall not want *any* good *t.*   Ps 34:10

incline not my heart to *any* evil *t.*   Ps 141:4

any t. it may be said, this is new   Ec 1:10

nothing put to it, nor *any t.* taken from it   Ec 3:14

heart not hasty to utter *any t.* before God   Ec 5:2

---

dead know not *any t.* nor have reward   Ec 9:5

is there *any t.* too hard for me   Jer 32:27

for the king is not he that can do *any t.*   Jer 38:5

nor *any t.* for which he hath sent me   Jer 42:21

speak *any t.* amiss against God   Da 3:29

let neither man nor beast taste *any t.*   Jon 3:7

if two shall agree touching *any t.*   M't 18:19

take *any t.* out of his house   M't 24:17;
  M'k 13:15

nor was *any t.* kept secret   M'k 4:22;
  Lu 8:17

if thou canst do *any t.* have compassion   M'k 9:22

if haply he might find *any t.* thereon   M'k 11:13

neither said they *any t.* to any man   M'k 16:8

if I have taken *any t.* from any man   Lu 19:8

lacked ye *any t.?* and they said, Nothing   Lu 22:35

without him was not *any t.* made   Joh 1:3

can *any* good *t.* come out of Nazareth   Joh 1:46

is no man that doeth *any t.* in secret   Joh 7:4

if ye ask *any t.* in my name, I will do it   Joh 14:14

I have never eaten *any t.* common   Ac 10:14

as tho' he needed *any t.* seeing he   Ac 17:25

nor against Cæsar have I offended *any t.*   Ac 25:8

if I committed *any t.* worthy of death   Ac 25:11

lay *any t.* to the charge of God's elect   Ro 8:33

owe no man *any t.* but to love one another   Ro 13:8

any t. whereby thy brother stumbleth   Ro 14:21

to know *any t.* save Jesus crucified   1Co 2:2

neither is he that planteth *any t.* nor   1Co 3:7

if any man think that he knoweth *any t.*   1Co 8:2

what say I then? that the idol is *any t.*   1Co 10:19

if learn *any t.* let them ask husbands   1Co 14:35

to whom ye forgive *any t.* I forgive, for if I forgave *any t.* I forgave in   2Co 2:10

not sufficient to think *any t.* of ourselves   2Co 3:5

giving no offence in *any t.* that ministry   2Co 6:3

if I have boasted *any t.* to him of you   2Co 7:14

neither circumcision availeth *any t.* nor   Ga 5:6

not having wrinkle, or *any* such *t.*   Eph 5:27

if in *any t.* ye be otherwise minded   Ph'p 3:15

so that we need not to speak *any t.*   1Th 1:8

if there be *any* other *t.* contrary   1Ti 1:10

he shall receive *any t.* of the Lord   Jas 1:7

if we ask *any t.* according to his will   1Jo 5:14

that they should not hurt *any* green *t.*   Re 9:4

in no wise enter *any t.* that defileth   Re 21:27

EVERY THING

every t. that is in the earth shall die   Ge 6:17

God remembered Noah and *every* living *t.*   Ge 8:1

every moving *t.* that liveth shall be meat   Ge 9:3

every t. whereon he sitteth, unclean   Le 15:4

every t. she sitteth on shall be unclean   Le 15:20

---

ye shall offer *every t.* upon his day   Le 23:37

every devoted *t.* is most holy to the Lord   Le 27:28

every t. devoted in Israel shall be thine   Nu 18:14;
  Eze 44:29

every t. that openeth the matrix be thine   Nu 18:15

every t. that may abide fire, make it go   Nu 31:23

then keep thee from *every* wicked *t.*   De 23:9

priests stood till *every t.* was finished   Jos 4:10

every t. that was vile they destroyed   1Sa 15:9

send unto me *every t.* ye can hear   2Sa 15:36

told *every t.* that had befallen him   Es 6:13

and his eyes seeth *every* precious *t.*   Job 28:10

he searcheth after *every* green *t.*   Job 39:8

I know that thou canst do *every t.*   Job 42:2

let *every t.* that hath breath praise   Ps 150:6

to the hungry *every* bitter *t.* is sweet   Pr 27:7

to *every t.* there is a season and a time   Ec 3:1

hath made *every t.* beautiful in his time   Ec 3:11

work into judgment with *every* secret *t.*   Ec 12:14

every t. sown by the brook shall wither   Isa 19:7

every t. shall live where rivers come   Eze 47:9

told *every t.* and what was befallen   M't 8:33

in *every t.* ye are enriched   1Co 1:5;
  2Co 9:11

as ye are bound in *every t.* in faith   2Co 8:7

and *every* high *t.* that exalteth itself   2Co 10:5

be subject to their husbands in *every t.*   Eph 5:24

in *every t.* by prayer and supplication   Ph'p 4:6

in *every t.* give thanks, for this is   1Th 5:18

THAT THING

hide from Abraham *that t.* which I do   Ge 18:17

and the Lord did *that t.* on the morrow   Ex 9:6

shall confess that he hath sinned in *that t.*   Le 5:5

which have committed *that* wicked *t.*   De 17:5

he charged them to tell no man *that t.*   Lu 9:21

if ye be not able to do *that t.* which is least   Lu 12:26

not himself in *that t.* which he alloweth   Ro 14:22

THIS THING

accepted thee concerning *this t.*   Ge 19:21

sawest thou that thou hast done *this t.*   Ge 20:10

I wot not who hath done *this t.* neither   Ge 21:26

done *this t.* and not withheld thy son   Ge 22:16

if wilt do *this t.* I will again feed flock   Ge 30:31

we cannot do *this t.* to give our sister   Ge 34:14

this is the *t.* I have spoken to Pharaoh   Ge 41:28

that we should do according to *this t.*   Ge 44:7

why have ye done *this t.* and saved   Ex 1:18

Moses said, Surely *this t.* is known   Ex 2:14

heard *this t.* he sought to slay Moses   Ex 2:15

to-morrow the Lord shall do *this t.*   Ex 9:5

observe *this t.* for an ordinance to thee   Ex 12:24

this is the *t.* the Lord   *Ex 16:16;*
commanded   *16:32; 35:4; Le 8:5; 9:6;*
17:2; Nu 30:1; 36:6; De 15:15; 24:18,
22
what is *this t.* thou doest to   *Ex 18:14*
the people
this t. is too heavy for thee,   *Ex 18:18*
thou art
if thou do *this t.* and God   *Ex 18:23*
command thee
this is the *t.* that thou shalt do *Ex 29:1*
to them
I will do *this t.* that thou hast *Ex 33:17*
spoken
if ye will do *this t.,* if ye will *Nu 32:20*
this t. Lord commands about *Nu 36:6*
daughters
in *this t.* ye did not believe   *De 1:32*
God
for *this t.* the Lord thy God *De 15:10*
shall bless
if *this t.* be true, tokens be *De 22:20*
not found
thro' *this t.* ye shall prolong *De 32:47*
your days
we were afraid, and have done *Jos 9:24*
this t.
have not rather done it for *Jos 22:24*
fear of *this t.*
said one to another, Who hath *J'g 6:29*
done *this t.?* Gideon hath done
this t.
let *this t.* be done for me, let *J'g 11:37*
me alone
this shall be the *t.* which we   *J'g 20:9*
will do
and *this* is the *t.* that ye shall *J'g 21:11*
do
why should my father hide   *1Sa 20:2*
this t. from
the Lord forbid that I should *1Sa 24:6*
do *this t.*
this t. is not good that thou *1Sa 26:16*
hast done
no punishment happen to   *1Sa 28:10*
thee for *this t.*
Lord hath done *this t.* unto *1Sa 28:18*
thee this day
requite, because ye have done *2Sa 2:6*
this t.
as thy soul liveth, I will not   *2Sa 11:11*
do *this t.*
say to Joab, let not *this t.*   *2Sa 11:25*
displease thee
the man that hath done *this* *2Sa 12:5*
t. shall die
because he did *this t.* and *2Sa 12:6*
had no pity
I will do *this t.* before all *2Sa 12:12*
Israel
he is thy brother, regard not *2Sa 13:20*
this t.
king doth speak *this t.* as *2Sa 14:13*
one faulty
I am come to speak of *this* *2Sa 14:15*
t. unto king
thy servant Joab hath done *2Sa 14:20*
this t.
why doth my lord delight in *2Sa 24:3*
this t.
is *this t.* done by my lord   *1Ki 1:27*
pleased Lord that Solomon *1Ki 3:10;*
asked *this t.*   *3:11*
had commanded him   *1Ki 11:16*
concerning *this t.*
return for *this t.* is   *1Ki 12:24;*
from me   *2Ch 11:4*
made two calves, *this t.* *1Ki 12:30*
became a sin
after *this t.* Jeroboam   *1Ki 13:33*
returned not
this t. became sin to   *1Ki 13:34*
Jeroboam
tell the king *this t.* I may not *1Ki 20:9*
do
do *this t.* take the kings *1Ki 20:24*
away
in *this t.* the Lord pardon   *2Ki 5:18*
king of Syria was troubled *2Ki 6:11*
for *this t.*
Lord make windows, might   *2Ki 7:2*
this t. be
this is the *t.* that ye shall do *2Ki 11:5;*
                   2Ch 23:4
Lord said, Ye shall not do *2Ki 17:12*
this t.
God forbid that I should do *1Ch 11:19*
this t.
why then doth my lord   *1Ch 21:3*
require *this t.*

and God was displeased with *1Ch 21:7*
this t.
I have sinned, because I have *1Ch 21:8*
done *this t.*
was in rage with him,   *2Ch 16:10*
because of *this t.*
when I heard *this t.* I rent my *Ezr 9:3*
garment
there is hope in Israel   *Ezr 10:2*
concerning *this t.*
we are many that have   *Ezr 10:13*
transgressed in *this t.*
what is *this t.* that ye do? will *Ne 2:19*
ye rebel
Lord will do *this t.* that he *Isa 38:7*
hath spoken
this is the *t.* that I command *Jer 7:23*
them
if ye do *this t.* then shall enter *Jer 22:4*
kings
therefore *this t.* is come upon *Jer 40:3*
you
Gedaliah said, Thou shalt *Jer 40:16*
not do *this t.*
oh do not *this* abominable *t.* *Jer 44:4*
that I hate
he looked to see her that had *M'k 5:32*
done *this t.*
see *this t.* which is come to *Lu 2:15*
pass
which of them should do *this* *Lu 22:23*
t.
sayest thou *this t.* of thyself *Joh 18:34*
why hast thou conceived *this* *Ac 5:4*
t.
for *this t.* was not done in a *Ac 26:26*
corner
attending continually upon *Ro 13:6*
this very *t.*
if I do *this t.* willingly, I *1Co 9:17*
have reward
for *this t.* I besought Lord *2Co 12:8*
thrice
being confident in *this* very *t.* *Ph'p 1:6*
that
this one *t.* I do, I press *Ph'p 3:13*
toward mark

UNCLEAN THING

if a soul touch any *unclean t.* *Le 5:2;*
                  7:21
flesh that toucheth *unclean t.* *Le 7:19*
not be eaten
take brother's wife, it is an *Le 20:21*
unclean t.
that he see no *unclean t.* in *De 23:14*
thee
and eat not any *unclean t.* *J'g 13:4;*
                13:7, 14
touch no *unclean t.* Isa 52:11; *2Co 6:17*
we are all as an *unclean t.* we *Isa 64:6*
all do fade
have never eaten any *t.*   *Ac 10:14*
unclean

THINGS

the Lord had blessed   *Ge 24:1*
Abraham in all *t.*
goodly *t.* of his master's (E) *Ge 24:10*
ten asses laden with good *t.* *Ge 45:23*
of Egypt
if sin thro' ignorance   *Le 4:2;*
concerning *t.* ought not be done *4:13,*
                  22, 27
best forget *t.* thine eyes have *De 4:9*
seen
with all lost *t.* of brother's he *De 22:3*
hath lost
an abundance of good *t.* (B) *De 28:11*
secret *t.* belong unto the *De 29:29*
Lord our God
t. that shall come on them *De 32:35*
make haste
the chief *t.* of the ancient *De 33:15*
mountains
took the *t.* which Micah had *J'g 18:27*
made
for then should ye go after *1Sa 12:21*
vain *t.*
but the people took the chief *1Sa 15:21*
of the *t.*
I offer thee three *t.*   *2Sa 24:12;*
               1Ch 21:10
Solomon brought in the *t.* *1Ki 7:51*
dedicated
Asa brought in the *t.*   *1Ki 15:15;*
               2Ch 15:18
Israel wrought wicked *t.* to *2Ki 17:11*
provoke

and these are ancient *t.* *1Ch 4:22*
the office over *t.* that were *1Ch 9:31*
made in pans
gold for *t.* of gold, silver for *1Ch 29:2*
t. of silver, brass for *t.* of
brass, iron for *t.* of iron
and also in Judah *t.* went *2Ch 12:12*
well
found precious *t.* (A)(R) *2Ch 20:25*
houses filled with good *t.* *Ne 9:25*
(A)(B)(E)(R)
let *t.* for purification be given *Es 2:3;*
                 2:12
doth marvellous *t.* without *Job 5:9*
number
the *t.* that my soul refuseth to *Job 6:7*
touch
cannot my taste discern *Job 6:30*
perverse *t.*
he discovereth deep *t.* out of *Job 12:22*
darkness
only do not two *t.* to me, *Job 13:20*
then will I
for thou writest bitter *t.* *Job 13:26*
against me
beholdeth all high *t.* is king *Job 41:34*
over pride
I have uttered *t.* too *Job 42:3*
wonderful for me
cut off tongue, that speaketh *Ps 12:3*
proud *t.*
thine eyes behold the *t.* that *Ps 17:2*
are equal
which speak grievous *t.* *Ps 31:18*
proudly
they laid to my charge *t.* I *Ps 35:11*
knew not
that seek my hurt, speak *Ps 38:12*
mischievous *t.*
I speak of the *t.* which I have *Ps 45:1*
made
thy right hand shall teach thee *Ps 45:4*
terrible *t.*
thou hast shewed thy people *Ps 60:3*
hard *t.*
by terrible *t.* wilt thou answer *Ps 65:5*
us
the God of Israel, who doth *Ps 72:18*
wondrous *t.*
marvellous *t.* did he in Egypt *Ps 78:12;*
                98:1
thou art great, and dost *Ps 86:10*
wondrous *t.*
glorious *t.* are spoken of thee, *Ps 87:3*
O city
how long utter and speak hard *Ps 94:4*
t.
had done terrible *t.* by the *Ps 106:22*
Red sea
to behold the *t.* that are in *Ps 113:6*
heaven
behold wondrous *t.* out of *Ps 119:18*
thy law
in great matters, or in *t.* too *Ps 131:1*
high for me
from the man that speaketh *Pr 2:12*
froward *t.*
I will speak of excellent *t.* of *Pr 8:6*
right *t.*
he shutteth his eyes to devise *Pr 16:30*
froward *t.*
I have written to thee *Pr 22:20*
excellent *t.*
shalt rejoice, when thy lips *Pr 23:16*
speak right *t.*
and thine heart shall utter *Pr 23:33*
perverse *t.*
his heart shall behold strange *Pr 23:33*
t. (A)(S)
two *t.* have I required of thee, *Pr 30:7*
deny not
there are three *t.* that are *Pr 30:15*
never satisfied
there be three *t.* that be too *Pr 30:18*
wonderful
for three *t.* the earth is *Pr 30:21*
disquieted
four *t.* which are little on the *Pr 30:24*
earth
there be three *t.* which go *Pr 30:29*
well, yea four
nor any remembrance of *t.* to *Ec 1:11*
come
to seek out wisdom and the *Ec 7:25*
reason of *t.*
sing to Lord, he hath done *Isa 12:5*
excellent *t.*
sing to Lord, thou hast done *Isa 25:1*
wonderful *t.*

make unto all people a feast *Isa 23:6* of fat *t.*

surely your turning of *t.* *Isa 29:16* upside down

which say, Prophesy not to *Isa 30:10* us right *t.*

but the liberal deviseth liberal *Isa 32:8* *t.* and by liberal *t.* shall he stand

shew the *t.* that are to come *Isa 41:23* hereafter

former *t.* come to pass, new *t.* *Isa 42:9* I declare

I will make crooked *t.* *Isa 42:16* straight

the *t.* that are coming and *Isa 44:7* shall come

ask me of *t.* to come *Isa 45:11* concerning my sons

I the Lord speak, I declare *t.* *Isa 45:19* that are right

I have shewed thee new *t.* *Isa 48:6* even hidden *t.*

eunuchs that choose the *t.* *Isa 56:4* that please me

thou didst terrible *t.* we *Isa 64:3* looked not for

all our pleasant *t.* are laid *Isa 64:11* waste

broth of abominable *t.* is in *Isa 65:4* their vessels

walked after *t.* that do not *Jer 2:8;* profit *16:19*

t. I have given them shall pass *Jer 8:13* away

planters shall eat them as *Jer 31:5* common *t.*

Jerusalem remembered her *La 1:7* pleasant *t.*

they have given her pleasant *t.* *La 1:11* for meat

thy prophets have seen foolish *La 2:14* *t.* for thee

I know *t.* that come in your *Eze 11:5* mind

like *t.* shall not come, nor *Eze 16:16* shall it be so

at same time *t.* come into *Eze 38:10* thy mind

he revealeth the deep and *Da 2:22* secret *t.*

speak marvellous *t.* against *Da 11:36* God of gods

carried into your temples my *Joe 3:5* goodly *t.*

how are the *t.* of Esau searched *Ob 6* out! how are his hidden *t.* sought up

I will shew unto him *Mic 7:15* marvellous *t.*

who hath despised the day of *Zec 4:10* small *t.*

morrow take thought for *t.* of *M't 6:34* itself

brings out of his treasure *t.* *M't 13:52* new and old

savourest not *t.* of God *M't 16:23;* *M'k 8:33*

render to Cæsar *t.* that are *M't 22:21;* Cæsar's, to God *t.* that are *M'k 12:17;* God's *Lu 20:25*

lusts of other *t.* choke the *M'k 4:19* word

but the *t.* which come out of *M'k 7:15* him defile

we have seen strange *t.* to-day *Lu 5:26*

call me Lord, and do not *t.* *Lu 6:46* I say

blessed eyes which see the *t.* *Lu 10:23* that ye see

in the abundance of the *t.* he *Lu 12:15* possesseth

and did commit *t.* worthy of *Lu 12:48* stripes

t. which are impossible with *Lu 18:27* men are

known the *t.* which belong to *Lu 19:42* thy peace

for the *t.* concerning me have *Lu 22:37* an end

all people beholding, *t.* done *Lu 23:48*

not known *t.* which are *Lu 24:18* come to pass

he expounded the *t.* *Lu 24:27* concerning himself

thou shalt see greater *t.* than *Joh 1:50* these

if I have told you earthly *t.* *Joh 3:12* heavenly *t.*

the Spirit will shew you *t.* to *Joh 16:13* come

speaking of *t.* pertaining to *Ac 1:3* kingdom

we cannot but speak the *t.* we *Ac 4:20* have seen

and why did the people *Ac 4:25* imagine vain *t.*

that ought of *t.* possessed was *Ac 4:32* his own

preaching *t.* concerning *Ac 8:12* kingdom of God

abstain from *t.* strangled *Ac 15:20;* *15:29*

abstain from *t.* offered *Ac 15:29* (E)(S)

she attended to the *t.* spoken *Ac 16:14* of Paul

Apollos taught diligently *t.* of *Ac 18:25* the Lord

persuading *t.* concerning the *Ac 19:8* kingdom of God

not knowing the *t.* that shall *Ac 20:22* befall me

men arise, speaking perverse *Ac 20:30* *t.*

teach distorted *t.* (B) *Ac 20:30*

that they keep from *t.* offered *Ac 21:25* to idols

neither can they prove the *t.* *Ac 24:13* whereof

saying none other *t.* than the *Ac 26:22* prophets

some believed the *t.* that *Ac 28:24* were spoken

invisible *t.* are clearly seen, *Ro 1:20* being understood by *t.* that are

for thou that judgest doest the *Ro 2:1* same *t.*

Gentiles do by nature *t.* *Ro 2:14* contained in law

approvest the *t.* that are more *Ro 2:18* excellent

mind the *t.* of the flesh, mind *t.* *Ro 8:5* of the Spirit

nor *t.* present, nor *t.* to come *Ro 8:38;* *1Co 3:22*

bring glad tidings of good *t.* *Ro 10:15* (E)(P)

mind not high *t.* *Ro 12:16*

provide *t.* honest *Ro 12:17*

follow after *t.* that make for *Ro 14:19* peace

whatsoever *t.* were written *Ro 15:4* aforetime

if Gentiles partakers of *Ro 15:27* spiritual *t.* their duty is to minister to them in carnal *t.*

God hath chosen foolish *t.* of *1Co 1:27* world, weak *t.* to confound *t.* mighty

base *t.* and *t.* despised hath *1Co 1:28* God chosen

the *t.* which God hath *1Co 2:9* prepared for them

the Spirit searcheth the deep *1Co 2:10* *t.* of God

what man knoweth *t.* of man, *1Co 2:11* so *t.* of God knoweth no man, but Spirit of God

might know *t.* freely given us *1Co 2:12* of God

which *t.* we speak, *1Co 2:13* comparing spiritual *t.*

man receiveth not *t.* of the *1Co 2:14* Spirit of God

will bring to light hidden *t.* of *1Co 4:5* darkness

much more *t.* that pertain to *1Co 6:3;* this life *6:4*

unmarried careth for *t.* of *1Co 7:32;* the Lord *7:34*

married careth for *t.* of the *1Co 7:33* world

as touching *t.* offered to *1Co 8:11* idols, we know

if we have sown spiritual *t.*, if *1Co 9:11* reap carnal *t.*

the *t.* which the Gentiles *1Co 10:20* sacrifice

when I became man, I put *1Co 13:11* away childish *t.*

even *t.* without life giving *1Co 14:7* sound

acknowledge *t.* that I write *1Co 14:37* to you

let all your *t.* be done with *1Co 16:14* charity

for we write none other *t.* *2Co 1:13* unto you

t. that I purpose, do I *2Co 1:17* purpose according

have renounced the hidden *t.* *2Co 4:2* of dishonesty

we look not at *t.* which are *2Co 4:18* seen, *t.* seen are temporal, *t.* not seen are eternal,

visible *t.* are transitory *2Co 4:18* (B)(P)(R)

every one may receive *t.* *2Co 5:10* done in body

old *t.* are passed away, all *t.* *2Co 5:17* are new

providing for honest *t.* in *2Co 8:21* sight of men

look on *t.* after outward *2Co 10:7* appearance

not boast of *t.* without our *2Co 10:13;* measure *10:15*

not to boast in another *2Co 10:16* man's line of *t.*

I will glory of *t.* which *2Co 11:30* concern mine

if I build again the *t.* I *Ga 2:18* destroyed

which *t.* are an allegory, for *Ga 4:24* these are two

so that ye cannot do the *t.* *Ga 5:17* that ye would

t. are out of place (P) *Eph 5:4*

ye, masters, do the same *t.* to *Eph 6:9* them

ye may approve *t.* that are *Ph'p 1:10* excellent

t. which happened have *Ph'p 1:12* fallen out

look not every man on his *Ph'p 2:4* own *t.* but every man also on the *t.* of others

of *t.* in heaven, *t.* in earth, *Ph'p 2:10* under earth

seek not the *t.* which are *Ph'p 2:21* Jesus Christ's

to write the same *t.* *Ph'p 3:1*

who mind earthly *t.* *Ph'p 3:19*

whatsoever *t.* are true, honest, *Ph'p 4:8* just, pure

full, having received *t.* sent *Ph'p 4:18* from you

whether *t.* in earth, or *t.* in *Col 1:20* heaven

which are shadow of *t.* to *Col 2:17;* come *Heb 10:1*

which *t.* have indeed a shew *Col 2:23* of wisdom

set affection on *t.* above, not *Col 3:2* on *t.* on earth

for which *t.* sake wrath of *Col 3:6* God cometh

ye also have suffered like *t.* *1Th 2:14* of your

will do the *t.* which we *2Th 3:4* command

speaking *t.* which they ought *1Ti 5:13* not

the *t.* which thou hast heard of *2Ti 2:2* me

continue in *t.* thou hast *2Ti 3:14* learned

thou shouldest set in order *t.* *Tit 1:5* wanting

teaching *t.* ought not for *Tit 1:11* lucre's sake

speak *t.* which become sound *Tit 2:1* doctrine

be temperate in all *t.* (N) *Tit 2:6*

give heed to *t.* we have heard *Heb 2:1*

faithful high priest in *t.* *Heb 2:17;* pertain to God *5:1*

learned obedience by *t.* he *Heb 5:8* suffered

we are persuaded better *t.* of *Heb 6:9* you, *t.* that accompany salvation

that by two immutable *t.* in *Heb 6:18* which it was

of *t.* we have spoken this *Heb 8:1* is the sum

to the example and shadow of *Heb 8:5* heavenly *t.*

patterns of *t.* in heaven be *Heb 9:23* purified, but heavenly *t.* with better sacrifices

now faith is the substance of *Heb 11:1* *t.* hoped for, the evidence of *t.* not seen

t. seen were not made of *t.* *Heb 11:3* which do appear

Noah being warned of God *Heb 11:7* of *t.* not seen

blessed Jacob and Esau *Heb 11:20* concerning *t.* to

that speaketh better *t*. than | Heb 12:24
that of Abel
t. in the sea are tamed of | Jas 3:7
mankind
did minister *t*. now reported; | 1Pe 1:12
which *t*. angels desire to look into
not redeemed with | 1Pe 1:18
corruptible *t*.
speak evil of *t*. they | 2Pe 2:12
understand not
neither the *t*. that are in the | 1Jo 2:15
world
revelation of Jesus Christ to | Re 1:1;
shew servants *t*. must shortly | 22:6
come to pass
write *t*. which thou hast seen, | Re 1:19
t. which are, *t*. which shall be
hereafter
to eat *t*. sacrificed to idols, | Re 2:14;
and fornication | 2:20
strengthen *t*. which remain, | Re 3:2
ready to die
I will shew thee the *t*. must be | Re 4:1
hereafter
sware by him who created | Re 10:6
heaven, earth, sea, and all *t*.
that therein are
for the former *t*. are passed | Re 21:4
away
take his part from *t*. written | Re 22:19
in this book

ALL THINGS

as green herb have I given you | Ge 9:3
all *t*.
the Lord hath blessed | Ge 24:1
Abraham in all *t*.
servant told Isaac all *t*. that | Ge 24:66
he had done
in all *t*. be circumspect | Ex 23:13
do according to all *t*. I | Ex 29:35
commanded
Aaron and sons did all *t*. | Le 8:36
commanded
Levites over all *t*. that belong | Nu 1:50
to it
purify all *t*. made of wood | Nu 31:20
and skins
I commanded you all *t*. ye | De 1:18
should do
as the Lord our God is in all *t*. | De 4:7
we call for
not do after all *t*. that we do | De 12:8
here
servedst not for the | De 28:47
abundance of all *t*.
shalt serve thine enemies in | De 28:48
want of all *t*.
eat them for want of all *t*. | De 28:57
secretly in siege
as we hearkened to Moses in | Jos 1:17
all *t*.
the spies told him all *t*. that | Jos 2:23
befell them
this was the manner, to | Ru 4:7
confirm all *t*.
perform all *t*. concerning | 1Sa 3:12
Eli's house
if thou hide any of all *t*. he | 1Sa 3:17
said to thee
and Jonathan shewed David | 1Sa 19:7
all those *t*.
Joab sent and told David all | 2Sa 11:18
t.
to know all *t*. that are in the | 2Sa 14:20
earth
he made a covenant ordered | 2Sa 23:5
in all *t*.
he did all *t*. as did the | 1Ki 21:26
Amorites
captains did according to all | 2Ki 11:9;
t. that Jehoiada commanded | 2Ch 23:8
Amaziah, according to all *t*. | 2Ki 14:3
that Joash did
they have seen all *t*. in my | 2Ki 20:15
house
all *t*. come of thee, and of | 1Ch 29:14
thine
Solomon brought all *t*. | 2Ch 5:1
dedicated
tithe of all *t*. brought they in | 2Ch 31:5
abundantly
the Lord made all *t*. | Ne 9:6;
| Ac 14:15; 17:24, 25; Col 1:16; Re 4:11
he beholdeth all high *t*. he is | Job 41:34
a king
thou hast put all *t*. under his | Ps 8:6;
feet | 1Co15:27; Eph 1:22
cry to God that performeth | Ps 57:2
all *t*. for me

precepts concerning all *t*. to | Ps 119:128
be right
wisdom is more precious than | Pr 3:15;
all *t*. | 8:11
the Lord hath made all *t*. for | Pr 16:4
himself
the great God that formed all | Pr 26:10
t.
they that seek Lord understand | Pr 28:5
all *t*.
all *t*. are full of labour, man | Ec 1:8
cannot
all *t*. have I seen in days of | Ec 7:15
my vanity
all *t*. come alike to all, there is | Ec 9:2
one event
an evil among all *t*. done under | Ec 9:3
the sun
but money answereth all *t*. | Ec 10:19
I am Lord that maketh all *t*. | Isa 44:24;
| 66:2
for he is the former of all *t*. | Jer 10:16;
| 51:19
heart deceitful above all *t*. and | Jer 17:9
wicked
if we do not even according | Jer 42:5
to all *t*.
wanted all *t*. and have been | Jer 44:18
consumed
I spake all *t*. the Lord hath | Eze 11:25
shewed
all creeping *t*. shake at my | Eze 38:20
presence
the first of all *t*. shall be the | Eze 44:30
priest's
forasmuch as iron subdueth | Da 2:40
all *t*.
I will consume all *t*. off the | Zep 1:2
land
all *t*. ye would that men | M't 7:12
do to you
all *t*. are delivered to me | M't 11:27;
| Lu 10:22
they shall gather all *t*. that | M't 13:41
offend
Elias shall restore all *t*. | M't 17:11;
| M'k 9:12
with man is impossible, but | M't 19:26;
with God all *t*. are possible | M'k 10:27;
| 14:36
all *t*. whatsoever ye ask in | M't 21:22
prayer
tell them bidden, all *t*. are | M't 22:4;
ready, come to the marriage | Lu 14:17
swears by it, and by all *t*. | M't 23:20
thereon
teaching them to observe all | M't 28:20
t. commanded
he expounded all *t*. to his | M'k 4:34
disciples
they told him all *t*. what they | M'k 6:30
had done
astonished, he hath done all | M'k 7:37
t. well
all *t*. are possible to him that | M'k 9:23
believeth
take heed, I have foretold | M'k 13:23
you all *t*.
praising God for all *t*. they | Lu 2:20
had heard
performed all *t*. according to | Lu 2:39
law of God
they wondered at all *t*. which | Lu 9:43
Jesus did
and behold, all *t*. are clean | Lu 11:41
unto you
all *t*. written concerning Son | Lu 18:31;
of man be accomplished | 21:22; 24:44;
| Joh 19:28
all *t*. were made by him | Joh 1:3
and hath given all *t*. into his | Joh 3:35;
hand | 13:3
when he is come, he will tell | Joh 4:25
us all *t*.
man who told me all *t*. that | Joh 4:29
ever I did
Father sheweth the Son all *t*. | Joh 5:20
he doeth
all *t*. that John spake of him | Joh 10:41
were true
Comforter shall teach you | Joh 14:26
all *t*. and bring all *t*. to
your remembrance
all *t*. I have heard, I have | Joh 15:15
made known
all *t*. that the Father hath, | Joh 16:15
are mine
we now are sure that thou | Joh 16:30
knowest all *t*.

that all *t*. thou hast given me, | Joh 17:7
are of thee
Jesus therefore knowing all *t*. | Joh 18:4;
| 19:28
Peter said, Lord, thou | Joh 21:17
knowest all *t*.
believed had all *t*. common | Ac 2:44;
| 4:32
till the times of restitution of | Ac 3:21
all *t*.
him shall ye hear in all *t*. he | Ac 3:22
shall say
to hear all *t*. commanded | Ac 10:33
thee of God
we are witnesses of all *t*. | Ac 10:39
which he did
all that believe are justified | Ac 13:39
from all *t*.
God who made heaven, | Ac 14:15
earth, and all *t*.
I have shewed you all *t*. how | Ac 20:35
ye ought
and there it shall be told thee | Ac 22:10
of all *t*.
believing all *t*. which are | Ac 24:14
written
touching all the *t*. whereof, I | Ac 26:2
am accused
we know that all *t*. work for | Ro 8:28
good
how shall he not also freely | Ro 8:32
give us all *t*.
of him, thro' him and to | Ro 11:36
him, are all *t*.
for one believeth that he may | Ro 14:2
eat all *t*.
all *t*. indeed are pure, but it | Ro 14:20
is evil for him
Spirit searcheth all *t*. deep | 1Co 2:10
things
but he that is spiritual | 1Co 2:15
judgeth all *t*.
no man glory in men, for all | 1Co 3:21
t. are yours
are the offscouring of all *t*. | 1Co 4:13
to this day
all *t*. are lawful, but all *t*. | 1Co 6:12;
are not expedient, all *t*. are | 10:23
lawful for me
one God the Father, of whom | 1Co 8:6
are all *t*. one Lord Jesus Christ,
by whom are all *t*.
suffer all *t*. | 1Co 9:12
made all *t*. to all men | 1Co 9:22
every man that striveth is | 1Co 9:25
temperate in all *t*.
even as I please all men in | 1Co 10:33
all *t*.
I praise you that ye | 1Co 11:2
remember me in all *t*.
but all *t*. are of God | 1Co 11:12;
| 2Co 5:18
charity beareth all *t*. | 1Co 13:7
believeth all *t*. hopeth all *t*.
endureth all *t*.
let all *t*. be done unto | 1Co 14:26
edifying
let all *t*. be done decently | 1Co14:40
and in order
when all *t*. be subdued, then | 1Co 15:28
the Son be subject to him that
put all *t*. under
know whether be obedient in | 2Co 2:9
all *t*.
for all *t*. are for your sakes, | 2Co 4:15
that grace
old things passed away, all *t*. | 2Co 5:17
become new
in all *t*. approving ourselves as | 2Co 6:4
ministers
as having nothing, yet | 2Co 6:10
possessing all *t*.
in all *t*. ye have approved | 2Co 7:11
yourselves
we spake all *t*. to you in | 2Co 7:14
truth
that I have confidence in you | 2Co 7:16
in all *t*.
that ye having all sufficiency | 2Co 9:8
in all *t*.
we have been manifest to | 2Co 11:6
you in all *t*.
in all *t*. I kept from being | 2Co 11:9
burdensome
but we do all *t*. for your | 2Co 12:19
edifying
cursed that continueth not in | Ga 3:10
all *t*.
gather together in one all *t*. | Eph 1:10
in Christ

worketh *all t.* after counsel | Eph 1:11
of his will
gave him to be head over | Eph 1:22
all t. to the church
God, who created *all t.* by | Eph 3:9
Jesus Christ
he ascended up, that he | Eph 4:10
might fill *all t.*
grow up unto him in *all t.* | Eph 4:15
which is head
all t. reproved are made | Eph 5:13
manifest
giving thanks always for *all* | Eph 5:20
t. unto God
shall make known to you *all* | Eph 6:21;
t. | Col 4:9
do *all t.* without murmurings | Ph'p 2:14
I count *all t.* loss for Christ | Ph'p 3:8
my Lord, for whom I have
suffered loss of *all t.*
he is able to subdue *all t.* to | Ph'p 3:21
himself
everywhere, and in *all t.* I | Ph'p 4:12
am instructed
I can do *all t.* thro' Christ | Ph'p 4:13
who strengtheneth
he is before *all t.* by him *all* | Col 1:17
t. consist
in *all t.* he might have the | Col 1:18
pre-eminence
and by him to reconcile *all t.* | Col 1:20
to himself
children, obey your parents in | Col 3:20
all t.
servants, obey in *all t.* your | Col 3:22
masters
prove *all t.* hold fast which is | 1Th 5:21
good
their wives must be faithful in | 1Ti 3:11
all t.
but godliness is profitable unto | 1Ti 4:8
all t.
in the sight of God who | 1Ti 6:13
quickeneth *all t.*
living God giveth richly *all t.* | 1Ti 6:17
to enjoy
Lord give thee understanding | 2Ti 2:7
in *all t.*
I endure *all t.* for the elect's | 2Ti 2:10
sake
watch thou in *all t.* endure | 2Ti 4:5
afflictions
unto the pure *all t.* are pure | Tit 1:15
in *all t.* shewing a pattern of | Tit 2:7
good
be obedient, please them well | Tit 2:9
in *all t.*
may adorn the doctrine of | Tit 2:10
God in *all t.*
whom he appointed heir of *all* | Heb 1:2
t.
upholding *all t.* by the word | Heb 1:3
of his power
put *all t.* in subjection under | Heb 2:8
his feet; but now we see not
all t. put under
for whom are *all t.* and by | Heb 2:10
whom are *all t.*
in *all t.* it behoved him to be | Heb 2:17
like brethren
he that built *all t.* is God | Heb 3:4
all t. are naked and opened | Heb 4:13
unto eyes
make *all t.* according to the | Heb 8:5
pattern
almost *all t.* by law purged | Heb 9:22
by blood
in *all t.* willing to live | Heb 13:18
honestly
above *all t.* my brethren, | Jas 5:12
swear not
the end of *all t.* is at hand, be | 1Pe 4:7
sober
above *all t.* have fervent | 1Pe 4:8
charity
that God in *all t.* may be | 1Pe 4:11
glorified
given us *all t.* that pertain | 2Pe 1:3
to life
all t. continue as from | 2Pe 3:4
beginning
have an unction, ye know *all* | 1Jo 2:20
t.
same anointing teacheth you | 1Jo 2:27
all t.
God greater than heart, | 1Jo 3:20
knoweth *all t.*
I wish above *all t.* that thou | 3Jo 2
prosper

who bare record of *all t.* that | Re 1:2
he saw
hast created *all t.* for thy | Re 4:11
pleasure
I make *all t.* new | Re 21:5
he shall inherit *all t.* | Re 21:7

THESE **THINGS**

told her mother's house *these* | Ge 24:28
t.
Jacob said, All *these t.* are | Ge 42:36
against me
when he be guilty in one of | Le 5:5;
these t. | 5:17
defile not yourselves in any of | Le 18:24
these t.
they committed all *these t.* | Le 20:23
if ye will not be reformed by | Le 26:23
these t.
these t. the burden of | Nu 4:15
Kohath
all born of the country shall | Nu 15:13
do *these t.*
these t. ye shall do to the | Nu 29:39
Lord
these t. shall be for a statute | Nu 35:29
when all *these t.* are come | De 4:30
upon me
all that do *these t.* are an | De 18:12
abomination
when all *these t.* are come | De 30:1
upon thee
we heard *these t.* our hearts | Jos 2:11
did melt
nor would he have shewed us | J'g 13:23
these t.
when his wife had told him | 1Sa 25:37
these t.
these t. did three mighty | 2Sa 23:17;
men | 1Ch 11:19
these t. did Benaiah | 2Sa 23:22;
| 1Ch 11:24
these t. did Araunah give to | 2Sa 24:23
the king
done all *these t.* at thy | 1Ki 18:36
word
proclaimed *these t.* thou | 2Ki 23:17
hast done
in *these t.* was Solomon | 2Ch 3:3
instructed
did not king Solomon sin by | Ne 13:26
these t.
how long wilt thou speak *these* | Job 8:2
t.
these t. hast thou hid in | Job 10:13
thine heart
lo, all *these t.* worketh God | Job 33:29
with man
doeth *these t.* shall never be | Ps 15:5
moved
I remember *these t.* I pour out | Ps 42:4
my soul
these t. hast thou done and I | Ps 50:21
kept silence
these six *t.* doth the Lord hate | Pr 6:16
these t. also belong to the | Pr 24:23
wise
for *these t.* God will bring to | Ec 11:9
judgment
O Lord, by *these t.* men live, | Isa 38:16
and in all *these t.* is the life of
my spirit
behold, who hath created | Isa 40:26
these t.
these t. will I do, and not | Isa 42:16
forsake them
I form the light, I the Lord | Isa 45:7
do all *these t.*
thou didst not lay *these t.* to | Isa 47:7
heart
these t. come to thee in a | Isa 47:9
moment
let the astrologers save thee | Isa 47:13
from *these t.*
which hath declared *these t.* | Isa 48:14
these t. are come unto thee | Isa 51:19
wilt thou refrain thyself for | Isa 64:12
these t.
I said after she had done all | Jer 3:7
these t.
doings have procured *these t.* | Jer 4:18
to thee
shall I not visit for *these t.* | Jer 5:9;
| 5:29; 9:9
your iniquities have turned | Jer 5:25
away *these t.*
in *these t.* do I delight, saith | Jer 9:24
the Lord

say, Wherefore come *these t.* | Jer 13:22
on me
thou hast made all *these t.* | Jer 14:22
for thy sins I have done | Jer 30:15
these t. to thee
for *these t.* I weep, mine eye | La 1:16
runneth
heart is faint, for *these t.* our | La 5:17
eyes are dim
seeing thou dost all these *t.* | Eze 16:30;
| 17:18
thou hast fretted me in all | Eze 16:43
these t.
know ye not what *these t.* | Eze 17:12
that doeth the like to any | Eze 18:10
one of *these t.*
I will do *these t.* unto thee, | Eze 23:30
because
wilt thou not tell what *these* | Eze 24:19
t. are to us
none that holdeth with me in | Da 10:21
these t.
all *these t.* shall be finished | Da 12:7
what shall be the end of *these* | Da 12:8
t.
who is wise, he shall | Ho 14:9
understand *these t.*
these are the *t.* which ye shall | Zec 8:16
do
for all *these* are *t.* that I hate | Zec 8:17
but while he thought on *these* | M't 1:20
t.
when Herod heard *these t.* he | M't 2:3
was troubled
all *these t.* do Gentiles seek, | M't 6:32;
knows that ye have need of | Lu 12:30
these t.
all *these t.* be added to you | M't 6:33;
| Lu 12:31
hid *these t.* from the wise | M't 11:25;
| Lu 10:21
Jesus saith, Have ye | M't 13:51
understood *these t.*
whence hath this man *these* | M't 13:56;
t. | M'k 6:2
these are the *t.* which defile | M't 15:20
a man
all *these t.* have I kept from | M't 19:20
my youth
by what authority dost thou | M't 21:23;
these t. | M'k 11:28; Lu 20:2
I will tell you by what | M't 21:24;
authority I do *these t.* | 21:27;
| M'k 11:29, 33; Lu 20:8
all *these t.* shall come on | M't 23:36
this generation
Jesus said, See ye not all | M't 24:2
these t.
when shall *these t.* be | M't 24:3;
| M'k 13:4; Lu 21:7
all *these t.* must come to | M't 24:6;
pass | Lu 21:9, 28
when ye shall see all *these* | M't 24:33;
t. know that it is near | M'k 13:29;
| Lu 21:31
till all *these t.* be fulfilled | M't 24:34;
| M'k 13:30
till day that *these t.* be | Lu 1:20
performed
Mary kept *these t.* and | Lu 2:19
pondered them
they could not answer him to | Lu 14:6
these t.
he asked what *these t.* meant | Lu 15:26
and they understood none of | Lu 18:34
these t.
to escape all *these t.* that | Lu 21:36
shall come
for if they do *these t.* in a | Lu 23:31
green tree
to-day is third day since | Lu 24:21
these t. were
ought not Christ to have | Lu 24:26
suffered *these t.*
and ye are witnesses of *these* | Lu 24:48
t.
he said to them, Take *these t.* | Joh 2:16
hence
what sign, seeing that thou | Joh 2:18
dost *these t.*
Nicodemus said, How can | Joh 3:9
these t. be
master of Israel, and knowest | Joh 3:10
not *these t.*
he had done *these t.* on the | Joh 5:16
sabbath day
if do *these t.* shew thyself to | Joh 7:4
world

these *t.* understood not his   *Joh 12:16*
disciples, they remembered
these *t.* were written
these *t.* said Esaias, when he   *Joh 12:41*
saw his glory
if ye know these *t.* happy   *Joh 13:17*
are ye if ye do
all these *t.* will they do unto   *Joh 15:21;*
you   *16:3*
these *t.* therefore the soldiers   *Joh 19:24*
did
these *t.* were done, that   *Joh 19:36*
scriptures should
we are his witnesses of these *t.*   *Ac 5:32*
these *t.* so   *Ac 7:1*
hath not my hand made all   *Ac 7:50*
these *t.*
when heard these *t.* were cut   *Ac 7:54*
to heart
pray that none of these *t.*   *Ac 8:24*
come on me
saith the Lord, who doth all   *Ac 15:17*
these *t.*
we would know what these   *Ac 17:20*
t. mean
these *t.* cannot be spoken   *Ac 19:36*
against
none of these *t.* move me,   *Ac 20:24*
neither count
Jews assented, saying these *t.*   *Ac 24:9*
were so
there be judged of these *t.*   *Ac 25:9*
before me
to make thee a witness of   *Ac 26:16*
these *t.*
king knoweth of these *t.*   *Ac 26:26*
before whom
what shall we then say to   *Ro 8:31*
these *t.*
men that doeth these *t.* shall   *Ro 10:5*
live by
for he that in these *t.* serveth   *Ro 14:18*
Christ
say I these *t.* as a man, or   *1Co 9:8*
saith law
I used none of these *t.* nor   *1Co 9:15*
have I written
these *t.* were our examples,   *1Co 10:6*
to intent
and who is sufficient for   *2Co 2:16*
these *t.*
because of these *t.* cometh   *Eph 5:6*
wrath of God
if be any praise, think on   *Ph'p 4:8*
these *t.*
above all these *t.* put on   *Col 3:14*
charity
put brethren remembrance of   *1Ti 4:6*
these *t.*
these *t.* command   *1Ti 4:11*
meditate on these *t.*   *1Ti 4:15*
these *t.* give in charge   *1Ti 5:7*
observe these *t.*   *1Ti 5:21*
these *t.* exhort   *1Ti 6:2;*
  Tit 2:15
flee these *t.*   *1Ti 6:11*
of these *t.* put them in   *2Ti 2:14*
remembrance
these *t.* I will that thou affirm   *Tit 3:8*
constantly, these *t.* are good
and profitable to men
for he of whom these *t.* are   *Heb 7:13*
spoken
brethren, these *t.* ought not to   *Jas 3:10*
be so
for if these *t.* be in you and   *2Pe 1:8*
abound
but he that lacketh these *t.* is   *2Pe 1:9*
blind
for if ye do these *t.* ye shall   *2Pe 1:10*
never fall
I will put you in   *2Pe 1:12*
remembrance of these *t.*
have these *t.* always in   *2Pe 1:15*
remembrance
seeing all these *t.* shall be   *2Pe 3:11*
dissolved
in his epistles, speaking in   *2Pe 3:16*
them of these *t.*
seeing ye know these *t.*   *2Pe 3:17*
before, beware
the feet of angel who shewed   *Re 22:8*
me these *t.*
to testify to you these *t.* in   *Re 22:16*
the churches
he which testifieth these *t.*   *Re 22:20*
saith, I come

THOSE **THINGS**

eat those *t.* wherewith   *Ex 29:33*
atonement made
in those *t.* which they allow   *Le 22:2*
unto me
those *t.* which are revealed   *De 29:29*
belong to us
children of Israel did secretly   *2Ki 17:9*
those *t.*
whoso will observe those *t.*   *Ps 107:43*
they shall
for all those *t.* hath mine   *Isa 66:2*
hand made, and all those *t.*
have been
approach to those *t.* that are   *Eze 42:14*
for people
desired to see those *t.* ye   *M't 13:17;*
see, and hear those *t.* ye hear   *Lu 10:24*
offer those *t.* which Moses   *M'k 1:44*
commanded
performance of those *t.* which   *Lu 1:45*
were told
wondered at those *t.* told by   *Lu 2:18*
shepherds
whose shall those *t.* be thou   *Lu 12:20*
hast provided
I do always those *t.* that   *Joh 8:29*
please him
but those *t.* he hath so fulfilled   *Ac 3:18*
gave heed to those *t.* which   *Ac 8:6*
Philip spake
spake against those *t.* which   *Ac 13:45*
were
they searched whether those   *Ac 17:11*
t. were so
and Gallio cared for none of   *Ac 18:17*
those *t.*
of those *t.* in which I will   *Ac 26:16*
appear to thee
more than those *t.* spoken by   *Ac 27:11*
Paul
to do those *t.* not convenient   *Ro 1:28*
calleth those *t.* which be not,   *Ro 4:17*
as though
what fruit in those *t.* whereof   *Ro 6:21*
ye are now ashamed, for the
end of those *t.* is death
I may glory in those *t.* which   *Ro 15:17*
pertain
I will not dare to speak of   *Ro 15:18*
any of those *t.*
eating of those *t.* offered to   *1Co 8:4;*
idols   *8:10*
besides those *t.* which are   *2Co 11:28*
without
it is a shame even to speak   *Eph 5:12*
of those *t.*
forgetting those *t.* which are   *Ph'p 3:13*
behind, reaching to those *t.*
which are before
those *t.* which ye have   *Ph'p 4:9*
learned and seen do
intruding into those *t.* hath   *Col 2:18*
not seen
seek those *t.* which are above   *Col 3:1*
was faithful for a testimony   *Heb 3:5*
of those *t.*
removing of those *t.* which   *Heb 12:27*
are shaken, that those *t.* which
cannot be shaken may remain
ye give not those *t.* which are   *Jas 2:16*
needful
do those *t.* pleasing in his   *1Jo 3:22*
sight
we lose not those *t.* we have   *2Jo 8*
wrought
speak evil of those *t.* they   *Jude 10*
know not
blessed are they that keep   *Re 1:3*
those *t.*
fear none of those *t.* thou   *Re 2:10*
shalt suffer
seal up those *t.* seven thunders   *Re 10:4*
uttered
dead were judged out of   *Re 20:12*
those *t.* written

UNCLEAN **THINGS**

they shall eat unclean *t.* in   *Ho 9:3*
Assyria

WHAT **THINGS**

tell thy son what *t.* I have   *Ex 10:2*
wrought
Father knows what *t.* ye have   *M't 6:8*
need of
should tell no man what *t.*   *M'k 9:9*
they had seen

began to tell them what *t.*   *M'k 10:32*
should happen
what *t.* soever ye desire   *M'k 11:24*
when ye pray
go, tell John what *t.* ye have   *Lu 7:22*
seen
what *t.* they said to him   *Lu 24:19*
concerning Jesus
and they told what *t.* were   *Lu 24:35*
done in the way
what *t.* he doth, these doth   *Joh 5:19*
the Son
they understood not what *t.*   *Joh 10:6*
they were
some told them what *t.*   *Joh 11:46*
Jesus had done
what *t.* God wrought among   *Ac 21:19*
Gentiles
what *t.* were gain to me, I   *Ph'p 3:7*
counted loss

THINGS'

For which *t.* sake the wrath of   *Col 3:6*
God

THINK

t. on me when it shall be well   *Ge 40:14*
them marry to whom they *t.*   *Nu 36:6*
best
t. that all the king's sons are   *2Sa 13:33*
dead
And now ye *t.* to withstand   *2Ch 13:8*
T. upon me, my God, for good   *Ne 5:19*
that thou and the Jews *t.* to   *Ne 6:6*
rebel
My God, *t.* thou upon Tobiah   *Ne 6:14*
T. not with thyself that thou   *Es 4:13*
shalt
why then should I *t.* upon a   *Job 31:1*
maid
one would *t.* the deep to be   *Job 41:32*
hoary
t. up treacheries all day (B)   *Ps 38:12*
will *t.* of all thy works (B)   *Ps 77:12;*
  143:5
that thou dost *t.* (R)   *Ps 144:3*
though a wise man *t.* to know   *Ec 8:17*
so, neither doth his heart *t.*   *Isa 10:7*
Which *t.* to cause my people   *Jer 23:27*
the thoughts that I *t.* toward   *Jer 29:11*
you
and thou shalt *t.* an evil   *Eze 38:10*
thought
and *t.* to change times and   *Da 7:25*
laws
t. only evil (B)   *Ho 7:15*
if so be that God will *t.* upon   *Jon 1:6*
t. evil in his heart (B)   *Zec 7:10*
If ye *t.* good, give me my   *Zec 11:12*
price
t. not to say within yourselves   *M't 3:9*
T. not that I am come to   *M't 5:17*
destroy
they *t.* that they shall be heard   *M't 6:7*
Wherefore *t.* ye evil in your   *M't 9:4*
hearts
T. not that I am come   *M't 10:34*
to send
How *t.* ye? if a man have an   *M't 18:12*
what *t.* ye? A certain man   *M't 21:28*
had
Saying, What *t.* ye of   *M't 22:42*
Christ? whose
in such an hour as ye *t.* not   *M't 24:44*
the Son
What *t.* ye? They answered   *M't 26:66*
heard the blasphemy: what   *M'k 14:64*
t. ye
cometh at an hour when ye *t.*   *Lu 12:40*
not
t. ye that they were sinners   *Lu 13:4*
above
I *t.* not (S)   *Lu 17:9*
in them ye *t.* ye have eternal   *Joh 5:39*
life
Do not *t.* that I will accuse   *Joh 5:45*
you to
What *t.* ye, that he will not   *Joh 11:56*
come to
will *t.* that he doeth God   *Joh 16:2*
service
Whom *t.* ye that I am? I am   *Ac 13:25*
not
not to *t.* that the Godhead is   *Ac 17:29*
like
I *t.* myself happy, king   *Ac 26:2*
Agrippa
not to *t.* of himself more   *Ro 12:3*
highly

more highly than he ought to *t.*   Ro 12:3

but to *t.* soberly, according as God   Ro 12:3

not to *t.* of men above that which is   1Co 4:6

For I *t.* that God hath set forth us   1Co 4:9

if any man *t.* that he behaveth   1Co 7:36

I *t.* also that I have the Spirit of   1Co 7:40

if any man *t.* that he knoweth any   1Co 8:2

which we *t.* to be less honourable   1Co 12:23

If any man *t.* himself to be   1Co 14:37

to *t.* any thing as of ourselves   2Co 3:5

I *t.* to be bold against some, which   2Co 10:2

which *t.* of us as if we walked   2Co 10:2

let him of himself *t.* this again   2Co 10:7

Let such an one *t.* this, that, such   2Co 10:11

say again, Let no man *t.* me a fool   2Co 11:16

man should *t.* of me above that   2Co 12:6

t. ye that we excuse ourselves unto   2Co 12:19

if a man *t.* himself to be something   Ga 6:3

above all that we ask or *t.*   Eph 3:20

is meet for me to *t.* this of you all   Ph'p 1:7

be any praise, *t.* on these things   Ph'p 4:8

that man *t.* that he shall receive   Jas 1:7

Do ye *t.* that the scripture saith in   Jas 4:5

t. it strange that ye run not with them   1Pe 4:4

t. it not strange concerning the fiery   1Pe 4:12

I *t.* it meet, as long as I am   2Pe 1:13

THINKEST

T. thou that David doth honour   2Sa 10:3; 1Ch 19:3

T. thou this to be right, that thou   Job 35:2

him, saying, What *t.* thou Simon   M't 17:25

Tell us therefore, What *t.* thou   M't 22:17

T. thou that I cannot now pray to   M't 26:53

Which now of these three, *t.* thou   Lu 10:36

desire to hear of thee what thou *t.*   Ac 28:22

And *t.* thou this, O man, that   Ro 2:3

THINKETH

Me *t.* the running of the foremost   2Sa 18:27

needy; yet the Lord *t.* upon me   Ps 40:17

For as he *t.* in his heart, so is he   Pr 23:7

let him that *t.* he standeth take   1Co 10:12

is not easily provoked, *t.* no evil   1Co 13:5

If any other man *t.* that he hath   Ph'p 3:4

THINKING

t., have brought good tidings   2Sa 4:10

t. David cannot come in hither   2Sa 5:6

became futile in *t.* (R)   Ro 1:21

THINKS

t. some days of more importance (P)   Ro 14:5

t. it unclean (A)(P)(R)   Ro 14:14

THIRD

commanded he the second and *t.*   Ge 32:19

saw Ephraim's children of *t.* generation   Ge 50:23

the *t.* and fourth generation   Ex 20:5; 34:7; Nu 14:18; De 5:9

that hate me

the *t.* row a ligure, an agate   Ex 28:19; 39:12

the camp of Ephraim in the *t.* rank   Nu 2:24

an Edomite shall enter in *t.* generation   De 23:8

the *t.* lot came up for Zebulun   Jos 19:10

he sent again a captain of the *t.* fifty   2Ki 1:13

the *t.* lot came forth to Haram   1Ch 24:8

the *t.* lot came forth to Zaccur   1Ch 25:10

the *t.* captain of host for the *t.* month   1Ch 27:5

Israel shall be the *t.* with Egypt   Isa 19:24

the *t.* was the face of a lion   Eze 10:14

another *t.* kingdom of brass   Da 2:39

shall be *t.* ruler in kingdom   Da 5:7; 16:29

in the *t.* chariot white horses   Zec 6:3

he went out about the *t.* hour   M't 20:3

likewise *t.* died   M't 22:26; M'k 12:21; Lu 20:31

it was *t.* hour, they crucified him   M'k 15:25

come in the *t.* watch, find them so   Lu 12:38

he sent the *t.* and they wounded him   Lu 20:12

seeing it is but the *t.* hour of the day   Ac 2:15

Eutychus fell down from the *t.* loft   Ac 20:9

be ready at the *t.* hour of the night   Ac 23:23

t. teachers (S)   1Co 12:28

such an one caught up to *t.* heaven   2Co 12:2

and the *t.* beast had a face as a man   Re 4:7

had opened the *t.* seal, I heard   Re 6:5

the *t.* beast

the *t.* angel sounded, there fell a star   Re 8:10

and behold, the *t.* woe cometh quickly   Re 11:14

and the *t.* angel followed them, saying   Re 14:9

the *t.* angel poured out his vial on rivers   Re 16:4

the *t.* foundation was a chalcedony   Re 21:19

THIRD *TIME*

the Lord called Samuel the *t. time*   1Sa 3:8

Saul sent messengers again the *t. time*   1Sa 19:21

do it the *t. time*, they did it   1Ki 18:34

let the sword be doubled the *t. time*   Eze 21:14

and he prayed the *t. time*   M't 26:44; M'k 14:41

the *t. time* Jesus shewed himself   Joh 21:14

saith the *t. time*, lovest thou me? Peter was grieved, because he said, the *t. time*   Joh 21:17

the *t. time* I am ready to come   2Co 12:14; 13:1

THIRD *YEAR*

t. year, which is the year of tithing   De 26:12

in *t. year* of Asa, did Baasha slay   1Ki 15:28; 15:33

word of Lord came to Elijah in *t. year*   1Ki 18:1

in *t. year*, Jehoshaphat came to king   1Ki 22:2

in *t. year* of Hoshea son of Elah   2Ki 18:1

in *t. year* sow ye and reap   2Ki 19:29; Isa 37:30

in *t. year* of Jehoshaphat's reign   2Ch 17:7

Ammonites paid the second and *t. year*   2Ch 27:5

in *t. year* of the reign of Ahasuerus   Es 1:3

in *t. year* of the reign of Jehoiakim   Da 1:1

in the *t. year* of the reign of Belshazzar   Da 8:1

in the *t. year* of Cyrus king of Persia   Da 10:1

THIRDLY

secondarily prophets, *t.* teachers   1Co 12:28

THIRST

our children and our cattle with *t.*   Ex 17:3

hunger, and in *t.* and in nakedness   De 28:48

heart, to add drunkenness to *t.*   De 29:19

and now shall I die for *t.* and fall   J'g 15:18

yourselves to die by famine and *t.*   2Ch 32:11

for them out of the rock for their *t.*   Ne 9:15

and gavest them water for their *t.*   Ne 9:20

their winepresses, and suffer *t.*   Job 24:11

in my *t.* they gave me vinegar to   Ps 69:21

the wild asses quench their *t.*   Ps 104:11

their multitude dried up with *t.*   Isa 5:13

and their tongue faileth for *t.*   Isa 41:17

They shall not hunger nor *t.*   Isa 49:10

there is no water, and dieth for *t.*   Isa 50:2

unshod, and thy throat from *t.*   Jer 2:25

down from thy glory, and sit in *t.*   Jer 48:18

to the roof of his mouth for *t.*   La 4:4

like a dry land, and slay her with *t.*   Ho 2:3

famine of bread, nor a *t.* for water   Am 8:11

virgins and young men faint for *t.*   Am 8:13

hunger and *t.* after righteousness   M't 5:6

drinketh, this water shall *t.* again   Joh 4:13

that I shall give him shall never *t.*   Joh 4:14

give me this water, that I *t.* not   Joh 4:15

that believeth on me shall never *t.*   Joh 6:35

If any man *t.* let him come unto   Joh 7:37

might be fulfilled, saith, I *t.*   Joh 19:28

feed him: if he *t.* give him drink   Ro 12:20

both hunger, and *t.* and are naked   1Co 4:11

watchings often, in hunger and *t.*   2Co 11:27

no more, neither *t.* any more   Re 7:16

THIRSTED

And the people *t.* there for water   Ex 17:3

And they *t.* not when he led them   Isa 48:21

THIRSTETH

My soul *t.* for God, for the living   Ps 42:2

my soul *t.* for thee, my flesh longeth   Ps 63:1

my soul *t.* after thee, as a thirsty   Ps 143:6

Ho, every one that *t.* come ye   Isa 55:1

THIRSTY

a little water to drink: for I am *t.*   J'g 4:19

now shall I die very *t.* (S)   J'g 15:18

is hungry, and weary, and *t.*   2Sa 17:29

longeth for thee in a dry and *t.* land   Ps 63:1

Hungry and *t.* their soul fainted   Ps 107:5

soul thirsteth after thee, as a *t.* land   Ps 143:6

and if he be *t.* give him water   Pr 25:21

As cold waters to a *t.* soul, so is good   Pr 25:25

brought water to him that *Isa 21:14*
was *t.*
or as when a *t.* man dreameth *Isa 29:8*
will cause the drink of the *t.* to *Isa 32:6*
fail
and the *t.* land springs of *Isa 35:7*
water
pour water upon him that is *t.* *Isa 44:3*
shall drink, but ye shall be *t.* *Isa 65:13*
wilderness, in a dry and *t.* *Eze 19:13*
ground
I was *t.* and ye gave me *M't 25:35*
drink
fed thee? or *t.* and gave thee *M't 25:37*
drink
I was *t.* and ye gave me no *M't 25:42*
drink

THIRTEEN

his son was *t.* years old *Ge 17:25*
hundred and threescore and *t.* *Nu 3:43;*
 3:46
t. young bullocks, two rams *Nu 29:13*
every bullock of the *t.* *Nu 29:14*
bullocks
t. cities and their villages *Jos 19:6*
the tribe of Benjamin, *t.* *Jos 21:4*
cities
Manasseh in Bashan, *t.* cities *Jos 21:6*
t. cities with their suburbs *Jos 21:19;*
 21:33
building his own house *t.* *1Ki 7:1*
years
their families were *t.* cities *1Ch 6:60*
Manasseh in Bashan *t.* cities *1Ch 6:62*
and brethren of Hosah were *1Ch 26:11*
t.
length of the gate, *t.* cubits *Eze 40:11*

THIRTEENTH

in the *t.* year they rebelled *Ge 14:4*
t. to Huppah, the fourteenth *1Ch 24:13*
The *t.* to Shubael, he, his *1Ch 25:20*
sons
scribes called on the *t.* day *Es 3:12*
upon the *t.* day of the twelfth *Es 3:13;*
 8:12
Adar, on the *t.* day of the same *Es 9:1*
the *t.* day of the month Adar *Es 9:17*
together on the *t.* day thereof *Es 9:18*
in the *t.* year of his reign *Jer 1:2*
the *t.* year of Josiah the son *Jer 25:3*

THIRTIETH

in the nine and *t.* year of *2Ki 15:13*
Uzziah
In the nine and *t.* year of *2Ki 15:17*
Azariah
seven and *t.* year of the *2Ki 25:27*
captivity of
five and *t.* year of the reign *2Ch 15:19*
of Asa
six and *t.* year of the reign of *2Ch 16:1*
Asa
two and *t.* year of Artaxerxes *Ne 5:14*
the two and *t.* year of *Ne 13:6*
Artaxerxes
seven and *t.* year of the *Jer 52:31*
captivity of
Now it came to pass in the *t.* *Eze 1:1*
year

THIRTY

the height of the ark was *t.* *Ge 6:15*
cubits
Salah lived *t.* years, and *Ge 11:14*
begat Eber
Peleg lived *t.* years, and *Ge 11:18*
begat Reu
Serug lived *t.* years, and *Ge 11:22*
begat Nahor
peradventure there shall be *t.* *Ge 18:30*
found, he said, I will not do it
if I find *t.* there
t. milch camels with their *Ge 32:15*
colts
Joseph was *t.* years old when *Ge 41:46*
he stood
shall give to their master *t.* *Ex 21:32*
shekels
the length of one curtain *t.* *Ex 26:8;*
cubits *36:15*
thy estimation shall be *t.* *Le 27:4*
shekels
from *t.* years old and upwards *Nu 4:3;*
 4:23, 30, 35, 39, 43, 47; 1Ch 23:3

Jair had *t.* sons, they had *t.* *J'g 10:4*
cities
Ibzan had *t.* sons and *t.* *J'g 12:9*
daughters he took in *t.*
daughters for his sons
Abdon had forty sons and *t.* *J'g 12:14*
nephews
brought *t.* companions to be *J'g 14:11*
with him
give you *t.* sheets, *t.* change *J'g 14:12*
of garments
t. linen tunics (B) *J'g 14:12*
ye shall give *t.* sheets, *t.* *J'g 14:13*
change of garments
Samson slew *t.* men, and *J'g 14:19*
took their spoil
to smite about *t.* men of *J'g 20:31;*
Israel *20:39*
Saul sat among about *t.* *1Sa 9:22*
persons
David was *t.* years old when *2Sa 5:4*
he began
three of the *t.* chief went *2Sa 23:13*
down
Beniah was more *2Sa 23:23;*
honourable than the *t.* *1Ch 11:15, 25;*
 27:6
Asahel. brother of Joab, was *2Sa 23:24*
one of the *t.*
provision for one day was *t.* *1Ki 4:22*
measures
height of house of Lord was *t.* *1Ki 6:2*
cubits
height of house of the forest *1Ki 7:2*
was *t.* cubits
the breadth of the porch was *t.* *1Ki 7:6*
cubits
a line of *t.* cubits did *1Ki 7:23*
compass it about
appointed to Hezekiah *t.* *2Ki 18:14*
talents
Adina a captain, and *t.* with *1Ch 11:42*
him
the number of them was *t.* *Ezr 1:9*
chargers
t. basons of gold, silver *Ezr 1:10*
basons
take from hence *t.* men with *Jer 38:10*
thee
t. chambers were on the *Eze 40:17*
pavement
the side chambers were *t.* in *Eze 41:6*
order
courts joined of *t.* cubits *Eze 46:22*
broad
they weighed for my price *t.* *Zec 11:12*
pieces
I took the *t.* pieces of silver *Zec 11:13;*
 M't 27:9
brought *t.* fold *M't 13:8;*
 13:23; M'k 4:8, 20
they covenanted with him *M't 26:15*
for *t.* pieces
Judas brought again the *t.* *M't 27:3*
pieces of silver
Jesus began to be about *t.* *Lu 3:23*
years of age
had rowed about twenty-five *Joh 6:19*
or *t.* furlongs

THIRTY ONE

kings Joshua subdued *t.* and *Jos 12:24*
one
in the *t.* and *one* year of *1Ki 16:23*
king Asa
Josiah eight years old, *2Ki 22:1;*
reigned *t.* and *one* years *2Ch 34:1*

THIRTY TWO

Reu lived *t. two* years, and *Ge 11:20*
begat Serug
Lord's tribute was *t. two* *Nu 31:40*
persons
t. two kings were with *1Ki 20:1;*
Ben-hadad *20:16*
king commanded his *t. two* *1Ki 22:31*
captains
Jehoram was *t. two* years old *2Ki 8:17;*
when he began to reign *2Ch 21:5, 20*

THIRTY THREE

all souls of sons and *Ge 46:15*
daughters, *t. three*
in blood of purifying *t. three* *Le 12:4*
days
David reigned in Jerusalem *t.* *2Sa 5:5;*
and *three* years *1Ki 2:11; 1Ch 3:4;*
 29:27

THIRTY FOUR

Eber lived *t. four* years, *Ge 11:16*
begat Peleg

THIRTY FIVE

Arphaxad lived *five* and *t.* *Ge 11:12*
years
Jehoshaphat was *t. five* *1Ki 22:42;*
years old when he began *2Ch 20:31*
to reign
made two pillars *t. five* *2Ch 3:15*
cubits high

THIRTY SIX

men of Ai smote *t. six* men *Jos 7:5*
of Israel

THIRTY SEVEN

Uriah the Hittite, *t. seven* *2Sa 23:39*
in all
in the *t.* and *seventh* year of *2Ki 13:10*
Joash

THIRTY EIGHT

over brook Zered *t. eight* *De 2:14*
years
in the *t.* and *eighth* year of *1Ki 16:29*
Asa
in the *t.* and *eighth* year of *2Ki 15:8*
Azariah
which had an infirmity *t. eight* *Joh 5:5*
years

THIRTY NINTH

Asa in the *t.* and *ninth* year *2Ch 16:12*
diseased

THIRTYFOLD

some sixtyfold, some *t.* *M't 13:8*
brought forth, some *t.* (S) *M'k 4:8*
forth fruit, some *t.* some *M'k 4:20*
sixty

THIS

t. same shall comfort us *Ge 5:29*
concerning work
saying, *T.* shall not be thine *Ge 15:4*
heir, but he shall
and I will speak yet but *Ge 18:32*
t. once
they said, *T.* one fellow came *Ge 19:9*
in to sojourn
because thou hast done *t.* *Ge 22:14*
as it is said to *t.* day *Ge 22:16*
thing
after *t.*, Abraham buried *Ge 23:19*
Sarah
willing to follow me unto *t.* *Ge 24:5*
land
unto thy seed will I give *t.* *Ge 24:7*
land
send me good speed *t.* day *Ge 24:12*
shalt thou be clear from *t.* *Ge 24:41*
my oath
And I came *t.* day unto the *Ge 24:42*
well
we will give thee *t.* also for *Ge 29:27*
the service
in *t.* will we consent unto *Ge 34:15*
you
sent coat, and said, *T.* have *Ge 37:32*
we found
bound a thread, saying, *T.* *Ge 38:28*
came out first
t. breach be upon thee *Ge 38:29*
T. is the thing which I have *Ge 41:28*
is not *t.* it in which my Lord *Ge 44:5*
drinketh
What deed is *t.* that ye have *Ge 44:15*
done
if ye take *t.* from me, and *Ge 44:29*
mischief befall
fed me all my life long unto *Ge 48:15*
t. day
and *t.* shall be a token unto *Ex 3:12*
thee
I will give *t.* people favour in *Ex 3:21*
in *t.* thou shalt know that I *Ex 7:17*
am Lord
neither did he set his heart to *Ex 7:23*
t. also
that ye shall keep *t.* service *Ex 12:25*
Aaron, *T.* is the ordinance *Ex 12:43*

T. shall be, when the Lord shall give   *Ex 16:8*

t. they shall give, each half a shekel   *Ex 30:13*

I also will do t. unto you: I will   *Le 26:16*

t. shall be thine of the most holy things from the fire   *Nu 18:9;*

alas, who shall live when God doth t.   *De 18:3*

Nu 24:23

T. is the offering made by fire   *Nu 28:3*

until ye came into t. place   *De 1:31; 11:5*

O that they were wise and understood t.   *De 32:29*

is not t. laid up in store with me   *De 32:34*

t. shall go with thee, t. shall not go   *J'g 7:4*

come up t. once, for he hath shewed all   *J'g 16:18*

neither hath the Lord chosen t.   *1Sa 16:8; 16:9*

and he saith, Let not Jonathan know t.   *1Sa 20:3*

that t. be no grief unto thee   *1Sa 25:31*

I will be more vile than t. (S)   *2Sa 6:22*

t. was a small thing in thy sight   *2Sa 7:19*

shall not Shimei be put to death for t.   *2Sa 19:21*

is not t. the blood of the men   *2Sa 23:17*

to judge t. thy great people   *1Ki 3:9*

t. was the cause that he lift his hand   *1Ki 11:27*

I will for t. afflict the seed of David   *1Ki 11:39*

by t. I know thou art a man of God   *1Ki 17:24*

I set t. before an hundred men   *2Ki 4:43*

under the hand of Judah unto t.   *2Ki 8:22*

glory of t. and tarry at home   *2Ki 14:10*

He shall not come into t. city   *2Ki 19:32*

at commandment of Lord came t. on Judah   *2Ki 24:3*

destroyed them utterly unto t. day   *1Ch 4:41*

on t. side Jordan westward in all   *1Ch 26:30*

because t. was in thine heart   *2Ch 1:11*

hast fulfilled it as it is t. day   *2Ch 6:15*

the Lord is able to give more than t.   *2Ch 25:9*

send his pleasure concerning t.   *Ezr 5:17*

let his house be made a dunghi'l for t.   *Ezr 6:11*

put such thing as t. in king's heart   *Ezr 7:27*

we fasted, and besought God for t.   *Ezr 8:23*

hast given us such deliverance as t.   *Ezr 9:13*

cannot stand before thee because of t.   *Ezr 9:15*

remember me concerning t.   *Ne 13:14; 13:22*

come to kingdom for such time as t.   *Es 4:14*

t. we have searched, so it is   *Job 5:27*

the hand of the Lord hath wrought t.   *Job 12:9*

upright men shall be astonied at t.   *Job 17:8*

for t. I make haste   *Job 20:2*

knowest not t.   *Job 20:4*

hear and let t. be your consolation   *Job 21:2*

in t. thou art not just, I will answer   *Job 33:12*

thinkest thou t. to be right   *Job 35:2*

t. shall be the portion of their cup   *Ps 11:6*

though war rise, in t. will I be confident   *Ps 27:3*

for t. shall every one that is godly pray   *Ps 32:6*

t. thou hast seen, keep not silence   *Ps 35:22*

by t. I know that thou favourest me   *Ps 41:11*

shall not God search t. out   *Ps 44:21*

for t. God is our God for ever   *Ps 48:14*

t. their way is their folly, yet their   *Ps 49:13*

now consider t. ye that forget God   *Ps 50:22*

turn back, t. I know, for God is for me   *Ps 56:9*

twice have I heard t. that power belongs   *Ps 62:11*

t. shall please the Lord better than ox   *Ps 69:31*

humble shall see t. and be glad   *Ps 69:32*

when I thought to know t. it was painful   *Ps 73:16*

the Lord heard t. and was wroth   *Ps 78:21; 78:59*

for t. was a statute for Israel   *Ps 81:4*

t. he ordained in Joseph for a testimony   *Ps 81:5*

neither doth a fool understand t.   *Ps 92:6*

let t. be reward of mine adversaries   *Ps 109:20*

T.. is my comfort in my affliction   *Ps 119:50*

I had, because I kept precepts   *Ps 119:56*

T. is my rest for ever   *Ps 132:14*

t. honour have all his saints   *Ps 149:9*

for t. a man is envied of his neighbour   *Ec 4:4*

t. hath more rest than the other   *Ec 6:5*

dost not inquire wisely concerning t.   *Ec 7:10*

it is good that thou take hold of t. also from t. withdraw not thine hand   *Ec 7:18*

t. have I found   *Ec 7:27; 7:29*

whether shall prosper, either t. or that   *Ec 11:6*

who hath required t. at your hand   *Isa 1:12*

he said, Lo, t. hath touched thy lips   *Isa 6:7*

but t. shall be with burning   *Isa 9:5*

zeal of the Lord of hosts will perform t.   *Isa 9:7*

surely t. iniquity shall not be purged   *Isa 22:14*

by t. iniquity of Jacob be purged   *Isa 27:9*

t. also cometh forth from the Lord   *Isa 28:29*

saying, Read t., I pray thee   *Isa 29:11; 29:12*

Forasmuch as t. people draw near   *Isa 29:13*

therefore have I cried concerning t.   *Isa 30:7*

who among them can declare t.   *Isa 43:9; 45:21*

remember t.   *Isa 46:8*

declare ye, tell t.   *Isa 48:20*

therefore hear now t.   *Isa 47:8; 48:1, 16; 51:21*

t. shall ye have of mine hand, ye shall   *Isa 50:11*

blessed is the man that doeth t.   *Isa 56:2*

wilt thou call t. a fast   *Isa 58:5*

is not t. the fast that I have chosen   *Isa 58:6*

when ye see t. your hearts rejoice   *Isa 66:14*

be astonished, O ye heavens, at t.   *Jer 2:12*

hast thou not procured t. unto thyself   *Jer 2:17*

for t. gird you with sackcloth, lament   *Jer 4:8*

for t. shall the earth mourn   *Jer 4:28*

how shall I pardon thee for t.   *Jer 5:7*

be avenged on such a nation as t.   *Jer 5:9; 5:29; 9:9*

but let him that glorieth, glory in t.   *Jer 9:24*

I will t. once cause them to know   *Jer 16:21*

I will bring upon t. city   *Jer 19:15*

was not t. to know me, saith the Lord   *Jer 22:16*

t. hath been thy manner from thy youth   *Jer 22:21*

how long t. be in heart of prophets   *Jer 23:26*

t. shall be covenant that I will make   *Jer 31:33*

I knew that t. was the word of Lord   *Jer 32:8*

I will bring them again into t. place   *Jer 32:37*

t. I recall to mind, therefore I hope   *La 3:21*

for t. our heart is faint, our eyes are dim   *La 5:17*

he said, Hast thou seen t.   *Eze 8:15; 8:17; 47:6*

t. was the iniquity of thy sister Sodom   *Eze 16:49*

in t. your fathers have blasphemed me   *Eze 20:27*

saith the Lord, t. shall not be the same   *Eze 21:26*

and when her sister Aholibah saw t.   *Eze 23:11*

t. cometh, ye shall know   *Eze 24:24; 33:33*

I will yet for t. be inquired of by Israel   *Eze 36:37*

t. gate shall be shut, no man shall enter   *Eze 44:2*

shall not find occasion against t. Daniel   *Da 6:5; 6:28*

t. shall be their derision in Egypt   *Ho 7:16*

t. liketh you, O children of Israel   *Am 4:5*

Lord repented for t. it shall not be   *Am 7:3; 7:6*

shall not the land tremble for t.   *Am 8:8*

saith the Lord that doth t.   *Am 9:12*

was not t. my saying in my country   *Jon 4:2*

the remnant of Baal from t. place   *Zep 1:4*

t. shall they have for their pride   *Zep 2:10*

t. shall come to pass if ye obey Lord   *Zec 6:15*

t. shall be the plague wherewith   *Zec 14:12; 14:15*

t. shall be the punishment of Egypt   *Zec 14:19*

t. hath been by your means   *Mal 1:9*

should I accept t. of your hands   *Mal 1:13*

The Lord will cut off the man that doth t.   *Mal 2:12*

t. is Elias, which was for to come   *M't 11:14*

but if ye had known that t. meaneth   *M't 12:7*

is not t. the carpenter's son   *M't 13:55; M'k 6:3; Lu 4:22; Joh 6:42*

Lord, t. shall not be unto thee   *M't 16:22*

t. that if good man of the house had known in   *M't 24:43; Lu 12:39*

what watch

shall also t. that t. woman hath done   *M't 26:13*

saying, Truly t. was the Son of God   *M't 27:54*

and if t. come to the governor's ears   *M't 28:14*

and the second is like, namely, t.   *M'k 12:31*

whereby shall I know t. for I am old   *Lu 1:18*

how shall t. be, seeing I know not a man   *Lu 1:34*

saying, What manner of child shall t. be   *Lu 1:66*

added yet t. above all, that he shut up John   *Lu 3:20*

have ye not read so much as t. what David   *Lu 6:3*

be sure of t.   *Lu 10:11*

in t. rejoice not   *Lu 10:20*

t. my son was dead and is alive again   *Lu 15:24*

take t. and divide it among yourselves   *Lu 22:17*

that t. must yet be accomplished in me   *Lu 22:37*

certainly t. was a righteous man   *Lu 23:47*

saying, T., was he of whom I spake   *Joh 1:15*

his disciples remembered he had said t.   *Joh 2:22*

on t. came his disciples, and marvelled   *Joh 4:27*

is not t. Christ   *Joh 4:29*

marvel not at t.   *Joh 5:28*

t. he said to prove him, for he himself knew   *Joh 6:6*

is not *t.* he whom they seek Joh 7:25
to kill
t. did not Abraham Joh 8:40
believest thou *t.* Joh 11:26
t. spake he not of himself, Joh 11:51
but prophesied
t. he said, not that he cared Joh 12:6
for the poor
for what intent he spake *t.* Joh 13:28
unto him
by *t.* all men know ye are my Joh 13:35
disciples
greater love hath no man Joh 15:13
than *t.*
by *t.* we believe thou camest Joh 16:30
from God
t. Jesus shall so come in like Ac 1:11
manner
what meaneth *t.* Ac 2:12
he seeing *t.* before Ac 2:31
t. Jesus hath God raised up, Ac 2:32
whereof we all
he hath shed forth *t.* which ye Ac 2:33
now see
when they heard *t.* they were Ac 2:37
pricked
ye men of Israel, why marvel Ac 3:12
ye at *t.*
they doubted whereunto *t.* Ac 5:24
would grow
that *t.* Jesus of Nazareth Ac 6:14
destroy *t.* place
t. Moses they refused, did Ac 7:35
God send
as for *t.* Moses, we wot not Ac 7:40
what is become
repent therefore of *t.* thy Ac 8:22
wickedness
the place of scripture which Ac 8:32
he read was *t.*
is not *t.* he that destroyed Ac 9:21
them which
when Gentiles heard *t.* they Ac 13:48
were glad
to *t.* agree .he words of the Ac 15:15
prophets
t. did she many days, but Ac 16:18
Paul turned
when they heard *t.* they were Ac 19:5
baptized
but *t.* I confess to thee, that Ac 24:14
after
thinkest thou *t.* O man, that Ro 2:3
judgest
knowing *t.* that our old man is Ro 6:6
crucified
not only *t.* but when Rebecca Ro 9:10
conceived
when therefore I have Ro 15:28
performed *t.*
t. I say, every one saith, I 1Co 1:12
am of Paul
my answer to them that 1Co 9:3
examine me is *t.*
in *t.* that I declare to you, I 1Co 11:17
praise you not
shall I praise you in *t.*? I 1Co 11:22
praise you not
have not knowledge, I speak 1Co 15:34
t. to shame
in *t.* we groan earnestly, 2Co 5:2
desiring
I speak not *t.* to condemn you 2Co 7:3
t. they did, not as we hoped, 2Co 8:5
but
let him of himself think *t.* 2Co 10:7;
again 10:11
t. also we wish, even your 2Co 13:9
perfection
t. would I learn of you, Ga 3:2
Received ye
law is fulfilled in one word, Ga 5:14
even in *t.*
t. I say therefore, and testify Eph 4:17
in Lord
for *t.* ye know, that no Eph 5:5
whoremonger
t. I pray, your love may Ph'p 1:9
abound
I know that *t.* shall turn to Ph'p 1:19
my salvation
when with you, *t.* we 2Th 3:10
commanded you
knowing *t.* 1Ti 1:9;
  Jas 1:3; 2Pe 1:20; 3:3
T. is a true saying, If a man 1Ti 3:1
desire
in doing *t.* thou shalt both 1Ti 4:16
save thyself
t. with an oath Heb 7:21

t. did he once Heb 7:27
But *t.* man, because he Heb 7:24
continueth
in *t.* the children of God are 1Jo 3:10
manifest
in *t.* was manifested the love 1Jo 4:9
of God
by *t.* we know we love children 1Jo 5:2
put in remembrance tho' once Jude 5
knew *t.*
t. thou hast, that thou hatest Re 2:6
the deeds

THIS *IS*

Adam said, *T. is* bone of my Ge 2:23
bones
t. is thy kindness, thou shalt Ge 20:13
shew me
Jacob said, *T. is* none other Ge 28:17
but the house of God, and
t. is the gate of heaven
when Jacob saw, he said, *T.* Ge 32:2
is God's host
Pharaoh said, Can we find Ge 41:38
such a one as *t. is*
not so, father, for *t. is* the Ge 48:18
firstborn
t. is my name for ever Ex 3:15
the magicians said, *T. is* the Ex 8:19
finger of God
t. is that which the Lord hath Ex 16:23
said
t. is that the Lord spake, Le 10:3
saying
t. is that belongeth to the Nu 8:24
Levites
t. is thine, the heave offering Nu 18:11
of gift
do no more such wickedness De 13:11
as *t. is*
and *t. is* the manner of the De 15:2
release
arise, anoint him, for *t. is* he 1Sa 16:12
forasmuch as *t. is* done of 1Ki 11:11
thee
t. is the sign the Lord hath 1Ki 13:3
spoken
t. is but a light thing in sight 2Ki 3:18
of Lord
t. is not the way, neither is 2Ki 6:19
this the city
O king, *t. is* the woman, and *t.* 2Ki 8:5
is her son
so that they shall not say, *T.* 2Ki 9:37
is Jezebel
t. is that king Ahaz 2Ch 28:22
t. is nothing but sorrow of Ne 2:2
heart
t. is God that brought thee Ne 9:18
out
behold, *t. is* the joy of his Job 8:19
way
I know that *t. is* with thee Job 10:13
t. is the place of him that Job 18:21
knoweth not
t. is the portion of a wicked Job 20:29;
man 27:13
t. is the generation of them Ps 24:6
that seek
t. is the hill God desireth to Ps 68:16
dwell in
t. is my infirmity, I will Ps 77:10
remember
they may know that *t. is* thy Ps 109:27
hand
t. is the Lord's doing Ps 118:23;
  M't 21:42
t. is my comfort in mine Ps 119:50
affliction
t. is my rest for ever, here Ps 132:14
will I
whereof it be said, See, *T. is* Ec 1:10
new
to rejoice in labour, *t. is* the Ec 5:19
gift of God
for *t. is* the whole duty of Ec 12:13
man
t. is my beloved, and *t. is* my Ca 5:16
friend
t. is known in all the earth Isa 12:5
t. is our God, we have waited Isa 25:9
for him
t. is all the fruit, to take away Isa 27:9
his sin
t. is the rest, and *t. is* the Isa 28:12
refreshing
saying, *T. is* the way, walk ye Isa 30:21
in it

for *t. is* as the waters of Noah Isa 54:9
unto me
t. is the heritage of servants Isa 54:17
of the Lord
as for me, *t. is* my covenant Isa 59:21
with them
t. is thy wickedness, it is Jer 4:18
bitter
t. is a nation that obeyeth not Jer 7:28
the Lord
t. is grief Jer 10:19
t. is thy lot Jer 13:25
t. is the name he shall be Jer 23:6;
called, The Lord our 33:16
Righteousness
t. is Zion, whom no man Jer 30:17
seeketh after
t. is Jerusalem, I set it in the Eze 5:5
midst
t. is a lamentation, shall be Eze 19:14
for a lamentation
t. is Pharaoh and all his Eze 31:18
multitude
t. is the writing that was Da 5:25
written
arise, depart, for *t. is* not Mic 2:10
your rest
t. is the rejoicing city that Zep 2:15
dwelt
t. is the curse that goeth forth Zec 5:3
t. is an ephah Zec 5:6
t. is wickedness Zec 5:8
t. is he that was spoken of by M't 3:3
Esaias
t. is beloved Son M't 3:17;
  17:5; M'k 9:7; Lu 9:35
for *t. is* the law and the M't 7:12
prophets
t. is he of whom it is M't 11:10;
written Lu 7:27
t. is Elias which was for to M't 11:14
come
t. is he had received seed by M't 13:19
the way
Jesus said, With men *t. is* M't 19:26
impossible
t. is the heir M't 21:38;
  M'k 12:7; Lu 20:14
t. is first commandment M't 22:38;
  M'k 12:30
Jesus said, Take, eat, *t. is* my M't 26:26
body
t. is my blood M't 26:28;
  M'k 14:22, 24; Lu 22:19, 20; 1Co 11:24,
  25
t. is one of them, he denied M'k 14:69
again
have known what manner of Lu 7:39
woman *t. is*
t. is your hour and the power Lu 22:53
of darkness
and *t. is* the record of John Joh 1:19
t. is he of whom I said, After Joh 1:30
me cometh
I bare record that *t. is* the Joh 1:34
Son of God
t. is condemnation, that Joh 3:19
light is come
that *t. is* indeed the Christ Joh 4:42;
  7:26, 41
t. is the work of God, that Joh 6:29
ye believe
t. is the Father's will which Joh 6:39;
sent me 6:40
t. is the bread which cometh Joh 6:50
from heaven
t. is that bread which came Joh 6:58
down from
t. is an hard saying, who can Joh 6:60
hear it
some said, *T. is* he Joh 9:9
t. is our son Joh 9:20
t. is my commandment, that Joh 15:12
ye love
t. is life eternal, that they Joh 17:3
might know
t. is that which was spoken by Ac 2:16
Joel
t. is that Moses which said Ac 7:37
unto Israel
t. is he in the church in Ac 7:38
wilderness
Saul increased, proving that *t.* Ac 9:22
is very Christ
t. is my covenant Ro 11:27;
  Heb 8:10; 10:16
t. is not to eat the Lord's 1Co 11:20
supper

THIS IS

obey your parents, for *t. is*   Eph 6:1
right
if I live, *t. is* the fruit of my   Ph'p 1:22
labour
for *t. is* well pleasing to the   Col 3:20
Lord
for *t. is* the will of God   1Th 4:3; 5:18
t. is a faithful saying   1Ti 1:15;
    3:1; 4:9; Tit 3:8
for *t. is* acceptable in the sight   1Ti 2:3
of God
t. is thankworthy, if a man   1Pe 2:19
endure
take patiently, *t. is* acceptable   1Pe 2:20
with God
t. is the message we have   1Jo 1:5; 3:11
and *t. is* the promise, even   1Jo 2:25
eternal life
t. is his commandment, that   1Jo 3:23
we should believe
and *t. is* that spirit of antichrist   1Jo 4:3
t. is the love of God, that we   1Jo 5:3
keep his commandments
and *t. is* the victory, even our   1Jo 5:4
faith
t. is he that came by water   1Jo 5:6
and blood
t. is the witness of God which   1Jo 5:9
he testified
t. is the record, that God   1Jo 5:11
hath given life
t. is the confidence that we   1Jo 5:14
have in him
t. is the true God, and eternal   1Jo 5:20
life
t. is love that we walk after   2Jo 6
his commandments
t. is a deceiver and an antichrist   2Jo 7
years were finished. T. is the   Re 20:5
first resurrection
into lake of fire, *t. is* the   Re 20:14
second death

IS THIS

Lord said to the woman,   Ge 3:13;
What *is t.* that thou hast done   12:18;
    26:10; 29:25
what man *is t.* that walketh   Ge 24:65
in the field
what *is t.* that God hath   Ge 42:28
done unto us
is t. your younger brother, of   Ge 43:29
whom
what deed *is t.* that ye have   Ge 44:15
done
saying, What *is t.*   Ex 13:14; J'g 18:24
wherefore *is t.* that thou hast   Ex 17:3
brought us
what trespass *is t.* ye   Jos 22:16
committed
what *is t.* thou hast done   J'g 15:11;
    2Sa 12:21
what wickedness *is t.* done   J'g 20:12
among you
what *is t.* come to the son   1Sa 10:11
of Kish
Saul said, Is *t.* thy voice, my   1Sa 24:16
son David
is t. the manner of man, O   2Sa 7:19
Lord God
is t. thy kindness to thy   2Sa 16:17
friend
what confidence *is t.* wherein   2Ki 18:19
nor *is t.* a work of one day   Ezr 10:13
or two
who *is t.* that darkeneth   Job 38:2
counsel
who *is t.* cometh out of the   Ca 3:6
wilderness
who *is t.* that cometh up from   Ca 8:5
the wilderness
is t. your joyous city, whose   Isa 23:7
antiquity
who *is t.* that cometh from   Isa 63:1
Edom, with
for who *is t.* that engaged his   Jer 30:21
heart
who *is t.* that cometh up as a   Jer 46:7
flood
is t. of thy whoredoms a   Eze 16:20
small matter
is not t. a brand plucked out   Zec 3:2
of the fire
and see what *is t.* that goeth   Zec 5:5
forth
saying, What manner of man *M't 8:27*;

is t. that the winds obey him   M'k 4:41;
    Lu 8:25
people said, Is not *t.* the son   M't 12:23
of David
who *is t.*   M't 21:10
what thing *is t.*   M'k 1:27
whence *is t.* to me, that mother   Lu 1:43
of my Lord
what a word *is t.* with   Lu 4:36
authority he
who *is t.* which speaketh   Lu 5:21
blasphemies
who *is t.* that forgiveth sin   Lu 7:49
also
but who *is t.* of whom I hear   Lu 9:9
such things
what *is t.* then that it is   Lu 20:17
written
what manner of saying *is t.*   Joh 7:36
he said
is t. your son, say was born   Joh 9:19
blind
what *is t.* that he saith unto   Joh 16:17;
us   16:18
for our rejoicing, *is t.* the   2Co 1:12
testimony
to me *is t.* grace given, to   Eph 3:8
preach to
pure religion and undefiled *is*   Jas 1:27
t.

THISTLE

the *t.* in Lebanon, a wild   2Ki 14:9;
beast trod down the *t.*   2Ch 25:18
thorn and *t.* come up on their   Ho 10:8
altars

THISTLES

thorns and *t.* shall it bring   Ge 3:18
forth
let *t.* grow instead of wheat   Job 31:40
lily among *t.* (B)   Ca 2:2
do men gather figs of *t.*   M't 7:16

THITHER

city is near, let me escape *t.*   Ge 19:20
haste thee, escape *t.* till thou   Ge 19:22
be come *t.*
do any thing till thou be come   Ge 19:22
t.
thou bring not my son *t.* again   Ge 24:6
that thou mayest bring in *t.*   Ex 26:33
the ark
that the slayer may flee *t.*   Nu 35:6;
    11:15; De 4:42; 19:3, 4; Jos 20:3, 9
thou shalt not go in *t.*   De 1:37;
    1:38, 39
unto his habitation, *t.* thou   De 12:5
shalt come
t. bring your burnt offerings   De 12:6;
    12:11
Israel went *t.* a whoring after   J'g 8:27
and *t.* fled all the men and   J'g 9:51
women
did to Israelites that came *t.*   1Sa 2:14
they carried the ark of God   1Sa 5:8
about *t.*
now let us go *t.*; peradventure   1Sa 9:6
they inquired if the man   1Sa 10:22
should come *t.*
make ready before it was   1Ki 6:7
brought *t.*
waters were divided hither   2Ki 2:8;
and *t.*   2:14
Elisha turned in *t.* to eat bread   2Ki 4:8;
    4:11
for *t.* the Syrians are come   2Ki 6:9
down
carry *t.* one of the priests   2Ki 17:27
whom
resort *t.* to us, God shall fight   Ne 4:20
for us
t. brought again the vessels of   Ne 13:9
the house
they came *t.* and were   Job 6:20
ashamed
the rain returneth not *t.*   Isa 55:10
again
he shall not return *t.* any   Jer 22:11
more
but to the land, *t.* shall they   Jer 22:27
not return
they went, *t.* was their spirit   Eze 1:20
to go
Israel shall come *t.* and take   Eze 11:18
away
because these waters shall   Eze 47:9
come *t.*

t. cause mighty ones to come   Joe 3:11
down
afraid to go *t.* but being   M't 2:22
warned
t. will the eagles be gathered   Lu 17:37
together
where I am, *t.* ye cannot   Joh 7:34;
come   7:36
to stone thee, and goest thou   Joh 11:8
t. again
Jesus oft-times resorted *t.*   Joh 18:2
with disciples
Judas cometh *t.* with lanterns   Joh 18:3
and torches
Philip ran *t.* to him, and heard   Ac 8:30
him
spake to the women which   Ac 16:13
resorted *t.*

THITHERWARD

And they turned *t.* and came   J'g 18:15
the way to Zion with their   Jer 50:5
faces *t.*
to be brought on my way *t.*   Ro 15:24
by you

THOMAS

T. and Matthew the publican   M't 10:3
T. and James the son of   M'k 3:18
Alphaeus
T., James the son of Alphaeus   Lu 6:15
said T. which is called   Joh 11:16
Didymus
T. saith unto him, Lord, we   Joh 14:5
know
But T. one of the twelve,   Joh 20:24
called
were within, and T. with   Joh 20:26
them
Then saith he to T., Reach   Joh 20:27
hither
T. answered and said unto   Joh 20:28
him
T. because thou hast seen me   Joh 20:29
Peter, and T. called Didymus   Joh 21:9
T., Bartholomew, and Matthew   Ac 1:13

THONGS

as they bound him with *t.*   Ac 22:25
Paul

THORN

or bore his jaw through with   Job 41:2
a *t.*
with a hook or spike   Job 41:2
(A)(E)(R)
pierce his jaw with a spur   Job 41:2
(B)
As a *t.* goeth up into the hand   Pr 26:9
of a
of the *t.* shall come up the fir   Isa 55:13
tree
grieving *t.* of all that are   Eze 28:24
round
a brier to prick (A)   Eze 28:24
the *t.* and the thistle shall   Ho 10:8
come up
upright is sharper than a *t.*   Mic 7:4
hedge
was given to me a *t.* in the   2Co 12:7
flesh

THORNS

T. also and thistles shall it   Ge 3:18
bring
If fire break out, and catch in   Ex 22:6
t. so
in your eyes, and *t.* in your   Nu 33:55
sides
in your sides, and *t.* in your   Jos 23:13
eyes
but they shall be as *t.* in your   J'g 2:3
sides
I will tear your flesh, with the *t.*   J'g 8:7
and *t.* of the wilderness and   J'g 8:16
briers
be all of them as *t.* thrust   2Sa 23:6
away
took Manasseh among the *t.*   2Ch 33:11
took Manasseh with hooks   2Ch 33:11
(A)(B)(R)
took Manasseh in chains   2Ch 33:11
(E)
and taketh it even out of the *t.*   Job 5:5
Before your pots can feel the   Ps 58:9
t. he

they are quenched as the fire *Ps 118:12* of *t.*

slothful man is as an hedge *Pr 15:19* of *t.*

T. and snares are in the way of *Pr 22:5*

all grown over with *t.* and *Pr 24:31* nettles

as the crackling of *t.* under a *Ec 7:6* pot

As the lily among *t.* so is my *Ca 2:2* love

lily among thistles (B) *Ca 2:2*

lily among brambles (R) *Ca 2:2*

there shall come up briers and *Isa 5:6* *t.*

upon all *t.* and upon all *Isa 7:19* bushes

it shall even be for briers and *Isa 7:23* *t.*

the land shall become briers *Isa 7:24* and *t.*

thither the fear of briers and *Isa 7:25* *t.*

it shall devour the briers and *Isa 9:18* *t.*

shall burn and devour his *t.* *Isa 10:17* and his

set the briers and *t.* against *Isa 27:4* me in

people shall come up *t.* and *Isa 32:13* briers

t. cut up shall they be *Isa 33:12* burned in the

t. shall come up in her *Isa 34:13* palaces

ground, and sow not among *t.* *Jer 4:3*

have sown wheat, but shall *Jer 12:13* reap *t.*

though briers and *t.* be with *Eze 2:6* thee

I will hedge up thy way with *t.* *Ho 2:6*

t. shall be in their tabernacles *Ho 9:6*

while they be folden together *Na 1:10* as *t.*

Do men gather grapes of *t.* or *M't 7:16* figs

And some fell among *t.* *M't 13:7* them

the *t.* sprung up, and choked *M't 13:7* them

also that received seed *M't 13:22* among the *t.*

when they had platted a *M't 27:29* crown of *t.*

And some fell among *t.* *M'k 4:7*

and the *t.* grew up, and *M'k 4:7* choked it

are they which are sown *M'k 4:18* among *t.*

platted a crown of *t.* and *M'k 15:17* put it

of *t.* men do not gather figs, *Lu 6:44* nor of

And some fell among *t.* *Lu 8:7*

t. sprang up with it, and *Lu 8:7* choked it

that which fell among *t.* are *Lu 8:14* they

the soldiers platted a crown *Joh 19:2* of *t.*

Jesus forth, wearing the *Joh 19:5* crown of *t.*

that which beareth *t.* and *Heb 6:8* briers is

THORNY

many *t.* griefs (N) *1Ti 6:10*

THOROUGHLY

shall cause him to be *t.* *Ex 21:19* healed

his images brake they in *2Ki 11:18* pieces

thoroughly (S) *Ps 51:2; Jer 6:9; 7:5; 50:34; Eze 16:9; M't 3:12; Lu 3:17; 2Co 11:6; 2Ti 3:17*

and *t.* purge away thy dross *Isa 1:25* (S)

THOSE

were giants in the earth in *t.* *Ge 6:4* days

lamp that passed between *t.* *Ge 15:17* pieces

And he overthrew *t.* cities, *Ge 19:25* and all

possess the gate of *t.* *Ge 24:60* which hate them

and said, Who are *t.* with thee *Ge 33:5*

gather all the food of *t.* good *Ge 41:35* years

came to buy corn among *t.* *Ge 42:5* that came

the days of *t.* which are *Ge 50:3* embalmed

And it came to pass in *t.* days *Ex 2:11*

thou do all *t.* wonders before *Ex 4:21* Pharaoh

they shall eat *t.* things *Ex 29:33* wherewith the

and of *t.* that devise cunning *Ex 35:35* work

all four, *t.* are unclean unto *Le 11:27* you

and *t.* things, before the Lord *Le 14:11*

and put them in the place of *Le 14:42* *t.* stones

that beareth any of *t.* things *Le 15:10* shall

whosoever toucheth *t.* things *Le 15:27* shall be

t. things which they hallow *Le 22:2* unto me

T. that were numbered of *Nu 1:21; 1:22, 23, 25, 27, 29, 31, 33, 35, 37, 39, 41, 43, 44, 45; 2:4, 13, 15, 21, 23, 26, 28, 30, 32; 3:22, 34, 43; 4:36, 38, 40, 42, 44, 45, 46, 48; 26:18, 22, 25, 27, 34, 37, 43, 47, 54, 62*

t. that pitch next to him shall *Nu 2:5* be

t. that were numbered thereof *Nu 2:6; 2:8, 11*

t. which pitch by him shall be *Nu 2:12*

t. that encamp by him shall be *Nu 2:27*

all *t.* that were numbered of *Nu 2:32*

But *t.* that encamp before the *Nu 3:38*

for *t.* that are to be redeemed *Nu 3:46*

And *t.* men said unto him *Nu 9:7*

all *t.* men were heads of the *Nu 13:3* children

t. men which have seen my *Nu 14:22* glory

t. men that did bring up the *Nu 14:37* evil

And *t.* that are to be *Nu 18:16* redeemed from a

t. that died in the plague *Nu 25:9* were twenty

according to *t.* that were *Nu 26:18; 26:22, 25, 27*

t. which ye let remain of *Nu 33:55* them shall

will put out *t.* nations before *De 7:22* thee

the judge that shall be in *t.* *De 17:9* days

the abominations of *t.* nations *De 18:9*

he shall flee unto one of *t.* *De 19:5* cities

judges, which shall be in *t.* *De 19:17* days

And *t.* which remain shall *De 19:20* hear, and

the priest that shall be in *t.* *De 26:3* days

the signs, and *t.* great miracles *De 29:3*

but *t.* things which are *De 29:29* revealed

with *t.* which are not a *De 32:21* people

t. that came down toward the *Jos 3:16* sea of

t. twelve stones, which they *Jos 4:20* took

and bring out *t.* five kings *Jos 10:22* unto me

brought forth *t.* five kings *Jos 10:23* unto him

brought out *t.* kings unto *Jos 10:24* Joshua

king of Hazor had heard *t.* *Jos 11:1* things

was the head of all *t.* *Jos 11:10* kingdoms

And all the cities of *t.* kings *Jos 11:12*

war a long time with all *t.* *Jos 11:18* kings

drive out the inhabitants of *Jos 17:12* *t.* cities

he that doth flee unto one of *Jos 20:4* *t.* cities

high priest that shall be in *t.* *Jos 20:6* days

nine cities out of *t.* two *Jos 21:16* tribes

which did *t.* great signs in *Jos 24:17* our sight

of the hand of *t.* that spoiled *J'g 2:16* them

the Lord left *t.* nations, *J'g 2:23* without

and retained *t.* three hundred *J'g 7:8* men

therefore restore *t.* lands *J'g 11:13* again

t. Ephraimites which were *J'g 12:5* escaped

In *t.* days there was no king *J'g 17:6; 18:1*

in *t.* days the tribe of the *J'g 18:1* Danites

it came to pass in *t.* days, *J'g 19:1* when

of God was there in *t.* days *J'g 20:27*

of Aaron, stood before it in *J'g 20:28* *t.* days

in *t.* days there was no king *J'g 21:25*

the Lord was precious in *t.* *1Sa 3:1* days

and judged Israel in all *t.* *1Sa 7:16* places

all *t.* signs came to pass that *1Sa 10:9* day

upon Saul when he heard *t.* *1Sa 11:6* tidings

Saul and all Israel heard *t.* *1Sa 17:11* words of

whom hast thou left *t.* few *1Sa 17:28* sheep

Saul's servants spake *t.* *1Sa 18:23* words in

Jonathan shewed him all *t.* *1Sa 19:7* things

according to all *t.* words in *1Sa 25:9*

came and told them all *t.* *1Sa 25:12* sayings

for *t.* nations were of old the *1Sa 27:8*

And it came to pass in *t.* *1Sa 28:1* days, that

had put away *t.* that had *1Sa 28:3* familiar

hath cut off *t.* that have *1Sa 28:9* familiar

where *t.* that were left behind *1Sa 30:9* stayed

they drave before *t.* other *1Sa 30:20* cattle

of Belial, of *t.* that went *1Sa 30:22* with David

be the names of *t.* that were *2Sa 5:14* born

which he counselled in *t.* *2Sa 16:23* days

let them be of *t.* that eat at *1Ki 2:7* thy table

name of the Lord, until *t.* days *1Ki 3:2*

t. officers provided victual for *1Ki 4:27*

t. did the priests and the *1Ki 8:4* Levites

upon *t.* did Solomon levy a *1Ki 9:21* tribute

when Ahab heard *t.* words, *1Ki 21:27* that he

shalt pour out into all *t.* *2Ki 4:4* vessels

wouldest thou smite *t.* whom *2Ki 6:22* thou

In *t.* days the Lord began to *2Ki 10:32* cut

In *t.* days the Lord began to *2Ki 15:37* send

did secretly *t.* things that *2Ki 17:9* were not

unto *t.* days the children of *2Ki 18:4* Israel

In *t.* days was Hezekiah sick *2Ki 20:1* unto

t. carried he into captivity *2Ki 24:15* from

and *t.* that dwelt among *1Ch 4:23* plants and

and cymbals for *t.* that *1Ch 16:42* should make

rest, and he had no war in *t.* *2Ch 14:6* years

t. times there was no peace *2Ch 15:5* to him

t. whom the king put in the *2Ch 17:19* fenced

on all the kingdoms of *t.* *2Ch 20:29* countries

the gods of the nations of *t.* *2Ch 32:13* lands

among all the gods of *t.* *2Ch 32:14* nations

In *t.* days Hezekiah was *2Ch 32:24* sick to

Even *t.* did Cyrus king of Persia bring   *Ezr 1:8*

t. which had been carried away, whom   *Ezr 2:1*

t. that were reckoned by genealogy   *Ezr 2:62*

because of the people of *t.* countries   *Ezr 3:3*

Then asked we *t.* elders, and said   *Ezr 5:9*

t. did Cyrus the king take out   *Ezr 5:14*

t. deliver thou before the God   *Ezr 7:19*

children of *t.* that had been carried   *Ezr 8:35*

themselves with the people of *t.* lands   *Ezr 9:2*

transgression of *t.* that had been   *Ezr 9:4*

and of *t.* that trembled at the   *Ezr 10:3*

congregation of *t.* that had been   *Ezr 10:8*

that bare burdens, with *t.* that laded   *Ne 4:17*

beside *t.* that came unto us from   *Ne 5:17*

in *t.* days the nobles of Judah sent   *Ne 6:17*

of *t.* that had been carried away, whom   *Ne 7:6*

register among *t.* that were reckoned   *Ne 7:64*

women, and *t.* that could understand   *Ne 8:3*

Now *t.* that sealed were, Nehemiah   *Ne 10:1*

In *t.* days saw I in Judah some   *Ne 13:15*

In *t.* days also saw I Jews that had   *Ne 13:23*

That in *t.* days, when the king   *Es 1:2*

In *t.* days, while Mordecai sat   *Es 2:21*

of *t.* which kept the door, were wroth   *Es 2:21*

the hands of *t.* that have the charge   *Es 3:9*

they would unto *t.* that hated them   *Es 9:5*

the number of *t.* that were slain in   *Es 9:11*

To set up on high *t.* that be low; that   *Job 5:11*

t. which mourn may be exalted to   *Job 5:11*

seeing he judgeth *t.* that are high   *Job 21:22*

are of *t.* that rebel against the light   *Job 24:13*

doth the grave *t.* which have sinned   *Job 24:19*

T. that remain of him shall be buried   *Job 27:15*

t. that put their trust in thee rejoice   *Ps 5:11*

t. that trouble me rejoice when I am   *Ps 13:4*

thee from *t.* that rise up against them   *Ps 17:7*

is a buckler to all *t.* that trust in him   *Ps 18:30*

subdued under me *t.* that rose up   *Ps 18:39*

liftest me up above *t.* that rise up   *Ps 18:48*

hand shall find out *t.* that hate thee   *Ps 21:8*

t. that wait upon the Lord they shall   *Ps 37:9*

Let all *t.* that seek thee rejoice and be   *Ps 40:16*

t. that have made a covenant with me   *Ps 50:5*

the heritage of *t.* that fear thy name   *Ps 61:5*

But *t.* that seek my soul, to destroy it   *Ps 63:9*

he bringeth out *t.* which are bound   *Ps 68:6*

the company of *t.* that published it   *Ps 68:11*

let not *t.* that seek thee be confounded   *Ps 69:6*

they talk to the grief of *t.* whom thou   *Ps 69:26*

Let all *t.* that seek thee rejoice and be   *Ps 70:4*

the tumult of *t.* that rise up against   *Ps 74:23*

preserve thou *t.* that are appointed to   *Ps 79:11*

T. that be planted in the house of the   *Ps 92:13*

to loose *t.* that are appointed to death   *Ps 102:20*

t. that remember his commandments   *Ps 103:18*

of all *t.* that carried them captives   *Ps 106:46*

him from *t.* that condemn his soul   *Ps 109:31*

Let *t.* that fear thee turn unto me   *Ps 119:79*

t. that have known thy testimonies   *Ps 119:79*

usest to do unto *t.* that love thy name   *Ps 119:132*

the scorning of *t.* that are at ease   *Ps 123:4*

Do good, O Lord, unto *t.* that be good   *Ps 125:4*

I grieved with *t.* that rise up against   *Ps 139:21*

As for the head of *t.* that compass me   *Ps 140:9*

as *t.* that have been long dead   *Ps 143:3*

raiseth up all *t.* that be bowed down   *Ps 145:14*

fear him, in *t.* that hope in his mercy   *Ps 147:11*

whole, as *t.* that go down into the pit   *Pr 1:12*

they are life unto *t.* that find   *Pr 4:22*

t. that seek me early shall find me   *Pr 8:17*

may cause *t.* that love me to inherit   *Pr 8:21*

spoil the soul of *t.* that spoiled them   *Pr 22:23*

death, and *t.* that are ready to be slain   *Pr 24:11*

A lying tongue hateth *t.* that are   *Pr 26:28*

and wine unto *t.* that be of heavy   *Pr 31:6*

are to come with *t.* that shall come   *Ec 1:11*

t. riches perish by evil travail   *Ec 5:14*

a woman among all *t.* have I not   *Ec 7:28*

deliver *t.* that are given to it   *Ec 8:8*

t. that look out of the windows   *Ec 12:3*

the lips of *t.* that are asleep to speak   *Ca 7:9*

and *t.* that keep the fruit thereof two   *Ca 8:12*

as the raiment of *t.* that are slain   *Isa 14:19*

him, as he smote *t.* that smote him   *Isa 27:7*

not pass over it; but it shall be for   *Isa 35:8*

In *t.* days was Hezekiah sick unto   *Isa 38:1*

gently lead *t.* that are with young   *Isa 40:11*

beside *t.* that are gathered unto him   *Isa 56:8*

yea, *t.* nations shall be utterly wasted   *Isa 60:12*

t. that remember thee in thy ways   *Isa 64:5*

in *t.* is continuance, and we shall   *Isa 64:5*

all *t.* things hath mine hand made   *Isa 66:2*

all *t.* things have been, saith   *Isa 66:2*

t. that escape of them unto the   *Isa 66:19*

in *t.* days, saith the Lord, they   *Jer 3:16*

In *t.* days the house of Judah   *Jer 3:18*

full wind from *t.* places shall come   *Jer 4:12*

Nevertheless in *t.* days, saith   *Jer 5:18*

it; the city, and *t.* that dwell therein   *Jer 8:16*

and famine, shall *t.* prophets be   *Jer 14:15*

the hand of *t.* that seek their life   *Jer 21:7*

t. will I let remain still in their own   *Jer 27:11*

In *t.* days they shall say no more   *Jer 31:29*

After *t.* days, saith the Lord, I will   *Jer 31:33*

If *t.* ordinances depart from   *Jer 31:36*

In *t.* days, and at that time, will   *Jer 33:15*

In *t.* days shall Judah be saved   *Jer 33:16*

t. women shall say, Thy friends   *Jer 38:22*

and *t.* that fell away, that fell to him   *Jer 39:9*

the hand of *t.* that seek their lives   *Jer 46:26*

hosts, from all *t.* that be about thee   *Jer 49:5*

scatter them toward all *t.* winds   *Jer 49:36*

In *t.* days, and in that time   *Jer 50:4; 50:20*

t. that fell away, and fell to the king   *Jer 52:15*

t. that I have swaddled and brought   *La 2:22*

The lips of *t.* that rose up against me   *La 3:62*

When *t.* went, these went; and when   *Eze 1:21*

and when *t.* stood, these stood; and   *Eze 1:21*

when *t.* were lifted up from the earth   *Eze 1:21*

that doeth not any of *t.* duties, but   *Eze 18:11*

T. that be near, and *t.* that be far   *Eze 22:5*

upon all *t.* that despise them round   *Eze 28:26*

that inhabit *t.* wastes of the land   *Eze 33:24*

hand of *t.* that served themselves of   *Eze 34:27*

prophesied in *t.* days many years   *Eze 38:17*

shall spoil *t.* that spoiled them, and   *Eze 39:10*

rob *t.* that robbed them, saith   *Eze 39:10*

t. that remain on the face of   *Eze 39:14*

round about, like *t.* windows   *Eze 40:25*

approach to *t.* things which are for   *Eze 42:14*

flame of the fire slew *t.* men that   *Da 3:22*

t. that walk in pride he is able to   *Da 4:37*

t. men which had accused Daniel   *Da 6:24*

In *t.* days I Daniel was mourning   *Da 10:2*

up, even for others beside *t.*   *Da 11:4*

And in *t.* times there shall many   *Da 11:14*

children, and *t.* that suck the breasts   *Joe 2:16*

t. days will I pour out my spirit   *Joe 2:29*

For, behold, in *t.* days, and in   *Joe 3:1*

to cut off *t.* of his that did escape   *Ob 14*

have delivered up *t.* of his that did   *Ob 14*

t. that have not sought the Lord   *Zep 1:6*

punish all *t.* that leap on the   *Zep 1:9*

since *t.* days were, when one came to   *Hag 2:16*

chariots, and *t.* that ride in them   *Hag 2:22*

spake unto *t.* that stood before him   *Zec 3:4*

hand of Zerubbabel with *t.* seven   *Zec 4:10*

even *t.* seventy years, did ye at   *Zec 7:5*

In *t.* days it shall come to pass   *Zec 8:23*

which shall not visit *t.* that be cut off   *Zec 11:16*

T. with which I was wounded in the   *Zec 13:6*

forth, and fight against *t.* nations   *Zec 14:3*

against *t.* that oppress the hireling   *Mal 3:5*

In *t.* days came John the Baptist   *M't 3:1*

t. were possessed with devils   *M't 4:24*

devils, and *t.* which were lunatick   *M't 4:24*

lunatick, and *t.* that had the palsy   *M't 4:24*

shew John again *t.* things which ye   *M't 11:4*

desired to see *t.* things which ye see   *M't 13:17*

and to hear *t*. things which *M't 13:17*
ye hear
t. things which proceed out *M't 15:18*
of the
with them *t*. that were lame, *M't 15:30*
blind
be of God, but *t*. that *M't 16:23*
be of men
will he do unto *t*. *M't 21:40*
husbandmen
miserably destroy *t*. wicked *M't 21:41*
men
and destroyed *t*. murderers *M't 22:7*
So *t*. servants went out into *M't 22:10*
to them that give suck in *t*. *M't 24:19*
days
except *t*. days should be *M't 24:22*
shortened
sake *t*. days shall be *M't 24:22*
shortened
after the tribulation of *t*. *M't 24:29*
days
Then all *t*. virgins arose, and *M't 25:7*
the lord of *t*. servants *M't 25:19*
cometh
and *t*. things that were done, *M't 27:54*
they
And it came to pass in *t*. *M'k 1:9*
days, that
cleansing *t*. things which *M'k 1:44*
Moses
then shall they fast in *t*. days *M'k 2:20*
about in beds *t*. that were *M'k 6:55*
sick
t. are they that defile the *M'k 7:15*
man
In *t*. days the multitude being *M'k 8:1*
very
disciples rebuked *t*. that *M'k 10:13*
brought
shall believe that *t*. things *M'k 11:23*
which he
But *t*. husbandmen said *M'k 12:7*
among
to them that give suck in *t*. *M'k 13:17*
days
For in *t*. days shall be *M'k 13:19*
affliction
the Lord had shortened *t*. *M'k 13:20*
days
in *t*. days, after that *M'k 13:24*
tribulation
a declaraton of *t*. things, which *Lu 1:1*
are
know the certainty of *t*. things *Lu 1:4*
after *t*. days his wife Elisabeth *Lu 1:24*
Mary arose in *t*. days, and *Lu 1:39*
went
t. things which were told her *Lu 1:45*
from
it came to pass in *t*. days, that *Lu 2:1*
wondered at *t*. things which *Lu 2:18*
were
marvelled at *t*. things which *Lu 2:33*
were
And in *t*. days he did eat *Lu 4:2*
nothing
and then shall they fast in *t*. *Lu 5:35*
days
And it came to pass in *t*. days *Lu 6:12*
that
sinners also love *t*. that love *Lu 6:32*
them
Among *t*. that are born of *Lu 7:28*
women
T. by the way side are they *Lu 8:12*
that
close, and told no man in *t*. *Lu 9:36*
days
any of *t*. things which they *Lu 9:36*
had seen
desired to see *t*. things which *Lu 10:24*
ye see
and to hear *t*. things which *Lu 10:24*
ye hear
then whose shall *t*. things be, *Lu 12:20*
which
Blessed are *t*. servants, whom *Lu 12:37*
them so, blessed are *t*. *Lu 12:38*
servants
Or *t*. eighteen, upon whom the *Lu 13:4*
a parable to *t*. which were *Lu 14:7*
bidden
t. men which were bidden *Lu 14:24*
shall
have done all *t*. things which *Lu 17:10*
are
t. mine enemies, which would *Lu 19:27*
not

that on one of *t*. days, as he *Lu 20:1*
taught
to them that give suck, in *t*. *Lu 21:23*
days
looking after *t*. things which *Lu 21:26*
are
touching *t*. things whereof ye *Lu 23:14*
accuse
in the temple *t*. that sold *Joh 2:14*
oxen
Then *t*. men when they had *Joh 6:14*
seen
where are *t*. thine accusers *Joh 8:10*
t. things which I have heard *Joh 8:26*
always *t*. things that please *Joh 8:29*
him
said Jesus to *t*. Jews which *Joh 8:31*
believed
which of *t*. works do ye *Joh 10:32*
stone me
Buy *t*. things that we have *Joh 13:29*
need of
name *t*. whom thou hast *Joh 17:11*
given me
t. that thou gavest me I *Joh 17:12*
have kept
t. days Peter stood up in the *Ac 1:15*
pour out in *t*. days of my Spirit *Ac 2:18*
But *t*. things, which God *Ac 3:18*
before had
Samuel and *t*. that follow *Ac 3:24*
after
And in *t*. days, when the *Ac 6:1*
number
made a calf in *t*. days, and *Ac 7:41*
offered
unto *t*. things which Philip *Ac 8:6*
spake
to pass in *t*. days, that she *Ac 9:37*
was
spake against *t*. things which *Ac 13:45*
were
Jews which were in *t*. quarters *Ac 16:3*
serjeants, saying, Let *t*. men *Ac 16:35*
go
noble than *t*. in Thessalonica *Ac 17:11*
daily, whether *t*. things were *Ac 17:11*
so
Gallio cared for none of *t*. *Ac 18:17*
things
when he had gone over *t*. *Ac 20:2*
parts
when we had accomplished *t*. *Ac 21:5*
days
t. days we took up our *Ac 21:15*
carriages
all may know that *t*. things, *Ac 21:24*
whereof
t. things in the which I will *Ac 26:16*
appear
saying none other things than *Ac 26:22*
t. which
t. things which were spoken *Ac 27:11*
by
teaching *t*. things which *Ac 28:31*
concern
t. things, which are not *Ro 1:28*
convenient
calleth *t*. things which be not *Ro 4:17*
as *t*. that are alive from the *Ro 6:13*
dead
fruit had ye then in *t*. things *Ro 6:21*
which
for the end of *t*. things is *Ro 6:21*
death
man, which doeth *t*. things *Ro 10:5*
shall live
in *t*. things which pertain to *Ro 15:17*
God
t. things which Christ hath *Ro 15:18*
not
eating of *t*. things that are *1Co 8:4*
offered
eat *t*. things which are *1Co 8:10*
offered to
much more *t*. members of *1Co 12:22*
the body
t. members of the body, *1Co 12:23*
which we
there come in *t*. that are *1Co 14:23*
unlearned
comforteth *t*. that are cast *2Co 7:6*
down
Beside *t*. things that are *2Co 11:28*
without
t. things which are done in *Eph 5:12*
secret
me, *t*. I counted loss for *Ph'p 3:7*
Christ

forgetting *t*. things are *Ph'p 3:13*
behind
reaching forth unto *t*. things *Ph'p 3:13*
which
help *t*. women which laboured *Ph'p 4:3*
with
T. things, which ye have both *Ph'p 4:9*
into *t*. things which he hath *Col 2:18*
not seen
Christ, seek *t*. things which are *Col 3:1*
all men, specially of *t*. that *1Ti 4:10*
believe
specially for *t*. of his own *1Ti 5:8*
house
instructing *t*., oppose *2Ti 2:25*
themselves
fierce, despisers of *t*. that are *2Ti 3:3*
good
testimony of *t*. things which *Heb 3:1*
were
t. who by reason of use have *Heb 5:14*
their
it is impossible for *t*. who *Heb 6:4*
were once
t. priests were made without *Heb 7:21*
needeth not daily, as *t*. high *Heb 7:27*
priests
the house of Israel after *t*. *Heb 8:10*
days
can never with *t*. sacrifices *Heb 10:1*
in *t*. sacrifices, is a *Heb 10:3*
remembrance
will make with them after *t*. *Heb 10:16*
days
removing of *t*. things, are *Heb 12:27*
shaken
t. things which cannot be *Heb 12:27*
shaken
For the bodies of *t*. beasts, *Heb 13:11*
whose
t. things which are needful to *Jas 2:16*
ensample unto *t*. that after *2Pe 2:6*
should
t. that were clean escaped *2Pe 2:18*
from
t. things that are pleasing in *1Jo 3:22*
his
lose not *t*. things we have *2Jo 8*
wrought
t. things which they know not *Jude 10*
t. things they corrupt *Jude 10*
themselves
t. things, are written therein *Re 1:3*
Fear none of *t*. things which *Re 2:10*
thou
t. days wherein Antipas was *Re 2:13*
my
t. beasts give glory and honour *Re 4:9*
t. men which have not the seal *Re 9:4*
in *t*. days shall men seek death *Re 9:6*
t. things which the seven *Re 10:4*
thunders
means of *t*. miracles which he *Re 13:14*
had
t. things which were written *Re 20:12*
in the

THOU

woman whom *t*. gavest to be *Ge 3:12*
with
if not restore *t*. shalt surely *Ge 20:7;*
die, *t*. and all that are thine *1Sa 22:16*
t. art our sister, be *t*. mother *Ge 24:60*
of thousands
t. art now the blessed of the *Ge 26:29*
Lord
none so discreet and wise as *Ge 41:39*
t. art
only in throne will I be *Ge 41:40*
greater than *t*.
t. shalt be near to me, *t*. and *Ge 45:10*
children
t. art he whom thy brethren *Ge 49:8*
shall praise
t. shalt come up, *t*. and *Ex 19:24*
Aaron
t. and all the company are *Nu 16:11*
gathered
be *t*. and they, and Aaron *Nu 16:16*
that thy servant may rest as *De 5:14*
well as *t*.
hath cast out nations mightier *De 7:1;*
than *t*. *20:1*
t. hast not known, *t*. nor thy *De 13:6;*
fathers *28:64*
that both *t*. and thy seed may *De 30:19*
live
to a neighbour that is better *1Sa 15:28*
than *t*.

he said, *T.* art more righteous than I — *1Sa 24:17*

blessed be *t.* that kept me from — *1Sa 25:33*

Nathan said to David, *T.* art the man — *2Sa 12:7*

then Absalom said, Of what city art *t.* — *2Sa 15:2*

t. and Ziba divide the land — *2Sa 19:29*

t. even *t.* knowest the hearts of all — *1Ki 8:39*

t. and thy father's house trouble Israel — *1Ki 18:18*

Who shall order the battle? he said *T.* — *1Ki 20:14*

that when I and *t.* rode after Ahab — *2Ki 9:25*

why meddle, that *t.* shouldest fall, even *t.* and Judah — *2Ki 14:10; 2Ch 25:19*

t. art the God, even *t.* alone of all the kingdoms — *2Ki 19:15; 19:19; Ne 9:6; Isa 37:20*

but *t.* art a God ready to pardon — *Ne 9:17*

t. and thy father's house shall be destroyed, who knoweth whether *t.* art — *Es 4:14*

the clouds which are higher than *t.* — *Job 35:5*

I will fear no evil, for *t.* art with me — *Ps 23:4*

it was *t.* a man, mine equal, my guide — *Ps 55:13*

t. hast tested us (B)(R) — *Ps 66:10*

t. art he that took me out my mother's bowels — *Ps 71:6*

t. even *t.* art to be feared, who may stand in thy sight when *t.* art angry — *Ps 76:7*

t. whose name is Jehovah, art most high — *Ps 83:18*

but *t.* art the same, thy years have no end — *Ps 102:27*

may know, that *t.*, Lord hast done it — *Ps 109:27*

t. art my God, and I will praise thee — *Ps 118:28*

t. art my hidingplace and my shield — *Ps 119:114*

arise into thy rest, *t.* and ark of strength — *Ps 132:8*

if I ascend up into heaven, *t.* art there — *Ps 139:8*

if make bed in hell, *t.* art there — *Ps 139:8*

that *t.* dost think (R) — *Ps 144:3*

tell me, O *t.* whom my soul loveth — *Ca 1:7*

t. art my servant, I have chosen — *Isa 41:9*

deliver me, for *t.* art my god — *Isa 44:17*

verily *t.* art a god that hidest thyself — *Isa 45:15*

who art *t.* that *t.* be afraid of man — *Isa 51:12*

t. art our father, *t.* Lord, art our father — *Isa 63:16*

come not near to me, I am holier than *t.* — *Isa 65:5*

those in whom *t.* trustest (E)(R) — *Jer 2:37*

t. shalt discontinue from thy heritage — *Jer 17:4*

there *t.* shalt die, *t.* and all thy friends — *Jer 20:6*

why will ye die, *t.* by sword — *Jer 27:13*

t. remainest for ever, thy throne — *La 5:19*

O *t.* that dwellest in the land, the time — *Eze 7:7*

they are more righteous than *t.* — *Eze 16:52*

it is *t.* that art become strong — *Da 4:22*

t. hast not humbled thine heart — *Da 5:22*

whence comest *t.* of what people art *t.* — *Jon 1:8*

t. that art named the house of Jacob — *Mic 2:7*

t. tower of the flock, to thee shall it come — *Mic 4:8*

art *t.* not from everlasting, O Lord — *Hab 1:12*

who art *t.* great mountain, before Zerubbabel — *Zec 4:7*

but *t.* when *t.* prayest, enter closet — *M't 6:6*

but *t.* when *t.* fastest, anoint thine head — *M't 6:17*

t. art Christ, Son of the living God — *M't 16:16; M'k 8:29; Lu 4:41; Joh 11:27*

nevertheless, not as I will, but as *t.* wilt — *M't 26:39*

t. also wast with Jesus — *M't 26:69; M'k 14:67*

hail *t.* that art highly favoured — *Lu 1:28*

art *t.* he that should come — *Lu 7:19; 7:20*

lest a more honourable than *t.* be bidden — *Lu 14:8*

how much owest *t.* unto my lord — *Lu 16:5; 16:7*

t. in lifetime receivedst good things but now he is comforted, *t.* art tormented — *Lu 16:25*

if *t.* hadst known, even *t.* in this thy day — *Lu 19:42*

to ask him, Who art *t.* — *Joh 1:19; 1:22; 8:25; 21:12*

Art *t.* Elias? Art *t.* that prophet — *Joh 1:21*

T. art Simon, thou shalt be called Cephas — *Joh 1:42*

art *t.* master of Israel, and knowest not — *Joh 3:10*

that *t.* being a Jew, askest drink of me — *Joh 4:9*

they said to him, Art *t.* also of Galilee — *Joh 7:52*

what sayest *t.* — *Joh 8:5*

t. art his disciple — *Joh 9:28*

t. hast seen him, he talketh with thee — *Joh 9:37*

I in them, and *t.* in me, that they may be — *Joh 17:23*

Art not *t.* one of this man's disciples — *Joh 18:17*

t. Lord, who knowest hearts of all — *Ac 1:24*

that *t.* art in the gall of bitterness — *Ac 8:23*

whereby *t.* and house shall be saved — *Ac 11:14*

t. child of the devil, *t.* enemy, wilt *t.* not cease to pervert right ways of Lord — *Ac 13:10*

T. art my Son, this day have I begotten thee — *Ac 13:33*

art not *t.* that Egyptian which madest — *Ac 21:38*

tell me, art *t.* a Roman? he said, Yea — *Ac 22:27*

I would not only *t.* but all that hear — *Ac 26:29*

t. therefore which teachest another — *Ro 2:21*

be *t.* an example of believers — *1Ti 4:12*

t. O man of God, flee these things — *1Ti 6:11*

be not *t.* ashamed of testimony — *2Ti 1:8*

t. therefore, my son, be strong in grace — *2Ti 2:1*

t. therefore receive him that is mine — *Ph'm 12*

t. Lord, hast laid foundation of earth — *Heb 1:10*

shall be changed, but *t.* are the same — *Heb 1:12*

who art *t.* that judgest another — *Jas 4:12*

t. art worthy to receive glory — *Re 4:11*

t. art worthy to take the book, and to open — *Re 5:9*

THOUGH

t. thou wouldest needs be gone — *Ge 31:30*

t. I had seen the face of God, and — *Ge 33:10*

and it was as *t.* it budded, and her — *Ge 40:10*

t. he wist it not, yet he is guilty — *Le 5:17*

And the swine *t.* he divide the hoof — *Le 11:7*

t. he be a stranger, or a sojourner — *Le 25:35*

unto you, as *t.* it were the corn of the — *Nu 18:27*

t. I walk in the imagination — *De 29:19*

t. they have iron chariots — *Jos 17:18*

chariots, and *t.* they be strong — *Jos 17:18*

T. thou detain me, I will not eat — *J'g 13:16*

t. I do them a displeasure — *J'g 15:3*

T. ye have done this, yet will I be — *J'g 15:7*

t. I be not like unto one of thine — *Ru 2:13*

t. it be in Jonathan my son — *1Sa 14:39*

side thereof, as *t.* I shot at a mark — *1Sa 20:20*

t. it were sanctified this day — *1Sa 21:5*

as *t.* he had not anointed with oil — *2Sa 1:21*

am this day weak, *t.* anointed king — *2Sa 3:39*

as *t.* they would have fetched wheat — *2Sa 4:6*

T. I should receive a thousand — *2Sa 18:12*

t. he turned not after Absalom — *1Ki 2:28*

t. he was not the firstborn, yet his — *1Ch 26:10*

t. he be not cleansed according to the — *2Ch 30:19*

t. there were of you cast out unto — *Ne 1:9*

t. at that time I had not set up — *Ne 6:1*

t. it was turned to the contrary — *Es 9:1*

T. thy beginning was small, yet thy — *Job 8:7*

t. I were righteous, yet would I — *Job 9:15*

T. I were perfect, yet would I — *Job 9:21*

have been as *t.* I had not been — *Job 10:19*

t. man be born like a wild ass's colt — *Job 11:12*

T. he slay me, yet will I trust in him — *Job 13:15*

T. the root thereof wax old in — *Job 14:8*

T. I speak, my grief is not — *Job 16:6*

and *t.* I forbear, what am I eased — *Job 16:6*

t. I entreated for the children's sake — *Job 19:17*

And *t.* after my skin worms destroy — *Job 19:26*

t. my reins be consumed within me — *Job 19:27*

T. his excellency mount up to — *Job 20:6*

T. wickedness be sweet in his mouth, *t.* he hide it under his tongue — *Job 20:12; Job 20:12*

T. he spare it, and forsake it not; but — *Job 20:13*

t. it be given him to be in safety — *Job 24:23*

t. he hath gained, when God taketh — *Job 27:8*

T. he heap up silver as the dust — *Job 27:16*

grave, *t.* they cry in his destruction — *Job 30:24*

young ones, as *t.* they were not hers — *Job 39:16*

t. I walk through the valley of — *Ps 23:4*

T. an host should encamp against — *Ps 27:3*

t. war should rise against me, in — *Ps 27:3*

t. he had been my friend or brother — *Ps 35:14*

T. he fall, he shall not be utterly — *Ps 37:24*

T. thou hast sore broken us in — *Ps 44:19*

we fear, *t.* the earth be removed — *Ps 46:2*

and *t.* the mountains be carried into — *Ps 46:2*

T. the waters thereof roar and be — *Ps 46:3*

t. the mountains shake with — *Ps 46:3*

T. while he lived he blessed his — *Ps 49:18*

T. ye have lien among the pots — *Ps 68:13*

T. he had commanded the clouds — *Ps 78:23*

t. thou tookest vengeance of their — *Ps 99:8*

T. the Lord be high, yet hath he — *Ps 138:6*

T. I walk in the midst of trouble — *Ps 138:7*

content, *t.* thou givest many gifts — *Pr 6:35*

T. hand join in hand, the wicked shall — *Pr 11:21*

t. hand join in hand, he shall not be — *Pr 16:5*

T. thou shouldest bray a fool *Pr 27:22*
in a
is perverse in his ways, *t.* he be *Pr 28:6*
rich
words: for *t.* he understand *Pr 29:19*
he will not
t. he live a thousand years *Ec 6:6*
twice told
T. a sinner do evil an hundred *Ec 8:12*
times
because *t.* a man labour to *Ec 8:17*
seek it
t. a wise man think to know it *Ec 8:17*
t. your sins be as scarlet, they *Isa 1:18*
shall
t. they be red like crimson, *Isa 1:18*
they
t. thy people Israel be as the *Isa 10:22*
sand
t. thou wast angry with me, *Isa 12:1*
thine
And *t.* the Lord give you the *Isa 30:20*
bread
men, *t.* fools, shall not err *Isa 35:8*
therein
thee, *t.* thou hast not known *Isa 45:4;*
me 45:5
T. Israel be not gathered, yet *Isa 49:5*
shall I
t. Abraham be ignorant of us *Isa 63:16*
For *t.* thou wash thee with *Jer 2:22*
nitre
T. thou clothest thyself with *Jer 4:30*
t. thou deckest thee with *Jer 4:30*
ornaments
t. thou rentest thy face with *Jer 4:30*
t. they say, The Lord liveth: *Jer 5:22*
surely
t. the waves thereof toss *Jer 5:22*
themselves
t. they roar, yet can they not *Jer 5:22*
pass over
t. they shall cry unto me, I *Jer 11:11*
will not
t. they speak fair words unto *Jer 12:6*
thee
t. our iniquities testify against *Jer 14:7*
us
T. Moses and Samuel stood *Jer 15:1*
before
t. Coniah the son of *Jer 22:24*
Jehoiakim
t. I make a full end of all *Jer 30:11*
nations
t. ye fight with the Chaldeans, *Jer 32:5*
ye
t. I taught them, rising up *Jer 32:33*
early and
For *t.* ye had smitten the *Jer 37:10*
whole
the Lord *t.* it cannot be *Jer 46:23*
searched
t. thou shouldest make thy *Jer 49:16*
nest
t. their land was filled with sin *Jer 51:5*
T. Babylon should mount up *Jer 51:53*
t. she should fortify the *Jer 51:53*
height of
But *t.* he cause grief, yet will *La 3:32*
t. briers, and thorns be with *Eze 2:6*
thee
looks, *t.* they be a rebellious *Eze 2:6;*
house 3:9
t. they cry in mine ears with *Eze 8:18*
a loud
t. they be a rebellious house *Eze 12:3*
shall he not see it, *t.* he shall *Eze 12:13*
die, there
T. these three men, Noah, *Eze 14:14*
Daniel, and
T. these three men were in *Eze 14:16;*
it, as I 14:18
T. Noah, Daniel, and Job, *Eze 14:20*
were in it
t. thou be sought for, yet *Eze 26:21*
shalt thou
t. thou set thine heart as the *Eze 28:2*
heart of
t. their terror was caused in *Eze 32:25*
t. they caused their terror in *Eze 32:26*
t. they were the terror of the *Eze 32:27*
mighty
t. thou knewest all this *Da 5:22*
t. we have rebelled against him *Da 9:9*
T. thou, Israel, play the harlot *Ho 4:15*
t. I have been a rebuker of *Ho 5:2*
them all
t. I have redeemed them, yet *Ho 7:13*
they

T. I have bound and *Ho 7:15*
strengthened
Yea, *t.* they have hired among *Ho 8:10*
T. they bring up their *Ho 9:12*
t. they bring forth, yet will I *Ho 9:16*
t. they called them to the *Ho 11:7*
most High
T. he be fruitful among his *Ho 13:15*
T. ye offer me burnt offerings *Am 5:22*
T. they dig into hell, thence *Am 9:2*
shall
t. they climb up to heaven, *Am 9:2*
thence
t. they hide themselves in the *Am 9:3*
top
t. they be hid from my sight in *Am 9:3*
t. they go into captivity before *Am 9:4*
their
T. thou exalt thyself as the eagle *Ob 4*
t. thou set thy nest among the *Ob 4*
stars
they shall be as *t.* they had *Ob 16*
not been
Beth-lehem Ephratah, *t.* thou *Mic 5:2*
be little
T. they be quiet, and likewise *Na 1:12*
T. I have afflicted thee, I will *Na 1:12*
afflict
will not believe, *t.* it be told *Hab 1:5*
you
t. it tarry, wait for it; because *Hab 2:3*
and Zidon, *t.* it be very wise *Zec 9:2*
be as *t.* I had not cast them *Zec 10:6*
off
t. all the people of the earth *Zec 12:3*
T. all men shall be offended *M't 26:33*
T. I should die with thee, *M't 26:35*
yet will
t. many false witnesses came *M't 26:60*
was as *t.* he would go to *Lu 9:53*
Jerusalem
T. he will not rise and give *Lu 11:8*
him
t. one rose from the dead *Lu 16:31*
T. I fear not God, nor regard *Lu 18:4*
man
him, *t.* he bear long with them *Lu 18:7*
as *t.* he would have gone *Lu 24:28*
further
T. Jesus himself baptized not *Joh 4:2*
on the ground, as *t.* he heard *Joh 8:6*
them
T. I bear record of myself, *Joh 8:14*
yet my
t. ye believe not me, believe *Joh 10:38*
t. he were dead, yet shall he *Joh 11:25*
live
t. he had done so many *Joh 12:37*
miracles
as *t.* by our own power or *Ac 3:12*
holiness
t. they found no cause of *Ac 13:28*
death in
t. a man declare it unto you *Ac 13:41*
as *t.* he needed any thing, *Ac 17:25*
seeing he
t. he be not far from every *Ac 17:27*
one of
as *t.* ye would enquire *Ac 23:15*
something
as *t.* they would enquire *Ac 23:20*
somewhat
as *t.* they would have cast *Ac 27:30*
anchors
whom, *t.* he hath escaped the *Ac 28:4*
sea
t. I have committed nothing *Ac 28:17*
against
believe, *t.* they be not *Ro 4:11*
circumcised
things which be not as *t.* they *Ro 4:17*
were
t. she be married to another *Ro 7:3*
Not as *t.* the word of God hath *Ro 9:6*
T. the number of the children *Ro 7:27*
t. ye have ten thousand *1Co 4:15*
instructors
as *t.* I would not come to *1Co 4:18*
you
judged already, as *t.* I were *1Co 5:3*
present
that have wives be as *t.* they *1Co 7:29*
had none
they that weep, as *t.* they *1Co 7:30*
wept not
that rejoice, as *t.* they *1Co 7:30*
rejoiced not
they that buy, as *t.* they *1Co 7:30*
possessed

t. there be that are called gods *1Co 8:5*
For *t.* I preach the gospel, I *1Co 9:16*
have
For *t.* I be free from all men, *1Co 9:19*
yet
T. I speak with the tongues *1Co 13:1*
of
And *t.* I have the gift of *1Co 13:2*
prophecy
t. I have all faith, so that I *1Co 13:2*
could
t. I bestow all my goods to *1Co 13:3*
feed
and *t.* I give my body to be *1Co 13:3*
burned
t. our outward man perish, *2Co 4:16*
yet the
t. we have known Christ *2Co 5:16*
after the
as *t.* God did beseech you by *2Co 5:20*
us
t. I made you sorry with a *2Co 7:8*
letter
I do not repent, *t.* I did repent *2Co 7:8*
sorry, *t.* it were but for a *2Co 7:8*
season
Wherefore, *t.* I wrote unto *2Co 7:12*
you, I
that, *t.* he was rich, yet for *2Co 8:9*
your sakes
t. we walk in the flesh, we do *2Co 10:3*
not war
t. I should boast somewhat *2Co 10:8*
more
as *t.* we reached not unto *2Co 10:14*
you
t. I be rude in speech, yet not *2Co 11:6*
in
reproach, as *t.* we had been *2Co 11:21*
weak
For *t.* I would desire to *2Co 12:6*
glory, I
chiefest apostles, *t.* I be *2Co 12:11*
nothing
t. the more abundantly I *2Co 12:15*
love you
For *t.* he was crucified *2Co 13:4*
through
is honest, *t.* we be as *2Co 13:7*
reprobates
But *t.* we, or an angel from *Ga 1:8*
heaven
T. it be but a man's *Ga 3:15*
covenant, yet
from a servant, *t.* he be lord of *Ga 4:1*
all
T. I might also have *Ph'p 3:4*
confidence in
Not as *t.* I had already *Ph'p 3:12*
attained
t. I be absent in the flesh, yet *Col 2:5*
am
as *t.* living in the world, are *Col 2:20*
ye subject
t. I might be much bold in *Ph'm 8*
Christ to
T. he were a Son, yet *Heb 5:8*
learned he
salvation, *t.* we thus speak *Heb 6:9*
t. they come out of the loins *Heb 7:5*
of
t. he sought it carefully *Heb 12:17*
with tears
t. a man say he hath faith *Jas 2:14*
the ships, which *t.* they be so *Jas 3:4*
great
ye greatly rejoice, *t.* now for a *1Pe 1:6*
season
that perisheth, *t.* it be tried *1Pe 1:7*
with fire
t. now ye see him not, yet *1Pe 1:8*
believing
t. some strange thing *1Pe 4:12*
happened unto
of these things, *t.* ye know *2Pe 1:12*
them
not as *t.* I wrote a new *2Jo 5*
commandment
in remembrance, *t.* ye once *Jude 5*
knew this

THOUGHT

I *t.* Surely the fear of God is *Ge 20:11*
not
saw her, he *t.* her to be an *Ge 38:15*
harlot
I had not *t.* to see thy face *Ge 48:11*
as for you, ye *t.* evil against *Ge 50:20*
me

the evil which he t. to do unto his   Ex 32:14
I t. to promote thee unto great   Nu 24:11
unto you, as I t. to do unto them   Nu 33:56
be not a t. in thy wicked heart   De 15:9
as he had t. to have done unto his   De 19:19
I verily t. that thou hadst utterly   J'g 15:2
by night, and t. to have slain me   J'g 20:5
I t. to advertise thee, saying, Buy   Ru 4:4
Eli t. she had been drunken   1Sa 1:13
for the asses, and take t. for us   1Sa 9:5
Saul t. to make David fall by the   1Sa 18:25
for he t., Something hath befallen   1Sa 20:26
who t. that I would have given him   2Sa 4:10
Amnon t. it hard for him to do   2Sa 13:2
hast thou t. such a thing against   2Sa 14:13
and to do what he t. good   2Sa 19:18
new sword t. to have slain David   2Sa 21:16
I t., He will surely come out to me   2Ki 5:11
every plan and t. (R)   1Ch 28:9
for he t. to make him king   2Ch 11:22
and t. to win them for himself   2Ch 32:1
But they t. to do me mischief   Ne 6:2
t. scorn to lay hands on Mordecai   Es 3:6
Now Haman t. in his heart, To   Es 6:6
despised in the t. of him that is at   Job 12:5
no t. can be withholden from   Job 42:2
We have t. of thy lovingkindness   Ps 48:9
Their inward t. is, that their houses   Ps 49:11
the inward t. of every one of them   Ps 64:6
When I t. to know this, it was too   Ps 73:16
I t. on my ways, and turned my   Ps 119:59
thou understandest my t. afar off   Ps 139:2
The t. of foolishness is sin   Pr 24:9
or if thou hast t. evil, lay thine   Pr 30:32
not the king, no not in thy t.   Ec 10:20
Surely as I have t. so shall it come   Isa 14:24
the evil that I t. to do unto them   Jer 18:8
and thou shalt think an evil t.   Eze 38:10
I t. it good to shew the signs   Da 4:2
king t. to set him over the whole   Da 6:3
declareth unto man what is his t.   Am 4:13
the Lord of hosts t. to do unto us   Zec 1:6
As I t. to punish you, when your   Zec 8:14
again have I t. in these days to do   Zec 8:15
Lord, and that t. upon his name   Mal 3:16
But while he t. on these things   M't 1:20
Take no t. for your life, what ye   M't 6:25
you by taking t. can add one cubit   M't 6:27
And why take ye t. for raiment   M't 6:28
take no t. saying, What shall we   M't 6:31
Take no t. for the morrow   M't 6:34
morrow shall take t. for the things   M't 6:34
take no t. how or what ye shall   M't 10:19
t. John a prophet (P)   M't 14:5
take no t. beforehand what ye   M'k 13:11
And when he t. thereon, he wept   M'k 14:72

neither t. I myself worthy to come   Lu 7:7
perceiving the t. of their heart   Lu 9:47
take ye no t. how or what thing ye   Lu 12:11
And he t. within himself, saying   Lu 12:17
Take no t. for your life, what ye   Lu 12:22
you with taking t. can add to his   Lu 12:25
is least, why take ye t. for the rest   Lu 12:26
they t. that the kingdom of God   Lu 19:11
they t. that he had spoken of   Joh 11:13
some of them t. because Judas had   Joh 13:29
happy to be t. worthy (B)(N)(P)   Ac 5:41
thou hast t. that the gift of God   Ac 8:20
t. of thine heart may be forgiven   Ac 8:22
While Peter t. on the vision   Ac 10:19
the angel; but t. he saw a vision   Ac 12:9
Paul t. not good to take him with   Ac 15:38
Should it be t. a thing incredible   Ac 26:8
I verily t. with myself, that I   Ac 26:9
as a child, I t. as a child   1Co 13:11
I t. it necessary to exhort the   2Co 9:5
every t. to the obedience of Christ   2Co 10:5
t. it not robbery to be equal with   Ph'p 2:6
I t. it necessary to (S)   Ph'p 2:25
we t. it good to be left at Athens   1Th 3:1
shall he be t. worthy, who hath   Heb 10:29

THOUGHTEST

thou t. that I was altogether such   Ps 50:21

THOUGHTFUL

if we are t. (B)   2Co 5:13

THOUGHTLESS

t. words (B)   Job 38:2
every t. word (N)   M't 12:36
be not t. (B)   Eph 5:17
foolishness of t. people (B)   1Pe 2:15

THOUGHTLESSNESS

thoughtlessness (B)   M'k 7:22

THOUGHTS

the t. of his heart was only evil   Ge 6:5
there were great t. of heart   J'g 5:15
the t. they were forming (B)   De 31:21
all the imaginations of the t.   1Ch 28:9
all of the t. (A)(B)   1Ch 28:9
of the t. of the heart of thy people   1Ch 29:18
t. of the hearts (B)(R)   1Ch 29:18
t. from the visions of the night   Job 4:13
broken off, even the t. of my heart   Job 17:11
do my t. cause me to answer   Job 20:2
I know your t. and the devices   Job 21:27
after God: God is not in all his t.   Ps 10:4
the t. of my heart (B)   Ps 19:14; 49:3
t. of his heart to all generations   Ps 33:11
and thy t. which are to us-ward   Ps 40:5
all their t. are against me for evil   Ps 56:5
Thy works! and thy t. are very deep   Ps 92:5
The Lord knoweth the t. of man   Ps 94:11
In the multitude of my t. within   Ps 94:19
I hate vain t.: but thy law do I   Ps 119:113
How precious are thy t. unto me   Ps 139:17
heart: try me, and know my t.   Ps 139:23

in that very day his t. perish   Ps 146:4
manufactures wicked t. (A)   Pr 6:18
The t. of the righteous are right   Pr 12:5
twisted t. he despised (B)   Pr 12:8
t. of the wicked are an abomination   Pr 15:26
and thy t. shall be established   Pr 16:3
The t. of the diligent tend only to   Pr 21:5
and the unrighteous man his t.   Isa 55:7
For my t. are not your t.   Isa 55:8
your ways, and my t. than your t.   Isa 55:9
blood: their t. are t. of iniquity   Isa 59:7
was not good, after their own t.   Isa 65:2
For I know their works and their t.   Isa 66:18
How long shall thy vain t. lodge   Jer 4:14
people, even the fruit of their t.   Jer 6:19
have performed the t. of his heart   Jer 23:20
I know the t. that I think toward   Jer 29:11
t. of peace, and not of evil, to   Jer 29:11
O king, thy t. came into thy mind   Da 2:29
mightest know the t. of thy heart   Da 2:30
t. upon my bed and the visions   Da 4:5
one hour, and his t. troubled him   Da 4:19
changed, and his t. troubled him   Da 5:6
let not thy t. trouble thee, nor   Da 5:10
my t. troubled (A)(B)(E)(R)   Da 7:28
they know not the t. of the Lord   Mic 4:12
And Jesus knowing their t. said   M't 9:4
Jesus knew their t. and said unto   M't 12:25
out of the heart proceed evil t.   M't 15:19
the heart of men, proceed evil t.   M'k 7:21
t. of many hearts may be revealed   Lu 2:35
But when Jesus perceived their t.   Lu 5:22
he knew their t. and said to the   Lu 6:8
knowing their t. said unto them   Lu 11:17
and why do t. arise in your hearts   Lu 24:38
and their t. the mean while   Ro 2:15
Lord knoweth the t. of the wise   1Co 3:20
renounced secret t. (A)   2Co 4:2
t. dwell on higher realm (N)   Col 3:2
a discerner of the t. and intents of   Heb 4:12
and are become judges of evil t.   Jas 2:4
searches men's t. (N)   Re 2:23

THOUSAND

I have given thy brother a t. pieces   Ge 20:16
of every tribe a t. send to war   Nu 31:4; 31:5, 6
suburbs of cities are t. cubits round about   Nu 35:4
Lord make you a t. times so many   De 1:11
God keepeth covenant to a t. generations   De 7:9
how should one chase a t.   De 32:30; Jos 23:10
men of Shechem died, about a t. men   J'g 9:49
Samson slew a t. men therewith   J'g 15:15; 15:16
hundred of a t. a t. out of ten thousand   J'g 20:10
ten cheeses to the captain of their t.   1Sa 17:18
Saul made David his captain over a t.   1Sa 18:13
Nabal had three t. sheep and a t. goats   1Sa 25:2
David took from him a t. chariots seven hundred horse   2Sa 8:4; 1Ch 18:4
though I should receive a t. shekels   2Sa 18:12

were a *t.* men of Benjamin	2Sa 19:17
with him	
a *t.* burnt offerings did	1Ki 3:4;
Solomon offer upon that altar	2Ch 1:6
Menahem gave Pul a *t.*	2Ki 15:19
talents	
carried away craftsmen and	2Ki 24:16
smiths a *t.*	
and the greatest was over a	1Ch 12:14
t.	
of Naphtali a *t.* captains,	1Ch 12:34
and with them	
word he commanded to a *t.*	1Ch 16:15
generations	
the children of Ammon sent	1Ch 19:6
a *t.* talents	
sacrificed sacrifices unto the	1Ch 29:21
Lord a *t.* bullocks, a *t.* rams,	
and a *t.* lambs	
Hezekiah did give a *t.*	2Ch 30:24
bullocks	
Cyrus did bring forth a *t.*	Ezr 1:9
chargers	
thirty basons of gold, and	Ezr 1:10
other vessels a *t.*	
he cannot answer him one of a	Job 9:3
t.	
if there be an interpreter,	Job 33:23
one of a *t.*	
Job had a *t.* yoke of oxen, a	Job 42:12
t. she asses	
the cattle on a *t.* hills are	Ps 50:10
mine	
a day in thy courts is better	Ps 84:10
than a *t.*	
a *t.* years in thy sight are as	Ps 90:4
yesterday	
a *t.* shall fall at thy side, ten	Ps 91:7
thousand	
though he live a *t.* years twice	Ec 6:6
told	
one man among a *t.* have I	Ec 7:28
found	
whereon there hang a *t.*	Ca 4:4
bucklers	
for the fruit was to bring a *t.*	Ca 8:11
pieces	
thou, O Solomon, must have a	Ca 8:12
t.	
were a *t.* vines, a *t.* silverlings	Isa 7:23
one *t.* shall flee at the rebuke	Isa 30:17
of one	
a little one shall become a *t.*	Isa 60:22
the man measured a *t.* cubits	Eze 47:3
he measured a *t.* and	Eze 47:4;
brought me	47:5
Belshazzar made a feast to a *t.*	Da 5:1
lords, drank wine before the *t.*	
city that went out by a *t.* shall	Am 5:3
leave	
one day is with the Lord as a	2Pe 3:8
t. years, and a *t.* years as one day	
and he bound Satan a *t.* years	Re 20:2
deceive nations no more, till *t.*	Re 20:3
years be	
and they reigned with Christ a	Re 20:4
t. years	
and when the *t.* years are	Re 20:7
expired	

ONE THOUSAND TWO HUNDRED AND SIXTY

they shall prophesy *one t. two*	Re 11:3
hundred and sixty days	
they should feed her *one t. two*	Re 12:6
hundred and sixty days	

ONE THOUSAND *TWO HUNDRED AND NINETY*

there shall be *one t. two*	Da 12:11
hundred and ninety days	

ONE THOUSAND THREE HUNDRED AND THIRTY FIVE

blessed that cometh to the *t.*	Da 12:12
three hundred and thirty five days	

ONE THOUSAND SIX HUNDRED

by the space of *one t. six*	Re 14:20
hundred furlongs	

TWO THOUSAND

measure on east side *two t.*	Nu 35:5
cubits, west side *two t.*,	
south side *two t.*	
space between you and the ark	Jos 3:4
two t.	
molten sea contained *two t.*	1Ki 7:26
baths	
deliver thee *two t.* horses if	2Ki 18:23;
thou be able to set riders upon	Isa 36:8
people gave *two t.* pounds of	Ne 7:72
silver	
about *two t.* swine were	M'k 5:13
choked in sea	

TWO THOUSAND TWO HUNDRED

fathers gave *two t. two*	Ne 7:71
hundred pounds of silver	

TWO THOUSAND THREE HUNDRED

to *two t. three hundred* days,	Da 8:14
sanctuary cleansed	

THREE THOUSAND

there fell of the people *three*	Ex 32:28
t.	
there went to Ai about *three t.*	Jos 7:4
men	
three t. went to bind Samson	J'g 15:11
were upon the roof *three t.*	J'g 16:27
men	
Saul chose *three t.* men of	1Sa 13:2
Israel	
then Saul took *three t.*	1Sa 24:2;
chosen men	26:2
Naboth had *three t.* sheep	1Sa 25:2
and a thousand goats	
Solomon spake *three t.*	1Ki 4:32
proverbs	
the molten sea held three *t.*	2Ch 4:5
baths	
his substance was *three t.*	Job 1:3
camels	
carried away captive *three t.*	Jer 52:28
Jews	
were added to them *three t.*	Ac 2:41
souls	

FOUR THOUSAND

slew of Israel about *four t.*	1Sa 4:2
men	
four t. porters, *four t.* praised	1Ch 23:5
Lord	
Solomon had *four t.* stalls	2Ch 9:25
for horses	
they that eat were *four t.*	M't 15:38;
	M'k 8:9
seven loaves among *four t.*	M't 16:10;
	M'k 8:20
leddest into the wilderness	Ac 21:38
four t. men	

FOUR THOUSAND FIVE HUNDRED

on the north side of the city	Eze 48:16;
four t. five hundred	48:30, 33, 34
measures, east side, south side,	
west side *four t. five hundred*	
measures	

FIVE THOUSAND

and he took about *five t.* men	Jos 8:12
they gleaned of them *five t.*	J'g 20:45
men	
and gave of gold *five t.*	1Ch 29:7
talents	
for offerings *five t.* small	2Ch 35:9
cattle	
they gave *five t.* pounds of	Ezr 2:69
silver	
they that had eaten were	M't 14:21
about *five t.*	
nor remember the five loaves	M't 16:9;
of the *five t.*	M'k 6:44; 8:19; Lu 9:14; Joh 6:10
number that believed were	Ac 4:4
about *five t.*	

FIVE THOUSAND FOUR HUNDRED

vessels of gold and silver	Ezr 1:11
five t. four hundred	

SIX THOUSAND

against Israel with *six t.*	1Sa 13:5
horsemen	
Naaman took *six t.* pieces of	2Ki 5:5
gold	
six t. were officers and judges	1Ch 23:4
for Job had *six t.* camels	Job 42:12

SIX THOUSAND SEVEN HUNDRED AND TWENTY

their asses, *six t. seven*	Ezr 2:67;
hundred and twenty	Ne 7:69

SEVEN THOUSAND

I left me *seven t.* in Israel	1Ki 19:18;
who have not bowed to Baal	Ro 11:4
children of Israel, being	1Ki 20:15
seven t.	
carried away men of might	2Ki 24:16
seven t.	
of Simeon, mighty men,	1Ch 12:25
seven t.	
David took from him *seven*	1Ch 18:4
t. horsemen	
David slew of the Syrians	1Ch 19:18
seven t. men	
I prepared *seven t.* talents of	1Ch 29:4
silver	
they offered *seven t.* sheep	2Ch 15:11
Hezekiah gave congregation	2Ch 30:24
seven t. sheep	
his substance also was *seven t.*	Job 1:3
sheep	
in earthquake were slain	Re 11:13
seven t. men	

SEVEN THOUSAND SEVEN HUNDRED

Arabians brought	2Ch 17:11
Jehoshaphat *seven t. seven*	
hundred rams, *seven t. seven*	
hundred he goats	

TEN THOUSAND

an hundred shall put *ten t.* to	Le 26:8
flight	
how should two put *ten t.* to	De 32:30
flight	
Lord came with *ten t.* of	De 33:2;
saints	Jude 14
They slew of them in Bezek	J'g 1:4
ten t. men	
they slew of Moab *ten t.* men,	J'g 3:29
all lusty	
Barak, go, and take *ten t.* men	J'g 4:6
of Naphtali	
he went up with *ten t.* men at	J'g 4:10;
his feet	4:14
and there remained to Gideon	J'g 7:3
ten t.	
there came up against Gibeah	J'g 20:34
ten t. men	
but now thou art worth *ten t.*	2Sa 18:3
of us	
sent them to Lebanon, *ten t.*	1Ki 5:14
a month	
leave to Jehoahaz *ten t.*	2Ki 13:7
footmen	
Amaziah slew of Edom *ten t.*	2Ki 14:7
he carried away even *ten t.*	2Ki 24:14
captives	
smote of the children of	2Ch 25:11
Seir *ten t.*	
ten t. left alive, did Judah	2Ch 25:12
carry away	
Ammonites gave Jotham *ten*	2Ch 27:5
t. measures of wheat, and	
ten t. of barley	
Hezekiah gave congregation	2Ch 30:24
ten t. sheep	
I will pay *ten t.* talents of silver	Es 3:9
ten t. shall fall at thy right	Ps 91:7
hand	
my beloved is the chiefest	Ca 5:10
among *ten t.*	

the breadth of the land shall *Eze 45:1;* be *ten t.*   *3:5; 48:9, 10, 13, 18*
ten t. times *ten t.* stood   *Da 7:10* before him
which owed him *ten t.*   *M't 18:24* talents
whether he be able with *ten t.*   *Lu 14:31* to meet
though you have *ten t.*   *1Co 4:15* instructors
than *ten t.* words in an   *1Co 14:19* unknown tongue
number of them was *ten t.*   *Re 5:11* times *ten t.*

TWELVE THOUSAND

all that fell of Ai were *twelve*   *Jos 8:25* *t.*
sent *twelve t.* men to   *J'g 21:10* Jabesh-gilead
Solomon had *twelve t.*   *1Ki 4:26;* horsemen   *10:26; 2Ch 1:14; 9:25*
of tribe of Juda, Reuben, Gad, *Re 7:5* sealed *twelve t.*
of Aser, Naphthalim, Manasses, *Re 7:6* sealed *twelve t.*
of Simeon, Levi, Issachar, were *Re 7:7* sealed *twelve t.*
of Zabulon, Joseph, Benjamin, *Re 7:8* sealed *twelve t.*
he measured the city *twelve t.* *Re 21:16* furlongs

FOURTEEN THOUSAND

for Job had *fourteen t.*   *Job 42:12* sheep

FOURTEEN THOUSAND SEVEN HUNDRED

that died in the plague   *Nu 16:49* *fourteen t. seven hundred*

SIXTEEN THOUSAND

the persons were *sixteen t.*   *Nu 31:40;*   *31:46*

SIXTEEN THOUSAND SEVEN HUNDRED AND FIFTY

Gold of offering *sixteen t.*   *Nu 31:52* *seven hundred and fifty*

SEVENTEEN THOUSAND TWO HUNDRED

sons of Jediel *seventeen t.*   *1Ch 7:11* *two hundred*

EIGHTEEN THOUSAND

destroyed of Israel *eighteen t.* *J'g 20:25* men
there fell of Benjamin   *J'g 20:44* *eighteen t.* men
of half tribe of Manasseh   *1Ch 12:31* *eighteen t.*
Abishai slew of the   *1Ch 18:12* Edomites *eighteen t.*
they gave of brass *eighteen t.* *1Ch 29:7* talents

TWENTY THOUSAND

David took from Hadadezer   *2Sa 8:4;* king of Zobah, *twenty t.*   *1Ch 18:4* footmen
the children of Ammon hired *2Sa 10:6* Syrians *twenty t.*
slaughter of Absalom's   *2Sa 18:7* company *twenty t.*
Solomon gave Hiram *twenty*   *1Ki 5:11;* *t.* measures of wheat   *2Ch 2:10* fathers gave to work *twenty*   *Ne 7:71;* *t.* drams   *7:72*
the chariots of God are *twenty* *Ps 68:17*
to meet him that cometh,   *Lu 14:31* with *twenty t.*

TWENTY-TWO THOUSAND

the number of Levites   *Nu 3:39* *twenty-two t.*

the firstborn males were   *Nu 3:43* *twenty-two t.*
of families of Simeonites   *Nu 26:14*
there returned of Gideon's   *J'g 7:3* army *twenty-two t.*
Benjamin destroyed of Israel *J'g 20:21* *twenty-two t.*
David slew of the Syrians   *2Sa 8:5;* *twenty-two t.* men   *1Ch 18:5*
Solomon offered *twenty-two* *1Ki 8:63;* *t.* oxen   *2Ch 7:5*
of Tola *twenty-two t.*   *1Ch 7:2*
of Bela *twenty-two t.*   *1Ch 7:7*

TWENTY-THREE THOUSAND

numbered of Levites   *Nu 26:62* *twenty-three t.*
and fell in one day *three* and *1Co 10:8* *twenty t.*

TWENTY-FOUR THOUSAND

died in the plague *twenty-four Nu 25:9* *t.*
twenty-four t. Levites to   *1Ch 23:4* forward the work
the officers that served were *1Ch 27:1* *twenty-four t.*

TWENTY-FIVE THOUSAND

destroyed of Benjamites   *J'g 20:35;* *twenty-five t.*   *20:46*
holy portion of land   *Eze 45:1;* *twenty-five t.* reeds in length *45:3, 5, 6;*   *48:8, 9, 10, 13*

TWENTY-SIX THOUSAND

Benjamin numbered   *J'g 20:15* *twenty-six t.*
of Asher, apt to war,   *1Ch 7:40* *twenty six t.*

TWENTY-SEVEN THOUSAND

a wall fell on *twenty-seven t.* *1Ki 20:30* men

TWENTY-EIGHT THOUSAND

Danites, expert in war,   *1Ch 12:35* *twenty-eight t.*

THIRTY THOUSAND

and the asses were *thirty t.* *Nu 31:39;*   *31:45*
Joshua chose *thirty t.* mighty *Jos 8:3* men
there fell of Israel *thirty t.* *1Sa 4:10* footmen
and the men of Judah were *1Sa 11:8* *thirty t.*
Philistines gathered *thirty t.* *1Sa 13:5* chariots
David gathered *thirty t.* chosen *2Sa 6:1* men
and the levy was *thirty t.* men *1Ki 5:13*

THIRTY-TWO THOUSAND

thirty-two t. women taken   *Nu 31:35* captives
Ammon hired *thirty-two t.*   *1Ch 19:7* chariots

THIRTY-TWO THOUSAND TWO HUNDRED

number of Manasseh   *Nu 1:35;* *thirty-two t. two hundred*   *2:21*

THIRTY-TWO THOUSAND FIVE HUNDRED

of Ephraim were numbered   *Nu 26:37* *thirty-two t. five hundred*

THIRTY-THREE THOUSAND

gave *thirty-three t.* bullocks   *2Ch 35:7*

THIRTY-FIVE THOUSAND

of Benjamin were *thirty-five t. Nu 1:37*

THIRTY-SIX THOUSAND

the beeves were *thirty* and   *Nu 31:38* six *t.*
pertained to congregation   *Nu 31:44* *thirty-six t.* beeves
the bands of soldiers were   *1Ch 7:4* *thirty-six t.*

THIRTY-SEVEN THOUSAND

of Naphtali *thirty* and *seven 1Ch 12:34* *t.*

THIRTY-EIGHT THOUSAND

Levites from thirty years,   *1Ch 23:3* *thirty-eight t.*

FORTY THOUSAND

about *forty t.* prepared for   *Jos 4:13* war
was there a shield seen among *J'g 5:8* *forty t.*
David slew *forty t.* horsemen *2Sa 10:18*
Solomon had *forty t.* stalls of *1Ki 4:26* horses
of Asher, expert in war,   *1Ch 12:36* *forty t.*
David slew of Syrians, *forty 1Ch 19:18* *t.* footmen

FORTY THOUSAND FIVE HUNDRED

of Ephraim were *forty t. five Nu 1:33;* *hundred*   *2:19*
of Gad were numbered *forty Nu 26:18* *t.* and *five hundred*

FORTY-ONE THOUSAND FIVE HUNDRED

of Asher numbered *forty-one Nu 1:41;* *t. five hundred*   *2:28*

FORTY-TWO THOUSAND

fell of Ephraimites *forty-two J'g 12:6* *t.*
whole congregation *forty-two Ezr 2:64;* *t.*   *Ne 7:66*

FORTY-THREE THOUSAND SEVEN HUNDRED AND THIRTY

of Reubenites *forty-three t.*   *Nu 26:7* *seven hundred and thirty*

FORTY-FOUR THOUSAND SEVEN HUNDRED AND SIXTY

of Reubenites to war   *1Ch 5:18* *forty-four t. seven hundred and sixty*

FORTY-FIVE THOUSAND FOUR HUNDRED

of Naphtali were *forty-five t. Nu 26:50* *four hundred*

FORTY-FIVE THOUSAND SIX HUNDRED

numbered of Benjamin   *Nu 26:41* *forty-five t. six hundred*

FORTY-FIVE THOUSAND SIX HUNDRED AND FIFTY

were numbered of Gad   *Nu 1:25;* *forty-five t. six hundred and fifty 2:15*

FORTY-SIX THOUSAND FIVE HUNDRED

of Reuben *forty-six t.* and   *Nu 1:21;* *five hundred*   *2:11*

FIFTY THOUSAND

the Lord smote *fifty t.* and   1Sa 6:19
seventy men
took of the Hagarites' sheep   1Ch 5:21
fifty t.
of Zebulun *fifty t.* could   1Ch 12:33
keep rank
the price of the book *fifty t.*   Ac 19:19
pieces

FIFTY-TWO THOUSAND SEVEN HUNDRED

of Manasseh *fifty-two t.* and   Nu 26:34
seven hundred

FIFTY-THREE THOUSAND FOUR HUNDRED

of Naphtali *fifty-three t. four*   Nu 1:43;
hundred   2:30

FIFTY-FOUR THOUSAND FOUR HUNDRED

of Issachar *fifty-four t.*   Nu 1:29;
four hundred   2:6

FIFTY-SEVEN THOUSAND FOUR HUNDRED

of Zebulun *fifty-seven t. four*   Nu 1:31;
hundred   2:8

FIFTY-NINE THOUSAND THREE HUNDRED

of Simeon *fifty-nine t. three*   Nu 1:23;
hundred   2:13

SIXTY THOUSAND

Shishak came with *sixty t.*   2Ch 12:3
horsemen

SIXTY THOUSAND FIVE HUNDRED

of Zebulunites, *sixty t.* and   Nu 26:27
five hundred

SIXTY-ONE THOUSAND

the booty was *sixty-one t.*   Nu 31:34
asses
they gave *sixty-one t.* drams   Ezr 2:69
of gold

SIXTY-TWO THOUSAND SEVEN HUNDRED

of tribe of Dan *sixty-two t.*   Nu 1:39;
seven hundred   2:26

SIXTY-FOUR THOUSAND THREE HUNDRED

of Issachar *sixty-four t.* and   Nu 26:25
three hundred

SIXTY-FOUR THOUSAND FOUR HUNDRED

of the Shuhamites *sixty-four*   Nu 26:43
t. four hundred

SEVENTY THOUSAND

there died of the people   2Sa 24:15
seventy t.
Solomon had *seventy t.* that   1Ki 5:15;
bare burdens   2Ch 2:2, 18
there fell of Israel *seventy t.*   1Ch 21:14

SEVENTY-TWO THOUSAND

booty of beeves was   Nu 31:33
seventy-two t.

SEVENTY-FOUR THOUSAND SIX HUNDRED

number of Judah *seventy-four*   Nu 1:27;
t. and *six hundred*   2:4

SEVENTY-FIVE THOUSAND

the booty was *seventy-five t.*   Nu 31:32
sheep
Jews slew of their foes   Es 9:16
seventy-five t.

SEVENTY-SIX THOUSAND FIVE HUNDRED

numbered of Judah   Nu 26:22
seventy-six t. five hundred

EIGHTY THOUSAND

Solomon had *eighty t.*   1Ki 5:15;
hewers in the mountains   2Ch 2:2, 18

EIGHTY-SEVEN THOUSAND

of Issachar, reckoned   1Ch 7:5
eighty-seven t.

THOUSAND THOUSAND

all they of Israel were a   1Ch 21:5
thousand t.
I have prepared a *thousand*   1Ch 22:14
t. talents of silver
the Ethiopian came with a   2Ch 14:9
thousand t.

TWO HUNDRED THOUSAND

carried away captive *two*   2Ch 28:8
hundred t.

TWO HUNDRED THOUSAND THOUSAND

army of horsemen *two*   Re 9:16
hundred thousand t.

TWO HUNDRED EIGHTY THOUSAND

out of Benjamin *two hundred*   2Ch 14:8
eighty t.

THOUSANDS

be thou the mother of *t.* of   Ge 24:60
millions
place such over them rulers   Ex 18:21;
of *t.*   18:25
shewing mercy to *t.* of them   Ex 20:6;
                       De 5:10
keeping mercy for *t.*, forgiving   Ex 34:7
iniquity
there were the princes of   Nu 1:16;
tribes, heads of *t.* in Israel   10:4;
          Jos 22:14, 21, 30
return, O Lord, to the many   Nu 10:36
t. of Israel
there were delivered out of   Nu 31:5
the *t.* of Israel
so I made them captains over   De 1:15;
t. Nu 31:14, 48, 52, 54; 1Sa 8:12; 22:7;
2Sa 18:1; 1Ch 12:20; 13:1; 15:25; 26:26;
   27:1; 28:1; 29:6; 2Ch 1:2; 17:14; 25:5
and they are the *t.* of   De 33:17
Manasseh
captains over *t.*   1Sa 8:12
therefore present yourselves   1Sa 10:19
by your *t.*
and to me they have ascribed   1Sa 18:8
but *t.*
will the son of Jesse make   1Sa 22:7
you captains of *t.*
I'll search him throughout   1Sa 23:23
the *t.* of Judah
the lords of the Philistines   1Sa 29:2
passed on by *t.*
and all the people came out   2Sa 18:4
by *t.*
t. of angels   Ps 68:17
low better than *t.* of gold   Ps 119:72
our sheep may bring forth by *t.*   Ps 144:13
thou shewest lovingkindness   Jer 32:18
to *t.*
thousand *t.* ministered unto   Da 7:10
him
tho' thou be little among the   Mic 5:2
t. of Judah
will the Lord be pleased with   Mic 6:7
t. of rams
how many *t.* of Jews which   Ac 21:20
believe
the number of them was   Re 5:11
thousand of *t.*

TEN THOUSANDS

they are the *ten t.* of   De 33:17
Ephraim

David slain his *ten t.*   1Sa 18:7;
         18:8; 21:11; 29:5
I will not be afraid of *ten t.* of   Ps 3:6
people
that our sheep may bring   Ps 144:13
forth *ten t.*
he shall cast down many *ten*   Da 11:12
t.
or be pleased with *ten t.* rivers   Mic 6:7
of oil
ten t. of angels (B)   Heb 12:22

THREAD

take from a *t.* even to a   Ge 14:23
shoelatchet
bound upon his hand a   Ge 38:28
scarlet *t.*
that had the scarlet *t.* upon   Ge 38:30
his hand
a blue *t.* (B)   Nu 15:38
shalt bind this line of scarlet   Jos 2:18
t.
as a *t.* of tow is broken when   J'g 16:9
them from off his arms like a   J'g 16:12
t.
Thy lips are like a *t.* of scarlet   Ca 4:3

THREADS

cut into *t.* (B)(R)   Ex 39:5

THREATEN

let us straitly *t.* them, that   Ac 4:17
they

THREATENED

So when they had further *t.*   Ac 4:21
them
again; when he suffered, he *t.*   1Pe 2:23
not

THREATENING

red and *t.* (A)(P)(R)   M't 16:3
t. and murderous desire (A)   Ac 9:1
things unto them, forbearing   Eph 6:9

THREATENINGS

because of *t.* of wicked (B)   Ps 55:3
And now, Lord, behold their   Ac 4:29
t.
And Saul, yet breathing out *t.*   Ac 9:1

THREATS

t. and murder (B)(N)(P)(R)   Ac 9:1

THREE

he looked, and lo, *t.* men   Ge 18:2
stood by him
and if he do not these *t.* unto   Ex 21:11
her
t. branches of the   Ex 25:32;
candlestick   37:18
t. bowls made like unto   Ex 25:33;
almonds   37:19
the height of the altar shall   Ex 27:1
be *t.* cubits   38:1
pillars *t.*, their sockets *t.*   Ex 27:14;
            27:15; 38:14, 15
take *t.* tenth deals of fine   Le 14:10;
flour for a meat offering Nu 15:9; 28:12
thy estimation for the female,   Le 27:6
t. shekels
come out, ye *t.* and they *t.*   Nu 12:4
came out
t. tenths deals for a bullock Nu 28:20;
         28:28; 29:3, 9, 14
ye shall give *t.* cities on this   Nu 35:14
side Jordan
Moses severed *t.* cities   De 4:41;
          19:2, 3, 7, 9
at the mouth of *t.* witnesses   De 17:6;
                   19:15
and Caleb drove thence the   Jos 15:14;
t. sons of Anak   J'g 1:20
t. men of each tribe to   Jos 18:4
describe the land
the *t.* companies blew the   J'g 7:20
trumpets
he divided the people into *t.*   J'g 9:43
companies
Hannah took with her *t.*   1Sa 1:24
bullocks

servant came with a   1Sa 2:13
fleshhook of *t.* teeth
Hannah bare *t.* sons and two 1Sa 2:21
daughters
meet thee *t.* men, one   1Sa 10:3
carrying *t.* kids, another
carrying *t.* loaves of bread
Saul put the people in *t.*   1Sa 11:11
companies
the *t.* eldest of Jesse's sons 1Sa 17:13;
followed Saul   17:14
I will shoot *t.* arrows on the 1Sa 20:20
side thereof
Saul died, and his *t.* sons   1Sa 31:6;
                                1Ch 10:6
they found Saul and his *t.*   1Sa 31:8
sons fallen
to Absalon there were born   2Sa 14:27
t. sons
Joab thrust *t.* darts through 2Sa 18:14
Absalom
Eleazar one of the *t.* mighty 2Sa 23:9;
                                1Ch 11:12
t. of the thirty chief went 2Sa 23:13
down to David
t. mighty brake through the 2Sa 23:16;
Philistines   23:17
Abishai brother of Joab   2Sa 23:18;
chief among *t.*   23:19
howbeit, he attained not to   2Sa 23:19;
the first *t.*   23:23
Benaiah had the name   2Sa 23:22
among *t.* mighty men
I offer thee *t.* things   2Sa 24:12;
                                1Ch 21:10
he built the inner court with 1Ki 6:36
t. rows
and there were windows in *t.* 1Ki 7:4
rows
it stood upon *t.* oxen looking 1Ki 7:25
toward the north, *t.* to the
west *t.* to the south, *t.* the east
t. pound of gold went to one 1Ki 10:17
shield
Lord hath called these *t.*   2Ki 3:10;
kings   3:13
the sons of Zeruiah were *t.* 1Ch 2:16
sons of Neariah, *t.*   1Ch 3:23
sons of Mushi, *t.*   1Ch 23:23
God gave Heman fourteen   1Ch 25:5
sons and *t.* daughters
let the foundations be laid   Ezr 6:4
with *t.* rows
were born to Job *t.* daughters Job 1:2;
                                42:13
the Chaldeans made out *t.*   Job 1:17
bands and fell
Job's *t.* friends heard of all Job 2:11
this evil
t. things which are never   Pr 30:15
satisfied
there be *t.* things too   Pr 30:18
wonderful for me
for *t.* things the earth is   Pr 30:21
disquieted
there be *t.* things which go Pr 30:29
well, yea four
two or *t.* berries in the top Isa 17:6
of the bough
though these *t.* men were in Eze 14:14;
it   14:16, 18
the little chambers were *t.* Eze 40:10;
on this side   40:21
side chambers were *t.* one   Eze 41:6
over another
t. gates, after names of   Eze 48:31;
tribes   48:32, 33, 34
did not we cast *t.* men bound Da 3:24
into fire
and Darius set over these *t.* Da 6:2
presidents
it had *t.* ribs in the mouth Da 7:5
between the teeth
t. of the first horns were   Da 7:8;
plucked up   7:20, 24
I Daniel was mourning *t.* full Da 10:2;
weeks   10:3
there shall stand up *t.* kings in Da 11:2
Persia
for *t.* transgressions   Am 1:3;
                    1:6, 9, 11, 13; 2:1, 4, 6
so two or *t.* cities wandered to Am 4:8
one city
t. shepherds I cut off in one Zec 11:8
month
hid in *t.* measures of meal   M't 13:33;
                                Lu 13:21
if thou wilt let us make here M't 17:4;
t. tabernacles   M'k 9:5; Lu 9:33

in mouth of two or *t.*   M't 18:16;
witnesses   2Co 13:1
where two or *t.* are gathered M't 18:20
in my name
which of these *t.* was   Lu 10:36
neighbour to him
say to him, Friend, lend me *t.* Lu 11:5
loaves
divided, *t.* against two, and Lu 12:52
two against *t.*
t. hours after, when his wife Ac 5:7
came in
behold, *t.* men seek thee   Ac 10:19;
                                11:11
come to meet us as far as the Ac 28:15
t. taverns
now abideth these *t.:* faith, 1Co 13:13
hope, charity
by two, or at most by *t.* and 1Co 14:27
that by course
let the prophets speak two   1Co 14:29
or *t.* and other
but before two or *t.* witnesses 1Ti 5:19
died under two or *t.*   Heb 10:28
witnesses
there are *t.* that bear record in 1Jo 5:7
heaven
t. bear witness in earth, and 1Jo 5:8
these *t.* agree
and *t.* measures of barley for a Re 6:6
penny
trumpet of *t.* angels who are Re 8:13
yet to sound
by these *t.* was the third part Re 9:18
of men killed
I saw *t.* unclean spirits like Re 16:13
frogs come
the great city was divided into Re 16:19
t. parts
on the east *t.* gates, on the Re 21:13
north *t.* gates, on the south *t.*
gates, and on the west *t.* gates

THREE *MONTHS*

about *t. months* after, it was Ge 38:24
told
was a goodly child, she hid   Ex 2:2
him *t. months*
ark continued in the house   2Sa 6:11;
of Obed-edom *t. months*   1Ch 13:14
wilt thou flee *t. months*   2Sa 24:13;
before thine enemies   1Ch 21:12
Jehoahaz son of Josiah   2Ki 23:31;
reigned *t. months* in   2Ch 36:2
Jerusalem
Jehoiachin reigned *t. months* 2Ki 24:8;
                                2Ch 36:9
there were yet *t. months* to Am 4:7
harvest
Moses was nourished up *t.*   Ac 7:20
months
Paul spake boldly the space of Ac 19:8
t. months
Paul abode in Greece *t.*   Ac 19:23
months
Moses hid *t. months* of his   Heb 11:23
parents

THREE *TIMES*

t. times keep a feast to me Ex 23:14
t. times in the year all males Ex 23:17;
appear before the Lord   De 16:16
smitten me these *t. times*   Nu 22:28;
                                22:32
the ass turned from me these   Nu 22:33
t. times
thou hast blessed them these   Nu 24:10
t. times
thou hast mocked me these *t.* J'g 16:15
times
David arose and bowed *t.*   1Sa 20:41
times
Solomon offered *t. times* a   1Ki 9:25
year
Elijah stretched himself on   1Ki 17:21
child *t. times*
times did Joash beat   2Ki 13:25
Hazael
offering *t. times* in the year 2Ch 8:13
kneeled on his knees *t. times* Da 6:10
a day
Daniel maketh his petition *t.* Da 6:13
times a day
this was done *t. times,* and Ac 11:10
drawn up

THREE YEARS

heifer of *t. years* old, a   Ge 15:9
she goat *t. years* old, and
a ram *t. years* old
fruit as uncircumcised *t.*   Le 19:23
years
it shall bring forth fruit for *t.* Le 25:21
years
at end of *t. years* bring tithe De 14:28
Abimelech had reigned *t.*   J'g 9:22
years
Absalom was in Geshur *t.*   2Sa 13:38
years
a famine in the days of   2Sa 21:1
David *t. years*
at end of *t. years* Shimei's 1Ki 2:39
servants ran
once in *t. years* came navy   1Ki 10:22;
of Tarshish, bringing gold   2Ch 9:21
and silver
Abijam reigned *t. years* in   1Ki 15:2;
Jerusalem   2Ch 13:2
they continued *t. years*   1Ki 22:1
without war
Assyrians besieged Samaria *t.* 2Ki 17:5
years
and at the end of *t. years*   2Ki 18:10
they took it
Jehoiakim became his servant   2Ki 24:1
t. years
choose thee either *t. years'* 1Ch 21:12
famine or three months to be
destroyed
made Rehoboam strong *t.*   2Ch 11:17
years, *t. years* they walked
in way of David
Abijah reigned *t. years* in   2Ch 13:2
Jerusalem
males, from *t. years* old and 2Ch 31:16
upward
unto Zoar, an heifer of *t.*   Isa 15:5
years old
within *t. years* as years of an Isa 16:14
hireling
as Isaiah walked barefoot *t.* Isa 20:3
years
as an heifer of *t. years* old Jer 48:34
so nourishing them *t. years* Da 1:5
and bring your tithes after *t.* Am 4:4
years
heaven shut up *t. years*   Lu 4:25;
                                Jas 5:17
these *t. years* I come seeking Lu 13:7
fruit, find none
t. years I ceased not to warn Ac 20:31
every one
after *t. years* I went up to Ga 1:18
Jerusalem

THREEFOLD

a *t.* cord is not quickly broken Ec 4:12

THREESCORE

an hundred *t.* and fifteen years Ge 25:7
Isaac was *t.* years old when Ge 25:26
she
all the souls were *t.* and six Ge 46:26
came into Egypt, were *t.* and Ge 46:27
ten
mourned for him *t.* and ten   Ge 50:3
days
water, and *t.* and ten palm   Ex 15:27
trees
hundred and *t.* and fifteen   Ex 38:25
shekels
of her purifying *t.* and six days Le 12:5
were *t.* and fourteen thousand Nu 1:27
were *t.* and two thousand and Nu 1:39;
                                2:26
were *t.* and fourteen thousand Nu 2:4
two hundred and *t.* and   Nu 3:43;
thirteen   3:46
hundred and *t.* and five   Nu 3:50
shekels
t. and sixteen thousand and Nu 26:22
five
t. and four thousand and   Nu 26:25
three
them, *t.* thousand and five   Nu 26:27
hundred
were *t.* and four thousand   Nu 26:43
t. and twelve thousand   Nu 31:33
beeves
And *t.* and one thousand   Nu 31:34
asses
six hundred and *t.* and   Nu 31:37
fifteen

Lord's tribute was *t.* and twelve	*Nu 31:38*
the Lord's tribute was *t.* and one	*Nu 31:39*
water, and *t.* and ten palm trees	*Nu 33:9*
t. cities, all the region of Argob	*De 3:4*
Egypt with *t.* and ten persons	*De 10:22*
which are in Bashan, *t.* cities	*Jos 13:30*
T. and ten kings, having their	*J'g 1:7*
thereof, even *t.* and seventeen men	*J'g 8:14*
had *t.* and ten sons of his body	*J'g 8:30*
which are *t.* and ten persons, reign	*J'g 9:2*
they gave him *t.* and ten pieces	*J'g 9:4*
Jerubbaal, being *t.* and ten persons	*J'g 9:5*
slain his sons, *t.* and ten persons	*J'g 9:18*
to the *t.* and ten sons of Jerubbaal	*J'g 9:24*
that rode on *t.* and ten ass colts	*J'g 12:14*
fifty thousand and *t.* and ten men	*1Sa 6:19*
three hundred and *t.* men died	*2Sa 2:31*
t. great cities with walls and	*1Ki 4:13*
fine flour, and *t.* measures of meal	*1Ki 4:22*
had *t.* and ten thousand that bare	*1Ki 5:15*
the length thereof was *t.* cubits	*1Ki 6:2*
hundred *t.* and six talents of gold	*1Ki 10:14*
and *t.* men of the people of the land	*2Ki 25:19*
whom he married when he was *t.*	*1Ch 2:21*
the towns thereof, even *t.* cities	*1Ch 2:23*
thousand seven hundred and *t.*	*1Ch 5:18*
and seven hundred and *t.*	*1Ch 9:13*
with their brethren, *t.* and eight	*1Ch 16:38*
t. and ten thousand men that drew	*1Ch 21:5*
were *t.* and two of Obed-edom	*1Ch 26:8*
t. and ten thousand men to bear	*2Ch 2:2*
t. and ten thousand of them to be	*2Ch 2:18*
the first measure was *t.* cubits	*2Ch 3:3*
six hundred and *t.* and six talents	*2Ch 9:13*
eighteen wives, and *t.* concubines	*2Ch 11:21*
and eight sons, and *t.* daughters	*2Ch 11:21*
chariots, and *t.* thousand horsemen	*2Ch 12:3*
brought, was *t.* and ten bullocks	*2Ch 29:32*
sabbath, to fulfil *t.* and ten years	*2Ch 36:21*
of Zaccai, seven hundred and *t.*	*Ezr 2:9*
two thousand three hundred and *t.*	*Ezr 2:64*
t. and one thousand drams of gold	*Ezr 2:69*
and height thereof *t.* cubits	*Ezr 6:3*
and the breadth thereof *t.* cubits	*Ezr 6:3*
him an hundred and *t.* males	*Ezr 8:10*
Shemaiah and with them *t.* males	*Ezr 8:13*
of Zaccai, seven hundred and *t.*	*Ne 7:14*
six hundred *t.* and seven	*Ne 7:18*
Bigvai, two thousand *t.* and seven	*Ne 7:19*
two thousand three hundred and *t.*	*Ne 7:66*
and *t.* and seven priests' garments	*Ne 7:72*
four hundred *t.* and eight valiant	*Ne 11:6*
of our years are *t.* years and ten	*Ps 90:10*
t. valiant men are about it, of	*Ca 3:7*
There are *t.* queens, and fourscore	*Ca 6:8*
and within *t.* and five years shall	*Isa 7:8*

and *t.* men of the people of the land	*Jer 52:25*
He made also posts of *t.* cubits	*Eze 40:14*
gold, whose height was *t.* cubits	*Da 3:1*
being about *t.* and two years old	*Da 5:31*
weeks, and *t.* and two weeks	*Da 9:25*
And after *t.* and two weeks shall	*Da 9:26*
indignation these *t.* and ten years	*Zec 1:12*
from Jerusalem about *t.* furlongs	*Lu 24:13*
his kindred, *t.* and fifteen souls	*Ac 7:14*
and horsemen *t.* and ten, and	*Ac 23:23*
two hundred *t.* and sixteen souls	*Ac 27:37*
the number under *t.* years old	*1Ti 5:9*
thousand two hundred and *t.* days	*Re 11:3; 12:6*
number is Six hundred *t.* and six	*Re 13:18*

THRESH

thou shalt *t.* the mountains	*Isa 41:15*
threshingfloor, it is time to *t.* her	*Jer 51:33*
Arise and *t.* O daughter of Zion	*Mic 4:13*
thou didst *t.* the heathen in anger	*Hab 3:12*

THRESHED

Gideon *t.* wheat by the winepress	*J'g 6:11*
fitches are not *t.* with a threshing	*Isa 28:27*
they have *t.* Gilead with threshing	*Am 1:3*

THRESHETH

he that *t.* in hope should be partaker	*1Co 9:10*

THRESHING

mourning in the *t.* floor (S)	*Ge 50:11*
And your *t.* shall reach unto	*Le 26:5*
and *t.* instruments and other	*2Sa 24:22*
the *t.* floor (B)(R)	*1Ki 22:10; 2Ch 18:9*
had made them like the dust by *t.*	*2Ki 13:7*
Now Ornan was *t.* wheat	*1Ch 21:20*
and the *t.* instruments for wood	*1Ch 21:23*
O my *t.* and the corn of my floor	*Isa 21:10*
not threshed with a *t.* instrument	*Isa 28:27*
because he will not ever be *t.* it	*Isa 28:28*
a new sharp *t.* instrument having	*Isa 41:15*
Gilead with *t.* instruments of iron	*Am 1:3*

THRESHINGFLOOR

And they came to the *t.* of Atad	*Ge 50:10*
as ye do the heave offering of the *t.*	*Nu 15:20*
as though it were the corn of the *t.*	*Nu 18:27*
Levites as the increase of the *t.*	*Nu 18:30*
produce of *t.* (A)(B)(E)(R)	*De 16:13*
winnoweth barley to night in the *t.*	*Ru 3:2*
when they came to Nachon's *t.*	*2Sa 6:6*
unto the Lord in the *t.* of Araunah	*2Sa 24:18*
David said, To buy the *t.* of thee	*2Sa 24:21*
David bought the *t.* and the oxen	*2Sa 24:24*
they came unto the *t.* of Chidon	*1Ch 13:9*
angel of the Lord stood by the *t.*	*1Ch 21:15*
unto the Lord in the *t.* of Ornan	*1Ch 21:18*

saw David, and went out of the *t.*	*1Ch 21:21*
Grant me the place of this *t.* that	*1Ch 21:22*
answered him in the *t.* of Ornan	*1Ch 21:28*
had prepared in the *t.* of Ornan	*2Ch 3:1*
The daughter of Babylon is like a *t.*	*Jer 51:33*
every *t.* (A)(B)(R)	*Ho 9:1*

THRESHINGFLOORS

Keilah, and they rob the *t.*	*1Sa 23:1*
like the chaff of the summer *t.*	*Da 2:35*

THRESHINGPLACE

angel of the Lord was by the *t.*	*2Sa 24:16*

THRESHOLD

and her hands were upon the *t.*	*J'g 19:27*
his hands were cut off upon the *t.*	*1Sa 5:4*
tread on the *t.* of Dagon in Ashdod	*1Sa 5:5*
she came to the *t.* of the door	*1Ki 14:17*
he was, to the *t.* of the house	*Eze 9:3*
and stood over the *t.* of the house	*Eze 10:4*
from off the *t.* of the house	*Eze 10:18*
and measured the *t.* of the gate	*Eze 40:6*
and the other *t.* of the gate, which	*Eze 40:6*
the *t.* of the gate by the porch of	*Eze 40:7*
setting of their *t.* by my thresholds	*Eze 43:8*
shall worship at the *t.* of the gate	*Eze 46:2*
waters issued out from under the *t.*	*Eze 47:1*
punish all those that leap on the *t.*	*Zep 1:9*

THRESHOLDS

the ward at the *t.* of the gates	*Ne 12:25*
setting of their threshold by my *t.*	*Eze 43:8*
desolation shall be in the *t.*	*Zep 2:14*

THREW

threw (R)	*Ex 9:10; 24:6, 8; Le 8:19; 9:12, 18; 2Ki 16:13; 2Ch 29:22; 30:16*
t. themselves on the loot (B)	*1Sa 14:32*
t. stones at him, and cast dust	*2Sa 16:13*
her down. So they *t.* her down	*2Ki 9:33*
t. down the high places and	*2Ch 31:1*
widow, and she *t.* in two mites	*M't 12:42*
devil *t.* him down, and tare him	*Lu 9:42*
clothes, and *t.* dust into the air	*Ac 22:23*

THREWEST

persecutors thou *t.* into the deeps	*Ne 9:11*

THRICE

T. in the year shall all your	*Ex 34:23*
Lord thy God *t.* in the year	*Ex 34:24*
And he smote *t.* and stayed	*2Ki 13:18*
thou shalt smite Syria but *t.*	*2Ki 13:19*
twice, year *t.* (S)	*Job 33:29*
crow, thou shalt deny me *t.*	*M't 26:34; 26:75*
twice, thou shalt deny me *t.*	*M'k 14:30; 14:72*
shalt *t.* deny that thou knowest	*Lu 22:34*
cock crow, thou shalt deny me *t.*	*Lu 22:61*
crow, till thou hast denied me *t.*	*Joh 13:38*

This was done *t*.; and the vessel   *Ac 10:16*

T. was I beaten with rods, once   *2Co 11:25*

t. I suffered shipwreck, a night   *2Co 11:25*

this thing I besought the Lord *t*.   *2Co 12:8*

THRILL

heart *t*. and rejoice (R)   *Isa 60:5*

THRIVE

he made him *t*. (B)   *2Ch 26:5*

THRIVED

they built and *t*. (B)   *2Ch 14:7*

THROAT

their *t*. is an open sepulchre; they   *Ps 5:9*

weary of my crying; my *t*. is dried   *Ps 69:3*

neither speak they through their *t*.   *Ps 115:7*

And put a knife to thy *t*. if thou   *Pr 23:2*

unshod, and thy *t*. from thirst   *Jer 2:25*

and took him by the *t*., saying   *M't 18:28*

Their *t*. is an open sepulchre   *Ro 3:13*

THROBS

my heart *t*. (A)(E)(R)   *Ps 38:10*

THRONE

only in the *t*. will I be greater   *Ge 41:40*

of Pharaoh that sitteth upon his *t*.   *Ex 11:5*

of Pharaoh that sat on his *t*.   *Ex 12:29*

sitteth upon the *t*. of his kingdom   *De 17:18*

make them inherit the *t*. of glory   *1Sa 2:8*

to set up the *t*. of David over Israel   *2Sa 3:10*

will stablish the *t*. of his kingdom   *2Sa 7:13*

thy *t*. shall be established for ever   *2Sa 7:16*

the king and his *t*. be guiltless   *2Sa 14:9*

me, and he shall sit upon my *t*.   *1Ki 1:13; 1:17*

who shall sit on the *t*. of my lord   *1Ki 1:20*

me, and he shall sit upon my *t*.   *1Ki 1:24*

who should sit on the *t*. of my lord   *1Ki 1:27*

he shall sit upon my *t*. in my stead   *1Ki 1:30*

he may come and sit upon my *t*.   *1Ki 1:35*

Solomon, and make his *t*. greater   *1Ki 1:37*

than the *t*. of my lord king David   *1Ki 1:37*

Solomon sitteth on the *t*. of   *1Ki 1:46*

and make his *t*. greater than thy *t*.   *1Ki 1:47*

given one to sit on my *t*. this day   *1Ki 1:48*

(said he) a man on the *t*. of Israel   *1Ki 2:4*

sat Solomon upon the *t*. of David   *1Ki 2:12*

and sat down on his *t*. and caused   *1Ki 2:19*

set me on the *t*. of David my father   *1Ki 2:24*

upon his *t*. shall there be peace   *1Ki 2:33*

the *t*. of David shall be established   *1Ki 2:45*

hast given him a son to sit on his *t*.   *1Ki 3:6*

son, whom I will set upon thy *t*. in   *1Ki 5:5*

he made a porch for the *t*. where he   *1Ki 7:7*

my father, and sit on the *t*. of Israel   *1Ki 8:20*

in my sight to sit on the *t*. of Israel   *1Ki 8:25*

will establish the *t*. of thy kingdom   *1Ki 9:5*

thee a man upon the *t*. of   *1Ki 9:9*

thee, to set thee on the *t*. of Israel   *1Ki 10:9*

the king made a great *t*. of ivory   *1Ki 10:18*

The *t*. had six steps, and the top of   *1Ki 10:19*

the top of the *t*. was round behind   *1Ki 10:19*

reign, as soon as he sat on his *t*.   *1Ki 16:11*

king of Judah sat each on his *t*.   *1Ki 22:10*

I saw the Lord sitting on his *t*.   *1Ki 22:19*

sons, and set him on his father's *t*.   *2Ki 10:3*

shall sit on the *t*. of Israel   *2Ki 10:30*

And he sat on the *t*. of the kings   *2Ki 11:19*

and Jeroboam sat upon his *t*.   *2Ki 13:13*

sons shall sit on the *t*. of Israel   *2Ki 15:12*

set his *t*. above the *t*. of the kings   *2Ki 25:28*

and I will stablish his *t*. for ever   *1Ch 17:12*

and his *t*. shall be established for   *1Ch 17:14*

establish the *t*. of his kingdom over   *1Ch 22:10*

to sit upon the *t*. of the kingdom of   *1Ch 28:5*

Solomon sat on the *t*. of the Lord   *1Ch 29:23*

and am set on the *t*. of Israel, as   *2Ch 6:10*

sight to sit upon the *t*. of Israel   *2Ch 6:16*

will I stablish the *t*. of thy kingdom   *2Ch 7:18*

in thee to set thee on his *t*.   *2Ch 9:8*

the king made a great *t*. of ivory   *2Ch 9:17*

And there were six steps to the *t*.   *2Ch 9:18*

gold, which were fastened to the *t*.   *2Ch 9:18*

Judah sat either of them on his *t*.   *2Ch 18:9*

I saw the Lord sitting upon his *t*.   *2Ch 18:18*

king upon the *t*. of the   *2Ch 23:20*

unto the *t*. of the governor on this   *Ne 3:7*

king Ahasuerus sat on the *t*. of his   *Es 1:2*

king sat upon his royal *t*. in the   *Es 5:1*

He holdeth back the face of his *t*.   *Job 26:9*

with kings are they on the *t*.; yea   *Job 36:7*

thou satest in the *t*. judging right   *Ps 9:4*

ever: he hath prepared his *t*.   *Ps 9:7*

temple, the Lord's *t*. is in heaven   *Ps 11:4*

Thy *t*. O God, is for ever and ever   *Ps 45:6*

God sitteth upon the *t*. of his   *Ps 47:8*

build up thy *t*. to all generations   *Ps 89:4*

are the habitation of thy *t*.   *Ps 89:14*

and his *t*. as the days of heaven   *Ps 89:29*

and his *t*. as the sun before me   *Ps 89:36*

and cast his *t*. down to the ground   *Ps 89:44*

Thy *t*. is established of old: thou   *Ps 93:2*

the *t*. of iniquity have fellowship   *Ps 94:20*

are the habitation of his *t*.   *Ps 97:2*

hath prepared his *t*. in the heavens   *Ps 103:19*

of thy body will I set upon thy *t*.   *Ps 132:11*

also upon thy *t*. for evermore   *Ps 132:12*

t. is established by righteousness   *Pr 16:12*

A king that sitteth in the *t*. of   *Pr 20:8*

and his *t*. is upholden by mercy   *Pr 20:28*

his *t*. shall be established in   *Pr 25:5*

his *t*. shall be established for ever   *Pr 29:14*

saw also the Lord sitting upon   *Isa 6:1*

upon the *t*. of David, and upon his   *Isa 9:7*

exalt my *t*. above the stars of God   *Isa 14:13*

in mercy shall the *t*. be established   *Isa 16:5*

a glorious *t*. to his father's house   *Isa 22:23*

there is no *t*. O daughter of   *Isa 47:1*

The heaven is my *t*. and the earth   *Isa 66:1*

set every one his *t*. at the entering   *Jer 1:15*

call Jerusalem the *t*. of the Lord   *Jer 3:17*

the kings that sit upon   *Jer 13:13*

do not disgrace the *t*. of thy glory   *Jer 14:21*

A glorious high *t*. from the   *Jer 17:12*

princes sitting upon the *t*. of David   *Jer 17:25*

that sittest upon the *t*. of David   *Jer 22:2*

kings sitting upon the *t*. of David   *Jer 22:4*

sitting upon the *t*. of David   *Jer 22:30*

that sitteth upon the *t*. of David   *Jer 29:16*

upon the *t*. of the house of Israel   *Jer 33:17*

not have a son to reign upon his *t*.   *Jer 33:21*

none to sit upon the *t*. of David   *Jer 36:30*

will set his *t*. upon these stones   *Jer 43:10*

I will set my *t*. in Elam, and will   *Jer 49:38*

set his *t*. above the *t*. of the kings   *Jer 52:32*

t. from generation to generation   *La 5:19*

thrust from kingly *t*. (B)   *La 5:20*

their heads was the likeness of a *t*.   *Eze 1:26*

upon the likeness of the *t*. was the   *Eze 1:26*

appearance of the likeness of a *t*.   *Eze 10:1*

the place of my *t*. and the place of   *Eze 43:7*

he was deposed from his kingly *t*.   *Da 5:20*

his *t*. was like the fiery flame   *Da 7:9*

Nineveh, and he arose from his *t*.   *Jon 3:6*

I will overthrow the *t*. of kingdoms   *Hag 2:22*

and shall sit and rule upon   *Zec 6:13*

he shall be a priest upon his *t*.   *Zec 6:13*

by heaven; for it is God's *t*.   *M't 5:34*

man shall sit in the *t*. of his glory   *M't 19:28*

heaven, sweareth by the *t*. of God   *M't 23:22*

shall he sit upon the *t*. of his glory   *M't 25:31*

unto him the *t*. of his father David   *Lu 1:32*

raise up Christ to sit on his *t*.   *Ac 2:30*

Heaven is my *t*. and earth is my   *Ac 7:49*

in royal apparel, sat upon his *t*.   *Ac 12:21*

Thy *t*. O God, is for ever and ever   *Heb 1:8*

come boldly unto the *t*. of grace   *Heb 4:16*

right hand of the *t*. of the Majesty   *Heb 8:1*

at the right hand of the *t*. of God   *Heb 12:2*

Spirits which are before his *t*.   *Re 1:4*

throne (S)   *Re 2:13; 4:4; 11:16; 13:2; 16:10*

will I grant to sit with me in my *t*.   *Re 3:21*

set down with my Father in his *t*.   *Re 3:21*

and, behold, a *t.* was set in heaven   Re 4:2
and one sat on the *t.*   Re 4:2
was a rainbow round about the *t.*   Re 4:3
about the *t.* were four and twenty   Re 4:4
out of the *t.* proceeded lightnings   Re 4:5
lamps of fire burning before the *t.*   Re 4:5
before the *t.* there was a sea of   Re 4:6
and the midst of the *t.*   Re 4:6
and round about the *t.* were four   Re 4:6
thanks to him that sat on the *t.*   Re 4:9
down before that sat on the *t.*   Re 4:10
and cast their crowns before the *t.*   Re 4:10
hand of him that sat on the *t.* a   Re 5:1
in the midst of the *t.* and of   Re 5:6
hand of him that sat upon the *t.*   Re 5:7
of many angels round about the *t.*   Re 5:11
unto him that sitteth upon the *t.*   Re 5:13
face of him that sitteth on the *t.*   Re 6:16
stood before the *t.* and before our God which sitteth upon the *t.*   Re 7:9 Re 7:10
angels stood round about the *t.*   Re 7:11
and fell before the *t.* on their faces   Re 7:11
are they before the *t.* of God   Re 7:15
he that sitteth on the *t.* shall dwell   Re 7:15
Lamb which is in the midst of the *t.*   Re 7:17
altar which was before the *t.*   Re 8:3
caught up unto God, and to his *t.*   Re 12:5
as it were a new song before the *t.*   Re 14:3
without fault before the *t.* of God   Re 14:5
from the *t.* saying, It is done   Re 16:17
worshipped God that sat on the *t.*   Re 19:4
a voice came out of the *t.* saying   Re 19:5
I saw a great white *t.* and him that   Re 20:11
he that sat upon the *t.* said, Behold   Re 21:5
proceeding out of the *t.* of God and   Re 22:1
the *t.* of God and of the Lamb shall   Re 22:3

THRONED

t. above the cherubim (B)(R)   1Sa 4:4

THRONES

For there are set *t.* of judgment   Ps 122:5
the *t.* of the house of David   Ps 122:5
raised up from their *t.* all the kings   Isa 14:9
sea shall come down from their *t.*   Eze 26:16
I beheld till the *t.* were cast down   Da 7:9
ye also shall sit upon twelve *t.*   M't 19:28
sit on *t.* judging the twelve tribes   Lu 22:30
whether they be *t.* or dominions   Col 1:16
thrones (S)   Re 4:4; 11:16
I saw *t.* and they sat upon them   Re 20:4

THRONG

multitude, lest they should *t.* him   M'k 3:9
large *t.* of disciples (B)   Lu 6:17
the multitude *t.* thee and press   Lu 8:45

THRONGED

people followed him, and *t.* him   M'k 5:24
But as he went the people *t.* him   Lu 8:42

THRONGING

Thou seest the multitude *t.* thee   M'k 5:31

THROUGH

is filled with violence *t.* them   Ge 6:13
Abram passed *t.* the land unto   Ge 12:6
walk *t.* the land in the length of it   Ge 13:17
looked *t.* a window (S)   Ge 26:8
I will pass *t.* all thy flock to day   Ge 30:32
that the land perish not *t.* the famine   Ge 41:36
of the field, *t.* all the land of Egypt   Ex 10:15
pass *t.* the land of Egypt this night   Ex 12:12
will pass *t.* to smite the Egyptians   Ex 12:23
God led them not *t.* the way of the   Ex 13:17
t. the way of the wilderness of the   Ex 13:18
ground *t.* the midst of the sea   Ex 14:16
of the Egyptians *t.* the pillar of fire   Ex 14:24
shall surely be stoned, or shot *t.*   Ex 19:13
lest they break *t.* unto the Lord to   Ex 19:21
people break *t.* to come up unto the   Ex 19:24
shall bore his ear *t.* with an awl   Ex 21:6
middle bar to shoot *t.* the boards   Ex 36:33
If a soul shall sin *t.* ignorance   Le 4:2
congregation, Israel sin *t.* ignorance   Le 4:13
and done somewhat *t.* ignorance   Le 4:22
the common people sin *t.* ignorance   Le 4:27
a trespass, and sin *t.* ignorance   Le 5:15
of thy seed pass *t.* the fire to Molech   Le 18:21
neither shall the sword go *t.* your land   Le 26:6
t. which we have gone to search it   Nu 13:32
land, which we passed *t.* to search it   Nu 14:7
And if any soul sin *t.* ignorance   Nu 15:27
law for him that sinneth *t.* ignorance   Nu 15:29
us pass, I pray thee, *t.* thy country   Nu 20:17
country; we will not pass *t.* the fields   Nu 20:17
or *t.* the vineyards, neither will we   Nu 20:17
any thing else, go *t.* on my feet   Nu 20:19
And he said, Thou shalt not go *t.*   Nu 20:20
to give Israel passage *t.* his border   Nu 20:21
Let me pass *t.* thy land: we will not   Nu 21:22
not suffer Israel to pass *t.* his border   Nu 21:23
and pierce them *t.* with his arrows   Nu 24:8
the tent, and thrust both of them *t.*   Nu 25:8
Israel, and the woman *t.* her belly   Nu 25:8
t. the counsel of Balaam, to commit   Nu 31:16
ye shall make it go *t.* the fire, and it   Nu 31:23
fire ye shall make go *t.* the water   Nu 31:23
and passed *t.* the midst of the sea   Nu 33:8
t. all that great and terrible wilderness   De 1:19
are to pass *t.* the coast of your brethren   De 2:4
thy walking *t.* this great wilderness   De 2:7
t. the way of the plain from Elath   De 2:8
Thou art to pass over *t.* Ar, the coast   De 2:18

Let me pass *t.* thy land; I will go   De 2:27
drink: only I will pass *t.* on my feet   De 2:28
thee out thence *t.* a mighty hand   De 5:15
t. that great and terrible wilderness   De 8:15
thou hast redeemed *t.* thy greatness   De 9:26
and thrust it *t.* his ear unto the door   De 15:17
son or his daughter to pass *t.* the fire   De 18:10
t. the nations which ye passed by   De 29:16
him to anger in the work of your hands   De 31:29
t. this thing ye shall prolong your days   De 32:47
smite *t.* the loins of them that rise   De 33:11
Pass *t.* the host, and command the   Jos 1:11
down by a cord *t.* the window   Jos 2:15
that the officers went *t.* the host   Jos 3:2
and they shall rise and go *t.* the land   Jos 18:4
Go and walk *t.* the land, and describe   Jos 18:8
the men went and passed *t.* the land   Jos 18:9
went up *t.* the mountains westward   Jos 18:12
all the people *t.* whom we passed   Jos 24:17
That *t.* them I may prove Israel   J'g 2:22
Then Ehud went forth *t.* the porch   J'g 3:23
and the travellers walked *t.* byways   J'g 5:6
pierced and stricken *t.* his temples   J'g 5:26
a window, and cried *t.* the lattice   J'g 5:28
And his young man thrust him *t.*   J'g 9:54
t. the wilderness unto the Red sea   J'g 11:16
Let me, I pray thee, pass *t.* thy land   J'g 11:17
they went along *t.* the wilderness   J'g 11:18
pray thee, *t.* thy land into my place   J'g 11:19
trusted not Israel to pass *t.* his coast   J'g 11:20
sent men *t.* all the tribes of Benjamin   J'g 20:12
And he passed *t.* mount Ephraim, and   1Sa 9:4
and passed *t.* the land of Shalisha   1Sa 9:4
then they passed *t.* the land of Shalim   1Sa 9:4
passed *t.* the land of the Benjamites   1Sa 9:4
Michal let David down *t.* a window   1Sa 19:12
sword, and thrust me *t.* therewith   1Sa 31:4
uncircumcised come and thrust me *t.*   1Sa 31:4
men walked all that night *t.* the plain   2Sa 2:29
over Jordan, and went *t.* all Bithron   2Sa 2:29
and gat them away *t.* the plain all   2Sa 4:7
daughter looked *t.* a window   2Sa 6:16
and made them pass *t.* the brickkiln   2Sa 12:31
thrust them *t.* the heart of Absalom   2Sa 18:14
And he went *t.* all the tribes of Israel   2Sa 20:14
T. the brightness before him were   2Sa 22:13
For by thee I have run *t.* a troop: by   2Sa 22:30
brake *t.* the host of the Philistines   2Sa 23:16
Go now *t.* all the tribes of Israel   2Sa 24:2
So when they had gone *t.* all the land   2Sa 24:8
Ahaziah fell down *t.* a lattice in his   2Ki 1:2

The way t. the wilderness of | 2Ki 3:8
Edom
break t., unto the king of | 2Ki 3:26
Edom
And Jehu sent t. all Israel: | 2Ki 10:21
and all the
and made his son to pass t. | 2Ki 16:3
the fire
and their daughters to pass | 2Ki 17:17
t. the fire
And he made his son pass t. | 2Ki 21:6
the fire
daughter to pass t. the fire | 2Ki 23:10
to Molech
t. the anger of the Lord, it | 2Ki 24:20
came to
sword, and thrust me t. | 1Ch 10:4
therewith
brake t. the host of the | 1Ch 11:18
Philistines
he went out again t. the | 2Ch 19:4
people from
they came t. the high gate | 2Ch 23:20
into
made a proclamation t. | 2Ch 24:9
Judah and
t. the country of Ephraim | 2Ch 30:10
their daughters, t. all the | 2Ch 31:18
congregation
that ran t. the midst of the | 2Ch 32:4
land
caused his children to pass t. | 2Ch 33:6
the fire
they prospered t. the | Ezr 6:14
prophesying of
they went t. the midst of the | Ne 9:11
sea
bring him on horseback t. the | Es 6:9
street
brought him on horseback t. | Es 6:11
the street
dreams, and terrifiest me t. | Job 7:14
visions
Yet t. the scent of water it | Job 14:9
will bud
the bow of steel shall strike | Job 20:24
him t.
know? can be judge t. the | Job 22:13
dark cloud
In the dark they dig t. | Job 24:16
houses
understanding he smiteth t. | Job 26:12
the proud
when by his light I walked t. | Job 29:3
darkness
I went out to the gate t. the | Job 29:7
city
his eyes: his nose pierceth t. | Job 40:24
snares
nose? or bore his jaw t. with | Job 41:2
a thorn
passeth t. the paths of the seas | Ps 8:8
wicked t. the pride of his | Ps 10:4
countenance
For by thee I have run t. a | Ps 18:29
troop; and
Their line is gone out t. all the | Ps 19:4
earth
t. the mercy of the most High | Ps 21:7
he shall
t. the valley of the shadow of | Ps 23:4
death
my bones waxed old t. my | Ps 32:3
roaring all
T. thee will we push down our | Ps 44:5
t. thy name will we tread them | Ps 44:5
under
T. God we shall do valiantly: | Ps 60:12
for he it
t. the greatness of thy power | Ps 66:3
shall
land: they went t. the flood on | Ps 66:6
foot
heads; we went t. fire and t. | Ps 66:12
water
thou didst march t. the | Ps 68:7
wilderness
their tongue walketh t. the | Ps 73:9
earth
the sea, and caused them to | Ps 78:13
pass t.
he went out t. the land of | Ps 81:5
Egypt
passing t. the valley of Baca | Ps 84:6
make it a
Lord, hast made me glad t. thy | Ps 92:4
work
t. the depths, as t. the | Ps 106:9
wilderness

and brought low t. | Ps 107:39
oppression
T. God we shall do | Ps 108:13
valiantly: for he it
My knees are weak t. | Ps 109:24
fasting; and
strike t. kings in the day of | Ps 110:5
his wrath
not: neither speak they t. | Ps 115:7
their throat
Thou t. thy commandments | Ps 119:98
hast
T. thy precepts, I get | Ps 119:104
understanding
Israel to pass t. the midst of | Ps 136:14
which led his people t. the | Ps 136:16
wilderness
of my house I looked t. my | Pr 7:6
casement
Passing t. the street near her | Pr 7:8
corner
Till a dart strike t. his liver; as | Pr 7:23
a bird
but t. knowledge shall the just | Pr 11:9
be
T. desire a man, having | Pr 18:1
separated
T. wisdom is an house builded | Pr 24:3
a dream cometh t. the | Ec 5:3
multitude of
t. idleness of the hands the | Ec 10:18
house
the hands the house droppeth | Ec 10:18
t.
shewing himself t. the lattice | Ca 2:9
And he shall pass t. Judah; he | Isa 8:8
shall
And they shall pass t. it, | Isa 8:21
hardly
T. the wrath of the Lord of | Isa 9:19
hosts is
one that is found shall be | Isa 13:15
thrust t.
are slain, thrust t. with a | Isa 14:19
sword
they wandered t. the | Isa 16:8
wilderness
As whirlwinds in the south | Isa 21:1
pass t.
Pass t. thy land as a river, O | Isa 23:10
daughter
I would go t. them, I would | Isa 27:4
burn
But they also have erred t. | Isa 28:7
wine
t. strong drink are out of the | Isa 28:7
way
have erred t. strong drink | Isa 28:7
are out of the way t. strong | Isa 28:7
drink
overflowing scourge shall | Isa 28:15;
pass t. | 28:18
For t. the voice of the Lord | Isa 30:31
shall the
none shall pass t. it for ever | Isa 34:10
and ever
When thou passest t. the | Isa 43:2
waters, I will
t. the rivers, they shall not | Isa 43:2
overflow
when thou walkest t. the fire, | Isa 43:2
thou
not when he led them t. the | Isa 48:21
deserts
hated, so that no man went | Isa 60:15
t. thee
Go t. go t. the gates; prepare | Isa 62:10
That led them t. the deep, as | Isa 63:13
an horse
of Egypt that led us t. the | Jer 2:6
wilderness
t. a land of deserts and of pits | Jer 2:6
t. a land of drought, and of the | Jer 2:6
shadow
t. a land that no man passed t. | Jer 2:6
t. the lightness of her whoredom | Jer 3:9
Run ye to and fro t. the streets | Jer 5:1
t. deceit they refuse to know | Jer 9:6
me
up so that none can pass t. | Jer 9:10
them
a wilderness that none passeth | Jer 9:12
t.
upon all high places t. the | Jer 12:12
wilderness
in no burden t. the gates of | Jer 17:24
this city
their daughters to pass t. the | Jer 32:35
fire unto

that are thrust t. in her streets | Jer 51:4
t. all her land the wounded | Jer 51:52
shall
t. the anger of the Lord it | Jer 52:3
came to
that our prayer should not pass | La 3:44
t.
stricken t. for want of the | La 4:9
fruits of the
the cup shall also pass t. unto | La 4:21
thee
and blood shall pass t. thee | Eze 5:17
ye shall be scattered t. the | Eze 6:8
countries
Go, t. the midst of the city | Eze 9:4
t. the midst of Jerusalem, and | Eze 9:4
set a
Go ye after him t. the city, and | Eze 9:5
smite
Dig thou t. the wall in their | Eze 12:5
sight, and
and in the even I digged t. | Eze 12:7
the wall
they shall dig t. the wall to | Eze 12:12
carry out
all estranged from me t. their | Eze 14:5
idols
noisome beasts to pass t. the | Eze 14:15
land
no man may pass t. because | Eze 14:15
of the
land. and say, Sword, go t. | Eze 14:17
the land
for it was perfect t. my | Eze 16:14
comeliness
cause them to pass t. the fire | Eze 16:21
for them
discovered t. thy whoredoms | Eze 16:36
with thy
and thrust thee t. with their | Eze 16:40
swords
and disperse them t. the | Eze 20:23
countries
t. the fire all that openeth | Eze 20:26
the womb
ye make your sons to pass t. | Eze 20:31
the fire
to pass for them t. the fire, | Eze 23:37
to devour
No foot of man shall pass t. | Eze 29:11
it, nor
foot of beast shall pass t. it, | Eze 29:11
neither
will disperse them t. the | Eze 29:12;
countries | 30:23
be desolate, that none shall | Eze 33:28
pass t.
My sheep wandered t. all the | Eze 34:6
they were dispersed t. the | Eze 36:19
countries
passing t. the land to bury | Eze 39:14
with the
the passengers that pass t. | Eze 39:15
the land
made t. all the house round | Eze 41:19
about
he brought me t. the entry, | Eze 46:19
which
and he brought me t. the | Eze 47:3
waters
and brought me t. the waters | Eze 47:4
a thousand, and brought me | Eze 47:4
t.
And t. his policy also he shall | Da 8:25
t. all the countries whither | Da 9:7
thou hast
strength t. his riches he shall | Da 11:2
stir up
come, and overflow, and pass | Da 11:10
t.
shall overflow and pass t. | Da 11:40
(S)
no strangers pass t. her any | Joe 3:17
more
led you forty years t. the | Am 2:10
wilderness
for I will pass t. thee, saith | Am 5:17
proclaimed and published t. | Jon 3:7
Nineveh
and have passed t. the gate, | Mic 2:13
and are
if he go t. both treadeth down | Mic 5:8
be cut down, when he shall | Na 1:12
pass t.
the wicked shall no more pass | Na 1:15
t. thee
that selleth nations t. her | Na 3:4
whoredoms
and familiar t. her witchcrafts | Na 3:4

shall march *t.* the breadth of the land	*Hab 1:6*
didst march *t.* the land in indignation	*Hab 3:12*
Thou didst strike *t.* with his staves	*Hab 3:14*
didst walk *t.* the sea with thine horses	*Hab 3:15*
horses, *t.* the heap of great waters	*Hab 3:15*
sent to walk to and fro *t.* the earth	*Zec 1:10*
have walked to and fro *t.* the earth	*Zec 1:11*
My cities *t.* prosperity shall yet be	*Zec 1:17*
run to and fro *t.* the whole earth	*Zec 4:10*
t. the two golden pipes empty	*Zec 4:12*
is their resemblance *t.* all the earth	*Zec 5:6*
might walk to and fro *t.* the earth	*Zec 6:7*
hence, walk to and fro *t.* the earth	*Zec 6:7*
So they walked to and fro *t.* the earth	*Zec 6:7*
that no man passed *t.* nor returned	*Zec 7:14*
no oppressor shall pass *t.* them any	*Zec 9:8*
drink, and make a noise as *t.* wine	*Zec 9:15*
their heart shall rejoice as *t.* wine	*Zec 10:7*
he shall pass *t.* the sea with affliction	*Zec 10:11*
that begat him shall thrust him *t.*	*Zec 13:3*
I will bring the third part *t.* the fire	*Zec 13:9*
where thieves break *t.* and steal	*M't 6:19*
thieves do not break *t.* nor steal	*M't 6:20*
devils *t.* the prince of the devils	*M't 9:34*
on the sabbath day *t.* the corn	*M't 12:1*
he walketh *t.* dry places, seeking	*M't 12:43*
camel to go *t.* the eye of a needle	*M't 19:24*
t. the corn fields on the sabbath	*M'k 2:23*
ran *t.* that whole region round	*M'k 6:55*
God of none effect *t.* your tradition	*M'k 7:13*
t. the midst of the coast of	*M'k 7:31*
thence, and passed *t.* Galilee	*M'k 9:30*
a camel to go *t.* the eye of a needle	*M'k 10:25*
carry any vessel *t.* the temple	*M'k 11:16*
T. the tender mercy of our God	*Lu 1:78*
sword shall pierce *t.* thy own soul	*Lu 2:35*
fame of him *t.* all the region	*Lu 4:14*
he passing *t.* the midst of them	*Lu 4:30*
let him down *t.* the tiling with his	*Lu 5:19*
that he went *t.* the corn fields	*Lu 6:1*
and went *t.* the towns, preaching	*Lu 9:6*
are subject unto us *t.* thy name	*Lu 10:17*
casteth out devils *t.* Beelzebub	*Lu 11:15*
I cast out devils *t.* Beelzebub	*Lu 11:18*
he walketh *t.* dry places, seeking	*Lu 11:24*
suffered his house to be broken *t.*	*Lu 12:39*
he went *t.* the cities and villages	*Lu 13:22*
woe unto him, *t.* whom they come	*Lu 17:1*
he passed *t.* the midst of Samaria	*Lu 17:11*
for a camel to go *t.* a needle's eye	*Lu 18:25*
Jesus entered, passed *t.* Jericho	*Lu 19:1*
that all men *t.* him might believe	*Joh 1:7*
the world *t.* him might be saved	*Joh 3:17*
And he must needs go *t.* Samaria	*Joh 4:4*

t. the midst of them, and so passed	*Joh 8:59*
Now ye are clean *t.* the word which	*Joh 15:3*
t. thine own name those whom	*Joh 17:11*
Sanctify them *t.* thy truth: thy	*Joh 17:17*
might be sanctified *t.* the truth	*Joh 17:19*
shall believe on me *t.* their word	*Joh 17:20*
ye might have life *t.* his name	*Joh 20:31*
after that he *t.* the Holy Ghost had	*Ac 1:2*
his name *t.* faith in his name	*Ac 3:16*
I wot that *t.* ignorance ye did it	*Ac 3:17*
preached *t.* Jesus the resurrection	*Ac 4:2*
that *t.* laying on of the apostles'	*Ac 8:18*
passing *t.* he preached in all	*Ac 8:40*
t. his name whosoever believeth	*Ac 10:43*
out, and passed on *t.* one street	*Ac 12:10*
when they had gone *t.* the isle unto	*Ac 13:6*
that *t.* this man is preached unto	*Ac 13:38*
t. much tribulation enter into	*Ac 14:22*
they passed *t.* Phenice and Samaria	*Ac 15:3*
we believe that *t.* the grace of the	*Ac 15:11*
and he went *t.* Syria and Cilicia	*Ac 15:41*
And as they went *t.* the cities, they	*Ac 16:4*
when they had passed *t.* Amphipolis	*Ac 17:1*
which had believed *t.* grace	*Ac 18:27*
having passed *t.* the upper coasts	*Ac 19:1*
when he had passed *t.* Macedonia	*Ac 19:21*
purposed to return *t.* Macedonia	*Ac 20:3*
who said to Paul *t.* the Spirit, that	*Ac 21:4*
I thank my God *t.* Jesus Christ	*Ro 1:8*
uncleanness *t.* the lusts of their	*Ro 1:24*
t. breaking the law dishonourest	*Ro 2:23*
blasphemed among the Gentiles *t.*	*Ro 2:24*
abounded *t.* my lie unto his glory	*Ro 3:7*
t. the redemption that is in Christ	*Ro 3:24*
a propitiation *t.* faith in his blood	*Ro 3:25*
past, *t.* the forbearance of God	*Ro 3:25*
faith, and uncircumcision *t.* faith	*Ro 3:30*
then make void the law *t.* faith	*Ro 3:31*
Abraham, or to his seed, *t.* the law	*Ro 4:13*
but *t.* the righteousness of	*Ro 4:13*
not at the promise of God *t.* unbelief	*Ro 4:20*
peace with God *t.* our Lord Jesus	*Ro 5:1*
shall be saved from wrath *t.* him	*Ro 5:9*
in God *t.* our Lord Jesus Christ	*Ro 5:11*
if *t.* the offence of one many be dead	*Ro 5:15*
grace reign *t.* righteousness	*Ro 5:21*
alive unto God *t.* Jesus Christ our	*Ro 6:11*
God is eternal life *t.* Jesus Christ	*Ro 6:23*
I thank God *t.* Jesus Christ our	*Ro 7:25*
do, in that it was weak *t.* the	*Ro 8:3*
if ye *t.* the Spirit do mortify the deeds	*Ro 8:13*
conquerors *t.* him that loved us	*Ro 8:37*
rather *t.* their fall salvation is come	*Ro 11:11*

now obtained mercy *t.* their unbelief	*Ro 11:30*
t. your mercy they also may obtain	*Ro 11:31*
and *t.* him, and to him, are	*Ro 11:36*
For I say, *t.* the grace given unto me	*Ro 12:3*
we *t.* patience and comfort of	*Ro 15:4*
t. the power of the Holy Ghost	*Ro 15:13*
I may glory *t.* Jesus Christ	*Ro 15:17*
T. mighty signs and wonders	*Ro 15:19*
be glory *t.* Jesus Christ for ever	*Ro 16:27*
Jesus Christ *t.* the will of God	*1Co 1:1*
I have begotten you *t.* the gospel	*1Co 4:15*
t. thy knowledge shall the weak	*1Co 8:11*
cloud, and all passed *t.* the sea	*1Co 10:1*
For now we see *t.* a glass, darkly	*1Co 13:12*
the victory *t.* our Lord Jesus Christ	*1Co 15:57*
you, when I shall pass *t.* Macedonia	*1Co 16:5*
for I do pass *t.* Macedonia	*1Co 16:5*
such trust have we *t.* Christ	*2Co 3:4*
t. the thanksgiving of many	*2Co 4:15*
that ye *t.* his poverty might be rich	*2Co 8:9*
causeth *t.* us thanksgiving to God	*2Co 9:11*
mighty *t.* God to the pulling down	*2Co 10:4*
beguiled Eve *t.* his subtilty	*2Co 11:3*
t. a window in basket was I let	*2Co 11:33*
t. the abundance of the revelations	*2Co 12:7*
he was crucified *t.* weakness	*2Co 13:4*
I *t.* the law am dead to the law	*Ga 2:19*
would justify the heathen *t.* faith	*Ga 3:8*
on the Gentiles *t.* Jesus Christ	*Ga 3:14*
the promise of the Spirit *t.* faith	*Ga 3:14*
son, then an heir of God *t.* Christ	*Ga 4:7*
t. infirmity of the flesh I preached	*Ga 4:13*
for we *t.* the Spirit wait for the hope	*Ga 5:5*
confidence in you *t.* the Lord	*Ga 5:10*
we have redemption *t.* his blood	*Eph 1:7*
toward us *t.* Christ Jesus	*Eph 2:7*
For by grace are ye saved *t.* faith	*Eph 2:8*
t. him we both have access by one	*Eph 2:18*
an habitation of God *t.* the Spirit	*Eph 2:22*
above all, and *t.* all, and in you all	*Eph 4:6*
t. the ignorance that is in them	*Eph 4:18*
to my salvation *t.* your prayer	*Ph'p 1:19*
Let nothing be done *t.* strife or	*Ph'p 2:3*
that which is *t.* the faith of Christ	*Ph'p 3:9*
hearts and minds *t.* Christ Jesus	*Ph'p 4:7*
I can do all things *t.* Christ which	*Ph'p 4:13*
we have redemption *t.* his blood	*Col 1:14*
peace *t.* the blood of his cross	*Col 1:20*
In the body of his flesh *t.* death	*Col 1:22*
any man spoil you *t.* philosophy	*Col 2:8*
ye are risen with him *t.* the faith	*Col 2:12*
you to salvation *t.* sanctification	*2Th 2:13*
consolation and good hope *t.* grace	*2Th 2:16*
pierced themselves *t.* with many	*1Ti 6:10*
immortality to light *t.* the gospel	*2Ti 1:10*
salvation *t.* faith which is in Christ	*2Ti 3:15*
manifested his word *t.* preaching	*Tit 1:3*

on us abundantly *t.* Jesus   *Tit 3:6*
Christ
that *t.* your prayers I shall be   *Ph'm 22*
given
their salvation perfect *t.*   *Heb 2:10*
sufferings
that *t.* death he might   *Heb 2:14*
destroy them
t. fear of death were all their   *Heb 2:15*
lifetime
hardened *t.* deceitfulness   *Heb 3:13*
of sin
who *t.* faith and patience   *Heb 6:12*
inherit
who *t.* the eternal Spirit   *Heb 9:14*
offered
t. the offering of the body   *Heb 10:10*
of Jesus
t. the veil, that is to say, his   *Heb 10:20*
flesh
T. faith we understand that   *Heb 11:3*
T. faith also Sara herself   *Heb 11:11*
received
T. faith he kept the passover   *Heb 11:28*
they passed *t.* the Red sea   *Heb 11:29*
as by dry
Who *t.* faith subdued   *Heb 11:33*
kingdoms
obtained a good report *t.*   *Heb 11:39*
faith
be stoned, or thrust *t.* with   *Heb 12:20*
a dart
t. the blood of the   *Heb 13:20*
everlasting
in his sight, *t.* Jesus Christ   *Heb 13:21*
t. sanctification of the Spirit,   *1Pe 1:2*
unto
of God *t.* faith unto salvation   *1Pe 1:5*
heaviness *t.* manifold   *1Pe 1:6*
temptations
in obeying the truth *t.* the   *1Pe 1:22*
Spirit
may be glorified *t.* Jesus   *1Pe 4:11*
Christ
faith with us *t.* the   *2Pe 1:1*
righteousness
unto you *t.* the knowledge of   *2Pe 1:2*
God
t. the knowledge of him that   *2Pe 1:3*
hath
that is in the world *t.* lust   *2Pe 1:4*
t. covetousness shall they with   *2Pe 2:3*
they allure *t.* the lusts of the   *2Pe 2:18*
flesh
t. much wantonness, those   *2Pe 2:18*
that
world *t.* the knowledge of the   *2Pe 2:20*
Lord
world, that we might live *t.* him   *1Jo 4:9*
an angel flying *t.* the midst of   *Re 8:13*
rich *t.* the abundance of her   *Re 8:3*
may enter in *t.* the gates into   *Re 22:14*

THROUGHLY

us make brick, and burn them   *Ge 11:3*
t.
Oh that my grief were *t.*   *Job 6:2*
weighed
Wash me *t.* from mine   *Ps 51:2*
iniquity
earth is *t.* dissolved (S)   *Isa 24:19*
They shall *t.* glean the remnant   *Jer 6:9*
if ye *t.* amend your ways and   *Jer 7:5*
your
if ye *t.* execute judgment   *Jer 7:5*
between
he shall *t.* plead their cause,   *Jer 50:34*
that
I *t.* washed away thy blood   *Eze 16:9*
from thee
he will *t.* purge his floor, and   *M't 3:12*
gather
he will *t.* purge his floor, and   *Lu 3:17*
will
been *t.* made manifest among   *2Co 11:6*
t. furnished unto all good   *2Ti 3:17*
works

THROUGHOUT

great plenty *t.* all the land of   *Ge 41:29*
Egypt
and went *t.* all the land of   *Ge 41:46*
Egypt
and a ruler *t.* all the land of   *Ge 45:8*
Egypt
abroad *t.* all the land of Egypt   *Ex 5:12*
may be blood *t.* all the land of   *Ex 7:19*
Egypt

was blood *t.* all the land of   *Ex 7:21*
Egypt
become lice *t.* all the land of   *Ex 8:16;*
Egypt   *8:17*
upon beast *t.* all the land of   *Ex 9:9*
Egypt
name may be declared *t.* all   *Ex 9:16*
the earth
herb of the field *t.* the land of   *Ex 9:22*
Egypt
hail smote *t.* all the land of   *Ex 9:25*
Egypt
a great cry *t.* all the land of   *Ex 11:6*
Egypt
feast to the Lord *t.* your   *Ex 12:14*
generations
burnt offerings *t.* your   *Ex 29:42*
generations
before the Lord *t.* your   *Ex 30:8*
generations
upon it *t.* your generations   *Ex 30:10*
and to his seed *t.* their   *Ex 30:21*
generations
oil unto me *t.* your   *Ex 30:31*
generations
me and you *t.* your   *Ex 31:13*
generations
the sabbath *t.* their   *Ex 31:16*
generations
and out from gate to gate *t.*   *Ex 32:27*
the camp
let any man be seen *t.* all the   *Ex 34:3*
mount
kindle no fire *t.* your   *Ex 35:3*
habitations
caused it to be proclaimed *t.*   *Ex 36:6*
the camp
t. the six branches going out   *Ex 37:19*
of the
priesthood *t.* their   *Ex 40:15*
generations
house of Israel, *t.* all their   *Ex 40:38*
journeys
your generations *t.* all your   *Le 3:17*
dwellings
a statute for ever *t.* their   *Le 7:36;*
generations   *10:9; 23:14, 31;*
  Nu 18:23
ever unto them *t.* their   *Le 17:7*
generations
all your dwellings *t.* your   *Le 23:21*
generations
the trumpet sound *t.* all your   *Le 25:9*
land
proclaim liberty *t.* all the   *Le 25:10*
land unto
him that bought it *t.* his   *Le 25:30*
generations
of Naphtali, *t.* their   *Nu 1:42*
generations
by his own standard, *t.* their   *Nu 1:52*
hosts
camp of Judah pitch, *t.* their   *Nu 2:3*
armies
and four hundred, *t.* their   *Nu 2:9*
armies
hundred and fifty, *t.* their   *Nu 2:16*
armies
and an hundred, *t.* their   *Nu 2:24*
armies
numbered of the camps *t.*   *Nu 2:32*
their hosts
t. their families, all the males   *Nu 3:39*
from a
Gershon, *t.* the houses of their   *Nu 4:22*
fathers
the sons of Gershon, *t.* their   *Nu 4:38*
families
numbered of them, *t.* their   *Nu 4:40*
families
of the sons of Merari, *t.* their   *Nu 4:42*
families
ordinance for ever *t.* your   *Nu 10:8*
generations
of all the camps *t.* their hosts   *Nu 10:25*
the people weep *t.* their   *Nu 11:10*
families
of their garments *t.* their   *Nu 15:38*
generations
and upward, *t.* their father's   *Nu 26:2*
house
every month *t.* the months of   *Nu 28:14*
the year
for every lamb, *t.* the seven   *Nu 28:21*
lambs
ye shall offer daily, *t.* the   *Nu 28:24*
seven days
unto one lamb, *t.* the seven   *Nu 28:29*
lambs

for one lamb, *t.* the seven   *Nu 29:4;*
lambs   *29:10*
a thousand *t.* all the tribes of   *Nu 31:4*
Israel
unto you *t.* your generations   *Nu 35:29*
in all
thy God giveth thee, *t.* thy   *De 16:18*
tribes
shalt have olive trees *t.* all   *De 28:40*
thy coasts
wherein thou trustedst, *t.* all   *De 28:52*
thy land
thee in all thy gates *t.* all thy   *De 28:52*
land
pursuers sought them *t.* all   *Jos 2:22*
the way
his fame was noised *t.* all the   *Jos 6:27*
country
up from Jericho *t.* mount   *Jos 16:1*
Beth-el
a prince *t.* all the tribes of   *Jos 22:14*
Israel
and led him *t.* all the land of   *Jos 24:3*
Canaan
he sent messengers *t.* all   *J'g 6:35*
Manasseh
against his fellow, even *t.* the   *J'g 7:22*
host
sent messengers *t.* all mount   *J'g 7:24*
Ephraim
and sent her *t.* all the country   *J'g 20:6*
of the
an hundred *t.* all the tribes of   *J'g 20:10*
Israel
a deadly destruction *t.* all the   *1Sa 5:11*
city
sent them *t.* all the coasts of   *1Sa 11:7*
Israel
Saul blew the trumpet *t.* all   *1Sa 13:3*
the land
no smith found *t.* all the   *1Sa 13:19*
land of Israel
out *t.* all the thousands of   *1Sa 23:23*
Judah
t. all Edom put he garrisons,   *2Sa 8:14*
and all
sent spies, *t.* all the tribes of   *2Sa 15:10*
Israel
were at strife *t.* all the tribes   *2Sa 19:9*
of Israel
for a fair damsel *t.* all the   *1Ki 1:3*
coasts
house finished *t.* all the parts   *1Ki 6:38*
thereof
made a proclamation *t.* all   *1Ki 15:22*
Judah
the land between them to   *1Ki 18:6*
pass *t.* it
there went a proclamation *t.*   *1Ki 22:36*
the host
of Assyria came up *t.* all the   *2Ki 17:5*
land
in their tents *t.* all the east   *1Ch 5:10*
land
their dwelling places *t.* their   *1Ch 6:54*
castles
t. their families were thirteen   *1Ch 6:60*
cities
the sons of Gershom *t.* their   *1Ch 6:62*
families
were given by lot, *t.* their   *1Ch 6:63*
families
t. the genealogy of them that   *1Ch 7:40*
were
were chief *t.* their   *1Ch 9:34*
generations
famous *t.* the house of their   *1Ch 12:30*
fathers
Joab departed, and went *t.*   *1Ch 21:4*
all Israel
Joab departed, and went *t.*   *1Ch 21:4*
all Israel
destroying *t.* all the coasts   *1Ch 21:12*
of Israel
of fame and of glory *t.* all   *1Ch 22:5*
countries
that ruled *t.* the house of   *1Ch 26:6*
their father
by month *t.* all the months of   *1Ch 27:1*
the year
and *t.* all the land of his   *2Ch 8:6*
dominion
children *t.* all the countries   *2Ch 11:23*
of Judah
run to and fro *t.* the whole   *2Ch 16:9*
earth
went about *t.* all the cities of   *2Ch 17:9*
Judah
put in the fenced cities *t.* all   *2Ch 17:19*
Judah

t. all the fenced cities of Judah — *2Ch 19:5*
and proclaimed a fast *t.* all Judah — *2Ch 20:3*
fathers, *t.* all Judah and Benjamin — *2Ch 25:5*
for them *t.* all the host — *2Ch 26:14*
shields
to make proclamation *t.* all Israel — *2Ch 30:5*
the king and his princes *t.* all Israel — *2Ch 30:6*
they did eat *t.* the feast seven days — *2Ch 30:22*
And thus did Hezekiah *t.* all Judah — *2Ch 31:20*
the idols *t.* all the land of Israel — *2Ch 34:7*
a proclamation *t.* all his kingdom — *2Ch 36:22*
a proclamation *t.* all his kingdom — *2Ch 36:22; Ezr 1:1*
And they made proclamation *t.* Judah — *Ezr 10:7*
shall be published *t.* all his empire — *Es 1:20*
Jews that were *t.* the whole kingdom — *Es 3:6*
cities *t.* all the provinces of the king — *Es 9:2*
his fame went out *t.* all the provinces — *Es 9:4*
and kept *t.* every generation — *Es 9:28*
and moon endure, *t.* all generations — *Ps 72:5*
thy years are *t.* all generations — *Ps 102:24*
memorial, O Lord, *t.* all generations — *Ps 135:13*
dominion endureth *t.* all generations — *Ps 145:13*
high places for sin, *t.* all thy borders — *Jer 17:3*
against him *t.* all my mountains — *Eze 38:21*
And his fame went *t.* all Syria — *M't 4:24*
fame spread abroad *t.* all the region — *M'k 1:28*
in their synagogues *t.* all Galilee — *M'k 1:39*
be preached *t.* the whole world — *M'k 14:9*
t. all the hill country of Judæa — *Lu 1:65*
great famine was *t.* all the land — *Lu 4:25*
of him went forth *t.* all Judæa — *Lu 7:17*
and *t.* all the region round about — *Lu 7:17*
he went *t.* every city and village — *Lu 8:1*
and published *t.* the whole city how — *Lu 8:39*
the people, teaching *t.* all Jewry — *Lu 23:5*
seam, woven from the top *t.* — *Joh 19:23*
scattered abroad *t.* the regions — *Ac 8:1*
had the churches rest *t.* all Judæa — *Ac 9:31*
as Peter passed *t.* all quarters, he — *Ac 9:32*
And it was known *t.* all Joppa — *Ac 9:42*
which was published *t.* all Judæa — *Ac 10:37*
be great dearth *t.* all the world — *Ac 11:28*
was published *t.* all the region — *Ac 13:49*
after they had passed *t.* Pisidia — *Ac 14:24*
when they had gone *t.* Phrygia — *Ac 16:6*
but almost *t.* all Asia, this Paul — *Ac 19:26*
among all the Jews *t.* the world — *Ac 24:5*
and *t.* all the coast of Judæa — *Ac 26:20*
is spoken of *t.* the whole world — *Ro 1:8*
might be declared *t.* all the earth — *Ro 9:17*
is in the gospel *t.* all the churches — *2Co 8:18*
church by Christ Jesus *t.* all ages — *Eph 3:21*
to the strangers scattered *t.* Pontus — *1Pe 1:1*

THROW

t. it toward heaven (R) — *Ex 9:8*
t. it against the altar (A)(R) — *Ex 29:16*

t. the blood (R) — *Le 1:5; 1:16; 3:2; 17:6; 2Ki 16:15*
ye shall *t.* down their altars — *J'g 2:2*
t. down the altar of Baal that — *J'g 6:25*
battered the wall, to *t.* it down — *2Sa 20:15*
And he said, T. her down. So — *2Ki 9:33*
and to destroy, and to *t.* down — *Jer 1:10*
to *t.* down, and to destroy, and to — *Jer 31:28*
shall *t.* down thine eminent place — *Eze 16:39*
and *t.* down all thy strong holds — *Mic 5:11*
They shall build, but I will *t.* down — *Mal 1:4*

THROWING

if he smite him with *t.* a stone — *Nu 35:17*
t. skirts over face (A)(R) — *Jer 13:26*
t. off his coat (B) — *M'k 10:50*

THROWN

rider hath he *t.* into the sea — *Ex 15:1; 15:21*
because he hath *t.* down his altar — *J'g 6:32*
his head shall be *t.* to thee over — *2Sa 20:21*
covenant, *t.* down thine — *1Ki 19:10; 19:14*
nor *t.* down any more for ever — *Jer 31:40*
which are *t.* down by the mounts — *Jer 33:4*
are fallen, her walls are *t.* down — *Jer 50:15*
he hath *t.* down in his wrath — *La 2:2*
hath *t.* down, and hath not pitied — *La 2:17*
leave thee *t.* into the wilderness — *Eze 29:5*
the mountains shall be *t.* down — *Eze 38:20*
and the rocks are *t.* down by him — *Na 1:6*
another, that shall not be *t.* down — *M't 24:2; M'k 13:22; Lu 21:6*
the devil had *t.* him in the midst — *Lu 4:35*
that great city Babylon be *t.* down — *Re 18:21*

THRUST

he shall surely *t.* you out hence — *Ex 11:1*
because they were *t.* out of Egypt — *Ex 12:39*
she *t.* herself unto the wall — *Nu 22:25*
tent, and *t.* both of them through — *Nu 25:8*
But if he *t.* him of hatred, or hurl — *Nu 35:20*
t. him suddenly without enmity — *Nu 35:22*
to *t.* thee out of the way which — *De 13:5*
to *t.* thee away from the Lord thy — *De 13:10*
t. it through his ear unto the door — *De 15:17*
he shall *t.* out the enemy from — *De 33:27*
right thigh, and *t.* it into his belly — *J'g 3:21*
t. the fleece together, and wringed — *J'g 6:38*
Zebul *t.* out Gaal and his brethren — *J'g 9:41*
his young man *t.* him through — *J'g 9:54*
they *t.* out Jephthah, and said — *J'g 11:2*
I may *t.* out all your right eyes — *1Sa 11:2*
and *t.* me through therewith — *1Sa 31:4*
come and *t.* me through — *1Sa 31:4*
and *t.* this sword in his fellow's side — *2Sa 2:16*
and *t.* them through the heart of — *2Sa 18:14*
be all of them as thorns *t.* away — *2Sa 23:6*
So Solomon *t.* out Abiathar from — *1Ki 2:27*
Gehazi came near to *t.* her away — *2Ki 4:27*
and *t.* me through therewith — *1Ch 10:4*

and they *t.* him out from thence — *2Ch 26:20*
Thou hast *t.* sore at me that — *Ps 118:13*
that is found shall be *t.* through — *Isa 13:15*
are slain, *t.* through with a sword — *Isa 14:19*
t. aside the innocent (A) — *Isa 29:21*
that are *t.* through in her streets — *Jer 51:4*
t. thee through with their swords — *Eze 16:40*
ye have *t.* with side and with — *Eze 34:21*
to *t.* them out of their possession — *Eze 46:18*
t. from kingly throne (B) — *Da 5:20*
Neither shall one *t.* another; they — *Joe 2:8*
begat him shall *t.* him through — *Zec 13:8*
rose up and *t.* him out of the city — *Lu 4:29*
would *t.* out a little from the land — *Lu 5:3*
heaven, shall be *t.* down to hell — *Lu 10:15*
of God, and you yourselves *t.* out — *Lu 13:28*
nails, and *t.* my hand into his side — *Joh 20:25*
thy hand, and *t.* it into my side — *Joh 20:27*
his neighbour wrong *t.* him away — *Ac 7:27*
not obey, but *t.* him from them — *Ac 7:39*
t. them into the inner prison — *Ac 16:24*
and now do they *t.* us out privily — *Ac 16:37*
it were possible, to *t.* in the ship — *Ac 27:39*
stoned, or *t.* through with a dart — *Heb 12:20*
T. in thy sickle, and reap — *Re 14:15*
cloud, *t.* in his sickle on the earth — *Re 14:16*
T. in thy sharp sickle, and gather — *Re 14:18*
the angel *t.* in his sickle into — *Re 14:19*

THRUSTETH

God *t.* him down, not man — *Job 32:13*

THRUSTING

t. them out of property (E)(R) — *Zec 46:18*

THUMB

and upon the *t.* of their right hand — *Ex 29:20*
and upon the *t.* of his right hand — *Le 8:23*
the *t.* of his right hand — *Le 14:14; 14:17, 25, 28*

THUMBS

upon the *t.* of their right hands — *Le 8:24*
cut off his *t.* and his great toes — *J'g 1:6*
t. and their great toes cut off — *J'g 1:7*

THUMMIN

of judgment the Urim and the T. — *Ex 28:30*
breastplate the Urim and the T. — *Le 8:8*
Let thy T. and thy Urim be with — *De 33:8*
a priest with Urim and with T. — *Ezr 2:63*
up a priest with Urim and T. — *Ne 7:65*

THUNDER

the Lord sent *t.* and hail, and — *Ex 9:23*
and the *t.* shall cease, neither shall — *Ex 9:29*
of heaven shall he *t.* upon them — *1Sa 2:10*
the Lord thundered with a great *t.* — *1Sa 7:10*
Lord, and he shall send *t.* and rain — *1Sa 12:17*
the Lord sent *t.* and rain that day — *1Sa 12:18*

But the *t.* or his power who | Job 26:14
can
away for the lightning of the | Job 28:26
t.
or a way for the lightning of | Job 38:25
t.
hast thou clothed his neck | Job 39:19
with *t.*
the *t.* of the captains, and | Job 39:25
thou *t.* with a voice like him | Job 40:9
voice of thy *t.* was in the | Ps 77:18
heaven
thee in the secret place of *t.* | Ps 81:7
voice of thy *t.* they hasted | Ps 104:7
away
visited of the Lord of hosts | Isa 29:6
with *t.*
as a *t.* of the Almighty | Eze 1:24
(B)(R)
Boanerges, The sons of *t.* | M'k 3:17
I heard, as it were the noise of | Re 6:1
t.
waters, and as a voice of a | Re 14:2
great *t.*
like peals of *t.* (S) | Re 19:6

THUNDERBOLTS

the hail, and their flocks to | Ps 78:48
hot *t.*

THUNDERCLAPS

lightnings and *t.* (S) | Re 4:5; 8:5; 11:19

THUNDERED

the Lord *t.* with a great | 1Sa 7:10
thunder
The Lord *t.* from heaven | 2Sa 22:14
The Lord also *t.* in the | Ps 18:13
heavens
and heard it, said that it *t.* | Joh 12:29

THUNDERETH

t. with the voice of his | Job 37:4
excellency
God *t.* marvellously with his | Job 37:5
voice
the God of glory *t.*: the Lord | Ps 29:3
is

THUNDERINGS

be no more mighty *t.* and hail | Ex 9:28
And all the people saw the *t.* | Ex 20:18
lightnings and *t.* and voices | Re 4:5
and there were voices, and *t.* | Re 8:5
were lightnings, and voices, | Re 11:19
and *t.*
and as the voice of mighty *t.* | Re 19:6

THUNDERS

t. and hail ceased, and the | Ex 9:33
rain
and the hail and the *t.* were | Ex 9:34
ceased
that there were *t.* and | Ex 19:16
lightnings
t. before his army (B) | Joe 2:11
cried, seven *t.* uttered their | Re 10:3
voices
seven *t.* had uttered their | Re 10:4
voices
things which the seven *t.* | Re 10:4
uttered
were voices, and *t.* and | Re 16:18
lightnings

THUS

T. the heavens and the earth | Ge 2:1
were
T. did Noah; according to all | Ge 6:22
that
T. were both the daughters | Ge 19:36
of Lot
with all other: *t.* she was | Ge 20:16
reproved
T. spake the man unto me; | Ge 24:30
that
she said, If it be so, why am | Ge 25:22
I *t.*
t. Esau despised his | Ge 25:34
birthright
If he said *t.*, The speckled | Ge 31:8
shall

if he said *t.*, The ringstraked | Ge 31:8
shall
T. God hath taken away the | Ge 31:9
cattle
T. they made a covenant at | Ge 31:32
T. I was; in the day the | Ge 31:40
drought
T. have I been twenty years | Ge 31:41
T. shall ye speak unto my lord | Ge 32:4
Thy servant Jacob saith *t.*, I | Ge 32:4
have
T. dwelt Esau in mount Seir: | Ge 36:8
Esau
T. his father wept for him | Ge 37:35
the way; and *t.* did he unto | Ge 42:25
them
T. saith thy son Joseph, | Ge 45:9
God hath
T. shalt thou say unto the | Ex 3:14
T. saith the Lord, Israel is my | Ex 4:22
son
T. saith the Lord God of Israel | Ex 5:1
T. saith Pharaoh, I will not | Ex 5:10
give
dealest thou *t.* with thy | Ex 5:15
servants
T. saith the Lord, In this thou | Ex 7:17
T. saith the Lord, Let my | Ex 8:1; 8:20
T. saith the Lord God of the | Ex 9:1;
| 9:13; 10:3
T. saith the Lord, About | Ex 11:4
midnight
t. shall ye eat it: with your | Ex 12:11
loins
T. did all the children of | Ex 12:50
Israel: as
hast thou dealt *t.* with us, to | Ex 14:11
carry
T. the Lord saved Israel that | Ex 14:30
day
T. shalt thou say to the house | Ex 19:3
of
T. thou shalt say unto the | Ex 20:22
t. shalt thou make for all the | Ex 26:17
t. shall it be for them both; | Ex 26:24
they
t. shalt thou do unto Aaron, | Ex 29:35
and to
T. saith the Lord God of | Ex 32:27
Israel
t. did he make for all the | Ex 36:22
boards
t. he did to both of them in | Ex 36:29
both the
T. was all the work of the | Ex 39:32
tabernacle
T. did Moses: according to | Ex 40:16
all that
T. shall ye separate the | Le 15:31
children of
T. shall Aaron come into | Le 16:3
the holy
t. do unto them, that they | Nu 4:19
may live
t. were they numbered of him, | Nu 4:49
as the
t. shalt thou do unto them, to | Nu 8:7
T. shalt thou separate the | Nu 8:14
Levites
T. shalt thou do unto the | Nu 8:26
Levites
T. were the journeyings of | Nu 10:28
if thou deal *t.* with me, kill | Nu 11:15
me
T. shall it be done for one | Nu 15:11
bullock
T. speak unto the Levites, | Nu 18:26
and say
T. ye also shall offer an | Nu 18:28
heave
T. saith thy brother Israel, | Nu 20:14
Thou
T. Edom refused to give | Nu 20:21
Israel
T. Israel dwelt in the land of | Nu 21:31
T. saith Balak the son of | Nu 22:16
Zippor
unto Balak, and *t.* thou shalt | Nu 23:5
speak
Go again into Balak, and say | Nu 23:16
t.
T. did your fathers, when I | Nu 32:8
sent
t. shall ye deal with them; ye | De 7:5
shall
T. I fell down before the Lord | De 9:25
forty
T. shalt thou do unto all the | De 20:15
the Lord done *t.* unto this | De 29:24
land

Do ye *t.* requite the Lord, O | De 32:6
said *t.*, There came men unto | Jos 2:4
me
once, T. shalt thou do six days | Jos 6:3
liest thou *t.* upon thy face | Jos 7:10
for *t.* saith the Lord God of | Jos 7:13
Israel
Israel, and *t.* and *t.* have I | Jos 7:20
done
t. shall the Lord do to all | Jos 10:25
your
according to their families | Jos 16:5
T. they gave to the children | Jos 21:13
of Aaron
them: *t.* were all these cities | Jos 21:42
T. saith the whole | Jos 22:16
congregation of
T. saith the Lord God of | Jos 24:2;
Israel | J'g 6:8
Why hast thou served us *t.* | J'g 8:1
T. was Midian subdued before | J'g 8:28
T. God rendered the | J'g 9:56
wickedness of
T. saith Jephthah, Israel took | J'g 11:15
not
t. the children of Ammon | J'g 11:33
were
askest thou *t.* after my name | J'g 13:18
T. dealeth Micah with me | J'g 18:4
and *t.* dealeth Micah with me | J'g 18:4
T. they inclosed the | J'g 20:43
Benjamites
T. saith the Lord, Did I | 1Sa 2:27
plainly
t. he spake, Come, and let us | 1Sa 9:9
go to
T. saith the Lord God of | 1Sa 10:19
Israel
T. shall ye say unto the men | 1Sa 11:9
If they say *t.* unto us, Tarry | 1Sa 14:9
until
But if they say *t.*, Come up | 1Sa 14:10
unto us
T. saith the Lord of hosts, I | 1Sa 15:2
T. shall ye say to David, | 1Sa 18:25
The king
If he say *t.* It is well: thy | 1Sa 20:7
servant
But if I say *t.* unto the | 1Sa 20:22
young man
t. shall ye say to him that | 1Sa 25:6
liveth in
doth my lord *t.* pursue after | 1Sa 26:18
his
I will yet be more vile than *t.* | 2Sa 6:22
T. saith the Lord, Shalt thou | 2Sa 7:5
T. saith the Lord of hosts, I | 2Sa 7:8
took
T. shalt thou say unto Joab | 2Sa 11:25
T. saith the Lord God of | 2Sa 12:7
Israel, I
T. saith the Lord, Behold, I | 2Sa 12:11
will
t. did he unto all the cities | 2Sa 12:31
of the
But if he *t.* say, I have no | 2Sa 15:26
delight
And *t.* said Shimei when he | 2Sa 16:7
cursed
T. and *t.* did Ahithophel | 2Sa 17:15
counsel
and *t.* and *t.* have I | 2Sa 17:15
counselled
for *t.* hath Ahithophel | 2Sa 17:21
counselled
Joab, I may not tarry *t.* with | 2Sa 18:14
thee
t. he said, O my son | 2Sa 18:33
Absalom
T. saith the Lord, I offer | 2Sa 24:12
thee
also *t.* said the king, Blessed | 1Ki 1:48
T. saith the king, Come forth | 1Ki 2:30
T. said Joab, and *t.* he | 1Ki 2:30
answered
T. they spake before the king | 1Ki 3:22
t. gave Solomon to Hiram | 1Ki 5:11
year by
the Lord done *t.* unto this land | 1Ki 9:8
for *t.* saith the Lord, the | 1Ki 11:31
God of
T. shalt thou speak unto this | 1Ki 12:10
t. shalt thou say unto them, | 1Ki 12:10
My
T. saith the Lord, Ye shall | 1Ki 12:24
not go
O altar, altar, *t.* saith the | 1Ki 13:2
Lord

Left		Middle		Right	
T. saith the Lord, Forasmuch as	1Ki 13:21	T. saith the Lord, Choose thee	1Ch 21:11	T. saith the Lord God of hosts, Go	Isa 22:15
t. shalt thou say unto her	1Ki 14:5	Ithamar; and t. were they divided	1Ch 24:4	When t. it shall be in the midst of	Isa 24:13
and t. shalt thou say unto her	1Ki 14:5	T. were they divided by lot, one sort	1Ch 24:5	Therefore t. saith the Lord God	Isa 28:16
T. saith the Lord God of Israel	1Ki 14:7	T. David the son of Jesse reigned	1Ch 29:26	t. saith the Lord, who redeemed	Isa 29:22
T. did Zimri destroy all the house	1Ki 16:12	T. Solomon made all these vessels	2Ch 4:18	t. saith the Holy One of Israel	Isa 30:12
For t. saith the Lord God of Israel	1Ki 17:14	T. all the work that Solomon made	2Ch 5:1	t. saith the Lord God, the Holy One	Isa 30:15
said unto him, T. saith Ben-hadad	1Ki 20:2	T. Solomon finished the house of the	2Ch 7:11	t. hath the Lord spoken unto me	Isa 31:4
T. speaketh Ben-hadad, saying	1Ki 20:5	the Lord done t. unto this land	2Ch 7:21	T. saith the great king, the king of	Isa 36:4
T. saith the Lord, Hast thou seen	1Ki 20:13	T. shalt thou answer the people	2Ch 10:10	T. saith the king, Let not Hezekiah	Isa 36:14
T. saith the Lord, Even by	1Ki 20:14	t. shalt thou say unto them, My	2Ch 10:10	t. saith the king of Assyria, Make	Isa 36:16
T. saith the Lord, Because the	1Ki 20:28	T. saith the Lord, Ye shall not go	2Ch 11:4	T. saith Hezekiah, This day is a	Isa 37:3
T. saith the Lord, Because thou	1Ki 20:42	T. saith the Lord, Ye have forsaken ye	2Ch 12:5	T. shall ye say unto your master	Isa 37:6
T. saith the Lord, Hast thou killed	1Ki 21:19	T. the children of Israel were	2Ch 13:18	T. saith the Lord, Be not afraid of	Isa 37:6
T. saith the Lord, In the place	1Ki 21:19	T. saith the Lord, With these thou	2Ch 18:10	T. shall ye speak to Hezekiah king	Isa 37:10
T. saith the Lord, With these shalt	1Ki 22:11	T. saith the king, Put this fellow	2Ch 18:26	T. saith the Lord God of Israel	Isa 37:21
T. saith the king, Put this fellow	1Ki 22:27	T. shall ye do in the fear of the	2Ch 19:9	t. saith the Lord concerning the	Isa 37:33
Now therefore t. saith the Lord	2Ki 1:4	T. saith the Lord unto you, Be not	2Ch 20:15	T. saith the Lord, Set thine house	Isa 38:1
T. saith the Lord, Is it not because	2Ki 1:6	T. saith the Lord God of David thy	2Ch 21:12	T. saith the Lord, the God of David	Isa 38:5
t. hath the king said, Come down	2Ki 1:11	T. they did day by day, and	2Ch 24:11	T. saith God the Lord, he that	Isa 42:5
T. saith the Lord, Forasmuch	2Ki 1:16	T. saith God, Why transgress ye	2Ch 24:20	now t. saith the Lord, that created	Isa 43:1
T. saith the Lord, I have healed	2Ki 2:21	T. Joash the king remembered not	2Ch 24:22	T. saith the Lord, your redeemer	Isa 43:14
T. saith the Lord, Make this valley	2Ki 3:16	t. did Hezekiah throughout	2Ch 31:20	T. saith the Lord, which maketh a	Isa 43:16
t. saith the Lord, Ye shall not see	2Ki 3:17	T. saith Sennacherib king of	2Ch 32:10	T. saith the Lord that made thee	Isa 44:2
t. saith the Lord, They shall eat	2Ki 4:43	T. the Lord saved Hezekiah	2Ch 32:22	T. saith the Lord the King of Israel	Isa 44:6
T. and t. said the maid that is of	2Ki 5:4	T. saith the Lord God of Israel	2Ch 34:23	T. saith the Lord, thy redeemer	Isa 44:24
T. saith the Lord, To-morrow	2Ki 7:1	T. saith the Lord, Behold, I will	2Ch 34:24	T. saith the Lord to his anointed	Isa 45:1
T. saith the Lord, I have anointed	2Ki 9:3	t. saith the Lord God of Israel	2Ch 34:26	T. saith the Lord, the Holy One of	Isa 45:11
T. saith the Lord God of Israel	2Ki 9:6	T. saith Cyrus king of Persia, All	2Ch 36:23	T. saith the Lord, The labour of	Isa 45:14
he said, T. and t. spake he to me	2Ki 9:12	T. saith Cyrus king of Persia, The	Ezr 1:2	For t. saith the Lord that created	Isa 45:18
T. saith the Lord, I have anointed	2Ki 9:12	and said t. unto them, Who hath	Ezr 5:3	T. shall they be unto thee with	Isa 47:15
T. saith the king, Is it peace	2Ki 9:18; 9:19	unto him, wherein was written Ezr 5:7 t.		T. saith the Lord, thy Redeemer	Isa 48:17; 49:7
T. Jehu destroyed Baal out	2Ki 10:28	and said unto them t., Who	Ezr 5:9	T. saith the Lord, In an acceptable	Isa 49:8
T. did Urijah the priest, according	2Ki 16:16	t. they returned us answer, saying	Ezr 5:11	T. saith the Lord God, Behold, I	Isa 49:22
T. saith the great king, the king	2Ki 18:19	therein was a record t. written	Ezr 6:2	t. saith the Lord, Even the captives	Isa 49:25
T. saith the king, Let not	2Ki 18:29	even t. be he shaken out, and	Ne 5:13	T. saith the Lord, Where is the bill	Isa 50:1
t. saith the king of Assyria, Make	2Ki 18:31	Did not your fathers t. and did	Ne 13:18	T. saith thy Lord the Lord, and	Isa 51:22
T. saith Hezekiah, This day is a	2Ki 19:3	T. cleansed I them from all	Ne 13:30	For t. saith the Lord, Ye have sold	Isa 52:3
T. shall ye say to your master	2Ki 19:6	T. shall there arise too much	Es 1:18	t. saith the Lord God, My people	Isa 52:4
T. saith the Lord, Be not afraid of	2Ki 19:6	t. came every maiden unto the	Es 2:13	T. saith the Lord, Keep ye	Isa 56:1
T. shall ye speak to Hezekiah king	2Ki 19:10	T. shall it be done to the man	Es 6:9	t. saith the Lord unto the eunuchs	Isa 56:4
T. saith the Lord God of Israel	2Ki 19:20	T. shall it be done unto the man	Es 6:11	for t. saith the high and lofty One	Isa 57:15
t. saith the Lord concerning	2Ki 19:32	T. the Jews smote all their enemies	Es 9:5	T. saith the Lord, As the new wine	Isa 65:8
T. saith the Lord, Set thine house	2Ki 20:1	hearts. T. did Job continually	Job 1:5	Therefore t. saith the Lord God	Isa 65:13
T. saith the Lord, the God of David	2Ki 20:5; 22:15	then are ye t. altogether vain	Job 27:12	T. saith the Lord, The heaven is	Isa 66:1
t. saith the Lord God of Israel	2Ki 21:12	T. I was as a man that heareth not	Ps 38:14	T. saith the Lord, Behold, I	Isa 66:12
T. saith the Lord, Behold, I will	2Ki 22:16	T. will I bless thee while I live	Ps 63:4	For t. saith the Lord; I remember	Jer 2:2
of the Lord, t. shall ye say to him	2Ki 22:18	If I say, I will speak t.; behold	Ps 73:15	T. saith the Lord, What iniquity	Jer 2:5
T. saith the Lord God of Israel	2Ki 22:18	T. my heart was grieved, and I	Ps 73:21	For t. saith the Lord to the men of	Jer 4:3
T. all Israel brought up the ark of	1Ch 15:28	T. they changed their glory into the	Ps 106:20	For t. hath the Lord said, The	Jer 4:27
T. saith the Lord, Thou shalt not	1Ch 17:4	T. they provoked him to anger with	Ps 106:29	them: t. shall it be done unto them	Jer 5:13
t. shalt thou say unto my servant	1Ch 17:7	T. were they defiled with their own	Ps 106:39	t. saith the Lord God of hosts,	Jer 5:14
T. saith the Lord of hosts, I took	1Ch 17:7	T. shall the man be blessed that	Ps 128:4	For t. hath the Lord of hosts said	Jer 6:6
T. the Lord preserved David	1Ch 18:6; 18:13	T. saith the Lord God, It shall	Isa 7:7		
T. saith the Lord, I offer thee	1Ch 21:10	spake t. to me with a strong hand	Isa 8:11		
		t. saith the Lord God of hosts	Isa 10:24		
		t. hath the Lord said unto me, Go,	Isa 21:6		
		For t. hath the Lord said unto me	Isa 21:6		

T. saith the Lord of hosts, *Jer 6:9*
They
T. saith the Lord, Stand ye in *Jer 6:16*
Therefore *t.* saith the Lord, *Jer 6:21*
Behold
T. saith the Lord, Behold, a *Jer 6:22*
people
T. saith the Lord of hosts, the *Jer 7:3*
God
Therefore *t.* saith the Lord *Jer 7:20*
God
T. saith the Lord of hosts, the *Jer 7:21*
God
say unto them, *T.* saith the *Jer 8:4*
Lord
t. saith the Lord of hosts *Jer 9:7; 9:15*
T. saith the Lord of hosts, *Jer 9:17*
Consider
T. saith the Lord, Even the *Jer 9:22*
T. saith the Lord, Let not the *Jer 9:23*
T. saith the Lord, Learn not *Jer 10:2*
T. shall ye say unto them *Jer 10:11*
For *t.* saith the Lord, *Jer 10:18*
Behold, I
T. saith the Lord God of *Jer 11:3*
Israel
Therefore *t.* saith the Lord, *Jer 11:11*
Behold
Therefore *t.* saith the Lord *Jer 11:21*
of the
t. saith the Lord of hosts, *Jer 11:22*
Behold
T. saith the Lord against all *Jer 12:14*
mine
T. saith the Lord unto me, Go *Jer 13:1*
T. saith the Lord, After this *Jer 13:9*
T. saith the Lord God of *Jer 13:12*
Israel
T. saith the Lord, Behold, I *Jer 13:13*
will
T. saith the Lord unto this *Jer 14:10*
people
T. have they loved to wander *Jer 14:10*
t. saith the Lord concerning *Jer 14:15*
t. saith the Lord, If thou *Jer 15:19*
return
t. saith the Lord concerning *Jer 16:3*
t. saith the Lord, Enter not *Jer 16:5*
into the
t. saith the Lord of hosts, the *Jer 16:9*
God
T. saith the Lord; Cursed be *Jer 17:5*
T. saith the Lord unto me; *Jer 17:19*
Go and
T. saith the Lord; Take *Jer 17:21*
heed to
saying, *T.* saith the Lord: *Jer 18:11*
Behold
Therefore *t.* saith the Lord; *Jer 18:13*
Ask ye
deal *t.* with them in the time *Jer 18:23*
of thine
T. saith the Lord, Go and get *Jer 19:1*
T. saith the Lord of hosts, the *Jer 19:3*
God
them, *T.* saith the Lord of *Jer 19:11*
hosts
T. will I do unto this place, *Jer 19:12*
saith
T. saith the Lord of hosts *Jer 19:15*
t. saith the Lord, Behold, I *Jer 20:4*
will
them, *T.* shall ye say to *Jer 21:3*
Zedekiah
T. saith the Lord God of *Jer 21:4*
Israel
thou shalt say, *T.* saith the *Jer 21:8*
Lord
house of David, *t.* saith the *Jer 21:12*
Lord
T. saith the Lord; Go down *Jer 22:1*
to the
T. saith the Lord; Execute ye *Jer 22:3*
t. saith the Lord unto the *Jer 22:6*
king's
Lord done *t.* unto this great *Jer 22:8*
city
For *t.* saith the Lord *Jer 22:11*
touching
t. saith the Lord touching *Jer 22:18*
t. saith the Lord concerning *Jer 22:18*
T. saith the Lord, Write ye *Jer 22:30*
this
t. saith the Lord God of *Jer 23:2*
Israel
Therefore *t.* saith the Lord *Jer 23:15*
of hosts

T. saith the Lord of hosts, *Jer 23:16*
Hearken
T. shall ye say every one to *Jer 23:35*
his
T. shalt thou say to the *Jer 23:37*
prophet
therefore *t.* saith the Lord *Jer 23:38*
T. saith the Lord, the God of *Jer 24:5*
t. saith the Lord, So will I *Jer 24:8*
give
t. saith the Lord of hosts; *Jer 25:8*
Because
t. saith the Lord God of *Jer 25:15*
Israel unto
T. saith the Lord of hosts, *Jer 25:27*
the God
T. saith the Lord of hosts; *Jer 25:28*
Ye shall
T. saith the Lord of hosts, *Jer 25:32*
Behold
T. saith the Lord; Stand in *Jer 26:2*
T. saith the Lord; If ye will *Jer 26:4*
not
T. saith the Lord of hosts; *Jer 26:18*
Zion
T. might we procure great *Jer 26:19*
evil
T. saith the Lord to me; Make *Jer 27:2*
T. saith the Lord of hosts, the *Jer 27:4*
God
T. shall ye say unto your *Jer 27:4*
masters
T. saith the Lord; Hearken *Jer 27:16*
not to
For *t.* saith the Lord of hosts *Jer 27:19*
t. saith the Lord of hosts, the *Jer 27:21*
God
T. speaketh the Lord of hosts *Jer 28:2*
T. saith the Lord; Even so *Jer 28:11*
will I
T. saith the Lord; Thou hast *Jer 28:13*
t. saith the Lord of hosts; the *Jer 28:14*
God
t. saith the Lord; Behold, I *Jer 28:16*
will
T. saith the Lord of hosts, the *Jer 29:4*
God
t. saith the Lord of hosts, the *Jer 29:8*
God
For *t.* saith the Lord, That *Jer 29:10*
after
that *t.* saith the Lord of the *Jer 29:16*
king
T. saith the Lord of hosts; *Jer 29:17*
Behold
T. saith the Lord of hosts, *Jer 29:21*
the God
T. shalt thou also speak to *Jer 29:24*
Shemaiah
T. speaketh the Lord of *Jer 29:25*
hosts, the
T. saith the Lord concerning *Jer 29:31*
Therefore *t.* saith the Lord; *Jer 29:32*
Behold
T. speaketh the Lord God of *Jer 30:2*
Israel
t. saith the Lord; We have *Jer 30:5*
heard a
t. saith the Lord, Thy bruise *Jer 30:12*
t. saith the Lord; Behold, I *Jer 30:18*
will
T. saith the Lord, The people *Jer 31:2*
For *t.* saith the Lord; Sing *Jer 31:7*
with
T. saith the Lord; A voice *Jer 31:15*
was
T. saith the Lord; Refrain *Jer 31:16*
thy
heard Ephraim bemoaning *Jer 31:18*
himself *t.*
T. saith the Lord of hosts *Jer 31:23*
T. saith the Lord, which *Jer 31:35*
giveth the
T. saith the Lord; If heaven *Jer 31:37*
above
T. saith the Lord, Behold, I *Jer 32:3*
will
T. saith the Lord of hosts, *Jer 32:14*
the God
t. saith the Lord of hosts, the *Jer 32:15*
God
t. saith the Lord; Behold, I *Jer 32:28*
will
And now therefore *t.* saith *Jer 32:36*
the Lord
t. saith the Lord: Like as I *Jer 32:42*
have
T. saith the Lord the maker *Jer 33:2*
For *t.* saith the Lord, the God *Jer 33:4*

T. saith the Lord; Again *Jer 33:10*
there
T. saith the Lord of hosts; *Jer 33:12*
Again
t. saith the Lord; David shall *Jer 33:17*
never
T. saith the Lord; If ye can *Jer 33:20*
break
t. they have despised my *Jer 33:24*
people, that
T. saith the Lord; If my *Jer 33:25*
covenant
T. saith the Lord, the God of *Jer 34:2*
Israel
T. saith the Lord; Behold, I *Jer 34:2*
will
T. saith the Lord of thee, *Jer 34:4*
Thou
T. saith the Lord, the God of *Jer 34:13*
Israel
t. saith the Lord; ye have not *Jer 34:17*
T. have we obeyed the voice *Jer 35:8*
T. saith the Lord of hosts *Jer 35:13*
t. saith the Lord God of *Jer 35:17*
hosts, the
T. saith the Lord of hosts, *Jer 35:18*
the God
Therefore *t.* saith the Lord *Jer 35:19*
of hosts
T. saith the Lord; Thou hast *Jer 36:29*
t. saith the Lord of *Jer 36:30*
Jehoiakim king
T. saith the Lord, the God of *Jer 37:7*
Israel
T. shall ye say to the king of *Jer 37:7*
Judah
T. saith the Lord; Deceive *Jer 37:9*
not
T. Jeremiah remained in the *Jer 37:21*
court
T. saith the Lord, He that *Jer 38:2*
T. saith the Lord, This city *Jer 38:3*
shall
t. he weakeneth the hands of *Jer 38:4*
T. saith the Lord, the God of *Jer 38:17*
T. saith the Lord of hosts, *Jer 39:16*
the God
T. saith the Lord, the God of *Jer 42:9*
Israel
T. saith the Lord of hosts, *Jer 42:15*
the God
For *t.* saith the Lord of *Jer 42:18*
hosts, the
t. came they even to *Jer 43:7*
Tahpanhes
T. saith the Lord of hosts *Jer 43:10*
T. saith the Lord of hosts, the *Jer 44:2*
God
now *t.* saith the Lord, the *Jer 44:7*
God
t. saith the Lord of hosts, the *Jer 44:11*
God
T. saith the Lord of hosts, *Jer 44:25*
the God
T. saith the Lord; Behold, I *Jer 44:30*
will
T. saith the Lord, the God of *Jer 45:2*
Israel
T. shalt thou say unto him, *Jer 45:4*
The
Lord saith *t.*; Behold, that *Jer 45:4*
which
T. saith the Lord; Behold, *Jer 47:2*
waters
Moab *t.* saith the Lord of *Jer 48:1*
hosts
t. saith the Lord; Behold, *Jer 48:40*
he shall
T. far is the judgment of *Jer 48:47*
Moab
t. saith the Lord; Hath Israel *Jer 49:1*
Edom, *t.* saith the Lord of *Jer 49:7*
hosts
For *t.* saith the Lord; *Jer 49:12*
Behold, they
t. saith the Lord; Arise, ye, *Jer 49:28*
go up to
T. saith the Lord of hosts; *Jer 49:35*
Behold
t. saith the Lord of hosts, the *Jer 50:18*
God
T. saith the Lord of hosts; *Jer 50:33*
The
T. saith the Lord; Behold, I *Jer 51:1*
will
T. the slain shall fall in the *Jer 51:4*
land of
t. saith the Lord of hosts, the *Jer 51:33*
God

t. saith the Lord; Behold, I   *Jer 51:36*
will
T. saith the Lord of hosts;   *Jer 51:58*
The
T. shall Babylon sink, and   *Jer 51:64*
shall
T. far are the words of   *Jer 51:64*
Jeremiah
T. Judah was carried away   *Jer 52:27*
captive
T. were their faces; and their   *Eze 1:11*
wings
unto them, *T.* saith the Lord   *Eze 2:4*
God
T. saith the Lord God;   *Eze 3:11*
whether
T. saith the Lord God; He   *Eze 3:27*
t. shall the children of Israel   *Eze 4:13*
eat
t. saith the Lord God; This is   *Eze 5:5*
t. saith the Lord God; Because   *Eze 5:7*
ye
t. saith the Lord God; Behold,   *Eze 5:8*
I
T. shall mine anger be   *Eze 5:13*
accomplished
T. saith the Lord God to   *Eze 6:3*
T. saith the Lord God; Smite   *Eze 6:11*
with
t. will I accomplish my fury   *Eze 6:12*
upon
t. saith the Lord God unto the   *Eze 7:2*
T. saith the Lord God; An evil   *Eze 7:5*
unto me, Speak; *T.* saith the   *Eze 11:5*
Lord
T. have ye said, O house of   *Eze 11:5*
Israel
Therefore *t.* saith the Lord   *Eze 11:7*
God
T. saith the Lord God;   *Eze 11:16*
Although I
T. saith the Lord God; I will   *Eze 11:17*
even
T. saith the Lord God; This   *Eze 12:10*
T. saith the Lord God of the   *Eze 12:19*
T. saith the Lord God; I   *Eze 12:23*
will make
T. saith the Lord God;   *Eze 12:28*
There shall
T. saith the Lord God; Woe   *Eze 13:3*
unto
Therefore *t.* saith the Lord   *Eze 13:8;*
God   *13:13*
T. will I accomplish my   *Eze 13:15*
wrath upon
T. saith the Lord God; Woe   *Eze 13:18*
to the
Wherefore *t.* saith the Lord   *Eze 13:20*
God
T. saith the Lord God; Every   *Eze 14:4*
man
T. saith the Lord God;   *Eze 14:6*
Repent, and
For *t.* saith the Lord God   *Eze 14:21*
Therefore *t.* saith the Lord   *Eze 15:6*
God
say, *T.* saith the Lord God   *Eze 16:3*
unto
T. wast thou decked with   *Eze 16:13*
gold and
and *t.* it was, saith the Lord   *Eze 16:19*
God
T. saith the Lord God;   *Eze 16:36*
Because
For *t.* saith the Lord God; I   *Eze 16:59*
will
T. saith the Lord God; A   *Eze 17:3*
great
T. saith the Lord God; Shall   *Eze 17:9*
it
Therefore *t.* saith the Lord   *Eze 17:19*
God
T. saith the Lord God; I   *Eze 17:22*
will also
T. saith the Lord God; Are   *Eze 20:3*
ye
T. saith the Lord God; In the   *Eze 20:5*
day
T. saith the Lord God; Yet   *Eze 20:27*
in this
T. saith the Lord God; Are   *Eze 20:30*
ye
t. saith the Lord God; Go   *Eze 20:39*
ye, serve
T. saith the Lord God;   *Eze 20:47*
Behold, I
T. saith the Lord; Behold, I   *Eze 21:3*
am
T. saith the Lord; Say, A   *Eze 21:9*
sword, a

t. saith the Lord God;   *Eze 21:24*
Because ye
T. saith the Lord God;   *Eze 21:26*
Remove the
T. saith the Lord God   *Eze 21:28*
concerning
T. saith the Lord God, The   *Eze 22:3*
city
t. saith the Lord God;   *Eze 22:19*
Because ye
T. saith the Lord God, when   *Eze 22:28*
T. were their names;   *Eze 23:4*
Samaria is
T. she committed her   *Eze 23:7*
whoredoms
t. thou calledst to   *Eze 23:21*
remembrance the
t. saith the Lord God;   *Eze 23:22*
Behold, I
T. will I make thy lewdness   *Eze 23:27*
to cease
t. saith the Lord God;   *Eze 23:28*
Behold, I
T. saith the Lord God; Thou   *Eze 23:32*
shalt
Therefore *t.* saith the Lord   *Eze 23:35*
God
t. have they done in the   *Eze 23:39*
midst of
t. saith the Lord God; I will   *Eze 23:46*
bring
T. will I cause lewdness to   *Eze 23:48*
cease out
t. saith the Lord God; Set on   *Eze 24:3*
Wherefore *t.* saith the Lord   *Eze 24:6*
God
Therefore *t.* saith the Lord   *Eze 24:9*
God
T. saith the Lord God;   *Eze 24:21*
Behold, I
T. Ezekiel is unto you a sign   *Eze 24:24*
according
T. saith the Lord God;   *Eze 25:3*
Because
For *t.* saith the Lord God;   *Eze 25:6*
Because
T. saith the Lord God;   *Eze 25:8;*
Because   *25:12*
t. saith the Lord God;   *Eze 25:13*
I will also
T. saith the Lord God;   *Eze 25:15*
Because the
t. saith the Lord God;   *Eze 25:16*
Behold, I
t. saith the Lord God;   *Eze 26:3*
Behold, I am
For *t.* saith the Lord God;   *Eze 26:7*
Behold
T. saith the Lord God to   *Eze 26:15*
Tyrus
t. saith the Lord God: When   *Eze 26:19*
I shall
T. saith the Lord God; O   *Eze 27:3*
Tyrus
T. saith the Lord God;   *Eze 28:2*
Because
Therefore *t.* saith the Lord   *Eze 28:6*
God
T. saith the Lord God; Thou   *Eze 28:12*
T. saith the Lord God;   *Eze 28:22*
Behold, I
T. saith the Lord God;   *Eze 28:25*
When I
T. saith the Lord God;   *Eze 29:3*
Behold, I
Therefore *t.* saith the Lord   *Eze 29:8*
God
Yet *t.* saith the Lord God;   *Eze 29:13*
At the
Therefore *t.* saith the Lord   *Eze 29:19*
God
T. saith the Lord God; Howl   *Eze 30:2*
ye
T. saith the Lord; They also   *Eze 30:6*
that
T. saith the Lord God; I   *Eze 30:10;*
will   *30:13*
T. will I execute judgments   *Eze 30:19*
in Egypt
Therefore *t.* saith the Lord   *Eze 30:22*
God
T. was he fair in his   *Eze 31:7*
greatness, in
Therefore *t.* saith the Lord   *Eze 31:10*
God
T. saith the Lord God; In   *Eze 31:15*
the day
To whom art thou *t.* like in   *Eze 31:18*
glory

T. saith the Lord God; I will   *Eze 32:3*
For *t.* saith the Lord God;   *Eze 32:11*
The sword of
T. ye speak, saying, If our   *Eze 33:10*
T. saith the Lord God; Ye   *Eze 33:25*
eat
Say thou *t.* unto them   *Eze 33:27*
T. saith the Lord God; As I   *Eze 33:27*
live
T. saith the Lord God unto   *Eze 34:2*
T. saith the Lord God;   *Eze 34:10*
Behold, I
t. saith the Lord God;   *Eze 34:11;*
Behold   *34:17*
t. saith the Lord God unto   *Eze 34:20*
them
T. shall they know that I the   *Eze 34:30*
Lord
T. saith the Lord God;   *Eze 35:3*
Behold, O
T. will I make mount Seir   *Eze 35:7*
most
T. with your mouth ye have   *Eze 35:13*
boasted
T. saith the Lord God: *Eze 35:14*
When the
T. saith the Lord God;   *Eze 36:2;*
Because   *36:3*
T. saith the Lord God to the   *Eze 36:4*
Therefore *t.* saith the Lord   *Eze 36:5*
God
T. saith the Lord God;   *Eze 36:6*
Behold, I
t. saith the Lord God; I have   *Eze 36:7*
lifted
T. saith the Lord God;   *Eze 36:13*
Because
T. saith the Lord God: I do   *Eze 36:22*
not
T. saith the Lord God; In   *Eze 36:33*
the day
T. saith the Lord God; I   *Eze 36:37*
will yet
T. saith the Lord God unto   *Eze 37:5*
these
T. saith the Lord God; Come   *Eze 37:9*
from
T. saith the Lord God   *Eze 37:12;*
    37:19, 21
T. saith the Lord God;   *Eze 38:3*
Behold, I
T. saith the Lord God; It   *Eze 38:10*
shall
T. saith the Lord God; In   *Eze 38:14*
that day
T. saith the Lord God; Art   *Eze 38:17*
thou he
T. will I magnify myself,   *Eze 38:23*
and sanctify
T. saith the Lord God;   *Eze 39:1*
Behold, I
T. shall they cleanse the   *Eze 39:16*
land
t. saith the Lord God; Speak   *Eze 39:17*
unto
T. ye shall be filled at my   *Eze 39:20*
table with
t. saith the Lord God; Now   *Eze 39:25*
will I
t. saith the Lord God; These   *Eze 43:18*
are
t. shalt thou cleanse and   *Eze 43:20*
purge it
T. saith the Lord God: O ye   *Eze 44:6*
house
T. saith the Lord God; No   *Eze 44:9*
stranger
T. saith the Lord God; Let it   *Eze 45:9*
T. saith the Lord God; In   *Eze 45:18*
the first
T. saith the Lord God; The   *Eze 46:1*
gate of
T. shall they prepare the   *Eze 46:15*
lamb, and
T. saith the Lord God; If   *Eze 46:16*
T. saith the Lord God; This   *Eze 47:13*
shall
T. Melzar took away the   *Da 1:16*
portion of
said *t.* unto him; Destroy   *Da 2:24*
not the
said *t.* unto him; I have found   *Da 2:25*
T. were the visions of mine   *Da 4:10*
head in
He cried aloud, and said *t.,*   *Da 4:14*
Hew
and said *t.* unto him, King   *Da 6:6*
Darius
they said *t.* unto it, Arise,   *Da 7:5*
devour

T. he said, The fourth beast shall | Da 7:23
upright ones with him; t. | Da 11:17
shall he do
T. shall he do in the most | Da 11:39
strong holds
t. judgment springeth up as | Ho 10:4
hemlock
T. saith the Lord; For | Am 1:3; 1:6, 11, 13
T. saith the Lord; For three | Am 2:1; 2:4, 6
Is it not even t. O ye children | Am 2:11
Therefore t. saith the Lord | Am 3:11
God
T. saith the Lord; As the | Am 3:12
shepherd
Therefore t. will I do unto | Am 4:12
thee, O
t. saith the Lord God; The | Am 5:3
city that
t. saith the Lord unto the | Am 5:4
house of
the Lord, saith t.; Wailing | Am 5:16
shall be
T. hath the Lord God shewed | Am 7:1; 7:4
T. he shewed me; and, behold | Am 7:7
For t. Amos saith, Jeroboam | Am 7:11
shall
t. saith the Lord; Thy wife | Am 7:17
shall
T. hath the Lord God shewed | Am 8:1
unto
T. saith the Lord concerning | Ob 1
T. saith the Lord; Behold, | Mic 2:3
against
T. saith the Lord, concerning | Mic 3:5
t. shall he deliver us from the | Mic 5:6
T. saith the Lord; Though | Na 1:12
they
yet t. shall they be cut down | Na 1:12
T. speaketh the Lord of hosts | Hag 1:2
therefore t. saith the Lord of | Hag 1:5
hosts
T. saith the Lord of hosts; | Hag 1:7
Consider
For t. saith the Lord of hosts; | Hag 2:6
Yet
T. saith the Lord of hosts; | Hag 2:11
Ask now
T. saith the Lord of hosts | Zec 1:3; 1:4
T. saith the Lord of hosts; I | Zec 1:14
am
Therefore t. saith the Lord; I | Zec 1:16
am
T. saith the Lord of hosts; | Zec 1:17
My
For t. saith the Lord of hosts; | Zec 2:8
After
T. saith the Lord of hosts; | Zec 3:7
If thou
T. speaketh the Lord of hosts | Zec 6:12; 7:9
T. the land was desolate after | Zec 7:14
them
T. saith the Lord of hosts; | Zec 8:2
I was
T. saith the Lord; I am | Zec 8:3
returned
T. saith the Lord of hosts; | Zec 8:4
There
T. saith the Lord of hosts; If | Zec 8:6
it be
T. saith the Lord of hosts; | Zec 8:7
Behold
T. saith the Lord of hosts; | Zec 8:9
Let
For t. saith the Lord of | Zec 8:14
hosts; As I
T. saith the Lord of hosts; | Zec 8:19
The fast
T. saith the Lord of hosts; It | Zec 8:20
shall
T. saith the Lord of hosts; In | Zec 8:23
those
T. saith the Lord my God; | Zec 11:4
Feed
t. saith the Lord of hosts, | Mal 1:4
They shall
t. ye brought an offering; | Mal 1:13
should I
for t. it is written by the | M't 2:5
prophet
for t. it becometh us to fulfil | M't 3:15
all
T. have ye the commandment | M't 15:6
be fulfilled, that t. it must | M't 26:54
be
this man t. speak blasphemies | M'k 2:7

T. hath the Lord dealt with | Lu 1:25
me in
Son, why hast thou t. dealt | Lu 2:48
with us
While he t. spake, there came | Lu 9:34
t. saying thou reproachest us | Lu 11:45
also
Even t. shall it be in the day | Lu 17:30
stood and prayed t. with | Lu 18:11
himself
when he had t. spoken, he | Lu 19:28
went
t. shall ye say unto him, | Lu 19:31
Because
answered and said, Suffer ye | Lu 22:51
t. far
and having said t. he gave up | Lu 23:46
And as they t. spake, Jesus | Lu 24:36
himself
when he had t. spoken, he | Lu 24:40
shewed
said unto them, T. it is | Lu 24:46
written
t. it behoved Christ to suffer | Lu 24:46
with his journey, sat t. on the | Joh 4:6
well
When he had t. spoken, he | Joh 9:6
spat on
when he t. had spoken, he | Joh 11:43
cried
If we let him t. alone, all | Joh 11:48
men will
When Jesus had t. said, he | Joh 13:21
was
when he had t. spoken, one | Joh 18:22
of the
when she had t. said, she | Joh 20:14
turned
And when he had t. spoken, | Ac 19:41
he
when he had t. spoken, he | Ac 20:36
kneeled
T. saith the Holy Ghost, So | Ac 21:11
shall
And as he t. spake for | Ac 26:24
himself
when he had t. spoken, the | Ac 26:30
king
when he had t. spoken, | Ac 27:35
he took
it, Why hast thou made me t. | Ro 9:20
t. are the secrets of his | 1Co 14:25
heart made
When I therefore was t. | 2Co 1:17
minded
because we t. judge, that if | 2Co 5:14
one died
as many as be perfect, be t. | Ph'p 3:15
minded
salvation, though we t. speak | Heb 6:9
when these things were t. | Heb 9:6
ordained
t. I saw the horses in the | Re 9:17
vision
be, because thou hast judged t. | Re 16:5
T. with violence shall that | Re 18:21
great

THYATIRA

a seller of purple, of the city | Ac 16:14
of T.
and unto T. and unto Sardis | Ro 1:11
the angel of the church in T. | Re 2:18
write
you I say, and unto the rest in | Re 2:24
T.

THYINE

silk, and scarlet, and all t. | Re 18:12
wood

THYSELF

separate t. I pray thee, from | Ge 13:9
me: if
the persons, and take the | Ge 14:21
goods to t.
and submit t. under her hands | Ge 16:9
brother: keep that thou hast | Ge 33:9
unto t.
yet exaltest thou t. against my | Ex 9:17
people
thou refuse to humble t. | Ex 10:3
before me
take heed to t. see my face | Ex 10:28
no more
why sittest thou t. alone, and | Ex 18:14
all the

thou art not able to perform | Ex 18:18
it t. alone
so shall it be easier for t. and | Ex 18:22
they
Thou shalt not bow down t. to | Ex 20:5
them
present t. there to me in the | Ex 34:2
top of the
Take heed to t. lest thou | Ex 34:12
make a
and make an atonement for t. | Le 9:7
and for
neighbour's wife to defile t. | Le 18:20
with her
with any beast to defile t. | Le 18:23
therewith
thou shalt love thy neighbour | Le 19:18
as t.
you, and thou shalt love him | Le 19:34
as t.
thee, that thou bear it not t. | Nu 11:17
alone
thou make t. altogether a | Nu 16:13
prince over
Only take heed to t. and keep | De 4:9
thy
shalt not bow down t. unto | De 5:9
them, nor
nations greater and mightier | De 9:1
than t.
Take heed to t. that thou | De 12:13
offer not thy
Take heed to t. that thou | De 12:19
forsake not
Take heed to t. that thou be | De 12:30
not
spoil thereof, shalt thou take | De 20:14
unto t.
go astray, and hide t. from | De 22:1
them
do likewise; thou mayest not | De 22:3
hide t.
by the way, and hide t. from | De 22:4
them
vesture, wherewith thou | De 22:12
coverest t.
when thou wilt ease t. | De 23:13
abroad, thou
thou shalt not anoint t. with | De 28:40
the oil
and cut down for t. there in | Jos 17:15
the land
Wash t. therefore, and anoint | Ru 3:3
thee
make not t. known unto the | Ru 3:3
man
redeem thou my right to t.; for | Ru 4:6
I
thee, take heed to t. until the | 1Sa 19:2
morning
abide in a secret place, and | 1Sa 19:2
hide t.
there be in me iniquity, slay | 1Sa 20:8
me t.
to the place where thou | 1Sa 20:19
didst hide t.
from avenging t. with thine | 1Sa 25:26
own hand
trees, that then thou shalt | 2Sa 5:24
bestir t.
hast confirmed to t. thy people | 2Sa 7:24
Israel
down on thy bed, and make | 2Sa 13:5
t. sick
I pray thee, feign t. to be a | 2Sa 14:2
mourner
and anoint not t. with oil, | 2Sa 14:2
but be as a
and thou t. wouldest have | 2Sa 18:13
set
wouldest have set t. against | 2Sa 18:13
me
merciful thou wilt shew t. | 2Sa 22:26
merciful
upright man thou wilt shew | 2Sa 22:26
t. upright
With the pure thou wilt | 2Sa 22:27
shew t. pure
froward thou wilt shew t. | 2Sa 22:27
unsavoury
strong therefore, and shew t. a | 1Ki 2:2
man
and whithersoever thou turnest | 1Ki 2:3
t.
and hast not asked for t. long | 1Ki 3:11
life
neither hast asked riches for | 1Ki 3:11
t. nor
t. understanding to discern | 1Ki 3:11
judgment

Come home with me, and refresh *t.* — *1Ki 13:7*

and disguise *t.* that thou be not known — *1Ki 14:2*

why feignest thou *t.* to be another — *1Ki 14:6*

hide *t.* by the brook Cherith, that is — *1Ki 17:3*

year, saying, Go, shew *t.* unto Ahab — *1Ki 18:1*

Go, strengthen *t.* and mark, and see — *1Ki 20:22*

thy judgment be; *t.* hast decided it — *1Ki 20:40*

sold *t.* to work evil in the sight of the — *1Ki 21:20*

go into an inner chamber to hide *t.* — *1Ki 22:25*

thou hast humbled *t.* before the Lord — *2Ki 22:19*

advise *t.* what word I shall bring — *1Ch 21:12*

asked wisdom and knowledge for *t.* — *2Ch 1:11*

go into an inner chamber to hide *t.* — *2Ch 18:24*

thou hast joined *t.* with Ahaziah — *2Ch 20:37*

house, which were better than *t.* — *2Ch 21:13*

and thou didst humble *t.* before God — *2Ch 34:27*

and humbledst *t.* before me — *2Ch 34:27*

Think not with *t.* that thou shalt — *Es 4:13*

prepare *t.* to the search of their — *Job 8:8*

thou shewest *t.* marvellous upon me — *Job 10:16*

dost thou restrain wisdom to *t.* — *Job 15:8*

Acquaint now *t.* with him, and be — *Job 22:21*

hand thou opposest *t.* against me — *Job 30:21*

Deck *t.* now with majesty — *Job 40:10*

and array *t.* with glory and beauty — *Job 40:10*

lift up *t.* because of the rage of mine — *Ps 7:6*

why hidest thou *t.* in times of trouble — *Ps 10:1*

merciful thou wilt shew *t.* merciful — *Ps 18:25*

man thou wilt shew *t.* upright — *Ps 18:25*

With the pure thou wilt shew *t.* pure — *Ps 18:26*

froward thou wilt shew *t.* froward — *Ps 18:26*

Stir up *t.* and awake to my judgment — *Ps 35:23*

Fret not *t.* because of evildoers — *Ps 37:1*

Delight *t.* also in the Lord; and he — *Ps 37:4*

fret not *t.* because of him who — *Ps 37:7*

fret not *t.* in any wise to do evil — *Ps 37:8*

thee, when thou doest well to *t.* — *Ps 40:18*

I was altogether such an one as *t.* — *Ps 50:21*

Why boastest thou *t.* in mischief, O — *Ps 52:1*

and hide not *t.* from my supplication — *Ps 55:1*

displeased; O turn *t.* to us again — *Ps 60:1*

branch that thou madest strong for *t.* — *Ps 80:15*

man whom thou madest strong for *t.* — *Ps 80:17*

turned *t.* from the fierceness of thine — *Ps 85:3*

long, Lord? wilt thou hide *t.* forever — *Ps 89:46*

whom vengeance belongeth, shew *t.* — *Ps 94:1*

Lift up *t.* thou judge of the earth — *Ps 94:2*

Who coverest *t.* with light as with a — *Ps 104:2*

Do this now, my son, and deliver *t.* — *Pr 6:3*

humble *t.* and make sure thy friend — *Pr 6:3*

Deliver *t.* as a roe from the hand of — *Pr 6:5*

thou be wise, thou shalt be wise for *t.* — *Pr 9:12*

Fret not *t.* because of evil men — *Pr 24:19*

and make it fit for *t.* in the field — *Pr 24:27*

Put not forth *t.* in the presence — *Pr 25:6*

Boast not *t.* of to morrow; for thou — *Pr 27:1*

hast done foolishly in lifting up *t.* — *Pr 30:32*

over much; neither make *t.* over wise — *Ec 7:16*

wise; why shouldest thou destroy *t.* — *Ec 7:16*

thou *t.* likewise hast cursed others — *Ec 7:22*

hide *t.* as it were for a little moment — *Isa 26:20*

at the lifting up of *t.* the nations — *Isa 33:3*

Verily thou art a God that hidest *t.* — *Isa 45:15*

Shake *t.* from the dust; arise, and sit — *Isa 52:2*

loose *t.* from the bands of thy neck — *Isa 52:2*

hast discovered *t.* to another than me — *Isa 57:8*

off, and didst debase *t.* even unto hell — *Isa 57:9*

thou hide not *t.* from thine own flesh — *Isa 58:7*

Then shalt thou delight *t.* in the Lord — *Isa 58:14*

people, to make *t.* a glorious name — *Isa 63:14*

Wilt thou refrain *t.* for these things — *Isa 64:12*

say, Stand by *t.* come not near to me — *Isa 65:5*

Hast thou not procured this unto *t.* — *Jer 2:17*

Though thou clothest *t.* with crimson — *Jer 4:30*

in vain shalt thou make *t.* fair — *Jer 4:30*

sackcloth, and wallow *t.* in ashes — *Jer 6:26*

And thou, even *t.* shalt discontinue — *Jer 17:4*

I will make thee a terror to *t.* and to — *Jer 20:4*

because thou closest *t.* in cedar — *Jer 22:15*

the redemption is thine; buy it for *t.* — *Jer 32:8*

And seekest thou great things for *t.* — *Jer 45:5*

Egypt, furnish *t.* to go into captivity — *Jer 46:19*

their valley: how long wilt thou cut *t.* — *Jer 47:5*

put up *t.* into thy scabbard, rest, and — *Jer 47:6*

give *t.* no rest; let not the apple of — *La 2:18*

Thou hast covered *t.* with a cloud — *La 3:44*

be drunken, and shalt make *t.* naked — *La 4:21*

me, Go, shut *t.* within thine house — *Eze 3:24*

thee, and madest to *t.* images of men — *Eze 16:17*

defiled *t.* in thine idols which thou — *Eze 22:4*

thou shalt take thine inheritance in *t.* — *Eze 22:16*

from whom thou didst wash *t.* — *Eze 23:40*

eyes, and deckedst *t.* with ornaments — *Eze 23:40*

thou hast lifted up *t.* in height, and — *Eze 31:10*

and prepare for *t.* thou, and all thy — *Eze 38:7*

Let thy gifts be to *t.* and give thy — *Da 5:17*

hast lifted up *t.* against the Lord of — *Da 5:23*

and to chasten *t.* before thy God, thy — *Da 10:12*

O Israel, thou hast destroyed *t.*; but — *Ho 13:9*

Though thou exalt *t.* as the eagle — *Ob 4*

house of Aphrah roll *t.* in the dust — *Mic 1:10*

Now gather *t.* in troops, O daughter — *Mic 5:1*

make *t.* many as the cankerworm — *Na 3:15*

make *t.* many as in the locusts — *Na 3:15*

Deliver *t.* O Zion, that dwellest with — *Zec 2:7*

be the Son of God, cast *t.* down — *M't 4:6*

Thou shalt not forswear *t.* but shalt — *M't 5:33*

shew *t.* to the priest, and offer — *M't 8:4*

Thou shalt love thy neighbour as *t.* — *M't 19:19; 22:39*

buildest it in three days, save *t.* — *M't 27:40*

shew *t.* to the priest, and offer for — *M'k 1:44*

Thou shalt love thy neighbour as *t.* — *M'k 12:31*

Save *t.* and come down from the — *M'k 15:30*

of God, cast *t.* down from hence — *Lu 4:9*

me this proverb, Physician, heal *t.* — *Lu 4:23*

but go, and shew *t.* to the priest — *Lu 5:14*

when thou *t.* beholdest not the beam — *Lu 6:42*

unto him, Lord, trouble not *t.*: for — *Lu 7:6*

thy mind; and thy neighbour as *t.* — *Lu 10:27*

and gird *t.* and serve me, till I have — *Lu 17:8*

be the king of the Jews, save *t.* — *Lu 23:37*

If thou be Christ, save *t.* and us — *Lu 23:39*

sent us. What sayest thou of *t.* — *Joh 1:22*

these things, shew *t.* to the world — *Joh 7:4*

him, Thou bearest record of *t.* — *Joh 8:13*

are dead: whom makest thou *t.* — *Joh 8:53*

thou, being a man, makest *t.* God — *Joh 10:33*

that thou wilt manifest *t.* unto us — *Joh 14:22*

Sayest thou this thing of *t.* or did — *Joh 18:34*

thou wast young, thou girdest *t.* — *Joh 21:18*

Go near, and join *t.* to this chariot — *Ac 8:29*

him, Gird *t.* and bind on thy sandals — *Ac 12:8*

Do *t.* no harm; for we are all here — *Ac 16:28*

take, and purify *t.* with them — *Ac 21:24*

that thou *t.* also walkest orderly — *Ac 21:24*

t. mayest take knowledge of all — *Ac 24:8*

Thou art permitted to speak for *t.* — *Ac 26:1*

a loud voice, Paul, thou art beside *t.* — *Ac 26:24*

another, thou condemnest *t.* — *Ro 2:1*

treasurest up unto *t.* wrath against — *Ro 2:5*

thou *t.* art a guide of the blind — *Ro 2:19*

another, teachest thou not *t.* — *Ro 2:21*

Thou shalt love thy neighbour as *t.* — *Ro 13:9*

thou faith? have it to *t.* before God — *Ro 14:22*

Thou shalt love thy neighbour as *t.* — *Ga 5:14*

considering *t.* lest thou also be — *Ga 6:1*

to behave *t.* in the house of God — *1Ti 3:15*

exercise *t.* rather unto godliness — *1Ti 4:7*

these things; give *t.* wholly to them — *1Ti 4:15*

Take heed unto *t.* and unto doing — *1Ti 4:16*

this thou shalt both save *t.* — *1Ti 4:16*

of other men's sins: keep *t.* pure — *1Ti 5:22*

godliness: from such withdraw *t.* — *1Ti 6:5*

Study to show *t.* approved unto — *2Ti 2:15*

showing *t.* a pattern of good works — *Tit 2:7*

Thou shalt love thy neighbour as *t.* — *Jas 2:8*

THWARTS

t. just man's testimony (B) — *Ex 23:8*

t. schemes of crafty (B) — *Job 5:12*

TIBERIAS

of Galilee, which is the sea of *Joh 6:1*
T.
there came other boats from *Joh 6:23*
T.
to the disciples at the sea of *Joh 21:1*
T.

TIBERIUS

year of the reign of T. Caesar *Lu 3:1*

TIBHATH

Likewise from T. and from *1Ch 18:8*
Chun

TIBNI

the people followed T. the *1Ki 16:21*
son of
people that followed T. the *1Ki 16:22*
son of
so T. died, and Omri *1Ki 16:22*
reigned

TIDAL

of Elam, and T. king of *Ge 14:1*
nations
Elam, and with T. king of *Ge 14:9*
nations

TIDINGS

when Laban heard the t. of *Ge 29:13*
Jacob
when the people heard these *Ex 33:4*
evil t.
heard this adverse message *Ex 33:4*
(B)
heard the t. that the ark of *1Sa 4:19*
God
the report (B) *1Sa 4:19; 2Sa 4:4*
and told the t. in the ears of *1Sa 11:4*
the news (A) *1Sa 11:4; 1Ki 2:28*
2Sa 4:4; 18:20, 25, 26, 31; Jer 37:5
          1Ch 10:9; Jer 37:5
him the t. of the men of *1Sa 11:5*
Jabesh
upon Saul when he heard *1Sa 11:6*
those t.
nor woman alive, to bring t. *1Sa 27:11*
to Gath
to carry the t. (E) *1Sa 31:9*
five years old when the t. came *2Sa 4:4*
the news (R) *2Sa 4:4; 1Ki 2:28*
thinking to have brought *2Sa 4:10*
good t.
have given him a reward for *2Sa 4:10*
his t.
good news (A) *2Sa 4:10;*
1Ki 1:42; 2Ki 7:9; Isa 41:27; Lu 1:19;
2:10; 8:1; Ac 13:32; 1Th 3:6
good news (B) *2Sa 4:10;*
18:19, 31; 1Ki 1:42; 2Ki 7:9; 1Ch 10:9;
          Isa 41:27; Lu 2:10; 8:1
good news (R) *2Sa 4:10;*
1Ki 1:42; 2Ki 7:9 ; 1Ch 10:9; Lu 1:19;
2:10; 8:1; Ac 13:32; Ro 10:15; 1Th 3:6
that t. came to David, *2Sa 13:30*
saying
me now run, and bear the *2Sa 18:19*
king t.
Thou shalt not bear t. this *2Sa 18:20*
day
the news (B) *2Sa 18:20;*
18:22, 25, 26; Jer 20:15; 37:5
but thou shalt bear t. *2Sa 18:20*
another day
but this day thou shalt bear *2Sa 18:20*
no t.
seeing that thou hast no t. *2Sa 18:22*
ready
be alone, there is t. in his *2Sa 18:25*
mouth
the king said, He also *2Sa 18:26*
bringeth t.
man and cometh with good *2Sa 18:27*
t.
the good reports (B) *2Sa 18:27*
Cushi said, T. my lord the *2Sa 18:31*
king
valiant man, and bringest *1Ki 1:42*
good t.
Then t. came to Joab: for *1Ki 2:28*
Joab
the report (B) *1Ki 2:28*
for I am sent to thee with *1Ki 14:6*
heavy t.

heavy news (A) *1Ki 14:6*
                1Ki 14:6
bad news (B) *2Ki 7:9*
this day is a day of good t. *2Ki 7:9*
and we
to carry t. unto their idols, *1Ch 10:9*
and to
proclaimed glad t. (A)(B)(E) *Ps 40:9*
He shall not be afraid of *Ps 112:7*
evil t.
evil report (B) *Ps 112:7*
O Zion, that bringest good t. *Isa 40:9*
get
O Jerusalem, that bringest *Isa 40:9*
good t.
one that bringeth good t. *Isa 41:27*
feet of him that bringeth good *Isa 52:7*
t.
that bringeth good t. of good, *Isa 52:7*
that
to preach good t. unto the *Isa 61:1*
meek
man who brought t. to my *Jer 20:15*
father
the news (R) *Jer 20:15; 37:5; Ac 11:22*
Jerusalem heard t. of them *Jer 37:5*
Arnad: for they have heard *Jer 49:23*
evil t.
bad news (A) *Jer 49:23*
that thou shalt answer, For *Eze 21:7*
the t.
But t. out of the east and *Da 11:44*
out of
rumors from the east and *Da 11:44*
north (A)
report from the east and *Da 11:44*
north (B)
feet of him that bringeth good *Na 1:15*
t.
thee, and to shew thee these *Lu 1:19*
glad t.
good news (N) *Lu 1:19;*
          2:10; 8:1; Ro 10:15; 1Th 3:6
good news (P) *Lu 1:19; 8:1; Ac 13:32*
I bring you good t. of great *Lu 2:10*
joy
glorious news (P) *Lu 2:10*
shewing the glad t. of the *Lu 8:1*
kingdom
told glad t. (B) *Ac 8:12*
t. of these things came unto *Ac 11:22*
rumors of this came (A) *Ac 11:22*
word of this came (B) *Ac 11:22*
news of this reached the *Ac 11:22*
church (N)
And we declare unto you *Ac 13:32*
glad t.
proclaim good t. (A) *Ac 16:10*
t. came unto the chief *Ac 21:31*
captain of
word came to the *Ac 21:31*
commandant (A)(R)
report reached the *Ac 21:31*
commandant (B)(N)(P)
and bring glad t. of good *Ro 10:15*
things
the glad, good news (B) *Ro 10:15*
bring glad t. of good things *Ro 10:15*
(E)(P)
proclaimed glad t. (A)(N) *1Th 2:9*
and brought us good t. of your *1Th 3:6*
faith
the good message (B) *1Th 3:6*
definite news (P) *1Th 3:6*

TIDY

swept and t. (N) *M't 12:44*

TIE

no yoke, and t. the kine to the *1Sa 6:7*
cart
and t. them about thy neck *Pr 6:21*

TIED

And they t. unto it a lace of *Ex 39:31*
blue
milch kine, and t. them to the *1Sa 6:10*
cart
but horses t. and asses t. and *2Ki 7:10*
straightway ye shall find an *M't 21:2*
ass t.
ye shall find a colt t. *M'k 11:2*
whereon
and found the colt t. by the *M'k 11:4*
door
your entering ye shall find a *Lu 19:30*
colt t.

TIERS

light in three t. (S) *1Ki 7:4; 7:5*

TIGHTENED

t. the belt of truth (A)(B) *Eph 6:14*

TIGLATH-PILESER

Israel came T. king of *2Ki 15:29*
Assyria
so Ahaz sent messengers to *2Ki 16:7*
T.
Ahaz went to Damascus to *2Ki 16:10*
meet T.

TIKVAH

wife of Shallum the son of *2Ki 22:14*
T.
and Jahaziah the son of T. *Ezr 10:15*
were

TIKVATH

the wife of Shallum the son *2Ch 34:22*
of T.

TILE

son of man, take thee a t. and *Eze 4:1*
lay it
get a clay tablet (B) *Eze 4:1*
take a brick (R) *Eze 4:1*

TILGATH-PILNESER

whom T. king of Assyria *1Ch 5:6*
carried
and the spirit of T. king of *1Ch 5:26*
Assyria
T. king of Assyria came *2Ch 28:20*
unto him

TILING

let him down through the t. *Lu 5:19*

TILL

was not a man to t. the ground *Ge 2:5*
put him in the garden to t. it *Ge 2:15*
(S)
t. thou return unto the ground *Ge 3:19*
to t. the ground from whence *Ge 3:23*
he
I cannot do any thing t. *Ge 19:22*
thou be
t. they roll the stone from the *Ge 29:8*
well's
house, t. Shelah my son be *Ge 38:11*
grown
give me a pledge, t. thou *Ge 38:17*
send it
t. thy people pass over, O *Ex 15:16*
Lord
t. the people pass over, which *Ex 15:16*
thou
no man leave of it t. the *Ex 16:19*
morning
And they laid it up t. the *Ex 16:24*
morning
t. Moses had done speaking *Ex 34:33*
with them
t. the day that it was taken *Ex 40:37*
up
t. Miriam was brought in *Nu 12:15*
again
stone them with stones, t. *De 17:5*
they die
thee t. thou be destroyed *De 28:45*
t. all the people that were men *Jos 5:6*
in the camp, t. they were whole *Jos 5:8*
t. we have drawn them from *Jos 8:6*
slaughter, t. they were *Jos 10:20*
consumed
they tarried t. they were *J'g 3:25*
ashamed
t. thou come unto Gaza, and *J'g 6:4*
left no
even t. thou come to Minnith *J'g 11:33*
Samson lay t. midnight, and *J'g 16:3*
arose
where her lord was, t. it was *J'g 19:26*
light
and abode there t. even before *J'g 21:2*
God
tarry for them t. they were *Ru 1:13*
grown

shalt thou tarry, *t.* I come to   *1Sa 10:8*
thee
will not sit down *t.* he come   *1Sa 16:11*
hither
t. I know what God will do   *1Sa 22:3*
for me
or ought else, *t.* the sun be   *2Sa 3:35*
down
servants, shall *t.* the land for   *2Sa 9:10*
him
taketh away dung, *t.* it be   *1Ki 14:10*
all gone
t. the blood gushed out upon   *1Ki 18:28*
them
they urged him *t.* he was   *2Ki 2:17*
ashamed
he sat on her knees, *t.* noon   *2Ki 4:20*
if we tarry *t.* the morning light   *2Ki 7:9*
Samaria, *t.* he had destroyed   *2Ki 10:17*
him
Aphek, *t.* thou have   *2Ki 13:17*
consumed
Syria *t.* thou hadst   *2Ki 13:19*
consumed it
t. he had filled Jerusalem   *2Ki 21:16*
from one
helped, *t.* he was strong   *2Ch 26:15*
help them, *t.* the work was   *2Ch 29:34*
ended
his people, *t.* there was no   *2Ch 36:16*
remedy
t. there stood up a priest with   *Ezr 2:63*
Urim
t. the matter came to Darius   *Ezr 5:5*
us *t.* thou hadst consumed us   *Ezr 9:14*
me over *t.* I come into Judah   *Ne 2:7*
t. we come in the midst   *Ne 4:11*
among
the morning *t.* the stars   *Ne 4:21*
appeared
t. there stood up a priest with   *Ne 7:65*
Urim
not be opened *t.* after the   *Ne 13:19*
sabbath
alone *t.* I swallow down my   *Job 7:19*
spittle
T. he fill thy mouth with   *Job 8:21*
laughing
t. he shall accomplish, as an   *Job 14:6*
t. the heavens be no more,   *Job 14:12*
they
will I wait, *t.* my change   *Job 14:14*
comes
t. I die I will not remove   *Job 27:5*
mine
Elihu had waited *t.* Job had   *Job 32:4*
spoken
out his wickedness *t.* thou   *Ps 10:15*
find none
turn again *t.* they were   *Ps 18:37*
consumed
t. every one submit himself   *Ps 68:30*
with
T. a dart strike through his   *Pr 7:23*
liver
a wise man keepeth it in *t.*   *Pr 29:11*
afterward
t. I might see what was that   *Ec 2:3*
good
nor awake my love, *t.* he please   *Ca 2:7;*
                       3:5
field to field, *t.* there be no   *Isa 5:8*
place
until night, *t.* wine inflame   *Isa 5:11*
them
not be purged from you *t.* ye   *Isa 22:14*
die
t. the Assyrian founded it for   *Isa 23:13*
them
t. ye be left as a beacon   *Isa 30:17*
upon the top
young asses that *t.* the   *Isa 30:24*
ground (S)
I reckoned *t.* morning, that,   *Isa 38:13*
as a
t. he have set judgment in the   *Isa 42:4*
give him no rest, *t.* he   *Isa 62:7*
establish
t. he make Jerusalem a praise   *Isa 62:7*
bury in Tophet, *t.* there be no   *Jer 7:32*
place
them, *t.* I have consumed   *Jer 9:16*
them
in Tophet, *t.* there be no   *Jer 19:11*
place to bury
t. he have performed the   *Jer 23:20*
thoughts
t. they be consumed from off   *Jer 24:10*
they shall *t.* it, and dwell   *Jer 27:11*
therein

they will destroy *t.* they have   *Jer 49:9*
enough
them, *t.* I have consumed   *Jer 49:37*
them
t. he had cast them out from   *Jer 52:3*
his
in prison *t.* the day of his   *Jer 52:11*
death
T. the Lord look down, and   *La 3:50*
behold
t. thou hast ended the days of   *Eze 4:8*
thy
even *t.* now have I not eaten   *Eze 4:14*
of that
t. I have caused my fury to   *Eze 24:13*
rest
t. iniquity was found in thee   *Eze 28:15*
t. ye have scattered them   *Eze 34:21*
abroad
t. the buriers have buried it   *Eze 39:15*
in the
And ye shall eat fat *t.* ye be   *Eze 39:19*
full, and
and drink blood *t.* ye be   *Eze 39:19*
drunken
t. a man come over against   *Eze 47:20*
before me, *t.* the time be   *Da 2:9*
changed
sawest *t.* that a stone was cut   *Da 2:34*
out
field, *t.* seven times pass over   *Da 4:23*
him
t. thou know that the most   *Da 4:25*
High
t. his hairs were grown like   *Da 4:33*
eagles
t. he knew that the most high   *Da 5:21*
God
laboured *t.* the going down of   *Da 6:14*
the
t. the wings thereof were   *Da 7:4*
plucked
t. the thrones were cast down   *Da 7:9*
beheld even *t.* the beast was   *Da 7:11*
slain
t. three whole weeks were   *Da 10:3*
fulfilled
t. the indignation be   *Da 11:36*
accomplished
and sealed *t.* the time of the   *Da 12:9*
end
But go thou thy way *t.* the   *Da 12:13*
end be
t. they acknowledge their   *Ho 5:15*
offence
t. he come and rain   *Ho 10:12*
righteousness
not have stolen *t.* they had   *Ob 5*
enough
t. he might see what would   *Jon 4:5*
gnaw not the bones *t.* the   *Zep 3:3*
morrow
not *t.* she had brought forth   *M't 1:25*
her
t. it came and stood over   *M't 2:9*
where the
T. heaven and earth pass, one   *M't 5:18*
jot
pass from the law, *t.* all be   *M't 5:18*
fulfilled
t. thou hast paid the   *M't 5:26*
uttermost
and there abide *t.* ye go   *M't 10:11*
thence
Israel, *t.* the Son of man be   *M't 10:23*
come
t. he send forth judgment   *M't 12:20*
meal, *t.* the whole was   *M't 13:33*
leavened
t. they see the Son of man   *M't 16:28*
coming
and I forgive him? *t.* seven   *M't 18:21*
times
prison, *t.* he should pay the   *M't 18:30*
debt
t. he should pay all that was   *M't 18:34*
due
t. I make thine enemies thy   *M't 22:44*
t. ye shall say, Blessed is he   *M't 23:39*
that
pass, *t.* all these things be   *M't 24:34*
fulfilled
abide, *t.* ye depart from that   *M'k 6:10*
place
t. they have seen the kingdom   *M'k 9:1*
of
t. the Son of man were risen   *M'k 9:9*
t. I make thine enemies thy   *M'k 12:36*

pass, *t.* all these things be   *M'k 13:30*
done
t. the day of his shewing unto   *Lu 1:80*
t. they see the kingdom of   *Lu 9:27*
God
straitened *t.* it be   *Lu 12:50*
accomplished
t. thou hast paid the very last   *Lu 12:59*
mite
t. I shall dig about it, and   *Lu 13:8*
dung it
meal, *t.* the whole was   *Lu 13:21*
leavened
and seek diligently *t.* she find   *Lu 15:8*
me, *t.* I have eaten and   *Lu 17:8*
drunken
said unto them, Occupy *t.* I   *Lu 19:13*
come
T. I make thine enemies   *Lu 20:43*
thy
not pass away, *t.* all be   *Lu 21:32*
fulfilled
crow, *t.* thou hast denied me   *Joh 13:38*
thrice
If I will that he tarry *t.* I   *Joh 21:22;*
come   *21:23*
T. another king arose, which   *Ac 7:18*
the cities, *t.* he came to   *Ac 8:40*
Cæsarea
even *t.* break of day, so he   *Ac 20:11*
departed
children, *t.* we were out of   *Ac 21:5*
the city
nor drink *t.* they had killed   *Ac 23:12*
Paul
nor drink *t.* they have killed   *Ac 23:21*
him
kept *t.* I might send him to   *Ac 25:21*
Cæsar
prophets, from morning *t.*   *Ac 28:23*
evening
the Lord's death *t.* he come   *1Co 11:26*
t. he hath put all enemies   *1Co 15:25*
under
t. the seed shall come to   *Ga 3:19*
whom
T. we all come in the unity   *Eph 4:13*
of the
offence *t.* the day of Christ   *Ph'p 1:10*
T. I come, give attendance   *1Ti 4:13*
t. his enemies be made his   *Heb 10:13*
footstool
have already hold fast *t.* I   *Re 2:25*
come
t. we have sealed the servants   *Re 7:3*
of
t. the seven plagues of the   *Re 15:8*
seven
t. the thousand years shall be   *Re 20:3*

TILLAGE

the work of the field for *t.*   *1Ch 27:26*
of the
the tithes in all the cities of   *Ne 10:37*
our *t.*
Much food is in the *t.* of the   *Pr 13:23*
poor

TILLED

t. with a hoe (B)   *Isa 7:25*
you, and ye shall be *t.* and   *Eze 36:9*
sown
And the desolate land shall   *Eze 36:34*
be *t.*
for whom it is *t.* (B)(E)   *Heb 6:7*
by whom it is *t.* (S)   *Heb 6:7*

TILLER

but Cain was a *t.* of the ground   *Ge 4:2*
I am a *t.* of the ground   *Zec 13:5*
(E)(R)
my Father is the *T.* (B)   *Joh 15:1*

TILLERS

t. of the soil (R)   *Joe 1:11*
tillers (B)   *M't 21:33;*
          21:34, 40; M'k 12:2

TILLEST

When thou *t.* the ground, it   *Ge 4:12*
shall

TILLETH

He that *t.* his land shall be   *Pr 12:11*
He that *t.* his land shall have   *Pr 28:19*
plenty

TILON

and Rinnah, Ben-hanan, and   1Ch 4:20
T.

TIMAEUS

blind Bartimæus, the son of   M'k 10:46
T.

TIMBER

and in carving of t. to work in   Ex 31:5
all
the stones of it, and the t.   Le 14:45
thereof
that can skill to hew t. like   1Ki 5:6
unto the
thy desire concerning t. of   1Ki 5:8
cedar
of cedar, and concerning t. of   1Ki 5:8
fir
prepared t. and stones to   1Ki 5:18
build the
rested on the house with t. of   1Ki 6:10
cedar
stones of Ramah, and the t.   1Ki 15:22
thereof
to buy t. and hewed stone to   2Ki 12:12
repair
to buy t. and hewn stone to   2Ki 22:6
repair
and t. of cedars, with   1Ch 14:1
masons and
t. also and stone have I   1Ch 22:14
prepared
and workers of stone and t.   1Ch 22:15
can skill to cut t. in Lebanon   2Ch 2:8
to prepare me t. in abundance   2Ch 2:9
thy servants, the hewers that   2Ch 2:10
cut t.
brass, in iron, in stone, and   2Ch 2:14
in t.
stones of Ramah, and the t.   2Ch 16:6
thereof
hewn stone, and t. for   2Ch 34:11
couplings
stones, and t. is laid in the   Ezr 5:8
walls
of great stones, and a row of   Ezr 6:4
new t.
let t. be pulled down from his   Ezr 6:11
house
he may give me t. to make   Ne 2:8
beams
thy stones and thy t. and thy   Eze 26:12
dust
beam out of the t. shall   Hab 2:11
answer it
the t. thereof and the stones   Zec 5:4
thereof

TIMBREL

timbrel (S)   Ge 31:27;
      1Sa 10:5; Isa 5:12
of Aaron, took a t. in her   Ex 15:20
hand
a tambourine (B)   Ex 15:20
They take the t. and harp   Job 21:12
tambourine and lyre (B)   Job 21:12
      Ps 149:3
tambourine (R)   Job 21:12
a psalm, and bring hither the   Ps 81:2
t.
sing praises unto him with   Ps 149:3
the t.
Praise him with the t. and   Ps 150:4
dance
praise him with a tambourine   Ps 150:4
(A)
timbrel (R)   Isa 5:12

TIMBRELS

women went out after her   Ex 15:20
with t.
tambourines (A)   Ex 15:20;
      2Sa 6:5; 1Ch 13:8
came out to meet him with t.   J'g 11:34
timbrels (A)(E)   1Sa 18:6;
      Isa 24:8; 30:32; Jer 31:4
timbrels (S)   1Sa 18:6;
      Isa 24:8; 30:32; Jer 31:4; Eze 28:13
harps, and on psalteries, and   2Sa 6:5
on t.
tambourines (A)   2Sa 6:5;
      1Ch 13:8; Ps 68:25
tambourines (R)   2Sa 6:5; 1Ch 13:8
and with psalteries, and with   1Ch 13:8
t.

were the damsels playing with   Ps 68:25
t.
timbrels (B)   Isa 24:8; 30:32

TIME

according to the t. of life   Ge 18:10;
                     18:14
t. that women go out to draw   Ge 24:11
water
from the t. he had made him   Ge 39:5
overseer
custody for some t. (A)(R)   Ge 40:4
the t. drew nigh that Israel   Ge 47:29
must die
only he shall pay for loss of   Ex 21:19
his t.
if beyond the t. of her   Le 15:25
separation
a wife besides the other in   Le 18:18
her life t.
them, by day t. in a pillar   Nu 13:20
grapes
what t. the fire devoured 250   Nu 14:14
of a cloud
men   Nu 26:10
the t. of your exodus (B)   De 16:6
such t. thou put the sickle to   De 16:9
the corn
at the t. of the going down   Jos 10:27;
of the sun Joshua   2Ch 18:34
commanded
their land did Joshua take at   Jos 10:42
one t.
all t. the house of God was   J'g 18:31
in Shiloh
since the t. I commanded   2Sa 7:11
judges
at the t. when kings go forth   2Sa 11:1
to battle
to this t. (S)   2Sa 15:34;
      1Ch 12:29; Isa 18:2, 7
against eight hundred he slew   2Sa 23:8
at one t.
is it t. to receive money and   2Ki 5:26
garments
were to come from t. to t.   1Ch 9:25
with them
peace, and at such a t.   Ezr 4:10;
      4:17; 7:12
people are many, and it is a   Ezr 10:13
t. of rain
when wilt thou return? I set   Ne 2:6
him a t.
what t. they wax warm they   Job 6:17
vanish
of judgment, who shall set me   Job 9:19
a t. to plead
it shall be accomplished   Job 15:32
before his t.
wicked, which were cut   Job 22:16
down out of t.
I reserved against the t. of   Job 38:23
trouble
knowest thou the t. they   Job 39:1;
bring forth   39:2
in a t. when thou mayest be   Ps 32:6
found
they shall not be ashamed in   Ps 37:19
the evil t.
Lord will deliver him in t. of   Ps 41:1
trouble
what t. I am afraid, I will   Ps 53:3
trust in thee
my prayer is to thee in an   Ps 69:13
acceptable t.
their t. should have endured   Ps 81:15
for ever
remember how short my t. is   Ps 89:47
until the t. that his word   Ps 105:19
came
proper t. (B)   Ps 145:15;
      Lu 1:20; 12:42; Ga 6:9
a t. to every purpose   Ec 3:1; 3:17; 8:6
a t. to be born, and a t. to die,   Ec 3:2
a t. to plant and a t. to pluck up
A t. to kill,
and a t. to heal; a t.
to break down, and a t.
to build up   Ec 3:3
A t. to weep,
and a t. to laugh; a t.
to mourn, and a t. to dance   Ec 3:4
A t. to castaway
stones, and a t. to gather,   Ec 3:5
a t. to embrace, and a t.

A t. to get, and   Ec 3:6
a t. to lose; a t. to
keep, and a t. to cast   Ec 3:7
A t. to rend,
and a t. to sew; a t.
to keep silent, and a t.   Ec 3:8
A t. to love,
and a t. to hate; a t.
of war, and a t. of peace
why shouldest thou die before   Ec 7:17
thy t.
a wise man's heart discerneth t.   Ec 8:5
and chance happeneth to   Ec 9:11
them all
the sons of men snared in an   Ec 9:12
evil t.
trapped in disastrous t. (B)   Ec 9:12
draweth near the t. of her   Isa 26:17
delivery
the t. it goeth forth it shall   Isa 28:19
take you
who hath declared this from   Isa 45:21
ancient t.
from the t. that it was, there   Isa 48:16
am I
in an acceptable t. have I   Isa 49:8;
heard thee in a day of   2Co 6:2
I the Lord will hasten it in   Isa 60:22
his t.
at the t. I visit shall be cast   Jer 6:15
down
crane and swallow observe t. of   Jer 8:7
coming
looked for a t. of health, and   Jer 8:15
behold
the Saviour thereof in t. of   Jer 14:8
trouble
the t. of healing, and behold   Jer 14:19
it is even the t. of Jacob's   Jer 30:7
trouble
the t. of their visitation   Jer 46:21; 50:27
the t. that I will visit him   Jer 49:8;
      50:31
who will appoint me the t.   Jer 49:19;
      50:44
Babylon like a floor, it is t. to   Jer 51:33
thresh
from t. to t. shalt thou eat it   Eze 4:10
t. was the t. of love, I spread   Eze 16:8
my skirt
as at the t. of thy reproach   Eze 16:57
of daughters
day is near, it shall be t. of   Eze 30:3
heathen
I know that ye would gain the   Da 2:8
t.
to speak before one, till t. be   Da 2:9
changed
Daniel desired that he would   Da 2:16
give him t.
what t. ye hear sound of   Da 3:5;
cornet   3:15
yet their lives were prolonged   Da 7:12
for a t.
t. came that saints possessed   Da 7:22
until a t. and the dividing of   Da 7:25;
t.   12:7
for a year, two years, and half   Da 7:25
a year (B)
at the t. of the end shall be the   Da 8:17
vision
relates to the final period (B)   Da 8:17;
      11:35; 12:4; 12:9
      Da 9:21
touched me about t. of   Da 11:24
evening oblation
he shall forecast his devices   Da 11:35
for a t.
to make them white, to the t.   Da 11:40
of the end
at t. of end shall king of the   Da 12:1
south
and there shall be a t. of   Da 12:4;
trouble   12:9
seal the book, even to t. of   Da 12:7
the end
a period, periods and
half-period (B)
the t. the daily sacrifice be   Da 12:11
taken away
it is t. to seek he Lord, till   Ho 10:12
he come
till the t. that she which   Mic 5:3
travaileth
is it t. to dwell in your ceiled   Hag 1:4
houses
that at evening t. it shall be   Zec 14:7
light

nor vine cast her fruit before the *t*.	*Mal 3:11*
about the *t*. they were carried away	*M't 1:11*
Herod enquired what *t*. star appeared	*M't 2:7*
art come to torment us before the *t*.	*M't 8:29*
torture us ahead of *t*. (B)(P)	*M't 8:29*
when the *t*. of the fruit drew near	*M't 21:34*
the proper *t*. (A)	*M't 24:45; Lu 1:20*
the proper *t*. (N)(P)	*M't 24:45; Lu 1:20; 12:42*
the master saith, My *t*. is at hand	*M't 26:18*
t. is fulfilled, repent and believe	*M'k 1:15*
have no root, and so endure but for a *t*.	*M'k 4:17*
this is a desert, the *t*. is far passed	*M'k 6:35*
for the *t*. of figs was not yet	*M'k 11:13*
watch, for ye know not when the *t*. is	*M'k 13:33*
Elisabeth's full *t*. came to be delivered	*Lu 1:57*
shewed him kingdoms in a moment of *t*.	*Lu 4:5*
favorable *t*. (A)	*Lu 4:13*
opportune *t*. (R)	*Lu 4:13*
but this woman, since the *t*. I came in	*Lu 7:45*
which in *t*. of temptation fall away	*Lu 8:13*
in *t*. of trial fall away (B)	*Lu 8:13*
In the mean *t*. when there were	*Lu 12:1*
not see me till the *t*. come when	*Lu 13:35*
knewest not the *t*. of thy visitation	*Lu 19:44*
my *t*. is not come, your *t*. is ready	*Joh 7:6*
t. cometh, that whosoever killeth you	*Joh 16:2*
the *t*. cometh when I shall no more speak	*Joh 16:25*
all the *t*. the Lord went in and out	*Ac 1:21*
when the *t*. of the promise drew nigh	*Ac 7:17*
in which *t*. Moses was born	*Ac 7:20*
spent *t*. in nothing else, but to tell	*Ac 17:21*
it is high *t*. to awake out of sleep	*Ro 13:11*
therefore judge nothing before the *t*.	*1Co 4:5*
defraud not, except consent for a *t*.	*1Co 7:5*
but this I say, brethren, the *t*. is short	*1Co 7:29*
one at a *t*. (N)	*1Co 14:27*
when *t*. had come (A)(B)(N)(P)(R)	*Ga 4:4*
the *t*. was ripe (N)	*Eph 1:10*
redeeming the *t*.	*Eph 5:16; Col 4:5*
make best use of *t*. (B)(P)(R)	*Eph 5:16; Col 4:5*
being taken from you for a short *t*.	*1Th 2:17*
that he might be revealed in his *t*.	*2Th 2:6*
be a *t*. of troubles (N)	*2Ti 3:1*
t. come, when they will not endure	*2Ti 4:3*
and the *t*. of my departure is at hand	*2Ti 4:6*
may find grace to help in *t*. of need	*Heb 4:16*
when for *t*. ye ought to be teachers	*Heb 5:12*
was a figure for the *t*. then present	*Heb 9:9*
imposed on them till *t*. of reformation	*Heb 9:10*
t. would fail me to tell of Gideon	*Heb 11:32*
a vapour that appeareth a little *t*.	*Jas 4:14*
what manner of *t*. the spirit of Christ	*1Pe 1:11*
pass *t*. of your sojourning here in fear	*1Pe 1:17*
at one *t*. were disobedient (S)	*1Pe 3:20*
he should no longer live the rest of his *t*.	*1Pe 4:2*
for the *t*. is at hand	*Re 1:3; 22:10*

sware, that there should be *t*. no longer	*Re 10:6*
t. of the dead, that they be judged	*Re 11:18*
he knoweth that he hath but a short *t*.	*Re 12:12*
nourished for a *t*. and times, and half a *t*.	*Re 12:14*
a period, periods, and a half period (B)	*Re 12:14*
or three years and a half (N)	*Re 12:14*

ANY TIME

the Levites may redeem	*Le 25:32*
if the slayer at *any t*. come without	*Nu 35:26*
sounded my father to-morrow *any t*.	*1Sa 20:12*
father had not displeased him at *any t*.	*1Ki 1:6*
angels shall bear thee up, lest at *any t*. thou dash thy foot	*M't 4:6; Lu 4:11*
lest at *any t*. the adversary deliver thee	*M't 5:25*
lest at *any t*. they should see	*M't 13:15; M'k 4:12*
nor transgressed I at *any t*. thy commandment	*Lu 11:29*
lest at *any t*. your hearts be overcharged	*Lu 21:34*
no man hath seen God at *any t*.	*Joh 1:18*
nor have ye heard his voice at *any t*.	*Joh 5:37*
nothing unclean hath at *any t*. entered	*Ac 11:8*
who goeth a warfare *any t*. at his charges	*1Co 9:7*
nor at *any t*. used we flattering words	*1Th 2:5*
to which of the angels said he at *any t*.	*Heb 1:5; 1:13*
lest at *any t*. we should let them slip	*Heb 2:1*
no man hath seen God at *any t*.	*1Jo 4:12*

AT THAT TIME

Balak was king of Moab *at that t*.	*Nu 22:4*
and I spake to you *at that t*.	*De 1:9*
I charged your judges *at that t*. saying	*De 1:16*
I commanded you *at that t*.	*De 1:18; 3:18*
I commanded Joshua *at that t*. saying	*De 3:21*
I besought the Lord *at that t*. saying	*De 3:23*
I stood between Lord and you *at that t*.	*De 5:5*
Lord hearkened to me *at that t*.	*De 9:19; 10:10*
the ark was *at that t*. with Israel	*1Sa 14:18*
Israel brought under *at that t*.	*2Ch 13:18*
could not keep the passover *at that t*.	*2Ch 30:3*
Israel kept the passover *at that t*.	*2Ch 35:17*
at that t. they shall call Jerusalem	*Jer 3:17*
at that t. they shall bring out the bones	*Jer 8:1*
at that t. cause branch of righteousness	*Jer 33:15*
at that t. shall Michael stand up	*Da 12:1*
will hide his face from them *at that t*.	*Mic 3:4*
at that t. I will search Jerusalem	*Zep 1:12*
at that t. I will undo all that afflict thee	*Zep 3:20*
at that t. will I bring you again, in time	*Zep 3:20*
himself was at Jerusalem *at that t*.	*Lu 23:7*
at that t. was a great persecution	*Ac 8:1*
at that t. ye were without Christ	*Eph 2:12*

IN THE TIME

came to pass *in the t*. of her travail	*Ge 38:27*

commanded *in the t*. of month Abib	*Ex 34:18*
let them deliver *in the t*. of tribulation	*J'g 10:14*
in the t. of wheat harvest Samson visited	*J'g 15:1*
in the t. of old age he was diseased	*1Ki 15:23*
in the t. of distress did he trespass	*2Ch 28:22*
in the t. of their trouble thou heardest	*Ne 9:27*
more than *in the t*. corn increased	*Ps 4:7*
as a fiery oven *in the t*. of thine anger	*Ps 21:9*
in the t. of trouble he shall hide me	*Ps 27:5*
he is their strength *in the t*. of trouble	*Ps 37:39*
cast me not off *in the t*. of old age	*Ps 71:9*
as cold of snow *in the t*. of harvest	*Pr 25:13*
confidence in unfaithful man *in the t*. of trouble	*Pr 25:19*
be our salvation *in the t*. of trouble	*Isa 33:2*
in the t. of trouble they will say	*Jer 2:27*
if they can save thee *in the t*. of trouble	*Jer 2:28*
in the t. of visitation shall be cast down	*Jer 8:12*
in the t. of visitation they perish	*Jer 10:15; 51:18*
not save them at all *in the t*. of trouble	*Jer 11:12*
I will not hear them *in the t*. that they cry	*Jer 11:14*
I will cause enemy to entreat thee well *in the t*. of evil,	*Jer 15:11*
in the t. of affliction	
deal with them *in the t*. of thine anger	*Jer 18:23*
handleth the sickle *in the t*. of harvest	*Jer 50:16*
in the t. when thou shalt be broken	*Eze 27:34*
perpetual hatred, *in the t*. of calamity, *in the t*. their iniquity	*Eze 35:5*
I will take away my corn *in the t*.	*Ho 2:9*
ask rain *in the t*. of the latter rain	*Zec 10:1*
in the t. of harvest I will say to reapers	*M't 13:30*
were many lepers *in the t*. of Eliseus	*Lu 4:27*

SAME TIME

Lord's anger was kindled the *same t*.	*Nu 32:10*
I prayed for Aaron also the *same t*.	*De 9:20*
Edom revolted, then Libnah revolted at *same t*.	*2Ki 8:22; 2Ch 21:10*
they offered the *same t*. 700 oxen	*2Ch 15:11*
Asa oppressed the people at *same t*.	*2Ch 16:10*
at the *same t*. came to them Tatnai	*Ezr 5:3*
gave them vineyards at the *same t*.	*Jer 39:10*
at the *same t*. shalt thou think evil	*Eze 38:10*
at the *same t*. my reason returned	*Da 4:36*
trouble, such as never was to that *same t*.	*Da 12:1*
the *same t*. there arose no small stir	*Ac 19:23*

THAT TIME

why did ye not recover in *that t*.	*J'g 11:26*
to-morrow by *that t*. the sun be hot	*1Sa 11:9*
since *that t*. hath it been in building	*Ezr 5:16*
to pass from *that t*. forth	*Ne 4:16; 13:21*
spoken concerning Moab since *that t*.	*Isa 16:13*
in *that t*. shall the present be brought	*Isa 18:7*

have I not told thee from *that* Isa 44:8
t.
who hath told it from *that t.* Isa 45:21
from *that t.* thine ear was not Isa 48:8
opened
that t. Israel shall come Jer 50:4
weeping
in *that t.* iniquity of Israel Jer 50:20
not be found
the prudent keep silence in Am 5:13
that t.
from *that t.* Jesus began to M't 4:17
preach
from *that t.* began to shew M't 16:21
his disciples
from *that t.* Judas sought M't 26:16
opportunity
since *that t.* kingdom of God Lu 16:16
is preached
from *that t.* many disciples Joh 6:66
went back
about *that t.* Herod stretched Ac 12:1
to vex

THIS TIME

this t. will my husband be Ge 29:34
joined
Pharaoh hardened his heart at Ex 8:32
this t.
I will at *this t.* send all my Ex 9:14
plagues
to-morrow about *this t.* I will Ex 9:18
cause rain
and Pharaoh said, I have Ex 9:27
sinned *this t.*
according to *this t.* it shall Nu 23:23
be said
nor would as at *this t.* have J'g 13:23
told us
for ye did not give unto them J'g 21:22
at *this t.*
for about *this t.* ye shall find 1Sa 9:13
him
the counsel is not good at 2Sa 17:7
this t.
not at *this t.* put thee to 1Ki 2:26
death
to-morrow *this t.* 1Ki 19:2;
    20:6; 2Ki 7:1, 18; 10:6
in all *this t.* was not I at Ne 13:6
Jerusalem
if thou thy peace at *this t.* art Es 4:14
come to kingdom for such a *t.* as
this
blessed be the Lord from Ps 113:2
this t. forth
we will bless the Lord from Ps 115:18
this t. forth
he will preserve thee from Ps 121:8
this t. forth
I have shewed new things Isa 48:6
from *this t.*
wilt thou not from *this t.* cry Jer 3:4
unto me
this is the *t.* of the Lord's Jer 51:6
vengeance
nor go haughtily, for *this t.* Mic 2:3
is evil
tribulation as was not since M't 24:21;
the beginning of world to M'k 13:19
this t.
shall receive an M'k 10:30;
hundredfold now in *this t.* Lu 18:30
how is it ye do not discern Lu 12:56
this t.
Lord, by *this t.* he stinketh Joh 11:39
wilt thou at *this t.* restore the Ac 1:6
kingdom
Felix answered, Go thy way Ac 24:25
for *this t.*
to declare at *this t.* his Ro 3:26
righteousness
that the sufferings of *this* Ro 8:18
present *t.*
at *this t.* will I come, Sara Ro 9:9
shall have a son
so at *this* present *t.* there is a Ro 11:5
remnant
his will was not to come at 1Co 16:12
this t.
that now at *this t.* your 2Co 8:14
abundance

TIMES

hath supplanted me these Ge 27:36
two *t.*
me, and changed my wages Ge 31:7
ten *t.*

thou hast changed my wages Ge 31:41
ten *t.*
himself to the ground seven *t.* Ge 33:3
five *t.* so much as any of Ge 43:34
theirs
Three *t.* thou shalt keep a Ex 23:14
feast unto
Three *t.* in the year all thy Ex 23:17
males
and sprinkle of the blood seven Le 4:6
t.
sprinkle it seven *t.* before the Le 4:17
Lord
therefore upon the altar seven Le 8:11
t.
cleansed from the leprosy seven Le 14:7
t.
of the oil with his finger seven Le 14:16
t.
oil that is in his left hand Le 14:27
seven *t.*
and sprinkle the house seven Le 14:51
t.
the blood with his finger Le 16:14
seven *t.*
upon it with his finger seven *t.* Le 16:19
ye use enchantment nor Le 19:26
observe *t.*
unto thee, seven *t.* seven years Le 25:8
punish you seven *t.* more for Le 26:18
your
bring seven *t.* more plagues Le 26:21
upon
punish you yet seven *t.* for Le 26:24
your
chastise you seven *t.* for your Le 26:28
sins
have tempted me now these Nu 14:22
ten *t.*
of the congregation seven *t.* Nu 19:4
thou hast smitten me these Nu 22:28
three *t.*
these thou smitten thine ass Nu 22:32
three *t.*
and turned from me these Nu 22:33
three *t.*
he went not, as at other *t.* to Nu 24:1
seek
altogether blessed them these Nu 24:10
three *t.*
you a thousand *t.* so many De 1:11
more
The Emims dwelt therein in *t.* De 2:10
past
and hated him not in *t.* past De 4:42
Three *t.* in a year shall all De 16:16
they
divination, or an observer of *t.* De 18:10
hearkened unto observers of *t.* De 18:14
ye shall compass the city seven Jos 6:4
t.
after the same manner seven Jos 6:15
t.
they compassed the city seven Jos 6:15
t.
began to move him at *t.* in J'g 13:25
the camp
hast mocked me these three J'g 16:15
t.
I will go out as at other *t.* J'g 16:20
before
against Gibeah, as at other *t.* J'g 20:30
the people, and kill, as at J'g 20:31
other *t.*
and called as other *t.* Samuel 1Sa 3:10
with his hand, as at other *t.* 1Sa 3:10
in his presence, as in *t.* past 1Sa 19:7
sat upon his seat, as at 1Sa 20:25
other *t.*
ground, bowed himself three 1Sa 20:41
t.
ye sought for David in *t.* past 2Sa 3:17
three *t.* in a year did 1Ki 9:25
Solomon
himself upon the child three 1Ki 17:21
t.
And he said, Go again seven 1Ki 18:43
t.
How many *t.* shall I adjure 1Ki 22:16
thee
and the child sneezed seven *t.* 2Ki 4:35
Go and wash in Jordan, 2Ki 5:10
seven *t.*
dipped himself seven *t.* in 2Ki 5:14
Jordan
shouldest have smitten five 2Ki 13:19
or six *t.*
Three *t.* did Joash beat him 2Ki 13:25

of ancient *t.* that I have 2Ki 19:25
formed it
fire, and observed *t.* and used 2Ki 21:6
men that had understanding 1Ch 12:32
of the *t.*
his people an hundred *t.* 1Ch 21:3
so many
and the *t.* that went over 1Ch 29:30
him, and
three *t.* in the year, even in 2Ch 8:13
those *t.* there was no 2Ch 15:5
peace to him
How many *t.* shall I adjure 2Ch 18:15
thee
also he observed *t.* and used 2Ch 33:6
in our cities come at Ezr 10:14
appointed *t.*
they said unto us ten *t.* From Ne 4:12
all
they sent unto me four *t.* after Ne 6:4
many *t.* didst thou deliver Ne 9:28
them
at *t.* appointed year by year Ne 10:34
the wood offering, at *t.* Ne 13:31
appointed
to the wise men, which knew Es 1:13
of Purim in their *t.* appointed Es 9:31
ten *t.* have ye reproached me Job 19:3
seeing *t.* are not hidden from Job 24:1
oppressed, a refuge in *t.* of Ps 9:9
trouble
hidest thou thyself in *t.* of Ps 10:1
trouble
in a furnace of earth, purified Ps 12:6
seven *t.*
My *t.* are in thy hand: deliver Ps 31:15
me
in their days, in the *t.* of old Ps 44:1
days of old, the years of Ps 77:5
ancient *t.*
Many *t.* did he deliver them; Ps 106:43
but
Seven *t.* a day do I praise Ps 119:164
thee because
For a just man falleth seven Pr 24:16
t. and
a sinner do evil an hundred *t.* Ec 8:12
shall be alone in his appointed Isa 14:31
t.
shall be the stability of thy *t.* Isa 33:6
ancient *t.* that I have formed Isa 37:26
it
from ancient *t.* the things Isa 46:10
that are
as in *t.* long past (B) Isa 51:9
heaven knoweth her appointed Jer 8:7
t.
he prophesieth of the *t.* that Eze 12:27
are far
he found them ten *t.* better Da 1:20
than all
changeth the *t.* and the Da 2:21
seasons
heat the furnace one seven *t.* Da 3:19
more
and let seven *t.* pass over him Da 4:16
let seven years pass over him Da 4:16
(B)
field, till seven *t.* pass over Da 4:23
him
and seven *t.* shall pass over Da 4:25;
thee   4:32
upon his knees three *t.* a day Da 6:10
maketh his petition three *t.* a Da 6:13
day
ten thousand *t.* ten thousand Da 7:10
stood
and think to change *t.* and Da 7:25
laws
think to change the sacred Da 7:25
seasons (B)
a time and *t.* and the Da 7:25
dividing of
a year, two years, and a half Da 7:25
year (B)
and the wall, even in Da 9:25
troublous *t.*
he that strengthened her in Da 11:6
these *t.*
in those *t.* there shall many Da 11:14
stand
shall be for a time, and an Da 12:7
half
a period, periods, and a half Da 12:7
period (B)
can yet not discern signs of *t.* M't 16:3
me, and I forgive him till M't 18:21
seven *t.*
I say not unto thee, Until M't 18:22
seven *t.*

but, until seventy *t.* seven   *M't 18:22*
trespass against thee seven *t.*   *Lu 17:4*
in a
even *t.* in a day turn again   *Lu 17:4*
to thee
the *t.* of the Gentiles be   *Lu 21:24*
fulfilled
you to know the *t.* or the   *Ac 1:7*
seasons
when the *t.* of refreshing shall   *Ac 3:19*
until the *t.* of restitution of   *Ac 3:21*
all
And this was done three *t.*   *Ac 11:10*
Who in *t.* past suffered all   *Ac 14:16*
nations
determined *t.* before   *Ac 17:26*
appointed
the *t.* of this ignorance God   *Ac 17:30*
winked
the *t.* past have not believed   *Ro 11:30*
God
in earlier *t.* (S)   *Ro 15:4*
five *t.* receive I forty stripes,   *2Co 11:24*
save
he which persecuted us in *t.*   *Ga 1:23*
past
observe days and months, and   *Ga 4:10*
t.
the dispensation of the   *Eph 1:10*
fulness of *t.*
the maturity of *t.* (A)(B)   *Eph 1:10*
our conversation in *t.* past in   *Eph 2:3*
of the *t.* and the seasons,   *1Th 5:1*
brethren
relative to periods and dates   *1Th 5:1*
(B)
latter *t.* some shall depart from   *1Ti 4:1*
Which in his *t.* he shall shew,   *1Ti 6:15*
who
the last days perilous *t.* shall   *2Ti 3:1*
come
troublous *t.* impending (B)   *2Ti 3:1*
hath in due *t.* manifested his   *Tit 1:3*
word
who at sundry *t.* and in   *Heb 1:1*
divers
manifest in these last *t.* for   *1Pe 1:20*
you
was ten thousand *t.* ten   *Re 5:11*
thousand
for a time, and *t.* and half a   *Re 12:14*
time
during a period, periods, and   *Re 12:14*
a half-period (B)

ALL TIMES

that he come not at *all t.*   *Le 16:2*
within the veil
maintain cause of his people   *1Ki 8:59*
at *all t.*
I will bless the Lord at *all t.*   *Ps 34:1*
his praise
trust in him at *all t.* ye people   *Ps 62:8*
pour out heart
blessed is he that doth   *Ps 106:3*
righteousness at *all t.*
for longing it hath to thy   *Ps 119:20*
judgments at *all t.*
let her breasts satisfy thee at   *Pr 5:19*
all t.
a friend loveth at *all t.* a   *Pr 17:17*
brother is born for

TIMID

made heart *t.*, broken (A)   *Job 23:16*
be not afraid or *t.* of heart (B)   *Isa 7:4*

TIMNA

T. was concubine to Eliphaz   *Ge 36:12*
Hemam; and Lotan's sister   *Ge 36:22*
was *T.*
Gatam, Kenaz, and *T.* and   *1Ch 1:36*
Amalek
Homam; and *T.* was Lotan's   *1Ch 1:39*
sister

TIMNAH

duke *T.*, duke Alvah, duke   *Ge 36:40*
and passed on to *T.*   *Jos 15:10*
Gibeah, and *T.*; ten cities   *Jos 15:57*
the dukes of Edom were;   *1Ch 1:51*
duke *T.*
and *T.* with the villages   *2Ch 28:18*
thereof

TIMNATH

up unto his sheepshearers to   *Ge 38:12*
T.

father in law goeth up to *T.*   *Ge 38:13*
place, which is by the way to   *Ge 38:14*
T.
Samson went down to *T.*   *J'g 14:1*
a woman in *T.* of the   *J'g 14:1;*
daughters   *14:2*
his father and his mother,   *J'g 14:5*
to *T.*
and came to the vineyards of   *J'g 14:5*
T.

TIMNATH-HERES

border of his inheritance in *T.*   *J'g 2:9*

TIMNATH-SERAH

asked, even *T.* in mount   *Jos 19:50*
Ephraim
border of his inheritance in   *Jos 24:30*
T.

TIMNITE

Samson, the son in law of the   *J'g 15:6*
T.

TIMON

T. and Parmenas, and Nicolas   *Ac 6:5*

TIMOTHEUS

disciple was there, named *T.*   *Ac 16:1*
but Silas and *T.* abode there   *Ac 17:14*
still
a commandment unto Silas   *Ac 17:15*
and *T.*
when Silas and *T.* were come   *Ac 18:5*
ministered unto him, *T.* and   *Ac 19:22*
Gaius of Derbe, and *T.*   *Ac 20:4*
T. my workfellow, and   *Ro 16:21*
Lucius
this cause have I sent unto   *1Co 4:17*
you *T.*
if *T.* come, see that he may   *1Co 16:10*
be with
even by me, and Silvanus   *2Co 1:19*
and *T.*
Paul and *T.* the servants of   *Ph'p 1:1*
Jesus
Jesus to send *T.* shortly   *Ph'p 2:19*
unto you
the will of God, and *T.* our   *Col 1:1*
brother
Silvanus and *T.* unto the   *1Th 1:1*
church
sent *T.* our brother, and   *1Th 3:2*
minister
But now when *T.* came from   *1Th 3:6*
you
Silvanus, and *T.* unto the   *2Th 1:1*
church

TIMOTHY

T. our brother, unto the   *2Co 1:1*
church
Unto *T.* my own son in the   *1Ti 1:2*
faith
charge I commit unto thee,   *1Ti 1:18*
son *T.*
O *T.* keep that which is   *1Ti 6:20*
committed
To *T.* my dearly beloved son   *2Ti 1:2*
and *T.* our brother, unto   *Ph'm 1*
Philemon
our brother *T.* is set at   *Heb 13:23*
liberty

TIN

the brass, the iron, the *t.* and   *Nu 31:22*
away thy dross, take away all   *Isa 1:25*
thy *t.*
all they are brass, and *t.* and   *Eze 22:18*
iron
brass, and iron, and lead,   *Eze 22:20*
and *t.*
with silver, iron, *t.* and lead,   *Eze 27:12*
they

TINGLE

every one that heareth it   *1Sa 3:11*
shall *t.*
heareth of it, both his ears   *2Ki 21:12*
shall *t.*
whosoever heareth, his ears   *Jer 19:3*
shall *t.*

TINKLING

and making a *t.* with their   *Isa 3:16*
feet

of their *t.* ornaments about   *Isa 3:18*
their feet
finery of their *t.* (A)(B)(R)   *Isa 3:18*
as sounding brass, or a *t.*   *1Co 13:1*
cymbal

TIP

the *t.* of the right ear of   *Ex 29:20*
Aaron
the *t.* of the right ear of his   *Ex 29:20*
sons
it upon the *t.* of Aaron's right   *Le 8:23*
ear
blood upon the *t.* of the right   *Le 8:24*
ear
put it upon the *t.* of the   *Le 14:14;*
right ear   *14:25*
put upon the *t.* of the right   *Le 14:17*
ear
upon the *t.* of the right ear of   *Le 14:28*
him
may dip the *t.* of his finger in   *Lu 16:24*
water

TIPHSAH

T. even to Azzah, over all the   *1Ki 4:24*
Then Menahem smote *T.*   *2Ki 15:16*
and all

TIRAS

and Tubal, and Meshech, and   *Ge 10:2;*
T.   *1Ch 1:5*

TIRATHITES

the *T.* the Shimeathites, and   *1Ch 2:55*

TIRE

the *t.* of thine head upon   *Eze 24:17*
thee, and
turban upon your head   *Eze 24:17*
(A)(B)(R)
bind the headtire upon thee   *Eze 24:17*
(E)

TIRED

painted her face, and *t.* her   *2Ki 9:30*
head
beautified her head (A)   *2Ki 9:30*
adorned her head (B)(R)   *2Ki 9:30*
attired her head (E)   *2Ki 9:30*
they have *t.* themselves out   *Jer 12:13*
(R)

TIRES

t. him to return to mouth (B)   *Pr 26:15*
and their round *t.* like the   *Isa 3:18*
moon
crescent head ornaments   *Isa 3:18*
(A)(B)(E)(R)
your *t.* shall be upon your   *Eze 24:23*
heads
turbans upon your heads   *Eze 24:23*
(A)(B)(R)
linen *t.* on heads (E)   *Eze 44:18*

TIRHAKAH

heard say of *T.* king of   *2Ki 19:9*
Ethiopia
say concerning *T.* king of   *Isa 37:9*
Ethiopia

TIRHANAH

concubine, bare Sheber, and   *1Ch 2:48*
T.

TIRIA

Jehaleleel; Ziph, and Ziphah,   *1Ch 4:16*
T.

TIRSHATHA

the *T.* said unto them, that   *Ezr 2:63;*
they   *Ne 7:56*
The *T.* gave to the treasure a   *Ne 7:70*
And Nehemiah, which is the *T.*   *Ne 8:9*
sealed were, Nehemiah, the *T.*   *Ne 10:1*

TIRZAH

Noah, Hoglah, Milcah, and   *Nu 26:33*
T.

and Hoglah, and Milcah, and _Nu 27:1_
T.
For Mahlah, T. and Hoglah _Nu 36:11_
The king of T. one: all the _Jos 12:24_
kings
and Noah, Hoglah, Milcah, _Jos 17:3_
and T.
and departed, and came to _1Ki 14:17_
T.
building of Ramah, and _1Ki 15:21_
dwelt in T.
Ahijah to reign over all _1Ki 15:23_
Israel in T.
his fathers, and was buried in _1Ki 16:6_
T.
Baasha to reign over Israel in _1Ki 16:8_
T.
as he was in T. drinking _1Ki 16:9_
himself
of Arza steward of his house _1Ki 16:9_
in T.
did Zimri reign seven days _1Ki 16:15_
in T.
with him, and they besieged _1Ki 16:17_
T.
years: six years reigned he _1Ki 16:23_
in T.
the son of Gadi went up _2Ki 15:14_
from T.
and the coasts thereof from _2Ki 15:16_
T.
art beautiful, O my love, as T. _Ca 6:4_

TISHBITE

And Elijah the T. who was of _1Ki 17:1_
the Lord came to Elijah the _1Ki 21:17;_
T.   _21:28_
of the Lord said to Elijah the _2Ki 1:3_
T.
And he said, It is Elijah the _2Ki 1:8_
T.
spake by his servant Elijah _2Ki 9:36_
the T.

TITHE

all the t. of the land, whether _Le 27:30_
concerning the t. of the herd, _Le 27:32_
or of
Lord, even a tenth part of _Nu 18:26_
the t.
within thy gates the t. of thy _De 12:17_
corn
truly t. all the increase of thy _De 14:22_
seed
t. of thy corn, of thy wine, _De 14:23_
and of
forth all the t. of thine _De 14:28_
increase
the t. of all things brought _2Ch 31:5_
they in
brought in the t. of oxen and _2Ch 31:6_
sheep
the t. of holy things which _2Ch 31:6_
were
the Levites shall bring up the _Ne 10:38_
t. of
brought all Judah the t. of _Ne 13:12_
the corn
for ye pay t. of mint and _M't 23:23_
anise
ye t. mint and rue and all _Lu 11:42_
manner

TITHES

hand. And he gave him t. of _Ge 14:20_
all
will at all redeem ought of _Le 27:31_
his t.
But the t. of the children of _Nu 18:24_
Israel
the t. which I have given you _Nu 18:26_
from
offering unto the Lord of all _Nu 18:28_
your t.
your t. and heave offerings of _De 12:6_
your
your t. and the heave _De 12:11_
offering of
the t. of thine increase the _De 26:12_
third
brought in the offerings and _2Ch 31:12_
the t.
the t. of our ground unto the _Ne 10:37_
the t. in all the cities of _Ne 10:37_
our
Levites, when the Levites _Ne 10:38_
take t.

bring up the tithe of the t. _Ne 10:38_
unto
for the firstfruits, and for _Ne 12:44_
the t.
the vessels, and the t. of the _Ne 13:5_
corn
and your t. after three years _Am 4:4_
robbed thee? In t. and _Mal 3:8_
offerings
ye all the t. into the _Mal 3:10_
storehouse
week, I give t. of all that I _Lu 18:12_
possess
to take t. of the people _Heb 7:5_
according to
from them received t. of _Heb 7:6_
Abraham
And here men that die receive _Heb 7:8_
t.
receiveth t. payed t. in _Heb 7:9_
Abraham

TITHING

made an end of t. all the _De 26:12_
tithes
third year, which is the year _De 26:12_
of t.

TITLE

said, What t. is that that I _2Ki 23:17_
see
whose likeness and t. (A) _M't 22:20_
And Pilate wrote a t. and _Joh 19:19_
put it
This t. then read many of _Joh 19:20_
the Jews

TITLES

let me give flattering t. unto _Job 32:21_
man
For I know not to give _Job 32:22_
flattering t.

TITTLE

one t. shall in no wise pass _M't 5:18_
from
not one smallest letter nor _M't 5:18_
one little hook (A)
not lose one single dot or _M't 5:18_
not a letter, not a stroke (N) _M't 5:18_
not lose one single dot or _M't 5:18_
comma (P)
not one iota, not a dot (R) _M't 5:18_
pass, than one t. of the law _Lu 16:17_
to fail
one dot of the law to become _Lu 16:17_
void (A)
one iota of the law to lapse _Lu 16:17_
(B)
one dot or stroke of law to _Lu 16:17_
lose its force (N)
a single point of the law to _Lu 16:17_
become a dead letter (P)
one dot of the law to become _Lu 16:17_
void (R)

TITUS

I found not T. my brother _2Co 2:13_
comforted us by the coming _2Co 7:6_
of T.
the more joyed we for the _2Co 7:13_
joy of T.
boasting, which I made _2Co 7:14_
before T.
Insomuch that we desired T. _2Co 8:6_
that
care into the heart of T. for _2Co 8:16_
you
Whether any do enquire of _2Co 8:23_
T. he
I desired T. and with him I _2Co 12:18_
sent
brother. Did T. make a gain _2Co 12:18_
of you
and took T. with me also _Ga 2:1_
But neither T. who was with _Ga 2:3_
me
to Galatia, T. unto Dalmatia _2Ti 4:10_
To T. mine own son after the _Tit 1:4_

TIZITE

and Joha his brother, the T. _1Ch 11:45_

TOAH

the son of Eliel the son of T. _1Ch 6:34_

TOB

and dwelt in the land of T. _J'g 11:3_
Jephthah out of the land of T. _J'g 11:5_

TOB-ADONIJAH

and Tobijah, and T., Levites _2Ch 17:8_

TOBIAH

of Delaiah, the children of T. _Ezr 2:60_
Horonite, and T. the servant _Ne 2:10;_
       _2:19_
Now T. the Ammonite was by _Ne 4:3_
him
pass, that when Sanballat, and _Ne 4:7_
T.
to pass, when Sanballat, and T. _Ne 6:1_
for T. and Sanballat had hired _Ne 6:12_
think thou upon T. and _Ne 6:14_
Sanballat
Judah sent many letters unto _Ne 6:17_
T.
the letters of T. came unto _Ne 6:17_
them
T. sent letters to put me in _Ne 6:19_
fear
the children of T. the children _Ne 7:62_
of our God, was allied unto T. _Ne 13:4_
the evil that Eliashib did for _Ne 13:7_
T.
forth all the household stuff of _Ne 13:8_
T.

TOBIJAH

and T. and Tob-adonijah, _2Ch 17:8_
Levites
even of Heldai, of T. and of _Zec 6:10_
shall be to Helem, and to T. _Zec 6:14_

TOCHEN

and T. and Ashan, five cities _1Ch 4:32_

TOE

upon the great t. of their _Ex 29:20_
right foot
upon the great t. of his right _Le 8:23;_
foot   _14:14, 17, 25, 28_

TOES

the great t. of their right feet _Le 8:24_
of his thumbs and his great t. _J'g 1:6_
thumbs and great t. cut off _J'g 1:7_
fingers, and on every foot _2Sa 21:20_
six t.
whose fingers and t. were _1Ch 20:6_
four and
whereas thou sawest the feet _Da 2:41_
and t.
And as the t. of the feet were _Da 2:42_
part of

TOGARMAH

Ashkenaz, and Riphath, and _Ge 10:3_
T.
Ashchenaz, and Riphath, and _1Ch 1:6_
T.
the house of T. traded in thy _Eze 27:14_
fairs
house of T. of the north _Eze 38:6_
quarters

TOGETHER

heaven be gathered t. unto one _Ge 1:9_
place
gathering, t. of the waters _Ge 1:10_
called he
and they sewed fig leaves t. _Ge 3:7_
them, that they might dwell t. _Ge 13:6_
so that they could not dwell t. _Ge 13:6_
were joined t. in the vale of _Ge 14:3_
Siddim
and they went both of them t. _Ge 22:6_
so they went both of them t. _Ge 22:8_
rose up and went t. to _Ge 22:19_
Beer-sheba
children struggled t. within _Ge 25:22_
her

the cattle should be gathered *t.* Ge 29:7
until all the flocks be gathered Ge 29:8
t.
Laban gathered *t.* all the men Ge 29:22
gather themselves *t.* against Ge 34:30
me
than that they might dwell *t.* Ge 36:7
put them all *t.* into ward Ge 42:17
three days
and said, Gather yourselves *t.* Ge 49:1
Gather yourselves *t.* and hear, Ge 49:2
ye
two men of the Hebrews Ex 2:13
strove *t.*
and gather the elders of Israel Ex 3:16
t.
and gathered *t.* all the elders Ex 4:29
of the
they gathered them *t.* upon Ex 8:14
heaps
the waters were gathered. Ex 15:8
And all the people answered *t.* Ex 19:8
And if men strive *t.* and one Ex 21:18
smite
five curtains shall be coupled Ex 26:3
t.
and couple the curtains *t.* with Ex 26:6
and couple the tent *t.* that it Ex 26:11
may be
they shall be coupled *t.* Ex 26:24
beneath
and they shall be coupled *t.* Ex 26:24
above
and so it shall be joined *t.* Ex 28:7
art of the apothecary, Ex 30:35
tempered *t.*
gathered themselves *t.* unto Ex 32:1
Aaron
gathered themselves *t.* unto Ex 32:26
him
of the children of Israel *t.* Ex 35:1
taches of brass to couple the Ex 36:18
tent *t.*
coupled *t.* at the head thereof Ex 36:29
shoulderpieces for it, to couple Ex 39:4
it *t.*
by the two edges was it Ex 39:4
coupled *t.*
gather thou all the congregation Le 8:3
t.
and the assembly was gathered Le 8:4
a man of Israel strove *t.* in Le 24:10
the camp
ye are gathered *t.* within Le 26:25
your cities
assembled all the congregation Nu 1:18
t.
gather the children of Israel *t.* Nu 8:9
congregation is to be gathered Nu 10:7
t.
the fish of the sea be Nu 11:22
gathered *t.* for
that are gathered *t.* against Nu 14:35
me
And they gathered themselves Nu 16:3
t.
all thy company are gathered Nu 16:11
t.
and they gathered themselves Nu 20:2
t.
and gather thou the assembly Nu 20:8
t.
Aaron gathered the Nu 20:10
congregation *t.*
unto Moses, Gather the Nu 21:16
people *t.*
but Sihon gathered all his Nu 21:23
people *t.*
Balaam, and he smote his Nu 24:10
hands *t.*
and swallowed them up *t.* Nu 26:10
with Korah
gathered themselves *t.* against Nu 27:3
unto me, Gather me the De 4:10
people *t.*
plough with an ox and an ass De 22:10
t.
sorts, as of woollen and linen De 22:11
t.
If brethren dwell *t.* and one of De 25:5
men strive *t.* one with De 25:11
another
Gather the people *t.* men, De 31:12
and
tribes of Israel were gathered De 33:5
t.
he shall push the people *t.* to De 33:17
the
people that were in Ai were Jos 8:16
called *t.*

That they gathered themselves Jos 9:2
t.
gathered themselves *t.* Jos 10:5
and went
mountains are gathered *t.* Jos 10:6
against us
when all these kings were met Jos 11:5
t.
came and pitched *t.* at the Jos 11:5
waters
they met *t.* in Asher on the Jos 17:10
north
of Israel assembled *t.* at Jos 18:1
Shiloh
gathered themselves *t.* at Jos 22:12
Shiloh
Sisera gathered *t.* all his J'g 4:13
chariots
of the east were gathered *t.* J'g 6:33
and thrust the fleece *t.* and J'g 6:38
wringed
of Israel gathered themselves J'g 7:23
t.
of Ephraim gathered J'g 7:24
themselves *t.*
the men of Shechem gathered J'g 9:6
t.
of Shechem were gathered *t.* J'g 9:47
children of Ammon were J'g 10:17
gathered *t.*
of Israel assembled J'g 10:17
themselves *t.*
but Sihon gathered all his J'g 11:20
people *t.*
Ephraim gathered themselves J'g 12:1
t.
Jephthah gathered *t.* all the J'g 12:4
men
Philistines gathered them *t.* J'g 16:23
for to
to Micah's house were J'g 18:22
gathered *t.*
did eat and drink both of J'g 19:6
them *t.*
and divided her, *t.* with her J'g 19:29
bones
was gathered *t.* as one man J'g 20:1
the city, knit *t.* as one man J'g 20:11
of Benjamin gathered J'g 20:14
themselves *t.*
gathered *t.* all the lords of the 1Sa 5:11
And they gathered *t.* to 1Sa 7:6
Mizpeh
Israel were gathered *t.* to 1Sa 7:7
Mizpeh
of Israel gathered themselves *t.* 1Sa 8:4
Samuel called the people *t.* 1Sa 10:17
unto
that two of them were not 1Sa 11:11
left *t.*
people were called *t.* after 1Sa 13:4
Saul to
Philistines gathered *t.* to 1Sa 13:5
fight
Philistines gathered 1Sa 13:11
themselves *t.*
And Saul gathered the people 1Sa 15:4
t.
Philistines gathered *t.* their 1Sa 17:1
armies
and were gathered *t.* at 1Sa 17:1
Shochoh
men of Israel were gathered 1Sa 17:2
t.
give me a man, that we may 1Sa 17:10
fight *t.*
Saul called all the people *t.* to 1Sa 23:8
war
all the Israelites were 1Sa 25:1
gathered *t.*
Philistines gathered their 1Sa 28:1
armies *t.*
Philistines gathered 1Sa 28:4
themselves *t.*
and Saul gathered all Israel *t.* 1Sa 28:4
and
But his servants, *t.* with the 1Sa 28:23
woman
the Philistines gathered *t.* all 1Sa 29:1
their
and all his men, that same 1Sa 31:6
day *t.*
and met *t.* by the pool of 2Sa 2:13
Gibeon
fellow's side; so they fell 2Sa 2:16
down *t.*
Benjamin gathered themselves 2Sa 2:25
t.
he had gathered all the 2Sa 2:30
people *t.*

David gathered *t.* all the 2Sa 6:1
chosen men
they gathered themselves *t.* 2Sa 10:15
told David, he gathered all 2Sa 10:17
Israel *t.*
it grew up *t.* with him, and 2Sa 12:3
with
gather the rest of the people 2Sa 12:28
t.
David gathered all the 2Sa 12:29
people *t.*
and they two strove *t.* in the 2Sa 14:6
field
would destroy me and my 2Sa 14:16
son *t.*
they were gathered *t.* and 2Sa 20:14
went also
they fell all seven *t.* and were 2Sa 21:9
put
were there gathered *t.* to 2Sa 23:9
battle
Philistines were gathered *t.* 2Sa 23:11
into a
we were *t.*; there was no 1Ki 3:18
stranger
and they two made a league 1Ki 5:12
t.
And Solomon gathered *t.* 1Ki 10:26
chariots
t. with the daughter of 1Ki 11:1
Pharaoh
and gathered the prophets *t.* 1Ki 18:20
unto
of Syria gathered all his host 1Ki 20:1
of Israel gathered the 1Ki 22:6
prophets *t.*
took his mantle, and wrapped 2Ki 2:8
it *t.*
hath called these three kings 2Ki 3:10;
t. 3:13
I and thou rode *t.* after Ahab 2Ki 9:25
his
Jehu gathered all the people 2Ki 10:18
t.
Saul and all his house died 1Ch 10:6
t.
Philistines were gathered *t.* 1Ch 11:13
So David gathered all Israel 1Ch 13:5
t.
And David gathered all 1Ch 15:3
Israel *t.*
and gather us *t.* and deliver 1Ch 16:35
us
of Ammon gathered 1Ch 19:7
themselves *t.*
David commanded to gather 1Ch 22:2
t. the
he gathered *t.* all the princes 1Ch 23:2
that were gathered *t.* to 2Ch 12:5
Jerusalem
they gathered *t.* at 2Ch 15:10
Jerusalem
of Israel gathered *t.* of 2Ch 18:5
prophets
And Judah gathered 2Ch 20:4
themselves *t.*
he gathered *t.* the priests and 2Ch 24:5
Amaziah gathered Judah *t.* 2Ch 25:5
Ahaz gathered *t.* the vessels 2Ch 28:24
of the
and gathered them *t.* into the 2Ch 29:4
east
the people gathered 2Ch 30:3
themselves *t.*
was gathered much people *t.* 2Ch 32:4
gathered them *t.* in the 2Ch 32:6
street
they have gathered *t.* the 2Ch 34:17
money
sent and gathered *t.* all the 2Ch 34:29
elders
whole congregation *t.* was Ezr 2:64
forty
gathered themselves *t.* as one Ezr 3:1
man
and his sons, the sons of Ezr 3:9
Judah, *t.*
they sang *t.* by course in Ezr 3:11
praising
we ourselves *t.* will build unto Ezr 4:3
and the Levites were purified Ezr 6:20
t.
gathered *t.* out of Israel chief Ezr 7:28
men
I gathered them *t.* to the river Ezr 8:15
that
should gather *t.* unto Ezr 10:7
Jerusalem
Benjamin gathered themselves Ezr 10:9
t.

all the wall was joined *t.* unto	Ne 4:6
conspired all of them *t.* to come	Ne 4:8
Come, let us meet *t.* in some one of	Ne 6:2
therefore, and let us take counsel *t.*	Ne 6:7
Let us meet *t.* in the house of God	Ne 6:10
mine heart to gather *t.* the nobles	Ne 7:5
whole congregation *t.* was forty	Ne 7:66
gathered themselves *t.* as one man	Ne 8:1
were gathered *t.* the chief of	Ne 8:13
the singers gathered themselves *t.*	Ne 12:28
And I gathered them *t.* and set	Ne 13:11
gather *t.* all the fair young virgins	Es 2:3
many maidens were gathered *t.*	Es 2:8
virgins were gathered *t.* the second	Es 2:19
Go gather *t.* all the Jews that are	Es 4:16
every city to gather themselves *t.*	Es 8:11
The Jews gathered themselves *t.*	Es 9:2
in Shushan gathered themselves *t.*	Es 9:15
provinces gathered themselves *t.*	Es 9:16
that were at Shushan assembled *t.*	Es 9:18
they had made an appointment *t.*	Job 2:11
There the prisoners rest *t.*; they	Job 3:18
my calamity laid in the balances *t.*	Job 6:2
and we should come *t.* in judgment	Job 9:32
have made me and fashioned me *t.*	Job 10:8
cut off, and shut up, or gather *t.*	Job 11:10
gathered themselves *t.* against me	Job 16:10
pit, when our rest *t.* is in the dust	Job 17:16
His troops come *t.* and raise up	Job 19:12
the poor of the earth hide *t.*	Job 24:4
the nettles they were gathered *t.*	Job 30:7
All flesh shall perish *t.* and man	Job 34:15
When the morning stars sang *t.*	Job 38:7
and the clods cleave fast *t.*	Job 38:38
Hide them in the dust *t.*; and bind	Job 40:13
sinews of his stones are wrapped *t.*	Job 40:17
pride, shut up *t.* as with a close seal	Job 41:15
they stick *t.* that they cannot be	Job 41:17
flakes of his flesh are joined *t.*	Job 41:23
and the rulers take counsel *t.*	Ps 2:2
aside, they are *t.* become filthy	Ps 14:3
they took counsel *t.* against me	Ps 31:13
He gathereth the waters of the sea *t.*	Ps 33:7
me, and let us exalt his name *t.*	Ps 34:3
and gathered themselves *t.*	Ps 35:15
the abjects gathered themselves *t.*	Ps 35:15
and brought to confusion *t.*	Ps 35:26
transgressors shall be destroyed *t.*	Ps 37:38
be ashamed and confounded *t.*	Ps 40:14
All that hate me whisper *t.* against	Ps 41:7
The princes are gathered *t.*	Ps 47:9
were assembled, they passed by *t.*	Ps 48:4
Both low and high, rich and poor *t.*	Ps 49:2
Gather my saints *t.* unto me	Ps 50:5
We took a sweet counsel *t.*	Ps 55:14
They gather themselves *t.* they hide	Ps 56:6
wait for my soul take counsel *t.*	Ps 71:10
hearts, Let us destroy them *t.*	Ps 74:8
have consulted *t.* with one consent	Ps 83:5
Mercy and truth are met *t.*	Ps 85:10
they compassed me about *t.*	Ps 88:17
They compassed me about *t.*	Ps 94:21
hands: let the hills be joyful *t.*	Ps 98:8
When the people are gathered *t.*	Ps 102:22
ariseth, they gather themselves *t.*	Ps 104:22
as a city that is compact *t.*	Ps 122:3
is for brethren to dwell *t.* in unity	Ps 133:1
are they gathered *t.* for war	Ps 140:2
gathered *t.* the outcasts of Israel	Ps 147:2
The rich and poor meet *t.*: the Lord is	Pr 22:2
poor and the deceitful man meet *t.*	Pr 29:13
and a time to gather stones *t.*	Ec 3:5
fool foldeth his hands *t.* and eateth his	Ec 4:5
if two lie *t.* then they have heat	Ec 4:11
Come now, and let us reason *t.* saith	Isa 1:18
and of the sinners shall be *t.*	Isa 1:28
spark, and they shall both burn *t.*	Isa 1:31
Take counsel *t.* and it shall come to	Isa 8:10
him, and join his enemies *t.*	Isa 9:11
they *t.* shall be against Judah	Isa 9:21
the young lion and the fatling *t.*	Isa 11:6
their young ones shall lie down *t.*	Isa 11:7
gather *t.* the dispersed of Judah	Isa 11:12
shall spoil them of the east *t.*	Isa 11:14
kingdoms of nations gathered *t.*	Isa 13:4
They shall be left *t.* unto the fowls	Isa 18:6
All thy rulers are fled *t.* they are	Isa 22:3
that are found in thee are bound *t.*	Isa 22:3
gathered *t.* the waters of the lower	Isa 22:9
And they shall be gathered *t.*	Isa 24:22
and he shall bring down their pride *t.*	Isa 25:11
t. with my dead body shall they arise	Isa 26:19
them, I would burn them *t.*	Isa 27:4
fall down, and they shall fail *t.*	Isa 31:3
the heavens shall be rolled *t.*	Isa 34:4
and all flesh shall see it *t.*	Isa 40:5
let us come near *t.* to judgment	Isa 41:1
and the pine, and the box tree *t.*	Isa 41:19
and consider, and understand *t.*	Isa 41:20
may be dismayed, and behold it *t.*	Isa 41:23
Let all the nations be gathered *t.*	Isa 43:9
they shall lie down *t.* they shall not	Isa 43:17
me in remembrance: let us plead *t.*	Isa 43:26
let them all be gathered *t.*	Isa 44:11
and they shall be ashamed *t.*	Isa 44:11
let righteousness spring up *t.* I	Isa 45:8
go to confusion *t.* that are makers	Isa 45:16
draw near *t.* ye that are escaped of	Isa 45:20
near; yea, let them take counsel *t.*	Isa 45:21
They stoop, they bow down *t.*	Isa 46:2
call unto them, they stand up *t.*	Isa 48:13
all these gather themselves *t.*	Isa 49:18
contend with me? let us stand *t.*	Isa 50:8
with the voice *t.* shall they sing	Isa 52:8
Break forth into joy, sing *t.* ye	Isa 52:9
they shall surely gather *t.* but	Isa 54:15
whosoever shall gather *t.* against	Isa 54:15
all they gather themselves *t.* they	Isa 60:4
Then thou shalt see, and flow *t.*	Isa 60:5
shall be gathered *t.* unto thee	Isa 60:7
tree, the pine tree, and the box *t.*	Isa 60:13
that have brought it *t.* shall drink	Isa 62:9
the iniquities of your fathers *t.*	Isa 65:7
The wolf and the lamb shall feed *t.*	Isa 65:25
the mouse, shall be consumed *t.*	Isa 66:17
they shall come *t.* out of the land of	Jer 3:18
cry, gather *t.*, and say, Assemble	Jer 4:5
the asembly of young men *t.*	Jer 6:11
with their fields and wives *t.*	Jer 6:12
the sons *t.* shall fall upon them	Jer 6:21
even the fathers and the sons *t.*	Jer 13:14
her that travaileth with child *t.*	Jer 31:8
shall flow *t.* to the goodness	Jer 31:12
dance, both young men and old *t.*	Jer 31:13
and in all the cities thereof *t.*	Jer 31:24
they did eat bread *t.* in Mizpah	Jer 41:1
mighty, and they are fallen both *t.*	Jer 46:12
turned back, and are fled away *t.*	Jer 46:21
with his priests and his princes *t.*	Jer 48:7
and his priests and his princes *t.*	Jer 49:3
Gather ye *t.* and come against	Jer 49:14
they and the children of Judah *t.*	Jer 50:4
Call *t.* the archers against	Jer 50:29
of Judah were oppressed *t.*	Jer 50:33
call *t.* against her the kingdoms of	Jer 51:27
They shall roar *t.* like lions: they	Jer 51:38
nations shall not flow *t.* any more	Jer 51:44
to lament; they languished *t.*	La 2:8
prophesy, and smite thine hands *t.*	Eze 21:14
I will also smite mine hands *t.* and	Eze 21:17
thou shalt not be brought *t.*	Eze 29:5
bones came *t.* bone to his bone	Eze 37:7
and the gold, broken to pieces *t.*	Da 2:35
king sent to gather *t.* the princes	Da 3:2
gathered *t.* unto the dedication of	Da 3:3
counsellors, being gathered *t.*	Da 3:27
presidents and princes assembled *t.*	Da 6:6
have consulted *t.* to establish	Da 6:7
they shall join themselves *t.*	Da 11:6
children of Israel be gathered *t.*	Ho 1:11
me, my repentings are kindled *t.*	Ho 11:8
gather yourselves *t.* round about	Joe 3:11
captivity, he and his princes *t.*	Am 1:15
Can two walk *t.* except they be	Am 3:3
them *t.* as the sheep of Bozrah	Mic 2:12
while they be folden *t.* as thorns	Na 1:10
melteth, and the knees smite *t.*	Na 2:10
Gather yourselves *t.* yea	Zep 2:1
yea, gather *t.*, O nation not desired	Zep 2:1
bow, out of him every oppressor *t.*	Zec 10:4
people of the earth be gathered *t.*	Zec 12:3
round about shall be gathered *t.*	Zec 14:14
before they came *t.* she was found	M't 1:18
priests and scribes of the people *t.*	M't 2:4

great multitudes were gathered t.   *M't 13:2*
Let both grow t. until the harvest   *M't 13:30*
Gather ye t. first the tares   *M't 13:30*
three are gathered t. in my name   *M't 18:20*
What therefore God hath joined t.   *M't 19:6; M'k 10:9*
gathered t. all as many as they   *M't 22:10*
they were gathered t.   *M't 22:34*
the Pharisees were gathered t.   *M't 22:41*
I have gathered thy children t.   *M't 23:37*
will the eagles be gathered t.   *M't 24:28*
gather t. his elect from the four   *M't 24:31*
Then assembled t. the chief priests   *M't 26:3*
when they were gathered t.   *M't 27:17*
and Pharisees came t. unto Pilate   *M't 27:62*
city was gathered t. at the door   *M'k 1:33*
many were gathered t.   *M'k 2:2*
and sinners sat also t. with Jesus   *M'k 2:15*
the multitude cometh t. again   *M'k 3:20*
apostles gathered themselves t.   *M'k 6:30*
them, and came t. unto him   *M'k 6:33*
came t. unto him the Pharisees   *M'k 7:1*
that the people came running t.   *M'k 9:25*
having heard them reasoning t.   *M'k 12:28*
gather t. his elect from the four   *M'k 13:27*
him, but their witness agreed not t.   *M'k 14:56*
neither so did their witness agree t.   *M'k 14:59*
and they call t. the whole band   *M'k 15:16*
great multitudes came t. to hear   *Lu 5:15*
measure, pressed down, and shaken   *Lu 6:38*
much people were gathered t.   *Lu 8:4*
he called his twelve disciples t.   *Lu 9:1*
the people were gathered thick t.   *Lu 11:29*
were gathered t. an innumerable   *Lu 12:1*
was bowed t. and could in no wise   *Lu 13:11*
I have gathered thy children t.   *Lu 13:34*
he calleth t. his friends and   *Lu 15:6*
her friends and her neighbours t.   *Lu 15:9*
the younger son gathered all t.   *Lu 15:13*
women be grinding t.   *Lu 17:35*
will the eagles be gathered t.   *Lu 17:37*
were set down t. Peter sat down   *Lu 22:55*
priests and the scribes came t.   *Lu 22:66*
Herod were made friends t.   *Lu 23:12*
he had called t. the chief priests   *Lu 23:13*
all the people that came t. to that   *Lu 23:48*
they talked t. of all these   *Lu 24:14*
they communed t. and reasoned   *Lu 24:15*
and found the eleven gathered t.   *Lu 24:33*
he that reapeth may rejoice t.   *Joh 4:36*
Therefore they gathered them t.   *Joh 6:13*
gather t. in one the children of God   *Joh 11:52*
they took counsel t. for to put   *Joh 11:53*
So they ran both t.: and the   *Joh 20:4*
but wrapped t. in a place by itself   *Joh 20:7*
There were t. Simon Peter   *Joh 21:2*
being assembled t. with them   *Ac 1:4*
When they therefore were come t.   *Ac 1:6*
of names t. were about an   *Ac 1:15*
abroad, the multitude came t.   *Ac 2:6*
all that believed were t.   *Ac 2:44*
Peter and John went up t.   *Ac 3:1*

all the people ran t. unto   *Ac 3:11*
were gathered t. at Jerusalem   *Ac 4:6*
rulers were gathered t.   *Ac 4:26*
people of Israel, were gathered t.   *Ac 4:27*
where they were assembled t.   *Ac 4:31*
it that ye have agreed t. to tempt   *Ac 5:9*
him, and called the council t.   *Ac 5:21*
called t. his kinsmen and near   *Ac 10:24*
and found many that were come t.   *Ac 10:27*
many were gathered t. praying   *Ac 12:12*
came almost the whole city t.   *Ac 13:44*
they went both t. into the   *Ac 14:1*
and had gathered the church t.   *Ac 14:27*
And the apostles and elders came t.   *Ac 15:6*
they had gathered the multitude t.   *Ac 15:30*
multitude rose up t. against them   *Ac 16:22*
arts brought their books t.   *Ac 19:19*
he called t. with the workmen   *Ac 19:25*
not wherefore they were come t.   *Ac 19:32*
disciples came t. to break bread   *Ac 20:7*
where they were gathered t.   *Ac 20:8*
multitude must needs come t.   *Ac 21:22*
was moved, and the people ran t.   *Ac 21:30*
certain of the Jews banded t.   *Ac 23:12*
Paul called the chief of the Jews t.   *Ac 28:17*
and when they were come t. he   *Ac 28:17*
I may be comforted t. with   *Ro 1:12*
they are t. become unprofitable   *Ro 3:12*
planted t. in the likeness of his   *Ro 6:5*
that we may be also glorified t.   *Ro 8:17*
groaneth and travaileth in pain t.   *Ro 8:22*
that all things work t. for good   *Ro 8:28*
strive t. with me in your prayers   *Ro 15:30*
that ye be perfectly joined t. in the   *1Co 1:10*
For we are labourers t. with God   *1Co 3:9*
when ye are gathered t. and my   *1Co 5:4*
come t. again, that Satan   *1Co 7:5*
that ye come t. not for the better   *1Co 11:17*
when ye come t. in the church, I   *1Co 11:18*
When ye come t. therefore into one   *1Co 11:20*
when ye come t. to eat, tarry one   *1Co 11:33*
ye come not t. unto condemnation   *1Co 11:34*
but God hath tempered the body t.   *1Co 12:24*
whole church be come t. into one   *1Co 14:23*
when ye came t. every one of you   *1Co 14:26*
Ye also helping t. by prayer for us   *2Co 1:11*
We then, as workers t. with him   *2Co 6:1*
Be ye not unequally yoked t. with   *2Co 6:14*
might gather t. in one all things   *Eph 1:10*
hath quickened us t. with Christ   *Eph 2:5*
And hath raised us up t.   *Eph 2:6*
made us sit t. in heavenly places   *Eph 2:6*
all the building fitly framed t.   *Eph 2:21*
In whom ye also are builded t. for   *Eph 2:22*
the whole body fitly joined t.   *Eph 4:16*
one mind striving t. for the faith   *Ph'p 1:27*
Brethren, be followers t. of me   *Ph'p 3:17*
he comforted, being knit t. in love   *Col 2:2*
hath he quickened t. with him   *Col 2:13*

ministered, and knit t.   *Col 2:19*
remain shall be caught up t. with   *1Th 4:17*
sleep, we should live t. with him   *1Th 5:10*
Wherefore comfort yourselves t.   *1Th 5:11*
and by our gathering t. unto him   *2Th 2:1*
the assembling of ourselves t.   *Heb 10:25*
Ye have heaped treasure t. for   *Jas 5:3*
being heirs t. of the grace of life   *1Pe 3:7*
is at Babylon, elected t. with you   *1Pe 5:13*
as a scroll when it is rolled t.   *Re 6:14*
he gathered them t. into a place   *Re 16:16*
Come and gather yourselves t. unto   *Re 19:17*
armies, gathered t. to make war   *Re 19:19*
Magog, to gather them t. to battle   *Re 20:8*

TOHU

the son of Elihu, the son of T.   *1Sa 1:1*

TOI

When T. king of Hamath heard   *2Sa 8:9*
T. sent Joram his son unto king   *2Sa 8:10*
for Hadadezer had wars with T.   *2Sa 8:10*

TOIL

our work and t. of our hands   *Ge 5:29*
hath made me forget all my t.   *Ge 41:51*
made them t. at the brickkiln (S)   *2Sa 12:31*
the bread of t. (A)(B)(E)(R)   *Ps 127:2*
all the t. (R)   *Ec 4:4; 4:6, 8; 1Th 2:9; 2Th 3:8*
however a man may t. (A)(R)   *Ec 8:17*
t. without rest (B)   *La 5:5*
they t. not, neither do they spin   *M't 6:28*
grow; they t. not, they spin not   *Lu 12:27*
in t. and hardship (A)(R)   *2Co 11:27*
t. and struggles (A)   *1Th 2:9; 2Th 3:8*

TOILED

Master, we have t. all the night   *Lu 5:5*

TOILING

t., depriving myself (R)   *Ec 4:8*
And he saw them t. in rowing; for   *M'k 6:48*

TOILS

the t. of his sin (R)   *Pr 5:22*
strain with which he t. (R)   *Ec 2:22*

TOKEN

This is the t. of the covenant which   *Ge 9:12*
a sign (B)   *Ge 9:12; 9:17; 17:11; Ex 13:16; Ps 86:17; 2Th 3:17*
a sign (R)   *Ge 9:13, 17; 17:11; Ex 3:12; Nu 17:10; Jos 2:12; Ps 86:17; M'k 14:44*
t. of a covenant between me   *Ge 9:13*
This is the t. of the covenant, which   *Ge 9:17*
t. of the covenant betwixt me and   *Ge 17:11*
this shall be a t. unto thee, that I   *Ex 3:12*
a sign   *Ex 3:12; Nu 17:10; Jos 2:12; Ps 86:17; Ph'p 1:28*
this will be your evidence (B)   *Ex 3:12*
the blood shall be to you for a t.   *Ex 12:13*
mark the homes (B)   *Ex 12:13*
shall be for a t. upon thine hand   *Ex 13:16*

TOKEN

a reminder upon your hand   Ex 13:16
(A)
be a mark (R)   Ex 13:16; 2Th 3:17
be kept for a t. against the   Nu 17:10
rebels
find them as a t. (B)   De 6:8; 11:18
father's house, and give me a   Jos 2:12
true (.)
give me a pledge (B)   Jos 2:12
Shew me a t. for good; that   Ps 86:17
they
see a t. of proof (B)   M't 12:38
betrayed him had given   M'k 14:44
them a t.
given them a signal   M'k 14:44
(A)(B)(N)
given them a sign (P)   M'k 14:44
this is a t. for you (B)   Lu 2:12
to them an evident t. of   Ph'p 1:28
perdition
for them this augurs   Ph'p 1:28
destruction (B)
a sure sign of their doom   Ph'p 1:28
sealed (N)
a clear omen of destruction   Ph'p 1:28
(R)
a manifest t. of the righteous   2Th 1:5
positive proof of just and   2Th 1:5
right judgment (A)
evidence of fair verdict (B)   2Th 1:5
which is the t. in every   2Th 3:17
epistle
this authenticates all my   2Th 3:17
letters (N)
my mark on all letters (P)   2Th 3:17

TOKENS

forth the t. of the damsel's   De 22:15
virginity
proofs of her virginity (B)   De 22:15
are the t. of my daughter's   De 22:17
virginity
evidences of her virginity   De 22:17;
(A)(B)   22:20
t. of virginity be not found   De 22:20
for the
evidence of chastity (B)   De 22:20
way? and do ye not know   Job 21:29
their t.
accept their testimony and   Job 21:29
evidences (A)
do you not accept their   Job 21:29
testimony (R)
uttermost parts are afraid at   Ps 65:8
thy t.
afraid of nature's signs (A)   Ps 65:8
stand in awe of thy signs (B)   Ps 65:8
afraid of thy signs (R)   Ps 65:8
sent t. and wonders into the   Ps 135:9
midst
sent signs and wonders   Ps 135:9
(A)(B)(R)
That frustrateth the t. of the   Isa 44:25
liars
who frustrates signs (A)   Isa 44:25
confounds the omens of   Isa 44:25
soothsayers (B)
frustrates omens of liars (R)   Isa 44:25

TOLA

sons of Issachar; T., and   Ge 46:13
Phuvah
of T., the family of the   Nu 26:23
Tolaites
defend Israel T. the son of   J'g 10:1
Puah
sons of Issachar were T., and   1Ch 7:1
sons of T., Uzzi, and   1Ch 7:2
Rephaiah
their father's house, to wit, of   1Ch 7:2
T.

TOLAD

Bilhah, and at Ezem, and at   1Ch 4:29
T.

TOLAITES

of Tola, the family of the T.   Nu 26:23

TOLD

Who t. thee that thou wast   Ge 3:11
naked
and t. his two brethren   Ge 9:22
without

escaped, and t. Abram the   Ge 14:13
Hebrew
t. all these things in their ears   Ge 20:8
the place of which God had t.   Ge 22:3
him
the place which God had t.   Ge 22:9
him of
that it was t. Abraham,   Ge 22:20
saying
t. them of her mother's house   Ge 24:28
these
eat, until I have t. mine   Ge 24:33
errand
servant, t. Isaac all things   Ge 24:66
that he
and t. him concerning the   Ge 26:32
well
her elder son were t. to   Ge 27:42
Rebekah
Jacob t. Rachel that he was   Ge 29:12
her
and she ran and t. her father   Ge 29:12
And he t. Laban all these   Ge 29:13
things
in that he t. him not that he   Ge 31:20
fled
t. Laban on the third day,   Ge 31:22
that
a dream, and he t. it his   Ge 37:5
brethren
dream, and t. it his brethren   Ge 37:9
And he t. it to his father,   Ge 37:10
and to
was t. Tamar, saying, Behold,   Ge 38:13
thy
that it was t. Judah, saying   Ge 38:24
chief butler t. his dream to   Ge 40:9
and Pharaoh t. them his   Ge 41:8
dream
we t. him, and he interpreted   Ge 41:12
to us
and I t. this unto the   Ge 41:24
magicians
t. him all that befell unto   Ge 42:29
them
we t. him according to the   Ge 43:7
tenor
we t. him the words of my   Ge 44:24
lord
t. him, saying, Joseph is yet   Ge 45:26
alive
t. him all the words of   Ge 45:27
Joseph
Joseph came and t. Pharaoh   Ge 47:1
that one t. Joseph, Behold, thy   Ge 48:1
one t. Jacob, and said,   Ge 48:2
Behold
Moses t. Aaron all the words   Ex 4:28
Aaron went in, and t. Pharaoh   Ex 5:1
it was t. the king of Egypt   Ex 14:5
that the
congregation came and t.   Ex 16:22
Moses
Moses t. his father in law all   Ex 18:8
that
Moses t. the words of the   Ex 19:9
people
Moses came and t. the people   Ex 24:3
all
Moses t. it unto Aaron, and to   Le 21:24
his
t. the people the words of   Nu 11:24
the Lord
ran a young man, and t.   Nu 11:27
Moses
t. him, and said, We came   Nu 13:27
unto
Moses t. these sayings unto   Nu 14:39
all
said unto Balak, T. not I   Nu 23:26
thee
t. the children of Israel   Nu 29:40
according
And it be t. thee, and thou   De 17:4
hast
And it was t. the king of   Jos 2:2
Jericho
t. him all things that befell   Jos 2:23
them
it was certainly t. thy servants   Jos 9:24
it was t. Joshua, saying, The   Jos 10:17
five
the children of Israel were t.   Jos 22:11
(S)
miracles which our fathers   J'g 6:13
t. us
there was a man that t. a   J'g 7:13
dream
And when they t. it to Jotham   J'g 9:7

by them: and it was t.   J'g 9:25
Abimelech
the field; and they t.   J'g 9:42
Abimelech
it was t. Abimelech, that all   J'g 9:47
the men
woman came and t. her   J'g 13:6
husband
was, neither t. he me his name   J'g 13:6
told (S)   J'g 13:10; 1Sa 11:9
at this time have t. us such   J'g 13:23
things
and t. his father and his   J'g 14:2
mother
he t. not his father or his   J'g 14:6
mother
he t. not them that he had   J'g 14:9
taken
my people, and hast not t. it   J'g 14:16
me
I have not t. it my father nor   J'g 14:16
my
on the seventh day, that he t.   J'g 14:17
her
she t. the riddle to the   J'g 14:17
children of
it was t. the Gazites, saying,   J'g 16:2
Samson
hast mocked me, and t. me   J'g 16:10;
lies   16:13
hast not t. me wherein thy   J'g 16:15
great
That he t. her all his heart   J'g 16:17
saw that he had t. her all his   J'g 16:18
heart
she t. her all that the man   Ru 3:16
had done
t. him that I will judge his   1Sa 3:13
house
Samuel t. him every whit, and   1Sa 3:18
hid
man came into the city, and   1Sa 4:13
t. it
man came in hastily, and t.   1Sa 4:14
Eli
Samuel t. all the words of the   1Sa 8:10
Lord
Lord had t. Samuel in his   1Sa 9:15
ear a
He t. us plainly that the   1Sa 10:16
asses
Samuel spake, he t. him not   1Sa 10:16
Samuel t. the people the   1Sa 10:25
manner
t. the tidings in the ears of   1Sa 11:4
t. him the tidings of the men   1Sa 11:5
side. But he t. not his father   1Sa 14:1
Then they t. Saul, saying,   1Sa 14:33
Behold
Jonathan t. him, and said, I   1Sa 14:43
did but
it was t. Samuel, saying, Saul   1Sa 15:12
came
they t. Saul, and the thing   1Sa 18:20
pleased
the servants of Saul t. him,   1Sa 18:24
saying
his servants t. David these   1Sa 18:26
words
and Jonathan t. David, saying   1Sa 19:2
Michal David's wife t. him,   1Sa 19:11
saying
and t. him all that Saul had   1Sa 19:18
done to
t. Saul, saying, Behold   1Sa 19:19
David is at
when it was t. Saul, he sent   1Sa 19:21
other
they t. David, saying, Behold   1Sa 23:1
it was t. Saul that David was   1Sa 23:7
come
was t. Saul that David was   1Sa 23:13
escaped
t. me that he dealeth very   1Sa 23:22
subtilly
they t. David; wherefore he   1Sa 23:25
came
that it was t. him, saying,   1Sa 24:1
Behold
came and t. him all those   1Sa 25:12
sayings
one of the young men t.   1Sa 25:14
Abigail
But she t. not her husband   1Sa 25:19
Nabal
she t. him nothing, less or   1Sa 25:36
more
his wife had t. him these   1Sa 25:37
things

t. Saul that David was fled to Gath	1Sa 27:4	messengers returned, t. the king	2Ki 7:15	So he t. me, and made me know the	Da 7:16
unto the young man that t. him	2Sa 1:5	king asked the woman, she t. him	2Ki 8:6	the vision, which t. is true	Da 8:26
the young man that t. him said, As	2Sa 1:6	t. him, saying, The man of God is	2Ki 8:7	the Lord, because he had t. them	Jon 1:10
said unto the young man that t. him	2Sa 1:13	He t. me that thou shouldest surely	2Ki 8:14	not believe, though it be t. you	Hab 1:5
And they t. David, saying, That the	2Sa 2:4	the watchman t. saying, The	2Ki 9:18	a lie, and have t. false dreams	Zec 10:2
they t. Joab, saying, Abner the son	2Sa 3:23	watchman t. saying, He came even	2Ki 9:20	into the city, and t. every thing	M't 8:33
When one t. me, saying, Behold	2Sa 4:10	they came again, and t. him	2Ki 9:36	and said unto him that t. him	M't 12:48
And it was t. king David	2Sa 6:12	there came a messenger, and t. him	2Ki 10:8	buried it, and went and t. Jesus	M't 14:12
When they t. it unto David	2Sa 10:5	t. the money that was found	2Ki 12:10	t. unto their lord all that was done	M't 18:31
was t. David, he gathered all Israel	2Sa 10:17	they gave the money, being t.	2Ki 12:11	Behold, I have t. you before	M't 24:25
conceived, and sent and t. David	2Sa 11:5	t. him the words of Rab-shakeh	2Ki 18:37	done, be t. for a memorial of her	M't 26:13
when they had t. David, saying	2Sa 11:10	the men of the city t. him, It is the	2Ki 23:17	shall ye see him; lo, I have t. you	M't 28:7
Then Joab sent and t. David all the	2Sa 11:18	hast t. thy servant that thou wilt	1Ch 17:25	t. it in the city, and in the country	M'k 5:14
Joab came to the king, and t. him	2Sa 14:33	t. David how the men were served	1Ch 19:5	they that saw it t. them how it	M'k 5:16
And one t. David, saying, Ahithophel	2Sa 15:31	it was t. David; and he gathered	1Ch 19:17	him, and t. him all the truth	M'k 5:33
and a wench went and t. them	2Sa 17:17	Solomon t. out threescore and ten	2Ch 2:2	t. him all things, both what they	M'k 6:30
and they went and t. king David	2Sa 17:17	which could not be t. nor numbered	2Ch 5:6	he answered and t. them, Elias	M'k 9:12
a lad saw them, and t. Absalom	2Sa 17:18	Solomon t. her all her questions	2Ch 9:2	t. them that had been with him	M'k 16:10
went and t. king David, and said	2Sa 17:21	from Solomon which he t. her	2Ch 9:2	they went and t. it unto the residue	M'k 16:13
a certain man saw it, and t. Joab	2Sa 18:10	of thy wisdom was not t. me	2Ch 9:6	which were t. her from the Lord	Lu 1:45
Joab said unto the man that t. him	2Sa 18:11	came some that t. Jehoshaphat	2Ch 20:2	was t. them concerning this child	Lu 2:17
watchman cried and t. the king	2Sa 18:25	Then Shaphan the scribe t. the king	2Ch 34:18	were t. them by the shepherds	Lu 2:18
And it was t. Joab, Behold, the king	2Sa 19:1	I t. them what they should	Ezr 8:17	and seen, as it was t. unto them	Lu 2:20
they t. unto all the people saying	2Sa 19:8	neither t. I any man what my God	Ne 2:12	it was t. him by certain which said	Lu 8:20
it was t. David what Rizpah	2Sa 21:11	neither had I as yet t. it to the Jews	Ne 2:16	went, and t. it in the city and in the	Lu 8:34
So God came to David, and t. him	2Sa 24:13	I t. them of the hand of my God	Ne 2:18	which saw it t. them by what means	Lu 8:36
they t. the king, saying, Behold	1Ki 1:23	who t. it unto Esther the queen	Es 2:22	t. him all that they had done	Lu 9:10
And it was t. Solomon, saying	1Ki 1:51	that they t. Haman, to see whether	Es 3:4	and t. no man in those days any of	Lu 9:36
t. king Solomon that Joab was fled	1Ki 2:29	he had t. them that he was a Jew	Es 3:4	some that t. him of the Galilæans	Lu 13:1
And they t. Shimei, saying, Behold	1Ki 2:39	chamberlains came and t. it her	Es 4:4	they t. him that Jesus of Nazareth	Lu 18:37
it was t. Solomon that Shimei had	1Ki 2:41	And Mordecai t. him of all that had	Es 4:7	t. all these things unto the eleven	Lu 24:9
that could not be t. nor numbered	1Ki 8:5	And Hatach came and t. Esther	Es 4:9	t. these things unto the apostles	Lu 24:10
Solomon t. her all her questions	1Ki 10:3	They t. to Mordecai Esther's words	Es 4:12	t. what things were done in	Lu 24:35
from the king, which he t. her not	1Ki 10:3	Esther t. them to return (S)	Es 4:15	if I have t. you earthly things	Joh 3:12
and, behold, the half was not t. me	1Ki 10:7	Haman t. them of the glory of his	Es 5:11	t. me all things that ever I did	Joh 4:29
his sons came and t. him all	1Ki 13:11	that Mordecai had t. of Bigthana	Es 6:2	He t. me all that ever I did	Joh 4:39
them they t. also to their father	1Ki 13:11	Haman t. Zeresh his wife and all	Es 6:13	and t. him, saying, Thy son liveth	Joh 4:51
and t. it in the city where the old	1Ki 13:25	Esther had t. what he was unto	Job 8:1	and t. the Jews that it was Jesus	Joh 5:15
which t. me that I should be king	1Ki 14:2	wise men have t. from their fathers	Job 15:18	a man that hath t. you the truth	Joh 8:40
Was it not t. my lord what I did	1Ki 18:13	Shall it be t. him that I speak? if a	Job 37:20	I have t. you already, and ye did	Joh 9:27
went to meet Ahab, and t. him	1Ki 18:16	our fathers have t. us, what work	Ps 44:1	them, I t. you, and ye believed not	Joh 10:25
Ahab t. Jezebel all that Elijah had	1Ki 19:1	the Edomite came and t. Saul	Ps 52 title	and t. them what things Jesus had	Joh 11:46
Ben-hadad sent out, and they t. him	1Ki 20:17	known, and our fathers have t. us	Ps 78:3	it were not so, I would have t. you	Joh 14:2
meet you, and t. you these words	2Ki 1:7	we spend our years as a tale that is t.	Ps 90:9	have t. you before it come to pass	Joh 14:29
she came and t. the man of God	2Ki 4:7	he live a thousand years twice t.	Ec 6:6	But these things have I t. you	Joh 16:4
hid it from me, and hath not t. me	2Ki 4:27	And it was t. the house of David	Isa 7:2	remember that I t. you of them	Joh 16:4
and t. him saying, The child is not	2Ki 4:31	t. him the words of Rabshakeh	Isa 36:22	I have t. you that I am he	Joh 18:8
one went in, and t. his lord, saying	2Ki 5:4	not been t. you from the beginning	Isa 40:21	t. the disciples that she had seen	Joh 20:18
man of God t. him and warned him	2Ki 6:10	have not I t. thee from that time	Isa 44:8	the prison, they returned, and t.	Ac 5:22
was t. him, saying, Behold, he is a	2Ki 6:13	who hath t. it from that time	Isa 45:21	Then came one and t. them, saying	Ac 5:25
they t. them, saying, We came to	2Ki 7:10	that which had not been t. them	Isa 52:15	t. glad tidings (B)	Ac 8:12
they t. it to the king's house within	2Ki 7:11	and t. all the words in the ears of	Jer 36:20	be t. thee what thou must do	Ac 9:6
		he t. them according to all these	Jer 38:27	t. how Peter stood before the gate	Ac 12:14
		and I t. the dream before them	Da 4:7	keeper of the prison t. this saying	Ac 16:36
		before him I t. the dream, saying	Da 4:8	serjeants t. these words unto	Ac 16:38
		and t. the sum of the matters	Da 7:1	it shall be t. thee of all things	Ac 22:10

he went and *t.* the chief captain   *Ac 22:26*
entered into the castle, and *t.* Paul   *Ac 23:16*
it was *t.* me how that the Jews   *Ac 23:30*
it shall be even as it was *t.* me   *Ac 27:25*
when he *t.* us your earnest desire   *2Co 7:7*
I *t.* you before, and foretell you   *2Co 13:2*
as I have also *t.* you in time past   *Ga 5:21*
walk of whom I have *t.* you often   *Ph'p 3:18*
we *t.* you before that we should   *1Th 3:4*
with you, I *t.* you these things   *2Th 2:5*
that they *t.* you there should be   *Jude 18*

TOLERABLE

It shall be more *t.* for the land   *M't 10:15*
fare better in the judgment (B)   *M't 10:15*
more bearable (N)   *M't 10:15; 11:22, 24; Lu 10:12, 14*
It shall be more *t.* for Tyre   *M't 11:22*
more endurable (A)   *M't 11:22; 11:24*
more endurable (B)   *M't 11:22; 11:24; M'k 6:11; Lu 10:12, 14*
more bearable (P)   *M't 11:22; 11:24*
it shall be more *t.* for the land of   *M't 11:24*
It shall be more *t.* for Sodom   *M'k 6:11*
it shall be more *t.* in that day for   *Lu 10:12*
it will be better (P)   *Lu 10:12; 10:14*
it shall be more *t.* for Tyre   *Lu 10:14*

TOLERANCE

goodness and *t.* (B)(N)   *Ro 2:4*

TOLERANT

t., and gentle when discipline is needed (N)   *2Ti 2:25*

TOLERATE

to *t.* (A)(B)(R)(S)   *Es 3:8; Ps 101:5*
not *t.* that woman (A)(B)(N)(P)(R)   *Re 2:20*

TOLL

then will they not pay *t.,* tribute   *Ezr 4:13*
t., tribute, and custom, was paid   *Ezr 4:20*
it shall not be lawful to impose *t.*   *Ezr 7:24*
sitting at the place of *t.* (E)   *M't 9:9*
receive *t.* or tribute (E)(N)(R)   *M't 17:25*
pay tax and *t.* (N)   *Ro 13:6*
t. to whom *t.* is due (B)   *Ro 13:7*

TOMB

tomb (A)   *Ge 23:6; De 34:6; J'g 8:32; 1Sa 10:2; 2Sa 2:32; 4:12; 17:23; 21:14; 1Ki 13:22; 2Ki 21:26; 23:17, 30; Isa 22:16; M't 27:60-61, 64; 28:1, 8; M'k 15:46; 16:2-3, 5, 8; Lu 23:53, 55; 24:1, 2, 9, 12, 22, 24; Joh 19:41-42; 20:1-4, 6, 8, 11; Ac 2:29; 7:16; 13:29*
tomb (B)   *J'g 8:32; 1Sa 10:2; 2Sa 17:23; M't 27:60-61, 64; 28:1, 8; M'k 15:46; 16:2-3, 5, 8; Lu 23:53, 55; 24:1-2, 9, 12, 22, 24; Joh 19:41-42; 20:2, 4, 6, 11; Ac 2:29; 7:16; 13:29*
in his own *t.* (A)   *2Ch 16:14*
grave, and shall remain in the *t.*   *Job 21:32*
hewn out of *t.* (R)   *Isa 22:16*
laid it in his own new *t.* which he   *M't 27:60*
tomb (E)   *M't 27:60; 28:8; M'k 15:46; 16:2-3, 5, 8; Lu 23:53, 55; 24:1-2, 9, 12, 22, 24; Joh 19:41-42; 20:1, 3-4, 6, 8, 11; Ac 2:29; 7:16; 13:29*
tomb (N)(P)(R)   *M't 27:60; 28:8; M'k 15:46; 16:2-3, 8; Lu 23:53; 24:1-*

2, 9, 22, 24; Joh 19:41-42; 20:1, 3-4, 6, 8, 11; Ac 2:29; 7:16; 13:29
up his corpse, and laid it in a *t.*   *M'k 6:29*
to be put in at *t.* (A)(E)(R)   *Re 11:9*

TOMBS

tombs (A)   *2Ki 23:16; 2Ch 21:20; 24:25; 28:27; 32:33; 35:24; M't 23:27, 29; Lu 11:47*
out of their *t.* (R)   *Jer 8:1*
with devils, coming out of the *t.*   *M't 8:28*
tombs (B)(N)(P)(R)   *M't 23:27; 23:29*
ye build the *t.* of the prophets   *M't 23:29*
t. were opened (A)(B)(E)(R)   *M't 27:52; 27:53*
there met him out of the *t.* a man   *M'k 5:2*
had his dwelling among the *t.*   *M'k 5:3*
and in the *t.* crying, and cutting   *M'k 5:5*
abode in any house, but in the *t.*   *Lu 8:27*
unseen *t.* (B)(E)(R)   *Lu 11:44*
who are in *t.* (A)(E)(R)   *Joh 5:28*

TONE

I change my *t.* of you (E)   *Ga 4:20*

TONES

give distinct *t.* (A)(B)(R)   *1Co 14:7*

TONGS

t. thereof, and the snuffdishes   *Ex 25:38*
the snuffers (A)(B)(R)   *Ex 25:38; Nu 4:9*
and his *t.* and his snuffdishes   *Nu 4:9*
and the lamps, and the *t.* of gold   *1Ki 7:49*
the lamps, and the *t.* made he of   *2Ch 4:21*
the snuffers (A)   *2Ch 4:21*
which he had taken with the *t.*   *Isa 6:6*
smith with the *t.* both worketh   *Isa 44:12*

TONGUE

every one after his *t.* after their   *Ge 10:5*
language (A)   *Ge 10:5; De 28:49; Ezr 4:7*
language (B)   *Ge 10:5; Ezr 4:7; Isa 3:8; Ne 13:24*
language (R)   *Ge 10:5*
slow of speech, and of a slow *t.*   *Ex 4:10*
Israel shall not a dog move his *t.*   *Ex 11:7*
whose *t.* thou shalt not understand   *De 28:49*
speech (B)   *De 28:49*
none moved his *t.* against any of   *Jos 10:21*
lappeth of the water with his *t.*   *J'g 7:5*
by me, and his word was in my *t.*   *2Sa 23:2*
letter was written in the Syrian *t.*   *Ezr 4:7*
and interpreted in the Syrian *t.*   *Ezr 4:7*
in the Ashdod *t.* (B)   *Ne 13:24*
every people in own *t.* (B)   *Es 1:22*
bondwomen, I had held my *t.*   *Es 7:4*
be hid from the scourge of the *t.*   *Job 5:21*
Teach me, and I will hold my *t.*   *Job 6:24*
Is there iniquity in my *t.?* cannot   *Job 6:30*
if I hold my *t.* I shall give up the   *Job 13:19*
thou choosest the *t.* of the crafty   *Job 15:5*
though he hide it under his *t.*   *Job 20:12*
asps: the viper's *t.* shall slay him   *Job 20:16*
wickedness, nor my *t.* utter deceit   *Job 27:4*
their *t.* cleaved to the roof of their   *Job 29:10*
my *t.* hath spoken in my mouth   *Job 33:2*
or his *t.* with a cord which thou   *Job 41:1*

sepulchre; they flatter with their *t.*   *Ps 5:9*
under his *t.* is mischief and vanity   *Ps 10:7*
the *t.* that speaketh proud things   *Ps 12:3*
said, With our *t.* will we prevail   *Ps 12:4*
He that backbiteth not with his *t.*   *Ps 15:3*
my *t.* cleaveth to my jaws; and thou   *Ps 22:15*
Keep thy *t.* from evil, and thy lips   *Ps 34:13*
And my *t.* shall speak of thy   *Ps 35:28*
and his *t.* talketh of judgment   *Ps 37:30*
my ways, that I sin not with my *t.*   *Ps 39:1*
burned: then spake I with my *t.*   *Ps 39:3*
my *t.* is the pen of a ready writer   *Ps 45:1*
to evil, and thy *t.* frameth deceit   *Ps 50:19*
my *t.* shall sing aloud of thy   *Ps 51:14*
Thy *t.* deviseth mischiefs; like a   *Ps 52:2*
words, O thou deceitful *t.*   *Ps 52:4*
arrows, and their *t.* a sharp sword   *Ps 57:4*
Who whet their *t.* like a sword, and   *Ps 64:3*
shall make their own *t.* to fall upon   *Ps 64:8*
and he was extolled with my *t.*   *Ps 66:17*
and the *t.* of thy dogs in the same   *Ps 68:23*
My *t.* also shall talk of thy   *Ps 71:24*
their *t.* walketh through the earth   *Ps 73:9*
spoken against me with a lying *t.*   *Ps 109:2*
My *t.* shall speak of thy word: for   *Ps 119:172*
lying lips, and from a deceitful *t.*   *Ps 120:2*
be done unto thee, thou false *t.*   *Ps 120:3*
laughter, and our *t.* with singing   *Ps 126:2*
let my *t.* cleave to the roof of my   *Ps 137:6*
For there is not a word in my *t.*   *Ps 139:4*
A proud look, a lying *t.* and hands   *Pr 6:17*
of the *t.* of a strange woman   *Pr 6:24*
t. of the just is as choice silver   *Pr 10:20*
but the forward *t.* shall be cut out   *Pr 10:31*
but the *t.* of the wise is health   *Pr 12:18*
but a lying *t.* is but for a moment   *Pr 12:19*
The *t.* of the wise useth knowledge   *Pr 15:2*
A wholesome *t.* is a tree of life: but   *Pr 15:4*
perversity in *t.* breaks (B)   *Pr 15:4*
answer of the *t.* is from the Lord   *Pr 16:1*
a liar giveth ear to a naughty *t.*   *Pr 17:4*
a perverse *t.* falleth into mischief   *Pr 17:20*
perverted *t.* fall into trouble (B)   *Pr 17:20*
and life are in the power of the *t.*   *Pr 18:21*
lying *t.* is a vanity tossed to and fro   *Pr 21:6*
keepeth his mouth and his *t.*   *Pr 21:23*
and a soft *t.* breaketh the bone   *Pr 25:15*
angry countenance a backbiting *t.*   *Pr 25:23*
A lying *t.* hateth those that   *Pr 26:28*
that he that flattereth with the *t.*   *Pr 28:23*
and in her *t.* is the law of kindness   *Pr 31:26*
honey and milk are under thy *t.*   *Ca 4:11*
their *t.* and their doings are against   *Isa 3:8*
their speech (A)(R)   *Isa 3:8*
destroy the *t.* of the Egyptian sea   *Isa 11:15*

and another *t*. will he speak   *Isa 28:11*
to this
and his *t*. as a devouring fire *Isa 30:27*
the *t*. of the stammerers shall *Isa 32:4*
of a stammering *t*. that thou *Isa 33:19*
canst
hart, and the *t*. of the dumb *Isa 35:6*
sing
none, and their *t*. faileth for *Isa 41:17*
thirst
knee shall bow, every *t*. shall *Isa 45:23*
swear
hath given me the *t*. of the *Isa 50:4*
learned
every *t*. that shall rise   *Isa 54:17*
against thee
a wide mouth, and draw out *Isa 57:4*
the *t*.
your *t*. hath muttered   *Isa 59:3*
perverseness
have taught their *t*. to speak lies *Jer 9:5*
Their *t*. is as an arrow shot *Jer 9:8*
out; it
and let us smite him with the *Jer 18:18*
t.
t. of the sucking child cleaveth *La 4:4*
people of a foreign *t*. (B)   *Eze 3:5*
make thy *t*. cleave to the roof *Eze 3:26*
of thy
and the *t*. of the Chaldeans *Da 1:4*
rock of every *t*. (B)   *Da 3:4*
by the sword for the rage of *Ho 7:16*
their *t*.
Then shall he say, Hold thy *t*. *Am 6:10*
their *t*. is deceitful in their *Mic 6:12*
mouth
holdest thy *t*. when the   *Hab 1:13*
wicked
shall a deceitful *t*. be found *Zep 3:13*
their *t*. shall consume away *Zec 14:12*
in their
and he spit, and touched his *M'k 7:33*
t.
and the string of his *t*. was *M'k 7:35*
loosed
and his *t*. loosed, and he *Lu 1:64*
spake, and
his finger in water, and cool *Lu 16:24*
my *t*.
called in the Hebrew *t*.   *Joh 5:2*
Bethesda
field is called in their proper *t*. *Ac 1:19*
their own dialect (A)(B)   *Ac 1:19*
in their own language (R)   *Ac 1:19*
hear we every man in our own *Ac 2:8*
t.
our own dialect (A)   *Ac 2:8*
our native speech (B)   *Ac 2:8*
our native language (N)   *Ac 2:8*
heart rejoice, and my *t*. was *Ac 2:26*
glad
spake unto them in the   *Ac 21:40*
Hebrew *t*.
in the Hebrew dialect (A)   *Ac 21:40*
in the Hebrew language (B) *Ac 21:40;*
   26:14
in the Jewish language (N) *Ac 21:40*
in the Hebrew language (R) *Ac 21:40;*
   22:2; 26:14
he spake in the Hebrew *t*. to *Ac 22:2*
them
in their own language (N)   *Ac 22:2*
and saying in the Hebrew *t*., *Ac 26:14*
Saul
and every *t*. shall confess to *Ro 14:11*
God
person with a foul *t*. (A)(P) *1Co 5:11*
he that speaketh in an   *1Co 14:2*
unknown *t*.
language of ecstasy (N)   *1Co 14:2;*
   14:4, 19
He that speaketh in an   *1Co 14:4*
unknown *t*.
except ye utter by the *t*.   *1Co 14:9*
words
ecstatic utterance (N)   *1Co 14:9;*
   14:26, 27
many *t*. in the world (A) *1Co 14:10*
him that speaketh in an   *1Co 14:13*
unknown *t*.
For if I pray in an   *1Co 14:14*
unknown *t*. my
thousand words in an   *1Co 14:19*
unknown *t*.
10,000 words in a strange *1Co 14:19*
language (A)
a psalm, hath a doctrine,   *1Co 14:26*
hath a *t*.
If any man speak in an   *1Co 14:27*
unknown *t*.

every *t*. should confess that *Ph'p 2:11*
Jesus
be religious, and bridleth not *Jas 1:26*
his *t*.
Even so the *t*. is a little   *Jas 3:5*
member
the *t*. is a fire, a world of   *Jas 3:6*
iniquity
so is the *t*. among our   *Jas 3:6*
members
But the *t*. can no man tame; it *Jas 3:8*
let him refrain his *t*. from   *1Pe 3:10*
evil
let us not love in word,   *1Jo 3:18*
neither in *t*.
out of every kindred, and *t*. *Re 5:9*
every tribe and language   *Re 5:9;*
(A)(N)   *14:6*
name in the Hebrew *t*. is   *Re 9:11*
Abaddon
the Greek *t*. hath his name *Re 9:11*
Apollyon
every nation, and kindred, and *Re 14:6*
t.
in the Hebrew *t*. Armageddon *Re 16:16*
gnawed *t*. in torment (A)   *Re 16:16*

TONGUES

their families, after their *t*.   *Ge 10:20;*
   10:31
languages (A)(R)   *Ge 10:20; 10:31*
languages (B)   *Ge 10:20*
in a pavilion from the strife *Ps 31:20*
of *t*.
dialects (B)   *Ps 31:20*
Destroy, O Lord, and divide *Ps 55:9*
their *t*.
confuse their speeches (B)   *Ps 55:9*
they lied unto him with their *Ps 78:36*
t.
sharpened their *t*. like a   *Ps 140:3*
serpent
that I will gather all nations *Isa 66:18*
and *t*.
they bend their *t*. like their *Jer 9:3*
bow for
that use their *t*. and say, He *Jer 23:31*
saith
they shall speak with new *t*. *M'k 16:17*
speak in new languages (A) *M'k 16:17*
there appeared unto them   *Ac 2:3*
cloven *t*.
began to speak with other *t*. as *Ac 2:4*
other languages (A)   *Ac 2:4; 10:40*
began to speak in foreign   *Ac 2:4*
languages (B)
different languages (P)   *Ac 2:4*
we do hear them speak in our *Ac 2:11*
t. the
our own languages (B)   *Ac 2:11*
our native language (P)   *Ac 2:11*
For they heard them speak   *Ac 10:46*
with *t*.
they spake with *t*. and   *Ac 19:6*
prophesied
spoke in foreign languages   *Ac 19:6*
(A)
with their *t*. they have used *Ro 3:13*
deceit
spirits; to another divers   *1Co 12:10*
kinds of *t*.
gifts of ecstatic utterance   *1Co 12:10;*
(N)   *12:28; 14:18, 39*
to another the interpretation *1Co 12:10*
of *t*.
governments, diversities of *t*. *1Co 12:28*
do all speak with *t*.? do all *1Co 12:30*
Though I speak with the *t*. *1Co 13:1*
of men
human and angelic language *1Co 13:1*
(B)
fail; whether there be *t*. they *1Co 13:8*
shall
I would that ye all spake   *1Co 14:5*
with *t*.
than he that speaketh with *t*. *1Co 14:5*
if I come unto you speaking *1Co 14:6*
with *t*.
ecstatic speech (N)   *1Co 14:6*
I speak with *t*. more than *1Co 14:18*
ye all
10,000 words in a strange *1Co 14:18*
language (A)
With men of other *t*. and   *1Co 14:21*
other lips
men of strange languages   *1Co 14:21*
(A)(B)
Wherefore *t*. are for a sign, *1Co 14:22*
not to

and all speak with *t*. and   *1Co 14:23*
there
and forbid not to speak   *1Co 14:39*
with *t*.
k.ndreds, and people and *t*. *Re 7:9*
stood
languages (A)   *Re 7:9; 10:11; 11:9*
languages (N)   *Re 7:9;*
   10:11; 11:9; 13:7; 17:15
every tribe and language (P) *Re 7:9;*
   13:7
many peoples, and nations, *Re 10:11*
and *t*.
languages (P) *Re 10:11; 11:9; 17:15*
of the people and   *Re 11:9*
kindreds and *t*.
all kindreds and nations   *Re 13:7; 17:15*
every dialect (B)   *Re 13:7; 17:15*
and they gnawed their *t*. for *Re 16:10*
pain
and multitudes, and nations, *Re 17:15*
and *t*.
nations and dialects (A)   *Re 17:15*

TOO

Is anything *t*. hard for the *Ge 18:14*
Lord
the household be *t*. little for *Ex 12:4*
the lamb
for this thing is *t*. heavy for *Ex 18:18*
thee
the work to make it, and *t*. *Ex 36:7*
much
alone, because it is *t*. heavy *Nu 11:14*
for me
Ye take *t*. much upon you, *Nu 16:3*
seeing
ye take *t*. much upon you, *Nu 16:7*
ye sons
people; for they are *t*. mighty *Nu 22:6*
for me
the cause that is *t*. hard for *De 1:17*
you, bring
was not one city *t*. strong for *De 2:36*
us
his name there be *t*. far from *De 12:21*
thee
And if the way be *t*. long for *De 14:24*
thee, so
or if the place be *t*. far from *De 14:24*
thee
arise a matter *t*. hard for thee *De 17:8*
in
mount Ephraim be *t*. narrow *Jos 17:15*
for thee
of Judah was *t*. much for   *Jos 19:9*
them
of Dan went out *t*. little for *Jos 19:47*
them
Is the iniquity of Peor *t*.   *Jos 22:17*
little for us
people that are with thee are *t*. *J'g 7:2*
many for
The people are yet *t*. many; *J'g 7:4*
bring them
saw that they were *t*. strong *J'g 18:26*
for him
for I am *t*. old to have an   *Ru 1:12*
husband
sons of Zeruiah be *t*. hard for *2Sa 3:39*
me
If the Syrians be *t*. strong *2Sa 10:11*
for me
children of Ammon be *t*.   *2Sa 10:11*
strong for
and if that had been *t*. little, *2Sa 12:8*
I would
me: for they were *t*. strong *2Sa 22:18*
for me
Lord God of my lord the   *1Ki 1:36*
king say so *t*.
t. little to receive the burnt *1Ki 8:64*
offerings
It is *t*. much for you to go *1Ki 12:28*
up to
because the journey is *t*. great *1Ki 19:7*
for thee
saw that the battle was *t*.   *2Ki 3:26*
sore for him
we dwell with thee is *t*. strait *2Ki 6:1*
for us
If the Syrians be *t*. strong *1Ch 19:12*
for me
children of Ammon be *t*.   *1Ch 19:12*
strong for
But the priests were *t*. few, *2Ch 29:34*
so that they
shall there arise *t*. much   *Es 1:18*
contempt

things *t.* wonderful for me,   *Job 42:3*
which I
me: for they were *t.* strong   *Ps 18:17*
for me
from him that is *t.* strong for   *Ps 35:10*
him
heavy burden they are *t.* heavy   *Ps 38:4*
for me
to know this, it was *t.* painful   *Ps 73:16*
for me
matters, or in things *t.* high   *Ps 131:1*
for me
Such knowledge is *t.* wonderful   *Ps 139:6*
for me
Wisdom is *t.* high for a fool;   *Pr 24:7*
he
three things which are *t.*   *Pr 30:18*
wonderful
shall even now be *t.* narrow   *Isa 49:19*
by reason
ears, The place is *t.* strait for   *Isa 49:20*
me
and there is nothing *t.* hard   *Jer 32:17*
for thee
flesh: is there anything *t.*   *Jer 32:27*
hard for me
all things ye are *t.*   *Ac 17:22*
superstitious

TOOK

Enoch was not, for God *t.* him   *Ge 5:24*
his mother *t.* him a wife out   *Ge 21:21*
of Egypt
God *t.* me from my father's   *Ge 24:7*
house
lord of the land *t.* us for   *Ge 42:30*
spies
Moses *t.* redemption money   *Nu 3:49;*
                       3:50
Lord *t.* of the spirit that was   *Nu 11:25*
on him
king Arad *t.* some of them   *Nu 21:1*
prisoners
I *t.* thee to curse mine   *Nu 23:11*
enemies, and lo
so I *t.* the chief of your tribes   *De 1:15*
only cattle we *t.* for a prey to   *De 2:35*
ourselves
there was not a city we *t.* not   *De 3:4*
from them
I *t.* your sin, the calf which ye   *De 9:21*
made
I *t.* this woman, found her   *De 22:14*
not a maid
then I coveted them, and *t.*   *Jos 7:21*
them
men *t.* of their victuals, and   *Jos 9:14*
asked not
I *t.* your father Abraham   *Jos 24:3*
from other side
Philistines *t.* Samson, put out   *J'g 16:21*
his eyes
the silver is with me, I *t.* it   *J'g 17:2*
no man *t.* them into his   *J'g 19:15*
house
man *t.* his concubine, and   *J'g 19:25*
brought her
I *t.* my concubine, and cut her   *J'g 20:6*
in pieces
a man *t.* off his shoe (S)   *Ru 4:7*
brought up, the priest *t.* for   *1Sa 2:14*
himself
the Philistines *t.* the ark of   *1Sa 5:1;*
God   *5:2*
Samuel *t.* vial of oil and   *1Sa 10:1*
poured on Saul
so Saul *t.* the kingdom over   *1Sa 14:47*
Israel
people *t.* of the spoil, sheep   *1Sa 15:21*
and oxen
Samuel *t.* horn of oil and   *1Sa 16:13*
anointed David
Saul *t.* him, would not let   *1Sa 18:2*
him go home
David *t.* the spear from   *1Sa 26:12*
Saul's bolster
I *t.* the crown and brought it   *2Sa 1:10*
hither
Uzzah *t.* hold of it for the   *2Sa 6:6*
oxen shook it
I *t.* thee from the sheepcote, to   *2Sa 7:8*
be ruler
mercy not depart, as I *t.* it   *2Sa 7:15*
from Saul
but *t.* the poor man's lamb   *2Sa 12:4*
and dressed it
Zadok the priest *t.* an horn   *1Ki 1:39*
of oil

she arose and *t.* my son from   *1Ki 3:20*
beside me
the cities my father *t.* I will   *1Ki 20:34*
restore
Jehu *t.* no heed to walk in   *2Ki 10:31*
the law
and *t.* him to Babylon (S)   *2Ki 25:7*
yet David *t.* the castle of   *1Ch 11:5*
Zion
t. away the Asherim   *2Ch 17:6;*
(A)(E)(R)   *31:1; 34:3, 7*
which *t.* Manasseh among   *2Ch 33:11*
thorns
vessels which   *Ezr 5:14;*
                       6:5
Nebuchadnezzar *t.*   *Es 2:7*
whom Mordecai *t.* for his own   *Es 2:7*
daughter
then *t.* Haman the apparel and   *Es 6:11*
the horse
t. on them, that they would   *Es 9:27*
keep Purim
he that *t.* me out of the womb   *Ps 22:9;*
                       71:6
fear *t.* hold on them there, and   *Ps 48:6*
pain
t. sweet counsel together, and   *Ps 55:14*
walked
he chose David, *t.* from   *Ps 78:70*
sheepfolds
I *t.* faithful witnesses to   *Isa 8:2*
record
with whom *t.* he counsel,   *Isa 40:14*
who instructed
then *t.* I the cup at Lord's   *Jer 25:17*
hand
in the day I *t.* them by the   *Jer 31:32;*
hand   *Heb 8:9*
even they *t.* Jeremiah out of   *Jer 39:14*
prison
he *t.* me by a lock of mine   *Eze 8:3*
head
he *t.* fire from between the   *Eze 10:7*
cherubims
heard trumpet, and, *t.* not   *Eze 33:5*
warning
Lord *t.* me as I followed the   *Am 7:15*
flock
I *t.* me two staves, beauty   *Zec 11:7*
and bands
I *t.* thirty pieces and cast to   *Zec 11:13*
the potter
himself *t.* our infirmities, and   *M't 8:17*
bare
like leaven which a woman   *M't 13:33;*
t.   *Lu 13:21*
foolish virgins *t.* no oil   *M't 25:3*
ve *t.* me in   *M't 25:35*
I was a stranger and ye *t.*   *M't 25:43*
me not in
the first *t.* a wife, and left   *M'k 12:20*
no seed
the second *t.* her and died   *M'k 12:21;*
                     Lu 20:29, 30
in the temple teaching, and   *M'k 14:49*
ye *t.* me not
that disciple *t.* her to his   *Joh 19:27*
own home
who was guide to them who   *Ac 1:16*
Jesus
Barnabas *t.* him, and declared   *Ac 9:27*
to them
t. with them John whose   *Ac 12:25*
surname was Mark
t. on them to call over   *Ac 19:13*
them which had
we *t.* and would have judged   *Ac 24:6*
by law
Paul thanked God and *t.*   *Ac 28:15*
courage
I went up and I *t.* Titus with   *Ga 2:1*
me also
t. upon him the form of a   *Ph'p 2:7*
servant
t. it out of the way, nailing it   *Col 2:14*
to his cross
he also himself *t.* part of the   *Heb 2:14*
same
t. joyfully the soiling of   *Heb 10:34*
your goods
he *t.* the book   *Re 5:7*
angel *t.* the censer   *Re 8:5*
I *t.* the little book out of   *Re 10:10*
angel's hand

TOOK AWAY

he *t.* away my birthright   *Ge 27:36*
a west wind *t.* away the   *Ex 10:19*
locusts

he *t.* not *away* pillar of   *Ex 13:22*
cloud by day
he shall restore that which ye *t.*   *Le 6:4*
away
Gideon *t. away*   *J'g 8:21*
their ornaments
Israel *t. away* my land when   *J'g 11:13*
they came
Israel *t.* not *away* the land of   *J'g 11:15*
Moab
David *t. away* the sheep and   *1Sa 27:9*
oxen
Shishak *t. away* the   *1Ki 14:26*
treasures
Asa *t. away* Sodomites out   *1Ki 15:12*
of land
they *t. away* the stones of   *1Ki 15:22*
Ramah
Josiah *t. away* the horses of   *2Ki 23:11*
the sun
all vessels the Chaldeans *t.*   *2Ki 25:14;*
away   *25:15; Jer 52:18-19*
Asa *t. away* the altars   *2Ch 14:3; 14:5*
Jehoshaphat *t. away* the high   *2Ch 17:6*
places
Hezekiah *t. away* altars in   *2Ch 30:14*
Jerusalem
Manasseh *t. away* the   *2Ch 33:15*
strange gods
I restored that which I *t.* not   *Ps 69:4*
away
the keepers *t. away* my veil   *Ca 5:7*
from me
I *t.* them *away* as I saw   *Eze 16:50*
good
and *t. away* the king *away* in my   *Ho 13:11*
wrath
the flood came and *t.* them   *M't 24:39*
all *away*
then they *t. away* the stone   *Joh 11:41*

TOOK UP

Balaam *t. up* his parable and   *Nu 23:7;*
said   *23:18; 24:3, 15, 20-21, 23*
the priests *t. up* the ark   *Jos 3:6;*
                       6:12; 1Ki 8:3
then the man *t. up* his   *J'g 19:28*
concubine
and the cook *t. up* the   *1Sa 9:24*
shoulder
they *t. up* Asahel and buried   *2Sa 2:32*
him
Mephibosheth's nurse *t.* him *up*   *2Sa 4:4*
and fled
and the prophet *t. up* the   *1Ki 13:29*
carcase
he *t. up* also the mantle of   *2Ki 2:13*
Elijah
the Shunammite *t. up* her son   *2Ki 4:37*
and went out
and he *t.* him *up* to him into   *2Ki 10:15*
the chariot
I *t. up* the wine and gave it to   *Ne 2:1*
the king
they *t.* Jeremiah *up* out of   *Jer 38:13*
the dungeon
then the spirit *t.* me *up*   *Eze 3:12;*
                     11:24; 43:5
the flame slew men that *t. up*   *Da 3:22*
Shadrach
so they *t. up* Jonah, and cast   *Jon 1:15*
him forth
they *t. up* the body of John   *M't 14:12;*
                     M'k 6:29
they *t. up* of the fragments   *M't 14:20;*
that remained   *15:37; M'k 6:43; 8:8, 20*
how many baskets ye *t. up*   *M't 16:9;*
                       6:10
he *t. up* the bed and went   *M'k 2:12*
forth
he *t.* them *up* in his arms   *M'k 10:16*
and blessed
t. him *up* in his arms and   *Lu 2:28*
blessed God
t. up stones to cast at him   *Joh 8:59;*
                       10:31
Pharaoh's daughter *t.* Moses   *Ac 7:21*
up
ye *t. up* the tabernacle of   *Ac 7:43*
Moloch
but Peter *t.* him *up,* saying,   *Ac 10:26*
Stand up
we *t. up* carriages and went   *Ac 21:15*
to Jerusalem
and a mighty angel *t. up* a   *Re 18:21*
stone

HE TOOK

Shechem saw her, he t. her, and lay	Ge 34:2
he t. it out, his hand was leprous	Ex 4:6
he t. the book of the covenant and read	Ex 24:7
and he t. the calf which they had made	Ex 32:20
he t. the veil off, until he came out	Ex 34:34
he t. all the fat on the inwards	Le 8:16; 8:25
he t. the elders of city and thorns	J'g 8:16
he t. ten men of the elders of the city	Ru 4:2
he t. a yoke of oxen, hewed them	1Sa 11:7
Saul saw any valiant man, he t. him	1Sa 14:52
he t. Agag king of the Amalekites alive	1Sa 15:8
he t. his staff in his hand and chose him	1Sa 17:40
he t. hold of her, lie with me	2Sa 13:11
he t. three darts, and thrust through	2Sa 18:14
he sent from above, he t. me	2Sa 22:17; Ps 18:16
he t. her son out of her bosom	1Ki 17:19
he t. the mantle of Elijah that fell	2Ki 2:14
he t. his eldest son and offered him for a	2Ki 3:27
he t. them from their hand	2Ki 5:24
he t. a thick cloth and dipped it in water	2Ki 8:15
and he t. unto him bow and arrows	2Ki 13:15
he t. him a potsherd to scrape himself	Job 2:8
slothful roasteth not that which he t.	Pr 12:27
he t. his brother by the heel in womb	Ho 12:3
he t. the seven loaves	M't 15:36; M'k 8:6
he t. the cup	M't 26:27; Lu 22:17; 1Co 11:25
he t. with him Peter, James, John	M't 26:37; Lu 9:28
he t. water and washed his hands	M't 27:24
and he t. the blind man by the hand	M'k 8:23
he t. a child and set him in the midst	M'k 9:36
he t. the five loaves and two fishes	Lu 9:16
he t. out two pence and gave to the host	Lu 10:35
and he t. bread	Lu 22:19; 24:30; Ac 27:35
he t. them the same hour and washed	Ac 16:33
he t. Paul's girdle and bound his hands	Ac 21:11
he t. not on him the nature of angels	Heb 2:16
he t. the blood of calves and of goats	Heb 9:19

THEY TOOK

they t. them wives which they chose	Ge 6:2
and they t. all the goods of Sodom	Ge 14:11
they t. Lot, Abram's brother's son	Ge 14:12
and they t. every man his censer	Nu 16:18
and they t. of the fruit of the land	De 1:25
people went up and they t. the city	Jos 6:20
king of Ai, they t. alive and brought	Jos 8:23
save Hivites, all other they t. in battle	Jos 11:19
they t. their daughters to be wives	J'g 3:6
they t. them alive and slew them	2Ki 10:14
they t. the young men to grind	La 5:13
I saw that they t. both one way	Eze 23:13

they t. his glory from him because they t. him for a prophet	Da 5:20 M't 21:46
so they t. the money, and did as taught	M't 28:15
they t. him, and killed him, and cast	M'k 12:8
they t. him, and led him	Lu 22:54; Joh 19:16
and they t. knowledge of them that	Ac 4:13
they t. him down from the tree and laid	Ac 13:29
they t. him, expounded way of God	Ac 18:26

TOOKEST

though thou t. vengeance of their	Ps 99:8
And t. thy broidered garments	Eze 16:18

TOOL

if thou lift up thy t. upon it, thou	Ex 20:25
and fashioned it with a graving t.	Ex 32:4
shalt not lift up any iron t. upon them	De 27:5
any t. of iron heard in the house	1Ki 6:7
produce a t. for work (B)	Isa 54:16

TOOTH

Eye for eye, t. for t. hand for	Ex 21:24
if he smite out his manservant's t.	Ex 21:27
or his maidservant's t.: he shall let	Ex 21:27
for breach, eye for eye, t. for	Le 24:20
t. for t., hand for hand, foot for foot	De 19:21
time of trouble is like a broken t.	Pr 25:19
An eye for an eye, and a t. for a t.	M't 5:38

TOOTH'S

shall let him go free for his t. sake	Ex 21:27

TOP

whose t. may reach unto heaven	Ge 11:4
and the t. of it reached to heaven	Ge 28:12
and poured oil upon the t. of it	Ge 28:18
I will stand on the t. of the hill	Ex 17:9
Hur went up to the t. of the hill	Ex 17:10
mount Sinai, on the t. of the mount	Ex 19:20
Lord called Moses up to the t. of.	Ex 19:20
like fire on the t. of the mount	Ex 24:17
there shall be an hole in the t. of it	Ex 28:32
gold the t. thereof, and the sides	Ex 30:3
there to me in the t. of the mount	Ex 34:2
both the t. of it, and the sides	Ex 37:26
up into the t. of the mountain	Nu 14:40
presumed to go up unto the hill t.	Nu 14:44
died there in the t. of the mount	Nu 20:28
to the t. of Pisgah, which looketh	Nu 21:20
from the t. of the rocks I see him	Nu 23:9
field of Zophim, to the t. of Pisgah	Nu 23:14
brought Balaam unto the t. of Peor	Nu 23:28
Get thee up into the t. of Pisgah	De 3:27
of thy foot unto the t. of thy head	De 28:35

and upon the t. of the head of him	De 33:16
to the t. of Pisgah, that is over	De 34:1
went up to the t. of mountain	Jos 15:8
was drawn from the t. of the hill	Jos 15:9
an altar upon the t. of this rock	J'g 6:26
stood in the t. of mount Gerizim	J'g 9:7
for him in the t. of the mountains	J'g 9:25
down from the t. of the mountains	J'g 9:36
gat them up to the t. of the tower	J'g 9:51
dwelt in the t. of the rock Etam	J'g 15:8
went to the t. of the rock Etam	J'g 15:11
carried them up to the t. of an hill	J'g 16:3
with Saul upon the t. of the house	1Sa 9:25
called Saul to the t. of the house	1Sa 9:26
stood on the t. of an hill afar off	1Sa 26:13
troop, and stood on the t. of an hill	2Sa 2:25
was come to the t. of the mount	2Sa 15:32
was a little past the t. of the hill	2Sa 16:1
a tent upon the t. of the house	2Sa 16:22
were upon the t. of the pillars	1Ki 7:17
the chapiters that were upon the t.	1Ki 7:18
that were upon the t. of the pillars	1Ki 7:19
the t. of the pillars was lily work	1Ki 7:22
in the t. of the base was there a	1Ki 7:35
and on the t. of the base the ledges	1Ki 7:35
were on the t. of the two pillars	1Ki 7:41
were upon the t. of the pillars round	1Ki 7:41
and the t. of the throne was round	1Ki 10:19
Elijah went up to the t. of Carmel	1Ki 18:42
behold, he sat on the t. of an hill	2Ki 1:9
under him on the t. of the stairs	2Ki 9:13
t. of the upper chamber of Ahaz	2Ki 23:12
that was on the t. of each of them	2Ch 3:15
were on the t. of the two pillars	2Ch 4:12
which were on the t. of the pillars	2Ch 4:12
brought them unto the t. of the rock	2Ch 25:12
cast down from the t. of the rock	2Ch 25:12
and touched the t. of the sceptre	Es 5:2
upon the t. of the mountains	Ps 72:16
sparrow alone upon the house t.	Ps 102:7
standeth in the t. of high places	Pr 8:2
he that lieth upon the t. of a mast	Pr 23:34
Lebanon: look from the t. of Amana	Ca 4:8
from the t. of Shenir and Hermon	Ca 4:8
established in the t. of mountains	Isa 2:2
in the t. of the uppermost bough	Isa 17:6
a beacon upon the t. of a mountain	Isa 30:17
shout from the t. of the mountains	Isa 42:11
for hunger in the t. of every street	La 2:19
poured out in the t. of every street	La 4:1
cropped off the t. of his young twigs	Eze 17:4

off from the *t.* of his young   *Eze 17:22*
twigs
she set it upon the *t.* of a   *Eze 24:7*
rock
set her blood upon the *t.* of a   *Eze 24:8*
rock
and make her like the *t.* of a   *Eze 26:4*
rock
will make thee like the *t.* of   *Eze 26:14*
a rock
his *t.* was among the thick   *Eze 31:3*
boughs
up his *t.* among the thick   *Eze 31:10*
boughs
up their *t.* among the thick   *Eze 31:14*
boughs
Upon the *t.* of the mountain   *Eze 43:12*
and the *t.* of Carmel shall   *Am 1:2*
wither
hide themselves in the *t.* of   *Am 9:3*
Carmel
in the *t.* of the mountains   *Mic 4:1*
in pieces at the *t.* of all the   *Na 3:10*
streets
with a bowl upon the *t.* of it   *Zec 4:2*
which are upon the *t.* thereof   *Zec 4:2*
in twain from the *t.* to the   *M't 27:51;*
bottom
seam, woven from the *t.*   *Joh 19:23*
throughout
leaning upon the *t.* of his   *Heb 11:21*
staff

TOPAZ

first row shall be a sardius, a   *Ex 28:17*
t.
first row was a sardius, a *t.*   *Ex 39:10*
t. of Ethiopia shall not equal   *Job 28:19*
it
sardius, *t.* and the diamond   *Eze 28:31*
the eighth, beryl; the ninth,   *Re 21:20*
a *t.*

TOPHER

between Paran, and *T.* and   *De 1:1*

TOPHET

T. is ordained of old; yea   *Isa 30:33*
have built the high places of   *Jer 7:31*
T.
that it shall no more be called   *Jer 7:32*
T.
for they shall bury in *T.* till   *Jer 7:32*
there
place shall no more be called   *Jer 19:6*
T.
and they shall bury them in   *Jer 19:11*
T.
and even make this city as *T.*   *Jer 19:12*
shall be defiled as the place   *Jer 19:13*
of *T.*
Then came Jeremiah from *T.*   *Jer 19:14*

TOPHETH

And he defiled *T.* which is   *2Ki 23:10*

TOPS

were the *t.* of the mountains   *Ge 8:5*
seen
going in the *t.* of the mulberry   *2Sa 5:24*
trees
to set upon the *t.* of the   *1Ki 7:16*
pillars
herb, as the grass on the   *2Ki 19:26*
house *t.*
in the *t.* of the mulberry   *1Ch 14:15*
trees
cut off as the *t.* of the ears   *Job 24:24*
of corn
into the *t.* of the ragged rocks   *Isa 2:21*
on the *t.* of their houses, and   *Isa 15:3*
in all the *t.* of the mountains   *Eze 6:13*
upon the *t.* of the mountains   *Ho 4:13*
chariots on the *t.* of mountains   *Joe 2:5*
shall

TORCH

smoking furnace, flaming *t.*   *Ge 15:17*
(A)(B)(E)(R)
put a *t.* between two tails (S)   *J'g 15:4*
and like a *t.* of fire in a sheaf   *Zec 12:6*
burning like a *t.*   *Re 8:10*
(A)(B)(E)(N)(P)(R)

TORCHES

t. inside (A)(B)(E)(R)   *J'g 7:16; 7:20*
Samson took *t.* and lighted   *J'g 15:4;*
the *t.* (S)   *15:5*
go burning *t.*   *Job 41:19*
(A)(B)(E)(R)
like *t.* moving   *Eze 1:13*
(A)(B)(E)(R)
eyes like flaming *t.*   *Da 10:6*
(A)(B)(E)(R)
chariots shall be with flaming *t.*   *Na 2:3*
chariots blaze with fire of steel   *Na 2:3*
(A)
chariots flash with steel (E)   *Na 2:3*
chariots flash like flame (R)   *Na 2:3*
they shall seem like *t.* they   *Na 2:4*
shall
with lanterns and *t.* and   *Joh 18:3*
weapons

TORE

tore (S)   *Ge 37:29;*
37:34; 44:13; Nu 14:6;
J'g 11:35; 14:6; 1Sa 15:27; 2Sa 1:11;
13:19; 1Ki 11:30; 14:8; 21:27; 2Ki 2:12;
5:7; 6:30; 11:14; 19:1; 22:11; 2Ch 23:13;
34:19; Ezr 9:3; Es 4:1; Job 1:20; 2:12;
Isa 37:1;   Jer 36:24; M't 26:65;
M'k 14:63; Ac 14:14; 16:22

TORMENT

t. him (A)(R)   *J'g 16:19*
t. my soul (R)   *Job 19:2*
lie down in *t.* (B)(R)   *Isa 50:11*
art thou come hither to *t.* us   *M't 8:29*
before
torture us ahead of time   *M't 8:29*
(B)(P)
thee by God, that thou *t.* me   *M'k 5:7*
not
don't torture me (P)   *M'k 5:7*
high? I beseech thee, *t.* me not   *Lu 8:28*
do not torture me (B)   *Lu 8:28*
they also come into this place   *Lu 16:28*
of *t.*
afflict, oppress *t.* (A)   *Ac 12:1*
out fear, because fear hath *t.*   *1Jo 4:18*
fear brings thought of   *1Jo 4:18*
punishment (A)
fear involves torture (B)   *1Jo 4:18*
fear hath punishment (E)   *1Jo 4:18*
fear brings pangs of   *1Jo 4:18*
punishment (N)
fear brings some of the   *1Jo 4:18*
torture of feeling guilty (P)
fear has to do with   *1Jo 4:18*
punishment (R)
their *t.* was as the *t.* of a   *Re 9:5*
scorpion
torture like that of a scorpion   *Re 9:5*
(B)(P)(R)
the smoke of their *t.*   *Re 14:11*
ascendeth up
smoke of their torture ascends   *Re 14:11*
forever (B)(P)
gnawed tongues in *t.* (A)   *Re 16:10*
so much *t.* and sorrow give   *Re 18:7*
her
impose on her torture (B)(P)   *Re 18:7*
mete out grief and *t.* (N)   *Re 18:7*
Standing afar off for fear of   *Re 18:10;*
her *t.*   *18:15*
dreading her torture (B)   *Re 18:10*
terror of her torture (B)   *Re 18:15*
through fear of her   *Re 18:15*
punishment (P)

TORMENTED

t. him (R)   *1Sa 16:14*
Amnon was *t.* (R)   *2Sa 13:2*
wicked man is *t.* (B)   *Job 15:20*
home sick of the palsy,   *M't 8:6*
grievously *t.*
distressed with intense pains   *M't 8:6*
(A)
paralyzed in great agony (B)   *M't 8:6*
racked with pain (N)   *M't 8:6*
in dreadful pain (P)   *M't 8:6*
in terrible distress (R)   *M't 8:6*
t. by a demon (A)(N)   *M't 15:22*
distressed and *t.* (A)   *Lu 2:48*
tongue; for I am *t.* in this   *Lu 16:24*
flame
I am in anguish in this flame   *Lu 16:24*
(A)(E)(R)

I am in agony in this fire   *Lu 16:24*
(N)(P)
he is comforted, and thou art   *Lu 16:25*
you are in anguish   *Lu 16:25*
(A)(B)(E)(R)
you who are in agony   *Lu 16:25*
(N)(P)
being destitute, afflicted, *t.*   *Heb 11:37*
cruelly treated (A)   *Heb 11:37*
maltreated (B)   *Heb 11:37*
ill-treated (E)(P)(R)   *Heb 11:37*
in misery (N)   *Heb 11:37*
that they should be *t.* five   *Re 9:5*
months
to torture them (B)(P)(R)   *Re 9:5*
these two prophets *t.* them   *Re 11:10*
that
had been vexing the dwellers   *Re 11:10*
on earth (B)
had brought such misery (P)   *Re 11:10*
he shall be *t.* with fire and   *Re 14:10*
brimstone
tortured with fire (B)(P)   *Re 14:10*
shall be *t.* day and night for   *Re 20:10*
ever
tortured day and night for   *Re 20:10*
timeless ages (B)(P)

TORMENTORS

wroth, and delivered him to   *M't 18:34*
the *t.*
to the torturers (A)   *M't 18:34*
to the scourgers (B)   *M't 18:34*
condemned the man to   *M't 18:34*
torture (N)
handed him over to jailers   *M't 18:34*
(P)(R)

TORMENTS

I wrestle with my *t.* (B)   *Job 30:18*
taken with divers diseases   *M't 4:24*
and *t.*
hell he lift up his eyes, being   *Lu 16:23*
in *t.*
suffering tortures in Hades   *Lu 16:23*
(B)

TORN

That which was *t.* of beasts I   *Ge 31:39*
torn (S)   *Ge 37:33;*
Le 13:45; Jos 9:4, 13; J'g 14:6; 1Sa 4:12;
15:28; 28:17; 2Sa 1:2; 18:31; 15:32;
1Ki 13:3, 5; 2Ki 5:8; 18:37; 22:19;
Ezr 9:5; Isa 36:22; Jer 41:5; Eze 30:16;
M't 27:51; M'k 15:38; Lu 23:45
Surely he is *t.* in pieces; and   *Ge 44:28*
I
If it be *t.* in pieces, then let   *Ex 22:13*
him
not make good that which   *Ex 22:13*
was *t.*
ye eat any flesh that is *t.* of   *Ex 22:31*
beasts
fat of that which is *t.* with   *Le 7:24*
beasts
or that which was *t.* with   *Le 17:15*
beasts
dieth of itself, or is *t.* with   *Le 22:8*
beasts
unto the lion, which hath *t.*   *1Ki 13:26*
him
eaten the carcase, nor *t.* the   *1Ki 13:28*
ass
carcases were *t.* in the midst   *Isa 5:25*
out thence shall be *t.* in pieces   *Jer 5:6*
dieth of itself, or is *t.* in   *Eze 4:14*
pieces
any thing that is dead of   *Eze 44:31*
itself, or *t.*
for he hath *t.* and he will heal   *Ho 6:1*
us
his dens with *t.* flesh (S)   *Na 2:12*
and ye brought that which   *Mal 1:13*
was *t.*
the unclean spirit had *t.* him   *M'k 1:26*

TORRENT

an overflowing *t.* (B)(R)   *Jer 47:2*

TORRENTS

t. of destruction (A)   *2Sa 22:5*

TORTOISE

mouse, and the *t.* after his kind	Le 11:29
the kinds of great lizard (A)(E)(R)	Le 11:29
every species of turtle (B)	Le 11:29

TORTURE

t. us ahead of time (B)(P)	M't 8:29
condemned to *t.* (N)	M't 18:34
don't *t.* me (P)	M'k 5:7
do not *t.* me (B)	Lu 8:28
fear involves *t.* (B)(P)	1Jo 4:18
t. like a scorpion (B)(P)(R)	Re 9:5
smoke of *t.* ascends (B)(P)	Re 14:11
impose on her *t.* (B)	Re 18:7
dreading her *t.* (B)	Re 18:10
terror of her *t.* (B)	Re 18:15

TORTURED

t. with fire (B)(P)	Ps 14:10; 20:10
and others were *t.* not accepting	Heb 11:35
stretched and broken on the wheel (B)	Heb 11:35
t. with filthy (A)(B)(N)	2Pe 2:7

TORTURERS

to the *t.* (A)	M't 18:34

TORTURES

suffering *t.* of Hades (B)	Lu 16:23

TOSS

violently turn and *t.* thee like	Isa 22:18
the waves thereof *t.* themselves	Jer 5:22

TOSSED

I am *t.* up and down as the locust	Ps 109:23
a vanity *t.* to and fro of them that	Pr 21:6
O thou afflicted, *t.* with tempest	Isa 54:11
On the midst of the sea, *t.* with waves	M't 14:24
exceedingly *t.* with a tempest	Ac 27:18
t. to and fro, and carried about	Eph 4:14
sea driven with the wind and *t.*	Jas 1:6

TOSSING

like the *t.* sea (R)	Isa 57:20
roaring of the *t.* sea (A)	Lu 21:25

TOSSINGS

I am full of *t.* to and fro unto	Job 7:4

TOTTERING

wall shall ye be, and as a *t.* fence	Ps 62:3

TOU

T. king of Hamath heard how	1Ch 18:9
for Hadarezer had war with *T.*	1Ch 18:10

TOUCH

it, neither shall ye *t* it, lest ye die	Ge 3:3
suffered I thee not to *t.* her	Ge 20:6
the mount, or *t.* the border of it	Ex 19:12
There shall not an hand *t.* it, but he	Ex 19:13
Or if a soul *t.* any unclean thing	Le 5:2
Or if he *t.* the uncleanness of man	Le 5:3
t. the flesh thereof shall be holy	Le 6:27
soul that shall *t.* any unclean thing	Le 7:21
and their carcase ye shall not *t.*	Le 11:8

whosoever doth *t.* them, when they	Le 11:31
she shall *t.* no hallowed thing	Le 12:4
but they shall not *t.* any holy thing	Nu 4:15
t. nothing of theirs, lest ye be	Nu 16:26
flesh, nor *t.* of their dead carcase	De 14:8
now therefore we may not *t.* them	Jos 9:19
men that they shall not *t.* thee	Ru 2:9
and he shall not *t.* thee any more	2Sa 14:10
that none *t.* the young man Absalom	2Sa 18:12
man that shall *t.* them must be	2Sa 23:7
T. not mine anointed, and do my	1Ch 16:22; Ps 105:15
and *t.* all that he hath, and he will	Job 1:11
and *t.* his bone and his flesh, and he	Job 2:5
in seven there shall no evil *t.* thee	Job 5:19
things that my soul refused to *t.* are	Job 6:7
t. the mountains, and they shall	Ps 144:5
from thence, *t.* no unclean thing	Isa 52:11
that *t.* the inheritance which I have	Jer 12:14
men could not *t.* their garments	La 4:14
it is unclean; depart, depart, *t.* not	La 4:15
and with his skirt do *t.* bread	Hag 2:12
by a dead body *t.* any of these	Hag 2:13
If I may but *t.* his garment, I shall	M't 9:21
might only *t.* the hem of his garment	M't 14:36
they pressed upon him for to *t.* him	M'k 3:10
If I may *t.* but his clothes, I shall be	M'k 5:28
t. if it were but the border of his	M'k 6:56
him, and besought him to *t.* him	M'k 8:22
to him, that he should *t.* them	M'k 10:13
whole multitude sought to *t.* him	Lu 6:19
t. not the burdens with one of your	Lu 11:46
also infants, that he would *t.* them	Lu 18:15
Jesus saith unto her, *T.* me not	Joh 20:17
is good for a man not to *t.* a woman	1Co 7:1
t. not the unclean thing; and I will	2Co 6:17
T. not; taste not; handle not	Col 2:21
destroyed the firstborn shall *t.*	Heb 11:28
And if so much as a beast *t.*	Heb 12:20

TOUCHED

us no hurt, as we have not *t.* thee	Ge 26:29
him, and *t.* the hollow of his thigh	Ge 32:25
he *t.* the hollow of Jacob's thigh	Ge 32:32
The soul which hath *t.* any such	Le 22:6
and upon him that *t.* a bone, or one	Nu 19:18
and whosoever hath *t.* any slain	Nu 31:19
t. the flesh and unleavened cakes	J'g 6:21
of men, whose hearts God had *t.*	1Sa 10:26
the wing of the one *t.* the one wall	1Ki 6:27
the other cherub *t.* the other wall	1Ki 6:27
their wings *t.* one another in	1Ki 6:27
then an angel *t.* him, and said unto	1Ki 19:5
and *t.* him, and said, Arise and eat	1Ki 19:7

let down, and *t.* the bones of Elisha	2Ki 13:21
near, and *t.* the top of the sceptre	Es 5:2
for the hand of God hath *t.* me	Job 19:21
and said, Lo, this hath *t.* thy lips	Isa 6:7
forth his hand, and *t.* my mouth	Jer 1:9
creatures that *t.* one another	Eze 3:13
earth, and *t.* not the ground	Da 8:5
but he *t.* me, and set me upright	Da 8:18
t. me about the time of the evening	Da 9:21
an hand *t.* me, which set me upon	Da 10:10
of the sons of men *t.* my lips	Da 10:16
t. me one like the appearance of a	Da 10:18
put forth his hand, and *t.* him	M't 8:3
he *t.* her hand, and the fever left her	M't 8:15
and *t.* the hem of his garment	M't 9:20
Then *t.* he their eyes, saying	M't 9:29
many as *t.* were made perfectly	M't 14:36
Jesus came and *t.* them, and said	M't 17:7
on them, and *t.* their eyes	M't 20:34
put forth his hand, and *t.* him, and	M'k 1:41
the press behind, and *t.* his garment	M'k 5:27
press, and said, Who *t.* my clothes	M'k 5:30
thee, and sayest thou, Who *t.* me	M'k 5:31
as many as *t.* him were made whole	M'k 6:56
ears, and he spit, and *t.* his tongue	M'k 7:33
he put forth his hand, and *t.* him	Lu 5:13
And he came and *t.* the bier	Lu 7:14
and *t.* the border of his garment	Lu 8:44
And Jesus said, Who *t.* me	Lu 8:45
thee, and sayest thou, Who *t.* me	Lu 8:45
Jesus said, Somebody hath *t.* me	Lu 8:46
people for what cause she had *t.* him	Lu 8:47
And he *t.* his ear, and healed him	Lu 22:51
And the next day we *t.* at Sidon	Ac 27:3
t. with feeling of our infirmities	Heb 4:15
unto the mount that might be *t.*	Heb 12:18

TOUCHETH

He that *t.* this man or his wife	Ge 26:11
whosoever *t.* the mount shall be	Ex 19:12
whatsoever *t.* the altar shall be holy	Ex 29:37
whatsoever *t.* them shall be holy	Ex 30:29
every one that *t.* them shall be holy	Le 6:18
the flesh that *t.* any unclean thing	Le 7:19
whosoever *t.* the carcase of them	Le 11:24
one that *t.* them shall be unclean	Le 11:26
whoso *t.* their carcase shall be	Le 11:27
which *t.* their carcase shall be	Le 11:36
he that *t.* the carcase thereof shall	Le 11:39
whosoever *t.* his bed shall wash his	Le 15:5
And he that *t.* the flesh of him	Le 15:7
whosoever *t.* any thing that was	Le 15:10
whomsoever he *t.* that hath	Le 15:11
that he *t.* which hath the issue	Le 15:12
whosoever *t.* her shall be unclean	Le 15:19
whosoever *t.* her bed shall wash his	Le 15:21

whosoever *t.* any thing that   *Le 15:22*
she
when he *t.* it, he shall be   *Le 15:23*
unclean
whosoever *t.* these things   *Le 15:27*
shall be
whoso *t.* any thing that is   *Le 22:4*
unclean
Or whosoever *t.* any creeping   *Le 22:5*
thing
He that *t.* the dead body of   *Nu 19:11*
any man
Whosoever *t.* the dead body   *Nu 19:13*
of any
And whosoever *t.* one that is   *Nu 19:16*
slain
he that *t.* the water of   *Nu 19:21*
separation
unclean person *t.* shall be   *Nu 19:22*
unclean
the soul that *t.* it shall be   *Nu 19:22*
unclean
of tow is broken when it *t.* the   *J'g 16:9*
fire
it *t.* thee, and thou art   *Job 4:5*
troubled
he *t.* the hills, and they   *Ps 104:32*
smoke
t. her shall not be innocent   *Pr 6:29*
wither, when the east wind   *Eze 17:10*
t. it
they break out, and blood *t.*   *Ho 4:2*
blood
God of hosts is he that *t.* the   *Am 9:5*
land
he that *t.* you *t.* the apple of   *Zec 2:8*
his eye
manner of woman this is, *t.*   *Lu 7:39*
him
and that wicked one *t.* him   *1Jo 5:18*
not

TOUCHING

Behold, thy brother Esau, as   *Ge 27:42*
t. thee
an atonement for him as *t.* his   *Lu 5:13*
sin
do unto the Levites *t.* their   *Nu 8:26*
charge
And as *t.* the matter which   *1Sa 20:23*
thou and I
As *t.* the words which thou   *2Ki 22:18*
hast heard
that *t.* any of the priests and   *Ezr 7:24*
Levites
T. the Almighty, we cannot   *Job 37:23*
find him
things which I have made *t.*   *Ps 45:1*
the king
a song of my beloved *t.* his   *Isa 5:1*
vineyard
them *t.* all their wickedness   *Jer 1:16*
And *t.* the house of the king   *Jer 21:11*
of Judah
For thus saith the Lord *t.*   *Jer 22:11*
Shallum
the vision is *t.* the whole   *Eze 7:13*
multitude
shall agree on earth as *t.* any   *M't 18:19*
thing
as *t.* the resurrection of the   *M't 22:31*
dead
And as *t.* the dead, that   *M'k 12:26*
they rise
no fault in this man *t.* those   *Lu 23:14*
things
ye intend to do as *t.* these   *Ac 5:35*
men
t. Peter (B)   *Ac 12:7*
As *t.* the Gentiles which   *Ac 21:25*
believe
T. the resurrection of the   *Ac 24:21*
dead I
t. the things whereof I am   *Ac 26:2*
accused
but as *t.* the election, they   *Ro 11:28*
as *t.* things offered unto idols   *1Co 8:1*
As *t.* our brother Apollos, I   *1Co 16:12*
greatly
as *t.* the ministering to the   *2Co 9:1*
saints
Hebrews; as *t.* the law, a   *Ph'p 3:5*
Pharisee
t. the righteousness which is   *Ph'p 3:6*
Barnabas, *t.* whom ye   *Col 4:10*
received
t. brotherly love ye need not   *1Th 4:9*
that

have confidence in the Lord *t.*   *2Th 3:4*
you

TOUCHY

love is not *t.* (A)(P)   *1Co 13:5*

TOW

as a thread of *t.* is broken   *J'g 16:9*
when it
a strand of rope snaps when   *J'g 16:9*
exposed to fire (B)
the strong shall be as *t.* and   *Isa 1:31*
extinct, they are quenched as   *Isa 43:17*
quenched like a lamp wick   *Isa 43:17*
(A)(B)

TOWARD

which goeth *t.* the east of   *Ge 2:14*
Assyria
journeyed, going on still *t.* the   *Ge 12:9*
south
and pitched his tent *t.* Sodom   *Ge 13:12*
Look now *t.* heaven, and tell   *Ge 15:5*
the stars
door, and bowed himself *t.*   *Ge 18:2*
the ground
thence, and looked *t.* Sodom   *Ge 18:16*
faces from thence, and went   *Ge 18:22*
t. Sodom
himself with his face *t.* the   *Ge 19:1*
ground
And he looked *t.* Sodom and   *Ge 19:28*
and *t.* all the land of the   *Ge 19:28*
plain
journeyed from thence *t.* the   *Ge 20:1*
south
Egypt, as thou goest *t.*   *Ge 25:18*
Assyria
from Beer-sheba, and went *t.*   *Ge 28:10*
Haran
of the flocks *t.* the   *Ge 30:40*
ringstraked
behold, it was not *t.* him as   *Ge 31:2*
before
that it is not *t.* me as before   *Ge 31:5*
and set his face *t.* the mount   *Ge 31:21*
Gilead
in his right hand *t.* Israel's   *Ge 48:13*
left hand
in his left hand *t.* Israel's   *Ge 48:13*
right hand
let Moses sprinkle it *t.* the   *Ex 9:8*
heaven in
throw it *t.* heaven (R)   *Ex 9:8*
and Moses sprinkled it up *t.*   *Ex 9:10*
heaven
Stretch forth thine hand *t.*   *Ex 9:22*
heaven
Stretched forth his rod *t.*   *Ex 9:23*
heaven
Stretch out thine hand *t.*   *Ex 10:21*
heaven
stretched forth his hand *t.*   *Ex 10:22*
heaven
that they looked *t.* the   *Ex 16:10*
wilderness
t. the mercy seat shall the   *Ex 25:20*
faces of
the side of the tabernacle *t.*   *Ex 26:35*
the south
t. the forepart thereof, over   *Ex 28:27*
and bowed his head *t.* the   *Ex 34:8*
earth
which is the north corner   *Ex 36:25*
underneath, *t.* the forepart of   *Ex 39:20*
it
lifted up his hand *t.* the people   *Le 9:22*
the part of his head *t.* his   *Le 13:41*
face
on the east side *t.* the rising   *Nu 2:3*
of the
before the tabernacle *t.* the   *Nu 3:38*
east
they looked *t.* the tabernacle   *Nu 16:42*
of the
which is before Moab, *t.* the   *Nu 21:11*
sunrising
which looketh *t.* Jeshimon   *Nu 21:20*
that looketh *t.* Jeshimon   *Nu 23:28*
he set his face *t.* the   *Nu 24:1*
wilderness
fierce anger of the Lord *t.*   *Nu 32:14*
Israel
Jericho eastward, *t.* the   *Nu 34:15*
sunrising

this side Jordan *t.* the   *De 4:41;*
sunrising   *4:47*
his eye shall be evil *t.* his   *De 28:54*
brother
and *t.* the wife of his bosom   *De 28:54*
t. the remnant of his children   *De 28:54*
which
be evil *t.* the husband of her   *De 28:56*
bosom
and *t.* her son, and *t.* her   *De 28:56*
daughter
t. her young one that cometh   *De 28:57*
out
t. her children which she   *De 28:57*
shall bear
sea *t.,* the going down of the   *Jos 1:4*
sun
on this side Jordan *t.* the   *Jos 1:15*
sunrising
came down *t.* the sea of the   *Jos 3:16*
plain
the spear that is in thy hand   *Jos 8:18*
t. Ai
that he had in his hand *t.* the   *Jos 8:18*
city
side Jordan *t.* the rising of   *Jos 12:1*
the sun
and all Lebanon, *t.* the   *Jos 13:5*
sunrising
From thence it passed *t.*   *Jos 15:4*
Azmon, the going down of the
the border went up *t.* Debir   *Jos 15:7*
from the
so northward, looking *t.*   *Jos 15:7*
Gilgal
passed *t.* the waters of   *Jos 15:7*
En-shemesh
t. the coast of Edom   *Jos 15:21*
southward
went out *t.* the sea to   *Jos 16:6*
Michmethah
border went over from   *Jos 18:13*
thence *t.* Luz
and went forth *t.* Geliloth   *Jos 18:17*
passed along *t.* the side over   *Jos 18:18*
And their border went up *t.*   *Jos 19:11*
the sea
from Sarid eastward *t.* the   *Jos 19:12*
sunrising
And their border was *t.*   *Jos 19:18*
Jezreel
t. the sunrising to   *Jos 19:27*
Beth-dagon
t. the north side of   *Jos 19:27*
Beth-emek
Judah upon Jordan *t.* the   *Jos 19:34*
and took the fords of Jordan *t.*   *J'g 3:28*
Moab
saying, Go and draw *t.* mount   *J'g 4:6*
Tabor
My heart is *t.* the governors of   *J'g 5:9*
Israel
acts *t.* the inhabitants of his   *J'g 5:11*
villages
Then their anger was abated *t.*   *J'g 8:3*
him
went up *t.* heaven from off   *J'g 13:20*
the altar
now the day draweth *t.*   *J'g 19:9*
evening
t. the side of mount Ephraim   *J'g 19:18*
over against Gibeah *t.* the   *J'g 20:43*
sunrising
turned and fled *t.* the   *J'g 20:45*
wilderness
toward (S)   *1Sa 9:14; 14:5; 25:20*
the valley of Zeboim *t.* the   *1Sa 13:18*
wilderness
he turned from him *t.*   *1Sa 17:30*
another
David hasted, and ran *t.* the   *1Sa 17:48*
army
works *t.* thee very good (S)   *1Sa 19:4*
if there be good *t.* David,   *1Sa 20:12*
and I
arose out of a place *t.* the   *1Sa 20:41*
south
the king's heart was *t.*   *2Sa 14:1*
Absalom
t. the way of the wilderness   *2Sa 15:23*
of the river of Gad, and *t.*   *2Sa 24:5*
Jazer
his servants coming on *t.*   *2Sa 24:20*
him
on the outside *t.* the great   *1Ki 7:9*
court
oxen, three looking *t.* the   *1Ki 7:25*
north

north, and three looking *t.* the west — *1Ki 7:25*

west, and three looking *t.* the south — *1Ki 7:25*

south, and three looking *t.* the east — *1Ki 7:25*

and spread forth his hands *t.* heaven — *1Ki 8:22*

eyes may be opened *t.* this house — *1Ki 8:29*

t. the place of which thou hast said — *1Ki 8:29*

thy servant shall make *t.* this place — *1Ki 8:29*

when they shall pray *t.* this place — *1Ki 8:30*

if they pray *t.* this place, and confess — *1Ki 8:35*

spread forth his hands *t.* this house — *1Ki 8:38*

shall come and pray *t.* this house — *1Ki 8:42*

Lord *t.* the city which thou hast — *1Ki 8:44*

and *t.* the house that I have built — *1Ki 8:44*

and pray unto thee *t.* their land — *1Ki 8:48*

some good thing *t.* the Lord God — *1Ki 14:13*

Go up now, look *t.* the sea — *1Ki 18:43*

I would not look *t.* thee, nor see — *2Ki 3:14*

king went the way *t.* the plain — *2Ki 25:4*

t. the east, west, north, and south — *1Ch 9:24*

both *t.* the east, and *t.* the west — *1Ch 12:15*

a day, and *t.* Asuppim two and two — *1Ch 26:17*

oxen, three looking *t.* the north — *2Ch 4:4*

north, and three looking *t.* the west — *2Ch 4:4*

west, and three looking *t.* the south — *2Ch 4:4*

south, and three looking *t.* the east — *2Ch 4:4*

and spread forth his hands *t.* heaven — *2Ch 6:13*

thy servant prayeth *t.* this place — *2Ch 6:20*

which they shall make *t.* this place — *2Ch 6:21*

if they pray *t.* this place, and confess — *2Ch 6:26*

they pray unto thee *t.* this city — *2Ch 6:34*

and pray *t.* their land, which thou — *2Ch 6:38*

t. the city which thou hast chosen — *2Ch 6:38*

and *t.* the house which I have built — *2Ch 6:38*

them whose heart is perfect *t.* him — *2Ch 16:9*

Judah came *t.* the watch tower — *2Ch 20:24*

done good in Israel, both *t.* God — *2Ch 24:16*

and *t.* his house — *2Ch 24:16*

the Levite, the porter *t.* the east — *2Ch 31:14*

mercy endureth for ever *t.* Israel — *Ezr 3:11*

against the water gate *t.* the east — *Ne 3:26*

hand upon the wall *t.* the dung gate — *Ne 12:31*

manner *t.* all that knew law — *Es 1:13*

held out the golden sceptre *t.* Esther — *Es 8:4*

dust upon their heads *t.* heaven — *Job 2:12*

stretch out thine hands *t.* him — *Job 11:13*

and stretch her wings *t.* the south — *Job 39:26*

will I worship *t.* thy holy temple — *Ps 5:7*

Mine eyes are ever *t.* the Lord; for — *Ps 25:15*

lift up my hands *t.* thy holy oracle — *Ps 28:2*

thy thoughts which are *t.* us (S) — *Ps 40:5*

his doing *t.* the children of men — *Ps 66:5*

cause thine anger *t.* us to cease — *Ps 85:4*

For great is thy mercy *t.* me — *Ps 86:13*

and his truth *t.* the house of Israel — *Ps 98:3*

is his mercy *t.* them that fear him — *Ps 103:11*

the Lord for all his benefits *t.* me — *Ps 116:12*

merciful kindness is great *t.* us — *Ps 117:2*

I will worship *t.* thy holy temple — *Ps 138:2*

The king's favour is *t.* a wise servant — *Pr 14:35*

they fly away as an eagle *t.* heaven — *Pr 23:5*

The wind goeth *t.* the south — *Ec 1:6*

and if the tree fall *t.* south, or — *Ec 11:3*

t. the north, in the place where the — *Ec 11:3*

Lebanon which looketh *t.* Damascus — *Ca 7:4*

beloved's, and his desire is *t.* me — *Ca 7:10*

went up *t.* Jerusalem to war against — *Isa 7:1*

of the Philistines *t.* the west — *Isa 11:14*

fear *t.* me is taught by the precept — *Isa 29:13*

turned his face *t.* the wall — *Isa 38:2*

to thee with their face *t.* the earth — *Isa 49:23*

great goodness *t.* the house of Israel — *Isa 63:7*

bowels and of thy mercies *t.* me — *Isa 63:15*

shall be known *t.* his servants — *Isa 66:14*

and his indignation *t.* his enemies — *Isa 66:14*

the face thereof is *t.* the north — *Jer 1:13*

proclaim these words *t.* the north — *Jer 3:12*

Set up the standard *t.* Zion: retire — *Jer 4:6*

t. the daughter of my people — *Jer 4:11*

me, and tried mine heart *t.* thee — *Jer 12:3*

mind could not be *t.* this people — *Jer 15:1*

perform my good word *t.* you — *Jer 29:10*

the thoughts that I think *t.* you — *Jer 29:11*

set thine heart *t.* the highway, even — *Jer 31:21*

corner of the horse gate *t.* the east — *Jer 31:40*

t. the north by the river Euphrates — *Jer 46:6*

will I scatter them *t.* all those winds — *Jer 49:36*

lift up thy hands *t.* him for the — *La 2:19*

straight, the one *t.* the other — *Eze 1:23*

thy face *t.* the siege of Jerusalem — *Eze 4:7*

thy face *t.* the mountains of Israel — *Eze 6:2*

than the wilderness *t.* Diblath — *Eze 6:14*

inner gate that looketh *t.* the north — *Eze 8:3*

thine eyes now the way *t.* the north — *Eze 8:5*

up mine eyes the way *t.* the north — *Eze 8:5*

house which was *t.* the north — *Eze 8:14*

backs *t.* the temple of the Lord — *Eze 8:16*

Lord, and their faces *t.* the east — *Eze 8:16*

they worshipped the sun *t.* the east — *Eze 8:16*

higher gate, which lieth *t.* the north — *Eze 9:2*

scatter *t.* every wind all that — *Eze 12:14*

So will I make my fury *t.* thee to rest — *Eze 16:42*

when I am pacified *t.* thee for all that — *Eze 16:63*

whose branches turned *t.* him — *Eze 17:6*

vine did bend her roots *t.* him — *Eze 17:7*

and shot forth her branches *t.* him — *Eze 17:7*

shall be scattered *t.* all winds — *Eze 17:21*

of man, set thy face *t.* the south — *Eze 20:46*

and drop thy word *t.* the south — *Eze 20:46*

man, set thy face *t.* Jerusalem — *Eze 21:2*

drop thy word *t.* the holy places — *Eze 21:2*

iniquities, and mourn one *t.* another — *Eze 24:23*

and lift up your eyes *t.* your idols — *Eze 33:25*

the gate which looketh *t.* the east — *Eze 40:6*

court that looked *t.* the north — *Eze 40:20*

of the gate that looketh *t.* the east — *Eze 40:22*

the gate *t.* the north, and *t.* the east — *Eze 40:23*

that he brought me *t.* the south — *Eze 40:24*

behold a gate *t.* the south: and he — *Eze 40:24*

gate in the inner court *t.* the south — *Eze 40:27*

from gate to gate *t.* the south — *Eze 40:27*

arches were *t.* the utter court — *Eze 40:31*

into the inner court *t.* the east — *Eze 40:32*

arches were *t.* the outward court — *Eze 40:34*

posts thereof were *t.* the utter court — *Eze 40:37*

their prospect was *t.* the south — *Eze 40:44*

having the prospect *t.* the north — *Eze 40:44*

whose prospect is *t.* the south — *Eze 40:45*

whose prospect is *t.* the north is — *Eze 40:46*

were *t.* the place that was left — *Eze 41:11*

one door *t.* the north — *Eze 41:11*

and another door *t.* the south — *Eze 41:11*

at the end *t.* the west was seventy — *Eze 41:12*

and of the separate place *t.* the east — *Eze 41:14*

face of a man was *t.* the palm tree — *Eze 41:19*

face of a young lion *t.* the palm tree — *Eze 41:19*

utter court, the way *t.* north — *Eze 42:1*

before the building *t.* the north — *Eze 42:1*

cubit: and their doors *t.* the north — *Eze 42:4*

t. the utter court on the forepart — *Eze 42:7*

the wall of the court *t.* the east — *Eze 42:10*

chambers which were *t.* the north — *Eze 42:11*

chambers that were *t.* the south — *Eze 42:12*

directly before the wall *t.* the east — *Eze 42:12*

he brought me forth *t.* the gate — *Eze 42:15*

whose prospect is *t.* the east — *Eze 42:15*

the gate that looketh *t.* the east — *Eze 43:1*

gate whose prospect is *t.* the east — *Eze 43:4*

and his stairs shall look *t.* the east — *Eze 43:17*

sanctuary which looketh *t.* the east — *Eze 44:1*

inner court that looketh *t.* the east — *Eze 46:1*

him the gate that looketh *t.* the east — *Eze 46:12*

priests, which looked *t.* the north — *Eze 46:19*

of the house stood *t.* the east — *Eze 47:1*

waters issue out *t.* the east country — *Eze 47:8*

border of the land *t.* the north side — *Eze 47:15*

t. the north five and twenty thousand — *Eze 48:10*

t. the west ten thousand in breadth — *Eze 48:10*

t. the east ten thousand in breadth — *Eze 48:10*

t. the south five and twenty thousand — *Eze 48:10*

t. the north two hundred and fifty — *Eze 48:17*

t. the south two hundred   *Eze 48:17*
and fifty
t. the east two hundred and   *Eze 48:17*
fifty
t. the west two hundred and   *Eze 48:17*
fifty
the oblation *t.* the east   *Eze 48:21*
border
and twenty thousand *t.* the   *Eze 48:21*
west
and to the river *t.* the great   *Eze 48:28*
sea
the high God hath wrought *t.*   *Da 4:2*
me
open in his chamber *t.*   *Da 6:10*
Jerusalem
ones *t.* the four winds of   *Da 8:8*
heaven
exceeding great, *t.* the south   *Da 8:9*
t. the east, and *t.* the pleasant   *Da 8:9*
land
deep sleep on my face *t.* the   *Da 8:18*
ground
my face, and my face *t.* the   *Da 10:9*
ground
unto me, I set my face *t.* the   *Da 10:15*
ground
be divided *t.* the four winds   *Da 11:4*
of heaven
his face *t.* the fort of his   *Da 11:19*
own land
shall return, and come *t.* the   *Da 11:29*
south
the Lord *t.* the children of   *Ho 3:1*
Israel
for judgment is *t.* you, because   *Ho 5:1*
ye
with his face *t.* the east sea   *Joe 2:20*
his hinder part *t.* the utmost   *Joe 2:20*
sea
will look again *t.* thy holy   *Jon 2:4*
temple
grisled go forth *t.* the south   *Zec 6:6*
country
these that go *t.* the north   *Zec 6:8*
country
tribes of Israel, shall be *t.* the   *Zec 9:1*
Lord
thereof *t.* the east and *t.* the   *Zec 14:4*
west
mountain shall remove *t.* the   *Zec 14:4*
north
the north, and half of it *t.* the   *Zec 14:4*
south
half of them *t.* the former sea   *Zec 14:8*
and half of them *t.* the   *Zec 14:8*
hinder sea
forth his hand *t.* his   *M't 12:49*
disciples
moved with compassion *t.*   *M't 14:14*
them
to dawn *t.* the first day of the   *M't 28:1*
week
moved with compassion *t.*   *M'k 6:34*
them
on earth peace, good will *t.*   *Lu 2:14*
men
himself, and is not rich *t.*   *Lu 12:21*
God
and journeying *t.* Jerusalem   *Lu 13:22*
for it is *t.* evening, and the   *Lu 24:29*
day is
went over the sea *t.*   *Joh 6:17*
Capernaum
looked stedfastly *t.* heaven as   *Ac 1:10*
he
go *t.* the south unto the way   *Ac 8:26*
that
to the Greeks, repentance *t.*   *Ac 20:21*
God
and faith *t.* our Lord Jesus   *Ac 20:21*
Christ
and was zealous *t.* God, as   *Ac 22:3*
ye all are
And have hope *t.* God, which   *Ac 24:15*
they
conscience void of offence *t.*   *Ac 24:16*
God
and *t.* men   *Ac 24:16*
t. the south west and north   *Ac 27:12*
west
to the wind, and made *t.*   *Ac 27:40*
shore
days: and so we went *t.*   *Ac 28:14*
Rome
burned in their lust one *t.*   *Ro 1:27*
another
God commendeth his love *t.*   *Ro 5:8*
us

t. thee, goodness, if thou   *Ro 11:22*
continue
of the same mind one *t.*   *Ro 12:16*
another
be likeminded one *t.* another   *Ro 15:5*
himself uncomely *t.* his virgin   *1Co 7:36*
t. you (S)   *2Co 1:12; 13:3*
be brought on my way *t.*   *2Co 1:16*
Judæa
word *t.* you was not yea and   *2Co 1:18*
nay
would confirm your love *t.*   *2Co 2:8*
him
is my boldness of speech *t.*   *2Co 7:4*
you
your fervent mind *t.* me   *2Co 7:7*
affection is more abundant   *2Co 7:15*
t. you
to make all grace abound *t.*   *2Co 9:8*
you
but being absent am bold *t.*   *2Co 10:1*
you
him by the power of God *t.*   *2Co 13:4*
you
was mighty in me *t.* the   *Ga 2:8*
Gentiles
hath abounded *t.* us in all   *Eph 1:8*
wisdom
in his kindness *t.* us through   *Eph 2:7*
supply your lack of service *t.*   *Ph'p 2:30*
me
I press *t.* the mark for the   *Ph'p 3:14*
prize
Walk in wisdom *t.* them that   *Col 4:5*
are
abound in love one *t.* another   *1Th 3:12*
t. all men, even as we do *t.*   *1Th 3:12*
you
indeed ye do it *t.* all the   *1Th 4:10*
brethren
ye may walk honestly *t.* them   *1Th 4:12*
that
the weak, be patient *t.* all   *1Th 5:14*
men
of you all *t.* each other   *2Th 1:3*
aboundeth
God our Saviour *t.* man   *Tit 3:4*
appeared
thou hast *t.* the Lord Jesus   *Ph'm 5*
and *t.* all saints   *Ph'm 5*
dead works, and of faith *t.*   *Heb 6:1*
God
which ye have shewed *t.* his   *Heb 6:10*
name
for conscience *t.* God endure   *1Pe 2:19*
grief
of a good conscience *t.* God   *1Pe 3:21*
then have we confidence *t.*   *1Jo 3:21*
God
manifested the love of God *t.*   *1Jo 4:9*
us

TOWEL

face wrapped in a *t.* (B)   *Joh 11:44*
and took a *t.* and girded   *Joh 13:4*
himself
wipe them with the *t.*   *Joh 13:5*
wherewith

TOWER

to, let us build us a city and a   *Ge 11:4*
t.
down to see the city and the *t.*   *Ge 11:5*
his tent beyond the *t.* of   *Ge 35:21*
Edar
peace, I will break down this *t.*   *J'g 8:9*
he beat down the *t.* of Penuel   *J'g 8:17*
men of the *t.* of Shechem   *J'g 9:46*
heard
men of the *t.* of Shechem were   *J'g 9:47*
men of the *t.* of Shechem died   *J'g 9:49*
also
that was a strong *t.* within the   *J'g 9:51*
city
gat them up to the top of the   *J'g 9:51*
t.
And Abimelech came unto the   *J'g 9:52*
t.
went hard unto the door of   *J'g 9:52*
the *t.*
my high *t.* and my refuge, my   *2Sa 22:3*
my stronghold (A)(R)   *2Sa 22:3*
my fort (B)   *2Sa 22:3*
He is the *t.* of salvation for   *2Sa 22:51*
his
when he came to the *t.* he   *2Ki 5:24*
took

there stood a watchman on the   *2Ki 9:17*
t.
from the *t.* of the watchman   *2Ki 17:9;*
to the   *18:8*
Judah came toward the   *2Ch 20:24*
watch *t.* in
even unto the *t.* of Meah they   *Ne 3:1*
sanctified it, unto the *t.* of   *Ne 3:1*
Hananeel
piece, and the *t.* of the   *Ne 3:11*
furnaces
t. which lieth out from the   *Ne 3:25*
king's
the east, and the *t.* that lieth   *Ne 3:26*
out
against the great *t.* that lieth   *Ne 3:27*
out
from beyond the *t.* of the   *Ne 12:38*
furnaces
fish gate, and the *t.* of   *Ne 12:39*
Hananeel
and the *t.* of Meah, even   *Ne 12:39*
unto the
of my salvation, and my high   *Ps 18:2*
t.
Thy neck is like the *t.* of David   *Ca 4:4*
Thy neck is as a *t.* of ivory;   *Ca 7:4*
thine
thy nose is as the *t.* of Lebanon   *Ca 7:4*
And upon every high *t.* and   *Isa 2:15*
upon
and built a *t.* in the midst of it   *Isa 5:2*
I have set thee for a *t.* and a   *Jer 6:27*
from the *t.* of Hananeel unto   *Jer 31:38*
from the *t.* of Syene even   *Eze 29:10*
unto the
from the *t.* of Syene shall   *Eze 30:6*
they fall
and thou, O *t.* of the flock   *Mic 4:8*
my watch, and set me upon   *Hab 2:1*
the *t.*
and from the *t.* of Hananeel   *Zec 14:10*
a winepress in it, and built a   *M't 21:33*
t.
built a watchtower   *M't 21:33;*
(A)(B)(N)(P)   *M'k 12:1*
place for the winefat, and   *M'k 12:1*
built a *t.*
upon whom the *t.* in Siloam   *Lu 13:4*
fell
which of you, intending to   *Lu 14:28*
build a *t.*

TOWERS

throughout their *t.* (S)   *1Ch 6:54; 27:25*
make about them walls, and   *2Ch 14:7*
t.
Uzziah built *t.* in Jerusalem   *2Ch 26:9*
at the
Also he built *t.* in the   *2Ch 26:10*
desert, and
be on the *t.* and upon the   *2Ch 26:15*
bulwarks
the forests he built castles   *2Ch 27:4*
and *t.*
broken, and raised it up to   *2Ch 32:5*
the *t.*
about her; tell the *t.* thereof   *Ps 48:12*
I am a wall, and my breasts   *Ca 8:10*
like *t.*
Hyenas cry in its *t.* (R)   *Isa 13:22*
they set up the *t.* thereof   *Isa 23:13*
great slaughter, when the *t.*   *Isa 30:25*
fall
the forts and *t.* shall be for   *Isa 32:14*
dens
where is he that counted the *t.*   *Isa 33:18*
of Tyrus, and break down her   *Eze 26:4*
t.
his axes he shall break down   *Eze 26:9*
thy *t.*
the Gammadims were in thy   *Eze 27:11*
t.
cities, and against the high *t.*   *Zep 1:16*
the nations; their *t.* are   *Zep 3:6*
desolate

TOWN

for her house was upon the   *Jos 2:15*
t. wall

the elders of the *t.* trembled   1Sa 16:4
at his
entering into a *t.* that hath   1Sa 23:7
gates
a place in some *t.* in the   1Sa 27:5
country
him that buildeth a *t.* with   Hab 2:12
blood
city or *t.* ye shall enter   M't 10:11
the hand, and led him out of   M'k 8:23
the *t.*
saying, Neither go into the *t.*   M'k 8:26
nor
nor tell it to any in the *t.*   M'k 8:26
were come out of every *t.* of   Lu 5:17
Galilee
out of the *t.* of Bethlehem,   Joh 7:42
where
the *t.* of Mary and her sister   Joh 11:1
Martha
Jesus was not yet come into   Joh 11:30
the *t.*
the *t.* clerk (P)   Ro 16:23

TOWNCLERK

And when the *t.* had   Ac 19:35
appeased the

TOWNS

these are their names, by   Ge 25:16
their *t.*
in all the *t.* (A)(B)(E)   Nu 21:25;
                             21:32
Jair went and took the   Nu 32:41
small *t.*
beside unwalled *t.* a great many   De 3:5
t. of Jair, which are in   Jos 13:30
Bashan
Ekron, with her *t.* and her   Jos 15:45
villages
Ashdod with her *t.* and her   Jos 15:47
villages
Gaza with her *t.* and her   Jos 15:47
villages
in Asher Beth-shean and her   Jos 17:11
t.
and Ibleam and her *t.*   Jos 17:11
the inhabitants of Dor and   Jos 17:11
her *t.*
inhabitants of En-dor and   Jos 17:11
her *t.*
inhabitants of Taanach and   Jos 17:11
her *t.*
inhabitants of Megiddo and   Jos 17:11
her *t.*
who are of Beth-shean and   Jos 17:16
her *t.*
of Beth-shean and her *t.*   J'g 1:27
nor Taanach and her *t.*   J'g 1:27
the inhabitants of Dor and   J'g 1:27
her *t.*
inhabitants of Ibleam and her   J'g 1:27
t.
inhabitants of Megiddo and   J'g 1:27
her *t.*
Israel dwelt in Heshbon and   J'g 11:26
her *t.*
and in Aroer and her *t.* and   J'g 11:26
in all
to him pertained the *t.* of   1Ki 4:13
Jair the
and Aram, with the *t.* of Jair   1Ch 2:23
with Kenath, and the *t.*   1Ch 2:23
thereof
in her *t.* and in all the suburbs   1Ch 5:16
were, Beth-el and the *t.*   1Ch 7:28
thereof
westward Gezer, with the *t.*   1Ch 7:28
thereof
Shechem also and the *t.*   1Ch 7:28
thereof
unto Gaza and the *t.* thereof   1Ch 7:28
Manasseh, Beth-shean and   1Ch 7:29
her *t.*
Taanach and her *t.*   1Ch 7:29
Megiddo and her *t.*   1Ch 7:29
Dor and her *t.*   1Ch 7:29
Ono, and Lod, with the *t.*   1Ch 8:12
thereof
Gath and her *t.* out of the   1Ch 18:1
hand of
him, Beth-el with the *t.*   2Ch 13:19
thereof
and Jeshanah with the *t.*   2Ch 13:19
thereof
and Ephrain with the *t.*   2Ch 13:19
thereof
that dwelt in the unwalled *t.*   Es 9:19

---

upon this city, and upon all   Jer 19:15
her *t.*
inhabited as *t.* without walls   Zec 2:4
Let us go into the next *t.*   M'k 1:38
that I
into the *t.* of Caesarea   M'k 8:27
Philippi
went through the *t.* preaching   Lu 9:6
they may go into the *t.* and   Lu 9:12
country

TRACED

t. my walking and resting (B)   Ps 139:3

TRACHONITIS

of Ituraea and of the region of   Lu 3:1
T.

TRACKS

interlacing her *t.* (B)   Jer 2:23

TRACT

the *t.* of land (A)(B)   Joh 4:5

TRADE

dwell and *t.* ye therein, and   Ge 34:10
get
acquire property (B)   Ge 34:10
dwell in the land, and *t.*   Ge 34:21
therein
stay and do business (B)   Ge 34:21
t. in the land (B)(R)   Ge 42:34
for their *t.* hath been to feed   Ge 46:32
cattle
their occupation (A)   Ge 46:32
Thy servants' *t.* hath been   Ge 46:34
about
profits from *t.* (B)   1Ki 10:15
carried unto the land of *t.*   Eze 17:4
(A)(R)(S)
by sharpness of *t.* (B)(R)   Eze 28:5
by unrighteousness of your   Eze 28:18
t. (A)(B)(R)
t. with this   Lu 19:13
(B)(E)(N)(P)(R)
Father's house a house of   Joh 2:16
t. (R)
by *t.* tent-makers   Ac 18:3
(E)(N)(P)(R)
occupation, *t.*   Ac 19:25;
(A)(B)(E)(R)   19:27
sailors, and as many as *t.* by   Re 18:17
sea
who live by seafaring (A)   Re 18:17
who work the sea for a living   Re 18:17
(B)
gain their living by the sea   Re 18:17
(E)
whose business is upon the   Re 18:17
sea (P)

TRADED

tin, and lead, they *t.* in thy   Eze 27:12
fairs
they *t.* the persons of men   Eze 27:13
house of Togarmah *t.* in thy   Eze 27:14
fairs
traded (S)   Eze 27:16; 27:19, 21-22, 27
t. in thy market wheat of   Eze 27:17
Minnith
talents went and *t.* with the   M't 25:16
same
did business with them   M't 25:16
(B)(N)(P)

TRADERS

Midianite *t.* (B)(R)   Ge 37:28
that which *t.* and merchants   2Ch 9:14
brought (S)
t. bargain over him   Job 41:6
(A)(B)(R)
t. are the honored of earth   Isa 23:8
(A)(B)(R)
carried into the land of *t.* (B)   Eze 17:4
the *t.* of thy merchandise   Eze 27:27
(S)

TRADES

men of similar *t.*   Ac 19:25
(A)(B)(N)(P)

TRADING

much every man had gained   Lu 19:15
by *t.*
made by buying and selling   Lu 19:15
(A)
what business they had   Lu 19:15
transacted (B)
what profit each had made   Lu 19:15
(N)(P)

TRADITION

transgress the *t.* of the elders   M't 15:2
commandment of God by   M't 15:3
your *t.*
of God of none effect by your   M't 15:6
t.
eat not, holding the *t.* of the   M'k 7:3
elder
according to the *t.* of the   M'k 7:5
elders
ye hold the *t.* of men, as the   M'k 7:8
that ye may keep your own *t.*   M'k 7:9
God of none effect through   M'k 7:13
your *t.*
vain deceit, after the *t.* of men   Col 2:8
not after the *t.* which he   2Th 3:6
received
received by *t.* from your   1Pe 1:18
fathers

TRADITIONAL

empty *t.* ways (N)   1Pe 1:18

TRADITIONS

keep the *t.*   1Co 11:2
(A)(E)(N)(P)(R)
zealous of the *t.* of my   Ga 1:14
fathers
hold the *t.* ye have been   2Th 2:15
taught

TRADESMEN

his fellow *t.* (A)   Ac 19:38

TRAFFIC

bands make *t.* of him (E)   Job 41:6
t. in sex (P)   Re 21:8

TRAFFICK

brother, and ye shall *t.* in the   Ge 42:34
land
ye shall do business in the   Ge 42:34
land (A)
you can trade in the land   Ge 42:34
(B)(R)
of the *t.* of the spice   1Ki 10:15
merchants
profits from trade with (B)   1Ki 10:15
and carried it into a land of   Eze 17:4
t.
carried into the land of trade   Eze 17:4
(A)(R)
carried into the land of   Eze 17:4
traders (B)
by thy *t.* hast thou increased   Eze 28:5
thy
by sharpness in trade (B)(R)   Eze 28:5
iniquities, by the iniquity of   Eze 28:18
thy *t.*
by the unrighteousness of   Eze 28:18
your trade (A)(B)(R)

TRAFFICKERS

t. are the honourable of the   Isa 23:8
earth
traders are the honored of   Isa 23:8
earth (A)(B)(R)

TRAILING

t. of his robe filled (B)   Isa 6:1

TRAIN

to Jerusalem with a very   1Ki 10:2
great *t.*
with a great retinue (R)   1Ki 10:2
a very great *t.* (E)   2Ch 9:1
T. up a child in the way he   Pr 22:6
should
Educate a child according to   Pr 22:6
life requirements (B)

up, and his *t.* filled the temple   *Isa 6:1*
the trailing of his robe filled   *Isa 6:1*
the temple (B)

TRAINED

captive, he armed his *t.*   *Ge 14:14*
servants
has been *t.* (R)   *M't 13:52*

TRAINING

has *t.* to engrave (S)   *2Ch 2:7*
rear them (tenderly) in *t.* (A)   *Eph 6:4*

TRAITOR

Iscariot, which was also the *t.*   *Lu 6:16*

TRAITORS

T., heady, highminded, lovers   *2Ti 3:4*

TRAMPLE

Wherefore *t.* ye my sacrifices   *1Sa 2:29*
(S)
dragon shalt thou *t.* under   *Ps 91:13*
feet
anger, and *t.* them in my fury   *Isa 63:3*
lest they *t.* them under their   *M't 7:6*
feet

TRAMPLED

t. upon them (B)   *J'g 10:8*
t. my life to the ground   *Ps 143:3*
(B)(R)
like a *t.* fountain (B)   *Pr 25:26*
trampled (S)   *Isa 5:5;*
14:19; 18:2, 7; 25:10; 28:3, 18; 63:18;
Jer 12:10; La 1:15; Eze 34:19; Da 8:13;
Mic 7:10
t. on him (A)(B)(E)(R)   *Da 8:7; 8:10*

TRAMPLING

t. under foot (B)   *Nu 14:41*

TRANCE

into a *t.* but having his eyes   *Nu 24:4;*
open   *24:16*
sees vision of the Almighty   *Nu 24:4;*
(A)(B)(E)(R)   *24:16*
they made ready, he fell into   *Ac 10:10*
a *t.*
and in a *t.* I saw a vision, A   *Ac 11:5*
certain
prayed in the temple, I was   *Ac 22:17*
in a *t.*

TRANQUIL

t. heart is life of flesh   *Pr 14:30*
(E)(R)

TRANQUILLITY

It may be a lengthening of thy   *Da 4:27*
t.

TRANSACTED

business they had *t.* (B)   *Lu 19:15*

TRANSCENDANT

such *t.* power (N)(R)   *2Co 4:7*

TRANSFER

t. the kingdom   *2Sa 3:10*
(A)(B)(E)(R)(S)

TRANSFERRED

I have in a figure *t.* to myself   *1Co 4:6*
priesthood never *t.* (B)   *Heb 7:24*

TRANSFIGURED

And was *t.* before them: and   *M't 17:2*
his
underwent a change (A)   *M't 17:2*
and he was *t.* before them   *M'k 9:2*

TRANSFORMED

ye *t.* by the renewing of your   *Ro 12:2*
mind

let God remold your minds   *Ro 12:2*
from within (P)
Satan himself is *t.* into an   *2Co 11:14*
angel
Satan masquerades as an   *2Co 11:14*
angel of light (A)(B)(N)(P)
Satan fashioneth himself   *2Co 11:14*
into an angel of light (E)
disguises himself as an   *2Co 11:14*
angel of light (R)
t. as ministers of   *2Co 11:15*
righteousness
his servants masquerade as   *2Co 11:15*
ministers of righteousness
(A)(B)
his ministers fashion   *2Co 11:15*
themselves as ministers of
righteousness (E)
his agents masquerade as   *2Co 11:15*
agents of good (N)
his agents have the   *2Co 11:15*
appearance of ministers of
righteousness (P)
his servants disguise as   *2Co 11:15*
servants of righteousness (R)

TRANSFORMING

t. themselves into the   *2Co 11:13*
apostles of
masquerading as apostles   *2Co 11:13*
(A)(N)
wearing the masks of   *2Co 11:13*
Christ's apostles (B)
fashioning themselves as   *2Co 11:13*
apostles (E)
they are counterfeits of the   *2Co 11:13*
real thing (P)
disguising themselves as   *2Co 11:13*
apostles (R)

TRANSGRESS

do ye *t.* the commandment   *Nu 14:41*
of the
trampling under foot the   *Nu 14:41*
Lord's direct order (B)
ye make the Lord's people to   *1Sa 2:24*
t.
Why ye the   *2Ch 24:20*
commandments of
If ye *t.*, I will scatter you   *Ne 1:8*
abroad
to *t.* against our God in   *Ne 13:27*
marrying
commit wickedness marrying   *Ne 13:27*
foreign women (B)
that my mouth shall not *t.*   *Ps 17:3*
ashamed which *t.* without   *Ps 25:3*
a piece of bread that man   *Pr 28:21*
will *t.*
a man will do wrong for a   *Pr 28:21*
piece of bread (B)(R)
and thou saidst, I will not *t.*   *Jer 2:20*
and them that *t.* against me   *Eze 20:38*
Come to Beth-el, and *t.*; at   *Am 4:4*
Gilgal
thy disciples *t.* the tradition   *M't 15:2*
do ye also *t.* the   *M't 15:3*
commandment
and circumcision dost *t.* the   *Ro 2:27*
law
break the law   *Ro 2:27*
(A)(B)(N)(P)(R)

TRANSGRESSED

I have not *t.* thy   *De 26:13*
commandments
and they have also *t.* my   *Jos 7:11*
covenant
because he hath *t.* the   *Jos 7:15*
covenant of
violated my covenant (B)   *Jos 7:15;*
  J'g 2:20
When ye have *t.* the   *Jos 23:16*
covenant of the
break the covenant (B)   *Jos 23:16*
transgress the covenant (R)   *Jos 23:16*
this people hath *t.* my   *J'g 2:20*
covenant
he said, Ye have *t.*: roll a   *1Sa 14:33*
great
for I have *t.* the   *1Sa 15:24*
commandment of
we have *t.* (B)   *1Ki 8:47*
wherein they have *t.* against   *1Ki 8:50*
thee
sinned against you (A)   *1Ki 8:50*
their God, but *t.* his   *2Ki 18:12*
covenant

Israel, who *t.* in thing   *1Ch 2:7*
accursed
violating the sacred things (B)   *1Ch 2:7*
t. against the God of their   *1Ch 5:25*
fathers
they broke faith with God   *1Ch 5:25*
(B)
they had *t.* against the Lord   *2Ch 12:2*
because of their   *2Ch 12:2*
unfaithfulness (B)
been unfaithful (R)   *2Ch 12:2; 36:14*
for he *t.* against the Lord   *2Ch 26:16*
his God
trespassed (A)   *2Ch 26:16;*
  36:14; Da 7:13
he was false to his God (R)   *2Ch 26:16*
naked, and *t.* sore against   *2Ch 28:19*
the Lord
had been faithless to God   *2Ch 28:19*
(R)
people, *t.* very much after   *2Ch 36:14*
all the
acted most unfaithfully (B)   *2Ch 36:14*
Ye have *t.* and have taken   *Ezr 10:10*
strange
acted wickedly and broken   *Ezr 10:10*
faith (A)
you have sinned (B)   *Ezr 10:10*
you have transgressed (R)   *Ezr 10:10*
many that have *t.* in this   *Ezr 10:13*
thing
because they have *t.* the laws   *Isa 24:5*
thy teachers have *t.* against   *Isa 43:27*
me
rebelled against me (B)   *Isa 43:27;*
  66:24; Jer 2:8, 29; 3:13
the men that have *t.* against   *Isa 66:24*
me
who have stepped over   *Isa 66:24*
against me (A)
rebelled against me (R)   *Isa 66:24;*
Jer 2:29; 3:13; Eze 2:3; Ho 7:13;
  Zep 3:11
the pastors also *t.* against me   *Jer 2:8*
ye all have *t.* against me, saith   *Jer 2:29*
rebelled and revolted against   *Jer 2:29*
me (A)
hast *t.* against the Lord thy   *Jer 3:13*
God
whereby they have *t.* against   *Jer 33:8*
me
sinned and rebelled against   *Jer 33:8*
me (A)(R)
the men that have *t.* my   *Jer 34:18*
covenant
We have *t.* and have rebelled   *La 3:42*
their fathers have *t.* against me   *Eze 2:3*
fathers have sinned against me   *Eze 2:3*
(B)
transgressions, whereby ye   *Eze 18:31*
have *t.*
Yea, all Israel have *t.* thy law   *Da 9:11*
they like men have *t.* the   *Ho 6:7*
covenant
because they have *t.* against   *Ho 7:13*
me
because they have *t.* my   *Ho 8:1*
covenant
wherein thou hast *t.* against   *Zep 3:11*
me
neither *t.* I at any time thy   *Lu 15:29*
never disobeyed your   *Lu 15:29*
commands (A)(R)
without ever neglecting your   *Lu 15:29*
order (B)
not once disobeying your   *Lu 15:29*
orders (N)(P)

TRANSGRESSEST

Mordecai, Why *t.* thou the   *Es 3:3*
king's

TRANSGRESSETH

his mouth *t.* not in judgment   *Pr 16:10*
Yea also, because he *t.* by   *Hab 2:5*
wine
Whosoever committeth sin *t.*   *1Jo 3:4*
Whosoever *t.* and abideth not in   *2Jo 9*

TRANSGRESSING

Lord thy God, in *t.* his   *De 17:2*
covenant
In *t.* and lying against the   *Isa 59:13*
Lord

TRANSGRESSION

forgiving iniquity and *t.* and   *Ex 34:7*
sin

forgiving iniquity and *t*. and *Nu 14:18*
by no
or if in *t*. against the Lord, *Jos 22:22*
(save
If it was in rebellion (R) *Jos 22:22*
is neither evil nor *t*. in mine *1Sa 24:11*
hand
evil or treason in my hands *1Sa 24:11*
(A)
carried away to Babylon for *1Ch 9:1*
their *t*.
for their unfaithfulness to *1Ch 9:1*
God (A)
because of unfaithfulness (B) *1Ch 9:1;*
10:13; 2Ch 29:19
because of unfaithfulness (R) *1Ch 9:1;*
10:13
So Saul died for his *t*. *1Ch 10:13*
which he
Saul died for his trespass *1Ch 10:13*
(A)
in his reign did cast away in *2Ch 29:19*
his *t*.
when he was faithless (R) *2Ch 29:19*
the *t*. of those that had been *Ezr 9:4*
violation of his will by *Ezr 9:4*
returned exiles (A)
because of faithlessness (R) *Ezr 9:4;*
10:6
he mourned because of the *t*. *Ezr 10:6*
exiles' faithlessness (A) *Ezr 10:6*
why dost thou not pardon my *Job 7:21*
t.
he have cast them away for *Job 8:4*
their *t*.
make me to know my *t*. and *Job 13:23*
my sin
My *t*. is sealed up in a bag *Job 14:17*
I am clean without *t*. I am *Job 33:9*
my wound is incurable *Job 34:6*
without *t*.
shall be innocent from the *Ps 19:13*
great *t*.
Blessed is he whose *t*. is *Ps 32:1*
forgiven
The *t*. of the wicked saith *Ps 36:1*
within
not for my *t*. nor for my sin, *Ps 59:3*
O Lord
will I visit their *t*. with the *Ps 89:32*
rod
Fools because of their *t*. and *Ps 107:17*
some were sick through their *Ps 107:17*
sinful ways (R)
The wicked is snared by the *t*. *Pr 12:13*
He that covereth a *t*. seeketh *Pr 17:9*
love
covers and forgives an offence *Pr 17:9*
(A)(B)(R)
He loveth *t*. that loveth strife *Pr 17:19*
and it is his glory to pass *Pr 19:11*
over a *t*.
look over an offence (B) *Pr 19:11*
For the *t*. of a land many are *Pr 28:2*
his mother, and saith, It is no *Pr 28:24*
t.
that is not sin (A) *Pr 28:24*
It is not wrong (B) *Pr 28:24*
t. of an evil man there is a *Pr 29:6*
snare
are multiplied, *t*. increaseth *Pr 29:16*
and a furious man aboundeth *Pr 29:22*
in *t*
abounds in wrong (B) *Pr 29:22*
t. thereof shall be heavy *Isa 24:20*
upon it
for the *t*. of my people was he *Isa 53:8*
are ye not children of *t*., a *Isa 57:4*
seed of
children of sin (B) *Isa 57:4*
children of *t*., offspring of *Isa 57:4*
deceit (R)
and shew my people their *t*. *Isa 58:1*
them that turn from *t*. in *Isa 59:20*
Jacob
who turn from sin (B) *Isa 59:20*
not deliver him in the day of *Eze 33:12*
his *t*.
the daily sacrifice by reason *Da 8:12*
of *t*.
sacrifice, and the *t*. of *Da 8:13*
desolation
to finish the *t*. and to make *Da 9:24*
an end
at Gilgal multiply *t*.: and bring *Am 4:4*
For the *t*. of Jacob is all this *Mic 1:5*
What is the *t*. of Jacob? Is it *Mic 1:5*
not
to declare unto Jacob his *t*. *Mic 3:8*
Jacob his rebellion (B) *Mic 3:8*

shall I give my firstborn for *Mic 6:7*
my *t*.
passeth by the *t*. of the *Mic 7:18*
remnant of
from which Judas by *t*. fell, *Ac 1:25*
that
for where no law is, there is *Ro 4:15*
no *t*.
after the similitude of Adam's *Ro 5:14*
t.
woman being deceived was in *1Ti 2:14*
the *t*.
every *t*. and disobedience *Heb 2:2*
received
the law: for sin is the *t*. of the *1Jo 3:4*
law
sin is lawbreaking (B) *1Jo 3:4*
sin is lawlessness (R) *1Jo 3:4*

TRANSGRESSIONS

their *t*. (E)(R) *Ge 50:17*
not; for he will not pardon *Ex 23:21*
your *t*.
because of their *t*. in all their *Le 16:16*
sins
and all their *t*. in all their *Le 16:21*
sins
not forgive your *t*. nor your *Jos 24:19*
sins
your rebellions (B) *Jos 24:19; Jer 5:6*
all their *t*. wherein they have *1Ki 8:50*
If I covered my *t*. as Adam *Job 31:33*
if thy *t*. be multiplied, what *Job 35:6*
doest
their *t*. that they have *Job 36:9*
exceeded
out in the multitude of their *t*. *Ps 5:10*
not the sins of my youth, nor *Ps 25:7*
my *t*.
I will confess my *t*. unto the *Ps 32:5*
Lord
Deliver me from all my *t*.: *Ps 39:8*
make
my sins (B) *Ps 39:8; Ga 3:19*
thy tender mercies blot out my *Ps 51:1*
t.
For I acknowledge my *t*.: and *Ps 51:3*
as for our *t*. thou shalt purge *Ps 65:3*
them
hath he removed our *t*. from *Ps 103:12*
us
blotteth out thy *t*. for mine *Isa 43:25*
own
blotted out, as a thick cloud, *Isa 44:22*
thy *t*.
your *t*. is your mother put *Isa 50:1*
away
But he was wounded for our *Isa 53:5*
t. he
our *t*. are multiplied before *Isa 59:12*
thee
for our *t*. are with us; and as *Isa 59:12*
for
because their *t*. are many, and *Jer 5:6*
their
her for the multitude of her *t*. *La 1:5*
yoke of my *t*. is bound by his *La 1:14*
hand
hast done unto me for all my *La 1:22*
t.
polluted any more with all *Eze 14:11*
their *t*.
All his *t*. that he hath *Eze 18:22*
committed
away from all his *t*. that he *Eze 18:28*
hath
turn yourselves from all *Eze 18:30*
your *t*.
Cast away from you all your *Eze 18:31*
t.
in that your *t*. are discovered *Eze 21:24*
If our *t*. and our sins be *Eze 33:10*
upon us
things, nor with any of their *Eze 37:23*
t.
according to their *t*. have I *Eze 39:24*
done
For three *t*. of Damascus, and *Am 1:3*
for
For three *t*. of Gaza, and for *Am 1:6*
four
For three *t*. of Tyrus, and for *Am 1:9*
four
For three *t*. of Edom, and for *Am 1:11*
four
For three *t*. of the children of *Am 1:13*
For three *t*. of Moab, and for *Am 2:1*
four

For three *t*. of Judah, and for *Am 2:4*
four
For three *t*. of Israel, and for *Am 2:6*
four
shall visit the *t*. of Israel *Am 3:14*
upon him
your manifold *t*. and your *Am 5:12*
mighty
the *t*. of Israel were found in *Mic 1:13*
thee
gift following many *t*. (A) *Ro 5:16*
It was added because of *t*. till *Ga 3:19*
the *t*. that were under the *Heb 9:15*
first

TRANSGRESSOR

and the *t*. for the upright *Pr 21:18*
the treacherous (A)(B)(E) *Pr 21:18;*
22:12
the faithless (R) *Pr 21:18; 22:12*
overthroweth the words of *Pr 22:12*
the *t*.
wast called a *t*. from the *Isa 48:8*
womb
I destroyed, I make myself a *Ga 2:18*
t.
a sinner (P) *Ga 2:18*
kill, thou art become a *t*. of *Jas 2:11*
the law
a lawbreaker (N) *Jas 2:11*

TRANSGRESSORS

But the *t*. shall be destroyed *Ps 37:38*
Then will I teach *t*. thy ways *Ps 51:13*
be not merciful to any wicked *Ps 59:5*
t.
I beheld the *t*. and was *Ps 119:158*
grieved
the treacherous (A) *Ps 119:158;*
Pr 2:22; 11:3, 6; 13:2; 23:28
The treacherous (B)(E) *Ps 119:158;*
The faithless (R) *Ps 119:158;*
Pr 13:15; 23:28
and the *t*. shall be rooted out *Pr 2:22*
of it
the treacherous (R) *Pr 2:22;*
11:3, 6; 13:2
the perverseness of *t*. shall *Pr 11:3*
destroy
t. shall be taken in their own *Pr 11:6*
the soul of the *t*. shall eat *Pr 13:2*
violence
favour: but the way of *t*. is *Pr 13:15*
hard
and increaseth the *t*. among *Pr 23:28*
men
the fool, and rewardeth *t*. *Pr 26:10*
the destruction of the *t*. and *Isa 1:28*
of the
rebels and sinners (A) *Isa 1:28; 46:8*
apostates and sinners (B) *Isa 1:28*
rebels and sinners (R) *Isa 1:28*
men: bring it again to mind, *Isa 46:8*
O ye *t*.
you apostates (B) *Isa 46:8*
and he was numbered with *Isa 53:12*
the *t*.
and made intercession for the *Isa 53:12*
t.
when the *t*. are come to the *Da 8:23*
full
when the wicked go to *Da 8:23*
extremes (B)
them: but the *t*. shall fall *Ho 14:9*
therein
And he was numbered with *M'k 15:28*
the *t*.
counted with outlaws *M'k 15:28;*
(B)(N) *Lu 22:37*
And he was reckoned among *Lu 22:37*
the *t*.
classed with wicked outlaws *Lu 22:37*
and criminals (A)
rated among criminals (B) *Lu 22:37*
and are convinced of the law *Jas 2:9*
as *t*.
convicted as violators and *Jas 2:9*
offenders (A)
convicted as culprits (B) *Jas 2:9*

TRANSIENT

a *t*. (B) *Ps 39:12*
the *t*. or alien (A) *Pr 7:5*
things seen are *t*. (R) *2Co 4:18*

TRANSITORINESS

all is *t.* (A)	Ec 12:10
under bondage of *t.* (B)	Ro 8:20

TRANSITORY

childhood and youth are *t.* (B)	Ec 11:10
t. never possess the everlasting (P)	1Co 15:50
visible things are *t.* (B)(P)	2Co 4:18
t. power of wealth (P)	1Ti 6:17

TRANSLATE

To *t.* the kingdom from the house	2Sa 3:10
transfer the kingdom (A)(B)(E)(R)	2Sa 3:10

TRANSLATED

Rabbi, *t.* teacher (A)(B)(N)(R)	Joh 1:38
t. meaning store (A)(B)	Joh 1:42
Barnabas, *t.* Son of (N)	Joh 4:36
Siloam *t.* Sent (S)	Joh 9:7
Tabitha *t.* Dorcas (B)	Ac 9:36
hath *t.* us into the kingdom of his	Col 1:13
transferred (A)(B)(R)	Col 1:13; Heb 11:5
reestablished us (N)	Col 1:13
his name when *t.* (A)	Heb 7:2
By faith, Enoch was *t.* that he	Heb 11:5
not found, because God had *t.* him	Heb 11:5
Enoch was taken up (R)	Heb 11:5

TRANSLATION

by *t.* king of righteousness (R)	Heb 7:2
for before his *t.* he had this	Heb 11:5
before he was taken to heaven (A)(N)(R)	Heb 11:5
previous to his passing over (B)	Heb 11:5

TRANSLUCENT

t. as glass (A)(B)	Re 21:21

TRANSPARENT

as *t.* crystal (B)	Eze 1:22
was pure gold, as it were *t.* glass	Re 21:21
gold as pure and translucent as glass (A)(B)	Re 21:21

TRANSPORTED

t. with delight in love (A)	Pr 5:19

TRAP

trap (S)	Job 18:9; Isa 8:14; Am 3:5
and a *t.* for him in the way	Job 18:10
for their welfare, let it become a *t.*	Ps 69:22
the hunter's *t.* (B)	Ps 91:3
keep me from the *t.* (A)(B)(R)	Ps 141:9
concealed a *t.* for me (B)(R)	Ps 142:3
for a *t.* and a snare (A)(B)(R)	Isa 8:14
they set a *t.* they catch men	Jer 5:26
they set a *t.* (A)(B)(E)(R)	Jer 5:26
a *t.* before me (B)	Jer 48:43; 48:44
a *t.* for him (A)(R)	Am 3:5
laid a *t.* under thee (S)	Ob 7
if eye serves as a *t.* (A)	M't 5:19; 5:30
like a *t.* or a moose (A)(B)(N)(P)	Lu 21:34
table he made a snare, and a *t.*	Ro 11:9

TRAPPED

t. in disastrous time (B)	Ec 9:12
t. and taken (B)	Isa 8:15
t. in holes (B)	Isa 42:22
wise men dumbfounded and *t.*	Jer 8:9
so you not be *t.* (B)	Joh 16:1

TRAPS

shall be snares and *t.* unto you	Jos 23:13
set *t.* for me (A)(B)(R)(S)	Ps 140:5
keep me from *t.* (S)	Ps 141:9

TRAVAIL

came to pass in the time of her *t.*	Ge 38:27
at the time of her delivery (B)	Ge 38:27
all the *t.* that had come upon them	Ex 18:8
all the hardships (A)(B)(R)	Ex 18:8
all the *t.* that hath befallen us	Nu 20:14
all the *t.* that has come upon us	Nu 20:14
all the adversity and birth pangs (A)	Nu 20:14
all the misery we have experienced (B)	Nu 20:14
and pain, as of a woman in *t.*	Ps 48:6
as a woman in childbirth (A)	Ps 48:6; Jer 6:24; 22:23; 49:24; 50:43; Mic 4:10
the throes of childbirth (B)	Ps 48:6
this sore *t.* hath God given to	Ec 1:13
a miserable business (A)	Ec 1:13
a trying task (B)	Ec 1:13; 2:23, 26
the unhappy business (R)	Ec 1:13
days are sorrows, and his *t.* grief	Ec 2:23
to the sinner he giveth *t.* to gather	Ec 2:26
I have seen the *t.* which God hath	Ec 3:10
the painful labor (A)	Ec 3:10
the business (R)	Ec 3:10
I considered all *t.* and every right	Ec 4:4
the painful effort in labor (A)	Ec 4:4; 4:6, 8
all toil (R)	Ec 4:4; 4:6, 8; 1Th 2:9; 2Th 3:8
hands full with *t.* and vexation	Ec 4:6
is also vanity, yea, it is a sore *t.*	Ec 4:8
But those riches perish by evil *t.*	Ec 5:14
riches lost by bad venture (A)(R)	Ec 5:14
I *t.* not, nor bring forth children	Isa 23:4
He shall see of the *t.* of his soul	Isa 53:11
see the results of His sufferings (B)	Isa 53:11
thou that didst not *t.* with child	Isa 54:1
Never writhed in childbirth (B)	Isa 54:1
heard a voice as of a woman in *t.*	Jer 4:31
us, and pain, as of a woman in *t.*	Jer 6:24
woman in labor (B)	Jer 6:24; 13:21; 22:23; 49:24; 50:43; Mic 4:10
sorrows take thee, as a woman in *t.*	Jer 13:21
thee, the pain as of a woman in *t.*	Jer 22:23
whether a man doth *t.* with child	Jer 30:6
man give birth to a child (A)	Jer 30:6
like a woman in labor (A)	Jer 30:6; Mic 4:9
can a man bear a child (B)	Jer 30:6
a woman in labor (R)	Jer 30:6
on his loins, as a woman in *t.*	Jer 30:6
have taken her, as a woman in *t.*	Jer 49:24
him, and pangs as of a woman in *t.*	Jer 50:43
compassed me with gall and *t.*	La 3:5
with bitterness, tribulation, and *t.* (A)	La 3:5
with bitterness and distress (B)	La 3:5
have taken thee as a woman in *t.*	Mic 4:9
of Zion, like a woman in *t.*	Mic 4:10
beginning of *t.* (N)	M't 24:8; M'k 13:8
A woman in *t.* hath sorrow (A)	Joh 16:21
woman when she gives birth	Joh 16:21
mother in childbirth has anguish (B)	Joh 16:21
a woman in labor (R)	Joh 16:21
pain of childbirth (P)	Joh 16:21
in labour and *t.* (E)	2Co 11:27

I *t.* in birth again until Christ be	Ga 4:19
am again suffering pangs (A)	Ga 4:19
once more suffer birth pains (B)	Ga 4:19
pain of child birth (P)	Ga 4:19
brethren, our labour and *t.*	1Th 2:9
toil and struggles (A)	1Th 2:9; 2Th 3:8
struggles and hard work (P)	1Th 2:9
as *t.* upon a woman with child	1Th 5:3
labor pains (A)	1Th 5:3
birth pangs of a pregnant woman (B)(R)	1Th 5:3
pangs upon a woman with child (P)	1Th 5:3
wrought with labour and *t.* night	2Th 3:8
we toiled and drudged (N)	2Th 3:8

TRAVAILED

Rachel *t.* and she had hard labour	Ge 35:16
pangs of childbirth (A)	Ge 35:16
felt the birth pangs (B)	Ge 35:16; 1Sa 4:19
It came to pass, when she *t.*	Ge 38:28
when she was in labor (A)(B)	Ge 38:28
dead, she bowed herself and *t.*	1Sa 4:19
her pain came upon her (A)(B)	1Sa 4:19; Isa 66:7
Before she *t.* she brought forth	Isa 66:7
as soon as Zion *t.* she brought forth	Isa 66:8
Zion was in labor (A)(B)	Isa 66:8

TRAVAILEST

forth and cry, thou that *t.* not	Ga 4:27
not feeling birth pains (A)(B)	Ga 4:27
never knew a mother's pangs (N)	Ga 4:27

TRAVAILETH

wicked man *t.* with pain all his	Job 15:20
suffers torment (A)	Job 15:20
tormented with anxiety (B)	Job 15:20
writhes in pain (R)	Job 15:20
he *t.* with iniquity, and hath	Ps 7:14
pregnant with mischief (A)(R)	Ps 7:14
conceived wrongdoing (B)	Ps 7:14
be in pain as a woman in *t.*	Isa 13:8
as a woman in childbirth (A)	Isa 13:8; 21:3
pangs and agony (R)	Isa 13:8
as the pangs of a woman that *t.*	Isa 21:3
like a woman giving birth (B)	Isa 21:3
her that *t.* with child together	Jer 31:8
her labors in childbirth (A)	Jer 31:8
woman with child is in labor (B)	Jer 31:8
she which hath *t.* hath brought forth	Mic 5:3
who is in labor (B)	Mic 5:3
t. in pain together until now	Ro 8:22
pains of labor until now (A)	Ro 8:22
sighing throes in unison (B)	Ro 8:22
in pangs of childbirth (R)	Ro 8:22

TRAVAILING

now will I cry like a *t.* woman	Isa 42:14
the sorrows of a woman in *t.*	Ho 13:13
pains of a woman in childbirth (R)	Ho 13:13
pangs of childbirth (R)	Ho 13:13
being with child cried, *t.* in birth	Re 12:2
cried out in birth pangs (A)	Re 12:2
agonizing in birth pangs of her delivery (B)	Re 12:2
in the anguish of her labor she cried to be delivered (N)	Re 12:2
cried out in labor and pains of bringing forth her child (P)	Re 12:2
pangs of childbirth (R)	Re 12:2

TRAVEL

t. on together (B)	Ge 33:12
cause to *t.* (B)	Eze 36:12; Lu 13:33
one day's *t.* (B)	Jon 3:4
t. over sea and land (A)(N)	M't 23:15

wearied by his *t.* (B)   *Joh 4:6*
Paul's companions in *t.*   *Ac 19:29*
chosen of the churches to *t.*   *2Co 8:19*
with us

TRAVELLED

Abram *t.* on (B)   *Ge 12:9*
he *t.* by stages (B)   *Ge 13:3; Ex 17:1*
Jacob *t.* on (B)   *Ge 29:1*
t. a day (B)   *Lu 2:44*
t. to a distant country (B)   *Lu 15:13*
as he *t.* he came (B)   *Ac 9:3*
Stephen *t.* as far as Phenice   *Ac 11:19*

TRAVELLER

there came a *t.* unto the rich   *2Sa 12:4*
man
but I opened my doors to   *Job 31:32*
the *t.*
I opened my door to   *Job 31:32*
wayfarers (B)(R)

TRAVELLERS

the *t.* walked through byways   *J'g 5:6*
strangers and *t.* (N)   *Heb 11:13*
as visitors and *t.* (B)   *1Pe 2:11*

TRAVELLETH

thy poverty come as one that *t.*   *Pr 6:11*
poverty shall come as a   *Pr 6:11;*
bandit (B)   *24:34*
poverty shall come as a   *Pr 6:11;*
robber (E)   *24:34*
poverty shall come like a   *Pr 6:11*
vagabond (R)
thy poverty come as one that *Pr 24:34*
t.
poverty shall come like a   *Pr 24:34*
robber (R)

TRAVELLING

O ye *t.* companies of   *Isa 21:13*
Dedanim
caravans of the Dedanites   *Isa 21:13*
(A)(B)(E)(R)
t. in the greatness of his   *Isa 63:1*
strength
striding triumphantly (A)   *Isa 63:1*
marching in the greatness of   *Isa 63:1*
His might (B)(E)(R)
is as a man *t.* into a far   *M't 25:14*
country
a man about to take a long   *M't 25:14*
journey (A)(R)
a man going abroad   *M't 25:14*
(B)(N)(P)
a man going into another   *M't 25:14*
country (E)
men *t.* with him (N)(R)   *Ac 9:7*
t. Jewish exorcists (A)(B)   *Ac 19:13*

TRAVELS

during all their *t.* (B)   *Ex 40:36*
in his *t.* he came (B)   *J'g 17:8*

TRAVERSE

t. through the land (B)   *Ge 13:17*
t. over sea and land (B)(R)   *M't 23:15*

TRAVERSING

art a swift dromedary *t.* her   *Jer 2:23*
ways
running hither and thither   *Jer 2:23*
(A)
entangling her walk (B)   *Jer 2:23*
interlacing her tracks (R)   *Jer 2:23*

TRAVESTY

upsetting faith with *t.* of gospel   *Ga 1:7*
(P)

TREACHERIES

think up *t.* all day (B)   *Ps 38:12*

TREACHEROUS

treacherous (A)   *Ps 119:158;*
    Pr 2:22; 11:3, 6; 13:2; 23:28
treacherous (B)   *Ps 119:158;*
    Pr 2:22; 11:3, 6; 13:2, 15; 23:28

treacherous (R)   *Pr 2:22; 11:3, 6; 13:2*
crookedness of *t.* (A)(R)   *Pr 11:3*
the treacherous (A)(B)(E)   *Pr 21:18;*
    22:12
t. dealer dealeth treacherously   *Isa 21:2*
t. dealers have dealt   *Isa 24:16*
treacherously
the deceivers deceive (B)   *Isa 24:16*
the *t.* dealers have dealt very   *Isa 24:16*
And her *t.* sister Judah saw it   *Jer 3:7*
false sister Judah (R)   *Jer 3:7;*
    3:8, 10-11
yet her *t.* sister Judah feared   *Jer 3:8*
not
faithless sister Judah (B)   *Jer 3:8;*
    3:10-11
her *t.* sister Judah hath not   *Jer 3:10*
herself more than *t.* Judah   *Jer 3:11*
adulterers, an assembly of *t.*   *Jer 9:2*
men
assembly of deceivers (B)   *Jer 9:2*
prophets are light and *t.*   *Zep 3:4*
persons

TREACHEROUSLY

act *t.* (R)   *Nu 31:16; Eze 20:27*
Shechem dealt *t.* with   *J'g 9:23*
Abimelech
I acted *t.* (B)(R)   *2Sa 18:13*
been untrue and dealt *t.*   *Ps 73:15*
(A)(E)
the treacherous dealer dealeth   *Isa 21:2*
t.
treacherous dealers have   *Isa 24:16*
dealt *t.*
dealers have dealt very *t.*   *Isa 24:16*
the deceivers deceive (B)   *Isa 24:16*
wast not spoiled; and dealest   *Isa 33:1*
t.
and they dealt not *t.* with thee   *Isa 33:1*
thou shalt make an end to   *Isa 33:1*
deal *t.*
they shall deal *t.* with thee   *Isa 33:1*
that thou wouldest deal very *t.*   *Isa 48:8*
as a wife *t.* departeth from   *Jer 3:20*
her
so have ye dealt *t.* with me   *Jer 3:20*
have dealt very *t.* against me   *Jer 5:11*
been altogether faithless to me   *Jer 5:11*
(B)(R)
are all they happy that deal   *Jer 12:1*
very *t.*
even they have dealt *t.* with   *Jer 12:6*
thee
her friends have dealt *t.* with   *La 1:2*
her
have dealt *t.* against the Lord   *Ho 5:7*
there have they dealt *t.* against   *Ho 6:7*
me
lookest thou upon them that   *Hab 1:13*
deal *t.*
we deal *t.* every man against   *Mal 2:10*
Judah hath dealt *t.* and an   *Mal 2:11*
Judah hath been faithless   *Mal 2:11;*
(B)(R)   *2:14*
against whom thou hast dealt   *Mal 2:14*
t.
been faithless (R)   *Mal 2:14; 2:15-16*
deal *t.* against the wife of his   *Mal 2:15*
youth
lest you be unfaithful (B)   *Mal 2:15;*
    2:16
to your spirit, that ye deal   *Mal 2:16*
not *t.*
they dealt *t.* (B)(R)   *Eze 39:23*

TREACHERY

iniquity of *t.* (A)(R)   *Le 26:40*
Ahaziah, There is *t.* O   *2Ki 9:23*
Ahaziah
Treason (B)   *2Ki 9:23*
found *t.* in Hoshea (A)(R)   *2Ki 17:4*
meditate *t.* all day (A)(R)   *Ps 38:12*
t. against me (R)   *Eze 17:20*
his *t.* (R)   *Eze 18:24; Da 9:7*
all their *t.* (A)(B)(R)   *Eze 39:26*
make *t.* to win out (B)   *Da 8:25*
the *t.* committed (R)   *Da 9:7*
execute through *t.* (B)   *M'k 14:1*

TREAD

land that he hath *t.* upon (S)   *De 1:36*
the soles of your feet shall *t.*   *De 11:24*
shall
upon all the land ye shall *t.*   *De 11:25*
upon
thou shalt *t.* upon their high   *De 33:29*
places

the sole of your feet shall *t.*   *Jos 1:3*
upon
t. on the threshold of Dagon   *1Sa 5:5*
t. their winepresses, and   *Job 24:11*
suffer
t. down the wicked in their   *Job 40:12*
place
let him *t.* down my life upon   *Ps 7:5*
will we *t.* them under that rise   *Ps 44:5*
it is that shall *t.* down our   *Ps 60:12*
enemies
shalt *t.* upon the lion and   *Ps 91:13*
adder
it is that shall *t.* down our   *Ps 108:13*
enemies
this at your hand, to *t.* my   *Isa 1:12*
courts
t. them down like the mire of   *Isa 10:6*
my mountains *t.* him under   *Isa 14:25*
foot
treaders shall *t.* out no wine   *Isa 16:10*
The foot shall *t.* it down, even   *Isa 26:6*
for I will *t.* them in mine   *Isa 63:3*
anger
I will *t.* down the people in   *Isa 63:6*
mine
shout, as they that *t.* the   *Jer 25:30*
grapes
none shall *t.* with shouting;   *Jer 48:33*
their
shall he *t.* down all thy streets   *Ex 26:1*
ye must *t.* down with your   *Eze 34:18*
feet the
shall *t.* it down, and break it   *Da 7:23*
and loveth to *t.* out the corn   *Ho 10:11*
t. upon the high places of the   *Mic 1:3*
and when he shall *t.* in our   *Mic 5:5*
palaces
thou shalt *t.* the olives, but   *Mic 6:15*
thou
go into clay, and *t.* the morter   *Na 3:14*
which *t.* down their enemies   *Zec 10:5*
in the
and ye shall *t.* down the   *Mal 4:3*
wicked
you power to *t.* on serpents   *Lu 10:19*
holy city shall they *t.* under   *Re 11:2*
foot

TREADER

the *t.* of grapes him that   *Am 9:13*
soweth

TREADERS

the *t.* shall tread out no wine   *Isa 16:10*

TREADETH

the ox when he *t.* out the corn   *De 25:4*
and *t.* upon the waves of the   *Job 9:8*
sea
morter, and as the potter *t.*   *Isa 41:25*
clay
like him that *t.* in the winefat   *Isa 63:2*
t. upon the high places of the   *Am 4:13*
earth
and when he *t.* within our   *Mic 5:6*
borders
t. down, and teareth in pieces   *Mic 5:8*
of the ox that *t.* out the corn   *1Co 9:9*
muzzle the ox that *t.* out the   *1Ti 5:18*
corn
and he *t.* the winepress of the   *Re 19:15*

TREADING

t. wine presses on the sabbath   *Ne 13:15*
and for the *t.* of lesser cattle   *Isa 7:25*
is a day of trouble, and of *t.*   *Isa 22:5*
down
as your *t.* is upon the poor   *Am 5:11*

TREASON

t. they perpetuated (B)   *Le 26:40*
and his *t.* that he wrought   *1Ki 16:20*
his conspiracy (B)(R)   *1Ki 16:20*
rent her clothes, and cried,   *2Ki 11:14*
T., T.
Conspiracy! Conspiracy! (B)   *2Ki 11:14*
rent their clothes, and said,   *2Ch 23:13*
T., T.
for his *t.* (B)(R)   *Eze 17:10*
t. against me (B)(R)   *Eze 17:20*

TREASURE

hath given you *t.* in your   *Ge 43:23*
sacks

TREASURE

they built for Pharaoh t. cities — Ex 1:11
store cities (B)(E)(R) — Ex 1:11
then ye shall be a peculiar t. — Ex 19:5
unto
my personal possession — Ex 19:5
(B)(E)(R)
shall open unto thee his good — De 28:12
t.
to the t. of the house of the — 1Ch 29:8
Lord
their ability unto to the t. of the — Ezr 2:69
work
be search made in the king's — Ezr 5:17
t.
it out of the king's t. house — Ezr 7:20
gave to the t. a thousand — Ne 7:70
drams of
gave to the t. of the work — Ne 7:71
twenty
to the chambers, into the t. — Ne 10:38
house
whose belly thou fillest with — Ps 17:14
thy hid t.
himself, and Israel for his — Ps 135:4
peculiar t.
his own possession (B)(E)(R) — Ps 135:4
house of the righteous is a — Pr 15:6
much t.
Lord than great t. and trouble — Pr 15:16
There is t. to be desired and — Pr 21:20
oil in
the peculiar t. of kings and of — Ec 2:8
the fear of the Lord is his t. — Isa 33:6
they have taken the t. and — Eze 22:25
vessels into the t. house of — Da 1:2
his god
spoil the t. of all pleasant — Ho 13:15
vessels
where your t. is, there will — M't 6:21;
your heart be — Lu 12:34
good t. of the heart bringeth — M't 12:35
forth
evil t. bringeth forth evil — M't 12:35
things
heaven is like unto t. hid in — M't 13:44
a field
out of his t. things new and — M't 13:52
old
and thou shalt have t. in — M't 19:21;
heaven — Lu 18:22
and thou shalt have t. in — M'k 10:21
heaven
good t. of his heart bringeth — Lu 6:45
forth
evil t. of his heart bringeth — Lu 6:45
forth
he that layeth up t. for — Lu 12:21
himself
t. in the heavens that faileth — Lu 12:33
not
who had the charge of all her — Ac 8:27
t.
we have this t. in earthen — 2Co 4:7
vessels
heaped t. together for the last — Jas 5:3

TREASURED

t. words of his mouth — Job 23:12
(B)(E)(R)
it shall not be t. nor laid up; — Isa 23:18
for
stored up or hoarded — Isa 23:18
(B)(R)
one t., one for common use — Ro 9:21
(N)

TREASURER

by the hand of Mithredath the — Ezr 1:8
t.
get thee unto this t. even — Isa 22:15
unto
the city t. — Ro 16:23
(A)(B)(E)(N)(R)

TREASURERS

the t. which are beyond the — Ezr 7:21
river
And I made t. over the — Ne 13:13
treasuries
judges, the t., the counsellors — Da 3:2;
  3:3

TREASURES

all sorts of master's t. — Ge 24:10
(A)(B)

me, and sealed up among my — De 32:34
t.
the seas, and of t. hid in the — De 33:19
sand
he put among the t. of the — 1Ki 7:51
house of
he took away the t. of the — 1Ki 14:26
house of
Lord, and the t. of the — 1Ki 14:26
king's house
In the t. of the house of the — 1Ki 15:18
Lord
and the t. of the king's — 1Ki 15:18
house, and
in the t. of the house of the — 2Ki 12:18
Lord
and in the t. in the king's — 2Ki 14:14;
house — 16:8
and in the t. of the king's — 2Ki 18:15
house
and all that was found in his — 2Ki 20:13
t.
among my t. that I have not — 2Ki 20:15
shewed
all the t. of the house of — 2Ki 24:13
the Lord
and the t. of the king's — 2Ki 24:13
house, and
Ahijah was over the t. of — 1Ch 26:20
the house
over the t. of the dedicated — 1Ch 26:20
things
were over the t. of the — 1Ch 26:22
house of the
the son of Moses, was ruler — 1Ch 26:24
were over all the t. of the — 1Ch 26:26
dedicated
over the king's t. was — 1Ch 27:25
Azmaveth the
among the t. of the house of — 2Ch 5:1
God
any matter, or concerning the — 2Ch 8:15
t.
took away the t. of the house — 2Ch 12:9
of the
and the t. of the king's house; — 2Ch 12:9
he
gold out of the t. of the — 2Ch 16:2
house of the
and the t. of the king's — 2Ch 25:24
house, the
and the t. of the house of — 2Ch 36:18
the Lord
and the t. of the king, and of — 2Ch 36:18
the t. were laid up in Babylon — Ezr 6:1
over the chambers for the t. — Ne 12:44
and dig for it more than for — Job 3:21
hid t.
laid up for his t. (S) — Job 20:26
entered into the t. of the — Job 38:22
snow
or hast thou seen the t. of — Job 38:22
the hail
and searchest for her as for hid — Pr 2:4
t.
substance, and I will fill their — Pr 8:21
t.
T. of wickedness profit — Pr 10:2
nothing: but
The getting of t. by a lying — Pr 21:6
tongue
neither is there any end of their — Isa 2:7
t.
people, and have robbed — Isa 10:13
their t.
their t. upon the bunches of — Isa 30:6
camels
and all that was found in his — Isa 39:2
t.
there is nothing among my t. — Isa 39:4
that I
I will give thee the t. of — Isa 45:3
darkness
bringeth forth the wind out — Jer 10:13
of his t.
Thy substance and thy t. will — Jer 15:13
I give
substance and all thy t. to the — Jer 17:3
spoil
and all the t. of the kings of — Jer 20:5
Judah
we have t. in the field, of — Jer 41:8
wheat
trusted in thy works and in — Jer 48:7
thy t.
that trusted in her t. saying, — Jer 49:4
Who
a sword is upon her t.; and — Jer 50:37
they

abundant in t., thine end is — Jer 51:13
come
bringeth forth the wind out — Jer 51:16
of his t.
t. in days of old — La 1:7
(A)(B)(E)(R)
gotten gold and silver into — Eze 28:4
thy t.
have power over the t. of — Da 11:43
gold and
Are there yet the t. of — Mic 6:10
wickedness
and when they had opened — M't 2:11
their t.
not up for yourselves t. upon — M't 6:19
earth
lay up for yourselves t. in — M't 6:20
heaven
whom are hid all the t. of — Col 2:3
wisdom
greater riches than the t. in — Heb 11:26
Egypt

TREASUREST

t. up unto thyself wrath against — Re 2:5

TREASURIES

treasuries (S) — 1Ki 15:18;
2Ki 12:18; 14:14; 16:8; 18:15; 20:13;
1Ch 26:20, 22, 24, 26; 27:25; 2Ch 5:1;
8:15; 16:2; Job 38:22; Pr 8:21; Eze 28:4;
  Isa 39:2; Jer 50:37
and t. of the house of God — 1Ch 9:26
thereof, and of the t. thereof — 1Ch 28:11
about, of the t. of the house — 1Ch 28:12
of God
of the t. of the dedicated — 1Ch 28:12
things
and he made himself t. for — 2Ch 32:27
silver
the new wine and the oil — Ne 13:12
unto the t.
And I made treasurers over — Ne 13:13
the t.
to bring it into the king's t. — Es 3:9
had promised to pay to the — Es 4:7
king's t.
he bringeth the wind out of — Ps 135:7
his t.

TREASURY

shall come into the t. of the — Jos 6:19
Lord
into the t. of the house of the — Jos 6:24
Lord
treasury (S) — 1Ch 29:8;
  Ezr 2:69; 7:70, 71
the house of the king under — Jer 38:11
the t.
lawful for to put them into — M't 27:6
the t.
and Jesus sat over against — M'k 12:41
the t.
the people cast money into — M'k 12:41
the t.
all they which have cast into — M'k 12:43
the t.
men casting their gifts into the — Lu 21:1
t.
These words spake Jesus in — Joh 8:20
the t.

TREAT

t. me so shabbily (B) — Ge 4:36
t. them shamefully (E) — Ac 14:5
double t. (P) — 2Co 1:15
t. their masters with respect — 1Ti 6:1
(P)

TREATED

treated (S) — Ge 12:16;
M't 22:6; Lu 18:32; 20:11; Ac 27:3;
  1Th 2:2
t. them shamefully — M't 22:6
(A)(E)(P)(R)
t. with contempt (A) — Lu 22:63; 23:11
t. with contempt (N) — Lu 23:11
shamefully t., laid waste (A) — Ac 8:3
t. Paul in a man-loving way — Ac 27:3
(A)(R)
as sheep (N) — Ro 8:36
t. like dirt the blood (P) — Heb 10:29
cruelly t. (A) — Heb 11:37

TREATETH

He evil t. the barren (S) — Jon 24:21

TREATING

t. body with respect (P)   1Th 4:4

TREATISE

The former t. have I made, O   Ac 1:1
The former account (A)   Ac 1:1
The former narrative (B)   Ac 1:1
In the first part of my work   Ac 1:1
(N)
In my first book (P)(R)   Ac 1:1

TREATMENT

noticed harsh t. (B)   Ge 16:11
forced them by harsh t. (B)   Ex 1:14

TREATY

make a t. with us (B)   Jos 9:6; 9:15
agreed to a t. (A)(B)(R)   1Ki 5:12
a t. between (B)   1Ki 15:19; 2Ch 16:3
when a t. has been made (B)   Da 11:23

TREK

moved ahead on their t. (B)   Ex 40:36

TREKKED

they t. on (B)   Ex 13:20

TREE

the fruit t. yielding fruit after   Ge 1:11
his
t. yielding fruit whose seed   Ge 1:12
was in
face of all the earth, and   Ge 1:29
every t.
is the fruit of a t. yielding   Ge 1:29
seed
grow every t. that is pleasant to   Ge 2:9
the
the t. of life also in the midst   Ge 2:9
of the
t. of knowledge of good and   Ge 2:9
evil
every t. of the garden thou   Ge 2:16
mayest
of the t. of the knowledge of   Ge 2:17
good
Ye shall not eat of every t. of   Ge 3:1
of the fruit of the t. which is   Ge 3:3
woman saw that the t. was good   Ge 3:6
a t. to be desired to make one   Ge 3:6
wise
Hast thou eaten of the t.   Ge 3:11
whereof
she gave me of the t. and I did   Ge 3:12
eat
and hast eaten of the t. of   Ge 3:17
which I
take also of the t. of life, and   Ge 3:22
eat
way, to keep the way of the t.   Ge 3:24
of life
and rest yourselves under the   Ge 18:4
t.
and he stood by them under   Ge 18:8
the t.
planted a tamarisk t.   Ge 21:33
(A)(B)(E)(R)
and of the hazel and chesnut   Ge 30:37
t.
buried beneath the terebinth   Ge 35:4
t. (B)
thee, and shall hang thee on   Ge 40:19
a t.
field, and brake every t. of the   Ex 9:25
field
shall eat every t. which   Ex 10:5
groweth for
the Lord shewed him a t.   Ex 15:25
which
or of the fruit of the t. is the   Le 27:30
Lord
eat nothing, made of the vine   Nu 6:4
t.
the hills, and under every   De 12:2
green t.
with the axe to cut down the   De 19:5
t.
for the t. of the field is man's   De 20:19
life
death, and thou hang him on   De 21:22
a t.
not remain all night upon the   De 21:23
t.

be before thee in the way in   De 22:6
any t.
When thou beatest thine   De 24:20
olive t.
the king of Ai he hanged on a   Jos 8:29
take his carcase down from   Jos 8:29
the t.
And she dwelt under the palm   J'g 4:5
t. of
they said unto the olive t.,   J'g 9:8
Reign
But the olive t. said, Should   J'g 9:9
And the trees said to the fig t.   J'g 9:10
But the fig t. said unto them   J'g 9:11
Gibeah under a pomegranate   1Sa 14:2
t.
Saul abode in Gibeah under a   1Sa 22:6
t. in
buried them under a t. at   1Sa 31:13
Jabesh
under his vine and under his   1Ki 4:25
fig t.
the cedar t. that is in Lebanon   1Ki 4:33
he made two cherubims of   1Ki 6:23
olive t.
the oracle he made doors of   1Ki 6:31
olive t.
The two doors also were of   1Ki 6:32
olive t.
door of the temple posts of   1Ki 6:33
olive t.
And the two doors were of fir   1Ki 6:34
t.
high hill, and under every   1Ki 14:23
green t.
and sat down under a juniper   1Ki 19:4
t.
he lay and slept under a   1Ki 19:5
juniper t.
and shall fell every good t.   2Ki 3:19
hills, and under every green t.   2Ki 16:4;
      17:10; 2Ch 28:4
vine, and every one of his fig   2Ki 18:31
t.
greater house he ceiled with   2Ch 3:5
fir t.
they were both hanged on a t.   Es 2:23
For there is a hope of a t. if   Job 14:7
it be cut
hope hath he removed like   Job 19:10
a t.
wickedness shall be broken   Job 24:20
as a t.
be like a t. planted by the rivers   Ps 1:3
himself like a green bay t.   Ps 37:35
like a green olive t. in the   Ps 52:8
house of God
shall flourish like the palm   Ps 92:12
She is a t. of life to them that   Pr 3:18
lay
fruit of the righteous is a t.   Pr 11:30
of life
the desire cometh, it is a t. of   Pr 13:12
life
A wholesome tongue is a t. of   Pr 15:4
life
Whoso keepeth the fig t. shall   Pr 27:18
eat
and if the t. fall toward the   Ec 11:3
south
the place where the t. falleth,   Ec 11:3
there
and the almond t. shall   Ec 12:5
flourish
As the apple t. among the trees   Ca 2:3
The fig t. putteth forth her   Ca 2:13
green
thy stature is like to a palm t.   Ca 7:7
I will go up to the palm t., I   Ca 7:8
will
raised thee up under the apple   Ca 8:5
t.
as a teil t. and as an oak,   Isa 6:13
whose
terebinth t. (A)(B)(E)(R)   Isa 6:13
as the shaking of an olive t.   Isa 17:6
two or
be as the shaking of an olive   Isa 24:13
t. and
as a falling of fig from the fig   Isa 34:4
t.
his vine, and every one of   Isa 36:16
his fig t.
chooseth a t. that will not   Isa 40:20
rot
wilderness the cedar, the   Isa 41:19
shittah t.
and the myrtle, and the oil t.   Isa 41:19

I will set in the desert the fir   Isa 41:19
t.
the pine, and the box t.   Isa 41:19
together
I fall down to the stock of a   Isa 44:19
t.
O forest, and every t. therein   Isa 44:23
the thorn shall come up the   Isa 55:13
fir t.
brier shall come up the   Isa 55:13
myrtle t.
eunuch say, Behold, I am a   Isa 56:3
dry t.
with idols under every green t.   Isa 57:5
shall come unto thee, the fir   Isa 60:13
t.
the pine t. and the box   Isa 60:13
together
as the days of a t. are the   Isa 65:22
days of
gardens behind one t. in the   Isa 66:17
midst
said, I see a rod of an almond   Jer 1:11
t.
and under every green t. thou   Jer 2:20
say to a t., You are my father   Jer 2:27
(A)(B)(S)
mountain and under every   Jer 3:6
green t.
the strangers under every   Jer 5:13
green t.
nor figs on the fig t. and the   Jer 8:13
leaf
one cutteth a t. out of the   Jer 10:3
forest
They are upright as the palm   Jer 10:5
t.
A green olive t. fair and of   Jer 11:16
goodly
Let us destroy the t. with the   Jer 11:19
fruit
be as a t. planted by the   Jer 17:8
waters
under every green t. and   Eze 6:13
under
What is the vine t. more than   Eze 15:2
any t.
As the vine t. among the   Eze 15:6
trees of
waters, and set it as a willow   Eze 17:5
t.
Lord have brought down the   Eze 17:24
high t.
have exalted the low t. have   Eze 17:24
have dried up the green t.   Eze 17:24
and have
and have made the dry t. to   Eze 17:24
flourish
green t. in thee, and every   Eze 20:47
dry t.
the rod of my son, as every   Eze 21:10
t.
nor any t. in the garden of   Eze 31:8
God was
t. of the field shall yield her   Eze 34:27
fruit
I will multiply the fruit of   Eze 36:30
the t.
a palm t. was between a   Eze 41:18
cherub
toward the palm t. on the   Eze 41:19
one side
toward the palm t. on the   Eze 41:19
other side
a t. in the midst of the earth   Da 4:10
the t. grew, and was strong   Da 4:11
Hew down the t. and cut off   Da 4:14
The t. that thou sawest, which   Da 4:20
grew
Hew the t. down, and destroy   Da 4:23
it; yet
leave the stump of the t. roots   Da 4:26
as the firstripe in the fig t. at   Ho 9:10
her
and his beauty shall be as the   Ho 14:6
olive t.
I am like a green fir t. From   Ho 14:8
me
vine waste, and barked my fig   Joe 1:7
t.
dried up, and the fig t.   Joe 1:12
languisheth
the pomegranate t., the palm   Joe 1:12
t.
the apple t. even all the trees   Joe 1:12
of
spring, for the t. beareth her   Joe 2:22
fruit
the fig t. and the vine do yield   Joe 2:22

under his vine and under his *Mic 4:4*
fig *t.*
the fig *t.* shall not blossom *Hab 3:17*
and the fig *t.* and the *Hag 2:19*
pomegranate
the olive *t.* hath not brought *Hag 2:19*
forth
under the vine and under the *Zec 3:10*
fig *t.*
Howl, fir *t.*; for the cedar is *Zec 11:2*
fallen
every *t.* which bringeth not *M't 3:10*
forth
good *t.* bringeth forth good *M't 7:17*
fruit
corrupt *t.* bringeth forth evil *M't 7:17*
fruit
good *t.* cannot bring forth *M't 7:18*
evil fruit
a corrupt *t.* bring forth good *M't 7:18*
fruit
every *t.* that bringeth not *M't 7:19*
forth
Either make the *t.* good, and *M't 12:33*
his
or else make the *t.* corrupt, *M't 12:33*
and his
for the *t.* is known by his *M't 12:33*
fruit
among herbs, and becometh *M't 13:32*
a *t.*
when he saw a fig *t.* in the *M't 21:19*
way he
presently the fig *t.* withered *M't 21:19*
away
How soon is the fig *t.* *M't 21:20*
withered
do this which is done to the *M't 21:21*
fig *t.*
Now learn a parable of the *M't 24:32;*
fig *t.* *M'k 13:28*
seeing a fig *t.* afar off *M'k 11:13*
having leaves
the fig *t.* dried up from the *M'k 11:20*
roots
fig *t.*, thou cursedst is *M'k 11:21*
withered
every *t.* therefore which *Lu 3:9*
bringeth
good *t.* bringeth not forth *Lu 6:43*
corrupt
corrupt *t.* bring forth good *Lu 6:43*
fruit
every *t.* is known by his own *Lu 6:44*
fruit
certain man had a fig *t.* *Lu 13:6*
planted
come seeking fruit on this fig *Lu 13:7*
t.
it grew, and waxed a great *t.* *Lu 13:19*
ye might say unto this *Lu 17:6*
sycamine *t.*
climbed up into a sycomore *t.* *Lu 19:4*
Behold the fig *t.* and all the *Lu 21:29*
trees
they do these things in a *Lu 23:31*
green *t.*
when thou wast under the fig *Joh 1:48*
t.
thee, I saw thee under the fig *Joh 1:50*
t.
whom ye slew and hanged on *Ac 5:30*
a *t.*
whom they slew and hanged *Ac 10:39*
on a *t.*
they took him down from the *Ac 13:29*
t.
and thou, being a wild olive *Ro 11:17*
t.
of the root and fatness of the *Ro 11:17*
olive
cut out of the olive *t.* which is *Ro 11:24*
wild
to nature into a good olive *t.* *Ro 11:24*
be graffed into their own *Ro 11:24*
olive *t.*
is every one that hangeth on a *Ga 3:13*
t.
Can the fig *t.* my brethren, *Jas 3:12*
bear
our sins in his own body, on *1Pe 2:24*
the *t.*
will I give to eat of the *t.* of life *Re 2:7*
a fig *t.* casteth her untimely *Re 6:13*
figs
nor on the sea, nor on any *t.* *Re 7:1*
any green thing, neither any *t.* *Re 9:4*
the river, was there the *t.* of *Re 22:2*
life

leaves of the *t.* were for the *Re 22:2*
healing
may have right to the *t.* of *Re 22:14*
life, and
from the words of the *t.* (S) *Re 22:19*

TREES

We may eat of the fruit of the *Ge 3:2*
t.
God amongst the *t.* of the *Ge 3:8*
garden
all the *t.* that were in the *Ge 23:17*
field, that
all the fruit of the *t.* which *Ex 10:15*
the hail
not any green thing in the *t.* *Ex 10:15*
and threescore and ten palm *Ex 15:27*
t.
burn their sacred *t.* (B) *Ex 34:13;*
De 12:3
planted all manner of *t.* for *Le 19:23*
food
first day the boughs of goodly *Le 23:40*
t.
branches of palm *t.* *Le 23:40*
and the boughs of thick *t.* *Le 23:40*
t. of the field shall yield their *Le 26:4*
fruit
neither shall the *t.* of the land *Le 26:20*
yield
t. of lign aloes which the Lord *Nu 24:6*
hath
as cedar *t.* beside the waters *Nu 24:6*
and threescore and ten palm *t.* *Nu 33:9*
vineyards, and olive *t.* which *De 6:11*
thou
and barley, and vines, and fig *t.* *De 8:8*
plant thee a grove of any *t.* *De 16:21*
near
thou shalt not destroy the *t.* *De 20:19*
the *t.* which thou knowest *De 20:20*
that they
they be not *t.* for meat, thou *De 20:20*
shalt
shall have olive *t.* throughout *De 28:40*
all
All thy *t.* and fruit of thy *De 28:42*
land
of Jericho, the city of palm *t.* *De 34:3*
unto
them, and hanged them on *Jos 10:26*
five *t.*
hanging upon the *t.* *Jos 10:26*
until evening
and they took them down off *Jos 10:27*
the *t.*
went up out of the city of *J'g 1:16*
palm *t.*
and possessed the city of palm *J'g 3:13*
t.
t. went forth on a time to *J'g 9:8*
anoint
and go to be promoted over the *J'g 9:9*
And the *t.* said to the fig tree, *J'g 9:10*
Come
and go to be promoted over *J'g 9:11*
Then said the *t.* unto the vine *J'g 9:12*
and go to be promoted over *J'g 9:13*
the *t.*
said all the *t.* unto the *J'g 9:14*
bramble
And the bramble said unto the *J'g 9:15*
t.
and cut down a bough from *J'g 9:48*
the *t.*
and cedar *t.*, and carpenters *2Sa 5:11*
over against the mulberry *t.* *2Sa 5:23*
in the tops of the mulberry *t.* *2Sa 5:24*
he spake of *t.* from the cedar *1Ki 4:33*
hew me cedar *t.* out of *1Ki 5:6*
Lebanon
Hiram gave Solomon cedar *t.* *1Ki 5:10*
fir *t.* according to all his *1Ki 5:10*
desire
figures of cherubims and *1Ki 6:29*
palm *t.*
carvings of cherubims and *1Ki 6:32*
palm *t.*
cherubims, and upon the palm *1Ki 6:32*
t.
thereon cherubims and palm *1Ki 6:35*
t.
cherubims, lions, and palm *t.* *1Ki 7:36*
furnished Solomon with cedar *1Ki 9:11*
t.
and fir *t.* and with gold, *1Ki 9:11*
according

Ophir great plenty of almug *1Ki 10:11*
t.
king made of the almug *t.* *1Ki 10:12*
pillars
there came no such almug *t.* *1Ki 10:12*
sycomore *t.* that are in the *1Ki 10:27*
vale
water, and felled all the good *2Ki 3:25*
t.
cut down the tall cedar *t.* *2Ki 19:23*
thereof
and the choice fir *t.* thereof *2Ki 19:23*
them over against the *1Ch 14:14*
mulberry *t.*
in the tops of the mulberry *1Ch 14:15*
Then shall the *t.* of the wood *1Ch 16:33*
sing
Also cedar *t.* in abundance *1Ch 22:4*
the olive *t.* and the *1Ch 27:28*
sycomore *t.*
as stones, and cedar *t.* made *2Ch 1:15*
he as
the sycomore *t.* that are in *2Ch 1:15*
the vale
also cedar *t.*, fir *t.* and almug *2Ch 2:8*
set thereon palm *t.* and chains *2Ch 3:5*
algum *t.* and precious stones *2Ch 9:10*
king made of the algum *t.* *2Ch 9:11*
terraces
cedar *t.* made he as the *2Ch 9:27*
sycomore
made he as the sycomore *t.* *2Ch 9:27*
to Jericho, the city of palm *2Ch 28:15*
t.
to bring cedar *t.* from Lebanon *Ezr 3:7*
to
and branches of thick *t.* to *Ne 8:15*
make
and fruit *t.* in abundance *Ne 9:25*
the firstfruits of all fruit of *Ne 10:35*
all *t.*
and the fruit of all manner *Ne 10:37*
of *t.* of
He lieth under the shady *t.* *Job 40:21*
The shady *t.* cover him with *Job 40:22*
lifted up axes upon the thick *t.* *Ps 74:5*
and their sycomore *t.* with *Ps 78:47*
frost
shall all the *t.* of the wood *Ps 96:12*
rejoice
The *t.* of the Lord are full *Ps 104:16*
of sap
the stork, the fir *t.* are her *Ps 104:17*
house
their vines also and their fig *Ps 105:33*
t.
and brake the *t.* of their *Ps 105:33*
coasts
hills; fruitful *t.* and all cedars *Ps 148:9*
I planted *t.* in them of all kind *Ec 2:5*
the wood that bringeth forth *t.* *Ec 2:6*
tree among the *t.* of the wood *Ca 2:3*
with all *t.* of frankincense *Ca 4:14*
as the *t.* of the wood are *Isa 7:2*
moved
the rest of the *t.* of his forest *Isa 10:19*
shall
Yea, the fir *t.* rejoice at thee *Isa 14:8*
and the choice fir *t.* thereof *Isa 37:24*
among the *t.* of the forest *Isa 44:14*
all the *t.* of the field shall *Isa 55:12*
clap their
might be called *t.* of *Isa 61:3*
righteousness
adultery with stones and *t.* *Jer 3:9*
(A)(B)(S)
eat up thy vines and thy fig *t.* *Jer 5:17*
Hew ye down *t.* and cast a *Jer 6:6*
mount
upon the *t.* of the field, and *Jer 7:20*
their groves by the green *t.* *Jer 17:2*
upon
a branch which is among the *Eze 15:2*
t. of
vine tree among the *t.* of the *Eze 15:6*
forest
t. of the field shall know that *Eze 17:24*
I the
every high hill, and all the *Eze 20:28*
thick *t.*
thy ship boards of fir *t.* of *Eze 27:5*
Senir
rivers unto all the *t.* of the *Eze 31:4*
field
above all the *t.* of the field *Eze 31:5*
the fir *t.* were not like his *Eze 31:8*
boughs
and the chestnut *t.* were not *Eze 31:8*
like his

so that all the *t.* of Eden, that | *Eze 31:9*
that none of all the *t.* by the | *Eze 31:14*
waters
neither their *t.* stand up in | *Eze 31:14*
all the *t.* of the field fainted | *Eze 31:15*
for
all the *t.* of Eden, the choice | *Eze 31:16*
in greatness among the *t.* of | *Eze 31:18*
Eden
brought down with the *t.* of | *Eze 31:18*
Eden
and upon each post were | *Eze 40:16*
palm *t.*
their arches, and their palm | *Eze 40:22*
t.
it had palm *t.* one on this | *Eze 40:26*
side, and
palm *t.* were upon the posts | *Eze 40:31;*
| *40:34, 37*
made with cherubims and | *Eze 41:18*
palm *t.*
were cherubims and palm *t.* | *Eze 41:20*
made
the temple, cherubims and | *Eze 41:25*
palm *t.*
windows and palm *t.* on the | *Eze 41:26*
one
were very many *t.* on the one | *Eze 47:7*
side
shall grow all *t.* for meat, | *Eze 47:12*
whose
I will destroy her vines and | *Ho 2:12*
her fig *t.*
even all the *t.* of the field, are | *Joe 1:12*
hath burned all the *t.* of the | *Joe 1:19*
field
your vineyards and your fig *t.* | *Am 4:9*
the fir *t.* shall be terribly | *Na 2:3*
shaken
strong holds shall be like fig *t.* | *Na 3:12*
he stood among the myrtle *t.* | *Zec 1:8*
that
that stood among the myrtle | *Zec 1:10;*
t. | *1:11*
two olive *t.* by it, one upon the | *Zec 4:3*
right
What are these two olive *t.* | *Zec 4:11*
upon the
ax is laid unto the root of | *M't 3:10*
the *t.*
cut down branches from the | *M't 21:8*
t. and
and said, I see men as *t.* | *M'k 8:24*
walking
cut down branches off the *t.* | *M'k 11:8*
axe is laid unto the root of the | *Lu 3:9*
t.
Behold the fig tree, and all | *Lu 21:29*
the *t.*
Took branches of palm *t.* | *Joh 12:13*
and
t. whose fruit withereth, | *Jude 12*
without
earth, neither the sea, nor the *t.* | *Re 7:3*
the third part of *t.* was burnt | *Re 8:7*
up
These are the two olive *t.* and | *Re 11:4*

TREMBLE

and shall *t.* and be in anguish | *De 2:25*
t. and shake (B) | *De 2:25*
faint, fear not, and do not *t.* | *De 20:3*
be not alarmed or terrified | *De 20:3*
(B)
those that *t.* at the | *Ezr 10:3*
commandment
nor *t.* before him (S) | *Es 5:9*
place, and the pillars thereof *t.* | *Job 9:6*
Rahab's helpers *t.* | *Job 9:13*
(B)(E)(R)
I *t.* before him (B) | *Job 23:15*
The pillars of heaven *t.* and | *Job 26:11*
the pillars of heaven sway | *Job 26:11*
(B)
t. with tumult (R) | *Ps 46:3*
Thou hast made the earth to *t.* | *Ps 60:2*
the land to quake (B)(R) | *Ps 60:2*
Lord reigneth; let the people *t.* | *Ps 99:1*
T., thou earth, at the | *Ps 114:7*
presence of
the keepers of the house shall | *Ec 12:3*
t.
the hills did *t.* and their | *Isa 5:25*
carcases
the mountains quake (B)(R) | *Isa 5:25*
the man that made the earth | *Isa 14:16*
to *t.*
tremble (B)(R) | *Isa 32:10; Eze 26:18*

T., ye women that are at | *Isa 32:11*
ease; be
nations may *t.* at thy presence | *Isa 64:2*
of the Lord, ye that *t.* at his | *Isa 66:5*
word
will ye not *t.* at my presence | *Jer 5:22*
at his wrath the earth shall *t.* | *Jer 10:10*
the earth quakes (B)(R) | *Jer 10:10*
they shall fear and *t.* for all | *Jer 33:9*
the land shall *t.* and sorrow: | *Jer 51:29*
for
people *t.* (A)(R) | *Eze 7:27*
shall *t.* at every moment, | *Eze 26:16*
and be
Now shall the isles *t.* in the | *Eze 26:18*
day of
the coast lands *t.* (A) | *Eze 26:18*
they shall *t.* at every | *Eze 32:10*
moment
men *t.* and fear before the | *Da 6:26*
God of
children shall *t.* from the west | *Ho 11:10*
shall *t.* as a bird out of | *Ho 11:11*
Egypt, and
all the inhabitants of the land | *Joe 2:1*
t.
before them; the heavens | *Joe 2:10*
shall *t.*
Shall not the land *t.* for this, | *Am 8:8*
and
the earth shakes (B) | *Am 8:8*
make you *t.* (B)(R) | *Hab 2:7*
curtains of the land of | *Hab 3:7*
Midian did *t.*
the devils also believe, and *t.* | *Jas 2:19*
demons believe and shudder | *Jas 2:19*
(B)(P)(R)

TREMBLED

And Isaac *t.* very exceedingly | *Ge 27:33*
the people that was in the | *Ex 19:16*
camp *t.*
earth *t.* and the heavens | *J'g 5:4*
dropped
his heart *t.* for the ark of | *1Sa 4:13*
God
and the spoilers they also *t.* | *1Sa 14:15*
elders of the town *t.* at his | *1Sa 16:4*
coming
was afraid, and his heart | *1Sa 28:5*
greatly *t.*
Then the earth shook and *t.* | *2Sa 22:8*
every one that *t.* at the words | *Ezr 9:4*
Then the earth shook and *t.* | *Ps 18:7*
the world: the earth *t.* and | *Ps 77:18*
shook
the world; the earth saw, and | *Ps 97:4*
t.
the mountains, and, lo, they *t.* | *Jer 4:24*
the whole land *t.* at the sound | *Jer 8:16*
t. and feared before him | *Da 5:19*
mountains saw thee, and | *Hab 3:10*
they *t.*
When I heard, my belly *t.*; | *Hab 3:16*
my
I *t.* in myself, that I might | *Hab 3:16*
rest in
for they *t.* and were amazed | *M'k 16:8*
Then Moses *t.* and durst not | *Ac 7:32*
Felix *t.* and answered, Go | *Ac 24:25*
thy

TREMBLES

the earth *t.* (B)(E)(R) | *Pr 30:21*
his soul *t.* (B)(E)(R) | *Isa 15:4*

TREMBLETH

At this also my heart *t.*, and | *Job 37:1*
He looketh on the earth, | *Ps 104:32*
and it *t.*
My flesh *t.* for fear of thee | *Ps 119:120*
contrite spirit, and *t.* at my | *Isa 66:2*
word

TREMBLING

t. shall take hold upon them | *Ex 15:15*
shall give thee there a *t.* | *De 28:65*
heart
and all the people followed | *1Sa 13:7*
him *t.*
And there was *t.* in the host | *1Sa 14:15*
quaked; so it was a very | *1Sa 14:15*
great *t.*
t. because of this matter, and | *Ezr 10:9*
Fear came upon me, and *t.* | *Job 4:14*
which

and *t.* taketh hold on my | *Job 21:6*
flesh
Lord with fear, and rejoice | *Ps 2:11*
with *t.*
Fearfulness and *t.* are come | *Ps 55:5*
upon
drunken the dregs of the cup | *Isa 51:17*
out of thine hand the cup of | *Isa 51:22*
t.
We have heard a voice of *t.* | *Jer 30:5*
drink thy water with *t.* and | *Eze 12:18*
with
shall clothe themselves with | *Eze 26:16*
t.
this word unto me, I stood *t.* | *Da 10:11*
When Ephraim spake *t.* he | *Ho 13:1*
I will make Jerusalem a cup | *Zec 12:2*
of *t.*
But the woman fearing and *t.* | *M'k 5:33*
she came *t.* and falling down | *Lu 8:47*
he *t.* and astonished said, Lord | *Ac 9:6*
and sprang in, and came *t.* | *Ac 16:29*
and in fear, and in much *t.* | *1Co 2:3*
with fear and *t.* ye received | *2Co 7:15*
him
with fear and *t.* in singleness | *Eph 6:5*
your own salvation with fear | *Ph'p 2:12*
and *t.*

TRENCH

he came to the *t.* as the | *1Sa 17:20*
host was
Saul lay in the *t.* and the | *1Sa 26:5*
people
Saul lay sleeping within the *t.* | *1Sa 26:7*
the city, and it stood in the | *2Sa 20:15*
t.
and he made a *t.* about the | *1Ki 18:32*
altar
and he filled the *t.* also with | *1Ki 18:35*
water
up the water that was in the | *1Ki 18:38*
t.
be cast into the *t.* (B) | *Ps 140:10*
enemies shall cast a *t.* about | *Lu 19:43*
thee

TRESPASS

What is my *t.*? what is my | *Ge 31:36*
sin, that
what is my sin (A) | *Ge 31:36*
what is my misdemeanor | *Ge 31:36;*
(B) | *50:17*
what is my offence (R) | *Ge 31:36*
the *t.* of thy brethren, and | *Ge 50:17*
their
your brother's crime (B) | *Ge 50:17*
their transgression (E)(R) | *Ge 50:17*
forgive the *t.* of thy servants | *Ge 50:17*
of the
For all manner of *t.* whether | *Ex 22:9*
it be
every unlawful deed (A) | *Ex 22:9*
every kind of misconduct (B) | *Ex 22:9*
every breach of trust (R) | *Ex 22:9*
he shall bring his *t.* offering | *Le 5:6*
unto
guilt offering (R) | *Le 5:6;*
5:7, 15-16, 18-19; 6:5-6, 17; 7:1-2, 5, 7,
37; 14:12-14, 17, 21, 24-25, 28; 19:21-22;
Nu 6:12; 18:9; 1Sa 6:3-4, 8, 17;
2Ki 12:16; Eze 40:39; 42:13; 44:29;
| *46:20*
then he shall bring for his *t.* | *Le 5:7*
which
guilt offering (A) | *Le 5:7;*
6:17; 1Sa 6:3-4, 8, 17; Eze 46:20
If a soul commit a *t.* and sin | *Le 5:15*
shall bring for his *t.* unto the | *Le 5:15*
Lord
of the sanctuary, for a *t.* | *Le 5:15*
offering
him with the ram of the *t.* | *Le 5:16*
offering
for a *t.* offering, unto the priest | *Le 5:18*
It is a *t.* offering; he hath | *Le 5:19*
certainly
and commit a *t.* against the | *Le 6:2*
Lord
if a person sins (B) | *Le 6:2*
commits a breach of faith (R) | *Le 6:2*
in the day of his *t.* offering | *Le 6:5*
bring his *t.* offering unto the | *Le 6:6*
Lord
for a *t.* offering, unto the priest | *Le 6:6*
sin offering, and as the *t.* | *Le 6:17*
offering
this is the law of the *t.* offering | *Le 7:1*

shall they kill the *t.* offering   *Le 7:2*
unto the Lord: it is a *t.* offering *Le 7:5*
sin offering is, so is the *t.*   *Le 7:7*
offering
and of the *t.* offering, and of   *Le 7:37*
lamb, and offer him for a *t.*   *Le 14:12*
offering
is the priest's, so is the *t.*   *Le 14:13*
offering
some of the blood of the *t.*   *Le 14:14;*
offering   *14:25*
upon the blood of the *t.*   *Le 14:17*
offering
take one lamb for a *t.*   *Le 14:21*
offering to be
take the lamb of the *t.*   *Le 14:24*
offering
shall kill the lamb of the *t.*   *Le 14:25*
offering
place of the blood of the *t.*   *Le 14:28*
offering
bring his *t.* offering unto the   *Le 19:21*
Lord
even a ram for a *t.* offering   *Le 19:21*
the ram of the *t.* offering   *Le 19:22*
before the
them to bear the iniquity of   *Le 22:16*
t.
sin of their trangression (B)   *Le 22:16;*
         Jos 22:16, 20, 31
fear iniquity and guilt (R)   *Le 22:16*
with their *t.* which they   *Le 26:40*
trespassed
with their treachery (R)   *Le 26:40;*
         Jos 22:16, 31
commit, to do a *t.* against the *Nu 5:6*
Lord
person guilty (R)   *Nu 5:6*
shall recompense his *t.* with the *Nu 5:7*
restitution for his wrong (R)   *Nu 5:7;*
         5:8
kinsman to recompense the *t.* *Nu 5:8*
unto
t. be recompensed unto the   *Nu 5:8*
Lord
and commit a *t.* against him   *Nu 5:12*
acts unfaithfully (R)   *Nu 5:12; 5:27*
have done *t.* against her   *Nu 5:27*
husband
of the first year for a *t.*   *Nu 6:12*
offering
for a guilt offering (B)   *Nu 6:12*
every *t.* offering of theirs,   *Nu 18:9*
which
to commit *t.* against the   *Nu 31:16*
Lord in
act treacherously (R)   *Nu 31:16;*
         Eze 20:27
children of Israel committed a   *Jos 7:1*
t. in
violated the dedicated portion   *Jos 7:1*
(B)
broke faith (R)   *Jos 7:1*
What *t.* is this ye have   *Jos 22:16*
committed
Achan the son of Zerah   *Jos 22:20*
commit a *t.*
have not committed this *t.*   *Jos 22:31*
against
any wise return him a *t.*   *1Sa 6:3*
offering
What shall be the *t.* offering   *1Sa 6:4*
which
ye return him for a *t.* offering *1Sa 6:8*
for a *t.* offering unto the   *1Sa 6:17*
Lord
forgive the *t.* of thine   *1Sa 25:28*
handmaid
any man *t.* against his   *1Ki 8:31*
neighbour
sins against his neighbor   *1Ki 8:31*
(A)(E)(R)
wrongs his neighbor (B)   *1Ki 8:31*
t. money and sin money was *2Ki 12:16*
not
money from the guilt   *2Ki 12:16*
offering (B)
Saul died for his *t.* (A)   *1Ch 10:13*
will he be a cause of *t.* to   *1Ch 21:3*
Israel
bring guilt upon Israel   *1Ch 21:3;*
(A)(B)(R)   *Ezr 10:10*
cause of guilt (E)   *1Ch 21:3;*
         Ezr 9:13; 10:19
warn them that they *t.* not   *2Ch 19:10*
against
be guilty before the Lord   *2Ch 19:10;*
(A)(B)   *28:13*
not be guilty (E)   *2Ch 19:10; Ezr 9:7*

---

incur guilt (B)(R)   *2Ch 19:10;*
   24:18; 28:13; Ezr 9:6, 7, 13; 10:10, 19
this do, and ye shall not *t.*   *2Ch 19:10*
and Jerusalem for this their   *2Ch 24:18*
t.
for their guiltiness (R)   *2Ch 24:18;*
         Ezr 9:6
add more to our sins and to   *2Ch 28:13*
our *t.*
our *t.* is great, and there is   *2Ch 28:13*
fierce
our *t.* is great (E)   *2Ch 28:13*
he *t.* yet more against the   *2Ch 28:22*
Lord
transgressed yet more (B)   *2Ch 28:22*
he became more faithless   *2Ch 28:22*
(R)
all his sins, and his *t.* and   *2Ch 33:19*
his rebellion (B)   *2Ch 33:19*
his faithlessness (R)   *2Ch 33:19;*
         Ezr 9:2
rulers hath been chief in this *t.* *Ezr 9:2*
first offenders of this sin (B)   *Ezr 9:2*
t. is grown up unto the   *Ezr 9:6*
heavens
guilt has grown (A)   *Ezr 9:6*
we been in a great *t.* unto this *Ezr 9:7*
day
been exceedingly guilty (A)   *Ezr 9:7;*
         9:13; 10:19
our evil deeds, and for our   *Ezr 9:13*
great *t.*
wives to increase the *t.* of   *Ezr 10:10*
Israel
a ram of the flock for their   *Ezr 10:19*
t.
because they have committed   *Eze 15:8*
a *t.*
have acted unfaithfully (B)   *Eze 15:8;*
         20:27
acted faithlessly (R)   *Eze 15:8*
will plead with him there for   *Eze 17:20*
his *t.*
for his treason (B)(R)   *Eze 17:20*
in his *t.* that he hath   *Eze 18:24*
trespassed
because of his unfaithfulness   *Eze 18:24*
(B)
his treachery (R)   *Eze 18:24; Da 9:7*
have committed a *t.* against   *Eze 20:27*
me
the sin offering and the *t.*   *Eze 40:39*
offering
his guilt offering (B)   *Eze 40:39;*
     42:13; 44:22; 46:20
the sin offering, and the *t.*   *Eze 42:13;*
         44:29
the priests shall boil the *t.*   *Eze 46:20*
offering
their *t.* that they have   *Da 9:7*
trespassed
because of their disloyalty   *Da 9:7*
show him his fault   *M't 18:15*
(A)(B)(E)(R)
grasp of everlasting *t.* (A)   *M'k 3:29*
If thy brother *t.* against thee,   *Lu 17:3*
rebuke
if your brother sins   *Lu 17:3;*
(A)(B)(E)(R)   *17:4*
if a brother wrongs you (N)   *Lu 17:3;*
         17:4
if a brother offends you (P)   *Lu 17:3*
if he *t.* against thee seven   *Lu 17:4*
times, in
if a brother wrongs you (P)   *Lu 17:4*
one man's *t.* death   *Ro 5:17*
(A)(E)(R)
law came to increase *t.*   *Ro 5:20*
(A)(B)(E)(R)
their *t.* means riches (R)   *Ro 11:12*
overtaken in any *t.* (E)(R)   *Ga 6:1*

TRESPASSED

certainly *t.* against the Lord   *Le 5:19*
he is certainly guilty (E)(R)   *Le 5:19*
trespass which they *t.* against *Le 26:40*
me
iniquity in their treachery   *Le 26:40*
(A)(R)
treason they perpetrated (B)   *Le 26:40*
unto him against whom he   *Nu 5:7*
hath *t.*
restitution for his wrongdoing   *Nu 5:7*
(A)(B)(R)
restitution for his guilt (E)   *Nu 5:7*
Because ye *t.* against me   *De 32:51*
among

---

you broke faith (A)(B)(R)   *De 32:51;*
         29:6
he *t.* (A)   *2Ch 26:16; 36:14; Da 7:13*
the sanctuary; for thou hast *2Ch 26:18*
you have done wrong (R)   *2Ch 26:18*
For our fathers have *t.* and   *2Ch 29:6*
done
have been unfaithful (R)   *2Ch 29:6*
t. against the Lord God of   *2Ch 30:7*
their
unfaithful to the Lord (A)   *2Ch 30:7*
who were faithless (R)   *2Ch 30:7*
but Amon *t.* more and more   *2Ch 33:23*
Amon multiplied his guilt   *2Ch 33:23*
(B)(R)
We have *t.* against our God   *Ezr 10:2*
broken faith (A)(R)   *Ezr 10:2*
sinned against the Lord (B)   *Ezr 10:2*
that he hath *t.* against me   *Eze 17:20*
for the treason against me   *Eze 17:20*
(B)(R)
in his trespass that he hath   *Eze 18:24*
for the treachery against me   *Eze 18:24*
(R)
because of their   *Eze 18:24*
unfaithfulness (B)
because they *t.* against me   *Eze 39:23*
they dealt treacherously   *Eze 39:23*
whereby they have *t.* against *Eze 39:26*
me
all the treachery they   *Eze 39:26*
practiced (B)(R)
that they have *t.* against thee   *Da 9:7*
the disloyalty they practiced   *Da 9:7*
(B)
because of the treachery   *Da 9:7*
committed (R)
my covenant, and *t.* against my *Ho 8:1*
law
who was delivered for our *t.*   *Ro 4:25;*
(E)(R)   *5:16*

TRESPASSES

we are before thee in our *t.*   *Ezr 9:15*
before you in our guilt   *Ezr 9:15*
(A)(B)(E)(R)
an one as goeth on still in his   *Ps 68:21*
t.
in their guilty doings—ways   *Ps 68:21*
(B)(R)
and all their *t.* whereby they *Eze 39:26*
have
all their treachery   *Eze 39:26*
(A)(B)(R)
For if ye forgive men their *t.* *M't 6:14*
forgive wrongs (N)   *M't 6:14; 6:15*
forgive failures (P)   *M't 6:14; 6:15*
But if ye forgive not men   *M't 6:15*
their *t.*
will your Father forgive your   *M't 6:15*
t.
not every one his brother   *M't 18:35*
their *t.*
forgive offences (A)   *M't 18:35*
heaven may forgive you   *M'k 11:25*
your *t.*
forgive failings and   *M'k 11:25;*
shortcomings (A)   *11:26*
which is in heaven forgive   *M'k 11:26*
your *t.*
forgive sins (P)   *M'k 11:26; Col 2:13*
not imputing their *t.* unto   *2Co 5:19*
them
not counting their sins   *2Co 5:19*
(A)(P)
no longer holding misdeeds   *2Co 5:19*
(N)
who were dead in *t.* and sin   *Eph 2:1*
dead in sins and wickedness   *Eph 2:1*
(N)
you were spiritually dead (P)   *Eph 2:1*
him, having forgiven you all   *Col 2:13*
t.
forgiven all sins (N)   *Col 2:13*

TRESPASSING

all that he hath done in *t.*   *Le 6:7*
therein
all he has done to become guilty *Le 6:7*
(A)(B)(E)(R)
land sinneth against me by *t.* *Eze 14:13*
sins against me acting   *Eze 14:13*
faithlessly (B)(R)

TRESSES

the king is held in the *t*. (S)   *Ca 7:5*

TRIAL

stood *t*. before the Assembly   *Nu 35:12*
(B)
appear before Assembly for *t*.   *Jos 20:6*
(B)
let me make a *t*. this once (S)   *J'g 6:39*
laugh at the *t*. of the innocent   *Job 9:23*
mocks at despair of innocent   *Job 9:23*
(B)
mocks at calamity of   *Job 9:23*
innocent (R)
come together in court *t*.   *Job 9:32*
(A)(B)(R)
Because it is a *t*. and what   *Eze 21:13*
if the
not be a testing (R)   *Eze 21:13*
t. of the Lord (E)   *M't 4:7;*
22:18; M'k 12:15; Lu 14:12; Ac 15:10;
                    1Co 10:9
must stand his *t*. (P)   *M't 5:21*
in time of *t*. fall way (B)   *Lu 8:13*
he was deprived of his *t*. (B)   *Ac 8:33*
why be a *t*. to God   *Ac 15:10;*
(A)(B)(R)   *1Co 10:9*
be put to *t*. (A)(N)(P)   *Ac 25:9*
I am standing *t*. (B)(P)(R) .   *Ac 26:6*
win verdict when on *t*. (N)   *Ro 3:4*
be put on *t*. by you (A)   *1Co 4:3*
no *t*. beyond what man can   *1Co 10:13*
bear (N)
How that in a great *t*. of   *2Co 8:2*
affliction
in the midst of severe   *2Co 8:2*
tribulation (A)
under ordeal of terrible   *2Co 8:2*
affliction (B)(E)
troubles been through (N)   *2Co 8:2*
most difficult circumstances   *2Co 8:2*
(P)
trial (S)   *Ga 4:14; Heb 3:8*
the day of *t*. (E)   *Heb 3:8*
others had *t*. of cruel   *Heb 11:36*
mockings
tests of mockings (B)(R)   *Heb 11:36*
had to face jeers (N)   *Heb 11:36*
exposed to tests of public   *Heb 11:36*
mockery (P)
That the *t*. of your faith. being   *1Pe 1:7*
faith may be tested (A)(B)   *1Pe 1:7*
proof of your faith (E)   *1Pe 1:7*
faith which has stood the test   *1Pe 1:7*
(N)
proving of your faith (P)   *1Pe 1:7*
the fiery *t*. which is to try you   *1Pe 4:12*
fiery ordeal to test you   *1Pe 4:12*
(A)(P)
fiery test being applied (B)   *1Pe 4:12*
fiery ordeal to prove you (R)   *1Pe 4:12*
the hour of *t*. (E)(P)(R)   *Re 3:10*

TRIALS

by *t*. (A)(R)   *De 4:34;*
  7:19; 29:3; Lu 22:28; Ac 20:19
trials (S)   *De 29:3;*
  Lu 22:28; Ac 20:19; Jas 1:2; 1Pe 1:6
my *t*. (B)(N)   *Lu 22:28;*
  Ac 20:19; Jas 1:2; 1Pe 1:6; 2Pe 2:9
comfort in *t*. (P)   *2Co 1:4*
t. of many kinds (B)(N)(P)(R)   *Jas 1:2*
distressed by various *t*.   *1Pe 1:6*
(B)(N)(R)

TRIBAL

the *t*. leaders (B)   *Nu 31:26*

TRIBE

the son of Hur, of the *t*. of   *Ex 31:2;*
Judah   *35:30; 38:22*
son of Ahisamach, of the *t*. of   *Ex 31:6;*
Dan   *35:34; 38:23*
daughter of Dibri, of the *t*. of   *Le 24:11*
Dan
there shall be a man of every *t*.   *Nu 1:4*
of the *t*. of Reuben   *Nu 1:5;*
1:21; 13:4; 34:14; Jos 13:15; 20:8; 21:7,
     36; 1Ch 6:63, 78; Re 7:5
of the *t*. of Simeon   *Nu 1:23;*
2:12; 10:16; 13:5; 34:20; Jos 19:1, 8
    21:4, 9; 2Ch 6:65; Re 7:5
of the *t*. of Gad   *Nu 1:25;*
2:14; 10:20; 13:15; 34:14; Jos 13:24;
20:8; 21:7, 38; 2Ch 6:63, 80; Re 7:5

of the *t*. of Judah   *Nu 1:27;*
7:12; 13:6; 34:19; Jos 7:1, 16, 18; 15:1,
20-21; 21:4, 9; 1Ki 12:20-21; 2Ki 17:18;
   2Ch 6:65; Ps 78:68; Re 5:5; 7:5
of the *t*. of Issachar   *Nu 1:29;*
2:5; 10:15; 13:7; 34:26; Jos 19:23; 21:6;
           1Ch 6:62, 72; Re 7:7
of the *t*. of Zebulun (Zabulon)   *Nu 1:31;*
2:7; 10:16; 13:10; 34:25; Jos 21:7, 34;
        2Ch 6:63, 77; Re 7:8
of the *t*. of Ephraim   *Nu 1:33;*
13:8; 34:24; Jos 16:8; 21:5, 20;
       1Ch 6:66; Ps 78:67
of the *t*. of Manasseh   *Nu 1:35;*
2:20; 10:23; 13:11; 32:33; 34:14, 23;
De 3:13; 29:8; Jos 1:12; 4:12; 12:6; 13:7,
29; 17:1; 18:7; 20:8; 21:5-6, 25, 27;
22:1, 7, 9-11, 13, 15, 21; 1Ch 5:18, 23,
26; 6:61-62, 70-71; 12:31, 37; 26:32;
        27:20-21; Re 7:6
of the *t*. of Benjamin   *Nu 1:37;*
2:22; 10:24; 13:9; 34:21; Jos 18:11, 21;
21:4, 17; J'g 20:12; 1Sa 9:21; 10:20-21;
1Ki 12:21; 1Ch 6:60, 65; Ac 13:21;
        Ro 11:1; Ph'p 3:5; Re 7:8
of the *t*. of Dan   *Nu 1:39;*
13:12; 34:22; Jos 19:40, 48; 21:5, 23;
              J'g 18:1, 30
of the *t*. of Asher (Aser)   *Nu 1:41;*
2:27; 10:26; 13:7; 34:27; Jos 10:24, 31;
  21:6, 30; 1Ch 6:62, 74; Lu 2:36; Re 7:6
of the *t*. of Naphtali   *Nu 1:43;*
(Nephtalim)   *2:29; 10:27; 13:14; 34:28;*
Jos 19:39; 21:6, 32; 1Ki 7:14; 1Ch 6:62,
               76; Re 7:6
Levites after the *t*. of their   *Nu 1:47*
fathers
Shalt not number the *t*. of   *Nu 1:49*
Levi
Bring the *t*. of Levi near, and   *Nu 3:6*
Cut not off the *t*. of the   *Nu 4:18*
families
every *t*. of their fathers shall   *Nu 13:2*
ye
of the *t*. of Joseph   *Nu 13:11;*
            36:5; Re 7:8
of the *t*. of Levi   *Nu 18:2;*
        1Ch 23:14; Re 7:7
the *t*. of thy father, bring thou   *Nu 18:2*
with
Of every *t*. a thousand   *Nu 31:4;*
                31:5-6
the half *t*. of Manasseh   *Nu 34:15;*
       Jos 14:2-3; 1Ch 6:61
take one prince of every *t*.   *Nu 34:18*
be put to the inheritance of   *Nu 36:3*
the *t*.
be put unto the inheritance   *Nu 36:4*
of the *t*.
inheritance of the *t*. of our   *Nu 36:4*
fathers
t. of their father shall they   *Nu 36:6*
marry
of Israel remove from *t*. to *t*.   *Nu 36:7*
inheritance of the *t*. of his   *Nu 36:7*
fathers
in any *t*. of the children of   *Nu 36:8*
Israel
of the family of the *t*. of her   *Nu 36:8*
father
remove from one *t*. to another   *Nu 36:9*
t.
the *t*. of the family of their   *Nu 36:12*
father.
twelve men of you, one of a *t*.   *De 1:23*
the Lord separated the *t*. of   *De 10:8*
Levi
all the *t*. of Levi, shall have   *De 18:1*
no part
man, or woman, or family,   *De 29:18*
or *t*.
of Israel, out of every *t*. a   *Jos 3:12*
man
of the people out of every *t*. a   *Jos 4:2*
man
of Israel, out of every *t*. a man   *Jos 4:4*
that the *t*. which the Lord   *Jos 7:14*
taketh
unto the *t*. of Levi he gave   *Jos 13:14;*
none   *13:33*
among you three men of each   *Jos 18:4*
t.
be a priest unto a *t*. and a   *J'g 18:19*
family
be today one *t*. lacking in   *J'g 21:3;*
Israel   *21:6, 1.*
but will give one *t*. to thy   *1Ki 11:13;*
son   *11:32, 36*
were left of the family of   *1Ch 6:61*
that *t*.

in what *t*. the stranger   *Eze 47:23*
sojourneth
spoken pertaineth to another   *Heb 7:1*
t.
of which *t*. Moses spake   *Heb 7:14*
nothing as to

TRIBES

t. clans (B)   *Ge 10:5; 10:20*
people, as one of the *t*. of   *Ge 49:16*
Israel
All these are the twelve *t*. of   *Ge 49:28*
Israel
according to the twelve *t*. of   *Ex 24:4*
Israel
they be according to the   *Ex 28:21*
twelve *t*.
name, according to the   *Ex 39:14*
twelve *t*.
princes of the *t*. of their   *Nu 1:16*
fathers
who were the princes of the *t*.   *Nu 7:2*
in his tents according to their   *Nu 24:2*
t.
names of the *t*. of their   *Nu 26:55*
fathers
spake unto the heads of the *t*.   *Nu 30:1*
throughout all the *t*. of Israel   *Nu 31:4*
and the chief fathers of the   *Nu 32:28*
t. of
according to the *t*. of your   *Nu 33:54*
fathers
commanded to give unto the   *Nu 34:1*
nine *t*.
two *t*. and the half   *Nu 34:15*
tribe received
to any of the sons of the   *Nu 36:3*
other *t*.
every one of the *t*. of the   *Nu 36:9*
children
and known among your *t*.   *De 1:13*
So I took the chief of your *t*.   *De 1:15*
wise
tens, and officers among your   *De 1:15*
t.
even all the heads of your *t*.   *De 5:23*
God shall choose out of all   *De 12:5*
your *t*.
Lord shall choose in one of   *De 12:14*
thy *t*.
God giveth thee, throughout   *De 16:18*
thy *t*.
hath chosen him out of all thy   *De 18:5*
t.
captains of your *t*., your   *De 29:10*
elders
unto evil out of all the *t*. of   *De 29:21*
Israel
unto me all the elders of   *De 31:28*
your *t*.
t. of Israel were gathered   *De 33:5*
together
twelve men out of the *t*. of   *Jos 3:12*
Israel
according to the number of the   *Jos 4:5*
t.
according unto the number of   *Jos 4:8*
the *t*.
be brought according to your   *Jos 7:14*
t.
and brought Israel by their *t*.   *Jos 7:16*
to their divisions by their *t*.   *Jos 11:23*
Joshua gave unto the *t*. of   *Jos 12:7*
Israel
for an inheritance unto the   *Jos 13:7*
nine *t*.
heads of the fathers of the *t*.   *Jos 14:1;*
           19:51; 21:1
for the nine *t*. and for the   *Jos 14:2*
half
had given the inheritance of   *Jos 14:3*
two *t*.
the children of Joseph were   *Jos 14:4*
two *t*.
And there remained seven *t*.   *Jos 18:2*
nine cities out of those two *t*.   *Jos 21:16*
throughout all the *t*. of Israel   *Jos 22:14*
to be an inheritance for your   *Jos 23:4*
t.
Joshua gathered all the *t*. of   *Jos 24:1*
Israel
not fallen unto them among   *J'g 18:1*
Israel
people, even of all the *t*. of   *J'g 20:2*
Israel
throughout all the *t*. of Israel   *J'g 20:10*
t. of Israel sent men through   *J'g 20:12*
all

is there among all the *t.* of Israel   *J'g 21:5*

What one is there of the *t.* of Israel   *J'g 21:8*

made a breach in the *t.* of Israel   *J'g 21:15*

choose him out of all the *t.* of Israel   *1Sa 2:28*

of the smallest of the *t.* of Israel   *1Sa 9:21*

before the Lord by your *t.*   *1Sa 10:19*

all the *t.* of Israel to come near   *1Sa 10:20*

made the head of the *t.* of Israel   *1Sa 15:17*

came all the *t.* of Israel to David   *2Sa 5:1*

I a word with any of the *t.* of Israel   *2Sa 7:7*

servant is of one of the *t.* of Israel   *2Sa 15:2*

spies throughout all the *t.* of Israel   *2Sa 15:10*

strife throughout all the *t.* of Israel   *2Sa 19:9*

he went through all the *t.* of Israel   *2Sa 20:14*

Go now through all the *t.* of Israel   *2Sa 24:2*

Israel, and all the heads of the *t.*   *1Ki 8:1*

no city out of all the *t.* of Israel   *1Ki 8:16*

and will give ten *t.* to thee   *1Ki 11:31*

chosen out of all the *t.* of Israel   *1Ki 11:32*

will give it unto thee, even ten *t.*   *1Ki 11:35*

did choose out of all the *t.* of Israel   *1Ki 14:21*

of the *t.* of the sons of Jacob   *1Ki 18:31*

I have chosen out of all *t.* of Israel   *2Ki 21:7*

Furthermore over the *t.* of Israel   *1Ch 27:16*

were the princes of the *t.* of Israel   *1Ch 27:22*

princes of Israel, princes of the *t.*   *1Ch 28:1*

and princes of the *t.* of Israel   *1Ch 29:6*

Israel, and all the heads of the *t.*   *2Ch 5:2*

no city among all the *t.* of Israel   *2Ch 6:5*

out of all the *t.* of Israel such as set   *2Ch 11:16*

chosen out of all the *t.* of Israel   *2Ch 12:13*

chosen before all the *t.* of Israel   *2Ch 33:7*

to the number of the *t.* of Israel   *Ezr 6:17*

t. of Israel to dwell in their tents   *Ps 78:55*

one feeble person among their *t.*   *Ps 105:37*

the *t.* go up, the *t.* of the Lord   *Ps 122:4*

that are the stay of the *t.* thereof   *Isa 19:13*

servant to raise up the *t.* of Jacob   *Isa 49:6*

sake, the *t.* of thine inheritance   *Isa 63:17*

and the *t.* of Israel his fellows   *Eze 37:19*

house of Israel according to their *t.*   *Eze 45:8*

according to the twelve *t.* of Israel   *Eze 47:13*

you according to the *t.* of Israel   *Eze 47:21*

with you among the *t.* of Israel   *Eze 47:22*

Now these are the names of the *t.*   *Eze 48:1*

serve it out of all the *t.* of Israel   *Eze 48:19*

As for the rest of the *t.* from the   *Eze 48:23*

divide by lot unto the *t.* of Israel   *Eze 48:29*

after the names of the *t.* of Israel   *Eze 48:31*

among the *t.* of Israel have I made   *Ho 5:9*

according to the oaths of the *t.*   *Hab 3:9*

of man, as of all the *t.* of Israel   *Zec 9:1*

judging the twelve *t.* of Israel   *M't 19:28*

shall all the *t.* of the earth mourn   *M't 24:30*

judging the twelve *t.* of Israel   *Lu 22:30*

Unto which promise our twelve *t.*   *Ac 26:7*

the twelve *t.* which are scattered   *Jas 1:1*

all the *t.* of the children of Israel   *Re 7:4*

are the names of the twelve *t.*   *Re 21:12*

TRIBESMEN

fellow *t.* of Saul (B)   *1Ch 12:2*

TRIBULATION

When thou art in *t.* and all these   *De 4:30*

when anguish is yours (B)   *De 4:30*

deliver you in the time of your *t.*   *J'g 10:14*

time of your distress (A)(B)(E)(R)   *J'g 10:14*

and let him deliver me out of all *t.*   *1Sa 26:24*

save me out of every difficulty (A)   *1Sa 26:24*

compassed with *t.* (A)   *La 3:5*

for when *t.* or persecution ariseth   *M't 13:21*

when affliction or troubles comes (A)   *M't 13:21*

trouble and persecution arises (B)   *M't 13:21*

trouble or persecution (R)   *M't 13:21*

For then shall be great *t.* such as   *M't 24:21*

such great sufferings as has never been (B)   *M't 24:21*

time of great distress (N)   *M't 24:21; 24:29; M'k 13:24*

there will be great misery (P)   *M't 24:21; 24:15, 29; M'k 13:24*

after the *t.* of those days   *M't 24:29*

after the affliction of those days (B)   *M't 24:29*

t., persecution (E)(R)   *M'k 4:17*

be in *t.* (E)(R)   *M'k 13:19*

after that *t.* the sun be darkened   *M'k 13:24*

after that distress (B)   *M'k 13:24*

In the world ye shall have *t.:* but   *Joh 16:33*

in the world you are under pressure (B)   *Joh 16:33*

you will have trouble (N)(P)   *Joh 16:33*

through much *t.* enter into   *Ac 14:22*

kingdom by way of many afflictions (B)   *Ac 14:22*

enter kingdom through great hardships (N)   *Ac 14:22*

T. and anguish upon every soul   *Ro 2:9*

affliction and anxiety to very human soul (B)   *Ro 2:9*

grinding misery upon everyone (N)   *Ro 2:9*

anger and wrath for those who rebel (P)   *Ro 2:9*

knowing that *t.* worketh patience   *Ro 5:3*

pressure, affliction, and hardship (A)   *Ro 5:3*

we exult in afflictions (B)   *Ro 5:3*

we exult in present sufferings (N)   *Ro 5:3*

even in trials and trouble (P)   *Ro 5:3*

shall *t.* or distress, or persecution   *Ro 8:35*

Affliction (B)   *Ro 8:35*

Can affliction or hardship separate us (N)   *Ro 8:35*

Can trouble, pain, or persecution (P)   *Ro 8:35*

Rejoicing in hope; patient in *t.*   *Ro 12:12*

as you endure afflictions (B)   *Ro 12:12*

in trouble stand firm (N)   *Ro 12:12*

when trials come endure them (P)   *Ro 12:12*

have *t.* in the flesh (E)   *1Co 7:28*

Who comforteth us in all our *t.*   *2Co 1:4*

encourages us in every trouble (A)   *2Co 1:4*

encourage those in every kind of distress (B)   *2Co 1:4*

affliction (E)   *2Co 1:4; 7:4; 1Th 3:4; 2Th 1:6*

comforts in all troubles (N)   *2Co 1:4*

comfort in trials (P)   *2Co 1:4*

I am exceeding joyful in all our *t.*   *2Co 7:4*

in all of our trouble (B)(N)(P)   *2Co 7:4*

before that we should suffer *t.*   *1Th 3:4*

suffer affliction (A)(R)   *1Th 3:4*

we are going to have trouble (B)   *1Th 3:4; Re 2:10*

bound to suffer hardship (N)   *1Th 3:4*

t. to them that trouble you   *2Th 1:6*

pay with distress and affliction (A)   *2Th 1:6*

repay with distress those who distress (B)   *2Th 1:6*

sending trouble on those who trouble you (N)   *2Th 1:6*

repay with affliction (R)   *2Th 1:6*

your brother, and companion in *t.*   *Re 1:9*

sharer in the distress (B)(P)   *Re 1:9*

share with you in suffering (N)   *Re 1:9*

thy works, and *t.* and poverty   *Re 2:9*

affliction, distress, and pressing trouble (A)   *Re 2:9*

I know your distress (B)   *Re 2:9*

I know how hard pressed you are (N)   *Re 2:9*

and ye shall have *t.* ten days   *Re 2:10*

ten days you will have affliction (A)   *Re 2:10*

afraid of the suffering to come (N)   *Re 2:10*

your distress will last ten days (P)   *Re 2:10*

adultery with her into great *t.*   *Re 2:22*

down to pressing distress, severe affliction (A)   *Re 2:22*

throw her into great distress (B)   *Re 2:22*

plunge her into terrible suffering (N)(P)   *Re 2:22*

they which came out of great *t.*   *Re 7:14*

who passed through the great ordeal (N)   *Re 7:14*

Come through the great oppression (P)   *Re 7:14*

TRIBULATIONS

of all your adversities and your *t.*   *1Sa 10:19*

all your troubles and distresses (A)(E)   *1Sa 10:19*

your calamities and miseries (B)   *1Sa 10:19*

only so, but we glory in *t.* also   *Ro 5:3*

rejoice in our sufferings (A)(P)(R)   *Ro 5:3*

exult in afflictions (B)   *Ro 5:3*

exult in our present sufferings (N)   *Ro 5:3*

joins in our troubles (P)   *Ro 5:3*

that ye faint not at my *t.* for you   *Eph 3:13*

our suffering in your behalf (A)(R)   *Eph 3:13*

these afflictions of mine (B)   *Eph 3:13*

not lose heart over sufferings (N)   *Eph 3:13*

persecutions and *t.* that ye endure   *2Th 1:4*

crushing distresses and afflictions (A)   *2Th 1:4*

persecutions and distresses (B)(R)   *2Th 1:4*

persecutions and afflictions (E)(R)   *2Th 1:4*

all the troubles you endure (N)   *2Th 1:4*

TRIBUNAL

seated on the *t.* (B)   *M't 27:19*

brought him before the *t.* (R)   *Ac 18:12*

drove him from the *t.* (R)   *Ac 18:16*

beat him in front of the *t.* (R)   *Ac 18:17*

stand at Cæsar's *t.* (B)(N)(R)   *Ac 25:10*

placed before God's *t.* (B)(N)   *Ro 14:10*

TRIBUNE

t. of the cohort (R)   *Ac 21:31*

TRIBUNES

the military *t.* (R)   *Ac 25:23*

TRIBUTARIES

found therein shall be *t.* unto *De 20:11* thee
dwelt among them, and *J'g 1:30* became *t.*
Beth-anath became *t.* unto *J'g 1:33* them
prevailed, so that they became *J'g 1:35* *t.*

TRIBUTARY

provinces, how is she become *t. La 1:1*

TRIBUTE

and became a servant unto *t. Ge 49:15*
submit to servitude (B) *Ge 49:15*
taskwork (E) *Ge 49:15;*
Jos 16:10; 17:13; J'g 1:28; 2Sa 20:24;
1Ki 4:6; 12:18; 2Ch 10:18; Pr 12:24
forced labor (R) *Ge 49:15;*
Jos 16:10; 17:13; J'g 1:28; 2Sa 20:24;
1Ki 4:6; 12:18; 2Ch 10:18; Pr 12:24
levy a *t.* unto the Lord of the *Nu 31:28* men
levy a tax (B) *Nu 31:28*
the Lord's *t.* of the sheep was *Nu 31:37* six
the Lord's *t.* was threescore *Nu 31:38*
which the Lord's *t.* was *Nu 31:39* threescore
the Lord's *t.* was thirty and *Nu 31:40* two
Moses gave the *t.* which was *Nu 31:41*
a *t.* of a freewill offering of *De 16:10* thine
forced labor (A) *De 16:10;*
17:13; J'g 1:28; 1Ki 4:6; 12:18;
2Ch 10:18; Pr 12:24
become bond servants (B) *De 16:10*
unto this day, and serve *Jos 16:10* under *t.*
that they put the Cananites *Jos 17:13;* to *t.* *J'g 1:28*
tribute (S) *J'g 3:15; 3:17-18;*
2Ch 17:5
And Adoram was over the *t. 2Sa 20:24*
the son of Abda was over the *1Ki 4:6* *t.*
conscript labor (A) *1Ki 4:6;*
9:21; 12:18; 2Ch 8:8
Solomon levy a *t.* of *1Ki 9:21* bondservice
forced levy of slaves (A) *1Ki 9:21;*
2Ch 8:8
raise a levy of bondservants *1Ki 9:21;* (E) *2Ch 8:8*
made a forced levy of slaves *1Ki 9:21;* (R) *2Ch 8:8*
sent Adoram, who was over *1Ki 12:18* the *t.*
put the land to a *t.* of an *2Ki 23:33* hundred
laid a fine on the land (B) *2Ki 23:33*
the Moabite brought *t.* (S) *1Ch 18:2;*
18:6
make to pay *t.* until this day *2Ch 8:8*
sent Hadoram that was over *2Ch 10:18* the *t.*
in charge of labor gangs *2Ch 10:18* (B)
brought presents, and *t. 2Ch 17:11* silver
put land under *t.* (B)(R) *2Ch 36:3*
then will they not pay toll, *t. Ezr 4:13*
not pay tax (B) *Ezr 4:13; 4:20; 7:24*
t. and custom, was paid unto *Ezr 4:20* them
even of the *t.* beyond the river *Ezr 6:8*
lawful to impose toll, *t.* or *Ezr 7:24* custom
borrowed money for the king's *Ne 5:4* *t.*
to pay the king's tax *Ne 5:4* (A)(B)(R)
Ahasuerus laid a *t.* upon the *Es 10:1* land
but the slothful shall be under *Pr 12:24* *t.*
they that receive *t.* money *M't 17:24* came
said, Doth not your master *M't 17:24* pay *t.*

collectors of temple tax *M't 17:24* (A)(B)(N)(P)
of the earth take custom or *M't 17:25* *t.*
pay taxes (B) *M't 17:25;*
22:17; M'k 12:14; Lu 23:2; Ro 13:6-7
receive toll or *t.* (E) *M't 17:25*
pay tax or toll (N)(P) *M't 17:25;*
22:17, 19; M'k 12:14; Lu 23:2; Ro 13:6-7
pay the tax (P) *M't 17:25;*
22:17, 19; M'k 12:14; Ro 13:6
Is it lawful to give *t.* unto *M't 22:17* Cæsar
Shew me the *t.* money. And *M't 22:19* they
It is lawful to give *t.* to *M'k 12:14* Cæsar, or
lawful for us to give *t.* unto *Lu 20:22* Cæsar
and forbidding to give *t.* to *Lu 23:2* Cæsar
For for this cause pay ye *t. Ro 13:6* also
for this reason pay taxes (A) *Ro 13:6*
t. to whom *t.* is due; custom *Ro 13:7* to
pay taxes to whom taxes is due *Ro 13:7* (A)(R)

TRICK

have Jesus arrested by some *M't 26:4* *t.* (N)(P)
think of some *t.* (P) *M'k 14:1*
he saw through their *t.* (N) *Lu 20:23*

TRICKED

astrologers *t.* him (N) *M't 2:16*

TRICKLETH

Mine eye *t.* down, and ceaseth *La 3:49*
my eyes overflow continually *La 3:49* (A)
my eyes keep flowing *La 3:49* unceasingly (B)
my eye poureth down (E) *La 3:49*
my eyes flow with rivers of *La 3:49* tears (R)

TRICKERY

did it with *t.* (A) *2Ki 10:19*
understanding dark *t.* (A) *Da 8:23*
cause *t.* to prosper (A) *Da 8:25*
aware of their *t.* (B) *Lu 20:23*
monster of *t.* and evil (P) *Ac 13:10*
renounced clever *t.* (P) *2Co 4:2*
ever shifting form of *t.* (A) *Eph 4:14*

TRICKINESS

catches wise in own *t.* (A) *Job 5:13*

TRIED

controversy and every stroke *De 21:5* be *t.*
t. before the congregation *Jos 20:6* (A)
perfect; the word of the *2Sa 22:31* Lord is *t.*
the promise of Lord proves *2Sa 22:31;* true (B) *Ps 18:30*
when he hath *t.* me, I shall *Job 23:10* come
when he has tested me (B) *Job 23:10*
is that Job may be *t.* unto *Job 34:36* the end
as silver *t.* in a furnace of earth *Ps 12:6*
purified in an earthen furnace *Ps 12:6* (B)
refined in a furnace (R) *Ps 12:6*
thou hast *t.* me, and shalt find *Ps 17:3*
thou hast proved my heart (E) *Ps 17:3*
perfect; the word of the Lord *Ps 18:30* is *t.*
the word of the Lord is *Ps 18:30* proven (B)
the promise of the Lord *Ps 18:30* proves true (R)
thou hast *t.* us, as silver is *t. Ps 66:10*
thou hast tested us (B)(R) *Ps 66:10*
your father *t.* me (S) *Ps 95:9*
came: the word of the Lord *Ps 105:19* *t.* him
The word of Lord showed *Ps 105:19* him right (B)

The word of the Lord tested *Ps 105:19* him (R)
a stone, and a *t.* stone, a *Isa 28:16* precious
a tested stone (A)(B)(R) *Isa 28:16*
me, and *t.* mine heart toward *Jer 12:3* thee
purified, and made white, and *Da 12:10* *t.*
purified, made white, and *Da 12:10* revived (B)
purifies themselves, make *Da 12:10* themselves white, and be refined (E)(R)
and will try them as gold is *t. Zec 13:9*
test them as gold is tested *Zec 13:9;* (A)(B) *Re 2:10*
I will refine them (E)(R) *Zec 13:9*
he *t.* to join himself with *Ac 9:26* disciples (B)
there be *t.* (B)(R) *Ac 25:9*
where I ought to be *t. Ac 25:10* (A)(B)(N)(R)
might triumph when *t.* (B) *Ro 3:4*
when he was *t.* offered up *Heb 11:17* Isaac
Abraham was put to the *Heb 11:17* test (A)(P)
Abraham when he was *Heb 11:17* tested (B)(R)
Abraham when the test *Heb 11:17* came (N)
or when he is *t.* he shall *Jas 1:12* receive
when he has stood the test *Jas 1:12* (A)(B)(E)(R)
faith which has stood the test *Jas 1:12* (N)
once his testing is complete *Jas 1:12* (P)
though it be *t.* with fire, might *1Pe 1:7*
tested and purified by fire *1Pe 1:7;* (A) *Re 3:18*
tested by fire (B)(R) *1Pe 1:7*
proved by fire (E) *1Pe 1:7*
thou hast *t.* them which say *Re 2:2*
have tested them (A)(R) *Re 2:2*
you have put them to the test *Re 2:2* (B)(R)
you have put to proof (N) *Re 2:2*
you into prison, that ye may *Re 2:10* be *t.*
you will be tested (B)(R) *Re 2:10*
your distress will last ten days *Re 2:10* (N)
to buy of me gold *t.* in the fire *Re 3:18*
buy fire tested gold (B) *Re 3:18*
gold refined in the fire *Re 3:18* (E)(N)(R)

TRIEST

my God, that thou *t.* the *1Ch 29:17* heart
dost test the heart (B) *1Ch 29:17*
that *t.* the reins and the *Jer 11:20* heart
who tests the heart (A) *Jer 11:20*
who tests the reins (B) *Jer 11:20*
that *t.* the righteous, and *Jer 20:12* seest the
who tests the righteous (B) *Jer 20:12*

TRIETH

For the ear *t.* words, as the *Job 34:3* mouth
the ear tests words (B) *Job 34:3*
for the righteous God *t.* the *Ps 7:9* hearts
The Lord *t.* the righteous: but *Ps 11:5*
who tests the righteous *Ps 11:5* (A)(B)(R)
put the righteous to the proof *Ps 11:5* (B)
for gold: but the Lord *t.* the *Pr 17:3* hearts
but God, which *t.* our hearts *1Th 2:4*
who tests our hearts *1Th 2:4* (A)(B)(R)
who proveth our hearts (E) *1Th 2:4*

TRIFLE

empty and worthless *t. De 32:47* (A)(R)
t. with (A) *Ro 2:4*

TRIM

and *t.* her nails (S)	*De 21:12*
t. the hair of (S)	*Eze 44:20*

TRIMMED

dressed his feet, nor *t.* his beard	*2Sa 19:24*
virgins arose, and *t.* their lamps	*M't 25:7*

TRIMMEST

Why *t.* thou thy way to seek love	*Jer 2:33*

TRIP

his *t.* successful (A)(B)	*Ge 24:21*
the *t.* successful (B)	*Ge 24:40*
is on a long *t.* (B)	*Nu 9:10*
he is on a *t.* (B)	*1Ki 18:27*
nothing for the *t.* (B)	*M'k 6:8*
come to me from a *t.* (B)	*Lu 11:6*
a rock to *t.* them up (N)	*Ro 9:33*

TRIPPING

I place in Zion a *t.* stone (B)	*Ro 9:33*

TRIUMPH

daughters of the uncircumcised	*2Sa 1:20*
daughters of the Philistines rejoice (A)(E)(R)	*2Sa 1:20*
daughters of the uncircumcised glory (B)	*2Sa 1:20*
let not mine enemies *t.* over me	*Ps 25:2*
my enemies exult over me (R)	*Ps 25:2*
my enemy does not exult over me (B)	*Ps 41:11*
unto God with the voice of *t.*	*Ps 47:1*
shout with loud songs of joy (R)	*Ps 47:1*
Philistia, *t.* thou because of me	*Ps 60:8*
Philistia, shout because of me (E)	*Ps 60:8*
I will *t.* in the works of thy hands	*Ps 92:4*
what my hands accomplished (B)	*Ps 92:4*
at works of my hands I sing for joy (R)	*Ps 92:4*
how long shall the wicked *t.*	*Ps 94:3*
how long shall wicked be jubilant (B)	*Ps 94:3*
how long shall wicked exult (R)	*Ps 94:3*
holy name, and to *t.* in thy praise	*Ps 106:47*
exult in praising thee (B)	*Ps 106:47*
glory in thy praise (R)	*Ps 106:47*
my shoes; over Philistia will I *t.*	*Ps 108:9*
over Philistia I will shout the victory (B)	*Ps 108:9*
over Philistia will I shout (E)	*Ps 108:9*
always causeth us to *t.* in Christ	*2Co 2:14*
leads us triumphantly on (B)	*2Co 2:14*

TRIUMPHANT

he is *t.* and victorious (R)	*Zec 9:9*

TRIUMPHANTLY

striding *t.* (A)	*Isa 63:1*

TRIUMPHED

the Lord, for he hath *t.* gloriously	*Ex 15:1; 15:21*

TRIUMPHING

That the *t.* of the wicked is short	*Job 20:5*
of them openly, *t.* over them in it	*Col 2:15*

TRIUMPHS

great *t.* giveth to (R)	*1Sa 22:51*

TRIVIAL

regards nothing as *t.* (B)	*Job 36:5*

TROAS

passing by Mysia came down to T.	*Ac 16:8*
Therefore loosing from T. we	*Ac 16:11*
going before tarried for us at T.	*Ac 20:5*
came unto them to T. in five days	*Ac 20:6*
I came to T. to preach Christ's	*2Co 2:12*
cloke that I left at T. with Carpus	*2Ti 4:13*

TRODDEN

give the land that he hath *t.* upon	*De 1:36*
land whereon thy feet have *t.* shall	*Jos 14:9*
soul, thou hast *t.* down strength	*J'g 5:21*
old way which wicked men have *t.*	*Job 22:15*
The lion's whelps have not *t.*	*Job 28:8*
hast *t.* down all them that err	*Ps 119:118*
thereof, and it shall be *t.* down	*Isa 5:5*
the pit; as a carcase *t.* under feet	*Isa 14:19*
a nation meted out and *t.* down	*Isa 18:2*
nation meted out and *t.* under foot	*Isa 18:7*
Moab shall be *t.* down under him	*Isa 25:10*
straw is *t.* down for the dunghill	*Isa 25:10*
of Ephraim, shall be *t.* under feet	*Isa 28:3*
then ye shall be *t.* down by it	*Isa 28:18*
I have *t.* the winepress alone	*Isa 63:3*
our adversaries have *t.* down thy	*Isa 63:18*
they have *t.* my portion under foot	*Jer 12:10*
hath *t.* under foot all my mighty	*La 1:15*
the Lord hath *t.* the virgin, the	*La 1:15*
which ye have *t.* with your feet	*Eze 34:19*
and the host to be *t.* under foot	*Da 8:13*
shall she be *t.* down as the mire of	*Mic 7:10*
out, and to be *t.* under foot of men	*M't 5:13*
it was *t.* down, and the fowls of	*Lu 8:5*
Jerusalem shall be *t.* down of	*Lu 21:24*
who hath *t.* under foot the Son of	*Heb 10:29*
winepress was *t.* without the city	*Re 14:20*

TRODE

their vineyards, and *t.* the grapes	*J'g 9:27*
and *t.* them down with ease over	*J'g 20:43*
trampled on (B)	*J'g 20:43; 2Ki 7:17, 20; 9:33; 14:9; 2Ch 25:18*
people *t.* upon him in the gate	*2Ki 7:17;*
trample on (A)	*2Ki 7:17; 7:20; 14:9; 2Ch 25:18*
horses: and he *t.* her under foot	*2Ki 9:33*
he drove over her (A)	*2Ki 9:33*
in Lebanon, and *t.* down the thistle	*2Ki 14:9; 2Ch 25:18*
that they *t.* one upon another	*Lu 12:1*

TROGYLLIUM

at Samos, and tarried at T.	*Ac 20:15*

TROOP

And Leah said, A *t.* cometh	*Ge 30:11*
victory and good fortune have come (A)	*Ge 30:11*
I am fortunate (B)(E)(R)	*Ge 30:11*
Gad, a *t.* shall overcome him: but	*Ge 49:19*
raiders will assail him (B)(R)	*Ge 49:19*
Shall I pursue after this *t.?* shall I	*1Sa 30:8*
shall I pursue these bandits (B)(R)	*1Sa 30:8*

down to this *t.* (E)	*1Sa 30:15*
after Abner, and became one *t.*	*2Sa 2:25*
became a band (E)	*2Sa 2:25*
and Joab came from pursuing a *t.*	*2Sa 3:22*
by thee I have run through a *t.:* by	*2Sa 22:30*
were gathered together into a *t.*	*2Sa 23:11*
gather into a combat group (R)	*2Sa 23:11*
the *t.* of the Philistines pitched in	*2Sa 23:13*
by thee I have run through a *t.*	*Ps 18:29*
that prepare a table for that *t.*	*Isa 65:11*
prepare a table for fortune (E)(R)	*Isa 65:11*
bring a *t.* suddenly upon them	*Jer 18:22*
the *t.* of robbers spoileth without	*Ho 7:1*
burglars, bandits who raid highways (B)(R)	*Ho 7:1*
and hath founded his *t.* in the earth	*Am 9:6*

TROOPS

the men of the *t.* (B)	*2Ch 25:13; Ezr 8:22*
The *t.* of Tema looked, the caravans of Tema (A)(B)(E)(R)	*Job 6:19*
His *t.* come together, and raise up	*Job 19:12*
assembled themselves by *t.* in	*Jer 5:7*
all the foreign *t.* (B)(R)	*Jer 50:37*
as *t.* of robbers wait for a man	*Ho 6:9*
as do bands of marauders (B)	*Ho 6:9*
Now gather thyself in *t.*	*Mic 5:1*
O daughter of *t.:* he hath laid	*Mic 5:1*
he will invade them with his *t.*	*Hab 3:16*
Herod and his *t.* (N)	*Lu 23:11*

TROPHIMUS

and of Asia, Tychicus, and T.	*Ac 20:4*
before with him in the city T.	*Ac 21:29*
but T. have I left at Miletum sick	*2Ti 4:20*

TROTH

plighted my *t.* (A)(B)	*Eze 16:8*

TROUBLE

noticed my *t.* (B)	*Ge 24:32*
not seen *t.* in Israel (B)	*Nu 23:21*
camp of Israel a curse, and *t.* us? the Lord shall *t.* thee this day	*Jos 6:18 Jos 7:25*
calamity (B)	*Jos 7:25; J'g 11:35; Job 5:6; Isa 65:23; Jer 2:27-28; 11:12*
thou art one of them that *t.* me	*J'g 11:35*
save me out of every *t.* (B)	*2Sa 4:9*
why stir up *t.* (B)(R)	*2Ki 14:10*
This day is a day of *t.* and of distress (B)	*2Ki 19:3; Job 15:24; Ps 59:16; 66:14; 69:17; 78:49; 81:7; 102:2; Isa 8:22; 46:7*
distress (B)	*2Ki 19:3; Job 38:23; Ps 31:7; 54:7; 59:16; 66:14; 77:2; 78:49; 81:7; 107:19, 28; 119:143; 143:11; Isa 8:22; 26:16; 46:7; Jer 30:7; 2Ti 2:9*
distress (R)	*2Ki 19:3; 2Ch 15:4; Job 15:24; Ps 31:9; 59:16; 69:17; 78:49; 81:7; Isa 8:22; 26:16; 37:3; Jer 30:7*
in my *t.* I have prepared for	*1Ch 22:14*
they in their *t.* did turn unto	*2Ch 15:4*
extremity (B)	*2Ch 15:4*
distress (E)	*2Ch 15:4; Job 15:24; Ps 31:9; 59:16; 66:14; 102:2; Isa 8:22*
and he hath delivered them to *t.*	*2Ch 29:8*
terror (A)	*2Ch 29:8; Ps 77:33; Isa 17:14; 65:23*
an object of horror (B)(R)	*2Ch 29:8*
to affright them, and to *t.* them	*2Ch 32:18*

are in great *t.* (A) — Ne 1:3
and in the time of their *t.* — Ne 9:27
when
suffering (A)(R) — Ne 9:27
let not all the *t.* seem little — Ne 9:32
before
adversity (B) — Ne 9:32;
Pr 25:19; Jer 14:8
hardship (R) — Ne 9:32
hid *t.* from eyes (B)(E) — Job 3:10
neither was I quiet; yet *t.* — Job 3:26
came
sow *t.* and mischief — Job 4:8
(A)(B)(E)(R)
doth *t.* spring out of the — Job 5:6
ground
Yet man is born unto *t.* as the — Job 5:7
you will forget *t.* (B) — Job 11:16
is of few days, and full of *t.* — Job 14:1
T. and anguish shall make — Job 15:24
him
his cry when *t.* cometh upon — Job 27:9
him
weep for him that was in *t.* — Job 30:25
quietness, who then can — Job 34:29
make *t.*
who can condemn him — Job 34:29
(B)(E)(R)
reserved against the time of — Job 38:23
t.
how are they increased that *t.* — Ps 3:1
me
adversaries (E) — Ps 3:1; 13:4; 60:11
many are my foes (R) — Ps 3:1
oppressed, a refuge in times of — Ps 9:9
t.
consider my *t.* which I suffer — Ps 9:13
afflicted (A) — Ps 9:13
suffer (R) — Ps 9:13
hidest thou thyself in times — Ps 10:1
of *t.*
you note *t.,* brief (A)(B)(R) — Ps 10:14
those that *t.* me rejoice when I — Ps 13:4
am
Lord hear thee in the day of *t.* — Ps 20:1
Be not far from me; for *t.* is — Ps 22:11
near
in the time of *t.* he shall hide — Ps 27:5
me
for thou hast considered my *t.* — Ps 31:7
affliction (A) — Ps 31:7; 2Ti 2:9
adversities (E) — Ps 31:7
affliction (R) — Ps 31:7
upon me, O Lord, for I am in — Ps 31:9
t.
I am in anguish (B) — Ps 31:9;
107:26; 116:3; Da 12:1
thou shalt preserve me from *t.* — Ps 32:7
is their strength in the time — Ps 37:39
of *t.*
Lord will deliver him in time — Ps 41:1
of *t.*
misfortune (B) — Ps 41:1
in the day of evil (E) — Ps 41:1
strength, a very present help in — Ps 46:1
t.
And call upon me in the day — Ps 50:15
of *t.*
he hath delivered me out of all — Ps 54:7
t.
t. in the midst (R) — Ps 55:10; 90:10
and refuge in the day of my *t.* — Ps 59:16
Give us help from *t.:* for — Ps 60:11
vain is
against the adversary (A) — Ps 60:11;
68:12
hath spoken, when I was in *t.* — Ps 66:14
from thy servant; for I am in — Ps 69:17
t.
They are not in *t.* as other — Ps 73:5
men
day of my *t.* I sought the Lord — Ps 77:2
in vanity, and their years in *t.* — Ps 78:33
end sudden disaster (B) — Ps 78:33
years in terror (E)(R) — Ps 78:33
wrath, and indignation, and *t.* — Ps 78:49
Thou calledst in *t.* and I — Ps 81:7
delivered
day of my *t.* I will call upon — Ps 86:7
thee
day of my anxiety (B) — Ps 86:7
I will be with him in *t.;* I will — Ps 91:15
deliver
respite from days of *t.* (R) — Ps 94:13
me in the day when I am in *t.* — Ps 102:2
a distressful day (B) — Ps 102:2
cried unto the Lord in their — Ps 107:6;
t. — 107:13
they cry unto the Lord in — Ps 107:19
their *t.*

their soul is melted because — Ps 107:26
of *t.*
they cry unto the Lord in — Ps 107:28
their *t.*
Give us help from *t.:* for — Ps 108:12
vain is the
upon me: I found *t.* and — Ps 116:3
sorrow
T. and anguish have taken — Ps 119:143
hold
Though I walk in the midst — Ps 138:7
of *t.*
him; I shewed before him my — Ps 142:2
t.
sake bring my soul out of *t.* — Ps 143:11
winketh causeth *t.* (R) — Pr 10:10
The righteous is delivered out — Pr 11:8
of *t.*
but the just shall come out of — Pr 12:13
t.
in the revenues of the wicked — Pr 15:6
is *t.*
great treasure and *t.* — Pr 15:16
therewith
lamentation (B) — Pr 15:16
perverted tongue fall into *t.* — Pr 17:20
(B)
in an unfaithful man in time — Pr 25:19
of *t.*
they are a *t.* unto me; I am — Isa 1:14
weary
an oppressive burden — Isa 1:14
(A)(B)(R)
behold *t.* and darkness, — Isa 8:22
dimness
And behold at eveningtide *t.* — Isa 17:14
For it is a day of *t.* and of — Isa 22:5
Lord, in *t.* have they visited — Isa 26:16
thee
into the land of *t.* and — Isa 30:6
anguish
our salvation also in the time — Isa 33:2
of *t.*
This day is a day of *t.* and of — Isa 37:3
a day of anguish (B) — Isa 37:3
answer, nor save him out of — Isa 46:7
his *t.*
in vain, nor bring forth for *t.* — Isa 65:23
calamity (E)(R) — Isa 65:23
in the time of their *t.* they — Jer 2:27
will say
can save thee in the time of — Jer 2:28
thy *t.*
a time of health, and behold — Jer 8:15
t.
terror (R) — Jer 8:15; 14:19
them at all in the time of their — Jer 11:12
t.
that they cry unto me for — Jer 11:14
their *t.*
the saviour thereof in time of — Jer 14:8
t.
the time of healing, and — Jer 14:19
behold *t.*
dismay, disaster, and terror — Jer 14:19
(A)
it is even the time of Jacob's — Jer 30:7
t.
t. and anxiety (A) — Jer 49:23
for in the day of *t.* they shall — Jer 51:2
be
day of calamity (A) — Jer 51:2
day of tumult (A)(B)(E) — Jer 7:7
neither shall the foot of man — Jer 32:13
t. them
nor the hoofs of beasts *t.* — Jer 32:13
them
the interpretation thereof, *t.* — Da 4:19
thee
let not thy thoughts *t.* thee, — Da 5:10
nor let
not alarmed at your thoughts — Da 5:10
(A)
and out of the north shall *t.* — Da 11:44
him
good, a strong hold in the day — Na 1:7
of *t.*
cause me to see *t.* (A)(R) — Hab 1:3
that I might rest in the day — Hab 3:16
of *t.*
of wrath, a day of *t.* and — Zec 1:15
distress
t. or persecution (B)(R) — M't 13:21
them, Why *t.* ye the woman — M't 26:10
T. or persecution — M'k 4:17
(A)(B)(N)(P)
healed of her *t.* (N)(P) — M'k 5:29; 5:34
said, Let her alone; why *t.* ye — M'k 14:6
her
unto him, Lord, *t.* not thyself — Lu 7:6

is dead; *t.* not the Master — Lu 8:49
shall answer and say, *T.* me — Lu 11:7
not
Do not disturb me (A) — Lu 11:7
Do not bother me (R)(N) — Lu 11:7
you will have *t.* (N)(P) — Joh 16:33
sentence is, that we *t.* not — Ac 15:19
them
Gentiles be not harrassed — Ac 15:19
(B)
impose no irksome — Ac 15:19
restrictions (N)
not put additional obstacles — Ac 15:19
in the way (P)
Jews, do exceedingly *t.* our — Ac 16:20
city
throwing our city in — Ac 16:20
confusion (A)
creating a disturbance — Ac 16:20
(B)(N)
T. not yourselves for his life — Ac 20:10
have no anxiety (R) — Ac 20:10
keep an eye on those who — Ro 16:17
cause *t.* (P)
such shall have *t.* in the flesh — 1Co 7:28
have tribulation in the flesh — 1Co 7:28
(E)
have pain and grief in bodily — 1Co 7:28
life (N)
comfort them which are in — 2Co 1:4
any *t.*
our *t.* which came to us in — 2Co 1:8
Asia
momentary *t.* (B) — 2Co 4:17
in all our *t.* (B)(N)(P) — 2Co 7:4
but there be some that *t.* you — Ga 1:7
were even cut off which *t.* you — Ga 1:12
who are unsettling you — 2Co 5:12
(B)(E)(R)
henceforth let no man *t.* me — 2Co 6:17
is no *t.* to me (N) — Ph'p 3:1
going to have *t.* (B) — 1Th 3:4; Re 2:10
tribulations to them that *t.* — 2Th 1:6
you
pay with *t.* (N) — 2Th 1:6
Wherein I suffer *t.* as an evil — 2Ti 2:9
doer
hardship (E)(N) — 2Ti 2:9
of bitterness springing up *t.* — Heb 12:15
you
cause a disturbance (B) — Heb 12:15
widows in *t.* (B) — Jas 1:27
suffering *t.* (B)(N)(P) — Jas 5:13

TROUBLED

Ye have *t.* me to make me to — Ge 34:30
stink
ruined me (A) — Ge 34:30
shocked me, and made me — Ge 34:30
odious (B)
the morning that his spirit — Ge 41:8
was *t.*
disturbed (B) — Ge 41:8;
1Sa 14:29; 2Ki 6:11; Ps 77:4
distressingly disturbed, and — Ge 45:3
dismayed (A)
were confounded (B) — Ge 45:3
dismayed (R) — Ge 45:3;
Ps 30:7; 83:17; 104:29
and *t.* the host of the — Ex 14:24
Eygptians
discomfited (A)(R) — Ex 14:24
brought on panic (B) — Ex 14:24
Joshua said, Why hast thou *t.* — Jos 7:25
us
Why did you bring calamity — Jos 7:25
I am sorely *t.* (R) — 1Sa 1:15
My father hath *t.* the land; — 1Sa 14:29
see
evil spirit from the Lord *t.* — 1Sa 16:14
him
terrified (B) — 1Sa 16:14; Ps 83:17; 90:7
tormented him (A) — 1Sa 16:14
Saul, and saw that he was — 1Sa 28:21
sore *t.*
he was sore distressed (B) — 1Sa 28:21
he was terrified (R) — 1Sa 28:21;
Job 23:15
feeble, and all the Israelites — 2Sa 4:1
were *t.*
fell into confusion (B) — 2Sa 4:1
Israel was dismayed (R) — 2Sa 4:1
was so *t.* (A) — 2Sa 13:2;
Ps 6:2-3, 10; Lu 6:18; Ac 5:16
he answered, I have not *t.* — 1Ki 18:18
Israel
king of Syria was sore *t.* for — 2Ki 6:11
this

Judah, and *t.* them in building	*Ezr 4:4*
discouraged Judah (R)	*Ezr 4:4*
it toucheth thee, and thou art *t.*	*Job 4:5*
you grow dismayed (B)	*Job 4:5*
you are impatient (R)	*Job 4:5*
why should not my spirit be *t.*	*Job 21:4*
why may I not be impatient (B)(R)	*Job 21:4*
Therefore am I *t.* at his presence	*Job 23:15*
I tremble before him (B)	*Job 23:15*
the people shall be *t.* at midnight	*Job 34:20*
people are shaken (A)(B)(R)	*Job 34:20*
my bones are *t.* (B)(E)(R)	*Ps 6:2; 6:10; Lu 6:18; Ac 5:16*
didst hide thy face, and I was *t.*	*Ps 30:7*
I felt disaster (B)	*Ps 30:7*
I am *t.*	*Ps 38:6*
I am bent (B)	*Ps 38:6*
I am bowed down and prostrate (R)	*Ps 38:6*
the waters thereof roar and be *t.*	*Ps 46:3*
waters roar and foam (A)	*Ps 46:3*
tremble with tumult (R)	*Ps 46:3*
dismayed (A)	*Ps 48:5*
amazed (B)	*Ps 48:5*
panic (R)	*Ps 48:5*
I remembered God, and was *t.*	*Ps 77:3*
my spirit faints (R)	*Ps 77:3*
I am so *t.* that I cannot speak	*Ps 77:4*
afraid: the depths also were *t.*	*Ps 77:16*
the depths shuddered (A)(B)	*Ps 77:16; Isa 32:11*
the depths were afraid (R)	*Ps 77:16*
Let them be confounded and *t.* for	*Ps 83:17*
anger, and by thy wrath are we *t.*	*Ps 90:7*
by thy wrath we are overwhelmed (R)	*Ps 90:7*
thou hidest thy face, they are *t.*	*Ps 90:7*
hidest thy face, they are *t.*	*Ps 104:29*
struck with despair (B)	*Ps 104:29*
the wicked is as a *t.* fountain	*Pr 25:26*
like a muddied, polluted fountain (A)(R)	*Pr 25:26*
like a trampled fountain (B)	*Pr 25:26*
Many days and years shall ye be *t.*	*Isa 32:10*
be shaken (B)	*Isa 32:10*
you will shudder (R)	*Isa 32:10*
are at ease: be *t.* ye careless ones	*Isa 32:11*
tremble (B)(R)	*Isa 32:11; Eze 26:18*
But the wicked are like *t.* sea	*Isa 57:20*
like the tossing sea (B)	*Isa 57:20*
my bowels are *t.* for him; I will	*Jer 31:20*
my heart yearns (A)(E)(R)	*Jer 31:20*
my emotions stir (B)	*Jer 31:20; La 2:11*
my bowels are *t.;* mine heart is	*La 1:20*
my vital parts are in tumult (A)(R)	*La 1:20*
my bowels are *t.,* my liver is poured	*La 2:11*
my emotions are deeply disturbed (A)	*La 2:11*
of the people of the land shall be *t.*	*Eze 7:27*
people tremble—palsied by terror (A)(R)	*Eze 7:27*
paralyzed by fear (B)	*Eze 7:27*
isles that are in the sea shall be *t.*	*Eze 26:18*
coastlands tremble (A)	*Eze 26:18*
lands are dismayed (E)	*Eze 26:18*
lands are dismayed (R)	*Eze 26:18; Da 4:19*
afraid, they shall be *t.* in their	*Eze 27:35*
their faces quiver (A)	*Eze 27:35*
they are appalled (R)	*Eze 27:35*
wherewith his spirit was *t.* and	*Da 2:1*
disturbed (B)	*Da 2:1; M't 2:3; Joh 5:7; 12:27; 13:21; 2Th 2:2*
my spirit was *t.* to know the dream	*Da 2:3*
and the visions of my head *t.* me	*Da 4:5*
made me afraid (R)	*Da 4:5*

one hour, and his thoughts *t.* him	*Da 4:19*
thoughts appalling him (B)	*Da 4:19*
his thoughts *t.* him, so that the	*Da 5:6*
thoughts alarmed him (B)	*Da 5:6; 7:28*
alarmed him (B)	*Da 5:6; 5:7; 7:15, 28; M't 24:6; M'k 13:7*
Then was king Belshazzar *t.* greatly.	*Da 5:9*
greatly perplexed (B)	*Da 5:9*
and the visions of my head *t.* me	*Da 7:15*
distressed (B)	*Da 7:15*
Daniel, my cogitations much *t.* me	*Da 7:28*
my thoughts *t.* (A)(B)(E)(R)	*Da 7:28*
they were *t.* because there was no	*Zec 10:2*
afflicted and hurt (A)	*Zec 10:2*
afflicted (B)(R)	*Zec 10:2*
afflicted (E)	*Zec 10:2; 2Co 7:5; 2Th 1:7*
had heard these things, he was *t.*	*M't 2:3*
greatly perturbed (N)	*M't 2:3; Lu 24:38; 1Pe 3:14*
greatly perturbed (R)	*M't 2:3*
they were *t.* saying, It is a spirit	*M't 14:26*
they were terrified (A)(P)	*M't 14:26*
cried out in terror (B)(N)	*M't 14:26*
see that ye be not *t.;* for all these	*M't 24:6*
don't be alarmed (N)(P)	*M't 24:6; M'k 13:7*
t. with remorse (A)(B)(N)(P)	*M't 27:3*
For they all saw him, and were *t.*	*M'k 6:50*
were agitated (A)	*M'k 6:50*
were frightened (B)	*M'k 6:50*
were terrified (N)(P)(R)	*M'k 6:50*
were scared out of their wits (P)	*M'k 6:51*
and rumours of wars, be ye not *t.*	*M'k 13:7*
distressed and *t.* (R)	*M'k 14:33*
when Zacharias saw him, he was *t.*	*Lu 1:12*
overcome with fear (N)	*Lu 1:12*
terribly agitated (P)	*Lu 1:12*
she was *t.* at his saying, and cast	*Lu 1:29*
Mary was deeply perturbed (N)(P)	*Lu 1:29*
t. with unclean spirits (N)(P)	*Lu 6:18*
careful and *t.* about many things	*Lu 10:41*
anxious and bustling about many (B)	*Lu 10:41*
fretting and fussing about many things (N)	*Lu 10:41*
worried and bothered about many (P)	*Lu 10:41*
Why are ye *t.?* and why do	*Lu 24:38*
Why are you so worried (P)	*Lu 24:38*
into the pool, and *t.* the water	*Joh 5:4*
stirred the water (B)	*Joh 5:4*
have no man, when the water is *t.*	*Joh 5:7*
water stirred up (P)	*Joh 5:7*
groaned in the spirit, was *t.*	*Joh 11:33*
disquieted (B)	*Joh 11:33*
was deeply moved (N)	*Joh 11:33*
deeply moved and visibly impressed (P)	*Joh 11:33*
Now is my soul *t.;* and what shall	*Joh 12:27*
my soul is in turmoil (N)	*Joh 12:27*
now comes the hour of heart break (P)	*Joh 12:27*
he was *t.* in spirit, and testified	*Joh 13:21*
in deep agitation of spirit	*Joh 13:21*
he was in anguish of soul (P)	*Joh 13:21*
Let not your heart be *t.:* ye believe	*Joh 14:1*
not let self be distressed (P)	*Joh 14:1; 14:27*
Let not your heart be *t.* neither let	*Joh 14:27*
unsettled or intimidated (B)	*Joh 14:27*
sore *t.* because (E)	*Ac 4:2*
out from us have *t.* you with words	*Ac 15:24*
caused you great distress (P)	*Ac 15:24*

disturbed (A)	*Ac 15:24; 2Th 2:2; 1Pe 3:14*
disturbed (N)	*Ac 15:24*
Paul, being sore *t.* (E)	*Ac 16:18*
they *t.* the people and the rulers of	*Ac 17:8*
aroused the emotions (B)	*Ac 17:8*
caused a great commotion (N)	*Ac 17:8*
succeeded in alarming the people (P)	*Ac 17:8*
disturbed (R)	*Ac 17:8*
if we are *t.* (A)(B)(P)	*2Co 1:6*
We are *t.* on every side, yet not	*2Co 4:8*
hard pressed on every side (N)	*2Co 4:8*
handicapped on all sides (P)	*2Co 4:8*
afflicted in every way (R)	*2Co 4:8; 7:5; 2Th 1:7*
rest, but we were *t.* on every side	*2Co 7:5*
oppressed in every way (A)	*2Co 7:5*
And to you who are *t.* rest with us	*2Th 1:7*
who are distressed (A)	*2Th 1:7*
or be *t.,* neither by spirit, nor by	*2Th 2:2*
alarm yourselves (N)	*2Th 2:2*
not be thrown off balance (P)	*2Th 2:2*
afraid of their terror, neither be *t.*	*1Pe 3:14*
not worry about them (P)	*1Pe 3:14*

TROUBLEDST

and *t.* the water with thy feet	*Eze 32:2*

TROUBLER

Achar, the *t.* of Israel, who	*1Ch 2:7*

TROUBLES

handle your *t.* (B)	*De 1:12*
evils and *t.* shall befall them	*De 31:17*
evils and *t.* are befallen them	*De 31:21*
your *t.* and distresses (A)(E)	*1Sa 10:19*
He shall deliver thee in six *t.:* yea	*Job 5:19*
The *t.* of my heart are enlarged	*Ps 25:17*
Israel, O God, out of all his *t.*	*Ps 25:22*
him, and saved him out of all his *t.*	*Ps 34:6*
delivereth them out of all their *t.*	*Ps 34:17*
hast shewed me great and sore *t.*	*Ps 71:20*
For my soul is full of *t.:* and my	*Ps 88:3*
tongue keepeth his soul from *t.*	*Pr 21:23*
because the former *t.* are forgotten	*Isa 65:16*
and there shall be famines and *t.*	*M'k 13:8*
joy in *t.* (P)	*Ro 5:3*
slight, little *t.* (N)(P)	*2Co 4:17*
all *t.* you endure (N)	*2Th 1:4*
be a time of *t.* (N)	*2Ti 3:1*

TROUBLEST

dead: why *t.* thou the Master any	*M'k 5:35*

TROUBLETH

an evil spirit from God *t.* thee	*1Sa 16:15*
him, Art thou he that *t.* Israel	*1Ki 18:17*
about thee, and sudden fear *t.* thee	*Job 22:10*
heart soft, and the Almighty *t.* me	*Job 23:16*
he that is cruel *t.* his own flesh	*Pr 11:17*
that *t.* his own house shall inherit	*Pr 11:29*
is greedy of gain *t.* his own house	*Pr 15:27*
is in thee, and no secret *t.* thee	*Da 4:9*
yet because this widow *t.* me	*Lu 18:5*
but he that *t.* you shall bear his	*Ga 5:10*

TROUBLING

There the wicked cease from *Job 3:17*
t.
the t. of the water stepped in *Joh 5:4*
was

TROUBLOUS

and the wall, even in t. times *Da 9:25*
t. times impending (B) *2Ti 3:1*

TROUGH

emptied her pitcher into the *Ge 24:20*
t.

TROUGHS

watering t. when the flocks *Ge 30:38*
came
filled the t. to water their *Ex 2:16*
father's

TROW

were commanded him? I t. not *Lu 17:9*

TRUCEBREAKERS

Without natural affection, t., *2Ti 3:3*
false

TRUE

we are t. men, thy servants *Ge 42:11*
are no
honest (B) *Ge 42:11;*
     42:31, 33; 2Co 6:8; Heb 10:22
honest (R) *Ge 42:11; 42:19, 31, 33-34*
If ye be t. men, let one of *Ge 42:19*
your
We are t. men; we are no *Ge 42:31*
spies
shall I know that ye are t. *Ge 42:33*
men
honest (A) *Ge 42:33; 42:34*
are no spies, but that ye are *Ge 42:34*
t. men
trustworthy (B) *Ge 42:34*
it be t. and the thing certain *De 17:4*
But if this thing be t. and the *De 22:20*
tokens
correct (B) *De 22:20*
house, and give me a t. token *Jos 2:12*
pledge of good faith (B) *Jos 2:12*
it is t. that I am thy near *Ru 3:12*
kinsman
art that God, and thy words *2Sa 7:28*
be t.
thy words are truth *2Sa 7:28;*
(A)(B)(E) *1Ki 22:16; Ps 119:160*
It was a t. report that I *1Ki 10:6*
heard in
tell me nothing but that *1Ki 22:16*
which is t.
nothing but the truth *1Ki 22:16*
(A)(B)(E)(R)
It was a t. report which I *2Ch 9:5*
heard in
Israel hath been without the *2Ch 15:3*
t. God
them right judgments, and t. *Ne 9:13*
laws
the judgments of the Lord are *Ps 19:9*
t.
Thy word is t. from the *Ps 119:160*
beginning
thy word is altogether truth *Ps 119:160*
(A)(B)(E)(R)
A t. witness delivereth souls: *Pr 14:25*
but a
a faithful witness delivers *Pr 14:25*
souls (B)
But the Lord is the t. God, *Jer 10:10*
he is the
Lord be a t. and faithful *Jer 42:5*
witness
hath executed t. judgment *Eze 18:8*
between
practices strict justice (B) *Eze 18:8*
Is it t. O Shadrach, Meshach, *Da 3:14*
and
said unto the king, T., O king *Da 4:37*
The thing is t. according to *Da 6:12*
the thing stands fast (B) *Da 6:12*
the morning which was told *Da 8:26*
is t.
and the thing was t. but the *Da 10:1*
time

Execute t. judgment, and shew *Zec 7:9*
sincere (A)(B) *M't 22:16; M'k 12:14*
honest (N)(P) *M't 22:16; M'k 12:14*
Master, we know that thou *M'k 12:14*
art t.
commit to your trust the t. *Lu 16:11*
riches
real (N) *Lu 16:11;*
Joh 1:9; 4:23; 6:32; 15:1; Ac 12:9;
     Heb 8:2; 1Jo 5:20
That was the t. Light, which *Joh 1:9*
lighteth
hath set to his seal that God *Joh 3:33*
is t.
when the t. worshippers shall *Joh 4:23*
genuine (B) *Joh 4:23;*
     Eph 4:24; Ph'p 4:3
herein is that saying t., One *Joh 4:37*
soweth
is verified (B) *Joh 4:37*
my judgment is t. (P) *Joh 5:30*
of myself, my witness is not t. *Joh 5:31*
testimony valid (A) *Joh 5:31;*
     5:32; 8:13, 17
testimony is reliable (B) *Joh 5:31*
which he witnesseth of me is *Joh 5:32*
t.
evidence on my behalf is *Joh 5:32*
valid (B)
my Father giveth you the t. *Joh 6:32*
bread
the real bread (B) *Joh 6:32*
glory of that sent him, the same *Joh 7:18*
is t.
is sincere (B) *Joh 7:18*
but he that sent me is t. *Joh 7:28*
whom ye
of thyself; thy record is not t. *Joh 8:13*
testimony valid (B)(N) *Joh 8:13;*
     8:14, 17
your evidence is not valid *Joh 8:13*
(P)
record of myself, yet my *Joh 8:14*
record is t.
my evidence is valid (P) *Joh 8:14*
yet if I judge, my judgment is *Joh 8:16*
t.
that the testimony of two *Joh 8:17*
men is t.
testimony of two persons *Joh 8:17*
valid (P)
he that sent me is t.; and I *Joh 8:26*
speak to
my sender is reliable (B) *Joh 8:26*
that John spake of this man *Joh 10:41*
were t.
I am the t. vine, and my *Joh 15:1*
Father is
I am the real vine (P) *Joh 15:1*
might know thee the only t. *Joh 17:3*
God
it bear record, and his *Joh 19:35*
record is t.
whose evidence is to be *Joh 19:35*
trusted (N)
he knoweth that he saith t. *Joh 19:35*
that ye
and we know that his *Joh 21:24*
testimony is t.
his witness is reliable (P) *Joh 21:24*
that it was t. which was done *Ac 12:9*
by the
was real (A)(B)(R) *Ac 12:9*
not knowing what the angel is *Ac 12:9*
doing (P)
let God be t. but every man a *Ro 3:4*
liar
But as God is t. our word *2Co 1:18*
toward
as God is trustworthy, *2Co 1:18*
faithful, and means what he
says (A)
as God is trustworthy (B) *2Co 1:18*
God is faithful (P)(R) *2Co 1:18*
report: as deceivers and yet t. *2Co 6:8*
truthful and honest (A) *2Co 6:8*
righteousness and t. holiness *Eph 4:24*
I intreat thee also, t. *Ph'p 4:3*
yokefellow
t. yokefellow (B) *Ph'p 4:3*
brethren, whatsoever things *Ph'p 4:8*
idols to serve the living and t. *1Th 1:9*
God
This is a t. saying, If a man *1Ti 3:1*
desire
trustworthy is the saying (B) *1Ti 3:1*
there is a popular saying (N) *1Ti 3:1*

This witness is t. Wherefore *Tit 1:13*
he told the truth (N) *Tit 1:13*
sanctuary, and of the t. *Heb 8:2*
tabernacle
real tabernacle (B)(P) *Heb 8:2; 9:24*
which are the figures of the *Heb 9:24*
t.
only a symbol of the reality *Heb 9:24*
(N)
Let us draw near with a t. *Heb 10:22*
heart in
in sincerity of heart (N) *Heb 10:22*
she considered God *Heb 11:11*
trustworthy and t. to his
word (A)(B)(P)
that this is the t. grace of *1Pe 5:12*
God
them according to the t. *2Pe 2:22*
proverb
which thing is t. in him and in *1Jo 2:8*
past, and the t. light now *1Jo 2:8*
shineth
that we may know him that is *1Jo 5:20*
t.
this is the real God and real *1Jo 5:20*
eternal life (P)
and we are in him that is t. *1Jo 5:20*
even in
This is the t. God, and *1Jo 5:20*
eternal life
and ye know that our record is *3Jo 12*
t.
saith he that is holy, he that is *Re 3:7*
t.
the faithful and t. witness, the *Re 3:14*
How long, O Lord, holy and t. *Re 6:10*
just and t. are thy ways, thou *Re 15:3*
King
t. and righteous are thy *Re 16:7*
judgments
t. and righteous are his *Re 19:2*
judgments
me, These are the t. sayings of *Re 19:9*
God
him was called Faithful and *Re 19:11*
T.
for these words are t. and *Re 21:5*
faithful
These sayings are faithful and *Re 22:6*
t.
reliable, worthy of confidence, *Re 22:6*
genuine (A)

TRULY

t. Lamech seventy and *Ge 4:24*
sevenfold
deal kindly and t. with my *Ge 24:49*
master
treat my master kindly and *Ge 24:49*
fairly (B)
and deal kindly and t. with *Ge 47:29*
me
deal loyally and faithfully *Ge 47:29;*
(A) *Jos 2:14*
but t. his younger brother *Ge 48:19*
shall be
But as t. as I live, all the *Nu 14:21*
earth
As t. as I live, saith the *Nu 14:28*
Lord, as ye
Thou shalt t. tithe all the *De 14:22*
increase
you shall surely tithe (A) *De 14:22*
will deal kindly and t. with *Jos 2:14*
thee
kindly and faithfully (B)(R) *Jos 2:14*
T. the Lord hath delivered *Jos 2:24*
into
if ye have done t. and *J'g 9:16*
sincerely, in
sincerely and honorably (A) *J'g 9:16;*
     9:19
ye then have dealt t. and *J'g 9:19*
sincerely
acted in good faith and honor *J'g 9:19*
(R)
but t. as the Lord liveth, and *1Sa 20:3*
as thy
For t. my words shall not be *Job 36:4*
false
T. my soul waiteth upon God *Ps 62:1*
T. God is good to Israel, even *Ps 73:1*
O Lord, t. I am thy servant; *Ps 116:16*
I am
they that deal t. are his *Pr 12:22*
delight
T. the light is sweet, and a *Ec 11:7*
pleasant

T. in vain is salvation hoped   *Jer 3:23*
for
t. in the Lord is the   *Jer 3:23*
salvation of
but I said, *T.* this is a grief,   *Jer 10:19*
and I
that the Lord hath *t.* sent   *Jer 28:9*
him
hath kept my judgments, to   *Eze 18:9*
deal *t.*
t. I am full of power by the   *Mic 3:8*
spirit
The harvest *t.* is plenteous,   *M't 9:37*
but the labourers
truly (A)   *M't 14:33;*
    M'k 12:32; Lu 9:27; 12:44; 21:3
truly (R)   *M't 14:33;*
M'k 12:14, 32; Lu 4:25, 27; 12:44; 21:3;
         Ac 4:27; 10:34
Elias *t.* shall first come, and   *M't 17:11*
saying, *T.* this was the Son   *M't 27:54*
of God
The spirit *t.* is ready, but   *M'k 14:38*
the flesh
T. this man was the Son of   *M'k 15:39*
God
Really this man was the Son   *M'k 15:39*
of God (A)
The harvest *t.* is great, but the   *Lu 10:2*
T. ye bear witness that ye   *Lu 11:48*
allow
teachest the way of God *t.*   *Lu 20:21*
teach way of God sincerely   *Lu 20:21*
(B)
t. the Son of man goeth, as it   *Lu 22:22*
thy husband: in that saidst   *Joh 4:18*
thou *t.*
many other signs *t.* did Jesus   *Joh 20:30*
For John *t.* baptized with water   *Ac 1:5*
For Moses *t.* said unto the   *Ac 3:22*
fathers
The prison *t.* found we shut   *Ac 5:23*
with
found the prison securely   *Ac 5:23*
locked (B)
T. the signs of an apostle   *2Co 12:2*
were
they *t.* were many priests,   *Heb 7:23*
because
And *t.* if they had been   *Heb 11:15*
mindful of
t. our fellowship is   *1Jo 1:3*
with Father

TRUMP

twinkling of an eye, at the   *1Co 15:52*
last *t.*
archangel, and with the *t.* of   *1Th 4:16*
God

TRUMPET

when the *t.* soundeth long,   *Ex 19:13*
they
the voice of the *t.* exceeding   *Ex 19:16*
loud
the voice of the *t.* sounded   *Ex 19:19*
long
lightnings, and the noise of   *Ex 20:18*
the *t.*
cause the *t.* of the jubile to   *Le 25:9*
sound
make the *t.* sound throughout   *Le 25:9*
all
And if they blow but with one   *Nu 10:4*
t.
when ye hear the sound of the   *Jos 6:5*
t.
people heard the sound of the   *Jos 6:20*
t.
that he blew a *t.* in the   *J'g 3:27*
mountain
upon Gideon, and he blew a *t.*   *J'g 6:34*
he put a *t.* in every man's   *J'g 7:16*
hand
When I blow with a *t.* I and all   *J'g 7:18*
Saul blew the *t.* throughout   *1Sa 13:3*
all the
So Joab blew a *t.* and all the   *2Sa 2:28*
people
and with the sound of the *t.*   *2Sa 6:15*
soon as ye hear the sound of   *2Sa 15:10*
the *t.*
Joab blew the *t.* and the   *2Sa 18:16*
people
blew a *t.* and said, We have   *2Sa 20:1*
no part
he blew a *t.* and they retired   *2Sa 20:22*
from

blow ye with the *t.* and say,   *1Ki 1:34*
God
they blew the *t.;* and all the   *1Ki 1:39*
people
when Joab heard the sound   *1Ki 1:41*
of the *t.*
he that sounded the *t.* was by   *Ne 4:18*
me
place, ye hear the sound of   *Ne 4:20*
the *t.*
he that it is the sound of the   *Job 39:24*
t.
the Lord with the sound of a *t.*   *Ps 47:5*
Blow up the *t.* in the new   *Ps 81:3*
moon, in
Praise him with the sound of   *Ps 150:3*
the *t.*
and when he bloweth a *t.* hear   *Isa 18:3*
ye
that the great *t.* shall be   *Isa 27:13*
blown
spare not, lift up thy voice   *Isa 58:1*
like a *t.*
and say, Blow ye the *t.* in the   *Jer 4:5*
land
heard, O my soul, the sound   *Jer 4:19*
of the *t.*
and hear the sound of the *t.*   *Jer 4:21*
and blow the *t.* in Tekoa, and   *Jer 6:1*
set up
Hearken to the sound of the *t.*   *Jer 6:17*
war, nor hear the sound of   *Jer 42:14*
the *t.*
blow the *t.* among the   *Jer 51:27*
nations
They have blown the *t.* even   *Eze 7:14*
to
blow the *t.* and warn the   *Eze 33:3*
people
heareth the sound of the *t.*   *Eze 33:4*
He heard the sound of the *t.*   *Eze 33:5*
if the watchman blow not   *Eze 33:6*
the *t.*
in Gibeah, and the *t.* in Ramah   *Ho 5:8*
Set the *t.* to thy mouth. He   *Ho 8:1*
shall
Blow ye the *t.* in Zion, and   *Joe 2:1*
sound
Blow the *t.* in Zion, sanctify a   *Joe 2:15*
fast
and with the sound of the *t.*   *Am 2:2*
Shall a *t.* be blown in the city   *Am 3:6*
A day of *t.* and alarm   *Zep 1:16*
against the
and the Lord God shall blow   *Zec 9:14*
the *t.*
alms, do not sound a *t.* before   *M't 6:2*
thee
angels with a great sound   *M't 24:31*
of a *t.*
if the *t.* give an uncertain   *1Co 14:8*
sound
for the *t.* shall sound, and   *1Co 15:52*
the dead
And the sound of a *t.* and   *Heb 12:19*
the voice
behind me a great voice, as of   *Re 1:10*
a *t.*
as it were of a *t.* talking with   *Re 4:1*
me
voices of the *t.* of the three   *Re 8:13*
angels
to the sixth angel which had   *Re 9:14*
the *t.*

TRUMPETER

hire a *t.* (P)   *M't 6:2*

TRUMPETERS

the princes and the *t.* by the   *2Ki 11:14*
king
as the *t.* and singers were as   *2Ch 5:13*
one
singers sang, and the *t.*   *2Ch 28:28*
sounded
musicians and of pipers and   *Re 18:22*
t.

TRUMPETS

a sabbath a memorial of   *Le 23:24*
blowing of *t.*
Make thee two *t.* of silver; of   *Nu 10:2*
the priests, shall blow with   *Nu 10:8*
the *t.*
ye shall blow an alarm with   *Nu 10:9*
the *t.*

blow with the *t.* over your   *Nu 10:10*
burnt
it is a day of blowing the *t.*   *Nu 29:1*
unto you
and the *t.* to blow in his hand   *Nu 31:6*
shall bear before the ark seven   *Jos 6:4*
t.
the priests shall blow with the   *Jos 6:4*
t.
priests bear seven *t.* of rams'   *Jos 6:6*
horns
seven priests bearing the seven   *Jos 6:8*
t.
the Lord, and blew with the *t.*   *Jos 6:8*
the priests that blew with the   *Jos 6:9*
t.
going on, and blowing with the   *Jos 6:9*
t.
And seven priests bearing   *Jos 6:13*
seven *t.*
continually, and blew with the   *Jos 6:13*
t.
going on, and blowing with   *Jos 6:13*
the *t.*
when the priests blew with   *Jos 6:16;*
the *t.*   *6:20*
victuals in their hand, and their   *J'g 7:8*
t.
blow ye the *t.* also on every   *J'g 7:18*
side of
and they blew the *t.* and brake   *J'g 7:19*
the three companies blew the   *J'g 7:20*
t.
the *t.* in their right hands to   *J'g 7:20*
blow
And the three hundred blew   *J'g 7:22*
the *t.*
blew with *t.* saying, Jehu is   *2Ki 9:13*
king
of the land rejoiced, and   *2Ki 11:14*
blew with
snuffers, basons, *t.,* any   *2Ki 12:13*
vessels of
and with cymbals, and with   *1Ch 13:8*
t.
did blow with the *t.* before   *1Ch 15:24*
the ark
sound of the cornet, and   *1Ch 15:28*
with *t.*
priests with *t.* continually   *1Ch 16:6*
before
with *t.* and cymbals for   *1Ch 16:42*
those that
twenty priests sounding with   *2Ch 5:12*
t.
they lifted up their voice   *2Ch 5:13*
with the *t.*
the priests sounded *t.* before   *2Ch 7:6*
them
his priests with sounding *t.*   *2Ch 13:12*
to cry
and the priests sounded   *2Ch 13:14*
with the *t.*
with shouting, and with *t.,*   *2Ch 15:14*
and with
harps and *t.* unto the house   *2Ch 20:28*
of the
the princes and the *t.,* by   *2Ch 23:13*
the king
land rejoiced, and sounded   *2Ch 23:13*
with *t.*
of David, and the priests   *2Ch 29:26*
with the *t.*
the song began also with   *2Ch 29:27*
the *t.*
the priests in their apparel   *Ezr 3:10*
with *t.*
certain of the priests' sons   *Ne 12:35*
with *t.*
Zechariah, and Hananiah,   *Ne 12:41*
with *t.*
He saith among the *t.,* Ha,   *Job 39:25*
ha; and
With *t.* and sound of cornet   *Ps 98:6*
make
and to them were given seven *t.*   *Re 8:2*
the seven *t.* prepared   *Re 8:6*
themselves to

TRUNKS

linen *t.* (B)   *Ex 28:42;*
     39:28; Le 6:10; 16:4

TRUST

and put your *t.* in my shadow   *J'g 9:15*
if in good faith (A)   *J'g 9:15*

Take refuge (B)   J'g 9:15;
Ps 2:12; 5:11; 11:1; 16:1; 17:7; 18:2;
31:1, 19; 34:22; 36:7; 61:4; 71:1; 73:28;
144:2; Pr 30:5; Isa 14:32; 30:2; 51:13;
Zep 3:12
take refuge in (E)   J'g 9:15;
Ru 2:12; 2Sa 22:3, 31; Ps 2:12; 5:11;
7:1; 11:1; 16:1; 17:7; 18:2, 30; 25:20;
31:1, 19; 34:22; 36:7; 37:40; 61:4; 62:8;
64:10; 71:1; 73:28; 91:2, 4; 118:8-9;
141:8; 144:2; Pr 30:5; Isa 14:32; 30:2-3;
57:13; Na 1:7; Zep 3:12
take refuge (R)   J'g 9:15;
Ru 2:12; 2Sa 22:3, 31; Ps 2:12; 5:11;
7:1; 11:1; 16:1; 17:7; 18:2, 30; 25:20;
31:1, 19; 34:22; 36:7; 37:40; 64:10;
71:1; 73:28; 91:2, 4; 118:8-9; 141:8;
144:2; Pr 30:5; Isa 14:32; 30:2; 57:13;
Na 1:7; Zep 3:12
put their t. in him (B)(R)   J'g 9:26
whose wings thou art come to   Ru 2:12
t.
come to shelter (B)   Ru 2:12
God of my rock; in him will   2Sa 22:3
I t.
a buckler to all them that t.   2Sa 22:31
in him
Now on whom dost thou t.   2Ki 18:20
that
rely (A)   2Ki 18:20; 18:21; Ph'p 3:4
confidence (B)   2Ki 18:20;
18:30; Job 4:18
rely (R)   2Ki 18:20;
18:21-22, 24, 30; Isa 36:5-7, 9, 15; 59:4;
2Co 1:9
of Egypt unto all that t. on   2Ki 18:21
him
me, We t. in the Lord our   2Ki 18:22
God
put thy t. on Egypt for   2Ki 18:24
chariots and
depend on Egypt (B)   2Ki 18:24
Hezekiah make you t. in   2Ki 18:30
the Lord
because they put their t. in   1Ch 5:20
him
relied on (A)   1Ch 5:20
Whereon do ye t. that ye   2Ch 32:10
abide in
he put no t. in his servants;   Job 4:18
and his
whose t. shall be a spider's   Job 8:14
web
he slay me, yet will I t. in   Job 13:15
him
I keep hoping (B)   Job 13:15
hope (E)   Job 13:15
hope (R)   Job 13:15;
Isa 51:5; Mt 12:21; Joh 5:45; Ro 15:12,
24; 1Co 16:7; 2Co 1:10, 13; 5:11; 13:6;
Ph'p 2:19; 2Ti 4:10; 6:17; 2Jo 12; 3Jo 14
he putteth no t. in his   Job 15:15
saints; yea
not him that is deceived t.   Job 15:31
in vanity
him; therefore t. thou in him   Job 35:14
Wilt thou t. him, because his   Job 39:11
will you depend on him (B)   Job 39:11
all they that put their t. in him   Ps 2:12
and put your t. in the Lord   Ps 4:5
that put their t. in thee rejoice   Ps 5:11
my God, in thee do I put my t.   Ps 7:1
thy name will put their t. in   Ps 9:10
thee
In the Lord put I my t.: how   Ps 11:1
say
O God: for in thee do I put   Ps 16:1
my t.
them which put their t. in thee   Ps 17:7
God, my strength, in whom I   Ps 18:2
will t.
buckler to all those that t. in   Ps 18:30
him
Some t. in chariots, and some   Ps 20:7
some boast of chariots (R)   Ps 20:7
O my God, I t. in thee: let me   Ps 25:2
ashamed; for I put my t. in   Ps 25:20
thee
In thee, O Lord, do I put my   Ps 31:1
t. let
lying vanities: but I t. in the   Ps 31:6
Lord
wrought for them that t. in   Ps 31:19
thee
none of them that t. in him   Ps 34:22
shall
children of men put their t.   Ps 36:7
under

T. in the Lord, and do good;   Ps 37:3
so
t. also in him; and he shall   Ps 37:5
bring it
save them, because they t. in   Ps 37:40
him
it, and fear, and shall t. in the   Ps 40:3
Lord
man that maketh the Lord his   Ps 40:4
t.
For I will not t. in my bow,   Ps 44:6
neither
They that t. in their wealth   Ps 49:6
I t. in the mercy of God for   Ps 52:8
ever and
half their days; but I will t.   Ps 55:23
in thee
time I am afraid, I will t. in   Ps 56:3
thee
have confidence (B)   Ps 56:3;
2Co 3:4; Ph'p 2:24; 3:4
his word, in God I have put my   Ps 56:4
t.
In God have I put my t.; I   Ps 56:11
will not
I will t. in the covert of thy   Ps 61:4
wings
T. in him at all times; ye   Ps 62:8
people
T. not in oppression, and   Ps 62:10
become
in the Lord, and shall t. in   Ps 64:10
him
In thee, O Lord, do I put my   Ps 71:1
t. let
thou art my t. from my youth   Ps 71:5
I have put my t. in the Lord   Ps 73:28
God
fortress: my God; in him will   Ps 91:2
I t.
and under his wings shalt thou   Ps 91:4
t.
O Israel t. thou in the Lord: Ps 115:9
he is
O house of Aaron, t. in the   Ps 115:10
Lord
Ye that fear the Lord, t. in   Ps 115:11
the Lord
It is better to t. in the Lord   Ps 118:8;
than   118:9
better to rely upon the Lord   Ps 118:8;
(B)   118:9
reproacheth me: for I t. in   Ps 119:42
thy word
They that t. in the Lord shall   Ps 125:1
be as
in thee is my t.; leave not my   Ps 141:8
soul
in thee do I t.: cause me to   Ps 143:8
know
my shield, and he in whom I   Ps 144:2
t.
Put not your t. in princes nor   Ps 146:3
T. in the Lord with all thine   Pr 3:5
heart
stronghold they t. (A)(B)(R)   Pr 21:22
That thy t. may be in the   Pr 22:19
Lord, I
t. in faithless man (B)(R)   Pr 25:19
he that putteth his t. in the   Pr 28:25
Lord
whoso putteth his t. in the   Pr 29:25
Lord shall
unto them that put their t. in   Pr 30:5
him
her husband doth safely t. in   Pr 31:11
her
I will t. and not be afraid: for   Isa 12:2
the poor of his people shall   Isa 14:32
t. in it
T. ye in the Lord for ever: for   Isa 26:4
and to t. in the shadow of   Isa 30:2
Egypt
the t. in the shadow of Egypt   Isa 30:3
your
shelter in the shadow of   Isa 30:3
Egypt (R)
t. in oppression   Isa 30:12
relied on them (B)   Isa 30:12
and t. in chariots, because they   Isa 31:1
now on whom dost thou t.   Isa 36:5
that thou
rely (B)   Isa 36:5; 36:7; 2Ch 1:9
king of Egypt to all that t. in   Isa 36:6
him
to me, We t. in the Lord, our   Isa 36:7
God
put thy t. on Egypt for   Isa 36:9
chariots and
put your reliance in (A)   Isa 36:9

T. ye not in lying words, The   Jer 7:4
temple
ye t. in lying words, that   Jer 7:8
cannot
wherein ye t. and unto the   Jer 7:14
place
and t. ye not in any brother   Jer 9:4
thou makest this people to t.   Jer 28:15
in a lie
and he caused you to t. in   Jer 29:31
a lie
thou hast put thy t. in me,   Jer 39:18
saith the
Pharaoh, and all them that t.   Jer 46:25
in him
alive; and let thy widows t. in   Jer 49:11
me
thou didst t. in thine own   Eze 16:15
beauty
if he t. to his own   Eze 33:13
righteousness
because thou didst t. in thy   Ho 10:13
way
and t. in the mountain of   Am 6:1
Samaria
T. ye not in a friend, put ye   Mic 7:5
not
he knoweth them that t. in him   Na 1:7
knows those who commit   Na 1:7
themselves to him (B)
shall t. in the name of the   Zep 3:12
Lord
in his name shall the   M't 12:21
Gentiles t.
set their hopes in him (A)   M't 12:21
nations hope in him (B)   M't 12:21
Gentiles hope (E)   M't 12:21; Ro 15:12
hope (N)   M't 12:21;
Joh 5:45; Ro 15:12, 24; 1Co 16:7;
2Co 1:10; 5:11; 13:6; Ph'p 2:10, 24;
1Ti 4:10; 6:17; Ph'm 22; 2Jo 12; 3Jo 14
hope (P)   M't 12:21;
Ro 15:12, 24; 1Co 16:7; Ph'p 2:19, 24;
Ph'm 22; 2Jo 12; 3Jo 14
he ought to t. (A)   M't 13:21
for them that t. in riches to   M'k 10:24
enter
commit to your t. the true   Lu 16:11
riches
you, even Moses, in whom ye   Joh 5:45
t.
Moses in whom ye are hoping   Joh 5:45
(B)(E)
confidence (P)   Joh 5:45;
2Co 3:4; Ph'p 3:4; 1Ti 6:17
in him shall the Gentiles t.   Ro 15:12
in him shall Gentiles hope   Ro 15:12
(A)(B)
for I t. to see you in my   Ro 15:24
journey
hope (A)   Ro 15:24;
1Co 16:7;   2Co 1:13;   5:11;   13:6;
Ph'p 2:19; 2Jo 12; 3Jo 14
hope (B)   Ro 15:24;
1Co 16:7;   2Co 1:10;   5:11;   13:6;
Ph'p 2:19;   1Ti 4:10;   6:17;   Ph'm 22;
2Jo 12;   3Jo 14
hope (E)   Ro 15:24;
1Co 16:7;   2Co 1:13;   5:11;   13:6;
Ph'p 2:19; 2Jo 12; 3Jo 14
I am discharging a t. (N)   1Co 9:17
but I t. to tarry a while with   1Co 16:7
you
that we should not t. in   2Co 1:9
ourselves
reliance (N)   2Co 1:9; 3:4
in whom we t. that he will   2Co 1:10
yet
set our hope (A)(E)   2Co 1:10;
1Ti 6:17
I t. ye shall acknowledge   2Co 1:13
even to
such is have we through Christ   2Co 3:4
to
such is the reliance and   2Co 3:4
confidence (A)
confidence (E)   2Co 3:4; Ph'p 3:4
confidence, confident (R)   2Co 3:4;
10:7; Ph'p 3:4
I t. also are made manifest in   2Co 5:11
If any man t. to himself that   2Co 10:7
we are
he
confident (A)   2Co 10:7; Ph'p 2:24
confident of his belonging to   2Co 10:7
Christ (B)
I t. that ye shall know that   2Co 13:6
But I t. in the Lord Jesus to   Ph'p 2:19
send

I *t.* in the Lord that I also   *Ph'p 2:24*
myself
whereof he might *t.* in the   *Ph'p 3:4*
flesh
to be put in *t.* with the gospel   *1Th 2:4*
which was committed to my *t.*   *1Ti 1:11*
because we *t.* in the living   *1Ti 4:10*
God
our hope set in the living God   *1Ti 4:10*
(E)
nor *t.* in uncertain riches, but   *1Ti 6:17*
that which is committed to   *1Ti 6:20*
thy *t.*
guard the deposit (B)   *1Ti 6:20*
for I *t.* that through your   *Ph'm 22*
prayers
again, I will put my *t.* in him   *Heb 2:13*
we *t.* we have a good   *Heb 13:18*
conscience
t. God with inward   *Jas 1:6*
reservations (P)
but I *t.* to come unto you, and   *2Jo 12*
But I *t.* I shall shortly see thee   *3Jo 14*

TRUSTED

gods, their rock in whom   *De 32:37*
they *t.*
took refuge (A)(B)(E)(R)   *De 32:37*
Sihon *t.* not Israel to pass   *J'g 11:20*
through
they *t.* unto the liers in wait   *J'g 20:36*
had confidence in (B)   *J'g 20:36.*
He *t.* in the Lord God of   *2Ki 18:5*
Israel; so
in which he *t.* (A)(E)(R)   *Job 18:14*
But I have *t.* in thy mercy; my   *Ps 13:5*
Our father *t.* in thee: they *t.*   *Ps 22:4*
they *t.* in thee, and were not   *Ps 22:5*
He *t.* on the Lord that he   *Ps 22:8*
would
he committed his cause to the   *Ps 22:8*
Lord (B)
I have *t.* also in the Lord;   *Ps 26:1*
therefore
my heart *t.* in him, and I am   *Ps 28:7*
helped
But I *t.* in thee, O Lord: I   *Ps 31:14*
said
because we have *t.* in his   *Ps 33:21*
holy name
own familiar friend, in whom   *Ps 41:9*
I *t.*
on whom I relied (B)   *Ps 41:9*
but *t.* in the abundance of his   *Ps 52:7*
riches
in God, and *t.* not in his   *Ps 78:22*
salvation
For thou hast *t.* in thy   *Isa 47:10*
wickedness
felt secure in wickedness   *Isa 47:10*
(B)(R)
forgotten me, and *t.* in   *Jer 13:25*
falsehood
because thou hast *t.* in thy   *Jer 48:7*
works
that *t.* in her treasures, saying   *Jer 49:4*
his servants that *t.* in him   *Da 3:28*
she *t.* not in the Lord; she   *Zep 3:2*
drew
He *t.* in God; let him deliver   *M't 27:43*
him
him all his armour wherein   *Lu 11:22*
he *t.*
he relied (A)(R)   *Lu 11:22*
he depended (B)   *Lu 11:22*
he pinned his faith (P)   *Lu 11:22*
unto certain which *t.* in   *Lu 18:9*
themselves
confiding in their own   *Lu 18:9*
righteousness (B)
confident in their own   *Lu 18:9*
goodness (P)
were sure of their own   *Lu 18:9*
goodness (R)
we *t.* that it had been he   *Lu 24:21*
which
hoping he was the one   *Lu 24:21*
(A)(P)(R)
we had hopes (B)(E)(R)   *Lu 24:21*
of his glory, who first *t.* in   *Eph 1:12*
Christ
first put our confidence in   *Eph 1:12*
(A)
put our hope in Christ   *Eph 1:12*
(B)(E)(N)(R)
In whom ye also *t.* after that   *Eph 1:13*
ye
adhered to and relied on (A)   *Eph 1:13*

holy women also, who *t.* in   *1Pe 3:5*
God
women of old who hoped in   *1Pe 3:5*
God (A)(B)(E)(R)
women who fixed hopes on him   *1Pe 3:5*
(N)

TRUSTEDST

walls come down, wherein   *De 28:52*
thou *t.*
thy fenced cities, wherein thou   *Jer 5:17*
t.
the land of peace, wherein   *Jer 12:5*
thou *t.*

TRUSTEES

under guardians and *t.*   *Ga 4:2*
(B)(N)(P)(R)

TRUSTEESHIP

entrusted with sacred *t.* (A)   *1Co 9:17*

TRUSTEST

confidence is this wherein   *2Ki 18:19*
thou *t.*
thou *t.* upon the staff of this   *2Ki 18:21*
bruised
God in whom thou *t.*   *2Ki 19:10*
deceive thee
confidence is this wherein   *Isa 36:4*
thou *t.*
thou *t.* in the staff of this   *Isa 36:6*
broken
Let not thy God, in whom   *Isa 37:10*
thou *t.*
those in whom thou *t.* (E)(R)   *Jer 2:37*

TRUSTETH

he *t.* that he can draw up   *Job 40:23*
Jordan
he is confident   *Job 40:23*
(A)(B)(E)(R)
For the king *t.* in the Lord   *Ps 21:7*
but he that *t.* in the Lord,   *Ps 32:10*
mercy
blessed is the man that *t.* in him   *Ps 34:8*
takes refuge in (E)(R)   *Ps 34:8; 57:1*
for my soul *t.* in thee: yea, in   *Ps 57:1*
soul takes refuge in (A)(B)   *Ps 57:1*
blessed is the man that *t.* in   *Ps 84:12*
thee
save thy servant that *t.* in thee   *Ps 86:2*
so is every one that *t.* in them   *Ps 115:8;*
   135:18
He that *t.* in his riches shall   *Pr 11:28*
fall
whoso *t.* in the Lord, happy   *Pr 16:20*
is he
He that *t.* in his own heart   *Pr 28:26*
is a fool
on thee: because he *t.* in thee   *Isa 26:3*
commits himself to you, leans   *Isa 26:3*
on you, and hopes confidently
in you (A)
Cursed be the man that *t.* in   *Jer 17:5*
man
Blessed is the man that *t.*   *Jer 17:7*
in Lord
the maker of his work *t.*   *Hab 2:18*
therein
indeed, and desolate, *t.* in God   *1Ti 5:5*
fixed her hope in God   *1Ti 5:5*
(A)(B)(E)(N)(P)(R)

TRUSTING

his heart is fixed, *t.* in the   *Ps 112:7*
Lord
t. you and believing (P)   *2Co 1:15*
t. me enough (P)   *1Ti 1:12*

TRUSTWORTHY

we are *t.* (B)   *Ge 42:34*
a *t.* man (A)   *1Ki 1:42*
removeth the speech of the   *Job 12:20*
t. (S)
God is *t.* (A)   *2Co 1:18*
t. is the saying (B)   *1Ti 3:1*
honest and *t.* (N)(P)   *Tit 2:10*
she considered God *t.* and   *Heb 11:11*
true to his word (A)(B)(P)

TRUSTY

removeth away the speech of   *Job 12:20*
the *t.*

TRUTH

my master of his mercy and   *Ge 24:27*
his *t.*
loving kindness and   *Ge 24:27*
steadfastness (B)
faithfulness (R)   *Ge 24:27;*
   32:10; Ex 34:6; De 32:4; Jos 24:14;
   2Sa 2:6; 15:20; 1Ki 2:4; 3:6; 2Ki 20:3;
   Ps 25:10; 26:3; 30:9; 33:4; 40:10-11;
   54:5; 57:3, 10; 61:7; 71:22; 85:10-11;
   86:15; 89:14, 49; 91:4; 98:3; 100:5;
   108:4; 111:8; 117:2; 119:30; 138:2;
   Pr 3:3; 14:22; 16:6; 20:28; Isa 16:5; 38:3,
   18-19; Ho 4:1; Mic 7:20; Zec 8:8
of all the *t.* which thou hast   *Ge 32:10*
shewed
mercies, lovingkindnesses,   *Ge 32:10*
faithfulness (A)
whether there be any *t.* in you   *Ge 42:16*
such as fear God, men of *t.*   *Ex 18:21*
hating
honest (B)   *Ex 18:21*
trustworthy (R)   *Ex 18:21*
and abundant in goodness and   *Ex 34:6*
t.
and, behold, if it be *t.* and the   *De 13:14*
thing
true and certain (A)   *De 13:14*
faithfulness (B)   *De 13:14;*
   Ps 33:4; 40:10; 54:5; 57:10; 71:22;
   89:14, 49; 91:4; 96:13; 98:3; 100:5;
   108:4; 111:9; 119:30; 138:2; Pr 3:3;
   16:6; 20:28; Isa 16:5; 38:18-19;
   Mic 7:20; 9:27; Lu 12:44; 21:3
a God of *t.* and without   *De 32:4*
iniquity
God of faithfulness (A)(E)   *De 32:4*
serve him in *t.* with all your   *1Sa 12:24*
heart
serve him faithfully (A)(R)   *1Sa 12:24*
faithfully (B)   *1Sa 12:24*
   2Ki 20:3
Of a *t.* women have been   *1Sa 21:5*
kept
shew kindness and *t.* unto you   *2Sa 2:6*
faithfulness (A)   *2Sa 2:6;*
   15:20; Ps 33:4; 54:5; 61:7; 89:49;
   Pr 12:22; Isa 38:18; 39:8; Ho 4:1
thy words are *t.* (A)(B)(E)   *2Sa 7:28;*
   1Ki 22:16; Ps 119:160
mercy and *t.* be with thee   *2Sa 15:20*
word of the Lord in thy   *1Ki 17:24*
mouth is *t.*
nothing but the *t.*   *1Ki 22:16*
(A)(B)(E)(R)
Of a *t.* Lord, the kings of   *2Ki 19:17*
Assyria
It is true (A)   *2Ki 19:17;*
   Job 9:2; Isa 37:18
truly (B)   *2Ki 19:17;*
   M'k 12:14; Lu 4:25; 3Jo 1
how I have walked before   *2Ki 20:3*
thee in *t.*
good, if peace and *t.* be in   *2Ki 20:19*
my days
peace and security (R)   *2Ki 20:19;*
   Isa 39:8; Jer 33:6
that thou say nothing but   *2Ch 18:15*
the *t.*
and right and *t.* before the   *2Ch 31:20*
Lord
right and faithful before God   *2Ch 31:20*
(E)
with words of peace and *t.*   *Es 9:30*
I know it is so of a *t.*: but   *Job 9:2*
how
and speaketh the *t.* in his heart   *Ps 15:2*
Lead me in thy *t.* and teach   *Ps 25:5*
me
paths of the Lord are mercy   *Ps 25:10*
and *t.*
redeemed me, O Lord, of *t.*   *Ps 31:5*
the faithful God (R)   *Ps 31:5*
because of *t.* and meekness   *Ps 45:4*
thou desirest *t.* in the inward   *Ps 51:6*
parts
send forth his mercy and his *t.*   *Ps 57:3*
be displayed because of the *t.*   *Ps 60:4*
O prepare mercy and *t.*   *Ps 61:7*
hear me, in the *t.* of thy   *Ps 69:13*
salvation
mercy and *t.* are met together   *Ps 85:10*
T. shall spring out of the earth   *Ps 85:11*
thou art plenteous in mercy   *Ps 86:15*
and *t.*
mercy and *t.* shall go before   *Ps 89:14*
thy face
his *t.* shall be thy shield and   *Ps 91:4*
buckler

he shall judge the people with *Ps 96:13*
his *t.*
he remembered his mercy and *Ps 98:3*
his *t.*
t. endureth to all generations *Ps 100:5;*
    117:2
are *t.* and justice (A)(E) *Ps 111:7*
I have chosen the way of *t.* *Ps 119:30*
and thy law is the *t.* *Ps 119:142;*
    119:151
thy word is *t.* (A)(B)(E)(R) *Ps 119:160*
Lord is God who keepeth *t.* *Ps 146:6*
for ever
keep faith forever (B)(R) *Ps 146:6*
let not mercy and *t.* forsake *Pr 3:3*
thee
my mouth shall speak *t.* *Pr 8:7*
he that speaks *t.* sheweth *Pr 12:17*
righteousness
the lip of *t.* shall be *Pr 12:19*
established for ever
truthful lips be established *Pr 12:19*
forever (A)(B)(R)
mercy and *t.* be to them that *Pr 14:22*
devise good
by mercy and *t.* iniquity is *Pr 16:6*
purged
mercy and *t.* preserve the *Pr 20:28*
king
make thee know certainty of *Pr 22:21*
the *t.* thou mightest answer
the words of *t.*
buy the *t.* and sell it not, also *Pr 23:23*
wisdom
what was written were words *Ec 12:10*
of *t.*
thy counsels are faithfulness *Isa 25:1*
and *t.*
nation which keepeth *t.* may *Isa 26:2*
enter in
keeps faith and troth with *Isa 26:2*
God (A)
keeps faith with God (E)(R) *Isa 26:2*
he shall bring forth judgment *Isa 42:3*
unto *t.*
or let them hear, and say, It is *Isa 43:9*
t.
nor any pleadeth for *t.* they *Isa 59:4*
speak lies
for *t.* is fallen in the street *Isa 59:14*
t. faileth, and he that *Isa 59:15*
departeth from evil
if there be any that seeketh the *Jer 5:1*
t.
O Lord, are not thine eyes *Jer 5:3*
upon the *t.*
t. is perished and cut off from *Jer 7:28*
mouth
not valiant for the *t.* on the *Jer 9:3*
earth
they will deceive and will not *Jer 9:5*
speak the *t.*
revealed abundance of peace *Jer 33:6*
and *t.*
king of heaven, all whose *Da 4:37*
works are *t.*
whose works are faithful and *Da 4:37*
right (A)
I asked him the *t.* of all this *Da 7:16;*
    7:19
and it cast down the *t.* to the *Da 8:12*
ground
which is noted in the *Da 10:21*
scripture of *t.*
and now will I shew thee the *Da 11:2*
t. Behold
there is not *t.* nor mercy in the *Ho 4:1*
land
thou wilt perform the *t.* to *Mic 7:20*
Jacob
Jerusalem shall be called a city *Zec 8:3*
of *t.*
the faithful city (R) *Zec 8:3*
speak ye every man the *t.* *Zec 8:16;*
execute the judgment of *t.* *Eph 4:25*
therefore love the *t.* and *Zec 8:19*
peace
the law of *t.* was in his mouth *Mal 2:6*
t. Lord, yet dogs eat the *M't 15:27*
crumbs
woman fearing told him all *M'k 5:33*
the *t.*
told him the whole story (P) *M'k 5:33*
but teachest the way of God *M'k 12:14*
in *t.*
Well, Master, thou hast said *M'k 12:32*
the *t.*
you are absolutely right *M'k 12:32*
(P)

of the Father, full of grace *Joh 1:14*
and *t.*
grace and *t.* came by Jesus *Joh 1:17*
Christ
he that doeth *t.* cometh to the *Joh 3:21*
light
the honest man comes to the *Joh 3:21*
light (N)
does what is true (R) *Joh 3:21*
the Father in spirit and in *t.* *Joh 4:23*
must worship him in spirit *Joh 4:24*
and in *t.*
worship in spirit and in *Joh 4:24*
reality (P)
and he bare witness unto the *Joh 5:33*
t.
This is of a *t.* that prophet *Joh 6:14*
said, Of a *t.* this is the *Joh 7:40*
Prophet
And ye shall know the *t.* and *Joh 8:32*
and the *t.* shall make you free *Joh 8:32*
a man that hath told you the *Joh 8:40*
t.
beginning, and abode not in *Joh 8:44*
the *t.*
because there is no *t.* in him *Joh 8:44*
because I tell you the *t.* ye *Joh 8:45*
believe
And if I say the *t.* why do ye *Joh 8:46*
not
I am the way, the *t.,* and *Joh 14:6*
the life
Even the Spirit of *t.,* whom *Joh 14:17*
the
the Father, even the Spirit *Joh 15:26*
of *t.*
Nevertheless I tell you the *t.* *Joh 16:7*
when he, the Spirit of *t.* is *Joh 16:13*
come, he
he will guide you into all *t.* *Joh 16:13*
for he
Sanctify them through thy *t.:* *Joh 17:17*
thy word is *t.* *Joh 17:17*
might be sanctified through *Joh 17:19*
the *t.*
I should bear witness unto *Joh 18:37*
the *t.*
Every one that is of the *t.* *Joh 18:37*
heareth
Pilate saith unto him, What *Joh 18:38*
is *t.*
but I speak forth the words *Ac 26:25*
of *t.*
who hold the *t.* in *Ro 1:18*
unrighteousness
who changed the *t.* of God *Ro 1:25*
into a lie
the judgment of God is *Ro 2:2*
according to *t.*
rests in all fairness (B) *Ro 2:2*
but unto them that do not obey *Ro 2:8*
the *t.*
which hast the form of the *t.* *Ro 2:20*
in the law
for if the *t.* of God hath more *Ro 3:7*
abounded
I say the *t.* in Christ, I lie not *Ro 9:1*
minister of circumcision for *t.* *Ro 15:8*
of God
God's truthfulness (R) *Ro 15:8*
with the unleavened bread of *1Co 5:8*
t.
know every hidden *t.* (N) *1Co 13:2*
utters secret *t.* (A) *1Co 14:2*
by manifestation of the *t.* *2Co 4:2*
even so our boasting I made *2Co 7:14*
is found a *t.*
as the *t.* of Christ is in me *2Co 11:10*
none shall stop
I shall not be a fool, for I *2Co 12:6*
will say the *t.*
we can do nothing against *t.* *2Co 13:8*
but for the *t.*
t. of the gospel might continue *Ga 2:5*
walked not according to *t.* of *Ga 2:14*
the gospel
that ye should not obey the *t.* *Ga 3:1;*
    5:7
your enemy, because I tell you *Ga 4:16*
the *t.*
because I am sincere with you *Ga 4:16*
(B)
speaking the *t.* in love, may *Eph 4:15*
grow
been taught by him as *t.* is in *Eph 4:21*
Jesus
for the fruit of the Spirit is in *Eph 5:9*
all *t.*
stand having loins girt about *Eph 6:14*
with *t.*

tightened the belt of *t.* *Eph 6:14*
(A)(B)
the secret *t.* (N) *Eph 6:19*
they received not love of *t.* *2Th 2:10*
might be damned, who *2Th 2:12*
believed not *t.*
chosen to salvation, thro' *2Th 2:13*
belief of *t.*
to come to the knowledge of *1Ti 2:4*
the *t.*
I speak the *t.* in Christ and lie *1Ti 2:7*
not
in faith and *t.* *1Ti 2:7*
(A)(B)(E)(P)(R)
deep *t.* of our faith (B)(N) *1Ti 3:9*
church, the pillar and ground *1Ti 3:15*
of *t.*
hidden *t.,* mystic secret *1Ti 3:16*
(A)(B)
to be received of them which *1Ti 4:3*
know *t.*
corrupt minds, and destitute of *1Ti 6:5*
the *t.*
who concerning the *t.* have *2Ti 2:18*
erred
give repentance to *2Ti 2:25*
acknowledging of *t.*
not able to come to knowledge *2Ti 3:7*
of *t.*
as Jannes and Jambres, so do *2Ti 3:8*
these resist *t.*
shall turn away their ears from *2Ti 4:4*
t.
according to the acknowledging *Tit 1:1*
of *t.*
commandments of men that *Tit 1:14*
turn from *t.*
after we received knowledge *Heb 10:26*
of *t.*
glory not, and lie not against *Jas 3:14*
the *t.*
if any of you err from the *t.* *Jas 5:19*
purified your souls in obeying *1Pe 1:22*
t.
way of *t.* shall be evil spoken *2Pe 2:2*
of
walk in darkness we lie and do *1Jo 1:6*
not *t.*
we deceive ourselves, the *t.* is *1Jo 1:8*
not in us
t. is not in him *1Jo 2:4*
is *t.* and is no lie *1Jo 2:27*
because ye know not *t.* but *1Jo 2:21*
because ye know it, and no lie
is of *t.*
and hereby we know that we *1Jo 3:19*
are of the *t.*
beareth witness, because the *1Jo 5:6*
Spirit is a *t.*
also all they that have known *2Jo 1*
the *t.*
came and testified of the *t.* in *3Jo 3*
thee
that we might be fellow-helpers *3Jo 8*
to the *t.*
hath good report of all men *3Jo 12*
and of the *t.*

IN TRUTH

serve him *in t.* *Jos 24:14; 1Sa 12:24*
if in *t.* ye anoint me king *J'g 9:15*
walk *in t.* *1Ki 2:4*
as he walked *in t.* *1Ki 3:6*
remember how I walked *in t.* *2Ki 20:3*
all his works are done *in t.* *Ps 33:4;*
    111:8
the Lord hath sworn *in t.* to *Ps 132:11*
David
Lord is nigh to all that call *Ps 145:18*
in t.
stay on the Holy One of *Isa 10:20*
Israel *in t.*
he shall sit upon it *in t.* *Isa 16:5*
judging and
mention of God of Israel, but *Isa 48:1*
not *in t.*
I will direct their work *Isa 61:8*
in t. and make
thou shalt swear, The Lord *Jer 4:2*
liveth *in t.*
I will be their God *in t.* and *Zec 8:8*
teachest way of God *in t.* *M't 22:16;*
    M'k 12:14
teach the way of God *M't 22:16*
truthfully (A)(R)
teach the way of God *M't 22:16*
honestly (B)(N)
teach the way of God *M't 22:16*
faithfully (P)

worship him in spirit and *in*   Joh 4:23;
t.   4:24
as we speak all things to you   2Co 7:14
in t.
whether *in t.* Christ is   Ph'p 1:18
preached
since ye knew the grace of   Col 1:6
God *in t.*
as it is *in t.* the word of God   1Th 2:13
let us not love in tongue, but   1Jo 3:18
in t.
the Son of the Father, *in t.*   2Jo 3
rejoiced, that I found of thy   2Jo 4;
children walking *in t.*   3Jo 4

IN *THE* TRUTH

hear me *in the t.* of thy   Ps 69:13
salvation
he was a murderer and abode   Joh 8:44
not *in the t.*
but charity rejoiceth *in the t.*   1Co 13:6
rejoices in the right (R)   1Co 13:6
tho' ye established *in the*   2Pe 1:12
present *t.*
elect lady, whom I love   2Jo 1;
in the t.   3Jo 1
even as thou walkest *in the t.*   3Jo 3

OF A TRUTH

of a t. women have been kept   1Sa 21:5
from us
of a t. Lord, the kings of   2Ki 19:17;
Assyria have destroyed   Isa 37:18
nations
I know it is so *of a t.* but how   Job 9:2
should man
of a t. many houses shall be   Isa 5:9
desolate
of a t. the Lord hath sent me   Jer 26:15
to you
of a t., your God is a God of   Da 2:47
gods
of a t. thou art the Son of   M't 14:33
God
truly (A)   M't 14:33;
  M'k 12:32; Lu 9:27; 12:44; 21:3
truly (R)   M't 14:33;
M'k 12:14, 32; Lu 4:25, 27; 12:44; 21:3;
  Ac 4:27; 10:34
but I tell you *of a t.*   Lu 4:25; 9:27
of a t. I say unto you he will   Lu 12:44;
make   21:3
of a t. this fellow also was   Lu 22:59
with him
this is *of a t.* that prophet   Joh 6:14;
  7:40
of a t. against thy holy child   Ac 4:27
Jesus
of a t. I perceive that God is   Ac 10:34
no respecter
will report that God is in   1Co 14:25
you *of a t.*

THY TRUTH

lead me in *thy t.* and teach me   Ps 25:5
I have walked in *thy t.*   Ps 26:3
shall the dust praise and   Ps 30:9
declare *thy t.*
and *thy t.* from the great   Ps 40:10
congregation
let *thy t.* continually preserve   Ps 40:11
me
send out thy light and *thy t.*   Ps 43:3
let them lead
to mine enemies, cut them off   Ps 54:5
in *thy t.*
and *thy t.* unto the clouds   Ps 57:10;
  108:4
I will praise *thy t.*   Ps 71:22
walk in *thy t.*   Ps 86:11
which thou swarest to David   Ps 89:49
in *thy t.*
praise thy name for *thy t.*   Ps 138:2
that go into pit cannot hope   Isa 38:18
for *thy t.*
father to children make   Isa 38:19
known *thy t.*
that we might understand *thy*   Da 9:13
t.
sanctify them through *thy t.*   Joh 17:17

WORD OF TRUTH

take not *word of t.* out of my   Ps 119:43
mouth
approving ourselves by the   2Co 6:7
word of t.

after him that ye heard the   Eph 1:13
word of t.
whereof ye heard before in the   Col 1:5
word of t.
rightly dividing the *word*   2Ti 2:15
of t.
of own will begat he us by   Jas 1:18
word of t.

TRUTH'S

for thy mercy, and for thy *t.*   Ps 115:1
sake
For the *t.* sake, that dwelleth in   2Jo 2
us

TRUTHFUL

t. and honest (A)   2Co 6:8

TRUTHFULLY

teach way of God *t.* (A)(R)   M't 22:16

TRUTHFULNESS

God's *t.* (R)   Ro 15:8

TRY

and I will *t.* them for thee   J'g 7:4
there
test (A)   J'g 7:4;
Pr 11:4;   Jer 9:7;   La 3:40;
  Zec 13:9;   1Co 3:13;   1Pe 4:12
test (B)   J'g 7:4;
2Ch 32:31; Job 12:11; Ps 11:4; 26:2;
139:23;   Jer 6:27;   17:10;   La 3:40;
Zec 13:9; 1Co 3:13; 1Pe 4:12; 1Jo 4:1;
  Re 3:10
test (R)   J'g 7:4;
Job 7:18;   Ps 11:4;   Jer 9:7;   La 3:40;
  Zec 13:9;   1Co 3:13;   1Jo 4:1
God left him, to *t.* him, that   2Ch 32:31
he
morning, and *t.* him every   Job 7:18
moment
testing (B)   Job 7:18
Doth not the ear *t.* words   Job 12:11
discriminate (A)   Job 12:11
his eyelids *t.* the children of   Ps 11:4
men
me; *t.* my reins and my heart   Ps 26:2
t. me, and know my   Ps 139:23
thoughts
thou mayest know and *t.* their   Jer 6:27
way
assay their ways (R)   Jer 6:27
I will melt them, and *t.* them   Jer 9:7
assay them (B)   Jer 9:7
Lord search the heart, I *t.*   Jer 17:10
the reins
Let us search and *t.* our ways   La 3:40
fall, to *t.* them, and to purge   Da 11:35
and will *t.* them as gold is   Zec 13:9
tried
t. the Spirit of the Lord (E)   Ac 5:9
the fire shall *t.* every man's   1Co 3:13
work
prove each man's work   1Co 3:13
(E)(P)
test each man's work (N)   1Co 3:13
fiery trial which is to *t.* you   1Pe 4:12
to prove you (E)   1Pe 4:12
to test your faith (P)   1Pe 4:12
t. the spirits whether they are   1Jo 4:1
prove the spirits (A)(E)   1Jo 4:1
test the spirits (N)(P)   1Jo 4:1
t. them that dwell upon the   Re 3:10
earth
to test its inhabitants (N)(P)   Re 3:10

TRYING

t. him (E)   M't 16:1;
19:3; 22:35; M'k 8:11; 10:2; Lu 11:16;
  Joh 8:6
t. the Lord's Spirit (A)   Ac 5:9
amateur talker *t.* (B)   Ac 17:18

TRYPHENA

Salute *T.* and Tryphosa, who   Ro 16:12

TRYPHOSA

Salute Tryphena, and *T.* who   Ro 16:12

TUBAL

and *T.,* and Meshech, and   Ge 10:2;
Tiras   1Ch 1:5

to *T.,* and Javan, to isles   Isa 66:19
afar off
T. and Meshech, they were   Eze 27:13
thy
There is Meshech, *T.,* and   Eze 32:26
all her
chief prince of Meshech and   Eze 38:2;
T.   38:3; 39:1

TUBAL-CAIN

And Zillah, she also bare *T.*   Ge 4:22
instructor
and the sister of *T.* was   Ge 4:22
Naamah

TUBERCULOSIS

tuberculosis (B)   Le 26:16; De 28:22

TUBES

golden *t.* or spouts   Zec 4:12
(A)(B)(E)

TUMBLED

bread *t.* into the host of   J'g 7:13
Midian

TUMORS

with *t.* (A)(B)   De 28:27
tumors (S)   De 28:27;
  1Sa 5:6, 9, 12; 6:4-5, 11, 17
with *t.* or boils (A)   1Sa 5:6
with *t.* (E)(R)   1Sa 5:6; 5:9, 12; 6:4-5

TUMULT

What meaneth the noise of   1Sa 4:14
this *t.*
What is the uproar (A)(R)   1Sa 4:14
I saw a great *t.* but I knew   2Sa 18:29
not
against me and thy *t.* is   2Ki 19:28
come up
your arrogance and careless   2Ki 19:28
ease (A)   Isa 37:29
your insolence has come to   2Ki 19:28
my ears (B)
thine arrogance came to my   2Ki 19:28
ears (E)
groan because of *t.* of my   2Ki 38:8
heart (R)
tremble with *t.* (R)   2Ki 46:3
waves, and the *t.* of the people   Ps 65:7
clamor of the nations (B)   Ps 65:7;
  74:23
the *t.* of those that rise up   Ps 74:23
against
For, lo, thine enemies make a   Ps 83:2
t.
enemies are ranting (B)   Ps 83:2
in the battle *t.* (A)(E)(R)   Isa 9:5
a day of *t.* (R)   Isa 22:5; Eze 7:7
the noise of the *t.* the people   Ps 33:3
fled
at thunderous noise peoples   Ps 33:3
flee (E)
thy *t.* is come up into mine   Ps 37:29
ears
your arrogance has come   Ps 37:29
up (B)(E)(R)
with the noise of a great *t.* he   Jer 11:16
hath
the roar of a great tempest   Jer 11:16
(A)(B)(E)
my vital parts are in *t.*   La 1:20
(A)(R)
a day of *t.* (A)(B)(E)   Eze 7:7
full of *t.* (A)(E)(R)   Eze 22:5
shall a *t.* arise among thy   Ho 10:14
people
and Moab shall die with *t.* with   Am 2:2
die amid the uproar (A)(R)   Am 2:2
a great *t.* from the Lord shall   Zec 14:13
great confusion,
discomfiture, panic (A)   Zec 14:13
great confusion from the   Zec 14:13
Lord (B)
day of great panic (E)   Zec 14:13
but that rather a *t.* was   M't 27:24
made, he
but rather a riot   M't 27:24
(A)(B)(N)(R)
and seeth the *t.* and them   M'k 5:38
that
bedlam, loud weeping and   M'k 5:38
wailing (B)

great commotion, loud crying and wailing (E)	*M'k 5:38*	To-morrow *t*. you, and get you	*Nu 14:25*	*t*. from evil ways and keep my commandments	*2Ki 17:13; Jer 18:8; 26:3; Zec 1:3-4*
a hubbub, weeping and wailing (P)	*M'k 5:38*	will not *t*. to the right hand nor	*Nu 20:17*	to *t*. the kingdom of Saul to him	*1Ch 12:23*
gathering was in a *t*. (A)(B)	*Ac 19:32*	we will not *t*. into the fields, or into	*Nu 21:22*	but Josiah would not *t*. his face	*2Ch 35:22*
not know the certainty for the *t*.	*Ac 21:34*	Balaam smote the ass, to *t*. her	*Nu 22:23*	if ye *t*. and keep my commandments	*Ne 1:9; Eze 3:20; 18:21; 33:11, 14, 19*
because of furore (A)	*Ac 21:34*	was no way to *t*. either to the right	*Nu 22:26*	*t*. their reproach on their own head	*Ne 4:4*
because of the uproar (E)	*Ac 21:34*	*t*. heart of Israelites (B)	*Nu 32:7*		
because of the hubbub (N)	*Ac 21:34*	if ye *t*. away from after him, he	*Nu 32:15*	*t*. their taunt upon own (A)(R)	*Ne 4:4*
neither with multitude, nor with *t*.	*Ac 24:18*	your border shall *t*. from the south	*Nu 34:4*	prophets testified to *t*. them to thee	*Ne 9:26*
without any crowd or uproar (A)	*Ac 24:18*	*T*. you, and take your journey	*De 1:7*	to which of the saints wilt thou *t*.	*Job 5:1*
not with mobs or riots (B)	*Ac 24:18*	*t*. you, and take your journey into	*De 1:40*	*t*. from him that he may rest till	*Job 14:6*
no mob and no disturbance (P)	*Ac 24:18*	long enough: *t*. you northward	*De 2:3*	he is in one mind, who can *t*. him	*Job 23:13*

and they that *t.* many to *Da 12:3*
righteousness
they will not frame their *Ho 5:4*
doings to *t.*
therefore *t.* thou to thy God, *Ho 12:6*
keep mercy
I will *t.* mine hand against *Am 1:8*
Ekron
ye who *t.* judgment to *Am 5:7*
wormwood
and I will *t.* your feasts into *Am 8:10*
mourning
let them *t.* every one from his *Jon 3:8*
evil way
will I *t.* to people a pure *Zep 3:9*
language
t. to strong hold ye prisoners *Zec 9:12*
of hope
I will *t.* mine hand upon the *Zec 13:7*
little ones
t. the heart of fathers to *Mal 4:6*
children
on right cheek, *t.* to him the *M't 5:39*
other
t. and I should heal them *M't 13:15*
(A)(E)(N)(P)(R)
to *t.* hearts of fathers to *Lu 1:17*
children
it shall *t.* to you for a *Lu 21:13*
testimony
t. to me to heal (N)(P)(R) *Joh 12:40*
t. around and return *Ac 3:19*
(A)(E)(N)(P)(R)
of life, lo we *t.* to the *Ac 13:46*
Gentiles
that ye should *t.* from these *Ac 13:46*
vanities
and to *t.* them from darkness *Ac 26:18*
to light
that they should repent and *t.* *Ac 26:20*
to God
each in his own *t.* *1Co 14:27*
(A)(B)(E)(R)
I know this shall *t.* to my *Ph'p 1:19*
salvation
commandments of men that *t.* *Tit 1:14*
from truth
and we *t.* about their whole *Jas 3:3*
body
t. a sinner from evil *Jas 5:20*
(A)(B)(N)
to *t.* from the holy *2Pe 2:21*
commandment
have power to *t.* waters to *Re 11:6*
blood

TURN *AGAIN*

if the raw flesh *t. again* and *Le 13:16*
be
therefore we *t. again* to thee *J'g 11:8*
now
she said, *T. again,* my *Ru 1:11;*
daughters *1:12*
I pray thee, *t. again* with *1Sa 15:25;*
me *15:30*
when Israel shall *t. again* *1Ki 8:33*
to thee
heart of this people *t. again* *1Ki 12:27*
to their lord
eat not, nor *t. again* by the *1Ki 13:9;*
same way *13:17*
go *t. again* to the king that *2Ki 1:6*
sent you
t. again and tell Hezekiah *2Ki 20:5*
t. again to Lord *2Ch 30:6*
if *t. again* *2Ch 30:9*
and man shall *t. again* into *Job 34:15*
dust
nor did I *t. again* till they *Ps 18:37*
were
displeased, O *t.* thyself to us *Ps 60:1*
again
t. us *again,* O Lord *Ps 80:3; 80:7, 19*
restore us again (A)(B)(R) *Ps 80:3;*
80:19; 85:4
but let them not *t. again* to *Ps 85:8*
that they *t.* not *again* to cover *Ps 104:9*
earth
t. again our captivity, as *Ps 126:4*
streams
t. again every one from his *Jer 25:5*
evil way
t. again, virgin of Israel, *t.* *Jer 31:21*
again to cities
try our ways and *t. again* to *La 3:40*
the Lord
t. again and thou shalt see *Eze 8:6;*
8:13, 15

he will *t. again,* he will have *Mic 7:19*
compassion
live with their children and *Zec 10:9*
t. again
lest they *t. again* and rend you *M't 7:6*
if not, it shall *t.* to you *again* *Lu 10:6*
and seven times in a day *t.* *Lu 17:4*
again to thee
how *t.* ye *again* to the weak *Ga 4:9*
elements

TURN *ASIDE*

I will now *t. aside* and see this *Ex 3:3*
sight
shall not *t. aside* to the right *De 5:32*
hand
ye *t. aside* and serve other *De 11:16;*
gods *11:28*
that he *t.* not *aside* from *De 17:20*
commandment
after my death ye will *t.* *De 31:29*
aside from
t. not *aside,* therefrom to the *Jos 23:6;*
right hand or left *1Sa 12:20-21*
ho, such a one, *t. aside,* sit *Ru 4:1*
down here
Asahel, *t. aside* and take his *2Sa 2:21*
armour
howbeit he refused to *t. aside* *2Sa 2:23*
the king said, *T. aside,* and *2Sa 18:30*
stand here
respecteth not such as *t. aside* *Ps 40:4*
to lies
I hate the work of them that *Ps 101:3*
t. aside
as for such as *t. aside* to *Ps 125:5*
crooked ways
to *t. aside* the needy from *Isa 10:2*
judgment
t. aside the just for a thing *Isa 29:21*
of nought
get out of way, *t. aside* out *Isa 30:11*
of path
to *t. aside* the right of a man *La 3:35*
before thee
and that *t.* aside the way of *Am 2:7*
the meek
and they *t. aside* the poor in *Am 5:12*
the gate
and that *t. aside* the stranger *Mal 3:5*
from right

TURN *AWAY*

tarry till thy brother's fury *t.* *Ge 27:44*
away
till thy brother's anger *t. away* *Ge 27:45*
from thee
if ye *t. away* from after him *Nu 32:15;*
De 30:17; Jos 22:16; 2Ch 7:19
they will *t. away* thy son from *De 7:4*
following
he hath spoken to *t.* you *away* *De 13:5*
from the Lord
multiply wives, that his heart *De 17:17*
t. not *away*
that he see no unclean thing *De 23:14*
and *t. away*
surely they will *t. away* *1Ki 11:2*
your heart
wilt thou *t. away* the face *2Ki 18:24;*
of one captain and trust *Isa 36:9*
on Egypt
go not up, *t. away* from *1Ch 14:14*
them
God, *t.* not *away* the face of *2Ch 6:42;*
thine anointed *Ps 132:10*
Amaziah *t. away* *2Ch 25:27*
from following Lord
make a covenant with God *2Ch 29:10;*
that wrath may *t. away* *30:8; Ps 106:23;*
Pr 24:18
Lord will not *t. away* his face *2Ch 30:9*
from you
t. away mine eyes from *Ps 119:37*
vanity
t. away my reproach which I *Ps 119:39*
fear
and lest thine infamy *t.* not *Pr 25:10*
away
but wise men *t. away* wrath *Pr 29:8*
t. away thine eyes from me *Ca 6:5*
if *t. away* thy foot from the *Isa 58:13*
sabbath
in her occasion who can *t.* her *Jer 2:24*
away
and thou shalt not *t. away* *Jer 3:19*
from me
saith Lord shall he *t. away* and *Jer 8:4*
not return

I stood to *t. away* wrath from *Jer 18:20*
them
I will *t. away* captivity *Jer 29:14;*
Zep 2:7
that I will not *t. away* from *Jer 32:40*
them
discovered iniquity, to *t. away* *La 2:14*
captivity
t. away your faces from *Eze 14:6*
abominations
for four I will not *t. away* the *Am 1:3,*
punishment *1:6, 9, 11, 13; 2:1, 4, 6*
God will *t. away* his fierce *Jon 3:9*
anger
and did *t.* many *away* from *Mal 2:6*
iniquity
borrow of thee, *t.* not thou *M't 5:42*
away
seeking to *t. away* the deputy *Ac 13:8*
from faith
t. away ungodliness from *Ro 11:26*
Jacob
traitors, heady, from such *2Ti 3:5*
they shall *t. away* their ears *2Ti 4:4*
from truth
how escape, if we *t. away* *Heb 12:25*
from him

TURN *BACK*

t. back cover that which *De 23:13*
comes from thee
I will put a hook in thy *2Ki 19:28;*
nose and *t.* thee *back* *Isa 37:29*
makest us to *t. back* from *Ps 44:10*
enemy
when I cry, then mine enemies *Ps 56:9*
t. back
hand stretched, who shall *t.* *Isa 14:27*
it *back*
neither will I *t. back* from it *Jer 4:28*
t. back thine hand as a *Jer 6:9*
grapegatherer
behold, I will *t. back* the *Jer 21:4*
weapons of war
flee ye, *t. back,* dwell deep, O *Jer 49:8*
inhabitants
and I will *t.* thee *back* *Eze 38:4; 39:2*
when I *t. back* your captivity *Zep 3:20*
not *t. back* to take up his *M'k 13:16*
garment

TURN *IN*

my lords, *t. in,* I pray you *Ge 19:2*
t. in, my lord, *t. in* to me, fear *J'g 4:18*
not
let us *t. in* to this city of the *J'g 19:11*
Jebusites
that the man of God shall *t.* *2Ki 4:10*
in
whoso is simple, let him *t. in* *Pr 9:4;*
hither *9:16*

TURN *TO THE LORD*

if thou *t. to the* Lord *De 4:30; 30:10*
in their trouble did *t. to the* *2Ch 15:4*
Lord
ends of the world shall *t. to* *Ps 22:27*
the Lord
let us try our ways and *t. to* *La 3:40*
the Lord
take with you words and *t. to* *Ho 14:2*
the Lord
rend your heart and *t. to the* *Joe 2:13*
Lord
many of Israel shall he *t. to* *Lu 1:16*
the Lord
nevertheless when it shall *t.* *2Co 3:16*
to the Lord

TURNED

a flaming sword which *t.* every *Ge 3:24*
way
Joseph *t.* about from them *Ge 42:24*
and wept
the rod which was *t.* to a *Ex 7:15*
serpent
waters in the river shall be *t.* *Ex 7:17;*
to blood *7:20; Ps 78:44; 105:29*
heart of Pharaoh *t.* against *Ex 14:5*
people
Lord *t.* from the evil (A) *Ex 32:14*
when hair is *t.* white *Le 13:3;*
10:17, 20, 25
t. and went by way of *Nu 21:33*
Bashan

ass saw me and *t.* three times | Nu 22:33
t. curse into a blessing | De 23:5; Ne 13:2
in that they are *t.* unto other gods | De 31:18
Lord *t.* from fierceness of his anger | Jos 7:26
and *t.* about to Karkaa (S) | Jos 15:3
they *t.* quckly out of the way | J'g 2:17
Samson took firebrands and *t.* tail to tail | J'g 15:4
they *t.* their backs before Israel | J'g 20:42
and thou shalt be *t.* into another man | 1Sa 10:6
even they also *t.* to be with Israelites | 1Sa 14:21
wh.thersoever he *t.* himself he vexed them | 1Sa 14:47
as Samuel *t.* about to go away, he laid | 1Sa 15:27
and David *t.* from him towards another | 1Sa 17:30
Asahel *t.* not from following Abner | 2Sa 2:19
victory that day was *t.* into mourning | 2Sa 19:2
howbeit the kingdom is *t.* about | 1Ki 2:15
Joab *t.* after Adonijah, tho' not after Absalom | 1Ki 2:28
king *t.* his face about, and blessed Israel | 1Ki 8:14
because his heart was *t.* from the Lord | 1Ki 11:9
so Naaman *t.* and went away in rage | 2Ki 5:12
Ahaz *t.* covert from house of Lord | 2Ki 16:18
t. his face to wall, and prayed | 2Ki 20:2; Isa 38:2
as Josiah *t.* himself he spied sepulchres | 2Ki 23:16
was no king like *t.* to the Lord like him | 2Ki 23:25
Lord *t.* not from the fierceness of his wrath | 2Ki 23:26
he *t.* the kingdom unto David | 1Ch 10:14
the wrath of the Lord *t.* from him | 2Ch 12:12
they *t.* from them and destroyed them not | 2Ch 20:10
for our fathers have *t.* their backs | 2Ch 29:6
t. the heart of the king of Assyria | Ezr 6:22
until the wrath of our God be *t.* from us | Ezr 10:14
neither *t.* they from their wicked works | Ne 9:35
though it was *t.* to contrary that Jews | Es 9:1
month which was *t.* to them from sorrow | Es 9:22
God *t.* me into hands of wicked | Job 16:11
whom I loved are *t.* against me | Job 19:19
yet his meat in his bowels is *t.*, the gall | Job 20:14
not *t.* aside (A)(E)(R) | Job 23:11
and under it is *t.* up as it were fire | Job 28:5
terrors are *t.* upon me, they pursue | Job 30:15
my harp is *t.* to mourning, and my organ | Job 30:31
if my step hath *t.* out of the way | Job 31:7
it is *t.* as clay to the seal, they stand as | Job 38:14
and sorrow is *t.* into joy before him | Job 41:22
terror *t.* into joy (A)(E)(R) | Job 41:22
and the Lord *t.* the captivity of Job | Job 42:10
the wicked shall be *t.* into hell | Ps 9:17
hast *t.* my mourning into dancing | Ps 30:11
he *t.* the sea into dry land | Ps 66:6
t. my hand against their adversaries | Ps 81:14
he *t.* their heart to hate his people | Ps 105:25
which *t.* the rock into a standing water | Ps 114:8

I *t.* my feet unto thy testimonies | Ps 119:59
mind utter things *t.* the wrong way (A) | Pr 23:33
and I *t.* myself to behold wisdom | Ec 2:12
night of my pleasure he *t.* into fear | Isa 21:4
Lebanon shall be *t.* into a fruitful field | Isa 29:17
streams thereof shall be *t.* into pitch | Isa 34:9
we have *t.* every one to his own way | Isa 53:6
sea be *t.* to you (A)(B)(E)(R) | Isa 60:5
he was *t.* to be their enemy | Isa 63:10
how art thou *t.* into degenerate plant | Jer 2:21
they have *t.* their back to me | Jer 2:27; 32:33
Judah *t.* to me with her whole heart | Jer 3:10
their houses shall be *t.* unto others | Jer 6:12
no man repented, every one *t.* to his course | Jer 8:6
should have *t.* them from evil way | Jer 23:22
and I shall be *t.* | Jer 31:18
after that I was *t.* | Jer 31:19
ye were now *t.* and had done right | Jer 34:15
ye *t.* and polluted my name | Jer 34:16
t. about and returned (S) | Jer 41:14
how hath Moab *t.* thee back with shame | Jer 48:39
Lord, mine heart is *t.* within me | La 1:20
against me is he *t.* he turneth his hand | La 3:3
our inheritance is *t.* to strangers | La 5:2
joy ceased, our dance is *t.* into mourning | La 5:15
turn us unto thee, and we shall be *t.* | La 5:21
they *t.* not when they went | Eze 1:9; 1:12; 10:11
a vine, whose branches *t.* toward him | Eze 17:6
she is *t.* unto me, I shall be replenished | Eze 26:2
my comeliness was *t.* into corruption | Da 10:8
by the vision my sorrows are *t.* upon me | Da 10:16
Ephraim is a cake not *t.* | Ho 7:8
Ephraim, mine heart is *t.* within me | Ho 11:8
sun shall be *t.* into darkness | Joe 2:31; Ac 2:20
for ye have *t.* judgment into gall | Am 6:12
that they *t.* from their evil way | Jon 3:10
cup of Lord's right hand be *t.* to thee | Hab 2:16
all the land shall be *t.* into a plain | Zec 14:10
Jesus *t.* about in the press | M'k 5:30
have *t.* again (A)(E)(P)(R) | Lu 22:32
Lord *t.* and looked upon Peter | Lu 22:61
your sorrow shall be *t.* into joy | Joh 16:20
God *t.* and gave them up to worship | Ac 7:42
all at Lydda saw him and *t.* to Lord | Ac 9:35
great number believed and *t.* to Lord | Ac 11:21
which from the Gentiles are *t.* to God | Ac 15:19
these that *t.* world upside down | Ac 17:6
t. aside to right (A)(E)(R) | 2Co 3:4:2
shew how ye *t.* to God from idols | 1Th 1:9
t. off into empty talk (B)(E) | 1Ti 1:6
and they shall be *t.* unto fables | 2Ti 4:4
t. to flight the armies of the aliens | Heb 11:34
lest that which is lame be *t.* out of way | Heb 12:13
yet are they *t.* with a very small helm | Jas 3:4
let your laughter be *t.* to mourning | Jas 4:9

dog is *t.* to his own vomit again | 2Pe 2:22

TURNED *AGAIN*

it was *t. again* as his other flesh | Ex 4:7
Ehud *t. again* from the quarries | J'g 3:19
Israel *t. again*, went whoring after Baalim | J'g 8:33
when Israel *t. again*, Benjamites amazed | J'g 20:41
so Samuel *t. again* after Saul, and Saul | 1Sa 15:31
I *t.* not *again* till I had consumed | 2Sa 22:38
the man *t. again* from his chariot | 2Ki 5:26
Lord *t. again* the captivity of Zion | Ps 126:1

TURNED *ASIDE*

the Lord saw that he *t. aside* to see | Ex 3:4
they have *t. aside* quickly | Ex 32:8; De 9:12, 16
he *t. aside* to see the lion's carcase | J'g 14:8
the kine *t.* not *aside* to the right | 1Sa 6:12
but *t. aside* after lucre, and took bribes | 1Sa 8:3
David *t.* not *aside* from any thing | 1Ki 15:5
a man *t. aside* and brought a man to me | 1Ki 20:39
Josiah *t.* not *aside* to right hand or | 2Ki 22:2
the paths of their way are *t. aside* | Job 6:18
t. aside like a deceitful bow | Ps 78:57
whither is thy beloved *t. aside* | Ca 6:1
a deceived heart hath *t.* him *aside* | Isa 44:20
he hath *t. aside* my ways | La 3:11
have *t. aside* unto vain jangling | 1Ti 1:6
are already *t. aside* after Satan | 1Ti 5:15

TURNED *AWAY*

because ye are *t. away* from Lord | Nu 14:43
wherefore Israel *t. away* from him | Nu 20:21
the anger of the Lord may be *t. away* | Nu 25:4
Phinehas *t.* my wrath *away* from Israel | Nu 25:11
his wives *t. away* his heart | 1Ki 11:3; 11:4
Ahab *t. away*, and would eat no bread | 1Ki 21:4
our fathers *t. away* their faces | 2Ch 29:6
which hath not *t. away* my prayer | Ps 66:20
yea, many a time *t.* he his | Ps 78:38
for all this his anger is not *t. away* | Isa 5:25; 9:12, 17, 21; 10:4
thy anger is *t. away* | Isa 12:1
nor *t.* I *away* | Isa 50:5
and judgment is *t. away* backward | Isa 59:14
your iniquities have *t. away* these things | Jer 5:25
thy feet are sunk, they are *t. away* back | Jer 38:22
wherefore have I seen them *t. away* back | Jer 46:5
shepherds have *t.* them *away* on mountains | Jer 50:6
let thy fury be *t. away* from Jerusalem | Da 9:16
for mine anger is *t. away* from him | Ho 14:4
the Lord hath *t. away* excellency of Jacob | Na 2:2
this Paul hath *t. away* much people | Ac 19:26
all they in Asia be *t. away* from me | 2Ti 1:15

TURNED *BACK*

people *t. back* upon the pursuers | Jos 8:20
Joshua at that time *t. back*, and took | Jos 11:10

Saul is *t. back* from following me | 1Sa 15:11
the bow of Jonathan *t.* not *back* | 2Sa 1:22
that thou hast *t.* their heart *back* | 1Ki 18:37
saw it was not king of Israel, they *t. back.* | 1Ki 22:33
when messengers *t. back,* why *t. back* | 2Ki 1:5
he *t. back* and looked on them | 2Ki 2:24
so the king of Assyria *t. back* | 2Ki 15:20
Ornan *t. back* and saw the angel | 1Ch 21:20
because they *t. back* from him | Job 34:27
when mine enemies are *t. back* | Ps 9:3
let them be *t. back* that devise | Ps 35:4; 70:2-3
our heart is not *t. back* from thy way | Ps 44:18
Ephraim *t. back* in day of battle | Ps 78:9
they *t. back* and tempted God | Ps 78:41; 78:57
and let them be *t. back* that hate Zion | Ps 129:5
shall be *t. back* that trust in images | Isa 42:17
the anger of the Lord is not *t. back* | Jer 4:8
they are *t. back* to iniquities of fathers | Jer 11:30
they also are *t. back,* and art fled away | Jer 46:21
he hath *t. me back,* made me faint | La 1:13
them that are *t. back* from the Lord | Zep 1:6
t. back to Jerusalem seeking him | Lu 2:45
one of lepers *t. back* and glorified God | Lu 17:15
she *t. herself back* and saw Jesus | Joh 20:14
in their hearts *t. back* into Egypt | Ac 7:39

TURNED *IN, INTO*

the two angels *t. in* unto Lot | Ge 19:3
Judah *t. in* to Hirah the Adullamite | Ge 38:1
when Sisera had *t. in* unto Jael | J'g 4:18
the Danites *t. in* thither and said to him | J'g 18:3
Elisha *t. in* thither to eat bread | 2Ki 4:8
he *t. into* the chamber and lay there | 2Ki 4:11

TURNEST

and whithersoever thou *t.* thyself | 1Ki 2:3
thou *t.* thy spirit against God | Job 15:13
Thou *t.* man to destruction | Ps 90:3

TURNETH

the soul that *t.* after such as have | Le 20:6
whose heart *t.* away this day from | De 29:18
Israel *t.* their backs before | Jos 7:8
And *t.* toward the sunrising to | Jos 19:27
And then the coast *t.* to Ramah | Jos 19:29
Tyre; and the coast *t.* to Hosah | Jos 19:29
And then the coast *t.* westward to | Jos 19:34
neither *t.* he back from the sword | Job 39:22
He *t.* rivers into a wilderness | Ps 107:33
He *t.* the wilderness into a standing | Ps 107:35
the way of the wicked he *t.* upside | Ps 146:9
A soft answer *t.* away wrath | Pr 15:1
whithersoever it *t.* it prospereth | Pr 17:8
he *t.* it whithersoever he will | Pr 21:1
As the door *t.* upon his hinges, so | Pr 26:14
that *t.* away his ear from hearing | Pr 28:9

beasts, and *t.* not away for any | Pr 30:30
south, and *t.* about unto the north | Ec 1:6
should I be as one that *t.* aside | Ca 1:7
the people *t.* not unto him that | Isa 9:13
it waste, and *t.* it upside down | Isa 24:1
that *t.* wise men backward | Isa 44:25
as a wayfaring man that *t.* aside | Jer 14:8
feeble, and *t.* herself to flee | Jer 49:24
yea, she sigheth, and *t.* backward | La 1:8
t. his hand against me all the day | La 3:3
t. away from his righteousness | Eze 18:24
man *t.* away from his wickedness | Eze 18:27
t. away from all his transgressions | Eze 18:28
day that he *t.* from his wickedness | Eze 33:12
righteous *t.* from his righteousness | Eze 33:18
and *t.* the shadow of death into | Am 5:8

TURNING

wiping it, and *t.* it upside down | 2Ki 21:13
gate, and at the *t.* of the wall | 2Ch 26:9
heart from *t.* unto the Lord God | 2Ch 36:13
the armoury at the *t.* of the wall | Ne 3:19
from the *t.* of the wall unto the door | Ne 3:20
of Azariah unto the *t.* of the wall | Ne 3:24
over against the *t.* of the wall | Ne 3:25
the *t.* away of the simple shall slay | Pr 1:32
perpetual *t.* away (A) | Pr 8:5
your *t.* of things upside down | Isa 29:16
two leaves apiece, two *t.* leaves | Eze 41:24
t. away he hath divided our fields | Mic 2:4
But Jesus *t.* unto them said | Lu 23:28
Peter, *t.* about, seeth the disciple | Joh 21:20
in *t.* away every one of you | Ac 3:26
t. him to the body said, Tabitha | Ac 9:40
variableness, neither shadow of *t.* | Jas 1:17
t. a man back from wandering (P) | Jas 5:20
t. the cities of Sodom into ashes | 2Pe 2:6
t. the grace of our God into | Jude 4

TURTLE

every species of *t.* (B) | Le 11:29
the voice of the *t.* is heard | Ca 2:12
turtledove (A)(B)(E)(R) | Ca 2:12; Jer 8:7
and the *t.* and the crane and | Jer 8:7

TURTLEDOVE

old, and a *t.* and a young pigeon | Ge 15:9
pigeon, or a *t.,* for a sin offering | Le 12:6
O deliver not the soul of thy *t.* unto | Ps 74:19
voice of the *t.* (A)(B)(E)(R)(S) | Ca 2:12; Jer 8:7

TURTLEDOVES

he shall bring his offering of *t.* | Le 1:14
two *t.* or two young pigeons, unto | Le 5:7
But if he be not able to bring two *t.* | Le 5:11
turtledoves (A)(B)(E)(R)(S) | Le 12:8; 15:29; Nu 6:10
And two *t.* or two young pigeons | Le 14:22
And he shall offer the one of the *t.* | Le 14:30
day she shall take to him two *t.* | Le 15:14
A pair of *t.* or two young pigeons | Lu 2:24

TURTLES

Lamb, then she shall bring two | Le 12:8
turtledoves (A)(B)(E)(R) | Le 12:8; 15:29; Nu 6:10
day she shall take unto her two *t.* | Le 15:29
eighth day he shall bring two *t.* | Nu 6:10

TURRET

a *t.* of silver (A)(B)(E) | Ca 8:9
t. of the temple (A) | M't 4:5

TUTORS

10,000 *t.* in Christ (B) | 1Co 4:15
But is under *t.* and governors | Ga 4:2
guardians, administrators, trustees (A) | Ga 4:2
guardians and trustees (B)(N)(P)(R) | Ga 4:2
guardians and stewards (E) | Ga 4:2

TWAIN

my son in law in the one of the *t.* | 1Sa 18:21
and shut the door upon them *t.* | 2Ki 4:33
wings; with *t.* he covered his face | Isa 6:2
and with *t.* he covered his feet | Isa 6:2
and with *t.* he did fly | Isa 6:2
when they cut the calf in *t.* | Jer 34:18
both *t.* shall come forth out of one | Eze 21:19
thee to go a mile, go with him *t.* | M't 5:41
wife: and they *t.* shall be one flesh | M't 19:5
Wherefore they are no more *t. but* | M't 19:6
Whether of them *t.* did the will of | M't 21:31
Whether of the *t.* will ye that I | M't 27:21
the veil of the temple was rent in *t.* | M't 27:51
And they *t.* shall be one flesh: so | M'k 10:8
so then they are no more *t.* but one | M'k 10:8
the veil of the temple was rent in *t.* | M'k 15:38
make in himself of *t.* one new man | Eph 2:15

TWELFTH

On the *t.* day Ahira the son of | Nu 7:78
before him, and he with the *t.* | 1Ki 19:19
In the *t.* year of Joram the son | 2Ki 8:25
In the *t.* year of Ahaz king of | 2Ki 17:1
in the *t.* month, on the seven | 2Ki 25:27
to Eliashib, the *t.* to Jakim | 1Ch 24:12
The *t.* to Hashabiah, he, his | 1Ch 25:19
The *t.* captain for the *t.* month | 1Ch 27:15
and in the *t.* year he began to | 2Ch 34:3
the *t.* day of the first month | Ezr 8:31
the *t.* year of king Ahasuerus | Es 3:7
to the *t.* month, that is, the | Es 3:7
thirteenth day of the *t.* month | Es 3:13
thirteenth day of the *t.* month | Es 8:12
Now in the *t.* month, that is | Es 9:1
in the *t.* month, in the five | Jer 52:31
in the *t.* day of the month | Eze 29:1
it came to pass in the *t.* year | Eze 32:1
t. month, in the first day of | Eze 32:1
came to pass also in the *t.* year | Eze 32:17
it came to pass in the *t.* year | Eze 33:21
a jacinth; the *t.* an amethyst | Re 21:20

TWELVE

nine hundred and *t.* years | Ge 5:8
T. years they served | Ge 14:4
t. princes shall he beget, and | Ge 17:20
t. princes according to their | Ge 25:16
Now the sons of Jacob were *t.* | Ge 35:22
Thy servants are *t.* brethren | Ge 42:13

We be *t.* brethren, sons of   *Ge 42:32*
our
these are the *t.* tribes of   *Ge 49:28*
Israel
where were *t.* wells of water   *Ex 15:27*
under the hill, and *t.* pillars   *Ex 24:4*
according to the *t.* tribes of   *Ex 24:4*
of the children of Israel, *t.*   *Ex 28:21*
be according to the *t.* tribes   *Ex 28:21*
of the children of Israel, *t.*   *Ex 39:14*
according to the *t.* tribes   *Ex 39:14*
and bake *t.* cakes thereof   *Le 24:5*
princes of Israel, being *t.* men   *Nu 1:44*
covered wagons, and *t.* oxen   *Nu 7:3*
of Israel: *t.* chargers of silver   *Nu 7:84*
t. silver bowls, *t.* spoons of   *Nu 7:84*
gold
The golden spoons were *t.* full   *Nu 7:86*
were *t.* bullocks, the rams *t.*   *Nu 7:87*
the lambs of the first year *t.*   *Nu 7:87*
of the goats for sin offering *t.*   *Nu 7:87*
house of their fathers *t.* rods   *Nu 17:2*
fathers' houses, even *t.* rods   *Nu 17:6*
ye shall offer *t.* young   *Nu 29:17*
bullocks
t. thousand armed for war   *Nu 31:5*
And threescore and *t.*   *Nu 31:33*
thousand
Lord's tribute was threescore   *Nu 31:38*
were *t.* fountains of water   *Nu 33:9*
and I took *t.* men of you, one   *De 1:23*
take you *t.* men out of the   *Jos 3:12*
Take you *t.* men out of the   *Jos 4:2*
t. stones, and ye shall carry   *Jos 4:3*
Then Joshua called the *t.* men   *Jos 4:4*
t. stones out of the midst of   *Jos 4:8*
Joshua set up *t.* stones in the   *Jos 4:9*
And those *t.* stones, which   *Jos 4:20*
and women, were *t.* thousand   *Jos 8:25*
t. cities with their villages   *Jos 18:24;*
   19:15
the tribe of Zebulun, *t.* cities   *Jos 21:7*
were by their lot *t.* cities   *Jos 21:40*
with her bones, into *t.* pieces   *J'g 19:29*
sent thither *t.* thousand men   *J'g 21:10*
by number *t.* of Benjamin   *2Sa 2:15*
and *t.* of the servants of   *2Sa 2:15*
David
of Ish-tob *t.* thousand men   *2Sa 10:6*
me now choose out *t.*   *2Sa 17:1*
thousand
had *t.* officers over all Israel   *1Ki 4:7*
and *t.* thousand horsemen   *1Ki 4:26*
a line of *t.* cubits did   *1Ki 7:15*
compass
It stood upon *t.* oxen, three   *1Ki 7:25*
sea, and *t.* oxen under the sea   *1Ki 7:44*
t. lions stood there on the   *1Ki 10:20;*
one   *2Ch 9:19*
t. thousand horsemen, whom   *1Ki 10:26*
on him, and rent it in *t.*   *1Ki 11:30*
pieces
to reign over Israel, *t.* years   *1Ki 16:23*
And Elijah took *t.* stones   *1Ki 18:31*
plowing with *t.* yoke of oxen   *1Ki 19:19*
of Judah, and reigned *t.* years   *2Ki 3:1*
Manasseh was *t.* years old   *2Ki 21:1*
when
the tribe of Zebulun, *t.* cities   *1Ch 6:63*
gates were two hundred and   *1Ch 9:22*
t.
brethren an hundred and *t.*   *1Ch 15:10*
his brethren and sons were *t.*   *1Ch 25:9;*
   25:10-20, 22-30
sons, and his brethren, were   *1Ch 25:31*
t.
and *t.* thousand horsemen   *2Ch 1:14*
It stood upon *t.* oxen, three   *2Ch 4:4*
One sea, and *t.* oxen under it   *2Ch 4:15*
and *t.* thousand horsemen   *2Ch 9:25*
With *t.* hundred chariots, and   *2Ch 12:3*
Manasseh was *t.* years old   *2Ch 33:1*
thousand eight hundred and *t.*   *Ezr 2:6*
of Jorah, an hundred and *t.*   *Ezr 2:18*
t. he goats, according to the   *Ezr 6:17*
I separated *t.* of the chief   *Ezr 8:24*
t. bullocks for all Israel,   *Ezr 8:35*
ninety
t. he goats for a sin offering   *Ezr 8:35*
t. years, I and my brethren   *Ne 5:14*
of Hariph, an hundred and *t.*   *Ne 7:24*
that she had been *t.* months   *Es 2:12*
the valley of salt *t.*   *Ps 60 title*
thousand
and *t.* brasen bulls that were   *Jer 52:20*
a fillet of *t.* cubits did   *Jer 52:21*
compass
altar shall be *t.* cubits long   *Eze 43:16*
t. broad, square in the four   *Eze 43:16*

to the *t.* tribes of Israel   *Eze 47:13*
end of *t.* months he walked in   *Da 4:29*
with an issue of blood *t.*   *M't 9:20*
years
called unto him his *t.*   *M't 10:1*
disciples
the names of the *t.* apostles   *M't 10:2*
are
These *t.* Jesus sent forth, and   *M't 10:5*
of commanding his *t.*   *M't 11:1*
disciples
that remained *t.* baskets full   *M't 14:20*
ye also shall sit upon *t.*   *M't 19:28*
thrones
judging the *t.* tribes of Israel   *M't 19:28*
took the *t.* disciples apart in   *M't 20:17*
Then one of the *t.* called   *M't 26:14*
Judas
was come, he sat down   *M't 26:20*
with the *t.*
lo, Judas, one of the *t.*   *M't 26:47*
came, and
me more than *t.* legions of   *M't 26:53*
angels
he ordained *t.* that they   *M'k 3:14*
should be
that were about him with the   *M'k 4:10*
t.
had an issue of blood *t.*   *M'k 5:25*
years
for she was of the age of *t.*   *M'k 5:42*
years
And he called unto him the *t.*   *M'k 6:7*
they took up *t.* baskets full of   *M'k 6:43*
ye up? They say unto him, T.   *M'k 8:19*
And he sat down, and called   *M'k 9:35*
the *t.*
he took again the *t.* and   *M'k 10:32*
began to
went out unto Bethany with   *M'k 11:11*
the *t.*
Judas Iscariot, one of the *t.,*   *M'k 14:10*
went
evening he cometh with the   *M'k 14:17*
t.
It is one of the *t.* that   *M'k 14:20*
dippeth
spake, cometh Judas, one   *M'k 14:43*
of the *t.*
when he was *t.* years old, they   *Lu 2:42*
of them he chose *t.* whom also   *Lu 6:13*
of God: and the *t.* were with   *Lu 8:1*
him
daughter, about *t.* years of age   *Lu 8:42*
having an issue of blood *t.*   *Lu 8:43*
years
he called his *t.* disciples   *Lu 9:1*
together
then came the *t.* and said unto   *Lu 9:12*
that remained to them *t.*   *Lu 9:17*
baskets
Then he took unto him the *t,*   *Lu 18:31*
being of the number of the *t,*   *Lu 22:3*
and the *t.* apostles with him   *Lu 22:14*
judging the *t.* tribes of Israel   *Lu 22:30*
one of the *t.* went before   *Lu 22:47*
them
filled *t.* baskets with the   *Joh 6:13*
fragments
Then said Jesus unto the *t.,*   *Joh 6:67*
Will ye
Have not I chosen you *t.* and   *Joh 6:70*
one
betray him, being one of the   *Joh 6:71*
t.
Are there not *t.* hours in the   *Joh 11:9*
day
But Thomas, one of the *t.*   *Joh 20:24*
called
Then the *t.* called the multitude   *Ac 6:2*
and Jacob begat the *t.*   *Ac 7:8*
patriarchs
And all the men were about *t.*   *Ac 19:7*
yet but *t.* days since I went up   *Ac 24:11*
to
Unto which promise our *t.*   *Ac 26:7*
tribes
seen of Cephas, then of the *t.*   *1Co 15:5*
to the *t.* tribes which are   *Jas 1:1*
scattered
of Juda were sealed *t.* thousand   *Re 7:5*
of Reuben were sealed   *Re 7:5*
t. thousand
of Gad were sealed *t.* thousand   *Re 7:5*
of Aser were sealed *t.* thousand   *Re 7:6*
Nepthalim were sealed *t.*   *Re 7:6*
thousand
Manasses were sealed *t.*   *Re 7:6*
thousand

of Simeon were sealed   *Re 7:7*
t. thousand
of Levi were sealed *t.*   *Re 7:7*
thousand
Issachar were sealed *t.*   *Re 7:7*
thousand
of Zabulon were sealed *t.*   *Re 7:8*
thousand
of Joseph were sealed *t.*   *Re 7:8*
thousand
Benjamin were sealed *t.*   *Re 7:8*
thousand
upon her head a crown of *t.*   *Re 12:1*
stars
great and high and had *t.*   *Re 21:12*
gates
at the gates *t.* angels, and   *Re 21:12*
names
of the *t.* tribes of the   *Re 21:12*
children of
wall of the city had *t.*   *Re 21:14*
foundations
the names of the *t.* apostles   *Re 21:14*
with the reed, *t.* thousand   *Re 21:16*
furlongs
the *t.* gates were *t.* pearls;   *Re 21:21*
every
life, which bare *t.* manner of   *Re 22:2*
fruits

TWENTIETH

the seven and *t.* day of the   *Ge 8:14*
month
the one and *t.* day of the   *Ex 12:18*
month at
on the *t.* day of the second   *Nu 10:11*
month
t. year of Jeroboam king of   *1Ki 15:9*
Israel
three and *t.* year of king   *2Ki 12:6*
Jehoash
In the three and *t.* year of   *2Ki 13:1*
Joash the
t. year of Jotham the son of   *2Ki 15:30*
Uzziah
the seven and *t.* day of the   *2Ki 25:27*
month
to Pethahiah, the *t.* to   *1Ch 24:16*
Jehezekel
The one and *t.* to Jachin,   *1Ch 24:17*
the two
to Jachin, the two and *t.* to   *1Ch 24:17*
Gamul
The three and *t.* to Delaiah   *1Ch 24:18*
the four and *t.* to Maaziah   *1Ch 24:18*
The *t.* to Eliathah, he, his   *1Ch 25:27*
sons
The one and *t.* to Hothir,   *1Ch 25:28*
he, his
The two and *t.* to Giddalti,   *1Ch 25:29*
he, his
The three and *t.* to   *1Ch 25:30*
Mahazioth, he
The four and *t.* to   *1Ch 25:31*
Romamti-ezer
the *t.* day of the   *2Ch 7:10*
seventh month
on the *t.* day of the   *Ezr 10:9*
month
the month Chisleu, in the *t.*   *Ne 1:1*
year
in the *t.* year of Artaxerxes the   *Ne 2:1*
two
from the *t.* year even unto the   *Ne 5:14*
two
on the three and *t.* day thereof   *Es 8:9*
day, that is the three and *t.*   *Jer 25:3*
year
and *t.* year of   *Jer 52:30*
Nebuchadrezzar
in the five and *t.* day of the   *Jer 52:31*
month
to pass in the seven and *t.*   *Eze 29:17*
year
five and *t.* year of our   *Eze 40:1*
captivity
four and *t.* day of the first   *Da 10:4*
month
and *t.* day of the sixth month   *Hag 1:15*
in the one and *t.* day of the   *Hag 2:1*
month
the *t.* day of the ninth   *Hag 2:10;*
month   *2:18*
four and *t.* day of the ninth   *Hag 2:20*
month
and *t.* day of the eleventh   *Zec 1:7*
month

TWENTY

peradventure there shall be	Ge 18:31
t.; I will not destroy it for	
this t. years have I been with	Ge 31:38;
thee	31:41
for a present for Esau, t.	Ge 32:14
he goats, t. rams	
ten bulls, t. she asses, and	Ge 32:15
ten foals	
they sold Joseph for t. pieces	Ge 37:28
of silver	
a shekel is t. gerahs	Ex 30:13;
Le 27:25; Nu 3:47; 18:16; Eze 45:12	
from t. years old and above	Ex 30:14;
38:26; Nu 1:3, 18, 20; 14:29; 26:2;	
32:11; 1Ch 23:24, 27; 2Ch 25:5; 31:17;	
	Ezr 3:8
estimation of the male from t.	Le 27:3
years	
from five years old to t. years,	Le 27:5
t. shekels	
not eat neither ten days, nor	Nu 11:19
t. days	
the shekel of the sanctuary is	Nu 18:16
t. gerahs	
Jabin oppressed Israel t. years	J'g 4:3
Jephthah smote from Aroer	J'g 11:33
even t. cities	
Samson judged Israel t.	J'g 15:20;
years	16:31
ark was in Kirjath-jearim t.	1Sa 7:2
years	
Jonathan and armour-bearer	1Sa 14:4
slew t. men	
Abner came to David with t.	2Sa 3:20
men	
Ziba had fifteen sons and t.	2Sa 9:10;
servants	19:17
Solomon's provision daily, t.	1Ki 4:23
oxen	
at the end of t. years, when	1Ki 9:10;
Solomon had built the	2Ch 8:1
two houses	
Solomon gave Hiram t. cities	1Ki 9:11
in Galilee	
brought the man of God t.	2Ki 4:42
loaves	
I even weighed t. basons of	Ezr 8:27
gold	
thy meat by weight, t. shekels	Eze 4:10
a day	
the length of the porch was	Eze 40:49
t. cubits	
the breadth of the door was t.	Eze 41:2
cubits	
when one came to an heap	Hag 2:16
of t. measures, there were but t.	
the length of the flying roll t.	Zec 5:2
cubits	
and sounded, and found it t.	Ac 27:28
fathoms	

TWENTY TWO

Jair judged Israel t. two years	J'g 10:3
Jeroboam reigned t. two	1Ki 14:20
years	
Ahab reigned over Israel	1Ki 16:29
t. two years	
Ahaziah was t. and two years	2Ki 8:26
old	
Amon t. two years old, when	2Ki 21:19
began to reign	
of his fathers' house t. two	1Ch 12:28
captains	
but Abijah begat t. and two	2Ch 13:21
sons	

TWENTY THREE, THIRD

Tola judged Israel t. three	J'g 10:2
years	
Jehoahaz was t. three years	2Ki 23:31
old	
Jair had t. three cities in	1Ch 2:22
Gilead	
from thirteenth year of Josiah	Jer 25:3
to t. third year	
in the t. third year of	Jer 52:30
Nebuchadnezzar	

TWENTY FOUR, FOURTH

offerings were t. and four	Nu 7:88
bullocks	
fingers and toes t. four in	2Sa 21:20
number	
Baasha reigned t. and four	1Ki 15:33
years	

consider from t. fourth day	Hag 2:18
and ninth	
round the throne were t. four	Re 4:4
seats, and on the seats t. four	
elders	
the t. four elders fell down	Re 5:8;
	11:16; 19:4

TWENTY FIVE, FIFTH

from t. five years old and	Nu 8:24
upward	
Jehoshaphat reigned t. and	1Ki 22:42;
five years in Jerusalem	2Ch 20:31
Amaziah was t. five years	2Ki 14:2;
old when he began to reign	2Ch 25:1
Jotham t. five years old	2Ki 15:33;
	2Ch 27:1, 8
Hezekiah t. five years old	2Ki 18:2;
	2Ch 29:1
Jehoiakim t. five years	2Ki 23:36;
	2Ch 36:5
the wall finished in t. fifth day	Ne 6:15
of Elul	
t. fifth day Evil-merodach	Jer 52:31
lifted up	

TWENTY SIXTH

in t. sixth year of Asa, Elah	1Ki 16:8
began to reign	

TWENTY SEVENTH

t. seventh day of second	Ge 8:14
month, earth dried	
t. seventh of Asa, Zimri	1Ki 16:10;
reigned	16:15
on t. seventh day of twelfth	2Ki 25:27
month	

TWENTY EIGHT

length of curtain t. eight	Ex 26:2;
cubits	36:9
Jehu reigned t. and eight	2Ki 10:36
years	
Rehoboam begat t. eight	2Ch 11:21
sons	

TWENTY NINE

Nahor lived t. nine years and	Ge 11:24
begat	
Amaziah reigned t. nine years	2Ki 14:2
Hezekiah t. nine years	2Ki 18:2;
	2Ch 25:1; 29:1

TWENTY'S

I will not destroy it for t.	Ge 18:31
sake	

TWICE

was doubled unto Pharaoh t.	Ge 41:32
t. as much as they gather daily	Ex 16:5
they gathered t. as much	Ex 16:22
bread	
with his rod he smote the	Nu 20:11
rock t.	
avoided out of his presence	1Sa 18:11
t.	
which had appeared unto him	1Ki 11:9
t.	
saved himself not once nor	2Ki 6:10
t.	
without Jerusalem once or t.	Ne 13:20
For God speaketh once, yea	Job 33:14
t., yet	
t., yea, thrice (S)	Job 33:29
Once have I spoken; yea,	Job 40:5
t.; but I	
gave Job t. as much as he	Job 42:10
had	
t. have I heard this; that	Ps 62:11
power	
he live a thousand years t. told	Ec 6:6
before the cock crow t. thou	M'k 14:30
shalt	
Before the cock crow t.	M'k 14:72
thou shalt	
I fast t. in the week, I give	Lu 18:12
tithes of	
without fruit, t. dead,	Jude 12
plucked up	

TWIGS

eat the t. of it (B)	Isa 27:10
cropped off the top of his	Eze 17:4
young t.	

shot forth leafy t. (A)	Eze 17:6
off from the top of his young	Eze 17:22
t. a	

TWILIGHT

David smote them from the	1Sa 30:17
t.	
they rose up in the t. to go	2Ki 7:5
unto	
they arose and fled in the t.	2Ki 7:7
the stars of the t. thereof be	Job 3:9
dark	
of the adulterer waiteth	Job 24:15
for the t.	
In the t. in the evening, in	Pr 7:9
and carry it forth in the t.	Eze 12:6
I brought it forth in the t. and	Eze 12:7
bear upon his shoulder in the	Eze 12:12
t.	

TWINED

with ten curtains of fine t.	Ex 26:1;
linen	36:8
and fine t. linen of cunning	Ex 26:31
work	
and scarlet, and fine t. linen	Ex 26:36;
27:16; 28:8; 36:35, 37; 38:18; 39:2, 5, 8	
shall be hangings of fine t.	Ex 27:9
linen	
height five cubits of fine t.	Ex 27:18
linen	
of scarlet, and fine t. linen,	Ex 28:6;
with	28:15
of the court were of fine t.	Ex 38:9
linen	
round about were of fine t.	Ex 38:16
linen	
purple, and scarlet, and t.	Ex 39:24
linen	
and linen breeches of fine t.	Ex 39:28
linen	
And a girdle of fine t. linen,	Ex 39:29
and blue	

TWINKLING

In a moment, in the t. of an	1Co 15:52
eye	

TWINS

behold, there were t. in her	Ge 25:24
womb	
that, behold, t. were in her	Ge 38:27
womb	
where of everyone bear t. and	Ca 4:2
like two young roes that are t.	Ca 4:5
whereof every one beareth t.	Ca 6:6
like two young roes that are t.	Ca 7:3

TWIST

t. everything that is right (B)	Mic 3:9
he is a moral t. (P)	Tit 3:11

TWISTED

t. and crooked race (B)	De 32:5
the t. are t. to thee (B)	2Sa 22:27
t. that which was right (B)	Job 33:27
nothing t. or crooked (B)(R)	Pr 8:8
man with t. thought (B)	Pr 12:8

TWITTED

elders t. him (B)	M't 27:41

TWITTERING

like a t. swallow (B)	Isa 38:14

TWO

And god made t. great lights	Ge 1:16
Lamech took unto him t.	Ge 4:19
wives	
lived an hundred sixty and t.	Ge 5:18
years	
nine hundred sixty and t.	Ge 5:20
years	
seven hundred eighty and t.	Ge 5:26
years	
an hundred eighty and t. years	Ge 5:28
t. of every sort shalt thou	Ge 6:19
bring	
t. of every sort that shall come	Ge 6:20
in unto	

of beasts that are not clean by *t.*   Ge 7:2

There went in *t.* and *t.* unto Noah   Ge 7:9

into the ark, *t.* and *t.* of all flesh   Ge 7:15

and told his *t.* brethren without   Ge 9:22

And unto Eber were born *t.* sons   Ge 10:25

begat Arphaxad *t.* years after the flood   Ge 11:10

And Reu lived *t.* and thirty years   Ge 11:20

Reu lived *t.* hundred and seven years   Ge 11:21

Serug lived *t.* hundred years   Ge 11:23

were *t.* hundred and five years   Ge 11:32

And there came *t.* angels to Sodom   Ge 19:1

I have *t.* daughters which have not   Ge 19:8

take thy wife, and thy *t.* daughters   Ge 19:15

upon the hand of his *t.* daughters   Ge 19:16

and his *t.* daughters with him   Ge 19:30

in a cave, he and his *t.* daughters   Ge 19:30

took *t.* of his young men with him   Ge 22:3

and *t.* bracelets for her hands of ten   Ge 24:22

her, *T.* nations are in thy womb   Ge 25:23

and *t.* manner of people shall   Ge 25:23

fetch me from thence *t.* good kids   Ge 27:9

hath supplanted me these *t.* times   Ge 27:36

Laban had *t.* daughters: the name   Ge 29:16

into the *t.* maidservants' tents   Ge 31:33

fourteen years for thy *t.* daughters   Ge 31:41

herds, and the camels, into *t.* bands   Ge 32:7

and now I am become *t.* bands   Ge 32:10

T. hundred she goats, and twenty   Ge 32:14

t. hundred ewes, and twenty rams   Ge 32:14

that night, and took his *t.* wives   Ge 32:22

and his *t.* womenservants   Ge 32:22

Rachel, and unto the *t.* handmaids   Ge 33:1

that *t.* of the sons of Jacob, Simeon   Ge 34:25

was wroth against *t.* of his officers   Ge 40:2

to pass at the end of *t.* full years   Ge 41:1

And unto Joseph were born *t.* sons   Ge 41:50

Slay my *t.* sons, if I bring him not   Ge 42:37

know that my wife bare me *t.* sons   Ge 44:27

these *t.* years hath the famine been in   Ge 45:6

born him in Egypt, were *t.* souls   Ge 46:27

and he took with him his *t.* sons   Ge 48:1

thy *t.* sons, Ephraim and Manasseh   Ge 48:5

couching down between *t.* burdens   Ge 49:14

t. men of the Hebrews strove   Ex 2:13

will not believe also these *t.* signs   Ex 4:9

and strike it on the *t.* side posts   Ex 12:7

and the *t.* side posts with the blood   Ex 12:22

the lintel, and on the *t.* side posts   Ex 12:23

much bread, *t.* omers for one man   Ex 16:22

on the sixth day the bread of *t.* days   Ex 16:29

her *t.* sons; of which the name   Ex 18:3

thy wife and her *t.* sons with her   Ex 18:6

if he continue a day or *t.* he shall   Ex 21:21

t. cubits and a half shall be   Ex 25:10

t. rings shall be in the one side of   Ex 25:12

and *t.* rings in the other side of it   Ex 25:12

t. cubits and a half shall be   Ex 25:17

shalt make *t.* cherubims of gold   Ex 25:18

in the *t.* ends of the mercy seat   Ex 25:18

cherubims on the *t.* ends thereof   Ex 25:19

from between the *t.* cherubims   Ex 25:22

t. cubits shall be the length thereof   Ex 25:23

a knop under *t.* branches of   Ex 25:35

T. tenons shall there be in one   Ex 26:17

boards; *t.* sockets under one board   Ex 26:19

under one board for his *t.* tenons   Ex 26:19

and *t.* sockets under another board   Ex 26:19

another board for his *t.* tenons   Ex 26:19

silver; *t.* sockets under one board   Ex 26:21

and *t.* sockets under another board   Ex 26:21

t. boards shalt thou make for of the tabernacle in the *t.* sides   Ex 26:23

they shall be for the *t.* corners   Ex 26:24

t. sockets under one board   Ex 26:25

and *t.* sockets under another board   Ex 26:25

tabernacle, for the *t.* sides westward   Ex 26:27

be upon the *t.* sides of the altar   Ex 27:7

It shall have the *t.* shoulderpieces   Ex 28:7

joined at the *t.* edges thereof   Ex 28:7

And thou shalt take *t.* onyx stones   Ex 28:9

engrave the *t.* stones with the   Ex 28:11

the *t.* stones upon the shoulders of   Ex 28:12

upon his *t.* shoulders for a   Ex 28:12

t. chains of pure gold at the ends   Ex 28:14

the breastplate *t.* rings of gold   Ex 28:23

put the *t.* rings on the *t.* ends of the   Ex 28:23

put the *t.* wreathen chains of gold   Ex 28:24

the *t.* rings which are on the ends   Ex 28:24

t. ends of the *t.* wreathen chains   Ex 28:25

thou shalt fasten in the *t.* ouches   Ex 28:25

thou shalt make *t.* rings of gold   Ex 28:26

put them upon the *t.* ends of   Ex 28:26

t. other rings of gold thou shalt   Ex 28:27

them on the *t.* sides of the ephod   Ex 28:27

and *t.* rams without blemish   Ex 29:1

with the bullock and the *t.* rams   Ex 29:3

the *t.* kidneys, and the fat   Ex 29:13; 29:22

t. lambs of the first year day by day   Ex 29:38

t. cubits shall be the height thereof   Ex 30:2

t. golden rings shalt thou make to   Ex 30:4

of it, by the *t.* corners thereof   Ex 30:4

upon the *t.* sides of it shalt thou   Ex 30:4

even *t.* hundred and fifty shekels   Ex 30:23

calamus *t.* hundred and fifty shekels   Ex 30:23

t. tables of testimony, tables   Ex 31:18

the *t.* tables of the testimony were   Ex 32:15

Hew thee *t.* tables of stone   Ex 34:1

he hewed *t.* tables of stone   Ex 34:4

in his hand the *t.* tables of stone   Ex 34:4

with the *t.* tables of testimony   Ex 34:29

One board had *t.* tenons, equally   Ex 36:22

boards; *t.* sockets under one board   Ex 36:24

under one board for his *t.* tenons   Ex 36:24

t. sockets under another board for   Ex 36:24

another board for his *t.* tenons   Ex 36:24

silver, *t.* sockets under one board   Ex 36:26

and *t.* sockets under another board   Ex 36:26

t. boards made he for the corners of   Ex 36:28

of the tabernacle in the *t.* sides   Ex 36:28

under every board *t.* sockets   Ex 36:30

t. cubits and a half was the length   Ex 37:1

even *t.* rings upon the one side of   Ex 37:3

t. rings upon the other side of it   Ex 37:3

t. cubits and a half was the length   Ex 37:6

And he made *t.* cherubims of gold   Ex 37:7

on the *t.* ends of the mercy seat   Ex 37:7

the cherubims on the *t.* ends   Ex 37:8

t. cubits was the length thereof   Ex 37:10

a knop under *t.* branches of   Ex 37:21

and *t.* cubits was the height of it   Ex 37:25

And he made *t.* rings of gold for it   Ex 37:27

crown thereof, by the *t.* corners of   Ex 37:27

upon the *t.* sides thereof, to be   Ex 37:27

t. thousand and four hundred shekels   Ex 38:29

by the *t.* edges was it coupled   Ex 39:4

t. ouches of gold, and *t.* gold rings   Ex 39:16

put the *t.* rings in the *t.* ends   Ex 39:16

they put the *t.* wreathen chains of   Ex 39:17

in the *t.* rings on the ends of   Ex 39:17

t. ends of the *t.* wreathen chains   Ex 39:18

they fastened in the *t.* ouches   Ex 39:18

And they made *t.* rings of gold   Ex 39:19

on the *t.* ends of the breastplate   Ex 39:19

they made *t.* other golden rings   Ex 39:20

them on the *t.* sides of the ephod   Ex 39:20

the *t.* kidneys, and the fat   Le 3:4; 3:10, 15

the *t.* kidneys, and the fat that   Le 4:9

t. turtledoves, or *t.* young pigeons   Le 5:7; 5:11

the *t.* kidneys, and the fat that   Le 8:2

t. rams, and a basket of unleavened   Le 8:2

and the *t.* kidneys, and their fat   Le 8:16; 8:25

she shall be unclean *t.* weeks, as in   Le 12:5

t. turtles, or *t.* young pigeons   Le 12:8

cleansed *t.* birds alive and clean   Le 14:4

he shall take *t.* he lambs without   Le 14:10

t. turtledoves, or *t.* young pigeons   Le 14:22

take to cleanse the house *t.* birds   Le 14:49

t. turtledoves, or *t.* young pigeons   Le 15:14

her *t.* turtles, or *t.* young pigeons   Le 15:29

after the death of the *t.* sons   Le 16:1

t. kids of the goats for a sin   Le 16:5

And he shall take the *t.* goats, and   Le 16:7

shall cast lots upon the *t.* goats   Le 16:8

t. tenth deals of fine flour mingled   Le 23:13

t. wave loaves, of *t.* tenth deals   Le 23:17

one young bullock, and *t.* rams   Le 23:18

t. lambs of the first year for a   Le 23:19

before the Lord, with the *t.* lambs   Le 23:20

t. tenths deals shall be in one cake   *Le* 24:5

And thou shalt set them in *t.* rows   *Le* 24:6

were thirty and *t.* thousand   *Nu* 1:35

thousand and *t.* hundred   *Nu* 1:35

t. thousand and seven hundred   *Nu* 1:39

were thirty and *t.* thousand   *Nu* 2:21

thousand and *t.* hundred   *Nu* 2:21

t. thousand and seven hundred   *Nu* 2:26

were six thousand and *t.* hundred   *Nu* 3:34

were twenty and *t.* thousand   *Nu* 3:39

were twenty and *t.* thousand   *Nu* 3:43

t. hundred and three score and   *Nu* 3:43

be redeemed of the *t.* hundred   *Nu* 3:46

were *t.* thousand seven hundred and   *Nu* 4:36

were *t.* thousand and six hundred   *Nu* 4:40

were three thousand and *t.* hundred   *Nu* 4:44

t. turtles, or *t.* young pigeons   *Nu* 6:10

a wagon for *t.* of the princes   *Nu* 7:3

T. wagons and four oxen he gave   *Nu* 7:7

t. oxen   *Nu* 7:17; 7:23, 29, 35, 41, 47, 53, 59, 65, 71, 77, 83

silver vessels weighed *t.* thousand   *Nu* 7:85

from between the *t.* cherubims   *Nu* 7:89

Or whether it were *t.* days, or   *Nu* 9:22

Make thee *t.* trumpets of silver   *Nu* 10:2

shall not eat one day, nor *t.* days   *Nu* 11:19

there remained *t.* of the men in   *Nu* 11:26

it were *t.* cubits high upon the face   *Nu* 11:31

bare it between *t.* upon a staff   *Nu* 13:23

offering *t.* tenth deals of flour   *Nu* 15:6

t. hundred and fifty princes of   *Nu* 16:2

t. hundred and fifty censers   *Nu* 16:17

the *t.* hundred and fifty men   *Nu* 16:35

and his *t.* servants were with him   *Nu* 22:22

devoured *t.* hundred and fifty men   *Nu* 26:10

twenty and *t.* thousand and   *Nu* 26:14

thousand and *t.* hundred   *Nu* 26:14

t. thousand and seven hundred   *Nu* 26:34

and *t.* thousand and five hundred   *Nu* 26:37

t. lambs of the first year without   *Nu* 28:3; 28:9

t. tenth deals of flour for a meat   *Nu* 28:9; 28:12

t. young bullocks, and one ram   *Nu* 28:11; 28:19, 27

and *t.* tenth deals for a ram   *Nu* 28:20; 29:3, 14

t. tenth deals unto one ram   *Nu* 28:28; 29:9

t. rams, and fourteen lambs   *Nu* 29:13

t. tenth deals to each ram of   *Nu* 29:14

twelve young bullocks, *t.* rams   *Nu* 29:17

third day eleven bullocks *t.* rams   *Nu* 29:20

fourth day ten bullocks, *t.* rams   *Nu* 29:23

the fifth day nine bullocks, *t.* rams   *Nu* 29:26

sixth day eight bullocks, *t.* rams   *Nu* 29:29

day seven bullocks, *t.* rams   *Nu* 29:32

And divide the prey into *t.* parts   *Nu* 31:27

and *t.* thousand persons in all   *Nu* 31:35

tribute was thirty and *t.* persons   *Nu* 31:40

The *t.* tribes and the half tribe have   *Nu* 34:15

on the east side *t.* thousand cubits   *Nu* 35:5

the south side *t.* thousand cubits   *Nu* 35:5

on the west side *t.* thousand cubits   *Nu* 35:5

the north side *t.* thousand cubits   *Nu* 35:5

ye shall add forty and *t.* cities   *Nu* 35:6

out of the hand of the *t.* kings   *De* 3:8

God hath done unto these *t.* kings   *De* 3:21

wrote them upon *t.* tables of stone   *De* 4:13

Bashan, *t.* kings of the Amorites   *De* 4:47

he wrote them in *t.* tables of stone   *De* 5:22

delivered unto me *t.* tables of stone   *De* 9:10

Lord gave me the *t.* tables of stone   *De* 9:11

and the *t.* tables of the covenant   *De* 9:15

were in my *t.* hands   *De* 9:15

I took the *t.* tables, and cast them   *De* 9:17

cast them out of my *t.* hands   *De* 9:17

How the *t.* tables of stone like   *De* 10:1

hewed *t.* tables of stone like unto   *De* 10:3

having the *t.* tables in mine hand   *De* 10:3

and cleaveth the cleft into *t.* claws   *De* 14:6

At the mouth of *t.* witnesses   *De* 17:6

the shoulder, and the *t.* cheeks   *De* 18:3

at the mouth of *t.* witnesses   *De* 19:15

If a man have *t.* wives, one beloved   *De* 21:15

and *t.* put ten thousand to flight   *De* 32:30

sent out of Shittim *t.* men to spy   *Jos* 2:1

And the woman took the *t.* men   *Jos* 2:4

unto the *t.* kings of the Amorites   *Jos* 2:10

So the *t.* men returned, and   *Jos* 2:23

t. thousand cubits by measure   *Jos* 3:4

the *t.* men that had spied out   *Jos* 6:22

let about *t.* or three thousand men   *Jos* 7:3

and *t.* hundred shekels of silver, and   *Jos* 7:21

to the *t.* kings of the Amorites   *Jos* 9:10

given the inheritance of *t.* tribes   *Jos* 14:3

children of Joseph were *t.* tribes   *Jos* 14:4

t. cities with their villages   *Jos* 15:60

twenty and *t.* cities with   *Jos* 19:30

nine cities out of those *t.* tribes   *Jos* 21:16

with her suburbs; *t.* cities   *Jos* 21:25; 21:27

even the *t.* kings of the Amorites   *Jos* 24:12

him a dagger which had *t.* edges   *J'g* 3:16

prey; to every man a damsel or *t.*   *J'g* 5:30

the people twenty and *t.* thousand   *J'g* 7:3

took *t.* princes of the Midianites   *J'g* 7:25

and took the *t.* kings of Midian   *J'g* 8:12

t. other companies ran upon   *J'g* 9:44

judged Israel twenty and *t.* years   *J'g* 10:3

let me alone *t.* months, that I may   *J'g* 11:37

and he sent her away for *t.* months   *J'g* 11:38

came to pass at the end of *t.* months   *J'g* 11:39

Ephraimites forty and *t.* thousand   *J'g* 12:6

put a firebrand between *t.* tails   *J'g* 15:4

they bound him with *t.* new cords   *J'g* 15:13

the gate of the city, and the *t.* posts   *J'g* 16:3

of the Philistines for my *t.* eyes   *J'g* 16:28

Samson took hold of the *t.* middle   *J'g* 16:29

took *t.* hundred shekels of silver   *J'g* 17:4

were with him *t.* asses saddled   *J'g* 19:10

day twenty and *t.* thousand men   *J'g* 20:21

and slew *t.* thousand men of them   *J'g* 20:45

he, and his wife, and his *t.* sons   *Ru* 1:1

the name of his *t.* sons Mahlon   *Ru* 1:2

and she was left, with her *t.* sons   *Ru* 1:3

the woman was left of her *t.* sons   *Ru* 1:5

her *t.* daughters in law with her   *Ru* 1:7

said unto her *t.* daughters in law   *Ru* 1:8

So they *t.* went until they came   *Ru* 1:19

t. did build the house of Israel   *Ru* 4:11

he had *t.* wives; the name of   *1Sa* 1:2

And the *t.* sons of Eli, Hophni   *1Sa* 1:3

bare three sons and *t.* daughters   *1Sa* 2:21

that shall come upon thy *t.* sons   *1Sa* 2:34

and *t.* sons of Eli, Hophni   *1Sa* 4:4; 4:11

and thy *t.* sons also, Hophni   *1Sa* 4:17

take *t.* milch kine, on which there   *1Sa* 6:7

took *t.* milch kine, and tied them   *1Sa* 6:10

thou shalt find *t.* men by Rachel's   *1Sa* 10:2

and give thee *t.* loaves of bread   *1Sa* 10:4

t. of them were not left together   *1Sa* 11:11

when he had reigned *t.* years over   *1Sa* 13:1

t. thousand were with Saul in   *1Sa* 13:2

names of his *t.* daughters were   *1Sa* 14:49

t. hundred thousand footmen   *1Sa* 15:4

two (S)   *1Sa* 18:21; *2Ki* 4:33; *Isa* 6:2; *Jer* 34:18; *Eze* 21:19; *M't* 5:41; 19:5-6; 21:31; 27:21; *M'k* 10:8; *Eph* 2:15

slew of the Philistines *t.* hundred men   *1Sa* 18:27

they *t.* made a covenant before   *1Sa* 23:18

and *t.* hundred abode by the stuff   *1Sa* 25:13

haste, and took *t.* hundred loaves   *1Sa* 25:18

t. bottles of wine, and five sheep   *1Sa* 25:18

t. hundred cakes of figs, and laid them   *1Sa* 25:18

David with his *t.* wives, Ahinoam   *1Sa* 27:3

and he went, and *t.* men with him   *1Sa* 28:8

And David's *t.* wives were taken   *1Sa* 30:5

t. hundred abode behind, which were   *1Sa* 30:10

of figs, and *t.* clusters of raisins   *1Sa* 30:12

and David rescued his *t.* wives   *1Sa* 30:18

David came to the *t.* hundred men   *1Sa* 30:21

David abode *t.* days in Ziklag   *2Sa* 1:1

up thither, and his *t.* wives also   *2Sa* 2:2

over Israel, and reigned *t.* years   *2Sa* 2:10

Saul's sons had *t.* men that were   *2Sa* 4:2

even with *t.* lines measured he   *2Sa* 8:2

the Syrians *t.* and twenty thousand   *2Sa* 8:5

There were *t.* men in one city; the   *2Sa* 12:1

it came to pass after *t.* full years   *2Sa* 13:23

And thy handmaid had *t.* sons   *2Sa* 14:6

and they *t.* strove together in   *2Sa* 14:6

t. hundred shekels after the king's   *2Sa* 14:26

dwelt *t.* full years in Jerusalem   *2Sa* 14:28

with Absalom went *t.* hundred men   *2Sa* 15:11

peace, and your *t.* sons with you   *2Sa* 15:27

have there with them their *t.* sons   *2Sa* 15:36

upon them *t.* hundred loaves of bread   *2Sa* 16:1

David sat between the *t.* gates   *2Sa* 18:24

the king took the *t.* sons of Rizpah   *2Sa 21:8*

he slew *t.* lionlike men of Moab   *2Sa 23:20*

what he did to the *t.* captains   *1Ki 2:5*

fell upon *t.* men more righteous   *1Ki 2:32*

t. of the servants of Shimei ran   *1Ki 2:39*

Then came there *t.* women   *1Ki 3:16*

the house, save we *t.* in the house   *1Ki 3:18*

said, Divide the living child in *t.*   *1Ki 3:25*

and they *t.* made a league together   *1Ki 5:12*

Lebanon, and *t.* months at home   *1Ki 5:14*

the oracle he made *t.* cherubims   *1Ki 6:23*

The *t.* doors also were of olive tree   *1Ki 6:32*

And the *t.* doors were of fir tree   *1Ki 6:34*

the *t.* leaves of the one door were   *1Ki 6:34*

the *t.* leaves of the other door were   *1Ki 6:34*

For he cast *t.* pillars of brass   *1Ki 7:15*

made *t.* chapiters of molten brass   *1Ki 7:16*

t. rows round about upon the one   *1Ki 7:18*

the chapiters upon the *t.* pillars   *1Ki 7:20*

the pomegranates were *t.* hundred   *1Ki 7:20*

the knops were cast in *t.* rows   *1Ki 7:24*

it contained *t.* thousand baths   *1Ki 7:26*

The *t.* pillars, and the   *1Ki 7:41*

the *t.* bowls of the chapiters   *1Ki 7:41*

were on top of the *t.* pillars   *1Ki 7:41*

t. networks, to cover the *t.* bowls   *1Ki 7:41*

pomegranates for the *t.* networks   *1Ki 7:42*

t. rows of pomegranates for one   *1Ki 7:42*

cover the *t.* bowls of the chapiters   *1Ki 7:42*

spread forth their *t.* wings over   *1Ki 8:7*

the ark save the *t.* tables of stone   *1Ki 8:9*

t. and twenty thousand oxen   *1Ki 8:63*

Solomon had built the *t.* houses   *1Ki 9:10*

king Solomon made *t.* hundred targets   *1Ki 10:16*

and *t.* lions stood beside the stays   *1Ki 10:19*

and they *t.* were alone in the field   *1Ki 11:29*

counsel, and made *t.* calves of gold   *1Ki 12:28*

reigned were *t.* and twenty years   *1Ki 14:20*

and reigned over Israel *t.* years   *1Ki 15:25*

to reign over Israel in Tirzah, *t.* years   *1Ki 16:8*

of Israel divided into *t.* parts   *1Ki 16:21*

of Shemer for *t.* talents of silver   *1Ki 16:24*

in Samaria twenty and *t.* years   *1Ki 16:29*

I am gathering *t.* sticks, that I   *1Ki 17:12*

long halt ye between *t.* opinions   *1Ki 18:21*

them therefore give us *t.* bullocks   *1Ki 18:23*

would contain *t.* measures of seed   *1Ki 18:32*

were thirty and *t.* kings with him   *1Ki 20:1*

and they were *t.* hundred   *1Ki 20:15*

hundred and thirty *t.*   *1Ki 20:15*

the thirty and *t.* kings that helped   *1Ki 20:16*

them the *t.* little flocks of kids   *1Ki 20:27*

set *t.* men, sons of Belial, before   *1Ki 21:10*

there came in *t.* men, children of   *1Ki 21:13*

his thirty and *t.* captains that had   *1Ki 22:31*

and reigned *t.* years over Israel   *1Ki 22:51*

burnt up the *t.* captains of the   *2Ki 1:14*

leave thee. And they *t.* went   *2Ki 2:6*

off: and they *t.* stood by Jordan   *2Ki 2:7*

they *t.* went over on dry ground   *2Ki 2:8*

clothes, and rent them in *t.* pieces   *2Ki 2:12*

forth *t.* she bears out of the wood   *2Ki 2:24*

tare forty and *t.* children of them   *2Ki 2:24*

come to take unto him my *t.* sons   *2Ki 4:1*

servant *t.* mules' burden of earth   *2Ki 5:17*

mount Ephraim *t.* young men   *2Ki 5:22*

silver, and *t.* changes of garments   *2Ki 5:22*

said, Be content, take *t.* talents   *2Ki 5:23*

bound *t.* talents of silver in *t.* bags   *2Ki 5:23*

with *t.* changes of garments   *2Ki 5:23*

laid them upon *t.* of his servants   *2Ki 5:23*

t. measures of barley for a shekel   *2Ki 7:1*

took therefore *t.* chariot horses   *2Ki 7:14*

and *t.* measures of barley for a shekel   *2Ki 7:16*

T. measures of barley for a shekel   *2Ki 7:18*

Thirty and *t.* years old was he   *2Ki 8:17*

T. and twenty years old was   *2Ki 8:26*

out to him *t.* or three eunuchs   *2Ki 9:32*

t. kings stood not before him   *2Ki 10:4*

Lay ye them in *t.* heaps at the   *2Ki 10:8*

t. and forty men; neither left   *2Ki 10:14*

t. parts of all you that go forth on   *2Ki 11:7*

t. and fifty years in Jerusalem   *2Ki 15:2*

Israel in Samaria, and   *2Ki 15:23*

reigned *t.* years

In the *t.* and fiftieth year of Azariah   *2Ki 15:27*

them molten images, even *t.* calves   *2Ki 17:16*

deliver the *t.* thousand horses   *2Ki 18:23*

t. courts of the house of the Lord   *2Ki 21:5*

Amon was twenty and *t.* years old   *2Ki 21:19*

he reigned *t.* years in Jerusalem   *2Ki 21:19*

made in the *t.* courts of the house   *2Ki 23:12*

the way of the gate between *t.* walls   *2Ki 25:4*

The *t.* pillars, one sea, and   *2Ki 25:16*

And unto Eber were born *t.* sons   *1Ch 1:19*

the father of Tekoa had *t.* wives   *1Ch 4:5*

of sheep *t.* hundred and fifty thousand   *1Ch 5:21*

of asses *t.* thousand, and of men an   *1Ch 5:21*

t. and twenty thousand and six   *1Ch 7:2*

twenty and *t.* thousand and thirty   *1Ch 7:7*

was twenty thousand and *t.* hundred   *1Ch 7:9*

thousand and *t.* hundred soldiers   *1Ch 7:11*

the gates were *t.* hundred and twelve   *1Ch 9:22*

was more honorable than the *t.*   *1Ch 11:21*

he slew *t.* lionlike men of Moab   *1Ch 11:22*

house twenty and *t.* captains   *1Ch 12:28*

the heads of them were *t.* hundred   *1Ch 12:32*

his brethren *t.* hundred and twenty   *1Ch 15:6*

the chief, and his brethren *t.* hundred   *1Ch 15:8*

Syrians *t.* and twenty thousand   *1Ch 18:5*

thirty and *t.* thousand chariots   *1Ch 19:7*

the *t.* and twentieth to Gamul   *1Ch 24:17*

was *t.* hundred fourscore and eight   *1Ch 25:7*

The *t.* and twentieth to Giddalti   *1Ch 25:29*

were threescore *t.* of Obed-edom   *1Ch 26:8*

day, and toward Asuppim *t.*   *1Ch 26:17*

the causeway, and *t.* at Parbar   *1Ch 26:18*

t. thousand and seven hundred chief   *1Ch 26:32*

made *t.* cherubims of image work   *2Ch 3:10*

he made before the house *t.* pillars   *2Ch 3:15*

T. rows of oxen were cast, when it   *2Ch 4:3*

the *t.* pillars, and the pommels, and   *2Ch 4:12*

which were on the top of the *t.* pillars   *2Ch 4:12*

t. wreaths to cover the *t.* pommels   *2Ch 4:12*

pomegranates on the *t.* wreaths   *2Ch 4:13*

t. rows of pomegranates on each   *2Ch 4:13*

to cover the *t.* pommels of   *2Ch 4:13*

nothing in the ark save the *t.* tables   *2Ch 5:10*

of twenty and *t.* thousand oxen   *2Ch 7:5*

even *t.* hundred and fifty, that bare   *2Ch 8:10*

king Solomon made *t.* hundred targets   *2Ch 9:15*

and *t.* lions standing by the stays   *2Ch 9:18*

and begat twenty and *t.* sons, and   *2Ch 13:21*

drew bows, *t.* hundred and fourscore   *2Ch 14:8*

with him *t.* hundred and fourscore   *2Ch 17:15*

t. hundred thousand mighty men of   *2Ch 17:16*

bow and shield *t.* hundred thousand   *2Ch 17:17*

Jehoram was thirty and *t.* years   *2Ch 21:5*

after the end of *t.* years, his bowels   *2Ch 21:19*

Thirty and *t.* years old was he when   *2Ch 21:20*

Forty and *t.* years old was Ahaziah   *2Ch 22:2*

And Jehoiada took for him *t.* wives   *2Ch 24:3*

and he reigned fifty and *t.* years in   *2Ch 26:3*

men of valour were *t.* thousand and six   *2Ch 26:12*

brethren *t.* hundred thousand   *2Ch 28:8*

rams, and *t.* hundred lambs   *2Ch 29:32*

t. courts of the house of the Lord   *2Ch 33:5*

Amon was *t.* and twenty years old   *2Ch 33:21*

and reigned *t.* years in Jerusalem   *2Ch 33:21*

t. thousand and six hundred small   *2Ch 35:8*

of Parosh, *t.* thousand an hundred   *Ezr 2:3*

thousand and hundred seventy and *t.*   *Ezr 2:3*

three hundred seventy and *t.*   *Ezr 2:6*

t. thousand eight hundred and twelve   *Ezr 2:6*

a thousand *t.* hundred fifty and four   *Ezr 2:7*

of Bani, six hundred forty and *t.*   *Ezr 2:10*

a thousand *t.* hundred twenty hundred twenty and *t.*   *Ezr 2:12*

Bigvai, *t.* thousand fifty and six   *Ezr 2:14*

Hashum, *t.* hundred twenty and three   *Ezr 2:19*

children of Azmaveth, forty and *t.*   *Ezr 2:24*

Michmas, an hundred twenty and *t.*   *Ezr 2:27*

and Ai, *t.* hundred twenty and three   *Ezr 2:28*

The children of Nebo, fifty and *t.*   *Ezr 2:29*

a thousand *t.* hundred fifty and four   *Ezr 2:31*
of Immer, a thousand fifty and *t.*   *Ezr 2:37*
thousand *t.* hundred forty and seven   *Ezr 2:38*
were three hundred ninety and *t.*   *Ezr 2:58*
of Nekoda, six hundred fifty and *t.*   *Ezr 2:60*
and *t.* thousand three hundred and   *Ezr 2:64*
among them *t.* hundred singing men   *Ezr 2:65*
their mules, *t.* hundred forty and five   *Ezr 2:66*
t. hundred rams, four hundred lambs   *Ezr 6:17*
and with him *t.* hundred males   *Ezr 8:4*
him *t.* hundred and eighteen males   *Ezr 8:9*
t. hundred and twenty Nethinims   *Ezr 8:20*
and *t.* vessels of fine copper   *Ezr 8:27*
is this a work of one day or *t.*   *Ezr 10:13*
t. and thirtieth year of Artaxerxes   *Ne 5:14*
the month Elul, in fifty and *t.* days   *Ne 6:15*
t. thousand an hundred seventy and *t.*   *Ne 7:8*
three hundred seventy and *t.*   *Ne 7:9*
of Arah, six hundred fifty and *t.*   *Ne 7:10*
t. thousand and eight hundred   *Ne 7:11*
a thousand *t.* hundred fifty and four   *Ne 7:12*
of Azgad, *t.* thousand three   *Ne 7:17*
three hundred twenty and *t.*   *Ne 7:17*
t. thousand threescore and seven   *Ne 7:19*
of Beth-azmaveth, forty and *t.*   *Ne 7:28*
an hundred and twenty and *t.*   *Ne 7:31*
men of the other Nebo, fifty and *t.*   *Ne 7:33*
a thousand *t.* hundred fifty and four   *Ne 7:34*
of Immer, a thousand fifty and *t.*   *Ne 7:40*
a thousand *t.* hundred forty and seven   *Ne 7:41*
were three hundred ninety and *t.*   *Ne 7:60*
of Nekoda, six hundred forty and *t.*   *Ne 7:62*
together was forty and *t.* thousand   *Ne 7:66*
t. hundred forty and five singing men   *Ne 7:67*
their mules, *t.* hundred forty and five   *Ne 7:68*
drams of gold, and *t.* thousand   *Ne 7:71*
and *t.* hundred pound of silver   *Ne 7:71*
gold, and *t.* thousand pound of silver   *Ne 7:72*
were eight hundred twenty and *t.*   *Ne 11:12*
the fathers *t.* hundred forty   *Ne 11:13*
and fathers hundred forty and *t.*   *Ne 11:13*
were *t.* hundred fourscore and four   *Ne 11:18*
were an hundred seventy and *t.*   *Ne 11:19*
t. great companies of them that   *Ne 12:31*
stood the *t.* companies of them that   *Ne 12:40*
t. and thirtieth year of Artaxerxes   *Ne 13:6*
t. of the king's chamberlains   *Es 2:21; 6:2*
keep these *t.* days according   *Es 9:27*
Only do not *t.* things unto me: then   *Job 13:20*
thee and against thy *t.* friends   *Job 42:7*
T. things have I required of thee   *Pr 30:7*
The horseleach hath *t.* daughters   *Pr 30:15*
T. are better than one; because   *Ec 4:9*
Again, if *t.* lie together, then they   *Ec 4:11*
against him, *t.* shall withstand him   *Ec 4:12*
Thy *t.* breasts are like *t.* young roes   *Ca 4:5*

As it were the company of *t.* armies   *Ca 6:13*
As it were the company of *t.* armies   *Ca 7:3*
Thy *t.* breasts are like *t.* young   *Ca 7:3*
that keep the fruit thereof *t.* hundred   *Ca 8:12*
for the *t.* tails of these smoking   *Isa 7:4*
nourish a young cow, and *t.* sheep   *Isa 7:21*
t. or three berries in the top   *Isa 17:6*
also a ditch between the *t.* walls for   *Isa 22:11*
I will give thee *t.* thousand horses, if   *Isa 36:8*
to open before him the *t.* leaved gates   *Isa 45:1*
these *t.* things shall come to thee   *Isa 47:9*
These *t.* things are come unto thee   *Isa 51:19*
my people have committed *t.* evils   *Jer 2:13*
you one of a city, and *t.* of a family   *Jer 3:14*
t. baskets of figs were set before the   *Jer 24:1*
Within *t.* full years will I bring again   *Jer 28:3*
within the space of *t.* full years   *Jer 28:11*
t. families the Lord hath chosen   *Jer 33:24*
by the gate betwixt the *t.* walls   *Jer 39:4*
way of the gate between the *t.* walls   *Jer 52:7*
The *t.* pillars, one sea, and twelve   *Jer 52:20*
eight hundred thirty and *t.* persons   *Jer 52:29*
t. wings of every one were joined   *Eze 1:11*
and *t.* covered their bodies   *Eze 1:11*
every one had *t.* which covered   *Eze 1:23*
son of man, appoint thee *t.* ways   *Eze 21:19*
the way, at the head of the *t.* ways   *Eze 21:21*
there were *t.* women, the daughters   *Eze 23:2*
hast said, These *t.* nations and   *Eze 35:10*
these *t.* countries shall be mine   *Eze 35:10*
they shall be no more *t.* nations   *Eze 37:22*
they be divided into *t.* kingdoms   *Eze 37:22*
and the posts thereof, *t.* cubits   *Eze 40:9*
porch of the gate were *t.* tables on   *Eze 40:39*
this side, and *t.* tables on that side   *Eze 40:39*
of the north gate, were *t.* tables   *Eze 40:40*
porch of the gate, were *t.* tables   *Eze 40:40*
the post of the door, *t.* cubits   *Eze 41:3*
and every cherub had *t.* faces   *Eze 41:18*
and the length thereof *t.* cubits   *Eze 41:22*
and the sanctuary had *t.* doors   *Eze 41:23*
And the doors had *t.* leaves apiece   *Eze 41:24*
leaves apiece, *t.* turning leaves   *Eze 41:24*
t. leaves for the one door   *Eze 41:24*
and *t.* leaves for the other door   *Eze 41:24*
to the lower settle shall be *t.* cubits   *Eze 43:14*
out of the flock, out of *t.* hundred   *Eze 45:15*
was a place on the *t.* sides westward   *Eze 46:19*
Israel: Joseph shall have *t.* portions   *Eze 47:13*
toward the north *t.* hundred and fifty   *Eze 48:17*
toward the south *t.* hundred and fifty   *Eze 48:17*
toward the east *t.* hundred and fifty   *Eze 48:17*
toward the west *t.* hundred and fifty   *Eze 48:17*

about threescore and *t.* years old   *Da 5:31*
the river a ram which had *t.* horns   *Da 8:3*
the *t.* horns were high; but one was   *Da 8:3*
came to the ram that had *t.* horns   *Da 8:6*
the ram, and brake his *t.* horns   *Da 8:7*
t. thousand and three hundred days   *Da 8:14*
ram thou sawest having *t.* horns   *Da 8:20*
and threescore and *t.* weeks shall   *Da 9:25*
after threescore and *t.* weeks shall   *Da 9:26*
there stood other *t.* the one on this   *Da 12:5*
thousand *t.* hundred and ninety days   *Da 12:11*
After *t.* days will he revive us   *Ho 6:2*
themselves in their *t.* furrows.   *Ho 10:10*
Israel, *t.* years before the earthquake   *Am 1:1*
Can *t.* walk together, except they   *Am 3:3*
out of the mouth of the lion *t.* legs   *Am 3:12*
So *t.* or three cities wandered unto   *Am 4:8*
t. olive trees by it, one upon the   *Zec 4:3*
What are these *t.* olive trees upon   *Zec 4:11*
What be these *t.* olive branches   *Zec 4:12*
through the *t.* golden pipes empty   *Zec 4:12*
These are the *t.* anointed ones   *Zec 4:14*
behold, there came out *t.* women   *Zec 5:9*
out from between *t.* mountains   *Zec 6:1*
And I took unto me *t.* staves   *Zec 11:7*
t. parts therein shall be cut off   *Zec 13:8*
from *t.* years old and under   *M't 2:16*
saw *t.* brethren, Simon called   *M't 4:18*
thence, he saw other *t.* brethren   *M't 4:21*
No man can serve *t.* masters   *M't 6:24*
met him *t.* possessed with devils   *M't 8:28*
t. blind men followed him, crying   *M't 9:27*
neither *t.* coats, neither shoes, nor   *M't 10:10*
t. tunics (R)   *M't 10:10*
t. sparrows sold for a farthing   *M't 10:29*
Christ, he sent *t.* of his disciples   *M't 11:2*
here but five loaves, and *t.* fishes   *M't 14:17*
the five loaves, and the *t.* fishes   *M't 14:19*
having *t.* hands or *t.* feet to be cast   *M't 18:8*
having *t.* eyes to be cast into hell   *M't 18:9*
then take with thee one or *t.* more   *M't 18:16*
the mouth of *t.* or three witnesses   *M't 18:16*
if *t.* of you shall agree on earth as   *M't 18:19*
For where *t.* or three are gathered   *M't 18:20*
Grant that my *t.* sons may sit   *M't 20:21*
indignation against the *t.* brethren   *M't 20:24*
t. blind men sitting by the way side   *M't 20:30*
Olives, then sent Jesus *t.* disciples   *M't 21:1*
A certain man had *t.* sons: and he   *M't 21:28*
On these *t.* commandments hang   *M't 22:40*
Then shall *t.* be in the field; the one shall   *M't 24:40*
T. women shall be grinding at the   *M't 24:41*
he gave five talents, to another *t.*   *M't 25:15*
likewise, he that had received *t.*   *M't 25:17*
he also gained the other *t.*   *M't 25:17*

that had received *t*. talents came	M't 25:22	
thou deliveredst unto me *t*. talents	M't 25:22	
I have gained *t*. other talents	M't 25:22	
that after *t*. days is the feast	M't 26:2	
Peter and the *t*. sons of Zebedee	M't 26:37	
At the last came *t*. false witnesses	M't 26:60	
the *t*. thieves crucified with him	M't 27:38	
they were about *t*. thousand	M'k 5:13	
to send them forth by *t*. and *t*.	M'k 6:7	
sandals; and not put on *t*. coats	M'k 6:9	
t. tunics (A)	M'k 6:9	
t. hundred pennyworth of bread	M'k 6:37	
knew, they say, Five and *t*. fishes	M'k 6:38	
the five loaves and the *t*. fishes	M'k 6:41	
t. fishes divided he among them all	M'k 6:41	
than having *t*. hands to go into hell	M'k 9:43	
having *t*. feet to be cast into hell	M'k 9:45	
having *t*. eyes to be cast into hell	M'k 9:47	
he sendeth forth *t*. of his disciples	M'k 11:1	
in a place where *t*. ways met	M'k 11:4	
widow, and she threw in *t*. mites	M'k 12:42	
After *t*. days was the feast of	M'k 14:1	
he sendeth forth *t*. of his disciples	M'k 14:13	
with him they crucify *t*. thieves	M'k 15:27	
in another form unto *t*. of them	M'k 16:12	
turtledoves, or *t*. young pigeons	Lu 2:24	
He that hath *t*. coats, let him impart	Lu 3:11	
t. tunics (A)	Lu 3:11	
saw *t*. ships standing by the lake	Lu 5:2	
calling unto him *t*. of his disciples	Lu 7:19	
creditor which had *t*. debtors	Lu 7:41	
neither have *t*. coats apiece	Lu 9:3	
more but five loaves and *t*. fishes	Lu 9:13	
took the five loaves and the *t*. fishes	Lu 9:16	
there talked with him *t*. men	Lu 9:30	
the *t*. men that stood with him	Lu 9:32	
seventy others, and sent them *t*.	Lu 10:1	
and sent them *t*. and *t*. before his face	Lu 10:1	
he departed, he took out *t*. pence	Lu 10:35	
five sparrows sold for *t*. farthings	Lu 12:6	
three against *t*. and *t*. against	Lu 12:52	
he said, A certain man had *t*. sons	Lu 15:11	
No servant can serve *t*. masters	Lu 16:13	
there shall be *t*. men in one bed	Lu 17:34	
T. women shall be grinding	Lu 17:35	
T. men shall be in the field	Lu 17:36	
T. men went up into the temple to	Lu 18:10	
Olives, he sent *t*. of his disciples	Lu 19:29	
widow casting in thither *t*. mites	Lu 21:2	
Lord, behold, here are *t*. swords	Lu 22:38	
there were also *t*. other, malefactors	Lu 23:32	
t. men stood by them in shining	Lu 24:4	
t. of them went that same day to a	Lu 24:13	
John stood, and *t*. of his disciples	Joh 1:35	
the *t*. disciples heard him speak	Joh 1:37	
One of the *t*. which heard John	Joh 1:40	
containing *t*. or three firkins apiece	Joh 2:6	

them: and he abode there *t*. days	Joh 4:40	
after *t*. days he departed thence	Joh 4:43	
T. hundred pennyworth of bread	Joh 6:7	
barley loaves, and *t*. small fishes	Joh 6:9	
that the testimony of *t*. men is true	Joh 8:17	
he abode *t*. days still in the same	Joh 11:6	
crucified him, and *t*. other with him	Joh 19:18	
And seeth *t*. angels in white sitting	Joh 20:12	
and *t*. other of his disciples	Joh 21:2	
but as it were *t*. hundred cubits	Joh 21:8	
t. men stood by them in white	Ac 1:10	
they appointed *t*., Joseph called	Ac 1:23	
of these *t*. thou hast chosen	Ac 1:24	
of Madian, where he begat *t*. sons	Ac 7:29	
they sent unto him *t*. men, desiring	Ac 9:38	
called *t*. of his household servants	Ac 10:7	
was sleeping between *t*. soldiers	Ac 12:6	
bound with *t*. chains: and the	Ac 12:6	
continued by the space of *t*. years	Ac 19:10	
he sent into Macedonia *t*. of them	Ac 19:22	
the space of *t*. hours cried out	Ac 19:34	
him to be bound with *t*. chains	Ac 21:33	
he called unto him *t*. centurions	Ac 23:23	
make ready *t*. hundred soldiers to	Ac 23:23	
spearmen *t*. hundred, at the third	Ac 23:33	
after *t*. years Porcius Festus came	Ac 24:27	
t. hundred threescore and sixteen	Ac 27:37	
into a place where *t*. seas met	Ac 27:41	
Paul dwelt *t*. whole years in	Ac 28:30	
for *t*. saith he, shall be one flesh	1Co 6:16	
let it be by *t*. or at the most	1Co 14:27	
Let the prophets speak *t*. or three	1Co 14:29	
the mouth of *t*. or three witnesses	2Co 13:1	
Abraham had *t*. sons, the one	Ga 4:22	
for these are the *t*. covenants	Ga 4:24	
wife, and they *t*. shall be one flesh	Eph 5:31	
For I am in a strait betwixt *t*.	Ph'p 1:23	
but before *t*. or three witnesses	1Ti 5:19	
That by *t*. immutable things	Heb 6:18	
mercy under *t*. or three witnesses	Heb 10:28	
the sharp sword with *t*. edges	Re 2:12	
there come *t*. woes more hereafter	Re 9:12	
t. hundred thousand thousand	Re 9:16	
under foot forty and *t*. months	Re 11:2	
give power unto my *t*. witnesses	Re 11:3	
t. hundred and threescore days	Re 11:3	
These are the *t*. olive trees	Re 11:4	
the *t*. candlesticks standing before	Re 11:4	
these *t*. prophets tormented them	Re 11:10	
thousand *t*. hundred and threescore	Re 12:6	
given *t*. wings of a great eagle	Re 12:14	
to continue forty and *t*. months	Re 13:5	
and he had *t*. horns like a lamb	Re 13:11	

TWO-EDGED

and a *t*. sword in their hand	Ps 149:6	
wormwood, sharp as a *t*. sword	Pr 5:4	
and sharper than any *t*. sword	Heb 4:12	
of his mouth went a sharp *t*. sword	Re 1:16	

TWOFOLD

make him *t*. more the child of hell	M't 23:15	

TYCHICUS

and of Asia, T. and Trophimus	Ac 20:4	
T., a beloved brother and faithful	Eph 6:21	
All my state and T. declare unto	Col 4:7	
And T. have I sent to Ephesus	2Ti 4:12	
send Artemas unto thee, or T.	Tit 3:12	

TYPE

Adam was a *t*. of (A)(R)	Ro 5:4	
visible *t*. of coming age (A)	Heb 9:9	

TYRANNUS

daily in the school of one T.	Ac 19:9	

TYRANT

the *t*. during years (B)	Job 15:20	
how the *t*. was stopped (B)	Isa 14:4	
the prey of the *t*. (R)	Isa 49:25	

TYRANTS

ruling *t*. are children (B)(R)	Isa 3:12	
the *t*. (B)	Isa 25:4; 25:5; 29:20; 49:25; 64:3; Jer 15:21	

TYRE

Ramah, and to the strong city T.	Jos 19:29	
Hiram king of T. sent messengers	2Sa 5:11	
And came to the strong hold of T.	2Sa 24:7	
Hiram king of T. sent his servants	1Ki 5:1	
sent and fetched Hiram out of T.	1Ki 7:13	
and his father was a man of T.	1Ki 7:14	
king of T. had furnished Solomon	1Ki 9:11	
Hiram came out from T. to see the	1Ki 9:12	
Hiram king of T.	1Ch 14:1	
sent messengers they of T. brought much cedar	1Ch 22:4	
sent to Huram the king of T.	2Ch 2:3	
the king of T. answered in writing	2Ch 2:11	
his father was a man of T. skilful	2Ch 2:14	
to them to T. to bring cedar trees	Ezr 3:7	
There dwelt men of T. also therein	Ne 13:16	
daughter of T. shall be there	Ps 45:12	
with the inhabitants of T.	Ps 83:7	
Philistia, and T. with Ethiopia	Ps 87:4	
The burden of T. Howl, ye ships	Isa 23:1	
be sorely pained at the report of T.	Isa 23:5	
hath taken this counsel against T.	Isa 23:8	
T. shall be forgotten seventy years	Isa 23:15	
years shall T. sing as an harlot	Isa 23:15	
years, that the Lord will visit T.	Isa 23:17	
ye to do with me, O T. and Zidon	Joe 3:4	
has been done in T. and Sidon	M't 11:21	
be more tolerable for T. and Sidon	M't 11:22	
into the coasts of T. and Sidon	M't 15:21	
they about T. and Sidon, a great	M'k 3:8	
into the borders of T. and Sidon	M'k 7:24	
departing from the coasts of T. and	M'k 7:31	
from the sea coast of T. and Sidon	Lu 6:17	

TYRE

works had been done in *T.*	*Lu 10:13*
be more tolerable for *T.* and Sidon	*Lu 10:14*
highly displeased with them of *T.*	*Ac 12:20*
sailed into Syria, and landed at *T.*	*Ac 21:3*
we had finished our course from *T.*	*Ac 21:7*

TYRUS

And all the kings of *T.* and all the	*Jer 25:22*
to the king of *T.* and to the king	*Jer 27:3*
and to cut off from *T.* and Zidon	*Jer 47:4*
T. hath said against Jerusalem	*Eze 26:2*
I am against thee, *T.*, and will	*Eze 26:3*
they shall destroy the walls of *T.*	*Eze 26:4*
will bring upon *T.* Nebuchadrezzar	*Eze 26:7*
Thus saith the Lord God to *T.*	*Eze 26:15*
man, take up a lamentation for *T.*	*Eze 27:2*
say unto *T.* thou that art situated	*Eze 27:3*
O *T.* thou hast said, I am of perfect	*Eze 27:3*
thy wise men, *T.*, that were in	*Eze 27:8*
saying, What city is like *T.*	*Eze 27:32*
of man, say unto the prince of *T.*	*Eze 28:2*
a lamentation upon the king of *T.*	*Eze 28:12*
to serve a great service against *T.*	*Eze 29:18*
he no wages, nor his army, for *T.*	*Eze 29:18*
Ephraim, as I saw *T.* is planted in	*Ho 9:13*
For three transgressions of *T.*	*Am 1:9*
I will send a fire on the wall of *T.*	*Am 1:10*
T. and Zidon, though it be	*Zec 9:2*
T. did build herself a strong hold	*Zec 9:3*

U

UCAL

Ithiel, even unto Ithiel and *U.*	*Pr 30:1*

UEL

of Bani; Maadai, Amram, and *U.*	*Ezr 10:34*

UGLY

u. and lean (B)	*Ge 41:3*
impudence and *u.* heart (B)	*1Sa 17:28*
people in an *u.* mood (B)	*1Sa 30:6*
with a very *u.* wound (B)	*Jer 14:17*
felt *u.* toward Tyrians (B)	*Ac 12:20*
u. blot on your company (N)	*2Pe 2:13*

ULAI

vision, and I was by the river of *U.*	*Da 8:2*
man's voice between the banks of *U.*	*Da 8:16*

ULAM

and his sons were *U.* and Rakem	*1Ch 7:16*
And the sons of *U.*; Bedan. These	*1Ch 7:17*
his brother were *U.* his firstborn	*1Ch 8:39*
the sons of *U.* were mighty men of	*1Ch 8:40*

ULCERS

boil breaking out with *u.* (S)	*Ex 9:9*
painful *u.* came (A)(B)(P)	*Re 16:2*
their anguish and *u.* (A)	*Re 16:11*

ULLA

And the sons of *U.*: Arah	*1Ch 7:39*

UMMAH

U. also, and Aphek, and Rehob	*Jos 19:30*

UNABLE

u. to support himself (A)	*Le 25:35*
u. to meet own obligation (B)	*Le 25:35*
u. to speak intelligently (P)	*M'k 7:32*

UNACCUSTOMED

as a bullock *u.* to the yoke	*Jer 31:18*

UNADULTERATED

unleavened bread of *u.* truth (P)	*1Co 5:8*
u. nourishing milk (B)	*1Pe 2:2*

UNADVISEDLY

so that he spake *u.* with his lips	*Ps 106:33*

UNAFFECTED

shared meals with *u.* joy (N)	*Ac 2:46*

UNAIDED

by one's *u.* mental powers (B)	*2Pe 1:20*

UNALTERABLE

by two *u.* facts (B)	*Heb 6:18*

UNAWARE

do not want you *u.* (B)	*Ro 1:13*

UNAWARES

Jacob stole away *u.* to Laban	*Ge 31:20*
slip away secretly (A)	*Ge 31:20*
outwitted Laban (R)	*Ge 31:20*
thou hast stolen away *u.* to me	*Ge 31:26*
stealing away (A)	*Ge 31:26*
which killeth any person at *u.*	*Nu 35:11*
unwittingly (E)	*Nu 35:11; 35:15; Jos 20:3, 9*
without intent (R)	*Nu 35:11; 35:15; Jos 20:9*
that killeth any person at *u.*	*Nu 35:15*
may flee	
accidentally (B)	*Nu 35:15; De 4:42; Jos 20:3, 9*
should kill his neighbour *u.*	*De 4:42*
slay unintentionally (A)	*De 4:42; Jos 20:9*
unintentionally (R)	*De 4:42*
killeth neighbour *u.* (E)	*De 19:4*
slayer that killeth any person *u.*	*Jos 20:3*
accidentally and (A)	*Jos 20:3*
unintentionally (A)	
unwittingly (R)	*Jos 20:3*
killeth any person at *u.* might flee	*Jos 20:9*
destruction come upon him at *u.*	*Ps 35:8*
and so that day come upon you *u.*	*Lu 21:34*
like a trap or a noose (A)	*Lu 21:34*
by a surprise like a trap (B)	*Lu 21:34*
suddenly as a snare (E)(R)	*Lu 21:34*
suddenly like a trap (N)	*Lu 21:34*
catch you like a springing trap (P)	*Lu 21:34*
of false brethren *u.* brought in	*Ga 2:4*
secretly smuggled in (A)	*Ga 2:4*
got in underhandedly (B)	*Ga 2:4*
brethren privately brought in (E)	*Ga 2:4*
stolen in (N)	*Ga 2:4*
wormed their way in (P)	*Ga 2:4*
slipped in (R)	*Ga 2:4*
some have entertained angels	*Heb 13:2*
u.	
without knowing it (A)(B)(N)	*Heb 13:2*

UNBLAMEABLE

there are certain men crept in *u.*	*Jude 4*
crept in stealthily (A)	*Jude 4*
certain people sneaked in (B)	*Jude 4*
crept in privately (E)	*Jude 4*
wormed their way in (N)	*Jude 4*
surreptitiously entered the church (P)	*Jude 4*
admission secretly gained (R)	*Jude 4*

UNBALANCED

u. and malicious men (B)	*2Th 3:2*
the ill-informed and *u.* (P)(R)	*2Pe 3:16*

UNBEARABLE

made our yoke *u.* (B)	*1Ki 12:4*

UNBECOMINGLY

act *u.* (A)	*1Co 13:5*

UNBELIEF

works there because of their *u.*	*M't 13:58*
said unto them, Because of your *u.*	*M't 17:20*
he marvelled because of their *u.*	*M'k 6:6*
Lord, I believe; help thou mine *u.*	*M'k 9:24*
upbraided them with their *u.* and	*M'k 16:14*
shall their *u.* make the faith of God	*Ro 3:3*
at the promise of God through *u.*	*Ro 4:20*
because of *u.* they were broken off	*Ro 11:20*
also, if they abide not still in *u.*	*Ro 11:23*
obtained mercy through their *u.*	*Ro 11:30*
God hath concluded them all in *u.*	*Ro 11:32*
because I did it ignorantly in *u.*	*1Ti 1:13*
be in any of you an evil heart of *u.*	*Heb 3:12*
they could not enter in because of *u.*	*Heb 3:19*
entered not in because of *u.*	*Heb 4:6*
fall after the same example of *u.*	*Heb 4:11*

UNBELIEVER

believer with *u.* (A)(B)(E)(N)(P)(R)	*2Co 6:15*
worse than an *u.* (A)(B)(E)(N)(R)	*1Ti 5:8*

UNBELIEVERS

him his portion with the *u.*	*Lu 12:46*
with brother, and that before the *u.*	*1Co 6:6*
in those that are unlearned, or *u.*	*1Co 14:23*
unequally yoked together with *u.*	*2Co 6:14*

UNBELIEVING

you (A)(B)(N)(P)	*M't 17:17*
the *u.* Jews stirred up the Gentiles	*Ac 14:2*
the *u.* husband is sanctified by the	*1Co 7:14*
u. wife is sanctified by the husband	*1Co 7:14*
But if the *u.* depart, let him depart	*1Co 7:15*
uninitiated or *u.* (B)	*1Co 14:13; 14:24*
are defiled and *u.* is nothing pure	*Tit 1:15*
to the *u.* (B)	*1Pe 2:7*
But the fearful, and *u.* and	*Re 21:8*

UNBLAMEABLE

to present you holy and *u.*	*Col 1:22*
faultless (A)	*Col 1:22*
blameless (B)	*Col 1:22*
without blemish (E)	*Col 1:22*
innocent (N)	*Col 1:22*
stablish your hearts *u.* in holiness	*1Th 3:13*
spotlessly (B)	*1Th 3:13*
faultless (N)	*1Th 3:13*

UNBLAMEABLY

justly and *u.* we behaved ourselves	*1Th 2:10*
irreproachable (B)	*1Th 2:10*
holily, righteousness, *u.* (E)	*1Th 2:10*

UNBLEMISHED

offered himself an *u.* sacrifice (A)	*Heb 9:14*
u. and unstained (P)	*1Pe 1:19*
u., above reproach (N)	*2Pe 3:14*
present you *u.* (A)	*Jude 24*

UNBRIDLED

abandoned to *u.* sensuality (A)	*Eph 4:19*
indulging in *u.* lusts (B)	*1Ti 4:3; 1Pe 4:3*
pervert grace into *u.* lust (B)	*Jude 4*

UNCERTAIN

For if the trumpet gave an *u.* sound	*Ac 14:8*
give *u.* voice (A)(E)	*Ac 14:8*
an indistinct sound (B)(R)	*Ac 14:8*
trumpet call not clear (N)(P)	*Ac 14:8*
nor trust in *u.* riches, but in	*1Ti 6:17*
transitory power of wealth (P)	*1Ti 6:17*

UNCERTAINLY

I therefore so run, not as *u.*	*1Co 9:26*

UNCERTAINTY

without *u.* and insincerity (R)	*Jas 3:17*

UNCHANGEABLE

his plan was *u.* (P)	*Heb 6:17*
u. character of purpose (R)	*Heb 6:17*
by two *u.* things (A)(R)	*Heb 6:18*
ever, hath an *u.* priesthood	*Heb 7:24*
priesthood never transferred (B)	*Heb 7:24*

UNCHANGEABLENESS

u. of purpose (A)(B)	*Heb 6:17*

UNCHANGING

u. was his purpose (N)(P)	*Heb 6:17*

UNCHASTE

an *u.* woman (S)	*Pr 6:26*
u. and profane (B)	*Heb 12:16*
the *u.* and adulterers (A)(B)	*Heb 13:4*
the *u.* (B)	*Re 22:15*

UNCHASTITY

other than *u.* (N)	*M't 5:32*
abstain from *u.* (B)(R)	*Ac 15:20*
unchastity (B)	*2Co 12:21; Eph 5:3*
no *u.* nor (B)	*Eph 5:5*
her *u.* (B)	*Re 2:21*
wine of her passionate *u.* (A)(B)	*Re 14:8*

UNCHRISTIAN

steer clear of *u.* babblings (P)	*2Ti 2:16*

UNCIRCUMCISED

And the *u.* man child whose flesh	*Ge 17:14*
give our sister to one that is *u.*	*Ge 34:14*
hear me, who am of *u.* lips	*Ex 6:12*
deficient and impeded speech (A)	*Ex 6:12; 6:30*
uncultured speech (B)	*Ex 6:12; 6:30*
I am of *u.* lips, and now shall	*Ex 6:30*
for no *u.* person shall eat thereof	*Ex 12:48*
shall count the fruit thereof as *u.*	*Le 19:23*
fruit inedible and forbidden (A)	*Le 19:23*
fruit inedible for you (B)	*Le 19:23*
forbidden fruit (R)	*Le 19:23*

three years shall it be as *u.* unto	*Le 19:23*
if then their *u.* hearts be humbled	*Le 26:41*
for they were *u.* because	*Jos 5:7*
to take a wife of the *u.* Philistines	*J'g 14:3*
and fall into the hand of the *u.*	*J'g 15:18*
over unto the garrison of these *u.*	*1Sa 14:6*
who is this *u.* Philistine, that	*1Sa 17:26*
this *u.* Philstine shall be as one of	*1Sa 17:36*
lest these *u.* come and thrust me	*1Sa 31:4*
the daughters of the *u.* triumph	*2Sa 1:20*
let these *u.* come and abuse me	*1Ch 10:4*
into thee the *u.* and the unclean	*Isa 52:1*
ear is *u.* and they cannot hearken	*Jer 6:10*
which are circumcised with the *u.*	*Jer 9:25*
for all these nations are *u.*	*Jer 9:26*
house of Israel are *u.* in the heart	*Jer 9:26*
Thou shalt die the deaths of the *u.*	*Jer 28:10*
thou shalt lie in the midst of the *u.*	*Jer 31:18*
down, and be thou laid with the *u.*	*Jer 32:19*
they lie *u.* slain by the sword	*Jer 32:21*
are gone down *u.* into the nether	*Jer 32:24*
All of them *u.* slain by the sword	*Jer 32:25; 32:26*
the mighty that are fallen of the *u.*	*Jer 32:27*
be broken in the midst of the *u.*	*Jer 32:28*
they shall lie with the *u.* and with	*Jer 32:29*
and they lie *u.* with them that be	*Jer 32:30*
shall be laid in the midst of the *u.*	*Jer 32:32*
u. in heart, and *u.* in flesh, to be	*Jer 44:7*
stranger, *u.* in heart, nor *u.* in flesh	*Jer 44:9*
Ye stiffnecked and *u.* in heart	*Ac 7:51*
Thou wentest in to men *u.*	*Ac 11:3*
which he had yet being *u.*	*Ro 4:11*
which he had being yet *u.*	*Ro 4:12*
let him not become *u.*	*1Co 7:18*

UNCIRCUMCISION

law, thy circumcision is made *u.*	*Ro 2:25*
if the *u.* keep the righteousness	*Ro 2:26*
shall not his *u.* be counted for	*Ro 2:26*
And shall not *u.* which is by nature	*Ro 2:27*
by faith, and *u.* through faith	*Ro 3:30*
or upon the *u.* also? for we say	*Ro 4:9*
he was in circumcision, or in *u.*	*Ro 4:10*
Not in circumcision, but in *u.*	*Ro 4:10*
Is any called in *u.*? let him not be	*1Co 7:18*
is nothing, and *u.* is nothing	*1Co 7:19*
gospel of the *u.* was committed unto	*Ga 2:7*
availeth any thing, nor *u.,* but faith	*Ga 5:6*
availeth any thing, nor *u.,* but a	*Ga 6:15*
who are called *U.* by that which	*Eph 2:11*
your sins and the *u.* of your flesh	*Col 2:13*
Greek nor Jew, circumcision nor *u.*	*Col 3:11*

UNCLE

the sons of Uzziel the *u.* of Aaron	*Le 10:4*
Either his *u.* or his uncle's son	*Le 25:49*
Saul's *u.* said, unto him and to his	*1Sa 10:14*
Saul's *u.* said, Tell me, I pray thee	*1Sa 10:15*
Saul said unto his *u.* He told us	*1Sa 10:16*

Abner, the son of Ner, Saul's *u.*	*1Sa 14:50*
David's *u.* was a counsellor	*1Ch 27:32*
of Abihail the *u.* of Mordecai	*Es 2:15*
Hanameel, thine *u.* shall come	*Jer 32:7*
And a man's *u.* shall take him up	*Am 6:10*

UNCLEAN

u. thing	*Le 3:2; 7:19, 21; 20:21; 22:4; J'g 13:4, 7, 14; Isa 52:11; 64:6; 2Co 6:17*
u. cattle	*Le 5:2*
u. creeping things	*Le 5:2*
unclean (B)	*Le 5:3; 15:32; 18:25; 21:3; Nu 6:12; 9:6; 19:20; Jer 19:13; Eze 23:38*
u. things	*Le 5:5; 20:21*
between *u.* and clean	*Le 10:10; 11:47; 20:25; De 12:15, 22; 15:22; Eze 22:26; 44:23*
u. to you	*Le 11:4; 11:5, 26-29, 31, 35, 38; De 14:7-8, 10, 19*
ye shall be *u.*	*Le 11:24*
u. until the even	*Le 11:24; 11:25, 27-28, 31-32, 39-40; 14:46; 15:5-8, 10-11, 16-17, 19, 21-23, 27; 17:15; 19:7-8, 10, 21-22*
shall be *u.*	*Le 11:26; 11:32-36*
make yourselves *u.*	*Le 11:43*
she shall be *u.*	*Le 12:2; 12:5; 15:25*
pronounce him *u.*	*Le 13:3; 13:8, 11, 15, 20, 22, 25, 27, 30, 44, 59*
he is *u.*	*Le 13:11; 13:14, 36, 44, 46; 15:2, 4, 9, 20, 24; 22:6; Nu 19:11, 13-14, 16, 20*
raw flesh is *u.*	*Le 13:15*
shall cry, *U.,* *u.*	*Le 13:45*
it is *u.*	*Le 13:51; 13:55; 14:44, 57; Nu 19:15*
that is in the house be made *u.*	*Le 14:36*
u. place	*Le 14:40; 14:41, 45*
made *u.*	*Le 22:5*
u. beast	*Le 27:11; 5:2; 7:21; 27:27; Nu 18:15*
not make himself *u.* for his father	*Nu 6:7*
be *u.* by reason of a dead body	*Nu 9:10; Hag 2:13*
for an *u.* person	*Nu 19:17; 19:22; Eph 5:5*
shall sprinkle upon the *u.*	*Nu 19:19*
that he sees no *u.* thing in thee	*De 23:14*
away ought thereof for any *u.* use	*De 26:14*
If the land of your possession be *u.*	*Jos 22:19*
none which was *u.* in any thing	*2Ch 23:19*
taking away *u.* things (B)	*2Ch 29:5*
excluded as *u.* (A)(R)	*Ezr 2:62; Ne 7:64*
an *u.* land with the filthiness of	*Ezr 9:11*
bring a clean thing out of an *u.*	*Job 14:4*
and their life is among the *u.*	*Job 36:14*
and to the clean, and to the *u.*	*Ec 9:2*
because I am a man of *u.* lips	*Isa 6:5*
in the midst of a people of *u.* lips	*Isa 6:5*
an *u.* cloth (S)	*Isa 30:22; La 1:17; Eze 18:6*
the *u.* shall not pass over it	*Isa 35:8*
thee the uncircumcised and the *u.*	*Isa 52:1*
unto them. Depart ye; it is *u.*	*La 4:15*
u. from her impurity (B)(E)(R)	*Eze 22:10*
they shall eat *u.* things in Assyria	*Ho 9:3*
die in a land *u.* (E)(R)	*Am 7:17*
touch any of these, shall it be *u.*	*Hag 2:13*
answered and said, It shall be *u.*	*Hag 2:13*
that which they offer there is *u.*	*Hag 2:14*
u. spirit	*Zec 13:2; M't 12:43; M'k 1:23, 26; 3:30; 5:2, 8; 7:25; Lu 8:29; 9:42; 11:24*
u. spirits	*M't 10:1; M'k 1:27; 3:11; 5:13; 6:7; Lu 4:36; 6:18; Ac 5:16; 8:7; Re 16:13*

makes him *u*. (P)   *M't 15:11; 15:20*
with *u*. hands (B)   *M'k 7:2*
u. to unhallowed (A)(P)   *M'k 7:20*
rebuked *u*. spirit   *M'k 9:25*
(A)(B)(E)(N)
which had a spirit of an *u*.   *Lu 4:33*
devil
any thing that is common or   *Lu 10:14*
u.
not call any man common or   *Lu 10:28*
u.
nothing common or *u*. hath at   *Lu 11:8*
any
that there is nothing *u*. of   *Ro 14:14*
itself
any thing to be *u*. to him it is   *Ro 14:14*
u.
else were your children *u*.   *1Co 7:14*
of an heifer sprinkling the *u*.   *Heb 9:13*
full of *u*. things (E)   *Re 17:4*
a cage of every *u*. and hateful   *Re 18:2*
bird
fort for *u*. spirit   *Re 18:2*
(B)(E)(N)(P)

UNCLEANNESS

Or if he touch the *u*. of man   *Le 5:3*
whatsoever *u*. it be that a man   *Le 5:3*
the Lord, having his *u*. upon   *Le 7:20*
him
as the *u*. of man, or any   *Le 7:21*
unclean
that is to be cleansed from his   *Le 14:19*
u.
And this shall be his *u*. in his   *Le 15:3*
issue
stopped from his issue, it is   *Le 15:3*
his *u*.
all the days of the issue of her   *Le 15:25*
u.
her period of *u*. (B)   *Le 15:25*
unclean, as the *u*. of her   *Le 15:26*
separation
the Lord for the issue of her   *Le 15:30*
u.
the children of Israel from   *Le 15:31*
their *u*.
they die not in their *u*. when   *Le 15:31*
they
of the *u*. of the children of   *Le 16:16*
Israel
among them in the midst of   *Le 16:16*
their *u*.
from the *u*. of the children of   *Le 16:19*
Israel
as she is put apart for her *u*.   *Le 18:19*
having his *u*. upon him, that   *Le 22:3*
soul
or a man of whom he may   *Le 22:5*
take *u*.
whatsoever *u*. he hath   *Le 22:5*
if thou hast not gone aside to   *Nu 5:19*
u.
had sexual relations (B)   *Nu 5:19*
water of *u*. (B)   *Nu 19:9;*
   19:20-21; 31:23
be unclean; his *u*. is yet   *Nu 19:13*
upon him
reason of *u*. that chanceth   *De 23:10*
him by
he hath found some *u*. in her   *De 24:1*
for she was purified from her   *2Sa 11:4*
u.
out all the *u*. that they   *2Ch 29:16*
found
from end to another with   *Ezr 9:11*
their *u*.
u. of people (E)   *Ezr 9:11*
me as the *u*. of a removed   *Eze 36:17*
woman
clean from all *u*. (A)(R)   *Eze 36:25*
According to their *u*. and   *Eze 39:24*
according
because of *u*. (A)(B)(E)(R)   *Mic 2:10*
of Jerusalem for sin and for   *Zec 13:1*
u.
of dead men's bones, and of   *M't 23:27*
all *u*.
every thing impure (A)   *M't 23:27*
impurity (B)   *M't 23:27;*
Ro 1:24; 6:19; 2Co 12:21; Ga 5:19;
   Eph 4:19; 5:3; Col 3:5
all kinds of filth (N)   *M't 23:27*
all kinds of rottenness (P)   *M't 23:27*
God also gave them up to *u*.   *Ro 1:24*
gave them up to sexual   *Ro 1:24*
impurity (A)

to vileness of own desires and   *Ro 1:24*
consequent degradation of their
own bodies (N)
to be playthings of their own   *Ro 1:24*
desires (P)
to lusts of their hearts to   *Ro 1:24;*
impurity (R)   *6:19; 2Co 12:21; Ga 5:19;*
   Eph 5:3; Col 3:5
yielded your members servants   *Ro 6:19*
to *u*.
to impurity (A)   *Ro 6:19;*
   2Co 12:21; Ga 5:19; Eph 4:19; 5:3;
   Col 3:5
impurity, lawlessness, making   *Ro 6:19*
moral anarchy (N)
and have not repented of   *2Co 12:21*
the *u*. and
not sorry for impurity,   *2Co 12:21*
immorality, lustfulness (P)
are these; Adultery,   *Ga 5:19*
fornication, *u*.
impurity (N)   *Ga 5:19; 1Th 4:7*
impurity of mind (P)   *Ga 5:19*
to work all *u*. with greediness   *Eph 4:19*
impure motives (B)   *Eph 4:19*
abandoned themselves to vice   *Eph 4:19*
(N)
any form of impurity (P)   *Eph 4:19;*
   1Th 4:7
given themselves up to   *Eph 4:19*
licentiousness (R)
But fornication, and all *u*.   *Eph 5:3*
indecency of any kind (N)   *Eph 5:3;*
   Col 3:5
sexual immorality (P)   *Eph 5:3*
upon the earth; fornication, *u*.   *Col 3:5*
dirtymindedness (P)   *Col 3:5*
not of deceit, nor of *u*. nor in   *1Th 2:3*
guile
For God hath not called us   *1Th 4:7*
unto *u*.
all *u*. (A)   *Jas 1:21*
after the flesh in the lust of   *2Pe 2:10*
u.
indulge in the lust of   *2Pe 2:10*
polluting passions (A)(B)
follow abominable lusts (N)   *2Pe 2:10*
lust of defiling passion (R)   *2Pe 2:10*

UNCLEANNESSES

will also save you from all   *Eze 36:29*
your *u*.

UNCLE'S

if a man shall lie with his *u*.   *Le 20:20*
wife
hath uncovered his *u*.   *Le 20:20*
nakedness
Either his uncle, or his *u*.   *Le 25:49*
son, may
that is, Esther his *u*.   *Es 2:7*
daughter
Hanameel mine *u*. son came   *Jer 32:8*
to me
the field of Hanameel my *u*.   *Jer 32:9*
son
the sight of Hanameel   *Jer 32:12*
mine *u*. son

UNCLOTHED

not for that we would be *u*.   *2Co 5:4*

UNCOMELY

behaveth himself *u*. toward a   *1Co 7:36*
virgin
our *u*. parts have more   *1Co 12:23*
abundant

UNCONDEMNED

They have beaten us openly   *Ac 16:37*
u.
a man that is a Roman, and   *Ac 22:25*
u.

UNCONTAMINATED

keep *u*. by world (P)   *Jas 1:27*

UNCONTROLLED

uncontrolled (A)(B)   *2Ti 3:3*

UNCORRECTED

u. by his father (P)   *Heb 12:7*

UNCORRUPTIBLE

changed the glory of the *u*.   *Ro 1:23*
God

UNCORRUPTNESS

in doctrine shewing *u*. gravity   *Tit 2:7*

UNCOVER

U. not your heads, neither rend   *Le 10:6*
kin to him, to *u*. their   *Le 18:6*
nakedness
of thy mother, shalt thou   *Le 18:7*
not *u*.
thou shalt not *u*. her   *Le 18:7;*
nakedness   *18:11, 15*
thy father's wife shalt thou not   *Le 18:8*
u.
nakedness thou shalt not *u*.   *Le 18:9;*
   18:10
nakedness thou shalt   *Le 18:9; 18:10*
not *u*.
not *u*. the nakedness of thy   *Le 18:12;*
father's   *18:14*
u. the nakedness of thy   *Le 18:13*
mother's
u. the nakedness of thy   *Le 18:15*
daughter
u. the nakedness of thy   *Le 18:16*
brother's
not *u*. the nakedness of a   *Le 18:17*
woman
daughter, to *u*. her nakedness   *Le 18:17*
to vex her, to *u*. her nakedness   *Le 18:18*
unto a woman to *u*. her   *Le 18:19*
nakedness
her sickness, and shall *u*. her   *Le 20:18*
u. the nakedness of thy   *Le 20:19*
mother's
shall not *u*. his head, nor rend   *Le 21:10*
Lord, and *u*. the woman's   *Nu 5:18*
head
uncover (S)   *De 22:30;*
Job 41:13; Isa 3:17; Jer 13:26; La 4:22;
   Eze 16:37; Ho 2:10; Mic 1:6; Na 3:5
and *u*. his feet, and lay thee   *Ru 3:4*
down
u. deep things   *Job 12:22*
(A)(B)(E)(R)
and grind meal: *u*. thy locks   *Isa 47:2*
make bare the leg, *u*. the   *Isa 47:2*
thigh
u. thy skirts (E)   *Jer 13:26*
u. your sins (A)(B)(E)(R)   *La 4:22*
u. nakedness (A)(B)(E)(R)   *Eze 16:37*
u. lewdness (A)(E)(R)   *Ho 2:10*
u. the foundations (E)(R)   *Mic 1:6*
for he shall *u*. the cedar work   *Zep 2:14*

UNCOVERED

and he was *u*. within his tent   *Ge 9:21*
nakedness be not *u*. (E)   *Ex 20:26*
wife hath *u*. his father's   *Le 20:11*
nakedness
he hath *u*. his sister's   *Le 20:17*
nakedness
and she hath *u*. the fountain   *Le 20:18*
of her
u. fountain of blood   *Le 20:18*
(A)(E)(R)
he hath *u*. his uncle's   *Le 20:20*
nakedness
he hath *u*. his brother's   *Le 20:21*
nakedness
and *u*. his feet, and laid her   *Ru 3:7*
down
who *u*. himself to-day in the   *2Sa 6:20*
eyes of
foot, even with their buttocks   *Isa 20:4*
u.
horsemen, and Kir *u*. the   *Isa 22:6*
shield
Thy nakedness shall be *u*. yea   *Isa 47:3*
u. your bed (A)(B)(E)(R)   *Isa 57:8*
uncovered (S)   *Isa 57:8;*
Jer 13:22; La 2:14; Eze 13:14; 16:36, 57;
   21:24; 22:10; 23:10, 18, 29; Ho 7:1
thy skirts *u*. (E)   *Jer 13:22*
bare, I have *u*. his   *Jer 49:10*
secret places
thine arm shall be *u*. and thou   *Eze 4:7*
foundations *u*. (E)   *Eze 13:14*
nakedness *u*. (A)(E)(R)   *Eze 16:36*
wickedness *u*.   *Eze 16:57;*
(A)(B)(E)(R)   *21:24; 22:10; 23:10*
also, and let thy foreskin be   *Hab 2:16*
u.

they *u.* the roof where he was *M'k 2:4*

or prophesieth with her head *1Co 11:5 u.*

that a woman pray unto God *1Co 11:13 u.*

UNCOVERETH

sister; for he *u.* his near kin *Le 20:19*

because he *u.* his father's skirt *De 27:20*

fellows shamelessly *u.* himself *2Sa 6:20*

he *u.* deep things (S) *Job 12:22*

UNCTION

ye have a *u.* from the Holy One *1Jo 2:20*

UNCULTIVATED

your *u.* vine (A) *Le 25:5; 25:11*

u. discussions (B) *2Ti 2:23*

UNCULTURED

u. speech (B) *Ex 6:12; 6:30*

UNDECIDED

thoughts of the *u.* in religion *Ps 119:113* (A)

u. to whom referred (B) *Joh 13:22*

UNDEFILED

Blessed are the *u.* in the way *Ps 119:1*

sister, my love, my dove, my *u. Ca 5:2*

My dove, my *u.* is but one; she *Ca 6:9*

who is holy, harmless, *u.* separate *Heb 7:26*

is honourable in all, and the bed *u.* *Heb 13:4*

Pure religion and *u.* before God *Jas 1:27*

an inheritance incorruptible, and *u.* *1Pe 1:4*

imperishable, *u.,* unfading (R) *1Pe 1:4*

UNDER

which were *u.* the firmament *Ge 1:7*

water *u.* the heaven be gathered *Ge 1:9*

the breath of life, from *u.* heaven *Ge 6:17*

hills, that were *u.* the whole heaven *Ge 7:19*

and submit thyself *u.* her hands *Ge 16:9*

and rest yourselves *u.* the tree *Ge 18:4*

and he stood by them *u.* the tree *Ge 18:8*

came they *u.* the shadow of my roof *Ge 19:8*

cast the child *u.* one of the shrubs *Ge 21:15*

I pray thee, thy hand *u.* my thigh *Ge 24:2; 47:29*

servant put his hand *u.* the thigh of *Ge 24:9*

Jacob hid them *u.* the oak which *Ge 35:4*

buried beneath Beth-el *u.* an oak *Ge 35:8*

to any thing that was *u.* his hand *Ge 39:23*

lay up corn *u.* the hand of Pharaoh *Ge 41:35*

blessings of the deep that lieth *u.* *Ge 49:25*

out from *u.* the burdens of *Ex 6:6; 6:7*

they took a stone, and put it *u.* him *Ex 17:12*

of Amalek from *u.* heaven *Ex 17:14*

from *u.* the hand of the Egyptians *Ex 18:10*

of that is in the water *u.* the earth *Ex 20:4*

with a rod, and he die *u.* his hand *Ex 21:20*

hateth thee lying *u.* his burden *Ex 23:5*

and builded an altar *u.* the hill *Ex 24:4*

and there was *u.* his feet as it were *Ex 24:10*

u. two branches of the same *Ex 25:35; 37:21*

of silver *u.* the twenty boards *Ex 26:19*

two sockets *u.* one board for *Ex 26:19; 26:21, 25*

two sockets *u.* one board for silver; two sockets *u.* one board *Ex 26:19 Ex 26:21*

two sockets *u.* one board, and two *Ex 26:25*

hang up the veil *u.* the taches *Ex 26:33*

u. the compass of the altar beneath *Ex 27:5*

thou make it *u.* the crown of it *Ex 30:4*

he made it *u.* the twenty boards *Ex 36:24*

two sockets *u.* one board for his *Ex 36:24*

two sockets *u.* another board for *Ex 36:24; 36:26*

two sockets *u.* one board, and two *Ex 36:26*

silver, *u.* every board two sockets *Ex 36:30*

of gold for it *u.* the crown thereof *Ex 37:27*

grate of network *u.* the compass *Ex 38:4*

any thing that was *u.* him shall be *Le 15:10*

it shall be seven days *u.* the dam *Le 22:27*

of whatsoever passeth *u.* the rod *Le 27:32*

u. the custody and charge of the sons *Nu 3:36*

u. the hand of Ithamar the son of *Nu 4:28; 4:33; 7:8*

in the fire which is *u.* the sacrifice *Nu 6:18*

clave asunder that was *u.* them *Nu 16:31*

the Lord, she fell down *u.* Balaam *Nu 22:27*

men of war which are *u.* our charge *Nu 31:49*

u. the hand of Moses and Aaron *Nu 33:1*

that are *u.* the whole heaven *De 2:25*

sea, *u.* Ashdoth-pisgah eastward *De 3:17*

near and stood *u.* the mountain *De 4:11*

all nations *u.* the whole heaven *De 4:19*

the plain *u.* the springs of Pisgah *De 4:49*

destroy their name from *u.* heaven *De 7:24*

out their name from *u.* heaven *De 9:14*

the hills, and *u.* every green tree *De 12:2*

of Amalek from *u.* heaven *De 25:19*

earth that is *u.* thee shall be iron *De 28:23*

blot out his name from *u.* heaven *De 29:20*

of my tent, and the silver *u.* it *Jos 7:21*

hid in his tent, and the silver *u.* it *Jos 7:22*

to the Hivite *u.* Hermon in the land *Jos 11:3*

of Lebanon *u.* mount Hermon *Jos 11:17*

from the south, *u.* Ashdoth-pisgah *Jos 12:3*

from Baal-gad *u.* mount Hermon *Jos 13:5*

unto this day, and serve *u.* tribute *Jos 16:10*

and set it up there *u.* an oak *Jos 24:26*

gathered their meat *u.* my table *J'g 1:7*

he did gird it *u.* his raiment upon *J'g 3:16*

that day *u.* the hand of Israel *J'g 3:30*

dwelt *u.* the palm tree of Deborah *J'g 4:5*

sat *u.* an oak which was in Ophrah *J'g 6:11*

brought it out utno him *u.* the oak *J'g 6:19*

to God this people were *u.* my hand *J'g 9:29*

u. whose wings thou art come to *Ru 2:12*

them, until they came *u.* Beth-car *1Sa 7:11*

u. a pomegranate tree which is in *1Sa 14:2*

therefore what is *u.* thine hand *1Sa 21:3*

is no common bread *u.* mine hand *1Sa 21:4*

here *u.* thine hand spear or sword *1Sa 21:8*

abode in Gibeah *u.* a tree in Ramah *1Sa 22:6*

buried them *u.* a tree at Jabesh *1Sa 31:13*

spear smote him *u.* the fifth rib *2Sa 2:23*

and smote him there *u.* the fifth rib *2Sa 3:27*

they smote him *u.* the fifth rib *2Sa 4:6*

were therein, and put them *u.* *2Sa 12:31*

u. harrows of iron, and *u.* axes of iron *2Sa 12:31*

part of the people *u.* the hand, of Joab *2Sa 18:2*

third part *u.* the hand of Abishai *2Sa 18:2*

third part *u.* the hand of Ittai *2Sa 18:2*

the mule went *u.* the thick boughs *2Sa 18:9*

the mule that was *u.* him went away *2Sa 18:9*

and darkness was *u.* his feet *2Sa 22:10*

Thou hast enlarged my steps *u.* me *2Sa 22:37*

yea, they are fallen *u.* my feet *2Sa 22:39*

me hast thou subdued *u.* me *2Sa 22:40*

bringeth down the people *u.* me *2Sa 22:48*

man *u.* his vine and *u.* his fig tree *1Ki 4:25*

put them *u.* the soles of his feet *1Ki 5:3*

u. the brim of it round about there *1Ki 7:24*

u. the laver were undersetters *1Ki 7:30*

u. the borders were four wheels *1Ki 7:32*

sea, and twelve oxen *u.* the sea *1Ki 7:44*

u. the wings of the cherubims *1Ki 8:6*

and found him sitting *u.* an oak *1Ki 13:14*

high hill, and *u.* every green tree *1Ki 14:23*

lay it on wood, and put no fire *u.* *1Ki 18:23*

of your gods, but put no fire *1Ki 18:25*

and sat down *u.* a juniper tree *1Ki 19:4*

he lay and slept *u.* a juniper tree *1Ki 19:5*

Edom revolted from *u.* the hand *2Ki 8:20; 8:22*

it *u.* him on the top of the stairs *2Ki 9:13*

the horses: and he trode her *u.* foot *2Ki 9:33*

they went out from *u.* the hand of *2Ki 13:5*

the name of Israel from *u.* heaven *2Ki 14:27*

the hills, and *u.* every green tree *2Ki 16:4; 2Ch 28:4*

off the brasen oxen that were *u.* it *2Ki 16:17*

from *u.* the hand of Pharaoh king *2Ki 17:7*

high hill, and *u.* every green tree *2Ki 17:10*

their bones *u.* the oak in Jabesh *1Ch 10:12*

the ark remaineth *u.* curtains *1Ch 17:1*

their manner, *u.* Aaron their father *1Ch 24:19*

the sons of Asaph *u.* the hands of *1Ch 25:2*

six, *u.* the hands of their father *1Ch 25:3*

were *u.* the hands of their father *1Ch 25:6*

it was *u.* the hand of Shelomith *1Ch 26:28*

from twenty years old and *u.* *1Ch 27:23*

u. it was the similitude of oxen *2Ch 4:3*

One sea, and twelve oxen *u.* *2Ch 4:15*

even *u.* the wings of the cherubims *2Ch 5:7*

Israel were brought *u.* at that time *2Ch 13:18*

revolted from *u.* the dominion of	2Ch 21:8
revolted from *u.* the hand of Judah	2Ch 21:10
did Libnah revolt from *u.* his hand	2Ch 21:10
u. the hand of Hananiah, one of	2Ch 26:11
And *u.* their hand was an army	2Ch 26:13
to keep *u.* the children of Judah	2Ch 28:10
overseers *u.* the hand of Cononiah	2Ch 31:13
u. him were Eden, and (S)	2Ch 31:15
the beast that was *u.* me to pass	Ne 2:14
made booths, and sat *u.* the booths	Ne 8:17
proud helpers do stoop *u.* him	Job 9:13
though he hide it *u.* his tongue	Job 20:12
are formed from *u.* the waters	Job 26:5
and the cloud is not rent *u.* them	Job 26:8
u. it is turned up as it were fire	Job 28:5
and seeth *u.* the whole heaven	Job 28:24
u. the nettles they were gathered	Job 30:7
He directeth it *u.* the whole heaven	Job 37:3
He lieth *u.* the shady trees	Job 40:21
whatsoever is *u.* the whole heaven is	Job 41:11
Sharp stones are *u.* him: he	Job 41:30
thou hast put all things *u.* his feet	Ps 8:6
u. his tongue is mischief and	Ps 10:7
hide me *u.* the shadow of thy wings	Ps 17:8
and darkness was *u.* his feet	Ps 18:9
Thou hast enlarged my steps *u.* me	Ps 18:36
to rise: they are fallen *u.* my feet	Ps 18:38
subdued *u.* me those that rose up	Ps 18:39
and subdueth the people *u.* me	Ps 18:47
their trust *u.* the shadow of thy wings	Ps 36:7
we tread them *u.* that rise up against	Ps 44:5
whereby the people fall *u.* thee	Ps 45:5
He shall subdue the people *u.* us	Ps 47:3
and the nations *u.* our feet	Ps 47:3
shall abide *u.* the shadow of	Ps 91:1
and *u.* his wings shalt thou trust	Ps 91:4
dragon shalt thou trample *u.* feet	Ps 91:13
into subjection *u.* their hand	Ps 106:42
adders' poison is *u.* their lips	Ps 140:3
who subdueth my people *u.* me	Ps 144:2
but the slothful shall be *u.* tribute	Pr 12:24
take away thy bed from *u.* thee	Pr 22:27
labour which he taketh *u.* the sun	Ec 1:3; 5:18
there is no new thing *u.* the sun	Ec 1:9
all things that are done *u.* heaven	Ec 1:13
the works that are done *u.* the sun	Ec 1:14
they should do *u.* the heaven all	Ec 2:3
and there was no profit *u.* the sun	Ec 2:11
work that is wrought *u.* the sun is	Ec 2:17
which I had taken *u.* the sun	Ec 2:18
shewed myself wise *u.* the sun	Ec 2:19
the labour which I took *u.* the sun	Ec 2:20
he hath laboured *u.* the sun	Ec 2:22
time to every purpose *u.* the heaven	Ec 3:1
u. the sun the place of judgment	Ec 3:16
that are done *u.* the sun	Ec 4:1
evil work that is done *u.* the sun	Ec 4:3
and I saw vanity *u.* the sun	Ec 4:7
the living which walk *u.* the sun	Ec 4:15
evil which I have seen *u.* the sun	Ec 5:13; 6:1; 10:5
what shall be after him *u.* the sun	Ec 6:12
the crackling of thorns *u.* the pot	Ec 7:6
every work that is done *u.* the sun	Ec 8:9
hath no better thing *u.* the sun	Ec 8:15
which God giveth him *u.* the sun	Ec 8:15
the work that is done *u.* the sun	Ec 8:17
all things that are done *u.* the sun	Ec 9:3
any thing that is done *u.* the sun	Ec 9:6
he hath given thee *u.* the sun	Ec 9:9
labour thou takest *u.* the sun	Ec 9:9
and saw *u.* the sun, that the race	Ec 9:11
wisdom have I seen also *u.* the sun	Ec 9:13
I sat down *u.* his shadow with great	Ca 2:3
His left hand is *u.* my head	Ca 2:6
honey and milk are *u.* thy tongue	Ca 4:11
His left hand should be *u.* my head	Ca 8:3
I raised thee up *u.* the apple tree	Ca 8:5
and let this ruin be *u.* thy hand	Isa 3:6
shall bow down *u.* the prisoners	Isa 10:4
they shall fall *u.* the slain. For	Isa 10:4
and *u.* his glory he shall kindle a	Isa 10:16
the worm is spread *u.* thee	Isa 14:11
pit; as a carcase trodden *u.* feet	Isa 14:19
my mountains tread him *u.* foot	Isa 14:25
meted out and trodden *u.* foot	Isa 18:7
also is defiled *u.* the inhabitants	Isa 24:5
Moab shall be trodden down *u.* him	Isa 25:10
of Ephraim, shall be trodden *u.* feet	Isa 28:3
u. falsehood have we hid ourselves	Isa 28:15
and hatch, and gather *u.* her shadow	Isa 34:15
with idols *u.* every green tree	Isa 57:5
valleys *u.* the clifts of the rocks	Isa 57:5
spread sackcloth and ashes *u.* him	Isa 58:5
high hill and *u.* every green tree	Jer 2:20
and *u.* every green tree, and	Jer 3:6
the strangers *u.* every green tree	Jer 3:13
earth, and from *u.* these heavens	Jer 10:11
have trodden my portion, *u.* foot	Jer 12:10
will not put their neck *u.* the yoke	Jer 27:8
that bring their neck *u.* the yoke	Jer 27:11
your necks *u.* the yoke of the king	Jer 27:12
pass again *u.* the hands of him	Jer 33:13
of the king *u.* the treasury	Jer 38:11
rags *u.* thine armholes *u.* the cords	Jer 38:12
fled stood *u.* the shadow of Heshbon	Jer 48:45
bulls that were *u.* the bases	Jer 52:20
trodden *u.* foot all my mighty men	La 1:15
crush *u.* his feet all the prisoners	La 3:34
them in anger from *u.* the heavens	La 3:66
U. his shadow we shall live among	La 4:20
Our necks are *u.* persecution	La 5:5
and the children fell *u.* the wood	La 5:13
the hands of a man *u.* their wings	Eze 1:8
u. the firmament were their wings	Eze 1:23
mountains, and *u.* every green tree	Eze 6:13
u. every thick oak, the place where	Eze 6:13
even *u.* the cherub, and fill	Eze 10:2
of a man's hand *u.* their wings	Eze 10:8
creatures that I saw *u.* the God of	Eze 10:8
hands of a man was *u.* their wings	Eze 10:21
and the roots thereof were *u.* him	Eze 17:6
u. it shall dwell all fowl of every	Eze 17:23
I will cause you to pass *u.* the rod	Eze 20:37
and burn also the bones *u.* it	Eze 24:5
u. his branches did all the beasts	Eze 31:6
and *u.* his shadow dwelt all great	Eze 31:6
that dwelt *u.* his shadow in	Eze 31:17
laid their swords *u.* their heads	Eze 32:27
u. these chambers was the entry	Eze 42:9
with boiling places *u.* the rows	Eze 46:23
issued out from *u.* the threshold	Eze 47:1
the waters came down from *u.*	Eze 47:1
beasts of field had shadow *u.* it	Da 4:12
let the beasts get way from *u.* it	Da 4:14
u. which the beasts of the field	Da 4:21
the kingdom *u.* the whole heaven	Da 7:27
and the host to be trodden *u.* foot	Da 8:13
for *u.* the whole heaven hath not	Da 9:12
gone a whoring from *u.* their God	Ho 4:12
u. oaks, and poplars and elms	Ho 4:13
They that dwell *u.* his shadow shall	Ho 14:7
The seed is rotten *u.* their clods	Joe 1:17
I am pressed *u.* you, as a cart is	Am 2:13
bread have laid a wound *u.* thee	Ob 7
booth, and sat *u.* it in the shadow	Jon 4:5
mountains shall be molten *u.* him	Mic 1:4
man *u.* his vine and *u.* his fig tree	Mic 4:4
u. the vine and *u.* the fig tree	Zec 3:10
be ashes *u.* the soles of your feet	Mal 4:3
from two years old and *u.*	M't 2:16
and to be trodden *u.* foot of men	M't 5:13
a candle, and put it *u.* a bushel	M't 5:15
they trample them *u.* their feet	M't 7:6
thou shouldest come *u.* my roof	M't 8:8
For I am a man *u.* authority	M't 8:9
having soldiers *u.* me: and I say	M't 8:9
her chickens *u.* her wings	M't 23:37
to be put *u.* a bushel, or *u.* a bed	M'k 4:21
air may lodge *u.* the shadow of it	M'k 4:32
shake off the dust *u.* your feet for	M'k 6:11
yet the dogs *u.* the table eat	M'k 7:28
thou shouldest enter *u.* my roof	Lu 7:6
I also am a man set *u.*	Lu 7:8
having *u.* me soldiers, and I say	Lu 7:8
a vessel, or putteth it *u.* a bed	Lu 8:16
neither *u.* a bushel, but on a	Lu 11:33
gather her brood *u.* her wings	Lu 13:34
out of the one part *u.* heaven	Lu 17:24
unto the other part *u.* heaven	Lu 17:24
when thou wast *u.* the fig tree, I	Joh 1:48
thee, I saw thee *u.* the fig tree	Joh 1:50
out of every nation *u.* heaven	Ac 2:5
none other name *u.* heaven given	Ac 4:12

of a great authority u. Candace	Ac 8:27
and bound themselves u. a curse	Ac 23:12
bound ourselves u. a great curse	Ac 23:14
we sailed u. Cyprus, because	Ac 27:4
we sailed u. Crete, over against	Ac 27:7
running u. a certain island which	Ac 27:16
u. colour as though they would have	Ac 27:30
Gentiles, that they are all u. sin	Ro 3:9
the poison of asps is u. their lips	Ro 3:13
saith to them who are u. the law	Ro 3:19
ye are not u. the law, but u. grace	Ro 6:14
we are not u. the law, but u. grace	Ro 6:15
but I am carnal, sold u. sin	Ro 7:14
bruise Satan u. your feet shortly	Ro 16:20
not be brought u. the power of any	1Co 6:12
sister is not u. bondage in such case	1Co 7:15
that are u. the law, as u. the law	1Co 9:20
gain them that are u. the law	1Co 9:20
to God, but u. the law to Christ	1Co 9:21
I keep u. my body, and bring it	1Co 9:27
all our fathers were u. the cloud	1Co 10:1
commanded to be u. obedience	1Co 14:34
hath put all enemies u. his feet	1Co 15:25; 15:27
he saith all things are put u. him	1Co 15:27
which did put all things u. him	1Co 15:27
unto him that put all things u. him	1Co 15:28
the governor u. Aretas the king	2Co 11:32
works of the law are u. the curse	Ga 3:10
hath concluded all u. sin, that	Ga 3:22
faith came, we were kept u. the law	Ga 3:23
we are no longer u. a schoolmaster	Ga 3:25
is u. tutors and governors until	Ga 4:2
u. the elements of the world	Ga 4:3
made of a woman, made u. the law	Ga 4:4
redeem them that were u. the law	Ga 4:5
ye that desire to be u. the law, do ye	Ga 4:21
of the Spirit, ye are not u. the law	Ga 5:18
And hath put all things u. his feet	Eph 1:22
in earth, and things u. the earth	Ph'p 2:10
every creature which is u. heaven	Col 1:23
number u. threescore years old	1Ti 5:9
servants as are u. the yoke count	1Ti 6:1
all things in subjection u. his feet	Heb 2:8
he put all in subjection u. him	Heb 2:8
left nothing that is not put u. him	Heb 2:8
see not yet all things put u. him	Heb 2:8
u. it the people received the law	Heb 7:11
the transgressions that were u. the	Heb 9:15
mercy u. two or three witnesses	Heb 10:28
trodden u. foot the Son of God	Heb 10:29
there, or sit here u. my footstool	Jas 2:3
u. the mighty hand of God	1Pe 5:6
keep ungodly u. chastisement (A)	2Pe 2:9
in everlasting chains u. darkness	Jude 6

nor in earth, neither u. the earth	Re 5:3
and on the earth, and u. the earth	Re 5:13
I saw u. the altar the souls of them	Re 6:9
shall they tread u. foot forty	Re 11:2
the sun, and the moon u. her feet	Re 12:1

UNDERESTIMATE

u. the wealth (A)(B)	Ro 2:4

UNDERGARMENT

the u. (B)	Ex 28:4; Le 8:7

UNDERGARMENTS

two u. (A)(B)	M't 10:10
two u. (B)	M'k 6:9; Lu 3:11
the u. (B)	Ac 9:39

UNDERGIRDING

up, they used helps, u. the ship	Ac 27:17

UNDERHANDED

eliminate u. ways (B)(R)	2Co 4:2

UNDERHANDEDLY

arrest Jesus u. (R)	M't 26:4
got in u. (B)	Ga 2:4

UNDERHANDEDNESS

vex with u. (B)	Nu 25:18
renounced u. (A)	2Co 4:2

UNDERLINGS

Christ's u. (N)	1Co 5:1

UNDERMINES

upsets and u. faith (A)(B)(P)	2Ti 2:14

UNDERNEATH

on the two sides of the ephod u.	Ex 28:27; 39:20
u. are the everlasting arms	De 33:27
u. they are ravage wolves (N)	M't 7:15

UNDERSETTERS

the four corners thereof had u.	1Ki 7:30
under the layer were u. molten	1Ki 7:30
were four u. to the four corners	1Ki 7:34
the u. were of the very base itself	1Ki 7:34

UNDERSKIRTS

the u. (A)	Ac 9:39

UNDERSTAND

may not u. one another's speech	Ge 11:7
canst u. a dream to interpret it	Ge 41:15
u. that these men have provoked	Nu 16:30
U. therefore this day, that the Lord	De 9:3
U. therefore, that the Lord thy	De 9:6
whose tongue thou shalt not u.	De 28:49
given to u. (A)(B)(R)	De 29:4
the Syrian language; for we u. it	2Ki 18:26
Lord made me u. in writing by his	1Ch 28:19
women, and those that could u.	Ne 8:3
caused the people to u. the law	Ne 8:7
and caused them to u. the reading	Ne 8:8
even to u. the words of the law	Ne 8:13
me to u. wherein I have erred	Job 6:24
and u. what he would say unto me	Job 23:5

thunder of his power who can u.	Job 26:14
neither do the aged u. judgment	Job 32:9
any u. the spreadings of the clouds	Job 36:29
see if there were any that did u.	Ps 14:2
Who can u. his errors? cleanse	Ps 19:12
see if there were any that did u.	Ps 53:2
They knew not, neither will they u.	Ps 82:5
not; neither doth a fool u. this	Ps 92:6
U. ye brutish among the people	Ps 94:8
u. the lovingkindness of the Lord	Ps 107:43
to u. the way of thy precepts	Ps 119:27
I u. more than the ancients	Ps 119:100
u. words of insight (R)	Pr 1:2
To u. a proverb, and the	Pr 1:6
shalt thou u. the fear of the Lord	Pr 2:5
Then shalt thou u. righteousness	Pr 2:9
O ye simple, u. wisdom: and, ye	Pr 8:5
of the prudent is to u. his way	Pr 14:8
and he will u. knowledge	Pr 19:25
how can a man then u. his own way	Pr 20:24
Evil men u. not judgment: but	Pr 28:5
they that seek the Lord u. all things	Pr 28:5
for though he u. he will not answer	Pr 29:19
people, Hear ye indeed, but u. not	Isa 6:9
and u. with the heart, and convert	Isa 6:10
whom shall he make to u. doctrine	Isa 28:9
be a vexation only to u. the report	Isa 28:19
also of the rash shall u. knowledge	Isa 32:4
tongue, that thou canst not u.	Isa 33:19
the Syrian language; for we u. it	Isa 36:11
and consider, and u. together	Isa 41:20
believe me, and u. that I am he	Isa 43:10
their hearts, that they cannot u.	Isa 44:18
they are shepherds that cannot u.	Isa 56:11
is the wise man, that may u. this	Jer 9:12
whose words thou canst not u.	Eze 3:6
make this man to u. the vision	Da 8:16
he said unto me, U. O son of man	Da 8:17
our iniquities, and u. thy truth	Da 9:13
therefore u. the matter and	Da 9:23
Know therefore and u. that from	Da 9:25
u. the words that I speak unto thee	Da 10:11
that thou didst set thine heart to u.	Da 10:12
make thee u. what shall befall thy	Da 10:14
they that u. among the people	Da 11:33
make many u. (R)	Da 11:33
and none of the wicked shall u.	Da 12:10
but the wise shall u.	Da 12:10
people that doth not u. shall fall	Ho 4:14
is wise, and he shall u. these things	Ho 14:9
Lord, neither u. they his counsel	Mic 4:12
they hear not, neither do they u.	M't 13:13
ye shall hear, and shall not u.	M't 13:14
and should u. with their heart, and	M't 13:15
and said unto them, Hear, and u.	M't 15:10
Do ye not yet u. neither whatsoever	M't 15:17
Do ye not yet u. neither remember	M't 16:9

How is it that ye do not *u.*   *M't 16:11*
that I
place, whoso readeth, let   *M't 24:15*
him *u.*
hearing they may hear, and   *M'k 4:12*
not *u.*
unto me every one of you, and *M'k 7:14*
u.
perceive ye not yet, neither   *M'k 8:17*
u.? have
them, How is it that ye do   *M'k 8:21*
not *u.*
(let him that readeth *u.)*   *M'k 13:14*
then let
not, neither *u.* I what thou   *M'k 14:68*
sayest
see, and hearing they might   *Lu 8:10*
not *u.*
that they might *u.* the   *Lu 24:45*
scriptures
Why do ye not *u.* my speech   *Joh 8:43*
nor *u.* with their heart, and   *Joh 12:40*
Because that thou mayest *u.*   *Ac 24:11*
that
ye shall hear, and shall not *u.*   *Ac 28:26*
u. with their heart, and   *Ac 28:27*
should be
that which I do I *u.* not (S)   *Ro 7:15*
they that have not heard   *Ro 15:21*
shall *u.*
Wherefore I give you to *u.*   *1Co 12:3*
that no
of prophecy, and *u.* all   *1Co 13:2*
mysteries
u. my knowledge in mystery   *Eph 3:4*
of
I would ye should *u.*   *Ph'p 1:12*
brethren
Through faith we *u.* that the   *Heb 11:3*
speak evil of things that they   *2Pe 2:12*
u.

UNDERSTANDEST

what *u.* thou, which is not in   *Job 15:9*
us
thou *u.* my thought afar off   *Ps 139:2*
not, neither *u.* what they say   *Jer 5:15*
said, *U.* thou what thou   *Ac 8:30*
readest

UNDERSTANDETH

and *u.* all the imaginations   *1Ch 28:9*
of the
God *u.* the way thereof, and   *Job 28:23*
he
Man that is in honour, and *u.*   *Ps 49:20*
not
They are all plain to him that   *Pr 8:9*
u.
knowledge is easy unto him   *Pr 14:6*
that *u.*
that he *u.* and knoweth me,   *Jer 9:24*
that I
word of the kingdom, and *u.*   *M't 13:19*
it not
he that heareth the word,   *M't 13:23*
and *u.* it
There is none that *u.* there is   *Ro 3:11*
none
for no man *u.* him; howbeit   *1Co 14:2*
in the
seeing he *u.* not what thou   *1Co 14:16*
sayest

UNDERSTANDING

of God, in wisdom, and in *u.*   *Ex 31:3*
spirit of God, in wisdom, in   *Ex 35:31*
u.
whom the Lord put wisdom   *Ex 36:1*
and *u.*
put dexterity and *u.* (B)   *Ex 36:1*
Take you wise men, and *u.*   *De 1:13*
your *u.* in the sight of the   *De 4:6*
nations
nation is a wise and *u.* people   *De 4:6*
neither is there any *u.* in   *De 32:28*
them
and she was a woman of good   *1Sa 25:3*
u.
Give thy servant an *u.* heart   *1Ki 3:9*
asked for thyself *u.* to discern   *1Ki 3:11*
given thee a wise and *u.* heart   *1Ki 3:12*
God gave Solomon wisdom   *1Ki 4:29*
and *u.*
he was filled with wisdom,   *1Ki 7:14*
and *u.*

were men that had *u.* of the   *1Ch 12:32*
times
the Lord give thee wisdom   *1Ch 22:12*
and *u.*
insight and *u.* (B)(E)(R)   *1Ch 22:12*
a man of *u.* (B)(E)(R)   *1Ch 27:32*
son, endued with prudence   *2Ch 2:12*
and *u.*
a cunning man, endued with   *2Ch 2:13*
u.
who had *u.* in the visions of   *2Ch 26:5*
God
and for Elnathan, men of *u.*   *Ezr 8:16*
us they brought us a man of   *Ezr 8:18*
u.
and all that could hear with *u.*   *Ne 8:2*
having knowledge, and   *Ne 10:28*
having *u.*
But I have *u.* as well as you;   *Job 12:3*
I am
wisdom; and in length of   *Job 12:12*
days *u.*
strength, he hath counsel   *Job 12:13*
and *u.*
taketh away the *u.* of the   *Job 12:20*
aged
thou hast hid their heart   *Job 17:4*
from *u.*
of my *u.* causeth me to   *Job 20:3*
answer
by his *u.* he smiteth through   *Job 26:12*
and where is the place of   *Job 28:12;*
u.   *28:20*
and to depart from evil is *u.*   *Job 28:28*
of the Almighty giveth them   *Job 32:8*
u.
hearken unto me, ye men of   *Job 34:10*
u.
If now thou hast *u.,* hear this   *Job 34:16*
Let men of *u.* tell me, and   *Job 34:34*
the earth? declare, if thou   *Job 38:4*
hast *u.*
or who hath given *u.* to the   *Job 38:36*
heart
neither hath he imparted to   *Job 39:17*
her *u.*
or as the mule, which have no   *Ps 32:9*
u.
the earth: sing ye praises with   *Ps 47:7*
u.
of my heart shall be of *u.*   *Ps 49:3*
a good *u.* have all they that   *Ps 111:10*
do his
Give me *u.* and I shall keep   *Ps 119:34*
thy
give me *u.* that I may learn   *Ps 119:73*
thy
more *u.* than all my teachers   *Ps 119:99*
Through thy precepts I get   *Ps 119:104*
u.
give me *u.* that I may know   *Ps 119:125*
thy
light: it giveth *u.* unto the   *Ps 119:130*
simple
give me *u.* and I shall live   *Ps 119:144*
give me *u.* according to thy   *Ps 119:169*
word
of great power: his *u.* is   *Ps 147:5*
infinite
u. is unlimited (B)   *Ps 147:5*
to perceive the words of *u.*   *Pr 1:2*
a man of *u.* shall attain unto   *Pr 1:5*
wise
and apply thine heart to *u.*   *Pr 2:2*
and liftest up thy voice for *u.*   *Pr 2:3*
mouth cometh knowledge and   *Pr 2:6*
u.
preserve thee, *u.* shall keep   *Pr 2:11*
thee
good *u.* in the sight of God and   *Pr 3:4*
and lean not unto thine own *u.*   *Pr 3:5*
and the man that getteth *u.*   *Pr 3:13*
earth: by *u.* hath he   *Pr 3:19*
established
of a father, and attend to know   *Pr 4:1*
u.
Get wisdom, get *u.:* forget it   *Pr 4:5*
not
and with all thy getting get *u.*   *Pr 4:7*
and bow thine ear to my *u.*   *Pr 5:1*
adultery with a woman lacketh   *Pr 6:32*
u.
sister; and call *u.* thy   *Pr 7:4*
kinswoman
youths, a young man void of *u.*   *Pr 7:7*
cry? and *u.* put forth her voice   *Pr 8:1*
and, ye fools, be ye of an *u.*   *Pr 8:5*
heart
wisdom: I am *u.;* I have   *Pr 8:14*
strength

as for him that wanteth *u.* she   *Pr 9:4*
live; and go in the way of *u.*   *Pr 9:6*
and the knowledge of the holy   *Pr 9:10*
is *u.*
as for him that wanteth *u.* she   *Pr 9:16*
In the lips of him that hath   *Pr 10:13*
u.
the back of him that is void   *Pr 10:13*
of *u.*
but a man of *u.* hath wisdom   *Pr 10:23*
but a man of *u.* holdeth his   *Pr 11:12*
peace
vain persons is void of *u.*   *Pr 12:11*
Good *u.* giveth favour: but   *Pr 13:15*
is slow to wrath is of great   *Pr 14:29*
u.
in the heart of him that hath   *Pr 14:33*
u.
that hath *u.* seeketh   *Pr 15:14*
knowledge
a man of *u.* walketh uprightly   *Pr 15:21*
he that heareth reproof   *Pr 15:32*
getteth *u.*
u. rather to be chosen than   *Pr 16:16*
silver
U. is a wellspring of life unto   *Pr 16:22*
A man void of *u.* striketh   *Pr 17:18*
hands
is before him that hath *u.;*   *Pr 17:24*
but the
and a man of *u.* is of an   *Pr 17:27*
excellent
his lips is esteemed a man of   *Pr 17:28*
u.
A fool hath no delight in *u.*   *Pr 18:2*
he that keepeth *u.* shall find   *Pr 19:8*
good
and reprove one that hath *u.*   *Pr 19:25*
but a man of *u.* will draw it   *Pr 20:5*
out
wandereth out of the way of   *Pr 21:16*
u.
no wisdom nor *u.* nor counsel   *Pr 21:30*
wisdom, and instruction, and   *Pr 23:23*
u.
and by *u.* it is established   *Pr 24:3*
vineyard of the man void of   *Pr 24:30*
u.
lacked *u.* (B)   *Pr 24:30*
by a man of *u.* and knowledge   *Pr 28:2*
the poor that hath *u.*   *Pr 28:11*
searcheth him
The prince that wanteth *u.* is   *Pr 28:16*
also
man, and have not the *u.* of a   *Pr 30:2*
man
nor yet riches to men of *u.*   *Ec 9:11*
nor yet
spirit of wisdom and *u.* the   *Isa 11:2*
spirit
shall make him of quick *u.* in   *Isa 11:3*
on fire: for it is a people of   *Isa 27:11*
no *u.*
u. of their prudent men shall   *Isa 29:14*
be hid
him that framed it. He had   *Isa 29:16*
no *u.*
erred in spirit shall come to   *Isa 29:24*
u.
and shewed to him the way   *Isa 40:14*
of *u.*
there is no searching of his   *Isa 40:28*
u.
is there knowledge nor *u.* to   *Isa 44:19*
say
feed you with knowledge and   *Jer 3:15*
u.
children, and they have none   *Jer 4:22*
u.
O foolish people, and without   *Jer 5:21*
u.
by *u.* and skill   *Jer 10:12*
(A)(B)(E)(R)(S)
stretched out the heaven by   *Jer 51:15*
his *u.*
with thine *u.* thou hast gotten   *Eze 28:4*
thee
in knowledge and *u.* science   *Da 1:4*
Daniel had *u.* in all visions   *Da 1:17*
in all matters of wisdom and   *Da 1:20*
u.
knowledge to them that know   *Da 2:21*
u.
mine *u.* returned unto me, and   *Da 4:34*
father light and *u.* and   *Da 5:11*
wisdom
and *u.* interpreting of dreams   *Da 5:12*
u. and excellent wisdom is   *Da 5:14*
found in

u. dark sentences, shall stand Da 8:23
up
come forth to give thee skill Da 9:22
and u.
the thing, and had u. of the Da 10:1
vision
And some of them of u. shall Da 11:35
fall
idols according to their own Ho 13:2
u.
under thee: there is none u. in Ob 7
him
and u. out of the mount of Esau Ob 8
have an u. with (B) M't 5:24
from the wise and u. M't 11:25
(E)(R)
said, Are ye also yet M'k 15:16
without u.
them, Are ye so without u. M'k 7:18
also
all the heart, and with all M'k 12:33
the u.
having had perfect u. of all Lu 1:3
things
him were astonished at his u. Lu 2:47
Then opened he their u. that Lu 24:45
they
a man of u. (E) Ac 13:7
Without u. covenant-breakers Ro 1:31
to nothing the u. of the 1Co 1:19
prudent
prayeth, but my u. is 1Co 14:14
unfruitful
and I will pray with the u. 1Co 14:15
also
and I will sing with the u. 1Co 14:15
also
rather speak five words with 1Co 14:19
my u.
Brethren, be not children in 1Co 14:20
u.
be ye children, but in u. be 1Co 14:20
men
eyes of your u. being Eph 1:18
enlightened
Having the u. darkened, Eph 4:18
being
u. what the will of the Lord Eph 5:17
is
peace of God, which passeth Ph'p 4:7
all u.
in all wisdom and spiritual u. Col 1:9
riches of the full assurance of Col 2:2
u.
u. neither what they say, nor 1Ti 1:7
Lord give thee u. in all things 2Ti 2:7
is come, and hath given us an 1Jo 5:20
u.
him that hath u. count the Re 13:18
number

UNDERSTANDINGLY

he dealt u. (A) 2Ch 11:23

UNDERSTOOD

knew not that Joseph u. them Ge 42:23
they were wise, that they u. De 32:29
this
they u. that the ark of the 1Sa 4:6
Lord
u. that Saul was come in very 1Sa 26:4
deed
Saul then u. (B) 1Sa 28:14
all the people and all Israel 2Sa 3:37
u. that
I u. God had not sent (R) Ne 6:12
I u. that this work (B) Ne 6:16
u. the words that were Ne 8:12
declared
u. of the evil that Eliashib did Ne 13:7
for
this, mine ear hath heard and Job 13:1
u. it
have I uttered that I u. not Job 42:3
of God; then u. I their end Ps 73:17
I heard a language that I u. Ps 81:5
not
Our fathers u. not thy Ps 106:7
wonders in
ye not u. from the Isa 40:21
foundations of
They have not known nor u.: Isa 44:18
for he
at the vision, but none u. it Da 8:27
I Daniel u. by books the Da 9:2
number of
and he u. the thing, and had Da 10:1
And I heard, but I u. not: Da 12:8
then said

them, Have ye u. all these M't 13:51
things
Then u. they how that he M't 16:12
bade
the disciples u. that he spake M't 17:13
unto
When Jesus u. it, he said M't 26:10
unto
But they u. not that saying M'k 9:32
u. not the saying which he Lu 2:50
spake
they u. not this saying, and it Lu 9:45
was
And they u. none of these Lu 18:34
things
u. not that he spake to them Joh 8:27
of
u. not what things they were Joh 10:6
which
These things u. not his Joh 12:16
disciples at
his brethren would have u. Ac 7:25
how
deliver them: but they u. not Ac 7:25
having u. that he was a Ac 23:27
Roman
when he u. that he was of Ac 23:34
Cilicia
u. by the things that are made Ro 1:20
I u. as a child, I thought as 1Co 13:11
a child
by the tongue words easy to 1Co 14:9
be u.
are some things hard to be u. 2Pe 3:16

UNDERTAKE

Lord, I am oppressed; u. for Isa 38:14
me

UNDERTOOK

Jews u. to do as they had Es 9:23
begun

UNDERWENT

u. a change (A) M't 17:2

UNDERWORLD

in depths of the u. (B) De 32:22
if I make the u. my (B) Ps 139:8

UNDESERVED

u. gift (B) Ro 1:5

UNDESERVING

u. servants (B) Lu 17:10

UNDILUTED

evil's u. power to deceive (P) 2Th 2:10

UNDISCIPLINED

u. eyes (A) 1Sa 3:16
son of an u. woman (B) 1Sa 20:30
an u. mischief (B) Jas 3:8

UNDISTRACTED

u., undivided devotion 1Co 7:35
(A)(R)

UNDISTURBED

calm, u. mind and heart (A) Pr 14:30
choice behavior, u. devotion 1Co 7:35
(B)

UNDIVIDED

undistracted, u. devotion 1Co 7:35
(A)(R)

UNDO

to u. the heavy burdens, and Isa 58:6
to let
that time I will u. all that Zep 3:19
afflict

UNDONE

thou art u., O people of Nu 21:29
Chemosh
he left nothing u. of all that Jos 11:15

Woe is me! for I am u. Isa 6:5
people of Chemosh are u. Jer 48:46
(A)(B)(E)(R)
done, and not to leave the M't 23:23;
other u. Lu 11:42

UNDRESSED

gather the grapes of thy vine Le 25:5
u.
your uncultivated vine (A) Le 25:5;
25:11
your unpruned vine (B) Le 25:5; 25:11
the grapes in it of thy vine u. Le 25:11

UNDYING

love with u. and Eph 6:24
incorruptible love (A)(R)

UNEDUCATED

u. and common (P)(R) Ac 4:13

UNENDING

the u. riches of Christ (A) Eph 3:8

UNEQUAL

are not your ways u. Eze 18:25;
18:29
unfair and unjust (A) Eze 18:25; 18:29
the Lord is not fair (B) Eze 18:25;
18:29
the Lord is not just (R) Eze 18:25;
25:29

UNEQUALLY

not u. yoked together with 2Co 6:14
do not unite with unbelievers 2Co 6:14
(N)
Don't link up with 2Co 6:14
unbelievers (P)(R)

UNERRING

be untainted u. (A) Ph'p 1:10

UNFADING

unsullied and u. 1Pe 1:4
(A)(B)(P)(R)
incorruptible, u. spirit 1Pe 3:4
(A)(E)(N)
u. garland of glory (N) 1Pe 5:4

UNFAILING

intense and u. love (A)(B)(R) 1Pe 4:8
love with u. love (P) Eph 6:24

UNFAIR

your people are u. (B) Ex 5:16
who despise u. profits (B) Ex 18:21
u. and unjust (A) Eze 18:25; 18:29
the u. judge (B) Lu 18:6
God is being u. (R) Ro 3:5
God is not u. (B)(P) 1Co 6:10

UNFAIRNESS

practice no u. (B) Le 19:15
every one practicing u. (B) De 25:16
builds his palace in u. (B) Jer 22:13

UNFAITHFUL

to become u. (B) 2Ch 21:11
had been u. (R) 2Ch 12:2; 36:14
have been u. (A)(R) 2Ch 29:6; 30:7
Confidence in an u. man in Pr 25:19
time of
trust in a faithless man Pr 25:19
(B)(R)
lest you be u. (B) Mal 2:15; 2:16
proving u. (P) 1Ti 5:12

UNFAITHFULLY

acted most u. (B) 2Ch 36:14
and dealt u. like their fathers Ps 78:57
acted u. (B) Eze 15:8; 20:27

UNFAITHFULNESS

your u. (B)(R) Nu 14:33
for their u. to God (A)(B)(R) 1Ch 9:1;
10:13; 2Ch 28:19

because of *u*. (B)   2Ch 12:2
u. of house of Ahab (R)   2Ch 21:13
because of *u*. (B)   Eze 18:24
except for *u*. (A)(B)(R)   M't 5:32

UNFASTEN

not fit to *u*. his shoes (N)   M'k 1:7

UNFASTENING

u. the cords of death (B)   Ac 2:24

UNFATHOMABLE

how *u*. are his judgments   Ro 11:33
(A)(P)

UNFATHOMLESS

the *u*. riches of Christ (N)   Eph 3:8

UNFEIGNED

by the Holy Ghost, by love *u*.   2Co 6:6
unpretended love (B)   2Co 6:6
by sincere love (N)   2Co 6:6
with genuine love (P)(R)   2Co 6:6
of a good conscience, and of   1Ti 1:5
faith *u*.
undisguised faith (B)   1Ti 1:5
faith that is genuine (N)(P)   1Ti 1:5
sincere faith (R)   2Ti 1:5
the *u*. faith that is in thee   2Ti 1:5
sincere and unqualified faith   2Ti 1:5
(A)
unalloyed faith (B)   2Ti 1:5
sincerity of your faith (N)   2Ti 1:5
Genuine faith (P)   2Ti 1:5
sincere faith (R)   2Ti 1:5
impartial and *u*. (A)(B)   Jas 3:17
Spirit unto *u*. love of the   1Pe 1:22
brethren
sincere affection (A)   1Pe 1:22

UNFERMENTED

u. batches of truth (B)   1Co 5:8

UNFIT

u. and worthless for (A)(B)(R)   Tit 1:16

UNFLAGGING

with *u*. energy (N)   Ro 12:11

UNFORMED

u. substance (A)(B)(E)(R)   Ps 139:16
yet being *u*. (S)   Ps 139:16

UNFRUITFUL

the word, and he becometh   M't 13:22
u.
unproductive (B)   M't 13:22
it proves barren (N)   M't 13:22;
                   M'k 4:19
it produces no crop (P)   M't 13:22;
                   M'k 4:19
choke the word, and it   M'k 4:19
becometh *u*.
it becomes fruitless (A)(B)   M'k 4:19
but my understanding is *u*.   1Co 14:14
my mind is unproductive   1Co 14:14
(A)(B)
my intellect lies fallow (N)   1Co 14:14
my mind is inactive (P)   1Co 14:14
with the *u*. works of darkness   Eph 5:11
fruitless deeds and   Eph 5:11
enterprises of darkness (A)
Fruitless doings of darkness   Eph 5:11
(B)
barren deeds of darkness   Eph 5:11
(N)
the activities of darkness (P)   Eph 5:11
necessary uses, that they be   Tit 3:14
not *u*.
they might be unproductive   Tit 3:14
(B)(N)
nor *u*. in the knowledge of our   2Pe 1:8
Lord
neither inactive nor   2Pe 1:8
reproductive (B)
useless or barren (N)   2Pe 1:8
complacent of unproductive   2Pe 1:8
(P)

UNGIRDED

he *u*. his camels, and gave   Ge 24:32
straw

UNGODLINESS

floods of *u*. (E)   2Sa 22:5; Ps 18:5
streams of *u*. (A)(B)   Ps 18:4
practicing profane *u*. (A)   Isa 32:6
have ploughed *u*. (B)   Ho 10:13
revealed from heaven against   Ro 1:18
all *u*.
impiety and wickedness (B)   Ro 1:18
godless wickedness (N)   Ro 1:18
godlessness and evil (P)   Ro 1:18
u. and wickedness (R)   Ro 1:18
and shall turn away *u*. from   Ro 11:26
Jacob
remove wickedness from   Ro 11:26
Jacob (N)
for they will increase unto   2Ti 2:16
more *u*.
stray further in godless   2Ti 2:16
courses (N)
further away from Christian   2Ti 2:16
living (P)
denying *u*. and worldly lusts   Tit 2:12
renounce godlessness (B)(P)   Tit 2:12
renounce godless ways (N)   Tit 2:12
renounce irreligion (R)   Tit 2:12

UNGODLY

floods of *u*. men made me   2Sa 22:5
afraid
torrents of destruction (A)   2Sa 22:5
the wicked (B)(R)   2Sa 22:5;
       2Ch 19:2; Ps 1:1; 3:7; 73:12
floods of ungodliness (E)   2Sa 22:5;
                      Ps 18:5
the ungodly (E)   2Sa 23:6
Shouldest thou help the *u*.   2Ch 19:2
the wicked (E)   2Ch 19:2;
         Ps 1:1, 4-6; 3:7; 73:12
God hath delivered me to   Job 16:11
the *u*.
the villains (B)   Job 16:11
dwellings of the *u*. (A)   Job 18:21;
              Ps 64:2; 75:10
dwellings of the *u*. (E)   Job 18:21;
                    29:17
wicked? and to princes, Ye   Job 34:18
are *u*.
the *u*. (B)   Job 34:18;
      Ps 28:3; 139:19; 145:20; 147:6
ye are vile (E) .   Job 34:18
you are worthless (R)   Job 34:18
walketh not in the counsel of   Ps 1:1
the *u*.
The *u*. are not so: but are like   Ps 1:4
the wicked (A)   Ps 1:4; 1:5
u. shall not stand in the   Ps 1:5
judgment
but the way of the *u*. shall   Ps 1:6
perish
hast broken the teeth of the *u*.   Ps 3:7
floods of *u*. men made me   Ps 18:4
afraid
streams of ungodliness (A)(B)   Ps 18:4
sorrows to the *u*. (B)   Ps 32:10
cause against an *u*. nation   Ps 43:1
a merciless people (B)   Ps 43:1
against an *u*. people (R)   Ps 43:1
the *u*. are estranged (A)   Ps 58:3
these are the *u*. who prosper   Ps 73:12
horns of the *u*. (B)   Ps 75:10;
         140:8; 146:9; Hab 3:13
An *u*. man diggeth up evil   Pr 16:27
a worthless man   Pr 16:27;
(A)(B)(E)(R)   19:28
An *u*. witness scorneth   Pr 19:28
judgment
on him that justifieth the *u*. his   Ro 4:5
who makes the *u*. righteous   Ro 4:5
(B)
the guilty (N)   Ro 4:5
the sinful (P)   Ro 4:5
in due time Christ died for the   Ro 5:6
u.
the wicked (N)   Ro 5:6
for the *u*. and for sinners, for   1Ti 1:9
the lawless and unruly (N)   1Ti 1:9
where shall the *u*. and the   1Pe 4:18
sinner
the impious and sinful   1Pe 4:18;
(B)(E)(N)   Jude 4
the wicked and the sinner   1Pe 4:18
(P)

in the flood upon the world of   2Pe 2:5
the *u*.
a godless world (B)(N)(R)   2Pe 2:5;
                 2:6; 3:7
the world and its wickedness   2Pe 2:5
(P)
unto those that after should   2Pe 2:6
live *u*.
the filthy lives of the godless   2Pe 2:6
(P)
the *u*. and lawless (A)   2Pe 2:7
keep *u*. under chastisement   2Pe 2:9
(A)
judgment and perdition of *u*.   2Pe 3:7
men
wicked men (B)   2Pe 3:7
u. men, turning the grace of   Jude 4
our God
to convince all that are *u*.   Jude 15
among
the godless desires (N)(P)   Jude 15;
                 Jude 18
the impious (R)   Jude 15
all their *u*. deeds which they   Jude 15
have
which they have *u*. committed   Jude 15
speeches which *u*. sinners   Jude 15
have
walk after their own *u*. lusts   Jude 18
impious passions (B)(R)   Jude 18

UNGRATEFUL

the *u*. (A)(B)(N)(P)(R)   2Ti 3:2

UNHALLOWED

unclean to *u*. (A)   M'k 7:20
common and *u*. (A)   Heb 10:29

UNHESITATINGLY

go *u*. (B)   Ac 10:20

UNHOLY

offer no *u*. incense (A)(B)   Ex 30:9
offered *u*. fire (B)   Le 10:1;
             Nu 3:4; 26:61
difference between holy and   Le 10:10
u.
the secular (B)   Le 10:10
the common (E)(R)   Le 10:10
for *u*. and profane, for   1Ti 1:9
murderers
the lawless (A)(B)(E)(N)   1Ti 1:9
u. and old womanish tales (B)   1Ti 4:7
u. empty discussions (A)   2Ti 2:16
to parents, unthankful, *u*.   2Ti 3:2
ungrateful (A)(B)(N)(P)(R)   2Ti 3:2
he was sanctified, and *u*.   Heb 10:29
thing
common and unhallowed   Heb 10:29
(A)
profaned the blood (N)(R)   Heb 10:29

UNICORN

as it were the strength of an   Nu 23:22;
u.   24:8
the wild ox (A)(E)(R)   Nu 23:22;
    24:8; Job 39:9-10; Ps 29:6; 92:10
the buffalo (B)   Nu 23:22; 24:8
Will the *u*. be willing to serve   Job 39:9
thee
Canst thou bind the *u*. with   Job 39:10
his
Lebanon and Sirion like a   Ps 29:6
young *u*.
an antelope (B)   Ps 29:6
thou exalt like the horn of an   Ps 92:10
u.

UNICORNS

his horns are like the horns   De 33:17
of *u*.
the wild ox (A)(B)(E)(R)   De 33:17;
         Ps 22:21; Isa 34:7
heard me from the horns of   Ps 22:21
the *u*.
the *u*. shall come down with   Isa 34:7
them

UNIFY

to *u*. all things (A)   Eph 1:10

UNINITIATED

the *u*. or unbelieving (B)   1Co 14:24

UNINSTRUCTED

u. persons (N)	1Co 14:13
who are u. (P)	1Co 14:16

UNINTELLIGIBLE

u. barbarous language (B)	Isa 33:19

UNINTENTIONAL

killing u. (B)(R)	De 19:4

UNINTENTIONALLY

sins u. (A)	Le 4:13
unintentionally (S)	Nu 35:11;
	35:15; De 4:42; Jos 20:3
slay u. (A)(R)	De 4:42; Jos 20:9
kills u. (A)(S)	De 19:4
any person u. (A)	Jos 20:3; 20:5

UNISON

Saul was in u. with David (B)	1Sa 18:1
sighing in throes of u. (A)	Ro 8:22

UNITE

u. my heart to fear thy name	Ps 86:11

UNITED

mine honour, be not thou u.	Ge 49:6
were u. as one man (A)(B)(R)	J'g 20:11
heart being u. with yours (B)	1Ch 12:17
with u. purpose (A)(B)	Ac 2:46
u. in the same mind (R)	1Co 1:10
who is u. to the Lord (A)(R)	1Co 6:17
u. by every ligament (B)	Eph 4:16

UNITES

who u. with a prostitute (B)	1Co 6:16
who u. with the Lord (B)	1Co 6:17

UNITS

u. of the army for war (A)(B)(R)	1Ch 7:4

UNITY

brethren to dwell together in u.	Ps 133:1
brothers to live harmoniously (B)	Ps 133:1
to keep the u. of the Spirit in harmony (A)	Eph 4:3
keep in harmony (P)	Eph 4:3
aim to be at one in the Spirit	Eph 4:3
we all come in the u. of the faith	Eph 4:13
attain to oneness in the faith (A)	Eph 4:13
in the u. of love (N)	Col 2:2
have u. of spirit (R)	1Pe 3:8

UNIVERSE

exhibition to the u. (B)	1Co 4:9
who fills the u. (B)	Eph 1:23
sustains u. by his almighty word	Heb 1:3

UNJUST

hating u. gain (A)(E)	Ex 18:21
me from the deceitful and u. man	Ps 43:1
and the hope of u. men perisheth	Pr 11:7
the expectation of the godless (A)	Pr 11:7
the wicked man (B)	Pr 11:7;
	29:27; 2Pe 2:9
the wicked (E)	Pr 11:7
the godless (R)	Pr 11:7
u. gain increaseth his substance	Pr 28:8
An u. man is an abomination	Pr 29:27
u. and wicked speaking (A)	Isa 58:9
unfair and u. (A)	Eze 18:25; 18:29
not; but the u. knoweth no shame	Zep 3:5

rain on the just and on the u.	M't 5:45
the wrongdoers (A)	M't 5:45
bad (N)	M't 5:45
dishonest (N)	M't 5:45
dishonest (P)	M't 5:45; Lu 18:6, 10
the lord commended the u. steward	Lu 16:8
dishonest manager (A)(B)	Lu 16:8
the unrighteous steward (E)	Lu 16:8;
	16:10; 16:6; 1Co 6:1; 1Pe 3:18; 2Pe 2:9;
	Re 22:11
dishonest (N)(R)	Lu 16:8; 16:10
rascally steward (P)	Lu 16:8
is u. in the least is u. also in much	Lu 16:10
unreliable (B)	Lu 16:10
the man who cheats (P)	Lu 16:10
said, Hear what the u. judge saith	Lu 18:6
unfair judge (B)	Lu 18:6
the unrighteous judge (R)	Lu 18:6
as other men are, extortioners, u.	Lu 18:11
dishonest (N)	Lu 18:11
crooked u. generation (A)	Ac 2:40
of the dead, both of the just and u.	Ac 24:15
wicked (N)	Ac 24:15; 2Pe 2:9
bad (P)	Ac 24:15
is God u. and wrong (A)(N)(R)	Ro 3:5
go to law before the u. and unrighteous (A)	1Co 6:1; 1Pe 3:18
before a pagan court (B)(N)(R)	1Co 6:1
the unrighteous (N)	1Co 6:1;
	1Pe 3:18; 2Pe 2:9
the unjust (N)	1Co 6:9
God would not be u. (N)(R)	1Co 6:10
our pride is not u. (P)	2Co 9:3
endures pain of u. suffering (B)	1Pe 2:19
suffered for sins, the just for the u.	1Pe 3:18
to reserve the u. unto the day	2Pe 2:9
keep the ungodly under chastisement (A)	2Pe 2:9
the wicked (P)	2Pe 2:9; Re 22:11
He that is u. let him be u. still	Re 22:11
the wrongdoer (B)	Re 22:11
the evil doer (N)	Re 22:11

UNJUSTLY

How long will ye judge u. and	Ps 82:2
of uprightness will he deal u.	Isa 26:10
he deals perversely (A)	Isa 26:10
he deals wrongfully (R)	Isa 26:10

UNKNOWN

eat u. of (A)	Le 22:14
this inscription, To The U. God	Ac 17:23
you worship as u. (A)(R)	Ac 17:23
he that speaketh in an u. tongue	1Co 14:2
a language of ecstasy (N)	1Co 14:2;
	14:4, 13, 19, 27
in an u. tongue edifieth himself	1Co 14:4
that speaketh in an u. tongue pray	1Co 14:13
if I pray in an u. tongue, my spirit	1Co 14:14
ten thousand words in an u. tongue	1Co 14:19
If any man speak in an u. tongue, let	1Co 14:27
As u. and yet well known; as dying	2Co 6:9
was u. by face unto the churches of	Ga 1:22

UNLADE

the ship was to u. her burden	Ac 21:3
unload her cargo (A)(N)(R)	Ac 21:3
discharge her cargo (B)(P)	Ac 21:3

UNLAWFUL

every u. deed (A)	Ex 22:9
an u. thing for a man that is a Jew	Ac 10:28
day to day with their u. deeds	2Pe 2:8

UNLEARNED

that they were u. and ignorant men	Ac 4:13

without schooling or skill (B)	Ac 4:13
untrained laymen (N)	Ac 4:13
uneducated and untrained (P)	Ac 4:13
uneducated and common men (R)	Ac 4:13
the u. (B)	Ro 1:14
the u. say Amen at thy giving of	1Co 14:16
not gifted in interpreting tongues (A)(B)(P)	1Co 14:16
the plain man (N)	1Co 14:16
who are uninstructed (P)	1Co 14:16
an outsider (R)	1Co 14:16; 14:23-24
there come in those that are u.	1Co 14:23
uninitiated or unbelieving (B)	1Co 14:23; 14:24
uninstructed persons (N)	1Co 14:23
one that believeth not, of one u.	1Co 14:24
foolish and u. questions avoid	2Ti 2:23
uncultural discussions (B)	2Ti 2:23
ignorant speculations (N)	2Ti 2:23
stupid, senseless controversies (R)	2Ti 2:23
that are u. and unstable wrest	2Pe 3:16
untaught and unsteady (B)	2Pe 3:16
the ignorant (N)(R)	2Pe 3:16
ill-informed and unbalanced (P)	2Pe 3:16

UNLEAVENED

did bake u. bread, and they did	Ge 19:3
night, roast with fire, and u. bread	Ex 12:8
Seven days shall ye eat u. bread	Ex 12:15
shall observe the feast of u. bread	Ex 12:17
ye shall eat u. bread, until the one	Ex 12:18
habitations shall ye eat u. bread	Ex 12:20
they baked u. cakes of the dough	Ex 12:39
Seven days thou shalt eat u. bread	Ex 13:6; 34:18; De 16:3
U. bread shall be eaten seven	Ex 13:7
shalt keep the feast of u. bread	Ex 23:15
thou shalt eat u. bread seven days	Ex 23:15
u. bread, and cakes u. tempered	Ex 29:2
and wafers u. anointed with oil	Ex 29:2
out of the basket of the u. bread	Ex 29:23
feast of u. bread shalt thou keep	Ex 34:18
u. cakes of fine flour mingled with	Le 2:4
oil, or u. wafers anointed with oil	Le 2:4
a pan, it shall be of fine flour u.	Le 2:5
with u. bread shall it be eaten	Le 6:16
u. cakes mingled with oil	Le 7:12
and u. wafers anointed with oil	Le 7:12
rams, and a basket of u. bread	Le 8:2
And out of the casket of u. bread	Le 8:26
he took one u. cake and a cake of	Le 8:26
the feast of u. bread unto the Lord	Le 23:6
seven days ye must eat u. bread	Le 23:6
and a basket of u. bread, cakes of	Nu 6:15
wafers of u. bread anointed with	Nu 6:15
Lord, with the basket of u. bread	Nu 6:17
and one u. cake out of the basket	Nu 6:19
one u. wafer, and shall put them	Nu 6:19
eat it with u. bread and bitter	Nu 9:11
seven days shall u. bread be eaten	Nu 28:17
Six days thou shalt eat u. bread	De 16:8
in the feast of u. bread, and De	16:16
u. cakes, and parched corn in	Jos 5:11
and u. cakes of an ephah of flour	J'g 6:19

Take the flesh and the *u.* cakes	*J'g 6:20*
touched the flesh and the *u.* cakes	*J'g 6:21*
the flesh and the *u.* cakes	*J'g 6:21*
kneaded it, and did bake *u.* bread	*1Sa 28:24*
did eat of the *u.* bread among their	*2Ki 23:9*
for the *u.* cakes, and for that which	*1Ch 23:29*
year, even in the feast of *u.* bread	*2Ch 8:13*
people to keep the feast of *u.* bread	*2Ch 30:13*
the feast of *u.* bread seven days	*2Ch 30:21; 35:17; Ezr 6:22*
seven days; *u.* bread shall be eaten	*Eze 45:21*
first day of the feast of *u.* bread	*M't 26:17*
of the passover, and of *u.* bread	*M'k 14:1*
the first day of *u.* bread, when they	*M'k 14:12*
Now the feast of *u.* bread drew nigh	*Lu 22:1*
Then came the day of *u.* bread	*Lu 22:7*
Then were the days of *u.* bread	*Ac 12:3*
Philippi after the days of *u.* bread	*Ac 20:6*
ye may be a new lump, as ye are *u.*	*1Co 5:7*
be new *u.* bread (P)	*1Co 5:7*
the *u.* bread of sincerity and truth	*1Co 5:8*
u. bread of unadulterated truth (P)	*1Co 5:8*

UNLESS

u. he wash his flesh with	*Le 22:6*
u. she had turned from me, surely	*Nu 22:33*
u. thou hadst spoken, surely	*2Sa 2:27*
u. I had believed to see the	*Ps 27:13*
U. the Lord had been my help, my	*Ps 94:17*
U. thy law had been my delights, I	*Ps 119:92*
u. they cause some to fall	*Pr 4:16*
u. ye have believed in vain	*1Co 15:2*

UNLIMITED

understanding is *u.* (B)	*Ps 147:5*
her strength *u.* (B)(S)	*Na 3:9*
u. seduction to evil (A)	*2Th 2:10*

UNLOAD

u. the cargo (S)	*Ac 21:3*

UNLOOSE

not worthy to stoop down and *u.*	*M'k 1:7*
whose shoes I am not worthy to *u.*	*Lu 3:16*
shoe's latchet I am not worthy to *u.*	*Joh 1:27*

UNLOVED

an *u.* and repugnant woman (A)(B)(R)	*Pr 30:23*

UNMARKED

like *u.* graves (N)(P)	*Lu 11:44*
four *u.* daughters (N)(P)(R)	*Ac 21:9*
perform *u.* deeds (P)	*Ro 1:28*
concerning the *u.* (N)(R)	*1Co 7:25*
not conceited and *u.* (B)	*1Co 13:5*

UNMARRIED

say therefore to the *u.* and widows	*1Co 7:8*
single (B)	*1Co 7:8; 7:11, 32*
and if she depart, let her remain *u.*	*1Co 7:11*
single (A)	*1Co 7:11*
He that is *u.* careth for the things	*1Co 7:32*
The *u.* woman careth for the things	*1Co 7:34*

UNMERCIFUL

natural affection, implacable, *u.*	*Ro 1:31*

UNMINDFUL

Rock that begat thee thou art *u.*	*De 32:18*

UNMIXED

with reverence, awe, and *u.* motives (B)	*Eph 6:5*
with *u.* motives (B)	*Col 3:22*

UNMOVEABLE

stuck fast, and remained *u.*	*Ac 27:41*
brethren, be ye stedfast, *u.*	*1Co 15:58*

UNNATURAL

indulged in *u.* vice (A)(N)(R)	*Jude 7*

UNNI

and Jehiel, and *u.,* Eliab	*1Ch 15:18; 15:20*
Also Bakbukiah and *U.* their	*Ne 12:9*

UNOCCUPIED

the highways were *u.* and the	*J'g 5:6*

UNOBJECTIONABLE

wholesome, *u.* message (B)	*Tit 2:8*

UNPARALLED

u. power (B)	*2Co 4:7*

UNPERFECT

did see my substance, yet being *u.*	*Ps 139:16*
unformed substance (A)(B)(E)(R)	*Ps 139:16*

UNPHILOSOPHICAL

utterly *u.* nonsense (A)	*1Co 1:23*

UNPLEASANT

it is a fact most *u.* (P)	*Heb 12:11*

UNPREPARED

come with me, and find you *u.*	*2Co 9:4*

UNPRETENDED

u. love (B)	*2Co 6:6*

UNPRETENTIOUS

impartial and *u.* (B)	*Jas 3:17*

UNPRINCIPLED

u. men (B)	*1Ki 21:10*
passionate and *u.* (P)	*2Ti 3:3*

UNPRODUCTIVE

my *u.* existence (B)	*Ec 7:15*
my mind is *u.* (A)(B)	*1Co 14:14*
be *u.* (B)(N)(P)	*Tit 3:14; 2Pe 1:8*

UNPROFITABLE

u. talk (E)	*Job 15:2*
Should he reason with *u.* talk	*Job 15:3*
pointless talk (B)	*Job 15:3*
your *u.* days (B)	*Ec 9:9*
cast ye the *u.* servant into outer	*M't 25:30*
good-for-nothing servant (A)	*M't 25:30*
useless servant (B)(N)(P)(R)	*M't 25:30*
you, say, We are *u.* servants	*Lu 17:10*
unworthy servants (A)(R)	*Lu 17:10*
undeserving servants (B)	*Lu 17:10*
servants and deserve no credit (N)	*Lu 17:10*
not much good as servants (P)	*Lu 17:10*

way, they are together become *u.*	*Ro 3:12*
have become utterly useless (B)	*Ro 3:12*
become debased (N)	*Ro 3:12*
the law: for they are *u.* and vain	*Tit 3:9*
they are futile and purposeless (B)	*Tit 3:9*
they settle nothing, and lead nowhere (P)	*Tit 3:9*
u. and futile (R)	*Tit 3:9*
Which in time past was to thee *u.*	*Ph'm 11*
useless to you (B)(R)	*Ph'm 11*
pretty useless in time past	*Ph'm 11*
with grief: for that is *u.* for you	*Heb 13:17*
hurtful to you (B)	*Heb 13:17*
that would bring you no advantage (N)(R)	*Heb 13:17*

UNPROFITABLENESS

for the weakness and *u.* thereof	*Heb 7:18*
ineffectiveness and uselessness (A)(B)(P)	*Heb 7:18*
impotent and useless (N)	*Heb 7:18*
weakness and uselessness (R)	*Heb 7:18*

UNPRUNED

your *u.* vines (B)(S)	*Le 25:5; 25:11*

UNPUNISHED

hand, the wicked shall not be *u.*	*Pr 11:2*
join in hand, he shall not be *u.*	*Pr 16:5*
is glad at calamities shall not be *u.*	*Pr 17:5*
A false witness shall not be *u.*	*Pr 19:5; 19:9*
name, and should ye be utterly *u.*	*Jer 25:29*
Ye shall not be *u.:* for I will call for	*Jer 25:29*
will not leave thee altogether *u.*	*Jer 30:11*
yet will I not leave thee wholly *u.*	*Jer 46:28*
thou he that shall altogether go *u.*	*Jer 49:12*
thou shalt not go *u.* but thou shalt	*Jer 49:12*

UNQUALIFIED

sincere and *u.* faith (A)	*1Ti 1:5*

UNQUENCHABLE

will burn up the chaff with *u.* fire	*M't 3:12*
fire that cannot be put out (A)(B)(P)	*M't 3:12*
fire that can never go out (N)	*M't 3:12*
the chaff he will burn with fire *u.*	*Lu 3:17*
fire that can never be extinguished (A)	*Lu 3:17*
fire that can never be put out (B)	*Lu 3:17*
fire that can never go out (N)	*Lu 3:17*
fire that cannot be put out (P)	*Lu 3:17*

UNRAVEL

solve riddle, *u.* knots (B)	*Da 5:12*

UNREASONABLE

u. verbiage (B)	*Job 39:16*
seemeth to me *u.* to send a prisoner	*Ac 25:27*
senseless and absurd (A)	*Ac 25:27*
it seems to me odd (B)	*Ac 25:27*
There is no sense (N)	*Ac 25:27*
It seems to me ridiculous (P)	*Ac 25:27*
delivered from *u.* and wicked men	*2Th 3:2*
perverse and wicked men (A)	*2Th 3:2*
unbalanced and malicious men (B)	*2Th 3:2*

UNREASONABLE

wrong-headed and wicked men (N) | 2Th 3:2
bigoted and wicked men (P) | 2Th 3:2
wicked and evil men (R) | 2Th 3:2

UNREBUKEABLE

commandment without spot, u. | 1Ti 6:14
unsullied, flawless, irreproachable (A) | 1Ti 6:14
sinless and irreproachable (B) | 1Ti 6:14
without spot, without reproach (E) | 1Ti 6:14
irreproachable and without fault (N) | 1Ti 6:14
clean and above reproach (P) | 1Ti 6:14
unstained and free from reproach (R) | 1Ti 6:14

UNRELIABLE

the u. messenger (B) | Pr 13:17
the u. steward (B) | Lu 16:8

UNRENEWED

discard old u. self (A) | Eph 4:22

UNREPROVEABLE

unblameable and u. in his sight | Col 1:22

UNRESERVEDLY

we speak u. (B) | 2Co 3:12

UNREST

u. to inhabitants (A)(R) | Jer 50:34

UNRESTRAINED

people were u. (A)(B) | Ex 32:25
u. (indecent) conduct (A) | M'k 7:22

UNRIGHTEOUS

the wicked to be an u. witness | Ex 23:1
to be a malicious witness (B)(R) | Ex 23:1
by the u. (B) | 2Sa 7:10
riseth up against me as the u. | Job 27:7
my opponent be as the perverse (B) | Job 27:7
my enemy be as the wicked (E)(R) | Job 27:7
destruction to the u. (A)(E) | Job 31:3
the hand of the u. and cruel man | Ps 71:4
from the hand of the wicked (B)(E)(R) | Ps 71:4
unto them that decree u. decrees | Isa 10:1
decree iniquitous decrees (R) | Isa 10:1
way, and the u. man his thoughts | Isa 55:7
the u. steward (E) | Lu 16:8; 16:10; 18:6; 1Co 6:1; 1Pe 3:18; 2Pe 2:9; Re 22:11
not been faithful in the u. mammon | Lu 16:11
faithful in matters of deceitful riches (B) | Lu 16:11
trustworthy with wealth of this world (N) | Lu 16:11
trusted to deal with wicked wealth (P) | Lu 16:11
the u. judge (R) | Lu 18:6
Is God u. who taketh vengeance | Ro 3:5
That God is unjust and wrong (A) | Ro 3:5
that God is wrong (B) | Ro 3:5
Is it unjust of God (N)(R) | Ro 3:5
God is being unfair (R) | Ro 3:5
the u. (A)(R) | 1Co 6:1; 1Pe 1:18; 2Pe 2:9
u. shall not inherit the kingdom of | 1Co 6:9
dishonest people (B) | 1Co 6:9
the unjust (N) | 1Co 6:9
the wicked (P) | 1Co 6:9
God is not u. to forget your work | Heb 6:10
God is not unfair (B)(P) | Heb 6:10
God would not be so unjust (N)(R) | Heb 6:10
shedding its u. fruit (A)(B)(E)(R) | Re 6:13

UNRIGHTEOUSNESS

Ye shall do no u. in judgment | Le 19:15
do no injustice in judgment (A)(R) | Le 19:15; 19:35
practice no unfairness in court | Le 19:15
Ye shall do no u. in judgment, in | Le 19:35
do no wrong in judgment (R) | Le 19:35
let not u. dwell (E) | Job 11:14
my rock, and there is no u. in him | Ps 92:15
that buildeth his house by u. | Jer 22:13
builds his palace in unfairness (B) | Jer 22:13
by u. of your trade (A)(B)(R) | Eze 28:18
friends of the mammon of u. | Lu 16:9
use deceitful wealth (B) | Lu 16:9
use worldly wealth (N) | Lu 16:9
use money, tainted as it is (P) | Lu 16:9
the same is true, and no u. is in him | Joh 7:18
in him is no deceit (B) | Joh 7:18
there is nothing false in him (N) | Joh 7:18
there is no dishonesty in him (P) | Joh 7:18
in him there is no falsehood (R) | Joh 7:18
all ungodliness and u. of men | Ro 1:18
impiety and wickedness (B) | Ro 1:18
godless wickedness (N) | Ro 1:18
the godlessness of evil (P) | Ro 1:18
ungodliness and wickedness (R) | Ro 1:18
of men, who hold the truth in u. | Ro 1:18
Being filled with all u. fornication | Ro 1:29
every sort of wickedness (B)(P)(R) | Ro 1:29
every kind of injustice (N) | Ro 1:29
but obey u. indignation and wrath | Ro 2:8
responsive to wickedness (A)(B)(R) | Ro 2:8
if our u. commend the righteousness | Ro 3:5
our wrongdoing (B) | Ro 3:5
our injustice (N) | Ro 3:5
our wickedness (P)(R) | Ro 3:5
as instruments of u. unto sin | Ro 6:13
we say then? Is there u. with God | Ro 9:14
Is there injustice upon God's part (A)(B)(N)(R) | Ro 9:14
do we conclude God is monstrously unfair (P) | Ro 9:14
hath righteousness with u. | 2Co 6:14
righteousness with lawlessness (B) | 2Co 6:14
righteousness and iniquity (E)(R) | 2Co 6:14
righteousness with wickedness (N) | 2Co 6:14
goodness and evil (P) | 2Co 6:14
deceivableness of u. in them that | 2Th 2:10
unlimited seduction to evil and all wicked deception (A) | 2Th 2:10
limitless deceit of wickedness (B) | 2Th 2:10
all the deception of sinfulness (N) | 2Th 2:10
all wicked deception (R) | 2Th 2:10
not the truth, but had pleasure in u. | 2Th 2:12
pleasure in wickedness (B) | 2Th 2:12
make sinfulness their deliberate choice (N) | 2Th 2:12
made evil their playfellow (P) | 2Th 2:12
For I will be merciful to their u. | Heb 8:12
merciful toward their wrongdoings (B) | Heb 8:12
merciful to their iniquities (E)(P)(R) | Heb 8:12
merciful to their wicked deeds (N) | Heb 8:12
And shall receive the reward of u. | 2Pe 2:13
reward of wickedness (B) | 2Pe 2:13
suffering wrong for wrongdoing (E)(R) | 2Pe 2:13
suffering hurt for the hurt they inflicted (N) | 2Pe 2:13
Bosor, who loved the wages of u. | 2Pe 2:15
loved the wages of wickedness (A)(B) | 2Pe 2:15
loved the hire of wrongdoing (E)(R) | 2Pe 2:15
take pay for doing wrong (N) | 2Pe 2:15
no objection to wickedness for pay (P) | 2Pe 2:15
sins, and to cleanse us from all u. | 1Jo 1:9
cleanse of every kind of wrong (N) | 1Jo 1:9
thoroughly clean from all evil (P) | 1Jo 1:9
All u. is sin: and there is a sin not | 1Jo 5:17
All wrongdoing is sin (A)(N)(R) | 1Jo 5:17
Every wrong is sin (B) | 1Jo 5:17
Every failure to obey God's laws is sin (P) | 1Jo 5:17

UNRIGHTEOUSLY

all that do u. are an abomination | De 25:16
everyone practicing unfairness (B) | De 25:16
all who act dishonestly (R) | De 25:16

UNRIPE

shake off his u. grape as the vine | Job 15:33

UNRULY

u., recalcitrant people (N) | Ro 10:21
brethren, warn them that are u. | 1Th 5:14
warn the disorderly (B)(E) | 1Th 5:14
admonish the careless (N) | 1Th 5:14
admonish the idle (R) | 1Th 5:14
for lawless and u. (A)(E)(N) | 1Ti 1:9
children not accused of riot or u. | Tit 1:6
accused of loose living and lawbreaking (P) | Tit 1:6
charged of being profligate or insubordinate (R) | Tit 1:6
there are many u. and vain talkers | Tit 1:10
out of control (N) | Tit 1:10; 1:6
will not recognize authority (P) | Tit 1:10
many insubordinate men (R) | Tit 1:10
it is an u. evil, full of deadly poison | Jas 3:8
a restless evil (A)(E)(R) | Jas 3:8
an undisciplined mischief (B) | Jas 3:8
an intractable evil (N) | Jas 3:8

UNSATIABLE

because thou wast u.; yea | Eze 16:28
you were not satisfied (A)(R) | Eze 16:28

UNSAVORY

I saw something u. (B)(R) | Jer 23:13

UNSAVOURY

froward thou wilt shew thyself u. | 2Sa 22:27
You will show yourself willful (A) | 2Sa 22:27
the twisted are twisted to thee (B) | 2Sa 22:27
with perverse show thyself froward (E) | 2Sa 22:27
with crooked show thyself perverse (R) | 2Sa 22:27
Can that which is u. be eaten | Job 6:6
Can that without taste be eaten (A) | Job 6:6
Can that which is insipid be eaten without salt (B) | Job 6:6
Can that without savour be eaten (E) | Job 6:6
Can the tasteless be eaten without salt (R) | Job 6:6

UNSCRUPULOUS

an u. grasping man (A) | Pr 3:31

UNSCRUPULOUSNESS

cunning of *u*. (A) — Lu 20:23
master of *u*. (A) — Ac 13:10

UNSEARCHABLE

doeth great things and *u*. — Job 5:9
praised; and his greatness is — Ps 145:3
u.
and the heart of kings is *u*. — Pr 25:3
how *u*. are his judgments, — Ro 11:33
and his
How unfathomable are his — Ro 11:33
judgments (A)
How inscrutable are his — Ro 11:33
judgments (N)
amazed at unfathomable — Ro 11:33
complexity of (P)
Gentiles the *u*. riches of — Eph 3:8
Christ
unending, boundless, — Eph 3:8
fathomless, incalculable, and
exhaustless riches in Christ (A)
the fathomless wealth of — Eph 3:8
Christ (B)
the unfathomable riches of — Eph 3:8
Christ (N)
the incalculable riches of — Eph 3:8
Christ (P)

UNSEEMLY

with men working that which — Ro 1:27
is *u*.
committing shameful acts (A) — Ro 1:27
committing shamelessness — Ro 1:27
with men (B)
behave indecently (N) — Ro 1:27
performed shameful horrors — Ro 1:27
(P)
committing shameful acts (R) — Ro 1:27
behave himself *u*. (S) — 1Co 7:36
Doth not behave itself *u*. — 1Co 13:5
seeketh not
act unbecomingly (A) — 1Co 13:5
not conceited and unmannerly — 1Co 13:5
(B)
nor rude (N)(R) — 1Co 13:5

UNSEEN

things seen and *u*. (A)(P) — Col 1:16

UNSELFISHNESS

known for *u*. (A) — Ph'p 4:5

UNSETTLE

u. your minds (N) — Ga 1:7

UNSETTLED

anxious mind—*u*. excited, — Lu 12:29
worried, in suspense (A)
u. or intimidated (B) — Joh 14:27
u. your minds — Ac 15:24
(B)(N)(P)(R)

UNSHAKEN

firm and *u*. to the end (A) — Heb 3:14

UNSHOD

Withhold thy foot from being — Jer 2:25
u.

UNSIGHTLY

make looks *u*. (B)(N) — M't 6:16

UNSKILFUL

every one that useth milk is — Heb 5:13
u. in
inexperienced (B) — Heb 5:13
without experience (E) — Heb 5:13
does not know what is right — Heb 5:13
(N)
is obviously immature (P) — Heb 5:13

UNSKILLED

if I am *u*. in speaking — 2Co 11:6
(A)(R)

UNSOUND

of *u*. mind (B) — De 32:28

UNSPEAKABLE

with *u*. yearnings and — Ro 8:26
groanings (A)
Thanks be unto God for his — 2Co 2:15
u. gift
indescribable, inexpressible, — 2Co 9:15
free gift (A)
Thanks for his gift beyond — 2Co 9:15
words (N)
his indescribable generosity — 2Co 9:15
(P)
his inexpressible gift (R) — 2Co 9:15
to paradise, and heard *u*. — 2Co 12:4
words
heard utterances beyond the — 2Co 12:4
power of man to put into
words (A)
heard ineffable sayings (B) — 2Co 12:4
heard words so secret that — 2Co 12:4
human lips may not repeat
them (N)
heard words that cannot, and — 2Co 12:4
indeed must not, be translated
in human speech (P)
heard things that cannot be — 2Co 12:4
told (R)
with joy *u*. and full of glory — 1Pe 1:8
exult and thrill with — 1Pe 1:8
inexpressible and glorious joy (A)
exult with inexpressible and — 1Pe 1:8
heavenly joy (B)
transported with a joy too — 1Pe 1:8
great for words (N)
a joy that words cannot — 1Pe 1:8
express, a hint of the glories
of heaven (P)
rejoice with unutterable and — 1Pe 1:8
exalted joy (R)

UNSPIRITUAL

u. nature, a slave to (N) — Ro 7:25
inflated by *u*. imaginations — Col 2:18
(P)
is earthly, *u*. (A)(R) — Jas 3:15
u., having not (N) — Jude 19

UNSPOILED

a fresh *u*. girl (P) — 2Co 11:2

UNSPOTTED

to keep himself *u*. from the — Jas 1:27
world
free fom the smut of the — Jas 1:27
world (B)
keep oneself untarnished by — Jas 1:27
the world (N)
keeping oneself — Jas 1:27
uncontaminated by the world (P)
oneself unstained from the — Jas 1:27
world (R)

UNSTABLE

U. as water, thou shalt not — Ge 49:4
excel
her ways are *u*. (S) — Pr 5:6
a double minded man is *u*. in — Jas 1:8
all
is unsteady in all his ways (B) — Jas 1:8
never can keep a steady course — Jas 1:8
(N)
will reveal instability at every — Jas 1:8
turn (P)
cease from sin; beguiling *u*. — 2Pe 2:14
souls
unsteady souls (B)(R) — 2Pe 2:14
unsteadfast souls (E) — 2Pe 2:14
that are unlearned and *u*. — 2Pe 3:16
wrest
untaught and unsteady twist — 2Pe 3:16
(B)
ignorant and unsteadfast — 2Pe 3:16
wrest (E)
ignorant and unstable — 2Pe 3:16
misinterpret (N)
ill-informed and unbalanced — 2Pe 3:16
distort (R)

UNSTAINED

u. and free from reproach — 1Ti 6:14
(R)
u. from the world (R) — Jas 1:27
unblemished and *u*. (P) — 1Pe 1:19

UNSTEADFAST

ignorant and *u*. wrest (E) — 2Pe 3:16

UNSTEADY

is *u*. in all his ways (B) — Jas 1:8
u. souls (B)(R) — 2Pe 2:14
the untaught and *u*. (B) — 2Pe 3:16

UNSTOPPED

and the ears of the deaf shall — Isa 35:5
be *u*.

UNSULLIED

may be *u*. and blameless (B) — Ph'p 1:10
u., flawless, irreproachable — 1Ti 6:14
(A)
u. and unfading (A)(B)(P) — 1Pe 1:4

UNSUSPECTING

the *u*. and simple-minded — Ro 16:18
(A)(B)

UNSWERVING

firm and *u*. (N) — Heb 10:23

UNTAINTED

be *u*., unerring (A) — Ph'p 1:10

UNTAKEN

remaineth the same veil *u*. — 2Co 3:14

UNTARNISHED

keep *u*. by world (N) — Jas 1:27

UNTAUGHT

u. and unsteady twist (B) — 2Pe 3:16

UNTEMPERED

others daubed it with *u*. — Eze 13:10
morter
daub it over with white — Eze 13:10;
wash (A)(B)(N) — 13:11, 14-15; 22:28
them which daub it with *u*. — Eze 13:11
morter
that ye have daubed with *u*. — Eze 13:14
morter
that have daubed it with *u*. — Eze 13:15
morter
have daubed them with *u*. — Eze 22:28
morter

UNTHANKFUL

is kind unto the *u*. and to the — Lu 6:35
evil
disobedient to parents, *u*. — 2Ti 3:2
unholy

UNTHINKING

an *u*. person (B) — Ps 92:6

UNTHINKINGLY

person *u*. utters an oath — Le 6:4
(B)(R)

UNTIE

sandal straps not fit to *u*. (B) — M'k 1:7

UNTIL

continually *u*. the tenth month — Ge 8:5
u. the waters were dried up — Ge 8:7
u. they have done drinking — Ge 24:19
u. I have told mine errand — Ge 24:33
and grew *u*. he became very — Ge 26:13
great
u. the fury brother's turn — Ge 27:44
U. thy brother's anger turn — Ge 27:45
u. I have done that which I — Ge 28:15
u. all the flocks be gathered — Ge 29:8
Laban, and stayed there *u*. — Ge 32:4
now
with him *u*. the breaking of — Ge 32:24
the day
u. he came near to his brother — Ge 33:3
u. I come unto my lord unto — Ge 33:14
Seir
held his peace *u*. they were — Ge 34:5
come
by her, *u*. his lord came — Ge 39:16
home
very much, *u*. he left — Ge 41:49
numbering

cattle from our youth even *u.* now   Ge 46:34

his feet, *u.* Shiloh come   Ge 49:10

foundation thereof even *u.* now   Ex 9:18

serve the Lord, *u.* we come thither   Ex 10:26

keep it up *u.* the fourteenth day of   Ex 12:6

nothing of it remain   Ex 12:10;
u. morning   12:15, 18, 22; 16:20, 23;
23:18; Le 7:15; 19:13; Nu 9:15; De 16:4;
J'g 19:25

the first day *u.* the seventh day   Ex 12:15

u. the one and twentieth day of the   Ex 12:18

u. they came to a land inhabited   Ex 16:35

u. they came unto the borders of   Ex 16:35

u. the going down of the sun   Ex 17:12

u. thou be increased, and inherit   Ex 23:30

for us, *u.* we come again unto you   Ex 24:14

u. he was gone into the tabernacle   Ex 33:8

he took the veil off, *u.* he came out   Ex 34:34

u. he went in to speak with him   Ex 34:35

u. the days of your consecration be   Le 8:33

shall be unclean *u.* the even   Le 11:24;
11:25, 27-28, 31-32, 39-40; 12:4; 14:46;
15:5-7, 10; 16-19, 21-23, 27; 17:15; 22:6;
Nu 19:7, 8, 10; 21:22

u. he come out, and have made an   Le 16:17

if ought remain *u.* the third day. it   Le 19:6

of the holy things, *u.* he be clean   Le 22:4

leave none of it *u.* the morrow   Le 22:30

u. the selfsame day that ye have   Le 23:14

eat of old fruit *u.* the ninth year   Le 25:22

u. her fruits come in ye shall   Le 25:22

bought it *u.* the year of jubile   Le 25:28

and upward even *u.* fifty years old   Nu 4:3

and upward *u.* fifty years old shalt   Nu 4:23

u. the days be fulfilled, in the   Nu 6:5

u. it come out at your nostrils, and   Nu 11:20

people, from Egypt even *u.* now   Nu 14:19

u. your carcases be wasted in   Nu 14:33

u. we have passed thy borders   Nu 20:17

way, *u.* we be past thy borders   Nu 21:22

u. there was none left him alive   Nu 21:35

not lie down *u.* he eat of the prey   Nu 23:24

u. Asshur shall carry thee away   Nu 24:22

u. all the generation, that had   Nu 32:13

u. we have brought them unto   Nu 32:17

u. the children of Israel have   Nu 32:18

u. he hath driven out his enemies   Nu 32:21

u. he stand before the congregation   Nu 35:12

u. the death of the high priest   Nu 35:28

land, *u.* the death of the priests   Nu 35:32

went, *u.* ye came into this place   De 1:31

u. we were come over the brook   De 2:14

u. all the generation of the men of   De 2:14

the host, *u.* they were consumed   De 2:15

u. I shall pass over Jordan into the   De 2:29

we smote him *u.* none was left   De 3:3

U. the Lord have given rest unto   De 3:20

you, and *u.* they also possess the land   De 3:20

u. they that are left, and hide   De 7:20

destruction, *u.* they be destroyed   De 7:23

thee, *u.* thou have destroyed them   De 7:24

u. ye came unto this place, ye have   De 9:7

even *u.* it was as small as dust   De 9:21

u. ye came into this place   De 11:5

war with thee, *u.* it be subdued   De 20:20

thee *u.* thy brother seek after it   De 22:2

for to do, *u.* thou be destroyed   De 28:20

and *u.* thou perish quickly   De 28:20

u. he have consumed thee from off   De 28:21

shall pursue thee *u.* thou perish   De 28:22

upon thee, *u.* thou be destroyed   De 28:24

neck, *u.* he have destroyed thee   De 28:48

of thy land, *u.* thou be destroyed   De 28:51

sheep *u.* he have destroyed thee   De 28:51

u. thy high and fenced walls come   De 28:52

upon thee, *u.* thou be destroyed   De 28:61

in a book, *u.* they were finished   De 31:24

of this song, *u.* they were ended   De 31:30

U. the Lord have given your days, *u.* the pursuers be returned   Jos 1:15

u. the pursuers were returned   Jos 2:16

u. all the people were passed   Jos 3:17

u. every thing was finished   Jos 4:10

u. ye were passed over, as the Lord   Jos 4:23

before us, *u.* we were gone over   Jos 4:23

of Israel, *u.* we were passed over   Jos 5:1

mouth, *u.* the day I bid you shout   Jos 6:10

the ark of the Lord *u.* the eventide   Jos 7:6

u. ye take away the accursed thing   Jos 7:13

the sword, *u.* they were consumed   Jos 8:24

u. he had utterly destroyed all   Jos 8:26

he hanged on a tree *u.* eventide   Jos 8:29

u. the people had avenged   Jos 10:13

upon the trees *u.* the evening   Jos 10:26

which remain *u.* this very day   Jos 10:27

u. he had left him none remaining   Jos 10:33

u. they left them none remaining   Jos 11:8

u. they had destroyed them   Jos 11:14

among the Israelites *u.* this day   Jos 13:13

u. he stand, before the congregation   Jos 20:6

u. the death of the high priest   Jos 20:6

u. he stood before the congregation   Jos 20:9

we are not cleansed *u.* this   Jos 22:17

u. ye perish from off this good land   Jos 23:13

u. he have destroyed you from off   Jos 23:15

u. they had destroyed Jabin king   J'g 4:24

in Israel, *u.* that I Deborah arose   J'g 5:7

u. I come unto thee, and bring   J'g 6:18

u. we shall have made ready a kid   J'g 13:15

u. the day of the captivity of   J'g 18:30

they tarried *u.* afternoon, and   J'g 19:8

and wept before the Lord *u.* even   J'g 20:23

fasted that day *u.* even, and offered   J'g 20:26

went *u.* they came to Beth-lehem   Ru 1:19

even from the morning *u.* now   Ru 2:7

she gleaned in the field *u.* even   Ru 2:17

u. they have ended all my   Ru 2:21

u. he shall have done eating   Ru 3:3

liveth: lie down *u.* the morning   Ru 3:13

she lay at his feet *u.* the morning   Ru 3:14

u. thou know how the matter   Ru 3:18

u. he have finished the thing   Ru 3:18

not go up *u.* the child be weaned   1Sa 1:22

tarry *u.* thou have weaned him   1Sa 1:23

her son suck *u.* she weaned him   1Sa 1:23

And Samuel lay *u.* the morning   1Sa 3:15

u. they came under Beth-car   1Sa 7:11

the people will not eat *u.* he come   1Sa 9:13

Ammonites *u.* the heat of the day   1Sa 11:11

Tarry *u.* we come to you; then we   1Sa 14:9

that eateth any food *u.* evening   1Sa 14:24

spoil them *u.* the morning light   1Sa 14:36

Havilah *u.* thou comest to Shur   1Sa 15:7

against them *u.* they be consumed   1Sa 15:18

to see Saul *u.* the day of his death   1Sa 15:35

u. thou come to the valley   1Sa 17:52

heed to thyself *u.* the morning   1Sa 19:2

u. he came to Naioth in Ramah   1Sa 19:23

with another, *u.* David exceeded   1Sa 20:41

less or more, *u.* the morning light   1Sa 25:36

u. they had no more power to   1Sa 30:4

and fasted *u.* even, for Saul   2Sa 1:12

were sojourners there *u.* this day   2Sa 4:3

from Geba *u.* thou come to Gazer   2Sa 5:25

Jericho *u.* your beards be grown   2Sa 10:5;
1Ch 19:5

u. all the people had done passing   2Sa 15:24

u. there come word from you to   2Sa 15:28

u. there be not one small stone   2Sa 17:13

befell thee from thy youth *u.* now   2Sa 19:7

king departed *u.* the day he came   2Sa 19:24

u. water dropped upon them out of   2Sa 21:10

not again *u.* I had consumed them   2Sa 22:38

u. his hand was weary   2Sa 23:10

u. he had made an end of building   1Ki 3:1

name of the Lord, *u.* those days   1Ki 3:2

u. the Lord put them under   1Ki 5:3

u. he had finished all the house   1Ki 6:22

u. I came, and mine eyes had seen   1Ki 10:7

u. he had cut off every male   1Ki 11:16

in Egypt *u.* the death of Solomon   1Ki 11:40

breathed, *u.* he had destroyed him   1Ki 15:29

u. the day that the Lord sendeth   1Ki 17:14

Baal from morning even *u.* noon   1Ki 18:26

u. the time of the offering of   1Ki 18:29

u. thou have consumed them   1Ki 22:11

of affliction, *u.* I come in peace   1Ki 22:27

u. an ass's head was sold for   2Ki 6:25

another, Why sit we here *u.* we die   2Ki 7:3

that she left the land, even *u.* now   2Ki 8:6

stedfastly, *u.* he was ashamed   2Ki 8:11

of the gate *u.* the morning   2Ki 10:8

u. he left him none remaining   2Ki 10:11

u. he had cast them out of his   2Ki 17:20

U. the Lord removed Israel out of	2Ki 17:23	U. I come and take you away to a	Isa 36:17	hast kept the good wine u. now	Joh 2:10
U. I come and take you away to a	2Ki 18:32	have laid up in store u. this day	Isa 39:6	u. they called the parents of him	Joh 9:18
u. he had cast them out from his	2Ki 24:20	u. the righteousness go forth as	Isa 62:1	U. the day in which he was taken	Ac 1:2
in their steads u. the captivity	1Ch 5:22	not return, u. he have executed	Jer 23:20	U. I make thy foes thy footstool	Ac 2:35
u. Solomon had built the house of	1Ch 6:32	u. the very time of his land come	Jer 27:7	u. the times of restitution of all	Ac 3:21
u. it was a great host, like the host	1Ch 12:22	u. I have consumed them by his	Jer 27:8	ago I was fasting u. this hour	Ac 10:30
u. thou hast finished all the work	1Ch 28:20	they be u. the day that I visit them	Jer 27:22	continued his speech u. midnight	Ac 20:7
make to pay tribute u. this day	2Ch 8:8	shall not return, u. he have done it	Jer 30:24	fifty years, u. Samuel the prophet	Ac 13:20
of the Lord, and u. it was finished	2Ch 8:16	u. he hath performed the intents of	Jer 30:24	continued his speech u. midnight	Ac 20:7
u. I came, and mine eyes had seen	2Ch 9:6	and there shall he be u. I visit him	Jer 32:5	u. an offering should be offered	Ac 21:26
u. his disease was exceeding great	2Ch 16:12	u. all the roll was consumed in the	Jer 36:23	conscience before God u. this day	Ac 23:1
push Syria u. they be consumed	2Ch 18:10	u. all the bread in the city were	Jer 37:21	eat nothing u. we have slain Paul	Ac 23:14
of affliction, u. I return in peace	2Ch 18:26	u. the day that Jerusalem was	Jer 38:28	For u. the law sin was in the world	Ro 5:13
against the Syrians u. the even	2Ch 18:34	famine, u. there be an end of them	Jer 44:27	travaileth in pain together u. now	Ro 8:22
u. thy bowels fall out by reason of	2Ch 21:15	a portion u. the day of his death	Jer 52:34	u. the fulness of the Gentiles	Ro 11:25
the chest, u. they had made an end	2Ch 24:10	more, u. he come whose right it is	Eze 21:27	u. the Lord come, who both will	1Co 4:5
u. the burnt offering was finished	2Ch 29:28	u. he came to me in the morning	Eze 33:22	will tarry at Ephesus u. Pentecost	1Co 16:8
u. the other priests had sanctified	2Ch 29:34	shall not be shut u. the evening	Eze 46:2	u. this day remaineth the same veil	2Co 3:14
u. they had utterly destroyed them	2Ch 31:1	u. thou know that the most High	Da 4:32	u. the time appointed of the father	Ga 4:2
burnt offerings and the fat u. night	2Ch 35:14	U. the Ancient of days came	Da 7:22	again u. Christ be formed in you	Ga 4:19
u. the wrath of the Lord arose	2Ch 36:16	u. a time, times and the dividing	Da 7:25	u. redemption of the purchased	Eph 1:14
u. the reign of the kingdom of	2Ch 36:20	desolate, u. the consummation	Da 9:27	gospel from the first day u. now	Ph'p 1:5
u. the land had enjoyed her	2Ch 36:21	the dough, u. it be leavened	Ho 7:4	it u. the day of Jesus Christ	Ph'p 1:6
even u. the reign of Darius king of	Ezr 4:5	u. the time, she which travaileth	Mic 5:3	let u. he be taken out of the way	2Th 2:7
u. another commandment shall be	Ezr 4:21	u. he plead my cause, and execute	Mic 7:9	u. the appearing of our Lord	1Ti 6:14
u. now hath it been in building	Ezr 5:16	u. the day that I rise up to the prey	Zep 3:8	u. I make thine enemies thy	Heb 1:13
u. ye weigh them before the chief	Ezr 8:29	u. the carrying away into Babylon	M't 1:17	them u. the time of reformation	Heb 9:10
astonied u. the evening sacrifice	Ezr 9:4	be thou there u. I bring thee word	M't 2:13	u. time of rectification (B)	Heb 9:10
u. the fierce wrath of our God for	Ezr 10:14	was there u. the death of Herod	M't 2:15	u. Christ should establish truth (P)	Heb 9:10
be opened u. the sun be hot	Ne 7:3	days of John the Baptist u. now	M't 11:12	u. he receive the early and latter	Jas 5:7
gate from the morning u. midday	Ne 8:3	and the law prophesied u. John	M't 11:13	u. the day dawn, and the day star	2Pe 1:19
u. the days of Johanan the son of	Ne 12:23	would have remained u. this day	M't 11:23	brother, is in darkness even u. now	1Jo 2:9
me secret, u. thy wrath be past	Job 14:13	both grow together u. the harvest	M't 13:30	u. their fellowservants also	Re 6:11
u. the day and night come to an	Job 26:10	u. the Son of man be risen again	M't 17:9	u. the words of God be fulfilled	Re 17:17
u. his iniquity be found to be hateful	Ps 36:2	say not unto thee, U. seven times	M't 18:22	u. thousand years were finished	Re 20:5
u. these calamities be overpast	Ps 57:1	times: but U. seventy times seven	M't 18:22		
u. I have shewed thy strength unto	Ps 71:18	u. the day that Noe entered into	M't 24:38; Lu 17:27	**UNTIMELY**	
U. I went into the sanctuary of God	Ps 73:17	And knew not u. the flood came	M't 24:39	a hidden u. birth I had not been	Job 3:16
u. the pit be digged for the wicked	Ps 94:13	u. that day when I drink it new	M't 26:29; M'k 14:25	was I not a miscarriage put hidden, and put away (A)	Job 3:26
and to his labour u. the evening	Ps 104:23	be made sure u. the third	M't 27:64	was I not a miscarriage put away (B)	Job 3:26
U. the time that his word came	Ps 105:19	among the Jews u. this day	M't 28:15	like the u. birth of a woman	Ps 58:8
u. I make thine enemies thy	Ps 110:1	the whole land u. the ninth hour	M'k 15:33	that an u. birth is better than	Ec 6:8
u. he see his desire upon his	Ps 112:8	u. the day that these things shall be	Lu 1:20	as a fig tree casteth her u. figs	Re 6:13
u. that he have mercy upon us	Ps 123:2	u. the time when ye shall say	Lu 13:35	shedding its unripe fruit (A)(B)(E)(P)	Re 6:13
U. I fine out a place for the Lord	Ps 132:5	after that which is lost, u. he find	Lu 15:4	sheds its winter fruit (R)	Re 6:13
take our fill of love u. the morning	Pr 7:18	and the prophets were u. John	Lu 16:16	**UNTOWARD**	
U. the day break, and the shadows	Ca 2:17; 4:6	u. the times of the Gentiles be	Lu 21:24	from this u. generation	Ac 2:40
u. I had brought him into my	Ca 3:11	u. it be fulfilled in the kingdom of	Lu 22:16	crooked, perverse, wicked, unjust generation (A)	Ac 2:40
nor awake my love, u. he please	Ca 8:4	u. the kingdom of God shall come	Lu 22:18	crooked generation (B)(E)(N)(R)	Ac 2:40
that continue u. night, till wine	Isa 5:11	over all the earth u. the ninth hour	Lu 23:44	perverse generation (P)	Ac 2:40
U. the cities be wasted without	Isa 6:11	u. ye be endued with power from	Lu 24:49	**UNTRAINED**	
u. the indignation be overpast	Isa 26:20			u. in schools (A)(N)(P)	Ac 4:13
U. the spirit be poured upon us	Isa 32:15			**UNTRUE**	
				been u. and dealt treacherously (A)(E)(R)	Ps 73:15
				mind utter things u. (A)	Pr 23:33
				UNTRUTH	
				lips speak u. (A)(B)	Job 27:4

UNUTTERABLE

u. exalted joy (R)   1Pe 1:8

UNVEILED

with u. face beholding (S)   2Co 3:18

UNWALLED

beside u. towns a great many   De 3:5
villages, that dwelt in the u.   Es 9:19
towns
will go up to the land of u.   Eze 38:11
villages

UNWASHEN

to eat with u. hands defileth   M't 15:20
not a
defiled, that is, with u. hands   M'k 7:2
elders, but eat bread with u.   M'k 7:5
hands

UNWEIGHED

And Solomon left all the   1Ki 7:47
vessels u.

UNWHOLESOME

u. worthless talk (A)   Eph 4:29

UNWISE

O foolish people and u.   De 32:6
senseless people (A)(R)   De 32:6
wisdom-lacking people (B)   De 32:6
he is an u. son; for he   Ho 13:13
should
foolish (B)   Ho 13:13
both to the wise, and to the u.   Ro 1:14
foolish (A)(E)(R)   Ro 1:14; Eph 5:17
the unlearned (B)   Ro 1:14
the simple (N)   Ro 1:14
ignorant savage (P)   Ro 1:14
the u. and witless   Eph 5:15
(A)(E)(R)
Wherefore be ye not u. but   Eph 5:17
thoughtless (B)   Eph 5:17
fools (N)   Eph 5:17
vague (P)   Eph 5:17

UNWITTINGLY

unwittingly (E)   Ge 35:11;
                                      35:15; Jos 20:3, 9
sin u. (A)(E)(R)   Le 4:2; 4:22, 27
sin u. (R)   Le 4:13
if a man eat of the holy thing   Le 22:14
u.
unknowingly (A)   Le 22:14
ignorantly (B)   Le 22:14
any person unawares and u.   Jos 20:3
u. killed (R)   Jos 20:3
unintentionally (A)   Jos 20:3; 20:5
without premeditation (B)   Jos 20:3;
                                              20:5
he smote his neighbour u.   Jos 20:5

UNWORLDLY

u., upright, blameless (A)(B)   1Th 2:10

UNWORTHILY

and drink this cup of the   1Co 11:27
Lord, u.
without proper reverence   1Co 11:27
(P)
For he that eateth and   1Co 11:29
drinketh u.
drinks without   1Co 11:29
discriminating and recognizing
with appreciation (A)
without due appreciation of   1Co 11:29
the body (B)
eats and drinks carelessly   1Co 11:29
(P)
eats and drinks without   1Co 11:29
discerning (R)

UNWORTHY

u. servants (A)(R)   Lu 17:10
u. of everlasting life   Ac 13:46
u. to judge the smallest   1Co 6:2
matters
nothing for u. ends (A)   Ph'p 2:3

UNYIELDING

u. people (A)(B)   Ro 10:21

UP

Lot said, U. get ye out of   Ge 19:14
this place
Joseph said, U. follow after   Ge 44:4
the men
up, make us gods that shall go   Ex 32:1
before us
rose u. early and got u.,   Nu 14:40
we be here and will go u.
go not u. for the Lord is not   Nu 14:42
among you
they presumed to go u. unto   Nu 14:44
the hill top
u. sanctify the people, and   Jos 7:13
say, Sanctify
u. for this is the day in which   J'g 4:14
the Lord
returned from battle before   J'g 8:13
sun u.
he said to his firstborn, U.   J'g 8:20
and slay them
up, thou and the people that   J'g 9:32
is with thee
as soon as sun is u. thou shalt   J'g 9:33
rise early
u. and let us be going, but   J'g 19:28
none answered
saying, U. that I may send   1Sa 9:26
thee away
as soon as ye be u. early,   1Sa 29:10
depart
when David was u. the word   2Sa 24:11
came
I am ready to die from my   Ps 88:15
youth u.
from the ground u. to the   Eze 41:16
windows
when sun was u. they   M't 13:6;
scorched, because they   M'k 4:6
these things I kept from my   M't 19:20
youth u.
all these I kept from my   Lu 18:21
youth u.
and they filled them u. to the   Joh 2:7
brim

UPBRAID

with whom ye did u. me,   J'g 8:15
saying
scoffed at me (A)   J'g 8:15
taunted me (B)(E)(R)   J'g 8:15
Then began he to u. the   M't 11:20
cities
began to reproach (B)   M't 11:20
began reproaching (P)   M't 11:20

UPBRAIDED

Jacob u. Laban (R)   Ge 31:36
u. him violently (R)   J'g 8:1
and u. them with their   M'k 16:14
unbelief
reproved and reproached   M'k 16:14
them (A)
chided their unbelief (B)   M'k 16:14
reproached them for   M'k 16:14
incredulity and dullness (N)
reproached them for their   M'k 16:14
lack of faith and reluctance to
believe (P)

UPBRAIDETH

to all men liberally, and u. not   Jas 1:5
without reproaching or   Jas 1:5
faultfinding (A)
without faultfinding (B)   Jas 1:5
neither refuses nor reproaches   Jas 1:5
anyone (N)
without making them foolish or   Jas 1:5
guilty (P)
without reproaching (R)   Jas 1:5

UPBUILDING

for their u. (A)   1Co 14:3; 2Co 10:8
for u. (R)   1Co 14:3
for u. of the church (B)(R)   1Co 14:12
for your u. (B)(R)   2Co 12:19
body for its u. in love (B)   Eph 4:12

UPHARSIN

written, Mene, Mene, Tekel,   Da 5:25
U.

UPHAZ

Tarshish, and gold   Jer 10:9
from U. the
were girded with fine gold of   Da 10:5
U.

UPHELD

his throne is u. (S)   Pr 20:28
unto me; and my fury, u. me   Isa 63:5

UPHOLD

and u. me with thy free spirit   Ps 51:12
sustain my soul (B)   Ps 51:12
Lord is with them that u. my   Ps 54:4
soul
U. me according unto thy   Ps 119:116
word
but honour shall u. the   Pr 29:23
humble in
I will u. thee with the right   Isa 41:10
hand of
Behold my servant, whom I   Isa 42:1
u.
I wondered there was none   Isa 63:5
to u.
They also that u. Egypt shall   Eze 30:6
fall

UPHOLDEN

Thy words have u. him that   Job 4:4
was
and his throne is u. by mercy   Pr 20:28

UPHOLDEST

me, thou u. me in mine   Ps 41:12
integrity

UPHOLDETH

but the Lord u. the righteous   Ps 37:17
for the Lord u. him with his   Ps 37:24
hand
after thee: thy right hand u.   Ps 63:8
me
Lord u. all that fall, and   Ps 145:14
raiseth

UPHOLDING

u. all things by the word of   Heb 1:3
his

UPPER

on the u. door post of the   Ex 12:7
houses
shall put a covering upon his   Le 13:45
u. lip
the nether or the u. millstone   De 24:6
And he gave her the u.   Jos 15:19
springs
unto Beth-horon the u.   Jos 16:5
Caleb gave her the u. springs   J'g 1:15
a lattice in his u. chamber that   2Ki 1:2
stood by the conduit of the   2Ki 18:17;
u. pool   Isa 36:2
the top of the u. chamber of   2Ki 23:12
Ahaz
Beth-horon the nether, and   1Ch 7:24
and of the u. chambers   1Ch 28:11
thereof
he overlaid the u. chambers   2Ch 3:9
with
also he built Beth-horon the   2Ch 8:5
u.
also stopped the u.   2Ch 32:30
watercourse of
the king's u. house (S)   Ne 3:25
end of the conduit of the u.   Isa 7:3
pool
Now the u. chambers were   Eze 42:5
shorter
shall lodge in the u. lintels of   Zep 2:14
it
shew you a large u. room   M'k 14:15;
furnished   Lu 22:12
they went up into an u. room   Ac 1:13
they laid her in an u. chamber   Ac 9:37
brought him into the u.   Ac 9:39
chamber
having passed through the u.   Ac 19:1
coasts
many lights in the u. chamber   Ac 20:8

UPPERMOST

u. basket there was of all manner	Ge 40:17
berries in the top of the *u.* bough	Isa 17:6
a forsaken bough, and an *u.* branch	Isa 17:9
love the *u.* rooms at feasts	M't 23:6
and the *u.* rooms at feasts	M'k 12:39
love the *u.* seats in synagogues	Lu 11:43

UPRIGHT

Noah was an *u.* man (B)	Ge 6:9
have I seen *u.* before me (B)	Ge 7:1
live and be *u.* (B)	Ge 17:1
lo, my sheaf arose, and also stood *u.*	Ge 37:7
the floods stood *u.* as an heap	Ex 15:8
of your yoke, and made you go *u.*	Le 26:13
erect (A)(B)(R)	Le 26:13
are *u.* and just (A)	De 4:8
more *u.* than I (A)	1Sa 24:17; Job 4:7
thou hast been *u.* and thy going	1Sa 29:6
you have been honest (R)	1Sa 29:6
was also *u.* before him, and	2Sa 22:24
blameless (A)	2Sa 22:24; Ps 19:13
perfect (E)	2Sa 22:24; 22:26; Ps 18:23, 25
blameless (R)	2Sa 22:24; 22:26; Job 12:4; Ps 18:23, 25; 19:13; Pr 11:20; 29:10, 27
merciful, and with the *u.* man	2Sa 22:26
thou wilt shew thyself *u.*	2Sa 22:26
the Levites were more *u.* in heart	2Ch 29:34
and that man was perfect and *u.*	Job 1:1
a perfect and an *u.* man, one that	Job 1:8; 2:3
If thou wert pure and *u.*	Job 8:6
never cast away an *u.* man (B)	Job 8:20
though I were *u.* (B)	Job 9:20; 9:21
just *u.* man is laughed to scorn	Job 12:4
U. men shall be astonied at this	Job 17:8
the *u.* person might (B)(R)	Job 23:7
God, which saveth the *u.* in heart	Ps 7:10
may privily shoot at the *u.* in heart	Ps 11:2
his countenance doth behold the *u.*	Ps 11:7
I was also *u.* before him, and	Ps 18:23
faultless (B)	Ps 18:23
thyself merciful; with an *u.* man	Ps 18:25
thou wilt shew thyself *u.*	Ps 18:25
perfect (B)	Ps 18:25
then shall I be *u.* and I shall	Ps 19:13
fallen: but we are risen, and stand *u.*	Ps 20:8
erect (B)	Ps 20:8
Good and *u.* is the Lord: therefore	Ps 25:8
for joy, all ye that are *u.* in heart	Ps 32:11
for praise is comely for the *u.*	Ps 33:1
thy righteousness to the *u.* in heart	Ps 36:10
slay such as be of *u.* conversation	Ps 37:14
Lord knoweth the days of the *u.*	Ps 37:18
perfect man, and behold the *u.*	Ps 37:37
watch the *u.* (B)	Ps 37:37
u. shall have dominion over them	Ps 49:14
and all the *u.* in heart shall glory	Ps 64:10
To shew that the Lord is *u.:* he is	Ps 92:15
all the *u.* in heart shall follow it	Ps 94:15
and gladness for the *u.* in heart	Ps 97:11
heart, in the assembly for the *u.*	Ps 111:1
generation of the *u.* shall be blessed	Ps 112:2
Unto the *u.* there ariseth light	Ps 112:4

O Lord, and *u.* are thy judgments	Ps 119:137
judgments fair (B)	Ps 119:137
to them that are *u.* in their hearts	Ps 125:4
the *u.* shall dwell in thy presence	Ps 140:13
sound wisdom for the *u.* (B)(R)	Pr 2:7; 3:32
For the *u.* shall dwell in the land	Pr 2:21
the *u.* shall inhabit (B)(R)	Pr 2:21
friendship with the *u.* (B)(E)(R)	Pr 3:32
of the Lord is strength to the *u.*	Pr 10:29
The integrity of the *u.* shall guide	Pr 11:3
righteousness of the *u.* shall deliver	Pr 11:6
By the blessing of the *u.* the city is	Pr 11:11
are *u.* in their way are his delight	Pr 11:20
mouth of the *u.* shall deliver them	Pr 12:6
keepeth him that is *u.* in the way	Pr 13:6
blameless (B)	Pr 13:6; 28:10
tabernacle of the *u.* shall flourish	Pr 14:11
the prayer of the *u.* is his delight	Pr 15:8
The highway of the *u.* is to depart	Pr 16:17
and the transgressor for the *u.*	Pr 21:18
as for the *u.* he directeth his way	Pr 21:29
the *u.* shall have good things	Pr 28:10
The bloodthirsty hate the *u.*	Pr 29:10
is *u.* in the way is abomination to	Pr 29:27
found, that God has made man *u.*	Ec 7:29
that which was written was *u.*	Ec 12:10
write rightly words of truth (A)	Ec 12:10
more than wine: the *u.* love thee	Ca 1:4
thou, most *u.* dost weigh the path	Isa 26:7
the righteous (R)	Isa 26:7
They are *u.* as the palm tree	Jer 10:5
but he touched me, and set me *u.*	Da 8:18
I speak unto thee, and stand *u.*	Da 10:11
kingdom, and *u.* ones with him	Da 11:17
and there is none *u.* among men	Mic 7:2
no one honest among men (B)	Mic 7:2
u. is sharper than a thorn hedge	Da 7:4
which is lifted up is not *u.* in him	Hab 2:4
to the wisdom of the *u.* (A)	Lu 1:17
an *u.* and devout man (B)(N)(P)	Lu 2:25
declare yourselves just and *u.* (A)	Lu 6:15
pretended to be *u.* (A)(B)(P)(R)	Lu 20:20
a good and *u.* man (B)(N)	Lu 23:50
a loud voice, Stand *u.* on thy feet	Ac 14:10
unworldly, *u.,* blameless (A)(B)	1Th 2:10
must be *u.* (A)(P)(R)	Tit 1:8
murdered the *u.* (B)	Jas 5:6
rescued *u.* Lot (B)	2Pe 2:7

UPRIGHTLY

He that walketh *u.* and worketh	Ps 15:2
walketh in integrity (B)	Ps 15:2
walks blamelessly (R)	Ps 15:2
who walk *u.* (R)	Ps 37:14
do ye judge *u.* O ye sons of men	Ps 58:1
speak righteousness (B)(E)	Ps 58:1
the congregation I will judge *u.*	Ps 75:2
render fair judgments (B)	Ps 75:2
judge with equity (R)	Ps 75:2

withhold from them that walk	Ps 84:11
is a buckler to them that walk *u.*	Pr 2:7
walking in integrity (B)	Pr 2:7
He that walketh *u.* walketh surely	Pr 10:9
walks in integrity (B)(R)	Pr 10:9
man of understanding walketh *u.*	Pr 15:21
Who so walketh *u.* shall be saved	Pr 28:18
Whoever walks wholeheartedly (B)	Pr 28:18
who walks in integrity (R)	Pr 28:18
righteously, and speaketh *u.*	Isa 33:15
they abhor him that speaketh *u.*	Am 5:10
speaks with integrity (B)	Am 5:10
who speaks the truth (B)(R)	Am 5:10
do good to him that walketh *u.*	Mic 2:7
who walks honestly (B)	Mic 2:7
they walked not *u.* according to	Ga 2:14

UPRIGHTNESS

or for the *u.* of thine heart, dost	De 9:5
and in *u.* of heart with thee	1Ki 3:6
in integrity of heart, and in *u.*	1Ki 9:4
the heart, and hast pleasure in *u.*	1Ch 29:17
u. of mine heart I have willingly	1Ch 29:17
thy hope, and the *u.* of thy ways	Job 4:6
shall be of the *u.* of my heart	Job 33:3
thousand, to shew unto man his *u.*	Job 33:23
judgment to the people in *u.*	Ps 9:8
Let integrity and *u.* preserve me	Ps 25:21
ever, and are done in truth and *u.*	Ps 111:8
I will praise thee with *u.* of heart	Ps 119:7
good; lead me into the land of *u.*	Ps 143:10
Who leave the paths of *u.* to walk	Pr 2:13
He that walketh in his *u.* feareth	Pr 14:2
for their *u.* (A)(B)	Pr 17:26
is the poor that walketh in his *u.*	Pr 28:6
The way of the just is *u.*	Isa 26:7
land of *u.* will he deal unjustly	Isa 26:10
beds, each one walking in his *u.*	Isa 57:2
peace and *u.* (A)(B)	Mal 2:6

UPRISING

my downsitting and mine *u.*	Ps 139:2

UPROAR

what is the *u.* (A)(R)	1Sa 4:14
noise of the city being in an *u.*	1Ki 1:41
die amid the *u.* (A)(R)	Am 2:2
u. of a multitude (A)(B)	Isa 13:4
there be an *u.* among the people	M't 26:5
lest there be an *u.* of the people	M'k 14:2
and set all the city on an *u.*	Ac 17:5
city in an *u.* (P)	Ac 19:29
called in question for this day's *u.*	Ac 19:40
this *u.* (N)	Ac 19:40
And after the *u.* was ceased, Paul	Ac 20:1
that all Jerusalem was in an *u.*	Ac 21:31
before these days madest an *u.*	Ac 21:38
without crowd or *u.* (A)	Ac 24:18

UPROOT

u. from the kingdom (P)	M't 13:41

UPROOTED

not be *u.* (R)	Jer 31:40
horns were *u.* (B)	Da 7:8

kingdom be *u.* (A)(B)   *Da 11:4*
be *u.* (B)(E)(N)(R)   *Lu 17:6*
twice dead and *u.* (B)(R)   *Jude 12*

UPSET

does it *u.,* displease you (A)   *Joh 6:61*
u. whole houses (B)(P)   *Tit 1:11*

UPSETTING

u. their minds (A)   *Ac 15:24*
u. faith with travesty of gospel *Ga 1:7* (P)
who are *u.* you (B)(E)(R)   *Ga 5:12*
u. whole families (R)   *Tit 1:11*

UPSETS

seriously *u.* brother (P)   *Ro 14:15*
u. and undermines faith   *2Ti 2:14*
(A)(B)(P)

UPSIDE

wiping it, and turning it *u.*   *2Ki 21:13*
way of the wicked he turneth *Ps 146:9*
u. down
mine utter *u.* down things (B)   *Pr 23:33*
waste, and turneth it *u.* down *Isa 24:1*
your turning of things *u.*   *Isa 29:16*
down shall
that have turned the world *u.*   *Ac 17:6*
down

UPWARD

Fifteen cubits *u.* did the   *Ge 7:20*
waters
from twenty years old and   *Ex 38:26*
u.
From twenty years old and *u.*   *Nu 1:3;*
all   *1:18, 20, 22, 24, 26, 28, 30, 32, 34,*
36, 38, 40, 42, 45; 8:24; 14:29; 26:2, 4,
32:11
every male from a month old *Nu 3:15;*
and *u.*   *3:22, 28, 34, 39-40, 43; 26:62*
from thirty years old and *u.*   *Nu 4:3;*
    4:23, 30, 35, 39, 43, 47
to Akrabbim, from the rock,   *J'g 1:36*
and *u.*
from his shoulders and *u.* he   *1Sa 9:2*
was
people from his shoulders   *1Sa 10:23*
and *u.*
were able to put on armour,   *2Ki 3:21*
and *u.*
root downward, and bear   *2Ki 19:30*
fruit *u.*
the age of thirty years and   *1Ch 23:3*
u.
the age of twenty years and *1Ch 23:24*
u.
males, from three years old *2Ch 31:16*
and *u.*
from twenty years old and *2Ch 31:17;*
u.   *Ezr 3:8*
unto trouble, as the sparks fly *Job 5:7*
u.
the spirit of man that goeth *u. Ec 3:21*
king and their God, and look *Isa 8:21*
u.
root downward, and bear   *Isa 37:31*
fruit *u.*
mine eyes fail with looking   *Isa 38:14*
u.
their wings were stretched *u.*   *Eze 1:11*
the appearance of his loins   *Eze 1:27*
even *u.*
from his loins even *u.* as the   *Eze 8:2*
a winding about still *u.* to the *Eze 41:7*
side
went still *u.* round about the *Eze 41:7*
breadth of the house was still *Eze 41:7*
u.
altar and *u.* shall be four   *Eze 43:15*
horns
you, consider from this day   *Hag 2:15*
and *u.*
Consider now from this day   *Hag 2:18*
and *u.*

UR

his nativity, in *U.* of the   *Ge 11:28*
Chaldees
with them from *U.* of the   *Ge 11:31*
Chaldees
thee out of *U.* of the Chaldees *Ge 15:7*

---

the Hararite, Eliphal the   *1Ch 11:35*
son of *U.*
him forth out of *U.* of the   *Ne 9:7*
Chaldees

URBANE

Salute *U.* our helper in Christ *Ro 16:9*

URGE

do not *u.* me to desert you   *Ru 1:16*
(A)(B)
the Pharisees began to *u.* him *Lu 11:53*
u. and constrain them (A)   *Lu 14:23*
u. to stand firm (P)   *Ac 14:22*

URGED

and he *u.* him, and he took   *Ge 33:11*
it
daily with her words, and *u.*   *J'g 16:16*
him
depart, his father in law *u.*   *J'g 19:7*
him
he *u.* him (A)   *1Sa 28:25*
they *u.* him till he was   *2Ki 2:17*
ashamed
u. him to eat (R)   *2Ki 4:8*
And he *u.* him to take it; but *2Ki 5:16*
he *u.* him, and bound two   *2Ki 5:23*
talents
u. the king (R)   *Jer 36:25*
u. disciples to embark (B)   *M't 14:22*
u. and insisted (A)(B)   *Lu 24:29*
I *u.* him strongly (N)(R)   *1Co 16:12*
we *u.* Titus (A)(R)   *2Co 8:6; 12:18*

URGENT

the Egyptians were *u.* upon   *Ex 12:33*
the king's commandment was *Da 3:22*
u.
they were *u.* with loud voices *Lu 23:23*
(S)

URGENTLY

I *u.* encouraged him (A)   *1Co 16:12*

URGES

his mouth *u.* him on   *Pr 16:26*
(A)(B)(E)(R)
controls, *u.,* impells us   *2Co 5:14*
(A)(B)(R)
refrain from sensual *u.* (B)   *1Pe 2:11*

URI

by name Bezaleel the son of   *Ex 31:2;*
U.   *35:30*
And Bezaleel the son of *U.*   *Ex 38:22*
the son
Geber the son of *U.* was in the *1Ki 4:19*
And Hur begat *U.* and *U.*   *1Ch 2:20*
begat
that Bezaleel the son of *U.*   *2Ch 1:5*
the son
Shallum, and Telem, and *U. Ezr 10:24*

URIAH

Eliam, the wife of *U.* the   *2Sa 11:3*
Hittite
saying, Send me *U.* the   *2Sa 11:6*
Hittite
And Joab sent *U.* to David   *2Sa 11:6*
And when *U.* was come unto *2Sa 11:7*
him
And David said to *U.,* Go   *2Sa 11:8*
down to
And *U.* departed out of the   *2Sa 11:8*
king's
U. slept at the door of the   *2Sa 11:10*
king's
U. went not down unto his   *2Sa 11:10*
house
David said unto *U.,* Camest *2Sa 11:10*
thou
U. said unto David, The   *2Sa 11:11*
ark, and
David said to *U.,* Tarry here *2Sa 11:12*
to-day
So *U.* abode in Jerusalem   *2Sa 11:12*
that day
Joab, and sent it by the hand *2Sa 11:14*
of *U.*
Set ye *U.* in the forefront of *2Sa 11:15*
he assigned *U.* unto a place *2Sa 11:16*
where

David; and *U.* the Hittite   *2Sa 11:17*
died also
Thy servant *U.* the Hittite is *2Sa 11:21;*
dead   *11:24*
the wife of *U.* heard that *U. 2Sa 11:26*
killed *U.* the Hittite with the *2Sa 12:9*
sword
taken the wife of *U.* the   *2Sa 12:10*
Hittite to
U. the Hittite: thirty and   *2Sa 23:39*
seven in
in the matter of *U.* the Hittite *1Ki 15:5*
U. the Hittite, Zabad the   *1Ch 11:41*
son of
the hand of Meremoth the son *Ezr 8:33*
of *U.*
witnesses to record, *U.* the   *Isa 8:2*
priest

URIAH'S

Lord struck the child that   *2Sa 12:15*
U. wife

URIAS

her that had been the wife of *M't 1:6*
U.

URIEL

Tahath his son, *U.* his son,   *1Ch 6:24*
Uzziah
the sons of Kohath; *U.* the   *1Ch 15:5*
chief
and for the Levites, for *U.,*   *1Ch 15:11*
Asaiah
the daughter of *U.* of Gibeah *2Ch 13:2*

URIJAH

Ahaz sent to *U.* the priest   *2Ki 16:10*
And *U.* the priest built an   *2Ki 16:11*
altar
U. the priest made it against *2Ki 16:11*
king
Ahaz commanded *U.* the   *2Ki 16:15*
priest
Thus did *U.* the priest,   *2Ki 16:16*
according to
repaired Meremoth the son of *Ne 3:4;*
U.   *3:21*
and Anaiah, and *U.* and   *Ne 8:4*
Hilkiah
U. the son of Shemaiah of   *Jer 26:20*
when *U.* heard it, he was   *Jer 26:21*
afraid
they fetched forth *U.* out of *Jer 26:23*
Egypt

URIM

the breastplate of judgment   *Ex 28:30*
the *U.*
he put in the breastplate the *U. Le 8:8*
judgment of *U.* before the   *Nu 27:21*
Lord
thy Thummim and thy *U.* be *De 33:8*
with
God of Israel, give *U.* (R)   *1Sa 14:41*
neither by dreams, nor by *U. 1Sa 28:6*
nor
till there stood up a priest   *Ezr 2:63;*
with *U.*   *Ne 7:65*

US

with *u.* even *u.* who are all of *De 5:3*
u. alive
if thou be Christ, save thyself *Lu 23:39*
and *u.*
even *u.* whom he hath called *Ro 9:24*
God hath set forth *u.* the   *1Co 4:9*
apostles
and will also raise up *u.* by   *1Co 6:14*
his own power
you have acknowledged *u.* in *2Co 1:14*
part
he which establisheth *u.* with *2Co 1:21*
you, is God
who hath reconciled *u.* to   *2Co 5:18*
himself by Christ
as ye have *u.* for an   *Ph'p 3:17*
ensample
let *u.* who are of the day be   *1Th 5:8*
sober
for God hath not appointed *u. 1Th 5:9*
to wrath
of his own will begat he *u.* by *Jas 1:18*
the word

ABOUT US

lick up all that are round *about u.*	*Nu 22:4*
came from heathen that are *about u.*	*Ne 5:17*
the heathen *about u.* saw these things	*Ne 6:16*
thy people a reproach to all *about u.*	*Da 9:16*

AFTER US

for they will come out *after u.*	*Jos 8:6*
be witness to our generations *after u.*	*Jos 22:27*
send her away, for she crieth *after u.*	*M't 15:23*

AGAINST US

he may seek occasion *against u.*	*Ge 43:18*
join our enemies and fight *against u.*	*Ex 1:10*
what are we that ye murmur *against u.*	*Ex 16:7*
your murmurings are not *against u.* but God	*Ex 16:8*
Sihon came *against u.*	*De 2:32; 29:7*
Og came out *against u.*	*De 3:1*
when men of Ai came out *against u.*	*Jos 8:5*
kings of the Amorites gathered *against u.*	*Jos 10:6*
rebel not against the Lord, nor *against u.*	*Jos 22:19*
why are ye come up *against u.*	*J'g 15:10*
delivered company that came *against u.*	*1Sa 30:23*
surely the men prevailed *against u.*	*2Sa 11:23*
the man that devised *against u.*	*2Sa 21:5*
great is the wrath of Lord *against u.*	*2Ki 22:13*
this great company that cometh *against u.*	*2Ch 20:12*
tread them under that rise *against u.*	*Ps 44:5*
remember not *against u.* former iniquities	*Ps 79:8*
Lord for us, when men rose up *against u.*	*Ps 124:2*
when their wrath was kindled *against u.*	*Ps 124:3*
no feller is come up *against u.*	*Isa 14:8*
our sins testify *against u.*	*Isa 59:12; Jer 14:7*
Lord pronounced this evil *against u.*	*Jer 16:10*
Nebuchadnezzar maketh war *against u.*	*Jer 21:2*
which say, Who shall come down *against u.*	*Jer 21:13*
but Baruch setteth thee on *against u.*	*Jer 43:3*
have opened their mouths *against u.*	*La 3:46*
rejected us, thou art very wroth *against u.*	*La 5:22*
confirmed his words he spake *against u.*	*Da 9:12*
Jesus said, Forbid him not, *against u.*	*M'k 9:40*
he that is not *against u.* is	*Lu 9:50*
if God be for us, who can be *against u.*	*Ro 8:31*
blotting out the handwriting *against u.*	*Col 2:14*
prating *against u.* with malicious words	*3Jo 10*

AMONG US

thou art a mighty prince *among u.*	*Ge 23:6*
saying, Is the Lord *among u.* or not	*Ex 17:7*
let my lord, I pray thee, go *among u.*	*Ex 34:9*
because our God is not *among us*	*De 31:17*
peradventure ye dwell *among u.*	*Jos 9:7; 9:22*
pass over and take possession *among u.*	*Jos 22:19*
we perceive the Lord is *among u.*	*Jos 22:31*

let not thy voice be heard *among u.*	*J'g 18:25*
when it cometh *among u.* it may save	*1Sa 4:3*
not *among u.* any can skill to hew timber	*1Ki 5:6*
he clappeth his hands *amongst u.*	*Job 34:37*
not *among u.* any that knoweth how long	*Ps 74:9*
cast in thy lot *among u.* let us have	*Pr 1:14*
who *among u.* shall dwell with the devouring fire	*Isa 33:14*
they will say, Is not the Lord *among u.*	*Mic 3:11*
a great prophet is risen up *among u.*	*Lu 7:16*
Word was made flesh and dwelt *among u.*	*Joh 1:14*
Lord Jesus went in and out *among u.*	*Ac 1:21*
God made choice *among u.* that Gentiles	*Ac 15:7*

AT US

if it first begin *at u.* what the end be	*1Pe 4:17*

BEFORE US

they said, Make us gods *before u.*	*Ex 32:23; Ac 7:40*
which shall go *before u.*	*De 1:22*
we will send men *before u.*	*De 2:33*
the Lord our God delivered him *before u.*	*Jos 4:23*
which he dried up from *before u.*	*Jos 8:6; 24:18*
they flee *before u.*; drave out *before u.*	
the Lord shall drive out *before u.*	*J'g 11:24*
smitten down *before u.* as at the first	*J'g 20:32; 20:39*
king may judge us and go out *before u.*	*1Sa 8:20*
Samuel said, Bid thy servant pass on *before u.*	*1Sa 9:27*
while the land is yet *before u.*	*2Ch 14:7*
cause Holy One of Israel cease *before u.*	*Isa 30:11*
to walk in his laws which he set *before u.*	*Da 9:10*
to lay hold on the hope set *before u.*	*Heb 6:18*
let us run the race that is set *before u.*	*Heb 12:1*

BEHIND US

also he is *behind u.*	*Ge 32:18; 32:20*

BETWEEN, BETWIXT US

let there be now an oath *betwixt u.*	*Ge 26:28*
that they may judge *betwixt u.* both	*Ge 31:37*
the God of Abraham judge *betwixt u.*	*Ge 31:53*
Lord made Jordan a border *between u.*	*Jos 22:25*
that it may be a witness *between u.*	*Jos 22:27; 22:28, 34*
Lord be witness *between u.*	*J'g 11:10; Jer 42:5*
neither is any daysman *betwixt u.*	*Job 9:33*
between u. and you, is a great gulf	*Lu 16:26*
put no difference *between u.* and them	*Ac 15:9*
middle wall of partition *between u.*	*Eph 2:14*

BY US

hath not the Lord spoken also *by u.*	*Nu 12:2*
this man of God which passeth *by u.*	*2Ki 4:9*
Jesus was preached among you *by u.*	*2Co 1:19*
are in him amen, to the glory of God *by u.*	*2Co 1:20*
manifest the savour of his knowledge *by u.*	*2Co 2:14*
to be the epistle of Christ, ministered *by u.*	*2Co 3:3*

as tho' God did beseech you *by u.* we pray	*2Co 5:20*
ye might receive damage *by u.*	*2Co 7:9*
which is administered *by u.* to glory	*2Co 8:19*

CONCERNING US

do according to all written *concerning u.*	*2Ki 22:13*

FOR US

now the Lord hath made room *for u.*	*Ge 26:22*
is there yet any inheritance *for u.*	*Ge 31:14*
better *for u.* to serve the Egyptians	*Ex 14:12*
tarry ye here *for u.* until we come again	*Ex 24:14*
better *for u.* to return into Egypt	*Nu 14:3*
fear not the people, for they are bread *for u.*	*Nu 14:9*
there was not one city too strong *for u.*	*De 2:36*
say, Who shall go up *for u.* to heaven	*De 30:12*
who shall go over sea *for u.*	*De 30:13*
art thou *for u.* or for our adversaries	*Jos 5:13*
is the iniquity of Peor too little *for u.*	*Jos 22:17*
who go up *for u.* against Canaanites	*J'g 1:1*
cease not to cry unto the Lord *for u.*	*1Sa 7:8*
come, lest my father take thought *for u.*	*1Sa 9:5*
it may be the Lord will work *for u.*	*1Sa 14:6*
if we flee they will not care *for u.*	*2Sa 18:3*
neither *for u.* shalt thou kill any man	*2Sa 21:4*
thou hast been careful *for u.*	*2Ki 4:13*
place where we dwell is too strait *for u.*	*2Ki 6:1*
as *for u.* the Lord is our God	*2Ch 13:10*
to seek of him a right way *for u.*	*Ezr 8:21*
resort, our God shall fight *for u.*	*Ne 4:20*
he shall choose our inheritance *for u.*	*Ps 47:4*
trust in him, God is a refuge *for u.*	*Ps 62:8*
strengthen that thou hast wrought *for u.*	*Ps 68:28*
the Lord hath done great things *for u.*	*Ps 126:3*
whom shall I send, and who will go *for u.*	*Isa 6:8*
Lord, thou wilt ordain peace *for u.*	*Isa 26:12*
let them take up a wailing *for u.*	*Jer 9:18*
hast smitten, and there is no healing *for u.*	*Jer 14:19*
inquire, I pray thee, of the Lord *for u.*	*Jer 21:2*
pray to the Lord our God *for u.*	*Jer 37:3; 42:2, 20*
as *for u.* our eyes as yet failed	*La 4:17*
Peter said, Lord, it is good *for u.* to be here	*M't 17:4; M'k 9:5; Lu 9:33*
not so, lest there be not enough *for u.*	*M't 25:9*
upper room, there make ready *for u.*	*M'k 14:15*
raised up horn of salvation *for u.*	*Lu 1:69*
for he that is not against us is *for u.*	*Lu 9:50*
for u. to whom it shall be imputed	*Ro 4:24*
while we were sinners, Christ died *for u.*	*Ro 5:8*
the Spirit maketh intercession *for u.*	*Ro 8:26*
if God be *for u.* who can be against us	*Ro 8:31*
spared not, but delivered him up *for u.* all	*Ro 8:32*
Christ also maketh intercession *for u.*	*Ro 8:34*
even Christ is sacrificed *for u.*	*1Co 5:7*

helping together by prayer 2Co 1:11
for u.
our light affliction 2Co 4:17
worketh *for u.*
he hath made him to be sin 2Co 5:21
for u.
Christ redeemed us, made a Ga 3:13
curse *for u.*
hath loved us, and given Eph 5:2
himself *for u.*
withal, praying *for u.* that God Col 4:3
would
who died *for u.* 1Th 5:10; 1Jo 3:16
pray *for u.* 1Th 5:25;
 2Th 3:1; Heb 13:18
who gave himself *for u.,* that Tit 2:14
he might
whither the forerunner is *for* Heb 6:20
u. entered
having obtained eternal Heb 9:12
redemption *for u.*
now to appear in the Heb 9:24
presence of God *for u.*
living way, which he hath Heb 10:20
consecrated *for u.*
God having provided some Heb 11:40
better thing *for u.*
because Christ hath suffered 1Pe 2:21;
for u. 4:1

FROM US

Abimelech said to Isaac, Go Ge 26:16
from u.
and to whom shall he go up 1Sa 6:20
from u.
number now, and see who is 1Sa 14:17
gone *from u.*
his wrath turn *from u.* 2Ch 29:10;
 Ezr 10:14
let us cast away their cords Ps 2:3
from u.
hath removed our Ps 103:12
transgressions *from u.*
therefore is judgment far *from* Isa 59:9
u.
we look for salvation, but it Isa 59:11
is far *from u.*
for thou hast hid thy face Isa 64:7
from u.
the anger of the Lord is not Jer 4:8
turned *from u.*
that Nebuchadrezzar may go Jer 21:2
up *from u.*
hide it not *from u.* we will Jer 38:25
not kill thee
to the day he was taken up Ac 1:22
from u.
heard that certain who went Ac 15:24
out *from u.*
nor by word, nor by letter as 2Th 2:2
from u.
they went out *from u.* but not 1Jo 2:19
of us

IN US

if Lord delight *in u.* he will Nu 14:8
bring us
what understand, thou, which Job 15:9
is not *in u.*
hast wrought all our works Isa 26:12
in u.
that they also may be one *in* Joh 17:21
u.
that the law might be fulfilled Ro 8:4
in u.
with the glory which shall be Ro 8:18
revealed *in u.*
ye might learn *in u.* not to 1Co 4:6
think
as sufferings of Christ 2Co 1:5
abound *in u.*
so death worketh *in u.* but 2Co 4:12
life in you
not straitened *in u.,* but in 2Co 6:12
yourselves
according to power that Eph 3:20
worketh *in u.*
by Holy Ghost which dwelleth 2Ti 1:14
in u.
the spirit that dwelleth *in u.* Jas 4:5
lusteth
truth is not *in u.;* word not *in* 1Jo 1:8;
u. 1:10
hereby we know that he 1Jo 3:24
abideth *in u.*
if we love, God dwelleth *in* 1Jo 4:12;
u. 4:13
for the truth's sake which 2Jo 2
dwelleth *in u.*

OF US

the man is become as one *of u.* Ge 3:22
and there lacketh not a man Nu 31:49
of u.
the inhabitants faint because Jos 2:24
of u.
our enemy, which slew many J'g 16:24
of u.
which *of u.* shall go up first J'g 20:18
to the battle
which *of u.* is for the king of 2Ki 6:11
Israel
we besought God he was Ezr 8:23
entreated *of u.*
the Lord hath been mindful Ps 115:12
of u.
he hath laid on him the Isa 53:6
iniquity *of u.* all
our father, tho' Abraham be Isa 63:16
ignorant *of u.*
anguish hath taken hold *of u.* Jer 6:24
and pain
yet thou, O Lord, art in the Jer 14:9
midst *of u.*
tho' he be not far from every Ac 17:27
one *of u.*
Abraham, who is the father *of* Ro 4:16
u. all
so account *of u.* as ministers 1Co 4:1
of Christ
lest Satan get an advantage 2Co 2:11
of u. for we
that the power may be of God, 2Co 4:7
and not *of u.*
some who think *of u.* as if 2Co 10:2
we walked
Jerusalem, which is the Ga 4:26
mother *of u.* all
but to every one *of u.* is given Eph 4:7
grace
ye became followers *of u.* and 1Th 1:6
of Lord
they themselves shew *of u.* 1Th 1:9
what entering in
ye received the word which 1Th 2:13
ye heard *of u.*
ye have good remembrance *of* 1Th 3:6
u. always
that as ye have received *of u.* 1Th 4:1
how to walk
not after tradition he received 2Th 3:6
of u.
the commandment *of u.* the 2Pe 3:2
apostles
were not *of u.* if had been *of* 1Jo 2:19
u. they might shew they were
not all *of u.*

ON US, UPON US

shouldest have brought Ge 26:10
guiltiness *upon u.*
therefore is this distress Ge 42:21
come *upon u.*
fall *upon u.* and take us for Ge 43:18
bondmen
lest he fall *upon u.* with Ex 5:3
pestilence
I beseech thee, lay not the Nu 12:11
sin *upon u.*
are not these evils come De 31:17
upon u.
let them live lest wrath be Jos 9:20
upon u.
they said, Rise thou and fall J'g 8:21
upon u.
his hand is sore *upon u.* and 1Sa 5:7
Dagon
yoke which he put *upon u.* 1Ki 12:4;
lighter 12:9; 2Ch 10:4, 9
some mischief will come *upon* 2Ki 7:9
u.
Lord our God made a 1Ch 15:13
breach *upon u.*
if when evil cometh *upon u.* 2Ch 20:9
as sword
for great is the wrath 2Ch 34:21
poured *upon u.*
by the good hand of our Ezr 8:18;
God *upon u.* 8:31
after all that is come *upon u.* Ezr 9:13
for our evil
the trouble little that hath Ne 9:32
come *upon u.*
thou art just in all that is Ne 9:33
brought *upon u.*
did not our God bring all Ne 13:18
this evil *upon u.*

that might lay his hand *upon* Job 9:33
u. both
lift up light of thy countenance Ps 4:6
upon u.
let thy mercy, O Lord, be Ps 33:22
upon u.
all this is come *upon u.* yet Ps 44:17
have we not
God bless us, cause his face to Ps 67:1
shine *upon u.*
the beauty of the Lord our Ps 90:17
God be *upon u.*
our eyes wait on Lord till he Ps 123:2
have mercy *upon u.*
have mercy *upon u.,* O Lord Ps 123:3;
have mercy *upon u.* M't 9:27; 20:30-31;
 Lu 17:13
until the Spirit be poured Isa 32:15
upon u.
fear and a snare is come *upon* La 3:47
u.
remember, O Lord, what is La 5:1
come *upon u.*
if our transgressions and sins Eze 33:10
be *upon u.*
therefore the curse is poured Da 9:11
upon u.
by bringing *upon u.* a great Da 9:12;
evil 10:13-14
and to hills, Fall *on u.* Ho 10:8;
 Lu 23:30; Re 6:16
for whose cause this evil is *on* Jon 1:7;
u. 1:8
they will say, None evil can Mic 3:11
come *upon u.*
he will turn and have Mic 7:19
compassion *upon u.*
his blood be *on u.* and our M't 27:25
children
look *on u.* Ac 3:4
or why look ye so earnestly *on* Ac 3:12
u. as though
this man's blood *upon u.* Ac 5:28
Spirit fell on them, as *on u.* Ac 11:15
at the beginning
Mary, who bestowed much Ro 16:6
labour *on u.*
which he shed *on u.* Tit 3:6
abundantly thro' Jesus
love the Father hath bestowed 1Jo 3:1
on u.

OVER US

said, Shalt thou indeed reign Ge 37:8
over u.
who made thee judge *over u.* Ex 2:14;
 Ac 7:27
thou make thyself a prince Nu 16:13
over u.
Israel said to Gideon, Rule J'g 8:22
over u.
the trees said to the olive tree, J'g 9:8
Reign *over u.*
to fig tree; to vine; to J'g 9:10;
bramble reign *over u.* 9:12, 14
but we will have a king *over* 1Sa 8:19;
u. 10:19
who said, Shall Saul reign 1Sa 11:12
over u.
in time past, when Saul was 2Sa 5:2
king *over u.*
and Absalom whom we 2Sa 19:10
anointed *over u.*
the kings whom thou hast set Ne 9:37
over u.
lips are our own, who is Lord Ps 12:4
over u.
other lords have had Isa 26:13
dominion *over u.*
servants have ruled *over u.* La 5:8
none to deliver
will not have this man to Lu 19:14
reign *over u.*

THROUGH US

causeth *through u.* 2Co 9:11
thanksgiving to God

TO, UNTO US

there is not a man to come Ge 19:31
in *unto u.*
said, What hast thou done Ge 20:9;
unto u. 26:10
let us take their daughters Ge 34:21
to u. for wives
brought an Hebrew *unto u.* Ge 39:14
to mock us
afraid, saying, What is this Ge 42:28;

that God hath done *unto u.*   *Jer 5:19*

thou mayest be *to u.* instead *Nu 10:31* of eyes

what goodness Lord shall do *Nu 10:32* *unto u.*

speak thou *unto u.* and we *De 5:27* will hear

but the things revealed *De 29:29* belong *unto u.*

go up to heaven and bring it *De 30:12* *unto u.*

shall go over the sea, and *De 30:13* bring it *unto u.*

we are in thy hand, as it *Jos 9:25;* seemeth good and right *J'g 10:15* do *unto u.*

let the man of God come *J'g 13:8* again *unto u.*

to do to him, as he hath *J'g 15:10* done *to u.*

go with us, be *to u.* a father *J'g 18:19* and priest

woe *unto u.*   *1Sa 4:8;*   *Jer 4:13; 6:4; La 5:16*

if they thus say *unto u.*, Tarry *1Sa 14:9* till we come

but the men were very good *1Sa 25:15* *unto u.*

they were a wall *unto u.* by *1Sa 25:16* night and day

bring again the ark of God *1Ch 13:8* *to u.*

the Jews which came from *Ezr 4:12* thee *to u.*

shall your brethren be sold *Ne 5:8* *unto u.*

let us choose *to u.* judgment, *Job 34:4* let us know

hast scattered, O turn thyself *Ps 60:1* *to u.* again

not *unto u.* O Lord, not *unto Ps 115:1* u.* but thy name

except had left *unto u.* a very *Isa 1:9* small remnant

unto u. a child is born, *unto u. Isa 9:6* a son is given

they shall say, Art thou *Isa 14:10* become like *unto u.*

the scourge shall not come *Isa 28:15* *unto u.*

prophesy not *unto u.* right *Isa 30:10* th'ngs, speak *unto u.* smooth

Lord be *unto u.* a place of *Isa 33:21* broad rivers

speak not *to u.* in the Jews' *Isa 36:11* language

reserveth *to u.* the appointed *Jer 5:24* weeks

spoken *to u.* in the name of *Jer 26:16* the Lord

for which the Lord shall send *Jer 42:5* thee *to u.*

as for the word thou hast *Jer 44:16* spoken *unto u.*

water for money, our wood is *La 5:4* sold *unto u.*

unto u. is this land given in *Eze 11:15* possession

tell us what these things are *Eze 24:19* *to u.*

but *unto u.* confusion of faces *Da 9:7;*   *9:8*

he shall come *unto u.* as the *Ho 6:3* rain

what then should a king do *to Ho 10:3* u.*

that the sea may be calm *Jon 1:11* *unto u.*

like as the Lord thought to do *Zec 1:6* *unto u.*

thou hast made them equal *M't 20:12* *unto u.*

saying, Lord, Lord, open *to M't 25:11;* u.*   *Lu 13:25*

what is that *to u.*? see thou *to M't 27:4* that

even as they delivered them *Lu 1:2* *unto u.*

which the Lord hath made *Lu 2:15* known *unto u.*

even the devils are subject *Lu 10:17* *unto u.*

speakest thou this parable *Lu 12:41* *unto u.*

neither can they pass *to u. Lu 16:26* that would

what sign shewest thou *unto Joh 2:18* u.*

that thou wilt manifest *Joh 14:22* thyself *unto u.*

---

what is this that he saith *Joh 16:17* *unto u.*

who received oracles to give *Ac 7:38* *unto u.*

to u. who did eat and drink *Ac 10:41* with him

God gave them the like gift *Ac 11:17* as *unto u.*

God hath fulfilled the same *Ac 13:33* *unto u.*

by the Holy Ghost which is *Ro 5:5* given *unto u.*

but *unto u.* it is the power of *1Co 1:18* God

Christ, who of God is made *1Co 1:30* *unto u.* wisdom

God revealed them *unto u.* by *1Co 2:10* his Spirit

but *to u.* there is but one God, *1Co 8:6* the Father

committed *to u.* word of *2Co 5:19* reconciliation

gave themselves *unto u.* by the *2Co 8:5* will of God

therefore as ye abound in *2Co 8:7* your love *to u.*

who declared *unto u.* your love *Col 1:8* in Spirit

that God would open *unto u.* a *Col 4:3* door

for *unto u.* was the gospel *Heb 4:2* preached

unto u. they did minister the *1Pe 1:12* things

TOWARD US

cause thine anger *toward u.* to *Ps 85:4* cease

his merciful kindness is great *Ps 117:2* *toward u.*

God commendeth his love *Ro 5:8* *toward u.*

wherein he hath abounded *Eph 1:8* *toward u.*

in his kindness *toward u. Eph 2:7* through Christ

manifested the love of God *1Jo 4:9* *toward u.*

UNDER US

he shall subdue the people *Ps 47:3* *under u.*

WITH US

no man is *with u.*; see, God *Ge 31:50* is witness

and make ye marriages *with Ge 34:9* u.* and give

ye shall dwell *with u.*; they *Ge 34:10;* dwell *with u.*   *34:23*

if thou send our brother *Ge 43:4;* *with us*   *44:26*

seeth that the lad is not *with Ge 44:30* u.*

the God of the Hebrews met *Ex 3:18;* *with u.*   *5:3*

wherefore hast thou dealt *Ex 14:11* thus *with u.*

speak thou *with u.*, let not *Ex 20:19* God speak *with u.*

is it not in that thou goest *Ex 33:16* *with u.*

come *with u.*, we will do thee *Nu 10:29* good

it shall be, if thou go *with u. Nu 10:32* that goodness

for it was well *with u.* in *Nu 11:18* Egypt

and the Lord is *with u.*, fear *Nu 14:9* them not

Balaam refuseth to come *Nu 22:14* *with u.*

the Lord made a covenant *De 5:2;* *with u.*   *5:3*

him that standeth here *with De 29:15* u.*, also him that is not *with u.* this day

therefore make a league *with Jos 9:6;* u.*   *9:11*

O my lord, if the Lord be *J'g 6:13* *with u.*

we turn again, that thou *J'g 11:8* mayest go *with u.*

they said, Hold thy peace and *J'g 18:19* go *with u.*

the ark of God shall not abide *1Sa 5:7* *with u.*

---

let my brother Amnon go *2Sa 13:26* *with u.*

shall go no more out *with u. 2Sa 21:17* to battle

there was no stranger *with u. 1Ki 3:18* in house

the Lord our God be *with u. 1Ki 8:57* as he was

they that be *with u.* are *2Ki 6:16;* more than they that be *2Ch 32:7*

behold, God is *with u.* 2Ch 13:12; 32:8

you have nothing to do *with u. Ezr 4:3* to build

wouldst not thou be angry *Ezr 9:14* *with u.* till thou

with u. are the greyheaded *Job 15:10* and aged

the Lord of hosts is *with u. Ps 46:7;*   *46:11*

wilt thou be angry *with u.* for *Ps 85:5* ever

he hath not dealt *with u. Ps 103:10* after our sins

come *with u.*; God is *with u. Pr 1:11;*   *Isa 8:10*

for our transgressions are *Isa 59:12* *with u.*

we are wise, the law of the *Jer 8:8* Lord is *with u.*

remember, break not thy *Jer 14:21* covenant *with u.*

that it may be well *with u. Jer 42:6* when we obey

found in Beth-el, there he *Ho 12:4* spake *with u.*

as our doings, so hath he *Zec 1:6* dealth *with u.*

being interpreted, is, God *M't 1:23* *with u.*

his sisters are all *with u. M't 13:56;*   *M'k 6:3*

now there were *with u. M't 22:25* seven brethren

son, why hast thou thus dealt *Lu 2:48* *with u.*

forbad him, because he *Lu 9:49* followeth not *with u.*

abide *with u.* *Lu 24:29*

while he talked *with u. Lu 24:32*

for he was numbered *with u. Ac 1:17* and had

his sepulchre is *with u.* unto *Ac 2:29* this day

to everyone that helpeth *1Co 16:16* *with u.*

who was chosen to travel *2Co 8:19* *with u.*

to you who are troubled, rest *2Th 1:7* *with u.*

have obtained like precious *2Pe 1:1* faith *with u.*

that ye may have fellowship *1Jo 1:3* *with u.*

would no doubt have *1Jo 2:19* continued *with u.*

the truth shall be *with u.* for *2Jo 2* ever

WITHIN US

did not our hearts burn *Lu 24:32* *within u.* while he opened

WITHOUT US

ye have reigned as kings *1Co 4:8* *without u.*

that they *without u.* not be *Heb 11:40* made perfect

USE

may be used in any other *u. Le 7:24*

neither shall ye *u. Le 19:26* enchantment

mayest *u.* them for the calling *Nu 10:2*

after which ye *u.* to go a *Nu 15:39* whoring

ought thereof for any *De 26:14* unclean *u.*

children of Judah the *u.* of *2Sa 1:18* the bow

u. both the right hand and *1Ch 12:2*

to the *u.* of every *1Ch 28:15* candlestick

that *u.* their tongues, and *Jer 23:31* say, He

shall *u.* this speech in the *Jer 31:23* land of

in vain shalt thou *u.* many *Jer 46:11* medicines

more *u.* it as a proverb in   *Eze 12:23*
Israel
shall *u.* this proverb against   *Eze 16:44*
thee
u. this proverb concerning the   *Eze 18:2*
more to *u.* this proverb in   *Eze 18:3*
Israel
of the two ways, to *u.*   *Eze 21:21*
divination
them which despitefully *u.*   *M't 5:44;*
you   *Lu 6:28*
when ye pray, *u.* not vain   *M't 6:7*
repetition
to *u.* them despitefully, and to   *Ac 14:5*
did change the natural *u.*   *Ro 1:26*
into that
leaving natural *u.* of the   *Ro 1:27*
woman
mayest be made free, *u.* it   *1Co 7:21*
rather
they that *u.* this world, as not   *1Co 7:31*
thus minded, did I *u.*   *2Co 1:17*
lightness
we *u.* great plainness of   *2Co 3:12*
speech
being present I *u.*   *2Co 13:10*
sharpness
u. not liberty for an occasion   *Ga 5:13*
to the
is good to the *u.* of edifying   *Eph 4:29*
is good, if a man *u.* it lawfully   *1Ti 1:8*
then let them *u.* the office of a   *1Ti 3:10*
deacon
u. a little wine, for thy   *1Ti 5:23*
stomach's
and meat for the master's *u.*   *2Ti 2:21*
those who by reason of *u.*   *Heb 5:14*
have
U. hospitality one to another   *1Pe 4:9*

USED

the ox hath *u.* to push in   *Ex 21:36*
time past
gold that was *u.* (S)   *Ex 38:24;*
   J'g 16:11
may be *u.* in any other use   *Le 7:24*
a beast, for so *u.* the young   *J'g 14:10*
men to do
whom he had *u.* as his friend   *J'g 14:20*
meal shall not be *u.* up (S)   *1Ki 17:14;*
   17:16
u. divination and   *2Ki 17:17*
enchantments
times, and *u.* enchantments   *2Ki 21:6;*
   2Ch 33:6
and *u.* witchcraft, and dealt   *2Ch 33:6*
with a
A wild ass *u.* to the wilderness   *Jer 2:24*
people of the land have *u.*   *Eze 22:29*
oppression
envy which thou hast *u.* out   *Eze 35:11*
of thy
multiplied vision, and *u.*   *Ho 12:10*
similitudes
and of the Pharisees *u.* to fast   *M'k 2:18*
in the same city *u.* sorcery   *Ac 8:9*
of them also which *u.*   *Ac 19:19*
curious arts
they *u.* helps, undergirding the   *Ac 27:17*
ship
their tongues they have *u.*   *Ro 3:13*
deceit
we have not *u.* this power   *1Co 9:12*
But I have *u.* none of these   *1Co 9:15*
things
time *u.* we flattering words   *1Th 2:5*
that have *u.* the office of a   *1Ti 3:13*
deacon
companions of them that   *Heb 10:33*
were so *u.*

USEFUL

everything is not *u.* (P)   *1Co 10:23*

USELESS

I kept *u.* (B)   *1Sa 25:21; Jas 1:26*
u. men (A)   *Job 11:11; Mal 3:14*
u. and a great misfortune (B)   *Ec 2:21*
every *u.* word (B)   *M't 12:36*
u. servant (B)(N)(P)(R)   *M't 25:30*
have become utterly *u.* (B)   *Ro 3:12*
not *u.* and fruitless (A)   *1Th 2:1*
promote *u.* speculations (A)   *1Ti 1:4*
u. to you (B)(P)(R)   *Ph'm 11*
impotent and *u.* (E)(N)   *Heb 7:18*
this man's religion is *u.* (P)   *Jas 1:26*
u. ways (A)(B)(R)   *1Pe 1:18*

USELESSLY

strength spent *u.* (B)   *Ex 26:20;*
   Ps 73:13; M't 15:9; Ga 2:2
come back to me *u.* (B)   *Isa 55:11*

USLESSNESS

uselessness (B)   *Ec 8:19; 4:7; Isa 41:29*
u. of ways of thinking (B)   *Eph 4:17*
ineffectiveness and *u.*   *Heb 7:18*
(A)(B)(P)(R)

USES

good works for necessary *u.*   *Tit 3:14*

USEST

as thou *u.* to do unto those   *Ps 119:132*
that

USETH

or that *u.* divination, or an   *De 18:10*
observer
be brought which the king *u.* to   *Es 6:8*
wear
of the wise *u.* knowledge   *Pr 15:2*
aright
The poor *u.* intreaties; but   *Pr 18:23*
that *u.* his neighbour's   *Jer 22:13*
service
every one that *u.* proverbs   *Eze 16:44*
shall
For one that *u.* milk is   *Heb 5:13*
unskilful

USING

Which all are to perish with   *Col 2:22*
the *u.*
not *u.* our liberty for a cloke   *1Pe 2:16*
of

USUALLY

more than *u.* (S)   *Da 3:19*

USURER

thou shalt not be to him as   *Ex 22:25*
an *u.*
as a creditor (A)(B)(E)(R)   *Ex 22:25*

USURP

nor to *u.* authority over the   *1Ti 2:12*
man
have authority over men   *1Ti 2:12*
(A)(R)
to domineer over the man   *1Ti 2:12*
(B)(N)
have dominion over the man   *1Ti 2:12*
(E)
in positions of authority over   *1Ti 2:12*
men (P)

USURY

shalt thou lay upon him *u.*   *Ex 22:25*
interest (A)(E)   *Ex 22:25;*
Le 25:36-37;   *De 23:19-20;*   *Ne 5:10;*
Ps 15:5;   *Pr 28:8; Eze 18:8, 17; 22:12;*
   M't 25:27;   *Lu 19:23*
interest (B)   *Ex 22:25;*
Le 25:36-37;   *De 23:19-20;*   *Ne 5:7;*
Ps 15:5; Pr 28:8; Eze 18:17; M't 25:27;
   Lu 19:23
interest (R)   *Ex 22:25;*
Le 25:36-37; De 23:19-20; Ne 5:7, 10;
Ps 15:5;   *Pr 28:8;*   *Eze 18:8, 13, 17;*
22:12; M't 25:27; Lu 19:23
Take thou no *u.* of him, or   *Le 25:36*
increase
not give him thy money upon   *Le 25:37*
u.
not lend upon *u.* to thy   *De 23:19*
brother
u. of money, *u.* of victuals   *De 23:19*
u. of any thing that is lent   *De 23:19*
upon
any thing that is lent upon *u.*   *De 23:19*
a stranger thou mayest lend   *De 23:20*
upon *u.*
thou shalt not lend upon *u.*   *De 23:20*
Ye exact *u.* every one of his   *Ne 5:7*
I pray you, let us leave off   *Ne 5:10*
this *u.*
putteth not out his money to   *Ps 15:5*
u.

He that by *u.* and unjust gain   *Pr 28:8*
as with the taker of *u.* so with   *Isa 24:2*
as with the creditor, so with   *Isa 24:2*
the debtor (A)(B)(E)(R)
so with the giver of *u.* to him   *Isa 24:2*
I have neither lent on *u.* nor   *Jer 15:10*
men
nor men have lent to me on   *Jer 15:10*
u.
thou hath not given forth   *Eze 18:8*
upon *u.*
Hath given forth upon *u.*   *Eze 18:13*
and hath
hath not received *u.* nor   *Eze 18:17*
increase
thou hast taken *u.* and   *Eze 22:12*
increase
have received mine own   *M't 25:27*
with *u.*
interest (N)(P)   *M't 25:27; Lu 19:23*
have required mine own with   *Lu 19:23*
u.

US-WARD

and thy thoughts which are to   *Ps 40:5*
u.
his power to *u.* who believed   *Eph 1:19*
but is longsuffering to *u.* not   *2Pe 3:9*

UTENSIL

every open *u.* (B)   *Nu 19:15; Ro 9:21*
I am like a worn-out *u.* (B)   *Ps 31:12*
a *u.* unto honor (B)   *2Ti 2:21*

UTENSILS

ministering *u.* (A)(B)   *Nu 4:12*
food bags and *u.* (A)   *1Sa 21:5*
u. in your sight (A)   *Job 18:3*
u. of gold (N)   *2Ti 2:20*

UTHAI

U. the son of Ammihud, the   *1Ch 9:4*
son
U. and Zabbud, and with   *Ezr 8:14*
them

UTMOST

the *u.* bound of the   *Ge 49:26*
everlasting hills
Arnon, which is in the *u.*   *Nu 22:36*
coast
might see the *u.* part of the   *Nu 22:41*
people
shalt see but the *u.* part of   *Nu 23:13*
them
the land of Judah, unto the *u.*   *De 34:2*
sea
and all that are in the *u.*   *Jer 9:26;*
corners   *25:23*
them that are in the *u.*   *Jer 49:32*
corners
against her from the *u.*   *Jer 50:26*
border
his hinder part toward the *u.*   *Joe 2:20*
sea
from the *u.* parts of the earth   *Lu 11:31*

UTTER

if he do not *u.* it, then he shall   *Le 5:1*
yours, if ye *u.* not this our   *Jos 2:14*
business
And if thou *u.* this our   *Jos 2:20*
business
Deborah: awake, awake, *u.* a   *J'g 5:12*
song
I appointed to *u.* destruction   *1Ki 20:42*
and *u.* words out of their   *Job 8:10*
heart
a wise man *u.* vain knowledge   *Job 15:2*
nor my tongue *u.* deceit   *Job 27:4*
lips shall *u.* knowledge clearly   *Job 33:3*
I will *u.* dark sayings of old   *Ps 78:2*
long shall they *u.* and speak   *Ps 94:4*
hard
Who can *u.* the mighty acts   *Ps 106:2*
of the
My lips shall *u.* praise,   *Ps 119:171*
when
shall abundantly *u.* the   *Ps 145:7*
memory
but a false witness will *u.* lies   *Pr 14:5*
put out in *u.* darkness (E)   *Pr 20:20*
heart shall *u.* perverse things   *Pr 23:33*
mind *u.* things untrue   *Pr 23:33*
(A)(B)

are full of labour: man cannot *Ec 1:8*
u.
hasty to *u.* any thing before *Ec 5:2*
God
and to *u.* error against the *Isa 32:6*
Lord
u. it even to the end of the *Isa 48:20*
earth
I will *u.* my judgments against *Jer 1:16*
u. his voice from his holy *Jer 25:30*
u. a parable unto the *Eze 24:3*
rebellious
were toward the *u.* court *Eze 40:31;*
40:37
brought me forth into the *u. Eze 42:1*
court
pavement was for the *u. Eze 42:3*
court
toward the *u.* court on the *Eze 42:7*
forepart
chambers that were in the *u. Eze 42:8*
court
goeth into them from the *u. Eze 42:9*
court
of the holy place into the *u. Eze 42:14*
court
they go forth into the *u. Eze 44:19*
court
even into the *u.* court of the *Eze 44:19*
people
bear them not out into the *Eze 46:20*
u. court
brought me forth into the *u. Eze 46:21*
court
u. gate by the way *Eze 47:2*
that looketh
Lord shall *u.* his voice before *Joe 2:11*
his
and *u.* his voice from *Joe 3:16;*
Jerusalem *Am 1:2*
he will make an *u.* end of *Na 1:8*
the place
he will make an *u.* end: *Na 1:9*
affliction
shall be no more *u.* *Zec 14:11*
destruction
u. things which have been *M't 13:35*
kept
you *u.* imposter (N) *Ac 13:10*
except ye *u.* by the tongue *1Co 14:9*
words
it is not lawful for a man to *2Co 12:4*
u.

UTTERANCE

took up prophetic *u.* (A) *Nu 24:20;*
24:21, 23
tongues, as the Spirit gave *Ac 2:4*
them *u.*
ye are enriched by him, in all *1Co 1:5*
u.
ecstatic *u.* (N) *1Co 14:9;*
12:10, 28; 14:18, 26-27, 39
in faith, and *u.* and *2Co 8:7*
knowledge
that *u.* may be given unto *Eph 6:19*
me, that
would open unto us a door of *Col 4:3*
u.

UTTERANCES

u. of a desperate man (B) *Job 6:26*
received living *u.* (A) *Ac 7:38*
u. of the prophets (A) *Ac 13:27*
entrusted with *u.* of God (B) *Ro 3:2*
u. beyond power of man (A) *2Co 12:4*
shameful *u.* (A) *Col 3:8*

UTTERED

vowed, or *u.* ought out of her *Nu 30:6*
lips
that which she *u.* with her lips *Nu 30:8*
Jephthah *u.* all his words *J'g 11:11*
before
and the most High *u.* his *2Sa 22:14*
voice
me, and *u.* my words to him *Ne 6:19*
To whom hast thou *u.* words *Job 26:4*
have I *u.* that I understood *Job 42:3*
not
he *u.* his voice, the earth *Ps 46:6*
melted
Which my lips have *u.* and *Ps 66:14*
Jahaz, have they *u.* their *Jer 48:34*
voice
waters, a noise of their voice *Jer 51:55*
is *u.*

the deep *u.* his voice, and *Hab 3:10*
lifted up
with groanings which cannot *Ro 8:26*
be *u.*
things to say, and hard to be *Heb 5:11*
u.
seven thunders *u.* their voices *Re 10:3*
seven thunders had *u.* their *Re 10:4*
voices
which the seven thunders *u.* *Re 10:4*

UTTERETH

For thy mouth *u.* thine *Job 15:5*
iniquity
Day unto day *u.* speech, and *Ps 19:2*
she *u.* her voice in the streets *Pr 1:20*
the city she *u.* her words, *Pr 1:21*
saying
and he that *u.* a slander, is a *Pr 10:18*
fool
A fool *u.* all his mind; but a *Pr 29:11*
wise
When he *u.* his voice, there *Jer 10:13;*
is a *51:16*
he *u.* his mischievous desire *Mic 7:3*

UTTERING

conceiving and *u.* from the *Isa 59:13*
heart
u. straight truth (A) *Ac 26:25*

UTTERLY

I will *u.* put out the *Ex 17:14*
remembrance of
father *u.* refuse to give her *Ex 22:17*
unto him
only, he shall be *u.* destroyed *Ex 22:20*
but thou shalt *u.* overthrow *Ex 23:24*
them
priest pronounce him *u.* *Le 13:44*
unclean
I abhor them, to destroy *Le 26:44*
them *u.*
that soul shall be *u.* cut off *Nu 15:31*
then I will *u.* destroy their *Nu 21:2*
cities
they *u.* destroyed them and *Nu 21:3*
their
husband hath *u.* made them *Nu 30:12*
void
and *u.* destroyed the men, and *De 2:34*
And we *u.* destroyed them, as *De 3:6*
u. destroying the men, women *De 3:6*
ye shall soon *u.* perish from *De 4:26*
off the
upon it, but shall be *u.* *De 4:26*
destroyed
smite them, and *u.* destroy them *De 7:2*
but thou shalt *u.* detest it, and *De 7:26*
and thou shalt *u.* abhor it; for *De 7:26*
it is a
Ye shall *u.* destroy all the *De 12:2*
places
destroying it *u.* and all that is *De 13:15*
But thou shalt *u.* destroy *De 20:17*
them
death ye will *u.* corrupt *De 31:29*
yourselves
and Og, whom ye *u.* destroyed *Jos 2:10*
they *u.* destroyed all that was *Jos 6:21*
in
until he had *u.* destroyed all *Jos 8:26*
taken Ai, and had *u.* destroyed *Jos 10:1*
it
the king thereof he *u.* *Jos 10:28*
destroyed
therein he *u.* destroyed that *Jos 10:35*
day
destroyed it *u.* and all the *Jos 10:37*
souls
and *u.* destroyed all the souls *Jos 10:39*
that
but *u.* destroyed all that *Jos 10:40*
breathed
of the sword, *u.* destroying *Jos 11:11*
them
he *u.* destroyed them, as *Jos 11:12*
Moses
that he might destroy them *Jos 11:20*
u.
destroyed them *u.* with their *Jos 11:21*
cities
tribute; but did not *u.* drive *Jos 17:13*
them out
Zephath, and *u.* destroyed it *J'g 1:17*
and did not *u.* drive them out *J'g 1:28*

thought that thou hadst *u.* *J'g 15:2*
hated her
Ye shall *u.* destroy every *J'g 21:11*
male
and *u.* destroy all that they *1Sa 15:3*
have
u. destroyed all the people *1Sa 15:8*
with the
good, and would not *u.* *1Sa 15:9*
destroy them
and refuse, that they *1Sa 15:9*
destroyed *u.*
and the rest we have *u.* *1Sa 15:15*
destroyed
Go and *u.* destroy the *1Sa 15:18*
sinners the
have *u.* destroyed the *1Sa 15:20*
Amalekites
which should have been *u.* *1Sa 15:21*
destroyed
his people Israel *u.* to abhor *1Sa 27:12*
him
is as the heart of a lion, *2Sa 17:10*
shall *u.* melt
they shall be *u.* burned with *2Sa 23:7*
fire in the
also were not able *u.* to *1Ki 9:21*
destroy
to all lands, by destroying *2Ki 19:11*
them *u.*
destroyed them *u.* unto this *1Ch 4:41*
day
Seir, *u.* to slay and destroy *2Ch 20:23*
them
until they had *u.* destroyed *2Ch 31:1*
them
nations, that my fathers *u.* *2Ch 32:14*
destroyed
thou didst not *u.* consume *Ne 9:31*
them
fall, he shall not be *u.* cast *Ps 37:24*
down
they are *u.* consumed with *Ps 73:19*
terrors
my lovingkindness will I not *Ps 89:33*
u. take
thy statutes: O forsake me *Ps 119:8*
not *u.*
word of truth *u.* out of my *Ps 119:43*
mouth
for love, it would *u.* be *Ca 8:7*
contemned
And the idols he shall *u.* *Isa 2:18*
abolish
man, and the land be *u.* *Isa 6:11*
desolate
shall *u.* destroy the tongue of *Isa 11:15*
shall be *u.* emptied, and *u.* *Isa 24:3*
spoiled
The earth is *u.* broken down *Isa 24:19*
he hath *u.* destroyed them, *Isa 34:2*
all lands by destroying them *Isa 37:11*
u.
and the young men shall *u.* *Isa 40:30*
fall
u. separated me from his *Isa 56:3*
people
yea, those nations shall be *u.* *Isa 60:12*
wasted
for every brother will *u.* *Jer 9:4*
supplant
I will *u.* pluck up and *Jer 12:17*
destroy that
Hast thou *u.* rejected Judah *Jer 14:19*
behold, I, even I, will *u.* *Jer 23:39*
forget you
about, and will *u.* destroy *Jer 25:9*
them
and should ye be *u.* *Jer 25:29*
unpunished
waste and *u.* destroy after *Jer 50:21*
them
up as heaps, and destroy her *Jer 50:26*
u.
men: destroy ye *u.* all her *Jer 51:3*
host
walls of Babylon shall be *u.* *Jer 51:58*
broken
But thou hast *u.* rejected us *La 5:22*
Slay *u.* old and young, both *Eze 9:6*
maids
shall it not *u.* wither, when *Eze 17:10*
the east
make themselves *u.* bald for *Eze 27:31*
thee
of Egypt *u.* waste and *Eze 29:10*
desolate
be broken and *u.* swept *Da 11:22*
away (A)(B)(R)

destroy, and *u.* to make | Da 11:44
away many
Israel: but I will *u.* take them | Ho 1:6
away
shall the king of Israel *u.* be | Ho 10:15
cut off
I will not *u.* destroy the house | Am 9:8
of
and say, We be *u.* spoiled | Mic 2:4
through thee; he is *u.* cut off | Na 1:15
will *u.* consume all things | Zep 1:2
from off
his right eye shall be *u.* | Zec 11:17
darkened
have become *u.* useless (B) | Ro 3:12
u. unphilosophical nonsense | 1Co 1:23
(A)
there is *u.* a fault among you | 1Co 6:7
u. dead and gone (P) | 1Co 15:18
and shall *u.* perish in their | 2Pe 2:12
own
she shall be *u.* burned with | Re 18:8
fire

UTTERMOST

in the *u.* edge of another | Ex 26:4
curtain
in the *u.* side of another | Ex 36:11
curtain
upon the *u.* edge of the | Ex 36:17
curtain
were in the *u.* parts of the | Nu 11:1
camp
a city in the *u.* of thy border | Nu 20:16
unto the *u.* sea shall your | De 11:24
coast be
was the *u.* part of the south | Jos 15:1
coast
of the sea at the *u.* part of | Jos 15:5
Jordan
the *u.* cities of the tribe of | Jos 15:21
the
tarried in the *u.* part of | 1Sa 14:2
Gibeah
from the *u.* part of the one | 1Ki 6:24
wing
wing unto the *u.* part of the | 1Ki 6:24
other
the *u.* part of the camp of | 2Ki 7:5
Syria
came to the *u.* part of the camp | 2Ki 7:8
out unto the *u.* part of the | Ne 1:9
heaven
and the *u.* parts of the earth for | Ps 2:8
thy
that dwell in the *u.* parts are | Ps 65:8
afraid
dwell in the *u.* parts of the sea | Ps 139:9
the *u.* part of the rivers of | Isa 7:18
Egypt
From the *u.* part of the earth | Isa 24:16
have
till thou hast paid the *u.* | M't 5:26
farthing
from the *u.* parts of the | M't 12:42
earth
from the *u.* part of the | M'k 13:27
earth
to the *u.* part of heaven | M'k 13:27
unto the *u.* part of the earth | Ac 1:8
I will know the *u.* of your | Ac 24:22
matter
wrath is come upon them to | 1Th 2:16
the *u.*
able also to save them to the | Heb 7:25
u.

UTTERS

person unthinkingly *u.* an oath | Le 6:4
(B)(R)
tongue *u.* wickedness (A)(E) | Isa 59:3

UZ

children of Aram; *U.* and | Ge 10:23
Hul
children of Dishan are these; | Ge 36:28
U.
Aram, and *U.*, and Hul, and | 1Ch 1:17
Gether
The sons of Dishan; *U.* and | 1Ch 1:42
Aran
There was a man in the land | Job 1:1
of *U.*
and all the kings of the land | Jer 25:20
of *U.*
that dwellest in the land of *U.* | La 4:21

UZAI

Palal the son of *U.* over | Ne 3:20
against

UZAL

Hadoram, and *U.* and Diklah | Ge 10:27
Hadoram also, and *U.* and | 1Ch 1:21
Diklah

UZZA

own house, in the garden of | 2Ki 21:18
his sepulchre in the garden | 2Ki 21:26
of *U.*
son, Shimei his son, *U.* his | 1Ch 6:29
son
he removed them, and begat | 1Ch 8:7
U.
and *U.* and Ahio drave the | 1Ch 13:7
cart
U. put forth his hand to hold | 1Ch 13:9
the Lord was kindled | 1Ch 13:10
against *U.*
Lord had made a breach | 1Ch 13:11
upon *U.*
The children of *U.* the | Ezr 2:49;
children of | Ne 7:51

UZZAH

U. and Ahio, the sons of | 2Sa 6:3
Abinadab
U. put forth his hand to the | 2Sa 6:6
ark of
the Lord was kindled against | 2Sa 6:7
U.
Lord had made a breach upon | 2Sa 6:8
U.

UZZEN-SHERAH

built Beth-horon and *U.* | 1Ch 7:24

UZZI

Bukki, and Bukki begat *U.* | 1Ch 6:5
U. begat Zerahiah, and | 1Ch 6:6
Zerahiah
Bukki his son, *U.* his son, | 1Ch 6:51
Zerahiah
sons of Tola; *U.* and Rephaiah | 1Ch 7:2
And the sons of *U.*; Izrahiah | 1Ch 7:3
sons of Bela; Ezbon, and *U.* | 1Ch 7:7
and Elah the son of *U.* the | 1Ch 9:8
son of
Zerahiah, the son of *U.* the son | Ezr 7:4
of
was *U.* the son of Bani, | Ne 11:22
the son
Joiarib, Mattenai; of | Ne 12:19
Jedaiah, *U.*
Eleazar, and *U.* and | Ne 12:42
Jehohanan

UZZIA

U. the Ashterathite, Shama | 1Ch 11:44

UZZIAH

the nine and thirtieth year of | 2Ki 15:13
U.
year of Jothan the son of *U.* | 2Ki 15:30
Jotham the son of *U.* to | 2Ki 15:32
reign
to all that his father *U.* had | 2Ki 15:34
done
Uriel his son, *U.* his son, and | 1Ch 6:24
was Jehonathan the son of | 1Ch 27:25
U.
all the people of Judah took | 2Ch 26:1
U.
Sixteen years old was *U.* | 2Ch 26:3
when he
the Ammonites gave gifts to | 2Ch 26:8
U.
U. built towers in Jerusalem | 2Ch 26:9
at
U. had an host of fighting | 2Ch 26:11
men
U. prepared for them | 2Ch 26:14
shields
And they withstood *U.* the | 2Ch 26:18
king
It appertaineth not unto | 2Ch 26:18
thee, *U.*

U. was wroth, and had a | 2Ch 26:19
censer in
U. the king was a leper | 2Ch 26:21
unto the
Now the rest of the acts of | 2Ch 26:22
U. first
So *U.* slept with his fathers | 2Ch 26:23
according to all his father *U.* | 2Ch 27:2
did
and Shemaiah, and Jehiel, | Ezr 10:21
and *U.*
of Judah; Athaiah the son of | Ne 11:4
U.
in the days of *U.* Jotham, Ahaz | Isa 1:1;
| Ho 1:1
In the year that king *U.* died I | Isa 6:1
saw
the son of Jotham the son of | Isa 7:1
U.
in the days of *U.* king of | Am 1:1
Judah
the earthquake in the days of | Zec 14:5
U.

UZZIEL

and Izhar, and Hebron, and | Ex 6:18;
U. | 1Ch 6:18
And the sons of *U.*; Mishael | Ex 6:22
the sons of *U.* the uncle of | Le 10:4
Aaron
and Izehar, Hebron, and *U.* | Nu 3:19
shall be Elizaphan the son of | Nu 3:30
U.
Rephaiah, and *U.* the sons of | 1Ch 4:42
Ishi
Amram, Izhar, and Hebron, | 1Ch 6:2;
and *U.* | 23:12
Ezbon, and Uzzi, and *U.* | 1Ch 7:7
Of the sons of *U.*; | 1Ch 15:10
Amminadab
Of the sons of *U.*; Micah | 1Ch 23:20
the first
Of the sons of *U.*: | 1Ch 24:24
Michah
Bukkiah, Mattaniah, *U.* | 1Ch 25:4
Shebuel
of Jeduthun; Shemaiah, and | 2Ch 29:14
U.
Next unto him repaired *U.* the | Ne 3:8
son

UZZIELITES

and the family of the *U.* | Nu 3:27
the Hebronites, and the *U.* | 1Ch 26:23

V

VACANT

a waste and *v.* void (A) | Jer 4:23

VAGABOND

a *v.* shalt thou be in the earth | Ge 4:12
wanderer (B)(E)(R) | Ge 4:12; 4:14
a fugitive and a *v.* in the earth | Ge 4:14
poverty came as a *v.* (R) | Pr 6:11
Then certain of the *v.* Jews | Ac 19:13
traveling Jewish exorcists | Ac 19:13
(A)(B)
strolling Jews, exorcists | Ac 19:13
(E)(N)
itinerant Jewish exorcists | Ac 19:13
(P)(R)

VAGABONDS

Let his children be | Ps 109:10
continually *v.*

VAGRANT

a *v.* and wanderer (B) | Ge 4:12

VAGUE

be not *v.* (P) | Eph 5:17

VAIN

let them not regard *v.* words | Ex 5:9
lying words (A)(E)(R) | Ex 5:9
trusting in lies (B) | Ex 5:9

take name of Lord thy God in *Ex 20:7*
v.
profanely (B)(R) *Ex 20:7; De 5:11*
ye shall sow your seed in *v.* *Ex 26:16*
your strength shall be spent in *Ex 26:20*
v.
uselessly (B) *Ex 26:20;*
Ps 73:13; M't 15:9; Ga 2:2
take name of the Lord in *v.* *De 5:11*
For it is not a *v.* thing for *De 32:47*
you
empty and worthless trifle *De 32:47*
(A)
meaningless word (B) *De 32:47*
Isa 1:13; Eph 5:6
trifle (R) *De 32:47*
Abimelech hired *v.* and light *J'g 9:4*
persons
worthless and foolhardy men *J'g 9:4*
(A)
lightheaded and foolhardy (B) *J'g 9:4*
worthless and reckless men (R) *J'g 9:4*
were gathered *v.* men to *J'g 11:3*
Jephthah
worthless (A) *J'g 11:3;*
1Sa 12:21; 2Sa 6:20; 2Ch 13:7; Pr 29:19;
Isa 30:7; La 4:17; Jas 1:26
renegades lined up with him *J'g 11:3*
(B)
worthless (R) *J'g 11:3; Job 11:11*
should you go after *v.* *1Sa 12:21*
things. They are *v.*
mere nothings-idols *1Sa 12:21*
he tried in *v.* to go (R) *1Sa 17:39*
in *v.* have I kept all that this *1Sa 25:21*
useless (B) *1Sa 25:21; Jas 1:26*
one of the *v.* fellows *2Sa 6:20*
worthless (B) *2Sa 6:20; Job 11:11*
vulgar (R) *2Sa 6:20*
v. idols (B) *1Ki 16:13; 16:26; Ps 31:6*
became *v.* and went after *2Ki 17:15*
false (A) *2Ki 17:15; Ps 26:4; Eze 13:7*
went after emptiness, *2Ki 17:15*
became empty (B)
false (R) *2Ki 17:15; Ps 26:4*
they are but *v.* words *2Ki 18:20*
empty words (A) *2Ki 18:20; Ps 2:1*
lip service (B) *2Ki 18:20*
mere words (R) *2Ki 18:20*
are gathered unto him *v.* men *2Ch 13:7*
good-for-nothing *2Ch 13:7*
ne'er-do-wells (B)
worthless scoundrels (E)(R) *2Ch 13:7*
wicked, why then labor I in *Job 9:29*
v.
For he knoweth *v.* men: he *Job 11:11*
seeth
useless men (A) *Job 11:11; Mal 3:14*
worthless men (B) *Job 11:11*
false men (E) *Job 11:11*
For *v.* man would be wise, *Job 11:12*
though
stupid man (A)(B)(R) *Job 11:12*
a wise man utter *v.* *Job 15:2*
knowledge
windy knowledge (A)(R) *Job 15:2*
pointless talk (B) *Job 15:2*
unprofitable talk (E) *Job 15:2*
Shall *v.* words have an end *Job 16:3*
futile (A) *Job 16:3;*
21:34; 1Co 3:20; Tit 3:9
empty words (B) *Job 16:3*
windy words (R) *Job 16:3*
How then comfort ye me in *Job 21:34*
v.
falsehood (B)(R) *Job 21:34*
then are ye thus altogether *Job 27:12*
v.
futility (B) *Job 27:12; Jer 2:5*
doth Job open his mouth in *Job 35:16*
v.
uselessly (A) *Job 35:16; M't 15:9*
empty talk (R) *Job 35:16*
her labour is in *v.* *Job 39:16*
unreasonable verbiage (B) *Job 39:16*
the hope of him is in *v.* *Job 41:9*
disappointed (A)(R) *Job 41:9*
disillusioned (B) *Job 41:9*
the people imagine a *v.* thing *Ps 2:1*
imagine an empty scheme (B) *Ps 2:1*
I have not sat with *v.* persons *Ps 26:4*
with deceptive men (B) *Ps 26:4*
men of falsehood (E) *Ps 26:4*
v. idols (A) *Ps 31:6*
An horse is a *v.* thing for *Ps 33:17*
safety
is devoid of value (A) *Ps 33:17*
every man walketh in a *v.* *Ps 39:6*
show

like a shadow in a pantomine *Ps 39:6*
(A)
trouble; for *v.* is the help of *Ps 60:11;*
man *108:12*
become not *v.* in robbery *Ps 62:10*
I have cleansed my heart in *Ps 73:13*
v.
hast thou made all men in *v.* *Ps 89:47*
emptiness, falsity, futility, *Ps 89:47*
frailty (A)
emptiness (B) *Ps 89:47; Jer 51:58*
I hate *v.* thoughts *Ps 119:113*
thoughts of the undecided *Ps 119:113*
in religion-double minded
people (A)
waverers (B) *Ps 119:113*
I hate men of a double *Ps 119:113*
mind (E)(R)
they labour in *v.* that build it *Ps 127:1*
the watchman waketh but in *Ps 127:1*
v.
futile (B) *Ps 127:1;*
1Co 3:20; 15:14, 17, 58; 1Th 2:1
it is *v.* for you to rise up *Ps 127:2*
early
thine enemies take thy name *Ps 139:20*
in *v.*
Surely in *v.* the net is spread *Pr 1:17*
he that followeth *v.* persons *Pr 12:11*
worthless pursuits (A)(R) *Pr 12:11*
he that followeth after *v.* *Pr 28:19*
persons
take the name of my God in *v.* *Pr 30:9*
profane the name of God *Pr 30:9*
(A)(R)
violate the name of God (B) *Pr 30:9*
beauty is *v.* *Pr 31:30*
beauty is passing (B) *Pr 31:30*
cometh in *v.* (B) *Ec 6:4*
increase *v.* glory (A) *Ec 6:11; 12:8*
all the days of his *v.* life *Ec 6:12*
his empty life (B) *Ec 6:12*
Bring no more *v.* oblations *Isa 1:13*
offerings of vanity-emptiness, *Isa 1:13*
falsity, vainglory, and futility (A)
offerings of vanity, *v.* glory *Isa 1:13*
(R)
the Egyptians shall help in *v.* *Isa 30:7*
worthless and empty (R) *Isa 30:7*
they are but *v.* words *Isa 36:5*
mere words (B)(R) *Isa 36:5*
he created it not in *v.* *Isa 45:18*
he created it not a worthless *Isa 45:18*
waste (A)
he created it not a waste *Isa 45:18*
(E)
he created it not a chaos *Isa 45:18;*
(R) *45:19*
Seek ye me in *v.* *Isa 45:19*
Seek ye me for nothing (A) *Isa 45:19;*
Ro 13:4
I have laboured in *v.* and in *Isa 49:4*
v.
they shall not labour in *v.* *Isa 65:23*
after vanity, and are become *v.* *Jer 2:5*
are become fruitless and *Jer 2:5*
worthless (A)
are become worthless (R) *Jer 2:5*
in *v.* have I smitten your *Jer 2:30*
children
Truly in *v.* is salvation hoped *Jer 3:23*
for
thy *v.* thoughts lodge within *Jer 4:14*
thee
grossly offensive thoughts (A) *Jer 4:14*
evil thoughts (R) *Jer 4:14*
in *v.* shalt thou make thyself *Jer 4:30*
fair
the founder melteth it in *v.* *Jer 6:29*
certainly in *v.* made he it *Jer 8:8*
made the law a falsehood (A) *Jer 8:8*
made it a fabrication (B) *Jer 8:8*
a lie (R) *Jer 8:8*
the customs of the people are *Jer 10:3*
v.
are false, empty, and futile *Jer 10:3*
(A)
the customs are false (B)(R) *Jer 10:3*
v. and without profit (B) *Jer 16:19*
they make you *v.* *Jer 23:16*
in *v.* shalt thou use many *Jer 46:11*
none shall return in *v.* *Jer 50:9*
returns not empty-handed *Jer 50:9*
(B)(R)
the people shall labour in *v.* *Jer 51:58*
shall labour for naught (R) *Jer 51:58*
have seen *v.* and foolish things *La 2:14*
seen falsehood and delusion *La 2:14*
(A)

seen an empty vision (B) *La 2:14;*
Eze 12:24
seen deceptive visions (R) *La 2:14*
failed for our *v.* help *La 4:17*
said in *v.* that I would do *Eze 6:10*
this evil
shall be any more a *v.* vision *Eze 12:24*
false, empty, and foolish *Eze 12:24*
vision (A)
false vision (E)(R) *Eze 12:24*
Have ye not seen a *v.* vision *Eze 13:7*
seen false visions (B) *Eze 13:7*
see delusive vision (R) *Eze 13:7*
v. visions (B) *Eze 13:9*
false dreams; they comfort in *Zec 10:2*
v.
they comfort with hot air (B) *Zec 10:2*
an empty consolation (R) *Zec 10:2*
have said, It is *v.* to serve *Mal 3:14*
God
when ye pray, use not *v.* *M't 6:7*
repetition
do not multiply words, *M't 6:7*
repeating the same ones over and
over, heaping up phrases like
Gentiles (A)
do not repeat and repeat like *M't 6:7*
pagans (B)
prayers go babbling on like *M't 6:7*
heathen (N)
rattle off long prayers like *M't 6:7*
pagans (P)
heap up empty phrases like *M't 6:7*
Gentiles (R)
in *v.* they do worship me *M't 15:9;*
M'k 7:7
the people imagine *v.* things *Ac 4:25*
became *v.* in their *Ro 1:21*
imaginations
until their stupid minds were *Ro 1:21*
dark (B)
their thinking ended in futility *Ro 1:21*
(N)(R)
plunged their silly minds still *Ro 1:21*
further (P)
he beareth not the sword in *v.* *Ro 13:4*
the sword without reason (B) *Ro 13:4*
it is not for nothing (N) *Ro 13:4*
every legitimate officer is no *Ro 13:4*
empty (P)
foolish and *v.* things *Ro 14:15*
(A)(E)(R)
thoughts of the wise, they are *1Co 3:20*
v.
arguments of the wise are *1Co 3:20*
futile (N)
are futile (R) *1Co 3:20; 15:17*
unless you have believed in *v.* *1Co 15:2*
without effect and all for *1Co 15:2*
nothing (A)
unlsss you believed baselessly *1Co 15:2*
(B)
faith had no meaning *1Co 15:2;*
behind it (P) *15:14*
bestowed upon me was not *1Co 15:10*
in *v.*
for nothing-fruitless, and *1Co 15:10*
without effect (A)
was not effective (B) *1Co 15:10*
has not proved a barren gift *1Co 15:10*
(P)
then is our preaching *v.* *1Co 15:14*
our preaching amounts to *1Co 15:14*
nothing (B)
preaching is null and void *1Co 15:14*
(N)
your faith is also *v.* *1Co 15:14*
be not raised, your faith is *1Co 15:17*
v.
your faith is mere *1Co 15:17*
delusion-futile, fruitless (A)
your faith has nothing in it *1Co 15:17*
(N)
your faith is futile (P) *1Co 15:17*
your labour is not in *v.* in *1Co 15:58*
the Lord
labor not futile-not wasted *1Co 15:58*
or to no purpose (B)
your labor cannot be lost *1Co 15:58*
(N)
nothing you do for him is *1Co 15:58*
ever lost or wasted (P)
receive not the grace of God *2Co 6:1*
in *v.*
not accept grace without using *2Co 6:1*
it (B)
do not let it go for nothing *2Co 6:1*
(N)
do not fail to use the grace of *2Co 6:1*
God (P)

boasting of you should not be | 2Co 9:3
in v.
be an empty boast | 2Co 9:3
(A)(B)(N)
made void (E) | 2Co 9:3
our pride in you is not | 2Co 9:3
unjustified (P)
I should run, or had run in v. | Ga 2:2
then Christ is dead in v. | Ga 2:21
Christ died groundlessly and | Ga 2:21
to no purpose (A)
Christ has died to no purpose | Ga 2:21
(B)(R)
Christ died for nothing | Ga 2:21
(N)(P)
many things in v.? if it be yet | Ga 3:4
in v.
bestowed upon you labour in | Ga 4:11
v.
wasted my efforts (B) | Ga 4:11
proved to be labor lost (N) | Ga 4:11
efforts over you have been | Ga 4:11
wasted (P)
Let us be desirous of v. glory | Ga 5:26
not be conceited (N)(R) | Ga 5:26
not ambitious of own | Ga 5:26
reputations (P)
man deceive you with v. | Eph 5:6
words
empty excuses and groundless | Eph 5:6
arguments (A)
with meaningless words (B) | Eph 5:6
with empty words (E)(R) | Eph 5:6
deceive you with shallow | Eph 5:6
arguments (N)
let no man fool you on this | Eph 5:6
point, however plausible his
argument (P)
not run in v. neither | Ph'p 2:16
laboured in v.
through philosophy and v. | Col 2:8
deceit
by empty deceitfulness (B)(R) | Col 2:8
by delusive speculations (N) | Col 2:8
spoils your faith through | Col 2:8
intellectualism or high sounding
nonsense (P)
in unto you, that it was not in | 1Th 2:1
v.
not useless and fruitless (A) | 1Th 2:1
was not fruitless (N) | 1Th 2:1
our visit to you was not a | 1Th 2:1
failure (P)
our labour be in v. | 1Th 3:5
fruitless and to no purpose | 1Th 3:5
(A)
labour might not be lost (N) | 1Th 3:5
have turned aside to v. | 1Ti 1:6
jangling
wandered away into v. | 1Ti 1:6
arguments (A)
empty talk (B) | 1Ti 1:6
turned aside into v. talking | 1Ti 1:6
(E)
gone astray in a wilderness of | 1Ti 1:6
words (N)
lost themselves in endless | 1Ti 1:6
words (R)
wandered away into v. | 1Ti 1:6
discussion (R)
avoiding profane and v. | 1Ti 6:20
babblings
irreligious and empty | 1Ti 6:20
discussions (P)
empty and worldly chatter | 1Ti 6:20;
(N)(R) | 2Ti 2:16
avoid the godless mixture of | 1Ti 6:20
contradictory notions (P)
shun profane and v. | 2Ti 2:16
babblings
unholy, empty discussions | 2Ti 2:16
(A)
steer clear of unchristian | 2Ti 2:16
babblings (P)
unruly and v. talkers and | Tit 1:10
deceivers
refractory, senseless talkers | Tit 1:10
(B)
talk wildly and lead men's | Tit 1:10
minds astray (N)
talk nonsense to deceive men's | Tit 1:10
minds (P)
empty talkers and deceivers | Tit 1:10
(R)
they are unprofitable and v. | Tit 3:9
are futile and purposeless (B) | Tit 3:9
steer clear of foolish | Tit 3:9
speculations (N)
steer clear of stupid arguments | Tit 3:9
(P)

unprofitable and futile (R) | Tit 3:9
this man's religion is v. | Jas 1:26
this man's religion is futile | Jas 1:26
(N)
this man's religion is useless | Jas 1:26
(P)
O v. man faith without works | Jas 2:20
is dead
faith is inactive, ineffective, | Jas 2:20
and worthless (A)
faith without works is | Jas 2:20
delinquent (B)
You quibbler, faith is barren | Jas 2:20
(N)(R)
think that the scripture saith in | Jas 4:5
v.
speaks to no purpose (A)(B) | Jas 4:5
your v. conversation | 1Pe 1:18
useless way of living (A) | 1Pe 1:18
useless ways (B) | 1Pe 1:18
v. manner of life (E) | 1Pe 1:18
empty folly of traditional | 1Pe 1:18
ways (N)
ransomed from futile ways | 1Pe 1:18
(P)(R)

VAINGLORY

be done through strife or v. | Ph'p 2:3
do nothing from factional | Ph'p 2:3
motives—through contentiousness,
strife, selfishness or for unworthy
ends—or prompted by conceit and
empty arrogance (A)
not act from factional | Ph'p 2:3
motives or out of vanity (B)
Rivalry and personal vanity | Ph'p 2:3
(N)(P)
Do nothing from selfishness | Ph'p 2:3
or conceit (R)

VAINLY

v. puffed up by his fleshly | Col 2:18
mind
who brags on visions and, | Col 2:18
though empty, is inflated by
his worldly mind (B)
bursting with futile conceit of | Col 2:18
worldly minds (N)
inflated by unspiritual | Col 2:18
imagination (P)
puffed up without reason by | Col 2:18
his sensuous mind (R)

VAJEZATHA

and Arisai, and Aridai, and V. | Es 9:9

VALE

together in the v. of Siddim | Ge 14:3
valley (A)(R) | Ge 14:3; 14:8, 10; 37:14
valley (B) | Ge 14:3; 14:8, 10
with them in the v. of Siddim | Ge 14:8
of Siddim was full of | Ge 14:10
slimepits
sent him out of the v. of | Ge 37:14
Hebron
in the hills, and in the v. and | De 1:7
lowland (A)(E) | De 1:7;
Jos 10:40; 1Ki 10:27; 2Ch 1:15;
Jer 33:13
the foothills (B) | De 1:7; Jos 10:40
the lowland (R) | De 1:7; Jos 10:40
of the south, and of the v. | Jos 10:40
sycomore trees that are in | 1Ki 10:27;
the v. | 2Ch 1:15
the Shephelah (foothills of | 1Ki 10:27
Judah) (B)
the Shephelah (foothills of | 1Ki 10:27;
Judah (R) | 2Ch 1:15; Jer 33:13
the lowland (B) | 2Ch 1:15; Jer 33:13
in the cities of the v. and in | Jer 33:13

VALIANT

v. men, warriors (B) | Jos 1:14
ten thousand men of the | J'g 21:10
most v. (S)
any strong man, or any v. | 1Sa 14:52
man
mighty or courageous man | 1Sa 14:52
(A)
brave and athletic man (B) | 1Sa 14:52
a mighty v. man, and a man | 1Sa 16:18
of war
mighty man of valor (E) | 1Sa 16:18
a man of war (R) | 1Sa 16:18

only be thou v. for me, and | 1Sa 18:17
fight
courageously (A) | 1Sa 18:17
bravely (B) | 1Sa 18:17
said to Abner, Art not thou | 1Sa 26:15
a v. man
All the v. men arose, and | 1Sa 31:12
went all
strengthened, and be ye v. | 2Sa 2:7
where he knew that v. men | 2Sa 11:16
were
be courageous, and be v. | 2Sa 13:28
courageous (A) | 2Sa 13:28; 2Ch 28:6
brave (B) | 2Sa 13:28
he also that is v., whose | 2Sa 17:10
heart
brave (A) | 2Sa 17:10
powerful (B) | 2Sa 17:10
they that are with him are v. | 2Sa 17:10
men
Jehoiada, the son of a v. | 2Sa 23:20
man
worthy man (B) | 2Sa 23:20
eight hundred thousand v. | 2Sa 24:9
men
able-bodied men (B) | 2Sa 24:9
Come in: for thou art a v. | 1Ki 1:42
man
trustworthy man (A) | 1Ki 1:42
a worthy man (E)(R) | 1Ki 1:42
tribe of Manasseh, of v. men | 1Ch 5:18
were v. men of might | 1Ch 7:2
mighty men of valor (A) | 1Ch 7:2; 7:5
powerful heroes (B) | 1Ch 7:2; 7:5
mighty men of valor (E) | 1Ch 7:2;
7:5; 28:1
mighty warriors (R) | 1Ch 7:2;
7:5; 2Ch 13:3
of Issachar were v. men of | 1Ch 7:5
might
They arose, all the v. men | 1Ch 10:12
mighty men (A) | 1Ch 10:12;
11:26; 28:1; Ca 3:7
flighting men (B) | 1Ch 10:12
the son of a v. man | 1Ch 11:22
Also the v. of the armies | 1Ch 11:26
were
mighty warriors (B) | 1Ch 11:26;
2Ch 13:3
mighty men (E)(R) | 1Ch 11:26; Ca 3:7
all the v. men, unto | 1Ch 28:1
Jerusalem
seasoned warriors (R) | 1Ch 28:1
with an army of v. men of | 2Ch 13:3
war
of the Lord, that were v. | 2Ch 26:17
men
men of courage (A) | 2Ch 26:17
courageous men (B) | 2Ch 26:17
men of valor (R) | 2Ch 26:17; 28:6
which were all v. men | 2Ch 28:6
able men (B) | 2Ch 28:6
threescore and eight v. men | Ne 11:6
threescore v. men are about it | Ca 3:7
are about it, of the v. of | Ca 3:7
Israel
the inhabitants like a v. man | Isa 10:13
their v. ones shall cry without | Isa 33:7
they are v. for the truth | Jer 9:3
strong (E) | Jer 9:3; 46:15
Why are thy v. men swept | Jer 46:15
away
the v. men are in scarlet | Na 2:3
waxed v. in fight | Heb 11:34
mighty in war (A)(E)(R) | Heb 11:34
grew powerful in war | Heb 11:34
(B)(N)
became strong men and | Heb 11:34
mighty warriors (P)

VALIANTEST

thousand men of the v. | J'g 21:10
sent the bravest men (A)(R) | J'g 21:10
sent warriors (B) | J'g 21:10

VALIANTLY

enemies: and Israel do v. | Nu 24:18
strength (B) | Nu 24:18
let us behave ourselves v. | 1Ch 19:13
courageously (A) | 1Ch 19:13
keep up courage | 1Ch 19:13
(B)(E)(R)
Through God we shall do v. | Ps 60:12;
108:13
right hand of the Lord | Ps 118:15;
doeth v. | 118:16

VALID

testimony v. (A)   Joh 5:31;
5:32; 8:13, 17
my evidence is v. (P)   Joh 8:14
message by angels was v. (B) Heb 2:2

VALLEY

in the v. (A)(B)(R)   Ge 14:3;
14:8, 10; 37:14
at the v. of Shaveh, which is   Ge 14:17
pitched his tent in the v. of   Ge 26:17
Gerar
Isaac's servants digged in the Ge 26:19
v.
the Canaanites dwelt in the v. Nu 14:25
and pitched in the v. of   Nu 21:12
Zared
from Bamoth in the v. that   Nu 21:20
is in
they went up unto the v. of   Nu 32:9
Eshcol
and came unto the v. of   De 1:24
Eshcol
unto the river Arnon half the De 3:16
v.
So we abode in the v. over   De 3:29
against
in the v. over against   De 4:46
Beth-peor, in
down the heifer unto a rough De 21:4
v.
off the heifer's neck there in De 21:4
the v.
heifer that is beheaded in the De 21:6
v.
and the plain of the v. of   De 34:3
Jericho
he buried him in a v. in the   De 34:6
land of
brought them unto the v. of   Jos 7:24
Achor
place was called, The v. of   Jos 7:26
Achor
was a v. between them and Ai Jos 8:11
that night into the midst of   Jos 8:13
the v.
and thou, Moon, in the v. of   Jos 10:12
Ajalon
the v. and in the borders of   Jos 11:2
Dor
unto the v. of Mizpeh   Jos 11:8
eastward
all the land of Goshen, and   Jos 11:16
the v.
of Israel, and the v. of the   Jos 11:16
same
Baal-gad in the v. of   Jos 11:17
Lebanon
from Baal-gad in the v. of   Jos 12:7
Lebanon
in the mount of the v.   Jos 13:19
And in the v. Beth-aram   Jos 13:27
toward Debir from the v. of   Jos 15:7
Achor
up by the v. of the son of   Jos 15:8
Hinnom
before the v. of Hinnom   Jos 15:8
westward
of the v. of the giants,   Jos 15:8
northward
in the v. Eshtaol, and Zoreah Jos 15:33
the land of the v. have   Jos 17:16
chariots
they who are of the v. of   Jos 17:16
Jezreel
before the v. of the son of   Jos 18:16
Hinnom
the v. of the giants on the   Jos 18:16
north
descended to the v. of   Jos 18:16
Hinnom, to the
Beth-hoglah, and the v. of   Jos 18:21
Keziz
are in the v. of Jiphthah-el   Jos 19:14
to the v. of Jiphthah-el   Jos 19:27
toward the
and in the south, and in the v. J'g 1:9
drive out the inhabitants of   J'g 1:19
the v.
suffer them to come down to J'g 1:34
the v.
he was sent on foot into the J'g 5:15
and pitched in the v. of   J'g 6:33
Jezreel
them, by the hill of Moreh, in J'g 7:1
the v.
Midian was beneath him in the J'g 7:8
v.

of the east lay along in the v. J'g 7:12
like
loved a woman in the v. of   J'g 16:4
Sorek
in the v. that lieth by   J'g 18:28
Beth-rehob
their wheat harvest in the v.   1Sa 6:13
that looketh to the v. of   1Sa 13:18
Zeboim
of Amalek, and laid wait in   1Sa 15:5
the v.
and pitched by the v. of Elah 1Sa 17:2
and there was a v. between   1Sa 17:3
them
of Israel, were in the v. of   1Sa 17:19
Elah
until thou come to the v.   1Sa 17:52
and to
thou slewest in the v. of Elah 1Sa 21:9
were on the other side of the 1Sa 31:7
v.
themselves in the v. of   2Sa 5:18;
Rephaim   5:22; 1Ch 14:9
of the Syrians in the v. of salt 2Sa 8:13
pitched in the v. of Rephaim 2Sa 23:13
some mountain, or into some 2Ki 2:16
v.
Lord, Make this v. full of   2Ki 3:16
ditches
yet that v. shall be filled with 2Ki 3:17
water
He slew of Edom in the v. of   2Ki 14:7
salt
in the v. of the children of   2Ki 23:10
Hinnom
the father of the v. of   1Ch 4:14
Charashim
even unto the east side of the 1Ch 4:39
v.
men of Israel that were in the 1Ch 10:7
v.
encamped in the v. of   1Ch 11:15
Rephaim
spread themselves abroad in   1Ch 14:13
the v.
of the Edomites in the v. of   1Ch 18:12
salt
in array in the v. of   2Ch 14:10
Zephathah
at the end of the v. (S)   2Ch 20:16
themselves in the v. of   2Ch 20:26
Berachah
was called, The v. of   2Ch 20:26
Berachah
went to the v. of salt, and   2Ch 25:11
smote of
at the v. gate, and at the   2Ch 26:9
turning of
in the v. of the son of   2Ch 28:3
Hinnom
fire in the v. of the son of   2Ch 33:6
Hinnom
west side of Gihon, in the v.   2Ch 33:14
even
came to fight in the v. of   2Ch 35:22
Megiddo
out by night by the gate of the Ne 2:13
v.
and entered by the gate of the Ne 2:15
v.
The v. gate repaired Hanun   Ne 3:13
Beer-sheba unto the v. of   Ne 11:30
Hinnom
Lod, and Ono, the v. of   Ne 11:35
craftsmen
The clods of the v. shall be   Job 21:33
sweet
He paweth in the v. and   Job 39:21
rejoiceth
through the v. of the shadow   Ps 23:4
of
smote of Edom in the v. of   Ps 60 title
salt
and mete out the v. of Succoth Ps 60:6;
108:7
Who passing through the v. of Ps 84:6
Baca
ravens of the v. shall pick it   Pr 30:17
out
of nuts to see the fruits of the Ca 6:11
v.
ears in the v. of Rephaim   Isa 17:5
The burden of the v. of vision Isa 22:1
God of hosts in the v. of   Isa 22:5
vision
which is on the head of the   Isa 28:4
fat v.
be wroth as in the v. of   Isa 28:21
Gibeon
Every v. shall be exalted, and Isa 40:4

As a beast goeth down into   Isa 63:14
the v.
v. of Achor a place for the   Isa 65:10
herds to
see thy way in the v. know   Jer 2:23
what
is in the v. of the son of   Jer 7:31
Hinnom
nor the v. of the son of   Jer 7:32;
Hinnom   19:6
but The v. of slaughter   Jer 7:32
they
unto the v. of the son of   Jer 19:2;
Hinnom   19:6
O inhabitant of the v. and   Jer 21:13
rock of
the whole v. of the dead   Jer 31:40
bodies, and
are in the v. of the son of   Jer 32:35
Hinnom
in the cities of the v. and in   Jer 32:44
off with the remnant of their Jer 47:5
v.
v. also shall perish, and the   Jer 48:8
plain
thy flowing v. O backsliding   Jer 49:4
midst of the v. which was full Eze 37:1
of
were very many in the open v. Eze 37:2
v. of the passengers on the   Eze 39:11
east of
shall call it The v. of   Eze 39:11
Hamon-gog
buried it in the v. of   Eze 39:15
Hamon-gog
bow of Israel in the v. of   Ho 1:5
Jezreel
the v. of Achor for a door of Ho 2:15
hope
down into the v. of   Joe 3:2
Jehoshaphat
come up to the v. of   Joe 3:12
Jehoshaphat
multitudes in the v. of   Joe 3:14
decision
Lord is near in the v. of   Joe 3:14
decision
and shall water the v. of   Joe 3:18
Shittim
the stones thereof into the v.   Mic 1:6
in the v. of Megiddon   Zec 12:11
and there shall be a very great Zec 14:4
v.
shall flee to the v. of the   Zec 14:5
mountains
the v. of the mountains shall   Zec 14:5
reach
Every v. shall be filled, and   Lu 3:5
every

VALLEYS

As the v. are they spread   Nu 24:6
forth
and depths that spring out of v. De 8:7
possess it, is a land of hills   De 11:11
and v.
Jordan, in the hills, and in the Jos 9:1
v.
In the mountains, and in the   Jos 12:8
v.
hills, but he is not God of   1Ki 20:28
the v.
they put to flight all them of   1Ch 12:15
the v.
over the herds that were in   1Ch 27:29
the v.
To dwell in the cliffs of the v. Job 30:6
or will he harrow the v.   Job 39:10
after thee
v. also are covered over with Ps 65:13
corn
they go down by the v. unto   Ps 104:8
He sendeth the springs into   Ps 104:10
the v.
of Sharon, and the lily of the Ca 2:1
v.
rest all of them in the   Isa 7:19
desolate v.
choicest v. shall be full of   Isa 22:7
chariots
head of the fat v. of them   Isa 28:1
that are
fountains in the midst of the   Isa 41:18
v.
slaying the children in the v. Isa 57:5
Wherefore gloriest thou in the Jer 49:4
v.
hills, to the rivers, and to the Eze 6:3
v.

the mountains like doves of *Eze 7:16*
the *v.*
in all the *v.* his branches are *Eze 31:12*
fallen
and fill the *v.* with thy height *Eze 32:5*
in thy hills, and in thy *v.* and *Eze 35:8*
in all
hills, to the rivers, and to *Eze 36:4;*
the *v.*   *36:6*
the *v.* shall be cleft, as wax *Mic 1:4*
before

VALOR

mighty man of *v.* (E) *1Sa 16:18*
mighty men of *v.* (A)(E) *1Ch 7:2;*
                                            7:35
men of *v.* (R) *2Ch 26:17; 26:6*

VALOUR

all the mighty men of *v.* and *Jos 1:14*
valiant men, warriors (B) *Jos 1:14*
thereof, and the mighty men of *Jos 6:2*
v.
her soldiers (B) *Jos 6:2*
thirty thousand mighty men of *Jos 6:3*
v.
men of war (B)(E)(R) *Jos 6:3*
him, and all the mighty men *Jos 10:7*
of *v.*
men, all lusty, and all men of *J'g 3:29*
v.
courageous men (A) *J'g 3:29*
healthy and vigorous men (B) *J'g 3:29*
strong, able-bodied men (R) *J'g 3:29*
with thee, and thou mighty *J'g 6:12*
man of *v.*
mighty men of courage (A) *J'g 6:12;*
1Ki 11:28; 1Ch 12:21; 2Ch 14:8; 17:13
mighty hero (B) *J'g 6:12; 1Ch 26:6*
Jephthah was a mighty man *J'g 11:1*
of *v.*
a mighty warrior (A) *J'g 11:1;*
1Ch 7:9, 40; 8:40; 2Ch 32:21
brave hero (B) *J'g 11:1*
mighty warrior (R) *J'g 11:1; 2Ch 32:21*
men from their coasts, men of *J'g 18:2*
v.
brave men (A) *J'g 18:2*
courageous men (B) *J'g 18:2*
able men (R) *J'g 18:2*
men; all these were men of *v. J'g 20:44*
warriors (B) *J'g 20:44*
the sword; all these were *J'g 20:46*
men of *v.*
Jeroboam was a mighty man *1Ki 11:28*
of *v.*
able men (B) *1Ki 11:28; 1Ch 26:30*
very able (R) *1Ki 11:28*
he was also a mighty man in *2Ki 5:1*
v. but
an outstanding man (B) *2Ki 5:1*
a great man (E)(R) *2Ki 5:1*
and all the mighty men of *v. 2Ki 24:14*
men of standing (B) *2Ki 24:14*
mighty men of *v.* famous *1Ch 5:24*
men, and
mighty men of strength of *1Ch 5:24*
mind and spirit (A)
brave warriors (B) *1Ch 5:24;*
7:7, 9, 40
mighty warriors (R) *1Ch 5:24;*
7:7, 9, 11, 40; 8:40
of their fathers, mighty men *1Ch 7:7;*
of *v.*   *7:9, 11*
powerful heroes (B) *1Ch 7:11;*
8:40; 12:21, 25, 28, 30
choice and mighty men of *v., 1Ch 7:40*
chief
of Ulam were mighty men of *1Ch 8:40*
v.
for they were all mighty *1Ch 12:21*
men of *v.*
mighty men of *v.* for the *1Ch 12:25*
war
mighty and brave warriors *1Ch 12:25*
(A)
Zadok, a young man mighty *1Ch 12:28*
of *v.*
eight hundred, mighty men *1Ch 12:30*
of *v.*
for they were mighty men of *1Ch 26:6*
v.
mighty men of ability and *1Ch 26:6;*
courage (A) *26:30-32*
men of great ability (R) *1Ch 26:6*
and his brethren, men of *v. 1Ch 26:30*
men of ability (R) *1Ch 26:30; 26:31-32*

among them mighty men of *1Ch 26:31*
v. at
mighty warriors (B) *1Ch 26:31;*
2Ch 13:3
his brethren, men of *v.* were *1Ch 26:32*
two
men of powers (B) *1Ch 26:32*
men, being mighty men of *v. 2Ch 13:3*
valiant men of war (R) *2Ch 13:3*
all these were mighty men of *2Ch 14:8*
v.
mighty men (B) *2Ch 14:8*
the men of war, mighty men *2Ch 17:13*
of *v.*
mighty courageous warriors *2Ch 17:13*
(B)
with him mighty men of *v. 2Ch 17:14*
three
brave men (B) *2Ch 17:14; 17:16-17*
thousand mighty men of *v. 2Ch 17:16*
Eliada a mighty man of *v. 2Ch 17:17*
mighty men of *v.* out of *2Ch 25:6*
Israel
strong and courageous men *2Ch 25:6;*
(B)   *26:12*
fathers of the mighty men *2Ch 26:12*
of *v.*
cut off all the mighty men *2Ch 32:21*
of *v.*
strong fighting men (B) *2Ch 32:21*
their brethren, mighty men of *Ne 11:14*
v.

VALUABLE

consider my own life *v.* (P) *Ac 20:24*
covenant *v.* by God (N) *Ga 3:17*

VALUATION

valuation (S) *Le 5:15;*
5:18; 6:6; 27:2-8, 13-17, 19, 23; Nu 18:16
at your *v.* (A)(R) *Le 27:2; 27:3*
a deduction shall be made *Le 27:18*
from thy *v.* (S)
according to his *v.* (S) *2Ki 23:35*

VALUATIONS

all thy *v.* (S) *Le 5:25; 27:27*

VALUE

priest, and the priest shall *v. Le 27:8*
him
that vowed shall the priest *v. Le 27:8*
him
evaluate (B) *Le 27:8*
And the priest shall *v.* it, *Le 27:12*
whether
priest shall *v.* it (R)(S) *Le 27:14*
lies, ye are all physicians of *Job 13:4*
no *v.*
worthless physicians (R) *Job 13:4*
is devoid of *v.* (A) *Job 33:17*
of more *v.* than many *M't 10:31*
sparrows
consequence (B) *M't 10:31*
worth more (N) *M't 10:31; Lu 12:7*
more valuable (P) *M't 10:31*
of the children of Israel did *M't 27:9*
did price (P) *M't 27:9*
of more *v.* than many *Lu 12:7*
sparrows
worth more (B)(P) *Lu 12:7*
my life of any *v.* (R) *Ac 20:24*
not steal things of small *v. Tit 2:10*
(A)

VALUED

v. in silver shekels (A)(R) *Le 5:15*
barley seed shall be *v.* at fifty *Le 27:16*
shekels
be *v.* with the gold of Ophir *Job 28:16*
neither shall it be *v.* with *Job 28:19*
pure gold
for what should he be *v.* (B) *Isa 2:22*
the price of him that was *v. M't 27:9*
he is properly *v.* by none (B) *1Co 2:15*

VALUEST

as thou *v.* it, who art the *Le 27:12*
priest, so

VANIAH

V., Meremoth, Eliashib *Ezr 10:36*

VANISH

time they wax warm, they *v. Job 6:17*
they dry up (B) *Job 6:17*
his name *v.* (B) *Ps 41:5*
every one shall *v.* (B) *Isa 2:18*
heavens shall *v.* away like *Isa 51:6*
smoke
marvel and *v.* (B) *Ac 13:41*
be knowledge, it shall *v. 1Co 13:8*
away
pass away (A)(R) *1Co 13:8*
lose its meaning (B) *1Co 13:8*
done away (E) *1Co 13:8*
waxeth old is ready to *v. Heb 8:13*
away
ripe for disappearance and to *Heb 8:13*
be dispensed with altogether
(A)(P)
disappear (N) *Heb 8:13*

VANISHED

v. from the community (B) *Nu 16:33*
memory of them has *v.* (B) *Ps 9:6*
jealousy long since *v.* (B) *Ec 9:6*
the prudent? is their wisdom *Jer 49:7*
v.
is counsel *v.* (A) *Jer 49:7*
wisdom faded (B) *Jer 49:7*
and he *v.* out of their sight *Lu 24:31*
he became invisible (B) *Lu 24:31*

VANISHETH

As the cloud is consumed and *Job 7:9*
v.
cloud dissolves and disappears *Job 7:9*
(B)
for a little time, and then *v. Jas 4:14*
away
disappears (A)(B) *Jas 4:14*
disappearing (N) *Jas 4:14*
dissolving in thin air (P) *Jas 4:14*

VANISHING

finish of the *v.* (A) *2Co 3:13*

VANITIES

me to anger with their *v. De 32:21*
idols (A)(R) *De 32:21; 1Ki 16:13, 26*
worthlessness (B) *De 32:21*
of Israel to anger with *1Ki 16:13;*
their *v.*   *16:26*
vain idols (B) *1Ki 16:13;*
16:26; Ps 31:6
hated them that regard lying *v. Ps 31:6*
vain idols (A) *Ps 31:6*
Vanity of *v.* saith the Preacher *Ec 1:2;*
12:8
vapor of vapors and futility of *Ec 1:2;*
futilities (A)   *12:8*
futility of futilities (B) *Ec 1:2; 12:8*
Preacher, vanity of *v.*: all is *Ec 1:2*
vanity
words there are also divers *v. Ec 5:7*
ruin in a flood of words (A) *Ec 5:7*
images, and with strange *v. Jer 8:19*
foreign idols (A)(B)(R) *Jer 8:19*
the stock is a doctrine of *v. Jer 10:8*
instruction of idols *Jer 10:8*
(A)(B)(E)(R)
any among the *v.* of the *Jer 14:22*
Gentiles
false gods of the nations (A) *Jer 14:22*
fallen gods of the nations (B) *Jer 14:22*
that observe lying *v.* forsake *Jon 2:8*
their
pay regard to false useless and *Jon 2:8*
worthless idols (A)
worthless idols (B) *Jon 2:8*
from these *v.* unto the living *Ac 14:15*
God
foolish and vain things (A) *Ac 14:15*
vain things (E)(R) *Ac 14:15*

VANITY

they followed *v.* and became *2Ki 17:15*
vain
went after emptiness and *2Ki 17:15*
became empty (B)
went after false idols and *2Ki 17:15*
became false (R)
I made to possess months of *Job 7:3*
v.
months of futile suffering (A) *Job 7:3*
months of misery (B)(E) *Job 7:3*
months of emptiness (R) *Job 7:3*

let me alone; for my days are *Job 7:16*
v.
my days are a breath, falsity, *Job 7:16*
futility (A)
my days are fleeting (B) *Job 7:16*
my days are a breath (R) *Job 7:16*
him that is deceived trust in *Job 15:31*
v.
futility (B) *Job 15:31;*
Ps 4:2; 119:37; Ec 5:10; 8:14; Jer 2:5
emptiness (R) *Job 15:31*
for v. shall be his *Job 15:31*
recompense
mischief, and bring forth v. *Job 15:35*
iniquity (A)(E) *Job 15:35; Ps 10:7*
deception (B) *Job 15:35*
evil (R) *Job 15:35*
If I have walked with v. or if *Job 31:5*
my
walked with lies (B) *Job 31:5*
faleshood (E) *Job 31:5;*
Ps 12:2; 24:4; 41:6; Pr 30:8; Jer 13:6, 8
falsehood (R) *Job 31:5;*
Pr 30:8; Eze 13:6
Surely God will not hear v. *Job 35:13*
neither
a baseless cry (B) *Job 35:13*
an empty cry (E)(R) *Job 35:13*
how long will ye love v. and *Ps 4:2*
seek
vain words (A) *Ps 4:2*
under his tongue is mischief *Ps 10:7*
and v.
trouble and sin (B) *Ps 10:7*
mischief and iniquity (E)(R) *Ps 10:7*
They speak v. every one with *Ps 12:2*
his
falsehood (B) *Ps 12:2;*
24:4; 41:6; 144:8; Pr 30:8
utter lies (B) *Ps 12:2 144:8, 11*
hath not lifted up his soul *Ps 24:4*
unto v.
faleshood (A) *Ps 24:4;*
41:6; Pr 30:8; Eze 13:6
what is false (B) *Ps 24:4*
at his best state is *Ps 39:5*
altogether v.
merely breath (A)(B) *Ps 39:5; 39:11*
breath (R) *Ps 39:5;*
62:9; 144:4; Isa 57:13
a moth: surely every man is *Ps 39:11*
v.
as a vapor (B) *Ps 39:11; Pr 21:6*
come to see me. he speaketh v. *Ps 41:6*
empty words (R) *Ps 41:6*
Surely men of low degree are *Ps 62:9*
v.
emptiness, futility, breath (A) *Ps 62:9;*
78:33; 94:11
emptiness (B) *Ps 62:9; Ec 2:23; 7:6*
a breath (R) *Ps 62:9;*
78:33; 94:11; 144:5; Isa 57:13
they are altogether lighter than *Ps 62:9*
v.
their days did he consume in *Ps 78:33*
v.
days disappear like a fog (B) *Ps 78:33*
thoughts of man, that they *Ps 94:11*
are v.
they are futile (A)(B) *Ps 94:11*
mine eyes from beholding v. *Ps 119:37*
Man is like to v.: his days are *Ps 144:4*
as
Whose mouth speaketh v. and *Ps 144:8*
deceit (A)(E) *Ps 144:8; 144:11*
children, whose mouth *Ps 144:11*
speaketh v.
Wealth gotten by v. shall be *Pr 13:11*
wealth acquired rashly (B) *Pr 13:11*
treasures by a lying tongue is a *Pr 21:6*
v.
is a vapor driven to and fro *Pr 21:6*
(A)
a fleeting vapor (R) *Pr 21:6*
that soweth iniquity shall reap *Pr 22:8*
v.
calamity and futility (A) *Pr 22:8*
reap nothing (B) *Pr 22:8*
reap calamity (E)(R) *Pr 22:8*
Remove far from me v. and *Pr 30:8*
lies
V. of vanities, saith the *Ec 1:2;*
Preacher *12:8*
vapor of vapors and futility of *Ec 1:2*
futilities (A)
futility of futilities (A)(B) *Ec 1:2;*
12:8
saith the Preacher, v. of *Ec 1:2;*
vanities *12:8*
saith the Preacher, all is v. *Ec 1:2*

all is futile (B) *Ec 1:2; 2:15; 12:8*
all is v. and vexation of spirit *Ec 1:14;*
2:17
worthlessness and chasing *Ec 1:14;*
wind (B) *2:19*
and, behold, this also is v. *Ec 2:1*
this also is worthless (B) *Ec 2:1; 2:11*
all was v. and vexation of *Ec 2:11*
spirit
in my heart, that this also is v. *Ec 2:15*
all is fruitless (B) *Ec 2:17*
under the sun. This is also v. *Ec 2:19*
This also is v. and a great evil *Ec 2:21*
useless and a great misfortune *Ec 2:21*
(B)
rest in the night. This is also v. *Ec 2:23*
also is v. and vexation of *Ec 2:26;*
spirit *4:16*
above a beast: for all is v. *Ec 3:19*
uselessness (B) *Ec 3:19; 4:7; Isa 41:29*
is also v. and vexation of spirit *Ec 4:4;*
6:9
futility and chasing wind (B) *Ec 4:4;*
4:16
and I saw v. under the sun *Ec 4:7*
This is also v., yea, it is a sore *Ec 4:8*
worthlessness and a sorry *Ec 4:8*
situation (B)
with increase: this is also v. *Ec 5:10*
this is v. and it is an evil *Ec 6:2*
disease
fruitlessness and a hurtful *Ec 6:2*
disease (B)
For he cometh in with v. and *Ec 6:4*
comes in futility (A) *Ec 6:4*
cometh in vain (B) *Ec 6:4*
futile and striving after wind *Ec 6:9*
(B)
be many things that increase *Ec 6:11*
v.
emptiness, falsity, vainglory, *Ec 6:11*
futility (A)
worthlessness (B) *Ec 6:11;*
Isa 40:17; Ho 12:11
laughter of the fool: this is also *Ec 7:6*
v.
have I seen in the days of my *Ec 7:15*
v.
my unproductive existence (B) *Ec 7:15*
they had so done: this is also *Ec 8:10*
v.
this is also ineffective (B) *Ec 8:10*
There is a v. which is done *Ec 8:14*
upon
said that this also is v. *Ec 8:14*
fruitlessness (B) *Ec 8:14*
all the days of the life of thy v. *Ec 9:9*
all the days of futility (A) *Ec 9:9*
your unprofitable days (B) *Ec 9:9*
the sun, all the days of thy v. *Ec 9:9*
be many. All that cometh is v. *Ec 11:8*
nothingness (B) *Ec 11:8; Zec 10:2*
for childhood and youth are *Ec 11:10*
v.
are transitory (B) *Ec 11:10*
all is futility-emptiness, falsity, *Ec 12:8*
vainglory, and transitoriness (A)
offerings of v., vain glory (A) *Isa 1:13*
draw iniquity with cords of v. *Isa 5:18*
cords of iniquity and *Isa 5:18*
falsehood (A)
worthless cords (B) *Isa 5:18*
cords of falsehood (E)(R) *Isa 5:18*
sift the nations with the *Isa 30:28*
sieve of v.
sieve of destruction *Isa 30:28*
(A)(B)(E)(R)
to him less than nothing, and *Isa 40:17*
v.
emptiness, waste, futility, *Isa 40:17*
worthlessness (A)
the judges of the earth as v. *Isa 40:23*
emptiness, falsity, futility *Isa 40:23;*
(A) *41:29; Jer 2:5; Hab 2:13*
look like nothing (B)(R) *Isa 40:23*
they are all v.; their works *Isa 41:29*
are
a delusion (R) *Isa 41:29;*
44:9; Eze 13:8
a graven image are all of *Isa 44:9*
them v.
confusion, chaos, *Isa 44:9*
worthlessness (A)
worthlessness (B) *Isa 44:9; Jer 10:15*
all away: v. shall take them *Isa 57:13*
a breath (E) *Isa 57:13*
of the finger, and speaking v. *Isa 58:9*
every form of false, harsh, *Isa 58:9*
unjust, and wicked speaking (A)

slanderous speech (B) *Isa 58:9*
speaking wickedly (E) *Isa 58:9*
speaking wickedness (R) *Isa 58:9*
they trust in v. and speak lies *Isa 59:4*
emptiness, worthlessness, *Isa 59:4*
futility (A)
trusted in confusion (B) *Isa 59:4*
rely on empty pleas (R) *Isa 59:4*
me, and have walked after v. *Jer 2:5*
went after worthlessness and *Jer 2:5*
became worthless (R)
They are v. and the work of *Jer 10:15*
errors
devoid of worth (A) *Jer 10:15*
worthless (B) *Jer 10:15; 51:18*
our fathers have inherited *Jer 16:19*
lies, v.
emptiness, futility, worthless *Jer 16:19*
things (A)
vain and without profit (B) *Jer 16:19*
they have burned incense to *Jer 18:15*
v.
to false gods (A)(B)(E)(R) *Jer 18:15*
They are v. the work of *Jer 51:18*
errors
worthless, emptiness, falsity, *Jer 51:18*
futility (A)
They have seen v. and lying *Eze 13:6*
Because ye have spoken v. *Eze 13:8*
false and delusive words (A) *Eze 13:8*
empty words (B) *Eze 13:8*
false visions (E) *Eze 13:8;*
13:23; 21:29; 22:28
be upon the prophets that see *Eze 13:9*
v.
empty, false, delusive visions *Eze 13:9*
(A)
vain visions (B) *Eze 13:9*
delusive vision (R) *Eze 13:9; 13:23*
ye shall see no more v. nor *Eze 13:23*
divine
false visions (A) *Eze 13:23;*
21:29; 22:28
illusions (B) *Eze 13:23*
Whiles they see v. unto thee *Eze 21:29*
false visions (B) *Eze 21:29*
false visions (R) *Eze 21:29; 22:28*
seeing v. and divining lies *Eze 22:28*
unto
empty visions (B) *Eze 22:28*
in Gilead? surely they are v. *Ho 12:11*
come to naught, be a mere *Ho 12:11*
waste (A)
come to naught (R) *Ho 12:11;*
Hab 2:13
weary themselves for very v. *Hab 2:13*
exhaust themselves for *Hab 2:13*
nothing (B)
For the idols have spoken *Zec 10:2*
v. and
utter nonsense (R) *Zec 10:2*
creature was made subject to *Ro 8:20*
v.
subject to frailty-futility, *Ro 8:20*
condemned to frustration (A)
brought under bondage of *Ro 8:20*
transitoriness (B)
victim of frustration (N) *Ro 8:20*
subject to futility (R) *Ro 8:20*
walk, in the v. of their mind *Eph 4:17*
uselessness of their ways of *Eph 4:17*
thinking (B)
good-for-nothing notions (N) *Eph 4:17*
blinded in a world of illusion *Eph 4:17*
(P)
futility of their minds (R) *Eph 4:17*
speak great swelling words of *2Pe 2:18*
v.
loud boasts of folly (A) *2Pe 2:18*
utter arrogant nonsense (B) *2Pe 2:18*
utter big, empty words (N) *2Pe 2:18*
high-sounding nonsense (P) *2Pe 2:18*
uttering loud boasts (R) *2Pe 2:18*

VANQUISHED

vanquished (S) *Ex 17:13;*
J'g 8:12; Ps 18:14

VAPOR

but a v. used to rise (B) *Ge 2:6*
man is as a v. (B) *Ps 39:11; Pr 21:6*
is a v. driven to and fro *Pr 21:6*
(A)(R)
v. of vapors (A) *Ec 1:2*

VAPORS

vapor of v. (A) *Ec 1:2*

VAPOUR

rain according to the *v.* *Job 36:27*
thereof
he distils his mist in rain *Job 36:27*
(R)
the cattle also concerning *Job 36:33*
the *v.*
cattle are told of his coming *Job 36:33*
storm (A)(B)(E)
blood, and fire, and *v.* of *Ac 2:19*
smoke
blood, fire, and smoky mist *Ac 2:19*
(B)
blood and fire and drifting *Ac 2:19*
smoke (N)
v. that appeareth for a little *Jas 4:14*
time
You are no more than a mist *Jas 4:14*
(N)
It is like a puff of smoke *Jas 4:14*
visible for a little while and then
dissolving into thin air (P)
you are a mist that appears a *Jas 4:14*
little while and then vanishes (R)

VAPOURS

He causeth the *v.* to ascend *Ps 135:7;*
Jer 10:13; 51:16
who makes the clouds arise *Ps 135:7*
(R)
Fire, and hail; snow and *v.* *Ps 148:8*
lightning, hail, fog and frost *Ps 148:8*
(A)(B)
fire and hail, snow and frost *Ps 148:8*
(R)
he makes the mist rise (R) *Jer 10:13;*
51:16

VARIABLENESS

with whom there is no *v.,* *Jas 1:17*
neither
no variation or shadow of *Jas 1:17*
inconsistency (A)(B)(E)(N)(P)(R)

VARIANCE

a man at *v.* against his *M't 10:35*
father
come to part asunder a man *M't 10:35*
from father (A)
bring division, a man *M't 10:35*
against father (B)
come to set a man against *M't 10:35*
father (N)(P)(R)
v., emulations, wrath, strife *Ga 5:20*
enmity (A)(E)(R) *Ga 5:20*
animosities (B) *Ga 5:20*
quarreling, quarrels (N)(P) *Ga 5:20*
without *v.* (E) *Jas 3:17*

VARIATION

no *v.* of inconsistency *Jas 1:17*
(A)(B)(E)(N)(P)(R)

VARIED

many and *v.* are thy works *Ps 104:24*
(A)
wisdom in all its *v.* forms *Eph 3:10*
(N)
fragmentary and *v.* fashion *Heb 1:1*
(P)
v., alien teachings (A) *Heb 13:9*
God's *v.* grace *1Pe 4:10*
(B)(N)(P)(R)

VARIETIES

v., endowments (A)(N)(R) *1Co 12:4*
v. of service (N)(R) *1Co 12:5*
distinctive *v.* of operations *1Co 12:6*
(A)
v. of things accomplished *1Co 12:6*
(B)
v. of workings (R) *1Co 12:6*

VARIETY

v. of miraculous powers (B) *Heb 2:4*

VARIOUS

various (S) *De 22:9;*
1Ch 29:2; 2Ch 16:14; Ps 78:45; 105:31;
Eze 16:16; 17:3; M't 24:7; M'k 13:8;
Lu 4:40; 2Ti 3:6; Tit 3:3; Heb 9:10;
13:9; Jas 1:2

v. or many colors *Eze 17:3*
(A)(B)(R)
v. diseases (A)(B)(R) *M't 4:24*
v. places (B)(R) *M't 24:7*
v. kinds of tongues *1Co 12:10*
(A)(B)(R)
gift of ecstatic utterances of *1Co 12:28*
v. kinds (N)
v. kinds of tongues (R) *1Co 12:28*
v. evil desires (A)(R) *2Ti 3:6*
v. desires (P) *Tit 3:3*
at *v.* times (B)(R) *Heb 1:1*
v. of miraculous powers *Heb 2:4*
(B)(R)
v. oblutions (B)(N)(R) *Heb 9:10*
v. temptations (A)(R) *Jas 1:2*
distressed by *v.* trials (E)(R) *1Pe 1:6*

VASE

a *v.* of preciousness (A) *Pr 20:15*
v. into honor (P) *Ro 9:21; 9:22*

VASHNI

sons of Samuel: the firstborn *1Ch 6:28*
V.

VASHTI

V. the queen made a feast for *Es 1:9*
bring *V.* the queen before the *Es 1:11*
king
the queen *V.* refused to come *Es 1:12*
unto the queen *V.* according *Es 1:15*
to law
V. the queen hath not done *Es 1:16*
wrong
commanded *V.* the queen to *Es 1:17*
That *V.* come no more *Es 1:19*
before king
he remembered *V.* and what she *Es 2:1*
maiden be queen instead of *V.* *Es 2:4*
and made her queen instead of *Es 2:17*
V.

VASSAL

young men shall be made *v.* *Isa 31:8*
(S)
how is she become a *v.* (S) *La 1:1*

VAST

to point out *v.* extent of sin *Ro 5:20*
(P)

VATS

v. overflowing with new wine *Pr 3:10*
(A)(B)(E)(R)
the *v.* overflow (S) *Joe 2:24; 3:13*

VAULT

v. over a wall (B) *2Sa 22:30*
buried in his own *v.* (B) *2Ch 16:14*

VAULTED

(brothel) *v.* place *Eze 16:24;*
(A)(B)(E)(R) *16:39*

VAUNT

lest Israel *v.* themselves against *J'g 7:2*
Israel boast about themselves *J'g 7:2*
(A)
lest Israel become boastful (B) *J'g 7:2*

VAUNTETH

charity *v.* not itself, is not *1Co 13:4*
puffed
love is not boastful or *1Co 13:4*
vainglorious (A)
love is not out for display *1Co 13:4*
(B)
love is never boastful *1Co 13:4*
(N)(R)
neither anxious to impress *1Co 13:4*
(P)

VAUNTS

who *v.* himself against me *Ps 55:12*
(B)

VEGETABLES

give them *v.* (A)(B)(R)(S) *Da 1:12;*
1:16

VEGETARIANS

be willing to be *v.* (P) *Ro 14:21*

VEGETATION

earth bring forth *v.* (S) *Ge 1:11; 1:12*

VEHEMENT

of fire, which hath a most *v.* *Ca 8:6*
flame
that God prepared a *v.* east *Jon 4:8*
wind
a sultry east wind *Jon 4:8*
(A)(B)(E)(R)
what fear, yea, what *v.* desire *2Co 7:11*

VEHEMENTLY

But he spake the more *v.* If *M'k 14:31*
asserted more insistently *M'k 14:31*
(B)
he insisted and repeated *M'k 14:31*
(N)
protested violently (P) *M'k 14:31*
stream beat *v.* upon that house *Lu 6:48*
torrent broke against that *Lu 6:48;*
house (A) *6:49*
river hurled itself against *Lu 6:48;*
that house (B) *6:49*
storm broke against that *Lu 6:48;*
house (E) *6:49*
river burst against that *Lu 6:48;*
house (N) *6:49*
water swept down upon that *Lu 6:48;*
house (P) *6:49*
stream broke against that *M'k 6:48;*
house (R) *6:49*
which the stream did beat *v.* *Lu 6:49*
v.
Pharisees began to urge him *Lu 11:53*
v.
provoke him to speak (A) *Lu 11:53*
undertook to heckle him *Lu 11:53*
fiercely (B)
assail him fiercely with *M'k 11:53*
questions (N)
press him hard to provoke *Lu 11:53*
him (R)
scribes stood and *v.* accused *Lu 23:10*
him
with all their might accusing *Lu 23:10*
him (B)
pressed the case against him *Lu 23:10*
vigorously (N)
making most violent *Lu 23:10*
accusations (P)

VEIL

therefore she took a *v.* and *Ge 24:65*
and covered her with a *v.* *Ge 38:14*
laid by her *v.* from her, and *Ge 38:19*
put on
And thou shalt make a *v.* of *Ex 26:31*
blue
thou shalt hang up the *v.* *Ex 26:33*
under
bring in thither within the *v.* *Ex 26:33*
v. shall divide unto you *Ex 26:33*
between
shalt set the table without *Ex 26:35*
the *v.*
of the congregation without *Ex 27:21*
the *v.*
the *v.* that is by the ark of the *Ex 30:6*
them, he put a *v.* on his face *Ex 34:33*
took the *v.* off, until he came *Ex 34:34*
out
Moses put the *v.* upon his *Ex 34:35*
face
seat, and the *v.* of the *Ex 35:12*
covering
he made a *v.* of blue, and *Ex 36:35*
purple
sanctuary, the sockets of *Ex 38:27*
the *v.*
skins, and the *v.* of the *Ex 39:34*
covering
and cover the ark with the *v.* *Ex 40:3*
and set up the *v.* of the *Ex 40:21*
covering
northward, without the *v.* *Ex 40:22*
of the congregation before *Ex 40:26*
the *v.*
before the *v.* of the sanctuary *Le 4:6*
before the Lord, even before *Le 4:17*
the *v.*

holy place within the *v.*   Le 16:2
before the
small, and bring it within the   Le 16:12
v.
and bring his blood within   Le 16:15
the *v.*
Only he shall not go in unto   Le 21:23
the *v.*
Without the *v.* of the   Le 24:3
testimony, in
shall take down the covering *v.*   Nu 4:5
of the altar, and within the *v.*   Nu 18:7
Bring the *v.* that thou hast   Ru 3:15
upon
And he made the *v.* of blue   2Ch 3:14
the keepers took away my *v.*   Ca 5:7
stripped me of my mantle   Ca 5:7
(B)(E)(R)
v. that is spread over all   Isa 25:7
nations
v. of the temple was rent in   M't 27:51;
twain   M'k 15:38; Lu 23:45
the curtain (A)(N)(P)(R)   M't 27:51;
   M'k 15:38; Lu 23:45
which put a *v.* over his face,   2Co 3:13
that
the same *v.* untaken away in   2Co 3:14
which *v.* is done away in   2Co 3:14
Christ
read, the *v.* is upon their heart   2Co 3:15
Lord, the *v.* shall be taken   2Co 3:16
away
entereth into that within the   Heb 6:19
v.
into the Holy of Holies (B)   Heb 6:19
in the innermost shrine of   Heb 6:19
heaven (P)
into the inner shrine behind   Heb 6:19
the curtain (R)
after the second *v.* the   Heb 9:3
tabernacle
the second curtain   Heb 9:3
(B)(N)(P)(R)
consecrated for us, through   Heb 10:20
the *v.*
through the curtain   Heb 10:20
(A)(B)(N)(P)(R)

VEILS

and gauze *v.* (B)   Isa 3:19
linen, and the hoods, and the   Isa 3:23
v.

VEIN

Surely there is a *v.* for the   Job 28:1
silver
a mine for silver   Job 28:1
(A)(B)(E)(R)

VENERABLE

v., sensible (A)(B)   Tit 2:2

VENERATED

Israel *v.* it (B)   J'g 8:27

VENGEANCE

v. shall be taken on him   Ge 4:15
sevenfold
execute *v.* (A)(E)(R)(S)   Le 26:25
v. gone out (B)   Nu 16:46
To me belongeth *v.* and   De 32:35
I will render *v.* to mine   De 32:41
enemies
will render *v.* to his   De 32:43
adversaries
retribution (B)   De 32:43;
   J'g 11:36; Ps 149:7; Isa 34:8; 35:4;
   Jer 46:10; 50:28; 51:6, 11; Eze 24:8;
   25:17; Mic 5:15; Na 1:2; 2Th 1:8;
   Heb 10:30
the Lord hath taken *v.* for   J'g 11:36
thee of
Lord hath avenged you (R)   J'g 11:36
from taking *v.* (R)   1Sa 25:26
shall rejoice when he seeth   Ps 58:10
the *v.*
when he sees the fair   Ps 58:10
punishment (B)
Lord God, to whom *v.*   Ps 94:1
belongeth
thou God of retribution (B)   Ps 94:1
O God, to whom *v.* belongeth,   Ps 94:1
shew
thou tookest *v.* of their   Ps 99:8
inventions

avenging (A)   Ps 99:8; Ac 28:4
make them pay for their evil   Ps 99:8
practices (B)
an avenger of their wrong   Ps 99:8
doings (R)
To execute *v.* upon the   Ps 149:7
heathen
he will not spare in the day of   Pr 6:34
v.
when he takes revenge (N)   Pr 6:34
For it is the day of the Lord's   Isa 34:8
v.
your God will come with *v.*   Isa 35:4
I will take *v.* and I will not   Isa 47:3
meet
he put on the garments of *v.*   Isa 59:17
Lord, and the day of *v.* of our   Isa 61:2
God
For the day of *v.* is in mine   Isa 63:4
heart
heart, let me see thy *v.* on   Jer 11:20;
them   20:12
a day of *v.* that he may   Jer 46:10
avenge him
for it is the *v.* of the Lord   Jer 50:15
take *v.* upon her: as she hath   Jer 50:15
declare in Zion *v.* of the   Jer 50:28
Lord
Lord our God, the *v.* of his   Jer 50:28
temple
for this is the time of the   Jer 51:6
Lord's *v.*
v. of the Lord, the *v.* of his   Jer 51:11
temple
thy cause, and take *v.* for   Jer 51:36
thee
require recompense (B)   Jer 51:36
Thou hast seen all their *v.* and   La 3:60
cause fury to come up to   Eze 24:8
take *v.*
the house of Judah by   Eze 25:12
taking *v.*
I will lay my *v.* upon Edom   Eze 25:14
they shall know my *v.* saith   Eze 25:14
taken *v.* with a despiteful   Eze 25:15
heart
great *v.* upon them with   Eze 25:17
furious
carry out my punishment   Eze 25:17
when I shall lay my *v.* upon   Eze 25:17
them
execute *v.* in anger and fury   Mic 5:15
upon
will take *v.* on his adversaries   Na 1:2
For these be the days of *v.*   Lu 21:22
a time of retribution (N)   Lu 21:22
the sea, yet *v.* suffereth not to   Ac 28:4
live
justice will not allow him to   Ac 28:4
live (B)(E)(N)(P)(R)
Is God unrighteous who taketh   Ro 3:5
v.
inflict his wrath (A)(R)   Ro 3:5
when he inflicts punishment   Ro 3:5
(B)
who visiteth with wrath (E)   Ro 3:5
to bring retribution (N)   Ro 3:5
God is unfair to punish us (P)   Ro 3:5
V. is mine; I will repay, saith   Ro 12:19
It is mine to punish (B)   Ro 12:19
for divine retribution (N)   Ro 12:19
in flaming fire taking *v.* on   2Th 1:8
them
do justice upon those who (N)   2Th 1:8
it will bring full justice (B)   2Th 1:8
V. belongeth unto me, I will   Heb 10:30
justice is mine (N)   Heb 10:30
suffering the *v.* of eternal fire   Jude 7
as an exhibit of perpetual   Jude 7
punishment (A)
suffering the punishment of   Jude 7
eternal fire (B)(E)(R)
they paid the penalty in eternal   Jude 7
fire (N)
a permanent warning of the fire   Jude 7
of judgment (P)

VENISON

Esau, because he did eat of   Ge 25:28
his *v.*
game (A)(B)(R)   Ge 25:28;
   27:3, 5, 7, 19, 25, 31, 33
to the field, and take me some   Ge 27:3
v.
went to the field to hunt for *v.*   Ge 27:5
Bring me *v.* and make me   Ge 27:7
savoury

sit and eat of my *v.* that thy   Ge 27:19
soul
to me, and I will eat of my   Ge 27:25
son's *v.*
father arise, and eat of his   Ge 27:31
son's *v.*
where is he that hath taken   Ge 27:33
v. and

VENOM

v. of creatures (B)   De 32:24;
   32:33; Ps 58:4; 140:3
dragons, and the cruel *v.* of   De 32:33
asps
v. of asps (A)(B)(N)(R)   Ro 3:13
full of deadly *v.* (N)   Jas 3:8

VENOMOUS

saw the *v.* beast hang on his   Ac 28:4
hand

VENT

belly is as wine which hath   Job 32:19
no *v.*
v. my wrath on enemies (R)   Isa 1:24

VENTURE

v. to take a nation (B)   De 4:34
v. to set the sale of (A)(S)   De 28:56
a certain man drew a bow   1Ki 20:34;
at a *v.*   2Ch 18:33
without specific aim (B)   1Ki 22:34
v. to converse with thee   Job 4:2
(B)(R)(S)
riches lost by bad *v.*   Ec 5:14
(A)(B)(R)
v. or dare to ask (A)   M't 22:46
did not *v.* to look (A)   Ac 7:32
v. in the theatre (N)(R)(S)   Ac 19:31
not *v.* to speak   Ro 15:18
(A)(E)(N)(R)
we *v.* to class (A)(B)(R)   2Co 10:12
did not *v.* to pronounce   Jude 9
sentence (B)

VENTURED

hath God *v.* to go (S)   De 4:34
my father *v.* his life (S)   J'g 9:17

VENTURING

v. to join (N)   Ac 5:13
v. into theatre (A)   Ac 19:31

VERBIAGE

unreasonable *v.* (B)   Job 39:16

VERDICT

nor turn aside from their *v.*   De 17:11
(A)(B)(R)
my *v.* is to muster nations (A)   Zep 3:8
this is the *v.* (B)   Joh 3:19
drinks *v.* of judgment (A)   1Co 11:29
God's fair *v.* (B)   2Th 1:5

VERIFIED

so shall your words be *v.* and   Ge 42:20
let thy word, I pray thee, be   1Ki 8:26
v.
God of Israel, let thy word   2Ch 6:17
be *v.*

VERIFY

to *v.* the promises (B)   Ro 15:8

VERILY

are *v.* guilty concerning our   Ge 42:21
brother
v. my sabbaths ye shall keep   Ex 31:13
v. thought thou hadst hated   J'g 15:2
her
v. our Lord made Solomon   1Ki 1:43
king
v. she hath no child, her   2Ki 4:14
husband
I will *v.* bring it for full price   1Ch 21:24
my acquaintance are *v.*   Job 19:13
estranged from me
do good, and *v.* thou shalt be   Ps 37:3
fed

v. every man at his best state   *Ps 39:5*
is vanity
v. there is a reward for the   *Ps 58:11*
righteous, *v.* he is a God
that judgeth in earth
v. God hath heard me, hath   *Ps 66:19*
attended
v. I have cleansed my heart   *Ps 73:13*
in vain
v. thou art God that hidest   *Isa 45:15*
thyself
v. it shall be well with thy   *Jer 15:11*
remnant, *v.* I will cause enemy
to entreat
v. I say unto you   *M't 5:18; 5:26;*
6:2, 5, 16; 8:10; 10:15, 23, 42; 11:11;
13:17; 16:28; 17:20; 18:3, 13, 18; 19:23;
28; 21:21, 31; 23:36; 24:2, 34, 47; 25:12,
40, 45; 26:13, 34; M'k 3:28; 6:11; 8:12;
9:1, 41; 10:15, 29; 11:23; 12:43; 13:30;
14:9, 18, 25, 30; 18:25; Lu 4:24; 11:51;
12:37; 13:35; 18:17, 29; 21:32; 23:43
Elias *v.* cometh first and   *M'k 9:12*
restoreth all
nay *v.* let them come and   *Ac 16:37*
fetch us
John *v.* baptized with baptism   *Ac 19:4*
of repentance
am *v.* a man which am a   *Ac 22:3*
Jew, born in Tarsus
I *v.* thought I ought to do   *Ac 26:9*
many times
for circumcision *v.* profiteth if   *Ro 2:25*
thou keep
v. their sound went into all   *Ro 10:18*
the earth
it hath pleased them *v.*   *Ro 15:27*
debtors they are
For I *v.* as absent in body   *1Co 5:3*
V. that, when I preach the   *1Co 9:18*
gospel
For thou *v.* givest thanks   *1Co 14:17*
well
v. righteousness should have   *Ga 3:21*
been
For *v.* when we were with   *1Th 3:4*
you, we
v. he took not on him the   *Heb 2:16*
nature of
Moses *v.* was faithful in all   *Heb 3:5*
his
For men *v.* swear by the   *Heb 6:16*
greater
v. they that are of the sons of   *Heb 7:5*
Levi
For there is *v.* a disannulling   *Heb 7:18*
of the
Then *v.* the first covenant had   *Heb 9:1*
also
For they *v.* for a few days   *Heb 12:10*
chastened
Who *v.* was foreordained   *1Pe 1:20*
before the
him *v.* is the love of God   *1Jo 2:5*
perfected

VERILY, VERILY

v., v. I say unto you   *Joh 1:51;*
5:19, 24-25; 6:26, 32, 47, 53; 8:34, 51,
58; 10:1, 7; 12:24; 13:16, 20-21; 14:12;
16:20, 23
v., v. I say unto thee   *Joh 3:3;*
5:11; 13:38; 21:18

VERITABLE

a *v.* plague (B)   *Ac 24:5*

VERITY

The works of his hands are *v.*   *Ps 111:7*
are truth and justice-faithful   *Ps 111:7*
and right (A)
are faithful and right (B)   *Ps 111:7*
are truth and justice (E)   *Ps 111:7*
are faithful and just (R)   *Ps 111:7*
of the Gentiles in faith and *v.*   *1Ti 2:7*
in faith and truth   *1Ti 2:7*
(A)(B)(E)(R)
in the true faith (N)   *1Ti 2:7*
to believe and know the truth   *1Ti 2:7*
(P)

VERMILION

with cedar, and painted with   *Jer 22:14*
v.
of the Chaldeans portrayed   *Eze 23:14*
with *v.*

VERMIN

v. and mice (B)   *Isa 66:17*

VERSED

who is *v.* in the kingdom   *M't 13:52*
(B)

VERY

made, and, behold, it was *v.*   *Ge 1:31*
good
And Cain was *v.* wroth, and   *Ge 4:5*
very (S)   *Ge 7:13;*
17:23, 26; 20:8; Ex 12:17, 41, 51;
Nu 22:3; De 32:48; Jos 5:11; 9:24;
J'g 10:9; 15:18; 1Sa 17:24; 21:12; 28:15,
20, 21; 31:4; 2Sa 1:26; 1Ch 10:4;
2Ch 28:19; Ne 13:8; Ps 6:3; 10; 38:8;
55:4; 118:18; Eze 27:35; 40:1; Da 6:14;
M't 8:13; 17:6; 21:15; M'k 6:51; 9:6;
Lu 2:9; 1Co 12:11; 2Co 5:5; 7:11
the woman that she was *v.*   *Ge 12:14*
fair
And Abram was *v.* rich in   *Ge 13:2*
cattle in
because their sin is *v.*   *Ge 18:20*
grievous
thing was *v.* grievous in   *Ge 21:11*
Abraham's
the damsel was *v.* fair to   *Ge 24:16*
look upon
and grew until he became *v.*   *Ge 26:13*
great
whether thou be my *v.* son   *Ge 27:21*
Esau or
he said, Art thou my *v.* son   *Ge 27:24*
Esau
Isaac trembled *v.* exceedingly   *Ge 27:33*
they were *v.* wroth, because he   *Ge 34:7*
and *v.* ill favoured and   *Ge 41:19*
leanfleshed
following; for it shall be *v.*   *Ge 41:31*
grievous
v. much, until he left   *Ge 41:49*
numbering
for the famine was *v.* sore,   *Ge 47:13*
so that
and it was a *v.* great   *Ge 50:9*
company
a great and *v.* sore   *Ge 50:10*
lamentation
multiplied, and waxed *v.*   *Ex 1:20*
mighty
only ye shall not go *v.* far   *Ex 8:28*
away
shall be a *v.* grievous murrain   *Ex 9:3*
And in *v.* deed for this cause   *Ex 9:16*
have
cause it to rain a *v.* grievous   *Ex 9:18*
hail
and fire with the hail, *v.*   *Ex 9:24*
grievous
v. grievous were they; before   *Ex 10:14*
them
Moses was *v.* great in the land   *Ex 11:3*
of
and herds, even *v.* much   *Ex 12:38*
cattle
thou shalt beat some of it *v.*   *Ex 30:36*
small
any man die *v.* suddenly by   *Nu 6:9*
him
the people with a *v.* great   *Nu 11:33*
plague
the man Moses was *v.* meek,   *Nu 12:3*
above
the cities are walled, and *v.*   *Nu 13:28*
great
very (S)   *Nu 14:7;*
2Sa 8:8; 12:2; 1Ki 4:29; 7:47; 16 20:2;
2Ch 11:12; 14:14; 16:12
Moses was *v.* wroth, and   *Nu 16:15*
said unto
promote thee unto *v.* great   *Nu 22:17*
honour
had a *v.* great multitude of   *Nu 32:1*
cattle
the Lord was *v.* angry with   *De 9:20*
Aaron
stamped it, and ground it *v.*   *De 9:21*
small
the cities which are *v.* far off   *De 20:15*
from
all the words of this law *v.*   *De 27:8*
plainly
shall get up above thee *v.*   *De 28:43*
high
and thou shalt come down *v.*   *De 28:43*
low

tender among you, and *v.*   *De 28:54*
delicate
But the word is *v.* nigh unto   *De 30:14*
thee
they are a *v.* froward   *De 32:20*
generation
be thou strong and *v.*   *Jos 1:7*
courageous
an heap *v.* far from the city   *Jos 3:16*
Adam
go not *v.* far from the city, but   *Jos 8:4*
be ye
From a *v.* far country thy   *Jos 9:9*
servants
by reason of the *v.* long   *Jos 9:13*
journey
We are *v.* far from you; when   *Jos 9:22*
ye
them with a *v.* great   *Jos 10:20*
slaughter
which remain until this *v.*   *Jos 10:27*
day
with horses and chariots *v.*   *Jos 11:4*
many
there remaineth yet *v.* much   *Jos 13:1*
land
your tents, and with *v.* much   *Jos 22:8*
cattle
iron and with *v.* much   *Jos 22:8*
raiment
Be ye therefore *v.* courageous   *Jos 23:6*
Moab: and Eglon was a *v.* fat   *J'g 3:17*
man
vineyards, with a *v.* great   *J'g 11:33*
slaughter
thou hast brought me *v.* low   *J'g 11:35*
of an angel of God, *v.*   *J'g 13:6*
terrible
the land, and, behold, it is *v.*   *J'g 18:9*
good
hath dealt *v.* bitterly with me   *Ru 1:20*
sin of the young men was *v.*   *1Sa 2:17*
great
Now Eli was *v.* old, and   *1Sa 2:22*
heard all
and there was a *v.* great   *1Sa 4:10*
slaughter
the city with a *v.* great   *1Sa 5:9*
destruction
hand of God was *v.* heavy   *1Sa 5:11*
there
so it was a *v.* great   *1Sa 14:15*
trembling
there was a *v.* great   *1Sa 14:20*
discomfiture
and the people were *v.* faint   *1Sa 14:31*
And Saul was *v.* wroth, and   *1Sa 18:8*
that he behaved himself *v.*   *1Sa 18:15*
wisely
have been to thee-ward *v.*   *1Sa 19:4*
good
but if he be *v.* wroth, then be   *1Sa 20:7*
sure
is told me that he dealeth *v.*   *1Sa 23:22*
subtilly
and the man was *v.* great,   *1Sa 25:2*
and he
But the men were *v.* good   *1Sa 25:15*
unto us
For in *v.* deed, as the Lord   *1Sa 25:34*
God of
him, for he was *v.* drunken   *1Sa 25:36*
that Saul was come in *v.* deed   *1Sa 26:4*
v. pleasant hast thou been   *2Sa 1:26*
unto
there was a *v.* sore battle that   *2Sa 2:17*
day
Then was Abner *v.* wroth for   *2Sa 3:8*
the woman was *v.* beautiful   *2Sa 11:2*
to look
bare unto David, and it was   *2Sa 12:15*
v. sick
and Jonadab was a *v.* subtil   *2Sa 13:3*
man
of all these things, he was *v.*   *2Sa 13:21*
wroth
and all his servants wept *v.*   *2Sa 13:36*
sore
a *v.* great heap of stones   *2Sa 18:17*
upon him
Now Barzillai was a *v.* aged   *2Sa 19:32*
man
for he was a *v.* great man   *2Sa 19:32*
for I have done *v.* foolishly   *2Sa 24:10*
And the damsel was *v.* fair   *1Ki 1:4*
and he also was a *v.* goodly   *1Ki 1:6*
man
and the king was *v.* old; and   *1Ki 1:15*
undersetters were of the *v.*   *1Ki 7:34*
base

to Jerusalem with a *v.* great *1Ki 10:2* train
and *v.* much gold, and *1Ki 10:2* precious
and of spices *v.* great store *1Ki 10:10*
I have been *v.* jealous *1Ki 19:10;* for the Lord *19:14*
he did *v.* abominably in *1Ki 21:26* following
of Israel, that it was *v.* *2Ki 14:26* bitter
the Lord was *v.* angry with *2Ki 17:18* Israel
shed innocent blood *v.* much *2Ki 21:16*
v. able men for the work of *1Ch 9:13*
brought David *v.* much brass *1Ch 18:8*
servant; for I have done *v.* *1Ch 21:8* foolishly
Lord; for *v.* great are his *1Ch 21:13* mercies
sons of Rehabiah were *v.* *1Ch 23:17* many
God in *v.* deed dwell with *2Ch 6:18* men on
with him, a *v.* great *2Ch 7:8* congregation
with a *v.* great company, and *2Ch 9:1*
they carried away *v.* much *2Ch 14:13* spoil
host, with *v.* many chariots *2Ch 16:8*
they made a *v.* great *2Ch 16:14* burning
king of Israel, who did *v.* *2Ch 20:35* wickedly
Lord delivered a *v.* great *2Ch 24:24* host
month, a *v.* great *2Ch 30:13* congregation
had given him substance *v.* *2Ch 32:29* much
and raised it up a *v.* great *2Ch 33:14* height
transgressed *v.* much after *2Ch 36:14* all the
a *v.* great congregation of *Ezr 10:1* men
children: for the people wept *Ezr 10:1* *v.* sore
We have dealt *v.* corruptly *Ne 1:7* against
heart. Then I was *v.* sore *Ne 2:2* afraid
stopped, then they were *v.* *Ne 4:7* wroth
I was *v.* angry when I heard *Ne 5:6* their
And there was *v.* great *Ne 8:17* gladness
therefore was the king *v.* *Es 1:12* wroth
asses, and a *v.* great household *Job 1:3*
saw that his grief was *v.* *Job 2:13* great
the grayheaded and *v.* aged *Job 15:10* men
said, I am young, and ye are *Job 32:6* *v.* old
their inward part is *v.* *Ps 5:9* wickedness
into that *v.* destruction let him *Ps 35:8* fall
a *v.* present help in trouble *Ps 46:1*
v. tempestuous round about *Ps 50:3* him
righteousness O God is *v.* *Ps 71:9* high
us: for we are brought *v.* low *Ps 79:8*
shalt establish in the *v.* *Ps 89:2* heavens
and thy thoughts are *v.* deep *Ps 92:5*
Thy testimonies are *v.* sure *Ps 93:5*
O Lord my God, thou art *v.* *Ps 104:1* great
but a few men in number; *v.* *Ps 105:12*
I am afflicted *v.* much *Ps 119:107*
are righteous and *v.* *Ps 119:138* faithful
Thy word is *v.* pure; *Ps 119:140* therefore
my cry; for I am brought *v.* *Ps 142:6* low
in that *v.* day his thoughts *Ps 146:4* perish
earth: his word runneth *v.* *Ps 147:15* swiftly
a matter separateth *v.* friends *Pr 17:9*
continual dropping in a *v.* *Pr 27:15* rainy
left unto us a *v.* small remnant *Isa 1:9*

hath a vineyard in a *v.* fruitful *Isa 5:1* hill
For yet a *v.* little while, and *Isa 10:25*
the pride of Moab; he is *v.* *Isa 16:6* proud
the remnant shall be *v.* small *Isa 16:14*
dealers have dealt *v.* *Isa 24:16* treacherously
It is not yet a *v.* little while *Isa 29:17*
he will be *v.* gracious unto *Isa 30:19* thee at the
because they are *v.* strong *Isa 31:1*
behold the land that is *v.* far *Isa 33:17* off
up the isles as a *v.* little *Isa 40:15* thing
hast thou *v.* heavily laid thy *Isa 47:6* yoke
thou wouldest deal *v.* *Isa 48:8* treacherously
and extolled, and be *v.* high *Isa 52:13*
Be not wroth *v.* sore, O Lord *Isa 64:9*
thy peace, and afflict us *v.* *Isa 64:12* sore
be ye *v.* desolate, saith the *Jer 2:12* Lord
I am pained at my *v.* heart; *Jer 4:19* my
dealt *v.* treacherously against *Jer 5:11* me
happy that deal *v.* *Jer 12:1* treacherously
breach, with a *v.* grievous *Jer 14:17* blow
Israel hath done a *v.* horrible *Jer 18:13* thing
born unto thee; making him *Jer 20:15* *v.* glad
One basket had *v.* good figs *Jer 24:2*
other basket had *v.* naughty *Jer 24:2* figs
I said, Figs; the good figs, *v.* *Jer 24:3* good
and the evil *v.* evil, that *Jer 24:3* cannot be
until the *v.* time of his land *Jer 27:7* come
wine and summer fruits *Jer 40:12* *v.* much
Egypt is like a *v.* fair heifer *Jer 46:20*
thou art *v.* wroth against us *La 5:22*
against me, even unto this *v.* *Eze 2:3* day
as if that were a *v.* little *Eze 16:47* thing
made *v.* glorious in the *Eze 27:25* midst of
art unto them as a *v.* lovely *Eze 33:32* song
were *v.* many in the open *Eze 37:2* valley
valley; and lo, they were *v.* *Eze 37:2* dry
set me upon a *v.* high *Eze 40:2* mountain
were *v.* many trees on the *Eze 47:7* one side
shall be a *v.* great multitude *Eze 47:9* of fish
the king was angry and *v.* *Da 2:12* furious
the king arose *v.* early in the *Da 6:19* morning
mouth that spake *v.* great *Da 7:20* things
the he goat waxed *v.* great *Da 8:8*
a *v.* great and mighty army *Da 11:25*
army; for his camp is *v.* great *Joe 2:11*
of the Lord is great and *v.* *Joe 2:11*
v. dark, and no brightness in *Am 5:20* it
exceedingly, and he was *v.* *Jon 4:1* angry
people shall labour in the *v.* *Hab 2:13* fire
weary themselves for *v.* *Hab 2:13* vanity
I am *v.* sore displeased with *Zec 1:15*
his staff in his hand for *v.* age *Zec 8:4*
and Zidon, though it be *v.* *Zec 9:2* wise
shall see it, and be *v.* *Zec 9:5* sorrowful
and there shall be a *v.* great *Zec 14:4* valley
But the *v.* hairs of your *M't 10:30* head are
made whole from that *v.* *M't 15:28* hour

child was cured from that *v.* *M't 17:18* hour
was done, they were *v.* sorry *M't 18:31*
a *v.* great multitude spread *M't 21:8* their
they shall deceive the *v.* elect *M't 24:24*
box of *v.* precious ointment *M't 26:7*
began to be sorrowful and *v.* *M't 26:37* heavy
the multitude being *v.* great *M'k 8:1*
ointment of spikenard *v.* *M'k 14:3* precious
be sore amazed, and to be *M'k 14:33* *v.* heavy
v. early in the morning the *M'k 16:2* first
rolled away: for it was *v.* *M'k 16:4* great
of all things from the *v.* first *Lu 1:3*
shake off the *v.* dust from your *Lu 9:5*
Even the *v.* dust of your city, *Lu 10:11* which
But even the *v.* hairs of your *Lu 12:7* head
till thou hast paid the *v.* last *Lu 12:59* mite
heard this, he was *v.* *Lu 18:23* sorrowful
sorrowful: for he was *v.* rich *Lu 18:23*
saw that he was *v.* sorrowful *Lu 18:24*
thou hast been faithful in a *Lu 19:17* *v.* little
were *v.* attentive to hear him *Lu 19:48*
v. early in the morning, they *Lu 24:1* came
indeed that this is the *v.* *Joh 7:26* Christ
was taken in adultery, in the *Joh 8:4* *v.* act
ointment of spikenard, *v.* *Joh 12:3* costly
else believe me for the *v.* *Joh 14:11* works' sake
proving that this is *v.* Christ *Ac 9:22*
he became *v.* hungry, and *Ac 10:10* would
that *v.* worthy deeds are done *Ac 24:2* unto
no wrong, as thou *v.* well *Ac 25:10* knowest
Esaias is *v.* bold, and saith, I *Ro 10:20* was
continually upon this *v.* thing *Ro 13:6*
it is a *v.* small thing that I *1Co 4:3* should
your zeal hath provoked *v.* *2Co 9:2* many
behind the *v.* chiefest *2Co 11:5* apostles
I behind the *v.* chiefest *2Co 12:11* apostles
I will *v.* gladly spend and be *2Co 12:15* spent
Being confident of this *v.* *Ph'p 1:6* thing, that
to esteem them *v.* highly in *1Th 5:13* love
the *v.* God of peace sanctify *1Th 5:23* you
he sought me out *v.* diligently *2Ti 1:17*
at Ephesus, thou knowest *v.* *2Ti 1:18* well
and not the *v.* image of the *Heb 10:1* things
turned about with a *v.* small *Jas 3:4* helm
that the Lord is *v.* pitiful, and *Jas 5:11* of

VESSEL

earthen *v.* wherein it is sodden *Le 6:28*
whether it be any *v.* of wood, *Le 11:32* or
whatsoever *v.* it be, wherein *Le 11:32* any
every earthen *v.* whereinto *Le 11:33* any of
in every such *v.* shall be *Le 11:34* unclean
the birds be killed in an *Le 14:5* earthen *v.*
pot (B) *Le 14:5*
an earthen *v.* over running *Le 14:50* water
And the *v.* of earth, that he *Le 15:12* toucheth
every *v.* of wood shall be *Le 15:12* rinsed in
take holy water in an earthen *Nu 5:17* *v.*

clay jar (B) *Nu 5:17*
And every open *v.* which *Nu 19:15*
hath no
open utensil (B) *Nu 19:15; Ro 9:21*
water shall be put thereto in *Nu 19:17*
a *v.*
a basin (B) *Nu 19:17*
but thou shalt not put any in *De 23:24*
thy *v.*
were sanctified this day in the *1Sa 21:5*
v.
I pray thee, a little water in *1Ki 17:10*
a *v.*
a jar (B) *1Ki 17:10; Ps 2:9*
unto her son, Bring me yet a · *2Ki 4:6*
v.
unto her, There is not a *v.* *2Ki 4:6*
more
them in pieces like a potter's *v.* *Ps 2:9*
like potter's ware (A) *Ps 2:9*
out of mind: I am like a *Ps 31:12*
broken *v.*
like a worn-out utensil (B) *Ps 31:12*
shall come forth a *v.* for the *Pr 25:4*
finer
like an earthen *v.* *Pr 26:23*
(A)(B)(E)(R)
it as the breaking of the *Isa 30:14*
potters' *v.*
bring an offering in a clean *Isa 66:20*
v. into
And the *v.* that he made of *Jer 18:4*
clay was
so he made it again another *Jer 18:18*
v. as
as one breaketh a potter's *v.* *Jer 19:11*
is he a *v.* wherein is no *Jer 22:28*
pleasure
and ye shall fall like a *Jer 25:34*
pleasant *v.*
and put them in an earthen *Jer 32:14*
v. that
hath not been emptied from *Jer 48:11*
v. to *v.*
have broken Moab like a *v.* *Jer 48:38*
wherein
he hath made me an empty *Jer 51:34*
v. he
and fitches, and put them in *Eze 4:9*
one *v.*
pin of it to hang any *v.* *Eze 15:3*
thereon
as a *v.* wherein is no pleasure *Ho 8:8*
carry any *v.* through the *M'k 11:16*
temple
household equipment (A) *M'k 11:16*
an implement (B) *M'k 11:16*
carrying goods (N) *M'k 11:16*
water pots (P) *M'k 11:16*
a candle, covereth it with a *v.* *Lu 8:16*
a basin (N)(P) *Lu 8:16*
kingship *v.* in me (N) *Lu 22:29*
there was set a *v.* full of *Joh 19:29*
vinegar
a jar of vinegar (N) *Joh 19:29*
a bowl of vinegar (P)(R) *Joh 19:29*
he is a chosen *v.* unto me, to *Ac 9:15*
bear
a chosen instrument *Ac 9:15*
(B)(N)(P)(R)
a certain *v.* descending unto *Ac 10:11*
him
a sheet (A)(B)(N)(P)(R) *Ac 10:11;*
10:16; 11:5
the *v.* was received up again *Ac 10:6*
into
saw a vision, A certain *v.* *Ac 11:5*
descend
lump to make one *v.* unto *Ro 9:21*
honour
a vase (P) *Ro 9:21*
to possess his *v.* in *1Th 4:4*
sanctification
his own body (A)(N)(P) *1Th 4:4*
his own wife (B)(R) *1Th 4:4*
he shall be a *v.* unto honour *2Ti 2:21*
utensil (B) *2Ti 2:21*
unto the wife, as unto the *1Pe 3:7*
weaker *v.*
pay honor to the woman's *1Pe 3:7*
body (N)(R)

VESSELS

best fruits in the land in your *Ge 43:11*
v.
sacks (A)(B) *Ge 43:11; 1Sa 9:7*
bags (R) *Ge 43:11*
both in *v.* of wood, and in *v.* *Ex 7:19*
of stone

containers (A)(B) *Ex 7:19*
shall he make it, with all *Ex 25:39*
these *v.*
utensils (A) *Ex 25:39;*
27:3, 19; 30:27, 28; 35:13, 16; 37:24;
38:30; 39:36, 37, 39, 40; 40:10; Le 8:11;
Nu 3:31; 4:10; 1Ch 9:28, 29; 2Ch 24:14;
28:24; 29:18, 19; Eze 40:10; 49:29;
M'k 7:4
utensils (B) *Ex 25:39;*
27:3, 19; 30:27, 28; 35:13, 16; 38:3, 30;
39:36, 37; 40:10; Le 8:11; Nu 3:31; 4:14;
7:1, 85; 1Ki 10:21, 25; 15:15; 1Ch 9:28;
2Ch 24:14; 25:24; 28:24; 29:18, 19; 36:7,
10; 18:19; Da 1:2; M'k 7:4; 2Co 4:7;
2Ti 2:20; Heb 9:21
utensils (R) *Ex 25:39;*
27:3, 19; 30:27, 28; 35:13, 16; 37:24;
38:3, 30; 39:36, 37, 39, 40; 40:10;
Le 8:11; Nu 4:10, 14, 15; 7:1; 1Ch 9:28,
29; 2Ch 24:14; 29:18, 19
v. thereof thou shalt make of *Ex 27:3*
brass
All the *v.* of the tabernacle in *Ex 27:19*
instruments (E) *Ex 27:19;*
39:40; Nu 3:36
And the table and all his *v.* *Ex 30:27*
and the candlestick and his *v.* *Ex 30:27*
And the altar with all his *v.* *Ex 30:28*
and his staves, and all his *v.* *Ex 35:13*
grate, his staves, and all his *Ex 35:16*
he made the *v.* which were *Ex 37:16*
upon
pure gold made he it, and all *Ex 37:24*
the *v.*
And he made all the *v.* of the *Ex 38:3*
altar
all the *v.* thereof made he of *Ex 38:3*
brass
for it, and all the *v.* of the *Ex 38:30*
altar
The table, and all the *v.* *Ex 39:36*
thereof
all the *v.* thereof, and the oil *Ex 39:37*
for
brass, his staves, and all his *v.* *Ex 39:39*
and all the *v.* of the service *Ex 39:40*
of the
articles (B) *Ex 39:40;*
Nu 18:3; 2Sa 8:10; 1Ki 7:45, 47, 48, 51;
8:4; 2Ki 12:13; 25:16; 1Ch 18:10;
2Ch 4:18; 5:5; 9:24; 15:18; Ezr 1:6;
Da 11:8; Re 18:12
hallow it, and all the *v.* *Ex 40:9*
thereof
furniture (A) *Ex 40:9;*
Nu 4:15, 16; 7:1; 1Ch 9:29
furniture (R) *Ex 40:9*
all his *v.* and sanctify the *Ex 40:10*
altar
anointed the altar and all his *Le 8:11*
v.
over all the *v.* thereof, and *Nu 1:50*
over all
furniture (E) *Nu 1:50; 4:15, 16; 7:1*
furnishings (R) *Nu 1:50; 19:18*
tabernacle, and all the *v.* *Nu 1:50*
thereof
the *v.* of the sanctuary *Nu 3:31*
wherewith
all the *v.* thereof, and all that *Nu 3:36*
accessories or instruments *Nu 3:36*
(A)(R)
accessories (B) *Nu 3:36; 4:10*
and the oil *v.* thereof, wherewith *Nu 4:9*
containers (B) *Nu 4:9; M't 25:4*
put it and all the *v.* thereof *Nu 4:10*
within
v. of the ministry (E)(R) *Nu 4:12*
shall put upon it all the *v.* *Nu 4:14*
thereof
the basons, all the *v.* of the *Nu 4:14*
altar
and all the *v.* of the sanctuary *Nu 4:15*
sanctuary, and in the *v.* *Nu 4:16*
thereof
equipment (B) *Nu 4:16;*
1Ch 22:19; 23:26; 28:13
the altar and all the *v.* thereof *Nu 7:1*
the silver *v.* weighed two *Nu 7:85*
thousand
come nigh the *v.* of the *Nu 18:3*
sanctuary
and upon all the *v.* and upon *Nu 19:18*
furniture (B) *Nu 19:18*
and gold, and *v.* of brass and *Jos 6:19*
iron
and the *v.* of brass and of *Jos 6:24*
iron

go unto the *v.* and drink of *Ru 2:9*
that
water jars (B) *Ru 2:9*
for the bread is spent in our *v.* *1Sa 9:7*
bag (B) *1Sa 9:7*
sacks (R) *1Sa 9:7*
the *v.* of the young men are *1Sa 21:5*
holy
food bags and utensils (A) *1Sa 21:5*
the kits (B) *1Sa 21:5*
brought with him *v.* of silver *2Sa 8:10*
articles (B) *2Sa 8:10;*
1Ki 10:25; 1Ch 18:10; 2Ch 9:24;
Re 18:12
and *v.* of gold, and *v.* of *2Sa 8:10*
brass
beds, and basons, and *2Sa 17:28*
earthen *v.*
pottery (B) *2Sa 17:28*
all these *v.* which Hiram *1Ki 7:45*
made
Solomon left all the *v.* *1Ki 7:47*
unweighed
Solomon made all the *v.* that *1Ki 7:48*
silver, and the gold, and the *1Ki 7:51*
v.
holy *v.* that were in the *1Ki 8:4*
tabernacle
Solomon's drinking *v.* were *1Ki 10:21*
of gold
all the *v.* of the house of the *1Ki 10:21*
forest
present, *v.* of silver, and *v.* *1Ki 10:25*
of gold
the Lord, silver, and gold, *1Ki 15:15*
and *v.*
Go, borrow thee *v.* abroad of *2Ki 4:3*
all
even empty *v.*; borrow not a *2Ki 4:3*
few
and shalt pour out into all *2Ki 4:4*
those *v.*
who brought the *v.* to her; and *2Ki 4:5*
to pass, when the *v.* were full *2Ki 4:6*
way was full of garments and *2Ki 7:15*
v.
equipment (A)(R) *2Ki 7:15*
supplies (B) *2Ki 7:15*
any *v.* of gold, or *v.* of *2Ki 12:13*
silver, of the
all the *v.* that were found in *2Ki 14:14*
all the *v.* that were made for *2Ki 23:4*
Baal
cut in pieces all the *v.* of *2Ki 24:13*
gold
all the *v.* of brass wherewith *2Ki 25:14*
they
all these *v.* was without *2Ki 25:16*
weight
articles (A) *2Ki 25:16;*
2Ch 9:24; Re 18:12
the charge of the ministering *1Ch 9:28*
v.
were appointed to oversee *1Ch 9:29*
the *v.*
vessels (S) *1Ch 9:29; 28:14*
and the pillars, and the *v.* of *1Ch 18:8*
brass
all manner of *v.* of gold and *1Ch 18:10*
silver
the holy *v.* of God, into the *1Ch 22:19*
house
any *v.* of it for the service *1Ch 23:26*
thereof
for all the *v.* of service in the *1Ch 28:13*
house
Solomon made all these *v.* in *2Ch 4:18*
great
Solomon made all the *v.* that *2Ch 4:19*
were
holy *v.* that were in the *2Ch 5:5*
tabernacle
the drinking *v.* of king *2Ch 9:20*
Solomon
all the *v.* of the house of the *2Ch 9:20*
forest
v. of silver, and *v.* of gold *2Ch 9:24*
dedicated, silver, and gold, *2Ch 15:18*
and *v.*
made *v.* for the house of the *2Ch 24:14*
Lord
even *v.* to minister, and to *2Ch 24:14*
offer
spoons, and *v.* of gold and *2Ch 24:14*
silver
all the *v.* that were found in *2Ch 25:24*
together the *v.* of the house *2Ch 28:24*
of God
cut in pieces the *v.* of the *2Ch 28:24*
house of

offering, with all the *v.* thereof — 2Ch 29:18
table, with all the *v.* thereof — 2Ch 29:18
Moreover all the *v.* which king — 2Ch 29:19
all kinds of attractive *v.* (A)(E)(R) — 2Ch 32:27
Nebuchadnezzar also carried *v.* of — 2Ch 36:7
goodly *v.* of the house of the Lord — 2Ch 36:10
all the *v.* of the house of God — 2Ch 36:18
destroyed all the goodly *v.* thereof — 2Ch 36:19
their hands with *v.* of silver — Ezr 1:6
Cyrus brought forth the *v.* of — Ezr 1:7
goblets (A)(R) — Ezr 1:7
cups (R) — Ezr 1:7
and ten, and other *v.* a thousand — Ezr 1:10
All the *v.* of gold and of silver were — Ezr 1:11
the *v.* also of gold and silver of the — Ezr 5:14
Take these *v.* go, carry them into — Ezr 5:15
golden and silver *v.* of the house — Ezr 6:5
The *v.* also that are given thee for — Ezr 7:19
silver, and the gold, and the *v.* — Ezr 8:25
and silver *v.* an hundred talents — Ezr 8:26
two *v.* of fine copper, precious as — Ezr 8:27
v. are holy also: and the silver — Ezr 8:28
the silver, and the gold, and the *v.* — Ezr 8:30
and the *v.* weighed in the house — Ezr 8:33
where are the *v.* of the sanctuary — Ne 10:39
the frankincense, and the *v.* — Ne 13:5
I again the *v.* of the house of God — Ne 13:9
they gave them drink in *v.* of gold — Es 1:7
v. being diverse one from another — Es 1:7
v. of bulrushes upon the waters — Isa 18:2
the issue, all *v.* of small quantity — Isa 22:24
the *v.* of cups, even to all the *v.* of — Isa 22:24
clean, that bear the *v.* of the Lord — Isa 52:11
abominable things is in their *v.* — Isa 65:4
they returned with their *v.* empty — Jer 14:3
v. of the Lord's house shall now — Jer 27:16
v. which are left in the house of — Jer 27:18
concerning the residue of the *v.* — Jer 27:19
concerning the *v.* that remain — Jer 27:21
bring again into this place all the *v.* — Jer 28:3
to bring again the *v.* of the Lord's — Jer 28:6
and put them in your *v.* and dwell — Jer 40:10
and shall empty his *v.* and break — Jer 48:12
and all their *v.* and their camels — Jer 49:29
goods (R) — Jer 49:29
all the *v.* of brass wherewith they — Jer 52:18
the brass of all these *v.* was without — Jer 52:20
the persons of men and *v.* of brass — Eze 27:13
part of the *v.* of the house of God — Da 1:2
he brought the *v.* into the treasure — Da 1:2
to bring the golden and silver *v.* — Da 5:2
Then they brought the golden *v.* — Da 5:3
have brought the *v.* of his house — Da 5:23

precious *v.* of silver and of gold — Da 11:8
spoil the treasure of all pleasant *v.* — Ho 13:15
to draw out fifty *v.* out of the press — Hag 2:16
bucketfuls (A) — Hag 2:16
measures (R) — Hag 2:16
gathered the good into *v.* but cast — M't 13:48
baskets (B) — M't 13:48
pails (N) — M't 13:48
barrels (P) — M't 13:48
wise took oil in their *v.* with — M't 25:4
took flasks of oil (B)(N)(P)(R) — M't 25:4
cups, and pots, and brazen *v.* — M'k 7:4
copper bowls (N) — M'k 7:4
basins (P) — M'k 7:4
v. of wrath fitted to destruction — Ro 9:22
agents (B) — Ro 9:22
a lovely vase (P) — Ro 9:22
of his glory on the *v.* of mercy — Ro 9:23
recipients (B) — Ro 9:33
the *v.* of service (S) — 1Co 9:28
have this treasure in earthen *v.* — 2Co 4:7
pots of earthenware (N) — 2Co 4:7; Re 2:27
earthenware jar (P) — 2Co 4:7
are not only *v.* of gold and of silver — 2Ti 2:20
utensils (N) — 2Ti 2:20
and all the *v.* of the ministry — Heb 9:21
as the *v.* of a potter shall they be — Re 2:27
as earthen pots are broken (A)(R) — Re 2:27
as clay jars (B) — Re 2:27
wood, and all manner *v.* of ivory — Re 18:12
manner *v.* of most precious wood — Re 18:12

VESTIBULE

went into the *v.* (A)(R) — J'g 3:23; 1Ki 6:3; 1Ch 28:11
made a *v.* of pillars (B) — 1Ki 7:6
the *v.* of the house (R) — 1Ki 7:12; 2Ch 3:4; 8:12; 15:8; 29:7, 17
the *v.* and the altar (B) — Eze 8:16
the *v.* (B)(R) — Eze 40:7; 40:48, 49; 41:25, 26; 44:3
the outer *v.* (A)(B)(R) — Eze 41:15
gone out into the *v.* (B) — M't 26:71
Solomon's *v.* (B) — Joh 10:23; Ac 3:11; 5:12

VESTMENTS

arrayed him in *v.* (A) — Ge 41:42
forth *v.* for all the worshippers — 2Ki 10:22
And he brought them forth *v.* — 2Ki 10:22

VESTRY

unto him that was over the *v.* — 2Ki 10:22
the wardrobe (B)(R) — 2Ki 10:22

VESTURE

upon the four quarters of thy *v.* — De 22:12
cloak (A)(B)(R) — De 22:12
them, and cast lots upon my *v.* — Ps 22:18
raiment (A)(R) — Ps 22:18
clothing (B) — Ps 22:18; Joh 19:24
as a *v.* shalt thou change them — Ps 102:26
garment (A) — Ps 102:26; Re 19:16
coat (B) — Ps 102:26
garment (E) — Ps 102:26; M't 27:35; Re 19:13, 16
raiment (R) — Ps 102:26
and upon my *v.* did they cast lots — M't 27:35
apparel (A) — M't 27:35
clothes (B)(N)(P) — M't 27:35
garments (B) — M't 27:35
and for my *v.* they did cast lots — Joh 19:24
clothing (A) — Joh 19:24
coat (E) · — Joh 19:24; 19:25

garments (N)(P) — Joh 19:24
as a *v.* shalt thou fold them up — Heb 1:12
mantle (A)(B)(E)(P)(R) — Heb 1:12
cloak (N) — Heb 1:12
clothed with a *v.* dipped in blood — Re 19:13
a robe (A) — Re 19:13
a robe (B)(R) — Re 19:13; 19:16
garment (N) — Re 19:13
cloak (P) — Re 19:13; 19:16
on his *v.* and on his thigh a name — Re 19:16

VESTURES

arrayed him in *v.* of fine linen — Ge 41:42
vestments (A) — Ge 41:42
fine linen garments (B) — Ge 41:42
garments (R) — Ge 41:42

VEX

Thou shalt neither *v.* a stranger — Ex 22:21
wrong (A)(E)(R) — Ex 22:21
not affront or maltreat an alien (B) — Ex 22:21
take a wife to her sister, to *v.* her — Le 18:18
a rival to (A)(B)(E)(R) — Le 18:18
in your land, ye shall not *v.* him — Le 19:33
suppress and mistreat him (A) — Le 19:33
maltreat (B) — Le 19:33
not do him wrong (E)(R) — Le 19:33
V. the Midianites, and smite — Nu 25:17
provoke (A)(B) — Nu 25:17
harass the Midianites (R) — Nu 25:17
For they *v.* you with their wiles — Nu 25:18
tormenting (B) — Nu 25:18
they harass you (R) — Nu 25:18
shall *v.* you in the land wherein — Nu 33:55
constant source of irritation (B) — Nu 33:55
trouble (E) — Nu 33:55; Eze 32:9
how will he then *v.* himself — 2Sa 12:18
harm (A)(B)(R) — 2Sa 12:18
God did *v.* them with all adversity — 2Ch 15:6
plagued (B) — 2Ch 15:6
every sort of distress (R) — 2Ch 15:6
How long will ye *v.* my soul — Job 19:2
torment (B) — Job 19:2
and *v.* them in his sore displeasure — Ps 2:5
troubles, terrifies, confounds (A) — Ps 2:5
terrifies by fury (B)(R) — Ps 2:5
us go up against Judah, and *v.* it — Isa 7:6
harass and terrify (A) — Isa 7:6
harass (B) — Isa 7:6
terrify (R) — Isa 7:6
and Judah shall not *v.* Ephraim — Isa 11:13
they *v.* me (B) — Jer 32:32; 44:3, 8
I will also *v.* the hearts of many — Eze 32:9
cause dismay (B) — Eze 32:9
and awake that shall *v.* thee — Hab 2:7
make you tremble (B)(R) — Hab 2:7
hands to *v.* certain of the church — Ac 12:1
afflict, oppress, torment (A) — Ac 12:1
laid violent hands on (B)(P)(R) — Ac 12:1
attacked (R) — Ac 12:1

VEXATION

shall send upon thee cursing, *v.* — De 28:20
confusion (A)(B)(R) — De 28:20
discomfiture (E) — De 28:20
anxiety and *v.* (R) — 1Sa 1:16
v. and rage (A)(E) — Job 5:2
my *v.* was weighed (A)(B)(E)(R) — Job 6:2
increase thy *v.* (R) — Job 10:17
note trouble, grief, *v.* (A)(R) — Ps 10:14
wicked see with *v.* (B) — Ps 112:10
all is vanity and *v.* of spirit — Ec 1:14
a striving after and feeding on wind (A) — Ec 1:14
chasing after wind (B) — Ec 1:14; 1:17; 2:11, 17; 2:26; 4:4, 6, 16; 6:9

striving after wind (E)(R) Ec 1:14;
1:17; 2:11, 17; 2:26; 4:4, 6, 16; 6:9
that this also is v. of spirit Ec 1:17
searching after wind and Ec 1:17;
feeding on it (A) 2:11, 17, 26; 4:4, 6,
16; 6:9
in more wisdom is v. Ec 1:18
(A)(B)(R)
all was vanity and v. of spirit Ec 2:11
for all is vanity and v. of Ec 2:17
spirit
labour, and of the v. of his Ec 2:22
heart
heart's striving he wearies Ec 2:22
himself (E)
striving of his heart (E) Ec 2:22
strain with which he toils (R) Ec 2:22
his work is v. (A)(B) Ec 2:23
also is vanity and v. of spirit Ec 2:26
This is also vanity and v. of Ec 4:4;
spirit 6:9
full with travail and v. of spirit Ec 4:6
this also is vanity and v. of Ec 4:16
spirit
hath much v. (R) Ps 5:17
shall not be such as was in her Isa 9:1
v.
who was in anguish (A)(B) Isa 9:1
that was in anguish (E)(R) Isa 9:1
shall be a v. only to Isa 28:19
understand
with terror (A) Isa 28:19
unmixed terror (B) Isa 28:19
naught but terror (E)(R) Isa 28:19
and shall howl for v. of Isa 65:14
spirit
anguish of soul (A) Isa 65:14
anguish of spirit (B) Isa 65:14
adding to my v. (B) Eze 8:17

VEXATIONS

but great v. were upon all the 2Ch 15:5
vexing afflictions and 2Ch 15:5
disturbances
many disturbances (B)(R) 2Ch 15:5
task v. (B) Ec 2:23

VEXED

were v. and alarmed (A) Ex 1:12
Egyptians v. us, and our Nu 20:15
fathers
Egyptians dealt evilly with us Nu 20:15
(A)
Egyptians mistreated us (B) Nu 20:15
Egyptians dealt ill with us Nu 20:15
(E)
Egyptians dealt harshly with Nu 20:15
us (R)
that oppressed them and v. J'g 2:18
them
crushed them (B) J'g 2:18
afflicted and oppressed them J'g 2:18
(R)
they v. and oppressed the J'g 10:8
children
trampled upon them (B) J'g 10:8
crushed and oppressed them J'g 10:8
(R)
so that his soul was v. unto J'g 16:16
death
wearied to death (B) J'g 16:16
he turned himself, he v. 1Sa 14:47
them
he made it worse for them 1Sa 14:47
(A)(E)(R)
he conquered them (B) 1Sa 14:47
Amnon was so v. that he fell 2Sa 13:2
sick
troubled (B) 2Sa 13:2;
Ps 6:2,3, 10; Lu 6:18; Ac 5:16
felt frustrated (B) 2Sa 13:2
so tormented (R) 2Sa 13:2
for her soul is v. within her 2Ki 4:27
soul in deep anxiety (B) 2Ki 4:27
soul in bitter distress (R) 2Ki 4:27
of their enemies, who v. them Ne 9:27
distressed (A)(E) Ne 9:27; 2Pe 2:7
made them suffer (R) Ne 9:27
Almighty, who hath v. my Job 27:2
soul
embittered my soul (B) Job 27:2
made my soul bitter (R) Job 27:2
heal me: for my bones are v. Ps 6:2
troubled (B) Ps 6:2; Lu 6:18; Ac 5:16
troubled (E)(R) Ps 6:2;
6:3, 10; Lu 6:18
My soul is also sore v.: but Ps 6:3
thou

---

disturbed (B) Ps 6:3
enemies be ashamed and sore Ps 6:10
v.
greatly dismayed (B) Ps 6:10
v. himself with strife (E) Pr 26:17
rebelled, and v. his holy Isa 63:10
Spirit
grieved (A)(B)(E) Isa 63:10
israel only v. me (B) Jer 32:20
which art infamous and much Eze 22:5
v.
full of tumult (A)(E)(R) Eze 22:5
abounding in rioting (B) Eze 22:5
death by oppression (E) Eze 22:5;
22:29
in thee have they v. the Eze 22:7
fatherless
wronged the fatherless Eze 22:7
(A)(R)
oppressed (B) Eze 22:7; 22:29
and have v. the poor and Eze 22:29
needy
oppressed (R) Eze 22:29
is grievously v. with a devil M't 15:22
miserably, distressingly, M't 15:22
cruelly tormented by a demon
(A)
badly demon possessed (B) M't 15:22;
17:15
tormented by a demon (N) M't 15:22
in a terrible state (P) M't 15:22; 17:15
severely possessed by a M't 15:22
demon (R)
for he is lunatick, and sore M't 17:15
v.
suffers terribly (A)(R) M't 17:15
suffereth grievously (E) M't 17:15
has bad fits (N) M't 17:15
v. at callousness (B) M'k 3:5
that were v. with unclean Lu 6:18
spirits
troubled with unclean spirits Lu 6:18
(N)(P)
v. and indignant (A) Ac 4:2
which were v. with unclean Ac 5:16
spirits
ill or harassed by unclean Ac 5:16
spirits (N)
suffering from evil spirits (P) Ac 5:16
afflicted with unclean spirits Ac 5:16
(R)
v. with the filthy conversation 2Pe 2:7
of
tortured (A)(B)(N)(R) 2Pe 2:7
wearied (B) 2Pe 2:7
sore distressed (E)(R) 2Pe 2:7
shocked by dissolute habits (N) 2Pe 2:7
v. his righteous soul from day 2Pe 2:8
to
suffering spiritual agonies (P) 2Pe 2:8

VEXING

v. him with handiwork De 31:29
(B)(R)
been v. dwellers on (B) Re 11:10

VIAL

Then Samuel took a v. of oil 1Sa 10:1
flask (B) 1Sa 10:1
poured out his v. upon the Re 16:2
earth
bowl (A)(B)(E)(N)(P)(R) Re 16:2;
16:3-4, 8, 10, 12, 17
poured out his v. upon the sea Re 16:3
poured out his v. upon the Re 16:4
rivers
poured out his v. upon the sun Re 16:8
poured out his v. upon the Re 16:10
seat
out his v. upon the great river Re 16:12
poured out his v. into the air Re 16:17

VIALS

and golden v. full of odours Re 5:8
bowls (A)(B)(E)(N)(P)(R) Re 5:8;
15:7; 16:1; 17:1; 21:9
seven golden v. full of the Re 15:7
wrath of
pour out the v. of the wrath Re 16:1
of God
angels which had the seven v. Re 17:1
the seven v. full of the seven Re 21:9
last

VICE

not in v. (N) Ro 13:13
leaven of malice and v. (B) 1Co 5:8

---

sexual v. (A) 2Co 12:2
no sexual v. (A) Eph 3:5
abandoned to v. (N)(P) Eph 4:19
unnatural v. (A)(R) Jude 7
filth of her lewdness and v. Re 17:4
(A)

VICIOUS

attention to a v. tongue (B) Pr 17:4
wrongdoing or v. crime (R) Ac 18:14

VICTIM

made a v. of frustration (N) Ro 8:20

VICTIMIZED

cleverly v. our race (P) Ac 7:19

VICTIMS

hates its v. (R) Pr 26:28
fell v. to poisonous snakes 1Co 10:9
(P)

VICTORIOUS

He is righteous and v. (B)(R) Zep 9:9
I myself was v. (N) Re 3:21

VICTOR'S

a v. wreath (A) 1Th 2:19

VICTORY

to give you v. (B)(R) De 20:4
great v. for Israel (B)(R) 1Sa 14:45
wrought great v. (E)(R) 1Sa 19:5
gave David v. (B)(E)(R) 2Sa 8:6;
8:14; 1Ch 18:6, 13
the v. that day was turned 2Sa 19:2
into
tht Lord, wrought a great v. 2Sa 23:10
and the Lord wrought a 2Sa 23:12
great v.
and the glory, and the v. 1Ch 29:11
the pre-eminence (B) 1Ch 29:11
own arm give v. Ps 44:3
holy arm, hath gotten him the Ps 98:1
v.
holy arm wrought salvation Ps 98:1
(A)(E)
He will swallow up death in Isa 25:8
v.
he send forth judgment unto M't 12:20
v.
Death is swallowed up in v. 1Co 15:54
thy sting? O grave, where is 1Co 15:55
thy v.
v. through our Lord Jesus 1Co 15:57
Christ
the v. that overcometh the 1Jo 5:4
world
I myself won the v. (P) Re 3:21
has won the v. (P) Re 5:5
had gotten the v. over the Re 15:2
beast

VICTUAL

prepared for themselves any Ex 12:39
v.
food (A) Ex 12:39;
1Ki 4:27; 2Ch 11:11
food (B) Ex 12:39;
J'g 20:10; 1Ki 4:27; 2Ch 11:11, 23
provisions (R) Ex 12:39;
J'g 20:10; 1Ki 4:27; 2Ch 11:23
to fetch v. for the people J'g 20:10
that they
provisions (A) J'g 20:10
those officers provided v. for 1Ki 4:27
king
captains in them, and store 2Ch 11:11
of v.
food (R) 2Ch 11:11
he gave them v. in 2Ch 11:23
abundance
supplies (A) 2Ch 11:23

VICTUALS

and Gomorrah, and all their Ge 14:11
v.
provisions (A) Ge 14:11;
Jos 1:11; 9:11; J'g 7:8; 1Sa 22:10;
1Ki 4:7; 11:18

provisions (B)   Ge 14:11;
Jos 1:11; 9:11, 14; 1Sa 22:10; 1Ki 4:7;
                1Ki 11:18
provisions (R)   Ge 14:11;
Jos 1:11; 9:11, 14; 1Sa 22:10; 1Ki 4:7;
                Lu 9:12
nor lend him thy v. for   Le 25:37
increase
food (A)   Le 25:37; Jos 9:14
food (B)   Le 25:37;
De 23:19; 1Ki 4:7; Ne 13:15; Jer 40:5;
     44:17; M't 14:15; Lu 9:12
food (R)   Le 25:37;
1Ki 11:18; Ne 13:15; Jer 40:5;
              M't 14:15
usury of money, usury of v.   De 23:19
people, saying, Prepare you   Jos 1:11
Take v. with you for the   Jos 9:11
journey
provisions (E)   Jos 9:11; 9:14; Lu 9:12
And the men took up their v.   Jos 9:14
the people took v. in their hand   J'g 7:8
any grain (A)(B)(E)(R)   J'g 10:31
and a suit of apparel, and   J'g 17:10
thy v.
your living (A)(R)   J'g 17:10
room and board (B)   J'g 17:10
and gave him v. and gave   1Sa 22:10
provided v. for the king and his   1Ki 4:7
appointed him v. and gave   1Ki 11:18
in the day wherein they sold   1Ki 13:15
v.
the produce (A)   1Ki 13:15
ware or any v. on the sabbath   Ne 10:31
day
captain of the guard gave him   Jer 40:5
v.
for then had we plenty of v.   Jer 44:17
villages, and buy themselves   M't 14:15
v.
food (E)   M't 14:15
food (N)(P)   M't 14:15; Lu 9:12
about, and lodge, and get v.   Lu 9:12

VIEW

What didst thou have in v.   Ge 20:10
(S)
Go v. the land, even Jericho   Jos 2:1
saying, Go up and v. the   Jos 7:2
country
went, and stood to v. afar off   2Ki 2:7
prophets were to v. at   2Ki 2:15
Jericho

VIEWED

And the men went up and v.   Jos 7:2
Ai
and I v. the people, and the   Ezr 8:15
priests
and v. the walls of Jerusalem   Ne 2:13
night by the brook, and v. the   Ne 2:15
wall ·

VIEWS

dared not to show my v. (B)   Job 32:6
do not criticize his v. (B)   Ro 14:1

VIGILANT

husband of one wife, v. sober   1Ti 3:2
Be sober, be v.; because your   1Pe 5:8

VIGILENCE

keep heart with all v. (A)(R)   Pr 4:23

VIGOR

thus v. abated (B)   De 34:7
lost their manly v. (B)(R)   Job 30:2

VIGOROUS

healthy and v. men (B)   J'g 3:29
instruction sound, fit, wise,   Tit 2:8
wholesome, v. (A)

VILE

done a v. thing in Israel (A)   Ge 34:7
thy brother should seem v.   De 25:3
low and worthless (B)   De 25:3
degraded (R)   De 25:3
do not do this v. thing (R)   J'g 19:23
this man do not so v. a thing   J'g 19:24
folly (A)
his sons made themselves v.   1Sa 3:13

bringing a curse upon   1Sa 3:13
themselves (A)(E)
blaspheming (R)   1Sa 3:13
but every thing that was v.   1Sa 15:9
more contemptible (R)   1Sa 15:9
I will yet be more v. than   2Sa 6:22
thus
lower (A)   2Sa 6:22
and reputed v. in your sight   Job 18:3
stupid (A)(B)(R)   Job 18:3
unclean (A)   Job 18:3
worthless and v. (A)(E)   Job 34:18
I am v.; what shall I answer   Job 40:4
thee
eyes a v. person is contemned   Ps 15:4
reprobate (B)(E)(R)   Ps 15:4
shamefully v. (A)   Pr 15:26
send forth a v. odor (A)   Ec 10:1
The v. person shall be no   Isa 32:5
more
fool (A)(B)(E)(R)   Isa 32:5; 32:6
the v. person will speak   Isa 32:6
villainy
she has done v. deeds (R)   Jer 11:15
forth the precious from the   Jer 15:19
v.
will make them like v. figs   Jer 29:17
and consider; for I am   Jer 29:17
become v.   La 1:11
abject (A)   La 1:11
abject, despised (B)   La 1:11
despised (R)   La 1:11
the v. abominations (B)   Eze 8:9
estate shall stand up a v.   Da 11:21
person
contemptuous and   Da 11:21
contemptible person (A)(R)
a disreputable person (B)   Da 11:21
make thy grave; for thou art   Na 1:14
v.
filth upon thee, and make thee   Na 3:6
v.
render you gazingstock   Na 3:6
(A)(B)(R)
took certain v. fellows (S)   Ac 17:5
gave them up unto v. affections   Ro 1:26
shameful (B)   Ro 1:26
dishonorable (R)   Ro 1:26
v. passions (E)   Ro 1:26
Who shall change our v.   Ph'p 3:21
body
humiliation, humiliated   Ph'p 3:21
(A)(B)
lowly (R)   Ph'p 3:21
v. and rebellious (P)   Tit 1:16
everything v., outgrowth of   Jas 1:21
evil (B)
everything v. (B)   Jas 1:27
in also a poor man in v.   Jas 2:2
raiment
shabby, shabbily (A)(B)(R)   Jas 2:2
the v. (N)   Re 21:8

VILELY

of the mighty is v. cast away   2Sa 1:21
defiled (A)(B)(R)   2Sa 1:21

VILENESS

of own desires (N)   Ro 1:24

VILER

men: they were v. than the   Job 30:8
earth

VILEST

when the v. men are exalted   Ps 12:8

VILLAGE

Go into the v. over against   M't 21:2
you
Go your way into the v. over   M'k 11:2
against
went throughout every city and   Lu 8:1
v.
entered into a v. of the   Lu 9:52
Samaritans
them. And they went to   Lu 9:56
another v.
that he entered into a certain   Lu 10:38
v.
And as he entered into a   Lu 17:12
certain v.
Go ye into the v. over   Lu 19:30
against you

same day to a v. called   Lu 24:13
Emmaus
And they drew nigh unto the   Lu 24:28
v.

VILLAGES

out of the v. and out of the   Ex 8:13
fields
houses of the v. which have   Le 25:31
no wall
Heshbon, and in all the v.   Nu 21:25
thereof
towns (A)   Nu 21:25
towns (B)(E)   Nu 21:25; 21:32
they took the v. thereof, and   Nu 21:32
drove
took Kenath, and the v.   Nu 32:4
thereof
the cities and the v. thereof   Jos 13:23
suburbs (B)   Jos 13:23;
13:28; 15:32, 36, 41, 44-47, 51, 54, 57,
59-60, 62; 16:9; 18:24, 28; 19:6-8, 15-16,
22-23, 30-31, 38-39, 48; 21:12; 2Ch 28:18
families, the cities, and their   Jos 13:28
v.
are twenty and nine, with   Jos 15:32
their v.
fourteen cities with their v.   Jos 15:36
sixteen cities with their v.   Jos 15:41
Mareshah; nine cities with   Jos 15:44
their v.
Ekron, with her towns and   Jos 15:45
her v.
that lay near Ashdod, with   Jos 15:46
their v.
Ashdod, with her towns and   Jos 15:47
her v.
Gaza with her towns and her   Jos 15:47
v.
Giloh; eleven cities with   Jos 15:51
their v.
and Zior; nine cities with   Jos 15:54
their v.
Timnah; ten cities with their   Jos 15:57
v.
Eltekon: six cities with their   Jos 15:59
v.
Ribbah; two cities with their   Jos 15:60
v.
En-gedi; six cities with their   Jos 15:62
v.
all the cities with their v.   Jos 16:9
Gaba; twelve cities with their   Jos 18:24
v.
fourteen cities with their v.   Jos 18:28
thirteen cities and their v.   Jos 19:6
Ashan; four cities and their v.   Jos 19:7
all the v. that were round   Jos 19:8
about
twelve cities with their v.   Jos 19:15
families, these cities with   Jos 19:16
their v.
Jordan: sixteen cities   Jos 19:22
with their v.
families, the cities and their   Jos 19:23
v.
twenty and two cities with   Jos 19:30
their v.
families, these cities with   Jos 19:31
their v.
nineteen cities with their v.   Jos 19:38
families, the cities and their   Jos 19:39
v.
families, these cities with   Jos 19:48
their v.
fields of the city, and the v.   Jos 21:12
thereof
The inhabitants of the v.   J'g 5:7
ceased
the inhabitants of his v. in   J'g 5:11
Israel
of fenced cities, and of   1Sa 6:18
country v.
And their v. were, Etam, and   1Ch 4:32
Ain
all their v. that were round   1Ch 4:33
about
fields of the city, and the v.   1Ch 6:56
thereof
dwelt in the v. of the   1Ch 9:16
Netophathites
by their genealogy in their v.   1Ch 9:22
brethren, which were in their   1Ch 9:25
v.
and the cities, and in the v.   1Ch 27:25
and Shocho with the v.   2Ch 28:18
thereof
and Timnah with the v.   2Ch 28:18
thereof

Gimzo also and the *v.* thereof: and   2Ch 28:18

together in some one of the *v.*   Ne 6:2

And for the *v.* with their fields   Ne 11:25

environs (B)   Ne 11:25; 11:27-28, 30-31; 12:28-29

Kiriath-arba, and the *v.* thereof   Ne 11:25

at Dibon, and in the *v.* thereof   Ne 11:25

at Jekabzeel, and in the *v.* thereof   Ne 11:25

Beer-sheba, and in the *v.* thereof   Ne 11:27

at Mekonah, and in the *v.* thereof   Ne 11:28

and in their *v.* at Lachish   Ne 11:30

at Azekah, and in the *v.* thereof   Ne 11:30

Aija, and Beth-el, and in their *v.*   Ne 11:31

and from the *v.* of Netophathi   Ne 12:28

for the singers had builded them *v.*   Ne 12:29

Therefore the Jews of the *v.*   Es 9:19

in the lurking places of the *v.*   Ps 10:8

the field; let us lodge in the *v.* (B)   Ca 7:11

let us lodge among the hennas   Ca 7:11

the *v.* that Kedar doth inhabit   Isa 42:11

encampments (B)   Isa 42:11

go up to the land of unwalled *v.*   Eze 38:11

with his staves the head of his *v.*   Hab 3:14

head of the enemy's hordes (A)   Hab 3:14

head of his warriors (B)(E)(R)   Hab 3:14

went about all the cities and *v.*   M't 9:35

that they may go into the *v.*   M't 14:15

And he went round about the *v.*   M'k 6:6

and into the *v.* and buy themselves   M'k 6:36

he entered, into the *v.* or cities, or   M'k 6:56

he went through the cities and *v.*   Lu 13:22

preached the gospel in many *v.*   Ac 8:25

many Samaritan communities (B)   Ac 8:25

VILLAINS

in the hands of *v.* (B)   Job 16:11

VILLAINY

For the vile person will speak *v.*   Isa 32:6

folly (A)(E)(R)   Isa 32:6; Jer 29:23

fool speak folly (A)   Isa 32:6

they have committed *v.* in Israel   Jer 29:23

a disgraceful thing (B)   Jer 29:23

the price of *v.* (N)   Ac 1:18

full of *v.* (B)(E)(R)   Ac 13:10

misdemeanor or *v.* (A)(E)   Ac 18:14

VINDICATE

to *v.* my holiness (B)   Nu 20:12

who *v.* me is near (B)(R)   Isa 50:8

I will *v.* the holiness (A)(B)   Eze 36:23

wanted to *v.* himself (N)   Lu 10:29

v. soon enough (N)   Lu 18:8

VINDICATED

man full of talk he *v.* (R)   Job 11:2

I shall be *v.* (B)(R)   Job 13:18

wisdom is *v.* by (B)   M't 11:19

thou mightest be *v.* (B)(N)   Ro 3:4

v. by the Spirit (B)(N)(R)   1Ti 3:16

VINDICATING

v. the righteous (R)   1Ki 8:32

VINDICATION

justice and *v.* (A)   Ps 7:6

my judgment of *v.* (B)   Ps 17:2

VINE

dream, behold, a *v.* was before me   Ge 40:9

And in the *v.* were three branches   Ge 40:10

Binding his foal unto the *v.*   Ge 49:11

his ass's colt unto the choice *v.*   Ge 49:11

the grapes of thy *v.* undressed   Le 25:5

the grapes in it of thy *v.* undressed   Le 25:11

eat nothing made of the *v.* tree   Nu 6:4

For their *v.* is of the *v.* of Sodom   De 32:32

Then said the trees unto the *v.*   J'g 9:12

the *v.* said unto them, Should   J'g 9:13

of any thing that cometh of *v.*   J'g 13:14

every man under his *v.* and   1Ki 4:25

to gather herbs, and found a wild *v.*   2Ki 4:39

eat ye every man of his own *v.* and   2Ki 18:31

and *v.* dressers in the mountains   2Ch 26:10

off his unripe grape as the *v.*   Job 15:33

hast brought a *v.* out of Egypt   Ps 80:8

and behold, and visit this *v.*   Ps 80:14

Thy wife, shall be as a fruitful *v.* by   Ps 128:3

to see whether the *v.* flourished   Ca 6:11

breasts shall be as clusters of the *v.*   Ca 7:8

let us see if the *v.* flourish, whether   Ca 7:12

and planted it with the choicest *v.*   Isa 5:2

languish, and the *v.* of Sibmah   Isa 16:8

weeping of Jazer the *v.* of Sibmah   Isa 16:9

wine mourneth, the *v.* languisheth   Isa 24:7

pleasant fields, for the fruitful *v.*   Isa 32:12

as the leaf falleth off from the *v.*   Isa 34:4

and eat ye every one of his *v.* and   Isa 36:16

Yet I have planted thee a noble *v.*   Jer 2:21

degenerate plant of a strange *v.*   Jer 2:21

glean the remnant of Israel as a *v.*   Jer 6:9

there shall be no grapes on the *v.*   Jer 8:13

O *v.* of Sibmah, I will weep for thee   Jer 48:32

What is the *v.* tree more than   Eze 15:2

As the *v.* tree among the trees   Eze 15:6

a spreading *v.* of low stature   Eze 17:6

so it became a *v.* and brought forth   Eze 17:6

this *v.* did bend her roots toward   Eze 17:7

fruit, that it might be a goodly *v.*   Eze 17:8

Thy mother is like a *v.* in thy blood   Eze 19:10

Israel is an empty *v.* he bringeth   Ho 10:1

as the corn, and grow as the *v.*   Ho 14:7

He hath laid my *v.* waste, and   Joe 1:7

The *v.* is dried up, and the fig tree   Joe 1:12

and the *v.* do yield their strength   Joe 2:22

sit every man under his *v.* and   Mic 4:4

out, and marred their *v.* branches   Na 2:2

as yet the *v.* and the fig tree   Hag 2:19

man his neighbour under the *v.*   Zec 3:10

the *v.* shall give her fruit, and   Zec 8:12

neither shall your *v.* cast her fruit   Mal 3:11

v. growers (N)   M't 21:33; M'k 12:2

henceforth of this fruit of the *v.*   M't 26:29

drink no more of the fruit of the *v.*   M'k 14:25

I will not drink of the fruit of the *v.*   Lu 22:18

I am the true *v.* and my Father is   Joh 15:1

of itself, except it abide in the *v.*   Joh 15:4

I am the *v.* ye are the branches: He   Joh 15:5

bear olive berries? either a *v.* figs   Jas 3:12

gather the clusters of the *v.*   Re 14:18

and gathered the *v.* of the earth   Re 14:19

VINEDRESSER

my Father is the *v.* (A)(P)(R)(S)   Joh 15:1

VINEDRESSERS

the land to be *v.* and husbandmen   2Ki 25:12

v. and soil-tillers (A)(B)(R)   2Ki 25:12

plowmen and *v.* (A)(B)(R)   2Ch 26:10

shall be your plowmen and your *v.*   Isa 61:5

the land for *v.* and for husbandmen   Jer 52:16

howl, O ye *v.* for the wheat   Joe 1:11

VINEGAR

no *v.* of wine, or *v.* of strong drink   Nu 6:3

bread, and dip thy morsel in the *v.*   Ru 2:14

my thirst they gave me *v.* to drink   Ps 69:21

As *v.* to the teeth, and as smoke to   Pr 10:26

and as *v.* upon nitre, so is he   Pr 25:20

v. to drink mingled with gall   M't 27:34

took a sponge, and filled it with *v.*   M't 27:48

ran and filled a spunge full of *v.*   M'k 15:36

coming to him, and offering him *v.*   Lu 23:36

there was set a vessel full of *v.*   Joh 19:29

and they filled a spunge with *v.*   Joh 19:29

When Jesus had received the *v.*   Joh 19:30

VINES

offerings of grains and *v.* (B)   Ex 22:29

place of seed, or of figs, or of *v.*   Nu 20:5

A land of wheat, and barley, and *v.*   De 8:8

He destroyed their *v.* with hail   Ps 78:47

He smote their *v.* also and their fig   Ps 105:33

the *v.* with the tender grape give a   Ca 2:13

v. blossom, bloom (B)(R)   Ca 2:13; 2:15; 7:12

the little foxes, that spoil the *v.*   Ca 2:15

for our *v.* have tender grapes   Ca 2:15

were a thousand *v.* at a thousand   Isa 7:23

they shall eat up thy *v.* and thy fig   Jer 5:17

yet plant *v.* upon the mountains   Jer 31:5

destroy her *v.* and her fig trees   Ho 2:12

neither shall fruit be in the *v.*   Hab 3:17

VINEYARD

husbandman, and he planted a *v.*   Ge 9:20

he planted a *v.* (A)(B)   Ge 9:20

shall cause a field or *v.* to be eaten   Ex 22:5

of the best of his own *v.* shall   Ex 22:5

manner thou shalt deal with thy *v.*   Ex 23:11

And thou shalt not glean thy *v.*   Le 19:10

thou gather every grape of thy *v.*   Le 19:10

six years thou shalt prune thy *Le 25:3*
v.
sow thy field, nor prune thy v. *Le 25:4*
man is he that hath planted a *De 20:6*
v.
Thou shalt not sow thy v. *De 22:9*
and the fruit of thy v. be *De 22:9*
defiled
thou comest into thy *De 23:24*
neighbour's v.
thou gatherest the grapes of *De 24:21*
thy v.
thou shalt plant a v. and *De 28:30*
shalt not
that Naboth the Jezreelite *1Ki 21:1*
had a v.
Give me thy v. that I may *1Ki 21:2*
have it
give thee for it a better v. *1Ki 21:2*
than it
Give me thy v. for money; or *1Ki 21:6*
else
I will give thee another v. for *1Ki 21:6*
it
I will not give thee my v. *1Ki 21:6*
I will give thee the v. of *1Ki 21:7*
Naboth
take possession of the v. of *1Ki 21:15*
Naboth
up to go down to the v. of *1Ki 21:16*
Naboth
behold, he is in the v. of *1Ki 21:18*
Naboth
the v. which thy right hand *Ps 80:15*
hath
and by the v. of the man void *Pr 24:30*
fruit of her hands she *Pr 31:16*
planteth a v.
but mine own v. have I not *Ca 1:6*
kept
Solomon had a v. at *Ca 8:11*
Baal-hamon
he let out the v. unto keepers *Ca 8:11*
My v. which is mine, is before *Ca 8:12*
me
of Zion is left as a cottage in a *Isa 1:8*
v.
ye have eaten up the v.; the *Isa 3:14*
spoil
song of my beloved touching *Isa 5:1*
his v.
hath a v. in a very fruitful hill *Isa 5:1*
I pray you, betwixt me and my *Isa 5:3*
v.
have been done more to my v. *Isa 5:4*
tell you what I will do to my v. *Isa 5:5*
v. of the Lord of hosts is the *Isa 5:7*
house
ten acres of v. shall yield one *Isa 5:10*
bath
sing ye unto her. A v. of red *Isa 27:2*
wine
Many pastors have destroyed *Jer 12:10*
my v.
house, nor sow seed, nor plant *Jer 35:7*
v.
neither have we v. nor field, *Jer 35:9*
nor
the field, and as plantings of a *Mic 1:6*
v.
to hire labourers into his v. *M't 20:1*
a day, he sent them into his *M't 20:2*
v.
unto them; Go ye also into *M't 20:4*
the v.
unto them, Go ye also into *M't 20:7*
the v.
the lord of the v. saith unto *M't 20:8*
his
said, Son, go work to day in *M't 21:28*
my v.
householder, which planted *M't 21:33*
a v.
cast him out of the v. and *M't 21:39*
slew him
the lord therefore of the v. *M't 21:40*
cometh
and will let out his v. unto *M't 21:41*
other
A certain man planted a v. *M'k 12:1*
and set
husbandmen, of the fruit of *M'k 12:2*
the v.
him, and cast him out of the *M'k 12:8*
v.
shall therefore the lord of the *M'k 12:9*
v. do
and will give the v. unto *M'k 12:9*
others

man had a fig tree planted in *Lu 13:6*
his v.
said he unto the dresser of his *Lu 13:7*
v.
A certain man planted a v. *Lu 20:9*
and let
give him of the fruit of the v. *Lu 20:10*
Then said the lord of the v., *Lu 20:13*
What
So they cast him out of the *Lu 20:15*
v. and
shall the lord of the v. do *Lu 20:15*
unto
and shall give the v. to others *Lu 20:16*
who planteth a v. and eateth *1Co 9:7*
not of

VINEYARDS

us inheritance of fields and *Nu 16:14*
v.
the fields, or through the v. *Nu 20:17*
turn into the fields, or into *Nu 21:22*
the v.
the Lord stood in a path of *Nu 22:24*
the v.
v. and olive trees, which thou *De 6:11*
Thou shalt plant v. and dress *De 28:39*
v. and oliveyards which ye *Jos 24:13*
planted
and gathered their v. and *J'g 9:27*
trode the
cities, and unto the plain of *J'g 11:33*
the v.
and came to the v. of Timnath *J'g 14:5*
corn, with the v. and olives *J'g 15:5*
saying, Go and lie in wait in *J'g 21:20*
the v.
then come ye out of the v. *J'g 21:21*
will take your fields, and your *1Sa 8:14*
v.
tenth of your seed, and of *1Sa 8:15*
your v.
give every one of you fields *1Sa 22:7*
and v.
garments, and oliveyards, and *2Ki 5:26*
v.
and wine, a land of bread *2Ki 18:32*
and v.
year sow ye, and reap, and *2Ki 19:29*
plant v.
the v. was Shimei the *1Ch 27:27*
Ramathite
over the increase of the v. *1Ch 27:27*
for the
We have mortgaged our lands, *Ne 5:3*
v.
and that upon our lands and v. *Ne 5:4*
other men have our lands and *Ne 5:5*
v.
even this day, their lands, their *Ne 5:11*
v.
wells digged, v. and oliveyards *Ne 9:25*
he beholdeth not the way of *Job 24:18*
the v.
And sow the fields, and *Ps 107:37*
plant v.
me houses; I planted me v. *Ec 2:4*
they made me the keeper of the *Ca 1:6*
v.
of camphire in the v. of *Ca 1:14*
En-gedi
Let us get up early to the v.: *Ca 7:12*
let us
in the v. there shall be no *Isa 16:10*
singing
and wine, a land of bread *Isa 36:17*
and v.
plant v. and eat the fruit *Isa 37:30*
thereof
they shall plant v. and eat *Isa 65:21*
the fruit
and v. shall be possessed *Jer 32:15*
again in
gave them v. and fields at the *Jer 39:10*
same
shall build houses, and plant *Eze 28:26*
v.
I will give her her v. from *Ho 2:15*
thence
when your gardens and your v. *Am 4:9*
ye have planted pleasant v. *Am 5:11*
but ye
And in all v. shall be wailing, *Am 5:17*
for I
and they shall plant v. and *Am 9:14*
drink
they shall plant v. but not *Zep 1:13*
drink

VINTAGE

threshing shall reach unto the *Le 26:5*
v.
the v. shall reach unto the *Le 26:5*
sowing
better than the v. of Abi-ezer *J'g 8:2*
they gather the v. of the *Job 24:6*
wicked
I have made their v. shouting *Isa 16:10*
to
grapes when the v. is done *Isa 24:13*
for the v. shall fail, the *Isa 32:10*
gathering
summer fruits and upon thy *Jer 48:32*
v.
as the grapegleanings of the v. *Mic 7:1*
the forest of the v. is come *Zec 11:2*
down

VIOL

And the harp, and the v. the *Isa 5:12*
That chant to the sound of the *Am 6:5*
v.

VIOLATE

do not v. rights of the *De 24:17*
immigrant or orphan (B)
v. the name of God (B) *Pr 30:9*
v. sanctity of sabbaths (A) *M't 12:5*

VIOLATED

v. dedicated portion (B) *Jos 7:1*
v. my covenant (B) *Jos 7:15; J'g 2:20*
v. father's couch (B) *1Ch 5:1*
v. your law (B) *Ps 119:126*
Her priests have v. my law *Eze 22:26*
v. law of Moses (R) *Heb 10:28*

VIOLATES

v. rights of immigrant (B) *De 24:17*

VIOLATING

v. sacred things (B) *1Ch 2:7*

VIOLATION

v. of his will (A) *Ezr 9:4*
in v. of the law (A) *Ac 18:13*
convicted as v. (A) *Jas 2:9*

VIOLENCE

and the earth was filled with *Ge 6:11*
v.
filled with lust and power *Ge 6:11;*
(B)   *6:13*
the earth is filled with v. *Ge 6:13*
through
implements of v. *Ge 49:5*
(A)(B)(E)(R)
or in a thing taken away *Le 6:2*
by v. or
robbery (A)(B)(E)(R) *Le 6:2;*
                         Eze 18:7, 12, 16, 18
saviour; thou savest me from *2Sa 22:3*
v.
Saviour from harm (B) *2Sa 22:3*
no guilt or v. in my hands *Job 16:17*
(A)(B)(E)(R)
he does v. (A) *Job 37:23*
him that loveth v. his soul *Ps 11:5*
hateth
I have seen v. and strife in the *Ps 55:9*
city
ye weigh the v. of your hands *Ps 58:2*
their soul from deceit and v. *Ps 72:14*
v. covereth them as a garment *Ps 73:6*
envy not a man of v. (E)(R) *Pr 3:31*
and drink the wine of v. *Pr 4:17*
but v. covereth the mouth *Pr 10:6;*
                                    10:11
of the transgressors shall eat v. *Pr 13:2*
minds plot oppression devise v. *Pr 24:2*
(A)(B)(R)
do no v. to his home (B)(R) *Pr 24:15*
A man that doeth v. to the *Pr 28:17*
blood
wilfully sheds blood (A) *Pr 28:17*
guilty of blood (B) *Pr 28:17*
laden with blood (E) *Pr 28:17*
because he had done no v. *Isa 53:9*
and the act of v. is in their *Isa 59:6*
hands

V. shall no more be heard in   *Isa 60:18*
thy
v. and spoil is heard in her;   *Jer 6:7*
before
I cried out, I cried *v.* and   *Jer 20:8*
spoil
no wrong, do no *v.* to the   *Jer 22:3*
stranger
for oppression, and for *v.* to   *Jer 22:17*
do it
The *v.* done to me and to my   *Jer 51:35*
flesh
come a rumour, and *v.* in the   *Jer 51:46*
land
V. is risen up into a rod of   *Eze 7:11*
crimes, and the city is full of   *Eze 7:23*
v.
they have filled the land with   *Eze 8:17*
v.
of the *v.* of all them that   *Eze 12:19*
dwell
hath spoiled none by *v.* hath   *Eze 18:7*
hath spoiled by *v.* hath not   *Eze 18:12*
steals (B)   *Eze 18:12*
neither hath spoiled by *v.*   *Eze 18:16*
spoiled his brother by *v.* and   *Eze 18:18*
filled the midst of thee with   *Eze 28:16*
v.
remove *v.* and spoil, and   *Eze 45:9*
execute
lies and *v.* (A)(R)   *Ho 12:1*
v. against the children of   *Joe 3:19*
Judah
who store up *v.* and robbery   *Am 3:10*
cause the seat of *v.* to come   *Am 6:3*
near
thy *v.* against thy brother Jacob   *Ob 10*
from the *v.* that is in their   *Jon 3:8*
hands
covet fields, and take them by   *Mic 2:2*
v.
seize them (A)(B)(E)   *Mic 2:2*
rich men thereof are full of *v.*   *Mic 6:12*
oppression (B)   *Mic 6:12*
even cry out unto thee of *v.*   *Hab 1:2*
for spoiling and *v.* are before   *Hab 1:3*
me
They shall come all for *v.*:   *Hab 1:9*
their
for the *v.* of the land, of the   *Hab 2:8*
city
the *v.* of Lebanon shall cover   *Hab 2:17*
thee
for the *v.* of the land, of the   *Hab 2:17*
city
fill their masters' houses with   *Zep 1:9*
v.
they have done *v.* to the law   *Zep 3:4*
one covereth *v.* with his   *Mal 2:16*
garment
covers clothing with cruelty   *Mal 2:16*
(B)
kingdom of heaven suffereth   *M't 11:12*
v.
has endured violent assault   *M't 11:12*
(A)
has been rushed (B)   *M't 11:12*
taken by storm (P)   *M't 11:12*
Do *v.* to no man, neither   *Lu 3:14*
accuse
never demand or enforce by   *Lu 3:14*
terrifying people or accusing
them wrongfully (A)
Do not extort (B)   *Lu 3:14*
No bullying; no blackmail   *Lu 3:14*
(N)
Don't bully people, don't bring   *Lu 3:14*
false charges (P)
and brought them without *v.*   *Ac 5:26*
force (B)   *Ac 5:26; 24:7; 27:41*
laid waste with *v.* (A)   *Ac 8:3*
the soldiers for the *v.* of the   *Ac 21:35*
people
with great *v.* took him away   *Ac 24:7*
out of
broken with the *v.* of the   *Ac 27:41*
waves
Quenched the *v.* of fire,   *Heb 11:34*
escaped
extinguishing raging fire   *Heb 11:34*
(A)
Quenched power of fire   *Heb 11:34*
(B)(E)
Quenched the fury of fire   *Heb 11:34*
(N)
Quenched the furious flame   *Heb 11:34*
of fire (P)
v. shall that great city   *Re 18:21*
Babylon be

VIOLENT

children of *v.* men (R)   *2Sa 7:10;*
  1Ch 17:9
more *v.* than the charges   *2Sa 19:43*
(A)(B)
delivered me from the *v.*   *2Sa 22:49*
man
v. dealing shall come down   *Ps 7:16*
upon
hast delivered me from the *v.*   *Ps 18:48*
man
v. men seek my life   *Ps 54:3*
(A)(B)(E)
the assemblies of *v.* men have   *Ps 86:14*
preserve me from the *v.*   *Ps 140:1;*
man   *140:4*
evil shall hunt the *v.* man to   *Ps 140:11*
envy not a *v.* man (B)   *Pr 3:31*
v. men win riches   *Pr 11:16*
(A)(B)(E)(R)
A *v.* man enticeth his   *Pr 16:29*
neighbour
v. perverting of judgment and   *Ec 5:8*
lay low boasting of *v.* (B)   *Isa 13:11*
most *v.* of nations (B)   *Eze 30:11*
and the *v.* take it by force   *M't 11:12*
making most *v.* accusations   *Lu 23:10*
(P)
laid *v.* hands on (B)(P)(R)   *Ac 12:1*
strife more *v.* (A)   *Ac 23:10*
using *v.* and abusive words   *Eph 6:9*
(A)
not (P)(R)(S)   *1Ti 3:3*

VIOLENTLY

servants had *v.* taken away   *Ge 21:25*
restore that which he took *v.*   *Le 6:4*
thine ass shall be *v.* taken   *De 28:31*
away
curse me *v.* (B)   *1Ki 2:8*
he hath *v.* taken away an   *Job 20:19*
house
they *v.* take away flocks, and   *Job 24:2*
feed
v. turn and toss thee like a   *Isa 22:18*
ball
v. taken away his tabernacle   *La 2:6*
of swine ran *v.* down a steep   *M't 8:32*
place
the herd ran *v.* down a steep   *M'k 5:13*
place
he protested *v.* (P)   *M'k 14:31*
the herd ran *v.* down a steep   *Lu 8:33*
strives *v.* to go in   *Lu 16:16*
(A)(E)(R)

VIOLS

the grave, and the noise of   *Isa 14:11*
thy *v.*
will not hear the melody of   *Am 5:23*
thy *v.*

VIPER

the *v.* and fiery flying serpent   *Isa 30:6*
is crushed breaketh out into a   *Isa 59:5*
v.
there came a *v.* out of the   *Ac 28:3*
heat

VIPERS

O generation of *v.* who hath   *M't 3:7;*
  Lu 3:7
O generation of *v.* how can   *M't 12:34*
ye generation of *v.* how can   *M't 23:33*

VIPER'S

asps: the *v.* tongue shall slay   *Job 20:16*
him

VIRGIN

was very fair to look upon, a   *Ge 24:16*
v.
v. cometh forth to draw   *Ge 24:43*
water
the maiden (A)   *Ge 24:43; Jer 31:13*
the girl (B)   *Ge 24:43*
for his sister a *v.* that is nigh   *Le 21:3*
take a *v.* to wife (B)   *Le 21:13*
he shall take a *v.* of his own   *Le 21:14*
people
an evil name upon a *v.* of   *De 22:19*
Israel

damsel that is a *v.* be   *De 22:23*
betrothed
If a man find a damsel that   *De 22:28*
is a *v.*
both the young man and the   *De 32:25*
v. the
the maid (B)   *De 32:25*
for she was a *v.*; and Amon   *2Sa 13:2*
for my lord the king a young   *1Ki 1:2*
v.
maiden (R)   *1Ki 1:2; Jer 31:13*
The *v.* the daughter of Zion   *2Ki 19:21*
hath
Behold, a *v.* shall conceive   *Isa 7:14*
a young woman (R)   *Isa 7:14*
O thou oppressed *v.* daughter   *Isa 23:12*
The *v.* the daughter of Zion,   *Isa 37:22*
hath
O *v.* daughter of Babylon, sit   *Isa 47:1*
For as a young man marrieth   *Isa 62:5*
a *v.*
v. daughter of my people is   *Jer 14:17*
broken
the *v.* of Israel hath done a   *Jer 18:13*
very
thou shalt be built, O *v.* of   *Jer 31:4*
Israel
shall the *v.* rejoice in the   *Jer 31:13*
dance
O *v.* of Israel turn again to   *Jer 31:21*
these
balm, O *v.* the daughter of   *Jer 46:11*
Egypt
the Lord hath trodden the *v.*   *La 1:15*
thee, O *v.* daughter of Zion   *La 2:13*
v. breasts handled (A)   *Eze 23:3*
v. bosoms handled (R)   *Eze 23:3; 23:8*
Lament like a *v.* girded with   *Joe 1:8*
The *v.* of Israel is fallen; she   *Am 5:2*
shall
Behold, a *v.* shall be with   *M't 1:23*
child
To a *v.* espoused to a man   *Lu 1:27*
whose
girl (N)   *Lu 1:27*
if a *v.* marry, she hath not   *1Co 7:28*
sinned
girl (R)   *1Co 7:28; 7:34*
also between a wife and a *v.*   *1Co 7:34*
himself uncomely toward his   *1Co 7:36*
v.
his heart that he will keep   *1Co 7:37*
his *v.*
you as a chaste *v.* to Christ   *2Co 11:2*
unspoiled girl (P)   *2Co 11:2*
pure bride (R)   *2Co 11:2*

VIRGINITY

he shall take a wife in her *v.*   *Le 21:13*
take a virgin to wife (B)   *Le 21:13*
forth the tokens of the   *De 22:15*
damsels *v.*
are the token of my   *De 22:17*
daughter's *v.*
tokens of *v.* be not found   *De 22:30*
for the
evidences of chastity (B)   *De 22:20*
bewail my *v.* I and my   *J'g 11:37*
fellows
and bewailed her *v.* upon the   *J'g 11:38*
they bruised the teats of their   *Eze 23:3*
v.
their virgin breasts were   *Eze 23:3*
handled (A)
her virgin bosoms handled   *Eze 23:3;*
(R)   *23:8*
the bruised the breasts of her   *Eze 23:8*
v.
they handled her girlish   *Eze 23:8*
bosom (A)(B)
husband seven years from her   *Lu 2:36*
v.
seven years from her   *Lu 2:36*
maidenhood (N)
after her girlhood seven years   *Lu 2:36*
(B)

VIRGINS

according to the dowry of *v.*   *Ex 22:17*
four hundred young *v.* that   *J'g 21:12*
had
the king's daughters that   *2Sa 13:18*
were *v.*
Let there be fair young *v.*   *Es 2:2*
sought
together all the fair young *v.*   *Es 2:3*
unto
maidens (B)   *Es 2:3; Ca 1:3*

VIRGINS

in his sight more than all the *v.* *Es 2:17*
maidens (A) *Es 2:17;*
2:19; Ca 1:3; La 1:4, 18; 2:10, 21;
Ac 21:9; 1Co 7:25
girls (B) *Es 2:7*
the *v.* were gathered together *Es 2:19*
the *v.* her companions that *Ps 45:14*
follow
therefore do the *v.* love thee *Ca 1:3*
maidens (R) *Ca 1:3;*
6:8; La 1:4, 18; 2:10, 21; M't 25:1, 7, 11
and *v.* without number *Ca 6:8*
harem daughters (B) *Ca 6:8*
up young men, nor bring up *Isa 23:4*
v.
priests sigh, her is afflicted *La 1:4*
my *v.* and my young men are *La 1:18*
the *v.* of Jerusalem hang down *La 2:10*
my *v.* and my young men are *La 2:21*
of heaven be likened unto ten *M't 25:1*
v.
girls (N) *M't 25:1; 25:7*
bridesmaids (P) *M't 25:1; 25:7, 11*
all those *v.* arose, and *M't 25:7*
trimmed
Afterward came also the *M't 25:11*
other *v.*
same man had four daughters *Ac 21:9*
v.
unmarried daughters *Ac 21:9*
(N)(P)(R)
Now concerning *v.* I have no *1Co 7:25*
the unmarried (R) *1Co 7:25*
with women; for they are *v.* *Re 14:4*
celibates (B)(P) *Re 14:4*
chaste (N)(R) *Re 14:4*

VIRGIN'S

and the *v.* name was Mary *Lu 1:27*
the girl's name was Mary *Lu 1:27*
(N)(P)

VIRTUE

throwing away your *v.* (B) *Eze 16:36*
that *v.* had gone out of him *M'k 5:30*
power
(A)(B)(E)(N)(P)(R) *Lu 6:19; 8:46*
for there went *v.* out of him *Lu 6:19*
perceive that *v.* has gone out *Lu 8:46*
of me
there be any *v.* and if there be *Ph'p 4:8*
any
praiseworthy (B)(P) *Ph'p 4:8*
excellent and admirable (N) *Ph'p 4:8*
worthy of praise (R) *Ph'p 4:8*
that hath called us to glory *2Pe 1:3*
and *v.*
excellence (A) *2Pe 1:3*
splendour and might (N) *2Pe 1:3*
glory and excellence (R) *2Pe 1:3*
diligence, add to your faith *v.* *2Pe 1:5*
and to *v.* knowledge *2Pe 1:5*

VIRTUOUS

know that thou art a *v.* *Ru 3:11*
woman
woman of strength, worth, *Ru 3:11*
bravery, capability (A)
a worthy woman (E) *Ru 3:11;*
Pr 12:4; 31:10
a woman of worth (R) *Ru 3:11*
A *v.* woman is a crown to her *Pr 12:4*
a wife of strength and *Pr 12:4;*
character (B) *31:10*
a good wife (R) *Pr 12:4; 31:10*
Who can find a *v.* woman *Pr 31:10*

VIRTUOUSLY

Many daughters have done *v.* *Pr 31:29*
nobly (B) *Pr 31:29*
worthily (E) *Pr 31:29*
excellently (R) *Pr 31:29*

VISAGE

his *v.* was so marred *Isa 52:14*
more than
face and whole appearance *Isa 52:14*
(A)
appearance (B)(R) *Isa 52:14*
Their *v.* is blacker than a *La 4:8*
coal
looks (B) *La 4:8*
the form of his *v.* was *Da 3:19*
changed

facial expression (A) *Da 3:19*
face distorted (B) *Da 3:19*
expression (R) *Da 3:19*

VISIBLE

does not come with *v.* display *Lu 17:20*
(A)
that are in earth, *v.* and *Col 1:16*
invisible
things seen (A) *Col 1:16*
made *v.* in human flesh (A) *1Ti 3:16*
v. symbol of present age *Heb 9:9*
(A)
not made of *v.* things *Heb 11:3*
(A)(B)
v. came from the invisible *Heb 11:3*
(N)
the life was made *v.* (N) *1Jo 1:2*
came in *v.* form to (A)(B) *1Jo 3:5*

VISION

Lord came unto Abram in a *Ge 15:1*
myself known unto him in a *Nu 12:6*
v.
saw the *v.* of the Almighty *Nu 24:4;*
24:16
sees *v.* of the Almighty *Nu 24:4;*
(A)(B)(E)(R) *24:16*
those days; there was no open *1Sa 3:1*
v.
Samuel feared to shew Eli the *1Sa 3:15*
v.
according to all this *v.* so did *2Sa 7:17;*
1Ch 17:15
they are written in the *v.* of *2Ch 32:32*
Isaiah
chased away as a *v.* of the *Job 20:8*
night
in a *v.* of the night, when *Job 33:15*
deep
thou spakest in *v.* to thy holy *Ps 89:19*
one
Where there is no *v.* the *Pr 29:18*
people
The *v.* of Isaiah the son of *Isa 1:1*
Amoz
grievous *v.* is declared unto *Isa 21:2*
me
The burden of the valley of *v.* *Isa 22:1*
God of hosts in the valley of *Isa 22:5*
v.
they err in *v.* they stumble in *Isa 28:7*
shall be as a dream of a night *Isa 29:7*
v.
the *v.* of all is become *Isa 29:11*
unto you as
they prophesy unto you a *Jer 14:14*
false *v.*
they speak a *v.* of their own *Jer 23:16*
heart
also find no *v.* from the Lord *La 2:9*
v. is touching the whole *Eze 7:13*
multitude
shall they seek a *v.* of the *Eze 7:26*
prophet
to the *v.* that I saw in the *Eze 8:4*
plain
brought me in a *v.* by the *Eze 11:24*
Spirit of
the *v.* that I had seen went *Eze 11:24*
up from
prolonged, and every *v.* *Eze 12:22*
faileth
at hand, and the effect of *Eze 12:23*
every *v.*
be no more any vain *v.* nor *Eze 12:24*
flattering
The *v.* that he seeth is for *Eze 12:27*
many
Have ye not seen a vain *v.* *Eze 13:7*
appearance of the *v.* which *Eze 43:3*
I saw
according to the *v.* that I saw *Eze 43:3*
when
were like the *v.* that I saw by *Eze 43:3*
revealed unto Daniel in a *Da 2:19*
night *v.*
and said, I saw in my *v.* by *Da 7:2*
night
Belshazzar a *v.* appeared unto *Da 8:1*
me
I saw in a *v.*; and it came to *Da 8:2*
pass
I saw in a *v.* and I was by the *Da 8:2*
river
shall be the *v.* concerning the *Da 8:13*

even I Daniel, had seen the *Da 8:15*
v. and
this man to understand the *v.* *Da 8:16*
the time of the end shall be *Da 8:17*
the *v.*
v. of the evening and the *Da 8:26*
morning
wherefore shut thou up the *v.* *Da 8:26*
I was astonished at the *v.* but *Da 8:27*
whom I had seen in the *v.* at *Da 9:21*
the matter, and consider the *v.* *Da 9:23*
and to seal up the *v.* and *Da 9:24*
prophecy
and had understanding of the *Da 10:1*
v.
and I Daniel alone saw the *v.* *Da 10:7*
that were with me saw not the *Da 10:7*
v.
left alone, and saw this great *v.* *Da 10:8*
for yet the *v.* is for many *Da 10:14*
days
by the *v.* my sorrows are *Da 10:16*
turned
themselves to establish the *v.* *Da 11:14*
The *v.* of Obadiah. Thus saith *Ob 1*
the
you, that ye shall not have *Mic 3:6*
a *v.*
The book of the *v.* of Nahum *Na 1:1*
Write the *v.* and make it *Hab 2:2*
plain
the *v.* is yet for an appointed *Hab 2:3*
time
be ashamed every one of his *Zec 13:4*
v.
Tell the *v.* to no man, until *M't 17:9*
he had seen a *v.* in the temple *Lu 1:22*
they had also seen a *v.* of *Lu 24:23*
angels
and to him said the Lord in a *Ac 9:10*
v.
seen in a *v.* a man named *Ac 9:12*
Ananias
He saw in a *v.* evidently about *Ac 10:3*
what this *v.* which he had *Ac 10:17*
seen
While Peter thought on the *v.* *Ac 10:19*
and in a trance I saw a *v.* a *Ac 11:5*
certain
angel; but thought he saw a *v.* *Ac 12:9*
a *v.* appeared to Paul in the *Ac 16:9*
night
And after he had seen the *v.* *Ac 16:10*
Lord to Paul in the night by a *Ac 18:9*
v.
disobedient unto the heavenly *Ac 26:19*
v.
I saw the horses in the *v.* and *Re 9:17*

VISIONS

unto Israel in the *v.* of the *Ge 46:2*
night
v. of Iddo the seer against *2Ch 9:29*
understanding in the *v.* of *2Ch 26:5*
God
thoughts from the *v.* of *Job 4:13*
the night
and terrifest me through *v.* *Job 7:14*
were opened, and I saw *v.* of *Eze 1:1*
God
brought me in the *v.* of God to *Eze 8:3*
false *v.* (E) *Eze 13:8;*
13:23; 21:29; 22:28
false, delusive *v.* (A)(B)(R) *Eze 13:9*
which see *v.* of peace for her *Eze 13:16*
false *v.* (A) *Eze 13:23; 21:29; 22:28*
empty *v.* (B) *Eze 22:28*
In the *v.* of God brought he *Eze 40:2*
me
and the *v.* were like the *Eze 43:3*
vision
understanding in all *v.* and *Da 1:17*
v. of thy head upon thy bed *Da 2:28*
and the *v.* of my head trouble *Da 4:5;*
me *7:15*
tell me the *v.* of my dream that *Da 4:9*
I
Thus were the *v.* of mine head *Da 4:10*
I saw in the *v.* of my head *Da 4:13*
upon my
and *v.* of his head upon his *Da 7:1*
bed
After this I saw in the night *v.* *Da 7:7*
I saw in the night *v.* and, *Da 7:13*
behold
I have multiplied *v.* and used *Ho 12:10*
your young men shall see *v.* *Joe 2:28;*
Ac 2:17
I will come to *v.* and *2Co 12:1*
revelations

VISIT

God will surely *v*. you, and bring — Ge 50:24
God will surely *v*. you, and ye shall — Ge 50:25;
the day when I *v*. I will *v*. their sin — Ex 13:19
Ex 32:34
I do *v*. the iniquity thereof upon it — Le 18:25
punish (B) — Le 18:25;
Jer 6:15; 9:9; 14:10; 49:8; Ho 9:9; Am 3:14
punish (R) — Le 18:25;
Ps 59:5; 89:32; Jer 5:9, 29; 6:15; 9:9; 14:10; 49:8; 50:31; Ho 2:13; 8:13; 9:9; Am 3:14
I will *v*. you with (B) — Le 26:16
and thou shalt *v*. thy habitation — Job 5:24
thou shouldest *v*. him every — Job 7:18
Israel, awake to *v*. all the heathen — Ps 59:5
heaven, and behold, and *v*. this — Ps 80:14
have regard (R) — Ps 80:14
Then will I *v*. their transgression — Ps 89:32
punish (A) — Ps 89:32;
Jer 5:9, 29; 6:15; 9:9; 14:10; 49:8; 50:31; La 4:22; Ho 8:13; 9:9; Am 3:14
people: O *v*. me with thy salvation — Ps 106:4
that the Lord will *v*. Tyre, and she — Isa 23:17
remember (A) — Isa 23:17
it; neither shall they *v*. it — Jer 3:16
remember (E)(R) — Jer 3:16
Shall I not *v*. for these things — Jer 5:9; 5:29
time that I *v*. them they shall be — Jer 6:15
Shall I not *v*. them for these things — Jer 9:9
their iniquity, and *v*. their sins — Jer 14:10
and *v*. me, and revenge me of my — Jer 15:15
v. upon you the evil of your doings — Jer 23:2
attend to you (R) — Jer 23:2
they be until the day that I *v*. them — Jer 27:22
remember (B) — Jer 27:22
at Babylon I will *v*. you — Jer 29:10
and there shall he be until I *v*. him — Jer 32:5
him, the time that I will *v*. him — Jer 49:8
is come, the time that I will *v*. thee — Jer 50:31
chasten (B) — Jer 50:31
he will *v*. thine iniquity, O daughter — La 4:22
punishment (R) — La 4:22
will *v*. upon her the days of Baalim — Ho 2:13
their iniquity, and *v*. their sins — Ho 8:13
their iniquity, he will *v*. their sins — Ho 9:9
shall *v*. the transgressions of Israel — Am 3:14
I will also *v*. the altars of Beth-el — Am 3:14
the Lord their God shall *v*. them — Zep 2:7
be mindful of them (R) — Zep 2:7
shall not *v*. those that be cut off — Zec 11:16
to *v*. his brethren the children — Ac 7:23
look in on (B) — Ac 7:23
God at the first did *v*. the Gentiles — Ac 15:14
Let us go again and *v*. our brethren — Ac 15:36
To *v*. the fatherless and widows in — Jas 1:27
look after (B) — Jas 1:27

VISITATION

visited after the *v*. of all men — Nu 16:29
what happens to all men happens to them (A) — Nu 16:29
usual experiences of all men are their (B) — Nu 16:29
visited after the fate of all men (R) — Nu 16:29
thy *v*. hath preserved my spirit — Job 10:12

your providence (A) — Job 10:12
thy care has preserved me (B)(R) — Job 10:12
And what will ye do in the day of *v*. — Isa 10:3
day of punishment (R) — Isa 10:3
the time of their *v*. they shall be — Jer 8:12
time of their punishment (A) — Jer 8:12;
10:15; 11:23; 51:18; Mic 7:4
when I punish them (R) — Jer 8:12
time of their *v*. they shall perish — Jer 10:15
time of their punishment (B) — Jer 10:15;
11:23; 23:12; 48:44; 51:18; Ho 9:7
time of their punishment (R) — Jer 10:15;
11:23; 23:12; 46:21; 48:44; 50:27; 51:18; Ho 9:7; Mic 7:4
Anathoth, even the year of their *v*. — Jer 11:23
them, even the year of their *v*. — Jer 23:12
upon them, and the time of their *v*. — Jer 46:21
upon Moab, the year of their *v*. — Jer 48:44
day is come, the time of their *v*. — Jer 50:27
time of their *v*. they shall perish — Jer 51:18
The days of *v*. are come, the — Ho 9:7
of thy watchmen and thy *v*. cometh — Mic 7:4
knewest not the time of thy *v*. — Lu 19:44
divinely visited (B) — Lu 19:44
did not recognize God's moment when it came (N) — Lu 19:44
behold, glorify God in the day of *v*. — 1Pe 2:12
in the day of inspection (A) — 1Pe 2:12
on the day he comes to hold assize (N) — 1Pe 2:12

VISITED

the Lord *v*. Sarah as he had said — Ge 21:1
came to (B) — Ge 21:1
I have surely *v*. you, and seen that — Ex 3:16
faithfully been present with (B) — Ex 3:16
observed you (R) — Ex 3:16
Lord had *v*. the children of Israel — Ex 4:31
Lord had looked upon (A) — Ex 4:31
had come to (B) — Ex 4:31
if they be *v*. after the visitation of — Nu 16:29
if what happens (A) — Nu 16:29
that Samson *v*. his wife with a kid — J'g 15:1
the Lord had *v*. his people in giving — Ru 1:6
And the Lord *v*. Hannah, so that she — 1Sa 2:21
it is not so, he hath *v*. in his anger — Job 35:15
punished in his anger (A) — Job 35:15
thou hath *v*. me in the night; thou — Ps 17:3
he shall not be *v*. with evil — Pr 19:23
after many days shall they be *v*. — Isa 24:22
punished (R) — Isa 24:22; Jer 6:6
hast thou *v*. and destroyed — Isa 26:14
Lord, in trouble have they *v*. — Isa 26:16
sought thee (B)(E)(R) — Isa 26:16
Thou shalt be *v*. of the Lord of — Isa 29:6
Jerusalem: this is the city to be *v*. — Jer 6:6
which must be punished (A)(B) — Jer 6:6
them away, and have not *v*. them — Jer 23:2
tended them (B)(E)(R) — Jer 23:2
After many days thou shall be *v*. — Eze 38:8
mustered (E)(R) — Eze 38:8
the Lord of hosts hath *v*. his flock — Zec 10:3
cares for (E)(R) — Zec 10:3
I was sick, and ye *v*. me: I — M't 25:36
and in prison, and ye *v*. me not — M't 25:43

hath *v*. and redeemed his people — Lu 1:68
dayspring from on high hath *v*. us — Lu 1:78
rise upon us (N) — Lu 1:78
and, That God hath *v*. his people — Lu 7:16
has risen upon us (N) — Lu 7:16

VISITEST

the son of man, that thou *v*. him — Ps 8:4
you care for him (A)(R) — Ps 8:4
thou carest for him (B) — Ps 8:4
Thou *v*. the earth, and waterest it — Ps 65:9
the son of man, that thou *v*. him — Heb 2:6
you graciously, helpfully care for, and visit and look after him (A) — Heb 2:6
lookest after him (B) — Heb 2:6
hast regard to him (N) — Heb 2:6
carest for him (R) — Heb 2:6

VISITETH

when he *v*. what shall I answer — Job 31:14
riseth up to judge (A) — Job 31:14

VISITING

v. the iniquity of the fathers upon — Ex 20:5; 34:7; Nu 14:18; De 5:9

VISITOR

only a *v*. (B)(R) — Lu 24:18

VISITORS

v. of Rome (B)(N)(P)(R) — Ac 2:10

VITAL

my *v*. parts are in tumult (A) — La 1:20

VITALS

your *v*. fall out (B) — 2Ch 21:15
he slashes open my *v*. (A) — Job 16:13

VITUPERATION

v. for *v*. (B) — 1Pe 3:9

VOCATION

walk worthy of the *v*. wherewith — Eph 4:1
walk worthy of the divine calling (A)(B)(E)(N)(R) — Eph 4:1
walk worthy of the high calling (P) — Eph 4:1

VOICE

they heard the *v*. of the Lord God — Ge 3:8
sound (A)(B)(R) — Ge 3:8; 3:10; Ex 32:18
I heard thy *v*. in the garden — Ge 3:10
hearkened unto the *v*. of thy wife — Ge 3:17
your wife's suggestion (B) — Ge 3:17
v. of thy brother's blood crieth unto — Ge 4:10
wives, Adah and Zillah, hear my *v*. — Ge 4:23
hearkened to the *v*. of Sarai — Ge 16:2
unto thee, hearken unto her *v*. — Ge 21:12
over against him, and lift up *v*. — Ge 21:16
wept audibly (B) — Ge 21:16; 29:11
And God heard the *v*. of the lad — Ge 21:17
God hath heard the *v*. of the lad — Ge 21:17
because thou hast obeyed my *v*. — Ge 22:18
that Abraham obeyed my *v*. — Ge 26:5
obey my *v*. according to that which — Ge 27:8
only obey my *v*. and go fetch me — Ge 27:13
word (A) — Ge 27:13
The *v*. is Jacob's *v*. but the hands — Ge 27:22

And Esau lifted up his *v.* and wept Ge 27:38
Now therefore, my son, obey my *v.* Ge 27:43
and lifted up his *v.* and wept Ge 29:11
me, and hath also heard my *v.* Ge 30:6
with me, and I cried with a loud *v.* Ge 39:14
I screamed (B) Ge 39:14
he heard that I lifted up my *v.* and Ge 39:15
as I lifted up my *v.* and cried, that Ge 39:18
they shall hearken to thy *v.* Ex 3:18
message (B) Ex 3:18; 19:5
me, nor hearken unto my *v.* Ex 4:1
my appeal (B) Ex 4:1
hearken to the *v.* of the first sign Ex 4:8
will believe the *v.* of the latter sign Ex 4:8
signs, neither hearken unto thy *v.*, Ex 4:9
should obey his *v.* to let Israel go Ex 5:2
hearken to the *v.* of the Lord Ex 15:26
Hearken now unto my *v.*, I Ex 18:19
to the *v.* of his father in law Ex 18:24
carried when he suggested (B) Ex 18:24
if ye will obey my *v.* indeed Ex 19:5
v. of the trumpet exceeding loud Ex 19:16
loud trumpet blast (A) Ex 19:16; 19:19
the *v.* of the trumpet sounded long Ex 19:19
and God answered him by a *v.* Ex 19:19
Beware of him, and obey his *v.* Ex 23:21
heed his suggestions (B) Ex 23:21
if thou shalt indeed obey his *v.* Ex 23:22
obey his word (B) Ex 23:22
all the people answered with one *v.* Ex 24:3
the people unanimously replied (B) Ex 24:3
v. of them that shout for mastery Ex 32:18
the *v.* of them that cry for being Ex 32:18
hear the *v.* of swearing, and is Le 5:1
he heard the *v.* of one speaking Nu 7:89
the congregation lifted up their *v.* Nu 14:1
and have not hearkened to my *v.* Nu 14:22
disregarded his word (B) Nu 14:22
he heard our *v.* and sent an angel Nu 20:16
he heard our plea (A) Nu 20:16
Lord hearkened to the *v.* of Israel Nu 21:3
heard Israel's request (B) Nu 21:3
Lord heard the *v.* of your words De 1:34
Lord would not hearken to your *v.* De 1:45
ye heard the *v.* of the words De 4:12
no similitude; only ye heard a *v.* De 4:12
and shalt be obedient unto his *v.* De 4:30
listen to him (B) De 4:30
v. of God speaking out of the midst De 4:33
he made thee to hear his *v.* that De 4:36
the thick darkness, with a great *v.* De 5:22
ye heard the *v.* out of the midst of De 5:23
we have heard his *v.* out of De 5:24
if we hear the *v.* of the Lord De 5:25
hath heard the *v.* of the living God De 5:26
Lord heard the *v.* of your words De 5:28
I listened to the words (B) De 5:28
heard the words of this people (R) De 5:28
I have heard the *v.* of the words of De 5:28
obedient unto the *v.* of the Lord De 8:20
him not, nor hearkened to his *v.* De 9:23

commandments, and obey his *v.* De 13:4
shalt hearken to the *v.* of the Lord De 13:18
hearken to the *v.* of the Lord De 15:5; 26:14; 28:1, 2; 30:10
not hear again the *v.* of the Lord De 18:16
will not obey the *v.* of his father De 21:18
or the *v.* of his mother, and De 21:18
rebellious, he will not obey our *v.* De 21:20
Lord heard our *v.* and looked on De 26:7
heard their cry (B) De 26:7
and to hearken unto his *v.* De 26:17
obey the *v.* of the Lord thy God De 27:10
all the men of Israel with a loud *v.* De 27:14
not hearken unto the *v.* of the Lord De 28:15
not unto the *v.* of the Lord De 28:45
not obey the *v.* of the Lord thy God De 28:62
obey his *v.* according to all that I De 30:2
return and obey the *v.* of the Lord De 30:8
that thou mayest obey his *v.* De 30:20
said, Hear, Lord, the *v.* of Judah De 33:7
they obeyed not the *v.* of the Lord Jos 5:6
nor make any noise with your *v.* Jos 6:10
hearkened unto the *v.* of a man Jos 10:14
have obeyed my *v.* in all that I Jos 22:2
we serve, and his *v.* will we obey Jos 24:24
but ye have not obeyed my *v.*: why J'g 2:2
obeyed my command (R) J'g 2:2
that the people lifted up their *v.* J'g 2:4
have not hearkened unto my *v.* J'g 2:20
but ye have not obeyed my *v.* J'g 6:10
lifted up his *v.* and cried, and said J'g 9:7
God hearkened to the *v.* of Manoah J'g 13:9
knew the *v.* of the young man J'g 18:3
Let not thy *v.* be heard among us J'g 18:25
hearken to the *v.* of their brethren J'g 20:13
listen to the demands of (B) J'g 20:13
they lifted up their *v.* and wept Ru 1:9; 1:14
moved, but her *v.* was not heard 1Sa 1:13
not unto the *v.* of their father 1Sa 2:25
not listen to father's warning (B) 1Sa 2:25
Hearken unto the *v.* of the people in 1Sa 8:7
therefore hearken unto their *v.* 1Sa 8:9
refused to obey the *v.* of Samuel 1Sa 8:19
declined to listen (B) 1Sa 8:19
Hearken unto their *v.* and make 1Sa 8:22
have hearkened unto your *v.* in all 1Sa 12:1
serve him, and obey his *v.*, 1Sa 12:14
ye will not obey the *v.* of the Lord 1Sa 12:15
the *v.* of the words of the Lord 1Sa 15:1
listen to the Lord's message (B) 1Sa 15:1
thou not obey the *v.* of the Lord 1Sa 15:19
I have obeyed the *v.* of the Lord 1Sa 15:20
as in obeying the *v.* of the Lord 1Sa 15:22
the people, and obeyed their *v.* 1Sa 15:24
hearkened unto the *v.* of Jonathan 1Sa 19:6
said, Is this thy *v.*, my son David 1Sa 24:16
And Saul lifted up his *v.* and wept 1Sa 24:16

I have hearkened to thy *v.* and 1Sa 25:35
And Saul knew David's *v.* and said 1Sa 26:17
Is this thy *v.* my son David 1Sa 26:17
David said, It is my *v.* my lord 1Sa 26:17
Samuel, she cried with a loud *v.* 1Sa 28:12
she screamed (A)(B) 1Sa 28:12
obeyedst not the *v.* of the Lord 1Sa 28:18
thine handmaid hath obeyed thy *v.* 1Sa 28:21
has obeyed you (A) 1Sa 28:21
unto the *v.* of thine handmaid 1Sa 28:22
obeyed your orders (B) 1Sa 28:22
and he hearkened unto their *v.* 1Sa 28:23
the words (A) 1Sa 28:23
him lifted up their *v.* and wept 1Sa 30:4
the king lifted up his *v.* and wept 2Sa 3:32
wept aloud (B) 2Sa 3:32
he would not hearken unto our *v.* 2Sa 12:18
he would not hearken unto her *v.* 2Sa 13:14
listen to her words (B) 2Sa 13:14
and lifted up their *v.* and wept 2Sa 13:36
all the country wept with a loud *v.* 2Sa 15:23
the king cried with a loud *v.*, O my 2Sa 19:4
any more the *v.* of singing men 2Sa 19:35
he did hear my *v.* out of his temple 2Sa 22:7
and the most High uttered his *v.* 2Sa 22:14
congregation of Israel with a loud *v.* 1Ki 8:55
the Lord heard the *v.* of Elijah; and 1Ki 17:22
But there was no *v.*, nor any 1Ki 18:26
that there was neither *v.* nor any 1Ki 18:29
and after the fire a still small *v.*, 1Ki 19:12
there came a *v.* unto him, and said 1Ki 19:13
he hearkened unto their *v.*, and did 1Ki 20:25
listened to their plan (B) 1Ki 20:25
hast not obeyed the *v.* of the Lord 1Ki 20:36
did not listen (B) 1Ki 20:36
there was neither *v.* nor hearing 2Ki 4:31
no man there, neither *v.* of man 2Ki 7:10
and if ye will hearken unto my *v.* 2Ki 10:6
obey me (A) 2Ki 10:6
listen to me (B) 2Ki 10:6
they obeyed not the *v.* of the Lord 2Ki 18:12
a loud *v.* in the Jews' language 2Ki 18:28
whom hast thou exalted thy *v.* 2Ki 19:22
by lifting up the *v.* with joy 1Ch 15:16
raise sounds of joy (R) 1Ch 15:16
lifted up their *v.* with the trumpets 2Ch 5:13
sware unto the Lord with a loud *v.* 2Ch 15:14
of Israel with a loud *v.* on high 2Ch 20:19
and their *v.* was heard, and their 2Ch 30:27
with a loud *v.* in the Jews' speech 2Ch 32:18
shouted it loudly (A)(B) 2Ch 32:18
their eyes, wept with a loud *v.* Ezr 3:12
answered and said with a loud *v.* Ezr 10:12
cried with a loud *v.* unto the Lord Ne 9:4
they lifted up their *v.* and wept Job 2:12
solitary, let not joyful *v.* come there Job 3:7
no joyful cry (R) Job 3:7
hear not the *v.* of the oppressor Job 3:18

the lion, and the v. of the fierce lion	Job 4:10
there was silence, and I heard a v.	Job 4:16
that he had hearkened unto my v.	Job 9:16
organ into the v. of them that weep	Job 30:31
I have heard the v. of thy words	Job 33:8
sound of their words (B)(R)	Job 33:8
hearken to the v. of my words	Job 34:16
Hear attentively the noise of his v.	Job 37:2
After it a v. roareth: he thundereth	Job 37:4
with the v. of his excellency	Job 37:4
not stay them when his v. is heard	Job 37:4
marvellously with his v.; great	Job 37:5
thou lift up thy v. to the clouds	Job 38:34
thou thunder with a v. like him	Job 40:9
I cried unto the Lord with my v.	Ps 3:4
I cry aloud (R)	Ps 3:4; 27:7
Hearken unto the v. of my cry, my	Ps 5:2
sound of my cry (A)(R)	Ps 5:2
My v. shalt thou hear in the	Ps 5:3
hath heard the v. of my weeping	Ps 6:8
he heard my v. out of his temple	Ps 18:6
and the Highest gave his v.	Ps 18:13
where their v. is not heard	Ps 19:3
no speech, nor words their v. (B)(R)	Ps 19:3
with the v. of thanksgiving	Ps 26:7
O Lord, when I cry with my v.	Ps 27:7
I cry aloud (A)(B)	Ps 27:7
Hear the v. of my supplications	Ps 28:2
heard the v. of my supplications	Ps 28:6
v. of the Lord is upon the waters	Ps 29:3
The v. of the Lord is powerful	Ps 29:4
the v. of the Lord is full of majesty	Ps 29:4
v. of the Lord breaketh the cedars	Ps 29:5
v. of the Lord divideth the flames	Ps 29:7
The v. of the Lord shaketh the	Ps 29:8
v. of the Lord maketh the hinds to	Ps 29:9
heardest the v. of my supplications	Ps 31:22
with the v. of joy and praise, with a	Ps 42:4
For the v. of him that reproacheth	Ps 44:16
words of the taunter and reviler (A)(R)	Ps 44:16
v. of the scoffer and scorner (B)	Ps 44:16
he uttered his v. the earth melted	Ps 46:6
unto God with the v. of triumph	Ps 47:1
Because of the v. of the enemy	Ps 55:3
the noise of the enemy (A)(R)	Ps 55:3
cry aloud: and he shall hear my v.	Ps 55:17
not hearken to the v. of charmers	Ps 58:5
Hear my v., O God, in my prayer	Ps 64:1
the v. of his praise to be heard	Ps 66:8
sound of his praise (B)(R)	Ps 66:8
attended to the v. of my prayer	Ps 66:19
lo, he doth send out his v.	Ps 68:33
and that a mighty v.	Ps 68:33
Forget not the v. of thine enemies	Ps 74:23
clamor of thy enemies (B)(R)	Ps 74:23
I cried unto God with my v.	Ps 77:1
unto God with my v.; and he gave	Ps 77:1
The v. of thy thunder was in	Ps 77:18
the crash of thy thunder (R)	Ps 77:18
a v. I had not known (R)	Ps 81:5
people would not hearken to my v.	Ps 81:11
attend to the v. of my supplications	Ps 86:6
the cry of my supplications (A)(R)	Ps 86:6
cry of my entreaty (B)	Ps 86:6
the floods have lifted up their v.	Ps 93:3
streams swirled up their roar (B)	Ps 93:3
hand. To-day if ye will hear his v.	Ps 95:7
the harp, and the v. of a psalm	Ps 98:5
By reason of the v. of my groaning	Ps 102:5
loud groaning (A)(R)	Ps 102:5
sound of my sighing (B)	Ps 102:5
hearkening unto the v. of his word	Ps 103:20
sound of his word (B)	Ps 103:20
at the v. of thy thunder they hasted	Ps 104:7
sound of thy thunder (R)	Ps 104:7
not unto the v. of the Lord	Ps 106:25
Lord, because he hath heard my v.	Ps 116:1
The v. of rejoicing and salvation is	Ps 118:15
the shout of joy (B)	Ps 118:15
Hear my v. according unto	Ps 119:149
Lord, hear my v.: let thine ears	Ps 130:2
thine ears be attentive to the v. of	Ps 130:2
give ear unto my v. when I cry	Ps 141:1
I cried unto the Lord with my v.	Ps 142:1
with my v. unto the Lord did I	Ps 142:1
she uttereth her v. in the streets	Pr 1:20
liftest up thy v. for understanding	Pr 2:3
not obeyed the v. of my teachers	Pr 5:13
understanding put forth her v.	Pr 8:1
and my v. is to the sons of man	Pr 8:4
my cry to the sons of men (R)	Pr 8:4
blesseth his friend with a loud v.	Pr 27:14
loudly praises and glorifies his neighbor (A)	Pr 27:14
a fool's v. is known by multitude of	Ec 5:3
should God be angry at thy v.	Ec 5:6
a bird of the air shall carry the v.	Ec 10:20
he shall rise up at the v. of the bird	Ec 12:4
The v. of my beloved! behold, he	Ca 2:8
the v. of the turtle is heard in our	Ca 2:12
me hear thy v.; for sweet is thy v.	Ca 2:14
v. of my beloved that knocketh	Ca 5:2
the companions hearken to thy v.	Ca 8:13
moved at the v. of him that cried	Isa 6:4
Also I heard the v. of the Lord	Isa 6:8
sound of one calling (B)	Isa 6:8
Lift up thy v. O daughter of	Isa 10:30
cry aloud in consternation (A)	Isa 10:30
shriek aloud (B)	Isa 10:30
cry aloud, O daughter of Gallim (R)	Isa 10:30
exalt the v. unto them, shake	Isa 13:2
their v. shall be heard even unto	Isa 15:4
They shall lift up their v. they shall	Isa 24:14
Give ye ear, and hear my v.	Isa 28:23
thy v. shall be, as of one that hath a	Isa 29:4
unto thee at the v. of thy cry	Isa 30:19
sound of your cry (A)(B)(R)	Isa 30:19
cause his glorious v. to be heard	Isa 30:30
through the v. of the Lord shall the	Isa 30:31
he will not be afraid of their v. nor	Isa 31:4
neither terrified at their shouting (B)(R)	Isa 31:4
hear my v. ye careless daughters	Isa 32:9
cried with a loud v. in the Jews'	Isa 36:13
whom hast thou exalted thy v.	Isa 37:23
The v. of him that crieth in	Isa 40:3
The v. said, Cry. And he said	Isa 40:6
tidings, lift up thy v. with strength	Isa 40:9
nor cause his v. to be heard in	Isa 42:2
and the cities thereof lift up their v.	Isa 42:11
with a v. of singing declare ye, tell	Isa 48:20
that obeyeth the v. of his servant	Isa 50:10
thanksgiving, and the v. of melody	Isa 51:3
Thy watchmen shall lift up the v.	Isa 52:8
with the v. together shall they sing	Isa 52:8
not, lift up thy v. like a trumpet	Isa 58:1
make your v. to be heard on high	Isa 58:4
the v. of weeping shall be no more	Isa 65:19
sound of weeping (A)(R)	Isa 65:19
heard in her, nor the v. of crying	Isa 65:19
nor the cry of distress (A)	Isa 65:19
A v. of noise from the city	Isa 66:6
a v. from the temple	Isa 66:6
a v. of the Lord that rendereth	Isa 66:6
and ye have not obeyed my v.	Jer 3:13
A v. was heard upon the high	Jer 3:21
have not obeyed the v. of the Lord	Jer 3:25
For a v. declareth from Dan	Jer 4:15
a message comes from Dan (B)	Jer 4:15
give out their v. against the cities	Jer 4:16
shout against the cities (B)	Jer 4:16
heard a v. as of a woman in travail	Jer 4:31
cry of a woman in travail (A)(R)	Jer 4:31
the v. of the daughter of Zion	Jer 4:31
cry of the daughter of Zion (A)	Jer 4:31
their v. roareth like the sea	Jer 6:23
sound like the roaring of the sea (R)	Jer 6:23
Obey my v. and I will be your God	Jer 7:23
that obeyeth not the v. of the Lord	Jer 7:28
the v. of mirth, the v. of gladness	Jer 7:34
the v. of the bridegroom, and	Jer 7:34
the v. of the bride: for the land	Jer 7:34
the v. of the cry of the daughter of	Jer 8:19
can men hear the v. of the cattle	Jer 9:10
the lowing of cattle (A)(B)(R)	Jer 9:10
and have not obeyed my v. neither	Jer 9:13
a v. of wailing is heard out of Zion	Jer 9:19
a sound of wailing (A)(R)	Jer 9:19
a mournful sound (B)	Jer 9:19
When he uttereth his v. there is a	Jer 10:13
the v. of tidings (E)	Jer 10:22
iron furnace, saying, Obey my v.	Jer 11:4
and protesting, saying, Obey my v.	Jer 11:7
the v. of mirth, the v. of gladness	Jer 16:9
the v. of the bridegroom, and	Jer 16:9
and the v. of the bride	Jer 16:9
that it obey not my v. then I will	Jer 18:10
hearken to the v. of them	Jer 18:19
hearken to my plea (R)	Jer 18:19
and lift up my v. in Bashan, and cry	Jer 22:20
that thou obeyedst not my v.	Jer 22:21
the v. of mirth, the v. of gladness	Jer 25:10
the v. of the bridegroom, and	Jer 25:10
and the v. of the bride, the sound	Jer 25:10

high, and utter his *v.* from   *Jer 25:30*
his holy
A *v.* of the cry of the   *Jer 25:36*
shepherds, and
obey the *v.* of the Lord your   *Jer 26:13*
God
We have heard a *v.* of   *Jer 30:5*
trembling
the cry of panic (R)   *Jer 30:5*
the *v.* of them that make   *Jer 30:19*
merry
A *v.* was heard in Ramah   *Jer 31:15*
Refrain thy *v.* from weeping   *Jer 31:16*
but they obeyed not thy *v.*   *Jer 32:23*
neither
The *v.* of joy, and the *v.* of   *Jer 33:11*
gladness
the *v.* of the bridegroom, and   *Jer 33:11*
and the *v.* of the bride, the   *Jer 33:11*
v. of them that shall say,   *Jer 33:11*
Praise the
we obeyed the *v.* of Jonadab   *Jer 35:8*
I beseech thee, the *v.* of the   *Jer 38:20*
Lord
Lord, and have not obeyed his   *Jer 40:3*
v.
we will obey the *v.* of the   *Jer 42:6*
Lord our
when we obey the *v.* of the   *Jer 42:6*
Lord our
neither obey the *v.* of the   *Jer 42:13*
Lord your
have not obeyed the *v.* of the   *Jer 42:21*
Lord
obeyed not the *v.* of the Lord   *Jer 43:4*
they obeyed not the *v.* of the   *Jer 43:7*
Lord
have not obeyed the *v.* of the   *Jer 44:23*
Lord
v. thereof shall go like a   *Jer 46:22*
serpent
sound like the rustling of a   *Jer 46:22*
serpent (A)
A *v.* of crying shall be from   *Jer 48:3*
sound of a cry (A)   *Jer 48:3*
Jahaz, have they uttered   *Jer 48:34*
their *v.*
v. of them that flee and   *Jer 50:28*
escape not
their *v.* shall roar like the   *Jer 50:42*
sea, and
sound of the roaring of the   *Jer 50:42*
sea (A)(R)
When he uttereth his *v.* there   *Jer 51:16*
is a
destroyed out of her the   *Jer 51:55*
great *v.*
a noise of their *v.* is uttered   *Jer 51:55*
Thou hast heard my *v.*: hide   *La 3:56*
not
thou hast heard my plea (R)   *La 3:56*
waters, as the *v.* of the   *Eze 1:24*
Almighty
as the thunder of the   *Eze 1:24*
Almighty (B)(R)
the *v.* of speech, as the noise   *Eze 1:24*
a *v.* from the firmament that   *Eze 1:25*
was
and I heard a *v.* of one   *Eze 1:28*
that spake
behind me a *v.* of a great   *Eze 3:12*
rushing
sound of a great earthquake   *Eze 3:12*
(R)
they cry in mine ears with a   *Eze 8:18*
loud *v.*
also in mine ears with a   *Eze 9:1*
loud *v.*
shouted loudly (B)   *Eze 9:1*
as the *v.* of the Almighty   *Eze 10:5*
God when
cried with a loud *v.* and   *Eze 11:13*
said, Ah
that his *v.* should no more be   *Eze 19:9*
heard
to lift up the *v.* with   *Eze 21:22*
shouting, to
a *v.* of a multitude being at   *Eze 23:42*
ease
sound of a careless crowd   *Eze 23:42*
(A)
sound of a carefree   *Eze 23:42*
multitude (R)
cause their *v.* to be heard   *Eze 27:30*
against
song of one that hath a   *Eze 33:32*
pleasant *v.*
and his *v.* was like a noise of   *Eze 43:2*
many
sound like many waters (R)   *Eze 43:2*

there fell a *v.* from heaven,   *Da 4:31*
saying
he cried with a lamentable *v.*   *Da 6:20*
cried in a tone of anguish and   *Da 6:20*
anxiety (B)(R)
the *v.* of the great words   *Da 7:11*
which the
sound of great words (A)(R)   *Da 7:11*
his proud words (B)   *Da 7:11*
I heard a man's *v.* between   *Da 8:16*
have we obeyed the *v.* of the   *Da 9:10*
Lord
that they might not obey thy   *Da 9:11*
v.
he doeth: for we obeyed not   *Da 9:14*
his *v.*
and the *v.* of his words like   *Da 10:6*
sound of his words   *Da 10:6;*
(A)(B)(R)   *10:9*
like the *v.* of a multitude   *Da 10:6*
Yet heard I the *v.* of his words   *Da 10:9*
when I heard the *v.* of his   *Da 10:9*
words
shall utter his *v.* before his   *Joe 2:11*
army
thunders before his army (B)   *Joe 2:11*
and utter his *v.* from   *Joe 3:16*
Jerusalem
roars from Jerusalem (B)   *Joe 3:16*
and utter his *v.* from   *Am 1:2*
Jerusalem
cried I, and thou heardest my *v.*   *Jon 2:2*
thee with the *v.* of   *Jon 2:9*
thanksgiving
and let the hills hear thy *v.*   *Mic 6:1*
The Lord's *v.* crieth unto the   *Mic 6:9*
city
lead her as with the *v.* of doves   *Na 2:7*
lamenting and moaning like   *Na 2:7*
doves (A)(R)
moaning like doves (B)   *Na 2:7*
v. of thy messengers shall no   *Na 2:13*
more
the deep uttered his *v.* and   *Hab 3:10*
lifted
my lips quivered at the *v.*   *Hab 3:16*
quivered at the sound   *Hab 3:16*
(A)(B)(R)
even the *v.* of the day of the   *Zep 1:14*
Lord
their *v.* shall sing in the   *Zep 2:14*
windows
noise wail in the windows   *Zep 2:14*
(B)
She obeyed not the *v.*; she   *Zep 3:2*
received
obeyed the *v.* of the Lord   *Hag 1:12*
their God
diligently obey the *v.* of the   *Zec 6:15*
Lord
v. of the howling of the   *Zec 11:3*
shepherds
cries of the shepherds (B)   *Zec 11:3*
wail of the shepherds (R)   *Zec 11:3*
a *v.* of the roaring of young   *Zec 11:3*
lions
In Rama was there a *v.* heard   *M't 2:18*
v. of one crying in the   *M't 3:3*
wilderness
And lo a *v.* from heaven,   *M't 3:17*
saying
any man hear his *v.* in the   *M't 12:19*
streets
and behold a *v.* out of the   *M't 17:5*
cloud
Jesus cried with a loud *v.*   *M't 27:46*
saying
cried aloud (N)   *M't 27:46;*
27:50; M'k 15:34, 37; Lu 1:42;
Ac 7:60; 14:10; Re 5:12; 14:9; 19:17
he had cried again with a   *M't 27:50*
loud *v.*
gave one more great cry   *M't 27:50;*
(P)   *M'k 15:37; Lu 23:46*
v. of one crying in the   *M'k 1:3*
wilderness
And there came a *v.* from   *M'k 1:11*
heaven
cried with a loud *v.*, he came   *M'k 1:26*
out of
with a loud cry left him (N)   *M'k 1:26*
let out a loud scream (P)   *M'k 1:26*
cried with a loud *v.* and said,   *M'k 5:7*
What
a *v.* came out of the cloud,   *M'k 9:7*
saying
hour Jesus cried with a loud   *M'k 15:34*
v.

Jesus cried with a loud *v.*   *M'k 15:37*
and gave
Jesus uttered a loud cry   *M'k 15:37*
(A)(R)
Jesus uttered a strong cry   *M'k 15:37*
(B)
And she spake out with a loud   *Lu 1:42*
v.
cried with a loud cry (A)(R)   *Lu 1:42;*
   4:33
v. of thy salutation sounded in   *Lu 1:44*
mine
sound of your salutation (A)   *Lu 1:44*
v. of one crying in the   *Lu 3:4*
wilderness
a *v.* came from heaven, which   *Lu 3:22*
said
devil and cried out with a   *Lu 4:33*
loud *v.*
cried out loudly (B)   *Lu 4:33*
with a loud *v.* said, What have   *Lu 8:28*
I to
shouted loudly (A)(B)   *Lu 8:28*
fell at his feet shouting (N)   *Lu 8:28*
let out a yell (P)   *Lu 8:28*
there came a *v.* out of the   *Lu 9:35*
cloud
when the *v.* was past, Jesus   *Lu 9:36*
was
certain woman lifted up her   *Lu 11:27*
v.
woman in the crowd   *Lu 11:27*
called out (N)
and with a loud *v.* glorified   *Lu 17:15*
God
loudly praising God (B)(N)   *Lu 17:15*
praise God with a loud *v.* for   *Lu 19:37*
all the
praise God loudly (A)   *Lu 19:37*
sing praise to God with loud   *Lu 19:37*
acclaim (B)
sing aloud the praises of God   *Lu 19:37*
(N)
shouted praises to God (P)   *Lu 19:37*
when Jesus had cried with a   *Lu 23:46*
loud *v.*
Jesus gave a great cry (P)   *Lu 23:46*
v. of one crying in the   *Joh 1:23*
wilderness
because of the bridegroom's   *Joh 3:29*
v.
shall hear the *v.* of the Son   *Joh 5:25*
of God
are in the graves shall hear   *Joh 5:28*
his *v.*
Ye have neither heard his *v.*   *Joh 5:37*
at any
openeth; and the sheep hear   *Joh 10:3*
his *v.*
follow him: for they know his   *Joh 10:4*
v.
they know not the *v.* of   *Joh 10:5*
strangers
and they shall hear my *v.*   *Joh 10:16*
My sheep hear my *v.* and I   *Joh 10:27*
know
listen to my call (B)   *Joh 10:27*
he cried with a loud *v.*,   *Joh 11:43*
Lazarus
called out strongly (B)   *Joh 11:43*
Then came there a *v.* from   *Joh 12:28*
heaven
This *v.* came not because of   *Joh 12:30*
me
that is of the truth heareth   *Joh 18:37*
my *v.*
lifted up his *v.* and said unto   *Ac 2:14*
them
they lifted up their *v.* to God   *Ac 4:24*
the *v.* of the Lord came unto   *Ac 7:31*
him
Then they cried out with a   *Ac 7:57*
loud *v.*
raised a great shout (A)   *Ac 7:57*
shouting loudly (B)   *Ac 7:57*
gave a great shout (N)   *Ac 7:57*
cried in ringing tones (P)   *Ac 7:57*
cried with a loud *v.*, Lord, lay   *Ac 7:60*
not
cried out loudly (A)(B)   *Ac 7:60*
spirits, crying with loud *v.*   *Ac 8:7*
came
made a great outcry (N)   *Ac 8:7*
and heard a *v.* saying unto him   *Ac 9:4*
hearing a *v.* but seeing no man   *Ac 9:7*
there came a *v.* to him, Rise,   *Ac 10:13*
Peter
the *v.* spake unto him again   *Ac 10:15*
the

And I heard a *v.* saying unto me | *Ac 11:7*
But the *v.* answered me again | *Ac 11:9*
And when she knew Peter's *v.* she | *Ac 12:14*
is the *v.* of a god, and not of a man | *Ac 12:22*
Said with a loud *v.*, Stand upright | *Ac 14:10*
shouted at him (A) | *Ac 14:10*
Paul cried with a loud *v.* saying | *Ac 16:28*
Paul shouted (A)(N) | *Ac 16:28*
called out loudly (B) | *Ac 16:28; 26:24*
one *v.* about the space of two hours | *Ac 19:34*
heard a *v.* saying unto me, Saul | *Ac 22:7*
heard not the *v.* of him that spake | *Ac 22:9*
shouldest hear the *v.* of his mouth | *Ac 22:14*
hear a message from his own lips (A) | *Ac 22:14*
Except it be for this one *v.* that I | *Ac 24:21*
death, I gave my *v.* against them | *Ac 26:10*
my vote was cast against them (A)(B)(E)(N)(P)(R) | *Ac 26:10*
I heard a *v.* speaking unto me, and | *Ac 26:14*
Festus said with a loud *v.*, Paul | *Ac 26:24*
called out loudly (A) | *Ac 26:24*
if I know not the meaning of the *v.* | *1Co 14:11*
not know the force of signification (A)(B) | *1Co 14:11*
know not the meaning of the sound (N) | *1Co 14:11*
meaning of the language (R) | *1Co 14:11*
that by my *v.* I might teach others | *1Co 14:19*
you now, and to change my *v.* | *Ga 4:20*
modify my tone (N) | *Ga 4:20*
with the *v.* of the archangel | *1Th 4:16*
shout of the archangel (A)(P) | *1Th 4:16*
the archangel's call (R) | *1Th 4:16*
saith, To-day if ye will hear his *v.* | *3:15; 4:7*
of a trumpet, and the *v.* of words | *Heb 12:19*
audible words (B) | *Heb 12:19*
which *v.* they that heard intreated | *Heb 12:19*
Whose *v.* then shook the earth | *Heb 12:26*
came such a *v.* to him from | *2Pe 1:17*
this *v.* which came from heaven we | *2Pe 1:18*
dumb ass speaking with man's *v.* | *2Pe 2:16*
and heard behind me a great *v.* as | *Re 1:10*
I turned to see the *v.* that spake | *Re 1:12*
his *v.* as the sound of many waters | *Re 1:15*
if any man hear my *v.* and open | *Re 3:20*
the first *v.* which I heard was as it | *Re 4:1*
angel proclaiming with a loud *v.* | *Re 5:2*
I hear the *v.* of many angels round | *Re 5:11*
Saying with a loud *v.* Worthy is the | *Re 5:12*
I heard a *v.* in the midst of the four | *Re 6:6*
I heard the *v.* of the fourth beast | *Re 6:7*
And they cried with a loud *v.* | *Re 6:10*
he cried with a loud *v.* to the four | *Re 7:2*
called aloud (N) | *Re 7:2*
And cried with a loud *v.* saying | *Re 7:10*
they shouted together (N) | *Re 7:10*
saying with a loud *v.* Woe, woe | *Re 8:13*
calling with a loud cry (N) | *Re 8:13*
I heard a *v.* from the four horns of | *Re 9:13*
cried with a loud *v.* as when a lion | *Re 10:3*

I heard a *v.* from heaven saying | *Re 10:4*
with a great shout (N) | *Re 10:4*
days of the *v.* of the seventh angel | *Re 10:7*
v. which I heard from heaven spake | *Re 10:8*
they heard a great *v.* from heaven | *Re 11:12*
I heard a loud *v.* saying in heaven | *Re 12:10*
And I heard a *v.* from heaven | *Re 14:2*
sounded like the noise of rushing water (N) | *Re 14:2*
a sound like the roar of a great waterfall, and heavy rolling thunder (P) | *Re 14:2*
as the *v.* of many waters, and | *Re 14:2*
and as the *v.* of a great thunder | *Re 14:2*
heard the *v.* of harpers harping | *Re 14:2*
Saying with a loud *v.* Fear God | *Re 14:7*
them, saying with a loud *v.* | *Re 14:9*
I heard a *v.* from heaven saying | *Re 14:13*
loud *v.* to him that sat on the cloud | *Re 14:15*
a great *v.* out of the temple saying | *Re 16:1*
a great *v.* out of the temple of | *Re 16:17*
he cried mightily with a strong *v.* | *Re 18:2*
I heard another *v.* from heaven | *Re 18:4*
the *v.* of harpers, and musicians | *Re 18:22*
sound of harpists (A)(P)(R) | *Re 18:22*
the *v.* of the bridegroom and | *Re 18:23*
I heard a great *v.* of much people | *Re 19:1*
shout of a great crowd (A) | *Re 19:1*
sounded like a roar of a vast throng (N)(P) | *Re 19:1*
And a *v.* came out of the throne | *Re 19:5*
it were the *v.* of a great multitude | *Re 19:6*
shout of a vast throng (A) | *Re 19:6*
sounded like a vast crowd (N) | *Re 19:6*
and as the *v.* of many waters | *Re 19:6*
like the boom of pounding waves (A) | *Re 19:6*
as the *v.* of mighty thunderings | *Re 19:6*
like the roar of terrific and mighty thunder peals (A) | *Re 19:6*
and he cried with a loud *v.* saying | *Re 19:17*
a great *v.* out of heaven saying | *Re 21:3*

VOICES

lifted up their *v.* and wept sore | *J'g 21:2*
people lifted up their *v.* and wept | *1Sa 11:4*
wept aloud (A)(R) | *1Sa 11:4*
wept audibly (B) | *1Sa 11:4*
And they lifted up their *v.* | *Lu 17:13*
And they were instant with loud *v.* | *Lu 23:23*
loud cries (A)(R) | *Lu 23:23*
shouting (N) | *Lu 23:23*
shouted him down (P) | *Lu 23:23*
v. of them and of the chief priests | *Lu 23:23*
their shouting won the day (P) | *Lu 23:23*
nor yet the *v.* of the prophets which | *Ac 13:27*
utterances of the prophets (A) | *Ac 13:27*
words of the prophets (N) | *Ac 13:27*
they lifted up their *v.* saying | *Ac 14:11*
they shouted (N)(P) | *Ac 14:11*
and then lifted up their *v.* and said | *Ac 22:22*
raised a great shout (P) | *Ac 22:22*
so many kinds of *v.* in the world | *1Co 14:10*
many tongues in the world (A) | *1Co 14:10*
many languages in the world (B)(R) | *1Co 14:10*
many kinds of sounds (N) | *1Co 14:10*
great variety of spoken sounds (P) | *1Co 14:10*

lightnings and thunderings and *v.* | *Re 4:5*
and there were *v.* and thunderings | *Re 8:5*
of the other *v.* of the trumpet | *Re 8:13*
seven thunders uttered their *v.* | *Re 10:4*
seven thunders had uttered their *v.* | *Re 10:4*
and there were great *v.* in heaven | *Re 11:15*
strong shouting arose (B) | *Re 11:15*
lightning and *v.* and thunderings | *Re 11:19*
there were *v.* and thunders | *Re 16:18*

VOID

the earth was without form, and *v.* | *Ge 1:2*
an empty waste (A) | *Ge 1:2*
empty (B) | *Ge 1:2; Jer 4:23*
made them *v.* on the day he heard | *Nu 30:12*
nullifies them (B) | *Nu 30:12; 30:13*
her husband hath made them *v.* | *Nu 30:12*
made them invalid (B) | *Nu 30:12*
or her husband may make it *v.* | *Nu 30:13*
annul (A) | *Nu 30:13*
make them *v.* after that he hath | *Nu 30:15*
nullify (A) | *Nu 30:15*
renounces them (B) | *Nu 30:15*
For they are a nation *v.* of counsel | *De 32:28*
unsound mind (B) | *De 32:28*
in a *v.* place in the entrance | *1Ki 22:10*
an open place (A)(E) | *1Ki 22:10; 2Ch 18:9*
the threshingfloor (B)(R) | *1Ki 22:10; 2Ch 18:9*
sat in a *v.* place at the entering in | *2Ch 18:9*
annul, render *v.* (A) | *Job 40:8*
made *v.* covenant of thy servant | *Ps 89:39*
despised, loathed, renounced covenant (A) | *Ps 89:39*
spurned the covenant (B) | *Ps 89:39*
renounced the covenant (R) | *Ps 89:39*
for they have made *v.* thy law | *Ps 119:126*
frustrated your law (A) | *Ps 119:126*
violated your law (B) | *Ps 119:126*
broken thy law (R) | *Ps 119:126*
a young man *v.* of understanding | *Pr 7:7*
senseless (B) | *Pr 7:7*
without sense (R) | *Pr 7:7; 10:13; 11:12; 12:11; 17:18; 24:30*
of him that is *v.* of understanding | *Pr 10:13*
without sense (A) | *Pr 10:13; 11:12; 12:11*
He that is *v.* of wisdom despiseth | *Pr 11:12*
lacks good sense (B) | *Pr 11:12; 12:11*
vain persons is *v.* of understanding | *Pr 12:11*
him that is *v.* of wisdom (E) | *Pr 15:21*
A man *v.* of understanding striketh | *Pr 17:18*
lacks good judgment (B) | *Pr 17:18*
of the man *v.* of understanding | *Pr 24:30*
lacked understanding (B) | *Pr 24:30*
it shall not return unto me *v.* but | *Isa 55:11*
come back to me uselessly (B) | *Isa 55:11*
return to me empty (R) | *Isa 55:11*
and, lo, it was without form, and *v.* | *Jer 4:23*
a waste and vacant (A) | *Jer 4:23*
make *v.* the counsel of Judah | *Jer 19:7*
She is empty, and *v.* and waste | *Na 2:10*
Desolation (A)(B)(R) | *Na 2:10*
conscience *v.* of offence toward God | *Ac 24:16*
make *v.* the law through faith | *Ro 3:31*
make the law of no effect (A)(E) | *Ro 3:31*
abrogated (B) | *Ro 3:31*
using faith to undermine law (N)(P) | *Ro 3:31*
overthrow the law by faith (R) | *Ro 3:31*

faith is made *v.* and the   Ro 4:14
promise
made little and empty of all   Ro 4:14
meaning (A)
faith is futile (B)   Ro 4:14
faith is empty (N)   Ro 4:14
make nonsense faith (P)   Ro 4:14
faith is null (R)   Ro 4:14
man should make my glorying   1Co 9:15
v.
rob me of the source of   1Co 9:15
honor (B)
make my boast an empty   1Co 9:15
boast (N)(P)
deprive me of my ground of   1Co 9:15
boasting (R)
preaching is null and *v.* (N)   1Co 15:14
do not make *v.* grace (E)   Ga 2:21
no one makes it *v.* (A)(B)(E)   Ga 3:15
cannot render null and *v.* (R)   Ga 3:17

VOLUME

in the *v.* of the book it is   Ps 40:7
written
roll of the book (E)(P)(R)   Ps 40:7;
                                           Heb 10:7
(in the *v.* of the book it is   Heb 10:7
written
in the roll of the book (B)   Heb 10:7
in the scroll (N)   Heb 10:7

VOLUNTARILY

peace offerings *v.* unto the   Eze 46:12
Lord
freewill (B)(E)(R)   Eze 46:12

VOLUNTARY

Offer it of his own *v.* will at the   Le 1:3
offering be a vow, or a *v.*   Le 7:16
offering
freewill offering (A)(B)(E)(R)   Le 7:16;
                                           Eze 46:12
shalt prepare a *v.* burnt   Eze 46:12
offering
you of your reward in a *v.*   Col 2:18
humility

VOLUNTEER

the *v.* growth (B)   Le 25:5

VOMIT

throw, *v.* (B)(E)(R)   Le 18:28
v., vomited (A)(B)(R)   Le 20:22
and he shall *v.* them up   Job 20:15
again
thou hast eaten shalt thou *v.*   Pr 23:8
up.
thou be filled therewith, and   Pr 25:16
v. it
a dog returned to his *v.*, so a   Pr 26:11
fool
drunken man staggereth in   Isa 19:14
his *v.*
For all tables are full of *v.* and   Isa 28:8
be drunken and *v.* (S)   Jer 25:27
Moab also shall wallow in   Jer 48:26
his *v.* and
dog is turned to his own *v.*   2Pe 2:22
again

VOMITED

it *v.* out Jonah upon the dry   Jon 2:10
land

VOMITETH

land itself *v.* out her   Le 18:25
inhabitants

VOPHSI

of Naphtali, Nahbi the son   Nu 13:14
of *V.*

VORACIOUS

they are *v.* wolves (B)   M't 7:15

VOTED

nor *v.* for their decision (P)   Lu 23:51

VOW

Jacob vowed a *v.*, saying, If   Ge 28:20
God

where thou vowedst a *v.* unto   Ge 31:13
me
the sacrifice of his offering be   Le 7:16
a *v.*
unto the lord to accomplish   Le 22:21
his *v.*
for a *v.* it shall not be   Le 22:23
accepted
a man shall make a singular *v.*   Le 27:2
shall separate themselves to *v.*   Nu 6:2
v. of a Nazarite, to separate   Nu 6:2
the days of the *v.* of his   Nu 6:5
separation
according to the *v.* which he   Nu 6:21
vowed
a sacrifice in performing a   Nu 15:3;
v. or   15:8
Israel vowed a *v.* unto the   Nu 21:2
Lord
If a man *v.* unto the Lord   Nu 30:2
v. unto the Lord, or swear   Nu 30:2
a woman also *v.* unto the   Nu 30:3
Lord
v. unto the Lord, and bind   Nu 30:3
her father hear her *v.* and her   Nu 30:4
bond
shall make her *v.* which she   Nu 30:8
vowed
But ever *v.* of a widow, and   Nu 30:9
of her
Every *v.* and every binding   Nu 30:13
oath to
vows which ye *v.* unto the   De 12:11
Lord
of the Lord thy God for any   De 23:18
v.
thou shalt *v.* unto the Lord   De 23:21
v. unto the Lord thy God   De 23:21
But if thou shalt forbear to   De 23:22
v. it
Jephthah vowed a *v.* unto the   J'g 11:30
according to his *v.* which he   J'g 11:39
had
And she vowed a *v.* and said,   1Sa 1:11
Lord the yearly sacrifice, and   1Sa 1:21
his *v.*
pray thee, let me go and pay   2Sa 15:7
my *v.*
servant vowed a *v.* while I   2Sa 15:8
abode
unto thee shall the *v.* be   Ps 65:1
performed
V. and pay unto the Lord   Ps 76:11
your
When thou vowest a *v.* unto   Ec 5:4
God
is it that thou shouldest not *v.*   Ec 5:5
that thou shouldest *v.* and not   Ec 5:5
pay
yea, they shall *v.* unto the   Isa 19:21
Lord
a *v.* unto the Lord, and   Isa 19:21
perform it
head in Cenchrea: for he had   Ac 18:18
a *v.*
four men which have a *v.* on   Ac 21:23
them

VOWED

And Jacob *v.* a vow, saying,   Ge 28:20
God
according to his ability that *v.*   Le 27:8
shall
law of the Nazarite who hath   Nu 6:21
v. and
according to the vow which   Nu 6:21
he *v.*
And Israel *v.* a vow unto the   Nu 21:2
Lord
at all an husband, when she *v.*   Nu 30:6
shall make her vow which she   Nu 30:8
v.
if she *v.* in her husband's   Nu 30:10
house
as thou hast *v.* unto the Lord   De 23:23
thy
I *v.* to their fathers (B)   Jos 1:6;
                                        5:6; Ps 95:11
Jephthah *v.* a vow unto the   J'g 11:30
Lord
to his vow which he had *v.*   J'g 11:39
And she *v.* a vow, and said,   1Sa 1:11
O Lord
I have *v.* unto the Lord, in   2Sa 15:7
Hebron
thy servant *v.* a vow while I   2Sa 15:8
abode
v. unto the mighty God of   Ps 132:2
Jacob

pay that which thou hast *v.*   Ec 5:4
perform our vows that we   Jer 44:25
have *v.*
I will pay that that I have *v.*   Jon 2:9
he *v.* to her (R)   M'k 6:23
I *v.* in my wrath (N)   Heb 3:11; 3:18

VOWEDST

and where thou *v.* a vow   Ge 31:13
unto me

VOWEST

nor any of thy vows which   De 12:17
thou *v.*
When thou *v.* a vow unto God,   Ec 5:4
defer

VOWETH

and *v.* and sacrificeth unto   Mal 1:14

VOWS

offer his oblation for all his *v.*   Le 22:18
beside all your *v.* and beside   Le 23:38
beside your *v.* and your   Nu 29:39
freewill
then all her *v.* shall stand, and   Nu 30:4
not any of her *v.* or of her   Nu 30:5
bonds
then her *v.* shall stand, and   Nu 30:7
then all her *v.* shall stand   Nu 30:12
out of her lips concerning   Nu 30:12
her *v.*
then he establisheth all her *v.*   Nu 30:14
your *v.* and your freewill   De 12:6
offerings
all your choice *v.* which ye   De 12:11
vow
nor any of thy *v.* which thou   De 12:17
and thy *v.* thou shalt take,   De 12:26
and go
thee, and thou shall pay thy   Job 22:27
v.
I will pay my *v.* before them   Ps 22:25
and pay thy *v.* unto the most   Ps 50:14
High
Thy *v.* are upon me, O God: Ps 56:12
I will
For thou, O God, hast heard   Ps 61:5
my *v.*
that I may daily perform my *v.*   Ps 61:8
offerings: I will pay thee my   Ps 66:13
v.
I will pay my *v.* unto the   Ps 116:14;
Lord   116:18
me; this day have I payed my   Pr 7:14
v.
holy, and after *v.* to make   Pr 20:25
enquiry
womb? and what, the son of   Pr 31:2
my *v.*
will surely perform our *v.*   Jer 44:25
that we
ye will surely accomplish   Jer 44:25
your *v.*
and surely perform your *v.*   Jer 44:25
sacrifice unto the Lord, and   Jon 1:16
made *v.*
thy solemn feasts, perform thy   Na 1:15
v.

VOYAGE

I perceive that this *v.* will be   Ac 27:10

VULGAR

one of the *v.* fellows (R)   2Sa 6:20

VULTURE

the *v.* and the kite after his   Le 11:14
kind
the whole species of falcon   Le 11:14
(A)(E)(R)
every species of buzzard (B)   Le 11:14
(A)(E)(R)
the kite, and the *v.* after his   De 14:13
kind
the buzzard (A)(B)(R)   De 14:13
the falcon (E)   De 14:13
the carrion *v.* (S)   De 14:17
the *v.* and hedgehog (R)   Zep 2:14

VULTURES

the *v.* also be gathered, every   Isa 34:15
the kites (A)(E)(R)   Isa 34:15
the vultures (B)   Isa 34:15

VULTURE'S

which the *v.* eye hath not seen	Job 28:7
the falcon's eye (A)(E)(R)	Joh 28:7
eagle's eye (B)	Joh 28:7

W

WAFER

and one *w.* out of the basket	Ex 29:23
a cake of oiled bread, and one *w.*	Le 8:26
the basket, and one unleavened *w.*	Nu 6:19

WAFERS

of it was like *w.* made with honey	Ex 16:31
w. unleavened anointed with oil	Ex 29:2
unleavened *w.* anointed with oil	Le 2:4; 7:12
w. of unleavened bread anointed	Nu 6:15

WAG

be astonished, and *w.* his head	Jer 18:16
shake the head (A)(B)(E)(R)	Jer 18:16
w. their head at the daughter	La 2:15
wave the hand (A)	La 2:15
shake the fist (B)(R)	La 2:15
her shall hiss, and *w.* his hand	Zep 2:15

WAGE

teaches to *w.* war (B)(E)(R)	Ps 144:1
Judah shall *w.* war (B)	Zec 14:14
a full day's *w.* (N)	M't 20:2; 20:10, 13
worker deserves his *w.* (B)	1Ti 5:18
by the error of Balaam's *w.* (B)	Jude 11

WAGES

tell me, what shall thy *w.* be	Ge 29:15
Appoint me thy *w.* and I will give	Ge 30:28
salary (A)	Ge 30:28
and changed my *w.* ten times	Ge 31:7
The speckled shall be thy *w.*	Ge 31:8
hast changd my *w.* ten times	Ge 31:41
me, and I will give thee thy *w.*	Ex 2:9
w. of him that is hired shall not	Le 19:13
a laborer longs for his *w.* (B)(E)(R)	Job 7:2
neighbour's service without *w.*	Jer 22:13
yet had he no *w.* nor his army	Eze 29:18
remuneration (A)	Eze 29:18
gained any returns (B)	Eze 29:18
and it shall be the *w.* for his army	Eze 29:19
and he that earneth *w.* earneth	Hag 1:6
earneth *w.* to put it into a bag	Hag 1:6
that oppress the hireling in his *w.*	Mal 3:5
and be content with your *w.*	Lu 3:14
allowance (A)	Lu 3:14
pay (N)(P)	Lu 3:14
And he that reapeth receiveth *w.*	Joh 4:36
the *w.* of crime (B)	Ac 1:18
w. counted as a favor (A)(B)(N)(P)(R)	Ro 4:4
For the *w.* of sin is death; but the	Ro 6:23
receive his own *w.* (R)	1Co 3:8
other churches taking *w.* of them	2Co 11:8
accepting support (A)(N)	2Co 11:8
taking pay (B)	2Co 11:8
workman deserves his *w.* (R)	1Ti 5:18
loved the *w.* of unrighteousness	2Pe 2:15
reward (A)	2Pe 2:15
pay (N)	2Pe 2:15; Joh 4:36
paid (P)	2Pe 2:15
Gain (R)	2Pe 2:15

WAGGING

by reviled him, *w.* their heads	M't 27:39
by railed on him, *w.* their heads	M'k 15:29

WAGON

a *w.* for two of the princes, and for	Nu 7:3

WAGONS

take you *w.* out of the land	Ge 45:19
Joseph gave them *w.* according to	Ge 45:21
when he saw the *w.* which Joseph	Ge 45:27
in the *w.* which Pharaoh had sent	Ge 46:5
before the Lord, six covered *w.*	Nu 7:3
Moses took the *w.* and the oxen	Nu 7:6
Two *w.* and four oxen he gave	Nu 7:7
four *w.* and eight oxen he gave	Nu 7:8
against thee with chariots *w.*	Eze 23:24

WAIL

wail (S)	Isa 13:6; 15:2, 3; 16:7; 23:6; 52:5; 65:14; Jer 4:8; 25:34; 47:2; 48:20, 31, 39; 49:3; 51:8; Eze 21:12; 30:2; Joe 1:5, 11, 13; Zec 11:2
w. for the multitude of Egypt	Eze 32:18
w. like a virgin (B)	Joe 1:8
Therefore I will *w.* and howl	Mic 1:8
w. in the windows (B)	Zep 2:14
w. of the shepherds (R)	Zec 11:3
kindreds of the earth shall *w.*	Re 1:7
beat their breasts, mourn, lament (A)	Re 1:7
beat their breasts (B)	Re 1:7
mourn over him (E)	Re 1:7
lament in remorse (N)	Re 1:7
bitter sorrow (P)	Re 1:7
weep, *w.* over her (A)(B)(E)(N)(P)(R)	Re 18:9

WAILED

when they *w.* upon their beds (S)	Ho 7:14
and them that wept and *w.* greatly	M'k 5:38

WAILING

and fasting, and weeping, and *w.*	Es 4:3
wailing (A)	Isa 15:8; Jer 25:36; Zep 1:10; Zec 11:3
will I take up a weeping and *w.*	Jer 9:10
haste, and take up a *w.* for us	Jer 9:18
a voice of *w.* is heard out of Zion	Jer 9:19
and teach your daughters *w.*	Jer 9:20
neither shall there be *w.* for them	Eze 7:11
bitterness of heart and bitter *w.*	Eze 27:31
in their *w.* they shall take up	Eze 27:32
W. shall be in all streets; and	Am 5:16
as are skilful of lamentation to *w.*	Am 5:16
And in all vineyards shall be *w.*	Am 5:17
I will make a *w.* like the dragons	Mic 1:8
be *w.* and gnashing of teeth	M't 13:42; 13:50
loud crying and *w.* (B)(E)(P)	M'k 5:38
of her torment, weeping and *w.*	Re 18:15
cried, weeping and *w.* saying	Re 18:19

WAILINGS

songs shall be *w.* (S)	Am 8:3

WAIST

the waist (B)	Ge 12:11; 28:42; 2Sa 20:8
girdle of his *w.* (A)(B)(E)(R)(S)	Isa 11:5
girdle about his *w.* (S)	M't 3:4; M'k 1:6

WAIT

if a man lie not in *w.*, but God	Ex 21:13
wait (B)	Ex 24:14; 2Ki 7:9; Hab 2:3; 1Co 11:33
shall *w.* on their priest's office	Nu 3:10
attend to (A)(B)(R)	Nu 3:10
in to *w.* upon the service of	Nu 8:24
perform the work (A)(R)	Nu 8:24
or hurl at him by laying of *w.*	Nu 35:20
him any thing without laying of *w.*	Nu 35:22
and lie in *w.* for him, and rise up	De 19:11
ye shall lie in *w.* against the city	Jos 8:4
ambush (B)	Jos 8:4; 8:13; J'g 9:25, 34, 43; 20:29, 33, 36-38; 1Sa 15:5; 22:8; Pr 7:12; Jer 9:8; Ac 23:16; 25:3
ambush (E)	Jos 8:4
ambush (R)	Jos 8:4; J'g 9:25, 35; 20:29, 33, 36-38; Jer 9:8; Ac 23:16, 21
liers in *w.* one west of the city	Jos 8:13
ambush (A)	Jos 8:13; J'g 9:25, 35; 20:29, 33, 36-38; Pr 7:12; Ac 25:3
wait (A)	J'g 6:18; 1:13; 1Sa 10:8; 14:9; 15:28; 2Ki 7:9; 1Co 11:33
set liers in *w.* for him in the top of	J'g 9:25
with thee, and lie in *w.* in the field	J'g 9:32
and they laid *w.* against Shechem	J'g 9:34
were with him, from lying in *w.*	J'g 9:35
laid *w.* in the field, and looked	J'g 9:43
laid *w.* for him all night in the gate	J'g 16:2
Now there were men lying in *w.*	J'g 16:9
having men hidden (B)	J'g 16:9
there were liers in *w.* abiding	J'g 16:12
Israel set liers in *w.* round about	J'g 20:29
liers in *w.* of Israel came forth	J'g 20:33
they trusted unto the liers in *w.*	J'g 20:36
liers in *w.* hasted, and rushed	J'g 20:37
liers in *w.* drew themselves along	J'g 20:37
men of Israel and the liers in *w.*	J'g 20:38
Go and lie in *w.* in the vineyards	J'g 21:20
hide in the vineyards (B)	J'g 21:20
wait (B)	Ru 1:13; 1Sa 10:8; Lu 24:49
wait (R)	Ru 1:13; 1Sa 1:23; 10:8; 14:9; 2Ki 7:9; Hab 2:3; 1Co 11:33
how he laid *w.* for him in the way	1Sa 15:2
waylaid (B)	1Sa 15:2; 22:13
Amalek, and laid *w.* in the valley	1Sa 15:5
my servant against me, to lie in *w.*	1Sa 22:8
should rise against me, to lie in *w.*	1Sa 22:13
I *w.* for the Lord any longer	2Ki 6:33
was to *w.* on the sons of Aaron	1Ch 23:28
and did not then *w.* by course	2Ch 5:11
the Levites *w.* upon their business	2Ch 13:10
and of such as lay in *w.* by the way	Ezr 8:31
ambushes (R)	Ezr 8:31
of my appointed time will I *w.*	Job 14:14
If I *w.* the grave is mine house	Job 17:13
if I look to Sheol (A)(E)(R)	Job 17:13
if I have laid *w.* at my neighbour	Job 31:9
lurked (B)	Job 31:9
and abide in the covert to lie in *w.*	Job 38:40
He lieth in *w.* secretly as a lion	Ps 10:9
he lieth in *w.* to catch the poor: he	Ps 10:9
none that *w.* on thee be ashamed	Ps 25:3

on thee do I w. all the day | Ps 25:5
preserve me; for I w. on thee | Ps 25:21
W. on the Lord: be of good | Ps 27:14
thine heart: w. I say, on the | Ps 27:14
Lord
Lord, and w. patiently for him | Ps 37:7
resign yourself to him (B) | Ps 37:7
but those that w. upon the | Ps 37:9
Lord
W. on the Lord, and keep | Ps 37:34
his way
And now, Lord, what w. I for | Ps 39:7
and I will w. on thy name; for | Ps 52:9
hope in thy name (E) | Ps 52:9
steps, when they w. for my | Ps 56:6
soul
For, lo, they lie in w. for my | Ps 59:3
soul
his strength will I w. upon thee | Ps 59:9
give heed to you (A) | Ps 59:9
My soul, w. thou only upon | Ps 62:5
God
eyes fail while I w. for my | Ps 69:3
God
Let not them that w. on thee | Ps 69:6
hope in thee (R) | Ps 69:6
and they that lay w. for my | Ps 71:10
soul
These w. all upon thee; that | Ps 104:27
thou
look to thee (R) | Ps 104:27; 123:2; 145:15
so our eyes w. upon the Lord | Ps 123:2
look to the Lord (A) | Ps 123:2
our eyes look to Jehovah (E) | Ps 123:2
I w. for the Lord, my soul | Ps 130:5
doth w.
The eyes of all w. upon thee | Ps 145:15
look expectantly to thee (B) | Ps 145:15
let us lay w. for blood, let us | Pr 1:11
lurk
And they lay w. for their own | Pr 1:18
blood
and lieth in w. at every corner | Pr 7:12
the wicked are to lie in w. for | Pr 12:6
blood
w. on the Lord, and he shall | Pr 20:22
save
She also lieth in w. as for a | Pr 23:28
prey
Lay not w. O wicked man, | Pr 24:15
against
And I will w. upon the Lord, | Isa 8:17
that
therefore will the Lord w. | Isa 30:18
that he
blessed are all they that w. for | Isa 30:18
him
they that w. upon the Lord | Isa 40:31
and the isles shall w. for his | Isa 42:4
law
not be ashamed that w. for | Isa 49:23
me
the isles shall w. upon me, | Isa 51:5
and on
w. for light, but behold | Isa 59:9
obscurity
look for the light (R) | Isa 59:9
Surely the isles shall w. for | Isa 60:9
me
they lay w. as he that setteth | Jer 5:26
but in heart he layeth his w. | Jer 9:8
therefore we will w. upon | Jer 14:22
thee: for
was unto me as a bear lying in | La 3:10
w.
Lord is good unto them that w. | La 3:25
quietly in for the salvation of | La 3:25
laid w. for us in the wilderness | La 4:19
as troops of robbers w. for a | Ho 6:9
man
like an oven, whiles they lie in | Ho 7:6
w.
and w. on thy God | Ho 12:6
continually
they all lie in w. for blood; | Mic 7:2
they
w. for the God of my | Mic 7:7
salvation
though it tarry, w. for it: | Hab 2:3
because
Therefore w. ye upon me, | Zep 3:8
saith the
a small ship should w. on him | M'k 3:9
Laying w. for him, and | Lu 11:54
seeking to
like men that w. for their | Lu 12:36
lord
wait (N) | Joh 21:22; 1Co 11:33

w. for the promise of the | Ac 1:4
Father
the Jews laid w. for him | Ac 20:3
by the lying in w. of the Jews | Ac 20:19
son heard of their lying in w. | Ac 23:16
ambush (N) | Ac 23:16; 25:3
for there lie in w. for him of | Ac 23:21
them
the Jews laid w. for the man | Ac 23:30
laying w. in the way to kill | Ac 25:3
then do we with patience w. | Ro 8:25
let us w. on our ministering | Ro 12:7
they which w. at the altar are | 1Co 9:13
those who tend (B) | 1Co 9:13
w. one for the other (E)(P) | 1Co 11:33
w. for the hope of | Ga 5:5
righteousness
anticipate (B) | Ga 5:5
whereby they lie in w. to | Eph 4:14
deceive
And to w. for his Son from | 1Th 1:10
heaven

WAITED

I have w. for thy salvation, | Ge 49:18
O Lord
w. on him (B) | 2Sa 13:17; M't 4:11; 8:15
and w. for the king by the | 1Ki 20:38
way
and she w. on Naaman's wife | 2Ki 5:2
and then they w. on their | 1Ch 6:32
office
performing their service | 1Ch 6:32
(A)(R)
rendering service (B) | 1Ch 6:32
they that w. with their | 1Ch 6:33
children
served (A)(R) | 1Ch 6:33
w. in the king's gate | 1Ch 9:18
eastward
assigned to the king's east | 1Ch 9:18
gate (A)
the gatekeepers (B)(R) | 1Ch 9:18
the priests w. on their offices | 2Ch 7:6
priests stood at their posts | 2Ch 7:6
(A)(B)(R)
These w. on the king, beside | 2Ch 17:19
those
these were in the king's | 2Ch 17:19
service (A)(R)
were the king's officers (B) | 2Ch 17:19
and the porters w. at every | 2Ch 35:15
gate
gatekeepers were at every | 2Ch 35:15
gate (A)
the doorkeepers (B) | 2Ch 35:15
priests and for the Levites | Ne 12:44
that w.
Levites who served (A) | Ne 12:44
Levite that ministered (R) | Ne 12:44
the companies of Sheba w. | Job 6:19
for them
and he is w. for of the | Job 15:22
sword
Unto me men gave ear, and | Job 29:21
w.
And they w. for me as for | Job 29:23
the rain
when I w. for light, there | Job 30:26
came
Elihu had w. till Job had | Job 32:4
spoken
Behold, I w. for your words | Job 32:11
When I had w. (for they | Job 32:16
I w. patiently for the Lord; and | Ps 40:1
he
they w. not for his counsel | Ps 106:13
wicked have w. for me to | Ps 119:95
destroy
my eyes w. for night | Ps 119:148
watches (B)
we have w. for him, and he | Isa 25:9
will
we have w. for him, we will | Isa 25:9
be glad
O Lord, have we w. for thee | Isa 26:8
we have w. for thee: be thou | Isa 33:2
their
when she saw that she had w. | Eze 19:5
of Maroth w. carefully for | Mic 1:12
good
poor of the flock that w. | Zec 11:11
upon me
who were watching me | Zec 11:11
(A)(B)(R)
also w. for the kingdom of | M'k 15:43
God

And the people w. for | Lu 1:21
Zacharias
himself w. for the kingdom | Lu 23:51
of God
them that w. on him | Ac 10:7
continually
personal attendants | Ac 10:7
(A)(B)(P)
And Cornelius w. for them | Ac 10:24
while Paul w. for them at | Ac 17:16
Athens
of God w. in the days of | 1Pe 3:20
Noah

WAITETH

the adulterer w. for the | Job 24:15
twilight
Our soul w. for the Lord; he | Ps 33:20
is
Truly my soul w. upon God: | Ps 62:1
from
Praise w. for thee, O God, in | Ps 65:1
Sion
My soul w. for the Lord more | Ps 130:6
than
he that w. on his master shall | Pr 27:18
be
prepared for him that w. for | Isa 64:4
him
Blessed is he that w. and | Da 12:12
cometh to
man, nor w. for the sons of | Mic 5:7
men
w. for the manifestation of | Ro 8:19
husbandman w. for the | Jas 5:7
precious

WAITING

cease w. upon the service | Nu 8:25
thereof
serve no more (A)(R) | Nu 8:25
retire from service (B) | Nu 8:25
gates, w. at the posts of my | Pr 8:34
doors
w. for the consolation of | Lu 2:25
Israel
w. expectantly (A) | Lu 3:15
him: for they were all w. for | Lu 8:40
him
w. for the moving of the water | Joh 5:3
w. for the adoption, to wit, the | Ro 8:23
w. for the coming of our Lord | 1Co 1:7
Jesus
and into the patient w. for | 2Th 3:5
Christ

WAITS

w. with eager longing (N)(R) | Ro 8:19

WAKE

a perpetual sleep, and not | Jer 51:39; 51:57
w.
w. up the mighty men, let all | Joe 3:9
whether we w. or sleep, we | 1Th 5:10
should

WAKED

with me came again, and w. | Zec 4:1
me

WAKENED

Let the heathen be w. | Joe 3:12
and come
a man that is w. out of his | Zec 4:1
sleep

WAKENETH

he w. morning by morning | Isa 50:4
w. mine ear to hear as the | Isa 50:4
learned

WAKETH

the watchman w. but in vain | Ps 127:1
I sleep, but my heart w.: it is | Ca 5:2
he w. morning by morning | Isa 50:4
(S)

WAKING

Thou holdest mine eyes w.: I | Ps 77:4
am

WALK

Arise, w. through the land in   Ge 13:17
traverse (B)   Ge 13:17
w. before me, and be thou   Ge 17:1
perfect
live in my presence (B)   Ge 17:1
The Lord, before whom I w.   Ge 24:40
will
fathers Abraham and Isaac   Ge 48:15
did w.
whether they will w. in my   Ex 16:4
law
follow my instructions or not   Ex 16:4
(B)
the way wherein they must w.   Ex 18:20
the way to behave (B)   Ex 18:20
and w. abroad upon his staff   Ex 21:19
shall ye w. in their ordinances   Le 18:3
follow their rules (B)   Le 18:3
mine ordinances, to w. therein   Le 18:4
ye shall not w. in the   Le 20:23
manners of
If ye w. in my statutes, and   Le 26:3
keep
I will w. among you, and will   Le 26:12
ye w. contrary unto me, and   Le 26:21
will
if you behave contrary to me   Le 26:21
(B)
but will w. contrary unto me   Le 26:23
will I also w. contrary unto   Le 26:24
you
unto me, but w. contrary   Le 26:27
unto me
behave in opposition to me   Le 26:27
(B)
Then I will w. contrary unto   Le 26:28
you
I will take measures against   Le 26:28
you (B)
Ye shall w. in all the ways   De 5:33
which
going strictly the whole course   De 5:33
ordered (B)
to w. in his ways, and to fear   De 8:6
him
w. after other gods, and serve   De 8:19
follow (B)   De 8:19;
13:4, 5; 1Ki 11:38; 16:31; 2Ki 23:3;
Ec 11:9; Jer 3:17; 7:6; 13:10; 16:12;
18:12; Eze 11:20; 33:15; 37:24
to w. in all his ways, and to   De 10:12
love
to w. in all his ways, and to   De 11:22
cleave
Ye shall w. after the Lord your   De 13:4
God
thy God commanded thee to w.   De 13:5
thy God, and to w. ever in his   De 19:9
ways
be thy God, and to w. in his   De 26:17
ways
Lord thy God, and w. in his   De 28:9
ways
I w. in the imaginations of   De 29:19
mine
though I walk in my   De 29:19
stubborn way (B)
Lord thy God to w. in his   De 30:16
ways
Go and w. through the land   Jos 18:8
God, and to w. in all his ways   Jos 22:5
the way of the Lord to w.   J'g 2:22
therein
in judgment, and w. by the   J'g 5:10
way
should w. before me for ever   1Sa 2:30
he shall w. before mine   1Sa 2:35
anointed
and thy sons w. not in thy ways   1Sa 8:5
behave (B)   1Sa 8:5;
M'k 7:5; Ro 8:1, 4; 13:13; 1Co 3:3;
Ga 5:16; Eph 4:17; Ph'p 3:17; 1Th 4:1
to w. in his ways, to keep his   1Ki 2:3
to w. before me in truth with   1Ki 2:4
if thou wilt w. in my ways, to   1Ki 3:14
keep
as thy father David did w.   1Ki 3:14
if thou wilt w. in my statutes   1Ki 6:12
my commandments to w. in   1Ki 6:12
them
thy servants that w. before   1Ki 8:23
thee
w. before me as thou hast   1Ki 8:25
walked
good way wherein they should   1Ki 8:36
w.
unto him, to w. in all his   1Ki 8:58
ways

Lord our God, to w. in his   1Ki 8:61
statutes
if thou wilt w. before me, as   1Ki 9:4
David
wilt w. in my ways, and do   1Ki 11:38
a light thing for him to w. in   1Ki 16:31
no heed to w. in the law of   2Ki 10:31
the Lord
observe the law (B)   2Ki 10:31; 34:31
the Lord, to w. after the lord   2Ki 23:3
that w. before thee with all   2Ch 6:14
heed to their way to w. in   2Ch 6:16
my law
good way, wherein they   2Ch 6:27
should w.
to w. in thy ways, so long as   2Ch 6:31
for thee, if thou wilt w.   2Ch 7:17
before me
the Lord, and to w. after   2Ch 34:31
the Lord
ye not to w. in the fear of our   Ne 5:9
God
conduct yourselves in reverence   Ne 5:9
(A)
into an oath, to w. in God's   Ne 10:29
law
The wicked w. on every side   Ps 12:8
the godless strut around (A)   Ps 12:8
the wicked prowl (R)   Ps 12:8; La 5:18
though I w. through the valley   Ps 23:4
for me, I will w. in mine   Ps 26:11
integrity
W. about Zion, and go round   Ps 48:12
I may w. before God in the   Ps 56:13
light
God, and refused to w. in his   Ps 78:10
law
they w. on in darkness   Ps 82:5
from them that w. uprightly   Ps 84:11
O Lord; I will w. in thy truth   Ps 86:11
they shall w., O Lord, in the   Ps 89:15
light
and w. not in my judgments   Ps 89:30
deviate from my judgments   Ps 89:30
I will w. within my house   Ps 101:2
with a
behave in my home (B)   Ps 101:2
feet have they, but they w.   Ps 115:7
not
I will w. before the Lord in   Ps 116:9
who w. in the law of the   Ps 119:1
Lord
no iniquity: they w. in his   Ps 119:3
ways
I will w. at liberty: for I   Ps 119:45
seek thy
I w. in the midst of trouble,   Ps 138:7
thou
know the way wherein I   Ps 143:8
should w.
w. not thou in the way with   Pr 1:15
them
buckler to them that w.   Pr 2:7
uprightly
to w. in the ways of darkness   Pr 2:13
thou mayest w. in the way of   Pr 2:20
good
shalt thou w. in thy way safely   Pr 3:23
the living which w. under the   Ec 4:15
sun
knoweth to w. before the living   Ec 6:8
and w. in the ways of thine   Ec 11:9
heart
ways, and we will w. in his   Isa 2:3
paths
let us w. in the light of the   Isa 2:5
Lord
w. with stretched forth necks   Isa 3:16
not w. in the way of this   Isa 8:11
people
That w. to go down into   Isa 30:2
Egypt
This is the way, w. ye in it,   Isa 30:21
when
but the redeemed shall w.   Isa 35:9
and they shall w. and not   Isa 40:31
faint
and spirit to them that w.   Isa 42:5
therein
for they would not w. in his   Isa 42:24
ways
w. in the light of your fire,   Isa 50:11
and in
brightness, but we w. in   Isa 59:9
darkness
entangling her w. (B)   Jer 2:23
neither shall they w. any more   Jer 3:17
follow the heart (R)   Jer 3:17;
13:10; 18:12; Eze 37:24

shall w. with the house of   Jer 3:18
Israel
is the good way, and w.   Jer 6:16
therein
they said, We will not w.   Jer 6:16
therein
into the field, nor w. by the   Jer 6:25
way
w. after other gods to your   Jer 7:6
hurt
w. after other gods whom ye   Jer 7:9
know
w. ye in all the ways that I   Jer 7:23
have
neighbour will w. with slanders   Jer 9:4
which w. in the imagination   Jer 13:10
of
and w. after other gods, to   Jer 13:10
serve
w. every one after   Jer 16:12
the imagination
we will w. after our own   Jer 18:12
devices
to w. in paths, in a way not   Jer 18:15
cast
commit adultery, and w. in   Jer 23:14
lies
hearken to me, to w. in my   Jer 26:4
law
cause them to w. by the rivers   Jer 31:9
us the way wherein we may w.   Jer 42:3
is desolate, the foxes w. upon   La 5:18
the foxes roam about (B)   La 5:18
That they may w. in   Eze 11:20
my statutes
W. ye not in the statutes of   Eze 20:18
your
w. in my statutes, and keep   Eze 20:19
my
w. in the statutes of life,   Eze 33:15
without
I will cause men to w. upon   Eze 36:12
you
travel (B)   Eze 36:12; Lu 13:33
cause you to w. in my   Eze 36:27
statutes
they shall also w. in my   Eze 37:24
judgments
chambers was a w. of ten   Eze 42:4
cubits
passageway (B)   Eze 42:4
passage (R)   Eze 42:4
those that w. in pride he is   Da 4:37
able to
to w. in his laws, which he set   Da 9:10
live in agreement with his   Da 9:10
laws (B)
follow his laws (R)   Da 9:10
They shall w. after the Lord;   Ho 11:10
he
go after the Lord (R)   Ho 11:10
right, and the just shall w. in   Ho 14:9
them
they shall w. every one in his   Joe 2:8
path
Can two w. together, except   Am 3:3
they
ways, and we will w. in his   Mic 4:2
paths
will w. every one in the name   Mic 4:5
of his
will w. in the name of the   Mic 4:5
Lord our
and to w. humbly with thy   Mic 6:8
God
Ahab, and ye w. in their   Mic 6:16
counsels
they shall stumble in their w.   Na 2:5
didst w. through the sea with   Hab 3:15
tread (B)   Hab 3:15; 3:19
me to w. upon mine high   Hab 3:19
places
that they shall w. like blind   Zep 1:17
men
to w. to and fro through the   Zec 1:10
earth
patrol the earth (A)(R)   Zec 1:10; 6:7
If thou wilt w. in my ways,   Zec 3:7
and if
to w. among these that stand   Zec 3:7
by
w. to and fro through the   Zec 6:7
earth
shall w. up and down in his   Zec 10:12
name
they shall glory in his name   Zec 10:12
(R)
thee: or to say, Arise, and w.   M't 9:5
and the lame w. the lepers   M't 11:5

the lame to *w.* and the blind	*M't 15:31*	
to see		
Arise, and take up thy bed,	*M'k 2:9*	
and *w.*		
Why *w.* not thy disciples	*M'k 7:5*	
according		
disciples refuse to follow	*M'k 7:5*	
ancient customs (P)		
thee: or to say, Rise up and *w.*	*Lu 5:23*	
how that the blind see, the	*Lu 7:22*	
lame *w.*		
the men that *w.* over them	*Lu 11:44*	
are not		
I must *w.* to day, and to-	*Lu 13:33*	
morrow		
journey on today (P)	*Lu 13:33*	
which desire to *w.* in long	*Lu 20:46*	
robes		
ye have one to another, as ye	*Lu 24:17*	
w.		
him, Rise, take up thy bed, and	*Joh 5:8*	
w.		
unto me, Take up thy bed,	*Joh 5:11*	
and *w.*		
thee, Take up thy bed, and *w.*	*Joh 5:12*	
for he would not *w.* in Jewry	*Joh 7:1*	
me shall not *w.* in darkness	*Joh 8:12*	
If any man *w.* in the day, he	*Joh 11:9*	
But if a man *w.* in the night,	*Joh 11:10*	
he		
W. while ye have the light,	*Joh 12:35*	
lest		
Christ of Nazareth rise up and	*Ac 3:6*	
w.		
we had made this man to *w.*	*Ac 3:12*	
all nations to *w.* in their own	*Ac 14:16*	
ways		
neither to *w.* after the	*Ac 21:21*	
customs		
nor observe the old customs	*Ac 21:21*	
(A)(P)(R)		
also *w.* in the steps of that	*Ro 4:12*	
faith		
living by the same sort of	*Ro 4:12*	
faith (P)		
follow the example of faith	*Ro 4:12*	
(R)		
should *w.* in newness of life	*Ro 6:4*	
conduct ourselves in a new way	*Ro 6:4*	
(B)		
set feet on a new path of life	*Ro 6:4*	
(N)		
rise to life on a new plane (P)	*Ro 6:4*	
who *w.* not after the flesh, but	*Ro 8:1;*	
	8:4	
conduct no longer under lower	*Ro 8:4*	
nature (N)		
Let us *w.* honestly, as in the	*Ro 13:13*	
day		
behave with decency (N)	*Ro 13:13*	
fling away things men do in	*Ro 13:13*	
the dark (P)		
conduct yourselves becomingly	*Ro 13:13*	
(R)		
are ye not carnal, and *w.* as	*1Co 3:3*	
men		
still on a natural plane (N)	*1Co 3:3*	
living just like men (P)	*1Co 3:3*	
behaving like ordinary men	*1Co 3:3*	
(R)		
called every one, so let him	*1Co 7:17*	
w.		
keep on conducting	*1Co 7:17*	
yourselves (B)		
For we *w.* by faith, not by	*2Co 5:7*	
sight		
faith is our guide (N)	*2Co 5:7*	
dwell in them, and *w.* in	*2Co 6:16*	
them		
live in them (R)	*2Co 6:16*	
For though we *w.* in the	*2Co 10:3*	
flesh, we		
spend our life in a body of	*2Co 10:3*	
flesh (B)		
fight on a spiritual level (P)	*2Co 10:3*	
W. in the Spirit, and ye shall	*Ga 5:16*	
not		
guided by the Spirit (N)	*Ga 5:16*	
live your life in the Spirit (P)	*Ga 5:16*	
Spirit, let us also *w.* in the	*Ga 5:25*	
Spirit		
let the Spirit direct you (N)	*Ga 5:25*	
centered in the Spirit, let us	*Ga 5:25*	
be guided by the Spirit (P)		
many as *w.* according to	*Ga 6:16*	
this rule		
take this principle as your	*Ga 6:16*	
guide (N)		
live by this principle (P)	*Ga 6:16*	
that we should *w.* in them	*Eph 2:10*	

enjoy life in them (B)	*Eph 2:10*	
that ye *w.* worthy of the	*Eph 4:1*	
vocation		
conduct yourselves worthy of	*Eph 4:1*	
calling (B)(P)		
live up to your calling (N)	*Eph 4:1*	
lead a life worthy of calling	*Eph 4:1;*	
(R)	*Col 1:10; 1Th 2:12*	
w. not as other Gentiles *w.*	*Eph 4:17*	
give up living like pagans (N)	*Eph 4:17*	
Do not live any longer as	*Eph 4:17*	
Gentiles (P)		
no longer live like Gentiles	*Eph 4:17*	
(R) *Ph'p 3:17, 18, Col 2:6;*	*1Th 4:1;*	
	2Th 3:11	
w. in love, as Christ also hath	*Eph 5:2*	
loved		
live in loving ways (B)	*Eph 5:2*	
live in love (N)(P)	*Eph 5:2*	
in the Lord: *w.* as children of	*Eph 5:8*	
light		
live as children of light (B)(P)	*Eph 5:8*	
live like men who are at home	*Eph 5:8*	
in daylight (R)		
See then that ye *w.*	*Eph 5:15*	
circumspectly		
conduct yourselves ever so	*Eph 5:15*	
carefully (B)		
conduct yourselves like	*Eph 5:15*	
sensible men, not like		
simpletons (N)		
live with a due sense of	*Eph 5:15*	
responsibility (P)		
let us *w.* by the same rule,	*Ph'p 3:16*	
let us		
moving in the same	*Ph'p 3:16*	
direction (B)		
let your conduct be	*Ph'p 3:16*	
consistent (N)		
mark them which *w.* so as ye	*Ph'p 3:17*	
have		
(For many *w.* of whom I	*Ph'p 3:18*	
have told		
many are living as enemies	*Ph'p 3:18*	
of the cross (B)		
That ye might *w.* worthy of	*Col 1:10*	
the Lord (B)		
live in a way worthy of the	*Col 1:10*	
Lord (B)		
Jesus the Lord, so *w.* ye in	*Col 2:6*	
him		
live in union with him (B)	*Col 2:6*	
live lives in union with him	*Col 2:6*	
(N)		
go on living in him (P)	*Col 2:6*	
W. in wisdom toward them	*Col 4:5*	
that		
conduct yourselves wisely	*Col 4:5*	
(B)(R)		
Be wise in your behaviour to	*Col 4:5*	
non-Christians (P)		
That ye would *w.* worthy of	*1Th 2:12*	
God		
deport yourselves worthy of	*1Th 2:12*	
God (B)		
live lives worthy of God	*1Th 2:12*	
(N)(P)		
ye ought to *w.* and to please	*1Th 4:1*	
God		
w. honestly toward them that	*1Th 4:12*	
are		
behaviour toward outsiders	*1Th 4:12*	
be honorable (B)		
command respect of outsiders	*1Th 4:12*	
(N)		
which *w.* among you	*2Th 3:11*	
disorderly		
you live neglecting your duty	*2Th 3:11*	
(B)		
living quite undisciplined	*2Th 3:11*	
lives (P)		
them that *w.* after the flesh in	*2Pe 2:10*	
yield to sensual polluting	*2Pe 2:10*	
passions (B)		
follow their abominable lusts	*2Pe 2:10*	
(N)(R)		
indulged all foulness of lower	*2Pe 2:10*	
natures (P)		
indulge in lust defiling	*2Pe 2:10*	
passions (P)		
with him, and *w.* in darkness	*1Jo 1:6*	
But if we *w.* in the light, as he	*1Jo 1:7*	
is in		
in him ought himself also so to	*1Jo 2:6*	
w.		
personally to live the way he	*1Jo 2:6*	
lived (B)		
binds himself to live as Christ	*1Jo 2:6*	
lived (N)		

professes living in God must	*1Jo 2:6*	
bear the stamp of Christ (P)		
we *w.* after his commandments	*2Jo 6*	
follow his commandments	*2Jo 6*	
(N)(R)		
live obedient to him (P)	*2Jo 6*	
the beginning, ye should *w.* in it	*2Jo 6*	
hear that my children *w.* in truth	*3Jo 4*	
leading the true life (B)	*3Jo 4*	
living the truth (N)(P)	*3Jo 4*	
follow the truth (R)	*3Jo 4*	
w. after their own ungodly	*Jude 18*	
lusts		
guided by impious passions	*Jude 18*	
(B)		
follow their own godless lusts	*Jude 18*	
(N)(R)		
live in their own godless	*Jude 18*	
desires (P)		
they shall *w.* with me in white	*Re 3:4*	
neither can see, nor hear, nor	*Re 9:20*	
w.		
lest he *w.* naked, and they	*Re 16:15*	
see his		
go around naked (B)(R)	*Re 16:15*	
keeps on his clothes, not go	*Re 16:15*	
naked (N)		
are saved shall *w.* in the light	*Re 21:24*	

WALKED

Enoch *w.* with God after he	*Ge 5:22*	
begat		
Enoch *w.* with God: and he	*Ge 5:24*	
generations, and Noah *w.* with	*Ge 6:9*	
God		
her maidens *w.* along by the	*Ex 2:5*	
river's		
children of Israel *w.* upon	*Ex 14:29*	
dry land		
they have *w.* contrary unto	*Le 26:40*	
treason they perpetrated	*Le 26:40*	
against me (B)		
I also have *w.* contrary unto	*Le 26:41*	
them		
w. forty years in the wilderness	*Jos 5:6*	
traveled (B)	*Jos 5:6*	
the way which their fathers *w.*	*J'g 2:17*	
the travellers *w.* through	*J'g 5:6*	
byways		
w. through the wilderness	*J'g 11:16*	
unto the		
And his sons *w.* not in his	*1Sa 8:3*	
ways		
sons conduct was not like his	*1Sa 8:3*	
(B)		
I have *w.* before you from	*1Sa 12:2*	
my		
and his men *w.* all that night	*2Sa 2:29*	
w. in a tent and in a	*2Sa 7:6*	
tabernacle		
moved about in a tent (A)	*2Sa 7:6*	
traveling about in a tent (B)	*2Sa 7:6*	
I have *w.* with all the children	*2Sa 7:7*	
moved with all the Israelites	*2Sa 7:7*	
(A)		
journeying with the whole	*2Sa 7:7;*	
nation (B)	*1Ch 17:6*	
and *w.* upon the roof of the	*2Sa 11:2*	
king's		
as he *w.* before thee in truth,	*1Ki 3:6*	
and		
me as thou hast *w.* before me	*1Ki 8:25*	
as David thy father *w.* in	*1Ki 9:4*	
integrity		
have not *w.* in my ways, to	*1Ki 11:33*	
do that		
followed my instructions	*1Ki 11:33*	
(B)		
And he *w.* in all the sins of	*1Ki 15:3*	
his		
guilty of all sins of his father	*1Ki 15:3*	
(B)		
and *w.* in the way of his	*1Ki 15:26*	
father		
going the way of his fathers	*1Ki 15:26;*	
(B)	*15:34*	
and *w.* in the way of	*1Ki 15:34*	
Jeroboam		
hast *w.* in the way of	*1Ki 16:2*	
Jeroboam		
he *w.* in all the way of	*1Ki 16:26*	
Jeroboam		
And he *w.* in all the ways of	*1Ki 22:43*	
Asa his		
and *w.* in the way of his	*1Ki 22:52*	
father		
and *w.* in the house to and	*2Ki 4:35*	
fro		
he *w.* in the way of the kings	*2Ki 8:18*	

he *w.* in the way of the house   *2Ki 8:27*
made Israel sin, but *w.*   *2Ki 13:6*
therein
made Israel sin: but he *w.*   *2Ki 13:11*
therein
But he *w.* in the way of the   *2Ki 16:3*
kings
w. in the statutes of the   *2Ki 17:8*
heathen
w. in the statutes of Israel   *2Ki 17:19*
followed the practices of   *2Ki 17:19*
Israel (B)
children of Israel *w.* in all   *2Ki 17:22*
the sins
w. before thee in truth and   *2Ki 20:3*
And he *w.* in all the way   *2Ki 21:21*
that his
in all the way that his father   *2Ki 21:21*
w. in
and *w.* not in the way of the   *2Ki 21:22*
Lord
and *w.* in all the way of   *2Ki 22:2*
David his
I have *w.* with all Israel   *1Ch 17:6*
thee whithersoever thou hast   *1Ch 17:8*
w.
law, as thou hast *w.* before   *2Ch 6:16*
me
before me, as David thy   *2Ch 7:17*
father *w.*
they *w.* in the way of David   *2Ch 11:17*
and
he *w.* in the first ways of his   *2Ch 17:3*
father
w. in his commandments,   *2Ch 17:4*
and not
And he *w.* in the way of   *2Ch 20:32*
Asa his
and he *w.* in the way of the   *2Ch 21:6*
kings
thou hast not *w.* in the   *2Ch 21:12*
ways of
hast *w.* in the way of the   *2Ch 21:13*
kings of
also *w.* in the ways of the   *2Ch 22:3*
house of
He *w.* also after their   *2Ch 22:5*
counsel, and
followed their counsel   *2Ch 22:5*
(A)(R)
following their advice (B)   *2Ch 22:5*
he *w.* in the ways of the   *2Ch 28:2*
kings of
w. in the ways of David his   *2Ch 34:2*
father
Mordecai *w.* every day before   *Es 2:11*
his light I *w.* through   *Job 29:3*
darkness
If I have *w.* with vanity, or if   *Job 31:5*
and mine heart *w.* after mine   *Job 31:7*
eyes
my heart gone the way my   *Job 31:7*
eyes invited (A)(R)
my thoughts followed my eyes   *Job 31:7*
(B)
thou *w.* in the search of the   *Job 38:16*
depth
for I have *w.* in mine integrity   *Ps 26:1*
eyes: and I have *w.* in thy   *Ps 26:3*
truth
and *w.* unto the house of   *Ps 55:14*
God in
they *w.* in their own counsels   *Ps 81:12*
and Israel had *w.* in my ways   *Ps 81:13*
In the way wherein I have   *Ps 142:3*
they
people that *w.* in darkness have   *Isa 9:2*
my servant Isaiah hath *w.*   *Isa 20:3*
naked
how I have *w.* before thee in   *Isa 38:3*
truth
and have *w.* after vanity, and   *Jer 2:5*
are
went after emptiness, falseness,   *Jer 2:5*
futility (A)
followed after futility (B)   *Jer 2:5*
went after worthlessness (R)   *Jer 2:5*
w. after things that do not   *Jer 2:8*
profit
following things that don't   *Jer 2:8*
profit (A)
pursued things that don't profit   *Jer 2:8*
(B)(R)
but *w.* in the counsels and in   *Jer 7:24*
and after whom they have *w.*   *Jer 8:2*
obeyed my voice, neither *w.*   *Jer 9:13*
therein
w. after the imagination of   *Jer 9:14*

followed their own hearts   *Jer 9:14*
(B)(R)
w. every one in the   *Jer 11:8*
imagination of
have *w.* after other gods, and   *Jer 16:11*
have
followed after foreign gods   *Jer 16:11*
(B)(R)
thy voice, neither *w.* in thy   *Jer 32:23*
law
have they feared, nor *w.* in   *Jer 44:10*
my law
of the Lord, nor *w.* in his   *Jer 44:23*
law, nor
statutes, they have not *w.* in   *Eze 5:6*
them
and have not *w.* in my statutes   *Eze 5:7*
for ye have not *w.* in my   *Eze 11:12*
statutes
hast thou not *w.* after their   *Eze 16:47*
ways
Hath *w.* in my statutes, and   *Eze 18:9*
hath
judgments, hath *w.* in my   *Eze 18:17*
statutes
they *w.* not in my statutes   *Eze 20:13*
and *w.* not in my statutes   *Eze 20:16*
they *w.* not in my statutes,   *Eze 20:21*
neither
hast *w.* in the way of thy   *Eze 23:31*
sister
hast *w.* up and down in   *Eze 28:14*
the midst
w. in the palace of the   *Da 4:29*
kingdom
he *w.* after the commandment   *Ho 5:11*
the which their fathers have *w.*   *Am 2:4*
even the old lion, *w.* and the   *Na 2:11*
lion's
We have *w.* to and fro   *Zec 1:11*
through the
patroled the earth (B)(R)   *Zec 1:11*
w. to and fro through the earth   *Zec 6:7*
patrol the earth (R)   *Zec 6:7*
he *w.* with me in peace and   *Mal 2:6*
equity
w. mournfully before the   *Mal 3:14*
Lord
he *w.* on the water, to go to   *M't 14:29*
Jesus
Now as he *w.* by the sea of   *M'k 1:16*
Galilee
the damsel arose, and *w.*, for   *M'k 5:42*
she
form unto two of them, as   *M'k 16:12*
they *w.*
looking upon Jesus as he *w.*   *Joh 1:36*
he
whole, and took up his bed,   *Joh 5:9*
and *w.*
back, and *w.* no more with   *Joh 6:66*
him
these things Jesus *w.* in Galilee   *Joh 7:1*
Jesus *w.* in the temple in   *Joh 10:23*
Solomon's
w. no more openly among   *Joh 11:54*
he leaping up stood, and *w.*   *Ac 3:8*
mother's womb, who never had   *Ac 14:8*
w.
on thy feet. And he leaped   *Ac 14:10*
and *w.*
as if we *w.* according to the   *2Co 10:2*
flesh
acting according to the flesh   *2Co 10:2*
(A)
behave in fleshly ways (B)   *2Co 10:2*
acting in a worldly fashion   *2Co 10:2*
(R)
you? *w.* we not in the same   *2Co 12:18*
spirit
act in the same spirit   *2Co 12:18*
(A)(R)
behaved in the same spirit   *2Co 12:18*
(B)
followed the same course   *2Co 12:18*
(N)
spirit? *w.* we not in the   *2Co 12:18*
same steps
they *w.* not uprightly   *Ga 2:14*
according to
in time past ye *w.* according   *Eph 2:2*
to the
once *w.* (B)   *Eph 2:3*
In the which ye also *w.* some   *Col 3:7*
time
we *w.* in lasciviousness, lusts   *1Pe 4:3*
also so to walk, even as he *w.*   *1Jo 2:6*
lived as Christ Himself lived   *1Jo 2:6*
(N)

WALKEDST

and *w.* whither thou   *Joh 21:18*
wouldest

WALKEST

and when thou *w.* by the way   *De 6:7;*
                        11:19
out, and *w.* abroad any   *1Ki 2:42*
whither
when thou *w.* through the fire   *Isa 43:2*
w. orderly, and keepest the   *Ac 21:24*
law
meat, now *w.* thou not   *Ro 14:15*
charitably
thee, even as thou *w.* in the   *3Jo 3*
truth

WALKETH

man is this that *w.* in the   *Ge 24:65*
field to
Lord thy God *w.* in the midst   *De 23:14*
behold, the king *w.* before   *1Sa 12:2*
you
own feet, and he *w.* upon a   *Job 18:8*
snare
and he *w.* in the circuit of   *Job 22:14*
heaven
iniquity, and *w.* with wicked   *Job 34:8*
men
that *w.* not in the counsel of the   *Ps 1:1*
He that *w.* uprightly, and   *Ps 15:2*
worketh
Surely every man *w.* in a vain   *Ps 39:6*
shew
and their tongue *w.* through   *Ps 73:9*
the pestilence that *w.* in   *Ps 91:6*
darkness
that *w.* in a perfect way,   *Ps 101:6*
he shall
who *w.* upon the wings of the   *Ps 104:3*
wind
the Lord; that *w.* in his ways   *Ps 128:1*
man, *w.* with a froward mouth   *Pr 6:12*
that *w.* uprightly *w.* surely   *Pr 10:9*
He that *w.* with wise men   *Pr 13:20*
shall be
He that *w.* in his uprightness   *Pr 14:2*
of understanding *w.* uprightly   *Pr 15:21*
the poor that *w.* in his   *Pr 19:1*
integrity
The just man *w.* in his   *Pr 20:7*
integrity
poor that *w.* in his uprightness   *Pr 28:6*
Whoso *w.* uprightly shall be   *Pr 28:18*
saved
but whoso *w.* wisely, he shall   *Pr 28:26*
be
but the fool *w.* in darkness: *Ec 2:14*
and I
when he that is a fool *w.* by   *Ec 10:3*
the way
He that *w.* righteously, and   *Isa 33:15*
that *w.* in darkness, and hath   *Isa 50:10*
no
w. in a way that was not good   *Isa 65:2*
in man that *w.* to direct his   *Jer 10:23*
steps
one that *w.* after the   *Jer 23:17*
imagination
whose heart *w.* after the   *Eze 11:21*
heart of
do good to him that *w.*   *Mic 2:7*
uprightly
he *w.* through dry places,   *M't 12:43;*
seeking   *Lu 11:24*
he that *w.* in darkness   *Joh 12:35*
knoweth
every brother that *w.*   *2Th 3:6*
disorderly
w. about, seeking whom   *1Pe 5:8*
he may
w. in darkness, and knoweth   *1Jo 2:11*
not
who *w.* in the midst of the   *Re 2:1*
seven

WALKING

of the Lord God *w.* in the   *Ge 3:8*
garden
he knoweth thy *w.* through this   *De 2:7*
w. in the statutes of David his   *1Ki 3:3*
in *w.* in the way of   *1Ki 16:19*
Jeroboam, and
and from *w.* up and down   *Job 1:7;*
in it   *2:2*
or the moon *w.* in brightness   *Job 31:26*

and princes w. as servants *Ec 10:7*
upon the
w. and mincing as they go *Isa 3:16*
he did so, w. naked and *Isa 20:2*
barefoot
each one w. in his uprightness *Isa 57:2*
revolters, w. with slanders *Jer 6:28*
loose, w. in the midst of the *Da 3:25*
fire
man w. in the spirit and *Mic 2:11*
falsehood
Jesus, w. by the sea of *M't 4:18*
Galilee
went unto them, w. on the *M't 14:25*
sea
the disciples saw him w. on *M't 14:26*
the sea
cometh unto them, w. upon *M'k 6:48*
the sea
when they saw him w. upon *M'k 6:49*
the sea
up, and said, I see men as *M'k 8:24*
trees, w.
and as he was w. in the *M'k 11:27*
temple
w. in all the commandments *Lu 1:6*
they see Jesus w. on the sea *Joh 6:19*
into the temple, w. and leaping *Ac 3:8*
saw him w. and praising God *Ac 3:9*
w. in the fear of the Lord, *Ac 9:31*
and in
not w. in craftiness, nor *2Co 4:2*
handling
scoffers, w. after their own *2Pe 3:3*
lusts
found of thy children w. in truth *2Jo 4*
w. after their own lusts *Jude 16*

WALL

selfwill they digged down a w. *Ge 49:6*
self-will they disabled an ox *Ge 49:6*
(A)
insolence they hamstrung an *Ge 49:6*
ox (B)
self-will they hocked an ox *Ge 49:6*
(E)
wantonness they hamstrung *Ge 49:6*
oxen (R)
whose branches run over the *Ge 49:22*
w.
waters were a w. unto them *Ex 14:22;*
them *14:29*
in sight are lower than the w. *Le 14:37*
which have no w. round *Le 25:31*
about
vineyards, a w. being on this *Nu 22:24*
side
this side, and a w. on that *Nu 22:24*
side
she thrust herself unto the w. *Nu 22:25*
Balaam's foot against the w. *Nu 22:25*
shall reach from the w. of the *Nu 35:4*
city
her house was upon the town *Jos 2:15*
w.
and she dwelt upon the w. *Jos 2:15*
w. of the city shall fall down *Jos 6:5*
flat
shout, that the w. fell down *Jos 6:20*
flat
I will smite David even to *1Sa 18:11*
the w.
to smite David even to the w. *1Sa 19:10*
with
he smote the javelin into the *1Sa 19:10*
w.
times, even upon a seat by *1Sa 20:25*
the w.
w. unto us both by night and *1Sa 25:16*
day
that pisseth against the w. *1Sa 25:22;*
25:34
his body to the w. of *1Sa 31:10*
Beth-shan
his sons from the w. of *1Sa 31:12*
Beth-shan
that they would shoot from *2Sa 11:20*
the w.
a millstone upon him from *2Sa 11:21*
the w.
Thebez? why went ye nigh *2Sa 11:21*
the w.
shooters shot from off the *2Sa 11:24*
w. upon
the roof over the gate unto *2Sa 18:24*
the w.
were with Joab battered the *2Sa 20:15*
w.

shall be thrown to thee over *2Sa 20:21*
the w.
by my God have I leaped *2Sa 22:30*
over a w.
the w. of Jerusalem round *1Ki 3:1*
about
that springeth out of the w. *1Ki 4:33*
And against the w. of the *1Ki 6:5*
house he
in the w. of the house he made *1Ki 6:6*
of the one touched the one w. *1Ki 6:27*
other cherub touched the *1Ki 6:27*
other w.
side posts were a fifth part of *1Ki 6:31*
the w.
of olive tree, a fourth part of *1Ki 6:33*
the w.
Millo, and the w. of *1Ki 9:15*
Jerusalem
him that pisseth against the *1Ki 14:10*
w.
not one that pisseth against *1Ki 16:11*
a w.
w. fell upon twenty and *1Ki 20:30*
seven
him that pisseth against the *1Ki 21:21*
w.
eat Jezebel by the w. of *1Ki 21:23*
Jezreel
for a burnt offering upon the *2Ki 3:27*
w.
chamber, I pray thee, on the *2Ki 4:10*
w.
Israel was passing by upon *2Ki 6:26*
the w.
he passed by upon the w. and *2Ki 6:30*
him that pisseth against the w. *2Ki 9:8*
her blood was sprinkled on *2Ki 9:33*
the w.
brake down the w. of *2Ki 14:13*
Jerusalem
of the people that are on the *2Ki 18:26*
w.
me to the men which sit on *2Ki 18:27*
the w.
Then he turned his face to *2Ki 20:2*
the w.
reaching to the w. of the *2Ch 3:11;*
house *3:12*
brake down the w. of *2Ch 25:23*
Jerusalem
and brake down the w. of *2Ch 26:6*
Gath
w. of Jabneh, and the w. of *2Ch 26:6*
Ashdod
turning of the w. and fortified *2Ch 26:9*
them
on the w. of Ophel he built *2Ch 27:3*
built up all the w. that was *2Ch 32:5*
broken
the towers, and another, *2Ch 32:5*
without
of Jerusalem that were on *2Ch 32:18*
built a w. without the city *2Ch 33:14*
of David
brake down the w. of *2Ch 36:19*
Jerusalem
this house, and to make up *Ezr 5:3*
this w.
a w. in Judah and in *Ezr 9:9*
Jerusalem
w. of Jerusalem also is broken *Ne 1:3*
and for the w. of the city, and *Ne 2:8*
by the brook, and viewed the *Ne 2:15*
w.
let us build up the w. of *Ne 2:17*
Jerusalem
Jerusalem unto the broad w. *Ne 3:8*
a thousand cubits on the w. *Ne 3:13*
w. of the pool of Siloah by *Ne 3:15*
the king's
the armoury at the turning of *Ne 3:19*
the w.
turning of the w. unto the *Ne 3:20*
door of the
of Azariah unto the turning of *Ne 3:24*
the w.
over against the turning of the *Ne 3:25*
w.
out, even unto the w. of Ophel *Ne 3:27*
heard that we builded the w. *Ne 4:1*
even break down their stone w. *Ne 4:3*
So built we the w.; and all the *Ne 4:6*
all the w. was joined together *Ne 4:6*
that we are not able to build *Ne 4:10*
the w.
I in the lower places behind *Ne 4:13*
the w.
we returned all of us to the w. *Ne 4:15*

They which builded on the w. *Ne 4:17*
we are separated upon the w. *Ne 4:19*
one
I continued in the work of *Ne 5:16*
this w.
heard that I had builded the w. *Ne 6:1*
which cause thou buildest the *Ne 6:6*
w. was finished in the twenty *Ne 6:15*
when the w. was built, and I had *Ne 7:1*
dedication of the w. of *Ne 12:27*
Jerusalem
people, and the gates, and *Ne 12:30*
the w.
the princes of Judah upon *Ne 12:31*
the w.
right hand upon the w. *Ne 12:31*
toward the
at the going up of the w. *Ne 12:37*
above the
the half of the people upon *Ne 12:38*
the w.
furnaces even unto the broad *Ne 12:38*
w.
them, Why lodge ye about *Ne 13:21*
the w.
by my God have I leaped *Ps 18:29*
over a w.
as a bowing w. shall ye be, *Ps 62:3*
and as
as an high w. in his own *Pr 18:11*
conceit
the stone w. thereof was *Pr 24:31*
broken
he standeth behind our w. he *Ca 2:9*
If she be a w. we will build *Ca 8:9*
upon
I am a w. and my breasts like *Ca 8:10*
high tower, upon every fenced *Isa 2:15*
w.
break down the w. thereof, and *Isa 5:5*
ye broken down to fortify *Isa 22:10*
the w.
ones is as a storm against the *Isa 25:4*
w.
swelling out in a high w. *Isa 30:13*
of the people that are on the *Isa 36:11*
w.
me to the men that sit upon *Isa 36:12*
the w.
turned his face toward the w. *Isa 38:2*
We grope for the w. like the *Isa 59:10*
blind
this people a fenced brasen *Jer 15:20*
w.
kindle a fire in the w. of *Jer 49:27*
Damascus
yea, the w. of Babylon shall *Jer 51:44*
fall
to destroy the w. of the *La 2:8*
daughter
the rampart and the w. to *La 2:8*
lament
O w. of the daughter of Zion, *La 2:18*
let
get it for a w. of iron between *Eze 4:3*
thee
I looked, behold a hole in the *Eze 8:7*
w.
me, Son of man, dig now in *Eze 8:8*
the w.
when I had digged in the w. *Eze 8:8*
pourtrayed upon the w. round *Eze 8:10*
Dig thou through the w. in *Eze 12:5*
their
I digged through the w. with *Eze 12:7*
mine
shall dig through the w. to *Eze 12:12*
carry
one built up a w. and, lo, *Eze 13:10*
others
will I break down the w. *Eze 13:14*
that ye
accomplish my wrath upon *Eze 13:15*
the w.
The w. is no more, neither *Eze 13:15*
they
saw men pourtrayed upon *Eze 23:14*
the w.
every w. shall fall to the *Eze 38:20*
ground
a w. on the outside of the *Eze 40:5*
house
he measured the w. of the *Eze 41:5*
house
they entered into the w. *Eze 41:6*
which
not hold in the w. of the *Eze 41:6*
house

The thickness of the w. which | Eze 41:9
was
w. of the building was five | Eze 41:12
cubits
all the w. round about | Eze 41:17
within and
made, and on the w. of the | Eze 41:20
temple
And the w. that was without | Eze 42:7
over
thickness of the w. of the | Eze 42:10
court
the way directly before the | Eze 42:12
w.
it had a w. round about, five | Eze 42:20
and the w. between me and | Eze 43:8
them
upon the plaister of the w. of | Da 5:5
shall be built again, and the | Da 9:25
w.
and make a w. that she shall | Ho 2:6
not
climb the w. like men of war | Joe 2:7
they shall run upon the w., they | Joe 2:9
will send a fire on the w. of | Am 1:7
Gaza
will send a fire on the w. of | Am 1:10
Tyrus
kindle a fire in the w. of | Am 1:14
Rabbah
and leaned his hand on the w. | Am 5:19
upon a w. made by a plumbline | Am 7:7
make haste to the w. thereof | Na 2:5
sea, and her w. was from the | Na 3:8
sea
the stone shall cry out of the | Hab 2:11
w.
will be unto her a w. of fire | Zec 2:5
round
let down by the w. in a basket | Ac 9:25
shall smite thee, thou whited | Ac 23:3
w.
a basket was I let down by | 2Co 11:33
the w.
broken down the middle w. | Eph 2:14
And had a w. great and | Re 21:12
high, and
the w. of the city had twelve | Re 21:14
gates thereof, and the w. | Re 21:15
thereof
And he measured the w. | Re 21:17
thereof
building of the w. was of | Re 21:18
jasper
foundations of the w. of the | Re 21:19
city

WALLED

sell a dwelling house in a w. | Le 25:29
city
w. city shall be established | Le 25:30
for ever
and the cities are w. and | Nu 13:28
are great and w. up to heaven | De 1:28

WALLET

five smooth stones in a | 1Sa 17:40
w. (S)
no w. (E) | M't 10:10; M'k 6:8; Lu 9:3
no w. (B)(E) | Lu 10:4
no w. (E)(P) | Lu 22:35; 22:36

WALLOW

sackcloth, and w. thyself in | Jer 6:26
ashes
roll in ashes (B)(R) | Jer 6:26
w. yourselves in the ashes, ye | Jer 25:34
roll in ashes (A)(B)(R) | Jer 25:34
Moab also shall w. in his | Jer 48:26
vomit
splash in own vomit (A)(B) | Jer 48:26
shall w. themselves in the | Eze 27:30
ashes

WALLOWED

Amasa w. in blood in the | 2Sa 20:12
midst of
on the ground and w. | M'k 9:20
foaming
rolling about (A)(B) | M'k 9:20
rolled about (N)(R) | M'k 9:20
writhed there (P) | M'k 9:20

WALLOWING

was washed to her w. in the | 2Pe 2:22
mire
rolls in the mud again (N) | 2Pe 2:22

WALLS

plague be in the w. of the | Le 14:37
house
plague be spread in the w. of | Le 14:39
cities were fenced with high w. | De 3:5
thy high and fenced w. come | De 28:52
down
great cities with w. and | 1Ki 4:13
brasen
against the w. of the house | 1Ki 6:5
round
be fastened in the w. of the | 1Ki 6:6
house
be built the w. of the house | 1Ki 6:15
within
the house, and the w. of the | 1Ki 6:15
ceiling
and the w. with boards of | 1Ki 6:16
cedar
he carved all the w. of the | 1Ki 6:29
house
on the w. (S) | 2Ki 4:10
way of the gate between two | 2Ki 25:4
w.
brake down the w. of | 2Ki 25:10
Jerusalem
to overlay the w. of the | 1Ch 29:4
houses
the w. thereof, and the doors | 2Ch 3:7
and graved cherubims on the | 2Ch 3:7
w.
fenced cities, with w. gates | 2Ch 8:5
make about them w. and | 2Ch 14:7
towers
and have set up the w. | Ezr 4:12
thereof
be builded, and the w. set up | Ezr 4:13
again
again, and the w. thereof set | Ezr 4:16
up
and timber is laid in the w. | Ezr 5:8
house, and to make up these | Ezr 5:9
w.
and viewed the w. of | Ne 2:13
Jerusalem
the w. of Jerusalem were made | Ne 4:7
up
Which make oil within their | Job 24:11
w.
build thou the w. of | Ps 51:18
Jerusalem
go about it upon the w. | Ps 55:10
thereof
Peace be within thy w. and | Ps 122:7
on top of the w. (R) | Pr 1:21
is broken down, and without | Pr 25:28
w.
keepers of the w. took away | Ca 5:7
my veil
breaking down the w. and of | Isa 22:5
also a ditch between the two | Isa 22:11
w.
fortress of the high fort of | Isa 25:12
thy w.
salvation will God appoint for | Isa 26:1
w.
thy w. are continually before | Isa 49:16
me
within my w. a place and a | Isa 56:5
name
of strangers shall build up | Isa 60:10
thy w.
thou shalt call thy w. | Isa 60:18
Salvation
I have set watchmen upon | Isa 62:6
thy w.
all the w., thereof round about | Jer 1:15
brasen w. against the whole | Jer 1:18
land
Go ye up upon her w. and | Jer 5:10
destroy
which besiege you without the | Jer 21:4
w.
by the gate betwixt the two w. | Jer 39:4
brake down the w. of | Jer 39:8
Jerusalem
are fallen, her w. are thrown | Jer 50:15
down
standard upon the w. of | Jer 51:12
Babylon
broad w. of Babylon shall be | Jer 51:58
utterly
way of the gate between the | Jer 52:7
two w.
brake down all the w. of | Jer 52:14
Jerusalem
of the enemy the w. of her | La 2:7
palaces

they shall destroy the w. of | Eze 26:4
Tyrus
set engines of war against thy | Eze 26:9
w.
thy w. shall shake at the | Eze 26:10
noise of
they shall break down thy w. | Eze 26:12
thine army were upon thy w. | Eze 27:11
round
hanged their shields, upon | Eze 27:11
thy w.
are talking against thee by | Eze 33:30
the w.
all of them dwelling without | Eze 38:11
the building, with the w. | Eze 41:13
thereof
and the w. thereof, were of | Eze 41:22
wood
like as were made upon the | Eze 41:25
w.
the day that thy w. are to be | Mic 7:11
built
inhabited as towns without w. | Zec 2:4
within four w. (P) | Lu 12:3
By faith the w. of Jericho | Heb 11:30
fell

WANDER

me to w. from my father's | Ge 20:13
house
children shall w. in the | Nu 14:33
wilderness
he made them w. in the | Nu 32:13
wilderness
he that maketh the blind to | De 27:18
w. out
causeth them to w. in a | Job 12:24
wilderness
unto God, they w. for lack | Job 38:41
of meat
then would I w. far off, and | Ps 55:7
remain
them w. up and down for | Ps 59:15
meat
them to w. in the wilderness | Ps 107:40
not w. from thy | Ps 119:10
commandments
shall w. every one to his | Isa 47:15
quarter
Thus have they loved to w. | Jer 14:10
that shall cause him to w. | Jer 48:12
And they shall w. from sea to | Am 8:12
sea

WANDERED

and w. in the wilderness of | Ge 21:14
of Israel w. in the wilderness | Jos 14:10
They w. in the wilderness in a | Ps 107:4
they w. through the wilderness | Isa 16:8
They have w. as blind men in | La 4:14
when they fled away and w. | La 4:15
My sheep w. through all the | Eze 34:6
or three cities w. unto one city | Am 4:8
w. away into vain arguments | 1Ti 1:6
(A)(R)
they w. about in sheepskins | Heb 11:37
they w. in deserts, and in | Heb 11:38

WANDERER

be a w. (B)(E)(R)(S) | Ge 4:12; 4:14

WANDERERS

be continually w. (S) | Ps 109:10
that I will send unto him w. | Jer 48:12
shall be w. among the nations | Ho 9:17

WANDEREST

under every green tree thou w. | Jer 2:20

WANDERETH

He w. abroad for bread, | Job 15:23
saying
The man that w. out of the | Pr 21:16
way of
As a bird that w. from her | Pr 27:8
nest, so
so is a man that w. from his | Pr 27:8
place
outcasts; bewray not him that | Isa 16:3
w.
none shall gather up him that | Jer 49:5
w.

WANDERING

behold, he was w. in the field   Ge 37:15
a w. Aramean was (B)(R)   De 26:5
As the bird by w. as the   Pr 26:2
swallow
the eyes than the w. of the   Ec 6:9
desire
as a w. bird cast out of the   Isa 16:2
nest
w. about from house to house   1Ti 5:13
w. stars, to whom is reserved   Jude 13

WANDERINGS

Thou tellest my w.: put thou   Ps 56:8
my

WANDERS

my mind reels and w. (A)   Isa 21:4

WANT

nakedness, and in w. of all   De 28:48
things
shall eat them for w. of all   De 28:57
things
a place where there is no w.   J'g 18:10
of
there is no w. of anything   J'g 19:19
embrace rock for w. of a   Job 24:8
shelter
For w. and famine they were   Job 30:3
seen any perish for w. of   Job 31:19
clothing
is my shepherd; I shall not w.   Ps 23:1
is no w. to them that fear him   Ps 34:9
Lord shall not w. any good   Ps 34:10
thing
and thy w. as an armed man   Pr 6:11
but fools die for w. of   Pr 10:21
wisdom
is destroyed for w. of   Pr 13:23
judgment
the belly of the wicked shall   Pr 13:25
w.
leads only to w. (B)(R)   Pr 14:23
but in the w. of people is the   Pr 14:28
every one that is hasty only to   Pr 21:5
w.
to the rich, shall surely come   Pr 22:16
to w.
and thy w. as an armed man   Pr 24:34
shall fail, none shall w. her   Isa 34:16
mate
never w. a man to sit upon   Jer 33:17
Levites w. a man before me   Jer 33:18
to offer
not w. a man to stand   Jer 35:19
before me for
for w. of the fruits of the field   La 4:9
they may w. bread and water   Eze 4:17
and w. of bread in all your   Am 4:6
places
she of her w. did cast in all   M'k 12:44
that
land; and he began to be in   Lu 15:14
w.
contributed of her lack and   Lu 21:4
w. (A)(E)
may be a supply for their w.   2Co 8:14
also may be a supply for   2Co 8:14
your w.
only supplieth the w. of the   2Co 9:12
saints
Not that I speak in respect   Ph'p 4:11
of w.

WANTED

we have w. all things, and   Jer 44:18
have
w. to see (P)   Lu 10:24
when they w. wine, the mother   Joh 2:3
I was present with you, and   2Co 11:9
w., I

WANTETH

for his need, in that which he   De 15:8
w.
for him that w. understanding   Pr 9:4
as for him that w.   Pr 9:16
understanding
of words there w. not sin: but   Pr 10:19
The prince that w.   Pr 28:16
understanding
so that he w. nothing for   Ec 6:2
his soul
round goblet, which w. not   Ca 7:2
liquor

WANTING

and all his priests: let none   2Ki 10:19
be w.
whosoever shall be w. he   2Ki 10:19
shall not
with words, yet they are w. to   Pr 19:7
him
which is w. cannot be   Ec 1:15
numbered
in the balances, and art found   Da 5:27
w.
set in order the things that are   Tit 1:5
that nothing be w. unto them   Tit 3:13
be perfect and entire, w.   Jas 1:4
nothing

WANTON

committed lewd and w. deed   J'g 20:6
(B)
the w. crime in Israel (R)   J'g 20:10
stretched forth necks and w.   Isa 3:16
eyes
with undisciplined flirtatious   J'g 3:16
and alluring eyes (A)
with ogling eyes (B)   J'g 3:16
glancing wantonly with their   J'g 3:16
eyes (R)
their w. hearts (R)   Eze 6:9
begun to wax w. against   1Ti 5:11
Christ
withdraw themselves against   1Ti 5:11
Christ (A)
spite of Christ (B)   1Ti 5:11
their passions draw them away   1Ti 5:11
from Christ (N)
pleasure on the earth, and been   Jas 5:5
w.
living in pleasures of   Jas 5:5
self-indulgence and self-
gratification (A)
given yourselves up to   Jas 5:5
pleasures (B)
lived delicately and taken   Jas 5:5
pleasure (E)
have indulged yourself to the   Jas 5:5
full (P)
lived in luxury and pleasure   Jas 5:5
(R)
w. ways of ungodly (A)   2Pe 2:7
waxed w. (E)(R)   Re 18:7

WANTONLY

ran w. after gods (B)   Ex 34:15; 34:16
dealt w. in Judah (E)(R)   2Ch 28:19
turn after idols w. (A)   Eze 6:9

WANTONNESS

in their w. they (R)   Ge 49:6
w. in Israel (R)   J'g 20:6
not in chambering and w.   Ro 13:13
not in
not in immorality and   Ro 13:13
debauchery (A)
not in prostitution and   Ro 13:13
debauch (B)
no debauchery or vice (N)   Ro 13:13
no getting drunk or playing   Ro 13:13
with sex (P)
not in debauchery and   Ro 13:13
licentiousness (R)
living in shameless, insolent w.   1Pe 4:3
(A)
through much w. those that   2Pe 2:18
were
beguile and lure through   2Pe 2:18
lustful desires (A)
through appeal to immoral   2Pe 2:18
passions (B)
entice in the lusts of the flesh   2Pe 2:18
(E)
make sensual lusts and   2Pe 2:18
debauchery a bait (N)
use the sensual pull of lower   2Pe 2:18
passions to attract (P)
entice with licentious   2Pe 2:18
passions (R)
pervert grace into w. (A)   Jude 4

WANTS

let all thy w. lie upon me;   J'g 19:20
only
and he that ministered to   Ph'p 2:25
my w.

WAR

these made w. with Bera king   Ge 14:2
of
when there falleth out any w.   Ex 1:10
the people repent when they   Ex 13:17
see w.
The Lord is a man of w.: the   Ex 15:3
the Lord is a warrior (B)   Ex 15:3
the Lord will have w. with   Ex 17:16
Amalek
There is a noise of w. in the   Ex 32:17
camp
able to go forth to w. in Israel   Nu 1:3;
1:20, 22, 24, 26, 28, 30, 32, 34, 36, 38,
40, 42
if ye go to w. in your land   Nu 10:9
against
that are able to go to w. in   Nu 26:2
Israel
some of yourselves unto the   Nu 31:3
w.
of Israel shall ye send to the   Nu 31:4
w.
twelve thousand armed for w.   Nu 31:5
And Moses sent them to the   Nu 31:6
w.
of Eleazar the priest, to the w.   Nu 31:6
men of w. which went to the   Nu 31:21
battle
soldiers (B)   Nu 31:21;
31:28, 32, 49, 53; Jos 5:4, 6; 8:1; 11:7;
2Ki 25:4, 19; Jer 38:4; 41:3, 16;
Eze 27:10; 39:20
them that took the w. upon   Nu 31:27
them
the men of w. which went   Nu 31:28
out to
warriors (A)   Nu 31:28; 31:49; 2Ki 25:4
which the men of w. had   Nu 31:32
caught
of them that went out to w.   Nu 31:36
men of w. which are under   Nu 31:49
our
the men of w. had taken   Nu 31:53
spoil
Shall your brethren go to w.   Nu 32:6
go armed before the Lord to   Nu 32:20
w.
over, every man armed for   Nu 32:27
w.
on every man his weapons of   De 1:41
w.
generation of the men of w.   De 2:14
were
fighting men (B)   De 2:14; 2:16; Joe 3:9
all the men of w. were   De 2:16
consumed
all that are meet for the w.   De 3:18
signs, and by wonders, and by   De 4:34
w.
but will make w. against   De 20:12
thee, then
in making w. against it to   De 20:19
take it
the city that maketh w. with   De 20:20
thee
When thou goest forth to w.   De 21:10
new wife, he shall not go out   De 24:5
to w.
forty thousand prepared for w.   Jos 4:13
even all the men of w. died in   Jos 5:4
all the people that were men of   Jos 5:6
w.
compass the city, all ye men of   Jos 6:3
w.
men of w. (B)(E)(R)   Jos 6:3
take all the people of w. with   Jos 8:1
thee
the fighting men (R)   Jos 8:1
arose, and all the people of w.   Jos 8:3
to
even the people of w. that   Jos 8:11
were
Gibeon, and made w. against   Jos 10:5
it
and all the people of w. with   Jos 10:7;
him   11:7
captains of the men of w.   Jos 10:24
which
armed forces (B)   Jos 10:24
Joshua made w. a long time   Jos 11:18
with
And the land rested from w.   Jos 11:23
even so is my strength now,   Jos 14:11
for w.
And the land had rest from w.   Jos 14:15
w.
he was a man of w. therefore   Jos 17:1
he

to go up to *w*. against them *Jos 22:12*
might know, to teach them *w*. *J'g 3:2*
judged Israel, and went out to *J'g 3:10*
w.
gods; then was *w*. in the gates *J'g 5:8*
the children of Ammon made *J'g 11:4;*
w.   *11:5*
doest me wrong to *w*. against *J'g 11:27*
me
appointed with weapons of *J'g 18:11*
w.
appointed with their weapons *J'g 18:16*
of *w*.
were appointed with weapons *J'g 18:17*
of *w*.
sword: all these were men of *J'g 20:17*
w.
not to each man his wife in *J'g 21:22*
the *w*.
and to make his instruments *1Sa 8:12*
of *w*.
was sore *w*. against the *1Sa 14:52*
Philistines
and a man of *w*. and *1Sa 16:18*
prudent in
and he a man of *w*. from his *1Sa 17:33*
youth
Saul set him over the men of *1Sa 18:5*
w.
there was *w*. again: and *1Sa 19:8*
David
called all the people together *1Sa 23:8*
to *w*.
Philistines make *w*. against *1Sa 28:15*
me
and the weapons of *w*. *2Sa 1:27*
perished
long *w*. between the house of *2Sa 3:1*
Saul
was *w*. between the house of *2Sa 3:6*
Saul
did, and how the *w*. *2Sa 11:7*
prospered
all the things concerning the *2Sa 11:18*
w.
end of telling the matters of *2Sa 11:19*
the *w*.
thy father is a man of *w*. and *2Sa 17:8*
will
Philistines had yet *w*. again *2Sa 21:15*
with
He teachth my hands to *w*. *2Sa 22:35*
and shed the blood of *w*. in *1Ki 2:5*
peace
put the blood of *w*. upon his *1Ki 2:5*
girdle
but they were men of *w*. and *1Ki 9:22*
there was *w*. between *1Ki 14:30;*
Rehoboam   *15:6*
there was *w*. between Abijam *1Ki 15:7*
there was *w*. between Asa *1Ki 15:16;*
and   *15:32*
or whether they be come out *1Ki 20:18*
for *w*.
continued three years without *1Ki 22:1*
w.
to the *w*. against Hazael king *2Ki 8:28*
of
hand of Jehoahaz his father *2Ki 13:25*
by *w*.
took Selah by *w*. and called *2Ki 14:7*
Israel came up to Jerusalem *2Ki 16:5*
to *w*.
counsel and strength for the *2Ki 18:20*
w.
that were strong and apt for *2Ki 24:16*
w.
men of *w*. fled by night by *2Ki 25:4*
the way
that was set over the men of *2Ki 25:19*
w.
in the days of Saul they *1Ch 5:10*
made *w*.
to shoot with bow, and *1Ch 5:18*
skilful in *w*.
threescore, that went out to *1Ch 5:18*
the *w*.
they made *w*. with the *1Ch 5:19*
Hagarites
slain, because the *w*. was of *1Ch 5:22*
God
were bands of soldiers for *w*. *1Ch 7:4*
fit to go out for *w*. and battle *1Ch 7:11*
of them that were apt to the *1Ch 7:40*
w. and
the mighty men, helpers of the *1Ch 12:1*
w.

and men of *w*. fit for the *1Ch 12:8*
battle
that were ready armed to *1Ch 12:23*
the *w*.
hundred, ready armed to the *1Ch 12:24*
w.
mighty men of valour for *1Ch 12:25*
the *w*.
forth to battle, expert in *w*. *1Ch 12:33*
with all instruments of *w*., *1Ch 12:33*
fifty
of the Danites expert in *w*. *1Ch 12:35*
twenty
battle, expert in *w*., forty *1Ch 12:36*
thousand
all manner of instruments *1Ch 12:37*
of *w*.
All these men of *w*. that *1Ch 12:38*
could
for Hadarezer had *w*. with *1Ch 18:10*
Tou
there arose *w*. at Gezer with *1Ch 20:4*
And there was *w*. again with *1Ch 20:5*
yet again there was *w*. at *1Ch 20:6*
Gath
thou hast been a man of *w*. *1Ch 28:3*
If thy people go out to *w*. *2Ch 6:34*
against
they were men of *w*. and chief *2Ch 8:9*
w. between Abijah and *2Ch 13:2*
Jeroboam
with an army of valiant men *2Ch 13:3*
of *w*.
mighty warriors (B) *2Ch 13:3;*
                  17:18; Jer 48:14
valiant men of *w*. (R) *2Ch 13:3*
and he had no *w*. in those *2Ch 14:6*
years
And there was no more *w*. *2Ch 15:19*
unto the
made no *w*. against *2Ch 17:10*
Jehoshaphat
and the men of *w*. mighty *2Ch 17:13*
men of
ready prepared for the *w*. *2Ch 17:18*
and we will be with thee in *2Ch 18:3*
the *w*.
son of Ahab king of Israel to *2Ch 22:5*
w.
choice men, able to go forth *2Ch 25:5*
to *w*.
men, that went out to *w*. by *2Ch 26:11*
bands
that made *w*. with mighty *2Ch 26:13*
power
them that came from the *w*. *2Ch 28:12*
And he set captains of *w*. *2Ch 32:6*
over the
and put captains of *w*. in all *2Ch 33:14*
the house wherewith I have *2Ch 35:21*
w.
in *w*. from the power of the *Job 5:20*
sword
changes and *w*. are against *Job 10:17*
me
against the day of battle *Job 38:23*
and *w*.
He teacheth my hands to *w*. *Ps 18:34*
though *w*. should rise against *Ps 27:3*
me
butter, but *w*. was in his *Ps 55:21*
heart
thou the people that delight *Ps 68:30*
in *w*.
but when I speak, they are for *Ps 120:7*
w.
are they gathered together for *Ps 140:2*
w.
teacheth my hands to *w*. *Ps 144:1*
teaches to wage *w*. *Ps 144:1*
(B)(E)(R)
and with good advice make *Pr 20:18*
w.
counsel thou shalt make thy *w*. *Pr 24:6*
is like a *w*. club (R) *Pr 25:18*
a time of *w*. and a time of *Ec 3:8*
peace
there is no discharge in that *Ec 8:8*
w.
no discharge in this battle (A) *Ec 8:8*
no furlough during battle (B) *Ec 8:8*
is better than weapons of *w*. *Ec 9:18*
hold swords, being expert in *w*. *Ca 3:8*
neither shall they learn *w*. any *Isa 2:4;*
                                       Mic 4:3
mighty man, and the man of *w*. *Isa 3:2*
word, and thy mighty in the *Isa 3:25*
w.
toward Jerusalem to *w*. against *Isa 7:1*
it

and from the grievousness of *Isa 21:15*
w.
I have counsel and strength *Isa 36:5*
for *w*.
come forth to make *w*. with *Isa 37:9*
thee
they that *w*. against thee *Isa 41:12*
shall be
stir up jealousy like a man *Isa 42:13*
of *w*.
like a warrior (A)(B) *Isa 42:13*
of the trumpet, the alarm of *Jer 4:19*
w.
shout of the battle (B) *Jer 4:19*
Prepare ye *w*. against her; arise *Jer 6:4*
set in array as men for *w*. *Jer 6:23*
against
king of Babylon maketh *w*. *Jer 21:2*
I will turn back the weapons *Jer 21:4*
of *w*. and of evil, and of *Jer 28:8*
pestilence
the hands of the men of *w*. *Jer 38:4*
that
soldiers (A) *Jer 38:4;*
                41:3 ,16; Eze 39:20
soldiers (R) *Jer 38:4; 41:3, 16*
saw them, and all the men of *Jer 39:4*
w.
found there, and the men of *Jer 41:3*
w.
even mighty men of *w*. and the *Jer 41:16*
Egypt, where we shall see no *Jer 42:14*
w.
mighty and strong men for *Jer 48:14*
the *w*.
cause an alarm of *w*. to be *Jer 49:2*
heard in
all the men of *w*. shall be cut *Jer 49:26*
off in
all her men of *w*. shall be cut *Jer 50:30*
off in
my battle axe and weapons *Jer 51:20*
of *w*.
and the men of *w*. are *Jer 51:32*
affrighted
all the men of *w*. fled, and *Jer 52:7*
went
had the charge of the men of *Jer 52:25*
w.
company make for him in *Eze 17:17*
the *w*.
engines of *w*. against thy *Eze 26:9*
walls
in thine army, thy men of *w*. *Eze 27:10*
all thy men of *w*. that are in *Eze 27:27*
thee
to hell with their weapons of *Eze 32:27*
w.
mighty men, and with all *Eze 39:20*
men of *w*.
all kinds of warriors (R) *Eze 39:20*
horn made *w*. with the saints *Da 7:21*
unto the end of the *w*. *Da 9:26*
desolations
shall climb the wall like men *Joe 2:7*
of *w*.
Prepare *w*. wake up the mighty *Joe 3:9*
let all the men of *w*. draw near *Joe 3:9*
by securely as men averse *Mic 2:8*
from *w*.
they even prepare *w*. against *Mic 3:5*
him
Judah shall wage *w*. (B) *Zec 14:14*
to make *w*. against another *Lu 14:31*
king
Herod with his men of *w*. set *Lu 23:11*
him
Herod and his troops (N) *Lu 23:11*
Herod joined his soldiers *Lu 23:11*
(N)(R)
who goeth to *w*. at his own *1Co 9:7*
(S)
flesh, we do not *w*. after the *2Co 10:3*
flesh
them mightest *w*. a good *1Ti 1:18*
warfare
wage a good warfare (A) *1Ti 1:18*
put up a splendid fight (B) *1Ti 1:18*
fight gallantly (N) *1Ti 1:18*
w. of words (B) *1Ti 6:4*
lusts that *w*. in your members *Jas 4:1*
arise from conflicting passions *Jas 4:1*
(P)
ye fight and *w*., yet ye have not *Jas 4:2*
you struggle with and fight one *Jas 4:2*
another (P)
lusts, which *w*. against the *1Pe 2:11*
soul
pit shall make *w*. against them *Re 11:7*

there was *w.* in heaven: *Re 12:7*
Michael
went to make *w.* with the   *Re 12:17*
remnant
who is able to make *w.* with   *Re 13:4*
him
him to make *w.* with the saints   *Re 13:7*
These make *w.* with the   *Re 17:14*
Lamb
he doth judge and make *w.*   *Re 19:11*
to make *w.* against him that   *Re 19:19*
sat
massed together for battle   *Re 19:19*
(P)

WARD

he put them in *w.* in the   *Ge 40:3*
house of
custody (A)   *Ge 40:3;*
  40:4, 7; 41:10; 42:17;   *Le 24:12;*
      Nu 15:34;
custody (B)   *Ge 40:3;*
      40:4, 7; 41:10; 42:17; *Le 24:12*
and they continued a season   *Ge 40:4*
in *w.*
with him in the *w.* of his   *Ge 40:7*
lord's
put me in *w.* in the captain   *Ge 41:10*
of the
he put them altogether into   *Ge 42:17*
w.
put them into prison (R)   *Ge 42:17*
they put him in *w.* that the   *Le 24:12*
mind
they put him in *w.* because it   *Nu 15:34*
was
put them in confinement   *Nu 15:34;*
  (B)   *2Sa 20:3*
put them in *w.* and fed them   *2Sa 20:3*
put them under guard   *2Sa 20:3*
(A)(R)
kept the *w.* of the house of   *1Ch 12:29*
Saul
kept their allegiance   *1Ch 12:29*
(A)(R)
maintaining loyalty (B)   *1Ch 12:29*
And they cast lots *w.* against   *1Ch 25:8*
against *w.* as well the small   *1Ch 25:8*
as the
of the going up, *w.* against   *1Ch 26:16*
w.
the man of God, *w.* over   *Ne 12:24*
against *w.*
porters keeping the *w.* at the   *Ne 12:25*
porters kept the *w.* of their   *Ne 12:45*
God
and the *w.* of the purification   *Ne 12:45*
I am set in my *w.* whole   *Isa 21:8*
nights
set in my station every night   *Isa 21:8*
(A)
my observation post (B)   *Isa 21:8*
I am stationed (R)   *Isa 21:8*
a captain of the *w.* was there   *Jer 37:13*
the put him in *w.* in chains   *Eze 19:9*
put them in a stronghold (B)   *Eze 19:9*
past the first and the second   *Ac 12:10*
w.
first guard, and the second   *Ac 12:10*
(A)(B)(E)(R)
first guard-post, then the   *Ac 12:10*
second (N)
first and second guard-points   *Ac 12:10*
(P)

WARDROBE

over the *w.* (B)(R)   *2Ki 10:22*
son of Harhas, keeper of the   *2Ki 22:14*
w.
son of Hasrah, keeper of the   *2Ch 34:22*
w.)

WARDS

house of the tabernacle, by *w.*   *1Ch 9:23*
having *w.* one against   *1Ch 26:12*
another
appointed the *w.* of the   *Ne 13:30*
priests and

WARE

the people of the land bring   *Ne 10:31*
w. or
brought fish, and all manner   *Ne 13:16*
of *w.*
sellers of all kind of *w.*   *Ne 13:20*
lodged

devils long time, and *w.*   *Lu 8:27*
no clothes
They were *w.* of it, and fled   *Ac 14:6*
unto
Of whom be thou *w.* also; for   *2Ti 4:15*

WARES

Gather up thy *w.* out of the   *Jer 10:17*
land
handle your *w.* (B)(R)   *Jer 27:9*
traded for your *w.*   *Jer 27:12;*
(A)(B)(E)(R)   27:14, 16, 19, 22, 27
of the *w.* of thy making   *Eze 27:16;*
      27:18
thy *w.* went forth out of the   *Eze 27:33*
seas
forth the *w.* that were in the   *Jon 1:5*
ship

WARFARE

their armies together for *w.*   *1Sa 28:1*
campaign (B)   *1Sa 28:1*
to fight against (R)   *1Sa 28:1*
her, that her *w.* is   *Isa 40:2*
accomplished
Who goeth a *w.* any time at   *1Co 9:7*
his
weapons of our *w.* are not   *2Co 10:4*
carnal
by them mightest war a good   *1Ti 1:18*
w.
put up a splendid fight (B)   *1Ti 1:18*

WARM

the king may get *w.* (S)   *1Ki 1:2*
the flesh of the child waxed   *2Ki 4:34*
w.
What time they wax *w.* they   *Job 6:17*
How thy garments are *w.*   *Job 37:17*
when
but how can one be *w.* alone   *Ec 4:11*
will take thereof, and *w.*   *Isa 44:15*
himself
Aha, I am *w.* I have seen the   *Isa 44:16*
fire
there shall not be a coal to   *Isa 47:14*
w. to
my compassion grows *w.*   *Ho 11:8*
and tender (R)
clothe you, but there is none   *Hag 1:6*
w.

WARMED

he were not *w.* with the   *Job 31:20*
fleece of
and *w.* himself at the fire   *M'k 14:54*
was cold: and they *w.*   *Joh 18:18*
themselves
stood with them, and *w.*   *Joh 18:18*
himself
Simon Peter stood and *w.*   *Joh 18:25*
himself
in peace, be ye *w.* and filled   *Jas 2:16*

WARMETH

the earth, and *w.* them in   *Job 39:14*
dust
yea, he *w.* himself, and saith,   *Isa 44:16*
Aha

WARMING

when she saw Peter *w.*   *M'k 14:67*
himself

WARN

I *w.* you (B)(R)   *De 8:19*
w. them that they trespass not   *2Ch 19:10*
nor speakest to *w.* the wicked   *Eze 3:18*
Yet if thou *w.* the wicked,   *Eze 3:19*
and he
if thou *w.* the righteous man   *Eze 3:21*
the trumpet, and *w.* the   *Eze 33:3*
people
my mouth, and *w.* them from   *Eze 33:7*
me
dost not speak to *w.* the   *Eze 33:8*
wicked
if thou *w.* the wicked of his   *Eze 33:9*
way to
w. you whom you should fear   *Lu 12:5*
(A)(E)(N)(R)
let him strongly *w.*   *Lu 16:28*
(B)(N)(P)(R)

I ceased not to *w.* every one   *Ac 20:31*
night
but as my beloved sons I *w.*   *1Co 4:14*
you
w. them that are unruly,   *1Th 5:14*
comfort
I *w.* every man   *Re 22:18*
(A)(B)(N)(R)

WARNED

of God told him and *w.* him   *2Ki 6:10*
of
Lord *w.* Israel (A)(B)(R)   *2Ki 17:13;*
    17:15; Ne 9:26; 13:15, 21
prophets *w.* them (B)   *Ne 9:26*
I *w.* them (B)   *Ne 13:21*
be *w.*, rulers of earth (B)(R)   *Ps 2:10*
by them is thy servant *w.*   *Ps 19:11*
shall surely live, because he is   *Eze 3:21*
w.
trumpet, and the people be   *Eze 33:6*
not *w.*
being *w.* of God in a dream   *M't 2:12*
that
being *w.* of God in a dream,   *M't 2:22*
he
w. you to flee from the wrath   *M't 3:7;*
      Lu 3:7
charged earnestly and *w.* (B)   *Ac 2:4*
w. from God by an holy   *Ac 10:22*
angel to
being *w.* of God of things   *Heb 11:7*
not seen

WARNING

whom shall I speak, and give   *Jer 6:10*
w.
mouth, and give them *w.*   *Eze 3:17*
from me
givest him not *w.* nor   *Eze 3:18*
speakest
because thou hast not given   *Eze 3:20*
him *w.*
a *w.* and a horror   *Eze 5:15*
(A)(B)(R)
of the trumpet, and taketh   *Eze 33:4*
not *w.*
of the trumpet, and took not   *Eze 33:5*
w.
taketh *w.* shall deliver his   *Eze 33:5*
soul
giving *w.* before it happens   *M'k 13:23*
(P)
w. every man, and teaching   *Col 1:28*
every
w. of punishment (B)(P)   *Jude 7*

WARNINGS

thy *w.* did extend to (B)   *Ne 9:34*
affirms *w.* to them (B)   *Job 33:16*
terrifies them with *w.* (R)   *Job 33:16*

WARP

Whether it be in the *w.* or   *Le 13:48;*
woof   13:49, 51-53, 56-59

WARPED

w. and crooked generation   *Ph'p 2:15*
(N)(P)
w. minds (P)   *1Ti 6:5*

WARRED

they *w.* against the Midianites   *Nu 31:7*
Moses divided from the men   *Nu 31:42*
that *w.*
Moab, arose and *w.* against   *Jos 24:9*
Israel
the acts of Jeroboam, how   *1Ki 14:19*
he *w.*
Samaria, and *w.* against it   *1Ki 20:1*
that he shewed, and how he   *1Ki 22:45*
w.
the king of Syria *w.* against   *2Ki 6:8*
Israel
how he *w.* and how he   *2Ki 14:28*
recovered
and *w.* against the Philistines   *2Ch 26:6*

WARRETH

No man that *w.* entangleth   *2Ti 2:4*
himself

WARRING

king of Assyria w. against   *2Ki 19:8;*
Libnah   *Isa 37:8*
w. against the law of my mind   *Ro 7:23*

WARRIOR

the Lord is a w. (B)   *Ex 15:3*
mighty w. (A)   *Jos 11:1;*
   1Ch 7:9, 40; 8:40; 2Ch 32:21
mighty w. (R)   *Jos 11:1; 2Ch 32:21*
like a w. (B)(R)   *Job 16:14*
battle of the w. is with   *Isa 9:5*
confused
like a w. (A)(B)   *Isa 42:13*

WARRIORS

the w. (A)   *Nu 31:28; 31:49; 2Ki 25:4*
valiant men, w. (B)   *Jos 1:14*
these were w. (B)   *Jos 20:44*
chosen men, which were w.   *1Ki 12:21*
brave w. (B)(R)   *1Ch 5:24; 7:7, 9, 40*
mighty w. (R)   *1Ch 7:2; 7:5; 2Ch 13:3*
mighty w. (B)   *1Ch 11:35; 2Ch 13:3*
mighty and brave w. (A)   *1Ch 12:25*
mighty w. (B)   *1Ch 26:31; 2Ch 13:3*
seasoned w. (R)   *1Ch 28:1*
chosen men, which were w.   *2Ch 11:1*
the mighty w. (B)   *2Ch 13:3;*
   17:18; Jer 48:14
mighty courageous w. (B)   *2Ch 17:4*
all kinds of w. (R)   *Eze 39:20*
head of his w. (B)(E)(R)   *Hab 3:14*

WARS

in the book of the w. of the   *Nu 21:14*
Lord
had not known all the w. of   *J'g 3:1*
Canaan
for Hadadezer had w. with   *2Sa 8:10*
Toi
the w. which were about him   *1Ki 5:3*
abundantly, and hast made   *1Ch 22:8*
great w.
there were w. between   *2Ch 12:15*
Rehoboam
henceforth thou shalt have w.   *2Ch 16:9*
the acts of Jotham, and all   *2Ch 27:7*
his w.
maketh w. to cease unto the   *Ps 46:9*
end of
shall hear of w. and rumours   *M't 24:6;*
of w.   *M'k 13:7*
ye shall hear of w. and   *Lu 21:9*
commotions
whence come w. and fightings   *Jas 4:1*

WAS

Enoch walked with God and   *Ge 5:24*
w. not
God w. with the lad, he grew   *Ge 21:20*
saw certainly the Lord w.   *Ge 26:28*
with thee
Jacob told Rachel, he w. her   *Ge 29:12*
father's
thus I w. in day, drought   *Ge 31:40*
consumed
and behold, Joseph w. not in   *Ge 37:29*
the pit
Lord w. with Joseph,   *Ge 39:2;*
prosperous   *39:22*
Moses drew near where God   *Ex 20:21*
w.
he w. not in the company of   *Nu 27:3*
Korah
as I w. with Moses, so I will   *Jos 1:5*
be with
God be with thee as he w.   *Jos 1:17*
with Moses
the Lord w. with Joshua, and   *Jos 6:27*
his fame noised
as yet I am as strong as I w.   *Jos 14:11*
for war
tell us, how w. this wickedness   *J'g 20:3*
they went where man of God   *1Sa 9:10*
w.
ewe lamb w. unto him as a   *2Sa 12:3*
daughter
counsel of Ahithophel w. as   *2Sa 16:23*
if a man
woman spake whose living   *1Ki 3:26*
child w.
God with us as he w. with   *1Ki 8:57*
our fathers
Lord w. not in wind; w. not   *1Ki 19:11;*
in earthquake; w. not in the fire   *19:12*

king discerned him that he   *1Ki 20:41*
w. of prophets
done to Ahab all that w. in   *2Ki 10:30*
my heart
Esther had told what he w. to   *Es 8:1*
her
I w. not in safety, neither   *Job 3:26*
had I rest
as I w. in the days of my   *Job 29:4*
youth
he passed away and lo he w.   *Ps 37:36*
not
thus I w. as a man that   *Ps 38:14*
heareth not
they were in great fear, where   *Ps 53:5*
no fear w.
dimness shall not be such as w.   *Isa 9:1*
in
this people w. not till   *Isa 23:13*
Assyrian founded it
W. it not thou (S)   *Isa 51:9; 51:10*
w. not Israel a derision unto   *Jer 48:27*
thee? w. he found among thieves
I w. no prophet, neither w. I   *Am 7:14*
a prophet's son, but I w. an
herdman
pray thee, Lord, w. not this   *Jon 4:2*
my saying
w. not Esau Jacob's brother   *Mal 1:2*
such as w. not since   *M't 24:21;*
beginning of world, or   *M'k 13:19*
they uncovered the roof where   *M'k 2:4*
he w.
always night and day he w. in   *M'k 5:5*
mountains
the baptism of John, w. it   *M'k 11:30;*
from heaven, or of men   *Lu 20:4*
Word w. with God; Word w.   *Joh 1:1*
God
that w. true light, that lighteth   *Joh 1:9*
every man
John cried, he w. before me   *Joh 1:15;*
   1:30
he that w. with thee beyond   *Joh 3:26*
Jordan
Son of man ascend up where   *Joh 6:62*
he w. before
verily before Abraham w. I   *Joh 8:58*
am
I am glad for your sakes I   *Joh 11:15*
w. not there
these things I said, because I   *Joh 16:4*
w. with you
the glory I had with thee   *Joh 17:5*
before the world w.
Thomas one of the twelve w.   *Joh 20:24*
not with them
full of fishes, yet w. not the   *Joh 21:11*
net broken
after sold, w. it not in thy own   *Ac 5:4*
power
with envy sold Joseph, but God   *Ac 7:9*
w. with him
what w. I that I could   *Ac 11:17*
withstand God
captain came near, demanded   *Ac 21:33*
who he w.
our word w. not yea and   *2Co 1:18;*
nay   *1:19*
I w. not a whit behind   *2Co 11:5*
chiefest apostles
our entrance unto you w. not   *1Th 2:1*
in vain
our exhortation w. not in   *1Th 2:3*
deceit, nor guile
folly shall be manifest as theirs   *2Ti 3:9*
also w.
now consider how great this   *Heb 7:4*
man w.
of whom the world w. not   *Heb 11:38*
worthy
forgetteth what manner of   *Jas 1:24*
man he w.
from him which is and which   *Re 1:4;*
w.   *1:8; 4:8*
beast w. and is not, yet is   *Re 17:8;*
   17:11

BEHOLD IT WAS

God saw every thing, behold   *Ge 1:31*
it w. good
God looked on earth, behold   *Ge 6:12*
it w. corrupt
in the morning, behold it w.   *Ge 29:25*
Leah
behold it w. not toward Jacob   *Ge 31:2*
as before
Pharaoh awoke and behold it   *Ge 41:7*
w. a dream

for behold it w. in the sack's   *Ge 42:27*
mouth
behold it w. burnt   *Le 10:16; 1Sa 30:3*
behold it w. dead, behold it   *1Ki 3:21*
w. my son

BEHOLD THERE WAS

behold there w. not one of   *Ex 9:7*
cattle of Israel dead
behold there w. a man told a   *J'g 7:13*
dream
behold there w. a swarm of   *J'g 14:8*
bees in the lion
behold there w. an image in   *1Sa 19:16*
the bed
behold there w. a cake baken   *1Ki 19:6*
on coals
behold there w. no man there   *2Ki 7:5;*
   7:10
behold there w. lifted up a   *Zec 5:7*
talent of lead
behold there w. a great   *M't 28:2*
earthquake

IT WAS

as he interpreted, so it w.   *Ge 41:13*
he it w. sold to all people of   *Ge 42:6*
the land
it w. not you that sent me, but   *Ge 45:8*
God
manna for they wist not what   *Ex 16:15*
it w.
it w. of Lord to harden   *Jos 11:20*
hearts
I brought Moses word as it   *Jos 14:7*
w. in my heart
so it w. when Israel had sown   *J'g 6:3*
it w. not of the king to slay   *2Sa 3:37*
Abner
saw a tumult, I knew not   *2Sa 18:29*
what it w.
is my brother's for it w. his   *1Ki 2:15*
his hand became as it w.   *1Ki 13:6*
before
perceived it w. not the king   *1Ki 22:33*
of Israel
left camp as it w. and fled for   *2Ki 7:7*
life
Esther gave command to   *Es 4:5*
Mordecai to know what it w.
and why it w.
then shall dust return to earth   *Ec 12:7*
as it w.
it w. but a little I passed from   *Ca 3:4*
them
as it w. to Israel in day he   *Isa 11:16*
came up
from the time that it w.   *Isa 48:16*
there am I
his w.; thus it w.   *Eze 16:15; 16:19*
went to see what it w. that   *M'k 5:14*
was done
they could not tell whence it   *Lu 20:7*
w.
began to inquire which of   *Lu 22:23*
them it w.
ruler tasted and knew not   *Joh 2:9*
whence it w.
he that was healed wist not   *Joh 5:13*
who it w.
knew not that it w. Jesus   *Joh 20:14;*
   21:4
disciples knowing it w. the   *Joh 21:12*
Lord
not as it w. by one that sinned,   *Ro 5:16*
so gift

THERE WAS

let there be light, and there w.   *Ge 1:3*
light
there w. not a man to till   *Ge 2:5*
ground
there w. not found an help   *Ge 2:20*
meet for him
there w. great cry for there   *Ex 12:30*
w. not an house where
there w. not one dead
there w. not a man Moses   *Nu 26:64*
numbered
there w. not one city too   *De 2:36;*
strong   *3:4*
there w. no strange god with   *De 32:12*
him
there w. not a man left in Ai   *Jos 8:17*
there w. not a word Joshua   *Jos 8:35*
read not
there w. not any left to   *Jos 11:11*
breathe

there w. not a city that made *Jos 11:19*
peace with Israel
host of Sisera fell, *there* w. *J'g 4:16*
not a man left
for *there* w. his house, there *1Sa 7:17*
he judged
there w. not a man that *2Ki 10:21*
came not
laid hands on her, and *there* *2Ki 11:16*
w. she slain
there w. not one of them left *Ps 106:11*
and *there* w. the hiding of his *Hab 3:4*
power
that as *there* w. a readiness *2Co 8:11*
to will

WASH

w. your feet and rest *Ge 18:4*
yourselves
tarry all night, and w. your *Ge 19:2*
feet
water to w. his feet, and the *Ge 24:32*
men's
daughter of Pharaoh came to *Ex 2:5*
w.
and let them w. their clothes *Ex 19:10*
and shalt w. them with water *Ex 29:4*
and w. the inwards of him, *Ex 29:17*
and his
his foot also of brass to w. *Ex 30:18*
withal
and his sons shall w. their *Ex 30:19*
hands
they shall w. with water, *Ex 30:20*
that they
they shall w. their hands and *Ex 30:21*
their
and w. them with water *Ex 40:12*
and put water there, to w. *Ex 40:30*
withal
and his legs shall he w. in water *Le 1:9*
But he shall w. the inwards *Le 1:13*
and
thou shalt w. that whereon it *Le 6:27*
was
he did w. the inwards and the *Le 9:14*
of them shall w. his clothes *Le 11:25;*
11:28
carcase of it shall w. his *Le 11:40*
clothes
and he shall w. his clothes *Le 13:6;*
13:34
w. the thing wherein the *Le 13:54*
plague is
of skin it be, which thou *Le 13:58*
shalt w.
to be cleansed shall w. his *Le 14:8*
clothes
and w. himself in water, that *Le 14:8*
he
and he shall w. his clothes, *Le 14:9*
also
also he shall w. his flesh in *Le 14:9*
water
in the house shall w. his *Le 14:47*
clothes
toucheth bed shall w. his *Le 15:5*
clothes
hath the issue shall w. his *Le 15:6;*
clothes *15:7*
he shall w. his clothes, and *Le 15:8*
bathe
of those things shall w. his *Le 15:10*
clothes
he shall w. his clothes, and *Le 15:11*
bathe
w. his clothes, and bathe his *Le 15:13*
flesh
he shall w. all his flesh in *Le 15:16*
water
her bed shall w. his clothes *Le 15:21*
she sat upon shall w. his *Le 15:22*
clothes
and shall w. his clothes, and *Le 15:27*
bathe
shall he w. his flesh in water *Le 16:4*
w. his flesh with water in the *Le 16:24*
holy
the scapegoat shall w. his *Le 16:26*
clothes
burneth them shall w. his *Le 16:28*
clothes
he shall both w. his clothes *Le 17:15*
if he w. them not, nor bathe *Le 17:16*
his
unless he w. his flesh with *Le 22:6*
water
and let them w. their clothes *Nu 8:7*

Then the priest shall w. his *Nu 19:7*
clothes
that burneth her shall w. his *Nu 19:8*
clothes
of the heifer shall w. his *Nu 19:10*
clothes
purify himself, and w. his *Nu 19:19*
clothes
of separation shall w. his *Nu 19:21*
clothes
w. your clothes on the *Nu 31:24*
seventh day
w. their hands over the heifer *De 21:6*
on, he shall w. himself with *De 23:11*
water
W. thyself therefore, and *Ru 3:3*
anoint
to w. the feet of the servants *1Sa 25:41*
of my
down to thy house, and w. *2Sa 11:8*
thy feet
Go and w. in Jordan seven *2Ki 5:10*
times
may I not w. in them, and be *2Ki 5:12*
clean
he saith to thee, W. and be *2Ki 5:13*
clean
and five on the left, to w. in *2Ch 4:6*
them
the sea was for the priests to *2Ch 4:6*
w. in
If I w. myself with snow *Job 9:30*
water, and
I will w. mine hands in *Ps 26:6*
innocency
W. me throughly from mine *Ps 51:2*
w. me, and I shall be whiter *Ps 51:7*
than
w. his feet in the blood of the *Ps 58:10*
W. you, make you clean; *Isa 1:16*
put away
though thou w. thee with nitre *Jer 2:22*
w. thine heart from wickedness *Jer 4:14*
purify your hearts from *Jer 4:14*
wickedness (B)
for whom thou didst w. *Eze 23:40*
thyself
anoint thine head, and w. thy *M't 6:17*
face
w. not their hands when they *M't 15:2*
eat
except they w. their hands oft, *M'k 7:3*
eat
except they w. they eat not *M'k 7:4*
began to w. his feet with tears *Lu 7:38*
him, Go, w. in the pool of *Joh 9:7*
Siloam
Go to the pool of Siloam, *Joh 9:11*
and w.
and began to w. the disciples' *Joh 13:5*
feet
him, Lord, dost thou w. my *Joh 13:6*
feet
him, Thou shalt never w. my *Joh 13:8*
feet
If I w. thee not, thou hast no *Joh 13:8*
part
needeth not save to w. his *Joh 13:10*
feet
also ought to w. one *Joh 13:14*
another's feet
be baptized, and w. away thy *Ac 22:16*
sins
Be cleansed from your sins *Ac 22:16*
(B)
Be clean from your sins as *Ac 22:16*
you call on his name (P)

WASHED

water, and they w. their feet *Ge 43:24*
And he w. his face, and went *Ge 43:31*
out
he w. his garments in wine *Ge 49:11*
people; and they w. their *Ex 19:14*
clothes
Aaron and his sons w. their *Ex 40:31*
hands
came near unto the altar, *Ex 40:32*
they w.
his sons, and w. them with *Le 8:6*
water
he w. the inwards and the legs *Le 8:21*
in
the plague, after that it is w. *Le 13:55*
it shall be w. the second time *Le 13:58*
shall be w. with water, and *Le 15:17*
be
purified and they w. their *Nu 8:21*
clothes

they w. their feet, and did *J'g 19:21*
eat and
David arose from the earth, *2Sa 12:20*
and w.
his beard, nor w. his clothes *2Sa 19:24*
one w. the chariot in the *1Ki 22:38*
pool of
his blood; and they w. his *1Ki 22:38*
armour
burnt offering they w. in them *2Ch 4:6*
w. out by a deluge (B)(E) *Job 22:16*
When I w. my steps with *Job 29:6*
butter
my steps were bathed in *Job 29:6*
dream (B)
and w. my hands in *Ps 73:13*
innocency
yet is not w. from their *Pr 30:12*
filthiness
I have w. my feet; how shall I *Ca 5:3*
rivers of waters, w. with milk *Ca 5:12*
Lord shall have w. away the *Isa 4:4*
filth
thou w. in water to supple *Eze 16:4*
thee
Then w. I thee with water *Eze 16:9*
I throughly w. away thy *Eze 16:9*
blood
where they w. the burnt *Eze 40:38*
offering
w. his hands before the *M't 27:24*
multitude
she hath w. my feet with tears *Lu 7:44*
he had not first w. before *Lu 11:38*
dinner
and w. and came seeing *Joh 9:7*
I went and w., and I received *Joh 9:11*
sight
mine eyes, and I w., and do *Joh 9:15*
see
He that is w. needeth not *Joh 13:10*
save to
So after he had w. their feet *Joh 13:12*
and Master, have w. your *Joh 13:14*
feet
whom when they had w. they *Ac 9:37*
laid
of the night, and w. their *Ac 16:33*
stripes
but ye are w. but ye are *1Co 6:11*
sanctified
if she have w. the saints' feet *1Ti 5:10*
and our bodies w. with pure *Heb 10:22*
water
sow that was w. to her *2Pe 2:22*
wallowing
w. us from our sins in his own *Re 1:5*
loosed and freed from our sins *Re 1:5*
(A)
freed us from our sins (B) *Re 1:5*
loose us from our sins (E) *Re 1:5*
freed from our sins (N)(R) *Re 1:5*
set us free from our sins (P) *Re 1:5*
and have w. their robes, and *Re 7:14*
made

WASHEST

thou w. away the *Job 14:19*
things which

WASHING

put water there for w. (S) *Ex 40:30*
somewhat dark after the w. *Le 13:56*
of it
roof he saw a woman w. *2Sa 11:2*
herself
that every one put them off *Ne 4:23*
for w.
which came up from the w. *Ca 4:2*
of sheep which go up from the *Ca 6:6*
w.
received to hold, as the w. of *M'k 7:4*
cups
of men, as the w. of pots and *M'k 7:8*
cups
of them, and were w. their nets *Lu 5:2*
cleanse it with the w. of *Eph 5:26*
water by
cleansing according to the *Eph 5:26*
word (B)
cleansed through the baptism *Eph 5:26*
of the word (P)
by the w. of regeneration, and *Tit 3:5*
cleansing of the new birth (A) *Tit 3:5*
bathing of regeneration (B) *Tit 3:5*
saved us through the water of *Tit 3:5*
rebirth (N)

by the cleansing power of the   *Tit 3:5*
new birth (P)
w. a dirty body (P)(R)   *1Pe 3:21*

WASHINGS

in meats and drinks, and   *Heb 9:10*
divers *w.*
various *w.* (A)(P)   *Heb 9:10*
various ablutions (B)(R)   *Heb 9:10*
various rites of cleansing   *Heb 9:10*
(N)

WASHBASIN

make a *w.* (B)   *Ex 30:18; 38:8; 40:7, 11*
Moab is my *w.* (B)(R)   *Ps 60:8; 108:9*

WASHBOWL

the *w.* and his (B)   *Ex 30:28*

WASHPOT

Moab is my *w.*   *Ps 60:8; 108:9*
Moab is my washbasin   *Ps 60:8;*
(B)(R)   *108:9*

WAST

Who told thee that thou *w.*   *Ge 3:11*
naked
ground; for out of it *w.* thou   *Ge 3:19*
taken
of God, and thou *w.* pleased   *Ge 33:10*
with me
manner when thou *w.* his   *Ge 40:13*
butler
w. a servant in the land of   *De 5:15*
Egypt
that thou *w.* a bondman in the   *De 15:15*
land
that thou *w.* a bondman in   *De 16:12*
Egypt
thou *w.* a stranger in his land   *De 23:7*
remember that thou *w.* a   *De 24:18*
bondman
thou *w.* a bondman in the   *De 24:22*
land of
thee, when thou *w.* faint and   *De 25:18*
weary
of Egypt, which thou *w.*   *De 28:60*
afraid of
with whose maidens thou *w.*   *Ru 3:2*
When thou *w.* little in thine   *1Sa 15:17*
own sight
w. thou not made the head   *1Sa 15:17*
of the
How *w.* thou not afraid to   *2Sa 1:14*
stretch
thou *w.* slain in thine high   *2Sa 1:25*
places
thou *w.* he that leddest out and   *2Sa 5:2;*
   1Ch 11:2
or *w.* thou made before the   *Job 15:7*
hills
Where *w.* thou when I laid   *Job 38:4*
thou it, because thou *w.* then   *Job 38:21*
born
thou *w.* a God that forgavest   *Ps 99:8*
them
Jordan, that thou *w.* driven   *Ps 114:5*
back
though thou *w.* angry with   *Isa 12:1*
me, thine
wherein thou *w.* made to serve   *Isa 14:3*
spoilest, and thou *w.* not   *Isa 33:1*
spoiled
Since thou *w.* precious in my   *Isa 43:4*
sight
and *w.* called a transgressor   *Isa 48:8*
from the
of youth, when thou *w.*   *Isa 54:6*
refused
hand; therefore thou *w.* not   *Isa 57:10*
grieved
as thou *w.* ashamed of   *Jer 2:36*
Assyria
O Babylon, and thou *w.* not   *Jer 50:24*
aware
day thou *w.* born thy navel   *Eze 16:4*
was not
neither *w.* thou washed in   *Eze 16:4*
water to
thou *w.* cast out in the open   *Eze 16:5*
field
person, in the day that thou   *Eze 16:5*
w. born
thee when thou *w.* in thy   *Eze 16:6*
blood

whereas thou *w.* naked and   *Eze 16:7*
bare
Thus *w.* thou decked with   *Eze 16:13*
gold and
thou *w.* exceeding beautiful   *Eze 16:13*
when thou *w.* naked and   *Eze 16:22*
bare
and *w.* polluted in thy blood   *Eze 16:22*
Assyrians, because thou *w.*   *Eze 16:28*
unsatiable
yet thou *w.* not satisfied   *Eze 16:29*
herewith
thou *w.* corrupted more than   *Eze 16:47*
they
in the place where thou *w.*   *Eze 21:30*
created
thou *w.* not purged, thou   *Eze 24:13*
shalt not
that *w.* inhabited of   *Eze 26:17*
seafaring men
which *w.* strong in the sea,   *Eze 26:17*
she and
thou *w.* replenished, and   *Eze 27:25*
made very
thee in the day that thou *w.*   *Eze 28:3*
created
thou *w.* upon the holy   *Eze 28:14*
mountain
Thou *w.* perfect in thy ways   *Eze 28:15*
from the
from the day that thou *w.*   *Eze 28:15*
created
even thou *w.* as one of them   *Ob 1:11*
Thou also *w.* with Jesus of   *M't 26:69*
Galilee
thou also *w.* with Jesus of   *M'k 14:67*
Nazareth
when thou *w.* under the fig   *Joh 1:48*
tree
Thou *w.* altogether born in   *Joh 9:34*
sins
When thou *w.* young, thou   *Joh 21:18*
girdedst
for thou *w.* slain, and hast   *Re 5:9*
redeemed
God Almighty, which art,   *Re 11:17*
and *w.*
Lord, which art, and *w.* and   *Re 16:5*
shalt

WASTE

an empty *w.* (A)(B)   *Ge 1:2; Jer 4:23*
earth was *w.* and void (E)   *Ge 1:2*
w. the eyes (A)(R)   *Le 26:16*
And I will make your cities   *Le 26:31*
w.
lay *w.* (A)   *Le 26:31; 26:32*
ruins (B)   *Le 26:31;*
   26:33; Isa 51:3; 58:12; Hag 1:9
be desolate, and your cities   *Le 26:33*
w.
we have laid them *w.* even   *Nu 21:30*
unto
ravaged (B)   *Nu 21:30*
and in the *w.* howling   *De 32:10*
wilderness
desert land (A)(E)(R)   *De 32:10*
The barrel of meal shall not   *1Ki 17:14*
w.
be empty (B)   *1Ki 17:14*
to lay *w.* fenced cities into   *2Ki 19:25*
ruinous
turn to rubbish heaps (B)   *2Ki 19:25*
ruinous heaps (E)   *2Ki 19:25*
heaps of ruins (R)   *2Ki 19:25*
of wickedness *w.* them any   *1Ch 17:9*
more
of my fathers' sepulchres, lieth   *Ne 2:3*
w.
how Jerusalem lieth *w.* and   *Ne 2:17*
lies in ruins (R)   *Ne 2:17*
in former time desolate and   *Job 30:3*
satisfy the desolate and *w.*   *Job 38:27*
ground
and laid *w.* his dwelling place   *Ps 79:7*
boar out of the wood doth *w.*   *Ps 80:13*
it
devours it (B)   *Ps 80:13*
ravage it (E)(R)   *Ps 80:13*
I will lay it *w.*: it shall not be   *Isa 5:6*
make it a desolation (B)   *Isa 5:6*
w. places of the fat ones shall   *Isa 5:17*
in the night Ar of Moab is   *Isa 15:1*
laid *w.*
the night Kir of Moab is laid   *Isa 15:1*
for it is laid *w.* so that there   *Isa 23:1*
is no

for your strength is laid *w.*   *Isa 23:14*
and maketh it *w.* and turneth   *Isa 24:1*
it
laid *w.* (E)   *Isa 24:3;*
   Jer 4:20; 25:26; 48:1, 15, 20; 49:3
The highways lie *w.* the   *Isa 33:8*
desolate (B)   *Isa 33:8; 34:10*
to generation it shall lie *w.*   *Isa 34:10*
Assyria have laid *w.* all the   *Isa 37:18*
nation
be to lay *w.* defenced cities   *Isa 37:26*
into
w., futility, worthlessness   *Isa 40:17*
(A)
images are wind and *w.* (B)   *Isa 41:29*
I will make *w.* mountains   *Isa 42:15*
he created it not a worthless   *Isa 45:18*
w. (A)(E)
they that made thee *w.* shall   *Isa 49:17*
go
your devastators (B)   *Isa 49:17*
thy destroyers (E)   *Isa 49:17*
thy *w.* and thy desolate   *Isa 49:19*
places
he will comfort all her *w.*   *Isa 51:3*
places
ye *w.* places of Jerusalem   *Isa 52:9*
thee shall build the old *w.*   *Isa 58:12*
places
they shall repair the *w.* cities   *Isa 61:4*
ruined cities (A)   *Isa 61:4*
our pleasant things are laid   *Isa 64:11*
w.
desirable places in ruins (A)   *Isa 64:11*
yelled, and they made his land   *Jer 2:15*
w.
and thy cities shall be laid *w.*   *Jer 4:7*
be destroyed (B)   *Jer 4:7;*
   Eze 6:6; Am 7:9
laid *w.* (A)   *Jer 4:20;*
   48:1; 49:3; Zec 11:2
laid *w.* (B)   *Jer 4:20*
   25:36; 48:1, 20; 49:3
a *w.* and vacant void (A)   *Jer 4:23*
earth a *w.* and void (E)(R)   *Jer 4:23*
land ruined and laid *w.*   *Jer 9:12*
(A)(B)(E)
laid *w.* my vineyard (B)   *Jer 12:10*
land a *w.* (A)(B)(R)   *Jer 25:11*
a perpetual *w.* (A)(B)(R)   *Jer 25:12*
should this city be laid *w.*   *Jer 27:17*
become a desolation (R)   *Jer 27:17*
Noph shall be *w.* and   *Jer 46:19*
desolate
become a desolation (B)(E)   *Jer 46:19*
laid *w.* (R)   *Jer 48:1; 48:20; 49:3*
a reproach, a *w.*, a curse   *Jer 49:13*
a *w.* (A)(B)(E)(R)   *Jer 49:13*
w. and utterly destroy after   *Jer 50:21*
them
Slay and utterly destroy   *Jer 50:21*
(A)(B)(E)
laying Babylon *w.* (R)   *Jer 51:55*
Moreover I will make thee *w.*   *Eze 5:14*
make you a desolation   *Eze 5:14*
(A)(B)(E)
dwellingplaces shall be laid *w.*   *Eze 6:6*
your altars may be laid *w.* and   *Eze 6:6*
are inhabited shall be laid *w.*   *Eze 12:20*
palaces, and he laid *w.* their   *Eze 19:7*
cities
be replenished, now she is   *Eze 26:2*
laid *w.*
of Egypt shall be desolate   *Eze 29:9*
and *w.*
of Egypt utterly *w.* and   *Eze 29:10*
desolate
among the cities that are   *Eze 29:12*
laid *w.*
I will make the land *w.* and   *Eze 30:12*
make desolate (A)(E)   *Eze 30:12*
I will lay thy cities *w.* and   *Eze 35:4*
thou
the *w.* and desolate and   *Eze 36:35*
ruined
so shall the *w.* cities be filled   *Eze 36:38*
with
which have been always *w.*   *Eze 38:8*
He hath laid my vine *w.* and   *Joe 1:7*
of Israel shall be laid *w.*   *Am 7:9*
and they shall build the *w.*   *Am 9:14*
cities
ruined and laid *w.* (A)   *Mic 2:4*
shall *w.* the land of Assyria   *Mic 5:6*
with
She is empty, and void, and   *Na 2:10*
w.
thee, and say, Nineveh is laid   *Na 3:7*
w.

Nineveh is ruined (B)   *Na 3:7*
a day of *w*. and desolation   *Zep 1:15*
(S)
I made their streets *w*. that   *Zep 3:6*
none
houses, and this house lie *w*.   *Hag 1:4*
this house lies in ruins   *Hag 1:4*
(A)(B)(R)
Because of mine house that is   *Hag 1:9*
w.
mountains and his inheritance   *Mal 1:3*
w.
To what purpose is this *w*.   *M't 26:8*
Why was this *w*. of the   *M'k 14:4*
ointment
laid *w*. the church with cruelty   *Ac 8:3*
and violence (A)(E)(R)
faith he once laid *w*. (B)   *Ga 1:23*
regard as *w*., consider as   *Ph'p 3:8*
rubbish (B)(P)
wealthy *w*. away (B)   *Jas 1:11*

WASTED

carcases be *w*. in the   *Nu 14:33*
wilderness
consumed (A)(E)   *Nu 14:33*
the Kenite shall be *w*. until   *Nu 24:22*
headed for destruction (B)   *Nu 24:22*
the men of war were *w*. out   *De 2:14*
from
perished (A)(R)   *De 2:14*
consumed (E)   *De 2:14*
And the barrel of meal *w*.   *1Ki 17:16*
not
was not spent (N)(R)   *1Ki 17:16*
w. the country of the   *1Ch 20:1*
children of
devastated (A)   *1Ch 20:1*
to devastate (B)   *1Ch 20:1*
ravaged the country (R)   *1Ch 20:1*
foundation *w*. away (R)   *Job 22:16*
they that *w*. us required of us   *Ps 137:3*
cities be *w*. without inhabitant   *Isa 6:11*
cities be made ruins (B)   *Isa 6:11*
the river shall be *w*. and dried   *Isa 19:5*
up
those nations shall be utterly   *Isa 60:12*
w.
utterly desolate (B)   *Isa 60:12*
perished (E)   *Isa 60:12*
and they are *w*. and desolate   *Jer 44:6*
the midst of the cities that   *Eze 30:7*
are *w*.
w. and destroyed (A)   *Ho 10:14*
The field is *w*. the land   *Joe 1:10*
mourneth
fields are desolate (B)   *Joe 1:10*
land mourneth; for the corn   *Joe 1:10*
is *w*.
there *w*. his substance with   *Lu 15:13*
riotous
squandered (B)(N)(P)(R)   *Lu 15:13*
unto him that he had *w*. his   *Lu 16:1*
goods
squandering (A)(N)   *Lu 16:1*
mismanaging (P)   *Lu 16:1*
nothing lost or *w*. (P)   *1Co 15:58*
the church of God, and *w*. it   *Ga 1:13*
make havoc and destroy it   *Ga 1:13*
(A)
devastated it (B)   *Ga 1:13*
tried to destroy it (N)(P)(R)   *Ga 1:13*
w. my efforts (B)(P)   *Ga 4:11*

WASTENESS

a day of *w*. and desolation, a   *Zep 1:15*
a day of ruin and devastation   *Zep 1:15*
(A)(R)
a day of wreck and   *Zep 1:15*
devastation (B)

WASTER

brother to him that is a great   *Pr 18:9*
w.
destroyer (A)(E)   *Pr 18:9*
he who destroys (B)(R)   *Pr 18:9*
I have created the *w*. to   *Isa 54:16*
destroy
devastator (A)(B)   *Isa 54:16*
ravager (R)   *Isa 54:16*

WASTES

the pathless *w*. (B)   *Ps 36:16*
And they shall build the old   *Isa 61:4*
w.
ancient ruins (A)(B)(R)   *Isa 61:4*

cities thereof shall be   *Jer 49:13*
perpetual *w*.
those *w*. of the land of   *Eze 33:24*
Israel
they that are in the *w*. shall   *Eze 33:27*
fall by
to the desolate *w*. and to the   *Eze 36:4*
cities
and the *w*. shall be builded   *Eze 36:10*
ruins rebuilt (B)   *Eze 36:10*
cities, and the *w*. shall be   *Eze 36:33*
builded

WASTETH

But man dieth, and *w*. away   *Job 14:10*
destruction that *w*. at noonday   *Ps 91:6*
He that *w*. his father, and   *Pr 19:26*

WASTING

sick man *w*. away (B)(R)   *Isa 10:18*
w. and destruction are in their   *Isa 59:7*
w. nor destruction within thy   *Isa 60:18*
outer nature is *w*. away (R)   *2Co 4:16*

WATCH

the Lord *w*. between me and   *Ge 31:49*
thee
in the morning *w*. the Lord   *Ex 14:24*
looked
in the beginning of the middle   *J'g 7:19*
w.
they had but newly set the *w*.   *J'g 7:19*
midst of the host in the   *1Sa 11:11*
morning *w*.
unto David's house, to *w*.   *1Sa 19:11*
him
the young man that kept the   *2Sa 13:34*
w.
keepers of the *w*. of the   *2Ki 11:5*
king's
guard (B)(R)   *2Ki 11:5; 11:6, 7*
shall ye keep the *w*. of the   *2Ki 11:6*
house
they shall keep the *w*. of the   *2Ki 11:7*
house
watch (S)   *1Ch 26:16; Ne 12:24, 25*
Judah came toward the *w*.   *2Ch 20:24*
tower
shall keep the *w*. of the Lord   *2Ch 23:6*
W. ye., and keep them,   *Ezr 8:29*
until ye
set a *w*. against them day and   *Ne 4:9*
of Jerusalem, every one in his   *Ne 7:3*
w.
that thou settest a *w*. over me   *Job 7:12*
dost thou not *w*. over my sin   *Job 14:16*
it is past, and as a *w*. in the   *Ps 90:4*
night
I *w*. and am as a sparrow   *Ps 102:7*
alone
than they that *w*. for   *Ps 130:6*
the morning
Set a *w*. O Lord, before my   *Ps 141:3*
mouth
discretion shall *w*. over you   *Pr 2:11*
(A)(E)(R)
eyes of Lord *w*. over (R)   *Pr 22:12*
table, *w*. in the watchtower   *Isa 21:5*
all that *w*. for iniquity are cut   *Isa 29:20*
off
a leopard shall *w*. over their   *Jer 5:6*
cities
so will I *w*. over them, to   *Jer 31:28*
build, and
I will *w*. over them for evil,   *Jer 44:27*
and not
stand by the way and *w*. (S)   *Jer 48:19*
make the *w*. strong, set up   *Jer 51:12*
w. the way, make thy loins   *Na 2:1*
strong
I will stand upon my *w*. and   *Hab 2:1*
set
will *w*. to see what he will say   *Hab 2:1*
fourth *w*. of the night Jesus   *M't 14:25*
went
w. therefore: for ye know   *M't 24:42*
not
in what *w*. the thief would   *M't 24:43*
come
W. therefore, for ye know   *M't 25:13*
neither
tarry ye here, and *w*. with me   *M't 26:38*
could ye not *w*. with me   *M't 26:40*
one hour
W. and pray, that ye enter   *M't 26:41*
not into
Ye have a *w*.: go our way,   *M't 27:65*
make

sealing the stone, and setting   *M't 27:66*
a *w*.
some of the *w*. came into   *M't 28:11*
the city
about the fourth *w*. of the   *M'k 6:48*
night
Take ye heed, *w*. and pray: *M'k 13:33*
for ye
and commanded the porter   *M'k 13:34*
to *w*.
W. ye therefore: for ye   *M'k 13:35*
know not
I say unto you I say unto   *M'k 13:37*
all, *W*.
unto death: tarry ye here,   *M'k 14:34*
and *w*.
couldest not thou *w*. one   *M'k 14:37*
hour
W. ye and pray, lest ye enter   *M'k 14:38*
into
keeping *w*. over their flock by   *Lu 2:8*
if he shall come in the   *Lu 12:38*
second *w*.
or come in the third *w*. and   *Lu 12:38*
find
W. ye therefore, and pray   *Lu 21:36*
always
Therefore *w*. and remember,   *Ac 20:31*
that
be always alert and on   *Ac 20:31;*
guard (A)   *1Co 16:13*
keep on the lookout (B)   *Ac 20:31*
be alert (R)   *Ac 20:31*
W. ye, stand fast in the   *1Co 16:13*
faith, quit
Be alert (B)   *1Co 16:13*
w. in the same with   *Col 4:2*
thanksgiving
others; but let us *w*. and be   *1Th 5:6*
sober
let us keep awake (A)   *1Th 5:6*
be on guard and composed   *1Th 5:6*
(B)
But *w*. thou in all things,   *2Ti 4:5*
endure
keep your head (B)   *2Ti 4:5*
always ready (R)   *2Ti 4:5*
they *w*. for your souls, as   *Heb 13:17*
they that
are attentive to your souls   *Heb 13:17*
(B)
sober, and *w*. unto prayer   *1Pe 4:7*
awake to the practice of   *1Pe 4:7*
prayer (B)
Keep sane (R)   *1Pe 4:7*
If therefore thou shalt not *w*.   *Re 3:3*
keep wide awake (A)(B)   *Re 3:3*

WATCHED

w. enviously David (S)   *1Sa 18:9*
when God *w*. over me (R)   *Job 29:2*
and they *w*. the house to   *Ps 59 title*
kill him
All my familiars *w*. for my   *Jer 20:10*
halting
that like as I have *w*. over   *Jer 31:28*
them
w. for a nation that could not   *La 4:17*
save
hath the Lord *w*. upon the   *Da 9:14*
evil
he would have *w*. and would   *M't 24:43*
not
w. for a chance to take (B)   *M't 26:16;*
  Lu 22:6
sitting down they *w*. him   *M't 27:36*
there
they *w*. him, whether he would   *M'k 3:2*
the scribes and Pharisees *w*.   *Lu 6:7*
him
he would have *w*., and not   *Lu 12:39*
have
the sabbath day, that they *w*.   *Lu 14:1*
him
they *w*. him, and sent forth   *Lu 20:20*
spies
they *w*. the gate day and night   *Ac 9:24*
to

WATCHER

you *w*. and keeper of men   *Job 7:20*
(A)(B)(E)(R)
a *w*. and an holy one came   *Da 4:13*
down
the king saw a *w*. and an holy   *Da 4:23*
one

WATCHERS

that *w.* come from a far country   *Jer 4:16*
besiegers (A)(B)(R)   *Jer 4:16*
matter is by the decree of the *w.*   *Da 4:17*
guardian-watcher (B)   *Da 4:17*

WATCHES

w. of the inhabitants of Jerusalem   *Ne 7:3*
were over against them in the *w.*   *Ne 12:9*
meditate on thee in the night *w.*   *Ps 63:6*
Mine eyes prevent the night *w.*   *Ps 119:148*
my eyes waited for night *w.* (B)   *Ps 119:148*
Lord *w.* over sojourners (R)   *Ps 146:9*
beginning of the *w.* pour out thine   *La 2:19*

WATCHEST

w. unto all my paths (S)   *Job 13:27*

WATCHETH

The wicked *w.* the righteous   *Ps 37:32*
the end is come: it *w.* for thee   *Eze 7:6*
Blessed is he that *w.* and keepeth   *Re 16:15*

WATCHFUL

Be *w.* and strengthen the things   *Re 3:2*

WATCHING

sat upon a seat by the wayside *w.*   *1Sa 4:13*
heareth me, *w.* daily at my gates   *Pr 8:34*
in our *w.* we have watched for   *La 4:17*
they that were with him, *w.* Jesus   *M't 27:54*
Lord when he cometh shall find *w.*   *Lu 12:37*
and *w.* thereunto with all   *Eph 6:18*

WATCHINGS

in tumults, in labours, in *w.* in   *2Co 6:5*
painfulness, in *w.* often, in hunger   *2Co 11:27*

WATCHMAN

the *w.* went up to the roof over the   *2Sa 18:24*
sentinel (B)   *2Sa 18:24; 18:25-27*
And the *w.* cried, and told the king   *2Sa 18:25*
the *w.* saw another man running   *2Sa 18:26*
and the *w.* called unto the porter   *2Sa 18:26*
And the *w.* said, Me thinketh   *2Sa 18:27*
there stood a *w.* on the tower   *2Ki 9:17*
the *w.* told, saying, The messenger   *2Ki 9:18*
And the *w.* told, saying, He came   *2Ki 9:20*
city, the *w.* waketh but in vain   *Ps 127:1*
sentry (B)   *Ps 127:1*
set a *w.* let him declare what he   *Isa 21:6*
W. what of the night   *Isa 21:11*
The *w.* said, The morning cometh   *Isa 21:12*
thee a *w.* unto the house of Israel   *Eze 3:17*
coasts, and set him for their *w.*   *Eze 33:2*
But if the *w.* see the sword come   *Eze 33:6*
thee a *w.* unto the house of Israel   *Eze 33:7*
w. of Ephraim was with my God   *Ho 9:8*
the *w.* opens (A)   *Joh 10:3*

WATCHMAN'S

blood will I require at the *w.* hand   *Eze 33:6*

WATCHMEN

w. of Saul in Gibeah of Benjamin   *1Sa 14:16*
outposts (B)   *1Sa 14:16*
from the tower of the *w.* to   *2Ki 17:9*
watchtower (A)(R)   *2Ki 17:9; 18:8*
from the tower of the *w.* to   *2Ki 18:8*
The *w.* that go about the city   *Ca 3:3*
The *w.* that went about the city   *Ca 5:7*
Thy *w.* shall lift up the voice   *Isa 52:8*
His *w.* are blind; they are all   *Isa 56:10*
I have set *w.* upon thy walls   *Isa 62:6*
I set *w.* over you, saying, Hearken   *Jer 6:17*
the *w.* upon the mount Ephraim   *Jer 31:6*
the watch strong, set up the *w.*   *Jer 51:12*
the day of thy *w.* and thy visitation   *Mic 7:4*

WATCHTOWER

the table, watch in the *w.* eat   *Isa 21:5*
I stand continually upon the *w.*   *Isa 21:8*
built a *w.* (A)(B)(N)(P)   *M't 21:33; M'k 12:1*

WATER

went out of Eden to *w.* the garden   *Ge 2:10*
a *w.*-deluge (B)   *Ge 6:17; 7:6, 10; 9:28*
found her by a fountain of *w.*   *Ge 16:7*
Let a little *w.* I pray you, be   *Ge 18:4*
and took bread, and a bottle of *w.*   *Ge 21:14*
And the *w.* was spent in the bottle   *Ge 21:15*
her eyes, and she saw a well of *w.*   *Ge 21:19*
went, and filled the bottle with *w.*   *Ge 21:19*
Abimelech because of a well of *w.*   *Ge 21:25*
by a well of *w.* at the time of   *Ge 24:11*
time that women go out to draw *w.*   *Ge 24:11*
I stand here by the well of *w.*   *Ge 24:13*
of the city come out to draw   *Ge 24:13*
thee, drink a little *w.* of thy pitcher   *Ge 24:17*
I will draw *w.* for thy camels also   *Ge 24:19*
ran again unto the well to draw *w.*   *Ge 24:20*
and *w.* to wash his feet, and   *Ge 24:32*
I stand by the well of *w.*   *Ge 24:43*
virgin cometh forth to draw *w.*   *Ge 24:43*
a little *w.* of thy pitcher to drink   *Ge 24:43*
down unto the well, and drew *w.*   *Ge 24:45*
Isaac digged again the wells of *w.*   *Ge 26:18*
found there a well of springing *w.*   *Ge 26:19*
herdmen, saying, The *w.* is ours   *Ge 26:20*
said unto him, We have found *w.*   *Ge 26:32*
w. ye the sheep, and go and feed   *Ge 29:7*
mouth: then we *w.* the sheep   *Ge 29:8*
was empty, there was no *w.* in it   *Ge 37:24*
and gave them *w.* and they washed   *Ge 43:24*
Unstable as *w.* thou shalt not excel   *Ge 49:4*
Because I drew him out of the *w.*   *Ex 2:10*
and they came and drew *w.* and   *Ex 2:16*
troughs to *w.* their father's flock   *Ex 2:16*
and also drew *w.* enough for us   *Ex 2:19*
shalt take of the *w.* of the river   *Ex 4:9*
the *w.* which thou takest out of   *Ex 4:9*
lo, he goeth out unto the *w.*   *Ex 7:15*
loathe to drink of the *w.* of the river   *Ex 7:18*
upon all their pools of *w.* that they   *Ex 7:19*
not drink of the *w.* of the river   *Ex 7:21*
digged round about the river for *w.*   *Ex 7:24*
for they could not drink of the *w.* of   *Ex 7:24*
lo, he cometh forth to the *w.*   *Ex 8:20*
nor sodden at all with *w.* but roast   *Ex 12:9*
in the wilderness, and found no *w.*   *Ex 15:22*
where were twelve wells of *w.*   *Ex 15:27*
was no *w.* for the people to drink   *Ex 17:1*
said, Give us *w.* that we may drink   *Ex 17:2*
the people thirsted there for *w.*   *Ex 17:3*
there shall come *w.* out of it   *Ex 17:6*
that is in the *w.* under the earth   *Ex 20:4*
shall bless thy bread, and thy *w.*   *Ex 23:25*
and shalt wash them with *w.*   *Ex 29:4*
and thou shalt put *w.* therein   *Ex 30:18*
they shall wash with *w.* that they   *Ex 30:20*
powder, and strawed it upon the *w.*   *Ex 32:20*
did neither eat bread, nor drink *w.*   *Ex 34:28*
the altar, and shalt put *w.* therein   *Ex 40:7*
and wash them with *w.*   *Ex 40:12*
and put *w.* there, to wash withal   *Ex 40:30*
and his legs shall he wash in *w.*   *Le 1:9*
the inwards and the legs with *w.*   *Le 1:13*
be both scoured, and rinsed in *w.*   *Le 6:28*
his sons, and wash them with *w.*   *Le 8:6*
the inwards and the legs in *w.*   *Le 8:21*
the *w.* hen (B)(R)   *Le 11:18; De 14:16*
is done, it must be put into *w.*   *Le 11:32*
on which such *w.* cometh shall be   *Le 11:34*
wherein there is plenty of *w.* shall   *Le 11:36*
But if any *w.* be put upon the seed   *Le 11:38*
an earthen vessel over running *w.*   *Le 14:5; 14:50*
was killed over the running *w.*   *Le 14:6*
and wash himself in *w.* that he   *Le 14:8*
he shall wash his flesh in *w.*   *Le 14:9*
in the running *w.* and sprinkle   *Le 14:51*
with the running *w.* and with *w.*   *Le 14:52*
and bathe himself in *w.*   *Le 15:5; 15:6-8, 10*
hath not rinsed his hands in *w.*   *Le 15:11*
his clothes, and bathe himself in *w.*   *Le 15:11*
vessel of wood shall be rinsed in *w.*   *Le 15:12*
and bathe his flesh in running *w.*   *Le 15:13*
he shall wash all his flesh in *w.*   *Le 15:16*
shall be washed with *w.* and be   *Le 15:17*
shall both bathe themselves in *w.*   *Le 15:18*
and bathe himself in *w.*   *Le 15:21; 15:22, 27*
shall he wash his flesh in *w.* and so   *Le 16:4*
shall wash his flesh with *w.* in the   *Le 16:24*
and bathe his flesh in *w.*   *Le 16:26; 16:28*
and bathe himself in *w.* and   *Le 17:15*
unless he wash his flesh with *w.*   *Le 22:6*
And the priest shall take holy *w.* in   *Nu 5:17*
shall take, and put it into the *w.*   *Nu 5:17*
bitter *w.* that causeth the curse   *Nu 5:18*
be thou free from this bitter *w.*   *Nu 5:19*
And this *w.* that causeth the curse   *Nu 5:22*
blot them out with the bitter *w.*   *Nu 5:23*
the woman to drink the bitter *w.*   *Nu 5:24*

the w. that causeth the curse shall *Nu 5:24*
cause the woman to drink the w. *Nu 5:26*
he hath made her to drink the w. *Nu 5:27*
the w. that causeth the curse shall *Nu 5:27*
Sprinkle w. of purifying upon *Nu 8:7*
and he shall bathe his flesh in w. *Nu 19:7*
her shall wash his clothes in w. *Nu 19:8*
bathe his flesh in w. and shall be *Nu 19:8*
of Israel for a w. of separation *Nu 19:9*
the w. of separation was not *Nu 19:13*
running w. shall be put thereto in *Nu 19:17*
take hyssop, and dip it in the w. *Nu 19:18*
clothes, and bathe himself in w. *Nu 19:19*
the w. of separation hath not been *Nu 19:20*
that sprinkleth the w. of separation *Nu 19:21*
that toucheth the w. of separation *Nu 19:21*
was no w. for the congregation *Nu 20:2*
neither is there any w. to drink *Nu 20:5*
it shall give forth his w. and thou *Nu 20:8*
forth to them w. out of the rock *Nu 20:8*
we fetch you w. out of this rock *Nu 20:10*
and the w. came out abundantly *Nu 20:11*
This is the w. of Meribah; because *Nu 20:13*
will we drink of the w. of the wells *Nu 20:17*
if I and my cattle drink of thy w. *Nu 20:19*
my word at the w. of Meribah *Nu 20:24*
is no bread, neither is there any w. *Nu 21:5*
together, and I will give them w. *Nu 21:16*
pour the w. out of his buckets, and *Nu 24:7*
sanctify me at the w. before their *Nu 27:14*
is the w. of Meribah in Kadesh in *Nu 27:14*
purified with the w. of separation *Nu 31:23*
ye shall make go through the w. *Nu 31:23*
Elim were twelve fountains of w. *Nu 33:9*
was no w. for the people to drink *Nu 33:14*
also buy w. of them for money *De 2:6*
and give me w. for money, that I *De 2:28*
good land, a land of brooks and w. *De 8:7*
drought, where there was no w. *De 8:15*
forth w. out of the rock of flint *De 8:15*
neither did eat bread nor drink w. *De 9:9*
did neither eat bread, nor drink w. *De 9:18*
he made the w. of the Red sea to *De 11:4*
drinketh w. of the rain of heaven *De 11:11*
pour it upon the earth as w. *De 12:16; 12:24*
shalt pour it upon the ground as w. *De 15:23*
met you not with bread and with w. *De 23:4*
on, he shall wash himself with w. *De 23:11*
wood unto the drawer of thy w. *De 29:11*
dried up the w. of the Red sea for *Jos 2:10*
to the brink of the w. of Jordan *Jos 3:8*

were dipped in the brim of the w. *Jos 3:15*
people melted, and became as w. *Jos 7:5*
and drawers of w. unto all the *Jos 9:21*
and drawers of w. for the house of *Jos 9:23*
drawers of w. for the congregation *Jos 9:27*
the fountain of the w. of Nephtoah *Jos 15:9*
land; give me also springs of w. *Jos 15:19*
unto the w. of Jericho on the east *Jos 16:1*
land; give me also springs of w. *J'g 1:15*
Give me a little w. to drink *J'g 4:19*
the clouds also dropped w. *J'g 5:4*
of archers in the places of drawing w. *J'g 5:11*
He asked w. and she gave him *J'g 5:25*
out of the fleece, a bowl full of w. *J'g 6:38*
bring them down unto the w. *J'g 7:4*
down the people unto the w. *J'g 7:5*
Every one that lappeth of the w. *J'g 7:5*
down upon their knees to drink w. *J'g 7:6*
jaw, and there came w. thereout *J'g 15:19*
drew w. and poured it out before *1Sa 7:6*
maidens going out to draw w. *1Sa 9:11*
I then take my bread, and my w. *1Sa 25:11*
and the cruse of w. and let us go *1Sa 26:11*
the cruse of w. from Saul's bolster *1Sa 26:12*
cruse of w. that was at his bolster *1Sa 26:16*
eat; and they made him drink w. *1Sa 30:11*
eaten no bread, nor drunk any w. *1Sa 30:12*
getteth up to the w. shaft (S) *2Sa 5:8*
break through of w. (A)(B) *2Sa 5:20*
and are as w. spilt on the ground *2Sa 14:14*
They be gone over the brook of w. *2Sa 17:20*
Arise, and pass quickly over the w. *2Sa 17:21*
until w. dropped upon them out of *2Sa 21:10*
of the w. of the well of Beth-lehem *2Sa 23:15; 1Ch 11:17*
and drew w. out of the well *2Sa 23:16; 1Ch 11:18*
bread nor drink w. in this place *1Ki 13:8*
Eat no bread, nor drink w. *1Ki 13:9*
will I eat bread nor drink w. with *1Ki 13:16*
eat no bread nor drink w. *1Ki 13:17; 13:22*
there he may eat bread and drink w. *1Ki 13:18*
bread in his house, and drank w. *1Ki 13:19*
hast eaten bread and drunk w. in *1Ki 13:22*
Israel, as a reed is shaken in the w. *1Ki 14:15*
I pray thee, a little w. in a vessel *1Ki 17:10*
and fed them with bread and w. *1Ki 18:4; 18:13*
unto all fountains of w. and unto *1Ki 18:5*
Fill four barrels with w. and pour *1Ki 18:33*
the w. ran round about the altar *1Ki 18:35*
he filled the trench also with w. *1Ki 18:35*
up the w. that was in the trench *1Ki 18:38*
coals, and a cruse of w. at his head *1Ki 19:6*
affliction and with w. of affliction *1Ki 22:27; 2Ch 18:26*
the w. is naught, and the ground *2Ki 2:19*
there was no w. for the host *2Ki 3:9*
poured w. on the hands of Elijah *2Ki 3:11*

that valley shall be filled with w. *2Ki 3:17*
good tree, and stop all wells of w. *2Ki 3:19*
there came w. by the way of Edom *2Ki 3:20*
and the country was filled with w. *2Ki 3:20*
and the sun shone upon the w. *2Ki 3:22*
the Moabites saw the w. on *2Ki 3:22*
they stopped all the wells of w. *2Ki 3:25*
beam the axe head fell into the w. *2Ki 6:5*
set bread and w. before them *2Ki 6:22*
a thick cloth, and dipped it in w. *2Ki 8:15*
drink their own w. (S) *2Ki 18:27; Isa 36:12*
and brought w. into the city *2Ki 20:20*
Assyria come, and find much w. *2Ch 32:4*
he did eat no bread, nor drink w. *Ezr 10:6*
against the w. gate toward the east *Ne 3:26*
street that was before the w. gate *Ne 8:1; 8:3*
and in the street of the w. gate *Ne 8:16*
forth w. for them out of the rock *Ne 9:15*
and gavest them w. for their thirst *Ne 9:20*
even unto the w. gate eastward *Ne 12:37*
of Israel with bread and with w. *Ne 13:2*
can the flag grow without w. *Job 8:11*
I wash myself with snow w. *Job 9:30*
through the scent of w. it will bud *Job 14:9*
which drinketh iniquity like w. *Job 15:16*
not given w. to the weary to drink *Job 22:7*
who drinketh up scorning like w. *Job 34:7*
he maketh small the drops of w. *Job 36:27*
a tree planted by the rivers of w. *Ps 1:3*
I w. my couch with my tears *Ps 6:6*
I am poured out like w. and all *Ps 22:14*
hart panteth after the w. brooks *Ps 42:1*
and thirsty land, where no w. is *Ps 63:1*
the river of God, which is full of w. *Ps 65:9*
went through fire and through w. *Ps 66:12*
as showers that w. the earth *Ps 72:6*
The clouds poured out w.: the *Ps 77:17*
Their blood have they shed like w. *Ps 79:3*
came round about me daily like w. *Ps 88:17*
the wilderness into a standing w. *Ps 107:35*
let it come into his bowels like w. *Ps 109:18*
turned the rock into a standing w. *Ps 114:8*
no fountains abounding with w. *Pr 8:24*
is as when one letteth out w. *Pr 17:14*
the heart of man is like deep w. *Pr 20:5*
of the Lord, as the rivers of w. *Pr 21:1*
he be thirsty, give him w. to drink *Pr 25:21*
As in w. face answereth to face, so *Pr 27:19*
the earth that is not filled with w. *Pr 30:16*
I made me pools of w. *Ec 2:6*
to w. therewith the wood that *Ec 2:6*
dross, thy wine mixed with w. *Isa 1:22*
and as a garden that hath no w. *Isa 1:30*
bread, and the whole stay of w. *Isa 3:1*
draw w. out of the wells of salvation *Isa 12:3*
for the bittern, and pools of w. *Isa 14:23*
I will w. thee with my tears *Isa 16:9*
brought w. to him that was thirsty *Isa 21:14*

two walls for the w. of the *Isa 22:11*
old pool
I will w. it every moment: lest *Isa 27:3*
or to take w. withal out of *Isa 30:14*
the pit
adversity, and the w. of *Isa 30:20*
affliction
as rivers of w. in a dry place *Isa 32:2*
and the thirsty land springs of *Isa 35:7*
w.
I have digged, and drunk w. *Isa 37:25*
When the poor and needy *Isa 41:17*
seek w.
make the wilderness a pool *Isa 41:18*
of w.
and the dry land springs of *Isa 41:18*
w.
pour w. upon him that is *Isa 44:3*
thirsty
as willows by the w. courses *Isa 44:4*
he drinketh no w. and is *Isa 44:12*
faint
by the springs of w. shall he *Isa 49:10*
guide
stinketh, because there is no *Isa 50:2*
w.
like a spring of w. whose *Isa 58:11*
waters
dividing the w. before them *Isa 63:12*
broken cisterns, that can hold *Jer 2:13*
no w.
and given us w. of gall to *Jer 8:14*
drink
and give them w. of gall to *Jer 9:15*
drink
thy loins, and put it not in w. *Jer 13:1*
came to the pits, and found no *Jer 14:3*
w.
and make them drink the w. *Jer 23:15*
of gall
in the dungeon there was no *Jer 38:6*
w.
mine eye runneth down with w. *La 1:16*
pour out thine heart like w. *La 2:19*
before
eye runneth down with rivers *La 3:48*
of w.
We have drunken our w. for *La 5:4*
money
shalt drink also w. by *Eze 4:11*
measure
and they shall drink w. by *Eze 4:16*
measure
That they may want bread *Eze 4:17*
and w.
and all knees shall be weak *Eze 7:17*
as w.
drink thy w. with trembling *Eze 12:18*
drink their w. with *Eze 12:19*
astonishment
neither wast thou washed in w. *Eze 16:4*
Then washed I thee with w. *Eze 16:9*
he might w. it by the furrows *Eze 17:7*
and all knees shall be weak *Eze 21:7*
as w.
set it on, and also pour w. *Eze 24:3*
into it
and thy dust in the midst of *Eze 26:12*
the w.
in their height, all that drink *Eze 31:14*
w.
of Lebanon, all that drink *Eze 31:16*
w.
also w. with thy blood the *Eze 32:6*
land
will I sprinkle clean w. upon *Eze 36:25*
you
us pulse to eat, and w. to *Da 1:12*
drink
that give me my bread and my *Ho 2:5*
w.
my wrath upon them that like *Ho 5:10*
w.
is cut off as the foam upon the *Ho 10:7*
w.
and shall w. the valley of *Joe 3:18*
Shittim
unto one city, to drink w. *Am 4:8*
famine of bread, not a thirst *Am 8:11*
for w.
let them not feed, nor drink w. *Jon 3:7*
Nineveh is of old like a pool of *Na 2:8*
w.
overflowing of the w. passed *Hab 3:10*
by
out of the pit wherein is no *Zec 9:11*
w.
I indeed baptize you with w. *M't 3:11*
unto

went up straightway out of *M't 3:16*
the w.
these little ones a cup of *M't 10:42*
cold w.
bid me come unto thee on *M't 14:28*
the w.
he walked on the w. to go to *M't 14:29*
Jesus
into the fire, and oft into the *M't 17:15*
w.
he took w. and washed his *M't 27:24*
hands
I indeed have baptized you *M'k 1:8*
with w.
coming up out of the w. he *M'k 1:10*
saw
you a cup of w. to drink in *M'k 9:41*
my name
you a man bearing a pitcher *M'k 14:13*
of w.
all, I indeed baptize you with *Lu 3:16*
w.
thou gavest me no w. for my *Lu 7:44*
feet
they were filled with w. and *Lu 8:23*
were in
wind and the raging of the w. *Lu 8:24*
commandeth even the winds *Lu 8:25*
and w.
may dip the tip of his finger *Lu 16:24*
in w.
meet you, bearing a pitcher *Lu 22:10*
of w.
them, saying, I baptize with *Joh 1:26*
w.
am I come baptizing with w. *Joh 1:31*
he that sent me to baptize *Joh 1:33*
with w.
them, Fill the waterpots with *Joh 2:7*
w.
tasted the w. that was made *Joh 2:9*
wine
servants which drew the w. *Joh 2:9*
knew
Except a man be born of w. *Joh 3:5*
and of
because there was must w. *Joh 3:23*
there
a woman of Samaria to draw *Joh 4:7*
w.
he would have given thee *Joh 4:10*
living w.
then hast thou that living w. *Joh 4:11*
Whosoever drinketh of this *Joh 4:13*
w. shall
whosoever drinketh of the w. *Joh 4:14*
that I
w. that I shall give him shall *Joh 4:14*
be in
him a well of w. springing up *Joh 4:14*
into
Sir, give me this w. that I *Joh 4:15*
thirst
Galilee, where he made the *Joh 4:46*
w. wine
waiting for the moving of the *Joh 5:3*
w.
into the pool, and troubled the *Joh 5:4*
w.
first after the troubling of the *Joh 5:4*
w.
when the w. is troubled, to put *Joh 5:7*
me
belly shall flow rivers of *Joh 7:38*
living w.
that he poureth w. into a *Joh 13:5*
bason
came there out blood and w. *Joh 19:34*
For John truly baptized with w. *Ac 1:5*
way, they came unto a certain *Ac 8:36*
w.
See, here is w.; what doth *Ac 8:36*
hinder
they went down both into the *Ac 8:38*
w.
they were come up out of the *Ac 8:39*
w.
Can any man forbid w. *Ac 10:47*
that these
said, John indeed baptized *Ac 11:16*
with w.
the washing of w. by the *Eph 5:26*
word
Drink no longer w. but use a *1Ti 5:23*
little
of calves and of goats, with *Heb 9:19*
w. and
our bodies washed with *Heb 10:22*
pure w.

at the same place sweet w. *Jas 3:11*
and bitter
both yield salt w. and fresh *Jas 3:12*
is, eight souls were saved by *1Pe 3:20*
w.
These are wells without w., *2Pe 2:17*
clouds
standing out of the w. and in *2Pe 3:5*
the w.
being overflowed with w. *2Pe 3:6*
perished
is he that came by w. and *1Jo 5:6*
blood
not by w. only, but by w. *1Jo 5:6*
and blood
earth, the spirit, and the w. *1Jo 5:8*
clouds they are without w. *Jude 12*
carried
out of his mouth w. as a *Re 12:15*
flood
swallowed up stream of w. *Re 12:16*
(A)(B)(E)(N)(P)(R)
and the w. thereof was dried *Re 16:12*
up
the fountain of the w. of life *Re 21:6*
freely
shewed me a pure river of w. *Re 22:1*
of life
will, let him take the w. of *Re 22:17*
life freely

WATERCOURSE

the upper w. of Gihon *2Ch 32:30*
w. for the overflowing of *Job 38:25*
waters
channel for the torrents of *Job 38:25*
rain (A)(R)
gullies for torrents of rain *Job 38:25*
(B)
channel for the waterflood *Job 38:25*
(E)

WATERCOURSES

they shall spring as willows by *Isa 44:4*
the w.

WATERED

w. the whole face of the *Ge 2:6*
ground
that it was well w. every *Ge 13:10*
where
out of that well they w. the *Ge 29:2*
flocks
the well's mouth, and w. the *Ge 29:3*
sheep
w. the flock of Laban his *Ge 29:10*
mother's
helped them, and w. their *Ex 2:17*
flock
enough for us, and w. the *Ex 2:19*
flock
watereth shall be w. also *Pr 11:25*
himself
and thou shalt be like a w. *Isa 58:11*
garden
their soul shall be as a w. *Jer 31:12*
garden
I have planted, Apollos w. *1Co 3:6*

WATEREDST

w. it with thy foot, as a *De 11:10*
garden of

WATEREST

Thou visitest the earth, and w. *Ps 65:9*
it
Thou w. the ridges thereof *Ps 65:10*

WATERETH

He w. the hills from his *Ps 104:13*
chambers
he that w. shall be watered *Pr 11:25*
w. the earth, and maketh it *Isa 55:10*
bring
any thing, neither he that w. *1Co 3:7*
planteth and he that w. are *1Co 3:8*
one

WATERFALL

sound like a great w. (P) *Re 14:2*

WATERFALLS

at the noise of thy w. (E) *Ps 42:7*

WATERFLOOD

Let not the w. overflow me   *Ps 69:15*

WATERING

in the gutters in the w.   *Ge 30:38*
troughs
by w. he wearieth the thick   *Job 37:11*
cloud
stall, and lead him away to   *Lu 13:15*
w.

WATERPOT

The woman then left her w.   *Joh 4:28*

WATERPOTS

were set there six w. of stone   *Joh 2:6*
unto them, Fill the w. with   *Joh 2:7*
water

WATERS

moved upon the face of the w.   *Ge 1:2*
firmament in the midst of the   *Ge 1:6*
w.
and let it divide the w. from   *Ge 1:6*
the w.
divided the w. which were   *Ge 1:7*
under
from the w. which were above   *Ge 1:7*
Let the w. under the heaven be   *Ge 1:9*
together of the w. called he   *Ge 1:10*
Seas
Let the w. bring forth   *Ge 1:20*
abundantly
the w. brought forth   *Ge 1:21*
abundantly
multiply, and fill the w. in the   *Ge 1:22*
seas
bring a flood of w. upon the   *Ge 6:17*
earth
the flood of w. was upon the   *Ge 7:6*
earth
ark, because of the w. of the   *Ge 7:7*
flood
that the w. of the flood were   *Ge 7:10*
upon
the w. increased, and bare up   *Ge 7:17*
w. prevailed, and were   *Ge 7:18*
increased
ark went upon the face of the   *Ge 7:18*
w.
w. prevailed exceedingly upon   *Ge 7:19*
cubits upward did the w.   *Ge 7:20*
prevail
the w. prevailed upon the   *Ge 7:24*
earth
the earth, and the w. asswaged   *Ge 8:1*
the w. returned from off the   *Ge 8:3*
earth
and fifty days the w. were   *Ge 8:3*
abated
the w. decreased continually   *Ge 8:5*
until
until the w. were dried up from   *Ge 8:7*
off
to see if the w. were abated   *Ge 8:8*
from
the w. were on the face of the   *Ge 8:9*
whole
Noah knew that the w. were   *Ge 8:11*
abated
w. were dried up from off the   *Ge 8:13*
earth
off any more by the w. of a   *Ge 9:11*
flood
the w. shall no more become a   *Ge 9:15*
flood
upon the w. which are in the   *Ex 7:17*
river
thine hand upon the w. of   *Ex 7:19*
Egypt
smote the w. that were in the   *Ex 7:20*
river
all the w. in the river were   *Ex 7:20*
turned
out his hand over the w. of   *Ex 8:6*
Egypt
dry land, and the w. were   *Ex 14:21*
divided
the w. were a wall unto them   *Ex 14:22*
on
w. may come upon the   *Ex 14:26*
Egyptians
the w. returned, and   *Ex 14:28*
covered the
the w. were a wall unto them   *Ex 14:29*

the w. were gathered together   *Ex 15:8*
they sank as lead in the   *Ex 15:10*
mighty w.
brought again the w. of the   *Ex 15:19*
sea
could not drink of the w. of   *Ex 15:23*
Marah
which when he had cast into   *Ex 15:25*
the w.
the w. were made sweet   *Ex 15:25*
and they encamped there by   *Ex 15:27*
the w.
shall ye eat of all that are in   *Le 11:9*
the w.
hath fins and scales in the w.   *Le 11:9*
of all that move in the w.   *Le 11:10*
and of
any living thing which is in   *Le 11:10*
the w.
hath no fins nor scales in the   *Le 11:12*
w.
living creature moveth in   *Le 11:46*
the w.
will not drink of the w. of   *Ne 21:22*
the well
and as cedar trees beside the   *Nu 24:6*
w.
and his seed shall be in many   *Nu 24:7*
w.
that is in the w. beneath the   *De 4:18;*
earth   *5:8*
to Jotbath, a land of rivers of   *De 10:7*
w.
shall eat of all that are in the   *De 14:9*
w.
Israel at the w. of   *De 32:51*
Meribah-Kadesh
didst strive at the w. of   *De 33:8*
Meribah
shall rest in the w. of the   *Jos 3:13*
Jordan
w. of the Jordan shall be cut   *Jos 3:13*
off
from the w. that come down   *Jos 3:13*
from
the w. which came down from   *Jos 3:16*
above
the w. of Jordan were cut off   *Jos 4:7*
before
the w. of Jordan were cut off   *Jos 4:7*
the w. of Jordan returned unto   *Jos 4:18*
God dried up the w. of   *Jos 4:23*
Jordan from
Lord had dried up the w. of   *Jos 5:1*
Jordan
pitched together at the w.   *Jos 11:5*
of Merom
against them by the w.   *Jos 11:7*
of Merom
toward the w. of   *Jos 15:7*
En-shemesh
out to the well of w. of   *Jos 18:15*
Nephtoah
in Taanach by the w. of   *J'g 5:19*
Megiddo
them the w. unto Beth-barah   *J'g 7:24*
took the w. unto Beth-barah   *J'g 7:24*
before me, as the breach of   *2Sa 5:20*
w.
and have taken the city of w.   *2Sa 12:27*
dark and thick clouds of   *2Sa 22:12*
he drew me out of many w.   *2Sa 22:17*
smote the w. and they were   *2Ki 2:8*
divided
and smote the w. and said,   *2Ki 2:14*
Where
when he also had smitten the   *2Ki 2:14*
w.
forth unto the spring of the   *2Ki 2:21*
w.
the Lord, I have healed these   *2Ki 2:21*
w.
the w. were healed unto this   *2Ki 2:22*
day
better than all the w. of   *2Ki 5:12*
Israel
ye every one the w. of his   *2Ki 18:31*
cistern
have digged and drunk   *2Ki 19:24*
strange w.
hand like the breaking forth   *1Ch 14:11*
of w.
men to stop the w. of the   *2Ch 32:3*
fountains
as a stone into the mighty w.   *Ne 9:11*
are poured out like the w.   *Job 3:24*
and sendeth w. upon the   *Job 5:10*
fields
remember it as w. that pass   *Job 11:16*
away

Behold, he withholdeth the   *Job 12:15*
w.
As the w. fail from the sea   *Job 14:11*
w. evaporate (A)(B)   *Job 14:11*
The w. wear the stones: thou   *Job 14:19*
and abundance of w. cover   *Job 22:11*
thee
He is swift as the w.; their   *Job 24:18*
portion
and heat consume the snow   *Job 24:19*
w.: so
are formed from under the w.   *Job 26:5*
He bindeth up the w. in his   *Job 26:8*
thick
compassed the w. with   *Job 26:10*
bounds
Terrors take hold on him as   *Job 27:20*
even the w. forgotten of the   *Job 28:4*
foot
he weigheth the w. by   *Job 28:25*
measure
My root was spread out by   *Job 29:19*
the w.
upon me as a wide breaking   *Job 30:14*
in of w.
breadth of the w. is   *Job 37:10*
straitened
for the overflowing of w.   *Job 38:25*
The w. are hid as with a   *Job 38:30*
stone
abundance of w. may cover   *Job 38:34*
thee
round about him were dark   *Ps 18:11*
w. and
Then the channels of w. were   *Ps 18:15*
seen
me, he drew me out of many   *Ps 18:16*
w.
he leadeth me beside the still   *Ps 23:2*
w.
voice of the Lord is upon the   *Ps 29:3*
w.
the Lord is upon many w.   *Ps 29:3*
surely in the floods of great w.   *Ps 32:6*
they
He gathereth the w. of the sea   *Ps 33:7*
Though the w. thereof roar   *Ps 46:3*
and be
Let them melt away as w.   *Ps 58:7*
which
the w. are come in unto my   *Ps 69:1*
soul
I am come into deep w.   *Ps 69:2*
where
hate me, and out of the deep   *Ps 69:14*
w.
and w. of a full cup are   *Ps 73:10*
wrung out
the heads of the dragons in   *Ps 74:13*
the w.
w. saw thee, O God, the   *Ps 77:16*
w. saw thee
sea, and thy path in the great   *Ps 77:19*
w.
he made the w. to stand as   *Ps 78:13*
an heap
caused w. to run down like   *Ps 78:16*
rivers
the rock, that the w. gushed   *Ps 78:20*
out
I proved thee at the w. of   *Ps 81:7*
Meribah
mightier than the noise of   *Ps 93:4*
many w.
beams of his chambers in the   *Ps 104:3*
w.
the w. stood above the   *Ps 104:6*
mountains
He turned their w. into   *Ps 105:29*
blood, and
the rock, and the w. gushed   *Ps 105:41*
out
And the w. covered their   *Ps 106:11*
enemies
angered him also at the w.   *Ps 106:32*
of strife
ships, that do business in   *Ps 107:23*
great w.
the flint into a fountain of w.   *Ps 114:8*
Rivers of w. run down   *Ps 119:136*
mine eyes
Then the w. had overwhelmed   *Ps 124:4*
us
proud w. had gone over our   *Ps 124:5*
soul
stretched the earth above   *Ps 136:6*
the w.
and deliver me out of great   *Ps 144:7*
w.

his wind to blow, and the *Ps 147:18*
w. flow
ye w. that be above the *Ps 148:4*
heavens
Drink w. out of thine own *Pr 5:15*
cistern
running w. out of thine own *Pr 5:15*
well
and rivers of w. in the streets *Pr 5:16*
that the w. should not pass his *Pr 8:29*
Stolen w. are sweet, and bread *Pr 9:17*
of a man's mouth are as deep *Pr 18:4*
w.
As cold w. to a thirsty soul, *Pr 25:25*
so is
hath bound the w. in a *Pr 30:4*
garment
Cast thy bread upon the w. *Ec 11:1*
a well of living w. and streams *Ca 4:15*
eyes of doves by the rivers of *Ca 5:12*
w.
Many w. cannot quench love *Ca 8:7*
the w. of Shiloah that go softly *Isa 8:6*
up upon them the w. of the *Isa 8:7*
river
the Lord, as the w. cover the *Isa 11:9*
sea
the w. of Nimrim shall be *Isa 15:6*
desolate
w. of Dimon shall be full of *Isa 15:9*
blood
like the rushing of mighty w. *Isa 17:12*
rush like the rushing of *Isa 17:13*
many w.
in vessels of bulrushes upon *Isa 18:2*
the w.
And the w. shall fail from the *Isa 19:5*
sea
they that spread nets upon the *Isa 19:8*
w.
gathered the w. of the lower *Isa 22:9*
pool
And by great w. the seed of *Isa 23:3*
Sihor
a flood of mighty w. *Isa 28:2*
overflowing
w. shall overflow the hiding *Isa 28:17*
place
high hill, rivers and streams *Isa 30:25*
of w.
Blessed ye that sow beside *Isa 32:20*
all w.
be given him; his w. shall be *Isa 33:16*
sure
the wilderness shall w. break *Isa 35:6*
out
every one the w. of his own *Isa 36:16*
cistern
measured the w. in the *Isa 40:12*
hollow of
When thou passest through *Isa 43:2*
the w.
sea, and a path in the mighty *Isa 43:16*
w.
because I give w. in the *Isa 43:20*
wilderness
come forth out of the w. of *Isa 48:1*
Judah
caused the w. to flow out of *Isa 48:21*
the rock
rock also, and the w. gushed *Isa 48:21*
out
the sea, the w. of the great *Isa 51:10*
deep
this is as the w. of Noah unto *Isa 54:9*
me
the w. of Noah should no *Isa 54:9*
more go
that thirsteth, come ye to the *Isa 55:1*
w.
whose w. cast up mire and *Isa 57:20*
dirt
spring of water, whose w. fail *Isa 58:11*
not
the fire causeth the w. to boil *Isa 64:2*
forsaken the fountain of *Jer 2:13*
living w.
of Egypt, to drink the w. of *Jer 2:18*
Sihor
to drink the w. of the river *Jer 2:18*
As a fountain casteth out her *Jer 6:7*
w.
Oh that my head were w. and *Jer 9:1*
mine
and our eyelids gush out with *Jer 9:18*
w.
is a multitude of w. in the *Jer 10:13*
heavens
have sent their little ones to *Jer 14:3*
the w.

me as a liar, and as a w. *Jer 15:18*
that fail
shall be as a tree planted by *Jer 17:8*
the w.
the Lord, the fountain of *Jer 17:13*
living w.
the cold flowing w. that *Jer 18:14*
come from
them to walk by the rivers of *Jer 31:9*
w.
by the great w. that are in *Jer 41:12*
Gibeon
whose w. are moved as the *Jer 46:7*
rivers
his w. are moved like the *Jer 46:8*
rivers
w. rise up out of the north *Jer 47:2*
for the w. also of Nimrim *Jer 48:34*
shall be
A drought is upon her w.; *Jer 50:38*
and they
O thou that dwellest upon *Jer 51:13*
many w.
is a multitude of w. in the *Jer 51:16*
heavens
her waves do roar like great *Jer 51:55*
W. flowed over mine head; *La 3:54*
then I
wings, like the noise of great *Eze 1:24*
w.
he placed it by great w. and *Eze 17:5*
set it
planted in a good soil by *Eze 17:8*
great w.
in thy blood, planted by the *Eze 19:10*
of branches by reason of *Eze 19:10*
many w.
thee, and great w. shall *Eze 26:19*
cover thee
have brought thee into great *Eze 27:26*
w.
by the seas in the depths of *Eze 27:34*
the w.
The w. made him great, the *Eze 31:4*
deep
because of the multitude of w. *Eze 31:5*
for his root was by great w. *Eze 31:7*
none of all the trees by the *Eze 31:14*
w. exalt
and the great w. were stayed *Eze 31:15*
troubledst the w. with thy *Eze 32:2*
feet and
thereof from beside the *Eze 32:13*
great w.
Then will I make their w. *Eze 32:14*
deep, and
and to have drunk of the *Eze 34:18*
deep w.
voice was like a noise of *Eze 43:2*
many w.
w. issued out from under the *Eze 47:1*
the w. came down from under *Eze 47:1*
there ran out w. on the right *Eze 47:2*
side
and he brought me through *Eze 47:3*
the w.
the w. were to the ancles *Eze 47:3*
and brought me through the *Eze 47:4*
w.
the w. were to the knees *Eze 47:4*
through; the w. were to the *Eze 47:4*
loins
for the w. were risen, w. to *Eze 47:5*
swim in
These w. issue out toward the *Eze 47:8*
east
the sea, the w. shall be healed *Eze 47:8*
these w. shall come thither *Eze 47:9*
their w. they issued out of *Eze 47:12*
even to the w. of strife in *Eze 47:19*
Kadesh
unto the w. of strife in *Eze 48:28*
Kadesh
was upon the w. of the river *Da 12:6;*
12:7
for the rivers of w. are dried *Joe 1:20*
up
rivers of Judah shall flow *Joe 3:18*
with w.
that calleth for the w. of the *Am 5:8*
sea
But let judgment run down as *Am 5:24*
he that calleth for the w. of *Am 9:6*
the sea
The w. compassed me about, *Joh 2:5*
even

as the w. that are poured *Mic 1:4*
down a
that had the w. round about it *Na 3:8*
Draw thee w. for the siege, *Na 3:14*
fortify
of the Lord, as the w. cover *Hab 2:14*
the sea
through the heap of great w. *Hab 3:15*
w. shall go out from *Zec 14:8*
Jerusalem
the sea, and perished in the *M't 8:32*
w.
him into the fire, and into the *M'k 9:22*
w.
in perils of w. in perils of *2Co 11:26*
robbers
his voice as the sound of *Re 1:15*
many w.
them unto living fountains of *Re 7:17*
w.
springs of living w. *Re 7:17*
(A)(B)(N)(P)(R)
and upon the fountains of w. *Re 8:10*
and the third part of the w. *Re 8:11*
became
and many men died of the w. *Re 8:11*
have power over w. to turn *Re 11:6*
them to
heaven, as the voice of many *Re 14:2*
w.
the sea, and the fountains of *Re 14:7*
w.
upon rivers and fountains of *Re 16:4*
w.
I heard the angel of the w. say *Re 16:5*
The w. which thou sawest, *Re 17:15*
where
and as the voice of many w. *Re 19:6*

IN, INTO WATERS

they sank as lead *in* the *Ex 15:10*
mighty w.
a tree when cast *into* w. they *Ex 15:25*
were sweet
eat. of all that are *in* w. what *Le 11:9;*
hath fins and scales *in* w. *11:10, 46;*
De 14:9
hath no fins nor scales *in* the *Le 11:12*
w. unclean
likeness of any fish *in* the w. *De 4:18;*
5:8
as the feet of priests rest *in* *Jos 3:13*
the w.
threwest a stone *into* the *Ne 9:11*
mighty w.
breakest the heads of dragons *Ps 74:13*
in w.
layeth the beams of his *Ps 104:3*
chambers *in* w.
the swine ran and perished *in* *M't 8:32*
the w.
oft it cast him into fire and *M'k 9:22*
into w.

MANY WATERS

and his seed shall be in *many* *Nu 24:7*
w.
drew me out of *many* w. *2Sa 22:17;*
Ps 18:16
the voice of the Lord is upon *Ps 29:3*
many w.
Lord mightier than the noise *Ps 93:4*
of *many* w.
many w. cannot quench love, *Ca 8:7*
nor floods
nations like the rushing of *Isa 17:13*
many w.
O thou that dwellest upon *Jer 51:13*
many w.
she was fruitful by reason of *Eze 19:10*
many w.
his voice like a noise of *Eze 43:2;*
many w. *Re 1:15; 14:2; 19:6*
great whore that sitteth on *Re 17:1*
many w.

WATERSKINS

tilt w. of heavens (R)(S) *Job 38:37*

WATERSPOUTS

unto deep at the noise of thy *Ps 42:7*
w.
cataracts (B)(R) *Ps 42:7*
waterfalls (E) *Ps 42:7*

WATERSPRINGS

and the w. into dry ground	Ps 107:33
springs (A)	Ps 107:33
pools of water (B)	Ps 107:33
springs of water (R)	Ps 107:33; 107:35
and dry ground, into w.	Ps 107:35

WAVE

shalt w. them before the Lord	Ex 29:24
for a w. offering before the Lord	Ex 29:24; 29:26; Le 7:30; 8:27; 9:21; 10:15; 14:24; 23:20; Nu 6:20
and w. it before the Lord	Ex 29:26
the breast of the w. offering	Ex 29:27
w. breast and the heave shoulder	Le 7:34; Nu 6:20
it for a w. offering before the Lord	Le 8:29
w. breast and heave shoulder shall	Le 10:14
w. breast shall they bring with the	Le 10:15
the fat, to w. it before the Lord	Le 10:15
and w. them before the Lord	Le 14:12
shall w. them before the Lord	Le 14:24
w. the sheaf before the Lord	Le 23:11
after sabbath the priest shall w.	Le 23:11
when ye w. the sheaf an he lamb	Le 23:12
the sheaf of the w. offering	Le 23:15
two w. loaves of two tenth deals	Le 23:17
priest shall w. them with the bread	Le 23:20
w. the offering before the Lord	Nu 5:25
And the priest shall w. them for a	Nu 6:20
the w. offerings of the children of	Nu 18:11
w. breast and as the right shoulder	Nu 18:18
w. the hand (A)	La 2:15
is like a w. of the sea driven with	Jas 1:6

WAVED

of the heave offering, which is w.	Ex 29:27
the breast may be w. for a wave	Le 7:30
w. them for a wave offering before	Le 8:27
w. it for a wave offering before the	Le 8:29
Aaron w. for a wave offering before	Le 9:21
for a trespass offering to be w.	Le 14:21

WAVER

his steps shall not w. (B)	De 37:31

WAVERERS

thoughts of w. (B)	Ps 119:113

WAVERETH

he that w. is like a wave of the sea	Jas 1:6
one who doubts (B)(R)	Jas 1:6
he that doubteth (E)	Jas 1:6
the doubter (N)	Jas 1:6
trusts God, but with inward reservations (P)	Jas 1:6

WAVERING

profession of our faith without w.	Heb 10:23
firm and unswerving (N)	Heb 10:23
without the slightest hesitation (P)	Heb 10:23
let him ask in faith, nothing w.	Jas 1:6
never a doubt (B)	Jas 1:6
nothing doubting (E)	Jas 1:6
without a doubt in his mind (N)	Jas 1:6
ask in sincere faith without secret doubts (P)	Jas 1:6
with no doubting (R)	Jas 1:6
w. individuals (A)(B)	Jas 4:8

WAVES

the w. were congealed (B)	Ex 15:8
the w. of death compassed me	2Sa 22:5
thy breakers (B)	2Sa 22:5
treadeth upon the w. of the sea	Job 9:8
here shall thy proud w. be stayed	Job 38:11
all thy w. and thy billows are gone	Ps 42:7
of the seas, the noise of their w.	Ps 65:7
hast afflicted me with all thy w.	Ps 88:7
when the w. thereof arise, thou	Ps 89:9
voice; the floods lift up their w.	Ps 93:3
yea, than the mighty w. of the sea	Ps 93:4
which lifteth up the w. thereof	Ps 107:25
so that the w. thereof are still	Ps 107:29
righteousness as the w. of the sea	Isa 48:18
divided the sea, whose w. roared	Isa 51:15
the w. thereof toss themselves, yet	Jer 5:22
the sea when the w. thereof roar	Jer 31:35
with the multitude of the w.	Jer 51:42
her w. do roar like great waters	Jer 51:55
the sea causeth his w. to come up	Eze 26:3
billows and thy w. passed over me	Joh 2:3
and shall smite the w. in the sea	Zec 10:11
the ship was covered with the w.	M't 8:24
midst of the sea, tossed with w.	M't 14:24
the w. beat into the ship, so that it	M'k 4:37
the sea and the w. roaring	Lu 21:25
roaring of the tossing sea (A)	Lu 21:25
roar and surge of the sea (N)	Lu 21:25
roar of the surging sea (P)	Lu 21:25
broken with the violence of the w.	Ac 27:41
Raging w. of the sea, foaming out	Jude 13

WAX

And my wrath shall w. hot, and I	Ex 22:24
my wrath shall burn (A)(R)	Ex 22:24; 32:10
my indignation shall burn (B)	Ex 22:24
that my wrath may w. hot against	Ex 32:10
my indignation shall flame (B)	Ex 32:10; 32:11
why doth thy wrath w. hot against	Ex 32:11
your wrath blaze hot (A)	Ex 32:11
my wrath shall burn hot (R)	Ex 32:11
not the anger of my lord w. hot	Ex 32:22
anger blaze hot (A)(B)	Ex 32:22
if a sojourner or stranger w. rich	Le 25:47
that dwelleth by him w. poor	Le 25:47
his eyes began to w. dim, that he	1Sa 3:2
What time they w. warm, they	Job 6:17
Though the root thereof w. old in	Job 14:8
root grows old (A)(R)	Job 14:8
roots age (B)	Job 14:8
my heart is like w.; it is melted in	Ps 22:14
as w. melteth before the fire, so let	Ps 68:2
The hills melted like w. at the	Ps 97:5
all of them shall w. old like a	Ps 102:26
the fatness of his flesh shall w. lean	Isa 17:4
neither shall his face now w. pale	Isa 29:22
they all shall w. old as a garment	Isa 50:9

WAXED

earth shall w. old like a garment	Isa 51:6
our hands w. feeble: anguish hath	Jer 6:24
shall be cleft, as w. before the fire	Mic 1:4
the love of many shall w. cold	M't 24:12
yourselves bags which w. not old	Lu 12:33
to w. wanton against Christ	1Ti 5:11
and seducers shall w. worse	2Ti 3:13
all shall w. old as doth a garment	Heb 1:11

WAXED

After I am w. old shall I have	Ge 18:12
And the man w. great, and went	Ge 26:13
the famine w. sore in the land of	Ge 41:56
multiplied and w. exceeding mighty	Ex 1:7
people multiplied, and w. very mighty	Ex 1:20
when the sun w. hot, it melted	Ex 16:21
long, and w. louder and louder	Ex 19:19
Moses' anger w. hot, and he cast	Ex 32:19
Is the Lord's hand w. short	Nu 11:23
Thy raiment w. not old upon thee	De 8:4
But Jeshurun w. fat, and kicked	De 32:15
Joshua w. old, and stricken in age	Jos 23:1
hath many children is w. feeble	1Sa 2:5
David w. stronger and stronger	2Sa 3:1
the house of Saul w. weaker	2Sa 3:1
Philistines: and David w. faint	2Sa 21:15
and the flesh of the child w. warm	2Ki 4:34
So David w. greater and greater	1Ch 11:9
Abijah w. mighty, and married	2Ch 13:21
And Jehoshaphat w. great	2Ch 17:12
Jehoiada w. old, and was full of	2Ch 24:15
their clothes w. not old, and	Ne 9:21
Mordecai w. greater and greater	Es 9:4
bones w. old through my roaring	Ps 32:3
Damascus is w. feeble, and	Jer 49:24
of them, and his hands w. feeble	Jer 50:43
Therefore the he goat w. very great	Da 8:8
horn, which w. exceeding great	Da 8:9
And it w. great, even to the host of	Da 8:10
For this people's heart is w. gross	M't 13:15
child grew, and w. strong in spirit	Lu 1:80; 2:40
and it grew, and w. a great tree	Lu 13:19
Then Paul and Barnabas w. bold	Ac 13:46
the heart of this people is w. gross	Ac 28:27
made strong, w. valiant in fight	Heb 11:34
merchants of the earth are w. rich	Re 18:3
w. wanton (E)(R)	Re 18:7

WAXEN

the cry of them is w. great before	Ge 19:13
If thy brother be w. poor	Le 25:25; 25:35
that dwelleth by thee be w. poor	Le 25:39
clothes are not w. old upon you	De 29:5
thy shoe is not w. old upon thy foot	De 29:5
and filled themselves, and w. fat	De 31:20

thou art w. fat, thou art grown   *De 32:15*

children of Israel were w. strong   *Jos 17:13*

are become great, and w. rich   *Jer 5:27*

They are w. fat, they shine: yea   *Jer 5:28*

thou hast increased and w. great   *Eze 16:7*

WAXETH

it w. old because of all mine   *Ps 6:7*

and w. old is ready to vanish   *Heb 8:13*

WAXING

w. confident by my bonds are   *Ph'p 1:14*

WAY

had perverted their w. (B)   *Ge 6:12*

if thou prosper my w. which I go   *Ge 24:42*

the w. of women upon me (R)   *Ge 31:35*

to give them provision for the w.   *Ge 42:25; 45:21*

led not thro' the w. of the Philistines   *Ex 13:17*

led the people thro' the w. of the wilderness   *Ex 13:18*

in a pillar of cloud to lead them the w.   *Ex 13:21*

shew them the w.   *Ex 18:20; Ne 9:19; Ps 107:4*

way (S)   *Nu 6:23; Jos 6:18; 23:12; Ps 37:8; M't 1:18; 5:18; 10:42; 14:31; Lu 13:11; 18:17; Ac 7:6; 13:34, 41; Ro 3:9; 10:6; Heb 4:4; Re 21:27*

was much discouraged because of the w.   *Nu 21:4*

there was no w. to turn to the right or left   *Nu 22:26*

by what w. we must go   *De 1:22; Jos 3:4*

remember the w. which the Lord led you   *De 8:2*

if the w. be too long for thee   *De 14:24*

shall henceforth return no more that w.   *De 17:16*

prepare thee a w.; the w. is long   *De 19:3; 19:6*

thou shalt go out one w. against them   *De 28:25*

ye will turn aside from w. I commanded   *De 31:29*

I am going the w. of all the earth   *Jos 23:14*

Lord preserved us in the w. we went   *Jos 24:17*

they ceased not from their stubborn w.   *J'g 2:19*

they robbed all that came along that w.   *J'g 9:25*

whether our w. we go shall be prosperous   *J'g 18:5*

before the Lord is your w. wherein ye go   *J'g 18:6*

to-morrow get you early on your w.   *J'g 19:9*

Turn again, my daughters, go your w.   *Ru 1:12*

kine took straight w. to Beth-shemesh   *1Sa 6:12*

peradventure he can shew us our w. to go   *1Sa 9:6*

give to the man of God to tell us our w.   *1Sa 9:8*

I will teach you the good and the right w.   *1Sa 12:23*

gone the w. which the Lord sent me   *1Sa 15:20*

servant will go little w. over Jordan   *2Sa 19:36*

I go the w. of all the earth, be strong   *1Ki 2:2*

that thou teach them the good w. to walk   *1Ki 8:36*

nor turn again by the same w.   *1Ki 13:9*

he went another w.; what w. went he   *1Ki 13:10; 13:12*

Ahab went one w. Obadiah another w.   *1Ki 18:6*

which w. went Spirit of Lord   *1Ki 22:24; 2Ch 18:22*

which w. shall we go? w. thro' wilderness   *2Ki 3:8*

take thy staff and go thy w.   *2Ki 4:29*

so he departed from him a little w.   *2Ki 5:19*

all the w. full of garments and vessels   *2Ki 7:15*

when thou hast taught them good w.   *2Ch 6:27*

to seek of him a right w. for us   *Ezr 8:21*

Go your w. eat the fat, and drink the   *Ne 8:10*

all the people went their w. to eat, and   *Ne 8:12*

light given to a man whose w. is hid   *Job 3:23*

wander where there is no w.   *Job 12:24; Ps 107:40*

go the w. whence I shall not return   *Job 16:22*

hast that marked the old w. which wicked   *Job 22:15*

but he knoweth the w. that I take   *Job 23:10*

God understands the w. thereof   *Job 28:23*

where is the w. where light dwelleth   *Job 38:19*

Lord knoweth w. of the righteous   *Ps 1:6*

kiss the Son, lest ye perish from the w.   *Ps 2:12*

he setteth himself in a w. that is not good   *Ps 36:4*

upright in the w. (E)   *Ps 37:14*

prepares his w. (A)(B)(E)(R)   *Ps 50:23*

he made a w. to his anger he spared not   *Ps 78:50*

I will behave wisely in a perfect w.   *Ps 101:2; 101:6*

make me understand w. of thy precepts   *Ps 119:27*

remove from me the w. of lying, and grant   *Ps 119:29*

I have chosen the w. of truth   *Ps 119:30*

I will run the w. of thy commandments   *Ps 119:32*

teach me, w. of thy statutes   *Ps 119:33; 143:8*

I hate every false w.   *Ps 119:104; 119:128*

see if there be any wicked w. in me   *Ps 139:24*

the w. of the wicked he turns upside down   *Ps 146:9*

he preserveth the w. of his saints   *Pr 2:8*

to deliver thee from the w. of evil man   *Pr 2:12*

the w. of the wicked is as darkness   *Pr 4:19*

are the w. of life   *Pr 6:23; 15:24; Jer 21:8*

near her corner, he went w. to her house   *Pr 7:8*

her house is w. to hell going down to death   *Pr 7:27*

who takes a crooked w. (A)   *Pr 10:9*

the w. of a fool is right in his own eyes   *Pr 12:15*

the w. of the wicked seduceth them   *Pr 12:26*

but the w. of the transgressors is hard   *Pr 13:15*

there is a w. which seemeth right   *Pr 14:12; 16:25*

the w. of the wicked is an abomination   *Pr 15:9*

is grievous to him that forsaketh the w.   *Pr 15:10*

w. of slothful man is an hedge of thorns; w. of the righteous is made plain   *Pr 15:19*

leadeth him into the w. that is not good   *Pr 16:29*

foolishness subverts his w. (A)(E)   *Pr 19:3*

the w. of man is forward and strange   *Pr 21:8*

mind utter things turned the wrong w. (A)   *Pr 23:33*

w. of an eagle, of, of a serpent, of a ship   *Pr 30:19*

such is the w. of an adulterous woman   *Pr 30:20*

knowest not what is the w. of the Spirit   *Ec 11:5*

go thy w. forth by the footsteps   *Ca 1:8*

they cause thee to err and destroy the w.   *Isa 3:12*

the w. of the just is uprightness   *Isa 26:7*

an highway and w. called w. of holiness   *Isa 35:8*

who shewed him the w. of understanding   *Isa 40:14*

Lord, who maketh a w. in the sea   *Isa 43:16; 51:10*

I will even make a w. in the wilderness   *Isa 43:19*

I will make all my mountains a w.   *Isa 49:11*

prepare a w.   *Isa 57:14*

the w. of peace they know not   *Isa 59:8; Ro 3:17*

cast up high w.   *Isa 62:10*

where is the good w. and walk therein   *Jer 6:16*

learn not w. of heathen, be not dismayed   *Jer 10:2*

I know that the w. of man is not in himself   *Jer 10:23*

wherefore doth the w. of the wicked prosper   *Jer 12:1*

to walk in paths, in a w. not cast up   *Jer 18:15*

I will give them one heart and one w.   *Jer 32:39*

Lord thy God may shew us the w.   *Jer 42:3*

they shall ask the w. to Zion with faces   *Jer 50:5*

appoint a w. that sword may come   *Eze 21:20*

then I saw that they took both one w.   *Eze 23:13*

glory of God came from the w. of the east   *Eze 43:2*

go thou thy w. till the end be: for thou   *Da 12:13*

and turn aside the w. of the meek   *Am 2:7*

keep the munition, watch the w.   *Na 2:1*

he shall prepare the w. before me   *Na 3:1*

broad is the w. that leads to destruction   *M't 7:13*

which go in the w. (S)   *M't 7:13*

and narrow is the w. which leadeth unto life   *M't 7:14*

so that no man might pass by that w.   *M't 8:28*

go not into the w. of the Gentiles   *M't 10:5*

we know thou art true, teachest w. of God in truth   *M't 22:16; M'k 12:14; Lu 20:21*

by what w. they might bring him in   *Lu 5:19*

there came down a certain priest that w.   *Lu 10:31*

when he was yet a great w. off, father saw   *Lu 15:20*

Zacchaeus ran to see him, was to pass that w.   *Lu 19:4*

but climbeth up some other w. is a thief   *Joh 10:1*

the w. ye know; I am the w. the truth   *Joh 14:4; 14:6*

Thomas saith, Lord, how can we know the w.   *Joh 14:5*

which shew to us the w. of salvation   *Ac 16:17*

expounded to him w. of God more perfectly   *Ac 18:26*

believeth not, but spake evil of that w.   *Ac 19:9*

there arose no small stir about that w.   *Ac 19:23*

after the w. which they call heresy   *Ac 24:14*

or an occasion to fall in brother's w.   *Ro 14:13*

with temptation make a w. to escape   *1Co 10:13*

shew I unto you a more excellent w.   *1Co 12:31*

former w. of life (N)(P)   *Eph 4:22*

our Lord Jesus direct our w. unto you   *1Th 3:11*

the w. into the holiest not yet manifest   *Heb 9:8*

by a living w. which he hath consecrated   *Heb 10:20*

she had sent them out another w.   *Jas 2:25*

useless *w.* of living　　　　*1Pe 1:18*
(A)(B)(P)(R)
the *w.* of truth shall be evil　　*2Pe 2:2*
spoken of
forsaken the right *w.*　　　　*2Pe 2:15*
following the *w.* of Balaam
better not known the *w.* of　　*2Pe 2:21*
righteousness
that *w.* of kings of the east　　*Re 16:12*
be prepared

WAY SIDE

where is harlot that was by　　*Ge 38:21*
the *w. side*
Eli sat on a seat by *w.* side　　*1Sa 4:13*
watching
the proud have spread a net　　*Ps 140:5*
by *w.* side
some seeds fell by the　　　　*M't 13:4;*
w. side, fowls came　*13:19; M'k 4:4, 15;*
　　　　　　　　　　　Lu 8:5, 12
two blind men sitting by the　*M't 20:30*
w. side
blind Bartimeus sat by the　*M'k 10:46;*
w. side begging　　　　　　*Lu 18:35*

BY THE WAY

if mischief befall him *by the*　*Ge 42:38*
w. ye go
Joseph said, See that ye fall　*Ge 45:24*
not out *by the w.*
Dan shall be a serpent *by the* *Ge 49:17*
w., an adder
by the w. in the inn the Lord　*Ex 4:24*
met him
get you into wilderness *by the Nu 14:25;*
w. of the Red sea　*21:4; De 1:2, 40; 2:1*
talk of them when walkest *by*　*De 6:7*
the w.　　　　　　　　　　*11:19*
what Amalek did to thee *by*　*De 25:17*
the w.
he met thee *by the w.*　　　*De 25:18;*
　　　　　　　　　　　　1Sa 15:2
Lord bring thee *by the w.*　　*De 28:68*
I spake
even all the men of war died　*Jos 5:4*
by the w.
they had not circumcized them　*Jos 5:7*
by the w.
not turn again *by the w.*　　*1Ki 13:9;*
　　　　　　　　　　　　13:17
a lion met him *by the w.*　　*1Ki 13:24*
and slew him
the prophet waited for the　　*1Ki 20:38*
king *by the w.*
there came water *by the w.* of　*2Ki 3:20*
Edom
I will turn thee back *by the*　*2Ki 19:28;*
w. by which thou camest　*Isa 37:29, 34*
of such as lay in wait *by the*　*Ezr 8:31*
w.
have ye not asked them that　*Job 21:29*
go *by the w.*
all they who pass *by the w.*　*Ps 80:12*
plucked her
all that pass *by the w.* spoil　*Ps 89:41*
him
when fools walk *by the w.*　　*Ec 10:3*
wisdom fails
bring blind *by the w.* they　*Isa 42:16*
knew not
the Lord God that leadeth　　*Isa 48:17*
thee *by the w.*
forsaken God when he led　　*Jer 2:17*
thee *by the w.*
walk not *by the w.* for sword *Jer 6:25*
of the enemy
glory of Lord came *by the w.*　*Eze 43:4*
of gate
prince shall enter *by the w.*　*Eze 44:3;*
of porch　　　　　　　　　　*46:2, 8*
he that entereth *by the w.* of　*Eze 46:9*
north gate
as a leopard *by the w.* will I　*Ho 13:7*
observe
if I send them fasting, they　　*M'k 8:3*
faint *by the w.*
by the w. he asked his　　　*M'k 8:27*
disciples, saying
what was it ye disputed *by*　　*M'k 9:33;*
the w.　　　　　　　　　　*9:34*
carry no shoes, salute no man　*Lu 10:4*
by the w.
heart burn while he talked　　*Lu 24:32*
with us *by the w.*
for I will not see you now *by* *1Co 16:7*
the w.

EVERY WAY

a flaming sword which turned　*Ge 3:24*
every w.
refrained my feet from *every*　*Ps 119:101*
evil *w.*
therefore I hate *every* false　*Ps 119:104;*
w.　　　　　　　　　　　　*119:128*
every w. of man right in his　*Pr 21:2*
own eyes
buildest eminent place in　　　*Eze 16:31*
every w.
much *every w.* because to them *Ro 3:2*
committed
every w. whether in pretence　*Ph'p 1:18*
or in truth

HIS WAY

all flesh had corrupted *his w.*　*Ge 6:12*
on earth
as for God *his w.* is perfect　*2Sa 22:31;*
　　　　　　　　　　　　Ps 18:30
condemning the wicked, to　　*1Ki 8:32;*
bring *his w.* on his own head　*2Ch 6:23*
behold, this is the joy of *his*　*Job 8:19*
w.
the righteous also shall hold　*Job 17:9*
on *his w.*
who shall declare *his w.* to　*Job 21:31*
his face
his w. have I kept and not　　*Job 23:11*
declined
who hath enjoined him *his*　　*Job 36:23*
w.
the meek will he teach *his w.*　*Ps 25:9*
because of him who prospereth *Ps 37:7*
in *his w.*
steps of good man, and he　　*Ps 37:23*
delighteth in *his w.*
wait on the Lord and keep　　*Ps 37:34*
his w. and he
wherewith shall a young man　*Ps 119:9*
cleanse *his w.*
Lord possessed me in　　　　*Pr 8:22*
beginning of *his w.*
righteousness of the perfect　*Pr 11:5*
direct *his w.*
wisdom of prudent is to　　　*Pr 14:8*
understand *his w.*
a man's heart deviseth *his w.*　*Pr 16:9*
he that keepeth *his w.*　　　*Pr 16:17*
preserveth his soul
the foolishness of man　　　　*Pr 19:3*
perverteth *his w.*
when he is gone *his w.* then　*Pr 20:14*
he boasteth
as for the upright, he　　　　*Pr 21:29*
directeth *his w.*
he shall make *his w.*　　　　*Isa 48:15*
prosperous
wicked forsake *his w.* and his　*Isa 55:7*
thoughts
the destroyer of the Gentiles is *Jer 4:7*
on *his w.*
to warn the wicked from *his*　*Eze 3:18*
wicked *w.*
and he turn not from *his*　　*Eze 3:19;*
wicked *w.*　　　　　　　　*33:8, 9*
he should not return from　　*Eze 13:22*
his wicked *w.*
the Lord hath *his w.* in the　*Na 1:3*
whirlwind
he beholdeth himself and　　　*Jas 1:24*
goeth *his w.*
who converteth sinner from　　*Jas 5:20*
error of *his w.*

IN THE WAY

I being *in the w.* the Lord　　*Ge 24:27*
led me
Blessed be the Lord who led　*Ge 24:48*
me *in the* right *w.*
the Lord was with me *in the*　*Ge 35:3*
w. I went
Rachel buried *in the w.* to　　*Ge 35:19;*
Ephrath　　　　　　　　　　*48:7*
Moses and Aaron stood *in the* *Ex 5:20*
w.
send angel before thee to　　　*Ex 23:20*
keep thee *in the w.*
who went *in the w.* before you　*De 1:33*
to search
because they met you not with　*De 23:4*
bread *in the w.*
Ahijah found Jeroboam *in*　　*1Ki 11:29*
the w.
his carcase was cast *in the*　*1Ki 13:24;*
w.　　　　　　　　　　　　*25:28*
he walked *in the w.* of his　　*1Ki 15:26;*
father　　　　　　　　　　　*22:52*
did evil in sight of Lord;　　*1Ki 15:34;*
walked *in the w.* of Jeroboam *16:2, 19,*
　　　　　　　　　　　26; 22:52
as Obadiah was *in the w.*　　*1Ki 18:7*
Elijah met him
he walked *in the w.* of the　　*2Ki 8:18*
kings of Israel　*16:2; 2Ch 21:6, 13*
he walked *in the w.* of the　　*2Ki 8:27*
house of Ahab
and walked not *in the w.* of　*2Ki 21:22*
the Lord
three years walked *in the w.*　*2Ch 11:17*
of David
he walked *in the w.* of Asa　*2Ch 20:32*
his father
to help us against the enemy　*Ezr 8:22*
in the w.
to give them light *in the w.*　*Ne 9:12*
they shall go
departed not by day to lead　*Ne 9:19*
them *in the w.*
snare laid and a trap for　　　*Job 18:10*
him *in the w.*
blessed, nor standeth *in the w.* *Ps 1:1*
of sinners
therefore will he teach sinners *Ps 25:8*
in the w.
him shall he teach *in the w.*　*Ps 25:12;*
　　　　　　　　　　　　32:8
and shall set us *in the w.* of　*Ps 85:13*
his steps
he weakened my strength in　*Ps 102:23*
the w.
he shall drink of the brook in　*Ps 110:7*
the w.
blessed are the undefiled *in the Ps 119:1*
w.
have rejoiced *in the w.* of thy *Ps 119:14*
testimonies
search me, and lead me *in*　*Ps 139:24*
the w. everlasting
in the w. have they privily　*Ps 142:3*
laid a snare
walk not thou *in the w.* with　*Pr 1:15*
them
thou mayest walk *in the w.* of *Pr 2:20*
good men
I have taught thee *in the w.* of *Pr 4:11*
wisdom
and go not *in the w.* of evil　*Pr 4:14*
men
I lead *in the w.* of　　　　　*Pr 8:20*
righteousness
live, and go *in the w.* of　　*Pr 9:6*
understanding
he is *in the w.* of life that　　*Pr 10:17*
keepeth instruction
in the w. of righteousness is　*Pr 12:28*
life
righteousness keepeth him that *Pr 13:6*
is upright *in the w.*
if it be found *in the w.* of　　*Pr 16:31*
righteousness
thorns and snares are *in the w.* *Pr 22:5*
of the froward
train up a child *in the w.* he　*Pr 22:6*
should go
be wise, and guide thy heart　*Pr 23:19*
in the w.
slothful man saith there is a　*Pr 26:13*
lion *in the w.*
upright *in the w.* is　　　　*Pr 29:27*
abomination to wicked
be afraid, and fears shall be in *Ec 12:5*
the w.
not walk *in the w.* of this　　*Isa 8:11*
people
in the w. of thy judgments we *Isa 26:8*
waited
went on frowardly *in the w.*　*Isa 57:17*
of his heart
which walked *in the w.* that　*Isa 65:2*
was not good
what hast thou to do in *the*　*Jer 2:18*
w. of Egypt or *in the w.* of
thou hast walked *in the w.*　*Eze 23:31*
of thy sister
so priests murder *in the w.* by *Ho 6:9*
consent
agree quickly whiles thou art　*M't 5:25*
in the w.
John came *in the w.* of　　　*M't 21:32*
righteousness
many spread garments *in the M'k 11:8;*
w. others strawed　*M't 21:8; Lu 19:36*
branches *in the w.*
to guide our feet *in the w.* of　*Lu 1:79*
peace

as thou art *in the w.* give diligence   *Lu 12:58*

Jesus that appeared to thee *in the w.*   *Ac 9:17*

how he had seen the Lord *in the w.*   *Ac 9:27*

they have gone *in the w.* of Cain   *Jude 11*

MY WAY

seeing the Lord hath prospered *my w.*   *Ge 24:56*

maketh *my w.* perfect   *2Sa 22:33; Ps 18:32*

fenced up *my w.* that I cannot pass   *Job 19:8*

why sayest *my w.* is hid from Lord   *Isa 40:27*

hear, O Israel, is not *my w.* equal   *Eze 18:25*

I go *my w.;* brought on *my w.*   *Joh 8:21; Ro 15:24*

to be brought on *my w.* to Jerusalem   *2Co 1:16*

OUT OF THE WAY

they have turned aside   *Ex 32:8;*

quickly *out of the w.*   *De 9:12, 16; J'g 2:17*

the ass turned aside *out of the w.*   *Nu 22:23*

cursed if ye turn aside *out of the w.*   *De 11:28*

thrust thee *out of the w.*   *De 13:5*

that maketh blind to wander *out of the w.*   *De 27:18*

they turn the needy *out of the w.*   *Job 24:4*

they are taken *out of the w.* and cut off   *Job 24:24*

if my step hath turned *out of the w.*   *Job 31:7*

wandereth *out of the w.* of understanding   *Pr 21:16*

thro' strong drink are *out of the w.*   *Isa 28:7*

get you *out of the w.* turn aside out   *Isa 30:11*

take stumblingblock *out of the w.*   *Isa 57:14*

but ye are departed *out of the w.*   *Mal 2:8*

all gone *out of the w.* none doth good   *Ro 3:12*

he took the handwriting *out of the w.*   *Col 2:14*

will let, till he be taken *out of the w.*   *2Th 2:7*

compassion on them that are *out of the w.*   *Heb 5:2*

lest that which is lame be turned *out of the w.*   *Heb 12:13*

OWN WAY

shall they eat the fruit of their *own w.*   *Pr 1:31*

how can a man understand his *own w.*   *Pr 20:24*

we have turned every one to his *own w.*   *Isa 53:6*

greedy dogs, they all look to their *own w.*   *Isa 56:11*

their *own w.* have I recompensed   *Eze 22:31*

defiled Israel by their *own w.* and doings   *Eze 36:17*

THEIR WAY

if children take heed to *their w.* to walk in truth   *1Ki 2:4; 8:25; 2Ch 6:16*

the paths of *their w.* are turned aside   *Job 6:18*

his troops raise up *their w.* against me   *Job 19:12*

I chose out *their w.* sat chief and dwelt   *Job 29:25*

let *their w.* be dark and slippery   *Ps 35:6*

this *their w.* is their folly, yet posterity   *Ps 49:13*

they have perverted *their w.* and forgot   *Jer 3:21*

that thou mayest know and try *their w.*   *Jer 6:27*

their w. shall be to them as slippery ways   *Jer 23:12*

I will do them after *their w.* according to their deserts   *Eze 7:27; 9:10; 11:21*

ye shall see *their w.* and their doings   *Eze 14:22*

as for them *their w.* is not equal   *Eze 33:17*

their w. was before me as uncleanness   *Eze 36:17*

according to *their w.* and doings I judged   *Eze 36:19*

being brought on *their w.* by the church   *Ac 15:3*

THIS WAY

if God will keep me in *this w.* I go   *Ge 28:20*

Moses looked *this w.* and that way   *Ex 2:12*

had no power to flee *this w.* or that   *Jos 8:20*

Elisha said, *This* is not the *w.* follow me   *2Ki 6:19*

saying, *This* is the *w.* walk ye in it   *Isa 30:21*

if he found any of *this w.* might bring   *Ac 9:2*

I persecuted *this w.* unto the death   *Ac 22:4*

THY WAY

the Lord will prosper *thy w.*   *Ge 24:40*

therefore, I pray, shew me *thy w.*   *Ex 33:13*

because *thy w.* is perverse before me   *Nu 22:32*

then thou shalt make *thy w.* prosperous   *Jos 1:8*

return on *thy w.* to the wilderness   *1Ki 19:15*

make *thy w.* straight before my face   *Ps 5:8*

teach me *thy w.,* lead me   *Ps 27:11; 86:11*

commit *thy w.* unto the Lord, trust in him   *Ps 37:5*

neither have our steps declined from *thy w.*   *Ps 44:18*

that *thy w.* may be known upon earth   *Ps 67:2*

thy w. O God, is in the sanctuary   *Ps 77:13*

thy w. is in the sea, thy path in great waters   *Ps 77:19*

and quicken thou me in *thy w.*   *Ps 119:37*

then shalt thou walk in *thy w.* safely   *Pr 3:23*

remove *thy w.* far from her, come not nigh   *Pr 5:8*

art wearied in the greatness of *thy w.*   *Isa 57:10*

see *thy w.* in the valley, what hast done   *Jer 2:23*

why trimmest thou *thy w.* to seek love   *Jer 2:33*

why gaddest thou about to change *thy w.*   *Jer 2:36*

thy w. have procured these things unto thee   *Jer 4:18*

I also will recompense *thy w.*   *Eze 16:43*

I will hedge up *thy w.* with thorns   *Ho 2:6*

because thou didst trust in *thy w.*   *Ho 10:13*

I send my messenger, who shall prepare *thy w.*   *M't 11:10; M'k 1:2; Lu 7:27*

WAYFARERS

I opened door to *w.* (B)(R)   *Job 31:32*

WAYFARING

he saw a *w.* man in the street   *J'g 19:17*

the *w.* man that was come unto him   *2Sa 12:4*

lie waste, the *w.* man ceaseth   *Isa 33:8*

the *w.* men, though fools   *Isa 35:8*

a lodging place of *w.* men   *Jer 9:2*

as a *w.* man that turneth aside to   *Jer 14:8*

WAYMARKS

Set thee up *w.* make thee high   *Jer 31:21*

WAYS

ye shall rise early and go on your *w.*   *Ge 19:2*

walk in all the *w.* Lord commanded   *De 5:33*

he walked in the *w.* of Asa his father   *1Ki 22:43*

he walked in all the *w.* of Manasseh   *2Ki 21:21*

he walked in *w.* of David   *2Ki 22:2; 2Ch 17:3; 34:2*

walked not in *w.* of Jehoshaphat   *2Ch 21:12*

he walked in the *w.* of the house of Ahab   *2Ch 22:3*

he walked in the *w.* of the kings of Israel   *2Ch 28:2*

they know not the *w.* of the light   *Job 24:13*

they raise up the *w.* of their destruction   *Job 30:12*

for his eyes are upon the *w.* of man   *Job 34:21*

Behemoth is the chief of the *w.* of God   *Job 40:19*

in whose heart are the *w.* of them   *Ps 84:5*

so are the *w.* of every one greedy of gain   *Pr 1:19*

to walk in the *w.* of darkness   *Pr 2:13*

whose *w.* are crooked, and they froward   *Pr 2:15*

wisdom's *w.* are *w.* of pleasantness and paths   *Pr 3:17*

her *w.* are moveable, canst not know them   *Pr 5:6*

the *w.* of man are before the Lord   *Pr 5:21*

go to the ant, consider her *w.* and be wise   *Pr 6:6*

let not thine heart decline to her *w.*   *Pr 7:25*

end thereof are the *w.* of death   *Pr 14:12; 16:25*

the *w.* of a man are clean in his own eyes   *Pr 16:2*

when a man's *w.* please the Lord, he makes   *Pr 16:7*

taketh a gift to pervert *w.* of judgment   *Pr 17:23*

wilfully goes in double and wrong *w.* (A)   *Pr 28:6*

she looketh well to the *w.* of her household   *Pr 31:27*

young man, walk in *w.* of thy heart   *Ec 11:9*

they shall feed in the *w.* and pastures   *Isa 49:9*

a swift dromedary traversing her *w.*   *Jer 2:23*

in the *w.* hast thou sat for them as Arabian   *Jer 3:2*

stand in the *w.* and see, ask for old paths   *Jer 6:16*

amend your *w.* and doings   *Jer 7:3; 7:5; 26:13*

walk in all the *w.* I have commanded you   *Jer 7:23*

if they diligently learn *w.* of my people   *Jer 12:16*

make your *w.* and your doings good   *Jer 18:11*

eyes are open on *w.* of sons of men   *Jer 32:19*

the *w.* of Zion do mourn, none come   *La 1:4*

search and try our *w.* and turn to Lord   *La 3:40*

are not your *w.* unequal   *Eze 18:25; 18:29*

there remember your *w.* and doings   *Eze 20:43*

not according to your wicked *w.* or doings   *Eze 20:44*

son of man appoint thee two *w.*   *Eze 21:19*

stood at head of two *w.* to use divination   *Eze 21:21*

saith the Lord, Consider your *w.*   *Hag 1:5; 1:7*

do to us according to our *w.* and doings   *Zec 1:6*

and the rough *w.* shall be made smooth   *Lu 3:5*

hast made known to me the *w.* of life   *Ac 2:28*

falsifying straight *w.* of Lord (R)   *Ac 13:10*

in *w.* that build up (A)   *1Co 14:12*

empty folly of traditional *w.*   *1Pe 1:18* (N)

wanton *w.* of ungodly (A)   *2Pe 2:7*

ANY WAYS

do *any w.* hide their eyes from   *Le 20:4* the man

if ye shall *any w.* make them   *Nu 30:15* void

any w. able to deliver their   *2Ch 32:13* lands

HIS WAYS

walk in *his w.* and fear him   *De 8:6; 26:17; 28:9; 30:16; 1Ki 2:3*

to walk in all *his w.* to love   *De 10:12;* him   *11:22; Jos 22:5; 1Ki 8:58*

to love the Lord and walk   *De 19:9* ever in *his w.*

all *his w.* are judgment   *De 32:4; Da 4:37*

Samuel's sons walked not in   *1Sa 8:3* *his w.*

David behaved wisely in *his*   *1Sa 18:14* *w.*

hear in heaven, give to every   *1Ki 8:39;* man according to *his w.*   *2Ch 6:30*

Abijah's acts and *his w.* are   *2Ch 13:22* written

Jotham prepared *his w.*   *2Ch 27:6* before the Lord

his w. are written in book   *2Ch 27:7;* of the kings   *28:26*

these are parts of *his w.*   *Job 26:14*

cause every man find   *Job 34:11* according to *his w.*

would not consider any of   *Job 34:27* *his w.*

his w. are always grievous   *Ps 10:5*

he made known *his w.* unto   *Ps 103:7* Moses

they do no iniquity, they   *Ps 119:3* walk in *his w.*

blessed is every one that   *Ps 128:1* walketh in *his w.*

the Lord is righteous in all   *Ps 145:17* *his w.*

envy not and choose none of   *Pr 3:31* *his w.*

he that perverteth *his w.* shall   *Pr 10:9* be known

he that is perverse in *his w.*   *Pr 14:2* despiseth

he that despiseth *his w.* shall   *Pr 19:16* die

lest thou learn *his w.* and get   *Pr 22:25* a snare

is better than he that is   *Pr 28:6* perverse in *his w.*

he that is perverse in *his w.*   *Pr 28:18* shall fall at once

he will teach us of *his w.*   *Isa 2:3; Mic 4:2*

for they would not walk in   *Isa 42:24* *his w.*

I will direct all *his w.* saith   *Isa 45:13* the Lord

I have seen *his w.* and will   *Isa 57:18* heal him

give every man according to   *Jer 17:10;* *his w.*   *32:19*

that he should return from   *Eze 18:23* *his w.*

I will judge Israel according   *Eze 18:30;* to *his w.*   *33:20*

is a snare of a fowler in all *his*   *Ho 9:8* *w.*

Lord will punish Jacob   *Ho 12:2* according to *his w.*

they shall march on every one   *Joe 2:7* in *his w.*

the hills did bow, *his w.* are   *Hab 3:6* everlasting

thou shalt go before Lord to   *Lu 1:76* prepare *his w.*

and *his w.* are past finding   *Ro 11:33* out

double-minded man is unstable   *Jas 1:8* in all *his w.*

so shall the rich man   *Jas 1:11* fade away in *his w.*

MY WAYS

if thou wilt walk in *my w.* as   *1Ki 3:14;* thy father David did walk   *11:38; Zec 3:7*

worshipped Milcom and not   *1Ki 11:33* walked in *my w.*

doth not he see *my w.* and   *Job 31:4* count my steps

I will take heed to *my w.* that   *Ps 39:1* I sin not

O that Israel had walked in   *Ps 81:13* *my w.*

they have not known *my w.*   *Ps 95:10; Heb 3:10*

O that *my w.* were directed to   *Ps 119:5* keep thy statutes

have declared *my w.* and   *Ps 119:26* thou heardest me

thought on *my w.* and turned   *Ps 119:59* my feet to thy

kept testimonies, all *my w.*   *Ps 119:168* are before thee

and art acquainted with all   *Ps 139:3* *my w.*

blessed are they that keep *my*   *Pr 8:32* *w.*

my son, let thine eyes observe   *Pr 23:26* *my w.*

neither are your ways *my w.*   *Isa 55:8* saith Lord

so are *my w.* higher than your   *Isa 55:9* ways

seek me daily and delight to   *Isa 58:2* know *my w.*

he hath inclosed *my w.* with   *La 3:9* hewn stone

he turned aside *my w.* and   *La 3:11* pulled me in pieces

are not *my w.* equal, your   *Eze 18:29* ways unequal

if thou wilt walk in *my w.* and   *Zec 3:7* keep

according as ye have not kept   *Mal 2:9* *my w.*

bring you into remembrance   *1Co 4:17* of *my w.*

OWN WAYS

I will maintain my *own w.*   *Job 13:15* before him

the backslider be filled with   *Pr 14:14* his *own w.*

honour him, not doing thine   *Isa 58:13* *own w.*

yea, they have chosen their   *Isa 66:3* *own w.*

then remember your *own*   *Eze 36:31* evil *w.*

be ashamed for your *own w.*   *Eze 36:32* O house of Israel

he suffered all nations to walk   *Ac 14:16* in *own w.*

THEIR WAYS

pray and turn from *their*   *2Ch 7:14* wicked *w.*

yet his eyes are upon *their*   *Job 24:23* *w.*

for such as turn to *their*   *Ps 125:5* crooked *w.*

call passengers who go right   *Pr 9:15* on *their w.*

since they return not from   *Jer 15:7* *their w.*

for mine eyes are upon all   *Jer 16:17* *their w.*

they caused them to stumble   *Jer 18:15* in *their w.*

comfort you when ye see   *Eze 14:23* *their w.*

yet hast thou not walked   *Eze 16:47* after *their w.*

I will punish them for *their w.*   *Ho 4:9* destruction and misery are in   *Ro 3:16* *their w.*

many shall follow *their*   *2Pe 2:2* pernicious *w.*

THY WAYS

thou shalt not prosper in *thy*   *De 28:29* *w.*

art old, thy sons walk not in   *1Sa 8:5* *thy w.*

may fear thee to walk in *thy*   *2Ch 6:31* *w.*

thy hope and the uprightness of   *Job 4:6* *thy w.*

we desire not the knowledge   *Job 21:14* of *thy w.*

is it gain to him thou makest   *Job 22:3* *thy w.* perfect

and the light shall shine   *Job 22:28* upon *thy w.*

shew me *thy w.* O Lord, teach   *Ps 25:4* me

then will I teach transgressors   *Ps 51:13* *thy w.*

charge has angels, to keep   *Ps 91:11* thee in all *thy w.*

I will have respect unto *thy*   *Ps 119:15* *w.*

in all *thy w.* acknowledge him,   *Pr 3:6* he direct

and let all *thy w.* be   *Pr 4:26* established

nor *thy w.* to that which   *Pr 31:3* destroyeth kings

why hast thou made us err   *Isa 63:17* from *thy w.*

those that remember thee in   *Isa 64:5* *thy w.*

thou hast taught the wicked   *Jer 2:33* *thy w.*

thou hast scattered *thy w.* to   *Jer 3:13* the strangers

judge thee according to *thy w.*   *Eze 7:3; 7:8*

corrupted more than they in   *Eze 16:47* all *thy w.*

then remember *thy w.* and be   *Eze 16:61* ashamed

according to *thy w.* shall they   *Eze 24:14* judge thee

thou wast perfect in *thy w.*   *Eze 28:15* from the day

the God in whose hand are all   *Da 5:23* *thy w.*

just and true are *thy w.* thou   *Re 15:3* king of saints

WAYSIDE

Eli sat upon a seat by the *w.*   *1Sa 4:13*

have spread a net by the *w.*   *Ps 140:5*

by the *w.* begging (S)   *M'k 10:46*

WE

been about cattle, *w.* and our   *Ge 46:34* fathers

w. not able, they are   *Nu 13:31* stronger than *w.*

the people is greater and taller   *De 1:28* than *w.*

that *w.* may be like all the   *1Sa 8:20* nations

w. will be with thee, be of   *Ezr 10:4* courage

w. his servants will arise and   *Ne 2:20* build

w. our sons and our daughters   *Ne 5:2* are many

w. after our ability have   *Ne 5:8* redeemed the Jews

w. are but of yesterday, know   *Job 8:9* nothing

w. are his people, sheep of his   *Ps 100:3* pasture

art thou also become weak   *Isa 14:10* as *w.*

w. are thine   *Isa 63:19*

for *w.* are many   *M'k 5:9*

why could not *w.* cast him out   *M'k 9:28*

that *w.* being delivered from   *Lu 1:74* enemies

w. be Abraham's seed, never   *Joh 8:33* in bondage

thou art his disciple, *w.* are   *Joh 9:28* Moses' disciples

are *w.* blind also; may be   *Joh 9:40;* one as *w.*   *17:11, 22*

and *w.* are his witnesses   *Ac 5:32; 10:39*

who received the Holy Ghost   *Ac 10:47* as well as *w.*

w. are men of like passions   *Ac 14:15* with you

w. or ever he come are ready   *Ac 23:15* to kill him

w. being many are one body   *Ro 12:5* in Christ

w. that are strong ought to   *Ro 15:1* bear infirmities

w. are labourers together with   *1Co 3:9* God

w. are fools, but ye are wise,   *1Co 4:10* *w.* are weak

being reviled, *w.* bless,   *1Co 4:12* persecuted, *w.* suffer it

one God, and *w.* in him; one   *1Co 8:6* Lord and *w.* by him

are not *w.* rather; *w.* are   *1Co 9:12;* one bread   *10:17*

do *w.* provoke Lord, are *w.*   *1Co 10:22*
stronger than he
that *w.* are your rejoicing, as   *2Co 1:14*
ye ours
w. that *w.* say not ye, should   *2Co 9:4*
be ashamed
that as he is Christ's, so are   *2Co 10:7*
w. Christ's
they may be found even as   *2Co 11:12*
w.
though *w.* or an angel from   *Ga 1:8*
heaven preach
w. when in *w.* were children, were   *Ga 4:3*
in bondage
now *w.* as Isaac, are the   *Ga 4:28*
children of promise
for *w.* are his workmanship in   *Eph 2:10*
Christ Jesus
w. which are alive shall be   *1Th 4:17*
caught in the clouds, and
so shall *w.* ever be with Lord
w. are not of the night nor of   *1Th 5:5*
darkness
whose house are *w.* if *w.* hold   *Heb 3:6*
fast confidence
w. are not of them who   *Heb 10:39*
draw back to perdition
w. are of God hereby *w.* know   *1Jo 4:6*
Spirit of truth
w. know that *w.* are of God   *1Jo 5:19*
and world lieth

WEAK

eyes *w.* and dull looking   *Ge 29:17*
(A)(R)
whether they be strong or *w.*   *Nu 13:18*
then shall I be *w.* and be as   *J'g 16:7;*
   16:11
I shall become *w.* and be like   *J'g 16:17*
any
And I am this day *w.*, though   *2Sa 3:39*
while he is weary and *w.*   *2Sa 17:2*
handed
and let not your hands be *w.*   *2Ch 15:7*
hast strengthened the *w.* hands   *Job 4:3*
upon me, O Lord: for I am *w.*   *Ps 6:2*
I am faint (A)   *Ps 6:2*
I am withered away (E)   *Ps 6:2*
I am languishing (R)   *Ps 6:2*
My knees are *w.* through   *Ps 109:24*
fasting
Art thou also become *w.* as   *Isa 14:10*
we
Strengthen ye in the *w.* hands   *Isa 35:3*
all knees shall be *w.* as water   *Eze 7:17;*
   21:7
How *w.* is thine heart, saith   *Eze 16:30*
the *w.* with your horns   *Eze 34:21*
(B)(R)
let the *w.* say, I am strong   *Joe 3:10*
is willing, but the flesh is *w.*   *M't 26:41*
truly is ready, but the flesh   *M'k 14:38*
is *w.*
ye ought to support the *w.*   *Ac 20:35*
being not *w.* in faith, he   *Ro 4:19*
considered
in that it was *w.* through the   *Ro 8:3*
flesh
Him that is *w.* in the faith   *Ro 14:1*
receive
another, who is *w.* eateth   *Ro 14:2*
herbs
or is offended, or is made *w.*   *Ro 14:21*
to bear the infirmities of the *w.*   *Ro 15:1*
chosen the *w.* things of the   *1Co 1:27*
world
we are *w.* but ye are strong   *1Co 4:10*
their conscience being *w.* is   *1Co 8:7*
defiled
stumblingblock to them that   *1Co 8:9*
are *w.*
the conscience of him which   *1Co 8:10*
is *w.*
shall the *w.* brother perish   *1Co 8:11*
and wound their *w.*   *1Co 8:12*
conscience
To the *w.* became I as *w.*   *1Co 9:22*
that I might gain the *w.*; I am   *1Co 9:22*
many are *w.* and sickly   *1Co 11:30*
among you
invalid (A)   *1Co 11:30*
feeble and sick (N)   *1Co 11:30*
feeble and sickly (P)   *1Co 11:30*
but his bodily presence is *w.*   *2Co 10:10*
as though we had been *w.*   *2Co 11:21*
Who is *w.* and I am not *w.*   *2Co 11:29*
for when I am *w.* then am I   *2Co 12:10*
strong

which to you-ward is not *w.*   *2Co 13:3*
but is
For we also are *w.* in him,   *2Co 13:4*
but we
when we are *w.* and ye are   *2Co 13:9*
strong
to the *w.* and beggarly elements   *Ga 4:9*
support the *w.* be patient   *1Th 5:14*
toward
w.-natured women (B)(R)   *2Ti 3:6*

WEAK HANDED

I will come on him while he   *2Sa 7:2*
is *w. handed*

WEAKEN

which didst *w.* the nations   *Isa 14:12*

WEAKENED

w. the hands of people of   *Ezr 4:4*
Judah
hands shall be *w.* from the   *Ne 6:9*
work
He *w.* my strength in the   *Ps 102:23*
way; he

WEAKENETH

w. the strength of the mighty   *Job 12:21*
he *w.* the hands of the men of   *Jer 38:4*
war

WEAKENING

a *w.* spirit (B)   *Lu 11:12; 13:11*

WEAKENS

my spirit *w.* (B)   *Ps 142:3*

WEAKER

the *w.* (B)   *Ge 30:42*
house of Saul waxed *w.* and *w.*   *2Sa 3:1*
tender scruples of *w.* men (N)   *Ro 15:1*
the wife, as unto the *w.* vessel   *1Pe 3:7*

WEAKHEARTED

that is *w.* (B)   *De 20:8*

WEAKNESS

see the *w.* of the land (R)   *Ge 42:9*
w. has seized me (B)   *2Sa 1:9*
borne our *w.* (A)   *Isa 53:4*
your human *w.* (B)(N)   *Ro 6:19*
helps our *w.* (A)(B)(N)(R)   *Ro 8:26*
w. of God is stronger than   *1Co 1:25*
men
I was with you in *w.* and in   *1Co 2:3*
fear
it is sown in *w.*; it is raised   *1Co 15:43*
in power
concerning my *w.*   *2Co 11:30*
(B)(E)(N)(P)(R)
not in my *w.* (B)(N)   *2Co 12:5; 12:10*
my strength is made perfect   *2Co 12:9*
in *w.*
though he was crucified   *2Co 13:4*
through *w.*
moral *w.* and physical   *Heb 5:2*
infirmity (A)
liable to *w.* (B)(P)(R)   *Heb 5:2*
for the *w.* and   *Heb 7:18*
unprofitableness
ineffectiveness and   *Heb 7:18*
uselessness (A)
impotent and useless (E)   *Heb 7:18*
w. and uselessness (R)   *Heb 7:18*
out of *w.* were made strong   *Heb 11:34*

WEAKNESSES

took our *w.* (B)   *M't 8:17*
bear the *w.* of (B)   *Ro 15:1*
not in my *w.*   *2Co 12:5; 12:10*
(E)(N)(P)(R)
feeling of our *w.*   *Heb 4:15*
(B)(N)(P)(R)

WEALTH

he has gotten all this *w.* (S)   *Ge 31:1*
wealth (B)   *Ge 31:16;*
Jos 22:8; *1Ki 10:23;* *1Ch 29:12;*
2Ch 32:27; *Es 1:4;* *5:11;* *Job 36:19;*
        Ps 52:7
their *w.* and all their little   *Ge 34:29*
ones

their *w.* (B)   *Ge 36:7; 1Ch 29:21*
mine hand hath gotten me this   *De 8:17*
he that giveth thee power to   *De 8:18*
get *w.*
a mighty man of *w.* of the   *Ru 2:1*
family
the *w.* which God shall give   *1Sa 2:32*
Israel
blessings I will give Israel   *1Sa 2:32*
(B)
prosperity (R)   *1Sa 2:32*
even of all the mighty men   *2Ki 15:20*
of *w.*
not asked riches, *w.*, or   *2Ch 1:11*
honour
I will give thee riches, and *w.*   *2Ch 1:12*
Hezekiah had great *w.* (A)   *2Ch 32:7*
nor seek their peace or their   *Ezr 9:12*
w.
seeking the *w.* of his people   *Es 10:3*
wealth (B)   *Job 5:5;*
6:22; *15:29;* *Pr 8:21;* *12:27;* *28:8;*
Ca 8:7; *Jer 15:13;* *17:3;* *Ho 12:8;*
         Mic 4:13
wealth (B)   *Job 5:5;*
6:22; *15:29;* *Pr 8:21;* *12:27;* *28:8;*
  Ca 8:7; *Jer 15:13;* *17:3;* *Ho 12:8;*
         Mic 4:13
wealth (A)   *Job 6:22;*
15:29; 20:18; Ps 17:14; Jer 17:3; Ho 12:8
give back his *w.*   *Job 20:10*
(A)(B)(E)(R)
They spend their days in *w.*   *Job 21:13*
and in
rejoiced because my *w.* was   *Job 31:25*
great
not increase thy *w.* by their   *Ps 44:12*
price
They that trust in their *w.* and   *Ps 49:6*
perish, and leave their *w.* to   *Ps 49:10*
others
W. and riches be in his   *Ps 112:3*
house
strangers be filled with thy *w.*   *Pr 5:10*
strangers filled with thy   *Pr 5:10*
strength (R)
rich man's *w.* is his strong   *Pr 10:15;*
city   *18:11*
poor, yet hath great *w.* (E)   *Pr 13:7*
W. gotten by vanity shall be   *Pr 13:11*
the *w.* of the sinner is laid up   *Pr 13:22*
crown of wise is their *w.*   *Pr 14:24*
(A)(B)
W. maketh many friends; but   *Pr 19:4*
house and *w.* are inherited   *Pr 19:14*
(B)(R)
do not toil to get *w.* (B)(R)   *Pr 23:4*
neither has eye satisfied with *w.*   *Ec 4:8*
(B)
w. retained by owner (B)   *Ec 5:13*
w. is lost in a bad venture (B)   *Ec 5:14*
God hath given riches and *w.*   *Ec 5:19*
to whom God hath given   *Ec 6:2*
riches, *w.*
the *w.* of Damascus (R)   *Isa 8:4*
w. of the people (A)(B)(R)   *Isa 10:14*
hoarded in secret (B)   *Isa 45:3*
eat *w.* of nations   *Isa 61:6*
(A)(B)(E)(R)
plunder your *w.* (B)   *Eze 26:12*
because of great *w.* (B)(R)   *Eze 27:12*
immense *w.* of every kind   *Eze 27:18*
(A)(B)(R)
your *w.* and wares (B)   *Eze 27:27*
your abundant *w.*   *Eze 27:33*
(A)(B)(R)
won for yourself great *w.*   *Eze 28:4*
(B)(R)
through his *w.* he (B)   *Da 11:2*
w. of all the heathen round   *Zec 14:14*
about
those who possess *w.*   *M't 10:23*
(A)(B)(N)
deceitfulness of *w.*   *M't 13:22*
(B)(N)(P)
wealth (B)   *M'k 8:14;*
18:24; Ro 2:4; 9:23; 11:33; 2Co 8:2;
Eph 1:7; 2:7; 3:8, 16; Ph'p 4:19;
         Col 1:27
put trust in *w.* (B)   *M'k 10:24*
use deceitful *w.* (B)(N)   *Lu 16:9*
trustworthy with *w.* of this   *Lu 16:11*
world (N)
wealth (A)   *Lu 18:24;*
  Ro 2:4; 9:23; 2Co 8:2; Col 2:2
that by this craft we have   *Ac 19:25*
our *w.*

underestimate his *w.* (A)(B)(N)   *Ro 2:4*

his own, but every one another's *w.*   *1Co 10:24*

the fathomless *w.* of Christ (B)   *Eph 3:8*

insatiable for *w.* (A)   *1Ti 3:3*

transitory power of *w.* (P)   *1Ti 6:17*

WEALTHY

broughtest us out into a *w.* place   *Ps 66:12*

brought us into a broad moist place—to abundance, refreshment, and open air (A)   *Ps 66:12*

brought us to an overflowing abundance (B)   *Ps 66:12*

brought us to an overflowing place (R)   *Ps 66:12*

get you up unto the *w.* nation   *Jer 49:31*

that is at ease (A)(E)(R)   *Jer 49:31*

that lives carelessly (B)   *Jer 49:31*

w. waste away (B)   *Jas 1:11*

WEANED

And the child grew, and was *w.*   *Ge 21:8*

the same day that Isaac was *w.*   *Ge 21:8*

will not go up until the child be *w.*   *1Sa 1:22*

tarry until thou have *w.* him   *1Sa 1:23*

gave her son suck until she *w.* him   *1Sa 1:23*

And when she had *w.* him, she   *1Sa 1:24*

Tahpenes *w.* in Pharaoh's house   *1Ki 11:20*

as a child that is *w.* of his mother   *Ps 131:2*

my soul is even as a *w.* child   *Ps 131:2*

w. child shall put his hand on   *Isa 11:8*

them that are *w.* from the milk   *Isa 28:9*

Now when she had *w.* Lo-ruhamah   *Ho 1:8*

WEAPON

smite him with an hand *w.* of   *Nu 35:18*

a paddle or spade (A)(B)   *Nu 35:18*

shalt have a paddle upon thy *w.*   *De 23:13*

man having his *w.* in his hand   *2Ch 23:10*

and with the other hand held a *w.*   *Ne 4:17*

He shall flee from the iron *w.* and   *Job 20:24*

produces *w.* for (A)(E)(R)   *Isa 54:17*

No *w.* that is formed against thee   *Isa 54:17*

with his destroying *w.* in his hand   *Eze 9:1*

man a slaughter *w.* in his hand   *Eze 9:2*

WEAPONS

therefore take, I pray thee, thy *w.*   *Ge 27:3*

w. of violence (A)(E)(R)   *Ge 49:5*

girded on every man his *w.* of war   *De 1:41*

shovel among thy *w.* (S)   *De 23:13*

six hundred men appointed with *w.*   *J'g 18:11*

men appointed with their *w.* of war   *J'g 18:16*

that were appointed with *w.* of war   *J'g 18:17*

w. and chariot equipment (B)   *1Sa 8:12*

Jonathan gave his *w.* to the lad (S)   *1Sa 20:40*

my sword nor my *w.* with me   *1Sa 21:8*

fallen, and the *w.* of war perished   *2Sa 1:27*

every man with his *w.* in his hand   *2Ki 11:8; 11:11; 2Ch 23:7*

he made *w.* in abundance (S)   *2Ch 32:5*

deadly *w.* (A)(B)(R)   *Ps 7:13*

Wisdom is better than *w.* of war   *Ec 9:18*

and the *w.* of his indignation   *Isa 13:5*

I will turn back the *w.* of war that   *Jer 21:4*

against thee, every one with his *w.*   *Jer 22:7*

forth the *w.* of his indignation   *Jer 50:25*

art my battle axe and *w.* of war   *Jer 51:20*

down to hell with their *w.* of war   *Eze 32:27*

shall set on fire and burn the *w.*   *Eze 39:9*

for they shall burn the *w.* with fire   *Eze 39:10*

with lanterns and torches and *w.*   *Joh 18:3*

w. of righteousness (P)   *Ro 6:13*

w. of our warfare are not carnal   *2Co 10:4*

WEAR

Thou wilt surely *w.* away both which   *Ex 18:18*

woman shall not *w.* that   *De 22:5*

not *w.* a garment of divers sorts   *De 22:11*

incense, to *w.* an ephod before me   *1Sa 2:28*

w. out your life (B)   *1Sa 2:33*

persons that did *w.* a linen ephod   *1Sa 22:18*

brought which the king useth to *w.*   *Es 6:8*

The waters *w.* the stones   *Job 14:19*

bread, and *w.* our own apparel   *Isa 4:1*

w. out the saints of the most High   *Da 7:25*

w. a rough garment to deceive   *Zec 13:4*

they that *w.* soft clothing are   *M't 11:8*

w. fine apparel (A)(P)   *Lu 7:25*

when the day began to *w.* away   *Lu 9:12*

outer man suffers *w.* and tear (P)   *2Co 4:16*

destined to be ruined by *w.* (B)   *Col 2:22*

they all shall *w.* out (B)   *Heb 1:11*

WEARETH

to him that *w.* the gay clothing   *Jas 2:3*

WEARIED

w. themselves to find the door   *Ge 19:11*

w. and grieved (A)   *Le 20:23*

his soul *w.* to death (B)   *J'g 16:16*

offering, nor *w.* thee with incense   *Isa 43:23*

hast *w.* me with thine iniquities   *Isa 43:24*

Thou art *w.* of the multitude of   *Isa 47:13*

w. in the greatness of thy way   *Isa 57:10*

soul is *w.* because of murderers   *Jer 4:31*

and they have *w.* thee, then   *Jer 12:5*

thou trustedst, they *w.* thee   *Jer 12:5*

She hath *w.* herself with lies   *Eze 24:12*

wherein have I *w.* thee? testify   *Mic 6:3*

w. the Lord with your words   *Mal 2:17*

ye say, Wherein have we *w.* him   *Mal 2:17*

be very *w.* (P)   *Lu 2:48*

being *w.* with his journey, sat   *Joh 4:6*

ye be *w.* and faint in your minds   *Heb 12:3*

w. with filthy (B)   *2Pe 2:7*

WEARIES

w. him (A)   *Pr 26:15*

he *w.* himself (B)   *Ec 2:22*

WEARIETH

by watering he *w.* the thick cloud   *Job 37:11*

w. to bring to mouth (E)   *Pr 26:15*

the foolish *w.* every one of them   *Ec 10:15*

WEARINESS

w. of workers (B)   *Ne 4:10*

much study is a *w.* of the flesh   *Ec 12:12*

said also, Behold, what a *w.* is it   *Mal 1:13*

In *w.* and painfulness, in   *2Co 11:27*

WEARING

priest in Shiloh, *w.* an ephod   *1Sa 14:3*

Jesus forth, *w.* the crown of thorns   *Joh 19:5*

w. discussion (A)   *1Ti 6:5*

plaiting the hair, and of *w.* of gold   *1Pe 3:3*

WEARISOME

and *w.* nights are appointed to me   *Job 7:3*

it seemed to me a *w.* task (R)   *Ps 73:16*

WEARS

w. him out (R)   *Pr 26:15*

WEARY

I am *w.* of my life because of   *Ge 27:46*

when thou wast faint and *w.*   *De 25:18*

w. and exhausted (B)(E)(R)   *De 25:18*

for he was fast asleep and *w.*   *J'g 4:21*

bread unto thy men that are *w.*   *J'g 8:15*

that were with him, came *w.*   *2Sa 16:14*

upon him while he is *w.* and weak   *2Sa 17:2*

The people is hungry, and *w.*   *2Sa 17:29*

Philistines until his hand was *w.*   *2Sa 23:10*

and there the *w.* be at rest   *Job 3:17*

My soul is *w.* of my life; I   *Job 10:1*

But now he hath made me *w.*   *Job 16:7*

not given water to the *w.* to drink   *Job 22:7*

I am *w.* with my groaning; all the   *Ps 6:6*

thine inheritance, when it was *w.*   *Ps 68:9*

I am *w.* of my crying: my throat   *Ps 69:3*

neither be *w.* of his correction   *Pr 3:11*

w. not to be rich (A)(E)   *Pr 23:4*

lest he be *w.* of thee, and so hate   *Pr 25:17*

unto me: I am *w.* to bear them   *Isa 1:14*

None shall be *w.* nor stumble   *Isa 5:27*

a small thing for you to *w.* men   *Isa 7:13*

but will ye *w.* my God also   *Isa 7:13*

that Moab is *w.* on the high place   *Isa 16:12*

ye may cause the *w.* to rest   *Isa 28:12*

shadow of a great rock in a *w.* land   *Isa 32:2*

earth, fainteth not, neither is *w.*   *Isa 40:28*

the youths shall faint and be *w.*   *Isa 40:30*

they shall run, and not be *w.;* and   *Isa 40:31*

thou hast been *w.* of me, O Israel   *Isa 43:22*

they are a burden to the *w.*   *Isa 46:1*

word in season to him that is *w.*   *Isa 50:4*

all they that seek her will not *w.*   *Jer 2:24*

the Lord; I am *w.* with holding in   *Jer 6:11*

w. themselves to commit iniquity   *Jer 9:5*

thee, I am *w.* with repenting   *Jer 15:6*

I was *w.* with forbearing, and   *Jer 20:9*

For I have satiated the *w.* soul   *Jer 31:25*

every *w.* soul (B)(R)   *Jer 31:25*

in the fire, and they shall be *w.*   *Jer 51:58*

upon her: and they shall be *w.*   *Jer 51:64*

w., not allowed to rest (A)(E)(R)   *La 5:5*

the people shall *w.* themselves for   *Hab 2:13*

her continual coming she *w.* me   *Lu 18:5*

And let us not be *w.* in well doing   *Ga 6:9*

brethren, be not *w.* in well doing   *2Th 3:13*

WEASEL

the *w.* and the mouse, and   *Le 11:29*

WEATHER

Fair w. cometh out of the north	Job 37:22
taketh away a garment in cold w.	Pr 25:20
evening, ye say, It will be fair w.	M't 16:2
morning, It will be foul w. to day	M't 16:3

WEAVE

and they that w. networks, shall be	Isa 19:9
eggs, and w. the spider's web	Isa 59:5
w. it together (S)	Mic 7:3

WEAVER

and in fine linen, and of the w.	Ex 35:35
I have cut off like a w. my life: he	Isa 38:12

WEAVER'S

of his spear was like a w. beam	1Sa 17:7
of whose spear was like a w. beam	2Sa 21:19
hand was a spear like a w. beam	1Ch 11:23
spear staff was like a w. beam	1Ch 20:5
days are swifter than a w. shuttle	Job 7:6

WEAVEST

If thou w. the seven locks of	J'g 16:13

WEB

locks of my head with the w.	J'g 16:13
pin of the beam and with the w.	J'g 16:14
whose trust shall be a spider's w.	Job 8:14
eggs, and weave the spider's w.	Isa 59:5

WEBS

w. shall not become garments	Isa 59:6

WEDDED

Ephraim is w. to his idols (B)	Ho 4:17

WEDDING

praised in w. song (A)	Ps 78:63
w. guests (A)(B)(P)(R)	M't 9:15
made a w. banquet (A)(B)(N)(P)	M't 22:2
them that were bidden to the w.	M't 22:3
marriage feast (E)(R)	M't 22:3
come to the w. (A)(B)(N)(R)	M't 22:4
The w. is ready, but they which	M't 22:8
banquet (B)	M't 22:8
the w. was furnished with guests	M't 22:10
which had not on a w. garment	M't 22:11
in hither not having a w. garment	M't 22:12
went in to the w. (N)	M't 25:10
when he will return from the w.	Lu 12:36
marriage feast (A)(E)(R)	Lu 12:36; 14:8
thou art bidden of any man to a w.	Lu 14:8
there was a w. (A)(B)(N)(P)	Joh 2:1; 2:2
w., wail over her (A)(B)(E)(N)(P)(R)	Re 18:9
the w. banquet (B)	Re 19:7; 19:9
the w. of the Lamb is come (N)(P)	Re 19:7
w.-supper of the Lamb (N)	Re 19:9
the w. feast (R)	Re 19:9

WEDGE

w. of gold of fifty shekels weight	Jos 7:21

bar of gold (A)(B)(R)	Jos 7:21
the w. of gold, and his sons, and his	Jos 7:24
bar of gold (B)(R)	Jos 7:24
a man than the golden w. of Ophir	Isa 13:12

WEDLOCK

as women that break w. and shed	Eze 16:38

WEEDS

widows w. (B)	Ge 38:14
and w. instead of barley (S)	Job 31:40
w. were wrapped about my head	Jon 2:5
sowed w. (B)	M't 13:29; 13:36, 38, 40

WEEK

Fulfil her w. and we will give thee	Ge 29:27
Jacob did so, and fulfilled her w.	Ge 29:28
the covenant with many for one w.	Da 9:27
and in the midst of the w. he shall	Da 9:27
toward the first day of the w.	M't 28:1
the morning the first day of the w.	M'k 16:2
risen early the first day of the w.	M'k 16:9
I fast twice in the w., I give tithes	Lu 18:12
Now upon the first day of the w.	Lu 24:1
the first day of the w. cometh Mary	Joh 20:1
being the first day of the w. when	Joh 20:19
And upon the first day of the w.	Ac 20:7
Upon the first day of the w. let every	1Co 16:2

WEEKS

thou shalt observe the feast of w.	Ex 34:22
then she shall be unclean two w.	Le 12:5
after your w. be out, ye shall have	Nu 28:26
Seven w. shalt thou number unto	De 16:9
begin to number the seven w. from	De 16:9
keep the feast of w. unto the Lord	De 16:10
in the feast of w. and in the feast	De 16:16; 2Ch 8:13
us the appoined w. of the harvest	Jer 5:24
Seventy w. are determined upon	Da 9:24
the Prince shall be seven w.	Da 9:25
and threescore and two w.	Da 9:25
threescore and two w. shall Messiah	Da 9:26
Daniel was mourning three full w.	Da 10:2
till three whole w. were fulfilled	Da 10:3

WEEP

mourn for Sarah, and to w. for her	Ge 23:2
and he sought where to w.; and he	Ge 43:30
people w. throughout their families	Nu 11:10
for they w. unto me, saying, Give	Nu 11:13
What aileth the people that they w.	1Sa 11:5
until they had no more power to w.	1Sa 30:4
daughters of Israel, w. over Saul	2Sa 1:24
thou didst fast and w. for the child	2Sa 12:21
rend thy clothes, and w. before me	2Ch 34:27
Lord your God; mourn not, nor w.	Ne 8:9
death: and his widows shall not w.	Job 27:15

Did not I w. for him was in	Job 30:25
organ into the voice of them that w.	Job 30:31
A time to w. and a time to laugh	Ec 3:4
to Dibon, the high places, to w.	Isa 15:2
I will w. bitterly, labour not	Isa 22:4
thou shalt w. no more: he will	Isa 30:19
the ambassadors of peace shall w.	Isa 33:7
that I might w. day and night for	Jer 9:1
my soul shall w. in secret places	Jer 13:17
and mine eye shall w. sore	Jer 13:17
W. ye not for the dead, neither	Jer 22:10
w. sore for him that goeth away	Jer 22:10
will w. for thee with the weeping of	Jer 48:32
For these things I w.; mine eye	La 1:16
neither shalt thou mourn nor w.	Eze 24:16
ye shall not mourn nor w. but ye	Eze 24:23
shall w. for thee with bitterness	Eze 27:31
Awake, ye drunkards, and w.	Joe 1:5
w. between the porch and the altar	Joe 2:17
ye it not at Gath, w. ye not at all	Mic 1:10
Should I w. in the fifth month	Zec 7:3
Why make ye this ado, and w.	M't 5:39
Blessed are ye that w. now: for ye	Lu 6:21
now! for ye shall mourn and w.	Lu 6:25
on her, and said unto her, W. not	Lu 7:13
he said, W. not; she is not dead	Lu 8:52
Daughters of Jerusalem, w. not for	Lu 23:28
but w. for yourselves, and for your	Lu 23:28
She goeth unto the grave to w.	Joh 11:31
you, That ye shall w. and lament	Joh 16:20
What meant ye to w. and to break	Ac 21:13
rejoice, and w. with them that w.	Ro 12:15
they that w. as though they wept	1Co 7:30
Be afflicted, and mourn, and w.	Jas 4:9
w. and howl for your miseries that	Jas 5:1
W. not: behold, the Lion of the tribe	Re 5:5
merchants of the earth shall w.	Re 18:11

WEEPEST

to her, Hannah, why w. thou	1Sa 1:8
unto her, Woman, why w. thou	Joh 20:13; 20:15

WEEPETH

w. and mourneth for Absalom	2Sa 19:1
And Hazael said, Why w. my lord	2Ki 8:12
He that goeth forth and w. bearing	Ps 126:6
She w. sore in the night, and her	La 1:2

WEEPING

were w. before the door of the	Nu 25:6
days of w. and mourning for Moses	De 34:8
husband went with her along w.	2Sa 3:16
they went up, w. as they went up	2Sa 15:30
the noise of the w. of the people	Ezr 3:13
w. and casting himself down	Ezr 10:1
and fasting, and w. and wailing	Es 4:3
My face is foul with w. and on my	Job 16:16

red, swollen with w.   *Job 16:16*
(A)(B)(E)(R)
Lord hath heard the voice of   *Ps 6:8*
my w.
w. may endure for a night, but   *Ps 30:5*
joy
and mingled my drink with   *Ps 102:9*
w.
one shall howl, w. abundantly   *Isa 15:3*
Luhith with w. shall they go it   *Isa 15:5*
up
I will bewail with the w. of   *Isa 16:9*
Jazer
did the Lord God of hosts   *Isa 22:12*
call to w.
voice of w. shall be no more   *Isa 65:19*
heard
w. and supplications of the   *Jer 3:21*
will I take up a w. and   *Jer 9:10*
wailing
They shall come with w. and   *Jer 31:9*
with
Ramah, lamentation, and   *Jer 31:15*
bitter w.
Rahel w. for her children   *Jer 31:15*
refused
Refrain thy voice from w. and   *Jer 31:16*
them, w. all along as he went   *Jer 41:6*
Luhith continual w. shall go   *Jer 48:5*
up
weep for thee with the w. of   *Jer 48:32*
Jazer
of Judah together, going and   *Jer 50:4*
w.
there sat women w. for   *Eze 8:14*
Tammuz
fasting, and with w. and with   *Joe 2:12*
with tears, with w. and with   *Mal 2:13*
crying
lamentation, and w. and great   *M't 2:18*
Rachel w. for her children   *M't 2:18*
shall be w. and gnashing of   *M't 8:12;*
teeth   *22:13; 24:51; 25:30;*
bedlam, loud w. (B)   *M'k 5:38*
stood at his feet behind him   *Lu 7:38*
w.
When Jesus therefore saw   *Joh 11:33*
her w.
Jews also w. which came   *Joh 11:33*
with her
be w. and moaning (B)   *Joh 16:20*
stood without at the   *Joh 20:11*
sepulchre w.
and all the widows stood by   *Ac 9:39*
him w.
often, and now tell you even   *Ph'p 3:18*
w.
fear of her torment, w. and   *Re 18:15*
wailing
w. and wailing, saying, Alas,   *Re 18:19*
alas

WEIGH

and found it to w. a talent of   *1Co 20:2*
gold
ye w. them before the chief of   *Ezr 8:29*
the
ye w. the violence of your hands   *Ps 58:2*
the
deal out violence (A)(B)(R)   *Ps 58:2*
dost w. the path of the just   *Isa 26:7*
direct, make level the path   *Isa 26:7*
(A)
smooth the path (B)(R)   *Isa 26:7*
w. silver in the balance, and   *Isa 46:6*
hire
then take thee balances to w.   *Eze 5:1*

WEIGHED

Abraham w. to Ephron the   *Ge 23:16*
silver
all the silver vessels w. two   *Nu 7:85*
thousand
and by him actions are w.   *1Sa 2:3*
spear's head w. six hundred   *1Sa 17:7*
shekel
he w. the hair of his head at   *2Sa 14:26*
two
spear w. three hundred   *2Sa 21:16*
shekels
And w. unto them the silver   *Ezr 8:25*
I even w. unto their hand six   *Ezr 8:26*
the vessels w. in the house of   *Ezr 8:33*
our
that my grief were throughly w.   *Job 6:2*
vexation was w.   *Job 6:2*
(A)(B)(E)(R)
silver be w. for the price   *Job 28:15*
thereof

Let me be w. in an even   *Job 31:6*
balance
and w. the mountains in   *Isa 40:12*
scales
w. him the money, even   *Jer 32:9*
seventeen
w. him the money in the   *Jer 32:10*
balances
Thou art w. in the balances   *Da 5:27*
they w. for my price thirty   *Zec 11:12*
pieces
hearts be w. down (R)   *Lu 21:34*

WEIGHETH

he w. the waters by measure   *Job 28:25*
eyes; but the Lord w. the   *Pr 16:2*
spirits
w. the hearts (S)   *Pr 21:2; 24:12*

WEIGHING

charges of silver w. an hundred   *Nu 7:85*
full of incense, w. ten shekels   *Nu 7:86*
apiece

WEIGHT

golden earring of half a   *Ge 24:22*
shekel w.
her hands of ten shekels w.   *Ge 24:22*
of gold
of his sack, our money in   *Ge 43:21*
full w.
of each shall there be a like   *Ex 30:34*
w.
in meteyard, in w. or in   *Le 19:35*
measure
deliver you your bread again   *Le 26:26*
by w.
w. whereof was an   *Nu 7:13;*
hundred   *7:19, 25, 61, 67, 73, 79*
charger of the w. of an   *Nu 7:31;*
hundred   *7:43, 55*
w. whereof was an hundred   *Nu 7:37;*
   7:49
bear alone the w. (R)(S)   *De 1:12*
shalt have a perfect and just   *De 25:15*
w.
wedge of gold of fifty shekels   *Jos 7:21*
w.
w. of the golden earrings that   *J'g 8:26*
he
w. of the coat was five   *1Sa 17:5*
thousand
the w. thereof was a talent   *2Sa 12:30*
of gold
hundred shekels after the   *2Sa 14:26*
king's w.
the w. of whose spear   *2Sa 21:16*
weighed
hundred shekels of brass in   *2Sa 21:16*
w.
neither was the w. of the   *1Ki 7:47*
brass
Now the w. of gold that   *1Ki 10:14*
came to
of all these vessels was   *2Ki 25:16*
without w.
six hundred shekels of gold   *1Ch 21:25*
by w.
brass in abundance without   *1Ch 22:3*
w.
and of brass and iron   *1Ch 22:14*
without w.
of gold by w. for things of   *1Ch 28:14*
gold, for
for all instruments of silver   *1Ch 28:14*
by w.
Even the w. for the   *1Ch 28:15*
candlesticks of
of gold, by w. for every   *1Ch 28:15*
candlestick
for the candlesticks of silver   *1Ch 28:15*
by w.
by w. he gave gold for the   *1Ch 28:16*
tables of
he gave gold by w. for every   *1Ch 28:17*
bason
silver by w. for every bason   *1Ch 28:17*
of
altar of incense refined gold   *1Ch 28:18*
by w.
And the w. of the nails was   *2Ch 3:9*
fifty
for the w. of the brass could   *2Ch 4:18*
not be
Now the w. of gold that   *2Ch 9:13*
came to
and the Levites the w. of the   *Ezr 8:30*
silver

By number and by w. of   *Ezr 8:34*
every one
and all the w. was written at   *Ezr 8:34*
that
To make the w. for the   *Job 28:25*
winds, and
Lord: but a just w. is his   *Pr 11:1*
delight
A just w. and balance are the   *Pr 16:11*
all these vessels was without   *Jer 52:20*
w.
thou shalt eat shall be by w.   *Eze 4:10*
and they shall eat bread by   *Eze 4:16*
w.
he cast the w. of lead upon the   *Zec 5:8*
aloes, about an hundred   *Joh 19:39*
pound w.
exceeding and eternal w. of   *2Co 4:17*
glory
let us lay aside every w. and   *Heb 12:1*
every stone about the w. of a   *Re 16:21*
talent

WEIGHTIER

omitted the w. matters of   *M't 23:23*
the law

WEIGHTS

Just balances, just w., a just   *Le 19:36*
shalt not have in thy bag   *De 25:13*
divers w.
all the w. of the bag are his   *Pr 16:11*
work
Divers w. and divers   *Pr 20:10*
measures
Divers w. are an abomination   *Pr 20:23*
unto
and with the bag of deceitful   *Mic 6:11*
w.
with deceitful w. (E)   *Mic 6:11*

WEIGHTY

A stone is heavy, and the   *Pr 27:3*
sand w.
his letters, say they, are w.   *2Co 10:10*

WELCOME

w. trials as friends (P)   *Jas 1:2*

WELDED

w. together in love (B)   *Col 2:2*

WELFARE

he asked them of their w.   *Ge 43:27*
they asked each other of their   *Ex 18:7*
w.
to king David, to enquire of   *1Ch 1:10*
his w.
the w. of the children of Israel   *Ne 2:10*
seeking the w. of his people   *Es 10:3*
(S)
my w. passeth away as a   *Job 30:15*
cloud
should have been for their w.   *Ps 69:22*
prosperity and w. are (A)   *Ps 112:3*
seeketh not the w. of this   *Jer 38:4*
people

WELL

If thou doest w. shalt thou not   *Ge 4:7*
be
if thou doest right (B)   *Ge 4:7*
if thou doest not w. sin lieth at   *Ge 4:7*
it may be w. with me for thy   *Ge 12:13*
sake
And he entreated Abram w.   *Ge 12:16*
for her
of Jordan, that it was w.   *Ge 13:10*
watered
the w. was called   *Ge 16:14*
Beer-lahai-roi
were old and w. stricken in   *Ge 18:11*
age
her eyes, and she saw a w.   *Ge 21:19*
of water
Abimelech because of a w. of   *Ge 21:25*
water
unto me, that I have digged   *Ge 21:30*
this w.
by a w. of water at the time   *Ge 24:11*
of the
I stand here by the w. of   *Ge 24:13*
water

she went down to the w. and filled — Ge 24:16
and ran again unto the w. to draw — Ge 24:20
ran out unto the man, unto the w. — Ge 24:29
he stood by the camels at the w. — Ge 24:30
And I came this day unto the w. — Ge 24:42
Behold, I stand by the w. of water — Ge 24:43
she went down unto the w. — Ge 24:45
from the way of the w. Lahai-roi — Ge 24:62
Isaac dwelt by the w. Lahai-roi — Ge 25:11
and found there a w. of springing — Ge 26:19
he called the name of the w. Esek — Ge 26:20
they digged another w. and strove — Ge 26:21
digged another w.; and for that they — Ge 26:22
there Isaac's servants digged a w. — Ge 26:25
told him concerning the w. — Ge 26:32
looked, and behold a w. in the field — Ge 29:2
for out of that w. they watered the — Ge 29:2
And he said unto them, Is he w. — Ge 29:6
And they said, He is w. and — Ge 29:6
was beautiful and w. favoured — Ge 29:17
beautiful and attractive (A) — Ge 29:17
lovely of form and face (B) — Ge 29:17
beautiful and well favored (E) — Ge 29:17
beautiful and lovely (R) — Ge 29:17
and I will deal w. with thee — Ge 32:9
I will do thee good (A)(E)(R) — Ge 32:9
I will treat you kindly (B) — Ge 32:9
see whether it be w. with thy — Ge 37:14
w. with the flocks; and bring me — Ge 37:14
a goodly person, and w. favoured — Ge 39:6
think on me when it shall be w. — Ge 40:14
the river seven w. favoured kine — Ge 41:2
the seven w. favoured and fat kine — Ge 41:4
kine. fatfleshed and w. favoured — Ge 41:18
Is your father w. the old man of — Ge 43:27
and it pleased Pharaoh w. and his — Ge 45:16
even a fruitful bough by a w. — Ge 49:22
God dealth w. with the midwives — Ex 1:20
Midian: and he sat down by a w. — Ex 2:15
brother? I know that he can speak w. — Ex 4:14
Thou has spoken w. I will see thy — Ex 10:29
as w. the stranger, as he that is born — Le 24:16
w. the stranger, as for one of your — Le 24:22
for it was w. with us in Egypt — Nu 11:18
it; for we are w. able to overcome it — Nu 13:30
the w. whereof the Lord spake unto — Nu 21:16
Spring up, O w.; sing ye unto it — Nu 21:17
The princes digged the w. the — Nu 21:18
not drink of the waters of the w. — Nu 21:22
of the sons of Joseph hath said w. — Nu 36:5
shall hear the small as w. as the great — De 1:17
And the saying pleased me w. — De 1:23
unto your brethren, as w. as unto you — De 3:20
that it may go w. with thee. and — De 4:40
maidservant may rest as w. as thou — De 5:14
that it may go w. with thee, in — De 5:16; 12:25, 28

w. said, all that they have spoken — De 5:28
that it might be w. with them — De 5:29
and that it may be w. with you — De 5:33
that it may be w. with thee, and — De 6:3; 6:18
shalt w. remember what the Lord — De 7:18
house, because he is w. with thee — De 15:16
They have w. spoken that which — De 18:17
Israel, that it may go w. with thee — De 19:13
his brethren's heart faint as w. as — De 20:8
that it may be w. with thee, and — De 22:7
w.-bred, delicately bred (A)(R) — De 28:54
of the Lord, as w. the stranger — Jos 8:33
to the w. of waters of Nephtoah — Jos 18:15
and pitched beside the w. of Harod — J'g 7:1
if ye have dealt w. with Jerubbaal — J'g 9:16
for me; for she pleaseth me w. — J'g 14:3
and she pleased Samson w. — J'g 14:7
sword, as w. the men of every city — J'g 20:48
thee, that it may be w. with thee — Ru 3:1
thee the part of a kinsman w. — Ru 3:13
said Saul to his servant, W. said — 1Sa 9:10
with his hand, and thou shalt be w. — 1Sa 16:16
me now that a man can play w. — 1Sa 16:17
so Saul was refreshed, and was w. — 1Sa 16:23
it pleased David w. to be the — 1Sa 18:26
came to a great w. that is in Sechu — 1Sa 19:22
If he say thus, It is w.; thy servant — 1Sa 20:7
that thou hast dealt w. with me — 1Sa 24:18
enemy, will he let him go w. — 1Sa 24:19
away
I know w. thou shalt surely be kin — 1Sa 24:20
shall have dealt w. with my lord — 1Sa 25:31
he said, W.; I will make a league — 2Sa 3:13
him again from the w. of Sirah — 2Sa 3:26
Israel, as w. to the women as men — 2Sa 6:19
devoureth one as w. as another — 2Sa 11:25
the saying pleased Absalom w. — 2Sa 17:4
which had a w. in his court — 2Sa 17:18
that they came out of the w. — 2Sa 17:21
and said unto the king, All is w. — 2Sa 18:28
then it had pleased thee w. — 2Sa 19:6
is all w. with you (A)(B)(E)(R) — 2Sa 20:9
the water of the w. of Beth-lehem — 2Sa 23:15; 1Ch 11:17
water out of the w. of Beth-lehem — 2Sa 23:16; 1Ch 11:18
W.; I will speak for thee unto the — 1Ki 2:18
thou didst w. that it was in thine — 1Ki 8:18
answered and said, It is w. spoken — 1Ki 18:24
And she said, It shall be w. — 2Ki 4:23
and say unto her, It is w. with thee — 2Ki 4:26
it is w. with thy husband — 2Ki 4:26
is it w. with the child — 2Ki 4:26
And she answered, It is w. — 2Ki 4:26
to met him, and said, Is all w. — 2Ki 5:21
And he said, All is w. My master — 2Ki 5:22
said one to another, We do not w. — 2Ki 7:9
and one said unto him, Is all w. — 2Ki 9:11
thou hast done w. in executing — 2Ki 10:30

out of his own w. (B) — 2Ki 18:31
and it shall be w. with you — 2Ki 25:24
ward, as w. the small as the great — 1Ch 25:8
cast lots, as w. the small as the great — 1Ch 26:13
thou didst w. in that it was in — 2Ch 6:8
and also in Judah things went w. — 2Ch 12:12
as w. to the great as to the small — 2Ch 31:15
even before the dragon w. and to — Ne 2:13
I have understanding as w. as you — Job 12:3
Mark w., O Job, hearken unto me — Job 33:31
Mark ye w. her bulwarks — Ps 48:13
when thou doest w. to thyself — Ps 49:18
gone; my steps had w. nigh slipped — Ps 73:2
So they did eat, and were w. filled — Ps 78:29
the valley of Baca make it a w. — Ps 84:6
As w. the singers as the players on — Ps 87:7
Thou hast dealt w. with thy — Ps 119:65
be, and it shall be w. with thee — Ps 128:2
and that my soul knoweth right w. — Ps 139:14
running waters out of thine own w. — Pr 5:15
of a righteous man is a w. of life — Pr 10:11
a fountain of life (B) — Pr 10:11
When it goeth w. with the — Pr 11:10
but with the w. advised is wisdom — Pr 13:10
the prudent man looketh w. to his — Pr 14:15
I saw, and considered it w.: I looked — Pr 24:32
flocks, and look w. to thy herds — Pr 27:23
There be three things which go w. — Pr 30:29
She looketh w. to the ways of her — Pr 31:27
be w. with them that fear God — Es 8:12
it shall not be w. with the wicked — Es 8:13
of gardens, a w. of living waters — Ca 4:15
Learn to do w.; seek judgment — Isa 1:17
learn to do right (A) — Isa 1:17
learn to do good (R) — Isa 1:17
that it shall be w. with him — Isa 3:10
instead of w. set hair baldness — Isa 3:24
of wines on the lees w. refined — Isa 25:6
not w. strengthen their mast — Isa 33:23
w. pleased for his righteousness — Isa 42:21
Lord unto me, Thou hast w. seen — Jer 1:12
you, that it may be w. unto you — Jer 7:23
Verily it shall be w. with thy — Jer 15:11
to entreat thee w. in the time of evil — Jer 15:11
and then it was w. with him — Jer 22:15
needy: then it was w. with him — Jer 22:16
so it shall be w. unto thee, and thy — Jer 38:20
take him, and look w. to him — Jer 39:12
and I will look w. unto thee — Jer 40:4
and it shall be w. with you — Jer 40:9
that it may be w. with us, when we — Jer 42:6
we plenty of victuals, and were w. — Jer 44:17
under it, and make it boil w. — Eze 24:5
consume the flesh, and spice it w. — Eze 24:10
and can play w. on an instrument — Eze 33:32
Son of man, mark w. and — Eze 44:5
mark w. the entering in of — Eze 44:5
shall inherit it, one as w. as another — Eze 47:14
was no blemish, but w. favoured — Da 1:4
the image which I have made w. — Da 3:15
Lord, Doest thou w. to be angry — Jon 4:4
thou w. to be angry for the gourd — Jon 4:9

he said, I do w. to be angry,   *Jon 4:9*
even

I thought in these days to do   *Zec 8:15*
w.

Son, in whom I am w.   *M't 3:17;*
pleased   *17:5; M'k 1:11*

well (S)   *M't 9:12;*
9:21, 22; 12:13; 14:36; 15:28, 31;
M'k 2:17; 5:28, 34; 6:56; 10:52; Lu 5:31;
6:10; 7:10; 8:48, 50; 17:19; Joh 5:4, 6, 9,
11, 14-15; Ac 4:9, 10; 9:34

is lawful to do w. on the   *M't 12:12*
sabbath

in whom my soul is w.   *M't 12:18*
pleased

w. did Esaias prophesy of   *M't 15:7*
you

W. done, thou good and   *M't 25:21*
faithful

him, W. done, good and   *M't 25:23*
faithful

W. hath Esaias prophesied of   *M'k 7:6*

Full w. ye reject the   *M'k 7:9*
commandment

He hath done all things w.   *M'k 7:37*

that he had answered them   *M'k 12:28*
w.

W., Master, thou hast said   *M'k 12:32*

were now w. stricken in years   *Lu 1:7*

and my wife w. stricken in   *Lu 1:18*
years

Son; in thee I am w. pleased   *Lu 3:22*

all men shall speak w. of you   *Lu 6:26*

And if it bear fruit, w.; and if   *Lu 13:9*
not, then

safe and w. (A)(B)   *Lu 15:27*

unto him, W. thou good   *Lu 19:17*
servant

said, Master, thou hast w.   *Lu 20:39*
said

and when men have w. drunk   *Joh 2:10*

when men have drunken freely   *Joh 2:10*
(A)(B)(E)(N)(R)

when men have had plenty to   *Joh 2:10*
drink (P)

Now Jacob's w. was there   *Joh 4:6*

his journey, sat thus on the w.   *Joh 4:6*

to draw with, and the w. is   *Joh 4:11*
deep

father Jacob, which gave us   *Joh 4:12*
the w.

a w. of water springing up   *Joh 4:14*
into

spring of water (A)(P)(R)   *Joh 4:14*

an inner spring (N)   *Joh 4:14*

Thou hast w. said, I have no   *Joh 4:17*

Say we not w. that thou art a   *Joh 8:48*

Lord, if he sleep, he shall do   *Joh 11:12*
w.

Master and Lord: and ye say   *Joh 13:13*
w.

but if w. why smitest thou   *Joh 18:23*
me

thou hast w. done that thou   *Ac 10:33*
art

the Holy Ghost as w. as we   *Ac 10:47*

ye shall do w. Fare ye w.   *Ac 15:29*

was w. reported of by the   *Ac 16:2*
brethren

wrong, as thou very w.   *Ac 25:10*
knowest

W. spake the Holy Ghost by   *Ac 28:25*

by patient continuance in w.   *Ro 2:7*
doing

W.; because of unbelief they   *Ro 11:20*

he will keep his virgin, doeth   *1Co 7:37*
w.

giveth her in marriage doeth   *1Co 7:38*
w.

a wife, as w. as other apostles   *1Co 9:5*

of them God was not w.   *1Co 10:5*
pleased

For thou verily givest   *1Co 14:17*
thanks w.

As unknown, and yet w.   *2Co 6:9*
known

ye might w. bear with him   *2Co 11:4*

if you behave w. (B)   *2Co 13:7*

zealously affect you, but not w.   *Ga 4:17*

Ye did run w.; who did hinder   *Ga 5:7*
you

let us not be weary in w. doing   *Ga 6:9*

acting nobly and doing right   *Ga 6:9*
(A)

what is right (B)   *Ga 6:9;*
  1Pe 2:20; 3:6, 17; 4:19

doing good (N)(P)   *Ga 6:9; 1Pe 4:19*

That it may be w. with thee   *Eph 6:3*

Notwithstanding ye have w.   *Ph'p 4:14*
done

do right (N)(R)   *Ph'p 4:14*

this is w. pleasing unto the   *Col 3:20*
Lord

be not weary in w. doing   *2Th 3:13*

One that ruleth w. his own   *1Ti 3:4*
house

children and their own houses   *1Ti 3:12*
w.

used the office of a deacon w.   *1Ti 3:13*

W. reported of for good   *1Ti 5:10*
works; if

the elders that rule w. be   *1Ti 5:17*
counted

a w.-balanced mind (A)   *2Ti 1:7*

me at Ephesus, thou knowest   *2Ti 1:18*
very w.

please them w. in all things   *Tit 2:9*

preached, as w. a unto them   *Heb 4:2*

such sacrifices God is w.   *Heb 13:16*
pleased

thy neighbour as thyself, ye do   *Jas 2:8*
w.

there is one God; thou doest   *Jas 2:19*
w.

for the praise of them that   *1Pe 2:14*
do w.

that with w. doing ye may put   *1Pe 2:15*
to

by doing right (A)(R)   *1Pe 2:15;*
  2:20; 3:6, 17; 4:19

your good conduct (N)   *1Pe 2:15*

how well you conduct   *1Pe 2:15*
yourselves (P)

when ye do w. and suffer for   *1Pe 2:20*
it, ye

ye are as long as ye do w. and   *1Pe 3:6*

ye suffer for w. doing, than   *1Pe 3:17*
for evil

of their souls to him in w.   *1Pe 4:19*
doing

Son, in whom I am w.   *2Pe 1:17*
pleased

ye do w. that ye take heed, as   *2Pe 1:19*
unto

after a godly sort, thou shalt do   *3Jo 6*
w.

WELLBELOVED

A bundle of myrrh is my w.   *Ca 1:13*

my beloved (A)(E)   *Ca 1:13; Ro 16:5*

my beloved one (B)   *Ca 1:13; Isa 5:1*

my beloved (R)   *Ca 1:13;*
  Isa 5:1; Ro 16:5

Now will I sing to my w. a   *Ca 5:1*
song of

My w. hath a vineyard in a   *Ca 5:1*
very

my greatly beloved (A)   *Ca 5:1*

yet therefore one son, his w.   *M'k 12:6*

a beloved son (A)(E)(R)   *M'k 12:6*

dearly loved one (B)   *M'k 12:6*

his own dear one (N)   *M'k 12:6*

Salute my w. Epaenetus, who   *Ro 16:5*
is the

w.-beloved children (A)   *Eph 5:1*

The elder unto the w. Gaius   *3Jo 1*

The esteemed (B)   *3Jo 1*

the beloved (E)(R)   *3Jo 1*

WELL-FAVORED

be a w. vine (S)   *Eze 17:8; 17:23*

WELLFAVOURED

whoredoms of the w. harlot   *Na 3:4*

WELLPLEASING

a sacrifice acceptable, w. to   *Ph'p 4:18*
God

you that which is w. in his   *Heb 13:21*
sight

WELLS

the w. which his father's   *Ge 26:15*
servants

Isaac digged again the w. of   *Ge 26:18*
water

where were twelve w. of   *Ex 15:27*
water

we drink of the water of the   *Nu 20:17*
w.

w. digged, which thou diggest   *De 6:11*
not

and stop all w. of water, and   *2Ki 3:19*

they stopped all the w. of   *2Ki 3:25*
water

the desert, and digged many   *2Ch 26:10*

w. digged, vineyards and   *Ne 9:25*

water out of the w. of   *Isa 12:3*
salvation

came to the w. (B)   *Jer 14:3*

These are w. without water   *2Pe 2:17*

WELL'S

great stone was upon the w.   *Ge 29:2*
mouth

rolled the stone from the w.   *Ge 29:3*
mouth

the stone again upon the w.   *Ge 29:3;*
mouth   *29:10*

roll the stone from the w.   *Ge 29:8*
mouth

a covering over the w.   *2Sa 17:19*
mouth

WELLSPRING

Understanding is a w. of life   *Pr 16:22*
unto

fountain of life (B)(R)   *Pr 16:22*

and the w. of wisdom as a   *Pr 18:4*
flowing

fountain of wisdom   *Pr 18:4*
(A)(B)(R)

WELTERING

w. in your blood (B)(E)(R)   *Eze 16:6*

WELTS

bruises, w., and raw wounds   *Isc 1:6*
(B)(R)

WEN

maimed, or having a w. or   *Le 22:22*
scurvy

having infected sores (B)   *Le 22:22*

having a discharge (R)   *Le 22:22*

WENCH

and a w. went and told them   *2Sa 17:17*

a maidservant (A)(E)(R)   *2Sa 17:17*

a servant girl (B)   *2Sa 17:17*

WENT

the Lord was with me in the   *Ge 35:3*
way I w.

in the first place w. standard   *Nu 10:14*
of Judah

went (S)   *Nu 11:30;*
J'g 9:48, 51; 19:28; 1Sa 24:22; 2Sa 4:7;
  17:23

him will I bring into land   *Nu 14:24*
whereto he w.

God's anger was kindled   *Nu 22:22*
because Balaam w.

Balaam w. not to seek for   *Nu 24:1*
enchantments

Phinehas w. after the man of   *Nu 25:8*
Israel

God bare thee in all the way   *De 1:31*
ye w.

w. to the children of Machir   *Jos 13:31*
(S)

he preserved us in all the   *Jos 24:17*
way we w.

so Simeon w. with Judah   *J'g 1:3*

Judah w. with Simeon his   *J'g 1:17*
brother

Samson's strength w. from   *J'g 16:19*
him

Saul's uncle said, Whither w.   *1Sa 10:14*
ye

there w. with Saul a band of   *1Sa 10:26*
men

man w. for an old man in   *1Sa 17:12*
days of Saul

but David w. to feed his   *1Sa 17:15*
father's sheep

David and men w. wherever   *1Sa 23:13*
they could

as long as we w. with them   *1Sa 25:15*
(S)

because they w. not with us,   *1Sa 30:22*
will not give

how w. the matter? I pray   *2Sa 1:4*
thee tell me

as he w. to recover his border   *2Sa 8:3;*
  1Ch 18:3

Lord preserved David   *2Sa 8:6;*
whithersoever he w.   *8:14; 1Ch 18:6, 13*

w. in their simplicity and 2Sa 15:11
knew nothing

as he *w.* thus he said, O my 2Sa 18:33
son Absalom

Solomon *w.* not fully after 1Ki 11:6
the Lord

and their father said, What 1Ki 13:12
way *w.* he

he *w.* after the man of God 1Ki 13:14
and found him

which way *w.* the Spirit 1Ki 13:22;
of the Lord 13:24; 2Ch 18:23

they *w.* not; they two *w.* on 1Ki 13:48;
2Ki 2:6

w. not my heart with thee 2Ki 5:26

he *w.* with them, they cut 2Ki 6:4
down wood

carried thence and *w.* and 2Ki 7:8
hid it

when he *w.* into his wife 1Ch 7:23

they *w.* from nation to 1Ch 16:20;
nation, kingdom to another Ps 105:13
people

so all Israel *w.* to their tents 2Ch 10:16

and also in Judah things *w.* 2Ch 12:12
well

people *w.* to house of Baal 2Ch 23:17
and brake

the rulers knew not whither I Ne 2:16
w.

in evening she *w.*, on morrow Es 2:14

I *w.* with them to the house of Ps 42:4
God

it *w.* ill with Moses for their Ps 106:32
sakes

a young man *w.* the way to her Pr 7:8
house

he *w.* on frowardly in way of Isa 57:17
his heart

they *w.* every one straight Eze 1:9
forward

they turned not when they *w.* Eze 1:12;
10:11

they *w.* on their four sides and Eze 1:17
returned

when those *w.* these *w.* those Eze 1:21
stood

for their heart *w.* after their Eze 20:16
idols

sleep *w.* from him (S) Da 2:1

she *w.* after her lovers and Ho 2:13
forgat

then *w.* Ephraim to the Ho 5:13
Assyrian

they *w.* to Baal-peor and Ho 9:10
separated

as they called them, so they *w.* Ho 11:2
from them

before him *w.* pestilence, Hab 3:5
burning coals

at the light of thine arrows, Hab 3:11
they *w.*

but afterwards he repented M't 21:29
and *w.*

he answered and said, I go, M't 21:30
sir, but *w.* not

while they *w.* to buy, the M't 25:10
bridegroom

they left their father and *w.* M'k 1:20
after him

w. to be taxed, every one of his Lu 2:3
city

but if one *w.* to them from Lu 16:30
the dead

that as they *w.* they were Lu 17:14
cleansed

Joseph *w.* to Pilate and Lu 23:52
begged body of

the Galileans also *w.* to the Joh 4:45
feast

every man *w.* to his own Joh 7:53
house

I *w.* and washed and I Joh 9:11
received sight

that he was come from God Joh 13:3
and *w.* to God

they *w.* backward and fell to Joh 18:6
the ground

then *w.* this saying among Joh 21:23
the brethren

w. every where preaching the Ac 8:4
word

Saul threatening *w.* unto the Ac 9:1
high priest

w. on their journey, Peter *w.* Ac 10:9
to pray

they *w.* both into synagogue Ac 14:1
of the Jews

and *w.* not with them to the Ac 15:38
work

as we *w.* to prayer, a damsel Ac 16:16
met us

as I *w.* to Damascus with Ac 26:12
authority

he *w.* preach, to spirits in 1Pe 3:19
prison

WENT *ABOUT*

the people *w.* about and Nu 11:8
gathered it

slingers *w.* about it and 2Ki 3:25
smote it

they *w.* about and taught the 2Ch 17:9
people

I *w.* about to cause my heart Ec 2:20
despair

the watchmen that *w.* about Ca 5:7
found me

Jesus *w.* about teaching M't 4:23
9:35; M'k 6:6

they *w.* about to slay him Ac 9:29;
21:31; 26:21

Jesus *w.* about doing good Ac 10:38
and healing

he *w.* about seeking some to Ac 13:11
lead him

WENT *ASIDE*

Jesus took them and *w.* aside Lu 9:10
privately

the chief captain *w.* aside Ac 23:19
privately

WENT *ASTRAY*

before I was afflicted I *w.* Ps 119:67
astray

when Israel *w.* astray after Eze 44:10;
idols 44:15

for the priests which *w.* not Eze 48:11
astray when Israel *w.* astray

as Levites *w.* astray

than of ninety-nine which *w.* M't 18:13
not astray

WENT *AWAY*

Samson *w.* away with doors J'g 16:3
of gates

and *w.* away with the pin of J'g 16:14
the beam

and his concubine *w.* away J'g 19:2
from him

mule that was under him *w.* 2Sa 18:9
away

Naaman was wroth, and 2Ki 5:11
w. away

queen of Sheba *w.* away to 2Ch 9:12
her land

he *w.* away sorrowful M't 19:22;
M'k 10:22

he *w.* away the second time M't 26:42
and prayed

he *w.* away the third time M't 26:44;
M'k 14:39

by reason of him many *w.* Joh 12:11
away

the disciples *w.* away to their Joh 20:10
own home

on the morrow Peter *w.* away Ac 10:23

WENT *BACK*

so he *w.* back and did eat 1Ki 13:19
and drink

king Joram *w.* back to be 2Ki 8:29
healed

from that time many disciples Joh 6:66
w. back

WENT *BEFORE*

Lord *w.* before them in a Ex 13:21
cloud

angel of God which *w.* before Ex 14:19
the camp

ark of covenant *w.* before Nu 10:33;
Jos 3:6

armed men *w.* before the Jos 6:9;
priests 6:13

one bearing a shield *w.* 1Sa 17:7;
before him 17:41

and Ahio *w.* before the ark 2Sa 6:4

Shobach *w.* before them 2Sa 10:16;
1Ch 19:16

when at Gibeon, Amasa *w.* 2Sa 20:8
before them

as they that *w.* before were Job 18:20
affrighted

the singers *w.* before the Ps 68:25
players

star which they saw *w.* before M't 2:9
them

multitudes *w.* before them M't 21:9;
cried, Hosanna to the son M'k 11:9
of David

they which *w.* before rebuked Lu 18:39

Judas *w.* before and drew Lu 22:47
near to kiss him

according to the prophecies 1Ti 1:18
which *w.* before

WENT *BEHIND*

the angel removed and *w.* Ex 14:19
behind

WENT *DOWN*

Abram *w.* down into Egypt to Ge 12:10
sojourn

when sun *w.* down, a Ge 15:17;
smoking furnace J'g 19:14; 2Sa 2:24
and burning lamp passed

brethren *w.* down; Benjamin Ge 42:3;
w. down 43:15

Moses *w.* down from the Ex 19:14;
mount and sanctified people 19:25;
32:15

w. down alive into the pit Nu 16:33

our fathers *w.* down and Nu 20:15;
dwelt a long time De 10:22; 26:5;
Jos 24:4

Israel *w.* down after Ehud J'g 3:27;
3:28

Barak *w.* down from mount J'g 4:14
Tabor

Gideon *w.* down with Phurah J'g 7:11
his servant

Samson *w.* down to Timnath J'g 14:1;
and saw a woman of the 14:5, 7

the men said to him before J'g 14:18
the sun *w.* down

Samson *w.* down to Ashkelon J'g 14:19
and slew thirty men

Ruth *w.* down unto the floor to Ru 3:6
Boaz

the Israelites *w.* down to 1Sa 13:20
sharpen

David's father's house *w.* 1Sa 22:1
down to him

David heard, and *w.* down to 2Sa 5:17
hold

Uriah *w.* not down to his 2Sa 11:9;
house 11:10, 13

a well in his court, whither 2Sa 17:18
they *w.* down

David *w.* down against the 2Sa 21:15
Philistines

three of thirty chief *w.* 2Sa 23:13;
down to David to cave 1Ch 11:15
of Adullam

Benaiah *w.* down and slew a 2Sa 23:20
lion in time of snow

Benaiah *w.* down to the 2Sa 23:21;
Egyptian, and slew him 1Ch 11:22, 23
with his own spear

Elijah *w.* down with him to 2Ki 1:15
the king

Elijah and Elisha *w.* down to 2Ki 2:2
Beth-el

Naaman *w.* down dipped 2Ki 5:14
himself in Jordan

Ahaziah *w.* down to see 2Ki 8:29;
Joram 2Ch 22:6

Jehoshaphat *w.* down to see 2Ch 18:2
Ahab

ointment that *w.* down to the Ps 133:2
skirts

I *w.* down into the garden of Ca 6:11
nuts

my people *w.* down aforetime Isa 52:4
into Egypt

then I *w.* down to the potter's Jer 18:3
house

in the day when he *w.* down Eze 31:15
to grave

they also *w.* down to hell Eze 31:17
with him

Jonah *w.* down to Joppa and Jon 1:3
found

I *w.* down to the bottoms of Jon 2:6
the mountains

this man *w.* down justified Lu 18:14
rather

an angel *w.* down and troubled Joh 5:4
the water

so Jacob w. down into Egypt Ac 7:15
and died
Philip w. down to Samaria, Ac 8:5
preached Christ
and they both w. down into Ac 8:38
the water
then Peter w. down to the Ac 10:21
men, and said
Herod w. down from Judaea Ac 12:19
to Caesarea
Paul w. down and embracing Ac 20:10
him

WENT FORTH

raven w. forth Ge 8:7
Noah w. forth and all out of Ge 8:18
ark
out of that land w. forth Ge 10:11
Ashur
w. forth from Ur Ge 11:31
they w. forth to go into land Ge 12:5
of Canaan
there w. forth a wind from the Nu 11:31
Lord
the princes w. forth to meet Nu 31:13;
them 33:1
trees w. forth to anoint a king J'g 9:8
over them
and he w. forth it fell out 2Sa 20:8
Elisha w. forth into the 2Ki 2:21
waters
he prospered whithersoever 2Ki 18:7
he w. forth
then w. Hanian forth that day Es 5:9
joyful
Satan w. forth from Job 1:12;
presence of Lord 2:7
angel of Lord w. forth and Isa 37:36
smote 185,000
the former things w. forth, Isa 48:3
I shewed them
Shallum who w. forth out of Jer 22:11
this place
thy renown w. forth among Eze 16:14
the heathen
her great scum w. not forth Eze 24:12
out of her
that which w. forth by an Am 5:3
hundred
burning coals w. forth at his Hab 3:5
feet
behold, a sower w. forth to M't 13:3
sow
ten virgins w. forth to meet M't 25:1
bridegroom
he arose and took up bed M'k 2:12
and w. forth
because for his name's sake 3Jo 7
they w. forth
he w. forth conquering and to Re 6:2
conquer

WENT HER WAY

woman w. her way and was no 1Sa 1:18
more sad
the woman of Samaria w. her Joh 4:28
way
when Martha had so said Joh 11:28
she w. her way

WENT HIS WAY

the Lord w. his way as soon Ge 18:33
as had
servant took Rebekah and w. Ge 24:61
his way
Esau did eat and drink and Ge 25:34
w. his way
Jethro w. his way into his Ex 18:27
own land
Balak; Saul w. his way Nu 24:25;
 1Sa 24:7
David w. on his way, Saul 1Sa 26:25
returned
every guest of Adonijah w. his 1Ki 1:49
way
Mordecai w. his way, did as Es 4:17
Esther commanded
the prophet Jeremiah w. his Jer 28:11
way
his enemy sowed tares and M't 13:25
w. his way
he passing thro' midst of Lu 4:30
them, w. his way
and w. his way and Lu 8:39
published great things
Judas w. his way and Lu 22:4
communed with priests

and the man believed, and Joh 4:50
w. his way
the eunuch w. on his way Ac 8:39
rejoicing
Ananias w. his way and Ac 9:17
entered the house

WENT IN, INTO

Noah w. into the ark and his Ge 7:7
sons with him
w. in two and two; w. in male Ge 7:9;
and female 7:16
the firstborn w. in and lay Ge 19:33
with her father
Joseph w. into the house to Ge 39:11
do business
Moses, Aaron w. in to Pharaoh Ex 5:1;
 7:10
w. into midst of sea on dry Ex 14:22
ground
the Egyptians w. in Ex 14:23;
after them 15:19
until Moses w. in to speak Ex 34:35
with him
when Aaron w. into the holy Le 16:23
place
the young men that were Jos 6:23
spies w. in
the haft also w. in after the J'g 3:22
blade
so the Levite w. in and dwelt J'g 17:10
with Micah
when the Levite w. in to J'g 19:15
lodge in Gibeah
Saul w. in to cover his feet 1Sa 24:3
then w. David in. before the 2Sa 7:18
Lord
Bath-sheba w. in unto the 1Ki 1:15
king
king of Israel disguised w. 1Ki 22:30
into the battle
Elisha w. in shut door and 2Ki 4:33
prayed
she w. in fell at his feet and 2Ki 4:37
took son
one w. in and told his lord 2Ki 5:4
Gehazi w. in and stood before 2Ki 5:25
his master
when they w. in to offer 2Ki 10:24
sacrifices
Uzziah w. into the temple 2Ch 26:16
of Lord
Azariah the priest w. in 2Ch 26:17
after him
so the children w. in and Ne 9:24
possessed
the king w. into the Es 7:7
palace-garden
until I w. into the sanctuary Ps 73:17
of God
Urijah fled and w. into Jer 26:21
Egypt
so I w. in; six men w. in Eze 8:10; 9:2
the man clothed with linen Eze 10:2;
w. in 10:3, 6
when they w. into captivity Eze 25:3
Israel w. into captivity for Eze 39:23
their iniquity
Daniel w. in and desired of the Da 2:16
king
to Arioch; he w. into his Da 2:24;
house to pray 6:10
the devils w. into the herd of M't 8:32
swine
a certain householder w. M't 21:33;
into a far country M'k 12:1; Lu 19:12;
 20:9
they that were ready w. in to M't 25:10
the marriage
w. into the holy city, and M't 27:53
appeared to many
David w. into the house of M'k 2:26;
God, did eat the shewbread Lu 6:4
Joseph w. in boldly to M'k 15:43
Pilate, craved body
Lot was to burn incense when Lu 1:9
he w. in
Mary arose and w. into the Lu 1:39
hill country
and he w. in to tarry with Lu 24:29
that disciple w. in with Jesus Joh 18:15
he saw linen clothes lying, Joh 20:5
yet w. not in
then w. in also that other Joh 20:8
disciple, and saw
all the time the Lord w. in and Ac 1:21
out

as Peter talked he w. in and Ac 10:27
found many
he departed and w. into Ac 12:17
another place
they w. into synagogue on Ac 13:14
the sabbath day
Paul w. into the synagogue Ac 17:2;
 17:10; 19:8
their sound w. into all the Ro 10:18
earth

WENT IN, UNTO A WOMAN

Abram w. in to Hagar, she Ge 16:4
conceived
Laban brought Leah to Ge 29:23
Jacob, he w. in to her
he w. in also unto Rachel Ge 29:30
w. in to Bilhah Ge 30:4
Judah saw Shuah and w. in Ge 38:2
to her
when Onan w. in to his Ge 38:9
brother's wife
Samson saw an harlot and w. J'g 16:1
in to her
Boaz w. in to Ruth, she Ru 4:13
conceived
David comforted Bath-sheba 2Sa 12:24
his wife, w. in unto her
Absalom w. in to his 2Sa 16:22
father's concubines
Ithra w. in to Abigail, 2Sa 17:25
Nahash's daughter
but David w. not in to them 2Sa 20:3
Hezron w. in to daughter of 1Ch 2:21
Machir
when Ephraim w. in to his 1Ch 7:23
wife, she conceived
yet they w. in unto her as a Eze 23:44
harlot

WENT OUT

Cain w. out from presence of Ge 4:16
Lord
Isaac w. out to meditate in Ge 24:63
the field
Dinah w. out to see daughters Ge 34:1
of land
Joseph washed his face and Ge 43:31
w. out
one w. out from me I saw Ge 44:28
him not since
Moses w. out to his brethren Ex 2:11;
 2:13
Aaron w. out from Pharaoh Ex 8:12;
 8:30; 9:33
all the hosts of the Lord w. Ex 12:41;
out 14:8
all the women w. out after Ex 15:20
Miriam
there w. out some people on Ex 16:27
sabbath day
Moses w. out to meet his Ex 18:7
father in law
every one w. out unto the Ex 33:7
tabernacle
there w. out fire from the Le 10:2
Lord
cloud was on them when Nu 10:34
they w. out
two men w. out into the Nu 11:26
tabernacle
Sihon w. out against Israel Nu 21:23
in wilderness
Og, the king of Bashan, Nu 21:33
w. out against them
behold, I w. out to Nu 22:32
withstand thee
none w. out, and none came in Jos 6:1
the men of Ai w. out against Jos 8:14;
Israel 8:17
the Canaanite w. out and all Jos 11:4
their hosts
they w. out, the Lord was J'g 2:15
against them
all that stood by him w. out J'g 3:19
from him
the master of the house w. J'g 19:23
out unto them
I w. out full and came home Ru 1:21
empty
ere the lamp of God w. out in 1Sa 3:3
the temple
I w. out after the bear, and 1Sa 17:35
smote him
David w. out where Saul 1Sa 18:5;
sent him 13:16; 19:8

at even he *w. out* to lie on   *2Sa 11:13*
his bed
they *w. out* every man from   *2Sa 13:9*
him
the day the king *w. out* of   *2Sa 19:19*
Jerusalem
they *w. out* at noon; *w. out*   *1Ki 20:16;*
first   *20:17*
the king of Israel *w. out* and   *1Ki 20:21*
smote the horses
the child *w. out* to his father   *2Ki 4:18*
to reapers
she went in and took up her   *2Ki 4:37*
son, and *w. out*
Gehazi *w. out* from his   *2Ki 5:27*
presence a leper
they *w. out* each in his   *2Ki 9:21*
chariot and met him
and the arrow *w. out* of   *2Ki 9:24*
Jehoram's heart
David *w. out* to meet them   *1Ch 12:17*
and said
David heard of it and *w. out*   *1Ch 14:8*
against them
Azariah *w. out* to meet Asa   *2Ch 15:2*
was no peace to him that *w.*   *2Ch 15:5*
out or came in
Jehu *w. out* to meet   *2Ch 19:2*
Jehoshaphat
be appointed singers to   *2Ch 20:21*
praise as they *w. out*
Josiah *w. out* against   *2Ch 35:20*
Pharaoh-necho
as the word *w. out* of the king's   *Es 7:8*
mouth
when I *w. out* to the gate   *Job 29:7*
thro' the city
fear terrify me, I *w.* not *out*   *Job 31:34*
at door
when he *w. out* thro' the land   *Ps 81:5*
of Egypt
Jeremiah *w. out* among people   *Jer 37:4*
took fire from the cherub and   *Eze 10:7*
w. out
the city that *w. out* by a   *Am 5:3*
thousand
neither any peace to him that   *Zec 8:10*
w. out
what *w.* ye *out* into the   *M't 11:7;*
wilderness to see   *11:8, 9; Lu 7:24-26*
a man who *w. out* early to   *M't 20:1*
hire labourers
he *w. out* at third hour;   *M't 20:3;*
sixth, eleventh   *20:5, 6*
those servants *w. out* into   *M't 22:10*
the highways
his friends *w. out* to lay hold   *M'k 3:21*
on him
the unclean spirits *w. out*   *M'k 5:13;*
and entered into the   *Lu 8:33; Ac 19:12*
swine
they *w. out* to see   *M'k 5:14; Lu 8:35*
for there *w.* virtue *out* of him   *Lu 6:19*
Peter *w. out* and wept   *Lu 22:62*
bitterly
they which heard it, *w. out*   *Joh 8:9*
one by one
Jesus hid himself and *w. out*   *Joh 8:59*
of the temple
Mary rose up hastily, and *w.*   *Joh 11:31*
out
Judas having received the   *Joh 13:30*
sop *w. out*
then *w. out* that other   *Joh 18:16*
disciple known to
all the time the Lord *w.* in   *Ac 1:21*
and *out*
certain *w. out* from us have   *Ac 15:24*
troubled you
Abraham *w. out*, not   *Heb 11:8*
knowing whither
they *w. out* from us, they *w.*   *1Jo 2:19*
out to be manifest that they

WENT OVER

there arose and *w. over* by   *2Sa 2:15*
number
they *w. over* Jordan before   *2Sa 19:17*
the king
Barzillai *w. over* Jordan   *2Sa 19:31*
with the king
so they two *w. over* on dry   *2Ki 2:8*
ground
Elisha smote the waters and   *2Ki 2:14*
w. over
these *w. over* Jordan when   *1Ch 12:15*
overflown
David's reign, and times   *1Ch 29:30*
that *w. over* him

other company *w. over*   *Ne 12:38*
against them
thy body as a street to them   *Isa 51:23*
that *w. over*

WENT THEIR WAY, WAYS

the children of Dan *w. their*   *J'g 18:26*
way
Amalekites burnt Ziklag and   *1Sa 30:2*
w. their way
all the people *w. their way* to   *Ne 8:12*
eat
they *w. their way* as a flock   *Zec 10:2*
that kept swine fled and *w.*   *M't 8:33*
their way
right I will give you, and they   *M't 20:4*
w. their way
they made light of it and *w.*   *M't 22:5*
their ways
they heard these words, they   *M't 22:22*
w. their way
w. their way and found colt   *M'k 11:4;*
  Lu 19:32
but some *w. their ways* to   *Joh 11:46*
Pharisees
as they *w.* on *their way* came   *Ac 8:36*
to water

WENT THROUGH

they *w. thro'* the midst of the   *Ne 9:11;*
sea on dry land   *Ps 66:6*
we *w. thro'* fire and through   *Ps 66:12*
water
forsaken, so that no man *w.*   *Isa 60:15*
thro' thee
he *w. thro'* corn fields on   *M'k 2:23;*
the sabbath, disciples began   *Lu 6:1*

WENT UP

and God *w. up* from   *Ge 17:22*
Abraham
God *w. up* from Jacob in   *Ge 35:13*
place he talked
w. up to father's bed, he *w. up*   *Ge 49:4*
to my couch
Moses, Aaron, Hur *w. up*   *Ex 17:10*
hill
Moses *w. up* to God   *Ex 19:3;*
  19:20; 24:13, 15; 34:4; De 10:3
so they *w. up*, and searched   *Nu 13:21*
the land
but the men that *w. up* with   *Nu 13:31*
him said
they *w. up* into mount Hor   *Nu 20:27;*
  33:38
w. up presumptuously into the   *De 1:43*
hill
so that the people *w. up* into   *Jos 6:20*
the city
brethren that *w. up* with me   *Jos 14:8*
made heart melt
Judah *w. up* and the Lord   *J'g 1:4*
delivered
the house of Joseph also *w.*   *J'g 1:22*
up against Beth-el
Barak and Deborah *w. up*   *J'g 4:10*
with 10,000 men
Gideon *w. up* thence to Penuel   *J'g 8:8;*
  8:11
Elkanah *w. up* out of his city   *1Sa 1:3;*
  1:7, 21
Hannah *w.* not *up* until child   *1Sa 1:22*
be weaned
the cry of the city *w. up* to   *1Sa 5:12*
heaven
David wept as he *w. up*   *2Sa 15:30*
barefoot
David *w. up* as the Lord   *2Sa 24:19;*
commanded   *1Ch 21:19*
Elijah *w. up* by whirlwind to   *2Ki 2:11*
heaven
Elisha *w. up* and lay on the   *2Ki 4:34;*
child   *4:35*
Hezekiah *w. up* into the   *2Ki 19:14;*
house of the Lord, and   *Isa 37:14*
Josiah *w. up* to house of   *2Ki 23:2;*
Lord   *2Ch 34:30*
Joab *w. up* first and was   *1Ch 11:6*
chief captain
children of the province that   *Ezr 2:1;*
w. up out of   *2:59; Ne 7:6, 61*
the captivity
they *w. up* in haste to   *Ezr 4:23*
Jerusalem to Jews
Ezra *w. up*   *Ezr 7:6*
this is the genealogy of them   *Ezr 8:1*
that *w. up*

priest that *w. up*   *Ne 12:1*
it *w. up* and down among   *Eze 1:13*
living creatures
and a thick cloud of incense   *Eze 8:11*
w. up
the glory of the Lord *w. up*   *Eze 10:4;*
  11:23, 24
he *w. up* and down among   *Eze 19:6*
the lions
Jesus *w. up* straightway out   *M't 3:16*
of the water
seeing the multitudes he *w. up*   *M't 5:1;*
into a mountain   *14:23; 15:29; Lu 9:28*
two men *w. up* into the temple   *Lu 18:10*
to pray
then *w.* he also *up* unto the   *Joh 7:10*
feast
as he *w. up* two men stood by   *Ac 1:10*
him
Peter and John *w. up* into the   *Ac 3:1*
temple
Peter *w. up* upon the   *Ac 10:9*
house top to pray
Paul *w. up* to Jerusalem   *Ac 24:11;*
  Ga 1:18; 2:1, 2
neither *w.* I *up* to Jerusalem   *Ga 1:17*
with them
they *w. up* on the breadth of   *Re 20:9*
the earth

WENT A WHORING

Israel *w. a whoring* after   *J'g 2:17;*
other gods   *8:33*
w. a whoring with their   *Ps 106:39*
inventions

WENTEST

thou *w. up* to thy father's bed   *Ge 49:4*
Lord, when thou *w.* out of   *J'g 5:4*
Seir
when thou *w.* to fight with the   *J'g 8:1*
asses which thou *w.* to seek   *1Sa 10:2*
with thee whithersoever thou   *2Sa 7:9*
w.
why *w.* thou not with thy   *2Sa 16:17*
friend
Wherefore *w.* not thou with   *2Sa 19:25*
me
thou *w.* forth before thy   *Ps 68:7*
people
even thither *w.* thou up to   *Isa 57:7*
offer
thou *w.* to the king with   *Isa 57:9*
ointment
thou *w.* after me in the   *Jer 2:2*
wilderness
even the way which thou *w.*   *Jer 31:21*
Thou *w.* forth for the   *Hab 3:13*
salvation of
Thou *w.* in to men   *Ac 11:3*
uncircumcised

WEPT

and lift up her voice, and *w.*   *Ge 21:16*
Esau lifted up his voice, and   *Ge 27:38*
w.
and lifted up his voice, and   *Ge 29:11*
w.
neck, and kissed him: and   *Ge 33:4*
they *w.*
Thus his father *w.* for him   *Ge 37:35*
himself about from them, and   *Ge 42:24*
w.
into his chamber, and *w.*   *Ge 43:30*
there
And he *w.* aloud   *Ge 45:2*
brother Benjamin's neck, and   *Ge 45:14*
w.
and Benjamin *w.* upon his   *Ge 45:14*
neck
his brethren, and *w.* upon   *Ge 45:15*
them
and *w.* on his neck a good   *Ge 46:29*
while
and *w.* upon him, and kissed   *Ge 50:1*
him
w. for him 70 days (E)(R)   *Ge 50:3*
Joseph *w.* when they spake   *Ge 50:17*
unto
child: and behold, the babe *w.*   *Ex 2:6*
children of Israel also *w.*   *Nu 11:4*
again
ye have *w.* in the ears of the   *Nu 11:18*
Lord
and have *w.* before him,   *Nu 11:20*
saying

cried; and the people w. that   Nu 14:1
night
returned and w. before the   De 1:45
Lord
the children of Israel w. for   De 34:8
Moses
people lifted up their voice,   J'g 2:4
and w.
And Samson's wife w.   J'g 14:16
before him
she w. before him the seven   J'g 14:17
days
and w. before the Lord until   J'g 20:23
even
came unto the house of God,   J'g 20:26
and w.
lifted up their voices, and w.   J'g 21:2
sore
they lifted up their voice, and   Ru 1:9
w.
lifted up their voice, and w.   Ru 1:14
again
therefore she w. and did not   1Sa 1:7
eat
prayed unto the Lord, and w.   1Sa 1:10
sore
people lifted up their voices,   1Sa 11:4
and w.
w. one with another, until   1Sa 20:41
David
Saul lifted up his voice, and   1Sa 24:16
w.
him lifted up their voice and   1Sa 30:4
w.
they mourned, and w. and   2Sa 1:12
fasted
and w. at the grave of Abner   2Sa 3:32
of Abner; and all the people   2Sa 3:32
w.
all the people w. again over   2Sa 3:34
him
child was yet alive, I fasted   2Sa 12:22
and w.
and lifted up their voice and   2Sa 13:36
w.
and all his servants w. very   2Sa 13:36
sore
all the country w. with a   2Sa 15:23
loud voice
mount Olivet, and w. as he   2Sa 15:30
went up
the chamber over the gate,   2Sa 18:33
and w.
ashamed: and the man of   2Ki 8:11
God w.
and w. over his face, and   2Ki 13:14
said, O my
thy sight. And Hezekiah w.   2Ki 20:3
sore
rent thy clothes, and w.   2Ki 22:19
before me
their eyes, w. with a loud   Ezr 3:12
voice
for the people w. very sore   Ezr 10:1
words, that I sat down and w.   Ne 1:4
For all the people w. when they   Ne 8:9
they lifted up their voice, and   Job 2:12
w.
When I w. and chastened my   Ps 69:10
soul
we w. when we remembered   Ps 137:1
Zion
thy sight. And Hezekiah w.   Isa 38:3
sore
he w. and made supplication   Ho 12:4
unto
And he went out, and w.   M't 26:75
bitterly
them that w. and wailed   M'k 5:38
greatly
when he thought thereon, he   M'k 14:72
w.
with him, as they mourned   M'k 16:10
and w.
to you, and ye have not w.   Lu 7:32
and w. and bewailed her: but   Lu 8:52
he
he beheld the city, and w.   Lu 19:41
over it
Peter went out, and w.   Lu 22:62
bitterly
Jesus w.   Joh 11:35
and as she w. she stooped   Joh 20:11
down
And they all w. sore, and fell   Ac 20:37
that weep, as though they w.   1Co 7:30
not
And I w. much, because no   Re 5:4
man

WERE

cannot do this, for that w. a   Ge 34:14
reproach
on the third day, when they   Ge 34:25
w. sore
Jacob said to all that w. with   Ge 35:2
him
gave all strange gods that w.   Ge 35:4
in hand
Israel saw they w. in evil case   Ex 5:19
since day they w. on earth to   Ex 10:6
this day
w. ye not afraid to speak   Nu 12:8
against Moses
we saw giants, we w. in our   Nu 13:33
own sight as grasshoppers,
so we w. in their sight
w. it not better for us to   Nu 14:3
return into Egypt
O that there w. such an heart   De 5:29
in them
for ye w. strangers in the   De 10:19
land of Egypt
whereas ye w. as the stars of   De 28:62
heaven
w. it not that I feared wrath   De 32:27
of enemy
O that they w. wise, that   De 32:29
they understood
I wist not whence they w.   Jos 2:4
mountains as if they w. men   J'g 9:36
passed Shalim, and there they   1Sa 9:4
w. not
where he knew that valiant   2Sa 11:16
men w.
we w. together, there was no   1Ki 3:18
stranger
straw brought they where the   1Ki 4:28
officers w.
Ahab did evil above all w.   1Ki 16:30;
before him   16:43
w. it not that I regard   2Ki 3:14
Jehoshaphat
but horses tied, and the tents   2Ki 7:10
as they w.
as many as w. of a free   2Ch 29:31
heart
though there w. of you cast out   Ne 1:9
for there w. that said, We, our   Ne 5:2;
sons   5:3, 4
nor their seed, whether they   Ne 7:61
w. of Israel
oh that I w. as in months   Job 29:2
past
a sojourner, as all my fathers   Ps 39:12
w.
take captives whose captives   Isa 14:2
they w.
they w. no gods, but work of   Isa 37:19
men's hands
Rachel weeping, because they   Jer 31:15
w. not
tho' Noah, Daniel, Job w.   Eze 14:14;
in it should deliver but   16:18, 20
own souls
before the heathen among   Eze 20:9
whom they w.
there w. but ten, there w. but   Hag 2:16
twenty
persecuted prophets which w.   M't 5:12
before you
read what David did, and   M't 12:3;
they that w. with him   12:4; M'k 2:25,
   26; Lu 6:3, 4
all men mused whether he w.   Lu 3:15
Christ
this man, if he w. a prophet,   Lu 7:39
would known
w. not ten cleansed, where   Lu 17:17
are the nine
if this man w. not of God   Joh 9:33
could do nothing
that if any man knew where   Joh 11:57
he w.
if ye w. of the world, world   Joh 15:19
would love
they which w. thou gavest   Joh 17:6
them me
they said, If he w. not a   Joh 18:30
malefactor
and w. not a little comforted   Ac 20:12
Jews assented, saying, These   Ac 24:9
things w. so
calleth things that be not as   Ro 4:17
tho' they w.
I will call them my people   Ro 9:25
that w. not
w. we all baptized into one   1Co 12:13
body (S)

if whole body w. an eye,   1Co 12:17
where w. hearing? If whole
w. hearing, where w. smelling
what they w. it maketh no   Ga 2:6
matter to me
w. by nature children of   Eph 2:3
wrath, as others
from even when we w. with   2Th 3:10
you
all things continue as they w.   2Pe 3:4
from beginning
till brethren killed as they w.   Re 6:11
fulfilled

AS IT WERE

it seemeth there is as it w. a   Le 14:35
plague
as it w. the company of two   Ca 6:13
armies
that draw sin as it w. with a   Isa 5:18
cart rope
as if staff lift up itself as it   Isa 10:15
w. no wood
hide thyself as it w. for a   Isa 26:20
little moment
and we hid as it w. our faces   Isa 53:3
from him
his sweat as it w. great drops   Lu 22:44
of blood
went up not openly, but as it   Joh 7:10
w. in secret
sought it as it w. by works of   Ro 9:32
the law
apostles, as it w. men   1Co 4:9
appointed to death
and his face was as it w. the   Re 10:1
sun
I saw one of his heads as it w.   Re 13:3
wounded
they sung as it w. a new song   Re 14:3
before throne
I saw as it w. a sea of glass   Re 15:2
with fire

IF IT WERE

if it w. so, why not my spirit   Job 21:4
be troubled
if it w. possible to deceive   M't 24:24
the very elect
they might touch if it w. the   M'k 6:56
border
if it w. not so, I would have   Joh 14:2
told you
if it w. a matter of wrong, O   Ac 18:14
ye Jews

WERT

If thou w. pure and upright;   Job 8:6
surely
O that thou w. as my brother   Ca 8:1
olive tree, w. graffed in   Ro 11:17
among them
For if thou w. cut out of the   Ro 11:24
olive tree
and w. graffed contrary to   Ro 11:24
nature into
nor hot: I would thou w. cold   Re 3:15
or hot

WEST

having Beth-el on the w. and   Ge 12:8
Hai
thou shalt spread abroad to   Ge 28:14
the w.
the w. side of the desert (S)   Ex 3:1
turned a mighty strong w.   Ex 10:19
wind
the w. side shall be hangings   Ex 27:12
of fifty
the w. side were hangings of   Ex 38:12
fifty
On the w. side shall be the   Nu 2:18
standard
this shall be your w. border   Nu 34:6
on the w. side two thousand   Nu 35:5
cubits
possess thou the w. and the   De 33:23
south
Beth-el and Ai, on the w. side   Jos 8:9
of Ai
and Ai, on the w. side, of the   Jos 8:12
city
liers in wait on the w. of the   Jos 8:13
city
in the borders of Dor on the   Jos 11:2
w.

on the east and on the *w.*   *Jos 11:3*
on this side Jordan on the *w.*   *Jos 12:7*
the *w.* border was to the great   *Jos 15:12*
sea
of Judah: this was the *w.*   *Jos 18:14*
quarter
and the border went out on   *Jos 18:15*
the *w.*
reacheth to Asher on the *w.*   *Jos 19:34*
side
and three looking toward the   *1Ki 7:25;*
w.   *2Ch 4:4*
toward the east, *w.* north   *1Ch 9:24*
the east, and toward the *w.*   *1Ch 12:15*
to the *w.* side of the city of   *2Ch 32:30*
David
on the *w.* side of Gihon, in   *2Ch 33:14*
from the east, nor from the *w.*   *Ps 75:6*
As far as the east is from   *Ps 103:12*
the *w.*
from the east, and from the *w.*   *Ps 107:3*
of the Philistines toward the   *Isa 11:14*
w.
east, and gather thee from the   *Isa 43:5*
w.
and from the *w.* that there is   *Isa 45:6*
none
and from the *w.* and these   *Isa 49:12*
the name of the Lord from   *Isa 59:19*
the *w.*
end toward the *w.* was   *Eze 41:12*
seventy
He turned about to the *w.*   *Eze 42:19*
side
city, from the *w.* side   *Eze 45:7*
westward
from the *w.* border unto the   *Eze 45:7*
east
w. side also shall be the   *Eze 47:20*
great sea
Hamath. This is the *w.* side   *Eze 47:20*
for these are his sides east   *Eze 48:1*
and *w.*
from the east side unto the   *Eze 48:2;*
w. side   *48:8*
the east side even unto the *w.*   *Eze 48:3;*
side   *48:6*
the east side unto the *w.*   *Eze 48:4;*
side   *48:5, 7-8, 23-27*
and toward the *w.* ten   *Eze 48:10*
thousand in
the *w.* side four thousand   *Eze 48:16;*
and five   *48:34*
toward the *w.* two hundred   *Eze 48:17*
and twenty thousand toward   *Eze 48:21*
the *w.*
an he goat came from the *w.*   *Da 8:5*
children shall tremble from   *Ho 11:10*
the *w.*
and from the *w.* country   *Zec 8:7*
toward the east and toward   *Zec 14:4*
the *w.*
shall come from the east and   *M't 8:11*
w.
east, and shineth even unto   *M't 24:27*
the *w.*
ye see a cloud rise out of the   *Lu 12:54*
w.
from the east, and from the   *Lu 13:29*
w.
toward the south *w.* and   *Ac 27:12*
north
toward the south and north   *Ac 27:12*
w.
gates; and on the *w.* three   *Re 21:13*
gates

WESTERN

And as for the *w.* border, ye   *Nu 34:6*
shall
unto the *w.* sea (S)   *De 11:24*

WESTWARD

southward, and eastward,   *Ge 13:14*
and *w.*
for the sides of the   *Ex 26:22;*
tabernacle *w.*   *36:27*
the tabernacle, for the two   *Ex 26:27*
sides *w.*
of the tabernacle for the   *Ex 36:32*
sides *w.*
pitch behind the tabernacle *w.*   *Nu 3:23*
of Pisgah, and lift up thine   *De 3:27*
eves *w.*
were on the side of Jordan *w.*   *Jos 5:1*
before the valley of Hinnom   *Jos 15:8*
w.

from Baalah *w.* unto mount   *Jos 15:10*
Seir
down *w.* to the coast of   *Jos 16:3*
Japhleti
Tappuah *w.* unto the river   *Jos 16:8*
Kanah
went up through the   *Jos 18:12*
mountains *w.*
and reacheth to Carmel *w.*   *Jos 19:26*
and to
coast turneth *w.* to   *Jos 19:34*
Aznoth-tabor
brethren on this side Jordan   *Jos 22:7*
w.
even unto the great sea *w.*   *Jos 23:4*
and *w.* Gezer, with the towns   *1Ch 7:28*
and Hosah the lot came   *1Ch 26:16*
forth *w.*
At Parbar *w.* four at the   *1Ch 26:18*
causeway
of Israel on this side Jordan   *1Ch 26:30*
w.
of the city, from the west   *Eze 45:7*
side *w.*
was a place on the two sides   *Eze 46:19*
eastward, and ten thousand   *Eze 48:18*
w.
and *w.* over against the five   *Eze 48:21*
I saw the ram pushing *w.* and   *Da 8:4*

WET

They are *w.* with the showers   *Job 24:8*
be *w.* with the dew of   *Da 4:15;*
heaven   *4:23*
w. thee with the dew of   *Da 4:25*
heaven
and his body was *w.* with the   *Da 4:33;*
dew   *5:21*

WHALE

Am I a sea, or a *w.* that thou   *Job 7:12*
sea monster (A)(E)(R)   *Job 7:12*
or a dragon (B)   *Job 7:12*
and thou art as a *w.* in the   *Eze 32:2*
seas
like a dragon in the seas   *Eze 32:2*
(A)(R)
or a crocodile in the seas (B)   *Eze 32:2*
like a monster in the seas   *Eze 32:2'*
(E)

WHALES

And God created great *w.* and   *Ge 1:21*
created great sea monsters   *Ge 1:21*
(A)(B)(E)(R)

WHALE'S

and three nights in the *w.*   *M't 12:40*
belly
the sea monster (A)(B)   *M't 12:40*

WHAT

W. mean these seven ewe   *Ge 21:29*
lambs
w. is that betwixt me and   *Ge 23:15*
thee
w. shall I do now to thee, my   *Ge 27:37*
son
discern thou *w.* is thine with   *Ge 31:32*
me
w. hast thou found of all   *Ge 31:37*
thy stuff
my master wotteth not *w.* is   *Ge 39:8*
with me
w. shall we say to my lord?   *Ge 44:16*
w. shall we speak
afar off, to wit *w.* would be   *Ex 2:4*
done to him
see *w.* I will do to Pharaoh   *Ex 6:1*
know not with *w.* we must   *Ex 10:26*
serve Lord
when son asketh, *W.* is this;   *Ex 13:14;*
w. are we   *16:7*
it is manna, for they wist not   *Ex 16:15*
w. it was
that I may know *w.* to do   *Ex 33:5*
unto thee
if ye shall say, *w.* shall we eat   *Le 25:20*
see the land *w.* it is, and the   *Nu 13:18*
people
w. the land is, and *w.* cities   *Nu 13:19;*
they be   *13:20*
it was not declared *w.* should   *Nu 15:34*
be done

w. is Aaron; *w.* hath Lord   *Nu 16:11;*
spoken   *23:17*
but *w.* the Lord saith, that   *Nu 24:13;*
will I speak   *1Ki 22:14; 2Ch 18:13*
w. the Lord did because of   *De 4:3*
Baal-peor
w. Lord did to Pharaoh; to   *De 7:18;*
Dathan   *11:6*
w. doth Lord require of   *De 10:12;*
Israel   *Mic 6:8*
w. man is there   *De 20:5; 20:6-8*
O Lord, *w.* shall I say, when   *Jos 7:8*
Israel
w. wouldest thou   *Jos 15:18;*
  J'g 1:14; 1Ki 1:16; M't 20:21
w. have you to do with the   *Jos 22:24*
Lord
thou shalt hear *w.* they say   *J'g 7:11*
w. hast thou to do with me to   *J'g 11:12*
fight
w. say ye; the priest said, *W.*   *J'g 18:8;*
do ye   *18:18*
w. have I more? *w.* is this?   *J'g 18:24*
w. aileth thee
mark the place, and he will   *Ru 3:4;*
W. is the thing Lord said to   *1Sa 3:17*
thee
and he said, *W.* is there done,   *1Sa 4:16*
my son
tell thee *w.* thou shalt do   *1Sa 10:8*
w. have I to do with you   *2Sa 16:10;*
  19:22
counsel among you *w.* we   *2Sa 16:20*
shall do
let us hear likewise *w.* he   *2Sa 17:5*
saith
I saw a tumult but I knew   *2Sa 18:29*
not *w.* it was
their father said, *W.* way   *1Ki 13:12*
went he
who cut off house of   *1Ki 14:14*
Jeroboam: *w.* even now
w. have I to do with thee   *1Ki 17:18;*
  2Ki 3:13; 2Ch 35:21; Joh 2:4
what (S)   *1Ki 18:9; 22:22;*
2Ch 18:20; 32:10; Mic 6:3; 6:6; Mal 1:2,
  6-7; 2:17; 3:7; M't 5:13; Ro 8:35
Elisha said, *W.* shall I do for   *2Ki 4:2;*
thee   *2:9*
w. hast thou to do with   *2Ki 9:18*
peace
w. said these men, from   *2Ki 20:14;*
whence   *Isa 39:3*
w. have they seen in thine   *2Ki 20:15;*
house   *Isa 39:4*
W. title is that that I see   *2Ki 23:17*
Jehoshaphat said, Take heed   *2Ch 19:6*
w. ye do
nor know *w.* to do, but our   *2Ch 20:12*
eyes are on thee
w. shall we do for the   *2Ch 25:9*
hundred talents given
w. shall we say after this   *Ezr 9:10;*
  Job 37:19
king said, for *w.* dost thou   *Ne 2:4*
make request
they said, *W.* thing is this ye   *Ne 2:19;*
do   *13:17*
to know *w.* it was, and why it   *Es 4:5*
was
w. wilt thou, queen Esther? *w.*   *Es 5:3;*
is thy request   *5:6; 7:2; 9:12*
w. is man, that thou   *Job 7:17;*
shouldest magnify him   *15:14; Ps 8:4;*
  144:3; Heb 2:6
w. shall I do unto thee, O   *Job 7:20*
thou preserver of men
who will say unto him, *W.*   *Job 9:12;*
dost thou   *Ec 8:4; Eze 12:9; Da 4:35*
let me speak, and let come   *Job 13:13*
on me *w.* will
w. then shall I do? *w.* shall   *Job 31:14;*
I answer him   *Lu 10:25; 12:17; 16:3*
let us know *w.* is good   *Job 34:4;*
  Mic 6:8
w. doest thou against him? *w.*   *Job 35:6*
doest to him
if thou be righteous, *w.* givest   *Job 35:7*
thou to him
w. man is he fears Lord   *Ps 25:12;*
  34:12; 89:48
I will hear *w.* God the Lord will   *Ps 85:8*
speak
w. shall be given unto thee,   *Ps 120:3*
w. done to thee
consider diligently *w.* is before   *Pr 23:1*
thee
lest thou know not *w.* to do in   *Pr 25:8*
the end

w. is his name? w. is his son's   Pr 30:4
name
w. my son? and w. the son of   Pr 31:2
my womb
I said of mirth, W. doeth it   Ec 2:2
W. shall one then answer the   Isa 14:32
he calleth watchman, W. of   Isa 21:11
the night
w. hast thou here? and whom   Isa 22:16
hast thou here
W. confidence is this wherein   Isa 36:4
thou
w. shall I say   Isa 38:15;
     Joh 12:27
therefore w. have I here, saith   Isa 52:5
the Lord
w. wilt thou do; w. wilt thou   Jer 4:30;
say   13:21
w. have I done? w. is done   Jer 8:6;
    48:19
W. is the high place   Eze 20:29
whereunto ye
O Ephraim, w. shall I do unto   Ho 6:4
thee
give them, O Lord, w. wilt   Ho 9:14
thou give them
w. have I to do any more with   Ho 14:8
idols
yea, and w. have ye to do with   Joe 3:4
me
declare unto man w. is his   Am 4:13
thought
he said, Amos, w. seest thou   Am 8:2
O my Lord, w. are these   Zec 1:9;
    4:4; 6:4
I said, W. be these   Zec 1:19;
    4:5, 13
w. is it   Zec 5:6
w. do you more than others   M't 5:47
take no thought w. ye shall   M't 6:25;
eat, or w. ye shall drink   6:31; Lu 12:22;
    29
with w. measure ye mete, it   M't 7:2
shall
w. have we to do with thee,   M't 8:29
Jesus thou Son of God   M'k 1:24; 5:7;
    Lu 4:34; 8:28
have ye not read w. David   M't 12:3;
did, when he was   M'k 2:25; Lu 6:3
an hungered
have forsaken all w. shall we   M't 19:27
have therefore
they said, W. is that to us?   M't 27:4
see thou to that
told w. they had done, and w.   M'k 6:30
they taught
for he wist not w. to say, they   M'k 9:6
were afraid
this cup, not w. I will, but w.   M'k 14:36
thou wilt
people asked w. shall we do   Lu 3:10;
then   12:17
the Lord said, unto w. are   Lu 7:31
they like
w. will I, if it be already   Lu 12:49
kindled
forgive them, they know not   Lu 23:34
w. they do
w. then   Joh 1:21
w. did he to thee   Joh 9:26
w. I should say, and w. I   Joh 12:49
should speak
w. is this that he saith, a   Joh 16:18
little while
w. is that to thee? follow   Joh 21:22;
thou me   21:23
brethren, w. shall we do   Ac 2:37; 4:16
Lord, w. wilt thou have me to   Ac 9:6;
do   22:10
w. is it, Lord   Ac 10:4
w. was I, that withstand   Ac 11:17
w. must I do   Ac 16:30
w. is it therefore   Ac 21:22
he said to them, to w. then   Ac 19:3
were ye baptized
w. shall we say   Ro 3:5; 4:1; 6:1; 7:7
w. then   Ro 3:9;
6:15; 8:31; 9:14, 30; 11:7; 1Co 10:19;
    14:15; Ph'p 1:18
    Ro 7:15
w. I would that do I not, but w.
I hate, that do I
w. will ye? shall I come with   1Co 4:21
a rod
that w. ye read or   2Co 1:13
acknowledge
But w. I do, that I will do,   2Co 11:12
that I may
yet w. I shall chose I wot not   Ph'p 1:22

understanding neither w. they   1Ti 1:7
say
consider w. I say, the Lord   2Ti 2:7
give understanding
w. shall I more say? time   Heb 11:32
would fail
ye know not w. shall be on   Jas 4:14
the morrow, for w. is your life
searching w. or w. manner of   1Pe 1:11
time
it doth not appear w. we shall   1Jo 3:2
be

WHATEVER

abide in w. state he is (S)   1Co 7:24

WHATSOEVER

w. Adam called every living   Ge 2:19
and w. creepeth upon the earth   Ge 8:19
and w. thou hast in the city   Ge 19:12
w. God hath said unto thee,   Ge 31:16
do
w. they did there, he was the   Ge 39:22
firstborn, w. openeth the   Ex 13:2
womb
ransom w. is laid upon him   Ex 21:30
w. toucheth the altar shall be   Ex 29:37
holy
w. toucheth them shall be   Ex 30:29
holy
w. uncleanness it be that a man   Le 5:3
w. a man shall pronounce   Le 5:4
W. shall touch the flesh   Le 6:27
thereof
W. soul it be that eateth any   Le 7:27
W. parteth the hoof, and is   Le 11:3
w. hath fins and scales in the   Le 11:9
W. hath no fins nor scales in   Le 11:12
w. goeth upon his paws,   Le 11:27
among all
upon w. any of them, when   Le 11:32
they
w. vessel it be, wherein any   Le 11:32
work is
w. is in it shall be unclean   Le 11:33
W. goeth upon the belly   Le 11:42
and w. goeth upon all fours   Le 11:42
or w. hath more feet among   Le 11:42
all
w. thing of skin it be, which   Le 13:58
thou
w. she sitteth upon shall be   Le 15:26
W. man there be of the house   Le 17:8;
of   17:10
w. man there be of the   Le 17:13
children
w. man he be that hath a   Le 21:18
blemish
w. uncleanness he hath   Le 22:5
W. he be of the house of   Le 22:18
Israel
w. hath a blemish, that shall   Le 22:20
ye
w. soul it be that shall not be   Le 23:29
w. soul it be that doeth any   Le 23:30
work in
even of w. passeth under the   Le 27:32
rod
w. any man giveth the priest,   Nu 5:10
it
and w. is first ripe in the   Nu 18:13
land
w. the unclean person   Nu 19:22
toucheth
I will do w. thou sayest unto   Nu 22:17
w. he sheweth me I will tell   Nu 23:3
then w. proceeded out of her   Nu 30:12
lips
w. the Lord our God forbad   De 2:37
us
man w. is right in his own   De 12:8
eyes
w. thy soul lusteth after,   De 12:15
according
eat flesh, w. thy soul lusteth   De 12:20
after
thy gates w. thy soul lusteth   De 12:21
after
w. hath not fins and scales ye   De 14:10
money for w. thy soul   De 14:26
lusteth
or for w. thy soul desireth   De 14:26
us w. seemeth good unto thee   J'g 10:15
w. cometh forth of the doors   J'g 11:31
of my
Do w. seemeth good unto   1Sa 14:36
thee
W. thy soul desireth, I will   1Sa 20:4
even

w. cometh to thine hand unto   1Sa 25:8
as w. the king did pleased all   2Sa 3:36
ready to do w. my lord the   2Sa 15:15
king
w. thou shalt require of me   2Sa 19:38
w. plague, w. sickness there be   1Ki 8:37
Sheba all her desire, w. she   1Ki 10:13;
asked   2Ch 9:12
that w. is pleasant in thine   1Ki 20:6
eyes
w. sore or w. sickness there   2Ch 6:28
be
w. shall seem good to thee   Ezr 7:18
And w. more shall be needful   Ezr 7:20
for the
w. Ezra the priest, the scribe   Ezr 7:21
W. is commanded by the God   Ezr 7:23
w. she desired was given   Es 2:13
do w. he commandeth them   Job 37:12
w. is under the whole   Job 41:11
heaven is mine
and w. he doeth shall prosper   Ps 1:3
w. passeth through the paths of   Ps 8:8
hath done w. he hath pleased   Ps 115:3
W. the Lord pleased, that did   Ps 135:6
w. my eyes desireth I kept not   Ec 2:10
w. God doeth, it shall be for   Ec 3:14
for he doeth w. pleaseth him   Ec 8:3
W. thy hand findeth to do, do   Ec 9:10
it
w. I command thee thou shalt   Jer 1:7
that w. thing the Lord shall   Jer 42:4
w. thing goeth forth out of   Jer 44:17
our
w. is more than these cometh   M't 5:37
of evil
w. ye would that men should   M't 7:12
into w. city or town   M't 10:11
ye enter
to give her w. she would ask   M't 14:7
by w. thou mightest be   M't 15:5
profited
w. entereth in at the mouth   M't 15:17
goeth
w. thou shalt bind on earth   M't 16:19
w. thou shalt loose on earth   M't 16:19
shall
have done unto him w. they   M't 17:12
listed
W. ye shall bind on earth   M't 18:18
w. ye shall loose on earth   M't 18:18
shall
and w. is right I will give you   M't 20:4
w. is right that shall ye   M't 20:7
receive
w. ye shall ask in prayer   M't 21:22
w. they bid you observe   M't 23:3
things w. I have commanded   M't 28:20
you
Ask of me w. thou wilt, and   M'k 6:22
W. thou shalt ask of me, I   M'k 6:23
will
by w. thou mightest be   M'k 7:11
profited by
w. thing from without   M'k 7:18
entereth
have done unto him w. they   M'k 9:13
listed
sell w. thou hast, and give   M'k 10:21
to the
do for us w. we shall desire   M'k 10:35
pass; he shall have w. he   M'k 11:23
saith
w. shall be given you in that   M'k 13:11
w. we have heard done in   Lu 4:23
w. house ye enter into, there   Lu 9:4
And into w. house ye enter,   Lu 10:5
first
into w. city ye enter, and   Lu 10:8;
they   10:10
w. thou spendest more, when   Lu 10:35
w. ye have spoken in darkness   Lu 12:3
W. he saith unto you, do it   Joh 2:5
made whole of w. disease he   Joh 5:4
had
w. thou wilt ask of God   Joh 11:22
w. I speak therefore, even as   Joh 12:50
w. ye shall ask in my name   Joh 14:13
remembrance, w. I have said   Joh 14:26
unto
friends, if ye do w.   Joh 15:14
I command
w. ye shall ask of the Father   Joh 15:16
w. he shall hear, that shall   Joh 16:13
he
W. ye shall ask the Father   Joh 16:23
in
w. thou hast given me are of   Joh 17:7
thee
in all things w. he shall say   Ac 3:22

to do *w.* thy hand and thy counsel — *Ac 4:28*
faith: for *w.* is not of faith is sin — *Ro 14:23*
w. things were written aforetime — *Ro 15:4*
ye assist her in *w.* business — *Ro 16:2*
W. is sold in the shambles — *1Co 10:25*
w. is set before you, eat, asking — *1Co 10:27*
w. ye do, do all to the glory of God — *1Co 10:31*
w. they were, it maketh no light — *Ga 2:6*
w. a man soweth, that shall he — *Ga 6:7*
w. doth make manifest is light — *Eph 5:13*
w. good thing any man — *Eph 6:8*
brethren, *w.* things are true — *Ph'p 4:8*
w. things are honest — *Ph'p 4:8*
w. things are just — *Ph'p 4:8*
w. things are pure — *Ph'p 4:8*
w. things are lovely — *Ph'p 4:8*
w. things are of good report — *Ph'p 4:8*
w. state I am, therewith to be — *Ph'p 4:11*
w. ye do in word or deed — *Col 3:17*
w. ye do, do it heartily, as — *Col 3:23*
w. we ask, we receive of him — *1Jo 3:22*
w. is born of God overcometh — *1Jo 5:4*
w. we ask we know that we — *1Jo 5:15*
w. thou doest to the brethren — *3Jo 5*
craftsman, of *w.* craft he be, shall — *Re 18:22*
w. worketh abomination, or maketh — *Re 21:27*

WHEAT

went in the days of *w.* harvest — *Ge 30:14*
the *w.* and the rie were not smitten — *Ex 9:32*
the firstfruits of *w.* harvest, and the — *Ex 34:22*
best of the wine, and of the *w.* — *Nu 18:12*
grain (A)(B)(E)(R) — *Nu 18:12; Pr 27:22*
A land of *w.* and barley, and — *De 8:8*
with the fat of kidneys of *w.* — *De 32:14*
his son Gideon threshed *w.* by — *J'g 6:11*
after, in the time of *w.* harvest — *J'g 15:1*
barley harvest and of *w.* harvest — *Ru 2:23*
were reaping their *w.* harvest in — *1Sa 6:13*
Is it not *w.* harvest to day? I will — *1Sa 12:17*
they would have fetched *w.* — *2Sa 4:6*
vessels, and *w.* and barley — *2Sa 17:28*
twenty thousand measures of *w.* — *1Ki 5:11*
Now Ornan was threshing *w.* — *1Ch 21:20*
and the *w.* for the meat offering — *1Ch 21:23*
thousand measures of beaten *w.* — *2Ch 2:10*
the *w.* and the barley, the oil — *2Ch 2:15*
and ten thousand measures of *w.* — *2Ch 27:5*
w., salt, wine, and oil, according — *Ezr 6:9*
and to an hundred measures of *w.* — *Ezr 7:22*
Let thistles grow instead of *w.* — *Job 31:40*
them also with the finest of the *w.* — *Ps 81:16*
filleth thee with the finest of the *w.* — *Ps 147:14*
bray a fool in a mortar among *w.* — *Pr 27:22*
an heap of *w.* set about with lilies — *Ca 7:2*
cast in the principal *w.* and — *Isa 28:25*
w. in rows (S) — *Isa 28:25*
They have sown *w.* but shall reap — *Jer 12:13*
What is the chaff to the *w.*? saith — *Jer 23:28*
for *w.* and for wine, and for oil — *Jer 31:12*
in the field, of *w.* and of barley — *Jer 41:8*
Take thou also unto thee *w.* — *Eze 4:9*
traded in thy market *w.* of Minnith — *Eze 27:17*

part of an ephah of an homer of *w.* — *Eze 45:13*
for the *w.* and for the barley — *Joe 1:11*
the floors shall be full of *w.* — *Joe 2:24*
ye take from him burdens of *w.* — *Am 5:11*
sabbath, that we may set forth *w.* — *Am 8:5*
yea, and sell the refuse of the *w.* — *Am 8:6*
and gather his *w.* into the garner — *M't 3:12; Lu 3:17*
and sowed tares among the *w.* — *M't 13:25*
ye root up also the *w.* with them — *M't 13:29*
sowed wild *w.* (A) — *M't 13:29*
but gather the *w.* into my barn — *M't 13:30*
through *w.* field (B) — *M'k 2:23*
said, An hundred measures of *w.* — *Lu 16:7*
you, that he may sift you as *w.* — *Lu 22:31*
a corn of *w.* fall into the ground — *Joh 12:24*
and cast out the *w.* into the sea — *Ac 27:38*
it may chance of *w.* or of some — *1Co 15:37*
A measure of *w.* for a penny — *Re 6:6*
and oil, and fine flour, and *w.* — *Re 18:13*

WHEATEN

of *w.* flour shalt thou make them — *Ex 29:2*

WHEEL

height of a *w.* was a cubit and half — *1Ki 7:32*
was like the work of a chariot *w.* — *1Ki 7:33*
God, make them like a *w.*; as — *Ps 83:13*
like whirling dust (A)(B)(E)(R) — *Ps 83:13*
and bringeth the *w.* over them — *Pr 20:26*
or the *w.* broken at the cistern — *Ec 12:6*
neither is a cart *w.* turned about — *Isa 28:27*
break it with the *w.* of his cart — *Isa 28:28*
behold one *w.* upon the earth — *Eze 1:15*
it were a *w.* in the middle of a *w.* — *Eze 1:16*
cherubim, one *w.* by one cherub — *Eze 10:9*
another *w.* by another cherub — *Eze 10:9*
a *w.* had been in the midst of a *w.* — *Eze 10:10*
unto them in my hearing, O *w.* — *Eze 10:13*
stretched and broken on *w.* (B) — *Heb 11:35*
w. of birth (A) — *Jas 3:6*
w. of nature (E) — *Jas 3:6*
w. of existence red hot (N) — *Jas 3:6*

WHEELS

took off their chariot *w.* that they — *Ex 14:25*
why tarry the *w.* of his chariots — *J'g 5:28*
And every base had four brasen *w.* — *1Ki 7:30*
under the borders were four *w.* — *1Ki 7:32*
axletrees of the *w.* were joined to — *1Ki 7:32*
work of the *w.* was like the work of — *1Ki 7:33*
and their *w.* like a whirlwind — *Isa 5:28*
he wrought a work on the *w.* — *Jer 18:3*
and at the rumbling of his *w.* — *Jer 47:3*
appearance of the *w.* and their — *Eze 1:16*
creatures went, the *w.* went by them — *Eze 1:19*
the earth, the *w.* were lifted up — *Eze 1:19; 1:21*
the *w.* were lifted up over against — *Eze 1:20*
of the living creature was in the *w.* — *Eze 1:20; 1:21*
noise of the *w.* over against them — *Eze 3:13*
Go in between the *w.* even under — *Eze 10:2*

Take fire from between the *w.* — *Eze 10:6*
went in, and stood beside the *w.* — *Eze 10:6*
the four *w.* by the cherubims — *Eze 10:9*
appearance of the *w.* was as — *Eze 10:9*
the *w.* were full of eyes round about — *Eze 10:12*
even the *w.* that they four had — *Eze 10:12*
As for the *w.* it was cried unto — *Eze 10:13*
cherubims went, the *w.* went by — *Eze 10:16*
the same *w.* also turned not from — *Eze 10:16*
out, the *w.* also were beside them — *Eze 10:19*
wings, and the *w.* beside them: — *Eze 11:22*
with chariots, wagons, and *w.* — *Eze 23:24*
of the horsemen, and of the *w.* — *Eze 26:10*
flame, and his *w.* as burning fire — *Da 7:9*
the noise of the rattling of the *w.* — *Na 3:2*

WHELP

Judah is a lion's *w.*: from the — *Ge 49:9*
cub (A)(B) — *Ge 49:9*
Dan is a lion's *w.*: he shall leap — *De 33:22*
the lion's *w.* and none made them — *Na 2:11*
where his cubs were (A)(R) — *Na 2:11*

WHELPS

as a bear robbed of her *w.* in the field — *2Sa 17:8*
robbed of her cubs (B)(R) — *2Sa 17:8; Pr 17:12*
the stout lion's *w.* are scattered — *Job 4:11*
The lion's *w.* have not trodden it — *Job 28:8*
Let a bear robbed of her *w.* meet a — *Pr 17:12*
lions: they shall yell as lions' *w.* — *Jer 51:38*
she nourished her *w.* among — *Eze 19:2*
she nourished her cubs (A) — *Eze 19:2; 19:3*
she brought one of her *w.*: it — *Eze 19:3*
she took another of her *w.* — *Eze 19:5*
as a bear that is bereaved of her *w.* — *Ho 13:8*
robbed of her cubs (A)(R) — *Ho 13:8*
tear in pieces enough for his *w.* — *Na 2:12*

WHEN

of the earth *w.* they were created — *Ge 2:4*
w. the woman saw that the tree — *Ge 3:6*
w. they were in the field, that Cain — *Ge 4:8*
W. thou tillest the ground, it — *Ge 4:12*
Adam, in the day *w.* they were created — *Ge 5:2*
w. men began to multiply on — *Ge 6:1*
w. the sons of God came in unto — *Ge 6:4*
w. the flood of waters was upon the — *Ge 7:6*
w. I bring a cloud over the earth, that — *Ge 9:14*
years old *w.* he departed out of Haran — *Ge 12:4*
w. he was come near to enter into — *Ge 12:11*
w. the Egyptians shall see thee — *Ge 12:12*
w. Abram was come into Egypt, the — *Ge 12:14*
w. Abram heard that his brother — *Ge 14:14*
w. the fowls came down upon the — *Ge 15:11*
And *w.* the sun was going down — *Ge 15:12*
w. the sun went down, and it was — *Ge 15:17*
w. she saw that she had conceived — *Ge 16:4; 16:5*
w. Sarai dealt hardly with her — *Ge 16:6*
w. Hagar bare Ishmael to Abram — *Ge 16:16*

w. Abram was ninety years old	Ge 17:1
w. he was circumcised in the flesh	Ge 17:24; 17:25
w. he saw them, he ran to meet	Ge 18:2
And w. the morning arose	Ge 19:15
w. they had brought them forth	Ge 19:17
the earth w. Lot entered into Zoar	Ge 19:23
w. God destroyed the cities of the	Ge 19:29
w. he overthrew the cities in	Ge 19:29
w. she lay down, nor w. she arose	Ge 19:33; 19:35
w. God caused me to wander from	Ge 20:13
w. his son Isaac was born unto him	Ge 21:5
And w. she had done giving him drink	Ge 24:19
w. he saw the earring and bracelets	Ge 24:30
a son to my master w. she was old	Ge 24:36
that w. the virgin cometh forth to draw	Ge 24:43
w. Abraham's servant heard their	Ge 24:52
w. she saw Isaac, she lighted off the	Ge 24:64
years old w. he took Rebekah to wife	Ge 25:20
w. her days to be delivered were	Ge 25:24
threescore years old w. she bare them	Ge 25:26
w. he had been there a long time	Ge 26:8
w. Esau heard the words of his father	Ge 27:34
w. thou shalt have the dominion	Ge 27:40
W. Esau saw that Isaac had blessed	Ge 28:6
w. Jacob saw Rachel the daughter	Ge 29:10
w. Laban heard the tidings of Jacob	Ge 29:13
w. the Lord saw that Leah was hated	Ge 29:31
w. Rachel saw that she bare Jacob no	Ge 30:1
W. Leah saw that she had left	Ge 30:9
w. Rachel had born Joseph	Ge 30:25
w. shall I provide for mine own	Ge 30:30
w. it shall come for my hire before	Ge 30:33
troughs w. the flocks came to drink	Ge 30:38
conceive w. they came to drink	Ge 30:38
w. the cattle were feeble, he put them	Ge 30:42
w. we are absent one from another	Ge 31:49
w. Jacob say them, he said, This	Ge 32:2
W. Esau my brother meeteth	Ge 32:17
speak unto Esau, w. ye find him	Ge 32:19
And w. he saw that he prevailed not	Ge 32:25
Canaan, w. he came from Padan-aram	Ge 33:18
And w. Shechem the son of Hamor the	Ge 34:2
came out of the field w. they heard it	Ge 34:7
w. they were sore, that two of the sons	Ge 34:25
w. thou fleddest from the face of Esau	Ge 35:1
w. he fled from the face of his	Ge 35:7
w. he came out of Padan-aram, and	Ge 35:9
w. she was in hard labour, that the	Ge 35:17
w. Israel dwelt in that land	Ge 35:22
w. his brethren saw that their father	Ge 37:4
w. they saw him afar off, even before	Ge 37:18
w. Joseph was come unto his	Ge 37:23
he was at Chezib, w. she bare him	Ge 38:5

w. he went in unto his brother's	Ge 38:9
W. Judah saw her, he thought her to	Ge 38:15
W. she was brought forth	Ge 38:25
w. she travailed, that the one put out	Ge 38:28
w. she saw that he had left his	Ge 39:13
w. he heard that I had lifted up my	Ge 39:15
w. his master heard the words of his	Ge 39:19
manner w. thou wast his butler	Ge 40:13
on me w. it shall be well with thee	Ge 40:14
W. the chief baker saw that	Ge 40:16
And w. they had eaten them up	Ge 41:21
years old w. he stood before Pharaoh	Ge 41:46
w. all the land of Egypt was famished	Ge 41:55
w. Jacob saw that there was corn in	Ge 42:1
w. he besought us, and we would not	Ge 42:21
w. both they and their father saw the	Ge 42:35
w. they had eaten up the corn	Ge 43:2
w. Joseph saw Benjamin with them	Ge 43:16
w. we came to the inn, that	Ge 43:21
w. Joseph came home, they brought	Ge 43:26
And w. they were gone out of the city	Ge 44:4
w. thou dost overtake them, say unto	Ge 44:4
w. we came up unto thy servant	Ge 44:24
w. I came to thy servant my	Ge 44:30
w. he seeth that the lad is not with us	Ge 44:31
w. he saw the wagons that Joseph had	Ge 45:27
w. Pharaoh shall call you	Ge 46:33
w. money failed in the land of Egypt	Ge 47:15
W. the year was ended, they came	Ge 47:18
w. I came from Padan, Rachel died by	Ge 48:7
w. yet there was but a little way	Ge 48:7
w. Joseph saw that his father laid his	Ge 48:17
w. Jacob had made an end of	Ge 49:33
w. the days of his mourning were past	Ge 50:4
And w. the inhabitants of the land	Ge 50:11
w. Joseph's brethren saw that their	Ge 50:15
Joseph wept w. they spake unto him	Ge 50:17
that, w. there falleth out any war	Ex 1:10
W. ye do the office of a midwife to the	Ex 1:16
and w. she saw him that he was a	Ex 2:2
And w. she could not longer hide him	Ex 2:3
w. she saw the ark among the flags	Ex 2:5
w. she had opened it, she saw	Ex 2:6
w. Moses was grown, that he went out	Ex 2:11
and w. he saw that there was no man	Ex 2:12
and w. he went out the second day	Ex 2:13
Now w. Pharaoh heard this thing	Ex 2:15
And w. they came to Reuel their father	Ex 2:18
w. the Lord saw that he turned aside	Ex 3:4
W. thou hast brought forth the	Ex 3:12
w. I came unto the children of Israel	Ex 3:13
that, w. ye go, ye shall not go	Ex 3:21
w. he took it out, behold, his hand was	Ex 4:6
w. he seeth thee, he will be glad in his	Ex 4:14

W. thou goest to return into Egypt	Ex 4:21
w. they heard that the Lord had	Ex 4:31
daily tasks, as w. they were straw	Ex 5:13
day w. the Lord spake unto Moses in	Ex 6:28
w. I stretch forth mine hand upon	Ex 7:5
years old, w. they spake unto Pharaoh	Ex 7:7
W. Pharaoh shall speak unto you	Ex 7:9
w. shall I intreat for thee, and	Ex 8:9
w. Pharaoh saw that there was respite	Ex 8:15
w. Pharaoh saw that the rain and the	Ex 9:34
and w. it was morning, the east wind	Ex 10:13
w. he shall let you go, he shall surely	Ex 11:1
w. I see the blood, I will pass over	Ex 12:13
you, w. I smite the land of Egypt	Ex 12:13
w. he seeth the blood upon the lintel	Ex 12:23
w. ye be come to the land which	Ex 12:25
w. your children shall say unto you	Ex 12:26
w. he smote the Egyptians	Ex 12:27
w. thou hast circumcised him, then	Ex 12:44
And w. a stranger shall sojourn	Ex 12:48
w. the Lord shall bring thee into	Ex 13:5
unto me w. I came forth out of Egypt	Ex 13:8
w. the Lord shall bring thee into	Ex 13:11
w. thy son asketh thee in time to	Ex 13:14
w. Pharaoh would hardly let us go	Ex 13:15
pass, w. Pharaoh had let the people go	Ex 13:17
the people repent w. they see war	Ex 13:17
w. Pharaoh drew nigh, the children of	Ex 14:10
w. I have gotten me honour upon	Ex 14:18
his strength w. the morning appeared	Ex 14:27
w. they came to Marah, they could not	Ex 15:23
w. he had cast into the waters, the	Ex 15:25
of Egypt, w. we sat by the flesh pots	Ex 16:3
and w. we did eat bread to the full	Ex 16:3
w. the Lord shall give you in the flesh	Ex 16:8
w. the dew that lay was gone up	Ex 16:14
And w. the children of Israel saw it	Ex 16:15
And w. they did mete it with an omer	Ex 16:18
w. the sun waxed hot, it melted	Ex 16:21
w. I brought you forth from the land	Ex 16:32
pass, w. Moses held up his hand	Ex 17:11
and w. he let down his hand	Ex 17:11
w. Jethro, the priest of Midian	Ex 18:1
w. Moses' father in law saw all that he	Ex 18:14
W. they have a matter, they come	Ex 18:16
w. the children of Israel were gone	Ex 19:1
people may hear w. I speak with thee	Ex 19:9
w. the trumpet soundeth long, they	Ex 19:13
And w. the voice of the trumpet	Ex 19:19
w. the people saw it, they removed	Ex 20:18
w. he crieth unto me, that I will	Ex 22:27

w. thou hast gathered in thy labours	Ex 23:16
w. he goeth in unto the holy place	Ex 28:29; 28:35
heart, w. he goeth in before the Lord	Ex 28:30
and w. he cometh out, that he die not	Ex 28:35
w. they come in unto the tabernacle	Ex 28:43
or w. they come near unto the altar to	Ex 28:43
w. he cometh into the tabernacle of	Ex 29:30
w. thou hast made an atonement for	Ex 29:36
w. he dresseth the lamps, he shall	Ex 30:7
w. Aaron lighteth the lamps at even	Ex 30:8
W. thou takest the sum of the Lord, w. thou numberest them	Ex 30:12 Ex 30:12
them, w. thou numberest them	Ex 30:12
w. they give an offering unto the Lord	Ex 30:15
W. they go into the tabernacle of the	Ex 30:20
or w. they come near to the altar to	Ex 30:20
w. he made an end of communing	Ex 31:18
w. the people saw that Moses delayed	Ex 32:1
w. Aaron saw it, he built an altar	Ex 32:5
w. Joshua heard the noise of	Ex 32:17
w. Moses saw that the people were	Ex 32:25
nevertheless in the day w. I visit I	Ex 32:34
w. the people heard these evil tidings	Ex 33:4
w. Moses went out unto the tabernacle	Ex 33:8
w. thou shalt go up to appear before	Ex 34:24
w. Moses came down from mount	Ex 34:29
w. he came down from the mount	Ex 34:29
w. Aaron and all the children of Israel	Ex 34:30
w. Moses went in before the Lord to	Ex 34:34
W. they went into the tent of	Ex 40:32
w. they came near unto the altar, they	Ex 40:32
w. the cloud was taken up from over	Ex 40:36
w. any will offer a meat offering unto	Le 2:1
and w. it is presented unto the priest	Le 2:8
W. the sin, which they have sinned	Le 4:14
W. a ruler hath sinned, and done	Le 4:22
w. he knoweth of it, then he shall be	Le 5:3; 5:4
w. he shall be guilty in one of	Le 5:5
the Lord in the day w. he is anointed	Le 6:20
w. it is baken, thou shalt bring it in	Le 6:21
w. there is sprinkled of the blood	Le 6:27
w. he presented them to minister unto	Le 7:35
w. all the people saw, they shouted	Le 9:24
w. ye go into the tabernacle of	Le 10:9
w. Moses heard that he was content	Le 10:20
doth touch them, w. they be dead	Le 11:31
any of them, w. they are dead	Le 11:32
w. the days of her purifying are	Le 12:6
W. a man shall have in the skin of	Le 13:2
w. the hair in the plague is turned	Le 13:3
W. the plague of leprosy is in a	Le 13:9
w. raw flesh appeareth in him	Le 13:14
And if, w. the priest seeth it, behold	Le 13:20
W. ye be come into the land	Le 14:34
To teach w. it is unclean, and	Le 14:57

and w. it is clean: this is the law of	Le 14:57
W. any man hath a running issue	Le 15:2
w. he that hath an issue is cleansed	Le 15:13
w. he toucheth it, he shall be unclean	Le 15:23
w. they defile my tabernacle that is	Le 15:31
w. they offered before the Lord, and	Le 16:1
w. he goeth in to make an atonement	Le 16:17
w. he hath made the end of reconciling	Le 16:20
put on w. he went into the holy place	Le 16:23
spue not you out also, w. ye defile it	Le 18:28
w. ye reap the harvest of your land	Le 19:9
And w. ye shall come into the land	Le 19:23
w. giveth of his seed unto Molech	Le 20:4
w. the sun is down, he shall be clean	Le 22:7
trespass, w. they eat their holy things	Le 22:16
W. a bullock, or a sheep, or a goat	Le 22:27
And w. ye will offer a sacrifice of	Le 22:29
W. ye be come into the land which	Le 23:10
offer that day w. ye wave the sheaf	Le 23:12
w. ye reap the harvest of your land	Le 23:22
w. ye have gathered in the fruit of the	Le 23:39
w. I brought them out of the land of	Le 23:43
w. he blasphemeth the name of the	Le 24:16
W. ye come into the land which I	Le 25:2
ye shall flee w. none pursueth you	Le 26:17
w. ye are gathered together within	Le 26:25
And w. I have broken the staff of your	Le 26:26
in your sabbaths, w. ye dwelt upon it	Le 26:35
and they shall fall w. none pursueth	Le 26:36
before a sword, w. none pursueth	Le 26:37
w. they be in the land of their enemies	Le 26:44
W. a man shall make a singular	Le 27:2
w. a man shall sanctify his house	Le 27:14
the field, w. it goeth out in the jubile	Le 27:21
And w. the tabernacle settleth forward	Nu 1:51
and w. the tabernacle is to be pitched	Nu 1:51
w. they offered strange fire before the	Nu 3:4
w. the camp setteth forward, Aaron	Nu 4:5
w. Aaron and his sons have made an	Nu 4:15
w. they approach unto the most holy	Nu 4:19
to see w. the holy things are covered	Nu 4:20
W. a man or a woman shall	Nu 5:6
w. the Lord doth make thy thigh to	Nu 5:21
And w. he hath made her to drink the	Nu 5:27
w. a wife goeth aside, to another	Nu 5:29
Or w. the spirit of jealousy cometh	Nu 5:30
W. either man or woman shall	Nu 6:2
brother, or for his sister, w. they die	Nu 6:7
w. the days of his separation are	Nu 6:13
altar, in the day w. it was anointed	Nu 7:84
And w. Moses was gone into	Nu 7:89
W. thou lightest the lamps, the	Nu 8:2

w. the children of Israel come nigh	Nu 8:19
w. the cloud was taken up from	Nu 9:17
And w. the cloud tarried long upon the	Nu 9:19
w. the cloud was a few days upon	Nu 9:20
w. the cloud abode from even unto	Nu 9:21
but w. it was taken, they journeyed	Nu 9:22
But w. they shall blow with them	Nu 10:3
W. ye blow an alarm, then the camps	Nu 10:5
W. ye blow an alarm the second time	Nu 10:6
w. the congregation is to be gathered	Nu 10:7
to their armies, w. they set forward	Nu 10:28
by day, w. they went out of the camp	Nu 10:34
came to pass, w. the ark set forward	Nu 10:35
w. it rested, he said, Return, O Lord	Nu 10:36
And w. the people complained, it	Nu 11:1
and w. Moses prayed unto the Lord	Nu 11:2
And w. the dew fell upon the camp	Nu 11:9
that, w. the spirit rested upon them	Nu 11:25
w. he cometh out of his mother's	Nu 12:12
W. ye be come into the land	Nu 15:2
w. thou preparest a bullock for a	Nu 15:8
W. ye come into the land whither I	Nu 15:18
w. ye eat of the bread of the land, ye	Nu 15:19
w. he sinneth by ignorance before the	Nu 15:28
And w. Moses heard it, he fell upon his	Nu 16:4
w. the congregation was gathered	Nu 16:42
W. ye take of the children of	Nu 18:26
W. ye have heaved the best thereof	Nu 18:30
w. ye have heaved from it the best of	Nu 18:32
the law, w. a man dieth in a tent	Nu 19:14
we had died w. our brethren died	Nu 20:3
w. we cried unto the Lord, he heard	Nu 20:16
And w. all the congregation saw that	Nu 20:29
And w. king Arad the Canaanite	Nu 21:1
bitten, w. he looketh upon it, shall live	Nu 21:8
w. he beheld the serpent of brass, he	Nu 21:9
And w. the ass saw the angel of	Nu 22:25; 22:27
And w. Balak heard that Balaam was	Nu 22:36
w. he came to him, behold, he stood	Nu 23:17
And w. Balaam, saw that it pleased	Nu 24:1
w. he looked upon Amalek, he took	Nu 24:20
Alas, who shall live w. God doeth it	Nu 24:23
And w. Phinehas, the son of Eleazar	Nu 25:7
w. they strove against the Lord	Nu 26:9
with Korah w. that company died	Nu 26:10
w. the fire devoured (S)	Nu 26:10
w. they offered strange fire before the	Nu 26:61
w. they numbered the children of	Nu 26:64
w. thou hast seen it, thou also shalt	Nu 27:13
w. ye bring a new meat offering unto	Nu 28:26
had at all a husband, w. she vowed	Nu 30:6
w. they saw the land of Jazer	Nu 32:1

w. I sent them from Kadesh-barnea	Nu 32:8	W. thou art come unto the land	De 17:14	w. all these things are come upon	De 30:1
For w. they went up unto the valley of	Nu 32:9	w. he sitteth upon the throne of his	De 17:18	W. all Israel is come to appear before	De 31:11
years old w. he died in mount Hor	Nu 33:39	W. thou art come into the land	De 18:9	w. I shall have brought them into	De 31:20
W. ye are passed over Jordan	Nu 33:51	W. the prophet speaketh in	De 18:22	w. many evils and troubles are	De 31:21
them, W. ye come into the land of	Nu 34:2	W. the Lord thy God hath cut off	De 19:1	w. Moses had made an end of writing	De 31:24
W. ye be come over Jordan unto	Nu 35:10	As w. a man goeth into the wood	De 19:5	W. the most High divided to	De 32:8
w. he meeteth him, he shall slay him	Nu 35:19	W. thou goest out to battle	De 20:1	w. he separated the sons of Adam, he	De 32:8
slay the murderer, w. he meeteth him	Nu 35:21	w. ye are come nigh unto the battle	De 20:2	And w. the Lord saw it, he abhorred	De 32:19
And w. the jubile of the children of	Nu 36:4	w. the officers have made an	De 20:9	w. he seeth that their power is	De 32:36
w. we departed from Horeb, we went	De 1:19	W. thou comest nigh unto a city	De 20:10	w. the heads of the people and	De 33:5
w. ye had girded on every man his	De 1:41	w. the Lord thy God hath delivered it	De 20:13	and twenty years old w. he died	De 34:7
w. we passed by from our brethren	De 2:8	W. thou shalt besiege a city a	De 20:19	w. it was dark, that the men went out	Jos 2:5
w. they had destroyed them from	De 2:12	W. thou goest forth to war against	De 21:10	sea for you, w. ye came out of Egypt	Jos 2:10
w. all the men of war were	De 2:16	w. he maketh his sons to inherit	De 21:16	w. the Lord hath given us the land	Jos 2:14
w. thou comest nigh over against the	De 2:19	w. they have chastened him, will not	De 21:18	w. we come into the land, thou shalt	Jos 2:18
w. he destroyed the Horims from	De 2:22	W. thou buildest a new house	De 22:8	W. ye see the ark of the covenant of	Jos 3:3
w. the Lord said unto me, Gather me	De 4:10	w. I came to her, I found her not a	De 22:14	W. ye are come to the brink of	Jos 3:8
w. thou seest the sun, and the moon	De 4:19	for as w. a man riseth against his	De 22:26	w. the people removed from their	Jos 3:14
W. thou shalt beget children	De 4:25	way, w. ye came forth out of Egypt	De 23:4	w. all the people were clean passed	Jos 4:1; 4:11
W. thou art in tribulation, and all	De 4:30	W. the host goeth forth against	De 23:9	w. your children ask their fathers	Jos 4:6
w. ye heard the voice out of the midst	De 5:23	w. evening cometh on, he shall wash	De 23:11	w. it passed over Jordan, the waters	Jos 4:7
of your words, w. ye spake unto me	De 5:28	w. the sun is down, he shall come into	De 23:11	w. the priests, that bare the ark of the	Jos 4:18
of them w. thou sitteth in thine house	De 6:7	w. thou wilt ease thyself abroad, thou	De 23:13	W. your children shall ask their	Jos 4:21
and w. thou walkest by the way	De 6:7	W. thou shalt vow a vow unto	De 23:21	w. all the kings of the Amorites	Jos 5:1
and w. thou liest down	De 6:7	w. thou comest into thy	De 23:24	w. they had done circumcising all	Jos 5:8
and w. thou risest up	De 6:7	W. thou comest into the standing	De 23:25	to pass, w. Joshua was by Jericho	Jos 5:13
w. the Lord thy God shall have	De 6:10	W. a man hath taken a wife	De 24:1	w. they make a long blast with	Jos 6:5
w. thou shalt have eaten and be full	De 6:11	w. she is departed out of his house	De 24:2	w. ye hear the sound of the trumpet	Jos 6:5
w. thy son asketh thee in time	De 6:20	W. a man hath taken a new wife	De 24:5	w. Joshua had spoken unto the people	Jos 6:8
W. the Lord thy God shall bring	De 7:1	W. thou dost lend thy brother any	De 24:10	w. the priests blew with the trumpets	Jos 6:16
w. the Lord thy God shall deliver	De 7:2	pledge again w. the sun goeth down	De 24:13	w. ye take of the accursed thing, and	Jos 6:18
W. thou hast eaten and art full	De 8:10	W. thou cuttest down thine	De 24:19	shouted w. the priests blew with the	Jos 6:20
Lest w. thou hast eaten and art full	De 8:12	W. thou beatest thine olive tree	De 24:20	w. the people heard the sound of the	Jos 6:20
w. thy herds and thy flocks multiply	De 8:13	W. thou gatherest the grapes of	De 24:21	w. Israel turneth their backs	Jos 7:8
W. I was gone up into the mount to	De 9:9	the ox w. he treadeth out the corn	De 25:14	W. I saw among the spoils a goodly	Jos 7:21
Likewise w. the Lord sent you from	De 9:23	w. men strive together one with	De 25:11	w. they come out against us, as	Jos 8:5
of them w. thou sittest in thine house	De 11:19	w. ye were come forth out of Egypt	De 25:17	shall be, w. ye have taken the city	Jos 8:8
and w. thou walkest by the way	De 11:19	thee, w. thou wast faint and weary	De 25:18	w. they had set the people, even all	Jos 8:13
w. thou liest down, and w. thou risest	De 11:19	w. the Lord thy God hath given thee	De 25:19	w. the king of Ai saw it that they	Jos 8:14
w. the Lord thy God hath brought	De 11:29	w. thou art come in unto the land	De 26:1	w. the men of Ai looked behind them	Jos 8:20
But w. ye go over Jordan, and dwell	De 12:10	w. we cried unto the Lord God of our	De 26:7	w. Joshua and all Israel saw that the	Jos 8:21
w. he giveth you rest from all your	De 12:10	W. thou hast made an end of	De 26:12	w. Israel had made an end of slaying	Jos 8:24
W. the Lord thy God shall enlarge	De 12:20	w. ye shall pass over Jordan unto	De 27:2	w. they were all fallen on the edge of	Jos 8:24
w. thou shalt do that which is right	De 12:25; 21:9	this law, w. thou art passed over	De 27:3	w. all the kings which were on this	Jos 9:1
w. thou doest that which is good	De 12:28	it shall be w. ye be gone over Jordan	De 27:4	w. the inhabitants of Gibeon heard	Jos 9:3
W. the Lord thy God shall cut off	De 12:29	people, w. ye are come over Jordan	De 27:12	far from you; w. ye dwell among us	Jos 9:22
W. thou shalt hearken to the voice	De 13:18	Blessed shalt thou be w. thou comest	De 28:6	w. Adoni-zedec king of Jerusalem	Jos 10:1
w. the Lord thy God hath blessed	De 14:24	blessed shalt thou be w. thou goest	De 28:6	in the day w. the Lord delivered up	Jos 10:12
w. there shall be no poor among	De 15:4	Cursed shalt thou be w. thou comest	De 28:19	w. Joshua and the children of Israel	Jos 10:20
shall not be grieved w. thou givest	De 15:10	cursed shalt thou be w. thou goest out	De 28:19	w. they brought out those kings onto	Jos 10:24
And w. thou sendest him out free	De 15:13	w. ye came unto this place, Sihon the	De 29:7	w. Jabin king of Hazor had heard	Jos 11:1
w. thou sendest him away free from	De 15:18	w. he heareth the words of this curse	De 29:19	w. all these kings were met together	Jos 11:5
w. thou camest forth out of the land	De 16:3	w. they see the plagues of that land	De 29:22		
		w. he brought them forth out of the	De 29:25		

w. Moses the servant of the Lord sent	Jos 14:7
w. the children of Israel were	Jos 17:13
W. they had made an end of dividing	Jos 19:49
w. he that doth flee unto one of those	Jos 20:4
w. Joshua sent them away also	Jos 22:7
w. they came unto the borders of	Jos 22:10
w. the children of Israel heard of it	Jos 22:12
w. they should so say to us or to	Jos 22:28
w. Phinehas the priest, and the princes	Jos 22:30
W. ye have transgressed the covenant	Jos 23:16
And w. they cried unto the Lord	Jos 24:7
it came to pass, w. she came to him	J'g 1:14
w. he shewed them the entrance into	J'g 1:25
w. Israel was strong, that they put the	J'g 1:28
w. the angel of the Lord spake these	J'g 2:4
And w. Joshua had let the people go	J'g 2:6
w. the Lord raised them up judges	J'g 2:18
w. the judge was dead, that they	J'g 2:19
nations which Joshua left w. he died	J'g 2:21
w. the children of Israel cried unto	J'g 3:9; 3:15
w. he had made an end to offer the	J'g 3:18
W. he was gone out, his servants came	J'g 3:24
w. they saw that, behold, the doors of	J'g 3:24
pass, w. he was come, that he blew a	J'g 3:27
sight of the Lord, w. Ehud was dead	J'g 4:1
w. he had turned in unto her into the	J'g 4:18
w. any man doth come and enquire	J'g 4:20
And w. he came into her tent, behold	J'g 4:22
w. the people willingly offered	J'g 5:2
Lord, w. thou wentest out of Seir	J'g 5:4
w. thou marchedst out of the field of	J'g 5:4
w. she had pierced and stricken	J'g 5:26
the sun w. he goeth forth in his might	J'g 5:31
And so it was, w. Israel had sown	J'g 6:3
w. the children of Israel cried unto	J'g 6:7
w. Gideon perceived that he was an	J'g 6:22
w. the men of the city arose early in	J'g 6:28
w. they enquired and asked, they said	J'g 6:29
And w. Gideon was come, behold	J'g 7:13
w. Gideon heard the telling of	J'g 7:15
w. I come to the outside of the camp	J'g 7:17
W. I blow with a trumpet, I and all	J'g 7:18
w. thou wentest to fight with	J'g 8:1
toward him, w. he had said	J'g 8:3
w. the Lord hath delivered Zeba and	J'g 8:7
W. I come again in peace, I will break	J'g 8:9
And w. Zeba and Zalmunna fled	J'g 8:12
And w. they told it to Jotham, he went	J'g 9:7
W. Abimelech had reigned three years	J'g 9:22
w. Zebul the ruler of the city heard	J'g 9:30
W. he and the people that is with him	J'g 9:33
And w. Gaal saw the people, he said to	J'g 9:36

And w. all the men of the tower of	J'g 9:46
And w. the men of Israel saw	J'g 9:55
w. the children of Ammon made	J'g 11:5
unto me now w. ye are in distress	J'g 11:7
w. they came up out of Egypt, from	J'g 11:13
But w. Israel came up from Egypt, and	J'g 11:16
w. I return in peace from the children	J'g 11:31
to pass, w. he saw her, that he rent his	J'g 11:35
w. I called you, ye delivered me not	J'g 12:2
And w. I saw that ye delivered me not	J'g 12:3
w. those Ephraimites which were	J'g 12:5
w. thy sayings come to pass we	J'g 13:17
w. the flame went up toward heaven	J'g 13:20
w. they saw him, that they brought	J'g 14:11
And w. he had set the brands on fire	J'g 15:5
w. he came unto Lehi, the Philistines	J'g 15:14
w. he had made an end of speaking	J'g 15:17
w. he had drunk, his spirit came again	J'g 15:19
w. it is day, we shall kill him	J'g 16:2
of tow is broken w. it toucheth the fire	J'g 16:9
thee, w. thine heart is not with me	J'g 16:15
w. she pressed him daily with her	J'g 16:16
w. Delilah saw that he had told her all	J'g 16:18
w. the people saw him, they praised	J'g 16:24
pass, w. their hearts were merry	J'g 16:25
w. he had restored the eleven hundred	J'g 17:3
who w. they came to mount Ephraim	J'g 18:3
W. they were by the house of Micah	J'g 18:3
W. ye go, ye shall come unto a people	J'g 18:10
w. they were a good way from the	J'g 18:22
w. Micah saw that they were too strong	J'g 18:26
days, w. there was no king in Israel	J'g 19:1
w. the father of the damsel saw him	J'g 19:3
w. they arose early in the morning	J'g 19:5
And w. the man rose up to depart, his	J'g 19:7; 19:9
w. they were by Jebus, the day was far	J'g 19:11
upon them w. they were by Gibeah	J'g 19:14
w. he went in, he sat him down in a	J'g 19:15
w. he had lifted up his eyes, he saw a	J'g 19:17
w. the day began to spring, they let	J'g 19:25
w. he was come into his house, he	J'g 19:29
w. they come to Gibeah of Benjamin	J'g 20:10
w. the men of Israel retired in the	J'g 20:39
w. the flame began to arise up out of	J'g 20:40
w. the men of Israel turned again	J'g 20:41
w. their fathers or their brethren	J'g 21:22
pass in the days w. the judges ruled	Ru 1:1
W. she saw that she was stedfastly	Ru 1:18
w. they were come to Beth-lehem, that	Ru 1:19
w. thou art athirst, go unto the	Ru 2:9
w. she was risen up to glean, Boaz	Ru 2:15

be, w. he lieth down, that thou shalt	Ru 3:4
And w. Boaz had eaten and drunk	Ru 3:7
And w. she held it, he measured six	Ru 3:15
And w. she came to her mother in law	Ru 3:16
w. he went in unto her, the Lord gave	Ru 4:13
w. the time was that Elkanah offered	1Sa 1:4
w. she went up to the house	1Sa 1:7
w. the time was come about after	1Sa 1:20
w. she had weaned him, she took	1Sa 1:24
that, w. any man offered sacrifice	1Sa 2:13
w. she came up with her husband to	1Sa 2:19
w. they were in Egypt in Pharaoh's	1Sa 2:27
w. Eli was laid down in his place	1Sa 3:2
w. I begin, I will also make an end	1Sa 3:12
w. they joined battle, Israel was	1Sa 4:2
w. the people were come into	1Sa 4:3
w. it cometh among us, it may save us	1Sa 4:3
w. the ark of the covenant of	1Sa 4:5
w. the Philistines heard the noise of	1Sa 4:6
w. he came, lo, Eli sat upon a seat by	1Sa 4:13
w. the man came into the city, and	1Sa 4:13
w. Eli heard the noise of the crying, he	1Sa 4:14
w. he made mention of the ark of God	1Sa 4:18
w. she heard the tidings that the ark	1Sa 4:19
W. the Philistines took the ark	1Sa 5:2
w. they of Ashdod arose early on the	1Sa 5:3
w. they arose early on the morrow	1Sa 5:4
w. the men of Ashdod saw that it was	1Sa 5:7
w. he had wrought wonderfully	1Sa 6:6
w. the five lords of the Philistines had	1Sa 6:16
And w. the Philistines heard that the	1Sa 7:7
w. the children of Israel heard it, they	1Sa 7:7
w. Samuel was old, that he made	1Sa 8:1
w. they said, Give us a king to	1Sa 8:6
w. they were come to the land of Zuph	1Sa 9:5
w. a man went to enquire of God	1Sa 9:9
and w. they were come into the city	1Sa 9:14
w. Samuel saw Saul, the Lord	1Sa 9:17
w. they were come down from the	1Sa 9:25
W. thou art departed from me to day	1Sa 10:2
w. thou art come thither to the city	1Sa 10:5
w. these signs are come unto thee	1Sa 10:7
w. he had turned his back to go from	1Sa 10:9
And w. they came thither to the hill	1Sa 10:10
w. all that knew him before time saw	1Sa 10:11
And w. he had made an end of	1Sa 10:13
w. we saw that they were no where	1Sa 10:14
w. Samuel had caused all the tribes	1Sa 10:20
W. he had caused the tribe of	1Sa 10:21
w. they sought him, he could not be	1Sa 10:21
w. he stood among the people, he was	1Sa 10:23
upon Saul w. he heard those tidings	1Sa 11:6
w. he numbered them in Bezek, the	1Sa 11:8

W. Jacob was come into Egypt   1Sa 12:8
w. they forgat the Lord their God, he   1Sa 12:9
w. ye saw that Nahash the king of the   1Sa 12:12
w. the Lord your God was your king   1Sa 12:12
and *w*. he had reigned two years over   1Sa 13:1
W. the men of Israel saw that they   1Sa 13:6
And *w*. they had numbered, behold   1Sa 14:17
w. they heard that the Philistines fled   1Sa 14:22
And *w*. the people were come into the   1Sa 14:26
not *w*. his father charged the people   1Sa 14:27
w. Saul saw any strong man, or any   1Sa 14:52
in the way, *w*. he came up from Egypt   1Sa 15:2
Israel, *w*. they came up out of Egypt   1Sa 15:6
w. Samuel rose early to meet Saul   1Sa 15:12
W. thou wast little in thine own   1Sa 15:17
w. they were come, that he looked on   1Sa 16:6
w. the evil spirit from God is upon   1Sa 16:16
w. the evil spirit from God was upon   1Sa 16:23
w. Saul and all Israel heard those   1Sa 17:11
w. they saw the man, fled from him   1Sa 17:24
heard *w*. he spake unto the men   1Sa 17:28
w. the words were heard which David   1Sa 17:31
w. he arose against me, I caught him   1Sa 17:35
w. the Philistine looked about, and   1Sa 17:42
w. the Philistine arose, and came   1Sa 17:48
w. the Philistines saw their champion   1Sa 17:51
w. Saul saw David go forth against   1Sa 17:55
w. he had made an end of speaking   1Sa 18:1
w. David was returned from the   1Sa 18:6
Wherefore *w*. Saul saw that he behaved   1Sa 18:15
w. Merab Saul's daughter should have   1Sa 18:19
w. his servants told David these words   1Sa 18:26
w. Saul sent messengers to take David   1Sa 19:14
And *w*. the messengers were come in   1Sa 19:16
and *w*. they saw the company of the   1Sa 19:20
w. it was told Saul, he sent other   1Sa 19:21
w. I have sounded my father about   1Sa 20:12
w. the Lord hath cut off the enemies   1Sa 20:15
And *w*. thou hast stayed three days   1Sa 20:19
hide thyself *w*. the business was in   1Sa 20:19
w. the new moon was come, the king   1Sa 20:24
w. the lad was come to the place of the   1Sa 20:37
in the day *w*. it was taken away   1Sa 21:6
w. his brethren and all his father's   1Sa 22:1
W. Saul heard that David was   1Sa 22:6
because they knew *w*. he fled   1Sa 22:17
w. Doeg the Edomite was there   1Sa 22:22
w. Abiathar the son of Ahimelech fled   1Sa 23:6
w. Saul heard that, he pursued after   1Sa 23:25
w. Saul was returned from following   1Sa 24:1

w. Saul looked behind him, David   1Sa 24:8
w. David had made an end of speaking   1Sa 24:16
as *w*. the Lord had delivered me   1Sa 24:18
And *w*. David's young men came, they   1Sa 25:9
with them, *w*. we were in the fields   1Sa 25:15
w. Abigail saw David, she hasted   1Sa 25:23
w. the Lord shall have done to my   1Sa 25:30
w. the Lord shall have dealt well with   1Sa 25:31
w. the wine was gone out of Nabal   1Sa 25:37
w. David heard that Nabal was dead   1Sa 25:39
w. the servants of David were come   1Sa 21:40
as *w*. one doth hunt a partridge in   1Sa 26:20
w. Saul saw the host of the Philistines   1Sa 28:5
And *w*. Saul enquired of the Lord   1Sa 28:6
w. the woman saw Samuel, she cried   1Sa 28:12
strength, *w*. thou goest on thy way   1Sa 28:22
w. David and his men were come to   1Sa 30:1
w. he had eaten, his spirit came again   1Sa 30:12
w. he had brought him down, behold   1Sa 30:16
w. David came near to the people, he   1Sa 30:21
w. David came to Ziklag, he sent of   1Sa 30:26
w. his armourbearer saw that Saul   1Sa 31:5
w. the men of Israel that were on the   1Sa 31:7
w. the Philstines came to strip the   1Sa 31:8
w. the inhabitants of Jabesh-gilead   1Sa 31:11
w. David was returned from   2Sa 1:1
w. he came to David, that he fell to the   2Sa 1:2
w. he looked behind him, he saw me   2Sa 1:7
old *w*. he began to reign over Israel   2Sa 2:10
down *w*. they were come to the hill of   2Sa 2:24
w. he had gathered all the people   2Sa 2:30
w. thou comest to see my face   2Sa 3:13
W. Joab and all the host that was   2Sa 3:23
w. Joab was come out from David, he   2Sa 3:26
w. Abner was returned to Hebron   2Sa 3:27
afterward *w*. David heard it, he said   2Sa 3:28
w. all the people came to cause David   2Sa 3:35
w. Saul's son heard Abner was dead   2Sa 4:1
w. the tidings came of Saul   2Sa 4:4
For *w*. they came into the house, he   2Sa 4:7
W. one told me, saying, Behold, Saul   2Sa 4:10
w. wicked men have slain a   2Sa 4:11
w. Saul was king over us, thou wast   2Sa 5:2
David was thirty years old *w*. he began   2Sa 5:4
w. the Philistines heard that they had   2Sa 5:17
w. David enquired of the Lord, he   2Sa 5:23
w. thou hearest the sound of a going   2Sa 5:24
And *w*. they came to Nachon's   2Sa 6:6
w. they that bare the ark of   2Sa 6:13
w. the king sat in his house   2Sa 7:1
w. thy days be fulfilled, and thou   2Sa 7:12
w. the Syrians of Damascus came to   2Sa 8:5
W. Toi king of Hamath heard that   2Sa 8:9

w. he returned from smiting of the   2Sa 8:13
w. they had called him unto David   2Sa 9:2
Now *w*. Mephibosheth, the son of   2Sa 9:6
W. they told it unto David, he sent to   2Sa 10:5
w. the children of Ammon saw that   2Sa 10:6; 10:14
w. David heard of it, he sent Joab, and   2Sa 10:7
W. Joab saw that the front of   2Sa 10:9
w. the Syrians saw that they were   2Sa 10:15
w. it was told David, he gathered all   2Sa 10:17
w. all the kings that were servants to   2Sa 10:19
time *w*. the kings go forth to battle   2Sa 11:1
w. Uriah was come unto him, David   2Sa 11:7
w. they had told David, saying, Uriah   2Sa 11:10
And *w*. David had called him, he did   2Sa 11:13
w. Joab observed the city, that he   2Sa 11:16
W. thou hast made an end of telling   2Sa 11:19
so nigh unto the city *w*. ye did fight   2Sa 11:20
w. the wife of Uriah heard that Uriah   2Sa 11:26
w. the mourning was past, David sent   2Sa 11:27
w. David saw that his servants   2Sa 12:19
w. he required, they set bread before   2Sa 12:20
w. the child was dead, thou didst   2Sa 12:21
w. thy father cometh to see thee, say   2Sa 13:5
and *w*. the king was come to see him   2Sa 13:6
w. she had brought them unto him to   2Sa 13:11
But *w*. king David heard of all these   2Sa 13:21
ye now *w*. Ammon's heart is merry   2Sa 13:28
and *w*. I say unto you, Smite Ammon   2Sa 13:28
w. the woman of Tekoah spake to the   2Sa 14:4
w. he polled his head, (for it was at   2Sa 14:26
w. he sent again the second time, he   2Sa 14:29
w. he had called for Absalom, he came   2Sa 14:33
w. any man that had a controversy   2Sa 15:2
w. any man came nigh to him to do   2Sa 15:5
w. David was come to the top of the   2Sa 15:32
w. David was a little past the top of   2Sa 16:1
And *w*. king David came to Bahurim   2Sa 16:5
thus said Shimei *w*. he cursed, Come   2Sa 16:7
w. Hushai the Archite, David's   2Sa 16:16
And *w*. Hushai was come to Absalom   2Sa 17:6
w. some of them be overthrown at the   2Sa 17:9
w. Absalom's servants came to the   2Sa 17:20
w. they had sought and could not find   2Sa 17:20
w. Ahithophel saw that his counsel   2Sa 17:23
w. David was come to Mahanaim   2Sa 17:27
w. the king gave all the captains   2Sa 18:5
W. Joab sent the king's servant, and   2Sa 18:29
steal away *w*. they flee in battle   2Sa 19:3
w. he was come to Jerusalem to   2Sa 19:25
w. the king was come over, the king   2Sa 19:39

W. they were at the great stone	2Sa 20:8	*W*. I am dead, then bury me in the	1Ki 13:31
w. the man saw that all the people	2Sa 20:12	it shall be, *w*. she cometh in, that she	1Ki 14:5
W. he was removed out of her, the	2Sa 20:13	*w*. Ahijah heard the sound of her feet	1Ki 14:6
w. he come near unto	2Sa 20:17	and *w*. thy feet enter into the city, the	1Ki 14:12
w. the Philistines had slain Saul	2Sa 21:12	*w*. she come to the threshold of the	1Ki 14:17
w. he defied Israel, Jonathan the son	2Sa 21:21	one years old *w*. he began to reign	1Ki 14:21
W. the waves of death compassed	2Sa 22:5	*w*. the king went into the house	1Ki 14:28
of the morning, *w*. the sun riseth	2Sa 23:4	it came to pass, *w*. Baasha heard	1Ki 15:21
w. they defied the Philistines that	2Sa 23:9	*w*. he reigned, that he smote all the	1Ki 15:29
So *w*. they had gone through all the	2Sa 24:8	*w*. he began to reign, as soon as he sat	1Ki 16:11
w. David was up in the morning,	2Sa 24:11	*w*. Zimri saw that the city was taken	1Ki 16:18
w. the angel stretched out his hand	2Sa 24:16	*w*. he came to the gate of the city	1Ki 17:10
w. he saw the angel that smote the	2Sa 24:17	*w*. Jezebel cut off the prophets of	1Ki 18:4
w. my lord the king shall sleep with	1Ki 1:21	and *w*. they said, He is not there	1Ki 18:10
w. he was come in before the king, he	1Ki 1:23	and so *w*. I come and tell Ahab	1Ki 18:12
And *w*. Joab heard the sound of the	1Ki 1:41	*w*. Jezebel slew the prophets of the	1Ki 18:13
to me *w*. I fled because of Absalom	1Ki 2:7	*w*. Ahab saw Elijah, that Ahab said	1Ki 18:17
in the day *w*. I went to Mahanaim	1Ki 2:8	*w*. midday was past, and they	1Ki 18:29
w. I rose in the morning to give my	1Ki 3:21	*w*. all the people saw it, they fell on	1Ki 18:39
but *w*. I had considered it in	1Ki 3:21	*w*. he saw that, he arose, and went for	1Ki 19:3
w. Hiram heard words of Solomon	1Ki 5:7	*w*. Elijah heard it, that he wrapped	1Ki 19:13
w. it was in building, was built of	1Ki 6:7	*w*. thou comest, anoint Hazael to be	1Ki 19:15
were cast in two rows, *w*. it was cast	1Ki 7:24	*w*. Ben-hadad heard this message	1Ki 20:12
w. the Lord made a covenant with	1Ki 8:9	*w*. Jezebel heard that Naboth was	1Ki 21:15
w. they came out of the land of Egypt	1Ki 8:9	*w*. Ahab heard that Naboth was dead	1Ki 21:16
w. the priests were come out of the	1Ki 8:10	to pass *w*. Ahab heard those words	1Ki 21:27
w. he brought them out of the land of	1Ki 8:21	*w*. thou shalt go into an inner	1Ki 22:25
w. they shall pray toward this	1Ki 8:30	*w*. the captains of the chariots	1Ki 22:32; 22:33
and *w*. thou hearest, forgive	1Ki 8:30	five years old *w*. he began to reign	1Ki 22:42; 2Ki 14:2; 23:36
W. thy people Israel be smitten down	1Ki 8:33	*w*. the messengers turned back unto	2Ki 1:5
W. heaven is shut up, and there is no	1Ki 8:35	*w*. the Lord would take up Elijah into	2Ki 2:1
there sin, *w*. thou afflictest them	1Ki 8:35	came to pass, *w*. they were gone over	2Ki 2:9
w. he shall come and pray toward this	1Ki 8:42	thou see me *w*. I am taken from thee	2Ki 2:10
w. thou broughtest our fathers out of	1Ki 8:53	*w*. he also had smitten the waters	2Ki 2:14
w. Solomon had made an end of	1Ki 8:54	*w*. the sons of the prophets which	2Ki 2:15
w. Solomon had finished the building	1Ki 9:1	*w*. they urged him till he was ashamed	2Ki 2:17
w. Solomon had built the two houses	1Ki 9:10	*w*. they came again to him	2Ki 2:18
w. the queen of Sheba heard of the	1Ki 10:1	it came to pass, *w*. Ahab was dead	2Ki 3:5
and *w*. she was come to Solomon, she	1Ki 10:2	came to pass, *w*. the minstrel played	2Ki 3:15
w. the queen of Sheba had seen all	1Ki 10:4	*w*. the meat offering was offered	2Ki 3:20
w. Solomon was old, that his	1Ki 11:4	*w*. all the Moabites heard that the	2Ki 3:21
w. David was in Edom, and Joab the	1Ki 11:15	*w*. they came to the camp of Israel	2Ki 3:24
w. Hadad heard in Egypt that David	1Ki 11:21	*w*. the king of Moab saw that	2Ki 3:26
a band, *w*. David slew them of Zobah	1Ki 11:24	*w*. thou art come in, thou shalt shut	2Ki 4:4
w. Jeroboam went out of Jerusalem	1Ki 11:29	came to pass, *w*. the vessels were full	2Ki 4:6
w. Jeroboam the son of Nebat, who	1Ki 12:2	and it shall be, *w*. he cometh to us	2Ki 4:10
So *w*. all Israel saw that the king	1Ki 12:16	*w*. he had called her, she stood before	2Ki 4:12
w. all Israel heard that Jeroboam was	1Ki 12:20	*w*. he had called her, she stood in the	2Ki 4:15
w. Rehoboam was come to Jerusalem	1Ki 12:21	*w*. the child was grown, it fell on	2Ki 4:18
w. king Jeroboam heard the saying of	1Ki 13:4	*w*. he had taken him, and brought	2Ki 4:20
w. he was gone, a lion met him by the	1Ki 13:24	*w*. the man of God saw her afar off	2Ki 4:25
w. the prophet that brought him back	1Ki 13:26		

w. she came to the man of God to the	2Ki 4:27
w. Elisha was come into the house	2Ki 4:32
w. she was come in unto him, he said	2Ki 4:36
Now *w*. this letter is come unto thee	2Ki 5:6
w. the king of Israel had read	2Ki 5:7
w. Elisha the man of God had heard	2Ki 5:8
w. he saith to thee, Wash, and be	2Ki 5:13
w. my master goeth into the house	2Ki 5:18
w. I bow down myself in the house of	2Ki 5:18
w. Naaman saw him running after	2Ki 5:21
w. he came to the tower, he took them	2Ki 5:24
w. the man turned again from his	2Ki 5:26
w. they came to Jordan, they cut down	2Ki 6:4
w. the servant of the man of God was	2Ki 6:15
w. they came down to him, Elisha	2Ki 6:18
w. they were come into Samaria	2Ki 6:20
w. he saw them, My father, shall I	2Ki 6:21
w. they had eaten and drunk, he sent	2Ki 6:23
w. the king heard the words of the	2Ki 6:30
w. the messenger cometh, shut	2Ki 6:32
w. they were come to the uttermost	2Ki 7:5
w. these lepers came to the uttermost	2Ki 7:8
W. they come out of the city, we	2Ki 7:12
who spake *w*. the king came down to	2Ki 7:17
w. the king asked the woman	2Ki 8:6
old was he *w*. he began to reign	2Ki 8:17
old was Ahaziah *w*. he began to reign	2Ki 8:26
w. he fought against Hazael king of	2Ki 8:29
w. thou comest thither, look out there	2Ki 9:2
w. he came, behold, the captains of	2Ki 9:5
w. he fought with Hazael king of	2Ki 9:15
w. Joram saw Jehu, that he said, Is it	2Ki 9:22
w. I and thou rode together after	2Ki 9:25
w. Ahaziah the king of Judah saw	2Ki 9:27
And *w*. Jehu was come to Jezreel	2Ki 9:30
w. he was come in, he did eat	2Ki 9:34
pass, *w*. the letter came to them, that	2Ki 10:7
w. he was departed thence, he lighted	2Ki 10:15
w. he came to Samaria, he slew all that	2Ki 10:17
And *w*. they went in to offer sacrifices	2Ki 10:24
w. Athaliah the mother of Ahaziah	2Ki 11:1
w. Athaliah heard the noise of the	2Ki 11:13
w. she looked, behold, the king stood	2Ki 11:14
was Jehoash *w*. he began to reign	2Ki 11:21
w. they saw that there was much	2Ki 12:10
and *w*. the man was let down, and	2Ki 13:21
old was he *w*. he began to reign	2Ki 15:2; 15:33; 18:2
old was Ahaz *w*. he began to reign	2Ki 16:2
And *w*. the king was come from	2Ki 16:12
w. they were come up, they came and	2Ki 18:17
w. they had called to the king, there	2Ki 18:18
w. he persuadeth you, saying, The	2Ki 18:32

to pass w. king Hezekiah	2Ki 19:1	
heard it		
w. he heard say of Tirhakah	2Ki 19:9	
king of		
w. they arose early in the	2Ki 19:35	
morning		
years old w. he began to	2Ki 21:1;	
reign	24:8	
two years old w. he began	2Ki 21:19	
to reign		
eight years old w. he began	2Ki 22:1;	
to reign	2Ch 34:1; 36:9	
w. the king had heard the	2Ki 22:11	
words of		
w. thou heardest what	2Ki 22:19	
I spake against		
him at Megiddo, w. he had	2Ki 23:29	
seen him		
three years old w. he began	2Ki 23:31	
to reign		
one years old w. he began to	2Ki 24:18	
reign, and		
w. all the captains of the	2Ki 25:23	
armies, they		
w. Bela was dead, Jobab the	1Ch 1:44	
son of		
And w. Jobab was dead,	1Ch 1:45	
Husham of		
w. Husham was dead, Hadad	1Ch 1:46	
the son		
w. Hadad was dead, Samlah	1Ch 1:47	
of		
w. Samlah was dead, Shaul	1Ch 1:48	
of		
w. Shaul was dead,	1Ch 1:49	
Baal-hanan the		
w. Ball-hanan was dead,	1Ch 1:50	
Hadad		
w. Azubah was dead, Caleb	1Ch 2:19	
took unto		
w. he was threescore years	1Ch 2:21	
old		
w. the genealogy of their	1Ch 5:7	
generations		
w. the Lord carried away	1Ch 6:15	
Judah and		
w. he went in to his wife, she	1Ch 7:23	
conceived		
w. his armourbearer saw that	1Ch 10:5	
Saul		
w. all the men of Israel that	1Ch 10:7	
were in		
w. the Philistines came to	1Ch 10:8	
strip the		
w. they had stripped him,	1Ch 10:9	
they took		
w. all Jabesh-gilead heard	1Ch 10:11	
all that the		
time past, even w. Saul was	1Ch 11:2	
king		
w. it had overflown all his	1Ch 12:15	
banks		
w. he came with the	1Ch 12:19	
Philistines		
w. they came unto the	1Ch 13:9	
threshingfloor		
w. the Philistines heard that	1Ch 14:8	
David		
And w. they had left their	1Ch 14:12	
gods there		
w. thou shalt hear a sound	1Ch 14:15	
of going		
w. god helped the Levites,	1Ch 15:26	
that bare		
w. David had made an end of	1Ch 16:2	
offering		
W. ye were but few, even a	1Ch 16:19	
few, and		
w. they went from nation to	1Ch 16:20	
nation		
w. thy days be expired that	1Ch 17:11	
thou		
w. the Syrians of Damascus	1Ch 18:5	
came		
w. Tou king of Hamath	1Ch 18:9	
heard how		
w. the children of Ammon	1Ch 19:6	
saw that		
w. David heard of it, he sent	1Ch 19:8	
Joab		
Now w. Joab saw that the	1Ch 19:10	
battle was		
w. the children of Ammon	1Ch 19:15	
saw that		
w. the Syrians saw that they	1Ch 19:16	
were		
w. David had put the battle	1Ch 19:17	
in array		
w. the servants of	1Ch 19:19	
Hadarezer saw that		

w. he defiled Israel, Jonathan	1Ch 20:7	
the son		
that time w. David saw that	1Ch 21:28	
the Lord		
w. David was old and full of	1Ch 23:1	
days, he		
of oxen were cast, w. it was	2Ch 4:3	
cast		
w. the Lord made a covenant	2Ch 5:10	
with		
of Israel, w. they came out	2Ch 5:10	
of Egypt		
w. the priests were come out	2Ch 5:11	
of the		
w. they lifted up their voice	2Ch 5:13	
with the		
heaven; and w. thou hearest,	2Ch 6:21	
forgive		
W. the heaven is shut up,	2Ch 6:26	
and there		
sin, w. thou dost afflict them	2Ch 6:26	
w. thou hast taught them the	2Ch 6:27	
good		
w. every one shall know his	2Ch 6:29	
own		
w. Solomon had made an end	2Ch 7:1	
of		
w. all the children of Israel	2Ch 7:3	
saw how		
w. David praised by their	2Ch 7:6	
ministry		
w. the queen of Sheba heard	2Ch 9:1	
of the		
w. she was come to Solomon,	2Ch 9:1	
she		
w. the queen of Sheba had	2Ch 9:3	
seen the		
w. Jeroboam the son of	2Ch 10:2	
Nebat, who		
w. all Israel saw that the	2Ch 10:16	
king would		
w. Rehoboam was come to	2Ch 11:1	
Jerusalem		
w. Rehoboam had	2Ch 12:1	
established the		
w. the Lord saw that	2Ch 12:7	
they humbled		
w. the king entered into the	2Ch 12:11	
house		
w. he humbled himself, the	2Ch 12:12	
wrath of		
forty years old w. he began	2Ch 12:13	
to reign		
w. Rehoboam was young and	2Ch 13:7	
w. Judah looked back,	2Ch 13:14	
behold, the		
w. they in their trouble did	2Ch 15:4	
turn		
w. Asa heard these words	2Ch 15:8	
w. they saw that the Lord his	2Ch 15:9	
God was		
w. Baasha heard it, that he	2Ch 16:5	
left off		
w. he was come to the king,	2Ch 18:14	
the king		
w. thou shalt go into an	2Ch 18:24	
inner		
w. the captains of the	2Ch 18:31;	
chariots	18:32	
w. they returned to	2Ch 19:8	
Jerusalem		
w. evil cometh upon us, as	2Ch 20:9	
the sword		
w. they came out of the land	2Ch 20:10	
of Egypt		
w. he had consulted with	2Ch 20:21	
the people		
w. they began to sing and to	2Ch 20:22	
w. they had made an end of	2Ch 20:23	
w. Judah came toward the	2Ch 20:24	
watch		
w. Jehoshaphat and his	2Ch 20:25	
people came		
w. they had heard that the	2Ch 20:29	
Lord		
and five years w. he began	2Ch 20:31	
to reign		
w. Jehoram was risen up to	2Ch 21:4	
two years old w. he began to	2Ch 21:5	
reign		
old was he w. he began to	2Ch 21:20	
reign		
was Ahaziah w. he began to	2Ch 22:2	
reign		
w. he fought with Hazael	2Ch 22:6	
king of		
w. he was come, he went out	2Ch 22:7	
with		
w. Jehu was executing	2Ch 22:8	
judgment		

w. they had slain him, they	2Ch 22:9	
buried		
w. Athaliah the mother of	2Ch 22:10	
Ahaziah		
w. he cometh in, and w. he	2Ch 23:7	
goeth out		
w. Athaliah heard the noise	2Ch 23:12	
of the		
w. she was come to the	2Ch 23:15	
entering of the		
seven years old w. he began to	2Ch 24:1	
reign		
and w. they saw that there	2Ch 24:11	
was much		
w. they had finished it, they	2Ch 24:14	
brought		
and was full of days w. he	2Ch 24:15	
died		
thirty years old was he w.	2Ch 24:15	
he died		
w. he died, he said, The Lord	2Ch 24:22	
look		
w. they were departed from	2Ch 24:25	
him		
five years old w. he began to	2Ch 25:1;	
reign	27:1; 36:5	
w. the kingdom was	2Ch 25:3	
established to		
old was Uzziah w. he began	2Ch 26:3	
to reign		
w. he was strong, his heart	2Ch 26:16	
was lifted		
twenty years old w. he began	2Ch 27:8;	
to reign	28:1; 33:21; 36:11	
to reign w. he was five and	2Ch 29:1	
twenty		
w. they had killed the rams	2Ch 29:22	
w. the burnt offering began	2Ch 29:27	
w. they had made an end of	2Ch 29:29	
offering		
w. all this was finished, all	2Ch 31:1	
Israel that		
w. Hezekiah and the princes	2Ch 31:8	
came		
w. Hezekiah saw that	2Ch 32:2	
Sennacherib		
w. he was come into the	2Ch 32:21	
house of his		
twelve years old w. he began	2Ch 33:1	
to reign		
w. he was in affliction, he	2Ch 33:12	
besought		
w. he had broken down the	2Ch 34:7	
altars and		
w. he had purged the land	2Ch 34:8	
w. they came to Hilkiah the	2Ch 34:9	
high		
w. they brought out the	2Ch 34:14	
money that		
w. the king had heard the	2Ch 34:19	
word of the		
w. thou heardest his words	2Ch 34:27	
against		
w. Josiah had prepared the	2Ch 35:20	
temple		
three years old w. he began	2Ch 36:2	
to reign		
w. the year was expired,	2Ch 36:10	
king		
w. they came to the house of	Ezr 2:68	
the Lord		
w. the seventh month was	Ezr 3:1	
come, and		
w. the builders laid the	Ezr 3:10	
foundation of		
w. they praised the Lord,	Ezr 3:11	
because the		
w. the foundation of this	Ezr 3:12	
house was		
w. the adversaries of Judah	Ezr 4:1	
Now w. the copy of king	Ezr 4:23	
now w. these things were done	Ezr 9:1	
w. I heard this thing, I rent	Ezr 9:3	
my		
w. Ezra had prayed, and w.	Ezr 10:1	
he had		
w. he came thither, he did	Eze 10:6	
eat no		
w. I heard these words, that	Ne 1:4	
I sat		
w. the city, the place of my	Ne 2:3	
fathers		
be? and w. wilt thou return	Ne 2:6	
W. Sanballat the Horonite	Ne 2:10	
and		
w. Sanballat the Horonite,	Ne 2:19	
and Tobiah		
w. Sanballat heard that we	Ne 4:1	
builded		

w. Sanballat, and Tobiah, and *Ne 4:7; 6:1*

w. the Jews which dwelt by them *Ne 4:12*

w. our enemies heard that it was *Ne 4:15*

w. I heard their cry and these *Ne 5:6*

w. all our enemies heard thereof *Ne 6:16*

w. the wall was built, and I had set *Ne 7:1*

w. the seventh month came *Ne 7:73*

w. he opened it, all the people stood *Ne 8:5*

w. they heard the words of the law *Ne 8:9*

w. they had made them a molten *Ne 9:18*

w. they cried unto thee, thou heardest *Ne 9:27*

w. they returned, and cried unto thee *Ne 9:28*

the Levites, w. the Levites take tithes *Ne 10:38*

w. they had heard the law, that they *Ne 13:3*

w. the gates of Jerusalem began to *Ne 13:19*

w. the king Ahasuerus sat on *Es 1:2*

W. he shewed the riches of his *Es 1:4*

w. these days were expired, the king *Es 1:5*

w. the heart of the king was merry *Es 1:10*

in their eyes, w. it shall be reported *Es 1:17*

w. the king's decree, which he shall *Es 1:20*

w. the wrath of king Ahasuerus was *Es 2:1*

w. her father and mother were dead *Es 2:7*

w. the kings commandment and his *Es 2:8*

and w. many maidens were gathered *Es 2:8*

w. every maid's turn was come *Es 2:12*

w. the turn of Esther, the daughter of *Es 2:15*

w. the virgins were gathered together *Es 2:19*

as w. she was brought up with him *Es 2:20*

w. inquisition was made of the matter *Es 2:23*

w. they spake daily unto him, and he *Es 3:4*

w. Haman saw that Mordecai bowed *Es 3:5*

W. Mordecai perceived all that was *Es 4:1*

w. the king saw Esther the queen *Es 5:2*

w. Haman saw Mordecai in the king's *Es 5:9*

w. he came home, he sent and called *Es 5:10*

w. the king's commandment *Es 9:1*

w. Esther came before the king, he *Es 9:25*

w. the days of their feasting were *Job 1:5*

was a day w. the sons of God came *Job 1:6; 2:1*

w. his sons and his daughters were *Job 1:13*

Now w. Job's three friends heard of *Job 2:11*

w. they lifted up their eyes afar off *Job 2:12*

the ghost w. I came out of the belly *Job 3:11*

glad, w. they can find the grave *Job 3:22*

night, w. deep sleep fallest upon men *Job 4:13*

afraid of destruction w. it cometh *Job 5:21*

the wild ass bray w. he hath grass *Job 6:5*

w. it is hot, they are consumed out of *Job 6:17*

W. I lie down, I say *Job 7:4*

W. shall I arise, and the night *Job 7:4*

W. I say, My bed shall comfort *Job 7:13*

w. thou mockest, shall no man make *Job 11:23*

W. a few years are come, then I *Job 16:22*

w. our rest together is in the dust *Job 17:16*

W. he is about to fill his belly, God *Job 20:23*

Even w. I remember I am afraid *Job 21:6*

w. the number of his months *Job 21:21* is cut off

W. men are cast down, then thou *Job 22:29*

w. he hath tried me, I shall come forth *Job 23:10*

w. I consider, I am afraid of him *Job 23:15*

w. God taketh away his soul *Job 27:8*

cry w. trouble cometh upon him *Job 27:9*

W. he made a decree for the rain, and *Job 28:26*

as in the days w. God preserved me *Job 29:2*

W. his candle shined upon my head *Job 29:3*

w. by his light I walked through *Job 29:3*

w. the secret of God was upon my *Job 29:4*

W. the Almighty was yet with *Job 29:5*

w. my children were about me *Job 29:5*

W. I washed my steps with butter *Job 29:6*

W. I went out to the gate through *Job 29:7*

w. I prepared my seat in the street *Job 29:7*

W. the ear heard me, then it *Job 29:11*

w. the eye saw me, it gave witness *Job 29:11*

W. I looked for good, then evil *Job 30:26*

w. I waited for light, there came *Job 30:26*

w. they contended with me *Job 31:13*

shall I do w. God raiseth up? and *Job 31:14*

w. he visiteth, what shall I answer *Job 31:14*

I saw my help in the gate *Job 31:21*

If I beheld the sun w. it shined or *Job 31:26*

lifted up myself w. evil found him *Job 31:29*

W. Elihu saw there was no answer in *Job 32:5*

W. I had waited, (for they spake not *Job 32:16*

night, w. deep sleep falleth upon men *Job 33:15*

W. he giveth quietness, who then can *Job 34:29*

w. he hideth his face, who then can *Job 34:29*

they cry not w. he bindeth them *Job 36:13*

w. people are cut off in their place *Job 36:20*

stay them w. his voice is heard *Job 37:4*

Dost thou know w. God disposed *Job 37:15*

warm, w. he quieteth the earth by the *Job 37:17*

wast thou w. I laid the foundations *Job 38:4*

W. the morning stars sang together *Job 38:7*

the sea with doors, w. it break forth *Job 38:8*

W. I made the cloud the garment *Job 38:9*

W. the dust groweth into hardness *Job 38:38*

W. they couch in their dens *Job 38:40*

w. his young ones cry unto God *Job 38:41*

w. the wild goats of the rock bring *Job 39:1*

thou mark w. the hinds do calve *Job 39:1*

thou the time w. they bring forth *Job 39:2*

W. he riseth up himself, the mighty *Job 41:25*

of Job, w. he prayed for his friends *Job 42:10*

w. his wrath is kindled but a little *Ps 2:12*

w. he fled from Absalom his son *Ps 3 title*

Hear me w. I call, O God of my *Ps 4:1*

hast enlarged me w. I was in distress *Ps 4:1*

the Lord will hear w. I call unto him *Ps 4:3*

W. I consider thy heavens, the *Ps 8:3*

W. mine enemies are turned back *Ps 9:3*

W. he maketh inquisition for *Ps 9:12*

poor, w. he draweth him into his net *Ps 10:9*

side w. the vilest men are exalted *Ps 12:8*

trouble me rejoice w. I am moved *Ps 13:4*

w. the Lord bringeth back the *Ps 14:7*

satisfied, w. I awake, with thy likeness *Ps 17:15*

Lord: let the king hear us w. we call *Ps 20:9*

w. thou shalt make ready thine arrows *Ps 21:12*

w. I was upon my mother's breasts *Ps 22:9*

but w. he cried unto me he heard *Ps 22:24*

W. the wicked, even mine enemies *Ps 27:2*

w. I cry with my voice: have mercy *Ps 27:7*

W. thou saidst, Seek ye my face: my *Ps 27:8*

W. my father and my mother *Ps 27:10*

my supplications, w. I cry unto thee *Ps 28:2*

w. I lift up my hands toward thy holy *Ps 28:2*

in my blood, w. I go down to the pit *Ps 30:9*

my supplications w. I cried unto thee *Ps 31:22*

W. I kept silence, my bones *Ps 32:3*

in a time w. thou mayest be found *Ps 32:6*

w. he changed his behaviour before *Ps 34 title*

w. they were sick, my clothing was *Ps 35:13*

nor condemn him w. he is judged *Ps 37:33*

w. the wicked are cut off, thou shalt *Ps 37:34*

w. my foot slippeth, they magnify *Ps 38:16*

W. thou with rebukes dost correct *Ps 39:11*

me, W. shall he die, and his name *Ps 41:5*

w. he goeth abroad, he telleth it *Ps 41:6*

w. shall I come and appear before *Ps 42:2*

W. I remember these things, I pour *Ps 47:4*

w. the iniquity of my heels shall *Ps 49:5*

Be not thou afraid w. one is made *Ps 49:16*

rich, w. the glory of his house is *Ps 49:16*

w. he dieth he shall carry nothing *Ps 49:18*

thee, w. thou doest well to thyself *Ps 49:18*

W. thou sawest a thief, then thou *Ps 50:18*

w. Nathan the prophet came unto *Ps 51 title*

mightest be justified w. thou speakest *Ps 51:4*

speakest, and be clear w. thou judgest *Ps 51:4*

w. Doeg the Edomite came and told *Ps 52 title*

W. God bringeth back the captivity of *Ps 53:6*

w. the Ziphims came and said to *Ps 54 title*

w. the Philistines took him in Gath *Ps 56 title*

my steps, w. they wait for my soul *Ps 56:6*

W. I cry unto thee, then shall mine *Ps 56:9*

w. he fled from Saul in the   Ps 57 title
cave
w. he bendeth his bow to   Ps 58:7
shoot his
rejoice w. he seeth the   Ps 58:10
vengeance
w. Saul sent, and they   Ps 59 title
watched the
w. he strove with Aram-   Ps 60 title
naharaim
w. Joab returned, and   Ps 60 title
smote of Edom
thee w. my heart is   Ps 61:2
overwhelmed
W. I remember thee upon my   Ps 63:6
bed
corn, w. thou hast so provided   Ps 65:9
for it
hath spoken, w. I was in   Ps 66:14
trouble
God w. thou wentest forth   Ps 68:7
before thy
w. thou didst march through   Ps 68:7
thine inheritance, w. it was   Ps 68:9
weary
W. the Almighty scattered   Ps 68:14
kings in
W. I wept, and chastened my   Ps 69:10
soul
forsake me not w. my strength   Ps 71:9
faileth
also w. I am old and   Ps 71:18
grayheaded
greatly rejoice w. I sing   Ps 71:23
unto thee
shall deliver the needy w. he   Ps 72:12
crieth
w. I saw the prosperity of the   Ps 73:3
wicked
w. I thought to know this, it   Ps 73:16
was too
a dream w. one awaketh; so,   Ps 73:20
O Lord
w. thou awakest, thou shalt   Ps 73:20
despise
W. I shall receive the   Ps 75:2
congregation
in thy sight w. once thou art   Ps 76:7
angry
W. God arose to judgment, to   Ps 76:9
save all
W. he slew them, then they   Ps 78:34
sought
w. he delivered them from the   Ps 78:42
W. God heard this, he was   Ps 78:59
wroth
w. he went out through the   Ps 81:5
land of
count, w. he writeth up the   Ps 87:6
people
w. the waves thereof arise,   Ps 89:9
thou stillest
are but as yesterday w. it is   Ps 90:4
past
W. the wicked spring as the   Ps 92:7
grass
and w. all the workers of   Ps 92:7
iniquity do
and ye fools, w. will ye be   Ps 94:8
wise
W. I said, My foot slippeth   Ps 94:18
W. your fathers tempted me   Ps 95:9
O w. wilt thou come unto me   Ps 101:2
w. he is overwhelmed, and   Ps 102 title
me in the day w. I am in   Ps 102:2
trouble
the day w. I call   Ps 102:2
answer me speedily
W. the Lord shall build up   Ps 102:16
Zion
W. the people are gathered   Ps 102:22
together
W. there were but a few   Ps 105:12
men in
W. they went from one nation   Ps 105:13
to
Egypt was glad w. they   Ps 105:38
departed
their affliction, w. he heard   Ps 106:44
their cry
w. he shall be judged, let him   Ps 109:7
be
gone like the shadow w. it   Ps 109:23
declineth
w. they looked upon me they   Ps 109:25
shaked
w. they arise, let them be   Ps 109:28
ashamed
W. Israel went out of Egypt   Ps 114:1

w. I have respect unto all thy   Ps 119:6
w. I shall have learned thy   Ps 119:7
righteous
w. thou shalt enlarge my   Ps 119:32
heart
fear thee will be glad w.   Ps 119:74
they see me
saying, W. wilt thou comfort   Ps 119:82
me
w. wilt thou execute   Ps 119:84
judgment on
w. thou hast taught me thy   Ps 119:171
but w. I speak, they are for   Ps 120:7
war
I was glad w. they said unto   Ps 122:1
me, Let
our side, w. men rose up   Ps 124:2
against us
w. their wrath was kindled   Ps 124:3
against
W. the Lord turned again the   Ps 126:1
yea, we wept, w. we   Ps 137:1
remembered Zion
the day w. I cried thou   Ps 138:3
answeredst me
w. they hear the words of thy   Ps 138:4
w. I was made in secret, and   Ps 139:15
w. as yet there was one of   Ps 139:16
them
w. I wake, I am still with   Ps 139:18
thee
ear unto my voice, w. I cry   Ps 141:1
unto thee
W. their judges are   Ps 141:6
overthrown in
as w. one cutteth and   Ps 141:7
cleaveth wood
A Prayer w. he was in   Ps 142 title
the cave
W. my spirit was   Ps 142:3
overwhelmed
I will mock w. your fear   Pr 1:26
cometh
W. your fear cometh as   Pr 1:27
desolation
w. distress and anguish cometh   Pr 1:27
upon
W. wisdom entereth into thine   Pr 2:10
W. thou liest down, thou shalt   Pr 3:24
not
of the wicked, w. it cometh   Pr 3:25
w. it is in the power of thine   Pr 3:27
hand to
will give; w. thou hast it by   Pr 3:28
thee
honour w. thou dost embrace   Pr 4:8
her
W. thou goest, thy steps shall   Pr 4:12
not be
w. thou runnest, thou shalt not   Pr 4:12
w. thy flesh and thy body are   Pr 5:11
w. thou art come into the hand   Pr 6:3
of
w. wilt thou arise out of thy   Pr 6:9
sleep
W. thou goest, it shall lead   Pr 6:22
thee
w. thou sleepest, it shall keep   Pr 6:22
thee
w. thou awakest, it shall talk   Pr 6:22
with
satisfy his soul w. he is hungry   Pr 6:30
W. there were no depths, I   Pr 8:24
was
w. there were no fountains   Pr 8:24
abounding
W. he prepared the heavens, I   Pr 8:27
w. he set a compass upon the   Pr 8:27
face of
W. he established the clouds   Pr 8:28
above
w. he strengthened the   Pr 8:28
fountains of
W. he gave to the sea his   Pr 8:29
decree that
w. he appointed the fountains   Pr 8:29
of the
W. pride cometh, then cometh   Pr 11:2
shame
W. a wicked man dieth, his   Pr 11:7
W. it goeth well with the   Pr 11:10
righteous
w. the wicked perish, there is   Pr 11:10
shouting
w. the desire cometh, it is a   Pr 13:12
tree of
w. thou perceivest not in him   Pr 14:7
the lips

W. a man's ways please the   Pr 16:7
Lord, he
strife is as w. one letteth out   Pr 17:14
water
w. he holdeth his peace, is   Pr 17:28
counted
W. the wicked cometh, then   Pr 18:3
cometh
but w. he is gone his way,   Pr 20:14
then he
W. the scorner is punished   Pr 21:11
w. the wise is instructed, he   Pr 21:11
receiveth
w. he bringeth it with a   Pr 21:27
wicked
and w. he is old, he will not   Pr 22:6
depart
W. thou sittest to eat with a   Pr 23:1
ruler
rejoice, w. thy lips speak right   Pr 23:16
things
not thy mother w. she is old   Pr 23:22
not thou upon the wine w. it   Pr 23:31
is red
w. it giveth his colour in the   Pr 23:31
cup
in the cup, w. it moveth itself   Pr 23:31
aright
w. shall I awake I will seek   Pr 23:35
it
w. thou hast found it, then   Pr 24:14
there
Rejoice not w. thine enemy   Pr 24:17
falleth
thine heart be glad w. he   Pr 24:17
stumbleth
w. thy neighbour hath put thee   Pr 25:8
to
W. he speaketh fair, believe   Pr 26:25
him
The wicked flee w. no man   Pr 28:1
pursueth
W. righteous men do rejoice,   Pr 28:12
there is
w. the wicked rise, a man is   Pr 28:12
hidden
W. the wicked rise, men hide   Pr 28:28
w. they perish, the righteous   Pr 28:28
increase
W. the righteous are in   Pr 29:2
authority, the
w. the wicked beareth rule, the   Pr 29:2
people
W. the wicked are multiplied   Pr 29:16
For a servant w. he reigneth   Pr 30:22
and a fool w. he is filled with   Pr 30:22
meat
odious woman w. she is   Pr 30:23
married
w. he sitteth among the elders   Pr 31:23
of the
woe to him that is alone w. he   Ec 4:10
falleth
Keep thy foot w. thou goest to   Ec 5:1
W. thou vowest a vow unto   Ec 5:4
God
W. goods increase, they are   Ec 5:11
increased
can tell him w. it shall be   Ec 8:7
W. I applied mine heart to   Ec 8:16
know
time, w. it falleth suddenly   Ec 9:12
upon them
w. he that is a fool walketh by   Ec 10:3
to thee, O land, w. thy king   Ec 10:16
is a child
land, w. thy king is the son   Ec 10:17
of nobles
w. thou shalt say, I have no   Ec 12:1
day w. the keepers of the   Ec 12:3
house shall
w. the sound of the grinding is   Ec 12:4
low
w. they shall be afraid of that   Ec 12:5
which is
my soul failed w. he spake: I   Ca 5:6
sought
w. I should find thee without, I   Ca 8:1
would
in the day w. she shall be   Ca 8:8
spoken for
W. ye come to appear before   Isa 1:12
me
w. ye spread forth your   Isa 1:15
hands, I will
w. ye make many prayers, I   Isa 1:15
will
w. he ariseth to shake terribly   Isa 2:19;
the   2:21

W. a man shall take hold of his   *Isa 3:6*

W. the Lord shall have washed   *Isa 4:4*

w. I looked that it should bring forth   *Isa 5:4*

in them, *w.* they cast their leaves   *Isa 6:13*

w. they shall say unto you, Seek   *Isa 8:19*

w. they shall be hungry, they shall   *Isa 8:21*

w. at the first he lightly afflicted   *Isa 9:1*

men rejoice *w.* they divide the spoil   *Isa 9:3*

w. the Lord hath performed his   *Isa 10:12*

be as *w.* a standard bearer fainteth   *Isa 10:18*

be as *w.* God overthrew Sodom and   *Isa 13:19*

w. it is seen that Moab is weary on   *Isa 16:12*

be as *w.* the harvestman gathereth   *Isa 17:5*

w. he lifteth up an ensign on   *Isa 18:3*

and *w.* he bloweth a trumpet, hear ye   *Isa 18:3*

afore the harvest, *w.* the bud is perfect   *Isa 18:5*

w. Sargon the king of Assyria sent   *Isa 20:1*

W. thus it shall be in the midst of   *Isa 24:13*

grapes *w.* the vintage is done   *Isa 24:13*

w. the Lord of hosts shall reign in   *Isa 24:23*

w. the blast of the terrible ones is   *Isa 25:4*

w. thy judgments are in the earth   *Isa 26:9*

w. thy hand is lifted up, they will not   *Isa 26:11*

w. they chastening was upon them   *Isa 26:16*

In measure, *w.* it shooteth forth, thou   *Isa 27:8*

w. he maketh all the stones of   *Isa 27:9*

W. the boughs thereof are withered   *Isa 27:11*

which *w.* he that looketh upon it seeth   *Isa 28:4*

w. the overflowing scourge   *Isa 28:15; 28:18*

W. he hath made plain the face   *Isa 28:25*

w. an hungry man dreameth   *Isa 29:8*

as *w.* a thirsty man dreameth   *Isa 29:8*

w. he seeth his children, the work   *Isa 29:23*

w. he shall hear it, he will answer   *Isa 30:19*

in it, *w.* ye turn to the right hand   *Isa 30:21*

hand, and *w.* ye turn to the left   *Isa 30:21*

the great slaughter, *w.* the towers fall   *Isa 30:25*

the night *w.* a holy solemnity is kept   *Isa 30:29*

w. one goeth with a pipe to come into   *Isa 30:29*

W. the Lord shall stretch out his   *Isa 31:3*

w. a multitude of shepherds is   *Isa 31:4*

even *w.* the needy speaketh right   *Isa 32:7*

W. it shall hail, coming down on the   *Isa 32:19*

w. thou shalt cease to spoil, thou shalt   *Isa 33:1*

w. thou shalt make an end to deal   *Isa 33:1*

w. king Hezekiah heard it, that he   *Isa 37:1*

And *w.* he heard it, he sent messengers   *Isa 37:9*

w. they arose early in the morning   *Isa 37:36*

w. he had been sick, and was   *Isa 38:9*

W. the poor and needy seek water   *Isa 41:17*

no counsellor, that *w.* I ask of them   *Isa 41:28*

W. thou passest through the   *Isa 43:2*

thou walkest through the fire   *Isa 43:2*

w. there was no strange god among   *Isa 43:12*

the day *w.* thou heardest them not   *Isa 48:7*

w. I call unto them, they stand up   *Isa 48:13*

thirsted not *w.* he led them through   *Isa 48:21*

w. I came, was there no man   *Isa 50:2*

w. I called, was there none to answer   *Isa 50:2*

w. the Lord shall bring again Zion   *Isa 52:8*

and *w.* we shall see him, there is no   *Isa 53:2*

w. thou shalt make his soul an   *Isa 53:10*

youth, *w.* thou wast refused, saith   *Isa 54:6*

W. thou criest, let thy companies   *Isa 57:13*

troubled sea, *w.* it cannot rest   *Isa 57:20*

w. thou seest the naked, that thou   *Isa 58:7*

W. the enemy shall come in like a   *Isa 59:19*

w. the melting fire burneth, the fire   *Isa 64:2*

W. thou didst terrible things which   *Isa 64:3*

because *w.* I called, ye did not answer   *Isa 65:12*

w. I spake, ye did not hear   *Isa 65:12*

because *w.* I called, none did   *Isa 66:4*

answer

w. I spake, they did not hear   *Isa 66:4*

w. ye see this, your heart shall rejoice   *Isa 66:14*

w. thou wentest after me in the   *Jer 2:2*

w. ye entered, ye defiled my land, and   *Jer 2:7*

God *w.* he led thee by the way   *Jer 2:17*

w. upon every high hill and under   *Jer 2:20*

thief is ashamed *w.* he is found   *Jer 2:26*

w. for all the causes whereby   *Jer 3:8*

w. ye be multiplied and increased   *Jer 3:16*

w. thou art spoiled, what wilt thou do   *Jer 4:30*

w. I had fed them to the full, they then   *Jer 5:7*

w. ye shall say, Wherefore doeth   *Jer 5:19*

Peace, peace; *w.* there is no peace   *Jer 6:14; 8:11*

ashamed *w.* they had committed   *Jer 6:15; 8:12*

W. I would comfort myself against   *Jer 8:18*

W. he uttereth his voice, there is a   *Jer 10:13*

w. thou doest evil, then thou   *Jer 11:15*

thou, O Lord, *w.* I plead with thee   *Jer 12:1*

thou say *w.* he shall punish thee   *Jer 13:21*

be made clean? *w.* shall it once be   *Jer 13:27*

W. they fast, I will not hear their   *Jer 14:12*

w. they offer burnt offering and an   *Jer 14:12*

w. thou shalt show this people all   *Jer 16:10*

and shall not see *w.* good cometh   *Jer 17:6*

and shall not see *w.* heat cometh   *Jer 17:8*

w. thou shalt bring a troop   *Jer 18:22*

w. king Zedekiah sent unto him   *Jer 21:1*

thou be *w.* pangs come upon thee   *Jer 22:23*

w. this people, or the prophet, or a   *Jer 23:33*

w. seventy years are accomplished   *Jer 25:12*

w. Jeremiah had made an end of   *Jer 26:8*

W. the princes of Judah heard these   *Jer 26:10*

w. Urijah heard it, he was all his   *Jer 26:21*

w. Uriah heard it, he was afraid, and   *Jer 26:21*

w. he carried away captive Jeconiah   *Jer 27:20*

w. the word of the prophet shall come   *Jer 28:9*

w. ye shall search for me with all   *Jer 29:13*

Israel, *w.* I went to cause him to rest   *Jer 31:2*

w. I shall bring again their captivity   *Jer 31:23*

the sea *w.* the waves thereof roar   *Jer 31:35*

w. I had delivered the evidence of the   *Jer 32:16*

w. Nebuchadnezzar king of Babylon   *Jer 34:1*

W. the king of Babylon's army fought   *Jer 34:7*

w. all the princes, and all the people   *Jer 34:10*

w. he hath served thee six years, thou   *Jer 34:14*

w. they cut the calf in twain   *Jer 34:18*

w. Nebuchadrezzar king of Babylon   *Jer 35:11*

W. Michaiah the son of Gemariah, the   *Jer 36:11*

w. Baruch read the book in the ears of   *Jer 36:13*

w. they had heard all the words, they   *Jer 36:16*

w. Jehudi had read three or four   *Jer 36:23*

w. the Chaldeans that besieged   *Jer 37:5*

w. the army of the Chaldeans   *Jer 37:11*

w. he was in the gate of Benjamin, a   *Jer 37:13*

W. Jeremiah was entered into   *Jer 37:16*

w. Ebed-melech the Ethiopian, one of   *Jer 38:7*

was there *w.* Jerusalem was taken   *Jer 38:28*

w. Zedekiah the king of Judah saw   *Jer 39:4*

w. they had taken him, they brought   *Jer 39:5*

w. he had taken him being bound in   *Jer 40:1*

Now *w.* all the captains of the forces   *Jer 40:7*

w. all the Jews that were in Moab   *Jer 40:11*

w. they came into the midst   *Jer 41:7*

But *w.* Johanan the son of Kareah   *Jer 41:11*

that *w.* all the people which were   *Jer 41:13*

w. we obey the voice of the Lord   *Jer 42:6*

you, *w.* ye shall enter into Egypt   *Jer 42:18*

w. ye sent me unto the Lord your   *Jer 42:20*

w. Jeremiah had made an end of   *Jer 43:1*

w. he cometh, he shall smite the land   *Jer 43:11*

w. we burned incense to the   *Jer 44:19*

w. he had written these words in a   *Jer 45:1*

W. he uttereth his voice, there is a   *Jer 51:16*

w. her waves do roar like great waters   *Jer 51:55*

w. he went with Zedekiah the king of   *Jer 51:59*

W. thou comest to Babylon, and shalt   *Jer 51:61*

w. thou hast made an end of reading   *Jer 51:63*

twenty years old *w.* he began to reign   *Jer 52:1*

w. her people fell into the hand of   *La 1:7*

w. they swooned as the wounded in   *La 2:12*

w. their soul was poured out into their   *La 2:12*

w. I cry and shout, he shutteth   *La 3:8*

pass *w.* the Lord commanded it not   *La 3:37*

w. they fled away and wandered   *La 4:15*

another; they turned not *w.* they went   *Eze 1:9*

and they turned not *w.* they went   *Eze 1:12; 1:17*

W. they went, they went upon their   *Eze 1:17*

w. the living creatures went   *Eze 1:19*

w. the living creatures were lifted up	*Eze 1:19*
W. those went, these went	*Eze 1:21*
w. those stood, these stood	*Eze 1:21*
w. those were lifted up from the earth	*Eze 1:21*
w. they went, I heard the noise of	*Eze 1:24*
w. they stood, they let down their	*Eze 1:24*
w. they stood, and had let down their	*Eze 1:25*
w. I saw it, I fell upon my face, and	*Eze 1:28*
into me *w.* he spake unto me	*Eze 2:2*
w. I looked, behold, an hand was sent	*Eze 2:9*
W. I say unto the wicked, Thou shalt	*Eze 3:18*
W. a righteous man doth turn from	*Eze 3:20*
w. I speak with thee, I will open thy	*Eze 3:27*
And *w.* thou hast accomplished them	*Eze 4:6*
w. the days of the siege are fulfilled	*Eze 5:2*
w. I have accomplished my fury in	*Eze 5:13*
w. I shall execute judgments in thee in	*Eze 5:15*
W. I shall send upon them the evil	*Eze 5:16*
w. ye shall be scattered through the	*Eze 6:8*
w. their slain men shall be among	*Eze 6:13*
w. I looked, behold a hole in the wall	*Eze 8:7*
w. I had digged in the wall, behold a	*Eze 8:8*
of the house, *w.* the man went in	*Eze 10:3*
the Almighty God *w.* he speaketh	*Eze 10:5*
that *w.* he had commanded the man	*Eze 10:6*
w. I looked, behold the four wheels	*Eze 10:9*
W. they went, they went upon their	*Eze 10:11*
w. the cherubims went, the wheels	*Eze 10:16*
w. the cherubims lifted up their wings	*Eze 10:16*
w. they stood, these stood	*Eze 10:17*
w. they were lifted up, these lifted up	*Eze 10:17*
w. they went out, the wheels also were	*Eze 10:19*
w. I prophesied, that Pelatiah the son	*Eze 11:13*
w. I shall scatter them among the	*Eze 12:15*
Lo, *w.* the wall is fallen, shall it not	*Eze 13:12*
w. he hath spoken a thing	*Eze 14:9*
w. the land sinneth against me by	*Eze 14:13*
w. I send my four sore judgments	*Eze 14:21*
w. ye see their ways and their doings	*Eze 14:23*
w. it was whole, it was meet for no	*Eze 15:5*
w. the fire hath devoured it	*Eze 15:5*
w. I set my face against them	*Eze 15:7*
w. I passed by thee, and saw thee	*Eze 16:6*
thee *w.* thou wast in thy blood, Live	*Eze 16:6*
w. I passed by thee, and looked upon	*Eze 16:8*
w. thou wast naked and bare, and	*Eze 16:22*
W. I shall bring again their captivity	*Eze 16:53*
W. thy sisters, Sodom and her	*Eze 16:55*
w. thou shalt receive thy sisters, thine	*Eze 16:61*
w. I am pacified toward thee for all	*Eze 16:63*
wither, *w.* the east wind toucheth it	*Eze 17:10*
w. lo, he had given his hand	*Eze 17:18*
W. the son hath done that which is	*Eze 18:19*

w. the righteous turneth away from	*Eze 18:24*
W. a righteous man turneth away	*Eze 18:26*
w. the wicked man turneth away	*Eze 18:27*
w. she saw that she had waited, and	*Eze 19:5*
In the day *w.* I chose Israel	*Eze 20:5*
w. I lifted up mine hand unto them	*Eze 20:5*
w. I had brought them into the land	*Eze 20:28*
For *w.* ye offer your gifts	*Eze 20:31*
w. ye make your sons to pass through	*Eze 20:31*
w. I bring you out from the people	*Eze 20:41*
w. I shall bring you into the land of	*Eze 20:42*
w. I have wrought with you for my	*Eze 20:44*
w. they say unto thee, Wherefore	*Eze 21:7*
w. iniquity shall have an end	*Eze 21:25*
w. their iniquity shall have an end	*Eze 21:29*
God, *w.* the Lord hath not spoken	*Eze 22:28*
played the harlot *w.* she was mine	*Eze 23:5*
And *w.* her sister Aholibah saw this	*Eze 23:11*
w. she saw men pourtrayed upon the	*Eze 23:14*
w. they had slain their children to	*Eze 23:39*
w. this cometh ye shall know that I	*Eze 24:24*
w. I take from them their strength	*Eze 24:25*
w. it was profaned; and against	*Eze 25:3*
land of Israel, *w.* it was desolate	*Eze 25:3*
Judah, *w.* they went into captivity	*Eze 25:3*
w. I shall lay my vengeance upon	*Eze 25:17*
w. he shall enter into thy gates, as	*Eze 26:10*
w. the wounded cry, *w.* the slaughter	*Eze 26:15*
W. I shall make thee a desolate city	*Eze 26:19*
w. I shall bring up the deep upon	*Eze 26:19*
W. I shall bring thee down with	*Eze 26:20*
W. thy wares went forth out of the	*Eze 27:33*
time *w.* thou shalt be broken by the	*Eze 27:34*
w. I shall have executed judgments in	*Eze 28:22*
W. I shall have gathered the house of	*Eze 28:25*
w. I have executed judgments upon	*Eze 28:26*
W. they took hold of thee by thy hand	*Eze 29:7*
and *w.* they leaned upon thee, thou	*Eze 29:7*
w. they shall look after them	*Eze 29:16*
w. the slain shall fall in Egypt, and	*Eze 30:4*
Lord, *w.* I have set a fire in Egypt	*Eze 30:8*
w. all her helpers shall be destroyed	*Eze 30:8*
w. I shall break there the yokes of	*Eze 30:18*
w. I shall put my sword into the hand	*Eze 30:25*
multitude of waters, *w.* he shot forth	*Eze 31:5*
the day *w.* he went down to the grave	*Eze 31:15*
w. I cast him down to hell with them	*Eze 31:16*
w. I shall put thee out, I will cover	*Eze 32:7*
w. I shall bring thy destruction	*Eze 32:9*
w. I shall brandish my sword before	*Eze 32:10*
W. I shall make the land of Egypt	*Eze 32:15*
w. I shall smite all them that dwell	*Eze 32:15*

W. I bring the sword upon a	*Eze 33:2*
w. he seeth the sword come upon the	*Eze 33:3*
W. I say unto the wicked, O wicked	*Eze 33:8*
W. I shall say to the righteous, that	*Eze 33:13*
w. I say unto the wicked, Thou shalt	*Eze 33:14*
W. the righteous turneth from his	*Eze 33:18*
w. I have laid the land most desolate	*Eze 33:29*
w. this cometh to pass, (lo, it will	*Eze 33:33*
of the field, *w.* they were scattered	*Eze 34:5*
w. I have broken the bands of their	*Eze 34:27*
among them, *w.* I have judged thee	*Eze 35:11*
W. the whole earth rejoiceth, I will	*Eze 35:14*
w. the house of Israel dwelt in their	*Eze 36:17*
And *w.* they entered unto the heathen	*Eze 36:20*
w. they said to them, These are	*Eze 36:20*
w. I shall be sanctified in you before	*Eze 36:23*
w. I beheld, lo, the sinews and the	*Eze 37:8*
w. I have opened your graves, O my	*Eze 37:13*
w. the children of thy people shall	*Eze 37:18*
w. my sanctuary shall be in the midst	*Eze 37:28*
day *w.* my people of Israel dwelleth	*Eze 38:14*
w. I shall be sanctified in thee, O Gog	*Eze 38:16*
w. Gog shall come against	*Eze 38:18*
w. any seeth a man's bone, then shall	*Eze 39:15*
w. they dwelt safely in their land, and	*Eze 39:26*
W. I have brought them again from	*Eze 39:27*
W. the priests enter therein	*Eze 42:14*
w. he had made an end of measuring	*Eze 42:15*
I saw *w.* I came to destroy the city	*Eze 43:3*
in the day *w.* they shall make it	*Eze 43:18*
W. thou hast made an end of	*Eze 43:23*
w. these days are expired, it shall be	*Eze 43:27*
w. ye offer my bread, the fat and the	*Eze 44:7*
far from me, *w.* Israel went astray	*Eze 44:10*
w. the children of Israel went astray	*Eze 44:15*
w. they enter in at the gates of the	*Eze 44:17*
w. they go forth into the utter court	*Eze 44:19*
w. they enter into the inner court	*Eze 44:21*
w. ye shall divide by lot the land for	*Eze 45:1*
w. the prince shall enter, he shall go	*Eze 46:8*
w. the people of the land shall come	*Eze 46:9*
in the midst of them, *w.* they go in	*Eze 46:10*
and *w.* they go forth, shall go forth	*Eze 46:10*
w. the man that had the line in his	*Eze 47:3*
w. I had returned, behold, at the bank	*Eze 47:7*
w. the children of Israel went astray	*Eze 48:11*
w. all the people heard the sound	*Da 3:7*
w. his heart was lifted up, and his	*Da 5:20*
w. Daniel knew that the writing was	*Da 6:10*
king, *w.* he heard these words	*Da 6:14*
w. he came to the den, he cried with	*Da 6:20*
pass, *w.* I saw, that I was at Shushan	*Da 8:2*

w. he was strong, the great horn was	*Da 8:8*	*w.* ye brought it home, I did blow upon	*Hag 1:9*	*W.* Jesus heard it, he marvelled, and	*M't 8:10*
w. I, even I Daniel, had seen	*Da 8:15*	with you *w.* ye came out of Egypt	*Hag 2:5*	*w.* Jesus was come into Peter's house	*M't 8:14*
w. he came, I was afraid, and fell	*Da 8:17*	*w.* one came to an heap of twenty	*Hag 2:16*	*W.* the even was come, they brought	*M't 8:16*
w. the transgressors are come to the	*Da 8:23*	*w.* one came to the pressfat for to	*Hag 2:16*	Now *w.* Jesus saw great multitudes	*M't 8:18*
And *w.* I heard the voice of his words	*Da 10:9*	*W.* they had sent unto the house of	*Zec 7:2*	*w.* he was entered into a ship	*M't 8:23*
w. he had spoken such words unto	*Da 10:15*	*W.* ye fasted and mourned in	*Zec 7:5*	*w.* he was come to the other side into	*M't 8:28*
w. he had spoken unto me, I was	*Da 10:19*	*w.* ye did eat, and *w.* ye did drink	*Zec 7:6*	*w.* they were come out, they went into	*M't 8:32*
w. I am gone forth, lo, the prince of	*Da 10:20*	*w.* Jerusalem was inhabited and in	*Zec 7:7*	*w.* they saw him, they besought him	*M't 8:34*
w. he shall stand up, his kingdom	*Da 11:4*	*w.* men inhabited the south	*Zec 7:7*	But *w.* the multitudes saw it, they	*M't 9:8*
w. he hath taken away the multitude	*Da 11:12*	*w.* your fathers provoked me to wrath	*Zec 8:14*	*w.* the Pharisees saw it, they said	*M't 9:11*
w. they shall fall, they shall be holpen	*Da 11:34*	*w.* the eyes of man, as of all	*Zec 9:1*	*w.* Jesus heard that, he said	*M't 9:12*
w. he held up his right hand and his	*Da 12:7*	*W.* I have bent Judah for me, filled	*Zec 9:13*	*w.* the bridegroom shall be taken	*M't 9:15*
and *w.* he shall have accomplished to	*Da 12:7*	*w.* they shall be in the siege both	*Zec 12:2*	*w.* he saw her, he said, Daughter, be	*M't 9:22*
w. she had weaned Lo-ruhamah, she	*Ho 1:8*	the *w.* any shall yet prophesy	*Zec 13:3*	*w.* Jesus came into the ruler's house	*M't 9:23*
day *w.* she came up out of the land of	*Ho 2:15*	thrust him through *w.* he prophesieth	*Zec 13:3*	*w.* the people were put forth	*M't 9:25*
your daughters *w.* they commit	*Ho 4:14*	of his vision, *w.* he hath prophesied	*Zec 13:4*	*w.* Jesus departed thence, two blind	*M't 9:27*
spouses *w.* they commit adultery	*Ho 4:14*	*w.* he fought in the day of battle	*Zec 14:3*	*w.* he was come into the house, the	*M't 9:28*
W. Ephraim saw is sickness	*Ho 5:13*	*w.* ye say, Every one that doeth evil is	*Mal 2:17*	But they, *w.* they were departed	*M't 9:31*
w. I returned the captivity of my	*Ho 6:11*	and who shall stand *w.* he appeareth	*Mal 3:2*	*w.* the devil was cast out, the dumb	*M't 9:33*
W. I would have healed Israel, then	*Ho 7:1*	that day *w.* I make up my jewels	*Mal 3:17*	*w.* he saw the multitudes, he	*M't 9:36*
W. they shall go, I will spread my	*Ho 7:12*	*W.* as his mother Mary was espoused	*M't 1:18*	*w.* he had called unto him his twelve	*M't 10:1*
w. they howled upon their beds	*Ho 7:14*	*w.* Jesus was born in Bethlehem of	*M't 2:1*	*w.* ye come into an house, salute it	*M't 10:12*
also to them *w.* I depart from them	*Ho 9:12*	*W.* Herod the king had heard these	*M't 2:3*	*w.* ye depart out of that house or city	*M't 10:14*
w. they shall bind themselves in their	*Ho 10:10*	And *w.* he had gathered all the chief	*M't 2:4*	*w.* they deliver you up, take no	*M't 10:19*
W. Israel was a child, then I	*Ho 11:1*	*w.* he had privily called the wise men	*M't 2:7*	*w.* they persecute you in this city	*M't 10:23*
w. he shall roar, then the children	*Ho 11:10*	*w.* ye have found him, bring me	*M't 2:8*	*w.* Jesus had made an end of	*M't 11:1*
W. Ephraim spake trembling	*Ho 13:1*	*W.* they had heard the king, they	*M't 2:9*	*w.* John had heard in the prison the	*M't 11:2*
but *w.* he offended in Baal, he died	*Ho 13:1*	*W.* they saw the star, they rejoiced	*M't 2:10*	*w.* the Pharisees saw it, they said	*M't 12:2*
w. they all upon the sword, they	*Joe 2:8*	*w.* they were come into the house, they	*M't 2:11*	David did, *w.* he was an hungred	*M't 12:3*
w. I shall bring again the captivity	*Joe 3:1*	*w.* they had opened their treasures	*M't 2:11*	*w.* he was departed thence, he went	*M't 12:9*
roar in the forest, *w.* he hath no prey	*Am 3:4*	*w.* they were departed, behold, the	*M't 2:13*	But *w.* Jesus knew it, he withdrew	*M't 12:15*
w. there were yet three months to the	*Am 4:7*	*W.* he arose, he took the young child	*M't 2:14*	*w.* the Pharisees heard it, they said	*M't 12:24*
w. your gardens and your vineyards	*Am 4:9*	Herod, *w.* he saw that he was mocked	*M't 2:16*	*W.* the unclean spirit is gone out	*M't 12:43*
w. they had made an end of eating	*Am 7:2*	*w.* Herod was dead, behold, an angel	*M't 2:19*	*w.* he is come, he findeth it empty	*M't 12:44*
W. will the new moon be gone	*Am 8:5*	*w.* he heard that Archelaus did reign	*M't 2:22*	*w.* he sowed, some seeds fell	*M't 13:4*
W. my soul fainted within me	*Jon 2:7*	*w.* he saw many of the Pharisees and	*M't 3:7*	And *w.* the sun was up, they were	*M't 13:6*
w. I was yet in my country	*Jon 4:2*	Jesus, *w.* he was baptized, went up	*M't 3:16*	*W.* any one heareth the word of the	*M't 13:19*
w. the morning rose the next day	*Jon 4:7*	*w.* he had fasted forty days and forty	*M't 4:2*	*w.* tribulation or persecution ariseth	*M't 13:21*
it came to pass, *w.* the sun did arise	*Jon 4:8*	*w.* the tempter came to him, he said	*M't 4:3*	But *w.* the blade was sprung up	*M't 13:26*
w. the morning is light, they practise	*Mic 2:1*	*w.* Jesus had heard that John was	*M't 4:12*	*w.* it is grown, it is the greatest	*M't 13:32*
w. the Assyrian shall come into	*Mic 5:5*	*w.* he was set, his disciples came unto	*M't 5:1*	the which *w.* a man hath found, he	*M't 13:44*
w. he shall tread in our palaces	*Mic 5:5*	*w.* men shall revile you, and not	*M't 5:11*	*w.* he hath found one pearl of great	*M't 13:46*
w. he cometh into our land	*Mic 5:6*	*w.* thou doest thine alms, do not	*M't 6:2*	*w.* it was full, they drew to shore	*M't 13:48*
w. he treadeth within our borders	*Mic 5:6*	But *w.* thou doest alms, let not thy left	*M't 6:3*	that *w.* Jesus had finished these	*M't 13:53*
w. they have gathered the summer	*Mic 7:1*	*w.* thou prayest, thou shalt not be	*M't 6:5*	*w.* he was come into his own country	*M't 13:54*
enemy: *w.* I fall, I shall arise	*Mic 7:8*	thou, *w.* thou prayest, enter into	*M't 6:6*	*w.* he would have put him to death, he	*M't 14:5*
w. I sit in darkness, the Lord shall be	*Mic 7:8*	*w.* thou hast shut thy door, pray to	*M't 6:6*	*w.* Herod's birthday was kept, they	*M't 14:6*
cut down *w.* he shall pass through	*Na 1:12*	*w.* ye pray, use not vain repetitions	*M't 6:7*	*w.* the people had heard departed	*M't 14:13*
w. the sun ariseth they flee away, and	*Na 3:17*	*w.* ye fast, be not, as the hypocrites	*M't 6:16*	*w.* the people had heard thereof, they	*M't 14:13*
w. the wicked devoureth the man that	*Hab 1:13*	*w.* thou fastest, anoint thine head	*M't 6:17*	*w.* it was evening, his disciples came	*M't 14:15*
I shall answer *w.* I am reproved	*Hab 2:1*	*w.* Jesus had ended these sayings	*M't 7:28*	*w.* he had sent the multitudes away	*M't 14:23*
W. I heard, my belly trembled; my	*Hab 3:16*	*W.* he was come down from	*M't 8:1*	*w.* the evening was come, he was	*M't 14:23*
w. he cometh up unto the people, he	*Hab 3:16*	*w.* Jesus was entered into Capernaum	*M't 8:5*		
w. I turn back your captivity before	*Zep 3:20*				

w. the disciples saw him walking on	M't 14:26
w. Peter was come down out of the	M't 14:29
w. he saw the wind boisterous, he was	M't 14:30
w. they were come into the ship, the	M't 14:32
w. they were gone over, they came	M't 14:34
w. the men of that place had their hands w. they eat bread	M't 14:35 M't 15:2
w. they saw the dumb to speak	M't 15:31
W. it is evening, ye say, it will be fair	M't 16:2
w. his disciples were come to	M't 16:5
Which w. Jesus perceived, he said	M't 16:8
W. Jesus came into the coasts of	M't 16:13
w. the disciples heard it, they fell on	M't 17:6
w. they had lifted up their eyes, they	M't 17:8
w. they were come to the multitude	M't 17:14
w. they were come to Capernaum	M't 17:24
w. he was come into the house	M't 17:25
w. thou hast opened his mouth, thou	M't 17:27
w. he had begun to reckon, one was	M't 18:24
w. his fellowservants saw what was	M't 18:31
that w. Jesus had finished these	M't 19:1
w. the young man heard that saying	M't 19:22
W. his disciples heard it, they were	M't 19:25
w. the Son of man shall sit in the	M't 19:28
w. he had agreed with the labourers	M't 20:2
So w. even was come, the lord of the	M't 20:8
w. they came that were hired about	M't 20:9
But w. the first came, they supposed	M't 20:10
And w. they had received it, they	M't 20:11
w. the ten heard it, they were moved	M't 20:24
w. they heard that Jesus passed by	M't 20:30
And w. they drew nigh unto w. he was come into Jerusalem, all	M't 21:1 M't 21:10
w. the chief priests and scribes saw	M't 21:15
w. he saw a fig tree in the way, he	M't 21:19
And w. the disciples saw it	M't 21:20
And w. he was come into the temple	M't 21:23
and ye, w. ye had seen it, repented not	M't 21:32
w. the time of the fruit drew near	M't 21:34
But w. the husbandmen saw the son	M't 21:38
W. the lord therefore of the w. the chief priests and Pharisees	M't 21:40 M't 21:45
w. they sought to lay hands on him	M't 21:46
But w. the king heard thereof, he was	M't 22:7
w. the king came in to see the guests	M't 22:11
W. they had heard these words, they	M't 22:22
the first, w. he had married a wife	M't 22:25
And w. the multitude heard this, they	M't 22:33
w. the Pharisees had heard that he	M't 22:34
w. he is made, ye make him	M't 23:15
Tell us, w. shall these things be	M't 24:3
W. ye therefore shall see the	M't 24:15
W. his branch is yet tender, and	M't 24:32
w. ye shall see all these things	M't 24:33

w. he cometh shall find so doing	M't 24:46
come in a day w. he looketh not for	M't 24:50
W. the Son of man shall come in	M't 25:31
w. saw we thee an hungered	M't 25:37
W. saw we thee a stranger, and	M't 25:38
Or w. saw we thee sick, or in	M't 25:39
w. saw we thee an hungered	M't 25:44
w. Jesus had finished all these	M't 26:1
w. Jesus was in Bethany, in the house	M't 26:6
But w. his disciples saw it, they had	M't 26:8
W. Jesus understood it, he said unto	M't 26:10
now w. the even was come, he sat	M't 26:20
until that day w. I drink it new	M't 26:29
And w. they had sung an hymn, they	M't 26:30
w. he was gone out into the porch	M't 26:71
W. the morning was come, all the	M't 27:1
w. they had bound him, they led him	M't 27:2
w. he saw that he was condemned	M't 27:3
w. he was accused of the chief	M't 27:12
w. they were gathered together	M't 27:17
W. he was set down on the judgment	M't 27:19
W. Pilate saw that he could prevail	M't 27:24
and w. he had scourged Jesus, he	M't 27:26
w. they had platted a crown of thorns	M't 27:29
w. they were come unto a place called	M't 27:33
w. he had tasted thereof, he would not	M't 27:34
w. they heard that, said, This man	M't 27:47
w. he had cried again with a loud	M't 27:50
w. the centurion, and they that were	M't 27:54
W. the even was come, there came a	M't 27:57
w. Joseph had taken the body, he	M't 27:59
Now, w. they were going, behold	M't 28:11
And w. they were assembled with the	M't 28:12
w. they saw him, they worshipped	M't 28:17
And w. he had gone a little farther	M'k 1:19
w. the unclean spirit had torn him	M'k 1:26
w. they were come out of the	M'k 1:29
w. the sun did set, they brought	M'k 1:32
w. they had found him, they said unto	M'k 1:37
w. they could not come nigh unto him	M'k 2:4
w. they had broken it up, they let	M'k 2:4
W. Jesus saw their faith, he said	M'k 2:5
immediately w. Jesus perceived in his	M'k 2:8
w. the scribes and Pharisees saw him	M'k 2:16
W. Jesus heard it, he saith unto	M'k 2:17
w. the bridegroom shall be taken	M'k 2:20
w. he had need, and was an	M'k 2:25
w. he had looked round about	M'k 3:5
w. they had heard what great things	M'k 3:8
unclean spirits, w. they saw	M'k 3:11
w. his friends heard of it, they went	M'k 3:21
w. the sun was up, it was scorched	M'k 4:6
w. he was alone, they that were	M'k 4:10

but w. they have heard, Satan	M'k 4:15
w. they have heard the word	M'k 4:16
w. affliction or persecution ariseth for	M'k 4:17
w. the fruit is brought forth	M'k 4:29
w. it is sown in the earth, is less	M'k 4:31
But w. it is sown, it groweth up	M'k 4:32
w. they were alone, he expounded all	M'k 4:34
the same day, w. the even was come	M'k 4:35
w. they had sent away the multitude	M'k 4:36
w. he was come out of the ship	M'k 5:2
w. he saw Jesus afar off, he ran and	M'k 5:6
w. he was come unto ship, he that	M'k 5:18
w. Jesus was passed over again by	M'k 5:21
and w. he saw him, he fell at his feet	M'k 5:22
W. she heard of Jesus, came in the	M'k 5:27
w. he was come in, he saith unto	M'k 5:39
w. he had put them all out, he taketh	M'k 5:40
And w. the sabbath day was come, he	M'k 6:2
w. ye depart thence, shake off the	M'k 6:11
w. Herod heard thereof, he said, It is	M'k 6:16
w. he heard him, he did many things	M'k 6:20
w. a convenient day was come, that	M'k 6:21
w. the daughter of the said Herodias	M'k 6:22
w. his disciples heard of it, they came	M'k 6:29
And Jesus, w. he came out, saw much	M'k 6:34
And w. the day was now far spent, his	M'k 6:35
w. they knew, they say. Five, and two	M'k 6:38
w. he had taken the five loaves and	M'k 6:41
And w. he had sent them away, he	M'k 6:46
w. even was come, the ship was in the	M'k 6:47
w. they saw him walking upon the	M'k 6:49
w. they had passed over, they came	M'k 6:53
w. they were come out of the ship	M'k 6:54
w. they saw some of his disciples eat	M'k 7:2
w. they come from the market, except	M'k 7:4
w. he had called all the people unto	M'k 7:14
w. he was entered into the house	M'k 7:17
w. she was come to her house, she	M'k 7:30
w. Jesus knew it, he saith unto	M'k 8:17
W. I brake the five loaves among	M'k 8:19
w. the seven among four thousand	M'k 8:20
w. he had spit on his eyes, and put his	M'k 8:23
w. he had turned about and looked	M'k 8:33
w. he had called the people unto him	M'k 8:34
w. he cometh in the glory of his	M'k 8:38
w. they had looked round about, they	M'k 9:8
w. he came to his disciples, he saw a	M'k 9:14
all the people, w. they beheld him	M'k 9:15
w. he saw him, straightway the spirit	M'k 9:20
W. Jesus saw the people came	M'k 9:25
w. he was come into the house, his	M'k 9:28

w. he had taken him in his arms, he — *M'k 9:36*
But *w.* Jesus saw it, he was much — *M'k 10:14*
w. he was gone forth into the way — *M'k 10:17*
w. the ten heard it, they began to be — *M'k 10:41*
w. he heard that it was Jesus of — *M'k 10:47*
w. they came nigh to Jerusalem — *M'k 11:1*
w. he had looked round about upon all — *M'k 11:11*
w. they were come from Bethany — *M'k 11:12*
w. he came to it, he found nothing but — *M'k 11:13*
w. even was come he went out of — *M'k 11:19*
things soever ye desire, *w.* ye pray — *M'k 11:24*
w. ye stand praying, forgive, if ye — *M'k 11:25*
w. they were come, they say unto him — *M'k 12:14*
therefore, *w.* they shall rise — *M'k 12:23*
For *w.* they shall rise from the dead — *M'k 12:25*
And *w.* Jesus saw that he answered — *M'k 12:34*
Tell us, *w.* shall these things be — *M'k 13:4*
sign *w.* all these things shall be — *M'k 13:4*
And *w.* ye shall heard of wars and — *M'k 13:7*
w. they shall lead you, and deliver — *M'k 13:11*
w. ye shall see the abomination of — *M'k 13:14*
W. her branch is yet tender, and — *M'k 13:28*
w. ye shall see these things come to — *M'k 13:29*
for ye know not *w.* the time is — *M'k 13:33*
w. the master of the house cometh — *M'k 13:35*
And *w.* they heard it, they were glad — *M'k 14:11*
w. they killed the passover, his — *M'k 14:12*
w. he had given thanks, he gave it to — *M'k 14:23*
And *w.* they had sung an hymn, they — *M'k 14:26*
w. he returned, he found them asleep — *M'k 14:40*
w. she saw Peter warming himself — *M'k 14:67*
And *w.* he thought thereon, he wept — *M'k 14:72*
Jesus, *w.* he had scourged him, to be — *M'k 15:15*
w. they had mocked him, they — *M'k 15:20*
And *w.* he had crucified him, they — *M'k 15:24*
w. the sixth hour was come, there was — *M'k 15:33*
w. they heard it, said, Behold, he — *M'k 15:35*
w. the centurion, which stood over — *M'k 15:39*
w. he was in Galilee, followed him — *M'k 15:41*
now *w.* the even was come, because it — *M'k 15:42*
w. he knew it of the centurion, he gave — *M'k 15:45*
w. the sabbath was past, Mary — *M'k 16:1*
And *w.* they looked, they saw that the — *M'k 16:4*
w. Jesus was risen early in the first — *M'k 16:9*
w. they had heard that he was alive — *M'k 16:11*
w. he went into the temple of the Lord — *Lu 1:9*
w. Zacharias saw him, he was — *Lu 1:12*
w. he came out, he could not speak — *Lu 1:22*
w. she saw him, she was troubled at — *Lu 1:29*
w. Elisabeth heard the salutation — *Lu 1:41*
w. Cyrenius was governor of Syria — *Lu 2:2*

w. they had seen it, they made known — *Lu 2:17*
w. eight days were accomplished — *Lu 2:21*
w. the days of her purification — *Lu 2:22*
w. the parents bought in the — *Lu 2:27*
w. they had performed all things — *Lu 2:39*
w. he was twelve years old, they — *Lu 2:42*
w. they had fulfilled the days, as they — *Lu 2:43*
w. they found him not, they turned — *Lu 2:45*
w. they saw him, they were amazed — *Lu 2:48*
w. all the people were — *Lu 3:21*
and *w.* they were ended, he afterward — *Lu 4:2*
w. the devil had ended all the — *Lu 4:13*
w. he had opened the book, he found — *Lu 4:17*
w. the heaven was shut up three — *Lu 4:25*
w. great famine was throughout — *Lu 4:25*
synagogue, *w.* they heard these — *Lu 4:28*
w. the devil had thrown him in the — *Lu 4:35*
Now *w.* the sun was setting, all they — *Lu 4:40*
And *w.* it was day, he departed and — *Lu 4:42*
w. he had left speaking, he said — *Lu 5:4*
w. they had this done, they inclosed a — *Lu 5:6*
W. Simon Peter saw it, he fell down — *Lu 5:8*
w. they had brought their ships to — *Lu 5:11*
w. he was in a certain city — *Lu 5:12*
w. they could not find by what way — *Lu 5:19*
w. he saw their faith, he said unto — *Lu 5:20*
w. Jesus perceived their thoughts — *Lu 5:22*
w. the bridegroom shall be taken — *Lu 5:35*
did, *w.* himself was an hungered — *Lu 6:3*
w. it was day, he called unto him — *Lu 6:13*
are ye *w.* men shall hate you — *Lu 6:22*
w. they shall separate you from — *Lu 6:22*
w. all men shall speak well of you — *Lu 6:26*
w. thou thyself beholdest not — *Lu 6:42*
w. the flood arose, the stream beat — *Lu 6:48*
w. he had ended all his sayings in — *Lu 7:1*
w. he heard of Jesus, he sent unto him — *Lu 7:3*
w. they came to Jesus, they besought — *Lu 7:4*
w. he was now not far from the house — *Lu 7:6*
W. Jesus heard these things, he — *Lu 7:9*
w. he came nigh to the gate of — *Lu 7:12*
And *w.* the Lord saw her, he had — *Lu 7:13*
W. the men were come unto him, they — *Lu 7:20*
And *w.* the messengers of John were — *Lu 7:24*
w. she knew that Jesus sat at meat in — *Lu 7:37*
w. the Pharisee which had bidden — *Lu 7:39*
w. they had nothing to pay, he frankly — *Lu 7:42*
And *w.* much people were gathered — *Lu 8:4*
w. he had said these things, he — *Lu 8:8*
w. they hear, receive the word — *Lu 8:13*
w. they have heard, go forth, — *Lu 8:14*
No man, *w.* he hath lighted a candle — *Lu 8:16*
w. he went forth to land, there met — *Lu 8:27*
W. he saw Jesus, he cried out, and — *Lu 8:28*
W. they that fed them saw what was — *Lu 8:34*
that, *w.* Jesus was returned — *Lu 8:40*

W. all denied, Peter and they that — *Lu 8:45*
w. the woman saw that she was not — *Lu 8:47*
w. Jesus heard it, he answered him — *Lu 8:50*
w. he came into the house, he suffered — *Lu 8:51*
w. ye go out of that city, shake off the — *Lu 9:5*
apostles, *w.* they were returned, told — *Lu 9:10*
the people, *w.* they knew it, followed — *Lu 9:11*
w. the day began to wear away, then — *Lu 9:12*
w. he shall come in his own glory — *Lu 9:26*
and *w.* they were awake, they saw his — *Lu 9:32*
w. the voice was past, Jesus — *Lu 9:36*
w. they were come down from the hill — *Lu 9:37*
w. the time was come that he — *Lu 9:51*
w. his disciples James and John saw — *Lu 9:54*
w. he saw him, he passed by on the — *Lu 10:31*
a Levite, *w.* he was at the place, came — *Lu 10:32*
w. he saw him, he had compassion on — *Lu 10:33*
on the morrow *w.* he departed, he — *Lu 10:35*
w. I come again, I will repay — *Lu 10:35*
w. he ceased, one of his disciples — *Lu 11:1*
W. ye pray, say, Our Father which — *Lu 11:2*
w. the devil was gone out, the dumb — *Lu 11:14*
W. a strong man armed keepeth — *Lu 11:21*
w. a stronger than he shall come — *Lu 11:22*
W. the unclean spirit is gone out — *Lu 11:24*
w. he cometh, he findeth it swept and — *Lu 11:25*
w. the people were gathered thick — *Lu 11:29*
No man, *w.* he hath lighted a candle — *Lu 11:33*
w. thine eye is single, thy whole — *Lu 11:34*
w. thine eye is evil, thy body also — *Lu 11:34*
w. the bright shining of a candle — *Lu 11:36*
w. the Pharisee saw it, he marvelled — *Lu 11:38*
w. they were gathered together an — *Lu 12:1*
w. they bring you the synagogues — *Lu 12:11*
w. he will return from the — *Lu 12:36*
that *w.* he cometh and knocketh — *Lu 12:36*
lord *w.* he cometh shall find watching — *Lu 12:37*
cometh at an hour *w.* ye think not — *Lu 12:40*
whom his lord *w.* he cometh shall find — *Lu 12:43*
come in a day *w.* he looketh not for — *Lu 12:46*
at and hour *w.* he is not aware, and will — *Lu 12:46*
W. ye see a cloud rise out of — *Lu 12:54*
w. ye see the south wind blow, ye — *Lu 12:55*
W. thou goest with thine — *Lu 12:58*
w. Jesus saw her, he called her to him — *Lu 13:12*
w. he had said these things, — *Lu 13:17*
all his
W. once the master of the house is — *Lu 13:25*
w. ye shall see Abraham, and — *Lu 13:28*
until the time come *w.* ye shall — *Lu 13:35*
w. he marked how they chose out the — *Lu 14:7*
W. thou art bidden of any man to — *Lu 14:8*
w. thou art bidden, go and sit down — *Lu 14:10*
w. he that bade thee cometh — *Lu 14:10*
W. thou makest a dinner or a — *Lu 14:12*

But *w.* thou makest a feast, call the — Lu 14:13

w. one of them that sat at meat with — Lu 14:15

w. he hath found it, he layeth it on his — Lu 15:5

And *w.* he cometh home, he calleth — Lu 15:6

w. she hath found it, she calleth her — Lu 15:9

w. he had spent all, there arose a — Lu 15:14

w. he came to himself, he said, How — Lu 15:17

w. he was yet a great way off, his — Lu 15:20

w. I am put out of the stewardship — Lu 16:4

w. ye fail, they may receive you — Lu 16:9

w. he is come from the field, Go and — Lu 17:7

w. ye shall have done all those — Lu 17:10

w. he saw them, he said unto them, Go — Lu 17:14

w. he saw that he was healed, turned — Lu 17:15

w. he was demanded of the Pharisees — Lu 17:20

w. the kingdom of God should — Lu 17:20

w. ye shall desire to see one of the — Lu 17:22

the day *w.* the Son of man is revealed — Lu 17:30

w. the Son of man cometh, shall he — Lu 18:8

w. his disciples saw it, they rebuked — Lu 18:15

w. Jesus heard these things, he — Lu 18:22

w. he heard this, he was very — Lu 18:23

w. Jesus saw that he was very — Lu 18:24

w. he was come near, he asked him — Lu 18:40

w. they saw it, gave praise unto God — Lu 18:43

And *w.* Jesus came to the place, he — Lu 19:5

w. they saw it, they all murmured — Lu 19:7

w. he was returned, having — Lu 19:15

w. he had thus spoken, he went before — Lu 19:28

w. he was come nigh to Bethphage — Lu 19:29

w. he was come nigh, even now at the — Lu 19:37

w. he was come near, he beheld — Lu 19:41

will reverence him *w.* they see him — Lu 20:13

w. the husbandmen saw him, they — Lu 20:14

And *w.* they heard it, they said, God — Lu 20:16

w. he calleth the Lord the God of — Lu 20:37

w. shall these things be? and what — Lu 21:7

w. these things shall come to pass — Lu 21:7

But *w.* ye shall hear of wars — Lu 21:9

w. ye see Jerusalem compassed — Lu 21:20

w. these things begin to come to pass — Lu 21:28

W. they now shoot forth, ye see — Lu 21:30

w. ye see these things come to pass — Lu 21:31

w. passover must be killed — Lu 22:7

w. ye are entered into the city, there — Lu 22:10

w. the hour was come, he sat — Lu 22:14

w. thou art converted, strengthen — Lu 22:32

W. I sent you without purse — Lu 22:35

w. he was at the place, he said unto — Lu 22:40

w. he rose up from prayer, and was — 22:45

W. they which were about him saw — Lu 22:49

W. I was daily with you in the temple — Lu 22:53

w. they had kindled a fire in the midst — Lu 22:55

And *w.* they had blindfolded him — Lu 22:64

W. Pilate heard of Galilee, he asked — Lu 23:6

W. Herod saw Jesus, he was glad — Lu 23:8

w. he had called together the chief — Lu 23:13

w. they were come to the place — Lu 23:33

w. thou comest into thy kingdom — Lu 23:42

w. Jesus had cried with a loud voice — Lu 23:46

w. the centurion saw what was done — Lu 23:47

unto you *w.* he was yet in Galilee — Lu 24:6

w. they found not his body, they came — Lu 24:23

w. he had thus spoken, he shewed — Lu 24:40

w. the Jews sent priests and — Joh 1:19

w. Jesus beheld him, he said, Thou art — Joh 1:42

w. thou was under the fig tree, I saw — Joh 1:48

w. they wanted wine, the mother of — Joh 2:3

W. the ruler of the feast had — Joh 2:9

w. men have well drunk, then that — Joh 2:10

w. he had made a scourge of small — Joh 2:15

W. therefore he was risen from — Joh 2:22

w. he was in Jerusalem at the — Joh 2:23

w. they saw the miracles which he did — Joh 2:23

How can a man be born *w.* he is old — Joh 3:4

W. therefore the Lord knew how — Joh 4:1

w. ye shall neither in this — Joh 4:21

w. the true worshippers shall — Joh 4:23

w. he is come, he will tell us all — Joh 4:25

w. the Samaritans were come unto — Joh 4:40

Then *w.* he was come into Galilee — Joh 4:45

W. he heard that Jesus was come out — Joh 4:47

hour *w.* he began to amend — Joh 4:52

w. he was come out of Judæa into — Joh 4:54

W. Jesus saw him lie, and knew that — Joh 5:6

no man, *w.* the water is troubled — Joh 5:7

w. the dead shall hear the voice of — Joh 5:25

W. Jesus then lifted up his eyes, and — Joh 6:5

w. he had given thanks, he distributed — Joh 6:11

W. they were filled, he said unto — Joh 6:12

w. they had seen the miracle that — Joh 6:14

W. Jesus therefore perceived that they — Joh 6:15

w. even was now come, his — Joh 6:16

So *w.* they had rowed about five and — Joh 6:19

w. the people which stood on the other — Joh 6:22

W. the people therefore saw that — Joh 6:24

w. they had found him on the other side — Joh 6:25

him, Rabbi, *w.* camest thou hither — Joh 6:25

disciples, *w.* they had heard this, said — Joh 6:60

W. Jesus knew in himself that his — Joh 6:61

W. he had said these words unto — Joh 7:9

w. his brethren were gone up, then — Joh 7:10

w. Christ cometh, no man knoweth — Joh 7:27

W. Christ cometh, will he do more — Joh 7:31

the people *w.* they heard this saying — Joh 7:40

w. they had set her in the midst — Joh 8:3

w. they continued asking him — Joh 8:7

W. Jesus had lifted up himself, and — Joh 8:10

W. ye have lifted up the Son — Joh 8:28

w. he speaketh a lie, he speaketh — Joh 8:44

night cometh, *w.* no man can work — Joh 9:4

W. he had thus spoken, he spat on — Joh 9:6

sabbath day *w.* Jesus made — Joh 9:14

w. he had found him, he said unto him — Joh 9:35

w. he putteth forth his own sheep — Joh 10:4

W. Jesus heard that, he said, This — Joh 11:4

W. he had heard therefore that he — Joh 11:6

w. Jesus came, he found that he had — Joh 11:17

w. she had so said, she went her way — Joh 11:28

w. they saw Mary, that she rose up — Joh 11:31

w. Mary was come where Jesus — Joh 11:32

W. Jesus therefore saw her — Joh 11:33

And *w.* he thus had spoken, he cried — Joh 11:43

w. they heard that Jesus was coming — Joh 12:12

Jesus, *w.* he had found a young ass — Joh 12:14

but *w.* Jesus was glorified, then — Joh 12:16

w. he called Lazarus out of his — Joh 12:17

w. he saw his glory, and spake of — Joh 12:41

w. Jesus knew that his hour was come — Joh 13:1

w. it is come to pass, ye may — Joh 13:19

W. Jesus had thus said, he was — Joh 13:21

I shall give a sop, *w.* I have dipped it — Joh 13:26

w. he had dipped the sop, he gave — Joh 13:26

w. he was gone out, Jesus said — Joh 13:31

w. it is come to pass, ye might — Joh 14:29

w. the Comforter is come, whom I — Joh 15:26

w. the time shall come, ye may — Joh 16:4

w. he is come, he will reprove the world — Joh 16:8

w. he, the Spirit of truth, is come — Joh 16:13

w. she is in travail hath sorrow — Joh 16:21

w. I shall no more speak unto you — Joh 16:25

W. Jesus had spoken these words, he — Joh 18:1

w. he had thus spoken, one or the — Joh 18:22

w. he had said this, he went out again — Joh 18:38

W. the chief priests therefore — Joh 19:6

W. Pilate therefore heard that — Joh 19:8; 19:13

w. they had crucified Jesus, took — Joh 19:23

W. Jesus therefore saw his mother — Joh 19:26

W. Jesus therefore had received — Joh 19:30

But *w.* they came to Jesus — Joh 19:33

Magdalene early, *w.* it was yet dark — Joh 20:1

w. she had thus said, she turned — Joh 20:14

w. the doors were shut where the — Joh 20:19

And *w.* he had so said, he shewed — Joh 20:20

disciples glad, *w.* they saw the Lord — Joh 20:20

w. he had said this, he breathed on — Joh 20:22

was not with them *w.* Jesus came — Joh 20:24

w. the morning was now come, Jesus — Joh 21:4

w. Simon Peter heard that it was the — Joh 21:7

w. they had dined, Jesus saith to — Joh 21:15

W. thou wast young, thou girdedst — Joh 21:18

w. thou shalt be old, thou shalt	Joh 21:18	eyes: and w. she saw Peter, she sat up	Ac 9:40
w. he had spoken this, he saith unto	Joh 21:19	w. he had called the saints and widows	Ac 9:41
W. they therefore were come together	Ac 1:6	w. he looked on him, he was afraid	Ac 10:4
w. he had spoken these things, while	Ac 1:9	w. the angel which spake unto	Ac 10:7
And w. they were come in, they	Ac 1:13	w. he had declared all these things	Ac 10:8
w. the day of Pentecost was	Ac 2:1	who, w. he cometh, shall speak unto	Ac 10:32
Now w. this was noised abroad, the	Ac 2:6	w. Peter was come up to Jerusalem	Ac 11:2
w. they heard this, they were pricked	Ac 2:37	which w. I had fastened mine eyes	Ac 11:6
w. Peter saw it, he answered unto the	Ac 3:12	W. they heard these things, they held	Ac 11:18
w. he was determined to let him go	Ac 3:13	w. they were come to Antioch, spake	Ac 11:20
w. the times of refreshing shall	Ac 3:19	w. he came, and had seen the grace	Ac 11:23
w. they had set them in the midst, they	Ac 4:7	w. he had found him, he brought him	Ac 11:26
Now w. they saw the boldness of Peter	Ac 4:13	w. he had apprehended him, and put	Ac 12:4
But w. they had commanded to go	Ac 4:15	w. Herod would have brought him	Ac 12:6
w. they had further threatened them	Ac 4:21	W. they were past the first and the	Ac 12:10
w. they heard that, they lifted up their	Ac 4:24	w. Peter was come to himself, he said	Ac 12:11
w. they had prayed, the place was	Ac 4:31	w. he had considered the thing, he	Ac 12:12
w. his wife, not knowing what was	Ac 5:7	w. she knew Peter's voice, she opened	Ac 12:14
w. they heard that, they entered into	Ac 5:21	w. they had opened the door, and saw	Ac 12:16
But w. the officers came, and found	Ac 5:22	w. Herod had sought for him	Ac 12:19
w. we had opened, we found no man	Ac 5:23	w. they had fulfilled their ministry	Ac 12:25
w. the high priest and the captain	Ac 5:24	w. they had fasted and prayed, and	Ac 13:3
w. they had brought them, they set	Ac 5:27	w. they were at Salamis, they	Ac 13:5
W. they heard that, they were cut to	Ac 5:33	w. they had gone through the isle	Ac 13:6
w. they had called the apostles, and	Ac 5:40	w. he saw what was done, believed	Ac 13:12
w. the number of disciples was	Ac 6:1	w. Paul and his company loosed from	Ac 13:13
w. they had prayed, they laid their	Ac 6:6	w. they departed from Perga, they	Ac 13:14
Abraham, w. he was in Mesopotamia	Ac 7:2	w. they dwelt as strangers in	Ac 13:17
w. his father was dead, he removed	Ac 7:4	w. he had destroyed seven nations in	Ac 13:19
after him, w. as yet he had no child	Ac 7:5	w. he had removed him, he raised up	Ac 13:22
w. Jacob heard that there was corn in	Ac 7:12	W. John had first preached before his	Ac 13:24
w. the time of the promise drew	Ac 7:17	w. they had fulfilled all that was	Ac 13:29
w. he was cast out, Pharaoh's daughter	Ac 7:21	w. the Jews were gone out of	Ac 13:42
w. he was full forty years old, it	Ac 7:23	w. the congregation was broken up	Ac 13:43
w. forty years were expired, there	Ac 7:30	w. the Jews saw the multitudes, they	Ac 13:45
W. Moses saw it, he wondered at the	Ac 7:31	w. the Gentiles heard this, they were	Ac 13:48
W. they heard these things they were	Ac 7:54	w. there was an assault made both	Ac 14:5
And w. he had said this, he fell asleep	Ac 7:60	w. the people saw what Paul had done	Ac 14:11
w. they believed Philip preaching	Ac 8:12	Which w. the apostles, Barnabas and	Ac 14:14
w. he was baptized, he continued with	Ac 8:13	And w. they had preached the gospel	Ac 14:21
w. the apostles which were at	Ac 8:14	w. they had ordained them elders in	Ac 14:23
Who, w. they were come down, prayed	Ac 8:15	w. they had preached the word in	Ac 14:25
w. Simon saw that through laying on	Ac 8:18	w. they had come, and had gathered	Ac 14:27
w. they had testified and preached the	Ac 8:25	W. therefore Paul and Barnabas had	Ac 15:2
w. they were come up out of water	Ac 8:39	w. they were come to Jerusalem, they	Ac 15:4
w. his eyes were opened, he saw no	Ac 9:8	w. there had been much disputing	Ac 15:7
w. he had received meat, he was	Ac 9:19	So w. they were dismissed, they came	Ac 15:30
w. Saul was come to Jerusalem, he	Ac 9:26	w. they had gathered the multitude	Ac 15:30
w. the brethren knew, they brought	Ac 9:30	Which w. they had read, they rejoiced	Ac 15:31
whom w. they had washed, they laid	Ac 9:37	w. they had gone throughout Phrygia	Ac 16:6
W. he was come, they brought him	Ac 9:39	w. she was baptized, and her	Ac 16:15
		w. her masters saw that the hope of	Ac 16:19
		w. they had laid many stripes upon	Ac 16:23
w. he had brought them into his	Ac 16:34
w. it was day, the magistrates sent the	Ac 16:35
w. they heard that they were Romans	Ac 16:38
w. they had seen the brethren, they	Ac 16:40
w. they had passed through	Ac 17:1
w. they found them not, they drew	Ac 17:6
the city, w. they heard these things	Ac 17:8
w. they had taken security of Jason	Ac 17:9
But w. the Jews of Thessalonica	Ac 17:13
w. he saw the city wholly given to	Ac 17:16
w. they heard of the resurrection of	Ac 17:32
w. Silas and Timotheus were come	Ac 18:5
w. they opposed themselves	Ac 18:6
w. Gallio was the deputy of Achaia	Ac 18:12
w. Paul was now about to open his	Ac 18:14
W. they desired him to tarry longer	Ac 18:20
w. he had landed at Cæsarea, and	Ac 18:22
w. Aquila and Priscilla had heard	Ac 18:26
w. he was disposed to pass into	Ac 18:27
w. he was come, helped them much	Ac 18:27
W. they heard this, they were baptized	Ac 19:5
w. Paul had laid his hands upon them	Ac 19:6
But w. divers were hardened	Ac 19:9
w. he had passed through Macedonia	Ac 19:21
And w. they heard these sayings, they	Ac 19:28
w. Paul would have entered in unto	Ac 19:30
But w. they knew that he was a Jew	Ac 19:34
w. the townclerk had appeased the	Ac 19:35
w. he had thus spoken, he dismissed	Ac 19:41
w. he had gone over those parts, and	Ac 20:2
w. the Jews laid wait for him, as he	Ac 20:3
w. the disciples came together	Ac 20:7
W. he therefore was come again, and	Ac 20:11
And w. he met with us at Assos	Ac 20:14
w. they were come to him, he said	Ac 20:18
w. he had thus spoken, he kneeled	Ac 20:36
Now w. we had discovered Cyprus	Ac 21:3
w. we had accomplished those	Ac 21:5
w. we had taken our leave one of	Ac 21:6
w. we had finished our course from	Ac 21:7
w. he was come unto us, he took Paul's	Ac 21:11
w. we heard these things, both we	Ac 21:12
w. he would not be persuaded, we	Ac 21:14
w. we were come to Jerusalem, the	Ac 21:17
w. he had saluted them, he declared	Ac 21:19
w. they heard it, they glorified the	Ac 21:20
And w. the seven days were almost	Ac 21:27
w. they saw him in the temple, stirred	Ac 21:27
w. they saw the chief captain and the	Ac 21:32
w. he could not know the certainty for	Ac 21:34
w. he came upon the stairs, so it	Ac 21:35
w. he had given him licence, Paul	Ac 21:40

w. there was made a great silence	Ac 21:40
w. they heard that he spake in	Ac 22:2
w. I could not see for the glory of	Ac 22:11
w. I was come again to Jerusalem	Ac 22:17
And w. the blood of thy martyr	Ac 22:20
W. the centurion heard that, he went	Ac 22:26
w. Paul perceived that the one part	Ac 23:6
w. he had so said, there arose	Ac 23:7
w. there arose a great dissension, the	Ac 23:10
w. it was day, certain of the Jews	Ac 23:12
w. Paul's sister's son heard of their	Ac 23:16
w. I would have known the cause	Ac 23:28
w. it was told me how that the Jews	Ac 23:30
Who, w. they came to Cæsarea, and	Ac 23:33
w. the governor had read the letter	Ac 23:34
w. he understood that he was of	Ac 23:34
w. thine accusers are also come	Ac 23:35
w. he was called forth, Tertullus	Ac 24:2
w. Felix heard these things, having	Ac 24:22
W. Lysias the chief captain shall	Ac 24:22
w. Felix came with his wife Drusilla	Ac 24:24
w. I have a convenient season, I will	Ac 24:25
w. Festus was come into the province	Ac 25:1
w. he had tarried among them more	Ac 25:6
w. he was come, the Jews which came	Ac 25:7
w. he had conferred with the council	Ac 25:12
w. they had been there many	Ac 25:14
About whom, w. I was at Jerusalem	Ac 25:15
w. they were come hither, without	Ac 25:17
Against whom w. the accusers stood	Ac 25:18
w. Paul had appealed to be reserved	Ac 25:21
w. Agrippa was come, and Bernice	Ac 25:23
w. I found that he had committed	Ac 25:25
w. they were put to death, I gave my	Ac 26:10
w. we were all fallen to the earth, I	Ac 26:14
w. he had thus spoken, the king rose	Ac 26:30
w. they were gone aside, they talked	Ac 26:31
W. it was determined that we	Ac 27:1
w. we had launched from thence, we	Ac 27:4
W. we had sailed over the sea of	Ac 27:5
w. we had sailed slowly many days	Ac 27:7
Now w. much time was spent	Ac 27:9
w. sailing was now dangerous	Ac 27:9
w. the south wind blew softly	Ac 27:13
w. the ship was caught, and could not	Ac 27:15
w. they had taken up, they used helps	Ac 27:17
w. neither sun nor stars in many days	Ac 27:20
w. the fourteenth night was come	Ac 27:27
w. they had gone a little further, they	Ac 27:28
w. they had let down the boat into the	Ac 27:30
And w. he had thus spoken, he took	Ac 27:35
w. he had broken it, he began to eat	Ac 27:35
w. they had eaten enough	Ac 27:38
w. it was day, they knew not	Ac 27:39

w. they had taken up the anchors, they	Ac 27:40
w. they were escaped, then they knew	Ac 28:1
w. Paul had gathered a bundle of	Ac 28:3
And w. the barbarians saw the	Ac 28:4
they looked w. he should have swollen	Ac 28:6
So w. this was done, others also	Ac 28:9
w. we departed, they laded us with	Ac 28:10
w. the brethren heard of us, they came	Ac 28:15
w. Paul saw, he thanked God, and	Ac 28:15
And w. we came to Rome	Ac 28:16
w. they were come together, he said	Ac 28:17
Who, w. they had examined me	Ac 28:18
w. the Jews spake against it, I was	Ac 28:19
w. they had appointed him a day	Ac 28:23
And w. they agreed not among	Ac 28:25
w. he had said these words, the Jews	Ac 28:29
w. they knew God, they glorified him	Ro 1:21
For w. the Gentiles, which have	Ro 2:14
In the day w. God shall judge	Ro 2:16
overcome w. thou art judged	Ro 3:4
w. he was in circumcision, or in	Ro 4:10
w. he was about an hundred years	Ro 4:19
w. we were yet without strength, in	Ro 5:6
if. w. we were enemies, we were	Ro 5:10
sin is not imputed w. there is no law	Ro 5:13
For w. ye were the servants of sin	Ro 6:20
For w. we were in the flesh, the	Ro 7:5
but w. the commandment came, sin	Ro 7:9
w. I would do good, evil is present	Ro 7:21
w. Rebecca also had conceived by one	Ro 9:10
w. I shall take away their sins	Ro 11:27
nearer than w. we believed	Ro 13:11
W. therefore I have performed this	Ro 15:28
w. I come unto you, I shall come in the	Ro 15:29
And I, brethren, w. I came to you	1Co 2:1
w. ye are gathered together, and my	1Co 5:4
w. ye so sin against the brethren, and	1Co 8:12
w. I preach the gospel I may make	1Co 9:18
w. I have preached to others, I myself	1Co 9:27
w. ye come together in the church, I	1Co 11:18
W. ye come together therefore into	1Co 11:20
w. he had given thanks, he brake it	1Co 11:24
he took the cup, w. he had supped	1Co 11:25
But w. we are judged, we are	1Co 11:32
w. ye come together to eat, tarry one	1Co 11:33
rest will I set in order w. I come	1Co 11:34
w. that which is perfect is come	1Co 13:10
W. I was child, I spake as a child	1Co 13:11
w. I became a man, I put away	1Co 13:11
w. thou shalt bless with the spirit	1Co 14:16
w. ye come together, every one of	1Co 14:26
w. he shall have delivered up the	1Co 15:24
w. he shall have put down all rule	1Co 15:24

w. he saith all things are put under	1Co 15:27
w. all things shall be subdued unto	1Co 15:28
So w. this corruptible shall have	1Co 15:54
there be no gatherings w. I come	1Co 16:2
w. I come, whomsoever ye shall	1Co 16:3
w. I shall pass through Macedonia	1Co 16:5
w. he shall have convenient time	1Co 16:12
W. I therefore was thus minded, I did	2Co 1:17
lest, w. I came, I should have sorrow	2Co 2:3
w. I came to Troas to preach Christ's	2Co 2:12
w. Moses is read, the veil is upon	2Co 3:15
w. it shall turn to the Lord	2Co 3:16
w. we were come into Macedonia, our	2Co 7:5
w. he told us your earnest desire	2Co 7:7
I may not be bold w. I am present	2Co 10:2
w. your obedience is fulfilled	2Co 10:6
in word by letters w. we are absent	2Co 10:11
we be also in deed w. we are present	2Co 10:11
w. your faith is increased, that we	2Co 10:15
And w. I was present with you, and	2Co 11:9
w. I am weak, then am I strong	2Co 12:10
w. I come, I shall not find you such as	2Co 12:20
w. I come again, my God will humble	2Co 12:21
For we are glad, w. we are weak	2Co 13:9
But w. it pleased God, who	Ga 1:15
w. they saw that the gospel of	Ga 2:7
And w. James, Cephas, and John, who	Ga 2:9
w. Peter was come to Antioch	Ga 2:11
w. they were come, he withdrew	Ga 2:12
But w. I saw that they walked not	Ga 2:14
so we, w. we were children, were in	Ga 4:3
But w. the fulness of the time was	Ga 4:4
w. ye knew not God, ye did service	Ga 4:8
and not only w. I am present	Ga 4:18
to be something, w. he is nothing	Ga 6:3
w. he raised him from the dead, and	Eph 1:20
Even w. we were dead in sins, hath	Eph 2:5
w. ye read, ye may understand my	Eph 3:4
good comfort, w. I know your state	Ph'p 2:19
w. ye see him again, ye may rejoice	Ph'p 2:28
w. I departed from Macedonia	Ph'p 4:15
W. Christ, who is our life, shall	Col 3:4
some time. w. ye lived in them	Col 3:7
w. this epistle is read among you	Col 4:16
w. we might have been burdensome	1Th 2:6
w. ye received the word of God which	1Th 2:13
w. we could no longer forbear, we	1Th 3:1
w. we were with you, we told you	1Th 3:4
w. I could no longer forbear, I sent	1Th 3:5
w. Timotheus came from you unto us	1Th 3:6
For w. they shall say, Peace	1Th 5:3
w. the Lord Jesus shall be	2Th 1:7
W. he shall come to be glorified	2Th 1:10
w. I was yet with you, I told ye these	2Th 2:5
even w. we were with you, this we	2Th 3:10

w. I went into Macedonia, that *1Ti 1:3* thou
for w. they have begun to *1Ti 5:11* wax
W. I call to remembrance the *2Ti 1:5*
But w. he was in Rome, he *2Ti 1:17* sought me
w. they will not endure sound *2Ti 4:3*
w. thou comest, bring with *2Ti 4:13* thee, and
W. I shall send Artemas unto *Tit 3:12*
w. he had by himself purged *Heb 1:3* our sins,
w. he bringeth in the *Heb 1:6* firstbegotten
W. your fathers tempted me *Heb 3:9*
some, w. they had heard, did *Heb 3:16* provoke
w. he had offered up prayers *Heb 5:7*
For w. for the time ye ought *Heb 5:12* to be
w. God made promise to *Heb 6:13* Abraham
father, w. Melchisedec met *Heb 7:10* him
he did once, w. he offered up *Heb 7:27* himself
of God w. he was about to *Heb 8:5* make the
w. I will make a new *Heb 8:8* covenant with
w. I took them by the hand to *Heb 8:9* lead
w. these things were thus *Heb 9:6* ordained
w. Moses had spoken every *Heb 9:12* precept to
w. he cometh into the world, *Heb 10:5* he saith
w. he said, Sacrifice and *Heb 11:8* offering and
w. he was called to go out *Heb 11:8* into a place
of a child w. she was *Heb 11:11* past age
Abraham, w. he was tried, *Heb 11:17* offered
w. he was a dying, blessed *Heb 11:21* both the
By faith Joseph, w. he died, *Heb 11:22* made
Moses, w. he was born, was *Heb 11:23* hid three
Moses, w. he was come to *Heb 11:24* years
w. she had received the *Heb 11:31* spies with
nor faint w. thou art *Heb 12:5* rebuked of him
w. he would have inherited *Heb 12:17*
w. ye fall into divers *Jas 1:2* temptations
w. he is tried, he shall receive *Jas 1:12*
Let no man say w. he is *Jas 1:13* tempted
w. he is drawn away of his *Jas 1:14* own lust
w. lust hath conceived, it *Jas 1:15* bringeth
sin, w. it is finished bringeth *Jas 1:15* forth
w. he had offered Isaac his *Jas 2:21* son upon
w. she had received the *Jas 2:25* messengers
w. it testified beforehand the *1Pe 1:11*
w. ye be buffeted for your *1Pe 2:20* faults, ye
w. ye do well and suffer for *1Pe 2:20* it, ye take
w. he was reviled, reviled not *1Pe 2:23* again
w. he suffered, he threatened *1Pe 2:23* not; but
w. once the longsuffering of *1Pe 3:20* God
w. we walked in lasciviousness, *1Pe 4:3* lusts
w. his glory shall be revealed *1Pe 4:13*
w. the chief Shepherd shall *1Pe 5:4* appear
w. we made known unto you *2Pe 1:16* the power
w. there came such a voice to *2Pe 1:17* him
w. we were with him in the *2Pe 1:18* holy
w. they speak great swelling *2Pe 2:18* words of

w. he shall appear, we may *1Jo 2:28* have
w. he shall appear, we shall *1Jo 3:2* be like
w. we love God, and keep his *1Jo 5:2*
w. the brethren came and *3Jo 3* testified of
w. I gave all diligence to write *Jude 3* unto
w. contending with the devil he *Jude 9*
w. they feast with you, feeding *Jude 12*
w. I saw him, I fell at his feet *Re 1:17* as
w. those beasts give glory and *Re 4:9*
And w. he had taken the book *Re 5:8*
I saw w. the Lamb opened one *Re 6:1* of
w. he had opened the second *Re 6:3* seal, I
w. he had opened the third *Re 6:5* seal, I
w. he had opened the fourth *Re 6:7* seal, I
w. he had opened the fifth seal, *Re 6:9* I
w. he had opened the sixth *Re 6:12* seal
w. she is shaken of a mighty *Re 6:13* wind
as a scroll w. it is rolled *Re 6:14* together
w. he had opened the seventh *Re 8:1* seal
scorpion, w. he striketh a man *Re 9:5*
a loud voice, as w. a lion *Re 10:3* roareth
w. he had cried, seven *Re 10:3* thunders
And w. the seven thunders had *Re 10:4*
w. he shall begin to sound, the *Re 10:7*
w. they shall have finished *Re 11:7* their
w. the dragon saw that he *Re 12:13* was
w. I saw her, I wondered with *Re 17:6* great
w. they behold the beast that *Re 17:8* was, and
w. he cometh, he must *Re 17:10* continue a
w. they shall see the smoke *Re 18:9* of their
w. they saw the smoke of her *Re 18:18* burning
w. the thousand years are *Re 20:7* expired
And w. I had heard and seen, *Re 22:8* I fell

WHENCE

ground from w. he was taken *Ge 3:23*
Sarai's maid, w. comest thou *Ge 16:8*
the land from w. thou camest *Ge 24:5*
unto them, My brethren, w. be *Ge 29:4* ye
he said unto them, W. come *Ge 42:7* ye
W. should I have flesh to *Nu 11:13* give unto
w. thou mayest see them *Nu 23:13*
land w. thou broughtest us out *De 9:28*
Egypt, from w. ye came out *De 11:10*
me, but I wist not w. they were *Jos 2:4*
Who are ye? and from w. *Jos 9:8* come ye
unto the city from w. he fled *Jos 20:6*
but I asked him not w. he was *J'g 13:6*
said unto him, W. comest *J'g 17:9* thou
goest thou? and w. comest *J'g 19:17* thou
whom I know not w. they be *1Sa 25:11*
belongest thou? w. art thou *1Sa 30:13*
unto him, From w. comest *2Sa 1:3* thou
man that told him, W. *2Sa 1:13* art thou
him, W. comest thou, Gehazi *2Ki 5:25*
not help thee, w. shall I help *2Ki 6:27* thee
and from w. came they *2Ki 20:14* unto thee
From all places w. ye shall *Ne 4:12* return
said unto Satan, W. comest *Job 1:7* thou
unto Satan, From w. comest *Job 2:2*
Before I go w. I shall not *Job 10:21* return

go the way w. I shall not *Job 16:22* return
W. then cometh wisdom *Job 28:20*
the hills, from w. cometh my *Ps 121:1* help
the place from w. the rivers *Ec 1:7* come
w. come the young and the *Isa 30:6* old lion
and from w. came they unto *Isa 39:3* thee
shalt not know from w. it *Isa 47:11* riseth
look unto the rock w. ye are *Isa 51:1* hewn
the hole of the pit w. ye are *Isa 51:1* digged
w. I caused you to be carried *Jer 29:14*
and w. comest thou? what is *Jon 1:8* thy
w. shall I seek comforters for *Na 3:7* thee
my house from w. I came *M't 12:44* out
thy field? from w. hath it *M't 13:27* tares
W. hath this man this wisdom *M't 13:54*
W. then hath this man all *M't 13:56* these
W. should we have so *M't 15:33* much bread
The baptism of John, w. *M't 21:25* was it
w. hath this man these things *M'k 6:2*
w. can a man satisfy these *M'k 8:4* men
Lord; and w. is he then his *M'k 12:37* son
And w. is this to me, that the *Lu 1:43*
unto my house w. I came *Lu 11:24* out
you, I know you not w. ye *Lu 13:25* are
tell you, I know you not w. *Lu 13:27* ye are
that they could not tell w. it *Lu 20:7* was
unto him, W. knowest thou *Joh 1:48* me
wine, and knew not w. it was *Joh 2:9*
but canst not tell w. it cometh *Joh 3:8*
w. then hast thou that living *Joh 4:11* water
W. shall we buy bread, that *Joh 6:5* these
Howbeit we know this man *Joh 7:27* w. he is
cometh, no man knoweth w. *Joh 7:27* he is
know me, and ye know w. I *Joh 7:28* am
for I know w. I came, and *Joh 8:14* whither
ye cannot tell w. I come, and *Joh 8:14*
fellow, we know not from w. *Joh 9:29* he is
that ye know not from w. he *Joh 9:30* is
saith unto Jesus, W. art thou *Joh 19:9*
to Antioch, from w. they had *Ac 14:26* been
w. also we look for the *Ph'p 3:20* Saviour
country from w. they came *Heb 11:15* out
from w. also he received *Heb 11:19* him in a
w. come wars and fightings *Jas 4:1*
therefore from w. thou art *Re 2:5* fallen
in white robes? and w. came *Re 7:13* they

WHENSOEVER

w. the stronger cattle did *Ge 30:41* conceive
w. ye will ye may do them *M'k 14:7* good
W. I take my journey into *Ro 15:24*

WHERE

of Havilah, w. there is gold *Ge 2:11*
and said unto him, W. art thou *Ge 3:9*
where (S)   *Ge 3:23;*
16:8; 24:5; 29:4; 32:17; 37:30; 42:7;
Nu 11:13; 23:13; De 1:28; 3:21; 4:27;
7:1; 11:10; 21:14; 28:21; J'g 17:9;
19:17; Ru 1:16; 1Sa 10:14; 25:11; 27:10;

2Sa 1:3, 13; 2:1; 13:13; 30:13; 1Ki 8:47;
18:10, 12; 21:18; 2Ki 5:25; 20:14;
2Ch 10:2; Ne 2:16; 4:12; Job 1:7; 2:2;
Isa 30:6; 39:3; 47:11; Jer 15:2; Eze 4:13;
47:9; Jon 1:8; Na 3:7; Zec 2:2; 5:10;
    M't 13:27, 54, 56; 15:33; 21:25

unto Cain, W. is Abel thy brother	Ge 4:9
place w. his tent had been at	Ge 13:3
that it was well watered every w.	Ge 13:10
look from the place w. thou art	Ge 13:14
unto him, W. is Sarah thy wife	Ge 18:9
W. are the men which came in to	Ge 19:5
place w. he stood before the Lord	Ge 19:27
before thee: dwell w. it pleaseth thee	Ge 20:15
the voice of the lad w. he is	Ge 21:17
w. is the lamb for a burnt offering	Ge 22:7
w. is he that hath taken venison	Ge 27:33
Bethel, w. anointedst the pillar	Ge 31:13
w. thou vowedst a vow unto me	Ge 31:13
field, w. he had spread his tent	Ge 33:19
in the place w. he talked with him	Ge 35:13
the place w. God spake with him	Ge 35:15
w. Abraham and Isaac sojourned	Ge 33:27
I pray thee, w. they feed their flocks	Ge 37:16
W. is the harlot, that was openly	Ge 38:21
w. the king's prisoners were bound	Ge 39:20
the place w. Joseph was bound	Ge 40:3
and he sought w. to weep; and he	Ge 43:30
w. is he? why is it that ye have	Ex 2:20
ye, get you straw w. ye can find it	Ex 5:11
Goshen, w. the children were	Ex 9:26
a token upon the houses w. ye	Ex 12:13
a house w. there was not one dead	Ex 12:30
w. were twelve wells of water	Ex 15:27
w. he encamped at the mount	Ex 18:5
the thick darkness w. God was	Ex 20:21
w. I record my name I will come	Ex 20:24
cubits, and the breadth fifty every w.	Ex 27:18
w. I will meet you, to speak	Ex 29:42
w. I will meet with thee	Ex 30:6
w. I will meet with thee: it	Ex 30:36
place, w. the ashes are poured out	Le 4:12
w. the ashes are poured out shall	Le 4:12
in the place w. they kill the burnt	Le 4:24
w. they kill the burnt offering	Le 4:33
place w. the burnt offering is killed	Le 6:25
place w. they kill the burnt offering	Le 7:2
place w. he shall kill the sin offering	Le 14:13
in the place w. the cloud abode	Nu 9:17
w. Ahiman, Sheshai, and Talmai	Nu 13:22
w. I will meet with you	Nu 17:4
w. was no way to turn either to the	Nu 22:26
w. was no water for the people to	Nu 33:14
place w. his lot falleth	Nu 33:54
w. thou hast seen how that the	De 1:31
drought, w. there was no water	De 8:15
w. thou sowedst thy seed	De 11:10
by the way w. the sun goeth down, in	De 11:30
of all Israel, w. he sojourned	De 18:6
one of thy gates, w. it liketh him best	De 23:16

W. are their gods, their rocks in	De 32:37
place w. the priests feet stood firm	Jos 4:3
place, w. ye shall lodge this night	Jos 4:3
unto the place w. they lodged	Jos 4:8
in the place w. the feet of the priests	Jos 4:9
w. he bowed, there he fell down	J'g 5:27
w. be all his miracles which our	J'g 6:13
W. is now thy mouth, wherewith	J'g 9:38
to sojourn w. he could find a place	J'g 17:8
to sojourn w. I could find a place	J'g 17:9
w. there is no want of any thing	J'g 18:10
man's house w. her lord was	J'g 19:26
w. they put themselves in array	J'g 20:22
out of the place w. she was	Ru 1:7
and w. thou lodgest, I will lodge	Ru 1:16
W. thou diest, will I die, and there	Ru 1:17
her, W. hath thou gleaned to-day	Ru 2:19
w. wroughtest thou? blessed be he	Ru 2:19
mark the place w. he shall lie	Ru 3:4
w. the ark of God was, and there,	1Sa 3:3
w. there was a great stone	1Sa 6:14
city w. the man of God was	1Sa 9:10
thee, w. the seer's house is	1Sa 9:18
God w. is the garrison of the	1Sa 10:5
when we saw that they were no w.	1Sa 10:14
out of the holes w. they hid	1Sa 14:11
my father in the field w. thou art	1Sa 19:3
said, W. are Samuel and David	1Sa 19:22
to the place w. thou didst hide	1Sa 20:19
and see his place w. his haunt is	1Sa 23:22
lurking places w. he hideth	1Sa 23:23
by the way, w. was a cave; and Saul	1Sa 24:3
the place w. Saul had pitched	1Sa 26:5
David beheld the place w. Saul	1Sa 26:5
And now see w. the king's spear is	1Sa 26:16
Besor, w. those that were left behind	1Sa 30:9
places w. David himself and	1Sa 30:31
to the place w. Asahel fell down	2Sa 2:23
the king said unto him, W. is he	2Sa 9:4
w. he knew that valiant men were	2Sa 11:16
the mount w. he worshipped	2Sa 15:32
said, And w. is thy master's son	2Sa 16:3
place w. he shall be found	2Sa 17:12
said, W. is Ahimaaz and Jonathan	2Sa 17:20
W. the people of Israel were slain	2Sa 18:7
w. the Philistines had hanged	2Sa 21:12
w. Elhanan the son of Jaare-oregim	2Sa 21:19
w. was a man of great stature, that	2Sa 21:20
w. was a piece of ground full of	2Sa 23:11
the place w. the officers were	1Ki 4:28
the throne w. he might judge	1Ki 7:7
his house w. he dwelt had	1Ki 7:8
in the city w. the old prophet dwelt	1Ki 13:25
him up into a loft w. he abode	1Ki 17:19
w. dogs licked the blood of Naboth	1Ki 21:19
said, W. is the Lord God of Elijah	2Ki 2:14
Shunem, w. was a great woman	2Ki 4:8
w. we dwelt with thee is too	2Ki 6:1
a place there, w. we may dwell	2Ki 6:2

the man of God said, W. fell it	2Ki 6:6
Go and spy w. he is, that I may	2Ki 6:13
W. are the gods of Hamath	2Ki 18:34
w. are the gods of Sepharvaim	2Ki 18:34
W. is the king of Hamath, and the	2Ki 19:13
w. the women wove hangings	2Ki 23:7
w. the priests had burned	2Ki 23:8
is Jebus; w. the Jebusites were	1Ch 11:4
abroad unto our brethren every w.	1Ch 13:2
Gath, w. was a man of great stature	1Ch 20:6
w. the Lord appeared unto David	2Ch 3:1
of Moses, w. the Lord commanded	2Ch 25:4
w. they were servants to him and his	2Ch 36:20
in any place w. he sojourneth	Ezr 1:4
w. the treasures were laid up in	Ezr 6:1
the place w. they offered sacrifices	Ezr 6:3
w. are the vessels of the sanctuary	Ne 10:39
w. aforetime they laid the meat	Ne 13:5
W. were white, green, and blue	Es 1:6
Who is he, and w. is he, that durst	Es 7:5
or w. were the righteous cut off	Job 4:7
thereof; if not, w. and who is he	Job 9:24
order, and w. the light is as darkness	Job 10:22
in a wilderness w. there is no way	Job 12:24
giveth up the ghost, and w. is he	Job 14:10
abroad for bread, saying, W. is it	Job 15:23
w. is now my hope? as for my	Job 17:15
have seen him shall say, W. is he	Job 20:7
say, W. is the house of the prince	Job 21:28
w. are the dwelling places of	Job 21:28
Oh that I knew w. I might find him	Job 23:3
w. he doth work, but I cannot behold	Job 23:9
and a place for gold w. they fine it	Job 28:1
But w. shall wisdom be found	Job 28:12
and w. is understanding	Job 28:12
w. is the place of understanding	Job 28:20
w. the workers of iniquity may	Job 34:22
W. is God my maker, who giveth	Job 35:10
broad place, w. there is no straitness	Job 36:16
W. wast thou when I laid the	Job 38:4
W. is the way w. light dwelleth	Job 38:19
darkness, w. is the place thereof	Job 38:19
it to rain on the earth, w. no man is	Job 38:26
and w. the slain are, there is she	Job 39:30
w. all the beasts of the field play	Job 40:20
language, w. their voice is not heard	Ps 19:3
the place w. thine honour dwelleth	Ps 26:8
say unto me, W. is thy God	Ps 42:3
say daily unto me, W. is thy God	Ps 42:10
there in great fear, w. no fear was	Ps 53:5
a dry and thirsty land, w. no water is	Ps 63:1
in deep mire, w. there is no standing	Ps 69:2
deep waters, w. the floods overflow me	Ps 69:2
W. is their God? let him be	Ps 79:10
w. I heard a language that I	Ps 81:5

herself *w.* she may lay her young — Ps 84:3
w. are thy former lovingkindnesses — Ps 89:49
W. the birds make their nests — Ps 104:17
the wilderness *w.* there is no way — Ps 107:40
heathen say, *W.* is now their God — Ps 115:2
W. no counsel is, the people fall — Pr 11:14
W. no oxen are, the crib is clean — Pr 14:4
is a dinner of herbs *w.* love is — Pr 15:17
W. no wood is, the fire goeth out — Pr 26:20
w. there is no talebearer, the strife — Pr 26:20
W. there is no vision the people — Pr 29:18
hasteth to his place *w.* he arose — Ec 1:5
W. the word of a king is, there is — Ec 8:4
in the city *w.* they had so done — Ec 8:10
place *w.* the tree falleth, there it — Ec 11:3
w. thou feedest, *w.* thou makest — Ca 1:7
w. there were a thousand vines at — Isa 7:23
and *w.* will ye leave your glory — Isa 10:3
W. are they? thy wise men — Isa 19:12
w. are thy wise men? and let them — Isa 19:12
to Ariel, the city *w.* David dwelt — Isa 29:1
w. the grounded staff shall pass — Isa 30:32
w. is the scribe? *w.* is the receiver — Isa 33:18
w. is he that counted the towers — Isa 33:18
the habitation of dragons, *w.* each — Isa 35:7
W. are the gods of Hamath — Isa 36:19
w. are the gods of Sepharvaim — Isa 36:19
W. is the king of Hamath, and the — Isa 37:13
left alone; these, *w.* had they been — Isa 49:21
W. is the bill of your mother's — Isa 50:1
and *w.* is the fury of the oppressor — Isa 51:13
lovedst their bed *w.* thou sawest it — Isa 57:8
W. is he that brought them up out — Isa 63:11
w. is he that put his holy Spirit — Isa 63:11
w. is thy zeal and thy strength, the — Isa 63:15
house *w.* our fathers praised thee — Isa 64:11
w. is the house that ye build unto — Isa 66:1
and *w.* is the place of my rest — Isa 66:1
W. is the Lord that brought us up — Jer 2:6
through, and *w.* no man dwelt — Jer 2:6
priests said not. *W.* is the Lord — Jer 2:8
w. are thy gods that thou hast made — Jer 2:28
see *w.* thou hast not been lien with — Jer 3:2
paths, *w.* is the good way, and walk — Jer 6:16
w. I set my name at the first — Jer 7:12
from the place *w.* I hid it — Jer 13:7
w. is the flock that was given thee — Jer 13:20
w. I will not shew you favour — Jer 16:13
W. is the word of the Lord? let it — Jer 17:15
country, *w.* ye were not born — Jer 22:26
in the land *w.* ye be strangers — Jer 35:7
and let no man know *w.* ye be — Jer 36:19
W. are now your prophets which — Jer 37:19
die for hunger in the place *w.* he — Jer 38:9
w. he gave judgment upon him — Jer 39:5
of Egypt, *w.* we shall see no war — Jer 42:14
w. he gave judgment upon him — Jer 52:9

mothers, *W.* is corn and wine — La 2:12
of Chebar, and I sat *w.* they sat — Eze 3:15
place *w.* they did offer sweet — Eze 6:13
w. was the seat of the image of — Eze 8:3
countries *w.* they shall come — Eze 11:16
w. ye have been scattered, and I — Eze 11:17
W. is the daubing wherewith ye — Eze 13:12
wither in the furrows *w.* it grew — Eze 17:10
in the place *w.* the king dwelleth that — Eze 17:16
out of the country *w.* they sojourn — Eze 20:38
in the place *w.* thou wast created — Eze 21:30
w. they have been scattered — Eze 34:12
w. they washed the burnt offering — Eze 40:38
w. the priests that approach — Eze 42:13
w. I will dwell in the midst of — Eze 43:7
place *w.* the priests shall boil — Eze 46:20
w. they shall bake the meat — Eze 46:20
w. the ministers of the house — Eze 46:24
So he came near *w.* I stood: and when — Da 8:17
the place *w.* it was said unto them — Ho 1:10
w. is any other that may save thee — Ho 13:10
among the people, *W.* is their God — Joe 2:17
upon the earth, *w.* no gin is for him — Am 3:5
unto me, *W.* is the Lord thy God — Mic 7:10
W. is the dwelling of the lions, and — Na 2:11
w. the lion, even the old lion — Na 2:11
place is not known *w.* they are — Na 3:17
land *w.* they have been put to shame — Zep 3:19
Your fathers, *w.* are they? and — Zec 1:5
I be a father, *w.* is mine honour — Mal 1:6
and if I be a master, *w.* is my fear — Mal 1:6
or, *W.* is the God of judgment — Mal 2:17
W. is he that is born King of — M't 2:2
of them *w.* Christ should be born — M't 2:4
stood over *w.* the young child was — M't 2:9
w. moth and rust doth corrupt — M't 6:19
w. thieves break through and steal — M't 6:19
w. neither moth nor rust doth — Mt 6:20
w. thieves do not break through — M't 6:20
w. your treasure is, there will your — M't 6:21
man hath not *w.* to lay his head — M't 8:20
w. they had not much earth — M't 13:5
For *w.* two or three are gathered — M't 18:20
reaping *w.* thou hast not sown — M't 25:24
and gathering *w.* thou hast not — M't 25:24
knewest that I reap *w.* I sowed — M't 25:26
and gather *w.* I have not strawed — M't 25:26
W. wilt thou that we prepare for — M't 26:17
w. the scribes and the elders were — M't 26:57
Come, see the place *w.* the Lord lay — M't 28:6
w. Jesus had appointed them — M't 28:16
uncovered the roof *w.* he was — M'k 2:4
ground, *w.* it had not much earth — M'k 4:5
the way side, *w.* the word is sown — M'k 4:15
and entereth in *w.* the damsel was — M'k 5:40
were sick, *w.* they heard he was — M'k 6:55
W. their worm dieth not — M'k 9:44; 9:46

W. their worm dieth not, and — M'k 9:48
without in a place *w.* two ways met — M'k 11:4
standing *w.* it ought not, (let him — M'k 13:14
W. wilt thou that we go and saith, *W.* is the guestchamber — M'k 14:12 / M'k 14:14
w. I shall eat the passover with my — M'k 14:14
of Joses beheld *w.* he was laid — M'k 15:47
behold the place *w.* they laid him — M'k 16:6
went forth, and preached every *w.* — M'k 16:20
w. he had been brought up — Lu 4:16
found the place *w.* it was written — Lu 4:17
said unto them, *W.* is your faith — Lu 8:25
the gospel, and healing every *w.* — Lu 9:6
of man hath not *w.* to lay his head — Lu 9:58
as he journeyed, came *w.* he was — Lu 10:33
no room *w.* to bestow my fruits — Lu 12:17
w. no thief approacheth, neither — Lu 12:33
w. your treasure is, there will your — Lu 12:34
ten cleansed? but *w.* are the nine — Lu 17:17
and said unto him, *W.* Lord — Lu 17:37
him, *W.* wilt thou that we prepare — Lu 22:9
into the house *w.* he entereth in — Lu 22:10
thee, *W.* is the guestchamber — Lu 22:11
w. I shall eat the passover with — Lu 22:11
Jordan *w.* John was baptizing — Joh 1:28
Master, (*w.* dwellest thou — Joh 1:38
They came and saw *w.* he dwelt — Joh 1:39
The wind bloweth *w.* it listeth — Joh 3:8
wind blows *w.* it will (A)(E)(N) — Joh 3:8
the place *w.* men ought to worship — Joh 4:20
Galilee, *w.* he made the water wine — Joh 4:46
the place *w.* they did eat bread — Joh 6:23
man ascend up *w.* he was before — Joh 6:62
at the feast, and said, *W.* is he — Joh 7:11
w. I am, thither ye cannot come — Joh 7:34; 7:36
town of Bethlehem *w.* David was — Joh 7:42
her, Woman, *w.* are those thine — Joh 8:10
said unto him, *W.* is thy Father — Joh 8:19
him, *W.* is he? He said, I know not — Joh 9:12
the place *w.* John at first baptized — Joh 10:40
days still in the same place *w.* he — Joh 11:6
in that place *w.* Martha met him — Joh 11:30
when Mary was come *w.* Jesus was — Joh 11:32
And said, *W.* have ye laid him — Joh 11:34
the place *w.* the dead was laid — Joh 11:41
if any man knew *w.* he were, he — Joh 11:57
w. Lazarus was which had been — Joh 12:1
and *w.* I am, there shall also my — Joh 12:26
that *w.* I am, there ye may be also — Joh 14:3
hast given me, be with me *w.* I am — Joh 17:24
w. was a garden, into the which he — Joh 18:1
W. the crucified him, and two — Joh 19:18
place *w.* Jesus was crucified was — Joh 19:20
the place *w.* he was crucified there — Joh 19:41

we know not *w*. they have | Joh 20:2
laid
feet, *w*. the body of Jesus | Joh 20:12
had lain
I know not *w*. they have | Joh 20:13
laid him
tell me *w*. thou hast laid | Joh 20:15
him, and I
w. the disciples were | Joh 20:19
assembled
w. abode both Peter and | Ac 1:13
James
all the house *w*. they were | Ac 2:2
sitting
w. they were assembled | Ac 4:31
of Madian, *w*. he begat two | Ac 7:29
sons
w. thou standest is holy | Ac 7:33
went every *w*. preaching the | Ac 8:4
word
come unto the house *w*. I | Ac 11:11
was
w. many were together praying | Ac 12:2
city *w*. we have preached | Ac 15:36
w. prayer was wont to be | Ac 16:13
made
w. was a synagogue of the | Ac 17:1
Jews
all men every *w*. to repent | Ac 17:30
days; *w*. we abode seven days | Ac 20:6
w. they were gathered together | Ac 20:8
men every *w*. against the | Ac 21:28
people
seat, *w*. I ought to be judged | Ac 25:10
falling into a place *w*. two | Ac 27:41
seas met
W. we found brethren, and | Ac 28:14
were
that every *w*. it is spoken | Ac 28:22
against
W. is boasting then? It is | Ro 3:27
for *w*. no law is, there is no | Ro 4:15
But *w*. sin abounded, grace | Ro 5:20
did
place *w*. it was said unto them | Ro 9:26
not *w*. Christ was named, | Ro 15:20
lest I
W. is the wise? *w*. is the | 1Co 1:20
scribe
w. is the disputer of this | 1Co 1:20
world
I teach every *w*. in every | 1Co 4:17
church
were an eye, *w*. were the | 1Co 12:17
hearing
hearing, *w*. were the | 1Co 12:17
smelling
one member, *w*. were the | 1Co 12:19
body
O death, *w*. is thy sting? O | 1Co 15:55
grave
sting? O grave, *w*. is thy | 1Co 15:55
victory
and *w*. the Spirit of the Lord | 2Co 3:17
is
W. is then the blessedness ye | Ga 4:15
every *w*. and in all things I | Ph'p 4:12
w. Christ sitteth on the right | Col 3:1
W. there is neither Greek nor | Col 3:11
that men pray every *w*. | 1Ti 2:8
w. a testament is, there must | Heb 9:16
also
w. remission of these is, | Heb 10:18
there is
w. envying and strife is, there | Jas 3:16
is
w. shall the ungodly and the | 1Pe 4:18
W. is the promise of his | 2Pe 3:4
coming
thy works, and *w*. thou | Re 2:13
dwellest
dwellest, even *w*. Satan's seat | Re 2:13
is
slain among you, *w*. Satan | Re 2:13
dwelleth
w. also our Lord was | Re 11:8
crucified
w. she hath a place prepared | Re 12:6
of
w. she is nourished for a | Re 12:14
time, and
w. the whore sitteth, are | Re 17:15
peoples
w. the beast and the false | Re 20:10
prophet

WHEREABOUT

thing of the business *w*. I send | 1Sa 2:2
thee

WHEREAS

W. thou hast searched all my | Ge 31:37
w. he was not worthy of death | De 19:6
w. ye were as the stars of | De 28:62
heaven
good, *w*. I have rewarded | 1Sa 24:17
thee evil
W. I have not dwelt in any | 2Sa 7:6
house
W. thou camest but | 2Sa 15:20
yesterday
W. it was in thine heart to | 1Ki 8:18
w. my father did lade you | 1Ki 12:11
with a
w. now thou shalt smite | 2Ki 13:19
Syria but
w. my father put a heavy | 2Ch 10:11
yoke
w. we have offended against | 2Ch 28:13
W. our substance is not cut | Job 22:20
down
w. also he that is born in his | Ec 4:14
W. thou hast prayed to me | Isa 37:21
W. thou hast been forsaken | Isa 60:15
w. the sword reached unto the | Jer 4:10
soul
W. ye say, The Lord saith it | Eze 13:7
W. thou wast naked and bare | Eze 16:7
w. none followeth thee to | Eze 16:34
commit
possess it; *w*. the Lord was | Eze 35:10
there
w. it lay desolate in the sight | Eze 36:34
w. thou sawest the feet and | Da 2:41
toes
w. thou sawest iron mixed | Da 2:43
with
w. the king saw a watcher | Da 4:23
and an
w. they commanded to leave | Da 4:26
w. four stood up for it, four | Da 8:22
W. Edom saith, We are | Mal 1:4
that *w*. I was blind, now I | Joh 9:25
see
w. there is among you envying | 1Co 3:3
W. ye know not what shall be | Jas 4:14
on
w. they speak against you as | 1Pe 2:12
w. they speak evil of you, as | 1Pe 3:16
of
W. angels, which are greater | 2Pe 2:11
in

WHEREBY

w. shall I know that I shall | Ge 15:8
inherit
drinketh, and *w*. indeed he | Ge 44:5
divineth
w. he may be made unclean | Le 22:5
w. an atonement shall be made | Nu 5:8
for
w. they murmur against you | Nu 17:5
w. the Lord thy God brought | De 7:19
thee
doings, *w*. thou hast forsaken | De 28:20
me
w. Jonathan knew that it was | 1Sa 20:33
w. the people fall under thee | Ps 45:5
w. they have made thee glad | Ps 45:8
w. thou didst confirm thine | Ps 68:9
w. backsliding Israel committed | Jer 3:8
w. the kings of Judah come | Jer 17:19
in
is his name *w*. he shall be | Jer 23:6
called
w. they have sinned against me | Jer 33:8
iniquities, *w*. they have sinned | Jer 33:8
w. they have transgressed | Jer 33:8
against
w. ye have transgressed: and | Eze 18:31
judgments *w*. they should | Eze 20:25
not live
w. they have trespassed | Eze 39:26
against
by the steps *w*. they went up | Eze 40:49
to it
the way of the gate *w*. he | Eze 46:9
came in
border, *w*. ye shall inherit | Eze 47:13
the land
w. they have reproached my | Zep 2:8
people
W. shall I know this? for I | Lu 1:18
w. the dayspring from on high | Lu 1:78
men, *w*. we must be saved | Ac 4:12
w. thou and all thy house | Ac 11:14
shall
w. we may give an account of | Ac 19:40

w. we cry, Abba, Father | Ro 8:15
thing *w*. thy brother | Ro 14:21
stumbleth
W. when ye read, ye may | Eph 3:4
w. they lie in wait to deceive | Eph 4:14
w. ye are sealed unto the day | Eph 4:30
w. he is able even to subdue | Ph'p 3:21
all
grace, *w*. we may serve God | Heb 12:28
W. are given unto us great | 2Pe 1:4
W. the world that then was | 2Pe 3:6
w. we know that it is the last | 1Jo 2:18
time

WHEREFORE

w. it is said, Even as Nimrod | Ge 10:9
W. the well was called | Ge 16:14
W. did Sarah laugh, saying, | Ge 18:13
Shall
W. she said unto Abraham, | Ge 21:10
Cast out
W. he called that place | Ge 21:31
w. standeth thou without? | Ge 24:31
for I
unto them, *W*. come ye to | Ge 26:27
me
w. then hast thou beguiled | Ge 29:25
W. didst thou flee away | Ge 31:27
secretly
yet, *w*. hast thou stolen my | Ge 31:30
W. is it that thou dost ask | Ge 32:29
after my
the Lord: *w*. he slew him | Ge 38:10
also
saying, *W*. look ye so sadly to | Ge 40:7
day
W. dealt ye so ill with me, as | Ge 43:6
to
W. have ye rewarded evil for | Ge 44:4
good
him, *W*. saith my lord these | Ge 44:7
words
W. shall we die before thine | Ge 47:19
eyes
w. they sold not their lands | Ge 47:22
w. the name of it was called | Ge 50:11
wrong, *W*. smitest thou thy | Ex 2:13
fellow
W. do ye, Moses and Aaron | Ex 5:4
W. have ye not fulfilled your | Ex 5:14
task
W. dealest thou thus with thy | Ex 5:15
w. hast thou so evil entreated | Ex 5:22
this
W. say unto the children of | Ex 6:6
Israel
w. hast thou dealt with us | Ex 14:11
W. criest thou unto me? | Ex 14:15
speak
W. the people did chide with | Ex 17:2
Moses
with me? *w*. do ye tempt the | Ex 17:2
Lord
W. is this that thou hast | Ex 17:3
brought
day: *w*. the Lord blessed the | Ex 20:11
W. the children of Israel | Ex 31:16
shall keep
W. should the Egyptians | Ex 32:12
speak
W. have ye not eaten the sin | Le 10:17
w. the priest shall pronounce | Le 13:25
him
W. ye shall do my statutes, | Le 25:18
and keep
w. are we kept back, that | Nu 9:7
we may
W. hast thou afflicted thy | Nu 11:11
servant
and *w*. have I not found | Nu 11:11
favour in
w. then were ye not afraid to | Nu 12:8
speak
w. hath the Lord brought us | Nu 14:3
into
W. now do ye transgress the | Nu 14:41
w. then lift ye up yourselves | Nu 16:3
w. have ye made us to come | Nu 20:5
up out
w. Israel turned away from | Nu 20:21
him
W. have ye brought us up out | Nu 21:5
of
W. it is said in the book of | Nu 21:14
W. they that speak in | Nu 21:27
proverbs
W. hast thou smitten thine | Nu 22:32
ass

w. camest thou not unto me? *Nu 22:37*	*w.* should I smite thee to the *2Sa 2:22*	*W.* then hast thou brought *Job 10:18*
am I	*w.* Abner with the hinder end *2Sa 2:23*	me
W. say, Behold, I give unto *Nu 25:12*	of the	*W.* do I take my flesh in my *Job 13:14*
him	*W.* hast thou gone in unto my *2Sa 3:7*	*W.* hidest thou thy face, and *Job 13:24*
W. said they, if we have *Nu 32:5*	*W.* they said, The blind and *2Sa 5:8*	*W.* we are counted as beasts *Job 18:3*
found grace	*W.* thou art great, O Lord *2Sa 7:22*	*W.* do the wicked live, *Job 21:7*
And *w.* discourage ye the *Nu 32:7*	*W.* Hanun took David's *2Sa 10:4*	become old
heart of	servants	*w.* I was afraid, and durst *Job 32:6*
W. it shall come to pass, if ye *De 7:12*	*W.* approached ye so nigh *2Sa 11:20*	not
W. Levi hath no part nor *De 10:9*	unto	*W.* Job, I pray thee, hear my *Job 33:1*
W. I command thee, saying *De 19:7*	*W.* hath thou despised the *2Sa 12:9*	*W.* I abhor myself, and *Job 42:6*
W. hath the Lord done thus *De 29:24*	now he is dead, *w.* should I *2Sa 12:23*	*W.* doth the wicked contemn *Ps 10:13*
W. the name of the place is *Jos 5:9*	fast	*W.* hidest thou thy face, and *Ps 44:24*
called	*W.* then hast thou thought *2Sa 14:13*	*W.* should I fear in the days of *Ps 49:5*
w. the hearts of the people *Jos 7:5*	such a	evil
melted	*W.* have thy servants set my *2Sa 14:31*	*W.* should the heathen say, *Ps 79:10;*
w. hast thou at all brought this *Jos 7:7*	field	Where *115:2*
w. liest thou thus upon thy *Jos 7:10*	say, *W.* am I come from *2Sa 14:32*	*W.* hast thou made all men *Ps 89:47*
face	Geshur	*W.* is there a price in the *Pr 17:16*
W. the name of that place *Jos 7:26*	*W.* goest thou also with us? *2Sa 15:19*	*W.* I perceive that there is *Ec 3:22*
W. our elders and all the *Jos 9:11*	return	nothing
inhabitants	then say, *W.* hast thou done *2Sa 16:10*	*W.* I praised the dead which are *Ec 4:2*
W. have ye beguiled us, *Jos 9:22*	so	*w.* should God be angry at thy *Ec 5:6*
saying	*W.* wilt thou run, my son *2Sa 18:22*	*w.* when I looked that it should *Isa 5:4*
W. Adoni-zedec king of *Jos 10:3*	*w.* then are ye the last to *2Sa 19:12*	*W.* it shall come to pass, *Isa 10:12*
Jerusalem	bring	that when
W. I also said, I will not drive *J'g 2:3*	*W.* wentest not thou with *2Sa 19:25*	*W.* my bowels shall sound *Isa 16:11*
them	me	*W.* glorify ye the Lord in the *Isa 24:15*
gods: *w.* I will deliver you no *J'g 10:13*	*w.* then should thy servant *2Sa 19:35*	*W.* hear the word of the *Isa 28:14*
more	be yet	Lord, ye
W. I have not sinned *J'g 11:27*	*W.* then be ye angry for this *2Sa 19:42*	*W.* the Lord said, *Isa 29:13*
against thee	*W.* David said unto the *2Sa 21:3*	Forasmuch as
W. passedst thou over to fight *J'g 12:1*	Gibeonites	*W.* thus saith the Holy One *Isa 30:12*
w. then are ye come up unto *J'g 12:3*	*W.* is my lord the king come *2Sa 24:21*	*w.* lift up thy prayer for the *Isa 37:4*
me	to	remnant
w. he called the name *J'g 15:19*	*W.* his servants said unto him, *1Ki 1:2*	*W.* when I came, was there no *Isa 50:2*
thereof	Let	*W.* do ye spend money for *Isa 55:2*
w. they called that place *J'g 18:12*	*W.* Nathan spake unto *1Ki 1:11*	that
W. she went forth out of the *Ru 1:7*	Bath-sheba	*W.* have we fasted, say they *Isa 58:3*
place	*W.* is this noise of the city *1Ki 1:41*	*w.* have we afflicted our soul *Isa 58:3*
W. it came to pass, when the *1Sa 1:20*	being	*W.* art thou red in thine *Isa 63:2*
time	*W.* the Lord said unto *1Ki 11:11*	apparel
W. the sin of the young men *1Sa 2:17*	Solomon	*W.* I will yet plead with you *Jer 2:9*
was	*W.* the king hearkened not *1Ki 12:15*	*W.* will ye plead with me? ye *Jer 2:29*
W. kick ye at my sacrifice *1Sa 2:29*	unto the	all
and at	*w.* all Israel made Omri, the *1Ki 16:16*	*w.* say my people, We are *Jer 2:31*
W. the Lord God of Israel *1Sa 2:30*	captain	lords
saith	*W.* he said unto the *1Ki 20:9*	*W.* a lion out of the forest *Jer 5:6*
W. hath the Lord smitten us to *1Sa 4:3*	messengers of	*W.* thus saith the Lord God of *Jer 5:14*
W. ye shall make images of *1Sa 6:5*	*w.* he said unto the driver of *1Ki 22:34*	*W.* doeth the Lord our God *Jer 5:19*
your	his	*W.* doth the way of the *Jer 12:1*
W. then do ye harden your *1Sa 6:6*	*W.* wilt thou go to him to *2Ki 4:23*	wicked
hearts	day	*w.* are all they happy that *Jer 12:1*
w. then speakest thou so to *1Sa 9:21*	*W.* he went again to meet *2Ki 4:31*	deal very
me	him	*W.* come these things upon *Jer 13:22*
W. he put forth the end of *1Sa 14:27*	*w.* consider, I pray you, and *2Ki 5:7*	me
the rod	*W.* hast thou rent thy clothes *2Ki 5:8*	*W.* hath the Lord *Jer 16:10*
W. then didst thou not obey *1Sa 15:19*	*W.* they arose and fled in the *2Ki 7:7*	pronounced
W. Saul sent messengers *1Sa 16:19*	twilight	*W.* came I forth out of the *Jer 20:18*
unto Jesse	*w.* came this mad fellow to *2Ki 9:11*	womb
W. when Saul saw that he *1Sa 18:15*	thee	*W.* hath the Lord done thus *Jer 22:8*
behaved	*W.* they came again, and told *2Ki 9:36*	*w.* are they cast out, he and *Jer 22:28*
W. Saul said to David, Thou *1Sa 18:21*	him	his
shalt this	*W.* they spake to the king of *2Ki 17:26*	*W.* their way shall be unto *Jer 23:12*
W. David arose and went, *1Sa 18:27*	Assyria	them
he and his	*w.* lift up thy prayers for the *2Ki 19:4*	*w.* should this city be laid *Jer 27:17*
w. then will thou sin against *1Sa 19:5*	remnant	waste
W. they say, Is Saul also *1Sa 19:24*	*W.* that place is called *1Ch 13:11*	*w.* do I see every man with *Jer 30:6*
W. cometh not the son of *1Sa 20:27*	Perez-uzza to	his
Jesse to	*W.* Hanun took David's *1Ch 19:4*	*W.* dost thou prophesy, and *Jer 32:3*
W. now send and fetch him *1Sa 20:31*	servants, and	say
unto me	*W.* Joab departed, and went *1Ch 21:4*	*W.* the princes were wroth *Jer 37:15*
W. shall he be slain? what *1Sa 20:32*	*W.* David blessed the Lord *1Ch 29:10*	with
hath	before all	*w.* should he slay thee, that *Jer 40:15*
w. then have ye brought him *1Sa 21:14*	*W.* all the men of Israel *2Ch 5:3*	all the
to me	assembled	*W.* my fury and mine anger *Jer 44:6*
w. he came down into a *1Sa 23:25*	*W.* now let the fear of the *2Ch 19:7*	was
rock, and	Lord be	*W.* commit ye this great evil *Jer 44:7*
W. Saul returned from *1Sa 23:28*	*W.* he did evil in the sight of *2Ch 22:4*	*W.* have I seen them dismayed *Jer 46:5*
pursuing after	the Lord	*W.* gloriest thou in the valleys *Jer 49:4*
W. hearest thou men's words *1Sa 24:9*	*W.* their anger was greatly *2Ch 25:10*	*W.* behold, the days come, *Jer 51:52*
w. the Lord reward thee *1Sa 24:19*	kindled	saith
good for that	*W.* the anger of the Lord *2Ch 25:15*	*W.* doth a living man *La 3:39*
W. let the young men find *1Sa 25:8*	was kindled	complain, a
favour in	*W.* the Lord his God *2Ch 28:5*	*W.* dost thou forget us forever *La 5:20*
w. she told him nothing, less *1Sa 25:36*	delivered him	*w.* as I live, saith the Lord *Eze 5:11*
or more	*W.* the wrath of the Lord was *2Ch 29:8*	God
w. then hast thou not kept *1Sa 26:15*	upon	*W.* I will bring the worst of *Eze 7:24*
thy	*w.* their brethren the Levites *2Ch 29:34*	*W.* thus saith the Lord God *Eze 13:20*
W. doth my lord thus pursue *1Sa 26:18*	did help	*W.* O harlot, hear the word *Eze 16:35*
after	*W.* the Lord brought upon *2Ch 33:11*	of the
w. Ziklag pertaineth unto the *1Sa 27:6*	them the	*w.* turn yourselves, and live *Eze 18:32*
w. then layest thou a snare for *1Sa 28:9*	*W.* the king said unto me, Why *Ne 2:2*	*W.* I caused them to go *Eze 20:10*
my	is	forth out of
W. then dost thou ask of me *1Sa 28:16*	*w.* Haman sought to destroy all *Es 3:6*	*W.* I gave them also statutes *Eze 20:25*
W. now return, and go in *1Sa 29:7*	*W.* they called these days *Es 9:26*	that
peace	*W.* is light given to him that *Job 3:20*	*W.* say unto the house of *Eze 20:30*
W. now rise up early in the *1Sa 29:10*	is in	Israel
together: *w.* that place was *2Sa 2:16*	*w.* thou contendest with me *Job 10:2*	*W.* sighest thou? that thou *Eze 21:7*
called		

W. I have delivered her unto	Eze 23:9	
W. thus saith the Lord God;	Eze 24:6	
Woe		
W. say unto them, Thus	Eze 33:25	
saith the		
W. I poured my fury upon	Eze 36:18	
them		
w. I have consumed them in	Eze 43:8	
mine		
W. at that time certain	Da 3:8	
W. O king, let my counsel be	Da 4:27	
W. king Darius signed	Da 6:9	
w. shut thou up the vision:	Da 8:26	
for it		
Knowest thou w. I come unto	Da 10:20	
thee		
w. should they say among the	Joe 2:17	
W. they cried unto the Lord	Jon 1:14	
w. lookest thou upon them	Hab 1:13	
that		
Yet ye say, W.? Because the	Mal 2:14	
w. one? That he might seek a	Mal 2:15	
W. if God so clothe the grass	M't 6:30	
of		
W. by their fruits ye shall	M't 7:20	
W. think ye evil in your	M't 9:4	
W. it is lawful to do well on	M't 12:12	
W. I say unto you, All	M't 12:31	
faith w. didst thou doubt	M't 14:31	
W. if thy hand or thy foot	M't 18:8	
offend		
W. they are no more twain,	M't 19:6	
but		
W. ye be witnesses unto	M't 23:31	
yourselves		
W. behold, I send unto you	M't 23:34	
W. if they shall say unto you	M't 24:26	
Friend, w. art thou come	M't 26:50	
W. that field was called, The	M't 27:8	
field		
W. neither thought I myself	Lu 7:7	
W. I say unto thee, Her sins	Lu 7:47	
W. then gavest not thou my	Lu 19:23	
hear: w. would ye hear it	Joh 9:27	
again		
W. of these men which have	Ac 1:21	
W. brethren, look ye out	Ac 6:3	
among		
is the cause w. ye are come	Ac 10:21	
W. he saith also in another	Ac 13:35	
psalm		
W. my sentence is, that we	Ac 15:19	
trouble		
w. they were come together	Ac 19:32	
W. if Demetrius, and the	Ac 19:38	
W. I take you to record this	Ac 20:26	
day		
w. they cried so against him	Ac 22:24	
w. he was accused of the	Ac 22:30	
Jews		
the cause w. they accused	Ac 23:28	
him		
w. he sent for him the	Ac 24:26	
oftener		
W. I have brought him forth	Ac 25:26	
before		
w. I beseech thee to hear me	Ac 26:3	
W. sirs, be of good cheer: for	Ac 27:25	
I		
W. I pray you to take some	Ac 27:34	
meat		
W. God also gave them up to	Ro 1:24	
W. as by man sin entered	Ro 5:12	
W. my brethren, ye also are	Ro 7:4	
W. the law is holy, and the	Ro 7:12	
W? Because they sought it	Ro 9:32	
not		
W. ye must needs be subject,	Ro 13:5	
not		
W. receive ye one another, as	Ro 15:7	
W. I beseech you, be ye	1Co 4:16	
followers		
W. if meat make my brother	1Co 8:13	
to		
W. let him that thinketh he	1Co 10:12	
W. my dearly beloved, flee	1Co 10:14	
from		
W. whosoever shall eat this	1Co 11:27	
bread		
W. my brethren, when ye	1Co 11:33	
come		
W. I give you to understand,	1Co 12:3	
that		
W. let him that speaketh in	1Co 14:13	
W. tongues are for a sign,	1Co 14:22	
not to		
W. brethren, covet to	1Co 14:39	
prophesy		
W. I beseech you that ye	2Co 2:8	
would		

W. we labour, that, whether	2Co 5:9	
W. henceforth know we no	2Co 5:16	
man		
W. come out from among	2Co 6:17	
them		
W. though I wrote unto you,	2Co 7:12	
I did		
W. shew ye to them, and	2Co 8:24	
before the		
W? because I love you not	2Co 11:11	
W. then serveth the law? It	Ga 3:19	
was		
W. the law was our	Ga 3:24	
schoolmaster		
W. thou art no more a servant	Ga 4:7	
W. I also, after I heard of	Eph 1:15	
W. remember, that ye being	Eph 2:11	
W. I desire that ye faint not	Eph 3:13	
at my		
W. he saith, When he	Eph 4:8	
ascended		
W. putting away lying, speak	Eph 4:25	
W. he saith, Awake thou	Eph 5:14	
that		
W. be ye not unwise, but	Eph 5:17	
W. take unto you the whole	Eph 6:13	
W. God also hath highly	Ph'p 2:9	
exalted		
W. my beloved, as ye have	Ph'p 2:12	
always		
W. if ye be dead with Christ	Col 2:20	
from		
W. we would have come unto	1Th 2:18	
you		
W. when we could no longer	1Th 3:1	
W. comfort one another with	1Th 4:18	
W. comfort yourselves	1Th 5:11	
together		
W. also we pray always for	2Th 1:11	
W. I put thee in remembrance	2Ti 1:6	
W. rebuke them sharply, that	Tit 1:13	
W. though I might be much	Ph'm 8	
bold		
W. in all things it behoved	Heb 2:17	
him to		
W. holy brethren, partakers of	Heb 3:1	
W. (as the Holy Ghost saith	Heb 3:7	
W. I was grieved with that	Heb 3:10	
W. he is able also to save	Heb 7:25	
w. it is of necessity that this	Heb 8:3	
man		
W. when he cometh into the	Heb 10:5	
w. God is not ashamed to	Heb 11:16	
be called		
W. seeing we also are	Heb 12:1	
compassed		
W. lift up the hands which	Heb 12:12	
hang		
W. we receiving a kingdom	Heb 12:28	
which		
W. Jesus also, that he might	Heb 13:12	
W. my beloved brethren, let	Jas 1:19	
W. lay apart all filthiness and	Jas 1:21	
W. he saith, God resisteth	Jas 4:6	
W. gird up the loins of your	1Pe 1:13	
mind		
W. laying aside all malice, and	1Pe 2:1	
W. also, it is contained in the	1Pe 2:6	
W. let them that suffer	1Pe 4:19	
according		
W. the rather, brethren, give	2Pe 1:10	
W. I will not be negligent to	2Pe 1:12	
put		
W. beloved, seeing that ye	2Pe 3:14	
look		
w. slew he him? Because his	1Jo 3:12	
W. if I come, I will	3Jo 10	
W. didst thou marvel? I will	Re 17:7	
tell		

WHEREIN

w. there is life, I have given	Ge 1:30	
every		
w. is the breath of life, from	Ge 6:17	
under		
of all flesh, w. is the breath of	Ge 7:15	
life		
the land w. thou art a	Ge 17:8	
stranger, all		
the land w. thou hast	Ge 21:23	
sojourned		
the land w. thou art a stranger	Ge 28:4	
the land w. they were	Ge 36:7	
strangers		
in the land w. his father was a	Ge 37:1	
w. they made them serve, was	Ex 1:14	
with		
pilgrimage, w. they were	Ex 6:4	
strangers		

of the houses, w. they shall eat	Ex 12:7	
it		
in the thing w. they dealt	Ex 18:11	
proudly		
shew them the way w. they	Ex 13:20	
must walk		
w. shall he sleep? and it shall	Ex 22:27	
w. shall it be known here	Ex 33:16	
that I		
w. he hath sinned, come to his	Le 4:23	
w. he erred and wist it not,	Le 5:18	
and it		
vessel w. it is sodden shall be	Le 6:28	
w. any work is done, it must	Le 11:32	
be put		
w. there is plenty of water,	Le 11:36	
shall be		
days w. the plague shall be in	Le 13:46	
him		
any thing of skin, w. the	Le 13:52	
plague is		
wash the thing w. the plague	Le 13:54	
is		
burn that w. the plague is	Le 13:57	
with fire		
land of Egypt, w. ye dwelt,	Le 18:3	
shall ye		
upon us, w. we have done	Nu 12:11	
foolishly		
foolishly, and w. we have	Nu 12:11	
sinned		
w. is no blemish, and upon	Nu 19:2	
which		
burnt all their cities w.	Nu 31:10	
they dwelt		
vex you in the land w. ye	Nu 33:55	
dwell		
shall not pollute the land w.	Nu 35:33	
ye are		
shall inhabit, w. I dwell	Nu 35:34	
A land w. thou shalt eat bread	De 8:9	
wilderness, w. were fiery	De 8:15	
serpents		
w. the nations which ye shall	De 12:2	
w. the Lord thy God hath	De 12:7	
blessed		
or sheep, w. is blemish, or any	De 17:1	
w. thou trustedst, throughout	De 28:52	
wilderness w. they chased	Jos 8:24	
them		
cave w. they had been hid	Jos 10:27	
w. the Lord's tabernacle	Jos 22:19	
land w. the children of	Jos 22:33	
Reuben		
us in all the way w. we went	Jos 24:17	
see w. his great strength lieth	J'g 16:5	
w. thy great strength lieth, and	J'g 16:6	
told me w. thy great strength	J'g 16:15	
lieth		
the Lord is your way w. ye go	J'g 18:6	
w. the jewels of gold were,	1Sa 6:15	
and put		
see w. this sin hath been this	1Sa 14:38	
day		
all the places w. I have walked	2Sa 7:7	
afflicted in all w. my father	1Ki 2:26	
was		
ark, w. is the covenant of the	1Ki 8:21	
the good way w. they should	1Ki 8:36	
walk		
w. they have transgressed	1Ki 8:50	
against		
sepulchre w. the man of	1Ki 13:31	
God is		
w. Jehoiada the priest	2Ki 12:2	
instructed		
w. the Lord commanded,	2Ki 14:6	
saying		
in their cities w. they dwelt	2Ki 17:29	
confidence is this w. thou	2Ki 18:19	
trustest		
w. this passover was holden	2Ki 23:23	
to the		
w. Solomon was instructed for	2Ch 3:3	
w. is the covenant of the	2Ch 6:11	
Lord		
good way, w. they should	2Ch 6:27	
walk		
w. Solomon had built the	2Ch 8:1	
house of		
the places w. he built high	2Ch 33:19	
places		
unto him, w. was written thus	Ezr 5:7	
W. was written, It is reported	Ne 6:6	
light in the way w. they	Ne 9:12	
should go		
light, and the way w. they	Ne 9:19	
should go		
them in the day w. they sold	Ne 13:15	
victuals		

w. the king had promoted him   *Es 5:11*
W. the king granted the Jews   *Es 8:11*
days w. the Jews rested from   *Es 9:22*
their
Let the day perish w. I was   *Job 3:3*
born, and
of the ice, and w. the snow is   *Job 6:16*
hid
me to understand w. I have   *Job 6:24*
erred
on the wilderness, w. there   *Job 38:26*
is no man
this mount Zion, w. thou hast   *Ps 74:2*
dwelt
to the days w. thou hast   *Ps 90:15*
afflicted us
and the years w. we have seen   *Ps 90:15*
evil
w. all the beasts of the forest   *Ps 104:20*
do
wide sea, w. are things   *Ps 104:25*
creeping
In the way w. I walked   *Ps 142:3*
have they
to know the way w. I should   *Ps 143:8*
walk
all my labour w. I have   *Ec 2:19*
laboured
w. I have shewed myself wise   *Ec 2:19*
under
w. he hath laboured under the   *Ec 2:22*
sun
worketh in that w. he laboureth   *Ec 3:9*
is a time w. one man ruleth   *Ec 8:9*
over
for w. is he to be accounted   *Isa 2:22*
of
bondage w. thou wast made   *Isa 14:3*
to
w. shall go no galley with   *Isa 33:21*
oars
confidence is this w. thou   *Isa 36:4*
trustest
w. thou hast laboured from   *Isa 47:12*
thy
did choose that w. I   *Isa 65:12*
delighted not
fenced cities, w. thou trustedst   *Jer 5:17*
called by my name, w. ye   *Jer 7:14*
trust, and
the land of peace, w. thou   *Jer 12:5*
trustedst
vanity, and things w. there is   *Jer 16:19*
no profit
Cursed be the day w. I was   *Jer 20:14*
born
not the day w. my mother   *Jer 20:14*
bare me
idol? is he a vessel w. is no   *Jer 22:28*
pleasure
way, w. they shall not stumble   *Jer 31:9*
roll w. thou hast read in the   *Jer 36:14*
ears of
pit w. Ishmael had cast all the   *Jer 41:9*
dead
shew us the way w. we may   *Jer 42:3*
walk
Moab like a vessel w. is no   *Jer 48:38*
pleasure
a land w. no man dwelleth   *Jer 51:43*
the countries w. ye are   *Eze 20:34*
scattered
countries w. ye have been   *Eze 20:41*
scattered
doings, w. ye have been   *Eze 20:43*
defiled
w. she had played the harlot   *Eze 23:19*
in the
enter into a city w. is made   *Eze 26:10*
a breach
thy blood the land w. thou   *Eze 32:6*
swimmest
w. they have sinned, and   *Eze 37:23*
will
servant, w. your fathers have   *Eze 37:25*
dwelt
their garments w. they   *Eze 42:14*
minister
their garments w. they   *Eze 44:19*
ministered
w. she burned incense to   *Ho 2:13*
them, and
Gentiles as a vessel w. is no   *Ho 8:8*
pleasure
w. are more than sixscore   *Jon 4:11*
thousand
thee? and w. I have wearied   *Mic 6:3*
thee
w. thou hast transgressed   *Zep 3:11*
against

prisoners out of the pit w. is   *Zec 9:11*
no water
Yet ye say, W. hast thou   *Mal 1:2*
loved us
W. have we despised thy name   *Mal 1:6*
W. have we polluted thee? In   *Mal 1:7*
that
ye say, W. have we wearied   *Mal 2:17*
him
But ye said, W. shall we   *Mal 3:7*
return
ye say, W. have we robbed   *Mal 3:8*
thee
w. most of his mighty works   *M't 11:20*
w. the Son of man cometh   *M't 25:13*
w. the sick of the palsy lay   *M'k 2:4*
w. thou hast been instructed   *Lu 1:4*
in the days w. he looked on   *Lu 1:25*
me
all his armour w. he trusted   *Lu 11:22*
w. never man before was laid   *Lu 23:53*
w. was never man yet laid   *Joh 19:41*
own tongue, w. we were born   *Ac 2:8*
into this land, w. ye now dwell   *Ac 7:4*
W. all manner of fourfooted   *Ac 10:12*
for w. thou judgest another   *Ro 2:1*
into this grace w. we stand   *Ro 5:2*
being dead w. we were held   *Ro 7:6*
same calling w. he was called   *1Co 7:20*
w. he is called, therein abide   *1Co 7:24*
have received, and w. ye   *1Co 15:1*
stand
that w. they glory, they may   *2Co 11:12*
be
For what is it w. ye were   *2Co 12:13*
inferior
w. he hath made us accepted   *Eph 1:6*
W. he hath abounded toward   *Eph 1:8*
us
W. in time past ye walked   *Eph 2:2*
drunk with wine, w. is excess   *Eph 5:18*
w. ye were also careful, but   *Ph'p 4:10*
w. also ye are risen with him   *Col 2:1*
W. I suffer trouble, as an evil   *2Ti 2:9*
W. God, willing more   *Heb 6:17*
first, w. was the candlestick   *Heb 9:2*
w. was the golden pot that   *Heb 9:4*
had
W. ye greatly rejoice, though   *1Pe 1:6*
w. few, that is, eight souls   *1Pe 3:20*
W. they think it strange that   *1Pe 4:4*
true grace of God w. ye stand   *1Pe 5:12*
w. the heavens being on fire   *2Pe 3:12*
w. dwelleth righteousness   *2Pe 3:13*
w. Antipas was my martyr   *Re 2:13*
w. were made rich all that   *Re 18:19*
had

WHEREINSOEVER

w. any is bold, (I speak   *2Co 11:21*

WHEREINTO

w. any of them falleth   *Le 11:33*
into the land w. he went   *Nu 14:24*
one w. his disciples entered   *Joh 6:22*

WHEREOF

w. I commanded thee that   *Ge 3:11*
thou
w. any of the blood is brought   *Le 6:30*
into
skin w. there is a hot   *Le 13:24*
burning, and
w. men bring an offering unto   *Le 27:9*
their camps, in the midst w. I   *Nu 5:3*
dwell
weight w. was   *Nu 7:19;*
    7:37, 49, 61, 67, 73, 79
well w. the Lord spake unto   *Nu 21:16*
Moses
to pass, w. he spake unto thee   *De 13:2*
itch w. thou canst not be   *De 28:27*
healed
by the way w. I spake unto   *De 28:68*
thee
w. the Lord spake in that   *De 14:12*
day
w. I spake unto you by the   *Jos 20:2*
hand of
w. they were possessed,   *Jos 22:9*
according
of the kingdom, w. Samuel   *1Sa 10:16*
spake
w. two thousand were with   *1Sa 13:2*
Saul in
weight w. was a talent of   *2Sa 12:30*
gold with

sick of this sickness w. he   *2Ki 13:14*
died
w. the Lord had said unto   *2K 17:12*
them
w. was according to the   *2Ch 3:8*
breadth
place w. thou hast said that   *2Ch 6:20*
thou
w. were made vessels for   *2Ch 24:14*
the house of
w. the Lord had said, In   *2Ch 33:4*
Jerusalem
w. one went on the right   *Ne 12:31*
hand upon
poison w. drinketh up my   *Job 6:4*
spirit
w. shall make glad the city of   *Ps 46:4*
God
midst w. they are fallen   *Ps 57:6*
themselves
great things for us; w. we are   *Ps 126:3*
glad
Is there any thing w. it may   *Ec 1:10*
be said
w. every one bear twins, and   *Ca 4:2*
none is
w. every one beareth twins, and   *Ca 6:6*
there
concerning this city, w. ye   *Jer 32:36*
say, it
this and, w. ye say, It is   *Jer 32:43*
desolate
and the famine, w. ye were   *Jer 42:16*
afraid
be destitute of that w. it was   *Eze 32:15*
full
this is the day w. I have   *Eze 39:8*
spoken
w. the word of the Lord came   *Da 9:2*
to
w. she hath said, These are   *Ho 2:12*
my
those things w. ye accuse him   *Lu 23:14*
raised up, w. we all are   *Ac 2:32*
witnesses
raised from the dead; w. we   *Ac 3:15*
are
new doctrine, w. thou   *Ac 17:19*
speakest, is
w. he hath given assurance   *Ac 17:31*
unto all
w. they were informed   *Ac 21:24*
concerning
all these things, w. we accuse   *Ac 24:8*
him
things w. they now accuse   *Ac 24:13*
of these things w. these   *Ac 25:11*
accuse me
things w. I am accused of the   *Ac 26:2*
Jews
he hath w. to glory; but not   *Ro 4:2*
before
w. ye are now ashamed   *Ro 6:21*
w. I may glory through Jesus   *Ro 15:17*
Christ
things w. ye wrote unto me   *1Co 7:1*
your bounty, w. ye had notice   *2Co 9:5*
before
W. I was made a minister   *Eph 3:7*
he hath w. he might trust in   *Ph'p 3:4*
the flesh
w. ye heard before in the word   *Col 1:5*
of
w. I Paul am made a minister   *Col 1:23*
W. I am made a minister   *Col 1:25*
they say, nor w. they affirm   *1Ti 1:7*
words, w. cometh envy, strife   *1Ti 6:4*
world to come, w. we speak   *Heb 2:5*
W. the Holy Ghost also is a   *Heb 10:15*
witness
chastisement w. all are   *Heb 12:8*
partakers
w. they have no right to eat   *Heb 13:10*
w. ye have heard that it should   *1Jo 4:3*

WHEREON

land w. thou liest, to thee   *Ge 28:13*
will
place w. thou standest is holy   *Ex 3:5*
also the ground w. they are   *Ex 8:21*
wash that w. it was sprinkled   *Le 6:27*
every thing, w. he sitteth   *Le 15:4*
sitteth on any thing w. he sat   *Le 15:6*
w. is the seed of copulation   *Le 15:17*
or on any thing w. she sitteth   *Le 15:23*
all the bed w. he lieth shall be   *Le 15:24*
bed w. she lieth all the days   *Le 15:26*
of
w. the soles of your feet shall   *De 11:24*
tread

place w. thou standest is holy *Jos 5:15*
land w. thy feet have trodden *Jos 14:9*
shall
Abel, w. they set down the *1Sa 6:18*
ark
tables w. the shewbread was *2Ch 4:19*
set
W. do ye trust, that ye *2Ch 32:10*
abide
upon the bed w. Esther was *Es 7:8*
him to be safety, w. he *Job 24:23*
resteth
w. there hang a thousand *Ca 4:4*
bucklers
w. if a man lean, it will go *Isa 36:6*
sticks w. thou writest shall *Eze 37:20*
be
a colt tied, w. never man sat *M'k 11:2*
the hill w. their city was built *Lu 4:29*
and took up that w. he lay *Lu 5:25*
a colt tied, w. never man sat *Lu 19:30*
to reap w. ye bestowed no *Joh 4:38*
labour

WHERESOEVER

to his foot, w. the priest *Le 13:12*
looketh
and sojourn w. thou canst *2Ki 8:1*
sojourn
w. any breach shall be found *2Ki 12:5*
W. I walked with all Israel *1Ch 17:6*
go w. it seemeth convenient *Jer 40:5*
w. the children of men dwelt *Da 2:38*
w. the carcase is, there will *M't 24:28*
W. this gospel shall be *M't 26:13;*
M'k 14:9
w. he taketh him, he teareth *M'k 9:18*
w. he shall go in, say ye to *M'k 14:14*
W. the body is, thither will *Lu 17:37*
the

WHERETO

w. might the strength of their *Job 30:2*
prosper in the thing w. I *Isa 51:11*
sent it
w. we have already attained *Ph'p 3:16*

WHEREUNTO

of the tribe w. they are *Nu 36:4*
received
perish from off the land w. ye *De 4:26*
go
w. the ark of the Lord hath *2Ch 8:11*
come
w. the king advanced him *Es 10:2*
w. I may continually resort *Ps 71:3*
the land w. they desire to *Jer 22:27*
return
w. I will not do any more the *Eze 5:9*
like
is the high place w. ye go *Eze 20:29*
w. shall I liken this *M't 11:16*
generation
W. shall we liken the *M'k 4:30*
kingdom
W. then shall I liken the men *Lu 7:31*
of
like? and w. shall I resemble *Lu 13:18*
it
W. shall I liken the kingdom *Lu 13:20*
of
of them w. this would grow *Ac 5:24*
for the work w. I have called *Ac 13:2*
them
nigh w. was the city of Lasea *Ac 27:8*
w. ye desire again to be in *Ga 4:9*
W. I also labour, striving *Col 1:29*
W. he called you by our *2Th 2:14*
gospel
W. I am ordained a preacher *1Ti 2:7*
doctrine, w. thou hast attained *1Ti 4:6*
w. thou art also called, and *1Ti 6:12*
W. I am appointed a preacher *2Ti 1:11*
w. also they were appointed *1Pe 2:8*
like figure w. even baptism *1Pe 3:21*
doth
w. ye do well that ye take *2Pe 1:19*
heed

WHEREUPON

w. any part of their carcase *Le 11:35*
pillars w. the house standeth *J'g 16:26*
of gold, w. the shewbread *1Ki 7:48*
was
W. the king took counsel, *1Ki 12:28*
and made

W. the princes of Israel and *2Ch 12:6*
the king
W. are the foundations *Job 38:6*
from the cherub, w. he was *Eze 9:3*
w. thou hast set thine *Eze 23:41*
incense and
that w. they set their minds, *Eze 24:25*
their sons
tables, w. they slew their *Eze 40:41*
sacrifices
w. also they laid the *Eze 40:42*
instruments
and the piece w. it rained not *Am 4:7*
W. he promised with an oath *M't 14:7*
to
W. certain Jews from Asia *Ac 24:18*
W. as I went to Damascus *Ac 26:12*
with
W. O king Agrippa, I was *Ac 26:19*
not
W. neither the first testament *Heb 9:18*
was

WHEREVER

wherever (S) *1Sa 14:47;*
18:5; 23:13; 2Sa 7:9; 8:6, 14; 15:20
1Ki 2:3; 8:44; Es 4:3; 8:17; Eze 1:12, 20;
21:16; 47:9; M't 8:19
w. the helmsman's whim *Jas 3:4*
determines (B)

WHEREWITH

blessing w. his father blessed *Ge 27:41*
him
thine hand, w. thou shalt do *Ex 4:17*
signs
may see the bread w. I have *Ex 16:32*
fed you
thy rod, w. thou smotest the *Ex 17:5*
river
things w. the atonement was *Ex 29:33*
made
of the sanctuary w. they *Nu 3:31*
minister
w. the odd number of them is *Nu 3:48*
to be
thereof, w. they minister unto *Nu 4:9*
it
w. they minister in the *Nu 4:12*
sanctuary
w. they minister about it, even *Nu 4:14*
w. they that were burnt had *Nu 16:39*
offered
w. they have beguiled you in *Nu 25:18*
her bond w. she hath bound *Nu 30:4*
her soul
bond w. she hath bound her *Nu 30:4*
soul
bonds w. she bound her *Nu 30:5*
soul
of her lips, w. she bound her *Nu 30:6*
soul
w. she bound her soul shall *Nu 30:7;*
stand *30:11*
lips, w. she bound her soul, *Nu 30:8*
of none
w. they have bound their souls *Nu 30:9*
throwing a stone, w. he may *Nu 35:17*
die
weapon of wood, w. he may *Nu 35:18*
die
with any stone, w. a man may *Nu 35:23*
die
w. the Lord was wroth against *De 9:19*
you
w. the Lord thy God hath *De 15:14*
blessed
of thy vesture, w. thou *De 22:12*
coverest
w. thine enemies shall *De 28:53;*
distress thee *28:55*
w. thine enemy shall distress *De 28:57*
thee
of thine heart w. thou shalt *De 28:67*
fear
w. Moses the man of God *De 33:1*
Blessed
w. he stretched out the spear, *Jos 8:26*
until
my Lord, w. shall I save Israel *J'g 6:15*
w. Abimelech hired vain and *J'g 9:4*
light
w. by me they honour God and *J'g 9:9*
man
is now thy mouth, w. thou *J'g 9:38*
saidst
w. thou mightest be bound to *J'g 16:6*
thee, w. thou mightest be *J'g 16:10*
bound

tell us w. we shall send it to his *1Sa 6:2*
w. they have forsaken me, and *1Sa 8:8*
served
for w. should he reconcile *1Sa 29:4*
himself
hatred w. he hated her was *2Sa 13:15*
greater
than the love w. he had *2Sa 13:15*
loved her
w. shall I make the atonement *2Sa 21:3*
w. I have made supplication *1Ki 8:59*
before
thereof, w. Baasha had *1Ki 15:22*
builded
in his sin w. he made Israel *1Ki 15:26;*
15:34; 16:26
to sin
w. he provoked the Lord *1Ki 15:30*
God of
w. thou hast provoked me to *1Ki 21:22*
anger
And the Lord said unto him, *1Ki 22:22*
W.
w. he fought against *2Ki 13:12*
Amaziah
his sin w. he made Judah to *2Ki 21:16*
sin
w. his anger was kindled *2Ki 23:26*
against
vessels of brass w. they *2Ki 25:14*
ministered
w. Solomon made the brasen *1Ch 18:8*
sea
w. David his father *2Ch 2:17*
had numbered
thereof, w. Baasha was *2Ch 16:6*
building
And the Lord said unto *2Ch 18:20*
him, W.
but against the house w. I *2Ch 35:21*
have war
w. thou didst testify against *Ne 9:34*
them
with speeches w. he can do *Job 15:3*
no good
w. they have reproached thee, *Ps 79:12*
O
W. thine enemies have *Ps 89:51*
reproached
w. they have reproached the *Ps 89:51*
strength, w. he hath girded *Ps 93:1*
himself
a girdle w. he is girded *Ps 109:19*
continually
w. to answer him that *Ps 119:42*
reproacheth
W. the mower filleth not his *Ps 129:7*
hand
crown w. his mother crowned *Ca 3:11*
him
w. ye may cause the weary *Isa 28:12*
to rest
w. the servants of the king of *Isa 37:6*
w. I said I would benefit *Jer 18:10*
them
w. their enemies, and they *Jer 19:9*
that seek
w. ye fight against the king of *Jer 21:4*
is the name w. she shall be *Jer 33:16*
called
vessels of brass w. they *Jer 52:18*
ministered
w. the Lord hath afflicted me *La 1:12*
in the
w. ye there hunt the souls to *Eze 13:20*
make
and oil, and honey, w. I fed *Eze 16:19*
thee
labour w. he served against *Eze 29:20*
it
lamentation w. they shall *Eze 32:16*
lament her
their idols w. they had *Eze 36:18*
polluted it
dreams, w. his spirit was *Da 2:1*
troubled
W. shall I come before the *Mic 6:6*
Lord
plague w. the Lord shall *Zec 14:12*
smite all
w. the Lord will smite the *Zec 14:18*
heathen
to him for the fear w. he *Mal 2:5*
feared me
savour, w. shall it be salted *M't 5:13*
w. soever they shall *M'k 3:28*
blaspheme
saltness, w. will ye season it *M'k 9:50*
savour, w. shall it be *Lu 14:34*
seasoned
Make ready w. I may sup, and *Lu 17:8*

with the towel w. he was girded   *Joh 13:5*
the love w. thou hast loved me may   *Joh 17:26*
things w. one may edify another   *Ro 14:19*
w. we ourselves are comforted of   *2Co 1:4*
w. he was comforted in you   *2Co 7:7*
w. I think to be bold against some   *2Co 10:2*
liberty w. Christ hath made us free   *Ga 5:1*
for his great love w. he loved us   *Eph 2:4*
of the vocation w. ye are called   *Eph 4:1*
w. ye shall be able to quench   *Eph 6:16*
joy w. we joy for your sakes before   *1Th 3:9*
w. he was sanctified, an unholy   *Heb 10:29*

WHEREWITHAL

w. shall a young man cleanse his   *Ps 119:9*
drink? or, W. shall we be clothed   *M't 6:31*

WHET

If I w. my glittering sword   *De 32:41*
he turn not, he will w. his sword   *Ps 7:12*
sharpen his sword (B)   *Ps 7:12*
Who w. their tongue like a sword   *Ps 64:3*
sharpened the tongue (B)   *Ps 64:3*
blunt, and he do not w. the edge   *Ec 10:10*
sharpen it (B)   *Ec 10:10*

WHETHER

see w. they have done altogether   *Ge 18:21*
to wit w. the Lord had made his   *Ge 24:21*
w. thou be my very son, Esau or not   *Ge 24:21*
w. stolen by day, or stolen by night   *Ge 31:39*
w. it be well with thy brethren, and   *Ge 37:14*
now w. it be thy son's coat or no   *Ge 37:32*
proved, w. there be any truth in you   *Ge 42:16*
the man w. ye had yet a brother   *Ge 43:6*
Egypt, and see w. they be yet alive   *Ex 4:18*
w. he be a stranger, or born in the   *Ex 12:19*
w. they will walk in my law, or no   *Ex 16:4*
w. it be beast or man, it shall not   *Ex 19:13*
W. he have gored a son, or have   *Ex 21:31*
hand alive, w. it be ox, or ass   *Ex 22:4*
to see w. he have put his hand   *Ex 22:8*
w. it be for ox, for ass, for sheep   *Ex 22:9*
cattle, w. ox or sheep, that is male   *Ex 34:19*
w. it be a male or female, he shall   *Le 3:1*
w. he hath seen or known of it   *Le 5:1*
w. it be a carcase of an unclean   *Le 5:2*
blood, w. it be of fowl or of beast   *Le 7:26*
w. it be any vessel of wood, or   *Le 11:32*
w. it be oven, or ranges for pots, they   *Le 11:35*
w. it be a woolen garment, or a linen   *Le 13:47*
W. it be in the warp, or woof, of   *Le 13:48*
w. in a skin, or any thing made of   *Le 13:48*
w. warp or woof, in woollen or in   *Le 13:52*
w. it be bare within or without   *Le 13:55*
w. his flesh run with his issue, or his   *Le 15:3*

w. it be one of your own country, or   *Le 16:29; 17:15*
w. she be born at home, or born   *Le 18:9*
And w. it be cow or ewe, ye shall not   *Le 22:28*
shall value it, w. it be good or bad   *Le 27:12*
estimate it, w. it be good or bad   *Le 27:14*
w. it be ox, or sheep; it is the   *Le 27:26*
w. of the seed of the land, or of the   *Le 27:30*
not search w. it be good or bad   *Le 27:33*
w. it was by day or by night   *Nu 9:21*
Or w. it were two days, or a month   *Nu 9:22*
w. my word shall come to pass unto   *Nu 11:23*
w. they be strong or weak, few or   *Nu 13:18*
they dwell in, w. it be good, or bad   *Nu 13:19*
w. in tents, or in strong holds   *Nu 13:19*
what the land is, w. it be fat or lean   *Nu 13:20*
lean, w. there be wood therein   *Nu 13:20*
w. he be born in the land, or   *Nu 15:30*
w. it be of men or beasts, shall be   *Nu 18:15*
w. there hath been any such thing as   *De 4:32*
w. thou wouldest keep his   *De 8:2*
to know w. ye love the Lord   *De 13:3*
a sacrifice, w. it be ox or sheep   *De 18:3*
w. they be young ones, or eggs   *De 22:6*
w. he be of thy brethren, or of thy   *De 24:14*
w. the gods which your fathers   *Jos 24:15*
w. they will keep the way of the Lord   *J'g 2:22*
know w. they would hearken unto the   *J'g 3:4*
W. is better for you, either that   *J'g 9:2*
may know w. our way which we go   *J'g 18:5*
not young men, w. poor or rich   *Ru 3:10*
Who can tell w. God will be gracious   *2Sa 12:22*
w. in death or life, even there also   *2Sa 15:21*
W. they be come out for peace   *1Ki 20:18*
or w. they be come out for war   *1Ki 20:18*
observe w. any thing would come   *1Ki 20:33*
w. I shall recover of this disease   *2Ki 1:2*
w. with many, or with them   *2Ch 14:11*
be put to death, w. small or great   *2Ch 15:13*
small or great, w. man or woman   *2Ch 15:13*
their seed, w. they were of Israel   *Ezr 2:59*
w. it be so, that a decree was made   *Ezr 5:17*
judgment w. it be unto death   *Ezr 7:26*
their seed, w. they were of Israel   *Ne 7:61*
w. Mordecai's matters would stand   *Es 3:4*
w. man or woman, shall come unto   *Es 4:11*
w. thou art come to the kingdom   *Es 4:14*
w. it be done against a nation, or   *Job 34:29*
w. thou refuse, or w. thou choose   *Job 34:33*
w. for correction, or for his land   *Job 37:13*
w. his work be pure, and w. it be   *Pr 20:11*
man, w. he rage or laugh, there is no   *Pr 29:9*
w. he shall be a wise man or a fool   *Ec 2:19*
is sweet, w. he eat little or much   *Ec 5:12*
knowest not w. shall prosper   *Ec 11:6*
or w. they both shall be alike good   *Ec 11:6*

things, w. it be good, or w. it be evil   *Ec 12:14*
and to see w. the vine flourished   *Ca 6:11*
flourish, w. the tender grape appear   *Ca 7:12*
and see w. a man doth travail   *Jer 30:6*
W. it be good, or w. it be evil, we   *Jer 42:6*
w. they hear, or w. they will forbear   *Eze 2:5; 2:7; 3:11*
or torn, w. it be fowl or beast   *Eze 44:31*
w. is easier, to say, Thy sins   *M't 9:5*
w. of them twain did the will   *M't 21:31*
for w. is greater, the gold or the   *M't 23:17*
w. is greater, the gift, or the altar   *M't 23:19*
thou tell us w. thou be the Christ   *M't 26:63*
W. of the twain will ye that I   *M't 27:21*
w. Elias will come to save him   *M't 27:49*
W. it is easier to say to the sick of   *M'k 2:9*
w. he would heal him on the   *M'k 3:2*
w. Elias will come to take him down   *M'k 15:36*
him w. he had been any while dead   *M'k 15:44*
w. he were the Christ, or not   *Lu 3:15*
W. is easier, to say, Thy sins   *Lu 5:23*
w. he would heal on the sabbath   *Lu 6:7*
w. he have sufficient to finish   *Lu 14:28*
it
w. he be able with ten thousand to   *Lu 14:31*
w. is greater, he that sitteth at   *Lu 22:27*
asked w. the man were a Galilaean   *Lu 23:6*
of the doctrine, w. it be of God   *Joh 7:17*
or w. I speak of myself   *Joh 7:17*
W. he be a sinner or no, I know   *Joh 9:25*
w. of these two thou hast   *Ac 1:24*
W. it be right in the sight of God   *Ac 4:19*
w. ye sold the land for so much   *Ac 5:8*
w. they were men or women   *Ac 9:2*
and asked w. Simon, which was   *Ac 10:18*
daily, w. those things were so   *Ac 17:11*
heard w. there be any Holy Ghost   *Ac 19:2*
him w. he would go to Jerusalem   *Ac 25:20*
ye obey; w. of sin unto death   *Ro 6:16*
w. prophecy, let us prophesy   *Ro 12:6*
w. we live, we live unto the   *Ro 14:8*
w. we die, we die unto the   *Ro 14:8*
w. we live therefore, or die   *Ro 14:8*
I know not w. I baptized any other   *1Co 1:16*
W. Paul, or Apollos, or Cephas   *1Co 3:22*
w. thou shalt save thy husband   *1Co 7:16*
man, w. thou shalt save thy wife   *1Co 7:16*
gods, w. in heaven or in earth   *1Co 8:5*
W. therefore ye eat, or drink, or   *1Co 10:31*
body, w. we be Jews or Gentiles   *1Co 12:13*
w. we be bond or free; and have   *1Co 12:13*
And w. one member suffer, all the   *1Co 12:26*
w. there be prophecies, they shall   *1Co 13:8*
w. there be tongues, they shall   *1Co 13:8*
w. there be knowledge, it shall   *1Co 13:8*
w. pipe or harp except they give a   *1Co 14:7*
Therefore w. it were I or they, so   *1Co 15:11*
And w. we be afflicted, it is for your   *2Co 1:6*
w. we be comforted, it is for your   *2Co 1:6*
w. ye be obedient in all things   *2Co 2:9*
w. present or absent, we may   *2Co 5:9*
he hath done, w. it be good or bad   *2Co 5:10*

w. we be beside ourselves, it is to	2Co 5:13	
w. we be sober, it is for your cause	2Co 5:13	
W. any do enquire of Titus, he is	2Co 8:23	
w. in the body, I cannot tell or w. out of the body, I cannot tell	2Co 12:2 2Co 12:2	
w. in the body, or out of the body	2Co 12:3	
yourselves, w. ye be in the faith	2Co 13:5	
the Lord, w. he be bond or free	Eph 6:8	
w. in pretence, or in truth, Christ	Ph'p 1:18	
body w. it be by life, or by death	Ph'p 1:20	
w. I come and see you, or else be	Ph'p 1:27	
w. they be thrones, or dominions	Col 1:16	
w. they be things in earth, or things	Col 1:20	
w. we wake or sleep, we should live	1Th 5:10	
taught, w. by word, or our epistle	2Th 2:15	
w. it be to the king, as supreme	1Pe 2:13	
try the spirits w. they are of God	1Jo 4:1	

WHICH

the waters w. were under the	Ge 1:7
waters w. were above the firmament	Ge 1:7
w. the waters brought forth	Ge 1:21
w. is upon the face of all the earth	Ge 1:29
in the w. is the fruit of a tree	Ge 1:29
ended his work w. he had made	Ge 2:2
from all his work w. he had made	Ge 2:2
from all his work w. God created	Ge 2:3
is it w. compasseth the whole land of	Ge 2:11
that is it w. goeth toward the east of	Ge 2:14
rib, w. the Lord God had taken	Ge 2:22
beast w. the Lord God had made	Ge 3:1
tree w. is in the midst of the garden	Ge 3:3
the tree, of w. I commanded thee	Ge 3:17
flaming sword w. turned every way	Ge 3:24
earth, w. hath opened her mouth	Ge 4:11
ground w. the Lord hath cursed	Ge 5:29
them wives of all w. they chose	Ge 6:2
became mighty men w. were of old	Ge 6:4
fashion w. thou shalt make it	Ge 6:15
w. was upon the face of the ground	Ge 7:23
window of the ark w. he had made	Ge 8:6
forth a raven, w. went forth to and fro	Ge 8:7
w. returned not again unto him any	Ge 8:12
life thereof, w. is the blood thereof	Ge 9:4
covenant w. I make between me	Ge 9:12
covenant w. is between me and you	Ge 9:15
the covenant, w. I have established	Ge 9:17
w. the children of men builded	Ge 11:5
w. they have imagined to do	Ge 11:6
altar, w. he had made there at	Ge 13:4
And Lot also, w. went with Abram	Ge 13:5
For all the land w. thou seest	Ge 13:15
and the king of Bela, w. is Zoar	Ge 14:2
vale of Siddim, w. is the salt sea	Ge 14:3
El-paran, w. is by the wilderness	Ge 14:6
w. is on the left hand of Damascus	Ge 14:15

of Shaveh, w. is the king's dale	Ge 14:17
w. hath delivered thine enemies	Ge 14:20
that w. the young men have eaten	Ge 14:24
of the men w. went with me	Ge 14:24
son's name, w. Hagar bare, Ishmael	Ge 16:15
is my covenant, w. ye shall keep	Ge 17:10
any stranger, w. is not of thy seed	Ge 17:12
w. Sarah shall bare unto thee at a	Ge 17:21
milk, and the calf w. he had dressed	Ge 18:8
the tent door, w. was behind him	Ge 18:10
a surety bear a child, w. am old	Ge 18:13
from Abraham that thing w. I do	Ge 18:17
that w. he hath spoken of him	Ge 18:19
to the cry of it, w. is come unto me	Ge 18:21
Lord, w. am but dust and ashes	Ge 18:27
w. came in to thee this night	Ge 19:5
daughters w. have not known man	Ge 19:8
sons in law, w. married his daughters	Ge 19:14
and thy two daughters, w. are here	Ge 19:15
w. thou hast shewed unto me	Ge 19:19
city for the w. thou hast spoken	Ge 19:21
and that w. grew upon the ground	Ge 19:25
the cities in the w. Lot dwelt	Ge 19:29
for the woman w. thou hast taken	Ge 20:3
is thy kindness, w. thou shalt show	Ge 20:13
which (S) Ge 20:13; 28:15; Ex 21:13; 30:4; Le 11:21; 18:3; Nu 13:27; 15:18; 35:25, 26; De 4:5, 14; 6:1; 9:28; 11:8, 10-11, 29; 12:29; 23:12, 20; 28:37, 63; 30:1, 3, 16, 18; 31:13; 32:47, 50; 1Sa 21:2; 1Ki 7:48; Ec 11:6; Eze 6:9; 12:16; 36:20, 22; 37:21; Da 9:7; Joe 3:7; M't 12:44; Ph'p 3:16	
set time of w. God had spoken to	Ge 21:2
w. she had born unto Abraham	Ge 21:9
well, w. Abimelech's servants had	Ge 21:25
seven ewe lambs w. thou hast set	Ge 21:29
the mountains w. I will tell thee of	Ge 22:2
to the place w. God had told him of	Ge 22:9
as the sand w. is upon the sea shore	Ge 22:17
w. he hath, w. is in the end of his	Ge 23:9
the silver, w. he had named in the	Ge 23:16
the field of Ephron, w. was in Machpelah, w. was before Mamre	Ge 23:17 Ge 23:17
field, and the cave w. was therein	Ge 23:17
w. took me from my father's house	Ge 24:7
my kindred, and w. spake unto me	Ge 24:7
the son of Milcah, w. she bare unto	Ge 24:24
w. had led me in the right way to	Ge 24:48
possess the gate of those w. hate them	Ge 24:60
years of Abraham's life w. he lived	Ge 25:7
the Hittite, w. is before Mamre	Ge 25:9
in the land w. I shall tell thee	Ge 26:2
oath w. I sware unto Abraham thy	Ge 26:3
the wells w. his father's servants	Ge 26:15
w. they had digged in the days of	Ge 26:18

by w. his father had called them	Ge 26:18
concerning the well w. they had	Ge 26:32
W. were a grief of mind unto Isaac	Ge 26:35
according to that w. I command	Ge 27:8
and the bread, w. she had prepared	Ge 27:17
of a field w. the Lord hath blessed	Ge 27:27
forget that w. thou hast done to him	Ge 27:45
w. are of the daughters of the land	Ge 27:46
land w. God gave unto Abraham	Ge 28:4
and took unto the wives w. he had	Ge 28:9
done that w. I have spoken to thee	Ge 28:15
this stone, w. I have set for a pillar	Ge 28:22
service w. thou shalt serve with me	Ge 29:27
knowest my service w. I have done	Ge 30:26
little w. thou hadst before I came	Ge 30:30
white appear w. was in the rods	Ge 30:37
set the rods w. he had pilled before	Ge 30:38
of that w. was our father's hath he	Ge 31:1
the rams w. leaped upon the cattle	Ge 31:10
the rams w. leap upon the cattle are	Ge 31:12
riches w. God hath taken from our	Ge 31:16
and all his goods w. he had gotten	Ge 31:18
w. he had gotten in Padan-aram	Ge 31:18
w. was torn of beasts I brought not	Ge 31:39
their children w. they have born	Ge 31:43
w. I have cast betwixt me and thee	Ge 31:51
other company w. is left shall escape	Ge 32:8
the Lord w. saidst unto me, Return	Ge 32:9
w. thou hast shewed unto thy	Ge 32:10
the sand, w. cannot be numbered	Ge 32:12
took of that w. came to his hand a	Ge 32:13
Israel eat not of the sinew w. shrank	Ge 32:32
w. is upon the hollow of the thigh	Ge 32:32
the children w. God hath graciously	Ge 33:5
thou by all this drove w. I met	Ge 33:8
Shechem, w. is in the land of Canaan	Ge 33:18
of Leah, w. she bare unto Jacob	Ge 34:1
w. things ought not to be done	Ge 34:7
asses, and that w. was in the city	Ge 34:28
the city, and that w. was in the field	Ge 34:28
was with me in the way w. I went	Ge 35:3
strange gods w. were in their hand	Ge 35:4
their earrings w. were in their ears	Ge 35:4
under the oak w. was by Shechem	Ge 35:4
Luz, w. is in the land of Canaan	Ge 35:6
And the land w. I gave Abraham	Ge 35:12
way to Ephrath, w. is Bethlehem	Ge 35:19
of Jacob, w. were born to him in	Ge 35:26
w. is Hebron, where Abraham and	Ge 35:27
w. were born unto him in the land	Ge 36:5
w. he had got in the land of Canaan	Ge 36:6

you, this dream w. I have dreamed — Ge 37:6
thing w. he did displeased the Lord — Ge 38:10
place, w. is by the way to Timnath — Ge 38:14
w. had brought him down thither — Ge 39:1
he had, save the bread w. he did eat — Ge 39:6
w. thou hast brought unto us — Ge 39:17
his wife, w. she spake unto him — Ge 39:19
that w. he did, the Lord made it to — Ge 39:23
of Egypt, w. were bound in prison — Ge 40:5
day w. was Pharaoh's birthday — Ge 40:20
w. I have spoken unto Pharaoh — Ge 41:28
w. shall be in the land of Egypt — Ge 41:36
in the second chariot w. he had — Ge 41:43
w. were in the land of Egypt — Ge 41:48
field, w. was round about every city — Ge 41:48
sons, w. Asenath, bare unto him — Ge 41:50
the dreams w. he dreamed of them — Ge 42:9
him by the way in the w. ye go — Ge 42:38
corn w. they had brought out — Ge 43:2
the present w. was in their hand — Ge 43:26
the Egyptians w. did eat with him — Ge 43:32
not this it in w. my lord drinketh — Ge 44:5
w. we found in our sacks' mouths — Ge 44:8
in w. there shall neither be earing — Ge 45:6
Joseph, w. he had said unto them — Ge 45:27
wagons w. Joseph had sent to carry — Ge 45:27
wagons w. Pharaoh had sent — Ge 46:5
w. they had gotten in the land — Ge 46:6
children of Israel, w. came into Egypt — Ge 46:8
of Leah, w. she bare unto Jacob — Ge 46:13
w. Asenath bare unto him — Ge 46:20
of Rachel, w. were born to Jacob — Ge 46:22
Bilhah, w. Laban gave unto Rachel — Ge 46:25
into Egypt, w. came out of his loins — Ge 46:26
Joseph, w. were born him in Egypt — Ge 46:27
w. came into Egypt, were threescore — Ge 46:27
w. were in the land of Canaan, are — Ge 46:81
for the corn w. they brought — Ge 47:14
their portion w. Pharaoh gave them — Ge 47:22
priests only, w. became not Pharaoh's — Ge 47:26
w. were born unto thee in the land of — Ge 48:5
issue, w. thou begettest after them — Ge 48:6
the God w. fed me all my life long — Ge 48:15
The angel w. redeemed me from all — Ge 48:16
w. I took out of the hand of — Ge 48:22
that w. shall befall you in the last — Ge 49:1
of Machpelah, w. is before Mamre — Ge 49:30
w. Abraham bought, with the field of — Ge 49:30
the days of those w. are embalmed — Ge 50:3
my grave w. I have digged for me — Ge 50:5
threshingfloor of Atad, w. is beyond — Ge 50:10
Abel-mizraim, w. is beyond Jordan — Ge 50:11
w. Abraham bought with the field — Ge 50:13
us all the evil w. we did unto him — Ge 50:15

land w. he sware unto Abraham — Ge 50:24
of Israel, w. came into Egypt — Ex 1:1
over Egypt, w. knew not Joseph — Ex 1:8
of w. the name of one was Shiphrah — Ex 1:15
of my people w. are in Egypt — Ex 3:7
and seen that w. is done to you in — Ex 3:16
my wonders w. I will do in the — Ex 3:20
water w. thou takest out of the river — Ex 4:9
unto my brethren w. are in Egypt — Ex 4:18
the men are dead w. sought thy life — Ex 4:19
w. I have put in thine hand — Ex 4:21
signs w. he had commanded him — Ex 4:28
the words w. the Lord had spoken — Ex 4:30
bricks, w. they did make heretofore — Ex 5:8
w. Pharaoh's taskmasters had set — Ex 5:14
God, w. bringeth you out from under — Ex 6:7
concerning the w. I did swear — Ex 6:8
are they w. spake to Pharaoh king — Ex 6:27
the rod w. was turned to a serpent — Ex 7:15
the waters w. are in the river — Ex 7:17
w. shall go up and come into thine — Ex 8:3
the frogs w. he had brought against — Ex 8:12
of Goshen, in w. my people dwell — Ex 8:22
is upon the cattle w. is in the field — Ex 9:3
beast w. shall be found in the field — Ex 9:19
signs w. I have done among — Ex 10:2
w. remaineth unto you from the hail — Ex 10:5
every tree w. groweth for you out of — Ex 10:5
w. neither thy fathers, nor thy — Ex 10:6
fruit of the trees w. the hail left — Ex 10:15
west wind, w. took away the locusts — Ex 10:19
Egypt, even darkness w. may be felt — Ex 10:21
and that w. remaineth of it until the — Ex 12:10
save that w. every man must eat — Ex 12:16
whosoever eateth that w. is leavened — Ex 12:19
the land w. the Lord will give you — Ex 12:25
dough w. they brought forth out of — Ex 12:39
day, in w. ye came out from Egypt — Ex 13:3
w. he sware unto thy fathers to give — Ex 13:5
of that w. the Lord did unto me — Ex 13:8
cometh of a beast w. thou hast — Ex 13:12
Lord w. he will shew to you to-day — Ex 14:13
w. went before the camp of Israel — Ex 14:19
work w. the Lord did put upon the — Ex 14:31
wrath w. consumed them as stubble — Ex 15:7
the people w. thou hast redeemed — Ex 15:13
pass over, w. thou hast purchased — Ex 15:16
w. thou hast made for thee to dwell — Ex 15:17
Lord, w. thy hands have established — Ex 15:17
w. when he had cast into the waters — Ex 15:25
wilt do that w. is right in his sight — Ex 15:26
diseases, w. I have brought upon the — Ex 15:26
of Sin, w. is between Elim and Sinai — Ex 16:1
shall prepare that w. they bring in — Ex 16:5

w. ye murmur against him — Ex 16:8
w. the Lord hath given you to eat — Ex 16:15
thing w. the Lord hath commanded — Ex 16:16
man for them w. are in his tents — Ex 16:16
This is that w. the Lord hath said — Ex 16:23
bake that w. ye will bake to-day — Ex 16:23
that w. remaineth over lay up for you — Ex 16:23
on the seventh day, w. is the sabbath — Ex 16:26
the thing w. the Lord commandeth — Ex 16:32
w. the name of the one was Gershom — Ex 18:3
w. the Lord had done to Israel — Ex 18:9
These are the words w. thou shalt — Ex 19:6
words w. the Lord commanded — Ex 19:7
priests also, w. come near to the Lord — Ex 19:22
w. have brought thee out of — Ex 20:2
the land w. the Lord thy God giveth — Ex 20:12
w. thou shalt set before them — Ex 21:1
w. another challengeth to be his — Ex 22:9
shall not make good that w. was torn — Ex 22:13
w. thou hast sown in the field — Ex 23:16
w. is in the end of the year — Ex 23:16
into the place w. I have prepared — Ex 23:20
thee, w. shall drive out the Hivite — Ex 23:28
the words w. the Lord hath said — Ex 24:3
of Israel, w. offered burnt offerings — Ex 24:5
w. the Lord hath made with you — Ex 24:8
commandments w. I have written — Ex 24:12
offering w. ye shall take of them — Ex 25:3
the testimony w. I shall give thee — Ex 25:16
w. are upon the ark of the testimony — Ex 25:22
of all things w. I will give thee in — Ex 25:22
w. was shewed thee in the mount — Ex 25:40
of the curtain w. coupleth the second — Ex 26:10
that w. remaineth in the length of the — Ex 26:13
w. was shewed thee in the mount — Ex 26:30
the veil, w. is before the testimony — Ex 27:21
the garments w. they shall make — Ex 28:4
girdle of the ephod, w. is upon it — Ex 28:8
w. are on the ends of the breastplate — Ex 28:24
w. is in the side of the ephod in ward — Ex 28:26
w. the children of Israel shall hallow — Ex 28:38
w. is waved, and w. is heaved up, of — Ex 29:27
even of that w. is for Aaron — Ex 29:27
and of that w. is for his sons — Ex 29:27
things w. I have commanded thee — Ex 29:35
w. thou shalt offer upon the altar — Ex 29:38
for the perfume w. thou shalt make — Ex 30:37
make us gods, w. shall go before us — Ex 32:1
w. are in the ears of your wives — Ex 32:2
earrings w. were in their ears — Ex 32:3
w. brought thee up out of the land — Ex 32:4
w. thou broughtest out of the land — Ex 32:7
of the way w. I commanded them — Ex 32:8
w. have brought up out of the land — Ex 32:8
w. thou hast brought forth out of the — Ex 32:11

of the evil w. he thought to do — Ex 32:14

took the calf w. they had made, and — Ex 32:20

Make us gods, w. shall go before us — Ex 32:23

out of thy book w. thou hast written — Ex 32:32

place of w. I have spoken unto thee — Ex 32:34

they made the calf, w. Aaron made — Ex 32:35

people w. thou hast brought up out — Ex 33:1

the land w. I sware unto Abraham — Ex 33:1

every one w. sought the Lord went out — Ex 33:7

w. was without the camp — Ex 33:7

in the first tables, w. thou brakest — Ex 34:1

people among w. thou art shall see — Ex 34:10

that w. I commanded thee this day — Ex 34:11

Israel that w. he was commanded — Ex 34:34

words w. the Lord hath commanded — Ex 35:1

the thing w. the Lord commanded — Ex 35:4

and brought that w. they had spun — Ex 35:25

w. the Lord had commanded to be — Ex 35:29

w. the children of Israel had brought — Ex 36:3

man from his work w. they made — Ex 36:4

w. the Lord commanded to make — Ex 36:5

the curtain w. was in the coupling — Ex 36:12

of the curtain w. coupleth the second — Ex 36:17

w. is toward the north corner, he made — Ex 36:25

the vessels w. were upon the table — Ex 37:16

w. assembled at the door of the — Ex 38:8

w. was on the side of the ephod — Ex 39:19

is on the fire w. is upon the altar — Le 1:8; 1:12

And that w. is left of the meat offering — Le 2:10

w. ye shall bring unto the Lord — Le 2:11

w. is by the flanks, and the caul — Le 3:4

w. is upon the wood that is on — Le 3:5

w. is by the flanks, and the caul — Le 3:10; 3:15

things w. ought not to be done — Le 4:2

for his sin, w. he hath sinned — Le 4:3

w. is in the tabernacle of the — Le 4:7

w. is at the door of the tabernacle — Le 4:7

w. is by the flanks, and the caul — Le 4:9

things w. should not be done — Le 4:13

sin, w. they have sinned against it — Le 4:14

of the altar w. is before the Lord — Le 4:18

w. is at the door of the tabernacle — Le 4:18

things w. should not be done — Le 4:22

things w. ought not to be done — Le 4:27

Or of his sin, w. he hath sinned — Le 4:28

for his sin w. he hath sinned — Le 4:28

Lord for his sin, w. he hath sinned — Le 5:6

his trespass, w. he hath committed — Le 5:7

offer that w. is for the sin offering — Le 5:8

him for his sin w. he hath sinned — Le 5:10

things w. are forbidden to be done — Le 5:17

that w. was delivered him to keep — Le 6:2

Or have found that w. was lost — Le 6:3

restore that w. he took violently — Le 6:4

thing w. he hath deceitfully gotten — Le 6:4

that w. was delivered him to keep — Le 6:4

or the lost thing w. he found — Le 6:4

that about w. he hath sworn falsely — Le 6:5

the ashes w. the fire hath consumed — Le 6:10

w. is upon the meat offering — Le 6:15

w. they shall offer unto the Lord in — Le 6:20

w. is by the flanks, and the caul — Le 7:4

burnt offering w. he hath offered — Le 7:8

w. he shall offer unto the Lord — Le 7:11

offerings, w. pertain unto the Lord — Le 7:21

the fat of that w. is torn with beasts — Le 7:24

of w. men offer an offering made by — Le 7:25

W. the Lord commanded to be — Le 7:36

W. the Lord commanded Moses in — Le 7:38

is the thing w. the Lord commanded — Le 8:5

of the blood w. was upon the altar — Le 8:30

And that w. remaineth of the flesh and — Le 8:32

w. the Lord commanded by the — Le 8:36

brought that w. Moses commanded — Le 9:5

is the thing w. the Lord commanded — Le 9:6

the sin offering, w. was for himself — Le 9:8

w. he sprinkled round about upon the — Le 9:12

w. was the sin offering for the — Le 9:15

offerings, w. was for the people — Le 9:18

w. he sprinkled upon the altar round — Le 9:18

and that w. covereth the inwards — Le 9:19

w. when all the people saw, they — Le 9:24

Lord, w. he commanded them not — Le 10:1

burning w. the Lord hath kindled — Le 10:6

statutes w. the Lord hath spoken — Le 10:11

w. are given out of the sacrifices of — Le 10:14

sons of Aaron w. were left alive — Le 10:16

These are the beasts w. ye shall eat — Le 11:2

any living thing w. is in the waters — Le 11:10

they w. ye shall have in abomination — Le 11:13

w. have legs above their feet — Le 11:21

creeping things, w. have four feet — Le 11:23

of every beast w. divideth the hoof — Le 11:26

Of all meat w. may be eaten — Le 11:34

that on w. such water cometh shall — Le 11:34

that w. toucheth their carcase shall be — Le 11:36

any sowing seed w. is to be sown — Le 11:37

if any beast, of w. ye may eat, die — Le 11:39

The flesh also, in w. even in the skin — Le 13:18

of skin if it be, w. thou shalt wash — Le 13:58

get that w. pertaineth to his cleansing — Le 14:32

w. I give to you for a possession — Le 14:34

w. in sight are lower than the wall — Le 14:37

the stones in w. the plague is — Le 14:40

that he toucheth w. hath the issue — Le 15:12

the mercy seat, w. is upon the ark — Le 16:2

of the sin offering, w. is for himself — Le 16:6

the goat upon w. the Lord's lot fell — Le 16:9

on w. the lot fell to be the scapegoat — Le 16:10

of the sin offering, w. is for himself — Le 16:11

w. he put on when he went into the — Le 16:23

thing w. the Lord hath commanded — Le 17:2

w. they offer in the open field — Le 17:5

the strangers w. sojourn among you — Le 17:8

w. hunteth and catcheth any beast — Le 17:13

soul that eateth that w. died of itself — Le 17:15

that w. was torn with beasts, whether — Le 17:15

w. if a man do, he shall live in them — Le 18:5

the land done, w. were before you — Le 18:27

w. were committed before you — Le 18:30

Lord for his sin, w. he hath done — Le 19:22

sin w. he hath done shall be forgiven — Le 19:22

w. brought you out of the land of — Le 19:36

I am the Lord w. sanctify you — Le 20:8

the nation, w. I cast out before you — Le 20:23

w. have separated you from other — Le 20:24

w. I have separated from you — Le 20:25

virgin w. hath had no husband — Le 21:3

I the Lord, w. sanctify you, am holy — Le 21:8

things w. they hallow unto me — Le 22:2

w. the children of Israel hallow unto — Le 22:3

The soul w. hath touched any such — Le 22:6

w. dieth of itself, or is torn with beasts — Le 22:8

Israel, w. they offer unto the Lord — Le 22:15

w. they will offer unto the Lord for a — Le 22:18

offer unto the Lord that w. is bruised — Le 22:24

I am the Lord w. hallow you — Le 22:32

w. ye shall proclaim to be holy — Le 23:2

w. ye shall proclaim in their seasons — Le 23:4

unto the land w. I give unto you — Le 23:10

w. ye shall proclaim to be holy — Le 23:37

offerings, w. ye give unto the Lord — Le 23:38

come into the land w. I give you — Le 25:2

That w. groweth of its own accord — Le 25:5

neither reap that w. groweth of itself — Le 25:11

he redeem that w. his brother sold — Le 25:25

then that w. is sold shall remain in — Le 25:28

w. have no wall round about them — Le 25:31

w. brought you forth out of the land — Le 25:38

w. I brought forth out of the land of — Le 25:42

thy bondmaids, w. thou shalt have — Le 25:44

with you, w. they begat in your land — Le 25:45

w. brought you forth out of — Le 26:13

w. shall rob you of your children, and — Le 26:22

enemies w. dwell therein shall — Le 26:32

trespass w. they trespassed against — Le 26:40

and laws w. the Lord made — Le 26:46

of w. they do not offer a sacrifice — Le 27:11

the Lord a field w. he hath bought — Le 27:22

w. is not of the fields of his — Le 27:22

w. should be the Lord's firstling — Le 27:26

devoted, w. shall be devoted of men — Le 27:29

w. the Lord commanded Moses for — Le 27:34

these men w. are expressed by their — Nu 1:17

w. Moses and Aaron numbered, and — Nu 1:44

those w. pitch by him shall be — Nu 2:12

those w. were numbered of	Nu 2:32	theirs, w. they shall render unto me	Nu 18:9	hundreds, w. came from the battle	Nu 31:14
the priests w. were anointed, whom	Nu 3:3	w. they shall offer unto the Lord	Nu 18:12	the men of war w. went to the battle	Nu 31:21
the court, w. is by the tabernacle	Nu 3:26	w. they shall bring unto the Lord	Nu 18:13	w. the Lord commanded Moses	Nu 31:21
w. Moses and Aaron numbered at	Nu 3:39	flesh, w. they bring unto the Lord	Nu 18:15	the men of war w. went out to battle	Nu 31:28
Israel, w. are more than the Levites	Nu 3:46	the sanctuary, w. is twelve gerahs	Nu 18:16	w. keep the charge of the tabernacle	Nu 31:30
the court, w. is by the tabernacle	Nu 4:26	w. the children of Israel offer unto	Nu 18:19	prey w. the men of war had caught	Nu 31:32
w. Moses and Aaron did number	Nu 4:37	for their service w. they serve	Nu 18:21	w. was the portion of them that went	Nu 31:36
confess their sin w. they have done	Nu 5:7	w. they offer as an heave offering	Nu 18:24	of w. the Lord's tribute was	Nu 31:38; 31:39, 40
Israel w. they bring unto the priest	Nu 5:9	the tithes w. I have given you from	Nu 18:26	w. was the Lord's heave offering	Nu 31:41
hands, w. is the jealousy offering	Nu 5:18	w. ye receive of the children	Nu 18:28	w. Moses divided from the men	Nu 31:42
in the w. he separateth himself	Nu 6:5	law w. the Lord hath commanded	Nu 19:2	w. kept the charge of the tabernacle	Nu 31:47
in the fire w. is under the sacrifice	Nu 6:18	and upon w. never came yoke	Nu 19:2	officers w. were over thousands	Nu 31:48
according to the vow w. he vowed	Nu 6:21	w. hath no covering bound upon it	Nu 19:15	men of war w. are under our charge	Nu 31:49
w. are heads of the thousands	Nu 10:4	unto the land w. I have given them	Nu 20:12	country w. the Lord smote before	Nu 32:4
w. was the reward of all the camps	Nu 10:25	unto the land w. I have given unto	Nu 20:24	land w. the Lord hath given them	Nu 32:7
unto the place of w. the Lord said	Nu 10:29	the Canaanite, w. dwelt in the south	Nu 21:1	land w. the Lord had given them	Nu 32:9
fish, w. we did eat in Egypt freely	Nu 11:5	the wilderness w. is before Moab	Nu 21:11	the land w. I sware unto Abraham	Nu 32:11
the land w. thou swarest unto their	Nu 11:12	w. is in the wilderness that cometh	Nu 21:13	w. hath proceeded out of your mouth	Nu 32:24
take of the spirit w. is upon thee	Nu 11:17	Pisgah, w. looketh toward Jeshimon	Nu 21:20	unto the cities w. they builded	Nu 32:38
despised the Lord w. is among you	Nu 11:20	Nophah, w. reacheth unto Medeba	Nu 21:30	the Amorite w. was in it	Nu 32:39
men w. were upon the face of	Nu 12:3	the Amorites, w. dwelt at Heshbon	Nu 21:34	w. went forth out of the land	Nu 33:1
w. I give unto the children of Israel	Nu 13:2	Pethor, w. is by the river of the land	Nu 22:5	firstborn, w. the Lord had smitten	Nu 33:4
w. Moses sent to spy out the land	Nu 13:16	w. covereth the face of the earth	Nu 22:11	w. is in the edge of the wilderness	Nu 33:6
w. the children of Israel cut down	Nu 13:24	the word w. I shall say unto thee	Nu 22:20	w. is before Baal-zephon	Nu 33:7
of the land w. they had searched	Nu 13:32	upon w. thou hast ridden ever since	Nu 22:30	wilderness of Zin, w. is Kadesh	Nu 33:36
through w. we have gone to search	Nu 13:32	Moab, w. is in the border of Arnon	Nu 22:36	Canaanite, w. dwelt in the south	Nu 33:40
of Anak, w. come of the giants	Nu 13:33	Arnon, w. is in the utmost coast	Nu 22:36	those w. ye let remain of them shall	Nu 33:55
w. were of them that searched	Nu 14:6	w. the Lord hath put in my mouth	Nu 23:12	This is the land w. ye shall inherit	Nu 34:13
w. we passed through to search it	Nu 14:7	said, w. heard the words of God	Nu 24:4	w. the Lord commanded to give	Nu 34:13
us; a land w. floweth with milk and	Nu 14:8	w. saw the vision of the Almighty	Nu 24:4	w. shall divide the land unto you	Nu 34:17
the signs w. I have shewed among	Nu 14:11	lign aloes w. the Lord hath planted	Nu 24:6	w. ye shall give unto the Levites	Nu 35:4; 35:6
nations w. have heard the fame of	Nu 14:15	messengers w. thou sentest unto	Nu 24:12	cities w. ye shall give to the Levites	Nu 35:7
the land w. he sware unto them	Nu 14:16	w. heard the words of God, and knew	Nu 24:16	the cities w. ye shall give shall be	Nu 35:8
all those men w. have seen my glory	Nu 14:22	w. saw the vision of the Almighty	Nu 24:16	to his inheritance w. he inheriteth	Nu 35:8
w. I did in Egypt and in the	Nu 14:22	w. was slain in the day of the plague	Nu 25:18	w. killeth any person at unawares	Nu 35:11
the land w. I sware unto their fathers	Nu 14:23	w. went forth out of the land of Egypt	Nu 26:4	And of these cities w. ye shall give	Nu 35:13
congregation, w. murmur against	Nu 14:27	w. were famous in the congregation	Nu 26:9	of Canaan, w. shall be cities of refuge	Nu 35:14
Israel, w. they murmur against me	Nu 14:27	land w. I have given unto the	Nu 27:12	w. was anointed with the holy oil	Nu 35:25
w. have murmured against me	Nu 14:29	W. may go out before them	Nu 27:17	a murderer, w. is guilty of death	Nu 35:31
w. I sware to make you dwell	Nu 14:30	and w. may go in before them, and	Nu 27:17	the land w. ye shall inhabit	Nu 35:34
ones, w. ye said should be a prey	Nu 14:31	and w. may lead them out	Nu 27:17	thing w. the Lord doth command	Nu 36:6
know the land w. ye have despised	Nu 14:31	w. may bring them in; that	Nu 27:17	w. the Lord commanded by	Nu 36:13
the days in w. ye search the land	Nu 14:34	not as sheep w. have no shepherd	Nu 27:17	w. Moses spake unto all Israel	De 1:1
w. Moses sent to search the land	Nu 14:36	fire w. ye shall offer unto the Lord	Nu 28:3	the Amorites, w. dwelt in Heshbon	De 1:4
w. were of the men that went to	Nu 14:38	w. was ordained in mount Sinai for	Nu 28:6	w. dwelt at Astaroth in Edrei	De 1:4
place w. the Lord hath promised	Nu 14:40	w. is for a continual burnt offering	Nu 28:23	the land w. the Lord sware unto	De 1:8
the Canaanites w. dwell in that hill	Nu 14:45	thing w. the Lord hath commanded	Nu 30:1	thing w. thou hast spoken is good	De 1:14
habitations w. I give unto you	Nu 15:2	shall make her vow w. she vowed	Nu 30:8	time all the things w. ye shall	De 1:18
w. the Lord hath spoken unto	Nu 15:22	and that w. she uttered with her lips	Nu 30:8	wilderness, w. ye saw by the way	De 1:19
after w. ye use to go a whoring	Nu 15:39	or all her bonds, w. are upon her	Nu 30:14	w. the Lord our God doth give unto	De 1:20
w. brought you out of the land of	Nu 15:41	w. the Lord commanded Moses	Nu 30:16	w. the Lord our God doth give us	De 1:25
For w. cause both thou and all thy	Nu 16:11	plains of Moab, w. are by Jordan	Nu 31:12	Lord your God w. goeth before you	De 1:30
Eliab: w. said, We will not come up	Nu 16:12			land, w. I sware to give unto your	De 1:35
w. is not of the seed of Aaron, come	Nu 16:40				

son of Nun, *w.* standeth before thee | De 1:38
ones, *w.* ye said should be a prey | De 1:39
w. in that day had no knowledge | De 1:39
Amorites, *w.* dwelt in that mountain | De 1:44
the children of Esau, *w.* dwelt in Seir | De 2:4
children of Esau, *w.* dwelt in Seir | De 2:8
W. also were accounted giants | De 2:11
w. the Lord gave unto them | De 2:12
the space in *w.* we came from | De 2:14
the children of Esau *w.* dwell in Seir | De 2:29
And the Avims *w.* dwelt in Hazerim | De 2:23
w. came forth out of Caphtor | De 2:23
the children of Esau *w.* dwell in Seir | De 2:29
Moabites *w.* dwell in Ar, did unto me | De 2:29
into the land *w.* the Lord our God | De 2:29
the spoil of the cities *w.* we took | De 2:35
Aroer, *w.* is by the brink of the river | De 2:36
the Amorites, *w.* dwelt at Heshbon | De 3:2
not a city *w.* we took not from them | De 3:4
W. Hermon the Sidonians call | De 3:9
land, *w.* we possessed at that time | De 3:12
w. is by the river Arnon, and half | De 3:12
w. was called the land of giants | De 3:13
w. is the border of the children of | De 3:16
your cities *w.* I have given you | De3:19
w. the Lord your God hath given | De 3:20
possession, *w.* I have given you | De 3:20
inherit the land *w.* thou shalt see | De 3:28
judgments, *w.* I teach you, for to do | De 4:1
unto the word *w.* I command you | De 4:2
Lord your God *w.* I command you | De 4:2
w. shall hear all these statutes, and | De 4:6
law, *w.* I set before you this day | De 4:8
the things *w.* thine eyes have seen | De 4:9
w. he commanded you to perform | De 4:13
w. the Lord thy God hath divided | De 4:19
w. the Lord thy God giveth thee for | De 4:21
covenant *w.* he made with you | De 4:23
w. the Lord thy God hath forbidden | De 4:23
w. neither see, nor hear, nor eat | De 4:28
fathers *w.* he sware unto them | De 4:31
that are past, *w.* were before thee | De 4:32
w. I command thee this day | De 4:40
w. the Lord thy God giveth thee | De 4:40
w. should kill his neighbour | De 4:42
law *w.* Moses set before the children | De 4:44
w. Moses spake unto the chilren of | De 4:45
w. were on this side Jordan toward | De 4:47
w. is by the bank of the river Arnon | De 4:48
unto mount Sion, *w.* is Hermon | De 4:48
w. I speak in your ears this day | De 5:1
God, *w.* brougth thee out of the land | De 5:6
land, *w.* the Lord thy God giveth | De 5:16
w. they have spoken unto thee | De 5:28
judgments, *w.* thou shalt teach them | De 5:31

them in the land *w.* I give them | De 5:31
w. the Lord your God commanded | De 5:33
in the land *w.* ye shall possess | De 5:33
w. the Lord your God commanded | De 6:1
commandments, *w.* I command thee | De 6:2
words, *w.* I command thee, this day | De 6:6
land *w.* he sware unto thy fathers | De 6:10
goodly cities, *w.* thou buildedst not | De 6:10
good things, *w.* thou filledst not | De 6:11
wells digged, *w.* thou diggedst not | De 6:11
olive trees, *w.* thou plantedst not | De 6:11
w. brought thee forth out of the | De 6:12
the people *w.* are round about you | De 6:14
w. he hath commanded thee | De 6:17
shalt do that *w.* is right and good | De 6:18
w. the Lord sware unto thy fathers | De 6:18
w. the Lord our God commanded | De 6:20
land *w.* he sware unto our fathers | De 6:23
w. he had sworn unto your fathers | De 7:8
w. keepeth covenant and mercy | De 7:9
w. I command thee this day, to do | De 7:11
land *w.* he sware unto thy fathers | De 7:12; 7:13
diseases of Egypt, *w.* thou knowest | De 7:15
w. the Lord thy God shall deliver | De 7:16
temptations *w.* thine eyes saw | De 7:19
commandments *w.* I command thee | De 8:1
land *w.* the Lord sware unto your | De 8:1
way *w.* the Lord thy God led thee | De 8:2
with manna, *w.* thou knewest not | De 8:3
good land *w.* he hath given thee | De 8:10
w. I command thee this day | De 8:11
w. brought thee forth out of the land | De 8:14
manna, *w.* thy fathers knew not | De 8:16
w. he sware unto thy fathers, as it | De 8:18
nations *w.* the Lord destroyeth | De 8:20
God, is he *w.* goeth over before thee | De 9:3
w. the Lord ṣware unto thy fathers | De 9:5
covenant *w.* the Lord made with | De 9:9
words *w.* the Lord spake with you | De 9:10
w. thou hast brought forth out | De 9:12
way *w.* the Lord had commanded | De 9:16
your sins *w.* ye sinned, in doing | De 9:18
your sin, the calf *w.* ye had made | De 9:21
the land *w.* I have given you | De 9:23
w. thou hast redeemed through thy | De 9:26
w. thou hast brought forth of | De 9:26
into the land *w.* he promised them | De 9:28
w. thou broughtest out by thy | De 9:29
in the first tables *w.* thou brakest | De 10:2
w. the Lord spake unto you in the | De 10:4
the tables in the ark *w.* I had made | De 10:5
w. I sware unto their fathers | De 10:11
w. I command thee this day | De 10:13
w. regardeth not persons, nor | De 10:17
terrible things, *w.* thine eyes have | De 10:21
your children *w.* have not known | De 11:2

known, and *w.* have not seen | De 11:2
acts, *w.* he did in the midst of Egypt | De 11:3
great acts of the Lord *w.* he | De 11:7
commandments *w.* I command you | De 11:8
w. the Lord sware unto your fathers | De 11:9
A land *w.* the Lord thy God careth | De 11:12
commandments *w.* I command you | De 11:13
good land *w.* the Lord giveth you | De 11:17
w. the Lord sware unto your fathers | De 11:21
commandments *w.* I command you | De 11:22
w. I command you this day | De 11:27
the way *w.* I command you this day | De 11:28
other gods, *w.* ye have not known | De 11:28
w. dwell in the champaign over | De 11:30
w. the Lord your God giveth you | De 11:31
judgments *w.* I set before you this | De 11:32
w. ye shall observe to do in the land | De 12:1
w. the Lord God of thy fathers hath | De 12:1
the nations *w.* ye shall possess | De 12:2
w. the Lord your God shall choose | De 12:5
w. the Lord your God giveth you | De 12:9; 12:10
w. the Lord your God shall choose | De 12:11
vows *w.* ye vowed unto the Lord | De 12:11
the place *w.* the Lord shall choose | De 12:14
Lord thy God *w.* he hath given thee | De 12:15
nor any of thy vows *w.* thou vowest | De 12:17
w. the Lord thy God shall choose | De 12:18
w. the Lord thy God hath chosen | De 12:21
flock, *w.* the Lord hath given thee | De 12:21
do that *w.* is right in the sight of the | De 12:25
Only thy holy things *w.* thou hast | De 12:26
the place *w.* the Lord shall choose | De 12:26
all these words *w.* I command thee | De 12:28
doest that *w.* is good and right in | De 12:28
abomination *w.* he hateth | De 12:31
other gods, *w.* thou hast not known | De 13:2
w. brought you out of the land of | De 13:5
of the way *w.* the Lord thy God | De 13:5
friend, *w.* is as thine own soul | De 13:6
other gods, *w.* thou hast not known | De 13:6
the people *w.* are round about you | De 13:7
w. brought thee out of the land of | De 13:10
w. the Lord thy God hath given | De 13:12
other gods, *w.* ye have not known | De 13:13
commandments *w.* I command thee | De 13:18
do that *w.* is right in the eyes of the | De 13:18
are the beasts *w.* ye shall eat | De 14:4
these are they of *w.* ye shall not eat | De 14:12
in the place *w.* he shall choose to | De 14:23
w. the Lord thy God shall choose | De 14:24
w. the Lord thy God shall choose | De 14:25
the widow, *w.* are within thy gates | De 14:29
work of thine hand *w.* thou doest | De 14:29

that *w.* is thine with thy brother   *De 15:3*

land *w.* the Lord thy God giveth   *De 15:4*

w. I command thee this day   *De 15:5*

land *w.* the Lord thy God giveth   *De 15:7*

for his need, in that *w.* he wanteth   *De 15:8*

the place *w.* the Lord shall choose   *De 15:20; 16:22*

w. thou sacrificedst the first day at   *De 16:4*

w. the Lord thy God giveth thee   *De 16:5*

w. the Lord thy God shall choose   *De 16:6*

place *w.* the Lord thy God shall   *De 16:7*

w. thou shalt give unto the Lord   *De 16:10*

w. the Lord thy God hath chosen   *De 16:11*

the place *w.* the Lord shall choose   *De 16:15*

God in the place *w.* he shall choose   *De 16:16*

Lord thy God *w.* he hath given thee   *De 16:17*

w. the Lord thy God giveth thee   *De 16:18*

That *w.* is altogether just shalt thou   *De 16:20*

land *w.* the Lord thy God giveth   *De 16:20*

thy God, *w.* thou shalt make thee   *De 16:21*

image; *w.* the Lord thy God hateth   *De 16:22*

w. the Lord thy God giveth thee   *De 17:2*

heaven, *w.* I have not commanded   *De 17:3*

w. have committed that wicked   *De 17:5*

w. the Lord thy God shall choose   *De 17:8*

sentence, *w.* they of that place   *De 17:10*

place *w.* the Lord shall choose   *De 17:10*

of the law *w.* they shall teach thee   *De 17:11*

judgment *w.* they shall tell thee   *De 17:11*

sentence *w.* they shall shew thee   *De 17:11*

land *w.* the Lord thy God giveth thee   *De 17:14*

over thee, *w.* is not thy brother   *De 17:15*

out of that *w.* is before the priests   *De 17:18*

the place *w.* the Lord shall choose   *De 18:6*

do, *w.* stand there before the Lord   *De 18:7*

that *w.* cometh of the sale of his   *De 18:8*

land *w.* the Lord thy God giveth   *De 18:9*

these nations, *w.* thou shalt possess   *De 18:14*

spoken that *w.* they have spoken   *De 18:17*

my words *w.* he shall speak in my   *De 18:19*

w. shall presume to speak a word in   *De 18:20*

w. I have not commanded him to   *De 18:20*

word *w.* the Lord hath not spoken   *De 18:21*

thing *w.* the Lord hath not spoken   *De 18:22*

w. the Lord thy God giveth thee   *De 19:2; 19:3*

the slayer, *w.* shall flee thither   *De 19:4*

land *w.* he promised to give unto   *De 19:8*

them, *w.* I command thee this day   *De 19:9*

land, *w.* the Lord thy God giveth thee   *De 19:10*

w. they of old time have set in thine   *De 19:14*

w. thou shalt inherit in the land   *De 19:14*

testify against him that *w.* is wrong   *De 19:16*

judges, *w.* shall be in those days   *De 19:17*

And those *w.* remain shall hear   *De 19:20*

w. brought thee up out of the land   *De 20:1*

w. the Lord thy God hath given   *De 20:14*

all the cities *w.* are very far off from   *De 20:15*

w. are not of the cities of these   *De 20:15*

w. the Lord thy God doth give thee   *De 20:16*

w. they have done unto their gods   *De 20:18*

Only the trees *w.* thou knowest that   *De 20:20*

land *w.* the Lord thy God giveth   *De 21:1*

cities *w.* are round about him that   *De 21:2*

the city *w.* is next unto the slain man   *De 21:3*

w. had not been wrought with   *De 21:3*

and *w.* hath not drawn in the yoke   *De 21:3*

valley, *w.* is neither eared nor sown   *De 21:4*

do that *w.* is right in the sight of the   *De 21:9*

his sons to inherit that *w.* he hath   *De 21:16*

the hated, *w.* is indeed the firstborn   *De 21:16*

w. will not obey the voice of his father   *De 21:18*

w. the Lord thy God giveth thee   *De 21:23*

of thy brother's, *w.* he hath lost   *De 22:3*

wear that *w.* pertaineth unto a man   *De 22:5*

fruit of thy seed *w.* thou hast sown   *De 22:9*

is a virgin, *w.* is not betrothed   *De 22:28*

and cover that *w.* cometh from thee   *De 23:13*

the servant *w.* is escaped from his   *De 23:15*

in that place *w.* he shall choose   *De 23:16*

That *w.* is gone out of thy lips thou   *De 23:23*

w. thou hast promised with thy   *De 23:23*

die, *w.* took her to be his wife   *De 24:3*

former husband, *w.* sent her away   *De 24:4*

w. the Lord thy God giveth thee for   *De 24:4*

cheer up his wife *w.* he hath taken   *De 24:5*

the firstborn *w.* she beareth shall   *De 25:6*

in the name of his brother *w.* is dead   *De 25:6*

land *w.* the Lord thy God giveth   *De 25:15; 25:19*

the land *w.* the Lord giveth thee for   *De 26:1*

w. thou shalt bring of thy land   *De 26:2*

place *w.* the Lord God shall choose   *De 26:2*

w. the Lord sware unto our father   *De 26:3*

w. thou, O Lord, hast given me   *De 26:10*

good thing *w.* the Lord hath given   *De 26:11*

third year, *w.* is the year of tithing   *De 26:12*

w. thou hast commanded me   *De 26:13*

and the land *w.* thou hast given us   *De 26:15*

above all nations *w.* he hath made   *De 26:19*

commandments *w.* I command you   *De 27:1*

w. the Lord thy God giveth thee   *De 27:2; 27:3*

stones, *w.* I command you this day   *De 27:4*

statutes, *w.* I command thee this day   *De 27:10*

commandments *w.* I command you   *De 28:1*

land *w.* the Lord thy God giveth   *De 28:8*

w. the Lord sware unto thy fathers   *De 28:11*

thy God, *w.* I command thee this day   *De 28:13*

words *w.* I command thee this day   *De 28:14*

statutes *w.* I command thee this day   *De 28:15*

nation *w.* thou knowest not eat up   *De 28:33*

sight of thine eyes, *w.* thou shalt see   *De 28:34*

thy king *w.* thou shalt set over thee   *De 28:36*

nation *w.* neither thou nor thy father   *De 28:36*

his statutes *w.* he commanded thee   *De 28:45*

w. the Lord shall send against thee   *De 28:48*

w. shall not regard the person, of   *De 28:50*

w. also shall not leave thee either   *De 28:51*

w. the Lord thy God hath given   *De 28:52; 28:53*

of his children *w.* he shall leave   *De 28:54*

w. would not adventure to set the   *De 28:56*

her children *w.* she shall hear   *De 28:57*

of Egypt, *w.* thou wast afraid of   *De 28:60*

w. is not written in the book of this   *De 28:61*

w. neither thou nor thy fathers   *De 28:64*

sight of thine eyes *w.* thou shall see   *De 28:67*

w. the Lord commanded Moses to   *De 29:1*

w. thine eyes have seen, the signs   *De 29:3*

w. the Lord thy God maketh with   *De 29:12*

through nations *w.* ye passed by   *De 29:16*

and gold, *w.* were among them   *De 29:17*

w. the Lord hath laid upon it   *De 29:22*

w. the Lord overthrew in his anger   *De 29:23*

w. he made with them when he   *De 29:25*

those things *w.* are revealed belong   *De 29:29*

the curse, *w.* I have set before thee   *De 30:1*

the land *w.* thy fathers possessed   *De 30:5*

that hate thee, *w.* persecuted thee   *De 30:7*

commandments *w.* I commanded   *De 30:8*

statutes *w.* are written in this book   *De 30:10*

commandment *w.* I command thee   *De 30:11*

w. the Lord sware unto thy fathers   *De 30:20*

w. I have commanded you   *De 31:5*

land *w.* the Lord hath sworn unto   *De 31:7*

w. bare the ark of the covenant of   *De 31:9*

God in the place *w.* he shall choose   *De 31:11*

children *w.* have not known any   *De 31:13*

evils *w.* they shall have wrought   *De 31:18*

land *w.* I sware unto their fathers   *De 31:20*

their imagination *w.* they go about   *De 31:21*

them into the land *w.* I sware   *De 31:21*

into the land *w.* I sware unto them   *De 31:23*

w. bare the ark of the covenant of   *De 31:25*

from the way *w.* I have commanded   *De 31:29*

then he forsook God *w.* made him   *De 32:15*

jealously with that *w.* is not God   *De 32:21*

with those *w.* are not a people   *De 32:21*

W. did eat the fat of their   *De 32:38*

all the words *w.* I testify among you	*De 32:46*	of Israel *w.* took it on the second day	*Jos 10:32*	of the Lord, *w.* our fathers made	*Jos 22:28*
w. ye shall command your children	*De 32:46*	*w.* the children of Israel smote	*Jos 12:1*	of Israel *w.* were with him, heard	*Jos 22:30*
Nebo, *w.* is in the land of Moab	*De 32:49*	*w.* is upon the bank of the river	*Jos 12:2*	*w.* the Lord your God hath given	*Jos 23:13*
Canaan, *w.* I give unto the children	*De 32:49*	*w.* is the border of the children of	*Jos 12:2*	things *w.* the Lord your God spake	*Jos 23:14*
land *w.* I give the children of Israel	*De 32:52*	*w.* was of the remnant of the giants	*Jos 12:4*	*w.* the Lord your God promised you	*Jos 23:15*
the land *w.* I sware unto Abraham	*De 34:4*	*w.* Joshua and the children of	*Jos 12:7*	*w.* the Lord your God hath given	*Jos 23:15*
the wonders, *w.* the Lord sent him	*De 34:11*	*w.* Joshua gave unto the tribes of	*Jos 12:7*	your God, *w.* he commanded you	*Jos 23:16*
the great terror *w.* Moses shewed	*De 34:12*	the king of Ai, *w.* is beside Beth-el	*Jos 12:9*	good land *w.* he hath given unto you	*Jos 23:16*
unto the land *w.* I do give to them	*Jos 1:2*	From Sihor, *w.* is before Egypt	*Jos 13:3*	according to that *w.* I did among	*Jos 24:5*
w. I sware unto their fathers to give	*Jos 1:6*	*w.* is counted to the Canaanite	*Jos 13:3*	*w.* dwelt on the other side Jordan	*Jos 24:8*
w. Moses my servant commanded	*Jos 1:7*	inheritance, *w.* Moses gave them	*Jos 13:8*	*w.* drave them out from before you	*Jos 24:12*
w. the Lord your God giveth you to	*Jos 1:11*	Amorites, *w.* reigned in Heshbon	*Jos 13:10*	you a land for *w.* ye did not labour	*Jos 24:13*
word *w.* Moses the servant of	*Jos 1:13*	*w.* reigned in Ashtaroth and Amorites, *w.* reigned in	*Jos 13:12* *Jos 13:21*	cities *w.* ye built not, and ye dwell	*Jos 24:13*
in the land *w.* Moses gave you on this	*Jos 1:14*	Heshbon and Reba, *w.* were dukes of Sihon	*Jos 13:21*	olive yards *w.* ye planted not do ye	*Jos 24:13*
w. the Lord your God giveth them	*Jos 1:15*	towns of Jair, *w.* are in Bashan	*Jos 13:30*	the gods *w.* your fathers served	*Jos 24:14;* *24:15*
w. Moses the Lord's servant gave	*Jos 1:15*	countries *w.* Moses did distribute	*Jos 13:32*	*w.* did those great signs in our sight	*Jos 24:17*
w. we are entered into thine house	*Jos 2:3*	*w.* the children of Israel inherited	*Jos 14:1*	the Amorites *w.* dwelt in the land	*Jos 24:18*
w. she had laid in order upon	*Jos 2:6*	*w.* Eleazar the priest, and Joshua	*Jos 14:1*	strange gods *w.* are among you	*Jos 24:23*
they *w.* pursued after them	*Jos 2:7*	*w.* Arba was a great man among the	*Jos 14:15*	words of the Lord *w.* he spake unto	*Jos 24:27*
oath *w.* thou hast made us swear	*Jos 2:17*	*w.* is on the south side of the river	*Jos 15:7*	*w.* is in mount Ephraim, on the north	*Jos 24:30*
window *w.* thou didst let us down by	*Jos 2:18*	*w.* is at the end of the valley of the	*Jos 15:8*	*w.* had known all the works of	*Jos 24:31*
oath *w.* thou hast made us to swear	*Jos 2:20*	to Baalah, *w.* is Kirjath-jearim	*Jos 15:9*	*w.* the children of Israel brought up	*Jos 24:32*
know the way by *w.* ye must go	*Jos 3:4*	of mount Jearim, *w.* is Chesalon	*Jos 15:10*	parcel of ground *w.* Jacob bought	*Jos 24:32*
the waters *w.* came down from above	*Jos 3:16*	father of Anak, *w.* city is Hebron	*Jos 15:13*	his son, *w.* was given him in mount	*Jos 24:33*
priests *w.* bare the ark of the covenant	*Jos 4:9*	Kerioth, and Hezron, *w.* is Hazor	*Jos 15:25*	Judah, *w.* lieth in the south of Arad	*J'g 1:16*
priests *w.* bare the ark stood in the	*Jos 4:10*	and Kirjath-sannah, *w.* is Debir	*Jos 15:49*	*w.* is the name thereof unto this	*J'g 1:26*
stones *w.* they took out of Jordan	*Jos 4:20*	and Kirjath-arba, *w.* is Hebron	*Jos 15:54*	land *w.* I sware unto your fathers	*J'g 2:1*
sea, *w.* he dried up from before us	*Jos 4:23*	Kirjath-baal, *w.* is Kirjath-jearim	*Jos 15:60*	after them, *w.* knew not the Lord	*J'g 2:10*
w. were on the side of Jordan	*Jos 5:1*	*w.* were on the other side Jordan	*Jos 17:5*	nor yet the works *w.* he had done	*J'g 2:10*
the Canaanites, *w.* were by the sea	*Jos 5:1*	tribes, *w.* had not yet received their	*Jos 18:2*	*w.* brought them out of the land of	*J'g 2:12*
men of war, *w.* came out of Egypt	*Jos 5:6*	*w.* the Lord God of your fathers	*Jos 18:3*	*w.* delivered them out of the hand of	*J'g 2:16*
land, *w.* the Lord sware unto their	*Jos 5:6*	*w.* Moses the servant of the Lord	*Jos 18:7*	the way *w.* their fathers walked in	*J'g 2:17*
w. Joshua sent to spy out Jericho	*Jos 6:25*	to the side of Luz, *w.* is Beth-el	*Jos 18:13*	my covenant *w.* I commanded their	*J'g 2:20*
Jericho to Ai, *w.* is beside Beth-aven	*Jos 7:2*	Kirjath-baal, *w.* is Kirjath-jearim	*Jos 18:14*	nations *w.* Joshua left when he died	*J'g 2:21*
my covenant *w.* I commanded them	*Jos 7:11*	and *w.* is in the valley of the giants	*Jos 18:16*	are the nations *w.* the Lord left	*J'g 3:1*
tribe *w.* the Lord taketh shall come	*Jos 7:14*	*w.* is over against the going up of	*Jos 18:17*	*w.* he commanded their fathers by	*J'g 3:4*
the family *w.* the Lord shall take	*Jos 7:14*	and Jebusi, *w.* is Jerusalem	*Jos 18:28*	made him a dagger *w.* had two edges	*J'g 3:16*
household *w.* the Lord shall take	*Jos 7:14*	they gave him the city *w.* he asked	*Jos 19:50*	*w.* he had made for himself alone	*J'g 3:20*
Lord *w.* he commanded Joshua	*Jos 8:27*	*w.* Eleazar the priest, and Joshua	*Jos 19:51*	*w.* slew of the Philistines six hundred	*J'g 3:31*
over *w.* no man hath lifted up any	*Jos 8:31*	and Kirjath-arba, *w.* is Hebron	*Jos 20:7*	was Sisera, *w.* dwelt in Harosheth	*J'g 4:2*
w. he wrote in the presence of	*Jos 8:32*	the priest, *w.* were of the Levites	*Jos 21:4*	*w.* was of the children of Hobab the	*J'g 4:11*
w. bare the ark of the covenant of	*Jos 8:33*	these cities *w.* are mentioned by	*Jos 21:9*	plain of Zaanaim, *w.* is by Kedesh	*J'g 4:11*
w. Joshua read not before all Jordan	*Jos 8:35*	*W.* the children of Aaron, being	*Jos 21:10*	in *w.* the Lord hath delivered Sisera	*J'g 4:14*
kings *w.* were on this side Jordan	*Jos 9:1*	father of Anak, *w.* city is Hebron	*Jos 21:11*	the dens *w.* are in the mountains	*J'g 6:2*
king of Bashan, *w.* was at Ashtaroth	*Jos 9:10*	Levites *w.* remained of the children	*Jos 21:20*	children of Israel, *w.* said unto them	*J'g 6:8*
And these bottles of wine *w.* we filled	*Jos 9:13*	*w.* were remaining of the families of	*Jos 21:40*	sat under an oak *w.* was in Ophrah	*J'g 6:11*
of the oath *w.* we sware unto them	*Jos 9:20*	land *w.* he sware to give unto their	*Jos 21:43*	miracles *w.* our fathers told us	*J'g 6:13*
in the place *w.* he should choose	*Jos 9:27*	good thing *w.* the Lord had spoken	*Jos 21:45*	the grove *w.* thou shalt cut down	*J'g 6:26*
more *w.* died with hailstones than	*Jos 10:11*	*w.* Moses the servant of the Lord	*Jos 22:4;* *22:5*	*w.* thing became a snare unto Gideon	*J'g 8:27*
the rest *w.* remained of them entered	*Jos 10:20*	Shiloh, *w.* is in the land of Canaan	*Jos 22:9*	goodness *w.* he had shewed unto	*J'g 8:35*
of the men of war *w.* went with him	*Jos 10:24*	from *w.* we are not cleansed until	*Jos 22:17*	*w.* are threescore and ten persons	*J'g 9:2*
mouth, *w.* remain until this very day	*Jos 10:27*				

and light persons, w. followed *J'g 9:4*
him

my wine, w. cheereth God and *J'g 9:13*
man

their brother, w. slew them *J'g 9:24*

w. aided him in the killing of *J'g 9:24*
his

Abimelech w. he did unto his *J'g 9:56*
father

w. are called Havoth-jair unto *J'g 10:4*
this

day w. are in the land of *J'g 10:4*
Gilead

land of the Amorites, w. is in *J'g 10:8*
Gilead

unto the gods w. ye have *J'g 10:14*
chosen

possess that w. Chemosh thy *J'g 11:24*
god

words of Jephthah w. he sent *J'g 11:28*
him

w. hath proceeded out of thy *J'g 11:36*
mouth

to his vow w. he had vowed *J'g 11:39*

those Ephraimites w. were *J'g 12:5*
escaped

the man of God w. thou didst *J'g 13:8*
send

unto them w. expounded the *J'g 14:19*
riddle

w. is in Lehi unto this day *J'g 15:19*

green withs w. had not been *J'g 16:8*
dried

of our country, w. slew many *J'g 16:24*
of us

pillars upon w. the house *J'g 16:29*
stood

and on w. it was borne up, *J'g 16:29*
of the one

So the dead w. he slew at his *J'g 16:30*
death

than they w. he slew in his *J'g 16:30*
life

from thee; about w. thou *J'g 17:2*
cursedst

man did that w. was right in *J'g 17:6*
his own

way w. we go shall be *J'g 18:5*
prosperous

w. were of the children of *J'g 18:16*
Dan, stood

have taken away my gods w. *J'g 18:24*
I made

took the things w. Micah had *J'g 18:27*
made

and the priest w. he had, and *J'g 18:27*
came

Micah's graven image, w. he *J'g 18:31*
made

against Jebus, w. is *J'g 19:10*
Jerusalem

Gibeah, w. belongeth to *J'g 19:14*
Benjamin

even, w. was also of mount *J'g 19:16*
Ephraim

young man w. is with thy *J'g 19:19*
servants

the thing w. we will do to *J'g 20:9*
Gibeah

children of Belial, w. are in *J'g 20:13*
Gibeah

w. were numbered seven *J'g 20:15*
hundred

W. of us shall go up first to *J'g 20:18*
the

of w. one goeth up to the *J'g 20:31*
house of

wait w. they had set beside *J'g 20:36*
Gibeah

them w. came out of the *J'g 20:42*
cities they

all w. fell that day of *J'g 20:46*
Benjamin were

Shiloh, w. is in the land of *J'g 21:12*
Canaan

them wives w. they had saved *J'g 21:14*
alive

w. is on the north side of *J'g 21:19*
Beth-el

did that w. was right in his *J'g 21:25*
own eyes

her, w. returned out of the *Ru 1:22*
country of

that w. the young men have *Ru 2:9*
drawn

w. thou knewest not *Ru 2:11*
heretofore

w. was our brother Elimelech's *Ru 4:3*

w. two did build the house of *Ru 4:11*
Israel

the seed w. the Lord shall give *Ru 4:12*
thee

Lord, w. hath not left thee *Ru 4:14*
this day

daughter in law w. loveth thee *Ru 4:15*

w. is better to thee than seven *Ru 4:15*

me my petition w. I asked of *1Sa 1:27*
him

for the loan w. is lent to the *1Sa 2:20*
Lord

offering, w. I have *1Sa 2:29*
commanded in

wealth w. God shall give *1Sa 2:32*
Israel

to that w. is in mine heart *1Sa 2:35*
and in my

at w. both the ears of every *1Sa 3:11*
one that

Eli all things w. I have *1Sa 3:12*
spoken

for the iniquity w. he *1Sa 3:13*
knoweth

w. dwelleth between the *1Sa 4:4*
cherubims

offering w. we shall return to *1Sa 6:4*
him

kine, on w. there hath come *1Sa 6:7*
no yoke

w. ye return him for a trespass *1Sa 6:8*

golden emerods w. the *1Sa 6:17*
Philistines

w. stone remaineth unto this *1Sa 6:18*
day in

cities w. the Philistines had *1Sa 7:14*
taken

to all the works w. they have *1Sa 8:8*
done

king w. ye shall have chosen *1Sa 8:18*
you

bidden, w. were about thirty *1Sa 9:22*
persons

Bring the portion w. I gave *1Sa 9:23*
thee

of w. I said unto thee, Set it *1Sa 9:23*
by thee

shoulder, and that w. was *1Sa 9:24*
upon it

Behold that w. is left; set it *1Sa 9:24*
before

asses w. thou wentest to seek *1Sa 10:2*

w. thou shalt receive of their *1Sa 10:4*
hands

that they w. remained were *1Sa 11:11*
scattered

w. he did to you and to your *1Sa 12:7*
fathers

w. brought forth your fathers *1Sa 12:8*
out of

w. the Lord will do before *1Sa 12:16*
your

w. ye have done in the sight *1Sa 12:17*
of the

things, w. cannot profit nor *1Sa 12:21*
deliver

as the sand w. is on the sea *1Sa 13:5*
shore in

thy God, w. he commanded *1Sa 13:13*
thee

that w. the Lord commanded *1Sa 13:14*
thee

pomegranate tree w. is in *1Sa 14:2*
Migron

w. Jonathan sought to go *1Sa 14:4*
over unto

w. Jonathan and his *1Sa 14:14*
armourbearer

land, w. a yoke of oxen *1Sa 14:14*
might plow

w. went up with them into *1Sa 14:21*

men of Israel w. had hid *1Sa 14:22*
themselves

of their enemies w. they *1Sa 14:30*
found

as the Lord liveth, w. saveth *1Sa 14:39*
Israel

I remember that w. Amalek *1Sa 15:2*
did to

the lowing of the oxen w. I *1Sa 15:14*
hear

gone the way w. the Lord *1Sa 15:20*
sent me

w. should have been utterly *1Sa 15:21*
destroyed

Samuel did not w. the Lord *1Sa 16:4*
spake

thy servants, w. are before *1Sa 16:16*
thee

thy son, w. is with the sheep *1Sa 16:19*

at Shochoh, w. belongeth to *1Sa 17:1*
Judah

words were heard w. David *1Sa 17:31*
spake

them in a shepherd's bag w. *1Sa 17:40*
he had

matter w. thou and I have *1Sa 20:23*
spoken

w. was the second day of *1Sa 20:27*
the month

out now the arrows w. I *1Sa 20:36*
shoot

of the arrow w. Jonathan *1Sa 20:37*
had shot

w. was set over the servants *1Sa 22:9*

as David, w. is the king's *1Sa 22:14*
son in law

his men, w. were about six *1Sa 23:13*
hundred

w. is on the south of *1Sa 23:19*
Jeshimon

the day of w. the Lord said *1Sa 24:4*
unto thee

now thy shepherds w. were *1Sa 25:7*
with us

this blessing w. thine *1Sa 25:27*
handmaid

w. sent thee this day to meet *1Sa 25:32*
me

be thou, w. hast kept me this *1Sa 25:33*
day

w. hath kept me back from *1Sa 25:34*
hurting

hand that w. she had brought *1Sa 25:35*
him

the son of Laish, w. was of *1Sa 25:44*
Gallim

Hachilah, w. is before *1Sa 26:1;*
Jeshimon   *26:3*

words w. thou spakest unto *1Sa 28:21*
me

by a fountain w. is in Jezreel *1Sa 29:1*

w. hath been with me these *1Sa 29:3*
days

to his place w. thou hast *1Sa 29:4*
appointed

w. were so faint that they *1Sa 30:10*
could not

the coast w. belongeth to *1Sa 30:14*
Judah

men, w. rode upon camels, *1Sa 30:17*
and fled

w. they drave before those *1Sa 30:20*
other

w. were so faint that they *1Sa 30:21*
could

that w. the Lord hath given *1Sa 30:23*
us

To them w. were in Beth-el, *1Sa 30:27*
and to

to them w. were in south *1Sa 30:27*
Ramoth

and to them w. were in *1Sa 30:27*
Jattir

and to them w. were in *1Sa 30:28*
Aroer

and to them w. were in *1Sa 30:28*
Siphmoth

and to them w. were in *1Sa 30:28*
Eshtemoa

to them w. were in Rachal, *1Sa 30:29*
and to

them w. were in the cities of *1Sa 30:29*

to them w. were in Hormah, *1Sa 30:30*
and to

and to them w. were in *1Sa 30:30*
Chor-ashan

and to them w. were in *1Sa 30:30*
Athach

to them w. were in Hebron, *1Sa 30:31*
and to

w. the Philistines had done *1Sa 31:11*
to Saul

w. pertained to Ish-bosheth *2Sa 2:15*
the son

Helkath-hazzurim, w. is in *2Sa 2:16*
Gibeon

of his father, w. is in *2Sa 2:32*
Beth-lehem

w. against Judah do shew *2Sa 3:8*
kindness

wife Michal, w. I espoused to *2Sa 3:14*
me

w. brought him again from *2Sa 3:26*
the well

thine enemy, w. sought thy life *2Sa 4:8*

w. spake unto David, saying, *2Sa 5:6*
Except

of Abinadab w. was at *2Sa 6:4*
Gibeah

Lord, w. chose me before thy *2Sa 6:21*
father

maidservants w. thou hast spoken 2Sa 6:22

w. shall proceed out of thy bowels 2Sa 7:12

w. thou redeemest to thee from 2Sa 7:23

W. also king David did dedicate 2Sa 8:11

of all nations w. he subdued 2Sa 8:11

hath yet a son, w. is lame on his feet 2Sa 9:3

Lord do that w. seemeth him good 2Sa 10:12

w. he had bought and nourished 2Sa 12:3

took the cakes w. she had made 2Sa 13:10

Baal-hazor, w. is beside Ephraim 2Sa 13:23

they shall quench my coal w. is left 2Sa 14:7

speak this thing as one w. is faulty 2Sa 14:13

w. cannot be gathered up again 2Sa 14:14

every man w. hath any suit or cause 2Sa 15:4

w. I have vowed unto the Lord, in 2Sa 15:7

left ten women, w. were concubines 2Sa 15:16

six hundred men w. came after 2Sa 15:18

my son w. came forth of my bowels 2Sa 16:11

w. he had left to keep the house 2Sa 16:21

w. he counselled in those days 2Sa 16:23

they w. be with him are valiant 2Sa 17:10

Bahurim, w. had a well in his court 2Sa 17:18

w. Amasa was a man's son, whose 2Sa 17:25

a pillar, w. is in the king's dale 2Sa 18:18

w. hath delivered up the men that 2Sa 18:28

w. this day have saved thy life 2Sa 19:5

a Benjamite, w. was of Bahurim 2Sa 19:16

remember that w. thy servant did 2Sa 19:19

that w. shall seem good unto thee 2Sa 19:38

set time w. he had appointed him 2Sa 20:5

the great stone w. is in Gibeon 2Sa 20:8

w. had stolen them from the street 2Sa 21:12

w. was of the sons of the giant 2Sa 21:16; 21:18

a people w. I knew not shall serve me 2Sa 22:44

of Bethlehem, w. is by the gate 2Sa 23:15

of the host, w. was with him 2Sa 24:2

God of that w. doth cost me nothing 2Sa 24:24

mighty men w. belonged to David 1Ki 1:8

of Zoheleth, w. is by En-rogel 1Ki 1:9

w. hath given one to sit on my 1Ki 1:48

word w. he spake concerning me 1Ki 2:4

w. cursed me with a grievous 1Ki 2:8

liveth, w. hath established me 1Ki 2:24

w. he spake concerning the house of 1Ki 2:27

the innocent blood, w. Joab shed 1Ki 2:31

wickedness w. thine heart is privy to 1Ki 2:44

w. went out, and fell upon him, that 1Ki 2:46

thy people w. thou hast chosen 1Ki 3:8

thee that w. thou hast not asked 1Ki 3:13

it was not my son, w. I did bear 1Ki 3:21

judgment w. the king had judged 1Ki 3:28

These were the princes w. he had 1Ki 4:2

w. provided victuals for the king 1Ki 4:7

w. had Taphath the daughter 1Ki 4:11

w. is by Zartanah beneath Jezreel 1Ki 4:12

son of Manasseh, w. are in Gilead 1Ki 4:13

region of Argob, w. is in Bashan 1Ki 4:13

the only officer w. was in the land 1Ki 4:19

sand w. is by the sea in multitude 1Ki 4:20

earth, w. had heard of his wisdom 1Ki 4:34

for the wars w. were about him 1Ki 5:3

w. hath given unto David a wise son 1Ki 5:7

thing w. thou sentest to me for 1Ki 5:8

Solomon's officers w. were over the 1Ki 5:16

w. ruled over the people that wrought 1Ki 5:16

month Zif, w. is the second month 1Ki 6:1

house w. king Solomon built 1Ki 6:2

this house w. thou art building 1Ki 6:12

w. I spake unto David thy father 1Ki 6:12

covered the altar w. was of cedar 1Ki 6:20

Bul, w. is the eighth month 1Ki 6:38

the porch, w. was of the like work 1Ki 7:8

chapters w. were upon the top of 1Ki 7:17

the belly w. was by the network 1Ki 7:20

chapters w. were upon the tops of 1Ki 7:41

w. Hiram made to king Solomon 1Ki 7:45

the things w. David his father 1Ki 7:51

out of the city of David, w. is Zion 1Ki 8:1

w. is the seventh month 1Ki 8:2

w. Moses put there at Horeb 1Ki 8:9

w. spake with his mouth unto Lord, w. he made with our fathers 1Ki 8:15 / 1Ki 8:21

w. thou spakest unto thy servant 1Ki 8:26

w. thy servant prayeth before thee 1Ki 8:28

the place of w. thou hast said prayer w. thy servant shall make 1Ki 8:29 / 1Ki 8:29

w. thou gavest unto their fathers 1Ki 8:34

w. thou hast given unto thy people 1Ki 8:36

w. shall know every man the plague 1Ki 8:38

land w. thou gavest unto our fathers 1Ki 8:40

house w. I have builded, is called by 1Ki 8:43

toward the city w. thou hast chosen 1Ki 8:44

enemies, w. led them away captive 1Ki 8:48

w. thou gavest unto their fathers 1Ki 8:48

the city w. thou hast chosen 1Ki 8:48

house w. I have built for thy name 1Ki 8:48

w. thou broughtest forth out 1Ki 8:51

w. he promised by the hand of Moses 1Ki 8:56

w. he commanded our fathers 1Ki 8:58

w. he offered unto the Lord, two 1Ki 8:63

desire w. he was pleased to do this house w. thou hast built statutes w. I have set before you 1Ki 9:1 / 1Ki 9:3 / 1Ki 9:6

of the land w. I have given them 1Ki 9:7

w. I have hallowed for my name 1Ki 9:7

And at this house w. is high cities w. Solomon had given him 1Ki 9:8 / 1Ki 9:12

are these w. thou hast given me 1Ki 9:13

the levy w. king Solomon raised 1Ki 9:15

w. Solomon desired to build in 1Ki 9:19

w. were not of the children of Israel 1Ki 9:20

w. bare rule over the people that 1Ki 9:23

unto her house w. Solomon had 1Ki 9:24

the altar w. he built unto the Lord 1Ki 9:25

Ezion-geber, w. is beside Eloth 1Ki 9:26

from the king w. he told her not 1Ki 10:3

by w. he went up into the house of 1Ki 10:5

exceedeth the fame w. I heard 1Ki 10:7

w. stand continually before thee 1Ki 10:8

w. delighted in thee, to set thee on 1Ki 10:9

w. the queen of Sheba gave to king 1Ki 10:10

w. Solomon gave her of his royal 1Ki 10:13

wisdom, w. God had put in his heart 1Ki 10:24

nations concerning w. the Lord said 1Ki 11:2

w. burnt incense and sacrificed unto 1Ki 11:8

w. had appeared unto him twice 1Ki 11:9

not that w. the Lord commanded 1Ki 11:10

w. I have commanded thee Jerusalem's sake w. I have chosen 1Ki 11:11 / 1Ki 11:13

w. gave him an house, and appointed 1Ki 11:18

w. fled from his lord Hadadezer 1Ki 11:23

the city w. I have chosen out of all 1Ki 11:32

to do that w. is right in mine eyes 1Ki 11:33

city w. I have chosen me to put my 1Ki 11:37

his heavy yoke w. he put upon us 1Ki 12:4

the old men, w. they had given him 1Ki 12:8

with him, and w. stood before him 1Ki 12:8

yoke w. thy father did put upon us 1Ki 12:9

w. the Lord spake by Ahijah Israel w. dwelt in the cities of Judah 1Ki 12:15 / 1Ki 12:17

chosen men, w. were warriors 1Ki 12:21

w. brought thee up out of the land 1Ki 12:28

w. were not of the sons of Levi 1Ki 12:31

the high places w. he had made 1Ki 12:32

upon the altar w. he had made month w. he had devised of his own 1Ki 12:33 / 1Ki 12:33

the sign w. the Lord hath spoken 1Ki 13:3

w. had cried against the altar hand, w. he put forth against him 1Ki 13:4 / 1Ki 13:4

sign w. the man of God had given 1Ki 13:5

the words w. he had spoken unto 1Ki 13:11

God went, w. came from Judah 1Ki 13:12

w. the Lord thy God commanded 1Ki 13:21

w. the Lord did say to thee, Eat no 1Ki 13:22

the lion, w. hath torn him, and slain 1Ki 13:26

of the Lord, w. he spake unto him 1Ki 13:26

For the saying w. he cried by the 1Ki 13:32

high places w. are in the cities of 1Ki 13:32

w. told me that I should be king 1Ki 14:2

that only w. was right in mine eyes 1Ki 14:8

land, w. he gave to their fathers 1Ki 14:15

w. he spake by the hand of his 1Ki 14:18

the days w. Jeroboam reigned were 1Ki 14:20

the city w. the Lord did choose out   *1Ki 14:21*

their sins w. they had committed   *1Ki 14:22*

nations w. the Lord cast out before   *1Ki 14:24*

shields of gold w. Solomon had made   *1Ki 14:26*

w. kept the door of the king's house   *1Ki 14:27*

father, w. he had done before him   *1Ki 15:3*

w. was right in the eyes of the Lord   *1Ki 15:5*

Asa did that w. was right in the eyes   *1Ki 15:11*

the things w. his father had dedicated   *1Ki 15:15*

the things w. himself had dedicated   *1Ki 15:15*

hosts w. he had against the cities   *1Ki 15:20*

did, and the cities w. he had built   *1Ki 15:23*

w. belonged to the Philistines   *1Ki 15:27*

w. he spake by his servant Ahijah   *1Ki 15:29*

sins of Jeroboam w. he sinned   *1Ki 15:30*

and w. he made Israel sin   *1Ki 15:30*

w. he spake against Baasha   *1Ki 16:12*

of Elah his son, by w. they sinned   *1Ki 16:13*

and by w. they made Israel to sin   *1Ki 16:13*

w. belonged to the Philistines   *1Ki 16:15*

his sins w. he sinned in doing evil   *1Ki 16:19*

his sin, w. he did, to make Israel   *1Ki 16:19*

the name of the city w. he built   *1Ki 16:24*

rest of the acts of Omri w. he did   *1Ki 16:27*

Baal, w. he had built in Samaria   *1Ki 16:32*

w. he spake by Joshua the son of   *1Ki 16:34*

to Zarephath, w. belongeth to Zidon   *1Ki 17:9*

of the Lord, w. he spake by Elijah   *1Ki 17:16*

w. was the governor of his house   *1Ki 18:3*

four hundred, w. eat at Jezebel's table   *1Ki 18:19*

took the bullock w. was given them   *1Ki 18:26*

leaped upon the altar w. was made   *1Ki 18:26*

Beer-sheba, w. belongeth to Judah   *1Ki 19:3*

knees w. have not bowed unto Baal   *1Ki 19:18*

every mouth w. hath not kissed   *1Ki 19:18*

and the army w. followed them   *1Ki 20:19*

w. my father took from thy father   *1Ki 20:34*

had a vineyard, w. was in Jezreel   *1Ki 21:1*

w. Naboth the Jezreelite had spoken   *1Ki 21:4*

letters w. she had sent unto them   *1Ki 21:11*

w. he refused to give thee   *1Ki 21:15*

king of Israel, w. is in Samaria   *1Ki 21:18*

Ahab, w. did sell himself to work   *1Ki 21:25*

of them, and speak that w. is good   *1Ki 22:13*

but that w. is true in the name of the   *1Ki 22:16*

W. way went the spirit of the   *1Ki 22:24*

the word w. he spake   *1Ki 22:38*

and the ivory house w. he made   *1Ki 22:39*

w. was right in the eyes of the Lord   *1Ki 22:43*

w. remained in the days of his father   *1Ki 22:46*

that bed on w. thou art gone up   *2Ki 1:4; 1:6*

was he w. came up to meet you   *2Ki 1:7*

off that bed on w. thou art gone up   *2Ki 1:16*

of the Lord w. Elijah had spoken   *2Ki 1:17*

of the acts of Ahaziah w. he did   *2Ki 1:18*

of the prophets w. were to view at   *2Ki 2:15*

the saying of Elijah w. he spake   *2Ki 2:22*

son of Nebat, w. made Israel to sin   *2Ki 3:3*

he said, W. way shall we go   *2Ki 3:8*

w. poured water on the hands of   *2Ki 3:11*

and thou shalt set aside that w. is full   *2Ki 4:4*

of God w. passeth by us continually   *2Ki 4:9*

at his hands that w. he brought   *2Ki 5:20*

place w. the man of God told him   *2Ki 6:10*

w. of us is for the king of Israel   *2Ki 6:11*

that remain, w. are left in the city   *2Ki 7:13*

w. the Syrians had cast away   *2Ki 7:15*

Edomites w. compassed him about   *2Ki 8:21*

w. the Syrians had given him   *2Ki 8:29; 9:15*

And Jehu said, Unto w. of all us   *2Ki 9:5*

second on horseback w. came to them   *2Ki 9:19*

going up to Gur, w. is by Ibleam   *2Ki 9:27*

w. he spake by his servant Elijah   *2Ki 9:36*

do thou that w. is good in thine eyes   *2Ki 10:5*

men of the city, w. brought them up   *2Ki 10:6*

w. the Lord spake concerning the   *2Ki 10:10*

that w. he spake by his servant   *2Ki 10:10*

of the Lord, w. he spake to Elijah   *2Ki 10:17*

executing that w. is right in mine eyes   *2Ki 10:30*

of Jeroboam, w. made Israel to sin   *2Ki 10:31*

Aroer, w. is by the river Arnon   *2Ki 10:33*

among the king's sons w. were slain   *2Ki 11:2*

by the way by the w. the horses came   *2Ki 11:16*

w. was right in the sight of the Lord   *2Ki 12:2*

house of Millo, w. goeth down to Silla   *2Ki 12:20*

w. was evil in the sight of   *2Ki 13:2*

son of Nebat, w. made Israel to sin   *2Ki 13:2*

w. was evil in the sight of the Lord   *2Ki 13:11*

w. he had taken out of the hand of   *2Ki 13:25*

w. is right in the sight of the Lord   *2Ki 14:3*

unto that w. is written in the book   *2Ki 14:6*

Beth-shemesh, w. belongeth to   *2Ki 14:11*

of the acts of Jehoash w. he did   *2Ki 14:15*

Azariah, w. was sixteen years old   *2Ki 14:21*

w. was evil in the sight of the Lord   *2Ki 14:24*

w. he spake by the hand of his   *2Ki 14:25*

prophet, w. was of Gath-hepher   *2Ki 14:25*

and Hamath, w. belonged to Judah   *2Ki 14:28*

w. was right in the sight of the Lord   *2Ki 15:3*

w. was evil in the sight of the Lord   *2Ki 15:9*

the Lord w. he spake unto Jehu   *2Ki 15:12*

and his conspiracy w. he made   *2Ki 15:15*

that w. was evil in the sight of   *2Ki 15:18; 15:24, 28*

w. was right in the sight of the Lord   *2Ki 15:34; 16:2*

king of Israel, w. rise up against me   *2Ki 16:7*

altar, w. was before the   *2Ki 16:14*

rest of the acts of Ahaz w. he did   *2Ki 16:19*

w. was evil in the sight of the Lord   *2Ki 17:2*

w. had brought them up out of the   *2Ki 17:7*

kings of Israel, w. they had made   *2Ki 17:8*

law w. I commanded your fathers   *2Ki 17:13*

and w. I sent to you by my servants   *2Ki 17:13*

w. he testified against them   *2Ki 17:15*

statutes of Israel w. they made   *2Ki 17:19*

all the sins of Jeroboam w. he did   *2Ki 17:22*

among them, w. slew some of them   *2Ki 17:25*

The nations w. thou hast removed   *2Ki 17:26*

high places w. the Samaritans had   *2Ki 17:29*

w. sacrificed for them in the   *2Ki 17:32*

w. the Lord commanded the   *2Ki 17:34*

commandment, w. he wrote for you   *2Ki 17:37*

w. was right in the sight of the Lord   *2Ki 18:3*

w. the Lord commanded Moses   *2Ki 18:6*

w. was the seventh year of Hoshea   *2Ki 18:9*

w. thou puttest on me will I bear   *2Ki 18:14*

w. Hezekiah king of Judah had   *2Ki 18:16*

w. is in the highway of the fuller's   *2Ki 18:17*

Hilkiah, w. was over the household   *2Ki 18:18*

Egypt, on w. if a man lean, it will go   *2Ki 18:21*

sent me to the men w. sit on the wall   *2Ki 18:27*

Hilkiah, w. was over the household   *2Ki 18:37*

Eliakim, w. was over the household   *2Ki 19:2*

words w. the Lord thy God hath   *2Ki 19:4*

of the words w. thou hast heard   *2Ki 19:6*

with w. the servants of the king of   *2Ki 19:6*

them w. my fathers have destroyed   *2Ki 19:12*

of Eden w. were in Thelasar   *2Ki 19:12*

w. dwellest between the cherubims   *2Ki 19:15*

w. hath sent him to reproach the   *2Ki 19:16*

That w. thou hast prayed to me   *2Ki 19:20*

by the way by w. thou camest   *2Ki 19:28*

year that w. springeth of the same   *2Ki 19:29*

done that w. is good in thy sight   *2Ki 20:3*

by w. it had gone down in the dial of   *2Ki 20:11*

that w. thy fathers have laid up in   *2Ki 20:17*

w. thou shalt beget, shall they take   *2Ki 20:18*

of the Lord w. thou hast spoken   *2Ki 20:19*

w. was evil in the sight of the Lord   *2Ki 21:2*

high places w. Hezekiah his father   *2Ki 21:3*

of the Lord, of w. the Lord said   *2Ki 21:4*

house, of w. the Lord said to David   *2Ki 21:7*

w. I have chosen out of all tribes   *2Ki 21:7*

of the land w. I gave their fathers   *2Ki 21:8*

Amorites did, w. were	2Ki 21:11
before him	
done that w. was evil in my	2Ki 21:15
sight	
w. was evil in the sight of	2Ki 21:16;
the Lord	21:20
of the acts of Amon w. he	2Ki 21:25
did	
w. was right in the sight of	2Ki 22:2
the Lord	
sum the silver w. is brought	2Ki 22:4
into the	
w. the keepers of the door	2Ki 22:4
have	
work w. is in the house of the	2Ki 22:5
Lord	
all that w. is written	2Ki 22:13
concerning us	
book w. the king of Judah	2Ki 22:16
hath	
w. sent you to enquire of	2Ki 22:18
the Lord	
the words w. thou hast	2Ki 22:18
heard	
evil w. I will bring upon this	2Ki 22:20
place	
covenant w. was found in the	2Ki 23:2
house	
w. were on a man's left hand	2Ki 23:8
at the	
w. is in the valley of the	2Ki 23:10
children of	
w. was in the suburbs, and	2Ki 23:11
burned	
w. the kings of Judah had	2Ki 23:12
made	
the altars w. Manasseh had	2Ki 23:12
made	
w. were on the right hand of	2Ki 23:13
w. Solomon the king of Israel	2Ki 23:13
had	
high place w. Jeroboam the	2Ki 23:15
son of	
Lord w. the man of God	2Ki 23:16
proclaimed	
man of God, w. came from	2Ki 23:17
Judah	
w. the kings of Israel had	2Ki 23:19
made to	
w. were written in the book	2Ki 23:24
that	
city Jerusalem w. I have	2Ki 23:27
chosen	
the house of w. I said, My	2Ki 23:27
name shall	
did that w. was evil in	2Ki 23:32;
the sight of	23:37
w. he spake by his servants	2Ki 24:2
blood; w. the Lord would not	2Ki 24:4
pardon	
w. was evil in the sight of the	2Ki 24:9
Lord	
w. Solomon king of Israel	2Ki 24:13
had made	
w. was evil in the sight of	2Ki 24:19
the Lord	
walls, w. is by the king's	2Ki 25:4
garden	
w. is the nineteenth year of	2Ki 25:8
king	
w. Solomon had made for the	2Ki 25:16
house	
w. were found in the city,	2Ki 25:19
and the	
w. mustered the people of	2Ki 25:19
the land	
w. smote Midian in the field	1Ch 1:46
of Moab	
w. three were born unto him of	1Ch 2:3
unto him Ephrath, w. bare	1Ch 2:19
him Hur	
w. was the father of Ziph	1Ch 2:42
of the scribes w. dwelt at	1Ch 2:55
Jabez	
w. were born unto him in	1Ch 3:1
Hebron	
granted him that w. he	1Ch 4:10
requested	
w. was the father of Eshton	1Ch 4:11
daughter of Pharaoh, w.	1Ch 4:18
Mered	
w. were left of the family of	1Ch 6:61
that tribe	
w. are called by their names	1Ch 6:65
these w. were chosen to be	1Ch 9:22
porters in	
brethren, w. were in the	1Ch 9:25
villages	
w. he committed against the	1Ch 10:13
Lord	

word of the Lord w. he kept	1Ch 10:13
not	
went to Jerusalem, w. is	1Ch 11:4
Jebus	
of Zion, w. is the city of	1Ch 11:5
David	
w. were expressed by name	1Ch 12:31
w. were men that had	1Ch 12:32
understanding	
fifty thousand, w. could	1Ch 12:33
keep rank	
and Levites w. are in their	1Ch 13:2
cities	
Kirjath-jearim, w. belonged	1Ch 13:6
of his children w. had in	1Ch 14:4
Jerusalem	
place, w. he had prepared for	1Ch 15:3
the word w. he commanded	1Ch 16:15
to a	
of the covenant w. he made	1Ch 16:16
Lord, w. he commanded	1Ch 16:40
Israel	
after thee, w. shall be of thy	1Ch 17:11
sons	
Lord do that w. is good in	1Ch 19:13
his sight	
seven thousand men w.	1Ch 19:18
fought in	
at w. time Sibbechai the	1Ch 20:4
w. he spake in the name of	1Ch 21:19
king do that w. is good in	1Ch 21:23
his eyes	
take that w. is thine for the	1Ch 21:24
Lord	
w. Moses made in the	1Ch 21:29
wilderness	
w. the Lord charged Moses	1Ch 22:13
with	
Of w. twenty and four	1Ch 23:4
thousand	
with the instruments w. I	1Ch 23:5
made	
and for that w. is baked in	1Ch 23:29
the pan	
in the pan, and for that w.	1Ch 23:29
is fried	
w. prophesied according to	1Ch 25:2
the order	
w. were over the treasures of	1Ch 26:22
W. Shelomith and his	1Ch 26:26
brethren	
w. David the king, and	1Ch 26:26
the chief	
w. came in and went out	1Ch 27:1
month by	
substance w. was king	1Ch 27:31
David's	
w. I have given to the house	1Ch 29:3
of my	
joy thy people, w. are present	1Ch 29:17
here	
for the w. I have made	1Ch 29:19
provision	
w. Moses the servant of the	2Ch 1:3
Lord	
to the place w. David had	2Ch 1:4
prepared	
w. was at the tabernacle of	2Ch 1:6
w. he placed in the chariot	2Ch 1:14
cities	
And the house w. I build is	2Ch 2:5
great	
house w. I am about to build	2Ch 2:9
shall	
in writing, w. he sent to	2Ch 2:11
Solomon	
device w. shall be put to him	2Ch 2:14
wine, w. my lord hath	2Ch 2:15
spoken of	
w. he overlaid with fine gold	2Ch 3:5
of oxen, w. did compass it	2Ch 4:3
round	
chapiters w. were on the top	2Ch 4:12
of the	
w. were on the top of the	2Ch 4:12
pillars	
chapiters w. were upon the	2Ch 4:13
pillars	
of the city of David, w. is	2Ch 5:2
Zion	
feast w. was in the seventh	2Ch 5:3
month	
and oxen, w. could not be told	2Ch 5:6
nor	
two tables w. Moses put	2Ch 5:10
therein	
Also the Levites w. were the	2Ch 5:12
singers	
his hands fulfilled that w. he	2Ch 6:4
spake	

thy son w. shall come forth	2Ch 6:9
out of	
w. keepest covenant, and	2Ch 6:14
shewest	
Thou w. hast kept with thy	2Ch 6:15
servant	
father that w. thou hast	2Ch 6:15;
promised	6:16
w. thou hast spoken unto thy	2Ch 6:17
less this house w. I have built	2Ch 6:18
w. thy servant prayeth before	2Ch 6:19
thee	
the prayer w. thy servant	2Ch 6:20
prayeth	
w. they shall make toward	2Ch 6:21
this	
w. thou gavest to them and to	2Ch 6:25
their	
w. thou hast given unto thy	2Ch 6:27
people	
w. thou gavest unto our	2Ch 6:31
fathers	
w. is not of thy people Israel	2Ch 6:32
house w. I have built is	2Ch 6:33
called by thy	
this city w. thou hast chosen	2Ch 6:34
house w. I have built for thy	2Ch 6:34
name	
for there is no man w.	2Ch 6:36
sinneth not	
w. thou gavest unto their	2Ch 6:38
fathers	
toward the city w. thou hast	2Ch 6:38
chosen	
house w. I have built for thy	2Ch 6:38
name	
thy people w. have sinned	2Ch 6:39
against	
w. David the king had made	2Ch 7:6
brasen altar w. Solomon had	2Ch 7:7
made	
people, w. are called by my	2Ch 7:14
name	
w. I have set before you, and	2Ch 7:19
shall go	
of my land w. I have given	2Ch 7:20
them	
w. I have sanctified for my	2Ch 7:20
name	
And this house, w. is high,	2Ch 7:21
shall be	
w. brought them forth out of	2Ch 7:22
w. Huram had restored to	2Ch 8:2
Solomon	
store cities, w. he built in	2Ch 8:4
Hamath	
the Jebusites, w. were not of	2Ch 8:7
Israel	
w. he had built before the	2Ch 8:12
porch	
from Solomon w. he told her	2Ch 9:2
his ascent by w. he went up	2Ch 9:4
into the	
a true report w. I heard in	2Ch 9:5
mine	
w. stand continually before	2Ch 9:7
thee	
w. delighted in thee to set thee	2Ch 9:8
on	
w. brought gold from Ophir	2Ch 9:10
that w. she had brought unto	2Ch 9:12
w. chapmen and merchants	2Ch 9:14
brought	
gold, w. were fastened to the	2Ch 9:18
throne	
counsel w. the old men gave	2Ch 10:8
him	
w. have spoken to me, saying,	2Ch 10:9
Ease	
w. he spake by the hand of	2Ch 10:15
Ahijah	
men, w. were warriors, to	2Ch 11:1
fight	
w. are in Judah and in	2Ch 11:10
Benjamin	
and for the calves w. he had	2Ch 11:15
made	
W. bare him children;	2Ch 11:19
Jeush, and	
w. bare him Abijah, and	2Ch 11:20
Attai, and	
cities w. pertained to Judah	2Ch 12:4
the shields of gold w.	2Ch 12:9
Solomom had	
Instead of w. king	2Ch 12:10
Rehoboam made	
the city w. the Lord had	2Ch 12:13
chosen out	

w. is in mount Ephraim, and 2Ch 13:4
said
w. Jeroboam made you for 2Ch 13:8
gods
the priests, w. minister unto 2Ch 13:10
the Lord
w. was good and right in the 2Ch 14:2
eyes of
cities w. he had taken from 2Ch 15:8
mount
time, of the spoil w. they 2Ch 15:11
had brought
w. he had made for himself 2Ch 16:14
in the
in the bed w. was filled with 2Ch 16:14
sweet
w. Asa his father had taken 2Ch 17:2
W. way went the spirit of 2Ch 18:23
the
in Hazazon-tamar; w. is 2Ch 20:2
En-gedi
w. thou hast given us to 2Ch 20:11
inherit
Seir, w. were come against 2Ch 20:22
Judah
w. they stripped off for 2Ch 20:25
themselves
w. was right in the sight of 2Ch 20:32
the Lord
w. was evil in the eyes of the 2Ch 21:6
Lord
the Edomites w. compassed 2Ch 21:9
him in
house, w. were better than 2Ch 21:13
thyself
of the wounds w. were given 2Ch 22:6
him
w. were in the house of God 2Ch 23:9
that none w. was unclean in 2Ch 23:19
any thing
w. was right in the sight of 2Ch 24:2
the Lord
the priest, w. stood above 2Ch 24:20
the people
kindness w. Jehoiada his 2Ch 24:22
father
w. was right in the sight of 2Ch 25:2
the Lord
talents w. I have given to the 2Ch 25:9
army
of the army w. Amaziah 2Ch 25:13
sent back
w. said unto me, Why hast 2Ch 25:15
thou
w. could not deliver their 2Ch 25:15
own
Beth-shemesh, w. 2Ch 25:21
belongeth to Judah
w. was right in the sight of 2Ch 26:4
the Lord
burial w. belonged to the 2Ch 26:23
kings
w. was right in the sight of 2Ch 27:2;
the Lord 28:1
in one day, w. were all 2Ch 28:6
valiant men
w. ye have taken captive of 2Ch 28:11
your
the men w. were expressed 2Ch 28:15
by name
the gods of Damascus, w. 2Ch 28:23
smote him
w. was right in the sight of 2Ch 29:2
the Lord
w. was evil in the eyes of the 2Ch 29:6
Lord
w. king Ahaz in his reign did 2Ch 29:19
cast
w. the congregation brought 2Ch 29:32
w. trespassed against the 2Ch 30:7
Lord God
w. he hath sanctified for ever 2Ch 30:8
w. they received of 2Ch 30:16
hands of the
holy things w. were 2Ch 31:6
consecrated unto
and that w. is left is this 2Ch 31:10
great store
over w. Cononiah the Levite 2Ch 31:12
was ruler
w. were in the fields of the 2Ch 31:19
suburbs of
that w. was good and right 2Ch 31:20
and truth
fountains w. were without 2Ch 32:3
the city
w. were the work of the 2Ch 32:19
hands of man

w. cut off all the mighty 2Ch 32:21
men of valour
w. was evil in the sight of 2Ch 33:22
the Lord
w. Hezekiah his father had 2Ch 33:3
broken
idol w. he had made, in the 2Ch 33:7
house of
of w. God had said to David 2Ch 33:7
and to
w. I have chosen before all 2Ch 33:7
the tribes
land w. I have appointed for 2Ch 38:8
your
w. took Manasseh among the 2Ch 33:11
thorns
w. was evil in the sight of 2Ch 33:22
the Lord
w. Manasseh his father had 2Ch 33:22
made
w. was right in the sight of the 2Ch 34:2
Lord
w. the Levites that kept the 2Ch 34:9
door
houses w. the kings of 2Ch 34:11
Judah had
w. they have read before the 2Ch 34:24
king of
the words w. thou hast 2Ch 34:26
heard
covenant w. are written in 2Ch 34:31
this book
all Israel, w. were holy unto 2Ch 35:3
the Lord
the house w. Solomon the 2Ch 35:3
son of
w. was written in the law of 2Ch 35:26
the Lord
w. was evil in the sight of 2Ch 36:5
the Lord
and his abominations w. he 2Ch 36:8
did
w. was found in him, behold, 2Ch 36:8
they are
w. was evil in the sight of 2Ch 36:9;
the Lord 36:12
w. he had hallowed in 2Ch 36:14
Jerusalem
house in Jerusalem, w. is in 2Ch 36:23
Judah
house at Jerusalem, w. is in Ezr 1:2
Judah
go up to Jerusalem, w. is in Ezr 1:3
Judah
(he is the God,) w. is in Ezr 1:3
Jerusalem
of the Lord w. is in Jerusalem Ezr 1:5
w. Nebuchadnezzar had Ezr 1:7
brought
of those w. had been carried Ezr 2:1
away
W. came with Zerubbabel Ezr 2:2
were they w. went up from Ezr 2:59
Tel-melah
w. took a wife of the Ezr 2:61
daughters of
of the Lord w. is at Jerusalem Ezr 2:68
of Assur, w. brought us up Ezr 4:2
hither
that the Jews w. came up Ezr 4:12
from
time: for w. cause was this Ezr 4:15
city
The letter w. ye sent unto us Ezr 4:18
hath
w. have ruled over all Ezr 4:20
countries
house of God w. is at Ezr 4:24
Jerusalem
the house of God w. is at Ezr 5:2
Jerusalem
w. were on this side the river Ezr 5:6
w. is builded with great stones Ezr 5:8
w. a great king of Israel Ezr 5:11
builded and
w. Nebuchadnezzar took out Ezr 5:14
house of God w. is at Ezr 5:16
Jerusalem
house, w. is there at Babylon Ezr 5:17
w. Nebuchadnezzar took forth Ezr 6:5
out
unto the temple w. is at Ezr 6:5
Jerusalem
w. are beyond the river, be ye Ezr 6:6
far
And that w. they have need of Ezr 6:9
both
the priests w. are at Jerusalem Ezr 6:9
house of God w. is at Ezr 6:12
Jerusalem

that w. Darius the king had Ezr 6:13
sent
w. was in the sixth year of Ezr 6:15
service of God, w. is at Ezr 6:18
Jerusalem
w. were come again out of Ezr 6:21
captivity
w. the Lord God of Israel had Ezr 7:6
w. was in the seventh year of Ezr 7:8
w. are minded of Ezr 7:13
their own freewill
law of thy God w. is in thine Ezr 7:14
hand
w. the king and his Ezr 7:15
counsellors
of their God w. is in Ezr 7:16
Jerusalem
of your God w. is in Ezr 7:17
Jerusalem
w. thou shalt have occasion to Ezr 7:20
treasurers w. are beyond the Ezr 7:21
river
w. may judge all the people Ezr 7:25
w. hath put such a thing as Ezr 7:27
this in
of the Lord w. is in Jerusalem Ezr 7:27
w. the king, and his Ezr 8:25
counsellors, and
w. were come out of captivity, Ezr 8:35
offered
W. thou hast commanded by Ezr 9:11
thy
land unto w. ye go to possess Ezr 9:11
it, is
w. have filled it from one end Ezr 9:11
all them w. have taken Ezr 10:14
strange wives
w. were left of the captivity Ne 1:2
w. I pray before thee now, day Ne 1:6
w. we have sinned against thee Ne 1:6
w. thou commandedst thy Ne 1:7
servant
place w. appertained to the Ne 2:8
house
Jerusalem, w. were broken Ne 2:13
down
of my God w. was good upon Ne 2:18
me
tower w. lieth out from the Ne 3:25
king's
of the rubbish w. are burned Ne 4:2
Even that w. they build, if a Ne 4:3
fox
when the Jews w. dwelt by Ne 4:12
them came
the Lord, w. is great and Ne 4:14
terrible
They w. builded on the wall, Ne 4:17
and they
men of the guard w. followed Ne 4:23
me
Jews, w. were sold unto the Ne 5:8
heathen
Now that w. was prepared for Ne 5:18
me
w. cause thou buildest the wall Ne 6:6
of them w. came up at the first Ne 7:5
they w. went up also from Ne 7:61
Tel-melah
w. took one of the daughters Ne 7:63
w. the rest of the people gave Ne 7:72
w. the Lord had commanded to Ne 8:1
w. they had made for the Ne 8:4
purpose
Nehemiah, w. is the Ne 8:9
Tirshatha
law w. the Lord had Ne 8:14
commanded
w. is exalted above all blessing Ne 9:5
w. thou hadst sworn to give Ne 9:15
them
w. thou hadst promised to Ne 9:23
their
slew thy prophets w. testified Ne 9:26
w. if a man do, he shall live in Ne 9:29
fat land w. thou gavest before Ne 9:35
w. was given by Moses the Ne 10:29
servant
w. was over the thanksgiving, Ne 12:8
he
gate, w. was over against Ne 12:37
them
w. was commanded to be Ne 13:5
given to the
w. they brought into Ne 13:15
Jerusalem on the

of Tyre also therein, w.   *Ne 13:16*
brought fish
(this is Ahasuerus w. reigned,   *Es 1:1*
from
w. was in Shushan the palace   *Es 1:2*
house w. belonged to king   *Es 1:9*
Ahasuerus
to the wise men, w. knew the   *Es 1:13*
times
and Media, w. saw the king's   *Es 1:14*
face
and w. sat the first in the   *Es 1:14*
kingdom
w. have heard of the deed of   *Es 1:18*
the king's decree w. he shall   *Es 1:20*
make
the maiden w. pleaseth the king   *Es 2:4*
be
w. had been carried away with   *Es 2:6*
maidens w. were meet to be   *Es 2:9*
given her
chamberlain, w. kept the   *Es 2:14*
concubines
tenth month., w. is the month   *Es 2:16*
Tebeth
of those w. kept the door, were   *Es 2:21*
wroth
servants, w. were in the king's   *Es 3:3*
month, w. is the month Adar   *Es 3:13*
city, w. was before the king's   *Es 4:6*
gate
king, w. is not according to   *Es 4:16*
the law
brought w. the king useth to   *Es 6:8*
wear
crown royal w. is set upon his   *Es 6:8*
head
w. Haman had made for   *Es 7:9*
Mordecai
ring, w. he had taken from   *Es 8:2*
Haman
w. he wrote to destroy the Jews   *Es 8:5*
w. are in all the king's   *Es 8:5*
provinces
writing w. is written in the   *Es 8:8*
king's
w. are from India unto   *Es 8:9*
Ethiopia
the Jews w. were in every city   *Es 8:11*
month, w. is the month Adar   *Es 8:12*
to the Jews w. are in Shushan   *Es 9:13*
w. was turned unto them from   *Es 9:22*
w. he devised against the Jews   *Es 9:25*
w. they had seen concerning   *Es 9:26*
this
matter, and w. had come unto   *Es 9:26*
them
night in w. it was said, There is   *Job 3:3*
a man
w. built desolate   *Job 3:14*
places for themselves
been; as infants w. never saw   *Job 3:16*
light
W. long for death, but it   *Job 3:21*
cometh
W. rejoice exceedingly, and   *Job 3:22*
are glad
thing w. I greatly feared is   *Job 3:25*
come upon
that w. I was afraid is come   *Job 3:25*
unto
w. made all my bones to   *Job 4:14*
shake
dust, w. are crushed before   *Job 4:19*
the moth
their excellency w. is in them   *Job 4:21*
go away
to w. of the saints wilt thou   *Job 5:1*
turn
W. doeth great things and   *Job 5:9*
those w. mourn may be   *Job 5:11*
exalted to
Can that w. is unsavoury be   *Job 6:6*
eaten
W. are blackish by reason of   *Job 6:16*
the ice
one that is desperate, w. are   *Job 6:26*
as wind
W. removeth the mountains   *Job 9:5*
w. overturneth them in his   *Job 9:5*
anger
W. shaketh the earth out of   *Job 9:6*
her place
W. commandeth the sun, and   *Job 9:7*
it riseth
W. alone spreadeth out the   *Job 9:8*
heavens
W. maketh Arcturus, Orion,   *Job 9:9*
and

W. doeth greater things past   *Job 9:10*
finding
and they are double to that   *Job 11:6*
w. is
things w. grow out of the   *Job 14:19*
dust of the
understandest thou, w. is not   *Job 15:9*
and he w. is born of a   *Job 15:14*
woman, that he
man, w. drinketh iniquity   *Job 15:16*
like water
and that w. I have seen I   *Job 15:17*
will declare
W. wise men have told from   *Job 15:18*
their
and in houses w. no man   *Job 15:28*
inhabiteth
w. are ready to become   *Job 15:28*
heaps
wrinkles, w. is a witness   *Job 16:8*
against me
they w. have seen him shall   *Job 20:7*
say
eye also w. saw him shall see   *Job 20:9*
him no
w. shall be down with him   *Job 20:11*
in the dust
That w. he laboured for   *Job 20:18*
shall he
away an house w. he builded   *Job 20:19*
not
he shall not save of that w.   *Job 20:20*
he desired
devices w. ye wrongfully   *Job 21:27*
imagine
way w. wicked men have   *Job 22:15*
trodden
W. were cut down out of   *Job 22:16*
time
W. said unto God, Depart   *Job 22:17*
from us
the words w. he would   *Job 23:5*
answer me
W. make oil within their   *Job 24:11*
walls, and
w. they had marked for   *Job 24:16*
themselves in
doth the grave those w. have   *Job 24:19*
sinned
and the son of man, w. is a   *Job 25:6*
worm
w. is with the Almighty will   *Job 27:11*
I not
w. they shall receive of the   *Job 27:13*
Almighty
There is a path w. no fowl   *Job 28:7*
knoweth
w. the vulture's eye hath not   *Job 28:7*
seen
cause w. I knew not I   *Job 29:16*
searched out
my belly is as wine w. hath no   *Job 32:19*
vent
that w. was right, and it   *Job 33:27*
profited me
W. goeth in company   *Job 34:8*
with the workers
That w. I see not teach thou   *Job 34:32*
me
the clouds w. are higher than   *Job 35:5*
thou
and that w. should be set on   *Job 36:16*
thy table
magnify his work, w. men   *Job 36:24*
behold
W. the clouds do drop and   *Job 36:28*
distil
doeth he, w. we cannot   *Job 37:5*
comprehend
of him w. is perfect in   *Job 37:16*
knowledge
w. is strong, and as a   *Job 37:18*
molten looking
the bright light w. is in the   *Job 37:21*
clouds
W. I have reserved against   *Job 38:23*
W. scattereth the east wind   *Job 38:24*
upon
W. leaveth her eggs in the   *Job 39:14*
earth
behemoth, w. I made with   *Job 40:15*
thee
with a cord w. thou lettest   *Job 41:1*
down
too wonderful for me, w. I   *Job 42:3*
knew not
spoken of me the thing w. is   *Job 42:8*
right
the chaff w. the wind driveth   *Ps 1:4*
away

Many there be w. say of my   *Ps 3:2*
soul
David, w. he sang unto the   *Ps 7 title*
Lord
w. saveth the upright in heart   *Ps 7:10*
fallen into the ditch w. he   *Ps 7:15*
made
the stars, w. thou hast ordained   *Ps 8:3*
to the Lord, w. dwelleth in   *Ps 9:11*
Zion
trouble w. I suffer of them that   *Ps 9:13*
hate
net w. they hid is their own   *Ps 9:15*
foot
by the judgment w. he   *Ps 9:16*
executeth
them w. put their trust in thee   *Ps 17:7*
from
soul from the wicked, w. is   *Ps 17:13*
thy sword
From men w. are thy hand, O   *Ps 17:14*
Lord
w. have their portion in this   *Ps 17:14*
life
enemy, and from them w.   *Ps 18:17*
hated me
W. is as a bridegroom coming   *Ps 19:5*
out of
device, w. they are not able to   *Ps 21:11*
perform
ashamed w. transgress without   *Ps 25:3*
w. speak peace to their   *Ps 28:3*
neighbours
w. speak grievous things   *Ps 31:18*
proudly
w. thou hast laid up for them   *Ps 31:19*
that
w. thou hast wrought for   *Ps 31:19*
them that
thee in the way w. thou shalt   *Ps 32:8*
go
the mule, w. have no   *Ps 32:9*
understanding
w. without cause they have   *Ps 35:7*
digged
w. deliverest the poor from   *Ps 35:10*
him that
w. hath pleasure in the   *Ps 35:27*
prosperity of
wonderful works w. thou hast   *Ps 40:5*
done
and thy thoughts w. are to   *Ps 40:5*
us-ward
I trusted, w. did eat of my   *Ps 41:9*
bread
they w. hate us spoil for   *Ps 44:10*
themselves
w. I have made touching the   *Ps 45:1*
king
that the bones w. thou hast   *Ps 51:8*
broken
W. will not hearken to the   *Ps 58:5*
voice of
away as waters w. run   *Ps 58:7*
continually
As a snail w. melteth, let   *Ps 58:8*
everyone of
for cursing and lying w.   *Ps 59:12*
they speak
not thou, O God, w. hadst cast   *Ps 60:10*
us off
w. didst not go out with our   *Ps 60:10*
armies
and truth, w. may preserve   *Ps 61:7*
him
W. by his strength setteth fast   *Ps 65:6*
W. stilleth the noise of the seas   *Ps 65:7*
the river of God, w. is full of   *Ps 65:9*
water
W. holdeth our soul in life   *Ps 65:9*
W. my lips have uttered, and   *Ps 66:14*
my
God, w. hath not turned   *Ps 66:20*
away my
he bringeth out those w. are   *Ps 68:6*
bound
the hill w. God desireth to   *Ps 68:16*
dwell in
w. thou hast wrought for us   *Ps 68:28*
heavens of heavens, w. were   *Ps 68:33*
of old
restored that w. I took not   *Ps 69:4*
away
w. should have been for their   *Ps 69:22*
welfare
w. hast shewed me great and   *Ps 71:20*
sore
my soul, w. thou hast   *Ps 71:23*
redeemed
w. thou hast purchased of old   *Ps 74:2*

inheritance, w. thou hast redeemed — Ps 74:2
W. we have heard and known — Ps 78:3
w. he commanded our fathers — Ps 78:5
even the children w. should be born — Ps 78:6
flies among them, w. devoured them — Ps 78:45
and frogs, w. destroyed them — Ps 78:45
w. his right hand had purchased — Ps 78:54
the tent w. he placed among men — Ps 78:60
Judah, the mount Zion w. he loved — Ps 78:68
like the earth w. he hath established — Ps 78:69
the blood of thy servants w. is shed — Ps 79:10
they w. pass by the way do pluck her — Ps 80:12
vineyard w. thy right hand hath — Ps 80:15
God, w. brought thee out of the land — Ps 81:10
W. perished at En-dor; they became — Ps 83:10
Lord shall give that w. is good; and — Ps 85:12
that they w. hate me may see — Ps 86:17
w. thou swarest unto David in thy — Ps 89:49
they are like the grass w. groweth up — Ps 90:5
hast made the Lord, w. is my refuge — Ps 91:9
thee, w. frameth mischief by a law — Ps 94:20
the people w. shall be created shall — Ps 102:18
place w. thou hast founded — Ps 104:8
the valleys, w. run among the hills — Ps 104:10
fowls w. sing among the branches — Ps 104:12
and bread w. strengtheneth man's — Ps 104:15
of Lebanon, w. he hath planted — Ps 104:16
the word w. he commanded to a — Ps 105:8
W. covenant he made with — Ps 105:9
w. had done great things in Egypt — Ps 106:21
idols: w. were a snare unto them — Ps 106:36
wind, w. lifteth up the waves thereof — Ps 107:25
w. may yield fruits of increase — Ps 107:37
him as the garment w. covereth him — Ps 109:19
W. turned the rock into a standing — Ps 114:8
the Lord w. made heaven and earth — Ps 115:15
into w. the righteous shall enter — Ps 118:20
The stone w. the builders refused is — Ps 118:22
is the day w. the Lord hath made — Ps 118:24
is the Lord, w. hath shewed us light — Ps 118:27
w. do err from thy commandments — Ps 119:21
Turn away my reproach w. I fear — Ps 119:39
commandments, w. I have loved — Ps 119:47; 119:48
w. thou hast caused me to hope — Ps 119:49
for me, w. are not after thy law — Ps 119:85
peace have they w. love thy law — Ps 119:165
the Lord, w. made heaven and earth — Ps 121:2
as mount Zion, w. cannot be moved — Ps 125:1
w. withereth afore it groweth up — Ps 129:6
Neither do they w. go by say, The — Ps 129:8
I w. by night stand in the house of the — Ps 134:1
of Zion, w. dwelleth at Jerusalem — Ps 135:21
To him w. divided the Red sea into — Ps 136:13

To him w. led his people through the — Ps 136:16
To him w. smote great kings; for his — Ps 136:17
will perfect that w. concerneth me — Ps 138:8
w. in continuance were fashioned — Ps 139:16
W. imagine mischiefs in their — Ps 140:2
oil, w. shall not break my head — Ps 141:5
the snares w. they have laid for me — Ps 141:9
w. teacheth my hands to war — Ps 144:1
W. made heaven, and earth, the sea — Ps 146:6
therein is: w. keepeth truth for ever — Ps 146:6
W. executeth judgment for — Ps 146:7
w. giveth food to the hungry — Ps 146:7
and to the young ravens. w. cry — Ps 147:9
hath made a decree w. shall not pass — Ps 148:6
w. taketh away the life of the owners — Pr 1:19
stranger w. flattereth with her words — Pr 2:16
W. forsaketh the guide of her youth — Pr 2:17
W. having no guide, overseer — Pr 6:7
stranger w. flattereth with her words — Pr 7:5
drink of the wine w. I have mingled — Pr 9:5
fair woman, w. is without discretion — Pr 11:22
not that w. he took in hunting — Pr 12:27
is a way w. seemeth right unto a man — Pr 14:12
that w. is in the midst of fools is made — Pr 14:33
that w. he hath given will he pay him — Pr 19:17
man who devoureth that w. is holy — Pr 20:25
landmark, w. thy fathers have set — Pr 22:28
set thine eyes upon that w. is not — Pr 23:5
morsel w. thou hast eaten shalt thou — Pr 23:8
honeycomb, w. is sweet to thy taste — Pr 24:13
w. the men of Hezekiah king of his — Pr 25:1
right hand, w. betrayeth itself — Pr 27:16
a sweeping rain w. leaveth no food — Pr 28:3
be three things w. are too wonderful — Pr 30:18
and for four w. it cannot bear — Pr 30:21
things w. are little upon the earth — Pr 30:24
There be three things w. go well, yea — Pr 30:29
A lion w. is strongest among beasts — Pr 30:30
thy ways to that w. destroyeth kings — Pr 31:3
his labour w. he taketh under the sun — Ec 1:3
that hath been, it is that w. shall be — Ec 1:9
w. is done is that w. shall be done — Ec 1:9
of old time, w. was before us — Ec 1:10
That w. is crooked cannot be made — Ec 1:15
and that w. is wanting cannot — Ec 1:15
w. they should do under the heaven — Ec 2:3
that w. hath been already done — Ec 2:12
seeing that w. now is in the days to — Ec 2:16
hated all my labour w. I had taken — Ec 2:18
despair of all the labour w. I took — Ec 2:20
a time to pluck up that w. is planted — Ec 3:2
w. God hath given to the sons of — Ec 3:10
That w. hath been is now; and that — Ec 3:15
that w. is to be hath already been — Ec 3:15
and God requireth that w. is past — Ec 3:15

For that w. befalleth the sons of men — Ec 3:19
praised the dead w. are already dead — Ec 4:2
than the living w. are yet alive — Ec 4:2
w. hath not yet been, who hath not — Ec 4:3
all the living w. walk under the sun — Ec 4:15
pay that w. thou hast vowed — Ec 5:4
evil w. I have seen under the sun — Ec 5:13
w. he may carry away in his hand — Ec 5:15
Behold that w. I have seen: it — Ec 5:18
days of his life, w. God giveth him — Ec 5:18
There is an evil w. I have seen — Ec 6:1
That w. hath been is named already — Ec 6:10
vain life w. he spendeth as a shadow — Ec 6:12
w. he hath made crooked — Ec 7:13
ten mighty men w. are in the city — Ec 7:19
That w. is far off, and exceeding — Ec 7:24
W. yet my soul seeketh, but I find — Ec 7:28
he knoweth not that w. shall be — Ec 8:7
that fear God, w. fear before him — Ec 8:12
prolong his days, w. are as a shadow — Ec 8:13
vanity w. is done upon the earth — Ec 8:14
w. God giveth him under the sun — Ec 8:15
w. he hath given thee under the sun — Ec 9:9
in thy labour w. thou takest under — Ec 9:9
an evil w. I have seen under the sun — Ec 10:5
error w. proceedeth from the ruler — Ec 10:5
and that w. hath wings shall tell — Ec 10:20
shall be afraid of what w. is high — Ec 12:5
and that w. was written was upright — Ec 12:10
w. are given from one shepherd — Ec 12:11
song of songs, w. is Solomon's — Ca 1:1
Behold his bed, w. is Solomon's — Ca 3:7
w. came up from the washing — Ca 4:2
are twins, w. feed among the lilies — Ca 4:5
of sheep w. go up from the washing — Ca 6:6
goblet, w. wanteth not liquor — Ca 7:2
Lebanon w. looketh toward Damascus — Ca 7:4
and old, w. I have laid up for thee — Ca 7:13
w. hath a most vehement flame — Ca 8:6
My vineyard, w. is mine, is before — Ca 8:12
w. he saw concerning Judah — Isa 1:1
of the oaks w. ye have desired — Isa 1:29
w. their own fingers have made — Isa 2:8
w. they made each for himself — Isa 2:20
they w. lead thee cause thee to err — Isa 3:12
W. justify the wicked for reward — Isa 5:23
w. he had taken with the tongs — Isa 6:6
of hosts, w. dwelleth in mount Zion — Isa 8:18
grievousness w. they have prescribed — Isa 10:1
the desolation w. shall come from far — Isa 10:3
w. shall stand for an ensign of the — Isa 11:10
of his people, w. shall be left — Isa 11:11; 11:16
w. Isaiah the son of Amoz did see — Isa 13:1
them w. shall not regard silver — Isa 13:17
ground, w. didst weaken the nations — Isa 14:12
and that w. they have laid up — Isa 15:7
shall be for flocks, w. shall lie down — Isa 17:2
that w. his fingers have made — Isa 17:8
w. they left because of the children — Isa 17:9

w. make a noise like the noise of the	Isa 17:12	
w. is beyond the rivers of Ethiopia	Isa 18:1	
w. the head or tail, branch or rush	Isa 19:15	
of hosts, w. he shaketh over	Isa 19:16	
w. he hath determined against it	Isa 19:17	
that w. I have heard of the Lord of	Isa 21:10	
together, w. have fled from far	Isa 22:3	
unto Shebna, w. is over the house	Isa 22:15	
w. keepeth the truth may enter in	Isa 26:2	
shall come w. were ready to perish	Isa 27:13	
w. are on the head of the fat	Isa 28:1	
w. as a tempest of hail and a	Isa 28:2	
w. is on the head of the fat valley	Isa 28:4	
w. when he that looketh upon it	Isa 28:4	
this people w. is in Jerusalem	Isa 28:14	
hosts, w. is wonderful in counsel	Isa 28:29	
w. men deliver to one that is	Isa 29:11	
W. say to the seers, See not	Isa 30:10	
w. hath been winnowed with	Isa 30:24	
be beaten down, w. smote with a rod	Isa 30:31	
w. the Lord shall lay upon him	Isa 30:32	
w. your own hands have made unto	Isa 31:7	
son, w. was over the house	Isa 36:3	
w. the Lord thy God hath heard	Isa 37:4	
delivered them w. my fathers have	Isa 37:12	
of Eden w. were in Telassar	Isa 37:12	
w. hath sent to reproach the living	Isa 37:17	
word w. the Lord hath spoken	Isa 37:22	
back by the way w. thou camest	Isa 37:29	
year that w. springeth of the same	Isa 37:30	
have done that w. is good in thy sight	Isa 38:3	
w. is gone down in the sun dial of	Isa 38:8	
by w. degrees it was gone down	Isa 38:8	
that w. thy fathers have laid up in	Isa 39:6	
w. thou shalt beget, shall they take	Isa 39:7	
of the Lord w. thou hast spoken	Isa 39:8	
earth, and that w. cometh out of it	Isa 42:5	
the Lord, w. maketh a way in the sea	Isa 43:16	
W. bringeth forth the chariot	Isa 43:17	
thee from the womb, w. will help thee	Isa 44:2	
w. he strengtheneth for himself	Isa 44:14	
the Lord, w. call thee by thy name	Isa 45:3	
w. are borne by me from the belly	Isa 46:3	
belly, w. are carried from the womb	Isa 46:3	
thee suddenly, w. thou shalt not know	Isa 47:11	
w. are called by the name of Israel	Isa 48:1	
w. swear by the name of the Lord	Isa 48:1	
w. among them hath declared	Isa 48:14	
thy God w. teacheth thee to profit	Isa 48:17	
w. leadeth thee by the way that thou	Isa 48:17	
The children w. thou shalt have, after	Isa 49:20	
w. of my creditors, is it to whom	Isa 50:1	
Art thou not it w. hath dried the sea	Isa 51:10	
son of man w. shall be made as grass	Isa 51:12	
w. hast drunk at the hand of	Isa 51:17	

w. have said to my soul, Bow down	Isa 51:23	
w. had not been told them shall	Isa 52:15	
that w. they had not heard shall they	Isa 52:15	
spend money for that w. is not bread	Isa 55:2	
your labour for that w. satisfieth not	Isa 55:2	
eat ye that w. is good, and let your	Isa 55:2	
it shall accomplish that w. I please	Isa 55:11	
Lord God w. gathereth the outcasts	Isa 56:8	
dogs w. can never have enough	Isa 56:11	
me, and the souls w. I have made	Isa 57:16	
that w. is crushed breaketh out into a	Isa 59:5	
words w. I have put in thy mouth	Isa 59:21	
the seed w. the Lord hath blessed	Isa 61:9	
w. the mouth of the Lord shall	Isa 62:2	
w. shall never hold their peace day	Isa 62:6	
for the w. thou hast laboured	Isa 62:8	
w. he hath bestowed on them	Isa 63:7	
terrible things w. we looked not for	Isa 64:3	
w. walketh in a way that was not	Isa 65:2	
W. remain among the graves	Isa 65:4	
w. eat swine's flesh, and broth	Isa 65:4	
W. say, Stand by thyself, come not	Isa 65:5	
w. have burned incense upon	Isa 65:7	
for ever in that w. I create	Isa 65:18	
and chose that in w. I delighted not	Isa 66:4	
the new earth, w. I will make, shall	Isa 66:22	
their gods, w. are yet no gods	Jer 2:11	
glory for that w. did not profit	Jer 2:11	
seen that w. backsliding Israel	Jer 3:6	
w. shall feed you with knowledge and	Jer 3:15	
w. thy sons and thy daughters should	Jer 5:17	
w. have eyes, and see not	Jer 5:21	
w. have ears, and hear not	Jer 5:21	
w. have placed the sand for	Jer 5:22	
w. is called by my name, and say	Jer 7:10	
w. is called by my name, become	Jer 7:11	
unto my place w. was in Shiloh	Jer 7:12	
house, w. is called by my name	Jer 7:14	
the place w. I gave to you and	Jer 7:14	
the house w. I called by my name	Jer 7:30	
w. is in the valley of the son	Jer 7:31	
w. I commanded them not, neither	Jer 7:31	
w. remain in all the places whither	Jer 8:3	
among you, w. will not be charmed	Jer 8:17	
my law w. I set before them	Jer 9:13	
w. their fathers taught them	Jer 9:14	
the Lord w. exercise lovingkindness	Jer 9:24	
punish all them w. are circumcised	Jer 9:25	
word w. the Lord speaketh unto	Jer 10:1	
W. I commanded your fathers	Jer 11:4	
to all w. I commanded you	Jer 11:4	
oath w. I have sworn unto your	Jer 11:5	
w. I commanded them to do	Jer 11:8	
w. refused to hear my words	Jer 11:10	
w. I made with their fathers	Jer 11:10	
w. they shall not be able to escape	Jer 11:11	
w. they have done against	Jer 11:17	
w. I have caused my people Israel to	Jer 12:14	
thou hast got, w. is upon thy loins	Jer 13:4	
w. I commanded thee to hide there	Jer 13:6	

people, w. refuse to hear my words	Jer 13:10	
w. walk in the imagination of their	Jer 13:10	
this girdle, w. is good for nothing	Jer 13:10	
for that w. he did in Jerusalem	Jer 15:4	
into a land w. thou knowest	Jer 15:14	
mine anger, w. shall burn upon you	Jer 15:14	
incurable, w. refuseth to be healed	Jer 15:18	
in the land w. thou knowest not	Jer 17:4	
in mine anger, w. shall burn for ever	Jer 17:4	
that w. came out of my lips was right	Jer 17:16	
by the w. they go out, and in all	Jer 17:19	
The word w. came to Jeremiah	Jer 18:1	
snow of Lebanon w. cometh from the	Jer 18:14	
w. is by the entry of the east gate	Jer 19:2	
the w. whosoever heareth, his ears	Jer 19:3	
w. I commanded not, nor spake it	Jer 19:5	
w. was by the house of the Lord	Jer 20:2	
w. shall spoil them, and take them	Jer 20:5	
the cities w. the Lord overthrew	Jer 20:16	
word w. came unto Jeremiah from	Jer 21:1	
w. besiege you without the walls	Jer 21:4	
w. say, Who shall come down against	Jer 21:13	
and cities w. are not inhabited	Jer 22:6	
w. reigned instead of Josiah his	Jer 22:11	
w. went forth out of this place; He	Jer 22:11	
cast into a land w. they know not	Jer 22:28	
over them w. shall feed them	Jer 23:4	
w. brought up the children of	Jer 23:7	
w. brought up and w. led the seed of	Jer 23:8	
W. think to cause my people to forget	Jer 23:27	
w. they tell every man to his	Jer 23:27	
shame. w. shall not be forgotten	Jer 23:40	
naughty figs, w. could not be eaten	Jer 24:2	
as the evil figs, w. cannot be eaten	Jer 24:8	
The w. Jeremiah the prophet spake	Jer 25:2	
words w. I have pronounced against	Jer 25:13	
w. Jeremiah hath prophesied	Jer 25:13	
of the isles w. are beyond the sea	Jer 25:22	
w. are upon the face of the earth	Jer 25:26	
sword w. I will send among you	Jer 25:27	
on the city w. is called by my name	Jer 25:29	
w. come to worship in the Lord's	Jer 26:2	
evil w. I purpose to do unto them	Jer 26:3	
in my law w. I have set before you	Jer 26:4	
of the evil w. he had pronounced	Jer 26:19	
the messengers w. come to Jerusalem	Jer 27:3	
kingdom w. will not serve the	Jer 27:8	
your sorcerers, w. speak unto you	Jer 27:9	
w. are left in the house of the Lord	Jer 27:18	
W. Nebuchadnezzar king of	Jer 27:20	
Azur the prophet, w. was of Gibeon	Jer 28:1	
thy words w. thou hast prophesied	Jer 28:6	
prophet w. prophesieth of peace	Jer 28:9	

elders *w.* were carried away captives	Jer 29:1
dreams *w.* ye caused to be dreamed	Jer 29:8
w. I sent unto them by my servants	Jer 29:19
w. prophesy a lie unto you in my	Jer 29:21
of Judah *w.* are in Babylon	Jer 29:22
w. I have not commanded them	Jer 29:23
w. maketh himself a prophet to you	Jer 29:27
The people *w.* were left of the sword	Jer 31:2
even the way *w.* thou wentest	Jer 31:21
w. my covenant they brake	Jer 31:32
w. giveth the sun for a light by day	Jer 31:35
w. divideth the sea when the waves	Jer 31:35
w. was the eighteenth year of	Jer 32:1
w. was in the king of Judah's	Jer 32:2
w. is in the country of Benjamin	Jer 32:8
both that *w.* was sealed according to	Jer 32:11
and custom, and that *w.* was open	Jer 32:11
of the purchase, both *w.* is sealed	Jer 32:14
and this evidence *w.* is open; and put	Jer 32:14
W. hast set signs and wonders in	Jer 32:20
w. thou didst swear to their fathers	Jer 32:22
w. they have done to provoke me to	Jer 32:32
w. is called by my name, to defile it	Jer 32:34
w. are in the valley of the son of	Jer 32:35
w. I commanded them not, neither	Jer 32:35
mighty things, *w.* thou knowest not	Jer 33:3
w. are thrown down by the mounts	Jer 33:4
w. shall hear all the good that I do	Jer 33:9
w. ye say shall be desolate without	Jer 33:10
w. is desolate without man	Jer 33:12
good thing *w.* I have promised	Jer 33:14
families *w.* the Lord hath chosen	Jer 33:24
The word *w.* came unto Jeremiah	Jer 34:1
former kings *w.* were before thee	Jer 34:5
all the people *w.* were at Jerusalem	Jer 34:8
w. had entered into the covenant	Jer 34:10
w. hath been sold unto thee	Jer 34:14
the house *w.* is called by my name	Jer 34:15
w. have not performed the words of	Jer 34:18
covenant *w.* they had made before	Jer 34:18
w. passed between the parts of the	Jer 34:19
army, *w.* are gone up from you	Jer 34:21
The word *w.* came unto Jeremiah	Jer 35:1
w. was by the chamber of the	Jer 35:4
w. was above the chamber of	Jer 35:4
in the land *w.* I have given to you	Jer 35:15
father, *w.* he commanded them	Jer 35:16
evil *w.* I purpose to do unto them	Jer 36:3
w. he had spoken unto him, upon a	Jer 36:4
w. thou hast written from my	Jer 36:6
the princes *w.* stood beside the king	Jer 36:21
w. Baruch wrote at the mouth of	Jer 36:27
w. Jehoiakim the king of Judah hath	Jer 36:28
w. Jehoiakim king of Judah had	Jer 36:32
Lord, *w.* he spake by the prophet	Jer 37:2

army, *w.* is come forth to help you	Jer 37:7
prophets, *w.* prophesied unto you	Jer 37:19
of Babylon's army, *w.* shall take it	Jer 38:3
w. was in the king's house, heard	Jer 38:7
of the Lord, *w.* I speak unto thee	Jer 38:20
of the people, *w.* had nothing	Jer 39:10
The word *w.* came to Jeremiah from	Jer 40:1
w. were carried away captive	Jer 40:1
chains *w.* were upon thine hand	Jer 40:4
of the forces *w.* were in the field	Jer 40:7
Chaldeans *w.* will come unto us	Jer 40:10
all the Jews *w.* are gathered unto	Jer 40:15
was it *w.* Asa the king had made for	Jer 41:9
the people *w.* were with Ishmael	Jer 41:13
of Chimham, *w.* is by Beth-lehem	Jer 41:17
for the *w.* the Lord thy God shall	Jer 42:5
of the forces *w.* were with him	Jer 42:8
sword, *w.* ye feared, shall overtake	Jer 42:16
for the *w.* he hath sent me unto you	Jer 42:21
for *w.* the Lord their God had sent	Jer 43:1
w. is at the entry of Pharaoh's	Jer 43:9
Jews *w.* dwell in the land of Egypt	Jer 44:1
w. dwell at Migdol, and at Tahpanhes	Jer 44:1
w. they have committed to provoke	Jer 44:3
w. they have committed in the land	Jer 44:9
w. are gone into the land of Egypt to	Jer 44:14
to the *w.* they desire to return	Jer 44:14
men *w.* knew that their wives had	Jer 44:15
people *w.* had given him that answer	Jer 44:20
of the abominations *w.* ye have	Jer 44:22
that *w.* I have built will I break	Jer 45:4
that *w.* I have planted I will pluck	Jer 45:4
The word *w.* came to Jeremiah	Jer 46:1
w. was by the river Euphrates in	Jer 46:2
w. Nebuchadrezzar king of Babylon	Jer 46:2; 49:28
nations *w.* have neither gates nor	Jer 49:31
neither gates nor bars *w.* dwell alone	Jer 49:31
w. shall make her land desolate	Jer 50:3
and done that *w.* he spake against	Jer 51:12
the Lord, *w.* destroyest all the earth	Jer 51:25
mouth that *w.* he hath swallowed up	Jer 51:44
The word *w.* Jeremiah the prophet	Jer 51:59
that *w.* was evil in the eyes of	Jer 52:2
walls, *w.* was by the king's garden	Jer 52:7
w. was the nineteenth year of	Jer 52:12
guard, *w.* served the king of Babylon	Jer 52:12
that *w.* was of gold in gold	Jer 52:19
and that *w.* was of silver in silver	Jer 52:19
w. king Solomon had made in the	Jer 52:20
w. had charge of the men of war	Jer 52:25
person, *w.* were found in the city	Jer 52:25
my sorrow, *w.* is done unto me	La 1:12
fire, *w.* devoureth round about	La 2:3
hath done that *w.* he had devised	La 2:17

the mountain of Zion, *w.* is desolate	La 5:18
w. was the fifth year of king	Eze 1:2
one had two, *w.* covered on this side	Eze 1:23
one had two, *w.* covered on that side	Eze 1:23
his righteousness *w.* he hath done	Eze 3:20
glory *w.* I saw by the river of Chebar	Eze 3:23
And the meat *w.* thou shalt eat shall	Eze 4:10
I not eaten of that *w.* dieth of itself	Eze 4:14
do in thee that *w.* I have not done	Eze 5:9
w. shall be for their destruction	Eze 5:16
and *w.* I will send to destroy you	Eze 5:16
heart, *w.* hath departed from me	Eze 6:9
eyes, *w.* go a whoring after their idols	Eze 6:9
evils *w.* they have committed in all	Eze 6:9
shall not return to that *w.* is sold	Eze 7:13
multitude thereof, *w.* shall not return	Eze 7:13
of jealousy, *w.* provoketh to jealousy	Eze 8:3
house *w.* was toward the north	Eze 8:14
abominations *w.* they commit here	Eze 8:17
gate, *w.* lieth toward the north	Eze 9:2
w. had the writer's inkhorn by his	Eze 9:3
men *w.* were before the house	Eze 9:6
w. had the inkhorn by his side	Eze 9:11
w. I saw by the river of Chebar	Eze 10:22
Lord's house, *w.* looketh eastward	Eze 11:1
W. say, It is not near; let us build	Eze 11:3
w. is on the east side of the city	Eze 11:23
w. have eyes to see, and see not	Eze 12:2
word *w.* I have spoken shall be done	Eze 12:28
w. daub it with untempered morter	Eze 13:11
w. prophesy concerning Jerusalem	Eze 13:16
and *w.* see visions of peace for her	Eze 13:16
w. prophesy out of their own heart	Eze 13:17
w. separateth himself from me	Eze 14:7
w. is among the trees of the forest	Eze 15:2
w. I have given to the fire for fuel	Eze 15:6
comeliness, *w.* I had put upon thee	Eze 16:14
of my silver, *w.* I had given thee	Eze 16:17
My meat also *w.* I gave thee, fine	Eze 16:19
w. are ashamed of thy lewd way	Eze 16:27
w. taketh strangers instead of her	Eze 16:32
w. thou didst give unto them	Eze 16:36
w. lothed their husbands and their	Eze 16:45
abominations *w.* thou hast done	Eze 16:51
also, *w.* hast judged thy sisters	Eze 16:52
Philistines *w.* despise thee round	Eze 16:57
w. hast despised the oath in	Eze 16:59
of feathers, *w.* had divers colours	Eze 17:3
and do that *w.* is lawful and right	Eze 18:5
his father's sins *w.* he hath done	Eze 18:14
w. is not good among his people	Eze 18:18
the son hath done that *w.* is lawful	Eze 18:19

and do that *w.* is lawful and right, he   *Eze 18:21*

doeth that *w.* is lawful and right, he   *Eze 18:27*

w. hath devoured her fruit, so that she   *Eze 19:14*

honey, *w.* is the glory of all lands   *Eze 20:6*

w. if a man do, he shall even live   *Eze 20:11; 20:13*

into the land *w.* I have given them   *Eze 20:15*

honey, *w.* is the glory of all lands   *Eze 20:15*

w. if a man do, he shall even live in   *Eze 20:21*

w. I lifted up mine hand to give it to   *Eze 20:28*

that *w.* cometh into your mind shall   *Eze 20:32*

for the *w.* I lifted up mine hand   *Eze 20:42*

w. entereth into their privy chambers   *Eze 21:14*

in thine idols *w.* thou hast made   *Eze 22:4*

w. art infamous and much vexed   *Eze 22:5*

dishonest gain *w.* thou hast made   *Eze 22:13*

thy blood *w.* hath been in the midst   *Eze 22:13*

W. were clothed with blue, captains   *Eze 23:6*

w. shall set against thee buckler and   *Eze 23:24*

w. put bracelets upon their hands   *Eze 23:42*

eyes, and that *w.* your soul pitieth   *Eze 24:21*

mouth be opened to him *w.* is escaped   *Eze 24:27*

from his cities *w.* are on his frontiers   *Eze 25:9*

her daughters *w.* are in the field   *Eze 26:6*

w. wast strong in the sea, she and   *Eze 26:17*

w. cause their terror to be on all   *Eze 26:17*

w. art a merchant for the people on   *Eze 27:3*

that *w.* thou spreadest forth to be thy   *Eze 27:7*

of E'ishah was that *w.* covered thee   *Eze 27:7*

company *w.* is in the midst of thee   *Eze 27:27*

w. hath said, My river is mine own   *Eze 29:3*

Israel *w.* bringeth their iniquity to   *Eze 29:16*

the strong, and that *w.* was broken   *Eze 30:22*

countries *w.* thou hast not known   *Eze 32:9*

w. caused terror in the land of the   *Eze 32:23*

w. are gone down uncircumcised   *Eze 32:24*

w. caused their terror in the land of   *Eze 32:24*

w. are gone down to hell with their   *Eze 32:27*

w. with their might are laid by them   *Eze 32:29*

w. are gone down with the slain   *Eze 32:30*

and do that *w.* is lawful and right   *Eze 33:14*

he hath done that *w.* is lawful and   *Eze 33:16*

do that *w.* is lawful and right, he shall   *Eze 33:19*

all their abominations *w.* they have   *Eze 33:29*

have ye healed that *w.* was sick   *Eze 34:4*

have ye bound up that *w.* was broken   *Eze 34:4*

ye brought again that *w.* was driven   *Eze 34:4*

have ye sought that *w.* was lost   *Eze 34:4*

I will seek that *w.* was lost, and bring   *Eze 34:16*

bring again that *w.* was driven away   *Eze 34:16*

and will bind up that *w.* was broken   *Eze 34:16*

and will strengthen that *w.* was sick   *Eze 34:16*

eat that *w.* ye have trodden with your   *Eze 34:19*

they drink that *w.* ye have fouled with   *Eze 34:19*

w. thou hast used out of thy hatred   *Eze 35:11*

blasphemies *w.* thou hast spoken   *Eze 35:12*

w. became a prey and derision to   *Eze 36:4*

w. have appointed my land into   *Eze 36:5*

w. the house of Israel had profaned   *Eze 36:21*

w. ye have profaned among   *Eze 36:22*

w. was profaned in the heathen   *Eze 36:23*

w. ye have profaned in the midst of   *Eze 36:23*

of the valley *w.* was full of bones   *Eze 37:1*

w. is in the hand of Ephraim   *Eze 37:19*

Israel, *w.* have been always waste   *Eze 38:8*

w. have gotten cattle and goods   *Eze 38:12*

w. prophesied in those days   *Eze 38:17*

of my sacrifice *w.* I have sacrificed   *Eze 39:19*

w. caused them to be led into   *Eze 39:28*

w. was as the frame of a city   *Eze 40:2*

on the gate, *w.* looketh toward the east   *Eze 40:6*

of the gate, *w.* was one reed broad   *Eze 40:6*

w. was at the porch of the gate   *Eze 40:40*

w. was at the side of the north gate   *Eze 40:44*

w. come near to the Lord to minister   *Eze 40:46*

w. was the breadth of the tabernacle   *Eze 41:1*

into the wall *w.* was of the house   *Eze 41:6*

w. was for the side chamber without   *Eze 41:9*

that *w.* was left was the place of the   *Eze 41:9*

separate place *w.* was behind it   *Eze 41:15*

w. was before the building toward   *Eze 42:1*

cubits *w.* were for the inner court   *Eze 42:3*

the pavement *w.* was for the utter   *Eze 42:3*

chambers *w.* were toward the north   *Eze 42:11*

w. are before the separate place   *Eze 42:13*

to those things *w.* are for the people   *Eze 42:14*

appearance of the vision *w.* I saw   *Eze 43:3*

seed of Zadok, *w.* approach unto me   *Eze 43:19*

sanctuary *w.* looketh toward the east   *Eze 44:1*

w. went astray away from me after   *Eze 44:10*

their abominations *w.* they have   *Eze 44:13*

w. shall come near to minister unto   *Eze 45:4*

cor *w.* is an homer of ten baths   *Eze 45:14*

w. was at the side of the gate   *Eze 46:19*

priests, *w.* looked toward the north   *Eze 46:19*

w. being brought forth into the sea   *Eze 47:8*

every thing that liveth, *w.* moveth   *Eze 47:9*

concerning the *w.* I lifted up mine   *Eze 47:14*

w. is between the border of   *Eze 47:16*

w. is by the coast of Hauran   *Eze 47:16*

w. shall beget children among you   *Eze 47:22*

be the offering *w.* ye shall offer   *Eze 48:8*

of Zadok; *w.* have kept my charge   *Eze 48:11*

w. went not astray when the   *Eze 48:11*

the midst of that *w.* is the prince's   *Eze 48:22*

This is the land *w.* ye shall divide   *Eze 48:29*

w. he carried into the land of Shinar   *Da 1:2*

meat, and of the wine *w.* he drank   *Da 1:5*

meat, nor with the wine *w.* he drank   *Da 1:8*

the children *w.* are of your sort   *Da 1:10*

w. did eat the portion of the king's   *Da 1:15*

w. was gone forth to slay the wise   *Da 2:14*

unto me the dream *w.* I have seen   *Da 2:26*

secret *w.* the king hath demanded   *Da 2:27*

w. smote the image upon his feet   *Da 2:34*

w. shall bear rule over all the   *Da 2:39*

w. shall never be destroyed   *Da 2:44*

image *w.* Nebuchadnezzar the king   *Da 3:2*

golden image *w.* thou hast set up   *Da 3:12*

the golden image *w.* I have set up   *Da 3:14*

worship the image *w.* I have made   *Da 3:15*

golden image *w.* thou hast set up   *Da 3:18*

w. speak anything amiss against   *Da 3:29*

I saw a dream *w.* made me afraid   *Da 4:5*

tree that thou sawest, *w.* grew   *Da 4:20*

under *w.* the beasts of the field dwelt   *Da 4:21*

w. is come upon my lord the king   *Da 4:24*

w. his father Nebuchadnezzar had   *Da 5:2*

of the temple *w.* was in Jerusalem   *Da 5:2*

house of God *w.* was at Jerusalem   *Da 5:3*

Daniel, *w.* art of the children of the   *Da 5:13*

w. see not, nor hear, nor know   *Da 5:23*

w. should be over the whole kingdom   *Da 6:1*

Medes and Persians, *w.* altereth   *Da 6:8; 6:12*

Daniel, *w.* is of the children of   *Da 6:13*

statute *w.* the king established   *Da 6:13*

those men *w.* had accused Daniel   *Da 6:24*

that *w.* shall not be destroyed   *Da 6:26*

w. had upon the back of it four   *Da 7:6*

the great words *w.* the horn spake   *Da 7:11*

dominion, *w.* shall not pass away   *Da 7:14*

that *w.* shall not be destroyed   *Da 7:14*

These great beasts, *w.* are four   *Da 7:17*

w. shall rise out of the earth   *Da 7:17*

w. was diverse from all the others   *Da 7:19*

w. devoured, brake in pieces   *Da 7:19*

and of the other *w.* came up   *Da 7:20*

earth, *w.* shall be diverse from all   *Da 7:23*

that *w.* appeared unto me at the first   *Da 8:1*

w. is in the province of Elam   *Da 8:2*

the river a ram *w.* had two horns   *Da 8:3*

w. I had seen standing before   *Da 8:6*

horn, *w.* waxed exceeding great   *Da 8:9*

said unto that certain saint *w.* spake   *Da 8:13*

w. called, and said, Gabriel, make this   *Da 8:16*

The ram *w.* thou sawest having   *Da 8:20*

the vision *w.* was told is true   *Da 8:26*

w. was made king over the realm of   *Da 9:1*

w. spake in thy name to our kings   *Da 9:6*

w. he set before us by his servants   *Da 9:10*

his words, *w.* he spake against us   *Da 9:12*

in all his works *w.* he doeth: Da 9:14
for we

the city *w.* is called by thy   Da 9:18
name

of the great river, *w.* is   Da 10:4
Hiddekel

touched me, *w.* set me upon   Da 10:10
my knees

that *w.* is noted in the   Da 10:21
scripture of

to his dominion *w.* he ruled   Da 11:4

estate, *w.* shall come with an   Da 11:7
army

w. by his hand shall be   Da 11:16
consumed

that *w.* his fathers have not   Da 11:24
done

prince *w.* standeth for the   Da 12:1
children

w. was upon the waters of   Da 12:6;
                               12:7

w. conceived, and bare him a   Ho 1:3
son

the sand *w.* cannot be   Ho 1:10
measured

and gold, *w.* they prepared for   Ho 2:8
Baal

will say to them *w.* are not   Ho 2:23
my people

made known that *w.* shall   Ho 5:9
surely be

That *w.* the palmerworm hath   Joe 1:4
left

and that *w.* the locust hath   Joe 1:4
left hath

and that *w.* the cankerworm   Joe 1:4
hath left

great army *w.* I sent among   Joe 2:25
you

w. he saw concerning Israel in   Am 1:1
the

w. shall devour the palaces of   Am 1:4

w. shall devour the palaces   Am 1:7;
thereof   1:10

w. shall devour the palaces of   Am 1:12

the *w.* their fathers have   Am 2:4
walked

w. I brought up from the land   Am 3:1

of Bashan *w.* oppress the   Am 4:1
poor

the poor, *w.* crush the needy   Am 4:1

w. say to their masters,   Am 4:1
Bring, and let

every cow at that *w.* is before   Am 4:3
her

word *w.* I take up against you   Am 5:1

and that *w.* went forth by an   Am 5:3
hundred

god, *w.* ye made for   Am 5:26
yourselves

w. are named chief of the   Am 6:1
nations

Ye *w.* rejoice in a thing of   Am 6:13
nought

w. say, Have we not taken   Am 6:13
to us horns

w. say. The evil shall not   Am 9:10
overtake nor

heathen, *w.* are called by my   Am 9:12
name

of their land *w.* I have given   Am 9:15
them

of Jerusalem, *w.* is in Sepharad   Ob 20

w. hath made the sea and the   Jon 1:9
dry

for the *w.* thou hast not   Jon 4:10
laboured

w. came up in a night, and   Jon 4:10
perished in

w. he saw concerning Samaria   Mic 1:1

evil, from *w.* ye shall not   Mic 2:3
remove

time that she *w.* travaileth   Mic 5:3
hath

and that *w.* thou deliverest   Mic 6:14
will I

shame shall cover her *w.* said   Mic 7:10
unto

w. dwell solitarily in the   Mic 7:14
wood

w. thou hast sworn unto our   Mic 7:20

w. camp in the hedges in cold   Na 3:17
day

The burden *w.* Habakkuk the   Hab 1:1

w. ye will not believe, though   Hab 1:5
it

w. shall march through the   Hab 1:6
breadth

his soul *w.* is lifted up is not   Hab 2:4
upright

him that increaseth that *w.* is   Hab 2:6
not his

spoil of beasts, *w.* made   Hab 2:17
them afraid

the Lord *w.* came unto   Zep 1:1
Zephaniah

w. fill their masters' houses   Zep 1:9
with

w. have wrought his judgment   Zep 2:3

that *w.* the ground bringeth   Hag 1:11
forth

that *w.* they offer there is   Hag 2:14
unclean

w. I commanded my servants   Zec 1:6

month, *w.* is the month Sebat   Zec 1:7

Judah, against *w.* thou hast   Zec 1:12
had

horns *w.* have scattered   Zec 1:19;
Judah   1:21

w. lifted up their horn over   Zec 1:21
the land

me unto the nations *w.* spoiled   Zec 2:8
you

lamps, *w.* are upon the top   Zec 4:2
thereof

w. run to and fro through   Zec 4:10
the whole

w. through the two golden   Zec 4:12
pipes

w. go forth from standing   Zec 6:5
before the

The black horses *w.* are therein   Zec 6:6
go

w. are come from Babylon   Zec 6:10

the priests *w.* were in the   Zec 7:3
house

the words *w.* the Lord hath   Zec 7:7
cried

and the words *w.* the Lord of   Zec 7:12
hosts

w. were in the day that the   Zec 8:9

w. tread down their enemies   Zec 10:5
in the

w. I had made with all the   Zec 11:10
people

w. shall not visit those that   Zec 11:16
be cut off

Lord, *w.* stretcheth forth the   Zec 12:1
heavens

Those with *w.* I was wounded   Zec 13:6

w. is before Jerusalem on the   Zec 14:4
east

day *w.* shall be known to the   Zec 14:7
Lord

of all the nations *w.* came   Zec 14:16
against

and ye brought that *w.* was   Mal 1:13
torn

w. hath in his flock a male   Mal 1:14

holiness of the Lord *w.* he   Mal 2:11
loved

w. I commanded unto him in   Mal 4:4

w. is conceived in her is of   M't 1:20
the Holy

fulfilled *w.* was spoken of   M't 1:22
the Lord

Emmanuel, *w.* being   M't 1:23
interpreted

lo, the star *w.* they saw in the   M't 2:9
east

fulfilled *w.* was spoken of the   M't 2:15

the time *w.* he had diligently   M't 2:16

that *w.* was spoken by Jeremy   M't 2:17

w. sought the young child's   M't 2:20
life

w. was spoken by the   M't 2:23
prophets

tree *w.* bringeth not forth   M't 3:10
good fruit

in Capernaum *w.* is upon the   M't 4:13
sea

fulfilled *w.* was spoken by   M't 4:14
Esaias

people *w.* sat in darkness saw   M't 4:16

w. sat in the region and   M't 4:16
shadow

those *w.* were possessed with   M't 4:24
devils

and those *w.* were lunatick,   M't 4:24
and those

Blessed are they *w.* do hunger   M't 5:6

w. are persecuted for   M't 5:10
righteousness

the prophets *w.* were before   M't 5:12
you

glorify your Father *w.* is in   M't 5:16
heaven

pray for them *w.* despitefully   M't 5:44
use

the children of your Father   M't 5:45
w. is in

For if ye love them *w.* love   M't 5:46
you

Father *w.* is in heaven is   M't 5:48
perfect

of your Father *w.* is in heaven   M't 6:1

Father *w.* seeth in secret   M't 6:4
himself

pray to thy Father *w.* is in   M't 6:6
secret

Father *w.* seeth in secret shall   M't 6:6

Our Father *w.* art in heaven   M't 6:9

unto thy Father *w.* is in   M't 6:18
secret

and thy Father, *w.* seeth in   M't 6:18
secret

W. of you by taking thought   M't 6:27
can

w. to-day is, and to-morrow   M't 6:30
is cast

not that *w.* is holy unto the   M't 7:6
dogs

w. is in heaven give good   M't 7:11
things

and many there be *w.* go in   M't 7:13
threat

narrow is the way, *w.* leadeth   M't 7:14

w. come to you in sheep's   M't 7:15

will of my Father *w.* is in   M't 7:21
heaven

w. built his house upon a   M't 7:24
rock

w. built his house upon the   M't 7:26
sand

w. was spoken by Esaias the   M't 8:17

w. had given such power unto   M't 9:8
men

that *w.* is put in to fill it up   M't 9:16
taketh

w. was diseased with an issue   M't 9:20

your Father *w.* speaketh in   M't 10:20
you

And fear not them *w.* kill   M't 10:28
the body

fear him *w.* is able to   M't 10:28
destroy

before my Father *w.* is in   M't 10:32;
heaven   10:33

those things *w.* ye do hear   M't 11:4

w. shall prepare thy way   M't 11:10
before

this is Elias, *w.* was for to   M't 11:14
come

works, *w.* were done in you,   M't 11:21
had

w. art exalted unto heaven   M't 11:23

works, *w.* have been done in   M't 11:23
thee

do that *w.* is not lawful to do   M't 12:2
upon

w. was not lawful for him to   M't 12:4
eat

neither for them *w.* were with   M't 12:4
him

was a man *w.* had his hand   M't 12:10
withered

w. was spoken by Esaias   M't 12:17

will of my Father *w.* in the   M't 12:50
heaven

w. saith, By hearing ye shall   M't 13:14
hear

to see those things *w.* ye see   M't 13:17

to hear those things *w.* ye   M't 13:17
hear

that *w.* was sown in his   M't 13:19
heart

is he *w.* received by the way   M't 13:19
side

w. also beareth fruit, and   M't 13:23
bringeth

unto a man *w.* sowed good   M't 13:24
seed in

a man took, and sowed in   M't 13:31

W. indeed is the least of all   M't 13:32
seeds

w. a woman took and hid in   M't 13:33
three

w. was spoken by the   M't 13:35
prophet

I will utter things *w.* have   M't 13:35
been kept

that offend, and them *w.* do   M't 13:41
iniquity

w. when a man hath found,   M't 13:44
he

W. when it was full, they drew to | M't 13:48
w. is instructed unto the kingdom | M't 13:52
w. bringeth forth out of his | M't 13:52
and them w. sat with him at meat | M't 14:9
Pharisees, w. were of Jerusalem | M't 15:1
Not that w. goeth into the mouth | M't 15:11
but that w. cometh out of the mouth | M't 15:11
w. my heavenly Father hath not | M't 15:13
w. proceed out of the mouth | M't 15:18
are the things w. defile a man | M't 15:20
crumbs w. fall from their masters' | M't 15:27
W. when Jesus perceived, he said | M't 16:8
but my Father w. is in heaven | M't 16:17
w. shall not taste of death, till | M't 16:28
a voice out of the cloud, w. said | M't 17:5
these little ones w. believe in me | M't 18:6
face of my Father w. is in heaven | M't 18:10
is come to save that w. was lost | M't 18:11
seeketh that w. is gone astray | M't 18:12
ninety and nine w. went not astray | M't 18:13
will of your Father w. is in heaven | M't 18:14
them of my Father w. is in heaven | M't 18:19
w. would take account of his | M't 18:23
w. owed him ten thousand talents | M't 18:24
w. owed him an hundred pence | M't 18:28
w. made them at the beginning | M't 19:4
marrieth her w. is put away doth | M't 19:9
w. were so born from their | M't 19:12
w. were made eunuchs of men | M't 19:12
w. have made themselves eunuchs | M't 19:12
He saith unto him, W?. Jesus | M't 19:18
That ye w. have followed me | M't 19:28
w. went out early in the morning | M't 20:1
w. have borne the burden | M't 20:12
w. was spoken by the prophet | M't 21:4
do this w. is done to the fig tree | M't 21:21
w. if ye tell me, I in like wise will | M't 21:24
householder, w. planted a | M't 21:33
w. shall render him the fruits in | M't 21:41
The stone w. the builders rejected | M't 21:42
w. made a marriage for his son | M't 22:2
Tell them w. are bidden, Behold, I | M't 22:4
they w. were bidden were not worthy | M't 22:8
w. had not on a wedding garment | M't 22:11
unto Cæsar the things w. are Cæsar's | M't 22:21
w. say that there is no resurrection | M't 22:23
w. was spoken unto you by God | M't 22:31
Then one of them, w. was a lawyer | M't 22:35
w. is the great commandment in | M't 22:36
is your Father, w. is in heaven | M't 23:9
unto you, ye blind guides, w. say | M't 23:16
blind guides. w. strain at a gnat | M't 23:24
first that w. is within the cup | M't 23:26
w. indeed appear beautiful | M't 23:27
of them w. killed the prophets | M't 23:31
stonest them w. are sent unto thee | M't 23:37

Then let them w. be in Judæa flee | M't 24:16
Let him w. is on the housetop not | M't 24:17
Neither let him w. is in the field | M't 24:18
ten virgins w. took their lamps | M't 25:1
Then he, w. had received the one | M't 25:24
give it unto him w. hath ten talents | M't 25:28
be taken away even that w. he hath | M't 25:29
Then Judas, w. betrayed him | M't 26:25
w. is shed for many for the | M't 26:28
one of them w. were with Jesus | M't 26:51
is it w. these witness against thee | M't 26:62
word of Jesus, w. said unto him | M't 26:75
Then Judas, w. had betrayed | M't 27:3
that w. was spoken by Jeremy | M't 27:9
or Jesus w. is called Christ | M't 27:17
then with Jesus w. is called Christ | M't 27:22
w. was spoken by the prophet | M't 27:35
also, w. were crucified with him | M't 27:44
bodies of the saints w. slept arose | M't 27:52
w. followed Jesus from Galilee | M't 27:55
Among w. was Mary Magdalene | M't 27:56
w. he had hewn out in the rock | M't 27:60
ye seek Jesus, w. was crucified | M't 28:5
w. shall prepare thy way before | M'k 1:2
those things w. Moses commanded | M'k 1:44
sick of the palsy, w. was borne of | M'k 2:3
sabbath day that w. is not lawful | M'k 2:24
w. is not lawful to eat but for the | M'k 2:26
gave also to them w. were with him | M'k 2:26
a man there w. had a withered hand | M'k 3:1
unto the man w. had the withered | M'k 3:3
Boanerges, w. is, The sons | M'k 3:17
Judas Iscariot, w. also betrayed | M'k 3:19
the scribes w. came down from | M'k 3:22
about on them w. sat about him | M'k 3:34
likewise w. are sown on stony ground | M'k 4:16
are they w. are sown among thorns | M'k 4:18
are they w. are sown on good ground | M'k 4:20
hid w. shall not be manifested | M'k 4:22
shall be taken even that w. he hath | M'k 4:25
w. when it is sown in the earth | M'k 4:31
w. had an issue of blood twelve years | M'k 5:25
w. said, Thy daughter is dead | M'k 5:35
w. is, being interpreted, Damsel | M'k 5:41
wisdom is this w. is given unto him | M'k 6:2
for their sakes w. sat with him | M'k 6:26
the scribes w. came from Jerusalem | M'k 7:1
be, w. they have received to hold | M'k 7:4
tradition, w. ye have delivered | M'k 7:13
but the things w. come out of him | M'k 7:15
That w. cometh out of the man, that | M'k 7:20
here, w. shall not taste of death | M'k 9:1
thee my son, w. hath a dumb spirit | M'k 9:17

man w. shall do a miracle in my | M'k 9:39
that they w. are accounted to rule | M'k 10:42
the fig tree w. thou cursedst | M'k 11:21
w. he saith shall come to pass | M'k 11:23
your Father also w. is in heaven | M'k 11:25
Father w. is in heaven forgive your | M'k 11:26
The stone w. the builders rejected | M'k 12:10
w. say there is no resurrection | M'k 12:18
as the angels w. are in heaven | M'k 12:25
W. is the first commandment of | M'k 12:28
w. love to go in long clothing | M'k 12:38
W. devour widows' houses | M'k 12:40
in two mites, w. make a farthing | M'k 12:42
they w. have cast into the treasury | M'k 12:43
the creation w. God created unto | M'k 13:19
not the angels w. are in heaven | M'k 13:32
One of you w. eateth with me | M'k 14:18
testament, w. is shed for many | M'k 14:24
what is it w. these witness against | M'k 14:60
w. lay bound with them that had | M'k 15:7
w. is, being interpreted, The place | M'k 15:22
scripture was fulfilled, w. saith | M'k 15:28
w. is, being interpreted, My God | M'k 15:34
centurion, w. stood over against | M'k 15:39
women w. came up with him unto | M'k 15:41
w. waited for the kingdom | M'k 15:43
sepulchre w. was hewn out | M'k 15:46
Jesus of Nazareth, w. was crucified | M'k 16:6
w. had seen him after he was risen | M'k 16:14
things w. are most surely believed | Lu 1:1
w. from the beginning were | Lu 1:2
w. shall be fulfilled in their | Lu 1:20
holy thing w. shall be born of thee | Lu 1:35
things w. were told her from the Lord | Lu 1:45
w. have been since the world | Lu 1:70
oath w. he sware to our father | Lu 1:73
of David, w. is called Bethlehem | Lu 2:4
great joy, w. shall be to all people | Lu 2:10
a Saviour w. is Christ the Lord | Lu 2:11
see this thing w. is come to pass | Lu 2:15
w. the Lord hath made known unto | Lu 2:15
w. was told them concerning the | Lu 2:17
things w. were told them by | Lu 2:18
w. was so named of the angel | Lu 2:21
that w. is said in the law of the Lord | Lu 2:24
W. thou has prepared before | Lu 2:31
those things w. were spoken of him | Lu 2:33
and for a sign w. shall be spoken | Lu 2:34
w. departed not from the temple | Lu 2:37
the saying w. he spake unto them | Lu 2:50
w. bringeth not forth good fruit is | Lu 3:9
more than that w. is appointed you | Lu 3:13
all the evils w. Herod had done | Lu 3:19
a voice came from heaven, w. | Lu 3:22 said
son of Joseph, w. was the son of Heli | Lu 3:23

W. was the son of	Lu 3:24; 3:25-38	w. also sat at Jesus' feet, and heard	Lu 10:39	things w. are impossible with men	Lu 18:27
w. proceeded out of his mouth	Lu 4:22	w. shall not be taken away from	Lu 10:42	knew they the things w. were spoken	Lu 18:34
man, w. had a spirit of an unclean	Lu 4:33	Our Father w. art in heaven	Lu 11:2	they w. went before rebuked him	Lu 18:39
one of the ships, w. was Simon's	Lu 5:3	W. of you shall have a friend	Lu 11:5	w. was the chief among the	Lu 19:2
w. were in the other ship	Lu 5:7	and the paps w. thou hast sucked	Lu 11:27	to seek and to save that w. was lost	Lu 19:10
of fishes w. they had taken	Lu 5:9	w. come in may see the light	Lu 11:33	w. I have kept laid up in a napkin	Lu 19:20
Zebedee, w. were partners with	Lu 5:10	light w. is in thee be not darkness	Lu 11:35	every one w. hath shall be given	Lu 19:26
w. were come out of every town of	Lu 5:17	he, that made that w. is without	Lu 11:40	w. would not that I should reign	Lu 19:27
a man w. was taken with a palsy	Lu 5:18	make that w. is within also	Lu 11:40	in the w. at your entering ye shall	Lu 19:30
is this w. speaketh blasphemies	Lu 5:21	ye are as graves w. appear not	Lu 11:44	the things w. belong unto thy peace	Lu 19:42
do ye that w. is not lawful to do on	Lu 6:2	prophets, w. was shed from the	Lu 11:50	The stone w. the builders rejected	Lu 20:17
hungred, and they w. were with	Lu 6:3	w. perished between the altar	Lu 11:51	w. should feign themselves just men	Lu 20:20
w. it is not lawful to eat but for the	Lu 6:4	the Pharisees, w. is hypocrisy	Lu 12:1	unto Cæsar the things w. be Cæsar's	Lu 20:25
man w. had the withered hand	Lu 6:8	w. ye have spoken in the ear, in	Lu 12:3	and unto God the things w. be God's	Lu 20:25
Judas Iscariot, w. also was the	Lu 6:16	w. after he hath killed hath power	Lu 12:5	w. deny that there is any	Lu 20:27
w. came to hear him, and to be	Lu 6:17	abundance of the things w. he	Lu 12:15	they w. shall be accounted worthy	Lu 20:35
I say unto you w. hear, Love your	Lu 6:27	things be, w. thou hast provided	Lu 12:20	w. desire to walk in long robes	Lu 20:46
do good to them w. hate you	Lu 6:27	w. neither have storehouse nor	Lu 12:24	W. devour widows' houses	Lu 20:47
for them w. despitefully use you	Lu 6:28	And w. of you with taking thought	Lu 12:25	As for these things w. ye behold	Lu 21:5
if ye love them w. love you what	Lu 6:32	be not able to do that thing w. is	Lu 12:26	in the w. there shall not be left one	Lu 21:6
ye do good to them w. do good to you	Lu 6:33	the grass w. is to-day in the field	Lu 12:28	w. all your adversaries shall not be	Lu 21:15
heart bringeth forth that w. is good	Lu 6:45	yourselves bags w. wax not old	Lu 12:33	them w. are in Judæa flee to	Lu 21:21
heart bringeth forth that w. is evil	Lu 6:45	servant, w. knew his lord's will	Lu 12:47	let them w. are in the midst of it	Lu 21:21
and do not the things w. I say	Lu 6:46	a woman w. had a spirit of infirmity	Lu 13:11	that all things w. are written	Lu 21:22
is like a man w. built a house	Lu 6:48	six days in w. men ought to work	Lu 13:14	those things w. are coming on	Lu 21:26
against w. the stream did beat	Lu 6:49	of mustard seed, w. a man took	Lu 13:19	drew nigh w. is called the Passover	Lu 22:1
they w. are gorgeously apparelled	Lu 7:25	leaven, w. a woman took and hid	Lu 13:21	is my body w. is given for you	Lu 22:19
w. shall prepare the way before	Lu 7:27	there are last w. shall be first	Lu 13:30	in my blood, w. is shed for you	Lu 22:20
woman in the city, w. was a	Lu 7:37	and there are first w. shall be last	Lu 13:30	w. of them it was that should do	Lu 22:23
w. had bidden him saw it, he	Lu 7:39	Jerusalem, w. killest the prophets	Lu 13:34	w. of them should be accounted	Lu 22:24
a certain creditor w. had two debtors	Lu 7:41	man before him w. had the dropsy	Lu 14:2	w. have continued with me in my	Lu 22:28
w. of them will love him most	Lu 7:42	W. of you shall have an ass or	Lu 14:5	w. were about him saw what would	Lu 22:49
Her sins, w. are many, are	Lu 7:47	a parable to those w. were bidden	Lu 14:7	the elders, w. were come to him	Lu 22:52
w. had been healed of evil spirits	Lu 8:2	men w. were bidden shall taste	Lu 14:24	w. also bewailed and lamented	Lu 23:27
w. ministered unto him of their	Lu 8:3	w. of you, intending to build	Lu 14:28	in the w. they shall say, Blessed	Lu 23:29
w. when they hear, receive the	Lu 8:13	go after that w. is lost, until he find	Lu 15:4	and the paps w. never gave suck	Lu 23:29
no root, w. for a while, believe	Lu 8:13	have found my sheep w. was lost	Lu 15:6	to the place w. is called Calvary	Lu 23:33
that w. fell among thorns are they	Lu 8:14	persons w. need no repentance	Lu 15:7	malefactors w. were hanged railed	Lu 23:39
w. when they have heard, go forth	Lu 8:14	have found the piece w. I had lost	Lu 15:9	beholding the things w. were done	Lu 23:48
w. in an honest and good heart	Lu 8:15	w. hath devoured thy living with	Lu 15:30	w. came with him from Galilee	Lu 23:55
they w. enter in may see the light	Lu 8:16	rich man, w. had a steward	Lu 16:1	the spices w. they had prepared	Lu 24:1
even that w. he seemeth to have	Lu 8:18	is faithful in that w. is least	Lu 16:10	w. told these things unto the	Lu 24:10
was told him by certain w. said	Lu 8:20	faithful in that w. is another man's	Lu 16:12	himself at that w. was come to pass	Lu 24:12
these w. hear the word of God	Lu 8:21	shall give you that w. is your own	Lu 16:12	w. was from Jerusalem about	Lu 24:13
w. is over against Galilee	Lu 8:26	they w. justify yourselves before	Lu 16:15	of all these things w. had happened	Lu 24:14
man w. had devils long time	Lu 8:27	for that w. is highly esteemed among	Lu 16:15	known the things w. are come to pass	Lu 24:18
They also w. saw it told them by	Lu 8:36	man w. was clothed in purple	Lu 16:19	w. was a prophet mighty in deed	Lu 24:19
w. had spent all her living upon	Lu 8:43	Lazarus, w. was laid at his gate	Lu 16:20	he w. should have redeemed Israel	Lu 24:21
w. shall not taste of death, till	Lu 9:27	crumbs, w. fell from the rich	Lu 16:21	w. were early at the sepulchre	Lu 24:22
men, w. were Moses and Elias	Lu 9:30	they w. would pass from hence to	Lu 16:26	angels, w. said that he was alive	Lu 24:23
w. he should accomplish at	Lu 9:31	w. of you, having a servant	Lu 17:7	w. were with us went to the sepulchre	Lu 24:24
of those things w. they had seen	Lu 9:36	those things, w. are commanded	Lu 17:10	the words w. I spake unto you	Lu 24:44
every one at all things w. Jesus did	Lu 9:43	done that w. was our duty to do	Lu 17:10	w. were written in the law of	Lu 24:44
w. of them should be greatest	Lu 9:46	that were lepers, w. stood afar off	Lu 17:12	w. lighteth every man that cometh	Joh 1:9
farewell, w. are at home at my	Lu 9:61	he w. shall be upon the housetop	Lu 17:31	W. were born, not of blood, nor of	Joh 1:13
dust of your city, w. cleaveth on	Lu 10:11	a judge, w. feared not God, neither	Lu 18:2		
Sidon, w. have been done in you	Lu 10:13	own elect, w. day and night	Lu 18:7		
w. art exalted to heaven, shalt	Lu 10:15	certain w. trusted in themselves	Lu 18:9		
eyes w. see the things that ye see	Lu 10:23				
desired to see those things w. ye	Lu 10:24				
to hear those things w. ye hear	Lu 10:24				
w. stripped him of his raiment	Lu 10:30				
W. now of these three, thinkest	Lu 10:36				

w. is in the bosom of the Father	Joh 1:18
w. were sent were of the Pharisees	Joh 1:24
w. taketh away the sin of the	Joh 1:29
a man w. is preferred before me	Joh 1:30
he w. baptizeth with the Holy Ghost	Joh 1:33
w. is to say, being interpreted	Joh 1:38
One of the two w. heard John	Joh 1:40
w. is, being interpreted, the Christ	Joh 1:41
w. is by interpretation, A stone	Joh 1:42
servants w. drew the water knew	Joh 2:9
well drunk then that w. is worse	Joh 2:10
and the word w. Jesus had said	Joh 2:22
they saw the miracles w. he did	Joh 2:23
That w. is born of the flesh is flesh	Joh 3:6
that w. is born of the Spirit is spirit	Joh 3:6
the Son of man w. is in heaven	Joh 3:13
w. standeth and heareth him	Joh 3:29
city of Samaria, w. is called Sychar	Joh 4:5
of me, w. am a woman of Samaria	Joh 4:9
Jacob, w. gave us the well	Joh 4:12
Messias cometh, w. is called	Joh 4:25
w. told me all things that ever I	Joh 4:29
w. testified, He told me all that ever	Joh 4:39
in the w. Jesus said unto him	Joh 4:53
w. is called in the Hebrew tongue	Joh 5:2
w. had an infirmity thirty and eight	Joh 5:5
w. said unto thee. Take up thy	Joh 5:12
Jesus, w. had made him whole	Joh 5:15
not the Father w. hath sent him	Joh 5:23
in the w. all that are in the graves	Joh 5:28
will of the Father w. hath sent me	Joh 5:30
witness w. he witnesseth of me is	Joh 5:32
works w. the Father hath given me	Joh 5:36
Father himself, w. hath sent me, hath	Joh 5:37
and they are they w. testify of me	Joh 5:39
w. receive honour one of another, and	Joh 5:44
of Galilee, w. is the sea of Tiberias	Joh 6:1
miracles w. he did on them that	Joh 6:2
lad here, w. hath five barley loaves	Joh 6:9
w. remained over and above unto	Joh 6:13
people w. stood on the other side	Joh 6:22
not for the meat w. perisheth, but	Joh 6:27
meat w. endureth unto everlasting	Joh 6:27
w. the Son of man shall give unto	Joh 6:27
is he w. cometh down from heaven	Joh 6:33
the Father's will w. hath sent me	Joh 6:39
all w. he hath given me I should lose	Joh 6:39
that every one w. seeth the Son	Joh 6:40
bread w. came down from heaven	Joh 6:41
except the Father w. hath sent me	Joh 6:44
save he w. is of God, he hath seen	Joh 6:46
bread w. cometh down from heaven	Joh 6:50
bread w. came down from heaven	Joh 6:51
w. I will give for the life of	Joh 6:51
bread w. came down from heaven	Joh 6:58
than these w. this man hath done	Joh 7:31
w. they that believe on him should	Joh 7:39
And they w. heard it, being convicted	Joh 8:9
those things w. I have heard of him	Joh 8:26
to those Jews w. believed on him	Joh 8:31
I speak that w. I have seen with	Joh 8:38
ye do that w. ye have seen with	Joh 8:38
the truth, w. I have heard of God	Joh 8:40
W. of you convinceth me of sin	Joh 8:46
our father Abraham, w. is dead	Joh 8:53
a man w. was blind from his birth	Joh 9:1
w. is by interpretation, Sent	Joh 9:7
w. before had seen him that he was	Joh 9:8
world, that they w. see not might see	Joh 9:39
that they w. see might be made blind	Joh 9:39
Pharisees w. were with him heard	Joh 9:40
things they were w. he spake	Joh 10:6
sheep I have, w. are not of this fold	Joh 10:16
My Father, w. gave them me, is	Joh 10:29
w. of those works do ye stone me	Joh 10:32
Mary w. anointed the Lord with	Joh 11:2
said Thomas, w. is called Didymus	Joh 11:16
God, w. should come into the world	Joh 11:27
Jews then w. were with her in the	Joh 11:31
Jews also weeping w. came with her	Joh 11:33
w. opened the eyes of the blind	Joh 11:37
because of the people w. stand by I	Joh 11:42
many of the Jews w. came to Mary	Joh 11:45
the things w. Jesus did, believed	Joh 11:45
where Lazarus was w. had been	Joh 12:1
Simon's son, w. should betray him	Joh 12:4
Philip. w. was of Bethsaida of Galilee	Joh 12:21
w. he spake, Lord, who hath	Joh 12:38
but the Father w. sent me, he	Joh 12:49
loved his own w. were in the world	Joh 13:1
the word w. ye hear is not mine	Joh 14:24
mine but the Father's w. sent me	Joh 14:24
the Comforter, w. is the Holy Ghost	Joh 14:26
the word w. I have spoken unto	Joh 15:3
the works w. none other man did	Joh 15:24
w. proceedeth from the Father	Joh 15:26
the work w. thou gavest me to do	Joh 17:4
w. I had with thee before the world	Joh 17:5
men w. thou gavest me out of the	Joh 17:6
them the words w. thou gavest me	Joh 17:8
for them w. thou hast given me	Joh 17:9
w. shall believe on me through their	Joh 17:20
glory w. thou gavest me I have	Joh 17:22
my glory, w. thou hast given me	Joh 17:24
a garden, into the w. he entered	Joh 18:1
Judas also, w. betrayed him, knew	Joh 18:2
w. betrayed him, stood with them	Joh 18:5
might be fulfilled, w. he spake	Joh 18:9
Of them w. thou gavest me have I	Joh 18:9
cup w. my Father hath given me	Joh 18:11
Caiaphas, w. was the high priest	Joh 18:13
he w. gave counsel to the Jews	Joh 18:14
w. was known unto the high priest	Joh 18:16
ask them w. heard me, what I have	Joh 18:21
the officers w. stood by struck Jesus	Joh 18:22
w. he spake signifying what death	Joh 18:32
w. is called in the Hebrew Golgotha	Joh 19:17
w. saith, They parted my raiment	Joh 19:24
the other w. was crucified with him	Joh 19:32
w. at the first came to Jesus by	Joh 19:39
w. came first to the sepulchre	Joh 20:8
him, Rabboni; w. is to say, Master	Joh 20:16
w. are not written in this book	Joh 20:30
of the fish w. ye have now caught	Joh 21:10
w. also leaned on his breast at	Joh 21:20
Lord, w. is he that betrayeth thee	Joh 21:20
w. testifieth of these things	Joh 21:24
many other things w. Jesus did	Joh 21:25
w. if they should be written every	Joh 21:25
the day in w. he was taken up	Ac 1:2
w. saith he, ye have heard of me	Ac 1:4
w. the Father hath put in his own	Ac 1:7
W. also said, Ye men of Galilee	Ac 1:11
w. is taken up from you, into	Ac 1:11
w. is from Jerusalem a sabbath	Ac 1:12
w. the Holy Ghost by the mouth of	Ac 1:16
w. was guide to them that took	Ac 1:16
these men w. have companied with us	Ac 1:21
Lord w. knowest the hearts of all men	Ac 1:24
w. Judas by transgression fell	Ac 1:25
not all these w. speak Galilæans	Ac 2:7
w. was spoken by the prophet Joel	Ac 2:16
w. God did by him in the midst of	Ac 2:22
forth this, w. ye now see and hear	Ac 2:33
the temple w. is called Beautiful	Ac 3:2
he w. sat for alms at the Beautiful	Ac 3:10
at that w. had happened unto him	Ac 3:10
as the lame man w. was healed held	Ac 3:11
the faith w. is by him hath given him	Ac 3:16
w. God before had shewed by	Ac 3:18
w. before was preached unto	Ac 3:20
W. God hath spoken by the mouth	Ac 3:21
soul, w. will not hear that	Ac 3:23
covenant w. God made with our	Ac 3:25
many of them w. heard the word	Ac 4:4
stone w. was set at nought of you	Ac 4:11
w. is become the head of the corner	Ac 4:11
man w. was healed standing with	Ac 4:14
the things w. we have seen and	Ac 4:20

glorified God for that *w*. was done	Ac 4:21
w. hast made heaven, and earth	Ac 4:24
things *w*. he possessed was his own	Ac 4:32
w. is being interpreted, The son	Ac 4:36
feet of them *w*. have buried thy	Ac 5:9
them *w*. were vexed with unclean	Ac 5:16
w. is the sect of the Sadducees	Ac 5:17
w. is called the synagogue of	Ac 6:9
and the spirit by *w*. he spake	Ac 6:10
they suborned men, *w*. said, We have	Ac 6:11
set up false witnesses, *w*. said, This	Ac 6:13
the customs *w*. Moses delivered us	Ac 6:14
into the land *w*. I shall shew thee	Ac 7:3
w. God had sworn to Abraham	Ac 7:17
king arose, *w*. knew not Joseph	Ac 7:18
In *w*. time Moses was born	Ac 7:20
of my people *w*. is in Egypt	Ac 7:34
of the angel *w*. appeared to him in	Ac 7:35
w. said unto the children of Israel	Ac 7:37
angel *w*. spake to him in the mount	Ac 7:38
w. brought us out of the land	Ac 7:40
figures *w*. ye made to worship	Ac 7:43
W. also our fathers that came after	Ac 7:45
W. of the prophets have not your	Ac 7:52
slain them *w*. shewed before of	Ac 7:52
the church *w*. was at Jerusalem	Ac 8:1
unto those things *w*. Philip spake	Ac 8:6
and seeing the miracles *w*. he	Ac 8:6
w. beforetime in the same city used	Ac 8:9
the miracles and signs *w*. were done	Ac 8:13
apostles *w*. were at Jerusalem	Ac 8:14
of these things *w*. ye have spoken	Ac 8:24
Jerusalem unto Gaza, *w*. is desert	Ac 8:26
of the scripture *w*. he read was this	Ac 8:32
men *w*. journeyed with him stood	Ac 9:7
into the street *w*. is called Straight	Ac 9:11
the disciples *w*. were at Damascus	Ac 9:19
them *w*. called on this name	Ac 9:21
the Jews *w*. dwelt at Damascus	Ac 9:22
W. when the brethren knew, they	Ac 9:30
to the saints *w*. dwelt at Lydda	Ac 9:32
w. had kept his bed eight years	Ac 9:33
w. by interpretation is called	Ac 9:36
works and almsdeeds *w*. she did	Ac 9:36
and garments *w*. Dorcas made	Ac 9:39
w. gave much alms to the people	Ac 10:2
the angel *w*. spake unto Cornelius	Ac 10:7
vision *w*. he had seen should mean	Ac 10:17
men *w*. were sent from Cornelius	Ac 10:17
Simon, *w*. was surnamed Peter	Ac 10:18
to the men *w*. were sent unto him	Ac 10:21
word *w*. God sent unto the children	Ac 10:36
w. was published throughout all	Ac 10:37
after the baptism *w*. John	Ac 10:37
things *w*. he did both in the land	Ac 10:39
w. was ordained of God to be	Ac 10:42
fell on all them *w*. heard the word	Ac 10:44
w. believed were astonished	Ac 10:45
w. have received the Holy Ghost	Ac 10:47
the *w*. when I had fastened mine	Ac 11:6
w. stood and said unto him, Send men	Ac 11:13
they *w*. were scattered abroad upon	Ac 11:19
w. when they were come to the church	Ac 11:20
w. was in Jerusalem	Ac 11:22
w. came to pass in the days	Ac 11:28
unto the brethren *w*. dwelt in Judæa	Ac 11:29
W. also they did, and sent it	Ac 11:30
true *w*. was done by the angel	Ac 12:9
w. opened to them of his own	Ac 12:10
w. had been brought up with Herod	Ac 13:1
W. was with the deputy of the	Ac 13:7
heart, *w*. shall fulfill all my will	Ac 13:22
the prophets *w*. are read every	Ac 13:27
of them *w*. came up with him from	Ac 13:31
the promise *w*. was made unto the	Ac 13:32
from *w*. ye could not be justified	Ac 13:39
you *w*. is spoken of in the prophets	Ac 13:40
work *w*. ye shall in no wise believe	Ac 13:41
those things *w*. were spoken by Paul	Ac 13:45
w. gave testimony unto the word	Ac 14:3
of Jupiter, *w*. was before, their city	Ac 14:13
W. when the apostles, Barnabas and	Ac 14:14
the living God, *w*. made heaven	Ac 14:15
God for the work *w*. they fulfilled	Ac 14:26
certain men *w*. came down from	Ac 15:1
the sect of the Pharisees *w*. believed	Ac 15:5
And God, *w*. knoweth the hearts	Ac 15:8
w. neither our fathers nor we	Ac 15:10
of David, *w*. is fallen down	Ac 15:16
w. from among the Gentiles are	Ac 15:19
brethren *w*. are of the Gentiles	Ac 15:23
certain *w*. went out from us have	Ac 15:24
from *w*. if ye keep yourselves, ye	Ac 15:29
W. when they had read, they rejoiced	Ac 15:31
of a certain woman, *w*. was a Jewess	Ac 16:1
W. was well reported of by	Ac 16:2
Jews *w*. were in those quarters	Ac 16:3
and elders *w*. were at Jerusalem	Ac 16:4
w. is the chief city of that part of	Ac 16:12
unto the women *w*. resorted thither	Ac 16:13
Thyatira, *w*. worshipped God, heard	Ac 16:14
the things *w*. were spoken of Paul	Ac 16:14
w. brought her masters much gain	Ac 16:16
God, *w*. shew unto us the way of	Ac 16:17
w. are not lawful for us to receive	Ac 16:21
But the Jews *w*. believed not, moved	Ac 17:5
of honourable women *w*. were	Ac 17:12
strangers *w*. were there, spent	Ac 17:21
in the *w*. he will judge the world	Ac 17:31
among the *w*. was Dionysius	Ac 17:34
much *w*. had believed through grace	Ac 18:27
on him *w*. should come after him	Ac 19:4
they *w*. dwelt in Asia heard the word	Ac 19:10
to call over them *w*. had evil spirits	Ac 19:13
and chief of the priests *w*. did so	Ac 19:14
of them also *w*. used curious arts	Ac 19:19
w. made silver shrines for Diana	Ac 19:24
no gods, *w*. are made with hands	Ac 19:26
chief of Asia, *w*. were his friends, sent	Ac 19:31
the image *w*. fell down from Jupiter	Ac 19:35
w. are neither robbers of churches	Ac 19:37
and the craftsmen *w*. are with him	Ac 19:38
w. befell me by the lying in wait	Ac 20:19
w. I have received of the Lord	Ac 20:24
w. the Holy Ghost hath made you	Ac 20:28
w. he hath purchased with his own	Ac 20:28
grace, *w*. is able to build you up	Ac 20:32
among all them *w*. are sanctified	Ac 20:32
most of all for the words *w*. he	Ac 20:38
evangelist, *w*. was one of the seven	Ac 21:8
daughters, virgins, *w*. did prophesy	Ac 21:9
of Jews there are *w*. believe	Ac 21:20
the Jews *w*. are among the Gentiles	Ac 21:21
four men *w*. have a vow on them	Ac 21:23
As touching the Gentiles *w*. believe	Ac 21:25
the Jews *w*. were of Asia, when they	Ac 21:27
w. before these days madest an	Ac 21:38
I am a man *w*. am a Jew of Tarsus	Ac 21:39
my defence *w*. I make now unto you	Ac 22:1
a man *w*. am a Jew, born in Tarsus	Ac 22:3
bring them *w*. were there bound unto	Ac 22:5
things *w*. are appointed for thee	Ac 22:10
report of all the Jews *w*. dwelt there	Ac 22:12
w. should have examined him	Ac 22:29
forty *w*. had made this conspiracy	Ac 23:13
w. have bound themselves with	Ac 23:21
after the way *w*. they call heresy	Ac 24:14
all things *w*. are written in	Ac 24:14
w. they themselves also allow	Ac 24:15
his wife Drusilla, *w*. was a Jewess	Ac 24:24
w. among you are able, go down	Ac 25:5
Jews *w*. came down from Jerusalem	Ac 25:7
Paul, *w*. they could not prove	Ac 25:7
w. is accused have the accusers face	Ac 25:16
and of one Jesus, *w*. was dead, whom	Ac 25:19
all men *w*. are here present with	Ac 25:24
and questions *w*. are among the Jews	Ac 26:3
w. was at first among mine own	Ac 26:4
W. knew me from the beginning, if	Ac 26:5
w. promise our twelve tribes	Ac 26:7
w. hope's sake, king Agrippa, I am	Ac 26:7
W. thing I also did in Jerusalem	Ac 26:10
me and them *w*. journeyed with me	Ac 26:13
of these things *w*. thou hast seen	Ac 26:16
in the *w*. I will appear unto thee	Ac 26:16
among them *w*. are sanctified by	Ac 26:18
w. the prophets and Moses did say	Ac 26:22
a place *w*. is called The fair havens	Ac 27:8

those things *w.* were spoken of by	Ac 27:11	are not all Israel, *w.* are of Israel	Ro 9:6	*W.* things also we spake, not	1Co 2:13
w. is an haven of Crete, and lieth	Ac 27:12	They *w.* are the children of the flesh	Ro 9:8	the words *w.* man's wisdom teacheth	1Co 2:13
a certain island *w.* is called Clauda	Ac 27:16	*w.* he had afore prepared unto	Ro 9:23	but *w.* the Holy Ghost teacheth	1Co 2:13
W. when they had taken up, they	Ac 27:17	my people, *w.* were not my people	Ro 9:25	to the grace of God *w.* is given	1Co 3:10
into the *w.* they were minded	Ac 27:39	and her beloved, *w.* was not beloved	Ro 9:25	that is laid, *w.* is Jesus Christ	1Co 3:11
w. could swim should cast themselves	Ac 27:43	*w.* followed not righteousness	Ro 9:30	man's work abide *w.* he hath built	1Co 3:14
w. had diseases in the island	Ac 28:9	the righteousness *w.* is of faith	Ro 9:30	of God is holy, *w.* temple ye are	1Co 3:17
w. had wintered in the isle	Ac 28:11	Israel, *w.* followed after the law of	Ro 9:31	of men above that *w.* is written	1Co 4:6
some believed the things *w.* were	Ac 28:24	the righteousness *w.* is of the law	Ro 10:5	of my ways *w.* be in Christ	1Co 4:17
those things *w.* concern the Lord	Ac 28:31	man *w.* doeth those things shall live	Ro 10:5	the speech of them *w.* are puffed up	1Co 4:19
W. he had promised afore by his	Ro 1:2	*w.* is of faith speaketh on this wise	Ro 10:6	that he *w.* is joined to a harlot is one	1Co 6:16
w. was made of the seed of David	Ro 1:3	the word of faith, *w.* we preach	Ro 10:8	of the Holy Ghost *w.* is in you	1Co 6:19
w. may be known of God is manifest	Ro 1:19	away his people *w.* he foreknew	Ro 11:2	*w.* ye have of God, and ye are not	1Co 6:19
into that *w.* is against nature	Ro 1:26	not obtained that *w.* he seeketh	Ro 11:7	and in your spirit, *w.* are God's	1Co 6:20
men working that *w.* is unseemly	Ro 1:27	to emulation them *w.* are my flesh	Ro 11:14	woman *w.* hath an husband that	1Co 7:2
recompence of their error *w.* was	Ro 1:27	on them *w.* fell, severity; but toward	Ro 11:22	upon you, but for that *w.* is comely	1Co 7:35
those things *w.* are not convenient	Ro 1:28	cut out of the olive tree *w.* is wild	Ro 11:24	man see thee *w.* hast knowledge	1Co 8:10
w. commit such things are worthy of	Ro 1:32	*w.* be the natural branches, be graffed	Ro 11:24	conscience of him *w.* is weak be	1Co 8:10
against them *w.* commit such things	Ro 2:2	God *w.* is your reasonable service	Ro 12:1	those things *w.* are offered to idols	1Co 8:10
that judgest them *w.* do such things	Ro 2:3	dissimulation. Abhor that *w.* is evil	Ro 12:9	they *w.* minister about holy things	1Co 9:13
the Gentiles, *w.* have not the law	Ro 2:14	cleave to that *w.* is good	Ro 12:9	and they *w.* wait at the altar are	1Co 9:13
W. shew the work of the law	Ro 2:15	Bless them *w.* persecute you: bless	Ro 12:14	that they *w.* preach the gospel should	1Co 9:14
a light of them *w.* are in darkness	Ro 2:19	do that *w.* is good, and thou shalt	Ro 13:3	that they *w.* run in a race run all	1Co 9:24
w. hast the form of knowledge and of	Ro 2:20	But if thou do that *w.* is evil, be	Ro 13:4	The cup of blessing *w.* we bless	1Co 10:16
Thou therefore *w.* teachest	Ro 2:21	and let not him *w.* eateth not judge	Ro 14:3	bread in. we break, is it not	1Co 10:16
not uncircumcision *w.* is by nature	Ro 2:27	after the things *w.* make for peace	Ro 14:19	not they *w.* eat of the sacrifices	1Co 10:18
he is not a Jew, *w.* is one outwardly	Ro 2:28	in that thing *w.* he alloweth	Ro 14:22	or that *w.* is offered in sacrifice to	1Co 10:19
w. is outward in the flesh	Ro 2:28	in those things *w.* pertain to God	Ro 15:17	that the things *w.* the Gentiles	1Co 10:20
But he is a Jew, *w.* is one inwardly	Ro 2:29	those things *w.* Christ hath not	Ro 15:18	or for that for *w.* I give thanks	1Co 10:30
w. is by faith of Jesus Christ unto all	Ro 3:22	*w.* cause also I have been much	Ro 15:22	they *w.* are approved may be made	1Co 11:19
justifier of him *w.* believeth in Jesus	Ro 3:26	poor saints *w.* are at Jerusalem	Ro 15:26	of the Lord that *w.* also I delivered	1Co 11:23
w. shall justify the circumcision	Ro 3:30	service *w.* I have for Jerusalem	Ro 15:31	same night in *w.* he was betrayed	1Co 11:23
of the faith *w.* he had yet being	Ro 4:11	you Phebe our sister, *w.* is a servant	Ro 16:1	this is my body, *w.* is broken for	1Co 11:24
that faith *w.* he had being yet	Ro 4:12	of the church *w.* is at Cenchrea	Ro 16:1	the same God *w.* worketh all in all	1Co 12:6
For if they *w.* are of the law be heirs	Ro 4:14	Salute them *w.* are of Aristobulus	Ro 16:10	of the body, *w.* seem to be more feeble	1Co 12:22
seed; not to that only *w.* is of the law	Ro 4:16	of Narcissus, *w.* are in the Lord	Ro 16:11	*w.* we think to be less honourable	1Co 12:23
also *w.* is of the faith of Abraham	Ro 4:16	Persis, *w.* laboured much in	Ro 16:12	honor to that part *w.* lacked	1Co 12:24
things *w.* be not as though they were	Ro 4:17	and the brethren *w.* are with them	Ro 16:14	But when that *w.* is perfect is come	1Co 13:10
according to that *w.* was spoken	Ro 4:18	and all the saints *w.* are with them	Ro 16:15	that *w.* is in part shall be done away	1Co 13:10
Holy Ghost, *w.* is given unto us	Ro 5:5	them *w.* cause divisions and offences	Ro 16:17	believe not, but for them *w.* believe	1Co 14:22
w. is by one man Jesus Christ	Ro 5:15	the doctrine *w.* ye have learned	Ro 16:17	the gospel *w.* I preached unto you	1Co 15:1
much more they *w.* receive abundance	Ro 5:17	have you wise unto that *w.* is good	Ro 16:19	*w.* also ye have received, and	1Co 15:1
For the woman *w.* hath an husband is	Ro 7:2	*w.* was kept secret since the world	Ro 16:25	*w.* also ye are saved, if ye keep in	1Co 15:2
sins, *w.* were by the law, did work in	Ro 7:5	the church of God *w.* is at Corinth	1Co 1:2	first of all that *w.* I also received	1Co 15:3
w. was ordained to life, I found to be	Ro 7:10	the grace of God *w.* is given you by	1Co 1:4	his grace *w.* was bestowed upon me	1Co 15:10
that *w.* is good made death unto me	Ro 7:13	by them *w.* are of the house of Chloe	1Co 1:11	but the grace of God *w.* was with me	1Co 15:10
death in me by that *w.* is good	Ro 7:13	unto us *w.* are saved it is the power	1Co 1:18	also *w.* are fallen asleep in Christ are	1Co 15:18
For that *w.* I do I allow not	Ro 7:15	them *w.* are called, both Jews	1Co 1:24	*w.* did put all things under him	1Co 15:27
If then I do that *w.* I would not, I	Ro 7:16	confound the things *w.* are mighty	1Co 1:27	they do *w.* are baptized for the dead	1Co 15:29
but how to perform that *w.* is good I	Ro 7:18	things *w.* are despised, hath God	1Co 1:28	*w.* I have in Christ Jesus our Lord	1Co 15:31
law of sin *w.* is in my members	Ro 7:23	things *w.* are not, to bring to	1Co 1:28	fool, that *w.* thou sowest is not	1Co 15:36
to them *w.* are in Christ Jesus	Ro 8:1	*w.* God ordained before the world	1Co 2:7	And that *w.* thou sowest, thou	1Co 15:37
the glory *w.* shall be revealed	Ro 8:18	*W.* none of the princes of this	1Co 2:8		
w. have the firstfruits of the Spirit	Ro 8:23	things *w.* God hath prepared	1Co 2:9		
with groanings *w.* cannot be uttered	Ro 8:26	the spirit of man *w.* is in him	1Co 2:11		
the love of God, *w.* is in Christ	Ro 8:39	world, but the spirit *w.* is of God	1Co 2:12		

that was not first w. is spiritual — 1Co 15:46
but that w. is natural; and afterward — 1Co 15:46
and afterward that w. is spiritual — 1Co 15:46
w. giveth us the victory through — 1Co 15:57
that w. was lacking on your part they — 1Co 16:17
church of God w. is at Corinth — 2Co 1:1
all the saints w. are in all Achaia — 2Co 1:1
comfort them w. are in any trouble — 2Co 1:4
w. is effectual in the enduring of — 2Co 1:6
same sufferings w. ye also suffer — 2Co 1:6
our trouble w. came to us in Asia — 2Co 1:8
but in God w. raiseth the dead — 2Co 1:9
Now he w. stablisheth us with you in — 2Co 1:21
the same w. is made sorry by me — 2Co 2:2
ye might know the love w. I have — 2Co 2:4
this punishment, w. was inflicted — 2Co 2:6
w. always causeth us to triumph in — 2Co 2:14
not as many, w. corrupt the word of — 2Co 2:17
w. glory was to be done away — 2Co 3:7
w. was made glorious had no glory — 2Co 3:10
that w. is done away was glorious — 2Co 3:11
more than w. remaineth is glorious — 2Co 3:11
as Moses, w. put a veil over his face — 2Co 3:13
to the end of that w. is abolished — 2Co 3:13
w. veil is done away in Christ — 2Co 3:14
the minds of them w. believe not — 2Co 4:4
we w. live are alway delivered — 2Co 4:11
he w. raised up the Lord Jesus shall — 2Co 4:14
For w. cause we faint not — 2Co 4:16
affliction, w. is but for a moment — 2Co 4:17
we look not at the things w. are seen — 2Co 4:18
but at the things w. are not seen — 2Co 4:18
the things w. are seen are temporal — 2Co 4:18
things w. are not seen are eternal — 2Co 4:18
with our house w. is from heaven — 2Co 5:2
them w. glory in appearance — 2Co 5:12
they w. live should not henceforth — 2Co 5:15
unto him w. died for them, and rose — 2Co 5:15
w. I made before Titus, is found a — 2Co 7:14
performance also of that w. ye have — 2Co 8:11
w. but the same earnest care into — 2Co 8:16
w. is administered by us to — 2Co 8:19
abundance w. is administered by us — 2Co 8:20
great confidence w. I have in you — 2Co 8:22
for w. I boast of you to them of — 2Co 9:2
He w. soweth sparingly shall reap — 2Co 9:6
he w. soweth bountifully shall reap — 2Co 9:6
w. causeth us thanksgiving — 2Co 9:11
w. long after you for the exceeding — 2Co 9:14
w. think of us as if we walked — 2Co 10:2
w. the Lord hath given us — 2Co 10:8
rule w. God hath distributed to us — 2Co 10:13
spirit, w. ye have not received — 2Co 11:4

gospel, w. ye have not accepted — 2Co 11:4
for that w. was lacking to me, the — 2Co 11:9
brethren w. came from Macedonia — 2Co 11:9
from them w. desire occasion — 2Co 11:12
That w. I speak, I speak it not — 2Co 11:17
that w. cometh upon me daily, the — 2Co 11:28
glory of the things w. concern mine — 2Co 11:30
Christ w. is blessed for evermore — 2Co 11:31
w. it is not lawful for a man to — 2Co 12:4
above that w. he seeth me to be — 2Co 12:6
bewail many w. have sinned — 2Co 12:21
and lasciviousness w. they have — 2Co 12:21
to them w. heretofore have sinned — 2Co 13:2
w. to you-ward is not weak — 2Co 13:3
that ye should do that w. is honest — 2Co 13:7
the power w. the Lord hath given — 2Co 13:10
And all the brethren w. are with me — Ga 1:2
W. is not another; but there be — Ga 1:7
you than that w. we have preached — Ga 1:8
the gospel w. was preached of me — Ga 1:11
to them w. are apostles before me — Ga 1:17
Now the things w. I write unto — Ga 1:20
of Judæa w. were in Christ — Ga 1:22
he w. persecuted us in times past now — Ga 1:23
the faith w. once he destroyed — Ga 1:23
that gospel, w. I preach among — Ga 2:2
but privately to them w. were of — Ga 2:2
liberty w. we have in Christ Jesus — Ga 2:4
same w. I also was forward to do — Ga 2:10
them w. were of the circumcision — Ga 2:12
again the things w. I destroyed — Ga 2:18
the life w. I now live in the flesh I — Ga 2:20
ye therefore that they w. are of faith — Ga 3:7
So then they w. be of faith are — Ga 3:9
w. are written in the book of — Ga 3:10
And to thy seed, w. is Christ — Ga 3:16
w. was four hundred and thirty years — Ga 3:17
been a law given w. could have — Ga 3:21
faith w. should afterward be revealed — Ga 3:23
unto them w. by nature are no gods — Ga 4:8
my temptation w. was in my flesh ye — Ga 4:14
W. thing are an allegory: for — Ga 4:24
Sinai w. gendereth to bondage — Ga 4:24
to bondage, w. is Agar — Ga 4:24
answereth to Jerusalem, w. now — Ga 4:25
But Jerusalem w. is above is free — Ga 4:26
is free, w. is the mother of us all — Ga 4:26
more children than she w. hath and — Ga 4:27
but faith w. worketh by love — Ga 5:6
were even cut off w. trouble you — Ga 5:12
manifest, w. are these; Adultery — Ga 5:19
of the w. I tell you before, as — Ga 5:21
w. do such thing shall not inherit — Ga 5:21
w. of spiritual, restore such an — Ga 6:1
to the saints w. are at Ephesus — Eph 1:1
good pleasure w. he hath — Eph 1:9
w. are in heaven, and w. are on — Eph 1:10
W. is the earnest of our — Eph 1:14

W. he wrought in Christ, when he — Eph 1:20
world, but also in that w. is to come — Eph 1:21
W. is his body, the fulness of him — Eph 1:23
w. God hath before ordained that — Eph 2:10
w. is called the Circumcision in — Eph 2:11
peace to you w. were far off — Eph 2:17
of God w. is given me to you-ward — Eph 3:2
W. in other ages was not made — Eph 3:5
w. from the beginning of the — Eph 3:9
w. he purposed in Christ Jesus our — Eph 3:11
my tribulations for you, w. is your — Eph 3:13
love of Christ, w. passeth knowledge — Eph 3:19
him in all things w. is the head — Eph 4:15
by that w. every joint supplieth — Eph 4:16
w. is corrupt according to — Eph 4:22
man, w. after God is created in — Eph 4:24
with his hands the thing w. is good — Eph 4:28
w. is good to the use of edifying — Eph 4:29
nor jesting, w. are not convenient — Eph 5:4
things w. are one of them in secret — Eph 5:12
w. is the first commandment — Eph 6:2
of the Spirit, w. is the word of God — Eph 6:17
w. I am an ambassador in bonds — Eph 6:20
in Christ Jesus w. are at Philippi — Ph'p 1:1
w. hath begun a good work in you — Ph'p 1:6
w. are by Jesus Christ, unto — Ph'p 1:11
things w. happened unto me have — Ph'p 1:12
to be with Christ; w. is far better — Ph'p 1:23
w. is to them an evident token of — Ph'p 1:28
the same conflict w. ye saw in me — Ph'p 1:30
you, w. was also in Christ Jesus — Ph'p 2:5
a name w. is above every — Ph'p 2:9
it is God w. worketh in you both — Ph'p 2:13
not the things w. are Jesus Christ's — Ph'p 2:21
w. worship God in the spirit — Ph'p 3:3
the righteousness w. is in the law — Ph'p 3:6
own righteousness w. is of the law — Ph'p 3:9
but that w. is the faith of Christ — Ph'p 3:9
righteousness w. is of God by faith — Ph'p 3:9
that for w. also I am apprehended — Ph'p 3:12
forgetting those things w. are behind — Ph'p 3:13
unto those things w. are before — Ph'p 3:13
and mark them w. walk so as ye — Ph'p 3:17
women, w. laboured with me in — Ph'p 4:3
God, w. passeth all understanding — Ph'p 4:7
things, w. ye have both learned — Ph'p 4:9
through Christ w. strengtheneth you — Ph'p 4:13
the things w. were sent from — Ph'p 4:18
The brethren w. are with me greet — Ph'p 4:21
brethren in Christ w. are at Colosse — Col 1:2
love w. ye have to all the saints — Col 1:4
For the hope w. is laid up for you — Col 1:5
W. is come unto you, as it is in all — Col 1:6

w. hath made us meet to be — Col 1:12
hope of the gospel, w. ye have heard — Col 1:23
w. was preached to every creature — Col 1:23
to every creature w. is under heaven — Col 1:23
that w. is behind of the afflictions of — Col 1:24
his body's sake, w. is the church — Col 1:24
of God w. is given to me for you — Col 1:25
Even the mystery w. hath been — Col 1:26
w. is Christ in you, the hope — Col 1:27
w. worketh in me mightily — Col 1:29
w. is the head of all principality — Col 2:10
against us, w. was contrary to us — Col 2:14
W. are a shadow of things to — Col 2:17
those things w. he hath not seen — Col 2:18
w. all the body by joints and bands — Col 2:19
W. all are to perish with the using — Col 2:22
W. thing have indeed a shew of — Col 2:23
seek those things w. are above — Col 3:1
members w. are upon the earth — Col 3:5
and covetousness, w. is idolatry — Col 3:5
w. things' sake the wrath of God — Col 3:6
the w. ye also walked some — Col 3:7
w. is renewed in knowledge after — Col 3:10
w. is the bond of perfectness — Col 3:14
w. also ye are called in one body — Col 3:15
for the wrong w. he hath done — Col 3:25
unto your servants that w. is just — Col 4:1
Christ, for w. I am also in bonds — Col 4:3
you all things w. are done here — Col 4:9
Jesus, w. is called Justus, who are — Col 4:11
w. have been a comfort unto me — Col 4:11
the brethren w. are in Laodicea — Col 4:15
and the church w. is in his house — Col 4:15
ministry w. thou hast received — Col 4:17
w. is in God the Father, and — 1Th 1:1
w. delivered us from the wrath — 1Th 1:10
but God w. trieth our hearts — 1Th 2:4
the word of God w. ye heard of us — 1Th 2:13
w. effectually worketh also in you — 1Th 2:13
God w. in Judæa are in Christ — 1Th 2:14
that w. is lacking in your faith — 1Th 3:10
the Gentiles w. knew not God — 1Th 4:5
brethren w. are in all Macedonia — 1Th 4:10
concerning them w. are asleep — 1Th 4:13
even as other w. have no hope — 1Th 4:13
them also w. sleep in Jesus will God — 1Th 4:14
w. are alive and remain unto — 1Th 4:15
not prevent them w. are asleep — 1Th 4:15
w. are alive and remain shall be — 1Th 4:17
know them w. labour among you — 1Th 5:12
but ever follow that w. is good — 1Th 5:15
things; hold fast that w. is good — 1Th 5:21
W. is a manifest token of the — 2Th 1:5
of God, for w. ye also suffer — 2Th 1:5
traditions w. ye have been taught — 2Th 2:15
our Father, w. hath loved us — 2Th 2:16
do the things w. we command you — 2Th 3:4
the tradition w. he received of us — 2Th 3:6

there are some w. walk among you — 2Th 3:11
w. is the token in every epistle — 2Th 3:17
Lord Jesus Christ, w. is our hope — 1Ti 1:1
endless genealogies, w. minister — 1Ti 1:4
than godly edifying w. is in faith — 1Ti 1:4
From w. some having served — 1Ti 1:6
w. was committed to my trust — 1Ti 1:11
faith and love w. is in Christ — 1Ti 1:14
to them w. should hereafter believe — 1Ti 1:16
prophecies w. went before on thee — 1Ti 1:18
w. some having put away — 1Ti 1:19
w. becometh women professing — 1Ti 2:10
good report of them w. are without — 1Ti 3:7
in the faith w. is in Christ Jesus — 1Ti 3:13
w. is the church of the living — 1Ti 3:15
w. God hath created to be received — 1Ti 4:3
w. believe and know the truth — 1Ti 4:3
now is, and of that w. is to come — 1Ti 4:8
w. was given thee by prophecy — 1Ti 4:14
speaking things w. they ought not — 1Ti 5:13
to the doctrine w. is according — 1Ti 6:3
w. drown men in destruction — 1Ti 6:9
w. while some coveted after, they — 1Ti 6:10
W. in his times he shall shew — 1Ti 6:15
light w. no man can approach unto — 1Ti 6:16
that w. is committed to thy trust — 1Ti 6:20
W. some professing have erred — 1Ti 6:21
of life w. is in Christ Jesus — 2Ti 1:1
w. dwelt first in thy grandmother — 2Ti 1:5
w. is in thee by the putting on of — 2Ti 1:6
w. was given us in Christ Jesus — 2Ti 1:9
w. cause I also suffer these things — 2Ti 1:12
w. I have committed unto him — 2Ti 1:12
words w. thou hast heard of me — 2Ti 1:13
and love w. is in Christ Jesus — 2Ti 1:13
thing w. was committed unto thee — 2Ti 1:14
the Holy Ghost w. dwelleth in us — 2Ti 1:14
w. are in Asia be turned away — 2Ti 1:15
the salvation w. is in Christ Jesus — 2Ti 2:10
sort are they w. creep into houses — 2Ti 3:6
w. came unto me at Antioch — 2Ti 3:11
thou in the things w. thou hast — 2Ti 3:14
w. are able to make thee wise — 2Ti 3:15
through faith w. is in Christ Jesus — 2Ti 3:15
w. the Lord, the righteous judge — 2Ti 4:8
the truth w. is after godliness — Tit 1:1
w. God, that cannot lie, promised — Tit 1:2
w. is committed unto me — Tit 1:3
teaching things w. they ought not — Tit 1:11
things w. become sound doctrine — Tit 2:1
righteousness w. we have done — Tit 3:5
W. he shed on us abundantly — Tit 3:6
they w. have believed in God might — Tit 3:8
w. thou hast toward the Lord — Ph'm 5
good thing w. is in you in Christ — Ph'm 8
enjoin thee that w. is convenient — Ph'm 8
W. in time past was to thee — Ph'm 11
w. of the angels said he at — Heb 1:5
to w. of the angels said he at any — Heb 1:13
to the things w. we have heard — Heb 2:1
w. at the first began to be spoken — Heb 2:3

for w. cause he is not ashamed — Heb 2:11
children w. God hath given me — Heb 2:13
thing w. were to be spoken after — Heb 3:5
we w. have believed do enter into — Heb 4:3
not an high priest w. cannot be — Heb 4:15
by the things w. he suffered — Heb 5:8
w. be the first principles of — Heb 5:12
earth w. drinketh in the rain that — Heb 6:7
that w. beareth thorns and briers — Heb 6:8
w. ye have shewed toward his — Heb 6:10
in w. it was impossible for God — Heb 6:18
W. hope we have as an anchor of — Heb 6:19
w. entereth into that within the veil — Heb 6:19
of Salem, w. is, King of peace — Heb 7:2
of w. no man gave attendance at — Heb 7:13
of w. tribe Moses spake nothing — Heb 7:14
by the w. we draw nigh unto God — Heb 7:19
men high priests w. have infirmity — Heb 7:28
of the oath, w. was since the law — Heb 7:28
things w. we have spoken this — Heb 8:1
the true tabernacle, w. the Lord — Heb 8:2
w. was established upon better — Heb 8:6
Now that w. decayeth and waxeth — Heb 8:13
the shewbread; w. is called — Heb 9:2
the tabernacle w. is called the — Heb 9:3
W. had the golden censer, and — Heb 9:4
seat; of w. we cannot now speak — Heb 9:5
blood, w. he offered for himself — Heb 9:7
W. was a figure for the time then — Heb 9:9
in w. were offered both gifts — Heb 9:9
W. stood only in meats and — Heb 9:10
they w. are called might receive — Heb 9:15
testament w. God hath enjoined — Heb 9:20
w. are the figures of the true — Heb 9:24
w. they offered year by year — Heb 10:1
w. are offered by the law — Heb 10:8
By the w. will we are sanctified — Heb 10:10
sacrifices, w. can never take away — Heb 10:11
w. he hath consecrated for us — Heb 10:20
w. shall devour the adversaries — Heb 10:27
in w. after ye were illuminated — Heb 10:32
w. hath great recompense of — Heb 10:35
things w. are seen were not made — Heb 11:3
were not made of things w. do appear — Heb 11:3
by w. he obtained witness that he — Heb 11:4
by the w. he condemned the world — Heb 11:7
of the righteousness w. is by faith — Heb 11:7
place w. he should after receive — Heb 11:8
looked for a city w. hath foundations — Heb 11:10
as the sand w. is by the sea shore — Heb 11:12
w. the Egyptians assaying to do — Heb 11:29
the sin w. doth so easily beset us — Heb 12:1
w. speaketh unto you as unto — Heb 12:5
fathers of our flesh w. corrected us — Heb 12:9
unto them w. are exercised thereby — Heb 12:11
lift up the hands w. hang down, and — Heb 12:12

lest that *w.* is lame be   Heb 12:13
turned out of
w. no man shall see the   Heb 12:14
Lord
words, *w.* voice they that   Heb 12:19
had heard
not endure that *w.* was   Heb 12:20
commanded
firstborn, *w.* are written in   Heb 12:23
heaven
those things *w.* cannot be   Heb 12:27
shaken
a kingdom *w.* cannot be   Heb 12:28
moved
and them *w.* suffer adversity,   Heb 13:3
as being
Remember them *w.* have the   Heb 13:7
rule over
w. have not profited them   Heb 13:9
that
right to eat *w.* serve the   Heb 13:10
tabernacle
that *w.* is wellpleasing in   Heb 13:21
his sight
twelve tribes *w.* are scattered   Jas 1:1
w. the Lord hath promised   Jas 1:12
to them
word, *w.* is able to save your   Jas 1:21
souls
w. he hath promised to them   Jas 2:5
that
name by the *w.* ye are called   Jas 2:7
things *w.* are needful to the   Jas 2:16
body
was fulfilled *w.* saith,   Jas 2:23
Abraham
the ships, *w.* though they be so   Jas 3:4
great
w. are made after the   Jas 3:9
similitude
w. is of you kept back by   Jas 5:4
fraud
the cries of them *w.* have   Jas 5:4
reaped are
we count them happy *w.*   Jas 5:11
endure
that he *w.* converteth the   Jas 5:20
sinner from
w. according to his abundant   1Pe 1:3
Of *w.* salvation the prophets   1Pe 1:10
have
Spirit of Christ *w.* was in   1Pe 1:11
them did
w. are now reported unto you   1Pe 1:12
by
w. things the angels desire to   1Pe 1:12
look
But as he *w.* hath called you   1Pe 1:15
is holy
of God, *w.* liveth and abideth   1Pe 1:23
for ever
word *w.* by the gospel is   1Pe 1:25
preached
therefore *w.* believe he is   1Pe 2:7
precious
but unto them *w.* be   1Pe 2:7
disobedient
the stone *w.* the builders   1Pe 2:7
disallowed
to them *w.* stumble at the   1Pe 2:8
word
W. in time past were not a   1Pe 2:10
people
w. had not obtained mercy   1Pe 2:10
lusts, *w.* war against the soul   1Pe 2:11
your good works, *w.* they   1Pe 2:12
shall behold
heart, in that *w.* is not   1Pe 3:4
corruptible
w. is in the sight of God of   1Pe 3:4
great
if ye be followers of that *w.*   1Pe 3:13
is good
By *w.* also he went and   1Pe 3:19
preached
W. sometime were disobedient,   1Pe 3:20
when
as of the ability *w.* God   1Pe 4:11
giveth
the fiery trial *w.* is to try you   1Pe 4:12
The elders *w.* are among you I   1Pe 5:1
exhort
the flock of God *w.* is among   1Pe 5:2
you
this voice *w.* came from   2Pe 1:18
heaven we
w. are greater in power   2Pe 2:11
and might
W. have forsaken the right   2Pe 2:15
way

in both *w.* I stir up your pure   2Pe 3:1
of the words *w.* were spoken   2Pe 3:2
before
heavens and the earth, *w.* are   2Pe 3:7
now
w. the heavens shall pass   2Pe 3:10
in *w.* are some things hard to   2Pe 3:16
be
w. they that are unlearned and   2Pe 3:16
That *w.* was from the   1Jo 1:1
beginning
w. we have heard, *w.* we have   1Jo 1:1
seen
w. we have looked upon, and   1Jo 1:1
life, *w.* was with the Father   1Jo 1:2
That *w.* we have seen and   1Jo 1:3
heard
message *w.* we have heard of   1Jo 1:5
him
w. ye had from the beginning   1Jo 2:7
the word *w.* ye have heard   1Jo 2:7
w. thing is true in him and in   1Jo 2:8
you
in you, *w.* ye have heard   1Jo 2:24
from the
If that *w.* ye have heard from   1Jo 2:24
the
w. ye have received of him   1Jo 2:27
abideth
by the Spirit *w.* he hath given   1Jo 3:24
us
God *w.* he hath testified of his   1Jo 5:9
Son
sin a sin *w.* is not unto death   1Jo 5:16
the truth's sake, *w.* dwelleth in   2Jo 2
us
w. we had from the beginning   2Jo 5
those things *w.* we have wrought   2Jo 8
W. have borne witness of thy   3Jo 6
remember his deeds *w.* he   3Jo 10
doeth
Beloved, follow not that *w.* is   3Jo 11
but that *w.* is good. He that   3Jo 11
doeth
faith *w.* was once delivered   Jude 3
unto the
angels *w.* kept not their first   Jude 6
estate
evil of those things *w.* they   Jude 10
know
w. they have ungodly   Jude 15
committed
w. ungodly sinners have   Jude 15
spoken
the words *w.* were spoken   Jude 17
before
w. God gave unto him, to shew   Re 1:1
thing *w.* must shortly come to   Re 1:1
those things *w.* are written   Re 1:3
therein
the seven churches *w.* are in   Re 1:4
Asia
w. is, and *w.* was and *w.* is to   Re 1:4
come
the seven Spirits, *w.* are before   Re 1:4
and they also *w.* pierced him   Re 1:7
w. is, and *w.* was, and *w.* is to   Re 1:8
come
the seven churches *w.* are in   Re 1:11
Asia
Write the things *w.* thou hast   Re 1:19
seen
hast seen, and the things *w.* are   Re 1:19
the things *w.* shall be hereafter   Re 1:19
w. thou sawest in my right   Re 1:20
hand
w. thou sawest are the seven   Re 1:20
thou canst not bear them *w.* are   Re 2:2
evil
tried *w.* say they are   Re 2:2
apostles
the Nicolaitanes, *w.* I also hate   Re 2:6
w. is in the midst of the   Re 2:7
paradise
first and the last, *w.* was   Re 2:8
dead and
of them *w.* say they are Jews   Re 2:9
those things *w.* thou shalt   Re 2:10
suffer
saith he *w.* hath the sharp   Re 2:12
sword
the Nicolaitanes, *w.* thing I   Re 2:15
hate
w. no man knoweth saving he   Re 2:17
that
Jezebel, *w.* calleth herself a   Re 2:20
he *w.* searcheth the reins and   Re 2:23
w. have not known the depths   Re 2:24
that *w.* ye have already hold   Re 2:25
fast till

and strengthen the things *w.*   Re 3:2
remain
Sardis *w.* have not defiled their   Re 3:4
w. say they are Jews, and are   Re 3:9
not
w. shall come upon all the   Re 3:10
world
hold that fast *w.* thou hast,   Re 3:11
that
of my God, *w.* is new   Re 3:12
Jerusalem
w. cometh down out of heaven   Re 3:12
from
first voice *w.* I heard was as it   Re 4:1
w. said, Come up hither, and I   Re 4:1
will
thee things *w.* must be   Re 4:1
hereafter
w. are the seven Spirits of God   Re 4:5
w. was and is, and is to come   Re 4:8
w. are the seven Spirits of God   Re 5:6
odours, *w.* are the prayers of   Re 5:8
saints
And every creature *w.* is in   Re 5:13
heaven
and for the testimony *w.* they   Re 6:9
held
the number of them *w.* were   Re 7:4
sealed
w. no man could number, of all   Re 7:9
God *w.* sitteth upon the   Re 7:10
throne
w. are arrayed in white robes   Re 7:13
These are they *w.* came out of   Re 7:14
great
For the Lamb *w.* is in the   Re 7:17
midst of
the seven angels *w.* stood   Re 8:2
before
golden altar *w.* was before the   Re 8:3
w. came with the prayers of the   Re 8:4
seven angels *w.* had the seven   Re 8:6
of the creatures *w.* are in the   Re 8:9
sea
three angels *w.* are yet to   Re 8:13
sound
men *w.* have not the seal of God   Re 9:4
w. is the angel of the   Re 9:11
bottomless pit
the golden altar *w.* is before   Re 9:13
God
sixth angel *w.* had the trumpet   Re 9:14
w. are bound in the great river   Re 9:14
w. are prepared for an hour,   Re 9:15
and a
w. issued out of their mouths   Re 9:18
rest of the men *w.* were not   Re 9:20
killed
w. neither can see, nor hear,   Re 9:20
nor
things *w.* the seven thunders   Re 10:4
the angel *w.* I saw stand upon   Re 10:5
sea, and the things *w.* are   Re 10:6
therein
the voice *w.* I heard from   Re 10:8
heaven
book *w.* is open in the hand   Re 10:8
of the
angel *w.* standeth upon the sea   Re 10:8
the court *w.* is without the   Re 11:2
temple
w. spiritually is called Sodom   Re 11:8
fear fell upon them *w.* saw   Re 11:11
them
w. sat before God on their   Re 11:16
seats
w. art, and wast, and art to   Re 11:17
come
destroy them *w.* destroy the   Re 11:18
earth
w. was ready to be delivered   Re 12:4
w. deceiveth the whole world   Re 12:9
w. accused them before our   Re 12:10
God
w. brought for the man child   Re 12:13
the flood *w.* the dragon cast   Re 12:16
out
w. keep the commandments   Re 12:17
of
beast *w.* I saw was like unto a   Re 13:2
dragon *w.* gave power unto the   Re 13:4
and them *w.* dwell therein to   Re 13:12
worship
miracles *w.* he had power to   Re 13:14
w. had the wound by a sword   Re 13:14
w. were redeemed from the   Re 14:3
earth
These are they *w.* are not   Re 14:4
defiled
are they *w.* follow the Lamb   Re 14:4

w. is poured out without mixture   Re 14:10
the dead w. die in the Lord from   Re 14:13
out of the temple w. is in heaven   Re 14:17
from the altar, w. had power over fire   Re 14:18
w. had the mark of the beast   Re 16:2
upon them w. worshipped his image   Re 16:2
O Lord, w. art, and wast, and   Re 16:5
w. hath power over these plagues   Re 16:9
w. go forth unto the kings of the   Re 16:14
seven angels w. had the seven   Re 17:1
w. hath the seven heads and ten   Re 17:7
here is the mind w. hath wisdom   Re 17:9
on w. the woman sitteth   Re 17:9
ten horns w. thou sawest are   Re 17:12
w. have received no kingdom   Re 17:12
The waters w. thou sawest, where   Re 17:15
ten horns w. thou sawest upon   Re 17:16
woman w. thou sawest is that   Re 17:18
w. reigneth over the kings of the   Re 17:18
in the cup w. she hath filled fill to her double   Re 18:6
things w. were dainty and goodly   Re 18:14
w. were made rich by her, shall   Re 18:15
w. did corrupt the earth with her   Re 19:2
they w. are called unto the marriage   Re 19:9
And the armies w. were in heaven   Re 19:14
with w. he deceived them that   Re 19:20
w. sword proceeded out of his   Re 19:21
that old serpent, w. is the Devil   Re 20:2
w. had not worshipped the beast   Re 20:4
nations w. are in the four quarters   Re 20:8
opened, w. in the book of life   Re 20:12
those things w. were written   Re 20:12
gave up the dead w. were in   Re 20:13
gave up the dead w. were in them   Re 20:13
in the lake w. burneth with fire   Re 21:8
brimstone: w. is the second death   Re 21:8
seven angels w. had the seven   Re 21:9
w. are the names of the twelve   Re 21:12
them w. are saved shall walk in   Re 21:24
w. are written in the Lamb's book of   Re 21:27
life, w. bare twelve manner of fruits   Re 22:2
the things w. must shortly be done   Re 22:6
angel w. shewed me these things   Re 22:8
w. keep the sayings of this book   Re 22:9
and he w. is filthy, let him be filthy   Re 22:11
the things w. are written in this book   Re 22:19
He w. testifieth these things saith   Re 22:20

WHILE

W. the earth remaineth, seedtime   Ge 8:22
w. he lingered, the men laid hold   Ge 19:16
from Isaac his son, w. he yet lived   Ge 25:6
w. he yet spake with them, Rachel   Ge 29:9
w. Joseph made himself known unto   Ge 45:1
and wept on his neck a good w.   Ge 46:29
w. my glory passeth by, that I will   Ex 33:22
thee with my hand w. I pass by   Ex 33:22

his face shone w. he talked with him   Ex 34:29
ignorance, w. he doeth somewhat   Le 4:27
the house all the w. that it is shut up   Le 14:46
w. she lieth desolate without them   Le 26:43
w. the flesh was yet between their   Nu 11:33
w. the children of Israel were in the   Nu 15:32
offering, w. I meet the Lord yonder   Nu 23:15
w. he was zealous for my sake among   Nu 25:11
pursue the slayer, w. his heart   De 19:6
w. I am yet alive with you this day   De 31:27
w. the children of Israel wandered   Jos 14:10
And Ehud escaped w. they tarried   J'g 3:26
W. Israel dwelt in Heshbon and her   J'g 11:26
seven days, w. their feast lasted   J'g 14:17
a w. after, in the time of the wheat   J'g 15:1
that beheld w. Samson made sport   J'g 16:27
came w. the flesh was in seething   1Sa 2:13
to pass, w. the ark abode in   1Sa 7:2
but stand thou still a w. that   1Sa 9:27
w. Saul talked unto the priest   1Sa 14:19
w. yet I live shew me the kindness   1Sa 20:14
the w. that David was in the hold   1Sa 22:4
all the w. they were in Carmel   1Sa 25:7
w. we were with them keeping the   1Sa 25:16
the w. he dwelleth in the country   1Sa 27:11
w. there was war between the house   2Sa 3:6
David to eat meat w. it was yet day   2Sa 3:35
house for a great w. to come   2Sa 7:19
w. the child was yet alive, we spake   2Sa 12:18
weep for the child, w. it was alive   2Sa 12:21
W. the child was yet alive, I fasted   2Sa 12:22
w. they were in the way, that tidings   2Sa 13:30
vow w. I abode at Geshur in Syria   2Sa 15:8
from Giloh, w. he offered sacrifices   2Sa 15:12
upon him w. he is weary and weak   2Sa 17:2
w. he was yet alive in the midst of   2Sa 18:14
sustenance w. he lay at Mahanaim   2Sa 19:32
thine enemies, w. they pursue thee   2Sa 24:13
w. thou yet talkest there with   1Ki 1:14
lo, w. she yet talked with the king   1Ki 1:22
w. he yet spake, behold, Jonathan   1Ki 1:42
beside me, w. thine handmaid slept   1Ki 3:20
in the house, w. it was in building   1Ki 6:7
Solomon his father w. he yet lived   1Ki 12:6
after a w. that the brook dried   1Ki 17:7
the mean w. that the heaven was   1Ki 18:45
And w. he yet talked with them   2Ki 6:33
Ziklag, w. he yet kept himself close   1Ch 12:1
servant's house for a great w. to   1Ch 17:17
w. that the sword of thine enemies   1Ch 21:12
Solomon his father w. he yet lived   2Ch 10:6
bars, w. the land is yet before us   2Ch 14:7

Lord is with you, w. ye be with him   2Ch 15:2
w. he was wroth with the priests, the   2Ch 26:19
w. he was yet young, he began   2Ch 34:3
w. they stand by, let them shut   Ne 7:3
w. Mordecai sat in the king's gate   Es 2:21
w. they were yet talking with him   Es 6:14
W. he was yet speaking   Job 1:16; 1:17-18
shall rain it upon him w. he   Job 20:23
is eating
They are exalted for a little w. but   Job 24:24
All the w. my breath is in me   Job 27:3
in pieces, w. there is none to deliver   Ps 7:2
w. they took counsel together against   Ps 31:13
yet a little w. and the wicked shall   Ps 37:10
bridle, w. the wicked is before me   Ps 39:1
me, w. I was musing the fire burned   Ps 39:3
w. they continually say unto me   Ps 42:3
w. they say daily unto me, Where is   Ps 42:10
Though w. he lived he blest his soul   Ps 49:18
Thus will I bless thee w. I live: I will   Ps 63:4
mine eyes fail w. I wait for my God   Ps 69:3
w. their meat was yet in their   Ps 78:30
w. I suffer thy terrors I am distracted   Ps 88:15
to my God w. I have my being   Ps 104:33
W. I live will I praise the Lord: I   Ps 146:2
unto my God w. I have any being   Ps 146:2
W. as yet he had not made the   Pr 8:26
Chasten thy son w. there is hope   Pr 19:18
She riseth also w. it is yet night   Pr 31:15
madness is in their heart w. they live   Ec 9:3
w. the evil days come not, nor   Ec 12:1
W. the sun or the light or the   Ec 12:2
W. the king sitteth at his table   Ca 1:12
For yet a very little w. and   Isa 10:25
w. it is yet in his hand he eateth it   Isa 28:4
Is it not yet a very little w.   Isa 29:17
Seek ye the Lord w. he may be found   Isa 55:6
call ye upon him w. he is near   Isa 55:6
have possessed it but a little w.   Isa 63:18
w. they are yet speaking, I will   Isa 65:24
w. ye look for light, he turn it into   Jer 13:16
is gone down w. it was yet day   Jer 15:9
w. he was yet shut up in the court   Jer 33:1
w. he was shut up in the court of the   Jer 39:15
now w. he was not yet gone back   Jer 40:5
yet a little w. and the time of her   Jer 51:33
w. they sought their meat to   La 1:19
to pass, w. they were slaying them   Eze 9:8
W. the word was in the king's   Da 4:31
for yet a little w. and I will avenge   Ho 1:4
For w. they be folden together as   Na 1:10
w. they are drunken as drunkards   Na 1:10
it is a little w. and I will shake the   Hag 2:6
away w. they stand upon their feet   Zec 14:12
But w. he thought on these things   M't 1:20
W. he spake these things unto them   M't 9:18
W. he yet talked to the people   M't 12:46

in himself, but dureth for a *M't 13:21*
w.
w. men slept his enemy *M't 13:25*
came
Nay; lest w. ye gather up *M't 13:29*
the tares
w. he sent the multitudes *M't 14:22*
away
W. he yet spake, behold, a *M't 17:5*
bright
And w. they abode in *M't 17:22*
Galilee, Jesus
W. the Pharisees were *M't 22:41*
gathered
W. the bridegroom *M't 25:5*
tarried they all
w. they went to buy, the *M't 25:10*
bridegroom
ye here, w. I go and pray *M't 26:36*
yonder
w. he yet spake, lo, Judas, *M't 26:47*
one of the
after a w. came unto him *M't 26:73*
they that
deceiver said, w. he was yet *M't 27:63*
alive
and stole him away w. we *M't 28:13*
slept
rising up a great w. before *M'k 1:35*
day, he
w. the bridegroom is with *M'k 2:19*
W. he yet spake, there came *M'k 5:35*
from
into a desert place, and rest *M'k 6:31*
a w.
w. he sent away the people *M'k 6:45*
and said, w. he taught in *M'k 12:35*
the temple
Sit ye here, w. I shall pray *M'k 14:32*
w. he yet spake cometh *M'k 14:43*
Judas, one of
whether he had been any w. *M'k 15:44*
dead
w. he executed the priest's office *Lu 1:8*
w. they were there, the days *Lu 2:6*
were
w. the bridegroom is with *Lu 5:34*
for a w. believe, and in time *Lu 8:13*
one
W. he yet spake, there cometh *Lu 8:49*
W. he thus spake, there came *Lu 9:34*
a cloud
w. they wondered every one at *Lu 9:43*
all
they had a great w. ago *Lu 10:13*
repented
w. the other is yet a great *Lu 14:32*
way off, he
And he would not for a w.: *Lu 18:4*
but
w. he yet spake, behold a *Lu 22:47*
multitude
And after a little w. another *Lu 22:58*
saw him
w. he yet spake, the cock *Lu 22:60*
crew
w. they communed together *Lu 24:15*
w. he talked with us by the *Lu 24:32*
way
w. he opened to us the *Lu 24:32*
scriptures
w. they yet believed not for *Lu 24:41*
joy, and
w. I was yet with you, that *Lu 24:44*
all things
w. he blessed them, he was *Lu 24:51*
mean w. his disciples prayed *Joh 4:31*
him
but w. I am coming. another *Joh 5:7*
Yet a little w. am I with you *Joh 7:33*
of him that sent me, w. it is *Joh 9:4*
day
Yet a little w. is the light *Joh 12:35*
with you
w. ye have the light, lest *Joh 12:35*
darkness
W. ye have light, believe in *Joh 12:36*
children, yet a little w. I am *Joh 13:33*
with you
Yet a little w. and the world *Joh 14:19*
seeth me
A little w. and ye shall not *Joh 16:16*
see me
again, a little w. and ye *Joh 16:16*
shall see me
A little w. and ye shall not *Joh 16:17*
see me
again, a little w. and ye *Joh 16:17*
shall see me

What is this that he saith, A *Joh 16:18*
little w.
A little w. and ye shall not *Joh 16:19*
see me
again, a little w. and ye *Joh 16:19*
shall see me
W. I was with them in the *Joh 17:12*
world
w. they beheld, he was taken *Ac 1:9*
up
w. they looked stedfastly *Ac 1:10*
toward
Dorcas made, w. she was with *Ac 9:39*
them
but w. they made ready, he *Ac 10:10*
fell into a
w. Peter doubted in himself *Ac 10:17*
what
W. Peter thought on the *Ac 10:19*
vision, the
W. Peter yet spake these *Ac 10:44*
words, the
that a good w. ago God made *Ac 15:7*
w. Paul waited for them at *Ac 17:16*
Athens
this tarried there yet a good *Ac 18:18*
w.
w. Apollos was at Corinth *Ac 19:1*
talked a long w. even till *Ac 20:11*
break of
w. I prayed in the temple, I *Ac 22:17*
was in a
in me, w. I stood before the *Ac 24:20*
council
W. he answered for himself, *Ac 25:8*
neither
w. the day was coming on *Ac 27:33*
but after they had looked a *Ac 28:6*
great w.
their thoughts the mean *Ro 2:15*
w. accusing
w. we were yet sinners, Christ *Ro 5:8*
died for
So then if, w. her husband *Ro 7:3*
liveth, she
For w. one saith, I am of *1Co 3:4*
Paul
eat no flesh w. the world *1Co 8:13*
standeth
I trust to tarry a w. with you *1Co 16:7*
W. we look not at the things *2Co 4:18*
which
w. we seek to be justified by *Ga 2:17*
Christ
in pleasure is dead w. she *1Ti 5:6*
liveth
which w. some coveted *1Ti 6:10*
after, they
daily, w. it is called To-day *Heb 3:13*
W. it is said, To-day if ye *Heb 3:15*
will
w. as the first tabernacle was *Heb 9:8*
yet
at all w. the testator liveth *Heb 9:17*
For yet a little w. and he *Heb 10:37*
that
W. they behold your chaste *1Pe 3:2*
w. the ark was preparing, *1Pe 3:20*
wherein
after that ye have suffered a *1Pe 5:10*
w.
deceivings w. they feast with *2Pe 2:13*
you
W. they promise them liberty, *2Pe 2:19*
they

WHILES

W.: they see vanity unto *Eze 21:29*
thee
w. they divine a lie unto *Eze 21:29*
thee
w. they minister in the gates *Eze 44:17*
of the
Belshazzar, w. he tasted the *Da 5:2*
wine
w. I was speaking and praying *Da 9:20*
Yea, w. I was speaking in *Da 9:21*
prayer
like an oven, w. they lie in *Ho 7:6*
wait
w. thou art in the way with *M't 5:25*
W. it remained, was it not thine *Ac 5:4*
W. by the experiment of this *2Co 9:13*

WHILST

put to death w. it is yet *J'g 6:31*
morning
the work cease, w. I leave it *Ne 6:3*

W. it is yet in his greenness, *Job 8:12*
and not
w. ye searched out what to *Job 32:11*
say
own nets, w. that I withal *Ps 141:10*
escape
W. their children remember *Jer 17:2*
their
w. we are at home in the *2Co 5:6*
body, we
w. he remembereth the *2Co 7:15*
obedience
w. ye were made a *Heb 10:33*
grazing stock both
w. ye became companions *Heb 10:33*
of them

WHIM

wherever the helmsmans w. *Jas 3:4*
determines (B)

WHIP

take and w. him (A)(R) *De 22:18*
A w. for the horse, a bridle *Pr 26:3*
for the
The noise of a w. and the *Na 3:2*
noise of

WHIPPING

after a w. (B) *Lu 23:16; 23:22*

WHIPS

father hath chastised you *1Ki 12:11*
with w.
flogged you with w. (B) *1Ki 12:11; 12:14*
father also chastised you *1Ki 12:14*
with w.
my father chastised you *2Ch 10:11; 10:14*
with w.

WHIRLETH

it w. about continually, and *Ec 1:6*
circles about continually (A) *Ec 1:6*
goes round and round (B)(R) *Ec 1:6*
turneth about continually (E) *Ec 1:6*

WHIRLING

like w. dust (A)(B)(E)(R) *Ps 83:13*
w. storm-clouds (P) *2Pe 2:17*

WHIRLWIND

up Elijah into heaven by a w. *2Ki 2:1*
Elijah went up by a w. into *2Ki 2:11*
heaven
a great w. (A) *Job 1:19*
windstorm, w. (A)(B) *Job 27:20*
Out of the south cometh the *Job 37:9*
w.
Lord answered Job out of the *Job 38:1*
w.
the Lord unto Job out of the *Job 40:6*
w.
shall take them away as with a *Ps 58:9*
w.
your destruction cometh as a *Pr 1:27*
w.
As the w. passeth, so is the *Pr 10:25*
wicked
flint, and their wheels like a *Isa 5:28*
w.
like a rolling thing before the *Isa 17:13*
w.
the w. shall take them away *Isa 40:24*
and the w. shall scatter them *Isa 41:16*
and with his chariots like a *Isa 66:15*
w.
and his chariots shall be as a *Jer 4:13*
w.
a w. of the Lord is gone forth *Jer 23:19*
forth in fury, even a grievous *Jer 23:19*
w.
great w. shall be raised up *Jer 25:32*
from
w. of the Lord goeth forth *Jer 30:23*
with fury
forth with fury, a continuing *Jer 30:23*
w.
a w. came out of the north, a *Eze 1:4*
shall come against him like a *Da 11:40*
w.
wind, and they shall reap the *Ho 8:7*
w.

chaff that is driven with the   *Ho 13:3*
w.
a tempest in the day of the   *Am 1:14*
w.
the Lord hath his way in the   *Na 1:3*
w.
came out as a w. to   *Hab 3:14*
scatter me
But I scattered them with a w.   *Zec 7:14*

WHIRLWINDS

As w. in the south pass   *Isa 21:1*
through
and shall go with w. of the   *Zec 9:14*
south

WHISPER

All that hate me w. together   *Ps 41:7*
and thy speech shall w. out of   *Isa 29:4*
words will w. (B)   *Isa 29:4*

WHISPERED

David saw that his servants   *2Sa 12:19*
w.
much w. discussion (A)(N)   *Joh 7:12*

WHISPERER

and a w. separateth chief   *Pr 16:28*
friends

WHISPERERS

debate, deceit, malignity; w.   *Ro 1:29*

WHISPERING

starting a w. campaign (B)   *Nu 14:36*

WHISPERINGS

w. swellings, tumults   *2Co 12:20*

WHIT

and all the spoil thereof   *De 13:16*
every w.
And Samuel told him every   *1Sa 3:18*
w.
I have made a man every w.   *Joh 7:23*
whole
wash his feet, but is clean   *Joh 13:10*
every w.
not a w. behind the very   *2Co 11:5*
chiefest

WHITE

every one that had some w.   *Ge 30:35*
in it
and pilled w. strakes in them   *Ge 30:37*
w. appear which was in the   *Ge 30:37*
rods
had three w. baskets on my   *Ge 40:16*
head
wine, and his teeth w. with   *Ge 49:12*
milk
and it was like coriander   *Ex 16:31*
seed, w.
the w. owl (S)   *Le 11:17*
the hair in the plague is   *Le 13:3*
turned w.
If the bright spot be w. in the   *Le 13:4*
skin
the hair thereof be not turned   *Le 13:4*
w.
if the rising be w. in the skin   *Le 13:10*
and it have turned the hair   *Le 13:10*
w. and
hath the plague: it is all   *Le 13:13*
turned w.
again and be changed unto w.   *Le 13:16*
if the plague be turned into   *Le 13:17*
w.
place of a boil there be a w.   *Le 13:19*
rising
or a bright spot, w. and   *Le 13:19*
somewhat
and the hair thereof be   *Le 13:20*
turned w.
there be no w. hairs therein   *Le 13:21*
that burneth have a w. bright   *Le 13:24*
spot
spot, somewhat reddish, or w.   *Le 13:24*
in the bright spot be turned   *Le 13:25*
w.
there be no w. hair in the   *Le 13:26*
bright
bright spots, even w. bright   *Le 13:38*
spots

---

skin of their flesh be darkish   *Le 13:39*
w.
or bald forehead, a w.   *Le 13:42*
reddish sore
rising of the sore be w.   *Le 13:43*
reddish in
Miriam became leprous, w.   *Nu 12:10*
as snow
Speak, ye that ride on w. asses   *J'g 5:10*
his presence a leper as w. as   *2Ki 5:27*
snow
brethren, being arrayed in w.   *2Ch 5:12*
linen
Where were w., green, and blue,   *Es 1:6*
and blue, and w., and black,   *Es 1:6*
marble
king in royal apparel of blue   *Es 8:15*
and w.
any taste in the w. of an egg   *Job 6:6*
in it, it was w. as snow is   *Ps 68:14*
Salmon
Let thy garments be always w.   *Ec 9:8*
My beloved is w. and ruddy   *Ca 5:10*
they shall be as w. as snow   *Isa 1:18*
the wine of Helbon, and w.   *Eze 27:18*
wool
whose garment was w. as snow   *Da 7:9*
to purge, and to make them   *Da 11:35*
w.
shall be purified, and made   *Da 12:10*
w. and
the branches thereof are made   *Joe 1:7*
w.
there red horses, speckled, and   *Zec 1:8*
w.
And in the third chariot w.   *Zec 6:3*
horses
and the w. go forth after them   *Zec 6:6*
not make one hair w. or   *M't 5:36*
black
his raiment was w. as the   *M't 17:2*
light
and his raiment w. as snow   *M't 28:3*
shining, exceeding w. as snow   *M'k 9:3*
as no fuller on earth can w.   *M'k 9:3*
them
side, clothed in a long w.   *M'k 16:5*
garment
his raiment was w. and   *Lu 9:29*
glistering
for they are w. already to   *Joh 4:35*
harvest
And seeth two angels in w.   *Joh 20:12*
sitting
two men stood by them in w.   *Ac 1:10*
as w. as snow; and his eyes   *Re 1:14*
His head and his hairs were w.   *Re 1:14*
like
as w. as snow; and his eyes   *Re 1:14*
were as
will give him a w. stone, and   *Re 2:17*
in the
and they shall walk with me in   *Re 3:4*
w.
shall be clothed in w. raiment   *Re 3:5*
w. raiment, that thou mayest   *Re 3:18*
be
sitting, clothed in w. raiment   *Re 4:4*
And I saw, and behold a w.   *Re 6:2*
horse
w. robes were given unto   *Re 6:11*
every one
clothed with w. robes, and   *Re 7:9*
palms
which are arrayed in w. robes   *Re 7:13*
made them w. in the blood of   *Re 7:14*
I looked, and behold a w.   *Re 14:14*
cloud
clothed in pure and w. linen   *Re 15:6*
arrayed in fine linen, clean   *Re 19:8*
and w.
opened and behold a w. horse   *Re 19:11*
followed him upon w. horses   *Re 19:14*
clothed in fine linen, w. and   *Re 19:14*
clean
I saw a great w. throne, and   *Re 20:11*
him

WHITED

for ye are like unto w.   *M't 23:27*
sepulchres
God shall smite thee, thou w.   *Ac 23:3*
wall

WHITER

me and I shall be w. than   *Ps 51:7*
snow
snow, they were w. than milk   *La 4:7*

WHITEWASH

daub it with w. (A)(B)(R)   *Eze 13:10;*
13:11, 14-15; 22:28

WHITHER

camest thou? and w. wilt thou   *Ge 16:8*
go
everyplace w. we shall come   *Ge 20:13*
thee in all places w. thou   *Ge 28:15*
goest
Whoso art thou? and w.   *Ge 32:17*
goest thou
child is not; and I, w. shall I   *Ge 37:30*
go
a place w. he shall flee   *Ex 21:13*
inhabitants of the land w.   *Ex 34:12*
thou
w. I bring you, shall ye not do   *Le 18:3*
w. I bring you to dwell   *Le 20:22*
therein
unto the land w. thou sentest   *Nu 13:27*
us
into the land w. I bring you   *Nu 15:18*
of his refuge, w. he was fled   *Nu 35:25;*
35:26
W. shall we go up? our   *De 1:28*
brethren
unto all the kingdoms w. thou   *De 3:21*
the land w. ye go to possess it   *De 4:5*
w. ye go over to possess it   *De 4:14*
w. the Lord shall lead you   *De 4:27*
the land w. ye go to possess it   *De 6:1*
land w. thou goest to possess   *De 7:1*
the land w. ye go to possess   *De 11:8*
it
w. thou goest in to possess it   *De 11:10*
the land, w. ye go to possess   *De 11:11*
it
land w. thou goest to   *De 11:29*
possess
w. thou goest to possess   *De 12:29*
them
then thou shalt let her go w.   *De 21:14*
she
w. thou shalt go forth   *De 23:12*
abroad
land w. thou goest to   *De 23:20*
possess
w. thou goest to possess it   *De 28:21*
nations w. the Lord shall   *De 28:37*
lead
land w. thou goest to possess   *De 28:63*
w. the Lord thy God hath   *De 30:1;*
30:3
land w. thou goest to possess   *De 30:16*
w. thou passest over Jordan   *De 30:18*
to
w. ye go over Jordan to   *De 31:13*
w. they go to be among them   *De 31:16*
w. ye go over Jordan to   *De 32:47*
possess
in the mount w. thou goest   *De 32:50*
up
out: w. the men went I wot not   *Jos 2:5*
W. goest thou? and whence   *J'g 19:17*
comest
for w. thou goest, I will go   *Ru 1:16*
and to his servant, W. went   *1Sa 10:14*
ye
W. have ye made a road to   *1Sa 27:10*
day
And David said, W. shall I go   *2Sa 2:1*
up
w. shall I cause my shame   *2Sa 13:13*
to go
seeing I go w. I may, return   *2Sa 15:20*
in his court; w. they went   *2Sa 17:18*
down
and go not forth thence any   *1Ki 2:36*
w.
out, and walkest abroad any   *1Ki 2:42*
w.
the land w. they were carried   *1Ki 8:47*
w. my lord hath not sent to   *1Ki 18:10*
shall carry thee w. I know   *1Ki 18:12*
w. he is gone down to   *1Ki 21:18*
possess
he said, Thy servant went no   *2Ki 5:25*
w.
the land w. they are carried   *2Ch 6:37*
w. they have carried them   *2Ch 6:38*
captives
w. he had fled from the   *2Ch 10:2*
presence of
And the rulers knew not w.   *Ne 2:16*
I went

W. the tribes go up, the tribes of	*Ps 122:4*	
W. shall I go from thy spirit	*Ps 139:7*	
or *w*. shall I flee from thy presence	*Ps 139:7*	
in the grave, *w*. thou goest	*Ec 9:10*	
W. is thy beloved gone, O thou	*Ca 6:1*	
w. is thy beloved turned aside	*Ca 6:1*	
w. we flee for help to be	*Isa 20:6*	
places *w*. I have driven them	*Jer 8:3*	
unto thee, *W*. shall we go forth	*Jer 15:2*	
lands *w*. he had driven them	*Jer 16:15*	
Tophet, *w*. the Lord had sent him	*Jer 19:14*	
the place *w*. they have led him	*Jer 22:12*	
countries *w*. I have driven them	*Jer 23:3*	
countries *w*. I had driven them	*Jer 23:8*	
all places *w*. I shall drive them	*Jer 24:9*	
city *w*. I have caused you to	*Jer 29:7*	
the places *w*. I have driven you	*Jer 29:14*	
nations *w*. I have driven them	*Jer 29:18; 30:11*	
w. I have driven them in mine	*Jer 32:37*	
w. it seemeth good and convenient	*Jer 40:4*	
all places *w*. they were driven	*Jer 40:12*	
in the place *w*. ye desire to go	*Jer 42:22*	
nations, *w*. they had been driven	*Jer 43:5*	
Egypt, *w*. ye be gone to dwell	*Jer 44:8*	
in all places *w*. thou goest	*Jer 45:5*	
nations *w*. I have driven them	*Jer 29:18; 30:11*	
nation *w*. the outcasts of Elam	*Jer 49:36*	
w. the spirit was to go, they	*Eze 1:12*	
Gentiles, *w*. I will drive them	*Eze 4:13*	
nations *w*. they shall be carried	*Eze 6:9*	
to the place *w*. the head looked	*Eze 10:11*	
among the heathen *w*. they	*Eze 12:16*	
people *w*. they were scattered	*Eze 29:13*	
unto the heathen, *w*. they went	*Eze 36:20*	
the heathen, *w*. they went	*Eze 36:21; 36:22*	
the heathen, *w*. they be gone	*Eze 37:21*	
live *w*. the river cometh	*Eze 47:9*	
w. thou hast driven them	*Da 9:7*	
the place *w*. ye have sold them	*Joe 3:7*	
Then said I, *W*. goest thou	*Zec 2:2*	
me, *W*. do these bear the ephah	*Zec 5:10*	
place, *w*. he himself would come	*Lu 10:1*	
nigh unto the village, *w*. they went	*Lu 24:28*	
whence it cometh, and *w*. it goeth	*Joh 3:8*	
was at the land *w*. they went	*Joh 6:21*	
W. will he go, that we shall not	*Joh 7:35*	
I know whence I came, and *w*. I go	*Joh 8:14*	
tell whence I come, and *w*. I go	*Joh 8:14*	
sins: *w*. I go, ye cannot come	*Joh 8:21*	
he saith, *W*. I go, ye cannot come	*Joh 8:22*	
darkness knoweth not *w*. he goeth	*Joh 12:35*	
Jews, *W*. I go, ye cannot come	*Joh 13:33*	
said unto him, Lord, *w*. goest thou	*Joh 13:36*	
W. I go, thou canst not follow me	*Joh 13:36*	
w. I go ye know, and the way ye	*Joh 14:4*	
we know not *w*. thou goest	*Joh 14:5*	
of you asketh me, *W*. goest thou	*Joh 16:5*	
temple, *w*. the Jews always resort	*Joh 18:20*	
and walkedst *w*. thou wouldest	*Joh 21:18*	
carry thee *w*. thou wouldest not	*Joh 21:18*	
W. the forerunner is entered	*Heb 6:20*	

went out, not knowing *w*. he went	*Heb 11:8*	
and knoweth not *w*. he goeth	*1Jo 2:11*	

WHITHERSOEVER

mayest prosper *w*. thou goest	*Jos 1:7*	
God is with thee *w*. thou goest	*Jos 1:9*	
w. thou sendest us, we will	*Jos 1:16*	
W. they went out, the hand of	*J'g 2:15*	
w. he turned himself, he vexed	*1Sa 14:47*	
David went out *w*. Saul sent him	*1Sa 18:5*	
Keilah, and went *w*. they could go	*1Sa 23:13*	
was with thee *w*. thou wentest	*2Sa 7:9*	
preserved David *w*. he went	*2Sa 8:6; 8:14*	
w. thou turnest thyself	*1Ki 2:3*	
w. thou shalt send them	*1Ki 8:44*	
he prospered *w*. he went forth	*2Ki 18:7*	
with thee *w*. thou hast walked	*1Ch 17:8*	
preserved David *w*. he went	*1Ch 18:6; 18:13*	
w. the king's commandment	*Es 4:3*	
w. the king's commandment and his	*Es 8:17*	
w. it turneth, it prospereth	*Pr 17:8*	
he turneth it *w*. he will	*Pr 21:1*	
W. the spirit was to go, they	*Eze 1:20*	
or on the left, *w*. thy face is set	*Eze 21:16*	
w. the rivers come	*Eze 47:9*	
will follow thee *w*. thou goest	*M't 8:19*	
And *w*. he entered, into	*M'k 6:56*	
I will follow thee *w*. thou goest	*Lu 9:57*	
me on my journey *w*. I go	*1Co 16:6*	
helm, *w*. the governor listeth	*Jas 3:4*	
follow the Lamb *w*. he goeth	*Re 14:4*	

WHO

W. told thee that thou wast	*Ge 3:11*	
brother's son, *w*. dwelt in Sodom	*Ge 14:12*	
W. would have said unto	*Ge 21:7*	
I wot not *w*. hath done this thing	*Ge 21:26*	
w. was born to Bethuel, son of	*Ge 24:15*	
w. hath left destitute my master	*Ge 24:27*	
Here am I; *w*. art thou, my son	*Ge 27:18*	
said unto him, *W*. art thou	*Ge 27:32*	
Isaac trembled and said, *W*.	*Ge 27:33*	
w. hath withheld from thee	*Ge 30:2*	
and said, *W*. are those with thee	*Ge 33:5*	
w. answered me in the day of my	*Ge 35:3*	
generations of Esau, *w*. is Edom	*Ge 36:1*	
are the sons of Esau, *w*. is Edom	*Ge 36:19*	
Seir, the Horite, *w*. inhabited the land	*Ge 36:20*	
w. smote Midian in the field of Moab	*Ge 36:35*	
The man, *w*. is the lord of the land	*Ge 42:30*	
tell *w*. put our money in our sacks	*Ge 43:22*	
sons, said, *W*. are these	*Ge 48:8*	
Ephraim's head, *w*. was younger	*Ge 48:14*	
old lion; *w*. shall rouse him up	*Ge 49:9*	
God of thy father, *w*. shall help thee	*Ge 49:25*	
w. shall bless thee with blessings of	*Ge 49:25*	
W. made thee a prince and a judge	*Ex 2:14*	
And Moses said unto God, *W*. am I	*Ex 3:11*	
him, *W*. hath made man's mouth	*Ex 4:11*	
or *w*. maketh the dumb, or deaf. or	*Ex 4:11*	
words of the Lord *w*. had sent him	*Ex 4:28*	
And Pharaoh said, *W*. is the Lord	*Ex 5:2*	
Moses and Aaron, *w*. stood in the way	*Ex 5:20*	
me, *w*. am of uncircumcised lips	*Ex 6:12*	

God: but *w*. are they that shall go	*Ex 10:8*	
w. passed over the houses of	*Ex 12:27*	
of Israel *w*. dwelt in Egypt	*Ex 12:40*	
W. is like unto thee, O Lord	*Ex 15:11*	
w. is like thee, glorious in holiness	*Ex 15:11*	
w. hath delivered you out of	*Ex 18:10*	
w. hath delivered the people from	*Ex 18:10*	
w. hath betrothed her to himself	*Ex 21:8*	
said, *W*. is on the Lord's side	*Ex 32:26*	
w. shall offer that which is for the sin	*Le 5:8*	
W. shall offer it before the Lord, and	*Le 12:7*	
as thou valuest it, *w*. art the priest	*Le 27:12*	
law of the Nazarite *w*. hath vowed	*Nu 6:21*	
w. were the princes of the tribes	*Nu 7:2*	
w. were defiled by the dead body of	*Nu 9:6*	
said, *W*. shall give us flesh to eat	*Nu 11:4*	
saying, *W*. shall give us flesh to eat	*Nu 11:18*	
so, *w*. is faithful in all mine house	*Nu 12:7*	
w. returned, and made all	*Nu 14:36*	
the Lord will shew *w*. are his	*Nu 16:5*	
and *w*. is holy; and will cause him	*Nu 16:5*	
w. had fought against the former	*Nu 21:26*	
W. can count the dust of Jacob	*Nu 23:10*	
as a great lion: *w*. shall stir him up	*Nu 24:9*	
w. shall live when God doeth this	*Nu 24:23*	
w. were weeping before the door	*Nu 25:6*	
w. strove against Moses and against	*Nu 26:9*	
w. were fifty and three thousand and	*Nu 26:47*	
w. numbered the children of Israel	*Nu 26:63*	
w. shall ask counsel for him after the	*Nu 27:21*	
war upon them, *w*. went out to battle	*Nu 31:27*	
W. went in the way before you, to	*De 1:33*	
w. shall hear report of thee	*De 2:25*	
w. hath God so nigh unto them	*De 4:7*	
the Amorites, *w*. dwelt at Heshbon	*De 4:46*	
w. are all of us here alive this day	*De 5:3*	
w. is there of all flesh, that hath	*De 5:26*	
W. led thee through that great and	*De 8:15*	
w. brought thee forth water out of	*De 8:15*	
W. fed thee in the wilderness with	*De 8:16*	
W. can stand before the children	*De 9:2*	
it be not known *w*. had slain him	*De 21:1*	
W. shall go up for us to heaven	*De 30:12*	
W. shall go over the sea for us	*De 30:13*	
W. said unto his father and to his	*De 33:9*	
w. rideth upon the heaven in thy	*De 33:26*	
w. is like unto thee, O people	*De 33:29*	
w. is the sword of thy excellency	*De 33:29*	
W. are ye? and from whence	*Jos 9:8*	
the hand of Israel, *w*. smote them	*Jos 11:8*	
of the Amorites, *w*. dwelt in Heshbon	*Jos 12:2*	
w. remained of the remnant of the	*Jos 13:12*	
W. answered, Give me a blessing	*Jos 15:19*	
they *w*. are of Beth-shean and her	*Jos 17:16*	
they *w*. are of the valley of Jezreel	*Jos 17:16*	

w. were of the children of *Jos 21:10*
Levi, had

W. shall go up for us against *J'g 1:1*

w. had seen all the great works *J'g 2:7*

up a deliverer w. delivered *J'g 3:9*
them

thee, O King, w. said, Keep *J'g 3:19*
silence

another, W. hath done this *J'g 6:29*
thing

w. also was gathered after him *J'g 6:35*

Then Jerubbaal, w. is Gideon *J'g 7:1*

w. had delivered them out of *J'g 8:34*
hands

Gaal said, W. is Abimelech *J'g 9:28*
and

w. is Shechem, that we shall *J'g 9:28*

W. is Abimelech, that we *J'g 9:38*
should

w. did with her according to *J'g 11:39*
his vow

said, W. hath done this *J'g 15:6*

w. made thereof a graven *J'g 17:4*
image

one of his sons, w. became his *J'g 17:5*
priest

a young man w. was a Levite *J'g 17:7*

w. when they came to mount *J'g 18:2*

him, W. brought thee hither *J'g 18:3*

father, w. was born unto *J'g 18:29*
Israel

w. took to him a concubine *J'g 19:1*
out of

W. is there among all the *J'g 21:5*
tribes

w. was of the kindred of *Ru 2:3*
Elimelech

w. hath not left off his *Ru 2:20*
kindness to

And he said, W. art thou? *Ru 3:9*

said, W. art thou, my daughter *Ru 3:16*

the Lord, w. shall intreat for *1Sa 2:25*
him

w. shall deliver us out of the *1Sa 4:8*
hand

W. is able to stand before *1Sa 6:20*
this holy

and said, But w. is their *1Sa 10:12*
father

w. himself saved you out of *1Sa 10:19*
all

W. is he that said, Shall Saul *1Sa 11:12*

now and see w. is gone from *1Sa 14:17*
us

w. hath wrought this great *1Sa 14:45*

man, w. is a cunning player *1Sa 16:16*
on harp

be, that the man w. killeth *1Sa 17:25*
him

for w. is this uncircumcised *1Sa 17:26*

David said unto Saul, W. *1Sa 18:18*
am I

to Jonathan, W. shall tell me *1Sa 20:10*

w. is so faithful among all *1Sa 22:14*
thy

is, and w. hath seen him *1Sa 23:22*
there

W. is David? and w. is the *1Sa 25:10*
son of

W. will go down with me to *1Sa 26:6*
Saul to

for w. can stretch forth his *1Sa 26:9*
hand

W. art thou that criest to *1Sa 26:14*
the king

and w. is like to thee in *1Sa 26:15*
Israel

w. hath preserved us, and *1Sa 30:23*
delivered

w. will hearken unto you in *1Sa 30:24*
this

And he said unto me, W. art *2Sa 1:8*
thou

w. clothed you in scarlet, *2Sa 1:24*
with other

w. put on ornaments of gold *2Sa 1:24*

Ish-bosheth, w. lay on a bed at *2Sa 4:5*

w. hath redeemed my soul out *2Sa 4:9*

w. thought that I would have *2Sa 4:10*
given

w. uncovered himself to-day *2Sa 6:20*
in the

W. am I, O Lord God? and *2Sa 7:18*
what is

the captain of their host, w. *2Sa 10:18*
died there

W. smote Abimelech the son *2Sa 11:21*

W. can tell whether God will *2Sa 12:22*
be

W. shall then say, Wherefore *2Sa 16:10*
hast

the Lord, w. is worthy to be *2Sa 22:4*
praised

For w. is God, save the *2Sa 22:32*
Lord

and w. is a rock, save our *2Sa 22:32*
God

the man w. was raised up on *2Sa 23:1*
high

Benaiah w. had done many *2Sa 23:20*
acts

w. shall sit on the throne of *1Ki 1:20;*
                                1:27

and w. hath made me an *1Ki 2:24*
house

w. fell upon two men more *1Ki 2:32*

for w. is able to judge this thy *1Ki 3:9*
so

w. keepest covenant and *1Ki 8:23*
mercy with

W. hast kept with thy servant *1Ki 8:24*

before them w. carried them *1Ki 8:50*
captive

w. brought forth their father's *1Ki 9:9*
out

Jeroboam w. was yet in *1Ki 12:2*
Egypt

w. have spoken to me, *1Ki 12:9*
saying

Adoram, w. was over the *1Ki 12:18*
tribute

w. was disobedient unto the *1Ki 13:26*
word of

David, w. kept my *1Ki 14:8*
commandments

w. followed me with all his *1Ki 14:8*
heart, to

w. shall cut off the house of *1Ki 14:14*

w. did sin, and w. made *1Ki 14:16*
Israel to

w. was of the inhabitants of *1Ki 17:1*
Gilead

w. was plowing with twelve *1Ki 19:19*
yoke

he said, W. shall order the *1Ki 20:14*
battle

the nobles w. were the *1Ki 21:11*
inhabitants

W. shall persuade Ahab *1Ki 22:20*
that he

of Nebat, w. made Israel to *1Ki 22:52*
sin

w. brought the vessels to her *2Ki 4:5*

w. spake when the king came *2Ki 7:17*

Had Zimri peace, w. slew his *2Ki 9:31*
master

and said, W. is on my *2Ki 9:32*
side? w.

slew him: but w. slew all *2Ki 10:9*
these

king of Judah, and said, W. *2Ki 10:13*
are ye

of Nebat, w. made Israel to *2Ki 10:29*
sin

Jeroboam, w. made Israel sin *2Ki 13:6*

son of Nebat, w. made Israel *2Ki 13:11;*
to sin   *14:24*

w. made Israel to sin *2Ki 15:9;*
                        15:18, 24, 28

w. brought you up out of *2Ki 17:36*
the land

W. are they among all the *2Ki 18:35*
gods

sons of Nebat, w. made *2Ki 23:15*
Israel to sin

w. proclaimed these words *2Ki 23:16*

w. transgressed in the thing *1Ch 2:7*

w. had three and twenty cities *1Ch 2:22*
in the

w. had the dominion in *1Ch 4:22*
Moab, and

w. dwelt in Aroer, even unto *1Ch 5:8*
Nebo

the Hagarites, w. fell by their *1Ch 5:10*
hand

Asaph, w. stood on his right *1Ch 6:39*
hand

w. built Beth-horon the *1Ch 7:24*
nether

w. is the father of Birzavith *1Ch 7:31*

and Shamed, w. built Ono *1Ch 8:12*

w. were heads of the fathers *1Ch 8:13*

w. drove way the inhabitants *1Ch 8:13*

w. were carried away to *1Ch 9:1*
Babylon for

W. hitherto waited in the *1Ch 9:18*
king's gate

w. was the firstborn of *1Ch 9:31*
Shallum

w. remaining in the chambers *1Ch 9:33*
were

w. strengthened themselves *1Ch 11:10*
with him

w. was one of the three *1Ch 11:12*
mighties

Benaiah w. had done many *1Ch 11:22*
acts

Amasai, w. was chief of the *1Ch 12:18*
captains

chosen, w. were expressed *1Ch 16:41*
by name

W. am I, O Lord God, and *1Ch 17:16*
what is

w. came and pitched before *1Ch 19:7*
Medeba

Israel w. were clothed in *1Ch 21:16*
sackcloth

to thee, w. shall be a man of *1Ch 22:9*
rest

Mahli came Eleazar, w. had *1Ch 24:28*
no sons

w. should prophesy with *1Ch 25:1*
harps

Jeduthun, w. prophesied with *1Ch 25:3*
a harp

w. with his brethren and sons *1Ch 25:9*

w. was mighty among the *1Ch 27:6*
thirty

w. then is willing to *1Ch 29:5*
consecrate

w. am I, and what is my *1Ch 29:14*
people

for w. can judge this thy *2Ch 1:10*
people

w. is able to build him an *2Ch 2:6*
house

w. am I then, that I should *2Ch 2:6*
build

w. hath given to David the *2Ch 2:12*
king a

w. hath with his hands fulfilled *2Ch 6:4*
that

w. were left after them in the *2Ch 8:8*
land

the son of Nebat, w. was in *2Ch 10:2*
Egypt

w. willingly offered himself *2Ch 17:16*
unto the

W. shall entice Ahab king *2Ch 18:19*

Lord, w. is with you in the *2Ch 19:6*
judgment

w. didst drive out the *2Ch 20:7*
inhabitants of

w. is mentioned in the book *2Ch 20:34*

of Israel w. did very *2Ch 20:35*
wickedly

w. sought the Lord with all *2Ch 22:9*
his

Uzziah, w. was sixteen years *2Ch 26:1*
old

w. had understanding in the *2Ch 26:5*
visions

w. smote him with a great *2Ch 28:5*
slaughter

w. therefore gave them up to *2Ch 30:7*

fountains, w. stopped all the *2Ch 32:4*
fountains

W. was there among all the *2Ch 32:14*
gods

w. sent unto him to enquire *2Ch 32:31*
of the

w. sent you to enquire of *2Ch 34:26*
the Lord

w. is with me, that he *2Ch 35:21*
destroy thee

w. had made him swear by *2Ch 36:13*
God

w. slew their young men *2Ch 36:17*
with the

W. is there among you of *2Ch 36:23;*
all his   *Ezr 1:3*

of the fathers, w. were *Ezr 3:12*
ancient men

W. hath commanded you to *Ezr 5:3*

W. commanded you to build *Ezr 5:9*
this

Chaldean, w. destroyed this *Ezr 5:12*
house

servants, w. desire to fear thy *Ne 1:11*
name

w. also laid the beams thereof *Ne 3:3*

of Mehetabel, w. was shut up *Ne 6:10*

w. is there, that, being as I *Ne 6:11*
am

W. came with Zerubbabel, *Ne 7:7*
Jeshua

the God, w. didst choose *Ne 9:7*
Abram

hand of their enemies, w. vexed them	Ne 9:27
w. saved them out of the hand of their	Ne 9:27
God, w. keepest covenant and mercy	Ne 9:32
like him, w. was beloved of his God	Ne 13:26
W. had been carried away from	Es 2:6
w. had taken her for his daughter	Es 2:15
w. told it unto Esther the queen	Es 2:22
the inner court, w. is not called	Es 4:11
w. knoweth whether thou art	Es 4:14
w. sought to lay hand on the king	Es 6:2
the king said, W. is in the court	Es 6:4
W. is he, and where is he, that	Es 7:5
w. had spoken good for the king	Es 7:9
day, w. are ready to raise up their	Job 3:8
gold, w. filled their houses with silver	Job 3:15
but w. can withhold himself from	Job 4:2
w. ever perished, being innocent	Job 4:7
W. giveth rain upon the earth, and	Job 5:10
w. hath hardened himself against	Job 9:4
taketh away, w. can hinder him	Job 9:12
w. will say unto him, What doest	Job 9:12
w. shall set me a time to plead	Job 9:19
thereof; if not, where, and w. is he	Job 9:24
together, then w. can hinder him	Job 11:10
w. knoweth not such things as that	Job 12:3
w. calleth upon God, and he	Job 12:4
W. knoweth not in all these that	Job 12:9
W. is he that will plead with me	Job 13:19
W. can bring a clean thing out of	Job 14:4
me in his wrath. w. hateth me	Job 16:9
w. is he that will strike hands	Job 17:3
as for my hope, w. shall see it	Job 17:15
W. shall declare his way to his	Job 21:31
w. shall repay him what he hath	Job 21:31
one mind, and w. can turn him	Job 23:13
so now, w. will make me a liar	Job 24:21
of his power w. can understand	Job 26:14
w. hath taken away my judgment	Job 27:2
the Almighty, w. hath vexed my soul	Job 27:2
W. cut up mallows by the bushes	Job 30:4
w. drinketh up scorning like water	Job 34:7
W. hath given him a charge over	Job 34:13
w. hath disposed the whole world	Job 34:13
w. then can make trouble	Job 34:29
his face, w. then can behold him	Job 34:29
maker, w. giveth songs in the night	Job 35:10
W. teacheth us more than the beasts	Job 35:11
his power: w. teacheth like him	Job 36:22
W. hath enjoined him his way	Job 36:23
or w. can say, Thou hast wrought	Job 36:23
W. is this that darkeneth counsel	Job 38:2
W. hath laid the measures thereof	Job 38:5
w. hath stretched the line upon it	Job 38:5
or w. laid the corner stone thereof	Job 38:6

Or w. shut up the sea with doors	Job 38:8
W. hath divided a watercourse	Job 38:25
w. hath begotten the drops of dew	Job 38:28
of heaven, w. hath gendered it	Job 38:29
W. hath put wisdom in the inward	Job 38:36
or w. hath given understanding to	Job 38:36
W. can number the clouds in	Job 38:37
w. can stay the bottles of heaven	Job 38:37
W. provideth for the raven his	Job 38:41
W. hath sent out the wild ass free	Job 39:5
w. hath loosed the bands of	Job 39:5
w. then is able to stand before me	Job 41:10
W. hath prevented me, that I	Job 41:11
W. can discover the face of his	Job 41:13
w. can come to him with his double	Job 41:13
W. can open the doors of his face	Job 41:14
not his like, w. is made without fear	Job 41:33
W. is he that hideth counsel	Job 42:3
say W. will shew us any good	Ps 4:6
grave w. shall give thee thanks	Ps 6:5
w. hast set thy glory above the	Ps 8:1
W. have said, With our tongue will	Ps 12:4
are our own: w. is lord over us	Ps 12:4
w. eat up my people as they eat	Ps 14:4
w. shall abide in thy tabernacle	Ps 15:1
w. shall dwell in thy holy hill	Ps 15:1
Lord, w. hath given me counsel	Ps 16:7
enemies, w. compass me about	Ps 17:9
w. spake unto the Lord the	Ps 18 title
the Lord w. is worthy to be praised	Ps 18:3
For w. is God save the Lord	Ps 18:31
or w. is a rock save our God	Ps 18:31
W. can understand his errors	Ps 19:12
W. shall ascend into the hill of	Ps 24:3
w. shall stand in his holy place	Ps 24:3
w. hath not lifted up his soul unto	Ps 24:4
W. is this King of glory	Ps 24:8; 24:10
w. drove him away, and he departed	Ps 34 title
say, Lord w. is like unto thee	Ps 35:10
of him w. prospereth in his way	Ps 37:7
the man w. bringeth wicked devices	Ps 37:7
knoweth not w. shall gather	Ps 39:6
w. is the health of my countenance	Ps 42:11; 43:5
w. eat up my people as they eat	Ps 53:4
lips: for w. say they, doth hear	Ps 59:7
W. will bring me into the strong	Ps 60:9
city? W. will lead me into Edom	Ps 60:9
W. whet their tongue like a sword	Ps 64:3
they say, W. shall see them	Ps 64:5
w. art the confidence of all the ends of	Ps 65:5
w. daily loadeth us with benefits	Ps 68:19
high, w. hast done great things	Ps 71:19
O God, w. is like unto thee	Ps 71:19
w. only doeth wondrous things	Ps 72:18
the ungodly, w. prosper in the world	Ps 73:12
w. may stand in thy sight when	Ps 76:7
w. is so great a God as our God	Ps 77:13
w. should arise and declare them to	Ps 78:6
W. said, Let us take to ourselves	Ps 83:12

W. passing through the valley of	Ps 84:6
w. in the heaven can be compared	Ps 89:6
w. among the sons of the mighty can	Ps 89:6
w. is a strong Lord like unto thee	Ps 89:8
W. knoweth the power of thine	Ps 90:11
W. will rise up for me against the	Ps 94:16
w. will stand up for me against the	Ps 94:16
W. forgiveth all thine iniquities	Ps 103:3
iniquities; w. healeth all thy diseases	Ps 103:3
W. redeemeth thy life from	Ps 103:4
w. crowneth thee with lovingkindness	Ps 103:4
W. satisfieth thy mouth with good	Ps 103:5
W. coverest thyself with light as with	Ps 104:2
w. stretchest out the heavens like a	Ps 104:2
W. layeth the beams of his chambers	Ps 104:3
w. maketh the clouds his chariot	Ps 104:3
w. walketh upon the wings of	Ps 104:3
W. maketh his angels spirits;	Ps 104:4
his	
W. laid the foundations of the earth	Ps 104:5
Joseph, w. was sold for a servant	Ps 105:17
W. can utter the mighty acts of	Ps 106:2
w. can shew forth all his praise	Ps 106:2
W. will bring me into the strong	Ps 108:10
city? w. will lead me into Edom	Ps 108:10
not thou, O God, w. hast cast us off	Ps 108:11
W. is like unto the Lord our God	Ps 113:5
Lord our God, w. dwelleth on high	Ps 113:5
W. humbleth himself to behold the	Ps 113:6
way, w. walk in the law of the Lord	Ps 119:1
servant, w. is devoted to thy fear	Ps 119:38
been the Lord w. was on our side	Ps 124:1; 124:2
w. hath not given us as a prey to their	Ps 124:6
the Lord, w. made heaven and earth	Ps 124:8
iniquities, O Lord, w. shall stand	Ps 130:3
W. smote the firstborn of Egypt, both	Ps 135:8
W. sent tokens and wonders into the	Ps 135:9
W. smote great nations, and slew	Ps 135:10
To him w. alone doeth great wonders	Ps 136:4
W. remembered us in our low estate	Ps 136:23
W. giveth food to all flesh: for his	Ps 136:25
w. said, Rase it, rase it, even to the	Ps 137:7
of Babylon, w. art to be destroyed	Ps 137:8
w. have purposed to overthrow my	Ps 140:4
w. subdueth my people under me	Ps 144:2
w. delivereth David his servant from	Ps 144:10
W. covereth the heaven with clouds	Ps 147:8
w. prepareth rain for the earth	Ps 147:8
w. maketh grass to grow upon the	Ps 147:8
w. can stand before his cold	Ps 147:17
W. leave the paths of uprightness	Pr 2:13
W. rejoice to do evil, and delight in	Pr 2:14

passengers w. go right on their ways	Pr 9:15
a wounded spirit w. can bear	Pr 18:14
but a faithful man w. can find	Pr 20:6
W. can say, I have made my heart	Pr 20:9
man w. devoureth that which is holy	Pr 20:25
his name w. dealeth in proud wrath	Pr 21:24
W. hath woe? w. hath sorrow	Pr 23:29
w. hath contentions? w. hath	Pr 23:29
w. hath wounds without cause	Pr 23:29
w. hath redness of eyes	Pr 23:29
w. knoweth the ruin of them both	Pr 24:22
As a mad man w. casteth firebrands	Pr 26:18
w. is able to stand before envy	Pr 27:4
W. hath ascended up into heaven	Pr 30:4
w. hath gathered the wind in his	Pr 30:4
w. hath bound the waters in a	Pr 30:4
w. hath established all the ends of	Pr 30:4
thee, and say, W. is the Lord	Pr 30:9
W. can find a virtuous woman	Pr 31:10
And w. knoweth whether he shall	Ec 2:19
w. can eat, or w. else can hasten	Ec 2:25
w. knoweth the spirit of man that	Ec 3:21
w. shall bring him to see what shall	Ec 3:22
w. hath not seen the evil work	Ec 4:3
w. will no more be admonished	Ec 4:13
w. knoweth what is good for man	Ec 6:12
for w. can tell a man what shall be	Ec 6:12
for w. can make that straight	Ec 7:13
exceeding deep, w. can find it out	Ec 7:24
W. is as the wise man? and	Ec 8:1
w. knoweth the interpretation of a	Ec 8:1
w. may say unto him, What doest	Ec 8:4
w. can tell him when it shall be	Ec 8:7
w. had come and gone from the place	Ec 8:10
be after him, w. can tell him	Ec 10:14
the works of God w. maketh all	Ec 11:5
shall return unto God w. gave	Ec 12:7
W. is this that cometh out of	Ca 3:6
W. is she that looketh forth as	Ca 6:10
the mother's house, w. would instruct me	Ca 8:2
W. is this that cometh up from	Ca 8:5
w. hath required this at your	Isa 1:12
shall I send, and w. will go for us	Isa 6:8
He w. smote the people in wrath	Isa 14:6
purposed, and w. shall disannul it	Isa 14:27
out and w. shall turn it back	Isa 14:27
W. hath taken this counsel against	Isa 23:8
w. fleeth from the noise of the fear	Isa 24:18
w. would set the briers and thorns	Isa 27:4
W. seeth us? and w. knoweth us	Isa 29:15
the Lord, w. redeemed Abraham	Isa 29:22
W. among us shall dwell with the	Isa 33:14
w. among us shall dwell with	Isa 33:14
W. are they among all the gods of	Isa 36:20
w. was over the household	Isa 37:2
W. hath measured the waters	Isa 40:12
W. hath directed the spirit of	Isa 40:13
w. instructed him, and taught him in	Isa 40:14
and behold w. hath created these	Isa 40:26
W. raised up the righteous man	Isa 41:2

W. hath wrought and done it	Isa 41:4
W. hath declared from the	Isa 41:26
W. is blind, but my servant	Isa 42:19
W. is blind, but my servant? perfect	Isa 42:19
W. among you will give ear	Isa 42:23
w. will hearken and hear for the time	Isa 42:23
W. gave Jacob for a spoil	Isa 42:24
w. among them can declare this	Isa 43:9
I will work, and w. shall let	Isa 43:13
And w. as I, shall call, and shall	Isa 44:7
W. hath formed a god, or molten	Isa 44:10
w. hath declared this from ancient	Isa 45:21
w. hath told it from that time	Isa 45:21
W. hath begotten me these	Isa 49:21
w. will contend with me? let us	Isa 50:8
w. is mine adversary? let him come	Isa 50:8
w. is he that shall condemn me	Isa 50:9
W. is among you that feareth	Isa 50:10
w. art thou, that thou shouldest be	Isa 51:12
thee; w. shall be sorry for thee	Isa 51:19
W. hath believed our report	Isa 53:1
w. shall declare his generation	Isa 53:8
W. are these that fly as a cloud	Isa 60:8
W. is this that cometh from Edom	Isa 63:1
That w. blesseth himself in the	Isa 65:16
W. hath heard such a thing	Isa 66:8
w. hath seen such things? Shall	Isa 66:8
w. have forsaken me, and have	Jer 1:16
occasion w. can turn her away	Jer 2:24
W. is the wise man, that may	Jer 9:12
w. is he to whom the mouth of	Jer 9:12
W. should not fear thee, O king	Jer 10:7
For w. shall have pity upon thee	Jer 15:5
or w. shall bemoan thee	Jer 15:5
or w. shall go aside to ask how thou	Jer 15:5
desperately wicked: w. can know	Jer 17:9
w. hath heard such things	Jer 18:13
w. was also chief governor in	Jer 20:1
w. brought tidings to my father	Jer 20:15
W. shall come down against us	Jer 21:13
w. shall enter into our habitations	Jer 21:13
w. hath stood in the counsel of the	Jer 23:18
w. hath marked his word	Jer 23:18
w. prophesied against this city and	Jer 26:20
w. slew him with the sword, and cast	Jer 26:23
w. is this that engaged his heart	Jer 30:21
w. wrote therein from the mouth of	Jer 36:32
W. is this that cometh up as a	Jer 46:7
saying, W. shall come unto me	Jer 49:4
and w. is a chosen man, that I may	Jer 49:19
w. is like me? and w. will appoint	Jer 49:19
w. is that shepherd that will stand	Jer 49:19
and w. is a chosen man, that I may	Jer 50:44
w. is like me? and w. will appoint	Jer 50:44
w. is that shepherd that will stand	Jer 50:44
w. mustered the people of the land	Jer 52:25
like the sea: w. can heal thee	La 2:13
W. is he that saith, and it cometh	La 3:37
with linen: w. took it, and went out	Eze 10:7
w. hath appointed your meat and	Da 1:10
w. hast given me wisdom and	Da 2:23
w. is that God that shall deliver	Da 3:15

w. hath sent his angel, and	Da 3:28
w. hath delivered Daniel from	Da 6:27
w. look to other gods, and love	Ho 3:1
w. ceaseth from raising after he hath	Ho 7:4
W. is wise, and he shall	Ho 14:9
very terrible; and w. can abide it	Joe 2:11
W. knoweth if he will return	Joe 2:14
w. was among the herdmen of	Am 1:1
lion hath roared, w. will not fear	Am 3:8
hath spoken, w. can but prophesy	Am 3:8
w. store up violence and robbery in	Am 3:10
Ye w. turn judgment to wormwood	Am 5:7
W. shall bring me down to the	Ob 3
W. can tell if God will turn	Jon 3:9
W. hate the good, and love the evil	Mic 3:2
w. pluck off their skin from off	Mic 3:2
W. also eat the flesh of my people	Mic 3:3
w. if he go through, both treadeth	Mic 5:8
the rod, and w. hath appointed it	Mic 6:9
W. is a God like unto thee, that	Mic 7:18
W. can stand before his	Na 1:6
w. can abide in the fierceness of his	Na 1:6
is laid waste; w. will bemoan her	Na 3:7
w. enlargeth his desire as hell	Hab 2:5
the solemn assembly, w. are of the	Zep 3:18
W. is left among you that saw	Hag 2:3
W. art thou, O great mountain	Zec 4:7
w. hath despised the day of small	Zec 4:10
W. is there even among you that	Mal 1:10
But w. may abide the day of his	Mal 3:2
w. shall stand when he appeareth	Mal 3:2
born Jesus, w. is called Christ	M't 1:16
w. hath warned you to flee from	M't 3:7
first, Simon, w. is called Peter	M't 10:2
Judas Iscariot, w. also betrayed	M't 10:4
enter, enquire w. in it is worthy	M't 10:11
said unto him, W. is my mother	M't 12:48
and w. are my brethren	M't 12:48
W. hath ears to hear, let him	M't 13:9; 13:43
all w. act wickedly (A)(N)	M't 13:41
W. when he had found one pearl	M't 13:46
W. is the greatest in the kingdom	M't 18:1
saying, W. then can be saved	M't 19:25
city was moved, saying, W. is this	M't 21:10
and w. gave thee this authority	M't 21:23
W. then is a faithful and wise	M't 24:45
w. called his own servants	M't 25:14
priest, w. was called Caiaphas	M't 26:3
Christ, W. is he that smote thee	M't 26:68
w. himself was Jesus' disciple	M't 27:57
w. also were in the ship mending	M'k 1:19
I know thee w. thou art, the Holy	M'k 1:24
w. can forgive sins but God only	M'k 2:7
W. is my mother, or my brethren	M'k 3:33
when they have heard the	M'k 4:16
W. had his dwelling among the	M'k 5:3
and said, W. touched my clothes	M'k 5:30
and sayest thou, W. touched me	M'k 5:31
w. should be the greatest	M'k 9:34
themselves, W. then can be saved	M'k 10:26

w. gave thee this authority to do — M'k 11:28
w. left his house, and gave authority — M'k 13:34
w. had committed murder in — M'k 15:7
one Simon a Cyrenian, w. passed — M'k 15:21
W. also, when he was in Galilee — M'k 15:41
W. shall roll us away the stone — M'k 16:3
with her, w. was called barren — Lu 1:36
w. hath warned you to flee from — Lu 3:7
I know thee w. thou art; the Holy — Lu 4:34
w. seeing Jesus fell on his face — Lu 5:12
saying, W. is this which speaketh — Lu 5:21
W. can forgive sins, but God alone — Lu 5:21
servant, w. was dear unto him — Lu 7:2
w. and what manner of woman — Lu 7:39
W. is this that forgiveth sins also — Lu 7:49
And Jesus said, W. touched me — Lu 8:45
and sayest thou, W. touched me — Lu 8:45
but w. is this, of whom I hear such — Lu 9:9
W. appeared in glory, and spake — Lu 9:31
no man knoweth w. the Son is — Lu 10:22
and w. the Father is, but the Son — Lu 10:22
Jesus. And w. is my neighbour — Lu 10:29
w. made me a judge or a divider — Lu 12:14
W. then is that faithful and wise — Lu 12:42
w. will commit to your trust — Lu 16:11
w. shall give you that which is your — Lu 16:12
the Pharisees also, w. were covetous — Lu 16:14
it said, W. then can be saved — Lu 18:26
W. shall not receive manifold — Lu 18:30
he sought to see Jesus w. he was — Lu 19:3
or w. is he that gave thee this — Lu 20:2
Prophesy, w. is it that smote thee — Lu 22:64
w. himself also was at Jerusalem — Lu 23:7
W. for a certain sedition made in — Lu 23:19
w. also himself waited for the — Lu 23:51
to ask him, W. art thou — Joh 1:19
said they unto them, W. art thou — Joh 1:22
w. coming after me is preferred — Joh 1:27
and w. it is that saith to thee — Joh 4:10
that was healed wist not w. it was — Joh 5:13
is an hard saying; w. can hear it — Joh 6:60
w. they were that believed not — Joh 6:64
and w. should betray him — Joh 6:64
a devil: w. goeth about to ki!l thee — Joh 7:20
people w. knoweth not the law — Joh 7:49
said they unto him, W. art thou — Joh 8:25
w. did sin, this man, or his parents — Joh 9:2
son, w. ye say was born blind — Joh 9:19
w. hath opened his eyes, we know — Joh 9:21
W. is he, Lord, that I might — Joh 9:36
be lifted up? w. is this Son of man — Joh 12:34
Lord, w. hath believed our report — Joh 12:38
he knew w. should betray him — Joh 13:11
w. it should be of whom he spake — Joh 13:24
saith unto him, Lord, w. is it — Joh 13:25
w. had made a fire of coals; for it — Joh 18:18
durst ask him, W. art thou — Joh 21:12
w. was surnamed Justus, and — Ac 1:23
W. seeing Peter and John about — Ac 3:3

W. by the mouth of thy servant — Ac 4:25
w. by the apostles was surnamed — Ac 4:36
rose up Theudas, w. was slain — Ac 5:36
W. made thee a ruler and a judge — Ac 7:27; 7:35
w. received the lively oracles to — Ac 7:38
W. found favour before God — Ac 7:46
W. have received the law by the — Ac 7:53
W. when they were come down — Ac 8:15
w. had the charge of all her — Ac 8:27
w. shall declare his generation — Ac 8:33
And he said, W. art thou, Lord — Ac 9:5
w. when he cometh, shall speak — Ac 10:32
w. went about doing good — Ac 10:38
w. did eat and drink with him — Ac 10:41
W. shall tell thee words, whereby — Ac 11:14
w. believed on the Lord Jesus — Ac 11:17
W. when he came, and had seen — Ac 11:23
w. called for Barnabas and Saul — Ac 13:7
Then Saul, w. is also called Paul — Ac 13:9
w. are his witnesses unto the — Ac 13:31
w. speaking to them, persuaded — Ac 13:43
a cripple w. never had walked — Ac 14:8
w. stedfastly beholding him and — Ac 14:9
W. in times past suffered all nations — Ac 14:16
w. persuaded the people, and — Ac 14:19
Lord, w. doeth all these things — Ac 15:17
w. shall also tell you the same — Ac 15:27
w. departed from them from — Ac 15:38
W. having received such a — Ac 16:24
w. coming thither went into — Ac 17:10
w. when he was come, helped — Ac 18:27
and Paul I know; but w. are ye — Ac 19:15
w. said to Paul through the — Ac 21:4
W. immediately took soldiers — Ac 21:32
demanded w. he was and what — Ac 21:33
W. said, Canst thou speak Greek — Ac 21:37
I answered, W. art thou, Lord — Ac 22:8
w. hath something to say unto thee — Ac 23:18
W. when they came to Caesarea — Ac 23:33
w. informed the governor against — Ac 24:1
W. also hath gone about to — Ac 24:6
W. ought to have been here before — Ac 24:19
And I said, W. art thou, Lord — Ac 26:15
w. received us, and lodged us — Ac 28:7
W. also honoured us with many — Ac 28:10
W. when they had examined me — Ac 28:18
w. hold truth in unrighteousness — Ro 1:18
W. changed the truth of God into — Ro 1:25
the Creator, w. is blessed for ever — Ro 1:25
W. knowing the judgment of God — Ro 1:32
W. will render to every man — Ro 2:6
To them w. by patient continuance — Ro 2:7
w. by the letter and circumcision — Ro 2:27
unrighteous w. taketh vengeance — Ro 3:5
it saith to them w. are under the law — Ro 3:19
w. are not of the circumcision — Ro 4:12
w. also walk in the steps of that — Ro 4:12
of Abraham; w. is father of us all — Ro 4:16
God, w. quickeneth the dead — Ro 4:17
W. against hope believed in hope — Ro 4:18
W. was delivered for our offences — Ro 4:25

w. is the figure of him that is — Ro 5:14
to him w. is raised from the dead — Ro 7:4
w. shall deliver me from the body — Ro 7:24
w. walk not after the flesh, but after — Ro 8:1; 8:4
w. hath subjected the same in hope — Ro 8:20
w. are the called according to his — Ro 8:28
be for us, w. can be against us — Ro 8:31
W. shall lay any thing to the — Ro 8:33
W. is he that condemneth? It is — Ro 8:34
w. is even at the right hand of — Ro 8:34
w. also maketh intercession for us — Ro 8:34
W. shall separate us from the — Ro 8:35
w. are Israelites; to whom — Ro 9:4
w. is over all, God blessed for ever — Ro 9:5
For w. hath resisted his will — Ro 9:19
w. art thou that repliest against — Ro 9:20
W. shall ascend into heaven — Ro 10:6
Or, W. shall descend into the deep — Ro 10:7
Lord, w. hath believed our report — Ro 10:16
w. have not bowed the knee to — Ro 11:4
w. hath known the mind of — Ro 11:34
or w. hath been his counsellor — Ro 11:34
Or w. hath first given to him, and it — Ro 11:35
another, w. is weak, eateth herbs — Ro 14:2
W. art thou that judgest another — Ro 14:4
that man w. eateth with offence — Ro 14:20
W. have for my life laid down — Ro 16:4
w. is the firstfruits of Achaia unto — Ro 16:5
w. bestowed much labour on us — Ro 16:6
w. are of note among the apostles — Ro 16:7
w. also were in Christ before me — Ro 16:7
Tryphosa, w. labour in the Lord — Ro 16:12
I Tertius, w. wrote this epistle — Ro 16:22
W. shall also confirm you unto — 1Co 1:8
w. of God is made unto us wisdom — 1Co 1:30
w. hath known the mind of — 1Co 2:16
W. then is Paul, and w. is Apollos — 1Co 3:5
w. both will bring to light the — 1Co 4:5
w. maketh thee to differ from — 1Co 4:7
w. is my beloved son, and faithful — 1Co 4:17
the Lord, w. shall bring you into — 1Co 4:17
to judge w. are least esteemed — 1Co 6:4
W. goeth a warfare any time — 1Co 9:7
w. planteth a vineyard, and eateth — 1Co 9:7
w. feedeth a flock, and eateth not — 1Co 9:7
w. will not suffer you to be — 1Co 10:13
w. shall prepare himself to — 1Co 14:8
W. comforteth us in all our — 2Co 1:4
W. delivered us from so great a — 2Co 1:10
w. was preached among you by — 2Co 1:19
W. hath also sealed us, and given — 2Co 1:22
w. is he then that maketh me — 2Co 2:2
w. is sufficient for these things — 2Co 2:16
W. also hath made us able — 2Co 3:6
w. is the image of God, should — 2Co 4:4
w. commanded the light to shine — 2Co 4:6
w. also hath given unto us the — 2Co 5:5
w. hath reconciled us to himself by — 2Co 5:18
him to be sin for us, w. knew no sin — 2Co 5:21
for you, w. have begun before — 2Co 8:10
w. was also chosen of the churches — 2Co 8:19
W. in presence am base among — 2Co 10:1

W. is weak, and I am not 2Co 11:29
weak
w. is offended, and I burn 2Co 11:29
not
w. raised him from the dead Ga 1:1
W. gave himself for our sins, Ga 1:4
that
w. separated me from my Ga 1:15
mother's
neither Titus, w. was with me Ga 2:3
w. came in privily to spy out Ga 2:4
our
of these w. seemed to be Ga 2:6
somewhat
for they w. seemed to be Ga 2:6
somewhat
and John, w. seemed to be Ga 2:9
pillars
We w. are Jews by nature, Ga 2:15
and not
w. loved me, and gave himself Ga 2:20
for
Galatians, w. hath bewitched Ga 3:1
you
he w. was of the bondwoman Ga 4:23
was born
w. did hinder you that ye Ga 5:7
should
them w. are of the household Ga 6:10
of faith
they themselves w. are Ga 6:13
circumcised
Jesus Christ, w. hath blessed Eph 1:3
us
purpose of him w. worketh Eph 1:11
all things
glory, w. first trusted in Eph 1:12
Christ
of his power to us-ward w. Eph 1:19
believe
w. were dead in trespasses Eph 2:1
and sins
But God, w. is rich in mercy, Eph 2:4
for his
w. are called Uncircumcision Eph 2:11
by
ye w. sometimes were far off Eph 2:13
our peace, w. hath made Eph 2:14
both
w. am less than the least of all Eph 3:8
w. created all things by Jesus Eph 3:9
and Father of all, w. is above Eph 4:6
W. being past feeling have Eph 4:19
given
covetous man, w. is an Eph 5:5
idolater
W. being in the form of God Ph'p 2:6
w. will naturally care for Ph'p 2:20
your
shame, w. mind earthly Ph'p 3:19
things
w. is for you a faithful Col 1:7
minister of
W. also declared unto us your Col 1:8
love
W. hath delivered us from the Col 1:13
W. is the image of the Col 1:15
invisible
w. is the beginning, the Col 1:18
firstborn
W. now rejoice in my Col 1:24
sufferings
w. hath raised him from the Col 2:12
dead
When Christ, w. is our life, Col 3:4
shall
w. is a beloved brother, and a Col 4:7
beloved brother, w. is one of Col 4:9
you
w. are of the circumcision Col 4:11
Epaphras, w. is one of you, a Col 4:12
of God, w. hath called you 1Th 2:12
unto his
W. both killed the Lord Jesus 1Th 2:15
But let us, w. are of the day, 1Th 5:8
be sober
W. died for us, that, whether 1Th 5:10
we
that calleth you, w. also will 1Th 5:24
do it
to you w. are troubled rest 2Th 1:7
with us
W. shall be punished with 2Th 1:9
W. opposeth and exalteth 2Th 2:4
himself
only he w. now letteth will let, 2Th 2:7
until he
all might be damned w. 2Th 2:12
believed

W. shall stablish you, and 2Th 3:3
keep
our Lord, w. hath enabled me 1Ti 1:12
W. was before a blasphemer 1Ti 1:13
W. will have all men to be 1Ti 2:4
saved
W. gave himself a ransom for 1Ti 2:6
all
God, w. is the Saviour of all 1Ti 4:10
men
w. labour in the word and 1Ti 5:17
doctrine
of God, w. quickeneth all 1Ti 6:13
things
w. before Pontius Pilate 1Ti 6:13
witnessed
w. is the only Potentate 1Ti 6:15
W. only hath immortality 1Ti 6:16
w. giveth us richly all things 1Ti 6:17
to
W. hath saved us, and called 2Ti 1:9
us
Christ, w. hath abolished 2Ti 1:10
death
w. shall be able to teach others 2Ti 2:2
w. hath chosen him to be a 2Ti 2:4
soldier
w. works on the land (P) 2Ti 2:6
W. concerning the truth have 2Ti 2:18
w. are taken captive by him at 2Ti 2:26
his
w. shall judge the quick and 2Ti 4:1
w. subvert whole houses, Tit 1:11
teaching
W. gave himself for us, that Tit 2:14
he
W. at sundry times and in Heb 1:1
divers
W. being the brightness of his Heb 1:3
W. maketh his angels spirits Heb 1:7
them w. shall be heirs of Heb 1:14
salvation
w. was made a little lower Heb 2:9
than
sanctifieth and they w. are Heb 2:11
sanctified
them w. through fear of Heb 2:15
death
W. was faithful to him Heb 3:2
that appointed
as he w. hath builded the Heb 3:3
house
For w., when they had heard Heb 3:16
(S)
W. can have compassion on Heb 5:2
W. in the days of his flesh, Heb 5:7
when
w. by reason of use have Heb 5:14
their senses
for those w. were once Heb 6:4
enlightened
w. through faith and Heb 6:12
patience inherit
w. have fled for refuge to lay Heb 6:18
hold
w. met Abraham returning Heb 7:1
from
Levi, w. receive the office of Heb 7:5
Levi also, w. receiveth tithes Heb 7:9
W. is made, not after the Heb 7:16
law of a
w. is holy, harmless, Heb 7:26
undefiled
W. needeth not daily, as Heb 7:27
those
Son, w. is consecrated for Heb 7:28
evermore
w. is set on the right hand of Heb 8:1
W. serve unto the example Heb 8:5
and
w. through the eternal Spirit Heb 9:14
w. hath trodden under foot Heb 10:29
of them w. draw back unto Heb 10:39
perdition
judge him faithful w. had Heb 11:11
promised
endured, as seeing him w. is Heb 11:27
invisible
W. through faith subdued Heb 11:33
w. for the joy that was set Heb 12:2
before
w. for one morsel of meat Heb 12:16
sold his
w. refused him that spake Heb 12:25
on earth
w. have spoken unto you the Heb 13:7
word
all of us often go wrong, the Jas 3:2
man w. never says a wrong is (N)
W. is a wise man and endued Jas 3:13

w. is able to save and to Jas 4:12
destroy
destroy: w. art thou that Jas 4:12
judgest
w. have reaped down your Jas 5:4
fields
w. have spoken in the name of Jas 5:10
W. are kept by the power of 1Pe 1:5
God
w. prophesied of the grace 1Pe 1:10
that
w. without respect of persons 1Pe 1:17
W. verily was foreordained 1Pe 1:20
before
W. by him do believe in God, 1Pe 1:21
that
w. hath called you out of 1Pe 2:9
darkness
W. did no sin, neither was 1Pe 2:22
guile
W. when he was reviled, 1Pe 2:23
reviled
W. his own self bare our sins 1Pe 2:24
women also, w. trusted in God 1Pe 3:5
w. is he that will harm you, 1Pe 3:13
if ye
w. is gone into heaven, and 1Pe 3:22
is on
W. shall give account to him 1Pe 4:5
that
w. am also an elder, and a 1Pe 5:1
witness
w. hath called us unto his 1Pe 5:10
eternal
w. privily shall bring in 2Pe 2:1
damnable
w. loved the wages of 2Pe 2:15
escaped from them w. live in 2Pe 2:18
error
W. is a liar but he that 1Jo 2:22
denieth
as Cain, w. was of that 1Jo 3:12
wicked one
he w. loveth God love his 1Jo 4:21
brother
W. is he that overcometh the 1Jo 5:5
w. confess not that Jesus Christ 2Jo 7
w. loveth to have the 3Jo 9
preeminence
w. were before of old ordained Jude 4
w. should walk after their own Jude 18
These be they w. separate Jude 19
themselves
W. bare record of the word of Re 1:2
Christ, w. is the faithful witness Re 1:5
John, w. am also your brother Re 1:9
w. walketh in the midst of the Re 2:1
martyr, w. was slain among Re 2:13
you
Antipas, w. witnessed (B) Re 2:13
w. taught Balac to cast a Re 2:14
w. hath his eyes like unto a Re 2:18
flame
throne, w. liveth for ever and Re 4:9
ever
W. is worthy to open the book Re 5:2
and w. shall be able to stand Re 6:17
W. are these (S) Re 7:13
w. was to rule all nations with Re 12:5
W. is like unto the beast Re 13:4
w. is able to make war with Re 13:4
him
w. worship the beast and his Re 14:11
W. shall not fear thee, O Lord Re 15:4
God w. liveth for ever and Re 15:7
ever
is the Lord God w. judgeth Re 18:8
her
w. have committed fornication Re 18:9

WHOLE

and watered the w. face of the Ge 2:6
the w. land of Havilah Ge 2:11
the w. land of Ethiopia Ge 2:13
that were under the w. heaven Ge 7:19
were on the face of the w. Ge 8:9
earth
them was the w. earth Ge 9:19
overspread
the w. earth was of one Ge 11:1
language
upon the face of the w. earth Ge 11:4
Is not the w. land before thee Ge 13:9
the w. age of Jacob was an Ge 47:28
hundred
covered the face of the w. Ex 10:15
earth
w. assembly of the Ex 12:6
congregation

the w. congregation of the children — Ex 16:2
to kill this w. assembly — Ex 16:3
the w. congregation of the children — Ex 16:10
and the w. mount quaked greatly — Ex 19:18
thou shalt burn the w. ram — Ex 29:18
the fat thereof, and the w. rump — Le 3:9
Even the w. bullock shall he — Le 4:12
the w. congregation of Israel sin — Le 4:13
shall offer one out of the w. oblation — Le 7:14
and Moses burnt the w. ram — Le 8:21
the w. house of Israel, bewail — Le 10:6
may redeem it within a w. year — Le 25:29
charge of the w. congregation — Nu 3:7
shalt gather the w. assembly — Nu 8:9
of a w. piece shalt thou make — Nu 10:2
But even a w. month, until it — Nu 11:20
that they may eat a w. month — Nu 11:21
the w. congregation said unto — Nu 14:2
according to your w. number, from — Nu 14:29
w. congregation, into the desert of — Nu 20:1
the w. congregation, journeyed — Nu 20:22
that are under the w. heaven — De 2:25
all nations under the w. heaven — De 4:19
of the Lord thy God of w. stones — De 27:6
the w. land thereof is brimstone — De 29:23
w. burnt sacrifice upon thine — De 33:10
in the camp, till they were w. — Jos 5:8
an altar of w. stones, over which — Jos 8:31
not to go down about a w. day — Jos 10:13
So Joshua took the w. land — Jos 11:23
w. congregation of the children of — Jos 18:1; 22:12
the w. congregation of the Lord — Jos 22:16
with the w. congregation of Israel — Jos 22:18
and was there four w. months — J'g 19:2
w. congregation sent some to — J'g 21:13
because my life is yet w. in me — 2Sa 1:9
good to the w. house of Benjamin — 2Sa 3:19
among the w. multitude of Israel — 2Sa 6:19
w. family is risen against thine — 2Sa 14:7
w. house be overlaid with gold — 1Ki 6:22
the w. altar that was by the oracle — 1Ki 6:22
w. kingdom out of his hand — 1Ki 11:34
the w. house of Ahab shall perish — 2Ki 9:8
blessed the w. congregation of — 2Ch 6:3
sought him with their w. desire — 2Ch 15:15
run to and fro through the w. earth — 2Ch 16:9
w. number of the chief of the fathers — 2Ch 26:12
w. assembly took counsel to keep — 2Ch 30:23
according to the w. law and the — 2Ch 33:8
w. congregation together was forty — Ezr 2:64; 7:66
the w. kingdom of Ahasuerus — Es 3:6
woundeth, and his hands make w. — Job 5:18
and seeth under the w. heaven — Job 28:24
who hath disposed the w. world — Job 34:13
directeth it under the w. heaven — Job 37:3
is under the w. heaven is mine — Job 41:11
thee, O Lord, with my w. heart — Ps 9:1
converting the w. person (A) — Ps 19:7
joy of the w. earth, is mount Zion — Ps 48:2
offering and w. burnt offering — Ps 51:19
w. earth be filled with his glory — Ps 72:19

presence of the Lord of the w. earth — Ps 97:5
he brake the w. staff of bread — Ps 105:16
praise the Lord with my w. heart — Ps 111:1
that seek him with the w. heart — Ps 119:2
my w. heart have I sought thee — Ps 119:10
shall observe it with my w. heart — Ps 119:34
thy favour with my w. heart — Ps 119:58
thy precepts with my w. heart — Ps 119:69
I cried with my w. heart; hear me — Ps 119:145
I will praise thee with my w. heart — Ps 138:1
w. as those that go down into — Pr 1:12
the w. disposing thereof is of — Pr 16:33
be shewed before the w. congregation — Pr 26:26
the conclusion of the w. matter — Ec 12:13
for this is the w. duty of man — Ec 12:13
w. head is sick, and the w. heart — Isa 1:5
the staff, the w. stay of bread — Isa 3:1
and the w. stay of water — Isa 3:1
the w. earth is full of his glory — Isa 6:3
his w. work upon mount Zion — Isa 10:12
indignation, to destroy the w. land — Isa 13:5
The w. earth is at rest, and is quiet — Isa 14:7
is purposed upon the w. earth — Isa 14:26
Rejoice not thou, w. Palestina — Isa 14:29
thou, w. Palestina, art dissolved — Isa 14:31
I am set in my ward w. nights — Isa 21:8
even determined upon the w. earth — Isa 28:22
God of the w. earth shall he — Isa 54:5
brasen walls against the w. land — Jer 1:18
turned unto me with her w. heart — Jer 3:10
cried; for the w. land is spoiled — Jer 4:20
The w. land shall be desolate — Jer 4:27
The w. city shall flee for the noise — Jer 4:29
even the w. seed of Ephraim — Jer 7:15
the w. land trembled at the sound — Jer 8:16
the w. land is made desolate — Jer 12:11
unto me the w. house of Israel — Jer 13:11
Israel and the w. house of Judah — Jer 13:11
man of contention to the w. earth — Jer 15:10
that cannot be made w. again — Jer 19:11
unto me with their w. heart — Jer 24:7
this w. land shall be a desolation — Jer 25:11
the w. valley of the dead bodies — Jer 31:40
my w. heart and with my w. soul — Jer 32:41
the w. house of the Rechabites — Jer 35:3
had smitten the w. army of — Jer 37:10
I will pluck up, even the w. land — Jer 45:4
hammer of the w. earth cut asunder — Jer 50:23
praise of the w. earth surprised — Jer 51:41
her w. land shall be confounded — Jer 51:47
of beauty, The joy of the w. earth — La 2:15
the w. remnant of thee will I — Eze 5:10
touching the w. multitude thereof — Eze 7:13
their w. body, and their backs and — Eze 10:12
when it was w. it was meet for no — Eze 15:5
beasts of the w. earth with thee — Eze 32:4
When the w. earth rejoiceth, I will — Eze 35:14

bones are the w. house of Israel — Eze 37:11
mercy upon the w. house of Israel — Eze 39:25
may keep the w. form thereof — Eze 43:11
the w. limit thereof round about — Eze 43:12
shall be for the w. house of Israel — Eze 45:6
mountain, and filled the w. earth — Da 2:35
him ruler over the w. province — Da 2:48
should be over the w. kingdom — Eze 6:1
to set him over the w. realm — Eze 6:3
and shall devour the w. earth — Eze 7:23
the kingdom under the w. heaven — Eze 7:27
west on the face of the w. earth — Da 8:5
for under the w. heaven hath not — Da 9:12
three w. weeks were fulfilled — Da 10:3
the strength of his w. kingdom — Da 11:17
away captive the w. captivity — Am 1:6
they delivered up the w. captivity — Am 1:9
against the w. family which I — Am 3:1
unto the Lord of the w. earth — Mic 4:13
w. land shall be devoured by — Zep 1:18
to and fro through the w. earth — Zec 4:10
stand by the Lord of the w. earth — Zec 4:14
forth over the face of the w. earth — Zec 5:3
robbed me, even the w. nation — Mal 3:9
thy w. body should be cast into — M't 5:29; 5:30
thy w. body shall be full of light — M't 6:22
w. body shall be full of darkness — M't 6:23
the w. herd of swine ran violently — M't 8:32
the w. city came out to meet Jesus — M't 8:34
that be w. need not a physician — M't 9:12
touch his garment, I shall be w. — M't 9:21
thy faith hath made thee w. — M't 9:22
woman was made w. from that — M't 9:22
it was restored w. like as the — M't 12:13
w. multitude stood on the shore — M't 13:2
of meal, till the w. was leavened — M't 13:33
as touched were made perfectly w. — M't 14:36
was made w. from that very hour — M't 15:28
the maimed to be w. the lame to — M't 15:31
if he shall gain the w. world, and — M't 16:26
shall be preached in the w. world — M't 26:13
unto him the w. band of soldiers — M't 27:27
They that are w. have no need of — M'k 2:17
hand was restored w. as the other — M'k 3:5
the w. multitude was by the sea — M'k 4:1
but his clothes, I shall be w. — M'k 5:28
thy faith hath made thee w. — M'k 5:34
peace, and be w. of thy plague — M'k 5:34
ran through that w. region round — M'k 6:55
as touched him were made w. — M'k 6:56
if he shall gain the w. world — M'k 8:36
way; thy faith hath made thee w. — M'k 10:52
is more than all w. burnt offerings — M'k 12:33
preached throughout the w. — M'k 14:9
scribes and the w. council — M'k 15:1
and they call together the w. band — M'k 16:16
was darkness over the w. land until — M'k 16:33
the w. multitude of the people — Lu 1:10
that are w. need not a physician — Lu 5:31

hand was restored w. as the other	Lu 6:10		w. Hagar the Egyptian, Sarah's	Ge 25:12
w. multitude sought to touch him	Lu 6:19		children, for w. I have served thee	Ge 30:26
servant w. that had been sick	Lu 7:10		is, a man in w. the spirit of God is	Ge 41:38
the w. multitude of the country	Lu 8:37		well, the old man of w. ye spake	Ge 43:27
published throughout the w. city	Lu 8:39		younger brother, of w. ye spake	Ge 43:29
thy faith hath made thee w.; go in	Lu 8:48		w. it is found shall be my servant	Ge 44:10
only, and she shall be made w.	Lu 8:50		he also with w. the cup is found	Ge 44:16
if he gain the w. world, and lose	Lu 9:25		your brother, w. ye sold into Egypt	Ge 45:4
thy w. body also is full of light	Lu 11:34		w. Laban gave to Leah his daughter	Ge 46:18
w. body therefore be full of light	Lu 11:36		w. God hath given me in this place	Ge 48:9
dark the w. shall be full of light	Lu 11:36		w. my fathers Abraham and Isaac	Ge 48:15
of meal, till the w. was leavened	Lu 13:21		art he w. thy brethren shall praise	Ge 49:8
thy faith hath made thee w.	Lu 17:19		by the hand of him w. thou wilt send	Ex 4:13
w. multitude of the disciples began	Lu 19:37		w. the Egyptians keep in bondage	Ex 6:5
dwell on the face of the w. earth	Lu 21:35		and Moses, to w. the Lord said	Ex 6:26
the w. multitude of them arose	Lu 23:1		Egyptians w. ye have seen to	Ex 14:13
believed, and his w. house	Joh 4:53		w. he had delivered out of the land	Ex 18:9
w. of whatsoever disease he had	Joh 5:4		w. the judges shall condemn,	Ex 22:9
unto him, Wilt thou be made w.	Joh 5:6		the people to w. thou shalt come	Ex 23:27
immediately the man was made w.	Joh 5:9		w. I have filled with the spirit	Ex 28:3
He that made me w. the same said	Joh 5:11		w. thou swarest by thine own self	Ex 32:13
him, Behold, thou art made w.	Joh 5:14		know w. thou wilt send with me	Ex 33:12
was Jesus, which had made him w.	Joh 5:15		gracious to w. I will be gracious	Ex 33:19
every whit w. on the sabbath day	Joh 7:23		mercy on w. I will shew mercy	Ex 33:19
and that the w. nations perish not	Joh 11:50		every one w. his spirit made willing	Ex 35:21
by what means he is made w.	Ac 4:9		every man, with w. was found blue	Ex 35:23
this man stand here before you w.	Ac 4:10		with w. was found shittim wood	Ex 35:24
saying pleased the w. multitude	Ac 6:5		in w. the Lord put wisdom	Ex 36:1
Jesus Christ maketh thee w.	Ac 9:34		it unto him to w. it appertaineth	Le 6:5
that a w. year they assembled	Ac 11:26		And the leper in w. the plague	Le 13:45
came almost the w. city together	Ac 13:44		him in w. is the plague of leprosy	Le 14:32
and elders, with the w. church	Ac 15:22		woman also with w. man shall lie	Le 15:18
w. city was filled with confusion	Ac 19:29		And the priest, w. he shall anoint	Le 16:32
two w. years in his own hired	Ac 28:30		w. he shall consecrate to minister	Le 16:32
spoken of throughout the w. world	Ro 1:8		after w. they have gone a	Le 17:7
that the w. creation groaneth	Ro 8:22		of w. he may take uncleanness	Le 22:5
of the w. church, saluteth you	Ro 16:23		unto the man to w. he sold it	Le 25:47
little leaven leaveneth the w. lump	1Co 5:6		my servants w. I brought forth	Le 25:55
If the w. body were an eye	1Co 12:17		w. I brought forth out of the	Le 26:45
If the w. were hearing	1Co 12:17		unto him of w. it was bought	Le 27:24
w. church become together into one	1Co 14:23		w. possession of the land belong	Le 27:24
he is a debtor to do the w. law	Ga 5:3		w. he consecrated to minister	Nu 3:3
little leaven leaveneth the w. lump	Ga 5:9		w. Moses and Aaron did number	Nu 4:41
w. family in heaven and earth is	Eph 3:15		w. Moses and Aaron numbered	Nu 4:45
the w. body fitly joined together	Eph 4:16		w. Moses and Aaron and the chief	Nu 4:46
Put on the w. armour of God, that ye	Eph 6:11		him against w. he hath trespassed	Nu 5:7
take unto you the w. armour of God	Eph 6:13		w. thou knowest to be the elders of	Nu 11:16
your w. spirit and soul and body	1Th 5:23		The people, among w. I am, are six	Nu 11:21
who subvert w. houses, teaching	Tit 1:11		woman w. he had married	Nu 12:1
put the w. world in wrong (N)	Heb 11:7		of w. the flesh is half consumed	Nu 12:12
whosoever shall keep the w. law	Jas 2:10		even him w. he hath chosen will	Nu 16:5
able also to bridle the w. body	Jas 3:2		the man w. the Lord doth choose	Nu 16:7
and we turn about their w. body	Jas 3:3		w. I shall choose, shall blossom	Nu 17:5
that it defileth the w. body	Jas 3:6		that he w. thou blessest is blessed	Nu 22:6
also for the sins of the w. world	1Jo 2:2		and he w. thou cursest is cursed	Nu 22:6
the w. world lieth in wickedness	1Jo 5:19			
which deceiveth the w. world	Re 12:9			
of the earth and of the w. world	Re 16:14			

WHOLEHEARTEDLY

conscious mind w. endorses (P)	Ro 7:22
love w. (N)	1Pe 1:22

WHOLESOME

A w. tongue is a tree of live: but	Pr 15:4
w. teaching (A)(B)(N)(P)	1Ti 1:10
and consent not to w. words, even	1Ti 6:3
pattern of w. teaching (A)(B)(E)(R)	2Ti 1:13
w. doctine (B)(N)	Tit 2:1
instruction be sound, fit, wise, w. (A)(B)	Tit 2:8
w. instruction (B)	Jude 4:3

WHOLLY

it will be w. severe (B)	Ge 41:31
the Lord; it shall be w. burnt	Le 6:22
offering shall be w. burnt	Le 6:23
not w. reap the corners of thy field	Le 19:9
they are w. given unto him out	Nu 3:9
spread over it a cloth w. of blue	Nu 4:6
For they are w. given unto me from	Nu 8:16
they have not w. followed me	Nu 32:11
they have w. followed the Lord	Nu 32:12
he hath w. followed the Lord	De 1:36
I w. followed the Lord my God	Jos 14:8
hast w. followed the Lord my God	Jos 14:9
that he w. followed the Lord	Jos 14:14
w. dedicated the silver unto	J'g 17:3
a burnt offering w. unto the Lord	1Sa 7:9
people w. at thy commandment	1Ch 28:21
full strength, being w. at ease and	Job 21:23
art w. gone up to the housetops	Isa 22:1
thee a noble vine, w. a right seed	Jer 2:21
is w. oppression in the midst of her	Jer 6:6
it shall be w. carried away captive	Jer 13:19
ye w. set your faces to enter into	Jer 42:15
I not leave thee w. unpunished	Jer 46:28
but it shall be w. desolate	Jer 50:13
and all the house of Israel w.	Eze 11:15
and it shall rise up w. as a flood	Am 8:8
and it shall rise up w. like a flood	Am 9:5
he saw the city w. given to idolatry	Ac 17:16
very God of peace sanctify you w.	1Th 5:23
give thyself w. to them; that	1Ti 4:15

WHOM

he put the man w. he had formed	Ge 2:8
The woman w. thou gavest to be	Ge 3:12
seed instead of Abel, w. Cain slew	Ge 4:25
will destroy man w. I have created	Ge 6:7
out of w. came Philistim	Ge 10:14
w. they shall serve, will I judge	Ge 15:14
him, w. Sarah bare to him, Isaac	Ge 21:3
only son Isaac, w. thou lovest	Ge 22:2
the Canaanites, among w. I dwell	Ge 24:3
the damsel to w. I shall say, Let	Ge 24:14
before w. I walk, will send his angel	Ge 24:40
woman w. the Lord hath appointed	Ge 24:44
Nahor's son, w. Milcah bare unto	Ge 24:44

shall I curse, *w.* God hath not   Nu 23:8
cursed
I defy, *w.* the Lord hath not   Nu 23:8
defiled
of *w.* cometh the family of the   Nu 26:5
w. her mother bare to Levi in   Nu 26:59
w. Moses and Aaron the   Nu 26:64
priest
of Nun, a man in *w.* is the   Nu 27:18
spirit
are they *w.* the Lord   Nu 34:29
commanded to
Let them marry to *w.* they   Nu 36:6
think best
w. Moses and the children of   De 4:46
Israel
people of *w.* thou art afraid   De 7:19
of the Anakims, *w.* thou   De 9:2
knowest
and of *w.* thou hast heard say   De 9:2
w. the Lord thy God shall   De 17:15
choose
w. he hated not in time past   De 19:4
between *w.* the controversy   De 19:17
Israel *w.* thou hast redeemed   De 21:8
man to *w.* thou dost lend   De 24:11
shall
flesh of his children *w.* he   De 28:55
shall
them, gods *w.* they knew not   De 29:26
and *w.* he had not given   De 29:26
unto them
land of them, *w.* he destroyed   De 31:4
to gods *w.* they knew not, to   De 32:17
new gods
newly up, *w.* your fathers   De 32:17
feared not
generation, children in *w.* is   De 32:20
no faith
gods, their rock in *w.* they   De 32:37
trusted
one, *w.* thou didst prove at   De 33:8
Massah
with *w.* thou didst strive at   De 33:8
waters
w. the Lord knew face to   De 34:10
face
and Og, *w.* ye utterly   Jos 2:10
destroyed
w. he had prepared of the   Jos 4:4
children
w. the Lord sware that he   Jos 5:6
w. he raised up in their stead   Jos 5:7
w. the children of Israel slew   Jos 10:11
enemies against *w.* ye fight   Jos 10:25
With *w.* the Reubenites and   Jos 13:8
w. Moses smote with the   Jos 13:21
princes
you this day *w.* ye will serve   Jos 24:15
the people through *w.* we   Jos 24:17
passed
shew thee the man *w.* thou   J'g 4:22
seekest
shall be, that of *w.* I say unto   J'g 7:4
thee
with *w.* ye did upbraid me,   J'g 8:15
saying
men were they *w.* ye slew at   J'g 8:18
Tabor
thirty daughters, *w.* he sent   J'g 12:9
abroad
w. he had used as his friend   J'g 14:20
them that danced, *w.* they   J'g 21:23
caught
with *w.* she had wrought, and   Ru 2:19
w. I wrought to day is Boaz   Ru 2:19
kinsman of *w.* Boaz spake   Ru 4:1
came by
unto *w.* he said, Ho, such a one   Ru 4:1
w. Tamar bare unto Judah, of   Ru 4:12
w. I shall not cut off from   1Sa 2:33
mine altar
and to *w.* shall he go up from   1Sa 6:20
us
Behold the man *w.* I spake to   1Sa 9:17
thee
on *w.* is all the desire of Israel   1Sa 9:20
See ye him *w.* the Lord hath   1Sa 10:24
I taken? or *w.* have I   1Sa 12:3
defrauded
w. have I oppressed? or of   1Sa 12:3
whose
w. have I wronged (B)(P)   1Sa 12:3;
      12:4
the king *w.* ye have chosen   1Sa 12:13
chosen, and *w.* ye have   1Sa 12:13
desired
unto me him *w.* I name unto   1Sa 16:3
thee

w. hast thou left those few   1Sa 17:28
sheep
of Israel, *w.* thou hast defied   1Sa 17:45
w. thou slewest in the valley   1Sa 21:9
of
After *w.* is the king of Israel   1Sa 24:14
come
after *w.* dost thou pursue?   1Sa 24:14
after a
w. I know not whence they   1Sa 25:11
be
men of my lord, *w.* thou   1Sa 25:25
didst send
up, *w.* I shall name unto thee   1Sa 28:8
W. shall I bring up unto   1Sa 28:11
thee
of *w.* they sang one to   1Sa 29:5
another
unto him, To *w.* belongest   1Sa 30:13
thou
w. they had made also to   1Sa 30:21
abide at
w. I commanded to feed my   2Sa 7:7
people
Saul, *w.* I put away before   2Sa 7:15
thee
w. God went to redeem for a   2Sa 7:23
people
the life of his brother *w.* he   2Sa 14:7
slew
Unto *w.* David said, If thou   2Sa 15:33
passest
but *w.* the Lord, and this   2Sa 16:18
people
And again, *w.* should I serve   2Sa 16:19
man *w.* thou seekest is as if   2Sa 17:3
all
Absalom, *w.* we anointed   2Sa 19:10
over us
w. he had left to keep the   2Sa 20:3
house
of Saul, *w.* the Lord did   2Sa 21:6
choose
w. she bare unto Saul,   2Sa 21:8
Armoni
w. she brought up for Adriel   2Sa 21:8
of the mighty men *w.* David   2Sa 23:8
had
hundred, *w.* he slew at one   2Sa 23:8
time
Amasa the son of Jether, *w.*   1Ki 2:5
he slew
son, *w.* I will set upon thy   1Ki 5:5
throne
daughter, *w.* he had taken to   1Ki 7:8
wife
w. the children of Israel also   1Ki 9:21
were
w. he bestowed in the cities   1Ki 10:26
for
w. Tahpenes weaned in   1Ki 11:20
Pharaoh's
w. I chose, because he kept   1Ki 11:34
my
prophet *w.* he had brought   1Ki 13:23
back
of Israel liveth, before *w.* I   1Ki 17:1
stand
upon the widow with *w.* I   1Ki 17:20
sojourn
of hosts liveth, before *w.* I   1Ki 18:15
stand
unto *w.* the word of the Lord   1Ki 18:31
came
And Ahab said, By *w.*? And   1Ki 20:14
he
w. I appointed to utter   1Ki 20:42
destruction
w. Jezebel his wife stirred   1Ki 21:25
up
the Amorites, *w.* the Lord   1Ki 21:26
cast out
by *w.* we may enquire of the   1Ki 22:8
Lord
of hosts liveth, before *w.*   2Ki 3:14
I stand
As the Lord liveth, before *w.*   2Ki 5:16
I stand
bring you to the man *w.* ye   2Ki 6:19
seek
those *w.* thou hast taken   2Ki 6:22
captive
her son, *w.* Elisha restored to   2Ki 8:5
life
of the men *w.* I have brought   2Ki 10:24
into
w. the Lord cast out from   2Ki 16:3;
before   17:8
heathen *w.* the Lord carried   2Ki 17:11
away

w. the Lord had charged   2Ki 17:15
them
priests *w.* ye brought from   2Ki 17:27
thence
priests *w.* they had carried   2Ki 17:28
away
the nations *w.* they carried   2Ki 17:33
away
of Jacob, *w.* he named   2Ki 17:34
Israel
w. the Lord had made a   2Ki 17:35
covenant
Now on *w.* dost thou trust,   2Ki 18:20
that
w. the king of Assyria his   2Ki 19:4
master
thy God in *w.* thou trustest   2Ki 19:10
deceive
W. hast thou reproached   2Ki 19:22
against *w.* hast thou exalted   2Ki 19:22
thy
w. the Lord cast out before   2Ki 21:2
the nations *w.* the Lord   2Ki 21:9
destroyed
priests, *w.* the kings of   2Ki 23:5
Judah had
w. Nebuchadnezzar king of   2Ki 25:22
of *w.* came the Philistines   1Ch 1:12
w. he married when he was   1Ch 2:21
w. Tilgath-pilneser carried   1Ch 5:6
w. God destroyed before   1Ch 5:25
them
they *w.* David set over the   1Ch 6:31
service
of Manasseh; Ashriel, *w.* she   1Ch 7:14
bare
w. the men of Gath that   1Ch 7:21
were born
w. David and Samuel the   1Ch 9:22
seer
of the mighty men *w.* David   1Ch 11:10;
had   11:11
w. I commanded to feed my   1Ch 17:6
people
w. God went to redeem to   1Ch 17:21
be his
w. thou hast redeemed out   1Ch 17:21
of
w. king David made rulers   1Ch 26:32
over
my son, *w.* alone God hath   1Ch 29:1
chosen
w. precious stones were   1Ch 29:8
found
w. I have made thee king   2Ch 1:11
w. David my father did   2Ch 2:7
provide
w. the children of Israel   2Ch 8:8
consumed
w. he bestowed in the chariot   2Ch 9:25
cities
w. the king put in fenced   2Ch 17:19
cities
by *w.* we may enquire of the   2Ch 18:7
Lord
w. thou wouldest not let   2Ch 20:10
Israel
w. the Lord had anointed to   2Ch 22:7
cut off
w. David had distributed in   2Ch 23:18
w. the Lord had cast out   2Ch 28:3;
before the   33:2
heathen, *w.* the Lord had   2Ch 33:9
destroyed
w. Nebuchadnezzar the king of   Ezr 2:1
of *w.* there were seven   Ezr 2:65
thousand
w. the great and noble   Ezr 4:10
Asnapper
w. he had made governor   Ezr 5:14
w. David and the princes had   Ezr 8:20
had wives by *w.* they had   Ezr 10:44
children
w. thou hast redeemed by thy   Ne 1:10
w. Nebuchadnezzar the king of   Ne 7:6
of *w.* there were seven   Ne 7:67
thousand
them for *w.* nothing is   Ne 8:10
prepared
kings *w.* thou hast set over us   Ne 9:37
w. Nebuchadnezzar the king of   Es 2:6
w. Mordecai, when her father   Es 2:7
w. he had appointed to attend   Es 4:5
to *w.* the king shall hold out   Es 4:11
man *w.* the king delighteth to   Es 6:6
honour
To *w.* would the king delight to   Es 6:6
do
w. the king delighteth to honour   Es 6:7;
      6:9, 11

before *w.* thou hast begun to   *Es 6:13*
fall
is hid, and *w.* God hath   *Job 3:23*
hedged in
happy is the man *w.* God   *Job 5:17*
correcteth
W. though I were righteous,   *Job 9:15*
yet
w. alone the earth was given   *Job 15:19*
w. I loved are turned against   *Job 19:19*
me
w. I shall see for myself,   *Job 19:27*
and mine
upon *w.* doth not his light   *Job 25:3*
arise
To *w.* hast thou uttered words   *Job 26:4*
me, in *w.* old age was   *Job 30:2*
perished
the covetous, *w.* the Lord   *Ps 10:3*
abhorreth
the excellent, in *w.* is all my   *Ps 16:3*
delight
God, my strength, in *w.* I will   *Ps 18:2*
trust
w. I have not known shall   *Ps 18:43*
serve me
my salvation; *w.* shall I fear   *Ps 27:1*
of my life; of *w.* shall be   *Ps 27:1*
afraid
w. the Lord imputeth not   *Ps 32:2*
iniquity
people *w.* he hath chosen for   *Ps 33:12*
his own
familiar friend, in *w.* I trusted   *Ps 41:9*
w. thou mayest make princes   *Ps 45:16*
in all
excellency of Jacob *w.* he loved   *Ps 47:4*
Blessed is the man *w.* thou   *Ps 65:4*
choosest
him *w.* thou hast smitten   *Ps 69:26*
grief of those *w.* thou hast   *Ps 69:26*
wounded
W. have I in heaven but thee   *Ps 73:25*
w. thou madest strong for   *Ps 80:17*
thyself
All nations *w.* thou hast made   *Ps 86:9*
w. thou rememberest no more   *Ps 88:5*
With *w.* my hand be   *Ps 89:21*
established
God, to *w.* vengeance   *Ps 94:1*
belongeth
O God, to *w.* vengeance   *Ps 94:1*
belongeth
is the man *w.* thou   *Ps 94:12*
chastenest, O.
Unto *w.* I sware in my wrath   *Ps 95:11*
that
w. thou hast made to play   *Ps 104:26*
therein
and Aaron *w.* he had chosen   *Ps 105:26*
w. the Lord commanded   *Ps 106:34*
them
w. they sacrificed unto the   *Ps 106:38*
idols of
w. he hath redeemed from the   *Ps 107:2*
hand
my shield, and he in *w.* I trust   *Ps 144:2*
son of man, in *w.* there is no   *Ps 146:3*
help
For *w.* the Lord loveth he   *Pr 3:12*
a father the son, in *w.* he   *Pr 3:12*
delighteth
not good from them to *w.* it   *Pr 3:27*
is due
prince *w.* thine eyes have seen   *Pr 25:7*
against *w.* there is no rising   *Pr 30:31*
up
For *w.* do I labour, and   *Ec 4:8*
bereave
man also to *w.* God hath given   *Ec 5:19*
A man to *w.* God hath given   *Ec 6:2*
riches
just men, unto *w.* it happeneth   *Ec 8:14*
to *w.* it happeneth according   *Ec 8:14*
to the
with the wife *w.* thou lovest all   *Ec 9:9*
Tell me, O thou *w.* my soul   *Ca 1:7*
loveth
I sought him *w.* my soul loveth   *Ca 3:1*
I will seek him *w.* my soul   *Ca 3:2*
loveth
the city found me: to *w.* I said   *Ca 3:3*
Saw ye him *w.* my soul loveth   *Ca 3:3*
I found him *w.* my soul loveth: *Ca 3:4*
I held
W. shall I send, and who will   *Isa 6:8*
them to *w.* this people shall   *Isa 8:12*
say
children *w.* the Lord hath   *Isa 8:18*
given me

to *w.* will ye flee for help   *Isa 10:3*
W. the Lord of hosts shall   *Isa 19:25*
bless
w. hast thou here, that thou   *Isa 22:16*
hast
thou *w.* the merchants of   *Isa 23:2*
Zidon, that
W. shall he teach knowledge   *Isa 28:9*
and *w.* shall he make to   *Isa 28:9*
To *w.* he said, This is the   *Isa 28:12*
rest
unto him from *w.* the children   *Isa 31:6*
now on *w.* dost thou trust,   *Isa 36:5*
that
w. the king of Assyria his   *Isa 37:4*
master
not thy God, in *w.* thou   *Isa 37:10*
trustest
W. hast thou reproached and   *Isa 37:23*
against *w.* hast thou exalted   *Isa 37:23*
thy
With *w.* took he counsel, and   *Isa 40:14*
who
To *w.* then will ye liken God   *Isa 40:18*
To *w.* then will ye liken me   *Isa 40:25*
servant, Jacob *w.* I have   *Isa 41:8*
chosen
Thou *w.* I have taken from the   *Isa 41:9*
Behold my servant, *w.* I   *Isa 42:1*
uphold
mine elect, in *w.* my soul   *Isa 42:1*
delighteth
he against *w.* we have sinned   *Isa 42:24*
and my servant *w.* I have   *Isa 43:10*
chosen
and Israel, *w.* I have chosen   *Isa 44:1*
and thou, Jesurun, *w.* I have   *Isa 44:2*
chosen
To *w.* will ye liken me, and   *Isa 46:5*
make
thee with *w.* thou hast   *Isa 47:15*
laboured
O Israel, in *w.* I will be   *Isa 49:3*
glorified
Holy One, to him *w.* man   *Isa 49:7*
despiseth
to him *w.* the nation   *Isa 49:7*
abhorreth
divorcement, *w.* I have put   *Isa 50:1*
away
creditors is it to *w.* I have sold   *Isa 50:1*
you
the sons *w.* she hath brought   *Isa 51:18*
forth
by *w.* shall I comfort thee   *Isa 51:19*
and to *w.* is the arm of the   *Isa 53:1*
Lord
Against *w.* do ye sport   *Isa 57:4*
yourselves
against *w.* make ye a wide   *Isa 57:4*
mouth
And of *w.* hast thou been   *Isa 57:11*
afraid or
As one *w.* his mother   *Isa 66:13*
comforteth
w. the word of the Lord   *Jer 1:12*
came in the
To *w.* shall I speak, and give   *Jer 6:10*
after other gods *w.* ye know   *Jer 7:9*
not
w. they have loved, and *w.* they   *Jer 8:2*
and after *w.* they have walked   *Jer 8:2*
and *w.* they have sought, and   *Jer 8:2*
w. they have worshipped: they   *Jer 8:2*
who is he to *w.* the mouth of   *Jer 9:12*
w. neither they nor their   *Jer 9:16*
fathers
unto *w.* they offer incense   *Jer 11:12*
people to *w.* they prophesy   *Jer 14:16*
against *w.* I have pronounced   *Jer 18:8*
w. neither they nor their   *Jer 19:4*
fathers
to *w.* thou hast prophesied   *Jer 20:6*
like a man *w.* wine hath   *Jer 23:9*
overcome
w. I have sent out of this   *Jer 24:5*
place
to *w.* I send thee, to drink it   *Jer 25:15*
unto *w.* the Lord hath sent   *Jer 25:17*
me
the prophets, *w.* I sent unto   *Jer 26:5*
you
unto *w.* it seemed meet unto   *Jer 27:5*
me
w. Nebuchadnezzar had   *Jer 29:1*
carried
w. Zedekiah king of Judah   *Jer 29:3*
sent
w. I have caused to be carried   *Jer 29:4*
away

w. I have sent from   *Jer 29:20*
Jerusalem to
w. the king of Babylon   *Jer 29:22*
roasted in
king, *w.* I will raise up unto   *Jer 30:9*
them
is Zion, *w.* no man seeketh   *Jer 30:17*
after
w. I have slain in mine anger   *Jer 33:5*
handmaids, *w.* they had let   *Jer 34:11*
go free
w. he had set at liberty at   *Jer 34:16*
their
w. Nebuchadrezzar king of   *Jer 37:1*
Babylon
w. they have cast into the   *Jer 38:9*
men of *w.* thou art afraid   *Jer 39:17*
w. the king of Babylon hath   *Jer 40:5*
made
w. the king of Babylon had   *Jer 41:2*
made
w. he had slain because of   *Jer 41:9*
w. Nebuzar-adan the captain   *Jer 41:10*
of the
w. he had recovered from   *Jer 41:16*
Ishmael
w. he had brought again   *Jer 41:16*
from
w. the king of Babylon made   *Jer 41:18*
Lord our God, to *w.* we send   *Jer 42:6*
thee
w. ye sent me to present your   *Jer 42:9*
Babylon, of *w.* ye are afraid   *Jer 42:11*
other gods, *w.* they knew not   *Jer 44:3*
I will pardon them *w.* I   *Jer 50:20*
reserve
people *w.* Nebuchadrezzar   *Jer 52:28*
carried
w. thou didst command that   *La 1:10*
they
from *w.* I am not able to rise   *La 1:14*
up
consider to *w.* thou hast done   *La 2:20*
w. we said, Under his shadow   *La 4:20*
we
any man upon *w.* is the mark   *Eze 9:6*
among *w.* I saw Jaazaniah   *Eze 11:1*
the son
Your slain *w.* ye have laid in   *Eze 11:7*
the
w. the inhabitants of   *Eze 11:15*
Jerusalem
sad, *w.* I have not made sad   *Eze 13:22*
w. thou hast borne unto me   *Eze 16:20*
with *w.* thou hast taken   *Eze 16:37*
pleasure
the heathen, among *w.* they   *Eze 20:9*
were
and with all on *w.* she doted   *Eze 23:7*
the Assyrians, upon *w.* she   *Eze 23:9*
doted
from *w.* thy mind is   *Eze 23:22*
alienated
the hand of them *w.* thou   *Eze 23:28*
hatest
from *w.* thy mind is alienated   *Eze 23:28*
their sons, *w.* they bare unto   *Eze 23:37*
me
unto *w.* a messenger was   *Eze 23:40*
sent
for *w.* thou didst wash   *Eze 23:40*
thyself
daughters *w.* ye have   *Eze 24:21*
left shall fall
people among *w.* they are   *Eze 28:25*
scattered
W. art thou like in thy   *Eze 31:2*
To *w.* art thou thus like in   *Eze 31:18*
glory
W. doest thou pass in   *Eze 32:19*
beauty? go
Art thou he of *w.* I have   *Eze 38:17*
spoken in
Children in *w.* was no blemish   *Da 1:4*
w. they might teach the   *Da 1:4*
learning
Unto *w.* the prince of the   *Da 1:7*
eunuchs
w. the prince of the eunuchs   *Da 1:11*
had
w. the king had ordained to   *Da 2:24*
Jews *w.* thou hast set over   *Da 3:12*
God *w.* we serve is able to   *Da 3:17*
deliver
in *w.* is the spirit of the holy   *Da 4:8;*
gods   *5:11*
w. the king Nebuchadnezzar   *Da 5:11*
thy
w. the king named   *Da 5:12*
Belteshazzar

w. the king my father brought | Da 5:13
before him: w. he would he | Da 5:19
slew
and w. he would he kept alive | Da 5:19
alive; and w. he would he set | Da 5:19
up
up; and w. he would he put | Da 5:19
down
of w. Daniel was first | Da 6:2
God w. thou servest | Da 6:16
continually
God, w. thou servest | Da 6:20
continually able to
before w. there were three of | Da 7:8
came up, and before w. three | Da 7:20
fell
w. I had seen in the vision at | Da 9:21
w. they shall not give the | Da 11:21
honour
a god w. his fathers knew | Da 11:38
not
w. he shall acknowledge and | Da 11:39
and thy judges of w. thou | Ho 13:10
saidst
the remnant w. the Lord shall | Joe 2:32
call
w. they have scattered among | Joe 3:2
to w. the house of Israel came | Am 6:1
by w. shall Jacob arise? for he | Am 7:2;
 | 7:5
w. hath not thy wickedness | Na 3:19
passed
to w. the reproach was a | Zep 3:18
burden
w. the former prophets have | Zec 1:4
These are they w. the Lord | Zec 1:10
hath
all the nations w. they knew | Zec 7:14
not
look upon me w. | Zec 12:10
they pierced
people against w. the Lord | Mal 1:4
hath
w. thou hast dealt | Mal 2:14
treacherously
w. ye seek, shall suddenly | Mal 3:1
come
of the covenant, w. ye delight | Mal 3:1
in
of Mary, of w. was born | M't 1:16
Jesus
Son, in w. I am well pleased | M't 3:17
w. if his son ask bread, will he | M't 7:9
give
he. of w. it is written, | M't 11:10
Behold, I
my servant, w. I have | M't 12:18
chosen
in w. my soul is well pleased | M't 12:18
w. do your children cast | M't 12:27
them out
W. do men say that I the | M't 16:13
Son of
them, But w. say ye that I | M't 16:15
am
Son, in w. I am well pleased | M't 17:5
w. do the kings of the earth | M't 17:25
take
that man by w. the offence | M't 18:7
cometh
saying, save they to w. it is | M't 19:11
given
for w. it is prepared of my | M't 20:23
Father
w. ye slew between the | M't 23:35
temple and
w. his lord hath made ruler | M't 24:45
over
w. his lord when he cometh | M't 24:46
shall
by w. the Son of man is | M't 26:24
betrayed
w. the children of Israel did | M't 27:9
people a prisoner, w. they | M't 27:15
would
W. will ye that I release | M't 27:17
unto you
Son in w. I am well pleased | M'k 1:11
and calleth unto him w. he | M'k 3:13
would
he said, It is John, w. I | M'k 6:16
prepared
them, W. do men say that I | M'k 8:27
am
them, But w. say ye that I | M'k 8:29
am
to them for w. it is | M'k 10:40
prepared
the elect's sake, w. he hath | M'k 13:20
chosen

by w. the Son of man is | M'k 14:21
betrayed
I know not this man of w. ye | M'k 14:71
speak
him w. ye call the King of | M'k 15:12
the Jews
among w. was Mary | M'k 15:40
Magdalene
out of w. he had cast seven | M'k 16:9
devils
twelve, w. also he named | Lu 6:13
apostles
Simon, w. he also named | Lu 6:14
Peter
to them of w. ye hope to | Lu 6:34
receive
I will shew you to w. he is | Lu 6:47
like
worthy for w. he should do this | Lu 7:4
This is he, of w. it is written | Lu 7:27
that he, to w. he forgave most | Lu 7:43
to w. little is given, the same | Lu 7:47
loveth
out of w. went seven devils | Lu 8:2
out of w. the devils were | Lu 8:35;
departed | 8:38
is this, of w. I hear such things | Lu 9:9
W. say the people that I am | Lu 9:18
them, But w. say ye that I am | Lu 9:20
he to w. the Son will reveal | Lu 10:22
him
by w. do your sons cast them | Lu 11:19
out
will forewarn you w. ye shall | Lu 12:5
fear
warn you w. you should | Lu 12:5
fear (A)(E)(N)(R)
w. the lord when he cometh | Lu 12:37
shall
w. his lord shall make ruler | Lu 12:42
over
w. his Lord when he cometh | Lu 12:43
shall
to w. men have committed | Lu 12:48
much
upon w. the tower in Siloam | Lu 13:4
fell
w. Satan hath bound, lo, | Lu 13:16
these
unto him, through w. they | Lu 17:1
come
to w. he had given the | Lu 19:15
money, that
that man by w. he is | Lu 22:22
betrayed
into prison, w. they had | Lu 23:25
desired
This was he of w. I spake, | Joh 1:15
He that
one among you, w. ye know | Joh 1:26
not
This is he of w. I said, After | Joh 1:30
me
Upon w. thou shalt see the | Joh 1:33
Spirit
of w. Moses in the law, and | Joh 1:45
Israelite indeed, in w. is no | Joh 1:47
guile
to w. thou barest witness, | Joh 3:26
behold
For he w. God hath sent | Joh 3:34
speaketh
he w. thou now hast is not | Joh 4:18
thy
so the Son quickeneth w. he | Joh 5:21
will
w. he sent him ye believed | Joh 5:38
you, even Moses, in w. ye | Joh 5:45
trust
believe on him w. he hath | Joh 6:29
sent
him, Lord, to w. shall we go | Joh 6:68
Is not this he, w. they seek to | Joh 7:25
kill
sent me is true, w. ye know | Joh 7:28
not
dead: w. makest thou thyself | Joh 8:53
of w. ye say, that he is your | Joh 8:54
God
unto w. the word of God | Joh 10:35
came
him, w. the Father hath | Joh 10:36
sanctified
behold, he w. thou lovest is | Joh 11:3
sick
dead, w. he raised from the | Joh 12:1
dead
w. he had raised from the | Joh 12:9
dead

to w. hath the arm of the | Joh 12:38
Lord
I know w. I have chosen: | Joh 13:18
but that
another, doubting of w. he | Joh 13:22
spake
one of his disciples, w. Jesus | Joh 13:23
loved
who it should be of w. he | Joh 13:24
spake
He it is, to w. I shall give a | Joh 13:26
sop
w. the world cannot receive | Joh 14:17
w. the Father will send in my | Joh 14:26
name
w. I will send unto you from | Joh 15:26
the
Jesus Christ, w. thou hast | Joh 17:3
sent
name those w. thou hast | Joh 17:11
given me
w. thou hast given me, be | Joh 17:24
with me
and said unto them, W. seek | Joh 18:4
ye
asked he them again, W. seek | Joh 18:7
ye
disciple standing by w. he | Joh 19:26
loved
shall look on him w. they | Joh 19:37
pierced
the other disciple, w. Jesus | Joh 20:2
loved
weepest thou? w. seekest | Joh 20:15
thou
disciples w. Jesus loved saith | Joh 21:7
unto
seeth the disciple w. Jesus | Joh 21:20
loved
unto the apostles w. he had | Ac 1:2
chosen
To w. also he shewed himself | Ac 1:3
alive
W. God hath raised up, | Ac 2:24
having
same Jesus, w. ye have | Ac 2:36
crucified
w. they laid daily at the gate of | Ac 3:2
w. ye delivered up, and denied | Ac 3:13
him
w. God hath raised from the | Ac 3:15
dead
made this man strong, w. ye | Ac 3:16
see
W. the heaven must receive | Ac 3:21
until
Christ of Nazareth, w. ye | Ac 4:10
crucified
w. God raised from the dead | Ac 4:10
on w. this miracle of healing | Ac 4:22
was
child Jesus, w. thou hast | Ac 4:27
anointed
the men w. ye put in prison | Ac 5:25
w. ye slew and hanged on a | Ac 5:30
tree
w. God hath given to them | Ac 5:32
that
to w. a number of men, about | Ac 5:36
four
w. we may appoint over this | Ac 6:3
W. they set before the apostles | Ac 6:6
to w. they shall be in bondage | Ac 7:7
This Moses w. they refused, | Ac 7:35
saying
To w. our fathers would not | Ac 7:39
obey
w. God drave out before the | Ac 7:45
face of
of w. ye have been the | Ac 7:52
betrayers
To w. they all gave heed, from | Ac 8:10
the
of w. speaketh the prophet this | Ac 8:34
I am Jesus w. thou persecutest | Ac 9:5
w. when they had washed, | Ac 9:37
they
said, Behold I am he w. ye | Ac 10:21
seek
w. they slew and hanged on a | Ac 10:39
tree
to w. also he gave testimony | Ac 13:22
w. think ye that I am? I am | Ac 13:25
not
But he, w. God raised again, | Ac 13:37
saw
to the Lord, on w. they | Ac 14:23
believed
upon w. my name is called | Ac 15:17

to w. we gave no commandment   Ac 15:24
Jesus w. I preach unto you, is   Ac 17:3
W. Jason hath received: and these   Ac 17:7
W. ye ignorantly worship   Ac 17:23
by that man w. he hath ordained   Ac 17:31
w. when Aquila and Priscilla had   Ac 18:26
you by Jesus w. Paul preacheth   Ac 19:13
the man in w. the evil spirit was   Ac 19:16
W. he called together with the   Ac 19:25
w. all Asia and world worshippeth   Ac 19:27
among w. I have gone preaching   Ac 20:25
disciple, with w. we should lodge   Ac 21:16
w. they supposed that Paul had   Ac 21:29
from w. also I received letters unto   Ac 22:5
of Nazareth, w. thou persecutest   Ac 22:8
W. I perceived to be accused   Ac 23:29
w. we took, and would have judged   Ac 24:6
w. thyself mayest take knowledge   Ac 24:8
About w. when I was at   Ac 25:15
w. I answered, It is not the manner   Ac 25:16
w. when the accusers stood up   Ac 25:18
dead, w. Paul affirmed to be alive   Ac 25:19
w. all the multitude of the Jews   Ac 25:24
w. I have no certain thing to write   Ac 25:26
I am Jesus w. thou persecutest   Ac 26:15
Gentiles, unto w. now I send thee   Ac 26:17
before w. also I speak freely   Ac 26:26
God, whose I am, and w. I serve   Ac 27:23
w. though he hath escaped the sea   Ac 28:4
to w. Paul entered in, and prayed   Ac 28:8
w. when Paul saw, he thanked God   Ac 28:15
to w. he expounded and testified   Ac 28:23
By w. we have received grace   Ro 1:5
Among w. are ye also the called   Ro 1:6
w. I serve with my spirit in the   Ro 1:9
W. God had set forth to be a   Ro 3:25
unto w. God imputed righteousness   Ro 4:6
to w. the Lord will not impute sin   Ro 4:8
before him w. he believed, even   Ro 4:17
us also, to w. it shall be imputed   Ro 4:24
By w. also we have access by faith   Ro 5:2
by w. we have now received   Ro 5:11
to w. ye yield yourselves servants   Ro 6:16
his servants ye are to w. ye obey   Ro 6:16
For w. he did foreknow, he also did   Ro 8:29
Moreover w. he did predestinate   Ro 8:30
w. he called, them he also   Ro 8:30
w. he justified, them he also   Ro 8:30
to w. pertaineth the adoption   Ro 9:4
of w. as concerning the flesh   Ro 9:5
have mercy on w. I will have mercy   Ro 9:15
on w. I will have compassion   Ro 9:15
he mercy on w. he will have mercy   Ro 9:18
mercy, and w. he will he hardeneth   Ro 9:18
Even us, w. he hath called, not of   Ro 9:24
him in w. they have not believed   Ro 10:14
in him of w. they have not heard   Ro 10:14

things: to w. be glory for ever   Ro 11:36
dues: tribute to w. tribute is due   Ro 13:7
custom to w. custom   Ro 13:7
fear to w. fear   Ro 13:9
honour to w. honour   Ro 13:9
with thy meat, for w. Christ died   Ro 14:15
To w. he was not spoken of, they   Ro 15:21
unto w. not only I give thanks, but   Ro 16:4
by w. ye were called unto   1Co 1:9
but ministers by w. ye believed   1Co 3:5
to be married to w. she will   1Co 7:39
of w. are all things, and we in him   1Co 8:6
by w. are all things, and we by   1Co 8:6
brother perish, for w. Christ died   1Co 8:11
upon w. the ends of the world are   1Co 10:11
of w. the greater part remain unto   1Co 15:6
w. he raised not up, if so be that   1Co 15:15
in w. we trust that he will yet   2Co 1:10
from them of w. I ought to rejoice   2Co 2:3
To w. ye forgive anything, I forgive   2Co 2:10
forgave many things, to w. I forgave it   2Co 2:10
In w. the god of this world hath   2Co 4:4
w. we have often times proved   2Co 8:22
but w. the Lord commendeth   2Co 10:18
another Jesus, w. we have not   2Co 11:4
any of them w. I sent unto you   2Co 12:17
To w. be glory for ever and ever   Ga 1:5
To w. we gave place by subjection   Ga 2:5
come to w. the promise was made   Ga 3:19
of w. I travail in birth again   Ga 4:19
by w. the world is crucified unto   Ga 6:14
In w. we have redemption through   Eph 1:7
In w. also we have obtained an   Eph 1:11
In w. ye also trusted, after that ye   Eph 1:13
in w. also after that ye believed   Eph 1:13
Among w. also we all had our   Eph 2:3
In w. all the building fitly framed   Eph 2:21
In w. ye also are builded together   Eph 2:22
In w. we have boldness and access   Eph 3:12
Of w. the whole family in heaven   Eph 3:15
w. the whole body fitly joined   Eph 4:16
W. I have sent unto you for   Eph 6:22
among w. ye shine as lights in the   Ph'p 2:15
for w. I have suffered the loss   Ph'p 3:8
walk, of w. I have told you often   Ph'p 3:18
In w. we have redemption through   Col 1:14
To w. God would make known what   Col 1:27
W. we preach, warning every man   Col 1:28
In w. are hid all the treasures of   Col 2:3
In w. also ye are circumcised   Col 2:11
W. I have sent unto you for   Col 4:8
w. ye received commandments   Col 4:10
w. he raised from the dead   1Th 1:10
w. the Lord shall consume with the   2Th 2:8
save sinners; of w. I am chief   1Ti 1:15
w. is Hymenæus and Alexander   1Ti 1:20
w. I have delivered unto Satan   1Ti 1:20
w. no man hath seen nor can see   1Ti 6:16
to w. be honour and power   1Ti 6:16
w. I serve from my forefathers   2Ti 1:3

I know w. I have believed, and am   2Ti 1:12
w. are Phygellus and Hermogenes   2Ti 1:15
of w. is Hymenæus and Philetus   2Ti 2:17
of w. thou hast learned them   2Ti 3:14
Of w. be thou ware also; for he   2Ti 4:15
to w. be glory for ever and ever   2Ti 4:18
w. I have begotten in my bonds   Ph'm 10
W. I have sent again: thou   Ph'm 12
W. I would have retained with me   Ph'm 13
w. he hath appointed heir of all   Heb 1:2
by w. also he made the worlds   Heb 1:2
became him, for w. are all things   Heb 2:10
and by w. are all things, in   Heb 2:10
with w. was he grieved forty years   Heb 3:17
to w. sware he that they should not   Heb 3:18
they to w. it was first preached   Heb 4:6
eyes of him with w. we have to do   Heb 4:13
Of w. we have many things to say   Heb 5:11
meet for them by w. it is dressed   Heb 6:7
To w. also Abraham gave a tenth   Heb 7:2
w. even the patriarch Abraham   Heb 7:4
of w. it is witnessed that he liveth   Heb 7:8
he of w. these things are spoken   Heb 7:13
Of w. it was said, That in Isaac   Heb 11:18
Of w. the world was not worthy   Heb 11:38
w. the Lord loveth he chasteneth   Heb 12:6
and scourgeth every son w. he   Heb 12:6
what son is he w. the father   Heb 12:7
to w. be glory for ever and ever   Heb 13:21
with w. if he come shortly, I will   Heb 13:23
lights, with w. is no variableness   Jas 1:17
W. having not seen, ye love   1Pe 1:8
w. though now ye see him not, yet   1Pe 1:8
Unto w. it was revealed, that not   1Pe 1:12
To w. coming, as unto a living   1Pe 2:4
By w. also he went and preached (S)   1Pe 3:19
w. be praise and dominion for ever   1Pe 4:11
about, seeking w. he may devour   1Pe 5:8
W. resist stedfast in the faith   1Pe 5:9
Son, in w. I am well pleased   2Pe 1:17
by reason of w. the way of truth   2Pe 2:2
w. the mist of darkness is reserved   2Pe 2:17
for of w. a man is overcome, of the   2Pe 2:19
not his brother w. he hath seen   1Jo 4:20
he love God w. he hath not seen   1Jo 4:20
her children, w. I love in the truth   2Jo 1
Gaius, w. I love in the truth   3Jo 1
w. if thou bring forward on their   3Jo 6
to w. is reserved the blackness of   Jude 13
to w. it was given to hurt the earth   Re 7:2
With w. the kings of the earth have   Re 17:2
the number of w. is as the sand   Re 20:8

WHOMSOEVER

With w. thou findest the gods   Ge 31:32
With w. of thy servants it be found   Ge 44:9

w. he toucheth that hath the | Le 15:11
w. I say unto thee, This shall | J'g 7:4
not go
w. the Lord our God shall | J'g 11:24
drive
giveth it to w. he will, and | Da 4:17
setteth
men, and giveth it to w. | Da 4:25;
he will | 4:32
appointeth over it w. he will | Da 5:21
to w. the Son will reveal him | M't 11:27
but on w. it shall fall, it will | M't 21:44
W. I shall kiss, that same is | M't 26:48;
he | M'k 14:44
one prisoner, w. they desired | M'k 15:6
me; and to w. I will I give it | Lu 4:6
For unto w. much is given, | Lu 12:48
of
w. it shall fall, it shall grind | Lu 20:18
receiveth w. I send receiveth | Joh 13:20
that on w. I lay hands, he | Ac 8:19
may
w. ye shall approve by your | 1Co 16:3

WHORE

daughter, to cause her to be | Le 19:29
a w.
harlot (A)(E)(R) | Le 19:29;
21:7, 9; De 22:21; 23:18; Pr 23:27;
Isa 57:3; Eze 16:28; Re 17:1, 15-16; 19:2
a prostitute (B) | Le 19:29; 21:7
shall not take a wife that is a | Le 21:7
w.
profane herself by playing the | Le 21:9
w.
harlot (B) | Le 21:9;
De 22:21; 23:18; Pr 23:27; Isa 57:3;
Eze 16:28; Re 17:1, 15-16; 19:2
to play the w. in her father's | De 22:21
house
no w. of the daughters of | De 23:17
Israel
cult prostitute (A)(E)(R) | De 23:17
temple prostitute (B) | De 23:17
shalt not bring the hire of a | De 23:18
w.
And his concubine played the | J'g 19:2
w.
was untrue to him (A) | J'g 19:2
played him false (E) | J'g 19:2
played the harlot (E) | J'g 19:2
For a w. is a deep ditch; and | Pr 23:27
a
seed of the adulterer and the | Isa 57:3
w.
hast played the w. also with | Eze 16:28
judgment of the great w. that | Re 17:1
where the w. sitteth, are | Re 17:15
peoples
these shall hate the w. and | Re 17:16
shall
for he hath judged the great | Re 19:2
w.

WHOREDOM

behold, she is with child by | Ge 38:24
w.
played the harlot (A) | Ge 38:24;
Le 20:5; Nu 25:1; Eze 16:17; 20:30;
Ho 4:10, 13-14, 18; 5:3
harlotry (B) | Ge 38:24;
Le 20:5; Jer 3:9; Eze 23:27; 43:7
harlotry (R) | Ge 38:24;
Jer 3:9; Eze 23:27; 43:7; Ho 1:2; 4:18;
6:10
lest the land fall to w. and | Le 19:29
full of wickedness (A) | Le 19:29
licentious and thoroughly | Le 19:29
wicked (R)
harlot (R) | Le 19:29
to commit w. with Molech, | Le 20:5
from
play the harlot (E) | Le 20:5;
Nu 25:1; Eze 16:17; 20:30
playing the harlot (R) | Le 20:5;
Nu 25:1; Eze 16:17; Ho 4:10, 13-14; 5:3
people began to commit w. | Nu 25:1
illicit relations (B) | Nu 25:1
through the lightness of her w. | Jer 3:9
the lewdness of thy w. and | Jer 13:27
thine
harlotry (A) | Jer 13:27;
Eze 23:27; 43:9; Ho 1:2; 4:11
lewd harlotries (B) | Jer 13:27
and didst commit w. with | Eze 16:17
them
played the harlot (B) | Eze 16:17
multiplied your w. (E) | Eze 16:29

unto thee on every side for | Eze 16:33
thy w.
harlotries (A) | Eze 16:33; 23:8
your embraces (B) | Eze 16:33
your harlotries (R) | Eze 16:33
commit ye w. after their | Eze 20:30
and poured their w. upon her | Eze 23:8
lavished their lusts upon her | Eze 23:8
(B)
and they defiled her with | Eze 23:17
their w.
their evil desire (A) | Eze 23:17
defiled her with their lust | Eze 23:17
(B)(R)
thy w. brought from the land | Eze 23:27
they, nor their kings, by their | Eze 43:7
w.
Now let them put away their | Eze 43:9
w.
idolatry (R) | Eze 43:9
land hath committed great w. | Ho 1:2
harlotry (B) | Ho 1:2; 4:13
they shall commit w. and | Ho 4:10
shall not
play the harlot (B) | Ho 4:10;
4:14; 5:3; 6:10
play the harlot (E) | Ho 4:10;
4:13-14, 18; 5:3
W. and wine and new wine | Ho 4:11
take
lust (B)(R) | Ho 4:11
your daughters shall commit | Ho 4:13
w.
daughters when they commit | Ho 4:14
w.
have committed w. continually | Ho 4:18
O Ephraim, thou committest | Ho 5:3
w.
there is the w. of Ephraim, | Ho 6:10
Israel
harlotry and idolatry (A) | Ho 6:10

WHOREDOMS

and bear your w. until your | Nu 14:33
your unfaithfulness (B)(R) | Nu 14:33
your iniquities (E) | Nu 14:33
as the w. of thy mother | 2Ki 9:22
Jezebel
witchcrafts (A) | 2Ki 9:22
harlotries and seductions (B) | 2Ki 9:22
her w. are many (E) | 2Ki 9:22
harlotries and sorceries (R) | 2Ki 9:22
to the w. of the house of | 2Ch 21:13
Ahab
harlotry (A) | 2Ch 21:13;
Jer 3:2; Eze 16:25-26, 29, 35; Ho 1:2;
2:2, 4; 4:12; 5:4
harlotry (B) | 2Ch 21:13;
Eze 16:20, 22, 25; 23:8, 29, 35; Ho 1:2,
2:2, 4; 4:12; 5:4
play the harlot (E) | 2Ch 21:13;
Eze 23:3, 43
unfaithfulness (R) | 2Ch 21:13
hast polluted the land with thy | Jer 3:2
w.
fornication and wickedness (B) | Jer 3:2
vile harlotry (R) | Jer 3:2;
Eze 16:25-26; 23:8, 11, 14, 18-19, 29, 35,
43; Ho 1:2; 2:2; 4:12; 5:4
Is this of thy w. a small | Eze 16:20
matter
harlotries (A) | Eze 16:20;
16:24, 36; 23:7-8, 11, 14, 18-19
harlotries (R) | Eze 16:20;
16:22, 36; 23:7; Na 3:4
thy w. thou hast not | Eze 16:22
remembered
that passed by, and multiplied | Eze 16:25
thy w.
hast increased thy w. to | Eze 16:26
provoke
thee from other women in | Eze 16:34
thy w.
play the harlot (R) | Eze 16:34; 23:3
none followeth thee to | Eze 16:34
commit w.
discovered through thy w. | Eze 16:36
with
And they committed w. in | Eze 23:3
Egypt
played the harlot (A) | Eze 23:3; 23:43
played the harlot (B) | Eze 23:3
they committed w. in their | Eze 23:3
youth
she committed her w. with | Eze 23:7
them
harlotries (A) | Eze 23:7; 23:14, 18
left she her w. brought from | Eze 23:8
Egypt

and in her w. more than her | Eze 23:11
sister
more wanton (B) | Eze 23:11
more than her sister in her w. | Eze 23:11
And that she increased her | Eze 23:14
w.
So she discovered her w. | Eze 23:18
Yet she multiplied her w. in | Eze 23:19
of thy w. shall be discovered | Eze 23:29
both thy lewdness and thy w. | Eze 23:29
thou also thy lewdness and | Eze 23:35
thy w.
Will they now commit w. | Eze 23:43
with her
commit adultery (B) | Eze 23:43
a wife of w. and children of w. | Ho 1:2
put away her w. out of her | Ho 2:2
sight
for they be the children of w. | Ho 2:4
of w. hath caused them to err | Ho 4:12
spirit of w. is in the midst of | Ho 5:4
them
the w. of the wellfavoured | Na 3:4
harlot
that selleth nations through her | Na 3:4
w.

WHOREMONGER

we know, that no w. nor | Eph 5:5
unclean
sexual vice (A) | Eph 5:5
unchastity (B) | Eph 5:5
fornicator (E) | Eph 5:5
given to fornication (N) | Eph 5:5
immoral (P)(R) | Eph 5:5

WHOREMONGERS

For w. for them that defile | 1Ti 1:10
immoral persons (A)(R) | 1Ti 1:10
the unchaste (B) | 1Ti 1:10
fornicators (E)(N) | 1Ti 1:10
sexually uncontrolled (P) | 1Ti 1:10
w. and adulterers God will | Heb 13:4
judge
the unchaste (A)(B) | Heb 13:4
fornicators (E)(N) | Heb 13:4
traffic in the bodies of others | Heb 13:4
(P)
the immoral (R) | Heb 13:4
and w. and sorcerers, and | Re 21:8
the lewd and adulterous (A) | Re 21:8
the lewd (B) | Re 21:8
fornicators (E)(N)(R) | Re 21:8
traffickers in sex (P) | Re 21:8
are dogs, and sorcerers, and | Re 22:15
w.
practice impurity (A) | Re 22:15
the unchaste (B) | Re 22:15
fornicators (E)(N)(R) | Re 22:15
the impure (P) | Re 22:15

WHORES

They give gifts to all w.: but | Eze 16:33
thou
harlots (A)(B)(E) | Eze 16:33
lovers (R) | Eze 16:33
themselves are separated with | Ho 4:14
w.
alone with prostitutes (A) | Ho 4:14
aside with harlots (B)(E)(R) | Ho 4:14

WHORE'S

thou hadst a w. forehead, thou | Jer 3:3
the brow of a prostitute (A) | Jer 3:3
the brow of an harlot (B) | Jer 3:3
a harlot's forehead (E) | Jer 3:3
a harlot's brow (R) | Jer 3:3

WHORING

and they go a w. after their | Ex 34:15
gods
play the harlot (A) | Ex 34:15;
34:16; Le 17:7; 20:5-6; 15:39; 31:16;
J'g 2:17; 8:33; 1Ch 5:25; 2Ch 21:13;
Ps 106:39; Eze 23:30; Ho 4:12; 9:1
ran wantonly after their | Ex 34:15;
gods (B) | 34:16
play the harlot (E) | Ex 34:15;
34:16; Le 17:7; 20:5-6; Nu 15:39;
De 31:16; J'g 2:17; 8:27, 33; 1Ch 5:25;
2Ch 21:13; Ps 73:27; 106:39; Eze 6:9;
23:30; Ho 4:12; 9:1
play the harlot (R) | Ex 34:15;
34:16; 17:7; 20:5; De 31:16; J'g 2:17;
8:27, 33; 1Ch 5:25; Ps 106:39;
Eze 23:30; Ho 9:1

daughters go a *w.* after their | Ex 34:16
gods
thy sons go a *w.* after their | Ex 34:16
gods
after whom they have gone a | Le 17:7
w.
adulterously courting (B) | Le 17:7
off, and all that go a *w.* after | Le 20:5
him
harlotry after Moloch (B) | Le 20:5
wizards, to go a *w.* after | Le 20:6
them, I
harlotry after them (B) | Le 20:6
after which ye used to go a | Nu 15:39
w.
led you into harlotry (B) | Nu 15:39
go after wantonly (R) | Nu 15:39
and go a *w.* after the gods of | De 31:16
play the harlot (B) | De 31:16;
Eze 23:30; Ho 9:1
but they went a *w.* after | J'g 2:17
other gods
worshiping other gods (B) | J'g 2:17
all israel went thither a *w.* | J'g 8:27
after it
paid homage to (A) | J'g 8:27
Israel venerated it (B) | J'g 8:27
again, and went a *w.* after | J'g 8:33
Baalim
turned to the Baals (B) | J'g 8:33
and went a *w.* after the gods | 1Ch 5:25
of the
turned adulterously after | 1Ch 5:25
other gods (B)
inhabitants of | 2Ch 21:13
Jerusalem go a *w.*
commit harlotry (B) | 2Ch 21:13
unfaithfulness (R) | 2Ch 21:13
all them that go a *w.* from | Ps 73:27
thee
play thee false (B)(R) | Ps 73:27
went a *w.* with their own | Ps 106:39
inventions
immoral in their practices | Ps 106:39
(A)(B)
which go a *w.* after their idols | Eze 6:9
turn after idols wantonly (A) | Eze 6:9
their adulterous hearts turned | Eze 6:9
from me (B)
their wanton hearts departed | Eze 6:9
from me (R)
hast gone a *w.* after the | Eze 23:30
heathen
gone a *w.* from under their | Ho 4:12
God
a spirit of harlotry led them | Ho 4:12
astray (B)(R)
thou hast gone a *w.* from thy | Ho 9:1
God

WHORISH

by means of a *w.* woman a | Pr 6:26
man is
a harlot (A)(B)(E)(R) | Pr 6:26
I am broken with their *w.* | Eze 6:9
heart
lewdness (A) | Eze 6:9
lewd heart (E) | Eze 6:9
their wanton heart (R) | Eze 6:9
work of an imperious *w.* | Eze 16:30
woman
domineering harlot (A) | Eze 16:30
a brazen faced harlot | Eze 16:30
(B)(R)
impudent harlot (E) | Eze 16:30

WHOSE

w. seed is in itself, upon the | Ge 1:11
earth
w. seed was in itself, after his | Ge 1:12
kind
in *w.* nostrils was the breath | Ge 7:22
of life
tower, *w.* top may reach unto | Ge 11:4
heaven
an Egyptian, *w.* name was | Ge 16:1
Hagar
w. flesh of his foreskin is not | Ge 17:14
W. daughter art thou? tell | Ge 24:23
me, I
Canaanites, in *w.* land I | Ge 24:37
dwell
and said, *W.* daughter art | Ge 24:47
thou
W. art thou? and whither | Ge 32:17
goest
thou? and *w.* are these | Ge 32:17
before thee

Adullamite, *w.* name was | Ge 38:1
Hirah
Canaanite, *w.* name was | Ge 38:2
Shuah
Er his firstborn, *w.* name was | Ge 38:6
Tamar
man, *w.* these are, am I with | Ge 38:25
child
Discern, I pray thee, *w.* | Ge 38:25
are these
man in *w.* hand the cup is | Ge 44:17
found
well: *w.* branches run over | Ge 49:22
the wall
the Lord, *w.* name is | Ex 34:14
Jealous, is a
every one *w.* heart stirred | Ex 35:21
him up
the women *w.* heart stirred | Ex 35:26
them up
w. heart made them willing to | Ex 35:29
bring
in *w.* heart the Lord had put | Ex 36:2
wisdom
one *w.* heart stirred him up to | Ex 36:2
come
man *w.* hair is fallen off his | Le 13:40
head
w. hand is not able to get | Le 14:32
that
and of him *w.* seed goeth | Le 15:32
from him
w. blood was brought in to | Le 16:27
make
w. head the anointing oil was | Le 21:10
poured
or a man *w.* seed goeth from | Le 22:4
him
woman, *w.* father was an | Le 24:10
Egyptian
and the man *w.* eyes are | Nu 24:3;
open | 24:15
a land *w.* stones are iron, and | De 8:9
out
out of *w.* hills thou mayest dig | De 8:9
brass
w. land the Lord thy God | De 19:1
giveth
a nation *w.* tongue thou shalt | De 28:49
not
w. heart turneth away this | De 29:18
day from
of the Amorites, in *w.* land | Jos 24:15
ye dwell
the captain of *w.* host was | J'g 4:2
Sisera
the Amorites, in *w.* land ye | J'g 6:10
dwell
son, *w.* name he called | J'g 8:31
Abimelech
of the Danites, *w.* name was | J'g 13:2
Manoah
valley of Sorek, *w.* name was | J'g 16:4
Delilah
mount Ephraim, *w.* name was | J'g 17:1
Micah
him in *w.* sight I shall find | Ru 2:2
grace
the reapers, *W.* damsel is this | Ru 2:5
under *w.* wings thou art come | Ru 2:12
to
kindred, with *w.* maidens thou | Ru 3:2
wast
w. name was Kish, the son of | 1Sa 9:1
Abiel
And he had a son, *w.* name | 1Sa 9:2
was Saul
of men, *w.* hearts God had | 1Sa 10:26
touched
his anointed: *w.* ox have I | 1Sa 12:3
taken
or *w.* ass have I taken | 1Sa 12:3
of *w.* hand have I received | 1Sa 12:3
any
w. height was six cubits and | 1Sa 17:4
a span
w. name was Jesse; and he | 1Sa 17:12
had
host, Abner, *w.* son is this | 1Sa 17:55
youth
Enquire *w.* son the stripling | 1Sa 17:56
is
W. son art thou, thou young | 1Sa 17:58
man
Maon, *w.* possessions were in | 1Sa 25:2
Carmel
a concubine, *w.* name was | 2Sa 3:7
Rizpah
his behalf, saying, *W.* is the | 2Sa 3:12
land

w. name is called by the name | 2Sa 6:2
of
of Saul a servant *w.* name was | 2Sa 9:2
Ziba
had a young son, *w.* name | 2Sa 9:12
was Micha
had a fair sister, *w.* name | 2Sa 13:1
was Tamar
had a friend, *w.* name was | 2Sa 13:3
Jonadab
one daughter, *w.* name was | 2Sa 14:27
Tamar
w. name was Shimei, the son | 2Sa 16:5
of Gera
Saul, in *w.* stead thou hast | 2Sa 16:8
reigned
w. heart is as the heart of a | 2Sa 17:10
lion
son, *w.* name was Ithra an | 2Sa 17:25
Israelite
w. name was Sheba, the son | 2Sa 20:1
of Bichri
weight of *w.* spear weighed | 2Sa 21:16
three
of *w.* spear was like a | 2Sa 21:19
weaver's beam
woman *w.* the living child | 1Ki 3:26
was unto
to his ways, *w.* heart thou | 1Ki 8:39
knowest
servant, *w.* mother's name | 1Ki 11:26
was Zeruah
a lord on *w.* hand the king | 2Ki 7:2
leaned
the lord on *w.* hand he | 2Ki 7:17
leaned to
w. son he had restored to life | 2Ki 8:1;
| 8:5
w. hand they delivered the | 2Ki 12:15
money to
is it not he, *w.* high places | 2Ki 18:22
and *w.* altars Hezekiah hath | 2Ki 18:22
taken
W. sisters were Zeruiah, and | 1Ch 2:16
Abigail
another wife, *w.* name was | 1Ch 2:26
Atarah
an Egyptian, *w.* name was | 1Ch 2:34
Jarha
w. number was in the days of | 1Ch 7:2
David
w. sister's name was | 1Ch 7:15
Maachah
Gibeon; *w.* wife's name was | 1Ch 8:29
Maachah
Azel had six sons, *w.* names | 1Ch 8:38;
are these | 9:44
Jehiel, *w.* wife's name was | 1Ch 9:35
Maachah
w. faces were like the faces of | 1Ch 12:8
lions
cherubims, *w.* name is called | 1Ch 13:6
w. spear staff was like a | 1Ch 20:5
weaver's beam
w. fingers and toes were four | 1Ch 20:6
w. brethren were strong men, | 1Ch 26:7
Elihu
ways, *w.* heart thou knowest | 2Ch 6:30
them *w.* heart is perfect | 2Ch 16:9
toward him
Lord was there, *w.* name was | 2Ch 28:9
Obed
all them *w.* spirit God had | Ezr 1:5
raised
unto one, *w.* name was | Ezr 5:14
Sheshbazzar
w. habitation is in Jerusalem | Ezr 7:15
sons of Adonikam, *w.* names | Ezr 8:13
are these
a certain Jew, *w.* name was | Es 2:5
Mordecai
the land of Uz, *w.* name was | Job 1:1
Job
light given to a man *w.* way | Job 3:23
is hid
of clay, *w.* foundation is in | Job 4:19
the dust
W. harvest the hungry eateth | Job 5:5
W. hope shall be cut off, and | Job 8:14
and *w.* trust shall be a spider's | Job 8:14
web
w. hand God bringeth | Job 12:6
abundantly
In *w.* hand is the soul of | Job 12:10
every living
w. foundation was overflown | Job 22:16
with a
and *w.* spirit came from thee | Job 26:4
w. fathers I would have | Job 30:1
disdained

Out of *w*. womb came the ice — Job 38:29

W. house I have made the — Job 39:6

In *w*. eyes a vile person is contemned — Ps 15:4

w. belly thou fillest with thy hid — Ps 17:14

In *w*. hands is mischief, and their — Ps 26:10

Blessed is he *w*. transgression is forgiven, *w*. sin is covered — Ps 32:1

and in *w*. spirit there is no guile — Ps 32:2

w. mouth must be held in with bit and — Ps 32:9

is the nation *w*. God is the Lord — Ps 33:12

not, and in *w*. mouths are no reproofs — Ps 38:14

w. teeth are spears and arrows, and — Ps 57:4

w. spirit was not stedfast with God. — Ps 78:8

that thou, *w*. name alone is Jehovah — Ps 83:18

is the man *w*. strength is in thee — Ps 84:5

in *w*. heart are the ways of them — Ps 84:5

W. feet they hurt with fetters: he was — Ps 105:18

W. mouth speaketh vanity — Ps 144:8

w. mouth speaketh vanity, and their — Ps 144:11

is that people, *w*. God is the Lord — Ps 144:15

help, *w*. hope is in the Lord his God — Ps 146:5

W. ways are crooked, and they — Pr 2:15

W. hatred is covered by deceit, his — Pr 26:26

a generation, *w*. teeth are as swords — Pr 30:14

For there is a man *w*. labour is in — Ec 2:21

w. heart is snares and nets — Ec 7:26

shall be as an oak *w*. leaf fadeth — Isa 1:30

man, *w*. breath is in his nostrils — Isa 2:22

W. arrows are sharp, and all their — Isa 5:28

as an oak, *w*. substance is in them — Isa 6:13

w. graven images did excel them — Isa 10:10

them captives, *w*. captives they were — Isa 14:2

w. land the rivers have spoiled — Isa 18:2; 18:7

city *w*. antiquity is of ancient days — Isa 23:7

city, *w*. merchants are princes — Isa 23:8

w. traffickers are the honourable of — Isa 23:8

peace, *w*. mind is stayed on thee — Isa 26:3

w. glorious beauty is a fading flower — Isa 28:1

w. breaking cometh suddenly at an — Isa 30:13

w. fire is in Zion, and his furnace in — Isa 31:9

is it not he, *w*. high places taken — Isa 36:7

and *w*. altars Hezekiah hath — Isa 36:7

the Chaldeans, *w*. cry is in the ships — Isa 43:14

w. right hand I have holden — Isa 45:1

the people in *w*. heart is my law — Isa 51:7

that divided the sea, *w*. waves roared — Isa 51:15

w. name is Holy; I dwell in the — Isa 57:15

rest, *w*. waters cast up mire and dirt — Isa 57:20

spring of water, *w*. waters fail not — Isa 58:11

nation *w*. language thou knowest not — Jer 5:15

and *w*. heart departed from the Lord — Jer 17:5

the Lord, and *w*. hope the Lord is — Jer 17:7

upon *w*. roofs they have burned — Jer 19:13

the hand of them *w*. face thou fearest — Jer 22:25

w. roofs they have offered incense — Jer 32:29

w. wickedness I have hid my face — Jer 33:5

w. name was Irijah, the son — Jer 37:13

know *w*. words shall stand, mine — Jer 44:28

w. waters are moved as the rivers — Jer 46:7

king, *w*. name is the Lord of hosts — Jer 46:18; 48:15

they *w*. judgment was not to drink — Jer 49:12

king, *w*. name is the Lord of hosts — Jer 51:57

w. words canst not understand — Eze 3:6

w. heart walketh after the heart of — Eze 11:21

w. branches turned toward him — Eze 17:6

him king, *w*. oath he despised — Eze 17:16

w. covenant he brake, even with — Eze 17:16

w. sight I made myself known unto — Eze 20:9

in *w*. sight I brought them out — Eze 20:14

in *w*. sight I brought them forth — Eze 20:22

w. day is come, when iniquity shall — Eze 21:25

more, until he come *w*. right it is — Eze 21:27

w. day is come, when their iniquity — Eze 21:29

w. flesh is as the flesh of asses — Eze 23:20

w. issue is like the issue of horses — Eze 23:20

city, to the pot *w*. scum is therein — Eze 24:6

and *w*. scum is not gone out of it — Eze 24:6

W. graves are set in the sides of — Eze 32:23

w. appearance was like the appearance — Eze 40:3

w. prospect is toward the south — Eze 40:45

w. prospect is toward the north — Eze 40:46

w. prospect is toward the east — Eze 42:15

gate *w*. prospect is toward the east — Eze 43:4

trees for meat, *w*. leaf shall not fade — Eze 47:12

gods, *w*. dwelling is not with — Da 2:11

Daniel, *w*. name was Belteshazzar — Da 2:26

image, *w*. brightness was excellent — Da 2:31

w. height was threescore cubits — Da 3:1

w. bodies the fire had no power — Da 3:27

w. name was Belteshazzar — Da 4:8

Daniel, *w*. name was Belteshazzar — Da 4:19

w. height reached unto the heaven — Da 4:20

W. leaves were fair, and the fruit — Da 4:21

upon *w*. branches the fowls of — Da 4:21

w. dominion is an everlasting — Da 4:34

all *w*. works are truth, and all his — Da 4:37

the God in *w*. hand thy breath — Da 5:23

and *w*. are all thy ways, hast thou not — Da 5:23

sit, *w*. garment was white as snow — Da 7:9

dreadful, *w*. teeth were of iron — Da 7:19

w. look was more stout than his — Da 7:20

w. kingdom is an everlasting kingdom — Da 7:27

w. name was called Belteshazzar — Da 10:1

w. loins were girded with fine gold of — Da 10:5

w. teeth are the teeth of a lion, and — Joe 1:6

w. height was like the height — Am 2:9

Lord, *w*. name is The God of hosts — Am 5:27

of the rock, *w*. habitation high — Ob 3

for *w*. cause this evil is upon us — Jon 1:7

w. cause this evil is upon us — Jon 1:8

w. goings forth have been from of old — Mic 5:2

w. rampart was the sea, and her — Na 3:8

the man *w*. name is The Branch — Zec 6:12

W. possessors slay them, and hold — Zec 11:5

w. shoes I am not worthy to bear — M't 3:11

W. fan is in his hand, and he will — M't 3:12

w. surname was Thaddæus — M't 10:3

W. is this image and — M't 22:20

W. wife shall she be of the seven — M't 22:28

think ye of Christ? *w*. son is he — M't 22:42

latchet of *w*. shoes I am not worthy — M'k 1:7

w. young daughter had an unclean — M'k 7:25

them, *W*. is this image and — M'k 12:16

w. wife shall she be of them? for — M'k 12:23

to a man *w*. name was Joseph — Lu 1:27

Jerusalem, *w*. name was Simeon — Lu 2:25

w. shoes I am not worthy to — Lu 3:16

W. fan is in his hand, and he will — Lu 3:17

w. right hand was withered — Lu 6:6

w. shall those things be, which — Lu 12:20

w. blood Pilate had mingled with — Lu 13:1

W. image and superscription — Lu 20:24

w. wife of them is she — Lu 20:33

w. name was Cleopas, answering — Lu 24:18

sent from God, *w*. name was John — Joh 1:6

w. shoe's latchet I am not worthy — Joh 1:27

w. son was sick at Capernaum — Joh 4:46

w. father and mother we know — Joh 6:42

w. own the sheep are not, seeth the — Joh 10:12

hair, *w*. brother Lazarus was sick — Joh 11:2

his kinsman *w*. ear Peter cut off — Joh 18:26

but cast lots for it, *w*. it shall be — Joh 19:24

W. soever sins ye remit, they are — Joh 20:23

w. soever sins ye retain, they are — Joh 20:23

young man's feet, *w*. name was Saul — Ac 7:58

Simon, *w*. surname was Peter — Ac 10:5; 10:32; 11:13

tanner, *w*. house is by the sea side — Ac 10:6

of John, *w*. surname was Mark — Ac 12:12

them John, *w*. surname was Mark — Ac 12:25

a Jew, *w*. name was Bar-jesus — Ac 13:6

w. shoes of his feet I am not — Ac 13:25

them John, *w*. surname was Mark — Ac 15:37

w. heart the Lord opened, that she — Ac 16:14

w. house joined hard to the — Ac 18:7

God, *w*. I am, and whom I serve — Ac 27:23

of the island, *w*. name was Publius — Ac 28:7

isle, *w*. sign was Castor and Pollux — Ac 28:11

w. praise is not of men, but of God — Ro 2:29

may come? *w*. damnation is just — Ro 3:8

W. mouth is full of cursing — Ro 3:14

are they *w*. iniquities are forgiven — Ro 4:7

forgiven, and *w*. sins are covered — Ro 4:7

W. are the fathers, and of whom — Ro 9:5

w. praise is in the gospel — 2Co 8:18

w. end shall be according to their — 2Co 11:15

before *w*. eyes Jesus Christ hath — Ga 3:1

W. end is destruction, *w*. God is — Ph'p 3:19

w. glory is in their shame, *Ph'p 3:19*
who
w. names are in the book of *Ph'p 4:3*
life
w. coming is after the working *2Th 2:9*
W. mouths must be stopped, *Tit 1:11*
who
w. house are we, if we hold *Heb 3:6*
fast the
w. carcases fell in the *Heb 3:17*
wilderness
cursing; w. end is to be *Heb 6:8*
burned
he w. descent is not counted *Heb 7:6*
from
w. builder and maker is *Heb 11:10*
God
W. voice then shook the *Heb 12:26*
earth: but
w. faith follow, considering *Heb 13:7*
the end
w. blood is brought into the *Heb 13:11*
holy
by w. stripes ye were healed *1Pe 2:24*
W. adorning, let it not be that *1Pe 3:3*
w. daughters ye are, as long as *1Pe 3:6*
ye
w. judgment now of a long *2Pe 2:3*
time
trees w. fruit withereth, *Jude 12*
without
w. name in the Hebrew tongue *Re 9:11*
is
w. names are not written in the *Re 13:8*
beast, w. deadly wound was *Re 13:12*
healed
w. names were not written in *Re 17:8*
from w. face the earth and *Re 20:11*

WHOSO

W. sheddeth man's blood, by *Ge 9:6*
man
w. toucheth their carcases *Le 11:27*
shall be
w. toucheth any thing that is *Le 22:4*
unclean
W. killeth any person, the *Nu 35:30*
W. killeth his neighbour *De 19:4*
ignorantly
w. followeth her, let him be *2Ch 23:14*
slain with
W. offereth praise glorifieth *Ps 50:23*
me: and
W. privily slandereth his *Ps 101:5*
neighbour
W. is wise, and will observe *Ps 107:43*
these
But w. hearkeneth unto me *Pr 1:33*
shall dwell
But w. committeth adultery *Pr 6:32*
with a
For w. findeth me findeth life *Pr 8:35*
W. is simple, let him turn in *Pr 9:4;*
    9:16
W. loveth instruction loveth *Pr 12:1*
W. despiseth the word shall *Pr 13:13*
be
w. trusteth in the Lord, happy *Pr 16:20*
is he
W. mocketh the poor *Pr 17:5*
reproacheth his
W. rewardeth evil for good, *Pr 17:13*
evil shall
W. findeth a wife findeth a *Pr 18:22*
good thing
W. provoketh him to *Pr 20:2*
anger sinneth
W. curseth his father or his *Pr 20:20*
mother
W. stoppeth his ears at the *Pr 21:13*
cry of the
W. keepeth his mouth and his *Pr 21:23*
W. boasteth himself of a false *Pr 25:14*
W. diggeth a pit shall fall *Pr 26:27*
therein
W. keepeth the fig tree *Pr 27:18*
shall eat the
W. keepeth the law is a wise *Pr 28:7*
son
W. causeth the righteous to *Pr 28:10*
go
w. confesseth and forsaketh *Pr 28:13*
them
W. walketh uprightly shall be *Pr 28:18*
saved
W. robbeth his father or his *Pr 28:24*
mother
but w. walketh wisely, he shall *Pr 28:26*
be

W. loveth wisdom rejoiceth his *Pr 29:3*
W. is partner with a thief *Pr 29:24*
hateth his
but w. putteth his trust in the *Pr 29:25*
Lord
w. pleaseth God shall escape *Ec 7:26*
from
W. keepeth the commandment *Ec 8:5*
shall
w. breaketh an hedge, *Ec 10:8*
serpent shall
W. removeth stones shall be hurt *Ec 10:9*
w. falleth not down and *Da 3:6;*
worshippeth   *3:11*
that w. will not come up of *Zec 14:17*
all the
w. shall receive one such *M't 18:5*
w. shall offend one of these *M't 18:6*
W. marrieth her which is put *M't 19:9*
W. therefore shall swear by *M't 23:20*
And w. shall swear by the *M't 23:21*
temple
w. readeth, let him *M't 24:15*
understand
W. curseth father or mother, *M'k 7:10*
let
W. eateth my flesh, and *Joh 6:54*
drinketh
w. looketh into the perfect *Jas 1:25*
law of
w. keepeth his word, in him *1Jo 2:5*
But w. hath this world's good *1Jo 3:17*

WHOSOEVER

W. slayeth Cain, vengeance *Ge 4:15*
shall
for w. eateth leavened bread *Ex 12:15*
from
w. toucheth the mount shall *Ex 19:12*
be
w. lieth with a beast shall *Ex 22:19*
surely
W. compoundeth any like it *Ex 30:33*
or w. putteth any of it upon *Ex 30:33*
W. shall make like unto that *Ex 30:38*
for w. doeth any work *Ex 31:14*
therein, that
w. doeth any work in the *Ex 31:15*
sabbath
W. hath any gold, let them *Ex 32:24*
break
W. hath sinned against me *Ex 32:33*
w. doeth work therein shall be *Ex 35:2*
w. is of a willing heart, let *Ex 35:5*
him
For w. eateth the fat of the *Le 7:25*
beast
w. toucheth the carcase of *Le 11:24*
them
w. beareth ought of the *Le 11:25*
carcase of
w. doth touch them, when *Le 11:31*
they be
w. toucheth his bed shall wash *Le 15:5*
w. toucheth any thing that *Le 15:10*
was
w. toucheth her shall be *Le 15:19*
unclean
w. toucheth her bed shall *Le 15:21*
wash
w. toucheth any thing that she *Le 15:22*
sat
w. toucheth those things shall *Le 15:27*
be
w. eateth it shall be cut off *Le 17:14*
w. shall commit any of these *Le 18:29*
w. lieth carnally with a *Le 19:20*
woman
W. he be of the children of *Le 20:2*
Israel
W. he be of thy seed in their *Le 21:17*
W. he be of all your seed *Le 22:3*
w. toucheth any creeping thing *Le 22:5*
w. offereth a sacrifice of peace *Le 22:21*
w. curseth his God shall bear *Le 24:15*
and w. is defiled by the dead *Nu 5:2*
or w. be among you in your *Nu 15:14*
W. cometh any thing near *Nu 17:13*
unto
w. toucheth the dead body *Nu 19:13*
of any
w. toucheth one that is slain *Nu 19:16*
w. hath killed any person *Nu 19:18*
w. hath touched any slain, *Nu 31:19*
purify
w. will not hearken unto my *De 18:19*
W. he be that doth rebel *Jos 1:18*
w. shall go out of the doors *Jos 2:19*
w. shall be with thee in the *Jos 2:19*

w. killeth any person at *Jos 20:9*
unawares
W. is fearful and afraid, let *J'g 7:3*
him
W. cometh not forth after *1Sa 11:7*
Saul
W. getteth up to the gutter *2Sa 5:8*
W. saith ought unto thee, *2Sa 14:10*
bring him
w. heareth it will say, There *2Sa 17:9*
is a
w. would, he consecrated *1Ki 13:33*
him
w. shall be wanting, he shall *2Ki 10:19*
w. heareth of it, both his *2Ki 21:12*
ears shall
w. smiteth the Jebusites first *1Ch 11:6*
shall
and w. had dedicated any *1Ch 26:28*
thing
w. cometh to *2Ch 13:9*
consecrate himself
w. would not seek the Lord *2Ch 15:13*
God
and w. else cometh into the *2Ch 23:7*
house
w. remaineth in any place *Ezr 1:4*
where
that w. shall alter this word *Ezr 6:11*
w. will not do the law of thy *Ezr 7:26*
God
w. would not come within *Ezr 10:8*
three
that w. whether man or *Es 4:11*
woman
w. toucheth her shall not be *Pr 6:29*
w. is deceived thereby is not *Pr 20:1*
wise
W. hideth her hideth the *Pr 27:16*
wind, and
w. shall gather together *Isa 54:15*
against
w. goeth therein shall not *Isa 59:8*
know
which w. heareth, his ears *Jer 19:3*
shall
Then w. heareth the sound of *Eze 33:4*
the
W. shall read this writing, and *Da 5:7*
w. shall ask a petition of any *Da 6:7*
God
w. shall call on the name of *Joe 2:32*
W. therefore shall break one *M't 5:19*
w. shall do and teach them *M't 5:19*
w. shall kill shall be in *M't 5:21*
danger
w. is angry with his brother *M't 5:22*
w. shall say to his brother *M't 5:22*
but w. shall say, Thou fool *M't 5:22*
w. looketh on a woman to *M't 5:28*
W. shall put away his wife *M't 5:31*
w. shall put away his wife *M't 5:32*
w. shall marry her that is *M't 5:32*
w. shall smite thee on thy *M't 5:39*
right
w. shall compel thee to go a *M't 5:41*
mile
w. heareth these sayings of *M't 7:24*
And w. shall not receive you *M't 10:14*
W. therefore shall confess *M't 10:32*
w. shall deny me before men *M't 10:33*
w. shall give to drink unto *M't 10:42*
w. shall not be offended in me *M't 11:6*
w. speaketh a word against *M't 12:32*
w. speaketh against the Holy *M't 12:32*
w. shall do the will of my *M't 12:50*
For w. hath, to him shall be *M't 13:12*
given
w. hath not, from him shall *M't 13:12*
be
W. shall say to his father or *M't 15:5*
w. will save his life shall *M't 16:25*
lose
w. will lose his life for my *M't 16:25*
W. therefore shall humble *M't 18:4*
W. shall put away his wife *M't 19:9*
w. will be great among you *M't 20:26*
w. will be chief among you *M't 20:27*
w. shall fall on this stone *M't 21:44*
shall
w. shall exalt himself shall *M't 23:12*
be
W. shall swear by the temple *M't 23:16*
w. shall swear by the gold of *M't 23:16*
W. shall swear by the altar *M't 23:18*
w. sweareth by the gift that *M't 23:18*
w. shall do the will of God *M'k 3:35*
w. shall not receive you, nor *M'k 6:11*
W. will come after me, let *M'k 8:34*
him

w. will save his life shall lose   *M'k 8:35*
w. shall lose his life for my   *M'k 8:35*
sake
W. therefore shall be   *M'k 8:38*
ashamed
W. shall receive one of such   *M'k 9:37*
w. shall receive me, receiveth   *M'k 9:37*
w. shall give you a cup of   *M'k 9:41*
water
w. shall offend one of these   *M'k 9:42*
W. shall put away his wife   *M'k 10:11*
W. shall not receive the   *M'k 10:15*
w. will be great among you   *M'k 10:43*
w. of you will be the   *M'k 10:44*
chiefest
That w. shall say unto this   *M'k 11:23*
W. cometh to me, and   *Lu 6:47*
w. shall not be offended in me   *Lu 7:23*
w. hath, to him shall be given   *Lu 8:18*
w. hath not, from him shall be   *Lu 8:18*
And w. will not receive you   *Lu 9:5*
For w. will save his life shall   *Lu 9:24*
w. will lose his life for my   *Lu 9:24*
sake
w. shall be ashamed of me   *Lu 9:26*
W. shall receive this child in   *Lu 9:48*
w. shall receive me receiveth   *Lu 9:48*
W. shall confess me   *Lu 12:8*
w. shall speak a word   *Lu 12:10*
against
w. exalteth himself shall be   *Lu 14:11*
w. doth not bear his cross   *Lu 14:27*
w. he be of you that forsaketh   *Lu 14:33*
not
W. putteth away his wife   *Lu 16:18*
w. marrieth her that is put   *Lu 16:18*
W. shall seek to save his life   *Lu 17:33*
W. shall lose his life shall   *Lu 17:33*
W. shall not receive the   *Lu 18:17*
W. shall fall upon that stone   *Lu 20:18*
w. believeth in him should   *Joh 3:15;*
  3:16
W. drinketh of this water   *Joh 4:13*
shall
But w. drinketh of the water   *Joh 4:14*
w. then first after the troubling   *Joh 5:4*
W. committeth sin is the   *Joh 8:34*
w. liveth and believeth in me   *Joh 11:26*
w. believeth on me should   *Joh 12:46*
not
w. killeth you will think that   *Joh 16:2*
w. maketh himself a king   *Joh 19:12*
w. shall call on the name of   *Ac 2:21*
w. believeth in him shall   *Ac 10:43*
w. among you feareth God, to   *Ac 13:26*
you
man, w. thou art that judgest   *Ro 2:1*
w. believeth on him shall not   *Ro 9:33*
W. believeth on him shall not   *Ro 10:11*
w. shall call upon the   *Ro 10:13*
W. therefore resisteth the   *Ro 13:2*
power
w. shall eat this bread, and   *1Co 11:27*
w. of you are justified by the   *Ga 5:4*
law
bear his judgment, w. he be   *Ga 5:10*
w. shall keep the whole law   *Jas 2:10*
w. therefore will be a friend   *Jas 4:4*
W. denieth the Son, the same   *1Jo 2:23*
W. committeth sin   *1Jo 3:4*
W. abideth in him sinneth not   *1Jo 3:6*
W. sinneth hath not seen him   *1Jo 3:6*
W. is born of God doth not   *1Jo 3:9*
w. doeth not righteousness is   *1Jo 3:10*
W. hateth his brother is a   *1Jo 3:15*
W. shall confess that Jesus is   *1Jo 4:15*
W. believeth that Jesus is   *1Jo 5:1*
w. is born of God sinneth not   *1Jo 5:18*
W. transgresseth, and abideth   *2Jo 9*
w. receiveth the mark of his   *Re 14:11*
name
w. was not found written in   *Re 20:15*
w. loveth and maketh a lie   *Re 22:15*
w. will. let him take the   *Re 22:17*
water of

WHY

unto Cain, W. art thou wroth   *Ge 4:6*
and w. is thy countenance   *Ge 4:6*
fallen
w. didst thou not tell me that   *Ge 12:18*
she
W. saidst thou, She is my   *Ge 12:19*
sister
she said, If it be so, w. am I   *Ge 25:22*
thus
w. should I be deprived also   *Ge 27:45*
of you
W. do you look one upon   *Ge 42:1*
another

w. should we die in thy   *Ge 47:15*
presence
W. have ye done this thing, and   *Ex 1:18*
w. is it that ye have left the   *Ex 2:20*
man
this great sight, w. the bush is   *Ex 3:3*
people? w. is it thou hast sent   *Ex 5:22*
me
W. have we done this, that we   *Ex 14:5*
unto them, W. chide ye with   *Ex 17:2*
me
why (S)   *Ex 17:3;*
Jos 7:10; 9:22; J'g 12:1, 3; 1Sa 4:3;
9:21; 15:19; 19:5; 20:27, 32; 21:14; 24:9;
26:15, 18; 28:9, 16; 2Sa 2:22; 11:20; 12:9,
23; 14:13, 31-32; 15:19; 16:10; 18:22;
19:12, 25, 35, 42; 24:21; 1Ki 1:41;
2Ki 5:8; 6:33; 9:11; Job 13:14, 24; 18:3;
Ps 79:10; 89:47; Pr 17:16; Isa 5:4;
Isa 5:4; 55:2; 58:3; 63:2; Jer 2:29, 31;
5:19; 12:1, 13; 22:12; 16:10; 20:18;
22:8, 28; 27:17; 30:6; 32:3; 40:15; 44:7;
46:5; 49:4; La 3:39; 5:20; Eze 21:7;
Da 10:20; Joe 2:17; Hab 1:13; Mal 2:14-
15; M't 9:4; 14:31; 26:50; Lu 5:22;
  Ro 9:32
w. sittest thou thyself alone   *Ex 18:14*
w. doth thy wrath wax hot   *Ex 32:11*
against
W. came we forth out of   *Nu 11:20*
Egypt
And w. have ye brought up   *Nu 20:4*
W. should the name of our   *Nu 27:4*
father
Now therefore w. should we   *De 5:25*
die
cause w. Joshua did circumcise   *Jos 5:4*
W. hast thou troubled us? the   *Jos 7:25*
W. hast thou given me but   *Jos 17:14*
one
my voice: w. have ye done this   *J'g 2:2*
W. abodest thou among the   *J'g 5:16*
and w. did Dan remain in   *J'g 5:17*
ships
W. is his chariot so long in   *J'g 5:28*
w. tarry the wheels of his   *J'g 5:28*
chariot
w. then is all this befallen us   *J'g 6:13*
W. hast thou served us thus,   *J'g 8:1*
that
Shechem, w. should we serve   *J'g 9:28*
him
w. are ye come unto me now   *J'g 11:7*
when
w. therefore did ye not   *J'g 11:26*
recover
W. askest thou thus after my   *J'g 13:18*
W. are ye come up against us   *J'g 15:10*
w. is this come to pass in   *J'g 21:3*
Israel
w. will ye go with me? are   *Ru 1:11*
there
w. then call ye me Naomi,   *Ru 1:21*
seeing
W. have I found grace in   *Ru 2:10*
thine
w. weepest thou? and w. eatest   *1Sa 1:8*
w. is thy heart grieved? am I   *1Sa 1:8*
not
unto them, W. do ye such   *1Sa 2:23*
things
you w. his hand is not   *1Sa 6:3*
removed
W. are ye come out to set   *1Sa 7:8*
your
said, W. camest thou down   *1Sa 17:28*
hither
W. hast thou deceived me   *1Sa 19:17*
so, and
Let me go; w. should I kill   *1Sa 19:17*
thee
w. should my father hide this   *1Sa 20:2*
for w. shouldest thou bring   *1Sa 20:8*
me to
w. art thou alone, and no   *1Sa 21:1*
man
W. have ye conspired   *1Sa 22:13*
against me
for w. should thy servant   *1Sa 27:5*
dwell in
W. hast thou deceived me   *1Sa 28:12*
W. hast thou disquieted me,   *1Sa 28:15*
to
w. is it that thou hast sent   *2Sa 3:24*
him
W. build ye not me an house   *2Sa 7:7*
of
w. then didst thou not go   *2Sa 11:10*
down

w. went ye nigh the wall?   *2Sa 11:21*
then say
W. art thou, being the king's   *2Sa 13:4*
son
him, W. should he go with   *2Sa 13:26*
thee
W. should this dead dog   *2Sa 16:9*
curse my
w. wentest thou not with thy   *2Sa 16:17*
w. didst thou not smite him   *2Sa 18:11*
there
w. speak ye not a word of   *2Sa 19:10*
bringing
W. are ye the last to bring   *2Sa 19:11*
the king
W. speakest thou any more   *2Sa 19:29*
of thy
w. should the king   *2Sa 19:36*
recompense it
W. have our brethren the   *2Sa 19:41*
men of
w. then did ye despise us, that   *2Sa 19:43*
w. wilt thou swallow up the   *2Sa 20:19*
w. doth my lord the king   *2Sa 24:3*
delight
in saying, W. hast thou done so   *1Ki 1:6*
w. then doth Adonijah reign   *1Ki 1:13*
And w. dost thou ask   *1Ki 2:22*
Abishag the
W. then hast thou not kept   *1Ki 2:43*
W. hath the Lord done this   *1Ki 9:8*
w. feignest thou thyself to be   *1Ki 14:6*
for w. shouldest thou   *1Ki 14:10*
meddle to
W. is thy spirit so sad, that   *1Ki 21:5*
thou
them, W. are ye now turned   *2Ki 1:5*
back
W. sit we here until we die   *2Ki 7:3*
Hazael said, W. weepeth my   *2Ki 8:12*
lord
W. repair ye not the breaches   *2Ki 12:7*
W. have ye not built me an   *1Ch 17:6*
house
w. then doth my lord require   *1Ch 21:3*
this
w. will he be a cause of   *1Ch 21:3*
trespass to
W. hath the Lord done thus   *2Ch 7:21*
unto
W. hast thou not required of   *2Ch 24:6*
W. transgress ye the   *2Ch 24:20*
W. hast thou sought after   *2Ch 25:15*
the gods
w. shouldest thou be smitten   *2Ch 25:16*
w. shouldest thou meddle to   *2Ch 25:19*
thine
W. should the king of   *2Ch 32:4*
Assyria come
w. should damage grow to the   *Ezr 4:22*
w. should there be wrath   *Ezr 7:23*
against
W. is thy countenance sad   *Ne 2:2*
w. should not my countenance   *Ne 2:3*
be
w. should the work cease,   *Ne 6:3*
whilst
W. is the house of God   *Ne 13:11*
forsaken
them, W. lodge ye about the   *Ne 13:21*
wall
W. transgressest thou the king's   *Es 3:3*
know what it was, and w. it   *Es 4:5*
was
W. died I not from the womb   *Job 3:11*
w. did I not give up the ghost   *Job 3:11*
W. did the knees prevent me   *Job 3:12*
or w. the breasts that I   *Job 3:12*
should suck
W. is light given to a man   *Job 3:23*
whose
w. hast thou set me as a   *Job 7:20*
mark
And w. dost thou not pardon   *Job 7:21*
my
be wicked, w. then labour I   *Job 9:29*
in vain
W. doth thine heart carry   *Job 15:12*
thee
W. do ye persecute me as   *Job 19:22*
God
W. persecute we him, seeing   *Job 19:28*
so, w. should not my spirit be   *Job 21:4*
W. seeing times are not   *Job 24:1*
hidden
w. then are ye thus   *Job 27:12*
altogether
w. then should I think upon a   *Job 31:1*
W. dost thou strive against   *Job 33:13*
him

W. do the heathen rage, and the	Ps 2:1
W. standest thou afar off, O Lord	Ps 10:1
w. hidest thou thyself in times of	Ps 10:1
My God, my God, *w.* hast thou	Ps 22:1
w. art thou so far from helping me	Ps 22:1
W. art thou cast down, O my soul	Ps 42:5
w. art thou disquieted in me	Ps 42:5
rock, *W.* hast thou forgotten me	Ps 42:9
w. go I mourning because of	Ps 42:9
W. art thou cast down, O my soul	Ps 42:11
w. art thou disquieted within me	Ps 42:11
strength: *w.* dost thou cast me off	Ps 43:2
w. go I mourning because of	Ps 43:2
W. art thou cast down, O my soul	Ps 43:5
w. art thou disquieted within me	Ps 43:5
Awake, *w.* sleepest thou, O Lord	Ps 44:23
W. boastest thou thyself in	Ps 52:1
W. leap ye, ye high hills? this	Ps 68:16
w. hast thou cast us off for ever	Ps 74:1
w. doth thine anger smoke against	Ps 74:1
W. withdrawest thou thy hand	Ps 74:11
W. hast thou then broken down	Ps 80:12
Lord *w.* castest thou off my soul	Ps 88:14
w. hidest thou thy face from me	Ps 88:14
w. wilt thou, my son, be ravished	Pr 5:20
w. should he take away thy bed	Pr 22:27
me; and *w.* was I then more wise	Ec 2:15
w. shouldest thou destroy thyself	Ec 7:16
w. shouldest thou die before thy	Ec 7:17
w. should I be as one that turneth	Ca 1:7
W. should ye be stricken any	Isa 1:5
W. sayest thou, O Jacob, and	Isa 40:27
w. hast thou made us to err from	Isa 63:17
homeborn slave? *w.* is he spoiled	Jer 2:14
W. trimmest thou thy way to	Jer 2:33
W. gaddest thou about so much	Jer 2:36
W. then is this people of	Jer 8:5
W. do we sit still? assemble	Jer 8:14
W. have they provoked me to	Jer 8:19
w. then is not the health of	Jer 8:22
w. shouldest thou be as a stranger	Jer 14:8
W. shouldest be as a man	Jer 14:9
w. hast thou smitten us, and	Jer 14:19
W. is my pain perpetual, and my	Jer 15:18
W. hast thou prophesied in	Jer 26:9
W. will ye die, thou and thy	Jer 27:13
w. hast thou not reproved Jeremiah	Jer 29:27
W. criest thou for thine affliction	Jer 30:15
W. hast thou written therein	Jer 36:29
W. are thy valiant men swept	Jer 46:15
w. then doth their king inherit	Jer 49:1
W.? doth not the son bear	Eze 18:19
w. will ye die, O house of Israel	Eze 18:31; 33:11
for *w.* should he see your faces	Da 1:10
W. is the decree so hasty	Da 2:15
him, *W.* hast thou done this	Jon 1:10
Now *w.* dost thou cry out aloud	Mic 4:9
W. dost thou show me iniquity	Hab 1:3
W.? saith the Lord of hosts	Hag 1:9
w. do we deal treacherously	Mal 2:10
w. take ye thought for raiment	M't 6:28
w. beholdest thou the mote that	M't 7:3
W. are ye fearful, O ye of little faith	M't 8:26

W. eateth your Master with	M't 9:11
W. do we and the Pharisees fast	M't 9:14
W. speakest thou unto them	M't 13:10
W. do thy disciples transgress	M't 15:2
W. do ye also transgress the	M't 15:3
W. reason ye among yourselves	M't 16:8
W. then say the scribes that Elias	M't 17:10
W. could not we cast him out	M't 17:19
W. did Moses then command	M't 19:7
W. callest thou me good? there is	M't 19:17
W. stand ye here all the day idle	M't 20:6
us, *W.* did ye not then believe him	M't 21:25
W. tempt ye me, ye hypocrites	M't 22:18
W. trouble ye the woman? for she	M't 26:10
said, *W.* what evil hath he done	M't 27:23
my God, *w.* hast thou forsaken me	M't 27:46
W. doth this man thus speak	M'k 2:7
W. reason ye these things in	M'k 2:8
W. do the disciples of John	M'k 2:18
w. do they on the sabbath day	M'k 2:24
W. are ye so fearful? how is it that	M'k 4:40
w. troublest thou the Master any	M'k 5:35
W. make ye this ado, and weep	M'k 5:39
W. walk not thy disciples	M'k 7:5
W. doth this generation seek	M'k 8:12
W. reason ye, because ye have no	M'k 8:17
W. say the scribes that Elias	M'k 9:11
W. could not we cast him out	M'k 9:28
W. callest thou me good? there is	M'k 10:18
man say unto you, *W.* do ye	M'k 11:3
W. then did ye not believe him	M'k 11:31
said unto them, *W.* tempt ye me	M'k 12:15
W. was this waste of the	M'k 14:4
Let her alone; *w.* trouble ye her	M'k 14:6
them, *W.* what evil hath he done	M'k 15:14
my God, *w.* hast thou forsaken	M'k 15:34
w. hast thou thus dealt with us	Lu 2:48
W. do ye eat and drink with	Lu 5:30
W. do the disciples of John fast	Lu 5:33
W. do ye that which is not lawful	Lu 6:2
w. beholdest thou the mote that is	Lu 6:41
w. call ye me, Lord, Lord, and do	Lu 6:46
w. take ye thought for the rest	Lu 12:26
w. even of yourselves judge ye not	Lu 12:57
down; *w.* cumbereth it the ground	Lu 13:7
him, *W.* callest thou me good	Lu 18:19
man ask you, *W.* do ye loose him	Lu 19:31
unto them, *W.* loose ye the colt	Lu 19:33
say, *W.* then believed ye him not	Lu 20:5
said unto them, *W.* tempt ye me	Lu 20:23
them, *W.* sleep ye? rise and pray	Lu 22:46
time, *W.* what evil hath he done	Lu 23:22
W. seek ye the living among	Lu 24:5
said unto them, *W.* are ye troubled	Lu 24:38
w. do thoughts arise in hearts	Lu 24:38
W. baptizest thou then, if thou be	Joh 1:25
thou? or, *W.* talkest thou with her	Joh 4:27
the law? *W.* go ye about to kill me	Joh 7:19
them, *W.* have ye not brought him	Joh 7:45

W. do ye not understand my	Joh 8:43
truth, *w.* do ye not believe me	Joh 8:46
W. herein is a marvellous thing	Joh 9:30
devil, and is mad; *w.* hear ye him	Joh 10:20
W. was not this ointment sold	Joh 12:5
Lord, *w.* cannot I follow thee now	Joh 13:37
W. askest thou me? ask them	Joh 18:21
but if well, *w.* smitest thou me	Joh 18:23
her, Woman, *w.* weepest thou	Joh 20:13; 20:15
w. stand ye gazing up into heaven	Ac 1:11
w. marvel ye at this? or *w.* look ye	Ac 3:12
W. did the heathen rage, and	Ac 4:25
w. hath Satan filled thine heart	Ac 5:3
w. hast thou conceived this thing	Ac 5:4
w. do ye wrong one to another	Ac 7:26
Saul, *w.* persecutest thou me	Ac 9:4
Sirs, *w.* do ye these things	Ac 14:15
Now therefore *w.* tempt ye God	Ac 15:10
Saul, Saul, *w.* persecutest thou me	Ac 22:7; 26:14
And now *w.* tarriest thou? arise	Ac 22:16
W. should it be thought a thing	Ac 26:8
w. yet am I also judged as a sinner	Ro 3:7
man seeth, *w.* doth he yet hope for	Ro 8:24
unto me, *W.* doth he yet find fault	Ro 9:19
it, *W.* hast thou made me thus	Ro 9:20
But *w.* dost thou judge thy brother	Ro 14:10
w. dost thou set at nought thy	Ro 14:10
w. dost thou glory, as if thou hadst	1Co 4:7
W. do ye not rather take wrong	1Co 6:7
w. do ye not rather suffer	1Co 6:7
w. is my liberty judged of	1Co 10:29
w. am I evil spoken of for that	1Co 10:30
w. are they then baptized for	1Co 15:29
w. stand ye in jeopardy every hour	1Co 15:30
w. compellest thou the Gentiles to	Ga 21:14
w. do I yet suffer persecution	Ga 5:11
w. as though living in the world	Col 2:20

WICK

shall be as a *w.* (S)	Isa 1:31; 43:17
quenched like a lamp *w.*	Isa 43:17 (A)(B)

WICKED

wilt destroy righteous with *w.*	Ge 18:23; 18:25
the bad (B)	Ge 18:23
Er was *w.*; my people *w.*	Ge 38:7; Ex 9:27
for I will not justify the *w.*	Ex 23:7
it is a *w.* thing, they shall be cut off	Le 20:17
a shameful thing (R)	Le 20:17
w. men have arisen (B)	De 13:13
be not a thought in thy *w.* heart	De 15:9
who have committed that *w.* thing	De 17:5
evil (E)	De 17:5; 23:9; Job 21:30; Pr 14:19; Eze 20:44; M't 12:45; Col 1:21
evil thing (R)	De 17:5; 23:9
and keep thee from every *w.* thing	De 23:9
evil (A)	De 23:9; Job 21:30; Ps 101:4; Eze 20:44
evil (B)	De 23:9; 2Ki 17:11; 2Ch 7:4; Job 21:30; Pr 11:21; 12:2, 13; Col 1:21
and condemn the *w.*	De 25:1; 1Ki 8:32
guilty (A)	De 25:1; Job 9:29; Isa 5:23; Na 1:3
guilty (B)	De 25:1; Job 9:29; 10:7; Isa 5:23; Na 1:3

guilty (R) *De 25:1;*
2Ch 6:23; Job 10:7; Na 1:3
do not commit such w. act *J'g 19:23*
(B)
a w. woman (A)(E)(S) *1Sa 1:16*
the w. shall be silent in *1Sa 2:9*
darkness
the godless (B) *1Sa 2:9*
wickedness proceedeth from *1Sa 24:13*
the w.
such a w. man (A) *1Sa 25:17*
w. men, base fellows *1Sa 30:22*
(A)(E)(R)
the wicked (B)(R) *2Sa 22:5;*
2Ch 19:2; Ps 1:1; 3:7; 73:12
w., godless, worthless (A) *2Sa 23:6*
Israel wrought w. things to *2Ki 17:11*
provoke
judge thy servant by *2Ch 6:23*
requiting the w.
if my people humble *2Ch 7:14;*
themselves and turn from *Eze 18:21;*
w. ways *33:11, 19*
the wicked (E) *2Ch 19:2;*
Ps 1:1, 4-6; 3:7; 73:12
shouldst thou help the w. (S) *2Ch 19:2*
the sons of Athaliah that w. *2Ch 24:7*
woman
the rebellious and w. city (S) *Ezr 4:12*
w. practices of people (B) *Ezr 9:11*
our kings not served thee, nor *Ne 9:35;*
turned from their w. ways *Eze 3:19;*
13:22
the adversary is this w. Haman *Es 7:6*
Haman's w. device return on *Es 9:25*
his head
there the w. cease from *Job 3:17*
troubling
he destroyeth the perfect and *Job 9:22*
the w.
if I be w. why labour in vain *Job 9:29;*
10:15
be condemned (R) *Job 10:15*
thou knowest that I am not *Job 10:7*
w.
against the w. (B) *Job 17:8*
wherefore do the w. live, *Job 21:7*
become old
w. is reserved to day of *Job 21:30*
destruction
let mine enemy be as the w. *Job 27:7*
is it fit to say to a king, *Job 34:18*
Thou art w.
worthless and vile (A) *Job 34:18*
ungodly (B) *Job 34:18;*
Ps 28:3; 139:19; 145:20; 147:6
that w. might be shaken out *Job 38:13*
of it
from the w. their light is *Job 38:15*
withholden
tread down the w. in their *Job 40:12*
place
advice of the w. (B) *Ps 1:1*
the wicked (A) *Ps 1:4; 1:5*
God is angry with w. every *Ps 7:11*
day
thou hast destroyed the w. for *Ps 9:5*
ever
the w. is snared in work of his *Ps 9:16*
hands
w. shall be turned into hell *Ps 9:17*
w. in pride doth persecute the *Ps 10:2*
poor
w. boasteth; w. will not seek *Ps 10:3;*
God *10:4*
wherefore doth the w. *Ps 10:13*
contemn God
w. bend bow, make ready *Ps 11:2*
arrow
the w. and violence his soul *Ps 11:5*
hateth
upon the w. he shall rain *Ps 11:6*
snares, fire
w. walk on every side when *Ps 12:8*
vilest men
keep me from the w. that *Ps 17:9*
oppress me
Lord, deliver my soul from *Ps 17:13*
the w.
and I will not sit with the w. *Ps 26:5*
when w. came upon me to eat *Ps 27:2*
my flesh
evil-doers (E) *Ps 27:2; Pr 17:4*
evil-doers (R) *Ps 27:2*
draw me not away with the w. *Ps 28:3*
let w. be ashamed and silent in *Ps 31:17*
grave
evil shall slay w. they that *Ps 34:21*
hate righteous

man who bringeth w. devices *Ps 37:7*
to pass
yet a little, w. shall not be *Ps 37:10;*
Pr 10:25
the evil-doer (B) *Ps 37:10;*
37:12, 14, 16, 35, 40; 39:1; Ec 8:13
w. plotteth; w. shall perish *Ps 37:12;*
37:20
w. have drawn out sword, they *Ps 37:14*
bent
is better than the riches of *Ps 37:16*
many w.
w. borroweth, and payeth not *Ps 37:21*
again
w. watcheth the righteous to *Ps 37:32*
slay him
when w. are cut off, thou *Ps 37:34*
shalt see it
seen the w. in great power, *Ps 37:35*
spreading
he shall deliver them from *Ps 37:40*
the w.
keep my mouth, while w. is *Ps 39:1*
before me
the w. are estranged from the *Ps 58:3*
womb
the ungodly (A) *Ps 58:3*
be not merciful to any w. *Ps 59:5*
transgressors
who treacherously plot evil *Ps 59:5*
(A)(R)
let the w. perish at presence of *Ps 68:2*
God
w. of the earth shall wring *Ps 75:8*
them out
when w. spring as grass, and *Ps 92:7*
flourish
sinners (B) *Ps 92:7; 94:3; 104:35*
Lord, how long shall the w. *Ps 94:3*
triumph
until the pit be digged for the *Ps 94:13*
w.
I will set no w. thing *Ps 101:3*
before eyes
I will not know a w. person *Ps 101:4*
no evil thing (E) *Ps 101:4*
I will early destroy all the w. *Ps 101:8*
of the land
sinners consumed, let w. be *Ps 104:35*
no more
the flame burnt up the w. *Ps 106:18*
the w. shall see it and be *Ps 112:10*
grieved
the w. have waited for me to *Ps 119:95*
destroy me
w. laid a snare for me, yet *Ps 119:110*
I erred not
thou puttest away all w. *Ps 119:119*
like dross
salvation is far from the w. *Ps 119:155*
surely thou wilt slay the w. *Ps 139:19*
and see if there be any w. *Ps 139:24*
way in me
baneful motive (B) *Ps 139:24*
further not his w. device *Ps 140:8*
lest they
their schemes (B) *Ps 140:8*
to practice w. works with *Ps 141:4*
men
let the w. fall into their own *Ps 141:10*
nets
but all the w. will he destroy *Ps 145:20*
he casteth w. down to the *Ps 147:6*
ground
w. shall be cut off from the *Pr 2:22*
earth
his iniquities shall take w. *Pr 5:22*
himself
worthless, w. man *Pr 6:12*
(A)(B)(E)(R)
a heart that deviseth w. *Pr 6:18*
imaginations
but the w. shall not inhabit *Pr 10:30*
the earth
the w. shall fall by his own *Pr 11:5*
wickedness
when w. dieth, his expectation *Pr 11:7*
perisheth
the w. man (B)(E) *Pr 11:7;*
29:27; 2Pe 2:9
righteous delivered; w. cometh *Pr 11:8*
in stead
and when the w. perish there *Pr 11:10*
is shouting
the w. worketh a deceitful *Pr 11:18*
work
w. shall not be unpunished *Pr 11:21;*
11:31
a man of w. devices will he *Pr 12:2*
condemn

w. are overthrown, and are *Pr 12:7;*
not *21:12*
the w. desireth the net of evil *Pr 12:12*
men
w. is snared by transgression *Pr 12:13*
of his lips
but the w. shall be filled with *Pr 12:21*
mischief
a w. messenger falleth into *Pr 13:17*
mischief
unreliable (B) *Pr 13:17*
bad (R) *Pr 13:17*
and a man of w. devices is *Pr 14:17*
hated
w. bow at the gate of the *Pr 14:19*
righteous
w. is driven away in his *Pr 14:32*
wickedness
the Lord is far from the w. *Pr 15:29*
even the w. for the day of evil *Pr 16:4*
a w. doer giveth heed to false *Pr 17:4*
lips
he that justifieth w. is an *Pr 17:15*
abomination
when w. cometh, then cometh *Pr 18:3*
contempt
wise king scattereth w. *Pr 20:26*
w. shall be ransom for the *Pr 21:18*
righteous
when he bringeth it with a w. *Pr 21:27*
mind
but the w. shall fall into *Pr 24:16*
mischief
neither be thou envious at the *Pr 24:19*
w.
take away w. from before king *Pr 25:5*
righteous man falling down *Pr 25:26*
before w.
a w. heart is like a potsherd *Pr 26:23*
covered
the w. flee when no man *Pr 28:1*
pursueth
they that forsake the law *Pr 28:4*
praise the w.
when w. arise *Pr 28:12; 28:28*
so is a w. ruler *Pr 28:15*
when the w. beareth rule *Pr 29:2*
people mourn
but the w. regardeth not to *Pr 29:7*
know it
his servants are w.; w. are *Pr 29:12;*
multiplied *29:16*
God shall judge the righteous *Ec 3:17*
and the w.
be not overmuch w. neither be *Ec 7:17*
foolish
I saw the w. buried, they were *Ec 8:10*
forgotten
but it shall not be well with *Ec 8:13*
the w.
which justify the w. for *Isa 5:23*
reward
with breath of his lips shall *Isa 11:4*
he slay w.
I will punish the w. for their *Isa 13:11*
iniquity
he deviseth w. devices to *Isa 32:7*
destroy the poor
he made his grave with the w. *Isa 53:9*
criminals (B) *Isa 53:9*
let w. forsake his way, let him *Isa 55:7*
return
w. like troubled sea which *Isa 57:20*
cannot rest
thou hast taught the w. ones *Jer 2:33*
thy ways
evil women (B) *Jer 2:33*
for the w. are not plucked *Jer 6:29*
away
she has comitted w. acts (B) *Jer 11:15*
the heart is deceitful and *Jer 17:9*
desperately w.
exceedingly perverse, corrupt, *Jer 17:9*
severely mortally sick (A)
utterly corrupt (B) *Jer 17:9*
exceedingly corrupt (E) *Jer 17:9*
desperately corrupt (R) *Jer 17:9*
he will give the w. to the *Jer 25:31*
sword
to warn the w. *Eze 3:18; 3:19; 33:8-9*
behold the w. abominations *Eze 8:9*
they do here
vile abominations (R) *Eze 8:9*
these men give w. counsel in *Eze 11:2*
this city
devise iniquity (B) *Eze 11:2*
have I any pleasure that the *Eze 18:23*
w. should die
not according to your w. *Eze 20:44*
ways nor doings

cut off righteousness and the   *Eze 21:3;*
w.   *21:4*
profane w. prince of Israel   *Eze 21:25*
whose day is come
if the w. restore the pledge,   *Eze 33:15*
he shall live
but the w. shall do wickedly   *Da 12:10*
the w. deeds of Samaria (R)   *Ho 7:1*
shall I count them pure with   *Mic 6:11*
w. balances
crooked balances (B)   *Mic 6:11*
deceitful weights (E)   *Mic 6:11*
Lord shall not at all acquit the   *Na 1:3*
w.
guilty (E)   *Na 1:3*
one come out of thee a w.   *Na 1:11*
counsellor
w. shall no more pass through   *Na 1:15*
thee
w. doth compass about the   *Hab 1:4*
righteous
the w. devoureth the man   *Hab 1:13*
more righteous
consume stumblingblocks with   *Zep 1:3*
the w.
shall discern between   *Mal 3:18*
righteous and w.
and ye shall tread down the w.   *Mal 4:3*
as ashes
more w. than himself, even   *M't 12:45;*
so shall it be to this w.   *Lu 11:26*
generation
evil generation (P)(R)   *M't 12:45;*
  13:49; 16:4
angels shall sever the w.   *M't 13:49*
from the just
a w. generation seeketh after   *M't 16:4*
a sign
thou w. servant   *M't 18:32;*
  25:26; Lu 19:22
contemptible slave (B)   *M't 18:32*
and by w. hands have ye slain   *Ac 2:23*
him
by lawless hands (B)(R)   *Ac 2:23*
by the hand of lawless men   *Ac 2:23*
(E)
crooked, w. generation (A)   *Ac 2:40*
if it were a matter of w.   *Ac 18:14*
lewdness
misdemeanor or villainy (A)   *Ac 18:14*
crookedness, w.   *Ac 18:14*
unscrupulousness (B)
the wicked (N)   *Ro 5:6*
therefore put away that w.   *1Co 5:13*
person
evildoer (N)   *1Co 5:13*
the wicked (P)   *1Co 6:9*
crooked and w. generation   *Ph'p 2:15*
(A)(B)
enemies in your mind by w.   *Col 1:21*
works
evil things (P)   *Col 1:21*
evil deeds (P)   *Col 1:21*
then shall that w. be revealed   *2Th 2:8*
the lawless one   *2Th 2:8*
(A)(B)(E)(R)
the lawless man (P)   *2Th 2:8*
the w. and the sinner (P)   *1Pe 4:18*
keep the w. (P)   *2Pe 2:9; Re 22:11*
the w. men (P)   *2Pe 3:7*
lies under the w. one (B)   *1Jo 5:19*
sharer of w. works (B)(E)(R)   *2Jo 11*

OF THE WICKED

place of the w. shall come to   *Job 8:22*
nought
the earth is given into the   *Job 9:24*
hand of the w.
shouldest shine upon counsel   *Job 10:3*
of the w.
but the eye of the w. shall   *Job 11:20*
fail
God turned me into the   *Job 16:11*
hands of the w.
villains (B)   *Job 16:11*
the light of the w. shall be   *Job 18:5*
put out
surely such are the dwellings   *Job 18:21*
of the w.
ungodly (A)   *Job 18:21; Ps 64:2; 75:10*
the unrighteous (E)   *Job 18:21; 29:17*
he triumphing of the w. is   *Job 20:5*
short
every hand of the w. shall   *Job 20:22*
come upon him
counsel of the w. is far from   *Job 21:16;*
me   *22:18*
how oft is candle of the w.   *Job 21:17;*
put out   *Pr 13:9; 24:20*

where are the dwelling   *Job 21:28*
places of the w.
and they gathered the vintage   *Job 24:6*
of the w.
I brake jaws of the w. and   *Job 29:17*
plucked
he preserveth not the life of   *Job 36:6*
the w.
thou hast fulfilled the   *Job 36:17*
judgment of the w.
let wickedness of the w. come   *Ps 7:9*
to an end
break thou the arm of the w.   *Ps 10:15*
man
the assembly of the w. have   *Ps 22:16*
enclosed me
evildoers (E)   *Ps 22:16; 64:2; 92:11*
evildoers (R)   *Ps 22:16*
transgression of the w. saith in   *Ps 36:1*
my heart
let not the hand of the w.   *Ps 36:11*
remove me
the arms of the w. shall be   *Ps 37:17*
broken
but the seed of the w. shall   *Ps 37:28*
be cut off
evildoers (B)   *Ps 37:28; 37:38*
the end of the w. shall be cut   *Ps 37:38*
off
because of the oppression of   *Ps 55:3*
the w.
wash his feet in the blood of   *Ps 58:10*
the w.
hide me from the counsel of   *Ps 64:2*
the w.
deliver me out of hand of the   *Ps 71:4;*
w. and cruel man   *74:19; 82:4; 97:10*
when I saw the prosperity of   *Ps 73:3*
the w.
all horns of the w. also will I   *Ps 75:10*
cut off
ungodly (B)   *Ps 75:10;*
  140:8; 146:9; Hab 3:13
how long accept the persons of   *Ps 82:2*
the w.
behold, and see the reward of   *Ps 91:8*
the w.
sinner's reward (B)   *Ps 91:8*
mine ears shall hear my desire   *Ps 92:11*
of the w.
evildoers (A)   *Ps 92:11*
mouth of the w. is opened   *Ps 109:2*
against me
desire of the w. shall perish   *Ps 112:10;*
  Pr 10:28
because of the w. that   *Ps 119:53*
forsake thy law
the hands of the w. have   *Ps 119:61*
robbed me
rod of the w. shall not rest   *Ps 125:3*
on just
Lord cut asunder cords of the   *Ps 129:4*
w.
keep me, from the hands of   *Ps 140:4*
the w.
grant not the desires of the   *Ps 140:8*
w.
the way of the w. he turns   *Ps 146:9*
upside down
who delight in frowardness of   *Pr 2:14*
the w.
delight in perverseness of   *Pr 2:14*
evil (A)(E)
be not afraid of the desolation   *Pr 3:25*
curse of the Lord is in the   *Pr 3:33*
house of the w.
enter not into the path of the   *Pr 4:14*
w.
way of the w. is as darkness   *Pr 4:19*
he casteth away the substance   *Pr 10:3*
of the w.
violence covereth mouth of   *Pr 10:6;*
the w.   *10:11*
but the name of the w. shall   *Pr 10:7*
rot
the fruit of the w. tendeth to   *Pr 10:16*
sin
the heart of the w. is little   *Pr 10:20*
worth
the fear of the w. it shall come   *Pr 10:24*
upon him
but the years of the w. shall   *Pr 10:27*
be shortened
the mouth of the w. speaketh   *Pr 10:32*
frowardness
the city is overthrown by   *Pr 11:11*
mouth of the w.
but the expectation of the w.   *Pr 11:23*
is wrath

but the counsels of the w. are   *Pr 12:5*
deceit
words of the w. are to lie in   *Pr 12:6*
wait for blood
but the tender mercies of the   *Pr 12:10*
w. are cruel
but the way of the w. seduceth   *Pr 12:26*
them
but the belly of the w. shall   *Pr 13:25*
want
the house of the w. shall be   *Pr 14:11*
overthrown
in the revenues of the w. is   *Pr 15:6*
trouble
sacrifice of the w. is an   *Pr 15:8;*
abomination   *21:27*
way of the w. is an   *Pr 15:9*
abominaton to Lord
the thoughts of the w. are an   *Pr 15:26*
abomination
the mouth of the w. poureth   *Pr 15:28*
out evil things
it is not good to accept person   *Pr 18:5*
of the w.
the mouth of the w.   *Pr 19:28*
devoureth iniquity
and the plowing of the w. is   *Pr 21:4*
sin
the robbery of the w. shall   *Pr 21:7*
destroy them
the soul of the w. desireth   *Pr 21:10*
evil
he wisely considereth the   *Pr 21:12*
house of the w.
Lord hath broken the staff of   *Isa 14:5*
the w.
they overpass the deeds of the   *Jer 5:28*
w.
wherefore doth way of the w.   *Jer 12:1*
prosper
I will deliver thee out of   *Jer 15:21*
hand of the w.
whirlwind fall on head of   *Jer 23:19;*
the w.   *30:23*
have strengthened the hands   *Eze 13:22*
of the w.
the wickedness of the w.   *Eze 18:20*
shall be on him
to bring thee upon the necks   *Eze 21:29*
of the w.
I will sell land into the hand   *Eze 30:12*
of the w.
evil men (A)(E)   *Eze 30:12*
I have no pleasure in the   *Eze 33:11*
death of the w.
as for the wickedness of the   *Eze 33:12*
w.
none of the w. shall   *Da 12:10*
understand
treasures of wickedness in   *Mic 6:10*
house of the w.
wound head out of house of   *Hab 3:13*
the w.
able to quench all fiery darts   *Eph 6:16*
of the w.
the evil one (B)(E)(N)(R)   *Eph 6:16*
vexed with the conversation of   *2Pe 2:7*
the w.
ungodly and lawless (A)   *2Pe 2:7*
the lawless (B)   *2Pe 2:7; 3:17*
lest be led away with error of   *2Pe 3:17*
the w.
the lawless (R)   *2Pe 3:17*

TO, UNTO THE WICKED

is not destruction to the w.   *Job 31:3*
unrighteous (A)(E)   *Job 31:3*
many sorrows shall be to the   *Ps 32:10*
w.
ungodly (B)   *Ps 32:10*
unto the w. God saith, What   *Ps 50:16*
hast thou
he that saith unto the w.,   *Pr 24:24*
Thou art
the upright is abomination to   *Pr 29:27*
the w.
one event to righteous and to   *Ec 9:2*
the w.
woe unto the w. it shall be ill   *Isa 3:11*
with him
let favour be showed to the   *Isa 26:10*
w. yet will
no peace, saith God, unto   *Isa 48:22;*
the w.   *57:21*
when I say unto the w.   *Eze 3:18;*
  33:8, 14
give it to the w. of the earth   *Eze 7:21*
for a spoil

WICKEDLY

And said, do not so *w.*   Ge 19:7;
   J'g 19:23
have behaved *w.* (B)   Ex 32:7
your sins which ye sinned in   De 9:18
doing *w.*
if ye shall still do *w.* be   1Sa 12:25
consumed
kept ways of the Lord and   2Sa 22:22;
have not *w.* departed from   Ps 18:21
my God
lo, I have sinned and have   2Sa 24:17
done *w.*
we have dealt *w.* (E)(R)   1Ki 8:47
Manasseh done *w.* above   2Ki 21:11
Amorites
we have sinned, done amiss,   2Ch 6:37;
dealt *w.*   Ne 9:33; Ps 106:6; Da 9:5, 15
Ahaziah king of Israel, did   2Ch 20:35
very *w.*
his mother was his counsellor   2Ch 22:3
to do *w.*
acted *w.* and broke faith (A)   Ezr 10:10
will you speak *w.* for God   Job 13:7
yea, surely God will not do   Job 34:12
w.
they speak *w.* concerning   Ps 73:8
oppression
the enemy hath done *w.* in the   Ps 74:3
sanctuary
for they speak against thee   Ps 139:20
w.
speaking *w.* (E)   Isa 58:9
such as do *w.* against the   Da 11:32
covenant
many purified, but wicked   Da 12:10
shall do *w.*
all that do *w.* shall be as   Mal 4:1
stubble
all who act *w.* (A)(N)   M't 13:41

WICKEDNESS

God saw that *w.* of men was   Ge 6:5
great
how can I do this great *w.*   Ge 39:9
and sin
great evil (A)   Ge 39:9
great crime (B)   Ge 39:9
it is *w.*   Le 18:17;
   20:14
it is incest (B)   Le 18:17; 20:14
land full of *w.*   Le 19:29
that there be no *w.* among   Le 20:14
you
for the *w.* of these nations   De 9:4; 9:5
Israel shall do no more any   De 13:11
such *w.*
evil (B)   De 13:11;
   17:2; 1Sa 12:17; 12:20; 1Ki 1:52
if there be any that hath   De 17:2
wrought *w.*
evil (R)   De 17:2;
   28:20;   1Sa 12:20;   1Ki 2:44;   21:25;
   2Ki 21:6; Ps 7:9; 28:4; 1Co 5:9
according to his *w.* (E)   De 25:2
because of the *w.* of thy   De 28:20
doings
evil-doing (B)   De 28:20
evil (B)   De 28:20; 1Sa 12:20; 2Ki 21:6
is as *w.* (B)   Jos 14:23
die alone because of *w.* (B)   Jos 22:20
God rendered the *w.* of   J'g 9:56
Abimelech
crime (R)   J'g 9:56
Israel said, Tell us, how was   J'g 20:3
this *w.*
what *w.* is this that is done   J'g 20:12
among you
you may see that your *w.* is   1Sa 12:17
great
ye have done all this *w.* yet   1Sa 12:20
turn not aside
w. proceedeth from the   1Sa 24:13
wicked
returned the *w.* of Nabal on   1Sa 25:39
his own head
evil-doing (E)(R)   1Sa 25:29;
   Pr 14:32; Ec 7:15
reward doer of evil according   2Sa 3:39
to his *w.*
neither shall the children of   2Sa 7:10;
w. afflict them any more   Ps 89:22
violent men (R)   2Sa 7:10; 1Ch 17:9
if *w.* be found in him, he   1Ki 1:52
shall die
knowest all *w.* thy heart is   1Ki 2:44
privy to
repent, saying, We have   1Ki 8:47
committed *w.*

sinned, done wrong, and   1Ki 8:47
transgressed (B)
dealt wickedly (E)   1Ki 8:47
perversely and wickedly (R)   1Ki 8:47
Ahab sold himself to work   1Ki 21:25
w.
Manasseh wrought much *w.*   2Ki 21:6
nor the children of *w.* waste   1Ch 17:9
them
commit *w.* by marrying foreign   Ne 13:27
women (B)
they that sow *w.* reap the   Job 4:8
same
trouble and mischief (A)   Job 4:8
sow trouble (B)(E)(R)   Job 4:8
he seeth *w.*   Job 11:11
iniquity (A)(E)(R)   Job 11:11
let no *w.* dwell in thy   Job 11:14
tabernacles
evil (A)   Job 11:14; Ps 55:15
unrighteousness (E)   Job 11:14
tho' *w.* be sweet in his   Job 20:12
mouth
w. be broken   Job 24:20
my lips shall not speak *w.*   Job 27:4
untruth (A)(B)   Job 27:4
falsehood (R)   Job 27:4
far be it from God that he   Job 34:10
should do *w.*
do wrong (B)   Job 34:10
art not a God that hath   Ps 5:4
pleasure in *w.*
their inward part is very *w.*   Ps 5:9
let the *w.* of the wicked come   Ps 7:9
to an end
seek out his *w.*   Ps 10:15
in hand is *w.* (A)(B)(E)   Ps 26:10
according to the *w.* of their   Ps 28:4
endeavours
thou hatest *w.*   Ps 45:7
your tongue devises *w.*   Ps 52:2
(A)(B)(E)
he strengthened himself in his   Ps 52:7
w.
w. is in midst thereof, deceit   Ps 55:11
and guile
w. is in their dwellings and   Ps 55:15
among them
yea, in heart you work *w.*   Ps 58:22
weigh violence
than to dwell in the tents of   Ps 84:10
w.
turns fruitful land into   Ps 107:34;
barrenness for *w.* of them   Jer 12:4
that dwell therein
for they eat the bread of *w.*   Pr 4:17
and *w.* is an abomination to my   Pr 8:7
lips
wrong-doing (A)   Pr 8:7; 14:32
treasures of *w.* profit nothing   Pr 10:2
but the wicked shall fall by his   Pr 11:5
own *w.*
a man shall not be established   Pr 12:3
by *w.*
but *w.* overthroweth the sinner   Pr 13:6
the wicked is driven away in   Pr 14:32
his *w.*
mischief-making (B)   Pr 14:32
it is abomination to kings to   Pr 16:12
commit *w.*
God overthroweth the wicked   Pr 21:12
for their *w.*
his *w.* shall be shewed before   Pr 26:26
congregation
she eateth and saith, I have   Pr 30:20
done no *w.*
no wrong (B)   Pr 30:20
saw place of judgment, that *w.*   Ec 3:16
was there
a wicked man prolongeth his   Ec 7:15
life in *w.*
evil-doing (A)   Ec 7:15
I applied my heart to know   Ec 7:25
the *w.* of folly
nor *w.* deliver those that are   Ec 8:8
given to it
for *w.* burneth as the fire   Isa 9:18
behold, ye smite with the fist   Isa 58:4
of *w.*
fast I have chosen, to loose   Isa 58:6
bands of *w.*
speaking *w.* (R)   Isa 58:9
tongue utters *w.* (A)(E)   Isa 59:3
thine own *w.* shall correct   Jer 2:19
O Jerusalem, wash thine heart   Jer 4:14
from *w.*
so she casteth out her *w.*   Jer 6:7
continually

see what I did for the *w.* of   Jer 7:12
my people
no man repented of *w.*   Jer 8:6
fornication and *w.* (B)   Jer 13:2
we acknowledge our *w.* and   Jer 14:20
iniquity
that none doth return from   Jer 23:14
his *w.*
from the city whose *w.* I   Jer 33:5
hid my face
have ye forgotten *w.* of your   Jer 44:9
kings; your own *w.* and *w.*
of your wives
if he turn not from *w.* he   Eze 3:19
shall die
she hath changed my judgment   Eze 5:6
into *w.*
violence is risen up into a rod   Eze 7:11
of *w.*
the *w.* of the wicked shall be   Eze 18:20
on him
turneth from the *w.* he hath   Eze 18:27
committed
I have driven him out for   Eze 31:11
his *w.*
in the day he turneth from   Eze 33:12;
his *w.*   33:19
the *w.* of Samaria was   Ho 7:1
discovered
evil-doings (B)   Ho 7:1
wicked deeds (R)   Ho 7:1
the *w.* of their doings I will   Ho 9:15
drive out
have ploughed *w.* and reaped   Ho 10:13
iniquity
ungodliness (B)   Ho 10:13
iniquity (R)   Ho 10:13
so shall Beth-el do to you   Ho 10:15
because of your *w.*
the vats overflow for their *w.*   Joe 3:13
is great
treasures of *w.* in house of   Mic 6:10
wicked
and he said, This is *w.* and he   Zec 5:8
cast it
they shall call them the border   Mal 1:4
of *w.*
yea, they that work *w.* are set   Mal 3:15
up
out of the heart proceedeth *w.*   M'k 7:22
deceit
but your inward part is full   Lu 11:39
of *w.*
master of every form of *w.*   Ac 13:10
(A)
accuse this man, if any *w.* in   Ac 25:5
him
criminal (A)   Ac 25:5
impiety and *w.* (B)(N)(R)   Ro 1:18
being filled with all *w.*, envy,   Ro 1:29
murder
every sort of *w.* (B)(P)(R)   Ro 1:29
responsive to *w.* (A)(B)(R)   Ro 2:8
our *w.* (P)(R)   Ro 3:5
remove *w.* (N)   Ro 11:26
nor with the leaven of malice   1Co 5:8
and *w.*
vice (B)   1Co 5:8
against spiritual *w.* in high   Eph 6:12
places
spiritual forces of evil (B)   Eph 6:12
pleasure in *w.* (B)   2Th 2:12
growth of *w.* (A)(E)(R)(S)   Jas 1:21
every trace of *w.* (A)(E)   1Pe 2:1
as a pretext of *w.*   1Pe 2:16
(A)(B)(E)
world and its *w.* (P)   2Pe 2:5
reward of *w.* (A)(B)   2Pe 2:13
no objection to *w.* (P)   2Pe 2:13
we know whole world lieth in   1Jo 5:19
w.
lies under the wicked one (B)   1Jo 5:19
poisoned earth with *w.* (P)   Re 19:2

THEIR WICKEDNESS

look not to *their w.* nor to   De 9:27
their sin
God shall cut them off in   Ps 94:23
their w.
God overthrows the wicked for   Pr 21:12
their w.
utter judgments, touching all   Jer 1:16
their w.
their evil (B)   Jer 1:16; La 1:22
for I will pour *their w.* upon   Jer 14:16
them
yea, in my house have I   Jer 23:11
found *their w.*
they are a desolation, because   Jer 44:3
of *their w.*

inclined not their ear to turn   *Jer 44:5*
from *their* w.
let all *their* w. come before   *La 1:22*
thee
consider not that I remember   *Ho 7:2*
all *their* w.
their evil-doings (B)   *Ho 7:2; 7:3*
their evil works (R)   *Ho 7:2*
make king glad with *their* w.   *Ho 7:3*
all *their* w. is in Gilgal, there   *Ho 9:15*
I hated them
cry against Nineveh, for *their*   *Jon 1:2*
w. is come up
Jesus perceived *their* w. and   *M't 22:18*
said
their malicious plot (A)   *M't 22:18*
their malice (B)(R)   *M't 22:18*

THY WICKEDNESS

the Lord shall return *thy* w.   *1Ki 2:44*
upon thee
your evil (A)(R)   *1Ki 2:44; Na 3:19*
is not *thy* w. great? iniquities   *Job 22:5*
infinite
thy w. may hurt a man as   *Job 35:8*
thou art
for thou hast trusted in *thy*   *Isa 47:10*
w.
hast polluted the land with   *Jer 3:2*
thy w.
this is *thy* w. for it is bitter to   *Jer 4:18*
thy heart
thou shalt be confounded for   *Jer 22:22*
all *thy* w.
it came to pass after all *thy*   *Eze 16:23*
w.
before *thy* w. was   *Eze 16:57*
discovered, as at the time
upon whom hath not *thy* w.   *Na 3:19*
passed
your wrongs (B)   *Na 3:19*
repent therefore of this *thy* w.   *Ac 8:22*
your depravity (A)   *Ac 8:22*
your crookedness (B)   *Ac 8:22*

WIDE

open thine hand w. unto him   *De 15:8*
thine hand w. unto thy   *De 15:11*
brother
give a w. place for my steps   *2Sa 22:37*
(P)(R)
the land was w. and quiet   *1Ch 4:40*
opened their mouth w. as   *Job 29:23*
for the
as a w. breaking in of   *Job 30:14*
waters
opened their mouth w.   *Ps 35:21*
against
open thy mouth w. and I will   *Ps 81:10*
fill
So is this great and w. sea   *Ps 104:25*
he that openeth w. his lips   · *Pr 13:3*
shall
a brawling woman in a w.   *Pr 21:9;*
house   *25:24*
against whom make ye a w.   *Isa 57:4*
mouth
I will build me a w. house   *Jer 22:14*
the gates shall be set w. open   *Na 3:13*
for w. is the gate, and   *M't 7:13*
broad is the
with w.-open hearts (B)   *2Co 6:11*

WIDENED

w. my bed (B)(R)   *Isa 57:8*

WIDENESS

the w. of twenty cubits   *Eze 41:10*
round

WIDOW

Remain a w. at thy father's   *Ge 38:11*
house
Ye shall not afflict any w. or   *Ex 22:22*
A w. or a divorced woman   *Le 21:14*
But if the priest's daughter be   *Le 22:13*
a w.
But every vow of a w. and of   *Nu 30:9*
her
judgment of the fatherless   *De 10:18*
and w.
and the fatherless, and the   *De 14:29;*
w.   *16:11, 14; 24:19-21; 26:13*
stranger, the fatherless, and   *De 26:12*
the w.

of the stranger, fatherless, and   *De 27:19*
w.
answered, I am indeed a w.   *2Sa 14:5*
woman
name was Zeruah, a w.   *1Ki 11:26*
woman
commanded a w. woman   *1Ki 17:9*
there to
the w. woman was there   *1Ki 17:10*
gathering
evil up on the w. with whom   *1Ki 17:20*
not: and doeth not good to   *Job 24:21*
the w.
caused the eyes of the w. to   *Job 31:16*
fail
They slay the w. and the   *Ps 94:6*
stranger
be fatherless, and his wife a   *Ps 109:9*
w.
he relieveth the fatherless and   *Ps 146:9*
w.
will establish the border of   *Pr 15:25*
the w.
the fatherless, plead for the w.   *Isa 1:17*
the cause of the w. come unto   *Isa 1:23*
them
I shall not sit as a w. neither   *Isa 47:8*
shall I
stranger, the fatherless, and the   *Jer 7:6*
w.
stranger, the fatherless, nor   *Jer 22:3*
the w.
how is she become as a w.!   *Jer 22:3*
she that
they vexed the fatherless and   *Eze 22:7*
the w.
shall they take for their   *Eze 44:22*
wives a w.
or a w. that had a priest   *Eze 44:22*
before
And oppress not the w. nor   *Zec 7:10*
the hireling in his wages, the   *Mal 3:5*
w.
And there came a certain   *M'k 12:42*
poor w.
That this poor w. hath   *M'k 12:43*
cast more in
a w. of about fourscore and   *Lu 2:37*
four
Sidon, unto a woman that was   *Lu 4:26*
a w.
of his mother, and she was a   *Lu 7:12*
w.
And there was a w. in that   *Lu 18:3*
city
Yet because this w. troubleth   *Lu 18:5*
me
w. casting in thither two   *Lu 21:2*
mites
w. hath cast in more than they   *Lu 21:3*
all
if any w. have children or   *1Ti 5:4*
nephews
that is a w. indeed, and desolate   *1Ti 5:5*
not a w. be taken into the   *1Ti 5:9*
number
I sit a queen, and am no w.   *Re 18:7*

WIDOWHOOD

and put on the garments of   *Ge 38:19*
her w.
the day of their death, living   *2Sa 20:3*
in w.
day, the loss of children, and   *Isa 47:9*
w.
remember the reproach of thy   *Isa 54:4*
w.

WIDOWS

w. weeds (B)   *Ge 38:14*
and your wives shall be w.   *Ex 22:24*
Thou hast sent w. away   *Job 22:9*
empty, and
in death: and his w. shall   *Job 27:15*
not weep
the fatherless, and a judge of   *Ps 68:5*
the w.
and their w. made no   *Ps 78:64*
lamentation
mercy on their fatherless and   *Isa 9:17*
w.
people, that w. may be their   *Isa 10:2*
prey
Their w. are increased to me   *Jer 15:8*
above
bereaved of their children,   *Jer 18:21*
and be w.

alive: and let thy w. trust in   *Jer 49:11*
me
fatherless, our mothers are as   *La 5:3*
w.
made her many w. in the   *Eze 22:25*
midst
many w. were in Israel in the   *Lu 4:25*
days
their w. were neglected in the   *Ac 6:1*
daily
all the w. stood by him   *Ac 9:39*
weeping
he had called the saints and w.   *Ac 9:41*
therefore to the unmarried   *1Co 7:8*
and w.
Honour w. that are w. indeed   *1Ti 5:3*
But the younger w. refuse: for   *1Ti 5:11*
or woman that believeth have   *1Ti 5:16*
w.
relieve them that are w. indeed   *1Ti 5:16*
fatherless and w. in their   *Jas 1:27*
affliction

WIDOW'S

And she put her w. garments   *Ge 38:14*
off
nor take the w. raiment to   *De 24:17*
pledge
was a w. son of the tribe of   *1Ki 7:14*
Naphtali
they take the w. ox for a   *Job 24:3*
pledge
I caused the w. heart to sing   *Job 29:13*
for joy

WIDOWS'

for ye devour w. houses, and   *M't 23:14*
for a
Which devour w. houses,   *M'k 12:40;*
and for a   *Lu 20:47*

WIFE

the name of Abraham's w.   *Ge 11:29*
was Sarai *11:31; 12:17, 20; 20:18; 24:36*
woman thou hast taken is a   *Ge 20:3*
man's w.
Hagar took a w. for Ishmael   *Ge 21:21*
out of Egypt
take a w. to my son Isaac   *Ge 24:4;*
           24:38
Abraham took a w. her name   *Ge 25:1*
was Keturah
if Jacob take a w. of   *Ge 27:46;*
daughters of Heth, what good   *28:1;*
shall my life do   *28:6*
Judah took a w. for Er his   *Ge 38:6*
firstborn
go in unto thy brother's w.   *Ge 38:8*
and marry her
his master's w. cast her eyes   *Ge 39:7*
upon Joseph
Levi, and took to w. a daughter   *Ex 2:1*
of Levi
not covet neighbour's w.   *Ex 20:17;*
          De 5:21
if his master have given him a   *Ex 21:4*
w.
if he take him another w. her   *Ex 21:10*
food, raiment
the nakedness of thy father's   *Le 18:8;*
w. shalt thou not uncover   *20:11;*
          De 27:20
son's w.   *Le 18:15*
brother's w.   *Le 18:16; 20:21*
neither shalt thou take a w. to   *Le 18:18*
her sister
not lie with thy neighbour's   *Le 18:20;*
w.   *20:10*
if man take w. and mother, it   *Le 20:14*
is sin
if a man lie with his uncle's   *Le 20:20*
priests shall not take a w. that   *Le 21:7*
is a whore
high priest take a w. in her   *Le 21:13*
virginity
if any man's w. go aside   *Nu 5:12; 5:29*
be a w. to one of the family   *Nu 36:8*
of the tribe
if the w. of thy bosom entice   *De 13:6*
thee
what man betrothed a w. not   *De 20:7*
taken her
if any man take a w. and hate   *De 22:13*
her
because he humbleth his   *De 22:24*
neighbour's w.

a man shall not take his   *De 22:30*
father's *w.*
man hath taken *w.* and find   *De 24:1*
uncleanness
she may go and be another   *De 24:2*
man's *w.*
taken a new *w.* he shall not   *De 24:5*
go out to war
the *w.* of the dead not marry a   *De 25:5*
stranger
if he like not to take his   *De 25:7*
brother's *w.*
then shall his brother's *w.*   *De 25:9*
come unto him
the *w.* of the one draweth   *De 25:11*
near to deliver
betroth a *w.* and another lie   *De 28:30*
with her
his eye be evil toward the *w.*   *De 28:54*
of his bosom
Deborah, *w.* of Lapidoth,   *J'g 4:4*
judged
Jael the *w.* of Heber the   *J'g 4:17;*
Kenite   *4:21; 5:24*
thou goest to take a *w.* of   *J'g 14:3*
uncircumcised
Samson's *w.* wept before   *J'g 14:16*
him, and said
but his *w.* was given to his   *J'g 14:20*
companion
cursed be he that giveth a *w.*   *J'g 21:18*
to Benjamin
buy it of Ruth the *w.* of the   *Ru 4:5*
dead
thou hast taken the *w.* of   *2Sa 12:10*
Uriah
be not known to be the *w.* of   *1Ki 14:2*
Jeroboam
Ahijah said, Come in, thou *w.*   *1Ki 14:6*
of Jeroboam
and she waited on Naaman's   *2Ki 5:2*
w.
w. of Jehoiada hid him   *2Ch 22:11*
from Athaliah
rejoice with the *w.* of thy   *Pr 5:18*
youth
so he that goeth in to his   *Pr 6:29*
neighbour's *w.*
a good *w.* (B)(R)   *Pr 12:4; 31:10*
whoso findeth a *w.* findeth a   *Pr 18:22*
good thing
contentions of a *w.* a   *Pr 19:13*
continual dropping
and a prudent *w.* is from the   *Pr 19:14*
Lord
live joyfully with the *w.* of thy   *Ec 9:9*
youth
more than children of the   *Isa 54:1*
married *w.*
Lord hath called thee as a *w.*   *Isa 54:6*
of youth
surely as a *w.* treacherously   *Jer 3:20*
departeth
every one neighed after his   *Jer 5:8*
neighbour's *w.*
the husband and the *w.* shall   *Jer 6:11*
be taken
thou shalt not take thee a *w.*   *Jer 16:2*
in this place
as a *w.* that committeth   *Eze 16:32*
adultery
nor hath defiled his   *Eze 18:6;*
neighbour's *w.*   *18:15*
defiled his neighbour's *w.*   *Eze 18:11;*
           22:11; 33:26
take unto thee a *w.* of   *Ho 1:2*
whoredoms
Israel served for a *w.* and   *Ho 12:12*
kept sheep
Lord witness between thee   *Mal 2:14*
and *w.* of thy youth, the
w. of thy covenant
let none deal treacherously   *Mal 2:15*
against his *w.*
of her that had been the *w.* of   *M't 1:6*
Urias
Herod bound John for sake   *M't 14:3*
of Philip's *w.*
that hath forsaken *w.* or   *M't 19:29;*
children for my name's sake   *M'k 10:29;*
           Lu 18:29
seven brethren, the first,   *M't 22:25;*
when he had   *M'k 12:20; Lu 20:29*
married a *w.* deceased
I have married a *w.* and   *Lu 14:20*
cannot come
remember Lot's *w.*   *Lu 17:32*
that one should have his   *1Co 5:1*
father's *w.*

let husband render to *w.* due   *1Co 7:3*
benevolence, and likewise
also *w.* to husband
the *w.* hath not power over   *1Co 7:4*
her own body
let not the *w.* depart from   *1Co 7:10*
her husband
if any brother hath a *w.* that   *1Co 7:12*
believeth not
unbelieving *w.* is sanctified   *1Co 7:14*
by the husband
what knowest thou, O *w.* if   *1Co 7:16*
thou shalt save
art thou loosed from a *w.*   *1Co 7:27*
seek not a *w.*
there is difference between *w.*   *1Co 7:34*
and virgin
the *w.* is bound as long as   *1Co 7:39*
husband liveth
for the husband is the head   *Eph 5:23*
of the *w.*
let every one love *w.* even as   *Eph 5:33*
himself; *w.* see that she
reverence her husband
possess his own *w.* (B)   *1Th 4:4*
win his *w.* in purity and honor   *1Th 4:4*
(S)
the husband of one *w.*   *1Ti 3:2;*
           3:12; Tit 1:6
a widow, having been the *w.*   *1Ti 5:9*
of one man
giving honour to *w.* as weaker   *1Pe 3:7*
vessel
I will shew the bride, the   *Re 21:9*
Lamb's *w.*

HIS WIFE

a man leave father   *Ge 2:24;*
and mother and   *M't 19:5; M'k 10:7*
cleave unto *his w.*
they were both naked, the   *Ge 2:25*
man and *his w.*
they shall say, This is *his*   *Ge 12:12*
w. and kill me
the men laid hold on the   *Ge 19:16*
hand of *his w.*
but *his w.* looked back from   *Ge 19:26*
behind him
now therefore, restore the man   *Ge 20:7*
his w.
and she became *his w.*   *Ge 24:67;*
           1Sa 25:42
and Isaac entreated the Lord   *Ge 25:21*
for *his w.*
the men of the place asked   *Ge 26:7*
him of *his w.*
he that toucheth this man or   *Ge 26:11*
his w. shall die
kept back thee, because thou   *Ge 39:9*
art *his w.*
then *his w.* shall go out with   *Ex 21:3*
him
he shall surely endow her to   *Ex 22:16*
be *his w.*
thou shalt not approach to   *Le 18:14*
his w.
and if he be jealous of *his w.*   *Nu 5:14;*
           5:30
the man shall bring *his w.* to   *Nu 5:15*
the priest
the statutes between a man   *Nu 30:16*
and *his w.*
she shall be *his w.* all his   *De 22:19;*
days   *22:29*
he shall cheer up *his w.* that   *De 24:5*
he hath taken
Manoah arose and went   *J'g 13:11*
after *his w.*
Samson visited *his w.* with a   *J'g 15:1*
kid
come and catch you every   *J'g 21:21*
man *his w.*
save to every man *his w.*   *1Sa 30:22*
and children
thou hast taken *his w.* to be   *2Sa 12:9*
thy wife
whom Jezebel *his w.* stirred   *1Ki 21:25*
up
the daughter of Ahab was *his*   *2Ki 8:18*
w.
Haman called his friends and   *Es 5:10*
his w.
and let *his w.* be a widow   *Ps 109:9*
if a man put away *his w.*   *Jer 3:1;*
M't 5:31-32; 19:9; M'k 10:11; Lu 16:18
the Pharisees said, Is it   *M't 19:3;*
lawful for man to put away   *M'k 10:2*
his w. for every cause
if the case of a man be so   *M't 19:10*
with *his w.*

seven brethren deceased,   *M't 22:25;*
and left *his w.* to his   *M'k 12:19;*
brother   *Lu 20:28*
and hate not *his w.* and   *Lu 14:26*
children
his w. also being privy to it   *Ac 5:2*
his w. not knowing what was   *Ac 5:7*
done, came in
Paul found Aquila with *his w.*   *Ac 18:2*
Priscilla
when Felix came with *his w.*   *Ac 24:24*
Drusilla
let every man have *his* own *w.*   *1Co 7:2*
and let not the husband put   *1Co 7:11*
away *his w.*
he careth how he may please   *1Co 7:33*
his w.
he that loveth *his w.* loveth   *Eph 5:28*
himself
shall be joined to *his w.*   *Eph 5:31*
so love *his w.*   *Eph 5:33*
and *his w.* hath made herself   *Re 19:7*
ready

MY WIFE

she became *my w.*; she is   *Ge 20:12;*
my w.   *26:7*
give me *my w.*; I love *my w.*   *Ge 29:21;*
           Ex 21:5
Samson said, I will go in to   *J'g 15:1*
my w.
saying, Deliver me *my w.*   *2Sa 3:14*
Michal
shall I go into my house to   *2Sa 11:11*
lie with *my w.*
my breath is strange to *my*   *Job 19:17*
w.
then let *my w.* grind unto   *Job 31:10*
another
so I spake, and at even *my*   *Eze 24:18*
w. died
she is not *my w.* nor am I her   *Ho 2:2*
husband
and *my w.* is well stricken in   *Lu 1:18*
years

THY WIFE

hast hearkened to the voice of   *Ge 3:17*
thy w.
why didst thou not tell me   *Ge 12:18*
she was *thy w.*
behold *thy w.* take her, and   *Ge 12:19*
go thy way
Sarah, *thy w.* shall bear thee   *Ge 17:19;*
a son   *18:10*
arise, take *thy w.* and thy   *Ge 19:15*
two daughters
Abimelech said, Of a surety   *Ge 26:9*
she is *thy w.*
one might lightly have lien   *Ge 26:10*
with *thy w.*
I, Jethro, am come unto thee,   *Ex 18:6*
and *thy w.*
that thou wouldest have her   *De 21:11*
to *thy w.*
thou shall go in to her, and   *De 21:13*
she shall be *thy w.*
taken the wife of Uriah to be   *2Sa 12:10*
thy w.
thy w. shall be as a fruitful   *Ps 128:3*
vine
thy w. shall be an harlot in   *Am 7:17*
the city
whether thou shalt save *thy*   *1Co 7:16*
w.

TO WIFE

I might have taken her to me   *Ge 12:19*
to w.
Shechem said, Get me this   *Ge 34:4*
damsel *to w.*
I pray you, give him her *to*   *Ge 34:8;*
w.   *34:12*
she was not given to Shelah   *Ge 38:14*
to w.
Pharaoh gave Joseph *to w.*   *Ge 41:45*
Asenath
take a virgin of his own   *Le 21:14*
people *to w.*
I gave my daughter to this   *De 22:16*
man *to w.*
Caleb said, To him will I   *Jos 15:16;*
give Achsah my daughter *to w.*   *15:17;*
           J'g 1:12-13
now therefore get her for me *to*   *J'g 14:2*
w.

Merab, her will I give thee *to*   1Sa 18:17
w.

give me Abishag the   1Ki 2:17
Shunamite, *to w.*

thistle said to the cedar, Give   2Ki 14:9;
thy daughter to my son *to w.*   2Ch 25:18

Jehoram had daughter of   2Ch 21:6
Ahab *to w.*

the seven had her *to w.*   M'k 12:23;
  Lu 20:33

the second took her *to w.* and   Lu 20:30
died

WIFE'S

And Adam called his *w.* name   Ge 3:20
Eve

they will slay me for my *w.*   Ge 20:11
sake

and his *w.* name was   Ge 36:39;
Mehetabel   1Ch 1:50

The nakedness of thy father's   Le 18:11
w.

and his *w.* sons grew up, and   J'g 11:2

whose *w.* name was Maachah   1Ch 8:29;
  9:35

house, he saw his *w.* mother   M't 8:14
laid

Simon's *w.* mother lay sick   M'k 1:30
of a

And Simon's *w.* mother was   Lu 4:38
taken

WILD

And he will be a *w.* man; his   Ge 16:12
hand

a *w.*-ass among men   Ge 16:12
(A)(B)(E)(R)

also send *w.* beasts among   Le 26:22
you

the *w.* ox (A)(E)(R)   Nu 23:22;
  24:8; Job 39:9, 10; Ps 29:6; 92:10

w. ox (S)   Nu 23:22;
  24:8; De 33:17; Job 39:9, 10; Ps 29:6;
  92:10

the fallow deer, and the *w.*   De 14:5
goat

the pygarg, and the *w.* ox, and   De 14:5

the *w.* ox (A)(B)(E)(R)   De 33:17;
  Ps 22:21; Isa 34:7

and to the *w.* beasts of the   1Sa 17:46
earth

upon the rocks of the *w.*   1Sa 24:2
goats

was as light of foot as a *w.*   2Sa 2:18
roe

gather herbs, and found a *w.*   2Ki 4:39
vine

gathered thereof *w.* gourds   2Ki 4:39
his lap

a *w.* beast that was in   2Ki 14:9;
Lebanon   2Ch 25:18

w. ass bray when he hath   Job 6:5
grass

may be born like a *w.* ass's   Job 11:12
colt

as *w.* asses in the desert, go   Job 24:5
they

w. goats of the rock bring   Job 39:1
forth

Who hath sent out the *w.* ass   Job 39:5
free

loosed the hands of the *w.* ass   Job 39:5

the *w.* ox (B)   Job 39:9; Ps 92:10

w. ox (S)   Job 39:9; 39:10; Ps 29:6

that the *w.* beast may break   Job 39:15
them

w. oxen (S)   Ps 22:21; Isa 34:7

in the *w.*-dog region (B)   Ps 44:19

the *w.* beasts of the field are   Ps 50:11
mine

w. beasts of the field doth   Ps 80:13
devour it

the *w.* asses quench their   Ps 104:11
thirst

hills are a refuge for the *w.*   Ps 104:18
goats

no vision the people run *w.*   Pr 29:18
(B)

and it brought forth *w.* grapes   Isa 5:2

grapes, brought it forth *w.*   Isa 5:4
grapes

w. beast of the desert shall   Isa 13:21
lie

the *w.* goats shall cry   Isa 13:21
(A)(E)

w. beasts of the islands shall   Isa 13:22
cry

a joy of *w.* asses, a pasture of   Isa 32:14

w. beasts of the desert shall   Isa 34:14
also

meet with the *w.* beasts   Isa 34:14
of the

shaggy *w.* goats (A)(B)(E)   Isa 34:14

the streets, as a *w.* bull in a   Isa 51:20
net

A *w.* ass used to the   Jer 2:24
wilderness

w. asses did stand in the high   Jer 14:6

the *w.* beasts of the desert   Jer 50:39

w. beasts of the islands shall   Jer 50:39
dwell

dwelling was with the *w.* asses   Da 5:21

Assyria, a *w.* ass alone by   Ho 8:9
himself

his *w.* beast shall tear them   Ho 13:8

his meat was locusts and *w.*   M't 3:4
honey

he did eat locusts and *w.*   M'k 1:6
honey

and was with the *w.* beasts   M'k 1:13

w. beasts, and creeping   Ac 10:12;
things   11:6

being a *w.* olive tree, wert   Ro 11:17
graffed

the olive tree which is *w.* by   Ro 11:24
nature

WILDERNESS

El-paran, which is by the *w.*   Ge 14:6
desert (B)   Ge 14:6;
16:7; 21:14, 20, 21; 36:24; Ex 3:18; 4:27;
5:1; 7:16; 8:27, 28; 13:18, 20; 14:3, 11,
12;. 15:22; 16:1, 2, 3, 10, 14, 32; 17:1;
18:5; 19:1, 2; Nu 20:4; 21:5, 11, 13, 23;
24:1; 32:13; 33:6, 8; De 1:19, 31, 40;
2:1, 7, 8, 26; 4:43; 8:15; 9:7, 28; 11:5;
25; Jos 1:4; 5:5; 8:15, 24; 12:8; 15:51;
16:1; 18:12; 20:8; 24:7; J'g 11:18; 20:42,
45, 47; 1Sa 13:18; 17:28; 23:14, 15, 24;
24:1; 25:1, 4, 14, 21; 26:2, 3; 2 Sa 2:24;
15:23, 28; 16:2; 17:16, 29; 1Ki 2:34;
9:18; 19:4, 15; 2 Ki 3:8; 1Ch 5:9; 6:78;
12:8; 21:29; Job 1:19; 24:5; 38:26; 39:6;
Ps 55:7; 74:14; 78:52; 106:9, 14; 107:4,
33, 35; Ca 3:6; Isa 14:17; 16:1, 8; 32:15;
33:9; 42:11; 43:20; 50:2; Jer 2:31; 4:11,
26; 9:10, 26; 13:24; 17:6; 50:12;
Eze 6:14; 20:13, 17, 18, 21, 23, 36;
23:42; Ho 2:3; 13:15; Joe 2:3; Am 2:10;
Zep 2:13; M't 3:3; 4:1; M'k 1:3, 4, 12;
8:14; Lu 3:2, 4; 4:1; 5:16; 7:24;
Joh 1:23; 3:14; 6:49; 11:54; Ac 7:36, 38,
42, 44; 13:18; 1Co 10:5; Heb 3:8, 17;
Re 12:14

by a fountain of water in the   Ge 16:7
w.

wandered in the *w.* of   Ge 21:14
Beer-sheba

and he grew, and dwelt in   Ge 21:20
the *w.*

And he dwelt in the *w.* of   Ge 21:21
Paran

that found the mules in the   Ge 36:24
w.

him into this pit that is in   Ge 37:22
the *w.*

desert-pit (B)   Ge 37:22

three days' journey into the   Ex 3:18
w. that

Go into the *w.* to meet Moses   Ex 4:27

may hold a feast unto me in   Ex 5:1
the *w.*

that they may serve me in the   Ex 7:16
w.

go three days' journey into the   Ex 8:27

to the Lord your God in the   Ex 8:28
w.

the way of the *w.* of the Red   Ex 13:18
sea

in Etham, in the edge of the   Ex 13:20
w.

the land, the *w.* hath shut them   Ex 14:3
in

taken us away to die in them *w.*   Ex 14:11

than that we should die in the   Ex 14:12
w.

they went out into the *w.* of   Ex 15:22
Shur

and they went three days in   Ex 15:22
the *w.*

of Israel came unto the *w.* of   Ex 16:1
Sin

against Moses and Aaron in   Ex 16:2
the *w.*

have brought us forth into this   Ex 16:3
w.

that they looked toward the   Ex 16:10
w.

upon the face of the *w.* there   Ex 16:14
lay a

wherewith I have fed you in   Ex 16:32
the *w.*

Israel journeyed from the *w.* of   Ex 17:1
Sin

his wife unto Moses into the   Ex 18:5
w.

came they into the *w.* of Sinai   Ex 19:1

Sinai, and had pitched in the   Ex 19:2
w.

unto the Lord, in the *w.* of   Le 7:38
Sinai

him go for a scapegoat into   Le 16:10
the *w.*

spake unto Moses in the *w.* of   Nu 1:1
Sinai

numbered them in the *w.* of   Nu 1:19
Sinai

before the Lord, in the *w.* of   Nu 3:4
Sinai

unto Moses in the *w.* of Sinai   Nu 3:14;
  9:1

month at even in the *w.* of   Nu 9:5
Sinai

journeys out of the *w.* of   Nu 10:12
Sinai

cloud rested in the *w.* of   Nu 10:12
Paran

how we are to encamp in the   Nu 10:31
w.

and pitched in the *w.* of   Nu 12:16
Paran

sent them from the *w.* of   Nu 13:3
Paran

from the *w.* of Zin unto   Nu 13:21
Rehob

unto the *w.* of Paran, to   Nu 13:26
Kadesh

would God we had died in   Nu 14:2
this *w.*

which I did in Egypt and in   Nu 14:22
the *w.*

into the *w.* by the way of the   Nu 14:25
Red sea

Your carcases shall fall in   Nu 14:29
this *w.*

carcases, they shall fall in   Nu 14:32
this *w.*

shall wander in the *w.* forty   Nu 14:33
years

your carcases be wasted in   Nu 14:33
the *w.*

in this *w.* they shall be   Nu 14:35
consumed

children of Israel were in the   Nu 15:32
w.

to kill us in the *w.* except   Nu 16:13
thou

wilderness (B)(E)(R)   Nu 20:1;
  27:14; 2Ch 26:10

of the Lord into this *w.*   Nu 20:4

us up out of Egypt to die in   Nu 21:5
the *w.*

in the *w.* which is before   Nu 21:11
Moab

which is in the *w.* that   Nu 21:13
cometh out

the *w.* they went to Mattanah   Nu 21:18

went out against Israel into   Nu 21:23
the *w.*

but he set his face toward the   Nu 24:1
w.

of Israel in the *w.* of Sinai   Nu 26:64

They shall surely die in the   Nu 26:65
w.

Our father died in the *w.* and   Nu 27:3

Meribah in Kadesh in the *w.*   Nu 27:14
of Zin

them wander in the *w.* forty   Nu 32:13
years

which is in the edge of the *w.*   Nu 33:6

the midst of the sea into the   Nu 33:8
w.

went three days' journey in   Nu 33:8
the *w.*

and encamped in the *w.* of   Nu 33:11
Sin

their journey out of the *w.*   Nu 33:12
of Sin

pitched in the *w.* of   Nu 33:15
Sinai

pitched in the *w.* of Zin,   Nu 33:36
which is

w. of Zin along by the coast of   Nu 34:3
Edom

Israel on this side Jordan in   De 1:1
the *w.*

all that great and terrible *w.*   De 1:19
And in the *w.* where thou hast   De 1:31
take your journey into the *w.*   De 1:40
by
took our journey into the *w.* by   De 2:1
thy walking through this great   De 2:7
w.
by the way of the *w.* of Moab   De 2:8
I sent messengers out of the   De 2:26
w. of
Bezer in the *w.* in the plain   De 4:43
through that great and terrible   De 8:15
w.
Lord thy God to wrath in the   De 9:7
w.
them out to slay them in the   De 9:28
w.
what he did unto you in the   De 11:5
w.
from the *w.* and Lebanon,   De 11:24
from the
and in the waste howling *w.*   De 32:10
Meribah-Kadesh, in the *w.* of   De 32:51
Zin
From the *w.* and this Lebanon   Jos 1:4
even
of war, died in the *w.* by the   Jos 5:4
way
that were born in the *w.* by the   Jos 5:5
way
and fled by the way of the *w.*   Jos 8:15
people that fled to the *w.*   Jos 8:20
turned
in the *w.* wherein they chased   Jos 8:24
them
in the *w.* and in the south   Jos 12:8
country
of Edom the *w.* of Zin   Jos 15:1
southward
In the *w.* Beth-arabah,   Jos 15:61
Middin
the *w.* that goeth up from   Jos 16:1
Jericho
were at the *w.* of Beth-aven   Jos 18:12
assigned Bezer in the *w.* upon   Jos 20:8
ye dwelt in the *w.* a long   Jos 24:7
season
of Judah into the *w.* of Judah   J'g 1:16
your flesh with the thorns of   J'g 8:7
the *w.*
and thorns of the *w.* and   J'g 8:16
briers
walked through the *w.* unto   J'g 11:16
they went along through the   J'g 11:18
w.
and from the *w.* even unto   J'g 11:22
Jordan
of Israel unto the way of the   J'g 20:42
w.
fled toward the *w.* unto the   J'g 20:45
rock of
fled to the *w.* unto the rock   J'g 20:47
with all the plagues in the *w.*   1Sa 14:8
valley of Zeboim toward the   1Sa 13:18
w.
thou left those few sheep in   1Sa 17:28
the *w.*
David abode in the *w.* in   1Sa 23:14
strong
in a mountain in the *w.* of   1Sa 23:14
Ziph
David was in the *w.* of Ziph   1Sa 23:15
in a
his men were in the *w.* of   1Sa 23:24
Maon
rock, and abode in the *w.* of   1Sa 23:25
Maon
plain (B)   1Sa 23:25;
            Joe 1:19; 2:22; Eze 34:25
after David in the *w.* of   1Sa 23:25
Maon
David is in the *w.* of En-gedi   1Sa 24:1
and went down to the *w.* of   1Sa 25:1
Paran
David heard in the *w.* that   1Sa 25:4
Nabal
sent messengers out of the   1Sa 25:14
w. to
all that this fellow hath in   1Sa 25:21
the *w.*
and went down to the *w.* of   1Sa 26:2
Ziph
to seek David in the *w.* of   1Sa 26:2
Ziph
But David abode in the *w.*   1Sa 26:3
and he
Saul came after him into the   1Sa 26:3
w.

by the way of the *w.* of   2Sa 2:24
Gibeon
over, toward the way of   2Sa 15:23
the *w.*
I will tarry in the plain of   2Sa 15:28
the *w.*
as be faint in the *w.* may   2Sa 16:2
drink
this night in the plains of   2Sa 17:16
the *w.*
and weary, and thirsty, in   2Sa 17:29
the *w.*
buried in his own house in the   1Ki 2:34
w.
Baalath, and Tadmor in the   1Ki 9:18
w.
went a day's journey into the   1Ki 19:4
w.
on thy way to the *w.* of   1Ki 19:15
Damascus
The way through the *w.* of   2Ki 3:8
Edom
unto the entering in the *w.*   1Ch 5:9
Bezer in the *w.* with her   1Ch 6:78
suburbs
unto David into the hold to   1Ch 12:8
the *w.*
Lord, which Moses made in   1Ch 21:29
the *w.*
of the Lord had made in the   2Ch 1:3
w.
And he built Tadmor in the   2Ch 8:4
the brook, before the *w.* of   2Ch 20:16
Jeruel
went forth into the *w.* of   2Ch 20:20
Tekoa
toward the watch tower in   2Ch 20:24
the *w.*
of God laid upon Israel in   2Ch 24:9
the *w.*
forsookest them not in the *w.*   Ne 9:19
came a great wind from the *w.*   Job 1:19
causeth them to wander in a   Job 12:24
w.
jungle (B)   Job 12:24
the *w.* yieldeth food for them   Job 24:5
and
wilderness (A)(B)(E)(R)   Job 24:5;
Ps 78:40; 102:6; 106:14; Isa 40:3; 41:19;
                                    51:3
fleeing into the *w.* in former   Job 30:3
time
the *w.* wherein there is no   Job 38:26
man
Whose house I have made the   Job 39:6
w.
voice of the Lord shaketh the   Ps 29:8
w.
Lord, shaketh the *w.* of Kadesh Ps 29:8
far off, and remain in the *w.*   Ps 55:7
when he was in the *w.* of   Ps 63 title
Judah
drop upon the pastures of the   Ps 65:12
w.
thou didst march through the   Ps 68:7
w.
They that dwell in the *w.* shall   Ps 72:9
to the people inhabiting the   Ps 74:14
w.
He clave the rocks in the *w.*   Ps 78:15
provoking most High in the   Ps 78:17
w.
Can God furnish a table in   Ps 78:19
the *w.*
oft did they provoke him in   Ps 78:40
the *w.*
guided them in the *w.* like a   Ps 78:52
flock
I am like a pelican of the *w.*   Ps 102:6
the depths, as through the *w.*   Ps 106:9
But lusted exceedingly in the   Ps 106:14
w.
them, to overthrow them in   Ps 106:26
the *w.*
wandered in *w.* in a solitary   Ps 107:4
way
He turneth rivers into a *w.*   Ps 107:33
and the
turneth the *w.* into a   Ps 107:35
standing
causeth them to wander in   Ps 107:40
pathless wastes (B)   Ps 107:40
led his people through the *w.*   Ps 136:16
is this that cometh out of the   Ca 3:6
w.
is this that cometh up from the   Ca 8:5
w.
That made the world a *w.*   Isa 14:17
of the land from Sela to the *w.*   Isa 16:1

they wandered through the *w.*   Isa 16:8
it for them that dwell in the   Isa 23:13
w.
forsaken, and left like a *w.*   Isa 27:10
high, and the *w.* be a fruitful   Isa 32:15
field
Sharon is like a *w.;* and   Isa 33:9
Bashan
w. and the solitary place be   Isa 35:1
glad
w. and dry land   Isa 35:1
(A)(B)(E)(R)
I will make the *w.* a pool of   Isa 41:18
water
Let the *w.* and the cities   Isa 42:11
thereof
because, I give waters in the   Isa 43:20
w.
the sea, I make the rivers a *w.*   Isa 50:2
and he will make her *w.* like   Isa 51:3
Eden
the deep, as an horse in the   Isa 63:13
w.
Thy holy cities are a *w.* Zion   Isa 64:10
is a
Zion is a *w.,* Jerusalem a   Isa 64:10
Egypt that led us through the   Jer 2:6
w.
A wild ass used to the *w.* that   Jer 2:24
Have I been a *w.* unto Israel   Jer 2:31
for them, as the Arabian in the   Jer 3:2
w.
wind of the high places in the   Jer 4:11
w.
and, lo, the fruitful place was   Jer 4:26
a *w.*
and for the habitations of the   Jer 9:10
w.
and is burned up like a *w.*   Jer 9:12
corners, that dwell in the *w.*   Jer 9:26
my pleasant portion a   Jer 12:10
desolate *w.*
all high places through the   Jer 12:12
w.
passeth away by the wind of   Jer 13:24
the *w.*
the parched places in the *w.*   Jer 17:6
yet surely I will make thee a   Jer 22:6
w.
places of the *w.* are dried up   Jer 23:10
of the nations shall be a *w.*   Jer 50:12
a desolation, a dry land, and   Jer 51:43
a *w.*
a steppe (B)   Jer 51:43
cruel, like the ostriches in the   La 4:3
w.
because of the sword of the *w.*   La 5:9
than the *w.* toward Diblath   Eze 6:14
out my fury upon them in   Eze 20:13
the *w.*
I make an end of them in the   Eze 20:17
w.
said unto their children in   Eze 20:18
the *w.*
my anger against them in   Eze 20:21
the *w.*
mine hand unto them also in   Eze 20:23
the *w.*
pleaded with your fathers in   Eze 20:36
the *w.*
were brought Sabeans from   Eze 23:42
the *w.*
and make her as a *w.* and set   Ho 2:3
her
Lord shall come up from   Ho 13:15
the *w.*
devoured the pastures of the   Joe 1:19;
w.   *1:20*
and behind them a desolate *w.*   Joe 2:3
for the pastures of the *w.* do   Joe 2:22
spring
and Edom shall be a desolate   Joe 3:19
w.
led you forty years through   Am 2:10
the *w.*
and offerings in the *w.* forty   Am 5:25
years
Hemath unto the river of the   Am 6:14
w.
brook of the Arabah (B)   Am 6:14
a desolation, and dry like   Zep 2:13
a *w.*
waste for the dragons of the   Mal 1:3
w.
The voice of one crying in the   M't 3:3;
w.   *M'k 1:3; Lu 3:4; Joh 1:23*
Jesus led up of the spirit in   M't 4:1
the *w.*
wilderness (A)(E)(R)   M't 24:26;
                                    Joh 6:31

John did baptize in the w. and   M'k 1:4
the spirit driveth him into   M'k 1:12
the w.
he was there in the w. forty   M'k 1:13
days
men with bread here in the w.   M'k 8:4
the son of Zacharias in the w.   Lu 3:2
was led by the Spirit, into the   Lu 4:1
w.
he withdrew himself into the w.   Lu 5:16
went ye out into the w. for to   Lu 7:24
see
lifted up the serpent in the w.   Joh 3:14
fathers did eat manna in the   Joh 6:49
w.
unto a country near to the w.   Joh 11:54
Red sea, and in the w. forty   Ac 7:36
years
he, that was in the church in   Ac 7:38
the w.
the space of forty years in the   Ac 7:42
w.
the tabernacle of witness in   Ac 7:44
the w.
suffered he their manners in   Ac 13:18
the w.
for they were overthrown in   1Co 10:5
the w.
w. and intentions (A)(N)   2Co 2:11
gone astray in a w. of words   1Ti 1:6
(N)
in the day of temptation in   Heb 3:8
the w.
whose carcases fell in the w.   Heb 3:17
go on deliberately and w.   Heb 10:26
sinning (A)(P)(R)
that she might fly into the   Heb 12:14
w.

IN THE WILDERNESS

my miracles which I did in   Nu 14:22
the w.
again leave them in the w.   Nu 32:15;
  Eze 29:5
desert (B)   Nu 32:15;
Pr 21:19; Isa 32:16; 41:19; 43:19;
Jer 2:2; 9:2; 48:6; Eze 20:13, 15;
Ho 13:5; M't 3:1; 15:33; Ac 7:30;
  2Co 11:26
remember the Lord led thee   De 8:2;
forty years in the w.   29:5; Jos 5:6;
  14:10
who fed thee in the w. with   De 8:16
manna
forty years didst thou sustain   Ne 9:21
them in w.
as in the day of temptation in   Ps 95:8
the w.
better dwell in the w. than   Pr 21:19
with
then judgment shall dwell in   Isa 32:16
the w.
for in the w. shall waters   Isa 35:6
break out
the voice of him that crieth   Isa 40:3;
in the w.   M't 3:3; M'k 1:3; Lu 3:4;
  Joh 1:23
I will plant in the w. the   Isa 41:19
cedar and oil tree
I will even make a way in   Isa 43:19
the w.
when they wentest after me   Jer 2:2
in the w.
oh that I had in the w. a   Jer 9:2
lodging place
people that were left found   Jer 31:2
grace in the w.
flee and be like the heath   Jer 48:6
in the w.
they laid wait for us in the w.   La 4:19
and now she is planted in   Eze 19:13
the w.
Israel rebelled against me in   Eze 20:13
the w.
I lifted my hand to them in   Eze 20:15;
the w.   20:23
and they shall dwell safely   Eze 34:25
in the w.
I found Israel like grapes in   Ho 9:10
the w.
I did not know thee in the w. in   Ho 13:5
the dry land
John came preaching in the w.   M't 3:1
whence should we have so   M't 15:33
much bread in the w.   M'k 8:4
leave the ninety and nine in the   Lu 15:4
w.

an angel appeared in the   Ac 7:30;
w.   7:38
I have been in perils in the   2Co 11:26
w.

INTO THE WILDERNESS

send him by a fit man into   Le 16:21
the w.
desert (B)   Le 16:21;
16:22; Eze 20:10, 35; M't 11:7; Lu 8:29;
  Ac 21:38; Re 12:6; 17:3
and he shall let go the goat   Le 16:22
into the w.
and I brought them into the   Eze 20:10
w.
I will bring you into the w.   Eze 20:35
of the people
I will allure her and bring her   Ho 2:14
into the w.
what went ye out into the   M't 11:7;
w. to see? a reed shaken with   Lu 7:24
wind
he was driven of the devil into   Lu 8:29
the w.
which leddest into the w.   Ac 21:38
4000 men
and the woman fled into the   Re 12:6;
w.   12:14
so he carried me in the spirit   Re 17:3
into the w.

WILES

For they vex you with their   Nu 25:18
w.
their underhandedness (B)   Nu 25:18
stand against the w. of the   Eph 6:11
devil
strategies and deceits of the   Eph 6:11
devil (A)
the devil's intrigues (B)   Eph 6:11
the devices of the devil (N)   Eph 6:11
the devil's methods of attack   Eph 6:11
(P)

WILFUL

show yourself w. (A)   2Sa 22:27
w. and contrary talk (A)   Pr 4:24
w. contrariness breaks (A)   Pr 15:4
w. and contrary tongue will   Pr 17:20
(A)
bold and w. (R)   2Pe 2:10

WILFULLY

comes w. upon another   Ex 21:14
(A)(R)
person does anything w. (A)   Nu 21:30
are w. obstinate (A)   Nu 22:32
w. goes in double and wrong   Pr 28:6
ways (A)
w. sheds blood (A)   Pr 28:17
For if we sin w. after that   Heb 10:26
we have
go on deliberately and   Heb 10:26
willingly sinning (A)(P)(R)
if we persist in sin after (N)   Heb 10:26

WILILY

They did work w. and went   Jos 9:4
They worked cunningly (A)   Jos 9:4
they proceeded with stratagem   Jos 9:4
(B)
they acted with cunning (R)   Jos 9:4

WILL

I w. make him an help meet   Ge 2:18
for him
I w. put enmity between thee   Ge 3:15
and the
I w. greatly multiply thy   Ge 3:16
sorrow and
I w. destroy man whom I have   Ge 6:7
created
I w. destroy them with the   Ge 6:13
earth
with thee w. I establish my   Ge 6:18
covenant
I w. cause it to rain upon the   Ge 7:4
that I have made w. I destroy   Ge 7:4
I w. not again, curse the   Ge 8:21
ground any
neither w. I again smite any   Ge 8:21
more

your blood of your lives w. I   Ge 9:5
require
hand of every beast w. I   Ge 9:5
require it
every man's brother w. I   Ge 9:5
require the
I w. establish my covenant   Ge 9:11
with you
I w. remember my covenant,   Ge 9:15
which is
I w. look upon it, that I may   Ge 9:16
remember
nothing w. be restrained from   Ge 11:6
them
house, unto a land that I w.   Ge 12:1
show thee
I w. make of thee a great   Ge 12:2
nation
I w. bless thee, and make thy   Ge 12:2
name
And I w. bless them that bless   Ge 12:3
thee
Unto thy seed w. I give this   Ge 12:7
land
w. kill me, but they w. save   Ge 12:12
thee alive
left hand, then I w. go to the   Ge 13:9
right
right hand, then I w. go the   Ge 13:9
left
to thee w. I give it, and to   Ge 13:15
thy seed for
I w. make thy seed as the   Ge 13:16
dust of the
breadth of it; for I w. give it   Ge 13:17
unto thee
I w. not take from a thread   Ge 14:23
even to a
I w. not take any thing that   Ge 14:23
is thine
whom they shall serve, w. I   Ge 15:14
judge
I w. multiply thy seed   Ge 16:10
exceedingly
And he w. be a wild man;   Ge 16:12
his hand
his hand w. be against every   Ge 16:12
man, and
I w. make my covenant   Ge 17:2
between me
and w. multiply thee   Ge 17:2
exceedingly
I w. make thee exceeding   Ge 17:6
fruitful
and I w. make nations of   Ge 17:6
thee, and
I w. establish my covenant   Ge 17:7
between
I w. give unto thee, and unto   Ge 17:8
thy
possession; and I w. be their   Ge 17:8
God
I w. bless her, and give thee   Ge 17:16
a son
I w. bless her, and she shall   Ge 17:16
be a
I w. establish my covenant   Ge 17:19
with him
blessed him and w. make   Ge 17:20
him fruitful
and w. multiply him   Ge 17:20
exceedingly
and I w. make him a great   Ge 17:20
nation
But my covenant w. I   Ge 17:21
establish with
I w. fetch a morsel of bread   Ge 18:5
said, I w. certainly return   Ge 18:10
unto thee
At the time apointed I w.   Ge 18:14
return
he w. command his children   Ge 18:19
and his
I w. go down now, and see   Ge 18:21
whether
come unto me; and if not, I   Ge 18:21
w. know
I w. spare all the place for   Ge 18:26
their sakes
forty and five, I w. not   Ge 18:28
destroy it
he said, I w. not do it for   Ge 18:29
forty's sake
not the Lord be angry, and I   Ge 18:30
w. speak
he said, I w. not do it, if I   Ge 18:30
find thirty
I w. not destroy it for   Ge 18:31
twenty's sake

and I *w.* speak yet but this once — Ge 18:32

said, I *w.* not destroy it for ten's sake — Ge 18:32

we *w.* abide in the street all night — Ge 19:2

sojourn, and he *w.* needs be a judge — Ge 19:9

w. we deal worse with thee, than with — Ge 19:9

For we *w.* destroy this place, because — Ge 19:13

for the Lord *w.* destroy this city — Ge 19:14

that I *w.* not overthrow this city, for — Ge 19:21

and we *w.* lie with him, that we may — Ge 19:32

and they *w.* slay me for my wife's sake — Ge 20:11

that all that hear *w.* laugh with me — Ge 21:6

of the bondwoman *w.* I make a nation — Ge 21:13

for I *w.* make him a great nation — Ge 21:18

And Abraham said, I *w.* swear — Ge 21:24

mountains which I *w.* tell thee of — Ge 22:2

and I and the lad *w.* go yonder and — Ge 22:5

son, God *w.* provide himself a lamb — Ge 22:8

That in blessing I *w.* bless thee — Ge 22:17

multiplying I *w.* multiply thy seed as — Ge 22:17

I *w.* give thee money for the field — Ge 23:13

I *w.* make thee swear by the Lord — Ge 24:3

woman *w.* not be willing to follow — Ge 24:5

Unto thy seed *w.* I give this land — Ge 24:7

woman *w.* not be willing to follow — Ge 24:8

and I *w.* give thy camels drink also — Ge 24:14; 24:46

w. draw water for thy camels also — Ge 24:19

I *w.* not eat, until I have told mine — Ge 24:33

the woman *w.* not follow me — Ge 24:39

w. send his angel with thee — Ge 24:40

and I *w.* also draw for thy camels — Ge 24:44

if ye *w.* deal kindly and truly with my — Ge 24:49

We *w.* call the damsel, and enquire at — Ge 24:57

with this man? And she said, I *w.* go — Ge 24:58

I *w.* be with thee, and *w.* bless thee — Ge 26:3

thy seed, I *w.* give all these countries — Ge 26:3

I *w.* perform the oath which I sware — Ge 26:3

I *w.* make thy seed to multiply as the — Ge 26:4

and *w.* give unto thy seed all these — Ge 26:4

for I am with thee, and *w.* bless thee — Ge 26:24

I *w.* make them savoury meat for thy — Ge 27:9

My father peradventure *w.* feel me — Ge 27:12

me, and I *w.* eat of my son's venison — Ge 27:25

then *w.* I slay my brother Jacob — Ge 27:41

then *w.* I send, and fetch thee from — Ge 27:45

thou liest, to thee *w.* I give it — Ge 28:13

w. keep thee in all places whither thou — Ge 28:15

and *w.* bring thee again into this land — Ge 28:15

for I *w.* not leave thee, until I have — Ge 28:15

a vow, saying, If God, *w.* be with me — Ge 28:20

and *w.* keep me in this way that I go — Ge 28:20

w. give me bread to eat, and raiment — Ge 28:20

I *w.* surely give the tenth unto thee — Ge 28:22

I *w.* serve thee seven years for Rachel — Ge 29:18

and we *w.* give thee this also for the — Ge 29:27

now therefore my husband *w.* love me — Ge 29:32

this time *w.* my husband be joined — Ge 29:34

she said, Now *w.* I praise the Lord — Ge 29:35

for the daughters *w.* call me blessed — Ge 30:13

now *w.* my husband dwell with me — Ge 30:20

me thy wages, and I *w.* give it — Ge 30:28

I *w.* again feed and keep thy flock — Ge 30:31

I *w.* pass through all thy flock to-day — Ge 30:32

to thy kindred; and I *w.* be with thee — Ge 31:3

I *w.* not pass over this heap to thee — Ge 31:52

and I *w.* deal well with thee — Ge 32:9

him, lest he *w.* come and smite me — Ge 32:11

thou saidst, I *w.* surely do thee good — Ge 32:12

I *w.* appease him with the present — Ge 32:20

me, and afterward I *w.* see his face — Ge 32:20

peradventure he *w.* accept of me — Ge 32:20

said, I *w.* not let thee go, except thou — Ge 32:26

and let us go, and I *w.* go before thee — Ge 33:12

them one day, all the flock *w.* die — Ge 33:13

his servant; and I *w.* lead on softly — Ge 33:14

what ye shall say unto me I *w.* give — Ge 34:11

I *w.* give according as ye shall say — Ge 34:12

But in this *w.* we consent unto you — Ge 34:15

If ye *w.* be as we be, that every male — Ge 34:15

Then *w.* we give our daughters unto — Ge 34:16

and we *w.* take your daughters to us — Ge 34:16

and we *w.* dwell with you — Ge 34:16

and we *w.* become one people — Ge 34:16

But if ye *w.* not hearken unto us, to — Ge 34:17

then *w.* we take our daughter and we *w.* be gone — Ge 34:17

herein *w.* the men consent unto us — Ge 34:22

unto them, and they *w.* dwell with us — Ge 34:23

I *w.* make there an altar unto God — Ge 35:3

to thee I *w.* give it, and to thy seed — Ge 35:12

seed after thee *w.* I give the land — Ge 35:12

come, and I *w.* send thee unto them — Ge 37:13

and we *w.* say, Some evil beast hath — Ge 37:20

see what *w.* become of his dreams — Ge 37:20

I *w.* go down into the grave unto my — Ge 37:35

I *w.* send thee a kid from the flock — Ge 38:17

and God *w.* shortly bring it to pass — Ge 41:32

the throne *w.* I be greater than thou — Ge 41:40

w. I deliver you your brother, and ye — Ge 42:34

and ye *w.* take Benjamin away — Ge 42:36

and I *w.* bring him to thee again — Ge 42:37

us, we *w.* go down and buy thee food — Ge 43:4

wilt not send him, we *w.* not go down — Ge 43:5

lad with me, and we *w.* arise and go — Ge 43:8

I *w.* be surety for him; of my hand — Ge 43:9

and we also *w.* be my lord's bondmen — Ge 44:9

be with us, then *w.* we go down — Ge 44:26

the lad is not with us, that he *w.* die — Ge 44:31

And there *w.* I nourish thee; for yet — Ge 45:11

I *w.* give you the good of the land of — Ge 45:18

I *w.* go and see him before I die — Ge 45:28

for I *w.* there make of thee a great — Ge 46:3

I *w.* go down with thee into Egypt — Ge 46:4

I *w.* also surely bring thee up again — Ge 46:4

I *w.* go up, and shew Pharaoh, and say — Ge 46:31

I *w.* give you for your cattle, if money — Ge 47:16

We *w.* not hide it from my lord, how — Ge 47:18

and we and our land *w.* be servants — Ge 47:19

and we *w.* be Pharaoh's servants — Ge 47:25

But I *w.* lie with my fathers, and thou — Ge 47:30

And he said, I *w.* do as thou hast said — Ge 47:30

I *w.* make thee fruitful, and multiply — Ge 48:4

and I *w.* make of thee a multitude of — Ge 48:4

w. give this land to thy seed after thee — Ge 48:4

thee, unto me, and I *w.* bless them — Ge 48:9

I *w.* divide them in Jacob and scatter — Ge 49:7

bury my father, and I *w.* come again — Ge 50:5

said, Joseph *w.* peradventure hate us — Ge 50:15

w. certainly requite all the evil which — Ge 50:15

I *w.* nourish you, and your little ones — Ge 50:21

and God *w.* surely visit you, and bring — Ge 50:24

God *w.* surely visit you, and ye shall — Ge 50:25

it for me, and I *w.* give thee thy wages — Ex 2:9

Moses said, I *w.* now turn aside, and — Ex 3:3

and I *w.* send thee unto Pharaoh, that — Ex 3:10

he said, Certainly I *w.* be with thee — Ex 3:12

I *w.* bring you up out of the affliction — Ex 3:17

the king of Egypt *w.* not let you go — Ex 3:19

And I *w.* stretch out my hand — Ex 3:20

which I *w.* do in the midst thereof — Ex 3:20

and after that he *w.* let you go — Ex 3:20

I *w.* give this people favour in — Ex 3:21

they *w.* not believe me, nor hearken — Ex 4:1

for they *w.* say, The Lord hath not — Ex 4:1

if they *w.* not believe thee, neither — Ex 4:8

w. believe the voice of the later sign — Ex 4:8

w. not believe also these two signs — Ex 4:9

and I *w.* be with thy mouth — Ex 4:12

thee, he *w.* be glad in his heart — Ex 4:14

and I *w.* be with thy mouth, and with — Ex 4:15

and *w.* teach you what ye shall do — Ex 4:15

but I *w.* harden his heart, that he — Ex 4:21

behold, I *w.* slay thy son, even thy — Ex 4:23

the Lord, neither *w.* I let Israel go — Ex 5:2

Pharaoh, I *w.* not give you straw — Ex 5:10

thou see what I w. do to | Ex 6:1
Pharaoh
I w. bring you out from under | Ex 6:6
and I w. rid you out of their | Ex 6:6
bondage
I w. redeem you with a | Ex 6:6
stretched out
I w. take you to me for a | Ex 6:7
people, and I
I w. be to you a God: and ye | Ex 6:7
shall
And I w. bring you unto the | Ex 6:8
land
and I w. give it you for an | Ex 6:8
heritage
I w. harden Pharaoh's heart | Ex 7:3
I w. smite with the rod that is | Ex 7:17
in mine
I w. smite all thy borders with | Ex 8:2
frogs
I w. let the people go, that they | Ex 8:8
may
I w. send swarms of flies upon | Ex 8:21
thee
And I w. sever in that day the | Ex 8:22
land of
I w. put a division between | Ex 8:23
my people
their eyes, and w. they not | Ex 8:26
stone us
We w. go three days' journey | Ex 8:27
into the
Pharaoh said, I w. let you go, | Ex 8:28
that ye
I w. entreat the Lord that the | Ex 8:29
swarms
I w. send at this time all my | Ex 9:14
plagues
I w. stretch out my hand, that | Ex 9:15
I may
I w. cause it to rain a very | Ex 9:18
grievous
I w. spread abroad my hands | Ex 9:29
unto the
I know that ye w. not yet fear | Ex 9:30
the Lord
w. I bring the locusts into thy | Ex 10:4
coast
We w. go with our young and | Ex 10:9
with our
flocks and with our herds w. | Ex 10:9
we go
I w. let you go, and your | Ex 10:10
little ones
well, I w. see thy face again | Ex 10:29
no more
Yet w. I bring one plague | Ex 11:1
more upon
afterwards he w. let you go | Ex 11:1
hence
About midnight w. I go out | Ex 11:4
into the
thee: and after that I w. go out | Ex 11:8
I w. pass through the land of | Ex 12:12
Egypt
w. smite all the firstborn in | Ex 12:12
the land
gods of Egypt I w. execute | Ex 12:12
judgment
I w. pass over you, and the | Ex 12:13
plague
the Lord w. pass through to | Ex 12:23
smite the
posts, the Lord w. pass over | Ex 12:23
the door
w. not suffer the destroyer to | Ex 12:23
come in
the land which the Lord w. | Ex 12:25
give you
and w. keep the passover to | Ex 12:48
the Lord
saying, God w. surely visit | Ex 13:19
you
Pharaoh w. say of the children | Ex 14:3
And I w. harden Pharaoh's | Ex 14:4
heart, that
and I w. be honoured upon | Ex 14:4
Pharaoh
Lord, which he w. shew to | Ex 14:13
you to day
I w. harden the hearts of the | Ex 14:17
I w. get me honour upon | Ex 14:17
Pharaoh
I w. sing unto the Lord, for he | Ex 15:1
hath
and I w. prepare him an | Ex 15:2
habitation
my father's God, and I w. | Ex 15:2
exalt him

said, I w. pursue, I w. | Ex 15:9
overtake
I w. divide the spoil; my lust | Ex 15:9
shall be
I w. draw my sword, my hand | Ex 15:9
shall
I w. put none of these | Ex 15:26
diseases upon
I w. rain bread from heaven | Ex 16:4
for you
they w. walk in my law, or no | Ex 16:4
bake that which ye w. bake to- | Ex 16:23
day
to-day, and seethe that ye | Ex 16:23
w. seethe
I w. stand before thee there | Ex 17:6
upon the
I w. stand on the top of the | Ex 17:9
hill
I w. utterly put out the | Ex 17:14
remembrance
the Lord w. have war with | Ex 17:16
Amalek
I w. give thee counsel, and | Ex 18:19
God shall
if ye w. obey my voice indeed | Ex 19:5
that the Lord hath spoken we | Ex 19:8
w. do
Lord w. come down in the | Ex 19:11
sight of all
for the Lord w. not hold him | Ex 20:7
guiltless
Speak thou with us, and we | Ex 20:19
w. hear
record my name I w. come | Ex 20:24
unto thee
come unto thee, and I w. | Ex 20:24
bless thee
my children; I w. not go out | Ex 21:5
free
I w. appoint thee a place | Ex 21:13
whither he
woman's husband w. lay upon | Ex 21:22
him
all unto me, I w. surely hear | Ex 22:23
their cry
and I w. kill you with the | Ex 22:24
sword
he crieth unto me, that I w. | Ex 22:27
hear
not: for I w. not justify the | Ex 23:7
wicked
he w. not pardon your | Ex 23:21
transgressions
I w. be an enemy unto thy | Ex 23:22
enemies
the Jebusites: and I w. cut | Ex 23:23
them off
I w. take sickness away | Ex 23:25
from the
the number of thy days I w. | Ex 23:26
fulfil
I w. send my fear before | Ex 23:27
thee, and
and w. destroy all the people | Ex 23:27
to whom
and I w. make all thy | Ex 23:27
enemies turn
And I w. send hornets before | Ex 23:28
thee
I w. not drive them out from | Ex 23:29
before
I w. drive them out from | Ex 23:30
before thee
I w. set thy bounds from the | Ex 23:31
Red sea
I w. deliver the inhabitants of | Ex 23:31
the land
it w. surely be a snare unto | Ex 23:33
thee
which the Lord hath said w. | Ex 24:3
we do
that the Lord hath said w. | Ex 24:7
we do
and I w. give thee tables of | Ex 24:12
stone
And there I w. meet with | Ex 25:22
thee, and
I w. commune with thee | Ex 25:22
from above
I w. give thee in | Ex 25:22
commandment
I w. meet you, to speak | Ex 29:42
thereunto
I w. meet with the children | Ex 29:43
of Israel
And I w. sanctify the | Ex 29:44
tabernacle
I w. sanctify also both Aaron | Ex 29:44
and his

And I w. dwell among the | Ex 29:45
children
of Israel, and w. be their | Ex 29:45
God
testimony, where I w. meet | Ex 30:6
with thee
where I w. meet with thee | Ex 30:36
and I w. make of thee a | Ex 32:10
great nation
I w. multiply your seed as | Ex 32:13
the stars
spoken of w. I give unto our | Ex 32:13
seed
and now I w. go up unto the | Ex 32:30
Lord
me, him I w. blot out of my | Ex 32:33
book
I visit I w. visit their sin | Ex 32:34
upon them
saying, Unto thy seed w. I give | Ex 33:1
it
And I w. send an angel before | Ex 33:2
thee
and I w. drive out the | Ex 33:2
Canaanite
I w. not go up in the midst of | Ex 33:3
thee
I w. come up into the midst of | Ex 33:5
thee
with thee, and I w. give thee | Ex 33:14
rest
I w. do this thing also that | Ex 33:17
thou hast
I w. make all my goodness | Ex 33:19
pass
I w. proclaim the name of | Ex 33:19
the Lord
and w. be gracious unto | Ex 33:19
whom I w. be
w. shew mercy to whom I w. | Ex 33:19
shew
that I w. put thee in a clift | Ex 33:22
of a rock
w. cover thee with my hand | Ex 33:22
while I
I w. take away mine hand, | Ex 33:23
and thou
I w. write upon these tables | Ex 34:1
the words
that w. by no means clear the | Ex 34:7
guilty
before all thy people I w. | Ex 34:10
do marvels
for it is a terrible thing that I | Ex 34:10
w. do
I w. cast out the nations | Ex 34:24
before thee
when any w. offer a meat | Le 2:1
offering
for to-day the Lord w. appear | Le 9:4
unto
I w. be sanctified in them that | Le 10:3
come
before all the people I w. be | Le 10:3
glorified
for I w. appear in a cloud | Le 16:2
upon the
I w. even set my face against | `Le 17:10
that
and w. cut him off from | Le 17:10
among his
I w. set my face against that | Le 20:5
man
I w. even set my face against | Le 20:6
that
and w. cut him off from | Le 20:6
among his
I w. give it unto you to | Le 20:24
possess it
offer other his oblation for all | Le 22:18
his vows
which they w. offer unto the | Le 22:18
Lord
at your own w. a male | Le 22:19
without
And when ye w. offer a | Le 22:29
sacrifice
the Lord, offer it at your own | Le 22:29
w.
I w. be hallowed among the | Le 22:32
children
w. I destroy from among his | Le 23:30
people
awaiting revelation of Lord's | Le 24:12
w. (A)(B)(R)
I w. command my blessing | Le 25:21
upon you
I w. give you rain in due | Le 26:4
season

I w. give peace in the land,   Le 26:6
and ye
I w. rid evil beasts out of the   Le 26:6
land
I w. have respect unto you,   Le 26:9
and make
I w. set my tabernacle among   Le 26:11
you
I w. walk among you   Le 26:12
and w. be your God, and ye   Le 26:12
shall
But if ye w. not hearken unto   Le 26:14
me
w. not do all these   Le 26:14
commandments
Ye w. not do all my   Le 26:15
commandments
I also w. do this unto you   Le 26:16
I w. even appoint over you   Le 26:16
terror
I w. set my face against you,   Le 26:17
and ye
if ye w. not yet for all this   Le 26:18
hearken
I w. punish you seven times   Le 26:18
more for
I w. break the pride of your   Le 26:19
power
and I w. make your heaven as   Le 26:19
iron
me, and w. not hearken   Le 26:21
unto me
I w. bring seven times more   Le 26:21
plagues
I w. also send wild beasts   Le 26:22
among
And if ye w. not be reformed   Le 26:23
by me
but w. walk contrary unto me   Le 26:23
Then w. I also walk contrary   Le 26:24
unto
w. punish you yet seven times   Le 26:24
for
And I w. bring a sword upon   Le 26:25
you
I w. send the pestilence among   Le 26:25
you
if ye w. not for all this   Le 26:27
hearken unto
Then I w. walk contrary unto   Le 26:28
you
I, w. chastise you seven times   Le 26:28
for
I w. destroy your high places,   Le 26:30
and cut
I w. make your cities waste,   Le 26:31
and bring
I w. not smell the savour of   Le 26:31
your
I w. bring the land into   Le 26:32
desolation
I w. scatter you among the   Le 26:33
heathen
and w. draw out a sword   Le 26:33
after you
I w. send a faintness into   Le 26:36
their hearts
Then w. I remember my   Le 26:42
covenant
with Abraham w. I remember   Le 26:42
and I w. remember the land   Le 26:42
I w. not cast them away,   Le 26:44
neither
neither w. I abhor them, to   Le 26:44
destroy
I w. for their sakes remember   Le 26:45
if he w. at all redeem it, then   Le 27:13
he shall
that sanctified it w. redeem   Le 27:15
his house
the field w. in any wise   Le 27:19
redeem it
And if he w. not redeem the   Le 27:20
field
if a man w. at all redeem   Le 27:31
ought of
of Israel: and I w. bless them   Nu 6:27
and I w. hear what the Lord   Nu 9:8
Lord w. command concerning   Nu 9:8
you
w. keep the passover unto the   Nu 9:14
Lord
which the Lord said, I w.   Nu 10:29
give it you
thou with us, and we w.   Nu 10:29
do thee good
And he said unto him, I w.   Nu 10:30
not go
I w. depart to mine own land,   Nu 10:30
and to

unto us, the same w. we do   Nu 10:32
unto thee
I w. come down and talk   Nu 11:17
with thee
I w. take of the spirit which   Nu 11:17
is upon
w. put it upon them; and   Nu 11:17
they shall
therefore the Lord w. give   Nu 11:18
you flesh
I w. give them flesh, that   Nu 11:21
they may eat
I the Lord w. make myself   Nu 12:6
known unto
and w. speak unto you in a   Nu 12:6
dream
With him w. I speak mouth   Nu 12:8
to mouth
he w. bring us into this land,   Nu 14:8
and give
How long w. this people   Nu 14:11
provoke me
how long w. it be ere they   Nu 14:11
believe me
I w. smite them with the   Nu 14:12
pestilence
and w. make of thee a   Nu 14:12
greater nation
they w. tell it to the   Nu 14:14
inhabitants of this
the fame of thee w. speak,   Nu 14:15
saying
him w. I bring into the land   Nu 14:24
whereunto
spoken in mine ears, so w. I   Nu 14:28
do to you
them w. I bring in, and   Nu 14:31
they shall
I w. surely do it unto all this   Nu 14:35
evil
and w. go up unto the place   Nu 14:40
which the
therefore the Lord w. not be   Nu 14:43
with you
w. make an offering by fire   Nu 15:3
unto the
and w. offer an offering   Nu 15:14
made by fire
morrow the Lord w. show how   Nu 16:5
are his
w. cause him to come near   Nu 16:5
unto him
chosen w. he cause to come   Nu 16:5
near unto
Eliab: which said, We w. not   Nu 16:12
come up
testimony, where I w. meet   Nu 17:4
with you
I w. make to cease from me   Nu 17:5
we w. not pass through the   Nu 20:17
fields
w. we drink of the water of   Nu 20:17
the wells
we w. go by the king's high   Nu 20:17
way
we w. not turn to the right   Nu 20:17
hand nor to
unto him, We w. go by the   Nu 20:19
high way
of thy water, then w. I pay   Nu 20:19
for it
I w. only, without doing any   Nu 20:19
thing else
then I w. utterly destroy their   Nu 21:2
cities
together, and I w. give them   Nu 21:16
water
we w. not turn into the fields,   Nu 21:22
or into
w. not drink of the waters of   Nu 21:22
the well
we w. go along by the king's   Nu 21:22
high way
I w. bring you word again, as   Nu 22:8
the Lord
For I w. promote thee unto   Nu 22:17
very great
I w. do whatsoever thou   Nu 22:17
sayest unto
what the Lord w. say unto   Nu 22:19
me more
displease thee, I w. get me   Nu 22:34
back again
Stand by thy burnt offering,   Nu 23:3
and I w. go
the Lord w. come to meet me   Nu 23:3
whatsoever he sheweth me I w.   Nu 23:3
tell thee
I w. bring thee unto another   Nu 23:27
place

it w. please God that thou   Nu 23:27
mayest
what the Lord saith, that w.   Nu 24:13
I speak
evil of my own w. (A)(R)   Nu 24:13
I w. advertise thee what this   Nu 24:14
people
he w. yet again leave them in   Nu 32:15
We w. build sheepfolds here   Nu 32:16
for our
But we ourselves w. go ready   Nu 32:17
armed
We w. not return unto our   Nu 32:18
houses
For we w. not inherit with   Nu 32:19
them on
said unto them, If ye w. do   Nu 32:20
this thing
ye w. go armed before the   Nu 32:20
Lord to war
w. go all of you armed over   Nu 32:21
Jordan
But if ye w. not do so,   Nu 32:23
behold, ye have
and be sure your sin w. find   Nu 32:23
you out
w. do as my lord   Nu 32:25
commandeth
thy servants w. pass over,   Nu 32:27
every man
Reuben w. pass with you   Nu 32:29
over Jordan
But if they w. not pass over   Nu 32:30
with you
said unto thy servants, so w.   Nu 32:31
we do
w. pass over armed before   Nu 32:32
the Lord
if ye w. not drive out the   Nu 33:55
inhabitants
and I w. make them rulers   De 1:13
over you
you, bring it unto me, and I   De 1:17
w. hear it
We w. send men before us,   De 1:22
and they
to him w. I give the land that   De 1:36
he hath
and unto them w. I give it,   De 1:39
and they
we w. go up and fight,   De 1:41
according to all
for I w. not give you of their   De 2:5
land, no
for I w. not give thee of their   De 2:9
land
for I w. not give thee of the   De 2:19
land of the
This day w. I begin to put the   De 2:25
dread
land: I w. go along by the high   De 2:27
way
I w. neither turn unto the right   De 2:27
hand
only I w. pass through on my   De 2:28
feet
for I w. deliver him, and all his   De 3:2
people
I w. make them hear my   De 4:10
words, that
he w. not forsake thee, neither   De 4:31
destroy
Lord w. not hold them   De 5:11
guiltless that
for this great fire w. consume   De 5:25
us: if we
unto thee; and we w. hear it,   De 5:27
and do it
and I w. speak unto thee all   De 5:31
For they w. turn away thy son   De 7:4
from
so w. the anger of the Lord be   De 7:4
kindled
he w. not be slack to him that   De 7:10
hateth
him, he w. repay him to his   De 7:10
face
And he w. love thee, and bless   De 7:13
thee
he w. also bless the fruit of   De 7:13
thy womb
the Lord w. take away from   De 7:15
thee all
and w. put none of the evil   De 7:15
diseases
w. lay them upon all them   De 7:15
that hate
for that w. be a snare unto   De 7:16
thee

God w. send the hornet among them — De 7:20
thy God w. put out those nations — De 7:22
I w. make of thee a nation mightier — De 9:14
I w. write on the tables the words — De 10:2
I w. give you the rain of your land — De 11:14
I w. send grass in thy fields for thy — De 11:15
w. the Lord drive out all these — De 11:23
if ye w. not obey the commandments — De 11:28
I w. eat flesh, because thy soul — De 12:20
their gods? even so w. I do likewise — De 12:30
I w. not go away from thee; because — De 15:16
man that w. do presumptuously, and — De 17:12
w. not hearken unto the priest that — De 17:12
I w. set a king over me, like as all the — De 17:14
God w. raise up unto thee a Prophet — De 18:15
I w. raise them up a Prophet from — De 18:18
and w. put my words in his mouth — De 18:18
w. not hearken unto my words — De 18:19
in my name, I w. require it of him — De 18:19
if it w. make no peace with thee — De 20:12
w. make war against thee, then thou — De 20:12
shalt let her go whither she w. — De 21:14
w. not obey the voice of his father — De 21:18
him, w. not hearken unto them — De 21:18
rebellious, he w. not obey our voice — De 21:20
thy God w. surely require it of thee — De 23:21
w. not perform the duty of my — De 25:7
w. not build up his brother's house — De 25:9
thy God w. set thee on high above all — De 28:1
w. smite thee with the botch of Egypt — De 28:27
that he w. not give to any of them — De 28:55
Lord w. make thy plagues wonderful — De 28:59
he w. bring upon thee all the diseases — De 28:60
them w. the Lord bring upon thee — De 28:61
so the Lord w. rejoice over you — De 28:63
The Lord w. not spare him, but then — De 29:20
Lord thy God w. turn thy captivity — De 30:3
w. return and gather thee from all — De 30:3
from thence w. the Lord thy God — De 30:4
and from thence w. he fetch thee — De 30:4
thy God w. bring thee into the land — De 30:5
he w. do thee good, and multiply thee — De 30:5
the Lord w. circumcise thine heart — De 30:6
God w. put all these curses upon thine — De 30:7
Lord thy God w. make thee plenteous — De 30:9
for the Lord w. again rejoice over thee — De 30:9
thy God, he w. go over before thee — De 31:3
and he w. destroy these nations from — De 31:3
he w. not fail thee, nor forsake thee — De 31:6
he w. be with thee, he w. not fail thee — De 31:8

and this people w. rise up, and go — De 31:16
and w. forsake me, and break my — De 31:16
I w. forsake them, and I w. hide my — De 31:17
so that they w. say in that day, Are — De 31:17
I w. surely hide my face in that day — De 31:18
then w. they turn unto other gods — De 31:20
unto them: and I w. be with thee — De 31:23
after my death ye w. utterly corrupt — De 31:29
evil w. befall you in the latter days — De 31:29
because ye w. do evil in the sight of — De 31:29
ear, O ye heavens, and I w. speak — De 32:1
I w. publish the name of the Lord — De 32:3
ask thy father, and he w. shew thee — De 32:7
thy elders, and they w. tell thee — De 32:7
he said, I w. hide my face from them — De 32:20
I w. see what their end shall be — De 32:20
I w. move them to jealousy with those — De 32:21
I w. provoke them to anger with a — De 32:21
I w. heap mischiefs upon them — De 32:23
I w. spend mine arrows upon them — De 32:23
I w. also send the teeth of beasts upon — De 32:24
I w. render vengeance to mine — De 32:41
and w. reward them that hate me — De 32:41
I w. make mine arrows drunk with — De 32:42
for he w. avenge the blood of his — De 32:43
and w. render vengeance to his — De 32:43
w. be merciful unto his land, and to — De 32:43
for the good w. of him that dwell in — De 33:16
saying, I w. give it unto thy seed: I — De 34:4
was with Moses, so I w. be with thee — Jos 1:5
I w. not fail thee, nor forsake thee — Jos 1:5
that thou commandest us we w. do — Jos 1:16
thou sendest us, we w. go unto — Jos 1:16
things, so w. we hearken unto thee — Jos 1:17
and w. not hearken unto thy words — Jos 1:18
that ye w. also shew kindness unto — Jos 2:12
that ye w. save alive my father, and — Jos 2:13
we w. deal kindly and truly with thee — Jos 2:14
We w. be blameless of this thine oath — Jos 2:17
upon his head, and we w. be guiltless — Jos 2:19
then we w. be quit of thine oath — Jos 2:20
the Lord w. do wonders among you — Jos 3:5
This day w. I begin to magnify thee in — Jos 3:7
I was with Moses, so I w. be with thee — Jos 3:7
and that he w. without fail drive out — Jos 3:10
neither w. I be with you any more — Jos 7:12
with me, w. approach unto the city — Jos 8:5
the first, that we w. flee before them — Jos 8:5
(For they w. come but after us) till we — Jos 8:6
for they w. say, they flee before us, as — Jos 8:6

first: therefore we w. flee before them — Jos 8:6
the Lord your God w. deliver it into — Jos 8:7
Ai; for I w. give it into thy hand — Jos 8:18
This we w. do to them — Jos 9:20
we w. even let them live, lest — Jos 9:20
about this time w. I deliver them up — Jos 11:6
w. I drive out before the children — Jos 13:6
if so be the Lord w. be with me, then I — Jos 14:12
w. I give Achsah my daughter to wife — Jos 15:16
I w. send them, and they shall rise — Jos 18:4
it w. be, seeing ye rebel to-day against — Jos 22:18
to-morrow he w. be wroth with the — Jos 22:18
Lord your God w. no more drive out — Jos 23:13
choose you this day whom ye w. serve — Jos 24:15
and my house, we w. serve the Lord — Jos 24:15
therefore w. we serve the Lord — Jos 24:18
he w. not forgive your transgressions — Jos 24:19
then he w. turn and do you hurt, and — Jos 24:20
Nay; but we w. serve the Lord — Jos 24:21
God w. we serve, and his voice w. — Jos 24:24
I likewise w. go with thee unto thy lot — J'g 1:3
to him w. I give Achsah my daughter — J'g 1:12
the city, and we w. shew thee mercy — J'g 1:24
I w. never break my covenant with — J'g 2:1
I w. not drive them out from before — J'g 2:3
w. not henceforth drive out any from — J'g 2:21
they w. keep the way of the Lord — J'g 2:22
And I w. draw unto thee to the river — J'g 4:7
and I w. deliver him into thine hand — J'g 4:7
If thou wilt go with me, then I w. go — J'g 4:8
wilt not go with me, then I w. not go — J'g 4:8
And she said, I w. surely go with thee — J'g 4:9
I w. shew thee the man whom thou — J'g 4:22
I, even I, w. sing unto the Lord — J'g 5:3
I w. sing praise to the Lord God of — J'g 5:3
Surely I w. be with thee, and thou — J'g 6:16
said, I w. tarry until thou come again — J'g 6:18
W. ye plead for Baal? w. ye save him — J'g 6:31
he that w. plead for him, let him be put — J'g 6:31
I w. put a fleece of wool in the floor — J'g 6:37
me, and I w. speak but this once — J'g 6:39
and I w. try them for thee there — J'g 7:4
men that lapped w. I save you — J'g 7:7
I w. tear your flesh with the thorns of — J'g 8:7
in peace, I w. break down this tower — J'g 8:9
unto them, I w. not rule over you — J'g 8:23
answered, We w. willingly give — J'g 8:25
wherefore I w. deliver you no more — J'g 10:13
What man is he that w. begin to fight — J'g 10:18
from before us, them w. we possess — J'g 11:24
I w. offer it up for a burnt offering — J'g 11:31
w. burn thine house upon thee with — J'g 12:1

detain me, I w. not eat of	J'g 13:16
thy bread	
I w. now put forth a riddle	J'g 14:12
unto you	
I w. give you thirty sheets	J'g 14:12
and thirty	
I w. go in to my wife into the	J'g 15:1
chamber	
done this, yet w. I be avenged	J'g 15:7
of you	
avenged of you, and after I	J'g 15:7
w. cease	
ye w. not fall upon me	J'g 15:12
yourselves	
but we w. bind thee fast, and	J'g 15:13
deliver	
hand: but surely we w. not	J'g 15:13
kill thee	
we w. give thee every one of	J'g 16:5
us eleven	
then my strength w. go from	J'g 16:17
me	
I w. go out as at other times	J'g 16:20
before	
therefore I w. restore it unto	J'g 17:3
thee	
I w. give thee ten shekels of	J'g 17:10
silver by	
We w. not turn aside hither	J'g 19:12
into the	
of Israel; we w. pass over to	J'g 19:12
Gibeah	
them I w. bring out now, and	J'g 19:24
humble	
We w. not any of us go to his	J'g 20:8
tent	
neither w. we any of us turn	J'g 20:8
into his	
the thing which we w. do to	J'g 20:9
Gibeah	
Gibeah; we w. go up by lot	J'g 20:9
against it	
And we w. take ten men of	J'g 20:10
an hundred	
we w. not give them of our	J'g 21:7
daughters	
complain, that we w. say	J'g 21:22
unto them	
we w. return with thee unto	Ru 1:10
thy people	
my daughters: why w. ye go	Ru 1:11
with me	
for whither thou goest, I w.	Ru 1:16
go: and	
and where thou lodgest, I w.	Ru 1:16
lodge	
w. I die, and there w. I be	Ru 1:17
buried	
and he w. tell thee what thou	Ru 3:4
shalt do	
All that thou sayest unto me I	Ru 3:5
w. do	
I w. do to thee all that thou	Ru 3:11
requirest	
if he w. perform unto thee the	Ru 3:13
but if he w. not do the part of	Ru 3:13
then w. I do the part of a	Ru 3:13
kinsman to	
thou know how the matter w.	Ru 3:18
fall	
for the man w. not be in rest,	Ru 3:18
until he	
thee. And he said, I w. redeem	Ru 4:4
it	
then I w. give him unto the	1Sa 1:11
Lord all	
I w. not go up until the child	1Sa 1:22
be	
and then I w. bring him, that	1Sa 1:22
he may	
He w. keep the feet of his	1Sa 2:9
saints, and	
he w. not have sodden flesh	1Sa 2:15
of thee	
now: and if not, I w. take it	1Sa 2:16
by force	
for them that honour me I w.	1Sa 2:30
honour	
days come, that I w. cut off	1Sa 2:31
thine arm	
And I w. raise me up a	1Sa 2:35
faithful priest	
I w. build him a sure house;	1Sa 2:35
and he	
Behold, I w. do a thing in	1Sa 3:11
Israel	
I w. perform against Eli all	1Sa 3:12
things	
when I begin, I w. also make	1Sa 3:12
an end	

him that I w. judge his house	1Sa 3:13
for ever	
peradventure he w. lighten his	1Sa 6:5
hand	
he w. deliver you out of the	1Sa 7:3
hand of the	
and I w. pray for you unto the	1Sa 7:5
Lord	
he w. save us out of the hand	1Sa 7:8
of the	
This w. be the manner of the	1Sa 8:11
king that	
w. take your sons, and	1Sa 8:11
appoint them	
he w. appoint him captains	1Sa 8:12
over	
w. set them to ear his ground,	1Sa 8:12
and to	
he w. take your daughters to	1Sa 8:13
be	
And he w. take your fields,	1Sa 8:14
and your	
And he w. take the tenth of	1Sa 8:15
your seed	
And he w. take your	1Sa 8:16
menservants	
He w. take the tenth of your	1Sa 8:17
sheep	
the Lord w. not hear you in	1Sa 8:18
that day	
Nay; but we w. have a king	1Sa 8:19
over us	
w. I give to the man of God,	1Sa 9:8
to tell us	
the people w. not eat until he	1Sa 9:13
come	
I w. send thee a man out of	1Sa 9:16
the land of	
to-day, and to-morrow I w.	1Sa 9:19
let thee go	
w. tell thee all that is in thine	1Sa 9:19
heart	
and they w. say unto thee,	1Sa 10:2
The asses	
they w. salute thee, and give	1Sa 10:4
thee two	
Spirit of the Lord w. come	1Sa 10:6
upon thee	
I w. come down unto thee, to	1Sa 10:8
offer	
with us, and we w. serve thee	1Sa 11:1
condition w. I make a	1Sa 11:2
covenant with	
to save us, we w. come out to	1Sa 11:3
thee	
To-morrow we w. come out	1Sa 11:10
unto you	
there with? and I w. restore	1Sa 12:3
it you	
of our enemies, and we w.	1Sa 12:10
serve him	
If ye w. fear the Lord, and	1Sa 12:14
serve him	
ye w. not obey the voice of	1Sa 12:15
the Lord	
the Lord w. do before your	1Sa 12:16
eyes	
I w. call unto the Lord, and	1Sa 12:17
he shall	
the Lord w. not forsake his	1Sa 12:22
people	
I w. teach you the good and	1Sa 12:23
the right	
The Philistines w. come	1Sa 13:12
down now	
may be that the Lord w.	1Sa 14:6
work for us	
we w. pass over unto these	1Sa 14:8
men	
we w. discover ourselves unto	1Sa 14:8
them	
then we w. stand still in our	1Sa 14:9
place	
and w. not go up unto them	1Sa 14:9
Come up unto us; then we	1Sa 14:10
w. go up	
up to us, and we w. shew	1Sa 14:12
you a thing	
my son w. be on the other	1Sa 14:40
side	
I w. tell thee what the Lord	1Sa 15:16
hath said	
unto Saul, I w. not return	1Sa 15:26
with thee	
also the Strength of Israel	1Sa 15:29
w. not lie	
go, I w. send thee to Jesse	1Sa 16:1
can I go? If Saul hear it, he	1Sa 16:2
w. kill me	

I w. shew thee what thou	1Sa 16:3
shalt do	
for we w. not sit down till	1Sa 16:11
he come	
kill me, then w. we be your	1Sa 17:9
servants	
the king w. enrich him with	1Sa 17:25
great	
and w. give him his	1Sa 17:25
daughters	
thy servant w. go and fight	1Sa 17:32
with this	
he w. deliver me out of the	1Sa 17:37
hand of	
and I w. give thy flesh unto	1Sa 17:44
the fowl	
This day w. the Lord deliver	1Sa 17:46
thee in	
I w. smite thee, and take	1Sa 17:46
thine head	
and I w. give the carcases of	1Sa 17:46
the host	
and he w. give you into our	1Sa 17:47
hands	
I w. smite David to the wall	1Sa 18:11
with it	
Merab, her w. I give thee to	1Sa 18:17
wife	
I w. give him her,	1Sa 18:21
that she may be a	
I w. go out and stand beside	1Sa 19:3
my father	
I w. commune with my father	1Sa 19:3
of the	
and what I see, that w. I tell	1Sa 19:3
thee	
my father w. do nothing	1Sa 20:2
either great	
but that he w. shew it me:	1Sa 20:2
and why	
desireth, I w. even do it for	1Sa 20:4
thee	
I w. shew it thee, and send	1Sa 20:13
thee away	
missed, because thy seat w.	1Sa 20:18
be empty	
I w. shoot three arrows on	1Sa 20:20
the side	
I w. send a land, saying, Go,	1Sa 20:21
find out	
till I know what God w. do	1Sa 22:3
for me	
w. the son of Jesse give every	1Sa 22:7
one	
I w. deliver the Philistines	1Sa 23:4
into thine	
W. the men of Keilah	1Sa 23:11
deliver me up	
w. Saul come down, as thy	1Sa 23:11
servant	
And the Lord said, He w.	1Sa 23:11
come down	
W. the men of Keilah	1Sa 23:12
deliver me and	
the Lord said, They w.	1Sa 23:12
deliver thee up	
the certainty, and I w. go	1Sa 23:23
with you	
I w. search him out	1Sa 23:23
throughout all the	
I w. deliver thine enemy into	1Sa 24:4
thine	
I w. not put forth mine	1Sa 24:10
hand against	
enemy, w. he let him go well	1Sa 24:19
away	
young men, and they w. shew	1Sa 25:8
thee	
w. certainly make my lord a	1Sa 25:28
sure	
Who w. go down with me to	1Sa 26:6
Saul	
Abishai said, I w. go down	1Sa 26:6
with thee	
I w. not smite him the	1Sa 26:8
second time	
for I w. no more do thee	1Sa 26:21
harm	
and so w. be his manner all	1Sa 27:11
the while	
w. I make thee keeper of	1Sa 28:2
mine head	
the Lord w. also deliver	1Sa 28:19
Israel with	
he refused, and said, I w.	1Sa 28:23
not eat	
I w. bring thee down to this	1Sa 30:15
company	
we w. not give them ought	1Sa 30:22
of the spoil	

who w. hearken unto you in *1Sa 30:24*
this
I also w. requite you this *2Sa 2:6*
kindness
it w. be bitterness in the *2Sa 2:26*
latter end
Well; I w. make a league *2Sa 3:13*
with thee
I w. save my people Israel out *2Sa 3:18*
of the
I w. arise and go, and w. *2Sa 3:21*
gather all
I w. doubtless deliver the *2Sa 5:19*
Philistines
therefore w. I play before the *2Sa 6:21*
Lord
I w. yet be more vile than *2Sa 6:22*
thus, and
w. be base in mine own sight *2Sa 6:22*
I w. appoint a place for my *2Sa 7:10*
people
w. plant them, that they may *2Sa 7:10*
dwell
that he w. make thee an *2Sa 7:11*
house
I w. set up thy seed after thee *2Sa 7:12*
and I w. establish his *2Sa 7:12*
kingdom
and I w. stablish the throne *2Sa 7:13*
of his
I w. be his father, and he *2Sa 7:14*
shall be my
I w. chasten him with the rod *2Sa 7:14*
of men
saying, I w. build thee an *2Sa 7:27*
house
for I w. surely shew thee *2Sa 9:7*
kindness
w. restore thee all the land of *2Sa 9:7*
Saul
I w. shew kindness unto *2Sa 10:2*
Hanun
thee, then w. I come and *2Sa 10:11*
help thee
soul liveth, I w. not do *2Sa 11:11*
this thing
and to-morrow I w. let thee *2Sa 11:12*
depart
I w. raise up evil *2Sa 12:11*
against thee out of
I w. take thy wives before *2Sa 12:11*
thine eyes
I w. do this thing before all *2Sa 12:12*
Israel
how w. he then vex himself, *2Sa 12:18*
if we tell
whether God w. be gracious *2Sa 12:22*
to me
for he w. not withhold me *2Sa 13:13*
from thee
and we w. destroy the heir *2Sa 14:7*
also
and I w. give charge *2Sa 14:8*
concerning thee
said, I w. now speak unto *2Sa 14:15*
the king
that the king w. perform the *2Sa 14:15*
request
For the king w. hear, to *2Sa 14:16*
deliver his
the Lord thy God w. be with *2Sa 14:17*
thee
Jerusalem, then w. I serve the *2Sa 15:8*
Lord
even there also w. thy *2Sa 15:21*
servant be
he w. bring me again, and *2Sa 15:25*
shew me
I w. tarry in the plain of the *2Sa 15:28*
Absalom, I w. be thy *2Sa 15:34*
servant, O king
so w. I now also be thy *2Sa 15:34*
servant
that the Lord w. look on my *2Sa 16:12*
affliction
that the Lord w. requite me *2Sa 16:12*
good
his w. I be, and with him w. *2Sa 16:18*
I abide
presence, so w. I be in thy *2Sa 16:19*
presence
and I w. arise and pursue *2Sa 17:1*
after David
w. come upon him while he is *2Sa 17:2*
weary
handed, and w. make him *2Sa 17:2*
afraid
flee; and I w. smite the king *2Sa 17:2*
only

And I w. bring back all the *2Sa 17:3*
people
and w. not lodge with the *2Sa 17:8*
people
and it w. come to pass, when *2Sa 17:9*
some of
that whosoever heareth it w. *2Sa 17:9*
say
and we w. light upon him as *2Sa 17:12*
the dew
and we w. draw it into the *2Sa 17:13*
river
I w. surely go forth with you *2Sa 18:2*
myself
we flee away, they w. not *2Sa 18:3*
care for us
if half of us die, w. they care *2Sa 18:3*
for us
them, What seemeth you best *2Sa 18:4*
I w. do
w. not tarry one with thee *2Sa 19:7*
this night
w. be worse unto thee than *2Sa 19:7*
all the evil
I w. saddle me an ass, that I *2Sa 19:26*
may ride
I w. feed thee with me in *2Sa 19:33*
Jerusalem
servant w. go a little way *2Sa 19:36*
over Jordan
I w. do to him that which *2Sa 19:38*
shall seem
require of me, that w. I do *2Sa 19:38*
for thee
only, and I w. depart from *2Sa 20:21*
the city
We w. have no silver nor *2Sa 21:4*
gold of Saul
ye shall say, that w. I do for *2Sa 21:4*
you
we w. hang them up unto the *2Sa 21:6*
Lord
And the king said, I w. give *2Sa 21:6*
them
God of my rock; in him w. I *2Sa 22:3*
trust
I w. call on the Lord, who is *2Sa 22:4*
worthy
and the Lord w. lighten my *2Sa 22:29*
darkness
Therefore I w. give thanks *2Sa 22:50*
unto thee
and I w. sing praises unto *2Sa 22:50*
thy name
I w. surely buy it of thee at *2Sa 24:24*
a price
neither w. I offer burnt *2Sa 24:24*
offerings
himself, saying, I w. be a king *1Ki 1:5*
I also w. come in after thee *1Ki 1:14*
even so w. I certainly do this *1Ki 1:30*
day
that he w. not slay his *1Ki 1:51*
servant with
If he w. shew himself a *1Ki 1:52*
worthy man
I w. not put thee to death *1Ki 2:8*
with the
king, for he w. not say thee *1Ki 2:17*
nay
I w. speak for thee unto the *1Ki 2:18*
king
mother: for I w. not say thee *1Ki 2:20*
nay
I w. not at this time put thee *1Ki 2:26*
to death
And he said, Nay; but I w. *1Ki 2:30*
die here
king hath said, so w. thy *1Ki 2:38*
servant do
did walk, then I w. lengthen *1Ki 3:14*
thy days
whom I w. set upon thy throne *1Ki 5:5*
in thy
thee. I w. give hire for thy *1Ki 5:6*
servants
I w. do all thy desire *1Ki 5:8*
concerning
I w. convey them by sea in *1Ki 5:9*
floats unto
w. cause them to be *1Ki 5:9*
discharged there
w. I perform my word *1Ki 6:12*
with thee
w. dwell among the children *1Ki 6:13*
of Israel
and w. not forsake my people *1Ki 6:13*
Israel
w. God indeed dwell on the *1Ki 8:27*
earth

I w. establish the throne of thy *1Ki 9:5*
w. not keep my *1Ki 9:6*
commandments and
w. I cut off Israel out of the *1Ki 9:7*
land
my name, w. I cast out of my *1Ki 9:7*
sight
w. turn away your heart after *1Ki 11:2*
their
I w. surely rend the *1Ki 11:11*
kingdom from
thee, and w. give it to thy *1Ki 11:11*
servant
I w. not do it for David thy *1Ki 11:12*
father's
I w. rend it out of the hand *1Ki 11:12*
of thy son
I w. not rend away all the *1Ki 11:13*
kingdom
w. give one tribe to thy son *1Ki 11:13*
for David
I w. rend the kingdom out *1Ki 11:31*
of the hand
and w. give ten tribes to *1Ki 11:31*
thee
I w. not take the whole *1Ki 11:34*
kingdom out
I w. make him prince all the *1Ki 11:34*
days of
I w. take the kingdom out *1Ki 11:35*
of his son's
w. give it unto thee, even *1Ki 11:35*
ten tribes
And unto his son w. I give *1Ki 11:36*
one tribe
I w. take thee, and thou *1Ki 11:37*
shalt reign
I w. be with thee, and build *1Ki 11:38*
thee a
David, and w. give Israel *1Ki 11:38*
unto thee
I w. for this afflict the seed *1Ki 11:39*
of David
us, lighter, and we w. serve *1Ki 12:4*
thee
they w. be thy servants for *1Ki 12:7*
ever
heavy yoke, I w. add to *1Ki 12:11*
your yoke
but I w. chastise you with *1Ki 12:11;*
scorpions *12:14*
heavy, and I w. add to your *1Ki 12:14*
yoke
thyself, and I w. give thee a *1Ki 13:7*
reward
thine house, I w. not go with *1Ki 13:8*
thee
neither w. I eat bread nor *1Ki 13:8;*
drink *13:16*
I w. bring evil upon the *1Ki 14:10*
house of
w. cut off from Jeroboam *1Ki 14:10*
him that
w. take away the remnant of *1Ki 14:10*
the
w. take away the posterity of *1Ki 16:3*
Baasha
w. make thy house like the *1Ki 16:3*
house
and I w. send rain upon the *1Ki 18:1*
earth
I w. surely shew myself unto *1Ki 18:15*
him to
I w. dress the other bullock, *1Ki 18:23*
and lay
I w. call on the name of the *1Ki 18:24*
Lord
mother, and then I w. *1Ki 19:20*
follow thee
I w. send my servants unto *1Ki 20:6*
for to thy servants at first I *1Ki 20:9*
w. do
I w. deliver it into thine *1Ki 20:13*
hand this day
king of Syria w. come up *1Ki 20:22*
against thee
we w. fight against them in *1Ki 20:25*
the plain
w. I deliver all this great *1Ki 20:28*
multitude
peradventure he w. save thy *1Ki 20:31*
life
took from thy father, I w. *1Ki 20:34*
restore
w. send thee away with this *1Ki 20:34*
covenant
I w. give thee for it a better *1Ki 21:2*
vineyard

w. give thee the worth of it in money *1Ki 21:2*

i w. not give thee the inheritance of *1Ki 21:4*

I w. not give thee another vineyard for it *1Ki 21:6*

I w. not give thee my vineyard *1Ki 21:6*

I w. give thee the vineyard of Naboth *1Ki 21:7*

Behold, I w. bring evil upon thee *1Ki 21:21*

and w. take thy posterity *1Ki 21:21*

and w. cut off from Ahab him that *1Ki 21:21*

w. make thine house like the house *1Ki 21:22*

I w. not bring the evil in his days *1Ki 21:29*

in his son's day w. I bring the evil *1Ki 21:29*

the Lord saith to me, that w. I speak *1Ki 22:14*

Lord, and said, I w. persuade him *1Ki 22:21*

I w. go forth, and I w. be a lying spirit *1Ki 22:22*

I w. disguise myself, and enter into *1Ki 22:30*

thy soul liveth, I w. not leave thee *2Ki 2:2; 4:30*

Lord w. take away thy master from *2Ki 2:3; 5*

he said, I w. go up: I am as thou art *2Ki 3:7*

w. deliver the Moabites also into your *2Ki 3:18*

I w. send a letter unto the king of *2Ki 5:5*

He w. surely come out to me *2Ki 5:11*

whom I stand, w. receive none *2Ki 5:16*

servant w. henceforth offer neither *2Ki 5:17*

I w. run after him, and take somewhat *2Ki 5:20*

And he answered, I will go *2Ki 6:3*

W. ye not shew me which of us is for *2Ki 6:11*

I w. bring you to the man whom ye *2Ki 6:19*

and we w. eat my son to-morrow *2Ki 6:28*

We w. enter into the city, then *2Ki 7:4*

light, some mischief w. come upon us *2Ki 7:9*

I w. now shew you what the Syrians *2Ki 7:12*

I w. cut off from Ahab him that *2Ki 9:8*

I w. make the house of Ahab like the *2Ki 9:9*

I w. requite thee in this plat, saith *2Ki 9:26*

and w. do all that thou shalt bid us *2Ki 10:5*

we w. not make any king: do thou *2Ki 10:5*

if ye w. hearken unto my voice, take *2Ki 10:6*

which thou puttest on me w. I bear *2Ki 18:14*

w. go into his hand, and pierce it *2Ki 18:21*

I w. deliver thee two thousand horses *2Ki 18:23*

The Lord w. surely deliver us, and *2Ki 18:30*

you saying, The Lord w. deliver us *2Ki 18:32*

thy God w. hear all the words of *2Ki 19:4*

w. reprove the words which the Lord *2Ki 19:4*

I w. send a blast upon him, and he *2Ki 19:7*

I w. cause him to fall by the sword in *2Ki 19:7*

and w. cut down the tall cedar trees *2Ki 19:23*

I w. enter into the lodgings of his *2Ki 19:23*

I w. put my hook in thy nose *2Ki 19:28*

I w. turn thee back by the way by *2Ki 19:28*

For I w. defend this city, to save it *2Ki 19:34*

thy tears: behold, I w. heal thee *2Ki 20:5*

I w. add unto thy days fifteen years *2Ki 20:6*

I w. deliver thee and this city out of *2Ki 20:6*

I w. defend this city for mine own *2Ki 20:6*

be the sign that the Lord w. heal me *2Ki 20:8*

Lord w. do the thing he hath spoken *2Ki 20:9*

In Jerusalem w. I put my name *2Ki 21:4*

of Israel, w. I put my name for ever *2Ki 21:7*

Neither w. I make the feet of Israel *2Ki 21:8*

if they w. observe to do according to *2Ki 21:8*

I w. stretch over Jerusalem the line of *2Ki 21:13*

I w. wipe Jerusalem as a man wipeth *2Ki 21:13*

I w. forsake the remnant of mine *2Ki 21:14*

I w. bring evil upon this place, and *2Ki 22:16*

I w. gather thee unto thy fathers *2Ki 22:20*

evil which I w. bring upon this place *2Ki 22:20*

I w. remove Judah also out of my *2Ki 23:27*

w. cast off this city Jerusalem which *2Ki 23:27*

He w. fall to his master Saul to the *1Ch 12:19*

I w. deliver them into thine hand *1Ch 14:10*

Unto thee w. I give the land of Canaan *1Ch 16:18*

I w. ordain a place for my people *1Ch 17:9*

and w. plant them, and they shall *1Ch 17:9*

I w. subdue all thine enemies *1Ch 17:10*

that the Lord w. build thee an house *1Ch 17:10*

that I w. raise up thy seed after thee *1Ch 17:11*

and I w. establish his kingdom *1Ch 17:11*

and I w. stablish his throne for ever *1Ch 17:12*

I w. be his father, and he shall be my *1Ch 17:13*

I w. not take my mercy away from *1Ch 17:13*

I w. settle him in mine house and in *1Ch 17:14*

I w. shew kindness unto Hanun the *1Ch 19:2*

strong for thee, then I w. help thee *1Ch 19:12*

w. he be a cause of trespass to Israel *1Ch 21:3*

I w. verily buy it for the full price *1Ch 21:24*

I w. not take that which is thine for *1Ch 21:24*

I w. therefore now make preparation *1Ch 22:5*

I w. give him rest from all his enemies *1Ch 22:9*

I w. give peace and quietness unto *1Ch 22:9*

be my son, and I w. be his father *1Ch 22:10; 28:6*

and I w. establish the throne of his *1Ch 22:10*

I w. establish his kingdom for ever *1Ch 28:7*

seek him, he w. be found of thee *1Ch 28:9*

forsake him, he w. cast thee off for *1Ch 28:9*

God, even my God w. be with thee *1Ch 28:20*

he w. not fail thee, nor forsake thee *1Ch 28:20*

w. be wholly at thy commandment *1Ch 28:21*

I w. give thee riches, and wealth, and *2Ch 1:12*

I w. give to thy servants, the hewers *2Ch 2:10*

w. cut wood out of Lebanon, as much *2Ch 2:16*

w. bring it to thee in floats by sea *2Ch 2:16*

w. God in every deed dwell with men *2Ch 6:18*

ways, then w. I hear from heaven *2Ch 7:14*

and w. forgive their sin *2Ch 7:14*

and w. heal their land *2Ch 7:14*

w. I stablish the throne of thy *2Ch 7:18*

w. I pluck them up by the roots out of *2Ch 7:20*

my name, w. I cast out of my sight *2Ch 7:20*

and w. make it to be a proverb and a *2Ch 7:20*

he put upon us, and we w. serve thee *2Ch 10:4*

them, they w. be thy servants for ever *2Ch 10:7*

upon you, I w. put more to your yoke *2Ch 10:11*

but I w. chastise you with scorpions *2Ch 10:11; 10:14*

your yoke heavy, but I w. add thereto *2Ch 10:14*

therefore I w. not destroy them *2Ch 12:7*

I w. grant them some deliverance *2Ch 12:7*

if ye seek him, he w. be found of you *2Ch 15:2*

if ye forsake him, he w. forsake you *2Ch 15:2*

and we w. be with thee in the war *2Ch 18:3*

for God w. deliver it into the king's *2Ch 18:5*

what my God saith, that w. I speak *2Ch 18:13*

the Lord, and said, I w. entice him *2Ch 18:20*

I w. go out, and be a lying spirit *2Ch 18:21*

Jehoshaphat, I w. disguise myself *2Ch 18:29*

and w. go to the battle; but put thou *2Ch 18:29*

them: for the Lord w. be with you *2Ch 20:17*

a great plague w. the Lord smite thy *2Ch 21:14*

them, therefore w. I sacrifice to them *2Ch 28:23*

he w. return to the remnant of you *2Ch 30:6*

w. not turn away his face from you *2Ch 30:9*

of Israel, w. I put my name for ever *2Ch 33:7*

Neither w. I any more remove the foot *2Ch 33:8*

so that they w. take heed to do all that *2Ch 33:8*

I w. bring evil upon this place *2Ch 34:24*

I w. gather thee to thy fathers *2Ch 34:28*

evil that I w. bring upon this place *2Ch 34:28*

together w. build unto the Lord God *Ezr 4:3*

then w. they not pay toll, tribute *Ezr 4:13*

And whosoever w. not do the law of *Ezr 7:26*

we also w. be with thee: be of good *Ezr 10:4*

I w. scatter you abroad among *Ne 1:8*

yet w. I gather them from thence *Ne 1:9*

w. bring them unto the place that *Ne 1:9*

ye do? w. ye rebel against the king *Ne 2:19*

The God of heaven, he w. prosper us *Ne 2:20*

we his servants w. arise and build *Ne 2:20*

Jews? w. they fortify themselves *Ne 4:2*

w. they sacrifice? w. they make an *Ne 4:2*

w. they revive the stones out of *Ne 4:2*

people had a w. to work (B) *Ne 4:6*

return unto us they w. be upon you *Ne 4:12*

w. ye even sell your brethren? or shall *Ne 5:8*

We w. restore them, and w. require *Ne 5:12*

of them; so w. we do as thou sayest *Ne 5:12*

temple: for they *w.* come to   *Ne 6:10* slay thee

in the night *w.* they come to   *Ne 6:10* slay thee

w. not forsake the house of   *Ne 10:39* our God

ye do so again, I *w.* lay   *Ne 13:21* hands on you

I *w.* pay ten thousand talents of   *Es 3:9* silver

and my maidens *w.* fast   *Es 4:16* likewise

so *w.* I go in unto the king,   *Es 4:16* which is not

w. do to-morrow as the king   *Es 5:8* hath said

W. he force the queen also   *Es 7:8* before me

hath, and he *w.* curse thee to   *Job 1:11* thy face

that a man hath *w.* he give for   *Job 2:4* his life

flesh, and he *w.* curse thee to   *Job 2:5* thy face

if there be any that *w.* answer   *Job 5:1* thee

Teach me, and I *w.* hold my   *Job 6:24* tongue

Therefore I *w.* not refrain my   *Job 7:11* mouth

I *w.* speak in the anguish of   *Job 7:11* my spirit

I *w.* complain in the   *Job 7:11* bitterness of my

God *w.* not cast away a   *Job 8:20* perfect man

neither *w.* he help the evil   *Job 8:20* doers

If he *w.* contend with him, he   *Job 9:3* cannot

who *w.* say unto him, What   *Job 9:12* doest

If God *w.* not withdraw   *Job 9:13* his anger

w. not suffer me to take my   *Job 9:18* breath

w. laugh at the trial of the   *Job 9:23* innocent

If I say, I *w.* forget my   *Job 9:27* complaint

I *w.* leave off my heaviness   *Job 9:27*

I *w.* leave my complaint upon   *Job 10:1* myself

I *w.* speak in the bitterness of   *Job 10:1* my soul

I *w.* say unto God, Do not   *Job 10:2* condemn

righteous, yet *w.* I not lift   *Job 10:15* up my head

also; *w.* he not then consider   *Job 11:11* it

W. ye speak wickedly for   *Job 13:7* God

W. ye accept his person? *w.*   *Job 13:8* ye

He *w.* surely reprove you, if   *Job 13:10* ye do

speak, and let come on me   *Job 13:13* what *w.*

Though he slay me, yet *w.* I   *Job 13:15* trust him

but I *w.* maintain mine own   *Job 13:15* ways

Who is he that *w.* plead   *Job 13:19* with me

then *w.* I not hide myself   *Job 13:20* from thee

Then call thou, and I *w.*   *Job 13:22* answer

be cut down, that it *w.* sprout   *Job 14:7* again

tender branch thereof *w.* not   *Job 14:7* cease

through the scent of water it   *Job 14:9* *w.* bud

days of my appointed time   *Job 14:14* *w.* I wait

Thou shalt call, and I *w.*   *Job 14:15* answer thee

I *w.* shew thee, hear me;   *Job 15:17* and that

that which I have seen I *w.*   *Job 15:17* declare

is he that *w.* strike hands with   *Job 17:3* me

How long *w.* it be ere ye   *Job 18:2* make an end

mark, and afterwards we *w.*   *Job 18:2* speak

How long *w.* ye vex my soul   *Job 19:2*

If indeed ye *w.* magnify   *Job 19:5* yourselves

W. he reprove thee for fear   *Job 22:4* of thee

w. he enter with thee into   *Job 22:4* judgment

W. he plead against me with   *Job 23:6* his great

who *w.* make me a liar, and   *Job 24:25* make my

w. not remove mine integrity   *Job 27:5* from me

I hold fast, and *w.* not let it   *Job 27:6* go

W. God hear his cry when   *Job 27:9* trouble

W. he delight himself in the   *Job 27:10* Almighty

w. he always call upon God   *Job 27:10*

I *w.* teach you by the hand   *Job 27:11* of God

with the Almighty *w.* I not   *Job 27:11* conceal

he *w.* not stretch out his   *Job 30:24* hand to the

to me: I also *w.* shew mine   *Job 32:10* opinion

neither *w.* I answer him with   *Job 32:14* your

I said, I *w.* answer my part,   *Job 32:17* I also

part, I also *w.* shew mine   *Job 32:17* opinion

I *w.* speak, that I may be   *Job 32:20* refreshed

I *w.* open my lips and   *Job 32:20* answer

I *w.* answer thee, that God   *Job 33:12* is greater

and he *w.* be favourable   *Job 33:26* unto him

w. render man his   *Job 33:26* righteousness

He *w.* deliver his soul from   *Job 33:28* going

hold thy peace, and I *w.*   *Job 33:31* speak

Yea, surely God *w.* not do   *Job 34:12* wickedly

w. the Almighty pervert   *Job 34:12* judgment

For he *w.* not lay upon man   *Job 34:23* more than

I *w.* not offend any more   *Job 34:31*

I have done iniquity, I *w.*   *Job 34:32* do no more

he *w.* recompense it,   *Job 34:33* whether thou

What advantage *w.* it be unto   *Job 35:3* thee

I *w.* answer thee, and thy   *Job 35:4* companions

Surely God *w.* not hear   *Job 35:13* vanity

neither *w.* the Almighty   *Job 35:13* regard it

and I *w.* shew thee that I   *Job 36:2* have yet to

I *w.* fetch my knowledge   *Job 36:3* from afar

w. ascribe righteousness to   *Job 36:3* my Maker

W. he esteem thy riches? no,   *Job 36:19* not gold

he *w.* not stay them when his   *Job 37:4* voice is

in plenty of justice: he *w.*   *Job 37:23* not afflict

for I *w.* demand of thee, and   *Job 38:3* answer

W. the unicorn be willing to   *Job 39:9* serve

or *w.* he harrow the valleys   *Job 39:10* after thee

that he *w.* bring home thy   *Job 39:12* seed

I *w.* lay mine hand upon my   *Job 40:4* mouth

have I spoken; but I *w.* not   *Job 40:5* answer

twice; but I *w.* proceed no   *Job 40:5* further

I *w.* demand of thee, and   *Job 40:7* declare thou

Then *w.* I also confess unto   *Job 40:14* thee that

W. he make many   *Job 41:3* supplications unto

w. he speak soft words unto   *Job 41:3* thee

W. he make a covenant with   *Job 41:4* thee

I *w.* not conceal his parts,   *Job 41:12* nor his

Hear, I beseech thee, and I   *Job 42:4* *w.* speak

I *w.* demand of thee, and   *Job 42:4* declare thou

for him *w.* I accept: lest I   *Job 42:8* deal with

I *w.* declare the decree: the   *Ps 2:7* Lord hath

I *w.* not be afraid of ten   *Ps 3:6* thousands of

w. ye turn my glory into shame   *Ps 4:2*

how long *w.* ye love vanity, and   *Ps 4:2* seek

the Lord *w.* hear when I call   *Ps 4:3* unto him

that say, Who *w.* shew us any   *Ps 4:6* good

I *w.* both lay me down in peace   *Ps 4:8*

and my God: for unto thee *w.* I   *Ps 5:2* pray

in the morning *w.* direct my   *Ps 5:3* prayer

my prayer unto thee, and *w.*   *Ps 5:3* look up

the Lord *w.* abhor the bloody   *Ps 5:6*

I *w.* come unto thy house in the   *Ps 5:7*

and in thy fear *w.* I worship   *Ps 5:7* toward

the Lord *w.* receive my prayer   *Ps 6:9*

If he turn not, he *w.* whet his   *Ps 7:12* sword

I *w.* praise the Lord according   *Ps 7:17* to his

w. sing praise to the name of   *Ps 7:17* the Lord

I *w.* praise thee, O Lord, with   *Ps 9:1* my

I *w.* shew forth all thy   *Ps 9:1* marvellous

I *w.* be glad and rejoice in thee   *Ps 9:2*

I *w.* sing praise to thy name, O   *Ps 9:2* thou

The Lord also *w.* be a refuge   *Ps 9:9* for the

thy name *w.* put their trust in   *Ps 9:10* thee

Zion: I *w.* rejoice in thy   *Ps 9:14* salvation

countenance, *w.* not seek after   *Ps 10:4* God

hideth his face; he *w.* never   *Ps 10:11* see it

said, With our tongue *w.* we   *Ps 12:4* prevail

needy, now *w.* I arise, saith   *Ps 12:5* the Lord

I *w.* set him in safety from   *Ps 12:5* him that

I *w.* sing unto the Lord,   *Ps 13:6* because he

offerings of blood *w.* I not   *Ps 16:4* offer

I *w.* bless the Lord, who hath   *Ps 16:7* given

I *w.* behold thy face in   *Ps 17:15* righteousness

I *w.* love thee, O Lord, my   *Ps 18:1* strength

my strength, in whom I *w.*   *Ps 18:2* trust

I *w.* call upon the Lord, who   *Ps 18:3* is worthy

my God *w.* enlighten my   *Ps 18:28* darkness

Therefore *w.* I give thanks   *Ps 18:49* unto thee

We *w.* rejoice in thy salvation,   *Ps 20:5* and in

name of our God we *w.* set up   *Ps 20:5* our

w. hear him from his holy   *Ps 20:6* heaven

w. remember the name of the   *Ps 20:7* Lord

so *w.* we sing and praise thy   *Ps 21:13* power

I *w.* declare thy name unto   *Ps 22:22* my

of the congregation *w.* I praise   *Ps 22:22* thee

I *w.* pay my vows before   *Ps 22:25* them that

shadow of death, I *w.* fear no   *Ps 23:4* evil

I *w.* dwell in the house of the   *Ps 23:6* Lord for

w. he teach sinners in the way *Ps 25:8*
The meek *w.* he guide in judgment *Ps 25:9*
and the meek *w.* he teach his way *Ps 25:9*
and he *w.* shew them his covenant *Ps 25:14*
neither *w.* I go in with dissemblers *Ps 26:4*
doers; and *w.* not sit with the wicked *Ps 26:5*
I *w.* wash mine hands in innocency *Ps 26:6*
so *w.* I compass thine altar, O Lord *Ps 26:6*
for me, I *w.* walk in mine integrity *Ps 26:11*
the congregations *w.* I bless the Lord *Ps 26:12*
against me, in this *w.* I be confident *Ps 27:3*
of the Lord, that *w.* I seek after *Ps 27:4*
therefore *w.* I offer in his tabernacle *Ps 27:6*
I *w.* sing, yea, I *w.* sing praises unto *Ps 27:6*
unto thee, Thy face, Lord, *w.* I seek *Ps 27:8*
me, then the Lord *w.* take me up *Ps 27:10*
over unto the *w.* of mine enemies *Ps 27:12*
Unto thee *w.* I cry, O Lord my rock *Ps 28:1*
and with my song *w.* I praise him *Ps 28:7*
The Lord *w.* give strength unto his *Ps 29:11*
Lord *w.* bless his people with peace *Ps 29:11*
I *w.* extol thee, O Lord; for thou hast *Ps 30:1*
I *w.* give thanks unto thee for ever *Ps 30:12*
I *w.* be glad and rejoice in thy mercy *Ps 31:7*
I *w.* confess my transgressions unto *Ps 32:5*
I *w.* instruct thee and teach thee in *Ps 32:8*
go: I *w.* guide thee with mine eye *Ps 32:8*
I *w.* bless the Lord at all times: his *Ps 34:1*
I *w.* teach you the fear of the Lord *Ps 34:11*
I *w.* give thee thanks in the great *Ps 35:18*
I *w.* praise thee among much people *Ps 35:18*
Lord *w.* not leave him in his hand *Ps 37:33*
For I *w.* declare mine iniquity *Ps 38:18*
iniquity; I *w.* be sorry for my sin *Ps 38:18*
I said, I *w.* take heed to my ways, that *Ps 39:1*
I *w.* keep my mouth with a bridle *Ps 39:1*
the Lord *w.* deliver him in time of *Ps 41:1*
The Lord *w.* preserve him, and *Ps 41:2*
him unto the *w.* of his enemies *Ps 41:2*
Lord *w.* strengthen him upon the bed *Ps 41:3*
w. I remember thee from the land of *Ps 42:6*
Lord *w.* command his lovingkindness *Ps 42:8*
I *w.* say unto God my rock, Why hast *Ps 42:9*
Then *w.* I go unto the altar of God *Ps 43:4*
upon the harp *w.* I praise thee, O God *Ps 43:4*
Through thee *w.* we push down our *Ps 44:5*
through thy name *w.* we tread them *Ps 44:5*
For I *w.* not trust in my bow, neither *Ps 44:6*
w. make thy name to be remembered *Ps 45:17*
Therefore *w.* not we fear, though the *Ps 46:2*
I *w.* be exalted among the heathen *Ps 46:10*

heathen, I *w.* be exalted in the earth *Ps 46:10*
God *w.* establish it for ever *Ps 48:8*
he *w.* be our guide even unto death *Ps 48:14*
I *w.* incline mine ear to a parable *Ps 49:4*
I *w.* open my dark saying upon the *Ps 49:4*
But God *w.* redeem my soul from *Ps 49:15*
and men *w.* praise thee, when thou *Ps 49:18*
Hear, O my people, and I *w.* speak *Ps 50:7*
Israel, and I *w.* testify against thee *Ps 50:7*
I *w.* not reprove thee for thy sacrifices *Ps 50:8*
I *w.* take no bullock out of thy house *Ps 50:9*
W. I eat the flesh of bulls, or drink *Ps 50:13*
w. deliver thee, and thou shalt glorify *Ps 50:15*
but I *w.* reprove thee, and set *Ps 50:21*
them in aright *w.* I shew the salvation of God *Ps 50:23*
w. I teach transgressors thy ways *Ps 51:13*
I *w.* praise thee for ever, because thou *Ps 52:9*
and I *w.* wait on thy name; for it is *Ps 52:9*
w. freely sacrifice unto thee *Ps 54:6*
I *w.* praise thy name, O Lord *Ps 54:6*
As for me, I *w.* call upon God; and the *Ps 55:16*
at noon, *w.* I pray, and cry aloud *Ps 55:17*
their days; but I *w.* trust in thee *Ps 55:23*
time I am afraid, I *w.* trust in thee *Ps 56:3*
in God *w.* I praise his word, in God I *Ps 56:4*
I *w.* not fear what flesh can do unto *Ps 56:4*
In God *w.* I praise his word *Ps 56:10*
in the Lord *w.* I praise his word *Ps 56:10*
I *w.* not be afraid what man can do *Ps 56:11*
God: I *w.* render praises unto thee *Ps 56:12*
of thy wings *w.* I make my refuge *Ps 57:1*
I *w.* cry unto God most high *Ps 57:2*
is fixed: I *w.* sing and give praise *Ps 57:7*
and harp: I myself *w.* awake early *Ps 57:8*
I *w.* praise thee, O Lord, among the *Ps 57:9*
I *w.* sing unto thee among the nations *Ps 57:9*
w. not hearken to the voice of *Ps 58:5*
of his strength *w.* I wait upon thee *Ps 59:9*
but I *w.* sing of thy power *Ps 59:16*
I *w.* sing aloud of thy mercy in the *Ps 59:16*
Unto thee, O my strength, *w.* I sing *Ps 59:17*
I *w.* rejoice, I *w.* divide Shechem, and *Ps 60:6*
over Edom *w.* I cast out my shoe *Ps 60:8*
Who *w.* bring me into the strong city *Ps 60:9*
city? who *w.* lead me unto Edom *Ps 60:9*
end of the earth *w.* I cry unto thee *Ps 61:2*
I *w.* abide in thy tabernacle for *Ps 61:4*
I *w.* trust in the covert of thy wings *Ps 61:4*
So *w.* I sing praise unto thy name for *Ps 61:8*
How long *w.* ye imagine mischief *Ps 62:3*
art my God; early *w.* I seek thee *Ps 63:1*
Thus *w.* I bless thee while I live *Ps 63:4*
I *w.* lift up my hands in thy name *Ps 63:4*
the shadow of thy wings *w.* I rejoice *Ps 63:7*

I *w.* go into thy house with burnt *Ps 66:13*
offerings: I *w.* pay thee my vows *Ps 66:13*
I *w.* offer unto thee burnt sacrifices of *Ps 66:15*
rams: I *w.* offer bullocks with goats *Ps 66:15*
and I *w.* declare what he hath done *Ps 66:16*
my heart, the Lord *w.* not hear me *Ps 66:18*
yea, the Lord *w.* dwell in it for ever *Ps 68:16*
said, I *w.* bring again from Bashan *Ps 68:22*
I *w.* bring my people again from the *Ps 68:22*
I *w.* praise the name of God with a *Ps 69:30*
w. magnify him with thanksgiving *Ps 69:30*
For God *w.* save Zion, and *w.* build *Ps 69:35*
But I *w.* hope continually *Ps 71:14*
and *w.* yet praise thee more and more *Ps 71:14*
I *w.* go in the strength of the Lord *Ps 71:16*
I *w.* mention of thy righteousness *Ps 71:16*
I *w.* also praise thee with the psaltery *Ps 71:22*
unto thee *w.* I sing with the harp *Ps 71:22*
If I say, I *w.* speak thus: behold, I *Ps 73:15*
the congregation I *w.* judge uprightly *Ps 75:2*
I *w.* declare for ever; I *w.* sing praises *Ps 75:9*
horns of the wicked also *w.* I cut off *Ps 75:10*
W. the Lord cast off for ever *Ps 77:7*
w. he be favourable no more *Ps 77:7*
I *w.* remember the years of the right *Ps 77:10*
I *w.* remember the works of the Lord *Ps 77:11*
I *w.* remember thy wonders of old *Ps 77:11*
I *w.* meditate also of all thy work *Ps 77:12*
I *w.* open my mouth in a parable *Ps 78:2*
I *w.* utter dark sayings of old *Ps 78:2*
We *w.* not hide them from their *Ps 78:4*
pasture *w.* give thee thanks for ever *Ps 79:13*
we *w.* shew forth thy praise to all *Ps 79:13*
So *w.* not we go back from thee *Ps 80:18*
us, and we *w.* call upon thy name *Ps 80:18*
people, and I *w.* testify unto thee *Ps 81:8*
open thy mouth wide, and I *w.* fill it *Ps 81:10*
How long *w.* ye judge unjustly *Ps 82:2*
know not, neither *w.* they understand *Ps 82:5*
house: they *w.* be still praising thee *Ps 84:4*
the Lord *w.* give grace and glory *Ps 84:11*
no good thing *w.* he withhold from *Ps 84:11*
I *w.* hear what God the Lord *w.* speak *Ps 85:8*
for he *w.* speak peace unto his people *Ps 85:8*
day of my trouble I *w.* call upon thee *Ps 86:7*
way, O Lord; I *w.* walk in thy truth *Ps 86:11*
I *w.* praise thee, O Lord my God *Ps 86:12*
I *w.* glorify thy name for evermore *Ps 86:12*
I *w.* make mention of Rahab *Ps 87:4*
I *w.* sing of the mercies of the Lord *Ps 89:1*
w. I make known thy faithfulness *Ps 89:1*
Thy seed *w.* I establish for ever *Ps 89:4*
And I *w.* beat down his foes before his *Ps 89:23*

I w. set his hand also in the sea — Ps 89:25
Also I w. make him my firstborn — Ps 89:27
My mercy w. I keep for him for — Ps 89:28
Then w. I visit their transgression — Ps 89:32
my loving kindness w. I not utterly — Ps 89:33
My covenant w. I not break — Ps 89:34
holiness that I w. not lie unto David — Ps 89:35
I w. say of the Lord, He is my refuge — Ps 91:2
my God; in him w. I trust — Ps 91:2
upon me, therefore w. I deliver him — Ps 91:14
I w. set him on high, because he hath — Ps 91:14
call upon me, and I w. answer him — Ps 91:15
I w. be with him in trouble — Ps 91:15
I w. deliver him, and honour him — Ps 91:15
With long life w. I satisfy him — Ps 91:16
w. triumph in the works of thy hands — Ps 92:4
and ye fools, when w. ye be wise — Ps 94:8
For the Lord w. not cast off his people — Ps 94:14
neither w. he forsake his inheritance — Ps 94:14
Who w. rise up for me against the — Ps 94:16
or who w. stand up for me against — Ps 94:16
To-day if ye w. hear his voice — Ps 95:7
I w. sing of mercy and judgment — Ps 101:1
unto thee, O Lord, w. I sing — Ps 101:1
I w. behave myself wisely in a perfect — Ps 101:2
I w. walk within my house with a — Ps 101:2
I w. set no wicked thing before mine — Ps 101:3
I w. not know a wicked person — Ps 101:4
his neighbour, him w. I cut off — Ps 101:5
and a proud heart w. not I suffer — Ps 101:5
I w. early destroy all the wicked — Ps 101:8
He w. regard the prayer of — Ps 102:17
He w. not always chide: neither — Ps 103:9
neither w. he keep his anger for ever — Ps 103:9
w. sing unto the Lord as long as I live — Ps 104:33
I w. sing praise to my God while I have — Ps 104:33
be sweet: I w. be glad in the Lord — Ps 104:34
Unto thee w. I give the land of Canaan — Ps 105:11
is wise, and w. observe these things — Ps 107:43
I w. sing and give praise, even with — Ps 108:1
and harp: I myself w. awake early — Ps 108:2
I w. praise thee, O Lord, among the — Ps 108:3
and I w. sing praises unto thee — Ps 108:3
I w. rejoice, I w. divide Shechem — Ps 108:7
over Edom w. I cast out my shoe — Ps 108:9
my shoe; over Philistia w. I triumph — Ps 108:9
Who w. bring me into the strong city — Ps 108:10
who w. lead me into Edom — Ps 108:10
I w. greatly praise the Lord with my — Ps 109:30
I w. praise him among the multitude — Ps 109:30
Lord hath sworn, and w. not repent — Ps 110:4
I w. praise the Lord with my whole — Ps 111:1
w. ever be mindful of his covenant — Ps 111:5
he w. guide his affairs with discretion — Ps 112:5

he w. bless us; he w. bless the house — Ps 115:12
he w. bless the house of Aaron — Ps 115:12
He w. bless them that fear the Lord — Ps 115:13
But we w. bless the Lord, from this — Ps 115:18
therefore w. I call upon him as long — Ps 116:2
I w. walk before the Lord in the land — Ps 116:9
I w. take the cup of salvation, and call — Ps 116:13
I w. pay my vows unto the Lord now — Ps 116:14; 116:18
I w. offer to thee the sacrifice of — Ps 116:17
and w. call upon the name of the Lord — Ps 116:17
The Lord is on my side; I w. not fear — Ps 118:6
name of the Lord w. I destroy them — Ps 118:10; 118:11-12
I w. go into them, and I w. praise the — Ps 118:19
I w. praise thee: for thou hast heard — Ps 118:21
made; we w. rejoice and be glad in it — Ps 118:24
Thou art my God, and I w. praise thee — Ps 118:28
thou art my God, I w. exalt thee — Ps 118:28
I w. praise thee with uprightness — Ps 119:7
I w. keep thy statutes: O forsake me — Ps 119:8
I w. meditate in thy precepts — Ps 119:15
I w. delight myself in thy statutes — Ps 119:16
statutes: I w. not forget thy word — Ps 119:16
I w. run the way of commandments — Ps 119:32
And I w. walk at liberty; for I seek — Ps 119:45
I w. speak of thy testimonies also — Ps 119:46
kings, and w. not be ashamed — Ps 119:46
And I w. delight myself in thy — Ps 119:47
My hands also w. I lift up unto thy — Ps 119:48
and I w. meditate in thy statutes — Ps 119:48
At midnight I w. rise to give thanks — Ps 119:62
but I w. keep thy precepts with my — Ps 119:69
They that fear thee w. be glad when — Ps 119:74
but I w. meditate in thy precepts — Ps 119:78
I w. never forget thy precepts — Ps 119:93
but I w. consider thy testimonies — Ps 119:95
I have sworn, and I w. perform it — Ps 119:106
w. keep thy righteous judgments — Ps 119:106
for I w. keep the commandments of — Ps 119:115
I w. have respect unto thy statutes — Ps 119:117
of man: so w. I keep thy precepts — Ps 119:134
me, O Lord: I w. keep thy statutes — Ps 119:145
w. lift up mine eyes unto the hills — Ps 121:1
He w. not suffer thy foot to be moved — Ps 121:3
he that keepeth thee w. not slumber — Ps 121:3
I w. now say, Peace be within thee — Ps 122:8
the Lord our God I w. seek thy good — Ps 122:9
I w. not come into the tabernacle — Ps 132:3
I w. not give sleep to mine eyes — Ps 132:4
We w. go into his tabernacles — Ps 132:7
we w. worship at his footstool — Ps 132:7
unto David; he w. not turn from it — Ps 132:11

of thy body w. I set upon thy throne — Ps 132:11
If thy children w. keep my covenant — Ps 132:12
here w. I dwell; for I have desired it — Ps 132:14
I w. abundantly bless her provision — Ps 132:15
I w. satisfy her poor with bread — Ps 132:15
I w. also clothe her priest with — Ps 132:16
There w. I make the home of David — Ps 132:17
His enemies w. I clothe with shame — Ps 132:18
For the Lord w. judge his people — Ps 135:14
w. repent himself concerning his — Ps 135:14
I w. praise thee with my whole heart — Ps 138:1
before the gods w. I sing — Ps 138:1
I w. worship toward thy holy temple — Ps 138:2
Lord w. perfect that which concerneth me — Ps 138:8
I w. praise thee; for I am wonderfully made — Ps 139:14
the Lord w. maintain the cause of afflicted — Ps 140:12
I w. sing a new song unto thee — Ps 144:9
ten strings w. I sing praise unto thee — Ps 144:9
I w. extol thee, my God — Ps 145:1
I w. bless thy name for ever — Ps 145:1
Every day w. I bless thee; and — Ps 145:2
and I w. praise thy name for ever and — Ps 145:2
I w. speak of the glorious honour — Ps 145:5
acts: and I w. declare thy greatness — Ps 145:6
He w. fulfil the desire of them that — Ps 145:19
w. hear their cry, and w. save them — Ps 145:19
but all the wicked w. he destroy — Ps 145:20
While I live w. I praise the Lord — Ps 146:2
I w. sing praises unto my God while I — Ps 146:2
w. beautify the meek with salvation — Ps 149:4
A wise man w. hear — Pr 1:5
and w. increase learning — Pr 1:5
ye simple ones, w. ye love simplicity — Pr 1:22
I w. pour out my spirit unto you — Pr 1:23
I w. make known my words unto you — Pr 1:23
I also w. laugh at your calamity — Pr 1:26
I w. mock when your fear cometh — Pr 1:26
call upon me, but I w. not answer — Pr 1:28
come again, and to-morrow I w. give — Pr 3:28
adulteress w. hunt for precious life — Pr 6:26
w. not spare in the day of vengeance — Pr 6:34
He w. not regard any ransom — Pr 6:35
neither w. he rest content — Pr 6:35
w. come home at the day appointed — Pr 7:20
for I w. speak of excellent things — Pr 8:6
and I w. fill their treasures — Pr 8:21
a wise man, and he w. love thee — Pr 9:8
to a wise man, and he w. be yet wiser — Pr 9:9
man, and he w. increase in learning — Pr 9:9
The Lord w. not suffer the soul of the — Pr 10:3
in heart w. receive commandments — Pr 10:8
man of wicked devices w. he condemn — Pr 12:2
A faithful witness w. not lie — Pr 14:5
but a false witness w. utter lies — Pr 14:5
neither w. he go unto the wise — Pr 15:12
The Lord w. destroy the house of the — Pr 15:25

w. establish the border of the   Pr 15:25
widow
of death; but a wise man w.   Pr 16:14
pacify it
a man w. sustain his infirmity   Pr 18:14
w. intreat the favour of the   Pr 19:6
prince
he hath given w. he pay him   Pr 19:17
again
and w. not so much as bring   Pr 19:24
it to his
a scorner, and the simple w.   Pr 19:25
beware
and he w. understand   Pr 19:25
knowledge
strife: but every fool w. be   Pr 20:3
meddling
The sluggard w. not plow by   Pr 20:4
reason of
man of understanding w. draw   Pr 20:5
it out
Most men w. proclaim every   Pr 20:6
one his
Say not thou, I w.   Pr 20:22
recompense evil
he turneth it whithersoever he   Pr 21:1
w.
he is old, he w. not depart   Pr 22:6
from it
For the Lord w. plead their   Pr 22:23
cause
he w. despise the wisdom of   Pr 23:9
thy words
shall I awake? I w. seek it yet   Pr 23:35
again
w. do so to him as he hath   Pr 24:29
done to me
I w. render to the man   Pr 24:29
according to
rolleth a stone, it w. return   Pr 26:27
upon him
yet w. not his foolishness   Pr 27:22
depart
gather it for him that w. pity   Pr 28:8
the poor
piece of bread that man w.   Pr 28:21
transgress
servant w. not be corrected   Pr 29:19
by words
he understand he w. not   Pr 29:19
answer
She w. do him good and not   Pr 31:12
evil all
Go to now, I w. prove thee   Ec 2:1
with mirth
fall, the one w. lift up his   Ec 4:10
fellow
who w. no more be   Ec 4:13
admonished
abundance of the rich w. not   Ec 5:12
suffer
and the living w. lay it to his   Ec 7:2
heart
I w. be wise; but it was far   Ec 7:23
from me
Surely the serpent w. bite   Ec 10:11
without
lips of a fool w. swallow up   Ec 10:12
himself
God w. bring thee into   Ec 11:9
judgment
Draw me, we w. run after thee   Ca 1:4
we w. be glad and rejoice in   Ca 1:4
thee
w. remember thy love more   Ca 1:4
than wine
We w. make thee borders of   Ca 1:11
gold with
I w. rise now, and go about the   Ca 3:2
city in
I w. seek him whom my soul   Ca 3:2
loveth
I w. get me to the mountain of   Ca 4:6
myrrh
What w. ye see in the   Ca 6:13
Shulamite
I said, I w. go up to the palm   Ca 7:8
tree
I w. take hold of the boughs   Ca 7:8
thereof
forth: there w. I give thee my   Ca 7:12
loves
wall, we w. build upon her a   Ca 8:9
palace of
w. inclose her with boards of   Ca 8:9
cedar
ye w. revolt more and more   Isa 1:5
hands, I w. hide mine eyes   Isa 1:15
from you

ye make many prayers, I w.   Isa 1:15
not hear
Ah, I w. ease me of mine   Isa 1:24
adversaries
I w. turn my head upon thee   Isa 1:25
And I w. restore thy judges as   Isa 1:26
at the
and he w. teach us of his ways   Isa 2:3
and we w. walk in his paths: Isa 2:3
for out
I w. give children to be their   Isa 3:4
princes
swear, saying, I w. not be an   Isa 3:7
healer
Lord w. enter into judgment   Isa 3:14
with the
the Lord w. smite with a scab   Isa 3:17
and the Lord w. discover their   Isa 3:17
secret
Lord w. take away the   Isa 3:18
bravery of their
We w. eat our own bread, and   Isa 4:1
wear
And the Lord w. create upon   Isa 4:5
every
Now w. I sing my well beloved   Isa 5:1
a song
I w. tell you what I w. do to   Isa 5:5
my
I w. take away the hedge   Isa 5:5
thereof, and
And I w. lay it waste: it shall   Isa 5:6
not be
I w. also command the clouds   Isa 5:6
that
And he w. lift up an ensign to   Isa 5:26
and w. hiss unto them   Isa 5:26
from the end of
shall I send, and who w. go for   Isa 6:8
us
If ye w. not believe, surely ye   Isa 7:9
shall
I w. not ask, neither w. I   Isa 7:12
tempt
men, but w. ye weary my God   Isa 7:13
also
I w. wait upon the Lord, that   Isa 8:17
hideth
house of Jacob, and I w. look   Isa 8:17
for him
of the Lord of hosts w.   Isa 9:7
perform this
but we w. build with hewn   Isa 9:10
stones
but we w. change them into   Isa 9:10
cedars
the Lord w. cut off from   Isa 9:14
Israel head
And what w. ye do in the day   Isa 10:3
of
from far? to whom w. ye flee   Isa 10:3
for help
and where w. ye leave your   Isa 10:3
glory
I w. send him against an   Isa 10:6
hypocritical
of my wrath w. I give him a   Isa 10:6
charge
I w. punish the fruit of the   Isa 10:12
stout heart
shalt say, O Lord, I w. praise   Isa 12:1
thee
I w. trust, and not be afraid   Isa 12:2
And I w. punish the world   Isa 13:11
for their
I w. cause the arrogancy of   Isa 13:11
the proud
and w. lay low the   Isa 13:11
haughtiness of the
I w. make a man more   Isa 13:12
precious than
Therefore I w. shake the   Isa 13:13
heavens, and
I w. stir up the Medes   Isa 13:17
against them
For the Lord w. have mercy   Isa 14:1
on Jacob
and w. yet choose Israel, and   Isa 14:1
set
thine heart, I w. ascend into   Isa 14:13
heaven
I w. exalt my throne above   Isa 14:13
the stars of
I w. sit also upon the mount   Isa 14:13
of the
I w. ascend above the   Isa 14:14
heights of the
I w. be like the most High   Isa 14:14
For I w. rise up against   Isa 14:22
them, saith

I w. also make it a   Isa 14:23
possession for the
I w. sweep it with the besom   Isa 14:23
of
That I w. break the Assyrian   Isa 14:25
in my
I w. kill thy root with   Isa 14:30
famine, and he
for I w. bring more upon   Isa 15:9
Dimon, lions
I w. bewail with the weeping   Isa 16:9
of Jazer
I w. water thee with my tears,   Isa 16:9
O
Lord said unto me, I w. take   Isa 18:4
my rest
and I w. consider in my   Isa 18:4
dwelling place
I w. set the Egyptians against   Isa 19:2
and I w. destroy the counsel   Isa 19:3
thereof
And the Egyptians w. I give   Isa 19:4
over into
if ye w. enquire, enquire ye: Isa 21:12
return
I w. weep bitterly, labour not   Isa 22:4
to
Lord w. carry thee away   Isa 22:17
with a
and w. surely cover thee   Isa 22:17
He w. surely violently turn   Isa 22:18
and toss
And I w. drive thee from thy   Isa 22:19
station
I w. call my servant Eliakim   Isa 22:20
the son
I w. clothe him with thy   Isa 22:21
robe, and
I w. commit thy government   Isa 22:21
into his
the key w. I lay upon his   Isa 22:22
shoulder
And I w. fasten him as a   Isa 22:23
nail in a sure
that the Lord w. visit Tyre,   Isa 23:17
and she
I w. exalt thee, I w. praise thy   Isa 25:1
name
he w. destroy in this   Isa 25:7
mountain the
He w. swallow up death in   Isa 25:8
victory
Lord God w. wipe away tears   Isa 25:8
from off
waited for him, and he w.   Isa 25:9
save us
him, we w. be glad and   Isa 25:9
rejoice in his
salvation w. God appoint for   Isa 26:1
walls and
spirit within me w. I seek   Isa 26:9
thee early
of the world w. learn   Isa 26:9
righteousness
yet w. he not learn   Isa 26:10
righteousness
of uprightness w. he deal   Isa 26:10
unjustly
w. not behold the majesty of   Isa 26:10
the Lord
thy hand is lifted up, they w.   Isa 26:11
not see
by thee only w. we make   Isa 26:13
mention of
keep it; I w. water it every   Isa 27:3
moment
hurt it, I w. keep it night and   Isa 27:3
day
them w. not have mercy on   Isa 27:11
them
formed them w. shew them   Isa 27:11
no favour
another tongue w. he speak   Isa 28:11
to this
Judgment also w. I lay to the   Isa 28:17
line, and
he w. not ever be threshing   Isa 28:28
Yet I w. distress Ariel, and   Isa 29:2
there shall
I w. camp against thee round   Isa 29:3
about
and w. lay siege against thee   Isa 29:3
with a
and I w. raise forts against thee   Isa 29:3
I w. proceed to do a   Isa 29:14
marvellous work
they w. carry their riches   Isa 30:6
upon the

children that w. not hear the *Isa 30:9*
law of
said, No; for we w. flee upon *Isa 30:16*
horses
We w. ride upon the swift; *Isa 30:16*
therefore
And therefore w. the Lord *Isa 30:18*
wait, that
you, and therefore w. he be *Isa 30:18*
exalted
he w. be very gracious unto *Isa 30:19*
thee at
he shall hear it, he w. answer *Isa 30:19*
thee
and in battles of shaking w. *Isa 30:32*
he fight
Yet he also is wise, and w. *Isa 31:2*
bring evil
evil, and w. not call back his *Isa 31:2*
words
but w. arise against the house *Isa 31:2*
of the
he w. not be afraid of their *Isa 31:4*
voice, nor
so w. the Lord of hosts *Isa 31:5*
defend
defending also he w. deliver it *Isa 31:5*
and passing over he w. *Isa 31:5*
preserve it
For the vile person w. speak *Isa 32:6*
villainy
and his heart w. work *Isa 32:6*
iniquity, to
he w. cause the drink of the *Isa 32:6*
thirsty to
Now w. I arise, saith the *Isa 33:10*
Lord; now
w. I be exalted; now w. I *Isa 33:10*
lift up
Lord w. be unto us a place of *Isa 33:21*
broad
the Lord is our king; he w. *Isa 33:22*
save us
your God w. come with *Isa 35:4*
vengeance
recompence; he w. come and *Isa 35:4*
save you
it w. go into his hand, and *Isa 36:6*
pierce it
I w. give thee two thousand *Isa 36:8*
horses
saying, The Lord w. surely *Isa 36:15*
deliver us
you, saying, The Lord w. *Isa 36:18*
deliver us
Lord thy God w. hear the *Isa 37:4*
words of
and w. reprove the words *Isa 37:4*
which the
I w. send a blast upon him, *Isa 37:7*
and he shall
I w. cause him to fall by the *Isa 37:7*
sword in
I w. cut down the tall cedars *Isa 37:24*
thereof
I w. enter into the height of *Isa 37:24*
his border
w. I put my hook in thy nose *Isa 37:29*
I w. turn thee back by the *Isa 37:29*
way by
For I w. defend this city to *Isa 37:35*
save it for
I w. add unto thy days *Isa 38:5*
fifteen years
And I w. deliver thee and this *Isa 38:6*
city
Assyria; and I w. defend this *Isa 38:6*
city
Lord w. do this thing that he *Isa 38:7*
hath
I w. bring again the shadow *Isa 38:8*
of the
he w. cut me off with pining *Isa 38:12*
sickness
as a lion, so w. he break all *Isa 38:13*
my bones
we w. sing my songs to the *Isa 38:20*
stringed
the Lord God w. come with *Isa 40:10*
strong
To whom then w. ye liken *Isa 40:18*
God? or
or what likeness w. ye *Isa 40:18*
compare unto
chooseth a tree that w. not *Isa 40:20*
rot
To whom then w. ye liken *Isa 40:25*
me, or shall
I w. strengthen thee *Isa 41:10*
yea, I w. help thee *Isa 41:10*

I w. uphold thee with the *Isa 41:10*
right hand of
Lord thy God w. hold thy *Isa 41:13*
right hand
unto thee, Fear not; I w. *Isa 41:13*
help thee
I w. help thee, saith the *Isa 41:14*
Lord, and thy
I w. make thee a new sharp *Isa 41:15*
threshing
I the Lord w. hear them, I the *Isa 41:17*
God
God of Israel w. not forsake *Isa 41:17*
them
I w. open rivers in high *Isa 41:18*
places, and
I w. make the wilderness a *Isa 41:18*
pool of
I w. p.ant in the wilderness *Isa 41:19*
the cedar
I w. set in the desert the fir *Isa 41:19*
tree, and
I w. give to Jerusalem one *Isa 41:27*
that
w. hold thine hand, and w. *Isa 42:6*
keep thee
my glory w. I not give to *Isa 42:8*
another
now w. I cry like a travailing *Isa 42:14*
woman
I w. destroy and devour at *Isa 42:14*
once
I w. make waste *Isa 42:15*
mountains and hills
and I w. make the rivers *Isa 42:15*
islands, and
islands, and I w. dry up the *Isa 42:15*
pools
I w. bring the blind by a *Isa 42:16*
way that
I w. lead them in paths that *Isa 42:16*
they have
I w. make darkness light *Isa 42:16*
before them
These things w. I do unto *Isa 42:16*
them, and
he w. magnify the law, and *Isa 42:21*
make it
Who among you w. give ear *Isa 42:23*
to this
who w. hearken and hear for *Isa 42:23*
the time
the waters, I w. be with thee *Isa 43:2*
therefore w. I give men for *Isa 43:4*
thee, and
I w. bring thy seed from the *Isa 43:5*
east
I w. say to the north, Give *Isa 43:6*
up; and to
hand: I w. work, and who *Isa 43:13*
shall let it
Behold, I w. do a new thing, *Isa 43:19*
now it
I w. make a way in the *Isa 43:19*
wilderness
sake, and w. not remember *Isa 43:25*
thy sins
from the womb, which w. *Isa 44:2*
help thee
For I w. pour water upon *Isa 44:3*
him that
I w. pour my spirit upon thy *Isa 44:3*
seed
for he w. take thereof, and *Isa 44:15*
warm
and I w. raise up the decayed *Isa 44:26*
places
Be dry, and I w. dry up thy *Isa 44:27*
rivers
and I w. loose the loins of *Isa 45:1*
kings
I w. go before thee, and make *Isa 45:2*
I w. break in pieces the gates *Isa 45:2*
of brass
w. give thee the treasures of *Isa 45:3*
darkness
and I w. direct all his ways *Isa 45:13*
and even to hoar hairs w. I *Isa 46:4*
carry you
carry you: I have made, and I *Isa 46:4*
w. bear
even I w. carry, and w. *Isa 46:4*
deliver you
To whom w. ye liken me, and *Isa 46:5*
make
stand, and I w. do all my *Isa 46:10*
pleasure
spoken it, I w. also bring it *Isa 46:11*
to pass

I have purposed it, I w. also *Isa 46:11*
do it
w. place salvation in Zion *Isa 46:13*
for Israel
shall be seen: I w. take *Isa 47:3*
vengeance
and I w. not meet thee as a *Isa 47:3*
man
see all this; and w. not ye *Isa 48:6*
declare it
name's sake w. I defer mine *Isa 48:9*
anger
for my praise w. I refrain for *Isa 48:9*
thee
even for mine own sake, w. *Isa 48:11*
I do it
I w. not give my glory unto *Isa 48:11*
another
he w. do his pleasure on *Isa 48:14*
Babylon
O Israel, in whom I w. be *Isa 49:3*
glorified
I w. also give thee for a light *Isa 49:6*
to the
and I w. preserve thee, and *Isa 49:8*
give thee
I w. make all my mountains *Isa 49:11*
a way
w. have mercy upon his *Isa 49:13*
afflicted
may forget, yet w. I not *Isa 49:15*
forget thee
I w. lift up mine hand to the *Isa 49:22*
Gentiles
w. contend with him that *Isa 49:25*
contendeth
with thee, and I w. save thy *Isa 49:25*
children
And I w. feed them that *Isa 49:26*
oppress thee
For the Lord God w. help me *Isa 50:7*
me: who w. contend with thee *Isa 50:8*
Behold, the Lord God w. help *Isa 50:9*
me
he w. comfort all her desolate *Isa 51:3*
places
w. make her wilderness like *Isa 51:3*
Eden
and I w. make my judgment *Isa 51:4*
to rest
But I w. put it into the hand *Isa 51:23*
of them
for the Lord God w. go *Isa 52:12*
before you
God of Israel w. be your *Isa 52:12*
reward
Therefore w. I divide him a *Isa 53:12*
portion
with great mercies w. I *Isa 54:7*
gather thee
everlasting kindness w. I have *Isa 54:8*
mercy
I w. lay thy stones with fair *Isa 54:11*
colours
And I w. make thy windows *Isa 54:12*
of agates
and I w. make an everlasting *Isa 55:3*
covenant
Lord, and he w. have mercy *Isa 55:7*
upon him
our God, for he w. *Isa 55:7*
abundantly pardon
unto them I w. give in mine *Isa 56:5*
house
I w. give them an everlasting *Isa 56:5*
name
w. I bring to my holy *Isa 56:7*
mountain
Yet w. I gather others to him, *Isa 56:8*
besides
Come ye, say they, I w. fetch *Isa 56:12*
wine
we w. fill ourselves with *Isa 56:12*
strong drink
I w. declare thy *Isa 57:12*
righteousness
For I w. not contend for *Isa 57:16*
ever, neither
neither w. I be always *Isa 57:16*
wroth: for the
have seen his ways, and w. *Isa 57:18*
heal him
I w. lead him also, and *Isa 57:18*
restore
saith the Lord; and I w. heal *Isa 57:19*
him
and I w. cause thee to ride *Isa 58:14*
upon the
his face from you, that he w. *Isa 59:2*
not hear

he *w.* repay, fury to his adversaries | Isa 59:18

to the islands he *w.* repay recompence | Isa 59:18

and I *w.* glorify the house of my glory | Isa 60:7

and kingdom that *w.* not serve thee | Isa 60:12

w. make the place of my feet glorious | Isa 60:13

I *w.* make thee an eternal excellency | Isa 60:15

For brass I *w.* bring gold, and for iron | Isa 60:17

and for iron I *w.* bring silver, and for | Isa 60:17

I *w.* also make thy officers peace | Isa 60:17

I the Lord *w.* hasten it in his time | Isa 60:22

and I *w.* direct their work in truth | Isa 61:8

I *w.* make an everlasting covenant | Isa 61:8

I *w.* greatly rejoice in the Lord | Isa 61:10

the Lord God *w.* cause righteousness | Isa 61:11

For Zion's sake I *w.* not hold my peace | Isa 62:1

and for Jerusalem's sake I *w.* not rest | Isa 62:1

Surely I *w.* no more give thy corn to | Isa 62:8

for I *w.* tread them in mine anger | Isa 63:3

and I *w.* stain all my raiment | Isa 63:3

I *w.* tread down the people in mine | Isa 63:6

I *w.* bring down their strength to the | Isa 63:6

I *w.* mention the lovingkindnesses | Isa 63:7

my people, children that *w.* not lie | Isa 63:8

I *w.* not silence, but *w.* recompense | Isa 65:6

therefore *w.* I measure their former | Isa 65:7

so *w.* I do for my servants' sakes, that | Isa 65:8

I *w.* bring forth a seed out of Jacob | Isa 65:9

w. I number you to the sword | Isa 65:12

And I *w.* rejoice in Jerusalem | Isa 65:19

that before they call, I *w.* answer | Isa 65:24

they are yet speaking, I *w.* hear | Isa 65:24

but to this man *w.* I look, even to him | Isa 66:2

I also *w.* choose their delusions | Isa 66:4

and *w.* bring their fears upon them | Isa 66:4

I *w.* extend peace to her like a river | Isa 66:12

comforteth, so *w.* I comfort you | Isa 66:13

the Lord *w.* come with fire, and with | Isa 66:15

and by his sword *w.* the Lord plead | Isa 66:16

I *w.* gather all nations and tongues | Isa 66:18

And I *w.* set a sign among them | Isa 66:19

I *w.* send those that escape of them | Isa 66:19

And I *w.* also take of them for priests | Isa 66:21

and the new earth, which I *w.* make | Isa 66:22

for I *w.* hasten my word to perform it | Jer 1:12

I *w.* call all the families of the | Jer 1:15

And I *w.* utter my judgments against | Jer 1:16

Wherefore I *w.* yet plead with you | Jer 2:9

your children's children *w.* I plead | Jer 2:9

and thou saidst, I *w.* not transgress | Jer 2:20

all they that seek her *w.* not weary | Jer 2:24

strangers, and after them *w.* I go | Jer 2:25

of their trouble they *w.* say, Arise | Jer 2:27

Wherefore *w.* ye plead with me? ye all | Jer 2:29

lords; we *w.* come no more unto thee | Jer 2:31

Behold, I *w.* plead with thee, because | Jer 2:35

W. he reserve his anger for ever | Jer 3:5

w. he keep it to the end? Behold, thou | Jer 3:5

I *w.* not cause mine anger to fall upon | Jer 3:12

Lord, and I *w.* not keep anger for ever | Jer 3:12

I *w.* take you one of a city, and two of | Jer 3:14

a family, and I *w.* bring you to Zion | Jer 3:14

I *w.* give you pastors according to | Jer 3:15

and I *w.* heal your backslidings | Jer 3:22

for I *w.* bring evil from the north | Jer 4:6

also *w.* I give sentence against them | Jer 4:12

desolate; yet *w.* I not make a full end | Jer 4:27

have purposed it, and *w.* not repent | Jer 4:28

neither *w.* I turn back from it | Jer 4:28

fair; thy lovers *w.* despise thee | Jer 4:30

despise thee, they *w.* seek thy life | Jer 4:30

seeketh the truth; and I *w.* pardon it | Jer 5:1

I *w.* get me unto the great men | Jer 5:5

and *w.* speak unto them; for they | Jer 5:5

I *w.* make my words in thy mouth | Jer 5:14

w. bring a nation upon you from far | Jer 5:15

I *w.* not make a full end with you | Jer 5:18

w. ye not tremble at my presence | Jer 5:22

and what *w.* ye do in the end thereof | Jer 5:31

I *w.* pour it out upon the children | Jer 6:11

for I *w.* stretch out my hand upon the | Jer 6:12

But they said, We *w.* not walk therein | Jer 6:16

But they said, We *w.* not hearken | Jer 6:17

I *w.* bring evil upon this people | Jer 6:19

I *w.* lay stumbling blocks before this | Jer 6:21

I *w.* cause you to dwell in this place | Jer 7:3

w. I cause you to dwell in this place | Jer 7:7

W. ye steal, murder, and commit | Jer 7:9

Therefore *w.* I do unto this house | Jer 7:14

And I *w.* cast you out of my sight | Jer 7:15

to me; for I *w.* not hear thee | Jer 7:16

Obey my voice, and I *w.* be your God | Jer 7:23

but they *w.* not hearken to thee | Jer 7:27

them; but they *w.* not answer thee | Jer 7:27

w. I cause to cease from the cities | Jer 7:34

w. I give their wives unto others | Jer 8:10

I *w.* surely consume them, saith the | Jer 8:13

I *w.* send serpents, cockatrices | Jer 8:17

which *w.* not be charmed, and they | Jer 8:17

for every brother *w.* utterly supplant | Jer 9:4

neighbour *w.* walk with slanders | Jer 9:4

w. deceive every one his neighbour | Jer 9:5

W. not speak the truth: they have | Jer 9:5

I *w.* melt them, and try them: for | Jer 9:7

For the mountains *w.* I take up a | Jer 9:10

I *w.* make Jerusalem heaps, and a | Jer 9:11

I *w.* make the cities of Judah desolate | Jer 9:11

I *w.* feed them, even this people | Jer 9:15

I *w.* scatter them also among | Jer 9:16

I *w.* send a sword after them, till I | Jer 9:16

that I *w.* punish all them that are | Jer 9:25

I *w.* sling out the inhabitants of the | Jer 10:18

w. distress them, that they may find it | Jer 10:18

be my people, and I *w.* be your God | Jer 11:4

I *w.* bring upon them all the words | Jer 11:8

I *w.* bring evil upon them, which they | Jer 11:11

unto me, I *w.* not hearken unto them | Jer 11:11

for I *w.* not hear them in the time | Jer 11:14

of hosts, Behold, I *w.* punish them | Jer 11:22

for I *w.* bring evil upon the men of | Jer 11:23

I *w.* pluck them out of their land | Jer 12:14

I have plucked them out I *w.* return | Jer 12:15

w. bring them again, every man to his | Jer 12:15

if they *w.* diligently learn the ways of | Jer 12:16

But if they *w.* not obey | Jer 12:17

I *w.* utterly pluck up and destroy | Jer 12:17

After this manner *w.* I mar the pride | Jer 13:9

I *w.* fill all the inhabitants of this | Jer 13:13

I *w.* dash them one against another | Jer 13:14

I *w.* not pity, nor spare, nor have | Jer 13:14

But if ye *w.* not hear it, my soul shall | Jer 13:17

I *w.* scatter them as the stubble | Jer 13:24

w. I discover thy skirts upon thy face | Jer 13:26

he *w.* now remember their iniquity | Jer 14:10

they fast, I *w.* not hear their cry | Jer 14:12

and an oblation, I *w.* not accept them | Jer 14:12

I *w.* consume them by the sword, and | Jer 14:12

but I *w.* give you assured peace in | Jer 14:13

I *w.* pour their wickedness upon them | Jer 14:16

God? therefore we *w.* wait upon thee | Jer 14:22

I *w.* appoint over them four kinds | Jer 15:3

I *w.* cause them to be removed into | Jer 15:4

therefore *w.* I stretch out my hand | Jer 15:6

I *w.* fan them with a fan in the gates | Jer 15:7

I *w.* bereave them of children | Jer 15:7

I *w.* destroy my people, since they | Jer 15:7

residue of them *w.* I deliver to the | Jer 15:9

verily I *w.* cause the enemy to entreat | Jer 15:11

treasures *w.* I give to the spoil | Jer 15:13

I *w.* make thee to pass with thine | Jer 15:14

return, then *w.* I bring thee again | Jer 15:19

I *w.* make thee unto this people as | Jer 15:20

I *w.* deliver thee out of the hand of | Jer 15:21

I *w.* redeem thee out of the hand of | Jer 15:21

I *w.* cause to cease out of this place | Jer 16:9

w. I cast you out of this land *Jer 16:13* into

where I w. not shew you *Jer 16:13* favour

I w. bring them again into *Jer 16:15* their land

I w. send for many fishers, *Jer 16:16* saith the

after w. I send for many *Jer 16:16* hunters, and

first I w. recompense their *Jer 16:18* iniquity

I w. this once cause them to *Jer 16:21* know

I w. cause them to know *Jer 16:21* mine hand

I w. give thy substance and all *Jer 17:3* thy

I w. cause thee to serve thine *Jer 17:4* enemies

But if ye w. not hearken *Jer 17:27* unto me

then w. I kindle a fire in the *Jer 17:27* gates

and there w. I cause thee to *Jer 18:2* hear my

I w. repent of the evil that I *Jer 18:8* thought

then w. I repent of the good *Jer 18:10*

but we w. walk after our *Jer 18:12* own devices

we w. every one do the *Jer 18:12* imagination of

W. a man leave the snow of *Jer 18:14* Lebanon

I w. scatter them as with an *Jer 18:17* east wind

I w. shew them the back, and *Jer 18:17* not the

I w. bring evil upon this *Jer 19:3* place, the

I w. make void the counsel of *Jer 19:7* Judah

I w. cause them to fall by the *Jer 19:7* sword

their carcases w. I give to *Jer 19:7* be meat for

I w. make this city desolate, *Jer 19:8* ande a

I w. cause them to eat the *Jer 19:9* flesh of

Even so w. I break this *Jer 19:11* people and

Thus w. I do unto this place, *Jer 19:12* saith the

I w. bring upon this city and *Jer 19:15* upon all

I w. make thee a terror to *Jer 20:4* thyself

I w. give all Judah into the *Jer 20:4* hand of

I w. deliver all the strength of *Jer 20:5* this

w. I give into the hand of *Jer 20:5* their enemies

I w. not make mention of *Jer 20:9* him, nor

Report, say they, and we w. *Jer 20:10* report it

Peradventure he w. be *Jer 20:10* enticed, and

if so be that the Lord w. deal *Jer 21:2* with us

I w. turn back the weapons of *Jer 21:4* war

I w. assemble them into the *Jer 21:4* midst of

And I myself w. fight against *Jer 21:5* you

I w. smite the inhabitants of *Jer 21:6* this city

I w. deliver Zedekiah king of *Jer 21:7* Judah

I w. punish you according to *Jer 21:14* the fruit

and I w. kindle a fire in the *Jer 21:14* forest

But if ye w. not hear these *Jer 22:5* words, I

surely I w. make thee a *Jer 22:6* wilderness

I w. prepare destroyers against *Jer 22:7* thee

I w. build me a wide house *Jer 22:14* and large

but thou saidst, I w. not hear *Jer 22:21*

And, I w. give thee in the *Jer 22:25* hand of them

I w. cast thee out, and thy *Jer 22:26* mother

I w. visit upon you the evil of *Jer 23:2* your

I w. gather the remnant of my *Jer 23:3* flock

w. bring them again to their *Jer 23:3* folds

And I w. set up shepherds *Jer 23:4* over them

that I w. raise unto David a *Jer 23:5* righteous

for I w. bring evil upon *Jer 23:12* them, even the

I w. feed them with *Jer 23:15* wormwood, and

I w. even forsake you, saith *Jer 23:33* the Lord

w. even punish that man and *Jer 23:34* his house

I, even I, w. utterly forget *Jer 23:39* you

and I w. forsake you, and *Jer 23:39* the city that

I w. bring an everlasting *Jer 23:40* reproach

so w. I acknowledge them *Jer 24:5* that are

I w. set mine eyes upon them *Jer 24:6* for

I w. bring them again to this *Jer 24:6* land

I w. build them, and not pull *Jer 24:6* them

I w. plant them, and not *Jer 24:6* pluck them

I w. give them an heart to *Jer 24:7* know me

be my people, and I w. be *Jer 24:7* their God

So w. I give Zedekiah the *Jer 24:8* king of

I w. deliver them to be *Jer 24:9* removed into

And I w. send the sword, the *Jer 24:10* famine

your hands; and I w. do you *Jer 25:6* no hurt

I w. send and take all the *Jer 25:9* families

and w. bring them against this *Jer 25:9* land

and w. utterly destroy them *Jer 25:9*

I w. take from them the *Jer 25:10* voice of mirth

that I w. punish the king of *Jer 25:12* Babylon

and w. make it perpetual *Jer 25:12* desolations

I w. bring upon that land all *Jer 25:13* my words

I w. recompense them *Jer 25:14* according to

sword that I w. send among *Jer 25:16* them

the sword which I w. send *Jer 25:27* among you

I w. call for a sword upon *Jer 25:29* all the

nations: he w. plead with all *Jer 25:31* flesh

w. give them that are wicked *Jer 25:31* to the

so be they w. hearken, and *Jer 26:3* turn every

If ye w. not hearken to me, to *Jer 26:4* walk

w. I make this house like *Jer 26:6* Shiloh

w. make this city a curse to *Jer 26:6* all the

and the Lord w. repent him *Jer 26:13* of the evil

w. not serve the same *Jer 27:8* Nebuchadnezzar

w. not put their neck under *Jer 27:8* the yoke

that nation w. I punish, saith *Jer 27:8* the Lord

those w. I let remain still in *Jer 27:11* their own

Why w. ye die, thou and thy *Jer 27:13* people

that w. not serve the king of *Jer 27:13* Babylon

then w. I bring them up, and *Jer 27:22* restore

w. I bring again into this *Jer 28:3* place all

w. bring again to this place *Jer 28:4* Jeconiah

for I w. break the yoke of the *Jer 28:4* king of

Even so w. I break the yoke *Jer 28:11* of

I w. cast thee from off the *Jer 28:16* face of the

be accomplished at Babylon *Jer 29:10* I w. visit

unto me, and I w. hearken *Jer 29:12* unto you

And I w. be found of you, *Jer 29:14* saith the

and I w. turn away your *Jer 29:14* captivity

I w. gather you from all the *Jer 29:14* nations

I w. bring you again into the *Jer 29:14* place

I w. send upon them the *Jer 29:17* sword, the

and w. make them like vile *Jer 29:17* figs, that

I w. persecute them with the *Jer 29:18* sword

w. deliver them to be *Jer 29:18* removed to all

I w. deliver them into the *Jer 29:21* hand of

w. punish Shemaiah the *Jer 29:32* Nehelamite

the good that I w. do for my *Jer 29:32* people

I w. bring again the captivity *Jer 30:3* of my

I w. cause them to return to *Jer 30:3* the land

I w. break his yoke from off *Jer 30:8* thy neck

w. burst thy bonds, and *Jer 30:8* strangers

king, whom I w. raise up unto *Jer 30:9* them

I w. save thee from afar, and *Jer 30:10* thy

yet w. I not make a full end *Jer 30:11* of thee

I w. correct thee in measure *Jer 30:11*

and w. not leave thee *Jer 30:11* altogether

prey upon thee w. I give for *Jer 30:16* a prey

For I w. restore health unto *Jer 30:17* thee

I w. heal thee of thy wounds, *Jer 30:17* saith

w. bring again the captivity *Jer 30:18* of Jacob's

I w. multiply them, and they *Jer 30:19* shall

I w. also glorify them, and *Jer 30:19* they shall

I w. punish all that oppress *Jer 30:20* them

and I w. cause him to draw *Jer 30:21* near

be my people, and I w. be *Jer 30:22* your God

w. I be the God of all the *Jer 31:1* families of

I w. build thee, and thou shalt *Jer 31:4* be

I w. bring them from the *Jer 31:8* north

with supplications w. I lead *Jer 31:9* them

I w. cause them to walk by the *Jer 31:9* rivers

that scattered Israel w. *Jer 31:10* gather him

for I w. turn their mourning *Jer 31:13* into joy

and w. comfort them, and *Jer 31:13* make them

I w. satiate the soul of the *Jer 31:14* priests

I w. surely have mercy upon *Jer 31:20* him

I w. sow the house of Israel *Jer 31:27* and the

so w. I watch over them, to *Jer 31:28* build, and

I w. make a new covenant *Jer 31:31* with the

that I w. make with the *Jer 31:33* house of

I w. put my law in their *Jer 31:33* inward parts

w. be their God, and they *Jer 31:33* shall be

for I *w.* forgive them their iniquity — Jer 31:34

I *w.* remember their sin no more — Jer 31:34

I *w.* also cast off all the seed of Israel — Jer 31:37

I *w.* give this city into the hand of — Jer 32:3; 32:28

I *w.* gather them out of all countries — Jer 32:37

I *w.* bring them again unto this place — Jer 32:37

and I *w.* cause them to dwell safely — Jer 32:37

be my people, and I *w.* be their God — Jer 32:38

And I *w.* give them one heart, and — Jer 32:39

I *w.* make an everlasting covenant — Jer 32:40

that I *w.* not turn away from them — Jer 32:40

but I *w.* put my fear in their hearts — Jer 32:40

I *w.* rejoice over them to do them — Jer 32:41

I *w.* plant them in this land assuredly — Jer 32:41

so *w.* I bring upon them all the good — Jer 32:42

I *w.* cause their captivity to return — Jer 32:44

I *w.* answer thee, and shew thee great — Jer 33:3

I *w.* bring it health and cure — Jer 33:6

I *w.* cure them, and *w.* reveal unto — Jer 33:6

And I *w.* cause the captivity of Judah — Jer 33:7

and *w.* build them, as at the first — Jer 33:7

I *w.* cleanse them from all their — Jer 33:8

and I *w.* pardon all their iniquities — Jer 33:8

I *w.* cause to return the captivity of — Jer 33:11

I *w.* perform that good thing which I — Jer 33:14

w. I cause the Branch of righteousness — Jer 33:15

so *w.* I multiply the seed of David my — Jer 33:22

Then *w.* I cast away the seed of Jacob — Jer 33:26

so that I *w.* not take any of his seed — Jer 33:26

for I *w.* cause their captivity to return — Jer 33:26

I *w.* give this city into the hand of — Jer 34:2

and they *w.* lament thee, saying, Ah — Jer 34:5

I *w.* make you to be removed into all — Jer 34:17

And I *w.* give the men that have — Jer 34:18

I *w.* even give them into hand of — Jer 34:20

his princes *w.* I give into the hand of — Jer 34:21

I *w.* command, saith the Lord — Jer 34:22

and I *w.* make the cities of Judah a — Jer 34:22

But they said, We *w.* drink no wine — Jer 35:6

W. ye not receive instruction to — Jer 35:13

I *w.* bring upon Judah and upon all — Jer 35:17

house of Judah *w.* hear all the evil — Jer 36:3

they *w.* present their supplication — Jer 36:7

w. return every one from his evil way — Jer 36:7

We *w.* surely tell the king all these — Jer 36:16

I *w.* punish him and his seed and his — Jer 36:31

and I *w.* bring upon them, and upon — Jer 36:31

unto Jeremiah, I *w.* ask thee a thing — Jer 38:14

this soul, I *w.* not put thee to death — Jer 38:16

neither *w.* I give thee into the hand — Jer 38:16

and we *w.* not put thee to death — Jer 38:25

I *w.* bring my words upon this city — Jer 39:16

But I *w.* deliver thee in that day — Jer 39:17

For I *w.* surely deliver thee, and thou — Jer 39:18

and I *w.* look well unto thee: but if it — Jer 40:4

I *w.* dwell at Mizpah, to serve — Jer 40:10

which *w.* come unto us: out ye — Jer 40:10

w. slay Ishmael the son of Nethaniah — Jer 40:15

I *w.* pray unto the Lord your God — Jer 42:4

answer you, I *w.* declare it unto you — Jer 42:4

I *w.* keep nothing back from you — Jer 42:4

we *w.* obey the voice of the Lord our — Jer 42:6

If ye *w.* still abide in this land, then — Jer 42:10

then *w.* I build you, and not — Jer 42:10

I *w.* plant you, and not pluck you up — Jer 42:10

And I *w.* shew mercies unto you — Jer 42:12

say, We *w.* not dwell in this land — Jer 42:13

but we *w.* go into the land of Egypt — Jer 42:14

of bread; and there *w.* we dwell — Jer 42:14

the evil that I *w.* bring upon them — Jer 42:17

so declare unto us, and we *w.* do it — Jer 42:20

I *w.* send and take Nebuchadrezzar — Jer 43:10

and *w.* set his throne upon these stones — Jer 43:10

I *w.* kindle a fire in the houses of the — Jer 43:12

I *w.* set my face against you for evil — Jer 44:11

And I *w.* take the remnant of Judah — Jer 44:12

For I *w.* punish them that dwell in the — Jer 44:13

Lord, we *w.* not hearken unto thee — Jer 44:16

But we *w.* certainly do whatsoever — Jer 44:17

We *w.* surely perform our vows that — Jer 44:25

ye *w.* surely accomplish your vows — Jer 44:25

Behold, I *w.* watch over them for evil — Jer 44:27

that I *w.* punish you in this place — Jer 44:29

I *w.* give Pharaoh-hophra king of — Jer 44:30

which I have built, *w.* I break down — Jer 45:4

which I have planted I *w.* pluck up — Jer 45:4

I *w.* bring evil upon all flesh, saith — Jer 45:5

thy life *w.* I give unto thee for a prey — Jer 45:5

I *w.* go up, and *w.* cover the earth — Jer 46:8

I *w.* destroy the city and the — Jer 46:8

I *w.* punish the multitude of No, and — Jer 46:25

And I *w.* deliver them into the hand — Jer 46:26

behold, I *w.* save thee from afar off — Jer 46:27

for I *w.* make a full end of all the — Jer 46:28

but I *w.* not make a full end of thee — Jer 46:28

yet *w.* I not leave thee wholly — Jer 46:28

for the Lord *w.* spoil the Philistines — Jer 47:4

how long *w.* it be ere thou be quiet — Jer 47:6

that I *w.* send onto him wanderers — Jer 48:12

Therefore *w.* I howl for Moab, and — Jer 48:31

and I *w.* cry out for all Moab; mine — Jer 48:31

I *w.* weep for thee with the weeping — Jer 48:32

I *w.* cause to cease in Moab, saith — Jer 48:35

I *w.* bring upon it, even upon Moab — Jer 48:44

w. I bring again the captivity of Moab — Jer 48:47

that I *w.* cause an alarm of war to be — Jer 49:2

I *w.* bring fear upon thee, saith the — Jer 49:5

I *w.* bring again the captivity — Jer 49:6

I *w.* bring the calamity of Esau upon — Jer 49:8

him, the time that I *w.* visit him — Jer 49:8

they *w.* destroy till they have enough — Jer 49:9

I *w.* preserve them alive; and let thy — Jer 49:11

I *w.* make thee small among — Jer 49:15

I *w.* bring thee down from — Jer 49:16

I *w.* suddenly make him run away — Jer 49:19

and who *w.* appoint me the time — Jer 49:19

who is that shepherd that *w.* stand — Jer 49:19

And I *w.* kindle a fire in the wall of — Jer 49:27

I *w.* scatter into all winds them that — Jer 49:32

I *w.* bring their calamity from all — Jer 49:32

I *w.* break the bow of Elam, the chief — Jer 49:35

upon Elam *w.* I bring the four winds — Jer 49:36

w. scatter them towards all those — Jer 49:36

For I *w.* cause Elam to be dismayed — Jer 49:37

I *w.* bring evil upon them, even my — Jer 49:37

and I *w.* send the sword after them — Jer 49:37

And I *w.* set my throne in Elam, and — Jer 49:38

w. destroy from thence the king and — Jer 49:38

I *w.* bring again the captivity of Elam — Jer 49:39

I *w.* raise and cause to come up — Jer 50:9

I *w.* punish the king of Babylon and — Jer 50:18

And I *w.* bring Israel again to his — Jer 50:19

I *w.* pardon them whom I reserve — Jer 50:20

is come, the time that I *w.* visit thee — Jer 50:31

I *w.* kindle a fire in his cities, and it — Jer 50:32

are cruel, and *w.* not shew mercy — Jer 50:42

I *w.* make them suddenly run away — Jer 50:44

and who *w.* appoint me the time — Jer 50:44

shepherd that *w.* stand before me — Jer 50:44

w. raise up against Babylon — Jer 51:1

And *w.* send unto Babylon fanners — Jer 51:2

he *w.* render unto her a recompense — Jer 51:6

Surely I *w.* fill thee with men — Jer 51:14

w. I break in pieces the nations — Jer 51:20

and with thee *w.* I destroy kingdoms — Jer 51:20

thee *w.* I break in pieces the horse — Jer 51:21

thee *w.* I break in pieces the chariot — Jer 51:21

w. I break in pieces man and woman — Jer 51:22

w. I break in pieces old and young — Jer 51:22

w. I break in pieces the young man — Jer 51:22

I *w.* also break in pieces with thee — Jer 51:23

w. I break in pieces the husbandman — Jer 51:23

w. I break in pieces captains — Jer 51:23

I *w*. render unto Babylon and to all — *Jer 51:24*

I *w*. stretch out mine hand upon thee — *Jer 51:25*

and *w*. make thee a burnt mountain — *Jer 51:25*

I *w*. plead thy cause, and take — *Jer 51:36*

I *w*. dry up her sea, and make her — *Jer 51:36*

In their heat I *w*. make their feasts — *Jer 51:39*

I *w*. make them drunken, that they — *Jer 51:39*

I *w*. bring them down like lambs — *Jer 51:40*

And I *w*. punish Bel in Babylon — *Jer 51:44*

I *w*. bring forth out of his mouth that — *Jer 51:44*

I *w*. do judgment upon the graven — *Jer 51:47*

I *w*. do judgment upon her graven — *Jer 51:52*

I *w*. make drunk her princes, and her — *Jer 51:57*

the evil that I *w*. bring upon her — *Jer 51:64*

my soul: therefore *w*. I hope in him — *La 3:24*

For the Lord *w*. not cast off for ever — *La 3:31*

yet *w*. he have compassion — *La 3:32*

them; he *w*. no more regard them — *La 4:16*

he *w*. no more carry thee away into — *La 4:22*

he *w*. visit thine iniquity, O daughter — *La 4:22*

of Edom; he *w*. discover thy sins — *La 4:22*

thy feet, and I *w*. speak unto thee — *Eze 2:1*

whether they *w*. hear, or whether they — *Eze 2:5*

or whether they *w*. forbear, for they — *Eze 2:5*

unto them, whether they *w*. hear — *Eze 2:7*

or whether they *w*. forbear: for they — *Eze 2:7*

house of Israel *w*. not hearken unto — *Eze 3:7*

for they *w*. not hearken unto me — *Eze 3:7*

saith the Lord; whether they *w*. hear — *Eze 3:11*

or whether they *w*. forbear — *Eze 3:11*

blood *w*. I require at thine hand — *Eze 3:18; 3:20*

plain, and I *w*. there talk with thee — *Eze 3:22*

I *w*. make thy tongue cleave to the — *Eze 3:26*

with thee, I *w*. open thy mouth — *Eze 3:27*

I *w*. lay bands upon thee, and thou — *Eze 4:8*

the Gentiles, whither I *w*. drive them — *Eze 4:13*

I *w*. break the staff of bread in — *Eze 4:16*

and I *w*. draw out a sword after them — *Eze 5:2*

w. execute judgments in the midst of — *Eze 5:8*

I *w*. do in thee that which I have not — *Eze 5:9*

I *w*. not do any more the like — *Eze 5:9*

and I *w*. execute judgments in thee — *Eze 5:10*

thee *w*. I scatter unto all the winds — *Eze 5:10*

therefore *w*. I also diminish thee — *Eze 5:11*

eye spare, neither *w*. I have any pity — *Eze 5:11*

I *w*. scatter a third part into all — *Eze 5:12*

and I *w*. draw out a sword after them — *Eze 5:12*

I *w*. cause my fury to rest upon them — *Eze 5:13*

and I *w*. be comforted: and they shall — *Eze 5:13*

I *w*. make thee waste, and a reproach — *Eze 5:14*

which I *w*. send to destroy you — *Eze 5:16*

I *w*. increase the famine upon you — *Eze 5:16*

and *w*. break your staff of bread — *Eze 5:16*

w. I send upon you famine and evil — *Eze 5:17*

and I *w*. bring the sword upon thee — *Eze 5:17*

I, even I, *w*. bring a sword upon you — *Eze 6:3*

and I *w*. destroy your high places — *Eze 6:3*

I *w*. cast down your slain men before — *Eze 6:4*

And I *w*. lay the dead carcases of the — *Eze 6:5*

I *w*. scatter your bones round about — *Eze 6:5*

Yet *w*. I leave a remnant, that ye may — *Eze 6:8*

w. I accomplish my fury upon them — *Eze 6:12*

So *w*. I stretch out my hand — *Eze 6:14*

and I *w*. send mine anger upon thee — *Eze 7:3*

w. judge thee according to thy ways — *Eze 7:3*

w. recompense upon thee all thine — *Eze 7:3*

not spare thee, neither *w*. have pity — *Eze 7:4*

w. recompense thy ways upon thee — *Eze 7:4*

Now *w*. I shortly pour out my fury — *Eze 7:8*

w. judge thee according to thy ways — *Eze 7:8*

w. recompense thee for all thine — *Eze 7:8*

not spare, neither *w*. I have pity — *Eze 7:9*

I *w*. recompense thee according to thy — *Eze 7:9*

I *w*. give it into the hands of the — *Eze 7:21*

My face *w*. I turn also from them — *Eze 7:22*

I *w*. bring the worst of the heathen — *Eze 7:24*

I *w*. also make the pomp of the strong — *Eze 7:24*

I *w*. do unto them after their way — *Eze 7:27*

to their deserts *w*. I judge them — *Eze 7:27*

Therefore *w*. I also deal in fury: mine — *Eze 8:18*

not spare, neither *w*. I have pity — *Eze 8:18; 9:10*

a loud voice, yet *w*. I not hear them — *Eze 8:18*

but I *w*. recompense their way upon — *Eze 9:10*

But I *w*. bring you forth out of the — *Eze 11:7*

I *w*. bring a sword upon you, saith — *Eze 11:8*

And I *w*. bring you out of the midst — *Eze 11:9*

and *w*. execute judgment among you — *Eze 11:9*

I *w*. judge you in the border of Israel — *Eze 11:10; 11:11*

yet *w*. I be to them as a little — *Eze 11:16*

I *w*. even gather you from the people — *Eze 11:17*

and I *w*. give you the land of Israel — *Eze 11:17*

And I *w*. give them one heart — *Eze 11:19*

and I *w*. put a new spirit within you — *Eze 11:19*

I *w*. take the stony heart out of their — *Eze 11:19*

and *w*. give them a heart of flesh — *Eze 11:19*

be my people, and I *w*. be their God — *Eze 11:20*

I *w*. recompense their way upon them — *Eze 11:21*

it may be they *w*. consider, though — *Eze 12:3*

My net also *w*. I spread upon him — *Eze 12:13*

I *w*. bring him to Babylon to the land — *Eze 12:13*

I *w*. scatter toward every wind all that — *Eze 12:14*

and *w*. draw out the sword after them — *Eze 12:14*

I *w*. leave a few men of them from the — *Eze 12:16*

I *w*. make this proverb to cease — *Eze 12:23*

I *w*. speak, and the word that I shall — *Eze 12:25*

O rebellious house, *w*. I say the word — *Eze 12:25*

and *w*. perform it, saith the Lord God — *Eze 12:25*

I *w*. even rend it with a stormy wind — *Eze 13:13*

w. I break down the wall that ye have — *Eze 13:14*

I *w*. accomplish my wrath upon the — *Eze 13:15*

w. say unto you, The wall is — *Eze 13:15*

W. ye hunt the souls of my — *Eze 13:18*

w. ye save the souls alive that come — *Eze 13:18*

w. ye pollute me among my people for — *Eze 13:19*

and I *w*. tear them from your arms — *Eze 13:20*

w. let the souls go, even the souls that — *Eze 13:20*

Your kerchiefs also *w*. I tear, and — *Eze 13:21*

w. deliver my people out of your hand — *Eze 13:23*

I the Lord *w*. answer him that cometh — *Eze 14:4*

I the Lord *w*. answer him by myself — *Eze 14:7*

I *w*. set my face against that man — *Eze 14:8*

w. make him a sign and a proverb — *Eze 14:8*

I *w*. cut him off from the midst of my — *Eze 14:8*

I *w*. stretch out my hand upon him — *Eze 14:9*

w. destroy him from the midst of my — *Eze 14:9*

w. I stretch out mine hand upon it — *Eze 14:13*

and *w*. break the staff of the bread — *Eze 14:13*

and *w*. send famine upon it — *Eze 14:13*

and *w*. cut off man and beast from it — *Eze 14:13*

or *w*. men take a pin of it to hang any — *Eze 15:3*

fuel, so *w*. I give the inhabitants of — *Eze 15:6*

And I *w*. set my face against them — *Eze 15:7*

And I *w*. make the land desolate — *Eze 15:8*

delivered thee unto the *w*. of them — *Eze 16:27*

therefore I *w*. gather all thy lovers — *Eze 16:37*

I *w*. even gather them round about — *Eze 16:37*

w. discover thy nakedness unto them — *Eze 16:37*

And I *w*. judge thee, as women that — *Eze 16:38*

and I *w*. give thee blood in fury and — *Eze 16:38*

I *w*. also give thee into their hand — *Eze 16:39*

I *w*. cause thee to cease from playing — *Eze 16:41*

So *w*. I make my fury toward thee — *Eze 16:42*

and I *w*. be quiet, and *w*. be no more — *Eze 16:42*

I also *w*. recompense thy way upon — *Eze 16:43*

then *w*. I bring again the captivity — *Eze 16:53*

I *w*. even deal with thee as thou hast — *Eze 16:59*

I *w*. remember my covenant with thee — *Eze 16:60*

I *w*. establish unto thee an everlasting — *Eze 16:60*

w. give them unto thee for daughters — *Eze 16:61*

I *w*. establish my covenant with thee — *Eze 16:62*

even it *w.* I recompense upon his own	Eze 17:19	and I *w.* set judgment before them	Eze 23:24	I *w.* make the land of Egypt utterly	Eze 29:10
And I *w.* spread my net upon him	Eze 17:20	And I *w.* set my jealousy against thee	Eze 23:25	I *w.* make the land of Egypt desolate	Eze 29:12
snare, and I *w.* bring him to Babylon	Eze 17:20	Thus *w.* I make thy lewdness to cease	Eze 23:27	I *w.* scatter the Egyptians among the	Eze 29:12
and *w.* plead with him there for his	Eze 17:20	I *w.* deliver thee into the hand of them	Eze 23:28	and *w.* disperse them through	Eze 29:12
I *w.* also take of the highest branch	Eze 17:22	I *w.* do these things unto thee	Eze 23:30	forty years *w.* I gather the Egyptians	Eze 29:13
branch of the high cedar, and *w.* set it	Eze 17:22	*w.* I give her cup into thine hand	Eze 23:31	I *w.* bring the captivity of Egypt	Eze 29:14
I *w.* crop off from the top of his young	Eze 17:22	*W.* they now commit whoredoms with	Eze 23:43	*w.* cause them to return into the land	Eze 29:14
and *w.* plant it upon an high mountain	Eze 17:22	I *w.* bring up a company upon them	Eze 23:46	for I *w.* diminish them, that they shall	Eze 29:15
of the height of Israel *w.* I plant it	Eze 17:23	and *w.* give them to be removed and	Eze 23:46	I *w.* give the land of Egypt unto	Eze 29:19
if the wicked *w.* turn from all his sins	Eze 18:21	Thus *w.* I cause lewdness to cease	Eze 23:48	day *w.* I cause the horn of the house	Eze 29:21
Therefore I *w.* judge you, O house of	Eze 18:30	I *w.* even make the pile for fire great	Eze 24:9	I *w.* give thee the opening of the	Eze 29:21
for why *w.* ye die, O house of Israel	Eze 18:31	and I *w.* do it: I *w.* not go back	Eze 24:14	I *w.* also make the multitude of Egypt	Eze 30:10
God, I *w.* not be enquired of by you	Eze 20:3; 20:31	neither *w.* I spare, neither *w.* I repent	Eze 24:14	And I *w.* make the rivers dry, and sell	Eze 30:12
I *w.* pour out my fury upon them	Eze 20:8	Behold, I *w.* profane my sanctuary	Eze 24:21	I *w.* make the land waste, and all that	Eze 30:12
w. be as the heathen, as the families	Eze 20:32	I *w.* deliver thee to the men of the east	Eze 25:4	I *w.* also destroy the idols, and I	Eze 30:13
fury poured out, *w.* I rule over you	Eze 20:33	*w.* make Rabbah a stable for camels	Eze 25:5	I *w.* cause their images to cease out	Eze 30:13
I *w.* bring you out from the people	Eze 20:34	I *w.* stretch out mine hand upon thee	Eze 25:7	I *w.* put a fear in the land of Egypt	Eze 30:13
w. gather you out of countries wherein	Eze 20:34	and *w.* deliver thee for a spoil to the	Eze 25:7	And I *w.* make Pathros desolate, and	Eze 30:14
I *w.* bring you into the wilderness	Eze 20:35	and I *w.* cut thee off from the people	Eze 25:7	desolate, and *w.* set fire in Zoan	Eze 30:14
there *w.* I plead with you face to face	Eze 20:35	and I *w.* cause thee to perish out of	Eze 25:7	Zoan, and *w.* execute judgments in No	Eze 30:14
so *w.* I plead with you, saith the Lord	Eze 20:36	I *w.* destroy thee; and thou shalt	Eze 25:7	And I *w.* pour my fury upon Sin	Eze 30:15
I *w.* cause you to pass under the rod	Eze 20:37	I *w.* open the side of Moab from the	Eze 25:9	and I *w.* cut off the multitude of No	Eze 30:15
I *w.* bring you into the bond of the	Eze 20:37	and *w.* give them in possession, that	Eze 25:10	And I *w.* set fire in Egypt: Sin shall	Eze 30:16
I *w.* purge out from among you the	Eze 20:38	I *w.* execute judgments upon Moab	Eze 25:11	*w.* I execute judgments in Egypt	Eze 30:19
I *w.* bring them forth out of the	Eze 20:38	I *w.* also stretch out mine hand upon	Eze 25:13	king of Egypt, and *w.* break his arms	Eze 30:22
also, if ye *w.* not hearken unto me	Eze 20:39	and *w.* cut off man and beast from it	Eze 25:13	I *w.* cause the sword to fall out of his	Eze 30:22
serve me: there *w.* I accept them	Eze 20:40	I *w.* make it desolate from Teman	Eze 25:13	I *w.* scatter the Egyptians among the	Eze 30:23; 30:26
there *w.* I require your offerings	Eze 20:40	I *w.* lay my vengeance upon Edom by	Eze 25:14	and *w.* disperse them through the	Eze 30:23
I *w.* accept you with your sweet	Eze 20:41	I *w.* stretch out mine hand upon the	Eze 25:16	I *w.* strengthen the arms of the king	Eze 30:24; 30:25
I *w.* be sanctified in you before the	Eze 20:41	I *w.* cut off the Cherethims, and	Eze 25:16	I *w.* break Pharaoh's arms, and he	Eze 30:24
I *w.* kindle a fire in thee, and it shall	Eze 20:47	I *w.* execute great vengeance upon	Eze 25:17	I *w.* therefore spread out my net over	Eze 32:3
w. draw forth my sword out of the	Eze 21:3	*w.* cause many nations to come up	Eze 26:3	Then *w.* I leave thee upon the land	Eze 32:4
w. cut off from thee the righteous	Eze 21:3; 21:4	I *w.* also scrape her dust from her	Eze 26:4	I *w.* cast thee forth upon the open	Eze 32:4
I *w.* also smite mine hands together	Eze 21:17	Behold, I *w.* bring upon Tyrus	Eze 26:7	*w.* cause all the fowls of the heaven to	Eze 32:4
I *w.* cause my fury to rest: I the Lord	Eze 21:17	I *w.* cause the noise of thy songs to	Eze 26:13	I *w.* fill the beasts of the whole earth	Eze 32:4
but he *w.* call to remembrance the	Eze 21:23	I *w.* make thee like the top of a rock	Eze 26:14	I *w.* lay thy flesh upon the mountains	Eze 32:5
I *w.* overturn, overturn, overturn, it	Eze 21:27	I *w.* make thee a terror, and thou shalt	Eze 26:21	I *w.* also water with thy blood the	Eze 32:6
right it is; and I *w.* give it him	Eze 21:27	I *w.* bring strangers upon thee	Eze 28:7	I *w.* cover the heaven, and make the	Eze 32:7
I *w.* judge thee in the place where	Eze 21:30	I *w.* cast thee as profane out of the	Eze 28:16	I *w.* cover the sun with a cloud, and	Eze 32:7
I *w.* pour out mine indignation upon	Eze 21:31	I *w.* destroy thee, O covering cherub	Eze 28:16	lights of heaven *w.* I make dark over	Eze 32:8
I *w.* blow against thee in the fire of thy	Eze 21:31	I *w.* cast thee to the ground	Eze 28:17	I *w.* also vex the hearts of many	Eze 32:9
the Lord have spoken it, and *w.* do it	Eze 22:14	I *w.* lay thee before kings, that they	Eze 28:17	I *w.* make many people amazed at thee	Eze 32:10
I *w.* scatter thee among the heathen	Eze 22:15	*w.* I bring forth a fire from	Eze 28:18	*w.* I cause thy multitude to fall	Eze 32:12
w. consume thy filthiness out of thee	Eze 22:15	I *w.* bring thee to ashes upon the	Eze 28:18	I *w.* destroy also all the beasts	Eze 32:13
I *w.* gather you into the midst of	Eze 22:19	I *w.* be glorified in the midst of thee	Eze 28:22	Then *w.* I make their waters deep	Eze 32:14
so *w.* I gather you in mine anger and	Eze 22:20	For I *w.* send into her pestilence, and	Eze 28:23	but his blood *w.* I require at	Eze 33:6
I *w.* leave you there, and melt you	Eze 22:20	But I *w.* put hooks in thy jaws, and	Eze 29:4	his blood *w.* I require at thine hand	Eze 33:8
I *w.* gather you, and blow upon you	Eze 22:21	I *w.* cause the fish of the rivers to	Eze 29:4	for why *w.* ye die, O house of Israel	Eze 33:11
I *w.* raise up thy lovers against thee	Eze 23:22	I *w.* bring thee up out of the midst of	Eze 29:4	I *w.* judge you every one after his	Eze 33:20
I *w.* bring them against thee on every	Eze 23:22	And I *w.* leave thee thrown into the	Eze 29:5	in the open field *w.* I give to the beasts	Eze 33:27
		I *w.* bring a sword upon thee, and	Eze 29:8	For I *w.* lay the land most desolate	Eze 33:28

thy words, but they *w.* not do them	Eze 33:31	and a new spirit *w.* I put within you	Eze 36:26	and *w.* be jealous for my holy name	Eze 39:25
this cometh to pass, (lo, it *w.* come	Eze 33:33	I *w.* take away the stony heart out of	Eze 36:26	*w.* I hide my face any more from	Eze 39:29
I *w.* require my flock at their hand	Eze 34:10	and I *w.* give you an heart of flesh	Eze 36:26	I *w.* dwell in the midst of the children	Eze 43:7
for I *w.* deliver my flock from their	Eze 34:10	I *w.* put my spirit within you, and	Eze 36:27	I *w.* dwell in the midst of them for	Eze 43:9
I, *w.* both search my sheep, and seek	Eze 34:11	be my people, and I *w.* be your God	Eze 36:28	I *w.* accept you, saith the Lord God	Eze 43:27
w. I seek out my sheep, and *w.* deliver	Eze 34:12	I *w.* also save you from all your	Eze 36:29	But I *w.* make them keepers of the	Eze 44:14
I *w.* bring them out from the people	Eze 34:13	I *w.* call for the corn, and *w.* increase	Eze 36:29	and we *w.* shew the interpretation	Da 2:4
w. bring them to their own land, and	Eze 34:13	I *w.* multiply the fruit of the tree, and	Eze 36:30	if ye *w.* not make known unto me the	Da 2:5; 2:9
I *w.* feed them in a good pasture, and	Eze 34:14	I *w.* also cause you to dwell in the	Eze 36:33	we *w.* shew the interpretation of it	Da 2:7
I *w.* feed my flock, and	Eze 34:15	Lord have spoken it, and I *w.* do it	Eze 36:36	I *w.* shew unto the king the	Da 2:24
I *w.* cause them to lie down	Eze 34:15	I *w.* yet for this be enquired of by the	Eze 36:37	*w.* make known unto the king	Da 2:25
I *w.* seek that which was lost, and	Eze 34:16	I *w.* increase them with men like a	Eze 36:37	we *w.* tell the interpretation thereof	Da 2:36
w. bind up that which was broken	Eze 34:16	I *w.* cause breath to enter into you	Eze 37:5	he *w.* deliver us out of thine hand, O	Da 3:17; 4:25, 32
w. strengthen that which was sick	Eze 34:16	And I *w.* lay sinews upon you, and	Eze 37:6	king that we *w.* not serve thy gods	Da 3:18
I *w.* destroy the fat and the strong	Eze 34:16	*w.* bring up flesh from you, and cover	Eze 37:6	and giveth it to whomsoever he *w.*	Da 4:17
I *w.* feed them with judgment	Eze 34:16	I *w.* open your graves, and cause	Eze 37:12	and he *w.* shew interpretation	Da 5:12
even I, *w.* judge between the fat cattle	Eze 34:20	I *w.* take the stick of Joseph, which is	Eze 37:19	I *w.* read the writing unto the king	Da 5:17
w. I save my flock, and they shall	Eze 34:22	*w.* put them with him, even with the	Eze 37:19	over it whomsover he *w.*	Da 5:21
I *w.* judge between cattle and cattle	Eze 34:22	I *w.* take the children of Israel from	Eze 37:21	servest continually, he *w.* deliver thee	Da 6:16
I *w.* set up one shepherd over them	Eze 34:23	*w.* gather them on every side, and	Eze 37:21	I *w.* make thee known what shall be in	Da 8:19
I the Lord *w.* be their God, and my	Eze 34:24	I *w.* make them one nation in the	Eze 37:22	*w.* I return to fight with the prince	Da 10:20
I *w.* make with them a covenant of	Eze 34:25	but I *w.* save them out of all their	Eze 37:23	*w.* shew thee that which is noted in	Da 10:21
w. cause the evil beast to cease out of	Eze 34:25	have sinned, and *w.* cleanse them	Eze 37:23	And now *w.* I shew thee the truth	Da 11:2
I *w.* make them and the places round	Eze 34:26	be my people, and I *w.* be their God	Eze 37:23	and do according to his *w.*	Da 11:3
I *w.* cause the shower to come down in	Eze 34:26	I *w.* make a covenant of peace with	Eze 37:26	king shall do according to his *w.*	Da 11:36
I *w.* raise up for them a plant of	Eze 34:29	I *w.* place them, and multiply them	Eze 37:26	I *w.* avenge the blood of Jezreel upon	Ho 1:4
I *w.* stretch out mine hand against	Eze 35:3	*w.* set my sanctuary in the midst of	Eze 37:26	*w.* cause to cease the kingdom of the	Ho 1:4
and I *w.* make thee most desolate	Eze 35:3	I *w.* be their God, and they shall be	Eze 37:27	I *w.* break the bow of Israel in	Ho 1:5
I *w.* lay thy cities waste, and thou	Eze 35:4	I *w.* turn thee back, and put hooks	Eze 38:4	I *w.* no more have mercy upon	Ho 1:6
I *w.* prepare thee unto blood	Eze 35:6	I *w.* bring thee forth, and all thine	Eze 38:4	but I *w.* utterly take them away	Ho 1:6
w. I make mount Seir most desolate	Eze 35:7	I *w.* go up to the land of unwalled	Eze 38:11	I *w.* have mercy upon the house	Ho 1:7
I *w.* fill his mountains with his slain	Eze 35:8	I *w.* go to them that are at rest, that	Eze 38:11	*w.* save them by the Lord their God	Ho 1:7
I *w.* make thee perpetual desolations	Eze 35:9	I *w.* bring thee against my land, that	Eze 38:16	*w.* not save them by bow, nor by	Ho 1:7
shall be mine, and we *w.* possess it	Eze 35:10	And I *w.* call for a sword against him	Eze 38:21	my people, and I *w.* not be your God	Ho 1:9
I *w.* even do according to thine anger	Eze 35:11	I *w.* plead against him with pestilence	Eze 38:22	*w.* not have mercy upon her children	Ho 2:4
I *w.* make myself known among them	Eze 35:11	and I *w.* rain upon him, and upon his	Eze 38:22	I *w.* go after my lovers, that give me	Ho 2:5
rejoiceth, I *w.* make thee desolate	Eze 35:14	*w.* I magnify myself, and sanctify	Eze 38:23	I *w.* hedge up thy way with thorns	Ho 2:6
it was desolate, so *w.* I do unto thee	Eze 35:15	and I *w.* be known in the eyes of many	Eze 38:23	*w.* go and return to my first husband	Ho 2:7
and I *w.* turn unto you, and ye shall	Eze 36:9	I *w.* turn thee back, and leave but the	Eze 39:2	*w.* I return, and take away my corn	Ho 2:9
I *w.* multiply men upon you, all the	Eze 36:10	*w.* cause thee to come up from the	Eze 39:2	*w.* recover my wool and my flax given	Ho 2:9
And I *w.* multiply upon you man and	Eze 36:11	*w.* bring thee upon the mountain of	Eze 39:2	And now *w.* I discover her lewdness in	Ho 2:10
I *w.* settle you after your old estates	Eze 36:11	and I *w.* smite thy bow out of thy left	Eze 39:3	I *w.* also cause all her mirth to cease	Ho 2:11
w. do better unto you than at your	Eze 36:11	and *w.* cause thine arrows to fall out	Eze 39:3	I *w.* destroy her vines and her fig	Ho 2:12
I *w.* cause men to walk upon you	Eze 36:12	I *w.* give thee unto the ravenous birds	Eze 39:4	and I *w.* make them a forest	Ho 2:12
w. I cause men to hear in thee the	Eze 36:15	I *w.* send a fire on Magog, and among	Eze 39:6	And I *w.* visit upon her the days of	Ho 2:13
I *w.* sanctify my great name, which	Eze 36:23	So *w.* I make my holy name known in	Eze 39:7	I *w.* allure her, and bring her into	Ho 2:14
For I *w.* take you from among the	Eze 36:24	and I *w.* not let them pollute my holy	Eze 39:7	I *w.* give her her vineyards from	Ho 2:15
and *w.* bring you into your own land	Eze 36:24	I *w.* give unto Gog a place there of	Eze 39:11	I *w.* take away the names of Baalim	Ho 2:17
w. I sprinkle clean water upon you	Eze 36:25	I *w.* set my glory among the heathen	Eze 39:21	day *w.* I make a covenant for them	Ho 2:18
from all your idols, *w.* I cleanse you	Eze 36:25	Now *w.* I bring again the captivity of	Eze 39:25	I *w.* break the bow and the sword	Ho 2:18
A new heart also *w.* I give you	Eze 36:26			and *w.* make them to lie down safely	Ho 2:18
				I *w.* betroth thee unto me for ever	Ho 2:19
				yea, I *w.* betroth thee unto me in	Ho 2:19

I w. even betroth thee unto me in	Ho 2:20	there w. I devour them like a lion	Ho 13:8	father w. go in unto the same maid	Am 2:7
in that day, I w. hear, saith the Lord	Ho 2:21	I w. be thy king: where is any	Ho 13:10	I w. punish you for all your iniquities	Am 3:2
I w. hear the heavens, and they	Ho 2:21	I w. ransom them from the power	Ho 13:14	W. a lion roar in the forest, when he	Am 3:4
I w. sow her unto me in the earth	Ho 2:23	I w. redeem them from death	Ho 13:14	w. a young lion cry out of his den	Am 3:4
I w. have mercy upon her that had	Ho 2:23	O death, I w. be thy plagues	Ho 13:14	Surely the Lord God w. do nothing	Am 3:7
I w. say to them which were not my	Ho 2:23	O grave, I w. be thy destruction	Ho 13:14	lion hath roared, who w. not fear	Am 3:8
another man: so w. I also be for thee	Ho 3:3	so w. we render the calves of our lips	Ho 14:2	I w. also visit the altars of Beth-el	Am 3:14
night, and I w. destroy thy mother	Ho 4:5	save us we w. not ride upon horses	Ho 14:3	I w. smite the winter house with the	Am 3:15
I w. also reject thee, that thou shalt	Ho 4:6	neither w. we say any more to	Ho 14:3	that he w. take you away with hooks	Am 4:2
God, I w. also forget thy children	Ho 4:6	I w. heal their backsliding	Ho 14:4	thus w. I do unto thee, O Israel	Am 4:12
w. I change their glory into shame	Ho 4:7	I w. love them freely; for mine anger	Ho 14:4	because I w. do this unto thee	Am 4:12
I w. punish them for their ways	Ho 4:9	I w. be as the dew unto Israel	Ho 14:5	w. be gracious unto the remnant of	Am 5:15
I w. not punish your daughters when	Ho 4:14	O Lord, to thee w. I cry: for the fire	Joe 1:19	w. pass through thee, saith the Lord	Am 5:17
now the Lord w. feed them as a lamb	Ho 4:16	Who knoweth if he w. return	Joe 2:14	and I w. not smell in your solemn	Am 5:21
w. not frame their doings to turn	Ho 5:4	w. the Lord be jealous for his land	Joe 2:18	meat offerings, I w. not accept them	Am 5:22
I w. pour out my wrath upon them	Ho 5:10	Lord w. answer and say unto his	Joe 2:19	neither w. I regard the peace offerings	Am 5:22
w. I be unto Ephraim as a moth	Ho 5:12	I w. send you corn, and wine, and oil	Joe 2:19	I w. not hear the melody of thy viols	Am 5:23
For I w. be unto Ephraim as a lion	Ho 5:14	I w. no more make you a reproach	Joe 2:19	w. I cause you to go into captivity	Am 5:27
w. tear and go away; I w. take away	Ho 5:14	But I w. remove far off from you the	Joe 2:20	w. I deliver up the city with all that	Am 6:8
I w. go and return to my place, till	Ho 5:15	and w. drive him into a land barren	Joe 2:20	he w. smite the great house with	Am 6:11
their affliction they w. seek me early	Ho 5:15	for the Lord w. do great things	Joe 2:21	rock? w. one plow there with oxen	Am 6:12
he hath torn us, and he w. heal us	Ho 6:1	he w. cause to come down for you the	Joe 2:23	I w. raise up against you a nation	Am 6:14
hath smitten, and he w. bind us up	Ho 6:1	And I w. restore to you the years that	Joe 2:25	I w. set a plumbline in the midst	Am 7:8
After two days w. he revive us	Ho 6:2	I w. pour out my spirit upon all flesh	Joe 2:28	I w. not again pass by them anymore	Am 7:8; 8:2
in the third day he w. raise us up	Ho 6:2	In those days w. I pour out my spirit	Joe 2:29	w. rise against the house of Jeroboam	Am 7:9
go, I w. spread my net upon them	Ho 7:12	I w. shew wonders in the heavens	Joe 2:30	When w. the new moon be gone	Am 8:5
I w. bring them down as the fowls of	Ho 7:12	I w. also gather all nations	Joe 3:2	I w. never forget any of their works	Am 8:7
I w. chastise them, as their	Ho 7:12	w. bring them down into the valley	Joe 3:2	I w. cause the sun to go down at noon	Am 8:9
how long w. it be ere they attain to	Ho 8:5	and w. plead with them there for my	Joe 3:2	I darken the earth in the clear day	Am 8:9
now w. I gather them, and they shall	Ho 8:10	w. ye render me a recompence	Joe 3:4	I w. turn your feasts into mourning	Am 8:10
now w. he remember their iniquity	Ho 8:13	speedily w. I return your recompence	Joe 3:4	I w. bring up sackcloth upon all loins	Am 8:10
but I w. send a fire upon his cities	Ho 8:14	I w. raise them out of the place	Joe 3:7	I w. make it as the mourning of an	Am 8:10
What w. ye do in the solemn day	Ho 9:5	w. return your recompence upon your	Joe 3:7	that I w. send a famine in the land	Am 8:11
he w. remember their iniquity	Ho 9:9	I w. sell your sons and your daughters	Joe 3:8	I w. slay the last of them with	Am 9:1
he w. visit their sins	Ho 9:9	there w. I sit to judge all the heathen	Joe 3:12	thence w. I bring them down	Am 9:2
yet w. I bereave them, that there shall	Ho 9:12	the Lord w. be the hope of his people	Joe 3:16	w. I search and take them out thence	Am 9:3
I w. drive them out of mine house	Ho 9:15	I w. cleanse their blood that I have	Joe 3:21	thence w. I command the serpent	Am 9:3
mine house, I w. love them no more	Ho 9:15	The Lord w. roar from Zion, and utter	Am 1:2	thence w. I command the sword	Am 9:4
yet w. I slay even the beloved fruit	Ho 9:16	I w. not turn away the punishment	Am 1:3	w. set mine eyes upon them for evil	Am 9:4
My God w. cast them away, because	Ho 9:17	I w. send a fire into the house of	Am 1:4	I w. destroy it from off the face of the	Am 9:8
I w. make Ephraim to ride; Judah	Ho 10:11	I w. break also the bar of Damascus	Am 1:5	I w. not utterly destroy the house of	Am 9:8
I w. not execute the fierceness of	Ho 11:9	I w. not turn away the punishment	Am 1:6	I w. command, and I w. sift the house	Am 9:9
I w. not return to destroy Ephraim	Ho 11:9	I w. send a fire on the wall of Gaza	Am 1:7	that day w. I raise up the tabernacle	Am 9:11
and I w. not enter into the city	Ho 11:9	And I w. cut off the inhabitant from	Am 1:8	and I w. raise up his ruins	Am 9:11
I w. place them in their houses	Ho 11:11	I w. turn mine hand against Ekron	Am 1:8	I w. build it as in the days of old	Am 9:11
and w. punish Jacob according to his	Ho 12:2	I w. not turn away the punishment	Am 1:9; 1:11, 13; 2:1, 4, 6	I w. bring again the captivity of my	Am 9:14
to his doings w. he recompense him	Ho 12:2	I w. send a fire on the wall of Tyrus	Am 1:10	And I w. plant them upon their land	Am 9:15
of Egypt w. yet make thee to dwell	Ho 12:9	But I w. send a fire upon Teman	Am 1:12	thence w. I bring thee down, saith the	Ob 4
Therefore I w. be unto them as a lion	Ho 13:7	But I w. kindle a fire in the wall of	Am 1:14	if so be that God w. think upon us	Jon 1:6
leopard by the way w. I observe them	Ho 13:7	But I w. send a fire upon Moab	Am 2:2	yet I w. look again toward thy holy	Jon 2:4
I w. meet them as a bear that is	Ho 13:8	I w. cut off the judge from the midst	Am 2:3	I w. sacrifice unto thee with the voice	Jon 2:9
and w. rend the caul of their heart	Ho 13:8	w. slay all the princes thereof with	Am 2:3		
		But I w. send a fire upon Judah	Am 2:5		

I *w.* pay that that I have   *Jon 2:9*
vowed
can tell if God *w.* turn and   *Jon 3:9*
repent
w. come down, and tread   *Mic 1:3*
upon the
I *w.* make Samaria as an heap   *Mic 1:6*
of the
and I *w.* pour down the stones   *Mic 1:6*
thereof
I *w.* discover the   *Mic 1:6*
foundations thereof
all the idols thereof *w.* I lay   *Mic 1:7*
desolate
Therefore I *w.* wail and howl   *Mic 1:8*
and howl, I *w.* go stripped   *Mic 1:8*
and naked
I *w.* make a wailing like the   *Mic 1:8*
dragons
Yet *w.* I bring an heir unto   *Mic 1:15*
thee
I *w.* prophesy unto thee of   *Mic 2:11*
wine
I *w.* surely assemble, O   *Mic 2:12*
Jacob, all of
I *w.* surely gather the   *Mic 2:12*
remnant of
I *w.* put them together as the   *Mic 2:12*
sheep
the Lord, but he *w.* not hear   *Mic 3:4*
them
he *w.* even hide his face from   *Mic 3:4*
them
w. they lean upon the Lord,   *Mic 3:11*
and say
and he *w.* teach us of his ways   *Mic 4:2*
ways, and we *w.* walk in his   *Mic 4:2*
paths
w. walk every one in the name   *Mic 4:5*
of his
we *w.* walk in the name of the   *Mic 4:5*
Lord
w. I assemble her that halteth   *Mic 4:6*
and I *w.* gather her that is   *Mic 4:6*
driven out
I *w.* make her that halted a   *Mic 4:7*
remnant
for I *w.* make thine horn   *Mic 4:13*
iron, and I
iron, and I *w.* make thy   *Mic 4:13*
hoofs brass
I *w.* consecrate their gain   *Mic 4:13*
unto the
Therefore *w.* he give them up,   *Mic 5:3*
until
I *w.* cut off thy horses out of   *Mic 5:10*
the midst
of thee, and I *w.* destroy thy   *Mic 5:10*
chariots
And I *w.* cut off the cities of   *Mic 5:11*
thy land
I *w.* cut off witchcrafts out   *Mic 5:12*
of thine
Thy graven images also *w.* I   *Mic 5:13*
cut off
I *w.* pluck up thy groves out   *Mic 5:14*
of the
of thee; so *w.* I destroy thy   *Mic 5:14*
cities
I *w.* execute vengeance in   *Mic 5:15*
anger
people, and he *w.* plead with   *Mic 6:2*
Israel
W. the Lord be pleased with   *Mic 6:7*
w. I make thee sick in   *Mic 6:13*
smiting thee
which thou deliverest *w.* I   *Mic 6:14*
give up
Therefore I *w.* look unto the   *Mic 7:7*
Lord
I *w.* wait for the God of my   *Mic 7:7*
salvation
of my salvation: My God *w.*   *Mic 7:7*
hear me
I *w.* bear the indignation of   *Mic 7:9*
the Lord
he *w.* bring me forth to the   *Mic 7:9*
light
w. I show unto him   *Mic 7:15*
marvellous things
He *w.* turn again, he   *Mic 7:19*
he *w.* have compassion upon   *Mic 7:19*
us
he *w.* subdue our iniquites;   *Mic 7:19*
and thou
Lord *w.* take vengeance on his   *Na 1:2*
and *w.* not all acquit the   *Na 1:3*
wicked
he *w.* make an utter end of the   *Na 1:8*
place

w. make an utter end: *Na 1:9*
affliction shall
thee, I will afflict thee no more   *Na 1:12*
now *w.* I break his yoke from   *Na 1:13*
off thee
and *w.* burst thy bonds in   *Na 1:13*
sunder
gods *w.* I cut off the graven   *Na 1:14*
image
I *w.* make thy grave: for thou   *Na 1:14*
art vile
I *w.* burn her chariots in the   *Na 2:13*
smoke
I *w.* cut off thy prey from the   *Na 2:13*
earth
w. discover thy skirts upon thy   *Na 3:5*
face
I *w.* shew the nations thy   *Na 3:5*
nakedness
w. cast abominable filth upon   *Na 3:6*
thee
and *w.* set thee as a   *Na 3:6*
gazingstock
is laid waste: who *w.* bemoan   *Na 3:7*
her
for I *w.* work a work in your   *Hab 1:5*
days
which ye *w.* not believe,   *Hab 1:5*
though it be
I *w.* stand upon my watch,   *Hab 2:1*
and set
and *w.* watch to see what he   *Hab 2:1*
w. say
it *w.* surely come, it *w.* not   *Hab 2:3*
tarry
he *w.* invade them with his   *Hab 3:16*
troops
Yet I *w.* rejoice in the Lord   *Hab 3:18*
I *w.* joy in the God of my   *Hab 3:18*
salvation
and he *w.* make my feet like   *Hab 3:19*
hind's
he *w.* make me to walk upon   *Hab 3:19*
mine
I *w.* utterly consume all things   *Zep 1:2*
from
I *w.* consume man and beast   *Zep 1:3*
I *w.* consume the fowls of the   *Zep 1:3*
heaven
I *w.* cut off man from off the   *Zep 1:3*
land
I *w.* also stretch out mine   *Zep 1:4*
hand upon
and I *w.* cut off the remnant   *Zep 1:4*
of Baal
that I *w.* punish the princes,   *Zep 1:8*
and the
same day also *w.* I punish all   *Zep 1:9*
I *w.* search Jerusalem with   *Zep 1:12*
candles
The Lord *w.* not do good   *Zep 1:12*
neither *w.* he do evil   *Zep 1:12*
And I *w.* bring distress upon   *Zep 1:17*
men
Philistines, I *w.* even destroy   *Zep 2:5*
thee
The Lord *w.* be terrible unto   *Zep 2:11*
them
he *w.* famish all the gods of   *Zep 2:11*
the earth
he *w.* stretch out his hand   *Zep 2:13*
against the
and *w.* make Nineveh a   *Zep 2:13*
desolation
midst thereof; he *w.* not do   *Zep 3:5*
iniquity
then *w.* I turn to the people a   *Zep 3:9*
pure
w. take away out of the midst   *Zep 3:11*
of thee
I *w.* also leave in the midst   *Zep 3:12*
of thee
he *w.* save, he *w.* rejoice over   *Zep 3:17*
thee
he *w.* rest in his love, he *w.*   *Zep 3:17*
joy over
I *w.* gather them that are   *Zep 3:17*
sorrowful
time I *w.* undo all that afflict   *Zep 3:19*
thee
I *w.* save her that halteth,   *Zep 3:19*
and gather
I *w.* get them praise and   *Zep 3:19*
fame in
At that time *w.* I bring you   *Zep 3:20*
again
I *w.* make you a name and a   *Zep 3:20*
praise

house: and I *w.* take pleasure   *Hag 1:8*
in it
and I *w.* be glorified, saith the   *Hag 1:8*
Lord
I *w.* shake the heavens, and   *Hag 2:6*
the earth
I *w.* shake all nations and the   *Hag 2:7*
desire
I *w.* fill this house with glory,   *Hag 2:7*
saith
in this place *w.* I give peace,   *Hag 2:9*
saith the
from this day *w.* I bless you   *Hag 2:19*
I *w.* shake the heavens and   *Hag 2:21*
the earth
I *w.* overthrow the throne of   *Hag 2:22*
I *w.* destroy the strength   *Hag 2:22*
and I *w.* overthrow the   *Hag 2:22*
chariots
w. I take thee, O   *Hag 2:23*
Zerubbabel, my
Lord, and *w.* make thee as a   *Hag 2:23*
signet
I *w.* turn unto you, saith the   *Zec 1:3*
Lord
me, I *w.* shew thee what these   *Zec 1:9*
be
w. be unto her a wall of fire   *Zec 2:5*
round
and *w.* be glory in the midst of   *Zec 2:5*
her
I *w.* shake mine hand upon   *Zec 2:9*
them
and I *w.* dwell in the midst   *Zec 2:10;*
of thee   *2:11*
I *w.* clothe thee with change of   *Zec 3:4*
I *w.* give thee places to walk   *Zec 3:7*
among
I *w.* bring forth my servant the   *Zec 3:8*
I *w.* engrave the graving   *Zec 3:9*
thereof
I *w.* remove the iniquity of   *Zec 3:9*
that land
I *w.* bring it forth, saith the   *Zec 5:4*
Lord of
if ye *w.* diligently obey the   *Zec 6:15*
voice of the
w. dwell in the midst of   *Zec 8:3*
Jerusalem
I *w.* save my people from the   *Zec 8:7*
east
And I *w.* bring them, and they   *Zec 8:8*
shall
be my people, and I *w.* be   *Zec 8:8*
their God
I *w.* not be unto the residue   *Zec 8:11*
of this
I *w.* cause the remnant of   *Zec 8:12*
this people
so *w.* I save you, and ye shall   *Zec 8:13*
be a
seek the Lord of hosts: I *w.*   *Zec 8:21*
go also
is a Jew, saying, We *w.* go   *Zec 8:23*
with you
Behold, the Lord *w.* cast her   *Zec 9:4*
out
and he *w.* smite her power in   *Zec 9:4*
the sea
and I *w.* cut off the pride of   *Zec 9:6*
And I *w.* take away his blood   *Zec 9:7*
out of
And I *w.* encamp about mine   *Zec 9:8*
house
I *w.* cut off the chariot from   *Zec 9:10*
Ephraim
that I *w.* render double unto   *Zec 9:12*
thee
I *w.* strengthen the house of   *Zec 10:6*
Judah
and I *w.* save the house of   *Zec 10:6*
Joseph
I *w.* bring them again to   *Zec 10:6*
place them
the Lord their God, and *w.*   *Zec 10:6*
hear them
I *w.* hiss for them, and gather   *Zec 10:8*
them
I *w.* sow them among the   *Zec 10:9*
people
I *w.* bring them again also   *Zec 10:10*
out of the
w. bring them into the land   *Zec 10:10*
of Gilead
I *w.* strengthen them in the   *Zec 10:12*
Lord
For I *w.* no more pity the   *Zec 11:6*
inhabitants
I *w.* deliver the men every   *Zec 11:6*
one into his

of their hand I *w.* not deliver them   *Zec 11:6*
And I *w.* feed the flock of slaughter   *Zec 11:7*
Then said I, I *w.* not feed you: that   *Zec 11:9*
I *w.* raise up a shepherd in the land   *Zec 11:16*
I *w.* make Jerusalem a cup of   *Zec 12:2*
w. I make Jerusalem a burdensome   *Zec 12:3*
I *w.* smite every horse with   *Zec 12:4*
I *w.* open mine eyes upon the house   *Zec 12:4*
and *w.* smite every horse of   *Zec 12:4*
In that day *w.* I make the governors   *Zec 12:6*
I *w.* seek to destroy all the nations   *Zec 12:9*
I *w.* pour upon the house of David   *Zec 12:10*
I *w.* cut off the names of the idols   *Zec 13:2*
and also I *w.* cause the prophets and   *Zec 13:2*
I *w.* turn mine hand upon the ones   *Zec 13:7*
And I *w.* bring the third part through   *Zec 13:9*
and *w.* refine them as silver is refined   *Zec 13:9*
and *w.* try them as gold is tried   *Zec 13:9*
on my name, and I *w.* hear them   *Zec 13:9*
I *w.* say, It is my people; and they   *Zec 13:9*
For I *w.* gather all nations against   *Zec 14:2*
the Lord *w.* smite all the people   *Zec 14:12*
that whoso *w.* not come up of all the   *Zec 14:17*
the Lord *w.* smite the heathen   *Zec 14:18*
we *w.* return and build the desolate   *Mal 1:4*
shall build, but I *w.* throw down   *Mal 1:4*
The Lord *w.* be magnified from the   *Mal 1:5*
w. he be pleased with thee, or accept   *Mal 1:8*
God that he *w.* be gracious unto us   *Mal 1:9*
w. he regard your persons? saith the   *Mal 1:9*
neither *w.* I accept an offering at your   *Mal 1:10*
w. not hear, and *w.* not lay it to heart   *Mal 2:2*
I *w.* even send a curse upon you   *Mal 2:2*
you, and I *w.* curse your blessings   *Mal 2:2*
Behold, I *w.* corrupt your seed, and   *Mal 2:3*
The Lord *w.* cut off the man that   *Mal 2:12*
or receiveth it with good *w.* at   *Mal 2:13*
Behold, I *w.* send my messenger   *Mal 3:1*
I *w.* come near to you to judgment   *Mal 3:5*
I *w.* be a swift witness against   *Mal 3:5*
unto me, and I *w.* return unto you   *Mal 3:7*
W. a man rob God? Yet ye have   *Mal 3:8*
if I *w.* not open you the windows of   *Mal 3:10*
I *w.* rebuke the devourer for your   *Mal 3:11*
I *w.* spare them, as a man spareth   *Mal 3:17*
I *w.* spare them, as a man spareth   *Mal 3:17*
I *w.* send you Elijah the prophet   *Mal 4:5*
Herod *w.* seek the young child to   *M't 2:13*
and he *w.* throughly purge his floor   *M't 3:12*
but he *w.* burn up the chaff with   *M't 3:12*
All these things *w.* I give thee, if thou   *M't 4:9*
me, and I *w.* make you fishers of men   *M't 4:19*

if any man *w.* sue thee at the law   *M't 5:40*
heavenly Father *w.* also forgive you   *M't 6:14*
neither *w.* your Father forgive your   *M't 6:15*
is, there *w.* your heart be also   *M't 6:21*
for either he *w.* hate the one, and love   *M't 6:24*
or else he *w.* hold to the one   *M't 6:24*
ask bread, *w.* he give him a stone   *M't 7:9*
ask a fish *w.* he give him a serpent   *M't 7:10*
he that doeth the *w.* of my Father   *M't 7:21*
Many *w.* say to me in that day, Lord   *M't 7:22*
And then *w.* I profess unto them, I   *M't 7:23*
I *w.* liken him unto a wise man   *M't 7:24*
him, saying, I *w.*; be thou clean   *M't 8:3*
unto him, I *w.* come and heal him   *M't 8:7*
I *w.* follow thee withersoever thou   *M't 8:19*
I *w.* have mercy, and not sacrifice   *M't 9:13*
but the days *w.* come, when   *M't 9:15*
he *w.* send forth labourers into his   *M't 9:38*
they *w.* deliver you up to the councils   *M't 10:17*
and they *w.* scourge you in their   *M't 10:17*
him *w.* I confess also before my Father   *M't 10:32*
him *w.* I also deny before my Father   *M't 10:33*
And if ye *w.* receive it, this is   *M't 11:14*
whomsoever the Son *w.* reveal him   *M't 11:27*
heavy laden, and I *w.* give you rest   *M't 11:28*
I *w.* have mercy, and not sacrifice   *M't 12:7*
w. he not lay hold on it, and lift it   *M't 12:11*
I *w.* put my spirit upon him, and he   *M't 12:18*
man? and then he *w.* spoil his house   *M't 12:29*
I *w.* return into my house from   *M't 12:44*
do the *w.* of my Father which is in   *M't 12:58*
of harvest I *w.* say to the reapers   *M't 13:30*
I *w.* open my mouth in parables   *M't 13:35*
I *w.* utter things which have been   *M't 13:35*
I *w.* not send them away fasting   *M't 15:32*
It *w.* be fair weather; for the sky is   *M't 16:2*
It *w.* be foul weather to day: for the   *M't 16:3*
upon this rock I *w.* build my church   *M't 16:18*
And I *w.* give unto thee the keys of   *M't 16:19*
If any man *w.* come after me, let   *M't 16:24*
w. save his life shall lose it   *M't 16:25*
w. lose his life for my sake shall find   *M't 16:25*
worked their *w.* upon him (N)   *M't 17:12*
so it is not the *w.* of your Father   *M't 18:14*
But if he *w.* not hear thee, then take   *M't 18:16*
with me, and I *w.* pay thee all   *M't 18:26; 18:29*
and whatsoever is right I *w.* give you   *M't 20:4*
I *w.* give unto this last, even as   *M't 20:14*
me to do what I *w.* with mine own   *M't 20:15*
whosoever *w.* be great among you   *M't 20:26*
whosoever *w.* be chief among you   *M't 20:27*

What *w.* ye that I shall do unto you   *M't 20:32*
and straightway he *w.* send them   *M't 21:3*
I also *w.* ask you one thing, which if   *M't 21:24*
I in like wise *w.* tell you by what   *M't 21:24*
he *w.* say unto us, Why did ye not then   *M't 21:25*
He answered and said, I *w.* not   *M't 21:29*
twain did the *w.* of his father   *M't 21:31*
saying, They *w.* reverence my son   *M't 21:37*
what *w.* he do unto those husbandmen   *M't 21:40*
He *w.* miserably destroy those wicked   *M't 21:41*
and *w.* let out his vineyard unto other   *M't 21:41*
shall fall, it *w.* grind him to powder   *M't 21:44*
themselves *w.* not move them   *M't 23:4*
there *w.* the eagles be gathered   *M't 24:28*
I *w.* make thee ruler over   *M't 25:21; 25:23*
unto them. What *w.* ye give me   *M't 26:15*
and I *w.* deliver him unto you   *M't 26:15*
I *w.* keep the passover at thy house   *M't 26:18*
I *w.* not drink henceforth of this fruit   *M't 26:29*
it is written, I *w.* smite the shepherd   *M't 26:31*
again, I *w.* go before you into Galilee   *M't 26:32*
of thee, yet *w.* I never be offended   *M't 26:33*
die with thee, yet *w.* I not deny thee   *M't 26:35*
nevertheless not as I *w.* but   *M't 26:39*
Whom *w.* ye that I release   *M't 27:17*
of the twain *w.* ye that I release   *M't 27:21*
from the cross, and we *w.* believe him   *M't 27:42*
deliver him if he *w.* have him   *M't 27:43*
whether Elias *w.* come to save him   *M't 27:49*
alive. After three days I *w.* rise again   *M't 27:63*
we *w.* persuade him, and secure you   *M't 28:14*
w. make you to become fishers of men   *M'k 1:17*
saith unto him, I *w.*; be thou clean   *M'k 1:41*
But the days *w.* come, when   *M'k 2:20*
spilled, and the bottles *w.* be marred   *M'k 2:22*
except he *w.* first bind the strong   *M'k 3:27*
and then he *w.* spoil his house   *M'k 3:27*
then *w.* ye know all the parables   *M'k 4:13*
thou wilt, and I *w.* give it thee   *M'k 6:22*
I *w.* give it thee, unto the half of my   *M'k 6:23*
I *w.* that thou give me by and by   *M'k 6:25*
houses, they *w.* faint by the way   *M'k 8:3*
Whosoever *w.* come after me, let   *M'k 8:34*
whosoever *w.* save his life shall   *M'k 8:35*
saltness, wherewith *w.* ye season it   *M'k 9:50*
whosoever *w.* be great among you   *M'k 10:43*
whosoever of you *w.* be chiefest   *M'k 10:44*
straightway, he *w.* send him hither   *M'k 11:3*
neither *w.* your Father which is in   *M'k 11:26*
I *w.* also ask of you one question   *M'k 11:29*
I *w.* tell you by what authority I do   *M'k 11:29*

he *w.* say, Why then did ye not believe	*M'k 11:31*
saying, They *w.* reverence my son	*M'k 12:6*
w. come and destroy the husbandmen	*M'k 12:9*
w. give the vineyard into others	*M'k 12:9*
whensoever ye *w.* ye may do them	*M'k 14:7*
he *w.* shew you a large upper room	*M'k 14:15*
I *w.* drink no more of the fruit of the	*M'k 14:25*
is written, I *w.* smite the shepherd	*M'k 14:27*
risen, I *w.* go before you into Galilee	*M'k 14:28*
all shall be offended, yet *w.* not I	*M'k 14:29*
thee, I *w.* not deny thee in any wise	*M'k 14:31*
nevertheless not what I *w.*	*M'k 14:36*
I *w.* destroy this temple that is made	*M'k 14:58*
and within three days I *w.* build	*M'k 14:58*
W. ye that I release unto you the	*M'k 15:9*
What *w.* ye then that I shall do	*M'k 15:12*
whether Elias *w.* come to take him	*M'k 15:36*
peace, good *w.* toward men	*Lu 2:14*
and he *w.* throughly purge his floor	*Lu 3:17*
w. gather the wheat into his garner	*Lu 3:17*
but the chaff he *w.* burn with fire	*Lu 3:17*
power *w.* I give thee, and the glory	*Lu 4:6*
and to whomsoever I *w.* give it	*Lu 4:6*
w. surely say unto me this proverb	*Lu 4:23*
at thy word I *w.* let down the net	*Lu 5:5*
him, saying, I *w:* be thou clean	*Lu 5:13*
days *w.* come, when the bridegroom	*Lu 5:35*
else the new wine *w.* burst the bottles	*Lu 5:37*
unto them, I *w.* ask you one thing	*Lu 6:9*
I *w.* shew you to whom he is like	*Lu 6:47*
which of them *w.* love him most	*Lu 7:42*
And whosoever *w.* not receive you	*Lu 9:5*
If any man *w.* come after me, let	*Lu 9:23*
whosoever *w.* save his life shall	*Lu 9:24*
whosoever *w.* lose his life for my sake	*Lu 9:24*
I *w.* follow thee whithersoever thou	*Lu 9:57*
also said, Lord, I *w.* follow thee	*Lu 9:61*
he to whom the Son *w.* reveal him	*Lu 10:22*
when I come again, I *w.* repay thee	*Lu 10:35*
Thy *w.* be done, as in heaven, so	*Lu 11:2*
Though he *w.* not rise and give him	*Lu 11:8*
because of his importunity he *w.* rise	*Lu 11:8*
that is a father, *w.* he give him a stone	*Lu 11:11*
w. he for a fish give him a serpent	*Lu 11:11*
an egg *w.* he offer him a scorpion	*Lu 11:12*
I *w.* return unto my house whence I	*Lu 11:24*
I *w.* send them prophets and apostles	*Lu 11:49*
I *w.* forewarn you whom ye shall fear	*Lu 12:5*
And he said, This *w.* I do	*Lu 12:18*
I *w.* pull down my barns, and build	*Lu 12:18*
there *w.* I bestow all my fruits and	*Lu 12:18*

I *w.* say to my soul, Soul, thou hast	*Lu 12:19*
how much more *w.* he clothe you	*Lu 12:28*
there *w.* your heart be also	*Lu 12:34*
and he *w.* return from the wedding	*Lu 12:36*
and *w.* come forth and serve them	*Lu 12:37*
he *w.* make him ruler over all that he	*Lu 12:44*
lord of that servant *w.* come in a day	*Lu 12:46*
not aware, and *w.* cut him in sunder	*Lu 12:46*
w. appoint him his portion with the	*Lu 12:46*
knew his lord's *w.* and prepared	*Lu 12:47*
much, of him they *w.* ask the more	*Lu 12:48*
what *w.* I if it be already kindled	*Lu 12:49*
wind blow, ye say, There *w.* be heat	*Lu 12:55*
I say unto you *w.* seek to enter in	*Lu 13:24*
hence: for Herod *w.* kill thee	*Lu 13:31*
w. not straightway pull him out on	*Lu 14:5*
I *w.* arise and go to my father	*Lu 15:18*
w. say unto him, Father, I have sinned	*Lu 15:18*
who *w.* commit to your trust the true	*Lu 16:11*
for either he *w.* hate the one, and love	*Lu 16:13*
or else he *w.* hold to the one	*Lu 16:13*
them from the dead, they *w.* repent	*Lu 16:30*
neither *w.* they be persuaded, though	*Lu 16:31*
impossible but that offences *w.* come	*Lu 17:1*
w. say unto him by and by, when he is	*Lu 17:7*
And *w.* not rather say unto him	*Lu 17:8*
The days *w.* come, when ye shall	*Lu 17:22*
thither *w.* the eagles be gathered	*Lu 17:37*
I *w.* avenge her, lest by her continual	*Lu 18:5*
that he *w.* avenge them speedily	*Lu 18:8*
We *w.* not have this man to reign	*Lu 19:14*
of thine own mouth *w.* I judge thee	*Lu 19:22*
I *w.* ask you one thing; and answer	*Lu 20:3*
he *w.* say, Why then believed ye him	*Lu 20:5*
Of men; all the people *w.* stone us	*Lu 20:6*
I *w.* send my beloved son: it may be	*Lu 20:13*
may be they *w.* reverence him when	*Lu 20:14*
shall fall, it *w.* grind him to powder	*Lu 20:18*
the days *w.* come in the which there	*Lu 21:6*
what sign *w.* there be when these	*Lu 21:7*
For I *w.* give you a mouth	*Lu 21:15*
you, I *w.* not any more eat thereof	*Lu 22:16*
I *w.* not drink of the fruit of the vine	*Lu 22:18*
If I tell you, ye *w.* not believe	*Lu 22:67*
ye *w.* not answer me, nor let me go	*Lu 22:68*
I *w.* therefore chastise him and let	*Lu 23:16*
I *w.* therefore chastise him	*Lu 23:22*
but he delivered Jesus to them *w.*	*Lu 23:28*
and in three days I *w.* raise it up	*Joh 2:19*
wind blows where it *w.* (A)(E)(N)	*Joh 3:8*
he is come, he *w.* tell us all things	*Joh 4:25*
is to do the *w.* of him that sent me	*Joh 4:34*

signs and wonders, ye *w.* not believe	*Joh 4:48*
and he *w.* shew him greater works	*Joh 5:20*
the Son quickeneth whom he *w.*	*Joh 5:21*
w. of the Father which sent me	*Joh 5:30*
And ye *w.* not come to me, that ye	*Joh 5:40*
in his own name, him ye *w.* receive	*Joh 5:43*
Do not think that I *w.* accuse you	*Joh 5:45*
cometh to me I *w.* in no wise cast out	*Joh 6:37*
but the *w.* of him that sent me	*Joh 6:38*
the Father's *w.* which hath sent me	*Joh 6:39*
this is the *w.* of him, that sent me	*Joh 6:40*
I *w.* raise him up at the last day	*Joh 6:40; 6:44; 54*
the bread that I *w.* give is my flesh	*Joh 6:51*
I *w.* give for the life of the world	*Joh 6:51*
the twelve, *W.* ye also go away	*Joh 6:67*
if any man do his *w.* he shall	*Joh 7:17*
w. he do more miracles than these	*Joh 7:31*
Whither *w.* he go, that we shall not	*Joh 7:35*
w. he go unto the dispersed among	*Joh 7:35*
said the Jews, *W.* he kill himself	*Joh 8:22*
the lusts of your father ye *w.* do	*Joh 8:44*
w. ye also be his disciples	*Joh 9:27*
and doeth his *w.* him he heareth	*Joh 9:31*
And a stranger *w.* they not follow	*Joh 10:5*
w. flee from him: for they know not	*Joh 10:5*
wilt ask of God, God *w.* give it thee	*Joh 11:12*
thus alone, all men *w.* believe on him	*Joh 11:48*
that he *w.* not come to the feast	*Joh 11:56*
serve me, him *w.* my Father honour	*Joh 12:26*
glorified it, and *w.* glorify it again	*Joh 12:28*
the earth, *w.* draw all men unto me	*Joh 12:32*
I *w.* lay down my life for thy sake	*Joh 13:37*
I *w.* come again, and receive you unto	*Joh 14:3*
that *w.* I do, that the Father may be	*Joh 14:13*
ask any thing in my name, I *w.* do it	*Joh 14:14*
I *w.* pray the Father, and he shall give	*Joh 14:16*
I *w.* not leave you comfortless	*Joh 14:18*
you comfortless; I *w.* come	*Joh 14:18*
I *w.* love him and *w.* manifest myself	*Joh 14:21*
a man love me, he *w.* keep my words	*Joh 14:23*
w. love him, and we *w.* come unto him	*Joh 14:23*
whom the Father *w.* send in my name	*Joh 14:26*
Hereafter I *w.* not talk much with you	*Joh 14:30*
ye shall ask what ye *w.* and it	*Joh 15:7*
me, they *w.* also persecute you	*Joh 15:20*
my sayings, they *w.* keep yours also	*Joh 15:20*
all these things *w.* they do unto you	*Joh 15:21*
I *w.* send unto you from the Father	*Joh 15:26*
w. think that he doeth God service	*Joh 16:2*
And these things *w.* they do unto you	*Joh 16:3*
the Comforter *w.* not come unto you	*Joh 16:7*

if I depart, I *w*. send him unto   *Joh 16:7*
you
he *w*. reprove the world of   *Joh 16:8*
sin, and of
come, he *w*. guide you into   *Joh 16:13*
all truth
and he *w*. shew you things to   *Joh 16:13*
come
but I *w*. see you again, and   *Joh 16:22*
your
Father in my name, he *w*.   *Joh 16:23*
give it you
that I *w*. pray the Father for   *Joh 16:26*
you
Father, I *w*. that they also,   *Joh 17:24*
whom
unto them thy name, and *w*.   *Joh 17:26*
declare it
w. ye therefore that I release   *Joh 18:39*
unto
hast laid him, and I *w*. take   *Joh 20:15*
him away
hand into his side, I *w*. not   *Joh 20:25*
believe
If I *w*. that he tarry till I   *Joh 21:22;*
come   *21:23*
God, I *w*. pour out my Spirit   *Ac 2:17*
upon all
I *w*. pour out in those days   *Ac 2:18*
of my
I *w*. shew wonders in heaven   *Ac 2:19*
above
determined *w*. and plan of   *Ac 2:23*
God (A)(N)
determined *w*. and   *Ac 2:23*
foreknowledge of God (B)
soul, which *w*. not hear that   *Ac 3:23*
prophet
your *w*. and purpose   *Ac 4:28*
(A)(P)(B)
be of men, it *w*. come to   *Ac 5:38*
nought
we *w*. give ourselves continually   *Ac 6:4*
to
they shall be in bondage *w*. I   *Ac 7:7*
judge
now come, I *w*. send thee into   *Ac 7:34*
Egypt
w. carry you away beyond   *Ac 7:43*
Babylon
what house *w*. ye build me?   *Ac 7:49*
saith the
w. shew him how great   *Ac 9:16*
things he
I *w*. give you the sure   *Ac 10:34*
mercies of
After this I *w*. return, and *w*.   *Ac 15:16*
build
w. build again the ruins   *Ac 15:16*
thereof, and I
the ruins thereof, and I *w*.   *Ac 15:16*
set it up
said, What *w*. this babbler   *Ac 17:18*
say
which he *w*. judge the world   *Ac 17:31*
in
w. hear thee again of this   *Ac 17:32*
matter
henceforth I *w*. go unto the   *Ac 18:6*
Gentiles
I *w*. be no judge of such   *Ac 18:15*
matters
but I *w*. return again unto   *Ac 18:21*
you
again unto you, if God *w*.   *Ac 18:21*
the complete *w*. of God (P)   *Ac 20:27*
The *w*. of the Lord be done   *Ac 21:14*
for they *w*. hear that thou art   *Ac 21:22*
come
for they *w*. not receive thy   *Ac 22:18*
testimony
I *w*. send thee far hence unto   *Ac 22:21*
we *w*. eat nothing until we   *Ac 23:14*
have slain
they *w*. neither eat nor drink   *Ac 23:21*
till they
I *w*. hear thee, said he, when   *Ac 23:35*
thine
I *w*. know the uttermost of   *Ac 24:22*
your
convenient season, I *w*. call   *Ac 24:25*
for thee
in the which I *w*. appear   *Ac 26:16*
unto thee
that this voyage *w*. be with   *Ac 27:10*
hurt
the Gentiles, and that they *w*.   *Ac 28:28*
hear it
Who *w*. render to every man   *Ro 2:6*
according

to whom the Lord *w*. not   *Ro 4:8*
impute sin
for a righteous man *w*. one die   *Ro 5:7*
for to *w*. is present with me   *Ro 7:18*
At this time *w*. I come, and   *Ro 9:9*
Sarah
I *w*. have mercy on whom   *Ro 9:15*
I have
mercy on whom I *w*. have   *Ro 9:15*
mercy
I *w*. have compassion on   *Ro 9:15*
whom I
on whom I *w*. have   *Ro 9:15*
compassion
mercy on whom he *w*. have   *Ro 9:18*
mercy
and whom he *w*. he hardeneth   *Ro 9:18*
For who hath resisted his *w*.   *Ro 9:19*
I *w*. call them my people,   *Ro 9:25*
which were
For he *w*. finish the work, and   *Ro 9:28*
cut it
a short work *w*. the Lord   *Ro 9:28*
make upon
I *w*. provoke you to jealousy   *Ro 10:19*
by them
by a foolish nation I *w*.   *Ro 10:19*
anger you
Vengeance is mine; I *w*.   *Ro 12:19*
repay, saith
For this cause I *w*. confess to   *Ro 15:9*
thee
I *w*. not dare to speak of any   *Ro 15:18*
of those
journey into Spain, I *w*. come   *Ro 15:24*
to you
fruit, I *w*. come by you into   *Ro 15:28*
Spain
I *w*. destroy the wisdom of   *1Co 1:19*
the wise
w. bring to nothing the   *1Co 1:19*
understanding
who both *w*. bring to light the   *1Co 4:5*
hidden
and *w*. make manifest the   *1Co 4:5*
counsels
But I *w*. come to you shortly   *1Co 4:19*
if the Lord *w*.   *1Co 4:19*
w. know not the speech of   *1Co 4:19*
them
What *w*. ye? shall I come   *1Co 4:21*
unto you
I *w*. not be brought under   *1Co 6:12*
the power
w. also raise up us by his   *1Co 6:14*
own power
let him do what he *w*. he   *1Co 7:36*
sinneth
heart that he *w*. keep his   *1Co 7:37*
virgin
to be married to whom she   *1Co 7:39*
w.
I *w*. eat no flesh while the   *1Co 8:13*
world
who *w*. not suffer you to be   *1Co 10:13*
tempted
w. with the temptation also   *1Co 10:13*
make a
rest *w*. I set in order when I   *1Co 11:34*
come
to every man severally as he   *1Co 12:11*
w.
is it then? I *w*. pray with   *1Co 14:15*
the spirit
and I *w*. pray with the   *1Co 14:15*
understanding
I *w*. sing with the spirit   *1Co 14:15*
and I *w*. sing with the   *1Co 14:15*
understanding
other lips *w*. I speak unto   *1Co 14:21*
this people
yet for all that *w*. they not   *1Co 14:21*
hear me
w. they not say that ye are   *1Co 14:23*
mad
down on his face he *w*.   *1Co 14:25*
worship God
And if they *w*. learn any   *1Co 14:35*
thing
some man *w*. say, How are   *1Co 15:35*
the dead
them *w*. I send to bring your   *1Co 16:3*
liberality
Now I *w*. come unto you,   *1Co 16:5*
when I shall
And it may be that I *w*.   *1Co 16:6*
abide, yea
I *w*. not see you now by the   *1Co 16:7*
way

I *w*. tarry at Ephesus until   *1Co 16:8*
Pentecost
but he *w*. come when he   *1Co 16:12*
shall have
we trust that he *w*.   *2Co 1:10*
deliver us
I *w*. dwell in them, and walk   *2Co 6:16*
in them
and I *w*. their God, and they   *2Co 6:16*
shall
unclean thing; and I *w*.   *2Co 6:17*
receive you
And *w*. be a Father unto you,   *2Co 6:18*
and ye
as there was a readiness to   *2Co 8:11*
w.
such *w*. we be also in deed   *2Co 10:11*
when we
we *w*. not boast of things   *2Co 10:13*
without our
unto you, and so *w*. I keep   *2Co 11:9*
myself
But what I do, that I *w*. do   *2Co 11:12*
that I may
glory after the flesh, I *w*.   *2Co 11:18*
glory also
I *w*. glory of the things   *2Co 11:30*
which concern
I *w*. come to visions and   *2Co 12:1*
revelations of
Of such an one *w*. I glory: *2Co 12:5*
yet of
of myself I *w*. not glory,   *2Co 12:5*
but in mine
not be a fool; for I *w*. say the   *2Co 12:6*
truth
w. I rather glory in mine   *2Co 12:9*
infirmities
and I *w*. not be burdensome   *2Co 12:14*
to you
I *w*. very gladly spend and   *2Co 12:15*
be spent
my God *w*. humble me   *2Co 12:21*
among you
that, if I come again, I *w*.   *2Co 13:2*
not spare
that ye *w*. be none otherwise   *Ga 5:10*
minded
design of his own *w*. (B)   *Eph 1:11*
purpose in sovereign *w*. (P)   *Eph 1:11*
but what the *w*. of the Lord   *Eph 5:17*
is
With good *w*. doing service   *Eph 6:7*
w. I perform it until the day   *Ph'p 1:6*
of Jesus
strife; and some also of good   *Ph'p 1:15*
w.
therein do rejoice, yea, and   *Ph'p 1:18*
w. rejoice
both to *w*. and to do of his   *Ph'p 2:13*
good
who *w*. naturally care for   *Ph'p 2:20*
your state
as I shall see how it *w*. go   *Ph'p 2:23*
with me
a shew of wisdom in *w*.   *Col 2:23*
worship
which sleep in Jesus *w*. God   *1Th 4:14*
bring
for this is the *w*. of God in   *1Th 5:18*
Christ
that calleth you, who also *w*.   *1Th 5:24*
do it
only he who now letteth *w*.   *2Th 2:7*
do it
w. do the things which we   *2Th 3:4*
command
Who *w*. have all men to be   *1Ti 2:4*
saved
I *w*. therefore that men pray   *1Ti 2:8*
against Christ, they *w*. marry   *1Ti 5:11*
I *w*. therefore that the   *1Ti 5:14*
younger
that *w*. be rich fall into   *1Ti 6:9*
temptation
if we deny him, he also *w*.   *2Ti 2:12*
deny us
w. increase unto more   *2Ti 2:16*
ungodliness
their word *w*. eat as doth a   *2Ti 2:17*
canker
if God *w*. give them   *2Ti 2:25*
repentance
and all that *w*. live godly in   *2Ti 3:12*
Christ

time *w.* come when they *w.* not   *2Ti 4:3*
endure
and *w.* preserve me unto his   *2Ti 4:18*
heavenly
these things I *w.* that thou   *Tit 3:8*
affirm
with mine own hand, I *w.*   *Ph'm 19*
repay it
I *w.* be to him a Father, and   *Heb 1:5*
he shall
I *w.* declare thy name unto   *Heb 1:12*
my
the church *w.* I sing praise   *Heb 1:12*
unto thee
And again, I *w.* put my trust   *Heb 1:13*
in him
saith, To-day if ye *w.* hear his   *Heb 3:7;*
voice   *3:15; 4:7*
And this *w.* we do, if God   *Heb 6:3*
permit
Saying, Surely blessing I *w.*   *Heb 6:14*
bless thee
and multiplying I *w.* multiply   *Heb 6:14*
thee
The Lord sware and *w.* not   *Heb 7:21*
repent
when I *w.* make a new   *Heb 8:8*
covenant
I *w.* make with the house of   *Heb 8:10*
Israel
I *w.* put my laws into their   *Heb 8:10*
mind
and I *w.* be to them a God,   *Heb 8:10*
and they
For I *w.* be merciful to their   *Heb 8:12*
iniquities *w.* I remember no   *Heb 8:12*
more
he, Lo, I come to do thy *w.*   *Heb 10:9*
O God
By the which *w.* we are   *Heb 10:10*
sanctified
covenant that I *w.* make   *Heb 10:16*
with them
I *w.* put my laws into their   *Heb 10:16*
hearts
and in their minds *w.* I   *Heb 10:16*
write them
and iniquities *w.* I   *Heb 10:17*
remember no more
me, I *w.* recompense, saith   *Heb 10:30*
the Lord
shall come *w.* come, and *w.*   *Heb 10:37*
not tarry
and adulterers God *w.* judge   *Heb 13:4*
I *w.* never leave thee, nor   *Heb 13:5*
forsake
I *w.* not fear what man shall   *Heb 13:6*
do unto
if he come shortly, I *w.* see   *Heb 13:23*
you
I *w.* shew thee my faith by   *Jas 2:18*
my works
where the *w.* of pilot directs (R)   *Jas 3:4*
therefore *w.* be a friend of the   *Jas 4:4*
Resist the devil, and he *w.*   *Jas 4:7*
flee from
to God, and he *w.* draw nigh   *Jas 4:8*
to you
to-morrow we *w.* go into   *Jas 4:13*
such a city
If the Lord *w.* we shall live   *Jas 4:15*
For he that *w.* love life, and   *1Pe 3:10*
see
And who is he that *w.* harm   *1Pe 3:13*
you, if ye
wrought the *w.* of the Gentiles   *1Pe 4:3*
I *w.* not be negligent to put   *2Pe 1:12*
you
I *w.* endeavour that ye may   *2Pe 1:15*
be able
not in old time by the *w.* of   *2Pe 1:21*
man
day of the Lord *w.* come as a   *2Pe 3:10*
thief
I *w.* remember his deeds which   *3Jo 10*
he
I *w.* not with ink and pen write   *3Jo 13*
I *w.* put you in remembrance   *Jude 5*
or else I *w.* come unto thee   *Re 2:5*
quickly
w. remove thy candlestick out   *Re 2:5*
of his
To him that overcometh *w.* I   *Re 2:7*
give to
and I *w.* give thee a crown of   *Re 2:10*
life
or else I *w.* come unto thee   *Re 2:16*
quickly
w. fight against them with the   *Re 2:16*
sword

To him that overcometh *w.* I   *Re 2:17*
give to
and *w.* give him a white stone,   *Re 2:17*
and in
Behold, I *w.* cast her into a   *Re 2:22*
bed, and
I *w.* kill her children with   *Re 2:23*
death
and I *w.* give unto every one of   *Re 2:23*
you
I *w.* put upon you none other   *Re 2:24*
burden
to whom *w.* I give power over   *Re 2:26*
And I *w.* give him the   *Re 2:28*
morning star
I *w.* come on thee as a thief   *Re 3:3*
know what hour I *w.* come upon   *Re 3:3*
thee
I *w.* not blot out his name out   *Re 3:5*
of the
but I *w.* confess his name   *Re 3:5*
before my
I *w.* make them of the   *Re 3:9*
synagoguue of
I *w.* make them to come and   *Re 3:9*
worship
I also *w.* keep thee from the   *Re 3:10*
hour of
Him that overcometh *w.* I   *Re 3:12*
make a
I *w.* write upon him the name   *Re 3:12*
of my
I *w.* write upon him my new   *Re 3:12*
name
I *w.* spue thee out of my   *Re 3:16*
mouth
I *w.* come in to him, and *w.*   *Re 3:20*
sup with
To him that overcometh *w.* I   *Re 3:21*
grant to
I *w.* shew thee things which   *Re 4:1*
must be
w. give power unto my two   *Re 11:3*
witnesses
And if any man *w.* hurt them   *Re 11:5*
all plagues, as often as they *w.*   *Re 11:6*
I *w.* shew unto thee the   *Re 17:1*
judgment of
I *w.* tell thee the mystery of   *Re 17:7*
and he *w.* dwell with them,   *Re 21:3*
and they
I *w.* give unto him that is   *Re 21:6*
athirst of
and I *w.* be his God, and he   *Re 21:7*
shall be
hither, I *w.* shew thee the   *Re 21:9*
bride, the
whosoever *w.* let him take   *Re 22:17*

WILL *OF* GOD

that do after the *w. of* your   *Ezr 7:18*
God
who shall do the *w. of God*   *M'k 3:35*
is my brother
born, not of the *w. of* man,   *Joh 1:13*
but *of God*
served his generation by the   *Ac 13:36*
w. of God
have a prosperous journey by   *Ro 1:10*
the *w. of God*
makes intercession according to   *Ro 8:7*
the *w. of God*
prove that acceptable and   *Ro 12:2*
perfect *w. of God*
I come to you with joy, by   *Ro 15:32*
the *w. of God*
Paul an apostle by the *w. of*   *1Co 1:1;*
God   *2Co 1:1; Eph 1:1; Col 1:1; 2Ti 1:1*
gave themselves to us by the   *2Co 8:5*
w. of God
deliver us from evil world by the   *Ga 1:4*
w. of God
doing the *w. of God* from the   *Eph 6:6*
heart
may stand complete in all the   *Col 4:12*
w. of God
for this is the *w. of God*   *1Th 4:3; 5:18*
after ye have done, the *w.*   *Heb 10:36*
of God
so is the *w. of God* that ye   *1Pe 2:15*
put to silence
for it is better if the *w. of*   *1Pe 3:17*
God be so
live, not to the lusts of men,   *1Pe 4:2*
but to *w. of God*
them that suffer according to   *1Pe 4:19*
the *w. of God*
he that doth the *w. of God*   *1Jo 2:17*
abideth

HIS WILL

and he doth according to *his*   *Da 4:35*
w.
he did according to *his w.;*   *Da 8:4;*
do *his w.*   *11:3, 16, 36*
neither did according to *his*   *Lu 12:47*
if any man will do *his w.* he   *Joh 7:17*
shall know
that thou shouldest know *his*   *Ac 22:14*
w.
knowest *his w.*   *Ro 2:18*
resisted *his w.*   *Ro 9:19*
he that hath power over *his*   *1Co 7:37*
own *w.*
his w. was not at all to   *1Co 16:12*
come at this time
according to the good pleasure   *Eph 1:5*
of *his w.*
made known to us the mystery   *Eph 1:9*
of *his w.*
might be filled with knowledge   *Col 1:9*
of *his w.*
are taken captive by him at   *2Ti 2:26*
his w.
perfect in every good work   *Heb 13:21*
his w.
if we ask according to *his w.*   *1Jo 5:14*
he hears
God put in their hearts to   *Re 17:17*
fulfil *his w.*

MY WILL

this cup, not *my w.* but thine   *Lu 22:42*
be done
found David, who shall fulfil   *Ac 13:22*
all *my w.*
if I do this thing against *my*   *1Co 9:17*
w.

OWN WILL

he shall offer it of his *own*   *Le 1:3*
voluntary *w.*
ye shall offer it as your *own*   *Le 19:5;*
w.   *22:19, 29*
he shall do according to his   *Da 11:16*
own w.
because I seek not mine *own*   *Joh 5:30*
w.
I came from heaven, not to   *Joh 6:38*
do mine *own w.*
who worketh after counsel of   *Eph 1:11*
his *own w.*
gifts of Holy Ghost, according   *Heb 2:4*
to his *own w.*
of his *own w.* begat he us by   *Jas 1:18*
word of truth

THY WILL

I delight to do *thy w.* O my   *Ps 40:8*
God
teach me to do *thy w.* thou   *Ps 143:10*
art my God
thy w. be done in earth   *M't 6:10;*
be done   *Lu 11:2*
if this cup may not pass, *thy*   *M't 26:42*
w. be done
lo, I come to do *thy w.* O   *Heb 10:7;*
God   *10:9*

WILLETH

wind bloweth where it *w.* (S)   *Joh 3:8*
So then it is not of him that   *Ro 9:16*
w.
where the pilot *w.* (S)   *Jas 3:4*

WILLING

the woman will not be *w.* to   *Ge 24:5*
follow
woman will not be *w.* to   *Ge 24:8*
follow thee
whosoever is of a *w.* heart, let   *Ex 35:5*
him
one whom his spirit made *w.*   *Ex 35:21*
as many as were *w.* hearted   *Ex 35:22*
of Israel brought a *w.*   *Ex 35:29*
offering
whose heart made them *w.* to   *Ex 35:29*
am *w.* to (S)   *2Sa 6:22*
he was not *w.* to take of his   *2Sa 12:4*
own (S)
perfect heart and with a *w.*   *1Ch 28:9*
mind
workmanship every *w.*   *1Ch 28:21*
skilful

who then is *w.* to consecrate *1Ch 29:5*
his
Will the unicorn be *w.* to *Job 39:9*
serve thee
uphold me with a *w.* spirit *Ps 51:12*
(S)
Thy people shall be *w.* in the *Ps 110:3*
day
If ye be *w.* and obedient, ye *Isa 1:19*
shall eat
w. to make her a publick *M't 1:19*
example
not *w.* to expose her (A)(E) *M't 1:19*
the spirit indeed is *w.* but *M't 26:41*
Pilate, *w.* to content the *M'k 15:15*
people
But he, *w.* to justify himself, *Lu 10:29*
said
Father, if thou be *w.* remove *Lu 22:42*
this
Pilate *w.* to release Jesus, *Lu 23:20*
spake
ye were *w.* for a season to *Joh 5:35*
rejoice
w. to show the Jews a *Ac 24:27*
pleasure
w. to do the Jews a pleasure *Ac 25:9*
w. to bear witness (B) *Ac 26:5*
But the centurion, *w.* to save *Ac 27:43*
Paul
if God, *w.* to show his wrath *Ro 9:22*
be *w.* to be vegetarians and *Ro 14:21*
teetotalers (P)
w. rather to be absent from *2Co 5:8*
power they were *w.* of *2Co 8:3*
themselves
also to be *w.* a year ago (S) *2Co 8:10*
For if there be first a *w.* *2Co 8:12*
mind
I know you are *w.* (P) *2Co 9:2*
were *w.* to have imparted unto *1Th 2:8*
you
to distribute, *w.* to *1Ti 6:18*
communicate
w. more abundantly to shew *Heb 6:17*
unto
in all things *w.* to live *Heb 13:18*
honestly
not *w.* that any should perish *2Pe 3:9*

WILLINGLY

every man that giveth it *w.* *Ex 25:2*
with
the people *w.* offered *J'g 5:2*
themselves
that offered themselves *w.* *J'g 5:9*
among
answered, We will *w.* give *J'g 8:25*
them
of the king's work, offered *w.* *1Ch 29:6*
rejoiced, for that they offered *1Ch 29:9*
w.
with perfect heart they *1Ch 29:9*
offered *w.*
should be able to offer so *w.* *1Ch 29:14*
after
I have *w.* offered all these *1Ch 29:17*
things
present here, to offer *w.* *1Ch 29:17*
unto thee
w. offered himself unto the *2Ch 17:16*
Lord
princes gave *w.* unto the *2Ch 35:8*
people
besides all that was *w.* offered *Ezr 1:6*
that *w.* offered a freewill *Ezr 3:5*
offering
offering *w.* for the house of *Ezr 7:16*
their God
that *w.* offered themselves to *Ne 11:2*
dwell
and worketh *w.* with her *Pr 31:13*
hands
For he doth not afflict *w.* nor *La 3:33*
because he *w.* walked after *Ho 5:11*
they *w.* received him into the *Joh 6:21*
ship
subject to vanity, not *w.* but *Ro 8:20*
For if I do this thing, *w.* I *1Co 9:17*
it were of necessity, but *w.* *Ph'm 14*
thereof, not by constraint, *1Pe 5:2*
but *w.*
For this they *w.* are ignorant of *2Pe 3:5*

WILLINGNESS

your *w.* (A)(B) *2Co 9:2*

WILLOW

waters and set it as a *w.* tree *Eze 17:5*

WILLOWS

thick trees, and *w.* of the *Le 23:40*
brook
the *w.* of the brook compass *Job 40:22*
him
We hanged our harps upon *Ps 137:2*
the *w.*
carry away to the brook of *Isa 15:7*
the *w.*
grass, as *w.* by the water *Isa 44:4*
courses

WILT

if thou *w.* take the left hand, *Ge 13:9*
then I
what *w.* thou give me, seeing I *Ge 15:2*
go
thou? and whither *w.* thou go *Ge 16:8*
W. thou also destroy the *Ge 18:23*
righteous
w. thou also destroy and not *Ge 18:24*
spare
w. thou destroy all the city *Ge 18:28*
for lack of
w. thou slay also a righteous *Ge 20:4*
nation
that thou *w.* not deal falsely *Ge 21:23*
with me
But if thou *w.* give it, I pray *Ge 23:13*
thee
unto her, *W.* thou go with *Ge 24:58*
this man
if thou *w.* do this thing for *Ge 30:31*
me, I will
What *w.* thou give me, that *Ge 38:16*
thou
W. thou give me a pledge, *Ge 38:17*
till thou
If thou *w.* send our brother *Ge 43:4*
with us
But if thou *w.* not send him, *Ge 43:5*
we will
the hand of him whom thou *Ex 4:13*
w. send
if thou *w.* not let my people *Ex 8:21*
go
let them go, and *w.* hold them *Ex 9:2*
still
people, that thou *w.* not let *Ex 9:17*
them go
long *w.* thou refuse to humble *Ex 10:3*
thyself
and if thou *w.* redeem it, *Ex 13:13*
then thou
w. diligently hearken to the *Ex 15:26*
voice
and *w.* do that which is right *Ex 15:26*
in his
w. give ear to his *Ex 15:26*
commandments
Thou *w.* surely wear away, *Ex 18:18*
both thou
And if thou *w.* make an altar *Ex 20:25*
of stone
now, if thou *w.* fogive their *Ex 32:32*
sin
know whom thou *w.* send with *Ex 33:12*
me
w. thou put out the eyes of *Nu 16:14*
these men
and *w.* thou be wroth with *Nu 16:22*
all the
If thou *w.* indeed, deliver this *Nu 21:2*
people
so that thou *w.* not hear, but *De 30:17*
shall be
what *w.* thou do unto thy great *Jos 7:9*
name
Caleb said unto her, What *w.* *J'g 1:14*
thou
If thou *w.* go with me, then *J'g 4:8*
I will go
but if thou *w.* not go with me, *J'g 4:8*
then I
If thou *w.* save Israel by mine *J'g 6:36*
hand
thou *w.* save Israel by mine *J'g 6:37*
hand
W. not thou possess that *J'g 11:24*
which
and if thou *w.* offer a burnt *J'g 13:16*
offering
If thou *w.* redeem it, redeem it *Ru 4:4*
but if thou *w.* not redeem it, *Ru 4:4*
then tell

thou *w.* indeed look on the *1Sa 1:11*
affliction
but *w.* give unto thine *1Sa 1:11*
handmaid a
How long *w.* thou be drunken *1Sa 1:14*
w. thou deliver them into *1Sa 14:37*
the hand
How long *w.* thou mourn for *1Sa 16:1*
Saul
then *w.* thou sin against *1Sa 19:5*
innocent
if thou *w.* take that, take it: *1Sa 21:9*
for there
thou *w.* not cut off my seed *1Sa 24:21*
after me
that thou *w.* not destroy my *1Sa 24:21*
name
know and consider what *1Sa 25:17*
thou *w.* do
by God; that thou *w.* neither *1Sa 30:15*
kill me
w. thou deliver them into *2Sa 5:19*
mine hand
w. thou not tell me? And *2Sa 13:4*
Amnon
Wherefore *w.* thou run, my *2Sa 18:22*
son
why *w.* thou swallow up the *2Sa 20:19*
thou *w.* shew thyself *2Sa 22:26*
merciful
man thou *w.* shew thyself *2Sa 22:26*
upright
the pure thou *w.* shew *2Sa 22:27*
thyself pure
thou *w.* shew thyself *2Sa 22:27*
unsavoury
And the afflicted people thou *2Sa 22:28*
w. save
or *w.* thou flee three months *2Sa 24:13*
before
And if thou *w.* walk in my *1Ki 3:14*
ways
if thou *w.* walk in my *1Ki 6:12*
statutes
And if thou *w.* walk before me *1Ki 9:4*
and *w.* keep my statutes and *1Ki 9:4*
my
w. hearken unto all that I *1Ki 11:38*
command
and *w.* walk in my ways, *1Ki 11:38*
and do that
If thou *w.* be a servant unto *1Ki 12:7*
this
and *w.* serve them, and answer *1Ki 12:7*
them
If thou *w.* give me half thine *1Ki 13:8*
house
W. thou go with me to battle *1Ki 22:4*
to
w. thou go with me against *2Ki 3:7*
Moab to
Wherefore *w.* thou go to him *2Ki 4:23*
to day
the evil that thou *w.* do unto *2Ki 8:12*
their strong holds *w.* thou set *2Ki 8:12*
on fire
men *w.* thou slay with the *2Ki 8:12*
sword
and *w.* dash their children, *2Ki 8:12*
and rip up
How then *w.* thou turn *2Ki 18:24*
away the face
w. thou deliver them into *1Ch 14:10*
mine hand
that thou *w.* build him an *1Ch 17:25*
house
if thou *w.* walk before me, as *2Ch 7:17*
David
king of Judah, *W.* thou go *2Ch 18:3*
with me
affliction, then thou *w.* hear *2Ch 20:9*
and help
O our God, *w.* thou not *2Ch 20:12*
judge them
But if thou *w.* go, do it, be *2Ch 25:8*
strong for
and when thou *w.* return *Ne 2:6*
unto her, What *w.* thou, queen *Es 5:3*
Esther
with thee, *w.* thou be grieved *Job 4:2*
to which of the saints *w.* thou *Job 5:1*
turn
How long *w.* thou not depart *Job 7:19*
from me
How long *w.* thou not speak *Job 8:2*
these
that thou *w.* not hold me *Job 9:28*
innocent
and *w.* thou bring me into *Job 10:9*
dust again

and thou *w*. not acquit me | Job 10:14
from mine
W. thou break a leaf driven | Job 13:25
to and
and *w*. thou pursue the dry | Job 13:25
stubble
w. have a desire to the work | Job 14:15
of thine
I know that thou *w*. bring me | Job 30:23
to death
w. thou condemn him that is | Job 34:17
most
W. thou hunt the prey for | Job 38:39
the lion
or *w*. thou leave thy labour | Job 39:11
to him
W. thou trust him, because | Job 39:11
his
W. thou believe him, that he | Job 39:12
will
W. thou also disannul my | Job 40:8
w. thou condemn me, that | Job 40:8
thou
w. thou take him for a | Job 41:4
servant for
W. thou play with him as | Job 41:5
with a bird
or *w*. thou bind him for thy | Job 41:5
maidens
Lord, *w*. thou bless the | Ps 5:12
righteous
with favour *w*. thou compass | Ps 5:12
him as
in his heart, Thou *w*. not | Ps 10:13
require it
w. prepare their heart, thou | Ps 10:17
w. cause
How long *w*. thou forget me, | Ps 13:1
O Lord
long *w*. thou hide thy face from | Ps 13:1
me
For thou *w*. not leave my | Ps 16:10
soul in hell
w. thou suffer thine Holy One | Ps 16:10
to see
Thou *w*. shew me the path of | Ps 16:11
life
thee, for thou *w*. hear me, O | Ps 17:6
God
thou *w*. shew thyself merciful | Ps 18:25
man thou *w*. shew thyself | Ps 18:25
upright
the pure thou *w*. shew thyself | Ps 18:26
pure
thou *w*. shew thyself froward | Ps 18:26
For thou *w*. save the afflicted | Ps 18:27
people
but *w*. bring down high looks | Ps 18:27
thou *w*. light my candle: the | Ps 18:28
Lord my
Lord, how long *w*. thou look | Ps 35:17
on
thou *w*. hear, O Lord my | Ps 38:15
God
thou *w*. not deliver him unto | Ps 41:2
the will
w. make all his bed in his | Ps 41:3
sickness
heart, O God, thou *w*. not | Ps 51:17
despise
w. not thou deliver my feet | Ps 56:13
from
W. not thou, O God, which | Ps 60:10
hadst
Thou *w*. prolong the king's life | Ps 61:6
in righteousness *w*. thou answer | Ps 65:5
us
Lord? *w*. thou be angry for | Ps 79:5
ever
how long *w*. thou be angry | Ps 80:4
against
O Israel, if thou *w*. hearken | Ps 81:8
unto me
W. thou be angry with us for | Ps 85:5
ever
w. thou draw out thine anger | Ps 85:5
to all
W. thou not revive us again: | Ps 85:6
that thy
upon thee: for thou *w*. answer | Ps 86:7
me
W. thou shew wonders to the | Ps 88:10
dead
Lord? *w*. thou hide thyself | Ps 89:46
for ever
O when *w*. thou come unto | Ps 101:2
me? I will
W. not thou, O God, who | Ps 108:11
hast cast

w. not thou, O God, go | Ps 108:11
forth with our
saying, When *w*. thou | Ps 119:82
comfort me
w. thou execute judgment on | Ps 119:84
them
midst of trouble, thou *w*. | Ps 138:7
revive me
Surely thou *w*. slay the | Ps 139:19
wicked, O God
My son, if thou *w*. receive my | Pr 2:1
words
why *w*. thou, my son, be | Pr 5:20
ravished
How long *w*. thou sleep, O | Pr 6:9
sluggard
when *w*. thou arise out of thy | Pr 6:9
sleep
W. thou set thine eyes upon | Pr 23:5
that
Thou *w*. keep him in perfect | Isa 26:3
peace
Lord, thou *w*. ordain peace | Isa 26:12
for us
shooteth forth, thou *w*. debate | Isa 27:8
with it
How then *w*. thou turn away | Isa 36:9
the face
w. thou make an end of me | Isa 38:12;
| 38:13
so *w*. thou recover me and | Isa 38:16
make
w. thou call this a fast and an | Isa 58:5
W. thou refrain thyself for | Isa 64:12
these
w. thou hold thy peace, and | Isa 64:12
afflict us
W. thou not from this time cry | Jer 3:4
unto
If thou *w*. return, O Israel, | Jer 4:1
saith the
and if thou *w*. put away thine | Jer 4:1
thou art spoiled, what *w*. thou | Jer 4:30
do
w. thou do in the swelling of | Jer 12:5
Jordan
What *w*. thou say when he | Jer 13:21
shall
w. thou not be made clean | Jer 13:27
w. thou be unto me as a | Jer 15:18
liar
How long *w*. thou go about, | Jer 31:22
O thou
w. thou not surely put me to | Jer 38:15
death
w. thou not hearken unto me | Jer 38:15
If thou *w*. assuredly go forth | Jer 38:17
unto the
But if thou *w*. not go forth | Jer 38:18
to the
valley; how long *w*. thou cut | Jer 47:5
thyself
thou *w*. bring the day that | La 1:21
thou hast
w. thou destroy all the residue | Eze 9:8
w. thou make a full end of | Eze 11:13
W. thou judge them, son of | Eze 20:4
man
w. thou judge them? cause | Eze 20:4
them to
thou son of man, *w*. thou | Eze 22:2
judge
w. thou judge the bloody city | Eze 22:2
w. thou judge Aholah and | Eze 23:36
Aholibah
W. thou not tell us these | Eze 24:19
things are
W. thou yet say before him | Eze 28:9
that
W. thou not shew us what | Eze 37:18
thou
O Lord: what *w*. thou give? | Ho 9:14
give them
w. cast all their sins into the | Mic 7:19
depths
Thou *w*. perform the truth to | Mic 7:20
Jacob
shall I cry, and thou *w*. not | Hab 1:2
hear
out of violence, and thou *w*. | Hab 1:2
not save
I said, Surely thou *w*. fear me | Zep 3:7
thou *w*. receive instructions; so | Zep 3:7
their
how long *w*. thou not have | Zec 1:12
mercy on
If thou *w*. walk in my ways, | Zec 3:7
and if
and if thou *w*. keep my charge | Zec 3:7

if thou *w*. fall down and | M't 4:9
worship me
w. thou say to thy brother, Let | M't 7:4
me pull
Lord, if thou *w*. thou canst | M't 8:2
make
W. thou then that we go and | M't 13:28
be it unto thee even as thou | M't 15:28
w.
if thou *w*. let us make here | M't 17:4
three
but if thou *w*. enter into life, | M't 19:17
keep
If thou *w*. be perfect, go | M't 19:21
and sell
he said unto her, What *w*. | M't 20:21
thou
Where *w*. thou that we | M't 26:17
prepare for
not as I will, but as thou *w*. | M't 26:39
If thou *w*. thou canst make | M'k 1:40
me
Ask of me whatsoever thou | M'k 6:22
w. and
What *w*. thou that I should | M'k 10:51
do unto
Where *w*. thou that we go | M'k 14:12
not what I will, but what | M'k 14:36
thou *w*.
If thou therefore *w*. worship | Lu 4:7
me, all
Lord, if thou *w*. thou canst | Lu 5:12
make
w. thou that we command fire | Lu 9:54
to
What *w*. thou that I shall do | Lu 18:41
unto
Where *w*. thou that we | Lu 22:9
prepare
and *w*. thou rear it up in | Joh 2:20
three days
him, *W*. thou be made whole | Joh 5:6
whatsoever thou *w*. ask of | Joh 11:22
God
W. thou lay down thy life | Joh 13:38
for my
that thou *w*. manifest thyself | Joh 14:22
unto us
w. thou at this time restore | Ac 1:6
again the
thou *w*. not leave my soul in | Ac 2:27
hell
neither *w*. thou suffer thine | Ac 2:27
Holy One
W. thou kill me as thou | Ac 7:28
diddest
Lord, what *w*. thou have me to | Ac 9:6
do
w. thou not cease to perverse | Ac 13:10
W. thou go up to Jerusalem | Ac 25:9
Thou *w*. say then unto me, | Ro 9:19
Why
Thou *w*. say then, The | Ro 11:19
branches
W. thou then not be afraid of | Ro 13:3
thou *w*. also do more than I | Ph'm 21
say
But *w*. thou know, O vain | Jas 2:20
man

WILY

plottings of the *w*. (B)(R) | Job 5:13

WIMPLES

and the *w*. and the crisping | Isa 3:22
pins
the shawls (A)(B)(E) | Isa 3:22
the cloaks (R) | Isa 3:22

WIN

thought to *w*. them for | 2Ch 32:1
himself
thinking to take them (A)(B) | 2Ch 32:1
make treachery to *w*. out (B) | Da 8:25
w. a wreath (A)(N)(R) | 1Co 9:25
but dung, that I may *w*. | Ph'p 3:8
Christ
gain (B)(R) | Ph'p 3:8
w. his wife in purity and honor | 1Th 4:4
(B)

WIND

God made a *w*. to pass over | Ge 8:1
blasted with the east *w*. | Ge 41:6;
sprung up | 41:23
empty ears blasted with the | Ge 41:27
east *w*.

Lord brought an east *w.* upon the   *Ex 10:13*

the east *w.* brought the locusts   *Ex 10:13*

turned a mighty strong west *w.*   *Ex 10:19*

sea to go back by a strong *w.*   *Ex 14:21*

Thou didst blow with thy *w.*   *Ex 15:10*

went forth a *w.* from the Lord, and   *Nu 11:31*

was seen upon the wings of the *w.*   *2Sa 22:11*

was black with clouds and *w.*   *1Ki 18:45*

and strong, *w.* rent the mountains   *1Ki 19:11*

but the Lord was not in the *w.*   *1Ki 19:11*

and after the *w.* an earthquake   *1Ki 19:11*

Ye shall not see *w.* neither shall   *2Ki 3:17*

a great *w.* from the wilderness   *Job 1:19*

a great whirlwind (A)   *Job 1:19*

is desperate, which are as *w.*   *Job 6:26*

O remember that my life is *w.*   *Job 7:7*

of thy mouth be like a strong *w.*   *Job 8:2*

and fill his belly with the east *w.*   *Job 15:2*

swept away by the *w.* (A)(B)(R)   *Job 15:30*

They are as stubble before the *w.*   *Job 21:18*

The east *w.* carrieth him away, and   *Job 27:21*

they pursue my soul as the *w.*   *Job 30:15*

Thou liftest me up to the *w.*; thou   *Job 30:22*

quieteth the earth by the south *w.*   *Job 37:17*

but the *w.* passeth, and cleanseth   *Job 37:21*

scattereth the east *w.* upon the earth   *Job 38:24*

chaff which the *w.* driveth away   *Ps 1:4*

he did fly upon the wings of the *w.*   *Ps 18:10*

small as the dust before the *w.*   *Ps 18:42*

Let them be as chaff before the *w.*   *Ps 35:5*

ships of Tarshish with an east *w.*   *Ps 48:7*

He caused an east *w.* to blow in the   *Ps 78:26*

power he brought in the south *w.*   *Ps 78:26*

a *w.* that passeth away, and   *Ps 78:39*

wheel; as the stubble before the *w.*   *Ps 83:13*

For the *w.* passeth over it, and it is   *Ps 103:16*

walketh upon the wings of the *w.*   *Ps 104:3*

and raiseth the stormy *w.*   *Ps 107:25*

bringeth the *w.* out of his treasuries   *Ps 135:7*

he caused his *w.* to blow   *Ps 147:18*

stormy *w.* fulfilling his word   *Ps 148:8*

his own house shall inherit the *w.*   *Pr 25:14*

like clouds and *w.* without rain   *Pr 25:14*

The north *w.* driveth away rain   *Pr 25:23*

hideth her hideth the *w.* and   *Pr 27:16*

hath gathered the *w.* in his fists   *Pr 30:4*

w. goeth toward the south, and   *Ec 1:6*

w. returneth again according to   *Ec 1:6*

feeding on *w.* (A)   *Ec 1:14*

chasing after *w.* (B)(E)(R)   *Ec 1:14;*
1:17; 2:11, 17; 2:26; 4:4, 6, 16; 6:9

futility and chasing *w.* (B)   *Ec 4:4; 4:16*

he that hath laboured for the *w.*   *Ec 5:16*

striving after *w.* (B)   *Ec 6:9*

observeth the *w.* shall not sow   *Ec 11:4*

what is the way of the *w.* (S)   *Ec 11:5*

Awake, O north *w.*; and come, thou   *Ca 4:16*

the wood are moved with the *w.*   *Isa 7:2*

with his mighty *w.* shall he shake   *Isa 11:15*

of the mountains before the *w.*   *Isa 17:13*

have as it were brought forth *w.*   *Isa 26:18*

he stayeth his rough *w.*   *Isa 27:8*

in the day of the east *w.*   *Isa 27:8*

be as an hiding place from the *w.*   *Isa 32:2*

I will send a *w.* upon him (S)   *Isa 37:7*

and the *w.* shall carry them away   *Isa 41:16*

molten images are *w.* and confusion   *Isa 41:29*

images are *w.* and waste (B)(R)   *Isa 41:29*

the *w.* shall carry them all away   *Isa 57:13*

iniquities, like the *w.* have taken   *Isa 64:6*

snuffeth up the *w.* at her pleasure   *Jer 2:24*

A dry *w.* of the high places in   *Jer 4:11*

w. from those places shall come   *Jer 4:12*

And the prophets shall become *w.*   *Jer 5:13*

forth the *w.* out of his treasures   *Jer 10:13*

away by the *w.* of the wilderness   *Jer 13:24*

snuffed up the *w.* like dragons   *Jer 14:6*

will scatter them as with an east *w.*   *Jer 18:17*

The *w.* shall eat up all thy pastors   *Jer 22:22*

up against me, a destroying *w.*   *Jer 51:1*

forth the *w.* out of his treasurers   *Jer 51:16*

part thou shalt scatter in the *w.*   *Eze 5:2*

scatter toward every *w.* all that are   *Eze 12:14*

fall; and a stormy *w.* shall   *Eze 13:11*

rend it with a stormy *w.* in my fury   *Eze 13:13*

when the east *w.* toucheth it   *Eze 17:10*

and the east *w.* dried up her fruit   *Eze 19:12*

the east *w.* hath broken thee in   *Eze 27:26*

he unto me, Prophesy unto the *w.*   *Eze 37:9*

son of man, and say to the *w.*   *Eze 37:9*

and the *w.* carried them away   *Da 2:35*

The *w.* hath bound her up in her   *Ho 4:19*

they have sown the *w.* and they   *Ho 8:7*

Ephraim feedeth on *w.*   *Ho 12:1*

and followeth after the east *w.*   *Ho 12:1*

brethren, an east *w.* shall come   *Ho 13:15*

the *w.* of the Lord shall come up   *Ho 13:15*

mountains, and createth the *w.*   *Am 4:13*

sent out a great *w.* into the sea   *Jon 1:4*

God prepared a vehement east *w.*   *Jon 4:8*

their faces shall sup up as the east *w.*   *Hab 1:9*

and the *w.* was in their wings   *Zec 5:9*

to see. A reed shaken with the *w.*   *M't 11:7; Lu 7:24*

with waves: for the *w.* was contrary   *M't 14:24*

But when he saw the *w.* boisterous   *M't 14:30*

come into the ship, the *w.* ceased   *M't 14:32*

And there arose a great storm of *w.*   *M'k 4:37*

And he arose, and rebuked the *w.*   *M'k 4:39*

the *w.* ceased, and there was a great   *M'k 4:39*

even the *w.* and the sea obey him   *M'k 4:41*

for the *w.* was contrary unto them   *M'k 6:48*

into the ship; and the *w.* ceased   *M'k 6:51*

down a storm of *w.* on the lake   *Lu 8:23*

rebuked the *w.* and the raging of   *Lu 8:24*

And when ye see the south *w.* blow   *Lu 12:55*

The *w.* bloweth where it listeth   *Joh 3:8*

w. blows where it will (A)(E)(N)   *Joh 3:8*

by reason of the great *w.* that blew   *Joh 6:18*

heaven as of a rushing mighty *w.*   *Ac 2:2*

the *w.* not suffering us, we sailed   *Ac 27:7*

And when the south *w.* blew softly   *Ac 27:13*

arose against it a tempestuous *w.*   *Ac 27:14*

and could not bear up into the *w.*   *Ac 27:15*

hoisted up the mainsail to the *w.*   *Ac 27:40*

and after one day the south *w.* blew   *Ac 28:13*

about with every *w.* of doctrine   *Eph 4:14*

wave of the sea driven with the *w.*   *Jas 1:6*

when she is shaken of a mighty *w.*   *Re 6:13*

the *w.* should not blow on the earth   *Re 7:1*

WINDING

they went up with *w.* stairs   *1Ki 6:8*

a *w.* about still upward to the side   *Eze 41:7*

w. about of the house went still   *Eze 41:7*

WINDOW

A *w.* shalt thou make to the ark   *Ge 6:16*

an opening in the ark all around (B)   *Ge 6:16*

a light make to the ark (E)   *Ge 6:16*

Noah opened the *w.* of the ark   *Ge 8:6*

the Philistines looked out at a *w.*   *Ge 26:8*

down by a cord through the *w.*   *Jos 2:15*

bind this line of thread in the *w.*   *Jos 2:18*

she bound the scarlet line in the *w.*   *Jos 2:21*

of Sisera looked out at a *w.*   *J'g 5:28*

let David down through a *w.*   *1Sa 19:12*

daughter looked through a *w.*   *2Sa 6:16*

her head, and looked out at a *w.*   *2Ki 9:30*

And he lifted up his face to *w.*   *2Ki 9:32*

And he said, Open the *w.* eastward   *2Ki 13:17*

looking out at a *w.* saw king David   *1Ch 15:29*

at the *w.* of my house I looked   *Pr 7:6*

sat in a *w.* a certain young man   *Ac 20:9*

through a *w.* in a basket was I let   *2Co 11:33*

WINDOWS

and the *w.* of heaven were opened   *Ge 7:11*

and the *w.* of heaven were stopped   *Ge 8:2*

he made *w.* of narrow lights   *1Ki 6:4*

And there were *w.* in three rows   *1Ki 7:4*

posts were square, with the *w.*   *1Ki 7:5*

Lord would make *w.* in heaven   *2Ki 7:2*

Lord should make *w.* in heaven   *2Ki 7:19*

that look out of the *w.* be darkened   *Ec 12:3*

he looketh forth at the *w.*   *Ca 2:9*

for the *w.* from on high are opened   *Isa 24:18*

I will make thy *w.* of agates   *Isa 54:12*

pinnacles of agates (B)(E)(R)   *Isa 54:12*

and as the doves to the *w.*   *Isa 60:8*

dove-cote openings (B)   *Isa 60:8*

For death is come up into our *w.*   *Jer 9:21*

chambers, and cutteth him out *w.*   *Jer 22:14*

narrow *w.* to the little chambers   *Eze 40:16*

and *w.* were round about inward   *Eze 40:16*

And their w. and their　　Eze 40:22
arches, and
were w. in it and in the　Eze 40:25;
arches　　　　　　　　　　40:29
thereof round about, like　Eze 40:25
those w.
were w. therein and in the　Eze 40:33
arches
and the w. to it round about　Eze 40:36
The door posts, and the　Eze 41:16
narrow w.
and from the ground up to　Eze 41:16
the w.
and the w. were covered　Eze 41:16
were narrow w. and palm　Eze 41:26
trees
his w. being open in his　　Da 6:10
chamber
shall enter in at the w. like a　Joe 2:9
thief
their voice shall sing in the w.　Zep 2:14
wail in the w. (B)　　　　　Zep 2:14
will not open you the w. of　Mal 3:10
heaven

WINDS

To make the weight for the　Job 28:25
w.
who makes w. messengers　Ps 104:4
(A)(E)(R)
I will scatter into all w. them　Jer 49:32
that
upon Elam will I bring the　Jer 49:36
four w.
scatter them toward all those　Jer 49:36
w.
of thee will I scatter into all　Eze 5:10
the w.
scatter a third part into all　Eze 5:12
the w.
shall be scattered toward all　Eze 17:21
w.
Come from the four w. O　Eze 37:9
breath
the four w. of the heaven　　Da 7:2
strove
ones toward the four w. of　Da 8:8
heaven
toward the four w. of heaven　Da 11:4
as the four w. of the heaven　Zec 2:6
the four w. of heaven　　　Zec 6:5
(B)(E)(R)
the floods came, and the w.　M't 7:25;
blew　　　　　　　　　　　7:27
and rebuked the w. and the　M't 8:26
sea
even the w. and the sea obey　M't 8:27
him
together his elect from the　M't 24:31;
four w.　　　　　　　　　M'k 13:27
commandeth even the w. and　Lu 8:25
water
because the w. were contrary　Ac 27:4
who makes his angels w.　　Heb 1:7
(A)(E)(N)(P)(R)
are driven of fierce w. yet are　Jas 3:4
they
without water, carried about　Jude 12
of w.
holding the four w. of the earth　Re 7:1

WINDSTORM

w., whirlwind (A)(B)　　　　Job 27:20

WINDY

w. knowledge (A)(R)　　　Job 15:2
w. words (R)　　　　　　Job 16:3
my escape from the w. storm　Ps 55:8

WINE

And he drank of the w. and　Ge 9:21
Noah awoke from his w. and　Ge 9:24
knew
Salem brought forth bread,　Ge 14:18
and w.
let us make our father drink　Ge 19:32
w.
they made their father drink　Ge 19:33
w.
make him drink w. this night　Ge 19:34
also
they made their father drink　Ge 19:35
w.
he brought him w. and he　Ge 27:25
drank
earth, and plenty of corn and　Ge 27:28
w.

corn and w. have I sustained　Ge 27:37
him
he washed his garments in w.　Ge 49:11
His eyes shall be red with w.　Ge 49:12
the fourth part of an hin of　Ex 29:40
w.
Do not drink w. nor strong　Le 10:9
drink
drink offering thereof shall be　Le 23:13
of w.
He shall separate himself from　Nu 6:3
w.
and shall drink no vinegar of　Nu 6:3
w.
that the Nazarite may drink w.　Nu 6:20
the fourth part of an hin of　Nu 15:5
w.
offer the third part of an hin　Nu 15:7
of w.
a drink offering half an hin　Nu 15:10
of w.
all the best of the w. and of　Nu 18:12
cause the strong w. to be　Nu 28:7
poured
offerings shall be half an hin　Nu 28:14
of w.
of thy land, thy corn, and thy　De 7:13
w.
gather in thy corn, and thy　De 11:14
w.
the tithe of thy corn, or of　De 12:17;
thy w.　　　　　　　　　14:23
for sheep, or for w. or for　De 14:26
strong
gathered in thy corn, and thy　De 16:13
w.
also of the corn, of the w. and　De 18:4
of
but shalt neither drink of the　De 28:39
w.
leave thee either corn, w. or　De 28:51
oil
neither have ye drunk w. or　De 29:6
strong
Their w. is the poison of　　De 32:33
dragons
and drank the w. of their　　De 32:38
drink
be upon a land of corn and　De 33:28
w.
and w. bottles, old, and rent　Jos 9:4
these bottles of w. which we　Jos 9:13
filled
Should I leave my w. which　J'g 9:13
and drink not w. nor strong　J'g 13:4
drink
now drink no w. nor strong　J'g 13:7
drink
let her drink w. or strong　J'g 13:14
drink
there is bread and w. also for　J'g 19:19
me
put away thy w. from thee　1Sa 1:14
drunk neither w. nor strong　1Sa 1:15
drink
ephah of flour, and a bottle　1Sa 1:24
of w.
another carrying a bottle of　1Sa 10:3
w.
with bread, and a bottle of　1Sa 16:20
w.
hundred loaves, two bottles　1Sa 25:18
of w.
when the w. was gone out of　1Sa 25:37
Nabal
piece of flesh, and a flagon of　2Sa 6:19
w.
Ammon's heart is merry with　2Sa 13:28
w.
summer fruits, and a bottle of　2Sa 16:1
w.
and the w. that such as be　2Sa 16:2
faint
own land, a land of corn　2Ki 18:32
and w.
fine flour, and the w. and　1Ch 9:29
the oil
bunches of raisins, and w.　1Ch 12:40
and oil
good piece of flesh, and a　1Ch 16:3
flagon of w.
of the vineyards for the w.　1Ch 27:27
cellars
and twenty thousand baths　2Ch 2:10
of w.
and the w. which my lord　2Ch 2:15
hath
store of victual, and of oil　2Ch 11:11
and w.

the firstfruits of corn, w. and　2Ch 31:5
oil
increase of corn, and w. and　2Ch 32:28
oil
God of heaven, wheat, salt, w.　Ezr 6:9
and to an hundred baths of　Ezr 7:22
w.
the king, that w. was before　Ne 2:1
him
and I took up the w. and gave it　Ne 2:1
the w. and the oil, that ye　Ne 5:11
exact
had taken of them bread and　Ne 5:15
w.
ten days store of all sorts of　Ne 5:18
w.
of w. and of oil, unto the　Ne 10:37
priests
offering of the corn, of the　Ne 10:39
new w.
tithes of the corn, the new w.　Ne 13:5
the new w. and the oil unto　Ne 13:12
some treading w. presses on　Ne 13:15
as also w. grapes, and figs　Ne 13:15
and royal w. in abundance　　Es 1:7
of the king was merry with w.　Es 1:10
unto Esther at the banquet of　Es 5:6
w.
second day at the banquet of　Es 7:2
arising from the banquet of w.　Es 7:7
in
into the place of the banquet of　Es 7:8
w.
and drinking w. in their　　Job 1:13;
eldest　　　　　　　　　　1:18
belly is as w. which hath no　Job 32:19
vent
their corn and their w.　　　Ps 4:7
increased
to drink the w. of　　　　　Ps 60:3
astonishment
there is a cup, and the w. is　Ps 75:8
red
man that shouteth by reason　Ps 78:65
of w.
w. that maketh glad the　　Ps 104:15
heart of
shall burst out with new w.　Pr 3:10
and drink the w. of violence　Pr 4:17
beasts; she hath mingled her w.　Pr 9:2
and drink of the w. which I　Pr 9:5
have
W. is a mocker, strong drink　Pr 20:1
is
he that loveth w. and oil shall　Pr 21:17
not
They that tarry long at the w.　Pr 23:30
they that go to seek mixed w.　Pr 23:30
Look not thou upon the w.　Pr 23:31
when
it is not for kings to drink w.　Pr 31:4
and w. unto those that be of　Pr 31:6
heavy
mine heart to give myself unto　Ec 2:3
w.
drink thy w. with a merry heart　Ec 9:7
for laughter, and w. maketh　Ec 10:19
merry
for thy love is better than w.　Ca 1:2
remember thy love more than　Ca 1:4
w.
much better is thy love than　Ca 4:10
w.
I have drunk my w. with my　Ca 5:1
milk
mingled w. is never missing　Ca 7:2
(B)(E)
like the best w. for my beloved　Ca 7:9
cause thee to drink of spiced　Ca 8:2
w.
dross, thy w. mixed with　Isa 1:22
water
until night, till w. inflame　Isa 5:11
them
pipe, and w. are in their　Isa 5:12
feasts
them that are mighty to drink　Isa 5:22
w.
tread out no w. in their　　Isa 16:10
presses
eating flesh, and drinking w.　Isa 22:13
The new w. mourneth, the　Isa 24:7
vine
shall not drink w. with a song　Isa 24:9
is a crying for w. in the　Isa 24:11
streets
ye unto her, A vineyard of　Isa 27:2
red w.
them that are overcome with　Isa 28:1
w.

they also have erred through *w.*   *Isa 28:7*
drink, they are swallowed up *Isa 28:7* of *w.*
they are drunken, but not *Isa 29:9* with *w.*
own land, a land of corn and *Isa 36:17* *w.*
their own blood, as with *Isa 49:26* sweet *w.*
and drunken, but not with *w.* *Isa 51:21*
buy *w.* and milk without *Isa 55:1* money
Come ye, say they, I will *Isa 56:12* fetch *w.*
the stranger shall not drink *Isa 62:8* thy *w.*
new *w.* is found in the cluster *Isa 65:8*
bottle shall be filled with *w.* *Jer 13:12*
every bottle shall be filled *Jer 13:12* with *w.*
like a man whom *w.* hath *Jer 23:9* overcome
Take the *w.* cup of this fury *Jer 25:15* at my
for wheat, and for *w.* and for *Jer 31:12* oil
chambers, and give them *w.* to *Jer 35:2* drink
of the Rechabites pots full of *Jer 35:5* *w.*
and I said unto them, Drink *Jer 35:5* ye *w.*
they said, We will drink no *w.* *Jer 35:6*
Ye shall drink no *w.* neither *Jer 35:6*
us, to drink no *w.* all our days *Jer 35:8*
his sons not to drink *w.* *Jer 35:14*
gather ye *w.* and summer *Jer 40:10* fruits
gathered *w.* and summer *Jer 40:12* fruits very
w. to fail from the *Jer 48:33* winepresses
the nations have drunken of *Jer 51:7* her *w.*
mothers, Where is corn and *w.* *La 2:12*
in the *w.* of Helbon, and *Eze 27:18* white wool
Neither shall any priest drink *Eze 44:21* *w.*
meat, and of the *w.* which he *Da 1:5* drank
nor with the *w.* which he *Da 1:8* drank
and the *w.* that they should *Da 1:16* drink
and drank *w.* before the *Da 5:1* thousand
Belshazzar, whiles he tasted the *Da 5:2* *w.*
They drank *w.* and praised the *Da 5:4*
concubines, have drunk *w.* in *Da 5:23* them
come flesh nor *w.* in my *Da 10:3* mouth
know that I have her corn, and *Ho 2:8* *w.*
and my *w.* in the season *Ho 2:9* thereof
shall hear the corn, and the *Ho 2:22* *w.*
other gods, and love flagons of *Ho 3:1* *w.*
Whoredom and *w.* and new *Ho 4:11*
and new *w.* take away the *Ho 4:11* heart
made him sick with bottles of *Ho 7:5* *w.*
themselves for corn and *w.* *Ho 7:14*
and the new *w.* shall fail in her *Ho 9:2*
They shall not offer *w.* *Ho 9:4* offerings
shall be as the *w.* of Lebanon *Ho 14:7*
and howl, all ye drinkers of *w.* *Joe 1:5*
because of the new *w.*; for it is *Joe 1:5* cut
the new *w.* is dried up, the *Joe 1:10* oil
I will send you corn, and *w.* *Joe 2:19* and
vats shall overflow with *w.* *Joe 2:24* and oil
sold a girl for *w.* that they *Joe 3:3* might
shall drop down new *w.* *Joe 3:18*
drink the *w.* of the condemned *Am 2:8*
ye gave the Nazarites *w.* to *Am 2:12* drink
but ye shall not drink *w.* of *Am 5:11* them

That drink *w.* in bowls, and *Am 6:6* anoint
the mountains shall drop *Am 9:13* sweet *w.*
plant vineyards, and drink *Am 9:14* the *w.*
I will prophesy unto thee of *Mic 2:11* *w.*
anoint thee with oil; and *Mic 6:15* sweet *w.*
but shalt not drink *w.* *Mic 6:15*
because he transgresseth by *w.* *Hab 2:5*
but not drink the *w.* thereof *Zep 1:13*
upon the new *w.* and upon *Hag 1:11* the oil
do touch bread, or pottage, *Hag 2:12* or *w.*
and make a noise as through *Zec 9:15* *w.*
cheerful, and new *w.* the *Zec 9:17* maids
heart shall rejoice as through *Zec 10:7* *w.*
men put new *w.* into old *M't 9:17* bottles
and the *w.* runneth out, and *M't 9:17*
they put new *w.* into new *M't 9:17* bottles
a *w.* drinker *M't 11:19* (A)(B)(N)(P)(R)
putteth new *w.* into old *M'k 2:22;* bottles *Lu 5:37*
the new *w.* doth burst the *M'k 2:22* bottles
and the *w.* is spilled, and the *M'k 2:22*
but new *w.* must be put into *M'k 2:22;* new *Lu 5:38*
the *w.* press (S) *M'k 12:1*
to drink *w.* mingled with *M'k 15:23* myrrh
drink neither *w.* nor strong *Lu 1:15* drink
the new *w.* will burst the *Lu 5:37* bottles
having drunk old *w.* *Lu 5:39* straightway
eating bread nor drinking *w.* *Lu 7:33*
his wounds, pouring in oil *Lu 10:34* and *w.*
when they wanted *w.* the *Joh 2:3* mother
saith unto him, They have no *Joh 2:3* *w.*
tasted the water that was *Joh 2:9* made *w.*
beginning doth set forth good *Joh 2:10* *w.*
hast kept the good *w.* until *Joh 2:10* now
where he made the water *w.* *Joh 4:46*
said, These men are full of *Ac 2:13* new *w.*
to eat flesh, nor to drink *w.* *Ro 14:21*
And be not drunk with *w.* *Eph 5:18* wherein
Not given to *w.* no striker, not *1Ti 3:3;* *Tit 1:7*
not given to much *w.* not *1Ti 3:8* greedy
use a little *w.* for thy *1Ti 5:23* stomach's
not given to much *w.*, teachers *Tit 2:3* of
lusts, excess of *w.* revellings *1Pe 4:3*
thou hurt not the oil and the *w.* *Re 6:6*
drink of the *w.* of the wrath *Re 14:8* of her
drink of the *w.* of the wrath *Re 14:10* of God
the cup of the *w.* of the *Re 16:19* fierceness
drunk with the *w.* of her *Re 17:2* fornication
have drunk of the *w.* of the *Re 18:3* wrath
and *w.* and oil, and fine *Re 18:13* flour, and

WINE *CELLARS*

the vineyards for the *w.* *1Ch 27:27* cellars

WINEBIBBER

and a *w.*, a friend of *M't 11:19;* publicans and *Lu 7:34*
wine drinker (A)(B) *M't 11:19;* *Lu 7:34*

a drinker (N) *M't 11:19; Lu 7:34*
a drunkard (P)(R) *M't 11:19; Lu 7:34*

WINEBIBBERS

Be not among *w.*; among *Pr 23:20*

WINEPRESS

and as the fulness of the *w.* *Nu 18:27*
and as the increase of the *w.* *Nu 18:30*
out of thy floor, and out of *De 15:14* thy *w.*
Gibeon threshed wheat by the *J'g 6:11* *w.*
Zeeb they slew at the *w.* of *J'g 7:25* Zeeb
of the barnfloor, or out of *2Ki 6:27* the *w.*
of it, and also made a *w.* *Isa 5:2* therein
tread in the *w.* (A)(B)(R) *Isa 63:2;* *M'k 12:1*
I have trodden the *w.* alone *Isa 63:3*
the daughter of Judah, as in a *La 1:15* *w.*
The floor and the *w.* shall not *Ho 9:2* feed
and digged a *w.* in it, and *M't 21:33* built a
great *w.* of the wrath of God *Re 14:19*
w. was trodden without the *Re 14:20* city
and blood came out of the *w.* *Re 14:20* even
treadeth the *w.* of the *Re 19:15* fierceness

WINEPRESSES

I saw Judah treading *w.* *Ne 13:15*
tread their *w.* and suffer *Job 24:11* thirst
caused wine to fail from the *Jer 48:33* *w.*
of Hananeel unto the king's *Zec 14:10* *w.*

WINES

a feast of *w.* on the lees, of fat *Isa 25:6*
of *w.* on the lees well refined *Isa 25:6*

WINESKIN

took old *w.* (A)(B)(E)(R) *Jos 9:4;* *9:13*
like a *w.* in smoke *Ps 119:83* (B)(E)(R)
bottle (S) *Ps 119:83;* *Jer 13:12; Hab 2:15*
put your *w.* (B) *Hab 2:15*

WINESKINS

like new *w.* (A)(B)(E)(R) *Job 32:19*
wineskins (S) *Job 32:19;* *M't 9:17; M'k 2:22; Lu 5:37-38*
old *w.* *M't 9:17;* (A)(B)(E)(N)(P)(R) *M'k 2:22;Lu 5:37*

WINEVAT

like him that treadeth in the *Isa 63:2* *w.*
winepress (A)(B)(R) *Isa 63:2;* *M'k 12:1*
gone to the *w.* *Hag 2:16* (A)(B)(E)(R)(S)
and digged a place for the *w.* *M'k 12:1*
winepress (E)(N)(P) *M'k 12:1*

WING

was the one *w.* of the cherub *1Ki 6:24*
cubits the other *w.* of the *1Ki 6:24* cherub
uttermost part of the one *w.* *1Ki 6:24* unto
w. of the one touched the one *1Ki 6:27* wall
w. of the other cherub *1Ki 6:27* touched the
one *w.* of the one cherub was *2Ch 3:11* five
other *w.* was likewise five *2Ch 3:11* cubits
reaching to the *w.* of the *2Ch 3:11* other
one *w.* of the other cherub *2Ch 3:12* was five

and the other w. was five cubits   2Ch 3:12

joining to w. of the other cherub   2Ch 3:12

there was none that moved the w.   Isa 10:14

it shall dwell all fowl of every w.   Eze 17:23

the w. or pinnacle of (A)(B)(E)(R)   Da 9:27

WINGED

and every w. fowl after his kind   Ge 1:21

the w. insects   Le 11:20; 11:21, 23

among w. insects (A)(B)(R)   Le 11:21

likeness of any w. fowl that flieth in   De 4:17

WINGS

and how I bare you on eagles' w.   Ex 19:4

cherubims stretch forth their w.   Ex 25:20

the mercy seat with their w.   Ex 25:20

the cherubims spread out their w.   Ex 37:9

and covered with their w. over   Ex 37:9

shall cleave it with the w. thereof   Le 1:17

her young, spreadeth abroad her w.   De 32:11

them, beareth them on her w.   De 32:11

under whose w. thou art come to   Ru 2:12

was seen upon the w. of the wind   2Sa 22:11

they stretched forth the w. of   1Ki 6:27

their w. touched one another in the   1Ki 6:27

even under the w. of the cherubims   1Ki 8:6

spread forth their two w. over   1Ki 8:7

cherubims, that spread out their w.   1Ch 28:18

w. of the cherubims were twenty   2Ch 3:11

The w. of these cherubims spread   2Ch 3:13

even under the w. of the cherubims   2Ch 5:7

cherubims spread forth their w.   2Ch 5:8

the goodly w. unto the peacocks   Job 39:13

or w. and feathers unto the ostrich   Job 39:13

stretch her w. toward the south   Job 39:26

hide me under the shadow of thy w.   Ps 17:8

he did fly upon the w. of the wind   Ps 18:10

trust under the shadow of thy w.   Ps 36:7

said, Oh that I had w. like a dove   Ps 55:6

in the shadow of thy w. will I   Ps 57:1

I will trust in the covert of thy w.   Ps 61:4

the shadow of thy w. will I rejoice   Ps 63:7

w. of a dove covered with silver   Ps 68:13

and under his w. shalt thou trust   Ps 91:4

walketh upon the w. of the wind   Ps 104:3

If I take the w. of the morning, and   Ps 139:9

for riches make themselves w.   Pr 23:5

which hath w. shall tell the matter   Ec 10:20

the seraphims: each one had six w.   Isa 6:2

the stretching out of his w. shall   Isa 8:8

Woe to the land shadowing with w.   Isa 18:1

shall mount up with w. as eagles   Isa 40:31

Give w. unto Moab, that it may   Jer 48:9

and shall spread his w. over Moab   Jer 48:40

and spread his w. over Bozrah: and   Jer 49:22

faces and every one had four w.   Eze 1:6

the hands of a man under their w.   Eze 1:8; 10:21

fear had their faces and their w.   Eze 1:8

Their w. were joined one to   Eze 1:9

their w. were stretched upward   Eze 1:11

two w. of every one were joined one   Eze 1:11

firmament were their w. straight   Eze 1:23

I heard the noise of their w. like   Eze 1:24

they stood, they let down their w.   Eze 1:24

stood, and had let down their w.   Eze 1:25

of the w. of the living creatures   Eze 3:13

the sound of the cherubims' w. was   Eze 10:5

of a man's hand under their w.   Eze 10:8

and their hands, and their w. and   Eze 10:12

the cherubims lifted up their w. to   Eze 10:16; 10:19

apiece, and every one four w.   Eze 10:21

did the cherubims lift up their w.   Eze 11:22

A great eagle with great w.   Eze 17:3

another great eagle with great w.   Eze 17:7

cherub with overshadowing w. (A)(B)   Eze 28:14

was like a lion, and had eagle's w.   Da 7:4

till the w. thereof were plucked   Da 7:4

the back of it four w. of a fowl   Da 7:6

wind hath bound her up in her w.   Ho 4:19

and the wind was in their w.   Zec 5:9

they had w. like the w. of a stork   Zec 5:9

arise with healing in his w.   Mal 4:2

healing in its beams (B)   Mal 4:2

her chickens under her w.   M't 23:37

gather her brood under her w.   Lu 13:34

four beasts had each of them six w.   Re 4:8

sound of their w. was as the sound   Re 9:9

noise made by w. (A)(B)(P)(R)   Re 9:9

given two w. of a great eagle   Re 12:14

WINK

away? and what do thy eyes w. at   Job 15:12

eyes flash (A)(B)(E)(R)   Job 15:12

them w. with the eye that hate me   Ps 35:19

WINKED

times of this ignorance God w. at   Ac 17:30

God ignored and allowed to pass unnoticed (A)   Ac 17:30

God paid no attention to those seasons of ignorance (B)   Ac 17:30

the times of ignorance God overlooked (E)(N)(P)(R)   Ac 17:30

WINKETH

He w. with his eyes, he speaketh   Pr 6:13

He that w. with the eye causeth   Pr 10:10

WINNETH

life: and he that w. souls is wise   Pr 11:30

captures human lives for God (A)   Pr 11:30

lawlessness takes away lives (R)   Pr 11:30

WINNOWED

threshed and w. one (A)(B)(R)   Isa 21:10

hath been w. with the shovel   Isa 30:24

where you had not w. (A)(B)(R)   M't 25:24; 25:26

WINNOWER

the w. in his hand (B)   M't 3:12

WINNOWERS

will send unto Babylon w. (S)   Jer 51:2

WINNOWETH

he w. barley to night in the   Ru 3:2

WINNOWING

his w.-bark in his hand (R)   M't 3:12

WINS

gracious woman w. honor (A)(B)(R)   Pr 11:16

WINTER

cold and heat, and summer and w.   Ge 8:22

thou hast made summer and w.   Ps 74:17

the w. is past, the rain is over   Ca 2:11

the beasts shall w. upon them   Isa 18:6

I will smite the w. house with the   Am 3:15

in summer and in w. shall it be   Zec 14:8

that your flight may not be in w.   M't 24:20; M'k 13:18

of the dedication, and it was w.   Joh 10:22

have was not commodious to w. in   Ac 27:12

attain to Phenice, and there to w.   Ac 27:12

I will abide, yea, and w. with you   1Co 16:6

thy diligence to come before w.   2Ti 4:21

for I have determined there to w.   Tit 3:12

sheds its w. fruit (R)   Re 6:13

WINTERED

which had w. in the isle   Ac 28:11

WINTERHOUSE

the king sat in the w. in the ninth   Jer 36:22

WIPE

w. out (B)   Ge 18:23; 18:24

w. off the face of earth (B)   De 6:15

w. them out (B)   De 9:14

do not w. out thy people (B)   De 9:26

w. out Baal (R)   2Ki 10:28

and I will w. Jerusalem as a man   2Ki 21:13

w. not out my good deeds that I   Ne 13:14

do not expunge benevolent service (B)   Ne 13:14

to slay, to w. out (A)   Es 8:11

Lord God will w. away tears from   Isa 25:8

did w. them with the hairs of her   Lu 7:38

on us, we do w. off against you   Lu 10:11

and to w. them with the towel   Joh 13:5

God shall w. away all tears from   Re 7:17; 21:4

WIPED

be w. out (B)   1Sa 26:10

w. out of existence (A)   Es 7:4

his reproach shall not be w. away   Pr 6:33

handiworks w. out (A)(R)   Eze 6:6

w. them with the hairs of her head   Lu 7:44

and w. his feet with her hair   Joh 11:2; 12:3

WIPETH

Jerusalem as a man w. a dish   2Ki 21:13

she eateth, and w. her mouth   Pr 30:20

WIPING

w. it and turning it upside   2Ki 21:13
down
w. out sins of the past (P)   Ro 3:25

WIRES

into thin plates and cut it into   Ex 39:3
w.
cut into threads (B)(R)   Ex 39:3

WISDOM

I have filled with the spirit   Ex 28:3
of w.
endowed with skill and good   Ex 28:3
judgment (A)
endowed with skill (B)   Ex 28:3;
               31:3, 6; 35:26, 31; 36:2
endowed with an able mind   Ex 28:3
(R)
with the spirit of God, in w.   Ex 31:3
are wise hearted I have put w.   Ex 31:6
whose heart stirred them up   Ex 35:26
in w.
with the spirit of God, in w.   Ex 35:31
hath he filled with w. of   Ex 35:35
heart
filled them with ability (R)   Ex 35:35
in whom the Lord put w. and   Ex 36:1
dexterity and understanding   Ex 36:1
(B)
put ability and intelligence (R)   Ex 36:1;
               36:2
in whose heart the Lord had   Ex 36:2
put w.
men of w. (B)   De 1:13
is your w. and your   De 4:6
understanding
w. lacking people (B)   De 32:6
of Nun was full of the spirit   De 34:9
of w.
according to the w. of an   2Sa 14:20
angel of
my lord has w. (A)(B)(R)   2Sa 14:20
went unto all the people in   2Sa 20:22
her w.
w. and perceptive mind (B)   1Ki 3:12
saw that the w. of God was   1Ki 3:28
in him
And God gave Solomon w.   1Ki 4:29
Solomon's w. excelled the w.   1Ki 4:30
of all
country, and all the w. of   1Ki 4:30
Egypt
people to hear the w. of   1Ki 4:34
Solomon
earth, which had heard of his   1Ki 4:34
w.
And the Lord gave Solomon   1Ki 5:12
w.
filled with w. and   1Ki 7:14
understanding
Sheba had seen all Solomon's   1Ki 10:4
w.
of the earth for riches and   1Ki 10:23
for w.
sought to Solomon, to hear   1Ki 10:24
his w.
and his w. are they not   1Ki 11:41
written
Only the Lord give thee w.   1Ch 22:12
insight and understanding   1Ch 22:12
(B)
discretion and   1Ch 22:12
understanding (E)(R)
Give me now w. and   2Ch 1:10
knowledge
but hast asked w. and   2Ch 1:11
knowledge
W. and knowledge is granted   2Ch 1:12
unto
Sheba had seen the w. of   2Ch 9:3
Solomon
land of thine acts, and of thy   2Ch 9:5
w.
before thee, and hear thy w.   2Ch 9:7
kings of the earth in riches   2Ch 9:22
and w.
of Solomon, to hear his w.   2Ch 9:23
he displayed w. (B)   2Ch 11:23
thou, Ezra after the w. of thy   Ezr 7:25
God
go away? they die, even   Job 4:21
without w.
and is w. driven quite from   Job 6:13
me
people, and w. shall die with   Job 12:2
you

with the ancient is w. and in   Job 12:12
With him is w. and strength   Job 12:13
With him is strength and   Job 12:16
w.: the
peace; and it should be your   Job 13:5
w.
dost thou restrain w. to thyself   Job 15:8
counselled him that hath no   Job 26:3
w.
But where shall w. be found   Job 28:12
Whence then cometh w.   Job 28:20
the fear of the Lord, that is   Job 28:28
w.
multitudes of years shall teach   Job 32:7
w.
should say, We have found   Job 32:13
out w.
peace, and I shall teach thee   Job 33:33
w.
and his words were without   Job 34:35
w.
greater w. than birds (B)   Job 35:11
he is mighty in strength and   Job 36:5
w.
hath put w. in the inward   Job 38:36
parts
Who can number the clouds   Job 38:37
in w.
God hath deprived her of w.   Job 39:17
of the righteous speaketh w.   Ps 37:30
thou shalt make me to know w.   Ps 51:6
we may apply our hearts   Ps 90:12
unto w.
in w. hast thou made them   Ps 104:24
all
and teach his senators w.   Ps 105:22
him that by w. made the   Ps 136:5
heavens
To know w. and instruction   Pr 1:2
fools despised w. and instruction   Pr 1:7
W. crieth without; she uttereth   Pr 1:20
thou incline thine ear unto w.   Pr 2:2
For the Lord giveth w.: out of   Pr 2:6
his
He layeth up sound w. for the   Pr 2:7
w. entereth into thine heart   Pr 2:10
Happy is the man that findeth   Pr 3:13
w.
Lord by w. hath founded the   Pr 3:19
earth
keep sound w. and discretion   Pr 3:21
Get w. get understanding: Pr 4:5
forget
w. is the principal thing   Pr 4:7
principal thing; therefore get   Pr 4:7
w.
My son, attend unto my w. and   Pr 5:1
Say unto w. Thou art my   Pr 7:4
sister
Doth not w. cry? and   Pr 8:1
understanding
O ye simple, understand w.; and   Pr 8:5
For w. is better than rubies   Pr 8:11
I w. dwell with prudence, and   Pr 8:12
find
Counsel is mine, and sound w.   Pr 8:14
W. hath builded her house, she   Pr 9:1
hath understanding w. is   Pr 10:13
found
man of understanding hath w.   Pr 10:23
mouth of the just bringeth   Pr 10:31
forth w.
shame: but for the lowly is   Pr 11:2
w.
commended according to his   Pr 12:8
w.
but with the well advised is w.   Pr 13:10
A scorner seeketh w. and   Pr 14:6
findeth
w. of the prudent is to   Pr 14:8
understand
crown of wise is their w. (R)   Pr 14:24
W. resteth in the heart of him   Pr 14:33
that
better is it to get w. than gold   Pr 16:16
price in the hand of a fool to   Pr 17:16
get w.
W. is before him that hath   Pr 17:24
and intermeddleth with all w.   Pr 18:1
getteth w. loveth his own soul   Pr 19:8
There is no w. nor   Pr 21:30
understanding
be rich: cease from thine own   Pr 23:4
w.
will despise the w. of thy   Pr 23:9
words
also w. and instruction and   Pr 23:23
through w. is an house   Pr 24:3
builded
W. is too high for a fool he   Pr 24:7

walks in godly W. (A)(B)(R)   Pr 28:26
Whoso loveth w. rejoiceth his   Pr 29:3
the rod and reproof give w.   Pr 29:15
I neither learned w. nor have   Pr 30:3
She openeth her mouth with   Pr 31:26
w.
search out by w. concerning   Ec 1:13
all
have gotten more w. than all   Ec 1:16
they
And gave my heart to know w.   Ec 1:17
For in much w. is much grief   Ec 1:18
acquainting mine heart with w.   Ec 2:3
also my w. remained with me   Ec 2:9
And I turned myself to behold   Ec 2:12
w.
Then I saw that w. excelleth   Ec 2:13
folly
is a man whose labour is in w.   Ec 2:21
a man that is good in his sight   Ec 2:26
w.
is not from w. (R)   Ec 7:10
W. is good with an inheritance   Ec 7:11
For w. is a defence, and   Ec 7:12
money is a
w. giveth life to them that   Ec 7:12
have it
W. strengtheneth the wise   Ec 7:19
more
All this have I proved by w.   Ec 7:23
to seek out w. and the reason   Ec 7:25
of
a man's w. maketh his face to   Ec 8:1
I applied mine heart to know   Ec 8:16
w.
nor device, nor knowledge, nor   Ec 9:10
w.
This w. have I seen also under   Ec 9:13
he by his w. delivered the city   Ec 9:15
said I, W. is better than   Ec 9:16
strength
the poor man's w. is despised   Ec 9:16
W. is better than weapons   Ec 9:18
of war
in reputation for w. and   Ec 10:1
honour
his w. faileth him, and he saith   Ec 10:3
but w. is profitable to direct   Ec 10:3
hand I have done it, and by   Isa 10:13
my w.
the spirit of w. and   Isa 11:2
understanding
w. of their wise men shall   Isa 29:14
perish
w. and knowledge shall be   Isa 33:6
the Lord; and what w. is in   Jer 8:9
them
not the wise man glory in his   Jer 9:23
w.
hath established the world by   Jer 10:12
his w.
Is w. no more in Teman? is   Jer 49:7
counsel
the prudent? Is their w.   Jer 49:7
vanished
hath established the world by   Jer 51:15
his w.
By thy great w. and by thy   Eze 28:5
traffick
swords against the beauty of   Eze 28:7
thy w.
and skilful in all w. and   Da 1:4
causing
skilful in w. (A)(E)(R)   Da 1:4
and skill in all learning and w.   Da 1:17
answered with counsel and w.   Da 2:14
ever: for w. and might are his   Da 2:20
he giveth w. unto the wise   Da 2:21
who hast given me w. and   Da 2:23
might
is not revealed to me for any   Da 2:30
w.
light and understanding and   Da 5:11
w.
like the w. of the gods, was   Da 5:11
found
and excellent w. is found in   Da 5:14
thee
But w. is justified of her   M't 11:19
children
w. is justified by works   M't 11:19
(B)(R)
earth to hear the w. of   M't 12:42;
Solomon   Lu 11:31
Whence hath this man this   M't 13:54
w. and
w. is this which is given unto   M'k 6:2
him

disobedient to the *w.* of the just — *Lu 1:17*
strong in spirit, filled with *w.* — *Lu 2:40*
Jesus increased in *w.* and stature — *Lu 2:52*
w. is justified of all her children — *Lu 7:35*
Therefore also said the *w.* of God — *Lu 11:49*
For I will give you a mouth and *w.* — *Lu 21:15*
full of the Holy Ghost and *w.* — *Ac 6:3*
they were not able to resist the *w.* — *Ac 6:10*
gave him favour and *w.* in the sight — *Ac 7:10*
in all the *w.* of the Egyptians — *Ac 7:22*
not with *w.* of words, lest the cross — *1Co 1:17*
I will destroy the *w.* of the wise — *1Co 1:19*
made foolish the *w.* of this world — *1Co 1:20*
For after that in the *w.* of God — *1Co 1:21*
the world by *w.* knew not God — *1Co 1:21*
sign, and the Greeks seek after *w.* — *1Co 1:22*
the power of God, and the *w.* of God — *1Co 1:24*
who of God is made unto us *w.* — *1Co 1:30*
with enticing words of man's *w.* — *1Co 2:4*
should not stand in the *w.* of men — *1Co 2:5*
we speak *w.* among them that are — *1Co 2:6*
yet not the *w.* of this world, nor of — *1Co 2:6*
we speak the *w.* of God in a — *1Co 2:7*
even the hidden *w.* which God — *1Co 2:7*
words which mean *w.* teacheth — *1Co 2:13*
w. of this world is foolishness with — *1Co 3:19*
not with fleshy *w.* but by the grace — *2Co 1:12*
not with worldly *w.* (B)(N)(P) — *2Co 1:12*
hath abounded toward us in all *w.* — *Eph 1:8*
you the spirit of *w.* and revelation — *Eph 1:17*
the church is manifold *w.* of God — *Eph 3:10*
the knowledge of his will in all *w.* — *Col 1:9*
and teaching every man in all *w.* — *Col 1:28*
Christ dwell in you richly in all *w.* — *Col 3:16*
Walk in *w.* toward them that are — *Col 4:5*
If any of you lack *w.* let him ask — *Jas 1:5*
This *w.* descendeth not from above — *Jas 3:15*
But the *w.* that is from above is — *Jas 3:17*
according to the *w.* given unto him — *2Pe 3:15*
and *w.* and strength, and honour — *Re 5:12*
Blessing, and glory, and *w.* — *Re 7:12*
Here is *w.* Let him that hath — *Re 13:18*
here is the mind which hath *w.* — *Re 17:9*

OF WISDOM

he should shew thee secrets *of* *w.* — *Job 11:6*
for the price *of* *w.* is above rubies — *Job 28:18*
my mouth shall speak *of* *w.* and meditation — *Ps 49:3*
fear of the Lord is the beginning *of* *w.* — *Ps 111:10; Pr 9:10*
to receive their instruction *of* *w.,* justice — *Pr 1:3*
I have taught thee in the way *of* *w.* — *Pr 4:11*
but fools die for want *of* *w.* — *Pr 10:21*
he that is void *of* *w.* despiseth neighbour — *Pr 11:12*
folly is joy to him that is destitute *of* *w.* — *Pr 15:21*

the fear of the Lord is the instruction *of* *w.* — *Pr 15:33*
the well spring *of* *w.* as a flowing brook — *Pr 18:4*
shall knowledge *of* *w.* be to thy soul — *Pr 24:14*
my heart had great experience *of* *w.* — *Ec 1:16*
thou sealest up the sum full *of* *w.* — *Eze 28:12*
in all matters *of* *w.* found them better — *Da 1:20*
the man *of* *w.* shall see thy name — *Mic 6:9*
O the depth *of* the *w.* of God — *Ro 11:33*
not with excellency of speech or *of* *w.* — *1Co 2:1*
to one is given by the Spirit the word *of* *w.* — *1Co 12:8*
in whom are hid all the treasures *of* *w.* — *Col 2:3*
which things have indeed a shew *of* *w.* — *Col 2:23*
shew his works with meekness *of* *w.* — *Jas 3:13*

THY WISDOM

do therefore according to *thy* *w.* — *1Ki 2:6*
it was a true report that I heard of *thy* *w.* — *1Ki 10:6*
thy *w.* and prosperity exceedeth the fame — *1Ki 10:7*
happy are these thy servants that hear *thy* *w.* — *1Ki 10:8; 2Ch 9:5, 7*
the half of *thy* *w.* was not told me — *2Ch 9:6*
doth the hawk fly by *thy* *w.* — *Job 39:26*
thy *w.* it hath perverted thee — *Isa 47:10*
with *thy* *w.* hast gotten thee riches — *Eze 28:4; 28:5*
hast corrupted *thy* *w.* by thy brightness — *Eze 28:17*

WISE

tree to be desired to make one *w.* — *Ge 3:6*
Pharaoh called the *w.* men — *Ge 41:8*
look out a man discreet and *w.* — *Ge 41:33*
an intelligent and prudent man (B) — *Ge 41:33*
so discreet and *w.* as thou art — *Ge 41:39*
Pharaoh also called the *w.* men — *Ex 7:11*
sages (B) — *Ex 7:11*
the gift blindeth the *w.* — *Ex 23:8*
blinds those who have sight (A)(E) — *Ex 23:8*
And all the *w.* men, that wrought — *Ex 36:4*
skilled artisans (B) — *Ex 36:4*
Take you *w.* men, and — *De 1:13*
men of wisdom (B) — *De 1:13; 1:15*
the chief of your tribes *w.* men — *De 1:15*
is a *w.* and understanding people — *De 4:6*
a gift doth blind the eyes of the *w.* — *De 16:19*
O that they were *w.* that they — *De 32:29*
Her *w.* ladies answered her, yea — *J'g 5:29*
and my lord is *w.* according to the — *J'g 14:20*
my lord has wisdom (A) — *J'g 14:20*
like the wisdom of the angel of God (B)(R) — *J'g 14:20*
for thou art a *w.* man, and knowest — *1Ki 2:9*
a *w.* and an understanding heart — *1Ki 3:12*
the living child, and in no *w.* slay it — *1Ki 3:27*
by no means (A)(R) — *1Ki 3:27*
hath given unto David a *w.* son — *1Ki 5:7*
Zechariah his son, a *w.* counsellor — *1Ch 26:14*
counseller, a *w.* man, and a scribe — *1Ch 27:32*
a man of understanding (B)(E)(R) — *1Ch 27:32*
given to David the king a *w.* son — *2Ch 2:12*
Then the king said to the *w.* men — *Es 1:13*

Then said his *w.* men and Zeresh — *Es 6:13*
He taketh the *w.* in their own — *Job 5:13*
He is *w.* in heart, and mighty in — *Job 9:4*
vain man would be *w.* though — *Job 11:12*
a *w.* man utter vain knowledge — *Job 15:2*
w. men have told from their fathers — *Job 15:18*
cannot find one *w.* man — *Job 17:10*
he that is *w.* may be profitable — *Job 22:2*
Great men are not always *w.* — *Job 32:9*
Hear my words, O ye *w.* men — *Job 34:2*
and let a *w.* man hearken unto me — *Job 34:34*
not any that are *w.* of heart — *Job 37:24*
Be *w.* now therefore, O ye kings — *Ps 2:10*
is sure, making *w.* the simple — *Ps 19:7*
he hath left off to be *w.* and to do — *Ps 36:3*
For he seeth that *w.* men die — *Ps 49:10*
and ye fools, when will ye be *w.* — *Ps 94:8*
Whoso is *w.* and will observe — *Ps 107:43*
w. man will hear, and will increase — *Pr 1:5*
man shall attain unto *w.* counsels — *Pr 1:5*
the words of the *w.* and their dark — *Pr 1:6*
Be not *w.* in thine own eyes: fear — *Pr 3:7*
The *w.* shall inherit glory: but — *Pr 3:35*
consider her ways, and be *w.* — *Pr 6:6*
Hear instruction, and be *w.* — *Pr 8:33*
rebuke a *w.* man, and he will love — *Pr 9:8*
Give instruction to a *w.* man — *Pr 9:9*
If thou be *w.* thou shalt be *w.* for — *Pr 9:12*
A *w.* son maketh a glad father — *Pr 10:1*
gatherest in summer is a *w.* son — *Pr 10:5*
The *w.* in heart will receive — *Pr 10:8*
W. men lay up knowledge — *Pr 10:14*
he that refraineth his lips is *w.* — *Pr 10:19*
be servant to the *w.* of heart — *Pr 11:29*
and he that winneth souls is *w.* — *Pr 11:30*
hearkeneth unto counsel is *w.* — *Pr 12:15*
but the tongue of the *w.* is health — *Pr 12:18*
A *w.* son heareth his father's — *Pr 13:1*
law of the *w.* is a fountain of life — *Pr 13:14*
He that walketh with *w.* men shall — *Pr 13:20*
shall be *w.*: but a companion of — *Pr 13:20*
the lips of the *w.* shall preserve — *Pr 14:3*
A *w.* man feareth, and departeth — *Pr 14:16*
The crown of the *w.* is their riches — *Pr 14:24*
crown of *w.* is their wealth (A)(B)(R) — *Pr 14:24*
favour is toward a *w.* servant — *Pr 14:35*
the *w.* useth knowledge aright — *Pr 15:2*
lips of the *w.* disperse knowledge — *Pr 15:7*
neither will he go unto the *w.* — *Pr 15:12*
A *w.* son maketh a glad father: but — *Pr 15:20*
The way of life is above to the *w.* — *Pr 15:24*
of life abideth among the *w.* — *Pr 15:31*
death: but a *w.* man will pacify it — *Pr 16:14*
w. in heart shall be called prudent — *Pr 16:21*
heart of the *w.* teacheth his mouth — *Pr 16:23*
A *w.* servant shall have rule over — *Pr 17:2*
A reproof entereth more into a *w.* — *Pr 17:10*
holdeth his peace, is counted *w.* — *Pr 17:28*
the ear of the *w.* seeketh knowledge — *Pr 18:15*
that thou mayest be *w.* in thy — *Pr 19:20*
is deceived thereby is not *w.* — *Pr 20:1*
A *w.* king scattereth the wicked — *Pr 20:26*

punished, the simple is made Pr 21:11 w.
and when the w. is instructed, Pr 21:11 he
and oil in the dwelling of the Pr 21:20 w.
A w. man scaleth the city of Pr 21:22
and hear the words of the w. Pr 22:17
My son, if thine heart be w. Pr 23:15 my
Hear thou, my son, and be w. Pr 23:19
he that begetteth a w. child Pr 23:24 shall
A w. man is strong; yea, a Pr 24:5 man of
by w. counsel thou shalt make Pr 24:6 thy
These things also belong to Pr 24:23 the w.
a w. reprover upon an Pr 25:12 obedient ear
lest he be w. in his own Pr 26:5 conceit
thou a man w. in his own Pr 26:12 conceit
be w. and make my heart Pr 27:11 glad
Whoso keepeth the law is a Pr 28:7 w. son
rich man is w. in his own Pr 28:11 conceit
snare: but w. men turn away Pr 29:8 wrath
a w. man contendeth with a Pr 29:9 foolish
but a w. man keepeth it in till Pr 29:11
earth, but they are exceeding Pr 30:24 w.
The w. man's eyes are in his Ec 2:14 head
me; and why was I then more Ec 2:15 w.
no remembrance of the w. Ec 2:16 more
how dieth the w. man? as the Ec 2:16 fool
he shall be a w. man or a fool Ec 2:19
wherein I have shewed myself Ec 2:19 w.
Better is a poor and w. child Ec 4:13
hath the w. more than the fool Ec 6:8
heart of the w. is in the house Ec 7:4 of
better to hear the rebuke of the Ec 7:5 w.
oppression maketh a w. man Ec 7:7 mad
neither make thyself over w. Ec 7:16
Wisdom strengtheneth the w. Ec 7:10
I said, I will be w.; but it was Ec 7:23 far
Who is as the w. man? and Ec 8:1
a w. man's heart discerneth Ec 8:5 both
though a w. man think to Ec 8:17 know it
that the righteous, and the w. Ec 9:1
neither yet bread to the w. nor Ec 9:11
there was found in it a poor Ec 9:15 w. man
The words of w. men are Ec 9:17 heard in
A w. man's heart is at his Ec 10:2 right
of a w. man's mouth are Ec 10:12 gracious
because the preacher was w. Ec 12:9 he
The words of the w. are as Ec 12:11 goads
unto them that are w. in their Isa 5:21 own
the w. counsellers of Isa 19:11 Pharaoh is
I am the son of the w. the Isa 19:11 son of
are they? where are thy w. Isa 19:12 man
the wisdom of their w. men Isa 29:14 shall
Yet he also is w. and will Isa 31:2 bring
that turneth w. men Isa 44:25 backward
they are w. to do evil, but to Jer 4:22 do
We are w. and the law of the Jer 8:8 Lord
w. men are ashamed, they are Jer 8:9
Who is the w. man, that may Jer 9:12

the w. man glory in his Jer 9:23 wisdom
among all the w. men of the Jer 10:7 nations
nor counsel from the w. nor Jer 18:18
her princes, and upon her w. Jer 50:35 men
drunk her princes, and her w. Jer 51:57 men
thy w. man, O Tyrus, that Eze 27:8 were in
Gebal and the w. men thereof Eze 27:9 were
destroy all the w. men of Da 2:12 Babylon
that the w. men should be Da 2:13 slain
to slay the w. men of Babylon Da 2:14
the rest of the w. men of Da 2:18 Babylon
he giveth wisdom unto the w. Da 2:21
to destroy the w. men of Da 2:24 Babylon
Destroy not the w. men of Da 2:24 Babylon
hath demanded cannot the w. Da 2:27 men
over all the w. men of Da 2:48 Babylon
bring in all the w. men of Da 4:6 Babylon
w. men of my kingdom are Da 4:18 able
said to the w. men of Babylon Da 5:7
Then came in all the king's w. Da 5:8 men
now the w. men, the Da 5:15 astrologers
And they that be w. shall Da 12:3 shine
but the w. shall understand Da 12:10
Who is w. and he shall Ho 14:9 understand
destroy the w. men out of Edom Ob 8
and Zidon, though it be very Zec 9:2 w.
there came w. men from the M't 2:1 east
he had privily called the w. M't 2:7 men
that he was mocked of the w. M't 2:16 men
diligently enquired of the w. M't 2:16 men
I will liken him unto a w. M't 7:24 man
be ye therefore w. as M't 10:16 serpents, and
hast hid these things from M't 11:25 the w.
learned and intelligent (B) M't 11:25
I in like w. will tell you by M't 21:24 what
unto you prophets, and w. M't 23:34 men
sages (B) M't 23:34
then is a faithful and w. M't 24:45 servant
prudent (B) M't 24:45; 25:2, 4, 8-9
And five of them were w. and M't 25:2 five
But the w. took oil in their M't 25:4 vessels
And the foolish said unto the M't 25:8 w.
the w. answered, saying, Not M't 25:9 so
hast hid these things from Lu 10:21 the w.
is that faithful and w. Lu 12:42 steward
both to the w. and to the Ro 1:14 unwise
Professing themselves to be w. Ro 1:22
should be w. in your own Ro 11:25 conceits
Be not w. in your own Ro 12:16 conceits
you w. unto that which is Ro 16:19 good
To God only w. be glory Ro 16:27 through
I will destroy the wisdom of 1Co 1:19 the w.
learned (B) 1Co 1:19; 1:27
Where is the w.? where is the 1Co 1:20 scribe
not many w. men after the 1Co 1:26 flesh

of the world to confound the 1Co 1:27 w.
as a w. masterbuilder, I have 1Co 3:10 laid
skilled architect (B) 1Co 3:10
skilled master builder (R) 1Co 3:10
you seemeth to be w. in this 1Co 3:18 world
become a fool, that he may 1Co 3:18 be w.
He taketh the w. in their 1Co 3:19 own
knoweth the thoughts of the 1Co 3:20 w.
sake, but ye are w. in Christ 1Co 4:10
there is not a w. man among 1Co 6:5 you
I speak as to w. men; judge 1Co 10:15 ye
among themselves, are not 2Co 10:12 w.
seeing ye yourselves are w. 2Co 11:19
not as fools, but as w. Eph 5:15
the only w. God, be honour 1Ti 1:17
to make thee w. unto 2Ti 3:15 salvation
instruction be sound, fit, w. Tit 2:8 (A)
Who is a w. man and endued Jas 3:13 with
To the only w. God our Jude 25 Saviour
there shall in no w. enter into Re 21:27 it any

WISE *WOMAN*

and Joab fetched thence a w. 2Sa 14:2 woman
then cried a w. woman out 2Sa 20:16 of the city, Hear
every w. woman buildeth her Pr 14:1 house

ANY WISE

if thou afflict them in any w. Ex 22:23
shalt in any w. rebuke thy Le 19:17 neighbour
if he will in any w. redeem Le 27:19 the field
shalt in any w. set him king De 17:15 over thee
thou shalt in any w. bury De 21:23 him that day
thou shalt in any w. let the De 22:7 dam go
in any w. keep from the Jos 6:28 accursed thing
else if ye do in any w. go Jos 23:12 back and cleave
in any w. send a trespass 1Sa 6:3 offering
howbeit let me go in any w. 1Ki 11:22
fret not thyself in any w. to do Ps 37:8 evil
I will not deny thee in any M'k 14:31 w.

IN NO WISE

the fat of beasts torn, in no w. Le 7:24 eat of it
give the child, and in no w. 1Ki 3:26; slay it 3:27
one tittle shall in no w. pass M't 5:18 from the law
he shall in no w. lose his M't 10:42 reward
a woman could in no w. lift Lu 13:11 up herself
shall in no w. enter therein Lu 18:17; Re 21:27
he that cometh to me, I will Joh 6:37 in no w. cast
a work which ye shall in no Ac 13:41 w. believe
are we better than they? no, in Ro 3:9 no w.

ON THIS WISE

on this w. ye shall bless Israel Nu 6:23
the birth of Jesus Christ was M't 1:18 on this w.
and on this w. shewed he Joh 21:1 himself
God spake on this w. that his Ac 7:6 seed

he said *on this w*. I will give   *Ac 13:24*
sure mercies
the righteousness speaketh *on*   *Ro 10:6*
this w.
he spake of the seventh day   *Heb 4:4*
on this w.

WISE-HEARTED

speak to all that are *w*.   *Ex 28:3*
I have put wisdom in all that   *Ex 31:6*
are *w*.
every *w*. among you shall   *Ex 35:10*
make all
all the women that were   *Ex 35:25*
w. did spin
then wrought every *w*. man   *Ex 36:1*
Moses called Aholiab and   *Ex 36:2*
every *w*. man
every *w*. man made ten   *Ex 36:8*
curtains

WISELY

Come on, let us deal *w*. with   *Ex 1:10*
them
deal shrewdly with them   *Ex 1:10*
(A)(B)(R)
sent him, and behaved   *1Sa 18:5*
himself *w*.
David had success (B)(R)   *1Sa 18:5*
And David behaved himself   *1Sa 18:14*
w.
David had success (B)   *1Sa 18:15*
that he behaved himself very   *1Sa 18:15*
w.
how capable and successful   *1Sa 18:15*
David was (A)
how capable David was (B)   *1Sa 18:15*
saw he had great success   *1Sa 18:15*
(R)
David behaved himself more   *1Sa 18:30*
w.
And he dealt *w*. and   *2Ch 11:23*
dispersed of
dealt understandingly (A)   *2Ch 11:23*
he displayed wisdom (B)   *2Ch 11:23*
charmers, charming never so   *Ps 58:5*
w.
casting spells so cunningly (A)   *Ps 58:5*
casting spells skillfully (B)   *Ps 58:5*
the cunning charmer (R)   *Ps 58:5*
they shall *w*. consider of his   *Ps 64:9*
doing
be in awe (B)   *Ps 64:9*
be in fear (E)(R)   *Ps 64:9*
behave myself *w*. in a perfect   *Ps 101:2*
way
carefully observe (B)   *Ps 101:2*
give heed to the way (R)   *Ps 101:2*
He that handeth a matter *w*.   *Pr 16:20*
shall
gives heed to the word   *Pr 16:20*
(E)(R)
The righteous man *w*.   *Pr 21:12*
considereth
but whoso walketh *w*. he   *Pr 28:26*
shall be
walks with skillful and godly   *Pr 28:26*
wisdom (A)
walks in wisdom (B)(R)   *Pr 28:26*
for thou dost not enquire *w*.   *Ec 7:10*
is not from wisdom you ask   *Ec 7:10*
(R)
steward, because he had done   *Lu 16:8*
w.
for acting shrewdly and   *Lu 16:8*
prudently (A)
for acting shrewdly (B)   *Lu 16:8*
for acting so astutely (N)   *Lu 16:8*
been so careful for his own   *Lu 16:8*
future (P)
for his prudence (R)   *Lu 16:8*

WISER

For he was *w*. than all men   *1Ki 4:31*
and maketh us *w*. than the   *Job 35:11*
fowls
greater wisdom than birds   *Job 35:11*
(B)
commandments hast made   *Ps 119:98*
me *w*.
a wise man, and he will be yet   *Pr 9:9*
w.
sluggard is *w*. in his own   *Pr 26:16*
conceit
Behold, thou art *w*. than   *Eze 28:3*
Daniel

w. than the children of light   *Lu 16:8*
foolishness of God is *w*. than   *1Co 1:25*
men

WISH

I am according to thy *w*. in   *Job 33:6*
God's
and put to shame that *w*. me   *Ps 40:14*
evil
Who desire my hurt (B)(R)   *Ps 40:14*
who delight in my hurt (E)   *Ps 40:14*
have more than heart could *w*.   *Ps 73:7*
could *w*. that myself were   *Ro 9:3*
accursed
and this also we *w*. even   *2Co 13:9*
your
I *w*. above all things that thou   *3Jo 2*

WISHED

and *w*. in himself to die, and   *Joh 4:8*
said
w. to see (N)   *Lu 10:24*
contradict nor *w*. (S)   *Lu 21:15*
of the stern, and *w*. for the   *Ac 27:29*
day

WISHING

to sin by *w*. a curse to his   *Job 31:30*
soul

WIST

for they *w*. not what it was   *Ex 16:15*
did not know (A)   *Ex 16:15;*
   34:29; Jos 2:4; 8:14; J'g 16:20; M'k 9:6;
   14:40; Joh 5:13
did not know (B)   *Ex 16:15;*
   Jos 2:4; 8:14; J'g 16:20; M'k 9:6; 14:40;
   Lu 2:49; Joh 5:13; Ac 23:5
knew not (E)   *Ex 16:15;*
   34:29; Le 5:17, 18; Jos 2:4; 8:14;
   J'g 16:20; M'k 9:6; 14:40; Lu 2:49;
   Joh 5:13; Ac 12:9; 23:5
did not know (R)   *Ex 16:15;*
   34:29; Le 5:17; Jos 2:4; 8:14; J'g 16:20;
   M'k 9:6; 14:40; Lu 2:49; Joh 5:13;
   Ac 12:9; 23:5
Moses *w*. not that the skin of   *Ex 34:29*
his
was not ware (B)   *Ex 34:29*
though he *w*. it not, yet is he   *Le 5:17*
guilty
not aware of (A)   *Le 5:17*
ignorant of (B)   *Le 5:17*
wherein he erred and *w*. it not   *Le 5:18*
unknowingly (A)(B)   *Le 5:18*
unwittingly (R)   *Le 5:18*
me, but I *w*. not whence they   *Jos 2:4*
were
he *w*. not that there were liers   *Jos 8:14*
in
w. not that the Lord was   *J'g 16:20*
departed
For he *w*. not what to say; for   *M'k 9:6*
they
did not know (N)   *M'k 9:6;*
   14:40; Lu 2:49; Joh 5:13
did not know (P)   *M'k 9:6;*
   14:40; Lu 2:49; Ac 23:5
neither *w*. they what to   *M'k 14:40*
answer
w. ye not that I must be about   *Lu 2:49*
my
see and know (A)   *Lu 2:49*
that was healed *w*. not who it   *Joh 5:13*
was
he had no idea (P)   *Joh 5:13*
w. not that it was true which   *Ac 12:9*
was
was not conscious of (A)   *Ac 12:9; 23:5*
imagining he was seeing a   *Ac 12:9*
vision (B)
he had no idea (N)   *12:9; 23:5*
not knowing (P)   *Ac 12:9*
Then said Paul, I *w*. not,   *Ac 23:5*
brethren

WIT

to *w*. whether the Lord had   *Ge 24:21*
made
to *w*. what would be done to   *Ex 2:4*
him
to *w*. for Machir the firstborn   *Jos 17:1*
of
to *w*. Abner the son of Ner,   *1Ki 2:32*
captain of

doors of the house, to *w*. of   *1Ki 7:50*
the temple
to *w*. for the prophet whom   *1Ki 13:23*
he had
to *w*. the golden calves that   *2Ki 10:29*
were in
of their father's house, to *w*.   *1Ch 7:2*
of Tola
to *w*. the chief fathers and   *1Ch 27:1*
To *w*. the two pillars, and the   *2Ch 4:12*
Israel, to *w*. with all the   *2Ch 25:7*
children of
to *w*. the army that was   *2Ch 25:10*
come
to *w*. for the morning and   *2Ch 31:3*
evening
cities, to *w*. Israel, the priests,   *Ne 11:3*
and the
to *w*. six months with oil of   *Es 2:12*
myrrh
To *w*. Jerusalem, and the   *Jer 25:18*
cities of
of them, to *w*. of a Jew his   *Jer 34:9*
brother
To *w*. the prophets of Israel   *Eze 13:16*
which
to *w*. the redemption of our   *Ro 8:23*
body
To *w*. that God was in Christ   *2Co 5:19*
do you to *w*. of the grace of   *2Co 8:1*
God

WITCH

Thou shalt not suffer a *w*. to   *Ex 22:18*
live
a woman who practices   *Ex 22:18*
sorcery (A)
a sorceress (B)(E)(R)   *Ex 22:18*
of times, or an enchanter, or   *De 18:10*
a *w*.
a sorcerer (A)(E)(R)   *De 18:10*

WITCHCRAFT

neither is *w*. bound (B)   *Nu 23:23*
For rebellion is as the sin of   *1Sa 15:23*
w.
fortunetelling (B)   *1Sa 15:23*
divination (R)   *1Sa 15:23*
used enchantments, and used   *2Ch 33:6*
w.
sorcery (A)(E)(R)   *2Ch 33:6;*
   Ga 5:20
fortunetelling and sorcery   *2Ch 33:6*
(B)
Idolatry, *w*., hatred, variance   *Ga 5:20*
magic (B)   *Ga 5:20*

WITCHCRAFTS

Jezebel and her *w*. are so   *2Ki 9:22*
many
the *w*. of thy mother (A)   *2Ki 9:22*
harlotries (B)(R)   *2Ki 9:22*
whoredoms (E)   *2Ki 9:22*
sorceries (R)   *2Ki 9:22*
will cut off *w*. out of thine   *Mic 5:12*
hand
sorceries (B)(R)   *Mic 5:12*
the mistress of *w*. that selleth   *Na 3:4*
deadly charms (A)   *Na 3:4*
seduction (B)   *Na 3:4*
charms (R)   *Na 3:4*
and families through her *w*.   *Na 3:4*
enchantments (A)   *Na 3:4*
harlotries (B)(R)   *Na 3:4*

WITH

Cain talked *w*. Abel   *Ge 4:8*
spirit not always strive *w*. man   *Ge 6:3*
earth filled *w*. violence   *Ge 6:9; 6:13*
I will destroy them *w*. the   *Ge 6:13*
earth
w. lower, second, and third   *Ge 6:16*
stories
w. thee will I establish my   *Ge 6:18;*
covenant   *9:11*
keep them alive *w*. thee   *Ge 6:19*
Bring forth *w*. thee every   *Ge 8:17;*
living thing   *9:10, 12*
went forth *w*. them from Ur   *Ge 11:31*
came out *w*. great substance   *Ge 15:14*
ceased to be *w*. Sarah after   *Ge 18:11*
his household came *w*. Jacob   *Ex 1:1*
the bush burned *w*. fire   *Ex 3:2*
I will be *w*. thy mouth   *Ex 4:12*
w. a strong hand will be   *Ex 6:1*
w. his head and his fat   *Le 1:12*

washed from w. water | Le 8:6
his flesh run w. the issue | Le 15:3
stone him w. stones | Le 20:2
w. the number of their names | Nu 1:2
w. the ensign of their fathers | Nu 2:2
the Lord spake w. Moses | Nu 3:1
the stranger that is w. him | De 1:16
meddle not w. them | De 2:5
I will be w. thee | Jos 1:5
neither will I be w. thee | Jos 7:12
w. no hands stayed on her (S) | La 4:6
a man w. authority (S) | Lu 7:8

WITH ALL HEART

to serve him w. all your | De 11:13;
heart | Jos 22:5; 1Sa 12:20, 24
love God w. all your heart | De 13:3;
6:5;   30:6;   M't 22:37;   M'k 12:30,   33;
| Lu 10:37
do them w. all the heart | De 26:16
unto Lord w. all thine heart | De 30:2;
| 30:10
walk before me w. all heart | 1Ki 2:4;
| 8:23
return to thee w. all their | 1Ki 8:48;
heart | 2Ki 23:25; 2Ch 6:38
David followed w. all his | 1Ki 14:8
heart
Jehu took no heed to walk | 2Ki 10:31
w. all heart
made covenant to walk | 2Ki 23:3;
before Lord w. all their | 2Ch 34:31
heart
seek God w. all the heart | 2Ch 15:12
sworn w. all the heart | 2Ch 15:15
sought Lord w. all the heart | 2Ch 22:9
he did it w. all his heart | 2Ch 31:21
praise thee w. all the heart | Ps 86:12
trust in Lord w. all the heart | Pr 8:5
when ye search w. all your | Jer 29:13
heart
be glad w. all the heart | Zep 3:14
if believe w. all the heart | Ac 8:37

WITH CHILD

Hagar, thou art w. child | Ge 16:11
were w. child by their father | Ge 19:36
Tamar thy daughter is w. | Ge 38:24
child
I am w. child | Ge 38:25; 2Sa 11:5
if men hurt woman w. child | Ex 21:22
Phinehas' wife was w. child | 1Sa 4:19
rip up women w. child | 2Ki 8:12
grow in womb of her w. child | Ec 11:5
woman w. child draweth | Isa 26:17
near
we have been w. child in pain | Isa 26:18
Sing, that didst not travail w. | Isa 54:1
child
whether man doth travail w. | Jer 30:6
child
the woman w. child | Jer 31:8
woman w. child be ripped | Ho 13:16
they ripped up women w. | Am 1:13
child
found w. child of the Holy | M't 1:18
Ghost
virgin shall be w. child | M't 1:23
woe to them that are w. | M't 24:19;
child in those days | M'k 13:17; Lu 21:23
with Mary, being great w. child | Lu 2:5
as travail upon woman w. | 1Th 5:3
child
she being w. child cried in | Re 12:2
travail

WITH GOD

Enoch walked w. God | Ge 5:22; 5:24
Noah walked w. God | Ge 6:9
as a prince hast power w. | Ge 32:28
God
people to meet w. God | Ex 19:17
wrought w. God this day | 1Sa 14:45
my house not so w. God | 2Sa 23:5
forbear meddling w. God | 2Ch 35:21
how can a man be just w. God | Job 9:2
I desire to reason w. God | Job 13:3
might plead for a man w. | Job 16:2
God
How man be justified w. God | Job 25:4
portion of wicked man w. | Job 27:13
God
should delight himself w. God | Job 34:9
enter into judgment w. God | Job 34:23
w. God is terrible majesty | Job 37:22
spirit is not stedfast w. God | Ps 78:8

Judah yet ruleth w. God | Ho 11:12
Jacob had power w. God | Ho 12:3
w. God all things are | M't 19:26;
possible | M'k 10:27; Lu 1:37; 8:27
found favor w. God | Lu 1:30
Jesus increased in favor w. | Lu 2:52
God
Word was w. God; Word was | Joh 1:1;
God | 1:2
himself equal w. God | Joh 5:18;
| Ph'p 2:6
no respect of persons w. God | Ro 2:11
by faith we have peace w. God | Ro 5:1
is there unrighteousness w. | Ro 9:14
God
we are labourers w. God | 1Co 3:9
wisdom of world foolishness | 1Co 3:19
w. God
every man therein abide w. | 1Co 7:24
God
is it a righteous thing w. God | 2Th 1:6
to
friendship of world enmity w. | Jas 4:4
God
take patiently is acceptable | 1Pe 2:20
w. God

WITH HER

gave unto her husband w. her | Ge 3:6
thy wife, two sons w. her | Ex 18:6
he dealt deceitfully w. her | Ex 21:8
deal w. her after manner of | Ex 21:9
if he lie w. her | Ex 22:16
and all w. her in the house | Jos 6:17
father did w. her according | J'g 11:39
to vow
Manoah was not w. her | J'g 13:9
minded to go w. her | Ru 1:18
delivered of child w. her | 1Ki 3:17
be glad w. her | Isa 66:10
Mary abode w. her three | Lu 1:56
months
neighbours rejoiced w. her | Lu 1:58
Why talkest w. her | Joh 4:27
Jesus w. her, comforted her | Joh 11:31

WITH HIM

master saw the Lord was w. | Ge 39:3
him
given w. him Aholiab | Ex 31:6;
| 38:23
w. him will I speak | Nu 12:8; Jer 32:4
God w. him | Nu 23:21;
Ge 39:3;   1Sa 3:19;   16:18;   18:12,   14;
2Ki 18:7; 1Ch 9:20; 11:9; 2Ch 1:1; 15:9;
    Joh 3:2; Ac 7:9; 10:38
w. him that standeth here | De 29:15
this day
w. him that is not here | De 29:15
was no strange god w. him | De 32:12
folly w. him | 1Sa 25:25
and w. him will I abide | 2Sa 16:18
all Israel w. him | 1Ki 8:65; 2Ch 7:8
the word of the Lord is w. him | 2Ki 3:12
that his hand might be w. | 2Ki 15:19
him
the Lord was w. him he | 2Ki 18:7;
prospered | 1Ch 9:20; 2Ch 1:1; 15:9
Lord be with you, while you | 2Ch 15:2
are w. him
be more with us than w. | 2Ch 32:7
him
w. him is an arm of flesh | 2Ch 32:8
the Lord be w. him | 2Ch 36:23; Ezr 7:3
w. him is wisdom | Job 12:13;
| 12:16
candle be put out w. him | Job 18:6
Acquaint now thyself w. him | Job 22:21
my mercy be w. him | Ps 89:24
I will be w. him in trouble | Ps 91:15
w. him is plenteous | Ps 130:7
redemption
I was w. him as one brought | Pr 8:30
up w. him
abide w. him of his labour | Ec 8:15
it should be well w. him | Isa 3:10
it shall be ill w. him | Isa 3:11
his reward is w. him | Isa 40:10; 62:11
w. him that is of contrite | Isa 57:15
spirit
it was well w. him | Jer 22:15; 22:16
he shall surely deal w. him | Eze 31:11
covenant was w. him of life | Mal 2:5
while in the way w. him | M't 5:25
that they should be w. him | M'k 3:14
prayed he might be w. him | M'k 5:18;
| Lu 8:38
hand of Lord was w. him | Lu 1:66

this man was w. him | Lu 22:56
miracles except God be w. him | Joh 3:2
will make our abode w. him | Joh 14:23
feareth is accepted w. him | Ac 10:35
away w. him | Ac 21:36
buried w. him | Ro 6:4; Col 3:12
live w. him | Ro 6:8;
| 2Co 13:4; 1Th 5:10; 2Ti 2:11
w. him freely give us all things | Ro 8:32
will God bring w. him | 1Th 4:14
reign w. him | 2Ti 2:12; Re 20:6
heirs w. him of the same | Heb 11:9
when w. him in the mount | 2Pe 1:18
I will sup w. him | Re 3:20
w. him an 144,000 | Re 14:1
they that are w. him are | Re 17:14
called

WITH ISRAEL

Amalek fought w. Israel | Ex 17:8
made a covenant w. Israel | Ex 34:27
Levites no inheritance w. Israel | De 18:1
God executed judgment w. | De 33:21
Israel
kings of Canaan fought w. | Jos 9:2
Israel
made peace w. Israel | Jos 10:1;
| 2Sa 10:19
Philistines fought w. Israel | 1Sa 13:5;
| 28:1; 2Sa 21:15
Lord very angry w. Israel | 2Ki 17:18
Lord is not w. Israel | 2Ch 25:7
Lord will plead w. Israel | Mic 6:2

WITH ME

woman gavest to be w. me | Ge 3:12
that it may be well w. me | Ge 12:13
men which went w. me | Ge 14:24
that hear will laugh w. me | Ge 21:6
swear not deal falsely w. me | Ge 21:23
if God be w. me | Ge 28:20; Jos 14:12
Abide w. me | Ge 29:19
for service w. me | Ge 29:27
will husband dwell w. me | Ge 30:20
how thy cattle were w. me | Ge 30:29
shall be counted stone w. me | Ge 30:33
God of my father been w. | Ge 31:5
me
discern what is thine w. me | Ge 31:32
Except God of Abraham was | Ge 31:42
w. me
thou wast pleased w. me | Ge 33:10
herds with young are w. me | Ge 33:15
leave some of the folk w. me | Ge 33:15
lie w. me | Ge 39:7; 39:12, 14; 2Sa 13:11
leave one of brethren w. me | Ge 42:33
wherefore dealt ye so ill w. me | Ge 43:6
send the lad w. me | Ge 43:8
these men shall dine w. me | Ge 43:16
if the lad be not w. me | Ge 44:34
deal kindly and truly w. me | Ge 47:29
Why chide ye w. me | Ex 17:2
not make w. me gods | Ex 20:23
whom will ye send w. me | Ex 33:12
If thy presence go not w. me | Ex 33:15
ye are sojourners w. me | Le 25:23
if ye deal thus w. me | Nu 11:15
Balak said, Come w. me | Nu 23:13
Lord was angry w. me | De 1:37;
| 3:26; 4:21
this laid up in store w. me | De 32:34
there is no God w. me | De 32:39
I and the people that are w. | Jos 8:5
me
brethren that went up w. me | Jos 14:8
Come w. me into my lot | J'g 1:3
If thou wilt go w. me | J'g 4:8
shew a sign thou talkest w. me | J'g 6:17
I and all that are w. me | J'g 7:18
What hast thou to do w. me | J'g 11:12
when thy heart is not w. me | J'g 16:15
the silver is w. me | J'g 17:2
dwell w. me | J'g 17:10
Thus dealeth Micah w. me | J'g 18:4
as ye dealt w. me | Ru 1:8
ye shall eat w. me today | 1Sa 9:19
pardon, turn w. me | 1Sa 15:25; 15:30
come w. me to the sacrifice | 1Sa 16:5
if ye be able to fight w. me | 1Sa 17:9
neither sword nor weapon w. | 1Sa 21:8
me
w. me shall be a safeguard | 1Sa 22:23
thou hast dealt well w. me | 1Sa 24:13
Who will go down w. me | 1Sa 26:6
tomorrow be w. me | 1Sa 28:19
Is not this David w. me | 1Sa 29:3
thy coming in w. me is good | 1Sa 29:6
Make thy league w. me | 2Sa 3:12

if thou passest on *w. me* — 2Sa 15:33
Wherefore wentest thou not *w. me* — 2Sa 19:25
I will feed thee *w. me* — 2Sa 19:33
Chimham shall go over *w. me* — 2Sa 19:38
w. me an everlasting covenant — 2Sa 23:5
what hast thou lacked *w. me* — 1Ki 11:22
come home *w. me* — 1Ki 13:7; 13:15
Wilt thou go *w. me* to battle — 1Ki 22:4; 2Ch 18:3
wilt go *w. me* against Moab — 2Ki 3:7
Come *w. me* see my zeal — 2Ki 10:16
Make an agreement *w. me* — 2Ki 18:31; Isa 36:16
that thine hand be *w. me* — 1Ch 4:10
as with David deal *w. me* — 2Ch 2:3
cunning men are *w. me* — 2Ch 2:7
meddling with God, who is *w. me* — 2Ch 35:21
chief men to go up *w. me* — Ezr 7:28
genealogy of them *w. me* — Ezr 8:1
king sent horsemen *w. me* — Ne 2:9
I arose and a few men *w. me* — Ne 2:12
I and half the rulers *w. me* — Ne 12:40
but it is not so *w. me* — Job 9:35
shew wherefore ye contend *w. me* — Job 10:2
Who is he that will plead *w. me* — Job 13:19
Are not mockers *w. me* — Job 17:2
who will strike hands *w. me* — Job 17:3
sea saith, It is not *w. me* — Job 28:14
when the Almighty was *w. me* — Job 29:5
when they contended *w. me* — Job 31:13
brought up *w. me* — Job 31:18
peace *w. me* — Ps 7:4
thou art *w. me* — Ps 23:4
O magnify the Lord *w. me* — Ps 34:3
Plead with them that strive *w. me* — Ps 35:1
in the night his song be *w. me* — Ps 42:8
that hath made covenant *w. me* — Ps 50:5
there were many *w. me* — Ps 55:18
that they may dwell *w. me* — Ps 101:6
commandments are ever *w. me* — Ps 119:98
shall deal bountifully *w. me* — Ps 142:7
I have peace offerings *w. me* — Pr 7:14
riches and honor are *w. me* — Pr 8:18
my wisdom it remained *w. me* — Ec 2:9
mother's children were angry *w. me* — Ca 1:6
Come *w. me* to Lebanon — Ca 4:8
though thou be angry *w. me* — Isa 12:1
he should make peace *w. me* — Isa 27:5
who will contend *w. me* — Isa 50:8
of people there were none *w. me* — Isa 63:3
wherefore will he plead *w. me* — Jer 2:29
ye dealt treacherously *w. me* — Jer 3:20
to them that contend *w. me* — Jer 18:19
Lord is *w. me* — Jer 20:11
womb to be always great *w. me* — Jer 20:17
do *w. me* as seemeth good — Jer 26:14
to come *w. me* into Babylon — Jer 40:4
as he was speaking *w. me* — Da 8:18
men *w. me* saw not the vision — Da 10:7
none holdeth *w. me* — Da 10:21
then it was better *w. me* — Ho 2:7
what have ye to do *w. me* — Joe 3:4
angel communed *w. me* — Zec 1:14
he walked *w. me* in peace — Mal 2:6
he that is not *w. me* — M't 12:30; Lu 11:23
gathereth not *w. me* — M't 12:30; Lu 11:23
because they continue *w. me* — M't 15:32; M'k 8:2
Lord have patience *w. me* — M't 18:26; 18:29
agree *w. me* for a penny — M't 20:13
he that dippeth his hand *w. me* in the dish — M't 26:23; M'k 14:20
Tarry here, watch *w. me* — M't 26:38
one of you which eateth *w. me* — M'k 14:18
my children *w. me* in bed — Lu 11:7
divide the inheritance *w. me* — Lu 12:13
rejoice *w. me* — Lu 15:6; 15:9; Ph'p 2:18
Son, thou art ever *w. me* — Lu 15:31
hand of him *w. me* on the tables — Lu 22:21
Ye have continued *w. me* in my — Lu 22:28
shalt be *w. me* in paradise — Lu 23:43
he that sent me is *w. me* — Joh 8:29
wash thee not, no part *w. me* — Joh 13:8
he that eateth bread *w. me* hath — Joh 13:18

been *w. me* from the beginning — Joh 15:27
not alone because the Father is *w. me* — Joh 16:32
that they may be *w. me* — Joh 17:24
ministered to them *w. me* — Ac 20:34
they that were *w. me* saw light — Ac 22:9; 22:11
go down *w. me* and accuse — Ac 25:5
them which journeyed *w. me* — Ac 26:13
evil is present *w. me* — Ro 7:21
strive *w. me* in your prayers — Ro 15:30
w. me it is a very small thing — 1Co 4:3
grace of God that was *w. me* — 1Co 15:10
they shall go *w. me* — 1Co 16:4
w. me should be yea, yea — 2Co 1:17
if they of Macedonia come *w. me* — 2Co 9:4
would ye could bear *w. me* — 2Co 11:1
all the brethren *w. me* — Ga 1:2; Ph'p 4:2
I took Titus *w. me* — Ga 2:1; 2:3, 21
served *w. me* in the gospel — Ph'p 2:22
as soon as I shall see how go *w. me* — Ph'p 2:23
women, who laboured *w. me* — Ph'p 4:3
no church communicated *w. me* — Ph'p 4:15
only Luke is *w. me* — 2Ti 4:11
none stood *w. me* — 2Ti 4:16
the Lord stood *w. me* — 2Ti 4:17
All *w. me* saluteth thee — Tit 3:15
see voice that spake *w. me* — Re 1:12
shall walk *w. me* in white — Re 3:4
sup with him he *w. me* — Re 3:10
grant to sit *w. me* in my throne — Re 3:21
I come quickly, my reward is *w. me* — Re 22:12

WITH *THEE*

my covenant is *w. thee* — Ge 17:4; Ex 34:27; De 29:12
he is a covering to all *w. thee* — Ge 20:16
God is *w. thee* in all thou doest — Ge 21:22
Lord will send his angel *w. thee* — Ge 24:40
I will be *w. thee* and bless thee — Ge 26:3
I am *w. thee* — Ge 26:24; 28:15; 31:3; 46:4; Ex 3:12; De 31:8, 23; J'g 6:16; Jos 1:5; 3:7; 1Ki 11:38; Isa 43:2
We saw that the Lord was *w. thee* — Ge 26:28
twenty years have I been *w. thee* — Ge 31:38
Who are those *w. thee* — Ge 33:5
Let me leave *w. thee* some — Ge 33:15
I will go down *w. thee* in Egypt — Ge 46:4
God shall be *w. thee* — Ex 18:19
I will meet *w. thee* — Ex 25:22; 30:6, 36
My presence shall go *w. thee* — Ex 33:14; De 31:6, 8; J'g 6:16
wages should not abide *w. thee* — Le 19:13
What men are these *w. thee* — Le 22:9
God hath been *w. thee* — De 2:7
God is *w. thee* — De 20:1; 31:6; Jos 1:9, 17; J'g 6:12; 2Sa 7:3, 9
against the city that maketh war *w. thee* — De 20:20
I shall be well *w. thee* — De 22:2
we will deal truly *w. thee* — Jos 2:14
whoso shall be *w. thee* in the house — Jos 2:19
I will go *w. thee* into thy lot — J'g 1:3
I will surely go *w. thee* — J'g 4:9
people *w. thee* are too many — J'g 7:2
This shall go *w. thee* — J'g 7:4
for God is *w. thee* — 1Sa 10:7; 1Ch 17:2; Lu 1:28
I am *w. thee* according to thy — 1Sa 14:7
the Lord be *w. thee* — 1Sa 17:27; 20:13; 1Ch 22:11, 16
Why alone, and no man *w. thee* — 1Sa 21:1
I will go down *w. thee* — 1Sa 26:6
so long as I have been *w. thee* — 1Sa 29:8
my hand shall be *w. thee* — 2Sa 3:12
I was *w. thee* — 2Sa 7:9; 1Ch 17:8
Hath Amon thy brother been *w. thee* — 2Sa 13:20
Why should he go *w. thee* — 2Sa 13:26
God will be *w. thee* — 2Sa 14:17; 1Ch 28:20

mercy and truth be *w. thee* — 2Sa 15:20
hast thou not *w. thee* Zadok — 2Sa 15:35
w. thee Shemei who cursed — 1Ki 2:8
I will not go in *w. thee* — 1Ki 13:8; 13:16
What have I to do *w. thee* — 1Ki 17:18; 2Ki 3:13; 2Ch 35:21; M'k 5:7; Lu 8:28; Joh 2:4
thou and Judah *w. thee* — 2Ki 14:10; 2Ch 25:19
Lord it is nothing *w. thee* — 2Ch 14:11
we will be *w. thee* — 2Ch 18:3; Ezr 10:4
I know that this is *w. thee* — Job 10:13
there is forgiveness *w. thee* — Ps 130:4
when I awake, I am *w. thee* — Ps 139:18
his heart is not *w. thee* — Pr 23:7
that we may seek him *w. thee* — Ca 6:1
I am *w. thee* — Isa 41:10; 43:5; Jer 1:8, 19; 15:20; 30:11; 46:28; Ac 18:10
many people *w. thee* — Eze 38:6; 38:9, 15; 39:4
Is there yet any *w. thee* — Am 6:10
men that were at peace *w. thee* — Ob 7
come, and all the saints *w. thee* — Zec 14:5
What have we to do *w. thee* — M't 8:29; M'k 1:24; Lu 4:34
take *w. thee* one or two more — M't 18:16
though I should die *w. thee* — M't 26:35; M'k 14:31
I am ready to go *w. thee* into — Lu 22:33
he that was *w. thee* beyond Jordan — Joh 3:26
glory I had *w. thee* before the world — Joh 17:5
We also go *w. thee* — Joh 21:3
Thy money perish *w. thee* — Ac 8:20
Grace be *w. thee* — 1Ti 6:21

WITH *THEM*

Thou shalt not go *w. them* — Nu 22:12
the Lord was *w. them* — J'g 1:22
do *w. them* what seemeth good — J'g 19:24
all the while we were *w. them* — 1Sa 25:16
have *w. them* their two sons — 2Sa 15:36
more than they that be *w. them* — 2Ki 6:16
all that were *w. them* — 1Ch 5:20
whether with many or *w. them* — 2Ch 14:11
do *w. them* as they would — Ne 9:24
walk not in the way *w. them* — Pr 1:15
neither desire to be *w. them* — Pr 24:1
w. them that go down to the pit — Eze 26:20; 31:14; 32:18, 24-25, 29
I the Lord am *w. them* — Eze 34:30; Zec 10:5
neither *w. them* more than one loaf — M'k 8:14
eleven and them *w. them* — Lu 24:33
while I was *w. them* in the world — Joh 17:12
was it not *w. them* that came — Heb 3:17
God himself shall be *w. them* — Re 21:3

WITH US

Let the damsel abide *w. us* — Ge 24:55
No man is *w. us*. God is witness — Ge 31:50
make ye marriages *w. us* — Ge 34:9
ye shall dwell *w. us* — Ge 34:10; 34:22-23
these men are peaceable *w. us* — Ge 34:21
if send our brother *w. us* — Ge 43:4; 44:26
seeth the lad is not *w. us* — Ge 44:30; 44:31
God of Hebrews met *w. us* — Ex 3:18; 5:3
Our cattle shall go *w. us* — Ex 10:26; 17:3
wherefore hast dealt *w. us* — Ex 14:11
Speak *w. us*; let not God speak *w. us* — Ex 20:19
come *w. us* — Nu 10:29; 10:32
it was well *w. us* in Egypt — Nu 11:18
the Lord is *w. us* — Nu 14:9
Balaam refuseth to go *w. us* — Nu 22:14
Lord made a covenant *w. us* — De 5:2; 5:3
him that is here *w. us*; him that is not *w. us* here this day — De 29:15
make a league *w. us* — Jos 9:6; 9:11
if Lord is *w. us* why is all — J'g 6:13
hold thy peace and go *w. us* — J'g 18:19
ark shall not abide *w. us* — 1Sa 5:7

Make covenant *w. us*; we will   *1Sa* 11:1
Doth not David hide *w. us*   *1Sa* 23:19
not go *w. us* to battle   *1Sa* 29:4; 29:9
let Amnon go *w. us*   *2Sa* 13:26
go no more *w. us* to battle   *2Sa* 21:17
The Lord our God be *w. us*   *1Ki* 8:57
they that be *w. us* more than   *2Ki* 6:16
talk not *w. us* in Jews'   *2Ki* 18:26
language
God is *w. us*   *2Ch* 13:12; 32:8
w. us are the grayheaded   *Job* 15:10
the Lord of hosts is *w. us*   *Ps* 46:7
be angry *w. us* for ever   *Ps* 85:5
He hath not dealt *w. us*   *Ps* 103:10
God is *w. us*   *Isa* 8:10
our transgressions are *w. us*   *Isa* 59:12
the law of the Lord is *w. us*   *Jer* 8:8
break not thy covenant *w. us*   *Jer* 14:21
be well *w. us* when we obey   *Jer* 42:6
doings, so he dealt *w. us*   *Zec* 1:6
interpreted is, God *w. us*   *M't* 1:23
his sisters *w. us*   *M't* 13:56; *M'k* 6:3
were *w. us* seven brethren   *M't* 22:25
Son, why hast thou dealt *w. us*   *Lu* 2:48
because he followeth not *w. us*   *Lu* 9:49
Abide *w. us*; the day is far   *Lu* 24:29
spent
while he talked *w. us* by the   *Lu* 24:32
way
For he was numbered *w. us*   *Ac* 1:17
which have companied *w. us*   *Ac* 1:21
all
witness *w. us* of his   *Ac* 1:22
resurrection
his sepulchre *w. us* unto this   *Ac* 2:29
day
went *w. us* certain disciples   *Ac* 21:16
Agrippa and all here were *w.*   *Ac* 25:24
us
chosen to travel *w. us*   *2Co* 8:19
you who are troubled, rest *w.*   *2Th* 1:7
us
obtained like precious faith *w.*   *2Pe* 1:1
us
may have fellowship *w. us*   *1Jo* 1:3
truth shall be *w. us* for ever   *2Jo* 2

WITH *YOU*

establish covenant *w. you*   *Ge* 9:9;
    9:11; *Le* 26:9; *J'g* 2:1
with every creature that is *w.*   *Ge* 9:10
you
give me a buryingplace *w. you*   *Ge* 23:4
we will dwell *w. you* one   *Ge* 34:16
people
my son not go down *w. you*   *Ge* 42:18
except your brother be *w. you*   *Ge* 43:3;
    43:5; 44:21
God shall be *w. you*   *Ge* 48:21
let little ones go *w. you*   *Ex* 10:24
carry up my bones *w. you*   *Ex* 13:19
Lord talked *w. you* from   *Ex* 20:22
heaven
covenant the Lord made *w.*   *Ex* 24:8;
you   *De* 4:23; 9:9; *2Ki* 17:38
Aaron and Hur are *w. you*   *Ex* 24:14
stranger that dwelleth *w. you*   *Le* 19:34;
    Nu 15:14
buy of their families *w. you*   *Le* 25:45
w. you a man of every tribe   *Nu* 1:4
names of men that stand *w.*   *Nu* 1:5
you
where I will meet *w. you*   *Nu* 17:4
refuses me leave to go *w.*   *Nu* 22:13
you
if God will pass *w. you* over   *Nu* 32:29
Jordan
Lord was angry *w. you*   *De* 9:8
Lord spake *w. you* in the   *De* 9:10
mount
he hath no inheritance *w.*   *De* 12:12
you
God is he that goeth *w. you*   *De* 20:4
while I was yet alive *w. you*   *De* 31:27
stones carry over Jordan *w.*   *Jos* 4:3
you
neither will I be *w. you* any   *Jos* 7:12
more
we make a league *w. you*   *Jos* 9:7
Take victuals *w. you* for   *Jos* 9:11
journey
Amorites fought *w. you*   *Jos* 24:8
the Lord deal kindly *w. you*   *Ru* 1:8
Boaz said the Lord be *w. you*   *Ru* 2:4
will I make a covenant *w.*   *1Sa* 11:2
you
that I may reason *w. you*   *1Sa* 12:7
come again I will go *w. you*   *1Sa* 22:23

What have I to do *w. you*   *2Sa* 16:10;
    19:22
I will surely go *w. you*   *2Sa* 18:2
your master's son *w. you*   *2Ki* 10:2
Is not the Lord *w. you*   *1Ch* 22:18
are *w. you* golden calves   *2Ch* 13:8
Lord is *w. you* while ye are   *2Ch* 15:2
with him
Lord who is *w. you* in   *2Ch* 19:6
judgment
The Lord will be *w. you*   *2Ch* 20:17
are there not sins *w. you*   *2Ch* 28:10
Let us build *w. you*   *Ezr* 4:2
wisdom will die *w. you*   *Job* 12:2
lest I deal *w. you* after your   *Job* 42:8
folly
everlasting covenant *w. you*   *Isa* 55:3
I will plead *w. you*   *Jer* 2:9;
    Eze 20:35-36
Will not make a full end *w.*   *Jer* 5:18
you
cannot I do *w. you* as a   *Jer* 18:6
potter
I am *w. you*   *Jer* 42:11; *Hag* 1:13; 2:4
what I have wrought *w. you*   *Eze* 20:44
should have inheritance *w.*   *Eze* 47:22
you
God deal wondrously *w. you*   *Joe* 2:26
God of hosts be *w. you*   *Am* 5:14
word I covenanted *w. you*   *Hag* 2:5
We will go *w. you*, for we   *Zec* 8:23
have heard God is *w. you*
how long shall I be *w. you*   *M't* 17:17;
    M'k 9:19; *Lu* 9:41
ye have poor *w. you* always   *M't* 26:11;
    M'k 14:7; *Joh* 12:8
when I drink it new *w. you*   *M't* 26:29
in kingdom
I sat daily *w. you* teaching   *M't* 26:55;
    M'k 14:49; *Lu* 22:53
I am *w. you* alway unto the   *M't* 28:20
end
to eat passover *w. you* before   *Lu* 22:15
I spake while I was *w. you*   *Lu* 24:44
Yet a little while am I *w.*   *Joh* 7:33;
you   13:33
Yet a little while is light *w.*   *Joh* 12:35
you
Have I been so long *w. you*   *Joh* 14:9
Comforter that he may abide   *Joh* 14:16
w. you
Spirit of truth dwelleth *w.*   *Joh* 14:17
you
have spoken, being present   *Joh* 14:25
w. you
Peace I leave *w. you*, my   *Joh* 14:27
peace I
Hereafter will not talk much   *Joh* 14:30
w. you
these things I said because I   *Joh* 16:4
was *w. you*
men of like passions *w. you*   *Ac* 14:15
manner I have been *w. you*   *Ac* 20:18
at all
Why incredible *w. you*   *Ac* 26:8
I may be comforted *w. you*   *Ro* 1:12
refreshed *w. you*   *Ro* 15:32
I was *w. you* in weakness   *1Co* 2:3
that we might reign *w. you*   *1Co* 4:8
be a partaker *w. you*   *1Co* 9:23
be *w. you* without fear   *1Co* 16:10
establisheth us *w. you* is God   *2Co* 1:21
ye are in our hearts to die *w.*   *2Co* 7:3
you
when *w. you* not chargeable   *2Co* 11:9;
    Ga 4:18
the God of peace shall be   *2Co* 13:11
w. you
that gospel might continue *w.*   *Ga* 2:5
you
desire to be present *w. you*   *Ga* 4:20
yet am I *w. you* in spirit   *Col* 2:5
w. you we told you   *1Th* 3:4; *2Th* 2:5
word be glorified *w. you*   *2Th* 3:1
when *w. you* we commanded   *2Th* 3:10
God dealeth *w. you* as with   *Heb* 12:7
sons
the church elected *w. you*   *1Pe* 5:13
while they feast *w. you*   *2Pe* 2:13

LAY WITH

the firstborn *lay w.* father   *Ge* 19:33;
    34:35
Jacob *lay w.* Leah   *Ge* 30:16
Shechem *lay w.* Dinah   *Ge* 34:2
Reuben *lay w.* Bilhah   *Ge* 35:22
man that *lay w.* woman   *De* 22:22
man that *lay w.* her die   *De* 22:25
man that *lay w.* her give fifty   *De* 22:29

heard they *lay w.* women   *1Sa* 2:22
he *lay w.* her   *2Sa* 11:4; 12:24
forced Tamar and *lay w.*   *2Sa* 13:14
her
in her youth *lay w.* her   *Eze* 23:8

LIE WITH

drink wine, we will *lie w.*   *Ge* 19:32
him
go thou in, and *lie w.* him   *Ge* 19:34
he shall *lie w.* thee to-night   *Ge* 30:15
lie w. me   *Ge* 39:7; 39:12; *2Sa* 13:11
came in unto me to *lie w.* me   *Ge* 39:14
if a man *lie w.* a maid   *Ex* 22:16
woman *w.* whom man shall lie   *Le* 15:18
if any man *lie w.* her   *Le* 15:24;
    Nu 5:13
lie carnally *w.* neighbour's   *Le* 18:20
wife
not *lie w.* mankind   *Le* 18:22; 20:13
not *lie w.* any beast   *Le* 18:22; 20:15
if man *lie w.* daughter in law   *Le* 20:12
if man *lie w.* woman in   *Le* 20:18
sickness
if man *lie w.* uncle's wife   *Le* 20:20
man find and *lie w.* her   *De* 22:23
if man force and *lie w.* her   *De* 22:25
if find damsel and *lie w.* her   *De* 22:28
betroth a wife and *lie w.* her   *De* 28:30
go to *lie w.* my wife   *2Sa* 11:11
he shall *lie w.* thy wives   *2Sa* 12:11
Come, *lie w.* me my sister   *2Sa* 13:11

LIETH WITH

whoso *lieth w.* beast shall die   *Ex* 22:19
lieth w. her is unclean   *Le* 15:33
lieth carnally *w.* bondmaid   *Le* 19:20
man that *lieth w.* father's wife   *Le* 20:11
lieth w. mankind as *lieth w.*   *Le* 20:13
woman
cursed that *lieth w.* father's   *De* 27:20
wife
lieth w. beast   *De* 27:21
lieth w. sister   *De* 27:22
lieth w. mother in law   *De* 27:23

LYING WITH

folly in *lying w.* Jacob's   *Ge* 34:7
daughter
kill every woman that hath   *Nu* 31:17
known man by *lying w.* him
all that hath not known man   *Nu* 31:18;
by *lying w.* him   31:35; *J'g* 21:12
if man be found *lying w.*   *De* 22:22
woman

WITHAL

and bowls thereof, to cover   *Ex* 25:29
w.
places for the staves to bear   *Ex* 30:4
it *w.*
and his foot also of brass, to   *Ex* 30:18
wash *w.*
of the sanctuary, to make it *w.*   *Ex* 36:3
covers to cover *w.* of pure   *Ex* 37:16
gold
places for the staves to bear   *Ex* 37:27
it *w.*
the sides of the altar, to bear   *Ex* 38:7
it *w.*
and put water there, to wash   *Ex* 40:30
w.
it be that a man shall be defiled   *Le* 5:3
w.
to reconcile *w.* in the holy   *Le* 6:30
place
feet, to leap *w.* upon the   *Le* 11:21
earth
shall be holy to praise the   *Le* 19:24
Lord *w.*
the bowls, and covers to cover   *Nu* 4:7
w.
in their right hands to blow *w.*   *J'g* 7:20
w. of a beautiful   *1Sa* 16:12
countenance
w. how he had slain all the   *1Ki* 19:1
that Manasseh had provoked   *2Ki* 23:26
him *w.*
to overlay the walls of the   *1Ch* 29:4
houses *w.*
vessels to minister, and to   *2Ch* 24:14
offer *w.*
to shoot arrows and great   *2Ch* 26:15
stones *w.*
array the man *w.* whom the   *Es* 6:9
king
him a potsherd to scrape   *Job* 2:8
himself *w.*

own nets, whilst that I w.   Ps 141:10
escape
they shall w. be fitted in thy   Pr 22:18
lips
or to take water w. out of   Isa 30:14
the pit
that thou shalt sow the   Isa 30:23
ground w.
I am baptized w. shall ye be   M'k 10:39
baptized
that ye mete w. it shall be   Lu 6:38
measured
not w. to signify the crimes   Ac 25:27
laid
is given to every man to   1Co 12:7
profit w.
W. praying also for us that   Col 4:3
God
w. they learn to be idle,   1Ti 5:13
wandering
But w. prepare me also a   Ph'm 22
lodging

WITHDRAW

unto the priest, W. thine   1Sa 14:19
hand
If God will not w. his anger   Job 9:13
W. thine hand far from me   Job 13:21
he may w. man from his   Job 33:17
purpose
W. thy foot from thy   Pr 25:17
neighbour's
also from this w. not thine   Ec 7:18
hand
neither shall thy moon w.   Isa 60:20
itself
and the stars shall w. their   Joe 2:10;
shining   3:15
w. yourselves from every   2Th 3:6
brother
godliness: from such w. thyself   1Ti 6:5

WITHDRAWEST

Why w. thou thy hand, even   Ps 74:11
thy

WITHDRAWETH

He w. not his eyes from the   Job 36:7

WITHDRAWN

w. the inhabitants of their   De 13:13
city
but my beloved and w. himself   Ca 5:6
not w. his hand from   La 2:8
destroying
hath w. his hand from   Eze 18:8
iniquity
he hath w. himself from them   Ho 5:6
And he was w. from them   Lu 22:41
about a

WITHDREW

Israel w. from after David (S)   2Sa 20:2
W. from me I will bear (S)   2Ki 18:14
and w. the shoulder, and   Ne 9:29
Nevertheless I w. mine hand   Eze 20:22
it, he w. himself from thence   M't 12:15
Jesus w. himself with his   M'k 3:7
disciples
he w. himself into the   Lu 5:16
wilderness
he w. and separated himself   Ga 2:12

WITHER

his leaf also shall not w.   Ps 1:3
grass, and w. as the green herb   Ps 37:2
up: the reeds and flags shall   Isa 19:6
w.
sown by the brooks, shall w.   Isa 19:7
earth w. (A)(R)   Isa 24:4; 40:7
blow upon them, and they   Isa 40:24
shall w.
and the herbs of every field w.   Jer 12:4
cut off the fruit thereof, that   Eze 17:9
it w.
w. in all the leaves of her   Eze 17:9
spring
shall it not utterly w. when   Eze 17:10
w. in the furrows where it   Eze 17:10
grew
and the top of Carmel shall w.   Am 1:2
wreath that will soon w.   1Co 9:25
(A)(N)

rich man w. and die (A)(N)   Jas 1:11
nothing can destroy, spoil, w.   1Pe 1:4
(N)

WITHERED

seven ears, w. thin, and   Ge 41:23
blasted
I am w. away (E)   Job 6:2
heart is smitten, and w. like   Ps 102:4
grass
and I am w. like grass   Ps 102:11
for the hay is w. away, the   Isa 15:6
grass
When the boughs thereof are   Isa 27:11
w.
it is w. it is become like a stick   La 4:8
strong rods were broken and   Eze 19:12
w.
all the trees of the field, are w.   Joe 1:12
joy is w. away from the sons   Joe 1:12
of men
broken down; for the corn is   Joe 1:17
w.
piece whereupon it rained not   Am 4:7
w.
and it smote the gourd that it   Jon 4:7
w.
a man which had his hand w.   M't 12:10
they had no root, they w.   M't 13:6
away
And presently the fig tree w.   M't 21:19
away
How soon is the fig tree w.   M't 21:20
away
man there which had a w.   M'k 3:1
hand
the man which had the w.   M'k 3:3
hand
because it had no root, it w.   M'k 4:6
away
which thou cursedst is w.   M'k 11:21
away
a man whose right hand was   Lu 6:6
w.
man which had the w. hand,   Lu 6:8
Rise
it w. because it lacked moisture   Lu 8:6
halt, w., waiting for the   Joh 5:3
moving of
cast forth as a branch, and is   Joh 15:6
w.

WITHERETH

down, it w. before any other   Job 8:12
herb
the evening it is cut down, and   Ps 90:6
w.
which w. afore it groweth up   Ps 129:6
The grass w. the flowers   Isa 40:7;
fadeth   40:8
burning heat, but it w. the   Jas 1:11
grass
The grass w. and the flower   1Pe 1:24
trees whose fruit w. without   Jude 12
fruit

WITHERING

oak shedding w. leaves (B)   Isa 1:30

WITHERS

whose leaf w. (A)(R)   Isa 1:30
flower w. (B)(E)   Isa 40:7

WITHHELD

nothing will be w. from them   Ge 11:6
(S)
I also w. thee from sinning   Ge 20:6
seeing thou hast not w. thy   Ge 22:12
son
hast not w. thy son, thine   Ge 22:16
only son
who hath w. from thee the   Ge 30:2
fruit of
Lord hath not w. his kindness   Ru 2:20
(S)
withheld (S)   1Sa 25:26;
Jer 3:3; 5:25; Eze 18:16; Joe 1:13;
  Am 4:7
If I have w. the poor from   Job 31:16
their
I w. not my heart from any   Ec 2:10
joy

WITHHELDEST

w. not thy manna from their   Ne 9:20

WITHHOLD

shall w. from thee his   Ge 23:6
sepulchre
w. thy help (S)   De 22:1; 22:3-4
for he will not w. me from   2Sa 13:13
thee
can w. himself from speaking   Job 4:2
W. not thou thy tender   Ps 40:11
mercies
good thing will he w. from   Ps 84:11
them
W. no good from them to   Pr 3:27
whom it
W. not correction from a   Pr 23:13
child
in the evening w. not thine   Ro 11:6
hand
W. thy foot from being unshod   Jer 2:25
the earth w. her fruit (S)   Hag 1:10

WITHHOLDEN

w. thee from coming to shed   1Sa 25:26
hast w. bread from the   Job 22:7
hungry
from the wicked their light is   Job 38:15
w.
no thought can be w. from   Job 42:2
thee
hast not w. the request of his   Ps 21:2
lips
the showers have been w.   Jer 3:3
your sins have w. good things   Jer 5:25
from
hath not w. the pledge,   Eze 18:16
neither
drink offering is w. from the   Joe 1:13
also I have w. the rain from   Am 4:7
you

WITHHOLDETH

he w. the waters, and they   Job 12:15
dry up
he that w. more than is meet   Pr 11:24
He that w. corn, the people   Pr 11:26
shall
what w. that he might be   2Th 2:6
revealed

WITHIN

pitch it w. and without with   Ge 6:14
pitch
and he was uncovered w. his   Ge 9:21
tent
Sarah laughed w. herself,   Ge 18:12
saying
be fifty righteous w. the city   Ge 18:24
Sodom fifty righteous w. the   Ge 18:26
city
children struggled together w.   Ge 25:22
of the men of the house   Ge 39:11
there w.
Yet w. three days shall   Ge 40:13;
Pharaoh   40:19
nor thy stranger that is w.   Ex 20:10
thy gate
w. and without shalt thou   Ex 25:11
overlay
in thither w. the veil of the   Ex 26:33
ark of
it with pure gold w. and   Ex 37:2
without
not brought in w. the holy   Le 10:18
place
whether it be bare w. or   Le 13:55
without
caused the house to be   Le 14:41
scraped w.
holy place w. the veil before   Le 16:2
small, and bring it w. the veil   Le 16:12
and bring his blood w. the   Le 16:15
veil
it w. a whole year after it is   Le 25:29
sold
w. a full year may he redeem   Le 25:29
it
redeemed w. the space of   Le 25:30
a year
gathered together w. your   Le 26:25
cities
w. a covering of badgers'   Nu 4:10
skins
of the altar, and w. the veil   Nu 18:7
thy stranger that is w. thy   De 5:14
gates
the Levite that is w. your   De 12:12
gates

Thou mayest not eat w. thy gates	De 12:17
and the Levite that is w. thy gates	De 12:18; 14:27; 16:11
and shalt lay it up w. thy gates	De 14:28
the widow, which are w. thy gates	De 14:29
of thy brethren w. any of thy gates	De 15:7
Thou shalt eat it w. thy gates: the	De 15:22
the passover w. any of thy gates	De 16:5
the widow, that are w. thy gates	De 16:14
w. any of thy gates which the Lord	De 17:2
matters of controversy w. thy gates	De 17:8
he shall not come w. the camp	De 23:10
that are in thy land w. thy gates	De 24:14
that they may eat w. thy gates, and	De 26:12
stranger that is w. thee shall get	De 28:43
thy stranger that is w. thy gates	De 31:12
The sword without, and terror w.	De 32:25
w. three days ye shall pass over	Jos 1:11
w. the inheritance of the children	Jos 19:1
inheritance w. the inheritance	Jos 19:9
w. the possession of the children	Jos 21:41
and lamp w. the pitchers	J'g 7:16
was a strong tower w. the city	J'g 9:51
came not w. the border of Moab	J'g 11:18
ye not recover them w. that time	J'g 11:26
declare it me w. the seven days	J'g 14:12
But it came to pass w. a while after	J'g 15:1
camest not w. the days appointed	1Sa 13:11
w. as it were an half acre of land	1Sa 14:14
Nabal's heart was merry w. him	1Sa 25:36
that his heart died w. him	1Sa 25:37
Saul lay sleeping w. the trench	1Sa 26:7
ark of God dwelleth w. curtains	2Sa 7:2
me the men of Judah w. three days	2Sa 20:4
house w. with boards of cedar	1Ki 6:15
he even built them for it w. even	1Ki 6:16
cedar of the house w. was carved	1Ki 6:18
oracle he prepared in the house w.	1Ki 6:19
the house w. with pure gold	1Ki 6:21
w. the oracle he made two cherubims	1Ki 6:23
cherubims w. the inner house	1Ki 6:27
and open flowers, w. and without	1Ki 6:29
overlaid with gold, w. and without	1Ki 6:30
had another court w. the porch	1Ki 7:8
sawed with saws, w. and without	1Ki 7:9
mouth of it w. the chapiter	1Ki 7:31
alone; for her soul is vexed w. her	2Ki 4:27
had sackcloth w. upon his flesh	2Ki 6:30
they told it to the king's house w.	2Ki 7:11
and he that cometh w. the ranges	2Ki 11:8
he overlaid it w. with pure gold	2Ch 3:4
sedition w. the same of old time	Ezr 4:15
would not come w. three days	Ezr 10:8
unto Jerusalem w. three days	Ezr 10:9
his servant lodge w. Jerusalem	Ne 4:22
the house of God, w. the temple	Ne 6:10

arrows of the Almighty are w. me	Job 6:4
and his soul w. him shall mourn	Job 14:22
my reins are consumed w. me	Job 19:27
but keep it still w. his mouth	Job 20:13
it is the gall of asps w. him	Job 20:14
Which make oil w. their walls	Job 24:11
the spirit w. me constraineth me	Job 32:18
my heart is melted w. me (S)	Ps 22:14
of the wicked saith w. my heart	Ps 36:1
My heart was hot w. me while	Ps 39:3
God: yea, thy law is w. my heart	Ps 40:8
hid thy righteousness w. my heart	Ps 40:10
God, my soul is cast down w. me	Ps 42:6
why art thou disquieted w. me	Ps 42:11; 43:5
king's daughter is all glorious w.	Ps 45:13
and renew a right spirit w. me	Ps 51:10
My heart is sore pained w. me	Ps 55:4
multitude of my thoughts w. me	Ps 94:19
walk w. my house with a perfect	Ps 101:2
deceit shall not dwell w. my house	Ps 101:7
all that is w. me, bless his holy	Ps 103:1
and my heart is wounded w. me	Ps 109:22
Our feet shall stand w. thy gates	Ps 122:2
Peace be w. thy walls, and prosperity	Ps 122:7
walls, and prosperity w. thy palaces	Ps 122:7
I will now say, Peace be w. thee	Ps 122:8
my spirit was overwhelmed w. me	Ps 142:3
is my spirit overwhelmed w. me	Ps 143:4
my heart w. me is desolate	Ps 143:4
hath blessed thy children w. thee	Ps 147:13
thing if thou keep them w. thee	Pr 22:18
lips, and layeth up deceit w. him	Pr 26:24
was a little city, and a few men w. it	Ec 9:14
thou hast doves' eyes w. thy locks	Ca 4:1
of a pomegranate w. thy locks	Ca 4:3
are thy temples w. thy locks	Ca 6:7
w. threescore and five years shall	Isa 7:8
W. three years, as the years of an	Isa 16:14
W. a year, according to the years	Isa 21:16
my spirit w. me will I seek thee	Isa 26:9
mine house and w. my walls a place	Isa 56:5
nor destruction w. thy borders	Isa 60:18
he that put his holy spirit w. him	Isa 63:11
thy vain thoughts lodge w.	Jer 4:14
Mine heart w. me is broken because	Jer 23:9
W. two full years will I bring	Jer 28:3
w. the space of two full years	Jer 28:11
mine heart is turned w. me	La 1:20
of fire round about w. it	Eze 1:27
it was written w. and without	Eze 2:10
Go, shut thyself w. thine house	Eze 3:24
the pestilence and the famine w.	Eze 7:15
and I will put a new spirit w. you	Eze 11:19
divination w. the house of Israel	Eze 12:24
and a new spirit will I put w. you	Eze 36:25
And I wll put my spirit w. you	Eze 36:27
porch of the gate w. was one reed	Eze 40:7

also the porch of the gate w.	Eze 40:8
posts w. the gate round about	Eze 40:16
w. were hooks, an hand broad	Eze 40:43
of the side chambers that were w.	Eze 41:9
wall round about w. and without	Eze 41:17
gates of the inner court, and w.	Eze 44:17
of any God or man w. thirty days	Da 6:12
but w. few days he shall be destroyed	Da 11:20
mine heart is turned w. me	Ho 11:8
When my soul fainteth w. me I	Jon 2:7
pot, and as flesh w. the caldron	Mic 3:3
and when he treadeth w. our borders	Mic 5:6
no breath w. (S)	Hab 2:19
princes w. her are roaring lions	Zep 3:3
formeth the spirit of man w. him	Zec 12:1
think not to say w. yourselves	M't 3:9
of the scribes said w. themselves	M't 9:3
For she said w. herself, If I may	M't 9:21
w. they are full of extortion	M't 23:25
first that which is w. the cup	M't 23:26
are w. full of dead men's bones	M't 23:27
but w. ye are full of hypocrisy and	M't 23:28
they so reasoned w. themselves	M'k 2:8
from w., out of the heart of men	M'k 7:21
All these evil things come from w.	M'k 7:23
had indignation w. themselves	M'k 14:4
w. three days I will build another	M'k 14:58
begin not to say w. yourselves, We	Lu 3:8
he spake w. himself saying, This	Lu 7:39
him began to say w. themselves	Lu 7:49
he from w. shall answer and say	Lu 11:7
make that which is w. also	Lu 11:40
w. four walls (P)	Lu 12:3
And he thought w. himself, saying	Lu 12:17
Then the steward said w. himself	Lu 16:3
the kingdom of God is w. you	Lu 17:21
but afterward he said w. himself	Lu 18:4
ground, and thy children w. thee	Lu 19:44
Did not our heart burn w. us. while	Lu 24:32
days again his disciples were w.	Joh 20:26
had opened, we found no man w.	Ac 5:23
we ourselves groan w. ourselves	Ro 8:23
do not ye judge them that are w.	1Co 5:12
were fightings, w. were fears	2Co 7:5
entereth into that w. the veil	Heb 6:19
and they were full of eyes w.	Re 4:8
on the throne a book written w.	Re 5:1

WITHOUT

earth was w. form, and void	Ge 1:2
pitch it within and w. with pitch	Ge 6:14
and told his two brethren w.	Ge 9:22
him forth, and set him w. the city	Ge 19:16
camels to kneel down w. the city by	Ge 24:11
wherefore standeth thou w.	Ge 24:31
Joseph is w. doubt rent in pieces	Ge 37:33
w. thee shall no man lift up his	Ge 41:44

numbering; for it was *w.*   *Ge 41:49*
number
Your lamb shall be *w.* blemish   *Ex 12:5*
then shall she go out free *w.*   *Ex 21:11*
money
and *w.* shalt thou overlay it   *Ex 25:11*
thou shalt set the table *w.* the   *Ex 26:35*
veil
of the congregation *w.* the   *Ex 27:21*
veil
bullock and two rams *w.*   *Ex 29:1*
blemish
thou burn with fire *w.* the   *Ex 29:14*
camp
and pitched it *w.* the camp   *Ex 33:7*
which was *w.* the camp   *Ex 33:7*
it with pure gold within and   *Ex 37:2*
w.
tabernacle northward, *w.* the   *Ex 40:22*
veil
let him offer a male *w.* blemish   *Le 1:3*
he shall bring it a male *w.*   *Le 1:10*
blemish
he shall offer it *w.* blemish   *Le 3:1*
before
female, he shall offer it *w.*   *Le 3:6*
blemish
a young bullock *w.* blemish   *Le 4:3*
unto
shall he carry forth *w.* the   *Le 4:12*
camp
forth the bullock *w.* the camp   *Le 4:21*
of the goats, a male *w.*   *Le 4:23*
blemish
of the goats, a female *w.*   *Le 4:28*
blemish
shall bring it a female *w.*   *Le 4:32*
blemish
a ram *w.* blemish out of the   *Le 5:15*
flocks
a ram *w.* blemish out of the   *Le 5:18;*
flock   *6:6*
carry forth the ashes *w.* the   *Le 6:11*
camp
he burnt with fire *w.* the camp   *Le 8:17*
for a burnt offering, *w.* blemish   *Le 9:2*
both of the first year, *w.*   *Le 9:3*
blemish
he burnt with fire *w.* the camp   *Le 9:11*
eat it *w.* leaven beside the   *Le 10:12*
altar
w. the camp shall his   *Le 13:46*
habitation
whether it be bare within or   *Le 13:55*
w.
take two he lambs *w.* blemish   *Le 14:10*
lamb of the first year *w.*   *Le 14:10*
blemish
into an unclean place *w.* the   *Le 14:40*
city
w. the city into an unclean   *Le 14:41*
place
shall one carry forth *w.* the   *Le 16:27*
camp
your own will a male *w.*   *Le 22:19*
blemish
an he lamb *w.* blemish of the   *Le 23:12*
first
seven lambs *w.* blemish of the   *Le 23:18*
first
W. the veil of the testimony   *Le 24:3*
him that hath cursed *w.* the   *Le 24:14*
camp
while she lieth desolate *w.*   *Le 26:43*
them
w. the camp shall ye put them   *Nu 5:3*
so, and put them out *w.* the   *Nu 5:4*
camp
lamb of the first year *w.*   *Nu 6:14*
blemish
and one ram *w.* blemish for   *Nu 6:14*
peace
w. the knowledge of the   *Nu 15:24*
congregation
him with stones *w.* the camp   *Nu 15:35*
brought him *w.* the camp   *Nu 15:36*
bring thee a red heifer *w.*   *Nu 19:2*
spot
may bring her forth *w.* the   *Nu 19:3*
camp
up *w.* the camp in a clean   *Nu 19:9*
place
w. doing any thing else, go   *Nu 20:19*
through
two lambs of the first year *w.*   *Nu 28:3;*
spot   *28:9*
lambs of the first year *w.* spot   *Nu 28:11*
they shall be unto you *w.*   *Nu 28:19;*
blemish   *28:31*

lambs of the first year *w.*   *Nu 29:2;*
blemish   *29:20, 23*
they shall be unto you *w.*   *Nu 29:8*
blemish
first year; they shall be *w.*   *Nu 29:13*
blemish
lambs of the first year *w.*   *Nu 29:17;*
spot   *29:26*
of the first year *w.* blemish   *Nu 29:29;*
   29:32, 36
forth to meet them *w.* the   *Nu 31:13*
camp
ye abide *w.* the camp seven   *Nu 31:19*
days
shall measure from *w.* the city   *Nu 35:5*
on
thrust him suddenly *w.*   *Nu 35:22*
enmity
him any thing *w.* laying of   *Nu 35:22*
wait
time come *w.* the border of   *Nu 35:26*
the city
find him *w.* the borders of   *Nu 35:27*
the city
thou shalt eat bread *w.*   *De 8:9*
scarceness
have a place also *w.* the   *De 23:12*
camp
shall not marry *w.* unto a   *De 25:5*
stranger
a God of truth and *w.* iniquity   *De 32:4*
The sword *w.* and terror   *De 32:25*
within
he will *w.* fail drive out from   *Jos 3:10*
before
left them *w.* the camp of   *Jos 6:23*
Israel
w. driving them out hastily   *J'g 2:23*
and their camels were *w.*   *J'g 6:5;*
number   *7:12*
shalt *w.* fail deliver the   *J'g 11:30*
children
left thee this day *w.* a   *Ru 4:14*
kinsman
blood to stay David *w.* a   *1Sa 19:5*
cause
overtake them, and *w.* fail   *1Sa 30:8*
recover
riseth even a morning *w.*   *2Sa 23:4*
clouds
for *w.* in the wall of the house   *1Ki 6:6*
he
and open flowers, within and   *1Ki 6:29*
w.
overlaid with gold, within   *1Ki 6:30*
and *w.*
sawed with saws, within and   *1Ki 7:9*
w.
oracle, and they were not seen   *1Ki 8:8*
w.
three years *w.* war between   *1Ki 22:1*
Syria and
Jehu appointed fourscore   *2Ki 10:24*
men *w.*
Have her forth *w.* the ranges   *2Ki 11:15*
the king's entry *w.* turned he   *2Ki 16:18*
come up *w.* the Lord against   *2Ki 18:25*
he burned them *w.* Jerusalem   *2Ki 23:6*
w. Jerusalem, unto the brook   *2Ki 23:6*
all these vessels was *w.*   *2Ki 25:16*
weight
but Seled died *w.* children   *1Ch 2:30*
and Jether died *w.* children   *1Ch 2:32*
nor offer burnt offerings *w.*   *1Ch 21:24*
cost
and of brass and iron *w.*   *1Ch 22:14*
weight
oracle; but they were not seen   *2Ch 5:9*
w.
people were *w.* number that   *2Ch 12:3*
came
Israel hath been *w.* the true   *2Ch 15:3*
God
w. a teaching priest, and *w.*   *2Ch 15:3*
law
and departed *w.* being   *2Ch 21:20*
desired
set it *w.* at the gate of the   *2Ch 24:8*
house
fountains which were *w.* the   *2Ch 32:3*
city
the towers, and another wall   *2Ch 32:5*
w.
built a wall *w.* the city of   *2Ch 33:14*
David
it be given them day by day *w.*   *Ezr 6:9*
fail
salt *w.* prescribing how much   *Ezr 7:22*
and we are not able to stand   *Ezr 10:13*
w.

ware lodged *w.* Jerusalem   *Ne 13:20*
once
him, to destroy him *w.* cause   *Job 2:3*
perish forever *w.* any   *Job 4:20*
regarding it
away? they die, even *w.*   *Job 4:21*
wisdom
marvellous things *w.* number   *Job 5:9*
is unsavoury be eaten *w.* salt   *Job 6:6*
shuttle, and are spent *w.* hope   *Job 7:6*
Can the rush grow up *w.*   *Job 8:11*
mire
can the flag grow *w.* water   *Job 8:11*
yea, and wonders *w.* number   *Job 9:10*
multiplieth my wounds *w.*   *Job 9:17*
cause
shadow of death, *w.* any   *Job 10:22*
order
shalt thou lift up thy faces   *Job 11:15*
w. spot
They grope in the dark *w.*   *Job 12:25*
light
the naked to lodge *w.*   *Job 24:7*
clothing
him to go naked *w.* clothing   *Job 24:10*
thou helped him that is *w.*   *Job 26:2*
power
I went mourning *w.* the sun   *Job 30:28*
clothing, or any poor *w.*   *Job 31:19*
covering
eaten the fruits thereof *w.*   *Job 31:39*
money
I am clean *w.* transgression, I   *Job 33:9*
am
is incurable *w.* transgression   *Job 34:6*
shall be taken away *w.* hand   *Job 34:20*
in pieces mighty men *w.*   *Job 34:24*
number
Job hath spoken *w.*   *Job 34:35*
knowledge
and his words were *w.*   *Job 34:35*
wisdom
multiplieth words *w.*   *Job 35:16*
knowledge
and they shall die *w.*   *Job 36:12*
knowledge
counsel by words *w.*   *Job 38:2*
knowledge
her labour is in vain *w.* fear   *Job 39:16*
not his like, who is made *w.*   *Job 41:33*
fear
that hideth counsel *w.*   *Job 42:3*
knowledge
him that *w.* cause is mine   *Ps 7:4*
enemy
which transgress *w.* cause   *Ps 25:3*
that did see me *w.* fled from   *Ps 31:11*
me
w. cause have they hid for me   *Ps 35:7*
w. cause they have digged for   *Ps 35:7*
my
the eye that hate me *w.* a   *Ps 35:19*
cause
prepare themselves *w.* my fault   *Ps 59:4*
They that hate me *w.* a cause   *Ps 69:4*
are
caterpillars, and that *w.*   *Ps 105:34*
number
and fought against me *w.* a   *Ps 109:3*
cause
perversely with me *w.* a   *Ps 119:78*
cause
have persecuted me *w.* a   *Ps 119:161*
cause
privily for the innocent *w.*   *Pr 1:11*
cause
Wisdom crieth *w.*; she uttereth   *Pr 1:20*
Strive not with a man *w.* cause   *Pr 3:30*
He shall die *w.* instruction   *Pr 5:23*
shall he be broken *w.* remedy   *Pr 6:15*
Now is she *w.* now in the   *Pr 7:12*
streets
fair woman which is *w.*   *Pr 11:22*
discretion
W. counsel purposes are   *Pr 15:22*
than great revenues *w.* right   *Pr 16:8*
that the soul be *w.* knowledge   *Pr 19:2*
There is a lion *w.* I shall be   *Pr 22:13*
slain
who hath wounds *w.* cause   *Pr 23:29*
Prepare thy work *w.* an make   *Pr 24:27*
it
against thy neighbour *w.*   *Pr 24:28*
cause
gift is like clouds and wind   *Pr 25:14*
w. rain
that is broken down, and *w.*   *Pr 25:28*
walls
be destroyed, and that *w.*   *Pr 29:1*
remedy

serpent will bite *w.* enchantment	*Ec 10:11*
concubines, and virgins *w.* number	*Ca 6:8*
when I should find thee *w.*	*Ca 8:1*
even great and fair, *w.* inhabitant	*Isa 5:9*
opened her mouth *w.* measure	*Isa 5:14*
the cities be wasted *w.* inhabitant	*Isa 6:11*
and the houses *w.* man and	*Isa 6:11*
W. me they shall bow down under	*Isa 10:4*
their valiant ones shall cry *w.*	*Isa 33:7*
now come up *w.* the Lord against	*Isa 36:10*
confounded world *w.* end	*Isa 45:17*
ye shall be redeemed *w.* money	*Isa 52:3*
oppressed them *w.* cause	*Isa 52:4*
and milk *w.* money and *w.* price	*Isa 55:1*
cities are burned *w.* inhabitant	*Jer 2:15*
have forgotten me days *w.* number	*Jer 2:32*
be laid waste, *w.* an inhabitant	*Jer 4:7*
the earth, and, lo, it was *w.* form	*Jer 4:23*
people, and *w.* understanding	*Jer 5:21*
Judah desolate, *w.* an inhabitant	*Jer 9:11*
to cut off the children from *w.*	*Jer 9:21*
will I give to the spoil *w.* price	*Jer 15:13*
which besiege you *w.* the walls	*Jer 21:4*
his neighbour's service *w.* wages	*Jer 22:13*
shall be desolate *w.* an inhabitant	*Jer 26:9*
say, It is desolate *w.* man or beast	*Jer 32:43*
be desolate *w.* man and *w.* beast	*Jer 33:10*
that are desolate, *w.* man and *w.* inhabitant, and *w.* beast	*Jer 33:10*
desolate *w.* man and *w.* beast	*Jer 33:12*
Judah a desolation *w.* inhabitant	*Jer 34:22*
offerings unto her, *w.* our men	*Jer 44:19*
and a curse, *w.* an inhabitant	*Jer 44:22*
and desolate *w.* an inhabitant	*Jer 46:19*
desolate, *w.* any to dwell therein	*Jer 48:9*
nation, that dwelleth *w.* care	*Jer 49:31*
a desolation *w.* an inhabitant	*Jer 51:29*
and an hissing, *w.* an inhabitant	*Jer 51:37*
of all these vessels was *w.* weight	*Jer 52:20*
w. strength before the pursuer	*La 1:6*
ceaseth not, *w.* any intermission	*La 3:49*
me sore, like a bird, *w.* cause	*La 3:52*
and it was written within and *w.*	*Eze 2:10*
sword is *w.* and the pestilence	*Eze 7:15*
w. cause all that I have done in it	*Eze 14:23*
w. great power or many people to	*Eze 17:9*
of life, *w.* committing iniquity	*Eze 33:15*
all of them dwelling *w.* walls	*Eze 38:11*
the forefront of the inner court *w.*	*Eze 40:19*
at the side *w.* as one goeth up to	*Eze 40:40*
w. the inner gate were the which was for the side chamber *w.*	*Eze 40:44* *Eze 41:9*
even unto the inner house, and *w.*	*Eze 41:17*
wall round about within and *w.*	*Eze 41:17*
upon the face of the porch *w.*	*Eze 41:25*
wall that was *w.* over against	*Eze 42:7*
of the house, *w.* the sanctuary	*Eze 43:21*
offer a kid of the goats *w.* blemish	*Eze 43:22*
offer a young bullock *w.* blemish	*Eze 43:23*
a ram out of the flock *w.* blemish	*Eze 43:23; 43:25*
take a young bullock *w.* blemish	*Eze 45:18*
and seven rams *w.* blemish daily	*Eze 45:23*
way of the porch of that gate	*Eze 46:2*
shall be six lambs *w.* blemish	*Eze 46:4*
and a ram *w.* blemish	*Eze 46:4*
be a young bullock *w.* blemish	*Eze 46:6*
a ram: they shall be *w.* blemish	*Eze 46:6*
a lamb of the first year *w.* blemish	*Eze 46:13*
led me about the way *w.* unto	*Eze 47:2*
a stone was cut out *w.* hands	*Da 2:34*
out of the mountain *w.* hands	*Da 2:45*
but he shall be broken *w.* hand	*Da 8:25*
w. his own reproach he shall	*Da 11:18*
days *w.* a king, and *w.* a prince	*Ho 3:4*
w. a sacrifice, and *w.* an image	*Ho 3:4*
w. an ephod, and *w.* teraphim	*Ho 3:4*
the troop of robbers spoileth *w.*	*Ho 7:1*
also is like a silly dove *w.* heart	*Ho 7:11*
my land, strong, and *w.* number	*Joe 1:6*
shall be inhabited as towns *w.* walls	*Zec 2:4*
angry with his brother *w.* a cause	*M't 5:22*
fall on the ground *w.* your Father	*M't 10:29*
mother and his brethren stood *w.*	*M't 12:46*
mother and thy brethren stand *w.*	*M't 12:47; Lu 8:20*
w. a parable spake he not unto	*M't 13:34; M'k 4:34*
A prophet is not *w.* honour, save	*M't 13:57*
Are ye also yet *w.* understanding	*M't 15:16*
Peter sat *w.* in the palace	*M't 26:69*
city, but was *w.* in desert places	*M'k 1:45*
and, standing *w.* sent unto him	*M'k 3:31*
and thy brethren *w.* seek for thee	*M'k 3:32*
unto them that are *w.* all these	*M'k 4:11*
A prophet is not *w.* honour, but in	*M'k 6:4*
There is nothing from *w.* a man	*M'k 7:15*
Are ye so *w.* understanding also	*M'k 7:18*
from *w.* entereth into the man	*M'k 7:18*
the colt tied by the door *w.* in a	*M'k 11:4*
will build another made *w.* hands	*M'k 14:58*
praying *w.* at the time of incense	*Lu 1:10*
enemies might serve him *w.* fear	*Lu 1:74*
a man that *w.* a foundation built	*Lu 6:49*
he that made that which is *w.*	*Lu 11:40*
ye begin to stand *w.* and to knock	*Lu 13:25*
a wife, and he die *w.* children	*Lu 20:28*
took a wife, and died *w.* children	*Lu 20:29*
When I sent you *w.* purse	*Lu 22:35*
w. him was not any thing made	*Joh 1:3*
He that is *w.* sin among you, let	*Joh 8:7*
for *w.* me ye can do nothing	*Joh 15:5*
law. They hated me *w.* a cause	*Joh 15:25*
But Peter stood at the door *w.*	*Joh 18:16*
now the coat was *w.* seam, woven	*Joh 19:23*
Mary stood *w.* at the sepulchre	*Joh 20:11*
the keepers standing *w.* before	*Ac 5:23*
and brought them *w.* violence	*Ac 5:26*
And he was three days *w.* sight	*Ac 9:9*
came I unto you *w.* gainsaying	*Ac 10:29*
prayer was made *w.* ceasing	*Ac 12:5*
he left not himself *w.* witness	*Ac 14:17*
w. any delay on the morrow	*Ac 25:17*
w. ceasing I make mention of you	*Ro 1:9*
so that they are *w.* excuse	*Ro 1:20*
W. understanding	*Ro 1:31*
w. natural affection, implacable	*Ro 1:31*
For as many as have sinned *w.* law	*Ro 2:12*
shall also perish *w.* law; and	*Ro 2:12*
make the faith of God *w.* effect	*Ro 3:3*
righteousness of God *w.* the law	*Ro 3:21*
by faith *w.* the deeds of the	*Ro 3:28*
imputeth righteousness *w.* works	*Ro 4:6*
For when we were yet *w.* strength	*Ro 5:6*
For *w.* the law sin was dead	*Ro 7:8*
I was alive *w.* the law once	*Ro 7:9*
how shall they hear *w.* a preacher	*Ro 10:14*
calling of God are *w.* repentance	*Ro 11:29*
Let love be *w.* dissimulation	*Ro 12:9*
ye have reigned as kings *w.* us	*1Co 4:8*
do to judge them also that are *w.*	*1Co 5:12*
But them that are *w.* God judgeth	*1Co 5:13*
that a man doeth is *w.* the body	*1Co 6:18*
I would have you *w.* carefulness	*1Co 7:32*
attend upon the Lord *w.* distraction	*1Co 7:35*
the gospel of Christ *w.* charge	*1Co 9:18*
To them that are *w.* law, as *w.* law	*1Co 9:21*
not *w.* law to God, but under the law	*1Co 9:21*
I might gain them that are *w.* law	*1Co 9:21*
neither is the man *w.* the woman	*1Co 11:11*
neither the woman *w.* the man in	*1Co 11:11*
even things *w.* life giving sound	*1Co 14:7*
none of them is *w.* signification	*1Co 14:10*
that he may be with you *w.* fear	*1Co 16:10*
w. were fightings, within were	*2Co 7:5*
boast of things *w.* our measure	*2Co 10:13*
boasting of things *w.* our measure	*2Co 10:15*
Beside those things that are *w.*	*2Co 11:28*
and *w.* blame before him in love	*Eph 1:4*
at that time ye were *w.* Christ	*Eph 2:12*
no hope, and *w.* God in the world	*Eph 2:12*
throughout all ages, world *w.* end	*Eph 3:21*
it should be holy and *w.* blemish	*Eph 5:27*
w. offence till the day of Christ	*Ph'p 1:10*
bold to speak the word *w.* fear	*Ph'p 1:14*
Do all things *w.* murmurings	*Ph'p 2:14*
w. wrangling (N)	*Ph'p 2:14*
the sons of God, *w.* rebuke, in the	*Ph'p 2:15*
the circumcision made *w.* hands	*Col 2:11*
wisdom toward them that are *w.*	*Col 4:5*
Remembering *w.* ceasing your work	*1Th 1:3*
also thank we God *w.* ceasing	*1Th 2:13*
honestly toward them that are *w.*	*1Th 4:12*
Pray *w.* ceasing	*1Th 5:17*
hands, *w.* wrath and doubting	*1Ti 2:8*
w. wrath (E)	*1Ti 2:8*
good report of them which are *w.*	*1Ti 3:7*
w. controversy great is the mystery	*1Ti 3:16*
w. preferring one before another	*1Ti 5:21*
keep this commandment *w.* spot	*1Ti 6:14*

w. ceasing, I have   2Ti 1:3
remembrance of
W. affection, trucebreakers   2Ti 3:3
w. thy mind would I do   Ph'm 14
nothing
tempted like as we are, yet   Heb 4:15
w. sin
W. father; w. mother   Heb 7:3
w. descent, having neither   Heb 7:3
w. all contradiction the less is   Heb 7:7
not w. an oath he was made   Heb 7:20
priest
priests were made w. an oath   Heb 7:21
not w. blood, which he   Heb 9:7
offered for
offered himself w. spot to   Heb 9:14
God
testament was dedicated w.   Heb 9:18
blood
and w. shedding of blood is   Heb 9:22
no
second time w. sin unto   Heb 9:28
salvation
profession of our faith w.   Heb 10:23
wavering
despised Moses' law died w.   Heb 10:28
mercy
w. faith it is impossible to   Heb 11:6
please
w. us should not be made   Heb 11:40
perfect
But if ye be w. chastisement   Heb 12:8
w. which no man shall see   Heb 12:14
the
conversation be w.   Heb 13:5
covetousness
for sin, are burned w. the   Heb 13:11
camp
own blood, suffered w. the   Heb 13:12
gate
therefore unto him w. the   Heb 13:13
camp
he shall have judgment w.   Jas 2:13
mercy
shew me thy faith w. thy works   Jas 2:18
man, that faith w. works is   Jas 2:20
dead
as the body w. the spirit is   Jas 2:26
dead
so faith w. works is dead also   Jas 2:26
w. partiality, and w.   Jas 3:17
hypocrisy
who w. respect of persons   1Pe 1:17
judgeth
lamb w. blemish and w. spot   1Pe 1:19
they also may w. the word be   1Pe 3:1
won
one to another w. grudging   1Pe 4:9
These are wells w. water,   2Pe 2:17
clouds
in peace, w. spot, and   2Pe 3:14
blameless
you, feeding themselves w.   Jude 12
fear
clouds they are w. water,   Jude 12
carried
w. fruit, twice dead, plucked   Jude 12
up
court which is w. the temple   Re 11:2
leave
w. fault before the throne of   Re 14:5
God
poured out w. mixture into   Re 14:10
the cup
winepress was trodden w. the   Re 14:20
city
For w. are dogs, and   Re 22:15
sorcerers

WITHS

they bind me with seven green   J'g 16:7
w.
seven fresh strong gutstrings,   J'g 16:7
still moist (A)
seven fresh, wood fiber cords   J'g 16:7
(B)
seven fresh bowstrings not   J'g 16:7;
dried (R)   16:8-9
brought up to her seven green   J'g 16:8
w.
seven fresh, strong bowstrings   J'g 16:8;
(A)   16:9
seven fiber cords not dried (B)   J'g 16:8
he brake the w. as a thread of   J'g 16:9
tow

WITHSTAND

I went out to w. thee,   Nu 22:32
because thy

and could not w. them   2Ch 13:7
to w. the kingdom of the   2Ch 13:8
Lord
so that none is able to w.   2Ch 20:6
thee
and no man could w. them; for   Es 9:2
against him, two shall w. him   Ec 4:12
the arms of the south shall   Da 11:15
not w.
shall there be any strength to   Da 11:15
w.
what was I, that I could w.   Ac 11:17
God
ye may be able to w. in the   Eph 6:13
evil day

WITHSTOOD

And they w. Uzziah the   2Ch 26:18
king, and
of the kingdom of Persia w.   Da 10:13
me
w. them, seeking to turn away   Ac 13:8
I w. him to the face, because   Ga 2:11
he was
as Jannes and Jambres w.   2Ti 3:8
Moses
for he hath greatly w.   2Ti 4:15
our words

WITLESS

has become w. (A)   Isa 19:11
the unwise and w.   Eph 5:15
(A)(E)(R)

WITNESS

that they may be a w. unto me   Ge 21:30
be for a w. between me and   Ge 31:44
thee
heap is a w. between me and   Ge 31:48
thee
see, God is w. betwixt me   Ge 31:50
and thee
This heap be w. and this   Ge 31:52
pillar
and this pillar be w. that I   Ge 31:52
will
shalt not bear false w.   Ex 20:16
against thy
then let him bring it for w.   Ex 22:13
and he
the wicked to be an   Ex 23:1
unrighteous w.
the voice of swearing, and is a   Le 5:1
w.
and there be no w. against her   Nu 5:13
the Lord in the tabernacle of   Nu 17:7
w.
went into the tabernacle of w.   Nu 17:8
before the tabernacle of w.   Nu 18:2
but one w. shall not testify   Nu 35:30
against
I call heaven and earth to w.   De 4:26
shalt thou bear false w.   De 5:20
against
at the mouth of one w. he   De 17:6
shall not
One w. shall not rise up   De 19:15
against a
a false w. rise up against any   De 19:16
man
if the w. be a false w. and   De 19:18
hath
that this song may be a w.   De 31:19
for me
shall testify against   De 31:21
them as a w.
song be a w. (A)(R)   De 31:21
may be there for a w. against   De 31:26
thee
But that it may be a w.   Jos 22:27
between us
but it is a w. between us and   Jos 22:28
you
be a w. between us that the   Jos 22:34
Lord is
this stone shall be a w. unto   Jos 24:27
us
it shall be therefore a w.   Jos 24:27
unto you
The Lord be w. between us, if   J'g 11:10
we
w. against me before the Lord   1Sa 12:3
The Lord is w. against you   1Sa 12:5
and his anointed is w. this   1Sa 12:5
day
And they answered, He is w.   1Sa 12:5
to bare w. against him, saying   1Ki 21:10

Israel, for the tabernacle of   2Ch 24:6
w.
bore w. among them (B)   2Ch 24:19
w. against you (B)   Job 15:6
which is a w. against me   Job 16:8
up in me beareth w. to my   Job 16:8
face
my w. is in heaven, and my   Job 16:19
record
the eye saw me, it gave w.   Job 29:11
to me
and as a faithful w. in heaven   Ps 89:37
A false w. that speaketh lies   Pr 6:19
righteousness; but a false w.   Pr 12:17
deceit
A faithful w. will not lie: but a   Pr 14:5
false
lie; but a false w. will utter   Pr 14:5
lies
A true w. delivereth souls;   Pr 14:25
but a
but a deceitful w. speaketh lies   Pr 14:25
A false w. shall not be   Pr 19:5; 19:9
An ungodly w. scorneth   Pr 19:28
judgment
A false w. shall perish: but   Pr 21:28
Be not a w. against thy   Pr 24:28
neighbour
that beareth false w. against   Pr 25:18
his
countenance doth w. against   Isa 3:9
them
it shall be for a sign and for   Isa 19:20
a w.
given him for a w. to the   Isa 55:4
people
sins w. against you (B)   Isa 59:12
I know, and am a w. saith   Jer 29:23
the Lord
The Lord be a true and   Jer 42:5
faithful w.
thing shall I take to w. for thee   La 2:13
bear w. (A)(B)   Am 3:13;
           1Jo 4:14; Re 22:16
the Lord God be w. against   Mic 1:2
you
the Lord hath been w.   Mal 2:14
between
a swift w. against the   Mal 3:5
sorcerers
to give w. (P)   M't 10:18;
    M'k 13:9; Lu 21:13; Re 12:11, 17
thefts, false w. blasphemies   M't 15:19
steal, Thou shalt not bare   M't 19:18
false w.
preached in all the world for   M't 24:14
a w.
sought false w. against Jesus   M't 26:59
is it which these w. against   M't 26:62
thee
many things they w. against   M't 27:13
thee
for a w. (B)   M'k 6:11
Do not bare false w.   M'k 10:19
Defraud not
sought for w. against Jesus   M'k 14:55
many bare false w. against   M'k 14:56
him
but their w. agreed not   M'k 14:56
together
and bare false w. against   M'k 14:57
him
neither so did their w.   M'k 14:59
agree
is it which these w. against   M'k 14:60
thee
many things they w. against   M'k 15:4
thee
all bare him w. and wondered   Lu 4:22
Truly ye bare w. that ye   Lu 11:48
allow the
Do not bare false w., Honour   Lu 18:20
thy
What need we any further w.   Lu 22:71
The same came for a w. to   Joh 1:7
bear
to bear w. of the Light, that all   Joh 1:7
was sent to bear w. of that   Joh 1:8
Light
John bare w. of him, and   Joh 1:15
cried
witness (S)   Joh 1:19;
1:32, 34; 8:13-14; 12:17; 19:35; Ro 10:2;
2Co 1:23;   8:3;   Col 4:13; 1Jo 5:7; 3Jo 12; Re 1:2
that he may w. (A)(R)   Joh 2:25
seen; and ye receive not our   Joh 3:11
w.
bear w. to what (R)   Joh 3:11

Jordan, to whom thou barest *w.* — Joh 3:26
Ye yourselves bear me *w.* that I — Joh 3:28
If I bear *w.* of myself — Joh 5:31
my *w.* is not true — Joh 5:31
is another that beareth *w.* of me — Joh 5:32
I know that the *w.* which he — Joh 5:32
and he bare *w.* unto the truth — Joh 5:33
I receive not human *w.* (A) — Joh 5:34
he bore *w.* (B) — Joh 5:34; Re 6:9
have greater *w.* than that of John — Joh 5:36
works that I do, bear *w.* of me — Joh 5:36
hath sent me, hath borne *w.* of me — Joh 5:37
they bear *w.* of me (R) — Joh 5:39
I am one that bear *w.* of myself — Joh 8:18
that sent me beareth *w.* of me — Joh 8:18
Father's name, they bear *w.* of me — Joh 10:25
ye also shall bear *w.* because ye — Joh 15:27
spoken evil, bear *w.* of the evil — Joh 18:23
I should bear *w.* unto the truth — Joh 18:37
who is bearing *w.* (A)(R) — Joh 21:24
be a *w.* with us of his resurrection — Ac 1:22
the apostles *w.* of the resurrection — Ac 4:33
tabernacle of *w.* in the wilderness — Ac 7:44
had given clear *w.* (P) — Ac 8:25
To him give all the prophets *w.* — Ac 10:43
he bore *w.* (A) — Ac 13:22
he left not himself without *w.* — Ac 14:17
knoweth the hearts, bare them *w.* — Ac 15:8
I bore *w.* (A)(B) — Ac 20:21
the high priest doth bear me *w.* — Ac 22:5
thou shalt be his *w.* unto all men — Ac 22:15
must thou bear *w.* also at Rome — Ac 23:11
willing to bear *w.* (B) — Ac 26:5
and a *w.* both of these things — Ac 26:16
For God is my *w.* whom I serve — Ro 1:9
their conscience also bearing *w.* — Ro 2:15
itself beareth *w.* with our spirit — Ro 8:16
not, my conscience bearing me *w.* — Ro 9:1
Thou shalt not bear false *w.* — Ro 13:9
we bore *w.* (N) — 1Co 15:15
a cloke of covetousness; God is *w.* — 1Th 2:5
fearing *w.* of our Lord (B) — 2Th 1:8
This *w.* is true. Wherefore rebuke — Tit 1:13
God also bearing them *w.* both — Heb 2:4
bearing *w.* (B)(N) — Heb 3:5
the Holy Ghost also is a *w.* to us — Heb 10:15
received *w.* (S) — Heb 11:2; 11:39
obtained *w.* that he was righteous — Heb 11:4
the rust of them shall be a *w.* — Jas 5:3
a *w.* of the sufferings of Christ — 1Pe 5:1
we have seen it, and bear *w.* — 1Jo 1:2
we bear *w.* (B) — 1Jo 4:14
And it is the Spirit that beareth *w.* — 1Jo 5:6
are three that bear *w.* in earth — 1Jo 5:8
If we receive the *w.* of men — 1Jo 5:9
the *w.* of God is greater — 1Jo 5:9
this is the *w.* of God which he hath — 1Jo 5:9
w. he has borne (A)(N) — 1Jo 5:9
Son of God hath the *w.* in himself — 1Jo 5:10
have borne *w.* of thy charity — 3Jo 6
Christ, who is the faithful *w.* — Re 1:5
Antipas my *w.* (A)(E)(N)(P)(R) — Re 2:13
the faithful and the true *w.* — Re 3:14
for the *w.* they had borne (R) — Re 6:9
holding fast their *w.* — Re 19:10
beheaded for the *w.* of Jesus — Re 20:4
sent angel to *w.* (B) — Re 22:16
I bear solemn *w.* (N) — Re 22:18
he who is *w.* (P) — Re 22:20

WITNESSED

has not *w.* mischief in (B) — Nu 23:21
Lord *w.* against me (B) — Ru 1:21
the men of Belial *w.* against him — 1Ki 21:13
w. to the message (B) — Ac 14:3
being *w.* by the law and the — Ro 3:21
Pontius Pilate *w.* a good confession — 1Ti 6:13
them, of whom it *w.* that he liveth — Heb 7:8
it is *w.* of him (A)(B)(P)(R) — Heb 7:17
Antipas, who *w.* (B) — Re 2:13

WITNESSES

be put to death by the mouth of *w.* — Nu 35:30
At the mouth of two *w.* — De 17:6
or three *w.* shall he that is worthy — De 17:6
The hands of the *w.* shall be first — De 17:7
sinneth: at the mouth of two *w.* — De 19:15
or at the mouth of three *w.* shall — De 19:15
Ye are *w.* against yourselves that — Jos 24:22
him. And they said, We are *w.* — Jos 24:22
Ye are *w.* this day, that I have — Ru 4:9
of his place: ye are *w.* this day — Ru 4:10
and the elders, said, We are *w.* — Ru 4:11
Thou renewest thy *w.* against me — Job 10:17
false *w.* are risen up against me — Ps 27:12
False *w.* did rise up; they laid — Ps 35:11
took unto me faithful *w.* to record — Isa 8:2
let them bring forth their *w.* that — Isa 43:9
Ye are my *w.* saith the Lord — Isa 43:10
ye are my *w.* saith the Lord — Isa 43:12
declared it? ye are even my *w.* — Isa 44:8
and they are their own *w.* — Isa 44:9
evidence, and sealed it, and took *w.* — Jer 32:10
presence of the *w.* that subscribed — Jer 32:12
the field for money, and take *w.* — Jer 32:25
take *w.* in the land of Benjamin — Jer 32:44
in the mouth of two or three *w.* — M't 18:16
ye be *w.* unto yourselves, that — M't 23:31
though many false *w.* came, yet — M't 26:60
At the last came two false *w.* — M't 26:60
what further need have we of *w.* — M't 26:65
What need we any further *w.* — M'k 14:63
And ye are *w.* of these things — Lu 24:48
and ye shall be *w.* unto me both in — Ac 1:8
raised up, whereof we all are *w.* — Ac 2:32
from the dead; whereof we are *w.* — Ac 3:15
And we are his *w.* of these things — Ac 5:32
And set up false *w.* which said — Ac 6:13
and the *w.* laid down their clothes — Ac 7:58
we are *w.* of all things which he did — Ac 10:39
but unto *w.* chosen before of God — Ac 10:41
who are his *w.* unto the people — Ac 13:31
and we are found false *w.* of God — 1Co 15:15
In the mouth of two or three *w.* — 2Co 13:1
Ye are *w.* and God also, how holily — 1Th 2:10
but before two or three *w.* — 1Ti 5:19
a good profession before *w.* — 1Ti 6:12
hast heard of me among many *w.* — 2Ti 2:2
mercy unto two or three *w.* — Heb 10:28

about with so great a cloud of *w.* — Heb 12:1
I will give power unto my two *w.* — Re 11:3

WITNESSETH

witness which he *w.* of me is true — Joh 5:32
the Holy Ghost *w.* in every city — Ac 20:23

WITNESSING

w. both to small and great, saying — Ac 26:22
the *w.* (A) — 1Co 1:6; 2Th 1:10
our *w.* of Christ (B) — 1Co 1:6; 1Th 1:10
w. of our conscience (B) — 2Co 1:12

WITS

scared out of their *w.* (P) — M'k 6:50

WIT'S

man, and are at their *w.* end — Ps 107:27
rulers at their *w.* end (E) — Da 5:9

WITTINGLY

head, guiding his hands *w.* — Ge 48:14
crossing his hands intentionally (A) — Ge 48:14
consciously directing his hands (B) — Ge 48:14
crossing his hands (R) — Ge 48:14

WITTY

find out knowledge of *w.* inventions — Pr 8:12
find out knowledge and discretion (A)(E)(R) — Pr 8:12
find out knowledge through deliberating (B) — Pr 8:12

WIVES

Lamech took unto him two *w.* — Ge 4:19
they took them *w.* of all they chose — Ge 6:2
give me my *w.* and children — Ge 30:26
if thou take other *w.* besides my daughters — Ge 31:50
our *w.* and children be a prey — Nu 14:3
nor shall he multiply *w.* to himself — De 17:17
if man have two *w.* one beloved, another — De 21:15
Gideon had seventy sons, had many *w.* — J'g 8:30
how shall we do for *w.* for them — J'g 21:7; 21:16
we may not give them *w.* of — J'g 21:18
Elkanah had two *w.* Hannah and Peninnah — 1Sa 1:2
they were also both of them David's *w.* — 1Sa 25:43
David took more *w.* out of Jerusalem — 2Sa 5:13
I gave thee thy master's *w.* into thy bosom — 2Sa 12:8
Solomon had 700 *w.*, princesses — 1Ki 11:3
his *w.* turned away his heart when he was old — 1Ki 11:4
he sent unto me for my *w.* and children — 1Ki 20:7
Ashur had two *w.* Helah and Naarah — 1Ch 4:5
the sons of Uzzi had many *w.* and sons — 1Ch 7:4
Shaharaim had two *w.* Hushim and Baara — 1Ch 8:8
Rehoboam loved Maachah above all his *w.* — 2Ch 11:21
he gave them victuals; he desired many *w.* — 2Ch 11:23
Jehoiada took for him two *w.* he begat sons — 2Ch 24:3
and our *w.* are in captivity for this — 2Ch 29:9
a covenant to put away all the *w.* — Ezr 10:3; 10:44
the *w.* also and children rejoice — Ne 12:43
I saw Jews that had married *w.* of Ashdod — Ne 13:23

the *w.* shall give to husbands honour	Es 1:20
take ye *w.* and take *w.* for your sons	Jer 29:6
to drink no wine, we, nor our *w.* nor sons	Jer 35:8
his *w.* and concubines drink therein	Da 5:2; 5:3
they eat, drank, they married *w.*	Lu 17:27
they brought us on our way with *w.*	Ac 21:5
that have *w.* be as tho' they had none	1Co 7:29
w. submit to own husbands as unto Lord	Eph 5:22; Col 3:18; 1Pe 3:1
so let the *w.* be to their own husbands	Eph 5:24
may be won by the conversation of *w.*	1Pe 3:1

THEIR WIVES

all their wealth, their little ones, and *their* w. took captive	Ge 34:29; 1Sa 30:3
they took their daughters to be *their* w.	J'g 3:6
all Judah with *their* w. stood	2Ch 20:13
that they would put away *their* w.	Ezr 10:19
a great cry of the people and of *their* w.	Ne 5:1
their w. and daughters entered into an oath	Ne 10:28
house spoiled, and *their* w. ravished	Isa 13:16
their w. shall be turned to others	Jer 6:12; 8:10
they shall have none to bury *their* w.	Jer 14:16
let *their* w. be bereaved of their children	Jer 18:21
have ye forgotten wickedness of *their* w.	Jer 44:9
men who knew *their* w. had burnt incense	Jer 44:15
nor take for *their* w. a widow	Eze 44:22
cast them and *their* w. into den of lions	Da 6:24
their w. shall mourn apart	Zec 12:12; 12:13-14
to love *their* w. as their own bodies	Eph 5:28
even so must *their* w. be grave, sober	1Ti 3:11

THY WIVES

I will take *thy* w. and he shall lie with *thy* w. in sight of the sun	2Sa 12:11
who saved this day the lives of *thy* w.	2Sa 19:5
thy silver and gold is mine, and *thy* w.	1Ki 20:3
thou shalt deliver me, *thy* w. and children	1Ki 20:5
Lord will unite thy people and *thy* w.	2Ch 21:14
so they shall bring *thy* w. and children	Jer 38:23
thy w. and concubines have drunk wine	Da 5:23

YOUR WIVES

take wagons for *your* w. and come	Ge 45:19
said to people, come not at *your* w.	Ex 19:15
your w. shall be widows, children fatherless	Ex 22:24
break off the golden earrings of *your* w.	Ex 32:2
your w. and your little ones and your cattle shall remain in your cities	De 3:19; Jos 1:14
your w. shall enter into covenant with Lord	De 29:11
fight for *your* w. and your houses	Ne 4:14
have ye forgotten wickedness of *your* w.	Jer 44:9
ye and *your* w. have both spoken	Jer 44:25
Moses suffered you to put away *your* w.	M't 19:8
husbands, love *your* w.	Eph 5:25; Col 3:19

WIVES'

refuse profane and old *w.* fables	1Ti 4:7

WIZARD

do not turn to mediums, *w.*	Le 19:31 (B)(R)
who turns to spirits and *w.*	Le 20:6 (B)
or that is a *w.* shall surely be put	Le 20:27
medium or fortune teller (B)	Le 20:27
a medium or *w.* (R)	Le 20:27
spirits, or a *w.* or a necromancer	De 18:11
provided necromancers and *w.* (B)	2Ki 21:6
dealt with mediums and *w.* (R)	2Ki 21:6
exterminated necromancers and *w.* (B)	2Ki 23:24
put away mediums and *w.* (R)	2Ki 23:24
encouraging mediums and *w.* (A)(B)(R)	2Ch 33:6
consult mediums and *w.* (A)(R)	Isa 8:19
to *w.* and fortunetellers (B)	Isa 19:3
to mediums and *w.* (R)	Isa 19:3

WIZARDS

neither seek after *w.* to be defiled	Le 19:31
and after *w.* to go a whoring after	Le 20:6
spirits, and the *w.* out of the land	1Sa 28:3
mediums and fortune tellers (B)	1Sa 28:3; 28:9
spirits, and the *w.* out of the land	1Sa 28:9
dealt with familiar spirits and *w.*	2Ki 21:6
with familiar spirits, and the *w.*	2Ki 23:24
with a familiar spirit, and with *w.*	2Ch 33:6
fortunetelling (B)	2Ch 33:6; Isa 8:19; 19:3
unto *w.* that peep, and that mutter	Isa 8:19
have familiar spirits and to the *w.*	Isa 19:3

WOE

w. to thee, Moab	Nu 21:29; Jer 48:46
w. unto us	1Sa 4:7; 4:8; Jer 4:13; 6:4; La 5:16
who hath *w.?* who hath sorrow	Pr 23:29
w. to him that is alone when he falls	Ec 4:10
w. to thee when thy king is a child	Ec 10:16
w. to their soul, for they rewarded evil	Isa 3:9
w. to the wicked, it shall be ill with him	Isa 3:11
w. to the multitude of many people	Isa 17:12
w. to the land shadowing with wings	Isa 18:1
w. to the crown of pride, to the drunkards	Isa 28:1
w. to Ariel	Isa 29:1
w. to the rebellious children	Isa 30:1
w. to thee that spoilest	Isa 33:1
w. to him that striveth with his Maker	Isa 45:9
w. to him that saith to father, What begettest	Isa 45:10
w. unto thee, O Jerusalem, wilt thou	Jer 13:27
w. to him that builds by unrighteousness	Jer 22:13
w. to the pastors that destroy the sheep	Jer 23:1
w. to Nebo	Jer 48:1
there was written, mourning and *w.*	Eze 2:10
w. to foolish prophets, that follow their spirit	Eze 13:3
w. to women that sew pillows to armholes	Eze 13:18
w., *w.* unto thee	Eze 16:23
w. to the bloody city	Eze 24:6; 24:9; Na 3:1

saith Lord, howl, *w.* worth the day	Eze 30:2
w. be to the shepherds that feed themselves	Eze 34:2
w. to you that desire the day of the Lord	Am 5:18
w. to him that increaseth that is not his	Hab 2:6
w. to him that coveteth an evil covetousness	Hab 2:9
w. to him that buildeth a town with blood	Hab 2:12
w. to him that giveth his neighbour drink	Hab 2:15
w. to him that saith to the wood, Awake	Hab 2:19
w. to the inhabitants of the sea coasts	Zep 2:5
w. to her that is filthy and polluted, to the	Zep 3:1
w. to thee Chorazin, *w.* to thee, Bethsaida, for if works had been done	M't 11:21; Lu 10:13
w. to the world because of offences *w.* to that man	M't 18:7; Lu 17:1
by whom the offence cometh	
w. unto you scribes and Pharisees, hypocrites	M't 23:13; 23:14-15, 23, 25, 27, 29; Lu 11:44
w. unto you, ye blind guides, which say	M't 23:16
w. unto that man by whom the Son of man is betrayed	M't 26:24; Lu 22:22
w. unto you that are rich, for ye have	Lu 6:25
w. to you that are full, *w.* to you that laugh	Lu 6:25
w. to you when all men speak well of you	Lu 6:26
but *w.* unto you, Pharisees	Lu 11:42; 11:43
he said, *W.* to you also, ye lawyers	Lu 11:46; 11:47, 52
I heard an angel, saying, *W. w.* to the inhabiters of the earth	Re 8:13; 12:12
one *w.* is past	Re 9:12
the second *w.* is past	Re 11:14

WOE *IS ME*

w. *is me*, that I sojourn in Mesech	Ps 120:5
w. *is me*, I am undone, I am of unclean lips	Isa 6:5
w. *is me* now, for my soul is wearied	Jer 4:31
w. *is me* for my hurt	Jer 10:19
w. *is me*, my mother	Jer 15:10
w. *is me*, for the Lord hath added grief	Jer 45:3
w. *is me*, I am as when they gathered fruit	Mic 7:1

WOE *UNTO ME*

if I be wicked, *w.* *unto me*, if righteous	Job 10:15
but I said, My leanness, *w.* *unto me*	Isa 24:16
w. *unto me* if I preach not the gospel	1Co 9:16

WOE *TO THEM*

w. *to them* that join house to house	Isa 5:8
w. *to them* that rise up early in the morning	Isa 5:11
w. *to them* that draw iniquity with cords	Isa 5:18
w. *to them* that call evil good and good evil	Isa 5:20
w. *to them* that are wise in their own eyes	Isa 5:21
w. *to them* that are mighty to drink wine	Isa 5:22
w. *to them* that decree unrighteous decrees	Isa 10:1
w. *to them* that seek deep to hide counsel	Isa 29:15
w. *to them* that go down to Egypt for help	Isa 31:1
w. *to them* for their day is come	Jer 50:27
w. *to them!* for they have fled from me	Ho 7:13
w. *to them* when I depart from them	Ho 9:12

w. *to them* that are at ease in Zion   *Am 6:1*

w. *to them* that devise iniquity *Mic 2:1*

w. *to them* which are with *M't 24:19*; child, and to them *M'k 13:17; Lu 21:23*

w. *to them*, they have gone in *Jude 11* way of Cain

WOEFUL

neither have I desired the w. *Jer 17:16* day

WOES

there came two w. more *Re 9:12* hereafter

WOKE

came and w. him (S)   *M't 8:25*

WOLF

Benjamin shall ravin as a w. *Ge 49:27*

w. also shall dwell with the *Isa 11:6* lamb

The w. and the lamb shall *Isa 65:25* feed

and a w. of the evenings *Jer 5:6* shall spoil

seeth the w. coming, and *Joh 10:12* leaveth

and the w. catcheth them *Joh 10:12*

WOLVES

are like w. ravening the prey *Eze 22:27*

more fierce than the evening *Hab 1:8* w.

her judges are evening w.; they *Zep 3:3*

but inwardly they are *M't 7:15* ravening w.

forth as sheep in the midst *M't 10:16* of w.

send you forth as lambs *Lu 10:3* among w.

grievous w. enter in among *Ac 20:29* you

WOMAN

made he a w. and brought her *Ge 2:22*

she shall be called *W*. *Ge 2:23* because she

he said unto the w. Yea, hath *Ge 3:1* God

w. said unto the serpent, We *Ge 3:2* may

serpent said unto the w. Ye *Ge 3:4* shall

the w. saw that the tree was *Ge 3:6* good

The w. whom thou gavest to be *Ge 3:12*

Lord God said unto the w., *Ge 3:13* What is

w. said, The serpent beguiled *Ge 3:13* me

put enmity between thee and *Ge 3:15* the w.

Unto the w. he said, I will *Ge 3:16* greatly

that thou art a fair w. to *Ge 12:11* look upon

the Egyptians beheld the w. *Ge 12:14* that she

w. was taken into Pharaoh's *Ge 12:15* house

for the w. which thou hast *Ge 20:3* taken

w. will not be willing to *Ge 24:5* follow me

if the w. will not be willing to *Ge 24:8* follow

Peradventure the w. will not *Ge 24:39* follow

same be the w. whom the *Ge 24:44* Lord

Shaul the son of a *Ge 46:10* Canaanitish w.

the w. conceived, and bare a *Ex 2:2* son

w. took the child, and nursed it *Ex 2:9*

But every w. shall borrow of *Ex 3:22* her

Shaul the son of a Canaanitish *Ex 6:15* w.

every w. of her neighbour, *Ex 11:2* jewels

men strive, and hurt a w. *Ex 21:22* with child

a pregnant w. (A)(B) *Ex 21:22; 1Sa 4:19; 2Ki 8:12*

If an ox gore a man or a w. *Ex 21:28*

that he hath killed a man or *Ex 21:29* a w.

every man and w. whose *Ex 35:29* heart

neither man nor w. make any *Ex 36:6* more

If a w. have conceived seed *Le 12:2*

If a man or w. have a plague *Le 13:29* upon

a man also or a w. have in *Le 13:38* the skin

The w. also with whom man *Le 15:18* shall

And if a w. have an issue, *Le 15:19* and her

if a w. have an issue of her *Le 15:25* blood

issue, of the man, and of the *Le 15:33* w.

not uncover the nakedness of *Le 18:17* a w.

not approach unto a w. to *Le 18:19* uncover

neither shall any w. stand *Le 18:23* before a

whosoever lieth carnally with *Le 19:20* a w.

as he lieth with a w. both of *Le 20:13* them

And if a w. approach unto *Le 20:16* any beast

thou shalt kill the w. and the *Le 20:16* beast

lie with a w. having her *Le 20:18* sickness

or w. that hath a familiar *Le 20:27* spirit

neither shall they take a w. *Le 21:7* put away

And the son of an Israelitish *Le 24:10* w.

and this son of the Israelitish *Le 24:10* w.

man or w. shall commit any *Nu 5:6* sin

shall set the w. before the *Nu 5:18* Lord

say unto the w. If no man *Nu 5:19* have lain

shall charge the w. with an *Nu 5:21* oath of

and the priest shall say unto *Nu 5:21* the w.

And the w. shall say, Amen, *Nu 5:22* amen

cause the w. to drink the bitter *Nu 5:24*

cause the w. to drink the *Nu 5:26* water

the w. shall be a curse among *Nu 5:27* her

And if the w. be not defiled, *Nu 5:28* but he

and shall set the w. before the *Nu 5:30* Lord

and this w. shall bear her *Nu 5:31* iniquity

either man or w. shall separate *Nu 6:2*

Ethiopian w. whom he had *Nu 12:1* married

for he had married an *Nu 12:1* Ethiopian w.

a Midianitish w. in the sight *Nu 25:6* of Moses

and the w. through her belly *Nu 25:8*

Midianitish w. that was slain *Nu 25:15*

a w. also vow a vow unto the *Nu 30:3* Lord

kill every w. that hath known *Nu 31:17* man

or an Hebrew w. be sold *De 15:12* unto thee

man or w. that hath wrought *De 17:2*

bring forth that man or that *De 17:5*

gates, even that man or that w. *De 17:5*

among the captives a *De 21:11* beautiful w.

The w. shall not wear that *De 22:5* which

I took this w. and when I *De 22:14* came to

young w. (A)(R) *De 22:15; 22:20-21, 24, 26*

found lying with a w. *De 22:22* married to an

both the man that lay with the *De 22:22* w.

and the w.; so shall thou put *De 22:22* away

The tender and delicate w. *De 28:56* among you

should be among you man, *De 29:18* or w.

w. took the two men, and hid *Jos 2:4* them

both man, and w. young and *Jos 6:21* old

house, and bring out thence *Jos 6:22* the w.

shall sell Sisera into the hand of *J'g 4:9* a w.

And a certain w. cast a piece *J'g 9:53* of a

men say not of me, A w. slew *J'g 9:54* him

for thou art the son of a *J'g 11:2* strange w.

of the Lord appeared unto the *J'g 13:3* w.

the w. came and told her *J'g 13:6* husband

angel of God came again unto *J'g 13:9* the w.

w. made haste, and ran, and *J'g 13:10* told

the man that spakest unto the *J'g 13:11* w.

I said unto the w. let her *J'g 13:13* beware

And the w. bare a son, and *J'g 13:24* called

and saw a w. in Timnath of *J'g 14:1*

I have seen a w. in Timnath *J'g 14:2* of the

never a w. among the *J'g 14:3* daughters

went down, and talked with the *J'g 14:7* w.

So his father went down unto *J'g 14:10* the w.

loved a w. in the valley of *J'g 16:4* Sorek

came the w. in the dawning *J'g 19:26* of the

the w. his concubine was *J'g 19:27* fallen

husband of the w. that was *J'g 20:4* slain

and every w. that hath lain *J'g 21:11* by man

and the w. was left of her two *Ru 1:5* sons

and, behold, a w. lay at his feet *Ru 3:8*

know that thou art a virtuous *Ru 3:11* w.

w. of worthy (A)(R) *Ru 3:11*

a worthy w. (E) *Ru 3:11; Pr 12:4; 31:10*

not be known that a w. came *Ru 3:14*

The Lord make the w. that is *Ru 4:11*

Lord shall give thee of this *Ru 4:12* young w.

lord, I am a w. of a *1Sa 1:15* sorrowful spirit

a wicked w. (A)(E)(R) *1Sa 1:16*

So the w. went her way, and *1Sa 1:18* did eat

So the w. abode, and gave her *1Sa 1:23* son

I am the w. that stood by *1Sa 1:26* thee here

The Lord give thee seed of *1Sa 2:20* this w.

but slay both man and w. *1Sa 15:3* infant and

Thou son of the perverse *1Sa 20:30* rebellious w.

she was a w. of good *1Sa 25:3* understanding

and left neither man nor w. *1Sa 27:9* alive

And David saved neither *1Sa 27:11* man nor w.

a w. that hath a familiar *1Sa 28:7* spirit

is a w. that hath a familiar *1Sa 28:7* spirit

and they came to the w. by *1Sa 28:8* night

the w. said unto him, Behold, *1Sa 28:9* thou

said the w. Whom shall I *1Sa 28:11* bring

when the w. saw Samuel, she cried	1Sa 28:11	when the king asked the w. she	2Ki 8:6	him, and pangs as of a w. in travail	Jer 50:43
and the w. spake to Saul, saying	1Sa 28:12	see now this cursed w. and bury her	2Ki 9:34	will I break in pieces man and w.	Jer 51:22
the w. said unto Saul, I saw gods	1Sa 28:13	both man and w. to every one a	1Ch 16:3	Jerusalem is as a menstrous w.	La 1:17
the w. came unto Saul, and saw that	1Sa 28:21	son of a w. of the daughters of Dan	2Ch 2:14	work of an imperious whorish w.	Eze 16:30
together with the w. compelled him	1Sa 28:23	small or great, whether man or w.	2Ch 15:13	hath come near to a menstrous w.	Eze 18:6
the w. had a fat calf in the house	1Sa 28:24	sons of Athaliah, that wicked w.	2Ch 24:7	unto a w. that playeth the harlot	Eze 23:44
day with a fault concerning this w.	2Sa 3:8	whether man or w. shall come	Es 4:11	unto Aholibah, the lewd w.	Eze 23:44
roof he saw a w. washing herself	2Sa 11:2	Man that is born of a w. is of few	Job 14:1	as the uncleanness of a w. removed w.	Eze 36:17
w. was very beautiful to look upon	2Sa 11:2	he which is born of a w. that he	Job 15:14	love a w. beloved of her friend	Ho 3:1
David sent and enquired after the w.	2Sa 11:3	can he be clean that is born of a w.	Job 25:4	sorrows of a travailing w. shall come	Ho 13:13
the w. conceived, and sent and told	2Sa 11:5	heart have been deceived by a w.	Job 31:9	have taken thee as a w. in travail	Mic 4:9
did not a w. cast a piece of	2Sa 11:21	and pain, as of a w. in travail	Ps 48:6	daughter of Zion, like a w. in travail	Mic 4:10
put now this w. out from me	2Sa 13:17	like the untimely birth of a w.	Ps 58:8	this is a w. that sitteth in the midst	Zec 5:7
and fetched thence a wise w.	2Sa 14:2	maketh the barren w. to keep house	Ps 113:9	whosoever looketh on a w. to lust	M't 5:28
be as a w. that had a long time	2Sa 14:2	deliver thee from the strange w.	Pr 2:16	a w. which was diseased with	M't 9:20
when the w. of Tekoah spake	2Sa 14:4	To keep thee from the evil w.	Pr 6:24	the w. was made whole from that	M't 9:22
answered, I am indeed a widow w.	2Sa 14:5	of the tongue of a strange w.	Pr 6:24	like unto leaven, which a w. took	M't 13:33
king said unto the w., Go to thine	2Sa 14:8	by means of a whorish w. a man is	Pr 6:26	a w. of Canaan came out of	M't 15:22
w. of Tekoah said unto the king	2Sa 14:9	committeth adultery with a w.	Pr 6:32	unto her, O w. great is thy faith	M't 15:28
the w. said, Let thine handmaid	2Sa 14:12	may keep thee from the strange w.	Pr 7:5	and last of all the w. died	M't 22:27
the w. said, Wherefore then hast	2Sa 14:13	met him a w. with the attire of	Pr 7:10	him a w. having an alabaster box of	M't 26:7
king answered, and said unto the w.	2Sa 14:18	A foolish w. is clamorous: she	Pr 9:13	unto them, Why trouble ye the w.	M't 26:10
the w. said, Let my lord the king	2Sa 14:18	A gracious w. retaineth honour	Pr 11:16	that this w. hath done, be told for	M't 26:13
the w. answered and said, As they	2Sa 14:19	gracious w. wins honor (A)(B)(R)	Pr 11:16	certain w. which had an issue	M'k 5:25
she was a w. of a fair countenance	2Sa 14:27	fair w. which is without discretion	Pr 11:22	But the w. fearing and trembling	M'k 5:33
the w. took and spread a covering	2Sa 17:19	A virtuous w. is a crown to her	Pr 12:4	a certain w. whose young daughter	M'k 7:25
Absalom's servants came to the w.	2Sa 17:20	Every wise w. buildeth her house	Pr 14:1	The w. was a Greek, a	M'k 7:26
And the w. said unto them, They be	2Sa 17:20	a pledge of him for a strange w.	Pr 20:16	if a w. shall put away her husband	M'k 10:12
Then cried a wise w. out of the city	2Sa 20:16	with a brawling w. in a wide house	Pr 21:9; 25:24	seed: last of all the w. died also	M'k 12:22
unto her, the w. said, Art thou Joab	2Sa 20:17	a contentious and an angry w.	Pr 21:19	came a w. having an alabaster box	M'k 14:3
And the w. said to Joab, Behold	2Sa 20:21	and a strange w. is a narrow pit	Pr 23:27	unto a w. that was a widow	Lu 4:26
the w. went unto all the people	2Sa 20:22	a pledge of him for a strange w.	Pr 27:13	behold, a w. in the city, which was	Lu 7:37
And the one w. said, O my lord, I	1Ki 3:17	a pledge of him for a strange w.	Pr 27:13	what manner of w. this is that	Lu 7:39
I and this w. dwell in one house	1Ki 3:17	Such is the way of an adulterous w.	Pr 30:20	he turned to the w. and said	Lu 7:44
that this w. was delivered also	1Ki 3:18	an odious w. when she is married	Pr 30:23	said unto Simon, Seest thou this w.	Lu 7:44
the other w. said, Nay; but	1Ki 3:22	Who can find a virtuous w.	Pr 31:10	this w. since the time I came	Lu 7:45
Then spake the w. whose the living	1Ki 3:26	a w. that feareth the Lord, she	Pr 31:30	this w. hath anointed my feet	Lu 7:46
name was Zeruah, a widow w.	1Ki 11:26	find more bitter than death the w.	Ec 7:26	he said to the w. Thy faith hath	Lu 7:50
shall feign herself to be another w.	1Ki 14:5	a w. among all those have I not	Ec 7:28	a w. having an issue of blood	Lu 8:43
a widow w. there to sustain thee	1Ki 17:9	a young w. shall (R)	Isa 7:14	the w. saw that she was not hid	Lu 8:47
widow w. was gathering of sticks	1Ki 17:10	be in pain as a w. that travaileth	Isa 13:8	a certain w. named Martha	Lu 10:38
that the son of the w. the mistress	1Ki 17:17	as the pangs of a w. that travaileth	Isa 21:3	certain w. of the company lifted up	Lu 11:27
the w. said to Elijah, Now by this	1Ki 17:24	Like as a w. with child, that draweth	Isa 26:17	there was a w. which had a spirit	Lu 13:11
Now there cried a certain w. of	2Ki 4:1	now will I cry like a travailing w.	Isa 42:14	W. thou art loosed from thine	Lu 13:12
to Shunem, where was a great w.	2Ki 4:8	or to the w. What hast thou	Isa 45:10	And ought not this w. being	Lu 13:16
the w. conceived, and bare a son	2Ki 4:17	Can a w. forget her sucking child	Isa 49:15	which a w. took and hid in three	Lu 13:21
there cried a w. unto him, saying	2Ki 6:26	as a w. forsaken and grieved	Isa 54:6	what w. having ten pieces of silver	Lu 15:8
This w. said unto me, Give thy son	2Ki 6:28	heard a voice as of a w. in travail	Jer 4:3	Last of all the w. died also	Lu 20:32
the king heard the words of the w.	2Ki 6:30	of Zion to a comely and delicate w.	Jer 6:2	him, saying, W. I know him not	Lu 22:57
Then spake Elisha unto the w.	2Ki 8:1	of us, and pain, as of a w. in travail	Jer 6:24	W. what have I to do with thee	Joh 2:4
And the w. arose, and did after the	2Ki 8:2	take thee, as a w. in travail	Jer 13:21	a w. of Samaria to draw water	Joh 4:7
the w. returned out of the land of	2Ki 8:3	thee, the pain as of a w. in	Jer 22:23	saith the w. of Samaria unto him	Joh 4:9
the w. whose son he had restored	2Ki 8:5	thee, the pain as of a w. in travail	Jer 22:23	of me, which am a w. of Samaria	Joh 4:9
O king, this is the w. and this	2Ki 8:5	hands on his loins, as a w. in travail	Jer 30:6	w. saith unto him, Sir, Thou hast	Joh 4:11
		lame, the w. with child and her that	Jer 31:8	The w. saith unto him, Sir, give	Joh 4:15
		earth, A w. shall compass a man	Jer 31:22	The w. answered and said, I have	Joh 4:17
		to cut off from you man and w.	Jer 44:7	The w. saith unto him, Sir, I	Joh 4:19
		be as the heart of a w. in her pangs	Jer 48:41; 49:22	W. believe me, the hour cometh	Joh 4:21
		have taken her, as a w. in travail	Jer 49:24	The w. saith unto him, I know that	Joh 4:25
				that he talked with the w.	Joh 4:27

The w. then left her waterpot | Joh 4:28
on him for the saying of the | Joh 4:39
w.
said unto the w., Now we | Joh 4:42
believe
brought unto him a w. taken | Joh 8:3
this w. was taken in adultery | Joh 8:4
and the w. standing in the | Joh 8:9
midst
saw none but the w. he said | Joh 8:10
unto
W. where are thine accusers | Joh 8:10
a w. when she is in travail | Joh 16:21
hath
his mother, W. behold thy | Joh 19:26
son
unto her, W., why weepest | Joh 20:13;
thou | 20:15
this w. was full of good works | Ac 9:36
Timotheus, the son of a | Ac 16:1
certain
a certain w. named Lydia, a | Ac 16:14
seller
a w. named Damaris, and | Ac 17:34
others
leaving the natural use of the | Ro 1:27
w.
w. which hath an husband is | Ro 7:2
bound
good for a man not to touch a | 1Co 7:1
w.
every w. have her own | 1Co 7:2
husband
the w. which hath an | 1Co 7:13
husband
w. careth for the things of | 1Co 7:34
the Lord
the head of the w. is the | 1Co 11:3
man
w. that prayeth or prophesieth | 1Co 11:5
if the w. be not covered, let | 1Co 11:6
her
it be a shame for a w. to be | 1Co 11:6
shorn
but the w. is the glory of the | 1Co 11:7
man
For the man is not of the w. | 1Co 11:8
but the w. of the man | 1Co 11:8
was the man created for the | 1Co 11:9
w.
but the w. for the man | 1Co 11:9
cause ought the w. to have | 1Co 11:10
power
neither is the man without | 1Co 11:11
the w.
neither the w. without the | 1Co 11:11
man
For as the w. of the man, | 1Co 11:12
even so
even so is the man also by | 1Co 11:12
the w.
a w. pray unto God | 1Co 11:13
uncovered
if a w. have long hair it is | 1Co 11:15
a glory
sent forth his son, made of a | Ga 4:4
w.
blinded in w. of illusion (P) | Eph 4:17
as travail upon a w. with child | 1Th 5:3
Let the w. learn in silence | 1Ti 2:11
I suffer not a w. to teach, nor | 1Ti 2:12
but the w. being deceived was | 1Ti 2:14
If any man or w. that | 1Ti 5:16
believeth have
thou sufferest that w. Jezebel | Re 2:20
a w. clothed with the sun, and | Re 12:1
w. which was ready to be | Re 12:4
delivered
w. fled into the wilderness, | Re 12:6
where
w. which brought forth the | Re 12:13
man
to the w. were given two | Re 12:14
wings
mouth water as a flood after | Re 12:15
the w.
the earth helped the w. and | Re 12:16
the dragon was wroth with | Re 12:17
the w.
a w. sit upon a scarlet | Re 17:3
coloured
w. was arrayed in purple and | Re 17:4
I saw the w. drunken with the | Re 17:6
tell thee the mystery of the w. | Re 17:7
mountains, on which the w. | Re 17:9
sitteth
w. which thou sawest is that | Re 17:18
great

WOMANISH

unholy, old w. tales (B) | 1Ti 4:7

WOMANKIND

not lie with mankind, as with | Le 18:22
w.

WOMAN'S

his pledge from the w. hand | Ge 38:20
according as the w. husband | Ex 21:22
will
Israelitish w. son blasphemed | Le 24:11
uncover the w. head, and put | Nu 5:18
jealously offering out of the w. | Nu 5:25
hand
shall a man put on a w. | De 22:5
garment
And this w. child died in the | 1Ki 3:19
night

WOMB

Two nations are in thy w. | Ge 25:23
and two
behold, there were twins in | Ge 25:24
her w.
Leah was hated, he opened | Ge 29:31
her w.
from thee the fruit of the w. | Ge 30:2
to her, and opened her w. | Ge 30:22
that, behold, twins were in | Ge 38:27
her w.
of the breasts, and of the w. | Ge 49:25
whatsoever openeth the w. | Ex 13:2
among
womb (S) | Ex 13:12;
    13:15; 34:19; Nu 3:12; 18:15
instead of such as open every | Nu 8:16
w.
he cometh out of his | Nu 12:12
mother's w.
will also bless the fruit of thy | De 7:13
w.
be a Nazarite unto God from | J'g 13:5
the w.
be a Nazarite to God from the | J'g 13:7
w.
unto God from my mother's | J'g 16:17
w.
there yet any more sons in my | Ru 1:11
w.
but the Lord had shut up her | 1Sa 1:5
w.
the Lord had shut up her w. | 1Sa 1:6
came I out of my mother's w. | Job 1:21
not up the doors of my | Job 3:10
mother's w.
Why died I not from the w. | Job 3:11
came from the w. (B)(R) | Job 3:11
brought me forth out of the | Job 10:18
w.
carried from the w. to the | Job 10:19
grave
The w. shall forget him; the | Job 24:20
worm
that made me in the w. | Job 31:15
make him
did not one fashion us in the | Job 31:15
w.
guided her from my | Job 31:18
mother's w.
as if it had issued out of the | Job 38:8
w.
Out of whose w. came the ice | Job 38:29
art he that took me out of the | Ps 22:9
w.
I was cast upon thee from | Ps 22:10
the w.
from my mother's w. (A)(E) | Ps 22:10
wicked are estranged from the | Ps 58:3
w.
have I been holden up from the | Ps 71:6
w.
my mother's w. (A)(B)(R) | Ps 71:6
from the w. of the morning | Ps 110:3
the fruit of the w. is his reward | Ps 127:3
hast covered me in my | Ps 139:13
mother's w.
The grave; and the barren w. | Pr 30:16
son? and what, the son of my | Pr 31:2
w.
As he came forth of his | Ec 5:15
mother's w.
the bones do grow in the w. of | Ec 11:5
her
have no pity on the fruit of | Isa 13:18
the w.

thee, and formed thee from | Isa 44:2
the w.
he that formed thee from the | Isa 44:24
w.
which are carried from the w. | Isa 46:3
called a transgressor from the | Isa 48:8
w.
Lord hath called me from the | Isa 49:1
w.
formed me from the w. to be | Isa 49:5
his
compassion on the son of | Isa 49:15
her w.
cause to bring forth, and shut | Isa 66:9
the w.
thou camest forth out of the w. | Jer 1:5
found thee in the w. | Jer 1:5
(A)(B)(R)(S)
he slew me not from the w. | Jer 20:17
her w. to be always great | Jer 20:17
with me
I forth out of the w. to see | Jer 20:18
labour
the fire all that openeth the | Eze 20:26
w.
from the birth, and from the | Ho 9:11
w.
give them a miscarrying w. | Ho 9:14
even the beloved fruit of their | Ho 9:16
w.
his brother by the heel in the | Ho 12:3
w.
so born from their mother's | M't 19:12
w.
Ghost, even from his mother's | Lu 1:15
w.
thou shalt conceive in thy w. | Lu 1:31
the babe leaped in her w. | Lu 1:41
and blessed is the fruit of thy | Lu 1:42
w.
the babe leaped in my w. for | Lu 1:44
joy
before he was conceived in the | Lu 2:21
w.
Every male that openeth the | Lu 2:23
w.
Blessed is the w. that bare | Lu 11:27
thee
second time into his mother's | Joh 3:4
w.
man lame from his mother's w. | Ac 3:2
was
a cripple from his mother's w. | Ac 14:8
yet the deadness of Sarah's w. | Ro 4:19
me from my mother's w. | Ga 1:15

WOMBS

Lord had fast closed up all | Ge 20:18
the w.
and the w. that never bare | Lu 23:29

WOMEN

and the w. also, and the | Ge 14:16
people
with Sarah after the manner | Ge 18:11
of w.
the time that w. go out to | Ge 24:11
draw water
for the custom of w. is upon | Ge 31:35
me
the way of w. upon me (R) | Ge 31:35
and saw the w. and the | Ge 33:5
children
office of a midwife to the | Ex 1:16
Hebrew w.
w. are not as the Egyptian w. | Ex 1:19
call to thee a nurse of the | Ex 2:7
Hebrew w.
all the w. went out after her | Ex 15:20
And they came, both men | Ex 35:22
and w.
all the w. that were wise | Ex 35:25
hearted
all the w. whose heart stirred | Ex 35:26
them
looking glasses of the w. | Ex 38:8
assembling
ten w. shall bake your bread | Le 26:26
in one
took all the w. of Midian | Nu 31:9
captives
Have ye saved all the w. alive | Nu 31:15
all the w. children, that have | Nu 31:18
not
of w. that had not known | Nu 31:35
man by
destroyed the men, and the w. | De 2:34
utterly destroying the men, w. | De 3:6

But the *w.* and the little ones   *De 20:14*
the people together, men, and   *De 31:12*
w.
fell that day, both of men and   *Jos 8:25*
w.
congregation of Israel, with   *Jos 8:35*
the *w.*
Blessed above *w.* shall Jael   *J'g 5:24*
the wife
blessed shall she be above *w.*   *J'g 5:24*
also, about a thousand men   *J'g 9:49*
and *w.*
and thither fled all the men   *J'g 9:51*
and *w.*
the house was full of men   *J'g 16:27*
and *w.*
about three thousand men   *J'g 16:27*
and *w.*
sword, with the *w.* and the   *J'g 21:10*
children
alive of the *w.* of   *J'g 21:14*
Jabesh-gilead
w. are destroyed out of   *J'g 21:16*
Benjamin
took them wives of the *w.* of   *Ru 1:4*
Moab
w. said unto Naomi, Blessed be   *Ru 4:14*
the *w.* her neighbours gave it a   *Ru 4:17*
name
how they lay with the *w.* that   *1Sa 2:22*
time of her death the *w.* that   *1Sa 4:20*
stood
thy sword hath made *w.*   *1Sa 15:33*
childless
thy mother be childless   *1Sa 15:33*
among *w.*
w. came out of all cities of   *1Sa 18:6*
Israel
w. answered one another as   *1Sa 18:7*
they
kept themselves at least from   *1Sa 21:4*
w.
Of a truth *w.* have been kept   *1Sa 21:5*
from us
edge of the sword, both men   *1Sa 22:19*
and *w.*
had taken the *w.* captives,   *1Sa 30:2*
that were
wonderful, passing the love of   *2Sa 1:26*
w.
as well to the *w.* as men, to   *2Sa 6:19*
every
the king left ten *w.* which   *2Sa 15:16*
were
voice of singing men and   *2Sa 19:35*
singing *w.*
and the king took the ten   *2Sa 20:3*
w. his
Then came there two *w.* that   *1Ki 3:16*
were
Solomon loved many strange   *1Ki 11:1*
w.
w. of the Moabites,   *1Ki 11:1*
Ammonites
and rip up their *w.* with child   *2Ki 8:12*
w. therein that were with   *2Ki 15:16*
child he
the *w.* wove hangings for the   *2Ki 23:7*
grove
thousand, *w.*, sons, and   *2Ch 28:8*
daughters
singing *w.* spake of Josiah   *2Ch 35:25*
in their
hundred singing men and   *Ezr 2:65*
singing *w.*
great congregation of men   *Ezr 10:1*
and *w.*
and five singing men and   *Ne 7:67*
singing *w.*
congregation both of men and   *Ne 8:2*
w.
before the men and the *w.* and   *Ne 8:3*
that had married *w.* (S)   *Ne 13:23*
him did outlandish *w.* cause   *Ne 13:26*
to sin
commit wickedness by   *Ne 13:27*
marrying foreign *w.* (B)
the queen made a feast for the   *Es 1:9*
w.
queen shall come abroad unto   *Es 1:17*
all *w.*
the palace, to the house of the   *Es 2:3*
w.
Chamberlain, keeper of the *w.*   *Es 2:3*
custody of Hegai, keeper of the   *Es 2:8*
w.
best place of the house of the   *Es 2:9*
w.
according to the manner of the   *Es 2:12*
w.

things for the purifying of the   *Es 2:12*
w.
house of the *w.* unto the king's   *Es 2:13*
house
into the second house of the   *Es 2:14*
w.
chamberlain, the keeper of the   *Es 2:15*
w.
king loved Esther above all the   *Es 2:17*
w.
young and old, little children·   *Es 3:13*
and *w.*
both little ones and *w.* and to   *Es 8:11*
take
as one of the foolish *w.*   *Job 2:10*
speaketh
all the land were no *w.*   *Job 42:15*
found so fair
were among thy honourable *w.*   *Ps 45:9*
mouth of strange *w.* is a deep   *Pr 22:14*
pit
Thine eyes shall behold   *Pr 23:33*
strange *w.*
Give not thy strength unto *w.*   *Pr 31:3*
nor
I gat me men singers and *w.*   *Ec 2:8*
singers
know not, O thou fairest   *Ca 1:8*
among *w.*
beloved, O thou fairest among   *Ca 5:9*
w.
gone, O thou fairest among *w.*   *Ca 6:1*
oppressors, and *w.* rule over   *Isa 3:12*
them
seven *w.* shall take hold of one   *Isa 4:1*
man
day shall Egypt be like unto   *Isa 19:16*
w.
the *w.* come, and set them on   *Isa 27:11*
fire
Rise up, ye *w.* that are at   *Isa 32:9*
ease; hear
shall ye be troubled, ye   *Isa 32:10*
careless *w.*
Tremble, ye *w.* that are at   *Isa 32:11*
ease; be
taught evil *w.* (B)   *Jer 2:33*
the *w.* knead their dough, to   *Jer 7:18*
make
ye, and call for the mourning   *Jer 9:17*
w.
send for cunning *w.* that they   *Jer 9:17*
may
hear the word of the Lord, O   *Jer 9:20*
ye *w.*
all the *w.* that are left in the   *Jer 38:22*
king of Judah's house
and those *w.* shall say, Thy   *Jer 38:22*
friends
committed unto him men, and   *Jer 40:7*
w.
and the *w.* and the children   *Jer 41:16*
Even men, and *w.* and children   *Jer 43:6*
and all the *w.* that stood by,   *Jer 44:15*
a great
to the men, and to the *w.*   *Jer 44:20*
and to all
and to all the *w.*, Hear the   *Jer 44:24*
word
her; and they shall become   *Jer 50:37*
as *w.*
hath failed; they became as   *Jer 51:30*
w.
Shall the *w.* eat their fruit   *La 2:20*
pitiful *w.* have sodden their   *La 4:10*
own
They ravished the *w.* in Zion   *La 5:11*
there sat *w.* weeping for   *Eze 8:14*
Tammuz
maids, and little children, and   *Eze 9:6*
w.
Woe to the *w.* that sew   *Eze 13:18*
pillows to all
from other *w.* in thy   *Eze 16:34*
whoredoms
judge thee, as *w.* that break   *Eze 16:38*
wedlock
upon thee in the sight of   *Eze 16:41*
many *w.*
there were two *w.* the   *Eze 23:2*
daughters
and she became famous   *Eze 23:10*
among *w.*
and unto Aholibah, the lewd   *Eze 23:44*
w.
after the manner of *w.* that   *Eze 23:45*
shed blood
that all *w.* may be taught   *Eze 23:48*
not to do

shall give him the daughter   *Da 11:17*
of *w.*
nor the desire of *w.* nor   *Da 11:37*
regard any
their *w.* with child shall be   *Ho 13:16*
ripped up
their pregnant *w.* (A)(R)   *Ho 13:16*
they have ripped up the *w.*   *Am 1:13*
with child
w. of my people have ye cast   *Mic 2:9*
out
people in the midst of thee   *Na 3:13*
are *w.*
behold, there came out two *w.*   *Zec 5:9*
men and old *w.* dwell in the   *Zec 8:4*
streets
houses rifled, and the *w.*   *Zec 14:2*
ravished
Among them that are born   *M't 11:11*
of *w.*
five thousand men, beside *w.*   *M't 14:21*
four thousand men, beside *w.*   *M't 15:38*
w. who are pregnant   *M't 24:19*
(A)(P)
Two *w.* shall be grinding at   *M't 24:41*
the mill
many *w.* were there   *M't 27:55*
beholding
answered and said unto the   *M't 28:5*
w.
were also *w.* looking on   *M'k 15:40*
afar off
other *w.* which came up   *M'k 15:41*
with him
blessed art thou among *w.*   *Lu 1:28*
said, Blessed art thou among   *Lu 1:42*
w.
Among those that are born of   *Lu 7:28*
w.
certain *w.* which had been   *Lu 8:2*
healed
two *w.* shall be grinding   *Lu 17:35*
together
company of people, and of   *Lu 23:27*
w.
w. that followed him from   *Lu 23:49*
Galilee
the *w.* also, which came with   *Lu 23:55*
him
and other *w.* that were with   *Lu 24:10*
them
and certain *w.* also of our   *Lu 24:22*
company
it even so as the *w.* had said   *Lu 24:24*
and supplication, with the *w.*   *Ac 1:14*
multitudes both of man and *w.*   *Ac 5:14*
haling men and *w.* committed   *Ac 8:3*
them to prison
were baptized, both men and   *Ac 8:12*
w.
whether they were men or *w.* he   *Ac 9:2*
the devout and honourable   *Ac 13:50*
w.
spake unto the *w.* which   *Ac 16:13*
resorted
and of the chief *w.* not a few   *Ac 17:4*
honourable *w.* which were   *Ac 17:12*
Greeks
into prisons both men and *w.*   *Ac 22:4*
their *w.* did change the   *Ro 1:26*
natural use
w. keep silence in the   *1Co 14:34*
churches
for *w.* to speak in the   *1Co 14:35*
church
help those *w.* which laboured   *Ph'p 4:3*
with
w. adorn themselves in modest   *1Ti 2:9*
which becometh *w.* professing   *1Ti 2:10*
godly myths, fit for old *w.* (N)   *1Ti 4:7*
The elder *w.* as the mothers;   *1Ti 5:2*
the younger
therefore that the younger *w.*   *1Ti 5:14*
marry
captive silly *w.* laden with sins   *2Ti 3:6*
weak-natured *w.* (B)(R)   *2Ti 3:6*
The aged *w.* likewise, that they   *Tit 2:3*
may teach the young *w.* to be   *Tit 2:4*
sober
W. received their dead   *Heb 11:35*
raised to
in the old time the holy *w.* also   *1Pe 3:5*
they had hair as the hair of *w.*   *Re 9:8*
which were not defiled with *w.*   *Re 14:4*

WOMEN'S

before the court of the *w.*   *Es 2:11*
house

WOMENSERVANTS

and w. and gave them unto	Ge 20:14
flocks, and menservants, and w.	Ge 32:5
his two w. and his eleven sons	Ge 32:22

WON

I have w. out (B)	Ge 30:8; 32:28
w. a name (S)	1Ch 11:20; 11:24
Out of the spoils w. in battles did	1Ch 26:27
brother offended is harder to be w.	Pr 18:19
w. for yourself great wealth (B)(R)	Eze 28:4
may without the word be w.	1Pe 3:1

WONDER

and giveth thee a sign of a w.	De 13:1
the sign or the w. come to pass	De 13:2
upon thee for a sign and for a w.	De 28:46
enquire of the w. that was done	2Ch 32:31
a sign (B)(R)	2Ch 32:31
I am as a w. unto many; but	Ps 71:7
a marvel (B)	Ps 71:7; Ac 13:41
a portent (R)	Ps 71:7; Isa 20:3
for a sign and w. upon Egypt	Isa 20:3
Stay yourselves, and w.; cry ye	Isa 29:9
be confounded (B)	Isa 29:9
Stupify yourselves and be a stupor (R)	Isa 29:9
even a marvellous work and a w.	Isa 29:14
wonderful and marvelous (R)	Isa 29:14
and the prophets shall w.	Jer 4:9
prophets astounded and dazed (A)	Jer 4:9
shall be astounded (B)(R)	Jer 4:9
and regard, and w. marvellously	Hab 1:5
be astonished! Astounded! (A)	Hab 1:5
be amazed (B)	Hab 1:5; Re 17:8
w. and be astounded (R)	Hab 1:5
fills eyes with w. (B)	M't 21:42
were full of w. (N)	Lu 2:33
do not w. at this (N)	Joh 5:26
and they were filled with w.	Ac 3:10
with awe and amazement (A)	Ac 3:10
why do you w. at this (R)	Ac 3:12
Behold, ye despisers, and w.	Ac 13:41
marvel and perish (A)	Ac 13:41
effects w. working power (B)	Ga 3:5
do not w., brethren (R)	1Jo 3:13
appeared a great w. in heaven	Re 12:1
a great sign (A)(P)	Re 12:1; 12:3
a potent (B)(N)(R)	Re 12:1; 12:3
appeared another w. in heaven	Re 12:3
followed the beast with w. (B)(R)	Re 13:3
another w. in heaven (A)	Re 15:1
I wondered with great w. (S)	Re 17:6
why do you w. (A)(E)(S)	Re 17:7
that dwell on the earth shall w.	Re 17:8
will be astonished (A)(P)(R)	Re 17:8
will marvel (R)	Re 17:8

WONDERED

w. that there was no intercessor	Isa 59:16
amazed (B)	Isa 59:16; Re 17:6
w. that there was none to uphold	Isa 63:5
amazed and appalled (A)	Isa 63:5
marvelled (B)	Isa 63:5; Lu 2:18; Ac 7:31
appalled (R)	Isa 63:5
thee; for they are men w. at	Zec 3:8
a sign or omen (A)	Zec 3:8
significant men (B)	Zec 3:8
men of good omen (R)	Zec 3:8
Insomuch that the multitude w.	M't 15:31
amazed (A)	M't 15:31; Ac 8:13
amazement (N)	M't 15:31
astonished (P)	M't 15:31
the governor w. greatly (R)	M't 27:14
beyond measure, and w.	M'k 6:51
astonished exceedingly (A)	M'k 6:51
amazement (B)	M'k 6:51; Lu 8:25
dumbfounded (N)	M'k 6:51

absolutely terrified (P)	M'k 6:51
utterly astounded (R)	M'k 6:51
w. at his delaying (A)(R)	Lu 1:2
w. what this greeting (N)	Lu 1:29
that heard it w. at those things	Lu 2:18
astounded and marvelled (A)	Lu 2:18; Ac 7:31
astonished (N)	Lu 2:18
amazed (P)	Lu 2:18; 4:22
and w. at the gracious words which	Lu 4:22
marvelled (A)	Lu 4:22; 8:25; 11:14; 24:41
they being afraid w. saying one	Lu 8:25
seized with alarm and	Lu 8:25
profound and reverent dread (A)	
marveled (B)	Lu 8:25; 11:14; Re 17:6
astonished (N)	Lu 8:25; 11:14
frightened and bewildered (P)	Lu 8:25
they w. every one at all things	Lu 9:43
marvelling (A)(R)	Lu 9:43
astonished (B)	Lu 9:43
dumb spake; and the people w.	Lu 11:14
amazement (P)	Lu 11:14; Re 17:6
noticed and w. (B)	Lu 11:38
they yet believed not for joy, and w.	Lu 24:41
remained in a maze (B)	Lu 24:41
astounded (N)	Lu 24:41
bewildered (R)	Lu 24:41
w. to find him talking (A)	Joh 4:27
Amazed and w. (R)	Ac 2:6
Moses saw it, he w. at the sight	Ac 7:31
and w. beholding the miracles	Ac 8:13
surprised (A)	Ac 8:13
carried away (N)	Ac 8:13
amazed (R)	Ac 8:13
and all the world w. after the beast	Re 13:3
in amazement and admiration (A)	Re 13:3
followed the beast in wonder (B)(R)	Re 13:3
went after the beast with wondering admiration (N)	Re 13:3
her, I w. with great admiration	Re 17:6
utterly amazed and wondered greatly (A)	Re 17:6
greatly astonished (N)	Re 17:6

WONDERFUL

have shown w. kindness (B)	Ge 19:19
the Lord will make thy plagues w.	De 28:59
extraordinary (A)(B)(R)	De 28:59
all his w. deeds (R)	J'g 6:13
seeing it is w.	J'g 13:18
thy love to me was w. passing	2Sa 1:26
am about to build shall be w. great	2Ch 2:9
marvelous (B)	2Ch 2:9; Ps 119:129
great and w. (S)	2Ch 2:9
things too w. for me, which I knew	Job 42:3
thy w. works which thou hast done	Ps 40:5
and his w. works that he hath done	Ps 78:4
w. works to the children of	Ps 107:8; 107:15, 21, 31
his w. works to be remembered	Ps 111:4
Thy testimonies are w.	Ps 119:129
Such knowledge is too w. for me	Ps 139:6
be three things which are too w.	Pr 30:18
and his name shall be called W.	Isa 9:6
for thou hast done w. things	Isa 25:1
marvels (B)	Isa 25:1
which is w. in counsel, and	Isa 28:29
w. and horrible thing is committed	Jer 5:30
an appealing thing (A)(R)	Jer 5:30
an astonishing thing (B)	Jer 5:30
name done many w. works	M't 7:22
mighty acts (A)(E)(R)	M't 7:22
many miracles (B)	M't 7:22
many great things (P)	M't 7:22
saw the w. things that he did	M't 21:15
it w. in our eyes (N)	M't 21:42

our tongues the w. works of God	Ac 2:11
excellencies of God (B)	Ac 2:11
great things God has done (N)	Ac 2:11
the magnificence of God (P)	Ac 2:11
many w. things (N)	Ac 5:12

WONDERFULLY

he had wrought w. among them	1Sa 6:6
done wonders (A)	1Sa 6:6
made them feel his power (B)	1Sa 6:6
be made sport of them (F)	1Sa 6:6
for I am fearfully and w. made	Ps 139:14
therefore she came down w.	La 1:9
come down singularly and astonishingly (A)	La 1:9
she fell grievously (B)	La 1:9
her fall is terrific (R)	La 1:9
and he shall destroy w. and shall	Da 8:24
destroy astonishingly (A)	Da 8:24
in astonishing ways cause ruin (B)	Da 8:24
cause fearful destruction (R)	Da 8:24

WONDERING

the man w. at her held his peace	Ge 24:21
gazing at her (A)(B)(R)	Ge 24:21
look at one another w. (B)	Ge 43:33
w. why he delayed (B)(P)	Lu 1:21
w. about the things (B)	Lu 2:33
on tiptoe of expectation, w. (N)	Lu 3:15
w. in himself at that which was	Lu 24:12
is called Solomon's, greatly w.	Ac 3:11
in utmost amazement (A)	Ac 3:11
running in astonishment (N)	Ac 3:11
astounded (R)	Ac 3:11

WONDEROUSLY

and the angel did w.; and Manoah	J'g 13:19
angel working wonders (A)(B)	J'g 13:19

WONDERS

smite Egypt with all my w. which	Ex 3:20
do all those w. before Pharaoh	Ex 4:21
signs (B)	Ex 4:21
miracles (R)	Ex 4:21; Ps 78:11, 43; 105:27
and my w. in the land of Egypt	Ex 7:3
work these my w. (B)	Ex 10:11
that my w. may be multiplied	Ex 11:9
mighty works (B)	Ex 11:9
did all these w. before Pharaoh	Ex 11:10
fearful in praises, doing w.	Ex 15:11
I will work such w. (B)	Ex 34:10
by signs, and by w. and by war	De 4:34
And the Lord shewed signs and w.	De 6:22
portents and marvels (B)	De 6:22
and the w. and the mighty hand	De 7:19
and with signs and with w.	De 26:8
the w. which the Lord sent him to	De 34:11
the Lord will do w. among you	Jos 3:5
marvelous things (B)	Jos 3:5; Ps 96:3
his w. and the judgments of	1Ch 16:12
miracles (A)	1Ch 16:12
marvels (B)	1Ch 16:12
signs and w. upon Pharaoh	Ne 9:10
marvelous things (A)(E)(R)	Ne 9:10; Ps 96:3
neither were mindful of thy w.	Ne 9:17
out; yea, and w. without number	Job 9:10
work w. against me (B)	Job 10:16
I will remember thy w. of old	Ps 77:11
miracles (B)	Ps 77:11; 105:5. 27; 106:7; 2Th 2:9; Re 13:13
Thou art the God that doest	Ps 77:14
his w. that he had shewed them	Ps 78:11
and his w. in the field of Zoan	Ps 78:43

Wilt thou shew w. to the dead	Ps 88:10	w. work of him which is	Job 37:16	he made the table of shittim	Ex 37:10
Shall thy w. be known in the	Ps 88:12	perfect		w.	
dark		and tell of all thy w. works	Ps 26:7	he made the staves of shittim	Ex 37:15
And the heavens shall praise	Ps 89:5	have I declared thy w. works	Ps 71:17	w.	
thy w.		of Israel, who only doeth w.	Ps 72:18	made the incense altar of	Ex 37:25
heathen, his w. among all	Ps 96:3	things		shittim w.	
people		name is near thy w. works	Ps 75:1	he made the staves of shittim	Ex 37:28
his w. and the judgments of	Ps 105:5	declared		w.	
them, and w. in the land of	Ps 105:27	and believed not for his w.	Ps 78:33	altar of burnt offering of	Ex 38:1
Ham		works		shittim w.	
Our fathers understood not	Ps 106:7	thou art great, and doest w.	Ps 86:10	he made the staves of shittim	Ex 38:6
thy w.		things		w.	
miracles (A)	Ps 106:7; Re 13:13	performed w. things (B)	Ps 98:1	lay the w. in order upon the fire	Le 1:7
the Lord, and his w. in the	Ps 107:24	him; talk ye of all his w. works	Ps 105:2	order upon the w. that is on the	Le 1:8
deep		marvelous deeds (A)	Ps 105:2	fire	
Who sent tokens and w. into	Ps 135:9	W. works in the land of	Ps 106:22	order on the w. that is on the	Le 1:12
To him who alone doeth	Ps 136:4	Ham, and		fire	
great w.		behold w. things out of thy	Ps 119:18	upon the w. that is upon the	Le 1:17
for w. in Israel from the Lord	Isa 8:18	law		fire	
signs and portents (B)(R)	Isa 8:18	so shall I talk of thy w.	Ps 119:27	is upon the w. that is on the	Le 3:5
signs and w. in the land of	Jer 32:20	works		fire	
Egypt		of thy majesty, and of thy	Ps 145:5	and burn him on the w. with	Le 4:12
with signs and with w. and	Jer 32:21	w. works		fire	
with		us according to all his w.	Jer 21:2	the priest shall burn w. on it	Le 6:12
w. that the high God hath	Da 4:2	works		every	
wrought				whether it be any vessel of w.	Le 11:32
and how mighty are his w.	Da 4:3	**WONDROUSLY**		and cedar w. and scarlet, and	Le 14:4; 14:49
he worketh signs and w. in	Da 6:27			and the cedar w. and the	Le 14:6
heaven		God, that hath dealth w. with	Joe 2:26	scarlet	
shall it be to the end of these	Da 12:6	you		the cedar w. and the hyssop	Le 14:51
w.				with the cedar w. and with	Le 14:52
And I will shew w. in the	Joe 2:30	**WONT**		every vessel of w. shall be	Le 15:12
heavens				rinsed	
signs (B)	Joe 2:30	ox were w. to push with his	Ex 21:29	whether there be w. therein	Nu 13:20
portents (R)	Joe 2:30	horn		shall take cedar w. and hyssop	Nu 19:6
cause them to seek w.	Mic 7:15	was I ever w. to do so unto	Nu 22:30	hair, and all things made of	Nu 31:20
and shall shew great signs	M't 24:24	thee		w.	
and w.		and his men were w. to	1Sa 30:31	him with an hand weapon of	Nu 35:18
rise, and shall shew signs	M'k 13:22	haunt		w.	
and w.		They were w. to speak in	2Sa 20:18	work of men's hands, w. and	De 4:28
Except ye see signs and w. ye	Joh 4:48	old time		stone	
will		seven times more than it was	Da 3:19	mount, and make thee an ark	De 10:1
portents (N)	Joh 4:48; Ac 2:19, 22	w.		of w.	
And I will shew w. in heaven	Ac 2:19	governor was w. to release	M't 27:15	And I made an ark of shittim	De 10:3
above		unto		w.	
you by miracles and w. and	Ac 2:22	and, as he was w. he taught	M'k 10:1	As when a man goeth into the	De 19:5
signs		them		w.	
and many w. and signs were	Ac 2:43	and went, as he was w. to	Lu 22:39	with his neighbour to hew w.	De 19:5
done		where prayer was w. to be	Ac 16:13	thou serve other gods, w. and	De 28:36
marvels (N)	Ac 2:43	made		stone	
miracles (P)	Ac 2:43; 14:3; Ro 15:19; 2Co 12:12; Heb 2:4			have known, even w. and	De 28:64
and that signs and w. may be	Ac 4:30	**WOOD**		stone	
done				hewer of thy w. unto the	De 29:11
were many signs and w.	Ac 5:12	Make thee an ark of gopher	Ge 6:14	drawer	
wrought		w.		and their idols, w. and stone,	De 29:17
wonderful things (N)	Ac 5:12	ark of resinous w. (B)	Ge 6:14	silver	
did great w. and miracles	Ac 6:8	clave the w. for the burnt	Ge 22:3	but let them be hewers of w.	Jos 9:21
among		offering		hewers of w. drawers of	Jos 9:23; 9:27
signs (N)	Ac 6:8; 15:12; Ro 12:19	took the w. of the burnt	Ge 22:6	water	
remarkable signs (P)	Ac 6:8; Re 13:13	offering		then get thee up to the w.	Jos 17:15
that he had shewed w. and	Ac 7:36	he said, Behold the fire, and	Ge 22:7	country	
signs		the w.		for it is a w. and thou shalt	Jos 17:18
miracles (N)	Ac 7:36; 14:3; 2Th 2:9; Heb 2:4; Re 13:13	and laid the w. in order, and	Ge 22:9	cut it	
granted signs and w. to be	Ac 14:3	bound		sacrifice with the w. of the	J'g 6:26
done		laid him on the altar upon the	Ge 22:9	grove	
declaring what miracles and	Ac 15:12	w.		and they clave the w. of the	1Sa 6:14
w. God		both in vessels of w. and in	Ex 7:19	cart	
Through mighty signs and w.	Ro 15:19	vessels		all they of the land came to	1Sa 14:25
by		and badgers' skins, and	Ex 25:5	a w.	
signs, and w. and mighty	2Co 12:12	shittim w.		the people were come into	1Sa 14:26
deeds		shall make an ark of shittim	Ex 25:10; 37:1	the w.	
marvels (N)	2Co 12:12	w.		in the wilderness of Ziph	1Sa 23:15
all power and signs and lying	2Th 2:9	shalt make staves of shittim	Ex 25:13; 25:28; 30:5	in a w.	
w.		w.		and went to David into the	1Sa 23:16
delusive marvels (A)	2Th 2:9	also make a table of shittim	Ex 25:23	w.	
witness, both with signs and	Heb 2:4	w.		and David abode in the w.	1Sa 23:18
w.		for the tabernacle of shittim	Ex 26:15; 36:20	with us in strong holds in	1Sa 23:19
signs and w. (A)(B)(E)(R)	Heb 2:4	w.		the w.	
by means of the w. (B)	Heb 13:14	thou shalt make bars of	Ex 26:26	of instruments made of fir w.	2Sa 6:5
And he doeth great w. so that	Re 13:13	shittim w.		battle was in the w. of	2Sa 18:6
he		four pillars of shittim w.	Ex 26:32	Ephraim	
great signs (E)(R)	Re 13:13	overlaid		the w. devoured more people	2Sa 18:8
performing w. (P)	Re 16:14	the hanging five pillars of	Ex 26:37	cast him into a great pit in	2Sa 18:17
		shittim w.		the w.	
WONDER-WORKERS		shalt make an altar of shittim	Ex 27:1	instruments of the oxen for	2Sa 24:22
		w.		w.	
wonder-workers (A)	1Co 12:28	staves of shittim w. and	Ex 27:6	covered them on the inside	1Ki 6:15
		overlay		with w.	
WONDROUS		of shittim w. shalt thou make	Ex 30:1	and lay it on w. and put no	1Ki 18:22; 18:23
		it		fire	
all his w. works (A)(B)(E)	J'g 6:13	and badgers' skins, and	Ex 35:7	And he put the w. in order	1Ki 18:33
him, talk ye of all his w.	1Ch 16:9	shittim w.		and cut	
works		with whom was found shittim	Ex 35:24	in pieces, and laid him on	1Ki 18:33
miracles (B)	1Ch 16:9; Ps 106:22	w.		the w.	
God thunders w. (B)(R)	Job 37:5	and in carving of w. to make	Ex 35:33	the burnt sacrifice, and on	1Ki 18:33
and consider the w. works	Job 37:14	any		the w.	
of God		and he made bars of shittim w.	Ex 36:31	the burnt sacrifice, and the	1Ki 18:38
		thereunto four pillars of	Ex 36:36	w.	
		shittim w.			
		And he made staves of shittim	Ex 37:4		
		w.			

forth two she bears out of the w.   2Ki 2:24

came to Jordan, they cut down w.   2Ki 6:4

work of men's hands, w. and stone   2Ki 19:18

shall the trees of the w. sing out   1Ch 16:33

the threshing instruments for w.   1Ch 21:23

of Tyre brought much cedar w. to   1Ch 22:4

of iron, and w. for things of w.   1Ch 29:2

And we will cut w. out of Lebanon   2Ch 2:16

made two cherubims of w. (S)   2Ch 3:10

the scribe stood upon a pulpit of w.   Ne 8:4

and the people, for the w. offering   Ne 10:34

And for the w. offering at times   Ne 13:31

as straw, and brass as rotten w.   Job 41:27

boar out of the w. doth waste it   Ps 80:13

As the fire burneth a w. and   Ps 83:14

shall all the trees of the w. rejoice   Ps 96:12

we found it in the fields of the w.   Ps 132:6

and cleaneth w. upon the earth   Ps 141:7

Where no w. is, there the fire   Pr 26:20

to burning coals, and w. to fire   Pr 26:21

the w. that bringeth forth trees   Ec 2:6

and he that cleaveth w. shall be   Ec 10:9

tree among the trees of the w.   Ca 2:3

a chariot of the w. of Lebanon   Ca 3:9

as the trees of the w. are moved   Isa 7:2

lift up itself, as if it were no w.   Isa 10:15

pile thereof is fire and much w.   Isa 30:33

work of men's hands, w. and stone   Isa 37:19

set up the w. of their graven image   Isa 45:20

for w. brass, and for stones   Isa 60:17

thy mouth fire, and his people w.   Jer 5:14

The children gather, w. and   Jer 7:18

Thou hast broken the yokes of w.   Jer 28:13

her with axes, as hewers of w.   Jer 46:22

for money; our w. is sold unto us   La 5:4

and the children fell under the w.   La 5:13

w. be taken thereof to do any work   Eze 15:3

countries, to serve w. and stone   Eze 20:32

Heap on w. kindle the fire   Eze 24:10

shall take no w. out of the field   Eze 39:10

door, ceiled with w. round about   Eze 41:16

altar of w. was three cubits high   Eze 41:22

and the walls thereof, were of w.   Eze 41:22

brass, of iron, of w. and of stone   Da 5:4

gold, of brass, iron, w. and stone   Da 5:23

ask senseless w. idols (A)(B)(R)   Ho 4:12

which dwell solitarily in the w.   Mic 7:14

him that saith to the w., Awake   Hab 2:19

up to the mountain, and bring w.   Hag 1:8

an hearth of fire among the w.   Zec 12:6

precious stones, w., hay, stubble   1Co 3:12

silver, but also of w. and of earth   2Ti 2:20

and brass, and stone, and of w.   Re 9:20

and scarlet, and all thyine w.   Re 18:12

manner vessels of most precious w.   Re 18:12

WOODCUTTER

no w. come up (A)(B)   Isa 14:8

WOODS

Herth w. (B)   1Sa 22:5

wilderness, and sleep in the w.   Eze 34:25

WOOF

Whether it be in the warp, or w.   Le 13:48; 13:49, 51-53, 56-59

WOOL

will put a fleece of w. in the floor   J'g 6:37

thousand rams., with the w.   2Ki 3:4

He giveth snow like w. he   Ps 147:16

She seeketh w. and flax, and   Pr 31:13

like crimson, they shall be as w.   Isa 1:18

the worm shall eat them like w.   Isa 51:8

the wine of Helbon, and white w.   Eze 27:18

fat, and ye clothe you with the w.   Eze 34:3

and no w. shall come upon them   Eze 44:17

hair of his head like the pure w.   Da 7:9

my w. and my flax, mine oil   Ho 2:5

will recover my w. and my flax   Ho 2:9

and scarlet w. and hyssop   Heb 9:19

and his hairs were white like w.   Re 1:14

WOOLLEN

whether it be a w. garment   Le 13:47; 13:48-49, 52, 59

garment mingled of linen and w.   Le 19:19

sorts, as of w. and linen together   De 22:11

WORD

go and bring me w. again   Ge 37:14; M't 2:8

let me speak a w.   Ge 44:18; 2Sa 14:12

Lord did according to w. of Moses   Ex 8:13

Israel did according to the w.   Ex 12:35 of Moses

Levi did according to the w.   Ex 32:28; Le 10:7

they brought back w. unto them   Nu 13:26

lodge here, I will bring you w.   Nu 22:8; De 1:22

yet the w. I shall say to thee, that do   Nu 22:20

w. I shall speak   Nu 22:35

w. God putteth   Nu 22:38

the Lord put a w. in Balaam's mouth   Nu 23:5

they brought us w. again, and said   De 1:25

not add unto the w. I command you   De 4:2

by every w. that proceedeth out of mouth of God   De 8:3; M't 4:4

prophets that presume to speak a w.   De 18:20

how shall we know the w.   De 18:21; Jer 28:9

by their w. every controversy be tried   De 21:5

the w. is nigh thee   Jos 30:14; Ro 10:8

remember the w. Moses commanded   Jos 1:13

was not a w. which Joshua read not   Jos 8:35

brought him w.   Jos 14:7

brought them w.   Jos 22:32

w. of Samuel came to all Israel   1Sa 4:1

he could not answer Abner a w.   2Sa 3:11

in all places spake I a w.   2Sa 7:7; 1Ch 17:6

w. thou hast spoken concerning thy servant   2Sa 7:25

till there come w. from you to certify me   2Sa 15:28

consulted the w. of God (A)(B)   2Sa 16:23

speak ye not a w. of bringing the king   2Sa 19:10

the king's w. prevailed   2Sa 24:4; 1Ch 21:4

Benaiah brought the king w.   1Ki 2:30; again   2Ki 22:9, 20; 2Ch 34:16, 28

the w. that I have heard is good   1Ki 2:42

hath not failed one w. of all his promise   1Ki 8:56

the people answered not a w.   1Ki 18:21; Isa 36:21

he smote according to the w. of Elisha   2Ki 6:18

hear the w. of the great king of Assyria   2Ki 18:28

mindful of the w. which he   1Ch 16:15; commanded to a thousand generations   Ps 105:8

advise that w. I shall bring to him   1Ch 21:12

remember w. commandedst Moses   Ne 1:8

he did according to w. of Memucan   Es 1:21

as the w. went out of the king's mouth   Es 7:8

they sat down, none spake a w. to Job   Job 2:13

by w. of thy lips, I have kept me   Ps 17:4

no speech, nor spoken w. (A)   Ps 19:3

the Lord gave the w.: great was the   Ps 68:11

remember the w. to thy servant   Ps 119:49

mine eyes fail for the w. of thy righteousness   Ps 119:123

there is not a w. in my tongue, but thou   Ps 139:4

a good w. maketh the heart glad   Pr 12:25

whoso despiseth the w. be destroyed   Pr 13:13

simple believeth every w. but prudent   Pr 14:15

w. spoken in due season, how good is it   Pr 15:23

a w. fitly spoken is like apples of gold in pictures of silver   Pr 25:11

where w. of a king is there is power   Ec 8:4

they despised w. of Holy One of Israel   Isa 5:24

speak w. and it shall not stand   Isa 8:10

the Lord sent a w. to Jacob   Isa 9:8

that make a man an offender for a w.   Isa 29:21

thine ears shall hear a w. behind thee   Isa 30:21

no counsellor could answer a w.   Isa 41:28

that confirmeth the w. of his servant   Isa 44:26

the w. is gone out of my mouth   Isa 45:23

know how to speak a w. in season   Isa 50:4

become wind, the w. is not in them   Jer 5:13

let ear receive w. of his mouth   Jer 9:20; 10:1

nor shall the w. perish from the prophet   Jer 18:18

for every man's w. shall be his burden   Jer 23:36

speak unto them, diminish not a w.   Jer 26:2

I have pronounced the w. saith the Lord   Jer 34:5

king said, Is there any w. from Lord   Jer 37:17

as for the w. thou hast spoken unto us   Jer 44:16

therefore hear w. at my mouth   Eze 3:17; 33:7

the w. that I shall speak shall come to pass   Eze 12:25

the w. that I have spoken shall be done   Eze 12:28

that they would confirm the w.   Eze 13:6

hear w. that cometh from the Lord   Eze 33:30

who have changed the king's w.   Da 3:28

the demand is by w. of the holy ones   Da 4:17

while the w. was in the king's   Da 4:31
mouth
for w. came to the king of   Jon 3:6
Nineveh
according to the w. I   Hag 2:5
covenanted with
speak the w. only, he shall be   M't 8:8
healed
whoso speaketh a w. against   M't 12:32;
the Son of man, it shall be   Lu 12:10
forgiven
of every idle w. men shall   M't 12:36
give account
when any one heareth the   M't 13:19;
w. of the kingdom   20:22-23; M'k 4:16,
    18, 20; Lu 8:15
when tribulation or   M't 13:21;
persecution ariseth, because   M'k 4:17
of the w.
Jesus answered woman not   M't 15:23
a w.
that every w. may be   M't 18:16;
established   2Co 13:1
no man was able to answer   M't 22:46
him a w.
Jesus answered him to never   M't 27:14
a w.
they did run to bring his   M't 28:8
disciples w.
the sower soweth the w.   M'k 4:14
Peter called to mind the w.   M'k 14:72
that Jesus
the Lord confirming the w.   M'k 16:20
with signs
all amazed, saying, What a w.   Lu 4:36
is this
say in a w. and my servant be   Lu 7:7
healed
Jesus a prophet mighty in w.   Lu 24:19
and deed
in beginning was the W. the   Joh 1:1
W. was with God, and the W.
was God
the W. was made flesh, and   Joh 1:14
dwelt among us
they believed the w. that   Joh 2:22;
Jesus said   4:50
w. I have spoken shall judge   Joh 12:48
him in last day
the w. which you hear is not   Joh 14:24
mine
are clean through the w. I   Joh 15:3
spake to you
remember the w. that I said   Joh 15:20
unto you
that w. might be fulfilled,   Joh 15:25
written in their law
who shall believe on me   Joh 17:20
through their w.
he received the living w. (B)   Ac 7:38
the w. which God sent to   Ac 10:36
Israel
speaking the w. (E)(R)   Ac 11:19
if ye have any w. of   Ac 13:15
exhortation
to you is the w. of this   Ac 13:26
salvation sent
Gentiles, by my mouth, should   Ac 15:7
hear w.
proclaiming the w. (A)   Ac 15:35
they received the w. with all   Ac 17:11
readiness
I commend you to the w. of   Ac 20:32
his grace
after that Paul had spoken   Ac 28:25
one w.
that in the w. of faith we   Ro 10:8
preach
make Gentiles obedient by w.   Ro 15:18
and deed
the w. of the cross (E)(R)   1Co 1:18
kingdom of God is not in w.   1Co 4:20
but in power
w. of wisdom, to another w.   1Co 12:8
of knowledge
our w. toward you was not   2Co 1:18
yea and nay
God committed to us w. of   2Co 5:19
reconciliation
such as we are in w. by   2Co 10:11
letters when absent
all the law was fulfilled in one   Ga 5:14
w.
let him that is taught in w.   Ga 6:6
communicate
cleanse with washing of   Eph 5:26
water by the w.
are bold to speak the w.   Ph'p 1:14
without fear

holding forth w. of life to   Ph'p 2:16
rejoice in day
heard w. of the truth of the   Col 1:5
gospel
let the w. of Christ dwell in   Col 3:16
you richly
whatsoever ye do in w. or   Col 3:17
deed, do in name
our gospel come not to you in   1Th 1:5
w. only
having received the w. in much   1Th 1:6
affliction
received it not as w. of men   1Th 2:13
but as in truth w. God
working effectually
be troubled, not by Spirit, nor   2Th 2:2
by w.
been taught, whether by w.   2Th 2:15
or our epistle
God comfort and stablish you   2Th 2:17
in every good w.
if any man obey not our w.   2Th 3:14
be thou an example of   1Ti 4:12
believers in w.
they who labour in the w.   1Ti 5:17
and doctrine
their w. will eat as doth a   2Ti 2:17
canker
preach w. be instant in season   2Ti 4:2
out of season
holding fast the faithul w. as   Tit 1:9
taught
upholding all things by w. of   Heb 1:3
his power
sustains universe by his   Heb 1:3
almighty w. (B)
if the w. spoken by angels   Heb 2:2
was stedfast
but the w. preached did not   Heb 4:2
profit them
first principles of God's w.   Heb 5:12
(A)(R)
is unskilful in the w. of   Heb 5:13
righteousness
the w. of the oath which was   Heb 7:28
since the law
entreated w. should not be   Heb 12:19
spoken any more
brethren, suffer the w. of   Heb 13:22
exhortation
receive with meekness   Jas 1:21
ingrafted w.
be doers of the w. and not   Jas 1:22
hearers only
if any be a hearer of the w.   Jas 1:23
and not a doer
if any offend not in w. is a   Jas 3:2
perfect man
as babes desire the sincere   1Pe 2:2
milk of the w.
even to them who stumble at   1Pe 2:8
the w. being
if any obey not the w. may   1Pe 3:1
without the w.
we have a more sure w. of   2Pe 1:19
prophecy
the heavens by the same w.   2Pe 3:7
are kept in store
our hands have handled the w.   1Jo 1:1
of life
let us not love in w. but in   1Jo 3:18
deed and truth
the Father, the W., and   1Jo 5:7
the Holy Ghost are one
because thou hast kept w. of   Re 3:10
my patience
they overcame by the w. of   Re 12:11
their testimony

WORD *OF GOD*

that I may shew thee the w.   1Sa 9:27
of God
the w. of God came to   1Ki 12:22
Shemaiah
the w. of God came to   1Ch 17:3
Nathan
every w. of God is pure, he is   Pr 30:5
a shield
the w. of our God shall stand   Isa 40:8
for ever
making the w. of God of   M'k 7:13
none effect
the w. of God came unto John   Lu 3:2
in wilderness
not by bread alone, but by   Lu 4:4
every w. of God
the people pressed on him to   Lu 5:1
hear the w. of God

parable is this: The seed is the   Lu 8:11
w. of God
my brethren are these that   Lu 8:21
hear the w. of God
blessed are they that hear the   Lu 11:28
w. of God
if he called them gods to   Joh 10:35
whom w. of God came
they spake the w. of God with   Ac 4:31
boldness
not reason we should leave the   Ac 6:2
w. of God
the w. of God increased in   Ac 6:7;
Jerusalem   12:24
that Samaria had received the   Ac 8:14
w. of God
the Gentiles had received the   Ac 11:1
w. of God
Sergius Paulus desired to hear   Ac 13:7
the w. of God
the whole city came to hear   Ac 13:44
the w. of God
w. of God should be first   Ac 13:46
spoken to you
so mightily grew w. of God   Ac 19:20
and prevailed
not as tho' w. of God hath   Ro 9:6
taken none effect
faith by hearing, hearing by   Ro 10:17
w. of God
came the w. of God out   1Co 14:36
from your
as many which corrupt the   2Co 2:17
w. of God
not handling the w. of God   2Co 4:2
deceitfully
and the sword of the Spirit,   Eph 6:17
which is the w. of God
which is given me to fulfil the   Col 1:25
w. of God
when ye received the w. of   1Th 2:13
God
it is sanctified by w. of God   1Ti 4:5
and prayer
but the w. of God is not bound   2Ti 2:9
that the w. of God be not   Tit 2:5
blasphemed
the w. of God is quick and   Heb 4:12
powerful
and have tasted the good w.   Heb 6:5
of God
the worlds were framed by   Heb 11:3
the w. of God
who have spoken to you the   Heb 13:7
w. of God
being born again by the w. of   1Pe 1:23
God
by the w. of God the heavens   2Pe 3:5
were of old
are strong, the w. of God   1Jo 2:14
abideth in you
who bare record of the w. of   Re 1:2
God
was in isle of Patmos for the   Re 1:9
w. of God
souls that were slain for w. of   Re 6:9
God
his name is called The W. of   Re 19:13
God
them that were beheaded for   Re 20:4
w. of God

HIS WORD

at *his* w. shall they go out,   Nu 27:21
and at *his* w. they shall come in
if a man vow a vow, he shall   Nu 30:2
not break *his* w.
only the Lord establish *his* w.   1Sa 1:23
and *his* w. was in my tongue   2Sa 23:2
that the Lord may continue *his*   1Ki 2:4
w.
Lord performed *his* w. he   1Ki 8:20;
spake, I am risen up   2Ch 6:10
no God in Israel, to inquire   2Ki 1:16
of *his* w.
that the Lord might perform   2Ch 10:15
his w.
in God that I praise *his* w. in   Ps 56:4;
him trust   56:10
hearkening unto the voice of   Ps 103:20
his w.
until the time that *his* w.   Ps 105:19
came
and they rebelled not against   Ps 105:28
his w.
they believed not *his* w. but   Ps 106:24
murmured
he sent *his* w. and healed   Ps 107:20
them

I wait for the Lord and in his Ps 130:5
w. do I hope
his w. runneth very swiftly Ps 147:15
he sendeth out his w. and Ps 147:18
melteth them
he sheweth his w. unto Ps 147:19
Jacob, his statutes
snow, vapour, stormy wind Ps 148:8
fulfilling his w.
hear, ye that tremble at his w. Isa 66:5
but his w. was in my heart as Jer 20:9
a fire
hath fulfilled his w. he La 2:17
commanded
he is strong that executeth his Joe 2:11
w.
he cast out the spirits with M't 8:16
his w.
astonished, for his w. was with Lu 4:32
power
many believed because of his Joh 4:41
own w.
ye have not his w. abiding in Joh 5:38
you
they that gladly received his Ac 2:41
w.
but hath in due times Tit 1:3
manifested his w.
whoso keepeth his w. in him is 1Jo 2:5
the love

MY WORD

whether my w. shall come to Nu 11:23
pass
because ye rebelled against Nu 20:24
my w.
then will I perform my w. 1Ki 6:12
with thee
no dew nor rain, but 1Ki 17:1
according to my w.
so shall my w. be that goeth Isa 55:11
out of mouth
I will look to him that Isa 66:2
trembleth at my w.
I will hasten my w. to perform Jer 1:12
it
he that hath my w. let him Jer 23:28
speak my w.
is not my w. like fire, saith Jer 23:29
the Lord
I am against the prophets Jer 23:30
that steal my w.
I will perform my good w. to Jer 29:10
you
but my w. shall not pass M't 24:35
away
he that heareth my w. and Joh 5:24
believeth
continue in my w. ye are my Joh 8:31
disciples indeed
to kill me because my w. hath Joh 8:37
no place in you
even because ye cannot hear Joh 8:43
my w.
hast kept my w. not denied my Re 3:8
name

THIS WORD

is not this the w. that we did Ex 14:12
tell thee
since the Lord spake this w. Jos 14:10
to Moses
they sent this w. to the king 2Sa 19:1
hast not spoken this w. against 1Ki 2:23
his life
this is the w. that the Lord 2Ki 19:21;
hath spoken Isa 16:13; 24:3; 37:22
that whosoever shall alter this Ezr 6:11
w.
swear they should do Ezr 10:5
according to this w.
if they speak not according Isa 8:20
to this w.
because ye despise this w. Isa 30:12
and trust in
because ye speak this w. Jer 5:14;
23:38
proclaim there this w. and say, Jer 7:2
Hear word
thou shalt speak unto them Jer 13:12
this w.
therefore shalt thou say this Jer 14:17
w. to them
go down, and speak there Jer 22:1
this w.
in the reign of Jehoiakim this Jer 26:1;
w. came from Lord 27:1; 34:8; 36:1

hear now this w. Jer 28:7
Am 3:1; 4:1; 5:1
when he had spoken this w. to Da 10:11
me
this is the w. of the Lord to Zec 4:6
Zerubbabel
they gave him audience to Ac 22:22
this w.
this is w. of promise, Sarah Ro 9:9
have a son
this w. yet once more Heb 12:27
signifieth
this is the w. which is preached 1Pe 1:25
to you

THY WORD

I would it might be Ge 30:34
according to thy w.
according to thy w. shall my Ge 41:40
people be ruled
he said, Be it according to thy Ex 8:10
w.
I have pardoned, according Nu 14:20
to thy w.
observed thy w. and kept De 33:9
covenant
I have done according to thy 1Ki 3:12
w.
let thy w. I pray thee, be 1Ki 8:26
verified
I have done all these things 1Ki 18:36
at thy w.
let thy w. be like the word 1Ki 22:13;
of one of them and speak 2Ch 18:12
what is good
by taking heed according to Ps 119:9
thy w.
thy w. have I hid in mine Ps 119:11
heart, not to sin
I will not forget thy w. Ps 119:16
that I may live, and keep Ps 119:17;
thy w. 119:101
quicken me according to Ps 119:25;
thy w. 119:107, 154
strengthen thou me Ps 119:28;
according to thy w. 119:116
stablish thy w. Ps 119:38
even thy salvation according Ps 119:41
to thy w.
I trust in thy w. Ps 119:42
comfort in affliction, for thy Ps 119:50
w. quickened me
be merciful to me according Ps 119:58;
to thy w. 119:65, 76
I went astray, but now have Ps 119:67
I kept thy w.
because I have hoped in thy Ps 119:74;
w. 119:147
I hope in thy w. Ps 119:81; 119:114
mine eyes fail for thy w. Ps 119:82
for ever, O Lord, thy w. is Ps 119:89
settled in heaven
that I might keep thy w. Ps 119:101
I rejoice at thy w. Ps 119:102
thy w. is a lamp Ps 119:105
mine eyes fail for thy w. Ps 119:123
order my steps in thy w. let Ps 119:133
not iniquity
thy w. is pure Ps 119:140
night watches, that I might Ps 119:148
meditate in thy w.
quicken me according to Ps 119:154
thy w.
I was grieved because they Ps 119:158
kept not thy w.
thy w. is true Ps 119:160
but my heart standeth in Ps 119:161
awe of thy w.
give me understanding Ps 119:169
according to thy w.
supplication, deliver me Ps 119:170
according to thy w.
my tongue shall speak of Ps 119:172
thy w.
hast magnified thy w. above Ps 138:2
thy name
thy w. was to me the joy of Jer 15:16
my heart
drop thy w. toward the Eze 20:46
south, prophesy
drop thy w. toward holy Eze 21:2
places, prophesy
drop not thy w. against house Am 7:16
of Isaac
thy bow was made naked, Hab 3:9
even thy w.
be it unto me according to thy Lu 1:38
w.

servant depart in peace, Lu 2:29
according to thy w.
nevertheless at thy w. I will let Lu 5:5
down the net
thine w. they were; they have Joh 17:6
kept thy w.
I have given them thy w. Joh 17:14
thy w. is truth Joh 17:17
with all boldness they may Ac 4:29
speak thy w.

WORDS

and thou shalt put w. in his Ex 4:15
mouth
more work; let them not regard Ex 5:9
vain w.
Moses returned the w. of the Ex 19:8
people
gift perverteth w. of righteous Ex 23:8;
De 16:19
the w. which were in the first Ex 34:1
tables
Moses wrote w. of the Ex 34:28;
covenant De 10:2
I sent to Sihon with w. of De 2:26
peace
thou shalt not go aside from De 28:14
any of the w.
keep the w. of his covenant De 29:9;
that ye may prosper 2Ki 23:3; 24:2;
2Ch 34:31
give ear, O heavens, hear, O De 32:1;
earth, the w. of my mouth Ps 54:2;
78:1; Pr 7:24
Saul was afraid of the w. of 1Sa 28:20
Samuel
the w. of men of Judah were 2Sa 19:43
fiercer
the w. of prophets declare 1Ki 22:13;
good to the king 2Ch 18:12
Elisha telleth the w. thou 2Ki 6:12
speakest
but they are but vain w. 2Ki 18:20;
Isa 36:5
to sing praises with the w. 2Ch 29:30
of David
encouraging w. (S) 2Ch 30:22
the people rested on the w. 2Ch 32:8
of Hezekiah
whether Mordecai's w. will Es 3:4
stand (S)
sent letters with w. of peace Es 9:30
and truth
do ye imagine to reprove w. Job 6:26
and speeches
shall the w. of thy mouth be Job 8:2
like a strong wind
a deluge of w. (B) Job 11:2
doth not the ear try w. Job 12:11; 34:3
thou lettest such w. go out Job 15:13
of thy mouth
shall vain w. have an end Job 16:3
I could heap up w. against Job 16:4
you
how long will it be ere ye Job 18:2
make an end of w.
how long will ye break me in Job 19:5
pieces with w.
I would know the w. he Job 23:5
would answer me
I have esteemed the w. of Job 23:12
his mouth more
he multiplieth w. without Job 35:16
knowledge
who is this that darkeneth Job 38:2
counsel by w.
no speech, nor spoken w. Ps 19:3
(B)(R)
let the w. of my mouth be Ps 19:14
acceptable
why so far from the w. of my Ps 22:1
roaring
the w. of his mouth are Ps 36:3
iniquity and deceit
w. of the taunter (A)(R) Ps 44:16
lovest all devouring w. O Ps 52:4
deceitful tongue
w. of his mouth were Ps 55:21
smoother than butter
for w. of their lips let them be Ps 59:12
taken
to understand the w. of the wise Pr 1:6
decline not from the w. of my Pr 4:5;
mouth 5:7
thou art snared with the w. of Pr 6:2
thy mouth
in multitude of w. there Pr 10:19
wanteth not sin

w. of wicked are to lie in wait *Pr 12:6*
for blood
the w. of the pure are *Pr 15:26*
pleasant w.
w. of a man's mouth are as *Pr 18:4*
deep waters
w. of a talebearer are as *Pr 18:8;*
wounds *26:22*
he pursueth them with w. *Pr 19:7*
causeth thee to err from w. *Pr 19:27*
of knowledge
overthrows the w. of the *Pr 22:12*
transgressor
bow down thine ear, hear w. *Pr 22:17*
of the wise
make thee know certainty of *Pr 22:21*
w. of truth that thou mightest
answer w. of truth
and thou shalt lose thy sweet *Pr 23:8*
w.
a servant will not be *Pr 29:19*
corrected by w.
fool's voice known by *Ec 5:3;*
multitude of w. *10:14*
the w. of a wise man's mouth *Ec 10:12*
are gracious
preacher sought to find out *Ec 12:10*
acceptable w. that was written,
even the w. of truth
w. of the wise are as goads *Ec 12:11*
and as nails
w. will whisper (B) *Isa 29:4*
is become as the w. of a *Isa 29:11*
book sealed
may be God will hear w. of *Isa 37:4*
Rabshakeh
uttering from the heart w. of *Isa 59:13*
falsehood
hear ye the w. of this *Jer 11:2;*
covenant *11:6*
because of Lord and w. of *Jer 23:9*
his holiness
w. of Jonadab son of Rechab *Jer 35:14*
are performed
remnant shall know whose *Jer 44:28*
w. shall stand
whose w. thou canst not *Eze 3:6*
understand
false and delusive w. (A) *Eze 13:8*
speak great w. against most *Da 7:25*
High
shut up the w. *Da 12:4*
the w. are closed up *Da 12:9*
I have slain them by w. of my *Ho 6:5*
mouth
take with you w. and turn to *Ho 14:2*
the Lord
answered with good and *Zec 1:13*
comfortable w.
ye not hear the w. the Lord *Zec 7:7*
hath cried
saying the same w. *M't 26:44;*
M'k 14:39
all wondered at gracious w. *Lu 4:22*
the w. I speak to you they *Joh 6:63*
are life
thou hast the w. of eternal *Joh 6:68*
life
These w. spake Jesus, and *Joh 17:1*
lifted up
I have given to them w. thou *Joh 17:8*
gavest me
with many other w. did he *Ac 2:40*
testify
Moses was mighty in w. and *Ac 7:22*
in deeds
he received the living w. (P) *Ac 7:38*
Cornelius was warned to *Ac 10:22*
hear w. of
send for Peter, who shall tell *Ac 11:14*
thee w.
to this agree the w. of the *Ac 15:15*
prophets
that certain have troubled *Ac 15:24*
you with w.
if it be a question of w. and *Ac 18:15*
names
to remember the w. of the *Ac 20:35*
Lord Jesus
sorrowing most of all for the *Ac 20:38*
w. he spake
I speak forth w. of truth and *Ac 26:25*
soberness
by good w. deceive hearts of *Ro 16:18*
the simple
not with wisdom of w. *1Co 1:17;*
2:4, 13
lofty w. of eloquence (A)(R) *1Co 2:1*
except ye utter w. easy to be *1Co 15:9*
understood

rather speak five w. with *1Co 14:19*
understanding
w. so secret human lips may *2Co 12:4*
not repeat (N)
let no man deceive you with *Eph 5:6*
vain w.
a wilderness of w. (N)(P) *1Ti 1:6*
nourished up in w. of faith *1Ti 4:6*
and doctrine
war of w. (B) *1Ti 6:4*
that they strive not about w. to *2Ti 2:14*
no profit
for he hath greatly withstood *2Ti 2:15*
our w.
be mindful of the w. spoken *2Pe 3:2*
by prophets
hear the w. of this prophecy *Re 1:3;*
22:18
These w. (S) *Re 22:6; 22:7, 9-10*
take away from the w. of *Re 22:19*
this prophecy

ALL THE WORDS

they told Jacob all the w. of *Ge 45:27*
Joseph
Moses told Aaron all the w. of *Ex 4:28*
the Lord
Moses told the people all the *Ex 24:3;*
w. *Nu 11:24*
Moses wrote all the w. of the *Ex 24:4*
Lord and rose
on the tables were written all *De 9:10*
the w.
keep all the w. *De 17:19*
write on stones all the w. of *De 27:3;*
this law *27:8*
cursed is he that confirmeth *De 27:26*
not all the w.
if thou wilt not observe to do *De 28:58*
all the w.
may do all the w. *De 29:29*
and observe to do all the w. *De 31:12*
of this law
Moses spake all the w. of *De 32:44*
this song
set your hearts to all the w. I *De 32:46*
testify
he read all the w. of the law, *Jos 8:34*
blessings
Samuel told all the w. of the *1Sa 8:10*
Lord
it may be the Lord will hear *2Ki 19:4;*
all the w. of Rabshakeh *Isa 37:17*
Josiah read all the w. of the *2Ki 23:2;*
covenant found in house *2Ch 34:30*
of Lord
all the w. of my mouth are *Pr 8:8*
righteousness
also take no need unto all the *Ec 7:21*
w. spoken
bring on them all the w. of *Jer 11:8*
this covenant
speak all the w. that I *Jer 26:2*
command thee
according to all the w. of *Jer 26:20*
Jeremiah
write all the w. I have spoken *Jer 30:2;*
36:2
Baruch wrote all the w. of *Jer 36:4;*
the Lord *36:32*
when Jeremiah had ended all *Jer 43:1*
the w. of Lord
speak to the people all the w. *Ac 5:20*
of this life

WORDS OF GOD

which heard the w. of God *Nu 24:4;*
24:16
Heman the king's seer in the *1Ch 25:5*
w. of God
every one that trembleth at the *Ezr 9:4*
w. of God
they rebelled against the w. *Ps 107:11*
of God
he whom God sent speaketh *Joh 3:34*
the w. of God
he that is of God heareth the *Joh 8:47*
w. of God
until the w. of God be *Re 17:17*
fulfilled

HIS WORDS

they hated him yet the more *Ge 37:8*
for his w.
thou heardest his w. out of *De 4:36*
the fire

Jephthah uttered all his w. *J'g 11:11*
before Lord
he let none of his w. fall to *2Sa 3:19*
the ground
but they despised his w. and *2Ch 36:16*
misused
and lay up his w. in thine *Job 22:22*
heart
he hath not directed his w. *Job 32:14*
against me
and his w. were without *Job 34:35*
wisdom
for he multiplieth his w. *Job 34:37*
against God
his w. softer than oil *Ps 55:21*
then believed they his w. *Ps 106:12*
he that hath knowledge *Pr 17:27*
spareth his w.
seest a man that is hasty in *Pr 29:20*
his w.
add not to his w. lest he *Pr 30:6*
reprove thee
the Lord will not call back his *Isa 31:2*
w.
let us not give heed to any of *Jer 18:18*
his w.
he hath confirmed his w. he *Da 9:12*
spake
land is not able to hear all his *Am 7:10*
w.
disciples were astonished at *M'k 10:24*
his w.
to catch him in his w. *M'k 12:13;*
Lu 20:20
they could not take hold of *Lu 20:26*
his w.
they remembered his w. and *Lu 24:8*
returned

MY WORDS

he said, hear now my w. *Nu 12:6;*
Job 34:2
I will make them hear my w. *De 4:10*
lay up my w. in your heart *De 11:18*
and I will put my w. in his *De 18:18*
mouth
whosoever will not hearken *De 18:19;*
to my w. I will *Jer 29:19; 35:13*
require it of him
and they uttered my w. to *Ne 6:19*
him
therefore my w. are swallowed *Job 6:3*
up
O that my w. were now *Job 19:23*
written
after my w. they spake not *Job 29:22*
again
hearken to all my w. *Job 33:1;*
34:16; Ac 2:14
my w. be of uprightness of *Job 33:3;*
heart *36:4*
give ear to my w. O Lord, *Ps 5:1*
consider
seeing thou castest my w. *Ps 50:17*
behind thee
every day they wrest my w. *Ps 56:5*
hear my w. for they are sweet *Ps 141:6*
I will make known my w. *Pr 1:23*
my son, if thou wilt receive my *Pr 2:1*
w.
let thine heart retain my w. and *Pr 4:4*
live
attend to my w. *Pr 4:20*
keep my w. *Pr 7:1*
I have put my w. in thy *Isa 51:16;*
mouth, and say *Jer 1:9*
my w. which I have put in *Isa 59:21*
thy mouth
I will make my w. in thy *Jer 5:14*
mouth fire
they have not hearkened to *Jer 6:19*
my w. nor law
which refused to hear my w. *Jer 11:10;*
13:10
there I will cause thee to hear *Jer 18:2*
my w.
that they might not hear my *Jer 19:15*
w.
if they caused my people to *Jer 23:22*
hear my w.
because ye have not heard my *Jer 25:8*
w.
I will bring upon that and all *Jer 25:13*
my w.
I will bring my w. on this *Jer 39:16*
city for evil
you may know my w. shall *Jer 44:29*
surely stand

thou shalt speak *my w.* to them Eze 2:7; 3:4, 10
there shall none of *my w.* be prolonged Eze 12:28
do not *my w.* do good to him that Mic 2:7
my w. did they not take hold of your Zec 1:6
whosoever be ashamed of M'k 8:38
me and *my w.* of him Son of man be ashamed Lu 9:26
but *my w.* shall not pass away M'k 13:31; Lu 21:33
because thou believest not *my w.* which shall be fulfilled Lu 1:20
how shall ye believe *my w.* Joh 5:47
if any man hear *my w.* and believe not Joh 12:47
he that receiveth not *my w.* one judgeth him Joh 12:48
will keep *my w.* Joh 14:23
my w. abide in you Joh 15:7

THEIR WORDS

their w. pleased Hamor and Shechem Ge 34:18
I believed not *their w.* until I came 2Ch 9:6
their line is gone out thro' all Ps 19:4; earth, *their w.* to end of world Ro 10:18
son of man, be not afraid of *their w.* Eze 2:6
their w. seemed to them as idle tales Lu 24:11

THESE WORDS

she spake to him according to *these w.* Ge 39:17
we told according to the tenor of *these w.* Ge 43:7
these are the w. thou shalt speak Ex 19:6; 19:7
God spake all *these w.* Ex 20:1; De 5:22
Lord said, Write thou these *w.* Ex 34:27; Jer 36:17
these are w. which the Lord hath commanded you to do De 6:6; 29:1
as he had made an end of speaking all *these w.* De 32:45; 1Sa 24:16
observe, hear all *these w.* De 12:28; Zep 8:9
David laid up *these w.* in his heart 1Sa 21:12
David stayed his servants with *these w.* 1Sa 24:7
according to all *these w.* so 2Sa 7:17; did Nathan speak to David 1Ch 17:15
hath my master sent me to 2Ki 18:27; thy master to speak *these w.* Isa 36:12
the man of God proclaimed *these w.* 2Ki 23:16
go proclaim *these w.* toward the north Jer 3:12
speak all *these w.* unto them Jer 7:27; 26:15
shew *these w.* Jer 16:10
but if ye will not hear *these w.* I swear Jer 22:5
prophesy all *these w.* Jer 25:30
Zedekiah said, Let no man know of *these w.* Jer 38:24
when he had written *these w.* Jer 45:1; 51:60
when thou shalt read all *these w.* Jer 51:61
these are the w. I spake unto you Lu 24:44
these w. spake his parents, feared Jews Joh 9:22
these are not w. of him that hath a devil Joh 10:21
ye men of Israel, hear *these w.* Jesus Ac 2:22
while Peter yet spake *these w.* Holy Ghost Ac 10:44
besought *these w.* might be preached to them Ac 13:42
when he had said *these w.* Jews departed Ac 28:29
comfort one another with *these w.* 1Th 4:18
for *these w.* are true and faithful Re 21:5

THY WORDS

every one shall receive of *thy w.* De 33:3
whosoever will not hearken to *thy w.* Jos 1:18
if we do not according to thy *w.* J'g 11:10
Manoah said, Now let *thy w.* come to J'g 13:12
I have transgressed *thy w.* 1Sa 15:24
Behold, I have hearkened to *thy w.* 1Sa 28:21
thou art that God, and *thy w.* be true 2Sa 7:28
I will come in and confirm *thy w.* 1Ki 1:14
for thou hast performed *thy w.* Ne 9:8
thy w. upheld him that was falling Job 4:4
I said that I would keep *thy w.* Ps 119:57
how sweet are *thy w.* to my taste Ps 119:103
the entrance of *thy w.* giveth light Ps 119:130
mine enemies have forgotten *thy w.* Ps 119:139
thou shalt lose *thy w.* sweet Pr 23:8
he will despise the wisdom of *thy w.* Pr 23:9
be not rash, therefore let *thy w.* be few Ec 5:2
thy w. were found and I did eat them Jer 15:16
hear *thy w.* but do them not Eze 33:31; 33:32
Daniel, from the first day *thy w.* were heard, and I am come for *thy w.* Da 10:12
by *thy w.* thou shalt be justified, by *thy w.* thou shalt be condemned M't 12:37

YOUR WORDS

kept in prison, that *your w.* be proved Ge 42:16
bring Benjamin, so shall *your w.* be verified Ge 42:20
let it be according to *your w.* Ge 44:10; Jos 2:21
Lord heard the voice of *your w.* De 1:34; 5:28
Behold, I waited for *your w.*; I gave ear Job 32:11
there is none that heareth *your w.* Isa 41:26
I will pray to God according to *your w.* Jer 42:4
have multiplied *your w.* against me Eze 35:13
ye have wearied the Lord with *your w.* Mal 2:17
your w. have been stout against me, saith Lord Mal 3:13
shall not receive you nor hear *your w.* M't 10:14

WORD'S

For *thy w.* sake, and according to 2Sa 7:21
persecution ariseth for the *w.* sake M'k 4:17

WORK

went into the house to w. (S) Ge 39:11
more w. be laid upon the men Ex 5:9
Go therefore now, and w. Ex 5:18
w. these my wonders (B) Ex 10:11
no manner of w. shall be done in Ex 12:16
saw that great w. which the Lord Ex 14:31
and the w. that they must do Ex 14:20
in it thou shalt not do any w. thou Ex 20:10
Six days thou shalt do thy w. and Ex 23:12
a paved w. of a sapphire stone Ex 24:10
beaten w. shalt thou make them Ex 25:18
of beaten w. shall the candlestick Ex 25:31
shall be one beaten w. of pure gold Ex 25:36
cherubims of cunning w. shalt Ex 26:1

fine twined linen of cunning w. Ex 26:31
fine twined linen, with cunning w. Ex 28:6
same, according to the w. thereof Ex 28:8
the w. of an engraver in stone, like Ex 28:11
wreathen w. shalt thou make them Ex 28:14
of judgment with cunning w. Ex 28:15
after the w. of the ephod thou shalt Ex 28:15
ends of wreathen w. of pure gold Ex 28:22
a binding of woven w. round about Ex 28:32
to w. in gold, and in silver Ex 31:4
w. in all manner of workmanship Ex 31:5
whosoever doeth any w. therein Ex 31:14
Six days may w. be done; but Ex 31:15
doeth any w. in the sabbath day Ex 31:15
art shall see the w. of the Lord Ex 34:10
I will w. such wonders (B) Ex 34:10
Six days thou shalt w. but on Ex 34:21
Six days shall w. be done, but Ex 35:2
whosoever doeth w. therein shall be Ex 35:2
offering to the w. of the tabernacle Ex 35:21
wood for any w. of the service Ex 35:24
to bring for all manner of w. Ex 35:29
to w. in gold, and in silver Ex 35:32
make any manner of cunning w. Ex 35:33
wisdom of heart, to w. all manner Ex 35:35
manner of w. of the engraver Ex 35:35
even of them that do any w. Ex 35:35
of those that devise cunning w. Ex 35:35
understanding to know how to w. Ex 36:1
all manner of w. for the service Ex 36:1
up to come unto the w. to do it Ex 36:2
brought for the w. of the service Ex 36:3
wrought all the w. of the sanctuary Ex 36:4
enough for the service of the w. Ex 36:5
man nor woman make any more w. Ex 36:6
had was sufficient for all the w. Ex 36:7
wrought the w. of the tabernacle Ex 36:8
cherubims of cunning w. made he Ex 36:8
made he it of cunning w. Ex 36:35
beaten w. made he the candlestick Ex 37:17
it was one beaten w. of pure gold Ex 37:22
to the w. of the apothecary Ex 37:29
gold that was occupied for the w. Ex 38:24
all the w. of the holy place Ex 38:24
w. it in the blue, and in the purple Ex 39:3
in the fine linen, with cunning w. Ex 39:3
same, according to the w. thereof Ex 39:5
like breastplate of cunning w. Ex 39:8
like the w. of the ephod: of gold Ex 39:8
ends, of wreathen w. of pure gold Ex 39:15
the robe of the ephod of woven w. Ex 39:22
of fine linen of woven w. for Aaron Ex 39:27
was all the w. of the tabernacle Ex 39:32
children of Israel made all the w. Ex 39:42
Moses did look upon all the w. Ex 39:43
gate. So Moses finished the w. Ex 40:33
wherein any w. is done, it must be Le 11:32

or in any *w.* that is made of   *Le 13:51* skin

and do no *w.* at all, whether   *Le 16:29* it be

Six days shall *w.* be done; but   *Le 23:3*

ye shall do no *w.* therein: it is   *Le 23:3*

ye shall do no servile *w.*   *Le 23:7;* therein   *23:8, 21, 25, 35-36*

ye shall do no *w.* in that   *Le 23:28* same day

that doeth any *w.* in that   *Le 23:30* same day

Ye shall do no manner of *w.*   *Le 23:31* therein   *23:36*

to do the *w.* in the tabernacle   *Nu 4:3;* of   *4:23, 30*

for the *w.* in the tabernacle   *Nu 4:35;*   *4:39, 43*

this *w.* of the candlestick was   *Nu 8:4*

flowers thereof, was beaten   *Nu 8:4*

shall do no manner of servile   *Nu 28:18* *w.*

ye shall do no servile *w.*   *Nu 28:25;*   *28:26; 29:1, 12, 35*

of skins, and all *w.* of goats   *Nu 31:20* hair

serve gods, the *w.* of men's   *De 4:28* hands

shalt labour, and do all thy *w.*   *De 5:13*

in it thou shalt not do any *w.*   *De 5:14* thou

thee in all the *w.* of thine   *De 14:29* hand

shalt do no *w.* with the   *De 15:19* firstling

God: thou shalt do no *w.*   *De 16:8* therein

thee in all the *w.* of thine   *De 24:19* hands

w. of the hands of the   *De 27:15* craftsman

to bless all the *w.* of thine   *De 28:12* hand

plenteous in every *w.* of thine   *De 30:9* hand

through the *w.* of your hands   *De 31:29*

and accept the *w.* of his hands   *De 33:11*

They did *w.* wilily, and went   *Jos 9:4*

be that the Lord will *w.* for us   *1Sa 14:6*

officers which were over the   *1Ki 5:16* *w.*

the people that wrought in   *1Ki 5:16* the *w.*

with gold fitted upon the   *1Ki 6:35* carved *w.*

porch, which was of the like   *1Ki 7:8* *w.*

cunning to *w.* all works in   *1Ki 7:14* brass

And nets of checker *w.*   *1Ki 7:17*

and wreaths of chain *w.*   *1Ki 7:17*

pillars were of lily *w.* in the   *1Ki 7:19* porch

the top of the pillars was lily   *1Ki 7:22* *w.*

was the *w.* of the pillars   *1Ki 7:22* finished

the *w.* of the bases was on   *1Ki 7:28* this

certain additions made of   *1Ki 7:29* thin *w.*

was round after the *w.* of the   *1Ki 7:31* base

And the *w.* of the wheels was   *1Ki 7:33* like

was like the *w.* of a chariot   *1Ki 7:33* wheel

made an end of doing all the   *1Ki 7:40* *w.*

ended all the *w.* that king   *1Ki 7:51* Solomon

that were over Solomon's *w.*   *1Ki 9:23*

the people that wrought in   *1Ki 9:23* the *w.*

to anger with the *w.* of his   *1Ki 16:7* hands

w. evil in the sight of the   *1Ki 21:20* Lord

did sell himself to *w.*   *1Ki 21:25* wickedness

the hands of them that did   *2Ki 12:11* the *w.*

but the *w.* of men's hands,   *2Ki 19:18* wood

the hand of the doers of the   *2Ki 22:5* *w.*

them give it to the doers of   *2Ki 22:5* the *w.*

the hand of them that do the   *2Ki 22:9* *w.*

and the wreathen *w.* and   *2Ki 25:17*

second pillar with wreathen   *2Ki 25:17* *w.*

all the *w.* of the place most   *1Ch 6:49* holy

able men for the *w.* of the   *1Ch 9:13* service

were over the *w.* of the   *1Ch 9:19* service

employed in that *w.* day and   *1Ch 9:33* night

as every day's *w.* required   *1Ch 16:37*

men for every manner of *w.*   *1Ch 22:15*

the *w.* of the house of the   *1Ch 23:4* Lord

the *w.* for the service of the   *1Ch 23:24;* house   *23:28; 28:13; 28:20*

did the *w.* of the field for   *1Ch 27:26* tillage

and tender, and the *w.* is   *1Ch 29:1* great

of *w.* to be made by the   *1Ch 29:5* hands

with the rulers of the king's   *1Ch 29:6* *w.*

a man cunning to *w.* in gold   *2Ch 2:7*

man of Tyre, skilful to *w.* in   *2Ch 2:14* gold

overseers to set the people a   *2Ch 2:18* *w.*

made two cherubims of   *2Ch 3:10* image *w.*

it like the *w.* of the brim of a   *2Ch 4:5* cup

Huram finished the *w.* that   *2Ch 4:11* he

all the *w.* that Solomon made   *2Ch 5:1*

all the *w.* of Solomon was   *2Ch 8:16* prepared

such as did the *w.* of the   *2Ch 24:12* service

and the *w.* was perfected by   *2Ch 24:13* them

till the *w.* was ended, and   *2Ch 29:34* until the

in every *w.* that he began in   *2Ch 31:21*

were the *w.* of the hands of   *2Ch 32:19* man

the men did the *w.*   *2Ch 34:12* faithfully

of all that wrought the *w.*   *2Ch 34:13* in any

ability unto the treasure of   *Ezr 2:69* the *w.*

to set forward the *w.* of the   *Ezr 3:8* house

ceased the *w.* of the house of   *Ezr 4:24* God

and this *w.* goeth fast on, and   *Ezr 5:8*

Let the *w.* of this house of   *Ezr 6:7* God

in the *w.* of the house of God   *Ezr 6:22*

is this a *w.* of one day or two   *Ezr 10:13*

nor to the rest that did the *w.*   *Ne 2:16*

their hands for this good *w.*   *Ne 2:18*

necks to the *w.* of their Lord   *Ne 3:5*

for the people had a mind to   *Ne 4:6* *w.*

people had a will to *w.* (B)   *Ne 4:6*

them, and cause the *w.* to   *Ne 4:11* cease

of my servants wrought in the   *Ne 4:16* *w.*

one of his hands wrought in   *Ne 4:17* the *w.*

The *w.* is great and large and   *Ne 4:19*

So we laboured in the *w.*: and   *Ne 4:21*

continued in the *w.* of this   *Ne 5:16* wall

were gathered thither unto   *Ne 5:16* the *w.*

I am doing a great *w.* so that   *Ne 6:3*

why should the *w.* cease, whilst   *Ne 6:3*

shall be weakened from the *w.*   *Ne 6:9*

this *w.* was wrought of our   *Ne 6:16* God

of the fathers gave unto the *w.*   *Ne 7:70*

gave to the treasure of the *w.*   *Ne 7:71*

all the *w.* of the house of our   *Ne 10:33* God

that did the *w.* of the house   *Ne 11:12*

and the singers, that did the   *Ne 13:10* *w.*

hast blessed the *w.* of his   *Job 1:10* hands

despise the *w.* of thine hands   *Job 10:3*

w. wonders against me (R)   *Job 10:16*

a desire to the *w.* of thine   *Job 14:15* hands

the left hand, where he doth   *Job 23:9* *w.*

desert, go they forth to their   *Job 24:5* *w.*

the *w.* of a man shall he   *Job 34:11* render

they all are the *w.* of his   *Job 34:19* hands

Then he sheweth them their   *Job 36:9* *w.*

thy heavens, the *w.* of thy   *Ps 8:3* fingers

snared in the *w.* of his own   *Ps 9:16* hands

them after the *w.* of their   *Ps 28:4* hands

nor the *w.* of his hands   *Ps 28:5* (B)(R)

what *w.* thou didst in their   *Ps 44:1* days

Yea, in heart ye *w.* wickedess   *Ps 58:2*

they break down the carved *w.*   *Ps 74:6*

establish thou the *w.* of our   *Ps 90:17* hands

w. of our hands establish   *Ps 90:17* thou it

me, proved me, and saw my   *Ps 95:9* *w.*

I hate the *w.* of them that   *Ps 101:3* turn

heavens are the *w.* of thy   *Ps 102:25* hands

and gold, the *w.* of men's   *Ps 115:4* hands

It is time for thee, Lord, to   *Ps 119:126* *w.*

and gold, the *w.* of men's   *Ps 135:15* hands

works with men that *w.*   *Ps 141:4* iniquity

I muse on the *w.* of thy   *Ps 143:5* hands

wicked worketh a deceitful *w.*   *Pr 11:18*

He also that is slothful in his   *Pr 18:9* *w.*

to the man according to his *w.*   *Pr 24:29*

w. that is wrought under the   *Ec 2:17* sun

find out the *w.* that God   *Ec 3:11* maketh

every purpose and for every *w.*   *Ec 3:17*

not seen the evil *w.* that is done   *Ec 4:3*

all travail, and every right *w.*   *Ec 4:4*

and destroy the *w.* of thine   *Ec 5:6* hands

applied my heart unto every *w.*   *Ec 8:9*

sentence against an evil *w.*   *Ec 8:11* is not

according to the *w.* of the   *Ec 8:14* wicked

to the *w.* of the righteous   *Ec 8:14*

cannot find out the *w.* that is   *Ec 8:17* done

for there is no *w.* nor device   *Ec 9:10*

bring every *w.* into judgment   *Ec 12:14*

w. of the hands of a cunning   *Ca 7:1*

worship the *w.* of their own   *Isa 2:8* hands

regard not the *w.* of the Lord   *Isa 5:12*

to the altars, the *w.* of his   *Isa 17:8* hands

Moreover they that *w.* in fine   *Isa 19:9* flax

Egypt to err in every *w.*   *Isa 19:14* thereof

shall there be any *w.* for   *Isa 19:15* Egypt

and Assyria the *w.* of my   *Isa 19:25* hands

marvellous *w.* among this   *Isa 29:14* people

a marvellous *w.* and a   *Isa 29:14* wonder

the *w.* say of him that made   *Isa 29:16*

his children, the *w.* of mine   *Isa 29:23* hands

the help of them that *w.*   *Isa 31:2* iniquity

and his heart will *w.* iniquity   *Isa 32:6*

the *w.* of righteousness shall   *Isa 32:17* be

the *w.* of men's hands, wood   *Isa 37:19*

I will *w.* and who shall let it   *Isa 43:13*

concerning the *w.* of my   *Isa 45:11* hands

Lord, and my *w.* with my   *Isa 49:4* God

my planting, the *w.* of my hands | Isa 60:21
and I will direct their *w.* in truth | Isa 61:8
with him, and his *w.* before him | Isa 62:11
and we all are the *w.* of thine hand | Isa 64:8
will I measure their former *w.* | Isa 65:7
long enjoy the *w.* of their hands | Isa 65:22
w. of the hands of the workman | Jer 10:3
the *w.* of the workman, and | Jer 10:9
are all the *w.* of cunning men | Jer 10:9
are vanity, and the *w.* of errors | Jer 10:15
neither do ye any *w.* but hallow | Jer 17:22
sabbath day, to do no *w.* therein | Jer 17:24
he wrought a *w.* on the wheels | Jer 18:3
in counsel, and mighty in *w.* | Jer 32:19
anger with the *w.* of their hands | Jer 32:30
the *w.* of the Lord deceitfully | Jer 48:10
this is the *w.* of the Lord God of | Jer 50:25
her according to her *w.* | Jer 50:29
declare in Zion the *w.* of the Lord | Jer 51:10
They are vanity, the *w.* of errors | Jer 51:18
according to the *w.* of their hands | La 3:64
the *w.* of the hands of the potter | La 4:2
their *w.* was like unto the colour | Eze 1:16
and their *w.* was as it were a wheel | Eze 1:16
be taken thereof to do any *w.* | Eze 15:3
is burned. It is meet for any *w.* | Eze 15:4
was whole. It was meet for no *w.* | Eze 15:5
less shall it be meet for any *w.* | Eze 15:5
thee also with broidered *w.* | Eze 16:10
linen, and silk, and broidered *w.* | Eze 16:13
the *w.* of an imperious whorish | Eze 16:30
Fine linen with broidered *w.* | Eze 27:7
and broidered *w.* and fine linen | Eze 27:16
in blue clothes, and broidered *w.* | Eze 27:24
ye *w.* abomination, and ye defile | Eze 33:26
with him he shall *w.* deceitfully | Da 11:23
a city of them that *w.* iniquity | Ho 6:8
all of it the *w.* of the craftsman | Ho 13:2
any more to the *w.* of our hands | Ho 14:3
and *w.* evil upon their beds | Mic 2:1
worship the *w.* of thine hands | Mic 5:13
marvellously; for I will *w.* | Hab 1:5
a *w.* in your days, which ye will | Hab 1:5
for he shall uncover the cedar *w.* | Zep 2:14
did *w.* in the house of the Lord | Hag 1:14
the land, saith the Lord, and *w.* | Hag 2:4
and so is every *w.* of their hands | Hag 2:14
that *w.* wickedness are set up | Mal 3:15
from me, ye that *w.* iniquity | M't 7:23
Son, go *w.* to-day in my vineyard | M't 21:28
hath wrought a good *w.* upon me | M't 26:10
he could there do no mighty *w.* | M'k 6:5
she hath wrought a good *w.* on me | M'k 14:6
days in which men ought to *w.* | Lu 13:14
mighty in *w.* (A) | Lu 24:19
worketh hitherto, and I *w.* | Joh 5:17
that we might *w.* the works of God | Joh 6:28
believe thee? what dost thou *w.* | Joh 6:30
I have done one *w.* and ye all | Joh 7:21
I must *w.* the works of him | Joh 9:4

night cometh, when no man can *w.* | Joh 9:4
For a good *w.* we stone thee not | Joh 10:33
finished the *w.* which thou gavest | Joh 17:4
wrapped his *w.* jacket about him (B)(N) | Joh 21:7
or this *w.* be of men, it will come | Ac 5:38
for the *w.* whereunto I have called | Ac 13:2
for I *w.* a *w.* in your days | Ac 13:41
a *w.* which ye shall in no wise | Ac 13:41
for the *w.* which they fulfilled | Ac 14:26
and went not with them to the *w.* | Ac 15:38
we had much *w.* to come by | Ac 27:16
shew the *w.* of the law written in | Ro 2:15
did *w.* in our members to bring | Ro 7:5
all things *w.* together for good | Ro 8:28
For he will finish the *w.* and cut | Ro 9:28
short *w.* will the Lord make upon | Ro 9:28
otherwise *w.* is no more *w.* | Ro 11:6
man's *w.* shall be made manifest | 1Co 3:13
fire shall try every man's *w.* | 1Co 3:13
If any man's *w.* abide which he | 1Co 3:14
If any man's *w.* shall be burned | 1Co 3:15
are not ye my *w.* in the Lord | 1Co 9:1
are many kinds of *w.* (N) | 1Co 12:6
abounding in the *w.* of the Lord | 1Co 15:58
for he worketh the *w.* of the Lord | 1Co 16:10
w. of generosity (N)(P) | 2Co 8:6
may abound to every good *w.* | 2Co 9:8
for the *w.* of the ministry, for | Eph 4:12
to *w.* all uncleanness with | Eph 4:19
which hath begun a good *w.* in you | Ph'p 1:6
w. out your own salvation with | Ph'p 2:12
for the *w.* of Christ he was nigh | Ph'p 2:30
being fruitful in every good *w.* | Col 1:10
and to *w.* with your own hands | Col 4:11
and the *w.* of faith with power | 2Th 1:11
of iniquity doth already *w.* | 2Th 2:7
you in every good word and *w.* | 2Th 2:17
that if any would not *w.* neither | 2Th 3:10
that with quietness they *w.* | 2Th 3:12
of a bishop, he desireth a good *w.* | 1Ti 3:1
diligently followed every good *w.* | 1Ti 5:10
and prepared unto every good *w.* | 2Ti 2:21
do the *w.* of an evangelist | 2Ti 4:5
shall deliver me from every evil *w.* | 2Ti 4:18
and unto every good *w.* reprobate | Tit 1:16
to be ready to every good *w.* | Tit 3:1
Make you perfect in every good *w.* | Heb 13:21
let patience have her perfect *w.* | Jas 1:4
but a doer of the *w.* this man shall | Jas 1:25
is confusion and every evil *w.* | Jas 3:16
according to every man's *w.* | 1Pe 1:17
w. out the number of the beast (N) | Re 13:18

WORK, WORKS OF GOD

the tables were the *w.* of God | Ex 32:16
consider the wondrous *w.* of God | Job 37:14
all men shall declare the *w.* of Ps | Ps 64:9
come see the *w.* of God, he is | Ps 66:5
terrible
that they might not forget the *w.* of God | Ps 78:7
consider the *w.* of God who can make | Ec 7:13

then I beheld all the *w.* of God | Ec 8:17
even so thou knowest not the *w.* of God | Ec 11:5
that we might work the *w.* of God | Joh 6:28
this is the *w.* of God that ye believe on me | Joh 6:29
that *w.* of God might be made manifest | Joh 9:3
we hear them speak the *w.* of | Ac 2:11
for meat destroy not the *w.* of God | Ro 14:20

HIS WORK

God ended *his w.* | Ge 2:2
rested from *his w.* | Ge 2:3
they came every man from *his w.* | Ex 36:4
he is the rock, *his w.* is perfect | De 32:4
an old man came from *his w.* at even | J'g 19:16
he will take asses and put to *his w.* | 1Sa 8:16
Hiram came and wrought all *his w.* | 1Ki 7:14
they dwelt with the king for *his w.* | 1Ch 4:23
he made no servants for *his w.* | 2Ch 8:9
Baasha let *his w.* cease | 2Ch 16:5
that we returned every man to *his w.* | Ne 4:15
an hireling looketh for the reward of *his w.* | Job 7:2
remember that thou magnify *his w.* | Job 36:24
that all men may know *his w.* | Job 37:7
thou renderest to every man according to *his w.* | Ps 62:12;
Pr 24:29
man goeth forth to *his w.* and labour | Ps 104:23
his w. is honourable and glorious | Ps 111:3
all the weights of the bag are *his w.* | Pr 16:11
whether *his w.* be pure or whether right | Pr 20:11
but as for the pure *his w.* is right | Pr 21:8
let him hasten *his w.* that we may see | Isa 5:19
the Lord hath performed *his* whole *w.* | Isa 10:12
that he may do *his w.*, *his* strange *w.* | Isa 28:21
behold, *his w.* is before him | Isa 40:10;
62:11
that bringeth forth an instrument for *his w.* | Isa 54:16
that giveth him not for *his w.* | Jer 22:13
the maker of *his w.* trusteth therein | Hab 2:18
who gave to every man *his w.* | M'k 13:34
my meat is to finish *his w.* | Joh 4:34
let every man prove *his* own *w.* | Ga 6:4
to give every man as *his w.* shall be | Re 22:12

OUR WORK

this shall comfort us concerning *our w.* | Ge 5:29

THY WORK

six days do all *thy w.* | Ex 20:9;
23:12; De 5:13
the Lord recompense *thy w.* | Ru 2:12
I will meditate also of all *thy w.* | Ps 77:12
let *thy w.* appear unto thy servants | Ps 90:16
Lord, has made me glad thro' *thy w.* | Ps 92:4
prepare *thy w.* without and make it fit | Pr 24:27
or shall *thy w.* say he hath no hands | Isa 45:9
for *thy w.* shall be rewarded, saith the Lord | Jer 31:16
revive *thy w.* in the midst of the years | Hab 3:2

YOUR WORK

not ought of *your* w. be diminished	Ex 5:11
for *your* w. shall be rewarded	2Ch 15:7
ye are nothing, *your* w. is nought	Isa 41:24
remember, *your* w. of faith, labour of love	1Th 1:3
God is not unrighteous to forget *your* w.	Heb 6:10

WORKED

worked (S)	De 21:3; M't 20:12; Ac 18:3
w. their will upon him (N)	M't 17:12

WORKER

was a man of Tyre, a w. in brass	1Ki 7:14
w. deserves support (B)(N)(P)	M't 10:10
w. deserves his wage (B)	1Ti 5:18

WORKERS

Moreover the w. with familiar spirits	2Ki 23:24
and w. of stone and timber	1Ch 22:15
weariness of w. (B)	Ne 4:10
punishment to the w. of iniquity	Job 31:3
in company with the w. of iniquity	Job 34:8
where the w. of iniquity may hide	Job 34:22
thou hatest all w. of iniquity	Ps 5:5
from me, all ye w. of iniquity	Ps 6:8
the w. of iniquity no knowledge	Ps 14:4
with the w. of iniquity, which speak	Ps 28:3
There are the w. of iniquity fallen	Ps 36:12
against the w. of iniquity	Ps 37:1
the w. of iniquity no knowledge	Ps 53:4
Deliver me from the w. of iniquity	Ps 59:2
insurrection of the w. of iniquity	Ps 64:2
all the w. of iniquity do flourish	Ps 92:7
w. of iniquity shall be scattered	Ps 92:9
w. of iniquity boast themselves	Ps 94:4
for me against the w. of iniquity	Ps 94:16
them forth with the w. of iniquity	Ps 125:5
and the gins of the w. of iniquity	Ps 141:9
shall be to the w. of iniquity	Pr 10:29; 21:15
from me, all ye w. of iniquity	Lu 13:27
w. of spiritual power (P)	1Co 12:28
teachers? are all w. of miracles	1Co 12:29
We then, as w. together with him	2Co 6:1
are false apsostles, deceitful w.	2Co 11:13
Beware of dogs, beware of evil w.	Ph'p 3:2

WORKETH

these things w. God oftentimes	Job 33:29
and w. righteousness, and speaketh	Ps 15:2
He that w. deceit shall not dwell	Ps 101:7
The wicked w. a deceitful work	Pr 11:18
and a flattering mouth w. ruin	Pr 26:28
and w. willingly with her hands	Pr 31:13
What profit hath he that w. in	Ec 3:9
with the tongs both w. in the coals	Isa 44:12
w. it with the strength of his arms	Isa 44:12
rejoiceth and w. righteousness	Isa 64:5
w. signs and wonders in heaven	Da 6:27

My Father w. hitherto, and I work	Joh 5:17
w. righteousness, is accepted	Ac 10:35
peace, to every man that w. good	Ro 2:10
to him that w. is the reward not	Ro 4:4
But to him that w. not, but	Ro 4:5
Because the law w. wrath; for	Ro 4:15
knowing tribulation w. patience	Ro 5:3
Love w. no ill to his neighbour	Ro 13:10
the same God which w. all in all	1Co 12:6
w. that one and the selfsame Spirit	1Co 12:11
he w. the work of the Lord, as I	1Co 16:10
So then death w. in us, but life in	2Co 4:12
w. for us a far more exceeding	2Co 4:17
godly sorrow w. repentance unto	2Co 7:10
the sorrow of the world w. death	2Co 7:10
Spirit, and w. miracles among you	Ga 3:5
but faith which w. by love	Ga 5:6
purpose of him who w. all things	Eph 1:11
spirit that now w. in the children	Eph 2:2
to the power that w. in us	Eph 3:20
is God which w. in you both to will	Ph'p 2:13
working, which w. in me mightily	Col 1:29
which effectually w. also in you	1Th 2:13
trying of your faith w. patience	Jas 1:3
w. not the righteousness of God	Jas 1:20
whatsoever w. abomination, or	Re 21:27

WORKFELLOW

Timotheus my w. and Lucius	Ro 16:21

WORKING

like a sharp rasor, w. deceitfully	Ps 52:2
w. salvation in the midst of	Ps 74:12
w. and denying myself (B)	Ec 4:8
in counsel, and excellent in w.	Isa 28:29
east shall be shut the six w. days	Eze 46:1
the Lord w. with them, and	M'k 16:20
men w. that which is unseemly	Ro 1:27
w. death in me by that which is	Ro 7:13
labour, w. with our own hands	1Co 4:12
have not we power to forbear w.	1Co 9:6
are diversities of w. (E)(R)	1Co 12:6
To another the w. of miracles	1Co 12:10
to the w. of his mighty power	Eph 1:19
me by the effectual w. of his power	Eph 3:7
to the effectual w. in the measure	Eph 4:16
w. with his hands the thing which	Eph 4:28
according to the w. whereby he is	Ph'p 3:21
striving according to his w. which	Col 1:29
faith in the w. of God (A)(E)(R)	Col 2:12
coming is after the w. of Satan	2Th 2:9
w. not at all, but are busybodies	2Th 3:11
his will. w. in you that which	Heb 13:21
the spirits of devils, w. miracles	Re 16:14

WORKMAN

engraver, and of the cunning w.	Ex 35:35
an engraver, and a cunning w.	Ex 38:23
work of the hands of a cunning w.	Ca 7:1
The w. melteth a graven image	Isa 40:19

seeketh unto him a cunning w. to	Isa 40:20
skilful w. (E)	Isa 40:20
the work of the hands of the w.	Jer 10:3
from Uphaz, the work of the w.	Jer 10:9
the w. made it; therefore it is not	Ho 8:6
for the w. is worthy of his meat	M't 10:10
w. deserves his wages (R)	1Ti 5:18
a w. that needeth not to be	2Ti 2:15

WORKMANSHIP

and in all manner of w.	Ex 31:3
to work in all manner of w.	Ex 31:5
and in all manner of w.	Ex 35:31
according to all the w. thereof	2Ki 16:10
be with thee for all manner of w.	1Ch 28:21
w. of thy tabrets and of thy pipes	Eze 28:13
For we are his w. created in	Eph 2:10

WORKMEN

But they gave that to the w.	2Ki 12:14
money to be bestowed on w.	2Ki 12:15
are w. with thee in abundance	1Ch 22:15
number of the w. according	1Ch 25:1
So the w. wrought, and the	2Ch 24:13
w. that had the oversight	2Ch 34:10
w. that wrought in the house	2Ch 34:10
and to the hand of the w.	2Ch 34:17
the w. in the house of God	Ezr 3:9
and the w. they are of men	Isa 44:11
with the w. of like occupation	Ac 19:25

WORKMEN'S

her right hand to the w. hammer	J'g 5:26

WORKS

fulfil your w. and your daily tasks	Ex 5:13
the Lord hath sent me to do all these w.	Nu 16:28
the Lord blessed thee in all the w.	De 2:7
a generation which knew not the w.	J'g 2:10
all his wondrous w. (A)(B)(E)	J'g 6:13
according to all the w. they have done	1Sa 8:8
told him all the w. the man of God did	1Ki 13:11
forsaken and provoked me to anger with all the w. of their hands	2Ki 22:17; 2Ch 34:25
nor turned they from their wicked w.	Ne 9:35
corrupt, they have done abominable w.	Ps 14:1
concerning the w. of men by word of lips	Ps 17:4
I will triumph in the w. of thy hands	Ps 92:4
the w. of the Lord are great, sought out	Ps 111:2
the w. of his hands are verity and judgment	Ps 111:7
forsake not the w. of thine own hands	Ps 138:8
to practise wicked w. with men that	Ps 141:4
let her own w. praise her in the gates	Pr 31:31
I have seen the w. that are done	Ec 1:14; 2:11
the w. of his hands (B)(R)	Isa 5:12
thou hast wrought all our w. in us	Isa 26:12
because ye have done all these w.	Jer 7:13
provoke me not to anger with the w. of your hands	Jer 25:6; 25:7; 44:8
recompense them according to their deeds and the w.	Jer 25:14; Re 2:23
of their hands	
that your w. may be abolished	Eze 6:6
honour him whose w. are truth	Da 4:37
remember their evil w. (R)	Ho 7:2

the *w.* of the house of Ahab   *Mic 6:16* are kept
John heard in prison the *w.*   *M't 11:2* of Christ
wisdom is justified by *w.*   *M't 11:19* (E)
his *w.* plainly shown (A)   *Joh 3:21*
w. may be manifest (E)   *Joh 3:21*
he will shew him greater *w.*   *Joh 5:20* than these
the *w.* which the Father hath   *Joh 5:36* given me, the same *w.* that
I do bear witness of me
thy disciples may see the *w.*   *Joh 7:3* thou doest
because I testify that the *w.*   *Joh 7:7* thereof are evil
if children, ye would do *w.* of   *Joh 8:39* Abraham
w. of your father   *Joh 8:41* (A)(B)(E)(N)
I must work the *w.* of him that   *Joh 9:4* sent me
the *w.* that I do in my   *Joh 10:25* Father's name
for which of these do ye   *Joh 10:32* stone me
if I do not the *w.*   *Joh 10:37*
believe the *w.*   *Joh 10:38*
he doeth the *w.* believe for   *Joh 14:10;* the *w.*   15:11
the *w.* that I do, shall he do,   *Joh 14:12* and greater *w.*
if I had not done among   *Joh 15:24* them the *w.*
they rejoiced in the *w.* of their   *Ac 7:41* hands
Gentiles do *w.* meet for   *Ac 26:20* repentance
w. prescribed by law   *Ro 3:20* (A)(E)(R)
by what law? of *w.*? nay, but   *Ro 3:27* of faith
for if Abraham were justified   *Ro 4:2* by *w.*
God imputeth righteousness   *Ro 8:6* without *w.*
not of *w.* but of him that   *Ro 9:11* calleth
not by faith, but as it were by   *Ro 9:32* the *w.* of the law
if by grace, then is it no more   *Ro 11:6* of *w.* But if it be of *w.* is it no
more of grace
let us therefore cast off the   *Ro 13:12* *w.* of darkness
miracles, signs, mighty *w.*   *2Co 12:12* (A)(E)(P)(R)
a man is not justified by *w.* of   *Ga 2:16* the law, for by *w.* of law no
flesh is justified
received ye the Spirit by the *w.*   *Ga 3:2* of the law
doeth he it by the *w.* of the law   *Ga 3:5* or by faith
as many as are of *w.* of the   *Ga 3:10* law, under curse
the *w.* of the flesh are manifest,   *Ga 5:19* adultery
not of *w.* lest any man should   *Eph 2:9* boast
with the unfruitful *w.* of   *Eph 5:11* darkness
and enemies in your mind by   *Col 1:21* wicked *w.*
to esteem in love for their *w.*   *1Th 5:13* sake
saved us, not according to our   *2Ti 1:9;* *w.*   *Tit 3:5*
who *w.* on the land (P)   *2Ti 2:6*
but in *w.* they deny God,   *Tit 1:16* being abominable
the heavens are the *w.* of thy   *Heb 1:10* hands
thou didst set him over the *w.*   *Heb 2:7* of thy hands
fathers saw my *w.* forty years   *Heb 3:9* in wilderness
the *w.* were finished from   *Heb 4:3* foundation
the foundation of repentance   *Heb 6:1* from dead *w.*
purge conscience from dead   *Heb 9:14* *w.* to serve God
if he have not *w.* can faith   *Jas 2:14* save him
faith without *w.* is dead,   *Jas 2:17;* being alone   20:26
I have *w.* shew: me thy faith   *Jas 2:18* without thy *w.*

was not Abraham justified by   *Jas 2:21* *w.*
and by *w.* was faith made   *Jas 2:22* perfect
ye see then that by *w.* a man   *Jas 2:24* is justified
was not Rahab the harlot   *Jas 2:25* justified by *w.*
show his *w.* in meekness (R)   *Jas 3:13*
the earth and the *w.* therein   *2Pe 3:10* burnt up
that he might destroy the *w.*   *1Jo 3:8* of devil
sharer of wicked *w.*   *2Jo 11* (B)(E)(R)
w. of ungodliness (E)(P)   *Jude 15*
w. of Nicolaitans   *Re 2:6* (A)(E)(N)(P)(R)
he that keepeth my *w.* to the   *Re 2:26* end
yet repented not of the *w.* of   *Re 9:20* their hands
double to her double,   *Re 18:6* according to her *w.*

HIS WORKS

his w. have been to thee very   *1Sa 19:4* good
Hezekiah prospered in all   *2Ch 32:30* *his w.*
and all *his w.* are done in   *Ps 33:4* truth
forget *his w.* and his   *Ps 78:11;* wonders   106:13
bless the Lord, all his *w.* in   *Ps 103:22* all places
the Lord shall rejoice in *his*   *Ps 104:31* *w.*
let them declare *his w.* with   *Ps 107:22* rejoicing
he shewed his people the   *Ps 111:6* power of *his w.*
his tender mercies are over   *Ps 145:9* all *his w.*
the Lord is holy in all *his w.*   *Ps 145:17*
the Lord possessed me before   *Pr 8:22* *his w.*
shall not he render to every   *Pr 24:12;* man according to *his w.*   *M'k 16:27;*   *2Ti 4:14*
a man should rejoice in his   *Ec 3:22* own *w.*
God is righteous in all *his w.*   *Da 9:14*
known to God are all *his w.*   *Ac 15:18*
rested the seventh day from   *Heb 4:4* all *his w.*
he also hath ceased from *his*   *Heb 4:10* own *w.*
seest how faith wrought with   *Jas 2:22* *his w.*
shew out of a good   *Jas 3:13* conversation *his w.*

THEIR WORKS

why let the people from *their*   *Ex 5:4* *w.*
thou shalt not do after *their*   *Ex 23:24* *w.*
according to these *their w.*   *Ne 6:14*
therefore he knoweth *their*   *Job 34:25* *w.*
he considereth all *their w.*   *Ps 33:15*
and they learned *their w.*   *Ps 106:35*
thus were they defiled with   *Ps 106:39* *their* own *w.*
and *their w.* are in the hand of   *Ec 9:1* God
their w. are in the dark, they   *Isa 29:15* say
they are vanity, *their w.* are   *Isa 41:29* nothing
nor shall they cover   *Isa 59:6* themselves with *their w., their w.*
are works of iniquity
I know *their w.* and their   *Isa 66:18* thoughts
I will never forget any of *their*   *Am 8:7* *w.*
God saw *their w.* that they   *Jon 3:10* turned
but do not ye after *their w.*   *M't 23:3*
all their *w.* they do to be seen   *M't 23:5* of men
whose end be according to   *2Co 11:15* *their w.*
and *their w.* do follow them   *Re 14:13*
the dead judged according   *Re 20:12;* to *their w.*   20:13

THY WORKS

who can do according to *thy*   *De 3:24* *w.*
the Lord shall bless thee in   *De 15:10* all *thy w.*
the Lord hath broken *thy w.*   *2Ch 20:37*
tell of all *thy* wondrous *w.*   *Ps 26:7;*   145:4
say to God, how terrible art   *Ps 66:3* thou in *thy w.*
trust in Lord, that I may   *Ps 73:28* declare all *thy w.*
nor are there any works like   *Ps 86:8* unto *thy w.*
O Lord, how great are *thy w.*   *Ps 92:5*
earth is satisfied with fruit   *Ps 104:13* of *thy w.*
O Lord, how manifold are   *Ps 104:24* *thy w.*
I remember, I meditate on all   *Ps 143:5* *thy w.*
all *thy w.* shall praise thee,   *Ps 145:10* O Lord
commit *thy w.* unto the Lord   *Pr 16:3*
for now God accepteth *thy w.*   *Ec 9:7*
I will declare *thy w.*; they   *Isa 57:12* shall not profit
because thou hast trusted in   *Jer 48:7* *thy w.*
shew me thy faith without *thy*   *Jas 2:18* *w.*
I know *thy w.*   *Re 2:2;*   2:9, 13, 19; 3:1, 8, 15
I have not found *thy w.* perfect   *Re 3:2* before God

WONDERFUL WORKS

many, O Lord, are thy   *Ps 40:5* *wonderful w.*
shewing his *wonderful w.*   *Ps 78:4* he hath done
would praise the Lord for   *Ps 107:8;* his *wonderful w.* to the   107:15, 21, 31 children of men
made his *wonderful w.* to be   *Ps 111:4* remembered
in thy name have done   *M't 7:22* *wonderful w.*
Cretes and Arabians, we do   *Ac 2:11* hear them speak in our tongues
the *wonderful w.* of God

WORK'S

highly in love for their *w.*   *1Th 5:13* sake

WORKS'

believe me for the very *w.*   *Joh 14:11* sake

WORLD

he hath set the *w.* upon them   *1Sa 2:8*
channels of sea appeared   *2Sa 22:16;* foundations of *w.* were   *Ps 18:15* discovered
the *w.* also shall not be   *1Ch 16:30* moved
deliver from the *w.* (B)   *1Ch 16:35*
he shall be chased out of the   *Job 18:18* *w.*
or who hath disposed the   *Job 34:13* whole *w.*
that they may do on the   *Job 37:12* face of the *w.*
he shall judge the *w.* in   *Ps 9:8;* righteousness   96:13; 98:9
deliver my soul from the men   *Ps 17:14* of the *w.*
their words to the end of the   *Ps 19:4;* *w.*   *Ro 10:18*
all the ends of the *w.* shall   *Ps 22:27* remember
the earth and the *w.* is the   *Ps 24:1;* Lord's and they that   98:7; Na 1:5 dwell therein
let the inhabitants of the *w.*   *Ps 33:8* stand in awe
give ear, all ye inhabitants of   *Ps 49:1* the *w.*
for the *w.* is mine   *Ps 50:12*
the lightnings lightened the *w.*   *Ps 77:18;*   97:4
thou hast founded the *w.* and   *Ps 89:11* its fulness
hadst formed the earth and the   *Ps 90:2* *w.*

w. also is established, it — Ps 93:1
cannot be moved
w. also shall be established, it — Ps 96:10
cannot be moved
while he had not made dust of — Pr 8:26
the *w.*
also he hath set the *w.* in their — Ec 3:11
heart
I will punish the *w.* for their — Isa 13:11
evil
he that made the *w.* as a — Isa 14:17
wilderness
nor fill the face of the *w.* — Isa 14:21
with cities
the *w.* languisheth and fadeth — Isa 24:4
away
Israel shall fill face of *w.* with — Isa 27:6
fruit
let the *w.* hear, and all that — Isa 34:1
come forth
shall not be confounded, *w.* — Isa 45:17
without end
devil sheweth him all — M't 4:8;
kingdoms of *w.* and glory of — Lu 4:5
them
ye are light of the *w.*: a — M't 5:14
city on a hill
the field is the *w.*, good seed — M't 13:38
are children
so shall it be in the end of — M't 13:40;
this *w.* — 13:49
what profited, if he gain — M't 16:26;
whole *w.* and lose own soul — M'k 8:36;
— Lu 9:25
woe to the *w.* because of — M't 18:7
offences
gospel of kingdom shall be — M't 24:14;
preached in all *w.* for — M'k 14:9
witness to all
which have been since *w.* — Lu 1:70;
began — Ac 3:21
a decree that all the *w.* should — Lu 2:1
be taxed
trustworthy with wealth of — Lu 16:11
this *w.* (N)
they that are worthy to — Lu 20:35
obtain that *w.*
he was in *w.*, the *w.* was — Joh 1:10;
made by him, the *w.* knew — Ac 17:24
him not
Lamb of God that takes — Joh 1:29
away sin of *w.*
God so loved the *w.* that he — Joh 3:16
gave his Son
that the *w.* through him — Joh 3:17
might be saved
Christ, the Saviour of the *w.* — Joh 4:42;
— 1Jo 4:14
bread of God is he that — Joh 6:33
giveth life unto the *w.*
my flesh, which I give for the — Joh 6:51
life of the *w.*
if thou do these things, shew — Joh 7:4
thyself to the *w.*
the *w.* cannot hate you, but — Joh 7:7
me it hateth
Jesus said, I am the light of — Joh 8:12;
the *w.* — 9:5
behold, the *w.* is gone after — Joh 12:19
him
I came not to judge, but to — Joh 12:47
save the *w.*
the Spirit, whom the *w.* — Joh 14:17
cannot receive
a little while and the *w.* — Joh 14:19
seeth me no more
wilt manifest thyself unto us — Joh 14:22
and not unto the *w.*
my peace, I give, not as the — Joh 14:27
w. giveth give I
that the *w.* may know I love — Joh 14:31
Father
if the *w.* hate you — Joh 15:18; 1Jo 3:13
if ye were of the *w.* the *w.* — Joh 15:19
would love his own
but the *w.* shall rejoice — Joh 16:20
I leave the *w.* and go to the — Joh 16:28
Father
be of good cheer, I have — Joh 16:33
overcome the *w.*
the glory I had with thee — Joh 17:5
before the *w.* was
thy name to men thou gavest — Joh 17:6
me out of the *w.*
I pray not for *w.* but for — Joh 17:9
them thou hast given me
w. hated them, because they — Joh 17:14
are not of the *w.*
thou shouldest not take them — Joh 17:15
out of the *w.*

they are not of the *w.* even — Joh 17:16
as I am not of *w.*
that the *w.* may believe — Joh 17:21;
thou hast sent me — 17:23
O Father, the *w.* hath not — Joh 17:25
known thee
Jesus answered, I spake — Joh 18:20
openly to the *w.*
I suppose *w.* could not — Joh 21:25
contain the books
these that turned the *w.* — Ac 17:6
upside down
Diana, whom Asia and the — Ac 19:27
w. worshippeth
a mover of sedition thro' the — Ac 24:5
w., a ringleader
your faith is spoken of thro' — Ro 1:8
the whole *w.*
for then how shall God judge — Ro 3:6
the *w.*
that all the *w.* may become — Ro 3:19
guilty
promise that he should be heir — Ro 4:13
of the *w.*
if the fall of them be the — Ro 11:12
riches of the *w.*
if casting away of them be — Ro 11:15
reconciling of *w.*
nonsense to dying *w.* (P) — 1Co 1:18
the *w.* by wisdom knew not — 1Co 1:21
God
wisdom which God ordained — 1Co 2:7
before the *w.*
we have received not spirit — 1Co 2:12
of the *w.*
or the *w.* of life, or death, all — 1Co 3:22
are yours
for we are made a spectacle — 1Co 4:9
to *w.*, and to angels
we are made as the filth of — 1Co 4:13
w. and offscouring
for then must ye needs go — 1Co 5:10
out of the *w.*
do ye not know that saints — 1Co 6:2
shall judge the *w.*
careth for the things that are — 1Co 7:33;
in the *w.* — 7:34
I will eat no flesh while the — 1Co 8:13
w. standeth
that we should not be — 1Co 11:32
condemned with *w.*
there is a new *w.* (N) — 2Co 5:17
God in Christ reconciling — 2Co 5:19
w. to himself
glory in the cross by whom — Ga 6:14
the *w.* is crucified to me,
and I to the *w.*
warped and diseased *w.* (P) — Ph'p 2:15
in Christ before the *w.* began — 2Ti 1:9;
— Tit 1:2
he put not in subjection the — Heb 2:5
w. to come
have tasted the powers of the — Heb 6:5
w. to come
put the whole *w.* in wrong — Heb 11:7
(N)
of whom the *w.* was not — Heb 11:38
worthy
to keep himself unspotted — Jas 1:27
from he *w.*
the tongue is a fire, a *w.* of — Jas 3:6
iniquity
friendship of *w.* is enmity with — Jas 4:4
God, a friend of the *w.* is
enemy of God
God spared not the old *w.* — 2Pe 2:5
bringing in the flood on the *w.*
of the ungodly
w. and its wickedness (P) — 2Pe 2:5
whereby the *w.* that then was, — 2Pe 3:6
perished
he is the propitiation for the — 1Jo 2:2
sins of *w.*
love not the *w.* — 1Jo 2:15
but is of the *w.* — 1Jo 2:16
the *w.* passeth away, and the — 1Jo 2:17
lusts thereof
w. knoweth us not, because it — 1Jo 3:1
knew him not
they are of the *w.* therefore — 1Jo 4:5
speak of the *w.*
what is born of God, — 1Jo 5:4;
overcometh *w.* — 5:5
whole *w.* lieth in wickedness — 1Jo 5:19
hour of temptation, come on — Re 3:10
all *w.*
I have everything I want in *w.* — Re 3:17
(N)
called Satan, who deceiveth the — Re 12:9
whole *w.*

all the *w.* wondered after the — Re 13:3
beast

IN, INTO THE WORLD

the ungodly who prosper in — Ps 73:12
the *w.*
this gospel be preached in — M't 26:13
the whole *w.*
receive hundredfold; in the — M'k 10:30;
w. to come eternal life — Lu 18:30
lighteth every man that comes — Joh 1:9
into the *w.*
was in the *w.* and the world — Joh 1:10
was made by him
God sent not his Son into the — Joh 3:17
w. to condemn world
light is come into the *w.* men — Joh 3:19
loved darkness
prophet that should come — Joh 6:14;
into the *w.* — 11:27
as long as I am in the *w.* I am — Joh 9:5
the light of world
I am come a light into the — Joh 12:46
w. that whosoever believeth
in me. ye shall have — Joh 16:33
tribulation, in me peace
I am no more in the *w.* — Joh 17:11
these are in the *w.*
while I was with them in the — Joh 17:12
w. I kept them
and for this cause came I — Joh 18:37
into the *w.*
as by one man sin entered — Ro 5:12
into the *w.*
for unto the law, sin was in — Ro 5:13
the *w.*
we know an idol is nothing in — 1Co 8:4
the *w.*
having no hope, without God — Eph 2:12
in the *w.*
gospel is come to you as it is — Col 1:6
in all the *w.*
Christ Jesus came into *w.* to — 1Ti 1:15
save sinners
seen of angels and believed — 1Ti 3:16
on in the *w.*
when he cometh into the *w.* — Heb 10:5
he saith
the same afflictions that are — 1Pe 5:9
in the *w.*
love not the things that are — 1Jo 2:15
in the *w.*
many false prophets are gone — 1Jo 4:1
out into the *w.*
antichrist, even now already is — 1Jo 4:3
it in the *w.*
because he is greater than he — 1Jo 4:4
that is in the *w.*
God sent Son into the *w.* that — 1Jo 4:9
we might live
many deceivers are entered into — 2Jo 7
the *w.*

THIS WORLD

it shall not be forgiven him — M't 12:32
in this *w.*
cares of this *w.* choke word — M't 13:22;
— M'k 4:19
for the children of this *w.* are — Lu 16:8
wiser than
Jesus said, The children of — Lu 20:34
this *w.* marry
ye are of this *w.* I am not of — Joh 8:23
this *w.*
for judgment I am come into — Joh 9:39
this *w.*
he that hateth life in this *w.* — Joh 12:25
shall keep it
now is the judgment of this — Joh 12:31
w. now shall the prince of
this *w.* be cast out
he should depart out of this — Joh 13:1
w. to the Father
for prince of this *w.* cometh, — Joh 14:30
nothing in me
because the prince of this *w.* — Joh 16:11
is judged
Jesus answered, My kingdom — Joh 18:36
is not of this *w.*: if my
kingdom were of this *w.*
be not conformed to this *w.* but — Ro 12:2
transformed
where is disputer of this *w.*? — 1Co 1:20
God made foolish the
wisdom of this *w.*
yet we speak not the wisdom — 1Co 2:6
of this *w.*
if any man seemeth to be — 1Co 3:18
wise in this *w.*

the wisdom of *this w.* is foolishness with God	1Co 3:19
yet not with the fornicators of *this w.*	1Co 5:10
they that use *this w.* as not abusing it	1Co 7:31
god of *this w.* hath blinded the minds	2Co 4:4
he might deliver us from *this* present evil *w.*	Ga 1:4
not only in *this w.* but in that to come	Eph 1:21
walked according to course of *this w.*	Eph 2:2
against rulers of the darkness of *this w.*	Eph 6:12
for we brought nothing into *this w.*	1Ti 6:7
charge them that are rich in *this w.*	1Ti 6:17
Demas having loved *this* present *w.*	2Ti 4:10
we should live godly in *this* present *w.*	Tit 2:12
God hath chosen the poor of *this w.*	Jas 2:5
because as he is, so are we in *this w.*	1Jo 4:17

WORLDLY

you judge by *w.* standards (N)	Joh 8:15
to be *w.*-minded is death (B)	Ro 8:6
w.-mindedness is hostile to God (B)	Ro 8:7
not with *w.* wisdom (B)(N)(P)	2Co 1:12
boast of *w.* things (A)(B)(R)	2Co 11:18
conceit of *w.* minds (A)(B)(N)(P)	Col 2:18
empty, *w.* chatter (N)(R)	1Ti 6:20; 2Ti 2:16
denying ungodliness and *w.* lusts	Tit 2:12
service, and a *w.* sanctuary	Heb 9:1
immoral and *w.* minded (N)	Heb 12:16
w. having not (B)(R)	Jude 19

WORLDS

King of all *w.* (N)	1Ti 1:17
by whom also he made the *w.*	Heb 1:2
the *w.* were framed by the word of	Heb 11:3

WORLD'S

being *w.* friend is (A)(P)	Jas 4:4
But whoso hath this *w.* good	1Jo 3:17

WORM

neither was there any *w.* therein	Ex 16:24
to the *w.*, Thou art my mother	Job 17:14
the *w.* shall feed sweetly on him	Job 24:20
How much less man, that is a *w.*	Job 25:6
the son of man, which is a *w.*	Job 25:6
But I am a *w.* and no man	Ps 22:6
the *w.* is spread under thee	Isa 14:11
Fear not, thou *w.* Jacob, and	Isa 41:14
the *w.* shall eat them like wool	Isa 51:8
for their *w.* shall not die, neither	Isa 66:24
But God prepared a *w.* when	Jon 4:7
moth, rust, *w.* consume (A)(E)(R)	M't 6:19
Where their *w.* dieth not	M'k 9:44; 9:46, 48
w. their way into homes (A)(P)	2Ti 3:6

WORMED

w. their way in (P)	Ga 2:4
w. their way in (N)	Jude 4

WORMS

and it bred *w.* and stank	Ex 16:20
grapes; for the *w.* shall eat them	De 28:39
My flesh is clothed with *w.*	Job 7:5
after my skin *w.* shall destroy this	Job 19:26

dust, and the *w.* shall cover them	Job 21:26
under thee, and the *w.* cover thee	Isa 14:11
of their holes like *w.* of the earth	Mic 7:17
he was eaten of *w.* and gave up	Ac 12:23

WORMWOOD

a root that beareth gall and *w.*	De 29:18
But her end is bitter as *w.*, sharp	Pr 5:4
them, even this people, with *w.*	Jer 9:15
I will feed them with *w.* and make	Jer 23:15
hath made me drunken with *w.*	La 3:15
my misery the *w.* and the gall	La 3:19
Ye who turn judgment to *w.*	Am 5:7
turned justice to *w.* (B)	Am 6:12
the name of the star is called *W.*	Re 8:11
part of the waters became *w.*	Re 8:11

WORMY

grew *w.* and rancid (B)	Ex 16:20
neither rancid or *w.* (R)	Ex 16:24

WORN

have *w.* themselves out (A)	Jer 12:13

WORRIED

sorely *w.* him (A)	Ge 49:23
w. about much serving (B)(P)	Lu 10:40
w. and bothered about (P)	Lu 10:41
anxious mind-unsettled excited, *w.*, in suspense (A)	Lu 12:29
why are you so *w.* (P)	Lu 24:38

WORRY

do not let this *w.* you (B)	2Sa 11:25
trouble and *w.* threaten (B)	Job 15:24
you are not to *w.* (N)(P)	Lu 12:29

WORSE

now will we deal *w.* with thee	Ge 19:9
that will be *w.* unto thee than all	2Sa 19:7
did *w.* that all that were before	1Ki 16:25
Judah was put to the *w.* before	2Ki 14:12
were put in the *w.* before Israel	1Ch 19:16; 19:19
thy people Israel be put to the *w.*	2Ch 6:24
Judah was put to the *w.* before	2Ch 25:22
to do *w.* than the heathen, whom	2Ch 33:9
they did *w.* than their fathers	Jer 7:26
have done *w.* than your fathers	Jer 16:12
faces *w.* liking than the children	Da 1:10
garment, and the rent is made *w.*	M't 9:16
of that man is *w.* than the first	M't 12:45
last error shall be *w.* than the first	M't 27:64
the old, and the rent is made *w.*	M'k 2:21
bettered, but rather grew *w.*	M'k 5:26
of that man is *w.* than the first	Lu 11:26
well drunk, then that which is *w.*	Joh 2:10
lest a *w.* thing come unto thee	Joh 5:14
if we eat not, are we the *w.*	1Co 8:8
not for the better, but for the *w.*	1Co 11:17
faith, and is *w.* than an infidel	1Ti 5:8
and seducers shall wax *w.* and *w.*	2Ti 3:13
w. (sterner, heavier) punishment (A)(B)(R)	Heb 10:29
the latter end is *w.* with them than	2Pe 2:20

WORSHIP

and the lad will go yonder and *w.*	Ge 22:5
of Israel; and *w.* ye afar off	Ex 24:1
For thou shalt *w.* no other god	Ex 34:14
shouldest be driven to *w.* them	De 4:19
and serve them, and *w.* them	De 8:19
and serve other gods, and *w.* them	De 11:16
and *w.* before the Lord thy God	De 26:10
w. other gods, and serve them	De 30:17
on his face to the earth, and did *w.*	Jos 5:14
went up out of his city yearly to *w.*	1Sa 1:3
with me, that I may *w.* the Lord	1Sa 15:25
that I may *w.* the Lord thy God	1Sa 15:30
and serve other gods and *w.* them	1Ki 9:6
the people went to *w.* before the one	1Ki 12:30
the house of Rimmon to *w.* there	2Ki 5:18
shall ye fear, and him shall ye *w.*	2Ki 17:36
w. before the altar in Jerusalem	2Ki 18:22
w. the Lord in the beauty of	1Ch 16:29
and serve other gods, and *w.* them	2Ch 7:19
Ye shall *w.* before one altar	2Ch 32:12
will I *w.* toward thy holy temple	Ps 5:7
the nations shall *w.* before thee	Ps 22:27
fat upon earth shall eat and *w.*	Ps 22:29
w. the Lord in the beauty of	Ps 29:2
he is thy Lord; and *w.* thou him	Ps 45:11
All the earth shall *w.* thee, and	Ps 66:4
shalt thou *w.* any strange god	Ps 81:9
shall come and *w.* before thee	Ps 86:9
O come, let us *w.* and bow down	Ps 95:6
O *w.* the Lord in the beauty of	Ps 96:9
of idols: *w.* him all ye gods	Ps 97:7
our God, and *w.* at his footstool	Ps 99:5
our God, and *w.* at his holy hill	Ps 99:9
we will *w.* at his footstool	Ps 132:7
I will *w.* toward thy holy temple	Ps 138:2
w. the work of their own hands	Isa 2:8
made each one for himself to *w.*	Isa 2:20
shall *w.* the Lord in the holy mount	Isa 27:13
Ye shall *w.* before this altar	Isa 36:7
a god: they fall down, yea, they *w.*	Isa 46:6
see and arise, princes also shall *w.*	Isa 49:7
all flesh come to *w.* before me	Isa 66:23
in at these gates to *w.* the Lord	Jer 7:2
gods, to serve them, and to *w.* them	Jer 13:10
gods to serve them, and to *w.* them	Jer 25:6
come to *w.* in the Lord's house	Jer 26:2
did we make her cakes to *w.* her	Jer 44:19
w. at the threshold of the gate	Eze 46:2
shall *w.* at the door of this gate	Eze 46:3
by the way of the north gate to *w.*	Eze 46:9
fall down and *w.* the golden image	Da 3:5; 3:10
nor *w.* the golden image which thou	Da 3:12
nor *w.* the golden image which I	Da 3:14
ye fall down and *w.* the image	Da 3:15
but if ye *w.* not, ye shall be cast	Da 3:15
nor *w.* the golden image which thou	Da 3:18
might not serve nor *w.* any god	Da 3:28

more w. the work of thine | Mic 5:13
hands
them that w. the host of | Zep 1:5
heaven
w. and that swear by the Lord | Zep 1:5
and men shall w. him, every | Zep 2:11
one
from year to year to w. the | Zec 14:16
King
unto Jerusalem to w. the | Zec 14:17
King
the east, and are come to w. | M't 2:2
him
that I may come and w. him | M't 2:8
also
if thou wilt fall down and w. | M't 4:9
me
Thou shalt w. the Lord thy | M't 4:10
God
But in vain do they w. me, | M't 15:9
teaching
Howbeit in vain do they w. | M'k 7:7
me
If thou therefore wilt w. me | Lu 4:7
Thou shalt w. the Lord thy God | Lu 4:8
have w. in the presence of | Lu 14:10
them
the place where men ought to | Joh 4:20
w.
yet at Jerusalem, w. the | Joh 4:21
Father
Ye w. ye know not what | Joh 4:22
we know what we w.: for | Joh 4:22
salvation
shall w. the Father in spirit | Joh 4:23
and in
is a Spirit: and they that w. | Joh 4:24
him
must w. him in spirit and in | Joh 4:24
truth
that came up to w. at the | Joh 12:20
feast
them up to w. the host of | Ac 7:42
heaven
which ye made to w. them | Ac 7:43
had come to Jerusalem for to | Ac 8:27
w.
Whom therefore ye ignorantly | Ac 17:23
w.
fellow persuadeth men to w. | Ac 18:13
God
I went up to Jerusalem for to | Ac 24:11
w.
so w. I the God of my | Ac 24:14
fathers
down on his face he will w. | 1Co 14:25
God
which w. God in the spirit | Ph'p 3:3
indeed a shew of wisdom in | Col 2:23
will w.
let all the angels of God w. | Heb 1:6
him
to come and w. before thy feet | Re 3:9
that
and w. him that liveth for ever | Re 4:10
they should not w. devils | Re 9:20
altar, and them that w. therein | Re 11:1
dwell upon the earth shall w. | Re 13:8
him
dwell therein to w. the first | Re 13:12
beast
not w. the image of the beast | Re 13:15
and w. him that made heaven | Re 14:7
If any man w. the beast and his | Re 14:9
who w. the beast and his | Re 14:11
image
shall come and w. before thee | Re 15:4
And I fell at his feet to w. | Re 19:10
him
w. God: for the testimony of | Re 19:16
Jesus
I fell down to w. before the | Re 22:8
feet of
the sayings of this book: w. | Re 22:9
God

WORSHIPFULLY

to be w. revered (A) | Ps 89:7

WORSHIPPED

down his head, and w. the | Ge 24:26
Lord
down my head, and w. the | Ge 24:48
Lord
heard their words, he w. the | Ge 24:52
Lord

they bowed their heads and w. | Ex 4:31
the people bowed the head | Ex 12:27
and w.
them a molten calf, and have | Ex 32:8
w. it
and all the people rose up | Ex 33:10
and w.
his head toward the earth, | Ex 34:8
and w.
and served other gods, and w. | De 17:3;
them | 29:26
interpretation thereof, that he | J'g 7:15
w.
w. before the Lord, and | 1Sa 1:19
returned
Lord. And he w. the Lord | 1Sa 1:28
there
after Saul; and Saul w. the | 1Sa 15:31
into the house of the Lord, | 2Sa 12:20
and w.
top of the mount, where he | 2Sa 15:32
w. God
upon other gods, and have w. | 1Ki 9:9
them
have w. Ashtoreth the | 1Ki 11:33
goddess of
went and served Baal, and | 1Ki 16:31
w. him
For he served Baal, and w. | 1Ki 22:53
him
and w. all the host of | 2Ki 17:16;
heaven, and | 21:3
that his father served, and | 2Ki 21:21
w. them
down their heads, and w. | 1Ch 29:20
the Lord
and w. and praised the Lord | 2Ch 7:3
hold on other gods, and w. | 2Ch 7:22
them
And all the congregation w. | 2Ch 29:28
him bowed themselves, and | 2Ch 29:29
w.
and they bowed their heads | 2Ch 29:30
and w.
and w. all the host of heaven | 2Ch 33:3
and w. the Lord with their | Ne 8:6
faces to
and w. the Lord their God | Ne 9:3
fell down upon the ground, | Job 1:20
and w.
in Horeb and w. the molten | Ps 106:19
image
w. the works of their own | Jer 1:16
hands
sought, and whom they have w. | Jer 8:2
served them, and have w. | Jer 16:11
them
w. other gods, and served them | Jer 22:9
they w. the sun toward the | Eze 8:16
east
and w. Daniel, and commanded | Da 2:46
fell down, and w. the golden | Da 3:7
image
mother, and fell down and w. | M't 2:11
him
there came a leper and w. him | M't 8:2
came a certain ruler, and w. | M't 9:18
him
were in the ship came and | M't 14:33
w. him
Then came she and w. him, | M't 15:25
saying
fell down, and w. him, | M't 18:26
saying, Lord
held him by the feet, and w. | M't 28:9
him
they w. him: but some | M't 28:17
doubted
Jesus afar off, he ran and w. | M'k 5:6
him
and bowing their knees w. | M'k 15:19
him
And they w. him, and returned | Lu 24:52
Our fathers w. in this | Joh 4:20
mountain
Lord, I believe. And he w. | Joh 9:38
him
fell down at his feet and w. | Ac 10:25
him
Thyatira, which w. God, | Ac 16:14
heard us
Neither is w. with men's | Ac 17:25
hands
named Justus, one that w. | Ac 18:7
God
and w. and served the creature | Ro 1:25

all that is called God, or that | 2Th 2:4
is w.
and w. leaning upon the top | Heb 11:21
and w. him that liveth for ever | Re 5:14
throne on their faces, and w. | Re 7:11
God
fell upon their faces, and w. | Re 11:16
God
w. the dragon which gave | Re 13:4
power
and they w. the beast, saying, | Re 13:4
Who
and upon them which w. his | Re 16:2
image
four beasts fell down and w. | Re 19:4
God
beast, and them that w. his | Re 19:20
image
which had not w. the beast, | Re 20:4
neither

WORSHIPPER

but if any man be a w. of | Joh 9:31
God, and
a w. of the great goddess | Ac 19:35
Diana

WORSHIPPERS

guards feet of w. (B) | 1Sa 2:9
he might destroy the w. of | 2Ki 10:19
Baal
all the w. of Baal came, so | 2Ki 10:21
that
vestments for all the w. of | 2Ki 10:22
Baal
said unto the w. of Baal, | 2Ki 10:23
Search
the Lord, but the w. of Baal | 2Ki 10:23
only
flesh of thy w. (B) | Ps 79:2; 85:8
true w. shall worship the | Joh 4:23
Father
the w. once purged should | Heb 10:2
have

WORSHIPPETH

and the host of heaven w. thee | Ne 9:6
yea, he maketh a god, and | Isa 44:15
w. it
he falleth down unto it, and | Isa 44:17
w. it
whoso falleth not down and w. | Da 3:6
And whoso falleth not down | Da 3:11
and w.
whom all Asia and the | Ac 19:27
world w.

WORSHIPPING

w. other gods (B) | J'g 2:17
w. in the house of Nisroch | 2Ki 19:37
his god
fell before the Lord, w. | 2Ch 20:18
the Lord
w. in the house of Nisroch | Isa 37:38
his god
w. him, and desiring a | M't 20:20
certain
were w. and fasting | Ac 13:2
(A)(B)(P)(R)
humility and w. of angels | Col 2:18

WORST

I will bring the w. of the | Eze 7:24
heathen

WORTH

money as it is w. he shall give | Ge 23:9
is w. four hundred shekels of | Ge 23:15
silver
unto him the w. of thy | Le 27:23
estimation
been w. a double hired | De 15:18
servant
thou art w. ten thousand of | 2Sa 18:3
us
give thee the w. of it in | 1Ki 21:2
money
and make my speech nothing | Job 24:25
w.
the heart of the wicked is | Pr 10:20
little w.

devoid of *w.* (A)   Jer 10:15
God; Howl ye, Woe *w.* the   Eze 30:2
day

WORTHIES

He shall recount his *w.*: they   Na 2:5
shall
his bravest men (A)   Na 2:5
his officers (B)(R)   Na 2:5
his nobles (E)   Na 2:5

WORTHILY

do thou *w.* in Ephratah, and   Ru 4:11
daughter have done *w.* (E)   Pr 31:29

WORTHLESS

w. fellows (S)   De 13:13;
1Sa 2:12;- 10:27; 25:17, 25; 30:22;
2Sa 16:7; 10:1; 23:6; 1Ki 21:10, 13
low and *w.* (A)   De 25:3
empty and *w.* trifle (A)   De 32:47
w. and foolhardy men (A)(R)   J'g 9:4
worthless (A)   J'g 9:4;
11:3; 2Sa 6:20; 2Ch 13:7
w. men (A)   J'g 11:3;
1Sa 12:21; 2Sa 6:20; 2Ch 13:7; Pr 28:19;
Isa 30:7; La 4:17; Jas 1:26
certain *w.* fellows (A)   J'g 19:22
w. men, fellows (S)   1Sa 2:12; 25:17;
2Sa 23:6; 1Ki 21:10
w. men (E)   1Sa 2:16; 10:27; 25:17, 25
w. fellows (A)(E)(R)   1Sa 10:27
w. characters (B)(S)   1Sa 30:22
the *w.* fellows (B)   2Sa 6:20; Job 11:11
w. fellow (B)   2Sa 16:7
w. fellow (B)(R)   2Sa 20:1
wicked, godless, *w.* (A)(B)   2Sa 23:6
w. men (A)(E)(R)   2Ch 13:7
w. men (B)   Job 11:11
w. physicians (R)   Job 13:4
w. and nameless men (A)(B)   Job 30:8
w. and vile (A)   Job 34:18
you are *w.* (R)   Job 34:18
w., wicked man   Pr 6:12
(A)(B)(E)(R)(S)
w. pursuits (A)(R)   Pr 12:11
a *w.* man (A)(B)(E)(R)   Pr 16:27;
19:28
this is *w.* (B)   Ec 2:1; 2:11
w. cards (B)   Isa 5:18
w. and empty (R)   Isa 30:7
he created it not a *w.* waste   Isa 45:18
(A)(E)
are become fruitless and *w.*   Jer 2:5
(A)(R)
they are *w.* (R)   Jer 10:15; 51:18
futility, *w.* things (A)   Jer 16:19
sons of the *w.* (A)(B)   Jer 30:8
w., falsity, futility (A)   Jer 51:18
false, useless, *w.* idols (A)(B)   Jon 2:8
w. tree bears bad fruit (A)   M't 7:17
w. elementary things (A)   Ga 4:9
unwholesome *w.* talk (A)   Eph 4:29
unfit and *w.* for (A)   Tit 1:16
faith is *w.* (A)   Jas 2:20

WORTHLESSNESS

w., chasing mind (B)   Ec 1:14; 2:19
w., a sorry situation (B)   Ec 4:8
worthlessness (B)   Ec 6:11;
Isa 40:17; Ho 12:11
waste, futility, *w.* (A)   Isa 40:17
chaos, *w.* (A)(B)   Isa 44:9
emptiness, *w.* (A)   Isa 59:4
went after *w.* and become   Jer 2:5
worthless (R)

WORTHY

I am not *w.* of the least of   Ge 32:10
all the
is *w.* of death to be put to   De 17:6
death
whereas he was not *w.* of   De 19:6
death
have committed a sin *w.* of   De 21:22
death
is in the damsel no sin *w.* of   De 22:26
death
wicked man be *w.* to be   De 25:2
beaten
woman of *w.* (A)(R)   Ru 3:11
a *w.* woman (E)   Ru 3:11;
Pr 12:4; 31:10

unto Hannah he gave a *w.*   1Sa 1:5
portion
ye are *w.* to die, because ye   1Sa 26:16
have
the Lord, who is *w.* to be   2Sa 22:4
praised
a *w.* man (B)   2Sa 23:20
will shew himself a *w.* man   1Ki 1:52
fields; for thou art *w.* of   1Ki 2:26
death
the Lord, who is *w.* to be   Ps 18:3
praised
saying, This man is *w.* to die   Jer 26:11
This man is not *w.* to die: Jer 26:16
for he hath spoken in the name
whose shoes I am not *w.* to   M't 3:11
bear
I am not *w.* that thou shouldest   M't 8:8
for the workman is *w.* of his   M't 10:10
meat
shall enter, enquire who in it   M't 10:11
is *w.*
if the house be *w.* let your   M't 10:13
peace
if it be not *w.* let your peace   M't 10:13
return
more than me is not *w.* of   M't 10:37
me
followeth after me, is not *w.*   M't 10:38
of me
which were bidden were not   M't 22:8
w.
shoes I am not *w.* to stoop   M'k 1:7
down
therefore fruits *w.* of   Lu 3:8
repentance
shoes I am not *w.* to unloose   Lu 3:16
he was *w.* for whom he should   Lu 7:4
do
I am not *w.* that thou shouldest   Lu 7:6
thought I myself *w.* to come   Lu 7:7
for the labourer is *w.* of his   Lu 10:7
hire
did commit things *w.* of   Lu 12:48
stripes
and no more *w.* to be called   Lu 15:19;
thy son   15:21
accounted *w.* to obtain that   Lu 20:35
world
accounted *w.* to escape all   Lu 21:36
these
nothing *w.* of death is done   Lu 23:15
unto
latchet I am not *w.* to unloose   Joh 1:27
were counted *w.* to suffer   Ac 5:41
shame
of his feet am not *w.* to   Ac 12:25
loose
laid to his charge *w.* of death   Ac 23:29
very *w.* deeds are done unto   Ac 24:2
committed any thing *w.* of   Ac 25:11
death
had committed nothing *w.* of   Ac 25:25
death
nothing *w.* of death or of   Ac 26:31
bonds
such things are *w.* of death   Ro 1:32
time are not *w.* to be   Ro 8:18
compared
that ye walk *w.* of the   Eph 4:1
vocation
conduct *w.* of the gospel   Eph 1:27
(N)(P)
w. of praise (R)   Ph'p 4:8
might walk *w.* of the Lord   Col 1:10
That ye would walk *w.* of   1Th 2:12
God, who
may be counted *w.* of the   2Th 1:5
kingdom
count you *w.* of this calling   2Th 1:11
saying, and *w.* of all   1Ti 1:15; 4:9
acceptation
be counted *w.* of double   1Ti 5:17
honour
The labourer is *w.* of his   1Ti 5:18
reward
their own masters *w.* of all   1Ti 6:1
honour
man was counted *w.* of more   Heb 3:3
glory
shall he be thought *w.* who   Heb 10:29
hath trampled
Of whom the world was not   Heb 11:38
w.
they blaspheme that *w.* name   Jas 2:7
with me in white: for they are   Re 3:4
w.
Thou art *w.* O Lord, to   Re 4:11
receive
Who is *w.* to open the book   Re 5:2

no man was found *w.* to open   Re 5:4
Thou art *w.* to take the book   Re 5:9
W. is the lamb that was slain   Re 5:12
blood to drink; for they are *w.*   Re 16:6
w. of confidence, genuine (A)   Re 22:6

WOT

I *w.* not who hath done this   Ge 21:26
thing
w. ye not that such a man as I   Ge 44:15
can
w. not what is become of him   Ex 32:1;
32:23
I *w.* that he whom thou   Nu 22:6
blessest is
whither the men went I *w.* not   Jos 2:5
I *w.* that through ignorance ye   Ac 3:17
did
we *w.* not what is become of   Ac 7:40
him
W. ye not what the scripture   Ro 11:2
saith
yet what I shall choose I *w.*   Ph'p 1:22
not

WOTTETH

my master *w.* not what is with   Ge 39:8
me

WOULD

Adam to see what he *w.* call   Ge 2:19
them
Who *w.* have said unto   Ge 21:7
Abraham
I *w.* that it might be   Ge 30:34
according
he besought us, and we *w.*   Ge 42:21
not hear
and ye *w.* not hear?   Ge 42:22
therefore, behold
certainly know that he *w.* say,   Ge 43:7
Bring your brother
leave his father, his father *w.*   Ge 44:22
die
afar off, to wit what *w.* be   Ex 2:4
done to him
neither *w.* he let the people go   Ex 8:32
neither *w.* he let the children   Ex 9:35
he *w.* not let the children of   Ex 10:20;
Israel   11:10
heart, and he *w.* not let them   Ex 10:27
go
when Pharaoh *w.* hardly let   Ex 13:15
us go
W. to God we had died by   Ex 16:3
w. God that all the Lord's   Nu 11:29
Lord *w.* put his spirit upon   Nu 11:29
them
W. God that we had died in   Nu 14:2
w. God we had died in the   Nu 14:2
wilderness
W. God that we had died   Nu 20:3
when
And Sihon *w.* not suffer   Nu 21:23
Israel to pass
If Balak *w.* give me his house   Nu 22:18
full of
I *w.* there were a sword in   Nu 22:29
mine
in mine hand, for now I *w.*   Nu 22:29
kill thee
If Balak *w.* give me his house   Nu 24:13
full of
Notwithstanding ye *w.* not go   De 1:26
up
and ye *w.* not hear, but   De 1:43
rebelled
Lord *w.* not hearken to your   De 1:45
voice
king of Heshbon *w.* not let us   De 2:30
pass
for your sakes, and *w.* not   De 3:26
hear me
a heart in them, that they *w.*   De 5:29
fear me
because he *w.* keep the oath   De 7:8
which he
ye *w.* not be obedient unto the   De 8:20
voice
the Lord had said he *w.*   De 9:25
destroy you
and the Lord *w.* not destroy   De 10:10
thee
God *w.* not hearken unto   De 23:5
Balaam
it of thee; and it *w.* be sin in   De 23:21
thee

w. not adventure to set the sole of	De 28:56
say, W. God it were even	De 28:67
say, W. God it were morning	De 28:67
I said, I w. scatter them into corners	De 32:26
I w. make the remembrance of them	De 32:26
they w. consider their latter end	De 32:29
that he w. not shew them the land	Jos 5:6
unto their fathers that he w. give us	Jos 5:6
w. to God we had been content	Jos 7:7
Canaanites w. dwell in that land	Jos 17:12
But I w. not hearken unto Balaam	Jos 24:10
Canaanites w. dwell in that land	J'g 1:27
for they w. not suffer them to come	J'g 1:34
Amorites w. dwell in mount Heres	J'g 1:35
w. not hearken unto their judges	J'g 2:17
to know whether they w. hearken	J'g 3:4
saved them alive, I w. not slay you	J'g 8:19
them, I w. desire a request from you	J'g 8:24
w. give me every man the earrings	J'g 8:24
w. to God this people were	J'g 9:29
then w. I remove Abimelech	J'g 9:29
the king of Edom w. not hearken	J'g 11:17
king of Moab: but he w. not consent	J'g 11:17
he w. not have received a burnt	J'g 13:23
neither w. he have shewed us all	J'g 13:23
nor w. as at this time have told us	J'g 13:23
he rent him as he w. have rent a kid	J'g 14:6
her father w. not suffer him to go in	J'g 15:1
But the man w. not tarry that night	J'g 19:10
the men w. not hearken to him	J'g 19:25
of Benjamin w. not hearken	J'g 20:13
W. ye tarry for them till they were	Ru 1:13
w. ye stay for them from having	Ru 1:13
then he w. answer him, Nay	1Sa 2:16
because the Lord w. slay them	1Sa 2:25
for now w. the Lord have established	1Sa 13:13
and w. not utterly destroy them	1Sa 15:9
and w. let him go no more home to his	1Sa 18:2
come upon thee, then w. not I tell it	1Sa 20:9
servants of the king w. not put forth	1Sa 22:17
was there, that he w. surely tell Saul	1Sa 22:22
but I w. not stretch forth mine hand	1Sa 26:23
But his armourbearer w. not; for he	1Sa 31:4
But Asahel w. not turn aside from	2Sa 2:21
though they w. have fetched wheat	2Sa 4:6
that I w. have given him a reward	2Sa 4:10
So David w. not remove the ark of	2Sa 6:10
knew ye not that they w. shoot from	2Sa 11:20
I w. more over have given unto thee	2Sa 12:8
but he w. not, neither did he eat	2Sa 12:17
he w. not hearken unto our voice	2Sa 12:18
he w. not hearken unto her voice	2Sa 13:14
me. But he w. not hearken unto her	2Sa 13:16
howbeit he w. not go, but blessed	2Sa 13:25
man that w. destroy me and my son	2Sa 14:16
king; but he w. not come to him	2Sa 14:29
second time, he w. not come unto me, and I w. do him	2Sa 14:29
justice	2Sa 15:4
I w. have given thee ten shekels of	2Sa 18:11
yet w. I not put forth mine hand	2Sa 18:12
w. God I had died for thee	2Sa 18:33
that one w. give me drink of the water	2Sa 23:15
nevertheless he w. not drink	2Sa 23:16
therefore he w. not drink it	2Sa 23:17
he w. dwell in the thick darkness	1Ki 8:12
whosoever w. he consecrated him	1Ki 13:33
as great as w. contain two measures of	1Ki 18:32
whether any thing w. come from him	1Ki 20:33
away his face, and w. eat no bread	1Ki 21:4
w. prophesy no good concerning me	1Ki 22:18
the ships. But Jehoshaphat w. not	1Ki 22:49
when the Lord w. take up Elijah into	2Ki 2:1
I w. not look toward thee, nor see	2Ki 3:14
W. God my lord were with the	2Ki 5:3
for he w. recover him of his leprosy	2Ki 5:3
the Lord w. make windows in heaven	2Ki 7:2
Yet the Lord w. not destroy Judah	2Ki 8:19
and w. not destroy them, neither	2Ki 13:23
But Amaziah w. not hear	2Ki 14:11
that he w. blot out the name of Israel	2Ki 14:27
Notwithstanding they w. not hear	2Ki 17:14
and w. not hear them, nor do them	2Ki 18:12
which the Lord w. not pardon	2Ki 24:4
But his armourbearer w. not; for he	1Ch 10:4
that one w. give me drink of the water	1Ch 11:17
but David w. not drink of it	1Ch 11:18
Therefore he w. not drink it	1Ch 11:19
congregation said that they w. do so	1Ch 13:4
neither w. the Syrians help	1Ch 19:19
he w. increase Israel like to the stars	1Ch 27:23
that he w. dwell in the thick darkness	2Ch 6:1
saw that the king w. not hearken	2Ch 10:16
that he w. not destroy him altogether	2Ch 12:12
whosoever w. not seek the Lord God of	2Ch 15:13
that he w. not prophesy good unto me	2Ch 18:17
w. not destroy the house of David	2Ch 21:7
them: but they w. not give ear	2Ch 24:19
But Amaziah w. not hear; for it came	2Ch 25:20
his people: but they w. not hearken	2Ch 33:10
Josiah w. not turn his face from him	2Ch 35:22
w. not come within three days	Ezr 10:8
that they w. put away their wives	Ezr 10:19
w. go into the temple to save his life	Ne 6:11
prophets that w. have put he in fear	Ne 6:14
they might do with them as they w.	Ne 9:24
hardened their neck, and w. not hear	Ne 9:29
yet w. they not give ear: therefore	Ne 9:30
we w. not give our daughters unto the	Ne 10:30
w. not buy it of them on the sabbath	Ne 11:31
that we w. leave the seventh year	Ne 11:31
whether Mordecai's matters w. stand	Es 3:4
To whom w. the king delight to do	Es 6:6
and province that w. assault them	Es 8:11
what they w. unto those that hated	Es 9:5
that they w. keep these two days	Es 9:27
I w. seek unto God	Job 5:8
and unto God w. I commit my cause	Job 5:8
it w. be heavier than the sand of the	Job 6:3
that God w. grant me the thing	Job 6:8
that it w. please God to destroy me	Job 6:9
that he w. let loose his hand, and cut	Job 6:9
I w. harden myself in sorrow	Job 6:10
I loathe it, I w. not live alway: let me	Job 7:16
surely now he w. awake for thee, and	Job 8:6
I were righteous, yet w. I not answer	Job 9:15
I w. make supplication to my judge	Job 9:15
w. I not believe that he had hearkened	Job 9:16
perfect, yet w. I not know my soul	Job 9:21
I w. despise my life	Job 9:21
Then w. I speak, and not fear him	Job 9:35
But oh that God w. speak, and open	Job 11:5
he w. shew thee the secrets of wisdom	Job 11:6
For vain man w. be wise, though man	Job 11:12
Surely I w. speak to the Almighty and	Job 13:3
ye w. altogether hold your peace	Job 13:5
I w. strengthen you with my mouth	Job 16:5
I w. order my cause before him, and	Job 23:4
I w. know the words which he w. answer me, and	Job 23:5
understand what he w. say unto me	Job 23:5
No; but he w. put strength in me	Job 23:6
spare; he w. fain flee out of his hand	Job 27:22
whose fathers I w. have disdained to	Job 30:1
and w. root out all mine increase	Job 31:12
Oh that one w. hear me! behold, my	Job 31:35
that the Almighty w. answer me, and	Job 31:35
Surely I w. take it upon my shoulder	Job 31:36
I w. declare unto him the number of	Job 31:37
as a prince w. I go near unto him	Job 31:37
in so doing my maker w. soon take me	Job 32:22
and w. not consider any of his ways	Job 34:27
Even so w. he have removed thee out	Job 36:16
one w. think the deep to be hoary	Job 41:32
on the Lord that he w. deliver him	Ps 22:8
their hearts, Ah, so w. we have it	Ps 35:25
if I w. declare and speak of	Ps 40:5
If I were hungry, I w. not tell thee	Ps 50:12
not sacrifice; else w. I give it	Ps 51:16
for then w. I fly away, and be at rest	Ps 55:6
Lo, then w. I wander far off	Ps 55:7

I w. hasten my escape from   Ps 55:8
then I w. have hid myself   Ps 55:12
from him
O God: for man w. swallow me   Ps 56:1
up
Mine enemies w. daily swallow   Ps 56:2
me up
reproach of him that w.   Ps 57:3
swallow me
w. destroy me, being mine   Ps 69:4
enemies
people w. not hearken to my   Ps 81:11
voice
and Israel w. none of me   Ps 81:11
he said that he w. destroy   Ps 106:23
them
men w. praise the Lord for   Ps 107:8;
                107:15, 21, 31
I have said that I w. keep thy   Ps 119:57
words
there was no man that w.   Ps 142:4
know me
counsel, and w. none of my   Pr 1:25
reproof
They w. none of my counsel;   Pr 1:30
they
I held him, and w. not let him   Ca 3:4
go
and thee without, I w. kiss thee   Ca 8:1
I w. lead thee and bring thee   Ca 8:2
into
mother's house, who w. instruct   Ca 8:2
me
w. cause thee to drink of   Ca 8:2
spiced wine
if a man w. give all the   Ca 8:7
substance of
for love, it w. utterly be   Ca 8:7
contemned
who w. set the briers and   Isa 27:4
thorns
I w. go through them   Isa 27:4
I w. burn them together   Isa 27:4
refreshing: yet they w. not   Isa 28:12
hear
be your strength: and ye w.   Isa 30:15
not
for they w. not walk in his   Isa 42:24
ways
that I w. not be wroth with   Isa 54:9
thee
I w. comfort myself against   Jer 8:18
sorrow
Who w. not fear thee, O king   Jer 10:7
for a glory: but they w. not   Jer 13:11
hear
wherewith I said I w. benefit   Jer 18:10
them
hand, yet, w. I pluck thee   Jer 22:24
hence
but ye w. not hear, saith the   Jer 29:19
Lord
the king that he w. not burn   Jer 36:25
the roll
but he w. not hear them   Jer 36:25
that he w. not cause me to   Jer 38:26
return to
w. they not leave some   Jer 49:9
gleaning
We w. have healed Babylon,   Jer 51:9
but she
w. not have believed that the   La 4:12
they w. have hearkened unto   Eze 3:6
thee
that I w. do this evil unto   Eze 6:10
them
hope that they w. confirm the   Eze 13:6
word
me, and w. not hearken unto   Eze 20:8
me
I w. pour out my fury upon   Eze 20:13
them
I w. not bring into the land   Eze 20:15
which I
I w. pour out my fury upon   Eze 20:21
them
I w. scatter them among the   Eze 20:23
heathen
that I w. bring thee against   Eze 38:17
them
heart that he w. not defile   Da 1:8
himself
of certainty that ye w. gain the   Da 2:8
time
of the king that he w. give   Da 2:16
him time
w. shew the king the   Da 2:16
interpretation

they w. desire mercies of the   Da 2:18
God of
before him: whom he w. he   Da 5:19
slew
and whom he w. he kept   Da 5:19
alive
and whom he w. he set up   Da 5:19
and whom he w. he put down   Da 5:19
I w. know the truth of the   Da 7:19
fourth
that he w. accomplish seventy   Da 9:2
years
When I w. have healed Israel   Ho 7:1
most High, none at all w. exalt   Ho 11:7
him
w. they not have stolen till they   Ob 5
had
he had said that he w. do   Jon 3:10
unto them
see what w. become of the city   Jon 4:5
as he cried, and they w. not   Zec 7:13
hear
that w. shut the doors for   Mal 1:10
nought
children, and w. not be   M't 2:18
comforted
him that w. borrow of thee   M't 5:42
turn not
ye w. that men should do to   M't 7:12
you
he w. depart out of their   M't 8:34
coasts
they w. have repented long   M't 11:21
ago in
it w. have remained until   M't 11:23
this day
ye w. not have condemned   M't 12:7
we w. see a sign from thee   M't 12:38
when he w. have put him to   M't 14:5
death
to give her whatsoever she w.   M't 14:7
ask
he w. shew them a sign from   M't 16:1
heaven
w. take account of his   M't 18:23
servants
he w. not: but went and cast   M't 18:30
him
wedding: and they w. not   M't 22:3
come
we w. not have been   M't 23:30
partakers with
w. I have gathered thy   M't 23:37
children
under her wings, and ye w.   M't 23:37
not
in what watch the thief w.   M't 24:43
come
come, he w. have watched   M't 24:43
w. not have suffered his   M't 24:43
house to be
people a prisoner, whom   M't 27:15
they w.
tasted thereof, he w. not   M't 27:34
drink
whether he w. heal on the   M'k 3:2
sabbath
and calleth unto him whom   M'k 3:13
he w.
that he w. not send them   M'k 5:10
away out
and w. have killed him; but   M'k 6:19
she
sat with him, he w. not reject   M'k 6:26
her
sea, and w. have passed by   M'k 6:48
them
and w. have no man know it   M'k 7:24
that he w. cast forth the devil   M'k 7:26
out of
would (S)   M'k 8:35; 10:43,44
he w. not that any man   M'k 9:30
should
Master, we w. that thou   M'k 10:35
shouldest
What w. ye that I should do   M'k 10:36
for you
And w. not suffer that any   M'k 11:16
man should
father, how he w. have him   Lu 1:62
called
That he w. grant unto us, that   Lu 1:74
we
w. thrust out a little from the   Lu 5:3
land
whether he w. heal on the   Lu 6:7
sabbath

ye w. that men should do to   Lu 6:31
you
that he w. come and heal his   Lu 7:3
servant
desired him that he w. eat   Lu 7:36
with him
w. have known who and what   Lu 7:39
manner
he w. not command them to   Lu 8:31
go out
that he w. suffer them to enter   Lu 8:32
into
him that he w. come into his   Lu 8:41
house
as though he w. go to   Lu 9:53
Jerusalem
whither he himself w. come   Lu 10:1
that he w. send forth   Lu 10:2
labourers
known what hour the thief   Lu 12:39
w. come
he w. have watched, and not   Lu 12:39
have
w. I have gathered thy   Lu 13:34
childen
under her wings, and ye w.   Lu 13:34
not
he w. fain have filled his   Lu 15:16
belly with
he was angry, and w. not go   Lu 15:28
in
which w. pass from hence to   Lu 16:26
you
to us, that w. come from   Lu 16:26
thence
And he w. not for a while   Lu 18:4
w. not lift up so much as his   Lu 18:13
eyes
infants, that he w. touch   Lu 18:15
them
which w. not that I should   Lu 19:27
reign
the stones w. immediately cry   Lu 19:40
out
were about him saw what w.   Lu 22:49
follow
as though he w. have gone   Lu 24:28
further
Jesus w. go forth into Galilee   Joh 1:43
he w. have given thee living   Joh 4:10
water
him that he w. tarry with   Joh 4:40
them
besought him that he w. come   Joh 4:47
down
Moses, ye w. have believed   Joh 5:46
me
he himself knew what he w. do   Joh 6:6
of the fishes as much as they   Joh 6:11
w.
w. come and take him by   Joh 6:15
force
for he w. and not walk in   Joh 7:1
Jewry
some of them w. have taken   Joh 7:44
him
ye w. do the works of   Joh 8:39
Abraham
God were your Father, ye w.   Joh 8:42
love me
wherefore w. ye hear it again   Joh 9:27
him, saying, Sir, we w. see   Joh 12:21
Jesus
if it were not so, I w. have   Joh 14:2
told you
If ye loved me, ye w.   Joh 14:28
rejoice, because
the world, the world w. love   Joh 15:19
his own
we w. not have delivered   Joh 18:30
him up
then w. my servants fight,   Joh 18:36
that I
he w. raise up Christ to sit on   Ac 2:30
his
of them where unto this w.   Ac 5:24
grow
he w. give it to him for a   Ac 7:5
possession
brethren w. have understood   Ac 7:25
that God
that God by his hand w.   Ac 7:25
deliver them
w. have set them at one again,   Ac 7:26
saying
To whom our fathers w. not   Ac 7:39
obey
that he w. come up and sit   Ac 8:31
with him

he w. not delay to come to them   Ac 9:38
very hungry, and w. have eaten   Ac 10:10
heart that w. cleave unto the Lord   Ac 11:23
Herod w. have brought him forth   Ac 12:6
w. have done sacrifice with the   Ac 14:13
Him w. Paul have to go forth with   Ac 16:3
sword, and w. have killed himself   Ac 16:27
w. know therefore what these things   Ac 17:20
reason w. that I should bear with you   Ac 18:14
when Paul w. have entered in unto   Ac 19:30
that he w. not adventure himself into   Ac 19:31
w. have made his defence unto the   Ac 19:33
he w. not spend the time in Asia   Ac 20:16
And when he w. not be persuaded   Ac 21:14
he w. have known the certainty   Ac 22:30
w. neither eat nor drink till they had   Ac 23:12
that ye w. enquire something more   Ac 23:15
ye w. enquire somewhat of him   Ac 23:20
when I w. have known the cause   Ac 23:28
w. have judged according to our   Ac 24:6
he w. send for him to Jerusalem   Ac 25:3
that he himself w. depart shortly   Ac 25:4
him whether he w. go to Jerusalem   Ac 25:20
I w. also hear the man myself   Ac 25:22
the beginning, if they w. testify   Ac 26:5
I w. to God, that not only thou   Ac 26:29
though they w. have cast anchors   Ac 27:30
examined me, w. have let me go   Ac 28:18
Now I w. not have you ignorant   Ro 1:13
good man some w. even dare to die   Ro 5:7
for what I w. that I do not   Ro 7:15
If then I do that which I w. not   Ro 7:16
For the good that I w. I do not   Ro 7:19
the evil which I w. not, that I do   Ro 7:19
Now if I do that I w. not, it is no   Ro 7:20
when I w. do good, evil is present   Ro 7:21
For I w. not, brethren, that ye   Ro 11:25
yet I w. have you wise unto that   Ro 16:19
they w. not have crucified the Lord   1Co 2:8
and I w. to God ye did reign   1Co 4:8
up, as though I w. not come to you   1Co 4:18
I w. that all men were even as I   1Co 7:7
I w. have you without carefulness   1Co 7:32
I w. not that ye should be ignorant   1Co 10:1
and I w. not that ye should have   1Co 10:20
I w. have you know, that the head   1Co 11:3
For if we w. judge ourselves, we   1Co 11:31
I w. not have you ignorant   1Co 12:1
I w. that ye all spake with tongues   1Co 14:5
For we w. not, brethren, have you   2Co 1:8
that I w. not come again to you in   2Co 2:1
you that ye w. confirm your love   2Co 2:8

not for that we w. be unclothed   2Co 5:4
intreaty, that we w. receive the gift   2Co 8:4
so he w. also finish in you the same   2Co 8:6
that they w. go before unto you   2Co 9:5
seem as if I w. terrify you by letters   2Co 10:9
W. to God ye could bear with me   2Co 11:1
For though I w. desire to glory   2Co 12:6
I shall not find you such as I w.   2Co 12:20
found unto you such as ye w. not   2Co 12:20
and w. pervert the gospel of Christ   Ga 1:7
they w. that we should remember the   Ga 2:10
This only w. I learn of you   Ga 3:2
foreseeing that God w. justify   Ga 3:8
w. have plucked out your own eyes   Ga 4:15
they w. exclude you, that ye w.   Ga 4:17
I w. they were even cut off which   Ga 5:12
cannot do the things that ye w.   Ga 5:17
That he w. grant you, according to   Eph 3:16
But I w. ye should understand   Ph'p 1:12
To whom God w. make known   Col 1:27
For I w. that ye knew what great   Col 2:1
that God w. open unto us a door of   Col 4:3
we w. not be chargeable unto any   1Th 2:9
That ye w. walk worthy of God, who   1Th 2:12
we w. have come unto you   1Th 2:18
God, so ye w. abound more and more   1Th 4:1
I w. not have you to be ignorant   1Th 4:13
our God w. count you worthy of this   2Th 1:11
that if any w. not work, neither let him eat   2Th 3:10
Whom I w. have retained with me   Ph'm 13
without thy mind w. I do nothing   Ph'm 14
then w. he not afterward have spoken   Heb 4:8
For then w. they not have ceased to be   Heb 10:2
the time w. fail me to tell of Gideon   Heb 11:32
he w. have inherited the blessing   Heb 12:17
w. no doubt have continued with us   1Jo 2:19
I w. not write with paper and ink   2Jo 12
forbiddeth them that w. and casteth   3Jo 10
hot: I w. thou wert cold or hot   Re 3:15
as many as w. not worship the image   Re 13:11

WOULDEST

and w. thou take away my sons   Ge 30:15
now, though thou w. needs be gone   Ge 31:30
thou w. take by force thy daughters   Ge 31:31
behold, hitherto thou w. not hear   Ex 7:16
burden, and w. forbear to help him   Ex 23:5
her, that thou w. have her to thy wife   De 21:11
thou w. keep his commandments   De 28:2
w. not obey the voice of the Lord thy   De 28:62
Caleb said unto her, What w. thou   Jos 15:18
w. not suffer the revengers of blood   2Sa 14:11

thyself w. have set thyself against me   2Sa 18:13
And the king said, What w. thou   1Ki 1:16
w. deliver thy servant into thy hand   1Ki 18:9
w. thou be spoken for to the king   2Ki 4:13
great thing, w. thou not have done it   2Ki 5:13
w. thou smite those whom thou hast   2Ki 6:22
Oh that thou w. bless me indeed, and   1Ch 4:10
and that thou w. keep me from evil   1Ch 4:10
that thou w. put thy name there   2Ch 6:20
whom thou w. not let Israel invade   2Ch 20:10
w. not thou be angry with us till thou   Ezr 9:14
that thou w. send me unto Judah   Ne 2:5
If thou w. seek into God betimes, and   Job 8:5
O that thou w. hide me in the grave   Job 14:13
that thou w. keep me secret, until thy   Job 14:13
that thou w. appoint me a set time   Job 14:13
that thou w. deal very treacherously   Isa 48:8
Oh that thou w. rend the heavens   Isa 64:1
that thou w. come down, that   Isa 64:1
w. send him to my father's house   Lu 16:27
w. have asked of him, and he would   Joh 4:10
if thou w. believe, thou shouldest   Joh 11:40
and walkest whither thou w.   Joh 21:18
carry thee whither thou w. not   Joh 21:18
thee that thou w. bring down Paul   Ac 23:20
thou w. hear us of thy clemency   Ac 24:4
Sacrifice and offering thou w. not   Heb 10:5
and offering for sin thou w. not   Heb 10:8

WOUND

burning, w. for w., stripe for stripe   Ex 21:25
I make alive; I w. and I heal   De 32:39
crush (A)   De 32:29
the blood ran out of the w.   1Ki 22:35
my w. is incurable without   Job 34:6
But God shall w. the head of   Ps 68:21
shatter the head (A)(R)   Ps 68:21
strike the head (B)(E)   Ps 68:21
he shall w. the heads over many   Ps 110:6
crush the chief heads (A)   Ps 110:6
A w. and dishonour shall be get   Pr 6:33
blueness of a w. cleaneth evil   Pr 20:30
and healeth the stroke of their w.   Isa 30:26
me for my hurt! my w. is grievous   Jer 10:19
with a very ugly w. (A)(R)   Jer 14:17
perpetual, and my w. incurable   Jer 15:18
incurable, and thy w. is grievous   Jer 30:12
thee with the w. of an enemy   Jer 30:14
sickness, and Judah saw his w.   Ho 5:13
heal you, nor cure you of your w.   Ho 5:13
bread have laid a w. under thee   Ob 7
her w. is incurable: for it is come   Mic 1:9
of thy bruise: thy w. is grievous   Na 3:19
and w. it in linen clothes with the   Joh 19:40
bound (A)(E)(R)   Joh 19:40
wrapped (B)(N)   Joh 19:40; Ac 5:6
the young men arose, w. him up   Ac 5:6
wrapped (E)(R)   Ac 5:6

WOUND

and w. their weak conscience, ye | 1Co 8:12
hurt (B) | 1Co 8:12
and his deadly w. was healed | Re 13:2
beast, whose deadly w. was healed | Re 13:12
which had the w. by a sword | Re 13:14

WOUNDED

man who w. me (S) | Ge 4:23
He that is w. in the stones | De 23:1
w. in his testicles (A) | De 23:1
crushed (B) | De 23:1
many were overthrown and w. | J'g 9:40
the w. of the Philistines fell down | 1Sa 17:52
he was sore w. of the archers | 1Sa 31:3
wounded (R) | 2Sa 10:18; 2Ch 22:5
consumed them, and w. them | 2Sa 22:39
so that in smiting he w. him | 1Ki 20:37
me out of the host; for I am w. | 1Ki 22:34
and the Syrians w. Joram | 2Ki 8:28
and he was w. of the archers | 1Ch 10:3
out of the host: for I am sore w. | 2Ch 18:33
the Syrians w. Joram (A)(B)(S) | 2Ch 22:5
leaving him severely w. (R) | 2Ch 24:25
Have me away; for I am w. | 2Ch 35:23
and the soul of the w. crieth out | Job 24:12
w. them that they were not able | Ps 18:38
smite them (E) | Ps 18:38
arrow: suddenly shall they be w. | Ps 64:7
grief of those whom thou hast w. | Ps 69:26
gossip about those w. (A) | Ps 69:26
smitten (E) | Ps 69:26; Re 13:3
and my heart is w. within me | Ps 109:22
pierced (B) | Ps 109:22; Isa 51:9; 53:5
stricken within me (R) | Ps 109:22
For she hath cast down many | Pr 7:26
but a w. spirit who can bear | Pr 18:14
a broken spirit (A)(B)(E)(R) | Pr 18:14
those that it w. (A)(E) | Pr 26:28
me, they smote me, they w. me | Ca 5:7
cut Rahab, and w. the dragon | Isa 51:9
pierce (E)(R) | Isa 51:9
he was w. for our transgressions | Isa 53:5
broken or w. spirit (A) | Isa 66:2
I have w. thee with the wound of | Jer 30:14
stricken (B) | Jer 30:14
there remained but w. men among | Jer 37:10
all her land the w. shall groan | Jer 51:52
swooned as the w. in the streets | La 2:12
sound of thy fall, when the w. cry | Eze 26:15
the w. shall be judged in the midst | Eze 28:23
groanings of a deadly w. man | Eze 30:24
the sword, they shall not be w. | Joe 2:8
was w. in the house of my friends | Zec 13:6
beaten (B) | Zec 13:6
and w. him in the head, and sent | M'k 12:4
w. him, and departed, leaving | Lu 10:30
pummeled (B) | Lu 10:30
beat him (E)(R) | Lu 10:30
and they w. him also, and cast | Lu 20:12
fled out of that house naked and w. | Ac 19:16
his heads as it were w. to death | Re 13:3

WOUNDEDST

thou w. the head out of the house | Hab 3:13

WOUNDETH

he w. and his hands make whole | Job 5:18

WOUNDING

for I have slain a man to my w. | Ge 4:23

WOUNDS

to be healed in Jezreel of the w. | 2Ki 8:29; 9:15
healed in Jezreel because of the w. (B) | 2Ch 22:6
leave him with many w. | 2Ch 24:25
multiplieth my w. without cause | Job 9:17
My w. stink and are corrupt | Ps 38:5
in heart, and bindeth up their w. | Ps 147:3
words of a talebearer are as w. | Pr 18:8
are dainty morsels (A)(E) | Pr 18:8; 26:22
are tempting morsels (B) | Pr 18:8
delicious morsels (R) | Pr 18:8
who hath w. without cause | Pr 23:29
words of a talebearer are as w. | Pr 26:22
delicious morsels (B)(R) | Pr 26:22
Faithful are the w. of a friend | Pr 27:6
but w. and bruises, and putrifying | Isa 1:6
bruises, welts, and raw w. (B)(R) | Isa 1:6
the w. of my people (B) | Isa 30:26
me continually is grief and w. | Jer 6:7
and I will heal thee of thy w. saith | Jer 30:17
What are these w. in thine hands | Zec 13:6
went to him, and bound up his w. | Lu 10:34

WOVE

women w. hangings for the grove | 2Ki 23:7

WOVEN

it shall have a binding of w. work | Ex 28:32
the robe of the ephod of w. work | Ex 39:22
of fine linen of w. work for Aaron | Ex 39:27
with w. strands (B) | Ps 118:27
seam, w. from the top throughout | Joh 19:23

WRANGLE

he shall not w. (R) | M't 12:19

WRANGLING

without w. (N) | Ph'p 2:14
envy, w., slander (B) | 1Ti 6:4
w. of men (A)(E)(N)(P)(R) | 1Ti 6:5

WRAP

than that he can w. himself in it | Isa 28:20
desire: so they w. it up | Mic 7:3

WRAPPED

her with a veil and w. herself | Ge 38:14
w. in a cloth behind the ephod | 1Sa 21:9
that he w. his face in his mantle | 1Ki 19:13
his mantle, and w. it together | 2Ki 2:8
His roots are w. about the heap | Job 8:17
the sinews of his stones are w. | Job 40:17
twisted like ropes (A) | Job 40:17
knit together (B)(E)(R) | Job 40:17
it is w. up for the slaughter | Eze 21:15
the weeds were w. about my head | Jon 2:5
he w. it in a clean linen cloth | M't 27:59
him down, and w. him in the linen | M'k 15:46
and w. him in swaddling clothes | Lu 2:7
the babe w. in swaddling clothes | Lu 2:12
it down, and w. it in linen | Lu 23:53
face w. in a (B)(N)(R) | Joh 11:44
w. in linen clothes (B)(N) | Joh 19:4; Ac 5:6
but w. together in a place by itself | Joh 20:7
w. his jacket about him (B)(N) | Joh 21:7
w. him up (E)(R)(S) | Ac 5:6

WRATH

cursed be their w. for it was cruel | Ge 49:7
anger (E) | Ge 49:7; 2Ch 29:10; Job 36:13; 37:8; Pr 14:29; 15:1; Isa 14:6; Jer 21:5; 32:37; 44:8
anger (R) | Ge 49:7; 2Sa 11:20; 2Ch 29:10; Es 2:1; 7:10; Job 36:13; Ps 37:8; Pr 14:29; 30:33; Isa 14:6; 44:8; Ga 5:20; Eph 4:26; 6:4; Col 3:8; 1Ti 2:8; Heb 11:27; Jas 1:19,20
lest w. come upon all the people | Le 10:6
indignation (B) | Le 10:6; Nu 1:53
that no w. be on congregation | Nu 1:53; 18:5
for there is w. gone out from the Lord | Nu 16:46
vengeance (B) | Nu 16:46
thou provokedst the Lord to w. | De 9:7; 9:22
anger (B) | De 9:7
Lord rooted them out in anger and w. | De 29:28
fury (B) | De 29:28
were it not I feared w. of the enemy | De 32:27
provocation (A)(E)(R) | De 32:27
taunt of the foe (B) | De 32:27
let them live, lest w. be upon us | Jos 9:20
and w. fell on all the congregation | Jos 22:20
if so be that the king's w. arise | 2Sa 11:20
anger (A) | 2Sa 11:20; 2Ch 28:13; 29:10; Job 36:13; 14:29; Pr 21:14; 27:4; Isa 14:6; Jer 44:8; Ro 9:22; Ga 5:20; Eph 6:4; 1Ti 2:8; Jas 1:20; Re 12:12
angry (B) | 2Sa 11:20; Eph 4:26; Jas 1:19
Lord turned not from great w. | 2Ki 23:26
anger (B) | 2Ki 23:26; 1Ch 27:24; 2Ch 19:10; 24:18; 28:13; 29:10; Es 2:1; 3:5; 7:10; Ps 37:8; Pr 14:29; 19:12; 21:14; 30:33; Jer 21:5; 32:37; Lu 21:23; Ro 2:5; Eph 4:31; 6:4; Col 3:8; 1Ti 2:8; Heb 11:27; Jas 1:20; Re 12:12
he finished not, because there fell w. | 1Ch 27:24
therefore is w. upon thee from Lord | 2Ch 19:2
indignation (B) | 2Ch 19:2; 32:25; Ezr 7:24; Job 21:20; 36:13; Eze 7:12; Zep 1:18; Zec 7:12; Ro 2:8; 4:15; 5:9; 9:22; Eph 2:3; 1Th 2:16; 5:9; Re 6:16
trespass not, and so w. come upon you | 2Ch 19:10
w. came upon Judah for this trespass | 2Ch 24:18
and there is fierce w. against Israel | 2Ch 28:13
that his fierce w. may turn from us | 2Ch 29:10
therefore there was w. upon him | 2Ch 32:25
our fathers had provoked God to w. | Ezr 5:12
why should there be w. against realm | Ezr 7:23
yet ye bring more w. upon Israel | Ne 13:18
thus shall there arise too much w. | Es 1:18
when the w. of the king was appeased | Es 2:1
Mordecai bowed not, Haman full of w. | Es 3:5
fury (R) | Es 3:5
was filled with w. (A)(E)(R) | Es 5:9
then was the king's w. pacified | Es 7:10
for w. killeth foolish man | Job 5:2
vexation and rage (A) | Job 5:2

vexation (E)   *Job 5:2; Pr 12:16; 27:3*

for *w*. brings punishments of *Job 19:29*
sword

he shall drink of *w*. of the   *Job 21:20*
Almighty

heap up *w*.

but the hypocrites in heart   *Job 36:13*
because there is *w*. beware *Ps 36:18*
lest he take

forsake *w*.   *Ps 37:8*

in *w*. they hate me   *Ps 55:3*

surely the *w*. of man shall *Ps 76:10*
praise the, the remainder of
w. shalt thou restrain

stretch thy hand against *w*. of *Ps 138:7*
enemies

the expectation of the wicked *Pr 11:23*
is *w*.

fool's *w*. presently known, but *Pr 12:16*
prudent

that is slow to *w*. is of great *Pr 14:29*
understanding

a soft answer turneth away *w*. *Pr 15:1*
but words

w. of a king is as messengers *Pr 16:14*
of death

the king's *w*. is as the roaring *Pr 19:12*
of a lion

a man of great *w*. suffer   *Pr 19:19*
punishment

a reward in bosom pacifieth *Pr 21:14*
strong *w*.

scorner who dealeth in proud *Pr 21:24*
w.

a fool's *w*. is heavier than   *Pr 27:3*
them both

w. is cruel, and anger is   *Pr 27:4*
outrageous

but wise men turn away *w*.   *Pr 29:8*

forcing of *w*. bringeth forth *Pr 30:33*
strife

he hath much *w*. with his   *Ec 5:17*
sickness

vexation (R)   *Ec 5:17*

the day of the Lord cometh *Isa 13:9*
with *w*.

he who smote people in *w*. *Isa 14:6*
with a stroke

in a little *w*. I hid my face *Isa 54:8*
from thee

I myself will fight against you *Jer 21:5*
in *w*.

whither I have driven them *Jer 32:37*
in great *w*.

in that ye provoke me to *w*. *Jer 44:8*
with idols

w. is on all the multitude *Eze 7:12*
thereof

and he reserveth *w*. for his *Na 1:2*
enemies

O Lord, in *w*. remember   *Hab 3:2*
mercy

gold shall not deliver in day *Zep 1:18*
of *w*.

therefore came a great *w*. *Zec 7:12*
from Lord

when your fathers provoked *Zec 8:14*
me to *w*.

to flee from *w*. to come *M't 3:7; Lu 3:7*

judgment (B)   *M't 3:7*

they were filled with *w*.   *Lu 4:28;*
                        Ac 19:28

rage (A)   *Lu 4:28*

for there shall be *w*. on this *Lu 21:23*
people

indignation, punishment,   *Lu 21:23*
retribution (A)

treasurest up *w*. against the *Ro 2:5*
day of *w*.

but to them that obey   *Ro 2:8*
unrighteousness, *w*.

anger and *w*. upon (P)   *Ro 2:9*

inflict his *w*. (A)(E)(R)   *Ro 3:5*

because law worketh *w*. where *Ro 4:15*
no law is

we shall be saved from *w*. *Ro 5:9*
through him

endured vessels of *w*. fitted to *Ro 9:22*
destruction

avenge not, but rather give *Ro 12:19*
place to *w*.

divine retribution (B)   *Ro 12:19*

he is the minister of God to *Ro 13:4*
execute *w*.

avenger of *w*. on him (E) *Ro 13:4*

must needs be subject, not only *Ro 13:15*
for *w*.

the works of the flesh are *w*. *Ga 5:20*
strife

---

we were by nature the   *Eph 2:3*
children of *w*.

let not the sun go down upon *Eph 4:26*
your *w*.

let all *w*., anger, and clamour *Eph 4:31*
be put away

fathers, provoke not your *Eph 6:4*
children to *w*.

put off all these, *w*., malice, *Col 3:8*
blasphemy

who delivered us from *w*. to *1Th 1:10*
come

retribution (B)   *1Th 1:10*

for *w*. is come on them to *1Th 2:16*
the uttermost

for God hath not appointed us *1Th 5:9*
to *w*.

lifting up holy hands without *1Ti 2:8*
w.

without *w*. (E)   *1Ti 2:8*

Moses not fearing the *w*. of *Heb 11:27*
the king

let every man be slow to   *Jas 1:19*
speak, slow to *w*.

w. of man worketh not   *Jas 1:20*
righteousness of God

and hide us from the *w*. of the *Re 6:16*
Lamb

devil is come down, having *Re 12:12*
great *w*.

made all nations drink wine of *Re 14:8;*
w.   18:3

WRATH *OF GOD*

the fierce *w*. *of God* is upon *2Ch 28:11*
you

indignation (B)   *2Ch 28:11;*
Ps 78:31; Ro 1:18; Eph 5:6; Re 14:10,
          19; 15:1; 16:1; 19:15

till *w*. *of God* be turned from *Ezr 10:14*
us

anger (B)   *Ezr 10:14*

the *w*. *of God* came upon *Ps 78:31*
them

anger (E)   *Ps 78:31*

but the *w*. *of God* abideth on *Joh 3:36*
him

w. *of God* is revealed from *Ro 1:18*
heaven

because of these things *w*. *of* *Eph 5:6;*
God cometh on children of *Col 3:6*
disobedience

shall drink of the wine of the *Re 14:10*
w. *of God*

and cast it into winepress of *Re 14:19*
the *w*. *of God*

for in them is filled up the *w*. *Re 15:1*
of God

seven golden vials full of the *Re 15:7*
w. *of God*

pour out the vials of *w*. *of God* *Re 16:1*
on earth

treadeth winepress of the *w*. *Re 19:15*
of God

DAY *OF* WRATH

goods flow away in *day of* *Job 20:28*
his *w*.

wicked brought forth to the *Job 21:30*
day of w.

Lord strike thro' kings in *day* *Ps 110:5*
of his w.

indignation (A)(B)   *Ps 110:5*

riches profit not in the *day* *Pr 11:4*
of w.

that day is a *day of w*. and *Zep 1:15*
trouble

treasurest up wrath again the *Ro 2:5*
day of w.

day of anger (B)   *Ro 2:5*

for the great *day* of his *w*. is *Re 6:17*
come

HIS WRATH

the Lord overthrew in *his w*. *De 29:23*

anger and indignation (B) *De 29:23*

nor executedst *his w*. upon *1Sa 28:18*
Amalek

indignation (B)   *1Sa 28:18;*
Ezr 8:22; Ps 2:5; 21:9; 78:38, 49;
                      Ro 9:22

the Lord turned not from *2Ki 23:26*
his w.

anger (B)   *2Ki 23:26;*
       2Ch 29:10; Job 20:23

his fierce *w*. may turn away *2Ch 29:10;*
                     30:8

---

his w. is against them that *Ezr 8:22*
forsake him

king arising from the banquet *Es 17:7*
in *his w*.

he teareth me in *his w*.   *Job 16:9*

God shall cast fury of *his w*. *Job 20:23*
on him

anger (R)   *Job 20:23; Pr 24:18*

then shall he speak to them in *Ps 2:5*
his w.

Lord shall swallow them up in *Ps 21:9*
his w.

he shall take them away in his *Ps 58:9*
w.

turned away anger, did not *Ps 78:38*
stir up all *his w*.

be cast on them the fierceness *Ps 78:49*
of *his w*.

had not Moses stood to turn *Ps 106:23*
away *his w*.

his w. against him that   *Pr 14:35*
causeth shame

lest the Lord turn away *his* *Pr 24:18*
w. from him

we heard of Moab's pride and *Isa 16:6*
his w.

Lord hath forsaken generation *Jer 7:29*
of *his w*.

at *his w*. the earth shall   *Jer 10:10*
tremble

I know *his w*., saith the Lord, *Jer 48:30*
shall not be so

hath thrown down in *his w*. *La 2:2*
the holds

I have seen affliction by the *La 3:1*
rod of *his w*.

because he kept *his w*. for *Am 1:11*
ever

what if God willing to shew *Ro 9:22*
his w.

the cup of wine of fierceness *Re 16:19*
of *his w*.

MY WRATH

my w. shall wax hot, I will *Ex 22:24*
kill you

indignation (B)   *Ex 22:24;*
32:10; Nu 25:11 ; Ps 95:11; Isa 10:6;
Eze 7:14; 22:31; 38:19; Ho 5:10;
                      Heb 3:11

let me alone, that *my w*. may *Ex 32:10*
wax hot

Phinehas hath turned *my w*. *Nu 25:11*
away

my w. shall not be poured out *2Ch 12:7*
on Jerusalem

anger (B) *2Ch 12:7; Ho 13:11; Heb 4:3*

unto whom I sware in *my w*. *Ps 95:11*

anger (R)   *Ps 95:11*

send him against the people of *Isa 10:6*
my w.

in *my w*. I smote thee, but *Isa 60:10*
had mercy

for *my w*. is on all the   *Eze 7:14*
multitude

thus will I accomplish *my w*. *Exe 13:15*
on the wall

blow against thee in fire of *Eze 21:31;*
my w.   22:21

I consumed them with the *Eze 22:31*
fire of *my w*.

for in the fire of *my w*. have *Eze 38:19*
I spoken

I will pour out *my w*. on   *Ho 5:10*
them

a king, and I took him away *Ho 13:11*
in *my w*.

I sware in *my w*. they shall *Heb 3:11*
not enter

as I have sworn in *my w*. if *Heb 4:3*
they enter

THY WRATH

sentest *thy w*. which consumed *Ex 15:7*
them

indignation (A)   *Ex 15:7;*
32:11; Ps 38:1; 85:3; 88:7; 102:10;
                     Re 11:18

fury (A)(R)   *Ex 15:7*

why doth *thy w*. wax hot *Ex 32:11*
against people

turn from *thy* fierce *w*. and *Ex 32:12*
repent of this

anger (A)   *Ex 32:12;*
Ps 85:3; 88:16; 90:7, 11; Jer 18:20;
                     Hab 3:8

keep me secret until *thy w*. *Job 14:13*
be past

cast abroad the rage of *thy*   *Job 40:11*
w.
anger (E)   *Job 40:11*
anger (R)   *Job 40:11;*
  Ps 38:1; 79:6; 102:10
O Lord, rebuke me not in *thy*   *Ps 38:1*
w.
pour out *thy w.* on the heathen   *Ps 79:6*
fury (A)   *Ps 79:6*
thou hast taken away all *thy*   *Ps 85:3*
w.
thy w. lieth hard on me   *Ps 88:7*
thy fierce *w.* goeth over me,   *Ps 88:16*
thy terrors
how long shall *thy w.* burn   *Ps 89:46*
like fire
and by *thy w.* are we troubled   *Ps 90:7*
for all our days are passed   *Ps 90:9*
away in *thy w.*
even according to thy fear, so   *Ps 90:11*
is *thy w.*
because of thy indignation   *Ps 102:10*
and *thy w.*
I stood to turn away *thy w.*   *Jer 18:20*
from them
was *thy w.* against the sea   *Hab 3:8*
thy w. is come   *Re 11:18*

WRATHFUL

thy w. anger take hold of   *Ps 69:24*
them
indignation (A)(B)(E)(R)   *Ps 69:24*
A *w.* man stirreth up strife   *Pr 15:18*
anger (A)(B)(R)   *Pr 15:18*
w. man (A)(B)(E)(R)   *Pr 22:24; 29:22*

WRATHS

debates, envyings, *w.*, strifes   *2Co 12:20*

WREATH

rows of pomegranates on   *2Ch 4:13*
each *w.*
network (A)(B)(E)(R)   *2Ch 4:13*
give head a *w.* of gracefulness   *Pr 4:9*
(A)
city full of *w.* of judgment (E)   *Eze 9:9*
win a *w.* (A)(N)(R)   *1Co 9:25*
victor's *w.* (A)   *1Th 2:19*

WREATHED

they are *w.* and come up upon   *La 1:14*
twined (A)   *La 1:14*
woven tight (B)   *La 1:14*
knit together (E)   *La 1:14*
fastened together (R)   *La 1:14*

WREATHEN

of *w.* work shalt thou make   *Ex 28:14*
them
twisted like cords (A)(R)   *Ex 28:14;*
  28:22; 39:17, 18
twined chains (B)   *Ex 28:14;*
  28:22, 25; 39:15
fasten the *w.* chains to the   *Ex 28:14*
ouches
the ends of *w.* work of pure   *Ex 28:22*
gold
shalt put the two *w.* chains   *Ex 28:24*
of gold
twisted (A)   *Ex 28:24; 28:25; 39:15*
of the two *w.* chains thou   *Ex 28:25*
shalt
the ends, of *w.* work of pure   *Ex 39:15*
gold
they put the two *w.* chains of   *Ex 39:17*
gold
of the two *w.* chains they   *Ex 39:18*
fastened
the *w.* work, and   *2Ki 25:17*
pomegranates
had the second pillar with *w.*   *2Ki 25:17*
work
network (A)(B)(E)(R)   *2Ki 25:17*

WREATHS

w. of chain work, for the   *1Ki 7:17*
chapiters
two *w.* to cover the two   *2Ch 4:12*
pommels
network (A)(B)(E)(R)   *2Ki 4:12; 4:13*
hundred pomegranates   *2Ch 4:13*
on two *w.*

WRECK

day of *w.* and devastation   *Zep 1:15*
(B)

WRENCHED

chains *w.* away (A)(R)   *M'k 5:4*

WREST

after many to *w.* judgment   *Ex 23:2*
shalt not *w.* the judgment of   *Ex 23:6*
thy
Thou shalt not *w.* judgment;   *De 16:19*
thou
not *w.* justice due the   *De 24:17*
sojourner of fatherless (A)(E)(R)
Every day they *w.* my words   *Ps 56:5*
W. property from (B)   *Eze 46:18*
are unlearned and unstable *w.*   *2Pe 3:16*

WRESTLE

I *w.* with my torments (B)   *Job 30:18*
For we *w.* not against flesh   *Eph 6:12*

WRESTLED

have I *w.* with my sister, and   *Ge 30:8*
there *w.* a man with him   *Ge 32:24*
until the
was out of joint, as he *w.*   *Ge 32:25*
with him

WRESTLING

w. for you in prayers (B)   *Col 4:12*

WRESTLINGS

With great *w.* have I wrestled   *Ge 30:8*

WRETCHED

O *w.* man that I am! who shall   *Ro 7:24*
be *w.* (R)   *Jas 4:9*
and knowest not that thou are   *Re 3:17*
w.

WRETCHEDNESS

sight; and let me not see my   *Nu 11:15*
w.

WRING

w. off his head, and burn it on   *Le 1:15*
and *w.* off his head from his   *Le 5:8*
neck
of the earth shall *w.* them out   *Ps 75:8*

WRINGED

and *w.* the dew out of the   *J'g 6:38*
fleece

WRINGING

the *w.* of the nose bringeth   *Pr 30:33*
forth

WRINKLE

spot, or *w.* or any such thing   *Eph 5:27*

WRINKLES

And thou hast filled me with   *Job 16:8*
w.

WRISTS

bracelets for her *w.* (S)   *Ge 24:22;*
  24:30, 47

WRITE

W. this for a memorial in a   *Ex 17:14*
book
will *w.* upon these tables the   *Ex 34:1*
words
unto Moses, *W.* thou these   *Ex 34:27*
words
priest shall *w.* these curses in   *Nu 5:23*
a
w. thou every man's name   *Nu 17:2*
upon
w. Aaron's name upon the   *Nu 17:3*
rod of

thou shalt *w.* them upon the   *De 6:9*
posts
I will *w.* on the tables the   *De 10:2*
words
shalt *w.* them upon the door   *De 11:20*
posts
he shall *w.* a copy of   *De 17:18*
this law
w. her a bill of divorcement   *De 24:1;*
  24:3
shall *w.* upon them all the   *De 27:3*
words
w. upon the stones all the   *De 27:8*
words
therefore *w.* ye this song for   *De 31:19*
you
the prophet, the son of   *2Ch 26:22*
Amoz, *w.*
we might *w.* the names of the   *Ezr 5:10*
men
make a sure covenant, and *w.*   *Ne 9:38*
it
W. ye also for the Jews, as it   *Es 8:8*
w. them upon the table of thine   *Pr 3:3;*
  7:3
and *w.* in it with a man's pen   *Isa 8:1*
that *w.* grievousness which   *Isa 10:1*
they
be few, that a child may *w.*   *Isa 10:19*
them
go, *w.* it before them in a   *Isa 30:8*
table
another shall *w.* with the   *Isa 44:5*
hand (S)
W. ye this man childless, a   *Jer 22:30*
man
W. thee all the words that I   *Jer 30:2*
have
parts, and *w.* it in their   *Jer 31:33*
hearts
w. therein all the words that I   *Jer 36:2*
have
How didst thou *w.* all these   *Jer 36:17*
words
w. in it all the former words   *Jer 36:28*
that
man, *w.* thee the name of the   *Eze 24:2*
day
take ye one stick, and *w.*   *Eze 37:16*
upon it
take another stick, and *w.*   *Eze 37:16*
upon it
w. it in their sight, that they   *Eze 43:11*
may
W. the vision, and make it   *Hab 2:2*
plain
to *w.* a bill of divorcement   *M'k 10:4*
very first, to *w.* unto thee in   *Lu 1:3*
order
and sit down quickly, and *w.*   *Lu 16:6*
fifty
Take thy bill, and *w.* fourscore   *Lu 16:7*
in the law, and the prophets,   *Joh 1:45*
did *w.*
W. not, The King of the   *Joh 19:21*
Jews
But that we *w.* unto them,   *Ac 15:20*
that
I have no certain thing to *w.*   *Ac 25:26*
had, I might have somewhat   *Ac 25:26*
to *w.*
I *w.* not these things to   *1Co 4:14*
shame you
that the things that I *w.*   *1Co 14:37*
unto you
we *w.* none others things unto   *2Co 1:13*
you
For to this end also did I *w.*   *2Co 2:9*
that I
is superfluous for me to *w.* to   *2Co 9:1*
you
I *w.* to them which   *2Co 13:2*
heretofore have
I *w.* these things being   *2Co 13:10*
absent, lest
the things which I *w.* unto   *Ga 1:20*
you
To *w.* the same things to you   *Ph'p 3:1*
ye need not that I *w.* unto you   *1Th 4:9*
have no need that I *w.* unto   *1Th 5:1*
token in every epistle: so I   *2Th 3:17*
w.
These things *w.* I unto thee   *1Ti 3:14*
mind, and *w.* them in their   *Heb 8:10*
hearts
and in their minds will I *w.*   *Heb 10:16*
them
beloved, I now *w.* unto you   *2Pe 3:1*

And these things w., we unto you   *1Jo 1:4*
these things w. I unto you, that ye sin not   *1Jo 2:1*
I w. no new commandment unto   *1Jo 2:7*
new comandment I w. unto you   *1Jo 2:8*
I w. unto you, little children   *1Jo 2:12*
I w. unto you, fathers, because ye   *1Jo 2:13*
I w. unto you, young men, because   *1Jo 2:13*
I w. unto you, little children   *1Jo 2:13*
Having many things to w. unto you   *2Jo 12*
I would not w. with paper and ink   *2Jo 12*
I had many things to w. but I will   *3Jo 13*
not with ink and pen w. unto thee   *3Jo 13*
to w. unto you of the common   *Jude 3*
needful for me to w. unto you   *Jude 3*
What thou seest, w. in a book   *Re 1:11*
W. the things which thou hast   *Re 1:19*
angel of the church of Ephesus w.   *Re 2:1*
angel of the church in Smyrna w.   *Re 2:8*
of the church in Pergamos w.   *Re 2:12*
angel of the church in Thyatira w.   *Re 2:18*
angel of the church in Sardis w.   *Re 3:1*
of the church in Philadelphia w.   *Re 3:7*
I will w. upon him the name of my   *Re 3:12*
I will w. upon him my new name   *Re 3:12*
the church of the Laodiceans w.   *Re 3:14*
their voices, I was about to w.   *Re 10:4*
thunders uttered, and w. them not   *Re 10:4*
W., Blessed are the dead which die   *Re 14:13*
W., Blessed are they which are   *Re 19:9*
W. for these words are true   *Re 21:5*

WRITER

they that handle the pen of the w.   *J'g 5:14*
my tongue is the pen of a ready w.   *Ps 45:1*
writer (P)   *Col 1:20*

WRITER'S

with a w. inkhorn by his side   *Eze 9:2*
had the w. inkhorn by his side   *Eze 9:3*

WRITES

Moses w. (A)(E)(N)(P)(R)   *Ro 4:6*

WRITEST

thou w. bitter things against me   *Job 13:26*
sticks whereon thou w. shall be in   *Eze 37:20*

WRITETH

count, when he w. up the people   *Ps 87:6*

WRITHE

w. and groan like a woman (B)(R)   *Mic 4:10*
I w. in pain (A)(B)(R)   *Jer 4:19*

WRITHED

never w. in childbirth (B)   *Isa 54:1*

WRITHES

w. in anguish (B)   *Jer 51:29*

WRITING

the w. was the w. of God, graven   *Ex 32:16*
pure gold, and wrote upon it a w.   *Ex 39:30*
according to the first w. the ten   *De 10:4*

an end of w. the words of this law   *De 31:24*
Lord made me understand in w.   *1Ch 28:19*
the king of Tyre answered in w.   *2Ch 2:11*
came a w. to him from Elijah the   *2Ch 21:12*
to the w. of David king of Israel   *2Ch 35:4*
to the w. of Solomon his son   *2Ch 35:4*
his kingdom, and put it also in w.   *2Ch 36:22;*
   Ezr 1:1
w. of the letter was written in   *Ezr 4:7*
every province according to the w.   *Es 1:22;*
   3:12
copy of the w. for a commandment   *Es 3:14*
the copy of the w. of the decree   *Es 4:8*
w. which is written in the king's   *Es 8:8*
every province according to the w.   *Es 8:9*
to the Jews according to their w.   *Es 8:9*
copy of the w. for a commandment   *Es 8:13*
two days according to their w.   *Es 9:27*
w. of Hezekiah king of Judah   *Isa 38:9*
in the w. of the house of Israel   *Eze 13:9*
Whosoever shall read this w.   *Da 5:7*
but they could not read the w.   *Da 5:8*
that they should read this w.   *Da 5:15*
now if thou canst read the w.   *Da 5:16*
I will read the w. unto the king   *Da 5:17*
from him; and this w. was written   *Da 5:24*
And this is the w. that was written   *Da 5:25*
the decree, and sign the w.   *Da 6:8*
king Darius signed the w. and   *Da 6:9*
Daniel knew that the w. was signed   *Da 6:10*
w. or book of truth (A)(B)(E)(R)   *Da 10:21*
let him give her a w. of divorcement   *M't 5:31*
to give a w. of divorcement, and to   *M't 19:7*
And he asked for a w. table   *Lu 1:63*
And the w. was, Jesus Of Nazareth   *Joh 19:19*

WRITINGS

if ye believe not his w. how shall   *Joh 5:47*
our w. (P)   *2Th 2:16*

WRITTEN

commandments which I have w.   *Ex 24:12*
stone, w. with the finger of God   *Ex 31:18*
tables were w. on both their sides   *Ex 32:15*
and on the other were they w.   *Ex 32:15*
out of thy book which thou hast w.   *Ex 32:32*
they were of them that were w.   *Nu 11:26*
stone w. with the finger of God   *De 9:10*
was w. according to all the words   *De 9:10*
this law that are w. in this book   *De 28:58*
is not w. in the book of this law   *De 28:61*
the curses that are w. in this book   *De 29:20*
covenant that are w. in this book   *De 29:21*
the curses that are w. in this book   *De 29:27*
statutes which are w. in this book   *De 30:10*
according to all that is w. therein   *Jos 1:8*
as it is w. in the book of the law of   *Jos 8:31*
all that is w. in the book of the law   *Jos 8:34*
not this w. in the book of Jashar   *Jos 10:13*
all that is w. in the book of the law   *Jos 23:6*
it is w. in the book of Jasher   *2Sa 1:18*

as it is w. in the law of Moses   *1Ki 2:3*
not w. in the book of the acts of   *1Ki 11:41*
w. in the book of the   *1Ki 14:19;*
chronicles   *14:29; 15:7, 23, 31; 16:5, 14, 20, 27, 22:39, 45; Ne 12:23; Es 2:3*
as it was w. in the letters which   *1Ki 21:11*
not w. in the book of the   *2Ki 1:18;*
chronicles   *8:23; 10:34; 12:19; 13:8, 12; 14:15, 18, 28; 15:6, 11, 15, 21, 26, 31, 36; 16:19; 20:20; 21:17, 25; 23:28; 24:5*
which is w. in the book of the law   *2Ki 14:6*
all that which is w. concerning us   *2Ki 22:13*
covenant that were w. in this book   *2Ki 23:3*
w. in the book of this covenant   *2Ki 23:21*
which were w. in the book of Hilkiah   *2Ki 23:24*
these w. by name came in the days   *1Ch 4:41*
were w. in the book of the kings of   *1Ch 9:1*
that is w. in the law of the Lord   *1Ch 16:40*
w. in the book of Samuel the seer   *1Ch 29:29*
not w. in the book of Nathan the   *2Ch 9:29*
not w. in the book of Shemaiah the   *2Ch 12:15*
w. in the story of the prophet Iddo   *2Ch 13:22*
w. in the book of the kings of Judah   *2Ch 16:11*
they are w. in the book of Jehu   *2Ch 20:34*
as it is w. in the law of Moses   *2Ch 23:18*
are w. in the story of the book   *2Ch 24:27*
w. in the law in the book of Moses   *2Ch 25:4*
w. in the book of the kings of Judah   *2Ch 25:26; 28:26*
w. in the book of the kings of Israel   *2Ch 27:7*
long time in such sort as it was w.   *2Ch 30:5*
passover otherwise than it was w.   *2Ch 30:18*
as it is w. in the law of the Lord   *2Ch 31:3*
they are w. in the vision of Isaiah   *2Ch 32:32*
w. in the book of the kings of Israel   *2Ch 33:18*
w. among the sayings of the seers   *2Ch 33:19*
do after all that is w. in this book   *2Ch 34:21*
the curses that are w. in this book   *2Ch 34:24*
covenant which are w. in this book   *2Ch 34:31*
as it is w. in the book of Moses   *2Ch 35:12*
they are w. in the lamentations   *2Ch 35:25*
was w. in the law of the Lord   *2Ch 35:26*
w. in the book of the kings   *2Ch 35:27;*
of Israel   *36:8*
as it is w. in the law of Moses   *Ezr 3:2*
feast of tabernacles, as it is w.   *Ezr 3:4*
letter was w. in the Syrian tongue   *Ezr 4:7*
was w. thus; Unto Darius the   *Ezr 5:7*
a roll, and therein was a record w.   *Ezr 6:2*
as it is w. in the book of Moses   *Ezr 6:18*
the weight was w. at that time   *Ezr 8:34*
Wherein was w. It is reported   *Ne 6:6*
at the first, and found w. therein   *Ne 7:5*
found w. in the law which the Lord   *Ne 8:14*
trees, to make booths, as it is w.   *Ne 8:15*
Lord our God, as it is w. in the law   *Ne 10:34*
of our cattle, as it is w. in the law   *Ne 10:36*
and therein was found w. that   *Ne 13:1*

w. among the laws of the Persians	Es 1:19
it be w. that they may be destroyed	Es 3:9
w. according to all that Haman had	Es 3:12
name of king Ahasuerus was it	Es 3:12
it was found w. that Mordecai	Es 6:2
let it be w. to reverse the letters	Es 8:5
which is w. in the king's name	Es 8:8
w. according to all that Mordecai	Es 8:9
as Mordecai had w. unto them	Es 9:23
Purim; and it was w. in the book	Es 9:32
not w. in the book of the chronicles	Es 10:2
Oh that my words were now w.	Job 19:23
that mine adversary had w. a book	Job 31:35
volume of the book it is w. of me	Ps 40:7
and not be w. with the righteous	Ps 69:28
be w. for the generation to come	Ps 102:18
thy book all my members were w.	Ps 139:16
upon them the judgment w.	Ps 149:9
not I w. to thee excellent things	Pr 22:20
that which was w. was upright	Ec 12:10
one that is w. among the living	Isa 4:3
it is w. before me: I will not keep	Isa 65:6
sin of Judah is w. with a pen	Jer 17:1
from me shall be w. in the earth	Jer 17:13
even all that is w. in this book	Jer 25:13
thou hast w. from my mouth	Jer 36:6
saying, Why hast thou w. therein	Jer 36:29
when he had w. these words in	Jer 45:1
words that are w. against Babylon	Jer 51:60
and it was w. within and without	Eze 2:10
there was w. therein lamentations	Eze 2:10
neither shall they be w. in the	Eze 13:9
him; and this writing was w.	Da 5:24
And this is the writing that was w.	Da 5:25
oath that is w. in the law of Moses	Da 9:11
As it is w. in the law of Moses, all	Da 9:13
that shall be found w. in the book	Da 12:1
I have w. to him the great things	Ho 8:12
and a book of remembrance was w.	Mal 3:16
for thus it is w. by the prophet	M't 2:5
It is w., Man shall not live by	M't 4:4
for it is w., He shall give his angels	M't 4:6
It is w. again, Thou shalt not tempt	M't 4:7
for it is w., Thou shalt worship	M't 4:10
For this is he, of whom it is w.	M't 11:10
It is w., My house shall be called	M't 21:13
Son of man goeth as it is w. of him	M't 26:24
it is w., I will smite the shepherd	M't 26:31
up over his head his accusation w.	M't 27:37
As it is w. in the prophets, Behold	M'k 1:2
it is w., This people honoureth me	M'k 7:6
how it is w. of the Son of man, that	M'k 9:12
they listed, as it is w. of him	M'k 9:13
it not w., My house shall be called	M'k 11:17
indeed goeth as it is w. of him	M'k 14:21
it is w., I will smite the shepherd	M'k 14:27
of his accusation was w. over	M'k 15:26
(As it is w. in the law of the Lord	Lu 2:23
As it is w. in the book of the words	Lu 3:4
It is w., That man shall not live by	Lu 4:4
it is w., Thou shalt worship the	Lu 4:8
it is w., He shall give his angels	Lu 4:10
he found the place where it was w.	Lu 4:17
This is he, of whom it is w., Behold	Lu 7:27
your names are w. in heaven	Lu 10:20
What is w. in the law? how readest	Lu 10:26
things that are w. by the prophets	Lu 18:31
It is w., My house is the house of	Lu 19:46
said, What is this then that is w.	Lu 20:17
that all things w. may be fulfilled	Lu 21:22
that is w. must yet be accomplished	Lu 22:37
a superscription was w. over him	Lu 23:38
which were w. in the law of Moses	Lu 24:44
is w. and thus it behoved Christ	Lu 24:46
remembered that it was w.	Joh 2:17
as it is w., He gave them bread	Joh 6:31
It is w. in the prophets, And	Joh 6:45
It is also w. in your law, that	Joh 8:17
Is it not w. in your law, I said, Ye	Joh 10:34
young ass, sat thereon; as it is w.	Joh 12:14
that these things were w. of him	Joh 12:16
be fulfilled that is w. in their law	Joh 15:25
it was w. in Hebrew, and Greek	Joh 19:20
What I have w. I have w.	Joh 19:22
which are not w. in this book	Joh 20:30
these are w. that ye might believe	Joh 20:31
if they should be w. every one, I	Joh 21:25
the books that should be w.	Joh 21:25
it is w. in the book of Psalms	Ac 1:20
it is w. in the book of the prophets	Ac 7:42
had fulfilled all that was w. of him	Ac 13:29
it is also w. in the second psalm	Ac 13:33
words of the prophets; as it is w.	Ac 15:15
we have w. and concluded that	Ac 21:25
for it is w., Thou shalt not speak	Ac 23:5
all things which are w. in the law	Ac 24:14
as it is w., The just shall live by	Ro 1:17
work of the law w. in their hearts	Ro 2:15
Gentiles through you, as it is w.	Ro 2:24
but every man a liar; as it is w.	Ro 3:4
it is w., There is none righteous	Ro 3:10
As it is w., I have made thee a	Ro 4:17
it was not w. for his sake alone	Ro 4:23
not under old code of w. regulations(A)	Ro 7:6
As it is w., For thy sake we are	Ro 8:36
As it is w., Jacob have I loved	Ro 9:13
As it is w., Behold, I lay in Sion a	Ro 9:33
it is w., How beautiful are the feet	Ro 10:15
(According as it is w., God hath	Ro 11:8
as it is w., There shall come out of	Ro 11:26
for it is w., Vengeance is mine	Ro 12:19
For it is w., As I live, saith	Ro 14:11
as it is w., The reproaches of them	Ro 15:3
For whatsoever things were w.	Ro 15:4
were w. for our learning, that we	Ro 15:4
as it is w., For this cause I will	Ro 15:9
I have w. the more boldly unto you	Ro 15:15
But as it is w., To whom he was not	Ro 15:21
it is w. I will destroy the wisdom	1Co 1:19
as it is w., He that glorieth	1Co 1:31
But as it is w., Eye hath not seen	1Co 2:9
For it is w., He taketh the wise in	1Co 3:19
of men above that which is w.	1Co 4:6
w. unto you not to keep company	1Co 5:11
For it is w. in the law of Moses	1Co 9:9
For our sakes, no doubt, this is w.	1Co 9:10
neither have I w. these things	1Co 9:15
as it is w., The people sat down to	1Co 10:7
they are w. for our admonition	1Co 10:11
In the law it is w., With men of	1Co 14:21
so it is w., The first man Adam was	1Co 15:45
to pass the saying that is w.	1Co 15:54
Ye are our epistle w. in our hearts	2Co 3:2
ministered by us, w. not with ink	2Co 3:3
w. and engraven in stones	2Co 3:7
according as it is w. I believed	2Co 4:13
As it is w., He that had gathered	2Co 8:15
(As it is w., He hath dispersed	2Co 9:9
for it is w. Cursed is every one	Ga 3:10
which are w. in the book of the law	Ga 3:10
for it is w., Cursed is every one	Ga 3:13
is w. that Abraham had two sons	Ga 4:22
For it is w. Rejoice, thou barren	Ga 4:27
large a letter I have w. unto you	Ga 6:11
I Paul have w. it with mine own	Ph'm 19
volume of the book it is w. of me	Heb 10:7
firstborn, which are w. in heaven	Heb 12:23
w. a letter unto you in a few words	Heb 13:22
Because it is w., Be ye holy	1Pe 1:16
I have w. briefly, exhorting	1Pe 5:12
given unto him hath w. unto you	2Pe 3:15
I have w. unto you, fathers	1Jo 2:14
I have w. unto you, young men	1Jo 2:14
I have not w. unto you, because ye	1Jo 2:21
These things have I w. unto you	1Jo 2:26; 5:13
those things which are w. therein	Re 1:3
and in the stone a new name w.	Re 2:17
book w. within and on the backside	Re 5:1
names are not w. in the book of life	Re 13:8
Father's name w. in their foreheads	Re 14:1
upon her forehead was a name w.	Re 17:5
names not w. in the book of life	Re 17:8
had a name w. that no man knew	Re 19:12
and on his thigh a name w.	Re 19:16
things which were w. in the books	Re 20:12
was not found w. in the book of life	Re 20:15
and names w. thereon, which are	Re 21:12
are w. in the Lamb's book of life	Re 21:27

plagues that are *w.* in this   Re 22:18
book
things which are *w.* in this   Re 22:19
book

WRONG

unto Abram, My *w.* be upon   Ge 16:5
thee
proposal seemed very *w.* (B)   Ge 21:11
did me much *w.* (A)   Ge 43:6
he said to him that did the *w.*   Ex 2:13
neither *w.* a stranger   Ex 22:21
(A)(E)(R)
not do him *w.* (E)(R)   Le 19:33
do not *w.* in judgment (R)   Le 19:35
against him that which is *w.*   De 19:16
doest me *w.* to war against   J'g 11:27
me
found nothing *w.* (B)   1Sa 29:3
your servant did *w.* (R)   2Sa 19:19
have sinned and done *w.* (B)   1Ki 8:47
I have done *w.* (A)(B)(R)   2Ki 18:14
there is no *w.* in mine hands   1Ch 12:17
suffered no man to do them   1Ch 16:21
w.
we have done *w.* (A)   2Ch 6:37
you have done *w.* (R)   2Ch 26:18
the queen hath not done *w.* to   Es 1:16
charged God of doing *w.*   Job 1:22
(B)(R)
Behold, I cry out of *w.* but I   Job 19:7
am
regards not *w.* done them   Job 24:12
(A)
declared him to be *w.*   Job 32:3
(A)(B)(R)
put me in the *w.* (R)   Job 40:8
without any *w.* (B)   Ps 59:4
avenger of *w.* doings (R)   Ps 99:8
suffered no man to do them   Ps 105:14
w.
mind utter things turned the   Pr 23:33
w. way (A)
wilfully goes in double and *w.*   Pr 28:6
ways (A)
and do no *w.* do no violence   Jer 22:3
and his chambers by *w.*   Jer 22:13
what *w.* have I done (B)(R)   Jer 37:18
O Lord, thou hast seen my *w.*   La 3:59
w. judgment proceedeth   Hab 1:4
Friend, I do thee no *w.*:   M't 20:13
didst not
And seeing one of them suffer   Ac 7:24
w.
why do ye *w.* one to another   Ac 7:26
he that did his neighbour *w.*   Ac 7:27
thrust
matter of *w.* or wicked   Ac 18:14
lewdness
have committed nothing *w.*   Ac 25:8
(B)
to the Jews have I done no   Ac 25:10
w.
is God unjust and *w.* (A)(B)   Ro 3:5
love cannot *w.* a (N)(R)   Ro 13:10
Why do ye not rather take *w.*   1Co 6:7
Nay, ye do *w.* and defraud,   1Co 6:8
and that
for his cause that had done   2Co 7:12
the *w.*
for his cause that suffered *w.*   2Co 7:12
to you? forgive me this *w.*   2Co 12:13
ye did me no *w.*   Ga 4:12
(A)(B)(E)(N)(R)
do something *w.* (N)   Ga 6:1
But he that doeth *w.* shall   Col 3:25
receive
for the *w.* which he hath   Col 3:25
done
w. his brother (E)(N)(R)   1Th 4:6
put the whole word in *w.* (N)   Heb 11:7
all of us often go *w.*, the man   Jas 3:2
who never says a *w.* is (N)
as an excuse for doing *w.*   1Pe 2:16
(P)
if you do *w.* (A)(B)(N)(R)   1Pe 2:20
suffering *w.* as the hire of   2Pe 2:13
wrong doing (E)(R)
take pay for doing *w.* (N)   2Pe 2:13
every *w.* is sin (B)   1Jo 5:17

WRONGDOER

sentencing the *w.* (B)   1Ki 8:32
if then I am a *w.* (A)(E)(R)   Ac 25:11
the wrongdoer (B)   Re 22:11

WRONGDOING

restitution for *w.* (A)(B)(R)   Nu 5:7
crime or *w.* (B)(R)   Ac 18:14
our *w.* (B)   Ro 3:5
merciful toward their *w.* (B)   Heb 8:12
a screen for *w.* (N)(P)   1Pe 2:16
loved the hire of *w.* (E)(R)   2Pe 2:13
all *w.* is sin (A)(N)(R)   1Jo 5:17

WRONGED

whom have I *w.* (B)(P)   1Sa 12:3; 12:4
hath *w.* none (A)   Eze 18:7; 18:12
w. the fatherless (A)(R)   Eze 22:7
we have *w.* no man, we have   2Co 7:2
If he hath *w.* thee, or oweth   Ph'm 18
thee

WRONGETH

against me *w.* his own soul   Pr 8:36

WRONGFULLY

which ye *w.* imagine against   Job 21:27
me
mine enemies *w.* rejoice over   Ps 35:19
me
that hate me *w.* are   Ps 38:19
multiplied
being mine enemies *w.* are   Ps 69:4
overthrown me *w.* (E)   Ps 119:78
they persecute me *w.* help   Ps 119:86
thou
he deals *w.* (R)   Isa 26:10
oppressed the stranger *w.*   Eze 22:29
Edom hath acted *w.* (B)   Eze 25:12
ram on the *w.* (A)   M't 5:45
accusing *w.* (A)   Lu 3:14
God endure grief, suffering *w.*   1Pe 2:19

WRONGS

w. his neighbor (B)   1Ki 8:31
your *w.* passed (B)   Na 3:19
if a brother *w.* you (N)   Lu 17:3; 18:4
if a brother *w.* you (P)   Lu 17:4

WROTE

Moses *w.* all the words of the   Ex 24:4
he *w.* upon the tables the   Ex 34:28
words of
pure gold, and *w.* upon it a   Ex 39:30
writing
And Moses *w.* their goings   Nu 33:2
he *w.* them in two tables of   De 5:22
stone
he *w.* on the tables, according   De 10:4
to
Moses *w.* this law, and   De 31:9
delivered it
Moses therefore *w.* this song   De 31:22
he *w.* there upon the stones a   Jos 8:32
copy
which he *w.* in the presence of   Jos 8:32
Joshua *w.* these words in the   Jos 24:26
book
w. down for the princes (S)   J'g 8:14
and *w.* it in a book, and laid   1Sa 10:25
it up
that David *w.* a letter to   2Sa 11:14
Joab, and
he *w.* in the letter, saying,   2Sa 11:15
Set ye
So she *w.* letters in Ahab's   1Ki 21:8
name
and she *w.* in the letters,   1Ki 21:9
saying
And Jehu *w.* letters, and sent   2Ki 10:1
Then he *w.* a letter the   2Ki 10:6
second time
commandment, which he *w.*   2Ki 17:37
for you
Levites, *w.* them before the   1Ch 24:6
king
w. letters also to Ephraim   2Ch 30:1
w. also letters to rail on the   2Ch 32:17
Lord
w. they unto him an   Ezr 4:6
accusation
days of Artaxerxes *w.* Bishlam   Ezr 4:7
Shimshai the scribe *w.* a letter   Ezr 4:8
Then *w.* Rehum the chancellor   Ezr 4:9
which he *w.* to destroy the Jews   Es 8:5
w. in the king Ahasuerus' name   Es 8:10
And Mordecai *w.* these things   Es 9:20
Mordecai *w.* with all authority   Es 9:29

w. from the mouth of   Jer 36:4
Jeremiah
I *w.* them with ink in the book   Jer 36:18
w. at the mouth of Jeremiah   Jer 36:27
w. from the mouth of   Jer 36:32
Jeremiah
Jeremiah *w.* in a book all the   Jer 51:60
evil
w. over against the candlestick   Da 5:5
saw the part of the hand that   Da 5:5
w.
king Darius *w.* unto all people   Da 6:25
he *w.* the dream, and told the   Da 7:1
sum
your heart he *w.* you this   M'k 10:5
precept
Master, Moses *w.* unto us,   M'k 12:19
If a
and *w.* saying, His name is   Lu 1:63
John
Master, Moses *w.* unto us, If   Lu 20:28
any
have believed me: for he *w.* of   Joh 5:46
me
with his finger *w.* on the   Joh 8:6
ground
down, and *w.* on the ground   Joh 8:8
And Pilate *w.* a title, and   Joh 19:19
put it on
these things, and *w.* these   Joh 21:24
things
they *w.* letters by them after   Ac 15:23
this
the brethren *w.* exhorting the   Ac 18:27
he *w.* a letter after this   Ac 23:25
manner
I Tertius, who *w.* this epistle   Ro 16:22
I *w.* unto you in an epistle not   1Co 5:9
to
the things whereof ye *w.* unto   1Co 7:1
me
And I *w.* this same unto you,   2Co 2:3
lest
I *w.* unto you with many tears   2Co 2:4
though I *w.* unto you, I did it   2Co 7:12
not
(as I *w.* afore in few words   Eph 3:3
in thy obedience I *w.* unto   Ph'm 21
thee
though I *w.* a new   2Jo 5
commandment
I *w.* unto the church: but   3Jo 9

WROTH

And Cain was very *w.*, and his   Ge 4:5
said unto Cain, Why art thou   Ge 4:6
w.
Jacob was *w.* and chode with   Ge 31:36
and they were very *w.* because   Ge 34:7
Pharaoh was *w.* against two of   Ge 40:2
his
Pharaoh was *w.* with his   Ge 41:10
servants
and Moses was *w.* with them   Ex 16:20
And Moses was very *w.* and   Nu 16:15
said
be *w.* with all the   Nu 16:22
congregation
Moses was *w.* with the   Nu 31:14
officers of
words, and was *w.* and sware   De 1:34
the Lord was *w.* with me for   De 3:26
your
the Lord was *w.* against you   De 9:19
he will be *w.* with the which   Jos 22:18
Saul was very *w.* and the   1Sa 18:8
saying
but if he be very *w.* then be   1Sa 20:7
sure
the Philistines were *w.* with   1Sa 29:4
him
was Abner very *w.* for the   2Sa 3:8
words
all these things, he was very   2Sa 13:21
w.
and shook, because he was *w.*   2Sa 22:8
Naaman was *w.* and went   2Ki 5:11
away
the man of God was *w.* with   2Ki 13:19
him
Then Asa was *w.* with the   2Ch 16:10
seer
Then Uzziah was *w.* and   2Ch 26:19
had a
while he was *w.* with the   2Ch 26:19
priests
of your fathers was *w.* with   2Ch 28:9
Judah

we builded the wall, he was *w.*   Ne 4:1
be stopped, then they were very   Ne 4:7
w.
therefore was the king very *w.*   Es 1:12
were *w.*, and sought to lay   Es 2:21
hand on
were shaken, because he was   Ps 18:7
w.
the Lord heard this, and was   Ps 78:21
w.
When God heard this, he was   Ps 78:59
w.
and was *w.* with his   Ps 78:62
inheritance
hast been *w.* with thine   Ps 89:38
anointed
he shall be *w.* as in the   Isa 28:21
valley of
I was *w.* with my people, I   Isa 47:6
have
that I would not be *w.* with   Isa 54:9
thee
ever, neither will I be always   Isa 57:16
w.
of his covetousness was I *w.*   Isa 57:17
I hid me, and was *w.* and he   Isa 57:17
went
thou art *w.*; for we have   Isa 64:5
sinned
Be not *w.* very sore, O Lord   Isa 64:9
the princes were *w.* with   Jer 37:15
Jeremiah
thou art very *w.* against us   La 5:22
was exceeding *w.* and sent   M't 2:16
forth
his lord was *w.* and   M't 18:34
delivered
the king heard thereof, he   M't 22:7
was *w.*
nations were *w.* (E)   Re 11:18
dragon was *w.* with the   Re 12:17
woman

WROUGHT

because he had *w.* folly in   Ge 34:7
Israel
what things I have *w.* in Egypt   Ex 10:2
twined linen, *w.* with   Ex 26:36;
needlework   27:16
Then *w.* Bezaleel and Aholiab   Ex 36:1
w. all the work of the   Ex 36:4
sanctuary
w. the work of the tabernacle   Ex 36:8
w. onyx stones inclosed in   Ex 39:6
ouches
they have *w.* confusion: their   Le 20:12
blood
and of Israel, What hath   Nu 23:23
God *w.*
gold of them, even all *w.*   Nu 31:51
jewels
abomination is *w.* among you   De 13:14
hath *w.* wickedness in the sight   De 17:2
such abomination is *w.* in   De 17:4
Israel
which hath not been *w.* with   De 21:3
she hath *w.* folly in Israel, to   De 22:21
play
the evils which they shall   De 31:18
have *w.*
because he hath *w.* folly in   Jos 7:15
Israel
folly that they have *w.* in   J'g 20:10
Israel
in law with whom she had *w.*   Ru 2:19
with whom I *w.* to-day is   Ru 2:19
Boaz
w. wonderfully among them   1Sa 6:6
Lord hath *w.* salvation in   1Sa 11:13
Israel
w. this great salvation in   1Sa 14:45
Israel
for he hath *w.* with God this   1Sa 14:45
day
the Lord *w.* a great salvation   1Sa 19:5
for all
I should have *w.* falsehood   2Sa 18:13
against
Lord *w.* a great victory that   2Sa 23:10
day
and the Lord *w.* a great   2Sa 23:12
victory
over the people that *w.* in the   1Ki 5:16
work
king Solomon, and *w.* all his   1Ki 7:14
work
was *w.* like the brim of a cup   1Ki 7:26
the people that *w.* in the work   1Ki 9:23

his treason that he *w.* are   1Ki 16:20
they
But Omri *w.* evil in the eyes   1Ki 16:25
of the
he *w.* evil in the sight of the   2Ki 3:2
Lord
that *w.* upon the house of   2Ki 12:11
the Lord
w. wicked things to provoke   2Ki 17:11
he *w.* much wickedness in the   2Ki 21:6
house of them that *w.* fine   1Ch 4:21
linen
set masons to hew *w.* stones   1Ch 22:2
linen, and *w.* cherubims   2Ch 3:14
thereon
and he *w.* that which was   2Ch 21:6
evil in
such as *w.* iron and brass to   2Ch 24:12
mend
So the workmen *w.* and the   2Ch 24:13
work
w. that which was good and   2Ch 31:20
right
he *w.* much evil in the sight   2Ch 33:6
of the
workmen that *w.* in the   2Ch 34:10
house of
all that *w.* the work in any   2Ch 34:13
manner
half of my servants *w.* in the   Ne 4:16
work
one of his hands *w.* in the   Ne 4:17
work
that this work was *w.* of our   Ne 6:16
God
and had *w.* great provocations   Ne 9:18
and they *w.* great   Ne 9:26
provocations
the hand of the Lord hath *w.*   Job 12:9
this
can say, Thou hast *w.*   Job 36:23
iniquity
thou hast *w.* for them that   Ps 31:19
trust in
within: her clothing is of *w.*   Ps 45:13
gold
that which thou hast *w.* for   Ps 68:28
us
How he had *w.* his signs in   Ps 78:43
Egypt
curiously *w.* in the lowest   Ps 139:15
parts of
the works that my hands had   Ec 2:11
w.
the work that is *w.* under the   Ec 2:17
sun is
also hast *w.* all our works in   Isa 26:12
us
we have not *w.* any   Isa 26:18
deliverance in
Who hath *w.* and done it,   Isa 41:4
calling
she hath *w.* lewdness with   Jer 11:15
many
he *w.* a work on the wheels   Jer 18:3
w. for my name's sake   Eze 20:9;
  20:14, 22
w. with you for my name's   Eze 20:44
sake
because they *w.* for me, saith   Eze 29:20
the high God hath *w.* toward   Da 4:2
me
unto us, for the sea *w.* and   Jon 1:11
was
sea *w.* and was tempestuous   Jon 1:13
which have *w.* his judgment   Zep 2:3
These last have *w.* but one   M't 20:12
hour
she hath *w.* a good work   M't 26:10
upon me
mighty works are *w.* by his   M'k 6:2
hands
she hath *w.* a good work on   M'k 14:6
me
manifest, that they are *w.* in   Joh 3:21
God
and wonders *w.* among the   Ac 5:12
people
God had *w.* among the   Ac 15:12
Gentiles
he abode with them, and *w.*   Ac 18:3
God *w.* special miracles by   Ac 19:11
God had *w.* among the   Ac 21:19
Gentiles by
w. in me all manner of   Ro 7:8
which Christ hath not *w.* by   Ro 15:18
me
that hath *w.* us for the   2Co 5:5
selfsame

what carefulness it *w.* in you,   2Co 7:11
yea
signs of an apostle, were *w.*   2Co 12:12
among
For he that *w.* effectually in   Ga 2:8
Which he *w.* in Christ, when   Eph 1:20
he
w. with labour and travail   2Th 3:8
night
w. righteousness, obtained   Heb 11:33
thou how faith *w.* with his   Jas 2:22
works
have *w.* the will of the Gentiles   1Pe 4:3
not those things which we have   2Jo 8
w.
the false prophet that *w.*   Re 19:20
miracles

WROUGHTEST

to-day? and where *w.* thou   Ru 2:19

WRUNG

the blood thereof shall be *w.*   Le 1:15
out
rest of the blood shall be *w.*   Le 5:9
out
of a full cup are *w.* out to   Ps 73:10
them
cup of trembling, and *w.*   Isa 51:17
them out

Y

YARDSTICK

what *y.* you measure (B)   M't 7:2

YARN

out of Egypt, and linen *y.*   1Ki 10:28
received the linen *y.* at a   1Ki 10:28;
price   2Ch 1:16
out of Egypt, and linen *y.*   2Ch 1:16

YE

ye shall be as gods knowing   Ge 3:5
good and evil
ye are they which justify   Lu 16:15
yourselves
ye are washed, *ye* are   1Co 6:11
sanctified, *ye* are justified in the
name of the Lord
ye are bought with a price,   1Co 6:20
glorify God in body
ye are our epistle written in   2Co 3:2
our hearts
ye are not straitened in us   2Co 6:12
but in your own
brethren, be as I am, for I am   Ga 4:12
as *ye* are
ye which are spiritual, restore   Ga 6:1
such an one
ye who sometimes were far   Eph 2:13
off are nigh
what is our joy, are not even   1Th 2:19
ye
ye are our glory   1Th 2:20
if *ye* stand fast in Lord   1Th 3:8
but *ye*, brethren, are not in   1Th 5:4
darkness
ye are all children of light and   1Th 5:5
of the day
but *ye*, brethren, be not   2Th 3:13
weary
but *ye* are a chosen generation   1Pe 2:9

YEA

Y. hath God said, Ye shall   Ge 3:1
y. I will bless her, and she   Ge 17:16
shall be
Y. I know that thou didst this   Ge 20:6
in
him? *y.* and he shall be   Ge 27:33
blessed
y. though he be as a stranger,   Le 25:35
or a
y. it shall be, that what   Nu 10:32
goodness
Y. he loved the people; all his   De 33:3
y. she returned answer to   J'g 5:29
herself
Y. I have obeyed the voice   1Sa 15:20
of the

y. though it were sanctified this   *1Sa 21:5*

y. see the skirts of thy robe in my   *1Sa 24:11*

unto the king, *Y.* let him take all   *2Sa 19:30*

y. they are fallen under my feet   *2Sa 22:39*

Y. I know it; hold your peace   *2Ki 2:3; 2:5*

y. and made his son to pass   *2Ki 16:3*

y. he reproved kings for their sakes   *1Ch 16:21*

y. himself hasted also to go out, because   *2Ch 26:20*

y. the hand of the princes and rulers   *Ezr 9:2*

y. even their servants bare rule   *Ne 5:15*

Y. also I continued in the work   *Ne 5:16*

y. in the night will they come to slay   *Ne 6:10*

Y. when they had made them   *Ne 9:18*

Y. forty years didst thou sustain   *Ne 9:21*

Y. Esther the queen did let no man   *Es 5:12*

y. they have slain the servants   *Job 1:15*

y. and slain the servants with   *Job 1:17*

y., all that a man hath will he give   *Job 2:4*

y. in seven there shall no evil touch   *Job 5:19*

y. I would harden myself in sorrow   *Job 6:10*

Y. ye overwhelm the fatherless   *Job 6:27*

y. return again, my righteousness is   *Job 6:29*

out; *y.* and wonders without number   *Job 9:10*

y. thou shalt be stedfast, and shalt   *Job 11:15*

y. thou shalt dig about thee, and thou   *Job 11:18*

y. many shall make suit unto thee   *Job 11:19*

y. who knoweth not such things as   *Job 12:3*

y. man giveth up the ghost, and where   *Job 14:10*

Y. thou castest off fear, and   *Job 15:4*

y. thine own lips testify against thee   *Job 15:6*

y. the heavens are not clean in his   *Job 15:15*

Y. the light of the wicked shall   *Job 18:5*

Y. young children despised me   *Job 19:18*

y. he shall be chased away as   *Job 20:8*

y. the glittering sword cometh out   *Job 20:25*

old, *y.* are mighty in power   *Job 21:7*

Y. the Almighty shall be thy   *Job 22:25*

y. the stars are not pure in his sight   *Job 25:5*

he prepared it, *y.* and searched it   *Job 28:27*

Y. whereto might the strength of fools, *y:* children of base men   *Job 30:2 Job 30:8*

I their song, *y.* I am their by word   *Job 30:9*

y. let my offspring be rooted out   *Job 31:8*

y. it is an iniquity to be punished   *Job 31:11*

Y. I attended unto you, and behold   *Job 32:12*

For God speaketh once, *y.* twice yet   *Job 33:14*

Y. his soul draweth near unto his   *Job 33:22*

Y. surely God will not do   *Job 34:12*

y. he doth establish them for ever   *Job 36:7*

not answer: *y.* twice; but I will   *Job 40:5*

y. as hard as a piece of the nether   *Job 41:24*

y. I have delivered him that without   *Ps 7:4*

y. let him tread down my life upon   *Ps 7:5*

y. and the beasts of the field   *Ps 8:7*

y. I have a goodly heritage   *Ps 16:6*

y. he did fly upon the wings of the   *Ps 18:10*

Y. he sent out his arrows   *Ps 18:14*

Y. thou liftest me up above those   *Ps 18:48*

than gold, *y.* than much fine gold   *Ps 19:10*

y. though I walk through the valley   *Ps 23:4*

Y. let none that wait on thee be   *Ps 25:3*

y. I will sing praises unto the Lord   *Ps 27:6*

y. the Lord breaketh the cedars   *Ps 29:5*

y. the Lord sitteth King for ever   *Ps 29:10*

with grief, *y.* my soul and my belly   *Ps 31:9*

y. the poor and the needy from him   *Ps 35:10*

y. the abjects gathered themselves   *Ps 35:15*

Y. they opened their mouth wide   *Ps 35:21*

y. let them say continually, Let the   *Ps 35:27*

y. thou shalt diligently consider his   *Ps 37:10*

y. I sought him, but he could not   *Ps 37:36*

God: *y.* thy law is within my heart   *Ps 40:8*

Y. mine own familiar friend   *Ps 41:9*

y. upon the harp will I praise thee   *Ps 43:4*

Y. for thy sake are we killed all   *Ps 44:22*

y. in the shadow of thy wings will   *Ps 57:1*

Y. in heart ye work wickedness   *Ps 58:2*

y. I will sing aloud of thy mercy   *Ps 59:16*

God: *y.* let them exceedingly rejoice   *Ps 68:3*

y. the Lord will dwell in it for ever   *Ps 68:16*

for men: *y.* for the rebellious also   *Ps 68:18*

Y. all kings shall fall down before   *Ps 72:11*

Y. they spake against God   *Ps 78:19*

y. many a time turned he his anger   *Ps 78:38*

Y. they turned back and tempted   *Ps 78:41*

Zeeb: *Y.* all their princes as Zebah   *Ps 83:11*

y. let them be put to shame   *Ps 83:17*

My soul longeth, *y.* even fainteth   *Ps 84:2*

Y. the sparrow hath found an   *Ps 84:3*

Y. the Lord shall give that which   *Ps 85:12*

y. the work of our hands establish   *Ps 90:17*

y. than the mighty waves of the sea   *Ps 93:4*

y. the Lord our God shall cut them   *Ps 94:23*

her, *y.* the set time, is come   *Ps 102:13*

y. all of them shall wax old like a   *Ps 102:26*

v. very few, and strangers in it   *Ps 105:12*

y. he reproved kings for their sakes   *Ps 105:14*

Y. they despised the pleasant land   *Ps 106:24*

Y. they sacrificed their sons   *Ps 106:37*

y. I will praise him among   *Ps 109:30*

righteous: *y.* our God is merciful   *Ps 116:5*

y. they compassed me about   *Ps 118:11*

y. I shall observe it with my heart   *Ps 119:34*

y. sweeter than honey to my mouth   *Ps 119:103*

above gold: *y.* above fine gold   *Ps 119:127*

Y. thou shalt see thy children's   *Ps 128:6*

y. we wept, when we remembered   *Ps 137:1*

Y. they shall sing in the ways   *Ps 138:5*

Y. the darkness hideth not from   *Ps 139:12*

y. happy is that people, whose God   *Ps 144:15*

Y. if thou criest after knowledge   *Pr 2:3*

and equity: *y.* every good path   *Pr 2:9*

y. thou shalt lie down, and thy sleep   *Pr 3:24*

y. seven are an abomination unto   *Pr 6:16*

y. many strong men have been slain   *Pr 7:26*

y. durable riches and righteousness   *Pr 8:18*

better than gold, *y.* than fine gold   *Pr 8:19*

y. even the wicked for the day   *Pr 16:4*

y. strife and reproach shall cease   *Pr 22:10*

Y. my reins shall rejoice, when thy   *Pr 23:16*

Y. thou shalt be as he that lieth   *Pr 23:34*

y. a man of knowledge increaseth   *Pr 24:5*

y. he shall give delight unto thy soul   *Pr 29:17*

y. four things say not, It is enough   *Pr 30:15*

for me, *y.* four which I know not   *Pr 30:18*

go well, *y.* four are comely in going   *Pr 30:29*

y. she reacheth forth her hands to the   *Pr 31:20*

y. my heart had great experience of   *Ec 1:16*

Y. I hated all my labour which I had   *Ec 2:18*

y. his heart taketh not rest in   *Ec 2:23*

y. they have all one breath; so that   *Ec 3:19*

Y. better is he than both they, which   *Ec 4:3*

y. he hath neither child nor   *Ec 4:8*

is also vanity, *y.* it is a sore travail   *Ec 4:8*

Y. though he live a thousand years   *Ec 6:6*

y. also from his withdrawal not   *Ec 7:18*

y. farther; though a wise man   *Ec 8:17*

y. also the heart of the sons of men   *Ec 9:3*

Y. also, when he that is a fool   *Ec 10:3*

y. he gave good heed, and sought   *Ec 12:9*

art, fair, my beloved, *y.* pleasant   *Ca 1:16*

y. drink abundantly, O beloved   *Ca 5:1*

most sweet: *y.* he is altogether lovely   *Ca 5:16*

y. the queens and the concubines   *Ca 6:9*

y. I should not be despised   *Ca 8:1*

y. when ye make many prayers   *Isa 1:15*

Y. ten acres of vineyard shall   *Isa 5:10*

y. they shall roar, and lay hold of   *Isa 5:29*

Y. the fir trees rejoice at thee   *Isa 14:8*

y. they shall vow a vow unto   *Isa 19:21*

y. the treacherous dealers have dealt   *Isa 24:16*

Y. in the way of thy judgments   *Isa 26:8*

y. with my spirit within me will I   *Isa 26:9*

y. the fire of thine enemies shall   *Isa 26:11*

y. it shall be at an instant suddenly   *Isa 29:5*

y. for the king it is prepared   *Isa 30:33*

v. upon all the houses of joy in   *Isa 32:13*

Y. they shall not be planted   *Isa 40:24*

y. they shall not be sown   *Isa 40:24*

y. their stock shall not take root in   *Isa 40:24*

y. I will help thee; *y.* I will uphold   *Isa 41:10*

y. do good, or do evil, that we may   *Isa 41:23*

y. there is none that sheweth   *Isa 41:26*

y. there is none that declareth   *Isa 41:26*

y. there is none that heareth your   *Isa 41:26*

he shall cry, *y.* roar; he shall   *Isa 42:13*

formed him; *y.* I have made him   *Isa 43:7*

y. before the day was I am he: and   *Isa 43:13*

y. there is no God; I know not any   *Isa 44:8*

y. he is hungry, and his strength   *Isa 44:12*

y. he kindleth it, and baketh *Isa 44:15*
y. he maketh a god, and *Isa 44:15*
y. he warmeth himself, and *Isa 44:16*
saith
y. also I have baked bread *Isa 44:19*
upon
y. let them take counsel *Isa 45:21*
together
they fall down, y. they *Isa 46:6*
worship
y. one shall cry unto him, yet *Isa 46:7*
can
y. I have spoken it, I will *Isa 46:11*
also bring
y. thy shame shall be seen: I *Isa 47:3*
will
Y. thou heardest not: *Isa 48:8*
y. thou
y. from that time that thine *Isa 48:8*
ear
have spoken; y. I have called *Isa 48:15*
him
y. they may forget, yet will I *Isa 49:15*
not
y. come, buy wine and milk *Isa 55:1*
without
devour, y. all ye beasts in the *Isa 56:9*
forest
y. they are greedy dogs *Isa 56:11*
which can
Y. truth faileth; and he that *Isa 59:15*
y. these nations shall be *Isa 60:12*
utterly
Y. they have chosen their own *Isa 66:3*
y. thou shalt go forth from *Jer 2:37*
him
y. they overpass the deeds of *Jer 5:28*
Y. the stork in the heaven *Jer 8:7*
them, y. they have taken root *Jer 12:2*
grow, y. they bring forth fruit *Jer 12:2*
y. they have called a *Jer 12:6*
multitude
Y. the hind also calved in *Jer 14:5*
y. both the prophet and the *Jer 14:18*
y. in my house have I found *Jer 23:11*
their
y. they are prophets of the *Jer 23:26*
deceit of
Y. thus saith the Lord of *Jer 27:21*
hosts
Y. I have loved thee with an *Jer 31:3*
was ashamed, y. even *Jer 31:19*
confounded
Y. I will rejoice over them to *Jer 32:41*
many to fall, y. one fell upon *Jer 46:16*
another
y. the wall of Babylon shall *Jer 51:44*
fall
y. she sigheth, and turneth *La 1:8*
desolate, y. more desolate *Eze 6:14*
than the
y. I said unto thee when thou *Eze 16:6*
wast in
y. I sware unto thee, and *Eze 16:8*
entered
y. I throughly washed away thy *Eze 16:9*
y. thou hast played the harlot *Eze 16:28*
y. be thou confounded also *Eze 16:52*
Y. behold, being planted, *Eze 17:10*
shall it
y. thou shalt shew her all her *Eze 22:2*
Y. I will gather you, and *Eze 22:21*
blow upon
y. they have oppressed the *Eze 22:29*
stranger
Aholibah? y. declare unto *Eze 23:36*
them
y. the isles that are in the *Eze 26:18*
sea shall
y. they shall dwell with *Eze 28:26*
confidence
Y. I will make many people *Eze 32:10*
amazed
Y. thou shalt be broken in *Eze 32:28*
the midst
y. my flock was scattered *Eze 34:6*
upon all
Y. I will cause men to walk *Eze 36:12*
upon
y. I will be their God, and *Eze 37:27*
they
Y. all the people of the land *Eze 39:13*
shall
Y. he magnified himself even *Da 8:11*
to the
Y. all Israel have transgressed *Da 9:11*
thy
Y. whiles I was speaking in *Da 9:21*
prayer

be unto thee; be strong, y. be *Da 10:19*
strong
y. also the prince of the *Da 11:22*
covenant
y. and he shall forecast his *Da 11:24*
devices
Y. they that feed of the *Da 11:26*
portion of
y. I will betroth thee unto me *Ho 2:19*
y. the fishes of the sea also *Ho 4:3*
shall
y. gray hairs are here and there *Ho 7:9*
Y. though they have hired *Ho 8:10*
among
y. woe also to them when I *Ho 9:12*
y. though they bring forth, yet *Ho 9:16*
will
Y. he had power over the *Ho 12:4*
angel, and
y. their altars are as heaps in *Ho 12:11*
y. joy and gladness from the *Joe 1:16*
house
y. the flocks of sheep are *Joe 1:18*
made
y. and nothing shall escape *Joe 2:3*
them
Y. the Lord will answer and *Joe 2:19*
say
Y. and what have ye to do *Joe 3:4*
with
y. and sell the refuse of the *Am 8:6*
wheat
y. thou shouldest not have *Ob 13*
looked
y. they shall drink, and they *Ob 16*
shall
y. let them turn every one *Jon 3:8*
from his
y. they shall all cover their *Mic 3:7*
lips
y. the world, and all that dwell *Na 1:5*
Y. also, because he *Hab 2:5*
transgresseth
y. gather together, O nation not *Zep 2:1*
y. as yet the vine, and the fig *Hag 2:19*
tree
Y. they made their hearts as *Zec 7:12*
Y. many people and strong *Zec 8:22*
nations
y. their children shall see it, *Zec 10:7*
and be
y. ye shall flee, like as ye fled *Zec 14:5*
from
Y. every pot in Jerusalem *Zec 14:21*
and in
y. I have cursed them already *Mal 2:2*
y. they that work wickedness *Mal 3:15*
are
y. they that tempt God are *Mal 3:15*
even
proud, y. and all that do *Mal 4:1*
wickedly
let your communication be, *M't 5:37*
Y., y.
They said unto him, Y. Lord *M't 9:28*
A prophet? y. I say unto you *M't 11:9*
much more
They say unto him, Y. Lord *M't 13:51*
Y. have ye never read, Out *M't 21:16*
of the
y. though many false *M't 26:60*
witnesses
Y. a sword shall pierce *Lu 2:35*
through
A prophet? Y. I say unto you *Lu 7:26*
Y. rather, blessed are they *Lu 11:28*
that
hell; y. I say unto you, Fear *Lu 12:5*
him
Y. and why even of *Lu 12:57*
yourselves judge
y. and his own life also, he *Lu 14:26*
cannot
Y. and certain women also of *Lu 24:22*
our
Y. Lord; I believe that thou *Joh 11:27*
art
y. the time cometh, that *Joh 16:2*
whosoever
the hour cometh, y. is now *Joh 16:32*
come
Y. Lord; thou knowest that *Joh 21:15; 21:16*
I
y. the faith which is by him *Ac 3:16*
hath
Y. and all the prophets from *Ac 3:24*
And she said, Y. for so much *Ac 5:8*
Y. ye took up the tabernacle *Ac 7:43*
of

Y. ye yourselves know, that *Ac 20:34*
these
art thou a Roman? He said, *Ac 22:27*
Y.
y. let God be true, but every *Ro 3:4*
man a
forbid: y. we establish the law *Ro 3:31*
died, y. rather, that is risen *Ro 8:34*
again
Y. he shall be holden up: for *Ro 14:4*
God
Y. so have I strived to *Ro 15:20*
preach the
chosen, y. and things which *1Co 1:28*
are not
things, y. the deep things of *1Co 2:10*
God
y. I judge not mine own self *1Co 4:3*
y. woe is unto me, if I *1Co 9:16*
preach not
Y. and we are found false *1Co 15:15*
witnesses
will abide, y. and winter with *1Co 16:6*
you
that with me there should be *2Co 1:17*
y. y.
toward you was not y. and *2Co 1:18*
nay
not y. and nay, but in him *2Co 1:19*
was y.
the promises of God in him *2Co 1:20*
are y.
y. though we have known *2Co 5:16*
Christ
y. what clearing of yourselves *2Co 7:11*
y. what indignation, y. what *2Co 7:11*
fear
y. what vehement desire *2Co 7:11*
y. what zeal, y. what revenge *2Co 7:11*
y. and exceedingly the more *2Co 7:13*
joyed
y. and beyond their power *2Co 8:3*
they were
y. they would exclude you, *Ga 4:17*
that ye
do rejoice, y. and will rejoice *Ph'p 1:18*
Y. and if I be offered upon *Ph'p 2:17*
Y. doubtless, and I count all *Ph'p 3:8*
y. and all that will live godly *2Ti 3:12*
Y. brother, let me have joy of *Ph'm 20*
y. moreover of bonds and *Heb 11:36*
Y., a man may say, Thou hast *Jas 2:18*
your y. be y., and your nay, *Jas 5:12*
nay
Y., all of you be subject one *1Pe 5:5*
to
Y., I think it meet, as long as *2Pe 1:13*
I am
y. and we also bear record; and *3Jo 12*
ye
Y. saith the Spirit, that they *Re 14:13*
may

YEAR

six hundredth y. of Noah's life *Ge 7:11*
in the six hundredth and first *Ge 8:13*
y.
in the thirteenth y. they *Ge 14:4*
rebelled
fourteenth y. came *Ge 14:5*
Chedorlaomer
thee at this set time in the *Ge 17:21*
next y.
in the same y. an *Ge 26:12*
hundredfold
bread for all their cattle for *Ge 47:17*
that y.
When that y. was ended, they *Ge 47:18*
came
they came unto him the *Ge 47:18*
second y.
be the first month of the y. to *Ex 12:2*
you
blemish, a male of the first y. *Ex 12:5*
in his season from y. to y. *Ex 13:10*
the seventh y. thou shalt let it *Ex 23:11*
rest
keep a feast unto me in the *Ex 23:14*
y.
which is in the end of the *Ex 23:16*
y. when
Three times in the y. all thy *Ex 23:17*
males
out from before thee in one *Ex 23:29*
y.
two lambs of the first y. day *Ex 29:38*
by day
upon the horns of it once in *Ex 30:10*
a y.

once in the *y.* shall he make — Ex 30:10
Thrice in the *y.* shall all your — Ex 34:23
the Lord thy God thrice in the *y.* — Ex 34:24
in the first month in the second *y.* — Ex 40:17
calf and a lamb, both of the first *y.* — Le 9:3
shall bring a lamb of the first *y.* — Le 12:6
one ewe lamb of the first *y.* without — Le 14:10
of Israel for all their sins once a *y.* — Le 16:34
in the fourth *y.* all the fruit thereof — Le 19:24
the fifth *y.* shall ye eat of the fruit — Le 19:25
lamb without blemish of the first *y.* — Le 23:12
without blemish of the first *y.* — Le 23:18
two lambs of the first *y.* for a — Le 23:19
unto the Lord seven days in the *y.* — Le 23:41
the seventh *y.* shall be a sabbath — Le 25:4
it is a *y.* of rest unto the land — Le 25:5
And ye shall hallow the fiftieth *y.* — Le 25:10
A jubile shall that fiftieth *y.* be — Le 25:11
In the *y.* of this jubile ye shall — Le 25:13
What shall we eat the seventh *y.* — Le 25:20
blessing upon you in the sixth *y.* — Le 25:21
ye shall sow the eighth *y.* and eat — Le 25:22
yet of old fruit until the ninth *y.* — Le 25:22
bought it until the *y.* of jubile — Le 25:28
within a whole *y.* after it is sold — Le 25:29
within a full *y.* may he redeem it — Le 25:29
within the space of a full *y.* — Le 25:30
shall go out in the *y.* of jubile — Le 25:33
serve thee unto the *y.* of jubile — Le 25:40
him that bought him from the *y.* — Le 25:50
sold to him unto the *y.* of jubile — Le 25:50
but few years unto the *y.* of jubile — Le 25:52
he shall go out in the *y.* of jubile — Le 25:54
his field from the *y.* of jubile — Le 27:17
even unto the *y.* of the jubile — Le 27:18; 27:23
In the *y.* of the jubile the field — Le 27:24
in the second *y.* after they were — Nu 1:1
bring a lamb of the first *y.* for — Nu 6:12
one he lamb of the first *y.* without — Nu 6:14
one ewe lamb of the first *y.* without — Nu 6:14
one ram, one lamb of the first *y.* — Nu 7:15; 7:33, 39, 63, 75, 81
he goats, five lambs of the first *y.* — Nu 7:17; 7:23, 29, 35, 41, 47, 53, 59, 65, 69, 71, 77, 83
one ram, one lamb of the first *y.* — Nu 7:21; 7:27, 45, 51, 57
the lambs of the first *y.* twelve — Nu 7:87
the lambs of the first *y.* sixty — Nu 7:88
of the second *y.* after they were — Nu 9:1
month, or a *y.* that the cloud — Nu 9:22
in the second *y.* that the cloud — Nu 10:11
each day for a *y.* shall ye bear your — Nu 14:34
shall bring a she goat of the first *y.* — Nu 15:27
lambs of the first *y.* without spot — Nu 28:3; 28:9, 11
throughout the months of the *y.* — Nu 28:14
and seven lambs of the first *y.* — Nu 28:19; 28:27; 29:2, 8, 13, 17, 20, 23, 26, 29, 32, 36
the fortieth *y.* after the children — Nu 33:38
it came to pass in the fortieth *y.* — De 1:3
from the begining of the *y.* — De 11:12
even unto the end of the *y.* — De 11:12

the field bringeth forth *y.* by *y.* — De 14:22
tithe of thine increase the same *y.* — De 14:28
The seventh *y.* the *y.* of release — De 15:9
the seventh *y.* thou shalt let him — De 15:12
before the Lord thy God *y.* by *y.* — De 15:20
Three times in a *y.* shall all thy — De 16:16
but he shall be free at home one *y.* — De 24:5
tithes of thine increase the third *y.* — De 26:12
which is the *y.* of tithing, and hast — De 26:12
in the solemnity of the *y.* of release — De 31:10
fruit of the land of Canaan that *y.* — Jos 5:12
that *y.* they vexed and oppressed — J'g 10:8
the Gileadite four days in a *y.* — J'g 11:40
ten shekels of silver by the *y.* — J'g 17:10
And as he did so *y.* by *y.* when she — 1Sa 1:7
brought it to him from *y.* to *y.* — 1Sa 2:19
he went from *y.* to *y.* in circuit to — 1Sa 7:16
Saul reigned one *y.*; and when he — 1Sa 13:1
of the Philistines was a full *y.* — 1Sa 27:7
after the *y.* was expired, at — 2Sa 11:1
of David three years, *y.* after *y.* — 2Sa 21:1
each man his month in a *y.* made — 1Ki 4:7
gave Solomon to Hiram *y.* by *y.* — 1Ki 5:11
and eightieth *y.* after the children — 1Ki 6:1
in the fourth *y.* of Solomon's reign — 1Ki 6:1
In the fourth *y.* was the foundation — 1Ki 6:37
in the eleventh *y.* in the month — 1Ki 6:38
three times in a *y.* did Solomon — 1Ki 9:25
that came to Solomon in one *y.* — 1Ki 10:14
horses, and mules, a rate *y.* by *y.* — 1Ki 10:25
in the fifth *y.* of king Rehoboam — 1Ki 14:25
the eighteeneth *y.* of king Jeroboam — 1Ki 15:1
in the twentieth *y.* of Jeroboam — 1Ki 15:9
the second *y.* of Asa king of Judah — 1Ki 15:25
the third *y.* of Asa king of Judah — 1Ki 15:28; 15:33
twenty and sixth *y.* of Asa king — 1Ki 16:8
twenty and seventh *y.* of Asa king — 1Ki 16:10; 16:15
thirty and first *y.* of Asa king of — 1Ki 16:23
thirty and eighth *y.* of Asa king of — 1Ki 16:29
Lord came to Elijah in the third *y.* — 1Ki 18:1
at the return of the *y.* the king — 1Ki 20:22
to pass at the return of the *y.* — 1Ki 20:26
And it came to pass in the third *y.* — 1Ki 22:2
the fourth *y.* of Ahab king of Israel — 1Ki 22:41
the seventeenth *y.* of Jehoshaphat — 1Ki 22:51
in the second *y.* of Jehoram the son — 2Ki 1:17
the eighteenth *y.* of Jehoshaphat — 2Ki 3:1
fifth *y.* of Joram the son of Ahab — 2Ki 8:16
twelfth *y.* of Joram the son of Ahab — 2Ki 8:25
he reigned one *y.* in Jerusalem — 2Ki 8:26
the eleventh *y.* of Joram the son of — 2Ki 9:29
the seventh *y.* Jehoiada sent — 2Ki 11:4

In the seventh *y.* of Jehu, Jehoash — 2Ki 12:1
three and twentieth *y.* of Jehoash — 2Ki 12:6
three and twentieth *y.* of Joash — 2Ki 13:1
thirty and seventh *y.* of Joash king — 2Ki 13:10
the land at the coming in of the *y.* — 2Ki 13:20
second *y.* of Joash son of Jehoahaz — 2Ki 14:1
fifteenth *y.* of Amaziah the son of — 2Ki 14:23
twenty and seventh *y.* of Jeroboam — 2Ki 15:1
thirty and eighth *y.* of Azariah king — 2Ki 15:8
nine and thirtieth *y.* of Uzziah — 2Ki 15:13
nine and thirtieth *y.* of Azariah — 2Ki 15:17
fiftieth *y.* of Azariah king of Judah — 2Ki 15:23
two and fiftieth *y.* of Azariah king — 2Ki 15:27
twentieth *y.* of Jotham the son of — 2Ki 15:30
the second *y.* of Pekah the son of — 2Ki 15:32
seventeenth *y.* of Pekah the son of — 2Ki 16:1
twelfth *y.* of Ahaz king of Judah — 2Ki 17:1
of Assyria, as he had done *y.* by *y.* — 2Ki 17:4
the ninth *y.* of Hoshea the king of — 2Ki 17:6
to pass in the third *y.* of Hoshea — 2Ki 18:1
the fourth *y.* of king Hezekiah — 2Ki 18:9
which was the seventh *y.* of Hoshea — 2Ki 18:9
even in the sixth *y.* of Hezekiah — 2Ki 18:10
that is the ninth *y.* of Hoshea king — 2Ki 18:10
the fourteenth *y.* of king Hezekiah — 2Ki 18:13
eat this *y.* such things as grow — 2Ki 19:29
the second *y.* that which springeth — 2Ki 19:29
in the third *y.* sow ye, and reap — 2Ki 19:29
in the eighteenth *y.* of king Josiah — 2Ki 22:3; 23:23
him in the eighty *y.* of his reign — 2Ki 24:12
to pass in the ninth *y.* of his reign — 2Ki 25:1
the eleventh *y.* of king Hezekiah — 2Ki 25:2
which is the nineteenth *y.* of king — 2Ki 25:8
and thirtieth *y.* of the captivity — 2Ki 25:27
in the *y.* that he began to reign — 2Ki 25:27
pass, that after the *y.* was expired — 1Ch 20:1
fortieth *y.* of the reign of David — 1Ch 26:31
throughout all the months of the *y.* — 1Ch 27:1
month, in the fourth *y.* of his reign — 2Ch 3:2
solemn feasts, three times in the *y.* — 2Ch 8:13
that came to Solomon in one *y.* — 2Ch 9:13
horses, and mules, a rate *y.* by *y.* — 2Ch 9:24
in the fifth *y.* of king Rehoboam — 2Ch 12:2
the eighteenth *y.* of king Jeroboam — 2Ch 13:1
the fifteenth *y.* of the reign of Asa — 2Ch 15:10
thirtieth *y.* of the reign of Asa — 2Ch 15:19
and thirtieth *y.* of Asa — 2Ch 16:1
Asa in the thirty and ninth *y.* of his — 2Ch 16:12
the one and fortieth *y.* of his reign — 2Ch 16:13
third *y.* of his reign he sent to his — 2Ch 17:7

he reigned one *y.* in Jerusalem   2Ch 22:2
And in the seventh *y.*   2Ch 23:1
Jehoiada strengthened himself
the house of your God from *y.*   2Ch 24:5
to *y.*
it came to pass at the end   2Ch 24:23
of the *y.*
the same *y.* an hundred   2Ch 27:5
talents of
pay unto him, both the   2Ch 27:5
second *y.*
He in the first *y.* of his reign   2Ch 29:3
For in the eighth *y.* of his   2Ch 34:3
reign
in the twelfth *y.* he began to   2Ch 34:3
purge
in the eighteenth *y.* of his   2Ch 34:8
reign
In the eighteenth *y.* of the   2Ch 35:19
reign of
when the *y.* was expired,   2Ch 36:10
king
the first *y.* of Cyrus king of   2Ch 36:22;
Persia   Ezr 1:1
in the second *y.* of their   Ezr 3:8
coming
unto the second *y.* of the   Ezr 4:24
reign
In the first *y.* of Cyrus the   Ezr 5:13;
king   6:3
the sixth *y.* of the reign of   Ezr 6:15
Darius
in the seventh *y.* of Artaxerxes   Ezr 7:7
was in the seventh *y.* of the   Ezr 7:8
king
month Chisleu, in the twentieth   Ne 1:1
y.
the twentieth *y.* of Artaxerxes   Ne 2:1
the twentieth *y.* even unto the   Ne 5:14
two
two and thirtieth *y.* of   Ne 5:14
Artaxerxes
we would leave the seventh   Ne 10:31
y.
at times appointed *y.* by *y.* to   Ne 10:34
burn
of all fruit of all trees, *y.* by   Ne 10:35
y.
two and thirtieth *y.* of   Ne 13:6
Artaxerxes
In the third *y.* of his reign, he   Es 1:3
made
in the seventh *y.* of his reign   Es 2:16
in the twelfth *y.* of king   Es 3:7
Ahasuerus
to their appinted time every *y.*   Es 9:27
be joined unto the days of the   Job 3:6
y.
crownest the *y.* with thy   Ps 65:11
goodness
In the *y.* that king Uzziah died   Isa 6:1
In the *y.* that king Ahaz died   Isa 14:28
y. that Tartan came unto   Isa 20:1
Ashdod
Within a *y.* according to the   Isa 21:16
years
add ye *y.* to *y.*; let them kill   Isa 29:1
and the *y.* of recompences for   Isa 34:8
the fourteenth *y.* of king   Isa 36:1
Hezekiah
Ye shall eat this *y.* such as   Isa 37:30
groweth
the second *y.* that which   Isa 37:30
springeth
in the third *y.* sow ye, and   Isa 37:30
reap
the acceptable *y.* of the Lord   Isa 61:2
and the *y.* of my redeemed is   Isa 63:4
come
in the thirteenth *y.* of his reign   Jer 1:2
end of the eleventh *y.* of   Jer 1:3
Zedekiah
even the *y.* of their visitation   Jer 11:23
not be careful in the *y.* of   Jer 17:8
drought
even the *y.* of their visitation   Jer 23:12
fourth *y.* of Jehoiakim the   Jer 25:1
son of
was the first *y.* of   Jer 25:1
Nebuchadrezzar
thirteenth *y.* of Josiah the   Jer 25:3
son of
that is the three and   Jer 25:3
twentieth *y.*
And it came to pass the   Jer 28:1
same *y.*
in the fourth *y.* and in the   Jer 28:1
fifth

this *y.* thou shalt die,   Jer 28:16
because thou
the prophet died the same *y.*   Jer 28:17
in the tenth *y.* of Zedekiah   Jer 32:1
king of
eighteenth *y.* of   Jer 32:1
Nebuchadrezzar
pass in the fourth *y.* of   Jer 36:1
Jehoiakim
to pass in the fifth *y.* of   Jer 36:9
Jehoiakim
In the ninth *y.* of Zedekiah   Jer 39:1
king of
And in the eleventh *y.* of   Jer 39:2
Zedekiah
in the fourth *y.* of   Jer 45:1
Jehoiakim the
smote in the fourth *y.* of   Jer 46:2
Jehoiakim
Moab, the *y.* of their   Jer 48:44
visitation
a rumour shall both come   Jer 51:46
one *y.*
in another *y.* shall come a   Jer 51:46
rumour
in the fourth *y.* of his reign   Jer 51:59
to pass in the ninth *y.* of his   Jer 52:4
reign
the eleventh *y.* of king   Jer 52:5
Zedekiah
the nineteenth *y.* of   Jer 52:12
Nebuchadrezzar
the seventh *y.* three thousand   Jer 52:28
Jews
eighteenth *y.* of   Jer 52:29
Nebuchadrezzar
and twentieth *y.* of   Jer 52:30
Nebuchadrezzar
and thirtieth *y.* of the   Jer 52:31
captivity
in the first *y.* of his reign   Jer 52:31
lifted up
it came to pass in the thirtieth   Eze 1:1
y.
the fifth *y.* of king   Eze 1:2
Jehoiachin's
appointed thee each day for a   Eze 4:6
y.
it came to pass in the sixth *y.*   Eze 8:1
it came to pass in the seventh   Eze 20:1
y.
in the ninth *y.* in the tenth   Eze 24:1
month
came to pass in the eleventh   Eze 26:1
y.
In the tenth *y.* in the tenth   Eze 29:1
month
pass in the seven and   Eze 29:17
twentieth *y.*
it came to pass in the   Eze 30:20;
eleventh *y.*   31:1
it came to pass in the twelfth   Eze 32:1
y.
came to pass also in the   Eze 32:17
twelfth *y.*
in the twelfth *y.* of our   Eze 33:21
captivity
and twentieth *y.* of our   Eze 40:1
captivity
in the beginning of the *y.* in   Eze 40:1
fourteenth *y.* after that the   Eze 40:1
city
of a lamb of the first *y.*   Eze 46:13
without
it shall be his to the *y.* of   Eze 46:17
liberty
third *y.* of the reign of   Da 1:1
Jehoiakim
even unto the first *y.* of king   Da 1:21
Cyrus
in the second *y.* of the reign of   Da 2:1
In the first *y.* of Belshazzar   Da 7:1
king
a *y.*, two years, and half a *y.*   Da 7:25
(B)
In the third *y.* of the reign of   Da 8:1
king
In the first *y.* of Darius the son   Da 9:1
In the first *y.* of his reign I   Da 9:2
Daniel
the third *y.* of Cyrus king of   Da 10:1
Persia
I in the first *y.* of Darius the   Da 11:1
Mede
offerings, with calves of a *y.*   Mic 6:6
old
the second *y.* of Darius the   Hag 1:1;
king   1:15
in the second *y.* of Darius,   Hag 2:10;
came   Zec 1:17

pass in the fourth *y.* of king   Zec 7:1
Darius
even go up from *y.* to *y.* to   Zec 14:16
worship
parents went to Jerusalem   Lu 2:41
every *y.*
fifteenth *y.* of the reign of   Lu 3:1
Tiberius
the acceptable *y.* of the Lord   Lu 4:19
Lord, let it alone this *y.* also,   Lu 13:8
till I
being the high priest that   Joh 11:49
same *y.*
but being high priest that *y.*   Joh 11:51
he
was the high priest that   Joh 18:13
same *y.*
that a whole *y.* they   Ac 11:26
assembled
he continued there a *y.* and   Ac 18:11
six
but also to be forward a *y.*   2Co 8:10
ago
Achaia was ready a *y.* ago   2Co 9:2
the high priest alone once   Heb 9:7
every *y.*
into the holy place every *y.*   Heb 9:25
with
they offered *y.* by *y.*   Heb 10:1
continually
again made of sins every *y.*   Heb 10:3
and continue there a *y.* and   Jas 4:13
buy
and a day, and a month, and   Re 9:15
a *y.*

YEARLY

as a *y.* hired servant shall he   Le 25:53
be
of Israel went *y.* to lament   J'g 11:40
is a feast of the Lord in   J'g 21:19
Shiloh *y.*
up out of his city *y.* to worship   1Sa 1:3
offer unto the Lord the *y.*   1Sa 1:21
sacrifice
husband to offer the *y.*   1Sa 2:19
sacrifice
there is a *y.* sacrifice there   1Sa 20:6
for all
charge ourselves *y.* with the   Ne 10:32
third
the fifteenth day of the same *y.*   Es 9:21

YEARN

bowels did *y.* upon his   Ge 43:30
brother

YEARNED

for her bowels *y.* upon her   1Ki 3:26
son

YEARNING

deep *y.* of Jesus Christ   Ph'p 1:9
(N)

YEARNINGS

with unspeakable *y.* and   Ro 8:26
groanings (A)

YEARS

for seasons, and for days, and   Ge 1:14
y.
lived an hundred and thirty *y.*   Ge 5:3
Seth were eight hundred *y.*   Ge 5:4
were nine hundred and thirty *y.*   Ge 5:5
Seth lived an hundred and five   Ge 5:6
y.
Enos eight hundred and seven   Ge 5:7
y.
were nine hundred and twelve *y.*   Ge 5:8
Enos lived ninety *y.* and begat   Ge 5:9
eight hundred and fifteen *y.*   Ge 5:10
were nine hundred and five *y.*   Ge 5:11
Cainan lived seventy *y.* and   Ge 5:12
begat
eight hundred and forty *y.* and   Ge 5:13
were nine hundred and ten *y.*   Ge 5:14
Mahalaleel lived sixty and five   Ge 5:15
y.
Jared eight hundred and thirty   Ge 5:16
y.
eight hundred ninety and five   Ge 5:17
y.
lived an hundred sixty and   Ge 5:18
two *y.*

he begat Enoch eight hundred *y.*   *Ge 5:19*
nine hundred sixty and two *y.*   *Ge 5:20*
Enoch lived sixty and five *y.*   *Ge 5:21*
Methuselah three hundred *y.*   *Ge 5:22*
three hundred sixty and five *y.*   *Ge 5:23*
an hundred eighty and seven *y.*   *Ge 5:25*
seven hundred eighty and two *y.*   *Ge 5:26*
nine hundred sixty and nine *y.*   *Ge 5:27*
an hundred eighty and two *y.*   *Ge 5:28*
five hundred ninety and five *y.*   *Ge 5:30*
hundred seventy and seven *y.*   *Ge 5:31*
Noah was five hundred *y.* old   *Ge 5:32*
shall be an hundred and twenty *y.*   *Ge 6:3*
Noah was six hundred *y.* old when   *Ge 7:6*
flood three hundred and fifty *y.*   *Ge 9:28*
were nine hundred and fifty *y.*   *Ge 9:29*
Shem was an hundred *y.* old   *Ge 11:10*
Arphaxad two *y.* after the flood   *Ge 11:10*
begat Arphaxad five hundred   *Ge 11:11*
Arphaxad lived five and thirty   *Ge 11:12*
Salah four hundred and three   *Ge 11:13*
Salah lived thirty *y.* and begat   *Ge 11:14*
Eber four hundred and three *y.*   *Ge 11:15*
And Eber lived four and thirty *y.*   *Ge 11:16*
Peleg four hundred and thirty *y.*   *Ge 11:17*
Peleg lived thirty *y.* and begat   *Ge 11:18*
begat Reu two hundred and nine *y.*   *Ge 11:19*
And Reu lived two and thirty   *Ge 11:20*
Serug two hundred and seven *y.*   *Ge 11:21*
Serug lived thirty *y.* and begat   *Ge 11:22*
he begat Nahor two hundred   *Ge 11:23*
Nahor lived nine and twenty *y.*   *Ge 11:24*
Terah an hundred and nineteen *y.*   *Ge 11:25*
Terah lived seventy *y.* and begat   *Ge 11:26*
were two hundred and five *y.*   *Ge 11:32*
Abram was seventy and five *y.* old   *Ge 12:4*
Twelve *y.* they served   *Ge 14:4*
Take me an heifer of three *y.* old   *Ge 15:9*
and a she goat of three *y.* old   *Ge 15:9*
and a ram of three *y.* old, and   *Ge 15:9*
shall afflict them four hundred *y.*   *Ge 15:13*
Abram had dwelt ten *y.* in the land   *Ge 16:3*
Abram was fourscore and six *y.* old   *Ge 16:16*
Abram was ninety *y.* old and nine   *Ge 17:1*
unto him that is an hundred *y.* old   *Ge 17:17*
Sarah, that is ninety *y.* old, bear   *Ge 17:17*
Abraham was ninety *y.* old and   *Ge 17:24*
his son was thirteen *y.* old   *Ge 17:25*
Abraham was an hundred *y.* old   *Ge 21:5*
and seven and twenty *y.* old   *Ge 23:1*
were the *y.* of the life of Sarah   *Ge 23:1*
days of the *y.* of Abraham's life   *Ge 25:7*
hundred threescore and fifteen *y.*   *Ge 25:7*
old age, an old man, and full of *y.*   *Ge 25:8*
are the *y.* of the life of Ishmael   *Ge 25:17*
hundred and thirty and seven *y.*   *Ge 25:17*
Isaac was forty *y.* old when he took   *Ge 25:20*
Isaac was threescore *y.* old when   *Ge 25:26*

Esau was forty *y.* old when he took   *Ge 26:34*
will serve thee seven *y.* for Rachel   *Ge 29:18*
Jacob served seven *y.* for Rachel   *Ge 29:20*
serve with me yet seven other *y.*   *Ge 29:27*
served with him yet seven other *y.*   *Ge 29:30*
twenty *y.* have I been with thee   *Ge 31:38*
have I been twenty *y.* in thy house   *Ge 31:41*
I served thee fourteen *y.* for thy   *Ge 31:41*
six *y.* for thy cattle: and thou hast   *Ge 31:41*
were an hundred and fourscore *y.*   *Ge 35:28*
Joseph, being seventeen *y.* old, was   *Ge 37:2*
to pass at the end of two full *y.*   *Ge 41:1*
The seven good kine are seven *y.*   *Ge 41:26*
the seven good ears are seven *y.*   *Ge 41:26*
came up after them are seven *y.*   *Ge 41:27*
wind shall be seven *y.* of famine   *Ge 41:27*
there come seven *y.* of great plenty   *Ge 41:29*
after them seven *y.* of famine   *Ge 41:30*
of Egypt in the seven plenteous *y.*   *Ge 41:34*
food of those good *y.* that come   *Ge 41:35*
against the seven *y.* of famine   *Ge 41:36*
Joseph was thirty *y.* old when he   *Ge 41:46*
in the seven plenteous *y.* the earth   *Ge 41:47*
up all the food of the seven *y.*   *Ge 41:48*
sons before the *y.* of famine came   *Ge 41:50*
And the seven *y.* of plenteousness   *Ge 41:53*
seven *y.* of dearth began to come   *Ge 41:54*
these two *y.* hath the famine been   *Ge 45:6*
and yet there are five *y.* in which   *Ge 45:6*
for yet there are five *y.* of famine   *Ge 45:11*
days of the *y.* of my pilgrimage are   *Ge 47:9*
are an hundred and thirty *y.*   *Ge 47:9*
the days of the *y.* of my life been   *Ge 47:9*
of the *y.* of the life of my fathers   *Ge 47:9*
in the land of Egypt seventeen *y.*   *Ge 47:28*
was an hundred forty and seven *y.*   *Ge 47:28*
lived an hundred and ten *y.*   *Ge 50:22*
being an hundred and ten *y.* old   *Ge 50:26*
the *y.* of the life of Levi were   *Ex 6:16*
an hundred thirty and seven *y.*   *Ex 6:16*
the *y.* of the life of Kohath were an   *Ex 6:18*
an hundred thirty and three *y.*   *Ex 6:18*
the *y.* of the life of Amram were an   *Ex 6:20*
hundred and thirty and seven *y.*   *Ex 6:20*
Moses was fourscore *y.* old   *Ex 7:7*
Aaron fourscore and three *y.* old   *Ex 7:7*
was four hundred and thirty *y.*   *Ex 12:40*
of the four hundred and thirty *y.*   *Ex 12:41*
of Israel did eat manna forty *y.*   *Ex 16:35*
servant, six *y.* he shall serve   *Ex 21:2*
and six *y.* thou shalt sow thy land   *Ex 23:10*
from twenty *y.* old and above, shall   *Ex 30:14*
from twenty *y.* old and upward   *Ex 38:26*
three *y.* shall it be as   *Le 19:23*
Six *y.* thou shalt sow thy field   *Le 25:3*
y. thou shalt prune thy vineyard   *Le 25:3*

number seven sabbaths of *y.* unto   *Le 25:8*
unto thee, seven times seven *y.*   *Le 25:8*
space of the seven sabbaths of *y.*   *Le 25:8*
be unto thee forty and nine *y.*   *Le 25:8*
the number of *y.* after the jubile   *Le 25:15*
the number of *y.* of the fruits   *Le 25:15*
According to the multitude of *y.*   *Le 25:16*
according to the fewness of *y.* thou   *Le 25:16*
according to the number of the *y.*   *Le 25:16*
shall bring forth fruit for three *y.*   *Le 25:21*
let him count the *y.* of the sale   *Le 25:27*
according unto the number of *y.*   *Le 25:50*
If there be yet many *y.* behind   *Le 25:51*
but few *y.* unto the year of jubile   *Le 25:52*
according unto his *y.* shall he give   *Le 25:52*
if he be not redeemed in *y.*   *Le 25:54*
twenty *y.* old even unto sixty *y.* old   *Le 27:3*
five *y.* old even unto twenty *y.* old   *Le 27:5*
a month old even unto five *y.* old   *Le 27:6*
if it be from sixty *y.* old and above   *Le 27:7*
according to the *y.* that remain   *Le 27:18*
From twenty *y.* old and upward   *Nu 1:3; 1:18, 20, 22, 24, 26, 28, 30, 32, 34, 36, 38, 40, 42, 45; 14:29; 26:2; 26:4; 32:11*
thirty *y.* old until fifty *y.* old   *Nu 4:3; 4:23, 30, 35, 39, 43, 47*
twenty and five *y.* old and upward   *Nu 8:24*
the age of fifty *y.* they shall cease   *Nu 8:25*
Hebron was built seven *y.* before   *Nu 13:22*
wander in the wilderness forty *y.*   *Nu 14:33; 32:13*
even forty *y.* and ye shall know   *Nu 14:34*
and twenty and three *y.* old   *Nu 33:39*
these forty *y.* the Lord thy God   *De 2:7*
Zered, was thirty and eight *y.*   *De 2:14*
thy God led thee these forty *y.*   *De 8:2*
did thy foot swell, these forty *y.*   *De 8:4*
end of three *y.* thou shalt bring   *De 14:28*
end of every seven *y.* thou shalt   *De 15:1*
unto thee, and serve thee six *y.*   *De 15:12*
to thee, in serving thee six *y.*   *De 15:18*
And I have led you forty *y.* in   *De 29:5*
hundred and twenty *y.* old this day   *De 31:2*
At the end of every seven *y.*   *De 31:10*
the *y.* of many generations   *De 32:7*
was an hundred and twenty *y.* old   *De 34:7*
children of Israel walked forty *y.*   *Jos 5:6*
Joshua was old and stricken in *y.*   *Jos 13:1*
Thou art old and stricken in *y.*   *Jos 13:1*
Forty *y.* old was I when Moses the   *Jos 14:7*
these forty and five *y.* even since   *Jos 14:10*
this day fourscore and five *y.* old   *Jos 14:10*
being an hundred and ten *y.* old   *Jos 24:29; J'g 2:8*
Chushan-rishathaim eight *y.*   *J'g 3:8*
And the land had rest forty *y.*   *J'g 3:11; 5:31*
the king of Moab eighteen *y.*   *J'g 3:14*
And the land had rest fourscore *y.*   *J'g 3:30*
twenty *y.* he mightily oppressed   *J'g 4:3*
into the hand of Midian seven *y.*   *J'g 6:1*
the second bullock of seven *y.* old   *J'g 6:25*
country was in quietness forty *y.*   *J'g 8:28*
Abimelech had reigned three *y.*   *J'g 9:22*

judged Israel twenty and three *J'g 10:2*
y.
judged Israel twenty and two *y.* *J'g 10:3*
eighteen *y.* all the children of *J'g 10:8*
coasts of Arnon, three *J'g 11:26*
hundred *y.*
And Jephthah judged Israel six *J'g 12:7*
y.
And he judged Israel seven *y.* *J'g 12:9*
Israel; and he judged Israel *J'g 12:11*
ten *y.*
and he judged Israel eight *y.* *J'g 12:14*
the hand of the Philistines *J'g 13:1*
forty *y.*
days of the Philistines twenty *J'g 15:20*
y.
And he judged Israel twenty *J'g 16:31*
y.
they dwelled there about ten *y.* *Ru 1:4*
Eli was ninety and eight *y.* *1Sa 4:15*
old
And he had judged Israel *1Sa 4:18*
forty *y.*
time was long; for it was *1Sa 7:3*
twenty *y.*
he had reigned two *y.* over *1Sa 13:1*
Israel
with me these days, or these *1Sa 29:3*
Saul's son was forty *y.* old *2Sa 2:10*
when
over Israel, and reigned two *2Sa 2:10*
y.
Judah was seven *y.* and six *2Sa 2:11*
He was five *y.* old when the *2Sa 4:4*
tidings
David was thirty *y.* old when *2Sa 5:4*
he
to reign, and he reigned forty *2Sa 5:4*
y.
he reigned over Judah seven *y.* *2Sa 5:5*
thirty and three *y.* over all *2Sa 5:5*
Israel
it came to pass after two *2Sa 13:23*
full *y.*
to Geshur, and was there *2Sa 13:38*
three *y.*
So Absalom dwelt two full *2Sa 14:28*
y. in
and it came to pass after *2Sa 15:7*
forty *y.*
aged man, even fourscore *y.* *2Sa 19:32*
old
I am this day fourscore *y.* *2Sa 19:35*
old
famine in the days of David *2Sa 21:1*
three *y.*
Shall seven *y.* of famine *2Sa 24:13*
come unto
David was old and stricken in *1Ki 1:1*
y.
reigned over Israel were forty *1Ki 2:11*
y.
seven *y.* reigned he in Hebron *1Ki 2:11*
thirty and three *y.* reigned he *1Ki 2:11*
in
came to pass at the end of *1Ki 2:39*
three *y.*
So was he seven *y.* in building *1Ki 6:38*
it
building his own house *1Ki 7:1*
thirteen *y.*
to pass at the end of *1Ki 9:10*
twenty *y.*
once in three *y.* came the *1Ki 10:22*
navy of
over all Israel was forty *y.* *1Ki 11:42*
reigned were two and twenty *1Ki 14:20*
y.
Rehoboam was forty and one *1Ki 14:21*
y. old
reigned seventeen *y.* in *1Ki 14:21*
Jerusalem
Three *y.* reigned he in *1Ki 15:2*
Jerusalem
And forty and one *y.* *1Ki 15:10*
reigned he in
and reigned over Israel two *1Ki 15:25*
y.
Israel in Tirzah, twenty *1Ki 15:33*
and four *y.*
reign over Israel in Tirzah, *1Ki 16:8*
two *y.*
to reign over Israel, twelve *1Ki 16:23*
y.
six *y.* reigned he in Tirzah *1Ki 16:23*
in Samaria twenty and two *1Ki 16:29*
y.
shall not be dew nor rain *1Ki 17:1*
these *y.*

they continued three *y.* *1Ki 22:1*
without war
thirty and five *y.* old when *1Ki 22:42*
he
he reigned twenty and five *y.* *1Ki 22:42*
in
and reigned two *y.* over *1Ki 22:51*
Israel
of Judah, and reigned twelve *2Ki 3:1*
y.
also come upon the land seven *2Ki 8:1*
y.
land of the Philistines seven *2Ki 8:2*
y.
Thirty and two *y.* old was he *2Ki 8:17*
when
he reigned eight *y.* in *2Ki 8:17*
Jerusalem
Two and twenty *y.* old was *2Ki 8:26*
Ahaziah
Samaria was twenty and *2Ki 10:36*
eight *y.*
hid in the house of the Lord *2Ki 11:3*
six *y.*
Seven *y.* old was Jehoash *2Ki 11:21*
when he
forty *y.* reigned he in *2Ki 12:1*
Jerusalem
Samaria, and reigned *2Ki 13:1*
seventeen *y.*
Samaria, and reigned sixteen *2Ki 13:10*
y.
twenty and five *y.* old when *2Ki 14:2*
he
twenty and nine *y.* in *2Ki 14:2*
Jerusalem
Jehoahaz king of Israel *2Ki 14:17*
fifteen *y.*
which was sixteen *y.* old, *2Ki 14:21*
and made
and reigned forty and one *y.* *2Ki 14:23*
Sixteen *y.* old was he when *2Ki 15:2*
two and fifty *y.* in Jerusalem *2Ki 15:2*
and reigned ten *y.* in *2Ki 15:17*
Samaria
in Samaria, and reigned two *2Ki 15:23*
y.
in Samaria, and reigned *2Ki 15:27*
twenty *y.*
Five and twenty *y.* old was *2Ki 15:33*
he when
he reigned sixteen *y.* in *2Ki 15:33*
Jerusalem
Twenty *y.* old was Ahaz *2Ki 16:2*
when he
reigned sixteen *y.* in *2Ki 16:2*
Jerusalem
in Samaria over Israel nine *y.* *2Ki 17:1*
Samaria, and besieged it *2Ki 17:5*
three *y.*
Twenty and five *y.* old was he *2Ki 18:2*
when
twenty and nine *y.* in *2Ki 18:2*
Jerusalem
at the end of three *y.* they *2Ki 18:10*
took it
will add unto thy days fifteen *2Ki 20:6*
y.
Manasseh was twelve *y.* old *2Ki 21:1*
when
fifty and five *y.* in Jerusalem *2Ki 21:1*
Amon was twenty and two *2Ki 21:19*
y. old
he reigned two *y.* in *2Ki 21:19*
Jerusalem
Josiah was eight *y.* old when *2Ki 22:1*
he
thirty and one *y.* in Jerusalem *2Ki 22:1*
Jehoahaz was twenty and *2Ki 23:31*
three *y.*
Jehoiakim was twenty and *2Ki 23:36*
five *y.*
reigned eleven *y.* in Jerusalem *2Ki 23:36*
became his servant three *y.* *2Ki 24:1*
Jehoiachin was eighteen *y.* *2Ki 24:8*
old
Zedekiah was twenty and *2Ki 24:18*
one *y.* old
he reigned eleven *y.* in *2Ki 24:18*
Jerusalem
when he was threescore *y.* *1Ch 2:21*
reigned seven *y.* and six *1Ch 3:4*
months
he reigned thirty and three *y.* *1Ch 3:4*
the age of thirty *y.* and *1Ch 23:3*
upward
the age of twenty *y.* and *1Ch 23:24*
upward
from twenty *y.* old and above *1Ch 23:27*

from twenty *y.* old and *1Ch 27:23*
under
he reigned over Israel was *1Ch 29:27*
forty *y.*
seven *y.* reigned he in *1Ch 29:27*
Hebron
and thirty and three *y.* *1Ch 29:27*
reigned he
to pass at the end of twenty *y.* *2Ch 8:1*
every three *y.* once came the *2Ch 9:21*
ships
Jerusalem over all Israel *2Ch 9:30*
forty *y.*
son of Solomon strong, *2Ch 11:17*
three *y.*
three *y.* they walked in the *2Ch 11:17*
way of
Rehoboam was one and *2Ch 12:13*
forty *y.* old
reigned seventeen *y.* in *2Ch 12:13*
Jerusalem
He reigned three *y.* in *2Ch 13:2*
Jerusalem
his days the land was quiet *2Ch 14:1*
ten *y.*
rest, and he had no war in *2Ch 14:6*
those *y.*
after certain *y.* he went down *2Ch 18:2*
to
he was thirty and five *y.* *2Ch 20:31*
old when
he reigned twenty and five *2Ch 20:31*
y. in
Jehoram was thirty and two *2Ch 21:5*
y. old
he reigned eight *y.* in *2Ch 21:5*
Jerusalem
of time, after the end of *2Ch 21:19*
two *y.*
Thirty and two *y.* old was *2Ch 21:20*
he
he reigned in Jerusalem *2Ch 21:20*
eight *y.*
Forty and two *y.* old was *2Ch 22:2*
Ahaziah
them hid in the house of *2Ch 22:12*
God six *y.*
Joash was seven *y.* old when *2Ch 24:1*
he
he reigned forty *y.* in *2Ch 24:1*
Jerusalem
an hundred and thirty *y.* old *2Ch 24:15*
was he
Amaziah was twenty and five *2Ch 25:1*
y. old
he reigned twenty and nine *y.* *2Ch 25:1*
from twenty *y.* old and above *2Ch 25:5*
Jehoahaz king of Israel *2Ch 25:25*
fifteen *y.*
Uzziah, who was sixteen *y.* *2Ch 26:1*
old
Sixteen *y.* old was Uzziah *2Ch 26:3*
when he
and he reigned fifty and two *2Ch 26:3*
y. in
Jotham was twenty and five *2Ch 27:1*
old
he reigned sixteen *y.* in *2Ch 27:1*
Jerusalem
He was five and twenty *y.* old *2Ch 27:8*
reigned sixteen *y.* in *2Ch 27:8*
Jerusalem
Ahaz was twenty *y.* old when *2Ch 28:1*
he reigned sixteen *y.* in *2Ch 28:1*
Jerusalem
when he was five and twenty *2Ch 29:1*
y. old
he reigned nine and twenty *y.* *2Ch 29:1*
from three *y.* old and *2Ch 31:16*
upward, even
from twenty *y.* old and *2Ch 31:17*
upward
Manasseh was twelve *y.* old *2Ch:33:1*
when
and he reigned fifty and five *2Ch 33:1*
y. in
Amon was two and twenty *2Ch 33:21*
y. old
and reigned two *y.* in *2Ch 33:21*
Jerusalem
Josiah was eight *y.* old when *2Ch 34:1*
he
in Jerusalem one and thirty *2Ch 34:1*
y.
Jehoahaz was twenty and *2Ch 36:2*
three *y.*
Jehoiakim was twenty and *2Ch 36:5*
five *y.*
he reigned eleven *y.* in *2Ch 36:5*
Jerusalem

Jehoiachin was eight *y.* old   *2Ch 36:9*
when
Zedekiah was one and   *2Ch 36:11*
twenty *y.* old
reigned eleven *y.* in   *2Ch 36:11*
Jerusalem
to fulfill threescore and ten   *2Ch 36:21*
y.
from twenty *y.* old and upward   *Ezr 3:8*
was builded these many *y.*   *Ezr 5:11*
ago
twelve *y.* I and my brethren   *Ne 5:14*
have
forty *y.* didst thou sustain them   *Ne 9:21*
in
Yet many *y.* didst thou forbear   *Ne 9:30*
of man? are thy *y.* as man's   *Job 10:5*
days
the number of *y.* is hidden   *Job 15:20*
to the
When a few *y.* are come,   *Job 16:22*
then I
and multitude of *y.* should   *Job 32:7*
teach
and their *y.* in pleasures   *Job 36:11*
number of his *y.* be searched   *Job 36:26*
out
lived Job an hundred and   *Job 42:16*
forty *y.*
with grief, and my *y.* with   *Ps 31:10*
sighing
and his *y.* as many generations   *Ps 61:6*
days of old, the *y.* of ancient   *Ps 77:5*
times
remember the *y.* of the right   *Ps 77:10*
hand
in vanity, and their *y.* in   *Ps 78:33*
trouble
For a thousand *y.* in thy sight   *Ps 90:4*
are
we spend our *y.* as a tale that   *Ps 90:9*
is
The days of our *y.* are   *Ps 90:10*
threescore *y.*
of strength they be fourscore   *Ps 90:10*
y.
the *y.* wherein we have seen   *Ps 90:15*
evil
Forty *y.* long was I grieved   *Ps 95:10*
with
y. are throughout all   *Ps 102:24*
generations
same, and thy *y.* shall have   *Ps 102:27*
no end
and the *y.* of thy life shall be   *Pr 4:10*
many
others, and thy *y.* unto the   *Pr 5:9*
cruel
the *y.* of thy life shall be   *Pr 9:11*
increased
y. of the wicked shall be   *Pr 10:27*
shortened
hundred children, and live   *Ec 6:3*
many *y.*
so that the days of his *y.* be   *Ec 6:3*
many
though he live a thousand *y.*   *Ec 6:6*
twice
But if a man live many *y.* and   *Ec 11:8*
nor the *y.* draw nigh, when   *Ec 12:1*
thou
within threescore and five.   *Isa 7:8*
shall
unto Zoar, an heifer of thee *y.*   *Isa 15:5*
old
Within three *y.* as the *y.* of   *Isa 16:14*
walked naked and barefoot   *Isa 20:3*
three *y.*
according to the *y.* of an   *Isa 21:16*
hireling
Tyre shall be forgotten   *Isa 23:15*
seventy *y.*
end of seventy *y.* shall Tyre   *Isa 23:15*
sing
to pass after the end of   *Isa 23:17*
seventy *y.*
days and *y.* shall ye be   *Isa 32:10*
troubled
I will add unto thy days   *Isa 38:5*
fifteen *y.*
deprived of the residue of   *Isa 38:10*
my *y.*
I shall go softly all my *y.* in   *Isa 38:15*
child shall die an hundred *y.*   *Isa 65:20*
old
the sinner being an hundred   *Isa 65:20*
y. old
the king of Babylon seventy   *Jer 25:11*
y.

when seventy *y.* are   *Jer 25:12*
accomplished
Within two full *y.* will I bring   *Jer 28:3*
within the space of two full   *Jer 28:11*
y.
after seventy *y.* be   *Jer 29:10*
accomplished
At the end of seven *y.* let ye   *Jer 34:14*
go
when he hath served thee six   *Jer 34:14*
y.
as an heifer of three *y.* old   *Jer 48:34*
Zedekiah was one and twenty   *Jer 52:1*
y.
he reigned eleven *y.* in   *Jer 52:1*
Jerusalem
upon thee the *y.* of their   *Eze 4:5*
iniquity
and art come even unto thy *y.*   *Eze 22:4*
shall it be inhabited forty *y.*   *Eze 29:11*
waste shall be desolate forty   *Eze 29:12*
y.
At the end of forty *y.* will I   *Eze 29:13*
gather
in the latter *y.* thou shalt   *Eze 38:8*
come
in those days many *y.* that I   *Eze 38:17*
would
shall burn them with fire   *Eze 39:9*
seven *y.*
so nourishing them three *y.*   *Da 1:5*
that at
let seven *y.* pass over him (B)   *Da 4:16*
about threescore and two *y.*   *Da 5:31*
a year, two *y.*, and half a year   *Da 7:25*
(B)
by books the number of the *y.*   *Da 9:2*
he would accomplish seventy *y.*   *Da 9:2*
and in the end of *y.* they shall   *Da 11:6*
join
continue more *y.* than the king   *Da 11:8*
come after certain *y.* with a   *Da 11:13*
great
after it, even to the *y.* of many   *Joe 2:2*
restore to you the *y.* that the   *Joe 2:25*
locust
two *y.* before the earthquake   *Am 1:1*
led you forty *y.* through the   *Am 2:10*
and your tithes after three *y.*   *Am 4:4*
in the wilderness forty *y.*   *Am 5:25*
thy work in the midst of the   *Hab 3:2*
y.
in the midst of the *y.* make   *Hab 3:2*
known
these threescore and ten *y.*   *Zec 1:12*
as I have done these so many   *Zec 7:3*
y.
even those seventy *y.* did ye all   *Zec 7:5*
the days of old, and as in   *Mal 3:4*
former *y.*
from two *y.* old and under   *M't 2:16*
with an issue of blood twelve   *M't 9:20*
y.
had an issue of blood twelve *y.*   *M'k 5:25*
for she was of the age of   *M'k 5:42*
twelve *y.*
both were now well stricken in   *Lu 1:7*
y.
and my wife well stricken in *y.*   *Lu 1:18*
had lived with an husband   *Lu 2:36*
seven *y.*
of about fourscore and four *y.*   *Lu 2:37*
when he was twelve *y.* old,   *Lu 2:42*
they
began to be about thirty *y.* of   *Lu 3:23*
age
shut up three *y.* and six   *Lu 4:25*
months
daughter, about twelve *y.* of age   *Lu 8:42*
having an issue of blood   *Lu 8:43*
twelve *y.*
much goods laid up for many   *Lu 12:19*
y.
these three *y.* I come seeking   *Lu 13:7*
fruit
had a spirit of infirmity   *Lu 13:11*
eighteen *y.*
hath bound, lo, these   *Lu 13:16*
eighteen *y.*
Lo, these many *y.* do I serve   *Lu 15:29*
thee
Forty and six *y.* was this   *Joh 2:20*
temple in
had an infirmity thirty and   *Joh 5:5*
eight *y.*
Thou art not yet fifty *y.* old   *Joh 8:57*
the man was above forty *y.*   *Ac 4:22*
old

entreat them evil four hundred   *Ac 7:6*
y.
And when he was full forty   *Ac 7:23*
old
And when forty *y.* were   *Ac 7:30*
expired
and in the wilderness forty *y.*   *Ac 7:36*
space of forty *y.* in the   *Ac 7:42*
wilderness
which had kept his bed eight   *Ac 9:33*
y.
And about the time of forty   *Ac 13:18*
y.
space of four hundred and   *Ac 13:20*
fifty *y.*
Benjamin, by the space of   *Ac 13:21*
forty *y.*
continued by the space of   *Ac 19:10*
two *y.*
the space of three *y.* I ceased   *Ac 20:31*
not
thou hast been of many *y.* a   *Ac 24:10*
judge
after many *y.* I came to   *Ac 24:17*
bring alms
after two *y.* Porcius Festus   *Ac 24:27*
came
Paul dwelt two whole *y.* in   *Ac 28:30*
his own
he was about an hundred *y.* old   *Ro 4:19*
a great desire these many *y.*   *Ro 15:23*
to
in Christ above fourteen *y.*   *2Co 12:2*
ago
Then after three *y.* I went up   *Ga 1:18*
to
fourteen *y.* after I went up   *Ga 2:1*
again
four hundred and thirty *y.*   *Ga 3:17*
after
and months, and times, and *y.*   *Ga 4:10*
number under threescore *y.* old   *1Ti 5:9*
the same, and thy *y.* shall   *Heb 1:12*
not fail
me, and saw my works forty   *Heb 3:9*
y.
whom was he grieved forty   *Heb 3:17*
y.
when he was come to *y.*   *Heb 11:24*
earth by the space of three *y.*   *Jas 5:17*
is with the Lord as a   *2Pe 3:8*
thousand *y.*
and a thousand *y.* as one day   *2Pe 3:8*
for three *y.* and a half (N)   *Re 12:14*
and bound him a thousand *y.*   *Re 20:2*
the thousand *y.* should be   *Re 20:3*
fulfilled
reigned with Christ a   *Re 20:4*
thousand *y.*
until the thousand *y.* were   *Re 20:5*
finished
shall reign with him a   *Re 20:6*
thousand *y.*
when the thousand *y.* are   *Re 20:7*
expired

YEAR'S

feast of ingathering at the *y.*   *Ex 34:22*
end
at every *y.* end that he polled   *2Sa 14:26*
it

YEARS'

came to pass at the seven *y.*   *2Ki 8:3*
end
Either three *y.* famine; or   *1Ch 21:2*
three

YELL

they shall *y.* as lions' whelps   *Jer 51:38*
growling like lion's whelps   *Jer 51:38*
(A)
growl like lion's whelps   *Jer 51:38*
(B)(E)(R)
let out a *y.* (P)   *Lu 8:28*

YELLED

lions roared upon him, and *y.*   *Jer 2:15*
made their voices heard (A)   *Jer 2:15*
made their voices resound (B)   *Jer 2:15*
roared loudly (R)   *Jer 2:15*

YELLOW

and there be in it a *y.* thin   *Le 13:30*
hair

and there be in it no *y*. hair   Le 13:32
the priest shall not seek for *y*.   Le 13:36
hair
and her feathers with *y*. gold   Ps 68:13

YES

He saith, *Y*. And when he   M't 17:25
was
and said unto him, *Y*., Lord   M'k 7:28
Gentiles? *Y*. of the Gentiles   Ro 3:29
also
Y. verily, their sound went   Ro 10:18
into

YESTERDAY

task in making brick both *y*.   Ex 5:14
to meat, neither *y*. nor   1Sa 20:27
to-day
Whereas thou camest but *y*.   2Sa 15:20
I have seen *y*. the blood of   2Ki 9:26
Naboth
For we are but of *y*. and know   Job 8:9
years in thy sight are but as *y*.   Ps 90:4
y. at the seventh hour the   Joh 4:52
fever
as thou diddest the Egyptian *y*.   Ac 7:28
Jesus Christ the same *y*. and   Heb 13:8
to-day

YESTERNIGHT

Behold, I lay *y*. with my   Ge 19:34
father
God of your father spake   Ge 31:29
unto me *y*.
of my hands, and rebuked   Ge 31:42
thee *y*.

YET

y. his days shall be an hundred   Ge 6:3
y. seven days, and I will cause   Ge 7:4
it
And he stayed *y*. other seven   Ge 8:10;
days   8:12
of the Amorites is not *y*. full   Ge 15:16
but Abraham stood *y*. before   Ge 18:22
And he spake unto him *y*.   Ge 18:29
again
and I will speak *y*. but this   Ge 18:32
once
And *y*. indeed she is my   Ge 20:12
sister
neither *y*. heard I of it, but   Ge 21:26
to-day
Isaac his son, while he *y*. lived   Ge 25:6
Jacob was *y*. scarce gone out   Ge 27:30
from
And he said, Lo, it is *y*. high   Ge 29:7
day
And while he *y*. spake with   Ge 29:9
them
serve with me *y*. seven other   Ge 29:27
years
with him *y*. other seven years   Ge 29:30
Is there *y*. any portion or   Ge 31:14
y. wherefore hast stolen my   Ge 31:30
gods
and they hated him *y*. the   Ge 37:5;
more   37:8
And he dreamed *y*. another   Ge 37:9
dream
And she *y*. again conceived   Ge 38:5
Y. within three days shall   Ge 40:13;
    40:19
Y. did not the chief butler   Ge 40:23
remember
man whether ye had *y*. a   Ge 43:6
brother
saying, Is your father *y*. alive   Ge 43:7
of whom ye spake? Is he *y*.   Ge 43:27
alive
is in good health, he is *y*.   Ge 43:28
alive
gone out of the city, and not   Ge 44:4
y. far off
house; for he was *y*. there   Ge 44:14
am Joseph; doth my father *y*.   Ge 45:3
live
y. there are five years, in the   Ge 45:6
which
for *y*. here are five years of   Ge 45:11
famine
told him, saying, Joseph is *y*.   Ge 45:26
alive
Joseph my son is *y*. alive: I   Ge 45:28
will go
thy face, because thou art *y*.   Ge 46:30
alive

when *y*. there was but a little   Ge 48:7
way
and see whether they be *y*.   Ex 4:18
alive
y. not ought of your work   Ex 5:11
shall
y. shall ye deliver the tale of   Ex 5:18
bricks
y. exaltest thou thyself against   Ex 9:17
ye will not *y*. fear the Lord   Ex 9:30
God
he sinned *y*. more, and   Ex 9:34
hardened
knowest thou not *y*. that   Ex 10:7
Egypt is
Y. will I bring one plague   Ex 11:1
more
from her, and *y*. no mischief   Ex 21:22
follow
Y. thou hast said, I know   Ex 33:12
thee by
brought *y*. unto him free   Ex 36:3
offerings
though he wist it not *y*. is he   Le 5:17
guilty
y. he cheweth not the cud   Le 11:7
Y. these may ye eat of every   Le 11:21
flying
his head, he is bald; *y*. is he   Le 13:40
clean
he is forehead bald; *y*. is he   Le 13:41
clean
eat *y*. of old fruit until the   Le 25:22
ninth year
If there be *y*. many years   Le 25:51
behind
ye will not *y*. for all this   Le 26:18
hearken
you *y*. seven times for your   Le 26:24
sins
y. for all that, when they be   Le 26:44
in the
y. he shall keep the passover   Nu 9:10
unto
flesh was *y*. between their   Nu 11:33
teeth
his uncleanness is *y*. upon   Nu 19:13
him
And Balak sent *y*. again   Nu 22:15
princes
y. the word which I shalt say   Nu 22:20
unto
y. in her youth in her   Nu 30:16
father's house
to augment *y*. the fierce anger   Nu 32:14
of
he will *y*. again leave them   Nu 32:15
in the
y. in this thing ye did not   De 1:32
believe
Y. they are thy people and   De 9:29
thine
not as *y*. come to the rest   De 12:9
the hoof, *y*. cheweth not the   De 14:8
cud
vineyard, and hath not *y*.   De 20:6
eaten of it
and *y*. these are the tokens   De 22:17
of my
Y. the Lord hath not given   De 29:4
you
while I am *y*. alive with you   De 31:27
this
y. thou shalt see the land   De 32:52
before
y. there shall be a place   Jos 3:4
between
there remaineth *y*. very much   Jos 13:1
land
This is the land that *y*.   Jos 13:2
remaineth
As *y*. I am as strong this day   Jos 14:11
as I
Y. the children of Manasseh   Jos 17:12
could
Y. it came to pass, when the   Jos 17:13
children
had not *y*. received their   Jos 18:2
inheritance
y. the hand of the house of   J'g 1:35
Joseph
nor *y*. the works which he had   J'g 2:10
y. they would not hearken   J'g 2:17
unto
is *y*. in Ophrah of the   J'g 6:24
Abi-ezrites
to death whilst it is *y*.   J'g 6:31
morning
The people are *y*. too many   J'g 7:4

with him, faint, *y*. pursuing   J'g 8:4
them
feared, because he was *y*. a   J'g 8:20
youth
y. Jotham the youngest son of   J'g 9:5
Y. ye have forsaken me,   J'g 10:13
and serve
y. will I be avenged of you   J'g 15:7
Y. he restored the money unto   J'g 17:4
his
Y. there is both straw and   J'g 19:19
Shall I *y*. again go out to   J'g 20:28
battle
and *y*. so they suffced them   J'g 21:14
not
are there *y*. any more sons   Ru 1:11
in my
the Lord called *y*. again,   1Sa 3:6
Samuel
Samuel did not *y*. know the   1Sa 3:7
Lord
word of the Lord *y*. revealed   1Sa 3:7
unto
y. protest solemnly unto them   1Sa 8:9
if the man shall *y*. come   1Sa 10:22
thither
y. turn not aside from   1Sa 12:20
following
As for Saul, he was *y*. in   1Sa 13:7
Gilgal
Y. they had a file for the   1Sa 13:21
mattocks
I have sinned: *y*. honour me   1Sa 15:30
now
There remaineth *y*. the   1Sa 16:11
youngest
Saul was *y*. the more afraid   1Sa 18:29
not only while *y*. I live shew   1Sa 20:14
me
enquired of the Lord *y*. again   1Sa 23:4
Go, I pray you, prepare *y*.   1Sa 23:22
and know
y. thou huntest my soul to   1Sa 24:11
take it
Y. a man is risen to pursue   1Sa 25:29
thee
because my life is *y*. whole in   2Sa 1:9
me
to eat meat while it was *y*.   2Sa 3:35
day
were *y*. sons and daughters   2Sa 5:13
born
the Philistines came up *y*.   2Sa 5:22
again
I will *y*. be more vile than   2Sa 6:22
thus
was *y*. a small thing in thy   2Sa 7:19
sight
there *y*. any that is left of the   2Sa 9:1
house
not *y*. any of the house of Saul   2Sa 9:3
Jonathan hath *y*. a son, which   2Sa 9:3
is
while the child was *y*. alive,   2Sa 12:18
we
While the child was *y*.   2Sa 12:22
alive, I fasted
y. doth he devise means,   2Sa 14:14
that his
y. would I not put forth   2Sa 18:12
mine hand
was *y*. alive in the midst of   2Sa 18:14
the oak
the son of Zadok *y*. again   2Sa 18:22
y. didst thou set thy servant   2Sa 19:28
among
what right therefore have I *y*.   2Sa 19:28
to cry
servant be *y*. a burden unto   2Sa 19:35
my
the Philistines had *y*. war   2Sa 21:15
again
there was *y*. a battle in   2Sa 21:20
Gath
y. he hath made with me an   2Sa 23:5
y. talkest there with the king   1Ki 1:14
while she *y*. talked with the   1Ki 1:22
king
And while he *y*. spake,   1Ki 1:42
behold
Y. have thou respect unto the   1Ki 8:28
prayer
Y. if they shall bethink   1Ki 8:47
themselves
Egypt; Hadad being *y*. a   1Ki 11:17
little child
Nebat, who was *y*. in Egypt,   1Ki 12:2
heard
Depart *y*. for three days, then   1Ki 12:5

Solomon his father while he *y.* lived   *1Ki 12:6*

y. thou hast not been as my servant   *1Ki 14:8*

Y. I have left me seven thousand in   *1Ki 19:18*

Y. I will send my servants unto   *1Ki 20:6*

And he said, Is he *y.* alive? he is   *1Ki 20:32*

There is *y.* one man, Micaiah   *1Ki 22:8*

burn incense *y.* in the high places   *1Ki 22:43*

y. that valley shall be filled with water   *2Ki 3:17*

unto her son, bring me *y.* a vessel   *2Ki 4:6*

And while he *y.* talked with them   *2Ki 6:33*

Y. the Lord would not destroy Judah   *2Ki 8:19*

Y. Edom revolted from under them from his presence as *y.*   *2Ki 8:22*

y. not like David his father   *2Ki 14:3*

as *y.* the people did sacrifice   *2Ki 14:4*

Y. the Lord testified against Israel   *2Ki 17:13*

Judah shall *y.* again take root   *2Ki 19:30*

while he *y.* kept himself close   *1Ch 12:1*

the Philistines *y.* again spread   *1Ch 14:13*

y. this was a small thing in thine   *1Ch 17:17*

y. again there was war at Gath   *1Ch 20:6*

y. his father made him the chief   *1Ch 26:10*

hath chosen, is *y.* young and tender   *1Ch 29:1*

neither *y.* hast asked long life   *2Ch 1:11*

y. so that thy children take heed   *2Ch 6:16*

y. if they pray toward this place, and   *2Ch 6:26*

Y. if they bethink themselves in the   *2Ch 6:37*

Solomon his father while he *y.* lived   *2Ch 10:6*

Y. Jeroboam the son of Nebat   *2Ch 13:6*

while the land is *y.* before us   *2Ch 14:7*

y. because thou didst rely on   *2Ch 16:8*

y. in his disease he sought not to   *2Ch 16:12*

There is *y.* one man, by whom we   *2Ch 18:7*

as *y.* the people had not prepared   *2Ch 20:33*

Y. he sent prophets to them, to bring   *2Ch 24:19*

And the people did *y.* corruptly   *2Ch 27:2*

trespass *y.* more against the Lord   *2Ch 28:22*

y. did they eat the passover   *2Ch 30:18*

this manner, neither *y.* believe him   *2Ch 32:15*

And his servants spake *y.* more   *2Ch 32:16*

y. unto the Lord their God only   *2Ch 33:17*

while he was *y.* young, he began   *2Ch 34:3*

the temple of the Lord was not *y.*   *Ezr 3:6*

in building, and *y.* it is not finished   *Ezr 5:16*

y. our God hath not fosaken us in   *Ezr 9:9*

for we remain *y.* escaped, as it is this   *Ezr 9:15*

y. now there is hope in Israel   *Ezr 10:2*

y. will I gather them from thence   *Ne 1:9*

neither had I as *y.* told it to   *Ne 2:16*

Y. now our flesh is as the flesh of our   *Ne 5:5*

y. for all this required not I the bread   *Ne 5:18*

Y. they sent unto me four times   *Ne 6:4*

Y. thou in thy manifold mercies   *Ne 9:19*

y. when they returned, and cried unto   *Ne 9:28*

y. they dealt proudly, and hearkened   *Ne 9:29*

Y. many years didst thou forbear   *Ne 9:30*

prophets: *y.* would they not give ear   *Ne 9:30*

y. ye bring more wrath upon Israel by   *Ne 13:18*

y. among many nations were there no   *Ne 13:26*

Esther had not *y.* shewed her   *Es 2:20*

Y. all this availeth me nothing   *Es 5:13*

they were *y.* talking with him   *Es 6:14*

Esther spake *y.* again before the   *Es 8:3*

While he was *y.* speaking   *Job 1:16; 1:17, 18*

neither was I quiet; *y.* trouble came   *Job 3:26*

Y. man is born to trouble, as   *Job 5:7*

Then should I *y.* have comfort   *Job 6:10*

y. thy latter end should greatly   *Job 8:7*

Whilst it is *y.* in his greenness   *Job 8:12*

righteous, *y.* would I not answer   *Job 9:15*

y. would I not believe that he had   *Job 9:16*

y. would I not know my soul   *Job 9:21*

Y. shalt thou plunge me in   *Job 9:31*

about; *y.* thou dost destroy me   *Job 10:8*

y. will I not lift up my head   *Job 10:15*

he slay me, *y.* will I trust in him   *Job 13:15*

Y. through the scent of water it will   *Job 14:9*

body, *y.* in my flesh shall I see God   *Job 19:26*

Y. he shall perish for ever like his   *Job 20:7*

Y. his meat in his bowels is turned   *Job 20:14*

Y. shall he be brought to the grave   *Job 21:32*

Y. he filled their houses with good   *Job 22:18*

y. God layeth not folly to them   *Job 24:12*

y. his eyes are upon their ways   *Job 24:23*

the Almighty was *y.* with me   *Job 29:5*

answer, and *y.* had condemned Job   *Job 32:3*

yea twice, *y.* man perceiveth it not   *Job 33:14*

y. judgment is before him   *Job 35:14*

anger; *y.* he knoweth it not in great   *Job 35:15*

have *y.* to speak on God's behalf   *Job 36:2*

Y. have I set my king upon my holy   *Ps 2:6*

For *y.* a little while, and the   *Ps 37:10*

y. have I not seen the righteous   *Ps 37:25*

Y. he passed away, and, lo, he was   *Ps 37:36*

needy; *y.* the Lord thinketh upon me   *Ps 40:17*

I shall *y.* praise him for the help   *Ps 42:5*

Y. the Lord will command his   *Ps 42:8*

for I shall *y.* praise him, who is   *Ps 42:5; 42:11*

y. have we not forgotten thee, neither   *Ps 44:17*

y. their posterity approve their   *Ps 49:13*

than oil, *y.* were they drawn swords   *Ps 55:21*

y. shall ye be as the wings of a dove   *Ps 68:13*

will *y.* praise thee more and more   *Ps 71:14*

sinned *y.* more against him   *Ps 78:17*

their meat was *y.* in their mouths   *Ps 78:30*

Y. they tempted and provoked   *Ps 78:56*

years, *y.* is their strength labour and   *Ps 90:10*

Y. they say, The Lord shall not see   *Ps 94:7*

Y. setteth he the poor on high from   *Ps 107:41*

Y. have I not declined from thy law   *Ps 119:51*

smoke *y.* do I not forget thy statutes   *Ps 119:83*

my hand; *y.* do I not forget thy law   *Ps 119:109*

me; *y.* I erred not from thy precepts   *Ps 119:110*

y. do not I forget thy precepts   *Ps 119:141*

me: *y.* thy commandments are my   *Ps 119:143*

y. do not I decline from thy   *Ps 119:157*

y. they have not prevailed   *Ps 129:2*

y. hath he respect unto the lowly   *Ps 138:6*

my substance, *y.* being unperfect   *Ps 139:16*

when as *y.* there was none of them   *Ps 139:16*

for *y.* my prayer also shall be in   *Ps 141:5*

Y. a little sleep, a little slumber   *Pr 6:10; 24:33*

While as *y.* he had not made   *Pr 8:26*

man, and he will be *y.* wiser   *Pr 9:9*

that scattereth and *y.* increaseth   *Pr 11:24*

maketh himself rich, *y.* hath nothing   *Pr 13:7*

himself poor, *y.* hath great riches   *Pr 13:7*

words, *y.* they are wanting to him   *Pr 19:7*

him, *y.* thou must do it again   *Pr 19:19*

awake? I will seek it *y.* again   *Pr 23:35*

y. will not his foolishness depart from   *Pr 27:22*

y. is not washed from their filthiness   *Pr 30:12*

y. they prepare meat in the summer   *Pr 30:25*

y. make they houses in the rocks   *Pr 30:26*

y. go they forth all of them by bands   *Pr 30:27*

riseth also while it is *y.* night   *Pr 31:15*

run into the sea; *y.* the sea is not full   *Ec 1:7*

y. acquainting mine heart with   *Ec 2:3*

y. shall he have rule over all my   *Ec 2:19*

y. to a man that hath not laboured   *Ec 2:21*

than the living which are *y.* alive   *Ec 4:2*

both they, which have not *y.* been   *Ec 4:3*

y. is there no end of all his labour   *Ec 4:8*

y. God giveth him not power to eat   *Ec 6:2*

twice told, *y.* hath he seen no good   *Ec 6:6*

and *y.* the appetite is not filled   *Ec 6:7*

Which *y.* my soul seeketh, but   *Ec 7:28*

y. surely I know that it shall be   *Ec 8:12*

to seek it out, *y.* he shall not find it   *Ec 8:17*

y. shall he not be able to find it   *Ec 8:17*

neither *y.* bread to the wise   *Ec 9:11*

y. riches to men of understanding   *Ec 9:11*

nor *y.* favour to men of skill   *Ec 9:11*

y. no man remembered that   *Ec 9:15*

y. let him remember the days of   *Ec 11:8*

But *y.* it shall be a tenth, and it   *Isa 6:13*

y. a remnant of them shall return   *Isa 10:22*

For *y.* a very little while, and   *Isa 10:25*

y. shall he remain at Nob that day   *Isa 10:32*

and will *y.* choose Israel, and set   *Isa 14:1*

Y. thou shalt be brought down to   *Isa 14:15*

Y. gleaning grapes shall be left in it   *Isa 17:6*

y. will he not learn righteousness   *Isa 26:10*

y. the defenced city shall be desolate   *Isa 27:10*

is *y.* in his hand he eateth it up   *Isa 28:4*

refreshing; *y.* they would not hear   *Isa 28:12*

Y. I will distress Ariel, and there   *Isa 29:2*

Is it not *y.* a very little while, and   *Isa 29:17*

y. shall not thy teachers be removed   *Isa 30:20*

Y. he also is wise, and will bring evil   *Isa 31:2*

fire round about, *y.* he knew not   *Isa 42:25*

burned him, *y.* he laid it not *Isa 42:25*
to heart
Y. now hear, O Jacob my   *Isa 44:1*
servant
y. they shall fear, and they   *Isa 44:11*
shall be
y. can he not answer, nor save *Isa 46:7*
him
the things that are not *y.*   *Isa 46:10*
done
y. surely my judgment is with *Isa 49:4*
y. shall I be glorious in the   *Isa 49:5*
eyes of
may forget, *y.* will I not   *Isa 49:15*
forget thee
y. we did esteem him stricken *Isa 53:4*
afflicted, *y.* he opened not his *Isa 53:7*
mouth
Y. it pleased the Lord to   *Isa 53:10*
bruise him
Y. will I gather others to   *Isa 56:8*
him
y. saidst thou not, There is   *Isa 57:10*
no hope
Y. they seek me daily, and   *Isa 58:2*
delight to
while they are *y.* speaking, I *Isa 65:24*
will
Wherefore I will *y.* plead with *Jer 2:9*
you
their gods, which are *y.* no   *Jer 2:11*
gods
Y. I had planted thee a noble *Jer 2:21*
vine
y. thine iniquity is marked   *Jer 2:22*
before me
y. my people have forgotten   *Jer 2:32*
me days
Y. thou sayest, Because I am *Jer 2:35*
y. return again to me, saith the *Jer 3:1*
Lord
y. her treacherous sister Judah *Jer 3:8*
And *y.* for all this her   *Jer 3:10*
treacherous
desolate; *y.* will I not make a *Jer 4:27*
full end
themselves, *y.* can they not   *Jer 5:22*
prevail
roar, *y.* can they not pass over *Jer 5:22*
it
of the fatherless, *y.* they   *Jer 5:28*
prosper
Y. they hearkened not unto   *Jer 7:26*
me, nor
Y. hear the word of the Lord *Jer 9:20*
Y. they obeyed not, nor   *Jer 11:8*
inclined their
y. let me talk with thee of thy *Jer 12:1*
y. thou, O Lord, art in the   *Jer 14:9*
midst of
not, *y.* they say, Sword and   *Jer 14:15*
famine
y. my mind could not be   *Jer 15:1*
toward this
sun is gone down while it is *y.* *Jer 15:9*
day
y. every one of them doth   *Jer 15:10*
curse me
Y. Lord, thou knowest all   *Jer 18:23*
their
y. surely I will make thee a   *Jer 22:6*
hand, *y.* would I pluck thee   *Jer 22:24*
hence
not sent these prophets, *y.*   *Jer 23:21*
they ran
spoken to them, *y.* they   *Jer 23:21*
prophesied
y. I sent them not, nor   *Jer 23:32*
commanded
Y. ye have not hearkened   *Jer 25:7*
unto me
y. they prophesy a lie in my *Jer 27:15*
name
y. will I not make a full end *Jer 30:11*
of
Thou shall *y.* plant vines upon *Jer 31:5*
As *y.* they shall use this   *Jer 31:23*
speech in
the measuring line shall *y.* go *Jer 31:39*
forth
y. they have not hearkened to *Jer 32:33*
receive
he was *y.* shut up in the court *Jer 33:1*
Y. hear the word of the Lord *Jer 34:4*
Y. they were not afraid, nor *Jer 36:24*
rent
y. should they rise up every   *Jer 37:10*
man in
while he was not *y.* gone   *Jer 40:5*
back

Y. a small number that   *Jer 44:28*
escape the
y. will I not leave thee   *Jer 46:28*
wholly
Y. will I bring again the   *Jer 48:47*
captivity of
y. a little while, and the time *Jer 51:33*
of
y. from me shall spoilers   *Jer 51:53*
come
y. will he have compassion   *La 3:32*
according
eyes as *y.* failed for our vain *La 4:17*
help
y. shall know that there hath *Eze 2:5*
been a
Y. if thou warn the wicked, *Eze 3:19*
and he
Y. will I leave a remnant, that *Eze 6:8*
ye may
sold, although they were *y.*   *Eze 7:13*
alive
turn thee *y.* again, and thou   *Eze 8:6;*
shalt   *8:13, 15*
a loud voice, *y.* will I not   *Eze 8:18*
hear them
y. will I be to them as a   *Eze 11:16*
little
Y. shall he not see it,   *Eze 12:13*
though he shall
Y., behold, therein shall be   *Eze 14:22*
left a
less shall it be meet *y.* for any *Eze 15:5*
work
and *y.* couldest not be   *Eze 16:28*
satisfied
and *y.* thou wast not   *Eze 16:29*
satisfied
Y. hast thou not walked after *Eze 16:47*
their
Y. say ye, Why? doth not   *Eze 18:19*
the son
Y. ye say, The way of the   *Eze 18:25*
Lord is not
Y. saith the house of Israel, *Eze 18:29*
The way
Y. also I lifted up my hand   *Eze 20:15*
unto
Y. in this your fathers have   *Eze 20:27*
Y. she multiplied her   *Eze 23:19*
whoredoms
Y. they went in unto her, as *Eze 23:44*
they
y. neither shalt thou mourn   *Eze 24:16*
nor weep
y. shalt thou never be found *Eze 26:21*
again
y. thou art a man, and not   *Eze 28:2*
God
Wilt thou *y.* say before him *Eze 28:9*
that
Y. thus saith the Lord God *Eze 29:13*
y. had he no wages, nor his *Eze 29:18*
army
y. shalt thou be brought   *Eze 31:18*
down with
y. have they borne their   *Eze 32:24;*
shame   *32:25*
Y. the children of thy people *Eze 33:17*
say
Y. ye say, The way of the   *Eze 33:20*
Lord is not
I will *y.* for this be enquired *Eze 36:37*
of by
Y. they shall be ministers in *Eze 44:11*
my
y. leave the stump of the roots *Da 4:23*
y. I will read the writing unto *Da 5:17*
y. their lives were prolonged *Da 7:12*
for a
y. made we not our prayer   *Da 9:13*
before the
Y. heard I the voice of his   *Da 10:9*
words: and
for *y.* the vision is for many *Da 10:14*
days
stand up *y.* three kings in   *Da 11:2*
Persia
for *y.* the end shall be at the *Da 11:27*
time
y. they shall fall by the   *Da 11:33*
sword, and
it is *y.* for a time appointed *Da 11:35*
y. he shall come to his end, *Da 11:45*
and none
for *y.* a little while, and I will *Ho 1:4*
Y. the number of the children *Ho 1:10*
of
Go *y.* love a woman beloved of *Ho 3:1*
of her friend, *y.* an adulteress *Ho 3:1*

Y. let no man strive, nor   *Ho 4:4*
reprove
the harlot, *y.* let not Judah   *Ho 4:15*
offend
y. could he not heal you, nor *Ho 5:13*
cure you
there upon him, *y.* he knoweth *Ho 7:9*
not
y. they have spoken lies   *Ho 7:13*
against me
y. do they imagine mischief *Ho 7:15*
against
their children, *y.* will I   *Ho 9:12*
bereave them
y. will I slay even the   *Ho 9:16*
beloved fruit of
but Judah *y.* ruleth with God *Ho 11:12*
Y. I am become rich, I have *Ho 12:8*
found
Egypt will *y.* make thee to   *Ho 12:9*
dwell
Y. I am the Lord thy God   *Ho 13:4*
from the
Y. destroyed I the Amorite   *Am 2:9*
before
y. I destroyed his fruit from *Am 2:9*
above
y. have ye not returned unto *Am 4:6*
me
when there was *y.* three months *Am 4:7*
y. have ye not returned unto *Am 4:8;*
         4:9, 11
the house, Is there *y.* any   *Am 6:10*
with thee
y. shall not the least grain fall *Am 9:9*
upon
y. I will look again toward thy *Jon 2:4*
holy
y. hast thou brought up my   *Jon 2:6*
life from
Y. forty days, and Nineveh   *Jon 3:4*
shall
when I was *y.* in my country *Jon 4:2*
Y. will I bring an heir unto   *Mic 1:15*
thee
y. will they lean upon the   *Mic 3:11*
Lord, and
y. out of thee shall he come *Mic 5:2*
forth unto
And there *y.* the treasures   *Mic 6:10*
of
many, *y.* thus shall they be cut *Na 1:12*
down
of water; *y.* they shall flee   *Na 2:8*
away
Y. was she carried away, she *Na 3:10*
vision is *y.* for an appointed *Hab 2:3*
time
Y. I will rejoice in the Lord, *Hab 3:18*
I will
Y. now be strong, O   *Hag 2:4*
Zerubbabel
Y. once, it is a little while,   *Hag 2:6*
and I
y. ye turned not to me, saith *Hag 2:17*
the Lord
Is the seed *y.* in the barn? *Hag 2:19*
yea
as *y.* the vine, and the fig   *Hag 2:19*
tree
Cry *y.* saying, Thus saith the *Zec 1:17*
through prosperity shall *y.* be *Zec 1:17*
the Lord shall *y.* comfort   *Zec 1:17*
Zion
and shall *y.* choose Jerusalem *Zec 1:17*
shall *y.* old men and old   *Zec 8:4*
women
It shall *y.* come to pass, that *Zec 8:20*
there
Take unto thee *y.* the   *Zec 11:15*
instruments
that when any shall *y.*   *Zec 13:3*
prophesy
Y. ye say, Wherein hast thou *Mal 1:2*
loved
saith the Lord: *y.* I loved   *Mal 1:2*
Jacob
Y. ye say. Wherefore?   *Mal 2:14*
Because the
y. is she thy companion, and *Mal 2:14*
the wife
Y. had he the residue of the *Mal 2:15*
spirit
Y. ye say, Wherein have we *Mal 2:17*
wearied
rob God? Y. have ye robbed *Mal 3:8*
me
Y. ye say, What have we   *Mal 3:13*
spoken so

y. for your body, what ye shall put	M't 6:25
y. your heavenly Father feedeth them	M't 6:26
y. I say unto you, That even Solomon	M't 6:29
coats, neither shoes, nor y. staves	M't 10:10
While he y. talked to the people	M't 12:46
Y. hath he not root in himself, but	M't 13:21
ye also y. without understanding	M't 15:16
Do ye not y. understand, that	M't 15:17
y. the dogs eat of the crumbs	M't 15:27
Do ye not y. understand, neither	M't 16:9
While he y. spake, behold, a bright	M't 17:5
from my youth up: what lack I y.	M't 19:20
come to pass, but the end is not y.	M't 24:6
When his branch is y. tender	M't 24:32
of thee y. will I never be offended	M't 26:33
die with thee, y. will I not deny	M't 26:35
And while he y. spake, lo, Judas	M't 26:47
witnesses came, y. found they none	M't 26:60
said, while he was y. alive	M't 27:63
While he y. spake, there came	M'k 5:35
y. for his oath's sake, and for their	M'k 6:26
y. the dogs under the table eat	M'k 7:28
perceive ye not y. neither	M'k 8:17
have ye your heart y. hardened	M'k 8:17
for the time of figs was not y.	M'k 11:13
Having y. therefore one son, his	M'k 12:6
be; but the end shall not be y.	M'k 13:7
When her branch is y. tender, and	M'k 13:28
all shall be offended, y. will not I	M'k 14:29
while he y. spake, cometh Judas	M'k 14:43
But Jesus y. answered nothing	M'k 15:5
Added y. this above all, that he	Lu 3:20
While he y. spake, there cometh	Lu 8:49
And as he was y. a-coming	Lu 9:42
y. because of his importunity he	Lu 11:8
y. I say unto you, that Solomon is all	Lu 12:27
commanded, and y. there is room	Lu 14:22
while the other is y. a great way off	Lu 14:32
the land, nor y. for the dunghill	Lu 14:35
when he was y. a great way off	Lu 15:20
y. thou never gavest me a kid, that I	Lu 15:29
Y. because this widow troubleth	Lu 18:5
him, Y. lackest thou one thing	Lu 18:22
colt tied whereon y. never man sat	Lu 19:30
written must y. be accomplished	Lu 22:37
And while he y. spake, behold	Lu 22:47
while he y. spake, the cock crew	Lu 22:60
no, nor y. Herod; for I sent you to	Lu 23:15
you when he was y. in Galilee	Lu 24:6
while they y. believed not for joy	Lu 24:41
unto you, while I as y. with you	Lu 24:44
thee? mine hour is not y. come	Joh 2:4
John was not y. cast into prison	Joh 3:24
mountain, nor y. at Jerusalem	Joh 4:21

y. no man said, What seekest	Joh 4:27
There are y. four months	Joh 4:35
unto them, My time is not y. come	Joh 7:6
I go not up y. unto this feast	Joh 7:8
for my time is not y. full come	Joh 7:8
and y. none of you keepeth the law	Joh 7:19
because his hour was not y. come	Joh 7:30
Y. a little while am I with you	Joh 7:33
the Holy Ghost was not y. given	Joh 7:39
that Jesus was not y. glorified	Joh 7:39
record of myself y. my record is true	Joh 8:14
y. if I judge, my judgment is true	Joh 8:16
him; for his hour was not y.	Joh 8:20
Y. ye have not known him; but I	Joh 8:55
Thou art not y. fifty years old, and	Joh 8:57
and y. he hath opened mine eyes	Joh 9:30
though he were dead, y. shall he live	Joh 11:25
Jesus was not y. come into	Joh 11:30
Y. a little while is the light with	Joh 12:35
them, y. they believed not on him	Joh 12:37
y. a little while I am with you	Joh 13:33
y. hast thou not known me, Philip	Joh 14:9
Y. a little while, and the world	Joh 14:19
unto you, being y. present with you	Joh 14:25
I have y. many things to say	Joh 16:12
y. I am not alone, because the Father	Joh 16:32
wherein was never man y. laid	Joh 19:41
when it was y. dark, unto the	Joh 20:1
clothes lying: y. went they not in	Joh 20:5
as y. they knew not the scripture	Joh 20:9
I am not y. ascended to my Father	Joh 20:17
have not seen, and y. have believed	Joh 20:29
so many y. was not the net broken	Joh 21:11
y. Jesus said not unto him, He shall	Joh 21:23
y. he promised that he would give	Ac 7:5
him, when as y. he had no child	Ac 7:5
as y. he was fallen upon none of	Ac 8:16
y. breathing out threatenings	Ac 9:1
While Peter y. spake these words	Ac 10:44
nor y. the voices of the prophets	Ac 13:27
y. desired they Pilate that he should	Ac 13:28
this tarried there y. a good while	Ac 18:18
nor y. blasphemers of your	Ac 19:37
y. brought up in this city at the feet	Ac 22:3
there are y. but twelve days since	Ac 24:11
the temple, nor y. against Caesar	Ac 25:8
y. vengeance suffereth not to live	Ac 28:4
w. was I delivered prisoner from	Ac 28:17
why y. am I also judged as a	Ro 3:7
which he had y. being uncircumcised	Ro 4:11
which he had being y. uncircumcised	Ro 4:12
y. the deadness of Sarah's womb	Ro 4:19
we were y. without strength	Ro 5:6
y. peradventure for a good man	Ro 5:7
while we were y. sinners, Christ	Ro 5:8
man seeth, why doth he y. hope	Ro 8:24
For the children being not y. born	Ro 9:11

me, Why doth he y. find fault	Ro 9:19
y. have now obtained mercy through	Ro 11:30
y. I would have you wise unto that	Ro 16:19
y. not the wisdom of this world, nor	1Co 2:6
y. he himself is judged of no man	1Co 2:15
hear it, neither y. nor are ye able	1Co 3:2
For ye are y. carnal: for whereas	1Co 3:3
shall be saved; y. so as by fire	1Co 3:15
y. am I not hereby justified; but he	1Co 4:4
Christ, y. have ye not many fathers	1Co 4:15
Y. not altogether with the	1Co 5:10
y. not I, but the Lord, Let not the wife	1Co 7:10
y. I give my judgment as one that	1Co 7:25
knoweth nothing y. as he ought	1Co 8:2
others, y. doubtless I am to you	1Co 9:2
y. have I made myself servant unto	1Co 9:19
many members y. but one body	1Co 12:20
and y. shew I unto you a more	1Co 12:31
Y. in the church I had rather	1Co 14:19
y. for all that will they not hear me	1Co 14:21
y. not I, but the grace of God which	1Co 15:10
is vain: ye are y. in your sins	1Co 15:17
we trust that he will y. deliver us	2Co 1:10
you I came not as y. unto Corinth	2Co 1:23
on every side, y. not distressed	2Co 4:8
y. the inward man is renewed day	2Co 4:16
y. now henceforth know we him	2Co 5:16
good report: as deceivers, and	2Co 6:8
As unknown, and y. well known	2Co 6:9
As sorrowful, y. alway rejoicing	2Co 6:10
as poor, y. making many rich	2Co 6:10
nothing, and y. possessing all things	2Co 6:10
y. for your sakes he became poor	2Co 8:9
Y. have I sent the brethren, lest	2Co 9:3
in speech, y. not in knowledge	2Co 11:6
y. as a fool receive me, that I may	2Co 11:16
y. of myself I will not glory, but in	2Co 12:5
y. he liveth by the power of God	2Co 13:4
for if I y. pleased men, I should	Ga 1:10
y. not I, but Christ liveth in me	Ga 2:20
things in vain if it be y. in vain	Ga 3:4
y. if it be confirmed, no man	Ga 3:15
if I y. preach circumcision	Ga 5:11
why do I y. suffer persecution	Ga 5:11
no man ever y. hated his own flesh	Eph 5:29
love may abound y. more and	Ph'p 1:9
y. what I shall choose I wot not	Ph'p 1:22
Y. I supposed it necessary to send	Ph'p 2:25
works, y. now hath he reconciled	Col 1:21
y. am I with you in the spirit	Col 2:5
nor y. of others, when we might have	1Th 2:6
when I was y. with you, I told you	2Th 2:5
Y. count him not as an enemy	2Th 3:15
for masteries, y. is he not crowned	2Ti 2:5

we believe not, *y.* he abideth faithful	2Ti 2:13
Y. for love's sake I rather beseech	Ph'm 9
not *y.* all things put under him	Heb 2:8
tempted like as we are, *y.* without sin	Heb 4:11
y. learned he obedience by the things	Heb 5:8
he was *y.* in the loins of his father	Heb 7:10
And it is *y.* far more evident	Heb 7:15
of all was not *y.* made manifest	Heb 9:8
first tabernacle was *y.* standing	Heb 9:8
Nor *y.* that he should offer himself	Heb 9:25
For *y.* a little while, and he that	Heb 10:37
by it he being dead *y.* speaketh	Heb 11:4
of God of things not seen as *y.*	Heb 11:7
Ye have not *y.* resisted unto blood	Heb 12:4
Y. once more I shake not	Heb 12:26
word, *Y.* once more, signifeth	Heb 12:27
y. offend in one point, he is guilty of	Jas 2:10
commit no adultery, *y.* if thou kill	Jas 2:11
y. are they turned about with a very	Jas 3:4
y. ye have not, because ye ask not	Jas 4:2
now ye see him not, *y.* believing	1Pe 1:8
Y. if any man suffer as a Christian	1Pe 4:16
not *y.* appear what we shall be	1Jo 3:2
Y. Michael the archangel, when	Jude 9
should rest *y.* for a little season	Re 6:11
angels, which are *y.* to sound	Re 8:13
by these plagues *y.* repented not	Re 9:20
that was, and is not, and *y.* is	Re 17:8
one is, and the other is not, *y.* come	Re 17:10
have received no kingdom as *y.*	Re 17:12

YIELD

not henceforth *y.* unto thee fruits	Ge 4:12
fat, and he shall *y.* royal dainties	Ge 49:20
deliver (A)	Ge 49:20
gather in its *y.* (A)(R)	Ex 23:10
it may *y.* unto you the increase	Le 19:25
produce (A)	Le 19:25; Isa 5:10
produce (B)	Le 19:25; 26:20; De 11:17; Ps 11:17; Isa 5:10; Ho 8:7; Jas 3:12
	85:12;
And the land shall *y.* her fruit	Le 25:19
and the land shall *y.* her increase	Le 26:4
trees of the field shall *y.* their fruit	Le 26:4
your land shall not *y.* her increase	Le 26:20
the trees of the land *y.* their fruits	Le 26:20
and that the land *y.* not her fruit	De 11:17
y. yourselves unto the Lord	2Ch 30:8
shall the earth *y.* her increase	Ps 67:6
and our land and shall *y.* her increase	Ps 85:12
which may *y.* fruits of increase	Ps 107:37
fair speech she caused him to *y.*	Pr 7:21
forces him along (A)	Pr 7:21
entices him (B)	Pr 7:21
of vineyard shall *y.* one bath	Isa 5:10
seed of an homer shall *y.* an ephah	Isa 5:10
tree of the field shall *y.* her fruit	Eze 34:27
and the earth shall *y.* her increase	Eze 34:27
and *y.* your fruit to my people of	Eze 36:8

stalk: the bud shall *y.* no meal	Ho 8:7
if so be it *y.* the strangers shall	Ho 8:7
and the vine do *y.* their strength	Joe 2:22
fail, and the field shall *y.* no meat	Hab 3:17
and did *y.* fruit that sprang up	M'k 4:8
But do not thou *y.* unto them	Ac 23:21
give in to them (B)	Ac 23:21
Neither *y.* ye your members as	Ro 6:13
but *y.* yourselves unto God, as	Ro 6:13
offer your members (B)	Ro 6:13
ye *y.* yourselves servants to obey	Ro 6:16
surrender to (A)	Ro 6:16
offer your members (B)	Ro 6:16
so now *y.* your members servants	Ro 6:19
offered members of your body (B)	Ro 6:19
might *y.* God a harvest (B)	Ro 7:4
y. death a harvest (B)	Ro 7:5
no fountain both *y.* salt water	Jas 3:12
produce-furnish (A)(B)	Jas 3:12
precious crop land may *y.* (N)	Jas 5:7
who *y.* to the sensual (B)	2Pe 2:10

YIELDED

y. up the ghost, and was gathered	Ge 49:33
breathed his last (A)(B)(R)	Ge 49:33
blossoms, and *y.* almonds	Nu 17:8
borne ripe almonds (B)	Nu 17:8
bore ripe almonds (R)	Nu 17:8
king's word, and *y.* their bodies	Da 3:28
giving up their bodies (B)	Da 3:28
with a loud voice, *y.* up the ghost	M't 27:50
gave up his spirit (A)	M't 27:50
dismissed his spirit (B)	M't 27:50
breathed his last (N)	M't 27:50
and choked it, and it *y.* no fruit	M'k 4:7
at his feet, and *y.* up the ghost	Ac 5:10
died (A)(R)	Ac 5:10
expired (B)	Ac 5:10
have *y.* your members servants	Ro 6:19
offer your members (B)	Ro 6:19
we *y.* and respected them (A)(B)(P)(R)	Heb 12:9
soil *y.* its produce (B)	Jas 5:18
and *y.* her fruit every month	Re 22:2

YIELDETH

it *y.* much increase unto the kings	Ne 9:3
the wilderness *y.* food for them and	Job 24:5
the root of the righteous *y.* fruit	Pr 12:12
afterward it *y.* the peaceable fruit	Heb 12:11

YIELDING

forth grass, the herb *y.* seed	Ge 1:11
fruit tree *y.* fruit after his kind	Ge 1:11
and herb *y.* seed after his kind	Ge 1:12
and the tree *y.* fruit, whose seed	Ge 1:12
is the fruit of a tree *y.* seed	Ge 1:29
for *y.* pacifieth great offences	Ec 10:4
neither shall cease from *y.* fruit	Jer 17:8

YIELDS

y. a rich harvest (A)(B)(N)(P)	Joh 12:24

YOKE

break his *y.* from off thy neck	Ge 27:40
I have broken the bands of your *y.*	Le 26:13
and upon which never came *y.*	Nu 19:2
which hath not drawn in the *y.*	De 21:3
shall put a *y.* of iron upon thy neck	De 28:48
on which there hath come no *y.*	1Sa 6:7
And he took a *y.* of oxen	1Sa 11:7
which a *y.* of oxen might plow	1Sa 14:14

Thy father made our *y.* grievous	1Ki 12:4; 2Ch 10:4
his heavy *y.* which he put upon us	1Ki 12:4
y. which thy father did put upon us	1Ki 12:9
Thy father made our *y.* heavy, but	1Ki 12:10; 2Ch 10:10
father did lade you with a heavy *y.*	1Ki 12:11
I will add to your *y.*: my father	1Ki 12:11
My father made your *y.* heavy, and	1Ki 12:14; 2Ch 10:14
and I will add to your *y.*	1Ki 12:14
plowing with twelve *y.* of oxen	1Ki 19:19
took a *y.* of oxen, and slew them	1Ki 19:21
his heavy *y.* that he put upon us	2Ch 10:4
y. that thy father did put upon us	2Ch 10:9
my father put a heavy *y.* upon you	2Ch 10:11
will put more to your *y.*: my father	2Ch 10:11
and five hundred *y.* of oxen	Job 1:3
and a thousand *y.* of oxen	Job 42:12
hast broken the *y.* of his burden	Isa 9:4
and his *y.* from off thy neck	Isa 10:27
and the *y.* shall be destroyed	Isa 10:27
shall his *y.* depart from off them	Isa 14:25
hast thou very heavily laid thy *w.*	Isa 47:6
free, and that ye brake every *y.*	Isa 58:6
away from the midst of thee the *y.*	Isa 58:9
of old time I have broken thy *y.*	Jer 2:20
have altogether broken the *y.*	Jer 5:5
the *y.* of the king of Babylon	Jer 27:8; 27:11, 12; 28:2
brake the *y.* of the king of Babylon	Jer 28:4
took the *y.* from off the prophet	Jer 28:10
I break the *y.* of Nebuchadnezzar	Jer 28:11
the prophet had broken the *y.*	Jer 28:12
a *y.* of iron upon the neck of all	Jer 28:14
break his *y.* from off thy neck	Jer 30:8
as a bullock unaccustomed to the *y.*	Jer 31:18
a husbandman and his *y.* of oxen	Jer 51:23
The *y.* of my transgressions is	La 1:14
that he bear the *y.* in his youth	La 3:27
have broken the bands of their *y.*	Eze 34:27
that take off the *y.* on their jaws	Ho 11:4
will I break his *y.* from off thee	Na 1:13
Take my *y.* upon you, and learn of	M't 11:29
For my *y.* is easy, and my burden	M't 11:30
I have bought five *y.* of oxen	Lu 14:19
y. upon the neck of the disciples	Ac 15:10
again with the *y.* of bondage	Ga 5:1
many servants as are under the *y.*	1Ti 6:1

YOKED

y. together with unbelievers	2Co 6:14

YOKEFELLOW

true *y.* help those women which	Ph'p 4:3

YOKES

Make thee bonds and *y.* and put	Jer 27:2
Thou hast broken the *y.* of wood	Jer 28:13
shalt make for them *y.* of iron	Jer 28:13
shall break there the *y.* of Egypt	Eze 30:18

YONDER

lad will go *y*. and worship	Ge 22:5
and scatter thou the fire *y*.	Nu 16:37
offering, while I meet the Lord *y*.	Nu 23:15
inherit with them on *y*. side Jordan	Nu 32:19
Behold, *y*. is that Shunammite	2Ki 4:25
Remove hence to *y*. place	M't 17:20
Sit ye here, while I go and pray *y*.	M't 26:36

YOU

shall be a space between *y*. and ark	Jos 3:4
but *y*. have no portion in Jerusalem	Ne 2:20
I could shake my head at *y*.	Job 16:4
iniquities separate between *y*. and God	Isa 59:2
put a new spirit within *y*.	Eze 11:19; 36:26,27
heathen about *y*. bear shame	Eze 36:7; 36:36
behold, I am pressed under *y*.	Am 2:13
y. only have I known of all families	Am 3:2
he that heareth *y*. heareth me; despiseth *y*. despiseth me	Lu 10:16
y. yourselves thrust out of the kingdom	Lu 13:28
name of God is blasphemed thro' *y*.	Ro 2:24
y. also helping by prayer for us	2Co 1:11
other men be eased and *y*. burdened	2Co 8:13
lest we, that we say not *y*. be ashamed	2Co 9:4
preach gospel in the regions beyond *y*.	2Co 10:16
for I seek not yours but *y*.	2Co 12:14
y. hath he quickened who were dead	Eph 2:1
in whom *y*. also are builded together	Eph 2:22
y. that were some time alienated	Col 1:21
y. being dead in sins hath quickened	Col 2:13

AFTER YOU

establish covenant with you, and seed *after y*.	Ge 9:9
take them as an inheritance for your children *after y*.	Le 25:46; 1Ch 28:8
I will draw out a sword *after y*.	Le 26:33
overflow them, as they pursued *after y*.	De 11:4
generation that shall rise up *after y*.	De 29:22
go on before; I come *after y*.	1Sa 25:19
the famine shall follow close *after y*.	Jer 42:16
which long *after y*.	2Co 9:14; Ph'p 1:8
Epaphroditus longed *after y*.	Ph'p 2:26

AGAINST YOU

he said, I have sinned *against y*.	Ex 10:16
I will set my face *against y*.	Le 26:17; Jer 44:11
whereby they murmur *against y*.	Nu 17:5
the Amorites came out *against y*.	De 1:44
I call heaven and earth to witness *against y*. this day	De 4:26; 30:19
I testify *against y*. that ye shall surely perish	De 8:19
I was afraid of anger wherewith Lord was wroth *against y*.	De 9:19; 11:17; Jos 23:16
men of Jericho fought came *against y*.	Jos 24:11
the Lord is witness *against y*.	1Sa 12:5; Mic 1:2
Nahash king of Ammonites came *against y*.	1Sa 12:12
hand of the Lord shall be *against y*.	1Sa 12:15
thus Ahithophel counselled *against y*.	2Sa 17:21

to cry alarm *against y*. O Israel	2Ch 13:12
I could heap up words *against y*.	Job 16:4
behold, I devise a device *against y*.	Jer 18:11
I myself will fight *against y*. in anger	Jer 21:5
Lord will repent of evil pronounced *against y*.	Jer 26:13
army of the Chaldeans that fight *against y*.	Jer 37:10
the king of Babylon shall not come *against y*.	Jer 37:19
the king cannot do any thing *against y*.	Jer 38:5
that my words shall stand *against y*.	Jer 44:29
Nebuchadrezzar hath conceived a purpose *against y*.	Jer 49:30
I am *against y*.; enemy said *against y*.	Eze 13:8; 36:2
Lord hath spoken *against y*.	Am 3:1; 5:1; Zep 2:5
I will raise up *against y*. a nation	Am 6:14
one shall take up a parable *against y*.	Mic 2:4
say all manner of evil *against y*.	M't 5:11
go into village over *against y*.; find an ass tied	M't 21:2; M'k 11:2; Lu 19:30
dust of your city we wipe off *against y*.	Lu 10:11
the rust shall be a witness *against y*.	Jas 5:3
whereas they speak *against y*. as evil doers	1Pe 2:12

AMONG, AMONGST YOU

put away strange gods *among y*. and be clean	Ge 35:2; Jos 24:23; 1Sa 7:3
I will set my tabernacle *amongst y*.	Le 26:11
walk *among y*. and will be your God	Le 26:12
send wild beast *among y*.; pestilence *among y*.	Le 26:22; 26:25
ye have despised the Lord who is *among y*.	Nu 11:20; 14:42; De 6:15; 7:21; Jos 3:10
who is there *among y*.	2Ch 36:23;
who *among y*. will give ear	Isa 42:23
who is *among y*. that feareth Lord	Isa 50:10
purge out from *among y*. the rebels	Eze 20:38
who is left *among y*. that saw this house	Hag 2:3
who is there *among y*. that would shut	Mal 1:10
it shall not be so *among y*.	M't 20:26; M'k 10:43
whosoever will be chief *among y*. let him be your servant	M't 20:27; 23:11; Lu 22:26
he that is least *among y*. shall be great	Lu 9:48
but I am *among y*. as he that serveth	Lu 22:27
but there standeth one *among y*.	Joh 1:26
he that is without sin *among y*. let him cast	Joh 8:7
look ye out *among y*. seven men	Ac 6:3
and whosoever *among y*. feareth God	Ac 13:26
let them who *among y*. are able, go down	Ac 25:5
that I might have fruit *among y*.	Ro 1:13
I say to every man that is *among y*.	Ro 12:3
that there be no divisions *among y*.	1Co 1:10
there are contentions *among y*.	1Co 1:11; 11:18
determined not to know any thing *among y*.	1Co 2:2
whereas there is *among y*. envying, strife	1Co 3:3
if any man *among y*. seemeth to be wise	1Co 3:18
is reported that there is fornication *among y*.	1Co 5:1

that he might be taken away from *among y*.	1Co 5:2
how say some *among y*. is no resurrection	1Co 15:12
Christ who was preached *among y*.	2Co 1:19
I Paul, who in presence am base *among y*.	2Co 10:1
lest my God will humble me *among y*.	2Co 12:21
let it not be once named amongst *y*.	Eph 5:3
what manner of men we were *among y*.	1Th 1:5
if any man *among y*. seem religious	Jas 1:26
any *among y*. afflicted; any sick *among y*.	Jas 5:13; 5:14
feed the flock of God which is *among y*.	1Pe 5:2
there shall be false teachers *among y*.	2Pe 2:1
Antipas, who was slain *among y*.	Re 2:13

BEFORE YOU

the land shall be *before y*. dwell	Ge 34:10
God send me *before y*. to preserve life	Ge 45:5; 45:7
look to it, for evil is *before y*.	Ex 10:10
these nations are defiled which I cast out *before y*.	Le 18:24; 20:23; Nu 33:52, 55; De 11:23; Jos 3:10; 9:24, 23:5, 9; 24:8, 12; J'g 6:9
men of land *before y*.	Le 18:27; 18:28, 30
your enemies shall fall *before y*.	Le 26:7; 26:8
the Canaanites are there *before y*.	Nu 14:43
and the land shall be subdued *before y*.	Nu 32:29
behold, I have set the land *before y*.	De 1:8
Lord who goeth *before y*. fight for you	De 1:30
which I set *before y*. this day	De 4:8; 11:32
I set *before y*. blessing and curse	De 11:26; 30:19
the Lord dried up Jordan *before y*.	Jos 4:23
I sent the hornet *before y*. which drave	Jos 24:12
behold, he is *before y*. make haste	1Sa 9:12
behold the king walketh *before y*.	1Sa 12:2
if ye forsake my statutes, which I have set *before y*.	2Ch 7:19; Jer 26:4; 44:10
for the Lord will go *before y*.	Isa 52:12
behold, I set *before y*. the way of life	Jer 21:8
so persecuted prophets that were *before y*.	M't 5:12
go into the kingdom of God *before y*.	M't 21:31
after I am risen I will go *before y*. into Galilee	M't 26:32; 28:7; M'k 14:28; 16:7
into whatsoever city ye enter, eat things as are set *before y*.	Lu 10:8; 1Co 10:27
this man stands here *before y*. whole	Ac 4:10

BY YOU

I will not be inquired of *by y*.	Eze 20:3; 20:31
I trust brought on my way *by y*.	Ro 15:24
if the world shall be judged *by y*.	1Co 6:2
his spirit was refreshed *by y*.	2Co 7:13
we hope that we shall be enlarged *by y*.	2Co 10:15

CONCERNING YOU

what Lord will command *concerning y*.	Nu 9:8
which the Lord spake *concerning y*.	Jos 23:14

the Lord hath said   *Jer 42:19*
concerning y.
this is the will of God   *1Th 5:18*
concerning y.

FOR YOU

as *for* y.   *Ge 44:17;*
50:20; Nu 14:32; De 1:40; Jos 23:9;
  Job 17:10
one ordinance shall be *for* y.   *Nu 15:15;*
  15:16
all that he did *for* y.   *De 1:30;*
  4:34; 1Sa 12:24
as *for* y. O house of Israel   *Eze 20:39;*
  34:17
I am *for* y. and I will turn to   *Eze 36:9*
you
there is but one decree. *for* y.   *Da 2:9*
day of Lord, to what end is it   *Am 5:18*
for y.
is it not *for* y. to know   *Mic 3:1*
judgment
is it time *for* y. to dwell in   *Hag 1:4*
ceiled
O priests, this commandment   *Mal 2:1*
is *for* y.
it shall be more tolerable for   *M't 11:22;*
Tyre and Sidon, than *for* y.   *Lu 10:14*
come, inherit the kingdom   *M't 25:34*
prepared *for* y.
what would ye that I should   *M'k 10:36*
do *for* y.
this is my body which is   *Lu 22:19*
given *for* y.
my blood which is shed for   *Lu 22:20;*
y.   *1Co 11:24*
I go to prepare a place *for* y.   *Joh 14:2;*
  14:3
I say, that I will pray the   *Joh 16:26*
Father *for* y.
not *for* y. to know times or   *Ac 1:7*
seasons
for this cause have I called   *Ac 28:20*
for y.
I thank my God through Christ   *Ro 1:8*
for y. all
is Christ divided? was Paul   *1Co 1:13*
crucified *for* y.
that our care *for* y. appear   *2Co 7:12;*
  8:16
by their prayer *for* y. which   *2Co 9:14;*
long after you   *Ph'p 1:4; Col 1:3, 9,*
  4:12; 2Th 1:11
I will gladly spend and be   *2Co 12:15*
spent *for* y.
I cease not to give thanks   *Eph 1:16;*
for y.   *1Th 1:2; 3:9; 2Th 1:3; 2:13*
at my tribulations *for* y.   *Eph 3:13;*
  Col 1:24
is not grievous, but *for* y. it   *Ph'p 3:1*
is safe
for the hope which is laid up   *Col 1:5*
for y.
dispensation which is given   *Col 1:25*
to me *for* y.
ye knew what great conflict I   *Col 2:1*
have *for* y.
that he hath a great zeal *for*   *Col 4:13*
y.
for that is unprofitable *for*   *Heb 13:17*
y.
to inheritance reserved in   *1Pe 1:4*
heaven *for* y.
cast your care on him, for he   *1Pe 5:7*
careth *for* y.

FROM YOU

seeing ye have sent me away   *Ge 26:27*
from y.
saying we are very far *from* y.   *Jos 9:22*
why his hand is not removed   *1Sa 6:3*
from y.
until there came word *from*   *2Sa 15:28*
y.
his wrath may turn away   *2Ch 30:8*
from y.
Lord not turn away face *from*   *2Ch 30:9*
y.
I will hide mine eyes *from* y.   *Isa 1:15*
but your sins have hid his face   *Isa 59:2*
from y.
have withholden good things   *Jer 15:25*
from y.
king's army which are gone   *Jer 34:21*
up *from* y.
I will keep nothing back *from*   *Jer 42:4*
y.

cast away *from* y. your   *Eze 18:31*
transgressions
remove far *from* y. the   *Joe 2:20*
northern army
I have withholden the rain   *Am 4:7*
from y.
kingdom of God shall be   *M't 21:43*
taken *from* y.
and your joy no man taketh   *Joh 16:22*
from y.
who is taken up *from* y. into   *Ac 1:11*
heaven
seeing you put it *from* y. lo,   *Ac 13:46*
we turn
came the word of God out   *1Co 14:36*
from y.
letters of commendation *from*   *2Co 3:1*
y.
let evil speaking be put away   *Eph 4:31*
from y.
from y. sounded out the   *1Th 1:8*
word
we being taken *from* y. a   *1Th 2:17*
short time
resist the devil, and he will flee   *Jas 4:7*
from y.

IN YOU

whether there be any truth   *Ge 42:16*
in y.
and let him also rejoice   *J'g 9:19*
in y.
I will be sanctified *in* y.   *Eze 20:41;*
  36:23
and I will put breath *in* y.   *Eze 37:6*
  37:14
I have no pleasure *in* y. saith   *Mal 1:10*
Lord
but the Spirit which   *M't 10:20*
speaketh *in* y.
if mighty works which were   *M't 11:21*
done *in* y.
ye have not his word abiding   *Joh 5:38*
in y.
that ye have not the love of   *Joh 5:42*
God *in* y.
except eat the flesh, ye have   *Joh 6:53*
no life *in* y.
he shall be *in* y.   *Joh 14:17; 14:20*
I *in* y.   *Joh 15:4*
if my words abide *in* y.   *Joh 15:7;*
  1Jo 2:14, 24
the Spirit dwelleth *in* y.   *Ro 8:9;*
  1Jo 2:27
if Christ be *in* y. the body is   *Ro 8:10*
dead
as much as lieth *in* y. live   *Ro 12:18*
peaceably
testimony of Christ is   *1Co 1:6*
confirmed *in* y.
temple of the Holy Ghost   *1Co 6:19*
which is *in* y.
will report that God is *in* y.   *1Co 14:25*
of a truth
I wrote this to you, having   *2Co 2:3;*
confidence *in* y. all   *7:16; 8:22; Ga 5:10*
life *in* y.; he was comforted   *2Co 4:12;*
in y.   *7:7*
would finish *in* y. the same   *2Co 8:6*
grace also
for the exceeding grace of   *2Co 9:14*
God *in* y.
which is not weak, but mighty   *2Co 13:3*
in y.
know ye not that Jesus   *2Co 13:5*
Christ is *in* y.
I travail, till Christ be   *Ga 4:19*
formed *in* y.
one God above all, and *in* y.   *Eph 4:6*
all
let mind be *in* y. which was   *Ph'p 2:5*
in Christ
it is God which worketh   *Ph'p 2:13*
in y. to will
which bringeth fruit, as also   *Col 1:6*
in y.
which is Christ *in* y. the hope   *Col 1:27*
of glory
let the word of Christ dwell   *Col 3:16*
in y. richly
which effectually worketh *in*   *1Th 2:13*
y.
we glory *in* y. in the churches   *2Th 1:4*
the name of Christ may be   *2Th 1:12*
glorified *in* y.
acknowledging every good   *Ph'm 6*
thing *in* y.
working *in* y. what is   *Heb 13:21*
well-pleasing

a reason of the hope that is   *1Pe 3:15*
in y.
if these things be *in* y. and   *2Pe 1:8*
abound
which thing is true in him and   *1Jo 2:8*
in y.
greater is he that is *in* y. than   *1Jo 4:4*
in world

OF YOU

why should I be deprived *of* y.   *Ge 27:45*
both
that only may be done *of* y.   *Ex 12:16*
ye came near unto me every   *De 1:22*
one *of* y.
the inhabitants faint because   *Jos 2:9*
of y.
hath done to these nations   *Jos 23:3*
because *of* y.
that all *of* y. have conspired   *1Sa 22:8*
against me
hearken, O people, every   *1Ki 22:28*
one *of* y.
what Ezra requires *of* y. it be   *Ezr 7:21*
done
there were *of* y. cast out to   *Ne 1:9*
heaven
ye shall be slain all *of* y.   *Ps 62:3*
they that escape *of* y. shall   *Eze 6:9*
remember
he shall receive *of* y. his   *Mic 1:11*
standing
which *of* y. by taking   *M't 6:27;*
thought can add one cubit   *Lu 12:25*
to stature
doth not each one *of* y. lead   *Lu 13:15*
his ox
which *of* y. convinceth me of   *Joh 8:46*
sin
I speak not *of* y. all, I know   *Joh 13:18*
whom I chose
God did by him in midst *of* y.   *Ac 2:22*
turning every one *of* y. from   *Ac 3:26*
iniquities
which was set at nought *of* y.   *Ac 4:11*
builders
by the mutual faith both *of* y.   *Ro 1:12*
and me
it hath been declared to me   *1Co 1:11*
of y.
such were some *of* y. but ye   *1Co 6:11*
are washed
the head to the feet, I have   *1Co 12:21*
no need *of* y.
every one *of* y. hath a   *1Co 14:46*
psalm, a doctrine
let every one *of* y. lay by him   *1Co 16:2*
in store
and our hope *of* y. is stedfast   *2Co 1:7*
if I have boasted any thing to   *2Co 7:14*
him *of* y.
for ye suffer, if a man take   *2Co 11:20*
of y.
did I make a gain *of* y.   *2Co 12:17;*
did Titus make gain *of* y.   *12:18*
this would I learn *of* y.   *Ga 3:2*
received ye
as many *of* y. as have been   *Ga 3:27*
baptized into
change my voice, I stand in   *Ga 4:20*
doubt *of* y.
beloved brother, who is one   *Col 4:9;*
of y.   *4:12*
neither *of* y. sought we glory   *1Th 2:6*
every one *of* y. should know   *1Th 4:4*
how to possess
having no evil thing to say *of*   *Tit 2:8*
y.
hire which is *of* y. kept back   *Jas 5:4*
by fraud
whereas they speak evil   *1Pe 3:16; 4:4*
of y.

OVER YOU

I will even appoint *over* y.   *Le 26:16*
terror
they that hate you shall reign   *Le 26:17*
over y.
as Lord rejoiced *over* y. to   *De 28:63*
do you good, he will rejoice
over y. to destroy you
I will not rule *over* y. nor my   *J'g 8:23*
son rule *over* y. Lord shall
rule *over* y.
is it better seventy reign *over* y.   *J'g 9:2*
or one
if in truth ye anoint me king   *J'g 9:15*
over y.

manner of king that shall   1Sa 8:11
reign over y.
behold, I have made a king   1Sa 12:1
over y.
behold, the Lord hath set a   1Sa 12:13
king over y.
ye sought David to be king   2Sa 3:17
over y.
Amariah the chief priest is   2Ch 19:11
over y.
also I set the watchmen over y.   Jer 6:17
saying
with fury poured out will I   Eze 20:33
rule over y.
the heaven over y. is stayed   Hag 1:10
from dew
man, who made me a divider   Lu 12:14
over y.
sin shall not have dominion   Ro 6:14
over y.
be partakers of this power   1Co 9:12
over y.
I am jealous over y. with   2Co 11:2
godly zeal
we were comforted over y. in   1Th 3:7
affliction
know them which are over y.   1Th 5:12
in the Lord
remember them that have   Heb 13:7
rule over y.
obey them that have the   Heb 13:17
rule over y.
salute them that have the   Heb 13:24
rule over y.

TO, UNTO YOU

every herb to y. it shall be   Ge 1:29
for meat
and take our daughters unto   Ge 34:9
y.
take you to me, and be to y. a   Ex 6:7
God
when your children shall say   Ex 12:26
unto y.
ye shall not make unto y.   Ex 20:23
gods of gold
it shall be unto y. most holy   Ex 30:36
will do this unto y. appoint   Le 26:16
terror
they shall be to y. for an   Nu 10:8
ordinance
be to y. a memorial; unto y.   Nu 10:10;
for a fringe   15:39
do unto y. as I thought to do   Nu 33:56
to them
if ye go in to them, and they   Jos 23:12
to y.
be not servants, as they have   1Sa 4:9
been to y.
unto y. O men, I call, and my   Pr 8:4
voice is
this iniquity shall be to y. as   Isa 30:13
a breach
to y. it is commanded, O   Da 3:4
people
unto y. that fear my name   Mal 4:2
shall sun
that men should do to y.   M't 7:12;
  Lu 6:31
according to your faith be it   M't 9:29
unto y.
it is given unto y. to know   M't 13:11;
the mysteries of the kingdom   M'k 4:11;
  Lu 8:10
unto y. that hear shall more   M'k 4:24
be given
unto y. is born this day a   Lu 2:11
Saviour
if ye do good to them which   Lu 6:33
do good to y.
I appoint unto y. a kingdom   Lu 22:29
as my Father
the promise is unto y. and   Ac 2:39
children
unto y. first, God raised up   Ac 3:26
his Son
came I unto y. without   Ac 10:29
gainsaying
to y. is the word of this   Ac 13:26
salvation sent
if not to others, doubtless I   1Co 9:2
am to y.
or came the word of God   1Co 14:36
unto y. only
a measure to reach even   2Co 10:13
unto y.
we are come as far as to y.   2Co 10:14
in preaching

but is to y. a token of   Ph'p 1:28
salvation
unto y. it is given not only   Ph'p 1:29
to believe
our gospel came not unto y. in   1Th 1:5
word
to y. who are troubled, rest   2Th 1:7
with us
unto y. that believe, he is   1Pe 2:7
precious
but unto y. I say, and to the   Re 2:24
rest

TOWARDS YOU

perform my good word   Jer 29:10
towards y.
I know the thoughts I think   Jer 29:11
towards y.
give ear, for judgment is   Ho 5:1
towards y.
our word towards y. was not   2Co 1:18
yea
inward affection is abundant   2Co 7:15
towards y.
able to make all grace abound   2Co 9:8
towards y.
but being absent am bold   2Co 10:1
towards y.
live by the power of God   2Co 13:4
towards y.
abound in love, as we do   1Th 3:12
towards y.

UPON YOU

the plague shall not be upon   Ex 12:13
y.
he may bestow upon y. a   Ex 32:29
blessing
anointing oil of the Lord is   Le 10:7
upon y.
they said, ye take too much   Nu 16:3;
upon y.   16:7
the Lord did not set his love   De 7:7
upon y.
as all good things are come   Jos 23:15
upon y.
from all places they will be   Ne 4:12
upon y.
the blessing of the Lord be   Ps 129:8
upon y.
Lord poured upon y. spirit of   Isa 29:10
sleep
he may have mercy upon y.   Isa 30:18;
  Jer 42:12
I will visit upon y. evil of   Jer 23:2
doings
therefore this thing is come   Jer 40:3
upon y.
I will blow upon y. in fire of   Eze 22:21
my wrath
that lo, the days shall come   Am 4:2
upon y.
before day of Lord's anger   Zep 2:2
come upon y.
upon y. may come righteous   M't 23:35
blood
the kingdom of God is come   Lu 11:20
upon y.
and so that day come upon y.   Lu 21:34
unawares
I send the promise of my   Lu 24:49
Father upon y.
walk, lest darkness come   Joh 12:35
upon y.
after the Holy Ghost is come   Ac 1:8
upon y.
not that I may cast a snare   1Co 7:35
upon y.
lest I bestowed upon y. labour   Ga 4:11
in vain
howl for miseries that shall   Jas 5:1
come upon y.
the Spirit of God resteth   1Pe 4:14
upon y.
I will put upon y. none other   Re 2:24
burden

WITH YOU

we will dwell with y. be one   Ge 34:16
people
behold, I die, but God shall be   Ge 48:21
with y.
shall carry up my bones   Ex 13:19
hence with y.
ye have seen that I have   Ex 20:22
talked with y.
tarry ye here, Aaron and Hur   Ex 24:14
are with y.

with y. shall be a man of every   Nu 1:4
tribe
the testimony, where I will   Nu 17:4
meet with y.
and that it may be well with y.   De 5:33
no part with y.; God goeth   De 12:12;
with y.   20:4
nor with y. only do I make   De 29:14
this covenant
neither will I be with y. any   Jos 7:12
more
and Boaz said, The Lord be   Ru 2:4
with y.
let my father and mother be   1Sa 22:3
with y.
come again to me, and I will   1Sa 22:23
go with y.
what have I to do with y.   2Sa 16:10;
  19:22
I will surely go forth with y.   2Sa 18:2
myself
seeing your master's sons are   2Ki 10:2
with y.
there be with y. none of   2Ki 10:23
servants of Lord
it shall be well with y.   2Ki 25:24;
  Jer 40:9
is not the Lord your God   1Ch 22:18
with y.
there are with y. golden   2Ch 13:8
calves
the Lord is with y. while ye   2Ch 15:2
be with him
for the Lord, who is with y.   2Ch 19:6
in judgment
fear not, for the Lord will   2Ch 20:17
be with y.
are there not with y. even   2Ch 28:10
with y. sins
let us build with y. we seek   Ezr 4:2
your God
let I deal with y. after your   Job 42:8
folly
cannot I do with y. as this   Jer 18:6
potter
for I am with y.   Jer 42:11;
  Hag 1:13; 2:4
there will I plead with y.   Eze 20:35;
  20:36
know I am Lord when I   Eze 20:44
have wrought with y.
the God of hosts shall be   Am 5:14
with y.
we will go with y. for God is   Zec 8:23
with y.
faithless perverse generation   M't 17:17;
how long be with y.   M'k 9:19; Lu 9:41
ye have the poor always   M't 26:11;
with y. but me ye have   Joh 12:8
when I drink it new w. y. in   M't 26:29
my Father's kingdom
I am with y. always to the   M't 28:20
end of the world
I spake to you, while I was   Lu 24:44
with y.
yet a little while am I with   Joh 7:33;
y. then I go to him that sent me   12:35;
  13:33
Jesus said, Have I been so   Joh 14:9
long with y.
Comforter, that he may abide   Joh 14:16
with y. for ever
he dwelleth with y.   Joh 14:17
being present with y.   Joh 14:25
peace I leave with y.   Joh 14:27
I was with y.   Joh 16:4
reason would I should bear   Ac 18:14
with y.
I have been with y. at all   Ac 20:18
seasons
I may be comforted together   Ro 1:12
with y.
that I may with y. be   Ro 15:32
refreshed
now the God of peace be   Ro 15:33;
with y. all. Amen   2Co 13:11; Ph'p 4:9
grace of our Lord Jesus   Ro 16:20;
Christ be with y.   16:24; 1Co 16:23;
Ph'p 4:23; Col 4:18; 5:28; 2Th 3:18;
2Ti 4:15; Tit 3:15; Heb 13:25; 2Jo 3;
  Re 22:21
I was with y. in weakness and   1Co 2:3
in fear
that we also might reign with   1Co 4:8
y.
see that he may be with y.   1Co 16:10
without fear
my love be with y. all in   1Co 16:24
Christ Jesus

he that establisheth us *with*   *2Co 1:21*
y. is God
shall raise us up and present   *2Co 4:14*
us *with y.*
ye are in our hearts to die and   *2Co 7:3*
live *with y.*
when I was present *with y.*   *2Co 11:9;*
  Ga 4:18, 20
I joy and rejoice *with y.* all   *Ph'p 2:17*
yet am I *with y.* in the spirit,   *Col 2:5*
joying
word may be glorified, as it is   *2Th 3:1*
with y.
Lord of peace be *with y.* all   *2Th 3:16*
God dealeth *with y.* as with   *Heb 12:7*
sons
peace be *with y.* all that are   *1Pe 5:14*
in Christ
spots and blemishes, while   *2Pe 2:13*
they feast *with y.*

TO YOU-WARD

which *to y.* is not weak   *2Co 13:3*
the grace of God given me *to*   *Eph 3:2*
y.

YOUNG

and a *y.* man to my hurt   *Ge 4:23*
which the *y.* men have eaten   *Ge 14:24*
and a turtledove, and a *y.*   *Ge 15:9*
pigeon
good, and gave it unto a *y.*   *Ge 18:7*
man
the house round, both old and   *Ge 19:4*
y.
took two of his *y.* men with   *Ge 22:3*
him
Abraham said unto his *y.* men   *Ge 22:5*
Abraham returned unto his   *Ge 22:19*
y. men
thy, she goats have not cast   *Ge 31:38*
their *y.*
and herds with *y.* are with   *Ge 33:13*
me
y. man deferred not to do the   *Ge 34:19*
there was there with us a *y.*   *Ge 41:12*
man
go with our *y.* and with our   *Ex 10:9*
old
There shall nothing cast their   *Ex 23:26*
y.
y. men of the children of   *Ex 24:5*
Israel
Take one *y.* bullock, and   *Ex 29:1*
Joshua, the son of Nun, a *y.*   *Ex 33:11*
man
of turtledoves, or of *y.* pigeons   *Le 1:14*
a *y.* bullock without blemish   *Le 4:3*
offer a *y.* bullock for the sin   *Le 4:14*
or two *y.* pigeons, unto the Lord   *Le 5:7*
two *y.* pigeons, then he that   *Le 5:11*
sinned
a *y.* calf for a sin offering   *Le 9:2*
a *y.* pigeon, or a turtledove   *Le 12:6*
two turtles, or two *y.* pigeons   *Le 12:8*
two *y.* pigeons, such as he is   *Le 14:22*
able
y. pigeons, such as he can get   *Le 14:30*
or two *y.* pigeons, and come   *Le 15:14*
before
or two *y.* pigeons, and bring   *Le 15:29*
them
a *y.* bullock for a sin offering   *Le 16:3*
kill it and her *y.* both in one   *Le 22:28*
day
one *y.* bullock, and two rams   *Le 23:18*
or two *y.* pigeons, to the   *Nu 6:10;*
priest 7:15, 21, 27, 33, 39, 45, 51, 57,
  63, 69, 75
One *y.* bullock, one ram, one   *Nu 7:81*
Then let them take a *y.* bullock   *Nu 8:8*
y. bullock shalt thou take   *Nu 8:8*
ran a *y.* man, and told   *Nu 11:27*
Moses
one of his *y.* men, answered   *Nu 11:28*
offer one *y.* bullock for a   *Nu 15:24*
burnt
and lift up himself as a *y.*   *Nu 23:24*
lion
y. bullocks, one ram   *Nu 28:11;*
  28:19, 27
one *y.* bullock, one ram, and   *Nu 29:2;*
  29:8
thirteen *y.* bullocks, two   *Nu 29:13*
rams
shall offer twelve *y.* bullocks   *Nu 29:17*

whether they be *y.* ones, or   *De 22:6*
eggs
and the dam sitting upon the   *De 22:6*
y.
not take the dam with the *y.*   *De 22:6*
dam go, and take the *y.* to   *De 22:7*
thee
old, nor shew favour to the   *De 28:50*
y.
toward her *y.* one that   *De 28:57*
cometh out
fluttereth over her *y.*   *De 32:11*
spreadeth
shall destroy both the *y.* man   *De 32:25*
both man and woman, *y.* and   *Jos 6:21*
old
y. men that were spies went   *Jos 6:23*
in
Take thy father's *y.* bullock,   *J'g 6:25*
even
a *y.* man of the men of   *J'g 8:14*
Succoth
unto the *y.* man his   *J'g 9:54*
armourbearer
his *y.* man thrust him through   *J'g 9:54*
a *y.* lion roared against him   *J'g 14:5*
feast; for so used the *y.* men   *J'g 14:10*
to do
a *y.* man out of   *J'g 17:7*
Beth-lehem-judah
y. man was unto him as one   *J'g 17:11*
of his
and the *y.* man became his   *J'g 17:12*
priest
the voice of the *y.* man the   *J'g 18:3*
Levite
the house of the *y.* man   *J'g 18:15*
the Levite
y. man which is with thy   *J'g 19:19*
servants
four hundred *y.* virgins, that   *J'g 21:12*
had
have I not charged the *y.* men   *Ru 2:9*
that which the *y.* men   *Ru 2:9*
have drawn
Boaz commanded his *y.* men   *Ru 2:15*
shalt keep fast by my *y.* men   *Ru 2:21*
as thou followedst not *y.* men   *Ru 3:10*
shall give thee of this *y.* woman   *Ru 4:12*
in Shiloh: and the child was *y.*   *1Sa 1:24*
the sin of the *y.* men was very   *1Sa 2:17*
great
your goodliest *y.* men, and   *1Sa 8:16*
your
Saul, a choice *y.* man and a   *1Sa 9:2*
goodly
y. maidens going out to draw   *1Sa 9:11*
son of Saul said unto the *y.*   *1Sa 14:1*
man
Jonathan said to the *y.* man   *1Sa 14:6*
that
Whose son art thou, thou *y.*   *1Sa 17:58*
man
But if I say thus unto the *y.*   *1Sa 20:22*
man
If the *y.* men have kept   *1Sa 21:4*
themselves
vessels of the *y.* men are holy   *1Sa 21:5*
And David sent out ten *y.*   *1Sa 25:5*
men
David said unto the *y.* men,   *1Sa 25:5*
Get
Ask thy *y.* men, and they will   *1Sa 25:8*
shew
let the *y.* men find favour in   *1Sa 25:8*
thine
And when David's *y.* men   *1Sa 25:9*
came
So David's *y.* men turned   *1Sa 25:12*
their way
But one of the *y.* men told   *1Sa 25:14*
Abigail
thine handmaid saw not the   *1Sa 25:25*
y. men
the *y.* men that follow my   *1Sa 25:27*
lord
let one of the *y.* men come   *1Sa 26:22*
over and
he said, I am a *y.* man of   *1Sa 30:13*
Egypt
save four hundred *y.* men,   *1Sa 30:17*
which
David said unto the *y.* man   *2Sa 1:5*
that
And the *y.* man that told him   *2Sa 1:6*
said
And David said unto the *y.*   *2Sa 1:13*
man
David called one of the *y.* men   *2Sa 1:15*
Let the *y.* men now arise, and   *2Sa 2:14*

lay thee hold on one of the *y.*   *2Sa 2:21*
men
And David commanded his *y.*   *2Sa 4:12*
men
Mephibosheth had a *y.* son   *2Sa 9:12*
all the *y.* men the king's   *2Sa 13:32*
sons
the *y.* man that kept the   *2Sa 13:34*
watch
bring the *y.* man Absalom   *2Sa 14:21*
again
summer fruit for the *y.* men   *2Sa 16:2*
to eat
gently for my sake with the   *2Sa 18:5*
y. man
none touch the *y.* man   *2Sa 18:12*
Absalom
y. man that bare Joab's   *2Sa 18:15*
armour
said, Is the *y.* man Absalom   *2Sa 18:29;*
safe   *18:32*
do thee hurt, be as that *y.*   *2Sa 18:32*
man is
for my lord the king a *y.*   *1Ki 1:2*
virgin
Solomon seeing the *y.* man   *1Ki 11:28*
that
consulted with the *y.* men   *1Ki 12:8*
y. men that were grown up   *1Ki 12:10*
with
after the counsel of the *y.*   *1Ki 12:14*
men
y. men of the princes of   *1Ki 20:14;*
  20:15, 17, 19
me, I pray thee, one of the *y.*   *2Ki 4:22*
men
two *y.* men of the sons of the   *2Ki 5:22*
Lord opened the eyes of the   *2Ki 6:17*
y. man
their *y.* men wilt thou slay   *2Ki 8:12*
with
So the *y.* man, even the   *2Ki 9:4*
even the *y.* man the prophet   *2Ki 9:4*
Zadok, a *y.* man mighty of   *1Ch 12:28*
valour
Solomon my son is *y.* and   *1Ch 22:5*
tender
hath chosen, is yet *y.* and   *1Ch 29:1*
tender
took counsel with the *y.* men   *2Ch 10:8*
y. men that were brought up   *2Ch 10:10*
with
after the advice of the *y.*   *2Ch 10:14*
men
when Rehoboam was *y.* and   *2Ch 13:7*
himself with a *y.* bullock   *2Ch 13:9*
while he was yet *y.* he began   *2Ch 34:3*
who slew their *y.* men with   *2Ch 36:17*
had no compassion upon *y.*   *2Ch 36:17*
man
both *y.* bullocks, and rams   *Ezr 6:9*
there be fair *y.* virgins sought   *Es 2:2*
together all the fair *y.* virgins   *Es 2:3*
perish, all Jews., both *y.* and   *Es 3:13*
old
camels, and *y.* dromedaries   *Es 8:10*
it fell upon the *y.* men and   *Job 1:19*
they
and the teeth of the *y.* lions   *Job 4:10*
Yea, *y.* children despised me   *Job 19:18*
The *y.* men saw me, and hid   *Job 29:8*
I am *y.* and ye are very old   *Job 32:6*
or fill the appetite of the *y.*   *Job 38:39*
lions
when his *y.* ones cry unto   *Job 38:41*
God
they bring forth their *y.* ones   *Job 39:3*
Their *y.* ones are in good   *Job 39:4*
liking
is hardened against her *y.*   *Job 39:16*
ones
Her *y.* ones also suck up   *Job 39:30*
blood
a *y.* lion lurking in secret   *Ps 17:12*
places
and Sirion like a *y.* unicorn   *Ps 29:6*
The *y.* lions do lack, and   *Ps 34:10*
suffer
I have been *y.* and now am old   *Ps 37:25*
out the great teeth of the *y.*   *Ps 58:6*
lions
The fire consumed their *y.*   *Ps 78:63*
men
following the ewes great with   *Ps 78:71*
y.
where she may lay her *y.* even   *Ps 84:3*
y. lion and the dragon shalt   *Ps 91:13*
thou
The *y.* lions roar after their   *Ps 104:21*
prey

shall a *y.* man cleanse his way   *Ps 119:9*

and to the *y.* ravens which cry   *Ps 147:9*

Both *y.* men, and maidens; old   *Ps 148:12*

y. man knowledge and discretion   *Pr 1:4*

a *y.* man void of understanding   *Pr 7:7*

glory of *y.* men is their strength   *Pr 20:29*

out, and the *y.* eagles shall eat it   *Pr 30:17*

Rejoice, O *y.* man, in thy youth   *Ec 11:9*

beloved is like a roe or a *y.* hart   *Ca 2:9*

roe or a *y.* hart upon the mountains   *Ca 2:17*

are like two *y.* roes that are twins   *Ca 4:5; 7:3*

be thou like to a roe or to a *y.* hart   *Ca 8:14*

lion, they shall roar like *y.* lions   *Isa 5:29*

a *y.* woman shall (R)   *Isa 7:14*

that a man shall nourish a *y.* cow   *Isa 7:21*

shall have no joy in their *y.* men   *Isa 9:17*

and the *y.* lion and the fatling   *Isa 11:6*

y. ones shall lie down together   *Isa 11:7*

shall dash the *y.* men to pieces   *Isa 13:18*

Ethiopians captives, *y.* and old   *Isa 20:4*

neither do I nourish up *y.* men   *Isa 23:4*

whence come the *y.* and old lion   *Isa 30:6*

riches upon shoulders of *y.* asses   *Isa 30:6*

y. asses that ear the ground shall eat   *Isa 30:24*

the *y.* lion roaring on his prey   *Isa 31:4*

his *y.* men shall be discomfited   *Isa 31:8*

gently lead those that are with *y.*   *Isa 40:11*

the *y.* men shall utterly fall   *Isa 40:30*

For as a *y.* man marrieth a virgin   *Isa 62:5*

The *y.* lions roared upon him   *Jer 2:15*

the assembly of *y.* men together   *Jer 6:11*

and the *y.* men from the streets   *Jer 9:21*

the *y.* men shall die by the sword   *Jer 11:22*

aaginst the mother of the *y.* men   *Jer 15:8*

their *y.* men be slain by the sword   *Jer 18:21*

the *y.* of the flock and of the herd   *Jer 31:12*

both *y.* men and old together   *Jer 31:13*

his chosen *y.* men are gone down to   *Jer 48:15*

her *y.* men shall fall in her streets   *Jer 49:26*

shall her *y.* men fall in the streets   *Jer 50:30*

spare ye not her *y.* men; destroy ye   *Jer 51:3*

will I break in pieces old and *y.*   *Jer 51:22*

in pieces the *y.* man and the maid   *Jer 51:22*

against me to crush my *y.* men   *La 1:15*

my *y.* men are gone into captivity   *La 1:18*

him for the life of thy *y.* children   *La 2:19*

y. and the old lie on the ground in   *La 2:21*

virgins and my *y.* men are fallen   *La 2:21*

they give suck to their *y.* ones   *La 4:3*

y. children ask bread, and no man   *La 4:4*

They took the *y.* men to grind   *La 5:13*

gate, the *y.* men from their music   *La 5:14*

Slay utterly old and *y.* both maids   *Eze 9:6*

off the top of his *y.* twigs, and   *Eze 17:4*

off from the top of his *y.* twigs   *Eze 17:22*

her whelps among *y.* lions   *Eze 19:2*

it became a *y.* lion, and it learned   *Eze 19:3*

whelps, and made him a *y.* lion   *Eze 19:5*

he became a *y.* lion, and learned   *Eze 19:6*

all of them desirable *y.* men   *Eze 23:6; 23:12, 23*

y. men of Aven and of Pi-beseth   *Eze 30:17*

of the field bring forth their *y.*   *Eze 31:6*

art like a *y.* lion of the nations   *Eze 32:2*

of Tarshish, with all the *y.* lions   *Eze 38:13*

face of a *y.* lion toward the palm   *Eze 41:19*

y. bullock for a sin offering   *Eze 43:19*

a *y.* bullock without blemish   *Eze 43:23; 45:18; 46:6*

shall also prepare a *y.* bullock   *Eze 43:25*

as a *y.* lion to the house of Judah   *Ho 5:14*

your *y.* men shall see visions   *Joe 2:28; Ac 2:17*

and of your *y.* men for Nazarites   *Am 2:11*

will a *y.* lion cry out of his den   *Am 3:4*

your *y.* men have I slain with   *Am 4:10*

virgins and *y.* men faint for thirst   *Am 8:13*

as a *y.* lion among the flocks of   *Mic 5:8*

the feedingplace of the *y.* lions   *Na 2:11*

sword shall devour thy *y.* lions   *Na 2:13*

her *y.* children also were dashed in   *Na 3:10*

Run, speak to this *y.* man, saying   *Zec 2:4*

shall make the *y.* men cheerful   *Zec 9:17*

a voice of the roaring of *y.* lions   *Zec 11:3*

neither shall seek the *y.* one   *Zec 11:16*

search diligently for the *y.* child   *M't 2:8*

stood over where the *y.* child was   *M't 2:9*

the *y.* child with Mary his mother   *M't 2:11*

take the *y.* child and his mother   *M't 2:13; 2:20*

seek the *y.* child to destroy him   *M't 2:13*

he took the *y.* child and his mother   *M't 2:14; 2:21*

which sought the *y.* child's life   *M't 2:20*

The *y.* man saith unto him, All   *M't 19:20*

the *y.* man heard that saying, he   *M't 19:22*

y. daughter had an unclean spirit   *M'k 7:25*

they brought *y.* children to him   *M'k 10:13*

followed him a certain *y.* man   *M'k 14:51*

and the *y.* men laid hold on him   *M'k 14:51*

saw a *y.* man sitting on the right   *M'k 16:5*

of turtledoves, or two *y.* pigeons   *Lu 2:24*

Y. man I say unto thee, Arise   *Lu 7:14*

when he had found a *y.* ass,   *Joh 12:14*

When thou wast *y.* thou girdedst   *Joh 21:18*

the *y.* men arose, wound him up   *Ac 5:6*

y. men came in, and found her   *Ac 5:10*

they cast out their *y.* children   *Ac 7:19*

their clothes at a *y.* man's feet   *Ac 7:58*

a certain *y.* man named Eutychus   *Ac 20:9*

they brought the *y.* man alive   *Ac 20:12*

this *y.* man unto the chief captain   *Ac 23:17*

prayed me to bring this *y.* man   *Ac 23:18*

then let the *y.* man depart   *Ac 23:22*

teach the *y.* women to be sober   *Tit 2:4*

Y. men likewise exhort to be because   *Tit 2:6*

I write unto you, *y.* men,   *1Jo 2:13*

written unto you, *y.* men, because   *1Jo 2:14*

YOUNGER

knew what his *y.* son had done   *Ge 9:24*

the firstborn said unto the *y.*   *Ge 19:31; 19:34*

and the *y.* arose, and lay with him   *Ge 19:35*

And the *y.*, she also bare a son   *Ge 19:38*

and the elder shall serve the *y.*   *Ge 25:23*

put them upon Jacob her *y.* son   *Ge 27:15*

sent and called Jacob her *y.* son   *Ge 27:42*

and the name of the *y.* was Rachel   *Ge 29:16*

years for Rachel the *y.* daughter   *Ge 29:18*

to give the *y.* before the firstborn   *Ge 29:26*

Is this your *y.* brother, of whom   *Ge 43:29*

Ephraim's head, who was the *y.*   *Ge 48:14*

his *y.* brother shall be greater   *Ge 48:19*

Kenaz, Caleb's *y.* brother, took it   *J'g 1:13*

son of Kenaz, Caleb's *y.* brother   *J'g 3:9*

is not her *y.* sister, fairer than she   *J'g 15:2*

and the name of the *y.* Michal   *1Sa 14:49*

over against their *y.* brethren   *1Ch 24:31*

y. than I have me in derision   *Job 30:1*

thy *y.* sister, that dwelleth at thy   *Eze 16:46*

thy sisters, thine elder and thy *y.*   *Eze 16:61*

the *y.* of them said to his father   *Lu 15:12*

the *y.* son gathered all together   *Lu 15:13*

among you, let him be as the *y.*   *Lu 22:26*

her, The elder shall serve the *y.*   *Ro 9:12*

and the *y.* men as brethren   *1Ti 5:1*

the *y.* as sisters, with all purity   *1Ti 5:2*

But the *y.* widows refuse: for when   *1Ti 5:11*

therefore that the *y.* women marry   *1Ti 5:14*

ye *y.* submit yourselves unto   *1Pe 5:5*

YOUNGEST

the *y.* is this day with our father   *Ge 42:13*

your *y.* brother come hither father   *Ge 42:15*

bring your *y.* brother unto me   *Ge 42:20; 42:34*

y. is this day with our father   *Ge 42:32*

and the *y.* according to his youth   *Ge 43:33*

cup, in the sack's mouth of the *y.*   *Ge 44:2*

at the eldest, and left at the *y.*   *Ge 44:12*

Except your *y.* brother come down   *Ge 44:23*

if our *y.* brother be with us, then   *Ge 44:26*

except our *y.* brother be with us   *Ge 44:26*

and in his *y.* son shall he set up   *Jos 6:26*

the *y.* son of Jerubbaal was left   *J'g 9:5*

said, There remaineth yet the *y.*   *1Sa 16:11*

And David was the *y.*: and   *1Sa 17:14*

gates thereof in his *y.* son Segub   *1Ki 16:34*

save Jehoahaz, the *y.* of his sons   *2Ch 21:17*

made Ahaziah his *y.* son king in   *2Ch 22:1*

YOUR

thereof, then *y.* eyes shall be opened   *Ge 3:5*

sea; into *y.* hand are they delivered   *Ge 9:2*

y. blood, of y. lives will I require	Ge 9:5
with you, and with y. seed after you	Ge 9:9
circumcise the flesh of y. foreskin	Ge 17:11
every man child in y. generations, he	Ge 17:12
my covenant shall be in y. flesh for	Ge 17:13
you, be fetched, and wash y. feet	Ge 18:4
of bread, and comfort ye y. hearts	Ge 18:5
therefore are ye come to y. servant	Ge 18:5
I pray you, unto y. servant's house	Ge 19:2
and tarry all night, and wash y. feet	Ge 19:2
rise up early, and go on y. ways	Ge 19:2
do ye to them as is good in y. eyes	Ge 19:8
y. mind that I should bury my dead	Ge 23:8
I see y. father's countenance, that it	Ge 31:5
my power I have served y. father	Ge 31:6
And y. father hath deceived me	Ge 31:7
taken away the cattle of y. father	Ge 31:9
the God of y. father spake unto me	Ge 31:29
Shechem longeth for y. daughter	Ge 34:8
give y. daughters unto us, and take	Ge 34:9
Let me find grace in y. eyes, and what	Ge 34:11
we will take y. daughters, and we	Ge 34:16
be clean, and change y. garments	Ge 35:2
y. sheaves stood round about	Ge 37:7
except y. youngest brother come	Ge 42:15
of you, and let him fetch y. brother	Ge 42:16
that y. words may be proved, whether	Ge 42:16
true men, let one of y. brethren	Ge 42:19
bound in the house of y. prison	Ge 42:19
corn for the famine of y. houses	Ge 42:19
bring y. youngest brother unto me	Ge 42:20
so shall y. words be verified, and ye	Ge 42:20
one of y. brethren here with me	Ge 42:33
food for the famine of y. households	Ge 42:33
bring y. youngest brother unto me	Ge 42:34
so will I deliver you y. brother, and	Ge 42:34
except y. brother be with you	Ge 43:3; 43:5
saying, Is y. father yet alive	Ge 43:7
would say, Bring y. brother down	Ge 43:7
best fruits in the land in y. vessels	Ge 43:11
And take double money in y. hand	Ge 43:12
again in the mouth of y. sacks	Ge 43:12
carry it again in y. hand	Ge 43:12
Take also y. brother, and arise, go	Ge 43:13
he may send away y. other brother	Ge 43:14
y. God, and the God of y. father	Ge 43:23
hath given you treasure in y. sacks	Ge 43:23
I had y. money. And he brought	Ge 43:23
Is y. father well, the old man of whom	Ge 43:27
Is this y. younger brother, of whom	Ge 43:29
let it be according unto y. words	Ge 44:10
get you up in peace unto y. father	Ge 44:17
Except y. youngest brother come	Ge 44:23
I am Joseph y. brother, whom ye sold	Ge 45:4
and to save y. lives by a great	Ge 45:7
y. eyes see, and the eyes of my brother	Ge 45:12
lade y. beasts, and go, get you into	Ge 45:17
take y. father, and y. households	Ge 45:18
the land of Egypt, for y. little ones	Ge 45:19
and for y. wives, and bring y. father	Ge 45:19
Also regard not y. stuff; for the good	Ge 45:20
shall say, What is y. occupation	Ge 46:33
his brethren, What is y. occupation	Ge 47:3
And Joseph said, Give y. cattle	Ge 47:16
I will give you for y. cattle, if money	Ge 47:16
I have bought you this day and y. land	Ge 47:23
and four parts shall be y. own, for seed	Ge 47:24
y. food, and for them of y. households	Ge 47:24
and for food for y. little ones	Ge 47:24
you again unto the land of y. fathers	Ge 48:21
and hearken unto Israel y. father	Ge 49:2
now I have found grace in y. eyes	Ge 50:4
I will nourish you, and y. little ones	Ge 50:21
God of y. fathers hath sent me unto	Ex 3:13
The Lord God of y. fathers	Ex 3:15; 3:16
upon y. sons, and upon y. daughters	Ex 3:22
works? get you unto y. burdens	Ex 5:4
ought of y. work shall be diminished	Ex 5:11
hasted them, saying, Fulfil y. works	Ex 5:13
y. daily tasks, as when there was	Ex 5:13
have ye not fulfilled y. task	Ex 5:14
ought from y. bricks of y. daily task	Ex 5:19
shall know that I am the Lord y. God	Ex 6:7
Go ye, sacrifice to y. God in the land	Ex 8:25
ve may sacrifice to the Lord y. God	Ex 8:28
unto them, Go, serve the Lord y. God	Ex 10:8
I will let you go, and y. little ones	Ex 10:10
have sinned against the Lord y. God	Ex 10:16
and intreat the Lord y. God, that he	Ex 10:17
let y. flocks and y. herds be stayed	Ex 10:24
let y. little ones also go with you	Ex 10:24
to his eating shall make y. count	Ex 12:4
Y. lamb shall be without blemish	Ex 12:5
y. lions girded, y. shoes on y. feet	Ex 12:11
and y. staff in y. hand	Ex 12:11
the Lord throughout y. generations	Ex 12:14
put away leaven out of y. houses	Ex 12:15
y. armies out of the land of Egypt	Ex 12:17
ye observe this day in y. generations	Ex 12:17
there be no leaven found in y. houses	Ex 12:19
in all y. habitations shall ye eat	Ex 12:20
you a lamb according to y. families	Ex 12:21
destroyer to come in unto y. houses to	Ex 12:23
when y. children shall say unto you	Ex 12:26
Also take y. flocks and y. herds	Ex 12:32
for you, and ye shall hold y. peace	Ex 14:14
he heareth y. murmurings against	Ex 16:7
y. murmurings which ye murmur	Ex 16:8
y. murmurings are not against us	Ex 16:8
for he hath heard y. murmurings	Ex 16:9
shall know that I am the Lord y. God	Ex 16:12
to the number of y. persons	Ex 16:16
of it to be kept for y. generations	Ex 16:32
Lord, to be kept for y. generations	Ex 16:33
the third day: come not at y. wives	Ex 19:15
that his fear may be before y. faces	Ex 20:20
and y. wives shall be widows	Ex 22:24
and y. children fatherless	Ex 22:24
he will not pardon y. transgressions	Ex 23:21
And ye shall serve the Lord y. God	Ex 23:25
inhabitants of the land into y. hand	Ex 23:31
offering throughout y. generations	Ex 29:42
the Lord throughout y. generations	Ex 30:8
upon it through y. generations	Ex 30:10
to make an atonement for y. soul	Ex 30:15; 30:16
unto me throughout y. generations	Ex 30:31
and you throughout y. generations	Ex 31:13
which are in the ears of y. wives	Ex 32:2
of y. sons, and of y. daughters	Ex 32:2
I will multiply y. seed as the stars of	Ex 32:13
spoken of will I give unto y. seed	Ex 32:13
I shall make an atonement for y. sin	Ex 32:30
all y. menchildren appear before the	Ex 34:23
no fire throughout y. habitations	Ex 35:3
ye shall bring y. offering of the cattle	Le 1:2
a perpetual statute for y. generations	Le 3:17
throughout all y. dwellings, that ye	Le 3:17
a statute for ever in y. generations	Le 6:18
or of beast, in any of y. dwellings	Le 7:26
of the sacrifices of y. peace offerings	Le 7:32
until the days of y. consecration be	Le 8:33
carry y. brethren from before	Le 10:4
his sons, Uncover not y. heads	Le 10:6
neither rend y. clothes; lest ye die	Le 10:6
but let y. brethren, the whole house	Le 10:6
for ever throughout y. generations	Le 10:9
not make y. selves abominable	Le 11:43
For I am the Lord y. God: ye shall	Le 11:44
of the land of Egypt, to be y. God	Le 11:45
a house of the land of y. possession	Le 14:34
ye shall afflict y. souls, and do no	Le 16:29
whether it be one of y. own country	Le 16:29
ye may be clean from all y. sins	Le 16:30
and ye shall afflict y. souls, by a	Le 16:31
to make an atonement for y. souls	Le 17:11
whether it be one of y. own country	Le 17:15

Say unto them, I am the Lord *Le 18:2*
y. God
walk therein: I am the Lord *y*. *Le 18:4*
God
neither any of *y*. own nation, *Le 18:26*
nor any
I am the Lord *y*. God *Le 18:30*
holy: for I the Lord *y*. God *Le 19:2*
am holy
my sabbaths: I am the lord *y*. *Le 19:3*
God
molten gods: I am the Lord *y*. *Le 19:4*
God
Lord, ye shall offer it at *y*. *Le 19:5*
own will
when ye reap the harvest of *y*. *Le 19:9*
land
and stranger: I am the Lord *Le 19:10*
y. God
thereof: I am the Lord *y*. *Le 19:25*
God
not round the corners of *y*. *Le 19:27*
heads
not make any cuttings in *y*. *Le 19:28*
flesh
defiled by them: I am the *Le 19:31*
Lord *y*. God
stranger sojourn with thee in *Le 19:33*
y. land
land of Egypt: I am the Lord *Le 19:34*
y. God
I am the Lord *y*. God, which *Le 19:36*
brought
be ye holy: for I am the Lord *Le 20:7*
y. God
I am the Lord *y*. God, whtch *Le 20:24*
have
shall not make *y*. souls *Le 20:25*
abominable
of all *y*. seed among *y*. *Le 22:3*
generations
Ye shall offer at *y*. own will a *Le 22:19*
male
make any offering thereof in *Le 22:24*
y. land
offer the bread of *y*. God of *Le 22:25*
any of
unto the Lord, offer it at *y*. *Le 22:29*
own will
of the land of Egypt, to be *y*. *Le 22:33*
God
of the Lord in all *y*. dwellings *Le 23:3*
sheaf of the firstfruits of *y*. *Le 23:10*
harvest
brought an offering unto *y*. *Le 23:14*
God
y. generations in all *y*. *Le 23:14*
dwellings
Ye shall bring out of *y*. *Le 23:17*
habitations
statute for ever in all *y*. *Le 23:21*
dwellings
throughout *y*. generations *Le 23:21*
when ye reap the harvest of *Le 23:22*
y. land
the stranger: I am the Lord *Le 23:22*
y. God
and ye shall afflict *y*. souls, and *Le 23:27*
offer
for you before the Lord *y*. *Le 23:28*
God
y. generations in all *y*. *Le 23:31*
dwellings
of rest, and ye shall afflict *y*. *Le 23:32*
souls
even, shall ye celebrate *y*. *Le 23:32*
sabbath
beside *y*. gifts, and beside all *Le 23:38*
y. vows
and beside all *y*. freewill *Le 23:38*
offerings
shall rejoice before the Lord *y*. *Le 23:40*
God
a statute for ever in *y*. *Le 23:41*
generations
That *y*. generations may know *Le 23:43*
that I
land of Egypt: I am the Lord *Le 23:43*
y. God
a statute for ever in *y*. *Le 24:3*
generations
as for one of *y*. own country *Le 24:22*
for I am the Lord *y*. God *Le 24:22*
sound throughout all *y*. land *Le 25:9*
thy God: for I am the Lord *y*. *Le 25:17*
God
and ye shall eat *y*. fill, and *Le 25:19*
dwell
And in all the land of *y*. *Le 25:24*
possession

I am the Lord *y*. God, which *Le 25:38*
brought
the land of Canaan, and to *Le 25:38*
be *y*. God
you, which they begat in *y*. *Le 25:45*
land
and they shall be *y*. *Le 25:45*
possession
inheritance for *y*. children *Le 25:46*
after you
they shall be *y*. bondmen for *Le 25:46*
ever
over *y*. brethren the children *Le 25:46*
of Israel
land of Egypt: I am the Lord *Le 25:55*
y. God
set up any image of stone in *y*. *Le 26:1*
land
unto it: for I am the Lord *y*. *Le 26:1*
God
y. threshing shall reach unto *Le 26:5*
and ye shall eat *y*. bread to *Le 26:5*
the full
to the full, and dwell in *y*. *Le 26:5*
land safely
shall the sword go through *y*. *Le 26:6*
land
And ye shall chase *y*. enemies *Le 26:7*
and *y*. enemies shall fall *Le 26:8*
before you
walk among you, and will be *Le 26:12*
y. God
I am the Lord *y*. God, which *Le 26:13*
brought
I have broken the bands of *y*. *Le 26:13*
yoke
or if *y*. soul abhor my *Le 26:15*
judgments, so
and ye shall sow *y*. seed in *Le 26:16*
vain
for *y*. enemies shall eat it *Le 26:16*
ye shall be slain before *y*. *Le 26:17*
enemies
you seven times for *y*. sins *Le 26:18*
I will break the pride of *y*. *Le 26:19*
power
y. heaven iron, and *y*. earth *Le 26:19*
as brass
And *y*. strength shall be spent *Le 26:20*
in vain
y. land shall not yield her *Le 26:20*
increase
plagues upon you according to *Le 26:21*
y. sins
of *y*. children, and destroy *y*. *Le 26:22*
cattle
and *y*. high ways shall be *Le 26:22*
desolate
you yet seven times for *y*. *Le 26:24*
sins
are gathered together within *Le 26:25*
y. cities
I have broken the staff of *y*. *Le 26:26*
bread
ten women shall bake *y*. *Le 26:26*
bread in one
deliver you *y*. bread again by *Le 26:26*
weight
chastise you seven times for *y*. *Le 26:28*
sins
and ye shall eat the flesh of *Le 26:29*
y. sons
the flesh of *y*. daughters shall *Le 26:29*
ye eat
I will destroy *y*. high places *Le 26:30*
and cut down *y*. images *Le 26:30*
cast *y*. carcases upon the *Le 26:30*
carcases
upon the carcases of *y*. idols *Le 26:30*
And I will make *y*. cities *Le 26:31*
waste
bring *y*. sanctuaries unto *Le 26:31*
desolation
smell the savour of *y*. sweet *Le 26:31*
odours
and *y*. enemies which dwell *Le 26:32*
therein
y. land shall be desolate, and *Le 26:33*
y. cities
and ye be in *y*. enemies' land *Le 26:34*
because it did not rest in *y*. *Le 26:35*
sabbaths
no power to stand before *y*. *Le 26:37*
enemies
land of *y*. enemies shall eat *Le 26:38*
you up
in their iniquity in *y*. *Le 26:39*
enemies' lands
If any man of you or of *y*. *Nu 9:10*
posterity

forever throughout *y*. *Nu 10:8*
generations
And if ye go to war in *y*. land *Nu 10:9*
against
remembered before the Lord *Nu 10:9*
y. God
ye shall be saved from *y*. *Nu 10:9*
enemies
of *y*. gladness, and in *y*. *Nu 10:10*
solemn days
and in the beginnings of *y*. *Nu 10:10*
months
the trumpet over *y*. burnt *Nu 10:10*
offerings
the sacrifices of *y*. peace *Nu 10:10*
offerings
you for a memorial before *y*. *Nu 10:10*
God
I am the Lord *y*. God *Nu 10:10*
until it come out at *y*. *Nu 11:20*
nostrils, an it
Y. carcases shall fall in this *Nu 14:29*
you, according to *y*. whole *Nu 14:29*
number
But *y*. little ones, which ye *Nu 14:31*
said
as for you, *y*. carcases, they *Nu 14:32*
shall
y. children shall wander in *Nu 14:33*
years and bear *y*. whoredoms *Nu 14:33*
until *y*. carcases be wasted *Nu 14:33*
shall ye bear *y*. iniquities, *Nu 14:34*
even forty
ye be not smitten before *y*. *Nu 14:42*
enemies
come into the land of *y*. *Nu 15:2*
habitations
offering, or in *y*. solemn feasts *Nu 15:3*
be among you in *y*. *Nu 15:14*
generations
ordinance for ever in *y*. *Nu 15:15*
generations
of *y*. dough for an heave *Nu 15:20*
offering
Of the first of *y*. dough ye *Nu 15:21*
shall give
an heave offering in *y*. *Nu 15:21*
generations
henceforward among *y*. *Nu 15:23*
generations
after *y*. own heart and *y*. *Nu 15:39*
own eyes
and be holy unto *y*. God *Nu 15:40*
I am the Lord *y*. God, which *Nu 15:41*
brought
to be *y*. God: I am the Lord *Nu 15:41*
y. God
bear the iniquity of *y*. *Nu 18:1*
priesthood
I have taken *y*. brethren the *Nu 18:6*
Levites
with thee shall keep *y*. priest's *Nu 18:7*
office
I have given *y*. priest's office *Nu 18:7*
unto
for ever throughout *y*. *Nu 18:23*
generations
you from them for *y*. *Nu 18:26*
inheritance
y. heave offering shall be *Nu 18:27*
reckoned
offering unto the Lord of all *Nu 18:28*
y. tithes
Out of all *y*. gifts ye shall *Nu 18:29*
offer
every place, ye and *y*. *Nu 18:31*
households
for it is *y*. reward for *y*. *Nu 18:31*
service in
Get you into *y*. land: for the *Nu 22:13*
Lord
And in the beginning of *y*. *Nu 28:11*
months ye
unto the Lord, after *y*. weeks *Nu 28:26*
be out
and ye shall afflict *y*. souls: ye *Nu 29:7*
shall
Lord, in *y*. set feasts, beside *Nu 29:39*
y. vows
y. freewill offerings, and for *Nu 29:39*
y. burnt
y. meat offerings, and for *y*. *Nu 29:39*
drink
offerings, and for *y*. peace *Nu 29:39*
offerings
both yourselves and *y*. *Nu 31:19*
captives
And purify all *y*. raiment, and *Nu 31:20*
all

wash y. clothes on the seventh day	Nu 31:24	the Lord y. God hath given them	De 3:20
Shall y. brethren go to war, and shall	Nu 32:6	all that the Lord y. God hath done	De 3:21
Thus did y. fathers, when I sent	Nu 32:8	Lord y. God he shall fight for you	De 3:22
ye are risen up in y. fathers' stead	Nu 32:14	Lord was wroth with me for y. sakes	De 3:26
and this land shall be y. possession	Nu 32:22	Lord God of y. fathers giveth you	De 4:1
and be sure y. sin will find you out	Nu 32:23	commandments of the Lord y. God	De 4:2
Build you cities for y. little ones	Nu 32:24	Y. eyes have seen what the Lord did	De 4:3
and folds for y. sheep	Nu 32:24	that did cleave unto the Lord y. God	De 4:4
hath proceeded out of y. mouth	Nu 32:24	is y. wisdom and y. understanding	De 4:6
for an inheritance among y. families	Nu 33:54	Lord was angry with me for y. sakes	De 4:21
to the tribes of y. fathers ye	Nu 33:54	ye shall not prolong y. days upon it	De 4:26
in y. eyes, and thorns in y. sides	Nu 33:55	to all that the Lord y. God did	De 4:34
Then y. south quarter shall be from	Nu 34:3	for you in Egypt before y. eyes	De 4:34
y. south border shall be the outmost	Nu 34:3	which I speak in y. ears this day	De 5:1
y. border shall turn from the south	Nu 34:4	the Lord spake unto all y. assembly	De 5:22
border: this shall be y. west border	Nu 34:6	the heads of y. tribes, and y. elders	De 5:23
And this shall be y. north border	Nu 34:7	the Lord heard the voice of y. words	De 5:28
Hor ye shall point out y. border	Nu 34:8	to them, Get you into y. tents again	De 5:30
this shall be y. north border	Nu 34:9	Lord y. God hath commanded you	De 5:32; 5:33
ye shall point out y. east border from	Nu 34:10	ye may prolong y. days in the land	De 5:33
this shall be y. land with the coasts	Nu 34:12	the Lord y. God commanded to teach	De 6:1
y. generations in all y. dwellings	Nu 35:29	Ye shall not tempt the Lord y. God	De 6:16
Turn you, and take y. journey, and go	De 1:7	commandments of the Lord y. God	De 6:17
The Lord sware unto y. fathers	De 1:8	which he had sworn unto y. fathers	De 7:8
The Lord y. God hath multiplied you	De 1:10	barren among you, or among y. cattle	De 7:14
The Lord God of y. fathers make you	De 1:11	which the Lord sware unto y. fathers	De 8:1
I myself alone bear y. cumbrance	De 1:12	the Lord destroyeth before y. face	De 8:20
and y. burden and y. strife	De 1:12	unto the voice of the Lord y. God	De 8:20
and known among y. tribes, and I	De 1:13	had sinned against the Lord y. God	De 9:16
So I took the chief of y. tribes	De 1:15	hands, and brake them before y. eyes	De 9:17
over tens, and officers among y. tribes	De 1:15	of all y. sins which ye sinned	De 9:18
And I charged y. judges at that time	De 1:16	And I took y. sin, the calf which ye	De 9:21
Hear the causes between y. brethren	De 1:16	the commandment of the Lord y. God	De 9:23
commandment of the Lord y. God	De 1:26	therefore the foreskin of y. heart	De 10:16
And we murmured in y. tents	De 1:27	For the Lord y. God is God of gods	De 10:17
Lord y. God which goeth before you	De 1:30	I speak not with y. children which	De 11:2
did for you in Egypt before y. eyes	De 1:30	chastisement of the Lord y. God	De 11:2
ye did not believe the Lord y. God	De 1:32	y. eyes have seen all the great acts	De 11:7
you out a place to pitch y. tents in	De 1:33	ye may prolong y. days in the land	De 11:9
the Lord heard the voice of y. words	De 1:34	Lord sware unto y. fathers to give	De 11:9
which I sware to give unto y. fathers	De 1:35	this day, to love the Lord y. God	De 11:13
was angry with me for y. sakes	De 1:37	with all y. heart and with all y. soul	De 11:13
Moreover y. little ones, which ye said	De 1:39	I will give you the rain of y. land	De 11:14
Y. children, which in that day had no	De 1:39	that y. heart be not deceived, and ye	De 11:16
take y. journey into the wilderness	De 1:40	my words in y. heart and in y. soul	De 11:18
lest ye be smitten before y. enemies	De 1:42	bind them for a sign upon y. hand	De 11:18
Lord would not hearken to y. voice	De 1:45	may be as frontlets between y. eyes	De 11:18
pass through the coast of y. brethren	De 2:4	And ye shall teach them y. children	De 11:19
The Lord y. God hath given you this	De 3:18	That y. days may be multiplied	De 11:21
pass over armed before y. brethren	De 3:18	and the days of y. children, in the	De 11:21
But y. wives, and y. little ones	De 3:19	Lord sware unto y. fathers to give	De 11:21
and y. cattle, for I know that ye have	De 3:19	to love the Lord y. God, to walk in all	De 11:22
shall abide in y. cities which I have	De 3:19	the soles of y. feet shall tread shall be	De 11:24
Lord have given rest unto y. brethren	De 3:20	the uttermost sea shall y. coast be	De 11:24
		the Lord y. God shall lay the fear of	De 11:25
		commandments of the Lord y. God	De 11:27; 11:28
		which the Lord y. God giveth you	De 11:31
		shall not do so unto the Lord y. God	De 12:4
		y. God shall choose out of all y. tribes	De 12:5
		y. burnt offerings, and y. sacrifices	De 12:6
		y. tithes, and heave offerings of y.	De 12:6
		and y. vows, and y. freewill offerings	De 12:6
		firstlings of y. herds and of y. flocks	De 12:6
		ye shall eat before the Lord y. God	De 12:7
		rejoice in all that ye put y. hand unto	De 12:7
		ye and y. household, wherein	De 12:7
		which the Lord y. God giveth you	De 12:9; 12:10
		rest from all y. enemies round about	De 12:10
		which the Lord y. God shall choose	De 12:11
		I command you: y. burnt offerings	De 12:11
		and y. sacrifices, y. tithes	De 12:11
		and the heave offerings of y. hand	De 12:11
		and all y. choice vows which ye vow	De 12:11
		shall rejoice before the Lord y. God	De 12:12
		ye, and y. sons, and y. daughters	De 12:12
		y. menservants, and y. maidservants	De 12:12
		The Levite that is within y. gate	De 12:12
		for the Lord y. God proveth you, to	De 13:3
		whether ye love the Lord y.	De 13:3
		with all y. heart and with all y. soul	De 13:3
		Ye shall walk after the Lord y. God	De 13:4
		turn you away from the Lord y. God	De 13:5
		are the children of the Lord y. God	De 14:1
		make any baldness between y. eyes	De 14:1
		day unto battle against y. enemies	De 20:3
		let not y. hearts faint, fear not, and	De 20:3
		y. God is he that goeth with you	De 20:4
		to fight for you against y. enemies	De 20:4
		should ye sin against the Lord y. God	De 20:18
		ye shall be sold unto y. enemies	De 28:68
		did before y. eyes in the land of Egypt	De 29:5
		y. clothes are not waxen old upon you	De 29:5
		know that I am the Lord y. God	De 29:6
		day all of you before the Lord y. God	De 29:10
		y. captains of y. tribes, y. elders	De 29:10
		y. officers, with all the men of Israel	De 29:10
		Y. little ones, y. wives, and thy	De 29:11
		y. children that shall rise up after you	De 29:22
		not prolong y. days upon the land	De 30:18
		shall gave them up before y. face	De 31:5
		may learn, and fear the Lord y. God	De 31:12
		and learn to fear the Lord y. God	De 31:13

of the covenant of the Lord y. God	De 31:26	to love the Lord y. God, and to walk	Jos 22:5	of bread, and afterward go y. way	J'g 19:5
elders of y. tribes, and y. officers	De 31:28	with all y. heart and with all y. soul	Jos 22:5	to-morrow get you early on y. way	J'g 19:9
anger through the work of y. hands	De 31:29	with much riches unto y. tents	Jos 22:8	take advice, and speak y. minds	J'g 19:30
up, whom y. fathers feared not	De 32:17	spoil of y. enemies with y. brethren	Jos 22:8	give here y. advice and counsel	J'g 20:7
and help you, and be y. protection	De 32:38	the land of y. possession be unclean	Jos 22:19	womb, that they may be y. husbands	Ru 1:11
Set y. hearts unto all the words	De 32:46	time to come y. children might speak	Jos 22:24	again, my daughters, go y. way	Ru 1:12
command y. children to observe	De 32:46	y. children make our children cease	Jos 22:25	for it grieveth me much for y. sakes	Ru 1:13
thing for you, because it is y. life	De 32:47	y. children may not say to our	Jos 22:27	not arrogancy come out of y. mouth	1Sa 2:3
shall prolong y. days in the land	De 32:47	all that the Lord y. God hath done	Jos 23:3	for I hear of y. evil dealings by all	1Sa 2:23
the sole of y. foot shall tread upon	Jos 1:3	the Lord y. God is he that hath fought	Jos 23:3	was on you all, and on y. lords	1Sa 6:4
down of the sun, shall be y. coast	Jos 1:4	to be an inheritance for y. tribes	Jos 23:4	ye shall make images of y. emerods	1Sa 6:5
Lord y. God giveth you to possess	Jos 1:11	the Lord y. God, he shall expel them	Jos 23:5	images of y. mice that mar the land	1Sa 6:5
The Lord y. God hath given you rest	Jos 1:13	and drive them from out of y. sight	Jos 23:5	from off y. gods, and from off y. land	1Sa 6:5
Y. wives, y. little ones, and y. cattle	Jos 1:14	Lord y. God hath promised unto you	Jos 23:5	then do ye harden y. hearts	1Sa 6:6
shall pass before y. brethren armed	Jos 1:14	But cleave unto the Lord y. God	Jos 23:8	unto the Lord with all y. hearts	1Sa 7:3
the Lord hath given y. brethren rest	Jos 1:15	Lord y. God, he it is that fighteth for	Jos 23:10	and prepare y. hearts unto the Lord	1Sa 7:3
which the Lord y. God giveth them	Jos 1:15	heed therefore unto y. selves	Jos 23:11	He will take y. sons, and appoint	1Sa 8:11
unto the land of y. possession	Jos 1:15	that ye love the Lord y. God	Jos 23:11	y. daughters to be confectionaries	1Sa 8:13
and that y. terror is fallen upon us	Jos 2:9	Lord y. God will no more drive out	Jos 23:13	he will take y. fields, and y. vineyards	1Sa 8:14
the Lord y. God, he is God in heaven	Jos 2:11	unto you, and scourges in y. sides	Jos 23:13	y. oliveyards, even the best of them	1Sa 8:14
and afterward may ye go y. way	Jos 2:16	and thorns in y. eyes, until ye perish	Jos 23:13	tenth of y. seed, and of y. vineyards	1Sa 8:15
according unto y. words, so be it	Jos 2:21	the Lord y. God hath given you	Jos 23:13	y. menservants, and y. maidservants	1Sa 8:16
of the covenant of the Lord y. God	Jos 3:3	in all y. hearts and in all y. souls	Jos 23:14	y. goodliest young men, and y. asses	1Sa 8:16
then ye shall remove from y. place	Jos 3:3	things which the Lord y. God spake	Jos 23:14	He will take the tenth of y. sheep	1Sa 8:17
hear the words of the Lord y. God	Jos 3:9	the Lord y. God promised you	Jos 23:15	cry out in that day because of y. king	1Sa 8:18
over before the ark of the Lord y. God	Jos 4:5	The Lord y. God hath given you	Jos 23:15	And ye have this day rejected y. God	1Sa 10:19
when y. children ask their fathers	Jos 4:6	the covenant of the Lord y. God	Jos 23:16	all y. adversities and y. tribulations	1Sa 10:19
y. children shall ask their fathers	Jos 4:21	Y. fathers dwelt on the other side of	Jos 24:2	by y. tribes, and by y. thousands	1Sa 10:19
Then ye shall let y. children know	Jos 4:22	I took y. father Abraham from	Jos 24:3	that I may thrust out all y. right eyes	1Sa 11:2
the Lord y. God dried up the waters	Jos 4:23	I brought y. fathers out of Egypt	Jos 24:6	I have hearkened unto y. voice	1Sa 12:1
as the Lord y. God did to the Red sea	Jos 4:23	Egyptians pursued after y. fathers	Jos 24:6	brought y. fathers up out of the land	1Sa 12:6
that ye might fear the Lord y. God for	Jos 4:24	y. eyes have seen what I have done in	Jos 24:7	which he did to you and to y. fathers	1Sa 12:7
nor make any noise with y. voice	Jos 6:10	and I gave them into y. hand	Jos 24:8	and y. fathers cried unto the Lord	1Sa 12:8
any word proceed out of y. mouth	Jos 6:10	and I delivered them into y. hand	Jos 24:11	brought forth y. fathers out of Egypt	1Sa 12:8
be brought according to y. tribes	Jos 7:14	the gods which y. fathers served	Jos 24:14; 24:15	you out of the hand of y. enemies	1Sa 12:11
y. God will deliver it into y. hand	Jos 8:7	forgive y. transgressions nor y. sins	Jos 24:19	when the Lord y. God was y. king	1Sa 12:12
say unto them, We are y. servants	Jos 9:11	incline y. heart unto the Lord God	Jos 24:23	continue following the Lord y. God	1Sa 12:14
ye not, but pursue after y. enemies	Jos 10:19	unto you, lest ye deny y. God	Jos 24:27	you, as it was against y. fathers	1Sa 12:15
y. God delivered them into y. hand	Jos 10:19	land which I sware unto y. fathers	J'g 2:1	which the Lord will do before y. eyes	1Sa 12:16
y. feet upon the necks of these kings	Jos 10:24	they shall be as thorns in y. sides	J'g 2:3	and see that y. wickedness is great	1Sa 12:17
shall the Lord do to all y. enemies	Jos 10:25	y. enemies the Moabites into y. hand	J'g 3:28	but serve the Lord with all y. heart	1Sa 12:20
the sea: this shall be y. south coast	Jos 15:4	said unto you, I am the Lord y. God	J'g 6:10	serve him in truth with all y. heart	1Sa 12:24
Lord God of y. fathers hath given you	Jos 18:3	delivered into y. hand the host of	J'g 7:15	be consumed, both ye and y. king	1Sa 12:25
shall be y. refuge from the avenger	Jos 20:3	delivered into y. hand the princes	J'g 8:3	ye come out to set y. battle in array	1Sa 17:8
Ye have not left y. brethren these	Jos 22:3	I will tear y. flesh with the thorns	J'g 8:7	kill me, then will we be y. servants	1Sa 17:9
commandment of the Lord y. God	Jos 22:3	also that I am y. bone and y. flesh	J'g 9:2	because ye have not kept y. master	1Sa 26:16
the Lord y. God hath given rest	Jos 22:4	come and put y. trust in my shadow	J'g 9:15	on ornaments of gold upon y. apparel	2Sa 1:24
hath given rest unto y. brethren	Jos 22:4	Shechem, because he is y. brother	J'g 9:18	shewed this kindness unto y. lord	2Sa 2:5
return ye, and get you unto y. tents	Jos 22:4	you in the time of y. tribulation	J'g 10:14	now let y. hands be strengthened	2Sa 2:7
and unto the land of y. possession	Jos 22:4	them before me, shall I be y. head	J'g 11:9	for y. master Saul is dead, and also	2Sa 2:7
		the Lord is y. way wherein ye go	J'g 18:6	Rend y. clothes, and gird you with	2Sa 3:31
		for God hath given it into y. hands	J'g 18:10		

require his blood of *y.* hand, and take — *2Sa 4:11*

at Jericho until *y.* beards be grown — *2Sa 10:5; 1Ch 19:5*

in peace, and *y.* two sons with you — *2Sa 15:27*

take with you the servants of *y.* lord — *1Ki 1:33*

Let *y.* heart therefore be perfect with — *1Ki 8:61*

from following me, ye or *y.* children — *1Ki 9:6*

turn away *y.* heart after their gods — *1Ki 11:2*

a heavy yoke, I will add to *y.* yoke — *1Ki 12:11*

My father made *y.* yoke heavy, and I — *1Ki 12:14*

and I will add to *y.* yoke: my father — *1Ki 12:14*

to *y.* tents O Israel; now see to thine — *1Ki 12:16*

nor fight against *y.* brethren — *1Ki 12:24*

And call ye on the name of *y.* gods — *1Ki 18:24*

call on the name of *y.* gods, but put — *1Ki 18:25*

Yea, I know it; hold ye *y.* peace — *2Ki 2:3; 2:5*

both ye, and *y.* cattle, and *y.* beasts — *2Ki 3:17*

deliver the Moabites into *y.* hand — *2Ki 3:18*

If it be *y.* minds, then let none go — *2Ki 9:15*

seeing *y.* master's sons are with you — *2Ki 10:2*

best and meetest of *y.* master's sons — *2Ki 10:3*

throne, and fight for *y.* master's house — *2Ki 10:3*

heads of the men *y.* master's sons — *2Ki 10:6*

I have brought into *y.* hands escape — *2Ki 10:24*

no more money of *y.* acquaintance — *2Ki 12:7*

Turn ye from *y.* evil ways, and keep — *2Ki 17:13*

law which I commanded *y.* fathers — *2Ki 17:13*

But the Lord *y.* God ye shall fear — *2Ki 17:39*

you out of the hand of all *y.* enemies — *2Ki 17:39*

you away to a land like *y.* own land — *2Ki 18:32*

Thus shall ye say to *y.* master, Thus — *2Ki 19:6*

the passover unto the Lord *y.* God — *2Ki 23:21*

yourselves, both ye and *y.* brethren — *1Ch 15:12*

of Canaan, the lot of *y.* inheritance — *1Ch 16:18*

Is not the Lord *y.* God with you? and — *1Ch 22:18*

Now set *y.* heart and *y.* soul to — *1Ch 22:19*

seek the Lord *y.* God; arise — *1Ch 22:19*

commandments of the Lord *y.* God — *1Ch 28:8*

inheritance for *y.* children after you — *1Ch 28:8*

Now bless the Lord *y.* God. And all — *1Ch 29:20*

upon you, I will put more to *y.* yoke — *2Ch 10:11*

My father made *y.* yoke heavy, but I — *2Ch 10:14*

every man to *y.* tents, O Israel: and — *2Ch 10:16*

go up, nor fight against *y.* brethren — *2Ch 11:4*

against the Lord God of *y.* fathers — *2Ch 13:12*

and let not *y.* hands be weak — *2Ch 15:7*

for *y.* work shall be rewarded — *2Ch 15:7*

they shall be delivered into *y.* hand — *2Ch 18:14*

y. brethren that dwell in their cities — *2Ch 19:10*

come upon you, and upon *y.* brethren — *2Ch 19:10*

Believe in the Lord *y.* God, so shall — *2Ch 20:20*

repair the house of *y.* God from year — *2Ch 24:5*

the Lord God of *y.* fathers was wroth — *2Ch 28:9*

he hath delivered them into *y.* hand — *2Ch 28:9*

you, sins against the Lord *y.* God — *2Ch 28:10*

ye have taken captive of *y.* brethren — *2Ch 28:11*

house of the Lord God of *y.* fathers — *2Ch 29:5*

and to hissing, as ye see with *y.* eyes — *2Ch 29:8*

like *y.* fathers, and like *y.* brethren — *2Ch 30:7*

not stiffnecked, as *y.* fathers were — *2Ch 30:8*

and serve the Lord *y.* God, that — *2Ch 30:8*

y. brethren and *y.* children shall find — *2Ch 30:9*

the Lord *y.* God is gracious — *2Ch 30:9*

y. God should be able to deliver you — *2Ch 32:14*

much less shall *y.* God deliver you — *2Ch 32:15*

which I have apointed for *y.* fathers — *2Ch 33:8*

not be a burden upon *y.* shoulders — *2Ch 35:3*

serve now the Lord *y.* God, and his — *2Ch 35:3*

by the houses of *y.* fathers — *2Ch 35:4*

after *y.* courses, according to — *2Ch 35:4*

families of the fathers of *y.* brethren — *2Ch 35:5*

and prepare *y.* brethren, that they — *2Ch 35:6*

for we seek *y.* God, as ye do; and we — *Ezr 4:2*

y. companions the Apharsachites — *Ezr 6:6*

altar of the house of *y.* God which is — *Ezr 7:17*

gold, that do after the will of *y.* God — *Ezr 7:18*

unto the Lord God of *y.* fathers — *Ezr 8:28*

not *y.* daughters unto their sons — *Ezr 9:12*

take their daughters unto *y.* sons — *Ezr 9:12*

an inheritance to *y.* children for ever — *Ezr 9:12*

unto the Lord God of *y.* fathers — *Ezr 10:11*

and fight for *y.* brethren, *y.* sons, and — *Ne 4:14*

y. daughters, *y.* wives, and *y.* houses — *Ne 4:14*

and will ye even sell *y.* brethren — *Ne 5:8*

day is holy unto the Lord *y.* God — *Ne 8:9*

Go *y.* way, eat the fat, and drink — *Ne 8:10*

for the joy of the Lord is *y.* strength — *Ne 8:10*

Hold *y.* peace, for the day is holy — *Ne 8:11*

bless the Lord *y.* God for ever — *Ne 9:5*

Did not *y.* fathers thus, and did not — *Ne 13:18*

give *y.* daughters unto their sons — *Ne 13:25*

take their daughters unto *y.* sons — *Ne 13:25*

a reward for me of *y.* substance — *Job 6:22*

but what doth *y.* arguing reprove — *Job 6:25*

and ye dig a pit for *y.* friend — *Job 6:27*

ye would altogether hold *y.* peace — *Job 13:5*

and it should be *y.* wisdom — *Job 13:5*

Y. remembrances are like unto — *Job 13:12*

ashes, *y.* bodies to bodies of clay — *Job 13:12*

Hold *y.* peace, let me alone, that I — *Job 13:13*

and my declaration with *y.* ears — *Job 13:17*

if *y.* souls were in my soul's stead — *Job 16:4*

on my lips should asswage *y.* grief — *Job 16:5*

beasts, and reputed vile in *y.* sight — *Job 18:3*

and let this be *y.* consolations — *Job 21:2*

and lay *y.* hand upon *y.* mouth — *Job 21:5*

I know *y.* thoughts, and the devices — *Job 21:27*

seeing in *y.* answers there remaineth — *Job 21:34*

Behold, I waited for *y.* word — *Job 32:11*

I gave ear to *y.* reasons, whilst ye — *Job 32:11*

will I answer him with *y.* speeches — *Job 32:14*

lest I deal with you after *y.* folly — *Job 42:8*

with *y.* own heart upon *y.* bed — *Ps 4:4*

and put *y.* trust in the Lord — *Ps 4:5*

Flee as a bird to *y.* mountain — *Ps 11:1*

seek him; *y.* heart shall live for ever — *Ps 22:26*

Lift up *y.* heads, O ye gates; and be — *Ps 24:7*

Lift up *y.* heads, O ye gates; even lift — *Ps 24:9*

he shall strengthen *y.* heart, all ye — *Ps 31:24*

O clap *y.* hands, all ye people — *Ps 47:1*

the violence of *y.* hands in the earth — *Ps 58:2*

Before *y.* pots can feel the thorns — *Ps 58:9*

people, pour out *y.* heart before him — *Ps 62:8*

increase, set not *y.* heart upon them — *Ps 62:10*

y. heart shall live that seek God — *Ps 69:32*

Lift not up *y.* horn on high: speak — *Ps 75:5*

Vow, and pay unto the Lord *y.* God — *Ps 76:11*

incline *y.* ears to the words of my — *Ps 78:1*

Harden not *y.* heart, as in the — *Ps 95:8*

When *y.* fathers tempted me, proved — *Ps 95:9*

of Canaan, the lot of *y.* inheritance — *Ps 105:11*

more and more, you and *y.* children — *Ps 115:14*

Lift up *y.* hands in the sanctuary — *Ps 134:2*

Put not *y.* trust in princes, nor in — *Ps 146:3*

I also will laugh at *y.* calamity — *Pr 1:26*

I will mock when *y.* fear cometh — *Pr 1:26*

When *y.* fear cometh as desolation — *Pr 1:27*

y. destruction cometh as a whirlwind — *Pr 1:27*

Y. country is desolate, *y.* cities are — *Isa 1:7*

y. land, strangers devour it in *y.* — *Isa 1:7*

is the multitude of *y.* sacrifices — *Isa 1:11*

who hath required this at *y.* hand — *Isa 1:12*

Y. new moons and *y.* appointed feasts — *Isa 1:14*

And when ye spread forth *y.* hands — *Isa 1:15*

not hear: *y.* hands are full of blood — *Isa 1:15*

put away the evil of *y.* doings from — *Isa 1:16*

though *y.* sins be as scarlet, they — *Isa 1:18*

the spoil of the poor is in *y.* houses — *Isa 3:14*

be *y.* fear, and let him be *y.* dread — *Isa 8:13*

and where will ye leave *y.* glory — *Isa 10:3*

Is this *y.* joyous city, whose antiquity — *Isa 23:7*

for *y.* strength is laid waste — *Isa 23:14*

y. covenant with death shall be — *Isa 28:18*

y. agreement with hell shall not stand — *Isa 28:18*

lest *y.* bands be made strong — *Isa 28:22*

deep sleep, and hath closed *y.* eyes — *Isa 29:10*

the prophets and *y.* rulers, the seers — *Isa 29:10*

Surely *y.* turning of things upside — *Isa 29:16*

the strength of Pharaoh be *y.* shame — *Isa 30:3*

in the shadow of Egypt *y.* confusion — *Isa 30:3*

in confidence shall be *y.* strength — *Isa 30:15*

which *y*. own hands have made unto	Isa 31:7
and gird sackcloth upon *y*. loins	Isa 32:11
y. spoil shall be gathered like	Isa 33:4
y. breath, as fire, shall devour you	Isa 33:11
y. God will come with vengeance	Isa 35:4
you away to a land like *y*. own land	Isa 36:17
Thus shall ye say unto *y*. master	Isa 37:6
comfort ye my people, saith *y*. God	Isa 40:1
the cities of Judah. Behold *y*. God	Isa 40:9
Lift up *y*. eyes on high, and behold	Isa 40:26
Produce *y*. cause, saith the Lord	Isa 41:21
bring forth *y*. strong reasons, saith	Isa 41:21
of nothing, and *y*. work of nought	Isa 41:24
there is none that heareth *y*. words	Isa 41:26
Thus saith the Lord, *y*. redeemer	Isa 43:14
For *y*. sake I have sent to Babylon	Isa 43:14
I am the Lord, *y*. Holy One	Isa 43:15
the creator of Israel, *y*. King	Isa 43:15
y. carriages were heavy laden; they	Isa 46:1
And even to *y*. old age I am he	Isa 46:4
the bill of *y*. mother's divorcement	Isa 50:1
y. iniquities have ye sold yourselves	Isa 50:1
for *y*. transgressions is *y*. mother put	Isa 50:1
walk in the light of *y*. fire, and in	Isa 50:11
Look unto Abraham *y*. father	Isa 51:2
Lift up *y*. eyes to the heavens	Isa 51:6
the God of Israel will be *y*. rereward	Isa 52:12
y. labour for that which satisfieth not	Isa 55:2
let *y*. soul delight itself in fatness	Isa 55:2
Incline *y*. ear, and come unto me	Isa 55:3
hear and *y*. soul shall live; and I	Isa 55:3
For my thoughts are not *y*. thoughts	Isa 55:8
neither are *y*. ways my ways, saith	Isa 55:8
so are my ways higher than *y*. ways	Isa 55:9
and my thoughts than *y*. thoughts	Isa 55:9
in the day of *y*. fast ye find pleasure	Isa 58:3
and exact all *y*. labours	Isa 58:3
to make *y*. voice to be heard on high	Isa 58:4
But *y*. iniquities have separated	Isa 59:2
y. God and *y*. sins have hid his face	Isa 59:2
For *y*. hands are defiled with blood	Isa 59:3
and *y*. fingers with iniquity	Isa 59:3
y. lips have spoken lies	Isa 59:3
y. tongue hath muttered perverseness	Isa 59:3
shall stand and feed *y*. flocks	Isa 61:5
be *y*. plowmen and *y*. vinedressers	Isa 61:5
For *y*. shame ye shall have double	Isa 61:7
Y. iniquities, and the iniquities of	Isa 65:7
iniquities of *y*. fathers together	Isa 65:7
ye shall leave *y*. name for a curse	Isa 65:15
Y. brethren that hated you, that cast	Isa 66:5
but he shall appear to *y*. joy, and	Isa 66:5
ye see this, *y*. heart shall rejoice	Isa 66:14
y. bones shall flourish like an herb	Isa 66:14

And they shall bring all *y*. brethren	Isa 66:20
so shall *y*. seed and *y*. name remain	Isa 66:22
What iniquity *y*. fathers found in me	Jer 2:5
with *y*. children's children will	Jer 2:9
In vain have I smitten *y*. children	Jer 2:30
y. own sword devoured *y*. prophets	Jer 2:30
for an inheritance unto *y*. fathers	Jer 3:18
and I will heal *y*. backslidings	Jer 3:22
Break up *y*. fallow ground, and sow	Jer 4:3
take away the foreskins of *y*. heart	Jer 4:4
it, because of the evil of *y*. doings	Jer 4:4
and served strange gods in *y*. land	Jer 5:19
Y. iniquities have turned away these	Jer 5:25
y. sins have withholden good things	Jer 5:25
and ye shall find rest for *y*. souls	Jer 6:16
y. burnt offerings are not acceptable	Jer 6:20
nor *y*. sacrifices sweet unto me	Jer 6:20
Amend *y*. ways and *y*. doings, and I	Jer 7:3
amend *y*. ways and *y*. doings, if ye	Jer 7:5
walk after other gods to *y*. hurt	Jer 7:6
in the land that I gave to *y*. fathers	Jer 7:7
become a den of robbers in *y*. eyes	Jer 7:11
which I gave to you and to *y*. fathers	Jer 7:14
as I have cast out all *y*. brethren	Jer 7:15
y. burnt offerings unto *y*. sacrifices	Jer 7:21
For I spake not unto *y*. fathers	Jer 7:22
Obey my voice, and I will be *y*. God	Jer 7:23
Since the day that *y*. fathers came	Jer 7:25
let *y*. ear receive the word at his	Jer 9:20
and teach *y*. daughters wailing	Jer 9:20
I commanded *y*. fathers in the day	Jer 11:4
be my people, and I will be *y*. God	Jer 11:4
which I have sworn unto *y*. fathers	Jer 11:5
I earnestly protested unto *y*. fathers	Jer 11:7
they shall be ashamed of *y*. revenues	Jer 12:13
Give glory to the Lord *y*. God, before	Jer 13:16
before *y*. feet stumble upon the dark	Jer 13:16
weep in secret places for *y*. pride	Jer 13:17
for *y*. principalities shall come down	Jer 13:18
even the crown of *y*. glory	Jer 13:18
Lift up *y*. eyes, and behold them that	Jer 13:20
this place in *y*. eyes, and in *y*. days	Jer 16:9
Because *y*. fathers have forsaken me	Jer 16:11
have done worse than *y*. fathers	Jer 16:12
known not, neither ye nor *y*. fathers	Jer 16:13
and upon the horns of *y*. altars	Jer 17:1
carry forth a burden out of *y*. houses	Jer 17:22
day, as I commanded *y*. fathers	Jer 17:22
and make *y*. ways and *y*. doings good	Jer 18:11
weapons of war that are in *y*. hands	Jer 21:4
it, because of the evil of *y*. doings	Jer 21:12
according to the fruit of *y*. doings	Jer 21:14
visit upon you the evil of *y*. doings	Jer 23:2

city that I gave you and *y*. fathers	Jer 23:39
hearkened, nor inclined *y*. ear to hear	Jer 25:4
evil way, and the evil of *y*. doings	Jer 25:5
unto you, and to *y*. fathers for ever	Jer 25:5
to anger with the works of *y*. hands	Jer 25:6
the works of *y*. hands to *y*. own hurt	Jer 25:7
for the days of *y*. slaughter	Jer 25:34
of *y*. dispersions are accomplished	Jer 25:34
city, as ye have heard with *y*. ears	Jer 26:11
now amend *y*. ways and *y*. doings	Jer 26:13
obey the voice of the Lord *y*. God	Jer 26:13
As for me, behold, I am in *y*. hand	Jer 26:14
to speak all these things in *y*. ears	Jer 26:15
Thus shall ye say unto *y*. masters	Jer 27:4
hearken not ye to *y*. prophets	Jer 27:9
to *y*. diviners, nor to *y*. dreamers	Jer 27:9
to *y*. enchanters, nor to *y*. sorcerers	Jer 27:9
to remove you far from *y*. land	Jer 27:10
Bring *y*. necks under the yoke of the	Jer 27:12
not to the words of *y*. prophets that	Jer 27:16
and take wives for *y*. sons	Jer 29:6
and give *y*. daughters to husbands	Jer 29:6
Let not *y*. prophets and *y*. diviners	Jer 29:8
hearken to *y*. dreams which ye	Jer 29:8
shall search for me with all *y*. heart	Jer 29:13
and I will turn away *y*. captivity, and	Jer 29:14
y. brethren that are not gone forth	Jer 29:16
and he shall slay them before *y*. eyes	Jer 29:21
be my people, and I will be *y*. God	Jer 30:22
I made a covenant with *y*. fathers in	Jer 34:13
y. fathers hearkened not unto me	Jer 34:14
wine, neither ye, nor *y*. sons for ever	Jer 35:6
but all *y*. days ye shall dwell in tents	Jer 35:7
amend *y*. doings, and go not after	Jer 35:15
I have given to you and to *y*. fathers	Jer 35:15
but ye have not inclined *y*. ear, nor	Jer 35:15
commandment of Jonadab *y*. father	Jer 35:18
now *y*. prophets which prophesied	Jer 37:19
king said, Behold, he is in *y*. hand	Jer 38:5
and oil, and put them in *y*. vessels	Jer 40:10
and dwell in *y*. cities that ye have	Jer 40:10
I will pray unto the Lord *y*. God	Jer 42:4
according to *y*. words; and it shall	Jer 42:4
present *y*. supplication before him	Jer 42:9
cause you to return to *y*. own land	Jer 42:12
obey the voice of the Lord *y*. God	Jer 42:13
If ye wholly set *y*. faces to enter into	Jer 42:15
ye dissembled in *y*. hearts, when ye	Jer 42:20
ye sent me unto the Lord *y*. God	Jer 42:20
obeyed the voice of the Lord *y*. God	Jer 42:21
not, neither they, ye, nor *y*. fathers	Jer 44:3
ye this great evil against *y*. souls	Jer 44:7

wrath with the works of *y*. Jer 44:8
hands
forgotten the wickedness of *y*. Jer 44:9
fathers
of their wives, and *y*. own Jer 44:9
wickedness
and the wickedness of *y*. Jer 44:9
wives
I set before you and before Jer 44:10
y. fathers
y. fathers, *y*. kings, and *y*. Jer 44:21
princes
because of the evil of *y*. Jer 44:22
doings, and
therefore is *y*. land a Jer 44:22
desolation, and
Ye and *y*. wives have both Jer 44:25
spoken
y. mouths, and fulfilled with Jer 44:25
y. hand
ye will surely accomplish *y*. Jer 44:25
vows
and surely perform *y*. vows Jer 44:25
and stand forth with *y*. Jer 46:4
helmets
Flee, save *y*. lives, and be like Jer 48:6
Y. mother shall be sore Jer 50:12
confounded
they have done in Zion in *y*. Jer 51:24
sight
And lest *y*. heart faint, and Jer 51:46
ye fear
and let Jerusalem come into Jer 51:50
y. mind
you, and will break *y*. staff of Eze 5:16
bread
you, and I will destroy *y*. high Eze 6:3
places
And *y*. altars shall be desolate Eze 6:4
and *y*. image shall be broken; Eze 6:4
and I
down *y*. slain men before *y*. Eze 6:4
idols
y. bones round about *y*. altars Eze 6:5
In all *y*. dwellingplaces the Eze 6:6
cities
that *y*. altars may be laid waste Eze 6:6
y. idols may be broken and Eze 6:6
cease
and *y*. images may be cut Eze 6:6
down
and *y*. works may be abolished Eze 6:6
let not *y*. eye spare, neither Eze 9:5
have ye
the things that come into *y*. Eze 11:5
mind
have multiplied *y*. slain in Eze 11:6
this city
Y. slain whom ye have laid Eze 11:7
in the
This city shall not be *y*. Eze 11:11
caldron
Say, I am *y*. sign: like as I Eze 12:11
have done
for in *y*. days, O rebellious Eze 12:25
house, will
by *y*. lying to my people that Eze 13:19
hear
to my people that hear *y*. Eze 13:19
lies
Behold, I am against *y*. Eze 13:20
pillows
and I will tear them from *y*. Eze 13:20
arms
Y. kerchiefs also will I tear Eze 13:21
and deliver my people out of Eze 13:21
y. hand
be no more in *y*. hand to be Eze 13:21
hunted
will deliver my people out of Eze 13:23
y. hand
and turn yourselves from *y*. Eze 14:6
idols
y. faces from all *y*. Eze 14:6
abominations
y. mother was an Hittite Eze 16:45
and *y*. father an Amorite Eze 16:45
shall return to *y*. former Eze 16:55
estate
way equal? are not *y*. ways Eze 18:25
unequal
ways equal? are not *y*. ways Eze 18:29
unequal
yourselves from all *y*. Eze 18:30
transgressions
so iniquity shall not be *y*. Eze 18:30
ruin
away from you all *y*. Eze 18:21
transgressions

them, saying, I am the Lord Eze 20:5
y. God
idols of Egypt: I am the Eze 20:7
Lord *y*. God
ye not in the statutes of *y*. Eze 20:18
fathers
I am the Lord *y*. God; walk Eze 20:19
in my
may know that I am the Eze 20:20
Lord *y*. God
in this *y*. fathers have Eze 20:27
blasphemed
after the manner of *y*. Eze 20:30
fathers
For when ye offer *y*. gifts, Eze 20:31
when ye
make *y*. sons to pass Eze 20:31
through the fire
pollute yourselves with all *y*. Eze 20:31
idols
And that which cometh into Eze 20:32
y. mind
Like as I pleaded with *y*. Eze 20:36
fathers
more with *y*. gifts, and with Eze 20:39
y. idols
and there will I require *y*. Eze 20:40
offerings
y. oblations, with all *y*. holy Eze 20:40
things
will accept you with *y*. sweet Eze 20:41
savour
up mine hand to give it to *y*. Eze 20:42
fathers
And there shall ye remember Eze 20:43
y. ways
and all *y*. doings, wherein ye Eze 20:43
have
shall lothe yourselves in *y*. Eze 20:43
own sight
all *y*. evils that ye have Eze 20:43
committed
not according to *y*. wicked Eze 20:44
ways
nor according to *y*. corrupt Eze 20:44
doings
made *y*. iniquity to be Eze 21:24
remembered
that *y*. transgressions are Eze 21:24
discovered
that in all *y*. doings *y*. sins do Eze 21:24
appear
be taught not to do after *y*. Eze 23:48
lewdness
they shall recompense *y*. Eze 23:49
lewdness
and ye shall bear the sins of Eze 23:49
y. idols
of *y*. strength, the desire of *y*. Eze 24:21
eyes
and that which *y*. soul Eze 24:21
pitieth
and *y*. sons and *y*. daughters Eze 24:21
whom
ye shall not cover *y*. lips, Eze 24:22
nor eat the
And *y*. tires shall be upon *y*. Eze 24:23
heads
and *y*. shoes upon *y*. feet: ye Eze 24:23
shall
ye shall pine away for *y*. Eze 24:23
iniquities
turn ye from *y*. evil ways; Eze 33:11
for why will
and lift up *y*. eyes toward *y*. Eze 33:25
idols, and
Ye stand upon *y*. sword, ye Eze 33:26
work
with *y*. feet the residue of *y*. Eze 34:18
pastures
ye must foul the residue with Eze 34:18
y. feet
which ye have trodden with Eze 34:19
y. feet
which ye have fouled with *y*. Eze 34:19
feet
pushed all the diseased with Eze 34:21
y. horns
men, and I am *y*. God, saith Eze 34:31
the Lord
Thus with *y*. mouth ye have Eze 35:13
boasted
have multiplied *y*. words Eze 35:13
against me
ye shall shoot forth *y*. Eze 36:8
branches
yield *y*. fruit to my people of Eze 36:8
Israel
I will settle you after *y*. old Eze 36:11
estates

unto you than at *y*. Eze 36:11
beginnings
I do not this for *y*. sakes, O Eze 36:22
house of
and will bring you into *y*. Eze 36:24
own land
all *y*. filthiness, and from all Eze 36:25
y. idols
away the stony heart out of Eze 36:26
y. flesh
in the land that I gave to *y*. Eze 36:28
fathers
be my people, and I will be Eze 36:28
y. God
save you from all *y*. Eze 36:29
uncleannesses
shall ye remember *y*. own Eze 36:31
evil ways
and *y*. doings that were not Eze 36:31
good
lothe yourselves in *y*. own Eze 36:31
sight for
y. iniquitites and for *y*. Eze 36:31
abominations
Not for *y*. sakes do I this, Eze 36:32
saith the
and confounded for *y*. own Eze 36:32
ways
cleansed you from all *y*. Eze 36:33
O my people, I will open *y*. Eze 37:12
graves
cause you to come up out of Eze 37:12
y. graves
when I have opened *y*. Eze 37:13
graves, O my
and brought you up out of *y*. Eze 37:13
graves
and I shall place you in *y*. Eze 37:14
own land
wherein *y*. fathers have Eze 37:25
dwelt
y. burnt offerings upon the Eze 43:27
altar
and *y*. peace offerings; and I Eze 43:27
will
it suffice you of all *y*. Eze 44:6
abominations
because of all *y*. Eze 44:7
abominations
every sort of *y*. oblations, Eze 44:30
shall be
unto the priest the first of *y*. Eze 44:30
dough
away *y*. exactions from my Eze 45:9
people
fifteen shekels, shall be *y*. Eze 45:12
maneh
mine hand to give it unto *y*. Eze 47:14
fathers
hath apointed *y*. meat and *y*. Da 1:10
drink
for why should he see *y*. faces Da 1:10
worse
the children which are of *y*. Da 1:10
sort
y. houses shall be made a Da 2:5
dunghill
it is, that *y*. God is a God of Da 2:47
gods
in these things, but Michael Da 10:21
y. prince
my people, and I will not be *y*. Ho 1:9
God
Say ye unto *y*. brethren, Ammi Ho 2:1
and to *y*. sisters, Ruhamah Ho 2:1
Plead with *y*. mother, plead; Ho 2:2
for she
y. daughters shall commit Ho 4:13
y. spouses shall commit Ho 4:13
adultery
I will not punish *y*. daughters Ho 4:14
when
nor *y*. spouses when they Ho 4:14
commit
heal you, nor cure you of *y*. Ho 5:13
wound
y. goodness is as a morning Ho 6:4
cloud
I saw *y*. fathers as the Ho 9:10
firstripe in the
in mercy, break up *y*. fallow Ho 10:12
ground
you because of *y*. great Ho 10:15
wickedness
the land. Hath this been in *y*. Joe 1:2
days
or even in the days of *y*. Joe 1:2
fathers
Tell ye *y*. children of it, and let Joe 1:3

let *y.* children tell their children | Joe 1:3
wine: for it is cut off from *y.* mouth | Joe 1:5
withholden from the house of *y.* God | Joe 1:13
into the house of the Lord *y.* God | Joe 1:14
turn ye even to me with all *y.* heart | Joe 2:12
rend *y.* heart, and not *y.* garments | Joe 2:13
and turn unto the Lord *y.* God: for he | Joe 2:13
drink offering unto the Lord *y.* God | Joe 2:14
Zion, and rejoice in the Lord *y.* God | Joe 2:23
praise and the name of the Lord *y.* God | Joe 2:26
and that I am the Lord *y.* God | Joe 2:27
and *y.* sons and *y.* daughters shall | Joe 2:28
y. old men shall dream dreams | Joe 2:28
y. young men shall see visions | Joe 2:28
y. recompence upon *y.* own head | Joe 3:4
and have carried into *y.* temple my | Joe 3:5
y. recompence upon *y.* own head | Joe 3:7
I will sell *y.* sons and *y.* daughters | Joe 3:8
Beat *y.* plowshares into swords | Joe 3:10
and *y.* pruning hooks into spears | Joe 3:10
ye know that I am the Lord *y.* God | Joe 3:17
I raised up of *y.* sons for prophets | Am 2:11
and of *y.* young men for Nazarites | Am 2:11
I will punish you for all *y.* iniquities | Am 3:2
hooks, and *y.* posterity with fishhooks | Am 4:2
and bring *y.* sacrifices every morning | Am 4:4
and *y.* tithes after three years | Am 4:4
you cleanness of teeth in all *y.* cities | Am 4:6
and want of bread in all *y.* places | Am 4:6
when *y.* gardens and *y.* vineyards | Am 4:9
and *y.* fig trees and *y.* olive trees | Am 4:9
y. young men have I slain with the | Am 4:10
and have taken away *y.* horses | Am 4:10
I have made the stink of *y.* camps | Am 4:10
to come up unto *y.* nostrils; yet have | Am 4:10
as *y.* treading is upon the poor | Am 5:11
I know *y.* manifold transgressions | Am 5:12
y. mighty sins: they afflict the just | Am 5:12
I hate, I despise *y.* feast days | Am 5:21
will not smell in *y.* solemn assemblies | Am 5:21
burnt offerings and *y.* meat offerings | Am 5:22
the peace offerings of *y.* fat beasts | Am 5:22
borne the tabernacle of *y.* Moloch | Am 5:26
Chiun *y.* images, the star of *y.* god | Am 5:26
or their border greater than *y.* border | Am 6:2
I will turn *y.* feasts into mourning | Am 8:10
and all *y.* songs into lamentation | Am 8:10
which ye shall not remove *y.* necks | Mic 2:3
and depart; for this is not *y.* rest | Mic 2:10
shall Zion for *y.* sake be plowed as | Mic 3:12
for I will work a work in *y.* days | Hab 1:5
turn back *y.* captivity before *y.* eyes | Zep 3:20

O ye, to dwell in *y.* ceiled houses | Hag 1:4
the Lord of hosts; Consider *y.* ways | Hag 1:5
is it not in *y.* eyes in comparison of it | Hag 2:3
hail in all the labours of *y.* hands | Hag 2:17
been sore displeased with *y.* fathers | Zec 1:2
Be ye not as *y.* fathers, unto whom | Zec 1:4
turn ye now from *y.* evil ways | Zec 1:4
and from *y.* evil doings. but they did | Zec 1:4
Y. fathers, where are they | Zec 1:5
did they not take hold of *y.* fathers | Zec 1:6
obey the voice of the Lord *y.* God | Zec 6:15
evil against his brother in *y.* heart | Zec 7:10
Let *y.* hands be strong, ye that hear | Zec 8:9
fear not, but let *y.* hands be strong | Zec 8:13
when *y.* fathers provoked me to wrath | Zec 8:14
of truth, and peace in *y.* gates | Zec 8:16
none of you imagine evil in *y.* hearts | Zec 8:17
And *y.* eyes shall see, and ye shall say | Mal 1:5
unto us: this hath been by *y.* means | Mal 1:9
will he regard *y.* persons? saith | Mal 1:9
will I accept an offering at *y.* hand | Mal 1:10
should I accept this of *y.* hand? saith | Mal 1:13
I will curse *y.* blessings; yea, I have | Mal 2:2
Behold I will corrupt *y.* seed | Mal 2:3
and spread dung upon *y.* faces | Mal 2:3
even the dung of *y.* solemn feasts | Mal 2:3
it with good will at *y.* hand | Mal 2:13
Therefore take heed to *y.* spirit, and | Mal 2:15
therefore take heed to *y.* spirit, that | Mal 2:16
have wearied the Lord with *y.* words | Mal 2:17
Even from the days of *y.* fathers | Mal 3:7
will rebuke the devourer for *y.* sakes | Mal 3:11
not destroy the fruits of *y.* ground | Mal 3:11
shall *y.* vine cast her fruit before time | Mal 3:11
Y. words have been stout against me | Mal 3:13
be ashes under the soles of *y.* feet | Mal 4:3
for great is *y.* reward in heaven | M't 5:12
Let *y.* light so shine before men | M't 5:16
that they may see *y.* good works | M't 5:16
and glorify *y.* Father which is in | M't 5:16
except *y.* righteousness exceed | M't 5:20
But let *y.* communication be, Yea | M't 5:37
Love *y.* enemies, bless them that | M't 5:44
ye may be the children of *y.* Father | M't 5:45
And if ye salute *y.* brethren only | M't 5:47
as *y.* Father which is in heaven is | M't 5:48
that ye do not *y.* alms before men | M't 6:1
ye have no reward of *y.* Father | M't 6:1
for *y.* Father knoweth what things | M't 6:8
y. heavenly Father will also forgive | M't 6:14
will *y.* Father forgive *y.* trespasses | M't 6:15
For where *y.* treasure is there will *y.* heart be also | M't 6:21
Take no thought for *y.* life, what ye | M't 6:25

nor yet for *y.* body, what ye shall | M't 6:25
y. heavenly Father feedeth them | M't 6:26
for *y.* heavenly Father knoweth | M't 6:32
cast ye *y.* pearls before swine | M't 7:6
give good gifts unto *y.* children | M't 7:11
how much more shall *y.* Father | M't 7:11
Wherefore think ye evil in *y.* hearts | M't 9:4
eateth *y.* Master with publicans | M't 9:11
According to *y.* faith be it unto you | M't 9:29
nor silver, nor brass in *y.* purses | M't 10:9
Nor script for *y.* journey, neither | M't 10:10
worthy, let *y.* peace come upon it | M't 10:13
worthy, let *y.* peace return to you | M't 10:13
not receive you, nor hear *y.* words | M't 10:14
city, shake off the dust of *y.* feet | M't 10:14
Spirit of *y.* Father which speaketh | M't 10:20
on the ground without *y.* Father | M't 10:29
hairs of *y.* head are all numbered | M't 10:30
ye shall find rest unto *y.* souls | M't 11:29
by whom do *y.* children cast them | M't 12:27
therefore they shall be *y.* judges | M't 12:27
blessed are *y.* eyes, for they see | M't 13:16
and *y.* ears, for they hear | M't 13:16
of God by *y.* tradition | M't 15:3
God of none effect by *y.* tradition | M't 15:6
Because of *y.* unbelief: for verily I | M't 17:20
Doth not *y.* master pay tribute | M't 17:24
will of *y.* Father which is in heaven | M't 18:14
ye from *y.* hearts forgive not every | M't 18:35
because of the hardness of *y.* hearts | M't 19:8
suffered you to put away *y.* wives | M't 19:8
among you, let him be *y.* minister | M't 20:26
among you, let him be *y.* servant | M't 20:27
for one is *y.* Master, even Christ | M't 23:8
no man *y.* father upon the earth | M't 23:9
for one is *y.* Father, which is in | M't 23:9
for one is *y.* Master, even Christ | M't 23:10
among you shall be *y.* servant | M't 23:11
up then the measure of *y.* fathers | M't 23:32
shall ye scourge in *y.* synagogues | M't 23:34
y. house is left unto you desolate | M't 23:38
that *y.* flight be not in the winter | M't 24:20
not what hour *y.* Lord doth come | M't 24:42
Give us of *y.* oil; for our lamps are | M't 25:8
Sleep on now, and take *y.* rest | M't 26:45
go *y.* way. make it as sure as you | M't 27:65
reason ye these things in *y.* hearts | M'k 2:8
shake off the dust under *y.* feet | M'k 6:11
that ye may keep *y.* own tradition | M'k 7:9
of none effect through *y.* tradition | M'k 7:13
have ye *y.* heart yet hardened | M'k 8:17
For the hardness of *y.* heart be | M'k 10:5

among you, shall be *y.* minister   M'k 10:43

Go *y.* way into the village over   M'k 11:2

y. Father also which is in heaven   M'k 11:25

may forgive you *y.* trespasses   M'k 11:25

neither will *y.* Father which is in   M'k 11:26

is in heaven forgive *y.* trespasses   M'k 11:26

that *y.* flight be not in the winter   M'k 13:18

Sleep on now, and take *y.* rest: it is   M'k 14:41

But go *y.* way, tell his disciples and   M'k 16:7

and be content with *y.* wages   Lu 3:14

is this scripture fulfilled in *y.* ears   Lu 4:21

and let down *y.* nets for a draught   Lu 5:4

What reason ye in *y.* hearts   Lu 5:22

and cast out *y.* name as evil   Lu 6:22

y. reward is great in heaven   Lu 6:23

ye have received *y.* consolation   Lu 6:24

Love *y.* enemies, do good to them   Lu 6:27

But love ye *y.* enemies, and do good   Lu 6:35

and *y.* reward shall be great   Lu 6:35

as *y.* Father also is merciful   Lu 6:36

shall men give into *y.* bosom   Lu 6:38

Go *y.* way, and tell John what things   Lu 7:22

unto them, Where is *y.* faith   Lu 8:25

Take nothing for *y.* journey   Lu 9:3

shake off the very dust from *y.* feet   Lu 9:5

sayings sink down into *y.* ears   Lu 9:44

Go *y.* ways, behold, I send you   Lu 10:3

there, *y.* peace shall rest upon it   Lu 10:6

go *y.* ways out into the streets of   Lu 10:10

Even the very dust of *y.* city   Lu 10:11

y. names are written in heaven   Lu 10:20

to give good gifts unto *y.* children   Lu 11:13

more shall *y.* heavenly Father   Lu 11:13

by whom do *y.* sons cast them out   Lu 11:19

therefore shall they be *y.* judges   Lu 11:19

y. inward part is full of ravening   Lu 11:39

the burdens with one of *y.* fingers   Lu 11:46

prophets, *y.* fathers killed them   Lu 11:47

ye allow the deeds of *y.* fathers   Lu 11:48

hairs of *y.* head are all numbered   Lu 12:7

Take no thought for *y.* life, what ye   Lu 12:22

y. Father knoweth that ye have   Lu 12:30

for it is *y.* Father's good pleasure   Lu 12:32

For where *y.* treasure is there will *y.* heart be also   Lu 12:34

Let *y.* loins be girded about   Lu 12:35

and *y.* lights burning   Lu 12:35

y. house is left unto you desolate   Lu 13:35

commit to *y.* trust the true riches   Lu 16:11

give you that which is *y.* own   Lu 16:12

but God knoweth *y.* hearts   Lu 16:15

at *y.* entering ye shall find a colt   Lu 19:30

Settle it therefore in *y.* hearts, not   Lu 21:14

y. adversaries shall not be able   Lu 21:15

shall not an hair of *y.* head perish   Lu 21:18

In *y.* patience possess ye *y.* souls   Lu 21:19

then look up, and lift up *y.* heads   Lu 21:28

for *y.* redemption draweth nigh   Lu 21:28

ye see and know of *y.* own selves   Lu 21:30

any time *y.* hearts be overcharged   Lu 21:34

but this is *y.* hour, and the power of   Lu 22:53

for yourselves, and for *y.* children   Lu 23:28

why do thoughts arise in *y.* hearts   Lu 24:38

Lift up *y.* eyes, and look on   Joh 4:35

Y. fathers did eat manna in   Joh 6:49

not as *y.* fathers did eat manna   Joh 6:58

but *y.* time is alway ready   Joh 7:6

It is also written in *y.* law, that the   Joh 8:17

seek me, and shall die in *y.* sins   Joh 8:21

you, that ye shall die in *y.* sins   Joh 8:24

that I am he, ye shall die in *y.* sins   Joh 8:24

which ye have seen with *y.* father   Joh 8:38

Ye do the deeds of *y.* father   Joh 8:41

If God were *y.* Father, ye would   Joh 8:42

Ye are of *y.* father the devil   Joh 8:44

the lusts of *y.* father ye will do   Joh 8:44

of whom ye say, that he is *y.* God   Joh 8:54

Y. father Abraham rejoiced to see   Joh 8:56

Is this *y.* son, who ye say was born   Joh 9:19

We see; therefore *y.* sin remaineth   Joh 9:41

Is it not written in *y.* law, I said   Joh 10:34

glad for *y.* sakes that I was not   Joh 11:15

not because of me, but for *y.* sakes   Joh 12:30

If I then, *y.* Lord, and Master   Joh 13:14

have washed *y.* feet; ye also ought   Joh 13:14

Let not *y.* heart be troubled   Joh 14:1; 14:27

all things to *y.* remembrance   Joh 14:26

and that *y.* joy might be full   Joh 15:11

and that *y.* fruit should remain   Joh 15:16

you, sorrow hath filled *y.* heart   Joh 16:6

y. sorrow shall be turned into joy   Joh 16:20

again, and *y.* heart shall rejoice   Joh 16:22

and *y.* joy no man taketh from you   Joh 16:22

receive, that *y.* joy may be full   Joh 16:24

and judge him according to *y.* law   Joh 18:31

unto the Jews, Behold *y.* King   Joh 19:14

unto them, Shall I crucify *y.* King   Joh 19:15

unto my Father, and *y.* Father   Joh 20:17

and to my God, and *y.* God   Joh 20:17

y. sons and *y.* daughters shall   Ac 2:17

and *y.* young men shall see visions   Ac 2:17

y. old men shall dream dreams   Ac 2:17

is unto you, and to *y.* children   Ac 2:39

ye did it, as did also *y.* rulers   Ac 3:17

that *y.* sins may be blotted out   Ac 3:19

A prophet shall the Lord *y.* God   Ac 3:22; 7:37

raise up unto you of *y.* brethren   Ac 3:22; 7:37

filled Jerusalem with *y.* doctrine   Ac 5:28

and the star of *y.* god Remphan   Ac 7:43

Ghost: as *y.* fathers did, so do ye   Ac 7:51

have not *y.* fathers persecuted   Ac 7:52

for I work a work in *y.* days   Ac 13:41

subverting *y.* souls, saying, Ye   Ac 15:24

passed by, and beheld *y.* devotions   Ac 17:23

also of *y.* own poets have said   Ac 17:28

Y. blood be upon *y.* own heads   Ac 18:6

and names, and of *y.* law   Ac 18:15

yet blasphemers of *y.* goddess   Ac 19:37

of *y.* own selves shall men arise   Ac 20:30

know uttermost of *y.* matter   Ac 24:22

meat; for this is for *y.* health   Ac 27:34

y. faith is spoken of throughout   Ro 1:8

therefore reign in *y.* mortal body   Ro 6:12

yield ye *y.* members as instruments   Ro 6:13

and *y.* members as instruments of   Ro 6:13

because of the infirmity of *y.* flesh   Ro 6:19

have yielded *y.* members servants   Ro 6:19

so now yield *y.* members servants   Ro 6:19

ye have *y.* fruit unto holiness   Ro 6:22

quicken *y.* mortal bodies by his   Ro 8:11

be wise in *y.* own conceits   Ro 11:25

they are enemies for *y.* sakes   Ro 11:28

through *y.* mercy they also may   Ro 11:31

y. bodies a living sacrifice   Ro 12:1

which is *y.* reasonable service   Ro 12:1

by the renewing of *y.* mind   Ro 12:2

Be not wise in *y.* own conceits   Ro 12:16

then *y.* good be evil spoken of   Ro 14:16

somewhat filled with *y.* company   Ro 15:24

together with me in *y.* prayers   Ro 15:30

For *y.* obedience is come abroad   Ro 16:19

I am glad therefore on *y.* behalf   Ro 16:19

bruise Satan under *y.* feet shortly   Ro 16:20

thank my God always on *y.* behalf   1Co 1:4

For ye see *y.* calling, brethren   1Co 1:26

That *y.* faith should not stand   1Co 2:5

myself and to Apollos for *y.* sakes   1Co 4:6

Y. glorifying is not good   1Co 5:6

I speak to *y.* shame. Is it so, that   1Co 6:5

and defraud, and that *y.* brethren   1Co 6:8

that *y.* bodies are the members of   1Co 6:15

ye not that *y.* body is the temple   1Co 6:19

of God, and ye are not *y.* own   1Co 6:19

therefore glorify God in *y.* body   1Co 6:20

and in *y.* spirit, which are God's   1Co 6:20

tempt you not for *y.* incontinency   1Co 7:5

else were *y.* children unclean   1Co 7:14

And this I speak for *y.* own profit   1Co 7:35

if we shall reap *y.* carnal things   1Co 9:11

Let *y.* women keep silence in the   1Co 14:34

vain, and *y.* faith is also vain   1Co 15:14

be not raised, *y.* faith is vain   1Co 15:17

ye are yet in *y.* sins   1Co 15:17

I protest by *y.* rejoicing which I   1Co 15:31

of God: I speak this to *y.* shame   1Co 15:34

ye know that *y.* labour is not   1Co 15:58

ye shall approve by *y.* letters   1Co 16:3

will I send to bring *y.* liberality   1Co 16:3

y. things be done with charity   1Co 16:14

that which was lacking on *y.* part   1Co 16:17

it is for *y.* consolation and   2Co 1:6

that we are *y.* rejoicing, even as ye   2Co 1:14

we have domination over *y.* faith   2Co 1:24

are helpers of *y.* joy: for by faith   2Co 1:24

would confirm *y*. love toward him — 2Co 2:8

for *y*. sakes forgave I it in ourselves — 2Co 2:10

y. servants for Jesus — 2Co 4:5

For all things are for *y*. sakes — 2Co 4:15

made manifest in *y*. consciences — 2Co 5:11

we be sober, it is for *y*. cause — 2Co 5:13

ye are straitened in *y*. own bowels — 2Co 6:12

when he told us *y*. earnest desire — 2Co 7:7

y. mourning, *y*. fervent mind — 2Co 7:7

we were comforted in *y*. comfort — 2Co 7:13

and in *y*. love to us, see that ye — 2Co 8:7

to prove the sincerity of *y*. love — 2Co 8:8

yet for *y*. sakes he became poor — 2Co 8:9

y. abundance may be a supply for — 2Co 8:14

also may be a supply for *y*. want — 2Co 8:14

and declaration of *y*. ready mind — 2Co 8:19

the churches, the proof of *y*. love — 2Co 8:24

and of our boasting on *y*. behalf — 2Co 8:24

know the forwardness of *y*. mind — 2Co 9:2

y. zeal hath provoked very many — 2Co 9:2

and make up beforehand *y*. bounty — 2Co 9:5

both minister bread for *y*. food — 2Co 9:10

and multiply *y*. seed sown — 2Co 9:10

the fruits of *y*. righteousness — 2Co 9:10

y. professed subjection unto — 2Co 9:13

y. liberal distribution unto them — 2Co 9:13

when *y*. obedience is fulfilled — 2Co 10:6

and not for *y*. destruction, I should — 2Co 10:8

when *y*. faith is increased, that we — 2Co 10:15

so *y*. minds should be corrupted — 2Co 11:3

dearly beloved, for *y*. edifying — 2Co 12:19

in the faith; prove *y*. own selves — 2Co 13:5

Know ye not *y*. own selves, how — 2Co 13:5

we wish, even *y*. perfection — 2Co 13:9

the Spirit of his Son into *y*. hearts — Ga 4:6

have plucked out *y*. own eyes — Ga 4:15

Am I therefore become *y*. enemy — Ga 4:16

that they may glory in *y*. flesh — Ga 6:13

Lord Jesus Christ be with *y*. spirit — Ga 6:18

truth, the gospel of *y*. salvation — Eph 1:13

of *y*. faith in the Lord Jesus — Eph 1:15

eyes of *y*. understanding being — Eph 1:18

tribulations for you, which is *y*. glory — Eph 3:13

that Christ may dwell in *y*. hearts — Eph 3:17

are called in one hope of *y*. calling — Eph 4:4

renewed in the spirit of *y*. mind — Eph 4:23

the sun go down upon *y*. wrath — Eph 4:26

proceed out of *y*. mouth — Eph 4:29

melody in *y*. heart to the Lord — Eph 5:19

yourselves unto *y*. own husbands — Eph 5:22

Husbands, love *y*. wives, even as — Eph 5:25

obey *y*. parents in the Lord — Eph 6:1

provoke not *y*. children to wrath — Eph 6:4

to them that are *y*. masters — Eph 6:5

in singleness of *y*. heart, as unto — Eph 6:5

that *y*. Master also is in heaven — Eph 6:9

y. loins girt about with truth — Eph 6:14

y. feet shod with the preparation — Eph 6:15

that he might comfort *y*. hearts — Eph 6:22

For *y*. fellowship in the gospel — Ph'p 1:5

that *y*. love may abound yet more — Ph'p 1:9

my salvation through *y*. prayer — Ph'p 1:19

with you all for *y*. furtherance and — Ph'p 1:25

y. rejoicing may be more abundant — Ph'p 1:26

y. conversation be as it becometh — Ph'p 1:27

I may hear of *y*. affairs, that ye — Ph'p 1:27

nothing terrified by *y*. adversaries — Ph'p 1:28

work out *y*. own salvation with fear — Ph'p 2:12

sacrifice and service of *y*. faith — Ph'p 2:17

comfort, when I know *y*. state — Ph'p 2:19

who will naturally care for *y*. state — Ph'p 2:20

but *y*. messenger, and he that — Ph'p 2:25

to supply *y*. lack of service toward — Ph'p 2:30

y. moderation be known unto all — Ph'p 4:5

let *y*. requests be made known unto — Ph'p 4:6

keep *y*. hearts and minds through — Ph'p 4:7

last *y*. care of me hath flourished — Ph'p 4:10

may abound unto *y*. account — Ph'p 4:17

my God shall supply all *y*. need — Ph'p 4:19

Since we heard of *y*. faith in Christ — Col 1:4

unto us *y*. love in the Spirit — Col 1:8

enemies in *y*. mind by wicked — Col 1:21

joying and beholding *y*. order — Col 2:5

stedfastness of *y*. faith in Christ — Col 2:5

And you, being dead in *y*. sins and — Col 2:13

and the uncircumcision of *y*. flesh — Col 2:13

no man beguile you of *y*. reward — Col 2:18

Set *y*. affection on things above — Col 3:2

y. life is hid with Christ in God — Col 3:3

Mortify therefore *y*. members — Col 3:5

communication out of *y*. mouth — Col 3:8

the peace of God rule in *y*. hearts — Col 3:15

singing with grace in *y*. hearts to — Col 3:16

yourselves unto *y*. own husbands — Col 3:18

Husbands, love *y*. wives, and be not — Col 3:19

Children, obey *y*. parents in all — Col 3:20

provoke not *y*. children to anger — Col 3:21

obey in all things *y*. masters — Col 3:22

unto *y*. servants that which is just — Col 4:1

y. speech be alway with grace — Col 4:6

that he might know *y*. estate — Col 4:8

and comfort *y*. hearts — Col 4:8

ceasing *y*. work of faith — 1Th 1:3

beloved, *y*. election of God — 1Th 1:4

we were among you for *y*. sake — 1Th 1:5

every place *y*. faith to God-ward — 1Th 1:8

like things of *y*. own countrymen — 1Th 2:14

to see *y*. face with great desire — 1Th 2:17

to comfort you concerning *y*. faith — 1Th 3:2

I sent to now *y*. faith, lest by — 1Th 3:5

brought us good tidings of *y*. faith — 1Th 3:6

affliction and distress by *y*. faith — 1Th 3:7

we joy for *y*. sakes before our God — 1Th 3:9

that we might see *y*. face — 1Th 3:10

that which is lacking in *y*. faith — 1Th 3:10

the end he may stablish *y*. hearts — 1Th 3:13

will of God, even *y*. sanctification — 1Th 4:3

quiet, and to do *y*. own business — 1Th 4:11

and to work with *y*. own hands — 1Th 4:11

I pray God *y*. whole spirit and soul — 1Th 5:23

that *y*. faith groweth exceedingly — 2Th 1:3

of God for *y*. patience and faith — 2Th 1:4

y. persecutions and tribulations — 2Th 1:4

Comfort *y*. hearts, and stablish you — 2Th 2:17

Lord direct *y*. hearts into the love — 2Th 3:5

for I trust that through *y*. prayers — Ph'm 22

Lord Jesus Christ be with *y*. spirit — Ph'm 25

Harden not *y*. hearts, as in — Heb 3:8

When *y*. fathers tempted me — Heb 3:9

hear his voice, harden not *y*. hearts — Heb 3:15; 4:7

forget *y*. work and labour of love — Heb 6:10

purge *y*. conscience from dead — Heb 9:14

joyfully the spoiling of *y*. goods — Heb 10:34

not away therefore *y*. confidence — Heb 10:35

ye be wearied and faint in *y*. minds — Heb 12:3

make straight paths for *y*. feet — Heb 12:13

Let *y*. conversation be without — Heb 13:5

for they watch for *y*. souls — Heb 13:17

trying of *y*. faith worketh patience — Jas 1:3

which is able to save *y*. souls — Jas 1:21

only, deceiving *y*. own selves — Jas 1:22

come unto *y*. assembly a man — Jas 2:2

envying and strife in *y*. hearts — Jas 3:14

y. lusts that war in *y*. members — Jas 4:1

ye may consume it upon *y*. lusts — Jas 4:3

Cleanse *y*. hands, ye sinners — Jas 4:8

and purify *y*. hearts, ye double-minded — Jas 4:8

y. laughter be turned to mourning — Jas 4:9

and *y*. joy to heaviness — Jas 4:9

For what is *y*. life? It is even — Jas 4:14

now ye rejoice in *y*. boastings — Jas 4:16

weep and howl for *y*. miseries — Jas 5:1

Y. riches are corrupted, and — Jas 5:2

and *y*. garments are motheaten — Jas 5:2

Y. gold and silver is cankered — Jas 5:3

shall eat *y*. flesh as it were fire — Jas 5:3

who have reaped down *y*. fields — Jas 5:4

ye have nourished *y*. hearts, as in a — Jas 5:5

ye also patient; stablish *y*. hearts — Jas 5:8

oath: but let *y*. yea be yea — Jas 5:12

and *y*. nay, nay; lest ye fall — Jas 5:12

Confess *y*. faults one to another — Jas 5:16

That the trial of *y*. faith, being — 1Pe 1:7

Receiving the end of *y*. faith — 1Pe 1:9

even the salvation of *y*. soul — 1Pe 1:9

gird up the loins of *y*. mind — 1Pe 1:13

to the former lusts in *y*. ignorance — 1Pe 1:14

time of *y*. sojourning here in fear — 1Pe 1:17

from *y*. vain conversation received — 1Pe 1:18

by tradition from *y*. fathers — 1Pe 1:18

y. faith and hope might be in God — 1Pe 1:21

Seeing ye have purified *y*. souls in — 1Pe 1:22

Having *y*. conversation honest — 1Pe 2:12

they may by *y*. good works, which — 1Pe 2:12

and not using *y*. liberty for a cloak — 1Pe 2:16

subject to *y*. masters with all fear — 1Pe 2:18

when ye be buffeted for *y*. faults — 1Pe 2:20

Shepherd and Bishop of *y*. souls — 1Pe 2:25
in subjection to *y*. own husbands — 1Pe 3:1
behold *y*. chaste conversation — 1Pe 3:2
that *y*. prayers be not hindered — 1Pe 3:7
the Lord God in *y*. hearts — 1Pe 3:15
accuse *y*. good conversation — 1Pe 3:16
of, but on *y*. part he is glorified — 1Pe 4:14
Casting all *y*. care upon him; for — 1Pe 5:7
because *y*. adversary the devil — 1Pe 5:8
are accomplished in *y*. brethren — 1Pe 5:9
add to *y*. faith virtue; and to — 2Pe 1:5
give diligence to make *y*. calling — 2Pe 1:10
the day star arise in *y*. hearts — 2Pe 1:19
both which I stir up *y*. pure minds — 2Pe 3:1
fall from *y*. own stedfastness — 2Pe 3:17
unto you, that *y*. joy may be full — 1Jo 1:4
because *y*. sins are forgiven you for — 1Jo 2:12
receive him not into *y*. house, neither — 2Jo 10
are spots in *y*. feasts of charity — Jude 12
yourselves on *y*. most holy faith — Jude 20
I John, who also am *y*. brother — Re 1:9
one of you according to *y*. works — Re 2:23
Go *y*. ways, and pour out the vials — Re 16:1

YOURS

the good of all the land of Egypt is *y*. — Ge 45:20
of your feet shall tread shall be *y*. — De 11:24
Our life for *y*. if ye utter not this our — Jos 2:14
for the battle is not *y*. but God's — 2Ch 20:15
strangers in a land that is not *y*. — Jer 5:19
poor: for *y*. is the kingdom of God — Lu 6:20
my saying, they will keep *y*. also — Joh 15:20
in men; for all things are *y*. — 1Co 3:21
or things to come; all are *y*. — 1Co 3:22
means this liberty of *y*. become a — 1Co 8:9
have refreshed my spirit and *y*. — 1Co 16:18
for I seek not *y*. but you — 2Co 12:14

YOURSELVES

your feet, and rest *y*. under the tree — Ge 18:4
be not grieved, nor angry with *y*. — Ge 45:5
Gather *y*. together, that I may tell — Ge 49:1
Gather *y*. together, and hear, *y*. — Ge 49:2
Take heed to *y*. that ye go not up — Ex 19:12
ye shall not make to *y*. according to — Ex 30:37
Consecrate *y*. to-day to the Lord — Ex 32:29
neither shall ye make *y*. unclean — Le 11:43
not make *y*. abominable — Le 11:43
ye shall therefore sanctify *y*. — Le 11:44
neither shall ye defile *y*. with any — Le 11:44
Defile not ye *y*. in any of these — Le 18:24
and that ye defile not *y*. therein — Le 18:30
idols, nor make to *y*. molten gods — Le 19:4
Sanctify *y*. therefore, and be ye — Le 20:7
Sanctify *y*. against to-morrow, and ye — Nu 11:18
lift ye up *y*. above the congregation — Nu 16:3
Separate *y*. from among this — Nu 16:21
Arm some of *y*. unto the war — Nu 31:3

lying with him, keep alive for *y*. — Nu 31:18
purify both *y*. and your captives on — Nu 31:19
take ye good heed unto *y*. therefore — De 2:4
ye therefore good heed unto *y*. — De 4:15
Lest ye corrupt *y*. and make you — De 4:16
Take heed unto *y*. lest ye forget — De 4:23
corrupt *y*. and make a graven image — De 4:25
Take heed to *y*. that your heart — De 11:16
greater nations and mightier than *y*. — De 11:23
ye shall not cut *y*. nor make any — De 14:1
and present *y*. in the tabernacle of — De 31:14
my death ye will utterly corrupt *y*. — De 31:29
and hide *y*. there three days, until — Jos 2:16
Sanctify *y*. for to-morrow the Lord — Jos 3:5
Keep *y*. from the accursed thing — Jos 6:18
lest ye make *y*. accursed, when ye — Jos 6:18
say, Sanctify *y*. against to-morrow — Jos 7:13
shall ye take for a prey unto *y*. — Jos 8:2
serve them, nor bow *y*. unto them — Jos 23:7
heed therefore unto *y*. — Jos 23:11
other gods, and bowed *y*. to them — Jos 23:16
Ye are witnesses against *y*. that ye — Jos 24:22
that ye will not fall upon me *y*. — J'g 15:12
to make *y*. fat with the chiefest of — 1Sa 2:29
Be strong, and quit *y*. like men — 1Sa 4:9
to you: quit *y*. like men, and fight — 1Sa 4:9
therefore present *y*. before the Lord — 1Sa 10:19
said, Disperse *y*. among the people — 1Sa 14:34
sanctify *y*. and come with me to — 1Sa 16:5
Choose you one bullock for *y*. — 1Ki 18:25
unto his servants, Set *y*. in — 1Ki 20:12
nor bow *y*. to them, nor serve them — 2Ki 17:35
sanctify *y*. both ye and your brethren — 2Ch 15:12
set *y*. stand ye still, and see — 2Ch 20:17
ye Levites, sanctify now *y*. — 2Ch 29:5
have consecrated *y*. unto the Lord — 2Ch 29:31
but yield *y*. unto the Lord — 2Ch 30:8
to give over *y*. to die by famine — 2Ch 32:11
And prepare *y*. by the houses of — 2Ch 35:4
So kill the passover, and sanctify *y*. — 2Ch 35:6
separate *y*. from the people of the — Ezr 10:11
daughters unto your sons, or for *y*. — Ne 13:25
that ye make *y*. strange to me — Job 19:3
ye will magnify *y*. against me — Job 19:5
Behold, all ye *y*. have seen it — Job 27:12
and offer up for *y*. a burnt offering — Job 42:8
Associate *y*. O ye people and ye — Isa 8:9
gird *y*. and ye shall be broken — Isa 8:9
Stay *y*. and wonder; cry ye out — Isa 29:9
Assemble *y*. and come; draw near — Isa 45:20
Remember this, and shew *y*. men — Isa 46:8
All ye, assemble *y*. and hear — Isa 48:14
them that are in darkness, Shew *y*. — Isa 49:9
for your iniquities have ye sold *y*. — Isa 50:1
that compass *y*. about with sparks — Isa 50:11
Ye have sold *y*. for nought — Isa 52:3

Against whom do ye sport *y*. — Isa 57:4
Enflaming *y*. with idols under every — Isa 57:5
and in their glory shall ye boast *y*. — Isa 61:6
Circumcise *y*. to the Lord, and take — Jer 4:4
Assemble *y*. and let us go into — Jer 4:5
gather *y*. to flee out of the midst of — Jer 6:1
assemble *y*. and let us enter into — Jer 8:14
to the queen. Humble *y*. sit down — Jer 13:18
Take heed to *y*. and bear no — Jer 17:21
and wallow *y*. in the ashes, ye — Jer 25:34
surely bring innocent blood upon *y*. — Jer 26:15
Deceive not *y*. saying, The — Jer 37:9
that ye might cut *y*. off, and — Jer 44:8
Put *y*. in array against Babylon — Jer 50:14
and turn *y*. from your idols — Eze 14:6
y. from all your transgressions — Eze 18:30
wherefore turn *y*. and live ye — Eze 18:32
defile not *y*. with the idols of Egypt — Eze 20:7
nor defile *y*. with their idols — Eze 20:18
ye pollute *y*. with all your idol — Eze 20:31
ye shall lothe *y*. in your own sight — Eze 20:43
and shall lothe *y*. in your own sight — Eze 36:31
of the field, Assemble *y*. and come — Eze 39:17
gather *y*. on every side to my — Eze 39:17
my charge in my sanctuary for *y*. — Eze 44:8
Sow to *y*. in righteousness, reap — Ho 10:12
Gird *y*. and lament, ye priests — Joe 1:13
Assemble *y*. and come, all ye — Joe 3:11
and gather *y*. together round about — Joe 3:11
Assemble *y*. upon the mountains of — Am 3:9
of your God, which ye made to *y*. — Am 5:26
Gather *y*. together, yea, gather — Zep 2:1
not ye eat for *y*. and drink for *y*. — Zec 7:6
And think not to say within *y*. — M't 3:9
up for *y*. treasures upon earth — M't 6:19
lay up for *y*. treasures in heaven — M't 6:20
why reason ye among *y*. because — M't 16:8
for ye neither go in *y*. neither suffer — M't 23:13
more the child of hell than *y*. — M't 23:15
Wherefore ye be witnesses unto *y*. — M't 23:31
to them that sell, and buy for *y*. — M't 25:9
Come ye *y*. apart into a desert — M'k 6:31
ye disputed among *y*. by the way — M'k 9:33
Have salt in *y*. and have peace one — M'k 9:50
But take heed to *y*.: for they shall — M'k 13:9
to say within *y*. We have Abraham — Lu 3:8
and ye *y*. touch not the burdens — Lu 11:46
ye entered not in *y*. and them that — Lu 11:52
provide *y*. bags which wax not old — Lu 12:33
And ye *y*. like unto men that wait — Lu 12:36
why even of *y*. judge ye not what — Lu 12:57
of God, and you *y*. thrust out of — Lu 13:28
to *y*. friends of the mammon — Lu 16:9
they which justify *y*. before men — Lu 16:15
Take heed to *y*.: If thy brother — Lu 17:3
them, Go shew *y*. unto the priests — Lu 17:14
And take heed to *y*. lest at any — Lu 21:34

Take this, and divide it among *y*.	Lu 22:17
weep, not for me, but weep for *y*.	Lu 23:28
Ye *y*. hear me witness, that I	Joh 3:28
unto them, Murmur not among *y*.	Joh 6:43
enquire among *y*. of that I said	Joh 16:19
midst of you, as ye *y*. also know	Ac 2:22
y. from this untoward generation	Ac 2:40
take heed to *y*. what ye intend to	Ac 5:35
y. unworthy of everlasting life	Ac 13:46
from which if ye keep *y*. ye shall	Ac 15:29
Trouble not *y*.; for his life is in him	Ac 20:10
Take heed therefore unto *y*.	Ac 20:28
Yea, ye *y*. know, that these hands	Ac 20:34
also *y*. to be dead indeed unto sin	Ro 6:11
but yield *y*. unto God, as those	Ro 6:13
whom ye yield *y*. servants to obey	Ro 6:16
Dearly beloved, avenge not *y*.	Ro 12:19
from among *y*. that wicked	1Co 5:13
not rather suffer *y*. to be defrauded	1Co 6:7
may give *y*. to fasting and prayer	1Co 7:5
Judge in *y*.: is it comely that a	1Co 11:13
That ye submit *y*. unto such	1Co 16:16
in you, yea, what clearing of *y*.	2Co 7:11
have approved *y*. to be clean in this	2Co 7:11
fools gladly, seeing ye *y*. are wise	2Co 11:19
Examine *y*. whether ye be in	2Co 13:5
and that not of *y*.: it is the gift of	Eph 2:8
Speaking to *y*. in psalms and	Eph 5:19
Submitting *y*. one to another	Eph 5:21
submit *y*. unto your own husbands	Eph 5:22; Col 3:18
For *y*. brethren, know our entrance	1Th 2:1
for *y*. know that we are appointed	1Th 3:3
for ye *y*. are taught of God to love	1Th 4:9
For ye know perfectly that the day	1Th 5:2
Wherefore comfort *y*. together	1Th 5:11
And be at peace among *y*.	1Th 5:13
that which is good, both among *y*.	1Th 5:15
ye withdraw *y*. from every brother	2Th 3:6
For *y*. know how ye ought to follow	2Th 3:7
knowing in *y*. that ye have in	Heb 10:34
as being *y*. also in the body	Heb 13:3
the rule over you, and submit *y*.	Heb 13:17
Are ye not then partial in *y*.	Jas 2:4
Submit *y*. therefore to God	Jas 4:7
Humble *y*. in the sight of the Lord	Jas 4:10
not fashioning *y*. according to the	1Pe 1:14
Submit *y*. to every ordinance	1Pe 2:13
arm *y*. likewise with the same mind	1Pe 4:1
have fervent charity among *y*.	1Pe 4:8
ye younger, submit *y*. unto the elder	1Pe 5:5
Humble *y*. therefore under the	1Pe 5:6
Little children, Keep *y*. from idols	1Jo 5:21
Look to *y*. that we lose not those	2Jo 8
building up *y*. on your most holy	Jude 20
Keep *y*. in the love of God, looking	Jude 21
gather *y*. together unto the supper	Re 19:17

YOUTH

of man's heart is evil from his *y*.	Ge 8:21
the *y*. (A)(B)	Ge 21:15
the youngest according to his *y*.	Ge 43:33
cattle from our *y*. even until now	Ge 46:34
her father's house, as in her *y*.	Le 22:13
in her father's house in her *y*.	Nu 30:3
yet in her *y*. in her father's house	Nu 30:16
But the *y*. drew not his sword	J'g 8:20
feared, because he was yet a *y*.	J'g 8:20
with him: for thou art but a *y*.	1Sa 17:33
and he a man of war from his *y*.	1Sa 17:33
for he was but a *y*. and ruddy	1Sa 17:42
host, Abner, whose son is this *y*.	1Sa 17:55
evil that befell thee from thy *y*.	2Sa 19:7
servant fear the Lord from my *y*.	1Ki 18:12
to possess the iniquities of my *y*.	Job 13:26
bones are full of the sin of his *y*.	Job 20:11
As I was in the days of my *y*.	Job 29:4
Upon my right hand rise the *y*.	Job 30:12
from my *y*. he was brought up	Job 31:18
shall return to the days of his *y*.	Job 33:25
They die in *y*. and their life is	Job 36:14
Remember not the sins of my *y*.	Ps 25:7
thou art my trust from my *y*.	Ps 71:5
thou hast taught me from my *y*.	Ps 71:17
and ready to die from my *y*. up	Ps 88:15
The days of his *y*. hast thou	Ps 89:45
thy *y*. is renewed like the eagle's	Ps 103:5
thou hast the dew of thy *y*.	Ps 110:3
man; so are children of the *y*.	Ps 127:4
have they afflicted me from my *y*.	Ps 129:1; 129:2
be as plants grown up in their *y*.	Ps 144:12
forsaketh the guide of her *y*.	Pr 2:17
rejoice with the wife of thy *y*.	Pr 5:18
following the *y*. (A)(B)(E)(R)	Ec 4:15
Rejoice, O young man, in thy *y*.	Ec 11:9
cheer thee in the days of thy *y*.	Ec 11:9
for childhood, and *y*. are vanity	Ec 11:10
thy Creator in the days of thy *y*.	Ec 12:1
thou hast laboured from thy *y*.	Isa 47:12
even thy merchants, from thy *y*.	Isa 47:15
shalt forget the shame of thy *y*.	Isa 54:4
and a wife of *y*. when thou wast	Isa 54:6
the kindness of thy *y*. the love	Jer 2:2
father, thou art the guide of my *y*.	Jer 3:4
labour of our fathers from our *y*.	Jer 3:24
from our *y*. even unto this day	Jer 3:25
been thy manner from thy *y*.	Jer 22:21
I did bear the reproach of my *y*.	Jer 31:19
done evil before me from their *y*.	Jer 32:30
hath been at ease from his *y*.	Jer 48:11
that he bear the yoke in his *y*.	La 3:27
from my *y*. up even till now have I	Eze 4:14
remembered the days of thy *y*.	Eze 16:22; 16:43
with thee in the days of thy *y*.	Eze 16:60
committed whoredoms in their *y*.	Eze 23:3

for in her *y*. they lay with her	Eze 23:8
to remembrance the days of her *y*.	Eze 23:19
the lewdness of thy *y*.	Eze 23:21
Egyptians for the paps of thy *y*.	Eze 23:21
sing there, as in the days of her *y*.	Ho 2:15
Israel was a *y*. (B)	Ho 11:1
for the husband of her *y*.	Joe 1:8
me to keep cattle from my *y*.	Zec 13:5
thee and the wife of thy *y*.	Mal 2:14
against the wife of his *y*.	Mal 2:15
have I kept from my *y*. up	M't 19:20
these have I observed from my *y*.	M'k 10:20
these have I kept from my *y*. up	Lu 18:21
my manner of life from my *y*.	Ac 26:4
Let no man despise thy *y*.; but be	1Ti 4:12

YOUTHFUL

Flee also *y*. lusts; but follow	2Ti 2:22

YOUTHS

some *y*. came (B)	2Ki 2:23
youths (S)	2Ki 2:23; 2:24; Da 1:4, 10, 13, 15, 17
I discerned among the *y*. a young	Pr 7:7
the *y*. shall faint and be weary	Isa 40:30

YOU-WARD

and more abundantly to *y*.	2Co 1:12
which to *y*. is not weak, but is	2Co 13:3
grace which is given me to *y*.	Eph 3:2

Z

ZAANAIM

his tent unto the plain of Z.	J'g 4:11

ZAANAN

inhabitant of Z. came not forth	Mic 1:11

ZAANANNIM

from Heleph, from Allon to Z.	Jos 19:33

ZAAVAN

of Ezer are these; Bilhan, and Z.	Ge 36:27

ZABAD

Nathan, and Nathan begat Z.	1Ch 2:36
And Z. begat Ephlal, and Ephlal	1Ch 2:37
And Z. his son, and Shuthelah	1Ch 7:21
the Hittite, Z. the son of Ahlai	1Ch 11:41
Z. the son of Shimeath an	2Ch 24:26
Mattaniah, and Jeremoth, and Z.	Ezr 10:27
Mattathah, Z., Eliphelet, Jeremai	Ezr 10:33
Mattithiah, Z., Zebina, Jadau	Ezr 10:43

ZABBAI

Hananiah, Z., and Athlai	Ezr 10:28
Baruch the son of Z. earnestly	Ne 3:20

ZABBUD

Uthai, and Z. and with them	Ezr 8:14

ZABDI

the son of Carmi, the son of Z.	Jos 7:1; 7:18
man by man; and Z. was taken	Jos 7:17

And Jakim, and Zichri, and Z.   1Ch 8:19

wine cellars was Z. the Shiphmite   1Ch 27:27

the son of Z. the son of Asaph   Ne 11:17

ZABDIEL

was Jashobeam the son of Z.   1Ch 27:2

and their overseer was Z. the son   Ne 11:14

ZABUD

Z. the son of Nathan was principal   1Ki 4:5

ZABULON

borders of Z. and Nephthalim   M't 4:13

The land of Z. and the land   M't 4:15

Of the tribe of Z. were sealed   Re 7:8

ZACCAI

The children of Z. seven hundred   Ezr 2:9; Ne 7:14

ZACCHAEUS

there was a man named Z.   Lu 19:2

and unto him, Z. make haste   Lu 19:5

Z. stood, and said unto the Lord   Lu 19:8

ZACCHUR

Hamuel his son, Z. his son   1Ch 4:26

ZACCUR

Reuben, Shammua the son of Z.   Nu 13:4

and Shoham, and Z. and Ibri   1Ch 24:27

Z. and Joseph, and Nethaniah   1Ch 25:2

The third to Z. he, his sons   1Ch 25:10

them builded Z. the son of Imri   Ne 3:2

Z., Sherebiah, Shebaniah   Ne 10:12

the son of Michaiah, the son of Z.   Ne 12:35

to them was Hanan the son of Z.   Ne 13:13

ZACHARIAH

Z. his son reigned in his stead   2Ki 14:29

did Z. the son of Jeroboam reign   2Ki 15:8

And the rest of the acts of Z.   2Ki 15:11

also was Abi, the daughter of Z.   2Ki 18:2

ZACHARIAS

blood of Z. son of Barachias   M't 23:35

a certain priest named Z. of the   Lu 1:5

And when Z. saw him, he was   Lu 1:12

angel said unto him, Fear not, Z.   Lu 1:13

And Z. said unto the angel   Lu 1:18

And the people waited for Z.   Lu 1:21

And entered into the house of Z.   Lu 1:40

they called him Z. after the name   Lu 1:59

And his father Z. was filled with   Lu 1:67

came unto John the son of Z.   Lu 3:2

of Abel unto the blood of Z.   Lu 11:51

ZACHER

And Gedor, and Ahio, and Z.   1Ch 8:31

ZADOK

And Z. the son of Ahitub, and   2Sa 8:17

And lo Z. also, and all the Levites   2Sa 15:24

the king said unto Z., Carry back   2Sa 15:25

king said also unto Z. the priest   2Sa 15:27

Z. therefore and Abiathar carried   2Sa 15:29

hast thou not there with thee Z.   2Sa 15:35

thou shalt tell it to Z. and Abiathar   2Sa 15:35

Then said Hushai unto Z. and to   2Sa 17:15

Then said Ahimaaz the son of Z.   2Sa 18:19; 18:22

running of Ahimaaz the son of Z.   2Sa 18:27

David sent to Z. and to Abiathar   2Sa 19:11

Z. and Abiathar were the priests   2Sa 20:25; 1Ki 4:4

Z. the priest, and Benaiah son   1Ki 1:8; 1:26

Call me Z. the priest, and Nathan   1Ki 1:32

let Z. the priest, and Nathan   1Ki 1:34

So Z. the priest, and Nathan   1Ki 1:38

And Z. the priest took an horn of oil   1Ki 1:39

hath sent with him Z. the priest   1Ki 1:44

And Z. the priest and Nathan   1Ki 1:45

Z. the priest did the king put   1Ki 2:35

Azariah the son of Z. the priest   1Ki 4:2

was Jerusha, the daughter of Z.   2Ki 15:33

Ahitub begat Z. and Z. begat   1Ch 6:8; 6:12

Z. his son, Ahimaaz his son   1Ch 6:53

son of Meshullam, the son of Z.   1Ch 9:11

And Z. a young man mighty of   1Ch 12:28

David called for Z. and Abiathar   1Ch 15:11

And Z. the priest, and his brethren   1Ch 16:39

And Z. the son of Ahitub   1Ch 18:16

both Z. of the sons of Eleazar   1Ch 24:3

and the princes, and Z. the priest   1Ch 24:6

presence of David the king, and Z.   1Ch 24:31

of Kemuel: of the Aaronites, Z.   1Ch 27:17

chief governor, and Z. to be priest   1Ch 29:22

was Jerushah, the daughter of Z.   2Ch 27:1

chief priest of the house of Z.   2Ch 31:10

The son of Shallum, the son of Z.   Ezr 7:2

repaired Z. the son of Baana   Ne 3:4

repaired Z. the son of Immer   Ne 3:29

Meshezabeel, Z., Jaddua   Ne 10:21

son of Meshullam, the son of Z.   Ne 11:11

the priest, and Z. the scribe   Ne 13:13

these are the sons of Z.   Eze 40:46

among the Levites that be of the seed of Z.   Eze 43:19

the sons of Z. that kept the charge   Eze 44:15

are sanctified of the sons of Z.   Eze 48:11

ZADOK'S

Ahimaaz Z. son, and Jonathan   2Sa 15:36

ZAHAM

Jeush, and Shamariah, and Z.   2Ch 11:19

ZAIR

So Joram went over to Z. and all   2Ki 8:21

ZALAPH

and Hanun the sixth son of Z.   Ne 3:30

ZALMON

got him up to mount Z.   J'g 9:48

Z. the Ahohite, Maharai the   2Sa 23:28

ZALMONAH

mount Hor, and pitched in Z.   Nu 33:41

And they departed from Z.   Nu 33:42

ZALMUNNA

am pursuing after Zebah and Z.   J'g 8:5

Are the hands of Zebah   J'g 8:6

and Z. now

Lord hath delivered Zebah and Z.   J'g 8:7

Zebah and Z. were in Karkor   J'g 8:10

And when Zebah and Z. fled, he   J'g 8:12

two kings of Midian, Zebah, and Z.   J'g 8:12

Behold Zebah and Z. with whom   J'g 8:15

Are the hands of Zebah and Z. now   J'g 8:15

Then said he unto Zebah, and Z.   J'g 8:18

Zebah and Z. said, Rise thou   J'g 8:21

arose, and slew Zebah, and Z.   J'g 8:21

their princes as Zebah, and as Z.   Ps 83:11

ZAMZUMMIMS

and the Ammonites call them Z.   De 2:20

ZANOAH

Z. and En-gannim, Tappuah   Jos 15:34

And Jezreel, and Jokdeam, and Z.   Jos 15:56

and Jekuthiel the father of Z.   1Ch 4:18

Hanun, and the inhabitants of Z.   Ne 3:13

Z., Adullam, and in their villages   Ne 11:30

ZAPHNATH-PAANEAH

called Joseph's name Z.   Ge 41:45

ZAPHON

and Z. the rest of the kingdom   Jos 13:27

ZARA

Judas begat Phares and Z. of   M't 1:3

ZARAH

and his name was called Z.   Ge 38:30

and Shelah, and Pharez, and Z.   Ge 46:12

ZAREAH

and at En-rimmoh, and at Z.   Ne 11:29

ZAREATHITES

of them came the Z. and the   1Ch 2:53

ZARED

and pitched in the valley of Z.   Nu 21:12

ZAREPHATH

Arise, get thee to Z. which   1Ki 17:9

So he arose and went to Z.   1Ki 17:10

of the Canaanites, even unto Z.   Ob 20

ZARETAN

the city Adam, that is beside Z.   Jos 3:16

ZARETH-SHAHAR

and Z. in the mount of the valley   Jos 13:19

ZARHITES

Of Zerah, the family of the Z.   Nu 26:13; 26:20

and he took the family of the Z.   Jos 7:17

he brought the family of the Z.   Jos 7:17

Sibbecai the Hushathite, of   1Ch 27:11
the Z.
the Netophathite, of the Z.   1Ch 27:13

ZARTANAH

which is by Z. beneath Jezreel   1Ki 4:12

ZARTHAN

ground between Succoth and   1Ki 7:46
Z.

ZATTHU

Parosh, Pahath-moab, Elam,   Ne 10:14
Z.

ZATTU

The children of Z. nine   Ezr 2:8
hundred
sons of Z.; Elioenai, Eliashib   Ezr 10:27
The children of Z. eight   Ne 7:13
hundred

ZAVAN

Ezer; Bilhan, and Z. and   1Ch 1:42
Jakan

ZAZA

sons of Jonathan; Peleth and   1Ch 2:33
Z.

ZEAL

slay them in his z. to the   2Sa 21:2
children
and see my z. for the Lord   2Ki 10:16
z. of the Lord of hosts shall   2Ki 19:31
do this
z. of thine house hath eaten   Ps 69:9;
me up   Joh 2:17
My z. hath consumed me,   Ps 119:139
because
The z. of the Lord of hosts will   Isa 9:7
z. of the Lord of hosts shall   Isa 37:32
do this
and was clad with z. as a   Isa 59:17
cloak
where is thy z. and thy   Isa 63:15
strength
I the Lord have spoken it in   Eze 5:13
my z.
burning with spiritual z.   Ac 18:25
(A)(P)
record that they have a z. of   Ro 10:2
God
z. and singleness of mind (A)   Ro 12:8
never lag, flag in z. (A)(R)   Ro 12:11
related your z. (B)(E)(R)   2Co 7:7
yea, what z. yea, what   2Co 7:11
revenge
by the z. of others (A)   2Co 8:8
your z. hath provoked very   2Co 9:2
many
Concerning z. persecuting the   Ph'p 3:6
that he hath a great z. for   Col 4:13
you

ZEALOT

Simon the Z. (S)   Ac 1:13

ZEALOUS

while he was z. for my sake   Nu 25:11
because he was z. for his   Nu 25:13
God,
and they are all z. of the law   Ac 21:20
and was z. toward God, as ye   Ac 22:3
all
as ye are z. of spiritual gifts   1Co 14:12
z. of the traditions of my   Ga 1:14
fathers
a peculiar people, z. of good   Tit 2:14
works
be z. to confirm your call (R)   2Pe 1:10
be z. therefore, and repent   Re 3:19

ZEALOUSLY

more z. proclaimed it   M'k 7:36
(A)(R)
z. cultivate (A)   1Co 12:31
They z. affect you, but not   Ga 4:17
well

z. trying to dazzle you   Ga 4:17
(A)(E)
good to be z. affected always   Ga 4:18
in a

ZEBADIAH

And Z. and Arad, and Ader   1Ch 8:15
And Z. and Meshullam, and   1Ch 8:17
and Z. the sons of Jeroham   1Ch 12:7
Jediael the second, Z. the   1Ch 26:2
third
Joab, and Z. his son after   1Ch 27:7
him
and Nethaniah, and Z. the   2Ch 17:8
Asahel
Z. the son of Ishmael, the   2Ch 19:11
ruler
Z. the son of Michael, and   Ezr 8:8
sons of Immer; Hanani, and   Ezr 10:20
Z.

ZEBAH

and I am pursuing after Z.   J'g 8:5
Are the hands of Z. and   J'g 8:6;
Zalmunna   8:15
when the Lord hath delivered   J'g 8:7
Z.
Now Z. and Zalmunna were   J'g 8:10
in
And when Z. and Zalmunna   J'g 8:12
fled
kings of Midian, Z. and   J'g 8:12
Zalmunna
Behold Z. and Zalmunna, with   J'g 8:15
said he unto Z. and Zalmunna   J'g 8:18
Z. and Zalmunna said, Rise   J'g 8:21
thou
slew Z. and Zalmunna, and   J'g 8:21
took
all their princes as Z. and as   Ps 83:11

ZEBAIM

the children of Pochereth of   Ezr 2:57;
Z.   Ne 7:59

ZEBEDEE

James the son of Z. and John   M't 4:21;
his   10:2; M'k 3:17
in a ship with Z. their father   M't 4:21
him Peter and the two sons   M't 26:37
of Z.
he saw James the son of   M'k 1:19
left their father Z. in the ship   M'k 1:20
James and John, the sons of   M'k 10:35;
Z.   Lu 5:10
and the sons of Z. and two   Joh 21:2
other

ZEBEDEE'S

came the mother of Z.   M't 20:20
children
and the mother of Z.   M't 27:56
children

ZEBINA

Zabad, Z., Jadan, and Joel   Ezr 10:43

ZEBOIIM

Shemeber king of Z. and the   Ge 14:2
king of Z. and the king of   Ge 14:8
Bela

ZEBOIM

Gomorrah, and Admah, and   Ge 10:19;
Z.   De 29:23
that looketh to the valley of   1Sa 13:18
Hadid, Z., Neballat   Ne 11:34
how shall I set thee as Z.   Ho 11:8

ZEBUDAH

And his mother's name was   2Ki 23:36
Z.

ZEBUL

And Z. his officer? serve the   J'g 9:28
men
when Z. the ruler of the city   J'g 9:30
heard
he said to Z. Behold, there   J'g 9:36
come

And Z. said unto him, Thou   J'g 9:36
seest
Then said Z. unto him, Where   J'g 9:38
is
Z. thrust out Gaal and his   J'g 9:41
brethren

ZEBULONITE

after him Elon, a Z., judged   J'g 12:11
and Elon the Z. died, and   J'g 12:12
was

ZEBULUN

and she called his name Z.   Ge 30:20
and Judah, and Issachar, and   Ge 35:23
sons of Z.; Sered, and Elon   Ge 46:14
shall dwell at the haven   Ge 49:13
Issachar, Z. and Benjamin   Ex 1:3
Of Z.; Eliab the son of Helon   Nu 1:9
Of the children of Z. by their   Nu 1:30
even of the tribe of Z. were   Nu 1:31
fifty
Then the tribe of Z. and Eliab   Nu 2:7
be captain of the children of Z.   Nu 2:7
Helon, prince of the children   Nu 7:24
of Z.
of the children of Z. was   Nu 10:16
Eliab
Of the tribe of Z. Gaddiel   Nu 13:10
sons of Z. after their families   Nu 26:26
of the tribe of the children   Nu 34:25
of Z.
Gad and Asher, and Dan   De 27:13
of Z. he said, Rejoice, Z. in   De 33:18
thy
came up for the children of   Jos 19:10
Z.
inheritance of the children of   Jos 19:16
Z.
reacheth to Z. and to the   Jos 19:27
valley
reacheth to Z. on the south   Jos 19:34
side
out of the tribe of Z. twelve   Jos 21:7
cities
out of the tribe of Z.   Jos 21:34
Jokneam
Z. drive out the inhabitants   J'g 1:30
Naphtali and of the children of   J'g 4:6
Z.
Barak called Z. and Naphtali   J'g 4:10
out of Z. they that handle the   J'g 5:14
pen
Z. and Naphtali were a people   J'g 5:18
that
and unto Z. and unto Naphtali   J'g 6:35
in Aijalon in the country of   J'g 12:12
Z.
and Judah, Issachar, and Z.   1Ch 2:1
out of the tribe of Z. twelve   1Ch 6:63
cities
were given out of the tribe of   1Ch 6:77
Z.
of Z. such as went forth to   1Ch 12:33
battle
even unto Issachar and Z.   1Ch 12:40
of Z. Ishmaiah the son of   1Ch 27:19
and Manasseh even unto Z.   2Ch 30:10
and Manasseh and of Z.   2Ch 30:11
humbled
Issachar and Z. had not   2Ch 30:18
cleansed
princes of Z. and the princes   Ps 68:27
of
he lightly afflicted the land of   Isa 9:1
Z.
unto the west side, Z. a   Ezr 48:26
portion
And by the border of Z.   Ezr 48:27
from the
gate of Issachar, one gate of   Ezr 48:33
Z.

ZEBULUNITES

These are the families of the   Nu 26:27
Z.

ZECHARIAH

were the chief, Jeiel, and Z.   1Ch 5:7
And Z. the son of   1Ch 9:21
Meshelemiah
And Gedor, and Ahio, and Z.   1Ch 9:37
Z., Ben, and Jaaziel, and   1Ch 15:18
And Z. and Aziel, and   1Ch 15:20

and Z. and Benaiah, and Eliezer	1Ch 15:24
the chief, and next to him Z.	1Ch 16:5
of the sons of Isshiah; Z.	1Ch 24:25
Z. the firstborn, Jediael the	1Ch 26:2
Tebaliah the third, Z. the fourth	1Ch 26:11
for Z. his son, a wise counseller	1Ch 26:14
in Gilead, Iddo the son of Z.	1Ch 27:21
and to Obadiah, and to Z.	2Ch 17:7
Then upon Jahaziel the son of Z.	2Ch 20:14
and Jehiel, and Z. and Azariah	2Ch 21:2
Spirit of God came upon Z. the son	2Ch 24:20
he sought God in the days of Z.	2Ch 26:5
was Abijah, the daughter of Z.	2Ch 29:1
sons of Asaph; Z. and Mattaniah	2Ch 29:13
and Z. and Meshullam, of the sons	2Ch 34:12
Hilkiah and Z. and Jehiel	2Ch 35:8
prophet, and Z. the son of Iddo	Ezr 5:1; 6:14
of the sons of Pharosh; Z.	Ezr 8:3
Z. the son of Bebai, and with him	Ezr 8:11
for Z. and for Meshullam, Mattaniah, Z. and Jehiel	Ezr 8:16 Ezr 10:26
Hashbadana, Z. and Meshullam	Ne 8:4
the son of Z. the son of Amariah	Ne 11:4
the son of Joiarib, the son of Z.	Ne 11:5
the son of Z. the son of Pashur	Ne 11:12
Of Iddo, Z. of Ginnethon	Ne 12:16
namely, Z. the son of Jonathan	Ne 12:35
Z. and Hananiah, with trumpets	Ne 12:41
and Z. the son of Jeberechiah	Isa 8:2
came the word of the Lord unto Z.	Zec 1:1; 1:7
the word of the Lord came unto Z.	Zec 7:1; 7:8

ZEDAD

forth of the border shall be to Z.	Nu 34:8
way of Hethlon, as men go to Z.	Eze 47:15

ZEDEKIAH

Z. the son of Chenaanah made	1Ki 22:11
Z. the son of Chenaanah went near	1Ki 22:24
stead, and changed his name to Z.	2Ki 24:17
Z. was twenty and one years old	2Ki 24:18
that Z. rebelled against the king	2Ki 24:20
unto the eleventh year of king Z.	2Ki 25:2
slew the sons of Z. before his eyes	2Ki 25:7
put out the eyes of Z. and bound	2Ki 25:7
second Jehoiakim, the third Z.	1Ch 3:15
Jeconiah his son. Z. his son	1Ch 3:16
Z. the son of Chenaanah had made	2Ch 18:10
Z. the son of Chenaanah came	2Ch 18:23
made Z. his brother king over	2Ch 36:10
Z. was one and twenty years old	2Ch 36:11
eleventh year of Z. the son of	Jer 1:3
king Z. sent unto him Pashur	Jer 21:1
them. Thus shall ye say to Z.	Jer 21:3
I will deliver Z. king of Judah	Jer 21:7
will I give Z. the king of Judah	Jer 24:8
come to Jerusalem unto Z. king of	Jer 27:3
I spake also to Z. king of Judah	Jer 27:12
in the beginning of the reign of Z.	Jer 28:1

(whom Z. king of Judah sent unto	Jer 29:3
and of Z. the son of Maaseiah	Jer 29:21
The Lord made thee like Z.	Jer 29:22
the Lord in the tenth year of Z.	Jer 32:1
For Z. king of Judah had shut him	Jer 32:3
Z. king of Judah shall not escape	Jer 32:4
And he shall lead Z. to Babylon	Jer 32:5
Go and speak to Z. king of Judah	Jer 34:2
of the Lord, O Z. king of Judah	Jer 34:4
spake all these words unto Z. king	Jer 34:6
the king Z. had made a covenant	Jer 34:8
Z. king of Judah and his princes	Jer 34:21
and Z. the son of Hananiah	Jer 36:12
king Z. the son of Josiah reigned	Jer 37:1
Z. the king sent Jehucal the son	Jer 37:3
Z. the king sent, and took him out	Jer 37:17
Jeremiah said unto king Z. What	Jer 37:18
Z. the king commanded that they	Jer 37:21
Z. the king said, Behold, he is in	Jer 38:5
Then Z. the king sent, and took	Jer 38:14
Jeremiah said unto Z. If I declare	Jer 38:15
So Z. the king sware secretly unto	Jer 38:16
Then said Jeremiah unto Z. Thus	Jer 38:17
Z. the king said unto Jeremiah, I	Jer 38:19
said Z. unto Jeremiah, Let no man	Jer 38:24
ninth year of Z. king of Judah	Jer 39:1
And in the eleventh year of Z.	Jer 39:2
when Z. the king of Judah saw	Jer 39:4
and overtook Z. in the plains of	Jer 39:5; 52:8
king of Babylon slew the sons of Z.	Jer 39:6
as I gave Z. king of Judah into	Jer 44:30
in the beginning of the reign of Z.	Jer 49:34
went with Z. the king of Judah	Jer 51:59
Z. was one and twenty years old	Jer 52:1
that Z. rebelled against the king	Jer 52:3
unto the eleventh year of king Z.	Jer 52:5
slew the sons of Z. before his eyes	Jer 52:10
Then he put out the eyes of Z.	Jer 52:11

ZEDEKIAH'S

Moreover he put out Z. eyes	Jer 39:7

ZEEB

of the Midianites, Oreb and Z.	J'g 7:25
Z. they slew at the winepress of Z.	J'g 7:25
heads of Oreb and Z. to Gideon	J'g 7:25
princes of Midian, Oreb and Z.	J'g 8:3
nobles like Oreb, and like Z.	Ps 83:11

ZELAH

Z. Eleph, and Jebusi, which is	Jos 18:28
in the country of Benjamin in Z.	2Sa 21:14

ZELEK

Z. the Ammonite, Nahari	2Sa 23:37
Z. the Ammonite, Naharai the	1Ch 11:39

ZELOPHEHAD

Z. the son of Hepher had no sons	Nu 26:33
the names of the daughters of Z.	Nu 26:33
Then came the daughters of Z.	Nu 27:1
The daughters of Z. speak right	Nu 27:7
the inheritance of Z. our brother	Nu 36:2
concerning the daughters of Z.	Nu 36:6
Moses, so did the daughters of Z.	Nu 36:10
the daughters of Z. were married	Nu 36:11
Z. the son of Hepher, the son	Jos 17:3
was Z. and Z. had daughters	1Ch 7:15

ZELOTES

of Alphaeus, and Simon called	Lu 6:15
Simon Z. and Judas the brother	Ac 1:13

ZELZAH

in the border of Benjamin at Z.	1Sa 10:2

ZEMARAIM

Beth-arabah, and Z. and Beth-el	Jos 18:22
Abijah stood up upon mount Z.	2Ch 13:4

ZEMARITE

and the Z. and the Hamathite	Ge 10:18; 1Ch 1:16

ZEMIRA

sons of Becher; Z. and Joash	1Ch 7:8

ZENAN

Z. and Hadashah, Migdal-gad	Jos 15:37

ZENAS

Bring Z. the lawyer and Apollos	Tit 3:13

ZEPHANIAH

priest, and Z. the second priest	2Ki 25:18; Jer 52:24
the son of Azariah, the son of Z.	2Ch 6:36; Jer 29:25
Z. the son of Maaseiah the priest	Jer 21:1; 37:3
And Z. the priest read this letter	Jer 29:29
came unto Z. the son of Cushi	Zep 1:1
the house of Josiah the son of Z.	Zec 6:10
Jedaiah, and to Hen the son of Z.	Zec 6:14

ZEPHATH

the Canaanites that inhabited Z.	J'g 1:17

ZEPHATHAH

in the valley of Z. at Mareshah	2Ch 14:10

ZEPHI

Eliphaz; Teman, and Omar, Z.	1Ch 1:36

ZEPHO

Eliphaz were Teman, Omar, Z.	Ge 36:11
duke Omar, duke Z., duke Kenaz	Ge 36:15

ZEPHON

families: of Z. the family of the	Nu 26:15

ZEPHONITES

of Zephon, the family of the   *Nu 26:15*
Z.

ZER

the fenced cities are Ziddim,   *Jos 19:35*
Z.

ZERAH

sons of Reuel; Nahath, and   *Ge 36:13*
Z.
Nahath, duke Z. duke   *Ge 36:17*
Shammah
and Jobab the son of Z. of   *Ge 36:33;*
Bozrah   *1Ch 1:44*
Of Z. the family of the   *Nu 26:13;*
Zarhites   *26:20*
the son of Z. of the tribe of   *Jos 7:1;*
   7:18
took Achan the son of Z.   *Jos 7:24*
and the
Did not Achan the son of Z.   *Jos 22:20*
of Reuel; Nahath, and   *1Ch 1:37*
Shammah
in law bare him Pharez and Z.   *1Ch 2:4*
sons of Z.; Zimri, and Ethan   *1Ch 2:6*
and Jamin, Jarib, Z. and   *1Ch 4:24*
Shaul
Iddo his son, Z. his son,   *1Ch 6:21*
Jeaterai
The son of Ethni, the son of   *1Ch 6:41*
Z.
of the sons of Z.; Jeuel and   *1Ch 9:6*
their
out against them Z. the   *2Ch 14:9*
Ethiopian
children of Z. the son of   *Ne 11:24*
Judah

ZERAHIAH

Uzzi begat Z. and Z. begat   *1Ch 6:6*
his son, Uzzi his son, Z. his   *1Ch 6:51*
son
The son of Z., the son of Uzzi   *Ezr 7:4*
Elihoenai the son of Z., and   *Ezr 8:4*

ZERED

and get you over the brook Z.   *De 2:13*
And we went over the brook   *De 2:13*
Z.
we were come over the brook   *De 2:14*
Z.

ZEREDA

an Ephrathite of Z.   *1Ki 11:26*
Solomon's

ZEREDATHAH

ground between Succoth and   *2Ch 4:17*
Z.

ZERERATH

host fled to Beth-shittah in Z.   *J'g 7:22*

ZERESH

for his friends, and Z. his wife   *Es 5:10*
said Z. his wife and his   *Es 5:14*
friends
Haman told Z. his wife and   *Es 6:13*
all his
said his wise men and Z. his   *Es 6:13*
wife

ZERETH

And the sons of Helah were   *1Ch 4:7*
Z.

ZERI

of Jeduthun; Gedaliah, and   *1Ch 25:3*
Z.

ZEROR

the son of Abiel, the son of Z.   *1Sa 9:1*

ZERUAH

whose mother's name was Z.   *1Ki 11:26*

ZERUBBABEL

and the sons of Pedaiah   *1Ch 3:19*
were, Z.
and the sons of Z.;   *1Ch 3:19*
Meshullam
Which came with Z.: Jeshua   *Ezr 2:2*
priests, and Z. the son of   *Ezr 3:2*
Shealtiel
began Z. the son of Shealtiel   *Ezr 3:8*
Then they came to Z. and to   *Ezr 4:2*
But Z. and Jeshua, and the   *Ezr 4:3*
rest
rose up Z. the son of Shealtiel   *Ezr 5:2*
Who came with Z., Jeshua   *Ne 7:7*
the Levites that went up with   *Ne 12:1*
Z.
And all Israel in the days of   *Ne 12:47*
Z.
by Haggai the prophet unto Z.   *Hag 1:1*
Then Z. the son of Shealtiel   *Hag 1:12*
Lord stirred up the spirit of   *Hag 1:14*
Z.
Speak now to Z. the son of   *Hag 2:2*
Yet now be strong, O Z.,   *Hag 2:4*
saith
Speak to Z. governor of   *Hag 2:21*
Judah
will I take thee, O Z., my   *Hag 2:23*
servant
is the word of the Lord unto   *Zec 4:6*
Z.
before Z. thou shalt become a   *Zec 4:7*
The hands of Z. have laid the   *Zec 4:9*
plummet in the hand of Z.   *Zec 4:10*

ZERUIAH

Abishai the son of Z. brother   *1Sa 26:6*
to
And Joab the son of Z. and   *2Sa 2:13*
were three sons of Z. there,   *2Sa 2:18*
Joab
the sons of Z. be too hard for   *2Sa 3:39*
me
the son of Z. was over the   *2Sa 8:16*
host
the son of Z. perceived that   *2Sa 14:1*
Then said Abishai the son of   *2Sa 16:9*
Z.
I to do with you, ye sons of   *2Sa 16:10*
Z.
sister to Z. Joab's mother   *2Sa 17:25*
the hand of Abishai the son   *2Sa 18:2*
of Z.
Abishai the son of Z.   *2Sa 19:21*
answered
ye sons of Z. that ye should   *2Sa 19:22*
this
the son of Z. succoured him   *2Sa 21:17*
son of Z. was chief among   *2Sa 23:18*
three
armourbearer to Joab the   *2Sa 23:37*
son of Z.
conferred with Joab the son of   *1Ki 1:7*
Z.
also what Joab the son of Z.   *1Ki 2:5*
did
priest, and for Joab the son   *1Ki 2:22*
of Z.
Whose sisters were Z. and   *1Ch 2:16*
Abigail
sons of Z.; Abishai, and   *1Ch 2:16*
Joab, and
Joab the son of Z. went first   *1Ch 11:6*
up
armourbearer to Joab the   *1Ch 11:39*
son of Z.
son of Z. slew of the   *1Ch 18:12*
Edomites
the son of Z. was over the   *1Ch 18:15*
host
Joab the son of Z. had   *1Ch 26:28*
dedicated
the son of Z. began to   *1Ch 27:24*
number

ZETHAM

the chief was Jehiel, and Z.   *1Ch 23:8*
Z. and Joel his brother,   *1Ch 26:22*
which

ZETHAN

and Chenaanah, and Z. and   *1Ch 7:10*

ZETHAR

Bigtha, and Abagtha, Z. and   *Es 1:10*

ZEUS

called Barnabas Z. (A)(B)(R)   *Ac 14:12;*
   14:13

ZIA

and Jorai, and Jachan, and   *1Ch 5:13*
Z.

ZIBA

a servant whose name was Z.   *2Sa 9:2*
king said unto him, Art thou   *2Sa 9:2*
Z.
Z. said unto the king,   *2Sa 9:3*
Jonathan
Z. said unto the king, Behold,   *2Sa 9:4*
he
Then the king called to Z.   *2Sa 9:9*
Saul's
Now Z. had fifteen sons and   *2Sa 9:10*
Then said Z. unto the king   *2Sa 9:11*
all that dwelt in the house of   *2Sa 9:12*
Z.
Z. the servant of   *2Sa 16:1*
Mephibosheth
king said unto Z. What   *2Sa 16:2*
meanest
Z. said, The asses be for the   *2Sa 16:2*
king's
Z. said unto the king, Behold   *2Sa 16:3*
Then said the king to Z.   *2Sa 16:4*
Behold
Z. said, I humbly beseech   *2Sa 16:4*
thee
and Z. the servant of the   *2Sa 19:17*
house
said, Thou and Z. divide the   *2Sa 19:29*
land

ZIBEON

the daughter of Z. the Hivite   *Ge 36:2*
the daughter of Z. Esau's   *Ge 36:14*
wife
and Shobal, and Z. and Anah   *Ge 36:20*
And these are the children of   *Ge 36:24*
Z.
as he fed the asses of Z. his   *Ge 36:24*
father
duke Shobal, duke Z., duke   *Ge 36:29*
Anah
and Shobal, and Z., and Anah   *1Ch 1:38*
the sons of Z.; Aiah, and   *1Ch 1:40*
Anah

ZIBIA

Hodesh his wife, Jobab, and   *1Ch 8:9*
Z.

ZIBIAH

And his mother's name was   *2Ki 12:1*
Z.
His mother's name also was   *2Ch 24:1*
Z. of

ZICHRI

Korah, and Nepheg, and Z.   *Ex 6:21*
And Jakim, and Z. and   *1Ch 8:19*
Zabdi
And Abdon, and Z. and   *1Ch 8:23*
Hanan
and Z. the sons of Jeroham   *1Ch 8:27*
the son of Micah, the son of   *1Ch 9:15*
Z.
and Joram his son, and Z.   *1Ch 26:25*
his son
was Eliezer the son of Z.   *1Ch 27:16*
him was Amasiah the son   *2Ch 17:16*
of Z.
and Elishaphat the son of Z.   *2Ch 23:1*
And Z. a mighty man of   *2Ch 28:7*
Ephraim
the son of Z. was their   *Ne 11:9*
overseer
Of Abijah, Z.   *Ne 12:17*

ZIDDIM

And the fenced cities are Z.   *Jos 19:35*

ZIDKIJAH

the son of Hachaliah, and Z.   *Ne 10:1*

ZIDON

and his border shall be unto Z.   Ge 49:13
and chased them unto great Z.   Jos 11:8
and Kanah, even unto great Z.   Jos 19:28
Accho, nor the inhabitants of Z.   J'g 1:31
gods of Syria, and the gods of Z.   J'g 10:6
because it was far from Z.   J'g 18:28
came to Dan-jaan, and about to Z.   2Sa 24:6
Zarephath, which belongeth to Z.   1Ki 17:9
And Canaan begat Z. his firstborn   1Ch 1:13
drink, and oil, unto them of Z.   Ezr 3:7
thou whom the merchants of   Isa 23:2
Be thou ashamed, O Z.   Isa 23:4
oppressed virgin, daughter of Z.   Isa 23:12
of Tyrus, and all the kings of Z.   Jer 25:22
and to the king of Z. by the hand   Jer 27:3
to cut off from Tyrus and Z. every   Jer 47:4
inhabitants of Z. and Arvad were   Eze 27:8
Son of man, set thy face against Z.   Eze 28:21
Behold, I am against thee, O Z.   Eze 28:22
ye to do with me, O Tyre, and Z.   Joe 3:4
Tyrus, and Z. through it be very   Zec 9:2

ZIDONIANS

The Z. also, and the Amalekites   J'g 10:12
after the manner of the Z. quiet   J'g 18:7
and they were far from the Z.   J'g 18:7
Ammonites, Edomites, Z. and   1Ki 11:1
Ashtoreth the goddess of the Z.   1Ki 11:5; 11:33
daughter of Ethbaal king of the Z.   1Ki 16:31
the abomination of the Z.   2Ki 23:13
for the Z. and they of Tyre brought   1Ch 22:4
north, all of them, and all the Z.   Eze 32:30

ZIF

reign over Israel, in the month Z.   1Ki 6:1
of the Lord laid, in the month Z.   1Ki 6:37

ZIHA

children of Z. the children of   Ezr 2:43; Ne 7:46
and Z. and Gispa were over   Ne 11:21

ZIKLAG

and Z. and Madmannah   Jos 15:31
And Z. and Beth-marcaboth   Jos 19:5
Then Achish gave him Z. that day   1Sa 27:6
Z. pertaineth unto the kings of   1Sa 27:6
and his men were come to Z.   1Sa 30:1
had invaded the south, and Z.   1Sa 30:1
smitten Z. and burnt it with fire   1Sa 30:1
Caleb; and we burned Z. with fire   1Sa 30:14
when David came to Z. he sent of   1Sa 30:26
David had abode two days in Z.   2Sa 1:1
hold of him, and slew him in Z.   2Sa 4:10
Bethuel, and at Hormah, and at Z.   1Ch 4:30
are they that came to David to Z.   1Ch 12:1
As he went to Z. there fell to him   1Ch 12:20
And at Z. and at Mekonah   Ne 11:28

ZILLAH

and the name of the other Z.   Ge 4:19
And Z. she also bare Tubal-cain   Ge 4:22
said unto his wives, Adah and Z.   Ge 4:23

ZILPAH

gave unto his daughter Leah   Ge 29:24
she took Z. her maid, and gave   Ge 30:9
Z. Leah's maid bare Jacob a son   Ge 30:10
and Z. Leah's maid bare Jacob a   Ge 30:12
the sons of Z. Leah's handmaid   Ge 35:26
with sons of Z. his father's wives   Ge 37:2
These are the sons of Z. whom   Ge 46:18

ZILTHAI

And Elienai, and Z. and Eliel   1Ch 8:20
and Z. captains of the thousands   1Ch 12:20

ZIMMAH

son, Jahath, his son Z. his son   1Ch 6:20
the son of Z. the son of Shimei   1Ch 6:42
Joah the son of Z. and Eden   2Ch 29:12

ZIMRAN

she bare him Z. and Jokshan   Ge 25:2
she bare Z. and Jokshan, and   1Ch 1:32

ZIMRI

the Midianitish woman was Z.   Nu 25:14
And his servant Z. captain of half   1Ki 16:9
And Z. went in and smote him   1Ki 16:10
Thus did Z. destroy all the house   1Ki 16:12
of Judah did Z. reign seven days   1Ki 16:15
Z. hath conspired, and hath also   1Ki 16:16
Z. saw that the city was taken   1Ki 16:18
the rest of the acts of Z. and his   1Ki 16:20
said, Had Z. peace, who slew his   2Ki 9:31
sons of Zerah; Z. and Ethan   1Ch 2:6
and Z.; and Z. begat Moza   1Ch 8:36; 9:42
And all the kings of Z.: and all the   Jer 25:25

ZIN

the wilderness of Z. unto Rehob   Nu 13:21
congregation, into the desert of Z.   Nu 20:1
commandment in the desert of Z.   Nu 27:14
in Kadesh in the wilderness of Z.   Nu 27:14
and pitched in the wilderness of Z.   Nu 33:36
shall be from the wilderness of Z.   Nu 34:3
of Akrabbim, and pass on to Z.   Nu 34:4
Kadesh, in the wilderness of Z.   De 32:51
of Edom the wilderness of Z.   Jos 15:1
passed along to Z. and ascended   Jos 15:3

ZINA

sons of Shimei were, Jahath, Z.   1Ch 23:10

ZION

David took the strong hold of Z.   2Sa 5:7
of the city of David, which is Z.   1Ki 8:1
daughter of Z. hath despised thee   2Ki 19:21
they that escape out of mount Z.   2Ki 19:31
David took the castle of Z.   1Ch 11:5
of the city of David, which is Z.   2Ch 5:2
my king upon my holy hill of Z.   Ps 2:6
to the Lord, which dwelleth in   Ps 9:11
in the gates of the daughter of Z.   Ps 9:14
of Israel were come out of Z.   Ps 14:7
and strengthen thee out of Z.   Ps 20:2
of the whole earth, is mount Z.   Ps 48:2
Let mount Z. rejoice, let the   Ps 48:11
Walk about Z. and go round   Ps 48:12
Out of Z. The perfection of beauty   Ps 50:2
good in thy good pleasure unto Z.   Ps 51:18
of Israel were come out of Z.   Ps 53:6
For God will save Z. and will   Ps 69:35
this mount Z. wherein thou hast   Ps 74:2
and his dwelling place in Z.   Ps 76:2
the mount Z. which he loved   Ps 78:68
every one of them in Z. appeareth   Ps 84:7
The Lord loveth the gates of   Ps 87:2
And of Z. it shall be said, This   Ps 87:5
Z. heard, and was glad; and   Ps 97:8
The Lord is great in Z.   Ps 99:2
arise, and have mercy upon   Ps 102:13
when the Lord shall build up   Ps 102:16
declare the name of the Lord in Z.   Ps 102:21
the rod of thy strength out of Z.   Ps 110:2
in the Lord shall be as mount Z.   Ps 125:1
turned again the captivity of Z.   Ps 126:1
The Lord shall bless thee out of Z.   Ps 128:5
and turned back that hate Z.   Ps 129:5
or the Lord hath chosen Z.   Ps 132:13
upon the mountains of Z.   Ps 133:3
and earth bless thee out of Z.   Ps 134:3
Blessed be the Lord out of Z.   Ps 135:21
we wept, when we remembered Z.   Ps 137:1
Sing us one of the songs of Z.   Ps 137:3
reign for ever, even thy God, O Z.   Ps 146:10
O Jerusalem; praise thy God, O Z.   Ps 147:12
let the children of Z. be joyful in   Ps 149:2
Go forth, O ye daughters of Z.   Ca 3:11
daughter of Z. is left as a cottage   Isa 1:8
Z. shall be redeemed with   Isa 1:27
for out of Z. shall go forth the law   Isa 2:3
the daughters of Z. are haughty   Isa 3:16
of the head of the daughters of Z.   Isa 3:17
to pass, that he that is left in Z.   Isa 4:3
the filth of the daughters of Z.   Isa 4:4
every dwelling place of mount Z.   Isa 4:5
hosts, which dwelleth in mount Z.   Isa 8:18
his whole work upon mount Z.   Isa 10:12
O my people that dwellest in Z.   Isa 10:24
the mount of the daughter of Z.   Isa 10:32; 16:1
and shout, thou inhabitant of Z.   Isa 12:6
That the Lord hath founded Z.   Isa 14:32
of the Lord of hosts, the mount Z.   Isa 18:7
of hosts shall reign in mount Z.   Isa 24:23
I lay in Z. for a foundation a stone   Isa 28:16
be, that fight against mount Z.   Isa 29:8
shall dwell in Z. at Jerusalem   Isa 30:19
come down to fight for mount Z.   Isa 31:4
the Lord, whose fire is in Z.   Isa 31:9